THE CIA WORLD FACTBOOK 2025–2026

CENTRAL INTELLIGENCE AGENCY

Skyhorse Publishing

Skyhorse Publishing books may be purchased in bulk at special discounts for sales promotion, corporate gifts, fundraising, or educational purposes. Special editions can also be created to specifications. For details, contact the Special Sales Department, Skyhorse Publishing, 307 West 36th Street, 11th Floor, New York, NY 10018 or info@skyhorsepublishing.com.

Visit our website at www.skyhorsepublishing.com.
Please follow our publisher Tony Lyons on Instagram @tonylyonsisuncertain.

10 9 8 7 6 5 4 3 2 1

Library of Congress Cataloging-in-Publication Data is available on file.

Cover design by Kai Texel

Print ISBN: 978-1-5107-8208-2
Ebook ISBN: 978-1-5107-8209-9

Printed in the United States of America

CONTENTS

COUNTRY PROFILES

A

B

C

D

E

F

G

A BRIEF HISTORY OF BASIC INTELLIGENCE AND *THE WORLD FACTBOOK*

The Intelligence Cycle is the process by which information is acquired, converted into intelligence, and made available to policymakers. ***Information*** *is raw data from any source, data that may be fragmentary, contradictory, unreliable, ambiguous, deceptive, or wrong.* ***Intelligence*** *is information that has been collected, integrated, evaluated, analyzed, and interpreted.* ***Finished intelligence*** *is the final product of the Intelligence Cycle ready to be delivered to the policymaker.*

The three types of finished intelligence are: basic, current, and estimative. Basic intelligence provides the fundamental and factual reference material on a country or issue. Current intelligence reports on new developments. Estimative intelligence judges probable outcomes. The three are mutually supportive: basic intelligence is the foundation on which the other two are constructed; current intelligence continually updates the inventory of knowledge; and estimative intelligence revises overall interpretations of country and issue prospects for guidance of basic and current intelligence. *The World Factbook*, *The President's Daily Brief*, and the *National Intelligence Estimates* are examples of the three types of finished intelligence.

The United States has carried on foreign intelligence activities since the days of George Washington but only since World War II have they been coordinated on a government-wide basis. Three programs have highlighted the development of coordinated basic intelligence since that time: (1) *the Joint Army Navy Intelligence Studies* (JANIS), (2) *the National Intelligence Survey* (NIS), and (3) *The World Factbook.*

1941

During World War II, intelligence consumers realized that the production of basic intelligence by different components of the US Government resulted in a great duplication of effort and conflicting information. The Japanese attack on Pearl Harbor in 1941 brought home to leaders in Congress and the executive branch the need for integrating departmental reports to national policymakers. Detailed and coordinated information was needed not only on such major powers as Germany and Japan, but also on places of little previous interest. In the Pacific Theater, for example, the Navy and Marines had to launch amphibious operations against many islands about which information was unconfirmed or nonexistent. Intelligence authorities resolved that the United States should never again be caught unprepared.

1943

In 1943, Gen. George B. Strong (G-2), Adm. H. C. Train (Office of Naval Intelligence – ONI), and Gen. William J. Donovan (Director of the Office of Strategic Services – OSS) decided that a joint effort should be initiated. A steering committee was appointed on 27 April 1943 that recommended the formation of a Joint Intelligence Study Publishing Board to assemble, edit, coordinate, and publish the *Joint Army Navy Intelligence Studies* (JANIS). JANIS was the first interdepartmental basic intelligence program to fulfill the needs of the US Government for an authoritative and coordinated appraisal of strategic basic intelligence. Between April 1943 and July 1947, the board published 34 JANIS studies. JANIS performed well in the war effort, and numerous letters of commendation were received, including a statement from Adm. Forrest Sherman, Chief of Staff, Pacific Ocean Areas, which said, "JANIS has become the indispensable reference work for the shore-based planners."

1946

The need for more comprehensive basic intelligence in the postwar world was well expressed in 1946 by George S. Pettee, a noted author on national security. He wrote in *The Future of American Secret Intelligence* (Infantry Journal Press, 1946, page 46) that world leadership in peace requires even more elaborate intelligence than in war. "The conduct of peace involves all countries, all human activities – not just the enemy and his war production."

1947–48

The Central Intelligence Agency was established on 26 July 1947 and officially began operating on 18 September 1947. Effective 1 October 1947, the Director of Central Intelligence assumed operational responsibility for JANIS. On 13 January 1948, the National Security Council issued Intelligence Directive (NSCID) No. 3, which authorized the *National Intelligence Survey* (NIS) program as a peacetime replacement for the wartime JANIS program. Before adequate NIS country sections could be produced, government agencies had to develop more comprehensive gazetteers and better maps. The US Board on Geographic Names (BGN) compiled the names; the Department of the Interior produced the gazetteers; and CIA produced the maps.

1954-present

The Hoover Commission's Clark Committee, set up in 1954 to study the structure and administration of the CIA, reported to Congress in 1955 that: "The National Intelligence Survey is an invaluable publication which provides the essential elements of basic intelligence on all areas of the world. There will always be a continuing requirement for keeping the Survey up-to-date." The *Factbook* was created as an annual summary and update to the encyclopedic NIS studies. The first classified *Factbook* was published in August 1962, and the first unclassified version was published in June 1971. The NIS program was terminated in 1973 except for the *Factbook*, map, and gazetteer components. The 1975 *Factbook* was the first to be made available to the public with sales through the US Government Printing Office (GPO). The *Factbook* was first produced on CD-ROM in 1995, and it was made available on the Internet in June 1997. The hardcopy version ceased publication in 2017. The year 2023 marked the 76th anniversary of the Central Intelligence Agency and the 80th year of *The World Factbook* and its two predecessor programs supporting the US Government.

DEFINITIONS AND NOTES

Abbreviations This information is included in the **Abbreviations** reference guide, which includes all abbreviations and acronyms used in the *Factbook*, with their expansions.

Acronyms An acronym is an abbreviation coined from the initial letter of each successive word in a term or phrase. In general, an acronym made up solely from the first letter of the major words in the expanded form is rendered in all capital letters (NATO from North Atlantic Treaty Organization; an exception would be ASEAN for Association of Southeast Asian Nations). In general, an acronym made up of more than the first letter of the major words in the expanded form is rendered with only an initial capital letter (Comsat from Communications Satellite Corporation; an exception would be NAM from Nonaligned Movement). Hybrid forms are sometimes used to distinguish between initially identical terms (ICC for International Chamber of Commerce and ICCt for International Criminal Court).

Administrative divisions This entry gives the numbers, designatory terms, and first-order administrative divisions as approved by the US Board on Geographic Names (BGN). Changes that have been reported but not yet acted on by the BGN are noted. Geographic names conform to spellings approved by the BGN with the exception of the omission of diacritical marks and special characters.

Age structure This entry provides the distribution of the population according to age. Information is included by sex and age group as follows: *0–14 years (children), 15–64 years (working age)*, and *65 years and over (elderly)*.

Agricultural products This entry provides a list of a country's most important agricultural products, listed by annual tonnage.

Air pollutants This entry refers to specified gases and particulates released by various sources, including animals, plants, goods, and processes.

particulate matter emissions - This entry provides the modeled annual mean concentration of particulate matter of less than 2.5 microns in diameter ($PM_{2.5}$) measured in micrograms per cubic meter of air. Exposure to $PM_{2.5}$ pollutants should not exceed an annual mean concentration of 10 micrograms per cubic meter, according to World Health Organization guidelines. Particulate matter are inhalable and respirable particles composed of sulphate, nitrates, ammonia, sodium chloride, black carbon, mineral dust, and water. Fine particles less than 2.5 microns pose the greatest health risks because they can penetrate the lungs and enter the bloodstream. Sources include combustion engines, solid-fuel combustion, and other industrial activities.

carbon dioxide emissions - This entry provides the annual quantity of carbon dioxide emissions for a country, as measured in megatons. Human-influenced sources include the burning of fossil fuels (including coal, natural gas, and oil), solid waste, trees, and other biological materials, as well as certain chemical processes, such as cement production. Natural sources include decomposition, ocean release, and respiration.

methane emissions - This entry provides the annual quantity of methane emissions for a country, as measured in megatons. Methane is emitted during the breakdown of organic material from human-influenced and natural processes. Human-influenced sources include the production and transport of coal, natural gas, and oil; the decay of organic waste in landfills; agricultural activities; stationary and mobile combustion; waste-water treatment; and certain industrial processes. Natural sources include the decay of plant material in wetlands, the seepage of gas from underground deposits, and the digestion of food by ruminants.

Airports This entry gives the total number of active airports or airfields and includes both civilian and military facilities. The runway(s) may be paved (concrete or asphalt surfaces) or unpaved (grass, earth, sand, or gravel surfaces). Airports or airfields that are closed are not included. Note that not all airports have accommodations for refueling, maintenance, or air traffic control.

Alcohol consumption per capita This entry provides information on alcohol consumption per capita (APC), which is the recorded amount of alcohol consumed per capita by persons aged 15 years and over in a calendar year, measured in liters of pure alcohol. APC is broken down further into beer, wine, spirits, and other subfields. Beer includes malt beers, wine includes wine made from grapes, spirits include all distilled beverages, and other includes one or several other alcoholic beverages, such as fermented beverages made from sorghum, maize, millet, rice, or cider, fruit wine, and fortified wine. APC only takes into account the consumption that is recorded from production, import, export, and sales data, primarily derived from taxation.

Area This entry includes three subfields. *Total area* is the sum of all land and water areas delimited by international boundaries and/or coastlines. *Land area* is the aggregate of all surfaces delimited by international boundaries and/or coastlines, excluding inland water bodies (lakes, reservoirs, rivers). *Water area* is the sum of the surfaces of all inland water bodies, such as lakes, reservoirs, or rivers, as delimited by international boundaries and/or coastlines.

Area - comparative This entry provides an area comparison based on total area equivalents. Most entities are compared with the entire US or one of the 50 states based on area measurements (1990 revised) provided by the US Bureau of the Census. The smaller entities are compared with Washington, DC (178 sq km, 69 sq mi) or The Mall in Washington, DC (0.59 sq km, 0.23 sq mi, 146 acres).

Area - rankings This entry, which appears only in the World Geography category, provides rankings for the earth's largest (or smallest) continents, countries, oceans, islands, mountain ranges, or other physical features.

Average household expenditures This entry refers to the average consumer expenditures on food, alcohol, and tobacco for the country specified in a given year. The data is presented as a percentage of all goods and services consumed in private settings for personal or household uses.

Background This entry provides a brief introduction to each country, highlighting information like geographic details, early inhabitants, key leaders, and major historical events.

Bathymetry Bathymetry is the study of the depth and floors of bodies of water. This field describes the major bathymetric features found on the ocean floor. Specific bathymetric features associated with each of the following categories are listed for each ocean.

- The *continental shelf* is a rather flat area of the sea floor adjacent to the coast that gradually slopes down from the shore to water depths of about 200 m (660 ft). It is narrow or nearly nonexistent in some places; in others, it extends for hundreds of miles.
- The *continental slope* is where the bottom drops off more rapidly until it meets the deep-sea floor (abyssal plain) at about 3,200 m (10,500 ft) water depth. The continental slope can be indented by submarine canyons, often associated with the outflow of major rivers. Another feature of the continental slope are alluvial fans or cones of sediments carried downstream to the ocean by major rivers and deposited down the slope.
- The *abyssal plains*, at depths of over 3,000 m (10,000 ft) and covering 70% of the ocean floor, are the largest habitat on earth. Despite their name, these "plains" are not uniformly flat and are interrupted by features like hills, valleys, and seamounts.
- The *mid-ocean ridge*, rising up from the abyssal plain, is a continuous range of undersea volcanic mountains that encircles the globe almost entirely underwater. It is the longest mountain range on Earth at over 64,000 km (40,000 mi) long, rising to an average depth of 2,400 m (8,000 ft). Mid-ocean ridges form at divergent plate boundaries where two tectonic plates are moving apart and magma creates new crust.

- *Seamounts* are submarine mountains at least 1,000 m (3,300 ft) high, formed from individual volcanoes on the ocean floor. They are distinct from the plate-boundary volcanic system of the mid-ocean ridges, because seamounts tend to be circular or conical. Flat-topped seamounts are known as "guyots."
- *Ocean trenches* are the deepest parts of the ocean floor and are created by the process of subduction, when tectonic plates move toward each other and one plate sinks (is subducted) under another.
- *Atolls* are the remains of dormant volcanic islands. In warm tropical oceans, coral colonies establish themselves on the margins of the island. Over time, the high elevation of the island collapses and erodes away to sea level, leaving behind an outline of the island in the form of the coral reef. The resulting island typically has a low elevation of sand and coral with an interior shallow lagoon.

Birth rate This entry gives the average annual births during a year per 1,000 persons in the population at midyear, which is also known as "crude birth rate." The birth rate is usually the dominant factor in determining the rate of population growth.

Broadband - fixed subscriptions This entry gives the total number of fixed-broadband subscriptions, as well as the number of subscriptions per 100 inhabitants. Fixed broadband is a physical wired connection to the Internet (e.g., coaxial cable, optical fiber) at speeds equal to or greater than 256 kilobits/second (256 kbit/s).

Broadcast media This entry provides information on the approximate number of public and private TV and radio stations in a country, as well as basic information on the availability of satellite and cable TV services.

Budget This entry includes *revenues* and *expenditures. Revenues* include central government receipts from taxes, social contributions, fees, and other income excluding grants. *Expenditures* are payments for operating activities of the central government, including wages for government employees, interest payments, subsidies, social benefits, and other outlays. Figures reported in local currency units have been converted to current US dollars using an average official exchange rate for the year indicated.

Capital This entry gives the *name* of the seat of government, its *geographic coordinates*, the *time difference* relative to **Coordinated Universal Time (UTC)** and the time observed in Washington, DC, and, if applicable, information on *daylight saving time* **(DST)**. Where appropriate, a special *time zone note* has been added to highlight those countries that have multiple time zones. Finally, *etymology* explains how the capital acquired its name.

Carbon dioxide emissions This field refers to the amount of carbon dioxide released in a country by burning coal, petroleum, and natural gas. Data are reported in metric tonnes of CO_2.

Child marriage This entry provides data on the prevalence of child marriage in a country. Data includes the percentage of women aged 20 to 24 years who were first married or in union before age 15, and before age 18; and men aged 20 to 24 years who were first married or in union before age 18.

Children under the age of 5 years underweight This entry gives the percent of children under five considered to be underweight. Underweight means weight-for-age is less than minus two standard deviations from the median of the World Health Organization Child Growth Standards among children under 5 years of age. This statistic is an indicator of the nutritional status of a community.

Citizenship This entry provides information related to the acquisition and exercise of citizenship; it includes four subfields:

citizenship by birth describes the acquisition of citizenship based on place of birth, known as *Jus soli*, regardless of the citizenship of parents.

citizenship by descent only describes the acquisition of citizenship based on the principle of *Jus sanguinis*, or by descent, where at least one parent is a citizen of the state and being born within the territorial limits of the state is not required. The majority of countries adhere to this practice. In some cases, citizenship is conferred through the father or mother exclusively.

dual citizenship recognized indicates whether a state permits a citizen to simultaneously hold citizenship in another state. Many states do not permit dual citizenship, and the voluntary acquisition of citizenship in another country is grounds for revocation of citizenship. Holding dual citizenship makes an individual legally obligated to more than one state and can negate the normal consular protections afforded to citizens outside their original country of citizenship.

residency requirement for naturalization lists the length of time an applicant is required to live in a country before applying for naturalization. In most countries, citizenship can be acquired through the legal process of naturalization. The requirements for naturalization vary but generally include no criminal record, good health, economic wherewithal, and a period of authorized residency.

Civil aircraft registration country code prefix This entry provides the one- or two-character alphanumeric code indicating the nationality of civil aircraft. An aircraft registration number consists of two parts: this alphanumeric code and a registration suffix of one-to-five characters for the specific aircraft. The prefix codes are based on radio call-signs allocated by the International Telecommunications Union (ITU) to each country. Since 1947, the International Civil Aviation Organization (ICAO) has managed code standards and their allocation.

Climate This entry includes a brief description of typical weather regimes throughout the year; in the World entry only, it includes four subfields that describe climate extremes:

ten driest places on earth (average annual precipitation) describes the annual average precipitation measured in both millimeters and inches for selected countries with climate extremes.

ten wettest places on earth (average annual precipitation) describes the annual average precipitation measured in both millimeters and inches for selected countries with climate extremes.

ten coldest places on earth (lowest average monthly temperature) describes temperature measured in both degrees Celsius and Fahrenheit, as well as the month of the year for selected countries with climate extremes.

ten hottest places on earth (highest average monthly temperature) describes the temperature measured both in degrees Celsius and Fahrenheit, as well the month of the year for selected countries with climate extremes.

Coal This field refers to a country's coal and metallurgical coke *production, consumption, exports, imports*, and *proven reserves*. These energy sources include anthracite, metallurgical, bituminous, subbituminous, lignite coal, and metallurgical coke. *Proven reserves* are the quantities of coal that have been assessed as commercially recoverable in the future based on known reservoirs and assuming current economic conditions. Data are reported in metric tons, and one metric ton is 1,000 kilograms.

Coastline This entry gives the total length of the boundary between the land area (including islands) and the sea.

Communications This category deals with the means of exchanging information and includes entries on telephones (fixed and mobile), telecommunication systems, broadcast media, Internet users, and broadband subscriptions.

Communications - note This entry includes miscellaneous communications information not included elsewhere.

Constitution This entry provides information on a country's constitution and includes two subfields, *history* and *amendments*.

history - the dates of previous constitutions and the main steps and dates in formulating and implementing the latest constitution. For countries with one to three previous constitutions, the years are listed; for those with four to nine previous, the entry is listed as "several previous," and for those with 10 or more, the entry is "many previous."

amendments - summarizes the process of amending a country's constitution – from proposal through passage – and the dates of amendments, which are treated in the same manner as the constitution dates. Where appropriate, summaries are composed from English-language translations of non-English constitutions, which derive from official or non-official translations or machine translators.

Terms commonly used to describe constitutional changes are "amended," "revised," or "reformed." In countries such as South Korea and Turkmenistan, sources differ as to whether changes are stated as new constitutions or are amendments/revisions to existing ones.

A few countries, including Canada, Israel, and the UK, have no single constitution document but have various written and unwritten acts, statutes, common laws, and practices that, when taken together, establish a body of fundamental principles or precedents for governance. Some regions (Hong Kong, Macau) and countries (Oman, Saudi Arabia) use the term "basic law" instead of constitution. A number of self-governing dependencies and territories have their own constitutions.

Contraceptive prevalence rate This field gives the percentage of women of reproductive age (15–49) who are married or in union and are using – or whose sexual partner is using – a method of contraception. The contraceptive prevalence rate is an indicator of health services, development, and women's empowerment. It is also useful in understanding, past, present, and future fertility trends, especially in developing countries.

Coordinated Universal Time (UTC) UTC is the international atomic time scale that serves as the basis of timekeeping for most of the world. The hours, minutes, and seconds represent the time of day at the Prime Meridian (0° longitude) located near Greenwich, England, UK, as reckoned from midnight. UTC is calculated by the Bureau International des Poids et Measures (BIPM) in Sevres, France. UTC is the basis for all civil time, with the world divided into time zones expressed as positive or negative differences from UTC. UTC is also referred to as "Zulu time." See the Standard Time Zones of the World map included with the **Reference Maps**.

Country data codes See **Data codes.**

Country map Maps have been produced from the best information available at the time of preparation. Names and/or boundaries may have subsequently changed.

Country name This entry includes all forms of a country's name approved by the US Board on Geographic Names (Italy is used as an example): *conventional long form* (Italian Republic), *conventional short form* (Italy), *local long form* (Repubblica Italiana), *local short form* (Italia), *former* (Kingdom of Italy), as well as the *abbreviation* (if applicable). Additionally, an *etymology* entry explains how the country acquired its name. See also the **Terminology** definition.

Credit ratings This entry provides the current bond ratings for a country or territory from each of the three major credit bureaus (Fitch, Moody's, and Standard & Poors). Rating factors include the current account balance, debt payment history and timeliness, banking and financial operations, future economic outlook, and national economic strength. These three credit agencies constitute more than 95% of the credit evaluation market globally and are the primary sovereign debt ratings considered by international and regional finance institutions.

Current account balance This entry records a country's net trade in goods and services, plus net earnings from rents, interest, profits, and dividends and net transfer payments (such as pension funds and worker remittances) to and from the rest of the world during the period specified. These figures are calculated on an exchange rate basis, i.e., not in purchasing power parity (PPP) terms.

Current health expenditure Current health expenditure (CHE) describes the share of spending on health in each country relative to the size of its economy. It includes expenditures corresponding to the final consumption of health care goods and services and excludes investment, exports, and intermediate consumption. **Note:** Current health expenditure replaces the former Health Expenditures field and is calculated differently.

Currently married women (ages 15–49) This field provides the percentage of married or in-union women among women of reproductive age (15–49).

Data codes This information is presented in Country Data Codes and Hydrographic Data Codes.

Daylight Saving Time (DST) This entry is included for those entities that have adopted a policy of adjusting the official local time forward, usually one hour, from Standard Time during summer months. Such policies are most common in mid-latitude regions.

Death rate This entry gives the average annual number of deaths during a year per 1,000 persons at midyear, which is also known as "crude death rate." The death rate, while only a rough indicator of the mortality situation in a country, accurately indicates the current mortality impact on population growth. This indicator is significantly affected by age distribution, and most countries will eventually show a rise in the overall death rate, in spite of continued decline in mortality at all ages, as declining fertility and increased lifespans result in an aging population.

Debt - external This entry gives the total public and private debt owed to nonresidents, repayable in internationally accepted currencies, goods, or services. Where indicated, these figures represent the present value of external debt – the sum of short-term debt and discounted outstanding service payments for long-term debt over the lifetime of the loans. Data are in current US dollars for the year indicated.

Demographic profile This entry describes a country's key demographic features and trends and how they vary among regional, ethnic, and socioeconomic sub-populations. Some of the topics addressed are population age structure, fertility, health, mortality, poverty, education, and migration.

Dependency ratios Dependency ratios are a measure of the age structure of a population. They calculate the number of individuals that are likely to be economically dependent on the support of others by contrasting the ratio of youths (ages 0–14) and the elderly (ages 65+) to the number of those in the working-age group (ages 15–64). Changes in the dependency ratio provide an indication of potential social support requirements resulting from changes in population age structures. As fertility levels decline, the dependency ratio initially falls because the proportion of youths decreases while the proportion of the population of working age increases. The dependency ratio then increases because the proportion of the population of working age starts to decline as the proportion of elderly persons continues to increase.

total dependency ratio - the ratio of combined youth population (ages 0–14) and elderly population (ages 65+) per 100 people of working age (ages 15–64). A high total dependency ratio indicates that the working-age population and the overall economy face a greater burden to support and provide social services for youth and elderly persons, who are often economically dependent.

youth dependency ratio - the ratio of the youth population (ages 0–14) per 100 people of working age (ages 15–64). A high youth dependency ratio indicates that a country will be spending more on schooling and other services for children.

elderly dependency ratio - the ratio of the elderly population (ages 65+) per 100 people of working age (ages 15–64). Increases in the elderly dependency ratio put added pressure on governments to fund pensions and healthcare.

potential support ratio - the number of working-age people (ages 15–64) per one elderly person (ages 65+). As a population ages, the potential support ratio tends to fall, meaning there are fewer potential workers to support the elderly.

Dependency status This entry describes the formal relationship between a particular nonindependent entity and an independent state.

Dependent areas This entry contains an alphabetical listing of all nonindependent entities associated in some way with a particular independent state.

Diplomatic representation The US Government has diplomatic relations with 190 independent states, including 188 of the 193 UN members (excluded UN members are Bhutan, Cuba, Iran, North Korea, and the US itself). In addition, the US has diplomatic relations with two independent states that are not in the UN – the Holy See and Kosovo – as well as with the EU.

Diplomatic representation from the US This entry includes the *chief of mission, embassy address, mailing address, telephone number, FAX number, email* and *website addresses, branch office* locations, *consulate general* locations, and *consulate* locations.

Diplomatic representation in the US This entry includes the *chief of mission, chancery address, telephone, FAX, email and website addresses, consulate general* locations, and *consulate* locations. The use of the annotated title Appointed Ambassador refers to a new ambassador who has presented his/her credentials to the secretary of state but not the US president. Such ambassadors fulfill all diplomatic functions except meeting with or appearing at functions attended by the president until such time as they formally present their credentials at a White House ceremony.

Disputes - international This entry includes a wide variety of situations that range from traditional bilateral boundary disputes to unilateral claims of one sort or another. References to other situations involving borders or frontiers may also be included, such as resource disputes, geopolitical questions, or irredentist issues; however, inclusion does not necessarily constitute official acceptance or recognition by the US Government.

Drinking water source This entry provides information about access to improved or unimproved drinking water sources available to segments of the population of a country. *Improved* drinking water - use of any of the following sources: piped water into dwelling, yard, or plot; public tap or standpipe; tubewell or borehole; protected dug well; protected spring; or rainwater collection. *Unimproved* drinking water - use of any of the following sources: unprotected dug well; unprotected spring; cart with small tank or drum; tanker truck; surface water, which includes rivers, dams, lakes, ponds, streams, canals or irrigation channels; or bottled water.

Economic overview This entry briefly describes five economic components for a given country:

national economy, including a brief economic history.

domestic markets, including labor and wage markets, as well as brief commentary on economic sector portfolios.

financial power and public finance, including brief discussions of financial market strengths and security, lending/exchange rates (especially if abnormalities exist), and foreign direct investments.

trade power and influence, including brief commentary on chief imports and exports.

regional strategy and efforts, including key partners, regional economic development efforts, and any underlying economic data integrity concerns.

Economy This category includes the entries dealing with the size, development, and management of productive resources such as land, labor, and capital.

Education expenditures This entry provides the public expenditure on education as a percent of GDP.

Electricity This field refers to a country's installed generating capacities, consumption, exports, imports, and transmission/distribution losses.

installed generating capacity - the total capacity of a country's currently operational electric power generation, expressed in kilowatts (kW). A kilowatt produces one hour of continuously run electricity, referred to commonly in many appliances as a kilowatt hour (kWh).

consumption - a country's total electricity generated annually plus any imports and minus exports, expressed in kWh.

exports - a country's total amount of exported electricity in kWh.

imports - a country's total amount of imported electricity in kWh.

transmission/distribution losses - the combined difference between the amount of electricity generated and/or imported and the amount consumed and/or exported.

Electricity access This entry provides information on access to electricity. Due to differences in definitions and methodology from different sources, data quality may vary from country to country. The data — collected from industry reports, national surveys, and international sources — consists of four subfields:

population without electricity provides an estimate of the number of citizens that do not have access to electricity.

electrification – total population is the percent of a country's total population with access to electricity.

electrification – urban areas is the percent of a country's urban population with access to electricity.

electrification – rural areas is the percent of a country's rural population with access to electricity.

Electricity generation sources This field refers a country's energy portfolio of *fossil fuels, nuclear, solar, wind, hydroelectricity, tide and wave, geothermal,* and *biomass and waste.* Portfolios are expressed as a percentage share of a country's total generating capacity.

Elevation This entry includes the *mean elevation* and the elevation extremes, or *lowest point* and *highest point.*

Energy This category includes entries dealing with the production, consumption, import, and export of various forms of energy, including electricity, crude oil, refined petroleum products, and natural gas.

Energy consumption per capita This entry refers to a country's total energy consumption per capita, including the consumption of petroleum, dry natural gas, coal, net nuclear, hydroelectric, and non-hydroelectric renewable electricity. Data are reported in British thermal units per person (Btu/person).

Entities For this website, "independent state" refers to a people politically organized into a sovereign state with a definite territory. "Dependencies" and "areas of special sovereignty" refer to a broad category of political entities that are associated in some way with an independent state. "Country" names used in the table of contents or for page headings are usually the short-form names as approved by the US Board on Geographic Names and may include independent states, dependencies, areas of special sovereignty, or other geographic entities. Some of the entities included in this website are not officially recognized by the US Government. The entities may be categorized as follows:

INDEPENDENT STATES

Afghanistan, Albania, Algeria, Andorra, Angola, Antigua and Barbuda, Argentina, Armenia, Australia, Austria, Azerbaijan, The Bahamas, Bahrain, Bangladesh, Barbados, Belarus, Belgium, Belize, Benin, Bhutan, Bolivia, Bosnia and Herzegovina, Botswana, Brazil, Brunei, Bulgaria, Burkina Faso, Burma, Burundi, Cambodia, Cameroon, Canada, Cape Verde, Central African Republic, Chad, Chile, China, Colombia, Comoros, Democratic Republic of the Congo, Republic of the Congo, Cook Islands, Costa Rica, Cote d'Ivoire, Croatia, Cuba, Cyprus, Czechia, Denmark, Djibouti, Dominica, Dominican Republic, Ecuador, Egypt, El Salvador, Equatorial Guinea, Eritrea, Estonia, Ethiopia, Fiji, Finland, France, Gabon, The Gambia, Georgia, Germany, Ghana, Greece, Grenada, Guatemala, Guinea, Guinea-Bissau, Guyana, Haiti, Holy See, Honduras, Hungary, Iceland, India, Indonesia, Iran, Iraq, Ireland, Israel, Italy, Jamaica, Japan, Jordan, Kazakhstan, Kenya, Kiribati, North Korea, South Korea, Kosovo, Kuwait, Kyrgyzstan, Laos, Latvia, Lebanon, Lesotho, Liberia, Libya, Liechtenstein, Lithuania, Luxembourg, Macedonia, Madagascar, Malawi, Malaysia, Maldives, Mali, Malta, Marshall Islands, Mauritania, Mauritius, Mexico, Federated States of Micronesia, Moldova, Monaco, Mongolia, Montenegro, Morocco, Mozambique, Namibia, Nauru, Nepal, Netherlands, NZ, Nicaragua, Niger, Nigeria, Niue, Norway, Oman, Pakistan, Palau, Panama, Papua New Guinea, Paraguay, Peru, Philippines, Poland, Portugal, Qatar, Romania, Russia, Rwanda, Saint Kitts and Nevis, Saint Lucia, Saint Vincent and the Grenadines, Samoa, San Marino, Sao Tome and Principe, Saudi Arabia, Senegal, Serbia, Seychelles, Sierra Leone, Singapore, Slovakia, Slovenia, Solomon Islands, Somalia, South Africa, South Sudan, Spain, Sri Lanka, Sudan, Suriname, Swaziland, Sweden, Switzerland, Syria, Tajikistan, Tanzania, Thailand, Timor-Leste, Togo, Tonga, Trinidad and Tobago, Tunisia, Turkey, Turkmenistan, Tuvalu, Uganda, Ukraine, UAE, UK, US, Uruguay, Uzbekistan, Vanuatu, Venezuela, Vietnam, Yemen, Zambia, Zimbabwe

OTHER

Taiwan, European Union

DEPENDENCIES AND AREAS OF SPECIAL SOVEREIGNTY

Australia - Ashmore and Cartier Islands, Christmas Island, Cocos (Keeling) Islands, Coral Sea Islands, Heard Island and McDonald Islands, Norfolk Island

China - Hong Kong, Macau
Denmark - Faroe Islands, Greenland
France - Clipperton Island, French Polynesia, French Southern and Antarctic Lands, New Caledonia, Saint Barthelemy, Saint Martin, Saint Pierre and Miquelon, Wallis and Futuna
Netherlands - Aruba, Curacao, Sint Maarten
New Zealand - Tokelau
Norway - Bouvet Island, Jan Mayen, Svalbard
UK - Akrotiri and Dhekelia, Anguilla, Bermuda, British Indian Ocean Territory, British Virgin Islands, Cayman Islands, Falkland Islands, Gibraltar, Guernsey, Jersey, Isle of Man, Montserrat, Pitcairn Islands, Saint Helena, South Georgia and the South Sandwich Islands, Turks and Caicos Islands
US - American Samoa, Baker Island*, Guam, Howland Island*, Jarvis Island*, Johnston Atoll*, Kingman Reef*, Midway Islands*, Navassa Island, Northern Mariana Islands, Palmyra Atoll*, Puerto Rico, Virgin Islands, Wake Island (* consolidated in United States Pacific Island Wildlife Refuges entry)
Antarctica
Gaza Strip
Paracel Islands
Spratly Islands
West Bank

OTHER ENTITIES
Oceans - Arctic Ocean, Atlantic Ocean, Indian Ocean, Pacific Ocean, Southern Ocean
World

Environment - current issues The following terms and abbreviations are used throughout the entry:

acidification - the lowering of soil and water pH due to acid precipitation and deposition usually through precipitation; this process disrupts ecosystem nutrient flows and may kill freshwater fish and plants dependent on more neutral or alkaline conditions (see acid rain).

acid rain - characterized as containing harmful levels of sulfur dioxide or nitrogen oxide; acid rain is damaging and potentially deadly to the earth's fragile ecosystems; acidity is measured using the pH scale where 7 is neutral, values greater than 7 are considered alkaline, and values below 5.6 are considered acid precipitation; note - a pH of 2.4 (the acidity of vinegar) has been measured in rainfall in New England.

biodiversity - also biological diversity; the relative number of species, diverse in form and function, at the genetic, organism, community, and ecosystem level; loss of biodiversity reduces an ecosystem's ability to recover from natural or man-induced disruption.

catchments - assemblages used to capture and retain rainwater and runoff; an important water management technique in areas with limited freshwater resources, such as Gibraltar.

DDT (dichloro-diphenyl-trichloro-ethane) - a colorless, odorless insecticide that has toxic effects on most animals; the use of DDT was banned in the US in 1972.

defoliants - chemicals which cause plants to lose their leaves artificially; often used in agricultural practices for weed control and may have detrimental impacts on human and ecosystem health.

deforestation - the destruction of vast areas of forest (e.g., unsustainable forestry practices, agricultural and range land clearing, and the over exploitation of wood products for use as fuel) without planting new growth.

desertification - the spread of desert-like conditions in arid or semi-arid areas, due to overgrazing, loss of agriculturally productive soils, or climate change.

dredging - the practice of deepening an existing waterway; also, a technique used for collecting bottom-dwelling marine organisms (e.g., shellfish) or harvesting coral, often causing significant destruction of reef and ocean-floor ecosystems.

ecosystems - ecological units composed of complex communities of organisms and their specific environments.

effluents - waste materials, such as smoke or sewage, that are released into the environment.

endangered species - a species that is threatened with extinction through hunting or habitat destruction.

freshwater - water with very low soluble mineral content; sources include lakes, streams, rivers, glaciers, and underground aquifers.

greenhouse gas - a gas that "traps" infrared radiation in the lower atmosphere causing surface warming; water vapor, carbon dioxide, nitrous oxide, methane, hydrofluorocarbons, and ozone are the primary greenhouse gases in the Earth's atmosphere.

groundwater - water sources found below the surface of the earth, often in naturally occurring reservoirs in permeable rock strata; the source for wells and natural springs.

Highlands Water Project - a series of dams constructed jointly by Lesotho and South Africa to redirect Lesotho's abundant water supply into a rapidly growing area in South Africa; it is the largest infrastructure project in southern Africa and also the most costly and controversial.

Inuit Circumpolar Conference (ICC) - represents the roughly 150,000 Inuits of Alaska, Canada, Greenland, and Russia in international environmental issues; a General Assembly convenes every three years to determine the focus of the ICC.

metallurgical plants - industries which specialize in the science, technology, and processing of metals; these plants produce highly concentrated and toxic wastes which can contribute to pollution of ground water and air when not properly disposed.

overgrazing - permanent plant loss due to too many animals grazing limited range land.

ozone shield - a layer of the atmosphere composed of ozone gas (O3) that resides approximately 25 miles above the Earth's surface and absorbs solar ultraviolet radiation that can be harmful to living organisms.

poaching - the illegal killing of animals or fish.

pollution - the contamination of an environment by man-made waste.

potable water - water that is safe to be consumed.

salination - the process through which fresh (drinkable) water becomes salt (undrinkable) water; also involves the accumulation of salts in topsoil caused by evaporation of excessive irrigation water, a process that can eventually render soil incapable of supporting crops.

siltation - occurs when water channels and reservoirs become clotted with silt and mud, a side effect of deforestation and soil erosion.

slash-and-burn agriculture - a rotating cultivation technique in which trees are cut down and burned in order to clear land for temporary agriculture; the land is used until its productivity declines at which point a new plot is selected and the process repeats.

soil degradation - damage to the land's productive capacity because of poor agricultural practices such as the excessive use of pesticides or fertilizers, soil compaction from heavy equipment, or erosion of topsoil, eventually resulting in reduced ability to produce agricultural products.

soil erosion - the removal of soil by the action of water or wind, compounded by poor agricultural practices, deforestation, overgrazing, and desertification.

ultraviolet (UV) radiation - a portion of the electromagnetic energy emitted by the sun and naturally filtered in the upper atmosphere by the ozone layer.

Environment - international agreements This entry separates country participation in international environmental agreements into two levels: *party to* and *signed, but not ratified.* Agreements are listed in alphabetical order by the abbreviated form of the full name.

Environmental agreements This information is presented in Selected International Environmental Agreements, which includes the name, abbreviation, date opened for signature, date entered into force, objective, and parties by category.

Ethnic groups This entry provides an ordered listing of ethnic groups starting with the largest and normally includes the percent of total population.

Exchange rates This entry provides the average annual price of a country's monetary unit for the time period specified, expressed in units of local currency per US dollar, as determined by international market forces or by official fiat. The International Organization for Standardization (ISO) 4217 alphabetic currency code for the national medium of exchange is presented in parenthesis. Closing daily exchange rates are not presented in *The World Factbook* but are used to convert stock values – e.g., the market value of publicly traded shares – to US dollars as of the specified date.

Executive branch This entry includes five subentries: *chief of state; head of government; cabinet; elections/appointments; election results. Chief of state* includes the name, title, and beginning date in office of the titular leader of the country who represents the state at official and ceremonial functions, but who may not be involved with the day-to-day activities of the government. *Head of government* includes the name and title of the person designated to manage the executive branch of the government, as well as the beginning date in office. *Cabinet* includes the official name and the method of member selection. *Elections/appointments* includes the process for accession to office, date of the last election, and date of the next election. *Election results* includes each candidate's political affiliation and percentage of direct popular vote or indirect legislative/parliamentary vote.

The executive branches in approximately 80% of the world's countries have separate chiefs of state and heads of government; for the remainder, the chief of state is also the head of government. In dependencies, territories, and collectivities of sovereign countries – except those of the US – representatives are appointed to serve as chiefs of state.

Heads of government in the majority of countries are appointed by the president, monarch, or the majority party in the legislative body. Excluding countries where the chief of state is also head of government, the head of government is directly elected through popular vote in only a few countries.

Most executive branches have a cabinet, or a group of advisers to the country's leader. The majority of cabinets are appointed by the chief of state or head of government, sometimes in consultation with the legislature. Legislatures independently elect cabinets in only about a dozen countries.

Exports This entry provides the total US dollar amount of merchandise exports on an f.o.b. (free on board) basis. These figures are calculated on an exchange rate basis, i.e., not in purchasing power parity (PPP) terms.

Exports - commodities This entry provides a listing of the highest-valued exported commodities.

Exports - partners This entry provides a rank ordering of trading partners starting with the most important; it sometimes includes the percentage of total dollar value.

Flag description This entry provides a written flag description. The flags of independent states are used by their dependencies unless there is an officially recognized local flag. Some disputed entities and other areas do not have flags.

Flag graphic Most country profiles include an image of the country's flag. The flags of independent states are used by their dependencies unless there is an officially recognized local flag. Some disputed entities and other areas do not have flags.

Food insecurity Three levels of food-related crises are described in this field: countries facing an *exceptional shortfall in aggregate food production/supplies* as a result of crop failure, natural disasters, import or distribution disruptions, excessive post-harvest losses, or other supply bottlenecks; countries with *widespread lack of access*, where a majority of the population is unable to procure food due to very low incomes, very high food prices, or restricted movement within the country; and countries with *severe localized food insecurity* due to a refugee influx, internally displaced persons, or combinations of crop failure and deep poverty.

GDP - composition, by end use This entry shows who does the spending in an economy: consumers, businesses, government, and foreigners. The distribution gives the percentage contribution to total GDP of *household consumption, government consumption, investment in fixed capital, investment in inventories, exports of goods and services, and imports of goods and services.* Figures may not total 100% due to rounding or gaps in data collection.

household consumption consists of expenditures by resident households, and by nonprofit institutions that serve households, on goods and services that individuals consume. This includes consumption of both domestically produced and foreign goods and services.

government consumption consists of government expenditures on goods and services. These figures exclude government transfer payments, such as interest on debt, unemployment, and social security.

investment in fixed capital consists of total business spending on fixed assets, such as factories, machinery, equipment, dwellings, and raw materials, which provide the basis for future production. It is measured gross of asset depreciation, i.e., it includes investment that merely replaces worn-out or scrapped capital. Earlier versions of *The World Factbook* referred to this concept as Investment (gross fixed), and that data now have been moved to this new field.

investment in inventories consists of net changes to the stock of outputs that are still held by the units that produce them, awaiting further sale to an end user, such as automobiles sitting on a dealer's lot or groceries on the store shelves. This figure may be positive or negative. If the stock of unsold output increases during the relevant time period, *investment in inventories* is positive, but, if the stock of unsold goods declines, it will be negative.

exports of goods and services consist of sales, barter, gifts, or grants of goods and services from residents to nonresidents.

imports of goods and services consist of purchases, barter, or receipts of gifts, or grants of goods and services to residents from nonresidents. *Exports* are treated as a positive, while imports are treated as a negative. Imports are entered as a negative item to offset the fact that the expenditure figures for consumption, investment, government, and exports also include expenditures on imports. These imports contribute directly to foreign GDP but only indirectly to domestic GDP. Because of this negative offset for imports of goods and services, the sum of the other five items, excluding imports, will always total more than 100 percent of GDP.

GDP - composition, by sector of origin This entry shows where production takes place in an economy. The distribution gives the percentage value-added contribution of *agriculture, industry,* and *services* to total GDP after adding outputs and subtracting intermediate inputs. Agriculture includes farming, fishing, hunting, and forestry. Industry includes mining, manufacturing, energy production, and construction. Services cover government activities, communications, transportation, finance, and all other private economic activities that do not produce material goods. Figures may not total 100 percent due to non-allocated consumption, including financial intermediary services indirectly measured (FISIM) not allocated by industry, and taxes less subsidies on products.

GDP (official exchange rate) This entry gives the gross domestic product (GDP) or value of all final goods and services produced within a nation in a given year. A nation's GDP at official exchange rates (OER) is the home-currency-denominated annual GDP figure divided by the bilateral average US exchange rate with that country in that year.

GDP methodology In the **Economy** category, GDP dollar estimates for countries are reported both on an official exchange rate (OER) and a purchasing power parity (PPP) basis.

The PPP method uses standardized international dollar price weights, which are applied to the quantities of final goods and services produced in a given economy. The data derived from the PPP method probably provide the best available starting point for comparisons of economic strength and well-being between countries. In contrast, the currency exchange rate method involves a variety of international and domestic financial forces that may not capture the value of domestic output. Whereas PPP estimates for OECD countries are quite reliable, PPP estimates for developing countries are often rough approximations.

GDP derived using the OER method should be used to calculate the share of items such as exports, imports, military expenditures, external debt, or the current account balance, because the dollar values presented in the *Factbook* for these items have been converted at official exchange rates, not at PPP. Comparison of OER

GDP with PPP GDP may also indicate whether a currency is over- or under-valued. If OER GDP is smaller than PPP GDP, the official exchange rate may be undervalued, and vice versa.

note: The numbers for GDP and other economic data should not be chained together from successive versions of the *Factbook* because of changes in the US dollar measurement, revisions of data from statistical agencies, use of new or different sources of information, and changes in national statistical methods and practices.

Geographic coordinates This entry includes rounded latitude and longitude figures for the centroid or center point of a country expressed in degrees and minutes; it is based on the locations provided in the Geographic Names Server (GNS), maintained by the National Geospatial-Intelligence Agency on behalf of the US Board on Geographic Names.

Geographic names This information is presented in list form in Geographic Names. It includes alternate, former, local, and regional names for one or more related *Factbook* entries. Spellings are normally, but not always, those approved by the US Board on Geographic Names (BGN). Alternate names and additional information are included in parentheses.

Geographic overview This entry, which appears only in the Geography category under the World entry, provides basic geographic information about the earth's oceans and continents. The entry also lists all of the countries that compose each continent.

Geography This category includes the entries dealing with the natural environment and the effects of human activity on it.

Geography - note This entry includes miscellaneous geographic information of significance not included elsewhere.

Geoparks United Nations Educational, Scientific and Cultural Organization (UNESCO) Global Geoparks are geographic areas with sites and landscapes of international geological significance. Global Geoparks use their geological heritage, in connection with all other aspects of the area's natural and cultural heritage, to enhance awareness and understanding of key environmental issues facing society.

Gini Index coefficient - distribution of family income This entry measures the degree of inequality in the distribution of family income in a country. The index is calculated from the Lorenz curve, in which cumulative family income is plotted against the number of families arranged from the poorest to the richest. The index is the ratio of (a) the area between a country's Lorenz curve and the 45 degree helping line to (b) the entire triangular area under the 45 degree line. The more nearly equal a country's income distribution, the closer its Lorenz curve to the 45 degree line and the lower its Gini index, e.g., a Scandinavian country with an index of 25. The more unequal a country's income distribution, the farther its Lorenz curve from the 45 degree line and the higher its Gini index, e.g., a Sub-Saharan country with an index of 50.

GNP Gross national product (GNP) is the value of all final goods and services produced within a nation in a given year, plus income earned by its citizens abroad, minus income earned by foreigners from domestic production. The *Factbook*, following current practice, uses GDP rather than GNP to measure national production. In certain countries, however, net remittances from citizens working abroad may be a significant component of the national economy.

Government This category includes the entries dealing with the system for the adoption and administration of public policy.

Government - note This entry includes miscellaneous government information of significance not included elsewhere.

Government type This entry lists the basic form of government for each country. Definitions of the governmental terms are as follows (note that for some countries more than one definition applies):

absolute monarchy - a form of government where the monarch rules unhindered by laws, constitution, or legally organized opposition.

anarchy - a condition of lawlessness or political disorder brought about by the absence of governmental authority.

authoritarian - a form of government in which state authority is imposed onto many aspects of citizens' lives.

commonwealth - a nation, state, or other political entity founded on law and united by a compact of the people for the common good.

communist - a system of government in which the state plans and controls the economy and a single – often authoritarian – party holds power; the state imposes controls and eliminates private ownership of property or capital, while claiming to make progress toward a higher social order in which people equally share all goods in a classless society.

confederacy (confederation) - a union by compact or treaty between states, provinces, or territories that creates a central government with limited powers; the constituent entities retain supreme authority, except in matters delegated to the central government.

constitutional - a government operating under an authoritative document (constitution) that sets forth the system of fundamental laws and principles that determine the nature, functions, and limits of that government.

constitutional democracy - a form of government in which the sovereign power of the people is spelled out in a governing constitution.

constitutional monarchy - a system of government in which a monarch is guided by a constitution whereby his/her rights, duties, and responsibilities are spelled out in written law or by custom.

democracy - a form of government in which the supreme power is retained by the people, but which is usually exercised indirectly through a system of representation and delegated authority periodically renewed.

democratic republic - a state in which the supreme power rests in the body of citizens entitled to vote for officers and representatives responsible to them.

dictatorship - a form of government in which a ruler or small clique wield absolute power (not restricted by a constitution or laws).

ecclesiastical - a government administrated by a church.

emirate - similar to a monarchy or sultanate, but a government in which the supreme power is in the hands of an emir (the ruler of a Muslim state); the emir may be an absolute overlord or a sovereign with constitutionally limited authority.

federal (federation) - a form of government in which sovereign power is formally divided – usually by means of a constitution – between a central authority and a number of constituent regions (states, colonies, or provinces), so that each region retains some management of its internal affairs; differs from a confederacy in that the central government exerts influence directly on both individuals and the regional units.

federal republic - a state in which the powers of the central government are restricted and in which the component parts (states, colonies, or provinces) retain a degree of self-government; ultimate sovereign power rests with the voters who chose their governmental representatives.

Islamic republic - a particular form of government adopted by some Muslim states; although such a state is, in theory, a theocracy, it remains a republic, but its laws are required to be compatible with the laws of Islam.

Maoism - the theory and practice of Marxism-Leninism developed in China by Mao Zedong (Mao Tse-tung), which states that a continuous revolution is necessary if the leaders of a communist state are to keep in touch with the people.

Marxism - the political, economic, and social principles espoused by 19th century economist Karl Marx; he viewed history as a progression from a class struggle of the proletariat (workers) exploited by capitalists (business owners), to a socialist "dictatorship of the proletariat," and finally to a classless society (communism).

Marxism-Leninism - an expanded form of communism developed by Vladimir Lenin from Karl Marx's doctrines; Lenin saw imperialism as the final stage of capitalism and shifted the focus of the workers' struggle from developed to underdeveloped countries.

monarchy - a government in which the supreme power is in the hands of a monarch who reigns over a state or territory, usually for life and by hereditary right; the monarch may be either a sole absolute ruler or a sovereign – such as a king, queen, or prince – with constitutionally limited authority.

oligarchy - a government in which a small group of individuals exercises control.
parliamentary democracy - a political system in which the party with the most votes in the legislature (parliament) selects the government – a prime minister, premier, or chancellor and the cabinet ministers; by this system, the government has a responsibility to the people as well as to the parliament.
parliamentary government (cabinet-parliamentary government) - a government in which a legislature or parliament nominates members of an executive branch (the cabinet and its leader – a prime minister, premier, or chancellor); this type of government can be dissolved at will by the parliament (legislature) through a no-confidence vote, or the leader of the cabinet may dissolve the parliament if it can no longer function.
parliamentary monarchy - a state headed by a monarch who is not actively involved in policy formation or implementation and may have only a ceremonial capacity; governmental leadership is carried out by a cabinet and its head – a prime minister, premier, or chancellor – who are drawn from a legislature (parliament).
presidential - a system of government where the executive branch exists separately from a legislature (to which it is generally not accountable).
republic - a representative democracy in which the people's elected deputies (representatives), not the people themselves, vote on legislation.
socialism - a government in which the means of planning, producing, and distributing goods is controlled by a central government that theoretically seeks a more just and equitable distribution of property and labor; in actuality, most socialist governments have ended up being no more than dictatorships over workers by a ruling elite.
sultanate - similar to a monarchy, but a government in which the supreme power is in the hands of a sultan (the head of a Muslim state); the sultan may be an absolute ruler or a sovereign with constitutionally limited authority.
theocracy - a form of government in which a deity is recognized as the supreme civil ruler, but ecclesiastical authorities interpret (bishops, mullahs, etc.) the deity's laws; a government subject to religious authority.
totalitarian - a government that seeks to subordinate the individual to the state by controlling not only all political and economic matters, but also the attitudes, values, and beliefs of its population.

Greenwich Mean Time (GMT) The mean solar time at the Greenwich Meridian, Greenwich, England, with the hours and days, since 1925, reckoned from midnight. GMT is now a historical term having been replaced by UTC on 1 January 1972. See **Coordinated Universal Time.**

Gross domestic product See **GDP**

Gross national product See **GNP**

Gross reproduction rate This entry presents the average number of daughters born alive that a group of women would have in their lifetime if the age-specific fertility rate were to apply to them in a given period, usually a calendar year. It is a measure of replacement fertility that indicates whether the current generation of daughters will replace the preceding generation of women.

Gross world product See **GWP**

GWP This entry gives the gross world product (GWP) or aggregate value of all final goods and services produced worldwide in a given year.

Heliports This entry gives the total number of heliports with helicopter pads and no runways available for fixed-wing aircraft.

Hospital bed density This entry provides the number of hospital beds per 1,000 people; it serves as a general measure of inpatient service availability. Hospital beds include inpatient beds available in public, private, general, and specialized hospitals and rehabilitation centers. In most cases, beds for both acute and chronic care are included.

Household income or consumption by percentage share Data on household income or consumption come from household surveys, with the results adjusted for household size. Nations use different standards and procedures in collecting and adjusting the data. Surveys based on income will normally show a more unequal distribution than surveys based on consumption.

Hydrographic data codes See **Data codes**

Illicit drugs This entry gives information on the five categories of illicit drugs – narcotics, stimulants, depressants (sedatives), hallucinogens, and cannabis. These categories include many drugs legally produced and prescribed by doctors as well as those illegally produced and sold outside medical channels.
Cannabis (*Cannabis sativa*) is the common hemp plant, which provides hallucinogens with some sedative properties, and includes marijuana (pot, Acapulco gold, grass, reefer), tetrahydrocannabinol (THC, Marinol), hashish (hash), and hashish oil (hash oil).
Coca (mostly *Erythroxylum coca*) is a bush with leaves that contain the stimulant used to make cocaine. Coca is not to be confused with cocoa, which comes from cacao seeds and is used in making chocolate, cocoa, and cocoa butter.
Cocaine is a stimulant derived from the leaves of the coca bush.
Depressants (sedatives) are drugs that reduce tension and anxiety and include chloral hydrate, barbiturates (Amytal, Nembutal, Seconal, phenobarbital), benzodiazepines (Librium, Valium), methaqualone (Quaalude), glutethimide (Doriden), and others (Equanil, Placidyl, Valmid).
Drugs are any chemical substances that effect a physical, mental, emotional, or behavioral change in an individual.
Drug abuse is the excessive use of any licit or illicit chemical substance that results in physical, mental, emotional, or behavioral impairment in an individual.
Hallucinogens are drugs that affect sensation, thinking, self-awareness, and emotion. Hallucinogens include LSD (acid, microdot), mescaline and peyote (mexc, buttons, cactus), amphetamine variants (PMA, STP, DOB), phencyclidine (PCP, angel dust, hog), phencyclidine analogues (PCE, PCPy, TCP), and others (psilocybin, psilocyn).
Hashish is the resinous exudate of the cannabis or hemp plant (*Cannabis sativa*).
Heroin is a semisynthetic derivative of morphine.
Mandrax is a trade name for methaqualone, a pharmaceutical depressant.
Marijuana is the dried leaf of the cannabis or hemp plant (*Cannabis sativa*).
Methaqualone is a pharmaceutical depressant, referred to as mandrax in Southwest Asia and Africa.
Narcotics are drugs that relieve pain, often induce sleep, and refer to opium, opium derivatives, and synthetic substitutes. Natural narcotics include opium (paregoric, parepectolin), morphine (MS-Contin, Roxanol), codeine (Tylenol with codeine, Empirin with codeine, Robitussin AC), and thebaine. Semisynthetic narcotics include heroin (horse, smack), and hydromorphone (Dilaudid). Synthetic narcotics include meperidine or Pethidine (Demerol, Mepergan), methadone (Dolophine, Methadose), and others (Darvon, Lomotil).
Opium is the brown, gummy exudate of the incised, unripe seedpod of the opium poppy.
Opium poppy (*Papaver somniferum*) is the source for the natural and semisynthetic narcotics.
Poppy straw is the entire cut and dried opium poppy-plant material, other than the seeds. Opium is extracted from poppy straw in commercial operations that produce the drug for medical use.
Qat (kat, khat) is a stimulant from the buds or leaves of *Catha edulis* that is chewed or drunk as tea.
Stimulants are drugs that relieve mild depression, increase energy and activity, and include cocaine (coke, snow, crack), amphetamines (Desoxyn, Dexedrine), ephedrine, ecstasy (clarity, essence, doctor, Adam), phenmetrazine (Preludin), methylphenidate (Ritalin), and others (Cylert, Sanorex, Tenuate).

Imports This entry provides the total US dollar amount of merchandise imports on a c.i.f. (cost, insurance, and freight) or f.o.b. (free on board) basis. These figures are calculated on an exchange rate basis, i.e., not in purchasing power parity (PPP) terms.

Imports - commodities This entry provides a listing of the highest-valued imported commodities.

Imports - partners This entry provides a rank ordering of trading partners starting with the most important; it sometimes includes the percentage of total dollar value.

Independence For most countries, this entry gives the date that sovereignty was achieved and from which nation, empire, or trusteeship. For the other countries, the date given may not represent "independence" in the strict sense, but rather some significant nationhood event such as the traditional founding date or the date of unification, federation, confederation, establishment, fundamental change in the form of government, or state succession. For a number of countries, the establishment of statehood was a lengthy evolutionary process occurring over decades or even centuries; in such cases, several significant dates are cited. Dependent areas include the notation "none" followed by the nature of their dependency status. See also the **Terminology** definition.

Industrial production growth rate This entry gives the annual percentage increase in industrial production (includes manufacturing, mining, and construction).

Industries This entry provides a rank ordering of industries starting with the largest by value of annual output.

Infant mortality rate This entry gives the number of deaths of infants under one year old in a given year per 1,000 live births in the same year. Data is provided for the *total* per 1,000 live births, as well as the number of *male* and *female* per 1,000 live births.

Inflation rate (consumer prices) This entry provides the annual inflation rate, as calculated by the percentage change in current consumer prices from the previous year's consumer prices.

International disputes see **Disputes - international**

International law organization participation This entry includes information on a country's acceptance of jurisdiction of the International Court of Justice (ICJ) and of the International Criminal Court (ICCt); 61 countries have accepted ICJ jurisdiction with reservations and 12 have accepted ICJ jurisdiction without reservations; 123 countries and the Palestine Liberation Organization have accepted ICCt jurisdiction. Appendix B: International Organizations and Groups explains the differing mandates of the ICJ and ICCt. Consult the online edition of *The World Factbook.*

International organization participation This entry lists in alphabetical order by abbreviation the international organizations in which a country is a member or participates in some other way.

International organizations This information is presented in International Organizations and Groups which includes the name, abbreviation, date established, aim, members by category, and, when available, contact information (including address, phone, fax, email address, and website address).

Internet country code This entry includes the two-letter codes maintained by the International Organization for Standardization (ISO) in the ISO 3166 Alpha-2 list and used by the Internet Assigned Numbers Authority (IANA) to establish country-coded top-level domains (ccTLDs).

Internet users This entry gives the *total* number of individuals within a country who can access the Internet at home, via any device type (computer or mobile) and connection. The *percent of population* with Internet access (the penetration rate) helps gauge how widespread Internet use is within a country. Statistics may include users who access the Internet at least several times a week and those who access it only once within a period of several months.

Introduction This category includes one entry, **Background.**

Investment (gross fixed) This entry records total business spending on fixed assets, such as factories, machinery, equipment, dwellings, and inventories of raw materials, which provide the basis for future production. It is the measured gross of the depreciation of the assets, meaning that it includes investment that merely replaces worn-out or scrapped capital.

Irrigated land This entry gives the number of square kilometers of land area that is artificially supplied with water.

Judicial branch This entry includes three subfields. The *highest court(s)* subfield includes the name(s) of a country's highest court(s), the number and titles of the judges, and the types of cases the court hears. A number of countries have separate constitutional courts. The *judge selection and term of office* subfield includes the organizations and associated officials responsible for nominating and appointing judges, and a brief description of the process. Also included are judges' tenures, which can range from a few years to lifelong appointments. The *subordinate courts* subfield lists the lower courts in a country's court system hierarchy. A few countries with federal-style governments also have separate state- or province-level court systems, though generally the systems all interact.

Labor force This entry contains the total labor force figure.

Land boundaries This entry contains the *total* length of all land boundaries and the individual lengths for each of the contiguous *border countries.* When available, official lengths published by national statistical agencies are used. Because surveying methods differ, contiguous countries may report different country border lengths.

Land use This entry lists three different types of land use for a country's total land area: *agricultural land, forest,* and *other.*

Agricultural land is further divided into *arable land* (cultivated for crops that are replanted after each harvest), *permanent crops* (crops that are not replanted after each harvest, including land under flowering shrubs, fruit trees, nut trees, and vines), and *permanent pastures and meadows* (used for at least five years to grow herbaceous forage, either cultivated or growing naturally). *Forest* is land spanning more than 0.5 hectare with trees higher than five meters and a canopy cover of more than 10%, including windbreaks, shelterbelts, and corridors of trees greater than 0.5 hectare and at least 20 m wide. Land classified as *other* includes built-up areas, roads and other transportation features, barren land, and wasteland.

Languages This entry provides a listing of languages spoken in each country and specifies any that are official national or regional languages. When data is available, the languages spoken in each country are broken down according to the percent of the total population speaking each language as a first language, unless otherwise noted. For those countries without available data, languages are listed in rank order based on prevalence, starting with the most-spoken language.

Legal system This entry provides descriptions of countries' legal systems, which are modeled on elements of five main types: civil law (including French law, the Napoleonic Code, Roman law, Roman-Dutch law, and Spanish law); common law (including United States law); customary law; mixed or pluralistic law; and religious law (including Islamic law). An additional type of legal system – international law, which governs nations' interactions – is also addressed below.

Civil Law - the most widespread type of legal system in the world, applied in various forms in approximately 150 countries. Also referred to as European continental law, it is derived mainly from the Roman *Corpus Juris Civilus* (Body of Civil Law), a collection of laws and legal interpretations compiled under the East Roman (Byzantine) Emperor Justinian I between A.D. 528 and 565. The major feature of civil law systems is that the laws are organized into systematic written codes. The sources recognized as authoritative are principally legislation – especially codifications in constitutions or government statutes – and secondarily custom.

Common Law - often called "English common law," England and Wales use the system in the UK, and it is also in force in approximately 80 countries with ties to the former British Empire. English common law reflects Biblical influences as well as remnants of legal systems imposed by early conquerors, including the Romans, Anglo-Saxons, and Normans. Some legal scholars attribute the system to King Henry II (r.1154–1189), who established the king's court to replace locally administered laws and made laws "common" to the entire English realm. The foundation of the system is "legal precedent," often referred to as *stare decisis* ("to stand by things decided"), in which judges must follow the precedent set by earlier court decisions.

Customary Law - as the name implies, this system is based on the customs of a community. It serves as the basis of or has influenced the laws in approximately 40 countries – mostly in Africa, but some in the Pacific Islands, Europe, and the Near East. Customary law is also referred to as "primitive law," "unwritten law," "indigenous law," and "folk law." The earliest legal systems were customary and usually developed in small agrarian and hunter-gatherer communities. Customary legal systems are seldom written down, regulate social relations, and are agreed upon by community members. If a law is broken, resolution tends to be reconciliatory rather than punitive.

European Union (EU) Law - a variant of international law unique to a subset of European countries. Also known as Community Law or supranational law, the rights of sovereign European nations are limited in relation to one another, with EU law operating in tandem with the 27 member states' legal systems. The European Court of Justice (ECJ), established in 1952 by the Treaty of Paris, has been largely responsible for the development of EU law. Fundamental principles include: *subsidiarity* - issues are handled by the smallest, lowest, or least centralized competent authority; *proportionality* - the EU may only act to the extent needed to achieve its objectives; *conferral* - the EU is a union of member states, and members grant all its authorities; *legal certainty* - requires that rules be clear and precise; and *precautionary principle* - if an action or policy might cause severe or irreversible harm to the public or the environment, in the absence of a scientific consensus that harm would not ensue, the burden of proof falls on those who advocate the action.

French Law - a type of codified civil law that is used in France and serves as the basis for or is mixed with other legal systems in approximately 50 countries in North Africa, the Near East, and French territories and dependencies. Prior to the French Revolution (1789–1799), laws in the northern areas of present-day France were mostly local customs based on privileges and exemptions granted by kings and feudal lords, while in the southern areas Roman law predominated. Napoleon Bonaparte introduced what is now called the Napoleonic Code or the Civil Code in the early 1800s; many of these major reforms remain, with extensive amendments, part of France's current legal structure. French law distinguishes between "public law," which relates to government, the French Constitution, public administration, and criminal law, and "private law," which covers issues between private citizens or corporations.

International Law - the body of customary and treaty rules accepted as legally binding by states in their relations with each other. There are three separate disciplines: public international law, which governs the relationship between provinces and international entities and includes treaty law, law of the sea, international criminal law, and international humanitarian law; private international law, which addresses legal jurisdiction; and supranational law, a legal framework of regional agreements. At present, the European Union is the only entity under a supranational legal system. Modern international law developed as European nation-states emerged beginning in the early 16th century. The sources are set out in Article 38-1 of the Statute of the International Court of Justice in the UN Charter.

Islamic Law - the most widespread type of religious law, it is the legal system in over 30 countries, particularly in the Near East but also in Central and South Asia, Africa, and Indonesia. In many countries, Islamic law operates in tandem with a civil law system and is embodied in the *sharia*, an Arabic word meaning "the right path." Sharia covers all aspects of public and private life and organizes them into five categories: obligatory, recommended, permitted, disliked, and forbidden. The primary sources of sharia law are the Qur'an and the Sunnah. Traditional Sunni Muslims also recognize the consensus of Muhammad's companions and Islamic jurists on certain issues, called *ijmas*, and various forms of reasoning, including analogy by legal scholars, referred to as *qiyas*. Shia Muslims reject ijmas and qiyas as sources of sharia law.

Mixed Law - also referred to as pluralistic law, mixed law consists of elements of some or all of the other main types of legal systems. The mixed systems of a number of countries came about when colonial powers overlaid their own legal systems on colonized regions but retained elements of the colonies' existing systems.

Napoleonic Civil Code - a type of civil law, referred to as the Civil Code or *Code Civil des Français*, that forms part of the French legal system and underpins the legal systems of Bolivia, Egypt, Lebanon, Poland, and the US state of Louisiana. The Civil Code was established under Napoleon Bonaparte, enacted in 1804, and officially designated the *Code Napoleon* in 1807. This legal system combined the Teutonic civil law tradition of France's northern provinces with the Roman law tradition of the southern and eastern regions. The Civil Code has similarities with the Roman *Body of Civil Law* (see Civil Law above). As enacted in 1804, the Code addressed personal status, property, and the acquisition of property, with later additions including civil procedures, commercial law, criminal law and procedures, and a penal code.

Religious Law - a legal system that stems from the sacred text of a religious tradition and in most cases professes to cover all aspects of life as part of devotional obligations. Inalterability is implied, because the word of God cannot be amended or legislated, but human elaboration allows for a detailed legal system. The main types of religious law are *sharia* in Islam, *halakha* in Judaism, and canon law in some Christian groups. Sharia is the most widespread (see Islamic Law) and is the sole system for some countries, including Iran, the Maldives, and Saudi Arabia. No country is fully governed by halakha, but Jewish people may decide to settle disputes through Jewish courts. Canon law is not considered a divine law because it is viewed as human law inspired by God. Canon law regulates the internal ordering of the Roman Catholic Church, the Eastern Orthodox Church, and the Anglican Communion.

Roman Law - a type of civil law developed in ancient Rome and practiced from the time of the city's founding (traditionally 753 B.C.) until the fall of the Western Empire in the 5th century A.D. Roman law remained the legal system of the Byzantine (Eastern Empire) until the fall of Constantinople in 1453. Preserved fragments of the first legal text, known as the Law of the Twelve Tables, date from the 5th century B.C. and contain specific provisions designed to change prevailing customary law. Later, emperors asserted their authority as the ultimate source of law. The basis for Roman law was the idea that the exact form – not the intention – of words or of actions produced legal consequences. A comprehensive code was published in the late sixth century A.D. (see Civil Law). Roman law served as the basis for legal systems developed in a number of continental European countries.

Roman-Dutch Law - a type of civil law based on Roman law as applied in the Netherlands. Roman-Dutch law is the foundation for legal systems in seven African countries, as well as Guyana, Indonesia, and Sri Lanka. It originated in the province of Holland and expanded throughout the Netherlands and was instituted in a number of sub-Saharan African countries during the Dutch colonial period. The Dutch jurist/philosopher Hugo Grotius was the first to attempt to reduce Roman-Dutch civil law into a system in his *Jurisprudence of Holland* (1620–21), and the Dutch historian/lawyer Simon van Leeuwen coined the term "Roman-Dutch law" in 1652. It replaced by the French Civil Code in 1809.

Spanish Law - a type of civil law that is often referred to as the Spanish Civil Code. It is the present legal system of Spain and the basis of legal systems in 12 countries, mostly in Central and South America. The Spanish Civil Code reflects a complex mixture of customary, Roman, Napoleonic, local, and modern codified law. The Visigoth invaders in the 5th to 7th centuries were the earliest major influence, and the Christian Reconquest of Spain in the 11th through 15th centuries saw the development of customary law, which combined canon (religious) and Roman law. During several centuries of Hapsburg and Bourbon rule, systematic recompilations of the existing national legal system were attempted, but these often conflicted with local and regional customary civil laws. A national civil law system was finally enacted in 1889 as the Spanish Civil Code, which separates public and private law. Public law includes constitutional law, administrative law, criminal law, process law, financial and tax law, and international public law. Private law includes civil law, commercial law, labor law, and international private law.

United States Law - a type of common law and the basis of the US legal system. This system has several layers, which is due in part to the division between federal and state law. The United States was originally founded as a union of 13 colonies that later became the first states. The US Constitution, implemented in 1789, began shifting power away from the states and toward the federal government, though the states today retain substantial legal authority. US law draws from four sources: *constitutional law*, *statutory law*, *administrative regulations*, and *case law*. Constitutional law is based on the US Constitution and serves as the supreme federal law, with state constitutions governing state law. US statutory law is legislation enacted by the US Congress and is codified in the United States Code. The 50 state legislatures have similar authority to enact state statutes. Administrative law is the authority delegated to federal and state executive agencies. Case law, also referred to as common law, covers areas where constitutional or statutory law is lacking. Case law is a collection of judicial decisions, customs, and general principles that began in England centuries ago, that were adopted in America at the time of the Revolution, and that continue to develop today.

Legislative branch This entry has three subfields. The *description* subfield provides the legislative structure (unicameral – single house; bicameral – an upper and a lower house); formal name(s); number of member seats; types of constituencies or voting districts (single seat, multi-seat, nationwide); electoral voting system(s); and member term of office. The elections subfield includes the dates of the last election and next election. The *election results* subfield lists *percent of vote by party/coalition* and *number of seats by party/coalition* in the last election (in bicameral legislatures, upper house results are listed first). In general, parties with less than four seats and less than four percent of the vote are aggregated and listed as "other," and non-party-affiliated seats are listed as "independent." Also, the entries for some countries include two sets of *percent of vote by party* and *seats by party*; the former reflects results following a formal election announcement, and the latter – following a mid-term or byelection – reflects changes in a legislature's political party composition.

Of the approximately 240 countries with legislative bodies, approximately two-thirds are unicameral, and the remainder, bicameral. The selection of legislative members is typically governed by a country's constitution and/or its electoral laws. In general, members can be directly elected by a country's eligible voters using a defined electoral system; indirectly elected or selected by its province, state, or department legislatures; or appointed by the country's executive body. Legislative members in many countries are selected both directly and indirectly, and the electoral laws of some countries reserve seats for women and various ethnic and minority groups.

Worldwide, the two predominant direct voting systems are plurality/majority and proportional representation. The most common of the several plurality/majority systems is simple majority vote, or first-past-the-post, in which the candidate receiving the most votes is elected. Another common plurality/majority system – absolute majority or two-round – requires that candidates win at least 50 percent of the votes to be elected. If none of the candidates meets that vote threshold in the initial election, a second poll or "runoff" is held for the two top vote getters, and the candidate receiving a simple vote majority is declared the winner. Other plurality/majority voting systems, referred to as preferential voting and generally used in multi-seat constituencies, are block vote and single non-transferable vote, in which voters cast their ballots by ranking their candidate preferences from highest to lowest.

Proportional-representation electoral systems – in contrast to plurality/majority systems – award legislative seats to political parties in approximate proportion to the number of votes each receives. For example, in a 100-member legislature, if Party A receives 50 percent of the total vote, Party B, 30 percent, and Party C, 20 percent, then Party A would be awarded 50 seats, Party B 30 seats, and Party C 20 seats. There are various forms of proportional representation and the degree of reaching proportionality varies.

Many countries – both unicameral and bicameral – use a mix of electoral methods, in which a portion of legislative seats are awarded using one system, such as plurality/majority, while the remaining seats are awarded by another system, such as proportional representation. Many countries with bicameral legislatures use different voting systems for the two chambers.

Life expectancy at birth This entry contains the average number of years a group of people born in the same year will live, if mortality at each age remains constant in the future.

Literacy This entry includes a *definition* of literacy and UNESCO's percentage estimates for populations aged 15 years and over, including *total population*, *males*, and *females*. There are no universal definitions and standards of literacy. Unless otherwise specified, all rates are based on the most common definition, which is the ability to read and write at a specified age.

Location This entry identifies the country's regional location, neighboring countries, and adjacent bodies of water.

Major aquifers This entry lists the major (mega) aquifer system(s) that underlie a country; many of these mega aquifers are so large that they extend under multiple countries. More than 30% of freshwater is held in underground aquifers.

Major lakes (area sq km) This entry describes one of the two major surface hydrological features of a country (the other is rivers). The entry contains a list of major natural lakes, defined as having an area of 500 sq km or greater. Lakes and rivers are the primary sources of surface freshwater.

Major ocean currents This field describes the major ocean currents, or the movement of water from one location to another. Currents are generally measured in meters per second or in knots (1 knot = 1.85 kilometers per hour or 1.15 miles per hour), and they affect the Earth's climate by driving warm water from the Equator and cold water from the poles. Oceanic currents are driven by three main factors:

1. *Tides* create ocean currents, which are strongest near the shore but also extend into bays and estuaries along the coast. These are called "tidal currents." Tidal currents change in a very regular pattern and can be predicted. In some locations, strong tidal currents can travel at speeds of eight knots or more.
2. *Winds* drive currents that are at or near the ocean's surface. Near coastal areas, winds tend to drive currents on a localized scale and can result in phenomena like coastal upwelling. On a more global scale, winds in the open ocean drive currents that circulate water for thousands of miles.
3. *Thermohaline circulation* is a process driven by density differences in water due to temperature (thermo) and salinity (haline) variations in different parts of the ocean. Currents driven by thermohaline circulation occur at both deep and shallow ocean levels and move much more slowly than tidal or surface currents.

Major rivers (by length in km) This entry describes one of the two major surface hydrological features of a country (the other feature is lakes). The entry includes a list of major rivers, defined as having a length of 1,000 km or greater. These rivers constitute major drainage basins or watersheds that capture the flow of the majority of surface water flow. Rivers and lakes are the primary sources of surface freshwater.

In instances where a river flows through more than one country, a note has been added to the field to indicate the country where the river starts and the country where it ends. An "[s]" after the country name indicates river source; an "[m]" after the country name indicates river mouth.

Major urban areas - population This entry provides the population of the capital and up to six major cities defined as urban agglomerations with populations of at least 750,000 people. An *urban agglomeration* is defined as comprising the city or town proper and also the suburban fringe or thickly settled territory lying outside of, but adjacent to, the boundaries of the city. For smaller countries lacking urban centers of 750,000 or more, only the population of the capital is presented.

Major watersheds (area sq km) This entry lists the major watersheds or catchment areas of major rivers in a country. Most of the watersheds listed have an area of at least 500,000 sq km, although some smaller but significant watersheds are also included. The watersheds are listed by the ocean into which they drain. When they drain into a named body of water other than the ocean, italics are used to identify the constituent part of an ocean (e.g., *Black Sea*). Some watersheds, known as *endorheic basins*, drain internally with no external flow to the ocean. Given the size of the largest watersheds, they are frequently located in more than one country.

Map references This entry includes the name of the *Factbook* reference map on which a country may be found. Note that boundary representations on these maps are not necessarily authoritative. The entry on **Geographic coordinates** may be helpful in finding some smaller countries.

Marine fisheries This entry describes the major fisheries in the world's oceans in terms of the area covered, their ranking in global catch, the main producing countries, and the principal species caught.

Maritime claims This entry includes the following claims, the definitions of which are excerpted from the United Nations Convention on the Law of the Sea (UNCLOS), which alone contains the full and definitive descriptions:

territorial sea - the sovereignty of a coastal state extends beyond its land territory and internal waters to an adjacent belt of sea, described as the territorial sea in the UNCLOS (Part II). This sovereignty extends to the air space over the territorial sea as well as its underlying seabed and subsoil; every state has the right to establish the breadth of its territorial sea up to a limit of 12 nautical miles. The normal baseline for measuring the breadth is the mean low-water line along the coast. Where the coasts of two states are opposite or adjacent to each other, neither state is entitled to extend its territorial sea beyond the median line.

contiguous zone - this is the zone along a coastal state's territorial sea, where a country may prevent infringement of its customs, fiscal, immigration, or sanitary laws and punish infringement of these laws. The contiguous zone may not extend beyond 24 nautical miles from the baselines from which the breadth of the territorial sea is measured (e.g., the US has claimed a 12-nautical mile contiguous zone in addition to its 12-nautical mile territorial sea). Where the coasts of two states are opposite or adjacent to each other, neither state is entitled to extend its contiguous zone beyond the median line.

exclusive economic zone (EEZ) - a zone beyond and adjacent to the territorial sea, in which a coastal state has sovereign rights for the purpose of exploring, exploiting, conserving, and managing natural resources and for the economic exploitation and exploration of the zone. Countries have jurisdiction over the establishment and use of artificial islands, installations, and structures; marine scientific research; and the protection and preservation of the marine environment. The outer limit of the EEZ cannot exceed 200 nautical miles from the baselines from which the breadth of the territorial sea is measured.

continental shelf - this includes the seabed and subsoil of the submarine areas that extend beyond a country's territorial sea to the outer edge of the continental margin, or to a distance of 200 nautical miles from the baselines from which the breadth of the territorial sea is measured. The continental margin includes the submerged prolongation of the landmass of the coastal state and consists of the seabed and subsoil of the shelf, the slope, and the rise. If the continental margin extends beyond 200 nautical miles from the baseline, coastal states may extend their claim to a distance of 350 nautical miles from the baseline or 100 nautical miles from the 2,500-meter isobath, which is a line connecting points of 2,500 meters in depth.

exclusive fishing zone - this term is not used in the UNCLOS, but some states have chosen not to claim an EEZ but rather to claim jurisdiction over the living resources off their coast; in such cases, the term "exclusive fishing zone" is often used; the breadth of this zone is normally the same as the EEZ or 200 nautical miles.

Maternal mortality ratio The maternal mortality ratio (MMR) is the annual number of female deaths per 100,000 live births, from any cause related to or aggravated by pregnancy or its management (excluding accidental or incidental causes). The MMR includes deaths during pregnancy, childbirth, or within 42 days of termination of pregnancy, irrespective of the duration and site of the pregnancy, for a specified year.

Median age This entry is the age that divides a population into two numerically equal groups; that is, half the people are younger than this age and half are older.

Member states This entry, which appears only in the European Union entry under the Government category, provides a listing of all of the European Union member countries, as well as their associated overseas countries and territories.

Merchant marine This entry provides the total and the number of each type of privately or publicly owned commercial ship for each country; military ships are not included. There are five types of merchant marine ships:

bulk carrier - for cargo such as coal, grain, cement, ores, and gravel
container ship - for loads in truck-size containers (a transportation system called containerization)
general cargo - also referred to as break-bulk containers, for a wide variety of packaged merchandise
oil tanker - for crude oil and petroleum products
other - includes chemical carriers, dredgers, liquefied natural gas (LNG) carriers, refrigerated cargo ships called reefers, tugboats, passenger vessels (cruise and ferry), and offshore supply ships

Military This category includes the entries dealing with a country's military structure, manpower, and expenditures.

Military - note This entry includes miscellaneous military information of significance not included elsewhere.

Military and security forces This entry lists the military and security forces subordinate to defense ministries or the equivalent (typically ground, naval, air, and marine forces), as well as those belonging to interior ministries or the equivalent (typically gendarmeries, border/coast guards, paramilitary police, and other internal security forces).

Military and security service personnel strengths This entry provides estimates of military and security service personnel strengths. The numbers are based on a wide range of publicly available information. Unless otherwise noted, military estimates focus on the major services (army, navy, air force, and where applicable, gendarmeries) and do not account for activated reservists or delineate military service members assigned to joint staffs or defense ministries.

Military deployments This entry lists military forces deployed to other countries or territories abroad. *The World Factbook* defines "deployed" as a permanently stationed force or a temporary deployment of greater than six months. Paramilitaries, police, contractors, mercenaries, proxy forces, and deployments smaller than 100 personnel are not included. Numbers provided are estimates only and should be considered paper strengths, not necessarily the current number of troops on the ground. In addition, some estimates, such as those from the US military, are significantly influenced by deployment policies, contingencies, or world events and may change suddenly. Where available, the organization or mission under which at least some of the forces are deployed is listed. The following terms and abbreviations are used throughout the entry:

AMISOM - Africa Union (AU) Mission in Somalia; UN-supported, AU-operated peacekeeping mission
BATUS - British Army Training Unit Suffield, Canada
BATUK - British Army Training Unit, Kenya
CSTO - Collective Security Treaty Organization
ECOMIG - ECOWUS Mission in The Gambia; Africa Union-European Union peacekeeping, stabilization, and training mission in Gambia
EUTM - European Union Training Mission
EUFOR - European Union Force Bosnia and Herzegovina (also known as Operation Althea)
EuroCorps - European multi-national corps headquartered in Strasbourg, France, consisting of troops from Belgium, France, Germany, Luxembourg, and Spain; Greece, Italy, Poland, Romania and Turkey are Associated Nations of EuroCorps
G5 Joint Force - G5 Sahel Cross-Border Joint Force composed of troops from Burkina Faso, Chad, Mali, Mauritania, and Niger
KFOR - the Kosovo Force; a NATO-led international peacekeeping force in Kosovo
MFO - Multinational Force & Observers Sinai, headquartered in Rome
MINUSCA - United Nations Multidimensional Integrated Stabilization Mission in the Central African Republic
MINUSMA - United Nations Multidimensional Integrated Stabilization Mission in Mali

MNJTF - Multinational Joint Task Force Against Boko Haram, composed of troops from Benin, Cameroon, Chad, Niger, and Nigeria with the mission of fighting Boko Haram in the Lake Chad Basin
MONUSCO - United Nations Organization Stabilization Mission in the Democratic Republic of the Congo
NATO - North American Treaty Organization, headquartered in Brussels, Belgium
Operation Barkhane - French-led counterinsurgency and counterterrorism mission in the Sahel alongside the G5 Joint Force; headquartered in N'Djamena, Chad, and supported by Canada, Denmark, Estonia, the European Union, Germany, Spain, the United Kingdom, and the US
Operation Inherent Resolve - US-led coalition to counter the Islamic State in Iraq and Syria and provide assistance and training to Iraqi security forces
UNAFIL - United Nations Interim Force in Lebanon
UNAMID - African Union - United Nations Hybrid Operation in Darfur, Sudan
UNDOF - United Nations Disengagement Observer Force, Golan (Israel-Syria border)
UNFICYP - United Nations Peacekeeping Force in Cyprus
UNISFA - United Nations Interim Security Force for Abyei (Sudan-South Sudan border)
UNMISS - United Nations Mission in the Republic of South Sudan
UNSOM - United Nations Assistance Mission in Somalia

Military equipment inventories and acquisitions This entry provides basic information on each country's military equipment inventories, as well as how they acquire their equipment; it is intended to show broad trends in major military equipment holdings, such as tanks and other armored vehicles, air defense systems, artillery, naval ships, helicopters, and fixed-wing aircraft. Arms acquisition information is an overview of major arms suppliers over a specific period of time, including second-hand arms delivered as aid, with a focus on major weapons systems. It is based on the type and number of weapon systems ordered and delivered and the financial value of the deal. For some countries, general information on domestic defense industry capabilities is provided.

Military expenditures This entry gives estimates for defense-related spending for the most recent year available as a percentage of gross domestic product (GDP). For countries with no military forces, this figure can include expenditures on public security and police.

Military service age and obligation This entry gives the required ages for voluntary or conscript military service and the length of service obligation.

Money figures All money figures are expressed in contemporaneous US dollars unless otherwise indicated.

Mother's mean age at first birth This entry provides the mean (average) age of mothers at the birth of their first child.

National air transport system This entry includes four subfields describing the air transport system of a given country, in terms of both structure and performance.

number of registered air carriers - the total number of air carriers registered with the country's national aviation authority and issued an air operator certificate as required by the Convention on International Civil Aviation

inventory of registered aircraft operated by air carriers - the total number of aircraft operated by all registered air carriers in the country

annual passenger traffic on registered air carriers - the total number of passengers carried by air carriers registered in the country, including both domestic and international passengers, in a given year

annual freight traffic on registered air carriers - the volume of freight, express, and diplomatic bags carried by registered air carriers and measured in metric tons times kilometers traveled. For statistical purposes, freight does not include passenger baggage.

National anthem A generally patriotic musical composition that evokes and eulogizes the history, traditions, or struggles of a nation or its people. National anthems can be officially recognized as a national song in a country's constitution or law, or simply through tradition. Although most anthems contain lyrics, some do not.

National heritage The United Nations Educational, Scientific, and Cultural Organization (UNESCO) designates World Heritage Sites as part of its mission to encourage the identification, protection, and preservation of cultural, historic, scientific, and natural heritage sites around the world that are considered to be of outstanding value to humanity. This entry includes two subfields: *total World Heritage Sites* and *selected World Heritage Site locales*. The former consists of natural sites (n), cultural sites (c), and mixed (m; natural and cultural) sites in a country; the latter presents a representative sample of the sites found within a country.

National holiday This entry gives the primary national day of celebration, usually an independence day.

National symbol(s) A national symbol is an emblem or object – often flora or fauna – that over time has come to be closely identified with a country or entity. Not all countries have national symbols; a few countries have more than one.

Nationality This entry provides the identifying terms for citizens, both *noun* and *adjective*.

Natural gas This field refers to a country's natural gas *production*, *consumption*, *exports*, *imports*, and *proven reserves*. *Proven reserves* are those quantities of natural gas that have been analyzed as commercially recoverable in the future based on known reservoirs and assuming current economic conditions. All data reflect only dry natural gas and exclude non-hydrocarbon gases, as well as vented, flared, and reinjected natural gas. Data are reported using cubic meters.

Natural hazards This entry lists potential natural disasters. For countries where volcanic activity is common, a *volcanism* subfield highlights historically active volcanoes.

Natural resources This entry lists a country's mineral, petroleum, hydropower, and other resources of commercial importance, such as rare earth elements (REEs). In general, products appear only if they make a significant contribution to the economy, or are likely to do so in the future.

Net migration rate This entry includes the figure for the difference between the number of persons entering and leaving a country during the year per 1,000 persons (based on midyear population). An excess of persons entering the country is referred to as net immigration (e.g., 3.56 migrants/1,000 population); an excess of persons leaving the country as net emigration (e.g., -9.26 migrants/1,000 population). The net migration rate indicates the contribution of migration to the overall level of population change. The net migration rate does not distinguish between economic migrants, refugees, and other types of migrants, nor does it distinguish between lawful migrants and undocumented migrants.

Nuclear energy This field describes nuclear energy used for production of electricity. The information covers all countries with operational nuclear reactors that are used to produce electricity; the information does not include research reactors. Subfields include the current *number of operational nuclear reactors*, the *number of nuclear reactors under construction*, the *net capacity of operational nuclear reactors* expressed in gigawatts (GW), the *percent of total electricity production* from nuclear energy, the *percent of total energy produced* from nuclear energy, and the *number of nuclear reactors permanently shut down*. Watts are a measure of power, describing the rate at which electricity is being used at a specific moment. A gigawatt is 1 billion watts.

Obesity - adult prevalence rate This entry gives the percentage of a country's population considered to be obese. Obesity is defined as an adult having a Body Mass Index (BMI) greater than or equal to 30.0. BMI is calculated by taking a person's weight in kg and dividing it by the person's squared height in meters.

Ocean volume This entry provides the estimated volume of each of the oceans in millions of cubic kilometers and the percentage of the World Ocean total volume.

People - note This entry includes miscellaneous demographic information of significance not included elsewhere.

People and Society This category includes entries dealing with national identity (including ethnicities, languages, and religions), demography (a variety of population statistics) and societal characteristics (health and education indicators).

Personal Names - Capitalization The *Factbook* capitalizes the surname or family name of individuals for the convenience of our users, who are faced with a world of different cultures and naming conventions. The need for capitalization, bold type, underlining, italics, or some other indicator of the individual's surname is apparent in the following examples: MAO Zedong, Fidel CASTRO Ruz, George W. BUSH, and TUNKU SALAHUDDIN Abdul Aziz Shah ibni Al-Marhum Sultan Hisammuddin Alam Shah. By knowing the surname, a short form without all capital letters can be used with confidence as in President Castro, Chairman Mao, President Bush, or Sultan Tunku Salahuddin. The same system of capitalization is extended to the names of leaders with surnames that are not commonly used such as King CHARLES III. For Vietnamese names, the given name is capitalized because officials are referred to by their given name rather than by their surname. For example, the president of Vietnam is Nguyen Xuan PHUC. His surname is Nguyen, but he is referred to by his given name – President PHUC.

Personal Names - Spelling The transliteration of personal names in the *Factbook* normally follows the US Board on Geographic Names' system for spelling place names. At times, however, a foreign leader expressly indicates a preference for, or the media or official documents regularly use, a spelling that differs from the transliteration derived from the US Government standard. In such cases, the *Factbook* uses the alternative spelling.

Personal Names - Titles The *Factbook* capitalizes any valid title (or short form of it) immediately preceding a person's name. A title standing alone is not capitalized.

Petroleum This field refers a country's *crude oil production, refined petroleum consumption, crude oil exports, crude oil imports,* and *crude oil proven reserves.*

Crude oil data represent crude oil (including lease condensate), oil sands liquids, natural gas plant liquids, and other liquids. Other liquids include biodiesel, ethanol, liquids produced from coal, gas, and oil shale, Orimulsion, blending components, and other hydrocarbons. Refined petroleum data represent asphalt, petroleum coke, aviation gasoline, lubricants, ethane, naphtha, paraffin wax, petrochemical feedstocks, unfinished oils, white spirits, and direct use of crude oil.

Crude oil production, refined petroleum consumption, crude oil exports, and *crude oil imports* data are reported in barrels per day (bbl/day), and one barrel of crude oil roughly equates to 42 gallons (roughly 159 liters). *Crude oil proven reserves* data are reported in barrels (bbl) and are those quantities of crude oil that have been analyzed as commercially recoverable in the future based on known reservoirs and assuming current economic conditions.

Petroleum See entries under **Refined petroleum products.**

Petroleum products See entries under **Refined petroleum products.**

Physician density This entry gives the number of medical doctors (physicians), including generalist and specialist medical practitioners, per 1,000 of the population. Medical doctors are defined as doctors that study, diagnose, treat, and prevent illness, disease, injury, and other physical and mental impairments in humans through the application of modern medicine. They also plan, supervise, and evaluate care and treatment plans by other health care providers.

Pipelines This entry gives the lengths and types of pipelines for transporting products like natural gas, crude oil, or petroleum products.

Piracy Piracy is defined by the 1982 United Nations Convention on the Law of the Sea as any illegal act of violence, detention, or depredation directed against a ship, aircraft, persons, or property in a place outside the jurisdiction of any state. Such criminal acts committed in the territorial waters of a littoral state are generally considered to be armed robbery against ships.

Political parties This entry includes a listing of significant political parties, coalitions, and electoral lists as of each country's last legislative election, unless otherwise noted. Parties that do not win a seat in national elections are usually not included.

Political structure This entry, which appears only in the European Union entry under the Government category, provides a definition for the entity that is the European Union.

Population This entry gives an estimate from the US Bureau of the Census based on statistics from population censuses, vital statistics registration systems, or sample surveys pertaining to the recent past and based on assumptions about future trends. This annual estimate does not reflect sudden population shifts due to conflicts, natural disasters, or other unexpected events.

Population below poverty line National estimates of the percentage of the population falling below the poverty line are based on surveys of sub-groups, with the results weighted by the number of people in each group. Definitions of poverty vary considerably among nations.

Population distribution This entry provides a summary description of the population dispersion within a country. While it may suggest population density, it does not provide density figures.

Population growth rate The average annual percent change in the population, resulting from a surplus (or deficit) of births over deaths and the balance of migrants entering and leaving a country. The rate may be positive or negative.

Population pyramid A population pyramid illustrates the age and sex structure of a country's population. The population is distributed along the horizontal axis, with males shown on the left and females on the right. The male and female populations are broken down into five-year age groups represented as horizontal bars along the vertical axis, with the youngest age groups at the bottom and the oldest at the top. The shape of the population pyramid gradually evolves over time based on fertility, mortality, and international migration trends.

Ports This entry gives the number of ports in a country based on harbor size, a classification that is derived from factors such as area, facilities, and wharf space. Ports are usually multi-use, with activities that can include container shipping, military transport, and ferry or cruise ship transit. The total number of oil terminals located at these ports is noted but does not include standalone facilities that may be separate from ports. Liquified natural gas terminals are not listed because they are usually located at a distance from ports for safety reasons.

Preliminary statement This entry, which appears only in the European Union entry under the Introduction, provides an explanation and justification for the inclusion of a separate European Union geographic entity.

Principality A sovereign state ruled by a monarch with the title of prince; principalities were common in the past, but today only three remain: Liechtenstein, Monaco, and the co-principality of Andorra.

Public debt This entry records the cumulative total of all government borrowings less repayments that are denominated in a country's home currency. Public debt should not be confused with external debt, which reflects the foreign currency liabilities of both the private and public sector and must be financed out of foreign exchange earnings.

Railways This entry states the *total* route length of the railway network and of its component parts by gauge, which is the measure of the distance between the inner sides of the load-bearing rails. The four typical types of gauges are: *broad, standard, narrow,* and *dual.* Other gauges are listed in a *note.* Some 60% of the world's railways use the standard gauge of 1.4 m (4.7 ft). Gauges vary by country and sometimes within countries. The choice of gauge during initial construction was mainly in response to local conditions and the intent of the builder. Narrow-gauge railways were cheaper to build and could negotiate sharper curves, broad-gauge railways gave greater stability and permitted higher speeds. Standard-gauge railways were a compromise between narrow and broad gauges.

Rare earth elements Rare earth elements or REEs are 17 chemical elements that are critical in many of today's high-tech industries. They include lanthanum, cerium, praseodymium, neodymium, promethium, samarium, europium, gadolinium, terbium, dysprosium, holmium, erbium, thulium, ytterbium, lutetium, scandium, and yttrium.

Real GDP (purchasing power parity) This entry gives the gross domestic product (GDP) or value of all final goods and services produced within a nation in a given year. A nation's GDP at purchasing power parity (PPP) exchange rates is the sum value of all goods and services produced in the country valued at prices prevailing in the United States in the year noted. This is the measure most economists prefer when looking at per-capita welfare and when comparing living conditions or use of resources across countries. Many countries do not formally participate in the World Bank's PPP project that calculates these measures, so the resulting GDP estimates for these countries may lack precision. For many developing countries, PPP-based GDP measures are multiples of the official exchange rate (OER) measure. The differences between the OER- and PPP-denominated GDP values for most of the wealthy industrialized countries are generally much smaller.

Real GDP growth rate This entry gives a country's real GDP annual growth rate, adjusted for seasonal unemployment and inflation. A country's growth rate is year-over-year, and not compounded.

Real GDP per capita This entry shows real GDP, divided by population as of 1 July for the same year.

Reference maps This section includes world and regional maps.

Refugees and internally displaced persons This entry includes those persons residing in a country as *refugees, internally displaced persons (IDPs)*, or *stateless persons*. Each country's refugee entry includes only countries of origin that are the source of refugee populations of 5,000 or more. The UN definition of a *refugee* is "a person who is outside his/her country of nationality or habitual residence; has a well-founded fear of persecution because of his/her race, religion, nationality, membership in a particular social group or political opinion; and is unable or unwilling to avail himself/herself of the protection of that country, or to return there, for fear of persecution." The term *internally displaced person* is not specifically covered in the 1951 UN Convention Relating to the Status of Refugees; it is used to describe people who have fled their homes for reasons similar to refugees, but who remain within their own national territory and are subject to the laws of that state. A *stateless person* is defined as someone who is not considered a national by any state, according to the 1954 UN Convention Relating to the Status of Stateless Persons.

Religions This entry is an ordered listing of religions by adherents, starting with the largest group, and sometimes includes the percentage of the total population. The core characteristics and beliefs of the world's major religions are described below.

Baha'i - Founded by Mirza Husayn-Ali (known as Baha'u'llah) in Iran in 1852, Baha'i faith emphasizes monotheism and believes in one eternal transcendent God. Its guiding focus is to encourage the unity of all peoples so that justice and peace may be achieved on earth. Baha'i revelation contends that the prophets of major world religions reflect some truth or element of the divine, believes all were manifestations of God given to specific communities in specific times, and believes that Baha'u'llah is an additional prophet meant to call all humankind. Bahais are an open community, located worldwide, with the greatest concentration of believers in South Asia.

Buddhism - Religion or philosophy inspired by the fifth-century-B.C. teachings of Siddhartha Gautama (also known as Gautama Buddha, or "the enlightened one"). Buddhism focuses on the goal of spiritual enlightenment centered on an understanding of Gautama Buddha's Four Noble Truths on the nature of suffering and on the Eightfold Path of spiritual and moral practice, to break the cycle of suffering. Buddhism ascribes to a karmic system of rebirth. Several schools and sects of Buddhism exist, differing often on the nature of the Buddha, the extent to which enlightenment can be achieved (for one or for all) and by whom (religious orders or laity).

Basic Groupings

Theravada Buddhism: The oldest Buddhist school, Theravada is practiced mostly in Sri Lanka, Cambodia, Laos, Burma, and Thailand, with minority representation elsewhere in Asia and the West. Theravadans follow the Pali Canon of Buddha's teachings, and believe that one may escape the cycle of rebirth, worldly attachment, and suffering for oneself; this process may take one or several lifetimes.

Mahayana Buddhism, including subsets Zen and Tibetan (Lamaistic) Buddhism: Forms of Mahayana Buddhism are common in East Asia and Tibet, and parts of the West. Mahayanas have additional scriptures beyond the Pali Canon and believe the Buddha is eternal and still teaching. Unlike Theravada Buddhism, Mahayana schools maintain that the Buddha-nature is present in all beings, and all will ultimately achieve enlightenment.

Hoa Hao: a minority tradition of Buddhism practiced in Vietnam that stresses lay participation, primarily by peasant farmers; it eschews expensive ceremonies and temples and relocates the primary practices into the home.

Christianity - Descending from Judaism, Christianity's central belief maintains that Jesus of Nazareth is the promised messiah of the Hebrew Scriptures, and that his life, death, and resurrection are salvific for the world. Christianity is one of the three monotheistic Abrahamic faiths, along with Islam and Judaism, that trace their spiritual lineage to Abraham of the Hebrew Scriptures. Christianity's sacred texts include the Hebrew Bible and the New Testament (or the Christian Gospels).

Basic Groupings

Catholicism (or Roman Catholicism): This is the oldest established western Christian church and the world's largest single religious body. It is supranational and recognizes a hierarchical structure with the Pope, or Bishop of Rome, as its head, located at the Vatican. Catholics believe the Pope is the divinely ordered head of the Church, from a direct spiritual legacy of Jesus's apostle Peter. Catholicism is composed of 23 particular Churches, or Rites – one Western (Roman or Latin-Rite) and 22 Eastern. The Latin Rite is by far the largest, making up about 98% of Catholic membership. Eastern-Rite Churches, such as the Maronite Church and the Ukrainian Catholic Church, are in communion with Rome although they preserve their own worship traditions, and their immediate hierarchy consists of clergy within their own rite. The Catholic Church has a comprehensive theological and moral doctrine specified for believers in its catechism, which makes it unique among most forms of Christianity.

The Church of Jesus Christ of Latter-day Saints: The Church was organized in 1830 and teaches that it is the restoration of Jesus Christ's original church. It embraces salvation through Christ, personal revelation, and has an open canon, including the King James Bible and the Book of Mormon, which is another testament of Christ's divinity. The Book of Mormon maintains that there was an appearance of Jesus in the New World following the Christian account of his resurrection, and that the Americas are uniquely blessed continents. The Church has a centralized doctrine and leadership structure but has volunteer lay clergy who oversee local congregations in 176 countries and territories.

Jehovah's Witnesses: This group structures its faith on the Christian Bible, but its rejection of the Trinity is distinct from mainstream Christianity. They believe that a Kingdom of God, the Theocracy, will emerge following Armageddon and usher in a new earthly society. Adherents are required to evangelize and follow a strict moral code.

Orthodox Christianity: The oldest established eastern form of Christianity, the Holy Orthodox Church, has a ceremonial head in the Bishop of Constantinople (Istanbul), also known as a Patriarch, but its various regional forms (e.g., Greek Orthodox, Russian Orthodox, Serbian Orthodox, Ukrainian Orthodox) are autocephalous (independent of Constantinople's authority and have their own Patriarchs). Orthodox churches are highly nationalist and ethnic. The Orthodox Christian faith shares many theological tenets with the Roman Catholic Church, but it diverges on some key premises and does not recognize the governing authority of the Pope.

Protestant Christianity: Protestant Christianity originated in the 16th century as an attempt to reform Roman Catholicism's practices, dogma, and theology. It encompasses several forms or denominations which are extremely varied in structure, beliefs, relationship to national governments, clergy, and governance. Many Protestant theologies emphasize the primary role of scripture in their faith, advocating individual interpretation of Christian texts without the mediation of a final religious authority such as the Roman Pope. The oldest Protestant denominations include Lutheranism, Calvinism (Presbyterianism), and Anglican Christianity (Episcopalianism), which have established liturgies, governing structure, and formal clergy. Other variants on Protestant Christianity, including Pentecostal movements and independent churches, may lack one or more of these elements, and their leadership and beliefs are individualized and dynamic.

Hinduism - Originating in the Vedic civilization of India (second and first millennium B.C.), Hinduism is an extremely diverse set of beliefs and practices with no single founder or religious authority. Hinduism has many scriptures; the Vedas, the Upanishads, and the Bhagavad-Gita are some of the most important. Hindus may worship one or many deities, usually with prayer rituals within their own home. The most common figures of devotion are the gods Vishnu, Shiva, and a mother goddess, Devi. Most Hindus believe the soul, or *atman*, is eternal, and goes through a cycle of birth, death, and rebirth (*samsara*) determined by one's positive or negative karma, or the consequences of one's actions. The goal of religious life is to learn to act so as to finally achieve liberation (*moksha*) of one's soul, escaping the rebirth cycle.

Islam - One of the three monotheistic Abrahamic faiths, Islam originated with the teachings of Muhammad in the seventh century. Muslims believe Muhammad is the final of all religious prophets (beginning with Abraham) and that the Qu'ran, which is the Islamic scripture, was revealed to him by God. Islam derives from the word "submission," and obedience to God is a primary theme in this religion. In order to live an Islamic life, believers must follow the five pillars, or tenets, of Islam, which are the testimony of faith (*shahada*), daily prayer (*salah*), giving alms (*zakah*), fasting during Ramadan (*sawm*), and the pilgrimage to Mecca (*hajj*).

Basic Groupings

The two primary branches of Islam are *Sunni* and *Shia*, which split from each other over a religio-political leadership dispute about the rightful successor to Muhammad. The Shia believe Muhammad's cousin and son-in-law, Ali, was the only divinely ordained Imam (religious leader), while the Sunni maintain that the first three caliphs after Muhammad were also legitimate authorities. In modern Islam, Sunnis and Shia continue to have different views of acceptable schools of Islamic jurisprudence and who is a proper Islamic religious authority. Islam also has an active mystical branch, Sufism, with various Sunni and Shia subsets.

Sunni Islam accounts for 87–90% of the world's Muslim population. It recognizes the Abu Bakr as the first caliph after Muhammad. Sunni has four schools of Islamic doctrine and law – Hanafi, Maliki, Shafi'i, and Hanbali – which uniquely interpret the *Hadith*, or recorded oral traditions of Muhammad. A Sunni Muslim may elect to follow any one of these schools, as all are considered equally valid.

Shia Islam represents 10–13% of Muslims worldwide, and its distinguishing feature is its reverence for Ali as an infallible, divinely inspired leader and as the first Imam after Muhammad. A majority of Shia are known as "Twelvers," because they believe that the 11 familial successor imams after Muhammad culminate in a 12th Imam (al-Mahdi) who is hidden in the world and will reappear at its end to redeem the righteous.

Variants

Ismaili faith: A sect of Shia Islam, its adherents are also known as "Seveners," because they believe that the rightful seventh Imam in Islamic leadership was Isma'il, the elder son of Imam Jafar al-Sadiq. Ismaili tradition awaits the return of the seventh Imam as the Mahdi, or Islamic messianic figure. Ismailis are located in various parts of the world, particularly South Asia and the Levant.

Alawi faith: Another Shia sect of Islam, the name reflects followers' devotion to the religious authority of Ali. Alawites are a closed, secretive religious group who assert that they are Shia Muslims, although outside scholars speculate their beliefs may have a syncretic mix with other faiths originating in the Middle East. Alawis live mostly in Syria, Lebanon, and Turkey.

Druze faith: A highly secretive tradition and a closed community that derives from the Ismaili sect of Islam; its core beliefs are thought to emphasize a combination of Gnostic principles asserting that the Fatimid caliph, al-Hakin, is the one who embodies the key aspects of goodness of the universe, which are the intellect, the word, the soul, the preceder, and the follower. The Druze have a key presence in Syria, Lebanon, and Israel.

Jainism - Originating in India, the Jain philosophy believes in an eternal human soul, the eternal universe, and a principle of "the own nature of things." It emphasizes compassion for all living things, seeks liberation of the human soul from reincarnation through enlightenment, and values personal responsibility due to the belief in the immediate consequences of one's behavior. Jain philosophy teaches non-violence and prescribes vegetarianism for monks and laity alike; its adherents are a highly influential religious minority in Indian society.

Judaism - One of the first known monotheistic religions, likely dating to between 2000-1500 B.C., Judaism is the native faith of the Jewish people, based upon the belief in a covenant of responsibility between a sole omnipotent creator God and Abraham, the patriarch of Judaism's Hebrew Bible, or *Tanakh*. Divine revelation of principles and prohibitions in the Hebrew Scriptures form the basis of Jewish law, or *halakhah*, which is a key component of the faith. While there are extensive traditions of Jewish halakhic and theological discourse, there is no final dogmatic authority in the tradition. Local communities have their own religious leadership. Modern Judaism has three basic categories of faith: Orthodox, Conservative, and Reform/Liberal. These differ in their views and observance of Jewish law, with the Orthodox representing the most traditional practice, and Reform/Liberal communities the most accommodating of individualized interpretations of Jewish identity and faith.

Shintoism - A native animist tradition of Japan, Shinto practice is based on the premise that every being and object has its own spirit or *kami*. Shinto practitioners worship several particular *kamis*, including the *kamis* of nature, and families often have shrines to their ancestors' *kamis*. Shintoism has no fixed tradition of prayers or prescribed dogma and is characterized by individual ritual. Respect for the *kamis* in nature is a key Shinto value. Prior to the end of World War II, Shinto was the state religion of Japan and bolstered the cult of the Japanese emperor.

Sikhism - Founded by the Guru Nanak (born 1469), Sikhism believes in a non-anthropomorphic, supreme, eternal, creator God; centering one's devotion to God is seen as a means of escaping the cycle of rebirth. Sikhs follow the teachings of Nanak and nine subsequent gurus. Their scripture, the Guru Granth Sahib – also known as the Adi Granth – is considered the living Guru, or final authority of Sikh faith and theology. Sikhism emphasizes equality of humankind and disavows caste, class, or gender discrimination.

Taoism - Chinese philosophy or religion based upon Lao Tzu's Tao Te Ching, which centers on belief in the Tao, or the way, as the flow of the universe and the nature of things. Taoism encourages a principle of non-force, or wu-wei, as the means to live harmoniously with the Tao. Taoists believe the esoteric world is made up of a perfect harmonious balance and nature, while in the manifest world – particularly in the body – balance is distorted. The Three Jewels of the Tao are compassion, simplicity, and humility and serve as the basis for Taoist ethics.

Zoroastrianism - Originating from the teachings of Zoroaster in about the ninth or 10th century B.C., Zoroastrianism may be the oldest continuing creedal religion. Its key beliefs center on a transcendent creator God, Ahura Mazda, and the concept of free will. The key ethical tenets of Zoroastrianism expressed in its scripture, the Avesta, are based on a dualistic worldview where one may prevent chaos if one chooses to serve God and exercises good thoughts, good words, and good deeds. Zoroastrianism is generally a closed religion and members are almost always born to Zoroastrian parents. Prior to the spread of Islam, Zoroastrianism dominated greater Iran. Today, though a minority, Zoroastrians remain primarily in Iran, India (where they are known as Parsi), and Pakistan.

Traditional beliefs

Animism: the belief that non-human entities contain souls or spirits.

Badimo: a form of ancestor worship of the Tswana people of Botswana.

Confucianism: an ideology that humans are perfectible through self-cultivation and self-creation; developed from teachings of the Chinese philosopher Confucius. Confucianism has strongly influenced the culture and beliefs of East Asian countries, including China, Japan, Korea, Singapore, Taiwan, and Vietnam.

Inuit beliefs: a form of shamanism (see below) based on the animistic principles of the Inuit or Eskimo peoples.

Kirant: the belief system of the Kirat, a people who live mainly in the Himalayas of Nepal. It is primarily a form of polytheistic shamanism but includes elements of animism and ancestor worship.

Pagan: a blanket term used to describe many unconnected belief practices throughout history, usually in reference to religions outside the Abrahamic category (monotheistic faiths including Judaism, Christianity, and Islam).

Shamanism: beliefs and practices promoting communication with the spiritual world. Shamanistic beliefs are organized around a shaman or medicine man who – as an intermediary between the human and spirit world – is believed to be able to heal the sick, communicate with the spirit world, and help souls into the afterlife through the practice of entering a trance. In shaman-based religions, the shaman is also responsible for leading sacred rites.

Spiritualism: the belief that souls and spirits communicate with the living usually through intermediaries called mediums.

Syncretic (fusion of diverse religious beliefs and practices)

Cao Dai: a nationalistic Vietnamese sect, officially established in 1926, that draws practices and precepts from Confucianism, Taoism, Buddhism, and Catholicism.

Chondogyo or the religion of the Heavenly Way: based on Korean shamanism, Buddhism, and Korean folk traditions, with some elements drawn from Christianity. Formulated in the 1860s, it holds that God lives in all of us and strives to convert society into a paradise on earth that will be populated by believers transformed into intelligent moral beings with a high social conscience.

Kimbanguism: a puritan form of the Baptist denomination founded by Simon Kimbangu in the 1920s in what is now the Democratic Republic of Congo. Adherents believe that salvation comes through Jesus' death and resurrection, like Christianity, but additionally that living a spiritually pure life following strict codes of conduct is required for salvation.

Modekngei: a hybrid of Christianity and ancient Palauan culture and oral traditions founded around 1915 on the island of Babeldaob. Adherents simultaneously worship Jesus Christ and Palauan goddesses.

Rastafarianism: an afro-centrist ideology and movement based on Christianity that arose in Jamaica in the 1930s; it believes that Haile Selassie I, Emperor of Ethiopia from 1930–74, was the incarnation of the second coming of Jesus.

Santeria: practiced in Cuba, the merging of the Yoruba religion of Nigeria with Roman Catholicism and native Indian traditions. Its practitioners believe that each person has a destiny and eventually transcends to merge with the divine creator and source of all energy, Olorun.

Voodoo/Vodun: a form of spirit and ancestor worship combined with some Christian faiths, especially Catholicism. Haitian and Louisiana Voodoo, which have included more Catholic practices, are separate from West African Vodun, which has retained a focus on spirit worship.

Non-religious

Agnosticism: the belief that most things are unknowable. In regard to religion, it is usually characterized as neither a belief nor non-belief in a deity.

Atheism: the belief that there are no deities of any kind.

Reserves of foreign exchange and gold This entry gives the dollar value for the stock of all financial assets that are available to the central monetary authority for use in meeting a country's balance of payments needs as of the end-date of the period specified. This category includes not only foreign currency and gold, but also a country's holdings of Special Drawing Rights in the International Monetary Fund, and its reserve position in the Fund.

Revenue from coal This entry refers to the economic profits, expressed as a percentage of a country's GDP, from the extraction of coal. These profits equal coal gross revenues minus cost(s) to extract the coal. Other sources may refer to this field as coal rents.

Revenue from forest resources This entry refers to the economic profits, expressed as a percentage of a country's GDP, from the harvesting of forests (e.g., lumber and timber industries). These profits equal forest gross revenues minus costs to harvest the forest. Other sources may refer to this field as forest rents.

Roadways This entry gives the *total* length of the road network and includes the length of the *paved* and *unpaved* portions.

Sanitation facility access This entry provides information about access to improved or unimproved sanitation facilities available to segments of the population of a country.

Improved sanitation - use of flush or pour-flush to a piped sewer system, septic tank, or pit latrine; ventilated improved pit (VIP) latrine; pit latrine with slab; or a composting toilet.

Unimproved sanitation - use of flush or pour-flush not piped to a sewer system, septic tank, or pit latrine; pit latrine without a slab or open pit; bucket; hanging toilet or hanging latrine; shared facilities of any type; no facilities; or bush or field.

School life expectancy (primary to tertiary education) School life expectancy (SLE) is the total number of years of schooling (primary to tertiary) that a child can expect to receive, assuming that the probability of his or her being enrolled in school at any particular future age is equal to the current enrollment ratio at that age. Caution must be maintained when utilizing this indicator in international comparisons, because a year or grade completed in one country is not necessarily the same in terms of educational content or quality as a year or grade completed in another country. SLE represents the expected number of years of schooling that will be completed, including years spent repeating one or more grades.

Sex ratio This entry includes the number of males for each female in five age groups – *at birth, under 15 years, 15–64 years, 65 years and over*, and for the *total population*.

Single Euro Payments Area (SEPA) This entry refers to the payment integration initiative and framework of the European Union (EU) that simplifies non-cash transfers, whether credit or debit, of the euro to both EU and non-EU member states.

Smart City A smart city uses information technology and data analysis to improve operational activities in the city and share information related to residents' use of city infrastructure.

Space agency/agencies This field provides the names of national space agencies.

Space launch site(s) This field provides the names and locations of identified commercial and government space launch sites.

Space program overview This field provides a general survey of a country's space program, including areas of expertise and focus, national goals, international cooperation, and commercial space sector activities if applicable.

Stateless person A stateless individual is not considered a national by any country. Estimates of the number of stateless people are inherently imprecise because few countries have procedures to identify them; the UN assesses that there are at least 10 million stateless people worldwide. Stateless people are counted in a country's overall population figure if they have lived there for a year.

Suffrage This entry gives the age at enfranchisement and whether the right to vote is universal or restricted.

Taxes and other revenues This entry records total taxes and other revenues received by the national government during the time period indicated, expressed as a percentage of GDP. Taxes include personal and corporate income taxes, value added taxes, excise taxes, and tariffs. Other revenues include social contributions (such as payments for social security and hospital insurance), grants, and net revenues from public enterprises. Normalizing the data, by dividing total revenues by GDP, enables easy comparisons across countries and provides an average rate at which all income (GDP) is paid to the national-level government for the supply of public goods and services.

Telecommunication systems This entry includes a brief general assessment of a country's telecommunications system with details on the domestic and international components. The following terms and abbreviations are used throughout the entry:

2G - is short for second-generation cellular network. After 2G was launched, the previous mobile wireless network systems were retroactively dubbed 1G. While radio signals on 1G networks are analog, radio signals on 2G networks are digital. Both systems use digital signaling to connect the radio towers (which listen to the devices) to the rest of the mobile system. 2G introduced cellular services like SMS, multimedia messaging, and digitally encrypted voice conversations. 2G is still useful because the FM modulation travels a long distance.

3G -is the third generation of wireless mobile telecommunications technology. It is the upgrade for 2.5G and 2.5G GPRS networks, for faster data transfer and better voice quality. This increased speed is based on a set of standards used for mobile devices and mobile telecommunications use services and networks that comply with the International Mobile Telecommunications-2000 (IMT-2000) specifications by the International Telecommunication Union. 3G finds application in wireless voice telephony, mobile Internet access, fixed wireless Internet access, video calls, and mobile TV.

4G - is the fourth generation of broadband cellular network technology, succeeding 3G. The first-release Long Term Evolution (LTE) standard was commercially deployed in Oslo, Norway, and Stockholm, Sweden in 2009, and has since been deployed throughout most parts of the world. Applications, include enhanced mobile web access, IP telephony, high-definition mobile TV, and video conferencing.

5G - is the fifth generation technology standard for cellular networks, which cellular phone companies began deploying worldwide in 2019; it is the planned successor to the 4G networks which provide connectivity to most current cellphones. Like its predecessors, 5G networks are cellular networks, in which the service area is divided into small geographical areas called cells. All 5G wireless devices in a cell are connected to the Internet and telephone network by radio waves through a local antenna in the cell. The main advantage of the new networks is that they will have greater bandwidth, allowing higher download speeds, eventually up to 10 gigabits per second (Gbit/s). Due to the increased bandwidth, the expectation is that the new networks will not just serve cellphones like existing cellular networks, but also be used as general Internet service providers for laptops and desktop computers, competing with existing ISPs such as cable Internet. Existing 4G cellphones will not be able to use the new networks, which will require new 5G-enabled wireless devices.

6G - is the sixth-generation wireless and the successor to 5G cellular technology. 6G networks will be able to use higher frequencies than 5G networks and provide substantially higher capacity and much lower latency. One of the goals of the 6G internet is to support one microsecond latency communications. This is 1,000 times faster – or 1/1000th the latency – than one millisecond throughput. It is important to note that 6G is still being developed. Some vendors are investing in the next-generation wireless standard, industry specifications for 6G-enabled network products remain years away.

7G - is the seventh-generation wireless and is the inevitable intelligent cellular technology. 7G networks will be able to use higher frequencies and provide substantially higher capacity and much lower latency in communications. 7G is still in development.

ADSL - Asymmetric Digital Subscriber Line (ADSL) is a type of digital subscriber line (DSL) that allows faster data transmission via copper service phone lines to a home or business. ADSL provides an "always on" connection and higher speeds than dial-up Internet can provide. In ADSL, bandwidth and bit rate (i.e., speed) are asymmetric, meaning greater toward the customer (downstream) than the reverse (upstream).

AngoSat 2 - geostationary communications satellite for ground communication and broadcasting infrastructure in Angola, operated by Angosat and built by the Russian company ISS Reshetnev.

Arabsat - Arab Satellite Communications Organization (Riyadh, Saudi Arabia).

Cellular telephone system - the telephones in this system are radio transceivers, with each instrument having its own private radio frequency and sufficient radiated power to reach the booster station in its area (cell), from which the telephone signal is fed to a telephone exchange.

Central American Microwave System - a trunk microwave radio relay system that links the countries of Central America and Mexico with each other.

Coaxial cable - a multichannel communication cable consisting of a central conducting wire, surrounded by and insulated from a cylindrical conducting shell; a large number of telephone channels can be made available within the insulated space by the use of a large number of carrier frequencies.

DSL - Digital Subscriber Line (DSL) is a family of technologies that are used to transmit digital data over telephone lines.

e-services - Electronic services rely on information and communication technologies (ICT); the three main components of e-services are the service provider, service receiver (or customer), and the channel for delivery, generally the Internet. E-services have expanded to e-health, e-commerce, e-fleet, and e-government, among other services. E-services are also linked to the development of IoT and smart city technology.

ECOWAS telecommunications - Economic Community of West African States regional telecommunications development program, focused on broadband infrastructure, landing of submarine cables, and the establishment of a single liberalized telecoms market.

Eutelsat - European Telecommunications Satellite Organization (Paris).

Fiber-optic cable - a multichannel communications cable using a thread of optical glass fibers as a transmission medium in which the signal (voice, video, etc.) is in the form of a coded pulse of light.

FTTX - Fiber to the x (FTTX) is a generic term for any broadband network architecture using optical fiber to provide all or part of the local loop used for last mile telecommunications. As fiber optic cables are able to carry much more data than copper cables, especially over long distances, copper telephone networks built in the 20th century are being replaced by fiber. FTTX is a general term for several configurations of fiber deployment, broadly organized into two groups: FTTN and FTTP /H/B. Fiber to the node (FTTN), also referred to as Fiber to the neighborhood, delivers fiber to within 300m (1,000 ft) of a customer's premises. Fiber to the premises (FTTP) can be further categorized as fiber to the home (FTTH) or fiber to the building/business (FTTB). FTTN (and FTTC, fiber to the curb (to less than 300m (1,000 ft of a customer's premises)) are seen as interim steps toward full FTTP.

Galileo - Chartered in 2016, Galileo is a global navigation satellite system (GNSS) created by the European Union through the European Space Agency (ESA), and operated by the European Union Agency for the Space Programme (EUSPA). Headquartered in Prague, Czechia, it has two ground operations centers: one in Fucino, Italy, and the other in Oberpfaffenhofen, Germany. The project is named after the Italian astronomer Galileo Galilei and aims to provide an independent high-precision positioning system. Galileo provides a global search and rescue (SAR) function as part of the MEOSAR system.

GPON - stands for Gigabyte Passive Optical Networks, which are networks that rely on optical cables to deliver information from a single feeding fiber from a provider - to multiple destinations - via the use of splitters. GPONs are currently the leading form of Passive Optical Networks (PON) and offer up to a 1:64 ratio on a single fiber. As opposed to a standard copper wire in most networks, GPONs are 95% more energy efficient.

GSM - a global system for mobile (cellular) communications devised by the Groupe Special Mobile of the pan-European standardization organization, Conference Europeanne des Posts et Telecommunications (CEPT) in 1982.

HF - high frequency; any radio frequency in the 3,000- to 30,000-kHz range.

HSPA - High Speed Packet Access (HSPA) is an amalgamation of two mobile protocols, High Speed Downlink Packet Access

(HSDPA) and High Speed Uplink Packet Access (HSUPA), that extends and improves the performance of existing 3G mobile telecommunication networks using the Wideband Code Division Multiple Access (WCDMA) protocols. A further improved 3rd Generation Partnership Project (3GPP) standard, Evolved High Speed Packet Access (also known as HSPA+), was released late in 2008 with subsequent worldwide adoption beginning in 2010. The newer standard allows bit-rates to reach as high as 337 Mbit/s in the downlink and 34 Mbit/s in the uplink. However, these speeds are rarely achieved in practice.

ICT - Information and communications technology (ICT) encompasses the capture, storage, retrieval, processing, display, representation, presentation, organization, management, security, transfer, and interchange of data and information; includes all categories of ubiquitous technology used for the gathering, storing, transmitting, retrieving, or processing of information.

Inmarsat - International Maritime Satellite Organization is a British satellite telecommunications company, offering global mobile services. It provides telephone and data services to users worldwide, via portable or mobile terminals that communicate with ground stations through 13 geostationary telecommunications satellites. Inmarsat's network provides communications services to a range of governments, aid agencies, media outlets, and businesses (especially in the shipping, airline, and mining industries) with a need to communicate in remote regions or where there is no reliable terrestrial network.

Intelsat - Intelsat Corporation (formerly International Telecommunications Satellite Organization, INTEL-SAT, INTELSAT) is a communications satellite services provider.

Intersputnik - International Organization of Space Communications (Moscow); first established in the former Soviet Union and the East European countries, it is now marketing its services worldwide with earth stations in North America, Africa, and East Asia.

IP - Internet Protocol (IP) is a communications protocol for computers connected to a network, especially the Internet, specifying the format for addresses and units of transmitted data; data traversing the Internet is divided into smaller pieces, called packets.

IoT - the Internet of Things is a system of interrelated computing devices, mechanical, and digital machines provided with unique identifiers (UIDs) and the ability to transfer data over a network without requiring human-to-human or human-to-computer interaction.

Iridium - the Iridium satellite constellation provides L band (long wavelength band) voice and data information coverage to satellite phones, pagers, and integrated transceivers over the entire surface of the earth. Iridium Communications owns and operates the constellation, additionally selling equipment and access to its services.

ITU - the International Telecommunication Union (ITU) is a United Nations specialized agency that is responsible for issues that concern information and communication technologies. Founded in 1865, the ITU is the oldest global international organization. The ITU coordinates the shared global use of the radio spectrum, promotes international cooperation in assigning satellite orbits, works to improve telecommunication infrastructure in the developing world, and assists in the development and coordination of worldwide technical standards. The ITU is also active in the areas of broadband Internet, latest-generation wireless technologies, aeronautical and maritime navigation, radio astronomy, satellite-based meteorology, convergence in fixed-mobile phone, Internet access, data, voice, TV broadcasting, and next-generation networks.

IXP - an Internet exchange point (IXP) is a physical location through which Internet infrastructure companies such as Internet service providers (ISPs) and content delivery networks (CDNs) connect with each other.

Kacific 1 - Kacific Broadband Satellites Group (Kacific) is a satellite operator providing high-speed broadband Internet service for the South East Asia and Pacific Islands regions. Its first Ka-band HTS satellite, Kacific1, was designed and built by Boeing and launched into geostationary orbit in December 2019.

Landline - communication wire or cable of any sort that is installed on poles or buried in the ground.

LTE - Long-Term Evolution (LTE) is a standard for wireless broadband communication for mobile devices and data terminals Based on the GSM/EDGE and UMTS/HSPA technologies, it increases communication capacity and speed using a different radio interface together with core network improvements.

LTE Advanced - (aka LTE A) is a mobile communication standard and a major enhancement of the Long Term Evolution (LTE) standard. It was submitted as a candidate 4G in late 2009 as meeting the requirements of the IMT-Advanced standard, and was standardized by the 3rd Generation Partnership Project (3GPP) in March 2011 as 3GPP Release 10.

LTE-TDD & LTE-FDD - There are two major differences between LTE-TDD and LTE-FDD: how data is uploaded and downloaded, and what frequency spectra the networks are deployed in. While LTE-FDD uses paired frequencies to upload and download data, LTE-TDD uses a single frequency, alternating between uploading and downloading data through time. The ratio between uploads and downloads on a LTE-TDD network can be changed dynamically, depending on whether more data needs to be sent or received. LTE-TDD and LTE-FDD also operate on different frequency bands, with LTE-TDD working better at higher frequencies, and LTE-FDD working better at lower frequencies.

M-commerce - short for mobile commerce, m-commerce is the use of wireless handheld devices like cellphones and tablets to conduct commercial transactions online, including the purchase and sale of products, online banking, and paying bills.

MNO - a mobile network operator (MNO), also known as a wireless service provider, wireless carrier, cellular company, or mobile network carrier, is a provider of wireless communications services that owns or controls all the elements necessary to sell and deliver services to an end user including radio spectrum allocation, wireless network infrastructure, back haul infrastructure, billing, customer care, provisioning computer systems, and marketing and repair organizations.

MNP - mobile number portability

MVNO - a mobile virtual network operator (MVNO) does not own the wireless network infrastructure over which it provides services to its customers. A MVNO enters into a business agreement with a mobile network operator (MNO) to obtain bulk access to network services at wholesale rates, then sets retail prices independently.

Medarabtel - the Middle East Telecommunications Project of the International Telecommunications Union (ITU) providing a modern telecommunications network, primarily by microwave radio relay, linking Algeria, Djibouti, Egypt, Jordan, Libya, Morocco, Saudi Arabia, Somalia, Sudan, Syria, Tunisia, and Yemen; it was initially started in Morocco in 1970 by the Arab Telecommunications Union (ATU) and was known at that time as the Middle East Mediterranean Telecommunications Network.

Microwave radio relay - transmission of long distance telephone calls and television programs by highly directional radio microwaves that are received and sent on from one booster station to another on an optical path.

NB-IoT - narrowband Internet of Things is a low-power, wide-area network (LPWAN) radio technology. NB-IoT improves the power consumption of user devices, system capacity, and spectrum efficiency.

NGN - The next-generation network is the evolution and migration of fixed and mobile network infrastructures from distinct, proprietary networks to converged networks on an IP. One network transports all information and services (voice, data, and media) by encapsulating these into IP packets, similar to those used on the Internet. The result is unrestricted, consistent and ubiquitous access for users to different service providers.

NMT - Nordic Mobile Telephone (NMT) is a first generation (1G) mobile cellular phone system based on analog technology that was developed jointly by the national telecommunications authorities of the Nordic countries (Denmark, Finland, Iceland, Norway, and Sweden). NMT-450 analog networks have been replaced with digital networks using the same cellular frequencies.

Orbita - a Russian television service; also the trade name of a packet-switched digital telephone network.

PanAmSat - PanAmSat Corporation (Greenwich, CT) was a satellite service provider.
Radio telephone communications - the two-way transmission and reception of sounds by broadcast radio on authorized frequencies using telephone handsets.
Satellite communication system - a communication system consisting of two or more earth stations and at least one satellite that provide long distance transmission of voice, data, and television; the system usually serves as a trunk connection between telephone exchanges; if the earth stations are in the same country, it is a domestic system.
Satellite earth station - a communications facility with a microwave radio transmitting and receiving antenna, and receiving and transmitting equipment required for communicating with satellites.
Satellite link - a radio connection between a satellite and an earth station permitting communication between them, either one-way (down link from satellite to earth station - television receive-only transmission) or two-way (telephone channels).
SHF - super high frequency; any radio frequency in the 3,000- to 30,000-MHz range.
Shortwave - radio frequencies (from 1.605 to 30 MHz) that fall above the commercial broadcast band and are used for communication over long distances.
SIM card - subscriber identity/identification module card, is a small, removable integrated circuit used in a mobile phone to store data unique to the user, such as an identification number, passwords, phone numbers, and messages.
Solidaridad - geosynchronous satellites in Mexico's system of international telecommunications in the Western Hemisphere.
Spectrum - spectrum management is the allocation and regulation of the electromagnetic spectrum into radio frequency (RF) bands, a procedure normally carried out by governments in most countries. Because radio propagation does not stop at national boundaries, governments have sought to harmonise the allocation of RF bands and their standardization. A spectrum auction is a process whereby a government uses an auction system to sell the rights to transmit signals over specific bands of the electromagnetic spectrum and to assign scarce spectrum resources.
Submarine cable - a cable designed for service under water.
TE North - A submarine cable linking Egypt with France, with a branching unit to Cyprus, developed by Alcatel-Lucent.
Telecommunication (telecom) - is the exchange of signs, signals, messages, words, images and sounds, or information of any nature by wire, radio, optical, or other electromagnetic systems (i.e., via the use of technology). Telecommunication occurs through a transmission medium, such as over physical media, for example, over electrical cable, or via electromagnetic radiation through space such as radio or light.
Teledensity (telephone density) - is the number of telephone connections for every hundred individuals living within an area. It varies widely between nations and also between urban and rural areas within a country. Telephone density correlates closely with the per capita GDP of an area and is also used as an indicator of the purchasing power of the middle class of a country or specific region.
Telefax - facsimile service between subscriber stations via the public switched telephone network or the international Datel network.
Telegraph - a telecommunications system designed for unmodulated electric impulse transmission.
Telephony - is the field of technology involving the development, application, and deployment of telecommunication services for the purpose of electronic transmission of voice, fax, or data, between distant parties. The history of telephony is intimately linked to the invention and development of the telephone.
Telex - a communication service involving teletypewriters connected by wire through automatic exchanges.
Trans-Caspian cable - Trans-Caspian Fiber Optic (TCFO) submarine cable; a project between AzerTelecom in Azerbaijan, KazTransCom of Kazakhstan, and Turkmentelekom in Turkmenistan for the construction of a fiber-optic cable in the Caspian Sea.
Tropospheric scatter - a form of microwave radio transmission in which the troposphere is used to scatter and reflect a fraction of the incident radio waves back to earth. Powerful, highly directional antennas are used to transmit and receive the microwave signals. Reliable over-the-horizon communications are realized for distances up to 600 miles in a single hop; additional hops can extend the range of this system for very long distances.
Trunk network - a network of switching centers, connected by multichannel trunk lines.
UHF - ultra high frequency; any radio frequency in the 300- to 3,000-MHz range.
VHF - very high frequency; any radio frequency in the 30- to 300-MHz range.
VNO - A virtual network operator (VNO) is a management services provider and a network services reseller of other telecommunication service providers. VNOs do not possess a telecom network infrastructure; however, they provide telecom services by acquiring the required capacity from other telecom carriers. These network providers are classified as virtual because they offer network services to clients without possessing the actual network. VNOs usually lease bandwidth at agreed wholesale rates from different telecom providers and then offer solutions to their direct customers.
VOD - video on demand (VOD) is a video media distribution system that allows users to access video entertainment without a traditional video entertainment device and without the constraints of a typical static broadcasting schedule.
VoIP - Voice over Internet Protocol (VoIP), also called IP telephony, refers to the delivery of voice communications and multimedia sessions over Internet Protocol (IP) networks, such as the Internet. The terms Internet telephony, broadband telephony, and broadband phone service specifically refer to the provisioning of communications services (voice, fax, text-messaging, voice-messaging) over the public Internet, rather than via the public switched telephone network (PSTN), also known as plain old telephone service (POTS).
VSAT - a VSAT (very-small-aperture terminal) is a two-way satellite ground station with a dish antenna that is smaller than 3.8 meters. The majority of VSAT antennas range from 75 cm to 1.2 m. Data rates, generally, range from 4 kbit/s up to 16 Mbit/s.
WACS - the West Africa Cable System is a submarine communications cable linking South Africa with the UK along the west coast of Africa and Europe; constructed by Alcatel-Lucent. The cable consists of four fiber pairs and is 14,530 Km in length with 14 landing points – 12 along the western coast of Africa and 2 in Europe – with termination in London, UK.
WiMAX - stands for Worldwide Interoperability for Microwave Access; it is a family of wireless broadband communication standards based on the IEEE 802.16 set of standards, which provide multiple physical layer (PHY) and Media Access Control (MAC) options.

Telephone numbers All telephone numbers in *The World Factbook* consist of the country code in brackets, the city or area code (where required) in parentheses, and the local number. The international access code, which varies from country to country, is not included.

Telephones - fixed lines This entry gives the *total* number of fixed telephone lines in use, as well as the number of *subscriptions per 100 inhabitants.*

Telephones - mobile cellular This entry gives the *total* number of mobile cellular telephone subscribers, as well as the number of *subscriptions per 100 inhabitants.* Note that because of the ubiquity of mobile phone use in developed countries, the number of subscriptions per 100 inhabitants can exceed 100.

Terminology Due to the highly structured nature of the *Factbook* database, some collective generic terms have to be used. For example, the word *Country* in the *Country name* entry refers to a wide variety of dependencies, areas of special sovereignty, uninhabited islands, and other entities, in addition to the traditional countries or independent states. *Military* is also used as an umbrella term for various civil defense, security, and defense activities. The *Independence* entry includes colonial independence dates and former ruling states, as well as other significant nationhood dates. These can include the date of founding, unification, federation, confederation, establishment, or state succession. The status of dependent areas is noted.

Terrain This entry contains a brief description of the topography of a country.

Terrorist group(s) This entry lists the US State Department-designated Foreign Terrorist Organizations (FTO) that are assessed to maintain a presence in each country. This includes cases where sympathizers, supporters, or associates of designated FTOs have carried out attacks or been arrested for terrorist-type activities in the country. See Appendix T: Terrorist Organizations for details on each FTO.

Time difference This entry is expressed in *The World Factbook* in two ways. First, it is stated as the difference in hours between the capital of an entity and **Coordinated Universal Time (UTC)** during Standard Time. Additionally, the time difference between the capital of an entity and Washington, D.C., is also provided. Note that the time difference assumes both locations are simultaneously observing Standard Time or Daylight Saving Time.

Time zones Ten countries (Australia, Brazil, Canada, Indonesia, Kazakhstan, Mexico, New Zealand, Russia, Spain, and the United States) and the island of Greenland observe more than one official time depending on the number of designated time zones within their boundaries. An illustration of world and country time zones can be seen in the Standard Time Zones of the World map included in the **World and Regional Maps** section of *The World Factbook*.

Tobacco use This entry measures the prevalence of tobacco use, whether smoked or smokeless or both, among persons 15 years and older for the total population, and separately for the male and female populations.

Total fertility rate This entry gives a figure for the average number of children that would be born per woman if all women lived to the end of their childbearing years and bore children according to a given fertility rate at each age. The total fertility rate (TFR) is a more direct measure of the level of fertility than the crude birth rate, since it refers to births per woman.

Total renewable water resources This entry provides the long-term average water availability for a country measured in cubic meters per year of precipitation, recharged ground water, and surface inflows from surrounding countries. It does not include water resource totals that have been reserved for upstream or downstream countries through international agreements. Note that these values are averages and do not accurately reflect the total available in any given year, which can vary greatly due to short-term and long-term climatic and weather variations.

Total water withdrawal This entry provides the annual quantity of water in cubic meters withdrawn for municipal, industrial, and agricultural purposes. Municipal sector use refers to the annual quantity of water withdrawn primarily for direct use by the population through the public distribution network. Industrial sector use refers to the annual quantity of self-supplied water withdrawn for industrial purposes. Agricultural sector use refers to the annual quantity of self-supplied water withdrawn for irrigation, livestock, and aquaculture purposes.

Trafficking in persons Trafficking in persons is modern-day slavery, involving victims who are forced, defrauded, or coerced into labor or sexual exploitation. The International Labor Organization (ILO), the UN agency charged with addressing labor standards, employment, and social protection issues, estimated in 2022 that 27.6 million people worldwide were victims of forced labor, bonded labor, forced child labor, sexual servitude, and involuntary servitude. Human trafficking is a multi-dimensional threat, depriving people of their human rights and freedoms, risking global health, promoting social breakdown, inhibiting development by depriving countries of their human capital, and helping fuel the growth of organized crime. In 2000, the US Congress passed the Trafficking Victims Protection Act (TVPA), reauthorized several times (the latest in 2022 became law in January 2023), which provides tools for the US to combat trafficking in persons, both domestically and abroad. One of the law's key components is the creation of the US Department of State's annual *Trafficking in Persons Report*, which assesses the government response in some 185 countries with a significant number of victims trafficked across their borders who are recruited, harbored, transported, provided, or obtained for forced labor or sexual exploitation. Countries in the annual report are rated in three tiers, based on government efforts to combat trafficking. The countries identified in this entry are those listed in the annual *Trafficking in Persons Report* as 'Tier 2 Watch List' or 'Tier 3' based on the following *tier rating* definitions:

Tier 2 Watch List countries do not fully meet the TVPA's minimum standards for the elimination of trafficking but are making significant efforts to do so, and for which:
– the estimated number of victims of severe forms of trafficking is very significant or is significantly increasing and the country is not taking proportional concrete actions; or,
– there is a failure to provide evidence of increasing efforts to combat severe forms of trafficking in persons from the previous year, including increased investigations, prosecutions, and convictions of trafficking crimes, increased assistance to victims, and decreasing evidence of complicity in severe forms of trafficking by government officials

Tier 3 countries do not fully meet the TVPA's minimum standards and are not making significant efforts to do so.

Transnational issues This category includes entries that deal with current issues going beyond national boundaries.

Transportation This category includes the entries dealing with the means for movement of people and goods.

Transportation - note This entry includes miscellaneous transportation information of significance not included elsewhere.

Under-5 mortality rate This entry indicates the probability a newborn would die before reaching exactly 5 years of age, expressed per 1,000 live births. Data is provided for the *total* number of children under 5 per 1,000 live births, as well as for the number of *male* and *female* children under 5 years of age per 1,000 live births.

Unemployment rate This entry contains the percentage of the labor force that is without jobs. Substantial underemployment might be noted.

Union name This entry, which appears only in the European Union entry under the Government category, provides the full name and abbreviation for the European Union.

Urbanization This entry provides two measures of the degree of urbanization of a population. *Urban population* describes the percentage of the total population living in urban areas, as defined by the country. *Rate of urbanization* describes the projected average rate of change of the size of the urban population over the given period of time. It is possible for a country with a 100% urban population to still display a change in the rate of urbanization (up or down). For example, a population of 100,000 that is 100% urban can change in size to 110,000 or 90,000 but remain 100% urban.

Additionally, the World entry includes a list of the *ten largest urban agglomerations*. An *urban agglomeration* is defined as the city or town proper and also the suburban fringe or thickly settled territory lying outside of, but adjacent to, the boundaries of the city.

UTC (Coordinated Universal Time) See entry for **Coordinated Universal Time.**

Waste and recycling This entry provides the amount of municipal solid waste a country produces annually and the amount of that waste that is recycled. Municipal solid waste consists of everyday items that are used and thrown away. Municipal solid waste – often referred to as trash or garbage – comes from homes, schools, hospitals, and businesses. Recycling is the process of collecting and processing materials that would otherwise be thrown away as trash and turning them into new products. This entry includes three subfields: *annual amount of municipal solid waste generated* (tons), *annual amount of municipal solid waste recycled* (tons), and *percent of municipal solid waste recycled.*

Waterways This entry gives the total length of navigable rivers, canals, and other inland bodies of water.

Weights and Measures This information is presented in Weights and Measures and includes mathematical notations (mathematical powers and names), metric interrelationships (prefix; symbol; length, weight, or capacity; area; volume), and standard conversion factors.

Wonders of the World This entry provides an introduction to the Seven Wonders of the Ancient World and the New Seven Wonders of the World.

World biomes A biome is a biogeographical designation describing a biological community of plants and animals that has formed in response to a physical environment and a shared regional climate. Biomes can extend over more than one continent. Different classification systems define different numbers of biomes. *The World Factbook* recognizes the following seven biomes used by NASA: Tundra, Coniferous Forest, Temperate Deciduous Forest, Rainforest, Grassland, Shrubland, and Desert.

Years All year references are for the calendar year (CY) unless indicated as fiscal year (FY). The calendar year is an accounting period of 12 months from 1 January to 31 December. The fiscal year is an accounting period of 12 months other than 1 January to 31 December.

Youth unemployment rate (ages 15–24) This entry gives the percentage of the total labor force aged 15–24 that is unemployed during a specified year.

AFGHANISTAN

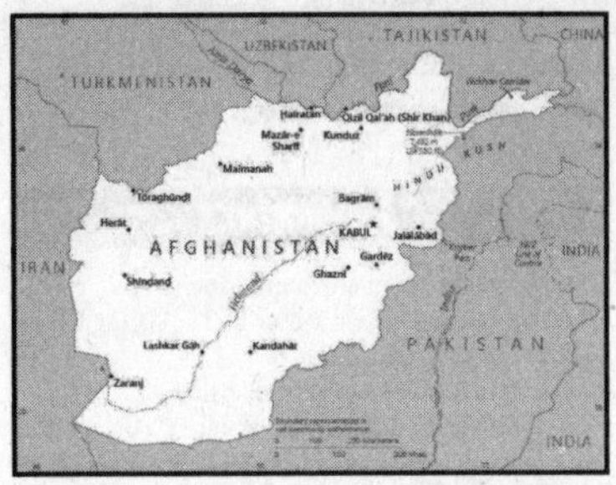

INTRODUCTION

Background: Ahmad Shah DURRANI unified the Pashtun tribes and founded Afghanistan in 1747. The country served as a buffer between the British and Russian Empires until it won independence from notional British control in 1919. A brief experiment in increased democracy ended in a 1973 coup and a 1978 communist countercoup. The Soviet Union invaded in 1979 to support the tottering Afghan communist regime, touching off a long and destructive war. Internationally supported anti-communist mujahidin rebels forced the USSR to withdraw in 1989. A series of subsequent civil wars saw Kabul finally fall in 1996 to the Taliban, a hardline Pakistani-sponsored movement. Following the 11 September 2001 terrorist attacks, a US and Allied military action toppled the Taliban for sheltering Usama BIN LADIN.

A UN-sponsored Bonn Conference in 2001 established a process for political reconstruction that included the adoption of a new constitution, a presidential election in 2004, and National Assembly elections in 2005. In 2004, Hamid KARZAI became the first democratically elected president of Afghanistan, and he was reelected in 2009. Ashraf Ghani AHMADZAI succeeded him as president in 2014 following a disputed election. The Taliban conducted an insurgency for two decades against the Afghan Government and forces from the United States and other countries. In February 2020, the US and the Taliban signed an agreement that led to the withdrawal of international forces in exchange for commitments on counterterrorism and other assurances. The Taliban took over Afghanistan on 15 August 2021.

The Taliban established an all-male interim leadership structure dominated by Pashtun clerics under the leadership of Haivatrullah AKHUNDZADA. The Taliban issued numerous edicts that constrained women's mobility, ability to study and work, and access to education beyond primary school. To date, no country has recognized the Taliban as the government of Afghanistan.

GEOGRAPHY

Location: Southern Asia, north and west of Pakistan, east of Iran

Geographic coordinates: 33 00 N, 65 00 E

Map references: Asia

Area: *total:* 652,230 sq km
land: 652,230 sq km
water: 0 sq km
comparison ranking: total 43

Area - comparative: almost six times the size of Virginia; slightly smaller than Texas

Land boundaries: *total:* 5,987 km
border countries (6): China 91 km; Iran 921 km; Pakistan 2,670 km; Tajikistan 1,357 km; Turkmenistan 804 km; Uzbekistan 144 km

Coastline: 0 km (landlocked)

Maritime claims: none (landlocked)

Climate: arid to semiarid; cold winters and hot summers

Terrain: mostly rugged mountains; plains in north and southwest

Elevation: *highest point:* Noshak 7,492 m
lowest point: Amu Darya 258 m
mean elevation: 1,884 m

Natural resources: natural gas, petroleum, coal, copper, chromite, talc, barites, sulfur, lead, zinc, iron ore, salt, precious and semiprecious stones, arable land

Land use: *agricultural land:* 58.1% (2018 est.)
agricultural land: arable land: 11.8% (2018)
agricultural land: permanent crops: 0.3% (2018)
agricultural land: permanent pasture: 46% (2018)
forest: 1.8% (2018 est.)
other: 40.1% (2018)

Irrigated land: 24,930 sq km (2020)

Major lakes (area sq km): *salt water lake(s):* Ab-e Istadah-ye Muqur (endorheic basin) - 520 sq km

Major rivers (by length in km): Amu Darya (shared with Tajikistan [s], Turkmenistan, and Uzbekistan [m]) - 2,620 km; Helmand river source (shared with Iran) - 1,130 km
note – [s] after country name indicates river source; [m] after country name indicates river mouth

Major watersheds (area sq km): Indian Ocean drainage: Indus (1,081,718 sq km)

Internal (endorheic basin) drainage: Amu Darya (534,739 sq km); Tarim Basin (1,152,448 sq km)

Population distribution: populations tend to cluster in the foothills and periphery of the rugged Hindu Kush range; smaller groups are found in many of the country's interior valleys; in general, the east is more densely settled, while the south is sparsely populated

Natural hazards: damaging earthquakes occur in Hindu Kush mountains; flooding; droughts

Geography - note: landlocked; the Hindu Kush mountains that run northeast to southwest divide the northern provinces from the rest of the country; the highest peaks are in the northern Vakhan (Wakhan Corridor)

PEOPLE AND SOCIETY

Population: *total:* 40,121,552
male: 20,301,066
female: 19,820,486 (2024 est.)
comparison rankings: female 37; male 37; total 36

Nationality: *noun:* Afghan(s)
adjective: Afghan

Ethnic groups: current, reliable statistical data on ethnicity in Afghanistan are not available; Afghanistan's 2004 Constitution cited Pashtun, Tajik, Hazara, Uzbek, Turkman, Baluch, Pashaie, Nuristani, Aymaq, Arab, Qirghiz, Qizilbash, Gujur, and Brahwui ethnicities; Afghanistan has dozens of other small ethnic groups

Languages: Afghan Persian or Dari (official, lingua franca) 77%, Pashto (official) 48%, Uzbeki 11%, English 6%, Turkmani 3%, Urdu 3%, Pashaie 1%, Nuristani 1%, Arabic 1%, Balochi 1%, other <1% (2020 est.)
major-language sample(s):
کتاب حقایق جهان، مرجعی ضروری برای اطلاعات اولیه (Dari)
د دنیا د حقائیقو کتاب، بنیادی معلوماتو لپاره ضروری سرچینه (Pashto)
note 1: percentages sum to more than 100% because many people are multilingual
note 2: Uzbeki, Turkmani, Pashaie, Nuristani, Balochi, and Pamiri are the third official languages in areas where the majority speaks them

Religions: Muslim 99.7% (Sunni 84.7 - 89.7%, Shia 10 - 15%), other <0.3% (2009 est.)

Age structure: *0-14 years:* 39.6% (male 8,062,407/female 7,818,897)
15-64 years: 57.5% (male 11,702,734/female 11,372,249)
65 years and over: 2.9% (2024 est.) (male 535,925/female 629,340)
2023 population pyramid:

Dependency ratios: *total dependency ratio:* 84.6
youth dependency ratio: 80.2
elderly dependency ratio: 4.8
potential support ratio: 22.5 (2021 est.)

Median age: *total:* 20 years (2024 est.)
male: 20 years
female: 20.1 years
comparison ranking: total 206

Population growth rate: 2.22% (2024 est.)
comparison ranking: 32

Birth rate: 34.2 births/1,000 population (2024 est.)
comparison ranking: 15

Death rate: 11.8 deaths/1,000 population (2024 est.)
comparison ranking: 19

Net migration rate: -0.1 migrant(s)/1,000 population (2024 est.)
comparison ranking: 99

Population distribution: populations tend to cluster in the foothills and periphery of the rugged Hindu Kush range; smaller groups are found in many of the country's interior valleys; in general, the east is more densely settled, while the south is sparsely populated

Urbanization: *urban population:* 26.9% of total population (2023)
rate of urbanization: 3.34% annual rate of change (2020-25 est.)

Major urban areas - population: 4.589 million KABUL (capital) (2023)

Sex ratio: *at birth:* 1.05 male(s)/female
0-14 years: 1.03 male(s)/female
15-64 years: 1.03 male(s)/female
65 years and over: 0.85 male(s)/female
total population: 1.02 male(s)/female (2024 est.)

Mother's mean age at first birth: 19.9 years (2015 est.)
note: data represents median age at first birth among women 25-49

Maternal mortality ratio: 620 deaths/100,000 live births (2020 est.)

comparison ranking: 8

Infant mortality rate: *total:* 101.3 deaths/1,000 live births (2024 est.)
male: 109.7 deaths/1,000 live births
female: 92.5 deaths/1,000 live births
comparison ranking: total 1

Life expectancy at birth: *total population:* 54.4 years (2024 est.)
male: 52.8 years
female: 56.1 years
comparison ranking: total population 227

Total fertility rate: 4.43 children born/woman (2024 est.)
comparison ranking: 17

Gross reproduction rate: 2.16 (2024 est.)

Contraceptive prevalence rate: 18.9% (2018)
note: percent of women aged 12-49

Drinking water source: *improved: urban:* 100% of population
improved: rural: 68.3% of population
improved: total: 76.5% of population
unimproved: urban: 0% of population
unimproved: rural: 31.7% of population
unimproved: total: 23.5% of population (2020 est.)

Current health expenditure: 15.5% of GDP (2020)

Physician density: 0.25 physicians/1,000 population (2020)

Hospital bed density: 0.4 beds/1,000 population (2017)

Sanitation facility access: *improved: urban:* 88.2% of population
rural: 52% of population
total: 61.4% of population
unimproved: urban: 11.8% of population
rural: 48% of population
total: 38.6% of population (2020 est.)

Obesity - adult prevalence rate: 5.5% (2016)
comparison ranking: 177

Alcohol consumption per capita: *total:* 0.01 liters of pure alcohol (2019 est.)
beer: 0 liters of pure alcohol (2019 est.)
wine: 0 liters of pure alcohol (2019 est.)
spirits: 0.01 liters of pure alcohol (2019 est.)
other alcohols: 0 liters of pure alcohol (2019 est.)
comparison ranking: total 183

Tobacco use: *total:* 23.3% (2020 est.)
male: 39.4% (2020 est.)
female: 7.2% (2020 est.)
comparison ranking: total 62

Children under the age of 5 years underweight: 19.1% (2018)
comparison ranking: 19

Currently married women (ages 15-49): 70.3% (2023 est.)

Child marriage: *women married by age 15:* 4.2%
women married by age 18: 28.3% (2017 est.)

Education expenditures: 2.9% of GDP (2020 est.)
comparison ranking: 162

Literacy: *definition:* age 15 and over can read and write
total population: 37.3%
male: 52.1%
female: 22.6% (2021)

School life expectancy (primary to tertiary education): *total:* 10 years
male: 13 years
female: 8 years (2018)

ENVIRONMENT

Environment - current issues: limited natural freshwater resources; inadequate supplies of potable water; soil degradation; overgrazing; deforestation (much of the remaining forests are being cut down for fuel and building materials); desertification; air and water pollution in overcrowded urban areas

Environment - international agreements: *party to:* Biodiversity, Climate Change, Climate Change-Kyoto Protocol, Climate Change-Paris Agreement, Comprehensive Nuclear Test Ban, Desertification, Endangered Species, Environmental Modification, Hazardous Wastes, Marine Dumping-London Convention, Nuclear Test Ban, Ozone Layer Protection
signed, but not ratified: Law of the Sea, Marine Life Conservation

Climate: arid to semiarid; cold winters and hot summers

Land use: *agricultural land:* 58.1% (2018 est.)
agricultural land: arable land: 11.8% (2018)
agricultural land: permanent crops: 0.3% (2018)
agricultural land: permanent pasture: 46% (2018)
forest: 1.8% (2018 est.)
other: 40.1% (2018)

Urbanization: *urban population:* 26.9% of total population (2023)
rate of urbanization: 3.34% annual rate of change (2020-25 est.)

Food insecurity: *severe localized food insecurity: due to civil conflict, population displacement, and economic slowdown* - between November 2021 and March 2022, during the winter lean season, the food insecurity situation was expected to deteriorate and the number of people in "Crisis" or above was likely to increase to 22.8 million, about 35% more than during the same season in 2020/21; following the developments of August 2021 in the country, the international aid flows, an important element of public spending, were halted; the food security situation and agricultural livelihoods in the country is likely to significantly deteriorate in the coming months due to cumulative and cascading impact of multiple shocks, including weather, conflict, economic crisis and the lingering effects of the COVID-19 pandemic (2022)

Revenue from forest resources: 0.2% of GDP (2018 est.)
comparison ranking: 94

Revenue from coal: 0.45% of GDP (2018 est.)
comparison ranking: 12

Air pollutants: *particulate matter emissions:* 62.49 micrograms per cubic meter (2019 est.)
carbon dioxide emissions: 8.67 megatons (2016 est.)
methane emissions: 90.98 megatons (2020 est.)

Waste and recycling: *municipal solid waste generated annually:* 5,628,525 tons (2016 est.)

Major lakes (area sq km): *salt water lake(s):* Ab-e Istadah-ye Muqur (endorheic basin) - 520 sq km

Major rivers (by length in km): Amu Darya (shared with Tajikistan [s], Turkmenistan, and Uzbekistan [m]) - 2,620 km; Helmand river source (shared with Iran) - 1,130 km
note – [s] after country name indicates river source; [m] after country name indicates river mouth

Major watersheds (area sq km): Indian Ocean drainage: Indus (1,081,718 sq km)

Internal (endorheic basin) drainage: Amu Darya (534,739 sq km); Tarim Basin (1,152,448 sq km)

Total water withdrawal: *municipal:* 200 million cubic meters (2020 est.)
industrial: 170 million cubic meters (2020 est.)
agricultural: 20 billion cubic meters (2020 est.)

Total renewable water resources: 65.33 billion cubic meters (2020 est.)

GOVERNMENT

Country name: *conventional long form:* Islamic Republic of Afghanistan (prior to 15 August 2021); current country name disputed
conventional short form: Afghanistan
local long form: Jamhuri-ye Islami-ye Afghanistan (prior to 15 August 2021; current country name is disputed)
local short form: Afghanistan
etymology: the name "Afghan" originally referred to the Pashtun people (today it is understood to include all the country's ethnic groups), while the suffix "-stan" means "place of" or "country"; so Afghanistan literally means the "Land of the Afghans"

Government type: theocratic; the United States does not recognize the Taliban Government

Capital: *name:* Kabul
geographic coordinates: 34 31 N, 69 11 E
time difference: UTC+4.5 (9.5 hours ahead of Washington, DC, during Standard Time)
daylight saving time: does not observe daylight savings time
etymology: named for the Kabul River, but the river's name is of unknown origin

Administrative divisions: 34 provinces (welayat, singular - welayat); Badakhshan, Badghis, Baghlan, Balkh, Bamyan, Daykundi, Farah, Faryab, Ghazni, Ghor, Helmand, Herat, Jowzjan, Kabul, Kandahar, Kapisa, Khost, Kunar, Kunduz, Laghman, Logar, Nangarhar, Nimroz, Nuristan, Paktika, Paktiya, Panjshir, Parwan, Samangan, Sar-e Pul, Takhar, Uruzgan, Wardak, Zabul

Independence: 19 August 1919 (from UK control over Afghan foreign affairs)

National holiday: *previous:* Independence Day, 19 August (1919); under the Taliban Government, 15 August (2022) is declared a national holiday, marking the anniversary of the victory of the Afghan jihad

Legal system: the Taliban is implementing its own interpretation of Islamic law, which is partially based on the Hanifi school of Islamic jurisprudence and have enforced strict punishments; before the Taliban takeover, Afghanistan had a mixed legal system of civil, customary, and Islamic law
(2021)

Constitution: *history:* several previous; latest ratified in 2004, but not currently enforced by the Taliban

International law organization participation: has not submitted an ICJ jurisdiction declaration; formerly accepted ICCt jurisdiction

Citizenship: *citizenship by birth:* no
citizenship by descent only: at least one parent must have been born in - and continuously lived in - Afghanistan
dual citizenship recognized: no
residency requirement for naturalization: 5 years

Suffrage: 18 years of age; universal

Executive branch: *chief of state:* Taliban Leader HAYBATULLAH Akhundzada (since 15 August 2021)
head of government: overall Taliban Leader HAYBATULLAH Akhundzada is the [so-called] Amir-ul Momineen of the Taliban and is seen by them as a head of government.
cabinet: the Taliban have announced a "cabinet" for the "caretaker government," including the "acting prime minister," "acting deputy prime ministers," and "ministers" who claim to represent 26 ministries
elections/appointments: the 2004 Afghan constitution directed that the president should be elected by majority popular vote for a 5-year term (eligible for a second term); election last held on 28 September 2019, and the Taliban have given no indication that they intend to reinstate elections or any other mechanism of democratic governance
note: the United States has not yet made a decision whether to recognize the Taliban or any other entity as the government of Afghanistan

Legislative branch: *note:* before August 2021, Afghanistan had a bicameral National Assembly that consisted of the House of Elders and House of the People; the parliament has been on hiatus since August 2021 and the Taliban has shown no interest in reviving it

Judicial branch: *highest court(s):* the Taliban are purported to have appointed clerics, including a "Chief Justice", to Afghanistan's Supreme Court
subordinate courts: provincial courts, religious courts, and specialty courts

Political parties: the Taliban Government enforces an authoritarian state and has banned other political parties; note - before 15 August 2021, the Ministry of Justice had licensed 72 political parties as of April 2019
the Taliban have banned other political parties but have allowed some party leaders, including the head of Hezb-e-Islami, Gulbuddin Hekmatyar, to continue to live and work in Afghanistan; Hekmatyar likely continues to enjoy some political support from loyalists; leaders of other parties, including Jamiat-e-Islami's Salahuddin Rabbani and Jumbesh's Rashid Dostum, operate from abroad but likely also command some following within Afghanistan; note - before 15 August 2021, the Ministry of Justice had licensed 72 political parties as of April 2019

International organization participation: Afghanistan is a member of the following organizations but Taliban representatives do not participate: ADB, CICA, CP, ECO, EITI (candidate country), FAO, G-77, IAEA, IBRD, ICAO, ICC (NGOs), ICCt, ICRM, IDA, IDB, IFAD, IFC, IFRCS, ILO, IMF, Interpol, IOC, IOM, IPU, ISO (correspondent), ITSO, ITU, ITUC (NGOs), MIGA, NAM, OIC, OPCW, OSCE (partner), SAARC, SACEP, SCO (dialogue member), UN, UNAMA, UNCTAD, UNESCO, UNHCR, UNIDO, UNWTO, UPU, WCO, WFTU (NGOs), WHO, WIPO, WMO, WTO

Diplomatic representation in the US: none

Note: the Afghan Embassy closed in March 2022

Diplomatic representation from the US: *embassy:* the United States does not maintain a presence in Afghanistan and its diplomatic mission to Afghanistan has relocated to Doha, Qatar

Flag description: three equal vertical bands of black (hoist side), red, and green, with the national emblem in white centered on the red band and slightly overlapping the other 2 bands; the center of the emblem features a mosque with pulpit and flags on either side, below the mosque are Eastern Arabic numerals for the solar year 1298 (1919 in the Gregorian calendar, the year of Afghan independence from the UK); this central image is circled by a border consisting of sheaves of wheat on the left and right, in the upper-center is an Arabic inscription of the Shahada (Muslim creed) below which are rays of the rising sun over the Takbir (Arabic expression meaning "God is great"), and at bottom center is a scroll bearing the name Afghanistan; black signifies the past, red is for the blood shed for independence, and green can represent either hope for the future, agricultural prosperity, or Islam
note 1: the United States has not recognized the Taliban or any other entity as the government of Afghanistan and, accordingly, continues to display the flag of Afghanistan as set forth in the country's constitution of 2004
note 2: Afghanistan had more changes to its national flag in the 20th century - 19 by one count - than any other country; the colors black, red, and green appeared on most of them

National symbol(s): lion; national colors: red, green, black

National anthem: *name:* "Milli Surood" (National Anthem)
lyrics/music: Abdul Bari JAHANI/Babrak WASA
note: adopted 2006

National heritage: *total World Heritage Sites:* 2 (both cultural)
selected World Heritage Site locales: Minaret of Jam; Buddhas of Bamyan
note: the monumental 6th- and 7th-century statues were destroyed by the Taliban in 2001

ECONOMY

Economic overview: extremely low-income South Asian economy; import drops, currency depreciation, disappearing central bank reserves, and increasing inflation after Taliban takeover; increasing Chinese trade; hit hard by COVID; ongoing sanctions

Real GDP (purchasing power parity): $80.416 billion (2022 est.)
$85.768 billion (2021 est.)
$108.209 billion (2020 est.)
note: data in 2021 dollars
comparison ranking: 103

Real GDP growth rate: -6.24% (2022 est.)
-20.74% (2021 est.)
-2.35% (2020 est.)
note: annual GDP % growth based on constant local currency
comparison ranking: 216

Real GDP per capita: $2,000 (2022 est.)
$2,100 (2021 est.)
$2,800 (2020 est.)
note: data in 2021 dollars
comparison ranking: 208

GDP (official exchange rate): $14.502 billion (2022 est.)
note: data in current dollars at official exchange rate

Inflation rate (consumer prices): 2.3% (2019 est.)
0.63% (2018 est.)
4.98% (2017 est.)
note: annual % change based on consumer prices
comparison ranking: 45

GDP - composition, by sector of origin: *agriculture:* 33.7% (2022 est.)
industry: 16.1% (2022 est.)
services: 45% (2022 est.)
note: figures may not total 100% due to non-allocated consumption not captured in sector-reported data
comparison rankings: services 168; industry 163; agriculture 9

GDP - composition, by end use: *household consumption:* 97.6% (2022 est.)
government consumption: 21.8% (2022 est.)
investment in fixed capital: 16.7% (2022 est.)
exports of goods and services: 18.4% (2022 est.)
imports of goods and services: -54.5% (2022 est.)
note: figures may not total 100% due to rounding or gaps in data collection

Agricultural products: wheat, milk, watermelons, grapes, potatoes, cantaloupes/melons, vegetables, rice, onions, apples (2022)
note: top ten agricultural products based on tonnage

Industries: small-scale production of bricks, textiles, soap, furniture, shoes, fertilizer, apparel, food products, non-alcoholic beverages, mineral water, cement; handwoven carpets; natural gas, coal, copper

Industrial production growth rate: -5.73% (2022 est.)
note: annual % change in industrial value added based on constant local currency
comparison ranking: 200

Labor force: 8.921 million (2023 est.)
note: number of people ages 15 or older who are employed or seeking work
comparison ranking: 60

Unemployment rate: 14.39% (2023 est.)
14.1% (2022 est.)
11.93% (2021 est.)
note: % of labor force seeking employment
comparison ranking: 186

Youth unemployment rate (ages 15-24): *total:* 18.1% (2023 est.)
male: 16.8% (2023 est.)
female: 30.4% (2023 est.)
note: % of labor force ages 15-24 seeking employment
comparison ranking: total 76

Population below poverty line: 54.5% (2016 est.)
note: % of population with income below national poverty line

Remittances: 2.55% of GDP (2022 est.)
2.24% of GDP (2021 est.)
3.95% of GDP (2020 est.)
note: personal transfers and compensation between resident and non-resident individuals/households/entities

Budget: *revenues:* $9.093 billion (2017 est.)
expenditures: $7.411 billion (2017 est.)
note: central government revenues (excluding grants) and expenses converted to US dollars at average official exchange rate for year indicated

Public debt: 7% of GDP (2017 est.)
comparison ranking: 198

Taxes and other revenues: 9.9% (of GDP) (2017 est.)
note: central government tax revenue as a % of GDP
comparison ranking: 180

Current account balance: -$3.137 billion (2020 est.)
-$3.792 billion (2019 est.)
-$3.897 billion (2018 est.)
note: balance of payments - net trade and primary/secondary income in current dollars
comparison ranking: 168

Exports: $1.476 billion (2020 est.)
$1.516 billion (2019 est.)
$1.609 billion (2018 est.)

note: balance of payments - exports of goods and services in current dollars
comparison ranking: 170

Exports - partners: Pakistan 57%, India 28%, China 3%, UAE 2%, Turkey 2% (2022)
note: top five export partners based on percentage share of exports

Exports - commodities: coal, cotton, grapes, gum resins, nuts (2022)
note: top five export commodities based on value in dollars

Imports: $6.983 billion (2020 est.)
$7.371 billion (2019 est.)
$7.988 billion (2018 est.)
note: balance of payments - imports of goods and services in current dollars
comparison ranking: 136

Imports - partners: UAE 21%, Kazakhstan 17%, Pakistan 17%, China 9%, Uzbekistan 9% (2022)
note: top five import partners based on percentage share of imports

Imports - commodities: wheat, tobacco, palm oil, packaged medicine, rice (2022)
note: top five import commodities based on value in dollars

Reserves of foreign exchange and gold: $9.749 billion (2020 est.)
$8.498 billion (2019 est.)
$8.207 billion (2018 est.)
note: holdings of gold (year-end prices)/foreign exchange/special drawing rights in current dollars
comparison ranking: 76

Debt - external: $2.14 billion (2022 est.)
note: present value of external debt in current US dollars
comparison ranking: 71

Exchange rates: afghanis (AFA) per US dollar -

Exchange rates: 76.814 (2020 est.)
77.738 (2019 est.)
72.083 (2018 est.)
68.027 (2017 est.)
67.866 (2016 est.)

ENERGY

Electricity access: *electrification - total population:* 85.3% (2022 est.)
electrification - urban areas: 95.9%
electrification - rural areas: 81.7%

Electricity: *installed generating capacity:* 627,000 kW (2022 est.)
consumption: 5.994 billion kWh (2022 est.)
imports: 5.881 billion kWh (2022 est.)
transmission/distribution losses: 717.333 million kWh (2022 est.)
comparison rankings: transmission/distribution losses 89; imports 43; consumption 125; installed generating capacity 146

Electricity generation sources: *fossil fuels:* 15.6% of total installed capacity (2022 est.)
solar: 9.6% of total installed capacity (2022 est.)
hydroelectricity: 74.8% of total installed capacity (2022 est.)

Coal: *production:* 4.885 million metric tons (2022 est.)
consumption: 1.545 million metric tons (2022 est.)
exports: 3.343 million metric tons (2022 est.)
imports: 4,000 metric tons (2022 est.)
proven reserves: 66 million metric tons (2022 est.)

Petroleum: *refined petroleum consumption:* 27,000 bbl/day (2022 est.)

Natural gas: *production:* 80.2 million cubic meters (2020 est.)
consumption: 80.2 million cubic meters (2020 est.)
proven reserves: 49.554 billion cubic meters (2021 est.)

Carbon dioxide emissions: 7.029 million metric tonnes of CO2 (2022 est.)
from coal and metallurgical coke: 3.125 million metric tonnes of CO2 (2022 est.)
from petroleum and other liquids: 3.904 million metric tonnes of CO2 (2022 est.)
from consumed natural gas: 167,000 metric tonnes of CO2 (2020 est.)
comparison ranking: total emissions 124

Energy consumption per capita: 2.686 million Btu/person (2022 est.)
comparison ranking: 178

COMMUNICATIONS

Telephones - fixed lines: *total subscriptions:* 146,000 (2021 est.)
subscriptions per 100 inhabitants: (2021 est.) less than 1
comparison ranking: total subscriptions 126

Telephones - mobile cellular: *total subscriptions:* 22.678 million (2021 est.)
subscriptions per 100 inhabitants: 57 (2021 est.)
comparison ranking: total subscriptions 57

Telecommunication systems: *general assessment:* Afghanistan's telecom sector is facing challenges providing adequate coverage to all of the population; prior to the Taliban regaining power, the World Bank and other donors supported the development of a nationwide fiber backbone and there is terrestrial cable connectivity to five neighboring countries; work on the 'Wakhan Corridor Fiber Optic Survey Project' to connect to China has faced obstacles because of Afghanistan's economic issues. (2021)
domestic: before the Taliban takeover in August 2021, less than 1 per 100 for fixed-line teledensity; 57 per 100 for mobile-cellular subscriptions (2021)
international: country code - 93; multiple VSAT's provide international and domestic voice and data connectivity (2019)

Broadcast media: under the Taliban government, independent media outlets have decreased in number and are probably self-censoring criticism of the Taliban and the Ministry of Information and Culture monitors all mass media in Afghanistan; television and radio are key media platforms; only about a fifth of Afghans use the internet, mostly through smartphones (2023)

Internet country code: .af

Internet users: *total:* 7.02 million (2020 est.)
percent of population: 18% (2020 est.)
comparison ranking: total 80

Broadband - fixed subscriptions: *total:* 26,570 (2020 est.)
subscriptions per 100 inhabitants: 0.1 (2020 est.)
comparison ranking: total 157

TRANSPORTATION

National air transport system: *number of registered air carriers:* 3 (2020)
inventory of registered aircraft operated by air carriers: 13
annual passenger traffic on registered air carriers: 1,722,612 (2018)
annual freight traffic on registered air carriers: 29.56 million (2018) mt-km

Civil aircraft registration country code prefix: YA

Airports: 67 (2024)
comparison ranking: 72

Heliports: 8 (2024)

Pipelines: 466 km gas (2013)

Roadways: *total:* 34,903 km
paved: 17,903 km
unpaved: 17,000 km (2021)
comparison ranking: total 94

Waterways: 1,200 km (2011) (chiefly Amu Darya, which handles vessels up to 500 DWT)
comparison ranking: 64

MILITARY AND SECURITY

Military and security forces: the Taliban claims authority over a Ministry of Defense and a National Army (aka Army of the Islamic Emirate of Afghanistan, Islamic Emirate Army, or Afghan Army); it has also formed police forces under a Ministry of Interior (2024)

Military expenditures: 3.3% of GDP (2019)
3.2% of GDP (2018)
3.3% of GDP (2017)
3.1% of GDP (2016)
2.9% of GDP (2015)
comparison ranking: 27

Military and security service personnel strengths: the Taliban claims that the defense forces have approximately 150,000 personnel; it also claims that over 50,000 personnel had been trained for the police forces (2024)

Military equipment inventories and acquisitions: the Taliban military/security forces are armed largely with US-provided equipment captured from the Afghan National Defense and Security Forces (2023)

Military service age and obligation: service is voluntary; there is no conscription (2023)
note: the Taliban dismissed nearly all women from the former Afghan National Defense and Security Forces, except those serving in detention facilities and assisting with body searches

Military - note: the Taliban's primary security threats include ISIS-Khorasan and anti-Taliban resistance elements (2023)

TERRORISM

Terrorist group(s): Haqqani Taliban Network; Harakat ul-Mujahidin; Harakat ul-Jihad-i-Islami; Islamic Jihad Union; Islamic Movement of Uzbekistan; Islamic State of Iraq and ash-Sham-Khorasan Province (ISIS-K); Islamic Revolutionary Guard Corps (IRGC)/Qods Force; Jaish-e-Mohammed; Jaysh al Adl (Jundallah); Lashkar i Jhangvi; Lashkar-e Tayyiba; al-Qa'ida; al-Qa'ida in the Indian Subcontinent (AQIS); Tehrik-e-Taliban Pakistan (TTP)
note 1: as of 2024, Afghanistan was assessed to be a place of global significance for terrorism, with approximately 20 designated and non-designated terrorist groups operating in the country
note 2: details about the history, aims, leadership, organization, areas of operation, tactics, targets, weapons, size, and sources of support of the group(s) appear(s) in the Terrorism reference guide

TRANSNATIONAL ISSUES

Refugees and internally displaced persons: *refugees (country of origin):* 59,486 (Pakistan) (mid-year 2022)

IDPs: 4.394 million (mostly Pashtuns and Kuchis displaced in the south and west due to natural disasters and political instability) (2022)

Trafficking in persons: tier rating: Tier 3 — Afghanistan does not fully meet the minimum standards for the elimination of trafficking and is not making significant efforts to do so, therefore, Afghanistan remained on Tier 3; for more details, go to: https://www.state.gov/reports/2024-trafficking-in-persons-report/afghanistan/

Illicit drugs: the world's largest supplier of opiates, but it is not a major supplier to the United States; 233,000 hectares (ha) of opium poppy cultivated in Afghanistan in 2022; opium from poppies used to produce morphine and heroin; also produces large quantities of methamphetamine, cannabis, and cannabis products such as hashish; one of the world's largest populations suffering from substance abuse; major source of precursor or essential chemicals used in the production of illicit narcotics. (2022)

AKROTIRI AND DHEKELIA

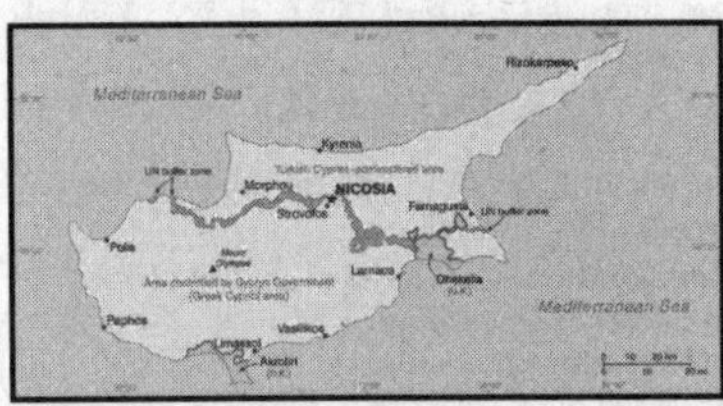

INTRODUCTION

Background: By terms of the 1960 Treaty of Establishment that created the independent Republic of Cyprus, the United Kingdom retained full sovereignty and jurisdiction over two areas of almost 254 square kilometers - Akrotiri and Dhekelia. The southernmost and smaller of the two is Akrotiri Sovereign Base Area, which is also referred to as the Western Sovereign Base Area. The larger area is the Dhekelia Sovereign Base Area, which is also referred to as the Eastern Sovereign Base Area. (2024)

GEOGRAPHY

Location: Eastern Mediterranean; Akrotiri is on a peninsula on the southwest coast of Cyprus; Dhekelia is on the southwest coast of Cyprus near Famagusta

Geographic coordinates: Akrotiri: 34 37 N, 32 58 E

Dhekelia: 34 59 N, 33 45 E

Map references: Middle East

Area: *total:* 254 sq km

Akrotiri: 123 sq km, includes salt and wetlands

Dhekelia: 131 sq km, area surrounds three Cypriot enclaves
comparison ranking: total 213

Area - comparative: Akrotiri: about 0.7 times the size of Washington, DC

Dhekelia: about three-quarters the size of Washington, DC

Land boundaries: border countries: Akrotiri: Cyprus 48 km

Dhekelia: Cyprus 108 km

Coastline: Akrotiri: 56.3 km

Dhekelia: 27.5 km

Climate: temperate; Mediterranean with hot, dry summers and cool winters

Geography - note: British extraterritorial rights also extended to several small off-post sites scattered across Cyprus; of the Sovereign Base Area land, 60% is privately owned and farmed, 20% is owned by the UK Ministry of Defense, and 20% is SBA Crown land

PEOPLE AND SOCIETY

Population: approximately 18,195 on the Sovereign Base Areas of Akrotiri and Dhekelia including 11,000 Cypriots and 7,195 Service and UK-based contract personnel and dependents (2020)

Languages: English, Greek
major-language sample(s):
Το Παγκόσμιο Βιβλίο Δεδομένων, η απαραίτητη πηγή βασικών πληροφοριών. (Greek)

ENVIRONMENT

Environment - current issues: Akrotiri: hunting around the salt lake; note - breeding place for loggerhead and green turtles; only remaining colony of griffon vultures is on the base

Dhekelia: netting and trapping of small migrant songbirds in the spring and autumn

Climate: temperate; Mediterranean with hot, dry summers and cool winters

GOVERNMENT

Country name: *conventional long form:* none
conventional short form: Akrotiri and Dhekelia
etymology: Akrotiri: named for the village that lies within the Western Sovereign Base Area of Cyprus

Dependency status: both are a special form of UK overseas territory; administered by an administrator who is also the Commander, British Forces Cyprus

Capital: *name:* Episkopi Cantonment in Akrotiri (base administrative center for Akrotiri and Dhekelia)
geographic coordinates: 34 40 N, 32 51 E
time difference: UTC+2 (7 hours ahead of Washington, DC, during Standard Time)
daylight saving time: + 1hr, begins last Sunday in March; ends last Sunday in October
etymology: "Episkopi" means "episcopal" in Greek and stems from the fact that the site previously served as the bishop's seat of an Orthodox diocese

Legal system: Laws applicable to the Cypriot population are, as far as possible, the same as the laws of the Republic of Cyprus (ROC); however, the SBA Administration has its own court system to deal with civil and criminal matters, its own police force responsible for civil law enforcement, and a Cyprus Joint Police Unit responsible for military law enforcement; SBA Police coordinate closely with ROC police and UN Peacekeeping Forces in Cyprus (UNFICYP); the SBA Police force is composed almost entirely of Greek Cypriots in ROC regions of the SBAs, and Turkish Cypriot officers in the small portion of Dhekelia administered by the Turkish Cypriots

Constitution: *history:* presented 3 August 1960, effective 16 August 1960 (The Sovereign Base Areas of Akrotiri and Dhekelia Order
in Council 1960 serves as a basic legal document)
amendments: amended 1966

Executive branch: *chief of state:* King CHARLES III (since 8 September 2022)
head of government: Administrator Air Vice-Marshall Peter J.M. SQUIRES (since 1 September 2022)
note: administrator reports to the British Ministry of Defense and is also Commander, British Forces Cyprus (BFC); the chief officer, an appointed civilian, is responsible for the day-to-day running of the civil government of the Sovereign Base Areas

Judicial branch: *highest court(s):* Senior Judges' Court (consists of several visiting judges from England and Wales)
judge selection and term of office: see entry for the United Kingdom
subordinate courts: Resident Judges' Court; Courts Martial

Diplomatic representation in the US: none (overseas territory of the UK)

Diplomatic representation from the US: *embassy:* none (overseas territory of the UK)

Flag description: the flag of the UK is used

National anthem: *note:* as a UK area of special sovereignty, "God Save the King" is official (see United Kingdom)

ECONOMY

Exchange rates: euros (EUR) per US dollar -

Exchange rates: 0.925 (2023 est.)
0.95 (2022 est.)
0.845 (2021 est.)
0.876 (2020 est.)
0.893 (2019 est.)

COMMUNICATIONS

Broadcast media: British Forces Service (BFBS) provides multi-channel satellite TV service as well as BFBS radio broadcasts to the Akrotiri Sovereign Base Area

MILITARY AND SECURITY

Military - note: Akrotiri: defense is the responsibility of the UK; Akrotiri (aka the Western Sovereign

Base Area) has a full Royal Air Force base, headquarters for British Forces Cyprus, and the Episkopi Cantonment

Dhekelia: defense is the responsibility of the UK; Dhekelia (aka the Eastern Sovereign Base Area) includes the Dhekelia Garrison and Ayios Nikolaos station connected by a roadway

TRANSNATIONAL ISSUES

Illicit drugs: NA

ALBANIA

INTRODUCTION

Background: After declaring independence from the Ottoman Empire in 1912, Albania experienced a period of political upheaval that led to a short-lived monarchy, which ended in 1939 when Italy conquered the country. Germany then occupied Albania in 1943, and communist partisans took over the country in 1944. Albania allied itself first with the USSR (until 1960) and then with China (until 1978). In the early 1990s, Albania ended communist rule and established a multiparty democracy.

Government-endorsed pyramid schemes in 1997 led to economic collapse and civil disorder, which only ended when UN peacekeeping troops intervened. In 1999, some 450,000 ethnic Albanians fled from Kosovo to Albania to escape the war with the Serbs. Albania joined NATO in 2009 and became an official candidate for EU membership in 2014.

GEOGRAPHY

Location: Southeastern Europe, bordering the Adriatic Sea and Ionian Sea, between Greece to the south and Montenegro and Kosovo to the north

Geographic coordinates: 41 00 N, 20 00 E

Map references: Europe

Area: *total:* 28,748 sq km
land: 27,398 sq km
water: 1,350 sq km
comparison ranking: total 144

Area - comparative: slightly smaller than Maryland

Land boundaries: *total:* 691 km
border countries: Greece 212 km; Kosovo 112 km; North Macedonia 181 km; Montenegro 186 km

Coastline: 362 km

Maritime claims: *territorial sea:* 12 nm
continental shelf: 200-m depth or to the depth of exploitation

Climate: mild temperate; cool, cloudy, wet winters; hot, clear, dry summers; interior is cooler and wetter

Terrain: mostly mountains and hills; small plains along coast

Elevation: *highest point:* Maja e Korabit (Golem Korab) 2,764 m
lowest point: Adriatic Sea 0 m
mean elevation: 708 m

Natural resources: petroleum, natural gas, coal, bauxite, chromite, copper, iron ore, nickel, salt, timber, hydropower, arable land

Land use: *agricultural land:* 42.8% (2018 est.)
arable land: 22.3% (2018 est.)
permanent crops: 3% (2018 est.)
permanent pasture: 17.4% (2018 est.)
forest: 28.8% (2018 est.)
other: 28.2% (2018 est.)

Irrigated land: 1,820 sq km (2020)

Major lakes (area sq km): *fresh water lake(s):* Lake Scutari (shared with Montenegro) - 400 sq km
note - largest lake in the Balkans

Major watersheds (area sq km): Atlantic Ocean drainage: *(Black Sea)* Danube (795,656 sq km)

Population distribution: a fairly even distribution, with somewhat higher concentrations of people in the western and central parts of the country

Natural hazards: destructive earthquakes; tsunamis occur along southwestern coast; floods; drought

Geography - note: strategic location along Strait of Otranto (links Adriatic Sea to Ionian Sea and Mediterranean Sea)

PEOPLE AND SOCIETY

Population: *total:* 3,107,100
male: 1,531,063
female: 1,576,037 (2024 est.)
comparison rankings: female 137; male 138; total 137

Nationality: *noun:* Albanian(s)
adjective: Albanian

Ethnic groups: Albanian 82.6%, Greek 0.9%, other 1% (including Vlach, Romani, Macedonian, Montenegrin, and Egyptian), unspecified 15.5% (2011 est.)
note: data represent population by ethnic and cultural affiliation

Languages: Albanian 98.8% (official - derived from Tosk dialect), Greek 0.5%, other 0.6% (including Macedonian, Romani, Vlach, Turkish, Italian, and Serbo-Croatian), unspecified 0.1% (2011 est.)
major-language sample(s):
Libri i fakteve boterore, burimi i pazevendesueshem per informacione elementare (Albanian)

Religions: Muslim 56.7%, Roman Catholic 10%, Orthodox 6.8%, atheist 2.5%, Bektashi (a Sufi order) 2.1%, other 5.7%, unspecified 16.2% (2011 est.)
note: all mosques and churches were closed in 1967 and religious observances prohibited; in November 1990, Albania began allowing private religious practice

Age structure: *0-14 years:* 18% (male 292,296/female 267,052)
15-64 years: 66.9% (male 1,023,515/female 1,055,388)
65 years and over: 15.1% (2024 est.) (male 215,252/female 253,597)

Dependency ratios: *total dependency ratio:* 48.2
youth dependency ratio: 24.1
elderly dependency ratio: 24.1
potential support ratio: 4.2 (2021 est.)

Median age: *total:* 36.3 years (2024 est.)
male: 34.8 years
female: 37.8 years
comparison ranking: total 91

Population growth rate: 0.16% (2024 est.)
comparison ranking: 181

Birth rate: 12.3 births/1,000 population (2024 est.)
comparison ranking: 141

Death rate: 7.4 deaths/1,000 population (2024 est.)
comparison ranking: 103

Net migration rate: -3.2 migrant(s)/1,000 population (2024 est.)
comparison ranking: 185

Population distribution: a fairly even distribution, with somewhat higher concentrations of people in the western and central parts of the country

Urbanization: *urban population:* 64.6% of total population (2023)
rate of urbanization: 1.29% annual rate of change (2020-25 est.)

Major urban areas - population: 520,000 TIRANA (capital) (2023)

Sex ratio: *at birth:* 1.06 male(s)/female
0-14 years: 1.09 male(s)/female
15-64 years: 0.97 male(s)/female
65 years and over: 0.85 male(s)/female
total population: 0.97 male(s)/female (2024 est.)

Mother's mean age at first birth: 26.6 years (2020 est.)

Maternal mortality ratio: 8 deaths/100,000 live births (2020 est.)
comparison ranking: 151

Infant mortality rate: *total:* 10.3 deaths/1,000 live births (2024 est.)
male: 11.3 deaths/1,000 live births
female: 9.2 deaths/1,000 live births
comparison ranking: total 130

Life expectancy at birth: *total population:* 79.9 years (2024 est.)
male: 77.3 years
female: 82.8 years
comparison ranking: total population 61

Total fertility rate: 1.55 children born/woman (2024 est.)
comparison ranking: 194

Gross reproduction rate: 0.75 (2024 est.)

Contraceptive prevalence rate: 46% (2017/18)

Drinking water source: *improved: urban:* 97.3% of population
rural: 96.4% of population
total: 97% of population
unimproved: urban: 2.7% of population
rural: 3.6% of population
total: 3% of population (2020 est.)

Current health expenditure: 6.7% of GDP (2018)

Physician density: 1.88 physicians/1,000 population (2020)

Hospital bed density: 2.9 beds/1,000 population (2013)

Sanitation facility access: *improved: urban:* 99.8% of population
rural: 100% of population
total: 99.9% of population
unimproved: urban: 0.2% of population
rural: 0.5% of population
total: 0.1% of population (2020 est.)

Obesity - adult prevalence rate: 21.7% (2016)
comparison ranking: 86

Alcohol consumption per capita: *total:* 4.4 liters of pure alcohol (2019 est.)
beer: 1.75 liters of pure alcohol (2019 est.)
wine: 1.15 liters of pure alcohol (2019 est.)
spirits: 1.43 liters of pure alcohol (2019 est.)
other alcohols: 0.08 liters of pure alcohol (2019 est.)
comparison ranking: total 90

Tobacco use: *total:* 22.4% (2020 est.)
male: 38.8% (2020 est.)
female: 6% (2020 est.)
comparison ranking: total 69

Children under the age of 5 years underweight: 1.5% (2017/18)
comparison ranking: 114

Currently married women (ages 15-49): 67.2% (2023 est.)

Child marriage: *women married by age 15:* 1.4%
women married by age 18: 11.8%
men married by age 18: 1.2% (2018 est.)

Education expenditures: 3.1% of GDP (2020 est.)
comparison ranking: 154

Literacy: *definition:* age 15 and over can read and write
total population: 98.4%
male: 98.7%
female: 98.2% (2021)

School life expectancy (primary to tertiary education): *total:* 14 years
male: 13 years
female: 15 years (2020)

ENVIRONMENT

Environment - current issues: deforestation; soil erosion; water pollution from industrial and domestic effluents; air pollution from industrial and power plants; loss of biodiversity due to lack of resources for sound environmental management

Environment - international agreements: *party to:* Air Pollution, Air Pollution-Nitrogen Oxides, Air Pollution-Sulphur 85, Biodiversity, Climate Change, Climate Change-Kyoto Protocol, Climate Change-Paris Agreement, Comprehensive Nuclear Test Ban, Desertification, Endangered Species, Hazardous Wastes, Law of the Sea, Ozone Layer Protection, Ship Pollution, Tropical Timber 2006, Wetlands
signed, but not ratified: none of the selected agreements

Climate: mild temperate; cool, cloudy, wet winters; hot, clear, dry summers; interior is cooler and wetter

Urbanization: *urban population:* 64.6% of total population (2023)
rate of urbanization: 1.29% annual rate of change (2020-25 est.)

Revenue from forest resources: 0.18% of GDP (2018 est.)
comparison ranking: 95

Revenue from coal: 0.03% of GDP (2018 est.)
comparison ranking: 40

Air pollutants: *particulate matter emissions:* 16.28 micrograms per cubic meter (2019 est.)
carbon dioxide emissions: 4.54 megatons (2016 est.)
methane emissions: 2.55 megatons (2020 est.)

Waste and recycling: *municipal solid waste generated annually:* 1,142,964 tons (2015 est.)

Major lakes (area sq km): *fresh water lake(s):* Lake Scutari (shared with Montenegro) - 400 sq km
note - largest lake in the Balkans

Major watersheds (area sq km): Atlantic Ocean drainage: *(Black Sea)* Danube (795,656 sq km)

Total water withdrawal: *municipal:* 230 million cubic meters (2020 est.)
industrial: 20 million cubic meters (2020 est.)
agricultural: 550 million cubic meters (2020 est.)

Total renewable water resources: 30.2 billion cubic meters (2020 est.)

GOVERNMENT

Country name: *conventional long form:* Republic of Albania
conventional short form: Albania
local long form: Republika e Shqiperise
local short form: Shqiperia
former: People's Socialist Republic of Albania
etymology: the English-language country name seems to be derived from the ancient Illyrian tribe of the Albani; the native name "Shqiperia" is derived from the Albanian word "Shqiponje" ("Eagle") and is popularly interpreted to mean "Land of the Eagles"

Government type: parliamentary republic

Capital: *name:* Tirana (Tirane)
geographic coordinates: 41 19 N, 19 49 E
time difference: UTC+1 (6 hours ahead of Washington, DC, during Standard Time)
daylight saving time: +1hr, begins last Sunday in March; ends last Sunday in October
etymology: the name Tirana first appears in a 1418 Venetian document; the origin of the name is unclear, but may derive from Tirkan Fortress, whose ruins survive on the slopes of Dajti mountain and which overlooks the city
Administrative divisions
12 counties (qarqe, singular - qark); Berat, Diber, Durres, Elbasan, Fier, Gjirokaster, Korce, Kukes, Lezhe, Shkoder, Tirane (Tirana), Vlore

Independence: 28 November 1912 (from the Ottoman Empire)

National holiday: Independence Day, 28 November (1912), also known as Flag Day

Legal system: civil law system except in the northern rural areas where customary law known as the "Code of Leke" is still present

Constitution: *history:* several previous; latest approved by the Assembly 21 October 1998, adopted by referendum 22 November 1998, promulgated 28 November 1998
amendments: proposed by at least one-fifth of the Assembly membership; passage requires at least a two-thirds majority vote by the Assembly; referendum required only if approved by two-thirds of the Assembly; amendments approved by referendum effective upon declaration by the president of the republic; amended several times, last in 2020

International law organization participation: has not submitted an ICJ jurisdiction declaration; accepts ICCt jurisdiction

Citizenship: *citizenship by birth:* no
citizenship by descent only: at least one parent must be a citizen of Albania
dual citizenship recognized: yes
residency requirement for naturalization: 5 years

Suffrage: 18 years of age; universal

Executive branch: *chief of state:* President Bajram BEGAJ (since 24 July 2022)
head of government: Prime Minister Edi RAMA (since 10 September 2013)
cabinet: Council of Ministers proposed by the prime minister, nominated by the president, and approved by the Assembly
elections/appointments: president indirectly elected by the Assembly for a 5-year term (eligible for a second term); a candidate needs three-fifths majority vote of the Assembly in 1 of 3 rounds or a simple majority in 2 additional rounds to become president; election last held in 4 rounds on 16, 23, and 30 May and 4 June 2022 (next election to be held in 2027); prime minister appointed by the president on the proposal of the majority party or coalition of parties in the Assembly
election results:
2022: Bajram BEGAJ elected president in the fourth round; Assembly vote - 78-4, opposition parties boycotted
2017: Ilir META elected president in the fourth round; Assembly vote - 87-2

Legislative branch: *description:* unicameral Assembly or Kuvendi (140 seats; members directly elected in multi-seat constituencies by open party-list proportional representation vote using the D'Hondt method; members serve 4-year terms)
elections: last held on 25 April 2021 (next to be held in 2025)
election results: percent of vote by party/coalition - PS 48.7%, PD-Alliance for Change 39.4%, LSI 6.8%, PSD 2.3%, other 2.8%; seats by party/coalition - PS 74, PD-Alliance for Change 59, LSI 4, PSD 3; composition - men 90, women 50, percentage 35.7%

Judicial branch: *highest court(s):* Supreme Court (consists of 19 judges, including the chief justice); Constitutional Court (consists of 9 judges, including the chairman)
judge selection and term of office: Supreme Court judges appointed by the High Judicial Council with the consent of the president to serve single 9-year terms; Supreme Court chairman is elected for a single 3-year term by the court members; appointments of Constitutional Court judges are rotated among the president, Parliament, and Supreme Court from a list of pre-qualified candidates (each institution selects

3 judges), to serve single 9-year terms; candidates are prequalified by a randomly selected body of experienced judges and prosecutors; Constitutional Court chairman is elected by the court members for a single, renewable 3-year term
subordinate courts: Courts of Appeal; Courts of First Instance; specialized courts: Court for Corruption and Organized Crime, Appeals Court for Corruption and Organized Crime (responsible for corruption, organized crime, and crimes of high officials)

Political parties: Alliance for Change (electoral coalition led by PD)
Democratic Party or PD
Party for Justice, Integration and Unity or PDIU (part of the Alliance for Change)
Social Democratic Party or PSD
Freedom Party of Albania or PL (formerly the Socialist Movement for Integration or LSI)
Socialist Party or PS

International organization participation: BSEC, CD, CE, CEI, EAPC, EBRD, EITI (compliant country), FAO, IAEA, IBRD, ICAO, ICC (national committees), ICCt, ICRM, IDA, IDB, IFAD, IFC, IFRCS, ILO, IMF, IMO, Interpol, IOC, IOM, IPU, ISO (correspondent), ITU, ITUC (NGOs), MIGA, NATO, OAS (observer), OIC, OIF, OPCW, OSCE, PCA, SELEC, UN, UNCTAD, UNESCO, UNHRC, UNIDO, UNOOSA, UNWTO, UPU, WCO, WFTU (NGOs), WHO, WIPO, WMO, WTO
note: Albania is an EU candidate country whose satisfactory completion of accession criteria is required before being granted full EU membership

Diplomatic representation in the US: *chief of mission:* Ambassador Ervin BUSHATI (since 15 September 2023)
chancery: 2100 S Street NW, Washington, DC 20008
telephone: [1] (202) 223-4942
FAX: [1] (202) 628-7342
email address and website:
embassy.washington@mfa.gov.al
http://www.ambasadat.gov.al/usa/en
consulate(s) general: New York

Diplomatic representation from the US: *chief of mission:* Ambassador (vacant); Chargé d'Affaires Nancy VANHORN (since August 2024)
embassy: Rruga Stavro Vinjau, No. 14, Tirana
mailing address: 9510 Tirana Place, Washington DC 20521-9510
telephone: [355] 4 2247-285
FAX: [355] 4 2232-222
email address and website:
ACSTirana@state.gov
https://al.usembassy.gov/

Flag description: red with a black two-headed eagle in the center; the design is claimed to be that of 15th-century hero Georgi Kastrioti SKANDERBEG, who led a successful uprising against the Ottoman Turks that resulted in a short-lived independence for some Albanian regions (1443-78); an unsubstantiated explanation for the eagle symbol is the tradition that Albanians see themselves as descendants of the eagle; they refer to themselves as "Shqiptare," which translates as "sons of the eagle"

National symbol(s): black double-headed eagle; national colors: red, black

National anthem: *name:* "Hymni i Flamurit" (Hymn to the Flag)
lyrics/music: Aleksander Stavre DRENOVA/ Ciprian PORUMBESCU
note: adopted 1912

National heritage: *total World Heritage Sites:* 4 (2 cultural, 1 natural, 1 mixed)
selected World Heritage Site locales: Butrint (c); Historic Berat and Gjirokastër (c); Primeval Beech Forests (n); Lake Ohrid Region (m)

ECONOMY

Economic overview: upper-middle -income Balkan economy; EU accession candidate; growth bolstered by tourism, services, construction, and private consumption; fiscal consolidation through revenue collection to address public debt; challenges include weak governance, corruption, climate adaptation, vulnerability to energy sector shocks, and emigration of workers

Real GDP (purchasing power parity): $49.592 billion (2023 est.)
$47.943 billion (2022 est.)
$45.723 billion (2021 est.)
note: data in 2021 dollars
comparison ranking: 126

Real GDP growth rate: 3.44% (2023 est.)
4.86% (2022 est.)
8.91% (2021 est.)
note: annual GDP % growth based on constant local currency
comparison ranking: 93

Real GDP per capita: $18,100 (2023 est.)
$17,300 (2022 est.)
$16,300 (2021 est.)
note: data in 2021 dollars
comparison ranking: 107

GDP (official exchange rate): $22.978 billion (2023 est.)
note: data in current dollars at official exchange rate

Inflation rate (consumer prices): 6.73% (2022 est.)
2.04% (2021 est.)
1.62% (2020 est.)
note: annual % change based on consumer prices
comparison ranking: 141

Credit ratings:

Moody's rating: B1 (2021)

Standard & Poors rating: B+ (2020)
note: The year refers to the year in which the current credit rating was first obtained.

GDP - composition, by sector of origin: *agriculture:* 18.3% (2023 est.)
industry: 21.2% (2023 est.)
services: 48% (2023 est.)
note: figures may not total 100% due to non-allocated consumption not captured in sector-reported data comparison rankings: services 154; industry 128; agriculture 42

GDP - composition, by end use: *household consumption:* 75.5% (2023 est.)
government consumption: 11.1% (2023 est.)
investment in fixed capital: 24.4% (2023 est.)
investment in inventories: 0.5% (2021 est.)
exports of goods and services: 39.6% (2023 est.)
imports of goods and services: -44.9% (2023 est.)
note: figures may not total 100% due to rounding or gaps in data collection

Agricultural products: milk, maize, tomatoes, potatoes, watermelons, wheat, grapes, olives, cucumbers/ gherkins, onions (2022)
note: top ten agricultural products based on tonnage

Industries: food; footwear, apparel and clothing; lumber, oil, cement, chemicals, mining, basic metals, hydropower

Industrial production growth rate: 4.03% (2023 est.)
note: annual % change in industrial value added based on constant local currency
comparison ranking: 76

Labor force: 1.388 million (2023 est.)
note: number of people ages 15 or older who are employed or seeking work
comparison ranking: 139

Unemployment rate: 11.58% (2023 est.)
11.59% (2022 est.)
12.47% (2021 est.)
note: % of labor force seeking employment
comparison ranking: 174

Youth unemployment rate (ages 15-24): *total:* 28.2% (2023 est.)
male: 29.1% (2023 est.)
female: 27% (2023 est.)
note: % of labor force ages 15-24 seeking employment
comparison ranking: total 32

Population below poverty line: 22% (2020 est.)
note: % of population with income below national poverty line

Gini Index coefficient - distribution of family income: 29.4 (2020 est.)
note: index (0-100) of income distribution; higher values represent greater inequality
comparison ranking: 126

Household income or consumption by percentage share: *lowest 10%:* 3.4% (2020 est.)
highest 10%: 22.8% (2020 est.)
note: % share of income accruing to lowest and highest 10% of population

Remittances: 8.57% of GDP (2023 est.)
9.23% of GDP (2022 est.)
9.58% of GDP (2021 est.)
note: personal transfers and compensation between resident and non-resident individuals/households/ entities

Budget: *revenues:* $5.319 billion (2021 est.)
expenditures: $4.4 billion (2021 est.)
note: central government revenues (excluding grants) and expenses converted to US dollars at average official exchange rate for year indicated

Public debt: 82.38% of GDP (2021 est.)
note: central government debt as a % of GDP
comparison ranking: 35

Taxes and other revenues: 18.2% (of GDP) (2021 est.)
note: central government tax revenue as a % of GDP
comparison ranking: 102

Current account balance: -$202.323 million (2023 est.)
-$1.117 billion (2022 est.)
-$1.37 billion (2021 est.)
note: balance of payments - net trade and primary/ secondary income in current dollars
comparison ranking: 110

Exports: $9.178 billion (2023 est.)
$7.057 billion (2022 est.)
$5.612 billion (2021 est.)
note: balance of payments - exports of goods and services in current dollars
comparison ranking: 118

Exports - partners: Italy 41%, Greece 10%, Spain 7%, Germany 5%, China 4% (2022)

note: top five export partners based on percentage share of exports

Exports - commodities: garments, footwear, iron alloys, electricity, crude petroleum (2022)
note: top five export commodities based on value in dollars

Imports: $10.373 billion (2023 est.)
$9.016 billion (2022 est.)
$8.004 billion (2021 est.)
note: balance of payments - imports of goods and services in current dollars
comparison ranking: 121

Imports - partners: Italy 25%, Turkey 14%, Greece 12%, China 10%, Germany 5% (2022)
note: top five import partners based on percentage share of imports

Imports - commodities: refined petroleum, garments, electricity, cars, raw iron bars (2022)
note: top five import commodities based on value in dollars

Reserves of foreign exchange and gold: $6.455 billion (2023 est.)
$5.266 billion (2022 est.)
$5.635 billion (2021 est.)
note: holdings of gold (year-end prices)/foreign exchange/special drawing rights in current dollars
comparison ranking: 104

Debt - external: $4.624 billion (2022 est.)
note: present value of external debt in current US dollars
comparison ranking: 54

Exchange rates: leke (ALL) per US dollar -

Exchange rates: 100.645 (2023 est.)
113.042 (2022 est.)
103.52 (2021 est.)
108.65 (2020 est.)
109.851 (2019 est.)

ENERGY

Electricity access: *electrification - total population:* 100% (2022 est.)

Electricity: *installed generating capacity:* 2.635 million kW (2022 est.)
consumption: 6.5 billion kWh (2022 est.)
exports: 2.123 billion kWh (2022 est.)
imports: 3.044 billion kWh (2022 est.)
transmission/distribution losses: 1.423 billion kWh (2022 est.)
comparison rankings: transmission/distribution losses 115; imports 54; exports 56; consumption 121; installed generating capacity 113

Electricity generation sources: *solar:* 0.6% of total installed capacity (2022 est.)
hydroelectricity: 99.4% of total installed capacity (2022 est.)

Coal: *production:* 379,000 metric tons (2022 est.)
consumption: 389,000 metric tons (2022 est.)
exports: 31,000 metric tons (2022 est.)
imports: 42,000 metric tons (2022 est.)
proven reserves: 522 million metric tons (2022 est.)

Petroleum: *total petroleum production:* 14,000 bbl/day (2023 est.)
refined petroleum consumption: 26,000 bbl/day (2022 est.)
crude oil estimated reserves: 150 million barrels (2021 est.)

Natural gas: *production:* 50.623 million cubic meters (2022 est.)
consumption: 50.623 million cubic meters (2022 est.)
proven reserves: 5.692 billion cubic meters (2021 est.)

Carbon dioxide emissions: 3.856 million metric tonnes of CO2 (2022 est.)
from coal and metallurgical coke: 608,000 metric tonnes of CO2 (2022 est.)
from petroleum and other liquids: 3.153 million metric tonnes of CO2 (2022 est.)
from consumed natural gas: 94,000 metric tonnes of CO2 (2022 est.)
comparison ranking: total emissions 144

Energy consumption per capita: 30.306 million Btu/person (2022 est.)
comparison ranking: 115

COMMUNICATIONS

Telephones - fixed lines: *total subscriptions:* 177,000 (2022 est.)
subscriptions per 100 inhabitants: 6 (2022 est.)
comparison ranking: total subscriptions 121

Telephones - mobile cellular: *total subscriptions:* 2.782 million (2022 est.)
subscriptions per 100 inhabitants: 98 (2022 est.)
comparison ranking: total subscriptions 143

Telecommunication systems: *general assessment:* Albania's small telecom market has experienced some significant changes in recent years; upgrades were made to the fixed-line infrastructure to support broadband services; fixed-line telephony use and penetration in Albania is declining steadily as subscribers migrate to mobile solutions; the mobile sector is well provided with LTE networks, while operators have invested in 5G; some of these efforts have been made in conjunction with neighboring Kosovo, with the intention of a seamless 5G corridor along the highway connecting the two countries; the country has long sought accession to the European Union (EU) which has benefited its telecoms sector through closer scrutiny of its regulatory regime and through the injection of funding to help modernize infrastructure (2021)
domestic: fixed-line approximately 7 per 100, teledensity continues to decline due to heavy use of mobile-cellular telephone services; mobile-cellular telephone use is widespread and generally effective, 92 per 100 for mobile-cellular (2021)
international: country code - 355; submarine cables for the Adria 1 and Italy-Albania provide connectivity to Italy, Croatia, and Greece; a combination submarine cable and land fiber-optic system, provides additional connectivity to Bulgaria, Macedonia, and Turkey; international traffic carried by fiber-optic cable and, when necessary, by microwave radio relay from the Tirana exchange to Italy and Greece (2019)

Broadcast media: Albania has more than 65 TV stations, including several that broadcast nationally; Albanian TV broadcasts are also available to Albanian-speaking populations in neighboring countries; many viewers have access to Italian and Greek TV broadcasts via terrestrial reception; Albania's TV stations have begun a government-mandated conversion from analog to digital broadcast; the government has pledged to provide analog-to-digital converters to low-income families affected by this decision; cable TV service is available; 2 public radio networks and roughly 78 private radio stations; several international broadcasters are available (2019)

Internet country code: .al

Internet users: *total:* 2.291 million (2021 est.)
percent of population: 79% (2021 est.)
comparison ranking: total 132

Broadband - fixed subscriptions: *total:* 508,937 (2020 est.)
subscriptions per 100 inhabitants: 18 (2020 est.)
comparison ranking: total 91

TRANSPORTATION

National air transport system: *number of registered air carriers:* 2 (2020)
inventory of registered aircraft operated by air carriers: 5
annual passenger traffic on registered air carriers: 303,137 (2018)

Civil aircraft registration country code prefix: ZA

Airports: 3 (2024)
comparison ranking: 184

Heliports: 9 (2024)

Pipelines: 498 km gas (a majority of the network is in disrepair and parts of it are missing), 249 km oil (2015)

Railways: *total:* 424 km (2017)
2021-All the trains in the country suspended
comparison ranking: total 119

Roadways: *total:* 3,581 km (2022)
comparison ranking: total 159

Waterways: 41 km (2011) (on the Bojana River)
comparison ranking: 114

Merchant marine: *total:* 69 (2023)
by type: general cargo 46, oil tanker 1, other 22
comparison ranking: total 110

Ports: *total ports:* 3 (2024)
large: 0
medium: 0
small: 1
very small: 2
ports with oil terminals: 0
key ports: Durres, Shengjin, Vlores

MILITARY AND SECURITY

Military and security forces: Republic of Albania Armed Forces (Forcat e Armatosura të Republikës së Shqipërisë (FARSH); aka Albanian Armed Forces (AAF)): Land Forces, Naval Force (includes Coast Guard), Air Forces

Ministry of Interior: Guard of the Republic, State Police (includes the Border and Migration Police) (2024)
note: the State Police are primarily responsible for internal security, including counterterrorism, while the Guard of the Republic protects senior state officials, foreign dignitaries, and certain state properties

Military expenditures: 2% of GDP (2024 est.)
1.7% of GDP (2023)
1.2% of GDP (2022)
1.2% of GDP (2021)
1.3% of GDP (2020)
comparison ranking: 68

Military and security service personnel strengths: approximately 7,000 total active-duty personnel (5,000 Army; 1,500 Navy; 500 Air Force) (2024)

Military equipment inventories and acquisitions: since joining NATO, the military has been in the process of modernizing by retiring its inventory of Soviet-era weapons and replacing them with

Western equipment, including donated and second-hand purchases (2023)

Military service age and obligation: 18-27 (up to 32 in some cases) for voluntary military service for men and women; conscription abolished 2010 (2024)
note: as of 2024, women comprised about 15% of the military's full-time personnel

Military - note: the Albanian Armed Forces (AAF) are responsible for defending the country's independence, sovereignty, and territory, assisting with internal security, providing disaster and humanitarian relief, and participating in international peacekeeping missions; the it is a small, lightly armed force that has been undergoing a modernization effort to improve its ability to fulfill NATO missions, including training and equipment purchases; the AAF has contributed small numbers of forces to several NATO missions since Albania joined NATO in 2009, including peacekeeping/stability missions in Afghanistan, Kosovo, and Iraq, and multinational battlegroups in Bulgaria and Latvia; it has also contributed to EU and UN missions (2024)

TERRORISM

Terrorist group(s): Islamic Revolutionary Guard Corps/Qods Force; Islamic State of Iraq and ash-Sham (ISIS)
note: details about the history, aims, leadership, organization, areas of operation, tactics, targets, weapons, size, and sources of support of the group(s) appear(s) in the Terrorism reference guide

TRANSNATIONAL ISSUES

Refugees and internally displaced persons: *refugees (country of origin):* 47,247 (Ukraine) (as of 30 January 2024)
stateless persons: 1,948 (2022)
note: 47,306 estimated refugee and migrant arrivals (January 2015-February 2024)

Illicit drugs: a source country for cannabis and an active transshipment point for Albanian narco-trafficking organizations moving illicit drugs into European markets

ALGERIA

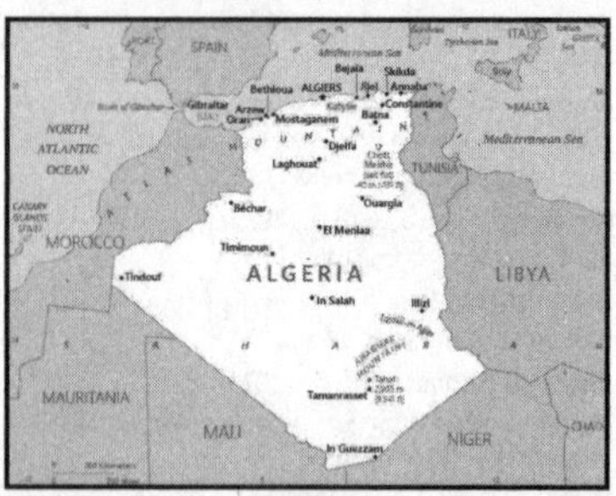

INTRODUCTION

Background: Algeria has known many empires and dynasties, including the ancient Numidians (3rd century B.C.), Phoenicians, Carthaginians, Romans, Vandals, Byzantines, over a dozen different Arab and Amazigh dynasties, Spaniards, and Ottoman Turks. Under the Turks, the Barbary pirates operated from North Africa and preyed on shipping, from about 1500 until the French captured Algiers in 1830. The French southward conquest of Algeria proceeded throughout the 19th century and was marked by many atrocities. A bloody eight-year struggle culminated in Algerian independence in 1962.

Algeria's long-dominant political party, the National Liberation Front (FLN), was established in 1954 as part of the struggle for independence and has since played a large role in politics, though it is falling out of favor with the youth and current President Abdelmadjid TEBBOUNE. The Government of Algeria in 1988 instituted a multi-party system in response to public unrest, but the surprising first-round success of the Islamic Salvation Front (FIS) in the 1991 legislative election led the Algerian military to intervene and postpone the second round of elections to prevent what the secular elite feared would be an extremist-led government from assuming power. An army crackdown on the FIS escalated into an FIS insurgency and intense violence from 1992-98 that resulted in over 100,000 deaths, many of which were attributed to extremist groups massacring villagers. The government gained the upper hand by the late 1990s, and FIS's armed wing, the Islamic Salvation Army, disbanded in 2000. FIS membership is now illegal.

In 1999, Abdelaziz BOUTEFLIKA won the presidency with the backing of the military, in an election that was boycotted by several candidates protesting alleged fraud. He won subsequent elections in 2004, 2009, and 2014. Widespread protests against his decision to seek a fifth term broke out in early 2019. BOUTEFLIKA resigned in April 2019, and in December 2019, Algerians elected former Prime Minister Abdelmadjid TEBBOUNE as the country's new president. A longtime FLN member, TEBBOUNE ran for president as an independent. In 2020, Algeria held a constitutional referendum on governmental reforms, which TEBBOUNE enacted in 2021. Subsequent reforms to the national electoral law introduced open-list voting to curb corruption. The new law also eliminated gender quotas in Parliament, and the 2021 legislative elections saw female representation plummet. The referendum, parliamentary elections, and local elections saw record-low voter turnout.

GEOGRAPHY

Location: Northern Africa, bordering the Mediterranean Sea, between Morocco and Tunisia

Geographic coordinates: 28 00 N, 3 00 E

Map references: Africa

Area: *total:* 2,381,740 sq km
land: 2,381,740 sq km
water: 0 sq km
comparison ranking: total 11

Area - comparative: slightly less than 3.5 times the size of Texas

Land boundaries: *total:* 6,734 km
border countries (6): Libya 989 km; Mali 1,359 km; Mauritania 460 km; Morocco 1,941 km; Niger 951 km; Tunisia 1,034 km

Coastline: 998 km

Maritime claims: *territorial sea:* 12 nm
contiguous zone: 24 nm
exclusive fishing zone: 32-52 nm

Climate: arid to semiarid; mild, wet winters with hot, dry summers along coast; drier with cold winters and hot summers on high plateau; sirocco is a hot, dust/sand-laden wind especially common in summer

Terrain: mostly high plateau and desert; Atlas Mountains in the far north and Hoggar Mountains in the south; narrow, discontinuous coastal plain

Elevation: *highest point:* Tahat 2,908 m
lowest point: Chott Melrhir -40 m
mean elevation: 800 m

Natural resources: petroleum, natural gas, iron ore, phosphates, uranium, lead, zinc

Land use: *agricultural land:* 17.4% (2018 est.)
arable land: 3.2% (2018 est.)
permanent crops: 0.4% (2018 est.)
permanent pasture: 13.8% (2018 est.)
forest: 0.8% (2018 est.)
other: 81.8% (2018 est.)

Irrigated land: 12,605 sq km (2016)

Major watersheds (area sq km): Atlantic Ocean drainage: Niger (2,261,741 sq km)

Internal (endorheic basin) drainage: Lake Chad (2,497,738 sq km)

Major aquifers: Lullemeden-Irhazer Aquifer System, Murzuk-Djado Basin, North Western Sahara Aquifer, Taoudeni-Tanezrouft Basin

Population distribution: the vast majority of the populace is found in the extreme northern part of the country along the Mediterranean Coast as shown in this population distribution map

Natural hazards: mountainous areas subject to severe earthquakes; mudslides and floods in rainy season; droughts

Geography - note: largest country in Africa but 80% desert; canyons and caves in the southern Hoggar Mountains and in the barren Tassili n'Ajjer area in the southeast of the country contain numerous examples of prehistoric art – rock paintings and carvings depicting human activities and wild and domestic animals (elephants, giraffes, cattle) – that date to the African Humid Period, roughly 11,000 to 5,000 years ago, when the region was completely vegetated

PEOPLE AND SOCIETY

Population: *total:* 47,022,473
male: 23,854,821
female: 23,167,652 (2024 est.)
comparison rankings: female 34; male 32; total 33

Nationality: *noun:* Algerian(s)
adjective: Algerian

Ethnic groups: Arab-Amazigh 99%, European less than 1%

note: although almost all Algerians are Amazigh in origin and not Arab, only a minority identify themselves as primarily Amazigh, about 15% of the total population; these people live mostly in the mountainous region of Kabylie east of Algiers and in several other communities; the Amazigh are also Muslim but identify with their Amazigh rather than Arab cultural heritage; some Amazigh have long agitated, sometimes violently, for autonomy; the government is unlikely to grant autonomy but has officially recognized Amazigh languages and introduced them into public schools

Languages: Arabic (official), French (lingua franca), Tamazight (official) (dialects include Kabyle (Taqbaylit), Shawiya (Tacawit), Mzab, Tuareg (Tamahaq))
major-language sample(s):
كتاب حقائق العالم، المصدر الذي لا يمكن الاستغناء عنه للمعلومات الأساسية
(Arabic)

Religions: Muslim (official; predominantly Sunni) 99%, other (includes Christian, Jewish, Ahmadi Muslim, Shia Muslim, Ibadi Muslim) <1% (2012 est.)

Demographic profile: For the first two thirds of the 20th century, Algeria's high fertility rate caused its population to grow rapidly. However, about a decade after independence from France in 1962, the total fertility rate fell dramatically from 7 children per woman in the 1970s to about 2.4 in 2000, slowing Algeria's population growth rate by the late 1980s. The lower fertility rate was mainly the result of women's rising age at first marriage (virtually all Algerian children being born in wedlock) and to a lesser extent the wider use of contraceptives. Later marriages and a preference for smaller families are attributed to increases in women's education and participation in the labor market; higher unemployment; and a shortage of housing forcing multiple generations to live together. The average woman's age at first marriage increased from about 19 in the mid-1950s to 24 in the mid-1970s to 30.5 in the late 1990s.
Algeria's fertility rate experienced an unexpected upturn in the early 2000s, as the average woman's age at first marriage dropped slightly. The reversal in fertility could represent a temporary fluctuation in marriage age or, less likely, a decrease in the steady rate of contraceptive use.
Thousands of Algerian peasants - mainly Berber men from the Kabylia region - faced with land dispossession and economic hardship under French rule migrated temporarily to France to work in manufacturing and mining during the first half of the 20th century. This movement accelerated during World War I, when Algerians filled in for French factory workers or served as soldiers. In the years following independence, low-skilled Algerian workers and Algerians who had supported the French (known as Harkis) emigrated en masse to France. Tighter French immigration rules and Algiers' decision to cease managing labor migration to France in the 1970s limited legal emigration largely to family reunification.
Not until Algeria's civil war in the 1990s did the country again experience substantial outmigration. Many Algerians legally entered Tunisia without visas claiming to be tourists and then stayed as workers. Other Algerians headed to Europe seeking asylum, although France imposed restrictions. Sub-Saharan African migrants came to Algeria after its civil war to work in agriculture and mining. In the 2000s, a wave of educated Algerians went abroad seeking skilled jobs in a wider range of destinations, increasing their presence in North America and Spain. At the same time, legal foreign workers principally from China and Egypt came to work in Algeria's construction and oil sectors. Illegal migrants from Sub-Saharan Africa, particularly Malians, Nigeriens, and Gambians, continue to come to Algeria in search of work or to use it as a stepping stone to Libya and Europe.
Since 1975, Algeria also has been the main recipient of Sahrawi refugees from the ongoing conflict in Western Sahara (today part of Morocco). More than 100,000 Sahrawis are estimated to be living in five refugee camps in southwestern Algeria near Tindouf.

Age structure: *0-14 years:* 30.8% (male 7,411,337/female 7,062,794)
15-64 years: 62.3% (male 14,846,102/female 14,441,034)
65 years and over: 6.9% (2024 est.) (male 1,597,382/female 1,663,824)
2023 population pyramid:

Dependency ratios: *total dependency ratio:* 58.5
youth dependency ratio: 48.7
elderly dependency ratio: 9.8
potential support ratio: 10.2 (2021 est.)

Median age: *total:* 29.1 years (2024 est.)
male: 28.8 years
female: 29.4 years
comparison ranking: total 146

Population growth rate: 1.54% (2024 est.)
comparison ranking: 62

Birth rate: 20.2 births/1,000 population (2024 est.)
comparison ranking: 67

Death rate: 4.4 deaths/1,000 population (2024 est.)
comparison ranking: 208

Net migration rate: -0.5 migrant(s)/1,000 population (2024 est.)
comparison ranking: 122

Population distribution: the vast majority of the populace is found in the extreme northern part of the country along the Mediterranean Coast as shown in this population distribution map

Urbanization: *urban population:* 75.3% of total population (2023)
rate of urbanization: 1.99% annual rate of change (2020-25 est.)

Major urban areas - population: 2.902 million ALGIERS (capital), 936,000 Oran (2022)

Sex ratio: *at birth:* 1.05 male(s)/female
0-14 years: 1.05 male(s)/female
15-64 years: 1.03 male(s)/female
65 years and over: 0.96 male(s)/female
total population: 1.03 male(s)/female (2024 est.)

Maternal mortality ratio: 78 deaths/100,000 live births (2020 est.)
comparison ranking: 76

Infant mortality rate: *total:* 18.7 deaths/1,000 live births (2024 est.)
male: 19.8 deaths/1,000 live births
female: 17.5 deaths/1,000 live births
comparison ranking: total 82

Life expectancy at birth: *total population:* 77.9 years (2024 est.)
male: 77.2 years
female: 78.7 years
comparison ranking: total population 85

Total fertility rate: 2.94 children born/woman (2024 est.)
comparison ranking: 49

Gross reproduction rate: 1.43 (2024 est.)

Contraceptive prevalence rate: 53.6% (2018/19)

Drinking water source: *improved: urban:* 99.6% of population
rural: 98.8% of population
total: 99.4% of population
unimproved: urban: 0.4% of population
rural: 1.2% of population
total: 0.6% of population (2020 est.)

Current health expenditure: 6.3% of GDP (2020)

Physician density: 1.72 physicians/1,000 population (2018)

Hospital bed density: 1.9 beds/1,000 population (2015)

Sanitation facility access: *improved: urban:* 98.3% of population
rural: 91.3% of population
total: 96.5% of population
unimproved: urban: 1.7% of population
rural: 8.7% of population
total: 3.5% of population (2020 est.)

Obesity - adult prevalence rate: 27.4% (2016)
comparison ranking: 38

Alcohol consumption per capita: *total:* 0.59 liters of pure alcohol (2019 est.)
beer: 0.31 liters of pure alcohol (2019 est.)
wine: 0.2 liters of pure alcohol (2019 est.)
spirits: 0.08 liters of pure alcohol (2019 est.)
other alcohols: 0 liters of pure alcohol (2019 est.)
comparison ranking: total 160

Tobacco use: *total:* 21% (2020 est.)
male: 41.3% (2020 est.)
female: 0.7% (2020 est.)
comparison ranking: total 80

Children under the age of 5 years underweight: 2.7% (2018/19)
comparison ranking: 93

Currently married women (ages 15-49): 56% (2023 est.)

Child marriage: *women married by age 18:* 3.8% (2019 est.)

Education expenditures: 7% of GDP (2020 est.)
comparison ranking: 21

Literacy: *definition:* age 15 and over can read and write
total population: 81.4%
male: 87.4%
female: 75.3% (2018)

ENVIRONMENT

Environment - current issues: air pollution in major cities; soil erosion from overgrazing and other poor farming practices; desertification; dumping of raw sewage, petroleum refining wastes, and other industrial effluents is leading to the pollution of rivers and coastal waters; Mediterranean Sea, in particular, becoming polluted from oil wastes, soil erosion, and fertilizer runoff; inadequate supplies of potable water

Environment - international agreements: *party to:* Biodiversity, Climate Change, Climate Change-Kyoto Protocol, Climate Change-Paris Agreement, Comprehensive Nuclear Test Ban, Desertification, Endangered Species, Environmental Modification, Hazardous Wastes, Law of the Sea, Ozone Layer Protection, Ship Pollution, Wetlands
signed, but not ratified: Nuclear Test Ban

Climate: arid to semiarid; mild, wet winters with hot, dry summers along coast; drier with cold winters and hot summers on high plateau; sirocco is a hot, dust/sand-laden wind especially common in summer

Urbanization: *urban population:* 75.3% of total population (2023)
rate of urbanization: 1.99% annual rate of change (2020-25 est.)

Revenue from forest resources: 0.1% of GDP (2018 est.)
comparison ranking: 113

Revenue from coal: 0% of GDP (2018 est.)
comparison ranking: 159

Air pollutants: *particulate matter emissions:* 22.68 micrograms per cubic meter (2019 est.)
carbon dioxide emissions: 150.01 megatons (2016 est.)
methane emissions: 49.94 megatons (2020 est.)

Waste and recycling: *municipal solid waste generated annually:* 12,378,740 tons (2016 est.)
municipal solid waste recycled annually: 990,299 tons (2013 est.)
percent of municipal solid waste recycled: 8% (2013 est.)

Major watersheds (area sq km): Atlantic Ocean drainage: Niger (2,261,741 sq km)

Internal (endorheic basin) drainage: Lake Chad (2,497,738 sq km)

Major aquifers: Lullemeden-Irhazer Aquifer System, Murzuk-Djado Basin, North Western Sahara Aquifer, Taoudeni-Tanezrouft Basin

Total water withdrawal: *municipal:* 3.6 billion cubic meters (2020 est.)
industrial: 190 million cubic meters (2020 est.)
agricultural: 6.67 billion cubic meters (2020 est.)

Total renewable water resources: 11.67 billion cubic meters (2020 est.)

GOVERNMENT

Country name: *conventional long form:* People's Democratic Republic of Algeria
conventional short form: Algeria
local long form: Al Jumhuriyah al Jaza'iriyah ad Dimuqratiyah ash Sha'biyah
local short form: Al Jaza'ir
etymology: the country name derives from the capital city of Algiers

Government type: presidential republic

Capital: *name:* Algiers
geographic coordinates: 36 45 N, 3 03 E
time difference: UTC+1 (6 hours ahead of Washington, DC, during Standard Time)
etymology: name derives from the Arabic "al-Jazair" meaning "the islands" and refers to the four islands formerly off the coast of the capital but joined to the mainland since 1525

Administrative divisions: 58 provinces (wilayas, singular - wilaya); Adrar, Ain Defla, Ain Temouchent, Alger (Algiers), Annaba, Batna, Bechar, Bejaia, Beni Abbes, Biskra, Blida, Bordj Badji Mokhtar, Bordj Bou Arreridj, Bouira, Boumerdes, Chlef, Constantine, Djanet, Djelfa, El Bayadh, El Meghaier, El Meniaa, El Oued, El Tarf, Ghardaia, Guelma, Illizi, In Guezzam, In Salah, Jijel, Khenchela, Laghouat, Mascara, Medea, Mila, Mostaganem, M'Sila, Naama, Oran, Ouargla, Ouled Djellal, Oum el Bouaghi, Relizane, Saida, Setif, Sidi Bel Abbes, Skikda, Souk Ahras, Tamanrasset, Tebessa, Tiaret, Timimoun, Tindouf, Tipaza, Tissemsilt, Tizi Ouzou, Tlemcen, Touggourt

Independence: 5 July 1962 (from France)

National holiday: Independence Day, 5 July (1962); Revolution Day, 1 November (1954)

Legal system: mixed legal system of French civil law and Islamic law; judicial review of legislative acts in ad hoc Constitutional Council composed of various public officials including several Supreme Court justices

Constitution: *history:* several previous; latest approved by referendum 1 November 2020
amendments: proposed by the president of the republic or through the president with the support of three fourths of the members of both houses of Parliament in joint session; passage requires approval by both houses, approval by referendum, and promulgation by the president; the president can forego a referendum if the Constitutional Council determines the proposed amendment does not conflict with basic constitutional principles; articles including the republican form of government, the integrity and unity of the country, and fundamental citizens' liberties and rights cannot be amended; amended 2002, 2008, 2016; last in 2020

International law organization participation: has not submitted an ICJ jurisdiction declaration; non-party state to the ICCt

Citizenship: *citizenship by birth:* no
citizenship by descent only: the mother must be a citizen of Algeria
dual citizenship recognized: no
residency requirement for naturalization: 7 years

Suffrage: 18 years of age; universal

Executive branch: *chief of state:* President Abdelmadjid TEBBOUNE (since 12 December 2019)
head of government: Prime Minister Nadir LARBAOUI (since 11 November 2023)
cabinet: Cabinet of Ministers appointed by the president
elections/appointments: president directly elected by absolute majority popular vote in two rounds if needed for a 5- year term (eligible for a second term); election last held on 7 September 2024 (next to be held in 2029); prime minister nominated by the president after consultation with the majority party in Parliament
election results:
2024: Abdelmadjid TEBBOUNE (NLF) 94.7%, Abdelaali Hassani CHERIF (MSP) 3.2%, Youcef AOUCHICHE (FFS) 2.2%
2019: (FLN) 58.1%, Abdelkader BENGRINA (El-Bina) 17.4%, Ali BENFLIS (Talaie El Hurriyet) 10.6%, Azzedine MIHOUBI (RND) 7.3%, Abdelaziz BELAID (Future Front) 6.7%

Legislative branch: *description:* bicameral Parliament consists of:
Council of the Nation or Majlis al-Umma (174 seats, statutory; 170 currently); two-thirds of members indirectly elected by simple majority vote by an electoral college composed of local assemblies within each wilaya, and one-third of members appointed by the president; members serve 6-year terms with one-half of the membership renewed every 3 years) National People's Assembly or al-Majlis al-Sha'abi al-Watani (407 seats, including 8 seats for Algerian diaspora); members directly elected in multi-seat constituencies by open-list proportional representation vote using the Hare quota method; members serve 5-year terms)
elections: Council of the Nation - last held on 5 February 2022 (next expected in 2025)
National People's Assembly - snap election held on 12 June 2021 (next to be held on 12 June 2026)
election results: Council of the Nation - percent of vote by party - NA; seats by party - FLN 54, RND 22, Future Front 7, National Construction Movement 5, FFS 4, other 6, independent 18, appointed 58; composition - men 163, women 7, percentage women 4.1%
National People's Assembly - percent of vote by party - NA; seats by party - FLN 98, MSP 65, RND 58, (Future Front) 48, Movement of National Construction 39, other 15, independent 84; composition - men 375, women 32, percentage women 7.9%; note - total Parliament percentage women 6.8%

Judicial branch: highest court(s): Supreme Court or Le Cour Suprême, (consists of 150 judges organized into 8 chambers: Civil, Commercial and Maritime, Criminal, House of Offenses and Contraventions, House of Petitions, Land, Personal Status, and Social; Constitutional Council (consists of 12 members including the court chairman and deputy chairman); note - Algeria's judicial system does not include sharia courts
judge selection and term of office: Supreme Court judges appointed by the High Council of Magistracy, an administrative body presided over by the president of the republic, and includes the republic vice-president and several members; judges appointed for life; Constitutional Council members - 4 appointed by the president of the republic, 2 each by the 2 houses of Parliament, 2 by the Supreme Court, and 2 by the Council of State; Council president and members appointed for single 6-year terms with half the membership renewed every 3 years
subordinate courts: appellate or wilaya courts; first instance or daira tribunals

Political parties: Algerian National Front or FNA
Algerian Popular Movement or MPA
Algeria's Hope Rally or TAJ
Dignity or El Karama
El-Infitah
El Mostakbal (Future Front)
Ennour El Djazairi Party (Algerian Radiance Party) or PED
Equity and Proclamation Party or PEP
Islamic Renaissance Movement or Ennahda Movement
Justice and Development Front or FJD
Movement for National Reform or El Islah
Movement of Society for Peace or MSP
National Construction Movement or El-Bina (Harakat El-Binaa El-Watani)
National Democratic Rally (Rassemblement National Democratique) or RND
National Front for Social Justice or FNJS
National Liberation Front or FLN
National Militancy Front or FMN
National Party for Solidarity and Development or PNSD
National Republican Alliance or ANR
New Dawn Party (El-Fajr El-Jadid)
New Generation (Jil Jadid)
Oath of 1954 or Ahd 54
Party of Justice and Liberty or PLJ
Rally for Culture and Democracy or RCD
Socialist Forces Front or FFS
Union for Change and Progress or UCP
Union of Democratic and Social Forces or UFDS
Vanguard of Liberties (Talaie El Hurriyet)
Workers Party or PT
Youth Party or PJ

note: a law banning political parties based on religion was enacted in March 1997

International organization participation: ABEDA, AfDB, AFESD, AMF, AMU, AU, BIS, CAEU, CD, FAO, G-15, G-24, G-77, IAEA, IBRD, ICAO, ICC (national committees), ICRM, IDA, IDB, IFAD, IFC, IFRCS, IHO, ILO, IMF, IMO, IMSO, Interpol, IOC, IOM, IPU, ISO, ITSO, ITU, ITUC (NGOs), LAS, MIGA, MONUSCO, NAM, OAPEC, OAS (observer), OIC, OPCW, OPEC, OSCE (partner), UN, UNCTAD, UNESCO, UNHCR, UNIDO, UNITAR, UNWTO, UPU, WCO, WHO, WIPO, WMO, WTO (observer)

Diplomatic representation in the US: *chief of mission:* Ambassador Sabri BOUKADOUM (since 27 February 2024)
chancery: 2118 Kalorama Road NW, Washington, DC 20008
telephone: [1] (202) 265-2800
FAX: [1] (202) 986-5906
email address and website:
mail@algerianembassy.org
https://www.algerianembassy.org/
consulate(s) general: New York

Diplomatic representation from the US: *chief of mission:* Ambassador Elizabeth Moore AUBIN (since 9 February 2022)
embassy: 05 Chemin Cheikh Bachir, Ibrahimi, El-Biar 16030, Alger
mailing address: 6030 Algiers Place, Washington DC 20521-6030
telephone: [213] (0) 770-08-2000
FAX: [213] (0) 770-08-2299
email address and website:
algierspd@state.gov
https://dz.usembassy.gov/

Flag description: two equal vertical bands of green (hoist side) and white; a red, five-pointed star within a red crescent centered over the two-color boundary; the colors represent Islam (green), purity and peace (white), and liberty (red); the crescent and star are also Islamic symbols, but the crescent is more closed than those of other Muslim countries because Algerians believe the long crescent horns bring happiness

National symbol(s): five-pointed star between the extended horns of a crescent moon, fennec fox; national colors: green, white, red

National anthem: *name:* "Kassaman" (We Pledge)
lyrics/music: Mufdi ZAKARIAH/Mohamed FAWZI
note: adopted 1962; ZAKARIAH wrote "Kassaman" as a poem while imprisoned in Algiers by French colonial forces

National heritage: *total World Heritage Sites:* 7 (6 cultural, 1 mixed)
selected World Heritage Site locales: Beni Hammad Fort (c); Djémila (c); Casbah of Algiers (c); M'zab Valley (c); Tassili n'Ajjer (m); Timgad (c); Tipasa (c)

ECONOMY

Economic overview: suffering oil and gas economy; lack of sector and market diversification; political instability chilling domestic consumption; poor credit access and declines in business confidence; COVID-19 austerity policies; delayed promised socio-economic reforms

Real GDP (purchasing power parity): $699.947 billion (2023 est.)
$672.379 billion (2022 est.)
$649.015 billion (2021 est.)
note: data in 2021 dollars
comparison ranking: 40

Real GDP growth rate: 4.1% (2023 est.)
3.6% (2022 est.)
3.8% (2021 est.)
note: annual GDP % growth based on constant local currency
comparison ranking: 75

Real GDP per capita: $15,300 (2023 est.)
$15,000 (2022 est.)
$14,700 (2021 est.)
note: data in 2021 dollars
comparison ranking: 123

GDP (official exchange rate): $239.899 billion (2023 est.)
note: data in current dollars at official exchange rate

Inflation rate (consumer prices): 9.32% (2023 est.)
9.27% (2022 est.)
7.23% (2021 est.)
note: annual % change based on consumer prices
comparison ranking: 169

Credit ratings: *note:* The year refers to the year in which the current credit rating was first obtained.

GDP - composition, by sector of origin: *agriculture:* 13.2% (2023 est.)
industry: 38% (2023 est.)
services: 45.1% (2023 est.)
note: figures may not total 100% due to non-allocated consumption not captured in sector-reported data comparison rankings: services 167; industry 35; agriculture 61

GDP - composition, by end use: *household consumption:* 41.2% (2023 est.)
government consumption: 16.9% (2023 est.)
investment in fixed capital: 33.2% (2023 est.)
investment in inventories: 4.6% (2023 est.)
exports of goods and services: 25.2% (2023 est.)
imports of goods and services: -21% (2023 est.)
note: figures may not total 100% due to rounding or gaps in data collection

Agricultural products: potatoes, wheat, milk, watermelons, onions, tomatoes, barley, vegetables, dates, oranges (2022)
note: top ten agricultural products based on tonnage

Industries: petroleum, natural gas, light industries, mining, electrical, petrochemical, food processing

Industrial production growth rate: 3.74% (2023 est.)
note: annual % change in industrial value added based on constant local currency
comparison ranking: 87

Labor force: 13.425 million (2023 est.)
note: number of people ages 15 or older who are employed or seeking work
comparison ranking: 47

Unemployment rate: 11.81% (2023 est.)
12.44% (2022 est.)
13.61% (2021 est.)
note: % of labor force seeking employment
comparison ranking: 177

Youth unemployment rate (ages 15-24): *total:* 30.8% (2023 est.)
male: 27.4% (2023 est.)
female: 46% (2023 est.)
note: % of labor force ages 15-24 seeking employment
comparison ranking: total 23

Average household expenditures: *on food:* 37.1% of household expenditures (2022 est.)
on alcohol and tobacco: 1% of household expenditures (2022 est.)

Remittances: 0.74% of GDP (2023 est.)
0.74% of GDP (2022 est.)
0.96% of GDP (2021 est.)
note: personal transfers and compensation between resident and non-resident individuals/households/entities

Budget: *revenues:* $55.185 billion (2019 est.)
expenditures: $64.728 billion (2019 est.)

Public debt: 27.5% of GDP (2017 est.)
note: data cover central government debt as well as debt issued by subnational entities and intra-governmental debt
comparison ranking: 172

Taxes and other revenues: 32.3% (of GDP) (2017 est.)
comparison ranking: 18

Current account balance: $5.424 billion (2023 est.)
$19.448 billion (2022 est.)
-$4.51 billion (2021 est.)
note: balance of payments - net trade and primary/secondary income in current dollars
comparison ranking: 34

Exports: $58.816 billion (2023 est.)
$69.242 billion (2022 est.)
$41.851 billion (2021 est.)
note: balance of payments - exports of goods and services in current dollars
comparison ranking: 64

Exports - partners: Italy 29%, Spain 12%, France 12%, US 5%, South Korea 5% (2022)
note: top five export partners based on percentage share of exports

Exports - commodities: natural gas, crude petroleum, refined petroleum, fertilizers, ammonia (2022)
note: top five export commodities based on value in dollars

Imports: $51.516 billion (2023 est.)
$46.63 billion (2022 est.)
$44.297 billion (2021 est.)
note: balance of payments - imports of goods and services in current dollars
comparison ranking: 66

Imports - partners: China 18%, France 14%, Italy 7%, Turkey 6%, Brazil 6% (2022)
note: top five import partners based on percentage share of imports

Imports - commodities: wheat, milk, plastics, corn, iron ore (2022)
note: top five import commodities based on value in dollars

Reserves of foreign exchange and gold: $81.217 billion (2023 est.)
$71.852 billion (2022 est.)
$56.211 billion (2021 est.)
note: holdings of gold (year-end prices)/foreign exchange/special drawing rights in current dollars
comparison ranking: 32

Debt - external: $671.248 million (2022 est.)
note: present value of external debt in current US dollars
comparison ranking: 88

Exchange rates: Algerian dinars (DZD) per US dollar -

Exchange rates: 135.843 (2023 est.)
141.995 (2022 est.)
135.064 (2021 est.)

126.777 (2020 est.)
119.354 (2019 est.)

ENERGY

Electricity access: *electrification - total population:* 100% (2022 est.)
electrification - urban areas: 100%
electrification - rural areas: 99.3%

Electricity: *installed generating capacity:* 21.706 million kW (2022 est.)
consumption: 77.786 billion kWh (2022 est.)
exports: 1.529 billion kWh (2022 est.)
imports: 391.148 million kWh (2022 est.)
transmission/distribution losses: 9.263 billion kWh (2022 est.)
comparison rankings: transmission/distribution losses 176; imports 96; exports 62; consumption 42; installed generating capacity 48

Electricity generation sources: *fossil fuels:* 99.2% of total installed capacity (2022 est.)
solar: 0.7% of total installed capacity (2022 est.)

Coal: *consumption:* 167,000 metric tons (2022 est.)
imports: 168,000 metric tons (2022 est.)
proven reserves: 223 million metric tons (2022 est.)

Petroleum: *total petroleum production:* 1.443 million bbl/day (2023 est.)
refined petroleum consumption: 428,000 bbl/day (2022 est.)
crude oil estimated reserves: 12.2 billion barrels (2021 est.)

Natural gas: *production:* 100.726 billion cubic meters (2022 est.)
consumption: 47.963 billion cubic meters (2022 est.)
exports: 49.583 billion cubic meters (2022 est.)
proven reserves: 4.504 trillion cubic meters (2021 est.)

Carbon dioxide emissions: 147.93 million metric tonnes of CO2 (2022 est.)
from coal and metallurgical coke: 501,000 metric tonnes of CO2 (2022 est.)
from petroleum and other liquids: 51.989 million metric tonnes of CO2 (2022 est.)
from consumed natural gas: 95.439 million metric tonnes of CO2 (2022 est.)
comparison ranking: total emissions 34

Energy consumption per capita: 58.473 million Btu/person (2022 est.)
comparison ranking: 83

COMMUNICATIONS

Telephones - fixed lines: *total subscriptions:* 5.576 million (2022 est.)
subscriptions per 100 inhabitants: 12 (2022 est.)
comparison ranking: total subscriptions 26

Telephones - mobile cellular: *total subscriptions:* 49.019 million (2022 est.)
subscriptions per 100 inhabitants: 109 (2022 est.)
comparison ranking: total subscriptions 35

Telecommunication systems: *general assessment:* Algeria has a steadily developing telecom infrastructure with growth encouraged by supportive regulatory measures and by government policies aimed at delivering serviceable internet connections across the country; mobile broadband is largely based on 3G and LTE, and the data rates are also low in global terms; LTE is available in all provinces, investment is required from the mobile network operators (MNOs) to improve the quality of service; the state has previously been hesitant to commit to 5G, instead encouraging the MNOs to undertake upgrades to LTE infrastructure before investing in commercial 5G services; in March 2022, the state is in the process of freeing up the requisite spectrum to enable the MNOs to launch 5G services sometime this year; fixed internet speeds remain slow (2022)
domestic: a limited network of fixed-lines with a teledensity of slightly less than 12 telephones per 100 persons has been offset by the rapid increase in mobile-cellular subscribership; mobile-cellular teledensity was approximately 106 telephones per 100 persons in 2020 (2021)
international: country code - 213; ALPAL-2 is a submarine telecommunications cable system in the Mediterranean Sea linking Algeria and the Spanish Balearic island of Majorca; ORVAL is a submarine cable to Spain; landing points for the TE North/TGN-Eurasia/SEACOM/SeaMeWe-4 fiber-optic submarine cable system that provides links to Europe, the Middle East, and Asia; MED cable connecting Algeria with France; microwave radio relay to Italy, France, Spain, Morocco, and Tunisia; Algeria part of the 4,500 Km terrestrial Trans Sahara Backbone network which connects to other fiber networks in the region; Alcomstat-1 satellite offering telemedicine network (2020)

Broadcast media: state-run Radio-Television Algerienne operates the broadcast media and carries programming in Arabic, Berber dialects, and French; use of satellite dishes is widespread, providing easy access to European and Arab satellite stations; state-run radio operates several national networks and roughly 40 regional radio stations

Internet country code: .dz

Internet users: *total:* 31.24 million (2021 est.)
percent of population: 71% (2021 est.)
comparison ranking: total 33

Broadband - fixed subscriptions: *total:* 3,790,459 (2020 est.)
subscriptions per 100 inhabitants: 9 (2020 est.)
comparison ranking: total 40

TRANSPORTATION

National air transport system: *number of registered air carriers:* 3 (2020)
inventory of registered aircraft operated by air carriers: 87
annual passenger traffic on registered air carriers: 6,442,442 (2018)
annual freight traffic on registered air carriers: 28.28 million (2018) mt-km

Civil aircraft registration country code prefix: 7T

Airports: 85 (2024)
comparison ranking: 60

Heliports: 9 (2024)

Pipelines: 2,600 km condensate, 16,415 km gas, 3,447 km liquid petroleum gas, 7,036 km oil, 144 km refined products (2013)

Railways: *total:* 4,020 km (2019)
comparison ranking: total 46

Roadways: *total:* 112,696 km (2020)
comparison ranking: total 46

Merchant marine: *total:* 119 (2022)
by type: bulk carrier 1, container ship 4, general cargo 11, oil tanker 14, other 89
comparison ranking: total 83

Ports: *total ports:* 17 (2024)
large: 2
medium: 1
small: 6
very small: 8
ports with oil terminals: 3
key ports: Alger, Annaba, Arzew, Arzew El Djedid, Bejaia, Mers El Kebir, Oran, Port Methanier, Skikda

MILITARY AND SECURITY

Military and security forces: Algerian People's National Army (ANP): Land Forces, Naval Forces (includes Coast Guard), Air Forces, Territorial Air Defense Forces, Republican Guard (under ANP but responsible to the President), National Gendarmerie

Ministry of Interior: General Directorate of National Security (national police) (2024)
note: the National Gendarmerie performs police functions outside urban areas under the auspices of the Ministry of National Defense; it is comprised of territorial, intervention/mobile, border guard, railway, riot control, and air support units; General Directorate of National Security share responsibility for maintaining law and order

Military expenditures: 9% of GDP (2023 est.)
4.8% of GDP (2022 est.)
5.6% of GDP (2021 est.)
6.7% of GDP (2020 est.)
6% of GDP (2019 est.)
comparison ranking: 2

Military and security service personnel strengths: approximately 225,000 armed forces personnel (100,000 Army; 15,000 Air Force/Air Defense; 10,000 Navy; 1,000 Republican Guard; 100,000 Gendarmerie) (2023)

Military equipment inventories and acquisitions: the ANP is one of the better-equipped militaries in North Africa; over the past decade, it has made large investments in more modern equipment, including armored vehicles, air defense systems, fighter aircraft, missiles, unmanned aerial vehicles, and warships, largely from Russia, its traditional supplier, but also China and Western European suppliers such as Germany (2023)

Military service age and obligation: 18 is the legal minimum age for voluntary military service for men and women; 19-30 years of age for mandatory national service for men (all Algerian men must register at age 17); service obligation reduced from 18 to 12 months in 2014 (2024)
note: conscripts comprise an estimated 70% of the military

Military - note: the ANP is responsible for external defense but also has some internal security responsibilities; key areas of concern include border and maritime security, terrorism, regional instability, and tensions with Morocco; Algeria supports the pro-independence Polisario Front in Western Sahara and accuses Morocco of supporting the Algerian separatist Movement for the Autonomy of Kabylie (MAK); border security and counterterrorism have received additional focus since the Arab Spring events of 2011 and the rise of terrorist threats emanating from Libya and the Sahel; the Army and Ministry of Defense (MND) paramilitary forces of the Gendarmerie and the border guards have beefed up their presence along the frontiers with Tunisia, Libya, Niger, and Mali to interdict and deter cross-border attacks by Islamist militant groups; the ANP and MND paramilitary forces have also increased counterterrorism

cooperation with some neighboring countries, particularly Tunisia, including joint operations
the ANP has also played a large role in the country's politics since independence in 1962, including coups in 1965 and 1991; it was a key backer of BOUTEFLIKA's election in 1999 and remained a center of power during his 20-year rule; the military was instrumental in BOUTEFLIKA's resignation in 2019, when it withdrew support and called for him to be removed from office (2024)

SPACE

Space agency/agencies: Algerian Space Agency (Agence Spatiale Algérienne, ASAL; established 2002) (2024)

Space launch site(s): none; note - in 1947, Algeria began hosting a French military rocket test site, which was the continent of Africa's first rocket launch site; it was called the Centre Interarmées d'Essais d'Engins Spéciaux (CIEES or Interarmy Special Vehicles Test Center) and was in service until 1967

Space program overview: has a national space policy and a national space research program with stated goals of supporting internal development, managing resource usage, mastering space technology, and reinforcing national sovereignty; builds and operates communications and remote sensing (RS) satellites; researching and developing a range of space-related capabilities, including satellites and satellite payloads, communications, RS, instrumentation, satellite image processing, and geo-spatial information; has bilateral relationships with a variety of foreign space agencies and industries, including those of Argentina, China, France, Germany, India, Russia, Ukraine, and the UK; also a member of the Arab Space Coordination Group, established by the UAE in 2019 (2024)
note: further details about the key activities, programs, and milestones of the country's space program, as well as government spending estimates on the space sector, appear in the Space Programs reference guide

TERRORISM

Terrorist group(s): al-Qa'ida in the Islamic Maghreb (AQIM); Islamic State of Iraq and ash-Sham (ISIS) – Algeria; al-Mulathamun Battalion (al-Mourabitoun)
note: details about the history, aims, leadership, organization, areas of operation, tactics, targets, weapons, size, and sources of support of the group(s) appear(s) in the Terrorism reference guide

TRANSNATIONAL ISSUES

Refugees and internally displaced persons: *refugees (country of origin):* more than 100,000 (Sahrawi, mostly living in Algerian-sponsored camps in the southwestern Algerian town of Tindouf); 7,345 (Syria) (mid-year 2022)

Trafficking in persons: tier rating: Tier 2 Watch list — Algeria does not fully meet the minimum standards for the elimination of trafficking but is making significant efforts to do so, therefore Algeria was upgraded to Tier 2 Watch List; for more details, go to: https://www.state.gov/reports/2024-trafficking-in-persons-report/algeria/

Illicit drugs: NA

AMERICAN SAMOA

INTRODUCTION

Background: Tutuila – the largest island in American Samoa – was settled by 1000 B.C., and the island served as a refuge for exiled chiefs and defeated warriors from the other Samoan islands. The Manu'a Islands, which are also now part of American Samoa, developed a traditional chiefdom that maintained autonomy by controlling oceanic trade. In 1722, Dutch explorer Jacob ROGGEVEEN was the first European to sail through the Manu'a Islands, and he was followed by French explorer Louis Antoine DE BOUGAINVILLE in 1768. Whalers and missionaries arrived in American Samoa in the 1830s, but American and European traders tended to favor the port in Apia – now in independent Samoa – over the smaller and less-developed Pago Pago on Tutuila. In the mid-1800s, a dispute arose in Samoa over control of the Samoan archipelago, with different chiefs gaining support from Germany, the UK, and the US. In 1872, the high chief of Tutuila offered the US exclusive rights to Pago Pago in return for US protection, but the US rejected this offer. As fighting resumed, the US agreed to the chief's request in 1878 and set up a coaling station at Pago Pago. In 1899, with continued disputes over succession, Germany and the US agreed to divide the Samoan islands, while the UK withdrew its claims in exchange for parts of the Solomon Islands. Local chiefs on Tutuila formally ceded their land to the US in 1900, followed by the chief of Manu'a in 1904. The territory was officially named "American Samoa" in 1911.

The US administered the territory through the Department of the Navy. In 1949, there was an attempt to organize the territory, granting it formal self-government, but local chiefs helped defeat the measure in the US Congress. Administration was transferred to the Department of the Interior in 1951, and in 1967, American Samoa adopted a constitution that provides significant protections for traditional Samoan land-tenure rules, language, and culture. In 1977, after four attempts, voters approved a measure to directly elect their governor. Nevertheless, American Samoa officially remains an unorganized territory, and people born in American Samoa are US nationals rather than US citizens.

GEOGRAPHY

Location: Oceania, group of islands in the South Pacific Ocean, about halfway between Hawaii and New Zealand

Geographic coordinates: 14 20 S, 170 00 W

Map references: Oceania

Area: *total:* 224 sq km
land: 224 sq km
water: 0 sq km
note: includes Rose Atoll and Swains Island
comparison ranking: total 216

Area - comparative: slightly larger than Washington, DC

Land boundaries: *total:* 0 km

Coastline: 116 km

Maritime claims: *territorial sea:* 12 nm
exclusive economic zone: 200 nm

Climate: tropical marine, moderated by southeast trade winds; annual rainfall averages about 3 m; rainy season (November to April), dry season (May to October); little seasonal temperature variation

Terrain: five volcanic islands with rugged peaks and limited coastal plains, two coral atolls (Rose Atoll, Swains Island)

Elevation: *highest point:* Lata Mountain 964 m
lowest point: Pacific Ocean 0 m

Natural resources: pumice, pumicite

Land use: *agricultural land:* 24.5% (2018 est.)
arable land: 15% (2018 est.)
permanent crops: 9.5% (2018 est.)
permanent pasture: 0% (2018 est.)
forest: 75.5% (2018 est.)
other: 0% (2018 est.)

Irrigated land: 0 sq km (2022)

Natural hazards: cyclones common from December to March
volcanism: limited volcanic activity on the Ofu and Olosega Islands; neither has erupted since the 19th century

Geography - note: Pago Pago has one of the best natural deepwater harbors in the South Pacific Ocean, sheltered by shape from rough seas and protected by peripheral mountains from high winds; strategic location in the South Pacific Ocean

PEOPLE AND SOCIETY

Population: *total:* 43,895
male: 21,804
female: 22,091 (2024 est.)
comparison rankings: female 211; male 211; total 211

Nationality: *noun:* American Samoan(s) (US nationals)
adjective: American Samoan

Ethnic groups: Pacific Islander 88.7% (includes Samoan 83.2%, Tongan 2.2%, other 3.3%), Asian 5.8% (includes Filipino 3.4%, other 2.4%), mixed 4.4%, other 1.1% (2020 est.)
note: data represent population by ethnic origin or race

Languages: Samoan 87.9% (closely related to Hawaiian and other Polynesian languages), English 3.3%, Tongan 2.1%, other Pacific Islander 4.1%, Asian languages 2.1%, other 0.5% (2020 est.)
note: most people are bilingual

Religions: Christian 98.3%, other <1%, unaffiliated <1% (2020 est.)

Age structure: *0-14 years:* 25.3% (male 5,738/female 5,387)
15-64 years: 66% (male 14,291/female 14,679)
65 years and over: 8.7% (2024 est.) (male 1,775/ female 2,025)
2023 population pyramid:

Dependency ratios: *total dependency ratio:* 52.3
youth dependency ratio: 41.9
elderly dependency ratio: 10.4
potential support ratio: 9.6 (2021)

Median age: *total:* 30 years (2024 est.)
male: 29.4 years
female: 30.6 years
comparison ranking: total 141

Population growth rate: -1.54% (2024 est.)
comparison ranking: 235

Birth rate: 15.7 births/1,000 population (2024 est.)
comparison ranking: 102

Death rate: 6.3 deaths/1,000 population (2024 est.)
comparison ranking: 145

Net migration rate: -24.8 migrant(s)/1,000 population (2024 est.)
comparison ranking: 229

Urbanization: *urban population:* 87.2% of total population (2023)
rate of urbanization: 0.26% annual rate of change (2020-25 est.)

Major urban areas - population: 49,000 PAGO PAGO (capital) (2018)

Sex ratio: *at birth:* 1.06 male(s)/female
0-14 years: 1.07 male(s)/female
15-64 years: 0.97 male(s)/female
65 years and over: 0.88 male(s)/female
total population: 0.99 male(s)/female (2024 est.)

Infant mortality rate: *total:* 9.7 deaths/1,000 live births (2024 est.)
male: 11.7 deaths/1,000 live births
female: 7.6 deaths/1,000 live births
comparison ranking: total 136

Life expectancy at birth: *total population:* 75.8 years (2024 est.)
male: 73.4 years
female: 78.5 years
comparison ranking: total population 122

Total fertility rate: 2.06 children born/woman (2024 est.)
comparison ranking: 97

Gross reproduction rate: 1 (2024 est.)

Drinking water source: *improved:*
total: 99.8% of population
unimproved:
total: 0.2% of population (2020 est.)
improved:
total: 99% of population
unimproved:
total: 1% of population (2020 est.)

Currently married women (ages 15-49): 53.5% (2023 est.)

ENVIRONMENT

Environment - current issues: limited supply of drinking water; pollution; waste disposal; coastal and stream alteration; soil erosion

Climate: tropical marine, moderated by southeast trade winds; annual rainfall averages about 3 m; rainy season (November to April), dry season (May to October); little seasonal temperature variation

Urbanization: *urban population:* 87.2% of total population (2023)
rate of urbanization: 0.26% annual rate of change (2020-25 est.)

Revenue from forest resources: 0% of GDP (2018 est.)
comparison ranking: 167

Revenue from coal: 0% of GDP (2018 est.)
comparison ranking: 83

Waste and recycling: *municipal solid waste generated annually:* 18,989 tons (2016 est.)

GOVERNMENT

Country name: *conventional long form:* American Samoa
conventional short form: American Samoa
former: Eastern Samoa
abbreviation: AS
etymology: the meaning of Samoa is disputed; some modern explanations are that the "sa" connotes "sacred" and "moa" indicates "center," so the name can mean "Holy Center"; alternatively, some assertions state that it can mean "place of the sacred moa bird" of Polynesian mythology; the name, however, may go back to Proto-Polynesian (PPn) times (before 1000 B.C.); a plausible PPn reconstruction has the first syllable as "sa'a" meaning "tribe or people" and "moa" meaning "deep sea or ocean" to convey the meaning "people of the deep sea"

Government type: unincorporated, unorganized Territory of the US with local self-government; republican form of territorial government with separate executive, legislative, and judicial branches

Dependency status: unincorporated, unorganized Territory of the US; administered by the Office of Insular Affairs, US Department of the Interior

Capital: *name:* Pago Pago
geographic coordinates: 14 16 S, 170 42 W
time difference: UTC-11 (6 hours behind Washington, DC, during Standard Time)
note: pronounced pahn-go pahn-go

Administrative divisions: none (territory of the US); there are no first-order administrative divisions as defined by the US Government, but there are 3 districts and 2 islands* at the second order; Eastern, Manu'a, Rose Island*, Swains Island*, Western

Independence: none (territory of the US)

National holiday: Flag Day, 17 April (1900)

Legal system: mixed legal system of US common law and customary law

Constitution: *history:* adopted 17 October 1960; revised 1 July 1967
amendments: proposed by either house of the Legislative Assembly; passage requires three-fifths majority vote by the membership of each house, approval by simple majority vote in a referendum, approval by the US Secretary of the Interior, and only by an act of the US Congress; amended several times, last in 2021

Citizenship: see United States

Note: in accordance with US Code Title 8, Section 1408, persons born in American Samoa are US nationals but not US citizens

Suffrage: 18 years of age; universal

Executive branch: *chief of state:* President Joseph R. BIDEN Jr. (since 20 January 2021)
head of government: Governor Lemanu Peleti MAUGA (since 3 January 2021)
cabinet: Cabinet consists of 12 department directors appointed by the governor with the consent of the Legislature or Fono
elections/appointments: president and vice president indirectly elected on the same ballot by an Electoral College of 'electors' chosen from each state to serve a 4-year term (eligible for a second term); under the US Constitution, residents of unincorporated territories, such as American Samoa, do not vote in elections for US president and vice president; however, they may vote in Democratic and Republican presidential primary elections; governor and lieutenant governor directly elected on the same ballot by absolute majority popular vote in 2 rounds if needed for a 4-year term (eligible for a second term); election last held on 3 November 2020 (next to be held in November 2024)
election results:
Lemanu Peleti MAUGA elected governor in first round; percent of vote - Lemanu Peleti MAUGA (independent) 60.3%, Gaoteote Palaie TOFAU (independent) 21.9%, I'aulualo Fa'afetai TALIA (independent) 12.3%

Legislative branch: *description:* bicameral Legislature or the American Samoa Fono consists of: Senate (18 seats; members indirectly selected by regional governing councils to serve 4-year terms)
House of Representatives (21 seats; 20 members in single- and multi-seat constituencies directly elected by simple majority popular vote and 1 decided by public meeting on Swains Island; members serve 2-year terms)
elections: Senate - last held on 8 November 2022 (next to be held in November 2024)
House of Representatives - last held on 8 November 2022 (next to be held on 5 November 2024)
election results: Senate - percent of vote by party - NA; seats by party - independent 18; composition - men 17, women 1; percentage women 5.6%
House of Representatives - percent of vote by party - NA; seats by party - NA; composition - men 20, women 1; percentage women 4.8%; total Legislature percentage women 5.1%
note: American Samoa elects 1 member by simple majority popular vote to serve a 2-year term as a delegate to the US House of Representatives; the delegate can vote when serving on a committee and when the House meets as the Committee of the Whole House, but not when legislation is submitted for a "full floor" House vote

Judicial branch: *highest court(s):* High Court of American Samoa (consists of the chief justice, associate chief justice, and 6 Samoan associate judges and organized into trial, family, drug, and appellate divisions); note - American Samoa has no US federal courts
judge selection and term of office: chief justice and associate chief justice appointed by the US Secretary

of the Interior to serve for life; Samoan associate judges appointed by the governor to serve for life
subordinate courts: district and village courts

Political parties: Democratic Party
Republican Party

International organization participation: AOSIS (observer), Interpol (subbureau), IOC, PIF (observer), SPC

Diplomatic representation in the US: none (territory of the US)

Diplomatic representation from the US: *embassy:* none (territory of the US)

Flag description: a large white triangle edged in red that is based on the fly side and extends to the hoist side and is charged with an eagle, all on a blue field; the red, white, and blue colors are those traditionally used by both the United States and Samoa; the brown and white American bald eagle flies toward the hoist side and carries 2 traditional Samoan symbols of authority, a war club known as a "fa'alaufa'i" (upper; left talon), and a coconut-fiber fly whisk known as a "fue" (lower; right talon); the combination of symbols broadly mimics that seen on the US Great Seal and reflects the relationship between the US and American Samoa

National symbol(s): a fue (coconut fiber fly whisk; representing wisdom) crossed with a to'oto'o (staff; representing authority); national colors: red, white, blue

National anthem: *name:* "Amerika Samoa" (American Samoa)
lyrics/music: Mariota Tiumalu TUIASOSOPO/ Napoleon Andrew TUITELELEAPAGA
note: local anthem adopted 1950; as a territory of the United States, "The Star-Spangled Banner" is official (see United States)

ECONOMY

Economic overview: tourism, tuna, and government services-based territorial economy; sustained economic decline; vulnerable tuna canning industry; large territorial government presence; minimum wage increases to rise to federal standards by 2036

Real GDP (purchasing power parity): $658 million (2016 est.)
$674.9 million (2015 est.)
$666.9 billion (2014 est.)
note: data are in 2016 dollars
comparison ranking: 212

Real GDP growth rate: 1.74% (2022 est.)
-0.78% (2021 est.)
4.41% (2020 est.)
note: annual GDP % growth based on constant local currency
comparison ranking: 148

Real GDP per capita: $11,200 (2016 est.)
$11,300 (2015 est.)
$11,200 (2014 est.)
comparison ranking: 143

GDP (official exchange rate): $871 million (2022 est.)
note: data in current dollars at official exchange rate

Inflation rate (consumer prices): -0.5% (2015 est.)
1.4% (2014 est.)
comparison ranking: 2

GDP - composition, by end use: *household consumption:* 71.3% (2022 est.)
government consumption: 49.7% (2016 est.)
investment in fixed capital: 7.3% (2016 est.)
investment in inventories: 5.1% (2016 est.)
exports of goods and services: 47% (2022 est.)
imports of goods and services: -77.7% (2022 est.)
note: figures may not total 100% due to rounding or gaps in data collection

Agricultural products: bananas, coconuts, vegetables, taro, breadfruit, yams, copra, pineapples, papayas; dairy products, livestock

Industries: tuna canneries (largely supplied by foreign fishing vessels), handicrafts

Labor force: 17,850 (2015 est.)
comparison ranking: 201

Budget: *revenues:* $249 million (2016 est.)
expenditures: $262.5 million (2016 est.)

Public debt: 12.2% of GDP (2016 est.)
comparison ranking: 196

Taxes and other revenues: 37.8% (of GDP) (2016 est.)
comparison ranking: 13

Exports: $409 million (2022 est.)
$332 million (2021 est.)
$427 million (2020 est.)
note: GDP expenditure basis - exports of goods and services in current dollars
comparison ranking: 192

Exports - partners: Australia 33%, South Korea 16%, Taiwan 8%, Kuwait 8%, Senegal 5% (2022)
note: top five export partners based on percentage share of exports

Exports - commodities: animal meal, packaged medicine, machinery, refined petroleum, insulated wire (2022)
note: top five export commodities based on value in dollars

Imports: $677 million (2022 est.)
$694 million (2021 est.)
$686 million (2020 est.)
note: GDP expenditure basis - imports of goods and services in current dollars
comparison ranking: 197

Imports - partners: Malaysia 27%, Singapore 24%, Fiji 12%, South Korea 9%, Taiwan 9% (2022)
note: top five import partners based on percentage share of imports

Imports - commodities: refined petroleum, fish, cars, paper containers, wood (2022)
note: top five import commodities based on value in dollars

Exchange rates: the US dollar is used

ENERGY

Electricity: *installed generating capacity:* 48,000 kW (2022 est.)
consumption: 157.326 million kWh (2022 est.)
transmission/distribution losses: 13.975 million kWh (2022 est.)
comparison rankings: transmission/distribution losses 21; consumption 195; installed generating capacity 194

Electricity generation sources: *fossil fuels:* 97.1% of total installed capacity (2022 est.)
solar: 2.9% of total installed capacity (2022 est.)

Petroleum: *refined petroleum consumption:* 3,000 bbl/day (2022 est.)

Carbon dioxide emissions: 391,000 metric tonnes of CO_2 (2022 est.)
from petroleum and other liquids: 391,000 metric tonnes of CO_2 (2022 est.)
comparison ranking: total emissions 191

Energy consumption per capita: 89.105 million Btu/person (2019 est.)
comparison ranking: 59

COMMUNICATIONS

Telephones - fixed lines: *total subscriptions:* 10,000 (2021 est.)
subscriptions per 100 inhabitants: 22 (2021 est.)
comparison ranking: total subscriptions 190

Telephones - mobile cellular: *total subscriptions:* 2,250 (2009 est.)
subscriptions per 100 inhabitants: 4 (2009 est.)
comparison ranking: total subscriptions 224

Telecommunication systems: *general assessment:* American Samoa Telecommunications Authority, ASTCA, supplies telecommunication services to the residents of the American Samoan islands, a territory of the United States, which are found in a remote area of the Pacific Ocean; the primary system between the islands consists of fiber-optic cables and satellite connections; over Independence Day weekend 2021, the undersea fiber-optic cable linking the Tutuila and Manu'a Islands failed, completely stranding the Manu'a Islands from all telecommunication services; telecommunication services were restored to the people of Manu'a islands through microwave link between Tutuila to the Manu'a Islands; the link is now providing a steady 1Gbps backhaul most of the time of the year with 600Mbps at four 9's availability, over this extremely long distance (2022)
domestic: nearly 22 per 100 fixed-line tele density (2021)
international: country code - 1-684; landing points for the ASH, Southern Cross NEXT and Hawaiki providing connectivity to New Zealand, Australia, American Samoa, Hawaii, California, and SAS connecting American Samoa with Samoa; satellite earth station - 1 (Intelsat-Pacific Ocean) (2019)

Broadcast media: 3 TV stations; multi-channel pay TV services are available; about a dozen radio stations, some of which are repeater stations

Internet country code: .as

Internet users: *total:* 18,135 (2021 est.)
percent of population: 40.3% (2021 est.)
comparison ranking: total 213

TRANSPORTATION

Airports: 3 (2024)
comparison ranking: 192

Roadways: *total:* 241 km (2016)
comparison ranking: total 207

Ports: *total ports:* 1 (2024)
large: 0
medium: 0
small: 1
very small: 0
ports with oil terminals: 1
key ports: Pago Pago Harbor

MILITARY AND SECURITY

Military - note: defense is the responsibility of the US

ANDORRA

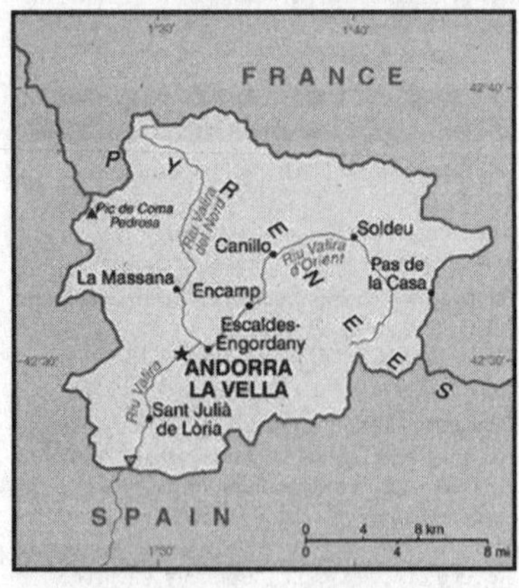

INTRODUCTION

Background: The landlocked Principality of Andorra – one of the smallest states in Europe and nestled high in the Pyrenees between the French and Spanish borders – is the last independent survivor of the Hispanic March states created by Frankish King Charlemagne in 795 after he halted the Moorish invasion of Spain. The March states were a series of buffer states to keep the Muslim Moors from advancing into Christian France. For 715 years, from 1278 to 1993, Andorrans lived under a unique co-principality, ruled by French and Spanish leaders (from 1607 onward, the French chief of state and the Bishop of Urgell). In 1993, this feudal system was modified with the introduction of a modern constitution; the co-princes remained as titular heads of state, but the government transformed into a parliamentary democracy.

Andorra's winter sports, summer climate, and duty-free shopping attract approximately 8 million people each year. Andorra has also become a wealthy international commercial center because of its mature banking sector and low taxes. As part of the effort to modernize its economy, Andorra has opened to foreign investment and engaged in other reforms, such as tax initiatives aimed at supporting broader infrastructure. Although not a member of the EU, Andorra enjoys a special relationship with the bloc that is governed by various customs and cooperation agreements, and Andorra uses the euro as its national currency.

GEOGRAPHY

Location: Southwestern Europe, Pyrenees mountains, on the border between France and Spain

Geographic coordinates: 42 30 N, 1 30 E

Map references: Europe

Area: *total:* 468 sq km
land: 468 sq km
water: 0 sq km
comparison ranking: total 195

Area - comparative: 2.5 times the size of Washington, DC

Land boundaries: *total:* 118 km
border countries (2): France 55 km; Spain 63 km

Coastline: 0 km (landlocked)

Maritime claims: none (landlocked)

Climate: temperate; snowy, cold winters and warm, dry summers

Terrain: rugged mountains dissected by narrow valleys

Elevation: *highest point:* Pic de Coma Pedrosa 2,946 m
lowest point: Riu Runer 840 m
mean elevation: 1,996 m

Natural resources: hydropower, mineral water, timber, iron ore, lead

Land use: *agricultural land:* 40% (2018 est.)
arable land: 1.7% (2018 est.)
permanent crops: 0% (2018 est.)
permanent pasture: 38.3% (2018 est.)
forest: 34% (2018 est.)
other: 26% (2018 est.)

Irrigated land: 0 sq km (2022)

Population distribution: population is unevenly distributed and is concentrated in the seven urbanized valleys that make up the country's parishes (political administrative divisions)

Natural hazards: avalanches

Geography - note: landlocked; straddles a number of important crossroads in the Pyrenees

PEOPLE AND SOCIETY

Population: *total:* 85,370
male: 43,652
female: 41,718 (2024 est.)
comparison rankings: female 199; male 199; total 199

Nationality: *noun:* Andorran(s)
adjective: Andorran

Ethnic groups: Spanish 34.3%, Andorran 32.1%, Portuguese 10%, French 5.6%, other 18% (2024 est.)
note: data represent population by country of birth

Languages: Catalan (official) 44.1%, Castilian 40.3%, Portuguese 13.5%, French 10%, English 3%, other 6.8% (2022 est.)
note: data represent mother tongue

Religions: Christian (predominantly Roman Catholic) 89.5, other 8.8%, unaffiliated 1.7% (2020 est.)

Age structure: *0-14 years:* 12% (male 5,276/female 4,954)
15-64 years: 67.7% (male 29,562/female 28,201)
65 years and over: 20.4% (2024 est.) (male 8,814/female 8,563)

Dependency ratios: *total dependency ratio:* 38.1
youth dependency ratio: 18.1
elderly dependency ratio: 20.1
potential support ratio: 5 (2021)

Median age: *total:* 48.8 years (2024 est.)
male: 48.7 years
female: 48.8 years
comparison ranking: total 4

Population growth rate: -0.12% (2024 est.)
comparison ranking: 205

Birth rate: 6.9 births/1,000 population (2024 est.)
comparison ranking: 224

Death rate: 8.1 deaths/1,000 population (2024 est.)
comparison ranking: 85

Net migration rate: 0 migrant(s)/1,000 population (2024 est.)
comparison ranking: 79

Population distribution: population is unevenly distributed and is concentrated in the seven urbanized valleys that make up the country's parishes (political administrative divisions)

Urbanization: *urban population:* 87.8% of total population (2023)
rate of urbanization: 0.11% annual rate of change (2020-25 est.)

Major urban areas - population: 23,000 ANDORRA LA VELLA (capital) (2018)

Sex ratio: *at birth:* 1.06 male(s)/female
0-14 years: 1.06 male(s)/female
15-64 years: 1.05 male(s)/female
65 years and over: 1.03 male(s)/female
total population: 1.05 male(s)/female (2024 est.)

Mother's mean age at first birth: 32.8 years (2019)

Infant mortality rate: *total:* 3.3 deaths/1,000 live births (2024 est.)
male: 3.4 deaths/1,000 live births
female: 3.2 deaths/1,000 live births
comparison ranking: total 200

Life expectancy at birth: *total population:* 83.8 years (2024 est.)
male: 81.6 years
female: 86.2 years
comparison ranking: total population 10

Total fertility rate: 1.47 children born/woman (2024 est.)
comparison ranking: 204

Gross reproduction rate: 0.71 (2024 est.)

Drinking water source: *improved: urban:* 100% of population
rural: 100% of population
total: 100% of population
(2020 est.)

Current health expenditure: 9.1% of GDP (2020)

Physician density: 3.63 physicians/1,000 population (2015)

Hospital bed density: 2.5 beds/1,000 population

Sanitation facility access: *improved: urban:* 100% of population
rural: 100% of population
total: 100% of population
(2020 est.)

Obesity - adult prevalence rate: 25.6% (2016)
comparison ranking: 50

Alcohol consumption per capita: *total:* 10.99 liters of pure alcohol (2019 est.)
beer: 3.59 liters of pure alcohol (2019 est.)
wine: 4.98 liters of pure alcohol (2019 est.)
spirits: 2.32 liters of pure alcohol (2019 est.)
other alcohols: 0 liters of pure alcohol (2019 est.)
comparison ranking: total 12

Tobacco use: *total:* 31.8% (2020 est.)
male: 35.3% (2020 est.)

female: 28.3% (2020 est.)
comparison ranking: total 23

Education expenditures: 2.9% of GDP (2021 est.)
comparison ranking: 163

Literacy: *definition:* age 15 and over can read and write
total population: 100%
male: 100%
female: 100% (2016)

ENVIRONMENT

Environment - current issues: deforestation; overgrazing of mountain meadows contributes to soil erosion; air pollution; wastewater treatment and solid waste disposal

Environment - international agreements: *party to:* Biodiversity, Climate Change, Climate Change-Paris Agreement, Comprehensive Nuclear Test Ban, Desertification, Hazardous Wastes, Ozone Layer Protection, Wetlands
signed, but not ratified: none of the selected agreements

Climate: temperate; snowy, cold winters and warm, dry summers

Urbanization: *urban population:* 87.8% of total population (2023)
rate of urbanization: 0.11% annual rate of change (2020-25 est.)

Revenue from forest resources: 0% of GDP (2018 est.)
comparison ranking: 191

Air pollutants: *particulate matter emissions:* 8.52 micrograms per cubic meter (2019 est.)
carbon dioxide emissions: 0.47 megatons (2016 est.)
methane emissions: 0.05 megatons (2020 est.)

Waste and recycling: *municipal solid waste generated annually:* 43,000 tons (2012 est.)

Total renewable water resources: 320 million cubic meters (2020 est.)

GOVERNMENT

Country name: *conventional long form:* Principality of Andorra
conventional short form: Andorra
local long form: Principat d'Andorra
local short form: Andorra
etymology: the origin of the country's name is obscure; the name may derive from the Arabic "ad-darra" meaning "the forest," a reference to its location as part of the Spanish March (defensive buffer zone) against the invading Moors in the 8th century; an alternate explanation is that the name originates from a Navarrese word "andurrial" meaning "shrub-covered land"

Government type: parliamentary democracy (since March 1993) that retains its chiefs of state in the form of a co-principality; the two princes are the President of France and Bishop of Seu d'Urgell, Spain

Capital: *name:* Andorra la Vella
geographic coordinates: 42 30 N, 1 31 E
time difference: UTC+1 (6 hours ahead of Washington, DC during Standard Time)
daylight saving time: +1hr, begins last Sunday in March; ends last Sunday in October
etymology: translates as "Andorra the Old" in Catalan

Administrative divisions: 7 parishes (parroquies, singular - parroquia); Andorra la Vella, Canillo, Encamp, Escaldes-Engordany, La Massana, Ordino, Sant Julia de Loria

Independence: 1278 (formed under the joint sovereignty of the French Count of Foix and the Spanish Bishop of Urgell)

National holiday: Our Lady of Meritxell Day, 8 September (1278)

Legal system: mixed legal system of civil and customary law with the influence of canon (religious) law

Constitution: *history:* drafted 1991, approved by referendum 14 March 1993, effective 28 April 1993
amendments: proposed by the coprinces jointly or by the General Council; passage requires at least a two-thirds majority vote by the General Council, ratification in a referendum, and sanctioning by the coprinces

International law organization participation: has not submitted an ICJ jurisdiction declaration; accepts ICCt jurisdiction

Citizenship: *citizenship by birth:* no
citizenship by descent only: the mother must be an Andorran citizen or the father must have been born in Andorra and both parents maintain permanent residence in Andorra
dual citizenship recognized: no
residency requirement for naturalization: 25 years

Suffrage: 18 years of age; universal

Executive branch: *chief of state:* Co-prince Emmanuel MACRON (since 14 May 2017); represented by Patrick STROZDA (since 14 May 2017); and Co-prince Archbishop Joan-Enric VIVES i Sicilia (since 12 May 2003); represented by Eduard Ibanez PULIDO (since 27 November 2023)
head of government: Prime Minister Xavier Espot ZAMORA (since 16 May 2019)
cabinet: Executive Council composed of head of government and 11 ministers designated by the head of government
elections/appointments: head of government indirectly elected by the General Council (Andorran parliament), formally appointed by the co-princes for a 4-year term; election last held on 2 April 2023 (next to be held in April 2027); the leader of the majority party in the General Council is usually elected head of government
election results:
2023: Xaviar Espot ZAMORA (DA) reelected head of government; percent of General Council vote - 57.1%
2019: Xaviar Espot ZAMORA (DA) elected head of government; percent of General Council vote - 60.7

Legislative branch: *description:* unicameral General Council of the Valleys or Consell General de les Valls (28 seats; 14 members directly elected in two-seat constituencies (7 parishes) by simple majority vote and 14 directly elected in a single national constituency by proportional representation vote; members serve 4-year terms); note - voters cast two separate ballots - one for national election and one for their parish
elections: last held on 2 April 2023 (next to be held in April 2027)
election results: percent of vote by party/coalition - DA, CC, L'A & ACCIO alliance 43.6%, C 21.4%, AE 16%, PS & SDP alliance 21.1%; seats by party/coalition - DA, CC, L'A & ACCIO alliance 17, C 5, AE 3, PS & SDP alliance 3; composition - men 14, women 14, percentage women 50%
note: voters cast two separate ballots – one for the national election and one for their parish

Judicial branch: *highest court(s):* Supreme Court of Justice of Andorra or Tribunal Superior de la Justicia d'Andorra (consists of the court president and 8 judges organized into civil, criminal, and administrative chambers); Constitutional Court or Tribunal Constitucional (consists of 4 magistrates)
judge selection and term of office: Supreme Court president and judges appointed by the Supreme Council of Justice, a 5-member judicial policy and administrative body appointed 1 each by the coprinces, 1 by the General Council, 1 by the executive council president, and 1 by the courts; judges serve 6-year renewable terms; Constitutional magistrates - 2 appointed by the coprinces and 2 by the General Council; magistrates' appointments limited to 2 consecutive 8-year terms
subordinate courts: Tribunal of Judges or Tribunal de Batlles; Tribunal of the Courts or Tribunal de Corts

Political parties: Action for Andorra or ACCIO
Committed Citizens or CC
Concord
Democrats for Andorra or DA
Forward Andorra or AE
Liberals of Andorra or L'A
Social Democratic Party or PS
Social Democracy and Progress or SDP
note: Andorra has several smaller parties at the parish level (one is Lauredian Union)

International organization participation: CE, FAO, ICAO, ICC (NGOs), ICCt, ICRM, IFRCS, Interpol, IOC, IPU, ITU, OIF, OPCW, OSCE, UN, UNCTAD, UNESCO, Union Latina, UNWTO, WCO, WHO, WIPO, WTO (observer)

Diplomatic representation in the US: *chief of mission:* Ambassador (vacant); Chargé d'Affaires Joan FORNER ROVIRA (since 20 August 2024); note - also Permanent Representative to the UN
chancery: 2 United Nations Plaza, 27th Floor, New York, NY 10017
telephone: [1] (212) 750-8064
FAX: [1] (212) 750-6630
email address and website:
contact@andorraun.org
https://www.exteriors.ad/en/embassies-of-andorra/andorra-usa-embassy

Diplomatic representation from the US: embassy: the US does not have an embassy in Andorra; the US ambassador to Spain is accredited to Andorra; US interests in Andorra are represented by the US Consulate General's office in Barcelona (Spain); mailing address: Paseo Reina Elisenda de Montcada, 23, 08034 Barcelona, Espana; telephone: [34] (93) 280-22-27; FAX: [34] (93) 280-61-75; email address: Barcelonaacs@state.gov

Flag description: three vertical bands of blue (hoist side), yellow, and red, with the national coat of arms centered in the yellow band; the latter band is slightly wider than the other 2 so that the ratio of band widths is 8:9:8; the coat of arms features a quartered shield with the emblems of (starting in the upper left and proceeding clockwise): Urgell, Foix, Bearn, and Catalonia; the motto reads VIRTUS UNITA FORTIOR (Strength United is Stronger); the flag combines the blue and red French colors with

the red and yellow of Spain to show Franco-Spanish protection
note: similar to the flags of Chad and Romania, which do not have a national coat of arms in the center, and the flag of Moldova, which does bear a national emblem

National symbol(s): red cow (breed unspecified); national colors: blue, yellow, red

National anthem: *name:* "El Gran Carlemany" (The Great Charlemagne)
lyrics/music: Joan BENLLOCH i VIVO/Enric MARFANY BONS
note: adopted 1921; the anthem provides a brief history of Andorra in a first person narrative

National heritage: *total World Heritage Sites:* 1 (cultural)
selected World Heritage Site locales: Madriu-Perafita-Claror Valley

ECONOMY

Economic overview: high GDP; low unemployment; non-EU Euro user; co-principality duty-free area between Spain and France; tourist hub but hit hard by COVID-19; modern, non-tax haven financial sector; looking for big tech investments; new member of SEPA and IMF

Real GDP (purchasing power parity): $5.168 billion (2023 est.)
$5.094 billion (2022 est.)
$4.65 billion (2021 est.)
note: data in 2021 dollars
comparison ranking: 183

Real GDP growth rate: 1.44% (2023 est.)
9.56% (2022 est.)
8.29% (2021 est.)
note: annual GDP % growth based on constant local currency
comparison ranking: 153

Real GDP per capita: $64,500 (2023 est.)
$63,800 (2022 est.)
$58,800 (2021 est.)
note: data in 2021 dollars
comparison ranking: 23

GDP (official exchange rate): $3.728 billion (2023 est.)
note: data in current dollars at official exchange rate

Inflation rate (consumer prices): -0.9% (2015 est.)
-0.1% (2014 est.)
comparison ranking: 1

Credit ratings: Fitch rating: A- (2022)

Moody's rating: Baa2 (2022)

Standard & Poors rating: BBB+ (2023)
note: The year refers to the year in which the current credit rating was first obtained.

GDP - composition, by sector of origin: *agriculture:* 0.5% (2023 est.)
industry: 11.4% (2023 est.)
services: 78.6% (2023 est.)
note: figures may not total 100% due to non-allocated consumption not captured in sector-reported data
comparison rankings: services 18; industry 184; agriculture 197

Agricultural products: small quantities of rye, wheat, barley, oats, vegetables, tobacco, sheep, cattle

Industries: tourism (particularly skiing), banking, timber, furniture

Industrial production growth rate: 3.88% (2023 est.)
note: annual % change in industrial value added based on constant local currency
comparison ranking: 83

Labor force: 39,750 (2016)
comparison ranking: 194

Unemployment rate: 3.7% (2016 est.)
4.1% (2015 est.)
comparison ranking: 70

Remittances: 0% of GDP (2023 est.)
0% of GDP (2022 est.)
1.59% of GDP (2021 est.)
note: personal transfers and compensation between resident and non-resident individuals/households/entities

Budget: *revenues:* $1.872 billion (2016)
expenditures: $2.06 billion (2016)

Public debt: 41% of GDP (2014 est.)
comparison ranking: 129

Taxes and other revenues: 69% (of GDP) (2016)
comparison ranking: 2

Current account balance: $583.199 million (2022 est.)
$467.435 million (2021 est.)
$448.869 million (2020 est.)
note: balance of payments - net trade and primary/secondary income in current dollars
comparison ranking: 63

Exports: $2.736 billion (2022 est.)
$2.414 billion (2021 est.)
$1.842 billion (2020 est.)
note: balance of payments - exports of goods and services in current dollars
comparison ranking: 157

Exports - partners: Spain 73%, France 6%, UK 3%, US 2%, Germany 2% (2022)
note: top five export partners based on percentage share of exports

Exports - commodities: paintings, integrated circuits, cars, orthopedic appliances, garments (2022)
note: top five export commodities based on value in dollars

Imports: $2.44 billion (2022 est.)
$2.143 billion (2021 est.)
$1.727 billion (2020 est.)
note: balance of payments - imports of goods and services in current dollars
comparison ranking: 166

Imports - partners: Spain 66%, France 12%, Germany 4%, China 3%, Italy 3% (2022)
note: top five import partners based on percentage share of imports

Imports - commodities: cars, refined petroleum, garments, electricity, beauty products (2022)
note: top five import commodities based on value in dollars

Exchange rates: euros (EUR) per US dollar -

Exchange rates: 0.925 (2023 est.)
0.95 (2022 est.)
0.845 (2021 est.)
0.876 (2020 est.)
0.893 (2019 est.)
note: while not an EU member state, Andorra has a 2011 monetary agreement with the EU to produce limited euro coinage—but not banknotes—that began enforcement in April 2012

ENERGY

Electricity access: *electrification - total population:* 100% (2022 est.)

COMMUNICATIONS

Telephones - fixed lines: *total subscriptions:* 51,000 (2022 est.)
subscriptions per 100 inhabitants: 64 (2022 est.)
comparison ranking: total subscriptions 154

Telephones - mobile cellular: *total subscriptions:* 114,000 (2022 est.)
subscriptions per 100 inhabitants: 142 (2022 est.)
comparison ranking: total subscriptions 191

Telecommunication systems: *general assessment:* Andorra has a modern telecommunications system with microwave radio relay connections between the exchanges and land line circuits to France and Spain (2023)
domestic: about 63 per 100 fixed-line, 110 per 100 mobile-cellular (2021)
international: country code - 376; landline circuits to France and Spain; modern system with microwave radio relay connections between exchanges (2023)

Broadcast media: 1 public TV station and 2 public radio stations; about 10 commercial radio stations; good reception of radio and TV broadcasts from stations in France and Spain; upgraded to terrestrial digital TV broadcasting in 2007; roughly 25 international TV channels available (2019)

Internet country code: .ad

Internet users: *total:* 74,260 (2021 est.)
percent of population: 94% (2021 est.)
comparison ranking: total 193

Broadband - fixed subscriptions: *total:* 37,000 (2020 est.)
subscriptions per 100 inhabitants: 48 (2020 est.)
comparison ranking: total 146

TRANSPORTATION

Civil aircraft registration country code prefix: C3

Heliports: 2 (2024)

Roadways: *total:* 320 km (2019)
comparison ranking: total 203

MILITARY AND SECURITY

Military and security forces: no regular military forces; Police Corps of Andorra (under the Ministry of Justice and Interior)

Military - note: defense is the responsibility of France and Spain

ANGOLA

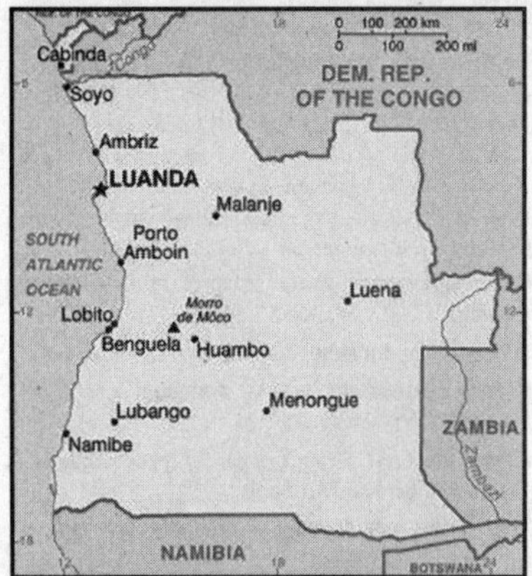

INTRODUCTION

Background: Bantu-speaking people settled in the area now called Angola in 6th century A.D.; by the 10th century various Bantu groups had established kingdoms, of which Kongo became the most powerful. From the late-14th to the mid-19th century, a Kingdom of Kongo stretched across central Africa from present-day northern Angola into the current Congo republics. It traded heavily with the Portuguese who, beginning in the 16th century, established coastal colonies and trading posts and introduced Christianity. Angola became a major hub of the transatlantic slave trade conducted by the Portuguese and other European powers – often in collaboration with local kingdoms, including the Kongo. The Angola area is estimated to have lost as many as 4 million people as a result of the slave trade. The Kingdom of Kongo's main rival was the Kingdom of Ndongo to its south, whose most famous leader was Nzingha Mbande, the 17th century diplomat to the Portuguese and later Queen, who successfully fought off Portuguese encroachment during her nearly 40- year reign. Smaller kingdoms, such as the Matamba and Ngoyo, often came under the control of the Kongo or Ndongo Kingdoms. During the Berlin Conference of 1884-85, Portugal and other European powers set Angola's modern borders, but the Portuguese did not fully control large portions of the territory. Portugal gained control of the Kingdom of Kongo in 1888 when Kongo's King Pedro V sought Portuguese military assistance in exchange for becoming a vassal. After a revolt in 1914, Portugal imposed direct rule over the colony and abolished the Kongo Kingdom.

The Angolan National Revolution began in 1961, and in 1975, Angola won its independence when Portugal's dictatorship fell, a collapse that occurred in part because of growing discontent over conflict in Angola and other colonies. Angola's multiple independence movements soon clashed, with the Popular Movement for Liberation of Angola (MPLA), led by Agostinho NETO, taking power and the National Union for the Total Independence of Angola (UNITA), led by Jonas SAVIMBI, emerging as its main competitor. After NETO's death in 1979, Jose Eduardo DOS SANTOS, also of the MPLA, became president. Over time, the Angolan civil war escalated and became a major Cold War conflict, with the Soviet Union and Cuba supporting the MPLA and the US and South Africa supporting UNITA. Up to 1.5 million lives may have been lost – and 4 million people displaced – during the more than a quarter-century of fighting. SAVIMBI's death in 2002 ended UNITA's insurgency and cemented the MPLA's hold on power. DOS SANTOS did not seek reelection in 2017 and supported Joao LOURENCO's successful bid to become president. LOURENCO was reelected in 2022. Angola scores low on human development indexes despite using its large oil reserves to rebuild since 2002.

GEOGRAPHY

Location: Southern Africa, bordering the South Atlantic Ocean, between Namibia and Democratic Republic of the Congo

Geographic coordinates: 12 30 S, 18 30 E

Map references: Africa

Area: *total:* 1,246,700 sq km
land: 1,246,700 sq km
water: 0 sq km
comparison ranking: total 24

Area - comparative: about eight times the size of Georgia; slightly less than twice the size of Texas

Land boundaries: *total:* 5,369 km
border countries (4): Democratic Republic of the Congo 2,646 km (of which 225 km is the boundary of discontiguous Cabinda Province); Republic of the Congo 231 km; Namibia 1,427 km; Zambia 1,065 km

Coastline: 1,600 km

Maritime claims: *territorial sea:* 12 nm
contiguous zone: 24 nm
exclusive economic zone: 200 nm

Climate: semiarid in south and along coast to Luanda; north has cool, dry season (May to October) and hot, rainy season (November to April)

Terrain: narrow coastal plain rises abruptly to vast interior plateau

Elevation: *highest point:* Moca 2,620 m
lowest point: Atlantic Ocean 0 m
mean elevation: 1,112 m

Natural resources: petroleum, diamonds, iron ore, phosphates, copper, feldspar, gold, bauxite, uranium

Land use: *agricultural land:* 45.7% (2018 est.)
arable land: 3.9% (2018 est.)
permanent crops: 0.3% (2018 est.)
permanent pasture: 41.5% (2018 est.)
forest: 54.3% (2018 est.)

Irrigated land: 860 sq km (2014)

Major rivers (by length in km): Rio Zambeze (Zambezi) (shared with Zambia [s], Namibia, Botswana, Zimbabwe, and Mozambique [m]) - 2,740 km; Rio Cubango (Okavango) river source (shared with Namibia and Botswana [m]) - 1,600 km
note – [s] after country name indicates river source; [m] after country name indicates river mouth

Major watersheds (area sq km): Atlantic Ocean drainage: Congo (3,730,881 sq km)

Indian Ocean drainage: Zambezi (1,332,412 sq km)

Internal (endorheic basin) drainage: Okavango Basin (863,866 sq km)

Major aquifers: Congo Basin, Upper Kalahari-Cuvelai-Upper Zambezi Basin

Population distribution: most people live in the western half of the country; urban areas account for the highest concentrations of people, particularly the capital of Luanda as shown in this population distribution map

Natural hazards: locally heavy rainfall causes periodic flooding on the plateau

Geography - note: the province of Cabinda is an exclave, separated from the rest of the country by the Democratic Republic of the Congo

PEOPLE AND SOCIETY

Population: *total:* 37,202,061
male: 18,196,058
female: 19,006,003 (2024 est.)
comparison rankings: female 39; male 42; total 40

Nationality: *noun:* Angolan(s)
adjective: Angolan

Ethnic groups: Ovimbundu 37%, Kimbundu 25%, Bakongo 13%, Mestico (mixed European and native African) 2%, European 1%, other 22%

Languages: Portuguese 71.2% (official), Umbundu 23%, Kikongo 8.2%, Kimbundu 7.8%, Chokwe 6.5%, Nhaneca 3.4%, Nganguela 3.1%, Fiote 2.4%, Kwanhama 2.3%, Muhumbi 2.1%, Luvale 1%, other 3.6% (2014 est.)
note: shares sum to more than 100% because some respondents gave more than one answer on the census

Religions: Roman Catholic 41.1%, Protestant 38.1%, other 8.6%, none 12.3% (2014 est.)

Demographic profile: More than two decades after the end of Angola's 27-year civil war, the country still faces a variety of socioeconomic problems, including poverty, high maternal and child mortality, and illiteracy. Despite the country's rapid post-war economic growth based on oil production, about 30 percent of Angolans live below the poverty line and unemployment is widespread, especially among the large young-adult population. Only about 70% of the population is literate, and the rate drops to around 60% for women. The youthful population - about 48% are under the age of 15 as of 2022 - is expected to continue growing rapidly with a fertility rate of more than 5 children per woman and a low rate of contraceptive use. Fewer than half of women deliver their babies with the assistance of trained health care personnel, which contributes to Angola's high maternal mortality rate.
Of the estimated 550,000 Angolans who fled their homeland during its civil war, most have returned home since 2002. In 2012, the UN assessed that conditions in Angola had been stable for several years and invoked a cessation of refugee status for Angolans. Following the cessation clause, some of those still in exile returned home voluntarily through UN repatriation programs, and others integrated into host countries.

Age structure: *0-14 years:* 46.9% (male 8,752,419/ female 8,701,422)

15-64 years: 50.7% (male 9,076,080/female 9,795,035)
65 years and over: 2.4% (2024 est.) (male 367,559/female 509,546)

Dependency ratios: *total dependency ratio:* 91.5
youth dependency ratio: 86.5
elderly dependency ratio: 5
potential support ratio: 20.1 (2021 est.)

Median age: *total:* 16.3 years (2024 est.)
male: 15.8 years
female: 16.8 years
comparison ranking: total 227

Population growth rate: 3.33% (2024 est.)
comparison ranking: 3

Birth rate: 41.1 births/1,000 population (2024 est.)
comparison ranking: 2

Death rate: 7.6 deaths/1,000 population (2024 est.)
comparison ranking: 99

Net migration rate: -0.2 migrant(s)/1,000 population (2024 est.)
comparison ranking: 105

Population distribution: most people live in the western half of the country; urban areas account for the highest concentrations of people, particularly the capital of Luanda as shown in this population distribution map

Urbanization: *urban population:* 68.7% of total population (2023)
rate of urbanization: 4.04% annual rate of change (2020-25 est.)

Major urban areas - population: 9.292 million LUANDA (capital), 959,000 Lubango, 905,000 Cabinda, 809,000 Benguela, 783,000 Malanje (2023)

Sex ratio: *at birth:* 1.03 male(s)/female
0-14 years: 1.01 male(s)/female
15-64 years: 0.93 male(s)/female
65 years and over: 0.72 male(s)/female
total population: 0.96 male(s)/female (2024 est.)

Mother's mean age at first birth: 19.4 years (2015/16 est.)
note: data represents median age at first birth among women 20-49

Maternal mortality ratio: 222 deaths/100,000 live births (2020 est.)
comparison ranking: 41

Infant mortality rate: *total:* 55.6 deaths/1,000 live births (2024 est.)
male: 60.7 deaths/1,000 live births
female: 50.3 deaths/1,000 live births
comparison ranking: total 13

Life expectancy at birth: *total population:* 62.9 years (2024 est.)
male: 60.8 years
female: 65.1 years
comparison ranking: total population 214

Total fertility rate: 5.7 children born/woman (2024 est.)
comparison ranking: 2

Gross reproduction rate: 2.81 (2024 est.)

Contraceptive prevalence rate: 13.7% (2015/16)

Drinking water source: *improved:* *urban:* 81.3% of population
rural: 36.5% of population
total: 66.5% of population
unimproved: *urban:* 18.7% of population
rural: 63.5% of population
total: 33.5% of population (2020 est.)

Current health expenditure: 2.9% of GDP (2020)

Physician density: 0.21 physicians/1,000 population (2018)

Sanitation facility access: *improved:* *urban:* 93.7% of population
rural: 30.3% of population
total: 72.7% of population
unimproved: *urban:* 6.3% of population
rural: 69.7% of population
total: 27.3% of population (2020 est.)

Obesity - adult prevalence rate: 8.2% (2016)
comparison ranking: 154

Alcohol consumption per capita: *total:* 5.84 liters of pure alcohol (2019 est.)
beer: 3.78 liters of pure alcohol (2019 est.)
wine: 0.72 liters of pure alcohol (2019 est.)
spirits: 1.27 liters of pure alcohol (2019 est.)
other alcohols: 0.08 liters of pure alcohol (2019 est.)
comparison ranking: total 73

Children under the age of 5 years underweight: 19% (2015/16)
comparison ranking: 20

Currently married women (ages 15-49): 55.7% (2023 est.)

Child marriage: *women married by age 15:* 7.9%
women married by age 18: 30.3%
men married by age 18: 6% (2016 est.)

Education expenditures: 2.4% of GDP (2020 est.)
comparison ranking: 178

Literacy: *definition:* age 15 and over can read and write
total population: 71.1%
male: 82.6%
female: 62.4% (2015)

ENVIRONMENT

Environment - current issues: overuse of pastures and subsequent soil erosion attributable to population pressures; desertification; deforestation of tropical rain forest, in response to both international demand for tropical timber and to domestic use as fuel, resulting in loss of biodiversity; soil erosion contributing to water pollution and siltation of rivers and dams; inadequate supplies of potable water

Environment - international agreements: *party to:* Biodiversity, Climate Change, Climate Change-Kyoto Protocol, Climate Change-Paris Agreement, Comprehensive Nuclear Test Ban, Desertification, Endangered Species, Hazardous Wastes, Law of the Sea, Marine Dumping-London Protocol, Ozone Layer Protection, Ship Pollution
signed, but not ratified: none of the selected agreements

Climate: semiarid in south and along coast to Luanda; north has cool, dry season (May to October) and hot, rainy season (November to April)

Urbanization: *urban population:* 68.7% of total population (2023)
rate of urbanization: 4.04% annual rate of change (2020-25 est.)

Revenue from forest resources: 0.36% of GDP (2018 est.)
comparison ranking: 75

Revenue from coal: 0% of GDP (2018 est.)
comparison ranking: 75

Air pollutants: *particulate matter emissions:* 27.16 micrograms per cubic meter (2019 est.)
carbon dioxide emissions: 34.69 megatons (2016 est.)
methane emissions: 23.28 megatons (2020 est.)

Waste and recycling: *municipal solid waste generated annually:* 4,213,644 tons (2012 est.)

Major rivers (by length in km): Rio Zambeze (Zambezi) (shared with Zambia [s], Namibia, Botswana, Zimbabwe, and Mozambique [m]) - 2,740 km; Rio Cubango (Okavango) river source (shared with Namibia and Botswana [m]) - 1,600 km
note – [s] after country name indicates river source; [m] after country name indicates river mouth

Major watersheds (area sq km): Atlantic Ocean drainage: Congo (3,730,881 sq km)

Indian Ocean drainage: Zambezi (1,332,412 sq km)

Internal (endorheic basin) drainage: Okavango Basin (863,866 sq km)

Major aquifers: Congo Basin, Upper Kalahari-Cuvelai-Upper Zambezi Basin

Total water withdrawal: *municipal:* 320 million cubic meters (2020 est.)
industrial: 240 million cubic meters (2020 est.)
agricultural: 150 million cubic meters (2020 est.)

Total renewable water resources: 148.4 billion cubic meters (2020 est.)

GOVERNMENT

Country name: *conventional long form:* Republic of Angola
conventional short form: Angola
local long form: Republica de Angola
local short form: Angola
former: People's Republic of Angola
etymology: name derived by the Portuguese from the title "ngola" held by kings of the Ndongo (Ndongo was a kingdom in what is now Angola)

Government type: presidential republic

Capital: *name:* Luanda
geographic coordinates: 8 50 S, 13 13 E
time difference: UTC+1 (6 hours ahead of Washington, DC, during Standard Time)
daylight saving time: does not observe daylight savings time
etymology: originally named "Sao Paulo da Assuncao de Loanda" (Saint Paul of the Assumption of Loanda), which over time was shortened and corrupted to just Luanda

Administrative divisions: 18 provinces (provincias, singular - provincia); Bengo, Benguela, Bie, Cabinda, Cuando Cubango, Cuanza-Norte, Cuanza-Sul, Cunene, Huambo, Huila, Luanda, Lunda-Norte, Lunda-Sul, Malanje, Moxico, Namibe, Uige, Zaire

Independence: 11 November 1975 (from Portugal)

National holiday: Independence Day, 11 November (1975)

Legal system: civil legal system based on Portuguese civil law; no judicial review of legislation

Constitution: *history:* previous 1975, 1992; latest passed by National Assembly 21 January 2010, adopted 5 February 2010
amendments: proposed by the president of the republic or supported by at least one third of the National Assembly membership; passage requires at least two-thirds majority vote of the Assembly subject to prior Constitutional Court review if requested by the president of the republic

International law organization participation: has not submitted an ICJ jurisdiction declaration; non-party state to the ICCt

Citizenship: *citizenship by birth:* no
citizenship by descent only: at least one parent must be a citizen of Angola
dual citizenship recognized: no
residency requirement for naturalization: 10 years

Suffrage: 18 years of age; universal

Executive branch: *chief of state:* President Joao Manuel Goncalves LOURENCO (since 26 September 2017)
head of government: President Joao Manuel Goncalves LOURENCO
cabinet: Council of Ministers appointed by the president
elections/appointments: the candidate of the winning party or coalition in the last legislative election becomes the president; president serves a 5-year term (eligible for a second consecutive or discontinuous term); last held on 24 August 2022 (next to be held in 2027)
election results: Joao Manuel Goncalves LOURENCO (MPLA) elected president by then winning party following the 24 August 2022 general election

Legislative branch: *description:* unicameral National Assembly or Assembleia Nacional (220 seats; members directly elected in a single national constituency and in multi-seat constituencies by closed list proportional representation vote; members serve 5- year terms)
elections: last held on 24 August 2022 (next to be held in 2027)
election results: percent of vote by party - MPLA 51.1%, UNITA 43.9%, FNLA 1.1%, PHA 1%, PRS 1.1%, other 1.7%; seats by party - MPLA 124, UNITA 90, FNLA 2, PHA 2, PRS 2; composition- men 135, women 85, percentage women 38.6%

Judicial branch: *highest court(s):* Supreme Court or Tribunal Supremo (consists of the court president, vice president, and a minimum of 16 judges); Constitutional Court or Tribunal Constitucional (consists of 11 judges)
judge selection and term of office: Supreme Court judges appointed by the president upon recommendation of the Supreme Judicial Council, an 18-member body chaired by the president; judge tenure NA; Constitutional Court judges - 4 nominated by the president, 4 elected by National Assembly, 2 elected by Supreme National Council, 1 elected by competitive submission of curricula; judges serve single 7-year terms
subordinate courts: provincial and municipal courts

Political parties: Broad Convergence for the Salvation of Angola Electoral Coalition or CASA-CE
Humanist Party of Angola or PHI
National Front for the Liberation of Angola or FNLA; note - party has two factions
National Union for the Total Independence of Angola or UNITA (largest opposition party)
Popular Movement for the Liberation of Angola or MPLA; note- ruling party in power since 1975
Social Renewal Party or PRS

International organization participation: ACP, AfDB, AU, CEMAC, CPLP, FAO, G-77, IAEA, IBRD, ICAO, ICRM, IDA, IFAD, IFC, IFRCS, ILO, IMF, IMO, Interpol, IOC, IOM, IPU, ISO (correspondent), ITSO, ITU, ITUC (NGOs), MIGA, NAM, OAS (observer), SADC, UN, UNCTAD, UNESCO, UNHCR, UNIDO, UNMISS, Union Latina, UNOOSA, UNWTO, UPU, WCO, WFTU (NGOs), WHO, WIPO, WMO, WTO

Diplomatic representation in the US: *chief of mission:* Ambassador Agostinho de Carvalho dos Santos VAN-DÚNEM (since 30 June 2023)
chancery: 2108 16th Street NW, Washington, DC 20009
telephone: [1] (202) 785-1156
FAX: [1] (202) 822-9049
email address and website:
info@angola.org
https://angola.org/
consulate(s) general: Houston, New York

Diplomatic representation from the US: *chief of mission:* Ambassador (vacant); Chargé d'Affaires Ambassador James Story (since 23 October 2024)
embassy: Rua Houari Boumedienne, #32, Luanda
mailing address: 2550 Luanda Place, Washington, DC 20521-2550
telephone: [244] (222) 64-1000
FAX: [244] (222) 64-1000
email address and website:
Consularluanda@state.gov
https://ao.usembassy.gov/

Flag description: two equal horizontal bands of red (top) and black with a centered yellow emblem consisting of a five-pointed star within half a cogwheel crossed by a machete (in the style of a hammer and sickle); red represents liberty and black the African continent; the symbols characterize workers and peasants

National symbol(s): Palanca Negra Gigante (giant black sable antelope); national colors: red, black, yellow

National anthem: *name:* "Angola Avante" (Forward Angola)
lyrics/music: Manuel Rui Alves MONTEIRO/Rui Alberto Vieira Dias MINGAO
note: adopted 1975

National heritage: *total World Heritage Sites:* 1 (cultural)
selected World Heritage Site locales: Mbanza-Kongo

ECONOMY

Economic overview: middle-income, oil-dependent African economy; widespread poverty; rising inflation and currency depreciation; seeking diversification through agricultural production; significant corruption in public institutions; major infrastructure investments from China and US; exited OPEC in 2023

Real GDP (purchasing power parity): $265.868 billion (2023 est.)
$263.611 billion (2022 est.)
$255.821 billion (2021 est.)
note: data in 2021 dollars
comparison ranking: 65

Real GDP growth rate: 0.86% (2023 est.)
3.05% (2022 est.)
1.2% (2021 est.)
note: annual GDP % growth based on constant local currency
comparison ranking: 169

Real GDP per capita: $7,200 (2023 est.)
$7,400 (2022 est.)
$7,400 (2021 est.)
note: data in 2021 dollars
comparison ranking: 158

GDP (official exchange rate): $84.723 billion (2023 est.)
note: data in current dollars at official exchange rate

Inflation rate (consumer prices): 13.64% (2023 est.)
21.36% (2022 est.)
25.75% (2021 est.)
note: annual % change based on consumer prices
comparison ranking: 192

Credit ratings: Fitch rating: CCC (2020)

Moody's rating: Caa1 (2020)

Standard & Poors rating: CCC+ (2020)
note: The year refers to the year in which the current credit rating was first obtained.

GDP - composition, by sector of origin: *agriculture:* 14.9% (2023 est.)
industry: 45.3% (2023 est.)
services: 39.7% (2023 est.)
note: figures may not total 100% due to non-allocated consumption not captured in sector-reported data
comparison rankings: services 194; industry 20; agriculture 56

GDP - composition, by end use: *household consumption:* 53.8% (2023 est.)
government consumption: 6.4% (2023 est.)
investment in fixed capital: 26.6% (2023 est.)
exports of goods and services: 39.9% (2023 est.)
imports of goods and services: -26.7% (2023 est.)
note: figures may not total 100% due to rounding or gaps in data collection

Agricultural products: cassava, bananas, maize, sweet potatoes, sugarcane, pineapples, tomatoes, onions, potatoes, citrus fruits (2022)
note: top ten agricultural products based on tonnage

Industries: petroleum; diamonds, iron ore, phosphates, feldspar, bauxite, uranium, and gold; cement; basic metal products; fish processing; food processing, brewing, tobacco products, sugar; textiles; ship repair

Industrial production growth rate: -7.18% (2023 est.)
note: annual % change in industrial value added based on constant local currency
comparison ranking: 204

Labor force: 15.223 million (2023 est.)
note: number of people ages 15 or older who are employed or seeking work
comparison ranking: 41

Unemployment rate: 14.62% (2023 est.)
14.69% (2022 est.)
15.8% (2021 est.)
note: % of labor force seeking employment
comparison ranking: 187

Youth unemployment rate (ages 15-24): *total:* 28.2% (2023 est.)
male: 30.7% (2023 est.)
female: 25.8% (2023 est.)
note: % of labor force ages 15-24 seeking employment
comparison ranking: total 30

Population below poverty line: 32.3% (2018 est.)
note: % of population with income below national poverty line

Gini Index coefficient - distribution of family income: 51.3 (2018 est.)
note: index (0-100) of income distribution; higher values represent greater inequality
comparison ranking: 9

Average household expenditures: *on food:* 49.6% of household expenditures (2022 est.)

on alcohol and tobacco: 1.5% of household expenditures (2022 est.)

Household income or consumption by percentage share: *lowest 10%:* 1.3% (2018 est.)
highest 10%: 39.6% (2018 est.)
note: % share of income accruing to lowest and highest 10% of population

Remittances: 0.01% of GDP (2023 est.)
0.01% of GDP (2022 est.)
0.02% of GDP (2021 est.)
note: personal transfers and compensation between resident and non-resident individuals/households/entities

Budget: *revenues:* $18.117 billion (2019 est.)
expenditures: $13.871 billion (2019 est.)
note: central government revenues and expenses (excluding grants/extrabudgetary units/social security funds) converted to US dollars at average official exchange rate for year indicated

Public debt: 65% of GDP (2017 est.)
comparison ranking: 64

Taxes and other revenues: 10.09% (of GDP) (2019 est.)
note: central government tax revenue as a % of GDP
comparison ranking: 179

Current account balance: $4.21 billion (2023 est.)
$11.763 billion (2022 est.)
$8.399 billion (2021 est.)
note: balance of payments - net trade and primary/secondary income in current dollars
comparison ranking: 38

Exports: $36.961 billion (2023 est.)
$50.12 billion (2022 est.)
$33.675 billion (2021 est.)
note: balance of payments - exports of goods and services in current dollars
comparison ranking: 72

Exports - partners: China 40%, India 9%, Netherlands 7%, France 7%, UAE 7% (2022)
note: top five export partners based on percentage share of exports

Exports - commodities: crude petroleum, natural gas, diamonds, ships, refined petroleum (2022)
note: top five export commodities based on value in dollars

Imports: $23.676 billion (2023 est.)
$28.564 billion (2022 est.)
$18.845 billion (2021 est.)
note: balance of payments - imports of goods and services in current dollars
comparison ranking: 89

Imports - partners: China 24%, Portugal 10%, Netherlands 8%, UAE 5%, India 4% (2022)
note: top five import partners based on percentage share of imports

Imports - commodities: refined petroleum, wheat, cars, poultry, palm oil (2022)
note: top five import commodities based on value in dollars

Reserves of foreign exchange and gold: $13.942 billion (2023 est.)
$13.655 billion (2022 est.)
$14.468 billion (2021 est.)
note: holdings of gold (year-end prices)/foreign exchange/special drawing rights in current dollars
comparison ranking: 68

Debt - external: $46.549 billion (2022 est.)
note: present value of external debt in current US dollars
comparison ranking: 13

Exchange rates: kwanza (AOA) per US dollar -

Exchange rates: 685.02 (2023 est.)
460.568 (2022 est.)
631.442 (2021 est.)
578.259 (2020 est.)
364.826 (2019 est.)

ENERGY

Electricity access: *electrification - total population:* 48.5% (2022 est.)
electrification - urban areas: 76.2%
electrification - rural areas: 7.3% (2018 est.)

Electricity: *installed generating capacity:* 7.588 million kW (2022 est.)
consumption: 14.986 billion kWh (2022 est.)
transmission/distribution losses: 1.954 billion kWh (2022 est.)
comparison rankings: transmission/distribution losses 125; consumption 83; installed generating capacity 76

Electricity generation sources: *fossil fuels:* 25% of total installed capacity (2022 est.)
solar: 0.1% of total installed capacity (2022 est.)
hydroelectricity: 74.6% of total installed capacity (2022 est.)
biomass and waste: 0.3% of total installed capacity (2022 est.)

Coal: *imports:* 3,000 metric tons (2022 est.)

Petroleum: *total petroleum production:* 1.175 million bbl/day (2023 est.)
refined petroleum consumption: 127,000 bbl/day (2022 est.)
crude oil estimated reserves: 7.783 billion barrels (2021 est.)

Natural gas: *production:* 5.514 billion cubic meters (2022 est.)
consumption: 1.397 billion cubic meters (2022 est.)
exports: 4.116 billion cubic meters (2022 est.)
proven reserves: 343.002 billion cubic meters (2021 est.)

Carbon dioxide emissions: 19.818 million metric tonnes of CO_2 (2022 est.)
from coal and metallurgical coke: 8,000 metric tonnes of CO_2 (2022 est.)
from petroleum and other liquids: 17.069 million metric tonnes of CO_2 (2022 est.)
from consumed natural gas: 2.741 million metric tonnes of CO_2 (2022 est.)
comparison ranking: total emissions 87

Energy consumption per capita: 9.61 million Btu/person (2022 est.)
comparison ranking: 151

COMMUNICATIONS

Telephones - fixed lines: *total subscriptions:* 94,000 (2022 est.)
subscriptions per 100 inhabitants: (2022 est.) less than 1
comparison ranking: total subscriptions 136

Telephones - mobile cellular: *total subscriptions:* 23.978 million (2022 est.)
subscriptions per 100 inhabitants: 67 (2022 est.)
comparison ranking: total subscriptions 54

Telecommunication systems: *general assessment:* Angola's telecom sector in recent years has benefited from political stability, which has encouraged foreign investment in the sector; the government and regulator have also set in train mechanisms to open up the telecom sector to new competitors, mobile services were launched in April 2022; the MNOs were slow to develop LTE services, instead relying on their GSM and 3G network capabilities; there has been slow progress in LTE network development, with only a small proportion of the country covered by network infrastructure; the Ministry of Telecommunications in early 2021 set up a 5G hub to assess 5G user cases; the regulator in November 2021 granted licenses to various companies offering 5G services, with spectrum in the 3.3-3.7GHz range having been set aside for such services (2022)
domestic: less than one fixed-line per 100 persons; mobile-cellular teledensity about 44 telephones per 100 persons (2021)
international: country code - 244; landing points for the SAT-3/WASC, WACS, ACE and SACS fiber-optic submarine cable that provides connectivity to other countries in west Africa, Brazil, Europe and Asia; satellite earth stations - 29, Angosat-2 satellite expected by 2021 (2019)

Broadcast media: state controls all broadcast media with nationwide reach; state-owned Televisao Popular de Angola (TPA) provides terrestrial TV service on 2 channels; a third TPA channel is available via cable and satellite; TV subscription services are available; state-owned Radio Nacional de Angola (RNA) broadcasts on 26 stations; approximately20 private radio stations broadcast locally

Internet country code: .ao

Internet users: *total:* 11.55 million (2021 est.)
percent of population: 33% (2021 est.)
comparison ranking: total 56

Broadband - fixed subscriptions: *total:* 230,610 (2020 est.)
subscriptions per 100 inhabitants: 0.7 (2020 est.)
comparison ranking: total 116

TRANSPORTATION

National air transport system: *number of registered air carriers:* 10 (2020)
inventory of registered aircraft operated by air carriers: 55
annual passenger traffic on registered air carriers: 1,516,628 (2018)
annual freight traffic on registered air carriers: 78.16 million (2018) mt-km

Civil aircraft registration country code prefix: D2

Airports: 106 (2024)
comparison ranking: 51

Heliports: 2 (2024)

Pipelines: 352 km gas, 85 km liquid petroleum gas, 1,065 km oil, 5 km oil/gas/water (2013)

Railways: *total:* 2,761 km (2022)
narrow gauge: 2,638 km (2022) 1.067-m gauge
123 km 0.600-mm gauge
comparison ranking: total 60

Roadways: *total:* 76,000 km
paved: 13,680 km (2020)
comparison ranking: total 67

Waterways: 1,300 km (2011)
comparison ranking: 57

Merchant marine: *total:* 64 (2023)
by type: general cargo 13, oil tanker 8, other 43
comparison ranking: total 112

Ports: *total ports:* 21 (2024)
large: 0

medium: 0
small: 8
very small: 13
ports with oil terminals: 17
key ports: Cabinda, Estrela Oil Field, Lobito, Luanda, Malongo Oil Terminal, Namibe, Palanca Terminal, Takula Terminal

MILITARY AND SECURITY

Military and security forces: Angolan Armed Forces (Forcas Armadas Angolanas, FAA): Army, Navy (Marinha de Guerra Angola, MGA), Angolan National Air Force (Forca Aerea Nacional Angolana, FANA; under operational control of the Army)

Ministry of Interior: National Police, Border Guard Police (2024)

Military expenditures: 1.3% of GDP (2023 est.)
1.3% of GDP (2022 est.)
1.4% of GDP (2021 est.)
1.7% of GDP (2020 est.)
1.8% of GDP (2019 est.)
comparison ranking: 104

Military and security service personnel strengths: approximately 100,000 active troops (mostly Army; 5-6,000 Air Force and Navy) (2023)

Military equipment inventories and acquisitions: most Angolan military weapons and equipment are of Russian or of Soviet-era origin; in recent years, Russia has been the principal supplier of military hardware to Angola (2023)

Military service age and obligation: 20-45 years of age for compulsory and 18-45 years for voluntary military service for men (registration at age 18 is mandatory); 20-45 years of age for voluntary service for women; 24-month conscript service obligation; Angolan citizenship required; the Navy is entirely staffed with volunteers (2023)

Military deployments: in 2023, Angola agreed to send 500 troops to the Democratic Republic of the Congo (DRC) for 12 months to oversee cantonment of a rebel group known as M23 (2023)

Military - note: the Angolan Armed Forces were created in 1991 under the Bicesse Accords signed between the Angolan Government and the National Union for the Total Independence of Angola (UNITA); the current force is responsible for country's external defense but also has some domestic security responsibilities, including border protection, expulsion of irregular migrants, and small-scale counterinsurgency operations against separatist groups; the Army and Air Force are some of the largest and better equipped forces in the region (2024)

SPACE

Space agency/agencies: National Space Program Office (Gabinete de Gestão do Programa Espacial Nacional, GGPEN; established 2013) (2024)

Space program overview: has a national space strategy with a focus on capacity building, developing space infrastructure, investing in domestic space sector, supporting socioeconomic growth, and establishing cooperation agreements with foreign technical and scientific institutions in the space industry; contracts with foreign companies to build and launch satellites; operates satellites; cooperates with a variety of foreign space agencies and industries, including those of France, Russia, and the US (2024)
note: further details about the key activities, programs, and milestones of the country's space program, as well as government spending estimates on the space sector, appear in the Space Programs reference guide

TRANSNATIONAL ISSUES

Refugees and internally displaced persons: *refugees (country of origin):* 9,272 (Guinea), 6,357 (Cote d'Ivoire), 5,725 (Mauritania) (2023); 22,841 (Democratic Republic of the Congo) (refugees and asylum seekers) (2024)

Illicit drugs: used as a transshipment point for cocaine destined for Western Europe and other African states, particularly South Africa

ANGUILLA

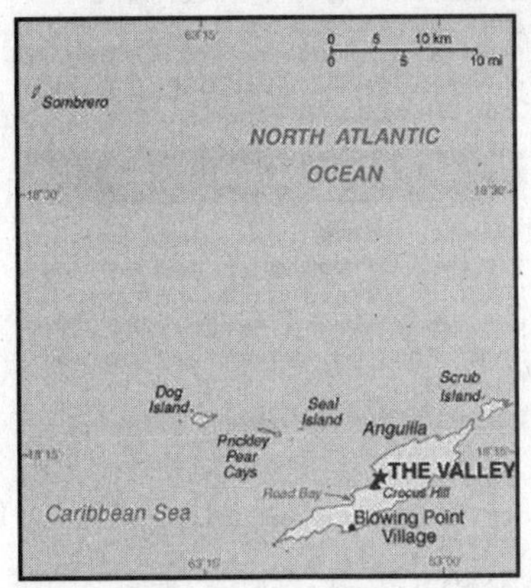

INTRODUCTION

Background: English settlers from Saint Kitts first colonized Anguilla in 1650. Great Britain administered the island until the early 19th century, when – against the wishes of the inhabitants – Anguilla was incorporated into a single British dependency along with Saint Kitts and Nevis. Several attempts at separation failed. In 1971, two years after a revolt, Anguilla was finally allowed to secede; this arrangement was formally recognized in 1980, when Anguilla became a separate British dependency. In 2017, Hurricane Irma caused extensive damage on the island, particularly to communications and residential and business infrastructure.

GEOGRAPHY

Location: Caribbean, islands between the Caribbean Sea and North Atlantic Ocean, east of Puerto Rico

Geographic coordinates: 18 15 N, 63 10 W

Map references: Central America and the Caribbean

Area: *total:* 91 sq km
land: 91 sq km
water: 0 sq km
comparison ranking: total 225

Area - comparative: about one-half the size of Washington, DC

Land boundaries: *total:* 0 km

Coastline: 61 km

Maritime claims: *territorial sea:* 12 nm
exclusive economic zone: 200 nm
exclusive fishing zone: 200 nm

Climate: tropical; moderated by northeast trade winds

Terrain: flat and low-lying island of coral and limestone

Elevation: *highest point:* Crocus Hill 73 m
lowest point: Caribbean Sea 0 m

Natural resources: salt, fish, lobster

Land use: *agricultural land:* 0% (2018 est.)
arable land: 0% (2018 est.)
permanent crops: 0% (2018 est.)
permanent pasture: 0% (2018 est.)
forest: 61.1% (2018 est.)
other: 38.9% (2018 est.)

Irrigated land: 0 sq km (2020)

Population distribution: most of the population is concentrated in The Valley in the center of the island; settlmement is fairly uniform in the southwest, but rather sparce in the northeast

Natural hazards: frequent hurricanes and other tropical storms (July to October)

Geography - note: the most northerly of the Leeward Islands in the Lesser Antilles

PEOPLE AND SOCIETY

Population: *total:* 19,416
male: 9,107
female: 10,309 (2024 est.)
comparison rankings: female 219; male 219; total 219

Nationality: *noun:* Anguillan(s)
adjective: Anguillan

Ethnic groups: African/Black 85.3%, Hispanic 4.9%, mixed 3.8%, White 3.2%, East Indian/Indian 1%, other 1.6%, unspecified 0.3% (2011 est.)
note: data represent population by ethnic origin

Languages: English (official)

Religions: Protestant 73.2% (includes Anglican 22.7%, Methodist 19.4%, Pentecostal 10.5%, Seventh Day Adventist 8.3%, Baptist 7.1%, Church of God 4.9%, Presbyterian 0.2%, Brethren 0.1%), Roman Catholic 6.8%, Jehovah's Witness 1.1%, other Christian 10.9%, other 3.2%, unspecified 0.3%, none 4.5% (2011 est.)

Age structure: *0-14 years:* 20.8% (male 2,056/female 1,992)
15-64 years: 67.5% (male 5,958/female 7,147)

65 years and over: 11.7% (2024 est.) (male 1,093/ female 1,170)

Dependency ratios: *total dependency ratio:* 38.6
youth dependency ratio: 24.4
elderly dependency ratio: 14.1
potential support ratio: 7.1 (2021)

Median age: *total:* 37.1 years (2024 est.)
male: 34.8 years
female: 39 years
comparison ranking: total 83

Population growth rate: 1.74% (2024 est.)
comparison ranking: 53

Birth rate: 11.8 births/1,000 population (2024 est.)
comparison ranking: 154

Death rate: 4.7 deaths/1,000 population (2024 est.)
comparison ranking: 204

Net migration rate: 10.3 migrant(s)/1,000 population (2024 est.)
comparison ranking: 9

Population distribution: most of the population is concentrated in The Valley in the center of the island; settlmement is fairly uniform in the southwest, but rather sparce in the northeast

Urbanization: *urban population:* 100% of total population (2023)
rate of urbanization: 0.47% annual rate of change (2020-25 est.)

Major urban areas - population: 1,000 THE VALLEY (capital) (2018)

Sex ratio: *at birth:* 1.03 male(s)/female
0-14 years: 1.03 male(s)/female
15-64 years: 0.83 male(s)/female
65 years and over: 0.93 male(s)/female
total population: 0.88 male(s)/female (2024 est.)

Infant mortality rate: *total:* 3 deaths/1,000 live births (2024 est.)
male: 3.9 deaths/1,000 live births
female: 2.1 deaths/1,000 live births
comparison ranking: total 208

Life expectancy at birth: *total population:* 82.6 years (2024 est.)
male: 80 years
female: 85.3 years
comparison ranking: total population 26

Total fertility rate: 1.72 children born/woman (2024 est.)
comparison ranking: 157

Gross reproduction rate: 0.85 (2024 est.)

Drinking water source: *improved:*
total: 97.5% of population
unimproved:
total: 2.5% of population (2017 est.)

Sanitation facility access: *improved:*
total: 99.1% of population
unimproved:
total: 0.9% of population (2017 est.)

Currently married women (ages 15-49): 46.1% (2023 est.)

Education expenditures: 4% of GDP (2020 est.)
comparison ranking: 119

ENVIRONMENT

Environment - current issues: supplies of potable water sometimes cannot meet increasing demand largely because of poor distribution system

Climate: tropical; moderated by northeast trade winds

Urbanization: *urban population:* 100% of total population (2023)
rate of urbanization: 0.47% annual rate of change (2020-25 est.)

GOVERNMENT

Country name: *conventional long form:* none
conventional short form: Anguilla
etymology: the name Anguilla means "eel" in various Romance languages (Spanish, Italian, Portuguese, French) and likely derives from the island's lengthy shape

Government type: parliamentary democracy (House of Assembly); self-governing overseas territory of the UK

Dependency status: overseas territory of the UK

Capital: *name:* The Valley
geographic coordinates: 18 13 N, 63 03 W
time difference: UTC-4 (1 hour ahead of Washington, DC, during Standard Time)
etymology: name derives from the capital's location between several hills

Administrative divisions: none (overseas territory of the UK)

Independence: none (overseas territory of the UK)

National holiday: Anguilla Day, 30 May (1967)

Legal system: common law based on the English model

Constitution: *history:* several previous; latest 1 April 1982
amendments: amended 1990, 2012, 2017, 2019

Citizenship: see United Kingdom

Suffrage: 18 years of age; universal

Executive branch: *chief of state:* King CHARLES III (since 8 September 2022); represented by Governor Julia CROUCH (since 11 September 2023)
head of government: Premier Dr. Ellis WEBSTER (since 30 June 2020)
cabinet: Executive Council appointed by the governor from among elected members of the House of Assembly
elections/appointments: the monarchy is hereditary; governor appointed by the monarch; following legislative elections, the leader of the majority party or majority coalition usually appointed premier by the governor

Legislative branch: *description:* unicameral House of Assembly (11 seats; 7 members directly elected in single-seat constituencies by simple majority vote, 2 appointed by the governor, and 2 ex-officio members - the attorney general and deputy governor; members serve five-year terms)
elections: last held on 29 June 2020 (next to be held in 2025)
election results: percent of vote by party - NA; seats by party - APM 7, AUF 4; composition - men 8, women 3, percentage women 27.3%

Judicial branch: *highest court(s):* the Eastern Caribbean Supreme Court (ECSC) is the superior court of the Organization of Eastern Caribbean States; the ECSC - headquartered on St. Lucia - consists of the Court of Appeal - headed by the chief justice and 4 judges - and the High Court with 18 judges; the Court of Appeal is itinerant, travelling to member states on a schedule to hear appeals from the High Court and subordinate courts; High Court judges reside in the member states, though none on Anguilla
judge selection and term of office: Eastern Caribbean Supreme Court chief justice appointed by Her Majesty, Queen ELIZABETH II; other justices and judges appointed by the Judicial and Legal Services Commission; Court of Appeal justices appointed for life with mandatory retirement at age 65; High Court judges appointed for life with mandatory retirement at age 62
subordinate courts: Magistrate's Court; Juvenile Court

Political parties: Anguilla Progressive Movement or APM; (formerly Anguilla United Movement or AUM)
Anguilla United Front or AUF

International organization participation: Caricom (associate), CDB, Interpol (subbureau), OECS, UNESCO (associate), UPU

Diplomatic representation in the US: none (overseas territory of the UK)

Diplomatic representation from the US: *embassy:* none (overseas territory of the UK); alternate contact is the US Embassy in Barbados [1] (246) 227-4000

Flag description: blue, with the flag of the UK in the upper hoist-side quadrant and the Anguillan coat of arms centered in the outer half of the flag; the coat of arms depicts three orange dolphins in an interlocking circular design on a white background with a turquoise-blue field below; the white in the background represents peace; the blue base symbolizes the surrounding sea, as well as faith, youth, and hope; the three dolphins stand for endurance, unity, and strength

National symbol(s): dolphin

National anthem: *name:* "God Bless Anguilla"
lyrics/music: Alex RICHARDSON
note: local anthem adopted 1981; as an overseas territory of the United Kingdom, "God Save the King" is official (see United Kingdom)

ECONOMY

Economic overview: small, tourism-dependent, territorial-island economy; very high public debt; COVID-19 crippled economic activity; partial recovery underway via tourism, benefitting from its high amount of timeshare residences; considering reopening oil refinery

Inflation rate (consumer prices): 1.3% (2017 est.)
-0.6% (2016 est.)
comparison ranking: 25

GDP - composition, by sector of origin: *agriculture:* 3% (2017 est.)
industry: 10.5% (2017 est.)
services: 86.4% (2017 est.)
comparison rankings: services 11; industry 190; agriculture 139

GDP - composition, by end use: *household consumption:* 74.1% (2017 est.)
government consumption: 18.3% (2017 est.)
investment in fixed capital: 26.8% (2017 est.)
exports of goods and services: 48.2% (2017 est.)
imports of goods and services: -67.4% (2017 est.)

Agricultural products: small quantities of tobacco, vegetables; cattle raising

Industries: tourism, boat building, offshore financial services

Industrial production growth rate: 4% (2017 est.)
comparison ranking: 77

Budget: *revenues:* $81.925 million (2017 est.)
expenditures: $72.352 million (2017 est.)
note: central government revenues and expenses (excluding grants/extrabudgetary units/social security funds) converted to US dollars at average official exchange rate for year indicated

Public debt: 20.1% of GDP (2015 est.)
comparison ranking: 185

Taxes and other revenues: 46.7% (of GDP) (2017 est.)
comparison ranking: 5

Current account balance: -$23.2 million (2017 est.)
-$25.3 million (2016 est.)
comparison ranking: 88

Exports: $7.9 million (2017 est.)
$3.9 million (2016 est.)
note: Data are in current year dollars and do not include illicit exports or re-exports.
comparison ranking: 219

Exports - partners: Chile 74%, Hungary 7%, Kyrgyzstan 3%, US 2%, Netherlands 2% (2022)
note: top five export partners based on percentage share of exports

Exports - commodities: packaged medicine, garments, vehicle parts/accessories, trucks, blank audio media (2022)
note: top five export commodities based on value in dollars

Imports: $186.2 million (2017 est.)
$170.1 million (2016 est.)
comparison ranking: 214

Imports - partners: Chile 48%, US 27%, Botswana 18%, Canada 1%, Japan 1% (2022)
note: top five import partners based on percentage share of imports

Imports - commodities: poultry, copper ore, refined petroleum, natural gas, fish (2022)
note: top five import commodities based on value in dollars

Reserves of foreign exchange and gold: $76.38 million (31 December 2017 est.)
$48.14 million (31 December 2015 est.)
comparison ranking: 190

Exchange rates: East Caribbean dollars (XCD) per US dollar -

Exchange rates: 2.7 (2023 est.)
2.7 (2022 est.)
2.7 (2021 est.)
2.7 (2020 est.)
2.7 (2019 est.)

ENERGY

Electricity access: *electrification - total population:* 100% (2020)

COMMUNICATIONS

Telephones - fixed lines: *total subscriptions:* 6,000 (2021 est.)
subscriptions per 100 inhabitants: 38 (2021 est.)
comparison ranking: total subscriptions 200

Telephones - mobile cellular: *total subscriptions:* 26,000 (2021 est.)
subscriptions per 100 inhabitants: 170 (2021 est.)
comparison ranking: total subscriptions 212

Telecommunication systems: *general assessment:* in the telecom sector, with declines seen in subscriber numbers (particularly for prepaid mobile services — the mainstay of short-term visitors) and revenue; fixed and mobile broadband services are two areas that have benefited from the crisis to a small extent as employees and students have resorted to working from home, but their contribution to the sector has been insufficient to offset steep falls in other areas of the market; one area of the telecom market that does not yet appear poised for growth is 5G mobile; governments, regulators, and even the mobile network operators have shown that they have little appetite for investing in 5G opportunities at the present time; network expansion and enhancements remain concentrated around improving LTE coverage; until the economies and markets stabilize, and overseas visitors return there is unlikely to be much momentum towards implementing 5G capabilities anywhere in the region (2021)
domestic: fixed-line teledensity is about 38 per 100 persons; mobile-cellular teledensity is roughly 170 per 100 persons (2021)
international: country code - 1-264; landing points for the SSCS, ECFS, GCN and Southern Caribbean Fiber with submarine cable links to Caribbean islands and to the US; microwave radio relay to island of Saint Martin/Sint Maarten (2019)

Broadcast media: 1 private TV station; multi-channel cable TV subscription services are available; about 10 radio stations, one of which is government-owned

Internet country code: .ai

Internet users: *total:* 13,056 (2021 est.)
percent of population: 81.6% (2021 est.)
comparison ranking: total 215

Broadband - fixed subscriptions: *total:* 5,000 (2018 est.)
subscriptions per 100 inhabitants: 35 (2018 est.)
comparison ranking: total 186

TRANSPORTATION

National air transport system: *number of registered air carriers:* 2 (2020)
inventory of registered aircraft operated by air carriers: 4

Civil aircraft registration country code prefix: VP-A

Airports: 1 (2024)
comparison ranking: 224

Roadways: *total:* 175 km
paved: 82 km
unpaved: 93 km (2004)
comparison ranking: total 211

Merchant marine: *total:* 2 (2023)
by type: other 2
comparison ranking: total 176

MILITARY AND SECURITY

Military - note: defense is the responsibility of the UK

TRANSNATIONAL ISSUES

Illicit drugs: transshipment point for South American narcotics destined for the US and Europe

ANTARCTICA

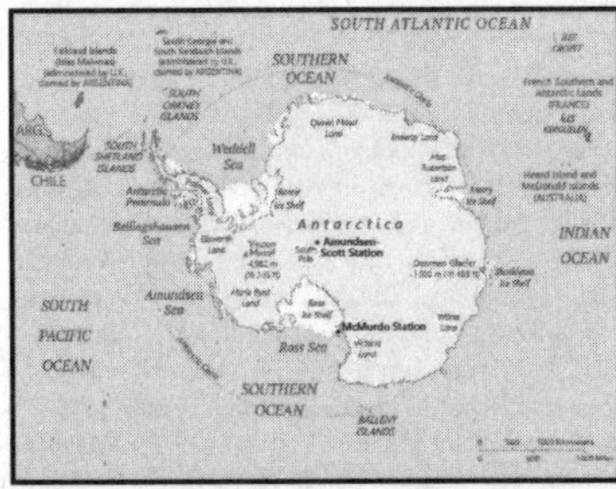

INTRODUCTION

Background: Speculation over the existence of a "southern land" was confirmed in the early 1820s when British and American commercial operators and British and Russian national expeditions began exploring the Antarctic Peninsula region and other areas south of the Antarctic Circle. In 1840, it was finally established that Antarctica was indeed a continent and not merely a group of islands or an area of ocean. Several exploration "firsts" were achieved in the early 20th century, but the area saw little human activity. Following World War II, however, the continent experienced an upsurge in scientific research. A number of countries have set up a range of year-round and seasonal stations, camps, and refuges to support scientific research in Antarctica. Seven have made territorial claims, with two maintaining the basis for a claim, but most countries do not recognize these claims. In order to form a legal framework for countries' activities on the continent, an Antarctic Treaty was negotiated that neither denies nor recognizes existing territorial claims; it was signed in 1959 and entered into force in 1961. Also relevant to Antarctic governance are the Environmental Protocol to the Antarctic Treaty and the Convention on the Conservation of Antarctic Marine Living Resources.

GEOGRAPHY

Location: continent mostly south of the Antarctic Circle

Geographic coordinates: 90 00 S, 0 00 E

Map references: Antarctic Region

Area: *total:* 14.2 million sq km
land: 14.2 million sq km (285,000 sq km ice-free, 13.915 million sq km ice-covered) (est.)
note: fifth-largest continent, following Asia, Africa, North America, and South America, but larger than Australia and the subcontinent of Europe

comparison ranking: total 2

Area - comparative: slightly less than 1.5 times the size of the US

Land boundaries: *note:* see entry on Disputes - international

Coastline: 17,968 km

Maritime claims: Australia, Chile, and Argentina claim Exclusive Economic Zone (EEZ) rights or similar over 200 nm extensions seaward from their continental claims, but like the claims themselves, these zones are not accepted by other countries; 22 of 29 Antarctic Treaty consultative parties have made no claims to Antarctic territory, although Russia and the United States have reserved the right to do so, and no country can make a new claim; also see the Disputes - international entry

Climate: the coldest, windiest, and driest continent on Earth; severe low temperatures vary with latitude, elevation, and distance from the ocean; East Antarctica is colder than West Antarctica because of its higher elevation; Antarctic Peninsula has the most moderate climate; higher temperatures occur in January along the coast and average slightly below freezing; summers characterized by continuous daylight, while winters bring continuous darkness; persistent high pressure over the interior brings dry, subsiding air that results in very little cloud cover

Terrain: about 99% thick continental ice sheet and 1% barren rock, with average elevations between 2,000 and 4,000 m; mountain ranges up to nearly 5,000 m; ice-free coastal areas include parts of southern Victoria Land, Wilkes Land, the Antarctic Peninsula area, and parts of Ross Island on McMurdo Sound; glaciers form ice shelves along about half of the coastline, and floating ice shelves constitute 11% of the area of the continent

Elevation: *highest point:* Vinson Massif 4,892 m
lowest point: Denman Glacier more than -3,500 m (-11,500 ft) below sea level
mean elevation: 2,300 m
note: the lowest known land point in Antarctica is hidden in the Denman Glacier; at its surface is the deepest ice yet discovered and the world's lowest elevation not under seawater

Natural resources: iron ore, chromium, copper, gold, nickel, platinum and other minerals, and coal and hydrocarbons have been found in small noncommercial quantities; mineral exploitation except for scientific research is banned by the Environmental Protocol to the Antarctic Treaty; krill, icefish, toothfish, and crab have been taken by commercial fisheries, which are managed through the Commission for the Conservation of Antarctic Marine Living Resources (CCAMLR)

Land use: *agricultural land:* 0% (2018 est.)

Natural hazards: katabatic (gravity-driven) winds blow coastward from the high interior; frequent blizzards form near the foot of the plateau; cyclonic storms form over the ocean and move clockwise along the coast; large icebergs may calve from ice shelf
volcanism: volcanic activity on Deception Island and isolated areas of West Antarctica; other seismic activity rare and weak

Geography - note: the coldest, windiest, highest (on average), and driest continent; during summer, more solar radiation reaches the surface at the South Pole than is received at the Equator in an equivalent period
mostly uninhabitable, 99% of the land area is covered by the Antarctic ice sheet, the largest single mass of ice on earth covering an area of 14 million sq km (5.4 million sq mi) and containing 26.5 million cu km (6.4 million cu mi) of ice (this is almost 62% of all of the world's fresh water); if all this ice were converted to liquid water, one estimate is that it would be sufficient to raise the height of the world's oceans by 58 m (190 ft)

PEOPLE AND SOCIETY

Population: no indigenous inhabitants, but staff is present at year-round and summer-only research stations
note: 56 countries have signed the 1959 Antarctic Treaty; 30 of those operate through their National Antarctic Program a number of seasonal-only (summer) and year-round research stations on the continent and its nearby islands south of 60 degrees south latitude (the region covered by the Antarctic Treaty); the population engaging in and supporting science or managing and protecting the Antarctic region varies from approximately 5,000 in summer to 1,100 in winter; in addition, approximately 1,000 personnel, including ship's crew and scientists doing onboard research, are present in the waters of the treaty region as of 2024, peak summer (December-February) maximum capacity in scientific stations - 4,713 total; Argentina 425, Australia 238, Belarus 15, Belgium 55, Brazil 64, Bulgaria 25, Chile 375, China 164, Czechia 32, Ecuador 35, Finland 16, France 136, France and Italy jointly 70, Germany 60, India 72, Italy 150, Japan 130, South Korea 158, New Zealand 85, Norway 60, Peru 30, Poland 41, Russia 211, South Africa 80, Spain 79, Sweden 16, Ukraine 15, United Kingdom 315, United States 1,495 , Uruguay 66 (2024)
winter (June-August) maximum capacity in scientific stations - 1,056 total; Argentina 221, Australia 52, Brazil 15, Chile 114, China 32, France 24, France and Italy jointly 13, Germany 9, India 48, Japan 40, Netherlands 10, South Korea 25, NZ 11, Norway 7, Poland 16, Russia 125, South Africa 15, Ukraine 12, UK 44, US 215, Uruguay 8 (2024)
in addition, during the austral summer, some nations have numerous occupied locations such as tent camps, summer-long temporary facilities, and mobile traverses in support of research

ENVIRONMENT

Environment - current issues: the discovery of a large Antarctic ozone hole in the earth's stratosphere (the ozone layer) - first announced in 1985 - spurred the signing of the Montreal Protocol in 1987, an international agreement phasing out the use of ozone-depleting chemicals; the ozone layer prevents most harmful wavelengths of ultra-violet (UV) light from passing through the earth's atmosphere; ozone depletion has been shown to harm a variety of Antarctic marine plants and animals (plankton); in 2016, a gradual trend toward "healing" of the ozone hole was reported; since the 1990s, satellites have shown accelerating ice loss driven by ocean change; although considerable uncertainty remains, scientists are increasing our understanding and ability to model potential impacts of ice loss

Climate: the coldest, windiest, and driest continent on Earth; severe low temperatures vary with latitude, elevation, and distance from the ocean; East Antarctica is colder than West Antarctica because of its higher elevation; Antarctic Peninsula has the most moderate climate; higher temperatures occur in January along the coast and average slightly below freezing; summers characterized by continuous daylight, while winters bring continuous darkness; persistent high pressure over the interior brings dry, subsiding air that results in very little cloud cover

GOVERNMENT

Country name: *conventional long form:* none
conventional short form: Antarctica
etymology: name derived from two Greek words meaning "opposite to the Arctic" or "opposite to the north"

Government type: Antarctic Treaty Summary - the Antarctic region is governed by a system known as the Antarctic Treaty system; the system includes: 1. the Antarctic Treaty, signed on 1 December 1959 and entered into force on 23 June 1961, which establishes the legal framework for the management of Antarctica, 2. Measures, Decisions, and Resolutions adopted at Antarctic Treaty Consultative Meetings, 3. The Convention for the Conservation of Antarctic Seals (1972), 4. The Convention on the Conservation of Antarctic Marine Living Resources (1980), and 5. The Protocol on Environmental Protection to the Antarctic Treaty (1991); the Antarctic Treaty Consultative Meetings operate by consensus (not by vote) of all consultative parties at annual Treaty meetings; by January 2024, there were 56 treaty member nations: 29 consultative and 27 non-consultative; consultative (decision-making) members include the seven nations that claim portions of Antarctica as national territory (some claims overlap) and 22 non-claimant nations; the US and Russia have reserved the right to make claims; the US does not recognize the claims of others; Antarctica is administered through meetings of the consultative member nations; measures adopted at these meetings are carried out by these member nations (with respect to their own nationals and operations) in accordance with their own national laws; the years in parentheses indicate when a consultative member-nation acceded to the Treaty and when it was accepted as a consultative member, while no date indicates the country was an original 1959 treaty signatory; claimant nations are - Argentina, Australia, Chile, France, NZ, Norway, and the UK; nonclaimant consultative nations are - Belgium, Brazil (1975/1983), Bulgaria (1978/1998), China (1983/1985), Czechia (1962/2014), Ecuador (1987/1990), Finland (1984/1989), Germany (1979/1981), India (1983/1983), Italy (1981/1987), Japan, South Korea (1986/1989), Netherlands (1967/1990), Peru (1981/1989), Poland (1961/1977), Russia, South Africa, Spain (1982/1988), Sweden (1984/1988), Ukraine (1992/2004), Uruguay (1980/1985), and the US; non-consultative members, with year of accession in parentheses, are - Austria (1987), Belarus (2006), Canada (1988), Colombia (1989), Costa Rica (2022) Cuba (1984), Denmark (1965), Estonia (2001), Greece (1987), Guatemala (1991), Hungary (1984), Iceland (2015), Kazakhstan (2015), North Korea (1987), Malaysia (2011), Monaco (2008), Mongolia (2015), Pakistan (2012), Papua New Guinea (1981), Portugal (2010), Romania (1971), San Marino (2023), Slovakia (1962/1993), Slovenia (2019), Switzerland (1990), Turkey (1996), and Venezuela (1999); note - Czechoslovakia acceded to the Treaty in 1962 and separated into the Czech Republic and Slovakia in 1993; Article 1 - area to be used for peaceful purposes only; military activity, such as weapons testing, is prohibited, but military personnel and equipment may be used for scientific research or any other peaceful purpose; Article 2 - freedom of scientific investigation and cooperation shall continue; Article 3 - free exchange of information and personnel, cooperation with the UN and other international agencies; Article 4 - does not recognize, dispute, or establish territorial claims and no new claims shall be asserted while the treaty is in force; Article 5 - prohibits nuclear explosions or disposal of radioactive wastes; Article 6 - includes under the treaty all land and ice shelves south of 60 degrees 00 minutes south and reserves high seas rights; Article 7 - treaty-state observers have free access, including aerial observation, to any area and may inspect all stations, installations, and equipment; advance notice of all expeditions and of the introduction of military personnel must be given; Article 8 - allows for jurisdiction over observers and scientists by their own states; Article 9 - frequent consultative meetings take place among member nations; Article 10 - treaty states will discourage activities by any country in Antarctica that are contrary to the treaty; Article 11 - disputes to be settled peacefully by the parties concerned or, ultimately, by the International Court of Justice; Articles 12, 13, 14 - deal with upholding, interpreting, and amending the treaty among involved nations; other agreements - some 200 measures adopted at treaty consultative meetings and approved by governments; the Protocol on Environmental Protection to the Antarctic Treaty was signed 4 October 1991 and entered into force 14 January 1998; this agreement provides for the protection of the Antarctic environment and includes five annexes that have entered into force: 1) environmental impact assessment, 2) conservation of Antarctic fauna and flora, 3) waste disposal and waste management, 4) prevention of marine pollution, 5) area protection and management; a sixth annex addressing liability arising from environmental emergencies has yet to enter into force; the Protocol prohibits all activities relating to mineral resources except scientific research; a permanent Antarctic Treaty Secretariat was established in 2004 in Buenos Aires, Argentina

Legal system: Antarctica is administered through annual meetings - known as Antarctic Treaty Consultative Meetings - which include consultative member nations, non-consultative member nations, observer organizations, and expert organizations; decisions from these meetings are carried out by these member nations (with respect to their own nationals and operations) in accordance with their own national laws; more generally, the Antarctic Treaty area and all areas south of 60 degrees south latitude, including all ice shelves and islands, are subject to a number of relevant legal instruments and procedures adopted by the states party to the Antarctic Treaty; note - US law, including certain criminal offenses by or against US nationals, such as murder, may apply extraterritoriality; some US laws directly apply to Antarctica; for example, the Antarctic Conservation Act, 16 U.S.C. section 2401 et seq., provides civil and criminal penalties for the following activities unless authorized by regulation or statute: the taking of native mammals or birds; the introduction of nonindigenous plants and animals; entry into specially protected areas; the discharge or disposal of pollutants; and the importation into the US of certain items from Antarctica; violation of the Antarctic Conservation Act carries penalties of up to $10,000 in fines and one year in prison; the National Science Foundation and Department of Justice share enforcement responsibilities; Public Law 95-541, the US Antarctic Conservation Act of 1978, as amended in 1996, requires expeditions from the US to Antarctica to notify, in advance, the Office of Ocean and Polar Affairs, Room 2665, Department of State, Washington, DC 20520, which reports such plans to other nations as required by the Antarctic Treaty; for more information, contact antarctica@state.gov

Flag description: unofficial; a True South flag, created in 2018, has quickly become popular for its simple yet elegant design and has been used by various National Antarctic Programs, Antarctic nonprofits, and expedition teams; the flag's meaning is described as horizontal stripes of navy and white representing the long days and nights at Antarctica's extreme latitude, with a lone white peak erupting from a field of snow and ice at the center; the long shadow it casts forms the shape of a compass arrow pointed south, an homage to the continent's legacy of exploration; together, the two center shapes create a diamond, symbolizing the hope that Antarctica will continue to be a center of peace, discovery, and cooperation for generations to come

ENERGY

Petroleum: *refined petroleum consumption:* 79.9 bbl/day (2022 est.)

Carbon dioxide emissions: 12,000 metric tonnes of CO2 (2022 est.)
from petroleum and other liquids: 12,000 metric tonnes of CO2 (2022 est.)
comparison ranking: total emissions 216

Energy consumption per capita: (2019)

COMMUNICATIONS

Telecommunication systems: *general assessment:*
general assessment: scientists with the United States Antarctic Program at McMurdo Station have a designated Starlink terminal, which has improved connectivity to carry out research; this was made possible through laser links between the SpaceX satellites in orbit that eliminate the need for ground stations at the poles, and makes Antarctica the seventh and final continent to receive Starlink internet coverage (2022)
(2022)
domestic: commercial cellular networks operating in a small number of locations (2019)
international: country code - none allocated; via satellite (including mobile Inmarsat and Iridium systems) to and from all research stations, ships, aircraft, and most field parties

Internet country code: .aq

Internet users: *total:* 4,400 (2021 est.)
percent of population: 100% (2021 est.)
comparison ranking: total 224

TRANSPORTATION

Airports: 30 (2024)
comparison ranking: 119

Heliports: 5 (2024)

Ports: *total ports:* 8 (2024)
large: 0
medium: 0
small: 1
very small: 7
ports with oil terminals: 0
key ports: Admiralty Bay, Andersen Harbor, Ellefsen Harbor, McMurdo Station, Melchior Harbor, Port Foster, Port Lockroy, Scotia Bay

Transportation - note: US coastal stations include McMurdo (77 51 S, 166 40 E) and Palmer (64 43 S, 64 03 W); government use only; all ships are subject to inspection in accordance with Article 7 of the Antarctic Treaty; ships must comply with relevant legal instruments and authorization procedures under the Antarctic Treaty (see "Legal System"); The Hydrographic Commission on Antarctica (HCA), a commission of the International Hydrographic Organization (IHO), coordinates and facilitates provision of accurate and appropriate charts and other aids to navigation; membership in HCA is open to any IHO Member State whose government has acceded to the Antarctic Treaty and which contributes resources or data to IHO Chart coverage of the area

MILITARY AND SECURITY

Military - note: the Antarctic Treaty of 1961 prohibits any measures of a military nature, such as the establishment of military bases and fortifications, the carrying out of military maneuvers, or the testing of any type of weapon; it permits the use of military personnel or equipment for scientific research or for any other peaceful purposes

ANTIGUA AND BARBUDA

INTRODUCTION

Background: The Siboney were the first people to inhabit the islands of Antigua and Barbuda in 2400 B.C., but the Arawaks populated the islands when Christopher COLUMBUS landed on his second voyage in 1493. Early Spanish and French settlements were succeeded by an English colony in 1667. Slavery, which provided labor on the sugar plantations on Antigua, was abolished in 1834. The islands became an independent state within the British Commonwealth of Nations in 1981. In 2017, Hurricane Irma passed over the island of Barbuda, devastating the island and forcing the evacuation of the population to Antigua. Almost all of the structures on Barbuda were destroyed and the vegetation stripped, but Antigua was spared the worst.

GEOGRAPHY

Location: Caribbean, islands between the Caribbean Sea and the North Atlantic Ocean, east-southeast of Puerto Rico

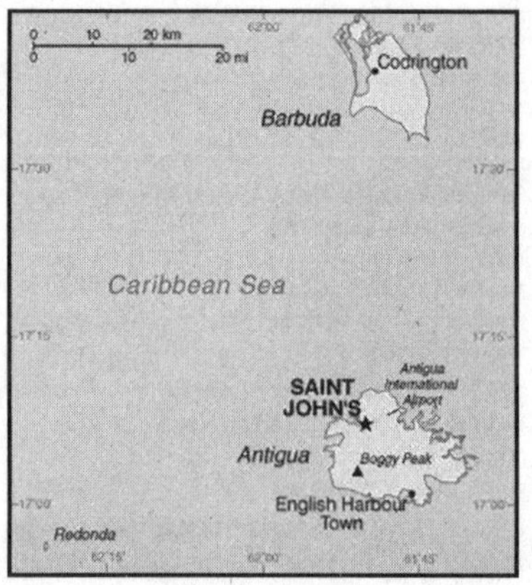

Geographic coordinates: 17 03 N, 61 48 W

Map references: Central America and the Caribbean

Area: *total:* 443 sq km (Antigua 280 sq km; Barbuda 161 sq km)
land: 443 sq km
water: 0 sq km
note: includes Redonda, 1.6 sq km
comparison ranking: total 200

Area - comparative: 2.5 times the size of Washington, DC

Land boundaries: *total:* 0 km

Coastline: 153 km

Maritime claims: *territorial sea:* 12 nm
contiguous zone: 24 nm
exclusive economic zone: 200 nm
continental shelf: 200 nm or to the edge of the continental margin

Climate: tropical maritime; little seasonal temperature variation

Terrain: mostly low-lying limestone and coral islands, with some higher volcanic areas

Elevation: *highest point:* Mount Obama 402 m
lowest point: Caribbean Sea 0 m

Natural resources: NEGL; pleasant climate fosters tourism

Land use: *agricultural land:* 20.5% (2018 est.)
arable land: 9% (2018 est.)
permanent crops: 2.3% (2018 est.)
permanent pasture: 9% (2018 est.)
forest: 18.8% (2018 est.)
other: 60.8% (2018 est.)

Irrigated land: 1.3 sq km (2012)

Population distribution: the island of Antigua is home to approximately 97% of the population; nearly the entire population of Barbuda lives in Codrington

Natural hazards: hurricanes and tropical storms (July to October); periodic droughts

Geography - note: Antigua has a deeply indented shoreline with many natural harbors and beaches; Barbuda has a large western harbor

PEOPLE AND SOCIETY

Population: *total:* 102,634
male: 48,311
female: 54,323 (2024 est.)
comparison rankings: female 192; male 197; total 194

Nationality: *noun:* Antiguan(s), Barbudan(s)
adjective: Antiguan, Barbudan

Ethnic groups: African descent 87.3%, mixed 4.7%, Hispanic 2.7%, White 1.6%, other 2.7%, unspecified 0.9% (2011 est.)
note: data represent population by ethnic group

Languages: English (official), Antiguan Creole (an English-based creole)

Religions: Protestant 68.3% (Anglican 17.6%, Seventh Day Adventist 12.4%, Pentecostal 12.2%, Moravian 8.3%, Methodist 5.6%, Wesleyan Holiness 4.5%, Church of God 4.1%, Baptist 3.6%), Roman Catholic 8.2%, other 12.2%, unspecified 5.5%, none 5.9% (2011 est.)

Age structure: *0-14 years:* 21.8% (male 11,384/female 11,034)
15-64 years: 67.6% (male 32,312/female 37,094)
65 years and over: 10.5% (2024 est.) (male 4,615/female 6,195)

Dependency ratios: *total dependency ratio:* 40.9
youth dependency ratio: 26.5
elderly dependency ratio: 14.4
potential support ratio: 7 (2020 est.)

Median age: *total:* 33.9 years (2024 est.)
male: 31.9 years
female: 35.7 years
comparison ranking: total 109

Population growth rate: 1.11% (2024 est.)
comparison ranking: 83

Birth rate: 14.9 births/1,000 population (2024 est.)
comparison ranking: 113

Death rate: 5.7 deaths/1,000 population (2024 est.)
comparison ranking: 171

Net migration rate: 2 migrant(s)/1,000 population (2024 est.)
comparison ranking: 49

Population distribution: the island of Antigua is home to approximately 97% of the population; nearly the entire population of Barbuda lives in Codrington

Urbanization: *urban population:* 24.3% of total population (2023)
rate of urbanization: 0.87% annual rate of change (2020-25 est.)

Major urban areas - population: 21,000 SAINT JOHN'S (capital) (2018)

Sex ratio: *at birth:* 1.05 male(s)/female
0-14 years: 1.03 male(s)/female
15-64 years: 0.87 male(s)/female
65 years and over: 0.74 male(s)/female
total population: 0.89 male(s)/female (2024 est.)

Maternal mortality ratio: 21 deaths/100,000 live births (2020)
comparison ranking: 120

Infant mortality rate: *total:* 13.6 deaths/1,000 live births (2024 est.)
male: 16.4 deaths/1,000 live births
female: 10.7 deaths/1,000 live births
comparison ranking: total 104

Life expectancy at birth: *total population:* 78.3 years (2024 est.)
male: 76.1 years
female: 80.5 years
comparison ranking: total population 80

Total fertility rate: 1.93 children born/woman (2024 est.)
comparison ranking: 116

Gross reproduction rate: 0.94 (2024 est.)

Drinking water source: *improved:* improved: total: 96.7% of population
unimproved: *unimproved:* total: 3.2% of population (2017 est.)

Current health expenditure: 5.6% of GDP (2020)

Physician density: 2.76 physicians/1,000 population (2017)

Hospital bed density: 2.9 beds/1,000 population (2017)

Sanitation facility access: *improved:* total: 91.7% of population
unimproved: *total:* 8.1% of population (2017 est.)

Obesity - adult prevalence rate: 18.9% (2016)
comparison ranking: 115

Alcohol consumption per capita: *total:* 11.88 liters of pure alcohol (2019 est.)
beer: 2.97 liters of pure alcohol (2019 est.)
wine: 3.95 liters of pure alcohol (2019 est.)
spirits: 4.55 liters of pure alcohol (2019 est.)
other alcohols: 0.41 liters of pure alcohol (2019 est.)
comparison ranking: total 6

Currently married women (ages 15-49): 31.5% (2023 est.)

Education expenditures: 3.8% of GDP (2021 est.)
comparison ranking: 126

Literacy: *definition:* age 15 and over has completed five or more years of schooling
total population: 99%
male: 98.4%
female: 99.4% (2015)

School life expectancy (primary to tertiary education): *total:* 15 years
male: 14 years
female: 16 years (2012)

ENVIRONMENT

Environment - current issues: water management - a major concern because of limited natural freshwater resources - is further hampered by the clearing of trees to increase crop production, causing rainfall to run off quickly

Environment - international agreements: *party to:* Biodiversity, Climate Change, Climate Change-Kyoto Protocol, Climate Change-Paris Agreement, Comprehensive Nuclear Test Ban, Desertification, Endangered Species, Environmental Modification, Hazardous Wastes, Law of the Sea, Marine Dumping-London Convention, Marine Dumping-London Protocol, Nuclear Test Ban, Ozone Layer Protection, Ship Pollution, Wetlands, Whaling
signed, but not ratified: none of the selected agreements

Climate: tropical maritime; little seasonal temperature variation

Urbanization: *urban population:* 24.3% of total population (2023)
rate of urbanization: 0.87% annual rate of change (2020-25 est.)

Revenue from forest resources: 0% of GDP (2018 est.)
comparison ranking: 163

Revenue from coal: 0% of GDP (2018 est.)
comparison ranking: 117

Air pollutants: *particulate matter emissions:* 8.3 micrograms per cubic meter (2019 est.)
carbon dioxide emissions: 0.56 megatons (2016 est.)
methane emissions: 0.22 megatons (2020 est.)

Waste and recycling: *municipal solid waste generated annually:* 30,585 tons (2012 est.)

Total water withdrawal: *municipal:* 10 million cubic meters (2020 est.)
industrial: 2.5 million cubic meters (2017 est.)
agricultural: 1.8 million cubic meters (2017 est.)

Total renewable water resources: 50 million cubic meters (2020 est.)

GOVERNMENT

Country name: *conventional long form:* none
conventional short form: Antigua and Barbuda
etymology: "antiguo" is Spanish for "ancient" or "old"; the island was discovered by Christopher COLUMBUS in 1493 and, according to tradition, named by him after the church of Santa Maria la Antigua (Old Saint Mary's) in Seville; "barbuda" is Spanish for "bearded" and the adjective may refer to the alleged beards of the indigenous people or to the island's bearded fig trees

Government type: parliamentary democracy under a constitutional monarchy; a Commonwealth realm

Capital: *name:* Saint John's
geographic coordinates: 17 07 N, 61 51 W
time difference: UTC-4 (1 hour ahead of Washington, DC, during Standard Time)
etymology: named after Saint John the Apostle

Administrative divisions: 6 parishes and 2 dependencies*; Barbuda*, Redonda*, Saint George, Saint John, Saint Mary, Saint Paul, Saint Peter, Saint Philip

Independence: 1 November 1981 (from the UK)

National holiday: Independence Day, 1 November (1981)

Legal system: common law based on the English model

Constitution: *history:* several previous; latest presented 31 July 1981, effective 31 October 1981 (The Antigua and Barbuda Constitution Order 1981)
amendments: proposed by either house of Parliament; passage of amendments to constitutional sections such as citizenship, fundamental rights and freedoms, the establishment, power, and authority of the executive and legislative branches, the Supreme Court Order, and the procedure for amending the constitution requires approval by at least two-thirds majority vote of the membership of both houses, approval by at least two-thirds majority in a referendum, and assent to by the governor general; passage of other amendments requires only two-thirds majority vote by both houses; amended 2009, 2011, 2018

International law organization participation: has not submitted an ICJ jurisdiction declaration; accepts ICCt jurisdiction

Citizenship: *citizenship by birth:* yes
citizenship by descent only: yes
dual citizenship recognized: yes
residency requirement for naturalization: 7 years

Suffrage: 18 years of age; universal

Executive branch: *chief of state:* King CHARLES III (since 8 September 2022); represented by Governor General Rodney WILLIAMS (since 14 August 2014)
head of government: Prime Minister Gaston BROWNE (since 13 June 2014)
cabinet: Council of Ministers appointed by the governor general on the advice of the prime minister
elections/appointments: the monarchy is hereditary; governor general appointed by the monarch on the advice of the prime minister; following legislative elections, the leader of the majority party or majority coalition usually appointed prime minister by the governor general

Legislative branch: *description:* bicameral Parliament consists of:
Senate (17 seats; members appointed by the governor general on the advice of the prime minister and leader of the opposition; members served 5-year terms)
House of Representatives (19 seats; members directly elected in single-seat constituencies by simple majority vote to serve 5-year terms; in addition, 1 ex-officio seat is allocated for the attorney general and 1 seat for the speaker of the House - elected by the House membership following its first post-election session)
elections: Senate - last appointed on 17 February 2023 (next appointments in 2028)
House of Representatives - last held on 18 January 2023 (next to be held in March 2028)
election results: Senate - composition - men 10, women 7, percentage women 41.2%
House of Representatives - percent of vote by party - ABLP 47.1%, UPP 45.2%, BPM 1.5%, independent 5.2%; seats by party - ABLP 9, UPP 6, BPM 1, independent 1; composition - men 17, women 1, percentage women 5.6%; total Parliament percentage women 22.9%

Judicial branch: *highest court(s):* the Eastern Caribbean Supreme Court (ECSC) is the superior court of the Organization of Eastern Caribbean States; the ECSC - headquartered on St. Lucia - consists of the Court of Appeal - headed by the chief justice and 4 judges - and the High Court with 18 judges; the Court of Appeal is itinerant, travelling to member states on a schedule to hear appeals from the High Court and subordinate courts; High Court judges reside in the member states, with 2 assigned to Antigua and Barbuda
judge selection and term of office: chief justice of Eastern Caribbean Supreme Court appointed by the His Majesty, King CHARLES III; other justices and judges appointed by the Judicial and Legal Services Commission; Court of Appeal justices appointed for life with mandatory retirement at age 65; High Court judges appointed for life with mandatory retirement at age 62
subordinate courts: Industrial Court; Magistrates' Courts

Political parties: Antigua Labor Party or ABLP
Barbuda People's Movement or BPM
Democratic National Alliance or DNA
Go Green for Life or GGL
United Progressive Party or UPP

International organization participation: ACP, ACS, AOSIS, C, Caricom, CDB, CELAC, FAO, G-77, IBRD, ICAO, ICC (NGOs), ICCt, ICRM, IDA, IFAD, IFC, IFRCS, ILO, IMF, IMO, IMSO, Interpol, IOC, IOM, ISO (subscriber), ITU, ITUC (NGOs), MIGA, NAM (observer), OAS, OECS, OPANAL, OPCW, Petrocaribe, UN, UNCTAD, UNESCO, UPU, WFTU (NGOs), WHO, WIPO, WMO, WTO

Diplomatic representation in the US: *chief of mission:* Ambassador Sir Ronald SANDERS (since 17 September 2015)
chancery: 3216 New Mexico Ave. NW, Washington, DC 20016
telephone: [1] (202) 362-5122
FAX: [1] (202) 362-5225
email address and website:
embantbar@aol.com
https://www.antigua-barbuda.org/Aghome01.htm
consulate(s) general: Miami, New York

Diplomatic representation from the US: *embassy:* the US does not have an embassy in Antigua and Barbuda; the US Ambassador to Barbados is accredited to Antigua and Barbuda

Flag description: red, with an inverted isosceles triangle based on the top edge of the flag; the triangle contains three horizontal bands of black (top), light blue, and white, with a yellow rising sun in the black band; the sun symbolizes the dawn of a new era, black represents the African heritage of most of the population, blue is for hope, and red is for the dynamism of the people; the "V" stands for victory; the successive yellow, blue, and white coloring is also meant to evoke the country's tourist attractions of sun, sea, and sand

National symbol(s): fallow deer; national colors: red, white, blue, black, yellow

National anthem: *name:* Fair Antigua, We Salute Thee
lyrics/music: Novelle Hamilton RICHARDS/Walter Garnet Picart CHAMBERS
note: adopted 1967; as a Commonwealth country, in addition to the national anthem, "God Save the King" serves as the royal anthem (see United Kingdom)

National heritage: *total World Heritage Sites:* 1 (cultural)
selected World Heritage Site locales: Antigua Naval Dockyard

ECONOMY

Economic overview: dual island-tourism and construction-driven economy; emerging "blue economy"; limited water supply and susceptibility to hurricanes limit activity; improving road infrastructure; friendly to foreign direct investment; looking at financial innovation in cryptocurrency and blockchain technologies

Real GDP (purchasing power parity): $2.703 billion (2023 est.)
$2.603 billion (2022 est.)
$2.376 billion (2021 est.)
note: data in 2021 dollars
comparison ranking: 197

Real GDP growth rate: 3.86% (2023 est.)
9.52% (2022 est.)
8.19% (2021 est.)
note: annual GDP % growth based on constant local currency
comparison ranking: 81

Real GDP per capita: $28,700 (2023 est.)
$27,800 (2022 est.)
$25,500 (2021 est.)
note: data in 2021 dollars
comparison ranking: 80

GDP (official exchange rate): $2.033 billion (2023 est.)
note: data in current dollars at official exchange rate

Inflation rate (consumer prices): 5.07% (2023 est.)
7.53% (2022 est.)
2.06% (2021 est.)
note: annual % change based on consumer prices
comparison ranking: 109

GDP - composition, by sector of origin: *agriculture:* 1.9% (2023 est.)
industry: 19.4% (2023 est.)
services: 67.8% (2023 est.)
note: figures may not total 100% due to non-allocated consumption not captured in sector-reported data comparison rankings: services 47; industry 140; agriculture 158

GDP - composition, by end use: *household consumption:* 53.5% (2017 est.)
government consumption: 15.2% (2017 est.)
investment in fixed capital: 23.9% (2017 est.)
investment in inventories: 0.1% (2017 est.)
exports of goods and services: 54.7% (2022 est.)
imports of goods and services: -62.9% (2022 est.)
note: figures may not total 100% due to rounding or gaps in data collection

Agricultural products: tropical fruits, milk, mangoes/guavas, eggs, lemons/limes, pumpkins/squash, vegetables, sweet potatoes, cassava, yams (2022)
note: top ten agricultural products based on tonnage

Industries: tourism, construction, light manufacturing (clothing, alcohol, household appliances)

Industrial production growth rate: 3.89% (2023 est.)
note: annual % change in industrial value added based on constant local currency
comparison ranking: 82

Unemployment rate: 11% (2014 est.)
comparison ranking: 168

Remittances: 2.43% of GDP (2023 est.)
1.86% of GDP (2022 est.)
2.83% of GDP (2021 est.)
note: personal transfers and compensation between resident and non-resident individuals/households/entities

Budget: *revenues:* $251.418 million (2014 est.)
expenditures: $266.044 million (2014 est.)
note: central government revenues and expenses (excluding grants/extrabudgetary units/social security funds) converted to US dollars at average official exchange rate for year indicated

Public debt: 86.8% of GDP (2017 est.)
comparison ranking: 30

Taxes and other revenues: 19.6% (of GDP) (2017 est.)
comparison ranking: 88

Current account balance: -$262.098 million (2023 est.)
-$296.147 million (2022 est.)
-$287.548 million (2021 est.)
note: balance of payments - net trade and primary/secondary income in current dollars
comparison ranking: 115

Exports: $1.217 billion (2023 est.)
$1.111 billion (2022 est.)
$705.697 million (2021 est.)
note: balance of payments - exports of goods and services in current dollars
comparison ranking: 177

Exports - partners: Suriname 28%, Poland 20%, Germany 13%, UK 8%, Barbados 5% (2022)
note: top five export partners based on percentage share of exports

Exports - commodities: refined petroleum, ships, gas turbines, soybean meal, liquor (2022)
note: top five export commodities based on value in dollars

Imports: $1.3 billion (2023 est.)
$1.234 billion (2022 est.)
$872.781 million (2021 est.)
note: balance of payments - imports of goods and services in current dollars
comparison ranking: 188

Imports - partners: US 57%, China 7%, Spain 4%, Brazil 4%, Finland 3% (2022)
note: top five import partners based on percentage share of imports

Imports - commodities: refined petroleum, ships, engine parts, plastic products, cars (2022)
note: top five import commodities based on value in dollars

Reserves of foreign exchange and gold: $364.367 million (2023 est.)
$396.506 million (2022 est.)
$367.512 million (2021 est.)
note: holdings of gold (year-end prices)/foreign exchange/special drawing rights in current dollars
comparison ranking: 172

Exchange rates: East Caribbean dollars (XCD) per US dollar -

Exchange rates: 2.7 (2023 est.)
2.7 (2022 est.)
2.7 (2021 est.)
2.7 (2020 est.)
2.7 (2019 est.)

ENERGY

Electricity access: *electrification - total population:* 100% (2022 est.)

Electricity: *installed generating capacity:* 97,000 kW (2022 est.)
consumption: 318.337 million kWh (2022 est.)
transmission/distribution losses: 37.847 million kWh (2022 est.)
comparison rankings: transmission/distribution losses 31; consumption 185; installed generating capacity 185

Electricity generation sources: *fossil fuels:* 94.2% of total installed capacity (2022 est.)
solar: 5.8% of total installed capacity (2022 est.)

Petroleum: *refined petroleum consumption:* 5,000 bbl/day (2022 est.)

Carbon dioxide emissions: 769,000 metric tonnes of CO_2 (2022 est.)
from petroleum and other liquids: 769,000 metric tonnes of CO_2 (2022 est.)
comparison ranking: total emissions 177

Energy consumption per capita: 114.469 million Btu/person (2022 est.)
comparison ranking: 42

COMMUNICATIONS

Telephones - fixed lines: *total subscriptions:* 27,000 (2021 est.)
subscriptions per 100 inhabitants: 29 (2021 est.)
comparison ranking: total subscriptions 168

Telephones - mobile cellular: *total subscriptions:* 184,000 (2021 est.)
subscriptions per 100 inhabitants: 197 (2021 est.)
comparison ranking: total subscriptions 185

Telecommunication systems: *general assessment:* the telecom sector has seen a decline in subscriber numbers (particularly for prepaid mobile services the mainstay of short term visitors) and revenue; fixed and mobile broadband services are two areas that have benefited from the crisis as employees and students have resorted to working from home; one area of the telecom market that is not prepared for growth is 5G mobile; governments, regulators, and even the mobile network operators have shown that they have not been investing in 5G opportunities at the present time; network expansion and enhancements remain concentrated around improving LTE coverage (2021)
domestic: fixed-line teledensity roughly 27 per 100 persons; mobile-cellular teledensity is about 200 per 100 persons (2021)
international: country code - 1-268; landing points for the ECFS and Southern Caribbean Fiber submarine cable systems with links to other islands in the eastern Caribbean; satellite earth stations - 1 Intelsat (Atlantic Ocean) (2019)

Broadcast media: state-controlled Antigua and Barbuda Broadcasting Service (ABS) operates 1 TV station; multi-channel cable TV subscription services are available; ABS operates 1 radio station; roughly 15 radio stations, some broadcasting on multiple frequencies

Internet country code: .ag

Internet users: *total:* 89,280 (2021 est.)
percent of population: 96% (2021 est.)
comparison ranking: total 191

Broadband - fixed subscriptions: *total:* 8,000 (2020 est.)
subscriptions per 100 inhabitants: 8 (2020 est.)
comparison ranking: total 181

TRANSPORTATION

National air transport system: *number of registered air carriers:* 1 (2020)
inventory of registered aircraft operated by air carriers: 10
annual passenger traffic on registered air carriers: 580,174 (2018)
annual freight traffic on registered air carriers: 290,000 (2018) mt-km

Civil aircraft registration country code prefix: V2

Airports: 3 (2024)
comparison ranking: 187

Heliports: 2 (2024)

Roadways: *total:* 1,170 km
paved: 386 km
unpaved: 784 km (2011)
comparison ranking: total 182

Merchant marine: *total:* 614 (2023)
by type: bulk carrier 24, container ship 109, general cargo 425, oil tanker 6, other 50
comparison ranking: total 36

Ports: *total ports:* 1 (2024)
large: 0
medium: 1
small: 0
very small: 0
ports with oil terminals: 1
key ports: St. John's

MILITARY AND SECURITY

Military and security forces: Antigua and Barbuda Defense Force (ABDF): Antigua and Barbuda Regiment, Air Wing, Coast Guard
Royal Police Force of Antigua and Barbuda (2024)

Military and security service personnel strengths: approximately 250 active military personnel (2024)

Military equipment inventories and acquisitions: the ABDF's equipment inventory is limited to small arms, light weapons, and soft-skin vehicles; the Coast Guard maintains ex-US patrol vessels and some smaller boats (2024)

Military service age and obligation: 18-23 years of age for voluntary military service for both men and women; no conscription (2023)

Military - note: the ABDF's responsibilities include providing for internal security and support to the police in maintaining law and order, interdicting narcotics smuggling, responding to natural disasters, and monitoring the country's territorial waters and maritime resources; established in 1981 from colonial forces originally created in 1897, it is one of the world's smallest militaries
the country has been a member of the Caribbean Regional Security System (RSS) since its creation in 1982; RSS signatories (Barbados, Dominica, Grenada, Guyana, Saint Kitts and Nevis, Saint Lucia, and Saint Vincent and the Grenadines) agreed to prepare contingency plans and assist one another, on request, in national emergencies, prevention of smuggling, search and rescue, immigration control, fishery protection, customs and excise control, maritime policing duties, protection of off-shore installations, pollution control, national and other disasters, and threats to national security (2024)

TRANSNATIONAL ISSUES

Illicit drugs: a transit point for cocaine and marijuana destined for North America, Europe, and elsewhere in the Caribbean; some local demand for cocaine and some use of synthetic drugs

ARCTIC OCEAN

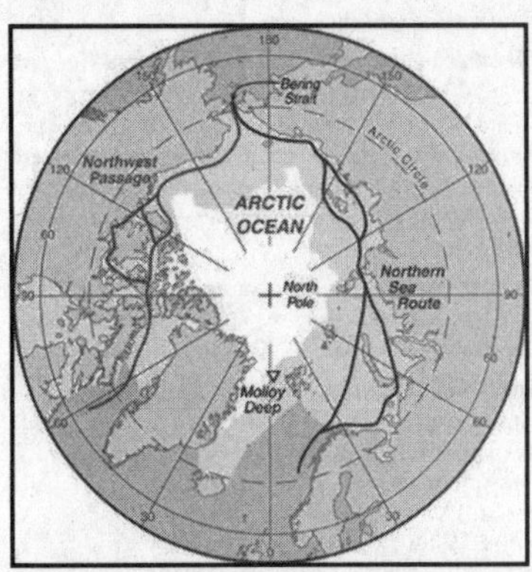

INTRODUCTION

Background: The Arctic Ocean is the smallest of the world's five ocean basins (after the Pacific Ocean, Atlantic Ocean, Indian Ocean, and the Southern Ocean). The Northwest Passage (US and Canada) and Northern Sea Route (Norway and Russia) are two important seasonal waterways. In recent years, the polar ice pack has receded in the summer allowing for increased navigation and raising the possibility of future sovereignty and shipping disputes among the Arctic coastal states affected (Canada, Denmark (Greenland), Iceland, Norway, Russia, US).

GEOGRAPHY

Location: body of water between Europe, Asia, and North America, mostly north of the Arctic Circle

Geographic coordinates: 90 00 N, 0 00 E

Map references: Arctic Region

Area: *total:* 15.558 million sq km
note: includes Barents Sea, Beaufort Sea, Chukchi Sea, East Siberian Sea, Greenland Sea, Kara Sea, Laptev Sea, Northwest Passage, Norwegian Sea, and other tributary water bodies

Area - comparative: slightly less than 1.5 times the size of the US

Coastline: 45,389 km

Climate: polar climate characterized by persistent cold and relatively narrow annual temperature range; winters characterized by continuous darkness, cold and stable weather conditions, and clear skies; summers characterized by continuous daylight, damp and foggy weather, and weak cyclones with rain or snow

Ocean volume: *ocean volume:* 18.75 million cu km
percent of World Ocean total volume: 1.4%

Major ocean currents: *two major, slow-moving, wind-driven currents (drift streams) dominate:* a clockwise drift pattern in the Beaufort Gyre in the western part of the Arctic Ocean and a nearly straight line Transpolar Drift Stream that moves eastward across the ocean from the New Siberian Islands (Russia) to the Fram Strait (between Greenland and Svalbard); sea ice that lies close to the center of the gyre can complete a 360 degree circle in about 2 years, while ice on the gyre periphery will complete the same circle in about 7-8 years; sea ice in the Transpolar Drift crosses the ocean in about 3 years

Elevation: *highest point:* sea level
lowest point: Molloy Deep -5,577 m
mean depth: -1,205 m
ocean zones: Composed of water and in a fluid state, the ocean is delimited differently than the solid continents. It is divided into three zones based on depth and light level. Sunlight entering the water may travel about 1,000 m into the oceans under the right conditions, but there is rarely any significant light beyond 200 m.
The upper 200 m (656 ft) of the ocean is called the euphotic, or "sunlight," zone. This zone contains the vast majority of commercial fisheries and is home to many protected marine mammals and sea turtles. Only a small amount of light penetrates beyond this depth.
The zone between 200 m (656 ft) and 1,000 m (3,280 ft) is usually referred to as the "twilight" zone, but is officially the dysphotic zone. In this zone, the intensity of light rapidly dissipates as depth increases. Such a minuscule amount of light penetrates beyond a depth of 200 m that photosynthesis is no longer possible.
The aphotic, or "midnight," zone exists in depths below 1,000 m (3,280 ft). Sunlight does not penetrate to these depths, and the zone is bathed in darkness.

Distance Sunlight Travels in the Ocean: Natural resources: sand and gravel aggregates, placer deposits, polymetallic nodules, oil and gas fields, fish, marine mammals (seals and whales)

Natural hazards: ice islands occasionally break away from northern Ellesmere Island; icebergs calved from glaciers in western Greenland and extreme northeastern Canada; permafrost in islands; virtually ice locked from October to June; ships subject to superstructure icing from October to May

Geography - note: major chokepoint is the southern Chukchi Sea (northern access to the Pacific Ocean via the Bering Strait); strategic location between North America and Russia; shortest marine link between the extremes of eastern and western Russia; floating research stations operated by the US and Russia; maximum snow cover in March or April about 20 to 50 centimeters over the frozen ocean; snow cover lasts about 10 months

ENVIRONMENT

Environment - current issues: climate change; changes in biodiversity; water pollution from use of toxic chemicals; endangered marine species include walruses and whales; fragile ecosystem slow to change and slow to recover from disruptions or damage; thinning polar icepack

Climate: polar climate characterized by persistent cold and relatively narrow annual temperature range; winters characterized by continuous darkness, cold and stable weather conditions, and clear skies; summers characterized by continuous daylight, damp and foggy weather, and weak cyclones with rain or snow

Marine fisheries: the Arctic fishery region (Region 18) is the smallest in the world with a catch of only 708 mt in 2019, although the Food and Agriculture Organization assesses that some Arctic catches are reported in adjacent regions; Russia and Canada were historically the major producers; in 2017, Canada, Denmark (Greenland), Iceland, Norway, Russia, and the US, along with the People's Republic of China, the European Union, Japan, and the Republic of Korea, agreed to a 16-year ban on fishing in the Central Arctic Ocean to allow for time to study the ecological system of these waters

Regional fisheries bodies: International Council for the Exploration of the Seas; Agreement to Prevent Unregulated High Seas Fisheries in the Central Arctic Ocean

GOVERNMENT

Country name: *etymology:* the name Arctic comes from the Greek word *arktikos* meaning "near the bear" or "northern," and that word derives from *arktos*, meaning "bear"; the name refers either to the constellation Ursa Major, the "Great Bear," which is prominent in the northern celestial sphere, or to the constellation Ursa Minor, the "Little Bear," which contains Polaris, the North (Pole) Star

TRANSPORTATION

Transportation - note: sparse network of air, ocean, river, and land routes; the Northwest Passage (North America) and Northern Sea Route (Eurasia) are important seasonal waterways

TRANSNATIONAL ISSUES

Disputes - international: *note:* record levels of summer melting of sea ice in the Arctic has renewed interest in maritime shipping lanes and sea floor exploration

ARGENTINA

INTRODUCTION

Background: In 1816, the United Provinces of the Río de la Plata declared their independence from Spain. After Bolivia, Paraguay, and Uruguay went their separate ways, the area that remained became Argentina. European immigrants heavily shaped the country's population and culture, with Italy and Spain providing the largest percentage of newcomers from 1860 to 1930. Until about the mid-20th century, much of Argentina's history was dominated by periods of internal political unrest and conflict between civilian and military factions.

After World War II, former President Juan Domingo PERÓN – the founder of the Peronist political movement – introduced an era of populism, serving three non-consecutive terms in office until his death in 1974. Direct and indirect military interference in government throughout the PERÓN years led to a military junta taking power in 1976. In 1982, the junta failed in its bid to seize the Falkland Islands (Islas Malvinas) by force from the United Kingdom. Democracy was reinstated in 1983 and has persisted despite numerous challenges, the most formidable of which was a severe economic crisis in 2001-02 that led to violent public protests and the successive resignations of several presidents. The years 2003-15 saw Peronist rule by Néstor KIRCHNER (2003-07) and his spouse Cristina FERNÁNDEZ DE KIRCHNER (2007-15), who oversaw several years of strong economic growth (2003-11) followed by a gradual deterioration in the government's fiscal situation and eventual economic stagnation and isolation. Argentina underwent a brief period of economic reform and international reintegration under Mauricio MACRI (2015-19), but a recession in 2018-19 and frustration with MACRI's economic policies ushered in a new Peronist government in 2019 led by President Alberto FERNÁNDEZ and Vice President Cristina FERNÁNDEZ DE KIRCHNER. Argentina's high public debts, its pandemic-related inflationary pressures, and systemic monetary woes served as the catalyst for the 2023 elections, culminating with President Javier MILEI's electoral success. Argentina has since eliminated half of its government agencies and is seeking shock therapy to amend taxation and monetary policies.

GEOGRAPHY

Location: Southern South America, bordering the South Atlantic Ocean, between Chile and Uruguay

Geographic coordinates: 34 00 S, 64 00 W

Map references: South America

Area: *total:* 2,780,400 sq km
land: 2,736,690 sq km
water: 43,710 sq km
comparison ranking: total 9

Area - comparative: slightly less than three-tenths the size of the US

Land boundaries: *total:* 11,968 km
border countries (5): Bolivia 942 km; Brazil 1,263 km; Chile 6,691 km; Paraguay 2,531 km; Uruguay 541 km

Coastline: 4,989 km

Maritime claims: *territorial sea:* 12 nm
contiguous zone: 24 nm
exclusive economic zone: 200 nm
continental shelf: 200 nm or to the edge of the continental margin

Climate: mostly temperate; arid in southeast; subantarctic in southwest

Terrain: rich plains of the Pampas in northern half, flat to rolling plateau of Patagonia in south, rugged Andes along western border

Elevation: *highest point:* Cerro Aconcagua (located in the northwestern corner of the province of Mendoza; highest point in South America) 6,962 m
lowest point: Laguna del Carbón (located between Puerto San Julián and Comandante Luis Piedra Buena in the province of Santa Cruz) -105 m
mean elevation: 595 m

Natural resources: fertile plains of the pampas, lead, zinc, tin, copper, iron ore, manganese, petroleum, uranium, arable land

Land use: *agricultural land:* 53.9% (2018 est.)
arable land: 13.9% (2018 est.)
permanent crops: 0.4% (2018 est.)
permanent pasture: 39.6% (2018 est.)
forest: 10.7% (2018 est.)
other: 35.4% (2018 est.)

Irrigated land: 23,600 sq km (2012)

Major lakes (area sq km): *fresh water lake(s):* Lago Buenos Aires (shared with Chile) - 2,240 sq km; Lago Argentino - 1,410 sq km; Lago Viedma - 1,090 sq km; Lago San Martín (shared with Chile) - 1,010 sq km; Lago Colhué Huapi - 800 sq km; Lago Fagnano (shared with Chile) - 590 sq km; Lago Nahuel Huapi - 550 sq km
salt water lake(s): Laguna Mar Chiquita - 1,850 sq km;

Major rivers (by length in km): Río de la Plata/Paraná river mouth (shared with Brazil [s], Paraguay, and Uruguay) - 4,880 km; Paraguay (shared with Brazil [s], and Paraguay [m]) - 2,549 km; Uruguay (shared with Brazil [s] and Uruguay [m]) - 1,610 km
note – [s] after country name indicates river source; [m] after country name indicates river mouth

Major watersheds (area sq km): Atlantic Ocean drainage: Paraná (2,582,704 sq km)

Major aquifers: Guaraní Aquifer System

Population distribution: one-third of the population lives in Buenos Aires; pockets of agglomeration occur throughout the northern and central parts of the country; Patagonia to the south remains sparsely populated

Natural hazards: San Miguel de Tucumán and Mendoza areas in the Andes subject to earthquakes; pamperos are violent windstorms that can strike the pampas and northeast; heavy flooding in some areas
volcanism: volcanic activity in the Andes Mountains along the Chilean border; Copahue (2,997 m) last erupted in 2000; other historically active volcanoes

include Llullaillaco, Maipo, Planchón-Peteroa, San José, Tromen, Tupungatito, and Viedma

Geography - note: *note 1:* second-largest country in South America (after Brazil); strategic location relative to sea lanes between the South Atlantic and the South Pacific Oceans (Strait of Magellan, Beagle Channel, Drake Passage); diverse geophysical landscapes range from tropical climates in the north to tundra in the far south; Cerro Aconcagua is the Western Hemisphere's tallest mountain, while Laguna del Carbón is the lowest point in the Western Hemisphere; shares Iguazú Falls, the world's largest waterfalls system, with Brazil
note 2: southeast Bolivia and northwest Argentina seem to be the original development site for peanuts

PEOPLE AND SOCIETY

Population: *total:* 46,994,384
male: 23,274,794
female: 23,719,590 (2024 est.)
comparison rankings: female 33; male 33; total 34

Nationality: *noun:* Argentine(s)
adjective: Argentine

Ethnic groups: European (mostly Spanish and Italian descent) and Mestizo (mixed European and Indigenous ancestry) 97.2%, Indigenous 2.4%, African descent 0.4% (2010 est.)

Languages: Spanish (official), Italian, English, German, French, indigenous (Quechua, Guarani, Mapudungun)
major-language sample(s):
La Libreta Informativa del Mundo, la fuente indispensable de información básica. (Spanish)

Religions: Roman Catholic 62.9%, Evangelical 15.3% (Pentecostal 13%, other Evangelical 2.3%), Jehovah's Witness and Church of Jesus Christ 1.4%, other 1.2% (includes Muslim, Jewish), none 18.9% (includes agnostic and atheist), unspecified 0.3% (2019 est.)

Demographic profile: Argentina's population continues to grow but at a slower rate because of its steadily declining birth rate. Argentina's fertility decline began earlier than in the rest of Latin America, occurring most rapidly between the early 20th century and the 1950s, and then becoming more gradual. Life expectancy has been improving, most notably among the young and the poor. While the population under age 15 is shrinking, the youth cohort - ages 15-24 - is the largest in Argentina's history and will continue to bolster the working-age population. If this large working-age population is well-educated and gainfully employed, Argentina is likely to experience an economic boost and possibly higher per capita savings and investment. Although literacy and primary school enrollment are nearly universal, grade repetition is problematic and secondary school completion is low. Both of these issues vary widely by region and socioeconomic group.
Argentina has been primarily a country of immigration for most of its history, welcoming European immigrants (often providing needed low-skilled labor) after its independence in the 19th century and attracting especially large numbers from Spain and Italy. More than 7 million European immigrants are estimated to have arrived in Argentina between 1880 and 1930, when it adopted a more restrictive immigration policy. European immigration also began to wane in the 1930s because of the global depression. The inflow rebounded temporarily following WWII and resumed its decline in the 1950s when Argentina's military dictators tightened immigration rules and European economies rebounded. Regional migration increased, however, supplying low-skilled workers escaping economic and political instability in their home countries. As of 2015, immigrants made up almost 5% of Argentina's population, the largest share in South America. Migration from neighboring countries accounted for approximately 80% of Argentina's immigrant population in 2015.
The first waves of highly skilled Argentine emigrant workers headed mainly to the United States and Spain in the 1960s and 1970s, driven by economic decline and repressive military dictatorships. The 2008 European economic crisis drove the return migration of some Argentinean and other Latin American nationals, as well as the immigration of Europeans to South America, where Argentina was a key recipient. In 2015, Argentina received the highest number of legal migrants in Latin America and the Caribbean. The majority of its migrant inflow came from Paraguay and Bolivia.

Age structure: *0-14 years:* 23.3% (male 5,632,983/female 5,301,778)
15-64 years: 63.9% (male 15,071,215/female 14,956,069)
65 years and over: 12.8% (2024 est.) (male 2,570,596/female 3,461,743)

Dependency ratios: *total dependency ratio:* 54.3
youth dependency ratio: 36
elderly dependency ratio: 18.2
potential support ratio: 5.5 (2021 est.)

Median age: *total:* 33.3 years (2024 est.)
male: 32.1 years
female: 34.6 years
comparison ranking: total 112

Population growth rate: 0.79% (2024 est.)
comparison ranking: 110

Birth rate: 15.2 births/1,000 population (2024 est.)
comparison ranking: 107

Death rate: 7.3 deaths/1,000 population (2024 est.)
comparison ranking: 107

Net migration rate: -0.1 migrant(s)/1,000 population (2024 est.)
comparison ranking: 98

Population distribution: one-third of the population lives in Buenos Aires; pockets of agglomeration occur throughout the northern and central parts of the country; Patagonia to the south remains sparsely populated

Urbanization: *urban population:* 92.5% of total population (2023)
rate of urbanization: 0.97% annual rate of change (2020-25 est.)

Major urban areas - population: 15.490 million BUENOS AIRES (capital), 1.612 million Córdoba, 1.594 million Rosario, 1.226 million Mendoza, 1.027 million San Miguel de Tucumán, 914,000 La Plata (2023)

Sex ratio: *at birth:* 1.07 male(s)/female
0-14 years: 1.06 male(s)/female
15-64 years: 1.01 male(s)/female
65 years and over: 0.74 male(s)/female
total population: 0.98 male(s)/female (2024 est.)

Maternal mortality ratio: 45 deaths/100,000 live births (2020 est.)
comparison ranking: 98

Infant mortality rate: *total:* 9 deaths/1,000 live births (2024 est.)
male: 9.9 deaths/1,000 live births
female: 7.9 deaths/1,000 live births
comparison ranking: total 140

Life expectancy at birth: *total population:* 78.8 years (2024 est.)
male: 75.8 years
female: 82 years
comparison ranking: total population 72

Total fertility rate: 2.15 children born/woman (2024 est.)
comparison ranking: 89

Gross reproduction rate: 1.04 (2024 est.)

Contraceptive prevalence rate: 70.1% (2019/20)

Drinking water source: *improved: urban:* 99.8% of population
unimproved: urban: 0.2% of population

Current health expenditure: 10% of GDP (2020)

Physician density: 4.06 physicians/1,000 population (2020)

Hospital bed density: 5 beds/1,000 population (2017)

Sanitation facility access: *improved: urban:* 100% of population

Obesity - adult prevalence rate: 28.3% (2016)
comparison ranking: 31

Alcohol consumption per capita: *total:* 7.95 liters of pure alcohol (2019 est.)
beer: 3.62 liters of pure alcohol (2019 est.)
wine: 2.88 liters of pure alcohol (2019 est.)
spirits: 0.72 liters of pure alcohol (2019 est.)
other alcohols: 0.72 liters of pure alcohol (2019 est.)
comparison ranking: total 45

Tobacco use: *total:* 24.5% (2020 est.)
male: 29.4% (2020 est.)
female: 19.6% (2020 est.)
comparison ranking: total 53

Children under the age of 5 years underweight: 1.7% (2018/19)
comparison ranking: 111

Currently married women (ages 15-49): 48.9% (2023 est.)

Child marriage: *women married by age 15:* 2.4%
women married by age 18: 15.5% (2020 est.)

Education expenditures: 5% of GDP (2020 est.)
comparison ranking: 79

Literacy: *definition:* age 15 and over can read and write
total population: 99%
male: 98.9%
female: 99.1% (2018)

School life expectancy (primary to tertiary education): *total:* 18 years
male: 17 years
female: 20 years (2020)

ENVIRONMENT

Environment - current issues: environmental problems (urban and rural) typical of an industrializing economy such as deforestation, soil degradation (erosion, salinization), desertification, air pollution, and water pollution

Environment - international agreements: *party to:* Antarctic-Environmental Protection, Antarctic-Marine Living Resources, Antarctic Seals, Antarctic Treaty, Biodiversity, Climate Change, Climate Change-Kyoto Protocol, Climate Change-Paris Agreement, Comprehensive Nuclear Test Ban, Desertification, Endangered Species, Environmental

Modification, Hazardous Wastes, Law of the Sea, Marine Dumping-London Convention, Nuclear Test Ban, Ozone Layer Protection, Ship Pollution, Wetlands, Whaling
signed, but not ratified: Marine Dumping-London Protocol, Marine Life Conservation

Climate: mostly temperate; arid in southeast; subantarctic in southwest

Urbanization: *urban population:* 92.5% of total population (2023)
rate of urbanization: 0.97% annual rate of change (2020-25 est.)

Revenue from forest resources: 0.09% of GDP (2018 est.)
comparison ranking: 115

Revenue from coal: 0% of GDP (2018 est.)
comparison ranking: 72

Air pollutants: *particulate matter emissions:* 12.04 micrograms per cubic meter (2019 est.)
carbon dioxide emissions: 201.35 megatons (2016 est.)
methane emissions: 120.66 megatons (2020 est.)

Waste and recycling: *municipal solid waste generated annually:* 17,910,550 tons (2014 est.)
municipal solid waste recycled annually: 1,074,633 tons (2010 est.)
percent of municipal solid waste recycled: 6% (2010 est.)

Major lakes (area sq km): *fresh water lake(s):* Lago Buenos Aires (shared with Chile) - 2,240 sq km; Lago Argentino - 1,410 sq km; Lago Viedma - 1,090 sq km; Lago San Martín (shared with Chile) - 1,010 sq km; Lago Colhué Huapi - 800 sq km; Lago Fagnano (shared with Chile) - 590 sq km; Lago Nahuel Huapi - 550 sq km
salt water lake(s): Laguna Mar Chiquita - 1,850 sq km;

Major rivers (by length in km): Río de la Plata/ Paraná river mouth (shared with Brazil [s], Paraguay, and Uruguay) - 4,880 km; Paraguay (shared with Brazil [s], and Paraguay [m]) - 2,549 km; Uruguay (shared with Brazil [s] and Uruguay [m]) - 1,610 km
note – [s] after country name indicates river source; [m] after country name indicates river mouth

Major watersheds (area sq km): Atlantic Ocean drainage: Paraná (2,582,704 sq km)

Major aquifers: Guaraní Aquifer System

Total water withdrawal: *municipal:* 5.85 billion cubic meters (2020 est.)
industrial: 4 billion cubic meters (2020 est.)
agricultural: 27.93 billion cubic meters (2020 est.)

Total renewable water resources: 876.24 billion cubic meters (2020 est.)

GOVERNMENT

Country name: *conventional long form:* Argentine Republic
conventional short form: Argentina
local long form: República Argentina
local short form: Argentina
etymology: originally the area was referred to as Tierra Argentina, i.e., "Land beside the Silvery River" or "silvery land," which referred to the massive estuary in the east of the country, the Río de la Plata (River of Silver); over time the name shortened to simply Argentina or "silvery"

Government type: presidential republic

Capital: *name:* Buenos Aires
geographic coordinates: 34 36 S, 58 22 W
time difference: UTC-3 (2 hours ahead of Washington, DC, during Standard Time)
etymology: the name translates as "fair winds" in Spanish and derives from the original designation of the settlement that would become the present-day city, "Santa Maria del Buen Aire" (Saint Mary of the Fair Winds)

Administrative divisions: 23 provinces (provincias, singular - provincia) and 1 autonomous city*; Buenos Aires, Catamarca, Chaco, Chubut, Ciudad Autonoma de Buenos Aires*, Cordoba, Corrientes, Entre Rios, Formosa, Jujuy, La Pampa, La Rioja, Mendoza, Misiones, Neuquen, Rio Negro, Salta, San Juan, San Luis, Santa Cruz, Santa Fe, Santiago del Estero, Tierra del Fuego - Antartida e Islas del Atlantico Sur (Tierra del Fuego - Antarctica and the South Atlantic Islands), Tucuman
note: the US does not recognize any claims to Antarctica

Independence: 9 July 1816 (from Spain)

National holiday: Revolution Day (May Revolution Day), 25 May (1810)

Legal system: civil law system based on West European legal systems; note - in mid-2015, Argentina adopted a new civil code, replacing the old one in force since 1871

Constitution: *history:* several previous; latest effective 11 May 1853
amendments: a declaration of proposed amendments requires two-thirds majority vote by both houses of the National Congress followed by approval by an ad hoc, multi-member constitutional convention; amended several times, last significant amendment in 1994

International law organization participation: has not submitted an ICJ jurisdiction declaration; accepts ICCt jurisdiction

Citizenship: *citizenship by birth:* yes
citizenship by descent only: yes
dual citizenship recognized: yes
residency requirement for naturalization: 2 years

Suffrage: 18-70 years of age; universal and compulsory; 16-17 years of age - optional for national elections

Executive branch: *chief of state:* President Javier Gerardo MILEI (since 10 December 2023)
head of government: President Javier Gerardo MILEI (since 10 December 2023)
cabinet: Cabinet appointed by the president
elections/appointments: president and vice president directly elected on the same ballot by qualified majority vote (to win, a candidate must receive at least 45% of votes or 40% of votes and a 10-point lead over the second place candidate; if neither occurs, a second round is held); the president serves a 4-year term (eligible for a second consecutive term); election last held on 22 October 2023 with a runoff held 19 November 2023 (next to be held in October 2027)
election results:
2023: Javier Gerardo MILEI elected president in second round; percent vote in first round - Sergio Tomás MASSA (FR) 36.7%, Javier Gerardo MILEI (PL) 30%, Patricia BULLRICH 23.8% (JxC/PRO), Juan SCHIARETTI (PJ) 6.8%, Myriam BREGMAN (PTS) 2.7%; percent of vote in second round - Javier Gerardo MILEI 55.7%, Sergio Tomás MASSA 44.3%
2019: Alberto Ángel FERNÁNDEZ elected president; percent of vote - Alberto Angel FERNÁNDEZ (TODOS) 48.1%, Mauricio MACRI (PRO) 40.4%, Roberto LAVAGNA (independent) 6.2%, other 5.3%

Legislative branch: *description:* bicameral National Congress or Congreso Nacional consists of:
Senate or Senado (72 seats; members directly elected from 24 provincial districts by closed-list proportional representation vote; 2 seats per district awarded to the party with the most votes and 1 seat per district to the party with the second highest votes; members serve 6-year terms with one-third of the membership renewed every 2 years) Chamber of Deputies or Cámara de Diputados (257 seats; members directly elected in multi-seat constituencies by closed-list proportional representation vote; members serve 4-year terms with one-half of the membership renewed every 2 years)
elections:
Senate - last held on 22 October 2023 (next to be held in October 2025)
Chamber of Deputies - last held on 22 October 2023 (next to be held in October 2025)
election results:
Senate - percent of vote by party/coalition - NA; seats by party/coalition - UP 12, LLA 8, JxC 2, other 2; composition - men 39, women 33, percentage women 45.8%
Chamber of Deputies - percent of vote by party/coalition - NA; seats by party/coalition - UP 58, LLA 35, JxC 31, NHP 4, other 2; composition - men 148, women 109, percentage women 42.4%; total National Congress percentage women 43.2%

Judicial branch: *highest court(s):* Supreme Court or Corte Suprema (consists of the court president, vice president, 2 judges, 1 vacancy)
judge selection and term of office: judges nominated by the president and approved by the Senate; ministers can serve until mandatory retirement at age 75; extensions beyond 75 require renomination by the president and approval by the Senate
subordinate courts: federal level appellate, district, and territorial courts; provincial level supreme, appellate, and first instance courts

Political parties: Avanza Libertad or AL
Civic Coalition ARI or CC-ARI
Consenso Federal (Federal Consensus) or CF
Frente Cívico por Santiago (Civic Front for Santiago)
Frente de Izquierda y de los Trabajadores – Unidad (Workers' Left Front) or FIT-U (coalition of leftist parties in lower house; includes PTS, PO, and MST)
Frente de la Concordia Misionero (Front for the Renewal of Social Concord) or FRCS
Frente Renovador (Renewal Front) or FR
Generación por un Encuentro Nacional (Generation for a National Encounter) or GEN
Hacemos por Córdoba (We do for Cordoba) or HC
Hacemos por Nuestro Pais (We Do For Our Country) or NHP
Juntos por el Cambio (Together for Change) or JxC (includes CC-ARI, PRO, and UCR); note - primary opposition coalition since 2019
Juntos Somos Río Negro (Together We Are Rio Negro) or JSRN
Partido Justicialista (Justicialist Party) or PJ
La Cámpora
La Libertad Avanza (The Liberty Advances) or LLA
Movimiento Popular Neuquino (Neuquén People's Movement) or MPN
Movimiento Socialista de los Trabajadores (Workers' Socialist Movement) or MST

Partido de los Trabajadores Socialistas (Socialist Workers' Party) or PTS
Partido Demócrata (Democratic Party) or PDN
Partido Libertario (Libertarian Party) or PL; note - party is also a founding member of the coalition La Libertad Avanza
Partido Obrero (Workers' Party) or PO
Partido Socialista or PS
Propuesta Republicana (Republican Proposal) or PRO
Unidad Federal (coalition of provencial parties in the lower house; includes FRCS and JSRN)
Unión Cívica Radical (Radical Civic Union) or UCR
Unión por la Patria (Union for the Homeland) or UP *(formerly Frente de Todos (Everyone's Front) or FdT)* (includes FR, La Cámpora, and PJ); note - ruling coalition since 2019; includes several national and provincial Peronist political parties
Vamos con Vos (Let's Go with You) or VcV

International organization participation: AfDB (nonregional member), Australia Group, BCIE, BIS, CAN (associate), CD, CABEI, CELAC, FAO, FATF, G-15, G-20, G-24, G-77, IADB, IAEA, IBRD, ICAO, ICC (national committees), ICCt, ICRM, IDA, IFAD, IFC, IFRCS, IHO, ILO, IMF, IMO, IMSO, Interpol, IOC, IOM, IPU, ISO, ITSO, ITU, ITUC (NGOs), LAES, LAIA, Mercosur, MIGA, MINURSO, MINUSTAH, NAM (observer), NSG, OAS, OPANAL, OPCW, Paris Club (associate), PCA, PROSUR, SICA (observer), UN, UNASUR, UNCTAD, UNDOF, UNESCO, UNFICYP, UNHCR, UNHRC, UNIDO, Union Latina (observer), UNOOSA, UNTSO, UNWTO, UPU, Wassenaar Arrangement, WCO, WFTU (NGOs), WHO, WIPO, WMO, WTO, ZC

Diplomatic representation in the US: *chief of mission:* Ambassador Gerardo WERTHEIN (since 17 June 2024)
chancery: 1600 New Hampshire Avenue NW, Washington, DC 20009
telephone: [1] (202) 238-6400
FAX: [1] (202) 332-3171
email address and website:
eeeuu@mrecic.gov.ar
https://eeeuu.cancilleria.gob.ar/en
consulate(s) general: Atlanta, Chicago, Houston, Los Angeles, Miami, New York

Diplomatic representation from the US: *chief of mission:* Ambassador Marc Robert STANLEY (since 24 January 2022)
embassy:
Avenida Colombia 4300, (C1425GMN) Buenos Aires
mailing address: 3130 Buenos Aires Place, Washington DC 20521-3130
telephone: [54] (11) 5777-4533
FAX: [54] (11) 5777-4240
email address and website:
Buenosairespublicaffairs@state.gov
https://ar.usembassy.gov/

Flag description: three equal horizontal bands of sky blue (top), white, and sky blue; centered in the white band is a radiant yellow sun with a human face (delineated in brown) known as the Sun of May; the colors represent the clear skies and snow of the Andes; the sun symbol commemorates the appearance of the sun through cloudy skies on 25 May 1810 during the first mass demonstration in favor of independence; the sun features are those of Inti, the Inca god of the sun

National symbol(s): Sun of May (a sun-with-face symbol); national colors: sky blue, white

National anthem: *name:* "Himno Nacional Argentino" (Argentine National Anthem)
lyrics/music: Vicente LOPEZ y PLANES/Jose Blas PARERA
note: adopted 1813; Vicente LOPEZ was inspired to write the anthem after watching a play about the 1810 May Revolution against Spain

National heritage: *total World Heritage Sites:* 12 (7 cultural, 5 natural)
selected World Heritage Site locales: Los Glaciares National Park (n); Jesuit Missions of the Guaranis (c); Iguazú National Park (n); Cueva de las Manos (c); Valdés Península (n); Ischigualasto/Talampaya National Parks (n); Jesuit Block and Estancias of Córdoba (c); Quebrada de Humahuaca (c); Qhapaq Ñan/Andean Road System (c)

ECONOMY

Economic overview: large diversified economy; financial risks from debt obligations, rapid inflation, and reduced investor appetites; resourcerich, export-led growth model; increasing trade relations with China; G20 and OAS leader; tendency to nationalize businesses and under-report inflation

Real GDP (purchasing power parity): $1.235 trillion (2023 est.)
$1.254 trillion (2022 est.)
$1.195 trillion (2021 est.)
note: data in 2021 dollars
comparison ranking: 28

Real GDP growth rate: -1.55% (2023 est.)
4.96% (2022 est.)
10.72% (2021 est.)
note: annual GDP % growth based on constant local currency
comparison ranking: 203

Real GDP per capita: $26,500 (2023 est.)
$27,100 (2022 est.)
$26,100 (2021 est.)
note: data in 2021 dollars
comparison ranking: 86

GDP (official exchange rate): $640.591 billion (2023 est.)
note: data in current dollars at official exchange rate

Inflation rate (consumer prices): 25.7% (2017 est.)
26.5% (2016 est.)
note: data are derived from private estimates
comparison ranking: 202

Credit ratings: Fitch rating: CCC (2020)

Moody's rating: Ca (2020)

Standard & Poors rating: CCC+ (2020)
note: The year refers to the year in which the current credit rating was first obtained.

GDP - composition, by sector of origin: *agriculture:* 6.1% (2023 est.)
industry: 25.1% (2023 est.)
services: 52.8% (2023 est.)
note: figures may not total 100% due to non-allocated consumption not captured in sector-reported data
comparison rankings: services 129; industry 95; agriculture 106

GDP - composition, by end use: *household consumption:* 67.2% (2023 est.)
government consumption: 15.8% (2023 est.)
investment in fixed capital: 19.1% (2023 est.)
investment in inventories: 0.4% (2023 est.)
exports of goods and services: 12.9% (2023 est.)
imports of goods and services: -14.1% (2023 est.)
note: figures may not total 100% due to rounding or gaps in data collection

Agricultural products: maize, soybeans, wheat, sugarcane, milk, barley, sunflower seeds, beef, sorghum, chicken (2022)
note: top ten agricultural products based on tonnage

Industries: food processing, motor vehicles, consumer durables, textiles, chemicals and petrochemicals, printing, metallurgy, steel

Industrial production growth rate: -0.35% (2023 est.)
note: annual % change in industrial value added based on constant local currency
comparison ranking: 158

Labor force: 21.906 million (2023 est.)
note: number of people ages 15 or older who are employed or seeking work
comparison ranking: 32

Unemployment rate: 6.18% (2023 est.)
6.81% (2022 est.)
8.74% (2021 est.)
note: % of labor force seeking employment
comparison ranking: 127

Youth unemployment rate (ages 15-24): *total:* 18% (2023 est.)
male: 16.9% (2023 est.)
female: 19.5% (2023 est.)
note: % of labor force ages 15-24 seeking employment
comparison ranking: total 77

Population below poverty line: 39.2% (2022 est.)
note: % of population with income below national poverty line

Gini Index coefficient - distribution of family income: 40.7 (2022 est.)
note: index (0-100) of income distribution; higher values represent greater inequality
comparison ranking: 40

Average household expenditures: *on food:* 23.1% of household expenditures (2022 est.)
on alcohol and tobacco: 1.9% of household expenditures (2022 est.)

Household income or consumption by percentage share: *lowest 10%:* 2% (2022 est.)
highest 10%: 29.8% (2022 est.)
note: % share of income accruing to lowest and highest 10% of population

Remittances: 0.25% of GDP (2023 est.)
0.2% of GDP (2022 est.)
0.18% of GDP (2021 est.)
note: personal transfers and compensation between resident and non-resident individuals/households/entities

Budget: *revenues:* $113.553 billion (2022 est.)
expenditures: $138.622 billion (2022 est.)
note: central government revenues (excluding grants) and expenses converted to US dollars at average official exchange rate for year indicated

Public debt: 57.6% of GDP (2017 est.)
comparison ranking: 86

Taxes and other revenues: 11.15% (of GDP) (2022 est.)
note: central government tax revenue as a % of GDP
comparison ranking: 175

Current account balance: -$21.494 billion (2023 est.)
-$4.29 billion (2022 est.)
$6.645 billion (2021 est.)

note: balance of payments - net trade and primary/secondary income in current dollars
comparison ranking: 200

Exports: $83.359 billion (2023 est.)
$103.002 billion (2022 est.)
$87.486 billion (2021 est.)
note: balance of payments - exports of goods and services in current dollars
comparison ranking: 53

Exports - partners: Brazil 15%, China 9%, US 8%, Chile 6%, India 5% (2022)
note: top five export partners based on percentage share of exports

Exports - commodities: soybean meal, corn, soybean oil, wheat, trucks (2022)
note: top five export commodities based on value in dollars

Imports: $92.574 billion (2023 est.)
$97.558 billion (2022 est.)
$72.392 billion (2021 est.)
note: balance of payments - imports of goods and services in current dollars
comparison ranking: 50

Imports - partners: China 21%, Brazil 20%, US 14%, Germany 3%, Paraguay 2% (2022)
note: top five import partners based on percentage share of imports

Imports - commodities: refined petroleum, vehicle parts/accessories, natural gas, fertilizers, cars (2022)
note: top five import commodities based on value in dollars

Reserves of foreign exchange and gold: $23.081 billion (2023 est.)
$44.795 billion (2022 est.)
$39.653 billion (2021 est.)
note: holdings of gold (year-end prices)/foreign exchange/special drawing rights in current dollars
comparison ranking: 42

Debt - external: $77.88 billion (2022 est.)
note: present value of external debt in current US dollars
comparison ranking: 9

Exchange rates: Argentine pesos (ARS) per US dollar -

Exchange rates: 296.258 (2023 est.)
130.617 (2022 est.)
94.991 (2021 est.)
70.539 (2020 est.)
48.148 (2019 est.)

ENERGY

Electricity access: *electrification - total population:* 100% (2022 est.)

Electricity: *installed generating capacity:* 46.82 million kW (2022 est.)
consumption: 127.98 billion kWh (2022 est.)
exports: 31 million kWh (2022 est.)
imports: 12.909 billion kWh (2022 est.)
transmission/distribution losses: 29.877 billion kWh (2022 est.)
comparison rankings: transmission/distribution losses 197; imports 20; exports 92; consumption 30; installed generating capacity 29

Electricity generation sources: *fossil fuels:* 65.3% of total installed capacity (2022 est.)
nuclear: 5.2% of total installed capacity (2022 est.)
solar: 2% of total installed capacity (2022 est.)
wind: 9.7% of total installed capacity (2022 est.)
hydroelectricity: 16.4% of total installed capacity (2022 est.)
biomass and waste: 1.5% of total installed capacity (2022 est.)

Nuclear energy: Number of operational nuclear reactors: 3 (2023)

Number of nuclear reactors under construction: 1 (2023)

Net capacity of operational nuclear reactors: 1.64GW (2023 est.)

Percent of total electricity production: 6.3% (2023 est.)

Coal: *production:* 1.318 million metric tons (2022 est.)
consumption: 3.391 million metric tons (2022 est.)
exports: 8,000 metric tons (2022 est.)
imports: 2.196 million metric tons (2022 est.)
proven reserves: 799.999 million metric tons (2022 est.)

Petroleum: *total petroleum production:* 807,000 bbl/day (2023 est.)
refined petroleum consumption: 706,000 bbl/day (2022 est.)
crude oil estimated reserves: 2.483 billion barrels (2021 est.)

Natural gas: *production:* 43.28 billion cubic meters (2022 est.)
consumption: 46.228 billion cubic meters (2022 est.)
exports: 3.422 billion cubic meters (2022 est.)
imports: 6.229 billion cubic meters (2022 est.)
proven reserves: 396.464 billion cubic meters (2021 est.)

Carbon dioxide emissions: 185.37 million metric tonnes of CO2 (2022 est.)
from coal and metallurgical coke: 5.392 million metric tonnes of CO2 (2022 est.)
from petroleum and other liquids: 89.464 million metric tonnes of CO2 (2022 est.)
from consumed natural gas: 90.515 million metric tonnes of CO2 (2022 est.)
comparison ranking: total emissions 32

Energy consumption per capita: 75.735 million Btu/person (2022 est.)
comparison ranking: 68

COMMUNICATIONS

Telephones - fixed lines: *total subscriptions:* 7.615 million (2022 est.)
subscriptions per 100 inhabitants: 17 (2022 est.)
comparison ranking: total subscriptions 21

Telephones - mobile cellular: *total subscriptions:* 60.236 million (2022 est.)
subscriptions per 100 inhabitants: 132 (2022 est.)
comparison ranking: total subscriptions 27

Telecommunication systems: *general assessment:* Argentina's ongoing problem with hyperinflation continues to distort the telecom market's performance, which shows strong growth in revenue but only modest gains in subscriber numbers each year; the fixed broadband segment has penetration levels only slightly higher than the fixed-line teledensity; nearly a quarter of the country's broadband connections are via DSL, although fiber is starting claim an increasing share of that market as networks expand across most of the main cities; mobile broadband continues to be the preferred platform for internet access, supported by high mobile penetration levels and nationwide LTE coverage; the first 5G service was launched in February 2021 using refarmed LTE frequencies; the anticipated 5G spectrum auctions should drive even stronger uptake in mobile broadband services; while the various fixed, mobile, and cable operators push to expand and enhance their services, the government is also making an active contribution towards boosting broadband connectivity around the country; its national connectivity plan 'Plan Conectar', launched in September 2020, provides funding for a range of programs to increase coverage; in August 2021, the telecom regulator announced the release funding to help operators accelerate the rollout of their broadband infrastructure and services (2021)
domestic: roughly 15 per 100 fixed-line and 130 per 100 mobile-cellular; microwave radio relay, fiber-optic cable, and a domestic satellite system with 40 earth stations serve the trunk network (2021)
international: country code - 54; landing points for the UNISUR, Bicentenario, Atlantis-2, SAm-1, and SAC, Tannat, Malbec and ARBR submarine cable systems that provide links to Europe, Africa, South and Central America, and US; satellite earth stations - 112 (2019)

Broadcast media: government owns a TV station and radio network; more than two dozen TV stations and hundreds of privately owned radio stations; high rate of cable TV subscription usage (2022)

Internet country code: .ar

Internet users: *total:* 39.15 million (2021 est.)
percent of population: 87% (2021 est.)
comparison ranking: total 25

Broadband - fixed subscriptions: *total:* 9,571,562 (2020 est.)
subscriptions per 100 inhabitants: 21 (2020 est.)
comparison ranking: total 20

TRANSPORTATION

National air transport system: *number of registered air carriers:* 6 (2020)
inventory of registered aircraft operated by air carriers: 107
annual passenger traffic on registered air carriers: 18,081,937 (2018)
annual freight traffic on registered air carriers: 311.57 million (2018) mt-km

Civil aircraft registration country code prefix: LV

Airports: 756 (2024)
comparison ranking: 9

Heliports: 144 (2024)

Pipelines: 29,930 km gas, 41 km liquid petroleum gas, 6,248 km oil, 3,631 km refined products (2013)

Railways: *total:* 17,866 km (2018)
comparison ranking: total 16

Roadways: *total:* 240,000 km
paved: 81,355 km
unpaved: 158,645 km (2017)
comparison ranking: total 18

Waterways: 11,000 km (2012)
comparison ranking: 13

Merchant marine: *total:* 201 (2023)
by type: container ship 1, bulk carrier 1 general cargo 8, oil tanker 33, other 158
comparison ranking: total 66

Ports: *total ports:* 37 (2024)
large: 1
medium: 2

small: 10
very small: 24
ports with oil terminals: 19
key ports: Buenos Aires, Campana, Concepcion del Uruguay, La Plata, Mar del Plata, Puerto Belgrano, Puerto Ingeniero White, Puerto Madryn, Rosario, San Sebastian Bay, Santa Fe, Ushuaia, Zarate

MILITARY AND SECURITY

Military and security forces: Armed Forces of the Argentine Republic (Fuerzas Armadas de la República Argentina): Argentine Army (Ejercito Argentino, EA), Navy of the Argentine Republic (Armada Republica, ARA; includes naval aviation and naval infantry), Argentine Air Force (Fuerza Aerea Argentina, FAA)

Ministry of Security: Gendarmería Nacional Argentina (National Gendarmerie), Coast Guard (Prefectura Naval) (2024)
note: all federal police forces are under the Ministry of Security

Military expenditures: 0.8% of GDP (2024 est.)
0.5% of GDP (2023 est.)
0.6% of GDP (2022 est.)
0.8% of GDP (2021 est.)
0.8% of GDP (2020 est.)
comparison ranking: 139

Military and security service personnel strengths: approximately 80,000 active-duty personnel (50,000 Army; 17,000 Navy, including about 3,500 marines); 13,000 Air Force); estimated 20,000 Gendarmerie (2023)

Military equipment inventories and acquisitions: the inventory of Argentina's armed forces is a mix of domestically-produced and mostly older imported weapons, largely from Europe and the US; in recent years, France and the US have been the leading suppliers of equipment; Argentina has an indigenous defense industry that produces air, land, and naval systems (2024)

Military service age and obligation: 18-24 years of age for voluntary military service for men and women; conscription suspended in 1995; citizens can still be drafted in times of crisis, national emergency, or war, or if the Defense Ministry is unable to fill all vacancies to keep the military functional (2024)
note: as of 2023, women comprised nearly 20% of the active duty military

Military deployments: 325 Cyprus (UNFICYP) (2024)

Military - note: the Argentine military's primary responsibilities are territorial defense and protecting the country's sovereignty; other duties include border security, countering narcotics trafficking, and other internal missions, such as disaster response and infrastructure development; it also conducts support operations in Antarctica to promote an active presence in areas of national territory that are sparsely populated; the military participates in both bilateral and multinational training exercises and supports UN peacekeeping operations
Argentina participates in the Tripartite Command, an interagency security mechanism created by Argentina, Brazil, and Paraguay to exchange information and combat transnational threats, including terrorism, in the Tri-Border Area; in addition, Argentina and Chile have a joint peacekeeping force known as the Combined Southern Cross Peacekeeping Force (FPC), designed to be made available to the UN; the FPC is made up of infantry, command and control, air, naval, and logistics support elements; Argentina has Major Non-NATO Ally (MNNA) status with the US, a designation under US law that provides foreign partners with certain benefits in the areas of defense trade and security cooperation
the Army and Navy were both created in 1810 during the Argentine War of Independence, while the Air Force was established in 1945; the military conducted coups d'état in 1930, 1943, 1955, 1962, 1966, and 1976; the 1976 coup, aka the "National Reorganization Process," marked the beginning of the so-called "Dirty War," a period of state-sponsored terrorism that saw the deaths or disappearances of thousands of Argentinians; the defeat in the 1983 Falklands War led to the downfall of the military junta (2024)

SPACE

Space agency/agencies: Argentina National Space Activities Commission (Comision Nacional de Actividades Espaciales, CONAE; formed in 1991); CONAE's predecessor was the National Commission for Space Research (Comisión Nacional de Investigaciones Espaciales, CNIE; formed in 1960) (2024)

Space launch site(s): Manuel Belgrano Space Center (Buenos Aires province): planned launch platform of the Tronador SLV (see Appendix S); Punta Indio Space Center (Buenos Aires province): test facility; Teofilo Tabanera Space Center (CETT; Cordoba Province): testing, mission control site (2024)

Space program overview: has a long history of involvement in the development of space-related capabilities, including rockets and satellites; develops, builds, and operates communications, remote sensing (RS), and scientific satellites, often in partnership with other countries; developing additional satellites with more advanced payloads; has a national space plan; contracts with commercial and other government space agencies for launches but has a domestic rocket program and is developing space launch vehicle (SLV) capabilities; cooperates with a broad range of space agencies and industries, including those of Brazil, China, the European Space Agency and its member states (particularly France, Italy), and the US; also has a commercial space industry, which includes efforts to design, build, and launch reusable small SLVs (2024)
note: further details about the key activities, programs, and milestones of the country's space program, as well as government spending estimates on the space sector, appear in the Space Programs reference guide

TERRORISM

Terrorist group(s): Hizballah
note: details about the history, aims, leadership, organization, areas of operation, tactics, targets, weapons, size, and sources of support of the group(s) appear(s) in the Terrorism reference guide

TRANSNATIONAL ISSUES

Refugees and internally displaced persons: *refugees (country of origin):* 217,742 (Venezuela) (economic and political crisis; includes Venezuelans who have claimed asylum, are recognized as refugees, or have received alternative legal stay) (2023)

Illicit drugs: counterfeiting, drug trafficking, and other smuggling offenses in the Tri-Border area; some money laundering organizations in the TBA have may have links to the terrorist organization Hizballah; a large producer of chemical precursors

ARMENIA

INTRODUCTION

Background: Armenia prides itself on being the first state to formally adopt Christianity (early 4th century). Armenia has existed as a political entity for centuries, but for much of its history it was under the sway of various empires, including the Roman, Byzantine, Arab, Persian, Ottoman, and Russian. During World War I, the Ottoman Empire instituted a policy of forced resettlement that, coupled with other harsh practices targeting its Armenian subjects, resulted in at least 1 million deaths; these actions have been widely recognized as constituting genocide. During the early 19th century, significant Armenian populations fell under Russian rule. Armenia declared its independence in 1918 in the wake of the Bolshevik Revolution in Russia, but it was conquered by the Soviet Red Army in 1920. Armenia, along with Azerbaijan and Georgia, was initially incorporated into the USSR as part of the Transcaucasian Federated Soviet Socialist Republic; in 1936, the republic was separated into its three constituent entities, which were maintained until the dissolution of the Soviet Union in 1991.

For over three decades, Armenia had a longstanding conflict with neighboring Azerbaijan about the status of the Nagorno-Karabakh region, which historically had a mixed Armenian and Azerbaijani population, although ethnic Armenians have constituted the majority since the late 19th century. In 1921, Moscow placed Nagorno-Karabakh within Soviet Azerbaijan as an autonomous oblast. In the late Soviet period, a separatist movement developed that sought to end Azerbaijani control over the region. Fighting over Nagorno-Karabakh began in 1988 and escalated after Armenia and Azerbaijan declared independence from the Soviet Union in 1991. By the time a cease-fire took effect in 1994, separatists with Armenian support controlled Nagorno-Karabakh and seven surrounding Azerbaijani territories. Armenia and Azerbaijan engaged in a second military conflict over Nagorno-Karabakh in 2020; Armenia lost control over much of the territory it had previously captured, returning the southern part of Nagorno-Karabakh and the territories around it to Azerbaijan.

In September 2023, Azerbaijan took military action to regain control over Nagorno-Karabakh; after an armed conflict that lasted only one day, nearly the entire ethnic Armenian population of Nagorno-Karabakh fled to Armenia.

Turkey closed its border with Armenia in 1993 in support of Azerbaijan during the first period of conflict with Armenia and has since maintained a closed border, leaving Armenia with closed borders both in the west (with Turkey) and east (with Azerbaijan). Armenia and Turkey engaged in intensive diplomacy to normalize relations and open the border in 2009, but the signed agreement was not ratified in either country. In 2015, Armenia joined the Eurasian Economic Union alongside Russia, Belarus, Kazakhstan, and Kyrgyzstan. In 2017, Armenia signed a Comprehensive and Enhanced Partnership Agreement (CEPA) with the EU.

In 2018, former President of Armenia (2008-18) Serzh SARGSIAN of the Republican Party of Armenia (RPA) tried to extend his time in power, prompting protests that became known as the "Velvet Revolution." After SARGSIAN resigned, the National Assembly elected the leader of the protests, Civil Contract party chief Nikol PASHINYAN, as the new prime minister. PASHINYAN's party has prevailed in subsequent legislative elections, most recently in 2021.

GEOGRAPHY

Location: Southwestern Asia, between Turkey (to the west) and Azerbaijan; note - Armenia views itself as part of Europe; geopolitically, it can be classified as falling within Europe, the Middle East, or both

Geographic coordinates: 40 00 N, 45 00 E

Map references: Asia

Area: *total:* 29,743 sq km
land: 28,203 sq km
water: 1,540 sq km
comparison ranking: total 142

Area - comparative: slightly smaller than Maryland

Land boundaries: *total:* 1,570 km
border countries (4): Azerbaijan 996 km; Georgia 219 km; Iran 44 km; Turkey 311 km

Coastline: 0 km (landlocked)

Maritime claims: none (landlocked)

Climate: highland continental, hot summers, cold winters

Terrain: Armenian Highland with mountains; little forest land; fast flowing rivers; good soil in Aras River valley

Elevation: *highest point:* Aragats Lerrnagagat' 4,090 m
lowest point: Debed River 400 m
mean elevation: 1,792 m

Natural resources: small deposits of gold, copper, molybdenum, zinc, bauxite

Land use: *agricultural land:* 59.7% (2018 est.)
arable land: 15.8% (2018 est.)
permanent crops: 1.9% (2018 est.)
permanent pasture: 42% (2018 est.)
forest: 9.1% (2018 est.)
other: 31.2% (2018 est.)

Irrigated land: 1,554 sq km (2020)

Major lakes (area sq km): *fresh water lake(s):* Lake Sevan - 1,360 sq km

Population distribution: most of the population is located in the northern half of the country; the capital of Yerevan is home to more than five times as many people as Gyumri, the second largest city in the country

Natural hazards: occasionally severe earthquakes; droughts

Geography - note: landlocked in the Lesser Caucasus Mountains; Sevana Lich (Lake Sevan) is the largest lake in this mountain range

PEOPLE AND SOCIETY

Population: *total:* 2,976,765
male: 1,456,415
female: 1,520,350 (2024 est.)
comparison rankings: female 138; male 139; total 139

Nationality: *noun:* Armenian(s)
adjective: Armenian

Ethnic groups: Armenian 98.1%, Yezidi 1.1%, other 0.8% (2022 est.)

Languages: Armenian (official) 97.9%, Kurmanji (spoken by Yezidi minority) 1%, other 1.1%; note - Russian is widely spoken (2011 est.)
major-language sample(s):
Աշխարհի Փաստագիրք, Անփոխարինելի Աղբյուր Հիմնական Տեղեկատվության. (Armenian)

Religions: Armenian Apostolic Christian 95.2%, other Christian 1.6%, other 0.9%, none 0.6%, unspecified 1.7% (2022 est.)

Demographic profile: Armenia's population peaked at nearly 3.7 million in the late 1980s but has declined sharply since independence in 1991, to just over 3 million in 2021, largely as a result of its decreasing fertility rate, increasing death rate, and negative net emigration rate. The total fertility rate (the average number of children born per woman) first fell below the 2.1 replacement level in the late 1990s and has hovered around 1.6-1.65 for over 15 years. In an effort to increase the country's birth rate, the government has expanded its child benefits, including a substantial increase in the lump sum payment for having a first and second child and a boost in the monthly payment to mothers of children under two. Reversing net negative migration, however, remains the biggest obstacle to stabilizing or increasing population growth. Emigration causes Armenia not only lose individuals but also the children they might have.
The emigration of a significant number of working-age people combined with decreased fertility and increased life expectancy is causing the elderly share of Armenia's population to grow. The growing elderly population will put increasing pressure on the government's ability to fund the pension system, health care, and other services for seniors. Improving education, creating more jobs (particularly in the formal sector), promoting labor market participation, and increasing productivity would mitigate the financial impact of supporting a growing elderly population.
Armenia has a long history of migration, some forced and some voluntary. Its large diaspora is diverse and dispersed around the world. Widely varying estimates suggest the Armenian diaspora may number anywhere from 5-9 million, easily outnumbering the number of Armenians living in Armenia. Armenians forged communities abroad from ancient Egypt, Greece and Rome to Russia and to the Americas, where they excelled as craftsmen, merchants, and in other occupations.
Several waves of Armenian migration occurred in the 20th century. In the aftermath of the 1915 Armenian genocide, hundreds of thousands of survivors fled to communities in the Caucasus (including present day Armenia), Lebanon, Syria, Iran, Europe, and Russia and established new communities in Africa and the Americas. In the 1930s, the Soviets deported thousands of Armenians to Siberia and Central Asia. After World War II, the Soviets encouraged the Armenian diaspora in France, the Middle East, and Iran to return the Armenian homeland in order to encourage population growth after significant losses in the male workforce during the war.
Following Armenian independence in 1991, the economic downturn and high unemployment prompted hundreds of thousands of Armenians to seek better economic opportunities primarily in Russia but also in the US, former Soviet states, and Europe. In the early 1990s, hundreds of thousands of Armenians fled from Azerbaijan to Armenia because of the ongoing Nagorno-Karbakh conflict, but many of them then emigrated again, mainly to Russia and the US. When the economy became more stable in the late 1990s, permanent emigration slowed, but Armenians continued to seek temporary seasonal work in Russia. The remittances families receive from relatives working abroad is vital to Armenian households and the country's economy.

Age structure: *0-14 years:* 17.7% (male 275,589/female 250,630)
15-64 years: 67% (male 991,490/female 1,004,101)
65 years and over: 15.3% (2024 est.) (male 189,336/female 265,619)

Dependency ratios: *total dependency ratio:* 49.6
youth dependency ratio: 30.6
elderly dependency ratio: 19.1
potential support ratio: 5.2 (2021 est.)

Median age: *total:* 38.9 years (2024 est.)
male: 37.6 years
female: 40.3 years
comparison ranking: total 70

Population growth rate: -0.42% (2024 est.)
comparison ranking: 217

Birth rate: 10.5 births/1,000 population (2024 est.)
comparison ranking: 177

Death rate: 9.6 deaths/1,000 population (2024 est.)
comparison ranking: 42

Net migration rate: -5.2 migrant(s)/1,000 population (2024 est.)

comparison ranking: 204

Population distribution: most of the population is located in the northern half of the country; the capital of Yerevan is home to more than five times as many people as Gyumri, the second largest city in the country

Urbanization: *urban population:* 63.7% of total population (2023)
rate of urbanization: 0.23% annual rate of change (2020-25 est.)

Major urban areas - population: 1.095 million YEREVAN (capital) (2023)

Sex ratio: *at birth:* 1.07 male(s)/female
0-14 years: 1.1 male(s)/female
15-64 years: 0.99 male(s)/female
65 years and over: 0.71 male(s)/female
total population: 0.96 male(s)/female (2024 est.)

Mother's mean age at first birth: 25.2 years (2019 est.)

Maternal mortality ratio: 27 deaths/100,000 live births (2020 est.)
comparison ranking: 116

Infant mortality rate: *total:* 11.6 deaths/1,000 live births (2024 est.)
male: 13.1 deaths/1,000 live births
female: 10 deaths/1,000 live births
comparison ranking: total 115

Life expectancy at birth: *total population:* 76.7 years (2024 est.)
male: 73.4 years
female: 80.1 years
comparison ranking: total population 102

Total fertility rate: 1.65 children born/woman (2024 est.)
comparison ranking: 172

Gross reproduction rate: 0.8 (2024 est.)

Contraceptive prevalence rate: 57.1% (2015/16)

Drinking water source: *improved:*
total: 100% of population
unimproved:
total: 0% of population (2020 est.)

Current health expenditure: 12.2% of GDP (2020)

Physician density: 4.4 physicians/1,000 population (2017)

Hospital bed density: 4.2 beds/1,000 population (2014)

Sanitation facility access: *improved: urban:* 100% of population
rural: 84.6% of population
total: 94.4% of population
unimproved: urban: 0% of population
rural: 15.4% of population
total: 5.6% of population (2020 est.)

Obesity - adult prevalence rate: 20.2% (2016)
comparison ranking: 101

Alcohol consumption per capita: *total:* 3.77 liters of pure alcohol (2019 est.)
beer: 0.52 liters of pure alcohol (2019 est.)
wine: 0.46 liters of pure alcohol (2019 est.)
spirits: 2.78 liters of pure alcohol (2019 est.)
other alcohols: 0.01 liters of pure alcohol (2019 est.)
comparison ranking: total 99

Tobacco use: *total:* 25.5% (2020 est.)
male: 49.4% (2020 est.)
female: 1.5% (2020 est.)
comparison ranking: total 45

Children under the age of 5 years underweight: 2.6% (2015/16)
comparison ranking: 95

Currently married women (ages 15-49): 64.8% (2023 est.)

Child marriage: *women married by age 15:* 0%
women married by age 18: 5.3%
men married by age 18: 0.4% (2016 est.)

Education expenditures: 2.8% of GDP (2021 est.)
comparison ranking: 167

Literacy: *definition:* age 15 and over can read and write
total population: 99.8%
male: 99.8%
female: 99.7% (2020)

School life expectancy (primary to tertiary education): *total:* 13 years
male: 13 years
female: 14 years (2021)

ENVIRONMENT

Environment - current issues: soil pollution from toxic chemicals such as DDT; deforestation; pollution of Hrazdan and Aras Rivers; the draining of Sevana Lich (Lake Sevan), a result of its use as a source for hydropower, threatens drinking water supplies; restart of Metsamor nuclear power plant in spite of its location in a seismically active zone

Environment - international agreements: *party to:* Air Pollution, Biodiversity, Climate Change, Climate Change-Kyoto Protocol, Climate Change-Paris Agreement, Comprehensive Nuclear Test Ban, Desertification, Endangered Species, Environmental Modification, Hazardous Wastes, Law of the Sea, Nuclear Test Ban, Ozone Layer Protection, Wetlands
signed, but not ratified: Air Pollution-Heavy Metals, Air Pollution-Multi-effect Protocol, Air Pollution-Persistent Organic Pollutants

Climate: highland continental, hot summers, cold winters

Urbanization: *urban population:* 63.7% of total population (2023)
rate of urbanization: 0.23% annual rate of change (2020-25 est.)

Revenue from forest resources: 0.28% of GDP (2018 est.)
comparison ranking: 82

Revenue from coal: 0% of GDP (2018 est.)
comparison ranking: 101

Air pollutants: *particulate matter emissions:* 34.13 micrograms per cubic meter (2019 est.)
carbon dioxide emissions: 5.16 megatons (2016 est.)
methane emissions: 2.91 megatons (2020 est.)

Waste and recycling: *municipal solid waste generated annually:* 492,800 tons (2014 est.)

Major lakes (area sq km): *fresh water lake(s):* Lake Sevan - 1,360 sq km

Total water withdrawal: *municipal:* 650 million cubic meters (2020 est.)
industrial: 190 million cubic meters (2020 est.)
agricultural: 1.99 billion cubic meters (2020 est.)

Total renewable water resources: 7.77 billion cubic meters (2020 est.)

GOVERNMENT

Country name: *conventional long form:* Republic of Armenia
conventional short form: Armenia
local long form: Hayastani Hanrapetut'yun
local short form: Hayastan
former: Armenian Soviet Socialist Republic, Armenian Republic
etymology: the etymology of the country's name remains obscure; according to tradition, the country is named after Hayk, the legendary patriarch of the Armenians and the great-great-grandson of Noah; Hayk's descendant, Aram, purportedly is the source of the name Armenia

Government type: parliamentary democracy; note - constitutional changes adopted in December 2015 transformed the government to a parliamentary system

Capital: *name:* Yerevan
geographic coordinates: 40 10 N, 44 30 E
time difference: UTC+4 (9 hours ahead of Washington, DC, during Standard Time)
etymology: name likely derives from the ancient Urartian fortress of Erebuni established on the current site of Yerevan in 782 B.C. and whose impressive ruins still survive

Administrative divisions: 11 provinces (marzer, singular - marz); Aragatsotn, Ararat, Armavir, Geghark'unik', Kotayk', Lorri, Shirak, Syunik', Tavush, Vayots' Dzor, Yerevan

Independence: *21 September 1991 (from the Soviet Union); notable earlier dates:* 321 B.C. (Kingdom of Armenia established under the Orontid Dynasty), A.D. 884 (Armenian Kingdom reestablished under the Bagratid Dynasty); 1198 (Cilician Kingdom established); 28 May 1918 (Democratic Republic of Armenia declared)

National holiday: Independence Day, 21 September (1991)

Legal system: civil law system

Constitution: *history:* previous 1915, 1978; latest adopted 5 July 1995
amendments:
proposed by the president of the republic or by the National Assembly; passage requires approval by the president, by the National Assembly, and by a referendum with at least 25% registered voter participation and more than 50% of votes; constitutional articles on the form of government and democratic procedures are not amendable; amended 2005, 2015, last in 2020; the Constitutional Reform Council formed in 2019 was dissolved in December 2021, and replaced by a new Constitutional Reform Council, whose members were officially appointed in late January 2022; the new council is expected to address the form of government, i.e. presidential or semi-presidential or parliamentary, and whether to merge the Court of Cassation with the Constitutional Court

International law organization participation: has not submitted an ICJ jurisdiction declaration; non-party state to the ICCt

Citizenship: *citizenship by birth:* no
citizenship by descent only: at least one parent must be a citizen of Armenia
dual citizenship recognized: yes
residency requirement for naturalization: 3 years

Suffrage: 18 years of age; universal

Executive branch: *chief of state:* President Vahagn KHACHATURYAN (since 13 March 2022)
head of government: Prime Minister Nikol PASHINYAN (since 10 September 2021)

cabinet: Council of Ministers appointed by the prime minister
elections/appointments: president indirectly elected by the National Assembly in 3 rounds if needed for a single 7-year term; election last held on 2 and 3 March 2022 (next election to be held in 2029); prime minister indirectly elected by majority vote in two rounds if needed by the National Assembly
election results:
2022: Vahagn KHACHATURYAN elected president in second round; note - Vahagn KHACHATURYAN (independent) ran unopposed and won the Assembly vote 71-0
2018: Armen SARKISSIAN elected president in first round; note - Armen SARKISSIAN (indpendent) ran unopposed and won the Assembly vote 90-10
note: Nikol PASHINYAN was first elected prime minister on 8 May 2018 and reelected on January 2019; in response to a political crisis that followed Armenia's defeat in the Second Nagorno-Karabakh War in late 2020, PASHINYAN called an early legislative election for 21 June 2021; his party won the election and PASHINYAN was elected prime minister for a third time; his election was confirmed by the president on 2 August 2021, and he was sworn in on 10 September 2021

Legislative branch: *description:* unicameral National Assembly (Parliament) or Azgayin Zhoghov (minimum 101 seats, with additional seats allocated as necessary and generally changing with each parliamentary convocation; current - 107 seats; members directly elected in single-seat constituencies by closed party-list proportional representation vote; members serve 5-year terms; four mandates are reserved for national minorities; no more than 70% of the top membership of a party list can belong to the same sex; political parties must meet a 5% threshold and alliances a 7% threshold to win seats; at least three parties must be seated in the Parliament)
elections: last held early on 20 June 2021 (next to be held in June 2026)
election results: percent of vote by party/coalition - Civil Contract 53.9%, Armenia Alliance 21%, I Have Honour Alliance 5.2%, other 19.9%; seats by party/coalition - Civil Contract 71, Armenia Alliance 29, I Have Honour Alliance 7; composition - men 68, women 39, percentage women 36.5%
note 1: additional seats allocated as necessary; the numbers usually change with each parliamentary convocation
note 2: four mandates are reserved for national minorities; no more than 70% of the top membership of a party list can belong to the same sex; political parties must meet a 5% threshold and alliances a 7% threshold to win seats; at least three parties must be seated in the Parliament

Judicial branch: *highest court(s):* Court of Cassation or Appeals Court (consists of the Criminal Chamber with a chairman and 5 judges and the Civil and Administrative Chamber with a chairman and 10 judges – with both civil and administrative specializations); Constitutional Court (consists of 9 judges)
judge selection and term of office: Court of Cassation judges nominated by the Supreme Judicial Council, a 10- member body of selected judges and legal scholars; judges appointed by the president; judges can serve until age 65; Constitutional Court judges - 4 appointed by the president, and 5 elected by the National Assembly; judges can serve until age 70
subordinate courts: criminal and civil appellate courts; administrative appellate court; first instance courts; specialized administrative and bankruptcy courts

Political parties: Armenia Alliance or HD
Armenian National Congress or ANC
Bright Armenia
Civil Contract or KP
Country To Live In
Homeland of Armenians
Homeland Party
I Have Honor Alliance (formerly known as the Republican Party of Armenia) PUD
Liberal Party
National Democratic Party
Prosperous Armenia or BHK
Republic Party (Hanrapetutyun Party)

International organization participation: ADB, BSEC, CD, CE, CIS, CSTO, EAEC (observer), EAEU, EAPC, EBRD, FAO, GCTU, IAEA, IBRD, ICAO, ICC, ICRM, IDA, IFAD, IFC, IFRCS, ILO, IMF, Interpol, IOC, IOM, IPU, ISO, ITSO, ITU, MIGA, NAM (observer), OAS (observer), OIF, OPCW, OSCE, PFP, UN, UNCTAD, UNESCO, UNIDO, UNIFIL, UNOOSA, UNWTO, UPU, WCO, WFTU (NGOs), WHO, WIPO, WMO, WTO

Diplomatic representation in the US: *chief of mission:* Ambassador Lilit MAKUNTS (since 15 September 2021)
chancery: 2225 R Street NW, Washington, DC 20008
telephone: [1] (202) 319-1976
FAX: [1] (202) 319-2982
email address and website: armembassyusa@mfa.am
https://usa.mfa.am/en/
consulate(s) general: Glendale (CA)

Diplomatic representation from the US: *chief of mission:* Ambassador Kristina A. KVIEN (since 21 February 2023)
embassy:
1 American Ave., Yerevan 0082
mailing address: 7020 Yerevan Place, Washington, DC 20521-7020
telephone: [374] (10) 464-700
FAX: [374] (10) 464-742
email address and website: acsyerevan@state.gov
https://am.usembassy.gov/

Flag description: three equal horizontal bands of red (top), blue, and orange; the color red recalls the blood shed for liberty, blue the Armenian skies as well as hope, and orange the land and the courage of the workers who farm it

National symbol(s): Mount Ararat, eagle, lion; national colors: red, blue, orange

National anthem: *name:* "Mer Hayrenik" (Our Fatherland)
lyrics/music: Mikael NALBANDIAN/Barsegh KANACHYAN
note: adopted 1991; based on the anthem of the Democratic Republic of Armenia (1918-1922) but with different lyrics

National heritage: *total World Heritage Sites:* 3 (3 cultural)
selected World Heritage Site locales: Monasteries of Haghpat and Sanahin; Monastery of Geghard and the Upper Azat Valley; Cathedral and Churches of Echmiatsin

ECONOMY

Economic overview: EEU-and CIS-member state but seeking more EU and US trade; business-friendly growth environments; stable monetary regime but vulnerable demand economy; key copper and gold exporter; persistent unemployment; large diaspora and remittances

Real GDP (purchasing power parity): $57.728 billion (2023 est.)
$53.108 billion (2022 est.)
$47.165 billion (2021 est.)
note: data in 2021 dollars
comparison ranking: 116

Real GDP growth rate: 8.7% (2023 est.)
12.6% (2022 est.)
5.8% (2021 est.)
note: annual GDP % growth based on constant local currency
comparison ranking: 7

Real GDP per capita: $20,800 (2023 est.)
$19,100 (2022 est.)
$16,900 (2021 est.)
note: data in 2021 dollars
comparison ranking: 100

GDP (official exchange rate): $24.212 billion (2023 est.)
note: data in current dollars at official exchange rate

Inflation rate (consumer prices): 1.98% (2023 est.)
8.64% (2022 est.)
7.18% (2021 est.)
note: annual % change based on consumer prices
comparison ranking: 35

Credit ratings: Fitch rating: B+ (2020)

Moody's rating: Ba3 (2019)
note: The year refers to the year in which the current credit rating was first obtained.

GDP - composition, by sector of origin: *agriculture:* 8.4% (2023 est.)
industry: 23.9% (2023 est.)
services: 59% (2023 est.)
note: figures may not total 100% due to non-allocated consumption not captured in sector-reported data comparison rankings: services 92; industry 108; agriculture 87

GDP - composition, by end use: *household consumption:* 65.3% (2023 est.)
government consumption: 14.1% (2023 est.)
investment in fixed capital: 20.8% (2023 est.)
investment in inventories: 0.6% (2023 est.)
exports of goods and services: 58.2% (2023 est.)
imports of goods and services: -58.9% (2023 est.)
note: figures may not total 100% due to rounding or gaps in data collection

Agricultural products: milk, potatoes, grapes, tomatoes, vegetables, wheat, watermelons, apricots, apples, barley (2022)
note: top ten agricultural products based on tonnage

Industries: brandy, mining, diamond processing, metal-cutting machine tools, forging and pressing machines, electric motors, knitted wear, hosiery, shoes, silk fabric, chemicals, trucks, instruments, microelectronics, jewelry, software, food processing

Industrial production growth rate: 5.51% (2023 est.)
note: annual % change in industrial value added based on constant local currency
comparison ranking: 46

Labor force: 1.356 million (2023 est.)

note: number of people ages 15 or older who are employed or seeking work
comparison ranking: 141

Unemployment rate: 8.59% (2023 est.)
8.61% (2022 est.)
10.01% (2021 est.)
note: % of labor force seeking employment
comparison ranking: 151

Youth unemployment rate (ages 15-24): *total:* 19% (2023 est.)
male: 21.5% (2023 est.)
female: 16% (2023 est.)
note: % of labor force ages 15-24 seeking employment
comparison ranking: total 71

Population below poverty line: 24.8% (2022 est.)
note: % of population with income below national poverty line

Gini Index coefficient - distribution of family income: 27.9 (2022 est.)
note: index (0-100) of income distribution; higher values represent greater inequality
comparison ranking: 137

Household income or consumption by percentage share: *lowest 10%:* 3.9% (2022 est.)
highest 10%: 23% (2022 est.)
note: % share of income accruing to lowest and highest 10% of population

Remittances: 7.64% of GDP (2023 est.)
10.43% of GDP (2022 est.)
11.22% of GDP (2021 est.)
note: personal transfers and compensation between resident and non-resident individuals/households/entities

Budget: *revenues:* $4.617 billion (2022 est.)
expenditures: $4.13 billion (2022 est.)
note: central government revenues (excluding grants) and expenses converted to US dollars at average official exchange rate for year indicated

Public debt: 46.55% of GDP (2022 est.)
note: central government debt as a % of GDP
comparison ranking: 118

Taxes and other revenues: 21.83% (of GDP) (2022 est.)
note: central government tax revenue as a % of GDP
comparison ranking: 67

Current account balance: -$510.104 million (2023 est.)
$150.994 million (2022 est.)
-$482.982 million (2021 est.)
note: balance of payments - net trade and primary/secondary income in current dollars
comparison ranking: 122

Exports: $14.13 billion (2023 est.)
$10.038 billion (2022 est.)
$5.012 billion (2021 est.)
note: balance of payments - exports of goods and services in current dollars
comparison ranking: 101

Exports - partners: Russia 41%, UAE 9%, China 7%, Georgia 4%, Switzerland 4% (2022)
note: top five export partners based on percentage share of exports

Exports - commodities: copper ore, gold, diamonds, tobacco, iron alloys (2022)
note: top five export commodities based on value in dollars

Imports: $14.279 billion (2023 est.)
$10.186 billion (2022 est.)
$6.12 billion (2021 est.)
note: balance of payments - imports of goods and services in current dollars
comparison ranking: 106

Imports - partners: Russia 23%, UAE 19%, China 10%, Georgia 5%, Iran 5% (2022)
note: top five import partners based on percentage share of imports

Imports - commodities: postage stamps/documents, cars, broadcasting equipment, refined petroleum, natural gas (2022)
note: top five import commodities based on value in dollars

Reserves of foreign exchange and gold: $3.607 billion (2023 est.)
$4.112 billion (2022 est.)
$3.23 billion (2021 est.)
note: holdings of gold (year-end prices)/foreign exchange/special drawing rights in current dollars
comparison ranking: 117

Debt - external: $6.028 billion (2022 est.)
note: present value of external debt in current US dollars
comparison ranking: 49

Exchange rates: drams (AMD) per US dollar -

Exchange rates: 392.476 (2023 est.)
435.666 (2022 est.)
503.77 (2021 est.)
489.009 (2020 est.)
480.445 (2019 est.)

ENERGY

Electricity access: *electrification - total population:* 100% (2022 est.)

Electricity: *installed generating capacity:* 3.893 million kW (2022 est.)
consumption: 7.393 billion kWh (2022 est.)
exports: 1.12 billion kWh (2022 est.)
imports: 362.079 million kWh (2022 est.)
transmission/distribution losses: 621.552 million kWh (2022 est.)
comparison rankings: transmission/distribution losses 86; imports 99; exports 66; consumption 116; installed generating capacity 100

Electricity generation sources: *fossil fuels:* 43.4% of total installed capacity (2022 est.)
nuclear: 30% of total installed capacity (2022 est.)
solar: 3.8% of total installed capacity (2022 est.)
hydroelectricity: 22.8% of total installed capacity (2022 est.)

Nuclear energy: Number of operational nuclear reactors: 1 (2023)

Net capacity of operational nuclear reactors: 0.42GW (2023 est.)

Percent of total electricity production: 31.1% (2023 est.)

Number of nuclear reactors permanently shut down: 1 (2023)

Coal: *production:* 60 metric tons (2022 est.)
consumption: 23,000 metric tons (2022 est.)
exports: 32.3 metric tons (2022 est.)
imports: 47,000 metric tons (2022 est.)
proven reserves: 317 million metric tons (2022 est.)

Petroleum: *refined petroleum consumption:* 14,000 bbl/day (2022 est.)

Natural gas: *consumption:* 2.861 billion cubic meters (2022 est.)
imports: 2.861 billion cubic meters (2022 est.)

Carbon dioxide emissions: 7.344 million metric tonnes of CO2 (2022 est.)
from coal and metallurgical coke: 62,000 metric tonnes of CO2 (2022 est.)
from petroleum and other liquids: 1.669 million metric tonnes of CO2 (2022 est.)
from consumed natural gas: 5.613 million metric tonnes of CO2 (2022 est.)
comparison ranking: total emissions 120

Energy consumption per capita: 60.957 million Btu/person (2022 est.)
comparison ranking: 78

COMMUNICATIONS

Telephones - fixed lines: *total subscriptions:* 366,000 (2022 est.)
subscriptions per 100 inhabitants: 13 (2022 est.)
comparison ranking: total subscriptions 102

Telephones - mobile cellular: *total subscriptions:* 3.761 million (2022 est.)
subscriptions per 100 inhabitants: 135 (2022 est.)
comparison ranking: total subscriptions 138

Telecommunication systems: *general assessment:* the telecom sector was able to post modest gains in the mobile and broadband segments; fixed-line services continue to decrease with the rollout of fiber networks; the fixed broadband market remains undeveloped due to the lack of infrastructure outside the main cities; mobile broadband is expected increase by 2026
(2024)
domestic: roughly 13 per 100 fixed-line and 135 per 100 mobile-cellular; reliable fixed-line and mobile-cellular services are available across Yerevan and in major cities and towns; mobile-cellular coverage available in most rural areas (2022)
international: country code - 374; Yerevan is connected to the Caucasus Cable System fiber-optic cable through Georgia and Iran to Europe; additional international service is available by microwave radio relay and landline connections to the other countries of the Commonwealth of Independent States, through the Moscow international switch, and by satellite to the rest of the world; satellite earth stations - 3 (2019)

Broadcast media: Armenia's government-run Public Television network operates alongside 100 privately owned TV stations that provide local to near nationwide coverage; three Russian TV companies are broadcast in Armenia under interstate agreements; subscription cable TV services are available in most regions; several major international broadcasters are available, including CNN; Armenian TV completed conversion from analog to digital broadcasting in late 2016; Public Radio of Armenia is a national, state-run broadcast network that operates alongside 18 privately owned radio stations
(2019)

Internet country code: .am

Internet users: *total:* 2.212 million (2021 est.)
percent of population: 79% (2021 est.)
comparison ranking: total 133

Broadband - fixed subscriptions: *total:* 430,407 (2020 est.)
subscriptions per 100 inhabitants: 15 (2020 est.)
comparison ranking: total 95

TRANSPORTATION

National air transport system: *number of registered air carriers:* 3 (2020)
inventory of registered aircraft operated by air carriers: 5

Civil aircraft registration country code prefix: EK

Airports: 11 (2024)
comparison ranking: 154

Heliports: 1 (2024)

Pipelines: 3,838 km gas (high and medium pressure) (2017)

Railways: *total:* 686 km (2017)
comparison ranking: total 101

Roadways: *total:* 7,700 km (2019)
urban: 3,780 km
non-urban: 3,920 km
comparison ranking: total 142

MILITARY AND SECURITY

Military and security forces: Armenian Republic Armed Forces: Armenian Army (includes land, air, air defense forces) (2024)
note: the Police of the Republic of Armenia is responsible for internal security, while the National Security Service is responsible for national security, intelligence activities, and border control

Military expenditures: 5.3% of GDP (2024 est.)
5.6% of GDP (2023 est.)
4.3% of GDP (2022 est.)
4.4% of GDP (2021 est.)
5% of GDP (2020 est.)
comparison ranking: 7

Military and security service personnel strengths: approximately 45,000 active troops (42,000 ground; 3,000 air/defense) (2023)

Military equipment inventories and acquisitions: the military's inventory includes mostly Russian and Soviet-era equipment; in recent years however, Armenia has looked to other countries besides Russia to provide military hardware, including France and India (2024)

Military service age and obligation: 18-27 for voluntary (men and women), contract (men and women) or compulsory (men) military service; contract military service is 3-12 months or 3 or 5 years; conscripts serve 24 months; men under the age of 36, who have not previously served as contract servicemen and are registered in the reserve, as well as women, regardless of whether they are registered in the reserve can be enrolled in contractual military service; all citizens aged 27 to 50 are registered in the military reserve and may be called to serve if mobilization is declared (2023)
note: in 2023, Armenia approved six-month voluntary service for women, after which they have the option to switch to a five-year contract; previously, women served on a contract basis; as of 2021, women made up about 10% of the active duty military

Military - note: the Armenian Armed Forces were officially established in 1992, although their origins go back to 1918; the modern military's missions include deterrence, territorial defense, crisis management, humanitarian assistance, and disaster response, as well as socio-economic development projects; territorial defense is its primary focus, particularly in regards to tensions with neighboring Azerbaijan; Armenia and Azerbaijan engaged in open conflicts over the Nagorno-Karabakh enclave in 1991-94 and 2020; Azerbaijan seized the entire enclave in 2023
Armenia has traditionally had close military ties with Russia and has hosted Russian military forces; it also had been a member of the Russian-led Collective Security Treaty Organization (CSTO) since 1994 and committed troops to CSTO's rapid reaction force until suspending its membership in 2024; Armenia has relations with NATO going back to 1992 when Armenia joined the North Atlantic Cooperation Council; in 1994, it joined NATO's Partnership for Peace program and has contributed to the NATO force in Kosovo, as well as the former NATO deployment in Afghanistan (2024)

TRANSNATIONAL ISSUES

Refugees and internally displaced persons: *refugees (country of origin):* 27,929 (Azerbaijan) (mid-year 2022)
IDPs: 8,400 (2022)
stateless persons: 816 (2022)

Illicit drugs: a transit country for illicit drugs with its location between source countries Afghanistan and Iran and the markets of Europe and Russia.

ARUBA

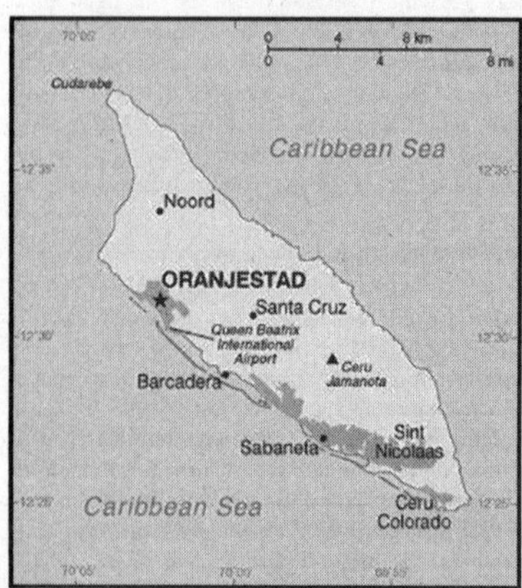

INTRODUCTION

Background: Discovered and claimed for Spain in 1499, Aruba was acquired by the Dutch in 1636. Three main industries have since dominated the island's economy: gold mining, oil refining, and tourism. A 19th-century gold rush was followed by prosperity brought on by the opening of an oil refinery in 1924. The last decades of the 20th century saw a boom in the tourism industry. Aruba seceded from the Netherlands Antilles in 1986 and became a separate, semi-autonomous member of the Kingdom of the Netherlands. Movement toward full independence was halted at Aruba's request in 1990.

GEOGRAPHY

Location: Caribbean, island in the Caribbean Sea, north of Venezuela

Geographic coordinates: 12 30 N, 69 58 W

Map references: Central America and the Caribbean

Area: *total:* 180 sq km
land: 180 sq km
water: 0 sq km
comparison ranking: total 218

Area - comparative: slightly larger than Washington, DC

Land boundaries: *total:* 0 km

Coastline: 68.5 km

Maritime claims: *territorial sea:* 12 nm
exclusive economic zone: 200 nm

Climate: tropical marine; little seasonal temperature variation

Terrain: flat with a few hills; scant vegetation

Elevation: *highest point:* Ceru Jamanota 188 m
lowest point: Caribbean Sea 0 m

Natural resources: NEGL; white sandy beaches foster tourism

Land use: *agricultural land:* 11.1% (2018 est.)
arable land: 11.1% (2018 est.)
permanent crops: 0% (2018 est.)
permanent pasture: 0% (2018 est.)
forest: 2.3% (2018 est.)
other: 86.6% (2018 est.)

Irrigated land: NA

Population distribution: most residents live in or around Oranjestad and San Nicolaas; most settlments tend to be located on the less mountainous western side of the island

Natural hazards: hurricanes; lies outside the Caribbean hurricane belt and is rarely threatened

Geography - note: a flat, riverless island renowned for its white sand beaches; its tropical climate is moderated by constant trade winds from the Atlantic Ocean; the temperature is almost constant at about 27 degrees Celsius (81 degrees Fahrenheit)

PEOPLE AND SOCIETY

Population: *total:* 125,063
male: 59,101
female: 65,962 (2024 est.)
comparison rankings: female 188; male 188; total 188

Nationality: *noun:* Aruban(s)
adjective: Aruban; Dutch

Ethnic groups: Dutch 78.7%, Colombian 6.6%, Venezuelan 5.5%, Dominican 2.8%, Haitian 1.3%, other 5.1% (2020 est.)
note: data represent population by nationality

Languages: Papiamento (official) (a creole language that mixes Portuguese, Spanish, Dutch, English,

French, African languages, and Arawak) 69.4%, Spanish 13.7%, English (widely spoken) 7.1%, Dutch (official) 6.1%, Chinese 1.5%, other 1.7%, unspecified 0.4% (2010 est.)

Religions: Roman Catholic 75.3%, Protestant 4.9% (includes Methodist 0.9%, Adventist 0.9%, Anglican 0.4%, other Protestant 2.7%), Jehovah's Witness 1.7%, other 12%, none 5.5%, unspecified 0.5% (2010 est.)

Age structure: *0-14 years:* 17.2% (male 10,815/female 10,747)
15-64 years: 65.7% (male 39,621/female 42,487)
65 years and over: 17.1% (2024 est.) (male 8,665/female 12,728)

Dependency ratios: *total dependency ratio:* 47.8
youth dependency ratio: 24.8
elderly dependency ratio: 23
potential support ratio: 4.4 (2021 est.)

Median age: *total:* 40.9 years (2024 est.)
male: 39.3 years
female: 42.4 years
comparison ranking: total 56

Population growth rate: 1.08% (2024 est.)
comparison ranking: 87

Birth rate: 11.6 births/1,000 population (2024 est.)
comparison ranking: 156

Death rate: 8.8 deaths/1,000 population (2024 est.)
comparison ranking: 68

Net migration rate: 8 migrant(s)/1,000 population (2024 est.)
comparison ranking: 11

Population distribution: most residents live in or around Oranjestad and San Nicolaas; most settlments tend to be located on the less mountainous western side of the island

Urbanization: *urban population:* 44.3% of total population (2023)
rate of urbanization: 0.77% annual rate of change (2020-25 est.)

Major urban areas - population: 30,000 ORANJESTAD (capital) (2018)

Sex ratio: *at birth:* 1.02 male(s)/female
0-14 years: 1.01 male(s)/female
15-64 years: 0.93 male(s)/female
65 years and over: 0.68 male(s)/female
total population: 0.9 male(s)/female (2024 est.)

Infant mortality rate: *total:* 11.5 deaths/1,000 live births (2024 est.)
male: 15.6 deaths/1,000 live births
female: 7.3 deaths/1,000 live births
comparison ranking: total 117

Life expectancy at birth: *total population:* 78.5 years (2024 est.)
male: 75.4 years
female: 81.6 years
comparison ranking: total population 78

Total fertility rate: 1.82 children born/woman (2024 est.)
comparison ranking: 137

Gross reproduction rate: 0.9 (2024 est.)

Drinking water source: *improved:*
total: 98.1% of population
unimproved:
total: 1.9% of population (2015 est.)

Sanitation facility access: *improved:*
total: 97.7% of population
unimproved:
total: 2.3% of population (2015 est.)

Currently married women (ages 15-49): 42.1% (2023 est.)

Education expenditures: 5.5% of GDP (2016 est.)
comparison ranking: 54

Literacy: *definition:* age 15 and over can read and write
total population: 97.8%
male: 97.8%
female: 97.8% (2018)

School life expectancy (primary to tertiary education): *total:* 14 years
male: 13 years
female: 14 years (2012)

ENVIRONMENT

Environment - current issues: difficulty in properly disposing of waste produced by large numbers of tourists; waste burning that occurs in the landfill causes air pollution and poses an environmental and health risk; ocean environmental damage due to plastic pollution

Climate: tropical marine; little seasonal temperature variation

Urbanization: *urban population:* 44.3% of total population (2023)
rate of urbanization: 0.77% annual rate of change (2020-25 est.)

Revenue from forest resources: 0% of GDP (2017 est.)
comparison ranking: 202

Air pollutants: *carbon dioxide emissions:* 0.88 megatons (2016 est.)

Waste and recycling: *municipal solid waste generated annually:* 88,132 tons (2013 est.)
municipal solid waste recycled annually: 9,695 tons (2013 est.)
percent of municipal solid waste recycled: 11% (2013 est.)

GOVERNMENT

Country name: *conventional long form:* Country of Aruba
conventional short form: Aruba
local long form: Land Aruba (Dutch); Pais Aruba (Papiamento)
local short form: Aruba
etymology: the origin of the island's name is unclear; according to tradition, the name comes from the Spanish phrase "oro huba" (there was gold), but in fact no gold was ever found on the island; another possibility is the native word "oruba," which means "well-situated"

Government type: parliamentary democracy; part of the Kingdom of the Netherlands

Dependency status: constituent country of the Kingdom of the Netherlands; full autonomy in internal affairs obtained in 1986 upon separation from the Netherlands Antilles; Dutch Government responsible for defense and foreign affairs

Capital: *name:* Oranjestad
geographic coordinates: 12 31 N, 70 02 W
time difference: UTC-4 (1 hour ahead of Washington, DC, during Standard Time)
etymology: translates as "orange town" in Dutch; the city is named after William I (1533-1584), Prince of Orange, the first ruler of the Netherlands

Administrative divisions: none (part of the Kingdom of the Netherlands)
note: Aruba is one of four constituent countries of the Kingdom of the Netherlands; the other three are the Netherlands, Curacao, and Sint Maarten

Independence: none (part of the Kingdom of the Netherlands)

National holiday: National Anthem and Flag Day, 18 March (1976)

Legal system: civil law system based on the Dutch civil code

Constitution: *history:* previous 1947, 1955; latest drafted and approved August 1985, enacted 1 January 1986 (regulates governance of Aruba but is subordinate to the Charter for the Kingdom of the Netherlands); in 1986, Aruba became a semi-autonomous entity within the Kingdom of the Netherlands

Citizenship: see the Netherlands

Suffrage: 18 years of age; universal

Executive branch: *chief of state:* King WILLEM-ALEXANDER of the Netherlands (since 30 April 2013); represented by Governor General Alfonso BOEKHOUDT (since 1 January 2017)
head of government: Prime Minister Evelyn WEVER-CROES (since 17 November 2017)
cabinet: Council of Ministers elected by the Legislature (Staten)
elections/appointments: the monarchy is hereditary; governor general appointed by the monarch for a 6-year term; prime minister and deputy prime minister indirectly elected by the Staten for 4-year term; election last held on 25 June 2021 (next to be held by June 2025)
election results: as leader of the majority party of the ruling coalition, Evelyn WEVER-CROES (MEP) elected prime minister; percent of Staten vote - NA

Legislative branch: *description:* unicameral Legislature or Staten (21 seats; members directly elected in a single nationwide constituency by proportional representation vote; members serve 4-year terms)
elections: last held on 25 June 2021 (next to be held in June 2025)
election results: percent of vote by party MEP 35.3%, AVP 31.3%, ROOTS 9.4%, MAS 8%, Accion21 5.8%; seats by party - MEP 9, AVP 7, ROOTS 2, MAS 2, Accion21 1; composition - men 13, women 8, percentage women - 38.1%

Judicial branch: *highest court(s):* Joint Court of Justice of Aruba, Curacao, Sint Maarten, and of Bonaire, Sint Eustatius and Saba or "Joint Court of Justice" (sits as a 3-judge panel); final appeals heard by the Supreme Court in The Hague, Netherlands
judge selection and term of office: Joint Court judges appointed for life by the monarch
subordinate courts: Court in First Instance

Political parties: Accion21
Aruban People's Party or AVP
Democratic Network or RED
Movimiento Aruba Soberano (Aruban Sovereignty Movement) or MAS
People's Electoral Movement Party or MEP
Pueblo Orguyoso y Respeta or POR
RAIZ (ROOTS)

International organization participation: ACS (associate), Caricom (observer), FATF, ILO, IMF, Interpol, IOC, ITUC (NGOs), UNESCO (associate), UNWTO (associate), UPU

Diplomatic representation in the US: none (represented by the Kingdom of the Netherlands)

Diplomatic representation from the US: *embassy:* the US does not have an embassy in Aruba; the Consul General to Curacao is accredited to Aruba

Flag description: *blue, with two narrow, horizontal, yellow stripes across the lower portion and a red, four-pointed star outlined in white in the upper hoist-side corner; the star represents Aruba and its red soil and white beaches, its four points the four major languages (Papiamento, Dutch, Spanish, English) as well as the four points of a compass, to indicate that its inhabitants come from all over the world; the blue symbolizes Caribbean waters and skies; the stripes represent the island's two main "industries"*: the flow of tourists to the sun-drenched beaches and the flow of minerals from the earth

National symbol(s): Hooiberg (Haystack) Hill; national colors: blue, yellow, red, white

National anthem: *name:* "Aruba Deshi Tera" (Aruba Precious Country)
lyrics/music: Juan Chabaya 'Padu' LAMPE/Rufo Inocencio WEVER
note: local anthem adopted 1986; as part of the Kingdom of the Netherlands, "Het Wilhelmus" is official (see Netherlands)

ECONOMY

Economic overview: small, tourism-dependent, territorial-island economy; very high public debt; COVID-19 crippled economic activity; partial recovery underway via tourism, benefitting from its high amount of timeshare residences; considering reopening oil refinery

Real GDP (purchasing power parity): $4.498 billion (2022 est.)
$4.072 billion (2021 est.)
$3.191 billion (2020 est.)
note: data in 2021 dollars
comparison ranking: 189

Real GDP growth rate: 10.46% (2022 est.)
27.64% (2021 est.)
-23.98% (2020 est.)
note: annual GDP % growth based on constant local currency
comparison ranking: 6

Real GDP per capita: $42,300 (2022 est.)
$38,200 (2021 est.)
$29,900 (2020 est.)
note: data in 2021 dollars
comparison ranking: 56

GDP (official exchange rate): $3.545 billion (2022 est.)
note: data in current dollars at official exchange rate

Inflation rate (consumer prices): 4.26% (2019 est.)
3.63% (2018 est.)
-1.03% (2017 est.)
note: annual % change based on consumer prices
comparison ranking: 90

Credit ratings: Fitch rating: BB (2020)

Standard & Poors rating: BBB+ (2013)
note: The year refers to the year in which the current credit rating was first obtained.

GDP - composition, by sector of origin: *agriculture:* 0% (2019 est.)
industry: 11.4% (2019 est.)
services: 78.3% (2019 est.)
note: figures may not total 100% due to non-allocated consumption not captured in sector-reported data comparison rankings: services 19; industry 185; agriculture 212

GDP - composition, by end use: *household consumption:* 53.8% (2022 est.)
government consumption: 19.9% (2022 est.)
investment in fixed capital: 20.6% (2022 est.)
exports of goods and services: 83.1% (2022 est.)
imports of goods and services: -77.3% (2022 est.)
note: figures may not total 100% due to rounding or gaps in data collection

Agricultural products: aloes; livestock; fish

Industries: tourism, petroleum transshipment facilities, banking

Unemployment rate: 7.7% (2016 est.)
comparison ranking: 143

Remittances: 1.08% of GDP (2022 est.)
1.16% of GDP (2021 est.)
1.37% of GDP (2020 est.)
note: personal transfers and compensation between resident and non-resident individuals/households/entities

Budget: *revenues:* $793 million (2019 est.)
expenditures: $782 million (2019 est.)

Public debt: 86% of GDP (2017 est.)
comparison ranking: 32

Taxes and other revenues: 25.2% (of GDP) (2017 est.)
comparison ranking: 44

Current account balance: $230.556 million (2022 est.)
$79.257 million (2021 est.)
-$316.455 million (2020 est.)
note: balance of payments - net trade and primary/secondary income in current dollars
comparison ranking: 67

Exports: $2.853 billion (2022 est.)
$2.201 billion (2021 est.)
$1.444 billion (2020 est.)
note: balance of payments - exports of goods and services in current dollars
comparison ranking: 156

Exports - partners: Colombia 40%, US 12%, Jordan 11%, Guyana 8%, Netherlands 6% (2022)
note: top five export partners based on percentage share of exports

Exports - commodities: tobacco, liquor, refined petroleum, scrap iron, orthopedic appliances (2022)
note: top five export commodities based on value in dollars

Imports: $2.429 billion (2022 est.)
$1.947 billion (2021 est.)
$1.644 billion (2020 est.)
note: balance of payments - imports of goods and services in current dollars
comparison ranking: 168

Imports - partners: US 39%, Netherlands 11%, Guyana 9%, Colombia 8%, China 5% (2022)
note: top five import partners based on percentage share of imports

Imports - commodities: refined petroleum, crude petroleum, tobacco, jewelry, other foods (2022)
note: top five import commodities based on value in dollars

Reserves of foreign exchange and gold: $1.544 billion (2022 est.)
$1.513 billion (2021 est.)
$1.213 billion (2020 est.)
note: holdings of gold (year-end prices)/foreign exchange/special drawing rights in current dollars
comparison ranking: 141

Exchange rates: Aruban guilders/florins per US dollar -

Exchange rates: 1.79 (2023 est.)
1.79 (2022 est.)
1.79 (2021 est.)
1.79 (2020 est.)
1.79 (2019 est.)

ENERGY

Electricity access: *electrification - total population:* 99.9% (2022 est.)
electrification - urban areas: 100%
electrification - rural areas: 100%

Electricity: *installed generating capacity:* 304,000 kW (2022 est.)
consumption: 809.548 million kWh (2022 est.)
transmission/distribution losses: 166.766 million kWh (2022 est.)
comparison rankings: transmission/distribution losses 61; consumption 165; installed generating capacity 165

Electricity generation sources: *fossil fuels:* 84.9% of total installed capacity (2022 est.)
solar: 1.2% of total installed capacity (2022 est.)
wind: 13.9% of total installed capacity (2022 est.)

Petroleum: *refined petroleum consumption:* 8,000 bbl/day (2022 est.)

Carbon dioxide emissions: 1.214 million metric tonnes of CO_2 (2022 est.)
from petroleum and other liquids: 1.214 million metric tonnes of CO_2 (2022 est.)
comparison ranking: total emissions 169

Energy consumption per capita: 161.715 million Btu/person (2022 est.)
comparison ranking: 24

COMMUNICATIONS

Telephones - fixed lines: *total subscriptions:* 35,000 (2021 est.)
subscriptions per 100 inhabitants: 33 (2021 est.)
comparison ranking: total subscriptions 164

Telephones - mobile cellular: *total subscriptions:* 141,000 (2021 est.)
subscriptions per 100 inhabitants: 132 (2021 est.)
comparison ranking: total subscriptions 188

Telecommunication systems: *general assessment:* the telecom sector has seen a decline in subscriber numbers (particularly for prepaid mobile services the mainstay of short term visitors) and revenue; fixed and mobile broadband services are two areas that have benefited from the crisis as employees and students have resorted to working from home; one area of the telecom market that is not prepared for growth is 5G mobile; governments, regulators, and even the mobile network operators have shown that they have not been investing in 5G opportunities at the present time; network expansion and enhancements remain concentrated around improving LTE coverage (2021)
domestic: 33 per 100 fixed-line telephone subscriptions and 130 per 100 mobile-cellular (2021)
international: country code - 297; landing points for the PAN-AM, PCCS, Deep Blue Cable, and Alonso de Ojeda submarine telecommunications cable system that extends from Trinidad and Tobago, Florida, Puerto Ricco, Jamaica, Guyana, Sint Eustatius &

Saba, Suriname, Dominican Republic, BVI, USVI, Haiti, Cayman Islands, the Netherlands Antilles, through Aruba to Panama, Venezuela, Colombia, Ecuador, Peru and Chile; extensive interisland microwave radio relay links (2019)

Broadcast media: 2 commercial TV stations; cable TV subscription service provides access to foreign channels; about 19 commercial radio stations broadcast (2017)

Internet country code: .aw

Internet users: *total:* 106,800 (2021 est.)
percent of population: 97% (2021 est.)
comparison ranking: total 187

Broadband - fixed subscriptions: *total:* 19,000 (2020 est.)
subscriptions per 100 inhabitants: 18 (2020 est.)
comparison ranking: total 167

TRANSPORTATION

National air transport system: *number of registered air carriers:* 3 (2020)
inventory of registered aircraft operated by air carriers: 19
annual passenger traffic on registered air carriers: 274,280 (2018)

Civil aircraft registration country code prefix: P4

Airports: 1 (2024)
comparison ranking: 220

Roadways: *total:* 1,000 km (2010)
comparison ranking: total 187

Merchant marine: *total:* 1 (2023)
by type: other 1
comparison ranking: total 182

Ports: *total ports:* 2 (2024)
large: 0
medium: 0
small: 1
very small: 1
ports with oil terminals: 1
key ports: Paardenbaai (Oranjestad), Sint Nicolaas Baai

MILITARY AND SECURITY

Military and security forces: no regular military forces; Aruban Militia (ARUMIL); Police Department for local law enforcement, supported by the Royal Netherlands Marechaussee (Gendarmerie), the Dutch Caribbean Police Force (Korps Politie Caribisch Nederland, KPCN), and the Dutch Caribbean Coast Guard (DCCG or Kustwacht Caribisch Gebied (KWCARIB)) (2024)

Military - note: defense is the responsibility of the Kingdom of the Netherlands; the Aruba security services focus on organized crime and terrorism; the Dutch Government controls foreign and defense policy; the Dutch Caribbean Coast Guard (DCCG) provides maritime security; the Dutch military maintains a presence on Aruba, including a marine company and a naval base (2024)

TRANSNATIONAL ISSUES

Refugees and internally displaced persons: *refugees (country of origin):* 17,085 (Venezuela) (2023)

Illicit drugs: northbound transshipment point for cocaine from Colombia and Venezuela; cocaine shipped to the United States, other Caribbean islands, Africa, and Europe

ASHMORE AND CARTIER ISLANDS

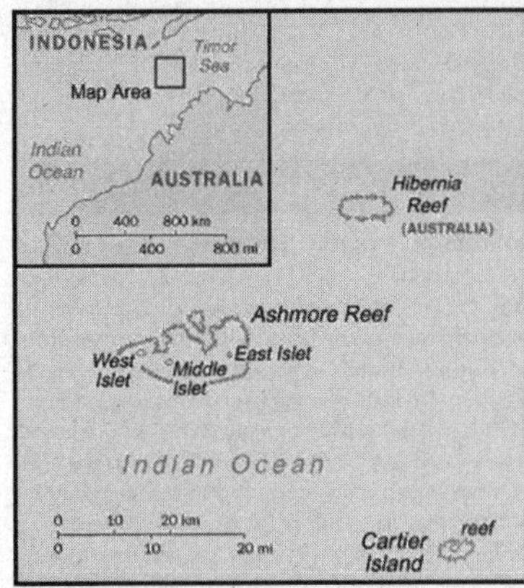

INTRODUCTION

Background: Indonesian fishermen have long fished in the area around Ashmore Reef and Cartier Island. British explorers were the first Europeans to see Cartier Island and Ashmore Reef in 1800 and 1811, respectively. American whalers frequently sailed by the islands in the 1850s and later settled to mine the phosphate deposits on Ashmore Reef, which were exhausted by 1891. The UK disputed US access to Ashmore Reef and formally annexed it in 1878. Cartier Island was annexed in 1909. In 1931, the UK transferred the islands to Australia, which accepted them in 1934 as part of Western Australia. In 1938, Australia transferred governance to the Northern Territory. During World War II, Cartier Island was used as a bombing range. In 1978, governance of Ashmore and Cartier Islands was moved to the federal government. Ashmore Reef and Cartier Island became marine reserves in 1983 and 2000 respectively.

In 1974, Australia and Indonesia signed a memorandum of understanding (MOU) to allow Indonesian fishermen to continue fishing around the islands. The MOU also allows Indonesian fishermen to visit the graves of past fishermen, replenish their fresh water, and shelter in the West Island Lagoon of Ashmore Reef. In the 1990s, Indonesia challenged Australia's claim to the islands, which was settled in a maritime boundary treaty in 1997. The islands were a popular first point of contact for migrants and refugees seeking to enter Australia, so in 2001, Australia declared the islands to be outside the Australian migration zone.

GEOGRAPHY

Location: Southeastern Asia, islands in the Indian Ocean, midway between northwestern Australia and Timor island; Ashmore Reef is 840 km west of Darwin and 610 km north of Broome; Cartier Islet is 70 km east of Ashmore Reef

Geographic coordinates: 12 25 S, 123 20 E
note - Ashmore Reef - 12 14 S, 123 05 E; Cartier Islet - 12 32 S, 123 32 E

Map references: Southeast Asia

Area: *total:* 5 sq km
land: 5 sq km
water: 0 sq km
note: includes Ashmore Reef (West, Middle, and East Islets) and Cartier Island
comparison ranking: total 247

Area - comparative: about eight times the size of the National Mall in Washington, DC

Land boundaries: *total:* 0 km

Coastline: 74.1 km

Maritime claims: *territorial sea:* 12 nm
contiguous zone: 24 nm
continental shelf: 200-m depth or to the depth of exploitation
exclusive fishing zone: 200 nm

Climate: tropical

Terrain: low with sand and coral

Elevation: *highest point:* Cartier Island 5 m
lowest point: Indian Ocean 0 m

Natural resources: fish

Land use: *agricultural land:* 0% (2018 est.)

Natural hazards: surrounded by shoals and reefs that can pose maritime hazards

Geography - note: Ashmore Reef National Nature Reserve established in August 1983; Cartier Island Marine Reserve established in 2000

PEOPLE AND SOCIETY

Population: *total:* (2021 est.) no indigenous inhabitants
note: Indonesian fishermen are allowed access to the lagoon and fresh water at Ashmore Reef's West Island; access to East and Middle Islands is by permit only

Population growth rate: 0.32% (2021 est.)

ENVIRONMENT

Environment - current issues: illegal killing of protected wildlife by traditional Indonesian fisherman, as well as fishing by non-traditional Indonesian vessels, are ongoing problems; sea level rise, changes in sea temperature, and ocean acidification are concerns; marine debris

Climate: tropical

Land use: *agricultural land:* 0% (2018 est.)

GOVERNMENT

Country name: *conventional long form:* Territory of Ashmore and Cartier Islands
conventional short form: Ashmore and Cartier Islands
etymology: named after British Captain Samuel ASHMORE, who first sighted his namesake island in 1811, and after the ship Cartier, from which the second island was discovered in 1800

Dependency status: territory of Australia; administered from Canberra by the Department of Regional Australia, Local Government, Arts and Sport

Legal system: the laws of the Commonwealth of Australia and the laws of the Northern Territory of Australia, where applicable, apply

Citizenship: see Australia

Diplomatic representation in the US: none (territory of Australia)

Diplomatic representation from the US: *embassy:* none (territory of Australia)

Flag description: the flag of Australia is used

MILITARY AND SECURITY

Military - note: defense is the responsibility of Australia

TRANSNATIONAL ISSUES

Illicit drugs: NA

ATLANTIC OCEAN

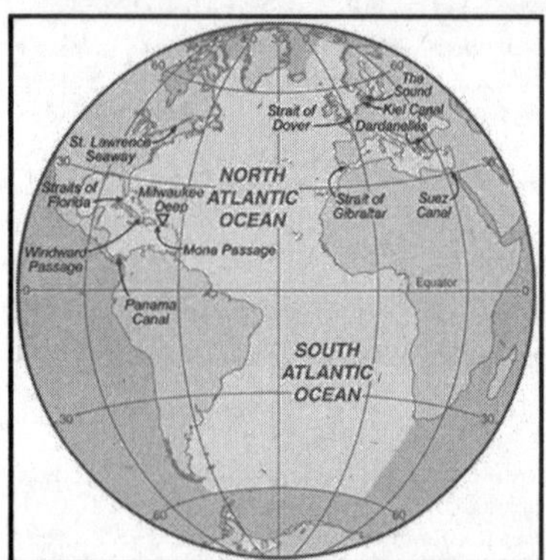

INTRODUCTION

Background: The Atlantic Ocean is the second largest of the world's five ocean basins (after the Pacific Ocean, but larger than the Indian Ocean, Southern Ocean, and Arctic Ocean). The Kiel Canal (Germany), Oresund (Denmark-Sweden), Bosporus (Turkey), Strait of Gibraltar (Morocco-Spain), and the Saint Lawrence Seaway (Canada-US) are important strategic access waterways. The decision by the International Hydrographic Organization in the spring of 2000 to delimit a fifth world ocean basin, the Southern Ocean, removed the portion of the Atlantic Ocean south of 60 degrees south latitude. For convenience and because of its immense size, the Atlantic Ocean is often divided at the Equator and designated as the North Atlantic Ocean and the South Atlantic Ocean.

GEOGRAPHY

Location: body of water between Africa, Europe, the Arctic Ocean, the Americas, and the Southern Ocean

Geographic coordinates: 0 00 N, 25 00 W

Map references: Map of the world oceans

Area: *total:* 85.133 million sq km
note: includes Baffin Bay, Baltic Sea, Black Sea, Caribbean Sea, Davis Strait, Denmark Strait, part of the Drake Passage, Hudson Bay, Hudson Strait, Gulf of Mexico, Labrador Sea, Mediterranean Sea, North Sea, almost all of the Scotia Sea, and other tributary water bodies

Area - comparative: about 7.5 times the size of the US

Coastline: 111,866 km

Climate: tropical cyclones (hurricanes) develop off the coast of Africa near Cabo Verde and move westward into the Caribbean Sea; hurricanes can occur from May to December but are most frequent from August to November

Ocean volume: *ocean volume:* 310,410,900 cu km
percent of World Ocean total volume: 23.3%

Major ocean currents: clockwise North Atlantic Gyre consists of the northward flowing, warm Gulf Stream in the west, the eastward flowing North Atlantic Current in the north, the southward flowing cold Canary Current in the east, and the westward flowing North Equatorial Current in the south; the counterclockwise South Atlantic Gyre composed of the southward flowing warm Brazil Current in the west, the eastward flowing South Atlantic Current in the south, the northward flowing cold Benguela Current in the east, and the westward flowing South Equatorial Current in the north

Elevation: *highest point:* sea level
lowest point: Puerto Rico Trench -8,605 m
mean depth: -3,646 m
ocean zones: Composed of water and in a fluid state, the ocean is delimited differently than the solid continents. It is divided into three zones based on depth and light level. Sunlight entering the water may travel about 1,000 m into the ocean under the right conditions, but there is rarely any significant light beyond 200 m.
The upper 200 m (656 ft) of the ocean is called the euphotic, or "sunlight," zone. This zone contains the vast majority of commercial fisheries and is home to many protected marine mammals and sea turtles. Only a small amount of light penetrates beyond this depth.
The zone between 200 m (656 ft) and 1,000 m (3,280 ft) is usually referred to as the "twilight" zone, but is officially the dysphotic zone. In this zone, the intensity of light rapidly dissipates as depth increases. Such a minuscule amount of light penetrates beyond a depth of 200 m that photosynthesis is no longer possible.
The aphotic, or "midnight," zone exists in depths below 1,000 m (3,280 ft). Sunlight does not penetrate to these depths, and the zone is bathed in darkness.

Natural resources: oil and gas fields, fish, marine mammals (seals and whales), sand and gravel aggregates, placer deposits, polymetallic nodules, precious stones

Natural hazards: icebergs common in Davis Strait, Denmark Strait, and the northwestern Atlantic Ocean from February to August and have been spotted as far south as Bermuda and the Madeira Islands; ships subject to superstructure icing in extreme northern Atlantic from October to May; persistent fog can be a maritime hazard from May to September; hurricanes (May to December)

Geography - note: major chokepoints include the Dardanelles, Strait of Gibraltar, access to the Panama and Suez Canals; strategic straits include the Strait of Dover, Straits of Florida, Mona Passage, The Sound (Oresund), and Windward Passage; the Equator divides the Atlantic Ocean into the North Atlantic Ocean and South Atlantic Ocean

ENVIRONMENT

Environment - current issues: endangered marine species include the manatee, seals, sea lions, turtles, and whales; unsustainable exploitation of fisheries (over fishing, unregulated bottom trawling, drift net fishing, discards, catch of non-target species); pollution (maritime transport, discharges, offshore drilling, oil spills, plastics from improperly disposed waste); municipal sludge pollution off eastern US, southern Brazil, and eastern Argentina; oil pollution in Caribbean Sea, Gulf of Mexico, Lake Maracaibo, Mediterranean Sea, and North Sea; industrial waste and municipal sewage pollution in Baltic Sea, North Sea, and Mediterranean Sea

Climate: tropical cyclones (hurricanes) develop off the coast of Africa near Cabo Verde and move westward into the Caribbean Sea; hurricanes can occur from May to December but are most frequent from August to November

Marine fisheries: *the Atlantic Ocean fisheries are the second most important in the world accounting for 25.8%, or 20,300,000 mt, of the global catch in 2020; of the seven regions delineated by the Food and Agriculture Organization in the Atlantic basin, the most important include the following:*
Northeast Atlantic region (Region 27) is the fourth most important in the world, producing 10.5% of the global catch or 8,310,000 mt in 2020; the region encompasses the waters north of 36º North latitude and east of 40º West longitude, with the major producers including Norway (3,528,240 mt), Russia (1,044,153 mt), Iceland (933,019 mt), UK (823,669 mt), and Denmark (641,927 mt); the region includes

the historically important fishing grounds of the North Sea, the Baltic Sea, and the Atlantic waters around Greenland, Iceland, and the British Isles; the principal catches include Atlantic cod, haddock, saithe (pollock), blue whiting, herring, and mackerel
Eastern Central Atlantic region (Region 34) is the second most important Atlantic fishery, and seventh largest in the world, producing more than 6.3% of the global catch or 4,950,000 mt in 2020; the region encompasses the waters between 36º North and 6º South latitude and east of 40º West longitude off the west coast of Africa, with the major producers including Morocco (1,419,872 mt), Mauritania (705,850 mt), Senegal (472,571 mt), Nigeria (451,768 mt), Ghana (303,001 mt), Cameroon (265,969 mt), and Sierra Leone (200,000 mt); the principal catches include pilchard, sardinellas, shad, and mackerel
Northwest Atlantic region (Region 21) is the fourth most important Atlantic fishery and eleventh in the world producing 1.9% of the global catch and 1,540,000 mt in 2020; it encompasses the waters north of 35º North latitude and west of 42º West longitude, including major fishing grounds over North America's continental shelf (the Grand Banks, Georges Bank, Flemish Cap, and Baffin Bay); the major producers include the US (927,777 mt), Canada (615,651 mt), and Greenland (179,990 mt); the principal catches include sea scallops, prawns, lobster, herring, and menhaden
Mediterranean and Black Sea region (Region 37) is a minor fishing region representing 1.5% or 1,190,000 mt of the world's total capture in 2020; the region encompasses all waters east of the Strait of Gibraltar, with the major producers including Turkey (686,650 mt), Italy (281,212 mt), Tunisia (129,325 mt), Spain (119,759 mt), and Russia (72,279 mt); the principal catches include European anchovy, European pilchard, gobies, and clams

Regional fisheries bodies: Commission for the Conservation of Southern Bluefin Tuna, Fishery Committee for the Eastern Central Atlantic, Fisheries Committee for the West Central Gulf of Guinea, General Fisheries Commission for the Mediterranean, International Commission for the Conservation of Atlantic Tunas, International Council for the Exploration of the Seas, Northwest Atlantic Fisheries Organization, North Atlantic Salmon Conservation Organization, North East Atlantic Fisheries Commission, Southeast Atlantic Fisheries Organization, Western Central Atlantic Fishery Commission

GOVERNMENT

Country name: *etymology:* name derives from the Greek description of the waters beyond the Strait of Gibraltar, *Atlantis thalassa*, meaning "Sea of Atlas"

TRANSPORTATION

Transportation - note: Kiel Canal and Saint Lawrence Seaway are two important waterways; significant domestic commercial and recreational use of Intracoastal Waterway on central and south Atlantic seaboard and Gulf of Mexico coast of US

AUSTRALIA

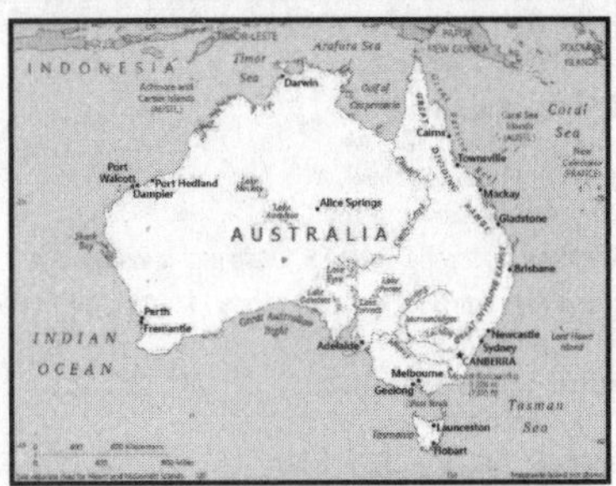

INTRODUCTION

Background: Aboriginal Australians arrived on the continent at least 60,000 years ago and developed complex hunter-gatherer societies and oral histories. Dutch navigators led by Abel TASMAN were the first Europeans to land in Australia in 1606, and they mapped the western and northern coasts. They named the continent New Holland but made no attempts to permanently settle it. In 1770, Englishman James COOK sailed to the east coast of Australia, named it New South Wales, and claimed it for Great Britain. In 1788 and 1825 respectively, Great Britain established New South Wales and then Tasmania as penal colonies. Great Britain and Ireland sent more than 150,000 convicts to Australia before ending the practice in 1868. As Europeans began settling areas away from the coasts, they came into more direct contact with Aboriginal Australians. Europeans also cleared land for agriculture, impacting Aboriginal Australians' ways of life. These issues, along with disease and a policy in the 1900s that forcefully removed Aboriginal children from their parents, reduced the Aboriginal Australian population from more than 700,000 pre-European contact to a low of 74,000 in 1933.

Four additional colonies were established in Australia in the mid-1800s: Western Australia (1829), South Australia (1836), Victoria (1851), and Queensland (1859). Gold rushes beginning in the 1850s brought thousands of new immigrants to New South Wales and Victoria, helping to reorient Australia away from its penal colony roots. In the second half of the 1800s, the colonies were all gradually granted self-government, and in 1901, they federated and became the Commonwealth of Australia. Australia contributed more than 400,000 troops to Allied efforts during World War I, and Australian troops played a large role in the defeat of Japanese troops in the Pacific in World War II. Australia severed most constitutional links with the UK in 1942 but remained part of the British Commonwealth. Australia's post-war economy boomed and by the 1970s, racial policies that prevented most non-Whites from immigrating to Australia were removed, greatly increasing Asian immigration to the country. In recent decades, Australia has become an internationally competitive, advanced market economy due in large part to economic reforms adopted in the 1980s and its proximity to East and Southeast Asia.

In the early 2000s, Australian politics became unstable with frequent attempts to oust party leaders, including five changes of prime minister between 2010 and 2018. As a result, both major parties instituted rules to make it harder to remove a party leader.

GEOGRAPHY

Location: Oceania, continent between the Indian Ocean and the South Pacific Ocean

Geographic coordinates: 27 00 S, 133 00 E

Map references: Oceania

Area: *total:* 7,741,220 sq km
land: 7,682,300 sq km
water: 58,920 sq km
note: includes Lord Howe Island and Macquarie Island
comparison ranking: total 7

Area - comparative: slightly smaller than the US contiguous 48 states

Land boundaries: *total:* 0 km

Coastline: 25,760 km

Maritime claims: *territorial sea:* 12 nm
contiguous zone: 24 nm
exclusive economic zone: 200 nm
continental shelf: 200 nm or to the edge of the continental margin

Climate: generally arid to semiarid; temperate in south and east; tropical in north

Terrain: mostly low plateau with deserts; fertile plain in southeast

Elevation: *highest point:* Mount Kosciuszko 2,228 m
lowest point: Lake Eyre -15 m
mean elevation: 330 m

Natural resources: alumina, coal, iron ore, copper, lithium, tin, gold, silver, uranium, nickel, tungsten, rare earth elements, mineral sands, lead, zinc, diamonds, opals, natural gas, petroleum
note 1: Australia is the world's largest net exporter of coal accounting for 26.5% of global coal exports in 2021; coal is the country's most abundant energy resource, and coal ranks as the second-largest export commodity from Australia in terms of revenue; in 2020, Australia held the third-largest recoverable coal reserves in the world behind the United States and Russia
note 2: Australia is by far the world's largest supplier of opals
note 3: Australia holds the largest uranium reserves in the world and was the second-largest global uranium producer behind Kazakhstan in 2020
note 4: Australia was the largest exporter of LNG in the world in 2020

Land use: *agricultural land:* 46.65% (2018 est.)
arable land: 4.03% (2018 est.)
permanent crops: 0.04% (2018 est.)
permanent pasture: 42.58% (2018 est.)
forest: 17.42% (2018 est.)
other: 33.42% (2018 est.)

Irrigated land: 15,210 sq km (2020)

Major lakes (area sq km): *fresh water lake(s):* Lake Alexandrina - 570 sq km
salt water lake(s): Lake Eyre - 9,690 sq km; Lake Torrens (ephemeral) - 5,780 sq km; Lake Gairdner - 4,470 sq km; Lake Mackay (ephemeral) - 3,494 sq km; Lake Frome - 2,410 sq km; Lake Amadeus (ephemeral) - 1,032 sq km

Major rivers (by length in km): River Murray - 2,508 km; Darling River - 1,545 km; Murrumbidgee River - 1,485 km; Lachlan River - 1,339 km; Cooper Creek - 1,113 km; Flinders River - 1,004 km

Major watersheds (area sq km): Indian Ocean drainage: *(Great Australian Bight)* Murray-Darling (1,050,116 sq km)

Internal (endorheic basin) drainage: Lake Eyre (1,212,198 sq km)

Major aquifers: Great Artesian Basin, Canning Basin

Population distribution: population is primarily located on the periphery, with the highest concentration of people residing in the east and southeast; a secondary population center is located in and around Perth in the west; of the States and Territories, New South Wales has, by far, the largest population; the interior, or "outback", has a very sparse population

Natural hazards: cyclones along the coast; severe droughts; forest fires
volcanism: volcanic activity on Heard and McDonald Islands

Geography - note: *note 1:* world's smallest continent but sixth-largest country; the largest country in Oceania, the largest country entirely in the Southern Hemisphere, and the largest country without land borders
note 2: the Great Dividing Range that runs along eastern Australia is that continent's longest mountain range and the third-longest land-based range in the world; the term "Great Dividing Range" refers to the fact that the mountains form a watershed crest from which all of the rivers of eastern Australia flow – east, west, north, and south
note 3: Australia is the only continent without glaciers; it is the driest inhabited continent on earth; the invigorating sea breeze known as the "Fremantle Doctor" affects the city of Perth on the west coast and is one of the most consistent winds in the world; Australia is home to 10% of the world's biodiversity, and a great number of its flora and fauna exist nowhere else in the world

PEOPLE AND SOCIETY

Population: *total:* 26,768,598
male: 13,305,110
female: 13,463,488 (2024 est.)
comparison rankings: female 55; male 54; total 54

Nationality: *noun:* Australian(s)
adjective: Australian

Ethnic groups: English 33%, Australian 29.9%, Irish 9.5%, Scottish 8.6%, Chinese 5.5%, Italian 4.4%, German 4%, Indian 3.1%, Australian Aboriginal 2.9%, Greek 1.7%, unspecified 4.7% (2021 est.)
note: data represent self-identified ancestry, with the option of reporting two ancestries

Languages: English 72%, Mandarin 2.7%, Arabic 1.4%, Vietnamese 1.3%, Cantonese 1.2%, other 15.7%, unspecified 5.7% (2021 est.)
note: data represent language spoken at home

Religions: Roman Catholic 20%, Protestant 18.1% (Anglican 9.8%, Uniting Church 2.6%, Presbyterian and Reformed 1.6%, Baptist 1.4%, Pentecostal 1%, other Protestant 1.7%), other Christian 3.5%, Muslim 3.2%, Hindu 2.7%, Buddhist 2.4%, Orthodox 2.3% (Eastern Orthodox 2.1%, Oriental Orthodox 0.2%), other 2.1%, none 38.4%, unspecified 7.3% (2021 est.)

Age structure: *0-14 years:* 18.3% (male 2,526,772/female 2,369,425)
15-64 years: 64.7% (male 8,688,023/female 8,640,671)
65 years and over: 17% (2024 est.) (male 2,090,315/female 2,453,392)

Dependency ratios: *total dependency ratio:* 53.7
youth dependency ratio: 28.2
elderly dependency ratio: 25.5
potential support ratio: 3.9 (2020 est.)

Median age: *total:* 38.1 years (2024 est.)
male: 36.9 years
female: 39.2 years
comparison ranking: total 77

Population growth rate: 1.13% (2024 est.)
comparison ranking: 81

Birth rate: 12.2 births/1,000 population (2024 est.)
comparison ranking: 142

Death rate: 6.8 deaths/1,000 population (2024 est.)
comparison ranking: 127

Net migration rate: 5.9 migrant(s)/1,000 population (2024 est.)
comparison ranking: 15

Population distribution: population is primarily located on the periphery, with the highest concentration of people residing in the east and southeast; a secondary population center is located in and around Perth in the west; of the States and Territories, New South Wales has, by far, the largest population; the interior, or "outback", has a very sparse population

Urbanization: *urban population:* 86.6% of total population (2023)
rate of urbanization: 1.27% annual rate of change (2020-25 est.)
note: data include Christmas Island, Cocos Islands, and Norfolk Island

Major urban areas - population: 5.235 million Melbourne, 5.121 million Sydney, 2.505 million Brisbane, 2.118 million Perth, 1.367 million Adelaide, 472,000 CANBERRA (capital) (2023)

Sex ratio: *at birth:* 1.06 male(s)/female
0-14 years: 1.07 male(s)/female
15-64 years: 1.01 male(s)/female
65 years and over: 0.85 male(s)/female
total population: 0.99 male(s)/female (2024 est.)

Mother's mean age at first birth: 28.7 years (2019 est.)

Maternal mortality ratio: 3 deaths/100,000 live births (2020 est.)
comparison ranking: 176

Infant mortality rate: *total:* 2.9 deaths/1,000 live births (2024 est.)
male: 3.2 deaths/1,000 live births
female: 2.7 deaths/1,000 live births
comparison ranking: total 211

Life expectancy at birth: *total population:* 83.5 years (2024 est.)
male: 81.3 years
female: 85.7 years
comparison ranking: total population 13

Total fertility rate: 1.73 children born/woman (2024 est.)
comparison ranking: 155

Gross reproduction rate: 0.84 (2024 est.)

Contraceptive prevalence rate: 66.9% (2015/16)
note: percent of women aged 18-44

Drinking water source: *improved: urban:* 100% of population
rural: 100% of population
total: 100% of population
(2020 est.)

Current health expenditure: 10.7% of GDP (2020)

Physician density: 4.13 physicians/1,000 population (2020)

Hospital bed density: 3.8 beds/1,000 population (2016)

Sanitation facility access: *improved: urban:* NA
rural: NA
total: 100% of population
unimproved: urban: NA
rural: NA
total: 0% of population (2020 est.)

Obesity - adult prevalence rate: 29% (2016)
comparison ranking: 27

Alcohol consumption per capita: *total:* 9.51 liters of pure alcohol (2019 est.)
beer: 3.71 liters of pure alcohol (2019 est.)
wine: 3.67 liters of pure alcohol (2019 est.)
spirits: 1.32 liters of pure alcohol (2019 est.)
other alcohols: 0.81 liters of pure alcohol (2019 est.)
comparison ranking: total 27

Tobacco use: *total:* 13.6% (2020 est.)
male: 15.6% (2020 est.)
female: 11.5% (2020 est.)
comparison ranking: total 114

Children under the age of 5 years underweight: NA

Currently married women (ages 15-49): 55.9% (2023 est.)

Education expenditures: 6.1% of GDP (2020 est.)
comparison ranking: 38

Literacy: *total population:* NA
male: NA
female: NA

School life expectancy (primary to tertiary education): *total:* 21 years
male: 20 years
female: 22 years (2020)

ENVIRONMENT

Environment - current issues: soil erosion from overgrazing, deforestation, industrial development, urbanization, and poor farming practices; limited natural freshwater resources; soil salinity rising due to the use of poor quality water; drought, desertification; clearing for agricultural purposes threatens the natural habitat of many unique animal and plant species; disruption of the fragile ecosystem has resulted in significant floral extinctions; the Great Barrier Reef off the northeast coast, the largest coral reef in the world, is threatened by increased shipping and its popularity as a tourist site; overfishing, pollution, and invasive species are also problems

Environment - international agreements: *party to:* Antarctic-Environmental Protection, Antarctic-Marine Living Resources, Antarctic Seals, Antarctic Treaty, Biodiversity, Climate Change, Climate Change-Kyoto Protocol, Climate Change-Paris Agreement, Comprehensive Nuclear Test Ban, Desertification, Endangered Species, Environmental Modification, Hazardous Wastes, Law of the Sea, Marine Dumping-London Convention,

Marine Dumping-London Protocol, Marine Life Conservation, Nuclear Test Ban, Ozone Layer Protection, Ship Pollution, Tropical Timber 2006, Wetlands, Whaling
signed, but not ratified: none of the selected agreements

Climate: generally arid to semiarid; temperate in south and east; tropical in north

Urbanization: *urban population:* 86.6% of total population (2023)
rate of urbanization: 1.27% annual rate of change (2020-25 est.)
note: data include Christmas Island, Cocos Islands, and Norfolk Island

Revenue from forest resources: 0.13% of GDP (2018 est.)
comparison ranking: 105

Revenue from coal: 0.78% of GDP (2018 est.)
comparison ranking: 7

Air pollutants: *particulate matter emissions:* 8.93 micrograms per cubic meter (2019 est.)
carbon dioxide emissions: 375.91 megatons (2016 est.)
methane emissions: 105.01 megatons (2020 est.)

Waste and recycling: *municipal solid waste generated annually:* 13.345 million tons (2015 est.)
municipal solid waste recycled annually: 5,618,245 tons (2015 est.)
percent of municipal solid waste recycled: 42.1% (2015 est.)

Major lakes (area sq km): *fresh water lake(s):* Lake Alexandrina - 570 sq km
salt water lake(s): Lake Eyre - 9,690 sq km; Lake Torrens (ephemeral) - 5,780 sq km; Lake Gairdner - 4,470 sq km; Lake Mackay (ephemeral) - 3,494 sq km; Lake Frome - 2,410 sq km; Lake Amadeus (ephemeral) - 1,032 sq km

Major rivers (by length in km): River Murray - 2,508 km; Darling River - 1,545 km; Murrumbidgee River - 1,485 km; Lachlan River - 1,339 km; Cooper Creek - 1,113 km; Flinders River - 1,004 km

Major watersheds (area sq km): Indian Ocean drainage: *(Great Australian Bight)* Murray-Darling (1,050,116 sq km)

Internal (endorheic basin) drainage: Lake Eyre (1,212,198 sq km)

Major aquifers: Great Artesian Basin, Canning Basin

Total water withdrawal: *municipal:* 2.29 billion cubic meters (2020 est.)
industrial: 2.89 billion cubic meters (2020 est.)
agricultural: 8.57 billion cubic meters (2020 est.)

Total renewable water resources: 492 billion cubic meters (2020 est.)

GOVERNMENT

Country name: *conventional long form:* Commonwealth of Australia
conventional short form: Australia
etymology: the name Australia derives from the Latin "australis" meaning "southern"; the Australian landmass was long referred to as "Terra Australis" or the Southern Land

Government type: federal parliamentary democracy under a constitutional monarchy; a Commonwealth realm

Capital: *name:* Canberra
geographic coordinates: 35 16 S, 149 08 E
time difference: UTC+10 (14 hours ahead of Washington, DC, during Standard Time)
daylight saving time: +1hr, begins first Sunday in October; ends first Sunday in April
time zone note: Australia has four time zones, including Lord Howe Island (UTC+10:30)
etymology: the name is claimed to derive from either Kambera or Camberry, which are names corrupted from the original native designation for the area "Nganbra" or "Nganbira"

Administrative divisions: 6 states and 2 territories*; Australian Capital Territory*, New South Wales, Northern Territory*, Queensland, South Australia, Tasmania, Victoria, Western Australia

Dependent areas: Ashmore and Cartier Islands, Christmas Island, Cocos (Keeling) Islands, Coral Sea Islands, Heard Island and McDonald Islands, Norfolk Island (6)

Independence: 1 January 1901 (from the federation of UK colonies)

National holiday: Australia Day (commemorates the arrival of the First Fleet of Australian settlers), 26 January (1788); ANZAC Day (commemorates the anniversary of the landing of troops of the Australian and New Zealand Army Corps during World War I at Gallipoli, Turkey), 25 April (1915)

Legal system: common law system based on the English model

Constitution: *history:* approved in a series of referenda from 1898 through 1900 and became law 9 July 1900, effective 1 January 1901
amendments: proposed by Parliament; passage requires approval of a referendum bill by absolute majority vote in both houses of Parliament, approval in a referendum by a majority of voters in at least four states and in the territories, and Royal Assent; proposals that would reduce a state's representation in either house or change a state's boundaries require that state's approval prior to Royal Assent; amended several times, last in 1977

International law organization participation: accepts compulsory ICJ jurisdiction with reservations; accepts ICCt jurisdiction

Citizenship: *citizenship by birth:* no
citizenship by descent only: at least one parent must be a citizen or permanent resident of Australia
dual citizenship recognized: yes
residency requirement for naturalization: 4 years

Suffrage: 18 years of age; universal and compulsory

Executive branch: *chief of state:* King CHARLES III (since 8 September 2022); represented by Governor General Samantha (Sam) MOSTYN (since 1 July 2024)
head of government: Prime Minister Anthony ALBANESE (since 23 May 2022)
cabinet: Cabinet nominated by the prime minister from among members of Parliament and sworn in by the governor general
elections/appointments: the monarchy is hereditary; governor general appointed by the monarch on the recommendation of the prime minister; following legislative elections, the leader of the majority party or majority coalition is sworn in as prime minister by the governor general

Legislative branch: *description:* bicameral Federal Parliament consists of:
Senate (76 seats; 12 members from each of the 6 states and 2 each from the 2 mainland territories; members directly elected in multi-seat constituencies by proportional representation vote; members serve 6-year terms with one-half of state membership renewed every 3 years and territory membership renewed every 3 years)
House of Representatives (151 seats; members directly elected in single-seat constituencies by majority preferential vote; members serve terms of up to 3 years)
elections: Senate - last held on 21 May 2022 (next to be held in May 2025)
House of Representatives - last held on 21 May 2022 (next to be held in May 2025)
election results: Senate - percent of vote by party/coalition - Liberal/National Coalition 40.7%, ALP 34.2%, Greens 14.5%, Pauline Hansen's One Nation 2.6%, Jacqui Lambee Network 2.6%, United Australia Party 1.3%, independent 3.9%; seats by party/coalition - Liberal/National Coalition 31, ALP 26, Australian Greens 11, Pauline Hansen's One Nation 2, Jacqui Lambee Network 2, United Australia Party 1, independent 3; composition - 33 men, 42 women; percentage women 56%
House of Representatives - percent of vote by party/coalition - ALP 50.9%, Coalition 36.4%, 7.9%, 2.6%, others less than 1%; seats by party/coalition - ALP 77, Coalition 55, independent 12, Greens 4, Katter's 1, Center Alliance 1, vacant 1; composition-92 men, 59 women; percentage women 39.1%; total Federal Parliament percentage women 44.7%

Judicial branch: *highest court(s):* High Court of Australia (consists of 7 justices, including the chief justice); note - each of the 6 states, 2 territories, and Norfolk Island has a Supreme Court; the High Court is the final appellate court beyond the state and territory supreme courts
judge selection and term of office: justices appointed by the governor-general in council for life with mandatory retirement at age 70
subordinate courts: subordinate courts: at the federal level: Federal Court; Federal Circuit and Family Court of Australia; at the state and territory level: Local Court - New South Wales; Magistrates' Courts – Victoria, Queensland, South Australia, Western Australia, Tasmania, Northern Territory, Australian Capital Territory; District Courts – New South Wales, Queensland, South Australia, Western Australia; County Court – Victoria; Family Court – Western Australia; Court of Petty Sessions – Norfolk Island

Political parties: Australian Greens Party or The Greens
Australian Labor Party or ALP
Centre Alliance (formerly known as the Nick Xenophon Team or NXT)
Jacqui Lambie Network or JLN
Katter's Australian Party
Liberal Party of Australia
The Nationals
One Nation or ONP
United Australia Party
note: the Labor Party is Australia's oldest political party, established federally in 1901; the present Liberal Party was formed in 1944; the Country Party was formed in 1920, renamed the National Country Party in 1975, the National Party of Australia in 1982, and since 2003 has been known as the Nationals; since the general election of 1949, the Liberal Party and the Nationals (under various names) when forming government have done so as a coalition

International organization participation: ADB, ANZUS, APEC, ARF, ASEAN (dialogue partner), Australia Group, BIS, C, CD, CP, EAS, EBRD, EITI (implementing country), FAO, FATF, G-20, IAEA, IBRD, ICAO, ICC (national committees), ICCt, ICRM, IDA, IEA, IFC, IFRCS, IHO, ILO, IMF, IMO, IMSO, Interpol, IOC, IOM, IPU, ISO, ITSO, ITU, ITUC (NGOs), MIGA, NEA, NSG, OECD, OPCW, OSCE (partner), Pacific Alliance (observer), Paris Club, PCA, PIF, SAARC (observer), Quad, SICA (observer), Sparteca, SPC, UN, UNCTAD, UNESCO, UNHCR, UNMISS, UNMIT, UNRWA, UNTSO, UNWTO, UPU, Wassenaar Arrangement, WCO, WFTU (NGOs), WHO, WIPO, WMO, WTO, ZC

Diplomatic representation in the US: *chief of mission:* Ambassador Kevin Michael RUDD (since 19 April 2023)
chancery: 1601 Massachusetts Avenue NW, Washington, DC 20036
telephone: [1] (202) 797-3000
FAX: [1] (202) 797-3168
email address and website:
info.us@dfat.gov.au
https://usa.embassy.gov.au/
consulate(s) general: Chicago, Honolulu, Houston, Los Angeles, New York, San Francisco

Diplomatic representation from the US: *chief of mission:* Ambassador Caroline KENNEDY (since 25 July 2022)
embassy: Moonah Place, Yarralumla, Australian Capital Territory 2600
mailing address: 7800 Canberra Place, Washington DC 20512-7800
telephone: [61] (02) 6214-5600
FAX: [61] (02) 9373-9184
email address and website:
AskEmbassyCanberra@state.gov
https://au.usembassy.gov/
consulate(s) general: Melbourne, Perth, Sydney

Flag description: blue with the flag of the UK in the upper hoist-side quadrant and a large seven-pointed star in the lower hoist-side quadrant known as the Commonwealth or Federation Star, representing the federation of the colonies of Australia in 1901; the star depicts one point for each of the six original states and one representing all of Australia's internal and external territories; on the fly half is a representation of the Southern Cross constellation in white with one small, five- pointed star and four larger, seven-pointed stars

National symbol(s): Commonwealth Star (seven-pointed Star of Federation), golden wattle tree (Acacia pycnantha), kangaroo, emu; national colors: green, gold

National anthem: *name:* Advance Australia Fair
lyrics/music: Peter Dodds McCORMICK
note 1: adopted 1984; although originally written in the late 19th century, the anthem was not used for all official occasions until 1984; as a Commonwealth country, in addition to the national anthem, "God Save the King" serves as the royal anthem (see United Kingdom)
note 2: the well-known and much-loved bush ballad "Waltzing Matilda" is often referred to as Australia's unofficial national anthem; the original lyrics were written in 1895 by Australian poet Banjo PATERSON, and were first published as sheet music in 1903; since 2012, a Waltzing Matilda Day has been held annually on 6 April, the anniversary of the first performance of the song in 1895

National heritage: *total World Heritage Sites:* 20 (4 cultural, 12 natural, 4 mixed); note - includes one site on Heard Island and McDonald Islands
selected World Heritage Site locales: Great Barrier Reef (n); Greater Blue Mountains Area (n); Fraser Island (n); Gondwana Rainforests (n); Lord Howe Island Group (n); Royal Exhibition Building and Carlton Gardens (c); Shark Bay (n); Sydney Opera House (c); Uluṟu-Kata Tjuṯa National Park (m); Kakadu National Park (m)

ECONOMY

Economic overview: highly developed, diversified, regionally and globally integrated economy; strong mining, manufacturing, and service sectors; net exporter driven by commodities to East Asian trade partners; "Future Made in Australia" program focused on green energy investments

Real GDP (purchasing power parity): $1.584 trillion (2023 est.)
$1.537 trillion (2022 est.)
$1.475 trillion (2021 est.)
note: data in 2021 dollars
comparison ranking: 20

Real GDP growth rate: 3.02% (2023 est.)
4.27% (2022 est.)
2.11% (2021 est.)
note: annual GDP % growth based on constant local currency
comparison ranking: 108

Real GDP per capita: $59,500 (2023 est.)
$59,100 (2022 est.)
$57,400 (2021 est.)
note: data in 2021 dollars
comparison ranking: 29

GDP (official exchange rate): $1.724 trillion (2023 est.)
note: data in current dollars at official exchange rate

Inflation rate (consumer prices): 5.6% (2023 est.)
6.59% (2022 est.)
2.86% (2021 est.)
note: annual % change based on consumer prices
comparison ranking: 118

Credit ratings: Fitch rating: AAA (2011)

Moody's rating: Aaa (2002)

Standard & Poors rating: AAA (2003)
note: The year refers to the year in which the current credit rating was first obtained.

GDP - composition, by sector of origin: *agriculture:* 2.4% (2023 est.)
industry: 27.4% (2023 est.)
services: 64.2% (2023 est.)
note: figures may not total 100% due to non-allocated consumption not captured in sector-reported data comparison rankings: services 63; industry 81; agriculture 150

GDP - composition, by end use: *household consumption:* 49.6% (2023 est.)
government consumption: 21.3% (2023 est.)
investment in fixed capital: 23.2% (2023 est.)
investment in inventories: 0.3% (2023 est.)
exports of goods and services: 26.7% (2023 est.)
imports of goods and services: -21.4% (2023 est.)
note: figures may not total 100% due to rounding or gaps in data collection

Agricultural products: wheat, sugarcane, barley, milk, rapeseed, cotton, sorghum, beef, oats, chicken (2022)
note: top ten agricultural products based on tonnage

Industries: mining, industrial and transportation equipment, food processing, chemicals, steel

Industrial production growth rate: 1.34% (2023 est.)
note: annual % change in industrial value added based on constant local currency
comparison ranking: 133

Labor force: 14.501 million (2023 est.)
note: number of people ages 15 or older who are employed or seeking work
comparison ranking: 44

Unemployment rate: 3.67% (2023 est.)
3.7% (2022 est.)
5.12% (2021 est.)
note: % of labor force seeking employment
comparison ranking: 69

Youth unemployment rate (ages 15-24): *total:* 8.6% (2023 est.)
male: 9.6% (2023 est.)
female: 7.5% (2023 est.)
note: % of labor force ages 15-24 seeking employment
comparison ranking: total 146

Population below poverty line: 13.4% (2020 est.)

Gini Index coefficient - distribution of family income: 34.3 (2018 est.)
note: index (0-100) of income distribution; higher values represent greater inequality
comparison ranking: 84

Average household expenditures: *on food:* 10.4% of household expenditures (2022 est.)
on alcohol and tobacco: 4.2% of household expenditures (2022 est.)

Household income or consumption by percentage share: *lowest 10%:* 2.7% (2018 est.)
highest 10%: 26.6% (2018 est.)
note: % share of income accruing to lowest and highest 10% of population

Remittances: 0.1% of GDP (2023 est.)
0.08% of GDP (2022 est.)
0.06% of GDP (2021 est.)
note: personal transfers and compensation between resident and non-resident individuals/households/entities

Budget: *revenues:* $431.371 billion (2022 est.)
expenditures: $447.119 billion (2022 est.)
note: central government revenues (excluding grants) and expenses converted to US dollars at average official exchange rate for year indicated

Public debt: 57.97% of GDP (2022 est.)
note: central government debt as a % of GDP
comparison ranking: 84

Taxes and other revenues: 23.6% (of GDP) (2022 est.)
note: central government tax revenue as a % of GDP
comparison ranking: 56

Current account balance: $21.384 billion (2023 est.)
$17.741 billion (2022 est.)
$49.092 billion (2021 est.)
note: balance of payments - net trade and primary/secondary income in current dollars
comparison ranking: 23

Exports: $447.508 billion (2023 est.)
$464.688 billion (2022 est.)
$389.158 billion (2021 est.)
note: balance of payments - exports of goods and services in current dollars
comparison ranking: 21

Exports - partners: China 29%, Japan 19%, South Korea 10%, India 7%, Taiwan 6% (2022)

note: top five export partners based on percentage share of exports

Exports - commodities: coal, iron ore, natural gas, gold, wheat (2022)
note: top five export commodities based on value in dollars

Imports: $363.573 billion (2023 est.)
$367.488 billion (2022 est.)
$299.549 billion (2021 est.)
note: balance of payments - imports of goods and services in current dollars
comparison ranking: 22

Imports - partners: China 28%, US 10%, South Korea 6%, Japan 6%, Singapore 5% (2022)
note: top five import partners based on percentage share of imports

Imports - commodities: refined petroleum, cars, garments, trucks, plastic products (2022)
note: top five import commodities based on value in dollars

Reserves of foreign exchange and gold: $61.703 billion (2023 est.)
$56.702 billion (2022 est.)
$57.878 billion (2021 est.)
note: holdings of gold (year-end prices)/foreign exchange/special drawing rights in current dollars
comparison ranking: 37

Exchange rates: Australian dollars (AUD) per US dollar -

Exchange rates: 1.505 (2023 est.)
1.442 (2022 est.)
1.331 (2021 est.)
1.453 (2020 est.)
1.439 (2019 est.)

ENERGY

Electricity access: *electrification - total population:* 100% (2022 est.)

Electricity: *installed generating capacity:* 101.35 million kW (2022 est.)
consumption: 250.005 billion kWh (2022 est.)
transmission/distribution losses: 11.481 billion kWh (2022 est.)
comparison rankings: transmission/distribution losses 184; consumption 20; installed generating capacity 16

Electricity generation sources: *fossil fuels:* 65.5% of total installed capacity (2022 est.)
solar: 15.2% of total installed capacity (2022 est.)
wind: 12% of total installed capacity (2022 est.)
hydroelectricity: 6.3% of total installed capacity (2022 est.)
biomass and waste: 1.1% of total installed capacity (2022 est.)

Coal: *production:* 465.865 million metric tons (2022 est.)
consumption: 107.624 million metric tons (2022 est.)
exports: 364.589 million metric tons (2022 est.)
imports: 657,000 metric tons (2022 est.)
proven reserves: 150.227 billion metric tons (2022 est.)

Petroleum: *total petroleum production:* 386,000 bbl/day (2023 est.)
refined petroleum consumption: 1.123 million bbl/day (2023 est.)
crude oil estimated reserves: 2.446 billion barrels (2021 est.)

Natural gas: *production:* 153.783 billion cubic meters (2022 est.)
consumption: 50.188 billion cubic meters (2022 est.)
exports: 106.072 billion cubic meters (2022 est.)
imports: 2.925 billion cubic meters (2022 est.)
proven reserves: 3.228 trillion cubic meters (2021 est.)

Carbon dioxide emissions: 415.177 million metric tonnes of CO_2 (2022 est.)
from coal and metallurgical coke: 173.542 million metric tonnes of CO_2 (2022 est.)
from petroleum and other liquids: 145.566 million metric tonnes of CO_2 (2022 est.)
from consumed natural gas: 96.069 million metric tonnes of CO_2 (2022 est.)
comparison ranking: total emissions 15

Energy consumption per capita: 236.653 million Btu/person (2022 est.)
comparison ranking: 12

COMMUNICATIONS

Telephones - fixed lines: *total subscriptions:* 6.409 million (2022 est.)
subscriptions per 100 inhabitants: 24 (2022 est.)
comparison ranking: total subscriptions 24

Telephones - mobile cellular: *total subscriptions:* 28.018 million (2022 est.)
subscriptions per 100 inhabitants: 107 (2022 est.)
comparison ranking: total subscriptions 49

Telecommunication systems: *general assessment:* the Australian telecom market since 2020 has been impacted by the pandemic, which forced many people to school and work from home and thus adopt fixed-line broadband services; internet traffic, both fixed and mobile, increased substantially as a result; in the fixed sector, there is an ongoing migration from copper-based platforms to fiber; the extension of fixed wireless access will mean that up to 120,000 premises currently dependent on satellite broadband will be able to access 5G-based fixed services; the fixed-line market has been falling steadily over the past five years; in the Australian fixed broadband market, there is a dynamic shift among customers to fiber networks; the DSL sector is steadily shrinking while subscribers on HFC infrastructure will continue to be provided by existing cable, with a steady migration to full fiber connectivity (2022)
domestic: 18 per 100 fixed-line telephone subscriptions and 105 per 100 mobile-cellular; more subscribers to mobile services than there are people; 90% of all mobile device sales are now smartphones, growth in mobile traffic brisk (2021)
international: country code - 61; landing points for more than 20 submarine cables including: the SeaMeWe-3 optical telecommunications submarine cable with links to Asia, the Middle East, and Europe; the INDIGO-Central, INDIGO West and ASC, North West Cable System, Australia-Papua New Guinea cable, CSCS, PPC-1, Gondwana-1, SCCN, Hawaiki, TGA, Basslink, Bass Strait-1, Bass Strait-2, JGA-S, with links to other Australian cities, New Zealand and many countries in southeast Asia, US and Europe; the H2 Cable, AJC, Telstra Endeavor, Southern Cross NEXT with links to Japan, Hong Kong, and other Pacific Ocean countries as well as the US; satellite earth stations - 10 Intelsat (4 Indian Ocean and 6 Pacific Ocean), 2 Inmarsat, 2 Globalstar, 5 other (2019)

Broadcast media: the Australian Broadcasting Corporation (ABC) runs multiple national and local radio networks and TV stations, as well as ABC Australia, a TV service that broadcasts in the Asia-Pacific region and is the main public broadcaster; Special Broadcasting Service (SBS), a second large public broadcaster, operates radio and TV networks broadcasting in multiple languages; several large national commercial TV networks, a large number of local commercial TV stations, and hundreds of commercial radio stations are accessible; cable and satellite systems are available (2022)

Internet country code: .au

Internet users: *total:* 24.96 million (2021 est.)
percent of population: 96% (2021 est.)
comparison ranking: total 35

Broadband - fixed subscriptions: *total:* 9,099,619 (2020 est.)
subscriptions per 100 inhabitants: 36 (2020 est.)
comparison ranking: total 23

TRANSPORTATION

National air transport system: *number of registered air carriers:* 25 (2020)
inventory of registered aircraft operated by air carriers: 583
annual passenger traffic on registered air carriers: 75,667,645 (2018)
annual freight traffic on registered air carriers: 2,027,640,000 (2018) mt-km

Civil aircraft registration country code prefix: VH

Airports: 2,180 (2024)
comparison ranking: 3

Heliports: 368 (2024)

Pipelines: 637 km condensate/gas, 30,054 km gas, 240 km liquid petroleum gas, 3,609 km oil, 110 km oil/gas/water, 72 km refined products (2013)

Railways: *total:* 32,606 km (2022) 3,448 km electrified
standard gauge: 18,007 km (2022) 1.435 mm
narrow gauge: 11,914 km (2022) 1.067 mm
broad gauge: 2,685 km (2022) 1.600 mm
comparison ranking: total 7

Roadways: *total:* 873,573 km
urban: 145,928 km
non-urban: 727,645 km (2015)
comparison ranking: total 9

Waterways: 2,000 km (2011) (mainly used for recreation on Murray and Murray-Darling River systems)
comparison ranking: 44

Merchant marine: *total:* 604 (2023)
by type: bulk carrier 2, general cargo 76, oil tanker 6, other 520
comparison ranking: total 37

Ports: *total ports:* 66 (2024)
large: 5
medium: 8
small: 24
very small: 29
ports with oil terminals: 38
key ports: Brisbane, Dampier, Darwin, Fremantle, Geelong, Hobart, Melbourne, Newcastle, Port Adelaide, Port Dalrymple, Port Kembla, Port Lincoln, Sydney

MILITARY AND SECURITY

Military and security forces: Australian Defense Force (ADF): Australian Army, Royal Australian Navy, Royal Australian Air Force (2024)
note: the Australian Federal Police (AFP) is an independent agency of the Attorney-General's Department; the AFP, state, and territorial police forces are responsible for internal security; the Australian Border Force is under the Department of Home Affairs

Military expenditures: 2% of GDP (2023 est.)
2% of GDP (2022)
2.1% of GDP (2021)
2.1% of GDP (2020)
2% of GDP (2019)
comparison ranking: 72

Military and security service personnel strengths: approximately 60,000 active troops (30,000 Army; 15,000 Navy; 15,000 Air Force) (2023)

Military equipment inventories and acquisitions: the military's inventory includes a mix of domestically produced and imported Western weapons systems; in recent years, the US has been the largest supplier of arms; the Australian defense industry produces a variety of land and sea weapons platforms; the defense industry also participates in joint development and production ventures with other Western countries, including the US and Canada (2024)
note: in 2023, the Australian defense ministry announced a new strategic review that called for the acquisition of more long-range deterrence capabilities, including missiles, submarines, and cyber tools; in early 2024, Australia announced a 10-year plan to more than double the number of the Navy's major surface combatant ships

Military service age and obligation: 17 years of age (with parental consent; 18 years of age to deploy) for voluntary military service for men and women; no conscription (abolished 1972) (2024)
note 1: as of July 2024, New Zealanders who are permanent residents and have lived in Australia for at least 12 months could apply to join the ADF; from January 2025, eligible permanent residents from Canada, the UK, and the US will also be able to apply
note 2: women have served in all roles, including combat arms, since 2013; in 2024, they comprised slightly more than 20% of the military

Military deployments: *note:* the number of Australian military forces varies by mission; since the 1990s, Australia has deployed more than 30,000 personnel on nearly 100 UN peacekeeping and coalition military operations around the World

Military - note: Australia has been part of the Australia, New Zealand, and US Security (ANZUS) Treaty since 1951; Australia is also a member of the Five Powers Defense Arrangements (FPDA), a series of mutual assistance agreements reached in 1971 embracing Australia, Malaysia, New Zealand, Singapore, and the UK
Australia has long-standing bi-lateral defense and security ties to the UK, including defense and security cooperation treaties in 2024 and 2013; in 2020, Australia and the UK signed a memorandum of understanding to cooperate on the building of a next generation of frigates for their respective navies; the Australia-UK Ministerial Consultations (AUKMIN) is their premier bilateral forum on foreign policy, defense, and security issues
Australia also has a long-standing military relationship with the US; Australian and US forces first fought together in France in 1918 and have fought together in every major US conflict since; Australia and the US signed an agreement in 2014 that allowed for closer bi-lateral defense and security cooperation, including rotations of US military forces and equipment to Australia; Australian military forces train often with US forces; Australia has Major Non-NATO Ally (MNNA) status with the US, a designation under US law that provides foreign partners with certain benefits in the areas of defense trade and security cooperation
in 2021, Australia, the UK, and the US announced an enhanced trilateral security partnership called "AUKUS" which would build on existing bilateral ties, including deeper integration of defense and security-related science, technology, industrial bases, and supply chains, as well as deeper cooperation on a range of defense and security capabilities; the first initiative under AUKUS was a commitment to support Australia in acquiring conventionally armed nuclear-powered submarines for the Royal Australian Navy
the ADF's missions include protecting Australia's borders and maritime interests, responding to domestic natural disasters, and deploying overseas for humanitarian, peacekeeping, and other security-related missions; it regularly participates in bi-lateral and multi-lateral exercises with foreign militaries; in 2024, it established a cyber command (2024)

SPACE

Space agency/agencies: Australian Space Agency (ASA; established 2018; headquarters opened in 2020); Defense Space Command (established 2022) (2024)

Space launch site(s): Whalers Way Orbital Launch Complex (commercial site, South Australia); Arnhem Space Center (commercial site, Northern Territory) (2024)

Space program overview: has a long history of involvement in space-related activities, including astronomy, rockets, satellites, and space tracking; develops, builds, operates, and tracks satellites, including communications, remote sensing (RS), navigational, and scientific/testing/research, often in partnership with other countries; develops other space technologies, including communications, RS capabilities, and telescopes; encouraging growth in domestic commercial space industry sector; cooperates with a variety of foreign space agencies and industries, including those of China, the European Space Agency/EU and their individual member states, India, Japan, New Zealand, South Korea, the UK, and the US; co-leads the Global Earth Observation System of Systems (2024)
note: further details about the key activities, programs, and milestones of the country's space program, as well as government spending estimates on the space sector, appear in the Space Programs reference guide

TERRORISM

Terrorist group(s): Islamic State of Iraq and ash-Sham (ISIS)
note: details about the history, aims, leadership, organization, areas of operation, tactics, targets, weapons, size, and sources of support of the group(s) appear(s) in the Terrorism reference guide

TRANSNATIONAL ISSUES

Refugees and internally displaced persons: *refugees (country of origin):* 12,180 (Iran), 8,741 (Afghanistan), 5,042 (Pakistan) (mid-year 2022)
stateless persons: 7,649 (2022)

Illicit drugs: amphetamine-type stimulants (ATS) and cannabis dominate the domestic illicit drug market and shown potential for expansion, with ATS accounting for the preponderance of detected imports; domestic heroin market is small, but also shown some growth; as of 2020, Malaysia was the primary embarkation point for heroin and ATS imports other than MDMA (ecstasy) for which South Korea was the primary embarkation point although MDMA is increasingly being produced domestically with number of detected labs nearly doubled. The US is the principal embarkation point for imported cannabis; Tasmania is one of the world's major suppliers of licit opiate products; government maintains strict controls over areas of opium poppy cultivation and output of poppy straw concentrate; major consumer of cocaine and amphetamines

AUSTRIA

INTRODUCTION

Background: Once the center of power for the large Austro-Hungarian Empire, Austria was reduced to a small republic after its defeat in World War I. Nazi Germany annexed Austria in 1938, and the victorious Allies then occupied the country in 1945. As a result, Austria's status remained unclear for a decade after World War II, until a State Treaty signed in 1955 ended the occupation, recognized Austria's independence, and forbade unification with Germany. A constitutional law that same year declared the country's "perpetual neutrality" as a condition for Soviet military withdrawal. Austria joined the EU in 1995, but the obligation to remain neutral kept it from joining NATO, although the country became a member of NATO's Partnership for Peace program in 1995. Austria entered the EU Economic and Monetary Union in 1999.

GEOGRAPHY

Location: Central Europe, north of Italy and Slovenia

Geographic coordinates: 47 20 N, 13 20 E

Map references: Europe

Area: *total:* 83,871 sq km
land: 82,445 sq km
water: 1,426 sq km
comparison ranking: total 114

Area - comparative: about the size of South Carolina; slightly more than two-thirds the size of Pennsylvania

Land boundaries: *total:* 2,524 km
border countries (8): Czech Republic 402 km; Germany 801 km; Hungary 321 km; Italy 404 km; Liechtenstein 34 km; Slovakia 105 km; Slovenia 299 km; Switzerland 158 km

Coastline: 0 km (landlocked)

Maritime claims: none (landlocked)

Climate: temperate; continental, cloudy; cold winters with frequent rain and some snow in lowlands and snow in mountains; moderate summers with occasional showers

Terrain: mostly mountains (Alps) in the west and south; mostly flat or gently sloping along the eastern and northern margins

Elevation: *highest point:* Grossglockner 3,798 m
lowest point: Neusiedler See 115 m
mean elevation: 910 m

Natural resources: oil, coal, lignite, timber, iron ore, copper, zinc, antimony, magnesite, tungsten, graphite, salt, hydropower

Land use: *agricultural land:* 38.4% (2018 est.)
arable land: 16.5% (2018 est.)
permanent crops: 0.8% (2018 est.)
permanent pasture: 21.1% (2018 est.)
forest: 47.2% (2018 est.)
other: 14.4% (2018 est.)

Irrigated land: 382 sq km (2016)

Major lakes (area sq km): *fresh water lake(s):* Lake Constance (shared with Switzerland and Germany) - 540 sq km

Major rivers (by length in km): Donau (Danube) (shared with Germany [s], Slovakia, Hungary, Croatia, Serbia, Bulgaria, Ukraine, Moldova, and Romania [m]) - 2,888 km
note – [s] after country name indicates river source; [m] after country name indicates river mouth

Major watersheds (area sq km): Atlantic Ocean drainage: Rhine-Maas (198,735 sq km), *(Black Sea)* Danube (795,656 sq km)

Population distribution: the northern and eastern portions of the country are more densely populated; nearly two-thirds of the populace lives in urban areas

Natural hazards: landslides; avalanches; earthquakes

Geography - note: *note 1:* landlocked; strategic location at the crossroads of central Europe with many easily traversable Alpine passes and valleys; major river is the Danube; population is concentrated on eastern lowlands because of steep slopes, poor soils, and low temperatures elsewhere
note 2: the world's largest and longest ice cave system at 42 km (26 mi) is the Eisriesenwelt (Ice Giants World) inside the Hochkogel mountain near Werfen, about 40 km south of Salzburg; ice caves are bedrock caves that contain yearround ice formations; they differ from glacial caves, which are transient and are formed by melting ice and flowing water within and under glaciers

PEOPLE AND SOCIETY

Population: *total:* 8,967,982
male: 4,392,898
female: 4,575,084 (2024 est.)
comparison rankings: female 99; male 102; total 100

Nationality: *noun:* Austrian(s)
adjective: Austrian

Ethnic groups: Austrian 80.8%, German 2.6%, Bosnian and Herzegovinian 1.9%, Turkish 1.8%, Serbian 1.6%, Romanian 1.3%, other 10% (2018 est.)
note: data represent population by country of birth

Languages: German (official nationwide) 88.6%, Turkish 2.3%, Serbian 2.2%, Croatian (official in Burgenland) 1.6%, other (includes Slovene, official in southern Carinthia, and Hungarian, official in Burgenland) 5.3% (2001 est.)
major-language sample(s):
Das World Factbook, die unverzichtbare Quelle für grundlegende Informationen. (German)

Religions: Roman Catholic 55.2%, Muslim 8.3%, Orthodox 4.9%, Evangelical Christian 3.8%, Jewish 0.1%, other 5.4%, none 22.4% (2021 est.)
note: data on Muslim is a 2016 estimate; data on other/none/unspecified are from 2012-2018 estimates

Age structure: *0-14 years:* 14.1% (male 648,639/ female 616,334)
15-64 years: 64.7% (male 2,904,587/female 2,898,339)
65 years and over: 21.2% (2024 est.) (male 839,672/ female 1,060,411)

Dependency ratios: *total dependency ratio:* 51.1
youth dependency ratio: 21.7
elderly dependency ratio: 29.4
potential support ratio: 3.4 (2021 est.)

Median age: *total:* 44.9 years (2024 est.)
male: 43.6 years
female: 46.3 years
comparison ranking: total 24

Population growth rate: 0.3% (2024 est.)
comparison ranking: 167

Birth rate: 9.3 births/1,000 population (2024 est.)
comparison ranking: 194

Death rate: 9.9 deaths/1,000 population (2024 est.)
comparison ranking: 37

Net migration rate: 3.5 migrant(s)/1,000 population (2024 est.)
comparison ranking: 32

Population distribution: the northern and eastern portions of the country are more densely populated; nearly two-thirds of the populace lives in urban areas

Urbanization: *urban population:* 59.5% of total population (2023)
rate of urbanization: 0.68% annual rate of change (2020-25 est.)

Major urban areas - population: 1.975 million VIENNA (capital) (2023)

Sex ratio: *at birth:* 1.05 male(s)/female
0-14 years: 1.05 male(s)/female
15-64 years: 1 male(s)/female
65 years and over: 0.79 male(s)/female
total population: 0.96 male(s)/female (2024 est.)

Mother's mean age at first birth: 29.7 years (2020 est.)

Maternal mortality ratio: 5 deaths/100,000 live births (2020 est.)
comparison ranking: 168

Infant mortality rate: *total:* 3.2 deaths/1,000 live births (2024 est.)
male: 3.6 deaths/1,000 live births
female: 2.7 deaths/1,000 live births
comparison ranking: total 201

Life expectancy at birth: *total population:* 82.7 years (2024 est.)
male: 80.1 years
female: 85.4 years
comparison ranking: total population 24

Total fertility rate: 1.52 children born/woman (2024 est.)
comparison ranking: 200

Gross reproduction rate: 0.74 (2024 est.)

Contraceptive prevalence rate: 79% (2019)
note: percent of women aged 16-49

Drinking water source: *improved: urban:* 100% of population
rural: 100% of population
total: 100% of population
(2020 est.)

Current health expenditure: 11.5% of GDP (2020)

Physician density: 5.29 physicians/1,000 population (2020)

Hospital bed density: 7.3 beds/1,000 population (2018)

Sanitation facility access: *improved: urban:* 100% of population
rural: 100% of population
total: 100% of population
(2020 est.)

Obesity - adult prevalence rate: 20.1% (2016)
comparison ranking: 105

Alcohol consumption per capita: *total:* 11.9 liters of pure alcohol (2019 est.)
beer: 6.3 liters of pure alcohol (2019 est.)
wine: 3.7 liters of pure alcohol (2019 est.)
spirits: 1.9 liters of pure alcohol (2019 est.)
other alcohols: 0 liters of pure alcohol (2019 est.)
comparison ranking: total 5

Tobacco use: *total:* 26.4% (2020 est.)
male: 27.7% (2020 est.)
female: 25% (2020 est.)
comparison ranking: total 42

Children under the age of 5 years underweight: NA

Currently married women (ages 15-49): 58.7% (2023 est.)

Education expenditures: 5.1% of GDP (2020 est.)
comparison ranking: 72

School life expectancy (primary to tertiary education): *total:* 16 years

male: 16 years
female: 16 years (2020)

ENVIRONMENT

Environment - current issues: some forest degradation caused by air and soil pollution; soil pollution results from the use of agricultural chemicals; air pollution results from emissions by coal- and oil-fired power stations and industrial plants and from trucks transiting Austria between northern and southern Europe; water pollution; the Danube, as well as some of Austria's other rivers and lakes, are threatened by pollution

Environment - international agreements: *party to:* Air Pollution, Air Pollution-Heavy Metals, Air Pollution-Nitrogen Oxides, Air Pollution-Persistent Organic Pollutants, Air Pollution-Sulphur 85, Air Pollution-Sulphur 94, Air Pollution-Volatile Organic Compounds, Antarctic Treaty, Biodiversity, Climate Change, Climate Change-Kyoto Protocol, Climate Change-Paris Agreement, Comprehensive Nuclear Test Ban, Desertification, Endangered Species, Environmental Modification, Hazardous Wastes, Law of the Sea, Nuclear Test Ban, Ozone Layer Protection, Ship Pollution, Tropical Timber 2006, Wetlands, Whaling
signed, but not ratified: Air Pollution-Multi-effect Protocol, Antarctic-Environmental Protection

Climate: temperate; continental, cloudy; cold winters with frequent rain and some snow in lowlands and snow in mountains; moderate summers with occasional showers

Urbanization: *urban population:* 59.5% of total population (2023)
rate of urbanization: 0.68% annual rate of change (2020-25 est.)

Revenue from forest resources: 0.07% of GDP (2018 est.)
comparison ranking: 123

Revenue from coal: 0% of GDP (2018 est.)
comparison ranking: 100

Air pollutants: *particulate matter emissions:* 11.51 micrograms per cubic meter (2019 est.)
carbon dioxide emissions: 61.45 megatons (2016 est.)
methane emissions: 6.34 megatons (2020 est.)

Waste and recycling: *municipal solid waste generated annually:* 4.836 million tons (2015 est.)
municipal solid waste recycled annually: 1,240,918 tons (2015 est.)
percent of municipal solid waste recycled: 25.7% (2015 est.)

Major lakes (area sq km): *fresh water lake(s):* Lake Constance (shared with Switzerland and Germany) - 540 sq km

Major rivers (by length in km): Donau (Danube) (shared with Germany [s], Slovakia, Hungary, Croatia, Serbia, Bulgaria, Ukraine, Moldova, and Romania [m]) - 2,888 km
note – [s] after country name indicates river source; [m] after country name indicates river mouth

Major watersheds (area sq km): Atlantic Ocean drainage: Rhine-Maas (198,735 sq km), *(Black Sea)* Danube (795,656 sq km)

Total water withdrawal: *municipal:* 720 million cubic meters (2020 est.)
industrial: 2.7 billion cubic meters (2020 est.)
agricultural: 720 million cubic meters (2020 est.)

Total renewable water resources: 77.7 billion cubic meters (2020 est.)

Geoparks: *total global geoparks and regional networks:* 3
global geoparks and regional networks: Ore of the Alps; Styrian Eisenwurzen; Karawanken/Karavanke (includes Slovenia) (2023)

GOVERNMENT

Country name: *conventional long form:* Republic of Austria
conventional short form: Austria
local long form: Republik Oesterreich
local short form: Oesterreich
etymology: the name Oesterreich means "eastern realm" and dates to the 10th century; the designation refers to the fact that Austria was the easternmost extension of both Bavaria and all German peoples; the word Austria is a Latinization of the German name

Government type: federal parliamentary republic

Capital: *name:* Vienna
geographic coordinates: 48 12 N, 16 22 E
time difference: UTC+1 (6 hours ahead of Washington, DC, during Standard Time)
daylight saving time: +1hr, begins last Sunday in March; ends last Sunday in October
etymology: the origin of the name is disputed but may derive from early Celtic settlements of the area; a plausible reconstructed Celtic name from several centuries B.C. is Vedunia (meaning "forest stream"), which in Old High German became *uuenia* (*wenia*), and later *wien* (its current German form) in New High German; another possibility is that the name stems from the Roman settlement Vindobona, established around 15 B.C., and its Celtic-derived name (likely from the Celtic *windo*, meaning "white, fair, or bright" and *bona* meaning "base, fortification, or settlement" to give a connotation of "white settlement" or "white fort"); archeological remains of the latter survive at many sites in the center of Vienna

Administrative divisions: 9 states (Bundeslaender, singular - Bundesland); Burgenland, Kaernten (Carinthia), Niederoesterreich (Lower Austria), Oberoesterreich (Upper Austria), Salzburg, Steiermark (Styria), Tirol (Tyrol), Vorarlberg, Wien (Vienna)

Independence: *no official date of independence:* 976 (Margravate of Austria established); 17 September 1156 (Duchy of Austria founded); 6 January 1453 (Archduchy of Austria acknowledged); 11 August 1804 (Austrian Empire proclaimed); 30 March 1867 (Austro-Hungarian dual monarchy established); 12 November 1918 (First Republic proclaimed); 27 April 1945 (Second Republic proclaimed)

National holiday: National Day (commemorates passage of the law on permanent neutrality), 26 October (1955)

Legal system: civil law system; judicial review of legislative acts by the Constitutional Court

Constitution: *history:* several previous; latest adopted 1 October 1920, revised 1929, replaced May 1934, replaced by German Weimar constitution in 1938 following German annexation, reinstated 1 May 1945
amendments: proposed through laws designated "constitutional laws" or through the constitutional process if the amendment is part of another law; approval required by at least a two-thirds majority vote by the National Assembly and the presence of one-half of the members; a referendum is required only if requested by one-third of the National Council or Federal Council membership; passage by referendum requires absolute majority vote; amended many times, last in 2020

International law organization participation: accepts compulsory ICJ jurisdiction; accepts ICCt jurisdiction

Citizenship: *citizenship by birth:* no
citizenship by descent only: at least one parent must be a citizen of Austria
dual citizenship recognized: no
residency requirement for naturalization: 10 years

Suffrage: 16 years of age; universal

Executive branch: *chief of state:* President Alexander VAN DER BELLEN (since 26 January 2017)
head of government: Chancellor Karl NEHAMMER (since 6 December 2021)
cabinet: Council of Ministers proposed by the chancellor and appointed by the president
elections/appointments: president directly elected by absolute majority popular vote in 2 rounds if needed for a 6-year term (eligible for a second term); election last held on 9 October 2022 (next to be held in 2028); chancellor appointed by the president but determined by the majority coalition parties in the Federal Assembly; vice chancellor appointed by the president on the advice of the chancellor
election results:
2022: Alexander VAN DER BELLEN reelected in first round; percent of vote - Alexander VAN DER BELLEN (independent) 56.7%, Walter ROSENKRANZ (FPO) 17.7%, Dominik WLAZNY (Beer Party) 8.3%, Tassilo WALLENTIN (independent) 8.1%, Gerald GROSZ (independent) 5.6%
2016: Alexander VAN DER BELLEN elected in second round; percent of vote in first round - Norbert HOFER (FPOe) 35.1%, Alexander VAN DER BELLEN (independent, allied with the Greens) 21.3%, Irmgard GRISS (independent) 18.9%, Rudolf HUNDSTORFER (SPOe) 11.3%, Andreas KHOL (OeVP) 11.1%, Richard LUGNER (independent) 2.3%; percent of vote in second round - Alexander VAN DER BELLEN 53.8%, Norbert HOFER 46.2%

Legislative branch: *description:* bicameral Federal Assembly or Bundesversammlung consists of:
Federal Council or Bundesrat (61 seats - currently 60; members appointed by state parliaments with each state receiving 3 to 12 seats in proportion to its population; members serve 5- or 6-year terms)
National Council or Nationalrat (183 seats; members directly elected in single-seat constituencies by proportional representation vote; members serve 5-year terms)
elections: Federal Council - last appointed in 2021
National Council - last held on 29 September 2019 (next to be held by 23 October 2024)
election results: Federal Council - percent of vote by party - OeVP 42.6%, SPOe 31.2%. FPOe 16.4%, The Greens 8.2%, NEOS 1.6%; seats by party - OeVP 26, SPOe 19, FPOe 10, The Greens 5, NEOS 1; composition - men 32, women 28, percentage women 46.7%
National Council - percent of vote by party - OeVP 37.5%, SPOe 21.2%, FPOe 16.2%, The Greens 13.9%, NEOS 8.1%, other 3.1%; seats by party - OeVP 71, SPOe 40, FPOe 31, The Greens 26, NEOS 15; composition - men 109, women 74, percentage women 41%; total Federal Assembly percentage women 42%

Judicial branch: *highest court(s):* Supreme Court of Justice or Oberster Gerichtshof (consists of 85 judges organized into 17 senates or panels of 5 judges each); Constitutional Court or Verfassungsgerichtshof (consists of 20 judges including 6 substitutes; Administrative Court or Verwaltungsgerichtshof - 2 judges plus other members depending on the importance of the case)
judge selection and term of office: Supreme Court judges nominated by executive branch departments and appointed by the president; judges serve for life; Constitutional Court judges nominated by several executive branch departments and approved by the president; judges serve for life; Administrative Court judges recommended by executive branch departments and appointed by the president; terms of judges and members determined by the president
subordinate courts: Courts of Appeal (4); Regional Courts (20); district courts (120); county courts

Political parties: Austrian People's Party or OeVP
Freedom Party of Austria or FPOe
The Greens - The Green Alternative
NEOS - The New Austria and Liberal Forum
Social Democratic Party of Austria or SPOe

International organization participation: ADB (nonregional member), AfDB (nonregional member), Australia Group, BIS, BSEC (observer), CD, CE, CEI, CERN, EAPC, EBRD, ECB, EIB, EMU, ESA, EU, FAO, FATF, G-9, IADB, IAEA, IBRD, ICAO, ICC (national committees), ICCt, ICRM, IDA, IEA, IFAD, IFC, IFRCS, IGAD (partners), ILO, IMF, IMO, Interpol, IOC, IOM, IPU, ISO, ITSO, ITU, ITUC (NGOs), MIGA, MINURSO, NEA, NSG, OAS (observer), OECD, OIF (observer), OPCW, OSCE, Paris Club, PCA, PFP, Schengen Convention, SELEC (observer), UN, UNCTAD, UNESCO, UNFICYP, UNHCR, UNIDO, UNIFIL, UNTSO, UNWTO, UPU, Wassenaar Arrangement, WCO, WFTU (NGOs), WHO, WIPO, WMO, WTO, ZC

Diplomatic representation in the US: *chief of mission:* Ambassador Petra SCHNEEBAUER (since 19 APRIL 2023)
chancery: 3524 International Court NW, Washington, DC 20008-3035
telephone: [1] (202) 895-6700
FAX: [1] (202) 895-6750
email address and website:
washington-ob@bmeia.gv.at
https://www.austria.org/
consulate(s) general: Los Angeles, New York
consulate(s): Chicago

Diplomatic representation from the US: *chief of mission:* Ambassador Victoria Reggie KENNEDY (since 12 January 2022)
embassy: Boltzmanngasse 16, 1090, Vienna
mailing address: 9900 Vienna Place, Washington DC 20521-9900
telephone: [43] (1) 31339 0
FAX: [43] (1) 31339 2017
email address and website:
ConsulateVienna@state.gov
https://at.usembassy.gov/

Flag description: three equal horizontal bands of red (top), white, and red; the flag design is certainly one of the oldest - if not the oldest - national banners in the world; according to tradition, in 1191, following a fierce battle in the Third Crusade, Duke Leopold V of Austria's white tunic became completely blood-spattered; upon removal of his wide belt or sash, a white band was revealed; the red-white-red color combination was subsequently adopted as his banner

National symbol(s): eagle, edelweiss, Alpine gentian; national colors: red, white

National anthem: *name:* "Bundeshymne" (Federal Hymn)
lyrics/music: Paula von PRERADOVIC/Wolfgang Amadeus MOZART or Johann HOLZER (disputed)
note 1: adopted 1947; the anthem is also known as "Land der Berge, Land am Strome" (Land of the Mountains, Land by the River); Austria adopted a new national anthem after World War II to replace the former imperial anthem composed by Franz Josef HAYDN, which had been appropriated by Germany in 1922 and was thereafter associated with the Nazi regime; a gender-neutral version of the lyrics was adopted by the Austrian Federal Assembly in fall 2011 and became effective 1 January 2012
note 2: the beloved waltz "The Blue Danube" ("An der schoenen, blauen Donau"), composed in 1866 by the Austrian composer Johann STRAUSS II, is consistently referred to as Austria's unofficial national anthem

National heritage: *total World Heritage Sites:* 12 (11 cultural, 1 natural)
selected World Heritage Site locales: Historic Salzburg (c); Palace and Gardens of Schönbrunn (c); Halstadt–Dachstein/Salzkammergut Cultural Landscape (c); Semmering railway (c); Historic Graz and Schloss Eggenberg (c); Wachau Cultural Landscape (c); Historic Vienna (c); Ferto/Neusiedlersee Cultural Landscape (c); Baden bei Wien (c); Primeval Beech Forests - Dürrenstein, Kalkalpen (n)

ECONOMY

Economic overview: one of the strongest EU and euro economies; diversified trade portfolios and relations; enormous trade economy; Russian energy dependence, but investing in alternative energy; aging labor force but large refugee population; large government debt

Real GDP (purchasing power parity): $590.354 billion (2023 est.)
$595.287 billion (2022 est.)
$567.987 billion (2021 est.)
note: data in 2021 dollars
comparison ranking: 43

Real GDP growth rate: -0.83% (2023 est.)
4.81% (2022 est.)
4.24% (2021 est.)
note: annual GDP % growth based on constant local currency
comparison ranking: 198

Real GDP per capita: $64,600 (2023 est.)
$65,800 (2022 est.)
$63,400 (2021 est.)
note: data in 2021 dollars
comparison ranking: 22

GDP (official exchange rate): $516.034 billion (2023 est.)
note: data in current dollars at official exchange rate

Inflation rate (consumer prices): 7.81% (2023 est.)
8.55% (2022 est.)
2.77% (2021 est.)
note: annual % change based on consumer prices
comparison ranking: 152

Credit ratings: Fitch rating: AA+ (2015)
Moody's rating: Aa1 (2016)
Standard & Poors rating: AA+ (2012)
note: The year refers to the year in which the current credit rating was first obtained.

GDP - composition, by sector of origin: *agriculture:* 1.3% (2023 est.)
industry: 26.3% (2023 est.)
services: 62.3% (2023 est.)
note: figures may not total 100% due to non-allocated consumption not captured in sector-reported data
comparison rankings: services 74; industry 88; agriculture 178

GDP - composition, by end use: *household consumption:* 51.8% (2023 est.)
government consumption: 20.3% (2023 est.)
investment in fixed capital: 24.4% (2023 est.)
investment in inventories: 0.9% (2023 est.)
exports of goods and services: 59.5% (2023 est.)
imports of goods and services: -56.6% (2023 est.)
note: figures may not total 100% due to rounding or gaps in data collection

Agricultural products: milk, sugar beets, maize, wheat, barley, potatoes, pork, grapes, triticale, apples (2022)
note: top ten agricultural products based on tonnage

Industries: construction, machinery, vehicles and parts, food, metals, chemicals, lumber and paper, electronics, tourism

Industrial production growth rate: -1.99% (2023 est.)
note: annual % change in industrial value added based on constant local currency
comparison ranking: 181

Labor force: 4.825 million (2023 est.)
note: number of people ages 15 or older who are employed or seeking work
comparison ranking: 90

Unemployment rate: 5.24% (2023 est.)
4.99% (2022 est.)
6.46% (2021 est.)
note: % of labor force seeking employment
comparison ranking: 99

Youth unemployment rate (ages 15-24): *total:* 10.9% (2023 est.)
male: 10.6% (2023 est.)
female: 11.3% (2023 est.)
note: % of labor force ages 15-24 seeking employment
comparison ranking: total 123

Population below poverty line: 14.8% (2021 est.)
note: % of population with income below national poverty line

Gini Index coefficient - distribution of family income: 30.7 (2021 est.)
note: index (0-100) of income distribution; higher values represent greater inequality
comparison ranking: 121

Average household expenditures: *on food:* 10.8% of household expenditures (2022 est.)
on alcohol and tobacco: 3.7% of household expenditures (2022 est.)

Household income or consumption by percentage share: *lowest 10%:* 2.8% (2021 est.)
highest 10%: 23.8% (2021 est.)
note: % share of income accruing to lowest and highest 10% of population

Remittances: 0.64% of GDP (2023 est.)
0.64% of GDP (2022 est.)
0.67% of GDP (2021 est.)
note: personal transfers and compensation between resident and non-resident individuals/households/entities

Budget: *revenues:* $212.218 billion (2022 est.)
expenditures: $225.52 billion (2022 est.)
note: central government revenues (excluding grants) and expenses converted to US dollars at average official exchange rate for year indicated

Public debt: 75.05% of GDP (2022 est.)
note: central government debt as a % of GDP
comparison ranking: 46

Taxes and other revenues: 26.24% (of GDP) (2022 est.)
note: central government tax revenue as a % of GDP
comparison ranking: 36

Current account balance: $13.686 billion (2023 est.)
-$1.29 billion (2022 est.)
$7.77 billion (2021 est.)
note: balance of payments - net trade and primary/secondary income in current dollars
comparison ranking: 24

Exports: $306.466 billion (2023 est.)
$292.012 billion (2022 est.)
$267.791 billion (2021 est.)
note: balance of payments - exports of goods and services in current dollars
comparison ranking: 31

Exports - partners: Germany 28%, US 7%, Italy 7%, Switzerland 5%, Hungary 5% (2022)
note: top five export partners based on percentage share of exports

Exports - commodities: cars, packaged medicine, vaccines, plastic products, electricity (2022)
note: top five export commodities based on value in dollars

Imports: $288.146 billion (2023 est.)
$290.277 billion (2022 est.)
$264.231 billion (2021 est.)
note: balance of payments - imports of goods and services in current dollars
comparison ranking: 29

Imports - partners: Germany 40%, Italy 7%, Czechia 5%, Switzerland 5%, Netherlands 4% (2022)
note: top five import partners based on percentage share of imports

Imports - commodities: cars, refined petroleum, gold, garments, broadcasting equipment (2022)
note: top five import commodities based on value in dollars

Reserves of foreign exchange and gold: $31.212 billion (2023 est.)
$33.078 billion (2022 est.)
$33.957 billion (2021 est.)
note: holdings of gold (year-end prices)/foreign exchange/special drawing rights in current dollars
comparison ranking: 60

Exchange rates: euros (EUR) per US dollar -

Exchange rates: 0.925 (2023 est.)
0.95 (2022 est.)
0.845 (2021 est.)
0.876 (2020 est.)
0.893 (2019 est.)

ENERGY

Electricity access: *electrification - total population:* 100% (2022 est.)

Electricity: *installed generating capacity:* 29.81 million kW (2022 est.)
consumption: 65.168 billion kWh (2022 est.)
exports: 19.882 billion kWh (2022 est.)
imports: 28.595 billion kWh (2022 est.)
transmission/distribution losses: 3.252 billion kWh (2022 est.)
comparison rankings: transmission/distribution losses 143; imports 7; exports 15; consumption 46; installed generating capacity 37

Electricity generation sources: *fossil fuels:* 25.1% of total installed capacity (2022 est.)
solar: 4.5% of total installed capacity (2022 est.)
wind: 11.7% of total installed capacity (2022 est.)
hydroelectricity: 51.2% of total installed capacity (2022 est.)
biomass and waste: 7.5% of total installed capacity (2022 est.)

Coal: *production:* 1.271 million metric tons (2022 est.)
consumption: 5.026 million metric tons (2022 est.)
exports: 2,000 metric tons (2022 est.)
imports: 4.152 million metric tons (2022 est.)

Petroleum: *total petroleum production:* 18,000 bbl/day (2023 est.)
refined petroleum consumption: 245,000 bbl/day (2023 est.)
crude oil estimated reserves: 35.2 million barrels (2021 est.)

Natural gas: *production:* 618.209 million cubic meters (2022 est.)
consumption: 8.136 billion cubic meters (2022 est.)
imports: 12.132 billion cubic meters (2022 est.)
proven reserves: 5.04 billion cubic meters (2021 est.)

Carbon dioxide emissions: 57.876 million metric tonnes of CO_2 (2022 est.)
from coal and metallurgical coke: 9.483 million metric tonnes of CO_2 (2022 est.)
from petroleum and other liquids: 32.758 million metric tonnes of CO_2 (2022 est.)
from consumed natural gas: 15.636 million metric tonnes of CO_2 (2022 est.)
comparison ranking: total emissions 55

Energy consumption per capita: 123.11 million Btu/person (2022 est.)
comparison ranking: 33

COMMUNICATIONS

Telephones - fixed lines: *total subscriptions:* 3.544 million (2022 est.)
subscriptions per 100 inhabitants: 40 (2022 est.)
comparison ranking: total subscriptions 36

Telephones - mobile cellular: *total subscriptions:* 11.035 million (2022 est.)
subscriptions per 100 inhabitants: 123 (2022 est.)
comparison ranking: total subscriptions 90

Telecommunication systems: *general assessment:* mature telecom market; the mobile market benefits from a growing number of Mobile Virtual Network Operators; the telcos as well as the government and regulator have been focused on delivering improved telecom infrastructure; the government has a program to provide a national gigabit service by 2030, delivered by private enterprise though with some state funding; this is based on fiber networks supported by 5G, with the Mobile Network Operators able to expand the reach of their 5G services following auctions held in March 2019 and September 2020; the fixed-line broadband market is still dominated by the DSL sector, while the cable broadband sector has held a steady share of connections in recent years; the fiber sector was slow to develop, and although fiber remains low there are plans to build out the network infrastructure (2021)
domestic: developed and efficient; 43 per 100 fixed telephone subscriptions; 122 per 100 mobile-cellular subscriptions (2021)
international: country code - 43; earth stations available in the Astra, Intelsat, Eutelsat satellite systems (2019)

Broadcast media: worldwide cable and satellite TV are available; the public incumbent ORF competes with three other major, several regional domestic, and up to 400 international TV stations; TV coverage is in principle 100%, but only 90% use broadcast media; Internet streaming not only complements, but increasingly replaces regular TV stations (2019)

Internet country code: .at

Internet users: *total:* 8.277 million (2021 est.)
percent of population: 93% (2021 est.)
comparison ranking: total 72

Broadband - fixed subscriptions: *total:* 2.606 million (2020 est.)
subscriptions per 100 inhabitants: 29 (2020 est.)
comparison ranking: total 49

Communications - note: *note 1:* the Austrian National Library contains important collections of the Imperial Library of the Holy Roman Empire and of the Austrian Empire, as well as of the Austrian Republic; among its more than 12 million items are outstanding holdings of rare books, maps, globes, papyrus, and music; its Globe Museum is the only one in the world
note 2: on 1 October 1869, Austria-Hungary introduced the world's first postal card - postal stationery with an imprinted stamp indicating the prepayment of postage; simple and cheap (sent for a fraction of the cost of a regular letter), postal cards became an instant success, widely produced in the millions worldwide
note 3: Austria followed up with the creation of the world's first commercial picture postcards - cards bearing a picture or photo to which postage is affixed - in May 1871; sent from Vienna, the image served as a souvenir of the city; together, postal cards and post cards served as the world's e-mails of the late 19th and early 20th centuries
note 4: Austria was also an airmail pioneer; from March to October of 1918, it conducted the world's first regular (daily) airmail service - between the imperial cities of Vienna, Krakow, and Lemberg - a combined distance of some 650 km (400 mi) (earlier airmail services had been set up in a few parts of the world but only for short stretches, and none lasted beyond a few days or weeks); an expansion of the route in June of 1918 allowed private mail to be flown to Kyiv, in newly independent Ukraine, which made the route the world's first regular international airmail service (covering a distance of some 1,200 km; 750 mi)

TRANSPORTATION

National air transport system: *number of registered air carriers:* 11 (2020)
inventory of registered aircraft operated by air carriers: 130
annual passenger traffic on registered air carriers: 12,935,505 (2018)
annual freight traffic on registered air carriers: 373.51 million (2018) mt-km

Civil aircraft registration country code prefix: OE

Airports: 61 (2024)
comparison ranking: 77

Heliports: 105 (2024)

Pipelines: 1,888 km gas, 594 km oil, 157 km refined products (2017)

Railways: *total:* 6,123 km (2022) 3,523 km electrified
comparison ranking: total 32

Roadways: *total:* 126,233 km (2022)
comparison ranking: total 41

Waterways: 358 km (2011)
comparison ranking: 99

Merchant marine: *total:* 1 (2023)
by type: other 1
comparison ranking: total 181

MILITARY AND SECURITY

Military and security forces: Austrian Armed Forces (Bundesheer): Land Forces, Air Forces, Cyber Forces, Special Operations Forces, Militia (reserves) (2024)
note 1: the federal police maintain internal security and report to the Ministry of the Interior
note 2: the militia is comprised of men and women who have done their basic military or training service and continue to perform a task in the armed forces; they are integrated into the military but have civilian jobs and only participate in exercises or operations; missions for the militia may include providing disaster relief, assisting security police, and protecting critical infrastructure (energy, water, etc.), as well as deployments on missions abroad

Military expenditures: 1% of GDP (2024 est.)
0.9% of GDP (2023 est.)
0.7% of GDP (2022)
0.8% of GDP (2021)
0.7% of GDP (2020)
comparison ranking: 124

Military and security service personnel strengths: approximately 14,000 regular troops; 8,000 civilians; 25,000 militia (2024)

Military equipment inventories and acquisitions: the military's inventory includes a mix of domestically produced and imported weapons systems from European countries and the US; the Austrian defense industry produces a range of equipment and partners with other countries (2024)

Military service age and obligation: registration requirement at age 17, the legal minimum age for voluntary military service; men above the age of 18 are subject to compulsory military service; women may volunteer; compulsory service is for 6 months, or optionally, alternative civil/community service (Zivildienst) for 9 months (2024)
note 1: as of 2023, women made up about 4% of the military's full-time personnel
note 2: in a January 2013 referendum, a majority of Austrians voted in favor of retaining the system of compulsory military service (with the option of alternative/non-military service) instead of switching to a professional army system

Military deployments: 170 Bosnia-Herzegovina (EUFOR stabilization force); 290 Kosovo (NATO/KFOR); 170 Lebanon (UNIFIL) (2024)

Military - note: the military's primary responsibilities are national defense and protecting Austria's neutrality; it also has some domestic security and disaster response responsibilities; each of the nine federal states has a military command that provides a link between the military and civil authorities; the main tasks of these commands include providing military assistance during disasters and supporting security police operations
the Austrian military contributes to international peacekeeping and humanitarian missions; Austria has been constitutionally militarily non-aligned since 1955 but is an EU member and actively participates in EU peacekeeping and crisis management operations under the EU Common Security and Defense Policy; Austria is not a member of NATO but joined NATO's Partnership for Peace framework in 1995 and participates in some NATO-led crisis management and peacekeeping operations; it has provided troops to international peacekeeping missions in Bosnia and Herzegovina (EU), Kosovo (NATO), and Lebanon (UN) in recent years; more than 100,000 Austrian military and civilian personnel have taken part in more than 50 international peace support and humanitarian missions since 1960 (2024)

SPACE

Space agency/agencies: Aerospace Agency (established in 1972 as the Austrian Space Agency) (2024)

Space program overview: has a national space program and is a member of the European Space Agency (ESA); develops, builds, operates, and tracks satellites, including remote sensing (RS) and research/scientific satellites; works closely with member states of ESA, the EU, and the commercial sector to develop a range of space capabilities and technologies, including applications for satellite payloads, space flight, and space research; has also cooperated with other foreign space agencies and industries, including those of China, India, Russia, and the US (2024)
note: further details about the key activities, programs, and milestones of the country's space program, as well as government spending estimates on the space sector, appear in the Space Programs reference guide

TERRORISM

Terrorist group(s): Islamic State of Iraq and ash-Sham (ISIS)
note: details about the history, aims, leadership, organization, areas of operation, tactics, targets, weapons, size, and sources of support of the group(s) appear(s) in the Terrorism reference guide

TRANSNATIONAL ISSUES

Refugees and internally displaced persons: *refugees (country of origin):* 68,700 (Syria), 43,725 (Afghanistan), 10,110 (Iraq), 8,684 (Somalia), 7,294 (Iran), 6,124 (Russia) (mid-year 2022); 84,135 (Ukraine) (as of 11 March 2024)
stateless persons: 3,219 (2022)

Illicit drugs: transshipment point for Southwest Asian heroin and South American cocaine destined for Western Europe; increasing consumption of European-produced synthetic drugs

AZERBAIJAN

INTRODUCTION

Background: Azerbaijan – a secular nation with a majority-Turkic and majority-Shia Muslim population – was briefly independent (from 1918 to 1920) following the collapse of the Russian Empire; it was subsequently incorporated into the Soviet Union for seven decades.

Beginning in 1988, Azerbaijan and Armenia fought over the Nagorno-Karabakh region, which was populated largely by ethnic Armenians but incorporated into Soviet Azerbaijan as an autonomous oblast in the early 1920s. In the late Soviet period, an ethnic- Armenian separatist movement sought to end Azerbaijani control over the region. Fighting over Nagorno-Karabakh escalated after Armenia and Azerbaijan gained independence from the Soviet Union in 1991. By the time a ceasefire took effect in 1994, separatists with Armenian support controlled Nagorno-Karabakh and seven surrounding Azerbaijani territories. After decades of cease-fire violations and sporadic flare-ups, a second sustained conflict began in 2020 when Azerbaijan tried to win back the territories it had lost in the 1990s. After significant Azerbaijani gains, Armenia returned the southern part of Nagorno-Karabakh and the surrounding territories to Azerbaijan. In September 2023, Azerbaijan took military action to regain the rest of Nagorno-Karabakh; after a conflict that lasted only one day, nearly the entire ethnic Armenian population of Nagorno-Karabakh fled to Armenia.

Since gaining its independence in 1991, Azerbaijan has significantly reduced the poverty rate and has directed some revenue from its oil and gas production to develop the country's infrastructure. However, corruption remains a burden on the economy, and Western observers and members of the country's political opposition have accused the government of authoritarianism. The country's leadership has remained in the ALIYEV family since Heydar ALIYEV, the most highly ranked Azerbaijani member of the Communist Party during the Soviet period, became president during the first Nagorno-Karabakh War in 1993.

GEOGRAPHY

Location: Southwestern Asia, bordering the Caspian Sea, between Iran and Russia, with a small European portion north of the Caucasus range

Geographic coordinates: 40 30 N, 47 30 E

Map references: Asia

Area: *total:* 86,600 sq km
land: 82,629 sq km
water: 3,971 sq km
note: includes the exclave of Naxcivan Autonomous Republic and the Nagorno-Karabakh region; the final status of the region has yet to be determined
comparison ranking: total 113

Area - comparative: about three-quarters the size of Pennsylvania; slightly smaller than Maine

Land boundaries: *total:* 2,468 km
border countries (5): Armenia 996 km; Georgia 428 km; Iran 689 km; Russia 338 km; Turkey 17 km

Coastline: 0 km (landlocked); note - Azerbaijan borders the Caspian Sea (713 km)

Maritime claims: none (landlocked)

Climate: dry, semiarid steppe

Terrain: large, flat Kur-Araz Ovaligi (Kura-Araks Lowland, much of it below sea level) with Great Caucasus Mountains to the north, Qarabag Yaylasi (Karabakh Upland) to the west; Baku lies on Abseron Yasaqligi (Apsheron Peninsula) that juts into Caspian Sea

Elevation: *highest point:* Bazarduzu Dagi 4,466 m
lowest point: Caspian Sea -28 m
mean elevation: 384 m

Natural resources: petroleum, natural gas, iron ore, nonferrous metals, bauxite

Land use: *agricultural land:* 57.6% (2018 est.)
arable land: 22.8% (2018 est.)
permanent crops: 2.7% (2018 est.)
permanent pasture: 32.1% (2018 est.)
forest: 11.3% (2018 est.)
other: 31.1% (2018 est.)

Irrigated land: 14,649 sq km (2020)

Major lakes (area sq km): *salt water lake(s):* Caspian Sea (shared with Iran, Russia, Turkmenistan, and Kazakhstan) - 374,000 sq km

Population distribution: highest population density is found in the far eastern area of the country, in and around Baku; apart from smaller urbanized areas, the rest of the country has a fairly light and evenly distributed population

Natural hazards: droughts

Geography - note: both the main area of the country and the Naxcivan exclave are landlocked

PEOPLE AND SOCIETY

Population: *total:* 10,650,239
male: 5,330,233
female: 5,320,006 (2024 est.)
comparison rankings: female 90; male 90; total 88

Nationality: *noun:* Azerbaijani(s)
adjective: Azerbaijani

Ethnic groups: Azerbaijani 91.6%, Lezghin 2%, Russian 1.3%, Armenian 1.3%, Talysh 1.3%, other 2.4% (2009 est.)
note: Nagorno-Karabakh, which is part of Azerbaijan on the basis of the borders recognized when the Soviet Union dissolved in 1991, was populated almost entirely by ethnic Armenians; Azerbaijan has over 80 ethnic groups

Languages: Azerbaijani (Azeri) (official) 92.5%, Russian 1.4%, Armenian 1.4%, other 4.7% (2009 est.)
major-language sample(s):
Dünya fakt kitabı, əsas məlumatlar üçün əvəz olunmaz mənbədir (Azerbaijani)
note: Russian is widely spoken

Religions: Muslim 97.3% (predominantly Shia), Christian 2.6%, other <0.1, unaffiliated <0.1 (2020 est.)
note: religious affiliation for the majority of Azerbaijanis is largely nominal, percentages for actual practicing adherents are probably much lower

Demographic profile: Azerbaijan's citizenry has over 80 ethnic groups. The far eastern part of the country has the highest population density, particularly in and around Baku. Apart from smaller urbanized areas, the rest of the country has a fairly light and evenly distributed population. Approximately 57% of the country's inhabitants lives in urban areas. While the population is continuing to grow, it is in the early stages of aging. The declining fertility rate – which has decreased from about 5.5 children per woman in the 1950s to less than the 2.1 replacement level in 2022 – combined with increasing life expectancy has resulted in the elderly making up a larger share of Azerbaijan's populace. The percentage of elderly residents and the slowed growth and eventual shrinkage of the working-age population could put pressure on the country's pension and healthcare systems.

Age structure: *0-14 years:* 22.3% (male 1,269,241/female 1,104,529)
15-64 years: 68.7% (male 3,659,441/female 3,656,493)
65 years and over: 9% (2024 est.) (male 401,551/female 558,984)
2023 population pyramid:

Dependency ratios: *total dependency ratio:* 44.2
youth dependency ratio: 34.7
elderly dependency ratio: 9.7
potential support ratio: 10.3 (2021 est.)

Median age: *total:* 34.3 years (2024 est.)
male: 32.8 years
female: 36 years
comparison ranking: total 104

Population growth rate: 0.43% (2024 est.)
comparison ranking: 156

Birth rate: 11.2 births/1,000 population (2024 est.)
comparison ranking: 161

Death rate: 6.4 deaths/1,000 population (2024 est.)
comparison ranking: 142

Net migration rate: -0.6 migrant(s)/1,000 population (2024 est.)
comparison ranking: 129

Population distribution: highest population density is found in the far eastern area of the country, in and around Baku; apart from smaller urbanized areas, the rest of the country has a fairly light and evenly distributed population

Urbanization: *urban population:* 57.6% of total population (2023)
rate of urbanization: 1.38% annual rate of change (2020-25 est.)
note: data include Nagorno-Karabakh

Major urban areas - population: 2.432 million BAKU (capital) (2023)

Sex ratio: *at birth:* 1.15 male(s)/female
0-14 years: 1.15 male(s)/female
15-64 years: 1 male(s)/female
65 years and over: 0.72 male(s)/female
total population: 1 male(s)/female (2024 est.)

Mother's mean age at first birth: 24 years (2019 est.)

Maternal mortality ratio: 41 deaths/100,000 live births (2020 est.)
comparison ranking: 102

Infant mortality rate: *total:* 10.9 deaths/1,000 live births (2024 est.)
male: 12.6 deaths/1,000 live births
female: 9 deaths/1,000 live births
comparison ranking: total 123

Life expectancy at birth: *total population:* 75.9 years (2024 est.)
male: 73.5 years
female: 78.6 years
comparison ranking: total population 120

Total fertility rate: 1.69 children born/woman (2024 est.)
comparison ranking: 167

Gross reproduction rate: 0.79 (2024 est.)

Drinking water source: *improved: urban:* 100% of population
rural: 93.3% of population
total: 97.1% of population
unimproved: urban: 0% of population
rural: 6.7% of population
total: 2.9% of population (2020 est.)

Current health expenditure: 4.6% of GDP (2020)

Physician density: 3.17 physicians/1,000 population (2019)

Hospital bed density: 4.8 beds/1,000 population (2014)

Sanitation facility access: *improved: urban:* 100% of population
unimproved: urban: 0% of population

Obesity - adult prevalence rate: 19.9% (2016)
comparison ranking: 107

Alcohol consumption per capita: *total:* 1.38 liters of pure alcohol (2019 est.)
beer: 0.36 liters of pure alcohol (2019 est.)
wine: 0.06 liters of pure alcohol (2019 est.)
spirits: 0.94 liters of pure alcohol (2019 est.)
other alcohols: 0.01 liters of pure alcohol (2019 est.)
comparison ranking: total 143

Tobacco use: *total:* 24% (2020 est.)
male: 47.9% (2020 est.)
female: 0.1% (2020 est.)
comparison ranking: total 58

Children under the age of 5 years underweight: 4.9% (2013)
comparison ranking: 75

Currently married women (ages 15-49): 62.9% (2023 est.)

Education expenditures: 4.3% of GDP (2020 est.)
comparison ranking: 108

Literacy: *definition:* age 15 and over can read and write
total population: 99.8%
male: 99.9%

female: 99.7% (2019)

School life expectancy (primary to tertiary education): *total:* 14 years
male: 13 years
female: 14 years (2021)

ENVIRONMENT

Environment - current issues: local scientists consider the Abseron Yasaqligi (Apsheron Peninsula) (including Baku and Sumqayit) and the Caspian Sea to be the ecologically most devastated area in the world because of severe air, soil, and water pollution; soil pollution results from oil spills, from the use of DDT pesticide, and from toxic defoliants used in the production of cotton; surface and underground water are polluted by untreated municipal and industrial wastewater and agricultural run-off

Environment - international agreements: *party to:* Air Pollution, Biodiversity, Climate Change, Climate Change-Kyoto Protocol, Climate Change-Paris Agreement, Comprehensive Nuclear Test Ban, Desertification, Endangered Species, Hazardous Wastes, Law of the Sea, Marine Dumping-London Convention, Ozone Layer Protection, Ship Pollution, Wetlands
signed, but not ratified: none of the selected agreements

Climate: dry, semiarid steppe

Urbanization: *urban population:* 57.6% of total population (2023)
rate of urbanization: 1.38% annual rate of change (2020-25 est.)
note: data include Nagorno-Karabakh

Revenue from forest resources: 0.02% of GDP (2018 est.)
comparison ranking: 139

Revenue from coal: 0% of GDP (2018 est.)
comparison ranking: 123

Air pollutants: *particulate matter emissions:* 24.64 micrograms per cubic meter (2019 est.)
carbon dioxide emissions: 37.62 megatons (2016 est.)
methane emissions: 44.87 megatons (2020 est.)

Waste and recycling: *municipal solid waste generated annually:* 2,930,349 tons (2015 est.)

Major lakes (area sq km): *salt water lake(s):* Caspian Sea (shared with Iran, Russia, Turkmenistan, and Kazakhstan) - 374,000 sq km

Total water withdrawal: *municipal:* 400 million cubic meters (2020 est.)
industrial: 570 million cubic meters (2020 est.)
agricultural: 11.6 billion cubic meters (2020 est.)

Total renewable water resources: 34.68 billion cubic meters (2020 est.)

GOVERNMENT

Country name: *conventional long form:* Republic of Azerbaijan
conventional short form: Azerbaijan
local long form: Azarbaycan Respublikasi
local short form: Azarbaycan
former: Azerbaijan Soviet Socialist Republic
etymology: the name translates as "Land of Fire" and refers to naturally occurring surface fires on ancient oil pools or from natural gas discharges

Government type: presidential republic

Capital: *name:* Baku (Baki, Baky)
geographic coordinates: 40 23 N, 49 52 E
time difference: UTC+4 (9 hours ahead of Washington, DC, during Standard Time)
daylight saving time: does not observe daylight savings time
etymology: the name derives from the Persian designation of the city "bad-kube" meaning "wind-pounded city" and refers to the harsh winds and severe snow storms that can hit the city
note: at approximately 28 m below sea level, Baku's elevation makes it the lowest capital city in the world

Administrative divisions: 66 districts (rayonlar; rayon - singular), 11 cities (saharlar; sahar - singular);
rayons: Abseron, Agcabadi, Agdam, Agdas, Agstafa, Agsu, Astara, Babak, Balakan, Barda, Beylaqan, Bilasuvar, Cabrayil, Calilabad, Culfa, Daskasan, Fuzuli, Gadabay, Goranboy, Goycay, Goygol, Haciqabul, Imisli, Ismayilli, Kalbacar, Kangarli, Kurdamir, Lacin, Lankaran, Lerik, Masalli, Neftcala, Oguz, Ordubad, Qabala, Qax, Qazax, Qobustan, Quba, Qubadli, Qusar, Saatli, Sabirabad, Sabran, Sadarak, Sahbuz, Saki, Salyan, Samaxi, Samkir, Samux, Sarur, Siyazan, Susa, Tartar, Tovuz, Ucar, Xacmaz, Xizi, Xocali, Xocavand, Yardimli, Yevlax, Zangilan, Zaqatala, Zardab
cities: Baku, Ganca, Lankaran, Mingacevir, Naftalan, Naxcivan (Nakhichevan), Saki, Sirvan, Sumqayit, Xankandi, Yevlax

Independence: 30 August 1991 (declared from the Soviet Union); 18 October 1991 (adopted by the Supreme Council of Azerbaijan)

National holiday: Republic Day (founding of the Democratic Republic of Azerbaijan), 28 May (1918)

Legal system: civil law system

Constitution: *history:* several previous; latest adopted 12 November 1995
amendments: proposed by the president of the republic or by at least 63 members of the National Assembly; passage requires at least 95 votes of Assembly members in two separate readings of the draft amendment six months apart and requires presidential approval after each of the two Assembly votes, followed by presidential signature; constitutional articles on the authority, sovereignty, and unity of the people cannot be amended; amended 2002, 2009, 2016

International law organization participation: has not submitted an ICJ jurisdiction declaration; non-party state to the ICCt

Citizenship: *citizenship by birth:* yes
citizenship by descent only: yes
dual citizenship recognized: no
residency requirement for naturalization: 5 years

Suffrage: 18 years of age; universal

Executive branch: *chief of state:* President Ilham ALIYEV (since 31 October 2003)
head of government: Prime Minister Ali ASADOV (since 8 October 2019)
cabinet: Council of Ministers appointed by the president and confirmed by the National Assembly
elections/appointments: president directly elected by absolute majority popular vote in 2 rounds (if needed) for a 7-year term; a single individual is eligible for unlimited terms; election last held on 7 February 2024 (next to be held in 2031); prime minister and first deputy prime minister appointed by the president and confirmed by the National Assembly; note - a constitutional amendment approved in a September 2016 referendum extended the presidential term from 5 to 7 years; a separate constitutional amendment approved in the same referendum also introduced the post of first vice president and additional vice-presidents, who are directly appointed by the president; however, no additional vice presidents have been appointed since the constitutional amendment was passed
election results:
2024: Ilham ALIYEV reelected president; percent of vote - Ilham ALIYEV (YAP) 92.1%, Zahid ORUJ (independent) 2.2%; on 16 February 2024, Ali ASADOV reappointed prime minister by parliamentary vote, 105-1
2018: Ilham ALIYEV reelected president in first round; percent of vote - Ilham ALIYEV (YAP) 86%, Zahid ORUJ (independent) 3.1%, other 10.9%
note: OSCE observers noted shortcomings in the election, including a restrictive political environment, limits on fundamental freedoms, a lack of genuine competition, and ballot box stuffing

Legislative branch: *description:* unicameral National Assembly or Milli Mejlis (125 seats, current 116; members directly elected in singleseat constituencies by simple majority vote to serve 5-year terms)
elections: last held on 1 September 2024 (next to be held in 2029)
election results: percent of vote by party - NA; seats by party - YAP 68, CSP 3, Justice, Law, Deomcracy Party 2, Azerbaijan Democratic Enlightenment Party 1, Azerbaijan National Independence Party 1, Democratic Reforms Party 1, Great Azerbaijan Party 1, Great Order Party 1, Motherland Party 1, National Front Party 1, Republican Alternative Party1, independents 44

Judicial branch: *highest court(s):* Supreme Court (consists of the chairman, vice chairman, and 23 judges in plenum sessions and organized into civil, economic affairs, criminal, and rights violations chambers); Constitutional Court (consists of 9 judges)
judge selection and term of office: Supreme Court judges nominated by the president and appointed by the Milli Majlis; judges appointed for 10 years; Constitutional Court chairman and deputy chairman appointed by the president; other court judges nominated by the president and appointed by the Milli Majlis to serve single 15-year terms
subordinate courts: Courts of Appeal (replaced the Economic Court in 2002); district and municipal courts

Political parties: Civic Solidarity Party or VHP
Democratic Reforms Party DiP
Great Order Party or BQP
Motherland Party or AVP
Party for Democratic Reforms or DIP
Republican Alternative Party or REAL
Unity Party or VƏHDƏT
Whole Azerbaijan Popular Front Party or BAXCP
New Azerbaijan Party (Yeni Azərbaycan Partiyasi) or YAP

International organization participation: ADB, BSEC, CD, CE, CICA, CIS, EAPC, EBRD, ECO, FAO, GCTU, GUAM, IAEA, IBRD, ICAO, ICC (NGOs), ICRM, IDA, IDB, IFAD, IFC, IFRCS, ILO, IMF, IMO, Interpol, IOC, IOM, IPU, ISO, ITSO, ITU, ITUC (NGOs), MIGA, NAM, OAS (observer), OIC, OPCW, OSCE, PFP, UN, UNCTAD, UNESCO, UNHCR, UNIDO, UNWTO, UPU, WCO, WFTU (NGOs), WHO, WIPO, WMO, WTO (observer)

Diplomatic representation in the US: *chief of mission:* Ambassador Khazar IBRAHIM (since 15 September 2021)
chancery: 2741 34th Street NW, Washington, DC 20008
telephone: [1] (202) 337-3500
FAX: [1] (202) 337-5911
email address and website:
azerbaijan@azembassy.us
https://washington.mfa.gov.az/en
consulate(s) general: Los Angeles

Diplomatic representation from the US: *chief of mission:* Ambassador Mark LIBBY (since 18 January 2024)
embassy: 111 Azadlig Avenue, AZ1007 Baku
mailing address: 7050 Baku Place, Washington, DC 20521-7050
telephone: [994] (12) 488-3300
FAX: [994] (12) 488-3330
email address and website:
BakuACS@state.gov
https://az.usembassy.gov/

Flag description: three equal horizontal bands of sky blue (top), red, and green; a vertical crescent moon and an eight-pointed star in white are centered in the red band; the blue band recalls Azerbaijan's Turkic heritage, red stands for modernization and progress, and green refers to Islam; the crescent moon and star are a Turkic insignia; the eight star points represent the eight Turkic peoples of the world

National symbol(s): flames of fire; national colors: blue, red, green

National anthem: *name:* "Azerbaijan Marsi" (March of Azerbaijan)
lyrics/music: Ahmed JAVAD/Uzeyir HAJIBEYOV
note: adopted 1992; although originally written in 1919 during a brief period of independence, "Azerbaijan Marsi" did not become the official anthem until after the dissolution of the Soviet Union

National heritage: *total World Heritage Sites:* 5 (4 cultural, 1 natural)
selected World Heritage Site locales: Walled City of Baku; Gobustan Rock Art Cultural Landscape; Historic Center of Sheki; Cultural Landscape of Khinalig People and "Koc Yolu" Transhumance Route

ECONOMY

Economic overview: oil-based economy; macroeconomic instabilities due to demand shocks; recent state bailout of largest lender; potential economic gains from Nagorno-Karabakh conflict; negatively impacted by COVID-19; investing in human capital to diversify and retain younger generation

Real GDP (purchasing power parity): $215.896 billion (2023 est.)
$213.497 billion (2022 est.)
$203.884 billion (2021 est.)
note: data in 2021 dollars
comparison ranking: 74

Real GDP growth rate: 1.12% (2023 est.)
4.71% (2022 est.)
5.62% (2021 est.)
note: annual GDP % growth based on constant local currency
comparison ranking: 161

Real GDP per capita: $21,300 (2023 est.)
$21,100 (2022 est.)
$20,100 (2021 est.)
note: data in 2021 dollars
comparison ranking: 98

GDP (official exchange rate): $72.356 billion (2023 est.)
note: data in current dollars at official exchange rate

Inflation rate (consumer prices): 8.79% (2023 est.)
13.85% (2022 est.)
6.65% (2021 est.)
note: annual % change based on consumer prices
comparison ranking: 163

Credit ratings: Fitch rating: BB+ (2016)

Moody's rating: Ba2 (2017)

Standard & Poors rating: BB+ (2016)
note: The year refers to the year in which the current credit rating was first obtained.

GDP - composition, by sector of origin: *agriculture:* 5.5% (2023 est.)
industry: 46.6% (2023 est.)
services: 39.1% (2023 est.)
note: figures may not total 100% due to non-allocated consumption not captured in sector-reported data comparison rankings: services 195; industry 18; agriculture 115

GDP - composition, by end use: *household consumption:* 53.2% (2023 est.)
government consumption: 14% (2023 est.)
investment in fixed capital: 14.9% (2023 est.)
investment in inventories: 3.5% (2023 est.)
exports of goods and services: 49% (2023 est.)
imports of goods and services: -34.6% (2023 est.)
note: figures may not total 100% due to rounding or gaps in data collection

Agricultural products: milk, wheat, potatoes, barley, tomatoes, watermelons, cotton, apples, onions, maize (2022)
note: top ten agricultural products based on tonnage

Industries: petroleum and petroleum products, natural gas, oilfield equipment; steel, iron ore; cement; chemicals and petrochemicals; textiles

Industrial production growth rate: 1.34% (2023 est.)
note: annual % change in industrial value added based on constant local currency
comparison ranking: 132

Labor force: 5.473 million (2023 est.)
note: number of people ages 15 or older who are employed or seeking work
comparison ranking: 78

Unemployment rate: 5.64% (2023 est.)
5.65% (2022 est.)
6.04% (2021 est.)
note: % of labor force seeking employment
comparison ranking: 111

Youth unemployment rate (ages 15-24): *total:* 13.5% (2023 est.)
male: 12% (2023 est.)
female: 15.3% (2023 est.)
note: % of labor force ages 15-24 seeking employment
comparison ranking: total 104

Population below poverty line: 4.9% (2015 est.)

Average household expenditures: *on food:* 42.4% of household expenditures (2022 est.)
on alcohol and tobacco: 2% of household expenditures (2022 est.)

Remittances: 3.87% of GDP (2023 est.)
5.01% of GDP (2022 est.)
2.78% of GDP (2021 est.)
note: personal transfers and compensation between resident and non-resident individuals/households/entities

Budget: *revenues:* $20.877 billion (2021 est.)
expenditures: $14.882 billion (2021 est.)
note: central government revenues (excluding grants) and expenses converted to US dollars at average official exchange rate for year indicated

Public debt: 16.82% of GDP (2021 est.)
note: central government debt as a % of GDP
comparison ranking: 192

Taxes and other revenues: 13.42% (of GDP) (2021 est.)
note: central government tax revenue as a % of GDP
comparison ranking: 152

Current account balance: $8.329 billion (2023 est.)
$23.478 billion (2022 est.)
$8.203 billion (2021 est.)
note: balance of payments - net trade and primary/secondary income in current dollars
comparison ranking: 29

Exports: $35.487 billion (2023 est.)
$47.274 billion (2022 est.)
$25.494 billion (2021 est.)
note: balance of payments - exports of goods and services in current dollars
comparison ranking: 75

Exports - partners: Italy 47%, Turkey 9%, Israel 4%, India 4%, Greece 4% (2022)
note: top five export partners based on percentage share of exports

Exports - commodities: crude petroleum, natural gas, refined petroleum, fertilizers, aluminum (2022)
note: top five export commodities based on value in dollars

Imports: $25.016 billion (2023 est.)
$21.274 billion (2022 est.)
$16.432 billion (2021 est.)
note: balance of payments - imports of goods and services in current dollars
comparison ranking: 86

Imports - partners: Russia 17%, Turkey 17%, China 10%, UAE 5%, Georgia 5% (2022)
note: top five import partners based on percentage share of imports

Imports - commodities: cars, refined petroleum, crude petroleum, wheat, packaged medicine (2022)
note: top five import commodities based on value in dollars

Reserves of foreign exchange and gold: $13.749 billion (2023 est.)
$11.338 billion (2022 est.)
$8.29 billion (2021 est.)
note: holdings of gold (year-end prices)/foreign exchange/special drawing rights in current dollars
comparison ranking: 89

Debt - external: $12.319 billion (2022 est.)
note: present value of external debt in current US dollars
comparison ranking: 34

Exchange rates: Azerbaijani manats (AZN) per US dollar -

Exchange rates: 1.7 (2023 est.)
1.7 (2022 est.)
1.7 (2021 est.)
1.7 (2020 est.)
1.7 (2019 est.)

ENERGY

Electricity access: *electrification - total population:* 100% (2022 est.)

Electricity: *installed generating capacity:* 7.71 million kW (2022 est.)
consumption: 23.827 billion kWh (2022 est.)
exports: 2.997 billion kWh (2022 est.)
imports: 137 million kWh (2022 est.)
transmission/distribution losses: 2.25 billion kWh (2022 est.)
comparison rankings: transmission/distribution losses 127; imports 109; exports 48; consumption 71; installed generating capacity 74

Electricity generation sources: *fossil fuels:* 93.6% of total installed capacity (2022 est.)
solar: 0.2% of total installed capacity (2022 est.)
wind: 0.3% of total installed capacity (2022 est.)
hydroelectricity: 5.5% of total installed capacity (2022 est.)
biomass and waste: 0.4% of total installed capacity (2022 est.)

Coal: *consumption:* 60,000 metric tons (2022 est.)
imports: 20,000 metric tons (2022 est.)

Petroleum: *total petroleum production:* 618,000 bbl/day (2023 est.)
refined petroleum consumption: 105,000 bbl/day (2022 est.)
crude oil estimated reserves: 7 billion barrels (2021 est.)

Natural gas: *production:* 34.175 billion cubic meters (2022 est.)
consumption: 11.759 billion cubic meters (2022 est.)
exports: 22.4 billion cubic meters (2022 est.)
imports: 67.711 million cubic meters (2022 est.)
proven reserves: 1.699 trillion cubic meters (2021 est.)

Carbon dioxide emissions: 36.187 million metric tonnes of CO2 (2022 est.)
from coal and metallurgical coke: 137,000 metric tonnes of CO2 (2022 est.)
from petroleum and other liquids: 12.982 million metric tonnes of CO2 (2022 est.)
from consumed natural gas: 23.068 million metric tonnes of CO2 (2022 est.)
comparison ranking: total emissions 66

Energy consumption per capita: 61.497 million Btu/person (2022 est.)
comparison ranking: 77

COMMUNICATIONS

Telephones - fixed lines: *total subscriptions:* 1.641 million (2022 est.)
subscriptions per 100 inhabitants: 16 (2022 est.)
comparison ranking: total subscriptions 58

Telephones - mobile cellular: *total subscriptions:* 11.068 million (2022 est.)
subscriptions per 100 inhabitants: 107 (2022 est.)
comparison ranking: total subscriptions 89

Telecommunication systems: *general assessment:* the telecom sector was one of the major contributors to Azerbaijan's non-oil GDP, overall development, growth, and investment; mobile usage rates reached 100% as far back as 2011, but have largely stagnated since then; the Mobile Network Operators (MNOs) are slowly extending the reach of their long-term evolution (LTE) networks around the country, and this increased coverage (along with access to faster data-based services) is expected to produce a moderate resurgence for both mobile and mobile broadband over the next few years as customers migrate from 3G to 4G. 5G services are still some ways off, as the demand for high-speed data and fast broadband can easily be met by existing capacity on LTE networks; fixed-line tele density continues to drop down each year as customers consolidate their telecommunications services around the mobile platform; yet the rate of decline is comparatively slow to other countries, since Azerbaijan has a relatively high proportion of (87%) of fixed-line broadband customers still on DSL; Fiber (12% of fixed broadband connections) is gradually being rolled out in urban areas, and this makes up the bulk of the (limited) growth being seen in the overall fixed broadband market; DSL's predominance, however, will serve to keep Azerbaijan's average access speeds in the sub-10Mbps range for the foreseeable future
(2024)
domestic: 16 fixed-lines subscriptions per 100 persons; mobile-cellular subscriptions of 107 telephones per 100 persons (2022)
international: country code - 994; Azerbaijan's largest mobile network operator (MNO) launched trial 5G mobile services in Baku on 27 December 2022 (2023)

Broadcast media: 3 state-run and 1 public TV channels; 4 domestic commercial TV stations and about 15 regional TV stations; cable TV services are available in Baku; 1 state-run and 1 public radio network operating; a small number of private commercial radio stations broadcasting; local FM relays of Baku commercial stations are available in many localities; note - all broadcast media is pro-government, and most private broadcast media outlets are owned by entities directly linked to the government

Internet country code: .az

Internet users: *total:* 8.6 million (2021 est.)
percent of population: 86% (2021 est.)
comparison ranking: total 68

Broadband - fixed subscriptions: *total:* 1,995,474 (2020 est.)
subscriptions per 100 inhabitants: 20 (2020 est.)
comparison ranking: total 58

TRANSPORTATION

National air transport system: *number of registered air carriers:* 42 (2020)
inventory of registered aircraft operated by air carriers: 44
annual passenger traffic on registered air carriers: 2,279,546 (2018)
annual freight traffic on registered air carriers: 44.09 million (2018) mt-km

Civil aircraft registration country code prefix: 4K

Airports: 32 (2024)
comparison ranking: 117

Heliports: 5 (2024)

Pipelines: 89 km condensate, 3,890 km gas, 2,446 km oil (2013)

Railways: *total:* 2,944.3 km (2017)
broad gauge: 2,944.3 km (2017) 1.520-m gauge (approx. 1,767 km electrified)
comparison ranking: total 59

Roadways: *total:* 24,981 km (2013)
note: total roadway length has increased significantly and continues to grow due to the recovery of Armenian-held territories and related reconstruction efforts. No updated figure is currently available.
comparison ranking: total 107

Merchant marine: *total:* 312 (2023)
by type: general cargo 40, oil tanker 44, other 228
comparison ranking: total 56

MILITARY AND SECURITY

Military and security forces: Azerbaijan Armed Forces: Land Forces, Air Forces, Navy Forces, State Border Service, Coast Guard

Ministry of Internal Affairs: Internal Troops, local police forces; Special State Protection Service (SSPS): National Guard (2024)
note: the Ministry of Internal Affairs and the State Security Service (intelligence, counterterrorism) are responsible for internal security; the SSPS is under the president and provides protective services to senior officials, foreign missions, significant state assets, government buildings, etc; the National Guard also serves as a reserve for the Army

Military expenditures: 4.5% of GDP (2023 est.)
4.5% of GDP (2022 est.)
5% of GDP (2021 est.)
5% of GDP (2020 est.)
3.8% of GDP (2019 est.)
comparison ranking: 12

Military and security service personnel strengths: estimates vary; approximately 60-75,000 active armed forces; approximately 15,000 Ministry of Internal Affairs troops (2023)

Military equipment inventories and acquisitions: Baku has been actively upgrading its equipment for over a decade with purchases from Belarus, Israel, Russia, and Turkey; while most of the military's equipment was once Soviet-era material, it now fields quantities of advanced equipment, including armored vehicles, artillery systems, air defense systems, tanks, and UAVs (2024)

Military service age and obligation: 18-25 years of age for compulsory military service for men; 18-35 years of age for voluntary/contractual service for men and women; 18 months service for conscripts, 36 months for voluntary/contractual service (2023)

Military - note: the Azerbaijani military was established in 1991, although its origins go back to 1918; much of the military's original equipment was acquired from former Soviet military forces that departed Azerbaijan by 1992; territorial defense is the military's primary focus, particularly with regards to neighboring Armenia; a secondary focus is guarding against Iran; Armenia and Azerbaijan engaged in open conflicts over the Nagorno-Karabakh enclave in 1991-94 and 2020; tensions continued following the 2020 conflict, and Azerbaijan seized the entire enclave in 2023
Turkey has been Azerbaijan's strongest military partner, a relationship that has included weapons transfers, technical advice, bilateral training exercises, and support during its conflicts with Armenia; Azerbaijan is not part of NATO but has had a cooperative relationship with it dating back to when it joined NATO's Partnership for Peace program in 1994 and has provided troops to NATO-led missions in Kosovo (1999-2008) and Afghanistan (2002-2014) (2024)

SPACE

Space agency/agencies: Azerbaijan National Aerospace Agency (NASA; Azərbaycan Milli Aerokosmik Agentliyi, MAKA; established in 1992 from the Kaspiy Scientific Center, established 1974); Space Agency of the Republic of Azerbaijan (Azercosmos; established 2010 as a state-owned satellite operating company) (2024)

Space program overview: national space program largely focused on the acquisition and operation of satellites; operates foreign-built communications and remote sensing (RS) satellites; has two satellite ground control stations; cooperates with a variety of foreign space agencies and commercial entities, including those of China, the European Space Agency (and individual member states such as France), Israel, Russia, Turkey, and the US; Azercosmos is the largest satellite operator in the Caucasus region (2024)
note: further details about the key activities, programs, and milestones of the country's space program, as well as government spending estimates on the space sector, appear in the Space Programs reference guide

TERRORISM

Terrorist group(s): Islamic State of Iraq and ash-Sham (ISIS); Islamic Revolutionary Guard Corps (IRGC)/Qods Force
note: details about the history, aims, leadership, organization, areas of operation, tactics, targets, weapons, size, and sources of support of the group(s) appear(s) in the Terrorism reference guide

TRANSNATIONAL ISSUES

Refugees and internally displaced persons: IDPs: 659,000 (conflict with Armenia over Nagorno-Karabakh; IDPs are mainly ethnic Azerbaijanis but also include ethnic Kurds, Russians, and Turks predominantly from occupied territories around Nagorno-Karabakh; includes IDPs' descendants, returned IDPs, and people living in insecure areas and excludes people displaced by natural disasters; around half the IDPs live in the capital Baku) (2022)
stateless persons: 3,585 (2022)

Illicit drugs: limited illicit cultivation of cannabis and opium poppy, mostly for CIS consumption; small government eradication program; transit point for Southwest Asian opiates bound for Russia and to a lesser extent the rest of Europe

BAHAMAS, THE

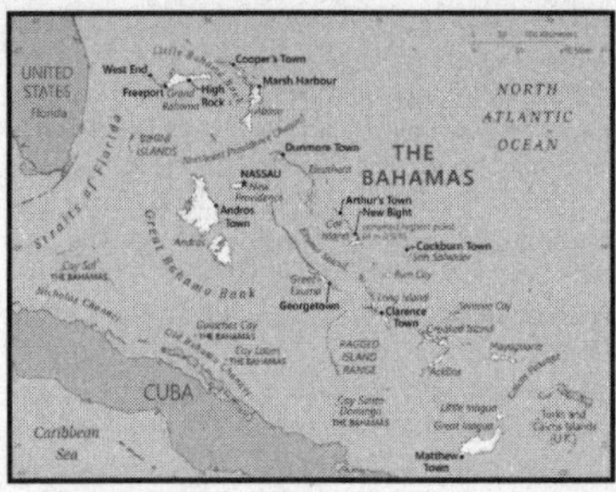

INTRODUCTION

Background: Lucayan Indians inhabited the Bahama islands when Christopher COLUMBUS first set foot in the New World in 1492. British settlement of the islands began in 1647; the islands became a colony in 1783. Piracy thrived in the 17th and 18th centuries because of The Bahamas' close proximity to shipping lanes. Since gaining independence from the UK in 1973, The Bahamas has prospered through tourism, international banking, and investment management, which comprise up to 85% of GDP. Because of its proximity to the US – the nearest Bahamian land-mass is only 80 km (50 mi) from Florida – the country is a major transshipment point for illicit trafficking to the US mainland, as well as to Europe. US law enforcement agencies cooperate closely with The Bahamas; the Drug Enforcement Administration, US Coast Guard, and US Customs and Border Protection assist Bahamian authorities with maritime security and law enforcement through Operation Bahamas, Turks and Caicos, or OPBAT.

GEOGRAPHY

Location: chain of islands in the North Atlantic Ocean, southeast of Florida, northeast of Cuba; note - although The Bahamas does not border the Caribbean Sea, geopolitically it is often designated as a Caribbean nation

Geographic coordinates: 24 15 N, 76 00 W

Map references: Central America and the Caribbean

Area: *total:* 13,880 sq km
land: 10,010 sq km
water: 3,870 sq km
comparison ranking: total 160

Area - comparative: slightly smaller than Connecticut

Land boundaries: *total:* 0 km

Coastline: 3,542 km

Maritime claims: *territorial sea:* 12 nm
exclusive economic zone: 200 nm

Climate: tropical marine; moderated by warm waters of Gulf Stream

Terrain: long, flat coral formations with some low rounded hills

Elevation: *highest point:* 1.3 km NE of Old Bight on Cat Island 64 m
lowest point: Atlantic Ocean 0 m

Natural resources: salt, aragonite, timber, arable land

Land use: *agricultural land:* 1.4% (2018 est.)
arable land: 0.8% (2018 est.)
permanent crops: 0.4% (2018 est.)
permanent pasture: 0.2% (2018 est.)
forest: 51.4% (2018 est.)
other: 47.2% (2018 est.)

Irrigated land: 10 sq km (2012)

Population distribution: most of the population lives in urban areas, with two-thirds living on New Providence Island where Nassau is located

Natural hazards: hurricanes and other tropical storms cause extensive flood and wind damage

Geography - note: strategic location adjacent to US and Cuba; extensive island chain of which 30 are inhabited

PEOPLE AND SOCIETY

Population: *total:* 410,862
male: 190,100
female: 220,762 (2024 est.)
comparison rankings: female 175; male 177; total 176

Nationality: *noun:* Bahamian(s)
adjective: **Bahamian**

Ethnic groups: African descent 90.6%, White 4.7%, mixed 2.1%, other 1.9%, unspecified 0.7% (2010 est.)
note: data represent population by racial group

Languages: English (official), Creole (among Haitian immigrants)

Religions: Protestant 69.9% (includes Baptist 34.9%, Anglican 13.7%, Pentecostal 8.9% Seventh Day Adventist 4.4%, Methodist 3.6%, Church of God 1.9%, Plymouth Brethren 1.6%, other Protestant 0.9%), Roman Catholic 12%, other Christian 13% (includes Jehovah's Witness 1.1%), other 0.6%, none 1.9%, unspecified 2.6% (2010 est.)

Age structure: *0-14 years:* 21.4% (male 41,675/ female 46,363)
15-64 years: 70% (male 132,626/female 154,866)
65 years and over: 8.6% (2024 est.) (male 15,799/ female 19,533)

Dependency ratios: *total dependency ratio:* 39.3
youth dependency ratio: 27.3
elderly dependency ratio: 11.9
potential support ratio: 8.4 (2021 est.)

Median age: *total:* 30.7 years (2024 est.)
male: 30.6 years
female: 30.7 years
comparison ranking: total 133

Population growth rate: 1.07% (2024 est.)
comparison ranking: 88

Birth rate: 13.1 births/1,000 population (2024 est.)
comparison ranking: 132

Death rate: 5.6 deaths/1,000 population (2024 est.)
comparison ranking: 175

Net migration rate: 3.2 migrant(s)/1,000 population (2024 est.)
comparison ranking: 34

Population distribution: most of the population lives in urban areas, with two-thirds living on New Providence Island where Nassau is located

Urbanization: *urban population:* 83.6% of total population (2023)
rate of urbanization: 1.02% annual rate of change (2020-25 est.)

Major urban areas - population: 280,000 NASSAU (capital) (2018)

Sex ratio: *at birth:* 1.03 male(s)/female
0-14 years: 0.9 male(s)/female
15-64 years: 0.86 male(s)/female
65 years and over: 0.81 male(s)/female
total population: 0.86 male(s)/female (2024 est.)

Maternal mortality ratio: 77 deaths/100,000 live births (2020 est.)
comparison ranking: 77

Infant mortality rate: *total:* 9.4 deaths/1,000 live births (2024 est.)
male: 10.5 deaths/1,000 live births
female: 8.2 deaths/1,000 live births
comparison ranking: total 138

Life expectancy at birth: *total population:* 76.7 years (2024 est.)
male: 75.1 years
female: 78.4 years
comparison ranking: total population 104

Total fertility rate: 1.44 children born/woman (2024 est.)
comparison ranking: 209

Gross reproduction rate: 0.71 (2024 est.)

Drinking water source: *improved:* total: 98.9% of population
unimproved: total: 1.1% of population (2017 est.)

Current health expenditure: 7.6% of GDP (2020)

Physician density: 1.94 physicians/1,000 population (2017)

Hospital bed density: 3 beds/1,000 population (2017)

Sanitation facility access: *improved:* total: 98.2% of population
unimproved: total: 1.8% of population (2017 est.)

Obesity - adult prevalence rate: 31.6% (2016)
comparison ranking: 21

Alcohol consumption per capita: *total:* 9.48 liters of pure alcohol (2019 est.)
beer: 3.66 liters of pure alcohol (2019 est.)
wine: 1.43 liters of pure alcohol (2019 est.)
spirits: 4.08 liters of pure alcohol (2019 est.)
other alcohols: 0.31 liters of pure alcohol (2019 est.)
comparison ranking: total 29

Tobacco use: *total:* 10.6% (2020 est.)
male: 18.8% (2020 est.)
female: 2.4% (2020 est.)
comparison ranking: total 134

Currently married women (ages 15-49): 38.9% (2023 est.)

Education expenditures: 2.8% of GDP (2021 est.)
comparison ranking: 164

ENVIRONMENT

Environment - current issues: coral reef decay; solid waste disposal

Environment - international agreements: *party to:* Biodiversity, Climate Change, Climate Change-Kyoto Protocol, Climate Change-Paris Agreement, Comprehensive Nuclear Test Ban, Desertification, Endangered Species, Hazardous Wastes, Law of the

Sea, Nuclear Test Ban, Ozone Layer Protection, Ship Pollution, Wetlands
signed, but not ratified: none of the selected agreements

Climate: tropical marine; moderated by warm waters of Gulf Stream

Urbanization: *urban population:* 83.6% of total population (2023)
rate of urbanization: 1.02% annual rate of change (2020-25 est.)

Revenue from forest resources: 0.01% of GDP (2018 est.)
comparison ranking: 147

Revenue from coal: 0% of GDP (2018 est.)
comparison ranking: 154

Air pollutants: *particulate matter emissions:* 5.2 micrograms per cubic meter (2019 est.)
carbon dioxide emissions: 1.79 megatons (2016 est.)
methane emissions: 0.23 megatons (2020 est.)

Waste and recycling: *municipal solid waste generated annually:* 264,000 tons (2015 est.)

Total water withdrawal: *municipal:* 30 million cubic meters (2020 est.)

Total renewable water resources: 700 million cubic meters (2020 est.)

GOVERNMENT

Country name: *conventional long form:* Commonwealth of The Bahamas
conventional short form: The Bahamas
etymology: name derives from the Spanish "baha mar," meaning "shallow sea," which describes the shallow waters of the Bahama Banks

Government type: parliamentary democracy under a constitutional monarchy; a Commonwealth realm

Capital: *name:* Nassau
geographic coordinates: 25 05 N, 77 21 W
time difference: UTC-5 (same time as Washington, DC, during Standard Time)
daylight saving time: +1hr, begins second Sunday in March; ends first Sunday in November
etymology: named after William III (1650-1702), king of England, Scotland, and Ireland, who was a member of the House of Nassau

Administrative divisions: 31 districts; Acklins Islands, Berry Islands, Bimini, Black Point, Cat Island, Central Abaco, Central Andros, Central Eleuthera, City of Freeport, Crooked Island and Long Cay, East Grand Bahama, Exuma, Grand Cay, Harbour Island, Hope Town, Inagua, Long Island, Mangrove Cay, Mayaguana, Moore's Island, North Abaco, North Andros, North Eleuthera, Ragged Island, Rum Cay, San Salvador, South Abaco, South Andros, South Eleuthera, Spanish Wells, West Grand Bahama

Independence: 10 July 1973 (from the UK)

National holiday: Independence Day, 10 July (1973)

Legal system: common law system based on the English model

Constitution: *history:* previous 1964 (preindependence); latest adopted 20 June 1973, effective 10 July 1973
amendments: proposed as an "Act" by Parliament; passage of amendments to articles such as the organization and composition of the branches of government requires approval by at least two-thirds majority of the membership of both houses of Parliament and majority approval in a referendum; passage of amendments to constitutional articles such as fundamental rights and individual freedoms, the powers, authorities, and procedures of the branches of government, or changes to the Bahamas Independence Act 1973 requires approval by at least three-fourths majority of the membership of both houses and majority approval in a referendum; amended many times, last in 2016

International law organization participation: has not submitted an ICJ jurisdiction declaration; non-party state to the ICCt

Citizenship: *citizenship by birth:* no
citizenship by descent only: at least one parent must be a citizen of The Bahamas
dual citizenship recognized: no
residency requirement for naturalization: 6-9 years

Suffrage: 18 years of age; universal

Executive branch: *chief of state:* King CHARLES III (since 8 September 2022); represented by Governor-General Cynthia A. PRATT (since 1 September 2023)
head of government: Prime Minister Philip Edward DAVIS (since 17 September 2021)
cabinet: Cabinet appointed by governor-general on recommendation of prime minister
elections/appointments: the monarchy is hereditary; governor-general appointed by the monarch on the advice of the prime minister; following parliamentary elections, the leader of the majority party or majority coalition is appointed prime minister by the governor-general; the prime minister recommends the deputy prime minister

Legislative branch: *description:* bicameral Parliament consists of:
Senate (16 seats; members appointed by the governor-general - 9 selected on the advice of the prime minister, 4 on the advice of the leader of the opposition party, and 3 on the advice of the prime minister in consultation with the opposition leader; members serve 5-year terms)
House of Assembly (39 seats statutory, 38 seats current; members directly elected in single-seat constituencies by simple majority vote to serve 5-year terms)
elections: Senate - last appointments on 7 October 2021 (next appointments by 31 October 2026)
House of Assembly - last held on 16 September 2021 (next to be held by September 2026)
election results: Senate - appointed: PLP 12, FNM 4; composition - men 12, women 4, percentage women 25%
House of Assembly - percent of vote by party - PLP 52.5%, FNM 36.2%; seats by party - PLP 32, FNM 7; composition - men 32, women 7, percentage women 18%; total Parliament percentage women 20%
note: Parliament sits for 5 years from the date of the last general election: the government may dissolve the parliament and call elections at any time

Judicial branch: *highest court(s):* Court of Appeal (consists of the court president and 6 justices, organized in 3-member panels); Supreme Court (consists of the chief justice and 19 justices)
judge selection and term of office: Court of Appeal president and Supreme Court chief justice appointed by the governor-general on the advice of the prime minister after consultation with the leader of the opposition party; other Court of Appeal and Supreme Court justices appointed by the governor general upon recommendation of the Judicial and Legal Services Commission, a 5-member body headed by the chief justice; Court of Appeal justices appointed for life with mandatory retirement normally at age 68 but can be extended until age 70; Supreme Court justices appointed for life with mandatory retirement normally at age 65 but can be extended until age 67
subordinate courts: Industrial Tribunal; Magistrates' Courts; Family Island Administrators (can also serve as magistrates)
note: The Bahamas is a member of the 15-member Caribbean Community but is not party to the agreement establishing the Caribbean Court of Justice as its highest appellate court; the Judicial Committee of the Privy Council (in London) serves as the final court of appeal for The Bahamas

Political parties: Coalition of Independents Party or COI
Democratic National Alliance or DNA
Free National Movement or FNM
Progressive Liberal Party or PLP

International organization participation: ACP, ACS, AOSIS, C, Caricom, CDB, CELAC, FAO, G-77, IADB, IAEA, IBRD, ICAO, ICC (NGOs), ICRM, IDA, IFAD, IFC, IFRCS, ILO, IMF, IMO, IMSO, Interpol, IOC, IOM, ISO (correspondent), ITSO, ITU, LAES, MIGA, NAM, OAS, OPANAL, OPCW, Petrocaribe, UN, UNCTAD, UNESCO, UNIDO, UNWTO, UPU, WCO, WHO, WIPO, WMO, WTO (observer)

Diplomatic representation in the US: *chief of mission:* Ambassador Wendall Kermith JONES (since 19 April 2022)
chancery: 600 New Hampshire Ave NW, Suite 530, Washington, DC 20037
telephone: [1] (202) 319-2660
FAX: [1] (202) 319-2668
email address and website:
embassy@bahamasembdc.org
https://www.bahamasembdc.org/
consulate(s) general: Atlanta, Miami, New York

Diplomatic representation from the US: *chief of mission:* Ambassador (vacant); Chargé d'Affaires Kimberly FURNISH (since June 2024)
embassy: 42 Queen Street, Nassau
mailing address: 3370 Nassau Place, Washington, DC 20521-3370
telephone: [1] (242) 322-1181
FAX: [1] (242) 356-7174
email address and website:
acsnassau@state.gov
https://bs.usembassy.gov/

Flag description: three equal horizontal bands of aquamarine (top), gold, and aquamarine, with a black equilateral triangle based on the hoist side; the band colors represent the golden beaches of the islands surrounded by the aquamarine sea; black represents the vigor and force of a united people, while the pointing triangle indicates the enterprise and determination of the Bahamian people to develop the rich resources of land and sea

National symbol(s): blue marlin, flamingo, Yellow Elder flower; national colors: aquamarine, yellow, black

National anthem: *name:* "March On, Bahamaland!"
lyrics/music: Timothy GIBSON
note: adopted 1973; as a Commonwealth country, in addition to the national anthem, "God Save the King" serves as the royal anthem (see United Kingdom)

ECONOMY

Economic overview: high-income tourism and financial services economy; major income inequality;

strong US bilateral relations; several tax relief programs; targeted investment in agriculture, energy, light manufacturing, and technology industries

Real GDP (purchasing power parity): $13.224 billion (2023 est.)
$12.884 billion (2022 est.)
$11.63 billion (2021 est.)
note: data in 2021 dollars
comparison ranking: 160

Real GDP growth rate: 2.64% (2023 est.)
10.78% (2022 est.)
15.4% (2021 est.)
note: annual GDP % growth based on constant local currency
comparison ranking: 120

Real GDP per capita: $32,000 (2023 est.)
$31,400 (2022 est.)
$28,500 (2021 est.)
note: data in 2021 dollars
comparison ranking: 75

GDP (official exchange rate): $14.339 billion (2023 est.)
note: data in current dollars at official exchange rate

Inflation rate (consumer prices): 3.05% (2023 est.)
5.61% (2022 est.)
2.9% (2021 est.)
note: annual % change based on consumer prices
comparison ranking: 61

Credit ratings: Moody's rating: Ba2 (2020)

Standard & Poors rating: BB- (2020): note: The year refers to the year in which the current credit rating was first obtained.

GDP - composition, by sector of origin: *agriculture:* 0.4% (2023 est.)
industry: 8.8% (2023 est.)
services: 80.8% (2023 est.)
note: figures may not total 100% due to non-allocated consumption not captured in sector-reported data
comparison rankings: services 13; industry 200; agriculture 199

GDP - composition, by end use: *household consumption:* 67.5% (2023 est.)
government consumption: 13% (2023 est.)
investment in fixed capital: 19.5% (2023 est.)
investment in inventories: 1.2% (2023 est.)
exports of goods and services: 39.7% (2023 est.)
imports of goods and services: -43% (2023 est.)
note: figures may not total 100% due to rounding or gaps in data collection

Agricultural products: sugarcane, grapefruits, vegetables, bananas, tomatoes, chicken, tropical fruits, oranges, coconuts, mangoes/guavas (2022)
note: top ten agricultural products based on tonnage

Industries: tourism, banking, oil bunkering, maritime industries, transshipment and logistics, salt, aragonite, pharmaceuticals

Industrial production growth rate: 10.34% (2023 est.)
note: annual % change in industrial value added based on constant local currency
comparison ranking: 14

Labor force: 242,000 (2023 est.)
note: number of people ages 15 or older who are employed or seeking work
comparison ranking: 174

Unemployment rate: 9.2% (2023 est.)
9.87% (2022 est.)
11.69% (2021 est.)
note: % of labor force seeking employment
comparison ranking: 160

Youth unemployment rate (ages 15-24): *total:* 23.6% (2023 est.)
male: 21.5% (2023 est.)
female: 26.7% (2023 est.)
note: % of labor force ages 15-24 seeking employment
comparison ranking: total 50

Remittances: 0.38% of GDP (2023 est.)
0.44% of GDP (2022 est.)
0.47% of GDP (2021 est.)

Budget: *revenues:* $2.606 billion (2022 est.)
expenditures: $3.102 billion (2022 est.)
note: central government revenues and expenses (excluding grants/extrabudgetary units/social security funds) converted to US dollars at average official exchange rate for year indicated

Public debt: 82.16% of GDP (2022 est.)
note: central government debt as a % of GDP
comparison ranking: 37

Taxes and other revenues: 16.43% (of GDP) (2022 est.)
note: central government tax revenue as a % of GDP
comparison ranking: 122

Current account balance: -$1.763 billion (2022 est.)
-$2.434 billion (2021 est.)
-$2.285 billion (2020 est.)
note: balance of payments - net trade and primary/secondary income in current dollars
comparison ranking: 154

Exports: $4.744 billion (2022 est.)
$3.33 billion (2021 est.)
$1.688 billion (2020 est.)
note: balance of payments - exports of goods and services in current dollars
comparison ranking: 141

Exports - partners: US 49%, Cote d'Ivoire 20%, Germany 9%, Thailand 7%, Poland 4% (2022)
note: top five export partners based on percentage share of exports

Exports - commodities: refined petroleum, ships, aluminum, postage stamps/documents, plastics (2022)
note: top five export commodities based on value in dollars

Imports: $5.692 billion (2022 est.)
$4.947 billion (2021 est.)
$3.411 billion (2020 est.)
note: balance of payments - imports of goods and services in current dollars
comparison ranking: 147

Imports - partners: US 59%, South Korea 6%, Germany 6%, China 5%, Brazil 4% (2022)
note: top five import partners based on percentage share of imports

Imports - commodities: refined petroleum, ships, cars, crude petroleum, coal tar oil (2022)
note: top five import commodities based on value in dollars

Reserves of foreign exchange and gold: $2.512 billion (2023 est.)
$2.609 billion (2022 est.)
$2.433 billion (2021 est.)
note: holdings of gold (year-end prices)/foreign exchange/special drawing rights in current dollars
comparison ranking: 125

Exchange rates: Bahamian dollars (BSD) per US dollar –

Exchange rates: 1 (2023 est.)
1 (2022 est.)
1 (2021 est.)
1 (2020 est.)
1 (2019 est.)

ENERGY

Electricity access: *electrification - total population:* 100% (2022 est.)

Electricity: *installed generating capacity:* 578,000 kW (2022 est.)
consumption: 2.021 billion kWh (2022 est.)
transmission/distribution losses: 10 million kWh (2022 est.)
comparison rankings: transmission/distribution losses 15; consumption 149; installed generating capacity 148

Electricity generation sources: *fossil fuels:* 99.8% of total installed capacity (2022 est.)
solar: 0.2% of total installed capacity (2022 est.)

Petroleum: *refined petroleum consumption:* 22,000 bbl/day (2022 est.)

Natural gas: *consumption:* 13.847 million cubic meters (2022 est.)
imports: 13.847 million cubic meters (2022 est.)

Carbon dioxide emissions: 3.431 million metric tonnes of CO2 (2022 est.)
from petroleum and other liquids: 3.409 million metric tonnes of CO2 (2022 est.)
from consumed natural gas: 22,000 metric tonnes of CO2 (2022 est.)
comparison ranking: total emissions 149

Energy consumption per capita: 115.318 million Btu/person (2022 est.)
comparison ranking: 40

COMMUNICATIONS

Telephones - fixed lines: *total subscriptions:* 86,000 (2022 est.)
subscriptions per 100 inhabitants: 21 (2022 est.)
comparison ranking: total subscriptions 142

Telephones - mobile cellular: *total subscriptions:* 404,000 (2022 est.)
subscriptions per 100 inhabitants: 99 (2022 est.)
comparison ranking: total subscriptions 177

Telecommunication systems: *general assessment:* the two local providers ensure good telecoms coverage across the archipelago; fiber-to-home investments have been prioritized with 5G adoption pending (2023)
domestic: 22 per 100 fixed-line, 115 per 100 mobile-cellular (2020)
international: country code - 1-242; landing points for the ARCOS-1, BICS, Bahamas 2-US, and BDSN fiber-optic submarine cables that provide links to South and Central America, parts of the Caribbean, and the US; satellite earth stations - 2; the Bahamas Domestic Submarine Network links all of the major islands; (2019)

Broadcast media: The Bahamas has 4 major TV providers that provide service to all major islands in the archipelago; 1 TV station is operated by government-owned, commercially run Broadcasting Corporation of the Bahamas (BCB) and competes freely with 4 privately owned TV stations; multi-channel cable TV subscription service is widely available; there are 32 licensed broadcast (radio) service providers, 31 are privately owned FM radio stations operating on New Providence, Grand Bahama Island, Abaco Island, and on smaller islands in the country; the BCB operates a multi-channel radio broadcasting network that has national coverage; the sector is regulated by the Utilities Regulation and Competition Authority (2019)

Internet country code: .bs

Internet users: *total:* 385,400 (2021 est.)
percent of population: 94% (2021 est.)
comparison ranking: total 173

Broadband - fixed subscriptions: *total:* 83,000 (2020 est.)
subscriptions per 100 inhabitants: 21 (2020 est.)
comparison ranking: total 130

TRANSPORTATION

National air transport system: *number of registered air carriers:* 5 (2020)
inventory of registered aircraft operated by air carriers: 35
annual passenger traffic on registered air carriers: 1,197,116 (2018)
annual freight traffic on registered air carriers: 160,000 (2018) mt-km

Civil aircraft registration country code prefix: C6

Airports: 55 (2024)
comparison ranking: 83

Heliports: 9 (2024)

Roadways: *total:* 2,700 km
paved: 1,620 km
unpaved: 1,080 km (2011)
comparison ranking: total 169

Merchant marine: *total:* 1,274 (2023)
by type: bulk carrier 345, container ship 39, general cargo 58, oil tanker 193, other 639
comparison ranking: total 19

Ports: *total ports:* 6 (2024)
large: 0
medium: 1
small: 1
very small: 4
ports with oil terminals: 4
key ports: Clifton Pier, Cockburn Town, Freeport, Matthew Town, Nassau, South Riding Point

MILITARY AND SECURITY

Military and security forces: Royal Bahamas Defense Force (RBDF): includes land, air, maritime elements; Royal Bahamas Police Force (RBPF) (2024)
note: the RBPF maintains internal security; both the RBDF and the RBPF, as well as the Department of Corrections, report to the Minister of National Security

Military expenditures: 0.8% of GDP (2023 est.)
0.8% of GDP (2022 est.)
0.9% of GDP (2021 est.)
0.9% of GDP (2020 est.)
0.7% of GDP (2019 est.)
comparison ranking: 140

Military and security service personnel strengths: approximately 1,700 active RBDF personnel (2024)

Military equipment inventories and acquisitions: most of the RBDF's major equipment inventory has been acquired from the Netherlands (2023)

Military service age and obligation: 18-30 years of age for voluntary service for men and women (18-60 for Reserves); no conscription (2024)

Military - note: established in 1980; the RBDF's primary responsibilities are disaster relief, maritime security, and counter-narcotics operations; it also provides security at a detention center for migrants and performs some domestic security functions, such as guarding embassies; the RBDF is a naval force, but includes a lightly-armed marine infantry/commando squadron for base and internal security, as well as a few light non-combat aircraft; the maritime element has coastal patrol craft and patrol boats; the RBDF maintains training relationships with the UK and the US (2024)

TRANSNATIONAL ISSUES

Illicit drugs: a transit point for illegal drugs bound for the United States; small scale illicit production of marijuana continues

BAHRAIN

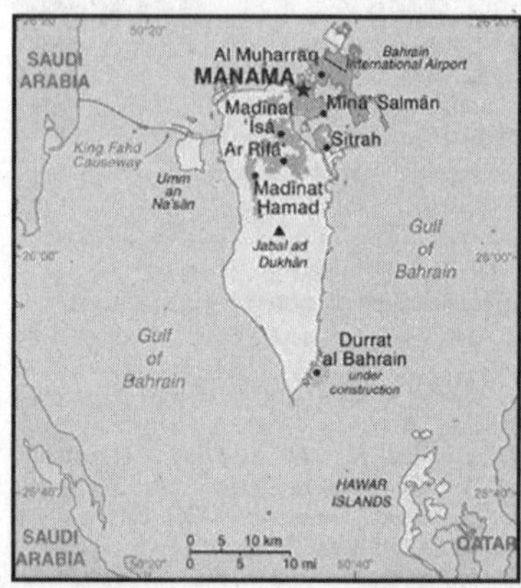

INTRODUCTION

Background: In 1783, the Sunni AL-KHALIFA family took power in Bahrain. In order to secure these holdings, it entered into a series of treaties with the UK during the 19th century that made Bahrain a British protectorate. The archipelago attained its independence in 1971. A steady decline in oil production and reserves since 1970 prompted Bahrain to take steps to diversify its economy, in the process developing petroleum processing and refining, aluminum production, and hospitality and retail sectors. It has also endeavored to become a leading regional banking center, especially with respect to Islamic finance. Bahrain's small size, central location among Gulf countries, economic dependence on Saudi Arabia, and proximity to Iran require it to play a delicate balancing act in foreign affairs among its larger neighbors. Its foreign policy activities usually fall in line with Saudi Arabia and the UAE. In 2022, the United States designated Bahrain as a major non-NATO ally.

The Sunni royal family has long struggled to manage relations with its Shia-majority population. In 2011, amid Arab uprisings elsewhere in the region, the Bahraini Government responded to similar pro-democracy and reform protests at home with police and military action, including deploying Gulf Cooperation Council security forces. Ongoing dissatisfaction with the political status quo continues to factor into sporadic clashes between demonstrators and security forces. In 2020, Bahrain and the United Arab Emirates signed the US-brokered Abraham Accords with Israel. In 2023, Bahrain and the United States signed the Comprehensive Security Integration and Prosperity Agreement to enhance cooperation across a wide range of areas, from defense and security to emerging technology, trade, and investment.

GEOGRAPHY

Location: Middle East, archipelago in the Persian Gulf, east of Saudi Arabia

Geographic coordinates: 26 00 N, 50 33 E

Map references: Middle East

Area: *total:* 760 sq km
land: 760 sq km
water: 0 sq km
comparison ranking: total 187

Area - comparative: 3.5 times the size of Washington, DC

Land boundaries: *total:* 0 km

Coastline: 161 km

Maritime claims: *territorial sea:* 12 nm
contiguous zone: 24 nm
continental shelf: extending to boundaries to be determined

Climate: arid; mild, pleasant winters; very hot, humid summers

Terrain: mostly low desert plain rising gently to low central escarpment

Elevation: *highest point:* Jabal ad Dukhan 135 m
lowest point: Persian Gulf 0 m

Natural resources: oil, associated and nonassociated natural gas, fish, pearls

Land use: *agricultural land:* 11.3% (2018 est.)
arable land: 2.1% (2018 est.)
permanent crops: 3.9% (2018 est.)
permanent pasture: 5.3% (2018 est.)
forest: 0.7% (2018 est.)
other: 88% (2018 est.)

Irrigated land: 40 sq km (2012)

Major aquifers: Arabian Aquifer System

Population distribution: smallest population of the Gulf States, but urbanization rate exceeds 90%; largest settlement concentration is found on the far northern end of the island in and around Manamah and Al Muharraq

Natural hazards: periodic droughts; dust storms

Geography - note: close to primary Middle Eastern petroleum sources; strategic location in Persian Gulf, through which much of the Western world's petroleum must transit to reach open ocean

PEOPLE AND SOCIETY

Population: *total:* 1,566,888
male: 940,022
female: 626,866 (2024 est.)
comparison rankings: female 159; male 154; total 155

Nationality: *noun:* Bahraini(s)
adjective: **Bahraini**

Ethnic groups: Bahraini 47.4%, Asian 43.4%, other Arab 4.9%, African 1.4%, North American 1.1%, Gulf Co-operative countries 0.9%, European 0.8%, other 0.1% (2020 est.)

Languages: Arabic (official), English, Farsi, Urdu
major-language sample(s):
العالم، المصدر الذي لا يمكن الاستغناء عنه للمعلومات الأساسية كتاب حقائق (Arabic)

Religions
Muslim 74.2%, other (includes Christian, Jewish, Hindu, Baha'i) 25.8% (2020 est.)

Age structure: *0-14 years:* 18.1% (male 143,399/ female 139,667)
15-64 years: 77.7% (male 762,190/female 454,616)
65 years and over: 4.3% (2024 est.) (male 34,433/ female 32,583)

Dependency ratios: *total dependency ratio:* 31.3
youth dependency ratio: 26.8
elderly dependency ratio: 4.6
potential support ratio: 21.8 (2021 est.)

Median age: *total:* 33.4 years (2024 est.)
male: 34.6 years
female: 31.2 years
comparison ranking: total 111

Population growth rate: 0.82% (2024 est.)
comparison ranking: 109

Birth rate: 12.2 births/1,000 population (2024 est.)
comparison ranking: 146

Death rate: 2.8 deaths/1,000 population (2024 est.)
comparison ranking: 226

Net migration rate: -1.2 migrant(s)/1,000 population (2024 est.)
comparison ranking: 151

Population distribution: smallest population of the Gulf States, but urbanization rate exceeds 90%; largest settlement concentration is found on the far northern end of the island in and around Manamah and Al Muharraq

Urbanization: *urban population:* 89.9% of total population (2023)
rate of urbanization: 1.99% annual rate of change (2020-25 est.)

Major urban areas - population: 709,000 MANAMA (capital) (2023)

Sex ratio: *at birth:* 1.03 male(s)/female
0-14 years: 1.03 male(s)/female
15-64 years: 1.68 male(s)/female
65 years and over: 1.06 male(s)/female
total population: 1.5 male(s)/female (2024 est.)

Maternal mortality ratio: 16 deaths/100,000 live births (2020 est.)
comparison ranking: 135

Infant mortality rate: *total:* 9.7 deaths/1,000 live births (2024 est.)
male: 11.3 deaths/1,000 live births
female: 8 deaths/1,000 live births
comparison ranking: total 135

Life expectancy at birth: *total population:* 80.4 years (2024 est.)
male: 78.1 years
female: 82.7 years
comparison ranking: total population 52

Total fertility rate: 1.65 children born/woman (2024 est.)
comparison ranking: 171

Gross reproduction rate: 0.81 (2024 est.)

water source
improved:
total: 100% of population
(2020 est.)

Current health expenditure: 4.2% of GDP (2020)

Physician density: 0.93 physicians/1,000 population (2015)

Hospital bed density: 1.7 beds/1,000 population (2017)

Sanitation facility access: *improved:*
total: 100% of population
(2020 est.)

Obesity - adult prevalence rate: 29.8% (2016)
comparison ranking: 25

Alcohol consumption per capita: *total:* 1.18 liters of pure alcohol (2019 est.)
beer: 0.4 liters of pure alcohol (2019 est.)
wine: 0.11 liters of pure alcohol (2019 est.)
spirits: 0.66 liters of pure alcohol (2019 est.)
other alcohols: 0.01 liters of pure alcohol (2019 est.)
comparison ranking: total 148

Tobacco use: *total:* 14.9% (2020 est.)
male: 25.3% (2020 est.)
female: 4.5% (2020 est.)
comparison ranking: total 104

Currently married women (ages 15-49): 43.8% (2023 est.)

Education expenditures: 2.2% of GDP (2020 est.)
comparison ranking: 183

Literacy: *definition:* age 15 and over can read and write
total population: 97.5%
male: 99.9%
female: 94.9% (2018)

School life expectancy (primary to tertiary education): *total:* 16 years
male: 16 years
female: 17 years (2019)

ENVIRONMENT

Environment - current issues: desertification resulting from the degradation of limited arable land, periods of drought, and dust storms; coastal degradation (damage to coastlines, coral reefs, and sea vegetation) resulting from oil spills and other discharges from large tankers, oil refineries, and distribution stations; lack of freshwater resources (groundwater and seawater are the only sources for all water needs); lowered water table leaves aquifers vulnerable to saline contamination; desalinization provides some 90% of the country's freshwater

Environment - international agreements: *party to:* Biodiversity, Climate Change, Climate Change-Kyoto Protocol, Climate Change-Paris Agreement, Comprehensive Nuclear Test Ban, Desertification, Endangered Species, Hazardous Wastes, Law of the Sea, Ozone Layer Protection, Ship Pollution, Wetlands
signed, but not ratified: none of the selected agreements

Climate: arid; mild, pleasant winters; very hot, humid summers

Urbanization: *urban population:* 89.9% of total population (2023)
rate of urbanization: 1.99% annual rate of change (2020-25 est.)

Revenue from forest resources: 0% of GDP (2018 est.)
comparison ranking: 160

Revenue from coal: 0% of GDP (2018 est.)
comparison ranking: 69

Air pollutants: *particulate matter emissions:* 51.82 micrograms per cubic meter (2019 est.)
carbon dioxide emissions: 31.69 megatons (2016 est.)
methane emissions: 15.47 megatons (2020 est.)

Waste and recycling: *municipal solid waste generated annually:* 951,943 tons (2016 est.)
municipal solid waste recycled annually: 76,155 tons (2012 est.)
percent of municipal solid waste recycled: 8% (2012 est.)

Major aquifers: Arabian Aquifer System

Total water withdrawal: *municipal:* 280 million cubic meters (2020 est.)
industrial: 10 million cubic meters (2020 est.)
agricultural: 140 million cubic meters (2020 est.)

Total renewable water resources: 120 million cubic meters (2020 est.)

GOVERNMENT

Country name: *conventional long form:* Kingdom of Bahrain
conventional short form: Bahrain
local long form: Mamlakat al Bahrayn
local short form: Al Bahrayn
former: Dilmun, Tylos, Awal, Mishmahig, Bahrayn, State of Bahrain
etymology: the name means "the two seas" in Arabic and refers to the water bodies surrounding the archipelago

Government type: constitutional monarchy

Capital: *name:* Manama
geographic coordinates: 26 14 N, 50 34 E
time difference: UTC+3 (8 hours ahead of Washington, DC, during Standard Time)
etymology: name derives from the Arabic "al-manama" meaning "place of rest" or "place of dreams"

Administrative divisions: 4 governorates (muhafazat, singular - muhafazah); Asimah (Capital), Janubiyah (Southern), Muharraq, Shamaliyah (Northern)
note: each governorate administered by an appointed governor

Independence: 15 August 1971 (from the UK)

National holiday: National Day, 16 December (1971); note - 15 August 1971 was the date of independence from the UK, 16 December 1971 was the date of independence from British protection

Legal system: mixed legal system of Islamic (sharia) law, English common law, Egyptian civil, criminal, and commercial codes; customary law

Constitution: *history:* previous 1973; latest adopted 14 February 2002, entry into force 14 February 2002
amendments: proposed by the king or by at least 15 members of either chamber of the National Assembly followed by submission to an Assembly committee for review and, if approved, submitted to the government for restatement as drafts; passage requires a two-thirds majority vote by the membership of both chambers and validation by the king; constitutional articles on the state religion (Islam), state language (Arabic), and the monarchy and "inherited rule" cannot be amended; amended 2012, 2017

International law organization participation: has not submitted an ICJ jurisdiction declaration; non-party state to the ICCt

Citizenship: *citizenship by birth:* no
citizenship by descent only: the father must be a citizen of Bahrain
dual citizenship recognized: no
residency requirement for naturalization: 25 years; 15 years for Arab nationals

Suffrage: 20 years of age; universal

Executive branch: *chief of state:* King HAMAD bin Isa Al-Khalifa (since 6 March 1999)
head of government: Prime Minister Crown Prince SALMAN bin Hamad Al-Khalifa (since 11 November 2020)
cabinet: Cabinet appointed by the monarch
elections/appointments: the monarchy is hereditary; prime minister appointed by the monarch

Legislative branch: *description:* bicameral National Assembly consists of:
Consultative Council or Majlis al-Shura (40 seats; members appointed by the king)
Council of Representatives or Majlis al-Nuwab (40 seats; members directly elected in single-seat constituencies by absolute majority vote in 2 rounds if needed; members serve 4-year renewable terms)
elections: Consultative Council - last appointments on 30 November 2022 (next appointments in 2026)
Council of Representatives - first round for 6 members held on 12 November 2022; second round for remaining 34 members held on 19 November 2022 (next to be held in November 2026)
election results: Consultative Council - all members appointed; composition - men 30, women 10, percentage women 25%
Council of Representatives - percent of vote by society - NA; seats by society - NA; composition - men 32, women 8, percentage women 20%; total National Assembly percentage women 23%

Judicial branch: *highest court(s):* Court of Cassation (consists of the chairman and 3 judges); Supreme Court of Appeal (consists of the chairman and 3 judges); Constitutional Court (consists of the president and 6 members); High Sharia Court of Appeal (court sittings include the president and at least one judge)
judge selection and term of office: Court of Cassation judges appointed by royal decree and serve for a specified tenure; Constitutional Court president and members appointed by the Higher Judicial Council, a body chaired by the monarch and includes judges from the Court of Cassation, sharia law courts, and Civil High Courts of Appeal; members serve 9-year terms; High Sharia Court of Appeal member appointments by royal decree for a specified tenure
subordinate courts: Civil High Courts of Appeal; middle and lower civil courts; High Sharia Court of Appeal; Senior Sharia Court; Administrative Courts of Appeal; military courts
note: the judiciary of Bahrain is divided into civil law courts and sharia law courts; sharia courts (involving personal status and family law) are further divided into Sunni Muslim and Shia Muslim; the Courts are supervised by the Supreme Judicial Council.

Political parties: *note:* political parties are prohibited, but political societies were legalized under a July 2005 law

International organization participation: ABEDA, AFESD, AMF, CAEU, CICA, FAO, G-77, GCC, IAEA, IBRD, ICAO, ICC (national committees), ICRM, IDA, IDB, IFC, IFRCS, IHO, ILO, IMF, IMO, IMSO, Interpol, IOC, IOM (observer), IPU, ISO, ITSO, ITU, ITUC (NGOs), LAS, MIGA, NAM, OAPEC, OIC, OPCW, PCA, UN, UNCTAD, UNESCO, UNIDO, UNOOSA, UNWTO, UPU, WCO, WFTU (NGOs), WHO, WIPO, WMO, WTO

Diplomatic representation in the US: *chief of mission:* Ambassador Abdulla bin Rashed AL KHALIFA (since 21 July 2017)
chancery: 3502 International Drive NW, Washington, DC 20008
telephone: [1] (202) 342-1111
FAX: [1] (202) 362-2192
email address and website:
ambsecretary@bahrainembassy.org
https://www.mofa.gov.bh/Default.aspx?language=en-US&tabid=7702
consulate(s) general: New York

Diplomatic representation from the US: *chief of mission:* Ambassador Steven C. BONDY (since 9 February 2022)
embassy: Building 979, Road 3119, Block 331, Zinj District, P.O. Box 26431, Manama
mailing address: 6210 Manama Place, Washington DC 20521-6210
telephone: [973] 17-242700
FAX: [973] 17-272594
email address and website:
ManamaConsular@state.gov
https://bh.usembassy.gov/

Flag description: red, the traditional color for flags of Persian Gulf states, with a white serrated band (five white points) on the hoist side; the five points represent the five pillars of Islam
note: until 2002, the flag had eight white points, but this was reduced to five to avoid confusion with the Qatari flag

National symbol(s): a red field surmounted by a white serrated band with five white points; national colors: red, white

National anthem: *name:* "Bahrainona" (Our Bahrain)
lyrics/music: unknown
note: adopted 1971; although Mohamed Sudqi AYYASH wrote the original lyrics, they were changed in 2002 following the transformation of Bahrain from an emirate to a kingdom

National heritage: *total World Heritage Sites:* 3 (all cultural)
selected World Heritage Site locales: Dilmun Burial Mounds; Qal'at al-Bahrain – Ancient Harbor and Capital of Dilmun; Bahrain Pearling Path

ECONOMY

Economic overview: growing, economically diverse Middle Eastern island economy; major recovery and balancing efforts to fulfill Economic Vision 2030; regional finance hub; increasing openness; high youth unemployment; water scarcity amid reservoir depletion

Real GDP (purchasing power parity): $85.491 billion (2023 est.)
$83.421 billion (2022 est.)
$79.531 billion (2021 est.)
note: data in 2021 dollars
comparison ranking: 101

Real GDP growth rate: 2.48% (2023 est.)
4.89% (2022 est.)
2.59% (2021 est.)
note: annual GDP % growth based on constant local currency
comparison ranking: 126

Real GDP per capita: $57,600 (2023 est.)
$56,700 (2022 est.)
$54,400 (2021 est.)
note: data in 2021 dollars
comparison ranking: 30

GDP (official exchange rate): $43.205 billion (2023 est.)
note: data in current dollars at official exchange rate

Inflation rate (consumer prices): 0.07% (2023 est.)
3.63% (2022 est.)
-0.61% (2021 est.)
note: annual % change based on consumer prices
comparison ranking: 7

Credit ratings: Fitch rating: B+ (2020)

Moody's rating: B2 (2018)

Standard & Poors rating: B+ (2017)
note: The year refers to the year in which the current credit rating was first obtained.

GDP - composition, by sector of origin: *agriculture:* 0.3% (2023 est.)
industry: 44.5% (2023 est.)
services: 51.1% (2023 est.)
note: figures may not total 100% due to non-allocated consumption not captured in sector-reported data
comparison rankings: services 141; industry 23; agriculture 203

GDP - composition, by end use: *household consumption:* 39.2% (2021 est.)
government consumption: 15.8% (2021 est.)
investment in fixed capital: 24.6% (2021 est.)
investment in inventories: 1% (2021 est.)
exports of goods and services: 89.7% (2021 est.)
imports of goods and services: -70.2% (2021 est.)
note: figures may not total 100% due to rounding or gaps in data collection

Agricultural products: lamb/mutton, dates, milk, chicken, tomatoes, fruits, sheep offal, eggs, sheepskins, cucumbers/gherkins (2022)
note: top ten agricultural products based on tonnage

Industries: petroleum processing and refining, aluminum smelting, iron pelletization, fertilizers, Islamic and offshore banking, insurance, ship repairing, tourism

Industrial production growth rate: -1.1% (2023 est.)
note: annual % change in industrial value added based on constant local currency
comparison ranking: 167

Labor force: 855,000 (2023 est.)
note: number of people ages 15 or older who are employed or seeking work
comparison ranking: 150

Unemployment rate: 1.16% (2023 est.)
1.33% (2022 est.)

1.55% (2021 est.)
note: % of labor force seeking employment
comparison ranking: 11

Youth unemployment rate (ages 15-24): *total:* 5.8% (2023 est.)
male: 2.9% (2023 est.)
female: 12.5% (2023 est.)
note: % of labor force ages 15-24 seeking employment
comparison ranking: total 170

Average household expenditures: *on food:* 13% of household expenditures (2022 est.)
on alcohol and tobacco: 0.4% of household expenditures (2022 est.)

Remittances: 0% of GDP (2023 est.)
0% of GDP (2022 est.)
0% of GDP (2021 est.)

Budget: *revenues:* $5.538 billion (2020 est.)
expenditures: $9.357 billion (2020 est.)
note: central government revenues and expenses (excluding grants/extrabudgetary units/social security funds) converted to US dollars at average official exchange rate for year indicated

Public debt: 115.52% of GDP (2020 est.)
comparison ranking: 13

Taxes and other revenues: 2.92% (of GDP) (2020 est.)
comparison ranking: 205

Current account balance: $2.699 billion (2023 est.)
$6.839 billion (2022 est.)
$2.602 billion (2021 est.)
note: balance of payments - net trade and primary/secondary income in current dollars comparison ranking: 45

Exports: $40.344 billion (2023 est.)
$44.58 billion (2022 est.)
$35.653 billion (2021 est.)
note: balance of payments - exports of goods and services in current dollars
comparison ranking: 71

Exports - partners: Saudi Arabia 15%, UAE 10%, US 9%, Japan 5%, India 4% (2022)
note: top five export partners based on percentage share of exports

Exports - commodities: aluminum, refined petroleum, iron ore, aluminum wire, iron blocks (2022)
note: top five export commodities based on value in dollars

Imports: $32.374 billion (2023 est.)
$33.066 billion (2022 est.)
$27.996 billion (2021 est.)
note: balance of payments - imports of goods and services in current dollars
comparison ranking: 77

Imports - partners: China 15%, UAE 12%, Brazil 9%, Australia 8%, India 7% (2022)
note: top five import partners based on percentage share of imports

Imports - commodities: iron ore, aluminum oxide, cars, gold, ships (2022)
note: top five import commodities based on value in dollars

Reserves of foreign exchange and gold: $5.118 billion (2023 est.)
$4.775 billion (2022 est.)
$4.993 billion (2021 est.)
note: holdings of gold (year-end prices)/foreign exchange/special drawing rights in current dollars
comparison ranking: 103

Exchange rates: Bahraini dinars (BHD) per US dollar –

Exchange rates: 0.376 (2023 est.)
0.376 (2022 est.)
0.376 (2021 est.)
0.376 (2020 est.)
0.376 (2019 est.)

ENERGY

Electricity access: *electrification - total population:* 100% (2022 est.)

Electricity: *installed generating capacity:* 6.983 million kW (2022 est.)
consumption: 34.515 billion kWh (2022 est.)
exports: 447.711 million kWh (2022 est.)
imports: 484.596 million kWh (2022 est.)
transmission/distribution losses: 1.063 billion kWh (2022 est.)
comparison rankings: transmission/distribution losses 100; imports 92; exports 79; consumption 63; installed generating capacity 78

Electricity generation sources: *fossil fuels:* 100% of total installed capacity (2022 est.)

Coal: *exports:* 2,000 metric tons (2022 est.)
imports: 94.7 metric tons (2022 est.)

Petroleum: *total petroleum production:* 189,000 bbl/day (2023 est.)
refined petroleum consumption: 72,000 bbl/day (2022 est.)
crude oil estimated reserves: 186.5 million barrels (2021 est.)

Natural gas: *production:* 18.005 billion cubic meters (2022 est.)
consumption: 17.924 billion cubic meters (2022 est.)
imports: 81.98 million cubic meters (2020 est.)
proven reserves: 81.383 billion cubic meters (2021 est.)

Carbon dioxide emissions: 43.343 million metric tonnes of CO2 (2022 est.)
from petroleum and other liquids: 8.185 million metric tonnes of CO2 (2022 est.)
from consumed natural gas: 35.163 million metric tonnes of CO2 (2022 est.)
comparison ranking: total emissions 61

Energy consumption per capita: 514.32 million Btu/person (2022 est.)
comparison ranking: 3

COMMUNICATIONS

Telephones - fixed lines: *total subscriptions:* 253,000 (2022 est.)
subscriptions per 100 inhabitants: 17 (2022 est.)
comparison ranking: total subscriptions 116

Telephones - mobile cellular: *total subscriptions:* 2.141 million (2022 est.)
subscriptions per 100 inhabitants: 145 (2022 est.)
comparison ranking: total subscriptions 148

Telecommunication systems: *general assessment:* Bahrain continues to develop its telecoms sector in a bid to develop its long-term Economic Vision 2030 strategy; this is a multi-faceted strategy aimed at developing a digital transformation across numerous sectors, including e-government, e-health, e-commerce, and e-banking; 5G services have become widely available since they were launched in 2020; Bahrain's telecom sector by the Fourth National Telecommunications Plan (initiated in 2016) which focuses on fiber optic infrastructure deployment and establishing affordable prices for high-speed access (2022)
domestic: approximately 18 per 100 fixed-line and 131 per 100 mobile-cellular; modern fiber-optic integrated services; digital network with rapidly expanding mobile-cellular telephones (2021)
international: country code - 973; Bahrain's Telecommunications Regulatory Authority (TRA) has made part of the C-band spectrum available for 5G private networks, in line with the goals outlined in its Workplan for the 2022-23 period (2023)

Broadcast media: state-run Bahrain Radio and Television Corporation (BRTC) operates 5 terrestrial TV networks and several radio stations; satellite TV systems provide access to international broadcasts; 1 private FM station directs broadcasts to Indian listeners; radio and TV broadcasts from countries in the region are available (2019)

Internet country code: .bh

Internet users: *total:* 1.5 million (2021 est.)
percent of population: 100% (2021 est.)
comparison ranking: total 144

Broadband - fixed subscriptions: *total:* 148,928 (2020 est.)
subscriptions per 100 inhabitants: 9 (2020 est.)
comparison ranking: total 123

TRANSPORTATION

National air transport system: *number of registered air carriers:* 6 (2020)
inventory of registered aircraft operated by air carriers: 42
annual passenger traffic on registered air carriers: 5,877,003 (2018)
annual freight traffic on registered air carriers: 420.98 million (2018) mt-km

Civil aircraft registration country code prefix: A9C

Airports: 3 (2024)
comparison ranking: 190

Heliports: 8 (2024)

Pipelines: 20 km gas, 54 km oil (2013)

Roadways: *total:* 4,122 km
paved: 3,392 km
unpaved: 730 km (2010)
comparison ranking: total 155

Merchant marine: *total:* 184 (2023)
by type: general cargo 12, oil tanker 3, other 169
comparison ranking: total 71

Ports: *total ports:* 4 (2024)
large: 0
medium: 3
small: 1
very small: 0
ports with oil terminals: 1
key ports: Al Manamah, Khalifa Bin Salman, Mina Salman, Sitrah

MILITARY AND SECURITY

Military and security forces: Bahrain Defense Force (BDF): Royal Bahraini Army (includes the Royal Guard), Royal Bahraini Navy, Royal Bahraini Air Force

Ministry of Interior: National Guard, Special Security Forces Command (SSFC), Coast Guard (2024)

note 1: the Royal Guard is officially under the command of the Army, but exercises considerable autonomy
note 2: the Ministry of Interior is responsible for internal security and oversees police and specialized security units responsible for maintaining internal order; the National Guard's primary mission is to guard critical infrastructure such as the airport and oil fields and is a back-up to the police; the Guard is under the Ministry of Interior but reports directly to the king

Military expenditures: 3.1% of GDP (2023 est.)
3.2% of GDP (2022 est.)
3.6% of GDP (2021 est.)
4.2% of GDP (2020 est.)
4% of GDP (2019 est.)
comparison ranking: 30

Military and security service personnel strengths: information varies; approximately 10,000 active personnel (7,500 Army; 1,000 Navy; 1,500 Air Force); approximately 3,000 National Guard (2023)

Military equipment inventories and acquisitions: the military's inventory consists of a mix of equipment acquired from a wide variety of suppliers; in recent years, the US has been the leading supplier of arms to Bahrain (2024)

Military service age and obligation: 18 years of age for voluntary military service; 18-55 to voluntarily join the reserves; no compulsory service (2024)

Military - note: the BDF is a small, but well-equipped military focused on territorial defense and support to internal security; its primary concern is Iran, both the conventional military threat and Tehran's support to regional terrorist groups; the BDF participates in multinational exercises and has conducted small deployments outside of the country; in 2015, for example, Bahrain joined the Saudi Arabia-led military intervention in Yemen, supplying a few hundred troops and combat aircraft
Bahrain's closest security partners are the US and Saudi Arabia; it hosts the US Naval Forces Central Command (USNAVCENT; established 1983), which includes the US 5th Fleet, several subordinate naval task forces, and the Combined Maritime Forces (established 2002), a coalition of more than 30 nations providing maritime security for regional shipping lanes; in 2003, the US granted Bahrain Major Non-NATO Ally status, a designation under US law that provides foreign partners with certain benefits in the areas of defense trade and security cooperation; Bahraini leaders have said that the security of Bahrain and Saudi Arabia are "indivisible"; Saudi Arabia sent forces to Bahrain to assist with internal security following the 2011 uprising; Bahrain also has close security ties to other Gulf Cooperation Council countries, particularly Kuwait and the United Arab Emirates, as well as the UK (2024)

SPACE

Space agency/agencies: Bahrain National Space Science Agency (NSSA; established 2014) (2024)

Space program overview: space program in nascent stages and is focused on developing the capabilities to build and operate satellites; the NSSA's mission includes promoting space science, technology, and research, building capacity in the fields of satellite manufacturing, tracking, control, data processing and analysis, and remote sensing, developing space-related programs and space policy, and facilitating international cooperation; cooperates with a variety of foreign agencies and commercial entities, including those of India, Italy, Japan, Saudi Arabia, the UK, the UAE, and the US; also a member of the Arab Space Coordination Group, established by the UAE in 2019 (2024)
note: further details about the key activities, programs, and milestones of the country's space program, as well as government spending estimates on the space sector, appear in the Space Programs reference guide

TERRORISM

Terrorist group(s): al-Ashtar Brigades; Islamic Revolutionary Guard Corps/Qods Force
note 1: details about the history, aims, leadership, organization, areas of operation, tactics, targets, weapons, size, and sources of support of the group(s) appear(s) in the Terrorism reference guide
note 2: in addition to the al-Ashtar Brigades and the IRGC/Qods Force, Saraya al-Mukhtar (aka The Mukhtar Brigade) is an Iran-backed terrorist organization based in Bahrain, reportedly receiving financial and logistic support from the IRGC; Saraya al-Mukhtar's self-described goal is to depose the Bahraini Government with the intention of paving the way for Iran to exert greater influence in Bahrain; the group was designated by the US as a Specially Designated Global Terrorist in Dec 2020

BANGLADESH

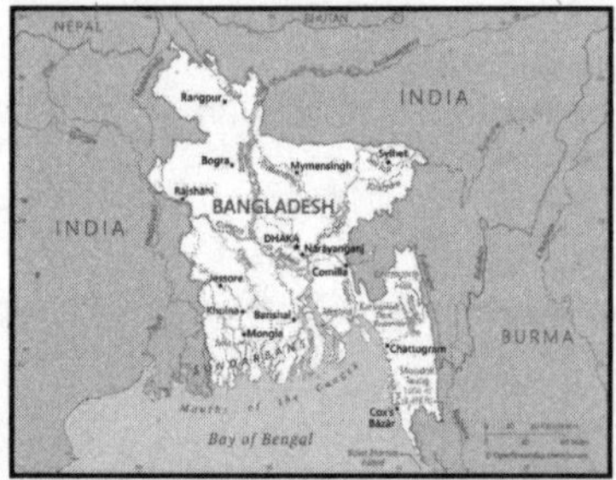

INTRODUCTION

Background: The huge delta region at the confluence of the Ganges and Brahmaputra River systems – now referred to as Bangladesh – was a loosely incorporated outpost of various empires for much of the first millennium A.D. Muslim conversions and settlement in the region began in the 10th century, primarily from Arab and Persian traders and preachers. Europeans established trading posts in the area in the 16th century. Eventually the area known as Bengal, which is primarily Hindu in the western section and mostly Muslim in the eastern half, became part of British India. After the partition of India in 1947, the Muslim-majority area became East Pakistan. Calls for greater autonomy and animosity between the eastern and western areas of Pakistan led to a Bengali independence movement. That movement, led by the Awami League (AL) and supported by India, won the independence war for Bangladesh in 1971.

The military overthrew the post-independence AL government in 1975, the first of a series of military coups that resulted in a military-backed government and the subsequent creation of the Bangladesh Nationalist Party (BNP) that took power in 1979. That government also ended in a coup in 1981, followed by military-backed rule until democratic elections were held in 1991. The BNP and AL alternated in power from 1991 to 2008, with the exception of a military-backed, emergency caretaker regime in 2007. The country returned to fully democratic rule in 2008 with the election of the AL and Prime Minister Sheikh HASINA. With the help of international development assistance, Bangladesh is on track to graduate from the UN's Least Developed Countries (LDC) list in 2026.

The economy has grown at an annual average of about 6.25% for the last two decades. Poverty declined from 11.8 percent in 2010 to 5.0 percent in 2022, based on the international poverty line of $2.15 a day (using 2017 Purchasing Power Parity exchange rate). Moreover, human development outcomes improved along many dimensions. The country made a rapid recovery from the COVID-19 pandemic, but faces several economic challenges.

GEOGRAPHY

Location: Southern Asia, bordering the Bay of Bengal, between Burma and India

Geographic coordinates: 24 00 N, 90 00 E

Map references: Asia

Area: *total:* 148,460 sq km
land: 130,170 sq km
water: 18,290 sq km
comparison ranking: total 94

Area - comparative: slightly larger than Pennsylvania and New Jersey combined; slightly smaller than Iowa

Land boundaries: *total:* 4,413 km
border countries (2): Burma 271 km; India 4,142 km

Coastline: 580 km

Maritime claims: *territorial sea:* 12 nm
contiguous zone: 18 nm
exclusive economic zone: 200 nm
continental shelf: to the outer limits of the continental margin

Climate: tropical; mild winter (October to March); hot, humid summer (March to June); humid, warm rainy monsoon (June to October)

Terrain: mostly flat alluvial plain; hilly in southeast

Elevation: *highest point:* Mowdok Taung 1,060 m
lowest point: Indian Ocean 0 m
mean elevation: 85 m

Natural resources: natural gas, arable land, timber, coal

Land use: *agricultural land:* 70.1% (2018 est.)
arable land: 59% (2018 est.)
permanent crops: 6.5% (2018 est.)
permanent pasture: 4.6% (2018 est.)
forest: 11.1% (2018 est.)
other: 18.8% (2018 est.)

Irrigated land: 81,270 sq km (2020)

Major rivers (by length in km): Brahmaputra river mouth (shared with China [s] and India) - 3,969 km; Ganges river mouth (shared with India [s]) - 2,704 km
note – [s] after country name indicates river source; [m] after country name indicates river mouth

Major watersheds (area sq km): Indian Ocean drainage: Brahmaputra (651,335 sq km), Ganges (1,016,124 sq km)

Major aquifers: Indus-Ganges-Brahmaputra Basin

Natural hazards: droughts; cyclones; much of the country routinely inundated during the summer monsoon season

Geography - note: *most of the country is situated on deltas of large rivers flowing from the Himalayas:* the Ganges unites with the Jamuna (main channel of the Brahmaputra) and later joins the Meghna to eventually empty into the Bay of Bengal

PEOPLE AND SOCIETY

Population: *total:* 168,697,184
male: 82,708,252
female: 85,988,932 (2024 est.)
comparison rankings: female 8; male 8; total 8

Nationality: *noun:* Bangladeshi(s)
adjective: Bangladeshi

Ethnic groups: Bengali at least 99%, other indigenous ethnic groups 1% (2022 est.)
note: Bangladesh's government recognizes 27 indigenous ethnic groups under the 2010 Cultural Institution for Small Anthropological Groups Act; other sources estimate there are about 75 ethnic groups

Languages: Bangla 98.8% (official, also known as Bengali), other 1.2% (2011 est.)
major-language sample(s):
বিশ্ব ফেসবুক, মৌলিক তথ্যের অপরিহার্য উৎস (Bangla)

Religions: Muslim 91%, Hindu 8%, other 1% (2022 est.)

Age structure: *0-14 years:* 25.1% (male 21,540,493/ female 20,800,712)
15-64 years: 67.1% (male 55,071,592/female 58,180,322)
65 years and over: 7.8% (2024 est.) (male 6,096,167/ female 7,007,898)

Dependency ratios: *total dependency ratio:* 47.7
youth dependency ratio: 39.1
elderly dependency ratio: 8.6
potential support ratio: 11.6 (2021 est.)

Median age: *total:* 29.6 years (2024 est.)
male: 28.7 years
female: 30.4 years
comparison ranking: total 144

Population growth rate: 0.89% (2024 est.)
comparison ranking: 103

Birth rate: 17.3 births/1,000 population (2024 est.)
comparison ranking: 88

Death rate: 5.5 deaths/1,000 population (2024 est.)
comparison ranking: 179

Net migration rate: -2.9 migrant(s)/1,000 population (2024 est.)
comparison ranking: 178

Urbanization: *urban population:* 40.5% of total population (2023)
rate of urbanization: 2.88% annual rate of change (2020-25 est.)

Major urban areas - population: 23.210 million DHAKA (capital), 5.380 million Chittagong, 955,000 Khulna, 962,000 Rajshahi, 964,000 Sylhet, 906,000 Bogra (2023)

Sex ratio: *at birth:* 1.04 male(s)/female
0-14 years: 1.04 male(s)/female
15-64 years: 0.95 male(s)/female
65 years and over: 0.87 male(s)/female
total population: 0.96 male(s)/female (2024 est.)

Mother's mean age at first birth: 18.6 years (2017/18 est.)
note: data represents median age at first birth among women 20-49

Maternal mortality ratio: 123 deaths/100,000 live births (2020 est.)
comparison ranking: 63

Infant mortality rate: *total:* 28.8 deaths/1,000 live births (2024 est.)
male: 31.3 deaths/1,000 live births
female: 26.3 deaths/1,000 live births
comparison ranking: total 52

Life expectancy at birth: *total population:* 75.2 years (2024 est.)
male: 73.1 years
female: 77.5 years
comparison ranking: total population 129

Total fertility rate: 2.07 children born/woman (2024 est.)
comparison ranking: 96

Gross reproduction rate: 1.01 (2024 est.)

Contraceptive prevalence rate: 62.7% (2019)

Drinking water source: *improved: urban:* 99% of population
rural: 98.7% of population
total: 98.9% of population
unimproved: urban: 1% of population
rural: 1.3% of population
total: 1.1% of population (2020 est.)

Current health expenditure: 2.6% of GDP (2020)

Physician density: 0.67 physicians/1,000 population (2020)

Hospital bed density: 0.8 beds/1,000 population (2016)

Sanitation facility access: *improved: urban:* 85.3% of population
rural: 73.5% of population
total: 78% of population
unimproved: urban: 14.7% of population
rural: 26.5% of population
total: 22% of population (2020 est.)

Obesity - adult prevalence rate: 3.6% (2016)
comparison ranking: 191

Alcohol consumption per capita: *total:* 0 liters of pure alcohol (2019 est.)
beer: 0 liters of pure alcohol (2019 est.)
wine: 0 liters of pure alcohol (2019 est.)
spirits: 0 liters of pure alcohol (2019 est.)
other alcohols: 0 liters of pure alcohol (2019 est.)
comparison ranking: total 187

Tobacco use: *total:* 34.7% (2020 est.)
male: 52.2% (2020 est.)
female: 17.1% (2020 est.)
comparison ranking: total 17

Children under the age of 5 years underweight: 22.6% (2019)
comparison ranking: 10

Currently married women (ages 15-49): 80.1% (2023 est.)

Child marriage: *women married by age 15:* 15.5%
women married by age 18: 51.4% (2019 est.)

Education expenditures: 2.1% of GDP (2021 est.)
comparison ranking: 186

Literacy: *definition:* age 15 and over can read and write
total population: 74.9%
male: 77.8%
female: 72% (2020)

School life expectancy (primary to tertiary education): *total:* 12 years
male: 12 years
female: 13 years (2020)

ENVIRONMENT

Environment - current issues: many people are landless and forced to live on and cultivate flood-prone land; waterborne diseases prevalent in surface water; water pollution, especially of fishing areas, results from the use of commercial pesticides; ground water contaminated by naturally occurring arsenic; intermittent water shortages because of falling water tables in the northern and central parts of the country; soil degradation and erosion; deforestation; destruction of wetlands; severe overpopulation with noise pollution

Environment - international agreements: *party to:* Biodiversity, Climate Change, Climate Change-Kyoto Protocol, Climate Change-Paris Agreement, Comprehensive Nuclear Test Ban, Desertification, Endangered Species, Environmental Modification, Hazardous Wastes, Law of the Sea, Nuclear Test Ban, Ozone Layer Protection, Ship Pollution, Wetlands
signed, but not ratified: none of the selected agreements

Climate: tropical; mild winter (October to March); hot, humid summer (March to June); humid, warm rainy monsoon (June to October)

Urbanization: *urban population:* 40.5% of total population (2023)
rate of urbanization: 2.88% annual rate of change (2020-25 est.)

Food insecurity: *severe localized food insecurity: due to economic constraints and high prices of important food items* - food insecurity is expected to remain fragile, given persisting economic constraints; domestic prices of wheat flour and palm oil, important food items, were at high levels in January 2023; the result of elevated international prices of energy, fuel and food, having been transmitted to the domestic markets (2023)

Revenue from forest resources: 0.08% of GDP (2018 est.)
comparison ranking: 120

Revenue from coal: 0.02% of GDP (2018 est.)
comparison ranking: 43

Air pollutants: *particulate matter emissions:* 45.99 micrograms per cubic meter (2019 est.)
carbon dioxide emissions: 84.25 megatons (2016 est.)
methane emissions: 59.3 megatons (2020 est.)

Waste and recycling: *municipal solid waste generated annually:* 14,778,497 tons (2012 est.)

Major rivers (by length in km): Brahmaputra river mouth (shared with China [s] and India) - 3,969 km; Ganges river mouth (shared with India [s]) - 2,704 km
note – [s] after country name indicates river source; [m] after country name indicates river mouth

Major watersheds (area sq km): Indian Ocean drainage: Brahmaputra (651,335 sq km), Ganges (1,016,124 sq km)

Major aquifers: Indus-Ganges-Brahmaputra Basin

Total water withdrawal: *municipal:* 3.6 billion cubic meters (2020 est.)
industrial: 770 million cubic meters (2020 est.)
agricultural: 31.5 billion cubic meters (2020 est.)

Total renewable water resources: 1.23 trillion cubic meters (2020 est.)

GOVERNMENT

Country name: *conventional long form:* People's Republic of Bangladesh
conventional short form: Bangladesh
local long form: Gana Prajatantri Bangladesh
local short form: Bangladesh
former: East Bengal, East Pakistan
etymology: the name - a compound of the Bengali words "Bangla" (Bengal) and "desh" (country) - means "Country of Bengal"

Government type: parliamentary republic

Capital: *name:* Dhaka
geographic coordinates: 23 43 N, 90 24 E
time difference: UTC+6 (11 hours ahead of Washington, DC, during Standard Time)
etymology: the origins of the name are unclear, but some sources state that the city's site was originally called "dhakka," meaning "watchtower," and that the area served as a watch-station for Bengal rulers

Administrative divisions: 8 divisions; Barishal, Chattogram, Dhaka, Khulna, Mymensingh, Rajshahi, Rangpur, Sylhet

Independence: 16 December 1971 (from Pakistan)

National holiday: Independence Day, 26 March (1971); Victory Day, 16 December (1971); note - 26 March 1971 is the date of the Awami League's declaration of an independent Bangladesh, and 16 December (Victory Day) memorializes the military victory over Pakistan and the official creation of the state of Bangladesh

Legal system: common law; since independence, statutory law enacted by the Parliament of Bangladesh has been the primary form of legislation; Bangladeshi law incorporates elements of English common law; Islamic law applies to Bangladeshi Muslims in family and inheritance laws, with Hindu personal law applying to Bangladeshi Hindus and Buddhists

Constitution: *history:* previous 1935, 1956, 1962 (preindependence); latest enacted 4 November 1972, effective 16 December 1972, suspended March 1982, restored November 1986
amendments: proposed by the House of the Nation; approval requires at least two-thirds majority vote of the House membership and assent of the president of the republic; amended many times, last in 2018

International law organization participation: has not submitted an ICJ jurisdiction declaration; accepts ICCt jurisdiction

Citizenship: *citizenship by birth:* no
citizenship by descent only: at least one parent must be a citizen of Bangladesh
dual citizenship recognized: yes, but limited to select countries
residency requirement for naturalization: 5 years

Suffrage: 18 years of age; universal

Executive branch: *chief of state:* President Mohammad Shahabuddin CHUPPI (since 24 April 2023)
head of government: Interim Prime Minister Muhammad YUNUS (since 8 August 2024)
cabinet: Cabinet selected by the prime minister, appointed by the president
elections/appointments: president indirectly elected by the National Parliament for a 5-year term (eligible for a second term); election last held on 13 February 2023 (next to be held by 2028); the president appoints as prime minister the majority party leader in the National Parliament
election results: President Mohammad Shahabuddin CHUPPI (AL) elected unopposed by the National Parliament; Sheikh HASINA reappointed prime minister for a fifth term following the 7 January 2024 parliamentary election

Legislative branch: *description:* unicameral House of the Nation or Jatiya Sangsad (350 seats; 300 members in single-seat territorial constituencies directly elected by simple majority vote; 50 members - reserved for women only - indirectly elected by the House of the Nation membership by proportional representation vote using single transferable vote method; all members serve 5-year terms); note - on 5 August 2024, Prime Minister Sheikh HASINA Wazed resigned, and the following day, President Mohammad Shahabuddin CHUPPI dissolved House of the Nation
elections: last held on 7 January 2024 (next to be held in 2026)
election results: percent of vote by party - NA; seats by party as of December 2023 - AL 306, JP 27, BNP 0, other 14, independent 3; composition - men 280, women 70, percentage women 20%
note: 50 seats are reserved for women only and are indirectly elected by the House of the Nation members using proportional representation

Judicial branch: *highest court(s):* Supreme Court of Bangladesh (organized into the Appellate Division with 7 justices and the High Court Division with 99 justices)
judge selection and term of office: chief justice and justices appointed by the president; justices serve until retirement at age 67
subordinate courts: civil courts include: Assistant Judge's Court; Joint District Judge's Court; Additional District Judge's Court; District Judge's Court; criminal courts include: Court of Sessions; Court of Metropolitan Sessions; Metropolitan Magistrate Courts; Magistrate Court; special courts/tribunals

Political parties: Awami League or AL
Bangladesh Jamaat-i-Islami or JIB
Bangladesh Nationalist Party or BNP
Islami Andolan Bangladesh
Jatiya Party or JP (Ershad faction)
Jatiya Party or JP (Manju faction)
National Socialist Party (Jatiya Samajtantrik Dal) or JSD
Workers Party or WP

International organization participation: ADB, ARF, BIMSTEC, C, CD, CICA (observer), CP, D-8, FAO, G-77, IAEA, IBRD, ICAO, ICC (national committees), ICRM, IDA, IDB, IFAD, IFC, IFRCS, IHO, ILO, IMF, IMO, IMSO, Interpol, IOC, IOM, IPU, ISO, ITSO, ITU, ITUC (NGOs), MIGA, MINURSO, MINUSCA, MONUSCO, NAM, OIC, OPCW, PCA, SAARC, SACEP, UN, UNAMID, UNCTAD, UNESCO, UNHCR, UNIDO, UNISFA, UNIFIL, UNMISS, UNOOSA, UNWTO, UPU, WCO, WFTU (NGOs), WHO, WIPO, WMO, WTO

Diplomatic representation in the US: *chief of mission:* Ambassador (vacant); Chargé d'Affaires DM Salahuddin MAHMUD (since 12 September 2024)
chancery: 3510 International Drive NW, Washington, DC 20008
telephone: [1] (202) 244-0183
FAX: [1] (202) 244-2771
email address and website:
mission.washington@mofa.gov.bd
Embassy of the People's Republic of Bangladesh, Washington, DC (mofa.gov.bd)
consulate(s) general: Los Angeles, Miami, New York

Diplomatic representation from the US: *chief of mission:* Ambassador (vacant); Chargé d'Affaires Helen LAFAVE (since July 2024)
embassy: Madani Avenue, Baridhara, Dhaka - 1212
mailing address: 6120 Dhaka Place, Washington DC 20521-6120
telephone: [880] (2) 5566-2000
FAX: [880] (2) 5566-2907
email address and website:
DhakaACS@state.gov
https://bd.usembassy.gov/

Flag description: green field with a large red disk shifted slightly to the hoist side of center; the red disk represents the rising sun and the sacrifice to achieve independence; the green field symbolizes the lush vegetation of Bangladesh

National symbol(s): Bengal tiger, water lily; national colors: green, red

National anthem: *name:* "Amar Shonar Bangla" (My Golden Bengal)
lyrics/music: Rabindranath TAGORE
note: adopted 1971; Rabindranath TAGORE, a Nobel laureate, also wrote India's national anthem

National heritage: *total World Heritage Sites:* 3 (2 cultural, 1 natural)
selected World Heritage Site locales: Bagerhat Historic Mosque (c); Ruins of the Buddhist Vihara at Paharpur (c); Sundarbans (n)

ECONOMY

Economic overview: one of the fastest growing emerging market economies; strong economic rebound following COVID-19; significant poverty reduction; exports dominated by textile industry; weakened exports and remittances resulted in declining foreign exchange reserves and 2022 IMF loan request

Real GDP (purchasing power parity): $1.413 trillion (2023 est.)
$1.336 trillion (2022 est.)
$1.248 trillion (2021 est.)
note: data in 2021 dollars
comparison ranking: 23

Real GDP growth rate: 5.78% (2023 est.)
7.1% (2022 est.)
6.94% (2021 est.)
note: annual GDP % growth based on constant local currency
comparison ranking: 35

Real GDP per capita: $8,200 (2023 est.)
$7,800 (2022 est.)
$7,400 (2021 est.)
note: data in 2021 dollars
comparison ranking: 154

GDP (official exchange rate): $437.415 billion (2023 est.)
note: data in current dollars at official exchange rate

Inflation rate (consumer prices): 9.88% (2023 est.)
7.7% (2022 est.)
5.55% (2021 est.)
note: annual % change based on consumer prices
comparison ranking: 177

Credit ratings: Fitch rating: BB- (2014)

Moody's rating: Ba3 (2012)

Standard & Poors rating: BB- (2010)
note: The year refers to the year in which the current credit rating was first obtained.

GDP - composition, by sector of origin: *agriculture:* 11% (2023 est.)
industry: 34.6% (2023 est.)
services: 51.1% (2023 est.)
note: figures may not total 100% due to non-allocated consumption not captured in sector-reported data
comparison rankings: services 142; industry 45; agriculture 72

GDP - composition, by end use: *household consumption:* 68.6% (2023 est.)
government consumption: 5.7% (2023 est.)
investment in fixed capital: 31% (2023 est.)
exports of goods and services: 13.2% (2023 est.)
imports of goods and services: -17.8% (2023 est.)
note: figures may not total 100% due to rounding or gaps in data collection

Agricultural products: rice, milk, potatoes, maize, sugarcane, onions, vegetables, jute, mangoes/guavas, tropical fruits (2022)
note: top ten agricultural products based on tonnage

Industries: cotton, textiles and clothing, jute, tea, paper, cement, fertilizer, sugar, light engineering

Industrial production growth rate: 8.37% (2023 est.)
note: annual % change in industrial value added based on constant local currency
comparison ranking: 26

Labor force: 74.914 million (2023 est.)
note: number of people ages 15 or older who are employed or seeking work
comparison ranking: 8

Unemployment rate: 5.06% (2023 est.)
5.25% (2022 est.)
5.82% (2021 est.)
note: % of labor force seeking employment
comparison ranking: 95

Youth unemployment rate (ages 15-24): *total:* 15.7% (2023 est.)
male: 13.5% (2023 est.)
female: 20.4% (2023 est.)
note: % of labor force ages 15-24 seeking employment
comparison ranking: total 92

Population below poverty line: 18.7% (2022 est.)
note: % of population with income below national poverty line

Gini Index coefficient - distribution of family income: 33.4 (2022 est.)
note: index (0-100) of income distribution; higher values represent greater inequality
comparison ranking: 99

Average household expenditures: *on food:* 52.7% of household expenditures (2022 est.)
on alcohol and tobacco: 2.1% of household expenditures (2022 est.)

Household income or consumption by percentage share: *lowest 10%:* 3.5% (2022 est.)
highest 10%: 27.4% (2022 est.)
note: % share of income accruing to lowest and highest 10% of population

Remittances: 5.26% of GDP (2023 est.)
4.67% of GDP (2022 est.)
5.33% of GDP (2021 est.)
note: personal transfers and compensation between resident and non-resident individuals/households/entities

Budget: *revenues:* $39.849 billion (2021 est.)
expenditures: $34.538 billion (2021 est.)
note: central government revenues and expenses (excluding grants/extrabudgetary units/social security funds) converted to US dollars at average official exchange rate for year indicated

Public debt: 33.1% of GDP (2017 est.)
comparison ranking: 162

Taxes and other revenues: 7.64% (of GDP) (2021 est.)
note: central government tax revenue as a % of GDP
comparison ranking: 192

Current account balance: $4.388 billion (2023 est.)
-$14.438 billion (2022 est.)
-$15.775 billion (2021 est.)
note: balance of payments - net trade and primary/secondary income in current dollars comparison ranking: 37

Exports: $58.885 billion (2023 est.)
$60.066 billion (2022 est.)
$49.291 billion (2021 est.)
note: balance of payments - exports of goods and services in current dollars
comparison ranking: 63

Exports - partners: US 18%, Germany 16%, UK 8%, Spain 7%, Poland 6% (2022)
note: top five export partners based on percentage share of exports

Exports - commodities: garments, footwear, fabric, textiles, jute yarn (2022)
note: top five export commodities based on value in dollars

Imports: $73.172 billion (2023 est.)
$93.635 billion (2022 est.)
$85.299 billion (2021 est.)
note: balance of payments - imports of goods and services in current dollars
comparison ranking: 54

Imports - partners: China 32%, India 17%, Singapore 6%, Malaysia 5%, Indonesia 5% (2022)
note: top five import partners based on percentage share of imports

Imports - commodities: refined petroleum, cotton fabric, cotton, fabric, fertilizers (2022)
note: top five import commodities based on value in dollars

Reserves of foreign exchange and gold: $21.86 billion (2023 est.)
$33.747 billion (2022 est.)
$46.166 billion (2021 est.)
note: holdings of gold (year-end prices)/foreign exchange/special drawing rights in current dollars
comparison ranking: 50

Debt - external: $53.63 billion (2022 est.)
note: present value of external debt in current US dollars
comparison ranking: 11

Exchange rates: taka (BDT) per US dollar –

Exchange rates: 106.309 (2023 est.)
91.745 (2022 est.)
85.084 (2021 est.)
84.871 (2020 est.)
84.454 (2019 est.)

ENERGY

Electricity access: *electrification - total population:* 99.4% (2022 est.)
electrification - urban areas: 100%
electrification - rural areas: 99.3%

Electricity: *installed generating capacity:* 22.449 million kW (2022 est.)
consumption: 99.553 billion kWh (2022 est.)
imports: 8.643 billion kWh (2022 est.)
transmission/distribution losses: 11.09 billion kWh (2022 est.)
comparison rankings: transmission/distribution losses 182; imports 29; consumption 36; installed generating capacity 44

Electricity generation sources: *fossil fuels:* 98.7% of total installed capacity (2022 est.)
solar: 0.5% of total installed capacity (2022 est.)
hydroelectricity: 0.8% of total installed capacity (2022 est.)

Nuclear energy: Number of nuclear reactors under construction: 2 (2023)

Coal: *production:* 754,000 metric tons (2022 est.)
consumption: 7.514 million metric tons (2022 est.)
imports: 5.62 million metric tons (2022 est.)
proven reserves: 3.26 billion metric tons (2022 est.)

Petroleum: *total petroleum production:* 13,000 bbl/day (2023 est.)
refined petroleum consumption: 160,000 bbl/day (2022 est.)
crude oil estimated reserves: 28 million barrels (2021 est.)

Natural gas: *production:* 24.62 billion cubic meters (2022 est.)
consumption: 30.384 billion cubic meters (2022 est.)
imports: 5.765 billion cubic meters (2022 est.)
proven reserves: 126.293 billion cubic meters (2021 est.)

Carbon dioxide emissions: 99.57 million metric tonnes of CO_2 (2022 est.)
from coal and metallurgical coke: 15.102 million metric tonnes of CO_2 (2022 est.)
from petroleum and other liquids: 25.09 million metric tonnes of CO_2 (2022 est.)
from consumed natural gas: 59.378 million metric tonnes of CO_2 (2022 est.)
comparison ranking: total emissions 42

Energy consumption per capita: 9.678 million Btu/person (2022 est.)
comparison ranking: 150

COMMUNICATIONS

Telephones - fixed lines: *total subscriptions:* 274,000 (2022 est.)
subscriptions per 100 inhabitants: (2022 est.) less than 1
comparison ranking: total subscriptions 111

Telephones - mobile cellular: *total subscriptions:* 180.198 million (2022 est.)
subscriptions per 100 inhabitants: 105 (2022 est.)
comparison ranking: total subscriptions 10

Telecommunication systems: *general assessment:* Bangladesh's economic resurgence over the last decade took a battering in 2020 and 2021 as a result of the Covid-19 pandemic; the country had been on track to move off the United Nation's Least Developed Countries list by 2026, however the crisis may have pushed that back a few years; the telecommunications sector experienced a set of challenges, with mobile data usage exploding at the same time as many consumers were being forced to curb their spending in other areas; the demand on data grew so large and so rapidly that Bangladesh came close to running out of bandwidth; at the start of 2020, Bangladesh was consuming around 900Gb/s on average, well below the 2,642GB/s capacity of its submarine cables; this ballooned to over 2,300Gb/s during the pandemic; Bangladesh was looking forward to adding 7,200Gb/s capacity when the SEA-ME-WE-6 submarine cable goes into service in mid-2024, but the sudden upsurge in downloads is forcing state-run company Bangladesh Submarine Cable Company Limited (BSCCL) to scramble to find alternatives before the country's internet supply is maxed out; the increased demand during the Covid-19 crisis also put pressure on the country's existing mobile networks, already under strain as a result of strong growth in the mobile broadband market coupled with significant untapped potential for mobile services in general across the country; this led to premium prices being paid at auction for spectrum in the 1800MHz and 2100MHz bands, most of which will be used to enhance and expand LTE services; a 5G spectrum auction had been anticipated for 2020, but low interest from the MNOs in going down that path when there are still so many areas waiting for LTE access means that 5G will likely be deferred until 2023 (2021)
domestic: fixed-line teledensity remains less than 1 per 100 persons; mobile-cellular telephone subscribership has been increasing rapidly and now exceeds 107 per 100 persons; mobile subscriber growth is anticipated over the next five years to 2023 (2021)
international: country code - 880; landing points for the SeaMeWe-4 and SeaMeWe-5 fiber-optic submarine cable system that provides links to Europe, the Middle East, and Asia; satellite earth stations - 6; international radiotelephone communications and landline service to neighboring countries (2019)

Broadcast media: state-owned Bangladesh Television (BTV) broadcasts throughout the country. Some channels, such as BTV World, operate via satellite. The government also owns a medium wave radio channel and some private FM radio broadcast news channels. Of the 41 Bangladesh approved TV stations, 26 are currently being used to broadcast. Of those, 23 operate under private management via cable distribution. Collectively, TV channels can reach more than 50 million people across the country.

Internet country code: .bd

Internet users: *total:* 66.3 million (2021 est.)
percent of population: 39% (2021 est.)
comparison ranking: total 15

Broadband - fixed subscriptions: *total:* 10,052,819 (2020 est.)
subscriptions per 100 inhabitants: 6 (2020 est.)
comparison ranking: total 19

TRANSPORTATION

National air transport system: *number of registered air carriers:* 6 (2020)
inventory of registered aircraft operated by air carriers: 30
annual passenger traffic on registered air carriers: 5,984,155 (2018)
annual freight traffic on registered air carriers: 63.82 million (2018) mt-km

Civil aircraft registration country code prefix: S2

Airports: 17 (2024)
comparison ranking: 143

Heliports: 35 (2024)

Pipelines: 2,950 km gas (2013)

Railways: *total:* 2,460 km (2014)
narrow gauge: 1,801 km (2014) 1.000-m gauge
broad gauge: 659 km (2014) 1.676-m gauge
comparison ranking: total 66

Roadways: *total:* 369,105 km
paved: 110,311 km
unpaved: 258,794 km (2018)
comparison ranking: total 16

Waterways: 8,370 km (2011) (includes up to 3,060 km of main cargo routes; network reduced to 5,200 km in the dry season)
comparison ranking: 18

Merchant marine: *total:* 558 (2023)
by type: bulk carrier 68, container ship 10, general cargo 170, oil tanker 162, other 148
comparison ranking: total 40

Ports: *total ports:* 2 (2024)
large: 0
medium: 1
small: 1
very small: 0
ports with oil terminals: 0
key ports: Chittagong, Mongla

MILITARY AND SECURITY

Military and security forces: Armed Forces of Bangladesh (aka Bangladesh Defense Force): Bangladesh Army, Bangladesh Navy, Bangladesh Air Force

Ministry of Home Affairs: Border Guard Bangladesh (BGB), Bangladesh Coast Guard, Rapid Action Battalion (RAB), Ansars, Village Defense Party (VDP) (2024)
note 1: the Armed Forces of Bangladesh are jointly administered by the Ministry of Defense (MOD) and the Armed Forces Division (AFD), both under the Prime Minister's Office; the AFD has ministerial status and parallel functions with MOD; the AFD is a joint coordinating headquarters for the three services and also functions as a joint command center during wartime; to coordinate policy, the prime minister and the president are advised by a six-member board, which includes the three service chiefs of staff, the principal staff officer of the AFD, and the military secretaries to the prime minister and president
note 2: the RAB, Ansars, and VDP are paramilitary organizations for internal security; the RAB is a joint task force founded in 2004 and composed of members of the police, Army, Navy, Air Force, and Border Guards seconded to the RAB from their respective units; its mandate includes internal security, intelligence gathering related to criminal activities, and government-directed investigations

Military expenditures: 1% of GDP (2023 est.)
1.1% of GDP (2022 est.)
1.2% of GDP (2021 est.)
1.3% of GDP (2020 est.)
1.4% of GDP (2019 est.)
comparison ranking: 126

Military and security service personnel strengths: information varies; approximately 160,000 total active personnel (130,000 Army; 15,000 Navy; 15,000 Air Force) (2023)

Military equipment inventories and acquisitions: much of the military's inventory is comprised of Chinese- and Russian-origin equipment; in recent years, China has been the leading provider of arms to Bangladesh (2024)

Military service age and obligation: *16-21 years of age for voluntary military service; Bangladeshi nationality and 10th grade education required; officers:* 17-21 years of age, Bangladeshi nationality, and 12th grade education required (2023)

Military deployments: approximately 1,400 Central African Republic (MINUSCA); 1,650 Democratic Republic of the Congo (MONUSCO; plus about 200 police); 120 Lebanon (UNIFIL); 100 Mali (MINUSMA; plus about 150 police); 1,600 South Sudan (UNMISS); 500 Sudan (UNISFA) (2024)
note: as of early 2024, Bangladesh had nearly 6,000 total military and police personnel deployed on UN missions

Military - note: the military's primary responsibility is external defense but it also has a domestic security role and has traditionally been a significant player in the country's politics, as well as its economy; following widespread domestic protests in September 2024, the Army was given law enforcement powers for 60 days, including making arrests, conducting searches, and dispersing unlawful assemblies; the military has a long history of participating in UN peacekeeping missions, which has provided operational experience and a source of funding; it runs an international institute for the training of peacekeepers; the military also conducts multinational and bilateral exercises with foreign partners, particularly India; it has commercial business interests in such areas as banking, food, hotels, manufacturing, real estate, and shipbuilding, and manages government infrastructure and construction projects (2024)

SPACE

Space agency/agencies: Bangladesh Space Research and Remote Sensing Organization (SPARRSO; established 1980) (2024)

Space program overview: has a modest space program focused on designing, building, and operating satellites, particularly those with remote sensing (RS) capabilities; researching a variety of other space-related capabilities and technologies; has a government-owned company for acquiring and operating satellites (Bangladesh Satellite Company Limited or BSCL, established in 2017); has relations with several foreign space agencies and commercial entities, including those of France, Japan, Russia, and the US (2024)
note: further details about the key activities, programs, and milestones of the country's space program, as well as government spending estimates on the space sector, appear in the Space Programs reference guide

TERRORISM

Terrorist group(s): Harakat ul-Jihad-i-Islami/ Bangladesh; Islamic State of Iraq and ash-Sham in Bangladesh (ISB); al- Qa'ida; al-Qa'ida in the Indian Subcontinent (AQIS)
note: details about the history, aims, leadership, organization, areas of operation, tactics, targets, weapons, size, and sources of support of the group(s) appear(s) in the Terrorism reference guide

TRANSNATIONAL ISSUES

Refugees and internally displaced persons: *refugees (country of origin):* 976,507 (Burma) (2024)
IDPs: 427,000 (conflict, development, human rights violations, religious persecution, natural disasters) (2022)
stateless persons: 929,606 (2022)

Illicit drugs: transit country for illegal drugs produced in neighboring countries; does not manufacture precursor chemicals with the exception of sulphuric acid, hydrochloric acid, and toluene

BARBADOS

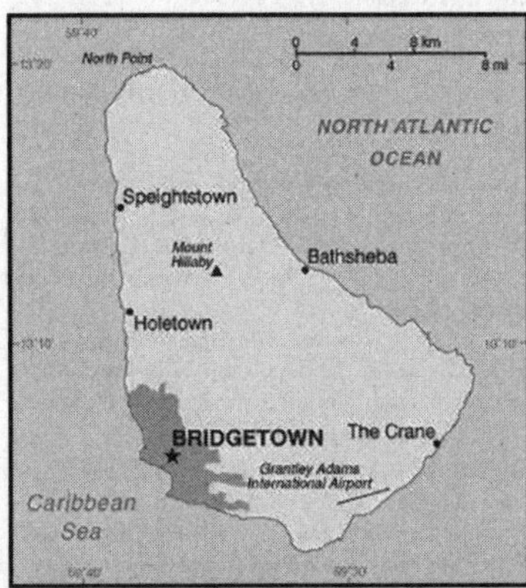

INTRODUCTION

Background: Barbados was uninhabited when first settled by the British in 1627. Enslaved Africans worked the sugar plantations established on the island, which initially dominated the Caribbean sugar industry. By 1720, Barbados was no longer a dominant force within the sugar industry, having been surpassed by the Leeward Islands and Jamaica. Slavery was abolished in 1834. The Barbadian economy remained heavily dependent on sugar, rum, and molasses production through most of the 20th century. The gradual introduction of social and political reforms in the 1940s and 1950s led to independence from the UK in 1966. In the 1990s, tourism and manufacturing surpassed the sugar industry in economic importance. Barbados became a republic in 2021, with the former Governor-General Sandra MASON elected as the first president.

GEOGRAPHY

Location: Caribbean, island in the North Atlantic Ocean, northeast of Venezuela

Geographic coordinates: 13 10 N, 59 32 W

Map references: Central America and the Caribbean

Area: *total:* 430 sq km
land: 430 sq km
water: 0 sq km
comparison ranking: total 201

Area - comparative: 2.5 times the size of Washington, DC

Land boundaries: *total:* 0 km

Coastline: 97 km

Maritime claims: *territorial sea:* 12 nm
exclusive economic zone: 200 nm

Climate: tropical; rainy season (June to October)

Terrain: relatively flat; rises gently to central highland region

Elevation: *highest point:* Mount Hillaby 336 m
lowest point: Atlantic Ocean 0 m

Natural resources: petroleum, fish, natural gas

Land use: *agricultural land:* 32.6% (2018 est.)
arable land: 25.6% (2018 est.)
permanent crops: 2.3% (2018 est.)
permanent pasture: 4.7% (2018 est.)
forest: 19.4% (2018 est.)
other: 48% (2018 est.)

Irrigated land: 50 sq km (2012)

Population distribution: most densely populated country in the eastern Caribbean; approximately one-third live in urban areas

Natural hazards: infrequent hurricanes; periodic landslides

Geography - note: easternmost Caribbean island

PEOPLE AND SOCIETY

Population: *total:* 304,139
male: 146,587
female: 157,552 (2024 est.)
comparison rankings: female 180; male 182; total 181

Nationality: *noun:* Barbadian(s) or Bajan (colloquial)
adjective: Barbadian or Bajan (colloquial)

Ethnic groups: African descent 92.4%, mixed 3.1%, White 2.7%, East Indian 1.3%, other 0.2%, unspecified 0.3% (2010 est.)

Languages: English (official), Bajan (English-based creole language, widely spoken in informal settings)

Religions: Protestant 66.4% (includes Anglican 23.9%, other Pentecostal 19.5%, Adventist 5.9%, Methodist 4.2%, Wesleyan 3.4%, Nazarene 3.2%, Church of God 2.4%, Baptist 1.8%, Moravian 1.2%, other Protestant 0.9%), Roman Catholic 3.8%, other Christian 5.4% (includes Jehovah's Witness 2.0%, other 3.4%), Rastafarian 1%, other 1.5%, none 20.6%, unspecified 1.2% (2010 est.)

Age structure: *0-14 years:* 16.6% (male 25,273/ female 25,284)
15-64 years: 67% (male 100,328/female 103,536)
65 years and over: 16.3% (2024 est.) (male 20,986/ female 28,732)

Dependency ratios: *total dependency ratio:* 49
youth dependency ratio: 25.6
elderly dependency ratio: 23.4
potential support ratio: 4.3 (2021 est.)

Median age: *total:* 41.4 years (2024 est.)
male: 40.3 years
female: 42.5 years
comparison ranking: total 50

Population growth rate: 0.23% (2024 est.)
comparison ranking: 173

Birth rate: 10.7 births/1,000 population (2024 est.)
comparison ranking: 172

Death rate: 8.1 deaths/1,000 population (2024 est.)
comparison ranking: 83

Net migration rate: -0.3 migrant(s)/1,000 population (2024 est.)
comparison ranking: 112

Population distribution: most densely populated country in the eastern Caribbean; approximately one-third live in urban areas

Urbanization: *urban population:* 31.4% of total population (2023)
rate of urbanization: 0.46% annual rate of change (2020-25 est.)

Major urban areas - population: 89,000 BRIDGETOWN (capital) (2018)

Sex ratio: *at birth:* 1.01 male(s)/female
0-14 years: 1 male(s)/female
15-64 years: 0.97 male(s)/female
65 years and over: 0.73 male(s)/female
total population: 0.93 male(s)/female (2024 est.)

Maternal mortality ratio: 39 deaths/100,000 live births (2020 est.)
comparison ranking: 106

Infant mortality rate: *total:* 9.6 deaths/1,000 live births (2024 est.)
male: 11.1 deaths/1,000 live births
female: 8.1 deaths/1,000 live births
comparison ranking: total 137

Life expectancy at birth: *total population:* 79 years (2024 est.)
male: 76.3 years
female: 81.8 years
comparison ranking: total population 68

Total fertility rate: 1.7 children born/woman (2024 est.)
comparison ranking: 163

Gross reproduction rate: 0.85 (2024 est.)

Contraceptive prevalence rate: 59.2% (2012)

Drinking water source: *improved:*
total: 98.8% of population
unimproved:
total: 2% of population (2020 est.)

Current health expenditure: 7.2% of GDP (2020)

Physician density: 2.49 physicians/1,000 population (2017)

Hospital bed density: 6 beds/1,000 population (2017)

Sanitation facility access: *improved:*
total: 100% of population

Obesity - adult prevalence rate: 23.1% (2016)
comparison ranking: 69

Alcohol consumption per capita: *total:* 9.94 liters of pure alcohol (2019 est.)
beer: 3.66 liters of pure alcohol (2019 est.)
wine: 1.36 liters of pure alcohol (2019 est.)
spirits: 4.75 liters of pure alcohol (2019 est.)
other alcohols: 0.17 liters of pure alcohol (2019 est.)
comparison ranking: total 22

Tobacco use: *total:* 8.5% (2020 est.)
male: 15% (2020 est.)
female: 1.9% (2020 est.)
comparison ranking: total 144

Currently married women (ages 15-49): 57.1% (2023 est.)

Education expenditures: 6.5% of GDP (2021 est.)
comparison ranking: 31

Literacy: *definition:* age 15 and over can read and write
total population: 99.6%
male: 99.6%
female: 99.6% (2014)

ENVIRONMENT

Environment - current issues: pollution of coastal waters from waste disposal by ships; soil erosion; illegal solid waste disposal threatens contamination of aquifers

Environment - international agreements: *party to:* Biodiversity, Climate Change, Climate Change-Kyoto Protocol, Climate Change-Paris Agreement, Comprehensive Nuclear Test Ban, Desertification, Endangered Species, Hazardous Wastes, Law of the Sea, Marine Dumping-London Convention, Marine Dumping-London Protocol, Ozone Layer Protection, Ship Pollution, Wetlands
signed, but not ratified: none of the selected agreements

Climate: tropical; rainy season (June to October)

Urbanization: *urban population:* 31.4% of total population (2023)
rate of urbanization: 0.46% annual rate of change (2020-25 est.)

Revenue from forest resources: 0.01% of GDP (2018 est.)
comparison ranking: 158

Revenue from coal: 0% of GDP (2018 est.)
comparison ranking: 58

Air pollutants: *particulate matter emissions:* 9.79 micrograms per cubic meter (2019 est.)
carbon dioxide emissions: 1.28 megatons (2016 est.)
methane emissions: 2.35 megatons (2020 est.)

Waste and recycling: *municipal solid waste generated annually:* 174,815 tons (2011 est.)
municipal solid waste recycled annually: 15,733 tons (2015 est.)
percent of municipal solid waste recycled: 9% (2015 est.)

Total water withdrawal: *municipal:* 20 million cubic meters (2020 est.)
industrial: 10 million cubic meters (2020 est.)
agricultural: 5 million cubic meters (2020 est.)

Total renewable water resources: 80 million cubic meters (2020 est.)

GOVERNMENT

Country name: *conventional long form:* none
conventional short form: Barbados
etymology: the name derives from the Portuguese "as barbadas," which means "the bearded ones" and can refer either to the long, hanging roots of the island's bearded fig trees or to the alleged beards of the indigenous Carib inhabitants

Government type: parliamentary republic; a Commonwealth realm

Capital: *name:* Bridgetown
geographic coordinates: 13 06 N, 59 37 W
time difference: UTC-4 (1 hour ahead of Washington, DC, during Standard Time)
etymology: named after a bridge constructed over the swampy area (known as the Careenage) around the Constitution River that flows through the center of Bridgetown

Administrative divisions: 11 parishes and 1 city*; Bridgetown*, Christ Church, Saint Andrew, Saint George, Saint James, Saint John, Saint Joseph, Saint Lucy, Saint Michael, Saint Peter, Saint Philip, Saint Thomas

Independence: 30 November 1966 (from the UK)

National holiday: Independence Day, 30 November (1966)

Legal system: English common law; no judicial review of legislative acts

Constitution: *history:* adopted 22 November 1966, effective 30 November 1966; Constitution (Amendment) (No. 2) Bill, 2021 establishes Barbados as a republic and revokes the earlier Order in Council
amendments: proposed by Parliament; passage of amendments to constitutional sections such as citizenship, fundamental rights and freedoms, and the organization and authorities of the branches of government requires two-thirds majority vote by the membership of both houses of Parliament; passage of other amendments only requires a majority vote of both houses; amended several times, last in 2021
note: following the transition to a republic in November 2021, the Government of Barbados in February 2022 began the process of establishing a constitution commission to review a new draft constitution

International law organization participation: accepts compulsory ICJ jurisdiction with reservations; accepts ICCt jurisdiction

Citizenship: *citizenship by birth:* yes
citizenship by descent only: yes
dual citizenship recognized: yes
residency requirement for naturalization: 5 years

Suffrage: 18 years of age; universal

Executive branch: *chief of state:* President Sandra MASON (since 30 November 2021)
head of government: Prime Minister Mia MOTTLEY (since 25 May 2018)
cabinet: Cabinet appointed by the president on the advice of the prime minister
elections/appointments: president elected by an electoral college of both Houses of Parliament for a 4-year renewable term; election last held on 20 October 2021 (next to be held in); following legislative elections, the leader of the majority party or leader of the majority coalition usually appointed prime minister by the president; the prime minister recommends the deputy prime minister
election results: Sandra MASON elected as first president on 20 October 2021

Legislative branch: *description:* bicameral Parliament consists of:
Senate (21 seats statutory - 21 current; members appointed by the president - 12 on the advice of the prime minister, 2 on the advice of the opposition leader, and 7 at the discretion of the president; members serve 5-year terms)
House of Assembly (30 seats; members directly elected in single-seat constituencies by simple majority vote to serve 5- year terms)
elections: Senate - last appointments on 4 February 2022 (next appointments in February 2027)
House of Assembly - last held on 19 January 2022 (next to be held in January 2027)
election results: Senate - appointed - BLP 12, independent 9; composition - men 13, women 8, percentage women
38.1%
House of Assembly - percent of vote by party - BLP 69%, DLP 26.5%, other 4.5%; seats by party - BLP 30; composition - men 22, women 8, percentage women 26.7%; note - total Parliament percentage women 32.7%
note: tradition dictates that the next election is held within 5 years of the last election, but constitutionally it is 5 years from the first seating of Parliament plus a 90-day grace period

Judicial branch: *highest court(s):* Supreme Court (consists of the High Court with 8 justices) and the Court of Appeal (consists of the High Court chief justice and president of the court and 4 justices; note - in 2005, Barbados acceded to the Caribbean Court of Justice as the final court of appeal, replacing that of the Judicial Committee of the Privy Council (in London)
judge selection and term of office: Supreme Court chief justice appointed by the president on the recommendation of the prime minister and opposition leader of Parliament; other justices appointed by the president on the recommendation of the Judicial and Legal Service Commission, a 5-member independent body consisting of the Supreme Court chief justice, the commission head, and presidential appointees recommended by the prime minister; justices serve until mandatory retirement at age 65
subordinate courts: Magistrates' Courts

Political parties: Alliance Party for Progress or APP
Barbados Labor Party or BLP
Democratic Labor Party or DLP

International organization participation: ACP, ACS, AOSIS, C, Caricom, CDB, CELAC, FAO, G-77, IADB, IBRD, ICAO, ICCt, ICRM, IDA, IFAD, IFC, IFRCS, ILO, IMF, IMO, Interpol, IOC, ISO, ITSO, ITU, ITUC (NGOs), LAES, MIGA, NAM, OAS, OPANAL, OPCW, UN, UNCTAD, UNESCO, UNHCR, UNIDO, UPU, WCO, WFTU (NGOs), WHO, WIPO, WMO, WTO

Diplomatic representation in the US: *chief of mission:* Ambassador Victor Anthony FERNANDES (since 18 September 2024)
chancery: 2144 Wyoming Avenue NW, Washington, DC 20008
telephone: [1] (202) 939-9200
FAX: [1] (202) 332-7467
email address and website:
washington@foreign.gov.bb
https://www.foreign.gov.bb/embassies-high-commissions-and-permanent-missions/
consulate(s) general: Miami, New York

Diplomatic representation from the US: *chief of mission:* Ambassador Roger F. NYHUS (since 19 January 2024) note - also accredited to Antigua and Barbuda, Dominica, Grenada, Saint Kitts and Nevis, Saint Lucia, and Saint Vincent and the Grenadines
embassy: Wildey Business Park, St. Michael BB 14006, Barbados, W.I.
mailing address: 3120 Bridgetown Place, Washington DC 20521-3120
telephone: (246) 227-4000
FAX: (246) 431-0179
email address and website:
bridgetownpublicaffairs@state.gov
https://bb.usembassy.gov/

Flag description: three equal vertical bands of ultramarine blue (hoist side), gold, and ultramarine blue with the head of a black trident centered on the gold band; the band colors represent the blue of the sea and sky and the gold of the beaches; the trident head represents independence and a break with the past (the colonial coat of arms contained a complete trident)

National symbol(s): Neptune's trident, pelican, Red Bird of Paradise flower (also known as Pride of Barbados); national colors: blue, yellow, black

National anthem: *name:* "The National Anthem of Barbados"
lyrics/music: Irving BURGIE/C. Van Roland EDWARDS
note: adopted 1966; the anthem is also known as "In Plenty and In Time of Need"

National heritage: *total World Heritage Sites:* 1 (cultural)
selected World Heritage Site locales: Historic Bridgetown and its Garrison

ECONOMY

Economic overview: largest Eastern Caribbean economy; dependent on US imports and currency strength; high Human Development Index; key tourism and financial sectors; declining but still very high public debt; cost-of-living and cost competitiveness vulnerabilities

Real GDP (purchasing power parity): $4.92 billion (2023 est.)
$4.708 billion (2022 est.)
$4.148 billion (2021 est.)
note: data in 2021 dollars
comparison ranking: 186

Real GDP growth rate: % (2023 est.)
13.48% (2022 est.)
-1.18% (2021 est.)
note: annual GDP % growth based on constant local currency
comparison ranking: 68

Real GDP per capita: $17,400 (2023 est.)
$16,700 (2022 est.)
$14,800 (2021 est.)
note: data in 2021 dollars
comparison ranking: 111

GDP (official exchange rate): $6.394 billion (2023 est.)
note: data in current dollars at official exchange rate

Inflation rate (consumer prices): 9.79% (2023 est.)
4.1% (2019 est.)
3.67% (2018 est.)
note: annual % change based on consumer prices
comparison ranking: 175

Credit ratings: Moody's rating: Caa1 (2019)

Standard & Poors rating: B- (2019)
note: The year refers to the year in which the current credit rating was first obtained.

GDP - composition, by sector of origin: *agriculture:* 1.4% (2023 est.)
industry: 13.1% (2023 est.)
services: 72.3% (2023 est.)
note: figures may not total 100% due to non-allocated consumption not captured in sector-reported data
comparison rankings: services 32; industry 175; agriculture 176

GDP - composition, by end use: *household consumption:* 75.6% (2022 est.)
government consumption: 11.8% (2022 est.)
investment in fixed capital: 16.5% (2022 est.)
investment in inventories: 0.2% (2022 est.)
exports of goods and services: 34.3% (2022 est.)
imports of goods and services: -42.2% (2022 est.)
note: figures may not total 100% due to rounding or gaps in data collection

Agricultural products: sugarcane, chicken, vegetables, milk, eggs, sweet potatoes, pork, coconuts, cantaloupes/melons, tropical fruits (2022)
note: top ten agricultural products based on tonnage

Industries: tourism, sugar, light manufacturing, component assembly for export

Industrial production growth rate: 3.64% (2023 est.)
note: annual % change in industrial value added based on constant local currency
comparison ranking: 88

Labor force: 146,000 (2023 est.)
note: number of people ages 15 or older who are employed or seeking work
comparison ranking: 179

Unemployment rate: 7.95% (2023 est.)
8.49% (2022 est.)
9.42% (2021 est.)
note: % of labor force seeking employment
comparison ranking: 146

Youth unemployment rate (ages 15-24): *total:* 24.9% (2023 est.)
male: 28.9% (2023 est.)
female: 20.3% (2023 est.)
note: % of labor force ages 15-24 seeking employment
comparison ranking: total 44

Remittances: 1.33% of GDP (2023 est.)
1.46% of GDP (2022 est.)
1.72% of GDP (2021 est.)
note: personal transfers and compensation between resident and non-resident individuals/households/entities

Budget: *revenues:* $1.269 billion (2015 est.)
expenditures: $1.664 billion (2015 est.)
note: central government revenues and expenses (excluding grants/extrabudgetary units/social security funds) converted to US dollars at average official exchange rate for year indicated

Public debt: 146.46% of GDP (2016 est.)
note: central government debt as a % of GDP
comparison ranking: 5

Taxes and other revenues: 27.39% (of GDP) (2016 est.)
note: central government tax revenue as a % of GDP
comparison ranking: 31

Current account balance: -$296.396 million (2017 est.)
-$452.39 million (2016 est.)
-$98.732 million (2015 est.)
note: balance of payments - net trade and primary/secondary income in current dollars
comparison ranking: 116

Exports: $2.228 billion (2017 est.)
$2.41 billion (2016 est.)
$2.358 billion (2015 est.)
note: balance of payments - exports of goods and services in current dollars
comparison ranking: 161

Exports - partners: US 23%, Jamaica 11%, Trinidad and Tobago 9%, Guyana 8%, Poland 6% (2022)
note: top five export partners based on percentage share of exports

Exports - commodities: liquor, packaged medicine, ships, paper labels, baked goods (2022)
note: top five export commodities based on value in dollars

Imports: $2.12 billion (2021 est.)
$2.213 billion (2017 est.)
$2.238 billion (2016 est.)
note: balance of payments - imports of goods and services in current dollars
comparison ranking: 176

Imports - partners: US 43%, China 8%, Trinidad and Tobago 7%, UK 5%, Netherlands 3% (2022)
note: top five import partners based on percentage share of imports

Imports - commodities: refined petroleum, plastic products, cars, railway cargo containers, packaged medicine (2022)
note: top five import commodities based on value in dollars

Reserves of foreign exchange and gold: $1.52 billion (2022 est.)
$1.673 billion (2021 est.)
$1.358 billion (2020 est.)
note: holdings of gold (year-end prices)/foreign exchange/special drawing rights in current dollars
comparison ranking: 146

Exchange rates: Barbadian dollars (BBD) per US dollar –

Exchange rates: 2 (2023 est.)
2 (2022 est.)
2 (2021 est.)
2 (2020 est.)
2 (2019 est.)
note: the Barbadian dollar is pegged to the US dollar

ENERGY

Electricity access: *electrification - total population:* 100% (2022 est.)

Electricity: *installed generating capacity:* 340,000 kW (2022 est.)
consumption: 1.02 billion kWh (2022 est.)
transmission/distribution losses: 65.871 million kWh (2022 est.)
comparison rankings: transmission/distribution losses 41; consumption 159; installed generating capacity 162

Electricity generation sources: *fossil fuels:* 92.1% of total installed capacity (2022 est.)
solar: 7.7% of total installed capacity (2022 est.)
biomass and waste: 0.2% of total installed capacity (2022 est.)

Coal: *imports:* 100 metric tons (2022 est.)

Petroleum: *total petroleum production:* 2,000 bbl/day (2023 est.)

refined petroleum consumption: 9,000 bbl/day (2022 est.)
crude oil estimated reserves: 1.978 million barrels (2021 est.)

Natural gas: *production:* 9.759 million cubic meters (2022 est.)
consumption: 15.813 million cubic meters (2022 est.)
imports: 6.054 million cubic meters (2022 est.)
proven reserves: 113.267 million cubic meters (2021 est.)

Carbon dioxide emissions: 1.347 million metric tonnes of CO2 (2022 est.)
from petroleum and other liquids: 1.316 million metric tonnes of CO2 (2022 est.)
from consumed natural gas: 31,000 metric tonnes of CO2 (2022 est.)
comparison ranking: total emissions 166

Energy consumption per capita: 68.271 million Btu/person (2022 est.)
comparison ranking: 74

COMMUNICATIONS

Telephones - fixed lines: *total subscriptions:* 121,000 (2022 est.)
subscriptions per 100 inhabitants: 43 (2022 est.)
comparison ranking: total subscriptions 131

Telephones - mobile cellular: *total subscriptions:* 323,000 (2022 est.)
subscriptions per 100 inhabitants: 115 (2022 est.)
comparison ranking: total subscriptions 179

Telecommunication systems: *general assessment:* the telecom sector has seen a decline in subscriber numbers (particularly for prepaid mobile services the mainstay of short term visitors) and revenue; fixed and mobile broadband services are two areas that have benefited from the crisis as employees and students have resorted to working from home; one area of the telecom market that is not prepared for growth is 5G mobile; governments, regulators, and even the mobile network operators have shown that they have not been investing in 5G opportunities at the present time; network expansion and enhancements remain concentrated around improving LTE coverage (2021)
domestic: fixed-line teledensity of roughly 43 per 100 persons; mobile-cellular telephone density about 113 per 100 persons (2021)
international: country code - 1-246; landing points for the ECFS and Southern Caribbean Fiber submarine cable with links to 15 other islands in the eastern Caribbean extending from the British Virgin Islands to Trinidad and Puerto Ricco; satellite earth stations - 1 (Intelsat - Atlantic Ocean); tropospheric scatter to Trinidad and Saint Lucia (2019)

Broadcast media: government-owned Caribbean Broadcasting Corporation (CBC) operates the lone terrestrial TV station; CBC also operates a multi-channel cable TV subscription service; roughly a dozen radio stations, consisting of a CBC-operated network operating alongside privately owned radio stations (2019)

Internet country code: .bb

Internet users: *total:* 240,800 (2021 est.)
percent of population: 86% (2021 est.)
comparison ranking: total 177

Broadband - fixed subscriptions: *total:* 128,000 (2020 est.)
subscriptions per 100 inhabitants: 45 (2020 est.)
comparison ranking: total 125

TRANSPORTATION

Civil aircraft registration country code prefix: 8P

Airports: 2 (2024)
comparison ranking: 198

Heliports: 1 (2024)

Pipelines: 33 km gas, 64 km oil, 6 km refined products (2013)

Roadways: *total:* 1,700 km
paved: 1,700 km (2015)
comparison ranking: total 175

Merchant marine: *total:* 272 (2023)
by type: bulk carrier 90, general cargo 149, oil tanker 5, other 28
comparison ranking: total 59

Ports: *total ports:* 1 (2024)
large: 0
medium: 0
small: 1
very small: 0
ports with oil terminals: 1
key ports: Bridgetown

MILITARY AND SECURITY

Military and security forces: Barbados Defense Force (BDF): The Barbados Regiment, The Barbados Coast Guard (2024)
note 1: the BDF also has a Youth Development Wing, which is comprised of the Barbados Cadet Corps and the Barbados Defense Force Sports Program
note 2: authority over the BDF is shared between the president and prime minister, with the president overseeing strategic direction and the prime minister responsible for operational leadership
note 3: the Barbados Police Service (TBPS) is the national police force; it is modeled after London's Metropolitan Police Service and divided into three territorial divisions

Military expenditures: 0.7% of GDP (2023 est.)
0.8% of GDP (2022 est.)
0.9% of GDP (2021 est.)
0.9% of GDP (2020 est.)
0.8% of GDP (2019 est.)
comparison ranking: 148

Military and security service personnel strengths: approximately 600 active personnel (2023)

Military equipment inventories and acquisitions: the Netherlands provide the BDF's major equipment inventory (maritime patrol boats) (2024)

Military service age and obligation: voluntary service only (men and women); 17 years, 9 months to 17 years, 11 months with letter of consent from a parent or guardian, or be in the age range of 18-25 years (18-30 for the Reserves) at the start of recruit training; citizens of Barbados by descent or naturalization (2024)

Military - note: formed in 1979, the Barbados Defense Force (BDF) is responsible for protecting national security, but it may also be called up to maintain internal public order in times of crisis, emergency, or other specific needs, such as special joint patrols with the police; it also provides humanitarian assistance and disaster response operations both domestically and regionally under the Caribbean Regional Security System (RSS); other duties include assisting with national development, such as through the training of the country's youth with the units of the Barbados Cadet Corps
Barbados has been a member of the RSS since its creation in 1982; RSS signatories (Antigua and Barbuda, Dominica, Grenada, Guyana, Saint Kitts and Nevis, Saint Lucia, and Saint Vincent and the Grenadines) agreed to prepare contingency plans and assist one another, on request, in national emergencies, prevention of smuggling, search and rescue, immigration control, fishery protection, customs and excise control, maritime policing duties, protection of offshore installations, pollution control, national and other disasters, and threats to national security; the RSS is headquartered in Barbados (2024)

TRANSNATIONAL ISSUES

Illicit drugs: a transit point for cocaine and marijuana destined for North America, Europe, and elsewhere in the Caribbean; some local demand for cocaine and some use of synthetic drugs

BELARUS

INTRODUCTION

Background: After seven decades as a constituent republic of the USSR, Belarus attained its independence in 1991. It has retained closer political and economic ties to Russia than any of the other former Soviet republics. In 1999, Belarus and Russia signed a treaty on a two-state union, envisioning greater political and economic integration. Although Belarus agreed to a framework to carry out the accord, serious implementation has yet to take place and negotiations on further integration have been contentious. Since taking office in 1994 as the country's first and only directly elected president, Alyaksandr LUKASHENKA has steadily consolidated his power through authoritarian means and a centralized economic system. Government restrictions on political and civil freedoms, freedom of speech and the press, peaceful assembly, and religion have remained in place. Restrictions on political freedoms have tightened in the wake of the disputed presidential election in 2020. The election results sparked large-scale protests as members of the opposition and civil society criticized the election's validity. LUKASHENKA has remained in power as the disputed winner of the presidential election after quelling protests in 2020. Since 2022, Belarus has facilitated Russia's war in Ukraine, which was launched in part from Belarusian territory.

GEOGRAPHY

Location: Eastern Europe, east of Poland

Geographic coordinates: 53 00 N, 28 00 E

Map references: Europe

Area: *total:* 207,600 sq km
land: 202,900 sq km
water: 4,700 sq km
comparison ranking: total 86

Area - comparative: slightly less than twice the size of Kentucky; slightly smaller than Kansas

Land boundaries: *total:* 3,599 km
border countries (5): Latvia 161 km; Lithuania 640 km; Poland 375 km; Russia 1,312 km; Ukraine 1,111 km

Coastline: 0 km (landlocked)

Maritime claims: none (landlocked)

Climate: cold winters, cool and moist summers; transitional between continental and maritime

Terrain: generally flat with much marshland

Elevation: *highest point:* Dzyarzhynskaya Hara 346 m
lowest point: Nyoman River 90 m
mean elevation: 160 m

Natural resources: timber, peat deposits, small quantities of oil and natural gas, granite, dolomitic limestone, marl, chalk, sand, gravel, clay

Land use: *agricultural land:* 43.7% (2018 est.)
arable land: 27.2% (2018 est.)
permanent crops: 0.6% (2018 est.)
permanent pasture: 15.9% (2018 est.)
forest: 42.7% (2018 est.)
other: 13.6% (2018 est.)

Irrigated land: 303 sq km (2020)

Major rivers (by length in km): Dnyapro (Dnieper) (shared with Russia [s] and Ukraine [m]) - 2,287 km
note – [s] after country name indicates river source; [m] after country name indicates river mouth

Major watersheds (area sq km): Atlantic Ocean drainage: *(Black Sea)* Dnieper (533,966 sq km)

Population distribution: a fairly even distribution throughout most of the country, with urban areas attracting larger and denser populations

Natural hazards: large tracts of marshy land

Geography - note: landlocked; glacial scouring accounts for the flatness of Belarusian terrain and for its 11,000 lakes

PEOPLE AND SOCIETY

Population: *total:* 9,501,451
male: 4,433,839
female: 5,067,612 (2024 est.)
comparison rankings: female 93; male 99; total 97

Nationality: *noun:* Belarusian(s)
adjective: Belarusian

Ethnic groups: Belarusian 83.7%, Russian 8.3%, Polish 3.1%, Ukrainian 1.7%, other 2.4%, unspecified 0.9% (2009 est.)

Languages: Russian (official) 71.4%, Belarusian (official) 26%, other 0.3% (includes small Polish- and Ukrainian-speaking minorities), unspecified 2.3% (2019 est.)
major-language sample(s):
Книга фактов о мире – незаменимый источник базовой информации. (Russian)

Religions: Orthodox 48.3%, Catholic 7.1%, other 3.5%, non-believers 41.1% (2011 est.)

Age structure: *0-14 years:* 16.1% (male 787,849/female 741,293)
15-64 years: 66.1% (male 3,073,507/female 3,204,088)
65 years and over: 17.8% (2024 est.) (male 572,483/female 1,122,231)

Dependency ratios: *total dependency ratio:* 50.8
youth dependency ratio: 25.4
elderly dependency ratio: 25.4
potential support ratio: 3.9 (2021 est.)

Median age: *total:* 42.1 years (2024 est.)
male: 39.5 years
female: 45 years
comparison ranking: total 46

Population growth rate: -0.42% (2024 est.)
comparison ranking: 216

Birth rate: 8.3 births/1,000 population (2024 est.)
comparison ranking: 210

Death rate: 13.3 deaths/1,000 population (2024 est.)
comparison ranking: 10

Net migration rate: 0.8 migrant(s)/1,000 population (2024 est.)
comparison ranking: 67

Population distribution: a fairly even distribution throughout most of the country, with urban areas attracting larger and denser populations

Urbanization: *urban population:* 80.7% of total population (2023)
rate of urbanization: 0.28% annual rate of change (2020-25 est.)

Major urban areas - population: 2.057 million MINSK (capital) (2023)

Sex ratio: *at birth:* 1.06 male(s)/female
0-14 years: 1.06 male(s)/female
15-64 years: 0.96 male(s)/female
65 years and over: 0.51 male(s)/female
total population: 0.88 male(s)/female (2024 est.)

Mother's mean age at first birth: 26.8 years (2019 est.)

Maternal mortality ratio: 1 deaths/100,000 live births (2020 est.)
comparison ranking: 186

Infant mortality rate: *total:* 2.1 deaths/1,000 live births (2024 est.)
male: 2.5 deaths/1,000 live births
female: 1.7 deaths/1,000 live births
comparison ranking: total 219

Life expectancy at birth: *total population:* 74.7 years (2024 est.)
male: 69.8 years
female: 80 years
comparison ranking: total population 138

Total fertility rate: 1.45 children born/woman (2024 est.)
comparison ranking: 208

Gross reproduction rate: 0.7 (2024 est.)

Contraceptive prevalence rate: 52.6% (2019)

Drinking water source: *improved: urban:* 100% of population
rural: 99.6% of population
total: 99.9% of population
unimproved: urban: 0% of population
rural: 0.4% of population
total: 0.1% of population (2020 est.)

Current health expenditure: 6.4% of GDP (2020)

Physician density: 4.54 physicians/1,000 population (2019)

Hospital bed density: 10.8 beds/1,000 population (2014)

Sanitation facility access: *improved: urban:* 99.9% of population
rural: 98.3% of population
total: 99.5% of population
unimproved: urban: 0.1% of population
rural: 1.7% of population
total: 0.5% of population (2020 est.)

Obesity - adult prevalence rate: 24.5% (2016)
comparison ranking: 58

Alcohol consumption per capita: *total:* 10.57 liters of pure alcohol (2019 est.)
beer: 2.26 liters of pure alcohol (2019 est.)
wine: 0.98 liters of pure alcohol (2019 est.)
spirits: 4.67 liters of pure alcohol (2019 est.)
other alcohols: 2.66 liters of pure alcohol (2019 est.)
comparison ranking: total 18

Tobacco use: *total:* 30.5% (2020 est.)
male: 47.4% (2020 est.)
female: 13.5% (2020 est.)
comparison ranking: total 30

Children under the age of 5 years underweight: NA

Currently married women (ages 15-49): 66.6% (2023 est.)

Child marriage: *women married by age 15:* 0.1%
women married by age 18: 4.7%
men married by age 18: 1.6% (2019 est.)

Education expenditures: 4.7% of GDP (2021 est.)
comparison ranking: 86

Literacy: *definition:* age 15 and over can read and write
total population: 99.9%
male: 99.9%
female: 99.9% (2019)

School life expectancy (primary to tertiary education): *total:* 15 years
male: 15 years
female: 15 years (2021)

ENVIRONMENT

Environment - current issues: soil pollution from pesticide use; southern part of the country contaminated with fallout from 1986 nuclear reactor accident at Chornobyl' in northern Ukraine

Environment - international agreements: *party to:* Air Pollution, Air Pollution-Nitrogen Oxides, Air Pollution-Sulphur 85, Antarctic-Environmental Protection, Antarctic Treaty, Biodiversity, Climate Change, Climate Change-Kyoto Protocol, Climate Change-Paris Agreement, Comprehensive Nuclear Test Ban, Desertification, Endangered Species,

Environmental Modification, Hazardous Wastes, Law of the Sea, Marine Dumping-London Convention, Nuclear Test Ban, Ozone Layer Protection, Ship Pollution, Wetlands
signed, but not ratified: none of the selected agreements

Climate: cold winters, cool and moist summers; transitional between continental and maritime

Urbanization: *urban population:* 80.7% of total population (2023)
rate of urbanization: 0.28% annual rate of change (2020-25 est.)

Revenue from forest resources: 1.02% of GDP (2018 est.)
comparison ranking: 52

Revenue from coal: 0% of GDP (2018 est.)
comparison ranking: 121

Air pollutants: *particulate matter emissions:* 15.48 micrograms per cubic meter (2019 est.)
carbon dioxide emissions: 58.28 megatons (2016 est.)
methane emissions: 17.19 megatons (2020 est.)

Waste and recycling: *municipal solid waste generated annually:* 4.28 million tons (2015 est.)
municipal solid waste recycled annually: 684,800 tons (2016 est.)
percent of municipal solid waste recycled: 16% (2016 est.)

Major rivers (by length in km): Dnyapro (Dnieper) (shared with Russia [s] and Ukraine [m]) - 2,287 km
note – [s] after country name indicates river source; [m] after country name indicates river mouth

Major watersheds (area sq km): Atlantic Ocean drainage: *(Black Sea)* Dnieper (533,966 sq km)

Total water withdrawal: *municipal:* 550 million cubic meters (2020 est.)
industrial: 410 million cubic meters (2020 est.)
agricultural: 370 million cubic meters (2020 est.)

Total renewable water resources: 57.9 billion cubic meters (2020 est.)

GOVERNMENT

Country name: *conventional long form:* Republic of Belarus
conventional short form: Belarus
local long form: Respublika Byelarus' (Belarusian)/ Respublika Belarus' (Russian)
local short form: Byelarus' (Belarusian)/ Belarus' (Russian)
former: Belorussian (Byelorussian) Soviet Socialist Republic
etymology: the name is a compound of the Belarusian words "bel" (white) and "Rus" (the Old East Slavic ethnic designation) to form the meaning White Rusian or White Ruthenian

Government type: presidential republic in name, although in fact a dictatorship

Capital: *name:* Minsk
geographic coordinates: 53 54 N, 27 34 E
time difference: UTC+2 (7 hours ahead of Washington, DC, during Standard Time)
etymology: the origin of the name is disputed; Minsk may originally have been located 16 km to the southwest, on the banks of Menka River; remnants of a 10th-century settlement on the banks of the Menka have been found

Administrative divisions: 6 regions (voblastsi, singular - voblasts') and 1 municipality* (horad); Brest, Homyel' (Gomel'), Horad Minsk* (Minsk City), Hrodna (Grodno), Mahilyow (Mogilev), Minsk, Vitsyebsk (Vitebsk)
note: administrative divisions have the same names as their administrative centers; Russian spelling provided for reference when different from Belarusian

Independence: 25 August 1991 (from the Soviet Union)

National holiday: Independence Day, 3 July (1944); note - 3 July 1944 was the date Minsk was liberated from German troops, 25 August 1991 was the date of independence from the Soviet Union

Legal system: civil law system; note - nearly all major codes (civil, civil procedure, criminal, criminal procedure, family, and labor) were revised and came into force in 1999 and 2000

Constitution: *history:* several previous; latest drafted between late 1991 and early 1994, signed 15 March 1994
amendments: proposed by the president of the republic through petition to the National Assembly or by petition of least 150,000 eligible voters; approval required by at least two-thirds majority vote in both chambers or by simple majority of votes cast in a referendum; amended 1996, 2004; note -one of several amendments passed in the February 2022 referendum - the presidential 5-year, two-term limit - will be imposed after the 2025 election

International law organization participation: has not submitted an ICJ jurisdiction declaration; non-party state to the ICCt

Citizenship: *citizenship by birth:* no
citizenship by descent only: at least one parent must be a citizen of Belarus
dual citizenship recognized: no
residency requirement for naturalization: 7 years

Suffrage: 18 years of age; universal

Executive branch: *chief of state:* President Alyaksandr LUKASHENKA (since 20 July 1994)
head of government: Prime Minister Roman GOLOVCHENKO (since 4 June 2020)
cabinet: Council of Ministers appointed by the president
elections/appointments: president directly elected by absolute majority popular vote in 2 rounds if needed for a 5-year term (no term limits); first election held on 23 June and 10 July 1994; according to the 1994 constitution, the next election should have been held in 1999; however, Alyaksandr LUKASHENKA extended his term to 2001 via a November 1996 referendum; subsequent election held on 9 September 2001; an October 2004 referendum ended presidential term limits and allowed the President LUKASHENKA to run and win a third term (19 March 2006); a fourth term (19 December 2010); a fifth term (11 October 2015); a sixth term (9 August 2020); next election to be held in 2025; prime minister and deputy prime ministers appointed by the president and approved by the National Assembly
election results:
2020: Alyaksandr LUKASHENKA reelected president; percent of vote - Alyaksandr LUKASHENKA (independent) 80.1%, Svyatlana TSIKHANOWSKAYA (independent) 10.1%, other 9.8%; note - widespread street protests erupted following announcement of the election results amid allegations of voter fraud
2015: Alyaksandr LUKASHENKA elected president; percent of vote - Alyaksandr LUKASHENKA (independent) 84.1%, Tatsyana KARATKEVIC (BSDPH) 4.4%, Sergey GAYDUKEVICH (LDP) 3.3%, other 8.2%.

Legislative branch: *description:* bicameral National Assembly or Natsyyalny Skhod consists of:
Council of the Republic or Savet Respubliki (65 seats statutory, currently 58; 56 members indirectly elected by regional and Minsk city councils and 8 members appointed by the president; members serve 4-year terms)
House of Representatives or Palata Pradstawnikow (110 seats; members directly elected in single-seat constituencies by absolute majority vote in 2 rounds if needed; members serve 4-year terms)
elections: Council of the Republic - indirect election last held on 4 April 2024 (next to be held in 2029)
House of Representatives - last held on 25 February 2024 (next to be held in 2028)
election results: Council of the Republic - percent of vote by party - NA; seats by party - independent 58, other 2; composition - men 42, women 16, percentage women 27.6%
House of Representatives - percent of vote by party - NA; seats by party - Belaya Rus 51, RPTS 8, CPB 7, LDPB 4, independent 40; composition - men 73, women 37, percentage women 33.6%; note - total National Assembly percentage women 31.5%

Judicial branch: *highest court(s):* Supreme Court (consists of the chairman and deputy chairman and organized into several specialized panels, including economic and military; number of judges set by the president of the republic and the court chairman); Constitutional Court (consists of 12 judges, including a chairman and deputy chairman)
judge selection and term of office: Supreme Court judges appointed by the president with the consent of the Council of the Republic; judges initially appointed for 5 years and evaluated for life appointment; Constitutional Court judges - 6 appointed by the president and 6 elected by the Council of the Republic; the presiding judge directly elected by the president and approved by the Council of the Republic; judges can serve for 11 years with an age limit of 70
subordinate courts: oblast courts; Minsk City Court; town courts; Minsk city and oblast economic courts

Political parties: Belaya Rus or BR
Republican Party of Labour and Justice or RPTS
Communist Party of Belarus or CBP
Liberal Democratic Party of Belarus or LDPB

International organization participation: BSEC (observer), CBSS (observer), CEI, CIS, CSTO, EAEC, EAEU, EAPC, EBRD, FAO, GCTU, IAEA, IBRD, ICAO, ICC (NGOs), ICRM, IDA, IFC, IFRCS, ILO, IMF, IMSO, Interpol, IOC, IOM, IPU, ISO, ITU, ITUC (NGOs), MIGA, NAM, NSG, OPCW, OSCE, PCA, PFP, SCO (dialogue member), UN, UNCTAD, UNESCO, UNIDO, UNIFIL, UNWTO, UPU, WCO, WFTU (NGOs), WHO, WIPO, WMO, WTO (observer), ZC

Diplomatic representation in the US: *chief of mission:* Ambassador (vacant; recalled by Belarus in 2008); Chargé d'Affaires Pavel SHIDLOWSKI (since 9 August 2022)
chancery: 1619 New Hampshire Avenue NW, Washington, DC 20009
telephone: [1] (202) 986-1606
FAX: [1] (202) 986-1805
email address and website:
usa@mfa.gov.by

Embassy of the Republic of Belarus in the United States of America (mfa.gov.by)

Diplomatic representation from the US: *chief of mission:* Ambassador (vacant); Chargé d'Affaires Peter KAUFMAN (since June 2023)
embassy: 46 Starovilenskaya Street, Minsk 220002
mailing address: 7010 Minsk Place, Washington DC 20521-7010
telephone: [375] (17) 210-12-83
FAX: [375] (17) 334-78-53
email address and website:
ConsularMinsk@state.gov
https://by.usembassy.gov/

Flag description: red horizontal band (top) and green horizontal band one-half the width of the red band; a white vertical stripe on the hoist side bears Belarusian national ornamentation in red; the red band color recalls past struggles from oppression, the green band represents hope and the many forests of the country

National symbol(s): no clearly defined current national symbol, the mounted knight known as Pahonia (the Chaser) is the traditional Belarusian symbol; national colors: green, red, white

National anthem: *name:* "My, Bielarusy" (We Belarusians)
lyrics/music: Mikhas KLIMKOVICH and Uladzimir KARYZNA/Nester SAKALOUSKI
note: music adopted 1955, lyrics adopted 2002; after the fall of the Soviet Union, Belarus kept the music of its Soviet-era anthem but adopted new lyrics; also known as "Dziarzauny himn Respubliki Bielarus" (State Anthem of the Republic of Belarus)

National heritage: *total World Heritage Sites:* 4 (3 cultural, 1 natural)
selected World Heritage Site locales: Bialowieza Forest (n); Mir Castle Complex (c); Architectural, Residential, and Cultural Complex of the Radziwill Family at Nesvizh (c)

ECONOMY

Economic overview: declining Russian energy subsidies will end in 2024; growing public debt; strong currency pressures have led to higher inflation; recent price controls on basic food and drugs; public sector wage increases and fragile private sector threaten household income gains and economic growth

Real GDP (purchasing power parity): $254.407 billion (2023 est.)
$244.89 billion (2022 est.)
$256.855 billion (2021 est.)
note: data in 2021 dollars
comparison ranking: 69

Real GDP growth rate: 3.89% (2023 est.)
-4.66% (2022 est.)
2.44% (2021 est.)
note: annual GDP % growth based on constant local currency
comparison ranking: 80

Real GDP per capita: $27,700 (2023 est.)
$26,500 (2022 est.)
$27,600 (2021 est.)
note: data in 2021 dollars
comparison ranking: 83

GDP (official exchange rate): $71.857 billion (2023 est.)
note: data in current dollars at official exchange rate

Inflation rate (consumer prices): 5% (2023 est.)
15.21% (2022 est.)
9.46% (2021 est.)
note: annual % change based on consumer prices
comparison ranking: 108

Credit ratings: Fitch rating: B (2018)

Moody's rating: B3 (2018)

Standard & Poors rating: B (2017)
note: The year refers to the year in which the current credit rating was first obtained.

GDP - composition, by sector of origin: *agriculture:* 7.3% (2023 est.)
industry: 32.5% (2023 est.)
services: 47.8% (2023 est.)
note: figures may not total 100% due to non-allocated consumption not captured in sector-reported data
comparison rankings: services 158; industry 53; agriculture 98

GDP - composition, by end use: *household consumption:* 54.7% (2023 est.)
government consumption: 18.1% (2023 est.)
investment in fixed capital: 21.9% (2023 est.)
investment in inventories: 2.2% (2023 est.)
exports of goods and services: 66.8% (2023 est.)
imports of goods and services: -66.2% (2023 est.)
note: figures may not total 100% due to rounding or gaps in data collection

Agricultural products: milk, sugar beets, potatoes, wheat, triticale, barley, maize, rapeseed, rye, apples (2022)
note: top ten agricultural products based on tonnage

Industries: metal-cutting machine tools, tractors, trucks, earthmovers, motorcycles, synthetic fibers, fertilizer, textiles, refrigerators, washing machines and other household appliances

Industrial production growth rate: 8.12% (2023 est.)
note: annual % change in industrial value added based on constant local currency
comparison ranking: 28

Labor force: 4.956 million (2023 est.)
note: number of people ages 15 or older who are employed or seeking work
comparison ranking: 89

Unemployment rate: 3.57% (2023 est.)
3.57% (2022 est.)
3.9% (2021 est.)
note: % of labor force seeking employment
comparison ranking: 64

Youth unemployment rate (ages 15-24): *total:* 10.2% (2023 est.)
male: 10.7% (2023 est.)
female: 9.8% (2023 est.)
note: % of labor force ages 15-24 seeking employment
comparison ranking: total 133

Population below poverty line: 4.8% (2020 est.)
note: % of population with income below national poverty line

Gini Index coefficient - distribution of family income: 24.4 (2020 est.)
note: index (0-100) of income distribution; higher values represent greater inequality
comparison ranking: 150

Average household expenditures: *on food:* 31.7% of household expenditures (2022 est.)
on alcohol and tobacco: 7.7% of household expenditures (2022 est.)

Household income or consumption by percentage share: *lowest 10%:* 4.4% (2020 est.)
highest 10%: 20.7% (2020 est.)
note: % share of income accruing to lowest and highest 10% of population

Remittances: 1.85% of GDP (2023 est.)
1.99% of GDP (2022 est.)
1.65% of GDP (2021 est.)
note: personal transfers and compensation between resident and non-resident individuals/households/entities

Budget: *revenues:* $20.609 billion (2022 est.)
expenditures: $20.856 billion (2022 est.)
note: central government revenues (excluding grants) and expenses converted to US dollars at average official exchange rate for year indicated

Public debt: 33.24% of GDP (2019 est.)
note: central government debt as a % of GDP
comparison ranking: 161

Taxes and other revenues: 11.23% (of GDP) (2022 est.)
note: central government tax revenue as a % of GDP
comparison ranking: 174

Current account balance: -$1.02 billion (2023 est.)
$2.539 billion (2022 est.)
$2.157 billion (2021 est.)
note: balance of payments - net trade and primary/secondary income in current dollars
comparison ranking: 142

Exports: $47.87 billion (2023 est.)
$46.878 billion (2022 est.)
$49.435 billion (2021 est.)
note: balance of payments - exports of goods and services in current dollars
comparison ranking: 68

Exports - partners: China 15%, Ukraine 12%, Poland 9%, Kazakhstan 8%, Lithuania 8% (2022)
note: top five export partners based on percentage share of exports

Exports - commodities: fertilizers, refined petroleum, rapeseed oil, wood, beef (2022)
note: top five export commodities based on value in dollars

Imports: $47.398 billion (2023 est.)
$42.289 billion (2022 est.)
$45.465 billion (2021 est.)
note: balance of payments - imports of goods and services in current dollars
comparison ranking: 69

Imports - partners: China 26%, Poland 15%, Germany 12%, Lithuania 12%, Turkey 9% (2022)
note: top five import partners based on percentage share of imports

Imports - commodities: cars, packaged medicine, fabric, plastic products, vehicle parts/accessories (2022)
note: top five import commodities based on value in dollars

Reserves of foreign exchange and gold: $8.118 billion (2023 est.)
$7.923 billion (2022 est.)
$8.425 billion (2021 est.)
note: holdings of gold (year-end prices)/foreign exchange/special drawing rights in current dollars
comparison ranking: 77

Exchange rates: Belarusian rubles (BYB/BYR) per US dollar -

Exchange rates: 3.007 (2023 est.)
2.626 (2022 est.)
2.539 (2021 est.)
2.44 (2020 est.)
2.092 (2019 est.)

ENERGY

Electricity access: *electrification - total population:* 100% (2022 est.)

Electricity: *installed generating capacity:* 11.508 million kW (2022 est.)
consumption: 35.516 billion kWh (2022 est.)
exports: 4.676 billion kWh (2022 est.)
imports: 4.287 billion kWh (2022 est.)
transmission/distribution losses: 2.717 billion kWh (2022 est.)
comparison rankings: transmission/distribution losses 134; imports 49; exports 39; consumption 60; installed generating capacity 63

Electricity generation sources: *fossil fuels:* 84.5% of total installed capacity (2022 est.)
nuclear: 12.1% of total installed capacity (2022 est.)
solar: 0.4% of total installed capacity (2022 est.)
wind: 0.5% of total installed capacity (2022 est.)
hydroelectricity: 1% of total installed capacity (2022 est.)
biomass and waste: 1.4% of total installed capacity (2022 est.)

Nuclear energy: Number of operational nuclear reactors: 2 (2023)

Net capacity of operational nuclear reactors: 2.22GW (2023 est.)

Percent of total electricity production: 28.6% (2023 est.)

Coal: *consumption:* 778,000 metric tons (2022 est.)
exports: 1.213 million metric tons (2022 est.)
imports: 2.467 million metric tons (2022 est.)

Petroleum: *total petroleum production:* 30,000 bbl/day (2023 est.)
refined petroleum consumption: 131,000 bbl/day (2022 est.)
crude oil estimated reserves: 198 million barrels (2021 est.)

Natural gas: *production:* 73.929 million cubic meters (2022 est.)
consumption: 16.683 billion cubic meters (2022 est.)
imports: 16.688 billion cubic meters (2022 est.)
proven reserves: 2.832 billion cubic meters (2021 est.)

Carbon dioxide emissions: 51.682 million metric tonnes of CO_2 (2022 est.)
from coal and metallurgical coke: 1.946 million metric tonnes of CO_2 (2022 est.)
from petroleum and other liquids: 17.32 million metric tonnes of CO_2 (2022 est.)
from consumed natural gas: 32.415 million metric tonnes of CO_2 (2022 est.)
comparison ranking: total emissions 56

Energy consumption per capita: 99.484 million Btu/person (2022 est.)
comparison ranking: 53

COMMUNICATIONS

Telephones - fixed lines: *total subscriptions:* 4.23 million (2022 est.)
subscriptions per 100 inhabitants: 44 (2022 est.)
comparison ranking: total subscriptions 33

Telephones - mobile cellular: *total subscriptions:* 11.771 million (2022 est.)
subscriptions per 100 inhabitants: 123 (2022 est.)
comparison ranking: total subscriptions 85

Telecommunication systems: *general assessment:* the government of Belarus has successfully promoted the migration to an all-internet protocol (IP) platform as part of a wider effort towards a digital transformation for the economy; the state-supported infrastructure operator has built an extensive fiber network which reaches all but the smallest settlements in the country; Belarus has the second highest fiber usage rate in Europe, behind only Iceland; long-term evolution (LTE) coverage is almost universal, while considerable progress has also been made in developing 5G services; telcos have had to invest in network infrastructure while managing a significant fall in the value of the local currency (particularly against the euro and the US dollar)
(2024)
domestic: fixed-line tele density 44 per 100 fixed-line; mobile-cellular tele density 123 telephones per 100 persons (2022)
international: country code - 375; Belarus is landlocked and therefore a member of the Trans-European Line (TEL), Trans-Asia-Europe (TAE) fiber-optic line, and has access to the Trans-Siberia Line (TSL); 3 fiber-optic segments provide connectivity to Latvia, Poland, Russia, and Ukraine; worldwide service is available to Belarus through this infrastructure; additional analog lines to Russia; Intelsat, Eutelsat, and Intersputnik earth stations; almost 31,000 base stations in service in 2019 (2020)

Broadcast media: 7 state-controlled national TV channels; Polish and Russian TV broadcasts are available in some areas; state-run Belarusian Radio operates 5 national networks and an external service; Russian and Polish radio broadcasts are available (2019)

Internet country code: .by

Internet users: *total:* 8.352 million (2021 est.)
percent of population: 87% (2021 est.)
comparison ranking: total 70

Broadband - fixed subscriptions: *total:* 3,255,552 (2020 est.)
subscriptions per 100 inhabitants: 35 (2020 est.)
comparison ranking: total 44

TRANSPORTATION

National air transport system: *number of registered air carriers:* 2 (2020)
inventory of registered aircraft operated by air carriers: 30
annual passenger traffic on registered air carriers: 2,760,168 (2018)
annual freight traffic on registered air carriers: 1.9 million (2018) mt-km

Civil aircraft registration country code prefix: EW

Airports: 46 (2024)
comparison ranking: 92

Heliports: 4 (2024)

Pipelines: 5,386 km gas, 1,589 km oil, 1,730 km refined products (2013)

Railways: *total:* 5,528 km (2014)
standard gauge: 25 km (2014) 1.435-m gauge
broad gauge: 5,503 km (2014) 1.520-m gauge (874 km electrified)
comparison ranking: total 34

Roadways: *total:* 86,600 km (2017)
comparison ranking: total 58

Waterways: 2,500 km (2011) (major rivers are the west-flowing Western Dvina and Neman Rivers and the south-flowing Dnepr River and its tributaries, the Berezina, Sozh, and Pripyat Rivers)
comparison ranking: 37

Merchant marine: *total:* 4 (2023)
by type: other 4
comparison ranking: total 171

MILITARY AND SECURITY

Military and security forces: Belarus Armed Forces: Army, Air and Air Defense Force, Special Operations Force, Special Troops (electronic warfare, signals, engineers, biological/chemical/nuclear protection troops, etc)

Ministry of Interior: State Border Troops, Militia, Internal Troops (2024)
note: in early 2023, President LUKASHENKA ordered the formation of a new volunteer paramilitary territorial defense force to supplement the Army

Military expenditures: 1.5% of GDP (2023 est.)
1.1% of GDP (2022 est.)
1.2% of GDP (2021 est.)
1.5% of GDP (2020 est.)
1.5% of GDP (2019 est.)
comparison ranking: 89

Military and security service personnel strengths: approximately 45-50,000 active-duty troops; information on the individual services varies, but reportedly includes about 25-30,000 Army, 15,000 Air/Air Defense, and 5,000 Special Operations forces (2023)

Military equipment inventories and acquisitions: the military's inventory is comprised mostly of Russian/Soviet-origin equipment, and in recent years Russia has continued to be the leading provider of arms; Belarus's defense industry manufactures some equipment (mostly modernized Soviet designs), including vehicles, guided weapons, and electronic warfare systems (2024)

Military service age and obligation: 18-27 years of age for compulsory military or alternative service; conscript service obligation is 12-18 months, depending on academic qualifications, and 24-36 months for alternative service, also depending on academic qualifications; 17-year-olds are eligible to become cadets at military higher education institutes, where they are classified as military personnel (2023)
note: conscripts can be assigned to the military, to the Ministry of Interior, or to the Ministry of Labor and Social Protection (alternative service)

Military - note: the military of Belarus is responsible for territorial defense; it is a mixed force of conscripts and professionals that is equipped with Russian or Soviet-era weapons; Russia is the country's closest security partner, a relationship that includes an integrated air and missile defense system and joint military training centers and exercises; Russia leases from Belarus a strategic ballistic missile defense site operated by Russian Aerospace Forces and a global communications facility for the Russian Navy; in 2020, the countries signed an agreement allowing for close security cooperation between the Belarusian Ministry of Interior and the Russian National Guard, including protecting public order and key government facilities and combating extremism and terrorism; in 2022, Belarus allowed Russian military forces to stage on its territory for their invasion of Ukraine and continues to supply arms and other aid to the Russian military, including logistical support, medical care, and airfields for Russian combat aircraft; in 2023, Belarus agreed to permit Russia to deploy nuclear weapons on its soil

Belarus has been a member of the Collective Security Treaty Organization (CSTO) since 1994 and has committed an airborne brigade to CSTO's rapid reaction force; the military trains regularly with other CSTO members (2023)

SPACE

Space agency/agencies: Belarus Space Agency (aka National Agency for Space Research; established 2009); National Academy of Sciences of Belarus (2024)

Space program overview: has a modest national space program focused on developing remote sensing (RS) satellites; jointly builds satellites with foreign partners; develops some space technologies and components for space equipment, including satellite payloads and associated technology, such as optics and imaging equipment; has cooperated with a variety of foreign space agencies and commercial entities, including those of Azerbaijan, China, Kazakhstan, Russia, and Ukraine; has a state-owned satellite company (2024)
note: further details about the key activities, programs, and milestones of the country's space program, as well as government spending estimates on the space sector, appear in the Space Programs reference guide

TRANSNATIONAL ISSUES

Refugees and internally displaced persons: *refugees (country of origin):* 42,785 (Ukraine) (as of 29 February 2024)
stateless persons: 5,626 (2022)

Trafficking in persons: tier rating: Tier 3 — Belarus does not fully meet the minimum standards for the elimination of trafficking and is not making significant efforts to do so, therefore, Belarus remained on Tier 3; for more details, go to: https://www.state.gov/reports/2024-trafficking-in-persons-report/belarus/

Illicit drugs: limited cultivation of opium poppy and cannabis, mostly for the domestic market; transshipment point for illicit drugs to and via Russia, and to the Baltics and Western Europe; a small and lightly regulated financial center; anti-money-laundering legislation does not meet international standards and was weakened further when know-your-customer requirements were curtailed in 2008; few investigations or prosecutions of money-laundering activities

BELGIUM

INTRODUCTION

Background: Belgium became independent from the Netherlands in 1830; it was occupied by Germany during World Wars I and II. The country prospered as a modern, technologically advanced European state and member of NATO and the EU. In recent years, longstanding tensions between the Dutch-speaking Flemish of the north and the French-speaking Walloons of the south have led to constitutional amendments granting these regions formal recognition and autonomy. The capital city of Brussels is home to numerous international organizations, including the EU and NATO.

GEOGRAPHY

Location: Western Europe, bordering the North Sea, between France and the Netherlands

Geographic coordinates: 50 50 N, 4 00 E

Map references: Europe

Area: *total:* 30,528 sq km
land: 30,278 sq km
water: 250 sq km
comparison ranking: total 140

Area - comparative: about the size of Maryland

Land boundaries: *total:* 1,297 km
border countries (4): France 556 km; Germany 133 km; Luxembourg 130 km; Netherlands 478 km

Coastline: 66.5 km

Maritime claims: *territorial sea:* 12 nm
contiguous zone: 24 nm
exclusive economic zone: geographic coordinates define outer limit
continental shelf: median line with neighbors

Climate: temperate; mild winters, cool summers; rainy, humid, cloudy

Terrain: flat coastal plains in northwest, central rolling hills, rugged mountains of Ardennes Forest in southeast

Elevation: *highest point:* Botrange 694 m
lowest point: North Sea 0 m
mean elevation: 181 m

Natural resources: construction materials, silica sand, carbonates, arable land

Land use: *agricultural land:* 44.1% (2018 est.)
arable land: 27.2% (2018 est.)
permanent crops: 0.8% (2018 est.)
permanent pasture: 16.1% (2018 est.)
forest: 22.4% (2018 est.)
other: 33.5% (2018 est.)

Irrigated land: 57 sq km (2013)

Major watersheds (area sq km): Atlantic Ocean drainage: Seine (78,919 sq km), Rhine-Maas (198,735 sq km)

Population distribution: most of the population concentrated in the northern two-thirds of the country; the southeast is more thinly populated; considered to have one of the highest population densities in the world; approximately 97% live in urban areas

Natural hazards: flooding is a threat along rivers and in areas of reclaimed coastal land, protected from the sea by concrete dikes

Geography - note: crossroads of Western Europe; most West European capitals are within 1,000 km of Brussels, the seat of both the EU and NATO

PEOPLE AND SOCIETY

Population: *total:* 11,977,634
male: 5,909,057
female: 6,068,577 (2024 est.)
comparison rankings: female 82; male 83; total 82

Nationality: *noun:* Belgian(s)
adjective: Belgian

Ethnic groups: Belgian 75.2%, Italian 4.1%, Moroccan 3.7%, French 2.4%, Turkish 2%, Dutch 2%, other 10.6% (2012 est.)

Languages: Dutch (official) 60%, French (official) 40%, German (official) less than 1%
major-language sample(s):
Het Wereld Feitenboek, een onmisbare bron van informatie. (Dutch)
The World Factbook, une source indispensable d'informations de base. (French)

Religions: Roman Catholic 57.1%, Protestant 2.3%, other Christian, 2.8%, Muslim 6.8%, other 1.7%, atheist 9.1%, nonbeliever/agnostic 20.2% (2018 est.)

Age structure: *0-14 years:* 16.9% (male 1,038,578/female 990,215)
15-64 years: 62.8% (male 3,796,844/female 3,730,784)
65 years and over: 20.2% (2024 est.) (male 1,073,635/female 1,347,578)

Dependency ratios: *total dependency ratio:* 56.5
youth dependency ratio: 26.1
elderly dependency ratio: 30.4
potential support ratio: 3.3 (2021 est.)

Median age: *total:* 42 years (2024 est.)
male: 40.8 years
female: 43.1 years
comparison ranking: total 47

Population growth rate: 0.53% (2024 est.)
comparison ranking: 148

Birth rate: 10.8 births/1,000 population (2024 est.)
comparison ranking: 169

Death rate: 9.5 deaths/1,000 population (2024 est.)
comparison ranking: 46

Net migration rate: 4 migrant(s)/1,000 population (2024 est.)
comparison ranking: 27

Population distribution: most of the population concentrated in the northern two-thirds of the country; the southeast is more thinly populated; considered to have one of the highest population densities in the world; approximately 97% live in urban areas

Urbanization: *urban population:* 98.2% of total population (2023)
rate of urbanization: 0.38% annual rate of change (2020-25 est.)

Major urban areas - population: 2.122 million BRUSSELS (capital), 1.057 million Antwerp (2023)

Sex ratio: *at birth:* 1.05 male(s)/female
0-14 years: 1.05 male(s)/female
15-64 years: 1.02 male(s)/female
65 years and over: 0.8 male(s)/female
total population: 0.97 male(s)/female (2024 est.)

Mother's mean age at first birth: 29.2 years (2020 est.)

Maternal mortality ratio: 5 deaths/100,000 live births (2020 est.)
comparison ranking: 166

Infant mortality rate: *total:* 3.1 deaths/1,000 live births (2024 est.)
male: 3.5 deaths/1,000 live births
female: 2.7 deaths/1,000 live births
comparison ranking: total 205

Life expectancy at birth: *total population:* 82.3 years (2024 est.)
male: 79.7 years
female: 85 years
comparison ranking: total population 30

Total fertility rate: 1.76 children born/woman (2024 est.)
comparison ranking: 145

Gross reproduction rate: 0.86 (2024 est.)

Contraceptive prevalence rate: 66.7% (2018)

Drinking water source: *improved:* *urban:* 100% of population
rural: 100% of population
total: 100% of population
(2020 est.)

Current health expenditure: 11.1% of GDP (2020)

Physician density: 6.08 physicians/1,000 population (2020)

Hospital bed density: 5.6 beds/1,000 population (2019)

Sanitation facility access: *improved:* *urban:* 100% of population
rural: 100% of population
total: 100% of population
(2020 est.)

Obesity - adult prevalence rate: 22.1% (2016)
comparison ranking: 82

Alcohol consumption per capita: *total:* 9.15 liters of pure alcohol (2019 est.)
beer: 4.35 liters of pure alcohol (2019 est.)
wine: 3.41 liters of pure alcohol (2019 est.)
spirits: 1.09 liters of pure alcohol (2019 est.)
other alcohols: 0.3 liters of pure alcohol (2019 est.)
comparison ranking: total 34

Tobacco use: *total:* 23.4% (2020 est.)
male: 25.8% (2020 est.)
female: 21% (2020 est.)
comparison ranking: total 61

Children under the age of 5 years underweight: 1% (2014/15)
comparison ranking: 117

Currently married women (ages 15-49): 43.2% (2023 est.)

Education expenditures: 6.7% of GDP (2020 est.)
comparison ranking: 25

School life expectancy (primary to tertiary education): *total:* 19 years
male: 18 years
female: 20 years (2020)

ENVIRONMENT

Environment - current issues: *intense pressures from human activities:* urbanization, dense transportation network, industry, extensive animal breeding and crop cultivation; air and water pollution also have repercussions for neighboring countries

Environment - international agreements: *party to:* Air Pollution, Air Pollution-Heavy Metals, Air Pollution-Multi-effect Protocol, Air Pollution-Nitrogen Oxides, Air Pollution-Persistent Organic Pollutants, Air Pollution-Sulphur 85, Air Pollution-Sulphur 94, Air Pollution-Volatile Organic Compounds, Antarctic-Environmental Protection, Antarctic-Marine Living Resources, Antarctic Seals, Antarctic Treaty, Biodiversity, Climate Change, Climate Change-Kyoto Protocol, Climate Change-Paris Agreement, Comprehensive Nuclear Test Ban, Desertification, Endangered Species, Environmental Modification, Hazardous Wastes, Law of the Sea, Marine Dumping-London Convention, Marine Dumping-London Protocol, Marine Life Conservation, Nuclear Test Ban, Ozone Layer Protection, Ship Pollution, Tropical Timber 2006, Wetlands, Whaling
signed, but not ratified: none of the selected agreements

Climate: temperate; mild winters, cool summers; rainy, humid, cloudy

Urbanization: *urban population:* 98.2% of total population (2023)
rate of urbanization: 0.38% annual rate of change (2020-25 est.)

Revenue from forest resources: 0.02% of GDP (2018 est.)
comparison ranking: 143

Revenue from coal: 0% of GDP (2018 est.)
comparison ranking: 132

Air pollutants: *particulate matter emissions:* 11.26 micrograms per cubic meter (2019 est.)
carbon dioxide emissions: 96.89 megatons (2016 est.)
methane emissions: 7.78 megatons (2020 est.)

Waste and recycling: *municipal solid waste generated annually:* 4.708 million tons (2015 est.)
municipal solid waste recycled annually: 1,614,985 tons (2015 est.)
percent of municipal solid waste recycled: 34.3% (2015 est.)

Major watersheds (area sq km): Atlantic Ocean drainage: Seine (78,919 sq km), Rhine-Maas (198,735 sq km)

Total water withdrawal: *municipal:* 740 million cubic meters (2020 est.)
industrial: 3.47 billion cubic meters (2020 est.)
agricultural: 50 million cubic meters (2020 est.)

Total renewable water resources: 18.3 billion cubic meters (2020 est.)

Geoparks: *total global geoparks and regional networks:* 2 (2024)
global geoparks and regional networks: Famenne-Ardenne; Schelde Delta (includes Netherlands) (2024)

GOVERNMENT

Country name: *conventional long form:* Kingdom of Belgium
conventional short form: Belgium
local long form: Royaume de Belgique (French)/Koninkrijk Belgie (Dutch)/Koenigreich Belgien (German)
local short form: Belgique/Belgie/Belgien
etymology: the name derives from the Belgae, an ancient Celtic tribal confederation that inhabited an area between the English Channel and the west bank of the Rhine in the first centuries B.C.

Government type: federal parliamentary democracy under a constitutional monarchy

Capital: *name:* Brussels
geographic coordinates: 50 50 N, 4 20 E
time difference: UTC+1 (6 hours ahead of Washington, DC, during Standard Time)
daylight saving time: +1hr, begins last Sunday in March; ends last Sunday in October
etymology: may derive from the Old Dutch *bruoc/broek*, meaning "marsh" and *sella/zele/sel* signifying "home" to express the meaning "home in the marsh"

Administrative divisions: *3 regions (French:* regions, singular - region; Dutch: gewesten, singular - gewest); Brussels-Capital Region, also known as Brussels Hoofdstedelijk Gewest (Dutch), Region de Bruxelles-Capitale (French long form), Bruxelles-Capitale (French short form); Flemish Region (Flanders), also known as Vlaams Gewest (Dutch long form), Vlaanderen (Dutch short form), Region Flamande (French long form), Flandre (French short form); Walloon Region (Wallonia), also known as Region Wallone (French long form), Wallonie (French short form), Waals Gewest (Dutch long form), Wallonie (Dutch short form)
note: as a result of the 1993 constitutional revision that furthered devolution into a federal state, there are now three levels of government (federal, regional, and linguistic community) with a complex division of responsibilities; the 2012 sixth state reform transferred additional competencies from the federal state to the regions and linguistic communities

Independence: 4 October 1830 (a provisional government declared independence from the Netherlands); 21 July 1831 (King LEOPOLD I ascended to the throne)

National holiday: Belgian National Day (ascension to the throne of King LEOPOLD I), 21 July (1831)

Legal system: civil law system based on the French Civil Code; note - Belgian law continues to be modified in conformance with the legislative norms mandated by the European Union; judicial review of legislative acts

Constitution: *history:* drafted 25 November 1830, approved 7 February 1831, entered into force 26 July 1831, revised 14 July 1993 (creating a federal state)
amendments: "revisions" proposed as declarations by the federal government in accord with the king or by Parliament followed by dissolution of Parliament and new elections; adoption requires two-thirds majority vote of a two-thirds quorum in both houses of the next elected Parliament; amended many times, last in 2019

International law organization participation: accepts compulsory ICJ jurisdiction with reservations; accepts ICCt jurisdiction

Citizenship: *citizenship by birth:* no

citizenship by descent only: at least one parent must be a citizen of Belgium
dual citizenship recognized: yes
residency requirement for naturalization: 5 years

Suffrage: 18 years of age; universal and compulsory

Executive branch: *chief of state:* King PHILIPPE (since 21 July 2013)
head of government: Prime Minister Alexander DE CROO (since 1 October 2020)
cabinet: Council of Ministers formally appointed by the monarch
elections/appointments: the monarchy is hereditary and constitutional; following legislative elections, the leader of the majority party or majority coalition usually appointed prime minister by the monarch and approved by Parliament
note - Alexander DE CROO resigned on 9 June 2024 following the parliamentary elections and is serving as prime minister in a caretaker status until a new prime minister is sworn into office

Legislative branch: *description:* bicameral Parliament consists of:
Senate or Senaat (in Dutch), Senat (in French) (60 seats; 50 members indirectly elected by the community and regional parliaments based on their election results, and 10 elected by the 50 other senators; members serve 5-year terms) Chamber of Representatives or Kamer van Volksvertegenwoordigers (in Dutch), Chambre des Representants (in French) (150 seats; members directly elected in multi-seat constituencies by proportional representation vote; members serve 5- year terms)
elections: Senate - last held 18 July 2024 (next to be held on 31 July 2029)
Chamber of Representatives - last held on 9 June 2024 (next to be held on 30 June 2029); note - elections coincided with the EU parliamentary elections
election results: Senate - percent of vote by party - N/A; seats by party - N-VA 10, MR 10, VB 8, PS 6, PVDA-PTB 6, CD&V 5, Les Engages 5, Open VLD 3, Ecolo 3, Vooruit 4; composition - men 32, women 28, percent percentage women 46.7%
Chamber of Representatives - percent of vote by party - N-VA 16.7%, VB 13.5%, MR 10.3%, PVDA-PTB 9.9%, Vooruit 8.1%, PS 8%, CD&V 8%, Les Engages 6.8%, Open VLD 5.5%, Green 4.7%, Ecolo 3%, Defi 1%; seats by party - N-VA 24, VB 20, MR 20, PS 16, PVDA+PTB 15, Les Engages 14, Vooruit 13, CD&V 11, Open VLD 7,Green 6, Ecolo 3, Defi 1; composition - men 86, women 64, percentage women 42.7%; total Parliament percentage women 42.9%
note: the 1993 constitutional revision that further devolved Belgium into a federal state created three levels of government (federal, regional, and linguistic community) with a complex division of responsibilities; this results in six governments, each with its own legislative assembly

Judicial branch: highest court(s): Constitutional Court or Grondwettelijk Hof (in Dutch) and Cour Constitutionelle (in French) (consists of 12 judges - 6 Dutch-speaking and 6 French-speaking); Supreme Court of Justice or Hof van Cassatie (in Dutch) and Cour de Cassation (in French) (court organized into 3 chambers: civil and commercial; criminal; social, fiscal, and armed forces; each chamber includes a Dutch division and a French division, each with a chairperson and 5-6 judges)
judge selection and term of office: Constitutional Court judges appointed by the monarch from candidates submitted by Parliament; judges appointed for life with mandatory retirement at age 70; Supreme Court judges appointed by the monarch from candidates submitted by the High Council of Justice, a 44-member independent body of judicial and nonjudicial members; judges appointed for life
subordinate courts: Courts of Appeal; regional courts; specialized courts for administrative, commercial, labor, immigration, and audit issues; magistrate's courts; justices of the peace

Political parties: Flemish parties: Christian Democratic and Flemish or CD&V
Vooruit or Forward (formerly Social Progressive Alternative or SP.A)
Groen or Green (formerly AGALEV, Flemish Greens)
New Flemish Alliance or N-VA
Open Flemish Liberals and Democrats or Open VLD
Vlaams Belang (Flemish Interest) or VB

Francophone parties: Ecolo (Francophone Greens)
Francophone Federalist Democrats or Defi
Les Engages (formerly Humanist and Democratic Center or CDH)
Reform Movement or MR
Socialist Party or PS
Workers' Party or PVDA-PTB

International organization participation: ADB (nonregional members), AfDB (nonregional members), Australia Group, Benelux, BIS, CD, CE, CERN, EAPC, EBRD, ECB, EIB, EITI (implementing country), EMU, ESA, EU, FAO, FATF, G-9, G-10, IADB, IAEA, IBRD, ICAO, ICC (national committees), ICCt, ICRM, IDA, IEA, IFAD, IFC, IFRCS, IGAD (partners), IHO, ILO, IMF, IMO, IMSO, Interpol, IOC, IOM, IPU, ISO, ITSO, ITU, ITUC (NGOs), MIGA, MONUSCO, NATO, NEA, NSG, OAS (observer), OECD, OIF, OPCW, OSCE, Pacific Alliance (observer), Paris Club, PCA, Schengen Convention, SELEC (observer), UN, UNCTAD, UNESCO, UNHCR, UNIDO, UNIFIL, UNRWA, UNTSO, UPU, Wassenaar Arrangement, WCO, WHO, WIPO, WMO, WTO, ZC

Diplomatic representation in the US: *chief of mission:* Ambassador (vacant); Chargé d'Affaires Sophie Chaska KARLSHAUSEN (since 31 August 2024)
chancery: 1430 K Street NW, Washington DC 20005
telephone: [1] (202) 333-6900
FAX: [1] (202) 338-4960
email address and website:
Washington@diplobel.fed.be
https://unitedstates.diplomatie.belgium.be/en
consulate(s) general: Atlanta, Los Angeles, New York

Diplomatic representation from the US: *chief of mission:* Ambassador Michael ADLER (since 15 March 2022)
embassy: Regentlaan 27 Boulevard du Regent, B-1000 Brussels
mailing address: 7600 Brussels Place, Washington DC 20521-7600
telephone: [32] (2) 811-4000
FAX: [32] (2) 811-4500
email address and website:
uscitizenBrussels@state.gov
https://be.usembassy.gov/

Flag description: three equal vertical bands of black (hoist side), yellow, and red; the vertical design was based on the flag of France; the colors are those of the arms of the duchy of Brabant (yellow lion with red claws and tongue on a black field)

National symbol(s): golden rampant lion; national colors: red, black, yellow

National anthem: *name:* "La Brabanconne" (The Song of Brabant)
lyrics/music: Louis-Alexandre DECHET [French] and Victor CEULEMANS [Dutch]/Francois VAN CAMPENHOUT
note: adopted 1830; according to legend, Louis-Alexandre DECHET, an actor at the theater in which the revolution against the Netherlands began, wrote the lyrics with a group of young people in a Brussels cafe

National heritage: *total World Heritage Sites:* 16 (15 cultural, 1 natural)
selected World Heritage Site locales: Belfries of Belgium (c); Historic Brugge (c); The Grand Place, Brussels (c); Major Town Houses of Victor Horta (c); Notre-Dame Cathedral, Tournai (c); Spa, Liege (c); Primeval Beech Forests - Sonian Wood (n); Stoclet Palace (c)

ECONOMY

Economic overview: high-income, core EU and eurozone economy; slow but steady growth supported by household consumption and energy shock recovery; high public debt and structural deficits linked to social spending; aging workforce with weak productivity growth and participation rates

Real GDP (purchasing power parity): $751.592 billion (2023 est.)
$741.47 billion (2022 est.)
$719.771 billion (2021 est.)
note: data in 2021 dollars
comparison ranking: 36

Real GDP growth rate: 1.37% (2023 est.)
3.01% (2022 est.)
6.93% (2021 est.)
note: annual GDP % growth based on constant local currency
comparison ranking: 155

Real GDP per capita: $63,600 (2023 est.)
$63,500 (2022 est.)
$62,100 (2021 est.)
note: data in 2021 dollars
comparison ranking: 26

GDP (official exchange rate): $632.217 billion (2023 est.)
note: data in current dollars at official exchange rate

Inflation rate (consumer prices): 4.05% (2023 est.)
9.6% (2022 est.)
2.44% (2021 est.)
note: annual % change based on consumer prices
comparison ranking: 81

Credit ratings: Fitch rating: AA- (2016)

Moody's rating: Aa3 (2011)

Standard & Poors rating: AA (2011)
note: The year refers to the year in which the current credit rating was first obtained.

GDP - composition, by sector of origin: *agriculture:* 0.8% (2023 est.)
industry: 18.4% (2023 est.)
services: 70.7% (2023 est.)
note: figures may not total 100% due to non-allocated consumption not captured in sector-reported data
comparison rankings: services 35; industry 150; agriculture 190

GDP - composition, by end use: *household consumption:* 51.4% (2023 est.)

government consumption: 24.2% (2023 est.)
investment in fixed capital: 24.6% (2023 est.)
investment in inventories: 0.7% (2023 est.)
exports of goods and services: 86.7% (2023 est.)
imports of goods and services: -87.6% (2023 est.)
note: figures may not total 100% due to rounding or gaps in data collection

Agricultural products: sugar beets, milk, potatoes, wheat, pork, lettuce, maize, chicken, barley, pears (2022)
note: top ten agricultural products based on tonnage

Industries: engineering and metal products, motor vehicle assembly, transportation equipment, scientific instruments, processed food and beverages, chemicals, pharmaceuticals, base metals, textiles, glass, petroleum

Industrial production growth rate: -1.95% (2023 est.)
note: annual % change in industrial value added based on constant local currency
comparison ranking: 179

Labor force: 5.432 million (2023 est.)
note: number of people ages 15 or older who are employed or seeking work
comparison ranking: 79

Unemployment rate: 5.51% (2023 est.)
5.56% (2022 est.)
6.26% (2021 est.)
note: % of labor force seeking employment
comparison ranking: 106

Youth unemployment rate (ages 15-24): *total:* 16.1% (2023 est.)
male: 17.8% (2023 est.)
female: 14.1% (2023 est.)
note: % of labor force ages 15-24 seeking employment
comparison ranking: total 89

Population below poverty line: 12.3% (2022 est.)
note: % of population with income below national poverty line

Gini Index coefficient - distribution of family income: 26.6 (2021 est.)
note: index (0-100) of income distribution; higher values represent greater inequality
comparison ranking: 142

Average household expenditures: *on food:* 13.5% of household expenditures (2022 est.)
on alcohol and tobacco: 3.9% of household expenditures (2022 est.)

Household income or consumption by percentage share: *lowest 10%:* 3.6% (2021 est.)
highest 10%: 21.9% (2021 est.)
note: % share of income accruing to lowest and highest 10% of population

Remittances: 2.29% of GDP (2023 est.)
2.3% of GDP (2022 est.)
2.34% of GDP (2021 est.)
note: personal transfers and compensation between resident and non-resident individuals/households/entities

Budget: *revenues:* $220.744 billion (2022 est.)
expenditures: $234.883 billion (2022 est.)
note: central government revenues (excluding grants) and expenses converted to US dollars at average official exchange rate for year indicated

Public debt: 94.04% of GDP (2022 est.)
note: central government debt as a % of GDP
comparison ranking: 26

Taxes and other revenues: 23.09% (of GDP) (2022 est.)
note: central government tax revenue as a % of GDP
comparison ranking: 61

Current account balance: -$6.205 billion (2023 est.)
-$5.304 billion (2022 est.)
$8.233 billion (2021 est.)
note: balance of payments - net trade and primary/secondary income in current dollars comparison ranking: 189

Exports: $535.174 billion (2023 est.)
$558.271 billion (2022 est.)
$527.746 billion (2021 est.)
note: balance of payments - exports of goods and services in current dollars
comparison ranking: 18

Exports - partners: Germany 19%, France 15%, Netherlands 14%, US 6%, Italy 5% (2022)
note: top five export partners based on percentage share of exports

Exports - commodities: natural gas, vaccines, refined petroleum, packaged medicine, cars (2022)
note: top five export commodities based on value in dollars

Imports: $545.471 billion (2023 est.)
$567.164 billion (2022 est.)
$516.8 billion (2021 est.)
note: balance of payments - imports of goods and services in current dollars
comparison ranking: 18

Imports - partners: Netherlands 19%, Germany 12%, France 9%, US 6%, China 6% (2022)
note: top five import partners based on percentage share of imports

Imports - commodities: natural gas, refined petroleum, cars, packaged medicine, vaccines (2022)
note: top five import commodities based on value in dollars

Reserves of foreign exchange and gold: $40.813 billion (2023 est.)
$41.274 billion (2022 est.)
$41.872 billion (2021 est.)
note: holdings of gold (year-end prices)/foreign exchange/special drawing rights in current dollars
comparison ranking: 53

Exchange rates: euros (EUR) per US dollar -

Exchange rates: 0.925 (2023 est.)
0.95 (2022 est.)
0.845 (2021 est.)
0.876 (2020 est.)
0.893 (2019 est.)

ENERGY

Electricity access: *electrification - total population:* 100% (2022 est.)

Electricity: *installed generating capacity:* 26.31 million kW (2022 est.)
consumption: 79.972 billion kWh (2022 est.)
exports: 23.877 billion kWh (2022 est.)
imports: 16.35 billion kWh (2022 est.)
transmission/distribution losses: 3.394 billion kWh (2022 est.)
comparison rankings: transmission/distribution losses 145; imports 15; exports 10; consumption 40; installed generating capacity 39

Electricity generation sources: *fossil fuels:* 29% of total installed capacity (2022 est.)
nuclear: 45.8% of total installed capacity (2022 est.)
solar: 7.7% of total installed capacity (2022 est.)
wind: 13% of total installed capacity (2022 est.)
hydroelectricity: -0.2% of total installed capacity (2022 est.) note: Belgium has negative net hydroelectric power generation based on losses from use of pumped storage hydropower
biomass and waste: 4.7% of total installed capacity (2022 est.)

Nuclear energy: Number of operational nuclear reactors: 5 (2023)

Net capacity of operational nuclear reactors: 3.91GW (2023 est.)

Percent of total electricity production: 41.2% (2023 est.)

Number of nuclear reactors permanently shut down: 3 (2023)

Coal: *production:* 1.27 million metric tons (2022 est.)
consumption: 4.869 million metric tons (2022 est.)
exports: 557,000 metric tons (2022 est.)
imports: 4.554 million metric tons (2022 est.)
proven reserves: 4.1 billion metric tons (2022 est.)

Petroleum: *total petroleum production:* 11,000 bbl/day (2023 est.)
refined petroleum consumption: 585,000 bbl/day (2023 est.)

Natural gas: *production:* 13.436 million cubic meters (2022 est.)
consumption: 15.347 billion cubic meters (2022 est.)
exports: 9.86 billion cubic meters (2022 est.)
imports: 25.327 billion cubic meters (2022 est.)

Carbon dioxide emissions: 116.271 million metric tonnes of CO2 (2022 est.)
from coal and metallurgical coke: 8.163 million metric tonnes of CO2 (2022 est.)
from petroleum and other liquids: 78.995 million metric tonnes of CO2 (2022 est.)
from consumed natural gas: 29.113 million metric tonnes of CO2 (2022 est.)
comparison ranking: total emissions 38

Energy consumption per capita: 205.444 million Btu/person (2022 est.)
comparison ranking: 18

COMMUNICATIONS

Telephones - fixed lines: *total subscriptions:* 2.953 million (2022 est.)
subscriptions per 100 inhabitants: 25 (2022 est.)
comparison ranking: total subscriptions 38

Telephones - mobile cellular: *total subscriptions:* 11.874 million (2022 est.)
subscriptions per 100 inhabitants: 102 (2022 est.)
comparison ranking: total subscriptions 84

Telecommunication systems: *general assessment:* mobile networks have been upgraded to support growing mobile data use among subscribers, with near-comprehensive LTE coverage; operators have also trialed 5G in preparation for launching services; the auction of 5G-suitable spectrum has been delayed to the beginning of 2022, while the onerous restrictions on radiation have meant that some 5G trials have been suspended; there is effective competition in Belgium between the DSL and cable platforms, while in recent years government support has also encouraged investment in fiber networks;

in a bid to encourage investment in under served areas, the regulator in 2018 amended the conditions by which market players grant wholesale access to copper and fiber infrastructure; in May 2019 it opened a further consultation on cost models for access to the networks of cablecos and fiber infrastructure (2021)
domestic: about 28 per 100 fixed-line and 101 per 100 mobile-cellular; nationwide mobile-cellular telephone system; extensive cable network; limited microwave radio relay network (2021)
international: country code - 32; landing points for Concerto, UK-Belgium, Tangerine, and SeaMeWe-3, submarine cables that provide links to Europe, the Middle East, Australia, and Asia; satellite earth stations - 7 (Intelsat - 3) (2019)

Broadcast media: a segmented market with the three major communities (Flemish, French, and German speaking) each having responsibility for their own broadcast media; multiple TV channels exist for each community; additionally, in excess of 90% of households are connected to cable and can access broadcasts of TV stations from neighboring countries; each community has a public radio network coexisting with private broadcasters

Internet country code: .be

Internet users: *total:* 10.92 million (2021 est.)
percent of population: 91% (2021 est.)
comparison ranking: total 57

Broadband - fixed subscriptions: *total:* 4,734,210 (2020 est.)
subscriptions per 100 inhabitants: 41 (2020 est.)
comparison ranking: total 34

TRANSPORTATION

National air transport system: *number of registered air carriers:* 7 (2020)
inventory of registered aircraft operated by air carriers: 117
annual passenger traffic on registered air carriers: 13,639,487 (2018)
annual freight traffic on registered air carriers: 1,285,340,000 (2018) mt-km

Civil aircraft registration country code prefix: OO

Airports: 49 (2024)
comparison ranking: 88

Heliports: 108 (2024)

Pipelines: 3,139 km gas, 154 km oil, 535 km refined products (2013)

Railways: *total:* 3,602 km (2020) 3,160 km electrified
comparison ranking: total 54

Roadways: *total:* 118,414 km
paved: 118,414 km (2015) (includes 1,747 km of expressways)
comparison ranking: total 42

Waterways: 2,043 km (2012) (1,528 km in regular commercial use)
comparison ranking: 43

Merchant marine: *total:* 198 (2023)
by type: bulk carrier 17, container ship 2, general cargo 16, oil tanker 21, other 142
comparison ranking: total 68

Ports: *total ports:* 7 (2024)
large: 1
medium: 2
small: 2
very small: 2
ports with oil terminals: 5
key ports: Antwerpen, Bruxelles, Ghent, Oostende, Zeebrugge

MILITARY AND SECURITY

Military and security forces: Belgian Armed Forces (Defensie or La Défense): Land Component, Marine (Naval) Component, Air Component, Medical Component (2024)
note: the Belgian Federal Police is the national police force and responsible for internal security and nationwide law and order, including migration and border enforcement; the force reports to the ministers of interior and justice

Military expenditures: 1.3% of GDP (2024 est.)
1.2% of GDP (2023)
1.2% of GDP (2022)
1.1% of GDP (2021)
1% of GDP (2020)
comparison ranking: 107

Military and security service personnel strengths: approximately 23,000 active-duty personnel (10,000 Land Component; 1,500 Marine Component; 5,000 Air Force Component; 1,500 Medical Component; 5,000 other, including joint staff, support, and training schools) (2024)

Military equipment inventories and acquisitions: the armed forces have a mix of weapons systems from European countries, Israel, and the US; Belgium has an export-focused defense industry that focuses on components and subcontracting (2024)

Military service age and obligation: 18 years of age for voluntary military service for men and women; conscription abolished in 1995 (2024)
note 1: in 2024, women comprised about 11% of the military's full-time personnel
note 2: foreign nationals 18-34 years of age who speak Dutch or French and are citizens of EU countries, Iceland, Lichtenstein, Norway, and Switzerland may apply to join the military

Military deployments: has about 1,000 personnel deployed on foreign missions, including more than 300 ground forces deployed in Eastern Europe, as well as air and naval assets, supporting NATO missions for the defense of NATO's eastern flank (2024)

Military - note: the Belgian military is a small, all-volunteer force equipped with modern Western equipment; its responsibilities include territorial defense, humanitarian/disaster relief, assistance to the police if required, international peacekeeping missions, and support to its NATO and EU security commitments, which Belgium considers vital components of its national security policy; outside of the country, the military operates almost always within an international organization or a coalition, such as its ongoing deployments to Africa for the EU and UN, eastern Europe as part of NATO's Enhanced Forward Presence mission, and the Middle East with an international coalition to combat the Islamic State of Iraq and ash-Sham; Belgium was one of the original 12 countries to sign the North Atlantic Treaty (also known as the Washington Treaty) establishing NATO in 1949; it hosts the NATO headquarters in Brussels; Belgium also cooperates with neighboring countries, such as Luxembourg and the Netherlands, in conducting joint patrols of their respective air spaces and in a composite combined special operations command with Denmark and the Netherlands (2024)

SPACE

Space agency/agencies: Royal Belgian Institute for Space Aeronomy-Interfederal Space Agency of Belgium (BIRA-IASB; established 1964; IASB added 2017); Belgium Federal Science Policy Office (BELSPO) (2024)

Space program overview: founding member of the European Space Agency (ESA), which acts as the de facto Belgian space agency as most programs are carried out under the ESA or bi-laterally with its member states; builds satellites, particularly research/ science/technology and remote sensing (RS) platforms; also researches, develops, and produces a wide variety of other space technologies, including telecommunications, optics, robotics, scientific instruments, and space launch vehicle (SLV) components; supports the ESA's SLV program with economic assistance (6% of the funding for the Ariane-5 SLV, for example), as well as legal, scientific, and technological expertise; hosts the European Space Security and Education Center (established 1968); participates in international astronomy efforts, particularly through the European Southern Observatory (ESO); participates in multiple ESA and EU space-related programs and research efforts; in addition to the ESA and EU and their individual country members, has cooperated with a variety foreign space agencies and commercial entities, including those of Argentina, China, India, Russia, South Africa, UAE, Vietnam, and the US (2024)
note: further details about the key activities, programs, and milestones of the country's space program, as well as government spending estimates on the space sector, appear in the Space Programs reference guide

TERRORISM

Terrorist group(s): Islamic Revolutionary Guard Corps/Qods Force; Islamic State of Iraq and ash-Sham (ISIS)
note: details about the history, aims, leadership, organization, areas of operation, tactics, targets, weapons, size, and sources of support of the group(s) appear(s) in the Terrorism reference guide

TRANSNATIONAL ISSUES

Refugees and internally displaced persons: *refugees (country of origin):* 20,086 (Syria), 7,049 (Afghanistan), 5,769 (Iraq) (mid-year 2022); 75,030 (Ukraine) (as of 29 February 2024)
stateless persons: 1,190 (2022)

Illicit drugs: a transit point for precursor chemicals from China and India destined for clandestine synthetic drug laboratories in the Netherlands and to some labs in Belgium; a primary entry point for cocaine into Europe; one of the top methamphetamine producers in Europe; a major source of precursor or essential chemicals used in the production of illicit narcotics

BELIZE

INTRODUCTION

Background: Belize was the site of several Mayan city states until their decline at the end of the first millennium A.D. The British and Spanish disputed the region in the 17th and 18th centuries; it formally became the colony of British Honduras in 1862. Territorial disputes between the UK and Guatemala delayed the independence of Belize until 1981. Guatemala refused to recognize the new nation until 1992, and the two countries are still involved in an ongoing border dispute. Tourism has become the mainstay of the economy. Current concerns include the country's heavy foreign debt burden, high crime rates, high unemployment combined with a majority youth population, growing involvement in the Mexican and South American drug trade, and one of the highest HIV/AIDS prevalence rates in Central America.

GEOGRAPHY

Location: Central America, bordering the Caribbean Sea, between Guatemala and Mexico

Geographic coordinates: 17 15 N, 88 45 W

Map references: Central America and the Caribbean

Area: *total:* 22,966 sq km
land: 22,806 sq km
water: 160 sq km
comparison ranking: total 151

Area - comparative: slightly smaller than Massachusetts

Land boundaries: *total:* 542 km
border countries (2): Guatemala 266 km; Mexico 276 km

Coastline: 386 km

Maritime claims: *territorial sea:* 12 nm in the north, 3 nm in the south; note - from the mouth of the Sarstoon River to Ranguana Cay, Belize's territorial sea is 3 nm; according to Belize's Maritime Areas Act, 1992, the purpose of this limitation is to provide a framework for negotiating a definitive agreement on territorial differences with Guatemala
exclusive economic zone: 200 nm

Climate: tropical; very hot and humid; rainy season (May to November); dry season (February to May)

Terrain: flat, swampy coastal plain; low mountains in south

Elevation: *highest point:* Doyle's Delight 1,124 m
lowest point: Caribbean Sea 0 m
mean elevation: 173 m

Natural resources: arable land potential, timber, fish, hydropower

Land use: *agricultural land:* 6.9% (2018 est.)
arable land: 3.3% (2018 est.)
permanent crops: 1.4% (2018 est.)
permanent pasture: 2.2% (2018 est.)
forest: 60.6% (2018 est.)
other: 32.5% (2018 est.)

Irrigated land: 35 sq km (2012)

Population distribution: approximately 25% to 30% of the population lives in the former capital, Belize City; over half of the overall population is rural; population density is slightly higher in the north and east

Natural hazards: frequent, devastating hurricanes (June to November) and coastal flooding (especially in south)

Geography - note: only country in Central America without a coastline on the North Pacific Ocean

PEOPLE AND SOCIETY

Population: *total:* 415,789
male: 205,895
female: 209,894 (2024 est.)
comparison rankings: female 176; male 175; total 175

Nationality: *noun:* Belizean(s)
adjective: Belizean

Ethnic groups: Mestizo 52.9%, Creole 25.9%, Maya 11.3%, Garifuna 6.1%, East Indian 3.9%, Mennonite 3.6%, White 1.2%, Asian 1%, other 1.2%, unknown 0.3% (2010 est.)
note: percentages add up to more than 100% because respondents were able to identify more than one ethnic origin

Languages: English 62.9% (official), Spanish 56.6%, Creole 44.6%, Maya 10.5%, German 3.2%, Garifuna 2.9%, other 1.8%, unknown 0.5% (2010 est.)
major-language sample(s):
La Libreta Informativa del Mundo, la fuente indispensable de información básica. (Spanish)
note: shares sum to more than 100% because some respondents gave more than one answer on the census

Religions: Roman Catholic 40.1%, Protestant 31.5% (includes Pentecostal 8.4%, Seventh Day Adventist 5.4%, Anglican 4.7%, Mennonite 3.7%, Baptist 3.6%, Methodist 2.9%, Nazarene 2.8%), Jehovah's Witness 1.7%, other 10.5% (includes Baha'i, Buddhist, Hindu, Church of Jesus Christ, Muslim, Rastafarian, Salvation Army), unspecified 0.6%, none 15.5% (2010 est.)

Demographic profile: Migration continues to transform Belize's population. About 16% of Belizeans live abroad, while immigrants constitute approximately 15% of Belize's population. Belizeans seeking job and educational opportunities have preferred to emigrate to the United States rather than former colonizer Great Britain because of the United States' closer proximity and stronger trade ties with Belize. Belizeans also emigrate to Canada, Mexico, and English-speaking Caribbean countries. The emigration of a large share of Creoles (Afro-Belizeans) and the influx of Central American immigrants, mainly Guatemalans, Salvadorans, and Hondurans, has changed Belize's ethnic composition. Mestizos have become the largest ethnic group, and Belize now has more native Spanish speakers than English or Creole speakers, despite English being the official language. In addition, Central American immigrants are establishing new communities in rural areas, which contrasts with the urbanization trend seen in neighboring countries. Recently, Chinese, European, and North American immigrants have become more frequent.
Immigration accounts for an increasing share of Belize's population growth rate, which is steadily falling due to fertility decline. Belize's declining birth rate and its increased life expectancy are creating an aging population. As the elderly population grows and nuclear families replace extended households, Belize's government will be challenged to balance a rising demand for pensions, social services, and healthcare for its senior citizens with the need to reduce poverty and social inequality and to improve sanitation.

Age structure: *0-14 years:* 27.7% (male 58,529/female 56,811)
15-64 years: 66.7% (male 135,903/female 141,503)
65 years and over: 5.5% (2024 est.) (male 11,463/female 11,580)

Dependency ratios: *total dependency ratio:* 49.7
youth dependency ratio: 42.3
elderly dependency ratio: 7.4
potential support ratio: 13.5 (2021 est.)

Median age: *total:* 26.8 years (2024 est.)
male: 26.4 years
female: 27.2 years
comparison ranking: total 162

Population growth rate: 1.47% (2024 est.)
comparison ranking: 67

Birth rate: 17.7 births/1,000 population (2024 est.)
comparison ranking: 81

Death rate: 5 deaths/1,000 population (2024 est.)
comparison ranking: 194

Net migration rate: 2 migrant(s)/1,000 population (2024 est.)
comparison ranking: 50

Population distribution: approximately 25% to 30% of the population lives in the former capital, Belize City; over half of the overall population is rural; population density is slightly higher in the north and east

Urbanization: *urban population:* 46.6% of total population (2023)
rate of urbanization: 2.3% annual rate of change (2020-25 est.)

Major urban areas - population: 23,000 BELMOPAN (capital) (2018)

Sex ratio: *at birth:* 1.05 male(s)/female
0-14 years: 1.03 male(s)/female

15-64 years: 0.96 male(s)/female
65 years and over: 0.99 male(s)/female
total population: 0.98 male(s)/female (2024 est.)

Maternal mortality ratio: 130 deaths/100,000 live births (2020 est.)
comparison ranking: 57

Infant mortality rate: *total:* 11.3 deaths/1,000 live births (2024 est.)
male: 12.4 deaths/1,000 live births
female: 10.1 deaths/1,000 live births
comparison ranking: total 120

Life expectancy at birth: *total population:* 74.3 years (2024 est.)
male: 72.6 years
female: 76.1 years
comparison ranking: total population 143

Total fertility rate: 2.05 children born/woman (2024 est.)
comparison ranking: 100

Gross reproduction rate: 1 (2024 est.)

Contraceptive prevalence rate: 51.4% (2015/16)

Drinking water source: *improved: urban:* 100% of population
rural: 99.4% of population
total: 99.7% of population
unimproved: urban: 0% of population
rural: 0.6% of population
total: 0.3% of population (2020 est.)

Current health expenditure: 6.9% of GDP (2020)

Physician density: 1.08 physicians/1,000 population (2018)

Hospital bed density: 1 beds/1,000 population (2017)

Sanitation facility access: *improved: urban:* 99.1% of population
rural: 95.7% of population
total: 97.3% of population
unimproved: urban: 0.9% of population
rural: 4.3% of population
total: 2.7% of population (2020 est.)

Obesity - adult prevalence rate: 24.1% (2016)
comparison ranking: 60

Alcohol consumption per capita: *total:* 5.93 liters of pure alcohol (2019 est.)
beer: 3.88 liters of pure alcohol (2019 est.)
wine: 0.68 liters of pure alcohol (2019 est.)
spirits: 1.19 liters of pure alcohol (2019 est.)
other alcohols: 0.17 liters of pure alcohol (2019 est.)
comparison ranking: total 72

Tobacco use: *total:* 8.5% (2020 est.)
male: 15.1% (2020 est.)
female: 1.8% (2020 est.)
comparison ranking: total 142

Children under the age of 5 years underweight: 4.6% (2015/16)
comparison ranking: 76

Currently married women (ages 15-49): 64.3% (2023 est.)

Child marriage: *women married by age 15:* 6.3%
women married by age 18: 33.5%
men married by age 18: 22.2% (2016 est.)

Education expenditures: 8.7% of GDP (2021 est.)
comparison ranking: 9

Literacy: *total population:* NA
male: NA
female: NA

School life expectancy (primary to tertiary education): *total:* 13 years
male: 12 years
female: 13 years (2021)

ENVIRONMENT

Environment - current issues: deforestation; water pollution, including pollution of Belize's Barrier Reef System, from sewage, industrial effluents, agricultural runoff; inability to properly dispose of solid waste

Environment - international agreements: *party to:* Biodiversity, Climate Change, Climate Change-Kyoto Protocol, Climate Change-Paris Agreement, Comprehensive Nuclear Test Ban, Desertification, Endangered Species, Hazardous Wastes, Law of the Sea, Ozone Layer Protection, Ship Pollution, Wetlands, Whaling
signed, but not ratified: none of the selected agreements

Climate: tropical; very hot and humid; rainy season (May to November); dry season (February to May)

Urbanization: *urban population:* 46.6% of total population (2023)
rate of urbanization: 2.3% annual rate of change (2020-25 est.)

Revenue from forest resources: 0.31% of GDP (2018 est.)
comparison ranking: 79

Revenue from coal: 0% of GDP (2018 est.)
comparison ranking: 107

Air pollutants: *particulate matter emissions:* 10.51 micrograms per cubic meter (2019 est.)
carbon dioxide emissions: 0.57 megatons (2016 est.)
methane emissions: 0.55 megatons (2020 est.)

Waste and recycling: *municipal solid waste generated annually:* 101,379 tons (2015 est.)

Total water withdrawal: *municipal:* 10 million cubic meters (2020 est.)
industrial: 20 million cubic meters (2020 est.)
agricultural: 70 million cubic meters (2020 est.)

Total renewable water resources: 21.73 billion cubic meters (2020 est.)

GOVERNMENT

Country name: *conventional long form:* none
conventional short form: Belize
former: British Honduras
etymology: may be named for the Belize River, whose name possibly derives from the Maya word "belix," meaning "muddy-watered"

Government type: parliamentary democracy (National Assembly) under a constitutional monarchy; a Commonwealth realm

Capital: *name:* Belmopan
geographic coordinates: 17 15 N, 88 46 W
time difference: UTC-6 (1 hour behind Washington, DC, during Standard Time)
etymology: the decision to move the capital of the country inland to higher and more stable land was made in the 1960s; the name chosen for the new city was formed from the union of two words: "Belize," the name of the longest river in the country, and "Mopan," one of the rivers in the area of the new capital that empties into the Belize River

Administrative divisions: 6 districts; Belize, Cayo, Corozal, Orange Walk, Stann Creek, Toledo

Independence: 21 September 1981 (from the UK)

National holiday: Battle of St. George's Caye Day (National Day), 10 September (1798); Independence Day, 21 September (1981)

Legal system: English common law

Constitution: *history:* previous 1954, 1963 (preindependence); latest signed and entered into force 21 September 1981; note - in July 2022, the government introduced a bill to establish the People's Constitutional Commission to review the constitution and to provide recommendations to the National Assembly
amendments: proposed and adopted by two-thirds majority vote of the National Assembly House of Representatives except for amendments relating to rights and freedoms, changes to the Assembly, and to elections and judiciary matters, which require at least three-quarters majority vote of the House; both types of amendments require assent of the governor general; amended several times, last in 2017

International law organization participation: has not submitted an ICJ jurisdiction declaration; accepts ICCt jurisdiction

Citizenship: *citizenship by birth:* yes
citizenship by descent only: yes
dual citizenship recognized: yes
residency requirement for naturalization: 5 years

Suffrage: 18 years of age; universal

Executive branch: *chief of state:* King CHARLES III (since 8 September 2022); represented by Governor-General Froyla TZALAM (since 27 May 2021)
head of government: Prime Minister John BRICEÑO (since 12 November 2020)
cabinet: Cabinet appointed by the governor general on the advice of the prime minister from among members of the National Assembly
elections/appointments: the monarchy is hereditary; governor-general appointed by the monarch; following legislative elections, the leader of the majority party or majority coalition usually appointed prime minister by the governor-general; prime minister recommends the deputy prime minister

Legislative branch: *description:* bicameral National Assembly consists of:
Senate (14 seats, including the president); members appointed by the governor-general - 6 on the advice of the prime minister, 3 on the advice of the leader of the opposition, and 1 each on the advice of the Belize Council of Churches and Evangelical Association of Churches, the Belize Chamber of Commerce and Industry and the Belize Better Business Bureau, non-governmental organizations in good standing, and the National Trade Union Congress and the Civil Society Steering Committee; 1 seat is held by the Senate president elected from among the Senate members or from outside the Senate; members serve 5-year terms
House of Representatives (32 seats; 31 members directly elected in single-seat constituencies by simple majority vote and the speaker, who may be designated from outside the government; members serve 5-year terms and the speaker serves at the pleasure of the government up to the full 5-year term)
elections: Senate - last appointed 11 November 2020 (next appointments in November 2025)

House of Representatives - last held on 11 November 2020 (next to be held in November 2025)
election results: Senate - all members appointed; composition - men 8, women 6, percentage women 42.9%
House of Representatives - percent of vote by party - PUP 59.6%, UDP 38.8%, other 1.6%; seats by party - PUP 26, UDP 5; composition - men 27, women 5, percentage women 15.6%; total percentage women in the National Assembly 23.9%

Judicial branch: *highest court(s):* Supreme Court of Judicature (consists of the Court of Appeal with the court president and 3 justices, and the Supreme Court with the chief justice and 10 justices); note - in 2010, Belize acceded to the Caribbean Court of Justice as the final court of appeal, replacing that of the Judicial Committee of the Privy Council in London
judge selection and term of office: Court of Appeal president and justices appointed by the governor-general upon advice of the prime minister after consultation with the National Assembly opposition leader; justices' tenures vary by terms of appointment; Supreme Court chief justice appointed by the governor-general upon the advice of the prime minister and the National Assembly opposition leader; other judges appointed by the governor-general upon the advice of the Judicial and Legal Services Section of the Public Services Commission and with the concurrence of the prime minister after consultation with the National Assembly opposition leader; judges can be appointed beyond age 65 but must retire by age 75; in 2013, the Supreme Court chief justice overturned a constitutional amendment that had restricted Court of Appeal judge appointments to as short as 1 year
subordinate courts: Magistrates' Courts; Family Court

Political parties: Belize People's Front or BPF
Belize Progressive Party or BPP (formed in 2015 from a merger of the People's National Party, elements of the Vision Inspired by the People, and other smaller political groups)
People's United Party or PUP
United Democratic Party or UDP
Vision Inspired by the People or VIP

International organization participation: ACP, ACS, AOSIS, C, Caricom, CD, CDB, CELAC, FAO, G-77, IADB, IAEA, IBRD, ICAO, ICC (NGOs), ICRM, IDA, IFAD, IFC, IFRCS, ILO, IMF, IMO, Interpol, IOC, IOM, ITU, LAES, MIGA, NAM, OAS, OPANAL, OPCW, PCA, Petrocaribe, SICA, UN, UNCTAD, UNESCO, UNIDO, UPU, WCO, WHO, WIPO, WMO, WTO

Diplomatic representation in the US: *chief of mission:* Ambassador Lynn Raymond YOUNG (since 7 July 2021)
chancery: 2535 Massachusetts Avenue NW, Washington, DC 20008-2826
telephone: [1] (202) 332-9636
FAX: [1] (202) 332-6888
email address and website:
reception.usa@mfa.gov.bz
https://www.belizeembassyusa.mfa.gov.bz/
consulate(s) general: Chicago, Los Angeles, Miami, New York

Diplomatic representation from the US: *chief of mission:* Ambassador Michelle KWAN (since 5 December 2022)
embassy: 4 Floral Park Road, Belmopan, Cayo
mailing address: 3050 Belmopan Place, Washington DC 20521-3050
telephone: (501) 822-4011
FAX: (501) 822-4012
email address and website:
ACSBelize@state.gov
https://bz.usembassy.gov/

Flag description: *royal blue with a narrow red stripe along the top and the bottom edges; centered is a large white disk bearing the coat of arms; the coat of arms features a shield flanked by two workers in front of a mahogany tree with the related motto SUB UMBRA FLOREO (I Flourish in the Shade) on a scroll at the bottom, all encircled by a green garland of 50 mahogany leaves; the colors are those of the two main political parties:* blue for the PUP and red for the UDP; various elements of the coat of arms - the figures, the tools, the mahogany tree, and the garland of leaves - recall the logging industry that led to British settlement of Belize
note: Belize's flag is the only national flag that depicts human beings; two British overseas territories, Montserrat and the British Virgin Islands, also depict humans

National symbol(s): Baird's tapir (a large, browsing, forest-dwelling mammal), keel-billed toucan, Black Orchid; national colors: red, blue

National anthem: *name:* Land of the Free
lyrics/music: Samuel Alfred HAYNES/Selwyn Walford YOUNG
note: adopted 1981; as a Commonwealth country, in addition to the national anthem, "God Save the King" serves as the royal anthem (see United Kingdom)

National heritage: *total World Heritage Sites:* 1 (natural)
selected World Heritage Site locales: Belize Barrier Reef Reserve System

ECONOMY

Economic overview: tourism- and agriculture-driven economy; strong post-pandemic rebound; innovative and ecological bond restructuring that significantly lowered public debt and expanded marine protections; central bank offering USD-denominated treasury notes; high mobility across borders

Real GDP (purchasing power parity): $5.257 billion (2023 est.)
$5.028 billion (2022 est.)
$4.624 billion (2021 est.)
note: data in 2021 dollars
comparison ranking: 182

Real GDP growth rate: 4.54% (2023 est.)
8.73% (2022 est.)
17.86% (2021 est.)
note: annual GDP % growth based on constant local currency
comparison ranking: 66

Real GDP per capita: $12,800 (2023 est.)
$12,400 (2022 est.)
$11,600 (2021 est.)
note: data in 2021 dollars
comparison ranking: 134

GDP (official exchange rate): $3.282 billion (2023 est.)
note: data in current dollars at official exchange rate

Inflation rate (consumer prices): 4.39% (2023 est.)
6.28% (2022 est.)
3.24% (2021 est.)
note: annual % change based on consumer prices
comparison ranking: 94

Credit ratings: Moody's rating: Caa3 (2020)

Standard & Poors rating: CCC+ (2020)
note: The year refers to the year in which the current credit rating was first obtained.

GDP - composition, by sector of origin: *agriculture:* 9% (2023 est.)
industry: 13.2% (2023 est.)
services: 63% (2023 est.)
note: figures may not total 100% due to non-allocated consumption not captured in sector-reported data
comparison rankings: services 68; industry 174; agriculture 84

GDP - composition, by end use: *household consumption:* 56.8% (2023 est.)
government consumption: 16.1% (2023 est.)
investment in fixed capital: 20.5% (2023 est.)
investment in inventories: 0.7% (2023 est.)
exports of goods and services: 53.6% (2023 est.)
imports of goods and services: -52.9% (2023 est.)
note: figures may not total 100% due to rounding or gaps in data collection

Agricultural products: sugarcane, maize, bananas, oranges, soybeans, sorghum, chicken, rice, beans, milk (2022)
note: top ten agricultural products based on tonnage

Industries: garment production, food processing, tourism, construction, oil

Industrial production growth rate: -4.52% (2023 est.)
note: annual % change in industrial value added based on constant local currency
comparison ranking: 197

Labor force: 190,000 (2023 est.)
note: number of people ages 15 or older who are employed or seeking work
comparison ranking: 178

Unemployment rate: 8.26% (2023 est.)
8.72% (2022 est.)
10.16% (2021 est.)
note: % of labor force seeking employment
comparison ranking: 148

Youth unemployment rate (ages 15-24): *total:* 17.4% (2023 est.)
male: 12.1% (2023 est.)
female: 26.2% (2023 est.)
note: % of labor force ages 15-24 seeking employment
comparison ranking: total 81

Remittances: 4.63% of GDP (2023 est.)
5.03% of GDP (2022 est.)
5.58% of GDP (2021 est.)
note: personal transfers and compensation between resident and non-resident individuals/households/entities

Budget: *revenues:* $554.405 million (2017 est.)
expenditures: $506.316 million (2017 est.)
note: central government revenues and expenses (excluding grants/extrabudgetary units/social security funds) converted to US dollars at average official exchange rate for year indicated

Public debt: 99% of GDP (2017 est.)
note: central government debt as a % of GDP
comparison ranking: 20

Taxes and other revenues: 21.34% (of GDP) (2017 est.)
note: central government tax revenue as a % of GDP
comparison ranking: 75

Current account balance: -$90.63 million (2023 est.)
-$235.566 million (2022 est.)
-$157.868 million (2021 est.)
note: balance of payments - net trade and primary/secondary income in current dollars comparison ranking: 95

Exports: $1.462 billion (2023 est.)
$1.369 billion (2022 est.)
$1.043 billion (2021 est.)
note: balance of payments - exports of goods and services in current dollars
comparison ranking: 171

Exports - partners: US 22%, UK 16%, Guatemala 10%, Spain 7%, Honduras 5% (2022)
note: top five export partners based on percentage share of exports

Exports - commodities: raw sugar, bananas, shellfish, bran, refined petroleum (2022)
note: top five export commodities based on value in dollars

Imports: $1.571 billion (2023 est.)
$1.574 billion (2022 est.)
$1.249 billion (2021 est.)
note: balance of payments - imports of goods and services in current dollars
comparison ranking: 184

Imports - partners: US 33%, China 23%, Guatemala 9%, Mexico 8%, Canada 3% (2022)
note: top five import partners based on percentage share of imports

Imports - commodities: refined petroleum, ships, tobacco, garments, plastic products (2022)
note: top five import commodities based on value in dollars

Reserves of foreign exchange and gold: $473.729 million (2023 est.)
$482.146 million (2022 est.)
$420.103 million (2021 est.)
note: holdings of gold (year-end prices)/foreign exchange/special drawing rights in current dollars
comparison ranking: 173

Debt - external: $1.176 billion (2022 est.)
note: present value of external debt in current US dollars
comparison ranking: 80

Exchange rates: Belizean dollars (BZD) per US dollar -

Exchange rates: 2 (2023 est.)
2 (2022 est.)
2 (2021 est.)
2 (2020 est.)
2 (2019 est.)

ENERGY

Electricity access: *electrification - total population:* 98.6% (2022 est.)
electrification - urban areas: 98.4%
electrification - rural areas: 97.1%

Electricity: *installed generating capacity:* 217,000 kW (2022 est.)
consumption: 443.175 million kWh (2022 est.)
imports: 283.8 million kWh (2022 est.)
transmission/distribution losses: 143.637 million kWh (2022 est.)
comparison rankings: transmission/distribution losses 56; imports 103; consumption 175; installed generating capacity 171

Electricity generation sources: *fossil fuels:* 18.7% of total installed capacity (2022 est.)
solar: 3.6% of total installed capacity (2022 est.)
hydroelectricity: 26.4% of total installed capacity (2022 est.)
biomass and waste: 51.3% of total installed capacity (2022 est.)

Coal: *imports:* (2022 est.) less than 1 metric ton

Petroleum: *total petroleum production:* 800 bbl/day (2023 est.)
refined petroleum consumption: 5,000 bbl/day (2022 est.)
crude oil estimated reserves: 6.7 million barrels (2021 est.)

Carbon dioxide emissions: 690,000 metric tonnes of CO_2 (2022 est.)
from petroleum and other liquids: 690,000 metric tonnes of CO_2 (2022 est.)
comparison ranking: total emissions 180

Energy consumption per capita: 30.71 million Btu/person (2022 est.)
comparison ranking: 114

COMMUNICATIONS

Telephones - fixed lines: *total subscriptions:* 19,000 (2021 est.)
subscriptions per 100 inhabitants: 5 (2021 est.)
comparison ranking: total subscriptions 176

Telephones - mobile cellular: *total subscriptions:* 264,000 (2021 est.)
subscriptions per 100 inhabitants: 66 (2021 est.)
comparison ranking: total subscriptions 180

Telecommunication systems: *general assessment:* Belize's fixed-line teledensity and mobile penetration remain lower than average for the region, a legacy of insufficient market competition and under investment in telecoms services; a significant investment in infrastructure, launching an LTE-A service at the end of 2016 and in mid-2017 completing a submarine cable to Ambergris Caye, enabling it to launch an FttP service in San Pedro; the nfrastructure has been updated from the legacy copper to fiber; investments have been made to provide high speed broadband to 80% of residences across Belize. (2021)
domestic: roughly 5 per 100 fixed-line and mobile-cellular teledensity of 66 per 100 persons; mobile sector accounting for over 90% of all phone subscriptions (2021)
international: country code - 501; landing points for the ARCOS and SEUL fiber-optic telecommunications submarine cable that provides links to South and Central America, parts of the Caribbean, and the US; satellite earth station - 8 (Intelsat - 2, unknown - 6) (2019)

Broadcast media: 8 privately owned TV stations; multi-channel cable TV provides access to foreign stations; about 25 radio stations broadcasting on roughly 50 different frequencies; state-run radio was privatized in 1998 (2019)

Internet country code: .bz

Internet users: *total:* 248,000 (2021 est.)
percent of population: 62% (2021 est.)
comparison ranking: total 176

Broadband - fixed subscriptions: *total:* 36,000 (2020 est.)
subscriptions per 100 inhabitants: 9 (2020 est.)
comparison ranking: total 147

TRANSPORTATION

National air transport system: *number of registered air carriers:* 2 (2020)
inventory of registered aircraft operated by air carriers: 28
annual passenger traffic on registered air carriers: 1,297,533 (2018)
annual freight traffic on registered air carriers: 3.78 million (2018) mt-km

Civil aircraft registration country code prefix: V3

Airports: 27 (2024)
comparison ranking: 124

Heliports: 5 (2024)

Roadways: *total:* 3,281 km
paved: 601 km
unpaved: 2,680 km (2017)
comparison ranking: total 161

Waterways: 825 km (2011) (navigable only by small craft)
comparison ranking: 77

Merchant marine: *total:* 774 (2023)
by type: bulk carrier 49, general cargo 410, oil tanker 64, other 251
comparison ranking: total 31

Ports: *total ports:* 2 (2024)
large: 0
medium: 0
small: 1
very small: 0
size unknown: 1
ports with oil terminals: 1
key ports: Belize City, Big Creek

MILITARY AND SECURITY

Military and security forces: Belize Defense Force (BDF): Army, Air Wing; Belize Coast Guard; Belize Police Department (2024)
note: the Ministry of National Defense and Border Security is responsible for oversight of the BDF and the Coast Guard, while the Ministry of Home Affairs and New Growth Industries has responsibility for the Belize Police Department and prisons; the Police Department is primarily responsible for internal security

Military expenditures: 0.9% of GDP (2023 est.)
1.1% of GDP (2022 est.)
1.3% of GDP (2021 est.)
1.5% of GDP (2020 est.)
1.4% of GDP (2019 est.)
comparison ranking: 134

Military and security service personnel strengths: approximately 1,500 BDF personnel; approximately 500 Coast Guard (2023)

Military equipment inventories and acquisitions: the military has a light inventory consisting mostly of UK- and US-origin equipment (2024)

Military service age and obligation: 18 years of age for voluntary military service; laws allow for conscription only if volunteers are insufficient, but conscription has never been implemented; initial service obligation is 12 years (2024)

Military - note: the Belize Defense Force (BDF) is responsible for external security but also provides some support to civilian authorities; it has limited powers of arrest within land and shoreline areas, while the Coast Guard has arrest powers and jurisdiction within coastal and maritime areas; the BDF traces its history back to the Prince Regent Royal Honduras Militia, a volunteer force established in 1817; the BDF was established in 1978 from the disbanded Police Special Force and the Belize Volunteer Guard to assist the resident British forces with the defense of Belize against Guatemala

the British Army has maintained a presence in Belize since its independence; the presence consists of a small training support unit that provides jungle training to troops from the UK and international partners (2024)

TRANSNATIONAL ISSUES

Illicit drugs: a significant drug trafficking and transit point between countries in South America and the United States; primary domestic use of narcotics is marijuana and some crack cocaine; a major source of precursor or essential chemicals used in the production of illicit narcotics

BENIN

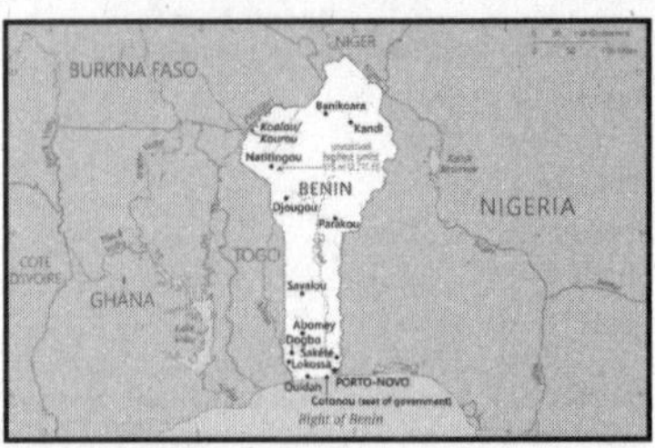

INTRODUCTION

Background: Present-day Benin is comprised of about 42 ethnic groups, including the Yoruba in the southeast, who migrated from what is now Nigeria in the 12th century; the Dendi in the north-central area, who came from Mali in the 16th century; the Bariba and the Fula in the northeast; the Ottamari in the Atakora mountains; the Fon in the area around Abomey in the south-central area; and the Mina, Xueda, and Aja, who came from Togo, on the coast. The Kingdom of Dahomey emerged on the Abomey plateau in the 17th century and was a regional power for much of the 18th and 19th centuries. The growth of Dahomey coincided with the growth of the Atlantic slave trade, and it became known as a major source of enslaved people. France began to control the coastal areas of Dahomey in the second half of the 19th century; the entire kingdom was conquered by 1894. French Dahomey achieved independence in 1960, and it changed its name to the Republic of Benin in 1975.

A succession of military governments ended in 1972 with the rise to power of Mathieu KEREKOU and a Marxist-Leninist government. A move to representative government began in 1989. Two years later, free elections ushered in former Prime Minister Nicephore SOGLO as president, marking the first successful transfer of power in Africa from a dictatorship to a democracy. KEREKOU returned to power after elections in 1996 and 2001. He stepped down in 2006 and was succeeded by Thomas YAYI Boni, a political outsider and independent, who won a second term in 2011. Patrice TALON, a wealthy businessman, took office in 2016; the space for pluralism, dissent, and free expression has narrowed under his administration. TALON won a second term in 2021.

GEOGRAPHY

Location: Western Africa, bordering the Bight of Benin, between Nigeria and Togo

Geographic coordinates: 9 30 N, 2 15 E

Map references: Africa

Area: *total:* 112,622 sq km
land: 110,622 sq km
water: 2,000 sq km
comparison ranking: total 102

Area - comparative: slightly smaller than Pennsylvania

Land boundaries: *total:* 2,123 km
border countries (4): Burkina Faso 386 km; Niger 277 km; Nigeria 809 km; Togo 651 km

Coastline: 121 km

Maritime claims: *territorial sea:* 200 nm; note: the US does not recognize this claim
continental shelf: 200 nm
exclusive fishing zone: 200 nm

Climate: tropical; hot, humid in south; semiarid in north

Terrain: mostly flat to undulating plain; some hills and low mountains

Elevation: *highest point:* unnamed elevation 675 m; located 2.5 km southeast of the town of Kotopounga
lowest point: Atlantic Ocean 0 m
mean elevation: 273 m

Natural resources: small offshore oil deposits, limestone, marble, timber

Land use: *agricultural land:* 31.3% (2018 est.)
arable land: 22.9% (2018 est.)
permanent crops: 3.5% (2018 est.)
permanent pasture: 4.9% (2018 est.)
forest: 40% (2018 est.)
other: 28.7% (2018 est.)

Irrigated land: 172 sq km (2017)

Major watersheds (area sq km): Atlantic Ocean drainage: Niger (2,261,741 sq km), Volta (410,991 sq km)

Population distribution: the population is primarily located in the south, with the highest concentration of people residing in and around the cities on the Atlantic coast; most of the north remains sparsely populated with higher concentrations of residents in the west as shown in this population distribution map

Natural hazards: hot, dry, dusty harmattan wind may affect north from December to March

Geography - note: sandbanks create difficult access to a coast with no natural harbors, river mouths, or islands

PEOPLE AND SOCIETY

Population: *total:* 14,697,052
male: 7,253,258
female: 7,443,794 (2024 est.)
comparison rankings: female 74; male 74; total 74

Nationality: *noun:* Beninese (singular and plural)
adjective: Beninese

Ethnic groups: Fon and related 38.4%, Adja and related 15.1%, Yoruba and related 12%, Bariba and related 9.6%, Fulani and related 8.6%, Ottamari and related 6.1%, Yoa-Lokpa and related 4.3%, Dendi and related 2.9%, other 0.9%, foreigner 1.9% (2013 est.)

Languages: 55 languages; French (official); Fon (a Gbe language), Yom (a Gur language) and Yoruba are the most important indigenous languages in the south; half a dozen regionally important languages in the north, including Bariba and Fulfulde

Religions: Muslim 27.7%, Roman Catholic 25.5%, Protestant 13.5% (Celestial 6.7%, Methodist 3.4%, other Protestant 3.4%), Vodoun 11.6%, other Christian 9.5%, other traditional religions 2.6%, other 2.6%, none 5.8% (2013 est.)

Demographic profile: Benin has a youthful age structure – almost 65% of the population is under the age of 25 as of 2022 – which is bolstered by high fertility and population growth rates. Benin's total fertility has been falling over time but remains high, declining from almost 7 children per women in 1990 to 5.4 in 2022. Benin's low contraceptive use and high unmet need for contraception contribute to the sustained high fertility rate. Although the majority of Beninese women use skilled health care personnel for antenatal care and delivery, the high rate of maternal mortality indicates the need for more access to high quality obstetric care.

Poverty, unemployment, increased living costs, and dwindling resources increasingly drive the Beninese to migrate. An estimated 4.4 million, more than 30%, of Beninese live abroad. Virtually all Beninese emigrants move to West African countries, particularly Nigeria and Cote d'Ivoire. Of the less than 1% of Beninese emigrants who settle in Europe, the vast majority live in France, Benin's former colonial ruler. With about 40% of the population living below the poverty line as of 2019, many desperate parents resort to sending their children to work in wealthy households as domestic servants (a common practice known as vidomegon), mines, quarries, or agriculture domestically or in Nigeria and other neighboring countries, often under brutal conditions. Unlike in other West African countries, where rural people move to the coast, farmers from Benin's densely populated southern and northwestern regions move to the historically sparsely populated central region to pursue agriculture. Immigrants from West African countries came to Benin in increasing numbers between 1992 and 2002 because of its political stability and porous borders.

Age structure: *0-14 years:* 45.3% (male 3,360,027/ female 3,294,201)
15-64 years: 52.2% (male 3,727,040/female 3,951,786)
65 years and over: 2.5% (2024 est.) (male 166,191/ female 197,807)

Dependency ratios: *total dependency ratio:* 84
youth dependency ratio: 78.3
elderly dependency ratio: 5.7
potential support ratio: 17.7 (2021 est.)

Median age: *total:* 17.2 years (2024 est.)
male: 16.6 years
female: 17.7 years
comparison ranking: total 223

Population growth rate: 3.29% (2024 est.)
comparison ranking: 4

Birth rate: 40.3 births/1,000 population (2024 est.)
comparison ranking: 3

Death rate: 7.6 deaths/1,000 population (2024 est.)
comparison ranking: 97

Net migration rate: 0.2 migrant(s)/1,000 population (2024 est.)
comparison ranking: 75

Population distribution: the population is primarily located in the south, with the highest concentration of people residing in and around the cities on the Atlantic coast; most of the north remains sparsely populated with higher concentrations of residents in the west as shown in this population distribution map

Urbanization: *urban population:* 50.1% of total population (2023)
rate of urbanization: 3.74% annual rate of change (2020-25 est.)

Major urban areas - population: 285,000 PORTO-NOVO (capital) (2018); 1.253 million Abomey-Calavi, 722,000 COTONOU (seat of government) (2022)

Sex ratio: *at birth:* 1.05 male(s)/female
0-14 years: 1.02 male(s)/female
15-64 years: 0.94 male(s)/female
65 years and over: 0.84 male(s)/female
total population: 0.97 male(s)/female (2024 est.)

Mother's mean age at first birth: 20.5 years (2017/18 est.)
note: data represents median age at first birth among women 25-49

Maternal mortality ratio: 523 deaths/100,000 live births (2020 est.)
comparison ranking: 13

Infant mortality rate: *total:* 52.9 deaths/1,000 live births (2024 est.)
male: 57.8 deaths/1,000 live births
female: 47.8 deaths/1,000 live births
comparison ranking: total 16

Life expectancy at birth: *total population:* 63 years (2024 est.)
male: 61.1 years
female: 65 years
comparison ranking: total population 213

Total fertility rate: 5.34 children born/woman (2024 est.)
comparison ranking: 5

Gross reproduction rate: 2.61 (2024 est.)

Contraceptive prevalence rate: 15.5% (2017/18)

Drinking water source: *improved: urban:* 79% of population
rural: 70.8% of population
total: 74.7% of population
unimproved: urban: 21% of population
rural: 29.2% of population
total: 25.3% of population (2020 est.)

Current health expenditure: 2.6% of GDP (2020)

Physician density: 0.07 physicians/1,000 population (2019)

Hospital bed density: 0.5 beds/1,000 population

Sanitation facility access: *improved: urban:* 56.3% of population
rural: 18.1% of population
total: 36.6% of population
unimproved: urban: 43.7% of population
rural: 81.9% of population
total: 63.4% of population (2020 est.)

Obesity - adult prevalence rate: 9.6% (2016)
comparison ranking: 142

Alcohol consumption per capita: *total:* 1.25 liters of pure alcohol (2019 est.)
beer: 0.81 liters of pure alcohol (2019 est.)
wine: 0.02 liters of pure alcohol (2019 est.)
spirits: 0.2 liters of pure alcohol (2019 est.)
other alcohols: 0.22 liters of pure alcohol (2019 est.)
comparison ranking: total 145

Tobacco use: *total:* 6.9% (2020 est.)
male: 11.8% (2020 est.)
female: 1.9% (2020 est.)
comparison ranking: total 157

Children under the age of 5 years underweight: 16.8% (2017/18)
comparison ranking: 28

Currently married women (ages 15-49): 68.3% (2023 est.)

Child marriage: *women married by age 15:* 9.4%
women married by age 18: 30.6%
men married by age 18: 4.8% (2018 est.)

Education expenditures: 3% of GDP (2020 est.)
comparison ranking: 159

Literacy: *definition:* age 15 and over can read and write
total population: 45.8%
male: 56.9%
female: 35% (2021)

School life expectancy (primary to tertiary education): *total:* 11 years
male: 12 years
female: 10 years (2020)

ENVIRONMENT

Environment - current issues: inadequate supplies of potable water; water pollution; poaching threatens wildlife populations; deforestation; desertification (the spread of the desert into agricultural lands in the north is accelerated by regular droughts)

Environment - international agreements: *party to:* Biodiversity, Climate Change, Climate Change-Kyoto Protocol, Climate Change-Paris Agreement, Comprehensive Nuclear Test Ban, Desertification, Endangered Species, Environmental Modification, Hazardous Wastes, Law of the Sea, Marine Dumping-London Convention, Nuclear Test Ban, Ozone Layer Protection, Ship Pollution, Tropical Timber 2006, Wetlands, Whaling
signed, but not ratified: none of the selected agreements

Climate: tropical; hot, humid in south; semiarid in north

Urbanization: *urban population:* 50.1% of total population (2023)
rate of urbanization: 3.74% annual rate of change (2020-25 est.)

Revenue from forest resources: 2.24% of GDP (2018 est.)
comparison ranking: 31

Revenue from coal: 0% of GDP (2018 est.)
comparison ranking: 54

Air pollutants: *particulate matter emissions:* 31.51 micrograms per cubic meter (2019 est.)
carbon dioxide emissions: 6.48 megatons (2016 est.)
methane emissions: 5.8 megatons (2020 est.)

Waste and recycling: *municipal solid waste generated annually:* 685,936 tons (1993 est.)
municipal solid waste recycled annually: 171,484 tons (2005 est.)
percent of municipal solid waste recycled: 25% (2005 est.)

Major watersheds (area sq km): Atlantic Ocean drainage: Niger (2,261,741 sq km), Volta (410,991 sq km)

Total water withdrawal: *municipal:* 150 million cubic meters (2020 est.)
industrial: 30 million cubic meters (2020 est.)
agricultural: 60 million cubic meters (2020 est.)

Total renewable water resources: 26.39 billion cubic meters (2020 est.)

GOVERNMENT

Country name: *conventional long form:* Republic of Benin
conventional short form: Benin
local long form: République du Benin
local short form: Benin
former: Dahomey, People's Republic of Benin
etymology: named for the Bight of Benin, the body of water on which the country lies

Government type: presidential republic

Capital: *name:* Porto-Novo (constitutional capital); Cotonou (seat of government)
geographic coordinates: 6 29 N, 2 37 E
time difference: UTC+1 (6 hours ahead of Washington, DC, during Standard Time)
etymology: the name Porto-Novo is Portuguese for "new port"; Cotonou means "by the river of death" in the native Fon language

Administrative divisions: 12 departments; Alibori, Atacora, Atlantique, Borgou, Collines, Couffo, Donga, Littoral, Mono, Oueme, Plateau, Zou

Independence: 1 August 1960 (from France)

National holiday: Independence Day, 1 August (1960)

Legal system: civil law system modeled largely on the French system and some customary law

Constitution: *history:* previous 1946, 1958 (preindependence); latest adopted by referendum 2 December 1990, promulgated 11 December 1990
amendments: proposed concurrently by the president of the republic (after a decision in the Council of Ministers) and the National Assembly; consideration of drafts or proposals requires at least three-fourths majority vote of the Assembly membership; passage requires approval in a referendum unless approved by at least four-fifths majority vote of the Assembly membership; constitutional articles

affecting territorial sovereignty, the republican form of government, and secularity of Benin cannot be amended; amended 2019

International law organization participation: has not submitted an ICJ jurisdiction declaration; accepts ICCt jurisdiction

Citizenship: *citizenship by birth:* no
citizenship by descent only: at least one parent must be a citizen of Benin
dual citizenship recognized: yes
residency requirement for naturalization: 10 years

Suffrage: 18 years of age; universal

Executive branch: *chief of state:* President Patrice TALON (since 6 April 2016)
head of government: President Patrice TALON
cabinet: Council of Ministers appointed by the president
elections/appointments: president directly elected by absolute majority popular vote in 2 rounds if needed for a 5- year term (eligible for a second term); last held on 11 April 2021 (next to be held on 12 April 2026); note - the president is both head of state and head of government
election results:
2021: Patrice TALON reelected president in the ; percent of vote - Patrice TALON (independent) 86.3%, Alassane SOUMANOU (FCBE) 11.4%, Corentin KOHOUE (The Democrats) 2.3%
2016: Patrice TALON elected president in second round; percent of vote in first round - Lionel ZINSOU (FCBE) 28.4%, Patrice TALON (independent) 24.8%, Sebastien AJAVON (independent) 23%, Abdoulaye Bio TCHANE (ABT) 8.8%, Pascal KOUPAKI (NC) 5.9%, other 9.1%; percent of vote in second round - Patrice TALON 65.4%, Lionel ZINSOU 34.6%

Legislative branch: *description:* unicameral National Assembly or Assemblee Nationale (109 seats; members directly elected in multiseat constituencies by party-list proportional representation vote; members serve 5-year terms except for the current members whose terms will end in 2026 to facilitate general elections)
elections: last held on 8 January 2023 (next to be held on 11 January 2027)
election results: percent of vote by party - Progressive Union for Renewal 37.6%, Bloc Republicain 29.2%, The Democrats 24%; seats by party - Progressive Union for Renewal 53, Bloc Republicain 28, The Democrats 28; composition- men 80, women 29, percentage women 26.6%
note: seat total includes 24 seats reserved for women

Judicial branch: *highest court(s):* Supreme Court or Cour Supreme (consists of the chief justice and 16 justices organized into an administrative division, judicial chamber, and chamber of accounts); Constitutional Court or Cour Constitutionnelle (consists of 7 members, including the court president); High Court of Justice (consists of the Constitutional Court members, 6 members appointed by the National Assembly, and the Supreme Court president); note - jurisdiction of the High Court of Justice is limited to cases of high treason by the national president or members of the government while in office
judge selection and term of office: Supreme Court president and judges appointed by the president of the republic upon the advice of the National Assembly; judges appointed for single renewable 5-year terms; Constitutional Court members - 4 appointed by the National Assembly and 3 by the president of the republic; members appointed for single renewable 5-year terms; other members of the High Court of Justice elected by the National Assembly; member tenure NA
subordinate courts: Court of Appeal or Cour d'Appel; Court for the Repression of Economic and Terrorism Infractions (CRIET) or Cour de Repression des Infractions Economiques et du Terrorisme; district courts; village courts; Assize courts

Political parties: African Movement for Development and Progress or MADEP
Benin Renaissance or RB
Cowrie Force for an Emerging Benin or FCBE
Democratic Renewal Party or PRD
Progressive Union for Renewal
Republican Bloc
Sun Alliance or AS
The Democrats
Union Makes the Nation or UN (includes PRD, MADEP)
note: approximately 20 additional minor parties

International organization participation: ACP, AfDB, AU, CD, ECOWAS, Entente, FAO, FZ, G-77, IAEA, IBRD, ICAO, ICCt, ICRM, IDA, IDB, IFAD, IFC, IFRCS, ILO, IMF, IMO, Interpol, IOC, IOM, IPU, ISO, ITSO, ITU, ITUC (NGOs), MIGA, MNJTF, MONUSCO, NAM, OAS (observer), OIC, OIF, OPCW, PCA, UN, UNAMID, UNCTAD, UNESCO, UNHCR, UNHRC, UNIDO, UNISFA, UNMIL, UNMISS, UNOCI, UNOOSA, UNWTO, UPU, WADB (regional), WAEMU, WCO, WFTU (NGOs), WHO, WIPO, WMO, WTO

Diplomatic representation in the US: *chief of mission:* Ambassador Jean-Claude Felix DO REGO (since 17 July 2020)
chancery: 2124 Kalorama Road NW, Washington, DC 20008
telephone: [1] (202) 232-6656
FAX: [1] (202) 265-1996
email address and website:
ambassade.washington@gouv.bj
https://beninembassy.us/

Diplomatic representation from the US: *chief of mission:* Ambassador Brian SHUKAN (since 5 May 2022)
embassy: 01BP 2012, Cotonou
mailing address:
2120 Cotonou Place, Washington DC 20521-2120
telephone: [229] 21-36-75-00
FAX: [229] 21-30-03-84
email address and website:
ACSCotonou@state.gov
https://bj.usembassy.gov/

Flag description: two equal horizontal bands of yellow (top) and red (bottom) with a vertical green band on the hoist side; green symbolizes hope and revival, yellow wealth, and red courage
note: uses the popular Pan-African colors of Ethiopia

National symbol(s): leopard; national colors: green, yellow, red

National anthem: *name:* "L'Aube Nouvelle" (The Dawn of a New Day)
lyrics/music: Gilbert Jean DAGNON
note: adopted 1960

National heritage: *total World Heritage Sites:* 2 (1 cultural, 1 natural)
selected World Heritage Site locales: Royal Palaces of Abomey (c); W-Arly-Pendjari Complex (n)

ECONOMY

Economic overview: robust economic growth; slightly declining but still widespread poverty; strong trade relations with Nigeria; cotton exporter; COVID-19 has led to capital outflows and border closures; WAEMU member with currency pegged to the euro; recent fiscal deficit and debt reductions

Real GDP (purchasing power parity): $52.51 billion (2023 est.)
$49.374 billion (2022 est.)
$46.468 billion (2021 est.)
note: data in 2021 dollars
comparison ranking: 122

Real GDP growth rate: 6.35% (2023 est.)
6.25% (2022 est.)
7.16% (2021 est.)
note: annual GDP % growth based on constant local currency
comparison ranking: 28

Real GDP per capita: $3,800 (2023 est.)
$3,700 (2022 est.)
$3,600 (2021 est.)
note: data in 2021 dollars
comparison ranking: 186

GDP (official exchange rate): $19.673 billion (2023 est.)
note: data in current dollars at official exchange rate

Inflation rate (consumer prices): 2.73% (2023 est.)
1.35% (2022 est.)
1.73% (2021 est.)
note: annual % change based on consumer prices
comparison ranking: 57

Credit ratings: Fitch rating: B (2019)

Moody's rating: B2 (2019)

Standard & Poors rating: B+ (2018)
note: The year refers to the year in which the current credit rating was first obtained.

GDP - composition, by sector of origin: *agriculture:* 25.4% (2023 est.)
industry: 17.3% (2023 est.)
services: 47.7% (2023 est.)
note: figures may not total 100% due to non-allocated consumption not captured in sector-reported data comparison rankings: services 161; industry 158; agriculture 18

GDP - composition, by end use: *household consumption:* 59% (2023 est.)
government consumption: 9.5% (2023 est.)
investment in fixed capital: 40.1% (2023 est.)
investment in inventories: 0.4% (2023 est.)
exports of goods and services: 21.2% (2023 est.)
imports of goods and services: -30.2% (2023 est.)
note: figures may not total 100% due to rounding or gaps in data collection

Agricultural products: cassava, yams, maize, oil palm fruit, cotton, rice, pineapples, soybeans, tomatoes, vegetables (2022)
note: top ten agricultural products based on tonnage

Industries: textiles, food processing, construction materials, cement

Industrial production growth rate: 7.29% (2023 est.)
note: annual % change in industrial value added based on constant local currency
comparison ranking: 32

Labor force: 4.964 million (2023 est.)
note: number of people ages 15 or older who are employed or seeking work

comparison ranking: 88

Unemployment rate: 1.45% (2023 est.)
1.47% (2022 est.)
1.69% (2021 est.)
note: % of labor force seeking employment
comparison ranking: 13

Youth unemployment rate (ages 15-24): *total:* 3.9% (2023 est.)
male: 3.2% (2023 est.)
female: 4.6% (2023 est.)
note: % of labor force ages 15-24 seeking employment
comparison ranking: total 186

Population below poverty line: 38.5% (2019 est.)
note: % of population with income below national poverty line

Gini Index coefficient - distribution of family income: 34.4 (2021 est.)
note: index (0-100) of income distribution; higher values represent greater inequality
comparison ranking: 82

Household income or consumption by percentage share: *lowest 10%:* 3.1% (2021 est.)
highest 10%: 27.2% (2021 est.)
note: % share of income accruing to lowest and highest 10% of population

Remittances: 1.19% of GDP (2023 est.)
1.32% of GDP (2022 est.)
1.31% of GDP (2021 est.)
note: personal transfers and compensation between resident and non-resident individuals/households/entities

Budget: *revenues:* $2.024 billion (2019 est.)
expenditures: $2.101 billion (2019 est.)

Public debt: 54.6% of GDP (2017 est.)
comparison ranking: 88

Taxes and other revenues: 17.1% (of GDP) (2017 est.)
comparison ranking: 114

Current account balance: -$734.659 million (2021 est.)
-$273.967 million (2020 est.)
-$575.593 million (2019 est.)
note: balance of payments - net trade and primary/secondary income in current dollars
comparison ranking: 128

Exports: $4.154 billion (2021 est.)
$3.506 billion (2020 est.)
$3.585 billion (2019 est.)
note: balance of payments - exports of goods and services in current dollars
comparison ranking: 144

Exports - partners: India 27%, Bangladesh 24%, UAE 23%, China 4%, Egypt 2% (2022)
note: top five export partners based on percentage share of exports

Exports - commodities: cotton, gold, coconuts/Brazil nuts/cashews, soybeans, oil seeds (2022)
note: top five export commodities based on value in dollars

Imports: $4.925 billion (2021 est.)
$3.942 billion (2020 est.)
$4.307 billion (2019 est.)
note: balance of payments - imports of goods and services in current dollars
comparison ranking: 152

Imports - partners: China 24%, India 14%, US 6%, UAE 6%, France 5% (2022)
note: top five import partners based on percentage share of imports

Imports - commodities: rice, refined petroleum, palm oil, cars, poultry (2022)
note: top five import commodities based on value in dollars

Reserves of foreign exchange and gold: $698.9 million (31 December 2017 est.)
$57.5 million (31 December 2016 est.)
comparison ranking: 149

Debt - external: $5.328 billion (2022 est.)
note: present value of external debt in current US dollars
comparison ranking: 53

Exchange rates: Communaute Financiere Africaine francs (XOF) per US dollar -

Exchange rates: 606.655 (2023 est.)
622.912 (2022 est.)
554.608 (2021 est.)
574.295 (2020 est.)
585.951 (2019 est.)

ENERGY

Electricity access: *electrification - total population:* 56.5% (2022 est.)
electrification - urban areas: 71.1%
electrification - rural areas: 45.5%

Electricity: *installed generating capacity:* 500,000 kW (2022 est.)
consumption: 1.502 billion kWh (2022 est.)
exports: 2 million kWh (2022 est.)
imports: 694 million kWh (2022 est.)
transmission/distribution losses: 317.697 million kWh (2022 est.)
comparison rankings: transmission/distribution losses 70; imports 87; exports 100; consumption 155; installed generating capacity 152

Electricity generation sources: *fossil fuels:* 98.4% of total installed capacity (2022 est.)
solar: 1.6% of total installed capacity (2022 est.)

Coal: *consumption:* 45,000 metric tons (2022 est.)
imports: 46,000 metric tons (2022 est.)

Petroleum: *refined petroleum consumption:* 46,000 bbl/day (2022 est.)
crude oil estimated reserves: 8 million barrels (2021 est.)

Natural gas: *consumption:* 182.131 million cubic meters (2022 est.)
imports: 182.131 million cubic meters (2022 est.)
proven reserves: 1.133 billion cubic meters (2021 est.)

Carbon dioxide emissions: 7.01 million metric tonnes of CO2 (2022 est.)
from coal and metallurgical coke: 102,000 metric tonnes of CO2 (2022 est.)
from petroleum and other liquids: 6.553 million metric tonnes of CO2 (2022 est.)
from consumed natural gas: 355,000 metric tonnes of CO2 (2022 est.)
comparison ranking: total emissions 125

Energy consumption per capita: 7.638 million Btu/person (2022 est.)
comparison ranking: 158

COMMUNICATIONS

Telephones - fixed lines: *total subscriptions:* 2,000 (2022 est.)
subscriptions per 100 inhabitants: (2022 est.) less than 1
comparison ranking: total subscriptions 217

Telephones - mobile cellular: *total subscriptions:* 14.55 million (2022 est.)
subscriptions per 100 inhabitants: 109 (2022 est.)
comparison ranking: total subscriptions 71

Telecommunication systems: *general assessment:* Benin's telecom market continues to be restricted by the poor condition of the country's fixed-line infrastructure; this has hampered the development of fixed-line voice and internet services, and there is negligible revenue derived from these sectors; mobile networks account for almost all internet connections, and also carry most voice traffic; there is promise for considerable change in the mobile sector; slow progress is being made in developing competition in the mobile sector; in May 2021 the government sought foreign companies to bid for a fourth mobile license; improved international internet connectivity has contributed to a reduction in end-user pricing, and provided the potential to transform many areas of the country's economy, bringing a greater proportion of the population into the orbit of internet commerce and connectivity; a 2,000km fiber project started in 2016 was finally completed in mid-2021, prompting the government to secure a loan to build additional fiber infrastructure connecting four of the country's 12 departments (2022)
domestic: fixed-line teledensity less than 1 per 100 people; mobile cellular subscriptions are 98 per 100 people (2021)
international: country code - 229; landing points for the SAT-3/WASC and ACE fiber-optic submarine cable that provides connectivity to Europe, and most West African countries; satellite earth stations - 7 (Intelsat-Atlantic Ocean) (2019)

Broadcast media: state-run Office de Radiodiffusion et de Television du Benin (ORTB) operates a TV station providing a wide broadcast reach; several privately owned TV stations broadcast from Cotonou; satellite TV subscription service is available; state-owned radio, under ORTB control, includes a national station supplemented by a number of regional stations; substantial number of privately owned radio broadcast stations; transmissions of a few international broadcasters are available on FM in Cotonou (2019)

Internet country code: .bj

Internet users: *total:* 4.42 million (2021 est.)
percent of population: 34% (2021 est.)
comparison ranking: total 104

Broadband - fixed subscriptions: *total:* 29,981 (2020 est.)
subscriptions per 100 inhabitants: 0.3 (2020 est.)
comparison ranking: total 155

TRANSPORTATION

National air transport system: *number of registered air carriers:* 1 (2015)
inventory of registered aircraft operated by air carriers: 1 (2015)
annual passenger traffic on registered air carriers: 112,392 (2015)
annual freight traffic on registered air carriers: 805,347 (2015) mt-km

Civil aircraft registration country code prefix: TY

Airports: 10 (2024)
comparison ranking: 158

Pipelines: 134 km gas

Railways: *total:* 438 km (2014)
narrow gauge: 438 km (2014) 1.000-m gauge
comparison ranking: total 115

Roadways: *total:* 16,000 km (2018)
comparison ranking: total 121

Waterways: 150 km (2011) (seasonal navigation on River Niger along northern border)
comparison ranking: 111

Merchant marine: *total:* 6 (2023)
by type: other 6
comparison ranking: total 165

Ports: *total ports:* 1 (2024)
large: 0
medium: 1
small: 0
very small: 0
ports with oil terminals: 1
key ports: Cotonou

MILITARY AND SECURITY

Military and security forces: Beninese Armed Forces (Forces Armees Beninoises, FAB; aka Benin Defense Forces): Land Force, Air Force, National Navy, National Guard (aka Republican Guard)

Ministry of Interior and Public Security: Republican Police (Police Republicaine, DGPR) (2024)
note: FAB is under the Ministry of Defense and is responsible for external security and supporting the DGPR in maintaining internal security, which has primary responsibility for enforcing law and maintaining order; the DGPR was formed in 2018 through a merger of police and gendarmes

Military expenditures: 0.5% of GDP (2023 est.)
0.7% of GDP (2022 est.)
0.7% of GDP (2021 est.)
0.5% of GDP (2020 est.)
0.5% of GDP (2019 est.)
comparison ranking: 159

Military and security service personnel strengths: approximately 12,000 active-duty troops, including about 3,000 National Guard; estimated 5,000 Republican Police (2024)

Military equipment inventories and acquisitions: the FAB is equipped with a small mix of mostly older or secondhand French, Soviet-era, and US equipment; in recent years, the EU, France, and the US have provided it with limited amounts of newer military hardware such as armored vehicles and helicopters (2024)

Military service age and obligation: 18-30 years of age for voluntary and selective compulsory military service for men and women; conscript service is 18 months (2024)

Military - note: in addition to its defense against external aggression duties, the Beninese Armed Forces (FAB) may be required to assist in maintaining public order and internal security under conditions defined by the country's president; it may also participate in economic development projects
a key focus for the security forces of Benin is countering infiltrations into the country by terrorist groups tied to al- Qa'ida and the Islamic State of Iraq and ash-Sham (ISIS) operating just over the border from northern Benin in Burkina Faso and Niger; in 2022, the Benin Government said it was "at war" after suffering a series of attacks from these groups; later that same year, President TALON pledged to increase the size of the military, modernize military equipment, and establish forward operating bases; as of 2024, Benin had sent approximately 7,000 troops to the north of the country to better secure its border on a full-time or seasonal basis; in addition, the FAB participates in the Multinational Joint Task Force (MNJTF) along with Cameroon, Chad, Niger, and Nigeria against Boko Haram and ISIS-West Africa in the general area of the Lake Chad Basin and along Nigeria's northeastern border
the FAB has a close working relationship with the Belgian armed forces; the Belgians offer military advice, training, and second-hand equipment donations, and deploy to Benin for limited military exercises (2024)

TERRORISM

Terrorist group(s): Jama'at Nusrat al Islam wal Muslimeen (JNIM); Islamic State in the Greater Sahara (ISIS-GS); Boko Haram
note: details about the history, aims, leadership, organization, areas of operation, tactics, targets, weapons, size, and sources of support of the group(s) appear(s) in the Terrorism reference guide

TRANSNATIONAL ISSUES

Trafficking in persons: tier rating: Tier 2 Watch list — Benin did not demonstrate overall increasing efforts to eliminate trafficking compared with the previous reporting period and was downgraded to Tier 2 Watch List; for more details, go to: https://www.state.gov/reports/2024-trafficking-in-persons-report/benin/

Illicit drugs: a significant transit and departure country for cocaine shipments in Africa destined for Europe

BERMUDA

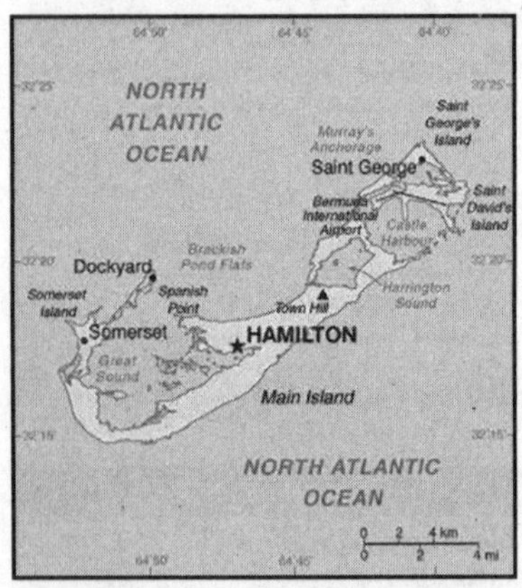

INTRODUCTION

Background: Bermuda was first settled in 1609 by shipwrecked English colonists heading for Virginia. Self-governing since 1620, Bermuda is the oldest and most populous of the British Overseas Territories. Vacationing on the island to escape North American winters first developed in Victorian times. Tourism continues to be important for the island's economy, although international business has overtaken it in recent years as Bermuda has developed into a highly successful offshore financial center. A referendum on independence from the UK was soundly defeated in 1995.

GEOGRAPHY

Location: North America, group of islands in the North Atlantic Ocean, east of South Carolina (US)

Geographic coordinates: 32 20 N, 64 45 W

Map references: North America

Area: *total:* 54 sq km
land: 54 sq km
water: 0 sq km
comparison ranking: total 229

Area - comparative: about one-third the size of Washington, DC

Land boundaries: *total:* 0 km

Coastline: 103 km

Maritime claims: *territorial sea:* 12 nm
exclusive economic zone: 200 nm
exclusive fishing zone: 200 nm

Climate: subtropical; mild, humid; gales, strong winds common in winter

Terrain: low hills separated by fertile depressions

Elevation: *highest point:* Town Hill 79 m
lowest point: Atlantic Ocean 0 m

Natural resources: limestone, pleasant climate fostering tourism

Land use: *agricultural land:* 14.8% (2018 est.)
arable land: 14.8% (2018 est.)
permanent crops: 0% (2018 est.)
permanent pasture: 0% (2018 est.)
forest: 20% (2018 est.)
other: 65.2% (2018 est.)

Irrigated land: NA

Population distribution: relatively even population distribution throughout

Natural hazards: hurricanes (June to November)

Geography - note: consists of about 138 coral islands and islets with ample rainfall, but no rivers or freshwater lakes; some land was leased by the US Government from 1941 to 1995

PEOPLE AND SOCIETY

Population: *total:* 72,800
male: 35,401
female: 37,399 (2024 est.)
comparison rankings: female 201; male 202; total 202

Nationality: *noun:* Bermudian(s)

adjective: Bermudian

Ethnic groups: African descent 52%, White 31%, mixed 9%, Asian 4%, other 4% (2010 est.)

Languages: English (official), Portuguese

Religions: Protestant 46.2% (includes Anglican 15.8%, African Methodist Episcopal 8.6%, Seventh Day Adventist 6.7%, Pentecostal 3.5%, Methodist 2.7%, Presbyterian 2.0%, Church of God 1.6%, Baptist 1.2%, Salvation Army 1.1%, Brethren 1.0%, other Protestant 2.0%), Roman Catholic 14.5%, Jehovah's Witness 1.3%, other Christian 9.1%, Muslim 1%, other 3.9%, none 17.8%, unspecified 6.2% (2010 est.)

Age structure: *0-14 years:* 16.4% (male 6,133/female 5,817)
15-64 years: 60.9% (male 22,247/female 22,113)
65 years and over: 22.7% (2024 est.) (male 7,021/female 9,469)

Dependency ratios: *total dependency ratio:* 52.9
youth dependency ratio: 22.8
elderly dependency ratio: 30.1
potential support ratio: 3.3 (2021)

Median age: *total:* 43.8 years (2024 est.)
male: 41.5 years
female: 46.3 years
comparison ranking: total 34

Population growth rate: 0.3% (2024 est.)
comparison ranking: 165

Birth rate: 10.9 births/1,000 population (2024 est.)
comparison ranking: 167

Death rate: 9.3 deaths/1,000 population (2024 est.)
comparison ranking: 50

Net migration rate: 1.4 migrant(s)/1,000 population (2024 est.)
comparison ranking: 59

Population distribution: relatively even population distribution throughout

Urbanization: *urban population:* 100% of total population (2023)
rate of urbanization: -0.2% annual rate of change (2020-25 est.)

Major urban areas - population: 10,000 HAMILTON (capital) (2018)

Sex ratio: *at birth:* 1.05 male(s)/female
0-14 years: 1.05 male(s)/female
15-64 years: 1.01 male(s)/female
65 years and over: 0.74 male(s)/female
total population: 0.95 male(s)/female (2024 est.)

Infant mortality rate: *total:* 2.1 deaths/1,000 live births (2024 est.)
male: 2.5 deaths/1,000 live births
female: 1.8 deaths/1,000 live births
comparison ranking: total 220

Life expectancy at birth: *total population:* 82.5 years (2024 est.)
male: 79.4 years
female: 85.7 years
comparison ranking: total population 29

Total fertility rate: 1.88 children born/woman (2024 est.)
comparison ranking: 125

Gross reproduction rate: 0.92 (2024 est.)

Contraceptive prevalence rate: NA

Drinking water source: *improved: urban:* 99.9% of population
rural: NA
total: 99.9% of population (2020)

Sanitation facility access: *improved: urban:* 99.9% of population
rural: NA
total: 99.9% of population (2020)

Currently married women (ages 15-49): 47.6% (2023 est.)

Education expenditures: 1.9% of GDP (2021 est.)
comparison ranking: 188

School life expectancy (primary to tertiary education): *total:* 13 years
male: 12 years
female: 13 years (2015)

ENVIRONMENT

Environment - current issues: dense population and heavy vehicle traffic create serious congestion and air pollution problems; water resources scarce (most obtained as rainwater or from wells); solid waste disposal; hazardous waste disposal; sewage disposal; overfishing; oil spills

Climate: subtropical; mild, humid; gales, strong winds common in winter

Urbanization: *urban population:* 100% of total population (2023)
rate of urbanization: -0.2% annual rate of change (2020-25 est.)

Air pollutants: *carbon dioxide emissions:* 0.61 megatons (2016 est.)

Waste and recycling: *municipal solid waste generated annually:* 82,000 tons (2012 est.)
municipal solid waste recycled annually: 1,640 tons (2012 est.)
percent of municipal solid waste recycled: 2% (2012 est.)

GOVERNMENT

Country name: *conventional long form:* none
conventional short form: Bermuda
former: Somers Islands
etymology: the islands making up Bermuda are named after Juan de BERMUDEZ, an early 16th century Spanish sea captain and the first European explorer of the archipelago

Government type: Overseas Territory of the UK with limited self-government; parliamentary democracy

Dependency status: overseas territory of the UK

Capital: *name:* Hamilton
geographic coordinates: 32 17 N, 64 47 W
time difference: UTC-4 (1 hour ahead of Washington, DC, during Standard Time)
daylight saving time: +1hr, begins second Sunday in March; ends first Sunday in November
etymology: named after Henry HAMILTON (ca. 1734-1796) who served as governor of Bermuda from 1788-1794

Administrative divisions: 9 parishes and 2 municipalities*; Devonshire, Hamilton, Hamilton*, Paget, Pembroke, Saint George*, Saint George's, Sandys, Smith's, Southampton, Warwick

Independence: none (overseas territory of the UK)

National holiday: Bermuda Day, 24 May; note - formerly known as Victoria Day, Empire Day, and Commonwealth Day

Legal system: English common law

Constitution: *history:* several previous (dating to 1684); latest entered into force 8 June 1968 (Bermuda Constitution Order 1968)
amendments: proposal procedure - NA; passage by an Order in Council in the UK; amended several times, last in 2012

International law organization participation: has not submitted an ICJ jurisdiction declaration; non-party state to the ICCt

Citizenship: *citizenship by birth:* no
citizenship by descent only: at least one parent must be a citizen of the UK
dual citizenship recognized: yes
residency requirement for naturalization: 10 years

Suffrage: 18 years of age; universal

Executive branch: *chief of state:* King CHARLES III (since 8 September 2022); represented by Governor Rena LALGIE (since 14 December 2020)
head of government: Premier David BURT (since 19 July 2017)
cabinet: Cabinet nominated by the premier, appointed by the governor
elections/appointments: the monarchy is hereditary; governor appointed by the monarch; following legislative elections, the leader of the majority party or majority coalition usually appointed premier by the governor

Legislative branch: *description:* bicameral Parliament consists of:
Senate (11 seats; 3 members appointed by the governor, 5 by the premier, and 3 by the opposition party; members serve 5-year terms)
House of Assembly (36 seats; members directly elected in single-seat constituencies by simple majority vote to serve up to 5-year terms)
elections: Senate - last appointments in 2022 (next appointments in 2027)
House of Assembly - last held on 1 October 2020 (next to be held by 2025)
election results: Senate - composition- men 5, women 6, percentage women 63.6%
House of Assembly - percent of vote by party - PLP 62.1%, OBA 32.3%, other 5.4%, independent 0.2%; seats by party - PLP 30, OBA 6; composition - men 28, women 7, percentage women 20%; total Parliament percentage women 28.3%

Judicial branch: *highest court(s):* Court of Appeal (consists of the court president and at least 2 justices); Supreme Court (consists of the chief justice, 4 puisne judges, and 1 associate justice); note - the Judicial Committee of the Privy Council (in London) is the court of final appeal
judge selection and term of office: Court of Appeal justice appointed by the governor; justice tenure by individual appointment; Supreme Court judges nominated by the Judicial and Legal Services Commission and appointed by the governor; judge tenure based on terms of appointment
subordinate courts: commercial court (began in 2006); magistrates' courts

Political parties: Free Democratic Movement or FDM
One Bermuda Alliance or OBA
Progressive Labor Party or PLP

International organization participation: Caricom (associate), ICC (NGOs), Interpol (subbureau), IOC, ITUC (NGOs), UPU, WCO

Diplomatic representation in the US: none (overseas territory of the UK)

Diplomatic representation from the US: *chief of mission:* Acting Consul General James SALLAY (since 20 August 2022)
embassy: US Consulate Bermuda, 16 Middle Road, Devonshire, DV 03, Bermuda
mailing address: 5300 Hamilton Place, Washington, DC 20520-5300
telephone: (441) 295-1342
FAX: (441) 295-1592
email address and website:
HamiltonConsulate@state.gov
https://bm.usconsulate.gov/
consulate(s) general: 16 Middle Road, Devonshire DV O3

Flag description: red, with the flag of the UK in the upper hoist-side quadrant and the Bermudian coat of arms (a white shield with a red lion standing on a green grassy field holding a scrolled shield showing the sinking of the ship Sea Venture off Bermuda in 1609) centered on the outer half of the flag; it was the shipwreck of the vessel, filled with English colonists originally bound for Virginia, that led to the settling of Bermuda
note: the flag is unusual in that it is only British overseas territory that uses a red ensign, all others use blue

National symbol(s): red lion

National anthem: *name:* Hail to Bermuda
lyrics/music: Bette JOHNS
note: serves as a local anthem; as a territory of the United Kingdom, "God Save the King" is official (see United Kingdom)

National heritage: *total World Heritage Sites:* 1 (cultural); note - excerpted from the UK entry
selected World Heritage Site locales: Historic Town of St George and Related Fortifications

ECONOMY

Economic overview: small, tourism- and construction-based, territorial-island economy; American import and tourist destination; known offshore banking hub; increasing inflation; major re-exportation and re-importation area

Real GDP (purchasing power parity): $6.349 billion (2022 est.)
$5.965 billion (2021 est.)
$5.659 billion (2020 est.)
note: data in 2021 dollars
comparison ranking: 174

Real GDP growth rate: 6.43% (2022 est.)
5.42% (2021 est.)
-6.84% (2020 est.)
note: annual GDP % growth based on constant local currency
comparison ranking: 26

Real GDP per capita: $99,800 (2022 est.)
$93,600 (2021 est.)
$88,600 (2020 est.)
note: data in 2021 dollars
comparison ranking: 7

GDP (official exchange rate): $7.828 billion (2022 est.)
note: data in current dollars at official exchange rate

Inflation rate (consumer prices): 1.9% (2017 est.)
1.4% (2016 est.)
comparison ranking: 33

Credit ratings: Fitch rating: N/A (2015)
Moody's rating: A2 (2016)
Standard & Poors rating: A+ (2015)
note: The year refers to the year in which the current credit rating was first obtained.

GDP - composition, by sector of origin: *agriculture:* 0.2% (2022 est.)
industry: 5.4% (2022 est.)
services: 90.5% (2022 est.)
note: figures may not total 100% due to non-allocated consumption not captured in sector-reported data comparison rankings: services 6; industry 212; agriculture 206

GDP - composition, by end use: *household consumption:* 47.2% (2022 est.)
government consumption: 11.9% (2022 est.)
investment in fixed capital: 12.1% (2022 est.)
exports of goods and services: 50.5% (2022 est.)
imports of goods and services: -25% (2022 est.)
note: figures may not total 100% due to rounding or gaps in data collection

Agricultural products: bananas, vegetables, citrus, flowers; dairy products, honey

Industries: international business, tourism, light manufacturing

Industrial production growth rate: 5.57% (2022 est.)
note: annual % change in industrial value added based on constant local currency
comparison ranking: 45

Labor force: 33,480 (2016 est.)
comparison ranking: 197

Unemployment rate: 7% (2017 est.)
7% (2016 est.)
comparison ranking: 137

Youth unemployment rate (ages 15-24): *total:* 29.3% (2014 est.)
male: 29.7%
female: 29%
comparison ranking: total 25

Remittances: 22.99% of GDP (2022 est.)
22.72% of GDP (2021 est.)
22.86% of GDP (2020 est.)
note: personal transfers and compensation between resident and non-resident individuals/households/entities

Budget: *revenues:* $999.2 million (2017 est.)
expenditures: $1.176 billion (2017 est.)

Public debt: 43% of GDP (FY14/15)
comparison ranking: 124

Taxes and other revenues: 16.3% (of GDP) (2017 est.)
comparison ranking: 125

Current account balance: $962.258 million (2021 est.)
$853.85 million (2020 est.)
$838.701 million (2019 est.)
note: balance of payments - net trade and primary/secondary income in current dollars
comparison ranking: 56

Exports: $1.136 billion (2021 est.)
$1.027 billion (2020 est.)
$1.605 billion (2019 est.)
note: balance of payments - exports of goods and services in current dollars
comparison ranking: 180

Exports - partners: Zambia 26%, US 16%, Angola 10%, France 10%, Tanzania 8% (2022)
note: top five export partners based on percentage share of exports

Exports - commodities: fertilizers, ships, liquor, vaccines, railway cargo containers (2022)
note: top five export commodities based on value in dollars

Imports: $1.925 billion (2021 est.)
$1.723 billion (2020 est.)
$2.224 billion (2019 est.)
note: balance of payments - imports of goods and services in current dollars
comparison ranking: 180

Imports - partners: US 34%, Norway 19%, South Korea 19%, China 5%, Canada 5% (2022)
note: top five import partners based on percentage share of imports

Imports - commodities: ships, refined petroleum, railway cargo containers, packaged medicine, cars (2022)
note: top five import commodities based on value in dollars

Exchange rates: Bermudian dollars (BMD) per US dollar -

Exchange rates: 1 (2023 est.)
1 (2022 est.)
1 (2021 est.)
1 (2020 est.)
1 (2019 est.)

ENERGY

Electricity access: *electrification - total population:* 100% (2022 est.)

Electricity: *installed generating capacity:* 173,000 kW (2022 est.)
consumption: 581.097 million kWh (2022 est.)
transmission/distribution losses: 42.493 million kWh (2022 est.)
comparison rankings: transmission/distribution losses 35; consumption 171; installed generating capacity 177

Electricity generation sources: *fossil fuels:* 99% of total installed capacity (2022 est.)
biomass and waste: 1% of total installed capacity (2022 est.)

Coal: *imports:* 54.3 metric tons (2022 est.)

Petroleum: *refined petroleum consumption:* 4,000 bbl/day (2022 est.)

Carbon dioxide emissions: 582,000 metric tonnes of CO_2 (2022 est.)
from petroleum and other liquids: 582,000 metric tonnes of CO_2 (2022 est.)
comparison ranking: total emissions 187

Energy consumption per capita: 124.882 million Btu/person (2022 est.)
comparison ranking: 32

COMMUNICATIONS

Telephones - fixed lines: *total subscriptions:* 25,000 (2021 est.)
subscriptions per 100 inhabitants: 39 (2021 est.)
comparison ranking: total subscriptions 171

Telephones - mobile cellular: *total subscriptions:* 68,000 (2021 est.)
subscriptions per 100 inhabitants: 106 (2021 est.)
comparison ranking: total subscriptions 200

Telecommunication systems: *general assessment:* the telecom sector has seen a decline in subscriber numbers (particularly for prepaid mobile services the mainstay of short term visitors) and revenue; fixed and mobile broadband services are two areas that have benefited from the crisis as employees and students

have resorted to working from home; one area of the telecom market that is not prepared for growth is 5G mobile; governments, regulators, and even the mobile network operators have shown that they have not been investing in 5G opportunities at the present time; network expansion and enhancements remain concentrated around improving LTE coverage (2021)
domestic: the system has a fixed-line teledensity of 39 per 100, coupled with a mobile-cellular teledensity of roughly 110 per 100 persons (2021)
international: country code - 1-441; landing points for the GlobeNet, Gemini Bermuda, CBUS, and the CB-1 submarine cables to the Caribbean, South America and the US; satellite earth stations - 3 (2019)

Broadcast media: 3 TV stations; cable and satellite TV subscription services are available; roughly 13 radio stations operating

Internet country code: .bm

Internet users: *total:* 64,000 (2021 est.)
percent of population: 100% (2021 est.)
comparison ranking: total 197

Broadband - fixed subscriptions: *total:* 23,000 (2020 est.)
subscriptions per 100 inhabitants: 37 (2020 est.)
comparison ranking: total 163

TRANSPORTATION

Civil aircraft registration country code prefix: VP-B

Airports: 1 (2024)
comparison ranking: 231

Roadways: *total:* 447 km
paved: 447 km (2010)
note: 225 km public roads; 222 km private roads
comparison ranking: total 197

Merchant marine: *total:* 122 (2023)
by type: container ship 15, oil tanker 8, other 99
comparison ranking: total 81

Ports: *total ports:* 4 (2024)
large: 0
medium: 1
small: 2
very small: 0
size unknown: 1
ports with oil terminals: 3
key ports: Freeport, Hamilton, Ireland Island, St. George

MILITARY AND SECURITY

Military and security forces: Royal Bermuda Regiment; Bermuda Police Service (2024)
note: the Royal Bermuda Regiment (aka "The Regiment") includes the Royal Bermuda Regiment Coast Guard

Military and security service personnel strengths: the Royal Bermuda Regiment has about 350 troops (2024)

Military equipment inventories and acquisitions: the Regiment is equipped with small arms (2024)

Military service age and obligation: men and women who are Commonwealth citizens and 18-45 years of age can volunteer for the Bermuda Regiment; service is for a minimum period of three years and two months from the date of enlistment; service can be extended only by volunteering or an executive order from the Governor; annual training commitment is about 30 days a year, which includes a two-week camp, weekends, and drill nights (2024)

Military - note: defense is the responsibility of the UK; the Royal Bermuda Regiment's responsibilities include maritime security of Bermuda's inshore waters, search and rescue, ceremonial duties, humanitarian/disaster assistance, security of key installations, and assisting the Bermuda Police with maintaining public order; it includes explosive ordnance disposal, diver, maritime, security police, and support units (2024)

BHUTAN

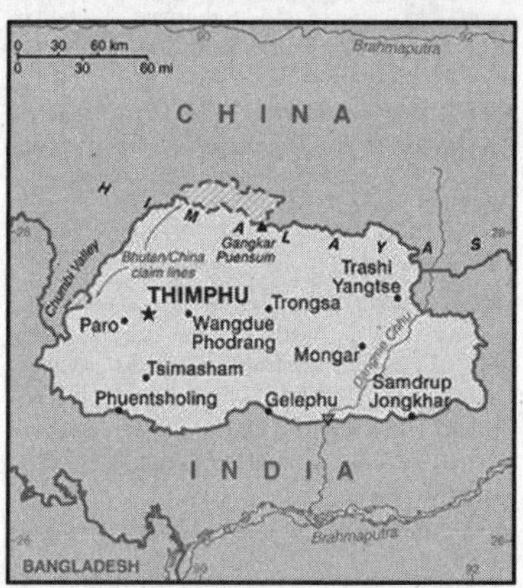

INTRODUCTION

Background: After Britain's victory in the 1865 Duar War, Britain and Bhutan signed the Treaty of Sinchulu, under which Bhutan would receive an annual subsidy in exchange for ceding land to British India. Ugyen WANGCHUCK – who had served as the de facto ruler of an increasingly unified Bhutan and had improved relations with the British toward the end of the 19th century – was named king in 1907. Three years later, a treaty was signed whereby the British agreed not to interfere in Bhutanese internal affairs, and Bhutan allowed Britain to direct its foreign affairs. Bhutan negotiated a similar arrangement with independent India in 1949. The Indo-Bhutanese Treaty of Friendship returned to Bhutan a small piece of the territory annexed by the British, formalized the annual subsidies the country received, and defined India's responsibilities in defense and foreign relations. Under a succession of modernizing monarchs beginning in the 1950s, Bhutan joined the UN in 1971 and slowly continued its engagement beyond its borders.

In 2005, King Jigme Singye WANGCHUCK unveiled the draft of Bhutan's first constitution – which introduced major democratic reforms – and held a national referendum for its approval. The King abdicated the throne in 2006 in favor of his son, Jigme Khesar Namgyel WANGCHUCK. In 2007, India and Bhutan renegotiated their treaty, eliminating the clause that stated that Bhutan would be "guided by" India in conducting its foreign policy, although Thimphu continues to coordinate closely with New Delhi. In 2008, Bhutan held its first parliamentary election in accordance with the constitution. Bhutan experienced a peaceful turnover of power following a parliamentary election in 2013, which resulted in the defeat of the incumbent party. In 2018, the incumbent party again lost the parliamentary election. In 2024, of the more than 100,000 ethnic Nepali – predominantly Lhotshampa – refugees who fled or were forced out of Bhutan in the 1990s, about 6,500 remain displaced in Nepal.

GEOGRAPHY

Location: Southern Asia, between China and India

Geographic coordinates: 27 30 N, 90 30 E

Map references: Asia

Area: *total:* 38,394 sq km
land: 38,394 sq km
water: 0 sq km
comparison ranking: total 136

Area - comparative: slightly larger than Maryland; about one-half the size of Indiana

Land boundaries: *total:* 1,136 km
border countries (2): China 477 km; India 659 km

Coastline: 0 km (landlocked)

Maritime claims: none (landlocked)

Climate: varies; tropical in southern plains; cool winters and hot summers in central valleys; severe winters and cool summers in Himalayas

Terrain: mostly mountainous with some fertile valleys and savanna

Elevation: *highest point:* Gangkar Puensum 7,570 m
lowest point: Drangeme Chhu 97 m
mean elevation: 2,220 m

Natural resources: timber, hydropower, gypsum, calcium carbonate

Land use: *agricultural land:* 13.6% (2018 est.)
arable land: 2.6% (2018 est.)
permanent crops: 0.3% (2018 est.)
permanent pasture: 10.7% (2018 est.)
forest: 85.5% (2018 est.)
other: 0.9% (2018 est.)

Irrigated land: 320 sq km (2012)

Natural hazards: violent storms from the Himalayas are the source of the country's Bhutanese name, which translates as Land of the Thunder Dragon; frequent landslides during the rainy season

Geography - note: landlocked; strategic location between China and India; controls several key Himalayan mountain passes

PEOPLE AND SOCIETY

Population: *total:* 884,546
male: 457,665
female: 426,881 (2024 est.)
comparison rankings: female 165; male 163; total 165

Nationality: *noun:* Bhutanese (singular and plural)
adjective: Bhutanese

Ethnic groups: Ngalop (also known as Bhote) 50%, ethnic Nepali 35% (predominantly Lhotshampas), indigenous or migrant tribes 15%

Languages: Sharchopkha 28%, Dzongkha (official) 24%, Lhotshamkha 22%, other 26% (includes foreign languages) (2005 est.)

Religions: Lamaistic Buddhist 75.3%, Indian- and Nepali-influenced Hinduism 22.1%, other 2.6% (2005 est.)

Age structure: *0-14 years:* 23.1% (male 104,771/female 99,981)
15-64 years: 70.2% (male 322,497/female 298,324)
65 years and over: 6.7% (2024 est.) (male 30,397/female 28,576)

Dependency ratios: *total dependency ratio:* 40.7
youth dependency ratio: 32.1
elderly dependency ratio: 8.6
potential support ratio: 11.1 (2021 est.)

Median age: *total:* 30.7 years (2024 est.)
male: 31.1 years
female: 30.3 years
comparison ranking: total 134

Population growth rate: 0.95% (2024 est.)
comparison ranking: 98

Birth rate: 15.3 births/1,000 population (2024 est.)
comparison ranking: 106

Death rate: 5.9 deaths/1,000 population (2024 est.)
comparison ranking: 158

Net migration rate: 0 migrant(s)/1,000 population (2024 est.)
comparison ranking: 92

Urbanization: *urban population:* 44.4% of total population (2023)
rate of urbanization: 2.52% annual rate of change (2020-25 est.)

Major urban areas - population: 203,000 THIMPHU (capital) (2018)

Sex ratio: *at birth:* 1.05 male(s)/female
0-14 years: 1.05 male(s)/female
15-64 years: 1.08 male(s)/female
65 years and over: 1.06 male(s)/female
total population: 1.07 male(s)/female (2024 est.)

Maternal mortality ratio: 60 deaths/100,000 live births (2020 est.)
comparison ranking: 92

Infant mortality rate: *total:* 24.3 deaths/1,000 live births (2024 est.)
male: 24.6 deaths/1,000 live births
female: 23.9 deaths/1,000 live births
comparison ranking: total 63

Life expectancy at birth: *total population:* 73.7 years (2024 est.)
male: 72.5 years
female: 75 years
comparison ranking: total population 147

Total fertility rate: 1.76 children born/woman (2024 est.)
comparison ranking: 147

Gross reproduction rate: 0.86 (2024 est.)

Contraceptive prevalence rate: NA

Drinking water source: *improved: urban:* 99.5% of population
rural: 100% of population
total: 99.8% of population
unimproved: urban: 0.5% of population
rural: 0% of population
total: 0.2% of population (2020 est.)

Current health expenditure: 4.4% of GDP (2020)

Physician density: 0.5 physicians/1,000 population (2020)

Hospital bed density: 1.7 beds/1,000 population (2012)

Sanitation facility access: *improved: urban:* 90.8% of population
rural: 83.1% of population
total: 86.4% of population
unimproved: urban: 9.2% of population
rural: 16.9% of population
total: 13.6% of population (2020 est.)

Obesity - adult prevalence rate: 6.4% (2016)
comparison ranking: 168

Alcohol consumption per capita: *total:* 0.07 liters of pure alcohol (2019 est.)
beer: 0.01 liters of pure alcohol (2019 est.)
wine: 0.05 liters of pure alcohol (2019 est.)
spirits: 0 liters of pure alcohol (2019 est.)
other alcohols: 0 liters of pure alcohol (2019 est.)
comparison ranking: total 179

Currently married women (ages 15-49): 62.8% (2023 est.)

Education expenditures: 7% of GDP (2021 est.)
comparison ranking: 22

Literacy: *definition:* age 15 and over can read and write
total population: 70.9%
male: 77.9%
female: 62.8% (2021)

School life expectancy (primary to tertiary education): *total:* 13 years
male: 13 years
female: 13 years (2018)

ENVIRONMENT

Environment - current issues: soil erosion; limited access to potable water; wildlife conservation; industrial pollution; waste disposal

Environment - international agreements: *party to:* Biodiversity, Climate Change, Climate Change-Kyoto Protocol, Climate Change-Paris Agreement, Desertification, Endangered Species, Hazardous Wastes, Nuclear Test Ban, Ozone Layer Protection, Wetlands
signed, but not ratified: Law of the Sea

Climate: varies; tropical in southern plains; cool winters and hot summers in central valleys; severe winters and cool summers in Himalayas

Urbanization: *urban population:* 44.4% of total population (2023)
rate of urbanization: 2.52% annual rate of change (2020-25 est.)

Revenue from forest resources: 1.89% of GDP (2018 est.)
comparison ranking: 37

Revenue from coal: 0% of GDP (2018 est.)
comparison ranking: 64

Air pollutants: *particulate matter emissions:* 26.1 micrograms per cubic meter (2019 est.)
carbon dioxide emissions: 1.26 megatons (2016 est.)
methane emissions: 1.11 megatons (2020 est.)

Waste and recycling: *municipal solid waste generated annually:* 111,314 tons (2007 est.)
municipal solid waste recycled annually: 957 tons (2016 est.)
percent of municipal solid waste recycled: 0.9% (2016 est.)

Total water withdrawal: *municipal:* 20 million cubic meters (2020 est.)
industrial: 3 million cubic meters (2019 est.)
agricultural: 320 million cubic meters (2020 est.)

Total renewable water resources: 78 billion cubic meters (2020 est.)

GOVERNMENT

Country name: *conventional long form:* Kingdom of Bhutan
conventional short form: Bhutan
local long form: Druk Gyalkhap
local short form: Druk Yul
etymology: named after the Bhotia, the ethnic Tibetans who migrated from Tibet to Bhutan; "Bod" is the Tibetan name for their land; the Bhutanese name "Druk Yul" means "Land of the Thunder Dragon"

Government type: constitutional monarchy

Capital: *name:* Thimphu
geographic coordinates: 27 28 N, 89 38 E
time difference: UTC+6 (11 hours ahead of Washington, DC, during Standard Time)
etymology: the origins of the name are unclear; the traditional explanation, dating to the 14th century, is that *thim* means "dissolve" and *phu* denotes "high ground" to express the meaning of "dissolving high ground," in reference to a local deity that dissolved before a traveler's eyes, becoming a part of the rock on which the present city stands

Administrative divisions: 20 districts (dzongkhag, singular and plural); Bumthang, Chhukha, Dagana, Gasa, Haa, Lhuentse, Mongar, Paro, Pemagatshel, Punakha, Samdrup Jongkhar, Samtse, Sarpang, Thimphu, Trashigang, Trashi Yangtse, Trongsa, Tsirang, Wangdue Phodrang, Zhemgang

Independence: 17 December 1907 (became a unified kingdom under its first hereditary king); 8 August 1949 (Treaty of Friendship with India maintains Bhutanese independence)

National holiday: National Day (Ugyen WANGCHUCK became first hereditary king), 17 December (1907)

Legal system: civil law based on Buddhist religious law

Constitution: *history:* previous governing documents were various royal decrees; first constitution drafted November 2001 to March 2005, ratified 18 July 2008
amendments: proposed as a motion by simple majority vote in a joint session of Parliament; passage requires at least a three-fourths majority vote in a joint session of the next Parliament and assent by the king

International law organization participation: has not submitted an ICJ jurisdiction declaration; non-party state to the ICCt

Citizenship: *citizenship by birth:* no
citizenship by descent only: the father must be a citizen of Bhutan
dual citizenship recognized: no
residency requirement for naturalization: 10 years

Suffrage: 18 years of age; universal

Executive branch: *chief of state:* King Jigme Khesar Namgyel WANGCHUCK (since 14 December 2006)
head of government: Prime Minister Tshering TOBGAY (since 28 January 2024)
cabinet: Council of Ministers or Lhengye Zhungtshog members nominated by the monarch in consultation with the prime minister and approved by the National Assembly; members serve 5-year terms
elections/appointments: the monarchy is hereditary but can be removed by a two-thirds vote of Parliament; leader of the majority party in Parliament is nominated as the prime minister, appointed by the monarch

Legislative branch: *description:* bicameral Parliament or Chi Tshog consists of:
non-partisan National Council or Gyelyong Tshogde (25 seats; 20 members directly elected in single-seat constituencies by simple majority vote and 5 members appointed by the king; members serve 5-year terms)
National Assembly or Tshogdu (47 seats; members directly elected in single-seat constituencies in a two-round system; in the primary round, contesting political parties are directly selected by simple majority vote; in the main round, the two top parties in the primary round field candidates who are directly elected by simple majority vote; members serve 5-year terms)
elections: National Council - last held on 20 April 2023 (next to be held in 2028)
National Assembly - first round held on 30 November 2023 with a runoff on 9 January 2024 (next to be held in 2028)
election results: National Council - seats by party - independent 20 (all candidates ran as independents) and 5 appointed by the king; composition - men 22, women 3, percentage women 12%
National Assembly - percent of vote by party in first round - PDP 42.5%, BTP 19.6%, DPT 14.9%, DNT 13.1% DTT 9.8%; percent of vote in second round - PDP 55%, BTP 45%; seats by party PDP 30, BTP 17; composition - men 45, women 2, percentage women 4.3%; total percentage women in Parliament 6.9%

Judicial branch: *highest court(s):* Supreme Court (consists of the chief justice and 4 associate justices); note - the Supreme Court has sole jurisdiction in constitutional matters
judge selection and term of office: Supreme Court chief justice appointed by the monarch upon the advice of the National Judicial Commission, a 4-member body to include the Legislative Committee of the National Assembly, the attorney general, the Chief Justice of Bhutan and the senior Associate Justice of the Supreme Court; other judges (drangpons) appointed by the monarch from among the High Court judges selected by the National Judicial Commission; chief justice serves a 5-year term or until reaching age 65 years, whichever is earlier; the 4 other judges serve 10-year terms or until age 65, whichever is earlier
subordinate courts: High Court (first appellate court); District or Dzongkhag Courts; sub-district or Dungkhag Courts

Political parties: Bhutan Peace and Prosperity Party (Druk Phuensum Tshogpa) or DPT
Bhutan Tendrel Party or BTP
Druk Thuendrel Tshogpa or DTT
People's Democratic Party or PDP
United Party of Bhutan (Druk Nyamrup Tshogpa) or DNT

International organization participation: ADB, BIMSTEC, CP, FAO, G-77, IBRD, ICAO, IDA, IFAD, IFC, IMF, Interpol, IOC, IOM (observer), IPU, ISO (correspondent), ITSO, ITU, MIGA, NAM, OPCW, SAARC, SACEP, UN, UNCTAD, UNESCO, UNIDO, UNISFA, UNTSO, UNWTO, UPU, WCO, WHO, WIPO, WMO, WTO (observer)

Diplomatic representation in the US: *chief of mission:* Ambassador/Permanent Representative to the United Nations (vacant); Chargé d'Affaires Phuntsho NORBU (since October 2022); note - also serving as the Deputy Permanent Representative to the UN
telephone: [1] (212) 682-2371
FAX: [1] (212) 661-0551
email address and website:
consulate.pmbny@mfa.gov.bt
https://www.mfa.gov.bt/pmbny/
consulate(s) general: 343 East, 43rd Street, New York, NY 10017
note - although Bhutan and the United States do not have diplomatic relations, the two countries established consular relations on 23 July 1986; the Consulate General of the Kingdom of Bhutan was established in New York with an officer from the Permanent Mission of the Kingdom of Bhutan to the United Nations holding dual accreditation as the Consul General with consular jurisdiction in the US

Diplomatic representation from the US: *embassy:* none; frequent informal contact is maintained via the US embassy in New Delhi (India) and Bhutan's Permanent Mission to the UN

Flag description: *divided diagonally from the lower hoist-side corner; the upper triangle is yellow and the lower triangle is orange; centered along the dividing line is a large black and white dragon facing away from the hoist side; the dragon, called the Druk (Thunder Dragon), is the emblem of the nation; its white color stands for purity and the jewels in its claws symbolize wealth; the background colors represent spiritual and secular powers within Bhutan:* the orange is associated with Buddhism, while the yellow denotes the ruling dynasty

National symbol(s): thunder dragon known as Druk Gyalpo; national colors: orange, yellow

National anthem: *name:* "Druk tsendhen" (The Thunder Dragon Kingdom)
lyrics/music: Gyaldun Dasho Thinley DORJI/Aku TONGMI
note: adopted 1953

ECONOMY

Economic overview: hydropower investments spurring economic development; Gross National Happiness economy; sharp poverty declines; low inflation; strong monetary and fiscal policies; stable currency; fairly resilient response to COVID-19; key economic and strategic relations with India; climate vulnerabilities

Real GDP (purchasing power parity): $10.981 billion (2022 est.)
$10.437 billion (2021 est.)
$9.995 billion (2020 est.)
note: data in 2021 dollars
comparison ranking: 166

Real GDP growth rate: 5.21% (2022 est.)
4.42% (2021 est.)
-10.22% (2020 est.)
note: annual GDP % growth based on constant local currency
comparison ranking: 45

Real GDP per capita: $14,000 (2022 est.)
$13,400 (2021 est.)
$12,900 (2020 est.)
note: data in 2021 dollars
comparison ranking: 129

GDP (official exchange rate): $2.898 billion (2022 est.)
note: data in current dollars at official exchange rate

Inflation rate (consumer prices): 4.23% (2023 est.)
5.64% (2022 est.)
7.35% (2021 est.)
note: annual % change based on consumer prices
comparison ranking: 89

GDP - composition, by sector of origin: *agriculture:* 14.7% (2022 est.)
industry: 31.8% (2022 est.)
services: 51.2% (2022 est.)
note: figures may not total 100% due to non-allocated consumption not captured in sector-reported data
comparison rankings: services 139; industry 57; agriculture 58

GDP - composition, by end use: *household consumption:* 57.6% (2022 est.)
government consumption: 21% (2022 est.)
investment in fixed capital: 55.2% (2022 est.)
investment in inventories: 0.1% (2022 est.)
exports of goods and services: 25.8% (2022 est.)
imports of goods and services: -60.1% (2022 est.)
note: figures may not total 100% due to rounding or gaps in data collection

Agricultural products: milk, rice, root vegetables, potatoes, maize, oranges, areca nuts, chilies/peppers, pumpkins/squash, bison milk (2022)
note: top ten agricultural products based on tonnage

Industries: cement, wood products, processed fruits, alcoholic beverages, calcium carbide, tourism

Industrial production growth rate: 5.6% (2022 est.)
note: annual % change in industrial value added based on constant local currency
comparison ranking: 44

Labor force: 430,000 (2023 est.)
note: number of people ages 15 or older who are employed or seeking work
comparison ranking: 161

Unemployment rate: 5.65% (2023 est.)
5.95% (2022 est.)
4.8% (2021 est.)
note: % of labor force seeking employment
comparison ranking: 112

Youth unemployment rate (ages 15-24): *total:* 29.2% (2023 est.)
male: 25.1% (2023 est.)
female: 33.1% (2023 est.)
note: % of labor force ages 15-24 seeking employment
comparison ranking: total 26

Population below poverty line: 12.4% (2022 est.)
note: % of population with income below national poverty line

Gini Index coefficient - distribution of family income: 28.5 (2022 est.)
note: index (0-100) of income distribution; higher values represent greater inequality
comparison ranking: 135

Household income or consumption by percentage share: *lowest 10%:* 3.6% (2022 est.)

highest 10%: 22.7% (2022 est.)
note: % share of income accruing to lowest and highest 10% of population

Remittances: 3.31% of GDP (2022 est.)
2.65% of GDP (2021 est.)
3.39% of GDP (2020 est.)
note: personal transfers and compensation between resident and non-resident individuals/households/entities

Budget: *revenues:* $740.333 million (2020 est.)
expenditures: $591.697 million (2020 est.)
note: central government revenues and expenses (excluding grants/extrabudgetary units/social security funds) converted to US dollars at average official exchange rate for year indicated

Public debt: 111.01% of GDP (2020 est.)
note: central government debt as a % of GDP
comparison ranking: 15

Taxes and other revenues: 12.28% (of GDP) (2020 est.)
note: central government tax revenue as a % of GDP
comparison ranking: 161

Current account balance: -$999.999 million (2023 est.)
-$805.723 million (2022 est.)
-$319.279 million (2021 est.)
note: balance of payments - net trade and primary/secondary income in current dollars
comparison ranking: 140

Exports: $815.05 million (2023 est.)
$791.342 million (2022 est.)
$739.514 million (2021 est.)
note: balance of payments - exports of goods and services in current dollars
comparison ranking: 187

Exports - partners: India 88%, Italy 5%, Nepal 2%, Colombia 2%, Singapore 1% (2022)
note: top five export partners based on percentage share of exports

Exports - commodities: iron alloys, dolomite, gypsum, cement, electricity (2022)
note: top five export commodities based on value in dollars

Imports: $1.754 billion (2023 est.)
$1.581 billion (2022 est.)
$1.027 billion (2021 est.)
note: balance of payments - imports of goods and services in current dollars
comparison ranking: 181

Imports - partners: India 75%, China 12%, Indonesia 5%, Thailand 2%, Singapore 1% (2022)
note: top five import partners based on percentage share of imports

Imports - commodities: computers, refined petroleum, electrical machinery, coke, wood charcoal (2022)
note: top five import commodities based on value in dollars

Reserves of foreign exchange and gold: $976.26 million (2021 est.)
$1.427 billion (2020 est.)
$1.238 billion (2019 est.)
note: holdings of gold (year-end prices)/foreign exchange/special drawing rights in current dollars
comparison ranking: 142

Debt - external: $2.514 billion (2022 est.)
note: present value of external debt in current US dollars
comparison ranking: 68

Exchange rates: ngultrum (BTN) per US dollar -

Exchange rates: 82.601 (2023 est.)
78.604 (2022 est.)
73.918 (2021 est.)
74.1 (2020 est.)
70.42 (2019 est.)

ENERGY

Electricity access: *electrification - total population:* 100% (2022 est.)

Electricity: *installed generating capacity:* 2.342 million kW (2022 est.)
consumption: 9.752 billion kWh (2022 est.)
exports: 6 billion kWh (2020 est.)
imports: 834.7 million kWh (2022 est.)
transmission/distribution losses: 83.626 million kWh (2022 est.)
comparison rankings: transmission/distribution losses 44; imports 84; consumption 104; installed generating capacity 118; exports 35

Electricity generation sources: *hydroelectricity:* 100% of total installed capacity (2022 est.)

Coal: *production:* 177,000 metric tons (2022 est.)
consumption: 325,000 metric tons (2022 est.)
exports: 100 metric tons (2022 est.)
imports: 148,000 metric tons (2022 est.)

Petroleum: *refined petroleum consumption:* 3,000 bbl/day (2022 est.)

Carbon dioxide emissions: 1.206 million metric tonnes of CO_2 (2022 est.)
from coal and metallurgical coke: 728,000 metric tonnes of CO_2 (2022 est.)
from petroleum and other liquids: 478,000 metric tonnes of CO_2 (2022 est.)
comparison ranking: total emissions 170

Energy consumption per capita: 60.788 million Btu/person (2022 est.)
comparison ranking: 79

COMMUNICATIONS

Telephones - fixed lines: *total subscriptions:* 20,000 (2022 est.)
subscriptions per 100 inhabitants: 3 (2022 est.)
comparison ranking: total subscriptions 173

Telephones - mobile cellular: *total subscriptions:* 742,000 (2022 est.)
subscriptions per 100 inhabitants: 95 (2022 est.)
comparison ranking: total subscriptions 169

Telecommunication systems: *general assessment:* the small land-locked Kingdom of Bhutan has only recently emerged from decades of isolation from the modern world; that, and its mountainous terrain, left the country far back in the field in terms of teledensity as well as access to the Internet; over the last decade, the country has undergone a significant transformation due to the opening of its borders, liberalization of its telecom sector, and the active support from the government towards increased competition in the mobile, broadband, and ISP segments; the relatively widespread availability of the mobile platform has caused an explosion in mobile broadband subscriber numbers, growing from zero to over 100% penetration in just ten years (between 2010 and 2019).; the onset of the Covid-19 crisis in 2020 caused the subscription rates to drop back a little; growth is projected to return in 2022 (along with the broader mobile market) as the overall economy recovers; the government opens up more to foreign investment, trade, and tourism; and network expansion continues – the recent (December 2021) launch of 5G services by both of the country's mobile operators being particularly noteworthy (2022)
domestic: approximately 3 to 100 fixed-line and 100 mobile cellular subscriptions per 100 people (2021)
international: country code - 975; international telephone and telegraph service via landline and microwave relay through India; satellite earth station - 1 Intelsat

Broadcast media: state-owned TV station established in 1999; cable TV service offers dozens of Indian and other international channels; first radio station, privately launched in 1973, is now state-owned; 5 private radio stations are currently broadcasting (2012)

Internet country code: .bt

Internet users: *total:* 670,800 (2021 est.)
percent of population: 86% (2021 est.)
comparison ranking: total 162

Broadband - fixed subscriptions: *total:* 3,189 (2020 est.)
subscriptions per 100 inhabitants: 0.4 (2020 est.)
comparison ranking: total 192

TRANSPORTATION

National air transport system: *number of registered air carriers:* 2 (2020)
inventory of registered aircraft operated by air carriers: 6
annual passenger traffic on registered air carriers: 275,849 (2018)
annual freight traffic on registered air carriers: 690,000 (2018) mt-km

Civil aircraft registration country code prefix: A5

Airports: 4 (2024)
comparison ranking: 179

Heliports: 8 (2024)

Roadways: *total:* 12,205 km (2017)
urban: 437 km
comparison ranking: total 131

MILITARY AND SECURITY

Military and security forces: Royal Bhutan Army (RBA; includes Royal Bodyguard of Bhutan, or RBG, and an air wing); National Militia

Ministry of Home and Cultural Affairs: Royal Bhutan Police (2024)

Military and security service personnel strengths: estimated 7-8,000 active personnel (2024)

Military equipment inventories and acquisitions: the Royal Bhutan Army is lightly armed with a mix of mostly older equipment originating from such suppliers as India, the former Soviet Union, Thailand, and others (2023)

Military service age and obligation: 18 years of age for voluntary military service for men and women; no conscription; militia training is compulsory for males aged 20-25, over a 3-year period (2023)
note: in 2021, the Royal Bhutan Army graduated from a year-long training course the first batch of 150 women to be allowed to serve in combat roles; previously, women were allowed to serve in medical and other non-combat roles

Military deployments: 190 Central African Republic (MINUSCA) (2024)

Military - note: the Army is responsible for external threats but also has some internal security functions such as conducting counterinsurgency operations, guarding forests, and providing security for prominent persons; Bhutan relies on India for military training, arms supplies, and the country's air defense (2024)

SPACE

Space agency/agencies: announced in 2018 that it intends to establish a space agency, but has not yet done so; has a Division of Telecom and Space (DoTS) under the GovTech Agency (2024)

Space program overview: has a small, recently established program focused on acquiring satellites and developing the capabilities to manufacture satellites; cooperates with India and the US (2024)
note: further details about the key activities, programs, and milestones of the country's space program, as well as government spending estimates on the space sector, appear in the Space Programs reference guide

BOLIVIA

INTRODUCTION

Background: Bolivia, named after independence fighter Simón BOLÍVAR, broke away from Spanish rule in 1825. Much of its subsequent history has consisted of a series of coups and countercoups, with the last coup occurring in 1980. Democratic civilian rule was established in 1982, but leaders have faced problems of deep-seated poverty, social unrest, and illegal drug production.

In 2005, Bolivians elected Movement Toward Socialism leader Evo MORALES as president – by the widest margin of any leader since 1982 – after he ran on a promise to change the country's traditional political class and empower the poor and indigenous majority. In 2009 and 2014, MORALES easily won reelection, and his party maintained control of the legislative branch. In 2016, MORALES narrowly lost a referendum to approve a constitutional amendment that would have allowed him to compete in the 2019 presidential election. A subsequent Supreme Court ruling stating that term limits violate human rights provided the justification for MORALES to run despite the referendum, but rising violence, pressure from the military, and widespread allegations of electoral fraud ultimately forced him to flee the country. An interim government, led by President Jeanine AÑEZ Chávez, held new elections in 2020, and Luis Alberto ARCE Catacora was elected president.

GEOGRAPHY

Location: Central South America, southwest of Brazil

Geographic coordinates: 17 00 S, 65 00 W

Map references: South America

Area: *total:* 1,098,581 sq km
land: 1,083,301 sq km
water: 15,280 sq km
comparison ranking: total 29

Area - comparative: slightly less than three times the size of Montana

Land boundaries: *total:* 7,252 km
border countries (5): Argentina 942 km; Brazil 3,403 km; Chile 942 km; Paraguay 753 km; Peru 1,212 km

Coastline: 0 km (landlocked)

Maritime claims: none (landlocked)

Climate: varies with altitude; humid and tropical to cold and semiarid

Terrain: rugged Andes Mountains with a highland plateau (Altiplano), hills, lowland plains of the Amazon Basin

Elevation: *highest point:* Nevado Sajama 6,542 m
lowest point: Rio Paraguay 90 m
mean elevation: 1,192 m

Natural resources: lithium, tin, natural gas, petroleum, zinc, tungsten, antimony, silver, iron, lead, gold, timber, hydropower

Land use: *agricultural land:* 34.3% (2018 est.)
arable land: 3.6% (2018 est.)
permanent crops: 0.2% (2018 est.)
permanent pasture: 30.5% (2018 est.)
forest: 52.5% (2018 est.)
other: 13.2% (2018 est.)

Irrigated land: 2,972 sq km (2017)

Major lakes (area sq km): *fresh water lake(s):* Lago Titicaca (shared with Peru) - 8,030 sq km
salt water lake(s): Lago Poopo - 1,340 sq km

Major watersheds (area sq km): Atlantic Ocean drainage: Amazon (6,145,186 sq km), Paraná (2,582,704 sq km)

Major aquifers: Amazon Basin

Population distribution: a high altitude plain in the west between two cordillera of the Andes, known as the Altiplano, is the focal area for most of the population; a dense settlement pattern is also found in and around the city of Santa Cruz, located on the eastern side of the Andes

Natural hazards: flooding in the northeast (March to April)
volcanism: volcanic activity in Andes Mountains on the border with Chile; historically active volcanoes in this region are Irruputuncu (5,163 m), which last erupted in 1995, and the Olca-Paruma volcanic complex (5,762 m to 5,167 m)

Geography - note: *note 1:* landlocked; shares control of Lago Titicaca, world's highest navigable lake (elevation 3,805 m), with Peru
note 2: the southern regions of Peru and the extreme northwestern part of Bolivia are considered to be the place of origin for the common potato, while southeast Bolivia and northwest Argentina seem to be the original development site for peanuts

PEOPLE AND SOCIETY

Population: *total:* 12,311,974
male: 6,192,774
female: 6,119,200 (2024 est.)
comparison rankings: female 80; male 81; total 80

Nationality: *noun:* Bolivian(s)
adjective: Bolivian

Ethnic groups: Mestizo (mixed White and Indigenous ancestry) 68%, Indigenous 20%, White 5%, Cholo/Chola 2%, African descent 1%, other 1%, unspecified 3%; 44% other Indigenous group, predominantly Quechua or Aymara (2009 est.)
note: results among surveys vary based on the wording of the ethnicity question and the available response choices; the 2001 national census did not provide "Mestizo" as a response choice, resulting in a much higher proportion of respondents identifying themselves as belonging to one of the available indigenous ethnicity choices; the use of "Mestizo" and "Cholo" varies among response choices in surveys, with surveys using the terms interchangeably, providing one or the other as a response choice, or providing the two as separate response choices

Languages: Spanish (official) 68.1%, Quechua (official) 17.2%, Aymara (official) 10.5%, Guarani (official) 0.6%, other 1.5%, unspecified 2.1%; note - Spanish and all Indigenous languages are official (2012 est.)
major-language sample(s):
La Libreta Informativa del Mundo, la fuente indispensable de información básica. (Spanish)

Religions: Roman Catholic 65%, Protestant 19.6% (Evangelical (non-specific) 11.9%, Evangelical Baptist 2.1%, Evangelical Pentecostal 1.8%, Evangelical Methodist 0.7%, Adventist 2.8%, Protestant (non-specific) 0.3%), Believer (not belonging to the church) 0.9%, other 4.8%, atheist 1.7%, agnostic 0.6%, none 6.1%, unspecified 1.3% (2023 est.)

Demographic profile: Bolivia ranks at or near the bottom among Latin American countries in several areas of health and development, including poverty, education, fertility, malnutrition, mortality, and life expectancy. On the positive side, more children are being vaccinated and more pregnant women are getting prenatal care and having skilled health practitioners attend their births.

Bolivia's income inequality is the highest in Latin America and one of the highest in the world. Public education is of poor quality, and educational opportunities are among the most unevenly distributed in Latin America, with girls and indigenous and rural children less likely to be literate or to complete primary school. The lack of access to education and family planning services helps to sustain Bolivia's high fertility rate—approximately three children per woman. Bolivia's lack of clean water and basic sanitation, especially in rural areas, contributes to health problems.

Between 7% and 16% of Bolivia's population lives abroad (estimates vary in part because of illegal migration). Emigrants primarily seek jobs and better wages in Argentina (the principal destination), the US, and Spain. In recent years, more restrictive immigration policies in Europe and the US have increased the flow of Bolivian emigrants to neighboring countries. Fewer Bolivians migrated to Brazil in 2015 and 2016 because of its recession; increasing numbers have been going to Chile, mainly to work as miners.

Age structure: *0-14 years:* 28.5% (male 1,792,803/female 1,718,081)
15-64 years: 64.5% (male 4,002,587/female 3,937,953)
65 years and over: 7% (2024 est.) (male 397,384/female 463,166)

Dependency ratios: *total dependency ratio:* 56.3
youth dependency ratio: 48.7
elderly dependency ratio: 12
potential support ratio: 8.3 (2021 est.)

Median age: *total:* 26.6 years (2024 est.)
male: 26.2 years
female: 27 years
comparison ranking: total 163

Population growth rate: 1% (2024 est.)
comparison ranking: 92

Birth rate: 17.6 births/1,000 population (2024 est.)
comparison ranking: 84

Death rate: 6.6 deaths/1,000 population (2024 est.)
comparison ranking: 130

Net migration rate: -1 migrant(s)/1,000 population (2024 est.)
comparison ranking: 143

Population distribution: a high altitude plain in the west between two cordillera of the Andes, known as the Altiplano, is the focal area for most of the population; a dense settlement pattern is also found in and around the city of Santa Cruz, located on the eastern side of the Andes

Urbanization: *urban population:* 71.2% of total population (2023)
rate of urbanization: 1.87% annual rate of change (2020-25 est.)

Major urban areas - population: 1.936 million LA PAZ (capital), 1.820 million Santa Cruz, 1.400 million Cochabamba (2022); 278,000 Sucre (constitutional capital) (2018)

Sex ratio: *at birth:* 1.05 male(s)/female
0-14 years: 1.04 male(s)/female
15-64 years: 1.02 male(s)/female
65 years and over: 0.86 male(s)/female
total population: 1.01 male(s)/female (2024 est.)

Mother's mean age at first birth: 21.1 years (2008 est.)
note: data represents median age at first birth among women 25-49

Maternal mortality ratio: 161 deaths/100,000 live births (2020 est.)
comparison ranking: 53

Infant mortality rate: *total:* 22.3 deaths/1,000 live births (2024 est.)
male: 24.5 deaths/1,000 live births
female: 20 deaths/1,000 live births
comparison ranking: total 68

Life expectancy at birth: *total population:* 72.5 years (2024 est.)
male: 71 years
female: 74 years
comparison ranking: total population 161

Total fertility rate: 2.2 children born/woman (2024 est.)
comparison ranking: 85

Gross reproduction rate: 1.07 (2024 est.)

Contraceptive prevalence rate: 66.5% (2016)

Drinking water source: *improved: urban:* 99.2% of population
rural: 80.2% of population
total: 93.5% of population
unimproved: urban: 0.8% of population
rural: 19.8% of population
total: 6.5% of population (2020 est.)

Current health expenditure: 7.9% of GDP (2020)

Physician density: 1.03 physicians/1,000 population (2017)

Hospital bed density: 1.3 beds/1,000 population (2017)

Sanitation facility access: *improved: urban:* 97.8% of population
rural: 48.4% of population
total: 83.1% of population
unimproved: urban: 2.2% of population
rural: 51.6% of population
total: 16.9% of population (2020 est.)

Obesity - adult prevalence rate: 20.2% (2016)
comparison ranking: 103

Alcohol consumption per capita: *total:* 2.98 liters of pure alcohol (2019 est.)
beer: 2.22 liters of pure alcohol (2019 est.)
wine: 0.14 liters of pure alcohol (2019 est.)
spirits: 0.54 liters of pure alcohol (2019 est.)
other alcohols: 0.08 liters of pure alcohol (2019 est.)
comparison ranking: total 115

Tobacco use: *total:* 12.7% (2020 est.)
male: 20.5% (2020 est.)
female: 4.8% (2020 est.)
comparison ranking: total 120

Children under the age of 5 years underweight: 3.4% (2016)
comparison ranking: 86

Currently married women (ages 15-49): 57.1% (2023 est.)

Child marriage: *women married by age 15:* 3.4%
women married by age 18: 19.7%
men married by age 18: 5.2% (2016 est.)

Education expenditures: 9.8% of GDP (2020 est.)
comparison ranking: 5

Literacy: *definition:* age 15 and over can read and write
total population: 92.5%
male: 96.5%
female: 88.6% (2015)

ENVIRONMENT

Environment - current issues: the clearing of land for agricultural purposes and the international demand for tropical timber are contributing to deforestation; soil erosion from overgrazing and poor cultivation methods (including slash-and-burn agriculture); desertification; loss of biodiversity; industrial pollution of water supplies used for drinking and irrigation

Environment - international agreements: *party to:* Biodiversity, Climate Change, Climate Change-Kyoto Protocol, Climate Change-Paris Agreement, Comprehensive Nuclear Test Ban, Desertification, Endangered Species, Hazardous Wastes, Law of the Sea, Marine Dumping-London Convention, Nuclear Test Ban, Ozone Layer Protection, Ship Pollution, Wetlands,
signed, but not ratified: Environmental Modification, Marine Life Conservation

Climate: varies with altitude; humid and tropical to cold and semiarid

Urbanization: *urban population:* 71.2% of total population (2023)
rate of urbanization: 1.87% annual rate of change (2020-25 est.)

Revenue from forest resources: 0.33% of GDP (2018 est.)
comparison ranking: 78

Revenue from coal: 0% of GDP (2018 est.)
comparison ranking: 171

Air pollutants: *particulate matter emissions:* 25.23 micrograms per cubic meter (2019 est.)
carbon dioxide emissions: 21.61 megatons (2016 est.)
methane emissions: 21.01 megatons (2020 est.)

Waste and recycling: *municipal solid waste generated annually:* 2,219,052 tons (2015 est.)
municipal solid waste recycled annually: 268,727 tons (2015 est.)
percent of municipal solid waste recycled: 12.1% (2015 est.)

Major lakes (area sq km): *fresh water lake(s):* Lago Titicaca (shared with Peru) - 8,030 sq km
salt water lake(s): Lago Poopo - 1,340 sq km

Major watersheds (area sq km): Atlantic Ocean drainage: Amazon (6,145,186 sq km), Paraná (2,582,704 sq km)

Major aquifers: Amazon Basin

Total water withdrawal: *municipal:* 140 million cubic meters (2020 est.)
industrial: 30 million cubic meters (2020 est.)
agricultural: 1.92 billion cubic meters (2020 est.)

Total renewable water resources: 574 billion cubic meters (2020 est.)

GOVERNMENT

Country name: *conventional long form:* Plurinational State of Bolivia
conventional short form: Bolivia
local long form: Estado Plurinacional de Bolivia
local short form: Bolivia
etymology: the country is named after Simón BOLÍVAR, a 19th-century leader in the South American wars for independence

Government type: presidential republic

Capital: *name:* La Paz (administrative capital); Sucre (constitutional [legislative and judicial] capital)

geographic coordinates: 16 30 S, 68 09 W
time difference: UTC-4 (1 hour ahead of Washington, DC, during Standard Time)
etymology: La Paz is a shortening of the original name of the city, Nuestra Señora de La Paz (Our Lady of Peace); Sucre is named after Antonio José de SUCRE (1795-1830), military hero in the independence struggle from Spain and the second president of Bolivia
note: at approximately 3,630 m above sea level, La Paz's elevation makes it the highest capital city in the world

Administrative divisions: 9 departments (departamentos, singular - departamento); Beni, Chuquisaca, Cochabamba, La Paz, Oruro, Pando, Potosi, Santa Cruz, Tarija

Independence: 6 August 1825 (from Spain)

National holiday: Independence Day, 6 August (1825)

Legal system: civil law system with influences from Roman, Spanish, canon (religious), French, and indigenous law

Constitution: *history:* many previous; latest drafted 6 August 2006 to 9 December 2008, approved by referendum 25 January 2009, effective 7 February 2009
amendments: proposed through public petition by at least 20% of voters or by the Plurinational Legislative Assembly; passage requires approval by at least two-thirds majority vote of the total membership of the Assembly and approval in a referendum; amended 2013

International law organization participation: has not submitted an ICJ jurisdiction declaration; accepts ICCt jurisdiction

Citizenship: *citizenship by birth:* yes
citizenship by descent only: yes
dual citizenship recognized: yes
residency requirement for naturalization: 3 years

Suffrage: 18 years of age; universal and compulsory

Executive branch: *chief of state:* President Luis Alberto ARCE Catacora (since 8 November 2020)
head of government: President Luis Alberto ARCE Catacora (since 8 November 2020)
cabinet: Cabinet appointed by the president
elections/appointments: president and vice president directly elected on the same ballot one of 3 ways: candidate wins at least 50% of the vote, or at least 40% of the vote and 10% more than the next highest candidate; otherwise a second round is held and the winner determined by simple majority vote; president and vice president are elected by majority vote to serve a 5-year term; no term limits (changed from two-consecutive-term limit by Constitutional Court in late 2017); election last held on 18 October 2020 (next to be held in October 2025)
election results:
2020: Luis Alberto ARCE Catacora elected president; percent of vote - Luis Alberto ARCE Catacora (MAS) 55.1%; Carlos Diego MESA Gisbert (CC) 28.8%; Luis Fernando CAMACHO Vaca (Creemos) 14%; other 2.1%
2019: Juan Evo MORALES Ayma reelected president; percent of vote - Juan Evo MORALES Ayma (MAS) 61%; Samuel DORIA MEDINA Arana (UN) 24.5%; Jorge QUIROGA Ramirez (POC) 9.1%; other 5.4%; note - MORALES resigned from office on 10 November 2019 over alleged election rigging; resignations of all his constitutionally designated successors followed, including the Vice President, President of the Senate, President of the Chamber of Deputies, and First Vice President of the Senate, leaving the Second Vice President of the Senate, Jeanine ANEZ Chavez, the highest-ranking official still in office; her appointment to the presidency was endorsed by Bolivia's Constitutional Court, and she served as interim president until the 8 November 2020 inauguration of Luis Alberto ARCE Catacora, who won the 18 October 2020 presidential election
note: the president is both chief of state and head of government

Legislative branch: *description:* bicameral Plurinational Legislative Assembly or Asamblea Legislativa Plurinacional consists of: Chamber of Senators or Camara de Senadores (36 seats; members directly elected in multi-seat constituencies by partylist proportional representation vote; members serve 5-year terms)
Chamber of Deputies or Camara de Diputados (130 seats; 70 members directly elected in single-seat constituencies by simple majority vote, 53 directly elected in single-seat constituencies by closed party-list proportional representation vote, and 7 (apportioned to non-contiguous, rural areas in 7 of the 9 states) directly elected in single-seat constituencies by simple majority vote; members serve 5-year terms)
elections: Chamber of Senators - last held on 18 October 2020 (next to be held in 2025)
Chamber of Deputies - last held on 18 October 2020 (next to be held in 2025)
election results: Chamber of Senators - percent of vote by party - NA; seats by party - MAS 21, ACC 11, Creemos 4; composition - men 16, women 20, percentage women 55.6%
Chamber of Deputies - percent of vote by party - NA; seats by party - MAS 75, ACC 39, Creemos 16; composition - men 70, women 60, percentage women 46.2%; total Plurinational Legislative Assembly percentage women - 48.2%

Judicial branch: *highest court(s):* Supreme Court or Tribunal Supremo de Justicia (consists of 12 judges or ministros organized into civil, penal, social, and administrative chambers); Plurinational Constitutional Tribunal (consists of 7 primary and 7 alternate magistrates); Plurinational Electoral Organ (consists of 7 members and 6 alternates); National Agro-Environment Court (consists of 5 primary and 5 alternate judges; Council of the Judiciary (consists of 3 primary and 3 alternate judges)
judge selection and term of office: Supreme Court, Plurinational Constitutional Tribunal, National Agro-Environmental Court, and Council of the Judiciary candidates pre-selected by the Plurinational Legislative Assembly and elected by direct popular vote; judges elected for 6-year terms; Plurinational Electoral Organ judges appointed - 6 by the Legislative Assembly and 1 by the president of the republic; members serve single 6-year terms
subordinate courts: National Electoral Court; District Courts (in each of the 9 administrative departments); agro-environmental lower courts

Political parties: Community Citizen Alliance or ACC
Front for Victory or FPV
Movement Toward Socialism or MAS
National Unity or UN
Revolutionary Left Front or FRI
Revolutionary Nationalist Movement or MNR
Social Democrat Movement or MDS
Third System Movement or MTS
We Believe or Creemos
note: We Believe or Creemos [Luis Fernando CAMACHO Vaca] is a coalition comprised of several opposition parties that participated in the 2020 election, which includes the Christian Democratic Party (PDC) and Solidarity Civic Unity (UCS)

International organization participation: CAN, CD, CELAC, FAO, G-77, IADB, IAEA, IBRD, ICAO, ICC (national committees), ICCt, ICRM, IDA, IFAD, IFC, IFRCS, ILO, IMF, IMO, Interpol, IOC, IOM, IPU, ISO (correspondent), ITSO, ITU, LAES, LAIA, Mercosur (associate), MIGA, MINUSTAH, MONUSCO, NAM, OAS, OPANAL, OPCW, PCA, UN, UN Security Council (temporary), UNAMID, UNASUR, UNCTAD, UNESCO, UNIDO, Union Latina, UNISFA, UNMIL, UNMISS, UNOCI, UNOOSA, UNWTO, UPU, WCO, WFTU (NGOs), WHO, WIPO, WMO, WTO

Diplomatic representation in the US: *chief of mission:* Ambassador (vacant); Chargé d'Affaires Henry BALDELOMAR CHÁVEZ (since 11 October 2023)
chancery: 3014 Massachusetts Ave., NW, Washington, DC 20008
telephone: [1] (202) 483-4410
FAX: [1] (202) 328-3712
email address and website:
embolivia.wdc@gmail.com
https://www.boliviawdc.org/en-us/
consulate(s) general: Houston, Los Angeles, Miami, New York

Diplomatic representation from the US: *chief of mission:* Ambassador (vacant); Chargé d'Affaires Debra HEVIA (since September 2023)
embassy: Avenida Arce 2780, Casilla 425, La Paz
mailing address: 3220 La Paz Place, Washington DC 20512-3220
telephone: [591] (2) 216-8000
FAX: [591] (2) 216-8111
email address and website:
ConsularLaPazACS@state.gov
https://bo.usembassy.gov/
note: in September 2008, the Bolivian Government expelled the US Ambassador to Bolivia, Philip GOLDBERG, and both countries have yet to reinstate their ambassadors

Flag description: three equal horizontal bands of red (top), yellow, and green with the coat of arms centered on the yellow band; red stands for bravery and the blood of national heroes, yellow for the nation's mineral resources, and green for the fertility of the land
note: similar to the flag of Ghana, which has a large black five-pointed star centered in the yellow band; in 2009, a presidential decree made it mandatory for a so-called wiphala - a square, multi-colored flag representing the country's indigenous peoples - to be used alongside the traditional flag

National symbol(s): llama, Andean condor, two national flowers: the cantuta and the patuju; national colors: red, yellow, green

National anthem: *name:* "Cancion Patriotica" (Patriotic Song)
lyrics/music: Jose Ignacio de SANJINES/Leopoldo Benedetto VINCENTI
note: adopted 1852

National heritage: *total World Heritage Sites:* 7 (6 cultural, 1 natural)
selected World Heritage Site locales: City of Potosi (c); El Fuerte de Samaipata (c); Historic Sucre

(c); Jesuit Missions of Chiquitos (c); Noel Kempff Mercado National Park (n); Tiahuanacu (c); Qhapaq Ñan/Andean Road System (c)

ECONOMY

Economic overview: resource-rich economy benefits during commodity booms; has bestowed juridical rights to Mother Earth, impacting extraction industries; increasing Chinese lithium mining trade relations; hard hit by COVID-19; increased fiscal spending amid poverty increases; rampant banking and finance corruption

Real GDP (purchasing power parity): $119.785 billion (2023 est.)
$116.927 billion (2022 est.)
$112.858 billion (2021 est.)
note: data in 2021 dollars
comparison ranking: 93

Real GDP growth rate: 2.44% (2023 est.)
3.61% (2022 est.)
6.11% (2021 est.)
note: annual GDP % growth based on constant local currency
comparison ranking: 128

Real GDP per capita: $9,700 (2023 est.)
$9,600 (2022 est.)
$9,300 (2021 est.)
note: data in 2021 dollars
comparison ranking: 147

GDP (official exchange rate): $45.85 billion (2023 est.)
note: data in current dollars at official exchange rate

Inflation rate (consumer prices): 2.58% (2023 est.)
1.75% (2022 est.)
0.74% (2021 est.)
note: annual % change based on consumer prices
comparison ranking: 53

Credit ratings: Fitch rating: B (2020)

Moody's rating: B2 (2020)

Standard & Poors rating: B+ (2020)
note: The year refers to the year in which the current credit rating was first obtained.

GDP - composition, by sector of origin: *agriculture:* 12.5% (2023 est.)
industry: 24.8% (2023 est.)
services: 51.3% (2023 est.)
note: figures may not total 100% due to non-allocated consumption not captured in sector-reported data
comparison rankings: services 138; industry 99; agriculture 63

GDP - composition, by end use: *household consumption:* 67.6% (2023 est.)
government consumption: 19.3% (2023 est.)
investment in fixed capital: 17.5% (2023 est.)
investment in inventories: -0.9% (2022 est.)
exports of goods and services: 27.3% (2023 est.)
imports of goods and services: -31.6% (2023 est.)
note: figures may not total 100% due to rounding or gaps in data collection

Agricultural products: sugarcane, soybeans, potatoes, maize, rice, sorghum, milk, chicken, plantains, wheat (2022)
note: top ten agricultural products based on tonnage

Industries: mining, smelting, electricity, petroleum, food and beverages, handicrafts, clothing, jewelry

Industrial production growth rate: 1% (2023 est.)
note: annual % change in industrial value added based on constant local currency
comparison ranking: 139

Labor force: 6.114 million (2023 est.)
note: number of people ages 15 or older who are employed or seeking work
comparison ranking: 73

Unemployment rate: 3.08% (2023 est.)
3.55% (2022 est.)
5.09% (2021 est.)
note: % of labor force seeking employment
comparison ranking: 50

Youth unemployment rate (ages 15-24): *total:* 5.3% (2023 est.)
male: 4.5% (2023 est.)
female: 6.3% (2023 est.)
note: % of labor force ages 15-24 seeking employment
comparison ranking: total 177

Population below poverty line: 39% (2020 est.)
note: % of population with income below national poverty line

Gini Index coefficient - distribution of family income: 40.9 (2021 est.)
note: index (0-100) of income distribution; higher values represent greater inequality
comparison ranking: 36

Average household expenditures: *on food:* 29% of household expenditures (2022 est.)
on alcohol and tobacco: 2.1% of household expenditures (2022 est.)

Household income or consumption by percentage share: *lowest 10%:* 1.8% (2021 est.)
highest 10%: 30.3% (2021 est.)
note: % share of income accruing to lowest and highest 10% of population

Remittances: 3.21% of GDP (2023 est.)
3.32% of GDP (2022 est.)
3.51% of GDP (2021 est.)
note: personal transfers and compensation between resident and non-resident individuals/households/entities

Budget: *revenues:* $11.796 billion (2019 est.)
expenditures: $14.75 billion (2019 est.)

Public debt: 49% of GDP (2017 est.)
note: data cover general government debt and includes debt instruments issued by government entities other than the treasury; the data include treasury debt held by foreign entities; the data include debt issued by subnational entities
comparison ranking: 108

Taxes and other revenues: 39.9% (of GDP) (2017 est.)
comparison ranking: 10

Current account balance: -$1.247 billion (2023 est.)
$939.089 million (2022 est.)
$1.582 billion (2021 est.)
note: balance of payments - net trade and primary/secondary income in current dollars
comparison ranking: 144

Exports: $11.975 billion (2023 est.)
$14.465 billion (2022 est.)
$11.596 billion (2021 est.)
note: balance of payments - exports of goods and services in current dollars
comparison ranking: 107

Exports - partners: India 16%, Brazil 14%, Argentina 13%, Colombia 8%, Japan 7% (2022)
note: top five export partners based on percentage share of exports

Exports - commodities: natural gas, gold, zinc ore, soybean meal, soybean oil (2022)
note: top five export commodities based on value in dollars

Imports: $13.13 billion (2023 est.)
$13.462 billion (2022 est.)
$10.187 billion (2021 est.)
note: balance of payments - imports of goods and services in current dollars
comparison ranking: 110

Imports - partners: Brazil 20%, China 19%, Chile 13%, Peru 9%, Argentina 6% (2022)
note: top five import partners based on percentage share of imports

Imports - commodities: refined petroleum, cars, pesticides, plastic products, trucks (2022)
note: top five import commodities based on value in dollars

Reserves of foreign exchange and gold: $1.8 billion (2023 est.)
$3.752 billion (2022 est.)
$4.73 billion (2021 est.)
note: holdings of gold (year-end prices)/foreign exchange/special drawing rights in current dollars
comparison ranking: 92

Debt - external: $9.862 billion (2022 est.)
note: present value of external debt in current US dollars
comparison ranking: 38

Exchange rates: bolivianos (BOB) per US dollar -

Exchange rates: 6.91 (2023 est.)
6.91 (2022 est.)
6.91 (2021 est.)
6.91 (2020 est.)
6.91 (2019 est.)

ENERGY

Electricity access: *electrification - total population:* 99.9% (2022 est.)
electrification - urban areas: 100%
electrification - rural areas: 95.6%

Electricity: *installed generating capacity:* 4.104 million kW (2022 est.)
consumption: 10.565 billion kWh (2022 est.)
transmission/distribution losses: 948.628 million kWh (2022 est.)
comparison rankings: transmission/distribution losses 95; consumption 102; installed generating capacity 98

Electricity generation sources: *fossil fuels:* 65% of total installed capacity (2022 est.)
solar: 3% of total installed capacity (2022 est.)
wind: 3.8% of total installed capacity (2022 est.)
hydroelectricity: 24.8% of total installed capacity (2022 est.)
biomass and waste: 3.4% of total installed capacity (2022 est.)

Coal: *consumption:* 9,000 metric tons (2022 est.)
imports: 9,000 metric tons (2022 est.)
proven reserves: 1 million metric tons (2022 est.)

Petroleum: *total petroleum production:* 58,000 bbl/day (2023 est.)
refined petroleum consumption: 87,000 bbl/day (2022 est.)
crude oil estimated reserves: 240.9 million barrels (2021 est.)

Natural gas: *production:* 13.76 billion cubic meters (2022 est.)

consumption: 3.055 billion cubic meters (2022 est.)
exports: 10.285 billion cubic meters (2022 est.)
proven reserves: 302.99 billion cubic meters (2021 est.)

Carbon dioxide emissions: 17.773 million metric tonnes of CO2 (2022 est.)
from coal and metallurgical coke: 24,000 metric tonnes of CO2 (2022 est.)
from petroleum and other liquids: 11.768 million metric tonnes of CO2 (2022 est.)
from consumed natural gas: 5.981 million metric tonnes of CO2 (2022 est.)
comparison ranking: total emissions 90

Energy consumption per capita: 24.229 million Btu/person (2022 est.)
comparison ranking: 126

COMMUNICATIONS

Telephones - fixed lines: *total subscriptions:* 550,000 (2021 est.)
subscriptions per 100 inhabitants: 5 (2021 est.)
comparison ranking: total subscriptions 87

Telephones - mobile cellular: *total subscriptions:* 12.034 million (2021 est.)
subscriptions per 100 inhabitants: 100 (2021 est.)
comparison ranking: total subscriptions 83

Telecommunication systems: *general assessment:* the structure of Bolivia's fixed telecom market is different from most other countries; local services are primarily provided by 15 telecom cooperatives; these are non-profit-making companies privately owned and controlled by their users; since the market was liberalized, the cooperatives have also provided long-distance telephony, while several also offer broadband and pay TV service; they have invested in network upgrades in a bid to improve services for customers, and to expand their footprints; Bolivia has a multi-carrier system wherein consumers can choose a long-distance carrier for each call by dialing the carrier's prefix; several operators have also adopted fixed-wireless technologies, and some rent fiber-optic capacity; the fixed broadband services remain expensive, though the cost of bandwidth is only a fraction of what it was only a few years ago; services are still unavailable in many rural and remote areas, and even in some of the major urban areas; being a landlocked country, Bolivia had no direct access to submarine cable networks, and relies on satellite services or terrestrial links across neighboring countries; in September 2020 a new cable running via Peru, has increased capacity and contributed to a dramatic fall in end-user prices; fixed broadband services are fast migrating from DSL to fiber, while there are also cable broadband services available in some major cities; in 2007 the focus was on providing telecom services in rural areas under a project known as 'Territory with Total Coverage'; this project aims to increase telecom coverage through mobile rather than through fixed networks; Bolivia has almost twenty times as many mobile phone subscribers as fixed line connections, and the trend towards fixed-mobile substitution continues; all the mobile companies offer 3G and LTE services; due to the poor quality, high cost, and poor reach of DSL, mobile networks have become the principal platform for voice services and data access; by early 2021 companies' networks reached more than 95% of the population; about 92% of all internet accesses are via smartphones (2021)
domestic: 4 per 100 fixed-line, mobile-cellular telephone use expanding rapidly and teledensity stands at 100 per 100 persons; most telephones are concentrated in La Paz, Santa Cruz, and other capital cities (2021)
international: country code - 591; Bolivia has no direct access to submarine cable networks and must therefore connect to the rest of the world either via satellite or through terrestrial links across neighboring countries; satellite earth station - 1 Intelsat (Atlantic Ocean) (2019)

Broadcast media: large number of radio and TV stations broadcasting with private media outlets dominating; state-owned and private radio and TV stations generally operating freely, although both pro-government and anti-government groups have attacked media outlets in response to their reporting (2019)

Internet country code: .bo

Internet users
total: 7.92 million (2021 est.)
percent of population: 66% (2021 est.)
comparison ranking: total 76

Broadband - fixed subscriptions: *total:* 931,918 (2020 est.)
subscriptions per 100 inhabitants: 8 (2020 est.)
comparison ranking: total 76

TRANSPORTATION

National air transport system: *number of registered air carriers:* 7 (2020)
inventory of registered aircraft operated by air carriers: 39
annual passenger traffic on registered air carriers: 4,122,113 (2018)
annual freight traffic on registered air carriers: 13.73 million (2018) mt-km

Civil aircraft registration country code prefix: CP

Airports: 200 (2024)
comparison ranking: 32

Heliports: 3 (2024)

Pipelines: 5,457 km gas, 51 km liquid petroleum gas, 2,511 km oil, 1,627 km refined products (2013)

Railways: *total:* 3,960 km (2019)
narrow gauge: 3,960 km (2014) 1.000-m gauge
comparison ranking: total 49

Roadways: *total:* 90,568 km
paved: 9,792 km
unpaved: 80,776 km (2017)
comparison ranking: total 55

Waterways: 10,000 km (2012) (commercially navigable almost exclusively in the northern and eastern parts of the country)
comparison ranking: 15

Merchant marine: *total:* 50 (2023)
by type: general cargo 30, oil tanker 2, other 18
comparison ranking: total 121

MILITARY AND SECURITY

Military and security forces: Bolivian Armed Forces (Fuerzas Armadas de Bolivia or FAB): Bolivian Army (Ejercito de Boliviano, EB), Bolivian Naval Force (Fuerza Naval Boliviana, FNB), Bolivian Air Force (Fuerza Aerea Boliviana, FAB)

Ministry of Government: National Police (Policía Nacional de Bolivia, PNB) (2024)

note: the PNB includes two paramilitary forces, the Anti-Narcotics Special Forces (Fuerza Especial de Lucha Contra el Narcotráfico, FELCN) and the Anti-Terrorist Group (GAT); the PNB is part of the reserves for the Armed Forces; the police and military share responsibility for border enforcement

Military expenditures: 1.2% of GDP (2023 est.)
1.3% of GDP (2022 est.)
1.4% of GDP (2021 est.)
1.4% of GDP (2020 est.)
1.4% of GDP (2019 est.)
comparison ranking: 118

Military and security service personnel strengths: approximately 40,000 active-duty military personnel; approximately 40,000 National Police (2023)

Military equipment inventories and acquisitions: the military is equipped with a mix of mostly older Brazilian, Chinese, European, and US equipment (2024)

Military service age and obligation: compulsory for all men between the ages of 18 and 22; men can volunteer from the age of 16, women from 18; service is for 12 months; Search and Rescue service can be substituted for citizens who have reached the age of compulsory military service; duration of this service is 24 months (2024)
note 1: foreign nationals 18-22 residing in Bolivia may join the armed forces; joining speeds the process of acquiring Bolivian citizenship by naturalization
note 2: as of 2022, women comprised about 8% of the Bolivian military's personnel

Military - note: the Bolivian Armed Forces (FAB) are responsible for territorial defense but also have some internal security duties, particularly counternarcotics and border security; the FAB shares responsibility for border enforcement with the National Police (PNB), and it may be called out to assist the PNB with maintaining public order in critical situations
Bolivia has a small naval force for patrolling some 5,000 miles of navigable rivers to combat narcotics trafficking and smuggling, provide disaster relief, and deliver supplies to remote rural areas, as well as for maintaining a presence on Lake Titicaca; the Navy also exists in part to cultivate a maritime tradition and as a reminder of Bolivia's defeat at the hands of Chile in the War of the Pacific (1879-1883), and its desire to regain access to the Pacific Ocean; every year on 23 March, the Navy participates in parades and government ceremonies commemorating the Día Del Mar (Day of the Sea) holiday that remembers the loss (2024)

SPACE

Space agency/agencies: Bolivian Space Agency (la Agencia Boliviana Espacial, ABE; established 2010 as a national public company) (2024)

Space program overview: has a small space program focused on acquiring and operating satellites; operates a telecommunications satellite and two ground stations; has cooperated with China and India and member states of the Latin American and Caribbean Space Agency (ALCE) (2024)
note: further details about the key activities, programs, and milestones of the country's space program, as well as government spending estimates on the space sector, appear in the Space Programs reference guide

TRANSNATIONAL ISSUES

Refugees and internally displaced persons: *refugees (country of origin)*: 16,350 (Venezuela) (2023)

Illicit drugs: the third-largest source country of cocaine and a major transit country for Peruvian cocaine; coca cultivation in 2021 totaled 39,700 hectares (ha); most cocaine is exported to other Latin American countries, especially Brazil, Paraguay, and Argentina, for domestic consumption, or for onward transit from those countries to West Africa and Europe, not the United States.

BOSNIA AND HERZEGOVINA

INTRODUCTION

Background: After four centuries of Ottoman rule over Bosnia and Herzegovina, Austria-Hungary took control in 1878 and held the region until 1918, when it was incorporated into the newly created Kingdom of Serbs, Croats, and Slovenes. After World War II, Bosnia and Herzegovina joined the Socialist Federal Republic of Yugoslavia (SFRY).

Bosnia and Herzegovina declared sovereignty in October 1991 and independence from the SFRY on 3 March 1992 after a referendum boycotted by ethnic Serbs. Bosnian Serb militias, with the support of Serbia and Croatia, then tried to take control of territories they claimed as their own. From 1992 to 1995, ethnic cleansing campaigns killed thousands and displaced more than two million people. On 21 November 1995, in Dayton, Ohio, the warring parties initialed a peace agreement, and the final agreement was signed in Paris on 14 December 1995.

The Dayton Accords retained Bosnia and Herzegovina's international boundaries and created a multiethnic and democratic government composed of two entities roughly equal in size: the predominantly Bosniak-Bosnian Croat Federation of Bosnia and Herzegovina and the predominantly Bosnian Serb-led Republika Srpska (RS). The Dayton Accords also established the Office of the High Representative to oversee the agreement's implementation. In 1996, the NATO-led Stabilization Force (SFOR) took over responsibility for enforcing the peace. In 2004, European Union peacekeeping troops (EUFOR) replaced SFOR. As of 2022, EUFOR deploys around 1,600 troops in Bosnia in a peacekeeping capacity. Bosnia and Herzegovina became an official candidate for EU membership in 2022.

GEOGRAPHY

Location: Southeastern Europe, bordering the Adriatic Sea and Croatia

Geographic coordinates: 44 00 N, 18 00 E

Map references: Europe

Area: *total:* 51,197 sq km
land: 51,187 sq km
water: 10 sq km
comparison ranking: total 128

Area - comparative: slightly smaller than West Virginia

Land boundaries: *total:* 1,543 km
border countries (3): Croatia 956 km; Montenegro 242 km; Serbia 345 km

Coastline: 20 km

Maritime claims: NA

Climate: hot summers and cold winters; areas of high elevation have short, cool summers and long, severe winters; mild, rainy winters along coast

Terrain: mountains and valleys

Elevation: *highest point:* Maglic 2,386 m
lowest point: Adriatic Sea 0 m
mean elevation: 500 m

Natural resources: coal, iron ore, antimony, bauxite, copper, lead, zinc, chromite, cobalt, manganese, nickel, clay, gypsum, salt, sand, timber, hydropower

Land use: *agricultural land:* 42.2% (2018 est.)
arable land: 19.7% (2018 est.)
permanent crops: 2% (2018 est.)
permanent pasture: 20.5% (2018 est.)
forest: 42.8% (2018 est.)
other: 15% (2018 est.)

Irrigated land: 30 sq km (2012)

Major watersheds (area sq km): Atlantic Ocean drainage: *(Black Sea)* Danube (795,656 sq km)

Population distribution: the northern and central areas of the country are the most densely populated

Natural hazards: destructive earthquakes

Geography - note: within Bosnia and Herzegovina's recognized borders, the country is divided into a joint Bosniak/Croat Federation (about 51% of the territory) and the Bosnian Serb-led Republika Srpska or RS (about 49% of the territory); the region called Herzegovina is contiguous to Croatia and Montenegro, and traditionally has been settled by an ethnic Croat majority in the west and an ethnic Serb majority in the east

PEOPLE AND SOCIETY

Population: *total:* 3,798,671
male: 1,852,164
female: 1,946,507 (2024 est.)
comparison rankings: female 130; male 132; total 131

Nationality: *noun:* Bosnian(s), Herzegovinian(s)
adjective: Bosnian, Herzegovinian

Ethnic groups: Bosniak 50.1%, Serb 30.8%, Croat 15.4%, other 2.7%, not declared/no answer 1% (2013 est.)
note: Republika Srpska authorities dispute the methodology and refuse to recognize the results; Bosniak has replaced Muslim as an ethnic term in part to avoid confusion with the religious term Muslim - an adherent of Islam

Languages: Bosnian (official) 52.9%, Serbian (official) 30.8%, Croatian (official) 14.6%, other 1.6%, no answer 0.2% (2013 est.)
major-language sample(s):
Knjiga svjetskih činjenica, neophodan izvor osnovnih informacija. (Bosnian)
Knjiga svetskih činjenica, neophodan izvor osnovnih informacija. (Serbian)
Knjiga svjetskih činjenica, nužan izvor osnovnih informacija. (Croatian)

Religions: Muslim 50.7%, Orthodox 30.7%, Roman Catholic 15.2%, atheist 0.8%, agnostic 0.3%, other 1.2%, undeclared/no answer 1.1% (2013 est.)

Age structure: *0-14 years:* 13.1% (male 257,444/female 240,209)
15-64 years: 68.3% (male 1,305,271/female 1,290,920)
65 years and over: 18.6% (2024 est.) (male 289,449/female 415,378)

Dependency ratios: *total dependency ratio:* 48
youth dependency ratio: 22.3
elderly dependency ratio: 27.1
potential support ratio: 3.7 (2021 est.)

Median age: *total:* 44.8 years (2024 est.)
male: 43.1 years
female: 46.5 years
comparison ranking: total 28

Population growth rate: -0.25% (2024 est.)
comparison ranking: 211

Birth rate: 8.2 births/1,000 population (2024 est.)
comparison ranking: 213

Death rate: 10.3 deaths/1,000 population (2024 est.)
comparison ranking: 32

Net migration rate: -0.4 migrant(s)/1,000 population (2024 est.)
comparison ranking: 118

Population distribution: the northern and central areas of the country are the most densely populated

Urbanization: *urban population:* 50.3% of total population (2023)
rate of urbanization: 0.61% annual rate of change (2020-25 est.)

Major urban areas - population: 346,000 SARAJEVO (capital) (2023)

Sex ratio: *at birth:* 1.07 male(s)/female
0-14 years: 1.07 male(s)/female
15-64 years: 1.01 male(s)/female
65 years and over: 0.7 male(s)/female

total population: 0.95 male(s)/female (2024 est.)

Mother's mean age at first birth: 27.7 years (2019 est.)

Maternal mortality ratio: 6 deaths/100,000 live births (2020 est.)
comparison ranking: 160

Infant mortality rate: *total:* 5 deaths/1,000 live births (2024 est.)
male: 5.1 deaths/1,000 live births
female: 4.9 deaths/1,000 live births
comparison ranking: total 176

Life expectancy at birth: *total population:* 78.5 years (2024 est.)
male: 75.5 years
female: 81.6 years
comparison ranking: total population 77

Total fertility rate: 1.38 children born/woman (2024 est.)
comparison ranking: 214

Gross reproduction rate: 0.67 (2024 est.)

Contraceptive prevalence rate: 45.8% (2011/12)

Drinking water source: *improved: urban:* 99.9% of population
rural: 100% of population
total: 99.9% of population
unimproved: urban: 0.1% of population
rural: 0% of population
total: 0.1% of population (2020 est.)

Current health expenditure: 9.8% of GDP (2020)

Physician density: 2.16 physicians/1,000 population (2015)

Hospital bed density: 3.5 beds/1,000 population (2014)

Sanitation facility access: *improved: urban:* 99.5% of population
unimproved: urban: 0.5% of population

Obesity - adult prevalence rate: 17.9% (2016)
comparison ranking: 118

Alcohol consumption per capita: *total:* 5.46 liters of pure alcohol (2019 est.)
beer: 4.19 liters of pure alcohol (2019 est.)
wine: 0.47 liters of pure alcohol (2019 est.)
spirits: 0.62 liters of pure alcohol (2019 est.)
other alcohols: 0.17 liters of pure alcohol (2019 est.)
comparison ranking: total 81

Tobacco use: *total:* 35% (2020 est.)
male: 42% (2020 est.)
female: 28% (2020 est.)
comparison ranking: total 15

Currently married women (ages 15-49): 63.8% (2023 est.)

Literacy: *definition:* age 15 and over can read and write
total population: 98.1%
male: 99.4%
female: 98.1% (2021)

School life expectancy (primary to tertiary education): *total:* 14 years
male: 14 years
female: 15 years (2014)

ENVIRONMENT

Environment - current issues: air pollution; deforestation and illegal logging; inadequate wastewater treatment and flood management facilities; sites for disposing of urban waste are limited; land mines left over from the 1992-95 civil strife are a hazard in some areas

Environment - international agreements: *party to:* Air Pollution, Biodiversity, Climate Change, Climate Change-Kyoto Protocol, Climate Change-Paris Agreement, Comprehensive Nuclear Test Ban, Desertification, Endangered Species, Hazardous Wastes, Law of the Sea, Marine Life Conservation, Nuclear Test Ban, Ozone Layer Protection, Wetlands
signed, but not ratified: none of the selected agreements

Climate: hot summers and cold winters; areas of high elevation have short, cool summers and long, severe winters; mild, rainy winters along coast

Urbanization: *urban population:* 50.3% of total population (2023)
rate of urbanization: 0.61% annual rate of change (2020-25 est.)

Revenue from forest resources: 0.49% of GDP (2018 est.)
comparison ranking: 66

Revenue from coal: 0.34% of GDP (2018 est.)
comparison ranking: 17

Air pollutants: *particulate matter emissions:* 26.19 micrograms per cubic meter (2019 est.)
carbon dioxide emissions: 21.85 megatons (2016 est.)
methane emissions: 2.92 megatons (2020 est.)

Waste and recycling: *municipal solid waste generated annually:* 1,248,718 tons (2015 est.)
municipal solid waste recycled annually: 12 tons (2015 est.)
percent of municipal solid waste recycled: 0% (2015 est.)

Major watersheds (area sq km): Atlantic Ocean drainage: *(Black Sea)* Danube (795,656 sq km)

Total water withdrawal: *municipal:* 310 million cubic meters (2020 est.)
industrial: 60 million cubic meters (2020 est.)

Total renewable water resources: 37.5 billion cubic meters (2020 est.)

GOVERNMENT

Country name: *conventional long form:* none
conventional short form: Bosnia and Herzegovina
local long form: none
local short form: Bosna i Hercegovina
former: People's Republic of Bosnia and Herzegovina, Socialist Republic of Bosnia and Herzegovina
abbreviation: BiH
etymology: the larger northern territory is named for the Bosna River; the smaller southern section takes its name from the German word "herzog," meaning "duke," and the ending "-ovina," meaning "land," forming the combination denoting "dukedom"

Government type: parliamentary republic

Capital: *name:* Sarajevo
geographic coordinates: 43 52 N, 18 25 E
time difference: UTC+1 (6 hours ahead of Washington, DC, during Standard Time)
daylight saving time: +1hr, begins last Sunday in March; ends last Sunday in October
etymology: the name derives from the Turkish noun *saray*, meaning "palace" or "mansion," and the term *ova*, signifying "plain(s)," to give a meaning of "palace plains" or "the plains about the palace"

Administrative divisions: 3 first-order administrative divisions - Brcko District (Brcko Distrikt) (ethnically mixed), Federation of Bosnia and Herzegovina (Federacija Bosne i Hercegovine) (predominantly Bosniak-Croat), Republika Srpska (predominantly Serb)

Independence: 1 March 1992 (from Yugoslavia); note - referendum for independence completed on 1 March 1992; independence declared on 3 March 1992

National holiday: Independence Day, 1 March (1992) and Statehood Day, 25 November (1943) - both observed in the Federation of Bosnia and Herzegovina entity; Victory Day, 9 May (1945) and Dayton Agreement Day, 21 November (1995) - both observed in the Republika Srpska entity
note: there is no national-level holiday

Legal system: civil law system; Constitutional Court review of legislative acts

Constitution: *history:* 14 December 1995 (constitution included as part of the Dayton Peace Accords); note - each of the political entities has its own constitution
amendments: decided by the Parliamentary Assembly, including a two-thirds majority vote of members present in the House of Representatives; the constitutional article on human rights and fundamental freedoms cannot be amended; amended several times, last in 2009

International law organization participation: has not submitted an ICJ jurisdiction declaration; accepts ICCt jurisdiction

Citizenship: *citizenship by birth:* no
citizenship by descent only: at least one parent must be a citizen of Bosnia and Herzegovina
dual citizenship recognized: yes, provided there is a bilateral agreement with the other state
residency requirement for naturalization: 8 years

Suffrage: 18 years of age, 16 if employed; universal

Executive branch: *chief of state:* Chairperson of the Presidency Denis BECIROVIC (chairperson since 16 March 2024; presidency member since 16 November 2022 - Bosniak seat); Zeljka CVIJANOVIC (presidency member since 16 November 2022 - Serb seat); Zeljko KOMSIC (presidency member since 20 November 2018 - Croat seat)
head of government: Chairperson of the Council of Ministers Borjana KRISTO (since 25 January 2023)
cabinet: Council of Ministers nominated by the council chairperson, approved by the state-level House of Representatives
elections/appointments: 3-member presidency (1 Bosniak and 1 Croat elected from the Federation of Bosnia and Herzegovina and 1 Serb elected from the Republika Srpska) directly elected by simple majority popular vote for a 4-year term (eligible for a second term but then ineligible for 4 years); the presidency chairpersonship rotates every 8 months with the new member of the presidency elected with the highest number of votes starting the new mandate as chair; election last held on 2 October 2022 (next to be held in October 2026); the chairperson of the Council of Ministers appointed by the presidency and confirmed by the state-level House of Representatives
election results:
2022: percent of vote - Denis BECIROVIC - (SDP BiH) 57.4% - Bosniak seat; Zeljko KOMSIC (DF) 55.8% - Croat seat; Zeljka CVIJANOVIC (SNSD) 51.7% - Serb seat
2018: percent of vote - Milorad DODIK (SNSD) 53.9% - Serb seat; Zeljko KOMSIC (DF) 52.6%

- Croat seat; Sefik DZAFEROVIC (SDA) 36.6% - Bosniak seat
note: President of the Federation of Bosnia and Herzegovina Lidija BRADARA (since 28 February 2023); Vice Presidents Refik LENDO (since 28 February 2023) and Igor STOJANOVIC (since 28 February 2023); President of the Republika Srpska Milorad DODIK (since 15 November 2022); Vice Presidents Camil DURAKOVIC (since 15 November 2022) and Davor PRANJIC (since 15 November 2022)

Legislative branch: *description:* bicameral Parliamentary Assembly or Skupstina consists of:
House of Peoples or Dom Naroda (15 seats - 5 Bosniak, 5 Croat, 5 Serb; members designated by the Federation of Bosnia and Herzegovina's House of Peoples and the Republika Srpska's National Assembly to serve 4-year terms)
House of Representatives or Predstavnicki Dom (42 seats to include 28 seats allocated to the Federation of Bosnia and Herzegovina and 14 to the Republika Srpska; members directly elected by proportional representation vote to serve 4-year terms)
elections: House of Peoples - last held on 2 October 2022 (next to be held in 2026)
House of Representatives - last held on 2 October 2022 (next to be held in 2026)
election results: House of Peoples - percent of vote by party/coalition - NA; seats by party/coalition - NA; composition - men 13, women 2, percentage women 13.3%
House of Representatives - percent of vote by party/coalition - SDA 17.2%, SNSD 16.3%, HDZ BiH 8.8%, SDP 8.2%, SDS 7.1%, DF-GS 6.4%, NiP 5%, PDP 4.6%, NS/HC 3.1%, NES 3%, For Justice and Order 2.1%, DEMOS 1.9%, US 1.6%, BHI KF 1.3%, other 13.4%; seats by party/coalition - SDA 9, SNSD 6, SDP 5, HDZ BiH 4, DF-GS 3, NiP 3, SDS 2, PDP 2, NS/HC 2, NES 2, For Justice and Order 1, DEMOS 1, US 1, BHI KF 1; composition - men 34, women 8, percentage women 19.1%; total Parliamentary Assembly percentage women 17.5%

Judicial branch: *highest court(s):* Bosnia and Herzegovina (BiH) Constitutional Court (consists of 9 members); Court of BiH (consists of 44 national judges and 7 international judges organized into 3 divisions - Administrative, Appellate, and Criminal, which includes a War Crimes Chamber)
judge selection and term of office: BiH Constitutional Court judges - 4 selected by the Federation of Bosnia and Herzegovina House of Representatives, 2 selected by the Republika Srpska's National Assembly, and 3 non-Bosnian judges selected by the president of the European Court of Human Rights; Court of BiH president and national judges appointed by the High Judicial and Prosecutorial Council; Court of BiH president appointed for renewable 6-year term; other national judges appointed to serve until age 70; international judges recommended by the president of the Court of BiH and appointed by the High Representative for Bosnia and Herzegovina; international judges appointed to serve until age 70
subordinate courts: the Federation has 10 cantonal courts plus a number of municipal courts; the Republika Srpska has a supreme court, 5 district courts, and a number of municipal courts

Political parties: Alliance of Independent Social Democrats or SNSD
Bosnian-Herzegovinian Initiative or BHI KF
Civic Alliance or GS
Croatian Democratic Union of Bosnia and Herzegovina or HDZ-BiH
Democratic Front or DF
Democratic Union or DEMOS
For Justice and Order
Our Party or NS/HC
Party for Democratic Action or SDA
Party of Democratic Progress or PDP
People and Justice Party or NiP
People's European Union of Bosnia and Herzegovina or NES
Serb Democratic Party or SDS
Social Democratic Party or SDP
United Srpska or US

International organization participation: BIS, CD, CE, CEI, EAPC, EBRD, FAO, G-77, IAEA, IBRD, ICAO, ICC (NGOs), ICCt, ICRM, IDA, IFAD, IFC, IFRCS, ILO, IMF, IMO, IMSO, Interpol, IOC, IOM, IPU, ISO, ITSO, ITU, ITUC (NGOs), MIGA, MONUSCO, NAM (observer), OAS (observer), OIC (observer), OIF (observer), OPCW, OSCE, PFP, SELEC, UN, UNCTAD, UNESCO, UNIDO, UNWTO, UPU, WCO, WHO, WIPO, WMO, WTO (observer)
note: Bosnia-Herzegovina is an EU candidate country whose satisfactory completion of accession criteria is required before being granted full EU membership

Diplomatic representation in the US: *chief of mission:* Ambassador Sven ALKALAJ (since 30 June 2023)
chancery: 2109 E Street NW, Washington, DC 20037
telephone: [1] (202) 337-1500
FAX: [1] (202) 337-1502
email address and website:
info@bhembassy.org
http://www.bhembassy.org/index.html
consulate(s) general: Chicago

Diplomatic representation from the US: *chief of mission:* Ambassador Michael J. MURPHY (since 23 February 2022)
embassy: 1 Robert C. Frasure Street, 71000 Sarajevo
mailing address: 7130 Sarajevo Place, Washington DC 20521-7130
telephone: [387] (33) 704-000
FAX: [387] (33) 659-722
email address and website:
sarajevoACS@state.gov
https://ba.usembassy.gov/
branch office(s): Banja Luka, Mostar

Flag description: a wide blue vertical band on the fly side with a yellow isosceles triangle abutting the band and the top of the flag; the remainder of the flag is blue with seven full five-pointed white stars and two half stars top and bottom along the hypotenuse of the triangle; the triangle approximates the shape of the country and its three points stand for the constituent peoples - Bosniaks, Croats, and Serbs; the stars represent Europe and are meant to be continuous (thus the half stars at top and bottom); the colors (white, blue, and yellow) are often associated with neutrality and peace, and traditionally are linked with Bosnia
note: one of several flags where a prominent component of the design reflects the shape of the country; other such flags are those of Brazil, Eritrea, and Vanuatu

National symbol(s): golden lily; national colors: blue, yellow, white

National anthem: *name:* "Drzavna himna Bosne i Hercegovine" (The National Anthem of Bosnia and Herzegovina)
lyrics/music: none officially/Dusan SESTIC
note: music adopted 1999; lyrics proposed in 2008 and others in 2016 were not approved

National heritage: *total World Heritage Sites:* 4 (3 cultural, 1 natural)
selected World Heritage Site locales: Old Bridge Area of Mostar (c); Mehmed Paša Sokolović Bridge (c); Stecci Medieval Tombstones Graveyards (c); Primeval Beech Forests - Janj Forest (n)

ECONOMY

Economic overview: import-dominated economy; remains consumption-heavy; lack of private sector investments and diversification; jointly addressing structural economic challenges; Chinese energy infrastructure investments; high unemployment; tourism industry impacted by COVID-19

Real GDP (purchasing power parity): $63.769 billion (2023 est.)
$62.717 billion (2022 est.)
$60.174 billion (2021 est.)
note: data in 2021 dollars
comparison ranking: 113

Real GDP growth rate: 1.68% (2023 est.)
4.23% (2022 est.)
7.39% (2021 est.)
note: annual GDP % growth based on constant local currency
comparison ranking: 149

Real GDP per capita: $19,900 (2023 est.)
$19,400 (2022 est.)
$18,400 (2021 est.)
note: data in 2021 dollars
comparison ranking: 101

GDP (official exchange rate): $27.055 billion (2023 est.)
note: data in current dollars at official exchange rate

Inflation rate (consumer prices): 1.98% (2021 est.)
-1.05% (2020 est.)
0.56% (2019 est.)
comparison ranking: 34

Credit ratings: Moody's rating: B3 (2012)
Standard & Poors rating: B (2011)
note: The year refers to the year in which the current credit rating was first obtained.

GDP - composition, by sector of origin: *agriculture:* 4.3% (2023 est.)
industry: 23.3% (2023 est.)
services: 56.4% (2023 est.)
note: figures may not total 100% due to non-allocated consumption not captured in sector-reported data comparison rankings: services 113; industry 113; agriculture 124

GDP - composition, by end use: *household consumption:* 71.9% (2023 est.)
government consumption: 19.9% (2023 est.)
investment in fixed capital: 22.1% (2022 est.)
investment in inventories: 4.7% (2023 est.)
exports of goods and services: 44.1% (2023 est.)
imports of goods and services: -56.9% (2023 est.)
note: figures may not total 100% due to rounding or gaps in data collection

Agricultural products: maize, milk, vegetables, potatoes, plums, wheat, apples, barley, chicken, pears (2022)
note: top ten agricultural products based on tonnage

Industries: steel, coal, iron ore, lead, zinc, manganese, bauxite, aluminum, motor vehicle assembly, textiles, tobacco products, wooden furniture, ammunition, domestic appliances, oil refining

Industrial production growth rate: -2.8% (2023 est.)
note: annual % change in industrial value added based on constant local currency
comparison ranking: 190

Labor force: 1.369 million (2023 est.)
note: number of people ages 15 or older who are employed or seeking work
comparison ranking: 140

Unemployment rate: 10.42% (2023 est.)
12.66% (2022 est.)
14.9% (2021 est.)
note: % of labor force seeking employment
comparison ranking: 165

Youth unemployment rate (ages 15-24): *total:* 26.5% (2023 est.)
male: 24.6% (2023 est.)
female: 30.1% (2023 est.)
note: % of labor force ages 15-24 seeking employment
comparison ranking: total 37

Population below poverty line: 16.9% (2015 est.)
note: % of population with income below national poverty line

Average household expenditures: *on food:* 29.2% of household expenditures (2022 est.)
on alcohol and tobacco: 8.3% of household expenditures (2022 est.)

Remittances: 10.53% of GDP (2023 est.)
10.52% of GDP (2022 est.)
10.47% of GDP (2021 est.)
note: personal transfers and compensation between resident and non-resident individuals/households/entities

Budget: *revenues:* $10.195 billion (2023 est.)
expenditures: $9.739 billion (2023 est.)
note: central government revenues (excluding grants) and expenses converted to US dollars at average official exchange rate for year indicated

Public debt: 41.74% of GDP (2022 est.)
note: central government debt as a % of GDP
comparison ranking: 127

Taxes and other revenues: 19.09% (of GDP) (2022 est.)
note: central government tax revenue as a % of GDP
comparison ranking: 92

Current account balance: -$760.467 million (2023 est.)
-$1.065 billion (2022 est.)
-$418.984 million (2021 est.)
note: balance of payments - net trade and primary/secondary income in current dollars
comparison ranking: 130

Exports: $11.942 billion (2023 est.)
$11.794 billion (2022 est.)
$10.058 billion (2021 est.)
note: balance of payments - exports of goods and services in current dollars
comparison ranking: 108

Exports - partners: Croatia 14%, Germany 14%, Serbia 13%, Italy 10%, Austria 9% (2022)
note: top five export partners based on percentage share of exports

Exports - commodities: aluminum, electricity, footwear, garments, plastic products (2022)
note: top five export commodities based on value in dollars

Imports: $15.398 billion (2023 est.)
$15.162 billion (2022 est.)
$12.738 billion (2021 est.)
note: balance of payments - imports of goods and services in current dollars
comparison ranking: 105

Imports - partners: Croatia 16%, Serbia 13%, Germany 8%, Italy 8%, China 7% (2022)
note: top five import partners based on percentage share of imports

Imports - commodities: refined petroleum, aluminum, garments, coal, cars (2022)
note: top five import commodities based on value in dollars

Reserves of foreign exchange and gold: $9.205 billion (2023 est.)
$8.762 billion (2022 est.)
$9.475 billion (2021 est.)
note: holdings of gold (year-end prices)/foreign exchange/special drawing rights in current dollars
comparison ranking: 87

Debt - external: $4.521 billion (2022 est.)
note: present value of external debt in current US dollars
comparison ranking: 55

Exchange rates: konvertibilna markas (BAM) per US dollar -

Exchange rates: 1.809 (2023 est.)
1.859 (2022 est.)
1.654 (2021 est.)
1.717 (2020 est.)
1.747 (2019 est.)

ENERGY

Electricity access: *electrification - total population:* 100% (2022 est.)

Electricity: *installed generating capacity:* 4.591 million kW (2022 est.)
consumption: 12.648 billion kWh (2022 est.)
exports: 6.856 billion kWh (2022 est.)
imports: 3.828 billion kWh (2022 est.)
transmission/distribution losses: 1.353 billion kWh (2022 est.)
comparison rankings: transmission/distribution losses 113; imports 50; exports 33; consumption 93; installed generating capacity 91

Electricity generation sources: *fossil fuels:* 69.3% of total installed capacity (2022 est.)
solar: 0.7% of total installed capacity (2022 est.)
wind: 2.3% of total installed capacity (2022 est.)
hydroelectricity: 27.7% of total installed capacity (2022 est.)
biomass and waste: 0.1% of total installed capacity (2022 est.)

Coal: *production:* 14.114 million metric tons (2022 est.)
consumption: 14.766 million metric tons (2022 est.)
exports: 739,000 metric tons (2022 est.)
imports: 1.425 million metric tons (2022 est.)
proven reserves: 2.264 billion metric tons (2022 est.)

Petroleum: *refined petroleum consumption:* 36,000 bbl/day (2022 est.)

Natural gas: *consumption:* 225.824 million cubic meters (2022 est.)
imports: 225.824 million cubic meters (2022 est.)

Carbon dioxide emissions: 25.762 million metric tonnes of CO_2 (2022 est.)
from coal and metallurgical coke: 20.191 million metric tonnes of CO_2 (2022 est.)
from petroleum and other liquids: 5.141 million metric tonnes of CO_2 (2022 est.)
from consumed natural gas: 430,000 metric tonnes of CO_2 (2022 est.)
comparison ranking: total emissions 78

Energy consumption per capita: 92.698 million Btu/person (2022 est.)
comparison ranking: 58

COMMUNICATIONS

Telephones - fixed lines: *total subscriptions:* 651,000 (2022 est.)
subscriptions per 100 inhabitants: 20 (2022 est.)
comparison ranking: total subscriptions 84

Telephones - mobile cellular: *total subscriptions:* 3.812 million (2022 est.)
subscriptions per 100 inhabitants: 118 (2022 est.)
comparison ranking: total subscriptions 137

Telecommunication systems: *general assessment:* the telecom market has been liberalized and a regulatory framework created based on the EU's regulatory framework for communications; although Bosnia-Herzegovina remains an EU candidate country, in July 2017 it applied amended mobile roaming charges to fit in with changes introduced across the Union; further roaming agreements were made in 2019 with other western Balkan countries; the fixed-line broadband network is comparatively underdeveloped, with the result that investments made in mobile upgrades to facilitate broadband connectivity in the country to a greater extent than is common elsewhere in Europe; internet services are available; DSL and cable are the main platforms for fixed-line connectivity, while fiber broadband as yet has only a small market presence; the three MNOs, each affiliated with one of the incumbent fixed-line operators, provide national coverage with 3G, though LTE coverage is only about 89%; their upgraded networks are helping to support broadband in rural areas where fixed-line infrastructure is insufficient; mobile data and mobile broadband offers will provide future revenue growth given the limited potential of mobile voice services; the MNOs tested LTE services under trial licenses from 2013, commercial launches were delayed until the award of spectrum in early 2019; the regulator stipulated that licenses must provide national coverage within five years; trials of 5G technology have been undertaken, though there are no plans to launch services commercially in the short term, given that the MNOs can continue to exploit the capacity of their existing LTE networks (2021)
domestic: fixed-line teledensity roughly 21 per 100 persons and mobile-cellular subscribership stands at 114 telephones per 100 persons (2021)
international: country code - 387; no satellite earth stations

Broadcast media: *3 public TV broadcasters:* Radio and TV of Bosnia and Herzegovina, Federation TV (operating 2 networks), and Republika Srpska Radio-TV; a local commercial network of 5 TV stations; 3 private, near-national TV stations and dozens of small independent TV broadcasting stations; 3 large public radio broadcasters and many private radio stations (2019)

Internet country code: .ba

Internet users: *total:* 2.508 million (2021 est.)
percent of population: 76% (2021 est.)
comparison ranking: total 128

Broadband - fixed subscriptions: *total:* 770,424 (2020 est.)
subscriptions per 100 inhabitants: 24 (2020 est.)
comparison ranking: total 78

TRANSPORTATION

National air transport system: *number of registered air carriers:* 1 (2020)
inventory of registered aircraft operated by air carriers: 1
annual passenger traffic on registered air carriers: 7,070 (2015)
annual freight traffic on registered air carriers: 87 (2015) mt-km

Civil aircraft registration country code prefix: T9

Airports: 13 (2024)
comparison ranking: 153

Heliports: 3 (2024)

Pipelines: 147 km gas, 9 km oil (2013)

Railways: *total:* 965 km (2014)
standard gauge: 965 km (2014) 1.435-m gauge (565 km electrified)
comparison ranking: total 91

Roadways: *total:* 8,619 km (2022)
comparison ranking: total 140

Waterways: 990 km (2022) (Sava River on northern border; open to shipping but use limited)
comparison ranking: 70

Ports: *total ports:* 1 (2024)
large: 0
medium: 0
small: 1
very small: 0
ports with oil terminals: 0
key ports: Neum

MILITARY AND SECURITY

Military and security forces: Armed Forces of Bosnia and Herzegovina (AFBiH or Oruzanih Snaga Bosne i Hercegovine, OSBiH): Army, Air, Air Defense forces organized into an Operations Command and a Support Command

Ministry of Security: Border Police (2024)

Military expenditures: 0.8% of GDP (2023 est.)
0.8% of GDP (2022)
0.9% of GDP (2021)
0.9% of GDP (2020)
0.8% of GDP (2019)
comparison ranking: 136

Military and security service personnel strengths: approximately 10,000 active-duty personnel (2023)

Military equipment inventories and acquisitions: the military's inventory is largely Soviet-era material with a smaller mix of mostly secondhand from other countries, particularly the US (2023)

Military service age and obligation: 18 years of age for voluntary military service; conscription abolished in 2005 (2024)
note: as of 2024, women made up about 9% of the military's full-time personnel

Military - note: the Armed Forces of Bosnia and Herzegovina (AFBiH) are comprised of the former Bosnian-Croat Army of the Federation of Bosnia and Herzegovina (Vojska Federacije Bosne i Hercegovin, VF) and the Bosnian-Serb Republic of Serbia Army (Vojska Republike Srpske, VRS); the two forces were unified under the 2006 Law on Defense, and the combined force includes each ethnic group; the 2006 law also established the country's Ministry of Defense the AFBiH is responsible for territorial defense, providing assistance to civil authorities during disasters or other emergencies, and participating in collective security and peace support operations; each of the AFBiH's three combat brigades are headquartered inside of their respective ethnicity territory, while its main headquarters is in Sarajevo; Bosnia and Herzegovina aspires to join NATO; it joined NATO's Partnership for Peace (PfP) program in 2007 and was invited to join NATO's Membership Action Plan in 2010; the AFBiH is undergoing a 10-year (2017-2027) defense modernization and reform program for preparing to join and integrate with NATO; it has contributed small numbers of troops to EU, NATO, and UN missions
NATO maintains a military headquarters in Sarajevo with the mission of assisting Bosnia and Herzegovina with the PfP program and promoting closer integration with NATO, as well as providing logistics and other support to the EU Force Bosnia and Herzegovina (EUFOR), which has operated in the country to oversee implementation of the Dayton/Paris Agreement since taking over from NATO's Stabilization Force (SFOR) in 2004; EUFOR has about 1,100 troops from 22 countries (2024)

TERRORISM

Terrorist group(s): Islamic Revolutionary Guard Corps/Qods Force
note: details about the history, aims, leadership, organization, areas of operation, tactics, targets, weapons, size, and sources of support of the group(s) appear(s) in the Terrorism reference guide

TRANSNATIONAL ISSUES

Refugees and internally displaced persons: IDPs: 91,000 (Bosnian Croats, Serbs, and Bosniaks displaced by inter-ethnic violence, human rights violations, and armed conflict during the 1992-95 war) (2022)
stateless persons: 48 (2022)
note: 153,304 estimated refugee and migrant arrivals (January 2015-March 2024)

Illicit drugs: drug trafficking groups are major players in the procurement and transportation of of large quantities of cocaine destined for European markets

BOTSWANA

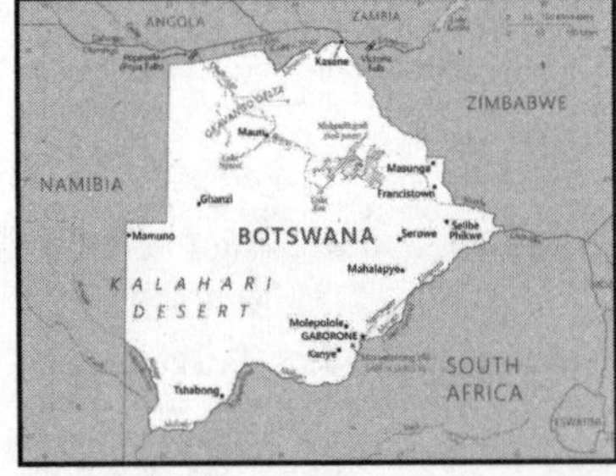

INTRODUCTION

Background: In the early 1800s, multiple political entities in what is now Botswana were destabilized or destroyed by a series of conflicts and population movements in southern Africa. By the end of this period, the Tswana ethnic group, who also live across the border in South Africa, had become the most prominent group in the area. In 1852, Tswana forces halted the expansion of white Afrikaner settlers who were seeking to expand their territory northwards into what is now Botswana. In 1885, Great Britain claimed territory that roughly corresponds with modern day Botswana as a protectorate called Bechuanaland. Upon independence in 1966, the British protectorate of Bechuanaland adopted the new name of Botswana, which means "land of the Tswana."

More than five decades of uninterrupted civilian leadership, progressive social policies, and significant capital investment have created an enduring democracy and upper-middle-income economy. The ruling Botswana Democratic Party has won every national election since independence; President Mokgweetsi Eric Keabetswe MASISI assumed the presidency in 2018 after the retirement of former President Ian KHAMA due to constitutional term limits. MASISI won his first election as president in 2019, and he is Botswana's fifth president since independence. Mineral extraction, principally diamond mining, dominates economic activity, though tourism is a growing sector due to the country's conservation practices and extensive nature preserves. Botswana has one of the world's highest rates of HIV/AIDS infection but also one of Africa's most progressive and comprehensive programs for dealing with the disease.

GEOGRAPHY

Location: Southern Africa, north of South Africa

Geographic coordinates: 22 00 S, 24 00 E

Map references: Africa

Area: *total:* 581,730 sq km
land: 566,730 sq km
water: 15,000 sq km
comparison ranking: total 50

Area - comparative: slightly smaller than Texas; almost four times the size of Illinois

Land boundaries: *total:* 4,347.15 km
border countries (4): Namibia 1,544 km; South Africa 1,969 km; Zambia 0.15 km; Zimbabwe 834 km

Coastline: 0 km (landlocked)

Maritime claims: none (landlocked)

Climate: semiarid; warm winters and hot summers

Terrain: predominantly flat to gently rolling tableland; Kalahari Desert in southwest

Elevation: *highest point:* Manyelanong Hill 1,495 m
lowest point: junction of the Limpopo and Shashe Rivers 513 m
mean elevation: 1,013 m

Natural resources: diamonds, copper, nickel, salt, soda ash, potash, coal, iron ore, silver

Land use: *agricultural land:* 45.8% (2018 est.)
arable land: 0.6% (2018 est.)
permanent crops: 0% (2018 est.)
permanent pasture: 45.2% (2018 est.)
forest: 19.8% (2018 est.)
other: 34.4% (2018 est.)

Irrigated land: 25 sq km (2014)

Major rivers (by length in km): Zambezi (shared with Zambia [s]), Angola, Namibia, Zimbabwe, and Mozambique [m]) - 2,740 km; Limpopo (shared with South Africa [s], Zimbabwe, and Mozambique [m]) - 1,800 km; Okavango river mouth (shared with Angola [s], and Namibia) - 1,600 km
note – [s] after country name indicates river source; [m] after country name indicates river mouth

Major watersheds (area sq km): Atlantic Ocean drainage: Orange (941,351 sq km)

Indian Ocean drainage: Zambezi (1,332,412 sq km)

Internal (endorheic basin) drainage: Okavango Basin (863,866 sq km)

Major aquifers: Lower Kalahari-Stampriet Basin, Upper Kalahari-Cuvelai-Upper Zambezi Basin

Population distribution: the population is primarily concentrated in the east with a focus in and around the captial of Gaborone, and the far central-eastern city of Francistown; population density remains low in other areas in the country, especially in the Kalahari to the west as shown in this population distribution map

Natural hazards: periodic droughts; seasonal August winds blow from the west, carrying sand and dust across the country, which can obscure visibility

Geography - note: landlocked; sparsely populated with most settlement concentrated in the southern and eastern parts of the country; geography dominated by the Kalahari Desert, which covers about 70% of the country, although the Okavango Delta brings considerable biodiversity as one of the largest inland deltas in the World

PEOPLE AND SOCIETY

Population: *total:* 2,450,668
male: 1,174,306
female: 1,276,362 (2024 est.)
comparison rankings: female 143; male 146; total 146

Nationality: *noun:* Motswana (singular), Batswana (plural)
adjective: Motswana (singular), Batswana (plural)

Ethnic groups: Tswana (or Setswana) 79%, Kalanga 11%, Basarwa 3%, other, including Kgalagadi and people of European ancestry 7%

Languages: Setswana 77.3%, Sekalanga 7.4%, Shekgalagadi 3.4%, English (official) 2.8%, Zezuru/Shona 2%, Sesarwa 1.7%, Sembukushu 1.6%, Ndebele 1%, other 2.8% (2011 est.)

Religions: Christian 79.1%, Badimo 4.1%, other 1.4% (includes Baha'i, Hindu, Muslim, Rastafarian), none 15.2%, unspecified 0.3% (2011 est.)

Demographic profile: Botswana has experienced one of the most rapid declines in fertility in Sub-Saharan Africa. The total fertility rate fell from more than 5 children per woman in the mid 1980s to approximately 2.4 in 2013, and remains at that level in 2022. The fertility reduction has been attributed to a host of factors, including higher educational attainment among women, greater participation of women in the workforce, increased contraceptive use, later first births, and a strong national family planning program. Botswana was making significant progress in several health indicators, including life expectancy and infant and child mortality rates, until being devastated by the HIV/ AIDs epidemic in the 1990s.
In 2021, Botswana had one of the highest HIV/AIDS prevalence rates in the world at close to 20%, however comprehensive and effective treatment programs have reduced HIV/AIDS-related deaths. The combination of declining fertility and increasing mortality rates because of HIV/AIDS is slowing the population aging process, with a narrowing of the youngest age groups and little expansion of the oldest age groups. Nevertheless, having the bulk of its population (about 60% as of 2022) of working age will only yield economic benefits if the labor force is healthy, educated, and productively employed.
Batswana have been working as contract miners in South Africa since the 19th century. Although Botswana's economy improved shortly after independence in 1966 with the discovery of diamonds and other minerals, its lingering high poverty rate and lack of job opportunities continued to push workers to seek mining work in southern African countries. In the early 1970s, about a third of Botswana's male labor force worked in South Africa (lesser numbers went to Namibia and Zimbabwe). Not until the 1980s and 1990s, when South African mining companies had reduced their recruitment of foreign workers and Botswana's economic prospects had improved, were Batswana increasingly able to find job opportunities at home.
Most Batswana prefer life in their home country and choose cross-border migration on a temporary basis only for work, shopping, visiting family, or tourism. Since the 1970s, Botswana has pursued an open migration policy enabling it to recruit thousands of foreign workers to fill skilled labor shortages. In the late 1990s, Botswana's prosperity and political stability attracted not only skilled workers but small numbers of refugees from neighboring Angola, Namibia, and Zimbabwe.

Age structure: *0-14 years:* 28.7% (male 355,583/female 348,863)
15-64 years: 65.2% (male 759,210/female 837,752)
65 years and over: 6.1% (2024 est.) (male 59,513/female 89,747)

Dependency ratios: *total dependency ratio:* 57.5
youth dependency ratio: 51.8
elderly dependency ratio: 5.7
potential support ratio: 13.8 (2021 est.)

Median age: *total:* 27.1 years (2024 est.)
male: 26 years
female: 28.3 years
comparison ranking: total 161

Population growth rate: 1.34% (2024 est.)
comparison ranking: 72

Birth rate: 19.6 births/1,000 population (2024 est.)
comparison ranking: 72

Death rate: 8.9 deaths/1,000 population (2024 est.)
comparison ranking: 62

Net migration rate: 2.7 migrant(s)/1,000 population (2024 est.)
comparison ranking: 42

Population distribution: the population is primarily concentrated in the east with a focus in and around the captial of Gaborone, and the far central-eastern city of Francistown; population density remains low in other areas in the country, especially in the Kalahari to the west as shown in this population distribution map

Urbanization: *urban population:* 72.9% of total population (2023)
rate of urbanization: 2.47% annual rate of change (2020-25 est.)

Major urban areas - population: 269,000 GABORONE (capital) (2018)

Sex ratio: *at birth:* 1.03 male(s)/female
0-14 years: 1.02 male(s)/female
15-64 years: 0.91 male(s)/female
65 years and over: 0.66 male(s)/female
total population: 0.92 male(s)/female (2024 est.)

Maternal mortality ratio: 186 deaths/100,000 live births (2020 est.)
comparison ranking: 48

Infant mortality rate: *total:* 23.7 deaths/1,000 live births (2024 est.)
male: 25.9 deaths/1,000 live births
female: 21.4 deaths/1,000 live births
comparison ranking: total 65

Life expectancy at birth: *total population:* 66.4 years (2024 est.)
male: 64.4 years
female: 68.6 years
comparison ranking: total population 201

Total fertility rate: 2.34 children born/woman (2024 est.)
comparison ranking: 75

Gross reproduction rate: 1.15 (2024 est.)

Contraceptive prevalence rate: 67.4% (2017)

Drinking water source: *improved: urban:* 98.1% of population
rural: 96.9% of population
total: 99.4% of population
unimproved: urban: 0.2% of population
rural: 3.1% of population
total: 0.6% of population (2020 est.)

Current health expenditure: 6.2% of GDP (2020)

Physician density: 0.38 physicians/1,000 population (2018)

Hospital bed density: 1.8 beds/1,000 population

Sanitation facility access: *improved: urban:* 94.9% of population
rural: 63% of population
total: 85.6% of population
unimproved: urban: 5.1% of population
rural: 37% of population
total: 14.4% of population (2020 est.)

Obesity - adult prevalence rate: 18.9% (2016)
comparison ranking: 114

Alcohol consumption per capita: *total:* 5.98 liters of pure alcohol (2019 est.)
beer: 2.93 liters of pure alcohol (2019 est.)
wine: 0.46 liters of pure alcohol (2019 est.)
spirits: 0.96 liters of pure alcohol (2019 est.)
other alcohols: 1.64 liters of pure alcohol (2019 est.)
comparison ranking: total 71

Tobacco use: *total:* 19.4% (2020 est.)
male: 30.4% (2020 est.)
female: 8.3% (2020 est.)
comparison ranking: total 90

Currently married women (ages 15-49): 45% (2023 est.)

Education expenditures: 8.7% of GDP (2020 est.)
comparison ranking: 10

Literacy: *definition:* age 15 and over can read and write
total population: 88.5%
male: 88%
female: 88.9% (2015)

School life expectancy (primary to tertiary education): *total:* 12 years
male: 12 years
female: 12 years (2021)

ENVIRONMENT

Environment - current issues: overgrazing; desertification; limited freshwater resources; air pollution

Environment - international agreements: *party to:* Biodiversity, Climate Change, Climate Change-Kyoto Protocol, Climate Change-Paris Agreement, Desertification, Endangered Species, Hazardous Wastes, Law of the Sea, Nuclear Test Ban, Ozone Layer Protection, Wetlands
signed, but not ratified: none of the selected agreements

Climate: semiarid; warm winters and hot summers

Urbanization: *urban population:* 72.9% of total population (2023)
rate of urbanization: 2.47% annual rate of change (2020-25 est.)

Revenue from forest resources: 0.23% of GDP (2018 est.)
comparison ranking: 88

Revenue from coal: 0.45% of GDP (2018 est.)
comparison ranking: 13

Air pollutants: *particulate matter emissions:* 12.82 micrograms per cubic meter (2019 est.)
carbon dioxide emissions: 6.34 megatons (2016 est.)
methane emissions: 5.73 megatons (2020 est.)

Waste and recycling: *municipal solid waste generated annually:* 210,854 tons (2010 est.)
municipal solid waste recycled annually: 2,109 tons (2005 est.)
percent of municipal solid waste recycled: 1% (2005 est.)

Major rivers (by length in km): Zambezi (shared with Zambia [s]), Angola, Namibia, Zimbabwe, and Mozambique [m]) - 2,740 km; Limpopo (shared with South Africa [s], Zimbabwe, and Mozambique [m]) - 1,800 km; Okavango river mouth (shared with Angola [s], and Namibia) - 1,600 km
note – [s] after country name indicates river source; [m] after country name indicates river mouth

Major watersheds (area sq km): Atlantic Ocean drainage: Orange (941,351 sq km)

Indian Ocean drainage: Zambezi (1,332,412 sq km)

Internal (endorheic basin) drainage: Okavango Basin (863,866 sq km)

Major aquifers: Lower Kalahari-Stampriet Basin, Upper Kalahari-Cuvelai-Upper Zambezi Basin

Total water withdrawal: *municipal:* 110 million cubic meters (2020 est.)
industrial: 30 million cubic meters (2020 est.)
agricultural: 80 million cubic meters (2020 est.)

Total renewable water resources: 12.24 billion cubic meters (2020 est.)

GOVERNMENT

Country name: *conventional long form:* Republic of Botswana
conventional short form: Botswana
local long form: Republic of Botswana
local short form: Botswana
former: Bechuanaland
etymology: the name Botswana means "Land of the Tswana" - referring to the country's largest ethnic group

Government type: parliamentary republic

Capital: *name:* Gaborone
geographic coordinates: 24 38 S, 25 54 E
time difference: UTC+2 (7 hours ahead of Washington, DC, during Standard Time)
etymology: named after GABORONE (ca. 1825-1931), a revered kgosi (chief) of the Tlokwa tribe, part of the larger Tswana ethnic group

Administrative divisions: 10 districts and 6 town councils*; Central, Chobe, Francistown*, Gaborone*, Ghanzi, Jwaneng*, Kgalagadi, Kgatleng, Kweneng, Lobatse*, North East, North West, Selebi-Phikwe*, South East, Southern, Sowa Town*

Independence: 30 September 1966 (from the UK)

National holiday: Independence Day (Botswana Day), 30 September (1966)

Legal system: mixed legal system of civil law influenced by the Roman-Dutch model and also customary and common law

Constitution: *history:* previous 1960 (pre-independence); latest adopted March 1965, effective 30 September 1966
amendments: proposed by the National Assembly; passage requires approval in two successive Assembly votes with at least two-thirds majority in the final vote; proposals to amend constitutional provisions on fundamental rights and freedoms, the structure and branches of government, and public services also requires approval by majority vote in a referendum and assent by the president of the republic; amended several times, last in 2021

International law organization participation: accepts compulsory ICJ jurisdiction with reservations; accepts ICCt jurisdiction

Citizenship: *citizenship by birth:* no
citizenship by descent only: at least one parent must be a citizen of Botswana
dual citizenship recognized: no
residency requirement for naturalization: 10 years

Suffrage: 18 years of age; universal

Executive branch: *chief of state:* President Duma BOKO (since 1 November 2024)
head of government: President Duma BOKO (since 1 November 2024)
cabinet: Cabinet appointed by the president
elections/appointments: president indirectly elected by the National Assembly for a 5-year term (eligible for a second term); election last held on 31 October 2024 (next to be held in October 2029); vice president appointed by the president
election results: National elections held in 2024 gave BOKO's UDC 35 seats in the National Assembly, which then selected BOKO as President

Legislative branch: *description:* unicameral Parliament consists of the National Assembly (65 seats; 58 members directly elected in singleseat constituencies by simple majority vote, 5 nominated by the president and indirectly elected by simple majority vote by the rest of the National Assembly, and 2 ex-officio members - the president and vice president of Botswana; elected members serve 5-year terms)
elections: last held on 23 October 2019 (next to be held by October 2024)
election results: percent of vote by party - BDP 52.7%, UDC 35.9%, BPF 4.4%, AP 5.1%, other 1.7%; seats by party - BDP 38, UDC 15, BPF 3, AP 1; composition- men 56, women 7, percentage women 11.1%
note: the House of Chiefs (Ntlo ya Dikgosi), an advisory body to the National Assembly, consists of 35 members – 8 hereditary chiefs from Botswana's principal tribes, 22 indirectly elected by the chiefs, and 5 appointed by the president; the House of Chiefs consults on issues including powers of chiefs, customary courts, customary law, tribal property, and constitutional amendments

Judicial branch: *highest court(s):* Court of Appeal, High Court (each consists of a chief justice and a number of other judges as prescribed by the Parliament)
judge selection and term of office: Court of Appeal and High Court chief justices appointed by the president and other judges appointed by the president upon the advice of the Judicial Service Commission; all judges appointed to serve until age 70
subordinate courts: Industrial Court (with circuits scheduled monthly in the capital city and in 3 districts); Magistrates Courts (1 in each district); Customary Court of Appeal; Paramount Chief's Court/Urban Customary Court; Senior Chief's Representative Court; Chief's Representative's Court; Headman's Court

Political parties: Alliance of Progressives or AP
Botswana Congress Party or BCP
Botswana Democratic Party or BDP
Botswana National Front or BNF [Duma BOKO]
Botswana Patriotic Front or BPF
Botswana Peoples Party or BPP
Botswana Republic Party or BRP
Umbrella for Democratic Change or UDC (various times the coalition has included the BPP, BCP, BNF and other parties)

International organization participation: ACP, AfDB, AU, C, CD, FAO, G-77, IAEA, IBRD, ICAO, ICCt, ICRM, IDA, IFAD, IFC, IFRCS, ILO, IMF, Interpol, IOC, IOM, IPU, ISO, ITSO, ITU, ITUC (NGOs), MIGA, MONUSCO, NAM, OPCW, SACU, SADC, UN, UNCTAD, UNESCO, UNIDO, UNWTO, UPU, WCO, WFTU (NGOs), WHO, WIPO, WMO, WTO

Diplomatic representation in the US: *chief of mission:* Ambassador Mpho Churchill MOPHUTING (since 18 September 2024)
chancery: 1531-1533 New Hampshire Avenue NW, Washington, DC 20036
telephone: [1] (202) 244-4990
FAX: [1] (202) 244-4164
email address and website:
info@botswanaembassy.org
http://www.botswanaembassy.org/

Diplomatic representation from the US: *chief of mission:* Ambassador Howard A. VAN VRANKEN (since 24 May 2023)

embassy: Embassy Drive, Government Enclave (off Khama Crescent), Gaborone
mailing address: 2170 Gaborone Place, Washington DC 20521-2170
telephone: [267] 395-3982
FAX: [267] 318-0232
email address and website:
ConsularGaborone@state.gov
https://bw.usembassy.gov/

Flag description: light blue with a horizontal white-edged black stripe in the center; the blue symbolizes water in the form of rain, while the black and white bands represent racial harmony

National symbol(s): zebra; national colors: light blue, white, black

National anthem: *name:* "Fatshe leno la rona" (Our Land)
lyrics/music: Kgalemang Tumedisco MOTSETE
note: adopted 1966

National heritage: *total World Heritage Sites:* 2 (1 cultural, 1 natural)
selected World Heritage Site locales: Tsodilo Hills (c); Okavango Delta (n)

ECONOMY

Economic overview: good economic governance and financial management; diamond-driven growth model declining; rapid poverty reductions; high unemployment, particularly among youth; COVID-19 sharply contracted the economy and recovery is slow; public sector wages have posed fiscal challenges

Real GDP (purchasing power parity): $46.742 billion (2023 est.)
$45.499 billion (2022 est.)
$43.133 billion (2021 est.)
note: data in 2021 dollars
comparison ranking: 129

Real GDP growth rate: 2.73% (2023 est.)
5.49% (2022 est.)
11.92% (2021 est.)
note: annual GDP % growth based on constant local currency
comparison ranking: 115

Real GDP per capita: $17,500 (2023 est.)
$17,300 (2022 est.)
$16,700 (2021 est.)
note: data in 2021 dollars
comparison ranking: 110

GDP (official exchange rate): $19.396 billion (2023 est.)
note: data in current dollars at official exchange rate

Inflation rate (consumer prices): 5.07% (2023 est.)
11.67% (2022 est.)
7.24% (2021 est.)
note: annual % change based on consumer prices
comparison ranking: 110

Credit ratings: Moody's rating: A2 (2020)

Standard & Poors rating: BBB+ (2020)
note: The year refers to the year in which the current credit rating was first obtained.

GDP - composition, by sector of origin: *agriculture:* 1.6% (2023 est.)
industry: 34.3% (2023 est.)
services: 59.4% (2023 est.)
note: figures may not total 100% due to non-allocated consumption not captured in sector-reported data
comparison rankings: services 90; industry 46; agriculture 172

GDP - composition, by end use: *household consumption:* 42.9% (2023 est.)
government consumption: 28.9% (2023 est.)
investment in fixed capital: 25.7% (2023 est.)
investment in inventories: 4.7% (2023 est.)
exports of goods and services: 31.7% (2023 est.)
imports of goods and services: -35.7% (2023 est.)
note: figures may not total 100% due to rounding or gaps in data collection

Agricultural products: milk, root vegetables, vegetables, maize, sorghum, beef, game meat, watermelons, cabbages, goat milk (2022)
note: top ten agricultural products based on tonnage

Industries: diamonds, copper, nickel, salt, soda ash, potash, coal, iron ore, silver; beef processing; textiles

Industrial production growth rate: 2.25% (2023 est.)
note: annual % change in industrial value added based on constant local currency
comparison ranking: 113

Labor force: 1.17 million (2023 est.)
note: number of people ages 15 or older who are employed or seeking work
comparison ranking: 143

Unemployment rate: 23.38% (2023 est.)
23.62% (2022 est.)
23.11% (2021 est.)
note: % of labor force seeking employment
comparison ranking: 202

Youth unemployment rate (ages 15-24): *total:* 45.4% (2023 est.)
male: 40.5% (2023 est.)
female: 51.5% (2023 est.)
note: % of labor force ages 15-24 seeking employment
comparison ranking: total 6

Population below poverty line: 16.1% (2015 est.)
note: % of population with income below national poverty line

Gini Index coefficient - distribution of family income: 53.3 (2015 est.)
note: index (0-100) of income distribution; higher values represent greater inequality
comparison ranking: 6

Household income or consumption by percentage share: *lowest 10%:* 1.5% (2015 est.)
highest 10%: 41.5% (2015 est.)
note: % share of income accruing to lowest and highest 10% of population

Remittances: 0.31% of GDP (2023 est.)
0.34% of GDP (2022 est.)
0.32% of GDP (2021 est.)
note: personal transfers and compensation between resident and non-resident individuals/households/entities

Budget: *revenues:* $5.989 billion (2022 est.)
expenditures: $5.099 billion (2022 est.)
note: central government revenues and expenses (excluding grants/extrabudgetary units/social security funds) converted to US dollars at average official exchange rate for year indicated

Public debt: 19.62% of GDP (2020 est.)
note: central government debt as a % of GDP
comparison ranking: 187

Taxes and other revenues: 19.65% (of GDP) (2022 est.)
note: central government tax revenue as a % of GDP
comparison ranking: 87

Current account balance: $606.394 million (2022 est.)
-$250.118 million (2021 est.)
-$1.531 billion (2020 est.)
note: balance of payments - net trade and primary/secondary income in current dollars
comparison ranking: 61

Exports: $8.9 billion (2022 est.)
$7.928 billion (2021 est.)
$4.703 billion (2020 est.)
note: balance of payments - exports of goods and services in current dollars
comparison ranking: 119

Exports - partners: UAE 27%, Belgium 18%, India 15%, South Africa 10%, Hong Kong 6% (2022)
note: top five export partners based on percentage share of exports

Exports - commodities: diamonds, copper ore, insulated wire, coal, cattle (2022)
note: top five export commodities based on value in dollars

Imports: $8.7 billion (2022 est.)
$9.252 billion (2021 est.)
$7.554 billion (2020 est.)
note: balance of payments - imports of goods and services in current dollars
comparison ranking: 128

Imports - partners: South Africa 61%, Namibia 9%, Belgium 5%, India 4%, Canada 4% (2022)
note: top five import partners based on percentage share of imports

Imports - commodities: diamonds, refined petroleum, trucks, raw sugar, plastic products (2022)
note: top five import commodities based on value in dollars

Reserves of foreign exchange and gold: $4.756 billion (2023 est.)
$4.279 billion (2022 est.)
$4.802 billion (2021 est.)
note: holdings of gold (year-end prices)/foreign exchange/special drawing rights in current dollars
comparison ranking: 94

Debt - external: $1.507 billion (2022 est.)
note: present value of external debt in current US dollars
comparison ranking: 76

Exchange rates: pulas (BWP) per US dollar -

Exchange rates: 13.596 (2023 est.)
12.369 (2022 est.)
11.087 (2021 est.)
11.456 (2020 est.)
10.756 (2019 est.)

ENERGY

Electricity access: *electrification - total population:* 75.9% (2022 est.)
electrification - urban areas: 95.5%
electrification - rural areas: 25%

Electricity: *installed generating capacity:* 738,000 kW (2022 est.)
consumption: 3.697 billion kWh (2022 est.)
exports: 2 million kWh (2022 est.)
imports: 1.662 billion kWh (2022 est.)
transmission/distribution losses: 591.813 million kWh (2022 est.)
comparison rankings: transmission/distribution losses 85; imports 63; exports 101; consumption 135; installed generating capacity 142

Electricity generation sources: *fossil fuels:* 99.8% of total installed capacity (2022 est.)
solar: 0.2% of total installed capacity (2022 est.)

Coal: *production:* 2.634 million metric tons (2022 est.)
consumption: 2.291 million metric tons (2022 est.)
exports: 539,000 metric tons (2022 est.)
imports: 1,000 metric tons (2022 est.)
proven reserves: 1.66 billion metric tons (2022 est.)

Petroleum: *refined petroleum consumption:* 21,000 bbl/day (2022 est.)

Carbon dioxide emissions: 8.145 million metric tonnes of CO2 (2022 est.)
from coal and metallurgical coke: 5.171 million metric tonnes of CO2 (2022 est.)
from petroleum and other liquids: 2.974 million metric tonnes of CO2 (2022 est.)
comparison ranking: total emissions 118

Energy consumption per capita: 39.265 million Btu/person (2022 est.)
comparison ranking: 102

COMMUNICATIONS

Telephones - fixed lines: *total subscriptions:* 92,000 (2022 est.)
subscriptions per 100 inhabitants: 3 (2022 est.)
comparison ranking: total subscriptions 138

Telephones - mobile cellular: *total subscriptions:* 4.348 million (2022 est.)
subscriptions per 100 inhabitants: 165 (2022 est.)
comparison ranking: total subscriptions 132

Telecommunication systems: *general assessment:* effective regulatory reform has made Botswana's telecom market one of the most liberalized in the region; there is a service-neutral licensing regime adapted to the convergence of technologies and services, and several operators now compete in all telecom sectors; Botswana has one of the highest mobile penetration rates in Africa; in a bid to generate new revenue streams and secure market share, the three mobile network operators have entered the underdeveloped broadband sector by adopting of 3G, LTE, and WiMAX technologies; in the fixed-line broadband market they compete with a large number of ISPs, some of which have rolled out their own wireless access infrastructure; the landlocked country depends on satellites for international bandwidth, and on other countries for transit capacity to the landing points of international submarine cables; the landing of additional cables in the region in recent years has improved the competitive situation in this sector, while prices for connectivity have fallen dramatically (2022)
domestic: fixed-line teledensity has declined in recent years and now stands at roughly 5 telephones per 100 persons; mobile-cellular teledensity is roughly 161 telephones per 100 persons (2021)
international: country code - 267; international calls are made via satellite, using international direct dialing; 2 international exchanges; digital microwave radio relay links to Namibia, Zambia, Zimbabwe, and South Africa; satellite earth station - 1 Intelsat (Indian Ocean)

Broadcast media: 2 TV stations - 1 state-owned and 1 privately owned; privately owned satellite TV subscription service is available; 2 state-owned national radio stations; 4 privately owned radio stations broadcast locally (2019)

Internet country code: .bw

Internet users: *total:* 1.924 million (2021 est.)
percent of population: 74% (2021 est.)
comparison ranking: total 134

Broadband - fixed subscriptions: *total:* 259,525 (2020 est.)
subscriptions per 100 inhabitants: 11 (2020 est.)
comparison ranking: total 111

TRANSPORTATION

National air transport system: *number of registered air carriers:* 1 (2020)
inventory of registered aircraft operated by air carriers: 6
annual passenger traffic on registered air carriers: 253,417 (2018)
annual freight traffic on registered air carriers: 110,000 (2018) mt-km

Civil aircraft registration country code prefix: A2

Airports: 122 (2024)
comparison ranking: 43

Railways: *total:* 888 km (2014)
narrow gauge: 888 km (2014) 1.067-m gauge
comparison ranking: total 94

Roadways: *total:* 31,747 km
paved: 9,810 km
unpaved: 21,937 km (2017)
comparison ranking: total 98

MILITARY AND SECURITY

Military and security forces: Botswana Defense Force (BDF): Ground Forces Command, Air Arm Command, Defense Logistics Command (2024)
note 1: both the BDF and the Botswana Police Service report to the Ministry of Defense and Security; the Botswana Police Service has primary responsibility for internal security; the BDF reports to the Office of the President through the minister of defense and security and has some domestic security responsibilities
note 2: the Ground Force Command includes a marine unit with boats and river craft for patrolling Botswana's internal waterways and supporting anti-poaching operations

Military expenditures: 2.6% of GDP (2023 est.)
2.8% of GDP (2022 est.)
3% of GDP (2021 est.)
3% of GDP (2020 est.)
2.8% of GDP (2019 est.)
comparison ranking: 42

Military and security service personnel strengths: approximately 10,000 active BDF personnel (2024)

Military equipment inventories and acquisitions: the BDF has a mix of mostly older weapons and equipment, largely of Western/European origin; in recent years, it has received limited amounts of material from several European countries and the US (2024)

Military service age and obligation: 18 is the legal minimum age for voluntary military service for men and women; no conscription (2024)

Military - note: the BDF's key functions include defending the country's territorial integrity on land and in the air, ensuring national security and stability, and aiding civil authorities in support of domestic missions such as disaster relief and anti-poaching; it participates in regional and international security operations
Bechuanaland/Botswana did not have a permanent military during colonial times, with the British colonial administrators relying instead on small, lightly armed constabularies such as the Bechuanaland Mounted Police, the Bechuanaland Border Police, and by the early 1960s, the Police Mobile Unit (PMU); after independence in 1966, Botswana militarized the PMU and gave it responsibility for the country's defense rather than create a conventional military force; however, turmoil in neighboring countries and numerous cross-border incursions by Rhodesian and South African security forces in the 1960s and 1970s demonstrated that the PMU was inadequate for defending the country and led to the establishment of the Botswana Defense Force (BDF) in 1977 (2024)

BOUVET ISLAND

INTRODUCTION

Background: This uninhabited volcanic island in Antarctica is almost entirely covered by glaciers, making it difficult to approach. Bouvet Island is recognized as the most remote island on Earth because it is furthest from any other point of land (1,639 km from Antarctica). The island was named after the French naval officer who discovered it in 1739, although no country laid claim to it until 1825, when the British flag was raised. A few expeditions visited the island in the late 19th century. In 1929, the UK waived its claim in favor of Norway, which had occupied the island two years previously. In 1971, Norway designated Bouvet Island and the adjacent territorial waters as a nature reserve. Since 1977, Norway has run an automated meteorological station and studied foraging strategies and distribution of fur seals and penguins on the island. In 2006, an earthquake weakened the station's foundation, causing it to be blown out to sea in a winter storm. Norway erected a new research station in 2014 that can hold six people for periods of two to four months.

GEOGRAPHY

Location: island in the South Atlantic Ocean, southwest of the Cape of Good Hope (South Africa)

Geographic coordinates: 54 26 S, 3 24 E

Map references: Antarctic Region

Area: *total:* 49 sq km
land: 49 sq km

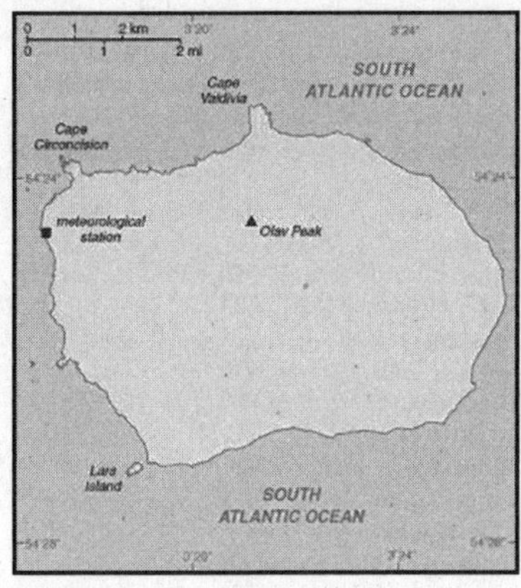

water: 0 sq km
comparison ranking: total 231

Area - comparative: about 0.3 times the size of Washington, DC

Land boundaries: *total:* 0 km

Coastline: 29.6 km

Maritime claims: *territorial sea:* 4 nm

Climate: antarctic

Terrain: volcanic; coast is mostly inaccessible

Elevation: *highest point:* Olavtoppen (Olav Peak) 780 m
lowest point: South Atlantic Ocean 0 m

Natural resources: none

Land use: *agricultural land:* 0% (2018 est.)
arable land: 0% (2018 est.)
permanent crops: 0% (2018 est.)
permanent pasture: 0% (2018 est.)
forest: 0% (2018 est.)
other: 100% (2018 est.)

Natural hazards: occasional volcanism, rock slides; harsh climate, surrounded by pack ice in winter

Geography - note: almost entirely covered by glacial ice (93%); declared a nature reserve by Norway; the distance from Bouvet Island to Norway is 12,776 km, which is almost one-third the circumference of the earth

PEOPLE AND SOCIETY

Population: *total:* uninhabited

ENVIRONMENT

Environment - current issues: none; almost entirely ice covered

Climate: antarctic

GOVERNMENT

Country name: *conventional long form:* none
conventional short form: Bouvet Island
etymology: named after the French naval officer Jean-Baptiste Charles BOUVET who discovered the island in 1739
note: pronounced boo-vay i-land

Dependency status: territory of Norway; administered by the Polar Department of the Ministry of Justice and Oslo Police

Legal system: the laws of Norway apply where applicable

Flag description: the flag of Norway is used

ECONOMY

Exports - partners: Singapore 76%, US 7%, Uzbekistan 5%, UK 2%, Brazil 1% (2022)
note: top five export partners based on percentage share of exports

Exports - commodities: fish, tensile testing machines, jewelry, paper, garments (2022)
note: top five export commodities based on value in dollars

Imports - partners: Singapore 72%, US 18%, Panama 3%, Indonesia 2%, Denmark 1% (2022)
note: top five import partners based on percentage share of imports

Imports - commodities: aluminum structures, animal products, cement, air pumps, electrical transformers (2022)
note: top five import commodities based on value in dollars

COMMUNICATIONS

Internet country code: .bv

Communications - note: has an automated meteorological station

MILITARY AND SECURITY

Military - note: defense is the responsibility of Norway

BRAZIL

INTRODUCTION

Background: After more than three centuries under Portuguese rule, Brazil gained its independence in 1822, maintaining a monarchical system of government until the abolition of slavery in 1888 and the subsequent proclamation of a republic by the military in 1889. Brazilian coffee exporters politically dominated the country until populist leader Getúlio VARGAS rose to power in 1930. VARGAS governed through various versions of democratic and authoritarian regimes from 1930 to 1945. Democratic rule returned in 1945 – including a democratically elected VARGAS administration from 1951 to 1954 – and lasted until 1964, when the military overthrew President João GOULART. The military regime censored journalists and repressed and tortured dissidents in the late 1960s and early 1970s. The dictatorship lasted until 1985, when the military regime peacefully ceded power to civilian rulers, and the Brazilian Congress passed its current constitution in 1988.

By far the largest and most populous country in South America, Brazil continues to pursue industrial and agricultural growth and development of its interior. Having successfully weathered a period of global financial difficulty in the late 20th century, Brazil was soon seen as one of the world's strongest emerging markets and a contributor to global growth under President Luiz Inácio LULA da Silva (2003-2010). The awarding of the 2014 FIFA World Cup and 2016 Summer Olympic Games – the first ever to be held in South America – to Brazil was symbolic of the country's rise. However, from about 2013 to 2016, Brazil was plagued by a sagging economy, high unemployment, and high inflation, only emerging from recession in 2017. Congress removed then-President Dilma ROUSSEFF (2011-2016) from office in 2016 for having committed impeachable acts against Brazil's budgetary laws, and her vice president, Michel TEMER, served the remainder of her second term. A money-laundering investigation, Operation Lava Jato, uncovered a vast corruption scheme and prosecutors charged several high-profile Brazilian politicians with crimes. Former President LULA was convicted of accepting bribes and served jail time (2018-19), although his conviction was overturned in 2021. LULA's revival became complete in 2022 when he narrowly defeated incumbent Jair BOLSONARO (2019-2022) in the presidential election. Positioning Brazil as an independent global leader on climate change and promoting sustainable development, LULA took on the 2024 G20 presidency, balancing the fight against deforestation with sustainable energy and other projects designed to alleviate poverty and promote economic growth, such as expanding fossil fuel exploration.

GEOGRAPHY

Location: Eastern South America, bordering the Atlantic Ocean

Geographic coordinates: 10 00 S, 55 00 W

Map references: South America

Area: *total:* 8,515,770 sq km
land: 8,358,140 sq km
water: 157,630 sq km

note: includes Arquipelago de Fernando de Noronha, Atol das Rocas, Ilha da Trindade, Ilhas Martin Vaz, and Penedos de Sao Pedro e Sao Paulo
comparison ranking: total 6

Area - comparative: slightly smaller than the US

Land boundaries: *total:* 16,145 km
border countries (10): Argentina 1,263 km; Bolivia 3,403 km; Colombia 1,790 km; French Guiana 649 km; Guyana 1,308 km; Paraguay 1,371 km; Peru 2,659 km; Suriname 515 km; Uruguay 1,050 km; Venezuela 2,137 km

Coastline: 7,491 km

Maritime claims: *territorial sea:* 12 nm
contiguous zone: 24 nm
exclusive economic zone: 200 nm
continental shelf: 200 nm or to edge of the continental margin

Climate: mostly tropical, but temperate in south

Terrain: mostly flat to rolling lowlands in north; some plains, hills, mountains, and narrow coastal belt

Elevation: *highest point:* Pico da Neblina 2,994 m
lowest point: Atlantic Ocean 0 m
mean elevation: 320 m

Natural resources: alumina, bauxite, beryllium, gold, iron ore, manganese, nickel, niobium, phosphates, platinum, tantalum, tin, rare earth elements, uranium, petroleum, hydropower, timber

Land use: *agricultural land:* 32.9% (2018 est.)
arable land: 8.6% (2018 est.)
permanent crops: 0.8% (2018 est.)
permanent pasture: 23.5% (2018 est.)
forest: 61.9% (2018 est.)
other: 5.2% (2018 est.)

Irrigated land: 69,029 sq km (2017)

Major lakes (area sq km): *fresh water lake(s):* Lagoa dos Patos - 10,140 sq km
salt water lake(s): Lagoa Mirim (shared with Uruguay) - 2,970 sq km

Major rivers (by length in km): Amazon river mouth (shared with Peru [s]) - 6,400 km; Río de la Plata/Paraná river source (shared with Paraguay, Argentina, and Uruguay [m]) - 4,880 km; Tocantins - 3,650 km; São Francisco - 3,180 km; Paraguay river source (shared with Argentina and Paraguay [m]) - 2,549 km; Rio Negro river mouth (shared with Colombia [s] and Venezuela) - 2,250 km; Uruguay river source (shared with Argentina and Uruguay [m]) - 1,610 km
note – [s] after country name indicates river source; [m] after country name indicates river mouth

Major watersheds (area sq km): Atlantic Ocean drainage: Amazon (6,145,186 sq km), Orinoco (953,675 sq km), Paraná (2,582,704 sq km), São Francisco (617,814 sq km), Tocantins (764,213 sq km)

Major aquifers: Amazon Basin, Guarani Aquifer System, Maranhao Basin

Population distribution: the vast majority of people live along, or relatively near, the Atlantic coast in the east; the population core is in the southeast, anchored by the cities of São Paolo, Brasília, and Rio de Janeiro

Natural hazards: recurring droughts in northeast; floods and occasional frost in south

Geography - note: *note 1:* largest country in South America and in the Southern Hemisphere; shares common boundaries with every South American country except Chile and Ecuador; most of the Pantanal, the world's largest tropical wetland, extends through the west central part of the country; shares Iguaçu Falls (Iguazú Falls), the world's largest waterfalls system, with Argentina
note 2: cassava (manioc) the sixth most important food crop in the world – after maize, rice, wheat, potatoes, and soybeans – probably originated in the west-central part of Brazil; pineapples are probably indigenous to the southern Brazil-Paraguay region
note 3: Rocas Atoll, located off the northeast coast of Brazil, is the only atoll in the South Atlantic

PEOPLE AND SOCIETY

Population: *total:* 220,051,512
male: 108,166,491
female: 111,885,021 (2024 est.)
comparison rankings: female 7; male 7; total 7

Nationality: *noun:* Brazilian(s)
adjective: Brazilian

Ethnic groups: mixed 45.3%, White 43.5%, Black 10.2%, Indigenous 0.6%, Asian 0.4% (2022 est.)

Languages: Portuguese (official and most widely spoken language); less common languages include Spanish (border areas and schools), German, Italian, Japanese, English, and many minor Amerindian languages
major-language sample(s):
O Livro de Fatos Mundiais, a fonte indispensável para informação básica. (Brazilian Portuguese)

Religions: Roman Catholic 52.8%, Protestant 26.7% (Evangelical 25.5%, other Protestant 1.2%), African-American cultist/Umbanda 1.8%, other 3%, agnostic/atheist 0.6%, none 13.6%, unspecified 1.4% (2023 est.)

Demographic profile: Brazil's rapid fertility decline since the 1960s is the main factor behind the country's slowing population growth rate, aging population, and fast-paced demographic transition. Brasilia has not taken full advantage of its large working-age population to develop its human capital and strengthen its social and economic institutions but is funding a study abroad program to bring advanced skills back to the country. The current favorable age structure will begin to shift around 2025, with the labor force shrinking and the elderly starting to compose an increasing share of the total population. Well-funded public pensions have nearly wiped out poverty among the elderly, and Bolsa Familia and other social programs have lifted tens of millions out of poverty. More than half of Brazil's population is considered middle class, but poverty and income inequality levels remain high; the Northeast, North, and Center-West, women, and black, mixed race, and indigenous populations are disproportionately affected. Disparities in opportunities foster social exclusion and contribute to Brazil's high crime rate, particularly violent crime in cities and favelas (slums).
Brazil has traditionally been a net recipient of immigrants, with its southeast being the prime destination. After the importation of African slaves was outlawed in the mid-19th century, Brazil sought Europeans (Italians, Portuguese, Spaniards, and Germans) and later Asians (Japanese) to work in agriculture, especially coffee cultivation. Recent immigrants come mainly from Argentina, Chile, and Andean countries (many are unskilled illegal migrants) or are returning Brazilian nationals. Since Brazil's economic downturn in the 1980s, emigration to the United States, Europe, and Japan has been rising but is negligible relative to Brazil's total population. The majority of these emigrants are well-educated and middle-class. Fewer Brazilian peasants are emigrating to neighboring countries to take up agricultural work.

Age structure: *0-14 years:* 19.6% (male 22,025,593/female 21,088,398)
15-64 years: 69.5% (male 75,889,089/female 77,118,722)
65 years and over: 10.9% (2024 est.) (male 10,251,809/female 13,677,901)

Dependency ratios: *total dependency ratio:* 43.1
youth dependency ratio: 29.4
elderly dependency ratio: 13.7
potential support ratio: 7.3 (2021 est.)

Median age: *total:* 35.1 years (2024 est.)
male: 34 years
female: 36.1 years
comparison ranking: total 101

Population growth rate: 0.61% (2024 est.)
comparison ranking: 138

Birth rate: 13.2 births/1,000 population (2024 est.)
comparison ranking: 131

Death rate: 7 deaths/1,000 population (2024 est.)
comparison ranking: 119

Net migration rate: -0.2 migrant(s)/1,000 population (2024 est.)
comparison ranking: 103

Population distribution: the vast majority of people live along, or relatively near, the Atlantic coast in the east; the population core is in the southeast, anchored by the cities of São Paolo, Brasília, and Rio de Janeiro

Urbanization: *urban population:* 87.8% of total population (2023)
rate of urbanization: 0.87% annual rate of change (2020-25 est.)

Major urban areas - population: 22.620 million São Paulo, 13.728 million Rio de Janeiro, 6.248 million Belo Horizonte, 4.873 million BRASÍLIA (capital), 4.264 million Recife, 4.212 million Porto Alegre (2023)

Sex ratio: *at birth:* 1.05 male(s)/female
0-14 years: 1.04 male(s)/female
15-64 years: 0.98 male(s)/female
65 years and over: 0.75 male(s)/female
total population: 0.97 male(s)/female (2024 est.)

Maternal mortality ratio: 72 deaths/100,000 live births (2020 est.)
comparison ranking: 86

Infant mortality rate: *total:* 12.9 deaths/1,000 live births (2024 est.)
male: 14.6 deaths/1,000 live births
female: 11.1 deaths/1,000 live births
comparison ranking: total 107

Life expectancy at birth: *total population:* 76.3 years (2024 est.)
male: 72.6 years
female: 80.1 years
comparison ranking: total population 113

Total fertility rate: 1.74 children born/woman (2024 est.)
comparison ranking: 151

Gross reproduction rate: 0.85 (2024 est.)

Contraceptive prevalence rate: 80.5% (2019)

Drinking water source: *improved: urban:* 99.8% of population
rural: 96.9% of population
total: 99.4% of population

unimproved: urban: 0.2% of population
rural: 3.1% of population
total: 0.6% of population (2020 est.)

Current health expenditure: 10.3% of GDP (2020)

Physician density: 2.31 physicians/1,000 population (2019)

Hospital bed density: 2.1 beds/1,000 population (2017)

Sanitation facility access: *improved: urban:* 94.1% of population
rural: 63.6% of population
total: 90.2% of population
unimproved: urban: 5.9% of population
rural: 36.4% of population
total: 9.8% of population (2020 est.)

Obesity - adult prevalence rate: 22.1% (2016)
comparison ranking: 81

Alcohol consumption per capita: *total:* 6.12 liters of pure alcohol (2019 est.)
beer: 3.84 liters of pure alcohol (2019 est.)
wine: 0.24 liters of pure alcohol (2019 est.)
spirits: 2 liters of pure alcohol (2019 est.)
other alcohols: 0.04 liters of pure alcohol (2019 est.)
comparison ranking: total 68

Tobacco use: *total:* 12.8% (2020 est.)
male: 16.2% (2020 est.)
female: 9.4% (2020 est.)
comparison ranking: total 119

Children under the age of 5 years underweight: NA

Currently married women (ages 15-49): 55.9% (2023 est.)

Education expenditures: 6% of GDP (2019 est.)
comparison ranking: 41

Literacy: *definition:* age 15 and over can read and write
total population: 94.7%
male: 94.4%
female: 94.9% (2022)

School life expectancy (primary to tertiary education): *total:* 16 years
male: 15 years
female: 16 years (2020)

ENVIRONMENT

Environment - current issues: deforestation in Amazon Basin destroys the habitat and endangers a multitude of plant and animal species indigenous to the area; illegal wildlife trade; illegal poaching; air and water pollution in Rio de Janeiro, Sao Paulo, and several other large cities; land degradation and water pollution caused by improper mining activities; wetland degradation; severe oil spills

Environment - international agreements: *party to:* Antarctic-Environmental Protection, Antarctic-Marine Living Resources, Antarctic Seals, Antarctic Treaty, Biodiversity, Climate Change, Climate Change-Kyoto Protocol, Climate Change-Paris Agreement, Comprehensive Nuclear Test Ban, Desertification, Endangered Species, Environmental Modification, Hazardous Wastes, Law of the Sea, Marine Dumping-London Convention, Nuclear Test Ban, Ozone Layer Protection, Ship Pollution, Tropical Timber 2006, Wetlands, Whaling
signed, but not ratified: Marine Dumping-London Protocol

Climate: mostly tropical, but temperate in south

Urbanization: *urban population:* 87.8% of total population (2023)
rate of urbanization: 0.87% annual rate of change (2020-25 est.)

Revenue from forest resources: 0.62% of GDP (2018 est.)
comparison ranking: 61

Revenue from coal: 0.01% of GDP (2018 est.)
comparison ranking: 51

Air pollutants: *particulate matter emissions:* 10.94 micrograms per cubic meter (2019 est.)
carbon dioxide emissions: 462.3 megatons (2016 est.)
methane emissions: 401.83 megatons (2020 est.)

Waste and recycling: *municipal solid waste generated annually:* 79,889,010 tons (2015 est.)
municipal solid waste recycled annually: 1,118,446 tons (2014 est.)
percent of municipal solid waste recycled: 1.4% (2014 est.)

Major lakes (area sq km): *fresh water lake(s):* Lagoa dos Patos - 10,140 sq km
salt water lake(s): Lagoa Mirim (shared with Uruguay) - 2,970 sq km

Major rivers (by length in km): Amazon river mouth (shared with Peru [s]) - 6,400 km; Río de la Plata/Paraná river source (shared with Paraguay, Argentina, and Uruguay [m]) - 4,880 km; Tocantins - 3,650 km; São Francisco - 3,180 km; Paraguay river source (shared with Argentina and Paraguay [m]) - 2,549 km; Rio Negro river mouth (shared with Colombia [s] and Venezuela) - 2,250 km; Uruguay river source (shared with Argentina and Uruguay [m]) - 1,610 km

note – [s] after country name indicates river source; [m] after country name indicates river mouth

Major watersheds (area sq km): Atlantic Ocean drainage: Amazon (6,145,186 sq km), Orinoco (953,675 sq km), Paraná (2,582,704 sq km), São Francisco (617,814 sq km), Tocantins (764,213 sq km)

Major aquifers: Amazon Basin, Guarani Aquifer System, Maranhao Basin

Total water withdrawal: *municipal:* 16.13 billion cubic meters (2020 est.)
industrial: 9.51 billion cubic meters (2020 est.)
agricultural: 41.42 billion cubic meters (2020 est.)

Total renewable water resources: 8.65 trillion cubic meters (2020 est.)

Geoparks: *total global geoparks and regional networks:* 6
global geoparks and regional networks: Araripe; Cacapava; Quarta Colonia; Serido; Southern Canyons Pathways; Uberaba (2024)

GOVERNMENT

Country name: *conventional long form:* Federative Republic of Brazil
conventional short form: Brazil
local long form: República Federativa do Brasil
local short form: Brasil
etymology: the country name derives from the brazilwood tree that used to grow plentifully along the coast of Brazil and that was used to produce a deep red dye

Government type: federal presidential republic

Capital: *name:* Brasília
geographic coordinates: 15 47 S, 47 55 W
time difference: UTC-3 (2 hours ahead of Washington, DC, during Standard Time)
time zone note: Brazil has four time zones, including one for the Fernando de Noronha Islands
etymology: name bestowed on the new capital of Brazil upon its inauguration in 1960; previous Brazilian capitals had been Salvador from 1549 to 1763 and Rio de Janeiro from 1763 to 1960

Administrative divisions: 26 states (estados, singular - estado) and 1 federal district* (distrito federal); Acre, Alagoas, Amapa, Amazonas, Bahia, Ceara, Distrito Federal*, Espirito Santo, Goias, Maranhao, Mato Grosso, Mato Grosso do Sul, Minas Gerais, Para, Paraiba, Parana, Pernambuco, Piaui, Rio de Janeiro, Rio Grande do Norte, Rio Grande do Sul, Rondonia, Roraima, Santa Catarina, Sao Paulo, Sergipe, Tocantins

Independence: 7 September 1822 (from Portugal)

National holiday: Independence Day, 7 September (1822)

Legal system: civil law; note - a new civil law code was enacted in 2002 replacing the 1916 code

Constitution: *history:* several previous; latest ratified 5 October 1988
amendments: proposed by at least one third of either house of the National Congress, by the president of the republic, or by simple majority vote by more than half of the state legislative assemblies; passage requires at least three-fifths majority vote by both houses in each of two readings; constitutional provisions affecting the federal form of government, separation of powers, suffrage, or individual rights and guarantees cannot be amended; amended many times, last in 2023

International law organization participation: has not submitted an ICJ jurisdiction declaration; accepts ICCt jurisdiction

Citizenship: *citizenship by birth:* yes
citizenship by descent only: yes
dual citizenship recognized: yes
residency requirement for naturalization: 4 years

Suffrage: voluntary between 16 to 18 years of age, over 70, and if illiterate; compulsory between 18 to 70 years of age; note - military conscripts by law cannot vote

Executive branch: *chief of state:* President Luiz Inácio LULA da Silva (since 1 January 2023)
head of government: President Luiz Inácio LULA da Silva (since 1 January 2023)
cabinet: Cabinet appointed by the president
elections/appointments: president and vice president directly elected on the same ballot by absolute majority popular vote in 2 rounds if needed for a 4-year term (eligible for a single consecutive term and additional terms after at least one term has elapsed); election last held on 2 October 2022 with runoff on 30 October 2022 (next to be held on 4 October 2026)
election results:
2022: Luiz Inácio LULA da Silva elected president in second round; percent of vote in first round - Luiz Inácio LULA da Silva (PT) 48.4%, Jair BOLSONARO (PSL) 43.2%, Simone Nassar TEBET (MDB) 4.2%, Ciro GOMES (PDT) 3%, other 1.2%; percent of vote in second round - Luiz Inácio LULA da Silva (PT) 50.9%, Jair BOLSONARO (PSL) 49.1%
2018: Jair BOLSONARO elected president in second round; percent of vote in first round - Jair BOLSONARO (PSL) 46%, Fernando HADDAD

(PT) 29.3%, Ciro GOMEZ (PDT) 12.5%, Geraldo ALCKMIN (PSDB) 4.8%, other 7.4%; percent of vote in second round - Jair BOLSONARO (PSL) 55.1%, Fernando HADDAD (PT) 44.9%
note - the president is both chief of state and head of government

Legislative branch: *description:* bicameral National Congress or Congresso Nacional consists of:
Federal Senate or Senado Federal (81 seats; 3 members each from 26 states and 3 from the federal district directly elected in multi-seat constituencies by simple majority vote to serve 8-year terms, with one-third and two-thirds of the membership elected alternately every 4 years)
Chamber of Deputies or Camara dos Deputados (513 seats; members directly elected in multi-seat constituencies by open party-list proportional representation vote to serve 4-year terms)
elections: Federal Senate - last held on 2 October 2022 for one-third of the Senate (next to be held on 4 October 2026 for two-thirds of the seats)
Chamber of Deputies - last held on 2 October 2022 (next to be held on 4 October 2026)
election results: Federal Senate - percent of vote by party - PL 25.4%, PSB 13.7%, PT 12.1%, PSD 11.4%, Progressistas 7.6%, Brazil Union 5.5%, PSC 4.3%, Republicans 4.3%, MDB 3.9%, other 11.8%; seats by party - PL 8, Brazil Union 5, PT 4, PP 3, Republicans 2, PSD 2, MDB 1, PSB 1, PSC 1
note - composition of the Federal Senate as of March 2024 - seats by party - PL 13, Brazil Union 12, MDB 10, PSD 10, PT 9, Progressistas 7, Podemos 6, PSDB 4, Republicans 3, PDT 2, Cidadania 1, PSB 1, PSC 1, PROS 1, REDE 1; composition - men 67, women 14, percentage women 17.3%
Chamber of Deputies - percent of vote by party - PL 16.6%, PT 12.1%, Brazil Union 9.3%, PP 8%, PSD 7.6%, MDB 7.2%, Republicans 7%, PSB 3.8%, PDT 3.5%, PSOL 3.5%, Podemos 3.3%, PSDB 3%, Avante 2%, PSC 1.8%, SD 1.6%, Cidadania 1.5%, Patriota 1.4%, PTB 1.3%, NOVO 1.2%, PCdoB 1.1%, PV 0.9%, PROS 0.7%, REDE 0.7%, other 0.9%; seats by party - PL 99, PT 69, Brazil Union 59, PP 47, MDB 42, PSD 42, Republicans 40, PDT 17, PSB 14, PSDB 13, Podemos 12, PSOL 12, Avante 7, PCdoB 6, PSC 6, PV 6, Cidadania 5, Patriota 4, SD 4, NOVO 3, PROS 3, REDE 2, PTB 1; composition - men 423, women 90, percentage women 17.5%; total National Congress percentage women 17.5%

Judicial branch: *highest court(s):* Supreme Federal Court or Supremo Tribunal Federal (consists of 11 justices)
judge selection and term of office: justices appointed by the president and approved by absolute majority by the Federal Senate; justices appointed to serve until mandatory retirement at age 75
subordinate courts: Tribunal of the Union, Federal Appeals Court, Superior Court of Justice, Superior Electoral Court, regional federal courts; state court system

Political parties: Act (Agir) (formerly Christian Labor Party or PTC)
Avante (formerly Labor Party of Brazil or PTdoB)
Brazil Union (União Brasil); note - founded from a merger between the Democrats (DEM) and the Social Liberal Party (PSL)
Brazilian Communist Party or PCB
Brazilian Democratic Movement or MDB
Brazilian Labor Party or PTB
Brazilian Renewal Labor Party or PRTB
Brazilian Labor Party or PTB
Brazilian Social Democracy Party or PSDB
Brazilian Socialist Party or PSB
Christian Democracy or DC (formerly Christian Social Democratic Party)
Cidadania (formerly Popular Socialist Party or PPS)
Communist Party of Brazil or PCdoB
Democratic Labor Party or PDT
Democratic Party or PSDC
Democrats or DEM (formerly Liberal Front Party or PFL); note - dissolved in February 2022
Green Party or PV
Liberal Party or PL [Valdemar Costa Neto] (formerly Party of the Republic or PR)
National Mobilization Party or PMN
New Party or NOVO
Patriota (formerly National Ecologic Party or PEN)
Podemos (formerly National Labor Party or PTN)
Progressive Party (Progressistas) or PP
Republican Social Order Party or PROS
Republicans (Republicanos) (formerly Brazilian Republican Party or PRB)
Social Christian Party or PSC
Social Democratic Party or PSD
Social Liberal Party or PSL
Socialism and Freedom Party or PSOL
Solidarity or SD
Sustainability Network or REDE
United Socialist Workers' Party or PSTU
Workers' Cause Party or PCO
Workers' Party or PT

International organization participation: AfDB (nonregional member), BIS, BRICS, CAN (associate), CD, CELAC, CPLP, FAO, FATF, G-15, G-20, G-24, G-5, G-77, IADB, IAEA, IBRD, ICAO, ICC (national committees), ICCt, ICRM, IDA, IFAD, IFC, IFRCS, IHO, ILO, IMF, IMO, IMSO, Interpol, IOC, IOM, IPU, ISO, ITSO, ITU, ITUC (NGOs), LAES, LAIA, LAS (observer), Mercosur, MIGA, MINURSO, MINUSTAH, MONUSCO, NAM (observer), NSG, OAS, OECD (enhanced engagement), OPANAL, OPCW, Paris Club (associate), PCA, PROSUR, SICA (observer), UN, UNASUR, UNCTAD, UNESCO, UNFICYP, UNHCR, UNHRC, UNIDO, UNISFA, UNIFIL, Union Latina, UNISFA, UNITAR, UNMIL, UNMISS, UNOCI, UNOOSA, UNRWA, UNWTO, UPU, WCO, WFTU (NGOs), WHO, WIPO, WMO, WTO

Diplomatic representation in the US: *chief of mission:* Ambassador Maria Luiza Ribeiro VIOTTI (since 30 June 2023)
chancery: 3006 Massachusetts Avenue NW, Washington, DC 20008
telephone: [1] (202) 238-2700
FAX: [1] (202) 238-2827
email address and website:
contact.washington@itamaraty.gov.br
https://www.gov.br/mre/pt-br/embaixada-washington
consulate(s) general: Atlanta, Boston, Chicago, Hartford (CT), Houston, Los Angeles, Miami, New York, Orlando, San Francisco

Diplomatic representation from the US: *chief of mission:* Ambassador Elizabeth Frawley BAGLEY (since 3 February 2023)
embassy: SES - Avenida das Nações, Quadra 801, Lote 03, 70403-900 - Brasília, DF
mailing address: 7500 Brasilia Place, Washington DC 20521-7500
telephone: [55] (61) 3312-7000
FAX: [55] (61) 3225-9136
email address and website:
BrasilliaACS@state.gov
https://br.usembassy.gov/
consulate(s) general: Recife, Porto Alegre, Rio de Janeiro, São Paulo
branch office(s): Belo Horizonte

Flag description: green with a large yellow diamond in the center bearing a blue celestial globe with 27 white five-pointed stars; the globe has a white equatorial band with the motto ORDEM E PROGRESSO (Order and Progress); the current flag was inspired by the banner of the former Empire of Brazil (1822-1889); on the imperial flag, the green represented the House of Braganza of Pedro I, the first Emperor of Brazil, while the yellow stood for the Habsburg Family of his wife; on the modern flag the green represents the forests of the country and the yellow rhombus its mineral wealth (the diamond shape roughly mirrors that of the country); the blue circle and stars, which replaced the coat of arms of the original flag, depict the sky over Rio de Janeiro on the morning of 15 November 1889 - the day the Republic of Brazil was declared; the number of stars has changed with the creation of new states and has risen from an original 21 to the current 27 (one for each state and the Federal District)
note: one of several flags where a prominent component of the design reflects the shape of the country; other such flags are those of Bosnia and Herzegovina, Eritrea, and Vanuatu

National symbol(s): Southern Cross constellation; national colors: green, yellow, blue

National anthem: *name:* "Hino Nacional Brasileiro" (Brazilian National Anthem)
lyrics/music: Joaquim Osorio Duque ESTRADA/ Francisco Manoel DA SILVA
note: music adopted 1890, lyrics adopted 1922; the anthem's music, composed in 1822, was used unofficially for many years before it was adopted

National heritage: *total World Heritage Sites:* 23 (15 cultural, 7 natural, 1 mixed)
selected World Heritage Site locales: Brasilia (c); Historic Salvador de Bahia (c); Historic Ouro Preto (c); Historic Olinda (c); Iguaçu National Park (n); Jesuit Missions of the Guaranis (c); Rio de Janeiro: Carioca Landscapes (c); Central Amazon Conservation Complex (n); Atlantic Forest South-East Reserves (n); Paraty and Ilha Grande – Culture and Biodiversity (m)

ECONOMY

Economic overview: upper-middle income, largest Latin American economy; Mercosur, BRICS, G20 member and OECD accession candidate; growth driven by strong domestic consumption; tax simplification reforms aimed at addressing business conditions and lagging productivity; high inequality in income and access to health and education

Real GDP (purchasing power parity): $4.016 trillion (2023 est.)
$3.902 trillion (2022 est.)
$3.788 trillion (2021 est.)
note: data in 2021 dollars
comparison ranking: 7

Real GDP growth rate: 2.91% (2023 est.)
3.02% (2022 est.)
4.76% (2021 est.)
note: annual GDP % growth based on constant local currency
comparison ranking: 112

Real GDP per capita: $18,600 (2023 est.)

$18,100 (2022 est.)
$17,700 (2021 est.)
note: data in 2021 dollars
comparison ranking: 105

GDP (official exchange rate): $2.174 trillion (2023 est.)
note: data in current dollars at official exchange rate

Inflation rate (consumer prices): 4.59% (2023 est.)
9.28% (2022 est.)
8.3% (2021 est.)
note: annual % change based on consumer prices
comparison ranking: 97

Credit ratings: Fitch rating: BB (2023)

Moody's rating: Ba2 (2016)

Standard & Poors rating: BB- (2018)
note: The year refers to the year in which the current credit rating was first obtained.

GDP - composition, by sector of origin: *agriculture:* 6.2% (2023 est.)
industry: 22.3% (2023 est.)
services: 58.9% (2023 est.)
note: figures may not total 100% due to non-allocated consumption not captured in sector-reported data comparison rankings: services 93; industry 121; agriculture 104

GDP - composition, by end use: *household consumption:* 63.3% (2023 est.)
government consumption: 18.2% (2023 est.)
investment in fixed capital: 16.5% (2023 est.)
investment in inventories: -0.5% (2023 est.)
exports of goods and services: 18.1% (2023 est.)
imports of goods and services: -15.7% (2023 est.)
note: figures may not total 100% due to rounding or gaps in data collection

Agricultural products: sugarcane, soybeans, maize, milk, cassava, oranges, chicken, rice, beef, wheat (2022)
note: top ten agricultural products based on tonnage

Industries: textiles, shoes, chemicals, cement, lumber, iron ore, tin, steel, aircraft, motor vehicles and parts, other machinery and equipment

Industrial production growth rate: 1.59% (2023 est.)
note: annual % change in industrial value added based on constant local currency
comparison ranking: 124

Labor force: 108.695 million (2023 est.)
note: number of people ages 15 or older who are employed or seeking work
comparison ranking: 5

Unemployment rate: 7.95% (2023 est.)
9.23% (2022 est.)
13.16% (2021 est.)
note: % of labor force seeking employment
comparison ranking: 145

Youth unemployment rate (ages 15-24): *total:* 17.9% (2023 est.)
male: 15.6% (2023 est.)
female: 20.9% (2023 est.)
note: % of labor force ages 15-24 seeking employment
comparison ranking: total 78

Population below poverty line: 4.2% (2016 est.)
note: approximately 4% of the population are below the "extreme" poverty line

Gini Index coefficient - distribution of family income: 52 (2022 est.)
note: index (0-100) of income distribution; higher values represent greater inequality
comparison ranking: 7

Average household expenditures: *on food:* 16.2% of household expenditures (2022 est.)
on alcohol and tobacco: 1.7% of household expenditures (2022 est.)

Household income or consumption by percentage share: *lowest 10%:* 1.2% (2022 est.)
highest 10%: 41% (2022 est.)
note: % share of income accruing to lowest and highest 10% of population

Remittances: 0.2% of GDP (2023 est.)
0.25% of GDP (2022 est.)
0.25% of GDP (2021 est.)
note: personal transfers and compensation between resident and non-resident individuals/households/entities

Budget: *revenues:* $578.267 billion (2022 est.)
expenditures: $666.279 billion (2022 est.)
note: central government revenues (excluding grants) and expenses converted to US dollars at average official exchange rate for year indicated

Public debt: 79.1% of GDP (2022 est.)
note: central government debt as a % of GDP
comparison ranking: 39

Taxes and other revenues: 14.73% (of GDP) (2022 est.)
note: central government tax revenue as a % of GDP
comparison ranking: 143

Current account balance: -$30.828 billion (2023 est.)
-$48.253 billion (2022 est.)
-$46.358 billion (2021 est.)
note: balance of payments - net trade and primary/secondary income in current dollars
comparison ranking: 203

Exports: $389.626 billion (2023 est.)
$380.619 billion (2022 est.)
$315.494 billion (2021 est.)
note: balance of payments - exports of goods and services in current dollars
comparison ranking: 22

Exports - partners: China 26%, US 11%, Argentina 5%, Netherlands 3%, Spain 3% (2022)
note: top five export partners based on percentage share of exports

Exports - commodities: soybeans, crude petroleum, iron ore, refined petroleum, corn (2022)
note: top five export commodities based on value in dollars

Imports: $346.639 billion (2023 est.)
$376.084 billion (2022 est.)
$306.087 billion (2021 est.)
note: balance of payments - imports of goods and services in current dollars
comparison ranking: 23

Imports - partners: China 24%, US 18%, Germany 5%, Argentina 5%, India 4% (2022)
note: top five import partners based on percentage share of imports

Imports - commodities: refined petroleum, fertilizers, vehicle parts/accessories, crude petroleum, pesticides (2022)
note: top five import commodities based on value in dollars

Reserves of foreign exchange and gold: $355.021 billion (2023 est.)
$324.673 billion (2022 est.)
$362.21 billion (2021 est.)
note: holdings of gold (year-end prices)/foreign exchange/special drawing rights in current dollars
comparison ranking: 11

Debt - external: $164.448 billion (2022 est.)
note: present value of external debt in current US dollars
comparison ranking: 4

Exchange rates: reals (BRL) per US dollar -

Exchange rates: 4.994 (2023 est.)
5.164 (2022 est.)
5.394 (2021 est.)
5.155 (2020 est.)
3.944 (2019 est.)

ENERGY

Electricity access: *electrification - total population:* 100% (2022 est.)
electrification - urban areas: 100%
electrification - rural areas: 97.3%

Electricity: *installed generating capacity:* 220.319 million kW (2022 est.)
consumption: 583.184 billion kWh (2022 est.)
exports: 4.979 billion kWh (2022 est.)
imports: 17.887 billion kWh (2022 est.)
transmission/distribution losses: 103.995 billion kWh (2022 est.)
comparison rankings: transmission/distribution losses 208; imports 12; exports 38; consumption 7; installed generating capacity 7

Electricity generation sources: *fossil fuels:* 9.9% of total installed capacity (2022 est.)
nuclear: 2.2% of total installed capacity (2022 est.)
solar: 4% of total installed capacity (2022 est.)
wind: 12.1% of total installed capacity (2022 est.)
hydroelectricity: 63.3% of total installed capacity (2022 est.)
biomass and waste: 8.4% of total installed capacity (2022 est.)

Nuclear energy: Number of operational nuclear reactors: 2 (2023)

Number of nuclear reactors under construction: 1 (2023)

Net capacity of operational nuclear reactors: 1.88GW (2023 est.)

Percent of total electricity production: 2.2% (2023 est.)

Coal: *production:* 15.644 million metric tons (2022 est.)
consumption: 32.787 million metric tons (2022 est.)
exports: 7,000 metric tons (2022 est.)
imports: 20.389 million metric tons (2022 est.)
proven reserves: 6.596 billion metric tons (2022 est.)

Petroleum: *total petroleum production:* 4.221 million bbl/day (2023 est.)
refined petroleum consumption: 3.027 million bbl/day (2022 est.)
crude oil estimated reserves: 12.715 billion barrels (2021 est.)

Natural gas: *production:* 22.67 billion cubic meters (2022 est.)
consumption: 31.654 billion cubic meters (2022 est.)
exports: 75.122 million cubic meters (2021 est.)
imports: 8.812 billion cubic meters (2022 est.)
proven reserves: 363.985 billion cubic meters (2021 est.)

Carbon dioxide emissions: 516.752 million metric tonnes of CO_2 (2022 est.)
from coal and metallurgical coke: 54.455 million metric tonnes of CO_2 (2022 est.)

from petroleum and other liquids: 404.548 million metric tonnes of CO_2 (2022 est.)
from consumed natural gas: 57.749 million metric tonnes of CO_2 (2022 est.)
comparison ranking: total emissions 12

Energy consumption per capita: 50.037 million Btu/person (2022 est.)
comparison ranking: 94

COMMUNICATIONS

Telephones - fixed lines: *total subscriptions:* 27.258 million (2022 est.)
subscriptions per 100 inhabitants: 13 (2022 est.)
comparison ranking: total subscriptions 9

Telephones - mobile cellular: *total subscriptions:* 212.926 million (2022 est.)
subscriptions per 100 inhabitants: 99 (2022 est.)
comparison ranking: total subscriptions 7

Telecommunication systems: *general assessment:* Brazil is one of the largest mobile and broadband markets in Latin America with healthy competition and pricing; 5G services was provided to all capital cities in July 2022, as well as about 35,500km of the national highway network; the country also has one of the largest fixed line broadband markets in Latin America, though broadband subscriptions is only slightly above the regional average, trailing behind Chile, Argentina, and Uruguay; amendments to the licensing regime adopted in October 2019 also require that ISPs which have switched to authorizations invest money saved from lighter regulations in the expansion of broadband services; the fixed line broadband market has seen rapid growth for a number of years, with a growing focus on fiber broadband; in 2019 the number of fiber accesses overtook DSL connections; the country is a key landing point for a number of important submarine cables connecting to the US, Central and South America, the Caribbean, Europe, and Africa; several new cable systems are due to come into service through to 2022, which will increase bandwidth and push down broadband prices for end-users; investments have also been made into terrestrial fiber cables between Brazil, Argentina, and Chile (2022)
domestic: fixed-line connections stand at roughly 13 per 100 persons; mobile-cellular teledensity roughly 102 per 100 persons (2021)
international: country code - 55; landing points for a number of submarine cables, including Malbec, ARBR, Tamnat, SAC, SAm-1, Atlantis -2, Seabras-1, Monet, EllaLink, BRUSA, GlobeNet, AMX-1, Brazilian Festoon, Bicentenario, Unisur, Junior, Americas -II, SAE x1, SAIL, SACS and SABR that provide direct connectivity to South and Central America, the Caribbean, the US, Africa, and Europe; satellite earth stations - 3 Intelsat (Atlantic Ocean), 1 Inmarsat (Atlantic Ocean region east), connected by microwave relay system to Mercosur Brazilsat B3 satellite earth station; satellites is a major communication platform, as it is almost impossible to lay fiber optic cable in the thick vegetation (2019)

Broadcast media: state-run Radiobras operates a radio and a TV network; more than 1,000 radio stations and more than 100 TV channels operating - mostly privately owned; private media ownership highly concentrated (2022)

Internet country code: .br

Internet users: *total:* 170.1 million (2021 est.)
percent of population: 81% (2021 est.)
comparison ranking: total 4

Broadband - fixed subscriptions: *total:* 36,344,670 (2020 est.)
subscriptions per 100 inhabitants: 17 (2020 est.)
comparison ranking: total 4

TRANSPORTATION

National air transport system: *number of registered air carriers:* 9 (2020)
inventory of registered aircraft operated by air carriers: 443
annual passenger traffic on registered air carriers: 102,109,977 (2018)
annual freight traffic on registered air carriers: 1,845,650,000 (2018) mt-km

Civil aircraft registration country code prefix: PP

Airports: 4,919 (2024)
comparison ranking: 2

Heliports: 1,768 (2024)

Pipelines: 5,959 km refined petroleum product (1,165 km distribution, 4,794 km transport), 11,696 km natural gas (2,274 km distribution, 9,422 km transport), 1,985 km crude oil (distribution), 77 km ethanol/petrochemical (37 km distribution, 40 km transport) (2016)

Railways: *total:* 29,849.9 km (2014)
standard gauge: 194 km (2014) 1.435-m gauge
narrow gauge: 23,341.6 km (2014) 1.000-m gauge (24 km electrified)
broad gauge: 5,822.3 km (2014) 1.600-m gauge (498.3 km electrified)
dual gauge: 492 km (2014) 1.600-1.000-m gauge
comparison ranking: total 9

Roadways: *total:* 2 million km
paved: 246,000 km
unpaved: 1.754 million km (2018)
comparison ranking: total 4

Waterways: 50,000 km (2012) (most in areas remote from industry and population)
comparison ranking: 2

Merchant marine: *total:* 888 (2023)
by type: bulk carrier 13, container ship 20, general cargo 38, oil tanker 27, other 790
comparison ranking: total 26

Ports: *total ports:* 45 (2024)
large: 4
medium: 7
small: 19
very small: 15
ports with oil terminals: 31
key ports: Belem, DTSE/Gegua Oil Terminal, Itajai, Port de Salvador, Porto Alegre, Recife, Rio de Janeiro, Rio Grande, Santos, Tubarao, Vitoria

MILITARY AND SECURITY

Military and security forces: Brazilian Armed Forces (Forças Armadas Brasileiras): Brazilian Army (Exercito Brasileiro, EB), Brazilian Navy (Marinha do Brasil, MB, includes Naval Aviation (Aviacao Naval Brasileira) and Marine Corps (Corpo de Fuzileiros Navais)), Brazilian Air Force (Forca Aerea Brasileira, FAB) (2024)

note: the three national police forces – the Federal Police, Federal Highway Police, and Federal Railway Police – have domestic security responsibilities and report to the Ministry of Justice and Public Security (Ministry of Justice); there are two distinct units within the state police forces: the civil police, which performs an investigative role, and the military police, charged with maintaining law and order in the states and the Federal District; despite the name, military police forces report to the Ministry of Justice, not the Ministry of Defense; the National Public Security Force (Forca Nacional de Seguranca Publica or SENASP) is a national police force made up of Military Police from various states

Military expenditures: 1.1% of GDP (2023 est.)
1.2% of GDP (2022 est.)
1.3% of GDP (2021 est.)
1.4% of GDP (2020 est.)
1.4% of GDP (2019 est.)
comparison ranking: 119

Military and security service personnel strengths: approximately 360,000 active military personnel (220,000 Army; 70,000 Navy; 70,000 Air Force); approximately 400,000 paramilitary security forces (2023)

Military equipment inventories and acquisitions: the Brazilian military's inventory consists of a mix of domestically produced and imported weapons, largely from Europe and the US; Brazil's defense industry designs and manufactures equipment for all three military services and for export; it also jointly produces equipment with other countries (2024)

Military service age and obligation: 18-45 years of age for compulsory military service for men (women exempted); only 5-10% of those inducted are required to serve; conscript service obligation is 10-12 months; 17-45 years of age for voluntary service (2024)
note: in 2024, women comprised approximately 10% of the Brazilian military

Military - note: the Brazilian Armed Forces (BAF) are the second largest military in the Western Hemisphere behind the US; they are responsible for external security and protecting the country's sovereignty but also have a considerable internal security role; the BAF's missions include patrolling and protecting the country's long borders and coastline and extensive territorial waters and river network, assisting with internal security, providing domestic disaster response and humanitarian assistance, and participating in multinational peacekeeping missions in the past decade, the BAF has mobilized thousands of troops to conduct counternarcotics operations, support the police in combating crime, assist with disease outbreaks and humanitarian missions, and provide security for major events such as the 2014 World Cup and the 2016 Summer Olympics; it has also cooperated regularly with neighboring countries such as Argentina and Paraguay on border security to combat smuggling and trafficking
Brazil has Major Non-NATO Ally (MNNA) status with the US, a designation under US law that provides foreign partners with certain benefits in the areas of defense trade and security cooperation
the origins of Brazil's military stretch back to the 1640s; Brazil provided a 25,000-man expeditionary force with air and ground units to fight with the Allies in the Mediterranean Theater during World War II; the Navy participated in the Battle of the Atlantic (2024)

SPACE

Space agency/agencies: Brazilian Space Agency (Agência Espacial Brasileira, AEB; established in 1994 when Brazil's space program was transferred from the military to civilian control); National Institute for Space Research (established, 1971; part of the Brazilian Ministry of Science, Technology and Innovations); Space Operations Command (Armed Forces); Department of Aerospace Science and Technology (DCTA; established in 1953 as a military space research program under the Brazilian Air Force) (2024)

Space launch site(s): Alcantara Launch Site (Maranhão state); Barreira do Inferno Launch Center (Rio Grande do Norte state) (2024)

Space program overview: has an active program with a long history; develops, builds, operates, and tracks satellites, including communications, remote sensing (RS), multi-mission, navigational, and scientific/testing/research; satellites are launched by foreign partners, but Brazil has a long-standing sounding (research) rocket and space launch vehicle (SLV) program and rocket launch facilities; cooperates with a variety of foreign space agencies and commercial entities, including those of Argentina, Canada, the European Space Agency and individual member states (particularly France and Germany), India, Japan, Russia, South Africa, South Korea, Ukraine, and the US; has a state-controlled communications company that operates Brazil's communications satellites and a growing commercial space sector with expertise in satellite technology (2024)
note: further details about the key activities, programs, and milestones of the country's space program, as well as government spending estimates on the space sector, appear in the Space Programs reference guide

TERRORISM

Terrorist group(s): Hizballah
note: details about the history, aims, leadership, organization, areas of operation, tactics, targets, weapons, size, and sources of support of the group(s) appear(s) in the Terrorism reference guide

TRANSNATIONAL ISSUES

Refugees and internally displaced persons: *refugees (country of origin):* 510,499 (Venezuela) (economic and political crisis; includes Venezuelans who have claimed asylum, are recognized as refugees, or received alternative legal stay) (2023)
IDPs: 5,600 (2022)
stateless persons: 12 (2022)

Illicit drugs: a significant drug transit and destination country for cocaine bound for Europe and other destinations including the United States; domestic drug use and addiction is a significant problem and it is second only to the United States in cocaine consumption; a major source of precursor or essential chemicals used in the production of illicit narcotics

BRITISH INDIAN OCEAN TERRITORY

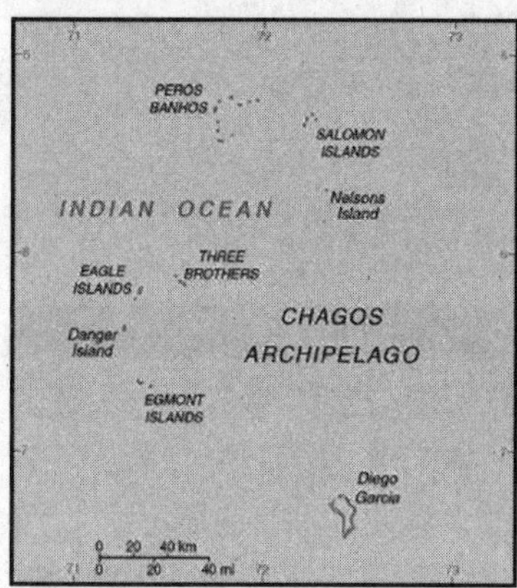

INTRODUCTION

Background: Formerly administered as part of the British Crown Colony of Mauritius, the British Indian Ocean Territory (BIOT) was established as an overseas territory of the UK in 1965. A number of the islands in the territory were later transferred to the Seychelles when it gained independence in 1976. Subsequently, BIOT has consisted of the six main island groups that make up the Chagos Archipelago. Only Diego Garcia, the largest and most southerly of the islands, is inhabited. It contains a joint UK-US naval support facility and hosts one of four dedicated ground antennas that assist in the operation of the Global Positioning System (GPS) navigation system – the others are on Kwajalein (Marshall Islands); at Cape Canaveral, Florida (US); and on Ascension Island (Saint Helena, Ascension, and Tristan da Cunha). The US Air Force also operates a telescope array on Diego Garcia as part of the Ground-Based Electro-Optical Deep Space Surveillance System (GEODSS) for tracking orbital debris, which can be a hazard to spacecraft and astronauts.
Between 1967 and 1973, the former agricultural workers who lived on the islands were relocated, primarily to Mauritius but also to the Seychelles. Negotiations with the UK between 1971 and 1982 resulted in the establishment of a trust fund to compensate the displaced islanders, known as Chagossians. Beginning in 1998, the islanders pursued a series of lawsuits against the British Government, seeking further compensation and the right to return to the territory. British court rulings in 2006 and 2007 invalidated immigration policies that had excluded the islanders from the archipelago, but in 2008, the House of Lords – the final court of appeal in the UK – ruled in favor of the British Government by overturning the lower court rulings and finding no right of return for the Chagossians. In 2015, the Permanent Court of Arbitration unanimously held that the marine protected area that the UK declared around the Chagos Archipelago in 2010 violated the UN Convention on the Law of the Sea.

In 2019, the International Court of Justice ruled in an advisory opinion that Britain's decolonization of Mauritius was not lawful because of continued Chagossian claims. A non-binding 2019 UN General Assembly vote demanded that Britain end its "colonial administration" of the Chagos Archipelago and that it be returned to Mauritius. UK officials continue to defend Britain's sovereignty over the islands and argue that the issue is a bilateral dispute between Mauritius and the UK that does not warrant international intervention.

GEOGRAPHY

Location: archipelago in the Indian Ocean, south of India, about halfway between Africa and Indonesia

Geographic coordinates: 6 00 S, 71 30 E;note - Diego Garcia 7 20 S, 72 25 E

Map references: Political Map of the World

Area: *total:* 60 sq km
land: 60 sq km (44 Diego Garcia)
water: 54,340 sq km
note: includes the entire Chagos Archipelago of 55 islands
comparison ranking: total 228

Area - comparative: land area is about one-third the size of Washington, DC

Land boundaries: *total:* 0 km

Coastline: 698 km

Maritime claims: *territorial sea:* 12 nm

Environment (Protection and Preservation) Zone: 200 nm

Climate: tropical marine; hot, humid, moderated by trade winds

Terrain: flat and low coral atolls (most areas do not exceed two m in elevation); sits atop the submarine volcanic Chagos- Laccadive Ridge

Elevation: *highest point:* ocean-side dunes on Diego Garcia 9 m
lowest point: Indian Ocean 0 m

Natural resources: coconuts, fish, sugarcane

Land use: *agricultural land:* 0% (2018 est.)
arable land: 0% (2018 est.)
permanent crops: 0% (2018 est.)
permanent pasture: 0% (2018 est.)
forest: 0% (2018 est.)
other: 100% (2018 est.)

Natural hazards: none; located outside routes of Indian Ocean cyclones

Geography - note: *note 1:* archipelago of 55 islands; Diego Garcia, the largest and southernmost island, occupies a strategic location in the central Indian Ocean; the island is the site of a joint US-UK military facility
note 2: Diego Garcia is the only inhabited island of the BIOT and one of only two British territories where traffic drives on the right, the other being Gibraltar

PEOPLE AND SOCIETY

Population: *total:* no indigenous inhabitants
note: approximately 1,200 former agricultural workers resident in the Chagos Archipelago, often referred to as Chagossians or Ilois, were relocated to Mauritius and the Seychelles in the 1960s and 1970s; approximately 3,000 UK and US military personnel and civilian contractors living on the island of Diego Garcia (2018)

ENVIRONMENT

Environment - current issues: wastewater discharge into the lagoon on Diego Garcia

Climate: tropical marine; hot, humid, moderated by trade winds

GOVERNMENT

Country name: *conventional long form:* British Indian Ocean Territory
conventional short form: none
abbreviation: BIOT
etymology: self-descriptive name specifying the territory's affiliation and location

Dependency status: overseas territory of the UK; administered by a commissioner, resident in the Foreign, Commonwealth, and Development Office in London

Capital: *name:* administered from London; often regarded as being on Diego Garcia
geographic coordinates: 7 18S, 12 24E
time difference: UTC+6 (12 hours ahead of Washington, DC, during Standard Time)

Legal system: the laws of the UK apply where applicable

Constitution: *history:* British Indian Ocean Territory (Constitution) Order 2004

Executive branch: *chief of state:* King CHARLES III (since 8 September 2022)
head of government: Commissioner Paul CANDLER (since 8 July 2021); Administrator Balraj DHANDA; note - both reside in the UK and are represented by Commander Colvin OSBORN, RN, Officer commanding British Forces on Diego Garcia (since January 2022)
cabinet: NA
elections/appointments: the monarchy is hereditary; commissioner and administrator appointed by the monarch

International organization participation: UPU

Diplomatic representation in the US: none (overseas territory of the UK)

Diplomatic representation from the US: *embassy:* none (overseas territory of the UK)

Flag description: white with six blue wavy horizontal stripes; the flag of the UK is in the upper hoist-side quadrant; the striped section bears a palm tree and yellow crown (the symbols of the territory) centered on the outer half of the flag; the wavy stripes represent the Indian Ocean; although not officially described, the six blue stripes may stand for the six main atolls of the archipelago

National anthem: *note:* as an overseas territory of the United Kingdom, "God Save the King" is official (see United Kingdom)

ECONOMY

Economic overview: small island territory economy; economic activity mainly on Diego Garcia with national military installations; recently settled disputes with Mauritius have increased oil exports; established marine reserve has limited commercial fishing

Exports - partners: Malta 42%, Brazil 11%, Switzerland 9%, France 8%, Egypt 6% (2022)
note: top five export partners based on percentage share of exports

Exports - commodities: ships, refined petroleum, asphalt, diamonds, jewelry (2022)
note: top five export commodities based on value in dollars

Imports - partners: US 34%, Switzerland 13%, China 11%, Italy 11%, France 7% (2022)
note: top five import partners based on percentage share of imports

Imports - commodities: ships, refined petroleum, diamonds, aircraft, aluminum (2022)
note: top five import commodities based on value in dollars

Exchange rates: the US dollar is used

COMMUNICATIONS

Telecommunication systems: *general assessment:* separate facilities for military and public needs are available (2018)
domestic: all commercial telephone services are available, including connection to the Internet (2018)
international: country code (Diego Garcia) - 246; landing point for the SAFE submarine cable that provides direct connectivity to Africa, Asia and near-by Indian Ocean island countries; international telephone service is carried by satellite (2019)

Broadcast media: Armed Forces Radio and Television Service (AFRTS) broadcasts over 3 separate frequencies for US and UK military personnel stationed on the islands

Internet country code: .io

Communications - note: Diego Garcia hosts one of four dedicated ground antennas that assist in the operation of the Global Positioning System (GPS) navigation system (the others are on Kwajalein (Marshall Islands), at Cape Canaveral, Florida (US), and on Ascension Island (Saint Helena, Ascension, and Tristan da Cunha))

TRANSPORTATION

Airports: 1 (2024)
comparison ranking: 227

Roadways: *note:* short section of paved road between port and airfield on Diego Garcia

Ports: *total ports:* 1 (2024)
large: 0
medium: 0
small: 0
very small: 1
ports with oil terminals: 1
key ports: Diego Garcia

MILITARY AND SECURITY

Military and security forces: no regular military forces

Military - note: defense is the responsibility of the UK; in November 2016, the UK extended the US lease on Diego Garcia until December 2036

BRITISH VIRGIN ISLANDS

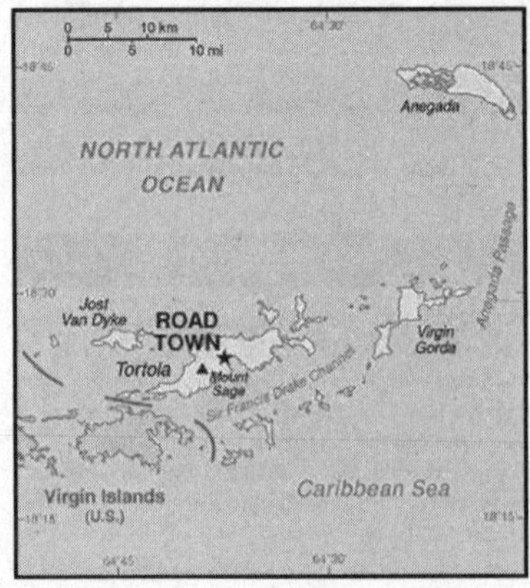

INTRODUCTION

Background: First inhabited by Arawak and later by Carib Indians, the Virgin Islands were settled by the Dutch in 1648 and then annexed by the English in 1672. The islands were part of the British colony of the Leeward Islands (1872-1960); they were granted autonomy in 1967. The economy is closely tied to the larger and more populous US Virgin Islands to the west, and the US dollar is the legal currency. In 2017, Hurricane Irma devastated the island of Tortola. An estimated 80% of residential and business structures were destroyed or damaged, communications disrupted, and local roads rendered impassable.

GEOGRAPHY

Location: Caribbean, between the Caribbean Sea and the North Atlantic Ocean, east of Puerto Rico

Geographic coordinates: 18 30 N, 64 30 W

Map references: Central America and the Caribbean

Area: *total:* 151 sq km
land: 151 sq km
water: 0 sq km
note: comprised of 16 inhabited and more than 20 uninhabited islands; includes the islands of Tortola, Anegada, Virgin Gorda, Jost van Dyke
comparison ranking: total 220

Area - comparative: about 0.9 times the size of Washington, DC

Land boundaries: *total:* 0 km

Coastline: 80 km

Maritime claims: *territorial sea:* 12 nm
exclusive fishing zone: 200 nm

Climate: subtropical; humid; temperatures moderated by trade winds

Terrain: coral islands relatively flat; volcanic islands steep, hilly

Elevation: *highest point:* Mount Sage 521 m
lowest point: Caribbean Sea 0 m

Natural resources: NEGL; pleasant climate, beaches foster tourism

Land use: *agricultural land:* 46.7% (2018 est.)
arable land: 6.7% (2018 est.)
permanent crops: 6.7% (2018 est.)
permanent pasture: 33.3% (2018 est.)
forest: 24.3% (2018 est.)
other: 29% (2018 est.)

Irrigated land: NA

Population distribution: a fairly even distribution throughout the inhabited islands, with the largest islands of Tortola, Anegada, Virgin Gorda, and Jost Van Dyke having the largest populations

Natural hazards: hurricanes and tropical storms (July to October)

Geography - note: strong ties to nearby US Virgin Islands and Puerto Rico

PEOPLE AND SOCIETY

Population: *total:* 40,102
male: 19,042
female: 21,060 (2024 est.)
comparison rankings: female 212; male 213; total 213

Nationality: *noun:* British Virgin Islander(s)
adjective: British Virgin Islander

Ethnic groups: African/Black 76.3%, Latino 5.5%, White 5.4%, mixed 5.3%, Indian 2.1%, East Indian 1.6%, other 3%, unspecified 0.8% (2010 est.)

Languages: English (official), Virgin Islands Creole

Religions: Protestant 70.2% (Methodist 17.6%, Church of God 10.4%, Anglican 9.5%, Seventh Day Adventist 9.0%, Pentecostal 8.2%, Baptist 7.4%, New Testament Church of God 6.9%, other Protestant 1.2%), Roman Catholic 8.9%, Jehovah's Witness 2.5%, Hindu 1.9%, other 6.2%, none 7.9%, unspecified 2.4% (2010 est.)

Age structure: *0-14 years:* 16.6% (male 3,298/female 3,351)
15-64 years: 71.3% (male 13,455/female 15,152)
65 years and over: 12.1% (2024 est.) (male 2,289/female 2,557)

Dependency ratios: *total dependency ratio:* 32.8
youth dependency ratio: 20.2
elderly dependency ratio: 12.6
potential support ratio: 8 (2021)

Median age: *total:* 38.5 years (2024 est.)
male: 38.1 years
female: 38.9 years
comparison ranking: total 74

Population growth rate: 1.82% (2024 est.)
comparison ranking: 47

Birth rate: 10.9 births/1,000 population (2024 est.)
comparison ranking: 168

Death rate: 5.5 deaths/1,000 population (2024 est.)
comparison ranking: 183

Net migration rate: 12.9 migrant(s)/1,000 population (2024 est.)
comparison ranking: 4

Population distribution: a fairly even distribution throughout the inhabited islands, with the largest islands of Tortola, Anegada, Virgin Gorda, and Jost Van Dyke having the largest populations

Urbanization: *urban population:* 49.7% of total population (2023)
rate of urbanization: 1.73% annual rate of change (2020-25 est.)

Major urban areas - population: 15,000 ROAD TOWN (capital) (2018)

Sex ratio: *at birth:* 1.05 male(s)/female
0-14 years: 0.98 male(s)/female
15-64 years: 0.89 male(s)/female
65 years and over: 0.9 male(s)/female
total population: 0.9 male(s)/female (2024 est.)

Infant mortality rate: *total:* 13.4 deaths/1,000 live births (2024 est.)
male: 16 deaths/1,000 live births
female: 10.7 deaths/1,000 live births
comparison ranking: total 105

Life expectancy at birth: *total population:* 80.1 years (2024 est.)
male: 78.6 years
female: 81.7 years
comparison ranking: total population 57

Total fertility rate: 1.38 children born/woman (2024 est.)
comparison ranking: 213

Gross reproduction rate: 0.67 (2024 est.)

Drinking water source: *improved:* total: 99.9% of population
unimproved: total: 0.1% of population (2020 est.)

Sanitation facility access: *improved: urban:* 97.5% of population
rural: 97.5% of population
total: 97.5% of population
unimproved: urban: 2.5% of population
rural: 2.5% of population
total: 2.5% of population (2015 est.)

Currently married women (ages 15-49): 46.6% (2023 est.)

Education expenditures: 2.6% of GDP (2020 est.)
comparison ranking: 172

School life expectancy (primary to tertiary education): *total:* 12 years
male: 12 years
female: 12 years (2018)

ENVIRONMENT

Environment - current issues: limited natural freshwater resources except for a few seasonal streams and springs on Tortola; most of the islands' water supply comes from desalination plants; sewage and mining/industry waste contribute to water pollution, threatening coral reefs

Climate: subtropical; humid; temperatures moderated by trade winds

Urbanization: *urban population:* 49.7% of total population (2023)
rate of urbanization: 1.73% annual rate of change (2020-25 est.)

Air pollutants: *carbon dioxide emissions:* 0.21 megatons (2016 est.)

Waste and recycling: *municipal solid waste generated annually:* 21,099 tons (2000 est.)

GOVERNMENT

Country name: *conventional long form:* none
conventional short form: British Virgin Islands
abbreviation: BVI
etymology: the myriad islets, cays, and rocks surrounding the major islands reminded explorer Christopher COLUMBUS in 1493 of Saint Ursula and her 11,000 virgin followers (Santa Ursula y las Once Mil Virgenes), which over time shortened to the Virgins (las Virgenes)

Government type: Overseas Territory of the UK with limited self-government; parliamentary democracy

Dependency status: overseas territory of the UK; internal self-governing

Capital: *name:* Road Town
geographic coordinates: 18 25 N, 64 37 W
time difference: UTC-4 (1 hour ahead of Washington, DC, during Standard Time)
etymology: name refers to the nautical term "roadstead" or "roads," a body of water less sheltered than a harbor but where ships can lie reasonably safely at anchor sheltered from rip currents, spring tides, or ocean swells

Administrative divisions: none (overseas territory of the UK)

Independence: none (overseas territory of the UK)

National holiday: Territory Day, 1 July (1956)

Legal system: English common law

Constitution: *history:* several previous; latest effective 15 June 2007 (The Virgin Islands Constitution Order 2007)
amendments: initiated by any elected member of the House of Assembly; passage requires simple majority vote by the elected members of the Assembly and assent by the governor on behalf of the monarch; amended 2015

Citizenship: see United Kingdom

Suffrage: 18 years of age; universal

Executive branch: *chief of state:* King CHARLES III (since 8 September 2022); represented by Governor Daniel PRUCE (since 29 January 2024)
head of government: Premier Dr. Natalio WHEATLEY (since 5 May 2022)
cabinet: Executive Council appointed by the governor from members of the House of Assembly
elections/appointments: the monarchy is hereditary; governor appointed by the monarch; following legislative elections, the leader of the majority party or majority coalition usually appointed premier by the governor
note; on 5 May 2022, Premier Andrew FAHIE was removed from office by a no confidence vote in House of Assembly following his arrest on drug trafficking and money laundering charges on 28 April 2022; Premier Dr. Natalio WHEATLEY sworn in as premier on 5 May 2022

Legislative branch: *description:* unicameral House of Assembly (15 seats; 13 members - 9 in single-seat constituencies and 4 members in a single, nationwide constituency directly elected by simple majority vote and 2 ex-officio members - the attorney general and the speaker - chosen from outside the House; members serve 4-year terms)
elections: last held on 24 April 2023 (next to be held in 2027)
election results: percent of vote by party - VIP 39.6%, NDP 29.1, PVIM 15.7%, PU 5%, independent 10.6%; seats by party - VIP 6, NDP 3, PVIM 3, PU 1; composition - men NA, women NA, percentage women NA%; note - percentages reflect 9 elected single seat constituencies, seat total includes four nationwide at-large elected members

Judicial branch: *highest court(s):* the Eastern Caribbean Supreme Court (ECSC) is the superior court of the Organization of Eastern Caribbean States; the ECSC - headquartered on St. Lucia - consists of the Court of Appeal - headed by the chief justice and 4 judges - and the High Court with 18 judges; the Court of Appeal is itinerant, traveling to member states on a schedule to hear appeals from the High Court and subordinate courts; High Court judges reside in the member states, with 3 in the British Virgin Islands
judge selection and term of office: Eastern Caribbean Supreme Court chief justice appointed by His Majesty, King Charles III; other justices and judges appointed by the Judicial and Legal Services Commission; Court of Appeal justices appointed for life with mandatory retirement at age 65; High Court judges appointed for life with mandatory retirement at age 62
subordinate courts: Magistrates' Courts

Political parties: National Democratic Party or NDP
Progressive Virgin Islands Movement or PVIM
Progressives United or PU
Virgin Islands Party or VIP

International organization participation: ACS (associate), Caricom (associate), CDB, Interpol (subbureau), IOC, OECS, UNESCO (associate), UPU

Diplomatic representation in the US: none (overseas territory of the UK)

Diplomatic representation from the US: *embassy:* none (overseas territory of the UK)

Flag description: blue with the flag of the UK in the upper hoist-side quadrant and the Virgin Islander coat of arms centered in the outer half of the flag; the coat of arms depicts a woman flanked on either side by a vertical column of six oil lamps above a scroll bearing the Latin word VIGILATE (Be Watchful); the islands were named by COLUMBUS in 1493 in honor of Saint Ursula and her 11 virgin followers (some sources say 11,000) who reputedly were martyred by the Huns in the 4th or 5th century; the figure on the banner holding a lamp represents the saint; the other lamps symbolize her followers

National symbol(s): zenaida dove, white cedar flower; national colors: yellow, green, red, white, blue

National anthem: *note:* as an overseas territory of the United Kingdom, "God Save the King" is official (see United Kingdom)

ECONOMY

Economic overview: British Caribbean island territorial economy; strong tourism and services industries; vulnerable to hurricanes; navigating public debt insolvency since 2008 Crisis; considered a tax haven; high electrification costs; major rum exporter

Real GDP (purchasing power parity): $500 million (2017 est.)
$490.2 million (2016 est.)
$481.1 million (2015 est.)
comparison ranking: 213

Real GDP growth rate: 2% (2017 est.)
1.9% (2016 est.)
1.8% (2015 est.)
comparison ranking: 140

Real GDP per capita: $34,200 (2017 est.)
comparison ranking: 72

GDP (official exchange rate): $1.38 billion (2018 est.)

Inflation rate (consumer prices): 4.2% (2022 est.)
2.8% (2021 est.)
0.4% (2020 est.)
comparison ranking: 87

GDP - composition, by sector of origin: *agriculture:* 0.2% (2017 est.)
industry: 6.8% (2017 est.)
services: 93.1% (2017 est.)
comparison rankings: services 1; industry 209; agriculture 208

GDP - composition, by end use: *household consumption:* 25.1% (2017 est.)
government consumption: 7.5% (2017 est.)
investment in fixed capital: 21.7% (2017 est.)
investment in inventories: 20.4% (2017 est.)
exports of goods and services: 94.7% (2017 est.)
imports of goods and services: -69.4% (2017 est.)

Agricultural products: fruits, vegetables; livestock, poultry; fish

Industries: tourism, light industry, construction, rum, concrete block, offshore banking center

Industrial production growth rate: 1.1% (2017 est.)
comparison ranking: 138

Unemployment rate: 2.9% (2015 est.)
comparison ranking: 40

Budget: *revenues:* $400 million (2017 est.)
expenditures: $400 million (2017 est.)

Taxes and other revenues: 38.9% (of GDP) (2017 est.)
comparison ranking: 12

Exports: $23 million (2017 est.)
$23 million (2015 est.)
note: Data are in current year dollars and do not include illicit exports or re-exports. comparison ranking: 216

Exports - partners: Malta 30%, Seychelles 29%, Switzerland 14% (2019)

Exports - commodities: aircraft, recreational boats, ships, hydrogen, halogens (2021)

Imports: $300 million (2017 est.)
$210 million (2016 est.)
comparison ranking: 208

Imports - partners: Germany 32%, United States 22%, Italy 9%, France 7%, Seychelles 7% (2019)

Imports - commodities: recreational boats, aircraft, refined petroleum, cars, furniture (2019)

Exchange rates: the US dollar is used

ENERGY

Electricity access: *electrification - total population:* 100% (2022 est.)

Electricity: *installed generating capacity:* 47,000 kW (2022 est.)
consumption: 161.368 million kWh (2022 est.)
transmission/distribution losses: 10.179 million kWh (2022 est.)
comparison rankings: transmission/distribution losses 18; consumption 194; installed generating capacity 195

Electricity generation sources: *fossil fuels:* 99.1% of total installed capacity (2022 est.)
solar: 0.2% of total installed capacity (2022 est.)
wind: 0.7% of total installed capacity (2022 est.)

Coal: *imports:* 20 metric tons (2022 est.)

Petroleum: *refined petroleum consumption:* 1,000 bbl/day (2022 est.)

Carbon dioxide emissions: 191,000 metric tonnes of CO_2 (2022 est.)
from petroleum and other liquids: 191,000 metric tonnes of CO_2 (2022 est.)
comparison ranking: total emissions 204

Energy consumption per capita: 87.47 million Btu/person (2022 est.)
comparison ranking: 61

COMMUNICATIONS

Telephones - fixed lines: *total subscriptions:* 23,000 (2021 est.)
subscriptions per 100 inhabitants: 73 (2021 est.)
comparison ranking: total subscriptions 172

Telephones - mobile cellular: *total subscriptions:* 38,000 (2021 est.)
subscriptions per 100 inhabitants: 121 (2021 est.)
comparison ranking: total subscriptions 210

Telecommunication systems: *general assessment:* the telecom sector has seen a decline in subscriber numbers (particularly for prepaid mobile services the mainstay of short term visitors) and revenue; fixed and mobile broadband services are two areas that have benefited from the crisis as employees and students have resorted to working from home; one major casualty may be the region's second largest telco operator, Digicel; the company filed for bankruptcy in the US in April 2020; it continues to operate in all of its Caribbean markets as it seeks to refinance billions of dollars of debt; the other major telco, regional incumbent Cable & Wireless Communications (CWC), is experiencing similar drops in subscriber numbers and revenue; CWC is expanding and enhancing its fixed and mobile networks in many of the countries it serves around the Caribbean, despite many locations being small islands with very small populations; one area of the telecom market that is not prepared for growth is 5G mobile; governments, regulators, and even the mobile network operators have shown that they have not been investing in 5G opportunities at the present time; network expansion and enhancements remain concentrated around improving LTE coverage. (2021)
domestic: fixed-line connections exceed 22 per 100 persons and mobile cellular subscribership is roughly 110 per 100 persons (2021)
international: country code - 1-284; landing points for PCCS, ECFS, CBUS, Deep Blue Cable, East-West, PAN-AM, Americas-1, Southern Caribbean Fiber, Columbus- IIb, St Thomas - St Croix System, Taino-Carib, and Americas I-North via submarine cable to Caribbean, Central and South America, and US (2019)

Broadcast media: 1 private TV station; multi-channel TV is available from cable and satellite subscription services; about a half-dozen private radio stations

Internet country code: .vg

Internet users: *total:* 24,087 (2021 est.)
percent of population: 77.7% (2021 est.)
comparison ranking: total 211

Broadband - fixed subscriptions: *total:* 6,738 (2020 est.)
subscriptions per 100 inhabitants: 22 (2020 est.)
comparison ranking: total 182

TRANSPORTATION

Civil aircraft registration country code prefix: VP-L

Airports: 3 (2024)
comparison ranking: 195

Heliports: 1 (2024)

Roadways: *total:* 200 km
paved: 200 km (2007)
comparison ranking: total 209

Merchant marine: *total:* 29 (2023)
by type: general cargo 3, other 26
comparison ranking: total 137

Ports: *total ports:* 1 (2024)
large: 0
medium: 1
small: 0
very small: 0
ports with oil terminals: 1
key ports: Road Harbor

MILITARY AND SECURITY

Military - note: defense is the responsibility of the UK

TRANSNATIONAL ISSUES

Illicit drugs: transshipment point for South American narcotics destined for the US and Europe; large offshore financial center makes it vulnerable to money laundering

BRUNEI

INTRODUCTION

Background: The Sultanate of Brunei's influence peaked between the 15th and 17th centuries, when its control extended over coastal areas of northwest Borneo and the southern Philippines. Internal strife over royal succession, colonial expansion of European powers, and piracy subsequently brought on a period of decline. In 1888, Brunei became a British protectorate; independence was achieved in 1984. The same family has ruled Brunei for over six centuries, and in 2017, the country celebrated the 50th anniversary of Sultan Hassanal BOLKIAH's accession to the throne. Brunei has one of the highest per-capita GDPs in the world, thanks to extensive petroleum and natural gas fields.

GEOGRAPHY

Location: Southeastern Asia, along the northern coast of the island of Borneo, bordering the South China Sea and Malaysia

Geographic coordinates: 4 30 N, 114 40 E

Map references: Southeast Asia

Area: *total:* 5,765 sq km
land: 5,265 sq km
water: 500 sq km
comparison ranking: total 172

Area - comparative: slightly smaller than Delaware

Land boundaries: *total:* 266 km
border countries (1): Malaysia 266 km

Coastline: 161 km

Maritime claims: *territorial sea:* 12 nm
exclusive economic zone: 200 nm or to median line

Climate: tropical; hot, humid, rainy

Terrain: flat coastal plain rises to mountains in east; hilly lowland in west

Elevation: *highest point:* Bukit Pagon 1,850 m
lowest point: South China Sea 0 m
mean elevation: 478 m

Natural resources: petroleum, natural gas, timber

Land use: *agricultural land:* 2.5% (2018 est.)
arable land: 0.8% (2018 est.)
permanent crops: 1.1% (2018 est.)
permanent pasture: 0.6% (2018 est.)
forest: 71.8% (2018 est.)
other: 25.7% (2018 est.)

Irrigated land: 10 sq km (2012)

Population distribution: the vast majority of the population is found along the coast in the western part of Brunei, which is separated from the eastern portion by Malaysia; the largest population concentration is in the far north on the western side of the Brunei Bay, in and around the capital of Bandar Seri Begawan

Natural hazards: typhoons, earthquakes, and severe flooding are rare

Geography - note: close to vital sea lanes through South China Sea linking Indian and Pacific Oceans; two parts physically separated by Malaysia; the eastern part, the Temburong district, is an exclave and is almost an enclave within Malaysia

PEOPLE AND SOCIETY

Population: *total:* 491,900
male: 239,140
female: 252,760 (2024 est.)
comparison rankings: female 173; male 173; total 173

Nationality: *noun:* Bruneian(s)
adjective: Bruneian

Ethnic groups: Malay 67.4%, Chinese 9.6%, other 23% (2021 est.)

Languages: Malay (Bahasa Melayu) (official), English, Chinese dialects
major-language sample(s):
Buku Fakta Dunia, sumber yang diperlukan untuk maklumat asas. (Malay)

Religions: Muslim (official) 82.1%, Christian 6.7%, Buddhist 6.3%, other 4.9% (2021 est.)

Demographic profile: Brunei is a small, oil-rich sultanate of less than half a million people, making it the smallest country in Southeast Asia by population. Its total fertility rate – the average number of births per woman – has been steadily declining over the last few decades, from over 3.5 in the 1980s to below replacement level today at nearly 1.8. The trend is due to women's increased years of education and participation in the workforce, which have resulted in later marriages and fewer children. Yet, the population continues to grow because of the large number of women of reproductive age and a reliance on foreign labor – mainly from Malaysia, Thailand, the Philippines, Indonesia, and South Asian countries – to fill low-skilled jobs.

Brunei is officially Muslim, and Malay is the official language. The country follows an official Malay national ideology, Malay Islamic Monarchy, which promotes Malay language and culture, Islamic values, and the monarchy. Only seven of Brunei's native groups are recognized in the constitution and are defined as "Malay" – Brunei Malays, Belait, Kedayan, Dusun, Bisayak, Lun Bawang, and Sama- Baiau. Together they make up about 66% percent of the population and are referred to as the Bumiputera. The Bumiputera are entitled to official privileges, including land ownership, access to certain types of employment (Royal Brunei Armed Forces and Brunei Shell Petroleum), easier access to higher education, and better job opportunities in the civil service.

Brunei's Chinese population descends from migrants who arrived when Brunei was a British protectorate (1888 and 1984). They are prominent in the nonstate commercial sector and account for approximately 10% of the population. Most Bruneian Chinese are permanent residents rather than citizens despite roots going back several generations. Many are stateless and are denied rights granted to citizens, such as land ownership, subsidized health care, and free secondary and university education. Because of the discriminatory policies, the number of Chinese in Brunei has shrunk considerably in the last 50 years. Native ethnic groups that are not included in the Bumiputera are not recognized in the constitution and are not officially identified as "Malay" or automatically granted citizenship. Foreign workers constitute some quarter of the labor force.

Age structure: *0-14 years:* 21.7% (male 54,924/female 51,710)
15-64 years: 70.8% (male 166,289/female 182,011)
65 years and over: 7.5% (2024 est.) (male 17,927/female 19,039)

Dependency ratios: *total dependency ratio:* 39.2
youth dependency ratio: 31.1
elderly dependency ratio: 8.1
potential support ratio: 12.4 (2021 est.)

Median age: *total:* 32.3 years (2024 est.)
male: 31.4 years
female: 33.1 years
comparison ranking: total 117

Population growth rate: 1.4% (2024 est.)
comparison ranking: 71

Birth rate: 15.8 births/1,000 population (2024 est.)
comparison ranking: 101

Death rate: 3.9 deaths/1,000 population (2024 est.)
comparison ranking: 218

Net migration rate: 2.1 migrant(s)/1,000 population (2024 est.)
comparison ranking: 48

Population distribution: the vast majority of the population is found along the coast in the western part of Brunei, which is separated from the eastern portion by Malaysia; the largest population concentration is in the far north on the western side of the Brunei Bay, in and around the capital of Bandar Seri Begawan

Urbanization: *urban population:* 79.1% of total population (2023)
rate of urbanization: 1.44% annual rate of change (2020-25 est.)

Major urban areas - population: 266,682 BANDAR SERI BEGAWAN (capital) (2021)
note: the boundaries of the capital city were expanded in 2007, greatly increasing the city area; the population of the capital increased tenfold

Sex ratio: *at birth:* 1.05 male(s)/female
0-14 years: 1.06 male(s)/female
15-64 years: 0.91 male(s)/female
65 years and over: 0.94 male(s)/female
total population: 0.95 male(s)/female (2024 est.)

Maternal mortality ratio: 44 deaths/100,000 live births (2020 est.)
comparison ranking: 99

Infant mortality rate: *total:* 10 deaths/1,000 live births (2024 est.)
male: 12.2 deaths/1,000 live births
female: 7.7 deaths/1,000 live births
comparison ranking: total 132

Life expectancy at birth: *total population:* 78.9 years (2024 est.)
male: 76.5 years
female: 81.3 years
comparison ranking: total population 71

Total fertility rate: *1.73 children born/woman (2024 est.) comparison ranking:* 153

Gross reproduction rate: 0.85 (2024 est.)

Contraceptive prevalence rate: NA

Drinking water source: *improved: urban:* 99.7% of population
total: 99.9% of population
unimproved: urban: 0.4% of population
total: 0.1% of population (2020)

Current health expenditure: 2.4% of GDP (2020)

Physician density: 1.61 physicians/1,000 population (2017)

Hospital bed density: 2.9 beds/1,000 population (2017)

Obesity - adult prevalence rate: 14.1% (2016)
comparison ranking: 129

Alcohol consumption per capita: *total:* 0.69 liters of pure alcohol (2019 est.)
beer: 0.66 liters of pure alcohol (2019 est.)
wine: 0.04 liters of pure alcohol (2019 est.)
spirits: 0 liters of pure alcohol (2019 est.)
other alcohols: 0 liters of pure alcohol (2019 est.)
comparison ranking: total 157

Tobacco use: *total:* 16.2% (2020 est.)
male: 30% (2020 est.)
female: 2.3% (2020 est.)
comparison ranking: total 100

Children under the age of 5 years underweight: NA

Currently married women (ages 15-49): 54.3% (2023 est.)

Education expenditures: 4.4% of GDP (2016 est.)
comparison ranking: 104

Literacy: *definition:* age 15 and over can read and write
total population: 97.6%
male: 98.3%
female: 96.9% (2021)

School life expectancy (primary to tertiary education): *total:* 14 years
male: 14 years
female: 14 years (2020)

ENVIRONMENT

Environment - current issues: no major environmental problems, but air pollution control is becoming a concern; seasonal trans-boundary haze from forest fires in Indonesia

Environment - international agreements: *party to:* Biodiversity, Climate Change, Climate Change-Kyoto Protocol, Climate Change-Paris Agreement, Comprehensive Nuclear Test Ban, Desertification, Endangered Species, Hazardous Wastes, Law of the Sea, Ozone Layer Protection, Ship Pollution
signed, but not ratified: none of the selected agreements

Climate: tropical; hot, humid, rainy

Urbanization: *urban population:* 79.1% of total population (2023)
rate of urbanization: 1.44% annual rate of change (2020-25 est.)

Revenue from forest resources: 0.05% of GDP (2018 est.)
comparison ranking: 129

Revenue from coal: 0% of GDP (2018 est.)
comparison ranking: 106

Air pollutants: *particulate matter emissions:* 6.86 micrograms per cubic meter (2019 est.)
carbon dioxide emissions: 7.66 megatons (2016 est.)
methane emissions: 8.4 megatons (2020 est.)

Waste and recycling: *municipal solid waste generated annually:* 216,253 tons (2016 est.)

Total water withdrawal: *municipal:* 150 million cubic meters (2020 est.)
agricultural: 10 million cubic meters (2020 est.)

Total renewable water resources: 8.5 billion cubic meters (2020 est.)

GOVERNMENT

Country name: *conventional long form:* Brunei Darussalam
conventional short form: Brunei
local long form: Negara Brunei Darussalam
local short form: Brunei
etymology: derivation of the name is unclear; according to legend, MUHAMMAD SHAH, who would become the first sultan of Brunei, upon discovering what would become Brunei exclaimed "Baru nah," which roughly translates as "there" or "that's it"

Government type: absolute monarchy or sultanate

Capital: *name:* Bandar Seri Begawan
geographic coordinates: 4 53 N, 114 56 E
time difference: UTC+8 (13 hours ahead of Washington, DC, during Standard Time)
etymology: named in 1970 after Sultan Omar Ali SAIFUDDIEN III (1914-1986; "The Father of Independence") who adopted the title of "Seri Begawan" (approximate meaning "honored lord") upon his abdication in 1967; "bandar" in Malay means "town" or "city"; the capital had previously been called Bandar Brunei (Brunei Town)

Administrative divisions: 4 districts (daerah-daerah, singular - daerah); Belait, Brunei dan Muara, Temburong, Tutong

Independence: 1 January 1984 (from the UK)

National holiday: National Day, 23 February (1984); note - 1 January 1984 was the date of independence from the UK, 23 February 1984 was the date of independence from British protection; the Sultan's birthday, 15 June

Legal system: mixed legal system based on English common law and Islamic law; note - in April 2019, the full sharia penal codes came into force and apply to Muslims and partly to non-Muslims in parallel with present common law codes

Constitution: *history:* drafted 1954 to 1959, signed 29 September 1959; note - some constitutional provisions suspended since 1962 under a State of Emergency, others suspended since independence in 1984
amendments: proposed by the monarch; passage requires submission to the Privy Council for Legislative Council review and finalization takes place by proclamation; the monarch can accept or reject changes to the original proposal provided by the Legislative Council; amended several times, last in 2010

International law organization participation: has not submitted an ICJ jurisdiction declaration; non-party state to the ICC

Citizenship: *citizenship by birth:* no
citizenship by descent only: the father must be a citizen of Brunei
dual citizenship recognized: no
residency requirement for naturalization: 12 years

Suffrage: 18 years of age for village elections; universal

Executive branch: *chief of state:* Sultan and Prime Minister Sir HASSANAL Bolkiah (since 5 October 1967)
head of government: Sultan and Prime Minister Sir HASSANAL Bolkiah (since 5 October 1967)
cabinet: Council of Ministers appointed and presided over by the monarch; note - 4 additional advisory councils appointed by the monarch are the Religious Council, Privy Council for constitutional issues, Council of Succession, and Legislative Council; Sultan and Prime Minister Sir HASSANAL Bolkiah is also Minister of Finance, Defense, and Foreign Affairs and Trade
elections/appointments: none; the monarchy is hereditary
note - the monarch is both chief of state and head of government

Legislative branch: *description:* unicameral Legislative Council or Majlis Mesyuarat Negara Brunei (up to 45 seats; up to 30 appointed; up to 15 representatives from the country's four districts: Brunei and Muara (up to seven members), Belait (up to three), Tutong (up to three), and Temburong (up to two)); members serve 5-year terms
elections: January 2023 - appointed by the sultan

election results: Legislative Council last appointed January 2023; composition - men 30, women 4, percentage women 11.8%

Judicial branch: *highest court(s):* Supreme Court (consists of the Court of Appeal and the High Court, each with a chief justice and 2 judges); Sharia Court (consists the Court of Appeals and the High Court); note - Brunei has a dual judicial system of secular and sharia (religious) courts; the Judicial Committee of Privy Council (in London) serves as the final appellate court for civil cases only
judge selection and term of office: Supreme Court judges appointed by the monarch to serve until age 65, and older if approved by the monarch; Sharia Court judges appointed by the monarch for life
subordinate courts: Intermediate Court; Magistrates' Courts; Juvenile Court; small claims courts; lower sharia courts

Political parties: National Development Party or NDP
note: the NDP is Brunei's only registered party, but does not have representation in the Legislative Council, which is appointed

International organization participation: ADB, APEC, ARF, ASEAN, C, CP, EAS, FAO, G-77, IAEA, IBRD, ICAO, ICC (NGOs), ICRM, IDA, IFRCS, ILO, IMF, IMO, IMSO, Interpol, IOC, ISO (correspondent), ITSO, ITU, NAM, OIC, OPCW, UN, UNCTAD, UNESCO, UNIFIL, UNWTO, UPU, WCO, WHO, WIPO, WMO, WTO

Diplomatic representation in the US: *chief of mission:* Ambassador Dato Paduka Haji SERBINI bin Haji Ali (since 28 January 2016)
chancery: 3520 International Court NW, Washington, DC 20008
telephone: [1] (202) 237-1838
FAX: [1] (202) 885-0560
email address and website:
info@bruneiembassy.org
http://www.bruneiembassy.org/index.html
consulate(s): New York

Diplomatic representation from the US: *chief of mission:* Ambassador Caryn R. McCLELLAND (since December 2021)
embassy: Simpang 336-52-16-9, Jalan Duta, Bandar Seri Begawan, BC4115
mailing address: 4020 Bandar Seri Begawan Place, Washington DC 20521-4020
telephone: (673) 238-7400
FAX: (673) 238-7533
email address and website:
ConsularBrunei@state.gov
https://bn.usembassy.gov/

Flag description: yellow with two diagonal bands of white (top, almost double width) and black starting from the upper hoist side; the national emblem in red is superimposed at the center; yellow is the color of royalty and symbolizes the sultanate; the white and black bands denote Brunei's chief ministers; the emblem includes five main components: a swallow-tailed flag, the royal umbrella representing the monarchy, the wings of four feathers symbolizing justice, tranquility, prosperity, and peace, the two upraised hands signifying the government's pledge to preserve and promote the welfare of the people, and the crescent moon denoting Islam, the state religion; the state motto "Always render service with God's guidance" appears in yellow Arabic script on the crescent; a ribbon below the crescent reads "Brunei, the Abode of Peace"

National symbol(s): royal parasol; national colors: yellow, white, black

National anthem: *name:* "Allah Peliharakan Sultan" (God Bless His Majesty)
lyrics/music: Pengiran Haji Mohamed YUSUF bin Pengiran Abdul Rahim/Awang Haji BESAR bin Sagap
note: adopted 1951

ECONOMY

Economic overview: almost exclusively an oil and gas economy; high income country; expansive and robust welfare system; the majority of the population works for the government; promulgating a nationalized halal brand; considering establishment of a bond market and stock exchange

Real GDP (purchasing power parity): $35.26 billion (2023 est.)
$34.771 billion (2022 est.)
$35.347 billion (2021 est.)
note: data in 2021 dollars
comparison ranking: 141

Real GDP growth rate: 1.41% (2023 est.)
-1.63% (2022 est.)
-1.59% (2021 est.)
note: annual GDP % growth based on constant local currency
comparison ranking: 154

Real GDP per capita: $77,900 (2023 est.)
$77,400 (2022 est.)
$79,400 (2021 est.)
note: data in 2021 dollars
comparison ranking: 12

GDP (official exchange rate): $15.128 billion (2023 est.)
note: data in current dollars at official exchange rate

Inflation rate (consumer prices): 0.36% (2023 est.)
3.68% (2022 est.)
1.73% (2021 est.)
note: annual % change based on consumer prices
comparison ranking: 11

GDP - composition, by sector of origin: *agriculture:* 1.2% (2023 est.)
industry: 61.8% (2023 est.)
services: 38.8% (2023 est.)
note: figures may not total 100% due to non-allocated consumption not captured in sector-reported data comparison rankings: services 197; industry 5; agriculture 179

GDP - composition, by end use: *household consumption:* 27.6% (2023 est.)
government consumption: 22.8% (2023 est.)
investment in fixed capital: 29.4% (2023 est.)
investment in inventories: 0.2% (2023 est.)
exports of goods and services: 76.5% (2023 est.)
imports of goods and services: -60% (2023 est.)
note: figures may not total 100% due to rounding or gaps in data collection

Agricultural products: chicken, eggs, fruits, rice, vegetables, beans, bananas, beef, pineapples, cucumbers/gherkins (2022)
note: top ten agricultural products based on tonnage

Industries: petroleum, petroleum refining, liquefied natural gas, construction, agriculture, aquaculture, transportation

Industrial production growth rate: -1.43% (2023 est.)
note: annual % change in industrial value added based on constant local currency
comparison ranking: 173

Labor force: 228,000 (2023 est.)
note: number of people ages 15 or older who are employed or seeking work
comparison ranking: 177

Unemployment rate: 5.27% (2023 est.)
5.19% (2022 est.)
4.91% (2021 est.)
note: % of labor force seeking employment
comparison ranking: 100

Youth unemployment rate (ages 15-24): *total:* 18.6% (2023 est.)
male: 16.2% (2023 est.)
female: 22.3% (2023 est.)
note: % of labor force ages 15-24 seeking employment
comparison ranking: total 73

Remittances: 0.01% of GDP (2023 est.)
0.01% of GDP (2022 est.)
0.01% of GDP (2021 est.)
note: personal transfers and compensation between resident and non-resident individuals/households/entities

Budget: *revenues:* $1.058 billion (2020 est.)
expenditures: $3.189 billion (2020 est.)

Public debt: 2.8% of GDP (2017 est.)
comparison ranking: 204

Taxes and other revenues: 18.5% (of GDP) (2017 est.)
comparison ranking: 97

Current account balance: $3.264 billion (2022 est.)
$1.57 billion (2021 est.)
$513.713 million (2020 est.)
note: balance of payments - net trade and primary/secondary income in current dollars
comparison ranking: 42

Exports: $14.411 billion (2022 est.)
$11.202 billion (2021 est.)
$6.886 billion (2020 est.)
note: balance of payments - exports of goods and services in current dollars
comparison ranking: 100

Exports - partners: Australia 19%, Japan 17%, China 16%, Singapore 14%, Malaysia 10% (2022)
note: top five export partners based on percentage share of exports

Exports - commodities: refined petroleum, natural gas, crude petroleum, hydrocarbons, fertilizers (2022)
note: top five export commodities based on value in dollars

Imports: $10.106 billion (2022 est.)
$9.219 billion (2021 est.)
$6.382 billion (2020 est.)
note: balance of payments - imports of goods and services in current dollars
comparison ranking: 123

Imports - partners: Malaysia 22%, UAE 11%, China 10%, Singapore 7%, Qatar 6% (2022)
note: top five import partners based on percentage share of imports

Imports - commodities: crude petroleum, refined petroleum, cars, coal, gas turbines (2022)
note: top five import commodities based on value in dollars

Reserves of foreign exchange and gold: $4.483 billion (2023 est.)
$5.035 billion (2022 est.)
$4.982 billion (2021 est.)
note: holdings of gold (year-end prices)/foreign exchange/special drawing rights in current dollars
comparison ranking: 102

Exchange rates: Bruneian dollars (BND) per US dollar -

Exchange rates: 1.343 (2023 est.)
1.379 (2022 est.)
1.344 (2021 est.)
1.38 (2020 est.)
1.364 (2019 est.)

ENERGY

Electricity access: *electrification - total population:* 100% (2022 est.)

Electricity: *installed generating capacity:* 1.265 million kW (2022 est.)
consumption: 5.24 billion kWh (2022 est.)
transmission/distribution losses: 513 million kWh (2022 est.)
comparison rankings: transmission/distribution losses 80; consumption 130; installed generating capacity 130

Electricity generation sources: *fossil fuels:* 100% of total installed capacity (2022 est.)

Coal: *consumption:* 1.203 million metric tons (2022 est.)
imports: 1.203 million metric tons (2022 est.)

Petroleum: *total petroleum production:* 95,000 bbl/day (2023 est.)
refined petroleum consumption: 17,000 bbl/day (2022 est.)
crude oil estimated reserves: 1.1 billion barrels (2021 est.)

Natural gas: *production:* 10.598 billion cubic meters (2022 est.)
consumption: 4.374 billion cubic meters (2022 est.)
exports: 6.12 billion cubic meters (2022 est.)
proven reserves: 260.515 billion cubic meters (2021 est.)

Carbon dioxide emissions: 12.172 million metric tonnes of CO_2 (2022 est.)
from coal and metallurgical coke: 1.419 million metric tonnes of CO_2 (2022 est.)
from petroleum and other liquids: 2.197 million metric tonnes of CO_2 (2022 est.)
from consumed natural gas: 8.557 million metric tonnes of CO_2 (2022 est.)
comparison ranking: total emissions 103

Energy consumption per capita: 466.111 million Btu/person (2022 est.)
comparison ranking: 5

COMMUNICATIONS

Telephones - fixed lines: *total subscriptions:* 122,000 (2022 est.)
subscriptions per 100 inhabitants: 27 (2022 est.)
comparison ranking: total subscriptions 130

Telephones - mobile cellular: *total subscriptions:* 529,000 (2022 est.)
subscriptions per 100 inhabitants: 118 (2022 est.)
comparison ranking: total subscriptions 173

Telecommunication systems: *general assessment:* Brunei's mobile market experienced drop-off in subscriber numbers in 2020; in 2022 there was a concerted effort to build out the fixed-line infrastructure while progressing towards introducing 5G mobile services, which was activated in June 2023; Brunei's fixed-line market is one of the few countries in the world to have displayed significant growth rather than a decline in teledensity in the last few years; this upward trend is set to continue as the new Unified National Network (UNN) works diligently to expand and enhance the fixed-line infrastructure around the country; strong growth was also seen in the fixed broadband space, on the back of those same infrastructure developments that are part of the Brunei Vision 2035 initiative; fixed broadband is starting from a relatively low base by international standards and is still only at 18%, leaving lots of room for growth; mobile and mobile broadband, on the other hand, are still suffering from the market contractions first felt in 2020; Brunei's 2G GSM network is shut down, with the spectrum to be reallocated to 3G, 4G, and potentially 5G use (2023)
domestic: 25 per 100 fixed-line, 136 per 100 mobile-cellular (2021)
international: country code - 673; landing points for the SEA-ME-WE-3, SJC, AAG, Lubuan-Brunei Submarine Cable via optical telecommunications submarine cables that provides links to Asia, the Middle East, Southeast Asia, Africa, Australia, and the US; satellite earth stations - 2 Intelsat (1 Indian Ocean and 1 Pacific Ocean) (2019)

Broadcast media: state-controlled Radio Television Brunei (RTB) operates 5 channels; 3 Malaysian TV stations are available; foreign TV broadcasts are available via satellite systems; RTB operates 5 radio networks and broadcasts on multiple frequencies; British Forces Broadcast Service (BFBS) provides radio broadcasts on 2 FM stations; some radio broadcast stations from Malaysia are available via repeaters

Internet country code: .bn

Internet users: *total:* 441,000 (2021 est.)
percent of population: 98% (2021 est.)
comparison ranking: total 170

Broadband - fixed subscriptions: *total:* 71,078 (2020 est.)
subscriptions per 100 inhabitants: 16 (2020 est.)
comparison ranking: total 134

TRANSPORTATION

National air transport system: *number of registered air carriers:* 1 (2020)
inventory of registered aircraft operated by air carriers: 10
annual passenger traffic on registered air carriers: 1,234,455 (2018)
annual freight traffic on registered air carriers: 129.35 million (2018) mt-km

Civil aircraft registration country code prefix: V8

Airports: 2 (2024)
comparison ranking: 200

Heliports: 14 (2024)

Pipelines: 33 km condensate, 86 km condensate/gas, 628 km gas, 492 km oil (2013)

Roadways: *total:* 2,976 km
paved: 2,559 km
unpaved: 417 km (2014)
comparison ranking: total 163

Waterways: 209 km (2012) (navigable by craft drawing less than 1.2 m; the Belait, Brunei, and Tutong Rivers are major transport links)
comparison ranking: 106

Merchant marine: *total:* 97 (2023)
by type: general cargo 18, oil tanker 2, other 77
comparison ranking: total 90

Ports: *total ports:* 5 (2024)
large: 0
medium: 0
small: 2
very small: 3
ports with oil terminals: 5
key ports: Bandar Seri Begawan, Kuala Belait, Lumut, Muara Harbor, Seria Oil Loading Terminal

MILITARY AND SECURITY

Military and security forces: Royal Brunei Armed Forces (RBAF) or Angkatan Bersenjata Diraja Brunei (ABDB): Royal Brunei Land Force (RBLF) or Tentera Darat Diraja Brunei (TDDB), Royal Brunei Navy (RBN) or Tentera Laut Diraja Brunei (TLDB), Royal Brunei Air Force (RBAirF) or Tentera Udara Diraja Brunei (TUDB)

Ministry of Home Affairs: Royal Brunei Police Force (RBPF) or Polis Diraja Brunei (PDB) (2024)
note: the Gurkha Reserve Unit (GRU) under the Ministry of Defense is a special guard force for the Sultan, the royal family, and the country's oil installations; the RBAF has a Joint Force Headquarters (JFHQ) to oversee joint/combined operations of the service branches

Military expenditures: 3% of GDP (2023 est.)
2.6% of GDP (2022 est.)
3.1% of GDP (2021 est.)
3.7% of GDP (2020 est.)
3.1% of GDP (2019 est.)
comparison ranking: 32

Military and security service personnel strengths: approximately 8,000 total active-duty troops (2024)

Military equipment inventories and acquisitions: the military's s inventory includes equipment and weapons systems from a wide variety of suppliers from Asia, Europe, and the US (2024)

Military service age and obligation: 17 years of age for voluntary military service; non-Malays are ineligible to serve (2024)
note: the Gurkha Reserve Unit (GRU) employs hundreds of Gurkhas from Nepal, the majority of whom are veterans of the British Army and the Singapore Police Force who have joined the GRU as a second career

Military - note: the Royal Brunei Armed Forces were formed in 1961 with British support as the Brunei Malay Regiment; "Royal" was added as an honorary title in 1965 and its current name was given in 1984; the military is responsible for ensuring the country's sovereignty and territorial integrity, as well as countering outside aggression, terrorism, and insurgency
Brunei has a long-standing defense relationship with the UK and hosts a British Army garrison, which includes a Gurkha battalion and a jungle warfare school; Brunei also hosts a Singaporean military training detachment
(2024)

TRANSNATIONAL ISSUES

Refugees and internally displaced persons: *stateless persons:* 20,863 (2022); note - thousands of stateless persons, often ethnic Chinese, are permanent residents and their families have lived in Brunei for generations; obtaining citizenship is difficult and requires individuals to pass rigorous tests on Malay culture, customs, and language; stateless residents receive an International Certificate of Identity, which enables them to travel overseas; the government is considering changing the law prohibiting non-Bruneians, including stateless permanent residents, from owning land

Trafficking in persons: tier rating: Tier 3 — Brunei does not fully meet the minimum standards for the elimination of trafficking and is not making significant efforts to do so, therefore, Brunei was downgraded to Tier 3; for more details, go to: https://www.state.gov/ reports/2024-trafficking-in-persons-report/brunei/

Illicit drugs: drug trafficking and illegally importing controlled substances are serious offenses in Brunei and carry a mandatory death penalty

BULGARIA

INTRODUCTION

Background: The Bulgars, a Central Asian Turkic tribe, merged with the local Slavic inhabitants in the late 7th century to form the first Bulgarian state. In succeeding centuries, Bulgaria struggled with the Byzantine Empire to assert its place in the Balkans, but by the end of the 14th century, the Ottoman Turks overran the country. Northern Bulgaria attained autonomy in 1878, and all of Bulgaria became independent from the Ottoman Empire in 1908. Having fought on the losing side in both World Wars, Bulgaria fell within the Soviet sphere of influence and became a People's Republic in 1946. Communist domination ended in 1990, when Bulgaria held its first multiparty election since World War II and began the contentious process of moving toward political democracy and a market economy while combating inflation, unemployment, corruption, and crime. The country joined NATO in 2004, the EU in 2007, and the Schengen Area for air and sea travel in 2024.

GEOGRAPHY

Location: Southeastern Europe, bordering the Black Sea, between Romania and Turkey: Geographic coordinates: 43 00 N, 25 00 E

Map references: Europe

Area: *total:* 110,879 sq km
land: 108,489 sq km
water: 2,390 sq km
comparison ranking: total 105

Area - comparative: almost identical in size to Virginia; slightly larger than Tennessee

Land boundaries: *total:* 1,806 km
border countries (5): Greece 472 km; Macedonia 162 km; Romania 605 km; Serbia 344 km; Turkey 223 km

Coastline: 354 km

Maritime claims: *territorial sea:* 12 nm
contiguous zone: 24 nm
exclusive economic zone: 200 nm

Climate: temperate; cold, damp winters; hot, dry summers

Terrain: mostly mountains with lowlands in north and southeast

Elevation: *highest point:* Musala 2,925 m
lowest point: Black Sea 0 m
mean elevation: 472 m

Natural resources: bauxite, copper, lead, zinc, coal, timber, arable land

Land use: *agricultural land:* 46.9% (2018 est.)
arable land: 29.9% (2018 est.)
permanent crops: 1.5% (2018 est.)
permanent pasture: 15.5% (2018 est.)
forest: 36.7% (2018 est.)
other: 16.4% (2018 est.)

Irrigated land: 987 sq km (2013)

Major rivers (by length in km): Dunav (Danube) (shared with Germany [s], Austria, Slovakia, Hungary, Croatia, Serbia, Ukraine, Moldova, and Romania [m]) - 2,888 km
note – [s] after country name indicates river source; [m] after country name indicates river mouth

Major watersheds (area sq km): Atlantic Ocean drainage: *(Black Sea)* Danube (795,656 sq km)

Population distribution: a fairly even distribution throughout most of the country, with urban areas attracting larger populations

Natural hazards: earthquakes; landslides

Geography - note: strategic location near Turkish Straits; controls key land routes from Europe to Middle East and Asia

PEOPLE AND SOCIETY

Population: *total:* 6,782,659
male: 3,303,491
female: 3,479,168 (2024 est.)
comparison rankings: female 106; male 107; total 107

Nationality: *noun:* Bulgarian(s)
adjective: Bulgarian

Ethnic groups: Bulgarian 78.5%, Turkish 7.8%, Roma 4.1%, other 1.2%, unspecified 9.4% (2021 est.) note: Romani populations are usually underestimated in official statistics and may represent 9–11% of Bulgaria's population

Languages: Bulgarian (official) 77.3%, Turkish 7.9%, Romani 3.5%, other 1%, unspecified 10.4% (2021 est.)
major-language sample(s):
Световен Алманах, незаменимият източник за основна информация. (Bulgarian): The World Factbook, the indispensable source for basic information.

Religions: Christian 64.7%, Muslim 9.8%, other 0.1%, none 4.7%, unspecified 20.7% (2021 est.)

Age structure: *0-14 years:* 13.8% (male 479,586/female 453,423)
15-64 years: 65.2% (male 2,250,962/female 2,171,279)
65 years and over: 21% (2024 est.) (male 572,943/female 854,466)

Dependency ratios: *total dependency ratio:* 57.3
youth dependency ratio: 22
elderly dependency ratio: 35.3
potential support ratio: 2.8 (2021 est.)

Median age: *total:* 45.1 years (2024 est.)
male: 43.3 years
female: 47 years
comparison ranking: total 19

Population growth rate: -0.66% (2024 est.)
comparison ranking: 226

Birth rate: 7.9 births/1,000 population (2024 est.)
comparison ranking: 216

Death rate: 14.2 deaths/1,000 population (2024 est.)
comparison ranking: 7

Net migration rate: -0.3 migrant(s)/1,000 population (2024 est.)
comparison ranking: 111

Population distribution: a fairly even distribution throughout most of the country, with urban areas attracting larger populations

Urbanization: *urban population:* 76.7% of total population (2023)
rate of urbanization: -0.28% annual rate of change (2020-25 est.)

Major urban areas - population: 1.288 million SOFIA (capital) (2023)

Sex ratio: *at birth:* 1.06 male(s)/female
0-14 years: 1.06 male(s)/female
15-64 years: 1.04 male(s)/female
65 years and over: 0.67 male(s)/female
total population: 0.95 male(s)/female (2024 est.)

Mother's mean age at first birth: 26.4 years (2020 est.)

Maternal mortality ratio: 7 deaths/100,000 live births (2020 est.)
comparison ranking: 158

Infant mortality rate: *total:* 7.7 deaths/1,000 live births (2024 est.)
male: 8.7 deaths/1,000 live births
female: 6.6 deaths/1,000 live births
comparison ranking: total 149

Life expectancy at birth: *total population:* 76.1 years (2024 est.)

male: 72.9 years
female: 79.4 years
comparison ranking: total population 118

Total fertility rate: 1.51 children born/woman (2024 est.)
comparison ranking: 202

Gross reproduction rate: 0.73 (2024 est.)

Contraceptive prevalence rate: NA

Drinking water source: *improved: urban:* 99.5% of population
rural: 97.4% of population
total: 99% of population
unimproved: urban: 0.5% of population
rural: 2.6% of population
total: 1% of population (2020 est.)

Current health expenditure: 8.5% of GDP (2020)

Physician density: 4.2 physicians/1,000 population (2018)

Hospital bed density: 7.5 beds/1,000 population (2017)

Sanitation facility access: *improved:*
total: 100% of population

Obesity - adult prevalence rate: 25% (2016)
comparison ranking: 53

Alcohol consumption per capita: *total:* 11.18 liters of pure alcohol (2019 est.)
beer: 4.44 liters of pure alcohol (2019 est.)
wine: 1.72 liters of pure alcohol (2019 est.)
spirits: 4.96 liters of pure alcohol (2019 est.)
other alcohols: 0.06 liters of pure alcohol (2019 est.)
comparison ranking: total 9

Tobacco use: *total:* 39% (2020 est.)
male: 40.9% (2020 est.)
female: 37.1% (2020 est.)
comparison ranking: total 7

Children under the age of 5 years underweight: 1.9% (2014)
comparison ranking: 106

Currently married women (ages 15-49): 57.3% (2023 est.)

Education expenditures: 4% of GDP (2020 est.)
comparison ranking: 117

Literacy: *definition:* age 15 and over can read and write
total population: 98.4%
male: 98.7%
female: 98.2% (2021)

School life expectancy (primary to tertiary education): *total:* 14 years
male: 13 years
female: 14 years (2020)

ENVIRONMENT

Environment - current issues: air pollution from industrial emissions; rivers polluted from raw sewage, heavy metals, detergents; deforestation; forest damage from air pollution and resulting acid rain; soil contamination from heavy metals from metallurgical plants and industrial wastes

Environment - international agreements: *party to:* Air Pollution, Air Pollution-Heavy Metals, Air Pollution-Multi-effect Protocol, Air Pollution-Nitrogen Oxides, Air Pollution-Persistent Organic Pollutants, Air Pollution-Sulphur 85, Air Pollution-Sulphur 94, Air Pollution-Volatile Organic Compounds, Antarctic-Environmental Protection, Antarctic-Marine Living Resources, Antarctic Treaty, Biodiversity, Climate Change, Climate Change-Kyoto Protocol, Climate Change-Paris Agreement, Comprehensive Nuclear Test Ban, Desertification, Endangered Species, Environmental Modification, Hazardous Wastes, Law of the Sea, Marine Dumping- London Convention, Marine Dumping-London Protocol, Nuclear Test Ban, Ozone Layer Protection, Ship Pollution, Tropical Timber 2006, Wetlands, Whaling
signed, but not ratified: none of the selected agreements

Climate: temperate; cold, damp winters; hot, dry summers

Urbanization: *urban population:* 76.7% of total population (2023)
rate of urbanization: -0.28% annual rate of change (2020-25 est.)

Revenue from forest resources: 0.22% of GDP (2018 est.)
comparison ranking: 90

Revenue from coal: 0.14% of GDP (2018 est.)
comparison ranking: 24

Air pollutants: *particulate matter emissions:* 17.29 micrograms per cubic meter (2019 est.)
carbon dioxide emissions: 41.71 megatons (2016 est.)
methane emissions: 6.77 megatons (2020 est.)

Waste and recycling: *municipal solid waste generated annually:* 3.011 million tons (2015 est.)
municipal solid waste recycled annually: 572,993 tons (2015 est.)
percent of municipal solid waste recycled: 19% (2015 est.)

Major rivers (by length in km): Dunav (Danube) (shared with Germany [s], Austria, Slovakia, Hungary, Croatia, Serbia, Ukraine, Moldova, and Romania [m]) - 2,888 km
note – [s] after country name indicates river source; [m] after country name indicates river mouth

Major watersheds (area sq km): Atlantic Ocean drainage: *(Black Sea)* Danube (795,656 sq km)

Total water withdrawal: *municipal:* 840 million cubic meters (2020 est.)
industrial: 3.48 billion cubic meters (2020 est.)
agricultural: 760 million cubic meters (2020 est.)

Total renewable water resources: 21.3 billion cubic meters (2020 est.)

GOVERNMENT

Country name: *conventional long form:* Republic of Bulgaria
conventional short form: Bulgaria
local long form: Republika Bulgaria
local short form: Bulgaria
former: Kingdom of Bulgaria, People's Republic of Bulgaria
etymology: named after the Bulgar tribes who settled the lower Balkan region in the 7th century A.D.

Government type: parliamentary republic

Capital: *name:* Sofia
geographic coordinates: 42 41 N, 23 19 E
time difference: UTC+2 (7 hours ahead of Washington, DC, during Standard Time)
daylight saving time: +1hr, begins last Sunday in March; ends last Sunday in October
etymology: named after the Saint Sofia Church in the city, parts of which date back to the 4th century A.D.

Administrative divisions: 28 provinces (oblasti, singular - oblast); Blagoevgrad, Burgas, Dobrich, Gabrovo, Haskovo, Kardzhali, Kyustendil, Lovech, Montana, Pazardzhik, Pernik, Pleven, Plovdiv, Razgrad, Ruse, Shumen, Silistra, Sliven, Smolyan, Sofia, Sofia-Grad (Sofia City), Stara Zagora, Targovishte, Varna, Veliko Tarnovo, Vidin, Vratsa, Yambol

Independence: 3 March 1878 (as an autonomous principality within the Ottoman Empire); 22 September 1908 (complete independence from the Ottoman Empire)

National holiday: Liberation Day, 3 March (1878)

Legal system: civil law

Constitution: *history:* several previous; latest drafted between late 1990 and early 1991, adopted 13 July 1991
amendments: proposed by the National Assembly or by the president of the republic; passage requires three-fourths majority vote of National Assembly members in three ballots; signed by the National Assembly chairperson; note - under special circumstances, a "Grand National Assembly" is elected with the authority to write a new constitution and amend certain articles of the constitution, including those affecting basic civil rights and national sovereignty; passage requires at least two-thirds majority vote in each of several readings; amended several times, last in 2023

International law organization participation: accepts compulsory ICJ jurisdiction with reservations; accepts ICCt jurisdiction

Citizenship: *citizenship by birth:* no
citizenship by descent only: at least one parent must be a citizen of Bulgaria
dual citizenship recognized: yes
residency requirement for naturalization: 5 years

Suffrage: 18 years of age; universal

Executive branch: *chief of state:* President Rumen RADEV (since 22 January 2017)
head of government: Caretaker Prime Minister Dimitar GLAVCHEV (since 9 April 2024)
cabinet: Council of Ministers nominated by the prime minister, elected by the National Assembly
elections/appointments: president and vice president elected on the same ballot by absolute majority popular vote in 2 rounds if needed for a 5-year term (eligible for a second term); election last held on 14 and 21 November 2021 (next to be held in fall 2026); chairman of the Council of Ministers (prime minister) elected by the National Assembly; deputy prime ministers nominated by the prime minister, elected by the National Assembly
election results:
2021: Rumen RADEV reelected president in second round; percent of vote in the first round - Rumen RADEV (independent) 49.4%, Anastas GERDZHIKOV (independent) 22.8%, Mustafa KARADAYI (DPS) 11.6%, Kostadin KOSTADINOV (Revival) 3.9%, Lozan PANOV (independent) 3.7%, other 8.6%; percent of vote in the second round - Rumen RADEV 66.7%, Anastas GERDZHIKOV 31.8%, neither 1.5%
2016: Rumen RADEV elected president in second round; percent of vote - Rumen RADEV (independent, supported by Bulgarian Socialist Party) 59.4%, Tsetska TSACHEVA (GERB) 36.2%, neither 4.5%

Legislative branch: *description:* unicameral National Assembly or Narodno Sabranie (240 seats; members directly elected in multi-seat constituencies by

open-list, proportional representation vote to serve 4-year terms)
elections: last held on 2 April 2023 (snap election to be held on 9 June 2024)
election results: percent of vote by party/coalition - GERB-SDS 25.4%, PP-DB 23.5%, Revival 13.6%, DPS 13.2%, BSP for Bulgaria 8.6%, ITN 3.9%, other 11.8%; seats by party/coalition GERB-SDS 69, PP-DB 64, Revival 37, DPS 36, BSP for Bulgaria 23, ITN 11; composition - men 179, women 61, percentage women 25.4%

Judicial branch: *highest court(s):* Supreme Court of Cassation (consists of a chairman and approximately 72 judges organized into penal, civil, and commercial colleges); Supreme Administrative Court (organized into 2 colleges with various panels of 5 judges each); Constitutional Court (consists of 12 justices); note - Constitutional Court resides outside the judiciary
judge selection and term of office: Supreme Court of Cassation and Supreme Administrative judges elected by the Supreme Judicial Council or SJC (consists of 25 members with extensive legal experience) and appointed by the president; judges can serve until mandatory retirement at age 65; Constitutional Court justices elected by the National Assembly and appointed by the president and the SJC; justices appointed for 9-year terms with renewal of 4 justices every 3 years
subordinate courts: appeals courts; regional and district courts; administrative courts; courts martial

Political parties: BSP for Bulgaria (electoral alliance of BSP, PKT, Ecoglasnost)
Bulgarian Rise or BV
Bulgarian Socialist Party or BSP
Citizens for the European Development of Bulgaria or GERB (alliance with SDS)
Democratic Bulgaria or DB (electoral alliance of Yes! Bulgaria, DSB, and The Greens)
Democrats for a Strong Bulgaria or DSB
Ecoglasnost
Green Movement or The Greens
Movement for Rights and Freedoms or DPS
Political Club Thrace or PKT
Revival
Stand Up.BG or IS.BG
There is Such a People or ITN
Union of Democratic Forces or SDS (alliance with GERB)
Yes! Bulgaria
We Continue the Change or PP
We Continue the Change and Democratic Bulgaria or PP-DB (electoral alliance of PP, DB, Yes! Bulgaria)

International organization participation: Australia Group, BIS, BSEC, CD, CE, CEI, CERN, EAPC, EBRD, ECB, EIB, EU, FAO, G- 9, IAEA, IBRD, ICAO, ICC (national committees), ICCt, ICRM, IDA, IFC, IFRCS, IHO (pending member), ILO, IMF, IMO, IMSO, Interpol, IOC, IOM, IPU, ISO, ITU, ITUC (NGOs), MIGA, NATO, NSG, OAS (observer), OIF, OPCW, OSCE, PCA, SELEC, UN, UNCTAD, UNESCO, UNHCR, UNHRC, UNIDO, UNMIL, UNOOSA, UNWTO, UPU, Wassenaar Arrangement, WCO, WFTU (NGOs), WHO, WIPO, WMO, WTO, ZC

Diplomatic representation in the US: *chief of mission:* Ambassador Georgi Velikov PANAYOTOV (since 7 June 2022)
chancery: 1621 22nd Street NW, Washington, DC 20008
telephone: [1] (202) 387 5770
FAX: [1] (202) 234-7973
email address and website:
office@bulgaria-embassy.org
https://www.bulgaria-embassy.org/en/homepage/
consulate(s) general: Chicago, Los Angeles, New York

Diplomatic representation from the US: *chief of mission:* Ambassador Kenneth MERTEN (since 7 April 2023)
embassy: 16, Kozyak Street, Sofia 1408
mailing address: 5740 Sofia Place, Washington, DC 20521-5740
telephone: [359] (2) 937-5100
FAX: [359] (2) 937-5209
email address and website:
acs_sofia@state.gov
https://bg.usembassy.gov/

Flag description: three equal horizontal bands of white (top), green, and red; the pan-Slavic white-blue-red colors were modified by substituting a green band (representing freedom) for the blue
note: the national emblem, formerly on the hoist side of the white stripe, has been removed

National symbol(s): lion; national colors: white, green, red

National anthem: *name:* "Mila Rodino" (Dear Homeland)
lyrics/music: Tsvetan Tsvetkov RADOSLAVOV
note: adopted 1964; composed in 1885 by a student en route to fight in the Serbo-Bulgarian War

National heritage: *total World Heritage Sites:* 10 (7 cultural, 3 natural)
selected World Heritage Site locales: Boyana Church (c); Madara Rider (c); Thracian Tomb of Kazanlak (c); Rock- Hewn Churches of Ivanovo (c); Rila Monastery (c); Ancient City of Nessebar (c); Thracian Tomb of Sveshtari (c); Srebarna Nature Reserve (n); Pirin National Park (n); Primeval Beech Forests of the Carpathians (n)

ECONOMY

Economic overview: upper-middle-income EU economy; currency pegged to the euro with accession pending; joined Schengen area as of March 2024; global events and internal political turmoil triggered export slump and stalled reforms; EU structural funds contributing to investment recovery; skilled labor shortage driven by emigration and aging population

Real GDP (purchasing power parity): $214.061 billion (2023 est.)
$210.181 billion (2022 est.)
$202.24 billion (2021 est.)
note: data in 2021 dollars
comparison ranking: 75

Real GDP growth rate: 1.85% (2023 est.)
3.93% (2022 est.)
7.66% (2021 est.)
note: annual GDP % growth based on constant local currency
comparison ranking: 146

Real GDP per capita: $33,300 (2023 est.)
$32,500 (2022 est.)
$29,400 (2021 est.)
note: data in 2021 dollars
comparison ranking: 74

GDP (official exchange rate): $101.584 billion (2023 est.)
note: data in current dollars at official exchange rate

Inflation rate (consumer prices): 9.44% (2023 est.)
15.33% (2022 est.)
3.3% (2021 est.)
note: annual % change based on consumer prices
comparison ranking: 173

Credit ratings: Fitch rating: BBB (2017)

Moody's rating: Baa1 (2020)

Standard & Poors rating: BBB (2019)
note: The year refers to the year in which the current credit rating was first obtained.

GDP - composition, by sector of origin: *agriculture:* 3% (2023 est.)
industry: 25.4% (2023 est.)
services: 59.3% (2023 est.)
note: figures may not total 100% due to non-allocated consumption not captured in sector-reported data
comparison rankings: services 91; industry 93; agriculture 138

GDP - composition, by end use: *household consumption:* 59.8% (2023 est.)
government consumption: 18.2% (2023 est.)
investment in fixed capital: 17.3% (2023 est.)
investment in inventories: 1.5% (2023 est.)
exports of goods and services: 60.9% (2023 est.)
imports of goods and services: -57.7% (2023 est.)
note: figures may not total 100% due to rounding or gaps in data collection

Agricultural products: wheat, maize, sunflower seeds, milk, barley, rapeseed, potatoes, grapes, tomatoes, chicken (2022)
note: top ten agricultural products based on tonnage

Industries: electricity, gas, water; food, beverages, tobacco; machinery and equipment, automotive parts, base metals, chemical products, coke, refined petroleum, nuclear fuel; outsourcing centers

Industrial production growth rate: 0.91% (2023 est.)
note: annual % change in industrial value added based on constant local currency
comparison ranking: 141

Labor force: 3.103 million (2023 est.)
note: number of people ages 15 or older who are employed or seeking work
comparison ranking: 107

Unemployment rate: 4.3% (2023 est.)
4.27% (2022 est.)
5.27% (2021 est.)
note: % of labor force seeking employment
comparison ranking: 83

Youth unemployment rate (ages 15-24): *total:* 12% (2023 est.)
male: 11.8% (2023 est.)
female: 12.2% (2023 est.)
note: % of labor force ages 15-24 seeking employment
comparison ranking: total 114

Population below poverty line: 20.6% (2022 est.)
note: % of population with income below national poverty line

Gini Index coefficient - distribution of family income: 39 (2021 est.)
note: index (0-100) of income distribution; higher values represent greater inequality
comparison ranking: 47

Average household expenditures: *on food:* 19.1% of household expenditures (2022 est.)
on alcohol and tobacco: 5.3% of household expenditures (2022 est.)

Household income or consumption by percentage share: *lowest 10%:* 2% (2021 est.)
highest 10%: 29.9% (2021 est.)

note: % share of income accruing to lowest and highest 10% of population

Remittances: 2.44% of GDP (2023 est.)
2.25% of GDP (2022 est.)
2.35% of GDP (2021 est.)
note: personal transfers and compensation between resident and non-resident individuals/households/entities

Budget: *revenues:* $33.1 billion (2022 est.)
expenditures: $35.619 billion (2022 est.)
note: central government revenues (excluding grants) and expenses converted to US dollars at average official exchange rate for year indicated

Public debt: 30.3% of GDP (2022 est.)
note: central government debt as a % of GDP
comparison ranking: 169

Taxes and other revenues: 21.8% (of GDP) (2022 est.)
note: central government tax revenue as a % of GDP
comparison ranking: 68

Current account balance: -$248.13 million (2023 est.)
-$591.65 million (2022 est.)
-$1.516 billion (2021 est.)
note: balance of payments - net trade and primary/secondary income in current dollars
comparison ranking: 113

Exports: $62.118 billion (2023 est.)
$60.712 billion (2022 est.)
$51.49 billion (2021 est.)
note: balance of payments - exports of goods and services in current dollars
comparison ranking: 58

Exports - partners: Germany 13%, Romania 13%, Italy 7%, Turkey 6%, Greece 6% (2022): note: top five export partners based on percentage share of exports

Exports - commodities: refined petroleum, natural gas, garments, wheat, refined copper (2022)
note: top five export commodities based on value in dollars

Imports: $58.79 billion (2023 est.)
$60.252 billion (2022 est.)
$50.048 billion (2021 est.)
note: balance of payments - imports of goods and services in current dollars
comparison ranking: 62

Imports - partners: Germany 10%, Russia 10%, Turkey 9%, Romania 7%, Greece 6% (2022)
note: top five import partners based on percentage share of imports

Imports - commodities: crude petroleum, natural gas, copper ore, cars, packaged medicine (2022)
note: top five import commodities based on value in dollars

Reserves of foreign exchange and gold: $46.334 billion (2023 est.)
$40.989 billion (2022 est.)
$39.188 billion (2021 est.)
note: holdings of gold (year-end prices)/foreign exchange/special drawing rights in current dollars
comparison ranking: 55

Debt - external: $14.277 billion (2022 est.)
note: present value of external debt in current US dollars
comparison ranking: 31

Exchange rates: leva (BGN) per US dollar –

Exchange rates: 1.809 (2023 est.)
1.86 (2022 est.)
1.654 (2021 est.)
1.716 (2020 est.)
1.747 (2019 est.)

ENERGY

Electricity access: *electrification - total population:* 100% (2022 est.)
electrification - urban areas: 100%
electrification - rural areas: 99.6%

Electricity: *installed generating capacity:* 12.031 million kW (2022 est.)
consumption: 35.369 billion kWh (2022 est.)
exports: 13.665 billion kWh (2022 est.)
imports: 1.47 billion kWh (2022 est.)
transmission/distribution losses: 2.616 billion kWh (2022 est.)
comparison rankings: transmission/distribution losses 132; imports 70; exports 22; consumption 61; installed generating capacity 59

Electricity generation sources: *fossil fuels:* 48.6% of total installed capacity (2022 est.)
nuclear: 32.8% of total installed capacity (2022 est.)
solar: 4% of total installed capacity (2022 est.)
wind: 3% of total installed capacity (2022 est.)
hydroelectricity: 7.2% of total installed capacity (2022 est.)
biomass and waste: 4.5% of total installed capacity (2022 est.)

Nuclear energy: Number of operational nuclear reactors: 2 (2023)

Net capacity of operational nuclear reactors: 2.01GW (2023 est.)

Percent of total electricity production: 40.3% (2023 est.)

Number of nuclear reactors permanently shut down: 4 (2023)

Coal: *production:* 35.516 million metric tons (2022 est.)
consumption: 35.97 million metric tons (2022 est.)
exports: 504,000 metric tons (2022 est.)
imports: 928,000 metric tons (2022 est.)
proven reserves: 2.366 billion metric tons (2022 est.)

Petroleum: *total petroleum production:* 4,000 bbl/day (2023 est.)
refined petroleum consumption: 101,000 bbl/day (2022 est.)
crude oil estimated reserves: 15 million barrels (2021 est.)

Natural gas: *production:* 20.837 million cubic meters (2022 est.)
consumption: 2.801 billion cubic meters (2022 est.)
exports: 2.75 million cubic meters (2020 est.)
imports: 2.911 billion cubic meters (2022 est.)
proven reserves: 5.663 billion cubic meters (2021 est.)

Carbon dioxide emissions: 43.234 million metric tonnes of CO2 (2022 est.)
from coal and metallurgical coke: 24.654 million metric tonnes of CO2 (2022 est.)
from petroleum and other liquids: 13.185 million metric tonnes of CO2 (2022 est.)
from consumed natural gas: 5.395 million metric tonnes of CO2 (2022 est.)
comparison ranking: total emissions 62

Energy consumption per capita: 107.943 million Btu/person (2022 est.)
comparison ranking: 45

COMMUNICATIONS

Telephones - fixed lines: *total subscriptions:* 691,000 (2022 est.)
subscriptions per 100 inhabitants: 10 (2022 est.)
comparison ranking: total subscriptions 82

Telephones - mobile cellular: *total subscriptions:* 7.964 million (2022 est.)
subscriptions per 100 inhabitants: 117 (2022 est.)
comparison ranking: total subscriptions 101

Telecommunication systems: *general assessment:* Bulgaria's telecom market was for some years affected by the difficult macroeconomic climate, as well as by relatively high unemployment and a shrinking population; these factors continue to slow investments in the sector, though revenue growth has returned since 2019; there still remains pressure on revenue growth, with consumers migrating from fixed-line voice telephony to mobile and VoIP alternatives, while the volume of SMS and MMS traffic has been affected by the growing use of alternative OTT messaging services; investing in network upgrades and its development of services based on 5G have stimulated other market players to invest in their own service provision; by the end of 2022 about 70% of the population is expected to be covered by 5G; the broadband market in Bulgaria enjoys excellent cross-platform competition; the share of the market held by DSL has fallen steadily as a result of customers being migrated to fiber networks; by early 2021 about 65% of fixed-line broadband subscribers were on fiber infrastructure; Bulgaria joins the U.S. State Department's Clean Network initiative in a bid to protect its 5G communications networks (2022)
domestic: fixed-line over 11 per 100 persons, mobile-cellular teledensity, fostered by multiple service providers, is over 115 telephones per 100 persons (2021)
international: country code - 359; Caucasus Cable System via submarine cable provides connectivity to Ukraine, Georgia and Russia; a combination submarine cable and land fiber-optic system provides connectivity to Italy, Albania, and Macedonia; satellite earth stations - 3 (1 Intersputnik in the Atlantic Ocean region, 2 Intelsat in the Atlantic and Indian Ocean regions) (2019)

Broadcast media: 4 national terrestrial TV stations with 1 state-owned and 3 privately owned; a vast array of TV stations are available from cable and satellite TV providers; state-owned national radio broadcasts over 3 networks; large number of private radio stations broadcasting, especially in urban areas

Internet country code: .bg

Internet users: *total:* 5.175 million (2021 est.)
percent of population: 75% (2021 est.)
comparison ranking: total 90

Broadband - fixed subscriptions: *total:* 2,115,053 (2020 est.)
subscriptions per 100 inhabitants: 30 (2020 est.)
comparison ranking: total 56

TRANSPORTATION

National air transport system: *number of registered air carriers:* 8 (2020)
inventory of registered aircraft operated by air carriers: 44
annual passenger traffic on registered air carriers: 1,022,645 (2018)

annual freight traffic on registered air carriers: 1.38 million (2018) mt-km

Civil aircraft registration country code prefix: LZ

Airports: 111 (2024)
comparison ranking: 48

Heliports: 8 (2024)

Pipelines: 2,765 km gas, 346 km oil, 378 km refined products (2017)

Railways: *total:* 4,029 km (2020) 2,871 km electrified
comparison ranking: total 45

Roadways: *total:* 19,117 km (2022)
note: does not include Category IV local roads
comparison ranking: total 116

Waterways: 470 km (2009)
comparison ranking: 92

Merchant marine: *total:* 78 (2023)
by type: bulk carrier 2, general cargo 13, oil tanker 8, other 55
comparison ranking: total 100

Ports: *total ports:* 2 (2024)
large: 1
medium: 0
small: 1
very small: 0
ports with oil terminals: 2
key ports: Burgas, Varna

MILITARY AND SECURITY

Military and security forces: Bulgarian Armed Forces (aka Bulgarian Army): Land Forces, Air Force, Navy

Ministry of Interior: General Directorate National Police (GDNP), General Directorate Border Police (GDBP), General Directorate for Combating Organized Crime (GDCOC), Fire Safety and Civil Protection General Directorate, Special Unit for Combating Terrorism (SOBT) (2024)
note: the GDMP includes the Gendarmerie, a special police force with military status deployed to secure important facilities, buildings and infrastructure, to respond to riots, and to counter militant threats

Military expenditures: 2.2% of GDP (2024 est.)
1.9% of GDP (2023)
1.6% of GDP (2022)
1.6% of GDP (2021)
1.6% of GDP (2020)
comparison ranking: 57

Military and security service personnel strengths: approximately 27,000 active-duty personnel (17,000 Army; 3,000 Navy; 7,000 Air Force) (2024)
note: in 2021, Bulgaria released a 10-year defense plan which called for an active military strength of 43,000

Military equipment inventories and acquisitions: the military's inventory consists mostly of Soviet-era equipment, although in recent years Bulgaria has procured limited amounts of more modern Western weapons systems (2023)

Military service age and obligation: 18-40 years of age for voluntary military service; conscription ended in 2007; service obligation 6-9 months (2023)
note 1: in 2021, women comprised about 17% of the Bulgarian military's full-time personnel
note 2: in 2020, Bulgaria announced a program to allow every citizen up to the age of 40 to join the armed forces for 6 months of military service in the voluntary reserve

Military - note: the Bulgarian military is responsible for guaranteeing Bulgaria's independence, sovereignty, and territorial integrity, providing support to international peace and security missions, and contributing to national security in peacetime, including such missions as responding to disasters or assisting with border security; the military trains regularly including in multinational exercises with regional partners and with NATO since Bulgaria joined the organization in 2004; it also participates in overseas peacekeeping and other security missions under the EU, NATO, and the UN; in 2022, Bulgaria established and began leading a NATO multinational battlegroup as part of an effort to boost NATO defenses in Eastern Europe following Russia's invasion of Ukraine; in 2021, Bulgaria approved a 10-year defense development program, which included calls for equipment upgrades and procurements, boosts in manpower, organizational reforms, and greater focus on such areas as cyber defense, communications, logistics support, and research and development
the Bulgarian military has participated in several significant conflicts since its establishment in 1878, including the Serbo-Bulgarian War (1885), the First Balkan War (1912-13), the Second Balkan War (1913), World War I (1915-1918), and World War II (1941-45); during the Cold War it was one of the Warsaw Pact's largest militaries with over 150,000 personnel and more than 200 Soviet-made combat aircraft (2024)

SPACE

Space agency/agencies: Space Research and Technology Institute - Bulgarian Academy of Sciences (SRTI-BAS; formed in 1987 but originated from the Central Laboratory for Space Research and the Bulgarian Aerospace Agency, which was established in 1969) (2024)

Space program overview: has a long history of involvement in space-related activities going back to the 1960s; develops, produces, and operates satellites, mostly with foreign partners; researches, develops, and produces other space technologies, including those related to astrophysics, remote sensing, data exploitation, optics, and electronics; has specialized in producing scientific instruments for space research; has more than 20 research institutes; Cooperating State of the European Space Agency (ESA) since 2015; cooperates with a variety of foreign space agencies and commercial entities, including those of the ESA and EU (and bi-laterally with their member states), India, Japan, Russia, and the US (2024)
note: further details about the key activities, programs, and milestones of the country's space program, as well as government spending estimates on the space sector, appear in the Space Programs reference guide

TERRORISM

Terrorist group(s): Islamic State of Iraq and ash-Sham (ISIS); Islamic Revolutionary Guard Corps/Qods Force
note: details about the history, aims, leadership, organization, areas of operation, tactics, targets, weapons, size, and sources of support of the group(s) appear(s) in the Terrorism reference guide

TRANSNATIONAL ISSUES

Refugees and internally displaced persons: *refugees (country of origin):* 22,226 (Syria) (mid-year 2022); 72,775 (Ukraine) (as of 8 March 2024)
stateless persons: 1,129 (2022)
note: 106,227 estimated refugee and migrant arrivals (January 2015-January 2024); Bulgaria is predominantly a transit country

Illicit drugs: source country for amphetamine tablets

BURKINA FASO

INTRODUCTION

Background: Many of Burkina Faso's ethnic groups arrived in the region between the 12th and 15th centuries. The Gurma and Mossi peoples established several of the largest kingdoms in the area and used horse-mounted warriors in military campaigns. Of the various Mossi kingdoms, the most powerful were Ouagadougou and Yatenga. In the late 19th century, European states competed for control of the region. France eventually conquered the area and established it as a French protectorate.

The country achieved independence from France in 1960 and changed its name to Burkina Faso in 1984. Repeated military coups were common in the country's first few decades. In 1987 Blaise COMPAORE deposed the president, established a government, and ruled for 27 years. In 2014, COMPAORE resigned after protests against his repeated efforts to amend the constitution's two-term presidential limit. An interim administration led a year-long transition, organizing presidential and legislative elections. In 2015, Roch Marc Christian KABORE was elected president, and he was reelected in 2020. In 2022, the military conducted two takeovers: In January, army colonel Paul Henri DAMIBA overthrew KABORE in a coup d'etat, and then in September, army captain Ibrahim TRAORE deposed DAMIBA and declared himself transition president. The transition government planned to hold elections by July 2024, but they may be delayed due to security concerns.

Terrorist groups – including groups affiliated with Al-Qa'ida and the Islamic State – began attacks in the country in 2016 and conducted attacks in the capital in 2016, 2017, and 2018. By early 2023, insecurity in Burkina Faso had displaced more than 2 million people and led to significant jumps in humanitarian needs and food insecurity. In addition to terrorism, the country faces a myriad of problems including high population growth, recurring drought, pervasive and perennial food insecurity, and limited natural resources. It is one of the world's poorest countries.

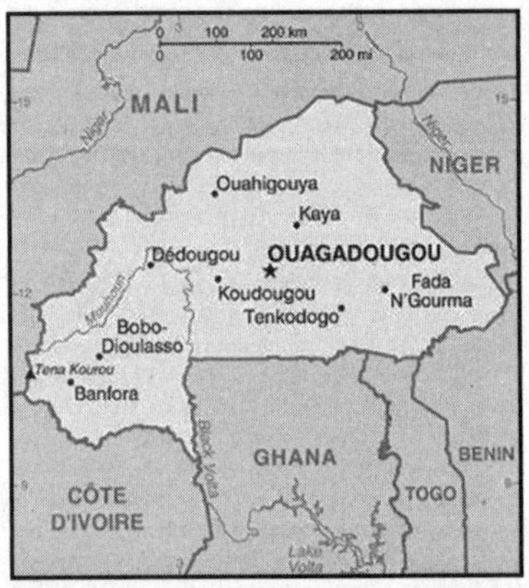

GEOGRAPHY

Location: Western Africa, north of Ghana

Geographic coordinates: 13 00 N, 2 00 W

Map references: Africa

Area: *total:* 274,200 sq km
land: 273,800 sq km
water: 400 sq km
comparison ranking: total 76

Area - comparative: slightly larger than Colorado

Land boundaries: *total:* 3,611 km
border countries (6): Benin 386 km; Cote d'Ivoire 545 km; Ghana 602 km; Mali 1325 km; Niger 622 km; Togo 131 km

Coastline: 0 km (landlocked)

Maritime claims: none (landlocked)

Climate: three climate zones including a hot tropical savanna with a short rainy season in the southern half, a tropical hot semi-arid steppe climate typical of the Sahel region in the northern half, and small area of hot desert in the very north of the country bordering the Sahara Desert

Terrain: mostly flat to dissected, undulating plains; hills in the west and southeast; occupies an extensive plateau with savanna that is grassy in the north and gradually gives way to sparse forests in the south

Elevation: *highest point:* Tena Kourou 749 m
lowest point: Mouhoun (Black Volta) River 200 m
mean elevation: 297 m

Natural resources: gold, manganese, zinc, limestone, marble, phosphates, pumice, salt

Land use: *agricultural land:* 44.2% (2018 est.)
arable land: 22% (2018 est.)
permanent crops: 37% (2018 est.)
permanent pasture: 21.93% (2018 est.)
forest: 19.3% (2018 est.)
other: 36.5% (2018 est.)

Irrigated land: 550 sq km (2016)

Major rivers (by length in km): Volta river source (shared with Ghana [m]) - 1,600 km
note – [s] after country name indicates river source; [m] after country name indicates river mouth

Major watersheds (area sq km): Atlantic Ocean drainage: Niger (2,261,741 sq km), Volta (410,991 sq km)

Population distribution: Most of the population is located in the center and south. Nearly one-third of the population lives in cities. The capital and largest city is Ouagadougou (Ouaga), with a population of 1.8 million as shown in this population distribution map
(2019)

Natural hazards: recurring droughts

Geography - note: landlocked savanna cut by the three principal rivers of the Black, Red, and White Voltas

PEOPLE AND SOCIETY

Population: *total:* 23,042,199
male: 11,297,749
female: 11,744,450 (2024 est.)
comparison rankings: female 59; male 59; total 59

Nationality: *noun:* Burkinabe (singular and plural)
adjective: **Burkinabe**

Ethnic groups: Mossi 53.7%, Fulani (Peuhl) 6.8%, Gurunsi 5.9%, Bissa 5.4%, Gurma 5.2%, Bobo 3.4%, Senufo 2.2%, Bissa 1.5%, Lobi 1.5%, Tuareg/Bella 0.1%, other 12.8%, foreign 0.7% (2021 est.)

Languages: Mossi 52.9%, Fula 7.8%, Gourmantche 6.8%, Dyula 5.7%, Bissa 3.3%, Gurunsi 3.2%, French (official) 2.2%, Bwamu 2%, Dagara 2%, San 1.7%, Marka 1.6%, Bobo 1.5%, Senufo 1.5%, Lobi 1.2%, other 6.6% (2019 est.)

Religions: Muslim 63.8%, Roman Catholic 20.1%, Animiste 9%, Protestant 6.2%, other 0.2%, none 0.7% (2019 est.)

Demographic profile: Burkina Faso has a young age structure – the result of declining mortality combined with steady high fertility – and continues to experience rapid population growth, which is putting increasing pressure on the country's limited arable land. Almost 65% of the population is under the age of 25 as of 2020, and the population is growing at 2.5% annually. Mortality rates, especially those of infants and children, have decreased because of improved health care, hygiene, and sanitation, but women continue to have an average of more than 4 children. Even if fertility were substantially reduced, today's large cohort entering their reproductive years would sustain high population growth for the foreseeable future. Only about a third of the population is literate and unemployment is widespread, dampening the economic prospects of Burkina Faso's large working-age population.
Migration has traditionally been a way of life for Burkinabe, with seasonal migration being replaced by stints of up to two years abroad. Cote d'Ivoire remains the top destination, although it has experienced periods of internal conflict. Under French colonization, Burkina Faso became a main labor source for agricultural and factory work in Cote d'Ivoire. Burkinabe also migrated to Ghana, Mali, and Senegal for work between the world wars. Burkina Faso attracts migrants from Cote d'Ivoire, Ghana, and Mali, who often share common ethnic backgrounds with the Burkinabe. Despite its food shortages and high poverty rate, Burkina Faso has become a destination for refugees in recent years and hosts about 33,600 Malian refugees as of October 2022.
(2018)

Age structure: *0-14 years:* 41.6% (male 4,868,488/female 4,727,316)
15-64 years: 55.1% (male 6,116,674/female 6,590,775)
65 years and over: 3.2% (2024 est.) (male 312,587/female 426,359)

Dependency ratios: *total dependency ratio:* 87.4
youth dependency ratio: 82.6
elderly dependency ratio: 4.8
potential support ratio: 20.9 (2021 est.)

Median age: *total:* 18.7 years (2024 est.)
male: 17.9 years
female: 19.5 years
comparison ranking: total 218

Population growth rate: 2.4% (2024 est.)
comparison ranking: 22

Birth rate: 31.9 births/1,000 population (2024 est.)
comparison ranking: 22

Death rate: 7.3 deaths/1,000 population (2024 est.)
comparison ranking: 110

Net migration rate: -0.6 migrant(s)/1,000 population (2024 est.)
comparison ranking: 123

Population distribution: Most of the population is located in the center and south. Nearly one-third of the population lives in cities. The capital and largest city is Ouagadougou (Ouaga), with a population of 1.8 million as shown in this population distribution map
(2019)

Urbanization: *urban population:* 32.5% of total population (2023)
rate of urbanization: 4.75% annual rate of change (2020-25 est.)

Major urban areas - population: 3.204 million OUAGADOUGOU (capital), 1.129 million Bobo-Dioulasso (2023)

Sex ratio: *at birth:* 1.03 male(s)/female
0-14 years: 1.03 male(s)/female
15-64 years: 0.93 male(s)/female
65 years and over: 0.73 male(s)/female
total population: 0.96 male(s)/female (2024 est.)

Mother's mean age at first birth: 20.1 years (2021 est.)
note: data represents median age at first birth among women 25-49

Maternal mortality ratio: 264 deaths/100,000 live births (2020 est.)
comparison ranking: 33

Infant mortality rate: *total:* 47 deaths/1,000 live births (2024 est.)
male: 51.1 deaths/1,000 live births
female: 42.7 deaths/1,000 live births
comparison ranking: total 20

Life expectancy at birth: *total population:* 64.2 years (2024 est.)
male: 62.3 years
female: 66.1 years
comparison ranking: total population 208

Total fertility rate: 4.02 children born/woman (2024 est.)
comparison ranking: 23

Gross reproduction rate: 1.98 (2024 est.)

Contraceptive prevalence rate: 35.3% (2020/21)

Drinking water source: *improved: urban:* 94.7% of population
rural: 71.3% of population
total: 78.5% of population
unimproved: urban: 5.3% of population
rural: 28.7% of population
total: 21.5% of population (2020 est.)

Current health expenditure: 6.7% of GDP (2020)

Physician density: 0.09 physicians/1,000 population (2019)

Hospital bed density: 0.4 beds/1,000 population

Sanitation facility access: *improved: urban:* 90.8% of population
rural: 37.7% of population
total: 54% of population
unimproved: urban: 9.2% of population
rural: 62.3% of population
total: 46% of population (2020 est.)

Obesity - adult prevalence rate: 5.6% (2016)
comparison ranking: 175

Alcohol consumption per capita: *total:* 7.28 liters of pure alcohol (2019 est.)
beer: 1 liters of pure alcohol (2019 est.)
wine: 0.08 liters of pure alcohol (2019 est.)
spirits: 0.31 liters of pure alcohol (2019 est.)
other alcohols: 5.88 liters of pure alcohol (2019 est.)
comparison ranking: total 57

Tobacco use: *total:* 14.3% (2020 est.)
male: 22.1% (2020 est.)
female: 6.4% (2020 est.)
comparison ranking: total 108

Children under the age of 5 years underweight: 17.5% (2021)
comparison ranking: 27

Currently married women (ages 15-49): 73.5% (2023)

Education expenditures: 5.5% of GDP (2020 est.)
comparison ranking: 58

Literacy: *definition:* age 15 and over can read and write
total population: 46%
male: 54.5%
female: 37.8% (2021)

School life expectancy (primary to tertiary education): *total:* 9 years
male: 9 years
female: 9 years (2020)

ENVIRONMENT

Environment - current issues: recent droughts and desertification severely affecting agricultural activities, population distribution, and the economy; overgrazing; soil degradation; deforestation (2019)

Environment - international agreements: *party to:* Biodiversity, Climate Change, Climate Change-Kyoto Protocol, Climate Change-Paris Agreement, Comprehensive Nuclear Test Ban, Desertification, Endangered Species, Hazardous Wastes, Law of the Sea, Marine Life Conservation, Ozone Layer Protection, Wetlands
signed, but not ratified: Nuclear Test Ban

Climate: three climate zones including a hot tropical savanna with a short rainy season in the southern half, a tropical hot semi-arid steppe climate typical of the Sahel region in the northern half, and small area of hot desert in the very north of the country bordering the Sahara Desert

Urbanization: *urban population:* 32.5% of total population (2023)
rate of urbanization: 4.75% annual rate of change (2020-25 est.)

Food insecurity: *severe localized food insecurity: due to civil insecurity in the north and high food prices* - according to the latest analysis, about 3.53 million people are projected to face acute food insecurity during the June to August 2023 lean season period; this would be a slight increase compared to the preceding year; food insecurity is primarily underpinned by worsening insecurity in Centre-Nord and Sahel regions, which, as of December 2022 (the latest data available), had displaced about 1.88 million people; high food prices further aggravate conditions of the most vulnerable households (2023)

Revenue from forest resources: 4.54% of GDP (2018 est.)
comparison ranking: 14

Revenue from coal: 0% of GDP (2018 est.)
comparison ranking: 165

Air pollutants: *particulate matter emissions:* 40.74 micrograms per cubic meter (2019 est.)
carbon dioxide emissions: 3.42 megatons (2016 est.)
methane emissions: 12.85 megatons (2020 est.)

Waste and recycling: *municipal solid waste generated annually:* 2,575,251 tons (2015 est.)
municipal solid waste recycled annually: 309,030 tons (2005 est.)
percent of municipal solid waste recycled: 12% (2005 est.)

Major rivers (by length in km): Volta river source (shared with Ghana [m]) - 1,600 km
note – [s] after country name indicates river source; [m] after country name indicates river mouth **Major watersheds (area sq km)**

Atlantic Ocean drainage: Niger (2,261,741 sq km), Volta (410,991 sq km)

Total water withdrawal: *municipal:* 380 million cubic meters (2020 est.)
industrial: 20 million cubic meters (2020 est.)
agricultural: 420 million cubic meters (2020 est.)

Total renewable water resources: 13.5 billion cubic meters (2020 est.)

GOVERNMENT

Country name: *conventional long form:* none
conventional short form: Burkina Faso
local long form: none
local short form: Burkina Faso
former: Upper Volta, Republic of Upper Volta
etymology: name translates as "Land of the Honest (Incorruptible) Men"

Government type: presidential republic

Capital: *name:* Ouagadougou
geographic coordinates: 12 22 N, 1 31 W
time difference: UTC 0 (5 hours ahead of Washington, DC, during Standard Time)
etymology: Ouagadougou is a Francophone spelling of the native name "Wogodogo," meaning "where people get honor and respect"

Administrative divisions: 13 regions; Boucle du Mouhoun, Cascades, Centre, Centre-Est, Centre-Nord, Centre-Ouest, Centre-Sud, Est, Hauts-Bassins, Nord, Plateau-Central, Sahel, Sud-Ouest

Independence: 5 August 1960 (from France)

National holiday: Republic Day, 11 December (1958); note - commemorates the day that Upper Volta became an autonomous republic in the French Community

Legal system: civil law based on the French model and customary law; in mid-2019, the National Assembly amended the penal code

Constitution: *history:* several previous; latest approved by referendum 2 June 1991, adopted 11 June 1991, temporarily suspended late October to mid-November 2014; initial draft of a new constitution to usher in the new republic was completed in January 2017 and a final draft was submitted to the government in December 2017; a constitutional referendum originally scheduled for adoption in March 2019 was postponed; on 1 March 2022 a transition charter was adopted, allowing military authorities to rule for three years and barring the transitional president from being an electoral candidate after the transition
amendments: proposed by the president, by a majority of National Assembly membership, or by petition of at least 30,000 eligible voters submitted to the Assembly; passage requires at least three-fourths majority vote in the Assembly; failure to meet that threshold requires majority voter approval in a referendum; constitutional provisions on the form of government, the multiparty system, and national sovereignty cannot be amended; amended several times

International law organization participation: has not submitted an ICJ jurisdiction declaration; accepts ICCt jurisdiction

Citizenship: *citizenship by birth:* no
citizenship by descent only: at least one parent must be a citizen of Burkina Faso
dual citizenship recognized: yes
residency requirement for naturalization: 10 years

Suffrage: 18 years of age; universal

Executive branch: *chief of state:* Transitional President Capt. Ibrahim TRAORE (since 30 September 2022)
head of government: Prime Minister Joachim KYLEM DE TAMBELA (since 21 October 2022)
cabinet: prior to the 2022 coups and adhoc suspension of laws and constitutional provisions, Council of Ministers appointed by the president on the recommendation of the prime minister
elections/appointments: prior to the 2022 coups and adhoc suspension of laws and constitutional provisions, president directly elected by absolute majority popular vote in 2 rounds if needed for a 5-year term (eligible for a second term); last held on 22 November 2020 (next were to be held by July 2024, but may be delayed by the transitional government due to security concerns); prime minister appointed by the president with consent of the National Assembly
election results:
2020: Roch Marc Christian KABORE reelected president in first round; percent of vote - Roch Marc Christian KABORE (MPP) 57.9%, Eddie KOMBOIGO (CDP) 15.5%, Zephirin DIABRE (UPC) 12.5%, other 14.1%
2015: Roch Marc Christian KABORE elected president in first round; percent of vote - Roch Marc Christian KABORE (MPP) 53.5%, Zephirin DIABRE (UPC) 29.6%, Tahirou BARRY (PAREN) 3.1%, Benewende Stanislas SANKARA (UNIRMS) 2.8%, other 10.9%
note - on 30 September 2022, a military junta, led by TRAORE, took power and ousted Transition President Lt. Col. Paul-Henri Sandaogo DAMIBA and took over as head of the Patriotic Movement for Safeguard and Restoration
note - Transitional President TRAORE appointed KYLEM DE TAMBELA Prime Minister on 21 October 2022; the position had been vacant since 30 September 2022 when the military ousted former Prime Minister Albert OUEDRAOGO

Legislative branch: *description:* prior to the 2022 coups and ad hoc suspension of laws and constitutional provisions, unicameral National Assembly (127 seats; 111 members directly elected in 13 multi-seat constituencies by party-list

proportional representation vote and 26 members elected in a nationwide constituency by proportional representation vote; members serve 5-year terms); 71-member Transitional Legislative Assembly (ALT) appointed by the military junta in 2022 indefinitely replaced the National Assembly
elections: last held on 22 November 2020 (next were to be held by July 2024 but have been delayed by the transitional government due to security concerns)
election results: percent of vote by party - NA; seats by party - NA; composition as of March 2024 - men 59, women 12, percentage women 16.9%
note: a series of coups in 2022 led to the ad hoc suspension of laws and constitutional provisions, including the unicameral National Assembly; a military junta in 2022 appointed the 71-member Transnational Legislative Assembly (ALT); a Transitional Charter, adopted in October 2022, provided for a transitional period that was extended in May 2024 until July 2029

Judicial branch: *highest court(s):* Supreme Court of Appeals or Cour de Cassation (consists of NA judges); Council of State (consists of NA judges); Constitutional Council or Conseil Constitutionnel (consists of the council president and 9 members)
judge selection and term of office: Supreme Court judge appointments mostly controlled by the president of Burkina Faso; judges have no term limits; Council of State judge appointment and tenure NA; Constitutional Council judges appointed by the president of Burkina Faso upon the proposal of the minister of justice and the president of the National Assembly; judges appointed for 9-year terms with one-third of membership renewed every 3 years
subordinate courts: Appeals Court; High Court; first instance tribunals; district courts; specialized courts relating to issues of labor, children, and juveniles; village (customary) courts

Political parties: Act Together
African Democratic Rally/Alliance for Democracy and Federation or ADF/RDA
Congress for Democracy and Progress or CDP
Convergence for Progress and Solidarity-Generation 3 or CPS-G3
Movement for the Future Burkina Faso or MBF
National Convention for Progress or CNP
New Era for Democracy or NTD
Pan-African Alliance for Refoundation or APR
Party for Democracy and Socialism/Metba or PDS/Metba
Party for Development and Change or PDC
Patriotic Rally for Integrity or RPI
Peoples Movement for Progress or MPP
Progressives United for Renewal or PUR
Union for Progress and Reform or UPC
Union for Rebirth - Sankarist Party or UNIR-PS

International organization participation: ACP, AfDB, AU (suspended), CD, EITI (compliant country), Entente, FAO, FZ, G-77, IAEA, IBRD, ICAO, ICC (NGOs), ICCt, ICRM, IDA, IDB, IFAD, IFC, IFRCS, ILO, IMF, Interpol, IOC, IOM, IPU, ISO, ITSO, ITU, ITUC (NGOs), MIGA, MINUSCA, MONUSCO, NAM, OIC, OIF, OPCW, PCA, UN, UNCTAD, UNESCO, UNIDO, UNISFA, UNITAR, UNMISS, UNOOSA, UNWTO, UPU, WADB (regional), WAEMU, WCO, WFTU (NGOs), WHO, WIPO, WMO, WTO

Diplomatic representation in the US: *chief of mission:* Ambassador (vacant); Chargé d'Affaires Edouard BOUDA (since 1 February 2024)
chancery: 2340 Massachusetts Avenue NW, Washington, DC 20008
telephone: [1] (202) 332-5577
FAX: [1] (202) 667-1882
email address and website:
contact@burkina-usa.org
https://burkina-usa.org/

Diplomatic representation from the US: *chief of mission:* Ambassador Joann M. LOCKARD (since 28 June 2024)
embassy: Secteur 15, Ouaga 2000, Avenue Sembene Ousmane, Rue 15.873, Ouagadougou
mailing address: 2440 Ouagadougou Place, Washington, DC 20521-2440
telephone: (226) 25-49-53-00
FAX: (226) 25-49-56-23
email address and website:
AmembOuaga@state.gov
https://bf.usembassy.gov/

Flag description: two equal horizontal bands of red (top) and green with a yellow five-pointed star in the center; red recalls the country's struggle for independence, green is for hope and abundance, and yellow represents the country's mineral wealth
note: uses the popular Pan-African colors of Ethiopia

National symbol(s): white stallion; national colors: red, yellow, green

National anthem: *name:* «Le Ditanye" (Anthem of Victory)
lyrics/music: Thomas SANKARA
note: adopted 1974; also known as «Une Seule Nuit» (One Single Night); written by the country's former president, an avid guitar player

National heritage: *total World Heritage Sites:* 3 (2 cultural, 1 natural)
selected World Heritage Site locales: Ruins of Loropéni (c); Ancient Ferrous Metallurgy Sites (c); W-Arly-Pendjari Complex (n)

ECONOMY

Economic overview: highly agrarian, low-income economy; limited natural resources; widespread poverty; terrorism disrupting potential economic activity; improving trade balance via increases in gold exports; economy inflating after prior deflation; growing public debt but still manageable

Real GDP (purchasing power parity): $57.152 billion (2023 est.)
$55.508 billion (2022 est.)
$54.539 billion (2021 est.)
note: data in 2021 dollars
comparison ranking: 119

Real GDP growth rate: 2.96% (2023 est.)
1.78% (2022 est.)
6.94% (2021 est.)
note: annual GDP % growth based on constant local currency
comparison ranking: 109

Real GDP per capita: $2,500 (2023 est.)
$2,400 (2022 est.)
$2,500 (2021 est.)
note: data in 2021 dollars
comparison ranking: 205

GDP (official exchange rate): $20.325 billion (2023 est.)
note: data in current dollars at official exchange rate

Inflation rate (consumer prices): 0.74% (2023 est.)
14.29% (2022 est.)
3.65% (2021 est.)
note: annual % change based on consumer prices
comparison ranking: 14

Credit ratings: Standard & Poors rating: B (2017)
note: The year refers to the year in which the current credit rating was first obtained.

GDP - composition, by sector of origin: *agriculture:* 16.3% (2023 est.)
industry: 29.3% (2023 est.)
services: 43.6% (2023 est.)
note: figures may not total 100% due to non-allocated consumption not captured in sector-reported data comparison rankings: services 176; industry 72; agriculture 51

GDP - composition, by end use: *household consumption:* 64.6% (2023 est.)
government consumption: 20% (2023 est.)
investment in fixed capital: 17.2% (2023 est.)
investment in inventories: 5.4% (2023 est.)
exports of goods and services: 28.9% (2023 est.)
imports of goods and services: -36% (2023 est.)
note: figures may not total 100% due to rounding or gaps in data collection

Agricultural products: sorghum, maize, fruits, vegetables, millet, cowpeas, cotton, groundnuts, sugarcane, rice (2022)
note: top ten agricultural products based on tonnage

Industries: cotton lint, beverages, agricultural processing, soap, cigarettes, textiles, gold

Industrial production growth rate: 1.95% (2023 est.)
note: annual % change in industrial value added based on constant local currency
comparison ranking: 116

Labor force: 8.577 million (2023 est.)
note: number of people ages 15 or older who are employed or seeking work
comparison ranking: 63

Unemployment rate: 5.29% (2023 est.)
5.35% (2022 est.)
5.11% (2021 est.)
note: % of labor force seeking employment
comparison ranking: 101

Youth unemployment rate (ages 15-24): *total:* 8% (2023 est.)
male: 7.6% (2023 est.)
female: 8.5% (2023 est.)
note: % of labor force ages 15-24 seeking employment
comparison ranking: total 152

Population below poverty line: 43.2% (2021 est.)
note: **% of population with income below national poverty line**

Gini Index coefficient - distribution of family income: 37.4 (2021 est.)
note: index (0-100) of income distribution; higher values represent greater inequality
comparison ranking: 60

Household income or consumption by percentage share: *lowest 10%:* 3% (2021 est.)
highest 10%: 30.2% (2021 est.)
note: % share of income accruing to lowest and highest 10% of population

Remittances: 2.85% of GDP (2023 est.)
2.78% of GDP (2022 est.)
2.91% of GDP (2021 est.)
note: personal transfers and compensation between resident and non-resident individuals/households/entities

Budget: *revenues:* $4.649 billion (2022 est.)
expenditures: $4.018 billion (2022 est.)

note: central government revenues (excluding grants) and expenses converted to US dollars at average official exchange rate for year indicated

Public debt: 62.53% of GDP (2022 est.)
note: central government debt as a % of GDP
comparison ranking: 74

Taxes and other revenues: 17.67% (of GDP) (2022 est.)
note: central government tax revenue as a % of GDP
comparison ranking: 105

Current account balance: -$1.404 billion (2022 est.)
$77.255 million (2021 est.)
$743.232 million (2020 est.)
note: balance of payments - net trade and primary/secondary income in current dollars
comparison ranking: 147

Exports: $5.814 billion (2022 est.)
$6.234 billion (2021 est.)
$5.356 billion (2020 est.)
note: balance of payments - exports of goods and services in current dollars
comparison ranking: 135

Exports - partners: Switzerland 74%, UAE 7%, Mali 4%, Singapore 2%, Cote d'Ivoire 2% (2022)
note: top five export partners based on percentage share of exports

Exports - commodities: gold, cotton, oil seeds, coconuts/Brazil nuts/cashews, zinc ore (2022)
note: top five export commodities based on value in dollars

Imports: $6.761 billion (2022 est.)
$5.835 billion (2021 est.)
$4.779 billion (2020 est.)
note: balance of payments - imports of goods and services in current dollars
comparison ranking: 137

Imports - partners: Cote d'Ivoire 16%, China 12%, Russia 7%, France 7%, Ghana 5% (2022)
note: top five import partners based on percentage share of imports

Imports - commodities: refined petroleum, electricity, packaged medicine, plastic products, natural gas (2022)
note: top five import commodities based on value in dollars

Reserves of foreign exchange and gold: $49 million (31 December 2017 est.)
$50.9 million (31 December 2016 est.)
comparison ranking: 191

Debt - external: $3.234 billion (2022 est.)
note: present value of external debt in current US dollars
comparison ranking: 64

Exchange rates: Communaute Financiere Africaine francs (XOF) per US dollar -

Exchange rates: 606.57 (2023 est.)
623.76 (2022 est.)
554.531 (2021 est.)
575.586 (2020 est.)
585.911 (2019 est.)

ENERGY

Electricity access: *electrification - total population:* 19.5% (2022 est.)
electrification - urban areas: 60.5%
electrification - rural areas: 3.4%

Electricity: *installed generating capacity:* 449,000 kW (2022 est.)
consumption: 2.11 billion kWh (2022 est.)
imports: 1.546 billion kWh (2022 est.)
transmission/distribution losses: 218.033 million kWh (2022 est.)
comparison rankings: transmission/distribution losses 64; imports 66; consumption 148; installed generating capacity 154

Electricity generation sources: *fossil fuels:* 68.4% of total installed capacity (2022 est.)
solar: 16% of total installed capacity (2022 est.)
hydroelectricity: 15.4% of total installed capacity (2022 est.)
biomass and waste: 0.3% of total installed capacity (2022 est.)

Coal: *exports:* (2022 est.) less than 1 metric ton
imports: 3 metric tons (2022 est.)

Petroleum: *refined petroleum consumption:* 36,000 bbl/day (2022 est.)

Carbon dioxide emissions: 4.989 million metric tonnes of CO_2 (2022 est.)
from petroleum and other liquids: 4.989 million metric tonnes of CO_2 (2022 est.)
comparison ranking: total emissions 134

Energy consumption per capita: 3.419 million Btu/person (2022 est.)
comparison ranking: 175

COMMUNICATIONS

Telephones - fixed lines: *total subscriptions:* 81,000 (2021 est.)
subscriptions per 100 inhabitants: (2021 est.) less than 1
comparison ranking: total subscriptions 144

Telephones - mobile cellular: *total subscriptions:* 24.678 million (2021 est.)
subscriptions per 100 inhabitants: 112 (2021 est.)
comparison ranking: total subscriptions 53

Telecommunication systems: *general assessment:* Burkina Faso's telecom sector in recent years has made some gains in providing the necessary infrastructure and bandwidth to support telecom services; an IXP completed in September 2020 increased international bandwidth capacity by a third, while in mid-2021 the government was able to start the second phase of a national fiber backbone project; this will link the capital city to an addition 145 municipalities, and provide additional connectivity to terrestrial cables in neighboring countries; the activities of the militants in side areas of the country jeopardize overall security, and render it difficult for the telcos to safeguard their networks and equipment; Burkina Faso joins G5 Sahel countries to eliminate roaming fees (2022)
domestic: fixed-line connections stand at less than 1 per 100 persons; mobile-cellular usage nearly 112 per 100, with multiple providers there is competition and the hope for growth from a low base; Internet penetration is 16% (2021)
international: country code - 226; satellite earth station - 1 Intelsat (Atlantic Ocean)

Broadcast media: since the official inauguration of Terrestrial Digital Television (TNT) in December 2017, Burkina Faso now has 14 digital TV channels among which 2 are state-owned; there are more than 140 radio stations (commercial, religious, community) available throughout the country including a national and regional state-owned network; the state-owned Radio Burkina and the private Radio Omega are among the most widespread stations and both include broadcasts in French and local languages (2019)

Internet country code: .bf

Internet users: *total:* 4.84 million (2021 est.)
percent of population: 22% (2021 est.)
comparison ranking: total 97

Broadband - fixed subscriptions: *total:* 13,979 (2020 est.)
subscriptions per 100 inhabitants: 0.1 (2020 est.)
comparison ranking: total 174

TRANSPORTATION

National air transport system: *number of registered air carriers:* 1 (2020)
inventory of registered aircraft operated by air carriers: 3
annual passenger traffic on registered air carriers: 151,531 (2018)
annual freight traffic on registered air carriers: 100,000 (2018) mt-km

Civil aircraft registration country code prefix: XT

Airports: 49 (2024)
comparison ranking: 90

Railways: *total:* 622 km (2014)
narrow gauge: 622 km (2014) 1.000-m gauge
note: another 660 km of this railway extends into Cote d'Ivoire
comparison ranking: total 107

Roadways: *total:* 15,304 km (2017)
paved: 3,642 km (2014)
unpaved: 11,662 km (2014)
comparison ranking: total 123

MILITARY AND SECURITY

Military and security forces: Armed Forces of Burkina Faso (FABF; aka National Armed Forces (FAN), aka Defense and Security Forces (Forces de Défense et de Sécurité or FDS)): Army of Burkina Faso (L'Armee de Terre, LAT), Air Force of Burkina Faso (Force Aerienne de Burkina Faso), National Gendarmerie, National Fire Brigade (Brigade Nationale de Sapeurs-Pompiers or BNSP); Homeland Defense Volunteers (Forcés de Volontaires de Défense pour la Patrie or VDP)
Ministry of Territorial Administration, Decentralization and Security (Ministère de l'Administration Territoriale, de la Décentralisation et de la Sécurité): National Police (2024)
note 1: the National Gendarmerie officially reports to the Ministry of Defense, but usually operates in support of the Ministry of Territorial Administration, Decentralization, and Security; the Gendarmerie's primary mission is counterterrorism; it is comprised of "legions" and mobile squadrons, including a Special Legion for combating organized crime and terrorism and providing security for high-level officials and government institutions; other government forces specializing in counterterrorism include the Army's Special Forces and the Multipurpose Intervention Unit of the National Police
note 2: the VDP is a lightly-armed civilian defense/militia force established in 2019 to act as auxiliaries to the Army; the volunteers receive two weeks of training and typically assist with carrying out surveillance, information-gathering, and escort duties, as well as local defense, and were to be based in each of the country's more than 300 municipalities; in 2022, the military government created a "Patriotic Watch and Defense Brigade" (La Brigade de Veille et

de Défense Patriotique or BVDP) under the FABF to coordinate the VDP recruits

Military expenditures: 4% of GDP (2023 est.)
2.9% of GDP (2022 est.)
2.4% of GDP (2021 est.)
2.4% of GDP (2020 est.)
2.2% of GDP (2019 est.)
comparison ranking: 17

Military and security service personnel strengths: approximately 15,500 personnel (10,000 Army; 500 Air Force; 5,000 National Gendarmerie) (2023)
note: in 2022, government authorities announced a special recruitment for up to 6,000 additional soldiers and 1,500 gendarmes to assist with its fight against terrorist groups operating in the country; the government also put out a recruitment call for up to 100,000 VDP volunteers, and as of 2023 claimed about 50,000 had volunteered (the VDP's original recruited strength was 15,000)

Military equipment inventories and acquisitions: the FABF has a mix of older, secondhand, and some modern equipment from a variety of suppliers, including China, Egypt, France, Russia, South Africa, Turkey, the UK, and the US (2024)

Military service age and obligation: 18-26 years of age for voluntary military service for men and women (2023)
note: the military government implemented an emergency law in 2023 that allows the president extensive powers to combat terrorist groups operating in the country, including conscripting citizens into the security services

Military - note: the FABF has a history of interference in the country's politics, having conducted eight coups since its formation in 1960-61, including the most recent in September 2022; several combat units were disbanded in 2011 following mutinies; while the FABF is responsible for external defense, it has an internal security role and can be called out to assist internal security forces in restoring public order, combating crime, securing the border, and counterterrorism; indeed, for more than a decade, its focus has largely been internal counterterrorism and counterinsurgency operations, and it is actively engaged in combat operations against terrorist groups affiliated with al-Qa'ida and the Islamic State of Iraq and ash- Sham (ISIS), particularly in the northern and eastern regions
in the north, Jama'at Nusrat al-Islam wal-Muslimin (JNIM), a coalition of al-Qa'ida linked militant groups that act as al- Qa'ida in the Land of the Islamic Magreb's (AQIM) arm in the Sahel, has exploited ethnic tensions and perceptions of state neglect, as well as grievances over corruption, patronage politics, social stratification, and land disputes; in 2024, JNIM was active in nearly all of the country's 13 provinces; the ISIS-Greater Sahara (ISIS-GS) terrorist group operates in the eastern part of the country (2024)

TERRORISM

Terrorist group(s): Ansarul Islam; Islamic State of Iraq and ash-Sham in the Greater Sahara (ISIS-GS); al-Mulathamun Battalion (al-Mourabitoun); Jama'at Nusrat al-Islam wal-Muslimin (JNIM)
note: details about the history, aims, leadership, organization, areas of operation, tactics, targets, weapons, size, and sources of support of the group(s) appear(s) in the Terrorism reference guide

TRANSNATIONAL ISSUES

Refugees and internally displaced persons: *refugees (country of origin):* 36,372 (Mali) (2023)
IDPs: 2,062,534 (2023)

Trafficking in persons: tier rating: Tier 2 Watch list — Burkina Faso did not demonstrate overall increasing efforts to eliminate trafficking compared with the previous reporting period and was downgraded to Tier 2 Watch List; for more details, go to: https://www.state.gov/reports/2024-trafficking-in-persons-report/burkina-faso/

BURMA

INTRODUCTION

Background: Burma is home to ethnic Burmans and scores of other ethnic and religious minority groups that have resisted external efforts to consolidate control of the country throughout its history. Britain conquered Burma over a period extending from the 1820s to the 1880s and administered it as a province of India until 1937, when Burma became a self-governing colony. Burma gained full independence in 1948. In 1962, General NE WIN seized power and ruled the country until 1988 when a new military regime took control.

In 1990, the military regime permitted an election but then rejected the results after the main opposition National League for Democracy (NLD) and its leader AUNG SAN SUU KYI (ASSK) won in a landslide. The military regime placed ASSK under house arrest until 2010. In 2007, rising fuel prices in Burma led pro-democracy activists and Buddhist monks to launch a "Saffron Revolution" consisting of large protests against the regime, which violently suppressed the movement. The regime prevented new elections until it had drafted a constitution designed to preserve the military's political control; it passed the new constitution in its 2008 referendum. The regime conducted an election in 2010, but the NLD boycotted the vote, and the military's political proxy, the Union Solidarity and Development Party, easily won; international observers denounced the election as flawed.

Burma nonetheless began a halting process of political and economic reforms. ASSK's return to government in 2012 eventually led to the NLD's sweeping victory in the 2015 election. With ASSK as the de facto head of state, Burma's first credibly elected civilian government drew international criticism for blocking investigations into Burma's military operations – which the US Department of State determined constituted genocide – against its ethnic Rohingya population. When the 2020 elections resulted in further NLD gains, the military denounced the vote as fraudulent. In 2021, the military's senior leader General MIN AUNG HLAING launched a coup that returned Burma to authoritarian rule, with military crackdowns that undid reforms and resulted in the detention of ASSK and thousands of pro-democracy actors.

Pro-democracy organizations have formed in the wake of the coup, including the National Unity Government (NUG). Members of the NUG include representatives from the NLD, ethnic minority groups, and civil society. In 2021, the NUG announced the formation of armed militias called the People's Defense Forces (PDF) and an insurgency against the military junta. As of 2024, PDF units across the country continued to fight the regime with varying levels of support from and cooperation with the NUG and other anti-regime organizations, including armed ethnic groups that have been fighting the central government for decades.

GEOGRAPHY

Location: Southeastern Asia, bordering the Andaman Sea and the Bay of Bengal, between Bangladesh and Thailand

Geographic coordinates: 22 00 N, 98 00 E

Map references: Southeast Asia

Area: *total:* 676,578 sq km
land: 653,508 sq km
water: 23,070 sq km
comparison ranking: total 42

Area - comparative: slightly smaller than Texas

Land boundaries: *total:* 6,522 km
border countries (5): Bangladesh 271 km; China 2,129 km; India 1,468 km; Laos 238 km; Thailand 2,416 km

Coastline: 1,930 km

Maritime claims: *territorial sea:* 12 nm
contiguous zone: 24 nm
exclusive economic zone: 200 nm
continental shelf: 200 nm or to the edge of the continental margin

Climate: tropical monsoon; cloudy, rainy, hot, humid summers (southwest monsoon, June to September); less cloudy, scant rainfall, mild temperatures, lower humidity during winter (northeast monsoon, December to April)

Terrain: central lowlands ringed by steep, rugged highlands

Elevation: *highest point:* Gamlang Razi 5,870 m
lowest point: Andaman Sea/Bay of Bengal 0 m
mean elevation: 702 m

Natural resources: petroleum, timber, tin, antimony, zinc, copper, tungsten, lead, coal, marble, limestone, precious stones, natural gas, hydropower, arable land

Land use: *agricultural land:* 19.2% (2018 est.)
arable land: 16.5% (2018 est.)
permanent crops: 2.2% (2018 est.)
permanent pasture: 0.5% (2018 est.)
forest: 48.2% (2018 est.)
other: 32.6% (2018 est.)

Irrigated land: 17,140 sq km (2020)

Major rivers (by length in km): Mekong (shared with China [s], Laos, Thailand, Cambodia, and Vietnam [m]) - 4,350 km; Salween river mouth (shared with China [s] and Thailand) - 3,060 km; Irrawaddy river mouth (shared with China [s]) - 2,809 km; Chindwin - 1,158 km
note – [s] after country name indicates river source; [m] after country name indicates river mouth

Major watersheds (area sq km): Indian Ocean drainage: Brahmaputra (651,335 sq km), Ganges (1,016,124 sq km), Irrawaddy (413,710 sq km), Salween (271,914 sq km)

Pacific Ocean drainage: Mekong (805,604 sq km)

Population distribution: population concentrated along coastal areas and in general proximity to the shores of the Irrawaddy River; the extreme north is relatively underpopulated

Natural hazards: destructive earthquakes and cyclones; flooding and landslides common during rainy season (June to September); periodic droughts

Geography - note: strategic location near major Indian Ocean shipping lanes; the north-south flowing Irrawaddy River is the country's largest and most important commercial waterway

PEOPLE AND SOCIETY

Population: *total:* 57,527,139
male: 28,387,831
female: 29,139,308 (2024 est.)
comparison rankings: female 27; male 27; total 27

Nationality: *noun:* Burmese (singular and plural)
adjective: Burmese

Ethnic groups: Burman (Bamar) 68%, Shan 9%, Karen 7%, Rakhine 4%, Chinese 3%, Indian 2%, Mon 2%, other 5%
note: the largest ethnic group — the Burman (or Bamar) — dominate politics, and the military ranks are largely drawn from this ethnic group; the Burman mainly populate the central parts of the country, while various ethnic minorities have traditionally lived in the peripheral regions that surround the plains in a horseshoe shape; the government recognizes 135 indigenous ethnic groups

Languages: Burmese (official): major-language sample(s):
ကမ္ဘာ့အချက်အလက်စာအုပ်- အခြေခံအချက်အလက်တွေအတွက် မရှိမဖြစ်တဲ့ အရင်းအမြစ်
(Burmese)
note: minority ethnic groups use their own languages

Religions: Buddhist 87.9%, Christian 6.2%, Muslim 4.3%, Animist 0.8%, Hindu 0.5%, other 0.2%, none 0.1% (2014 est.)
note: religion estimate is based on the 2014 national census, including an estimate for the non-enumerated population of Rakhine State, which is assumed to mainly affiliate with the Islamic faith; as of December 2019, Muslims probably make up less than 3% of Burma's total population due to the large outmigration of the Rohingya population since 2017

Demographic profile: Burma's 2014 national census – the first in more than 30 years – revealed that the country's total population is approximately 51.5 million, significantly lower than the Burmese Government's prior estimate of 61 million. The Burmese Government assumed that the 2% population growth rate between 1973 and 1983 remained constant and that emigration was zero, ignoring later sample surveys showing declining fertility rates and substantial labor migration abroad in recent decades. These factors reduced the estimated average annual growth rate between 2003 and 2014 to about .9%. Among Southeast Asian countries, Burma's life expectancy is among the lowest and its infant and maternal mortality rates are among the highest. The large difference in life expectancy between women and men has resulted in older age cohorts consisting of far more women than men.
Burma's demographic transition began in the 1950s, when mortality rates began to drop. Fertility did not start to decrease until the 1960s, sustaining high population growth until the decline accelerated in the 1980s. The birth rate has held fairly steady from 2000 until today. Since the 1970s, the total fertility rate (TFR) has fallen more than 60%, from almost 6 children per woman to 2.2 in 2016. The reduced TFR is largely a result of women marrying later and more women never marrying, both being associated with greater educational attainment and labor force participation among women. TFR, however, varies regionally, between urban and rural areas, by educational attainment, and among ethnic groups, with fertility lowest in urban areas (where it is below replacement level).
The shift in Burma's age structure has been slow (45% of the population is still under 25 years of age) and uneven among its socioeconomic groups. Any economic boost from the growth of the working-age population is likely to take longer to develop, to have a smaller impact, and to be distributed unequally. Rural poverty and unemployment continue to drive high levels of internal and international migration. The majority of labor migration is internal, mainly from rural to urban areas. The new government's growing regional integration, reforms, and improved diplomatic relations are increasing the pace of international migration and destination choices. As many as 4-5 million Burmese, mostly from rural areas and several ethnic groups, have taken up unskilled jobs abroad in agriculture, fishing, manufacturing, and domestic service. Thailand is the most common destination, hosting about 70% of Burma's international migrants, followed by Malaysia, China, and Singapore.
Burma is a patchwork of more than 130 religious and ethnic groups, distinguishing it as one of the most diverse countries in the region. Ethnic minorities face substantial discrimination, and the Rohingya, the largest Muslim group, are arguably the most persecuted population in the country. The Burmese Government and the Buddhist majority see the Rohingya as a threat to identity, competitors for jobs and resources, terrorists, and some still resent them for their alliance with Burma's British colonizers during its 19th century. Since at least the 1960s, they have been subjected to systematic human rights abuses, violence, marginalization, and disenfranchisement, which authorities continue to deny. Despite living in Burma for centuries, many Burmese see the Rohingya as illegal Bengali immigrants and refer to them Bengalis. As a result, the Rohingya have been classified as foreign residents and stripped of their citizenship, rendering them one of the largest stateless populations in the world.
Hundreds of thousands of Burmese from various ethnic groups have been internally displaced (an estimated 644,000 as of year-end 2016) or have fled to neighboring countries over the decades because of persecution, armed conflict, rural development projects, drought, and natural disasters. Bangladesh has absorbed the most refugees from Burma, with an estimated 33,000 officially recognized and 200,000 to 500,000 unrecognized Rohingya refugees, as of 2016. An escalation in violation has caused a surge in the inflow of Rohingya refugees since late August 2017, raising the number to an estimated 870,000. As of June 2017, another approximately 132,500 refugees, largely Rohingya and Chin, were living in Malaysia, and more than 100,000, mostly Karen, were housed in camps along the Burma-Thailand border.

Age structure: *0-14 years:* 24.4% (male 7,197,177/female 6,843,879)
15-64 years: 68.5% (male 19,420,361/female 19,998,625)
65 years and over: 7.1% (2024 est.) (male 1,770,293/female 2,296,804)

Dependency ratios: *total dependency ratio:* 46
youth dependency ratio: 36.3
elderly dependency ratio: 9.7
potential support ratio: 10.3 (2021 est.)

Median age: *total:* 30.8 years (2024 est.)
male: 29.9 years
female: 31.6 years
comparison ranking: total 131

Population growth rate: 0.71% (2024 est.)
comparison ranking: 123

Birth rate: 15.7 births/1,000 population (2024 est.)
comparison ranking: 103

Death rate: 7.3 deaths/1,000 population (2024 est.)
comparison ranking: 108

Net migration rate: -1.4 migrant(s)/1,000 population (2024 est.)
comparison ranking: 155

Population distribution: population concentrated along coastal areas and in general proximity to the shores of the Irrawaddy River; the extreme north is relatively underpopulated

Urbanization: *urban population:* 32.1% of total population (2023)

rate of urbanization: 1.85% annual rate of change (2020-25 est.)

Major urban areas - population: 5.610 million RANGOON (Yangon) (capital), 1.532 million Mandalay (2023)

Sex ratio: *at birth:* 1.06 male(s)/female
0-14 years: 1.05 male(s)/female
15-64 years: 0.97 male(s)/female
65 years and over: 0.77 male(s)/female
total population: 0.97 male(s)/female (2024 est.)

Mother's mean age at first birth: 24.7 years (2015/16 est.)
note: data represents median age at first birth among women 25-49

Maternal mortality ratio: 179 deaths/100,000 live births (2020 est.)
comparison ranking: 50

Infant mortality rate: *total:* 32.1 deaths/1,000 live births (2024 est.)
male: 35.4 deaths/1,000 live births
female: 28.5 deaths/1,000 live births
comparison ranking: total 42

Life expectancy at birth: *total population:* 70.3 years (2024 est.)
male: 68.5 years
female: 72.1 years
comparison ranking: total population 177

Total fertility rate: 1.97 children born/woman (2024 est.)
comparison ranking: 109

Gross reproduction rate: 0.96 (2024 est.)

Contraceptive prevalence rate: 52.2% (2015/16)

Drinking water source: *improved: urban:* 95.4% of population
rural: 80.7% of population
total: 85.3% of population
unimproved: urban: 4.6% of population
rural: 19.3% of population
total: 14.7% of population (2020 est.)

Current health expenditure: 3.7% of GDP (2020)

Physician density: 0.74 physicians/1,000 population (2019)

Hospital bed density: 1 beds/1,000 population (2017)

Sanitation facility access: *improved: urban:* 93.9% of population
rural: 81.3% of population
total: 85.2% of population
unimproved: urban: 6.1% of population
rural: 18.7% of population
total: 14.8% of population (2020 est.)

Obesity - adult prevalence rate: 5.8% (2016)
comparison ranking: 173

Alcohol consumption per capita: *total:* 2.06 liters of pure alcohol (2019 est.)
beer: 0.5 liters of pure alcohol (2019 est.)
wine: 0.02 liters of pure alcohol (2019 est.)
spirits: 1.55 liters of pure alcohol (2019 est.)
other alcohols: 0 liters of pure alcohol (2019 est.)
comparison ranking: total 128

Tobacco use: *total:* 44.1% (2020 est.)
male: 68.5% (2020 est.)
female: 19.7% (2020 est.)
comparison ranking: total 2

Children under the age of 5 years underweight: 19.1% (2017/18)
comparison ranking: 18

Currently married women (ages 15-49): 57.5% (2023 est.)

Child marriage: *women married by age 15:* 1.9%
women married by age 18: 16%
men married by age 18: 5% (2016 est.)

Education expenditures: 2.1% of GDP (2019 est.)
comparison ranking: 184

Literacy: *definition:* age 15 and over can read and write
total population: 89.1%
male: 92.4%
female: 86.3% (2019)
note: most public schools were closed immediately after the coup in 2021, and attendance has remained low since schools reopened; literacy is expected to decline from 2019 to 2023

School life expectancy (primary to tertiary education): *total:* 11 years
male: 10 years
female: 11 years (2018)

ENVIRONMENT

Environment - current issues: deforestation; industrial pollution of air, soil, and water; inadequate sanitation and water treatment contribute to disease; rapid depletion of the country's natural resources

Environment - international agreements: *party to:* Biodiversity, Climate Change, Climate Change-Kyoto Protocol, Climate Change-Paris Agreement, Comprehensive Nuclear Test Ban, Desertification, Endangered Species, Hazardous Wastes, Law of the Sea, Nuclear Test Ban, Ozone Layer Protection, Ship Pollution, Tropical Timber 2006, Wetlands
signed, but not ratified: none of the selected agreements

Climate: tropical monsoon; cloudy, rainy, hot, humid summers (southwest monsoon, June to September); less cloudy, scant rainfall, mild temperatures, lower humidity during winter (northeast monsoon, December to April)

Urbanization: *urban population:* 32.1% of total population (2023)
rate of urbanization: 1.85% annual rate of change (2020-25 est.)

Food insecurity: *severe localized food insecurity: due to conflict, political instability, and economic constraints* - the political crisis, following the military takeover on 1 February 2021, resulted in increased tensions and unrest throughout the country; the current uncertain political situation may further compromise the fragile situation of vulnerable households and the Rohingya IDPs residing in the country; armed conflict between the military and non-state armed groups led to population displacements, disrupted agricultural activities and limited access for humanitarian support especially in Rakhine, Chin, Kachin, Kayin, Kayah and Shan states; income losses and a decline in remittances, due to the impact of the COVID-19 pandemic, have affected the food security situation of vulnerable households; domestic prices of Emata rice, the most consumed variety in the country, were at high levels in May 2022, constraining access to a key staple food (2022)

Revenue from forest resources: 1.69% of GDP (2018 est.)
comparison ranking: 38

Revenue from coal: 0.01% of GDP (2018 est.)
comparison ranking: 50

Air pollutants: *particulate matter emissions:* 27.16 micrograms per cubic meter (2019 est.)
carbon dioxide emissions: 25.28 megatons (2016 est.)
methane emissions: 42.2 megatons (2020 est.)

Waste and recycling: *municipal solid waste generated annually:* 4,677,307 tons (2000 est.)

Major rivers (by length in km): Mekong (shared with China [s], Laos, Thailand, Cambodia, and Vietnam [m]) - 4,350 km; Salween river mouth (shared with China [s] and Thailand) - 3,060 km; Irrawaddy river mouth (shared with China [s]) - 2,809 km; Chindwin - 1,158 km
note – [s] after country name indicates river source; [m] after country name indicates river mouth

Major watersheds (area sq km): Indian Ocean drainage: Brahmaputra (651,335 sq km), Ganges (1,016,124 sq km), Irrawaddy (413,710 sq km), Salween (271,914 sq km)
Pacific Ocean drainage: Mekong (805,604 sq km)

Total water withdrawal: *municipal:* 3.32 billion cubic meters (2019 est.)
industrial: 500 million cubic meters (2019 est.)
agricultural: 29.57 billion cubic meters (2019 est.)

Total renewable water resources: 1.2 trillion cubic meters (2020 est.)

GOVERNMENT

Country name: *conventional long form:* Union of Burma
conventional short form: Burma
local long form: Pyidaungzu Thammada Myanma Naingngandaw (translated as the Republic of the Union of Myanmar)
local short form: Myanma Naingngandaw
former: Socialist Republic of the Union of Burma, Union of Myanmar
etymology: both "Burma" and "Myanmar" derive from the name of the majority Burman (Bamar) ethnic group
note: since 1989 the military authorities in Burma and the deposed parliamentary government have promoted the name Myanmar as a conventional name for their state; the US Government has not officially adopted the name

Government type: military regime

Capital: *name:* Rangoon (aka Yangon, continues to be recognized as the primary Burmese capital by the US Government); Nay Pyi Taw is the administrative capital
geographic coordinates: 16 48 N, 96 10 E
time difference: UTC+6.5 (11.5 hours ahead of Washington, DC, during Standard Time)
etymology: Rangoon/Yangon derives from the Burmese words yan and koun, which mean "danger" and "no more" respectively and provide the meaning of "end of strife"; Nay Pyi Taw translates as: "Abode of Royals" or "the capital city of a kingdom"

Administrative divisions: 7 regions (taing-myar, singular - taing), 7 states (pyi ne-myar, singular - pyi ne), 1 union territory
regions: **Ayeyarwady (Irrawaddy), Bago, Magway, Mandalay, Sagaing, Tanintharyi, Yangon (Rangoon)**
states: **Chin, Kachin, Kayah, Karen, Mon, Rakhine, Shan**
union territory: Nay Pyi Taw

Independence: 4 January 1948 (from the UK)

National holiday: Independence Day, 4 January (1948); Union Day, 12 February (1947)

Legal system: mixed legal system of English common law (as introduced in codifications designed for colonial India) and customary law

Constitution: *history:* previous 1947, 1974 (suspended until 2008); latest drafted 9 April 2008, approved by referendum 29 May 2008
amendments: proposals require at least 20% approval by the Assembly of the Union membership; passage of amendments to sections of the constitution on basic principles, government structure, branches of government, state emergencies, and amendment procedures requires 75% approval by the Assembly and approval in a referendum by absolute majority of registered voters; passage of amendments to other sections requires only 75% Assembly approval; military granted 25% of parliamentary seats by default; amended 2015

International law organization participation: has not submitted an ICJ jurisdiction declaration; non-party state to the ICCt

Citizenship: *citizenship by birth:* no
citizenship by descent only: both parents must be citizens of Burma
dual citizenship recognized: no
residency requirement for naturalization: none
note: an applicant for naturalization must be the child or spouse of a citizen

Suffrage: 18 years of age; universal

Executive branch: *chief of state:* Prime Minister, State Administration Council Chair, Sr. Gen. MIN AUNG HLAING (since 1 August 2021)
head of government: Prime Minister, State Administration Council Chair, Sr. Gen. MIN AUNG HLAING (since 1 August 2021)
cabinet: Cabinet appointments shared by the president and the commander-in-chief; note - on 2 February 2021, the military leadership replaced the Cabinet with the State Administrative Council (SAC), which is the official name of the military government in Burma
elections/appointments: prior to the military takeover in 2021, president was indirectly elected by simple majority vote by the full Assembly of the Union from among 3 vice-presidential candidates nominated by the Presidential Electoral College (consists of members of the lower and upper houses and military members); the other 2 candidates become vice presidents (president elected for a 5-year term); general election last held on 8 November 2020; the military junta has pledged to hold new general elections but has repeatedly announced delays
election results:
2020: the National League for Democracy (NLD) won 396 seats across both houses, well above the 322 required for a parliamentary majority, which would have ensured that its preferred candidates would be elected president and second vice president in the Presidential Electoral College; however, on 1 February 2021 the military claimed the results of the election were illegitimate and launched a coup d'état that deposed State Counsellor AUNG San SUU KYI and President WIN MYINT of the NLD, causing military-affiliated Vice President MYINT SWE (USDP) to become Acting President; MYINT SWE subsequently handed power to coup leader MIN AUNG HLAING; WIN MYINT and other key leaders of the ruling NLD party were placed under arrest following the military takeover
2018: WIN MYINT elected president in an indirect by-election held on 28 March 2018 after the resignation of HTIN KYAW; Assembly of the Union vote for president - WIN MYINT (NLD) 403, MYINT SWE (USDP) 211, HENRY VAN THIO (NLD) 18, 4 votes canceled (636 votes cast)
state counsellor: State Counselor AUNG SAN SUU KYI (since 6 April 2016); note - under arrest since 1 February 2021; formerly served as Minister of Foreign Affairs and Minister for the Office of the President
note 1: the military took over the government on 1 February 2021 and declared a state of emergency
note 2: prior to the military takeover, the a state counsellor served the equivalent term of the president and was similar to a prime minister in that the holder acted as a link between the parliament and the executive branch

Legislative branch: *description:* bicameral Assembly of the Union or Pyidaungsu consisted of:
House of Nationalities or Amyotha Hluttaw, (224 seats; 168 members directly elected in single-seat constituencies by absolute majority vote with a second round if needed and 56 appointed by the military; members served 5-year terms)
House of Representatives or Pyithu Hluttaw, (440 seats, currently 433; 330 members directly elected in single-seat constituencies by simple majority vote and 110 appointed by the military; members served 5-year terms)
elections: House of Nationalities - last held on 8 November 2020
House of Representatives - last held on 8 November 2020
election results: House of Nationalities - percent of vote by party - NLD 61.6%, USDP 3.1%, ANP 1.8%, MUP 1.3%, KySPD 1.3%, other 5.9%, military appointees 25%; seats by party - NLD 138, USDP 7, ANP 4, MUP 3, KySPD 3, SNLD 2, TNP 2, other 2, vacant 7 (canceled due to insurgency), military appointees 56
House of Representatives - percent of vote by party - NLD 58.6%, USDP 5.9%, SNLD 3.0%, other 7.5%, military 25%; seats by party - NLD 258, USDP 26, SNLD 13, ANP 4, PNO 3, TNP 3, MUP 2, KySPD 2, other 4, vacant 15 (canceled due to insurgency), military appointees 110
note 1: the Assembly of the Union was dissolved on 1 February 2021 after a military coup led by Sr. General MIN AUNG HLAING; it was replaced by the State Administration Council
note 2: the military junta overturned the results of the 8 November legislative elections

Judicial branch: *highest court(s):* Supreme Court of the Union (consists of the chief justice and 7-11 judges)
judge selection and term of office: chief justice and judges nominated by the president, with approval of the Lower House, and appointed by the president; judges normally serve until mandatory retirement at age 70
subordinate courts: High Courts of the Region; High Courts of the State; Court of the Self-Administered Division; Court of the Self-Administered Zone; district and township courts; special courts (for juvenile, municipal, and traffic offenses); courts martial

Political parties: Arakan National Party or ANP
Democratic Party or DP
Kayah State Democratic Party or KySDP
Kayin People's Party or KPP
Kokang Democracy and Unity Party or KDUP
La Hu National Development Party or LHNDP
Lisu National Development Party or LNDP
Mon Unity Party (formed in 2019 from the All Mon Region Democracy Party and Mon National Party)
National Democratic Force or NDF
National League for Democracy or NLD
National Unity Party or NUP
Pa-O National Organization or PNO
People's Party
Shan Nationalities Democratic Party or SNDP
Shan Nationalities League for Democracy or SNLD
Ta'ang National Party or TNP
Tai-Leng Nationalities Development Party or TNDP
Union Solidarity and Development Party or USDP
Unity and Democracy Party of Kachin State or UDPKS
Wa Democratic Party or WDP
Wa National Unity Party or WNUP
Zomi Congress for Democracy or ZCD
note: more than 90 political parties participated in the 2020 elections; political parties continued to function after the 2021 coup, although some political leaders have been arrested by the military regime; in 2023, the regime announced a new law with several rules and restrictions on political parties and their ability to participate in elections; dozens of parties refused to comply with the new rules; the regime's election commission has subsequently banned more than 80 political parties, including the National League for Democracy

International organization participation: ADB, ARF, ASEAN, BIMSTEC, CP, EAS, EITI (candidate country), FAO, G-77, IAEA, IBRD, ICAO, ICRM, IDA, IFAD, IFC, IFRCS, IHO, ILO, IMF, IMO, Interpol, IOC, IOM, IPU, ISO (correspondent), ITU, ITUC (NGOs), NAM, OPCW (signatory), SAARC (observer), UN, UNCTAD, UNESCO, UNIDO, UNWTO, UPU, WCO, WHO, WIPO, WMO, WTO

Diplomatic representation in the US: *chief of mission:* Ambassador (vacant); Chargé d'Affaires THET WIN (since 22 June 2022)
chancery: 2300 S Street NW, Washington, DC 20008
telephone: [1] (202) 332-3344
FAX: [1] (202) 332-4351
email address and website:
washington-embassy@mofa.gov.mm
https://www.mewashingtondc.org/
consulate(s) general: Los Angeles

Diplomatic representation from the US: *chief of mission:* Ambassador (vacant); Chargé d'Affaires Susan STEVENSON (since 10 July 2023)
embassy: 110 University Avenue, Kamayut Township, Rangoon
mailing address: 4250 Rangoon Place, Washington DC 20521-4250
telephone: [95] (1) 753-6509
FAX: [95] (1) 751-1069
email address and website:
ACSRangoon@state.gov
https://mm.usembassy.gov/

Flag description: design consists of three equal horizontal stripes of yellow (top), green, and red; centered on the green band is a large white five-pointed star that partially overlaps onto the adjacent colored stripes; the design revives the triband colors used by Burma from 1943-45, during the Japanese occupation

National symbol(s): chinthe (mythical lion); national colors: yellow, green, red, white

National anthem: *name:* «Kaba Ma Kyei" (Till the End of the World, Myanmar)
lyrics/music: SAYA TIN
note: adopted 1948; Burma is among a handful of non-European nations that have anthems rooted in indigenous traditions; the beginning portion of the anthem is a traditional Burmese anthem before transitioning into a Western-style orchestrated work

National heritage: *total World Heritage Sites:* 2 (both cultural)
selected World Heritage Site locales: Pyu Ancient Cities; Bagan

ECONOMY

Economic overview: prior to COVID-19 and the February 2021 military coup, massive declines in poverty, rapid economic growth, and improving social welfare; underdevelopment, climate change, and unequal investment threaten progress and sustainability planning; since coup, foreign assistance has ceased from most funding sources

Real GDP (purchasing power parity): $290.507 billion (2023 est.)
$287.624 billion (2022 est.)
$276.462 billion (2021 est.)
note: data in 2021 dollars
comparison ranking: 62

Real GDP growth rate: 1% (2023 est.)
4.04% (2022 est.)
-12.02% (2021 est.)
note: annual GDP % growth based on constant local currency
comparison ranking: 165

Real GDP per capita: $5,300 (2023 est.)
$5,300 (2022 est.)
$5,100 (2021 est.)
note: data in 2021 dollars
comparison ranking: 175

GDP (official exchange rate): $64.815 billion (2023 est.)
note: data in current dollars at official exchange rate

Inflation rate (consumer prices): 8.83% (2019 est.)
6.87% (2018 est.)
4.57% (2017 est.)
note: annual % change based on consumer prices
comparison ranking: 164

GDP - composition, by sector of origin: *agriculture:* 20.4% (2023 est.)
industry: 38.1% (2023 est.)
services: 41.5% (2023 est.)
note: figures may not total 100% due to non-allocated consumption not captured in sector-reported data
comparison rankings: services 187; industry 34; agriculture 39

GDP - composition, by end use: *household consumption:* 59.2% (2017 est.)
government consumption: 13.8% (2017 est.)
investment in fixed capital: 33.5% (2017 est.)
investment in inventories: 1.5% (2017 est.)
exports of goods and services: 21.4% (2017 est.)
imports of goods and services: -28.6% (2017 est.)

Agricultural products: rice, sugarcane, vegetables, beans, maize, groundnuts, fruits, plantains, coconuts, onions (2022)
note: top ten agricultural products based on tonnage

Industries: agricultural processing; wood and wood products; copper, tin, tungsten, iron; cement, construction materials; pharmaceuticals; fertilizer; oil and natural gas; garments; jade and gems

Industrial production growth rate: 1.53% (2023 est.)
note: annual % change in industrial value added based on constant local currency
comparison ranking: 128

Labor force: 22.884 million (2023 est.)
note: number of people ages 15 or older who are employed or seeking work
comparison ranking: 30

Unemployment rate: 2.84% (2023 est.)
2.83% (2022 est.)
4.34% (2021 est.)
note: % of labor force seeking employment
comparison ranking: 39

Youth unemployment rate (ages 15-24): *total:* 9.7% (2023 est.)
male: 10.3% (2023 est.)
female: 8.9% (2023 est.)
note: % of labor force ages 15-24 seeking employment
comparison ranking: total 138

Population below poverty line: 24.8% (2017 est.)
note: **% of population** with income below national poverty line

Gini Index coefficient - distribution of family income: 30.7 (2017 est.)
note: index (0-100) of income distribution; higher values represent greater inequality
comparison ranking: 120

Average household expenditures: *on food:* 56.4% of household expenditures (2022 est.)
on alcohol and tobacco: 0.6% of household expenditures (2022 est.)

Household income or consumption by percentage share: *lowest 10%:* 3.8% (2017 est.)
highest 10%: 25.5% (2017 est.)
note: % share of income accruing to lowest and highest 10% of population

Remittances: 2.31% of GDP (2023 est.)
2.03% of GDP (2022 est.)
1.93% of GDP (2021 est.)
note: personal transfers and compensation between resident and non-resident individuals/households/entities

Budget: *revenues:* $10.945 billion (2019 est.)
expenditures: $10.22 billion (2019 est.)
note: central government revenues (excluding grants) and expenses converted to US dollars at average official exchange rate for year indicated

Public debt: 33.6% of GDP (2017 est.)
comparison ranking: 159

Taxes and other revenues: 6.02% (of GDP) (2019 est.)
note: central government tax revenue as a % of GDP
comparison ranking: 200

Current account balance: $67.72 million (2019 est.)
-$2.561 billion (2018 est.)
-$4.917 billion (2017 est.)
note: balance of payments - net trade and primary/secondary income in current dollars
comparison ranking: 75

Exports: $20.4 billion (2021 est.)
$17.523 billion (2019 est.)
$15.728 billion (2018 est.)
note: balance of payments - exports of goods and services in current dollars
comparison ranking: 90

Exports - partners: China 36%, Thailand 13%, Germany 6%, Japan 6%, US 4% (2022)
note: top five export partners based on percentage share of exports

Exports - commodities: garments, precious stones, natural gas, dried legumes, rice (2022)
note: top five export commodities based on value in dollars

Imports: $23.1 billion (2021 est.)
$17.356 billion (2019 est.)
$18.664 billion (2018 est.)
note: balance of payments - imports of goods and services in current dollars
comparison ranking: 91

Imports - partners: China 45%, Thailand 16%, Singapore 14%, Malaysia 4%, Indonesia 4% (2022)
note: top five import partners based on percentage share of imports

Imports - commodities: refined petroleum, fabric, synthetic fabric, crude petroleum, fertilizers (2022)
note: top five import commodities based on value in dollars

Reserves of foreign exchange and gold: $7.67 billion (2020 est.)
$5.824 billion (2019 est.)
$5.646 billion (2018 est.)
note: holdings of gold (year-end prices)/foreign exchange/special drawing rights in current dollars
comparison ranking: 85

Exchange rates: kyats (MMK) per US dollar -

Exchange rates: 1,381.619 (2020 est.)
1,518.255 (2019 est.)
1,429.808 (2018 est.)
1,360.359 (2017 est.)
1,234.87 (2016 est.)

ENERGY

Electricity access: *electrification - total population:* 73.7% (2022 est.)
electrification - urban areas: 93.9%
electrification - rural areas: 62.8%

Electricity: *installed generating capacity:* 6.993 million kW (2022 est.)
consumption: 15.473 billion kWh (2022 est.)
exports: 1.317 billion kWh (2022 est.)
transmission/distribution losses: 3.591 billion kWh (2022 est.)
comparison rankings: transmission/distribution losses 149; exports 65; consumption 82; installed generating capacity 77

Electricity generation sources: *fossil fuels:* 50.6% of total installed capacity (2022 est.)
solar: 0.5% of total installed capacity (2022 est.)
hydroelectricity: 47.6% of total installed capacity (2022 est.)
biomass and waste: 1.3% of total installed capacity (2022 est.)

Coal: *production:* 1.268 million metric tons (2022 est.)
consumption: 1.453 million metric tons (2022 est.)
exports: 89,000 metric tons (2022 est.)
imports: 305,000 metric tons (2022 est.)
proven reserves: 252 million metric tons (2022 est.)

Petroleum: *total petroleum production:* 7,000 bbl/day (2023 est.)
refined petroleum consumption: 148,000 bbl/day (2022 est.)
crude oil estimated reserves: 139 million barrels (2021 est.)

Natural gas: *production:* 16.78 billion cubic meters (2022 est.)
consumption: 3.788 billion cubic meters (2022 est.)
exports: 13.099 billion cubic meters (2022 est.)

imports: 219.822 million cubic meters (2021 est.)
proven reserves: 637.129 billion cubic meters (2021 est.)

Carbon dioxide emissions: 31.347 million metric tonnes of CO2 (2022 est.)
from coal and metallurgical coke: 2.693 million metric tonnes of CO2 (2022 est.)
from petroleum and other liquids: 21.174 million metric tonnes of CO2 (2022 est.)
from consumed natural gas: 7.48 million metric tonnes of CO2 (2022 est.)
comparison ranking: total emissions 72

Energy consumption per capita: 9.244 million Btu/person (2022 est.)
comparison ranking: 153

COMMUNICATIONS

Telephones - fixed lines: *total subscriptions:* 535,000 (2022 est.)
subscriptions per 100 inhabitants: (2022 est.) less than 1
comparison ranking: total subscriptions 89

Telephones - mobile cellular: *total subscriptions:* 57.807 million (2022 est.)
subscriptions per 100 inhabitants: 107 (2022 est.)
comparison ranking: total subscriptions 30

Telecommunication systems: *general assessment:* Burma, one of the least developed telecom markets in Asia, saw growth in mobile and broadband services through expanded foreign access and investment in the 2010s and roll outs 4G and limited 5G network infrastructures; infrastructure expansion has been challenged by armed conflict, severe weather events, unreliable electricity, inefficient bureaucracy, and decreased foreign investment since the 2021 military coup; digital divide affects rural areas; fixed broadband remains low due to number of fixed-lines and widespread installation of the mobile network platforms; multiple m-banking platforms; tests for NB-IoT; benefit from launch of regional satellite; government censors online content and restricts Internet and mobile network quality in political crisis (2023)
domestic: fixed-line is just under 1 per 100, while mobile-cellular is roughly 126 per 100 (2021)
international: country code - 95; landing points for the SeaMeWe-3, SeaMeWe-5, AAE-1 and Singapore-Myanmar optical telecommunications submarine cable that provides links to Asia, the Middle East, Africa, Southeast Asia, Australia and Europe; satellite earth stations - 2, Intelsat (Indian Ocean) and ShinSat (2019)

Broadcast media: government controls all domestic broadcast media; 2 state-controlled TV stations with 1 of the stations controlled by the armed forces; 2 pay-TV stations are joint state-private ventures; 1 state-controlled domestic radio station and 9 FM stations that are joint state-private ventures; transmissions of several international broadcasters are available in parts of Burma; the Voice of America (VOA), Radio Free Asia (RFA), BBC Burmese service, the Democratic Voice of Burma (DVB), and Radio Australia use shortwave to broadcast in Burma; VOA, RFA, and DVB produce daily TV news programs that are transmitted by satellite to audiences in Burma; in March 2017, the government granted licenses to 5 private broadcasters, allowing them digital free-to-air TV channels to be operated in partnership with government-owned Myanmar Radio and Television (MRTV) and will rely upon MRTV's transmission infrastructure; following the February 2021 military coup, the regime revoked the media licenses of most independent outlets, including the free-to-air licenses for DVB and Mizzima (2022)

Internet country code: .mm

Internet users: *total:* 23.76 million (2021 est.)
percent of population: 44% (2021 est.)
comparison ranking: total 37

Broadband - fixed subscriptions: *total:* 688,185 (2020 est.)
subscriptions per 100 inhabitants: 1 (2020 est.)
comparison ranking: total 81

TRANSPORTATION

National air transport system: *number of registered air carriers:* 8 (2020)
inventory of registered aircraft operated by air carriers: 42
annual passenger traffic on registered air carriers: 3,407,788 (2018)
annual freight traffic on registered air carriers: 4.74 million (2018) mt-km

Civil aircraft registration country code prefix: XY

Airports: 73 (2024)
comparison ranking: 70

Heliports: 6 (2024)

Pipelines: 3,739 km gas, 1321 km oil (2017)

Railways: *total:* 5,031 km (2008)
narrow gauge: 5,031 km (2008) 1.000-m gauge
comparison ranking: total 39

Roadways: *total:* 157,000 km (2013)
paved: 57,840 km (2017)
unpaved: 99,160 km (2017)
comparison ranking: total 33

Waterways: 12,800 km (2011)
comparison ranking: 11

Merchant marine: *total:* 101 (2023)
by type: bulk carrier 1, general cargo 44, oil tanker 5, other 51
comparison ranking: total 89

Ports: *total ports:* 7 (2024)
large: 0
medium: 0
small: 5
very small: 2
ports with oil terminals: 3
key ports: Bassein, Mergui, Moulmein Harbor, Rangoon, Sittwe

MILITARY AND SECURITY

Military and security forces: Burmese Defense Service (aka Armed Forces of Burma, Myanmar Army, Royal Armed Forces, the Tatmadaw, or the Sit-Tat): Army (Tatmadaw Kyi), Navy (Tatmadaw Yay), Air Force (Tatmadaw Lay); People's Militia

Ministry of Home Affairs: Burma (People's) Police Force, Border Guard Forces/Police (2023)
note 1: under the 2008 constitution, the Tatmadaw was given control over the appointments of senior officials to lead the Ministry of Defense, the Ministry of Border Affairs, and the Ministry of Home Affairs; in March 2022, a new law gave the commander-in-chief of the Tatmadaw the authority to appoint or remove the head of the police force
note 2: the Burma Police Force is primarily responsible for internal security; the Border Guard Police is administratively part of the Burma Police Force but operationally distinct; both are under the Ministry of Home Affairs, which is led by an active-duty military general and controlled by the military

Military expenditures: 3.9% of GDP (2023 est.)
3.6% of GDP (2022 est.)
3.5% of GDP (2021 est.)
3% of GDP (2020 est.)
4.1% of GDP (2019 est.)
comparison ranking: 22

Military and security service personnel strengths: estimates vary widely, from approximately 150,000 to as many as 400,000 active military personnel (2023)

Military equipment inventories and acquisitions: the Burmese military inventory is comprised mostly of older Chinese and Russian/Soviet-era equipment with a smaller mix of more modern acquisitions from a variety of countries; in recent years, China and Russia have been the leading suppliers of military hardware; Burma has a limited defense industry, including some shipbuilding and production of ground force equipment that is largely based on Chinese and Russian designs (2024)

Military service age and obligation: 18-35 years of age (men) and 18-27 years of age (women) for voluntary and conscripted military service; 24-month service obligation; conscripted professional men (ages 18-45) and women (ages 18-35), including doctors, engineers, and mechanics, serve up to 36 months; service terms may be extended to 60 months in an officially declared emergency (2024)
note: in February 2024, the military government announced that the People's Military Service Law requiring mandatory military service would go into effect; the Service Law was first introduced in 2010 but had not previously been enforced; the military government also said that it intended to call up about 60,000 men and women annually for mandatory service; during the ongoing insurgency, the military has recruited men 18-60 to serve in local militias

Military - note: since the country's founding, the Tatmadaw has been heavily involved in domestic politics and the national economy; it ran the country for five decades following a military coup in 1962; prior to the most recent coup in 2021, the military already controlled three key security ministries (Defense, Border, and Home Affairs), one of two vice presidential appointments, 25% of the parliamentary seats, and had a proxy political party, the Union Solidarity and Development Party (USDP); it owns and operates two business conglomerates that have over 100 subsidiaries; the business activities of these conglomerates include banking and insurance, hotels, tourism, jade and ruby mining, timber, construction, real estate, and the production of palm oil, sugar, soap, cement, beverages, drinking water, coal, and gas; some of the companies supply goods and services to the military, such as food, clothing, insurance, and cellphone service; the military also manages a film industry, publishing houses, and television stations
the Tatmadaw's primary operational focus is internal security, and it is conducting counterinsurgency operations against anti-regime forces that launched an armed rebellion following the 2021 coup and an array of ethnic armed groups (EAGs), some of which have considerable military capabilities; as of 2024, the Tatmadaw was reportedly engaged in combat operations in 10 of its 14 regional commands; it has been accused of committing atrocities in the conduct of its campaign against the pro-democracy movement and opposition forces

the military is supported by pro-government militias; some are integrated within the Tatmadaw's command structure as Border Guard Forces, which are organized as battalions with a mix of militia forces, EAGs, and government soldiers that are armed, supplied, and paid by the Tatmadaw; other pro-military government militias are not integrated within the Tatmadaw command structure but receive direction and some support from the military and are recognized as government militias; a third type of pro-government militias are small community-based units that are armed, coordinated, and trained by local Tatmadaw forces and activated as needed; the military regime has attempted to raise new militia units to help combat the popular uprising

EAGs have been fighting for self-rule against the Burmese Government since 1948; there are approximately 20 such groups operating in Burma with strengths of a few hundred up to 30,000 estimated fighters; some are organized along military lines with "brigades" and "divisions" and armed with heavy weaponry, including artillery; they control large tracts of the country's territory, primarily in the border regions; key groups include the United Wa State Army, Karen National Union, Kachin Independence Army, Arakan Army, Ta'ang National Liberation Army, and the Myanmar Nationalities Democratic Alliance Army

the opposition National Unity Government claims its armed wing, the People's Defense Force (PDF), has more than 60,000 fighters loosely organized into battalions; in addition, several EAGs have cooperated with the NUG and supported local PDF groups (2024)

TRANSNATIONAL ISSUES

Refugees and internally displaced persons: IDPs: 1.975 million (government offensives against armed ethnic minority groups near its borders with China and Thailand, natural disasters, forced land evictions) (2023)
stateless persons: 600,000 (2022); note - Rohingya Muslims, living predominantly in Rakhine State, are Burma's main group of stateless people; the Burmese Government does not recognize the Rohingya as a "national race" and stripped them of their citizenship under the 1982 Citizenship Law, categorizing them as "non-nationals" or "foreign residents;" under the Rakhine State Action Plan drafted in October 2014, the Rohingya must demonstrate their family has lived in Burma for at least 60 years to qualify for a lesser naturalized citizenship and the classification of Bengali or be put in detention camps and face deportation; native-born but non-indigenous people, such as Indians, are also stateless; the Burmese Government does not grant citizenship to children born outside of the country to Burmese parents who left the country illegally or fled persecution, such as those born in Thailand; the number of stateless persons has decreased dramatically because hundreds of thousands of Rohingya have fled to Bangladesh since 25 August 2017 to escape violence

Trafficking in persons: tier rating: Tier 3 — Burma does not fully meet the minimum standards for the elimination of trafficking and is not making significant efforts to do so, therefore, Burma remained on Tier 3; for more details, go to: https://www.state.gov/reports/2024-trafficking-in-persons-report/burma/

Illicit drugs: source of precursor or essential chemicals used in the production of illicit narcotics; narcotics produced in Burma trafficked throughout the region, with routes extending beyond Southeast Asia to Australia, New Zealand, and Japan; largest opium poppy cultivator globally with an estimated 47,100 hectares grown in 2023; not a major source or transit country for drugs entering the United States; domestic consumption of synthetic drug cocktails such as Yaba, "Happy Water," and "Wei Tiong" (mixtures of drugs including caffeine, methamphetamine, tramadol, and MDMA) popular among the younger population and domestic drug consumption substantial and widespread. (2021)

BURUNDI

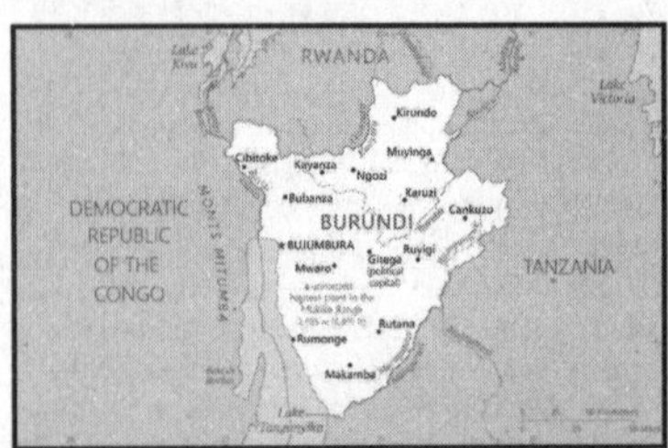

INTRODUCTION

Background: Established in the 1600s, the Burundi Kingdom has had borders similar to those of modern Burundi since the 1800s. Burundi's two major ethnic groups, the majority Hutu and minority Tutsi, share a common language and culture and largely lived in peaceful cohabitation under Tutsi monarchs in pre-colonial Burundi. Regional, class, and clan distinctions contributed to social status in the Burundi Kingdom, yielding a complex class structure. German colonial rule in the late 19th and early 20th centuries and Belgian rule after World War I preserved Burundi's monarchy. Seeking to simplify administration, Belgian colonial officials reduced the number of chiefdoms and eliminated most Hutu chiefs from positions of power. In 1961, the Burundian Tutsi king's oldest son, Louis RWAGASORE, was murdered by a competing political faction shortly before he was set to become prime minister, triggering increased political competition that contributed to later instability.

Burundi gained its independence from Belgium in 1962 as the Kingdom of Burundi. Revolution in neighboring Rwanda stoked ethnic polarization as the Tutsi increasingly feared violence and loss of political power. A failed Hutu-led coup in 1965 triggered a purge of Hutu officials and set the stage for Tutsi officers to overthrow the monarchy in 1966 and establish a Tutsi-dominated republic. A Hutu rebellion in 1972 resulted in the deaths of several thousand Tutsi civilians and sparked brutal Tutsi-led military reprisals against Hutu civilians which ultimately killed 100,000-200,000 people. International pressure led to a new constitution in 1992 and democratic elections in 1993. Tutsi military officers feared Hutu domination and assassinated Burundi's first democratically elected president, Hutu Melchior NDADAYE, in 1993 after only 100 days in office, sparking a civil war. In 1994, his successor, Cyprien NTARYAMIRA, died when the Rwandan president's plane he was traveling on was shot down, which triggered the Rwandan genocide and further entrenched ethnic conflict in Burundi. The internationally brokered Arusha Agreement, signed in 2000, and subsequent cease-fire agreements with armed movements ended the 1993-2005 civil war. Burundi's second democratic elections were held in 2005, resulting in the election of Pierre NKURUNZIZA as president. He was reelected in 2010 and again in 2015 after a controversial court decision allowed him to circumvent a term limit. President Evariste NDAYISHIMIYE – from NKURUNZIZA's ruling party – was elected in 2020.

GEOGRAPHY

Location: Central Africa, east of the Democratic Republic of the Congo, west of Tanzania

Geographic coordinates: 3 30 S, 30 00 E

Map references: Africa

Area: *total:* 27,830 sq km
land: 25,680 sq km
water: 2,150 sq km
comparison ranking: total 146

Area - comparative: slightly smaller than Maryland

Land boundaries: *total:* 1,140 km
border countries (3): Democratic Republic of the Congo 236 km; Rwanda 315 km; Tanzania 589 km

Coastline: 0 km (landlocked)

Maritime claims: none (landlocked)

Climate: equatorial; high plateau with considerable altitude variation (772 m to 2,670 m above sea level); average annual temperature varies with altitude from 23 to 17 degrees Celsius but is generally moderate; average annual rainfall is about 150 cm with two wet seasons (February to May and September to November) and two dry seasons (June to August and December to January)

Terrain: hilly and mountainous, dropping to a plateau in east, some plains

Elevation: *highest point:* unnamed elevation on Mukike Range 2,685 m
lowest point: Lake Tanganyika 772 m
mean elevation: 1,504 m

Natural resources: nickel, uranium, rare earth oxides, peat, cobalt, copper, platinum, vanadium, arable land, hydropower, niobium, tantalum, gold, tin, tungsten, kaolin, limestone

Land use: *agricultural land:* 73.3% (2018 est.)
arable land: 38.9% (2018 est.)
permanent crops: 15.6% (2018 est.)
permanent pasture: 18.8% (2018 est.)
forest: 6.6% (2018 est.)
other: 20.1% (2018 est.)

Irrigated land: 230 sq km (2012)

Major lakes (area sq km): *fresh water lake(s):* Lake Tanganyika (shared with Democratic Republic of Congo, Tanzania, and Zambia) - 32,000 sq km

Major watersheds (area sq km):Atlantic Ocean drainage: Congo (3,730,881 sq km), *(Mediterranean Sea)* Nile (3,254,853 sq km)

Population distribution: one of Africa's most densely populated countries; concentrations tend to be in the north and along the northern shore of Lake Tanganyika in the west; most people live on farms near areas of fertile volcanic soil as shown in this population distribution map

Natural hazards: flooding; landslides; drought

Geography - note: landlocked; straddles crest of the Nile-Congo watershed; the Kagera, which drains into Lake Victoria, is the most remote headstream of the White Nile

PEOPLE AND SOCIETY

Population: *total:* 13,590,102
male: 6,755,456
female: 6,834,646 (2024 est.)
comparison rankings: female 77; male 77; total 77

Nationality: *noun:* Burundian(s)
adjective: **Burundian**

Ethnic groups: Hutu, Tutsi, Twa, South Asian: Languages: Kirundi (official), French (official), English (official, least spoken), Swahili (2008 est.)
major-language sample(s):

Igitabo Mpuzamakungu c'ibimenyetso bifatika, isoko ntabanduka ku nkuru z'urufatiro. (Kirundi): *note:* data represent languages read and written by people 10 years of age or older; spoken Kirundi is nearly universal

Religions: Christian 93.9% (Roman Catholic 58.6%, Protestant 35.3% [includes Adventist 2.7% and other Protestant religions 32.6%]), Muslim 3.4%, other 1.3%, none 1.3% (2016-17 est.)

Demographic profile: Burundi is a densely populated country with a high population growth rate, factors that combined with land scarcity and poverty place a large share of its population at risk of food insecurity. About 90% of the population relies on subsistence agriculture. Subdivision of land to sons, and redistribution to returning refugees, results in smaller, overworked, and less-productive plots. Food shortages, poverty, and a lack of clean water contribute to a 60% chronic malnutrition rate among children. A lack of reproductive health services has prevented a significant reduction in Burundi's maternal mortality and fertility rates, which are both among the world's highest. With almost two-thirds of its population under the age of 25 and a birth rate of about 5 children per woman as of 2022, Burundi's population will continue to expand rapidly for decades to come, putting additional strain on a poor country.
Historically, migration flows into and out of Burundi have consisted overwhelmingly of refugees from violent conflicts. In the last decade, more than a half million Burundian refugees returned home from neighboring countries, mainly Tanzania. Reintegrating the returnees has been problematic due to their prolonged time in exile, land scarcity, poor infrastructure, poverty, and unemployment. Repatriates and existing residents (including internally displaced persons) compete for limited land and other resources. To further complicate matters, international aid organizations reduced their assistance because they no longer classified Burundi as a post-conflict country. Conditions deteriorated when renewed violence erupted in April 2015, causing another outpouring of refugees. In addition to refugee out-migration, Burundi has hosted thousands of refugees from neighboring countries, mostly from the Democratic Republic of the Congo and lesser numbers from Rwanda.

Age structure: *0-14 years:* 42.3% (male 2,895,275/female 2,848,286)
15-64 years: 54.4% (male 3,662,688/female 3,727,022)
65 years and over: 3.4% (2024 est.) (male 197,493/female 259,338)

Dependency ratios: *total dependency ratio:* 95.2
youth dependency ratio: 90.4
elderly dependency ratio: 4.8
potential support ratio: 20.7 (2021 est.)

Median age: *total:* 18.4 years (2024 est.)
male: 18 years
female: 18.7 years
comparison ranking: total 220

Population growth rate: 2.81% (2024 est.)
comparison ranking: 11

Birth rate: 34.6 births/1,000 population (2024 est.)
comparison ranking: 14

Death rate: 5.7 deaths/1,000 population (2024 est.)
comparison ranking: 174

Net migration rate: -0.7 migrant(s)/1,000 population (2024 est.)
comparison ranking: 137

Population distribution: one of Africa's most densely populated countries; concentrations tend to be in the north and along the northern shore of Lake Tanganyika in the west; most people live on farms near areas of fertile volcanic soil as shown in this population distribution map

Urbanization: *urban population:* 14.8% of total population (2023)
rate of urbanization: 5.43% annual rate of change (2020-25 est.)

Major urban areas - population: 1.207 million BUJUMBURA (capital) (2023)

Sex ratio: *at birth:* 1.03 male(s)/female
0-14 years: 1.02 male(s)/female
15-64 years: 0.98 male(s)/female
65 years and over: 0.76 male(s)/female
total population: 0.99 male(s)/female (2024 est.)

Mother's mean age at first birth: 21.5 years (2016/17 est.)
note: data represents median age at first birth among women 25-49

Maternal mortality ratio: 494 deaths/100,000 live births (2020 est.)
comparison ranking: 14

Infant mortality rate: *total:* 35.7 deaths/1,000 live births (2024 est.)
male: 39.7 deaths/1,000 live births
female: 31.5 deaths/1,000 live births
comparison ranking: total 36

Life expectancy at birth: *total population:* 68.1 years (2024 est.)
male: 66 years
female: 70.3 years
comparison ranking: total population 192

Total fertility rate: 4.9 children born/woman (2024 est.)
comparison ranking: 10

Gross reproduction rate: 2.41 (2024 est.)

Contraceptive prevalence rate: 28.5% (2016/17)

Drinking water source: *improved: urban:* 98.7% of population
rural: 78.9% of population
total: 81.6% of population
unimproved: urban: 1.3% of population
rural: 21.1% of population
total: 18.4% of population (2020 est.)

Current health expenditure: 6.5% of GDP (2020)

Physician density: 0.07 physicians/1,000 population (2020)

Hospital bed density: 0.8 beds/1,000 population (2014)

Sanitation facility access: *improved: urban:* 87.4% of population
rural: 53.7% of population
total: 58.4% of population
unimproved: urban: 12.6% of population
rural: 46.3% of population
total: 41.6% of population (2020 est.)

Obesity - adult prevalence rate: 5.4% (2016)
comparison ranking: 178

Alcohol consumption per capita: *total:* 4.07 liters of pure alcohol (2019 est.)
beer: 1.84 liters of pure alcohol (2019 est.)
wine: 0 liters of pure alcohol (2019 est.)
spirits: 0 liters of pure alcohol (2019 est.)
other alcohols: 2.23 liters of pure alcohol (2019 est.)
comparison ranking: total 95

Tobacco use: *total:* 11.8% (2020 est.)
male: 17.4% (2020 est.)
female: 6.1% (2020 est.)
comparison ranking: total 123

Children under the age of 5 years underweight: 27.6% (2022)
comparison ranking: 6

Currently married women (ages 15-49): 54.1% (2023 est.)

Child marriage: *women married by age 15:* 2.8%
women married by age 18: 19%
men married by age 18: 1.4% (2017 est.)

Education expenditures: 5% of GDP (2020 est.)
comparison ranking: 77

Literacy: *definition:* age 15 and over can read and write
total population: 74.7%
male: 81.3%
female: 68.4% (2021)

School life expectancy (primary to tertiary education): *total:* 11 years
male: 11 years
female: 11 years (2018)

ENVIRONMENT

Environment - current issues: soil erosion as a result of overgrazing and the expansion of agriculture into marginal lands; deforestation (little forested land remains because of uncontrolled cutting of trees for fuel); habitat loss threatens wildlife populations

Environment - international agreements: *party to:* Biodiversity, Climate Change, Climate Change-Kyoto Protocol, Climate Change-Paris Agreement, Comprehensive Nuclear Test Ban, Desertification, Endangered Species, Hazardous Wastes, Ozone Layer Protection, Wetlands
signed, but not ratified: Law of the Sea, Nuclear Test Ban

Climate: equatorial; high plateau with considerable altitude variation (772 m to 2,670 m above sea level); average annual temperature varies with altitude from 23 to 17 degrees Celsius but is generally moderate; average annual rainfall is about 150 cm with two wet seasons (February to May and September to November) and two dry seasons (June to August and December to January)

Urbanization: *urban population:* 14.8% of total population (2023)
rate of urbanization: 5.43% annual rate of change (2020-25 est.)

Food insecurity: *widespread lack of access: due to the effects of weather* - according to the latest estimates, about 1.2 million people are estimated to be facing Crisis levels of acute food insecurity between June and September 2023, unchanged year on year; the main drivers are the lingering impact of floods in northern areas in late 2022 and high food prices due, in part, to the depreciation of the local currency (2022)

Revenue from forest resources: 10.31% of GDP (2018 est.)
comparison ranking: 3

Revenue from coal: 0% of GDP (2018 est.)
comparison ranking: 126

Air pollutants: *particulate matter emissions:* 28 micrograms per cubic meter (2019 est.)
carbon dioxide emissions: 0.5 megatons (2016 est.)
methane emissions: 1.42 megatons (2020 est.)

Waste and recycling: *municipal solid waste generated annually:* 1,872,016 tons (2002 est.)

Major lakes (area sq km): *fresh water lake(s):* Lake Tanganyika (shared with Democratic Republic of Congo, Tanzania, and Zambia) - 32,000 sq km

Major watersheds (area sq km):Atlantic Ocean drainage: Congo (3,730,881 sq km), *(Mediterranean Sea)* Nile (3,254,853 sq km)

Total water withdrawal: *municipal:* 40 million cubic meters (2020 est.)
industrial: 20 million cubic meters (2020 est.)
agricultural: 220 million cubic meters (2020 est.)

Total renewable water resources: 12.54 billion cubic meters (2020 est.)

GOVERNMENT

Country name: *conventional long form:* Republic of Burundi
conventional short form: Burundi
local long form: République du Burundi (French)/ Republika y'u Burundi (Kirundi)
local short form: Burundi
former: Urundi, German East Africa, Ruanda-Urundi, Kingdom of Burundi
etymology: name derived from the pre-colonial Kingdom of Burundi (17th-19th century)

Government type: presidential republic

Capital: *name:* Gitega (political capital), Bujumbura (commercial capital)
geographic coordinates: 3 25 S, 29 55 E
time difference: UTC+2 (7 hours ahead of Washington, DC, during Standard Time)
etymology: the naming origins for both Gitega and Bujumbura are obscure; Bujumbura's name prior to independence in 1962 was Usumbura
note: in January 2019, the Burundian parliament voted to make Gitega the political capital of the country while Bujumbura would remain its economic capital; as of 2023, the government's move to Gitega remains incomplete

Administrative divisions: *18 provinces; Bubanza, Bujumbura Mairie, Bujumbura Rural, Bururi, Cankuzo, Cibitoke, Gitega, Karuzi, Kayanza, Kirundo, Makamba, Muramvya, Muyinga, Mwaro, Ngozi, Rumonge, Rutana, Ruyigi; note- a law was passed in March 2023 reducing the number of provinces to five:* Buhumuza, Bujumbura, Burunga, Butanyerera, Gitega, with full implementation by 2025.

Independence: 1 July 1962 (from UN trusteeship under Belgian administration)

National holiday: Independence Day, 1 July (1962)

Legal system: mixed legal system of Belgian civil law and customary law

Constitution: *history:* several previous, ratified by referendum 28 February 2005
amendments: proposed by the president of the republic after consultation with the government or by absolute majority support of the membership in both houses of Parliament; passage requires at least two-thirds majority vote by the Senate membership and at least four-fifths majority vote by the National Assembly; the president can opt to submit amendment bills to a referendum; constitutional articles including those on national unity, the secularity of Burundi, its democratic form of government, and its sovereignty cannot be amended; amended 2018 (amendments extended the presidential term from 5 to 7 years, reintroduced the position of prime minister, and reduced the number of vice presidents from 2 to 1)

International law organization participation: has not submitted an ICJ jurisdiction declaration; withdrew from ICCt in October 2017

Citizenship: *citizenship by birth:* no
citizenship by descent only: the father must be a citizen of Burundi
dual citizenship recognized: no
residency requirement for naturalization: 10 years

Suffrage: 18 years of age; universal

Executive branch: *chief of state:* President Evariste NDAYISHIMIYE (since 18 June 2020)
head of government: Minister Gervais NDIRAKOBUCA (since 7 September 2022)
cabinet: Council of Ministers appointed by president
elections/appointments: president directly elected by absolute majority popular vote in 2 rounds if needed for a 7-year term (eligible for a second term); election last held on 20 May 2020 (next to be held in May 2027); vice presidents nominated by the president, endorsed by Parliament; note - a 2018 constitutional referendum, effective for the 2020 election, increased the presidential term from 5 to 7 years with a 2-consecutive-term limit, reinstated the position of the prime minister position, and reduced the number of vice presidents from 2 to 1
election results:
2020: Evariste NDAYISHIMIYE elected president; percent of vote - Evariste NDAYISHIMIYE (CNDD-FDD) 71.5%, Agathon RWASA (CNL) 25.2%, Gaston SINDIMWO (UPRONA) 1.7%, other 1.6%
2015: Pierre NKURUNZIZA reelected president; percent of vote - Pierre NKURUNZIZA (CNDD-FDD) 69.4%, Agathon RWASA (Hope of Burundians - Amizerio y'ABARUNDI) 19%, other 11.6%

Legislative branch: *description:* bicameral Parliament or Parlement consists of:
Senate or Inama Nkenguzamateka (39 seats in the July 2020 election); 36 members indirectly elected by an electoral college of provincial councils using a three-round voting system, which requires a two-thirds majority vote in the first two rounds and simple majority vote for the two leading candidates in the final round; 3 seats reserved for Twas, and 30% of all votes reserved for women; members serve 5-year terms)
National Assembly or Inama Nshingamateka (123 seats in the May 2020 election; 100 members directly elected in multi-seat constituencies by proportional representation vote and 23 co-opted members; 60% of seats allocated to Hutus and 40% to Tutsis; 3 seats reserved for Twas; 30% of total seats reserved for women; members serve 5-year terms)
elections: Senate - last held on 20 July 2020 (next to be held in 2025)
National Assembly - last held on 20 May 2020 (next to be held in 2025)
election results: Senate - percent of vote by party - CNDD-FDD 87.2%, Twa 7.7%, CNL 2.6%, UPRONA 2.6%; seats by party - CNDD-FDD 34, Twa 3, CNL 1, UPRONA 1; composition - men 23, women 16, percentage women 37.2%
National Assembly - percent of vote by party - CNDD-FDD 70.9%, CNL 23.4%, UPRONA 2.5%, other (co-opted Twa) 3.2%; seats by party - CNDD-FDD 86, CNL 32, Twa 3, UPRONA 2; composition - men 76, women 47, percentage women 38.2%; note - total Parliament percentage women 38%

Judicial branch: *highest court(s):* Supreme Court (consists of 9 judges and organized into judicial, administrative, and cassation chambers); Constitutional Court (consists of 7 members)
judge selection and term of office: Supreme Court judges nominated by the Judicial Service Commission, a 15-member body of judicial and legal profession officials), appointed by the president and confirmed by the Senate; judge tenure NA; Constitutional Court judges appointed by the president and confirmed by the Senate and serve 6-year nonrenewable terms
subordinate courts: Courts of Appeal; County Courts; Courts of Residence; Martial Court; Commercial Court

Political parties: Council for Democracy and the Sustainable Development of Burundi or CODEBU
Front for Democracy in Burundi-Sahwanya or FRODEBU-Sahwanya
National Council for the Defense of Democracy - Front for the Defense of Democracy or CNDD-FDD
National Congress for Liberty or CNL
National Liberation Forces or FNL
Union for National Progress (Union pour le Progress Nationale) or UPRONA

International organization participation: ACP, AfDB, ATMIS, AU, CEMAC, CEPGL, CICA, COMESA, EAC, FAO, G-77, IBRD, ICAO, ICGLR, ICRM, IDA, IFAD, IFC, IFRCS, ILO, IMF, Interpol, IOC, IOM, IPU, ISO (correspondent), ITU, ITUC (NGOs), MIGA, NAM, OIF, OPCW, UN, UNCTAD, UNESCO, UNHRC, UNIDO, UNISFA, UNMISS, UNWTO, UPU, WCO, WHO, WIPO, WMO, WTO

Diplomatic representation in the US: *chief of mission:* Ambassador Jean Bosco BAREGE (since 27 February 2024)
chancery: 2233 Wisconsin Avenue NW, Washington, DC 20007
telephone: [1] (202) 342-2574

FAX: [1] (202) 342-2578
email address and website: burundiembusadc@gmail.com
Burundi Embassy Washington D.C. (burundiembassy-usa.com)

Diplomatic representation from the US: *chief of mission:* Ambassador Lisa PETERSON (since 27 June 2024)
embassy: No 50 Avenue Des Etats-Unis, 110-01-02, Bujumbura
mailing address: 2100 Bujumbura Place, Washington DC 20521-2100
telephone: [257] 22-207-000
FAX: [257] 22-222-926
email address and website:
BujumburaC@state.gov:
https://bi.usembassy.gov/

Flag description: divided by a white diagonal cross into red panels (top and bottom) and green panels (hoist side and fly side) with a white disk superimposed at the center bearing three red six-pointed stars outlined in green arranged in a triangular design (one star above, two stars below); green symbolizes hope and optimism, white purity and peace, and red the blood shed in the struggle for independence; the three stars in the disk represent the three major ethnic groups: Hutu, Twa, Tutsi, as well as the three elements in the national motto: unity, work, progress

National symbol(s): lion; national colors: red, white, green

National anthem: *name:* "Burundi Bwacu" (Our Beloved Burundi)
lyrics/music: Jean-Baptiste NTAHOKAJA/Marc BARENGAYABO
note: adopted 1962

ECONOMY

Economic overview: highly agrarian, low-income Sub-Saharan economy; declining foreign assistance; increasing fiscal insolvencies; dense and still growing population; COVID-19 weakened economic recovery and flipped two years of deflation

Real GDP (purchasing power parity): $11.347 billion (2023 est.)
$11.048 billion (2022 est.)
$10.848 billion (2021 est.)
note: data in 2021 dollars
comparison ranking: 165

Real GDP growth rate: 2.7% (2023 est.)
1.85% (2022 est.)
3.1% (2021 est.)
note: annual GDP % growth based on constant local currency
comparison ranking: 118

Real GDP per capita: $900 (2023 est.)
$900 (2022 est.)
$900 (2021 est.)
note: data in 2021 dollars
comparison ranking: 222

GDP (official exchange rate): $2.642 billion (2023 est.)
note: data in current dollars at official exchange rate

Inflation rate (consumer prices): 26.94% (2023 est.)
18.8% (2022 est.)
8.4% (2021 est.)
note: annual % change based on consumer prices
comparison ranking: 203

GDP - composition, by sector of origin: *agriculture:* 25.2% (2023 est.)
industry: 9.6% (2023 est.)
services: 48.8% (2023 est.)
note: figures may not total 100% due to non-allocated consumption not captured in sector-reported data comparison rankings: services 153; industry 195; agriculture 19

GDP - composition, by end use: *household consumption:* 75.6% (2023 est.)
government consumption: 30.5% (2023 est.)
investment in fixed capital: 13% (2023 est.)
exports of goods and services: 5.3% (2023 est.)
imports of goods and services: -24.3% (2023 est.)
note: figures may not total 100% due to rounding or gaps in data collection

Agricultural products: cassava, bananas, sweet potatoes, vegetables, beans, potatoes, maize, sugarcane, fruits, rice (2022)
note: top ten agricultural products based on tonnage

Industries: light consumer goods (sugar, shoes, soap, beer); cement, assembly of imported components; public works construction; food processing (fruits)

Industrial production growth rate: 2.75% (2023 est.)
note: annual % change in industrial value added based on constant local currency
comparison ranking: 110

Labor force: 5.722 million (2023 est.)
note: number of people ages 15 or older who are employed or seeking work
comparison ranking: 76

Unemployment rate: 0.93% (2023 est.)
0.92% (2022 est.)
1.11% (2021 est.)
note: % of labor force seeking employment
comparison ranking: 5

Youth unemployment rate (ages 15-24): *total:* 1.7% (2023 est.)
male: 2.2% (2023 est.)
female: 1.3% (2023 est.)
note: % of labor force ages 15-24 seeking employment
comparison ranking: total 197

Gini Index coefficient - distribution of family income: 37.5 (2020 est.)
note: index (0-100) of income distribution; higher values represent greater inequality
comparison ranking: 58

Household income or consumption by percentage share: *lowest 10%:* 2.9% (2020 est.)
highest 10%: 29.9% (2020 est.)
note: % share of income accruing to lowest and highest 10% of population

Remittances: 1.83% of GDP (2023 est.)
1.45% of GDP (2022 est.)
1.74% of GDP (2021 est.)
note: personal transfers and compensation between resident and non-resident individuals/households/entities

Budget: *revenues:* $713.694 million (2021 est.)
expenditures: $506.147 million (2021 est.)
note: central government revenues and expenses (excluding grants/extrabudgetary units/social security funds) converted to US dollars at average official exchange rate for year indicated

Public debt: 51.7% of GDP (2017 est.)
comparison ranking: 100

Taxes and other revenues: 15.64% (of GDP) (2021 est.)
comparison ranking: 133

Current account balance: -$362.645 million (2018 est.)
-$373.389 million (2017 est.)
-$339.695 million (2016 est.)
note: balance of payments - net trade and primary/secondary income in current dollars
comparison ranking: 118

Exports: $285.105 million (2018 est.)
$270.686 million (2017 est.)
$315 million (2017 est.)
note: balance of payments - exports of goods and services in current dollars
comparison ranking: 197

Exports - partners: UAE 32%, Democratic Republic of the Congo 14%, China 5%, Sudan 5%, Germany 4% (2022)
note: top five export partners based on percentage share of exports

Exports - commodities: gold, coffee, tea, rare earth ores, tobacco (2022)
note: top five export commodities based on value in dollars

Imports: $905.294 million (2018 est.)
$885.422 million (2017 est.)
$1.295 billion (2017 est.)
note: balance of payments - imports of goods and services in current dollars
comparison ranking: 193

Imports - partners: China 15%, UAE 14%, Saudi Arabia 13%, Tanzania 12%, India 7% (2022)
note: top five import partners based on percentage share of imports

Imports - commodities: refined petroleum, fertilizers, packaged medicine, cement, plastic products (2022)
note: top five import commodities based on value in dollars

Reserves of foreign exchange and gold: $90.35 million (2023 est.)
$158.53 million (2022 est.)
$266.164 million (2021 est.)
note: holdings of gold (year-end prices)/foreign exchange/special drawing rights in current dollars
comparison ranking: 188

Debt - external: $444.292 million (2022 est.)
note: present value of external debt in current US dollars
comparison ranking: 92

Exchange rates: Burundi francs (BIF) per US dollar –

Exchange rates: 2,574.052 (2023 est.)
2,034.307 (2022 est.)
1,975.951 (2021 est.)
1,915.046 (2020 est.)
1,845.623 (2019 est.)

ENERGY

Electricity access: *electrification - total population:* 10.3% (2022 est.)
electrification - urban areas: 64%
electrification - rural areas: 1.7%

Electricity: *installed generating capacity:* 114,000 kW (2022 est.)
consumption: 415.198 million kWh (2022 est.)
imports: 101 million kWh (2022 est.)
transmission/distribution losses: 40 million kWh (2022 est.)
comparison rankings: transmission/distribution losses 33; imports 110; consumption 177; installed generating capacity 184

Electricity generation sources: *fossil fuels:* 33.9% of total installed capacity (2022 est.)
solar: 2.3% of total installed capacity (2022 est.)

hydroelectricity: 62.1% of total installed capacity (2022 est.)
biomass and waste: 1.7% of total installed capacity (2022 est.)

Coal: *imports:* 9,000 metric tons (2022 est.)

Petroleum: *refined petroleum consumption:* 6,000 bbl/day (2022 est.)

Carbon dioxide emissions: 800,000 metric tonnes of CO2 (2022 est.)
from coal and metallurgical coke: 5,000 metric tonnes of CO2 (2022 est.)
from petroleum and other liquids: 795,000 metric tonnes of CO2 (2022 est.)
comparison ranking: total emissions 176

Energy consumption per capita: 961,000 Btu/person (2022 est.)
comparison ranking: 193

COMMUNICATIONS

Telephones - fixed lines: *total subscriptions:* 15,000 (2022 est.)
subscriptions per 100 inhabitants: (2022 est.) less than 1
comparison ranking: total subscriptions 182

Telephones - mobile cellular: *total subscriptions:* 7.471 million (2022 est.)
subscriptions per 100 inhabitants: 58 (2022 est.)
comparison ranking: total subscriptions 107

Telecommunication systems: *general assessment:* Burundi provides an attractive telecom market given its high population density and existing low subscription rates for all services; one downside for investors is that the country has a very low economic output,and an unconducive business environment; disposable income is also very low, and fixed-line infrastructure is poor outside the main urban areas; this is a greater motivation for investors to focus on improving mobile networks than in expanding fixed-line infrastructure; to overcome difficulties associated with the poor telecom infrastructure, the government has supported a number of prominent telcos building a national fiber backbone network; this network offers onward connectivity to submarine cable infrastructure landings in Kenya and Tanzania; the first sections of this network were switched on in early 2014, and additional provinces have since been connected; in addition, the government in early 2018 kick-started the Burundi Broadband project, which aims to deliver national connectivity by 2025; based on this improved infrastructure the government and ITU have developed an ICT strategy to make use of telecoms to promote the country's socio-economic development through to 2028; progress made by Tanzania with its own national backbone network has benefited Burundi, which has been provided with onward connectivity to most countries in the region; International bandwidth capacity has continued to increase in recent years, including a 38% increase in the nine months to September 2021, resulting in lower retail prices for consumers; two of the mobile operators have launched 3G and LTE services to capitalize on the growing demand for internet access; the number of mobile subscribers increased 7% in the third quarter of 2021, quarter-on-quarter; similar growth is expected for the next two years at least, which will help bring the mobile level closer to the average for the region (2022); Burundi's Telecommunications Regulation and Control Agency (ARCT) has recently published its roadmap for the deployment of 5G services in the country, setting out a target of July 2024 for the introduction of commercial services. (2022)
domestic: fixed-line connections stand at less than 1 per 100 persons; mobile-cellular usage is about 62 per 100 persons (2021)
international: country code - 257; satellite earth station - 1 Intelsat (Indian Ocean); the government, supported by the World Bank, has backed a joint venture with a number of prominent telecoms to build a national fiber backbone network, offering onward connectivity to submarine cable infrastructure landings in Kenya and Tanzania (2019)

Broadcast media: state-controlled Radio Television Nationale de Burundi (RTNB) operates a TV station and a national radio network; 3 private TV stations and about 10 privately owned radio stations; transmissions of several international broadcasters are available in Bujumbura (2019)

Internet country code: .bi

Internet users: *total:* 754,000 (2021 est.)
percent of population: 5.8% (2021 est.)
comparison ranking: total 158

Broadband - fixed subscriptions: *total:* 4,230 (2020 est.)
subscriptions per 100 inhabitants: 0.04 (2020 est.)
comparison ranking: total 190

TRANSPORTATION

Civil aircraft registration country code prefix: 9U

Airports: 6 (2024)
comparison ranking: 173

Roadways: *total:* 12,000 km
paved: 1,500 km (2020)
comparison ranking: total 132

Waterways: 673 km (2022) (mainly on Lake Tanganyika between Bujumbura, Burundi's principal port, and lake ports in Tanzania, Zambia, and the Democratic Republic of the Congo)
comparison ranking: 83

MILITARY AND SECURITY

Military and security forces: Burundi National Defense Force (BNDF; Force de Defense Nationale du Burundi or FDNB): Land Force (la Force Terrestre), the Navy Force (la Force de la Marine), the Air Force (la Force Aérienne) and Specialized Units (des Unités Spécialisées)

Ministry of Interior, Community Development, and Public Security: Burundi National Police (Police Nationale du Burundi) (2024)
note 1: the Naval Force is responsible for monitoring Burundi's 175-km shoreline on Lake Tanganyika; the Specialized Units include a special security brigade for the protection of institutions (aka BSPI), commandos, special forces, and military police
note 2: in 2022, Burundi created a new reserve force (Force de réserve et d'appui au développement, FRAD); the FRAD's duties include organizing paramilitary trainings, supporting other components in protecting the integrity of the national territory, conceiving and implementing development projects, and operationalizing national and international partnerships

Military expenditures: 3.7% of GDP (2023 est.)
2.8% of GDP (2022 est.)
2% of GDP (2021 est.)
2.1% of GDP (2020 est.)
3% of GDP (2019 est.)
comparison ranking: 23

Military and security service personnel strengths: approximately 25-30,000 active-duty troops, the majority of which are ground forces (2023)

Military equipment inventories and acquisitions: the military has a mix of mostly older weapons and equipment typically of French, Russian, and Soviet origin, and a smaller selection of more modern secondhand equipment from such countries as China, South Africa, and the US (2024)

Military service age and obligation: 18 years of age for voluntary military service for men and women (2023)

Military deployments: 760 Central African Republic (MINUSCA); up to 3,000 in Somalia (ATMIS; note - foreign troop contingents under ATMIS are drawing down towards a final exit in December 2024) (2024)
note: Burundi deployed military troops to the Democratic Republic of the Congo (DRC) in 2022 as part of an East African regional force; as of 2024, as many as 1,000 troops reportedly remained in the DRC

Military - note: the FDNB is responsible for defending Burundi's territorial integrity and protecting its sovereignty; it has an internal security role, including maintaining and restoring public order if required; the FDNB also participates in providing humanitarian/disaster assistance, countering terrorism, narcotics trafficking, piracy, and illegal arms trade, and protecting the country's environment; the FDNB conducts limited training with foreign partners such as Russia and participates in regional peacekeeping missions, most recently in the Central African Republic, the Democratic Republic of the Congo (DRC), and Somalia; these missions have provided the force some operational experience and funding; in recent years the FDNB has conducted operations against anti-government rebel groups based in the neighboring DRC that have carried out sporadic attacks in Burundi, such as the such as National Forces of Liberation (FNL), the Resistance for the Rule of Law-Tabara (aka RED Tabara), and Popular Forces of Burundi (FPB or FOREBU)
the Arusha Accords that ended the 1993-2005 civil war created a unified military by balancing the predominantly Tutsi ex-Burundi Armed Forces (ex-FAB) and the largely Hutu dominated armed movements and requiring the military to have a 50/50 ethnic mix of Tutsis and Hutus (2024)

TRANSNATIONAL ISSUES

Refugees and internally displaced persons: *refugees (country of origin):* 87,157 (Democratic Republic of the Congo) (refugees and asylum seekers) (2024)
IDPs: 76,987 (some ethnic Tutsis remain displaced from intercommunal violence that broke out after the 1993 coup and fighting between government forces and rebel groups; violence since April 2015) (2023)
stateless persons: 767 (mid-year 2021)

CABO VERDE

INTRODUCTION

Background: The Portuguese discovered and colonized the uninhabited islands of Cabo Verde in the 15th century; Cabo Verde subsequently became a trading center for African slaves and later an important coaling and resupply stop for whaling and transatlantic shipping. The fusing of European and various African cultural traditions is reflected in Cabo Verde's Crioulo language, music, and pano textiles. After gaining independence in 1975, a one-party system was established and maintained until multi-party elections were held in 1990. Cabo Verde continues to sustain one of Africa's most stable democratic governments and relatively stable economies, maintaining a currency pegged first to the Portuguese escudo and then to the euro since 1998. Repeated droughts during the second half of the 20th century caused significant hardship and prompted heavy emigration. As a result, Cabo Verde's expatriate population – concentrated in Boston, Massachusetts and Western Europe – is greater than its domestic one.

Most Cabo Verdeans have both African and Portuguese antecedents. Cabo Verde's population descends from its first permanent inhabitants in the late 15th-century – a preponderance of West African slaves, a small share of Portuguese colonists, and even fewer Italians and Spaniards. Among the nine inhabited islands, population distribution is varied. The islands in the east are very dry and are home to the country's growing tourism industry. The more western islands receive more precipitation and support larger populations, but agriculture and livestock grazing have damaged their soil fertility and vegetation. For centuries, the country's overall population size has fluctuated significantly, as recurring periods of famine and epidemics have caused high death tolls and emigration.

GEOGRAPHY

Location: Western Africa, group of islands in the North Atlantic Ocean, west of Senegal: Geographic coordinates: 16 00 N, 24 00 W

Map references: Africa: Area: *total:* 4,033 sq km
land: 4,033 sq km
water: 0 sq km
comparison ranking: total 175

Area - comparative: slightly larger than Rhode Island

Land boundaries: *total:* 0 km

Coastline: 965 km

Maritime claims: *territorial sea:* 12 nm
contiguous zone: 24 nm
exclusive economic zone: 200 nm
measured from claimed archipelagic baselines

Climate: temperate; warm, dry summer; precipitation meager and erratic

Terrain: steep, rugged, rocky, volcanic

Elevation: *highest point:* Mt. Fogo (a volcano on Fogo Island) 2,829 m
lowest point: Atlantic Ocean 0 m

Natural resources: salt, basalt rock, limestone, kaolin, fish, clay, gypsum

Land use: *agricultural land:* 18.6% (2018 est.)
arable land: 11.7% (2018 est.)
permanent crops: 0.7% (2018 est.)
permanent pasture: 6.2% (2018 est.)
forest: 21% (2018 est.)
other: 60.4% (2018 est.)

Irrigated land: 35 sq km (2012)

Population distribution: among the nine inhabited islands, population distribution is variable; islands in the east are very dry and are only sparsely settled to exploit their extensive salt deposits; the more southerly islands receive more precipitation and support larger populations, but agriculture and livestock grazing have damaged the soil fertility and vegetation; approximately half of the population lives on Sao Tiago Island, which is the location of the capital of Praia; Mindelo, on the northern island of Sao Vicente, also has a large urban population as shown in this population distribution map

Natural hazards: prolonged droughts; seasonal harmattan wind produces obscuring dust; volcanically and seismically active
volcanism: Fogo (2,829 m), which last erupted in 1995, is Cabo Verde's only active volcano

Geography - note: strategic location 500 km from west coast of Africa near major north-south sea routes; important communications station; important sea and air refueling site; one of four North Atlantic archipelagos that make up Macaronesia; the others are Azores (Portugal), Canary Islands (Spain), and Madeira (Portugal)

PEOPLE AND SOCIETY

Population: *total:* 611,014
male: 297,106
female: 313,908 (2024 est.)
comparison rankings: female 171; male 171; total 171

Nationality: *noun:* Cabo Verdean(s)
adjective: Cabo Verdean

Ethnic groups: Creole (Mulatto) 71%, African 28%, European 1%

Languages: Portuguese (official), Crioulo (a Portuguese-based creole language with two main dialects)

Religions: Roman Catholic 72.5%, Protestant 4% (includes Adventist 1.9%, Nazarene 1.8%, Assembly of God 0.2%, God is Love 0.1%), Christian Rationalism 1.7%, Muslim 1.3%, Jehovah's Witness 1.2%, Church of Jesus Christ 1%, other Christian 1.3%, other 1.2%, none 15.6%, no response 0.4% (2021 est.)

Demographic profile: Cabo Verde's population descends from its first permanent inhabitants in the late 15th-century – a preponderance of West African slaves, a small share of Portuguese colonists, and even fewer Italians, Spaniards, and Portuguese Jews. Over the centuries, the country's overall population size has fluctuated significantly, as recurring periods of famine and epidemics have caused high death tolls and emigration.

Labor migration historically reduced Cabo Verde's population growth and still provides a key source of income through remittances. Expatriates probably outnumber Cabo Verde's resident population, with most families having a member abroad. Cabo Verdeans have settled in the US, Europe, Africa, and South America. The largest diaspora community in New Bedford, Massachusetts, dating to the early 1800s, is a byproduct of the transatlantic whaling industry. Cabo Verdean men fleeing poverty at home joined the crews of US whaling ships that stopped in the islands. Many settled in New Bedford and stayed in the whaling or shipping trade, worked in the textile or cranberry industries, or operated their own transatlantic packet ships that transported compatriots to the US. Increased Cabo Verdean emigration to the US coincided with the gradual and eventually complete abolition of slavery in the archipelago in 1878.

During the same period, Portuguese authorities coerced Cabo Verdeans to go to Sao Tome and Principe and other Portuguese colonies in Africa to work as indentured laborers on plantations. In the 1920s, when the US implemented immigration quotas, Cabo Verdean emigration shifted toward Portugal, West Africa (Senegal), and South America (Argentina). Growing numbers of Cabo Verdean labor migrants headed to Western Europe in the 1960s and 1970s. They filled unskilled jobs in Portugal, as many Portuguese sought out work opportunities in the more prosperous economies of northwest Europe. Cabo Verdeans eventually expanded their emigration to the Netherlands, where they worked in the shipping industry. Migration to the US resumed under relaxed migration laws. Cabo Verdean women also began migrating to southern Europe to become domestic workers, a trend that continues today and has shifted the gender balance of Cabo Verdean emigration.

Emigration has declined in more recent decades due to the adoption of more restrictive migration policies in destination countries. Reduced emigration along with a large youth population, decreased mortality rates, and increased life expectancies, has boosted population growth, putting further pressure on domestic employment and resources. In addition, Cabo Verde has attracted increasing numbers of migrants in recent decades, consisting primarily of people from West Africa, Portuguese-speaking African countries, Portugal, and China. Since the 1990s, some West African migrants have used Cabo Verde as a stepping stone for illegal migration to Europe.

Age structure: *0-14 years:* 26.4% (male 80,973/female 80,129)
15-64 years: 67.2% (male 201,084/female 209,676)
65 years and over: 6.4% (2024 est.) (male 15,049/female 24,103)

Dependency ratios: *total dependency ratio:* 47.2
youth dependency ratio: 39.2
elderly dependency ratio: 8
potential support ratio: 12.5 (2021 est.)

Median age: *total:* 28.8 years (2024 est.)
male: 27.9 years
female: 29.6 years
comparison ranking: total 149

Population growth rate: 1.16% (2024 est.)
comparison ranking: 78

Birth rate: 17.9 births/1,000 population (2024 est.)
comparison ranking: 79

Death rate: 5.7 deaths/1,000 population (2024 est.)
comparison ranking: 168

Net migration rate: -0.6 migrant(s)/1,000 population (2024 est.)
comparison ranking: 124

Population distribution: among the nine inhabited islands, population distribution is variable; islands in the east are very dry and are only sparsely settled to exploit their extensive salt deposits; the more southerly islands receive more precipitation and support larger populations, but agriculture and livestock grazing have damaged the soil fertility and vegetation; approximately half of the population lives on Sao Tiago Island, which is the location of the capital of Praia; Mindelo, on the northern island of Sao Vicente, also has a large urban population as shown in this population distribution map

Urbanization: *urban population:* 68% of total population (2023)
rate of urbanization: 1.83% annual rate of change (2020-25 est.)

Major urban areas - population: 168,000 PRAIA (capital) (2018)

Sex ratio: *at birth:* 1.03 male(s)/female
0-14 years: 1.01 male(s)/female
15-64 years: 0.96 male(s)/female
65 years and over: 0.62 male(s)/female
total population: 0.95 male(s)/female (2024 est.)

Maternal mortality ratio: 42 deaths/100,000 live births (2020 est.)
comparison ranking: 101

Infant mortality rate: *total:* 22.4 deaths/1,000 live births (2024 est.)
male: 26.3 deaths/1,000 live births
female: 18.4 deaths/1,000 live births
comparison ranking: total 67

Life expectancy at birth: *total population:* 74.3 years (2024 est.)
male: 72 years
female: 76.7 years
comparison ranking: total population 144

Total fertility rate: 2.1 children born/woman (2024 est.)
comparison ranking: 95

Gross reproduction rate: 1.03 (2024 est.)

Contraceptive prevalence rate: 55.8% (2018)

Drinking water source: *improved: urban:* 100% of population
rural: 90% of population
total: 96.7% of population
unimproved: urban: 0% of population
rural: 10% of population
total: 3.3% of population (2020 est.)

Current health expenditure: 6% of GDP (2020)

Physician density: 0.83 physicians/1,000 population (2018)

Hospital bed density: 2.1 beds/1,000 population

Sanitation facility access: *improved: urban:* 91.7% of population
rural: 73.3% of population
total: 85.6% of population
unimproved: urban: 8.3% of population
rural: 26.7% of population
total: 14.4% of population (2020 est.)

Obesity - adult prevalence rate: 11.8% (2016)
comparison ranking: 134

Alcohol consumption per capita: *total:* 4.7 liters of pure alcohol (2019 est.)
beer: 2.28 liters of pure alcohol (2019 est.)
wine: 1.82 liters of pure alcohol (2019 est.)
spirits: 0.6 liters of pure alcohol (2019 est.)
other alcohols: 0 liters of pure alcohol (2019 est.)
comparison ranking: total 86

Tobacco use: *total:* 11.4% (2020 est.)
male: 17.3% (2020 est.)
female: 5.4% (2020 est.)
comparison ranking: total 127

Children under the age of 5 years underweight: NA

Currently married women (ages 15-49): 46.9% (2023 est.)

Education expenditures: 7.6% of GDP (2020 est.)
comparison ranking: 15

Literacy: *definition:* age 15 and over can read and write
total population: 90.8%
male: 94.2%
female: 87.4% (2021)

School life expectancy (primary to tertiary education): *total:* 13 years
male: 12 years
female: 13 years (2018)

ENVIRONMENT

Environment - current issues: deforestation due to demand for firewood; water shortages; prolonged droughts and improper use of land (overgrazing, crop cultivation on hillsides lead to desertification and erosion); environmental damage has threatened several species of birds and reptiles; illegal beach sand extraction; overfishing

Environment - international agreements: *party to:* Biodiversity, Climate Change, Climate Change-Kyoto Protocol, Climate Change-Paris Agreement, Comprehensive Nuclear Test Ban, Desertification, Endangered Species, Environmental Modification, Hazardous Wastes, Law of the Sea, Marine Dumping-London Convention, Nuclear Test Ban, Ozone Layer Protection, Ship Pollution, Wetlands
signed, but not ratified: none of the selected agreements

Climate: temperate; warm, dry summer; precipitation meager and erratic

Urbanization: *urban population:* 68% of total population (2023)
rate of urbanization: 1.83% annual rate of change (2020-25 est.)

Revenue from forest resources: 0.38% of GDP (2018 est.)
comparison ranking: 72

Revenue from coal: 0% of GDP (2018 est.)
comparison ranking: 125

Air pollutants: *particulate matter emissions:* 31.08 micrograms per cubic meter (2019 est.)
carbon dioxide emissions: 0.54 megatons (2016 est.)
methane emissions: 0.13 megatons (2020 est.)

Waste and recycling: *municipal solid waste generated annually:* 132,555 tons (2012 est.)

Total water withdrawal: *municipal:* 1.6 million cubic meters (2017 est.)
industrial: 400,000 cubic meters (2017 est.)
agricultural: 30 million cubic meters (2020 est.)

Total renewable water resources: 300 million cubic meters (2020 est.)

GOVERNMENT

Country name: *conventional long form:* Republic of Cabo Verde
conventional short form: Cabo Verde
local long form: Republica de Cabo Verde
local short form: Cabo Verde
etymology: the name derives from Cap-Vert (Green Cape) on the Senegalese coast, the westernmost point of Africa and the nearest mainland to the islands

Government type: parliamentary republic

Capital: *name:* Praia
geographic coordinates: 14 55 N, 23 31 W
time difference: UTC-1 (4 hours ahead of Washington, DC, during Standard Time)
etymology: the earlier Portuguese name was Villa de Praia ("Village of the Beach"); it became just Praia in 1974 (prior to full independence in 1975)

Administrative divisions: 22 municipalities (concelhos, singular - concelho); Boa Vista, Brava, Maio, Mosteiros, Paul, Porto Novo, Praia, Ribeira Brava, Ribeira Grande, Ribeira Grande de Santiago, Sal, Santa Catarina, Santa Catarina do Fogo, Santa Cruz, Sao Domingos, Sao Filipe, Sao Lourenco dos Orgaos, Sao Miguel, Sao Salvador do Mundo, Sao Vicente, Tarrafal, Tarrafal de Sao Nicolau

Independence: 5 July 1975 (from Portugal)

National holiday: Independence Day, 5 July (1975)

Legal system: civil law system of Portugal

Constitution: *history:* previous 1981; latest effective 25 September 1992
amendments: proposals require support of at least four fifths of the active National Assembly membership; amendment drafts require sponsorship of at least one third of the active Assembly membership; passage requires at least two-thirds majority vote by the Assembly membership; constitutional sections, including those on national independence, form of government, political pluralism, suffrage, and human rights and liberties, cannot be amended; revised 1995, 1999, 2010

International law organization participation: has not submitted an ICJ jurisdiction declaration; accepts ICCt jurisdiction

Citizenship: *citizenship by birth:* no
citizenship by descent only: at least one parent must be a citizen of Cabo Verde
dual citizenship recognized: yes
residency requirement for naturalization: 5 years

Suffrage: 18 years of age; universal

Executive branch: *chief of state:* President Jose Maria Pereira NEVES (since 9 November 2021)
head of government: Prime Minister Jose Ulisses CORREIA e SILVA (since 22 April 2016)
cabinet: Council of Ministers appointed by the president on the recommendation of the prime minister
elections/appointments: president directly elected by absolute majority popular vote in 2 rounds if

needed for a 5-year term (eligible for a second term); election last held on 17 October 2021 (next to be held in October 2026); prime minister nominated by the National Assembly and appointed by the president
election results:
2020: Jose Maria Pereira NEVES elected president; percent of vote - Jose Maria Pereira NEVES (PAICV) 51.7%, Carlos VEIGA (MPD) 42.4%, Casimiro DE PINA (independent) 1.8%, Fernando Rocha DELGADO (independent) 1.4%, Helio SANCHES (independent) 1.14%, Gilson ALVES (independent) 0.8%, Joaquim MONTEIRO (independent) 3.4%
2016: Jorge Carlos FONSECA reelected president; percent of vote - Jorge Carlos FONSECA (MPD) 74.1%, Albertino GRACA (independent) 22.5%, other 3.4%

Legislative branch: *description:* unicameral National Assembly or Assembleia Nacional (72 seats; members directly elected in multi-seat constituencies by proportional representation vote; members serve 5-year terms)
elections: last held on 18 April 2021 (next to be held in April 2026)
election results: percent of vote by party MPD 50.2%, PAICV 39.6%, UCID 9.0%, other 1.2%; seats by party - MPD 38, PAICV 30, UCID 4; composition - men 44, women 28, percentage women 38.9%

Judicial branch: *highest court(s):* Supreme Court of Justice (consists of the chief justice and at least 7 judges and organized into civil, criminal, and administrative sections)
judge selection and term of office: judge appointments - 1 by the president of the republic, 1 elected by the National Assembly, and 3 by the Superior Judicial Council (SJC), a 16-member independent body chaired by the chief justice and includes the attorney general, 8 private citizens, 2 judges, 2 prosecutors, the senior legal inspector of the Attorney General's office, and a representative of the Ministry of Justice; chief justice appointed by the president of the republic from among peers of the Supreme Court of Justice and in consultation with the SJC; judges appointed for life
subordinate courts: appeals courts, first instance (municipal) courts; audit, military, and fiscal and customs courts

Political parties: African Party for Independence of Cabo Verde or PAICV
Democratic and Independent Cabo Verdean Union or UCID
Democratic Christian Party or PDC
Democratic Renewal Party or PRD
Movement for Democracy or MPD
Party for Democratic Convergence or PCD
Party of Work and Solidarity or PTS
Social Democratic Party or PSD

International organization participation: ACP, AfDB, AOSIS, AU, CD, CPLP, ECOWAS, FAO, G-77, IAEA, IBRD, ICAO, ICCt (signatory), ICRM, IDA, IFAD, IFC, IFRCS, ILO, IMF, IMO, Interpol, IOC, IOM, IPU, ITSO, ITU, ITUC (NGOs), MIGA, NAM, OIF, OPCW, UN, UNCTAD, UNESCO, UNIDO, Union Latina, UNWTO, UPU, WCO, WHO, WIPO, WMO, WTO

Diplomatic representation in the US: *chief of mission:* Ambassador Jose Luis do Livramento MONTEIRO ALVES DE BRITO (since 23 December 2020)
chancery: 3415 Massachusetts Avenue NW, Washington, DC 20007
telephone: [1] (202) 965-6820
FAX: [1] (202) 965-1207
email address and website:
embassy.wdc@mnec.gov.cv
https://www.embcv-usa.gov.cv/
consulate(s) general: Boston

Diplomatic representation from the US: *chief of mission:* Ambassador Jennifer ADAMS (since 10 September 2024)
embassy: Rua Abilio Macedo 6, Praia
mailing address: 2460 Praia Place, Washington DC 20521-2460
telephone: [238] 260-8900
FAX: [238] 261-1355
email address and website:
PraiaConsular@state.gov:
https://cv.usembassy.gov/

Flag description: five unequal horizontal bands; the top-most band of blue - equal to one half the width of the flag - is followed by three bands of white, red, and white, each equal to 1/12 of the width, and a bottom stripe of blue equal to one quarter of the flag width; a circle of 10 yellow, five-pointed stars is centered on the red stripe and positioned 3/8 of the length of the flag from the hoist side; blue stands for the sea and the sky, the circle of stars represents the 10 major islands united into a nation, the stripes symbolize the road to formation of the country through peace (white) and effort (red)

National symbol(s): ten, five-pointed, yellow stars; national colors: blue, white, red, yellow

National anthem: *name:* "Cantico da Liberdade" (Song of Freedom)
lyrics/music: Amilcar Spencer LOPES/Adalberto Higino Tavares SILVA
note: adopted 1996

National heritage: *total World Heritage Sites:* 1 (cultural)
selected World Heritage Site locales: Cidade Velha; Historic Center of Ribeira Grande

ECONOMY

Economic overview: stable, middle-income, developing island economy; strong GDP growth led by tourism sector recovery; sustained poverty reduction through PEDS II development plan; high reliance on foreign remittances and aid to finance external debt

Real GDP (purchasing power parity): $4.903 billion (2023 est.)
$4.663 billion (2022 est.)
$3.971 billion (2021 est.)
note: data in 2021 dollars
comparison ranking: 187

Real GDP growth rate: 5.15% (2023 est.)
17.44% (2022 est.)
7.03% (2021 est.)
note: annual GDP % growth based on constant local currency
comparison ranking: 49

Real GDP per capita: $8,200 (2023 est.)
$7,900 (2022 est.)
$6,800 (2021 est.)
note: data in 2021 dollars
comparison ranking: 155

GDP (official exchange rate): $2.587 billion (2023 est.)
note: data in current dollars at official exchange rate

Inflation rate (consumer prices): 7.93% (2022 est.)
1.86% (2021 est.)
0.61% (2020 est.)
note: annual % change based on consumer prices
comparison ranking: 153

Credit ratings: Fitch rating: B- (2020)
Standard & Poors rating: B (2013)
note: The year refers to the year in which the current credit rating was first obtained.

GDP - composition, by sector of origin: *agriculture:* 4.5% (2023 est.)
industry: 10.7% (2023 est.)
services: 70.6% (2023 est.)
note: figures may not total 100% due to non-allocated consumption not captured in sector-reported data
comparison rankings: services 36; industry 189; agriculture 122

GDP - composition, by end use: *household consumption:* 74.7% (2023 est.)
government consumption: 20.4% (2023 est.)
investment in fixed capital: 19.4% (2023 est.)
exports of goods and services: 39.7% (2023 est.)
imports of goods and services: -54.1% (2023 est.)
note: figures may not total 100% due to rounding or gaps in data collection

Agricultural products: sugarcane, tomatoes, coconuts, pulses, goat milk, vegetables, bananas, milk, cabbages, potatoes (2022)
note: top ten agricultural products based on tonnage

Industries: food and beverages, fish processing, shoes and garments, salt mining, ship repair

Industrial production growth rate: 1.18% (2023 est.)
note: annual % change in industrial value added based on constant local currency
comparison ranking: 135

Labor force: 257,000 (2023 est.)
note: number of people ages 15 or older who are employed or seeking work
comparison ranking: 171

Unemployment rate: 11.99% (2023 est.)
12.27% (2022 est.)
13.91% (2021 est.)
note: % of labor force seeking employment
comparison ranking: 178

Youth unemployment rate (ages 15-24): *total:* 28.7% (2023 est.)
male: 24.9% (2023 est.)
female: 34.1% (2023 est.)
note: % of labor force ages 15-24 seeking employment
comparison ranking: total 27

Population below poverty line: 35.2% (2015 est.)
note: % of population with income below national poverty line

Gini Index coefficient - distribution of family income: 42.4 (2015 est.)
note: index (0-100) of income distribution; higher values represent greater inequality
comparison ranking: 33

Household income or consumption by percentage share: *lowest 10%:* 2.2% (2015 est.)
highest 10%: 32.3% (2015 est.)
note: % share of income accruing to lowest and highest 10% of population

Remittances: 12.24% of GDP (2023 est.)
13.6% of GDP (2022 est.)
15.33% of GDP (2021 est.)
note: personal transfers and compensation between resident and non-resident individuals/households/entities

Budget: *revenues:* $574.917 million (2017 est.)
expenditures: $503.059 million (2017 est.)

note: central government revenues (excluding grants) and expenses converted to US dollars at average official exchange rate for year indicated

Public debt: 125.8% of GDP (2017 est.)
comparison ranking: 10

Taxes and other revenues: 18.39% (of GDP) (2020 est.)
note: central government tax revenue as a % of GDP
comparison ranking: 99

Current account balance: -$82.487 million (2023 est.)
-$69.634 million (2022 est.)
-$250.632 million (2021 est.)
note: balance of payments - net trade and primary/secondary income in current dollars
comparison ranking: 93

Exports: $951.224 million (2023 est.)
$860.578 million (2022 est.)
$465.348 million (2021 est.)
note: balance of payments - exports of goods and services in current dollars
comparison ranking: 182

Exports - partners: Spain 56%, Portugal 12%, Italy 9%, US 6%, India 5% (2022)
note: top five export partners based on percentage share of exports

Exports - commodities: fish, shellfish, garments, natural gas, scrap iron (2022)
note: top five export commodities based on value in dollars

Imports: $1.424 billion (2023 est.)
$1.31 billion (2022 est.)
$1.117 billion (2021 est.)
note: balance of payments - imports of goods and services in current dollars
comparison ranking: 185

Imports - partners: Portugal 41%, Spain 12%, China 8%, Netherlands 7%, Togo 5% (2022)
note: top five import partners based on percentage share of imports

Imports - commodities: refined petroleum, fish, plastic products, milk, cars (2022)
note: top five import commodities based on value in dollars

Reserves of foreign exchange and gold: $816.554 million (2023 est.)
$704.63 million (2022 est.)
$769.65 million (2021 est.)
note: holdings of gold (year-end prices)/foreign exchange/special drawing rights in current dollars
comparison ranking: 148

Debt - external: $1.46 billion (2022 est.)
note: present value of external debt in current US dollars
comparison ranking: 78

Exchange rates: Cabo Verdean escudos (CVE) per US dollar –

Exchange rates: 101.805 (2023 est.)
104.863 (2022 est.)
93.218 (2021 est.)
96.796 (2020 est.)
98.495 (2019 est.)

ENERGY

Electricity access: *electrification - total population:* 97.1% (2022 est.)
electrification - urban areas: 95.3%
electrification - rural areas: 96.9%

Electricity: *installed generating capacity:* 204,000 kW (2022 est.)
consumption: 327 million kWh (2022 est.)
transmission/distribution losses: 106 million kWh (2022 est.)
comparison rankings: transmission/distribution losses 51; consumption 184; installed generating capacity 172

Electricity generation sources: *fossil fuels:* 83.1% of total installed capacity (2022 est.)
solar: 2.1% of total installed capacity (2022 est.)
wind: 14.8% of total installed capacity (2022 est.)

Petroleum: *refined petroleum consumption:* 4,000 bbl/day (2022 est.)

Carbon dioxide emissions: 681,000 metric tonnes of CO_2 (2022 est.)
from petroleum and other liquids: 681,000 metric tonnes of CO_2 (2022 est.)
comparison ranking: total emissions 181

Energy consumption per capita: 16.298 million Btu/person (2022 est.)
comparison ranking: 136

COMMUNICATIONS

Telephones - fixed lines: *total subscriptions:* 57,000 (2022 est.)
subscriptions per 100 inhabitants: 10 (2022 est.)
comparison ranking: total subscriptions 152

Telephones - mobile cellular: *total subscriptions:* 589,000 (2022 est.)
subscriptions per 100 inhabitants: 99 (2022 est.)
comparison ranking: total subscriptions 172

Telecommunication systems: *general assessment:* LTE reaches almost 40% of the population; regulator awards commercial 4G licenses and starts 5G pilot; govt. extends USD 25 million for submarine fiber-optic cable project linking Africa to Portugal and Brazil (2020)
domestic: 9 per 100 fixed-line teledensity and nearly 100 per 100 mobile-cellular (2021)
international: country code - 238; landing points for the Atlantis-2, EllaLink, Cabo Verde Telecom Domestic Submarine Cable Phase 1, 2, 3 and WACS fiber-optic transatlantic telephone cable that provides links to South America, Africa, and Europe; HF radiotelephone to Senegal and Guinea-Bissau; satellite earth station - 1 Intelsat (Atlantic Ocean) (2019)

Broadcast media: state-run TV and radio broadcast network plus a growing number of private broadcasters; Portuguese public TV and radio services for Africa are available; transmissions of a few international broadcasters are available (2019)

Internet country code: .cv

Internet users: *total:* 413,000 (2021 est.)
percent of population: 70% (2021 est.)
comparison ranking: total 171

Broadband - fixed subscriptions: *total:* 24,839 (2020 est.)
subscriptions per 100 inhabitants: 5 (2020 est.)
comparison ranking: total 160

TRANSPORTATION

National air transport system: *number of registered air carriers:* 2 (2020)
inventory of registered aircraft operated by air carriers: 5
annual passenger traffic on registered air carriers: 140,429 (2018)
annual freight traffic on registered air carriers: 1,728,152 (2015) mt-km

Civil aircraft registration country code prefix: D4

Airports: 10 (2024)
comparison ranking: 157

Roadways: *total:* 1,350 km
paved: 932 km
unpaved: 418 km (2013)
comparison ranking: total 178

Merchant marine: *total:* 44 (2023)
by type: general cargo 14, oil tanker 2, other 28
comparison ranking: total 122

Ports: *total ports:* 2 (2024)
large: 0
medium: 0
small: 1
very small: 1
ports with oil terminals: 1
key ports: Porto da Praia, Porto Grande

MILITARY AND SECURITY

Military and security forces: Cabo Verdean Armed Forces (FACV): National Guard (GN; serves as the army and includes a small air component), Cabo Verde Coast Guard (Guardia Costeira de Cabo Verde, GCCV) (2024)
note: the National Police are under the Ministry of Internal Affairs

Military expenditures: 0.6% of GDP (2023 est.)
0.5% of GDP (2022 est.)
0.5% of GDP (2021 est.)
0.5% of GDP (2020 est.)
0.5% of GDP (2019 est.)
comparison ranking: 156

Military and security service personnel strengths: the military has approximately 1,000-1,200 personnel (2023)

Military equipment inventories and acquisitions: the FACV has a limited amount of mostly dated or second-hand equipment, largely from China, some European countries, and the former Soviet Union (2024)

Military service age and obligation: 18-35 years of age for male and female selective compulsory military service; 24-month conscript service obligation; 17 years of age for voluntary service (with parental consent) (2024)

Military - note: the FACV is responsible for territorial defense; it also has an internal security role in collaboration with the police if required; its duties include monitoring and patrolling the country's air and maritime spaces, participating in training exercises, conducting search and rescue, countering narcotics and other forms of illicit trafficking, and supporting the police and civil society (2024)

TRANSNATIONAL ISSUES

Refugees and internally displaced persons: *stateless persons:* 115 (2022)

Illicit drugs: narcotraffickers transit cocaine, cannabis, and other drugs to Africa and Europe; domestic trafficking contributes to increased consumption of illicit substances;

CAMBODIA

INTRODUCTION

Background: Most Cambodians consider themselves to be Khmers, descendants of the Angkor Empire that extended over much of Southeast Asia and reached its zenith between the 10th and 13th centuries. Attacks by the Thai and Cham (from present-day Vietnam) weakened the empire, ushering in a long period of decline. The king placed the country under French protection in 1863, and it became part of French Indochina in 1887. Following Japanese occupation in World War II, Cambodia gained full independence from France in 1953. In 1975, after a seven-year struggle, communist Khmer Rouge forces captured Phnom Penh and evacuated all cities and towns. At least 1.5 million Cambodians died from execution, forced hardships, or starvation during the Khmer Rouge regime under POL POT. A 1978 Vietnamese invasion drove the Khmer Rouge into the countryside, began a 10-year Vietnamese occupation, and touched off 13 years of internecine warfare in which a coalition of Khmer Rouge, Cambodian nationalists, and royalist insurgents, with assistance from China, fought the Vietnamese-backed People's Republic of Kampuchea (PRK).

The 1991 Paris Agreements ended the country's civil war and mandated democratic elections, which took place in 1993 and ushered in a period of multi-party democracy with a constitutional monarchy. King Norodom SIHANOUK was reinstated as head of state, and the Cambodian People's Party (CPP) and the royalist FUNCINPEC party formed a coalition government. Nevertheless, the power-sharing arrangement proved fractious and fragile, and in 1997, a coup led by CPP leader and former PRK prime minister HUN SEN dissolved the coalition and sidelined FUNCINPEC. Despite further attempts at coalition governance, the CPP has since remained in power through elections criticized for lacking fairness, political and judicial corruption, media control, and influence over labor unions, all of which have been enforced with violence and intimidation. HUN SEN remained as prime minister until 2023, when he transferred power to his son, HUN MANET. HUN SEN has subsequently maintained considerable influence as the leader of the CPP and the Senate. The CPP has also placed limits on civil society, press freedom, and freedom of expression. Despite some economic growth and considerable investment from China over the past decade, Cambodia remains one of East Asia's poorest countries.

The remaining elements of the Khmer Rouge surrendered in 1999. A UN-backed special tribunal established in Cambodia in 1997 tried some of the surviving Khmer Rouge leaders for crimes against humanity and genocide. The tribunal concluded in 2022 with three convictions.

GEOGRAPHY

Location: Southeastern Asia, bordering the Gulf of Thailand, between Thailand, Vietnam, and Laos

Geographic coordinates: 13 00 N, 105 00 E

Map references: Southeast Asia

Area: *total:* 181,035 sq km
land: 176,515 sq km
water: 4,520 sq km
comparison ranking: total 90

Area - comparative: one and a half times the size of Pennsylvania; slightly smaller than Oklahoma

Land boundaries: *total:* 2,530 km
border countries (3): Laos 555 km; Thailand 817 km; Vietnam 1158 km

Coastline: 443 km

Maritime claims: *territorial sea:* 12 nm
contiguous zone: 24 nm
exclusive economic zone: 200 nm
continental shelf: 200 nm

Climate: tropical; rainy, monsoon season (May to November); dry season (December to April); little seasonal temperature variation

Terrain: mostly low, flat plains; mountains in southwest and north

Elevation: *highest point:* Phnum Aoral 1,810 m
lowest point: Gulf of Thailand 0 m
mean elevation: 126 m

Natural resources: oil and gas, timber, gemstones, iron ore, manganese, phosphates, hydropower potential, arable land

Land use: *agricultural land:* 32.1% (2018 est.)
arable land: 22.7% (2018 est.)
permanent crops: 0.9% (2018 est.)
permanent pasture: 8.5% (2018 est.)
forest: 56.5% (2018 est.)
other: 11.4% (2018 est.)

Irrigated land: 3,540 sq km (2012)

Major lakes (area sq km): *fresh water lake(s):* Tonle Sap - 2,700-16,000 sq km

Major rivers (by length in km): Mekong (shared with China [s], Burma, Thailand, Laos, and Vietnam [m]) - 4,350 km
note – [s] after country name indicates river source; [m] after country name indicates river mouth

Major watersheds (area sq km): Pacific Ocean drainage: Mekong (805,604 sq km)

Population distribution: population concentrated in the southeast, particularly in and around the capital of Phnom Penh; further distribution is linked closely to the Tonle Sap and Mekong Rivers

Natural hazards: monsoonal rains (June to November); flooding; occasional droughts

Geography - note: a land of paddies and forests dominated by the Mekong River and Tonle Sap (Southeast Asia's largest freshwater lake)

PEOPLE AND SOCIETY

Population: *total:* 17,063,669
male: 8,277,588
female: 8,786,081 (2024 est.)
comparison rankings: female 73; male 73; total 73

Nationality: *noun:* Cambodian(s)
adjective: **Cambodian**

Ethnic groups: Khmer 95.4%, Cham 2.4%, Chinese 1.5%, other 0.7% (2019-20 est.)

Languages: Khmer (official) 95.8%, minority languages 2.9%, Chinese 0.6%, Vietnamese 0.5%, other 0.2% (2019 est.)
major-language sample(s):
សៀវភៅហេតុការណ៍នៅលើពិភពលោក។
ទីតាំងពត៌មានមូលដ្ឋានគ្រឹះយ៉ាងសំខាន់។. (Khmer)

Religions: Buddhist (official) 97.1%, Muslim 2%, Christian 0.3%, other 0.5% (2019 est.)

Demographic profile: Cambodia is a predominantly rural country with among the most ethnically and religiously homogenous populations in Southeast Asia: more than 95% of its inhabitants are Khmer and more than 95% are Buddhist. The population's size and age structure shrank and then rebounded during the 20th century as a result of conflict and mass death. During the Khmer Rouge regime between 1975 and 1979 as many as 1.5 to 2 million people are estimated to have been killed or died as a result of starvation, disease, or overwork – a loss of about 25% of the population. At the same time, emigration was high, and the fertility rate sharply declined. In the 1980s, after the overthrow of the Khmer Rouge, fertility nearly doubled and reached pre-Khmer Rouge levels of close to 7 children per woman, reflecting in part higher infant survival rates. The baby boom was followed by a sustained fertility decline starting in the early 1990s, eventually decreasing from 3.8 in 2000 to 2.9 in 2010, although the rate varied by income, education, and rural versus urban location. Despite continuing fertility reduction, Cambodia still has a youthful population that is likely to maintain population growth through population momentum. Improvements have also been made in mortality, life expectancy, and contraceptive prevalence, although reducing malnutrition among children remains stalled. Differences in health indicators are pronounced between urban and rural areas, which experience greater poverty.

Cambodia is predominantly a country of migration, driven by the search for work, education, or marriage. Internal migration is more prevalent than international migration, with rural to urban migration being the most common, followed by rural to rural migration. Urban migration focuses on the pursuit of unskilled or semi-skilled jobs in Phnom Penh, with men working mainly in the construction industry and women working in garment factories. Most Cambodians who migrate abroad do so illegally using brokers because it is cheaper and faster than through formal channels, but doing so puts them at risk of being trafficked for forced labor or sexual exploitation.Young Cambodian men and women migrate short distances across the Thai border using temporary passes to work in agriculture, while others migrate long distances primarily into Thailand and Malaysia for work in agriculture, fishing, construction, manufacturing, and domestic service. Cambodia was a refugee sending country in the 1970s and 1980s as a result of the brutality of the Khmer Rouge regime, its ousting by the Vietnamese invasion, and the resultant civil war. Tens of thousands of Cambodians fled to Thailand; more than 100,000 were resettled in the US in the 1980s. Cambodia signed a multi-million dollar agreement with Australia in 2014 to voluntarily resettle refugees seeking shelter in Australia. However, the deal has proven to be a failure because of poor conditions and a lack of support services for the few refugees willing to accept the offer.

Age structure: *0-14 years:* 28.9% (male 2,497,056/female 2,436,618)
15-64 years: 65.8% (male 5,456,941/female 5,765,206)
65 years and over: 5.3% (2024 est.) (male 323,591/female 584,257)

Dependency ratios: *total dependency ratio:* 53.4
youth dependency ratio: 45
elderly dependency ratio: 8.5
potential support ratio: 11.8 (2021 est.)

Median age: *total:* 27.9 years (2024 est.)
male: 26.9 years
female: 28.9 years
comparison ranking: total 154

Population growth rate: 0.99% (2024 est.)
comparison ranking: 93

Birth rate: 18.2 births/1,000 population (2024 est.)
comparison ranking: 77

Death rate: 5.7 deaths/1,000 population (2024 est.)
comparison ranking: 173

Net migration rate: -2.6 migrant(s)/1,000 population (2024 est.)
comparison ranking: 173

Population distribution: population concentrated in the southeast, particularly in and around the capital of Phnom Penh; further distribution is linked closely to the Tonle Sap and Mekong Rivers

Urbanization: *urban population:* 25.6% of total population (2023)
rate of urbanization: 3.06% annual rate of change (2020-25 est.)

Major urban areas - population: 2.281 million PHNOM PENH (capital) (2023)

Sex ratio: *at birth:* 1.04 male(s)/female
0-14 years: 1.02 male(s)/female
15-64 years: 0.95 male(s)/female
65 years and over: 0.55 male(s)/female
total population: 0.94 male(s)/female (2024 est.)

Mother's mean age at first birth: 23.3 years (2021-22 est.)
note: data represents median age at first birth among women 25-49

Maternal mortality ratio: 218 deaths/100,000 live births (2020 est.)
comparison ranking: 42

Infant mortality rate: *total:* 27.9 deaths/1,000 live births (2024 est.)
male: 31.3 deaths/1,000 live births
female: 24.4 deaths/1,000 live births
comparison ranking: total 54

Life expectancy at birth: *total population:* 71.4 years (2024 est.)
male: 69.6 years
female: 73.3 years
comparison ranking: total population 169

Total fertility rate: 2.17 children born/woman (2024 est.)
comparison ranking: 88

Gross reproduction rate: 1.06 (2024 est.)

Contraceptive prevalence rate: 56.3% (2014)

Drinking water source: *improved: urban:* 99.3% of population
rural: 80.6% of population
total: 85.1% of population
unimproved: urban: 0.7% of population
rural: 19.4% of population
total: 14.9% of population (2020 est.)

Current health expenditure: 7.5% of GDP (2020)

Physician density: 0.19 physicians/1,000 population (2014)

Hospital bed density: 1.9 beds/1,000 population (2016)

Sanitation facility access: *improved: urban:* 100% of population
rural: 69.3% of population
total: 76.8% of population
unimproved: urban: 0% of population
rural: 30.7% of population
total: 23.2% of population (2020 est.)

Obesity - adult prevalence rate: 3.9% (2016)
comparison ranking: 188

Alcohol consumption per capita: *total:* 4.56 liters of pure alcohol (2019 est.)
beer: 4.12 liters of pure alcohol (2019 est.)
wine: 0.03 liters of pure alcohol (2019 est.)
spirits: 0.41 liters of pure alcohol (2019 est.)
other alcohols: 0 liters of pure alcohol (2019 est.)
comparison ranking: total 87

Tobacco use: *total:* 21.1% (2020 est.)
male: 36.1% (2020 est.)
female: 6% (2020 est.)
comparison ranking: total 79

Children under the age of 5 years underweight: 16.3% (2022)
comparison ranking: 29

Currently married women (ages 15-49): 66.4% (2023 est.)

Education expenditures: 3.1% of GDP (2020 est.)
comparison ranking: 155

Literacy: *definition:* age 15 and over can read and write
total population: 83.9%
male: 88.4%
female: 79.8% (2021)

ENVIRONMENT

Environment - current issues: illegal logging activities throughout the country and strip mining for gems in the western region along the border with Thailand have resulted in habitat loss and declining biodiversity (in particular, destruction of mangrove swamps threatens natural fisheries); soil erosion; in rural areas, most of the population does not have access to potable water; declining fish stocks because of illegal fishing and overfishing; coastal ecosystems choked by sediment washed loose from deforested areas inland

Environment - international agreements: *party to:* Biodiversity, Climate Change, Climate Change-Kyoto Protocol, Climate Change-Paris Agreement, Comprehensive Nuclear Test Ban, Desertification, Endangered Species, Hazardous Wastes, Marine Life Conservation, Ozone Layer Protection, Ship Pollution, Tropical Timber 2006, Wetlands, Whaling
signed, but not ratified: Law of the Sea

Climate: tropical; rainy, monsoon season (May to November); dry season (December to April); little seasonal temperature variation

Urbanization: *urban population:* 25.6% of total population (2023)
rate of urbanization: 3.06% annual rate of change (2020-25 est.)

Revenue from forest resources: 0.84% of GDP (2018 est.)
comparison ranking: 57

Revenue from coal: 0% of GDP (2018 est.)
comparison ranking: 87

Air pollutants: *particulate matter emissions:* 17.8 micrograms per cubic meter (2019 est.)
carbon dioxide emissions: 9.92 megatons (2016 est.)
methane emissions: 14.88 megatons (2020 est.)

Waste and recycling: *municipal solid waste generated annually:* 1.089 million tons (2014 est.)

Major lakes (area sq km): *fresh water lake(s):* Tonle Sap - 2,700-16,000 sq km

Major rivers (by length in km): Mekong (shared with China [s], Burma, Thailand, Laos, and Vietnam [m]) - 4,350 km
note – [s] after country name indicates river source; [m] after country name indicates river mouth

Major watersheds (area sq km): Pacific Ocean drainage: Mekong (805,604 sq km)

Total water withdrawal: *municipal:* 100 million cubic meters (2020 est.)
industrial: 30 million cubic meters (2020 est.)
agricultural: 2.05 billion cubic meters (2020 est.)

Total renewable water resources: 476.1 billion cubic meters (2020 est.)

GOVERNMENT

Country name: *conventional long form:* Kingdom of Cambodia
conventional short form: Cambodia
local long form: Preahreacheanachakr Kampuchea (phonetic transliteration)
local short form: Kampuchea
former: Khmer Republic, Democratic Kampuchea, People's Republic of Kampuchea, State of Cambodia
etymology: the English name Cambodia is an anglicization of the French Cambodge, which is the French transliteration of the native name Kampuchea

Government type: parliamentary constitutional monarchy

Capital: *name:* Phnom Penh
geographic coordinates: 11 33 N, 104 55 E
time difference: UTC+7 (12 hours ahead of Washington, DC, during Standard Time)
etymology: Phnom Penh translates as "Penh's Hill" in Khmer; the city takes its name from the present Wat Phnom (Hill Temple), the tallest religious structure in the city, whose establishment, according to legend, was inspired in the 14th century by a pious nun, Daun PENH

Administrative divisions: 24 provinces (khett, singular and plural) and 1 municipality (krong, singular and plural)
provinces: Banteay Meanchey, Battambang, Kampong Cham, Kampong Chhnang, Kampong Speu, Kampong Thom, Kampot, Kandal, Kep, Koh

Kong, Kratie, Mondolkiri, Oddar Meanchey, Pailin, Preah Sihanouk, Preah Vihear, Prey Veng, Pursat, Ratanakiri, Siem Reap, Stung Treng, Svay Rieng, Takeo, Tbong Khmum
municipalities: Phnom Penh (Phnum Penh)

Independence: 9 November 1953 (from France)

National holiday: Independence Day, 9 November (1953)

Legal system: civil law system (influenced by the UN Transitional Authority in Cambodia) customary law, Communist legal theory, and common law

Constitution: *history:* previous 1947; latest promulgated 21 September 1993
amendments: proposed by the monarch, by the prime minister, or by the president of the National Assembly if supported by one fourth of the Assembly membership; passage requires two-thirds majority of the Assembly membership; constitutional articles on the multiparty democratic form of government and the monarchy cannot be amended; amended several times, latest 2022

International law organization participation: accepts compulsory ICJ jurisdiction with reservations; accepts ICCt jurisdiction

Citizenship: *citizenship by birth:* no
citizenship by descent only: at least one parent must be a citizen of Cambodia
dual citizenship recognized: yes
residency requirement for naturalization: 7 years

Suffrage: 18 years of age; universal

Executive branch: *chief of state:* King Norodom SIHAMONI (since 29 October 2004)
head of government: Prime Minister HUN MANET (since 22 August 2023)
cabinet: Council of Ministers named by the prime minister and appointed by the monarch
elections/appointments: monarch chosen by the 9-member Royal Council of the Throne from among all eligible males of royal descent; following legislative elections, a member of the majority party or majority coalition named prime minister by the Chairman of the National Assembly and appointed by the monarch
note: MANET succeeded his father, HUN SEN, who had been prime minister since 1985

Legislative branch: *description:* bicameral Parliament of Cambodia consists of:
Senate (62 seats; 58 indirectly elected by parliamentarians and commune councils, 2 indirectly elected by the National Assembly, and 2 appointed by the monarch; members serve 6-year terms)
National Assembly (125 seats; members directly elected in multi-seat constituencies by proportional representation vote; members serve 5-year terms)
elections: Senate - last held on 25 February 2024 (next to be held in February 2030)
National Assembly - last held on 23 July 2023 (next to be held in July 2028)
election results: Senate - percent of vote by party - CPP 86%, KWP 12%; seats by party - CPP 57; KWP 3; independent 2; composition - men 50, women 12, percentage women 19.4%
National Assembly - percent of vote by party - CPP 82.4%, FUNCINPEC 9.2%, KNUP 1.7%, CYP 1.3%, other 5.4% (14 other parties received votes); seats by party - CPP 120, FUNCINPEC 5; composition - men 108, women 17, percentage women 13.6%
note: the EU, UN, and US condemned the July 2023 National Assembly election as neither free nor fair

Judicial branch: *highest court(s):* Supreme Council (organized into 5- and 9-judge panels and includes a court chief and deputy chief); Constitutional Court (consists of 9 members); note - in 1997, the Cambodian Government requested UN assistance in establishing trials to prosecute former Khmer Rouge senior leaders for crimes against humanity committed during the 1975-1979 Khmer Rouge regime; the Extraordinary Chambers of the Courts of Cambodia (also called the Khmer Rouge Tribunal) was established in 2006 and began hearings for the first case in 2009; court proceedings remain ongoing in 2021
judge selection and term of office: Supreme Court and Constitutional Council judge candidates recommended by the Supreme Council of Magistracy, a 17-member body chaired by the monarch and includes other high-level judicial officers; judges of both courts appointed by the monarch; Supreme Court judges appointed for life; Constitutional Council judges appointed for 9-year terms with one-third of the court renewed every 3 years
subordinate courts: Appellate Court; provincial and municipal courts; Military Court

Political parties: Candlelight Party or CP
Cambodian People's Party or CPP
Khmer Will Party or KWP
note 1: 18 parties registered to run in the 2023 parliamentary election
note 2: the Cambodian Government disqualified the Candlelight Party, the main opposition party, from the July 2023 election

International organization participation: ADB, ARF, ASEAN, CICA, EAS, FAO, G-77, IAEA, IBRD, ICAO, ICRM, IDA, IFAD, IFC, IFRCS, ILO, IMF, IMO, Interpol, IOC, IOM, IPU, ISO (correspondent), ITU, MIGA, NAM, OIF, OPCW, PCA, UN, UNAMID, UNCTAD, UNESCO, UNIDO, UNIFIL, UNISFA, UNMISS, UNWTO, UPU, WCO, WFTU (NGOs), WHO, WIPO, WMO, WTO

Diplomatic representation in the US: *chief of mission:* Ambassador KEO Chhea (since 19 April 2022)
chancery: 4530 16th Street NW, Washington, DC 20011
telephone: [1] (202) 726-7742
FAX: [1] (202) 726-8381
email address and website:
camemb.usa@mfaic.gov.kh
https://www.embassyofcambodiadc.org/

Diplomatic representation from the US: *chief of mission:* Ambassador (vacant); Chargé d'Affaires Bridgette L. WALKER (since August 2024)
embassy: #1, Street 96, Sangkat Wat Phnom, Khan Daun Penh, Phnom Penh
mailing address: 4540 Phnom Penh Place, Washington DC 20521-4540
telephone: [855] (23) 728-000
FAX: [855] (23) 728-700
email address and website:
ACSPhnomPenh@state.gov
https://kh.usembassy.gov/

Flag description: three horizontal bands of blue (top), red (double width), and blue with a white, three-towered temple, representing Angkor Wat, outlined in black in the center of the red band; red and blue are traditional Cambodian colors
note: only national flag to prominently incorporate an actual identifiable building into its design (a few other national flags - those of Afghanistan, San Marino, Portugal, and Spain - show small generic buildings as part of their coats of arms on the flag)

National symbol(s): Angkor Wat temple, kouprey (wild ox); national colors: red, blue

National anthem: *name:* "Nokoreach" (Royal Kingdom)
lyrics/music: CHUON NAT/F. PERRUCHOT and J. JEKYLL
note: adopted 1941, restored 1993; the anthem, based on a Cambodian folk tune, was restored after the defeat of the Communist regime

National heritage: *total World Heritage Sites:* 4 (all cultural)
selected World Heritage Site locales: Angkor; Temple of Preah Vihear; Sambor Prei Kuk; Koh Ker: Archaeological Site of Ancient Lingapora or Chok Gargyar

ECONOMY

Economic overview: one of the fastest growing economies; tourism and clothing exports; substantial manufacturing and construction sectors; COVID-19 declines and the suspension of EU market preferential access; massive reductions in poverty, but rural areas remain disproportionately poor

Real GDP (purchasing power parity): $85.9 billion (2023 est.)
$81.499 billion (2022 est.)
$77.442 billion (2021 est.)
note: data in 2021 dollars
comparison ranking: 100

Real GDP growth rate: 5.4% (2023 est.)
5.24% (2022 est.)
3.03% (2021 est.)
note: annual GDP % growth based on constant local currency
comparison ranking: 40

Real GDP per capita: $5,100 (2023 est.)
$4,900 (2022 est.)
$4,700 (2021 est.)
note: data in 2021 dollars
comparison ranking: 178

GDP (official exchange rate): $31.773 billion (2023 est.)
note: data in current dollars at official exchange rate

Inflation rate (consumer prices): 2.13% (2023 est.)
5.34% (2022 est.)
2.92% (2021 est.)
note: annual % change based on consumer prices
comparison ranking: 41

Credit ratings: Moody's rating: B2 (2007)

Standard & Poors rating: N/A (2014)
note: The year refers to the year in which the current credit rating was first obtained.

GDP - composition, by sector of origin: *agriculture:* 21.5% (2023 est.)
industry: 38.5% (2023 est.)
services: 33.4% (2023 est.)
note: figures may not total 100% due to non-allocated consumption not captured in sector-reported data
comparison rankings: services 207; industry 32; agriculture 32

GDP - composition, by end use: *household consumption:* 41.8% (2023 est.)
government consumption: 8.1% (2023 est.)
investment in fixed capital: 15.3% (2023 est.)
investment in inventories: 0.7% (2023 est.)
exports of goods and services: 73.1% (2023 est.)

imports of goods and services: -40.4% (2023 est.)
note: figures may not total 100% due to rounding or gaps in data collection

Agricultural products: cassava, rice, maize, sugarcane, vegetables, oil palm fruit, rubber, bananas, jute, pork (2022)
note: top ten agricultural products based on tonnage

Industries: tourism, garments, construction, rice milling, fishing, wood and wood products, rubber, cement, gem mining, textiles

Industrial production growth rate: 4.3% (2023 est.)
note: annual % change in industrial value added based on constant local currency
comparison ranking: 57

Labor force: 9.175 million (2023 est.)
note: number of people ages 15 or older who are employed or seeking work
comparison ranking: 58

Unemployment rate: 0.24% (2023 est.)
0.25% (2022 est.)
0.4% (2021 est.)
note: % of labor force seeking employment
comparison ranking: 2

Youth unemployment rate (ages 15-24): *total:* 0.8% (2023 est.)
male: 0.7% (2023 est.)
female: 0.9% (2023 est.)
note: % of labor force ages 15-24 seeking employment
comparison ranking: total 200

Population below poverty line: 16.5% (2016 est.)

Average household expenditures: *on food:* 41.4% of household expenditures (2022 est.)
on alcohol and tobacco: 1.9% of household expenditures (2022 est.)

Remittances: 8.81% of GDP (2023 est.)
8.87% of GDP (2022 est.)
9.42% of GDP (2021 est.)
note: personal transfers and compensation between resident and non-resident individuals/households/entities

Budget: *revenues:* $5.9 billion (2020 est.)
expenditures: $4.666 billion (2020 est.)
note: central government revenues (excluding grants) and expenses converted to US dollars at average official exchange rate for year indicated

Public debt: 30.4% of GDP (2017 est.)
comparison ranking: 168

Taxes and other revenues: 16.36% (of GDP) (2021 est.)
note: central government tax revenue as a % of GDP
comparison ranking: 124

Current account balance: $552.607 million (2023 est.)
-$7.582 billion (2022 est.)
-$10.893 billion (2021 est.)
note: balance of payments - net trade and primary/secondary income in current dollars
comparison ranking: 64

Exports: $27.753 billion (2023 est.)
$25.497 billion (2022 est.)
$20.178 billion (2021 est.)
note: balance of payments - exports of goods and services in current dollars
comparison ranking: 82

Exports - partners: US 36%, Vietnam 10%, Germany 7%, Japan 5%, Canada 5% (2022)
note: top five export partners based on percentage share of exports

Exports - commodities: garments, trunks and cases, footwear, cassava, shoes (2022)
note: top five export commodities based on value in dollars

Imports: $29.42 billion (2023 est.)
$34.759 billion (2022 est.)
$32.816 billion (2021 est.)
note: balance of payments - imports of goods and services in current dollars
comparison ranking: 81

Imports - partners: China 30%, Thailand 19%, Singapore 18%, Vietnam 13%, Switzerland 3% (2022)
note: top five import partners based on percentage share of imports

Imports - commodities: gold, refined petroleum, fabric, plastic products, vehicle parts/accessories (2022)
note: top five import commodities based on value in dollars

Reserves of foreign exchange and gold: $17.801 billion (2022 est.)
$20.27 billion (2021 est.)
$21.328 billion (2020 est.)
note: holdings of gold (year-end prices)/foreign exchange/special drawing rights in current dollars
comparison ranking: 64

Exchange rates: riels (KHR) per US dollar –

Exchange rates: 4,110.653 (2023 est.)
4,102.038 (2022 est.)
4,098.723 (2021 est.)
4,092.783 (2020 est.)
4,061.149 (2019 est.)

ENERGY

Electricity access: *electrification - total population:* 92.3% (2022 est.)
electrification - urban areas: 99%
electrification - rural areas: 88%

Electricity: *installed generating capacity:* 3.204 million kW (2022 est.)
consumption: 11.001 billion kWh (2022 est.)
imports: 3.566 billion kWh (2022 est.)
transmission/distribution losses: 1.38 billion kWh (2022 est.)
comparison rankings: transmission/distribution losses 114; imports 52; consumption 99; installed generating capacity 106

Electricity generation sources: *fossil fuels:* 49.2% of total installed capacity (2022 est.)
solar: 4.5% of total installed capacity (2022 est.)
hydroelectricity: 45.4% of total installed capacity (2022 est.)
biomass and waste: 1% of total installed capacity (2022 est.)

Coal: *production:* 113,000 metric tons (2022 est.)
consumption: 2.215 million metric tons (2022 est.)
imports: 2.265 million metric tons (2022 est.)

Petroleum: *refined petroleum consumption:* 73,000 bbl/day (2022 est.)

Carbon dioxide emissions: 14.396 million metric tonnes of CO2 (2022 est.)
from coal and metallurgical coke: 4.063 million metric tonnes of CO2 (2022 est.)
from petroleum and other liquids: 10.333 million metric tonnes of CO2 (2022 est.)
comparison ranking: total emissions 96

Energy consumption per capita: 12.831 million Btu/person (2022 est.)
comparison ranking: 145

COMMUNICATIONS

Telephones - fixed lines: *total subscriptions:* 38,000 (2022 est.)
subscriptions per 100 inhabitants: (2022 est.) less than 1
comparison ranking: total subscriptions 162

Telephones - mobile cellular: *total subscriptions:* 19.505 million (2022 est.)
subscriptions per 100 inhabitants: 116 (2022 est.)
comparison ranking: total subscriptions 65

Telecommunication systems: general assessment: Cambodia's mobile-dominated telecoms sector spent much of 2020 battling two major challenges: the global pandemic, and the government's retraction of trial licenses for the rollout of 5G; citing concerns about waste and inefficiency occurring if each operator built a separate 5G infrastructure in order to maximize their own network's coverage (and, presumably, to capture greater market share), the regulator withdrew the licenses that the operators had been using for their 5G trials; this was despite all of the operators having already announced a successful completion of their trials; more than a year later, the market is still waiting on the government to release its 5G policy and roadmap, along with the allocation of spectrum and approvals to permit commercial operation; there is little expectation of any further progress happening before the start of 2022; the mobile network operators have maintained their focus and investment strategies on upgrading and expanding their existing LTE networks around the country, and to 5G-enable their base stations; when the 5G market eventually arrives, the underlying infrastructure will at least be ready to support a rapid adoption of the higher-value applications and services; the mobile market fell back slightly during 2020 and 2021 (in terms of total subscriber numbers) as the Covid-19 crisis wore on, but it remains in relatively good health as mobile users increased their data usage over the period; the mobile broadband market experienced a small but very rare contraction in 2020, although rates were already very high in this area; there is likely to be a quick rebound to previous levels once economic conditions stabilize, followed by a modest rates of growth over the next five years; the number of fixed telephony lines in service continues to fall sharply as customers migrate to mobile platforms for both voice and data; the lack of any widespread fixed-line infrastructure has had a flow-on effect in the fixed-line broadband market, a sector that also remains largely under-developed (2021)
domestic: fixed-line connections stand at less than 1 per 100 persons; mobile-cellular usage, aided by competition among service providers, is about 120 per 100 persons (2021)
international: country code - 855; landing points for MCT and AAE-1 via submarine cables providing communication to Asia, the Middle East, Europe and Africa; satellite earth station - 1 Intersputnik (Indian Ocean region) (2019)

Broadcast media: mixture of state-owned, joint public-private, and privately owned broadcast media; 27 TV broadcast stations with most operating on multiple channels, including 1 state-operated station broadcasting from multiple locations, 11 stations either jointly operated or privately owned with some broadcasting from several locations; multi-channel cable and satellite systems are available (2019); 84 radio broadcast stations - 1 state-owned broadcaster with multiple stations and a large mixture of public and private broadcasters; one international broadcaster is available (2019) as well as one Chinese joint venture television station with the Ministry of Interior; several television and radio operators broadcast online only (often via Facebook) (2019)

Internet country code: .kh

Internet users: *total:* 10.2 million (2021 est.)
percent of population: 60% (2021 est.)
comparison ranking: total 58

Broadband - fixed subscriptions: *total:* 233,732 (2020 est.) Slowly increase as focus is on mobile internet
subscriptions per 100 inhabitants: 1 (2020 est.)
comparison ranking: total 114

TRANSPORTATION

National air transport system: *number of registered air carriers:* 6 (2020)
inventory of registered aircraft operated by air carriers: 25
annual passenger traffic on registered air carriers: 1,411,059 (2018)
annual freight traffic on registered air carriers: 680,000 (2018) mt-km

Civil aircraft registration country code prefix: XU

Airports: 13 (2024)
comparison ranking: 150

Heliports: 1 (2024)

Railways: *total:* 642 km (2014)
narrow gauge: 642 km (2014) 1.000-m gauge
note: under restoration
comparison ranking: total 106

Roadways: *total:* 61,810 km
paved: 15,000 km
unpaved: 46,810 km (2021)
comparison ranking: total 77

Waterways: 3,700 km (2012) (mainly on Mekong River)
comparison ranking: 30

Merchant marine: *total:* 195 (2023)
by type: container ship 2, general cargo 123, oil tanker 18, other 52
comparison ranking: total 69

Ports: *total ports:* 2 (2024)
large: 0
medium: 1
small: 0
very small: 1
ports with oil terminals: 1
key ports: Kampong Saom, Phsar Ream

MILITARY AND SECURITY

Military and security forces: Royal Cambodian Armed Forces (RCAF): Royal Cambodian Army, Royal Khmer Navy, Royal Cambodian Air Force, Royal Gendarmerie; the National Committee for Maritime Security (2024)
note 1: the National Committe for Maritime Security performs coast guard functions and has representation from military and civilian agencies
note 2: the Cambodian National Police are under the Ministry of Interior

Military expenditures: 2.1% of GDP (2022 est.)
2.3% of GDP (2021 est.)
2.3% of GDP (2020 est.)
2.2% of GDP (2019 est.)
2.2% of GDP (2018 est.)
comparison ranking: 61

Military and security service personnel strengths: information varies; approximately 100,000 total active troops including less than 5,000 Navy and Air Force personnel; approximately 10,000 Gendarmerie (2023)

Military equipment inventories and acquisitions: the RCAF is armed largely with older Chinese and Russian-origin equipment; in recent years it has received limited amounts of more modern equipment from several suppliers, particularly China (2024)
note: in December 2021, the US Government halted arms-related trade with Cambodia, citing deepening Chinese military influence, corruption, and human rights abuses by the government and armed forces; the policy of denial applied to licenses or other approvals for exports and imports of defense articles and defense services destined for or originating in Cambodia, with exceptions (on a case-by-case basis) related to conventional weapons destruction and humanitarian demining activities

Military service age and obligation: 18 is the legal minimum age for compulsory and voluntary military service (conscription only selectively enforced since 1993; service is for 18 months); women may volunteer (2024)

Military deployments: 340 Central African Republic (MINUSCA); 180 Lebanon (UNIFIL) (2024)

Military - note: the RCAF's primary responsibilities are border, coastal, and internal security; since 2016, the RCAF has regularly conducted a small annual training exercise known as "Golden Dragon" with the military of China, its closest security partner
the RCAF was re-established in 1993 under the first coalition government from the merger of the Cambodian Government's military forces (Cambodian People's Armed Forces) and the two non-communist resistance forces (Sihanoukist National Army, aka National Army for Khmer Independence, and the Khmer People's National Liberation Armed Forces); thousands of communist Khmer Rouge fighters began surrendering by 1994 under a government amnesty program and the last of the Khmer Rouge forces (National Army of Democratic Kampuchea) were demobilized or absorbed into the RCAF in 1999
Cambodia continues to be one of the most densely landmine-contaminated countries in the world; by the early 1990s, various aid organizations estimated there were 8-10 million landmines scattered throughout the country, with a particularly heavy concentration on a 1,000-km (620-mile) strip along the northwest Thai-Cambodia border known as the "K5 belt"; the mines were laid during Cambodia's decades-long war by the Cambodian army, the Vietnamese, the Khmer Rouge, the non-communist fighters, and US forces; part of Cambodia's defense policy is demining the territory with the intent of having the entire country cleared of unexploded ordnances by 2035; over 1 million landmines and over 3 million explosives were discovered and removed from 1992 to 2018; in 2018, the Cambodian government and Cambodian Mine Action and Victim Assistance Authority (CMAA), a government agency, launched the National Mine Action Strategy for 2018-2025 (2024)

TRANSNATIONAL ISSUES

Refugees and internally displaced persons: *stateless persons:* 75,000 (2022)

Trafficking in persons: tier rating: Tier 3 — Cambodia does not fully meet the minimum standards for the elimination of trafficking and is not making significant efforts to do so, therefore, Cambodia remained on Tier 3; for more details, go to: https://www.state.gov/reports/2024-trafficking-in-persons-report/cambodia/

Illicit drugs: a significant transshipment country for Burma-sourced methamphetamine and heroin and a location for large-scale ketamine production; transnational criminal organizations (TCO's) use Cambodia as both a transit and destination for illicit drugs; precursor chemicals from mainly China used at domestic clandestine laboratories operated by TCOs for the manufacturing of methamphetamine, ketamine, and other synthetic drugs
(2021)

CAMEROON

INTRODUCTION

Background: Powerful chiefdoms ruled much of the area of present-day Cameroon before it became a German colony known as Kamerun in 1884. After World War I, the territory was divided between France and the UK as League of Nations mandates. French Cameroon became independent in 1960 as the Republic of Cameroon. The following year, the southern portion of neighboring British Cameroon voted to merge with the new country to form the Federal Republic of Cameroon. In 1972, a new constitution replaced the federation with a unitary state, the United Republic of Cameroon. The country has generally enjoyed stability, which has enabled the development of agriculture, roads, and railways, as well as a petroleum industry. Nonetheless, unrest and violence in the country's two western, English-speaking regions have persisted since 2016. Movement toward democratic reform is slow, and political power remains firmly in the hands of President Paul BIYA.

GEOGRAPHY

Location: Central Africa, bordering the Bight of Biafra, between Equatorial Guinea and Nigeria

Geographic coordinates: 6 00 N, 12 00 E

Map references: Africa

Area: *total:* 475,440 sq km
land: 472,710 sq km
water: 2,730 sq km
comparison ranking: total 56

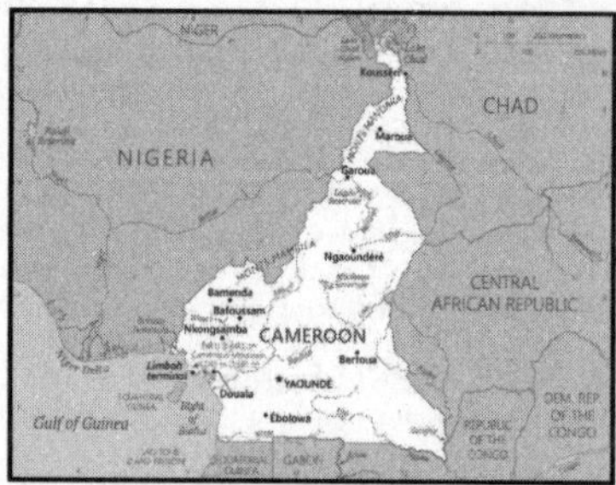

Area - comparative: slightly larger than California; about four times the size of Pennsylvania

Land boundaries: *total:* 5,018 km
border countries (6): Central African Republic 901 km; Chad 1,116 km; Republic of the Congo 494 km; Equatorial Guinea 183 km; Gabon 349 km; Nigeria 1975 km

Coastline: 402 km

Maritime claims: *territorial sea:* 12 nm
contiguous zone: 24 nm

Climate: varies with terrain, from tropical along coast to semiarid and hot in north

Terrain: diverse, with coastal plain in southwest, dissected plateau in center, mountains in west, plains in north

Elevation: *highest point:* Fako on Mont Cameroun 4,045 m
lowest point: Atlantic Ocean 0 m
mean elevation: 667 m

Natural resources: petroleum, bauxite, iron ore, timber, hydropower

Land use: *agricultural land:* 20.6% (2018 est.)
arable land: 13.1% (2018 est.)
permanent crops: 3.3% (2018 est.)
permanent pasture: 4.2% (2018 est.)
forest: 41.7% (2018 est.)
other: 37.7% (2018 est.)

Irrigated land: 290 sq km (2012)

Major lakes (area sq km): *fresh water lake(s):* Lake Chad (endorheic lake shared with Niger, Nigeria, and Chad) - 10,360-25,900 sq km
note - area varies by season and year to year

Major watersheds (area sq km): Atlantic Ocean drainage: Congo (3,730,881 sq km), Niger (2,261,741 sq km)

Internal (endorheic basin) drainage: Lake Chad (2,497,738 sq km)

Major aquifers: Lake Chad Basin

Population distribution: population concentrated in the west and north, with the interior of the country sparsely populated as shown in this population distribution map

Natural hazards: volcanic activity with periodic releases of poisonous gases from Lake Nyos and Lake Monoun volcanoes
volcanism: Mt. Cameroon (4,095 m), which last erupted in 2000, is the most frequently active volcano in West Africa; lakes in Oku volcanic field have released fatal levels of gas on occasion, killing some 1,700 people in 1986

Geography - note: sometimes referred to as the hinge of Africa because of its central location on the continent and its position at the westsouth juncture of the Gulf of Guinea; throughout the country there are areas of thermal springs and indications of current or prior volcanic activity; Mount Cameroon, the highest mountain in Sub-Saharan west Africa, is an active volcano

PEOPLE AND SOCIETY

Population: *total:* 30,966,105
male: 15,429,588
female: 15,536,517 (2024 est.)
comparison rankings: female 51; male 50; total 51

Nationality: *noun:* Cameroonian(s)
adjective: Cameroonian

Ethnic groups: Bamileke-Bamu 22.2%, Biu-Mandara 16.4%, Arab-Choa/Hausa/Kanuri 13.5%, Beti/Bassa, Mbam 13.1%, Grassfields 9.9%, Adamawa-Ubangi, 9.8%, Cotier/Ngoe/Oroko 4.6%, Southwestern Bantu 4.3%, Kako/Meka 2.3%, foreign/other ethnic group 3.8% (2022 est.)

Languages: 24 major African language groups, English (official), French (official)
major-language sample(s):
The World Factbook, une source indispensable d'informations de base. (French)

Religions: Roman Catholic 33.1%, Muslim 30.6%, Protestant 27.1% other Christian 6.1%, animist 1.3%, other 0.7%, none 1.2% (2022 est.)

Demographic profile: Cameroon has a large youth population, with more than 60% of the populace under the age of 25 as of 2020. Fertility is falling but remains at a high level, especially among poor, rural, and uneducated women, in part because of inadequate access to contraception. Life expectancy remains low at about 55 years due to the prevalence of HIV and AIDs and an elevated maternal mortality rate, which has remained high since 1990. Cameroon, particularly the northern region, is vulnerable to food insecurity largely because of government mismanagement, corruption, high production costs, inadequate infrastructure, and natural disasters. Despite economic growth in some regions, poverty is on the rise, and is most prevalent in rural areas, which are especially affected by a shortage of jobs, declining incomes, poor school and health care infrastructure, and a lack of clean water and sanitation. Underinvestment in social safety nets and ineffective public financial management also contribute to Cameroon's high rate of poverty. The activities of Boko Haram, other armed groups, and counterinsurgency operations have worsened food insecurity in the Far North region.
International migration has been driven by unemployment (including fewer government jobs), poverty, the search for educational opportunities, and corruption. The US and Europe are preferred destinations, but, with tighter immigration restrictions in these countries, young Cameroonians are increasingly turning to neighboring states, such as Gabon and Nigeria, South Africa, other parts of Africa, and the Near and Far East. Cameroon's limited resources make it dependent on UN support to host more than 480,000 refugees and asylum seekers as of December 2022. These refugees and asylum seekers are primarily from the Central African Republic and Nigeria. Internal and external displacement have grown dramatically in recent years. Boko Haram's attacks and counterattacks by government forces in the Far North since 2014 have increased the number of internally displaced people. Armed conflict between separatists and Cameroon's military in the Northwest and Southwest since 2016 have displaced hundreds of thousands of the country's Anglophone minority.

Age structure: *0-14 years:* 41.5% (male 6,477,438/ female 6,364,987)
15-64 years: 55.3% (male 8,488,522/female 8,638,519)
65 years and over: 3.2% (2024 est.) (male 463,628/ female 533,011)

Dependency ratios: *total dependency ratio:* 82.3
youth dependency ratio: 77.3
elderly dependency ratio: 4.9
potential support ratio: 20.3 (2021 est.)

Median age: *total:* 18.9 years (2024 est.)
male: 18.6 years
female: 19.2 years
comparison ranking: total 216

Population growth rate: 2.71% (2024 est.)
comparison ranking: 14

Birth rate: 34.7 births/1,000 population (2024 est.)
comparison ranking: 13

Death rate: 7.4 deaths/1,000 population (2024 est.)
comparison ranking: 102

Net migration rate: -0.3 migrant(s)/1,000 population (2024 est.)
comparison ranking: 114

Population distribution: population concentrated in the west and north, with the interior of the country sparsely populated as shown in this population distribution map

Urbanization: *urban population:* 59.3% of total population (2023)
rate of urbanization: 3.43% annual rate of change (2020-25 est.)

Major urban areas - population: 4.509 million YAOUNDE (capital), 4.063 million Douala (2023)

Sex ratio: *at birth:* 1.03 male(s)/female
0-14 years: 1.02 male(s)/female
15-64 years: 0.98 male(s)/female
65 years and over: 0.87 male(s)/female
total population: 0.99 male(s)/female (2024 est.)

Mother's mean age at first birth: 20.1 years (2018 est.)
note: data represents median age at first birth among women 25-49

Maternal mortality ratio: 438 deaths/100,000 live births (2020 est.)
comparison ranking: 21

Infant mortality rate: *total:* 46.1 deaths/1,000 live births (2024 est.)
male: 50.8 deaths/1,000 live births
female: 41.3 deaths/1,000 live births
comparison ranking: total 23

Life expectancy at birth: *total population:* 64.2 years (2024 est.)
male: 62.3 years
female: 66.1 years
comparison ranking: total population 209

Total fertility rate: 4.44 children born/woman (2024 est.)
comparison ranking: 16

Gross reproduction rate: 2.19 (2024 est.)

Contraceptive prevalence rate: 19.3% (2018)

Drinking water source: *improved: urban:* 95.1% of population
rural: 56.2% of population
total: 78.6% of population
unimproved: urban: 4.9% of population

rural: 43.8% of population
total: 21.4% of population (2020 est.)

Current health expenditure: 3.8% of GDP (2020)

Physician density: 0.13 physicians/1,000 population (2019)

Hospital bed density: 1.3 beds/1,000 population

Sanitation facility access: *improved: urban:* 83.2% of population
rural: 27.7% of population
total: 59.7% of population
unimproved: urban: 16.8% of population
rural: 72.3% of population
total: 40.3% of population (2020 est.)

Obesity - adult prevalence rate: 11.4% (2016)
comparison ranking: 135

Alcohol consumption per capita: *total:* 4.09 liters of pure alcohol (2019 est.)
beer: 2.36 liters of pure alcohol (2019 est.)
wine: 0.16 liters of pure alcohol (2019 est.)
spirits: 0.01 liters of pure alcohol (2019 est.)
other alcohols: 1.56 liters of pure alcohol (2019 est.)
comparison ranking: total 94

Tobacco use: *total:* 7.3% (2020 est.)
male: 13.2% (2020 est.)
female: 1.4% (2020 est.)
comparison ranking: total 155

Children under the age of 5 years underweight: 11% (2018/19)
comparison ranking: 53

Currently married women (ages 15-49): 54.2% (2023 est.)

Child marriage: *women married by age 15:* 10.7%
women married by age 18: 29.8%
men married by age 18: 2.9% (2018 est.)

Education expenditures: 3.2% of GDP (2020 est.)
comparison ranking: 152

Literacy: *definition:* age 15 and over can read and write
total population: 77.1%
male: 82.6%
female: 71.6% (2018)

School life expectancy (primary to tertiary education): *total:* 12 years
male: 13 years
female: 11 years (2016)

ENVIRONMENT

Environment - current issues: waterborne diseases are prevalent; deforestation and overgrazing result in erosion, desertification, and reduced quality of pastureland; poaching; overfishing; overhunting

Environment - international agreements: *party to:* Biodiversity, Climate Change, Climate Change-Kyoto Protocol, Climate Change-Paris Agreement, Comprehensive Nuclear Test Ban, Desertification, Endangered Species, Environmental Modification, Hazardous Wastes, Law of the Sea, Ozone Layer Protection, Ship Pollution, Tropical Timber 2006, Wetlands, Whaling
signed, but not ratified: Nuclear Test Ban

Climate: varies with terrain, from tropical along coast to semiarid and hot in north

Urbanization: *urban population:* 59.3% of total population (2023)
rate of urbanization: 3.43% annual rate of change (2020-25 est.)

Food insecurity: *severe localized food insecurity: due to civil insecurity, high food prices, and floods* - according to a November 2022 analysis (the latest available), about 3.6 million people were estimated to be acutely food insecure between October and December 2022, as a result of conflict, sociopolitical unrest and high food prices, as well as floods that caused people displacements, damaged standing crops and prevented access to fields (2023)

Revenue from forest resources: 2.5% of GDP (2018 est.)
comparison ranking: 27

Revenue from coal: 0% of GDP (2018 est.)
comparison ranking: 183

Air pollutants: *particulate matter emissions:* 56.37 micrograms per cubic meter (2019 est.)
carbon dioxide emissions: 8.29 megatons (2016 est.)
methane emissions: 30.71 megatons (2020 est.)

Waste and recycling: *municipal solid waste generated annually:* 3,270,617 tons (2013 est.)
municipal solid waste recycled annually: 13,082 tons (2009 est.)
percent of municipal solid waste recycled: 0.4% (2009 est.)

Major lakes (area sq km): *fresh water lake(s):* Lake Chad (endorheic lake shared with Niger, Nigeria, and Chad) - 10,360-25,900 sq km note - area varies by season and year to year

Major watersheds (area sq km): Atlantic Ocean drainage: Congo (3,730,881 sq km), Niger (2,261,741 sq km)

Internal (endorheic basin) drainage: Lake Chad (2,497,738 sq km)

Major aquifers: Lake Chad Basin

Total water withdrawal: *municipal:* 250 million cubic meters (2020 est.)
industrial: 100 million cubic meters (2020 est.)
agricultural: 740 million cubic meters (2020 est.)

Total renewable water resources: 283.15 billion cubic meters (2020 est.)

GOVERNMENT

Country name: *conventional long form:* Republic of Cameroon
conventional short form: Cameroon
local long form: République du Cameroun (French)/ Republic of Cameroon (English)
local short form: Cameroun/Cameroon
former: Kamerun, French Cameroon, British Cameroon, Federal Republic of Cameroon, United Republic of Cameroon
etymology: in the 15th century, Portuguese explorers named the area near the mouth of the Wouri River the Rio dos Camaroes (River of Prawns) after the abundant shrimp in the water; over time the designation became Cameroon in English; this is the only instance where a country is named after a crustacean

Government type: presidential republic

Capital: *name:* Yaounde
geographic coordinates: 3 52 N, 11 31 E
time difference: UTC+1 (6 hours ahead of Washington, DC, during Standard Time)
etymology: founded as a German colonial settlement of Jaunde in 1888 and named after the local Yaunde (Ewondo) people

Administrative divisions: 10 regions (regions, singular - region); Adamaoua, Centre, East (Est), Far North (Extreme-Nord), Littoral, North (Nord), North-West (Nord-Ouest), West (Ouest), South (Sud), South-West (Sud-Ouest)

Independence: 1 January 1960 (from French-administered UN trusteeship)

National holiday: State Unification Day (National Day), 20 May (1972)

Legal system: mixed legal system of English common law, French civil law, and customary law

Constitution: *history:* several previous; latest effective 18 January 1996
amendments: proposed by the president of the republic or by Parliament; amendment drafts require approval of at least one third of the membership in either house of Parliament; passage requires absolute majority vote of the Parliament membership; passage of drafts requested by the president for a second reading in Parliament requires two-thirds majority vote of its membership; the president can opt to submit drafts to a referendum, in which case passage requires a simple majority; constitutional articles on Cameroon's unity and territorial integrity and its democratic principles cannot be amended; amended 2008

International law organization participation: accepts compulsory ICJ jurisdiction; non-party state to the ICCt

Citizenship: *citizenship by birth:* no
citizenship by descent only: at least one parent must be a citizen of Cameroon
dual citizenship recognized: no
residency requirement for naturalization: 5 years

Suffrage: 20 years of age; universal

Executive branch: *chief of state:* President Paul BIYA (since 6 November 1982)
head of government: Prime Minister Joseph NGUTE (since 4 January 2019)
cabinet: Cabinet proposed by the prime minister, appointed by the president
elections/appointments: president directly elected by simple majority popular vote for a 7-year term (no term limits); election last held on 7 October 2018 (next to be held in October 2025); prime minister appointed by the president
election results:
2018: Paul BIYA reelected president; percent of vote - Paul BIYA (CPDM) 71.3%, Maurice KAMTO (MRC) 14.2%, Cabral LIBII (Univers) 6.3%, other 8.2%
2011: Paul BIYA reelected president; percent of vote - Paul BIYA (CPDM) 78.0%, John FRU NDI (SDF) 10.7%, Garga Haman ADJI 3.2%, other 8.1% (2018)

Legislative branch: *description:* bicameral Parliament or Parlement consists of:
Senate or Senat (100 seats; 70 members indirectly elected by regional councils and 30 appointed by the president; members serve 5-year terms)
National Assembly or Assemblee Nationale (180 seats; members directly elected in 49 single and multi-seat constituencies by simple majority vote to serve 5-year terms)
elections: Senate - last held on 12 March 2023 (next to be held in 2028)
National Assembly - last held on 9 February 2020 (next to be held 28 February 2025)
election results: Senate - percent of vote by party - CDPM 100%; seats by party - CDPM 100; composition - men 69, women 31, percentage women 31%
National Assembly - percent of vote by party - NA; seats by party - CPDM 152, UNDP 7, SDF 5, PCRN 5, UDC 4, FSNC 3, MDR 2, UMS 2; composition

- men 119, women 61, percentage women 33.9%; total Parliament percentage women 51.1%
note: 13 National Assembly seats were vacant after the 9 February 2020 election due to violence in northwest and southwest regions; CDPM won those seats in a 22 March 2020 election

Judicial branch: *highest court(s):* Supreme Court of Cameroon (consists of 9 titular and 6 surrogate judges and organized into judicial, administrative, and audit chambers); Constitutional Council (consists of 11 members)
judge selection and term of office: Supreme Court judges appointed by the president with the advice of the Higher Judicial Council of Cameroon, a body chaired by the president and includes the minister of justice, selected magistrates, and representatives of the National Assembly; judge term NA; Constitutional Council members appointed by the president for renewable 6-year terms
subordinate courts: Parliamentary Court of Justice (jurisdiction limited to cases involving the president and prime minister); appellate and first instance courts; circuit and magistrates' courts

Political parties: Alliance for Democracy and Development
Cameroon People's Democratic Movement or CPDM
Cameroon People's Party or CPP
Cameroon Renaissance Movement or MRC
Cameroonian Democratic Union or UDC
Cameroonian Party for National Reconciliation or PCRN
Front for the National Salvation of Cameroon or FSNC
Movement for the Defense of the Republic or MDR
Movement for the Liberation and Development of Cameroon or MLDC
National Union for Democracy and Progress or UNDP
Progressive Movement or MP
Social Democratic Front or SDF
Union of Peoples of Cameroon or UPC
Union of Socialist Movements

International organization participation: ACP, AfDB, AU, BDEAC, C, CEMAC, EITI (compliant country), FAO, FZ, G-77, IAEA, IBRD, ICAO, ICRM, IDA, IDB, IFAD, IFC, IFRCS, IHO, ILO, IMF, IMO, IMSO, Interpol, IOC, IOM, IPU, ISO, ITSO, ITU, ITUC (NGOs), LCBC, MIGA, MNJTF, MONUSCO, NAM, OIC, OIF, OPCW, PCA, UN, UNCTAD, UNESCO, UNHRC, UNIDO, UNMISS, UNWTO, UPU, WCO, WFTU (NGOs), WHO, WIPO, WMO, WTO

Diplomatic representation in the US: *chief of mission:* Ambassador Henri ETOUNDI ESSOMBA (since 27 June 2016)
chancery: 2349 Massachusetts Avenue NW, Washington, DC 20008
telephone: [1] (202) 265-8790
FAX: [1] (202) 387-3826
email address and website:
mail@cameroonembassyusa
Cameroon Embassy in Washington DC, USA (cameroonembassyusa.org)

Diplomatic representation from the US: *chief of mission:* Ambassador Christopher J. LAMORA (since 21 March 2022)
embassy: Avenue Rosa Parks, Yaoundé
mailing address: 2520 Yaounde Place, Washington, DC 20521-2520
telephone: [237] 22251-4000
FAX: [237] 22251-4000, Ext. 4531
email address and website:
YaoundeACS@state.gov
https://cm.usembassy.gov/
branch office(s): Douala

Flag description: three equal vertical bands of green (hoist side), red, and yellow, with a yellow five-pointed star centered in the red band; the vertical tricolor recalls the flag of France; red symbolizes unity, yellow the sun, happiness, and the savannahs in the north, and green hope and the forests in the south; the star is referred to as the "star of unity"
note: uses the popular Pan-African colors of Ethiopia

National symbol(s): lion; national colors: green, red, yellow

National anthem: *name:* "O Cameroun, Berceau de nos Ancetres" (O Cameroon, Cradle of Our Forefathers)
lyrics/music: Rene Djam AFAME, Samuel Minkio BAMBA, Moise Nyatte NKO'O [French], Benard Nsokika FONLON [English]/Rene Djam AFAME
note: adopted 1957; Cameroon's anthem, also known as "Chant de Ralliement" (The Rallying Song), has been used unofficially since 1948 and officially adopted in 1957; the anthem has French and English versions whose lyrics differ

National heritage: *total World Heritage Sites:* 2 (both natural)
selected World Heritage Site locales: Dja Faunal Reserve; Sangha Trinational Forest

ECONOMY

Economic overview: largest CEMAC economy with many natural resources; recent political instability and terrorism reducing economic output; systemic corruption; poor property rights enforcement; increasing poverty in northern regions

Real GDP (purchasing power parity): $138.925 billion (2023 est.)
$133.59 billion (2022 est.)
$128.969 billion (2021 est.)
note: data in 2021 dollars
comparison ranking: 85

Real GDP growth rate: 3.99% (2023 est.)
3.58% (2022 est.)
3.34% (2021 est.)
note: annual GDP % growth based on constant local currency
comparison ranking: 78

Real GDP per capita: $4,800 (2023 est.)
$4,800 (2022 est.)
$4,700 (2021 est.)
note: data in 2021 dollars
comparison ranking: 179

GDP (official exchange rate): $47.946 billion (2023 est.)
note: data in current dollars at official exchange rate

Inflation rate (consumer prices): 7.38% (2023 est.)
6.25% (2022 est.)
2.27% (2021 est.)
note: annual % change based on consumer prices
comparison ranking: 146

Credit ratings: Fitch rating: B (2006)

Moody's rating: B2 (2016)

Standard & Poors rating: B- (2020)
note: The year refers to the year in which the current credit rating was first obtained.

GDP - composition, by sector of origin: *agriculture:* 16.7% (2023 est.)
industry: 25.2% (2023 est.)
services: 51.6% (2023 est.)
note: figures may not total 100% due to non-allocated consumption not captured in sector-reported data comparison rankings: services 135; industry 94; agriculture 48

GDP - composition, by end use: *household consumption:* 73.3% (2023 est.)
government consumption: 11.3% (2023 est.)
investment in fixed capital: 17.5% (2023 est.)
investment in inventories: -0.1% (2023 est.)
exports of goods and services: 18.3% (2023 est.)
imports of goods and services: -20.3% (2023 est.)
note: figures may not total 100% due to rounding or gaps in data collection

Agricultural products: cassava, plantains, oil palm fruit, maize, taro, tomatoes, sorghum, sugarcane, bananas, vegetables (2022)
note: top ten agricultural products based on tonnage

Industries: petroleum production and refining, aluminum production, food processing, light consumer goods, textiles, lumber, ship repair

Industrial production growth rate: 3.8% (2023 est.)
note: annual % change in industrial value added based on constant local currency
comparison ranking: 84

Labor force: 11.965 million (2023 est.)
note: number of people ages 15 or older who are employed or seeking work
comparison ranking: 49

Unemployment rate: 3.65% (2023 est.)
3.69% (2022 est.)
3.95% (2021 est.)
note: % of labor force seeking employment
comparison ranking: 68

Youth unemployment rate (ages 15-24): *total:* 6.4% (2023 est.)
male: 6% (2023 est.)
female: 7% (2023 est.)
note: % of labor force ages 15-24 seeking employment
comparison ranking: total 164

Population below poverty line: 37.5% (2014 est.)
note: % of population with income below national poverty line

Gini Index coefficient - distribution of family income: 42.2 (2021 est.)
note: index (0-100) of income distribution; higher values represent greater inequality
comparison ranking: 34

Average household expenditures: *on food:* 45.2% of household expenditures (2022 est.)
on alcohol and tobacco: 2% of household expenditures (2022 est.)

Household income or consumption by percentage share: *lowest 10%:* 2.1% (2021 est.)
highest 10%: 31.1% (2021 est.)
note: % share of income accruing to lowest and highest 10% of population

Remittances: 0.78% of GDP (2023 est.)
1.29% of GDP (2022 est.)
0.96% of GDP (2021 est.)
note: personal transfers and compensation between resident and non-resident individuals/households/entities

Budget: *revenues:* $6.385 billion (2021 est.)
expenditures: $5.592 billion (2021 est.)
note: central government revenues and expenses (excluding grants/extrabudgetary units/social security

funds) converted to US dollars at average official exchange rate for year indicated

Public debt: 36.9% of GDP (2017 est.)
comparison ranking: 143

Taxes and other revenues: 11.35% (of GDP) (2021 est.)
note: central government tax revenue as a % of GDP
comparison ranking: 172

Current account balance: -$1.505 billion (2022 est.)
-$1.794 billion (2021 est.)
-$1.512 billion (2020 est.)
note: balance of payments - net trade and primary/secondary income in current dollars
comparison ranking: 150

Exports: $8.641 billion (2022 est.)
$7.447 billion (2021 est.)
$6.124 billion (2020 est.)
note: balance of payments - exports of goods and services in current dollars
comparison ranking: 122

Exports - partners: Netherlands 19%, France 15%, India 14%, Spain 10%, China 8% (2022)
note: top five export partners based on percentage share of exports

Exports - commodities: crude petroleum, natural gas, wood, cocoa beans, gold (2022)
note: top five export commodities based on value in dollars

Imports: $9.759 billion (2022 est.)
$9.025 billion (2021 est.)
$7.212 billion (2020 est.)
note: balance of payments - imports of goods and services in current dollars
comparison ranking: 126

Imports - partners: China 39%, France 8%, India 6%, Belgium 4%, UAE 4% (2022)
note: top five import partners based on percentage share of imports

Imports - commodities: refined petroleum, wheat, garments, rice, plastic products (2022)
note: top five import commodities based on value in dollars

Reserves of foreign exchange and gold: $5.133 billion (2022 est.)
$4.3 billion (2021 est.)
$3.962 billion (2020 est.)
note: holdings of gold (year-end prices)/foreign exchange/special drawing rights in current dollars
comparison ranking: 97

Debt - external: $9.612 billion (2022 est.)
note: present value of external debt in current US dollars
comparison ranking: 40

Exchange rates: Cooperation Financiere en Afrique Centrale francs (XAF) per US dollar -

Exchange rates: 606.57 (2023 est.)
623.76 (2022 est.)
554.531 (2021 est.)
575.586 (2020 est.)
585.911 (2019 est.)

ENERGY

Electricity access: *electrification - total population:* 71% (2022 est.)
electrification - urban areas: 94%
electrification - rural areas: 25%

Electricity: *installed generating capacity:* 1.763 million kW (2022 est.)
consumption: 6.311 billion kWh (2022 est.)
imports: 58.1 million kWh (2020 est.)
transmission/distribution losses: 1.811 billion kWh (2022 est.)
comparison rankings: transmission/distribution losses 123; consumption 123; installed generating capacity 125; imports 112

Electricity generation sources: *fossil fuels:* 37.6% of total installed capacity (2022 est.)
solar: 0.3% of total installed capacity (2022 est.)
hydroelectricity: 61.6% of total installed capacity (2022 est.)
biomass and waste: 0.5% of total installed capacity (2022 est.)

Coal: *imports:* 90.9 metric tons (2022 est.)

Petroleum: *total petroleum production:* 54,000 bbl/day (2023 est.)
refined petroleum consumption: 40,000 bbl/day (2022 est.)
crude oil estimated reserves: 200 million barrels (2021 est.)

Natural gas: *production:* 2.595 billion cubic meters (2022 est.)
consumption: 877.058 million cubic meters (2022 est.)
exports: 1.768 billion cubic meters (2022 est.)
proven reserves: 135.071 billion cubic meters (2021 est.)

Carbon dioxide emissions: 7.239 million metric tonnes of CO2 (2022 est.)
from petroleum and other liquids: 5.518 million metric tonnes of CO2 (2022 est.)
from consumed natural gas: 1.721 million metric tonnes of CO2 (2022 est.)
comparison ranking: total emissions 122

Energy consumption per capita: 4.656 million Btu/person (2022 est.)
comparison ranking: 171

COMMUNICATIONS

Telephones - fixed lines: *total subscriptions:* 929,000 (2022 est.)
subscriptions per 100 inhabitants: 3 (2022 est.)
comparison ranking: total subscriptions 72

Telephones - mobile cellular: *total subscriptions:* 23.107 million (2022 est.)
subscriptions per 100 inhabitants: 83 (2022 est.)
comparison ranking: total subscriptions 56

Telecommunication systems: *general assessment:* Cameroon was for many years one of the few countries in Africa with only two competing mobile operators; the investment programs among operators over the next few years aims to considerably boost mobile broadband services in rural areas of the country, many of which are under served by fixed-line infrastructure; the government has also been supportive, having launched its 'Cameroon Digital 2020' program, aimed at improving connectivity nationally; improved submarine and terrestrial cable connectivity has substantially increased international bandwidth, in turn leading to reductions in access prices for consumers; other projects such as Acceleration of the Digital Transformation of Cameroon are aimed at developing the digital economy (2022)
domestic: only a little above 3 per 100 persons for fixed-line subscriptions; mobile-cellular usage has increased sharply, reaching a subscribership base of roughly 83 per 100 persons (2021)
international: country code - 237; landing points for the SAT-3/WASC, SAIL, ACE, NCSCS, Ceiba-2, and WACS fiberoptic submarine cable that provides connectivity to Europe, South America, and West Africa; satellite earth stations - 2 Intelsat (Atlantic Ocean) (2019)

Broadcast media: government maintains tight control over broadcast media; state-owned Cameroon Radio Television (CRTV), broadcasting on both a TV and radio network, was the only officially recognized and fully licensed broadcaster until August 2007, when the government issued licenses to 2 private TV broadcasters and 1 private radio broadcaster; about 70 privately owned, unlicensed radio stations operate under "administrative tolerance," meaning the stations could be subject to closure at any time (2019)

Internet country code: .cm

Internet users: *total:* 12.42 million (2021 est.)
percent of population: 46% (2021 est.)
comparison ranking: total 54

Broadband - fixed subscriptions: *total:* 722,579 (2020 est.)
subscriptions per 100 inhabitants: 3 (2020 est.)
comparison ranking: total 79

TRANSPORTATION

National air transport system: *number of registered air carriers:* 1 (2020)
inventory of registered aircraft operated by air carriers: 3
annual passenger traffic on registered air carriers: 265,136 (2018)
annual freight traffic on registered air carriers: 70,000 (2018) mt-km

Civil aircraft registration country code prefix: TJ

Airports: 37 (2024)
comparison ranking: 108

Heliports: 1 (2024)

Pipelines: 53 km gas, 5 km liquid petroleum gas, 1,107 km oil, 35 km water (2013)

Railways: *total:* 987 km (2014)
narrow gauge: 987 km (2014) 1.000-m gauge
note: railway connections generally efficient but limited; rail lines connect major cities of Douala, Yaounde, Ngaoundere, and Garoua; passenger and freight service provided by CAMRAIL
comparison ranking: total 89

Roadways: *total:* 77,589 km
paved: 5,133 km
unpaved: 72,456 km (2019)
comparison ranking: total 66

Waterways: (2010) (major rivers in the south, such as the Wouri and the Sanaga, are largely non-navigable; in the north, the Benue, which connects through Nigeria to the Niger River, is navigable in the rainy season only to the port of Garoua)

Merchant marine: *total:* 198 (2023)
by type: bulk carrier 2, general cargo 91, oil tanker 42, other 63
comparison ranking: total 67

Ports: *total ports:* 7 (2024)
large: 0
medium: 1
small: 0
very small: 5
size unknown: 1
ports with oil terminals: 5

key ports: Douala, Ebome Marine Terminal, Kole Oil Terminal, Kome Kribi 1 Marine Terminal, Kribi Deep Sea Port, Limboh Terminal, Moudi Marine Terminal

MILITARY AND SECURITY

Military and security forces: Cameroon Armed Forces (Forces Armees Camerounaises, FAC): Army (L'Armee de Terre), Navy (Marine Nationale Republique, MNR, includes naval infantry or fusiliers marin), Air Force (Armee de l'Air du Cameroun, AAC), National Gendarmerie (Gendamerie Nationale, GN), National Firefighting Corps (Corps National de Sapeurs-Pompiers, CNSP), Presidential Guard (Garde Présidentielle du Cameroun, GP)
General Delegation for National Security (Délégation Générale à la Sûreté Nationale or DGSN): Cameroon Police (2024)
note 1: the Police and the National Gendarmerie are responsible for internal security; the Gendarmerie conducts administrative, criminal, and military investigative functions; other missions include customs, air and maritime surveillance, and road traffic control; in times of conflict, it participates in internal defense
note 2: the Army includes the Rapid Intervention Brigade (Brigade d'Intervention Rapide or BIR), which maintains its own command and control structure and reports directly to the Chief of Defense staff and the Presidency; the BIR includes airborne/airmobile, amphibious, armored reconnaissance, artillery, and counterterrorism forces, as well as support elements, such as intelligence

Military expenditures: 1% of GDP (2023 est.)
1% of GDP (2022 est.)
1% of GDP (2021 est.)
1% of GDP (2020 est.)
1.4% of GDP (2019 est.)
comparison ranking: 123

Military and security service personnel strengths: information varies; approximately 45-50,000 active-duty troops (30-35,000 ground forces, including the Rapid Intervention Battalion/BIR and Presidential Guard; 2,000 Navy; 1,000 Air Force; 10,000 Gendarmerie) (2023)
note: the BIR has approximately 10,000 personnel

Military equipment inventories and acquisitions: the FAC inventory is comprised of mostly older or second-hand equipment, with a smaller mix of more modern weapons systems; suppliers have included China, Israel, Russia, South Africa, the US, and several Western European countries (2023)

Military service age and obligation: 18-23 years of age for voluntary military service for men and women; no conscription; high school graduation required; service obligation 4 years (2023)

Military deployments: 750 (plus about 350 police) Central African Republic (MINUSCA) (2024)
note: Cameroon has committed approximately 2,000-2,500 troops to the Multinational Joint Task Force (MNJTF) against Boko Haram and other terrorist groups operating in the general area of the Lake Chad Basin and along Nigeria's northeast border; national MNJTF troop contingents are deployed within their own country territories, although cross-border operations occur occasionally

Military - note: the FAC ground forces (Army and the Rapid Intervention Battalion) are largely focused on internal security, particularly the threat from the terrorist groups Boko Haram and ISIS-West Africa along its frontiers with Nigeria and Chad (Far North region) and, since 2016, an insurgency from armed Anglophone separatist groups in the North-West and South-West regions; in addition, the FAC often deploys ground units to the border region with the Central African Republic to counter intrusions from armed militias and bandits; the Navy's missions include protecting Cameroon's oil installations, combatting crime and piracy in the Gulf of Guinea, and patrolling the country's lakes and rivers; the FAC's small Air Force supports both the ground and naval forces (2024)

TERRORISM

Terrorist group(s): Boko Haram; Islamic State of Iraq and ash-Sham – West Africa
note: details about the history, aims, leadership, organization, areas of operation, tactics, targets, weapons, size, and sources of support of the group(s) appear(s) in the Terrorism reference guide

TRANSNATIONAL ISSUES

Refugees and internally displaced persons: *refugees (country of origin):* 354,725 (Central African Republic), 121,172 (Nigeria) (2024)
IDPs: 1.066 million (2023) (includes far north, northwest, and southwest)

CANADA

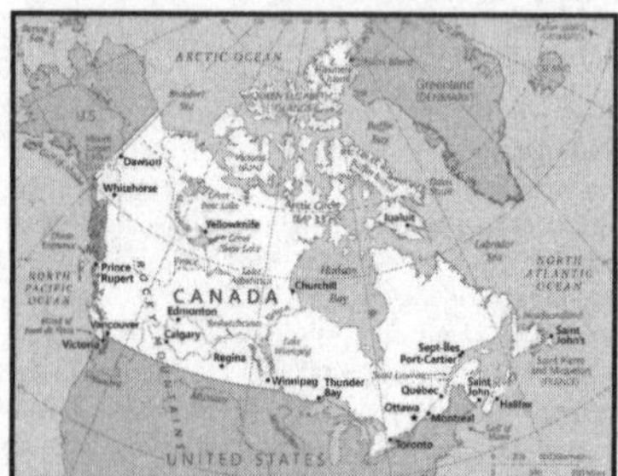

INTRODUCTION

Background: A land of vast distances and rich natural resources, Canada became a self-governing dominion in 1867, while retaining ties to the British crown. Canada gained legislative independence from Britain in 1931 and formalized its constitutional independence from the UK when it passed the Canada Act in 1982. Economically and technologically, the nation has developed in parallel with the US, its neighbor to the south across the world's longest international border. Canada faces the political challenges of meeting public demands for quality improvements in health care, education, social services, and economic competitiveness, as well as responding to the particular concerns of predominantly francophone Quebec. Canada also aims to develop its diverse energy resources while maintaining its commitment to the environment.

GEOGRAPHY

Location: Northern North America, bordering the North Atlantic Ocean on the east, North Pacific Ocean on the west, and the Arctic Ocean on the north, north of the conterminous US

Geographic coordinates: 60 00 N, 95 00 W

Map references: North America

Area: *total:* 9,984,670 sq km
land: 9,093,507 sq km
water: 891,163 sq km
comparison ranking: total 3

Area - comparative: slightly larger than the US

Land boundaries: *total:* 8,892 km
border countries: US 8,891 km (includes 2,475 km with Alaska); Denmark (Greenland) 1.3 km

Coastline: 202,080 km
note: the Canadian Arctic Archipelago - consisting of 36,563 islands, several of them some of the world's largest - contributes to Canada easily having the longest coastline in the world

Maritime claims: *territorial sea:* 12 nm
contiguous zone: 24 nm
exclusive economic zone: 200 nm
continental shelf: 200 nm or to the edge of the continental margin

Climate: varies from temperate in south to subarctic and arctic in north

Terrain: mostly plains with mountains in west, lowlands in southeast

Elevation: *highest point:* Mount Logan 5,959 m
lowest point: Atlantic/Pacific/Arctic Oceans 0 m
mean elevation: 487 m

Natural resources: bauxite, iron ore, nickel, zinc, copper, gold, lead, uranium, rare earth elements, molybdenum, potash, diamonds, silver, fish, timber, wildlife, coal, petroleum, natural gas, hydropower

Land use: *agricultural land:* 6.8% (2018 est.)
arable land: 4.7% (2018 est.)
permanent crops: 0.5% (2018 est.)
permanent pasture: 1.6% (2018 est.)
forest: 34.1% (2018 est.)
other: 59.1% (2018 est.)

Irrigated land: 9,045 sq km (2015)

Major lakes (area sq km): *fresh water lake(s):* Huron* - 35,972 sq km; Great Bear Lake - 31,328 sq km; Superior* - 28,754 sq km; Great Slave Lake - 28,568 sq km; Lake Winnipeg - 24,387 sq km; Erie* - 12,776 sq km; Ontario* - 9,790 sq km; Lake Athabasca - 7,935 sq km; Reindeer Lake - 6,650 sq km; Nettilling Lake - 5,542 sq km
note - Great Lakes* area shown as Canadian waters

Major rivers (by length in km): Mackenzie - 4, 241 km; Yukon river source (shared with the US [m]) - 3,185 km; Saint Lawrence river mouth (shared with US) - 3,058 km; Nelson - 2,570 km; Columbia river source (shared with the US [m]) - 1,953 km; Churchill - 1,600 km; Fraser - 1,368 km; Ottawa - 1,271 km; Athabasca - 1,231 km; North Saskatchewan - 1,220 km; Liard - 1,115 km
note – [s] after country name indicates river source; [m] after country name indicates river mouth

Major watersheds (area sq km): Atlantic Ocean drainage: Mississippi* *(Gulf of Mexico)* (3,202,185 sq km, Canada only 32,000 sq km), Nelson *(Hudson Bay)* (1,093,141 sq km), Saint Lawrence* (1,049,636 sq km, Canada only 839,200 sq km)

Arctic Ocean drainage: Mackenzie (1,706,388 sq km)

Pacific Ocean drainage: Yukon* (847,620 sq km, Canada only 823,800 sq km), Columbia* (657,501 sq km, Canada only 103,000 sq km)
note - watersheds shared with the US shown with *

Major aquifers: Northern Great Plains Aquifer

Population distribution: vast majority of Canadians are positioned in a discontinuous band within approximately 300 km of the southern border with the United States; the most populated province is Ontario, followed by Quebec and British Columbia

Natural hazards: continuous permafrost in north is a serious obstacle to development; cyclonic storms form east of the Rocky Mountains, a result of the mixing of air masses from the Arctic, Pacific, and North American interior, and produce most of the country's rain and snow east of the mountains
volcanism: the vast majority of volcanoes in Western Canada's Coast Mountains remain dormant

Geography - note: *note 1:* second-largest country in world (after Russia) and largest in the Americas; strategic location between Russia and US via north polar route; approximately 90% of the population is concentrated within 160 km (100 mi) of the US border
note 2: Canada has more fresh water than any other country and almost 9% of Canadian territory is water; Canada has at least 2 million and possibly over 3 million lakes – that is more than all other countries combined

PEOPLE AND SOCIETY

Population: *total:* 38,794,813
male: 19,234,729
female: 19,560,084 (2024 est.)
comparison rankings: female 38; male 38; total 37

Nationality: *noun:* Canadian(s)
adjective: Canadian

Ethnic groups: Canadian 15.6%, English 14.7%, Scottish 12.1%, French 11%, Irish 12.1%, German 8.1%, Chinese 4.7%, Italian 4.3%, First Nations 1.7%, Indian 3.7%, Ukrainian 3.5%, Metis 1.5% (2021 est.)
note: percentages add up to more than 100% because respondents were able to identify more than one ethnic origin

Languages: English (official) 87.1%, French (official) 29.1%, Chinese languages 4.2%, Spanish 3.2%, Punjabi 2.6%, Arabic 2.4%, Tagalog 2.3%, Italian 1.5% (2022 est.)
major-language sample(s):
The World Factbook, the indispensable source for basic information. (English)
The World Factbook, une source indispensable d'informations de base. (French)

Religions: Christian 53.3%, Muslim 4.9%, Hindu 2.3%, Sikh 2.1%, Buddhist 1%, Jewish 0.9%, Traditional (North American Indigenous) 0.2%, other religions and traditional spirituality 0.6%, none 34.6% (2021 est.)

Age structure: *0-14 years:* 15.5% (male 3,098,478/female 2,929,148)
15-64 years: 63.4% (male 12,382,422/female 12,227,512)
65 years and over: 21% (2024 est.) (male 3,753,829/female 4,403,424)

Dependency ratios: *total dependency ratio:* 52.1
youth dependency ratio: 23.9
elderly dependency ratio: 28.2
potential support ratio: 3.6 (2021 est.)

Median age: *total:* 42.6 years (2024 est.)
male: 41.4 years
female: 43.8 years
comparison ranking: total 40

Population growth rate: 0.71% (2024 est.)
comparison ranking: 125

Birth rate: 10 births/1,000 population (2024 est.)
comparison ranking: 186

Death rate: 8.2 deaths/1,000 population (2024 est.)
comparison ranking: 82

Net migration rate: 5.3 migrant(s)/1,000 population (2024 est.)
comparison ranking: 19

Population distribution: vast majority of Canadians are positioned in a discontinuous band within approximately 300 km of the southern border with the United States; the most populated province is Ontario, followed by Quebec and British Columbia

Urbanization: *urban population:* 81.9% of total population (2023)
rate of urbanization: 0.95% annual rate of change (2020-25 est.)

Major urban areas - population: 6.372 million Toronto, 4.308 million Montreal, 2.657 million Vancouver, 1.640 million Calgary, 1.544 million Edmonton, 1.437 million OTTAWA (capital) (2023)

Sex ratio: *at birth:* 1.05 male(s)/female
0-14 years: 1.06 male(s)/female
15-64 years: 1.01 male(s)/female
65 years and over: 0.85 male(s)/female
total population: 0.98 male(s)/female (2024 est.)

Mother's mean age at first birth: 29.4 years (2019 est.)

Maternal mortality ratio: 11 deaths/100,000 live births (2020 est.)
comparison ranking: 142

Infant mortality rate: *total:* 4.3 deaths/1,000 live births (2024 est.)
male: 4.5 deaths/1,000 live births
female: 4 deaths/1,000 live births
comparison ranking: total 185

Life expectancy at birth: *total population:* 84.2 years (2024 est.)
male: 81.9 years
female: 86.6 years
comparison ranking: total population 5

Total fertility rate: 1.58 children born/woman (2024 est.)
comparison ranking: 189

Gross reproduction rate: 0.77 (2024 est.)

Drinking water source: *improved: urban:* 99.3% of population
rural: 99.1% of population
total: 99.2% of population
unimproved: urban: 0.7% of population
rural: 0.9% of population
total: 0.8% of population (2020 est.)

Current health expenditure: 12.9% of GDP (2020)

Physician density: 2.44 physicians/1,000 population (2019)

Hospital bed density: 2.5 beds/1,000 population (2019)

Sanitation facility access: *improved: urban:* 99.1% of population
rural: 98.9% of population
total: 99% of population
unimproved: urban: 0.9% of population
rural: 1.1% of population
total: 1% of population (2020 est.)

Obesity - adult prevalence rate: 29.4% (2016)
comparison ranking: 26

Alcohol consumption per capita: *total:* 8 liters of pure alcohol (2019 est.)
beer: 3.5 liters of pure alcohol (2019 est.)
wine: 2 liters of pure alcohol (2019 est.)
spirits: 2.1 liters of pure alcohol (2019 est.)
other alcohols: 0.4 liters of pure alcohol (2019 est.)
comparison ranking: total 44

Tobacco use: *total:* 13% (2020 est.)
male: 15.3% (2020 est.)
female: 10.7% (2020 est.)
comparison ranking: total 117

Currently married women (ages 15-49): 52.2% (2023 est.)

Education expenditures: 5.2% of GDP (2020 est.)
comparison ranking: 70

School life expectancy (primary to tertiary education): *total:* 17 years
male: 16 years
female: 17 years (2020)

ENVIRONMENT

Environment - current issues: metal smelting, coal-burning utilities, and vehicle emissions impacting agricultural and forest productivity; air pollution and resulting acid rain severely affecting lakes and damaging forests; ocean waters becoming contaminated due to agricultural, industrial, mining, and forestry activities

Environment - international agreements: *party to:* Air Pollution, Air Pollution-Heavy Metals, Air Pollution-Multi-effect Protocol, Air Pollution-Nitrogen Oxides, Air Pollution-Persistent Organic Pollutants, Air Pollution-Sulphur 85, Air Pollution-Sulphur 94, Antarctic-Environmental Protection, Antarctic-Marine Living Resources, Antarctic Treaty, Biodiversity, Climate Change, Climate Change-Paris Agreement, Comprehensive Nuclear Test Ban, Desertification, Endangered Species, Environmental Modification, Hazardous Wastes, Law of the Sea, Marine Dumping-London Convention, Marine Dumping-London Protocol, Nuclear Test Ban, Ozone Layer Protection, Ship Pollution, Wetlands
signed, but not ratified: Air Pollution-Volatile Organic Compounds, Marine Life Conservation

Climate: varies from temperate in south to subarctic and arctic in north

Urbanization: *urban population:* 81.9% of total population (2023)
rate of urbanization: 0.95% annual rate of change (2020-25 est.)

Revenue from forest resources: 0.08% of GDP (2018 est.)
comparison ranking: 119

Revenue from coal: 0.08% of GDP (2018 est.)
comparison ranking: 27

Air pollutants: *particulate matter emissions:* 6.39 micrograms per cubic meter (2019 est.)
carbon dioxide emissions: 544.89 megatons (2016 est.)
methane emissions: 101.82 megatons (2020 est.)

Waste and recycling: *municipal solid waste generated annually:* 25,103,034 tons (2014 est.)
municipal solid waste recycled annually: 5,168,715 tons (2008 est.)
percent of municipal solid waste recycled: 20.6% (2008 est.)

Major lakes (area sq km): *fresh water lake(s):* Huron* - 35,972 sq km; Great Bear Lake - 31,328 sq km; Superior* - 28,754 sq km; Great Slave Lake - 28,568 sq km; Lake Winnipeg - 24,387 sq km; Erie* - 12,776 sq km; Ontario* - 9,790 sq km; Lake Athabasca - 7,935 sq km; Reindeer Lake - 6,650 sq km; Nettilling Lake - 5,542 sq km
note - Great Lakes* area shown as Canadian waters

Major rivers (by length in km): Mackenzie - 4, 241 km; Yukon river source (shared with the US [m]) - 3,185 km; Saint Lawrence river mouth (shared with US) - 3,058 km; Nelson - 2,570 km; Columbia river source (shared with the US [m]) - 1,953 km; Churchill - 1,600 km; Fraser - 1,368 km; Ottawa - 1,271 km; Athabasca - 1,231 km; North Saskatchewan - 1,220 km; Liard - 1,115 km
note – [s] after country name indicates river source; [m] after country name indicates river mouth

Major watersheds (area sq km): Atlantic Ocean drainage: Mississippi* *(Gulf of Mexico)* (3,202,185 sq km, Canada only 32,000 sq km), Nelson *(Hudson Bay)* (1,093,141 sq km), Saint Lawrence* (1,049,636 sq km, Canada only 839,200 sq km)

Arctic Ocean drainage: Mackenzie (1,706,388 sq km)

Pacific Ocean drainage: Yukon* (847,620 sq km, Canada only 823,800 sq km), Columbia* (657,501 sq km, Canada only 103,000 sq km)
note - watersheds shared with the US shown with *

Major aquifers: Northern Great Plains Aquifer

Total water withdrawal: *municipal:* 4.87 billion cubic meters (2020 est.)
industrial: 27.51 billion cubic meters (2020 est.)
agricultural: 3.86 billion cubic meters (2020 est.)

Total renewable water resources: 2.9 trillion cubic meters (2020 est.)

Geoparks: *total global geoparks and regional networks:* 5
global geoparks and regional networks: Perce; Stonehammer; Tumbler Ridge; Cliffs of Fundy; Discovery (2023)

GOVERNMENT

Country name: *conventional long form:* none
conventional short form: Canada
etymology: the country name likely derives from the St. Lawrence Iroquoian word "kanata" meaning village or settlement

Government type: federal parliamentary democracy (Parliament of Canada) under a constitutional monarchy; a Commonwealth realm; federal and state authorities and responsibilities regulated in constitution

Capital: *name:* Ottawa
geographic coordinates: 45 25 N, 75 42 W
time difference: UTC-5 (same time as Washington, DC, during Standard Time)
daylight saving time: +1hr, begins second Sunday in March; ends first Sunday in November
time zone note: Canada has six time zones
etymology: the city lies on the south bank of the Ottawa River, from which it derives its name; the river name comes from the Algonquin word "adawe" meaning "to trade" and refers to the indigenous peoples who used the river as a trade highway

Administrative divisions: 10 provinces and 3 territories*; Alberta, British Columbia, Manitoba, New Brunswick, Newfoundland and Labrador, Northwest Territories*, Nova Scotia, Nunavut*, Ontario, Prince Edward Island, Quebec, Saskatchewan, Yukon*

Independence: 1 July 1867 (union of British North American colonies); 11 December 1931 (recognized by UK per Statute of Westminster)

National holiday: Canada Day, 1 July (1867)

Legal system: common law system except in Quebec, where civil law based on the French civil code prevails

Constitution: *history:* consists of unwritten and written acts, customs, judicial decisions, and traditions dating from 1763; the written part of the constitution consists of the Constitution Act of 29 March 1867, which created a federation of four provinces, and the Constitution Act of 17 April 1982
amendments: proposed by either house of Parliament or by the provincial legislative assemblies; there are 5 methods for passage though most require approval by both houses of Parliament, approval of at least two thirds of the provincial legislative assemblies and assent and formalization as a proclamation by the governor general in council; the most restrictive method is reserved for amendments affecting fundamental sections of the constitution, such as the office of the monarch or the governor general, and the constitutional amendment procedures, which require unanimous approval by both houses and by all the provincial assemblies, and assent of the governor general in council; amended 11 times, last in 2011 (Fair Representation Act, 2011)

International law organization participation: accepts compulsory ICJ jurisdiction with reservations; accepts ICCt jurisdiction

Citizenship: *citizenship by birth:* yes
citizenship by descent only: yes
dual citizenship recognized: yes
residency requirement for naturalization: minimum of 3 of last 5 years resident in Canada

Suffrage: 18 years of age; universal

Executive branch: *chief of state:* King CHARLES III (since 8 September 2022); represented by Governor General Mary SIMON (since 6 July 2021)
head of government: Prime Minister Justin Pierre James TRUDEAU (since 4 November 2015)
cabinet: Federal Ministry chosen by the prime minister usually from among members of his/her own party sitting in Parliament
elections/appointments: the monarchy is hereditary; governor general appointed by the monarch on the advice of the prime minister for a 5-year term; following legislative elections, the leader of the majority party or majority coalition in the House of Commons generally designated prime minister by the governor general
note: the governor general position is largely ceremonial

Legislative branch: *description:* bicameral Parliament or Parlement consists of:
Senate or Senat (105 seats; members appointed by the governor general on the advice of the prime minister and can serve until age 75)
House of Commons or Chambre des Communes (338 seats; members directly elected in single-seat constituencies by simple majority vote with terms up to 4 years)
elections: Senate - last appointed in July 2021
House of Commons - last held on 20 September 2021 (next to be held on or before 20 October 2025)
election results: Senate - composition - men 43, women 54, percentage women 55.7% (8 seats are vacant)
House of Commons - percent of vote by party - CPC 33.7%, Liberal Party 32.6%, NDP 17.8%, Bloc Quebecois 7.7%, Greens 2.3%, other 5.9%; seats by party - Liberal Party 159, CPC 119, NDP 25, Bloc Quebecois 32, Greens 2, independent 1; composition - men 234, women 102; percentage women 30.4%; total Parliament percentage women 35.2%

Judicial branch: *highest court(s):* Supreme Court of Canada (consists of the chief justice and 8 judges); note - in 1949, Canada abolished all appeals beyond its Supreme Court, which prior to that time, were heard by the Judicial Committee of the Privy Council (in London)
judge selection and term of office: chief justice and judges appointed by the prime minister in council; all judges appointed for life with mandatory retirement at age 75
subordinate courts: federal level: Federal Court of Appeal; Federal Court; Tax Court; federal administrative tribunals; Courts Martial; provincial/territorial level: provincial superior, appeals, first instance, and specialized courts; note - in 1999, the Nunavut Court - a circuit court with the power of a provincial superior court, as well as a territorial court - was established to serve isolated settlements

Political parties: Bloc Quebecois
Conservative Party of Canada or CPC
Green Party
Liberal Party
New Democratic Party or NDP
People's Party of Canada

International organization participation: ADB (nonregional member), AfDB (nonregional member), APEC, Arctic Council, ARF, ASEAN (dialogue partner), Australia Group, BIS, C, CD, CDB, CE (observer), EAPC, EBRD, EITI (implementing country), FAO, FATF, G-7, G-8, G-10, G-20, IADB, IAEA, IBRD, ICAO, ICC (national committees), ICCt, ICRM, IDA, IEA, IFAD, IFC, IFRCS, IGAD (partners), IHO, ILO, IMF, IMO, IMSO, Interpol, IOC, IOM, IPU, ISO, ITSO, ITU, ITUC (NGOs), MIGA, MINUSTAH, MONUSCO, NAFTA, NATO, NEA, NSG, OAS, OECD, OIF, OPCW, OSCE, Pacific Alliance (observer), Paris Club, PCA, PIF (partner), UN, UNCTAD, UNESCO, UNFICYP, UNHCR, UNMISS, UNRWA, UNTSO, UPU, USMCA, Wassenaar Arrangement, WCO, WFTU (NGOs), WHO, WIPO, WMO, WTO, ZC

Diplomatic representation in the US: *chief of mission:* Ambassador Kirsten HILLMAN (since 17 July 2020)
chancery: 501 Pennsylvania Avenue NW, Washington, DC 20001
telephone: [1] (844) 880-6519
FAX: [1] (202) 682-7738
email address and website:
ccs.scc@international.gc.ca
https://www.international.gc.ca/country-pays/us-eu/washington.aspx?lang=eng
consulate(s) general: Atlanta, Boston, Chicago, Dallas, Denver, Detroit, Los Angeles, Miami, Minneapolis, New York, San Francisco, Seattle
trade office(s): Houston, Palo Alto (CA), San Diego; note - there are trade offices in the Consulates General

Diplomatic representation from the US: *chief of mission:* Ambassador David L. COHEN (since December 2021)
embassy: 490 Sussex Drive, Ottawa, Ontario K1N 1G8
mailing address: 5480 Ottawa Place, Washington DC 20521-5480
telephone: [1] (613) 688-5335
FAX: [1] (613) 241-7845
email address and website:
OttawaNIV@state.gov
https://ca.usembassy.gov/
consulate(s) general: Calgary, Halifax, Montreal, Quebec City, Toronto, Vancouver
consulate(s): Winnipeg

Flag description: two vertical bands of red (hoist and fly side, half width) with white square between them; an 11-pointed red maple leaf is centered in the white square; the maple leaf has long been a Canadian symbol

National symbol(s): maple leaf, beaver; national colors: red, white

National anthem: *name:* "O Canada"
lyrics/music: Adolphe-Basile ROUTHIER [French], Robert Stanley WEIR [English]/Calixa LAVALLEE
note: adopted 1980; originally written in 1880, "O Canada" served as an unofficial anthem many years before its official adoption; the anthem has French and English versions whose lyrics differ; as a Commonwealth realm, in addition to the national anthem, "God Save the King" serves as the royal anthem (see United Kingdom)

National heritage: *total World Heritage Sites:* 22 (10 cultural, 11 natural, 1 mixed) (2021)
selected World Heritage Site locales: L'Anse aux Meadows (c); Canadian Rocky Mountain Parks (n); Dinosaur Provincial Park (n); Historic District of Old Quebec (c); Old Town Lunenburg (c); Wood Buffalo National Park (n); Head- Smashed-In Buffalo Jump (c); Gros Morne National Park (n); Pimachiowin Aki (m)

ECONOMY

Economic overview: one of the world's leading developed economies; globally integrated commercial and financial markets; largest US trading partner; key energy, forestry, manufacturing and service industries; inflation recovering following interest rate hikes; government priorities include climate policy, immigration and affordable housing

Real GDP (purchasing power parity): $2.238 trillion (2023 est.)
$2.215 trillion (2022 est.)
$2.133 trillion (2021 est.)
note: data in 2021 dollars
comparison ranking: 16

Real GDP growth rate: 1.07% (2023 est.)
3.82% (2022 est.)
5.29% (2021 est.)
note: annual GDP % growth based on constant local currency
comparison ranking: 163

Real GDP per capita: $55,800 (2023 est.)
$56,900 (2022 est.)
$55,800 (2021 est.)
note: data in 2021 dollars
comparison ranking: 34

GDP (official exchange rate): $2.14 trillion (2023 est.)
note: data in current dollars at official exchange rate

Inflation rate (consumer prices): 3.88% (2023 est.)
6.8% (2022 est.)
3.4% (2021 est.)
note: annual % change based on consumer prices
comparison ranking: 78

Credit ratings: Fitch rating: AA+ (2020)
Moody's rating: Aaa (2002)
Standard & Poors rating: AAA (2002)
note: The year refers to the year in which the current credit rating was first obtained.

GDP - composition, by sector of origin: *agriculture:* 1.8% (2020 est.)
industry: 22.5% (2020 est.)
services: 69.6% (2020 est.)
note: figures may not total 100% due to non-allocated consumption not captured in sector-reported data
comparison rankings: services 39; industry 119; agriculture 166

GDP - composition, by end use: *household consumption:* 55.2% (2023 est.)
government consumption: 21.2% (2023 est.)
investment in fixed capital: 22.9% (2023 est.)
investment in inventories: 1% (2023 est.)
exports of goods and services: 33.5% (2023 est.)
imports of goods and services: -33.9% (2023 est.)
note: figures may not total 100% due to rounding or gaps in data collection

Agricultural products: wheat, rapeseed, maize, barley, milk, soybeans, potatoes, oats, peas, lentils (2022)
note: top ten agricultural products based on tonnage

Industries: transportation equipment, chemicals, processed and unprocessed minerals, food products, wood and paper products, fish products, petroleum, natural gas

Industrial production growth rate: -0.9% (2023 est.)
note: annual % change in industrial value added based on constant local currency
comparison ranking: 165

Labor force: 22.11 million (2023 est.)
note: number of people ages 15 or older who are employed or seeking work
comparison ranking: 31

Unemployment rate: 5.37% (2023 est.)
5.28% (2022 est.)
7.53% (2021 est.)
note: % of labor force seeking employment
comparison ranking: 103

Youth unemployment rate (ages 15-24): *total:* 10.6% (2023 est.)
male: 11.4% (2023 est.)
female: 9.8% (2023 est.)
note: % of labor force ages 15-24 seeking employment
comparison ranking: total 129

Gini Index coefficient - distribution of family income: 31.7 (2019 est.)
note: index (0-100) of income distribution; higher values represent greater inequality
comparison ranking: 112

Average household expenditures: *on food:* 9.5% of household expenditures (2022 est.)
on alcohol and tobacco: 3.7% of household expenditures (2022 est.)

Household income or consumption by percentage share: *lowest 10%:* 2.9% (2019 est.)
highest 10%: 24.4% (2019 est.)
note: % share of income accruing to lowest and highest 10% of population

Remittances: 0.04% of GDP (2023 est.)
0.04% of GDP (2022 est.)
0.04% of GDP (2021 est.)
note: personal transfers and compensation between resident and non-resident individuals/households/entities

Budget: *revenues:* $393.642 billion (2022 est.)
expenditures: $399.8 billion (2022 est.)
note: central government revenues (excluding grants) and expenses converted to US dollars at average official exchange rate for year indicated

Public debt: 61.42% of GDP (2022 est.)
note: central government debt as a % of GDP
comparison ranking: 77

Taxes and other revenues: 12.83% (of GDP) (2022 est.)
note: central government tax revenue as a % of GDP
comparison ranking: 156

Current account balance: -$13.255 billion (2023 est.)
-$7.622 billion (2022 est.)
$256.504 million (2021 est.)
note: balance of payments - net trade and primary/secondary income in current dollars
comparison ranking: 197

Exports: $717.677 billion (2023 est.)
$731.81 billion (2022 est.)
$626.676 billion (2021 est.)
note: balance of payments - exports of goods and services in current dollars
comparison ranking: 13

Exports - partners: US 75%, China 4%, Japan 2%, UK 2%, Mexico 1% (2022)
note: top five export partners based on percentage share of exports

Exports - commodities: crude petroleum, cars, natural gas, refined petroleum, gold (2022)
note: top five export commodities based on value in dollars

Imports: $726.139 billion (2023 est.)
$728.732 billion (2022 est.)
$626.558 billion (2021 est.)
note: balance of payments - imports of goods and services in current dollars
comparison ranking: 11

Imports - partners: US 56%, China 11%, Mexico 4%, Germany 3%, Japan 2% (2022)
note: top five import partners based on percentage share of imports

Imports - commodities: cars, refined petroleum, vehicle parts/accessories, trucks, crude petroleum (2022)
note: top five import commodities based on value in dollars

Reserves of foreign exchange and gold: $117.551 billion (2023 est.)
$106.952 billion (2022 est.)
$106.615 billion (2021 est.)
note: holdings of gold (year-end prices)/foreign exchange/special drawing rights in current dollars
comparison ranking: 28

Exchange rates: Canadian dollars (CAD) per US dollar -

Exchange rates: 1.35 (2023 est.)
1.302 (2022 est.)
1.254 (2021 est.)
1.341 (2020 est.)
1.327 (2019 est.)

ENERGY

Electricity access: *electrification - total population:* 100% (2022 est.)

Electricity: *installed generating capacity:* 158.973 million kW (2022 est.)
consumption: 553.261 billion kWh (2022 est.)
exports: 65.225 billion kWh (2022 est.)
imports: 14.116 billion kWh (2022 est.)
transmission/distribution losses: 33.626 billion kWh (2022 est.)
comparison rankings: transmission/distribution losses 199; imports 18; exports 2; consumption 8; installed generating capacity 8

Electricity generation sources: *fossil fuels:* 17.2% of total installed capacity (2022 est.)
nuclear: 12.9% of total installed capacity (2022 est.)
solar: 0.9% of total installed capacity (2022 est.)
wind: 6% of total installed capacity (2022 est.)
hydroelectricity: 61.5% of total installed capacity (2022 est.)
biomass and waste: 1.5% of total installed capacity (2022 est.)

Nuclear energy: Number of operational nuclear reactors: 19 (2023)

Net capacity of operational nuclear reactors: 13.7GW (2023 est.)

Percent of total electricity production: 13.7% (2023 est.)

Number of nuclear reactors permanently shut down: 6 (2023)

Coal: *production:* 43.024 million metric tons (2022 est.)
consumption: 17.138 million metric tons (2022 est.)
exports: 29.114 million metric tons (2022 est.)
imports: 6.444 million metric tons (2022 est.)
proven reserves: 6.582 billion metric tons (2022 est.)

Petroleum: *total petroleum production:* 5.692 million bbl/day (2023 est.)
refined petroleum consumption: 2.454 million bbl/day (2023 est.)
crude oil estimated reserves: 170.3 billion barrels (2021 est.)

Natural gas: *production:* 187.686 billion cubic meters (2022 est.)
consumption: 130.316 billion cubic meters (2022 est.)
exports: 84.928 billion cubic meters (2022 est.)
imports: 27.481 billion cubic meters (2022 est.)
proven reserves: 2.067 trillion cubic meters (2021 est.)

Carbon dioxide emissions: 572.82 million metric tonnes of CO2 (2022 est.)
from coal and metallurgical coke: 25.74 million metric tonnes of CO2 (2022 est.)
from petroleum and other liquids: 290.996 million metric tonnes of CO2 (2022 est.)
from consumed natural gas: 256.084 million metric tonnes of CO2 (2022 est.)
comparison ranking: total emissions 11

Energy consumption per capita: 315.581 million Btu/person (2022 est.)
comparison ranking: 7

COMMUNICATIONS

Telephones - fixed lines: *total subscriptions:* 11.312 million (2022 est.)
subscriptions per 100 inhabitants: 29 (2022 est.)
comparison ranking: total subscriptions 16

Telephones - mobile cellular: *total subscriptions:* 35.082 million (2022 est.)
subscriptions per 100 inhabitants: 91 (2022 est.)
comparison ranking: total subscriptions 44

Telecommunication systems: *general assessment:* the Canadian telecom market continues to show steady development as operators invest in network upgrades; much of the investment among telcos has been channeled into LTE infrastructure to capitalize on consumer demand for mobile data services, while there has also been further investment in 5G; investment programs have also been supported by regulatory efforts to ensure that operators have spectrum available to develop 5G services; an investment in fixed-line infrastructure, focused on FttP and, among cable broadband providers; government policy has encouraged the extension of broadband to rural and regional areas, with the result that services are almost universally available and the emphasis now is on improving service speeds to enable the entire population to benefit from the digital economy and society; cable broadband is the principal access platform, followed by DSL; the mobile rate remains comparatively low by international standards; Canadians have provided for LTE and LTE-A infrastructure; despite topographical challenges and the remoteness of many areas, the major players effectively offer 99% population coverage with LTE; operators now provide up to 70% population coverage with 5G (2024)
domestic: Nearly 29 per 100 fixed-line and 91 per 100 mobile-cellular teledensity (2022)
international: country code - 1; landing points for the Nunavut Undersea Fiber Optic Network System, Greenland Connect, Persona, GTT Atlantic, and Express, KetchCan 1 Submarine Fiber Cable system, St Pierre and Miquelon Cable submarine cables providing links to the US and Europe; satellite earth stations - 7 (5 Intelsat - 4 Atlantic Ocean and 1 Pacific Ocean, and 2 Intersputnik - Atlantic Ocean region) (2019)

Broadcast media: 2 public TV broadcasting networks, 1 in English and 1 in French, each with a large number of network affiliates; several private-commercial networks also with multiple network affiliates; overall, about 150 TV stations; multi-channel satellite and cable systems provide access to a wide range of stations including US stations; mix of public and commercial radio broadcasters with the Canadian Broadcasting Corporation (CBC), the public radio broadcaster, operating 4 radio networks, Radio Canada International, and radio services to indigenous populations in the north; roughly 1,119 licensed radio stations (2016)

Internet country code: .ca

Internet users: *total:* 35.34 million (2021 est.)
percent of population: 93% (2021 est.)
comparison ranking: total 28

Broadband - fixed subscriptions: *total:* 15,825,813 (2020 est.)
subscriptions per 100 inhabitants: 42 (2020 est.)
comparison ranking: total 16

TRANSPORTATION

National air transport system: *number of registered air carriers:* 51 (2020)
inventory of registered aircraft operated by air carriers: 879
annual passenger traffic on registered air carriers: 89.38 million (2018)
annual freight traffic on registered air carriers: 3,434,070,000 (2018) mt-km

Civil aircraft registration country code prefix: C

Airports: 1,425 (2024)
comparison ranking: 5

Heliports: 481 (2024)

Pipelines: 840,000 km oil and gas (2020)

Railways: *total:* 49,422 km (2021) note: 129 km electrified (2021)
standard gauge: 49,422 km (2021) 1.435-m gauge
comparison ranking: total 5

Roadways: *total:* 1,042,300 km
paved: 415,600 km (includes 17,000 km of expressways)
unpaved: 626,700 km (2011)
comparison ranking: total 8

Waterways: 636 km (2011) (Saint Lawrence Seaway of 3,769 km, including the Saint Lawrence River of 3,058 km, shared with United States)
comparison ranking: 85

Merchant marine: *total:* 716 (2023)
by type: bulk carrier 22, container ship 1, general cargo 78, oil tanker 15, other 600
comparison ranking: total 32

Ports: *total ports:* 284 (2024)
large: 4
medium: 14
small: 58
very small: 149
size unknown: 59
ports with oil terminals: 59
key ports: Argentia, Canaport (St. John), Halifax, Hamilton, Montreal, New Westminster, Pond Inlet, Prince Rupert, Quebec, Sept Iles, St. John, Sydney, Thunder Bay, Toronto, Trois Rivieres, Vancouver, Victoria Harbor, Windsor

MILITARY AND SECURITY

Military and security forces: Canadian Forces: Canadian Army, Royal Canadian Navy, Royal Canadian Air Force; Department of Fisheries and Oceans: Coast Guard (2024)
note 1: the CAF is comprised of both a Regular Force and a Reserve Force; the Reserve Force is part of all three services (Army, Navy, and Air Force) and is considered an integral component of the CAF; reservists are primarily parttime service positions; they may volunteer for full-time employment or deployment on operations; they typically serve one or more evenings a week and/or during weekends at locations close to home; the Reserve Force is comprised of the Primary Reserve, Canadian

Rangers, Cadet Organizations Administration and Training Service, and the Supplementary Reserve; the Canadian Rangers are part of the Army Reserve Force and provide a limited presence in Canada's northern, coastal, and isolated areas for sovereignty, public safety, and surveillance roles
note 2: the Royal Canadian Mounted Police (RCMP or "Mounties") are under the Department of Public Safety; only Ontario, Quebec, and Newfoundland and Labrador have provincial police forces, but the Royal Newfoundland Constabulary contracts policing in regions of the province to the RCMP; the RCMP and municipal forces provide coverage for other provinces and territories; some Indigenous reserves provide Indigenous policing; provincial and municipal police report to their respective provincial authorities

Military expenditures: 1.4% of GDP (2024)
1.3% of GDP (2023)
1.2% of GDP (2022)
1.3% of GDP (2021)
1.4% of GDP (2020)
comparison ranking: 100

Military and security service personnel strengths: approximately 70,000 active armed forces personnel (23,000 Army; 12,000 Navy; 12,000 Air Force; 23,000 other) (2024)
note: the Army also has approximately 19,000 part-time volunteer soldiers in the Reserve Force, including about 5,500 Rangers

Military equipment inventories and acquisitions: the CAF's inventory is a mix of domestically produced equipment and imported weapons systems from Australia, Europe, Israel, and the US; in recent years, the leading supplier has been the US; Canada's defense industry develops, maintains, and produces a range of equipment, including aircraft, combat vehicles, naval vessels, and associated components (2024)

Military service age and obligation: 17 years of age for voluntary male and female military service (with parental consent); 16 years of age for Reserve and Military College applicants; Canadian citizenship or permanent residence status required; maximum 34 years of age; service obligation 3-9 years (2023)
note 1: Canada opened up all military occupations to women in 2001; women in 2023 comprised about 16% of the CAF
note 2: the CAF offers waivers to foreign nationals applying for military service only in exceptional cases — to individuals on international military exchanges, for example, or to candidates who have specialized skills in high demand

Military deployments: the CAF has approximately 1,000 military personnel forward deployed for NATO air, land, and sea missions in the European theater, including a ground task force in Latvia; it also contributes smaller numbers of air, ground, and naval forces to a variety of other NATO and international missions (2024)
note: in 2024, Canada announced plans to have a full 2,000-person brigade deployed to Latvia by 2026

Military - note: the Canadian Armed Forces (CAF) are responsible for external security; the CAF's core missions include detecting, deterring, and defending against threats to or attacks on Canada; the military also provides assistance to civil authorities and law enforcement as needed for such missions as counterterrorism, search and rescue, and responding to natural disasters or other major emergencies; it regularly participates in bilateral and multinational training exercises with a variety of partners, including NATO (Canada is one of the original members) and the US; the CAF also contributes to international peacekeeping, stability, humanitarian, combat, and capacity building operations with the UN, NATO, and other security partners
Canada is part of the North American Aerospace Defense Command (NORAD; established 1958); NORAD is a Canada-US bi-national military command responsible for monitoring and defending North American airspace; traditionally, a CAF officer has served as the deputy commander of NORAD; Canada's defense relationship with the US extends back to the Ogdensburg Declaration of 1940, when the two countries formally agreed on military cooperation, including the establishment of the Permanent Joint Board on Defense (PJBD), which continues to be the highest-level bilateral defense forum between Canada and the US
British troops withdrew from Canada in 1871 as part of the UK-US Treaty of Washington; following the withdrawal, the first Canadian militia, known as the Royal Canadian Regiment, was organized in 1883 to protect Canadian territory and defend British interests abroad, which it did in the South African War (1899-1902), Canada's first overseas conflict; militia units formed the backbone of the more than 425,000 Canadian soldiers that went to Europe during World War I in what was called the Canadian Expeditionary Force; the Royal Canadian Navy was created in 1910, while the Canadian Air Force was established in 1920 and became the Royal Canadian Air Force in 1924; the Canadian Army was officially founded in 1942; a unified Canadian Armed Forces was created in 1968 (2024)

SPACE

Space agency/agencies: Canadian Space Agency (CSA; established 1989) (2024)

Space launch site(s): Churchill Rocket Research Range (sounding rockets; Manitoba); constructing a private, commercial space launch site in Nova Scotia (2023)

Space program overview: has a substantial program, a national space strategy, and a long history of developing space-related technologies; designs, builds, operates, and tracks communications, remote sensing (RS), multi-mission, and scientific/testing satellites; has an astronaut program (train in the US); designs, builds, or contributes to a variety of other space-related programs, including space telescopes, planetary probes, sensors, and robotic systems (such as the Canadian-made robotic arms used on the US Space Shuttle and the International Space Station); participates in international space efforts and cooperates with a variety of foreign space agencies and commercial entities, including those of Argentina, Brazil, the European Space Agency (ESA)/EU (and their member states), India, and particularly the US; ESA Cooperating State since 1979; has a robust commercial space sector that is involved in satellite communications, optics, space exploration, navigation, and space science (2024)
note: further details about the key activities, programs, and milestones of the country's space program, as well as government spending estimates on the space sector, appear in the Space Programs reference guide

TERRORISM

Terrorist group(s): Islamic State of Iraq and ash-Sham (ISIS); Hizballah
note: details about the history, aims, leadership, organization, areas of operation, tactics, targets, weapons, size, and sources of support of the group(s) appear(s) in the Terrorism reference guide

TRANSNATIONAL ISSUES

Refugees and internally displaced persons: *refugees (country of origin):* 22,400 (Venezuela) (refugees and migrants) (2020); 5,254 (Iran) (mid-year 2021)
stateless persons: 4,323 (2022)

Illicit drugs: transnational criminal organizations trafficked cocaine, opium, methamphetamine, other synthetic drugs, and prescription drugs (some of which transited the United States) to Canada for domestic consumption; a source of synthetic drugs (including synthetic opioids), cannabis, and MDMA trafficked to the United States; a major source of precursor or essential chemicals used in the production of illicit narcotics

CAYMAN ISLANDS

INTRODUCTION

Background: The British colonized the Cayman Islands during the 18th and 19th centuries, and Jamaica – also a British colony at the time – administered the islands after 1863. In 1959, the islands became a territory within the Federation of the West Indies. When the Federation dissolved in 1962, the Cayman Islands chose to remain a British dependency. The territory has transformed itself into a significant offshore financial center.

GEOGRAPHY

Location: Caribbean, three-island group (Grand Cayman, Cayman Brac, Little Cayman) in Caribbean Sea, 240 km south of Cuba and 268 km northwest of Jamaica

Geographic coordinates: 19 30 N, 80 30 W

Map references: Central America and the Caribbean

Area: *total:* 264 sq km
land: 264 sq km
water: 0 sq km
comparison ranking: total 210

Area - comparative: 1.5 times the size of Washington, DC

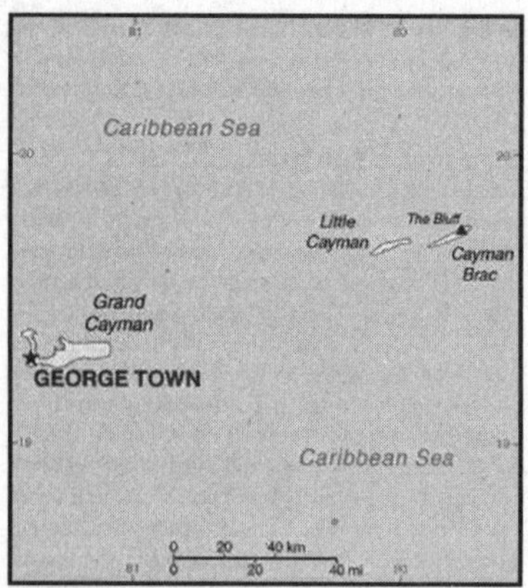

Land boundaries: *total:* 0 km

Coastline: 160 km

Maritime claims: *territorial sea:* 12 nm
exclusive economic zone: 200 nm
exclusive fishing zone: 200 nm

Climate: tropical marine; warm, rainy summers (May to October) and cool, relatively dry winters (November to April)

Terrain: low-lying limestone base surrounded by coral reefs

Elevation: *highest point:* 1 km SW of The Bluff on Cayman Brac 50 m
lowest point: Caribbean Sea 0 m

Natural resources: fish, climate and beaches that foster tourism

Land use: *agricultural land:* 11.2% (2018 est.)
arable land: 0.8% (2018 est.)
permanent crops: 2.1% (2018 est.)
permanent pasture: 8.3% (2018 est.)
forest: 52.9% (2018 est.)
other: 35.9% (2018 est.)

Irrigated land: NA

Population distribution: majority of the population resides on Grand Cayman

Natural hazards: hurricanes (July to November)

Geography - note: important location between Cuba and Central America

PEOPLE AND SOCIETY

Population: *total:* 66,653
male: 32,379
female: 34,274 (2024 est.)
comparison rankings: female 203; male 204; total 204

Nationality: *noun:* Caymanian(s)
adjective: Caymanian

Ethnic groups: Cayman Islander 35.4%, Jamaican 24.8%, Filipino 5.5%, British 5.3%, American 5.2%, Honduran 4.2%, Canadian 3.3%, Indian 2.1%, Cuban 1.6%, Nicaraguan 1%, other 11.1%, unspecified 0.5% (2021 est.)
note: data represent population by country of birth

Languages: English (official) 88.8%, Spanish 3.9%, Filipino 3.8%, other 2.8%, unspecified 0.7% (2021 est.)
note: data represent main language spoken at home

Religions: Protestant 60.8% (includes Church of God 19.5%, Seventh Day Adventist 8.7%, non-denominational 8.3%, Baptist 6.9%, Pentecostal 6.8%, Presbyterian/United Church 5.7%, Anglican 2.8%, Wesleyan Holiness 1.5%, Methodist 0.5%), Roman Catholic 13.6%, Hindu 1.7%, Jehovah's Witness 0.9%, other 4.8%, none 16.7%, unspecified 1.4% (2021 est.)

Age structure: *0-14 years:* 17.4% (male 5,845/female 5,767)
15-64 years: 65.9% (male 21,480/female 22,456)
65 years and over: 16.7% (2024 est.) (male 5,054/female 6,051)

Dependency ratios: *total dependency ratio:* 32.6
youth dependency ratio: 22.3
elderly dependency ratio: 10.4
potential support ratio: 9.6 (2021)

Median age: *total:* 41.2 years (2024 est.)
male: 40.3 years
female: 42 years
comparison ranking: total 51

Population growth rate: 1.75% (2024 est.)
comparison ranking: 51

Birth rate: 11.5 births/1,000 population (2024 est.)
comparison ranking: 158

Death rate: 6.1 deaths/1,000 population (2024 est.)
comparison ranking: 149

Net migration rate: 12.1 migrant(s)/1,000 population (2024 est.)
comparison ranking: 5

Population distribution: majority of the population resides on Grand Cayman

Urbanization: *urban population:* 100% of total population (2023)
rate of urbanization: 1.13% annual rate of change (2020-25 est.)

Major urban areas - population: 35,000 GEORGE TOWN (capital) (2018)

Sex ratio: *at birth:* 1.02 male(s)/female
0-14 years: 1.01 male(s)/female
15-64 years: 0.96 male(s)/female
65 years and over: 0.84 male(s)/female
total population: 0.95 male(s)/female (2024 est.)

Infant mortality rate: *total:* 7.3 deaths/1,000 live births (2024 est.)
male: 8.8 deaths/1,000 live births
female: 5.7 deaths/1,000 live births
comparison ranking: total 154

Life expectancy at birth: *total population:* 82.5 years (2024 est.)
male: 79.8 years
female: 85.2 years
comparison ranking: total population 27

Total fertility rate: 1.82 children born/woman (2024 est.)
comparison ranking: 136

Gross reproduction rate: 0.9 (2024 est.)

Drinking water source: *improved: urban:* 97.4% of population
total: 97.4% of population
unimproved: urban: 2.6% of population
total: 2.6% of population (2015 est.)

Sanitation facility access: *improved: urban:* 95.6% of population
total: 95.6% of population
unimproved: urban: 4.4% of population
total: 4.4% of population (2015 est.)

Currently married women (ages 15-49): 51.4% (2023 est.)

Education expenditures: 2.1% of GDP (2019)
comparison ranking: 185

Literacy: *total population:* 98.9%
male: 98.7%
female: 99% (2021)

ENVIRONMENT

Environment - current issues: no natural freshwater resources; drinking water supplies are met by reverse osmosis desalination plants and rainwater catchment; trash washing up on the beaches or being deposited there by residents; no recycling or waste treatment facilities; deforestation (trees being cut down to create space for commercial use)

Climate: tropical marine; warm, rainy summers (May to October) and cool, relatively dry winters (November to April)

Urbanization: *urban population:* 100% of total population (2023)
rate of urbanization: 1.13% annual rate of change (2020-25 est.)

Revenue from forest resources: 0% of GDP (2018 est.)
comparison ranking: 199

Revenue from coal: 0% of GDP (2018 est.)
comparison ranking: 127

Air pollutants: *carbon dioxide emissions:* 0.55 megatons (2016 est.)

Waste and recycling: *municipal solid waste generated annually:* 60,000 tons (2014 est.)
municipal solid waste recycled annually: 12,600 tons (2013 est.)
percent of municipal solid waste recycled: 21% (2013 est.)

GOVERNMENT

Country name: *conventional long form:* none
conventional short form: Cayman Islands
etymology: the islands' name comes from the native Carib word "caiman," describing the marine crocodiles living there

Government type: parliamentary democracy; self-governing overseas territory of the UK

Dependency status: overseas territory of the UK

Capital: *name:* George Town (on Grand Cayman)
geographic coordinates: 19 18 N, 81 23 W
time difference: UTC-5 (same time as Washington, DC, during Standard Time)
etymology: named after English King GEORGE III (1738-1820)

Administrative divisions: 6 districts; Bodden Town, Cayman Brac and Little Cayman, East End, George Town, North Side, West Bay

Independence: none (overseas territory of the UK)

National holiday: Constitution Day, the first Monday in July (1959)

Legal system: English common law and local statutes

Constitution: *history:* several previous; latest approved 10 June 2009, entered into force 6 November 2009 (The Cayman Islands Constitution Order 2009)
amendments: amended 2016, 2020

Citizenship: see United Kingdom

Suffrage: 18 years of age; universal

Executive branch: *chief of state:* King CHARLES III (since 8 September 2022); represented by Governor Jane OWEN (since 21 April 2023)
head of government: Premier Juliana O'CONNOR-CONNOLLY (since 15 November 2023)
cabinet: Cabinet selected from the Parliament and appointed by the governor on the advice of the premier
elections/appointments: the monarchy is hereditary; governor appointed by the monarch; following legislative elections, the leader of the majority party or majority coalition appointed premier by the governor

Legislative branch: *description:* unicameral Parliament (21 seats; 19 members directly elected by majority vote and 2 ex-officio members - the deputy governor and attorney general - appointed by the governor; members serve 4-year terms)
elections: last held on 14 April 2021 (next to be held in 2025)
election results: percent of vote by party - independent 79.1%, PPM 19.6%; elected seats by party - independent 12, PPM 7; ex-officio members 2; composition - men 16, women 5, percentage women 23.8%

Judicial branch: *highest court(s):* Court of Appeal (consists of the court president and at least 2 judges); Grand Court (consists of the court president and at least 2 judges); note - appeals beyond the Court of Appeal are heard by the Judicial Committee of the Privy Council (in London)
judge selection and term of office: Court of Appeal and Grand Court judges appointed by the governor on the advice of the Judicial and Legal Services Commission, an 8-member independent body consisting of governor appointees, Court of Appeal president, and attorneys; Court of Appeal judges' tenure based on their individual instruments of appointment; Grand Court judges normally appointed until retirement at age 65 but can be extended until age 70
subordinate courts: Summary Court

Political parties: Cayman Islands Peoples Party or CIPP
People's Progressive Movement or PPM

International organization participation: Caricom (associate), CDB, Interpol (subbureau), IOC, UNESCO (associate), UPU

Diplomatic representation in the US: none (overseas territory of the UK)

Diplomatic representation from the US: *embassy:* none (overseas territory of the UK); consular services provided through the US Embassy in Jamaica

Flag description: a blue field with the flag of the UK in the upper hoist-side quadrant and the Caymanian coat of arms centered on the outer half of the flag; the coat of arms includes a crest with a pineapple, representing the connection with Jamaica, and a turtle, representing Cayman's seafaring tradition, above a shield bearing a golden lion, symbolizing Great Britain, below which are three green stars (representing the three islands) surmounting white and blue wavy lines representing the sea; a scroll below the shield bears the motto HE HATH FOUNDED IT UPON THE SEAS

National symbol(s): green sea turtle

National anthem: *name:* "Beloved Isle Cayman"
lyrics/music: Leila E. ROSS
note: adopted 1993; served as an unofficial anthem since 1930; as an overseas territory of the United Kingdom, in addition to the local anthem, "God Save the King" is official (see United Kingdom)

ECONOMY

Economic overview: dominant offshore banking territory; services sector accounts for over 85% of economic activity; recently adopted a fiscal responsibility framework to combat tax evasion and money laundering; large tourism sector; does not have any welfare system; high standard of living

Real GDP (purchasing power parity): $5.467 billion (2022 est.)
$5.199 billion (2021 est.)
$4.956 billion (2020 est.)
note: data in 2021 dollars
comparison ranking: 181

Real GDP growth rate: 5.16% (2022 est.)
4.9% (2021 est.)
-4.95% (2020 est.)
note: annual GDP % growth based on constant local currency
comparison ranking: 48

Real GDP per capita: $79,600 (2022 est.)
$76,300 (2021 est.)
$73,600 (2020 est.)
note: data in 2021 dollars
comparison ranking: 11

GDP (official exchange rate): $6.601 billion (2022 est.)
note: data in current dollars at official exchange rate

Inflation rate (consumer prices): 2% (2017 est.)
-0.63% (2016 est.)
-2.35% (2015 est.)
note: annual % change based on consumer prices
comparison ranking: 36

Credit ratings: Moody's rating: Aa3 (1997)
note: The year refers to the year in which the current credit rating was first obtained.

GDP - composition, by sector of origin: *agriculture:* 0.5% (2022 est.)
industry: 8.2% (2022 est.)
services: 85.4% (2022 est.)
note: figures may not total 100% due to non-allocated consumption not captured in sector-reported data comparison rankings: services 12; industry 204; agriculture 198

GDP - composition, by end use: *household consumption:* 62.3% (2017 est.)
government consumption: 2.6% (2020 est.)
investment in fixed capital: 22.1% (2017 est.)
investment in inventories: 0.1% (2017 est.)
exports of goods and services: 59.6% (2020 est.)
imports of goods and services: -45.8% (2020 est.)
note: figures may not total 100% due to rounding or gaps in data collection

Agricultural products: vegetables, fruit; livestock; turtle farming

Industries: tourism, banking, insurance and finance, construction, construction materials, furniture

Industrial production growth rate: 3.45% (2022 est.)
note: annual % change in industrial value added based on constant local currency
comparison ranking: 97

Unemployment rate: (2008)
(2004)

Youth unemployment rate (ages 15-24): *total:* 13.8% (2015 est.)
male: 16.4%
female: 11.4%
comparison ranking: total 100

Remittances: 0.15% of GDP (2022 est.)
0.17% of GDP (2021 est.)
0.16% of GDP (2020 est.)
note: personal transfers and compensation between resident and non-resident individuals/households/entities

Budget: *revenues:* $874.5 million (2017 est.)
expenditures: $766.6 million (2017 est.)

Taxes and other revenues: 38.9% (of GDP) (2017 est.)
comparison ranking: 11

Current account balance: -$821.404 million (2021 est.)
-$827.492 million (2020 est.)
-$646.843 million (2019 est.)
note: balance of payments - net trade and primary/secondary income in current dollars
comparison ranking: 133

Exports: $4.054 billion (2021 est.)
$3.951 billion (2020 est.)
$4.205 billion (2019 est.)
note: balance of payments - exports of goods and services in current dollars
comparison ranking: 147

Exports - partners: Malta 30%, Norway 22%, Seychelles 16%, Grenada 8%, US 5% (2022)
note: top five export partners based on percentage share of exports

Exports - commodities: ships, aircraft, refined petroleum, natural gas, broadcasting equipment (2022)
note: top five export commodities based on value in dollars

Imports: $2.743 billion (2021 est.)
$2.51 billion (2020 est.)
$2.743 billion (2019 est.)
note: balance of payments - imports of goods and services in current dollars
comparison ranking: 165

Imports - partners: US 47%, Italy 19%, Turkey 7%, Germany 6%, Switzerland 4% (2022)
note: top five import partners based on percentage share of imports

Imports - commodities: ships, refined petroleum, diamonds, cars, gold (2022)
note: top five import commodities based on value in dollars

Reserves of foreign exchange and gold: $216.8 million (2020 est.)
$183.5 million (2019 est.)
$162.074 million (2018 est.)
note: holdings of gold (year-end prices)/foreign exchange/special drawing rights in current dollars
comparison ranking: 178

Exchange rates: Caymanian dollars (KYD) per US dollar -

Exchange rates: 0.833 (2021 est.)
0.833 (2020 est.)
0.833 (2019 est.)
0.833 (2018 est.)
0.833 (2017 est.)

ENERGY

Electricity access: *electrification - total population:* 100% (2022 est.)

Electricity: *installed generating capacity:* 175,000 kW (2022 est.)
consumption: 697.351 million kWh (2022 est.)

transmission/distribution losses: 2.117 million kWh (2022 est.)
comparison rankings: transmission/distribution losses 6; consumption 166; installed generating capacity 176

Electricity generation sources: *fossil fuels:* 96.9% of total installed capacity (2022 est.)
solar: 3.1% of total installed capacity (2022 est.)

Petroleum: *refined petroleum consumption:* 5,000 bbl/day (2022 est.)

Carbon dioxide emissions: 718,000 metric tonnes of CO_2 (2022 est.)
from petroleum and other liquids: 718,000 metric tonnes of CO_2 (2022 est.)
comparison ranking: total emissions 179

Energy consumption per capita: 144.845 million Btu/person (2022 est.)
comparison ranking: 29

COMMUNICATIONS

Telephones - fixed lines: *total subscriptions:* 36,000 (2021 est.)
subscriptions per 100 inhabitants: 53 (2021 est.)
comparison ranking: total subscriptions 163

Telephones - mobile cellular: *total subscriptions:* 100,000 (2021 est.)
subscriptions per 100 inhabitants: 147 (2021 est.)
comparison ranking: total subscriptions 194

Telecommunication systems: *general assessment:* the telecom sector has seen a decline in subscriber numbers (particularly for prepaid mobile services the mainstay of short term visitors) and revenue; fixed and mobile broadband services are two areas that have benefited from the crisis as employees and students have resorted to working from home; one area of the telecom market that is not prepared for growth is 5G mobile; governments, regulators, and even the mobile network operators have shown that they have not been investing in 5G opportunities at the present time; network expansion and enhancements remain concentrated around improving LTE coverage (2021)
domestic: 53 per 100 fixed-line and 150 per 100 mobile-cellular (2021)
international: country code - 1-345; landing points for the Maya-1, Deep Blue Cable, and the Cayman-Jamaica Fiber System submarine cables that provide links to the US and parts of Central and South America; satellite earth station - 1 Intelsat (Atlantic Ocean) (2019)

Broadcast media: 4 TV stations; cable and satellite subscription services offer a variety of international programming; government-owned Radio Cayman operates 2 networks broadcasting on 5 stations; 10 privately owned radio stations operate alongside Radio Cayman

Internet country code: .ky

Internet users: *total:* 55,148 (2021 est.)
percent of population: 81.1% (2021 est.)
comparison ranking: total 199

Broadband - fixed subscriptions: *total:* 3,200 (2020 est.)
subscriptions per 100 inhabitants: 49 (2020 est.)
comparison ranking: total 191

TRANSPORTATION

National air transport system: *number of registered air carriers:* 1 (2020)
inventory of registered aircraft operated by air carriers: 6

Civil aircraft registration country code prefix: VP-C

Airports: 3 (2024)
comparison ranking: 188

Heliports: 5 (2024)

Roadways: *total:* 785 km
paved: 785 km (2007)
comparison ranking: total 190

Merchant marine: *total:* 130 (2023)
by type: bulk carrier 29, container ship 3, general cargo 1, oil tanker 20, other 77
comparison ranking: total 77

Ports: *total ports:* 2 (2024)
large: 0
medium: 0
small: 0
very small: 2
ports with oil terminals: 2
key ports: Cayman Brac, Georgetown

MILITARY AND SECURITY

Military and security forces: no regular military forces; Royal Cayman Islands Police Service

Military - note: defense is the responsibility of the UK

TRANSNATIONAL ISSUES

Illicit drugs: major offshore financial center vulnerable to drug trafficking money laundering

CENTRAL AFRICAN REPUBLIC

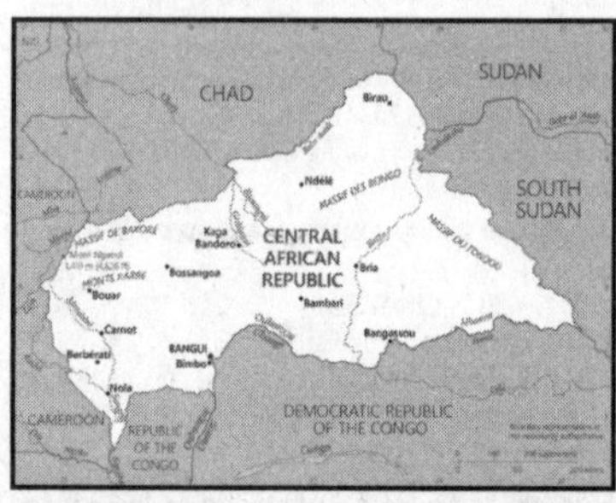

INTRODUCTION

Background: The Central African Republic (CAR) is a perennially weak state that sits at the crossroads of ethnic and linguistic groups in the center of the African continent. Among the last areas of Sub-Saharan Africa to be drawn into the world economy, its introduction into trade networks around the early 1700s fostered significant competition among its population. The local population sought to benefit from the lucrative Atlantic, trans-Saharan, and Indian Ocean trade in enslaved people and ivory. Slave raids aided by the local populations fostered animosity between ethnic groups that remains today. The territory was established as a French colony named Ubangui-Shari in 1903, and France modeled its administration of the colony after the Belgian Congo, subcontracting control of the territory to private companies that collected rubber and ivory. Although France banned the domestic slave trade in CAR in the 1910s, the private companies continued to exploit the population through forced labor. The colony of Ubangi-Shari gained independence from France as the Central African Republic in 1960, but the death of independence leader Barthelemy BOGANDA six months prior led to an immediate struggle for power.

CAR's political history has since been marred by a series of coups, the first of which brought Jean-Bedel BOKASSA to power in 1966. Widespread corruption and intolerance for any political opposition characterized his regime. In an effort to prolong his mandate, BOKASSA named himself emperor in 1976 and changed the country's name to the Central African Empire. His regime's economic mismanagement culminated in widespread student protests in 1979 that were violently suppressed by security forces. BOKASSA fell out of favor with the international community and was overthrown in a French-backed coup in 1979. After BOKASSA's departure, the country's name once again became the Central African Republic.

CAR's fifth coup in 2013 unseated President Francois BOZIZE after the Seleka, a mainly Muslim rebel coalition, seized the capital and forced BOZIZE to flee the country. The Seleka's widespread abuses spurred the formation of mainly Christian self-defense groups that called themselves the anti-Balaka, which have also committed human rights abuses against Muslim populations in retaliation. Since the rise of these groups, conflict in CAR has become increasingly ethnoreligious, although focused on identity rather than religious ideology. Elections in 2016 installed independent candidate Faustin-Archange TOUADERA as president; he was reelected in 2020. A peace agreement signed in 2019 between the government and the main armed factions has had little effect, and armed groups remain in control of large swaths of the country's territory. TOUADERA's United Hearts Movement has governed the country since 2016, and a new constitution approved by referendum on 30 July 2023 effectively ended term limits, creating the potential for TOUADERA to extend his rule.

GEOGRAPHY

Location: Central Africa, north of Democratic Republic of the Congo

Geographic coordinates: 7 00 N, 21 00 E

Map references: Africa

Area: *total:* 622,984 sq km
land: 622,984 sq km
water: 0 sq km
comparison ranking: total 47

Area - comparative: slightly smaller than Texas; about four times the size of Georgia

Land boundaries: *total:* 5,920 km
border countries (5): Cameroon 901 km; Chad 1556 km; Democratic Republic of the Congo 1,747 km, Republic of the Congo 487 km; South Sudan 1055 km; Sudan 174 km

Coastline: 0 km (landlocked)

Maritime claims: none (landlocked)

Climate: tropical; hot, dry winters; mild to hot, wet summers

Terrain: vast, flat to rolling plateau; scattered hills in northeast and southwest

Elevation: *highest point:* Mont Ngaoui 1,410 m
lowest point: Oubangui River 335 m
mean elevation: 635 m

Natural resources: diamonds, uranium, timber, gold, oil, hydropower

Land use: *agricultural land:* 8.1% (2018 est.)
arable land: 2.9% (2018 est.)
permanent crops: 0.1% (2018 est.)
permanent pasture: 5.1% (2018 est.)
forest: 36.2% (2018 est.)
other: 55.7% (2018 est.)

Irrigated land: 10 sq km (2012)

Major rivers (by length in km): Oubangui (Ubangi) river [s] (shared with Democratic Republic of Congo and Republic of Congo [m]) - 2,270 km
note – [s] after country name indicates river source; [m] after country name indicates river mouth

Major watersheds (area sq km):Atlantic Ocean drainage: Congo (3,730,881 sq km), *(Mediterranean Sea)* Nile (3,254,853 sq km)

Internal (endorheic basin) drainage: Lake Chad (2,497,738 sq km)

Major aquifers: Congo Basin, Lake Chad Basin

Population distribution: majority of residents live in the western and central areas of the country, especially in and around the capital of Bangui as shown in this population distribution map

Natural hazards: hot, dry, dusty harmattan winds affect northern areas; floods are common

Geography - note: landlocked; almost the precise center of Africa

PEOPLE AND SOCIETY

Population: *total:* 5,650,957
male: 2,814,497
female: 2,836,460 (2024 est.)
comparison rankings: female 119; male 117; total 117

Nationality: *noun:* Central African(s)
adjective: Central African

Ethnic groups: Baya 28.8%, Banda 22.9%, Mandjia 9.9%, Sara 7.9%, M'Baka-Bantu 7.9%, Arab-Fulani (Peuhl) 6%, Mbum 6%, Ngbanki 5.5%, Zande-Nzakara 3%, other Central African Republic ethnic groups 2%, non-Central African Republic ethnic groups .1% (2003 est.)

Languages: French (official), Sangho (lingua franca and national language), tribal languages

Religions: Roman Catholic 34.6%, Protestant 15.7%, other Christian 22.9%, Muslim 13.8%, ethnic religionist 12%, Baha'i 0.2%, agnostic/atheist 0.7% (2020 est.)
note: animistic beliefs and practices strongly influence the Christian majority

Demographic profile: The Central African Republic's (CAR) humanitarian crisis has worsened since the coup of March 2013. CAR's high mortality rate and low life expectancy are attributed to elevated rates of preventable and treatable diseases (including malaria and malnutrition), an inadequate health care system, precarious food security, and armed conflict. Some of the worst mortality rates are in western CAR's diamond mining region, which has been impoverished because of government attempts to control the diamond trade and the fall in industrial diamond prices. To make matters worse, the government and international donors have reduced health funding in recent years. The CAR's weak educational system and low literacy rate have also suffered as a result of the country's ongoing conflict. Schools are closed, qualified teachers are scarce, infrastructure, funding, and supplies are lacking and subject to looting, and many students and teachers have been displaced by violence. Rampant poverty, human rights violations, unemployment, poor infrastructure, and a lack of security and stability have led to forced displacement internally and externally. Since the political crisis that resulted in CAR's March 2013 coup began in December 2012, approximately 600,000 people have fled to Chad, the Democratic Republic of the Congo, and other neighboring countries, while another estimated 515,000 were displaced internally as of December 2022. The UN has urged countries to refrain from repatriating CAR refugees amid the heightened lawlessness.
(2019)

Age structure: *0-14 years:* 38.5% (male 1,113,795/ female 1,063,971)
15-64 years: 58% (male 1,613,770/female 1,662,522)
65 years and over: 3.5% (2024 est.) (male 86,932/ female 109,967)

Dependency ratios: *total dependency ratio:* 102.8
youth dependency ratio: 97.7
elderly dependency ratio: 5.1
potential support ratio: 19.7 (2021 est.)

Median age: *total:* 20.4 years (2024 est.)
male: 19.7 years
female: 21.2 years
comparison ranking: total 202

Population growth rate: 1.76% (2024 est.)
comparison ranking: 50

Birth rate: 31.9 births/1,000 population (2024 est.)
comparison ranking: 21

Death rate: 11.3 deaths/1,000 population (2024 est.)
comparison ranking: 21

Net migration rate: -3.1 migrant(s)/1,000 population (2024 est.)
comparison ranking: 180

Population distribution: majority of residents live in the western and central areas of the country, especially in and around the capital of Bangui as shown in this population distribution map

Urbanization: *urban population:* 43.6% of total population (2023)
rate of urbanization: 3.32% annual rate of change (2020-25 est.)

Major urban areas - population: 958,000 BANGUI (capital) (2023)

Sex ratio: *at birth:* 1.03 male(s)/female
0-14 years: 1.05 male(s)/female
15-64 years: 0.97 male(s)/female
65 years and over: 0.79 male(s)/female
total population: 0.99 male(s)/female (2024 est.)

Maternal mortality ratio: 835 deaths/100,000 live births (2020 est.)
comparison ranking: 4

Infant mortality rate: *total:* 80.5 deaths/1,000 live births (2024 est.)
male: 86.4 deaths/1,000 live births
female: 74.5 deaths/1,000 live births
comparison ranking: total 3

Life expectancy at birth: *total population:* 56.4 years (2024 est.)
male: 55.1 years
female: 57.7 years
comparison ranking: total population 226

Total fertility rate: 3.94 children born/woman (2024 est.)
comparison ranking: 25

Gross reproduction rate: 1.94 (2024 est.)

Contraceptive prevalence rate: 17.8% (2019)

Drinking water source: *improved: urban:* 83.9% of population
rural: 47.5% of population
total: 62.9% of population
unimproved: urban: 16.1% of population
rural: 52.5% of population
total: 37.1% of population (2020 est.)

Current health expenditure: 9.4% of GDP (2020)

Physician density: 0.07 physicians/1,000 population (2018)

Hospital bed density: 1 beds/1,000 population (2011)

Sanitation facility access: *improved: urban:* 53.8% of population
rural: 12.4% of population
total: 29.9% of population
unimproved: urban: 46.2% of population
rural: 87.6% of population
total: 70.1% of population (2020 est.)

Obesity - adult prevalence rate: 7.5% (2016)
comparison ranking: 159

Alcohol consumption per capita: *total:* 0.94 liters of pure alcohol (2019 est.)
beer: 0.55 liters of pure alcohol (2019 est.)
wine: 0.04 liters of pure alcohol (2019 est.)
spirits: 0.02 liters of pure alcohol (2019 est.)
other alcohols: 0.33 liters of pure alcohol (2019 est.)
comparison ranking: total 152

Children under the age of 5 years underweight: 20.5% (2019)
comparison ranking: 15

Currently married women (ages 15-49): 64.7% (2023 est.)

Child marriage: *women married by age 15:* 25.8%
women married by age 18: 61%
men married by age 18: 17.1% (2019 est.)

Education expenditures: 2.2% of GDP (2020 est.)
comparison ranking: 182

Literacy: *definition:* age 15 and over can read and write
total population: 37.5%
male: 49.2%

female: 26.2% (2020)

School life expectancy (primary to tertiary education): *total:* 7 years
male: 8 years
female: 6 years (2012)

ENVIRONMENT

Environment - current issues: water pollution; tap water is not potable; poaching and mismanagement have diminished the country's reputation as one of the last great wildlife refuges; desertification; deforestation; soil erosion

Environment - international agreements: *party to:* Biodiversity, Climate Change, Climate Change-Kyoto Protocol, Climate Change-Paris Agreement, Comprehensive Nuclear Test Ban, Desertification, Endangered Species, Hazardous Wastes, Nuclear Test Ban, Ozone Layer Protection, Tropical Timber 2006, Wetlands
signed, but not ratified: Law of the Sea

Climate: tropical; hot, dry winters; mild to hot, wet summers

Urbanization: *urban population:* 43.6% of total population (2023)
rate of urbanization: 3.32% annual rate of change (2020-25 est.)

Food insecurity: *exceptional shortfall in aggregate food production/supplies: due to internal conflict and high food prices* - according to the latest analysis, issued in November 2022, the number of people in Crisis and above is estimated at 2.7 million between September 2022 and March 2023; this is mainly attributed to the impact of civil insecurity and high food prices; persisting insecurity and population displacements continue to affect agricultural activities and limit farmers' access to crop growing areas and agricultural inputs; elevated international prices of fuel and fertilizers, largely imported, have reportedly led to a lower use of agricultural inputs in 2022, especially among smallholder farmers, with a negative impact on yields (2023)

Revenue from forest resources: 8.99% of GDP (2018 est.)
comparison ranking: 5

Revenue from coal: 0% of GDP (2018 est.)
comparison ranking: 71

Air pollutants: *particulate matter emissions:* 27.2 micrograms per cubic meter (2019 est.)
carbon dioxide emissions: 0.3 megatons (2016 est.)
methane emissions: 22.44 megatons (2020 est.)

Waste and recycling: *municipal solid waste generated annually:* 1,105,983 tons (2014 est.)

Major rivers (by length in km): Oubangui (Ubangi) river [s] (shared with Democratic Republic of Congo and Republic of Congo [m]) - 2,270 km
note – [s] after country name indicates river source; [m] after country name indicates river mouth

Major watersheds (area sq km):Atlantic Ocean drainage: Congo (3,730,881 sq km), *(Mediterranean Sea)* Nile (3,254,853 sq km)

Internal (endorheic basin) drainage: Lake Chad (2,497,738 sq km)

Major aquifers: Congo Basin, Lake Chad Basin

Total water withdrawal: *municipal:* 60 million cubic meters (2020 est.)
industrial: 10 million cubic meters (2020 est.)
agricultural: 400,000 cubic meters (2017 est.)

Total renewable water resources: 141 billion cubic meters (2020 est.)

GOVERNMENT

Country name: *conventional long form:* Central African Republic
conventional short form: none
local long form: République centrafricaine
local short form: none
former: Ubangi-Shari, Central African Empire
abbreviation: CAR
etymology: self-descriptive name specifying the country's location on the continent; "Africa" is derived from the Roman designation of the area corresponding to present-day Tunisia "Africa terra," which meant "Land of the Afri" (the tribe resident in that area), but which eventually came to mean the entire continent

Government type: presidential republic

Capital: *name:* Bangui
geographic coordinates: 4 22 N, 18 35 E
time difference: UTC+1 (6 hours ahead of Washington, DC, during Standard Time)
etymology: established as a French settlement in 1889 and named after its location on the northern bank of the Ubangi River; the Ubangi itself was named from the native word for the "rapids" located beside the outpost, which marked the end of navigable water north from Brazzaville

Administrative divisions: 14 prefectures (prefectures, singular - prefecture), 2 economic prefectures* (prefectures economiques, singular - prefecture economique), and 1 commune**; Bamingui-Bangoran, Bangui**, Basse-Kotto, Haute-Kotto, Haut-Mbomou, Kemo, Lobaye, Mambere-Kadei, Mbomou, Nana-Grebizi*, Nana-Mambere, Ombella-Mpoko, Ouaka, Ouham, Ouham-Pende, Sangha-Mbaere*, Vakaga

Independence: 13 August 1960 (from France)

National holiday: Republic Day, 1 December (1958)

Legal system: civil law system based on the French model

Constitution: *history:* several previous; latest constitution passed by a national referendum on 30 July 2023 and validated by the Constitutional Court on 30 August 2023; note - the new constitution was proposed by President Faustin-Archange Touadéra, extended the presidential term from 5 to 7 years, removed term limits, and will allow President Touadéra to run again in 2025; opposition parties denounced the changes, claiming they were created to facilitate a "life precedency" for Touadéra
amendments: proposals require support of the government, two thirds of the National Council of Transition, and assent by the "Mediator of the Central African" crisis; passage requires at least three-fourths majority vote by the National Council membership; non-amendable constitutional provisions include those on the secular and republican form of government, fundamental rights and freedoms, amendment procedures, or changes to the authorities of various high-level executive, parliamentary, and judicial officials

International law organization participation: has not submitted an ICJ jurisdiction declaration; accepts ICCt jurisdiction

Citizenship: *citizenship by birth:* no
citizenship by descent only: least one parent must be a citizen of the Central African Republic
dual citizenship recognized: yes
residency requirement for naturalization: 35 years

Suffrage: 18 years of age; universal

Executive branch: *chief of state:* President Faustin-Archange TOUADÉRA (since 30 March 2016)
head of government: Prime Minister Félix MOLOUA (since 7 February 2022)
cabinet: Council of Ministers appointed by the president
elections/appointments: president directly elected for 5-year term; election last held 27 December 2020 (next to be held in December 2025); constitutional referendum in July 2023 removed term limits and institutes 7-year terms; note - presidential and partial legislative elections were held on 27 December 2020; voting was disrupted in some areas, delaying the first round of legislative elections until 14 March 2021; constituencies that did vote on 27 December 2020 held runoff elections for their legislators
election results:
2020: Faustin-Archange TOUADÉRA reelected president in first round; percent of vote - Faustin-Archange TOUADÉRA (independent) 53.9%, Anicet Georges DOLOGUELE (URCA) 21%, other 25.1%
2015: Faustin-Archange TOUADÉRA elected president in the second round; percent of vote in first round - Anicet-Georges DOLOGUELE (URCA) 23.7%, Faustin-Archange TOUADÉRA (independent) 19.1%, Desire KOLINGBA (RDC) 12%, Martin ZIGUELE (MLPC) 11.4%, other 33.8%; percent of vote in second round - Faustin-Archange TOUADÉRA 62.7%, Anicet-Georges DOLOGUELE 37.3%

Legislative branch: *description:* unicameral National Assembly or Assemblee Nationale (140 seats; members directly elected in single-seat constituencies by absolute majority vote with a second round if needed; members serve 5-year terms)
elections: last held in December 2020 through July 2021 (next to be held 31 December 2025); note - on 27 December 2020, the day of first round elections, voting in many electoral areas was disrupted by armed groups; on 13 February 2021, President TOUADERA announced that new first round elections would be held on 27 February 2021 for those areas controlled by armed groups and the second round on 14 March 2021; ultimately, two additional rounds were held on 23 May and 25 July 2021 in areas that continued to suffer from election security problems
election results: percent of vote by party - NA; seats by party - MCU 63, MOUNI 9, URCA 7, MLPC 7, RDC 5, KNK 3, PATRIE 3, CDE 2, RDD 2, MDD 2, PGD 2, PAD 2, CANE 2, other 11, independent 20; composition - men 124, women 16, percentage women 11.4%; note - several members of other parties and independent candidates joined the MCU following the opening session of the National Assembly; as of 21 September 2021, the MCU held 86 seats
note: in accordance with article 98 of the constitution published in August 2023, the parliamentary term has increased from five to seven years and will be first applied to the legislature due to be elected in late 2025

Judicial branch: *highest court(s):* Supreme Court or Cour Supreme (consists of NA judges); Constitutional Court (consists of 9 judges, at least 3 of whom are women)

judge selection and term of office: Supreme Court judges appointed by the president; Constitutional Court judge appointments - 2 by the president, 1 by the speaker of the National Assembly, 2 elected by their peers, 2 are advocates elected by their peers, and 2 are law professors elected by their peers; judges serve 7-year non-renewable terms
subordinate courts: high courts; magistrates' courts

Political parties: Action Party for Development or PAD
African Party for Radical Transformation and Integration of States or PATRIE
Alliance for Democracy and Progress or ADP
Be Africa ti e Kwe (also known as Central Africa for Us All or BTK)
Central African Democratic Rally or RDC
Central African Party for Integrated Development or PCDI
Democratic Movement for the Renewal and Evolution of Central Africa or MDREC
Kodro Ti Mo Kozo Si Movement or MKMKS
Movement for Democracy and Development or MDD
Movement for the Liberation of the Central African People or MLPC
National Convergence (also known as Kwa Na Kwa or KNK)
National Movement of Independents or MOUNI
National Union for Democracy and Progress or UNDP
National Union of Republican Democrats or UNADER
New Impetus for Central Africa or CANE
Party for Democracy and Solidarity - Kélémba or KPDS
Party for Democratic Governance or PGD
Path of Hope or CDE
Renaissance for Sustainable Development or RDD
Socialist Party or PS
Transformation Through Action Initiative or ITA
Union for Central African Renewal or URCA
Union for Renaissance and Development or URD
United Hearts Movement or MCU

International organization participation: ACP, AfDB, AU, BDEAC, CEMAC, EITI (compliant country) (suspended), FAO, FZ, G-77, IAEA, IBRD, ICAO, ICCt, ICRM, IDA, IFAD, IFC, IFRCS, ILO, IMF, Interpol, IOC, IOM, ITSO, ITU, ITUC (NGOs), LCBC, MIGA, NAM, OIC (observer), OIF, OPCW, UN, UNCTAD, UNESCO, UNIDO, UNWTO, UPU, WCO, WHO, WIPO, WMO, WTO

Diplomatic representation in the US: *chief of mission:* Ambassador Martial NDOUBOU (since 17 September 2018)
chancery: 2704 Ontario Road NW, Washington, DC 20009
telephone: [1] (202) 483-7800
FAX: [1] (202) 332-9893
email address and website:
centrafricwashington@yahoo.com
https://www.usrcaembassy.org/

Diplomatic representation from the US: *chief of mission:* Ambassador Patricia A. MAHONEY (since 8 April 2022)
embassy: Avenue David Dacko, Bangui
mailing address: 2060 Bangui Place, Washington DC 20521-2060
telephone: [236] 2161-0200
FAX: [236] 2161-4494
email address and website:
https://cf.usembassy.gov/

Flag description: four equal horizontal bands of blue (top), white, green, and yellow with a vertical red band in center; a yellow five-pointed star to the hoist side of the blue band; banner combines the Pan-African and French flag colors; red symbolizes the blood spilled in the struggle for independence, blue represents the sky and freedom, white peace and dignity, green hope and faith, and yellow tolerance; the star represents aspiration towards a vibrant future

National symbol(s): elephant; national colors: blue, white, green, yellow, red

National anthem: *name:* "La Renaissance" (The Renaissance)
lyrics/music: Barthelemy BOGANDA/Herbert PEPPER
note: adopted 1960; Barthelemy BOGANDA wrote the anthem's lyrics and was the first prime minister of the autonomous French territory

National heritage: *total World Heritage Sites:* 2 (natural)
selected World Heritage Site locales: Manovo-Gounda St. Floris National Park; Sangha Trinational Forest

ECONOMY

Economic overview: enormous natural resources; extreme poverty; weak public institutions and infrastructure; political and gender-based violence have led to displacement of roughly 25% of population; Bangui-Douala corridor blockade reduced activity and tax collection; strong agricultural performance offset COVID-19 downturn

Real GDP (purchasing power parity): $5.849 billion (2023 est.)
$5.798 billion (2022 est.)
$5.769 billion (2021 est.)
note: data in 2021 dollars
comparison ranking: 177

Real GDP growth rate: 0.87% (2023 est.)
0.5% (2022 est.)
0.98% (2021 est.)
note: annual GDP % growth based on constant local currency
comparison ranking: 168

Real GDP per capita: $1,000 (2023 est.)
$1,000 (2022 est.)
$1,100 (2021 est.)
note: data in 2021 dollars
comparison ranking: 221

GDP (official exchange rate): $2.555 billion (2023 est.)
note: data in current dollars at official exchange rate

Inflation rate (consumer prices): 2.98% (2023 est.)
5.58% (2022 est.)
4.26% (2021 est.)
note: annual % change based on consumer prices
comparison ranking: 59

GDP - composition, by sector of origin: *agriculture:* 28.6% (2023 est.)
industry: 20.7% (2023 est.)
services: 40.5% (2023 est.)
note: figures may not total 100% due to non-allocated consumption not captured in sector-reported data
comparison rankings: services 190; industry 132; agriculture 12

GDP - composition, by end use: *household consumption:* 97.4% (2023 est.)
government consumption: 8.3% (2023 est.)
investment in fixed capital: 14.6% (2023 est.)
investment in inventories: 9.2% (2023 est.)
exports of goods and services: 14.4% (2023 est.)
imports of goods and services: -29% (2023 est.)
note: figures may not total 100% due to rounding or gaps in data collection

Agricultural products: cassava, groundnuts, yams, coffee, maize, sesame seeds, bananas, taro, sugarcane, beef (2022)
note: top ten agricultural products based on tonnage

Industries: gold and diamond mining, logging, brewing, sugar refining

Industrial production growth rate: -10.28% (2023 est.)
note: annual % change in industrial value added based on constant local currency
comparison ranking: 209

Labor force: 2.114 million (2023 est.)
note: number of people ages 15 or older who are employed or seeking work
comparison ranking: 125

Unemployment rate: 6.29% (2023 est.)
6.34% (2022 est.)
6.68% (2021 est.)
note: % of labor force seeking employment
comparison ranking: 128

Youth unemployment rate (ages 15-24): *total:* 10.7% (2023 est.)
male: 9.7% (2023 est.)
female: 11.8% (2023 est.)
note: % of labor force ages 15-24 seeking employment
comparison ranking: total 127

Population below poverty line: 68.8% (2021 est.)
note: % of population with income below national poverty line

Gini Index coefficient - distribution of family income: 43 (2021 est.)
note: index (0-100) of income distribution; higher values represent greater inequality
comparison ranking: 31

Household income or consumption by percentage share: *lowest 10%:* 2.1% (2021 est.)
highest 10%: 33.1% (2021 est.)
note: % share of income accruing to lowest and highest 10% of population

Remittances: 0% of GDP (2023 est.)
0% of GDP (2022 est.)
0% of GDP (2021 est.)

Budget: *revenues:* $360.48 million (2021 est.)
expenditures: $293.459 million (2021 est.)
note: central government revenues and expenses (excluding grants/extrabudgetary units/social security funds) converted to US dollars at average official exchange rate for year indicated

Public debt: 52.9% of GDP (2017 est.)
comparison ranking: 95

Taxes and other revenues: 8.21% (of GDP) (2021 est.)
note: central government tax revenue as a % of GDP
comparison ranking: 189

Current account balance: -$163 million (2017 est.)
-$97 million (2016 est.)
comparison ranking: 107

Exports: $293.074 million (2022 est.)
$332.869 million (2021 est.)

$353.021 million (2020 est.)
note: GDP expenditure basis - exports of goods and services in current dollars
comparison ranking: 196

Exports - partners: UAE 40%, Italy 11%, Pakistan 10%, China 10%, France 6% (2022)
note: top five export partners based on percentage share of exports

Exports - commodities: gold, wood, diamonds, vehicle parts/accessories, electrical machinery (2022)
note: top five export commodities based on value in dollars

Imports: $784.669 million (2022 est.)
$778.395 million (2021 est.)
$799.195 million (2020 est.)
note: GDP expenditure basis - imports of goods and services in current dollars
comparison ranking: 196

Imports - partners: Cameroon 28%, US 8%, China 7%, France 6%, South Korea 5% (2022)
note: top five import partners based on percentage share of imports

Imports - commodities: refined petroleum, engines, aircraft, prefabricated buildings, packaged medicine (2022)
note: top five import commodities based on value in dollars

Reserves of foreign exchange and gold: $374.405 million (2022 est.)
$483.872 million (2021 est.)
$432.524 million (2020 est.)
note: holdings of gold (year-end prices)/foreign exchange/special drawing rights in current dollars
comparison ranking: 169

Debt - external: $552.586 million (2022 est.)
note: present value of external debt in current US dollars
comparison ranking: 89

Exchange rates: Cooperation Financiere en Afrique Centrale francs (XAF) per US dollar -

Exchange rates: 606.57 (2023 est.)
623.76 (2022 est.)
554.531 (2021 est.)
575.586 (2020 est.)
585.911 (2019 est.)

ENERGY

Electricity access: *electrification - total population:* 15.7% (2022 est.)
electrification - urban areas: 34.7%
electrification - rural areas: 1.6%

Electricity: *installed generating capacity:* 38,000 kW (2022 est.)
consumption: 141.105 million kWh (2022 est.)
transmission/distribution losses: 10 million kWh (2022 est.)
comparison rankings: transmission/distribution losses 17; consumption 196; installed generating capacity 199

Electricity generation sources: *fossil fuels:* 0.7% of total installed capacity (2022 est.)
hydroelectricity: 99.3% of total installed capacity (2022 est.)

Coal: *imports:* 0.7 metric tons (2022 est.)
proven reserves: 3 million metric tons (2022 est.)

Petroleum: *refined petroleum consumption:* 2,000 bbl/day (2022 est.)

Carbon dioxide emissions: 316,000 metric tonnes of CO2 (2022 est.)
from petroleum and other liquids: 316,000 metric tonnes of CO2 (2022 est.)
comparison ranking: total emissions 196

Energy consumption per capita: 881,000 Btu/person (2022 est.)
comparison ranking: 194

COMMUNICATIONS

Telephones - fixed lines: *total subscriptions:* 2,000 (2021 est.)
subscriptions per 100 inhabitants: (2021 est.) less than 1
comparison ranking: total subscriptions 215

Telephones - mobile cellular: *total subscriptions:* 1.831 million (2021 est.)
subscriptions per 100 inhabitants: 34 (2021 est.)
comparison ranking: total subscriptions 153

Telecommunication systems: *general assessment:* given the poor fixed-line infrastructure in most countries across Africa, voice and data services across the region are greatly dependent on mobile networks; in the majority of markets, including those with better developed fixed infrastructure such as South Africa, Nigeria, and Kenya, up to 98% of all voice and data connections are via mobile networks; during the last two to three years, national governments and telecom regulators have striven to improve fixed infrastructure with the wider aim of developing economic growth based on digital services and connectivity; this work is principally focused on delivering fiber-based connectivity; since the amount of copper infrastructure (DSL or HFC) used for broadband is so negligible, governments and private firms, including telcos are investing in fiber rather than in older technologies; while supporting broadband to premises, health centers, and government buildings, the new fiber infrastructure is mainly being deployed to provide mobile platforms and to support the rapid growth in data traffic (2022)
domestic: very limited telephone service with less than 1 fixed-line connection per 100 persons; 34 per 100 mobilecellular subscribers (2020)
international: country code - 236; satellite earth station - 1 Intelsat (Atlantic Ocean)

Broadcast media: government-owned network, Radiodiffusion Television Centrafricaine, provides limited domestic TV broadcasting; state-owned radio network is supplemented by a small number of privately owned broadcast stations as well as a few community radio stations; transmissions of at least 2 international broadcasters are available (2017)

Internet country code: .cf

Internet users: *total:* 605,000 (2021 est.)
percent of population: 11% (2021 est.)
comparison ranking: total 165

Broadband - fixed subscriptions: *total:* 499 (2019 est.) Data available for 2019 only.
subscriptions per 100 inhabitants: 0.01 (2019 est.)
comparison ranking: total 210

TRANSPORTATION

National air transport system: *number of registered air carriers:* 2 (2020)
inventory of registered aircraft operated by air carriers: 2
annual passenger traffic on registered air carriers: 46,364 (2015)
annual freight traffic on registered air carriers: 0 (2015) mt-km

Civil aircraft registration country code prefix: TL

Airports: 43 (2024)
comparison ranking: 94

Roadways: *total:* 24,000 km
paved: 700 km
unpaved: 23,300 km (2018)
comparison ranking: total 110

Waterways: 2,800 km (2011) (the primary navigable river is the Ubangi, which joins the River Congo; it was the traditional route for the export of products because it connected with the Congo-Ocean railway at Brazzaville; because of the warfare on both sides of the River Congo from 1997, importers and exporters preferred routes through Cameroon)
comparison ranking: 36

MILITARY AND SECURITY

Military and security forces: Central African Armed Forces (Forces Armees Centrafricaines, FACA): Army (includes an air squadron, Escadrille Centrafricaine)

Ministry of Interior: National Gendarmerie (Gendarmerie Nationale), National Police (2023)
note 1: the Special Republican Protection Group (Groupement Spécial Chargé de la Protection Républicaine or GSPR) is part of the Army per a March 2022 decree, but reports to the president; the GSPR provides protection to the head of state
note 2: in 2019-2021, the CAR established three Mixed Special Security units (Unités Spéciales Mixtes de Sécurité or USMS), regionally based battalion-sized units comprised of about 40% government and 60% rebel soldiers formed to provide security along transportation corridors and at mining sites; the units were intended to be transitional in nature with a scheduled deployment time of two years; in addition, since mid-2021 the FACA have frequently recruited local militias, mostly former anti-balaka and seleka fighters, whom they pay to help track and attack rebels hiding in the bush

Military expenditures: 1.8% of GDP (2023 est.)
1.7% of GDP (2022 est.)
1.8% of GDP (2021 est.)
1.8% of GDP (2020 est.)
1.7% of GDP (2019 est.)
comparison ranking: 78

Military and security service personnel strengths: estimates vary; up to 15,000 FACA troops; estimated 15-20,000 Gendarmerie and National Police (2023)

Military equipment inventories and acquisitions: most of the military's heavy weapons and equipment were destroyed or captured during the 2012–2014 civil war; prior to the war, most of its equipment was of French, Russian, or Soviet origin; in recent years, it has received some secondhand equipment from China and Russia, including light weapons, as well as some armored vehicles, unmanned aerial vehicles, and helicopters (2024)
note: the CAR was under a UNSC arms embargo from 2013-July 2024

Military service age and obligation: 18 years of age for military service; no conscription although the constitution provides for the possibility of conscription in the event of an imminent threat to the country (2023)

Military - note: the 2013 coup resulted in the institutional collapse of the FACA; its forces were overwhelmed and forced to flee to neighboring countries; it has been estimated that only 10% of the FACA returned after the coup, and the FACA has struggled to rebuild in the years of instability since, despite significant foreign assistance; considerable portions of the country remain outside state control and are ungoverned, with the presence of multiple armed actors creating insecurity in much of the country

in late 2020 and early 2021, the Coalition des Patriotes pour le Change (CPC), a loose coalition of armed groups comprised largely of former Seleka and anti-Balaka fighters, attacked the capital Bangui; CAR Government forces, along with Russian private military contractors and Rwandan troops, repelled the attack while the CPC retreated to its rear bases and into neighboring countries and continued conducting attacks; as of 2023, the CAR Government claimed to have restored authority across much of the country, including the capital, although armed groups, including some not affiliated with CPC, continued to carry out violent activities in regions outside the capital, threatening local stability; forces on both sides have been accused of abuses and atrocities in the fighting

in 2018, the UN Security Council approved Russian security assistance for the CAR to help train and advise FACA personnel, as well as transport them to operational areas, provide logistical support, and assist with medical evacuation; in addition to teams of military trainers, Russia sent private military contractors to provide assistance to the FACA; the Russians have also performed other security roles such as guarding mines and government officials; some Russian contractors and the CAR forces they supported have been accused of carrying out indiscriminate killings, using excessive force against civilians, and looting

the UN Multidimensional Integrated Stabilization Mission in the Central African Republic (MINUSCA) has operated in the country since 2014; its mission includes providing security, protecting civilians, facilitating humanitarian assistance, disarming and demobilizing armed groups, and supporting the country's fragile transitional government; as of early 2024, MINUSCA had more than 16,000 military and police personnel

the European Union Training Mission in the Central African Republic (EUTM-RCA) has operated in the country since 2016, providing advice, training, and educational programs to the country's security forces; the EU mission has trained five FACA territorial infantry battalions and one amphibious infantry battalion; France and Rwanda have also provided assistance to the FACA; France suspended its support in 2021, but Rwanda continued providing troops and military training as of 2024 (2024)

TRANSNATIONAL ISSUES

Refugees and internally displaced persons: *refugees (country of origin):* 28,217 (Sudan) (refugees since 15 April 2023), 6,707 (Democratic Republic of the Congo) (2024)

IDPs: 490,868 (clashes between army and rebel groups since 2005; tensions between ethnic groups) (2023)

Trafficking in persons: tier rating: Tier 2 Watch list — The Central African Republic did not demonstrate overall increasing efforts to eliminate trafficking compared with the previous reporti`ng period and was downgraded to Tier 2 Watch List; for more details, go to: https://www.state.gov/reports/2024-trafficking-in-persons-report/central-african-republic/

CHAD

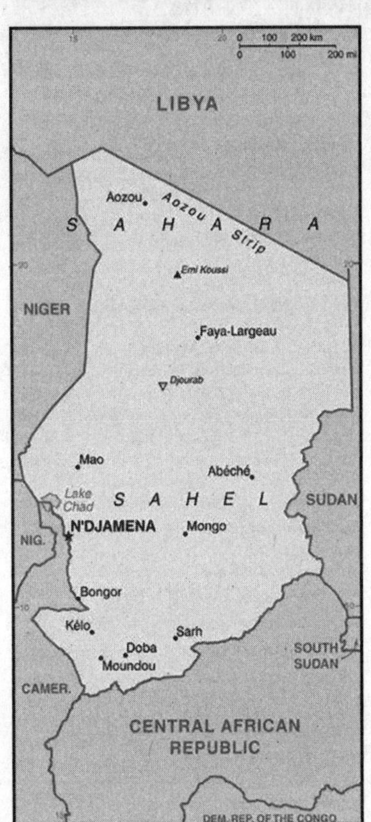

INTRODUCTION

Background: Chad emerged from a collection of powerful states that controlled the Sahelian belt starting around the 9th century. These states focused on controlling trans-Saharan trade routes and profited mostly from the slave trade. The Kanem-Bornu Empire, centered around the Lake Chad Basin, existed between the 9th and 19th centuries, and at its peak, the empire controlled territory stretching from southern Chad to southern Libya and included portions of modern-day Algeria, Cameroon, Niger, Nigeria, and Sudan. The Sudanese warlord Rabih AZ-ZUBAYR used an army comprised largely of slaves to conquer the Kanem-Bornu Empire in the late 19th century. In southeastern Chad, the Bagirmi and Ouaddai (Wadai) kingdoms emerged in the 15th and 16th centuries and lasted until the arrival of the French in the 19th and 20th centuries. France began moving into the region in the late 1880s and defeated the Bagirmi kingdom in 1897, Rabih AZ-ZUBAYR in 1900, and the Ouddai kingdom in 1909. In the arid regions of northern Chad and southern Libya, an Islamic order called the Sanusiyya (Sanusi) relied heavily on the trans-Saharan slave trade and had upwards of 3 million followers by the 1880s. The French defeated the Sanusiyya in 1910 after years of intermittent war. By 1910, France had incorporated the northern arid region, the Lake Chad Basin, and southeastern Chad into French Equatorial Africa.

Chad achieved its independence in 1960 and then saw three decades of instability, oppressive rule, civil war, and a Libyan invasion. With the help of the French military and several African countries, Chadian leaders expelled Libyan forces during the 1987 "Toyota War," so named for the use of Toyota pickup trucks as fighting vehicles. In 1990, Chadian general Idriss DEBY led a rebellion against President Hissene HABRE. Under DEBY, Chad approved a constitution and held elections in 1996. Shortly after DEBY was killed during a rebel incursion in 2021, a group of military officials – led by DEBY's son, Mahamat Idriss DEBY – took control of the government. The military officials dismissed the National Assembly, suspended the Constitution, and formed a Transitional Military Council (TMC), while pledging to hold democratic elections by October 2022. A national dialogue in August-October 2022 culminated in decisions to extend the transition for up to two years, dissolve the TMC, and appoint Mahamat DEBY as Transitional President; the transitional authorities held a constitutional referendum in December 2023 and claimed 86 percent of votes were in favor of the new constitution. The transitional authorities have announced plans to hold elections by October 2024.

Chad has faced widespread poverty, an economy severely weakened by volatile international oil prices, terrorist-led insurgencies in the Lake Chad Basin, and several waves of rebellions in northern and eastern Chad. In 2015, the government imposed a state of emergency in the Lake Chad Basin following multiple attacks by the terrorist group Boko Haram, now known as ISIS-West Africa. The same year, Boko Haram conducted bombings in N'Djamena. In 2019, the Chadian government also declared a state of emergency in the Sila and Ouaddai regions bordering Sudan and in the Tibesti region bordering Niger, where rival ethnic groups are still fighting. The army has suffered heavy losses to Islamic terror groups in the Lake Chad Basin.

GEOGRAPHY

Location: Central Africa, south of Libya

Geographic coordinates: 15 00 N, 19 00 E

Map references: Africa

Area: *total:* 1.284 million sq km

land: 1,259,200 sq km
water: 24,800 sq km
comparison ranking: total 22

Area - comparative: almost nine times the size of New York state; slightly more than three times the size of California

Land boundaries: *total:* 6,406 km
border countries (6): Cameroon 1,116 km; Central African Republic 1,556 km; Libya 1,050 km; Niger 1,196 km; Nigeria 85 km; Sudan 1,403 km

Coastline: 0 km (landlocked)

Maritime claims: none (landlocked)

Climate: tropical in south, desert in north

Terrain: broad, arid plains in center, desert in north, mountains in northwest, lowlands in south

Elevation: *highest point:* Emi Koussi 3,445 m
lowest point: Djourab 160 m
mean elevation: 543 m

Natural resources: petroleum, uranium, natron, kaolin, fish (Lake Chad), gold, limestone, sand and gravel, salt

Land use: *agricultural land:* 39.6% (2018 est.)
arable land: 3.9% (2018 est.)
permanent crops: 0% (2018 est.)
permanent pasture: 35.7% (2018 est.)
forest: 9.1% (2018 est.)
other: 51.3% (2018 est.)

Irrigated land: 300 sq km (2012)

Major lakes (area sq km): *fresh water lake(s):* Lake Chad (endorheic lake shared with Niger, Nigeria, and Cameroon) - 10,360-25,900 sq km
note - area varies by season and year to year

Major watersheds (area sq km): Atlantic Ocean drainage: Niger (2,261,741 sq km)

Internal (endorheic basin) drainage: Lake Chad (2,497,738 sq km)

Major aquifers: Lake Chad Basin, Nubian Aquifer System

Population distribution: the population is unevenly distributed due to contrasts in climate and physical geography; the highest density is found in the southwest, particularly around Lake Chad and points south; the dry Saharan zone to the north is the least densely populated as shown in this population distribution map

Natural hazards: hot, dry, dusty harmattan winds occur in north; periodic droughts; locust plagues

Geography - note: *note 1:* Chad is the largest of Africa's 16 landlocked countries
note 2: not long ago, geologically speaking, what is today the Sahara was green savannah teeming with wildlife; during the African Humid Period, roughly 11,000 to 5,000 years ago, a vibrant animal community, including elephants, giraffes, hippos, and antelope lived there; the last remnant of the "Green Sahara" exists in the Lakes of Ounianga (oo-nee-ahn-ga) in northern Chad, a series of 18 interconnected freshwater, saline, and hypersaline lakes now protected as a World Heritage site
note 3: Lake Chad, the most significant water body in the Sahel, is a remnant of a former inland sea, paleolake Mega- Chad; at its greatest extent, sometime before 5000 B.C., Lake Mega-Chad was the largest of four Saharan paleolakes that existed during the African Humid Period; it covered an area of about 400,000 sq km (150,000 sq mi), roughly the size of today's Caspian Sea

PEOPLE AND SOCIETY

Population: *total:* 19,093,595
male: 9,464,699
female: 9,628,896 (2024 est.)
comparison rankings: female 65; male 65; total 65

Nationality: *noun:* Chadian(s)
adjective: Chadian

Ethnic groups: Sara (Ngambaye/Sara/Madjingaye/Mbaye) 30.5%, Kanembu/Bornu/Buduma 9.8%, Arab 9.7%, Wadai/Maba/Masalit/ Mimi 7%, Gorane 5.8%, Masa/Musseye/Musgum 4.9%, Bulala/Medogo/Kuka 3.7%, Marba/Lele/Mesme 3.5%, Mundang 2.7%, Bidiyo/Migaama/Kenga/Dangleat 2.5%, Dadjo/Kibet/Muro 2.4%, Tupuri/Kera 2%, Gabri/Kabalaye/Nanchere/ Somrai 2%, Fulani/Fulbe/Bodore 1.8%, Karo/Zime/Peve 1.3%, Baguirmi/Barma 1.2%, Zaghawa/Bideyat/Kobe 1.1%, Tama/Assongori/Mararit 1.1%, Mesmedje/Massalat/Kadjakse 0.8%, other 4.6%, unspecified 1.7% (2014-15 est.)

Languages: French (official), Arabic (official), Sara (in south), more than 120 languages and dialects
major-language sample(s):
The World Factbook, une source indispensable d'informations de base. (French)
كتاب حقائق العالم، المصدر الذي لا يمكن الاستغناء عنه للمعلومات الأساسية
(Arabic)

Religions: Muslim 52.1%, Protestant 23.9%, Roman Catholic 20%, animist 0.3%, other Christian 0.2%, none 2.8%, unspecified 0.7% (2014-15 est.)

Demographic profile: Despite the start of oil production in 2003, around 40% of Chad's population lived below the poverty line as of 2018. The population will continue to grow rapidly because of the country's very high fertility rate and large youth cohort – more than 65% of the populace is under the age of 25 as of 2022 – although the mortality rate is high and life expectancy is low. Chad has the world's second highest maternal mortality rate as of 2017. Among the primary risk factors are poverty, anemia, rural habitation, high fertility, poor education, and a lack of access to family planning and obstetric care. Impoverished, uneducated adolescents living in rural areas are most affected. To improve women's reproductive health and reduce fertility, Chad will need to increase women's educational attainment, job participation, and knowledge of and access to family planning. Less than a quarter of women are literate, less than 10% use contraceptives, and more than 40% undergo genital cutting.
As of December 2022, more than 403,000 refugees from Sudan and more than 120,000 from the Central African Republic strain Chad's limited resources and create tensions in host communities. Thousands of new refugees fled to Chad in 2013 to escape worsening violence in the Darfur region of Sudan. The large refugee populations are hesitant to return to their home countries because of continued instability. Chad was relatively stable in 2012 in comparison to other states in the region, but past fighting between government forces and opposition groups and inter-communal violence have left more than 380,000 of its citizens displaced in the eastern part of the country as of 2022.

Age structure: *0-14 years:* 45.8% (male 4,428,132/female 4,323,398)
15-64 years: 51.7% (male 4,831,744/female 5,031,383)
65 years and over: 2.5% (2024 est.) (male 204,823/female 274,115)

Dependency ratios: *total dependency ratio:* 98.7
youth dependency ratio: 94.7
elderly dependency ratio: 4
potential support ratio: 24.9 (2021 est.)

Median age: *total:* 16.7 years (2024 est.)
male: 16.3 years
female: 17.2 years
comparison ranking: total 225

Population growth rate: 3.01% (2024 est.)
comparison ranking: 8

Birth rate: 39.2 births/1,000 population (2024 est.)
comparison ranking: 7

Death rate: 9 deaths/1,000 population (2024 est.)
comparison ranking: 60

Net migration rate: -0.1 migrant(s)/1,000 population (2024 est.)
comparison ranking: 101

Population distribution: the population is unevenly distributed due to contrasts in climate and physical geography; the highest density is found in the southwest, particularly around Lake Chad and points south; the dry Saharan zone to the north is the least densely populated as shown in this population distribution map

Urbanization: *urban population:* 24.4% of total population (2023)
rate of urbanization: 4.1% annual rate of change (2020-25 est.)

Major urban areas - population: 1.592 million N'DJAMENA (capital) (2023)

Sex ratio: *at birth:* 1.04 male(s)/female
0-14 years: 1.02 male(s)/female
15-64 years: 0.96 male(s)/female
65 years and over: 0.75 male(s)/female
total population: 0.98 male(s)/female (2024 est.)

Mother's mean age at first birth: 18.1 years (2014/15 est.)
note: data represents median age at first birth among women 20-49

Maternal mortality ratio: 1,063 deaths/100,000 live births (2020 est.)
comparison ranking: 2

Infant mortality rate: *total:* 62.5 deaths/1,000 live births (2024 est.)
male: 68.1 deaths/1,000 live births
female: 56.7 deaths/1,000 live births
comparison ranking: total 7

Life expectancy at birth: *total population:* 60 years (2024 est.)
male: 58.1 years
female: 62 years
comparison ranking: total population 222

Total fertility rate: 5.24 children born/woman (2024 est.)
comparison ranking: 6

Gross reproduction rate: 2.57 (2024 est.)

Contraceptive prevalence rate: 8.1% (2019)

Drinking water source: *improved: urban:* 90.2% of population
rural: 51.9% of population
total: 60.9% of population
unimproved: urban: 9.8% of population
rural: 48.1% of population
total: 39.1% of population (2020 est.)

Current health expenditure: 5.4% of GDP (2020)

Physician density: 0.06 physicians/1,000 population (2020)

Sanitation facility access: *improved: urban:* 57.5% of population
rural: 4.9% of population
total: 17.3% of population
unimproved: urban: 42.5% of population
rural: 95.1% of population
total: 82.7% of population (2020 est.)

Obesity - adult prevalence rate: 6.1% (2016)
comparison ranking: 171

Alcohol consumption per capita: *total:* 0.55 liters of pure alcohol (2019 est.)
beer: 0.37 liters of pure alcohol (2019 est.)
wine: 0.01 liters of pure alcohol (2019 est.)
spirits: 0.01 liters of pure alcohol (2019 est.)
other alcohols: 0.16 liters of pure alcohol (2019 est.)
comparison ranking: total 162

Tobacco use: *total:* 8.3% (2020 est.)
male: 13.8% (2020 est.)
female: 2.7% (2020 est.)
comparison ranking: total 147

Children under the age of 5 years underweight: 18.9% (2022)
comparison ranking: 21

Currently married women (ages 15-49): 70.6% (2023 est.)

Child marriage: *women married by age 15:* 24.2%
women married by age 18: 60.6%
men married by age 18: 8.1% (2019 est.)

Education expenditures: 2.9% of GDP (2021 est.)
comparison ranking: 161

Literacy: *definition:* age 15 and over can read and write French or Arabic
total population: 26.8%
male: 35.4%
female: 18.2% (2021)

School life expectancy (primary to tertiary education): *total:* 7 years
male: 9 years
female: 6 years (2015)

ENVIRONMENT

Environment - current issues: inadequate supplies of potable water; improper waste disposal in rural areas and poor farming practices contribute to soil and water pollution; desertification

Environment - international agreements: *party to:* Biodiversity, Climate Change, Climate Change-Kyoto Protocol, Climate Change-Paris Agreement, Comprehensive Nuclear Test Ban, Desertification, Endangered Species, Hazardous Wastes, Law of the Sea, Nuclear Test Ban, Ozone Layer Protection, Wetlands
signed, but not ratified: Marine Dumping-London Convention

Climate: tropical in south, desert in north

Urbanization: *urban population:* 24.4% of total population (2023)
rate of urbanization: 4.1% annual rate of change (2020-25 est.)

Food insecurity: *widespread lack of access: due to civil insecurity and shortfall in cereal production* - according to the latest analysis, about 1.86 million people are projected to experience acute food insecurity during the June to August 2023 lean season period; this would be an improvement compared to the previous year, mostly due to the higher year-on-year cereal output in 2022 after the below average 2021 production; acute food insecurity is underpinned by persisting insecurity in the Lac and Tibesti regions, which had displaced over 380 000 people by April 2023; furthermore, elevated food prices due to high fuel costs and localized crop losses during the 2022 floods are aggravating food insecurity (2023)

Revenue from forest resources: 3.81% of GDP (2018 est.)
comparison ranking: 19

Revenue from coal: 0% of GDP (2018 est.)
comparison ranking: 73

Air pollutants: *particulate matter emissions:* 41.15 micrograms per cubic meter (2019 est.)
carbon dioxide emissions: 1.02 megatons (2016 est.)
methane emissions: 30.69 megatons (2020 est.)

Waste and recycling: *municipal solid waste generated annually:* 1,358,851 tons (2010 est.)

Major lakes (area sq km): *fresh water lake(s):* Lake Chad (endorheic lake shared with Niger, Nigeria, and Cameroon) - 10,360-25,900 sq km
note - area varies by season and year to year

Major watersheds (area sq km): Atlantic Ocean drainage: Niger (2,261,741 sq km)

Internal (endorheic basin) drainage: Lake Chad (2,497,738 sq km)

Major aquifers: Lake Chad Basin, Nubian Aquifer System

Total water withdrawal: *municipal:* 100 million cubic meters (2020 est.)
industrial: 100 million cubic meters (2020 est.)
agricultural: 670 million cubic meters (2020 est.)

Total renewable water resources: 45.7 billion cubic meters (2020 est.)

GOVERNMENT

Country name: *conventional long form:* Republic of Chad
conventional short form: Chad
local long form: République du Tchad/Jumhuriyat Tshad
local short form: Tchad/Tshad
etymology: named for Lake Chad, which lies along the country's western border; the word "tsade" means "large body of water" or "lake" in several local native languages
note: the only country whose name is composed of a single syllable with a single vowel

Government type: presidential republic

Capital: *name:* N'Djamena
geographic coordinates: 12 06 N, 15 02 E
time difference: UTC+1 (6 hours ahead of Washington, DC, during Standard Time)
etymology: name taken from the Arab name of a nearby village, Nijamina, meaning "place of rest"

Administrative divisions: 23 provinces (provinces, singular - province); Barh-El-Gazel, Batha, Borkou, Chari-Baguirmi, Ennedi-Est, Ennedi-Ouest, Guera, Hadjer-Lamis, Kanem, Lac, Logone Occidental, Logone Oriental, Mandoul, Mayo-Kebbi-Est, Mayo-Kebbi-Ouest, Moyen-Chari, N'Djamena, Ouaddai, Salamat, Sila, Tandjile, Tibesti, Wadi-Fira

Independence: 11 August 1960 (from France)

National holiday: Independence Day, 11 August (1960)

Legal system: mixed legal system of civil and customary law

Constitution: *history:* several previous; latest adopted by National Transitional Council 27 June 2023, approved by referendum 17 December, verified by Chad Supreme Court 28 December, promulgated 1 January 2024
amendments: previous process: proposed as a revision by the president of the republic after a Council of Ministers (cabinet) decision or by the National Assembly; approval for consideration of a revision requires at least three-fifths majority vote by the Assembly; passage requires approval by referendum or at least two-thirds majority vote by the Assembly

International law organization participation: has not submitted an ICJ jurisdiction declaration; accepts ICCt jurisdiction

Citizenship: *citizenship by birth:* no
citizenship by descent only: both parents must be citizens of Chad
dual citizenship recognized: Chadian law does not address dual citizenship
residency requirement for naturalization: 15 years

Suffrage: 18 years of age; universal

Executive branch: *chief of state:* President Mahamat Idriss DÉBY (since 6 May 2024)
head of government: Prime Minister Allamaye HALINA (since 23 May 2024)
cabinet: Council of Ministers
elections/appointments: president directly elected by absolute majority popular vote in 2 rounds if needed for a 5-year term (no term limits); election last held on 6 May 2024 (next to be held NA)
election results:
2024: Mahamat Idriss DÉBY elected president; percent of vote - Mahamat Idriss DÉBY (MPS) 61%, Succes MASRA (Transformers) 18.5%, Albert PADACKE 16.9%, other 3.6%
2021: Lt. Gen. Idriss DÉBY reelected transitional president; percent of vote - Lt. Gen. Idriss DÉBY (MPS) 79.3%, Pahimi PADACKET Albert (RNDT) 10.3%, Lydie BEASSEMDA (Party for Democracy and Independence) 3.2%, other 7.2%
note: on 20 April 2021; President Idriss DÉBY died of injuries sustained following clashes between government forces and insurgents in northern Chad; following his death, Mahamat Idriss DÉBY , his son, took control of the country, established a Transitional Military Council which was dissolved in October 2022, and was elected president by popular vote in May 2024

Legislative branch: *description:* bicameral Parliament to replace unicameral National Assembly and to consist of:
Senate - representing the Autonomous Communities - NA seats (members indirectly elected by electoral college of provincial and communal councilors for 6-year renewable terms)
National Assembly NA seats (members directly elected by popular vote to serve 5-year renewable terms)
elections: last held for National Assembly on 6 May 2011 (first elections for new Parliament expected in late 2024)
election results: 6 May 2011: percent of vote by party - NA; seats by party - NA; composition - men 64, women 29, percent of women 31.2%
note: the Transitional Military Council dissolved the National Assembly in September 2021 and replaced it with the National Transitional Council (CNT) in October 2022; the CNT serves as an interim

parliament for the country and is tasked with preparations for elections in late 2024

Judicial branch: *highest court(s):* Supreme Court (consists of the chief justice, 3 chamber presidents, and 12 judges or councilors and divided into 3 chambers); Supreme Council of the Judiciary (consists of the Judiciary president, vice president and 13 members)
judge selection and term of office: Supreme Court chief justice selected by the president; councilors - 8 designated by the president and 7 by the speaker of the National Assembly; chief justice and councilors appointed for life; Supreme Council of the Judiciary - with the exception of the Judiciary president and vice president, members are elected for single renewable 4-year terms
subordinate courts: High Court of Justice; Courts of Appeal; tribunals; justices of the peace

Political parties: Chadian Convention for Peace and Development or CTPD
Federation Action for the Republic or FAR
National Rally for Development and Progress or Viva-RNDP
National Union for Democracy and Renewal or UNDR
Party for Unity and Reconstruction or PUR
Patriotic Salvation Movement or MPS
Rally for Democracy and Progress or RDP
Rally of Chadian Nationalists/Awakening or RNDT/Le Reveil
Social Democratic Party for a Change-over of Power or PDSA
Union for Democracy and the Republic or UDR
Union for Renewal and Democracy or URD

TRANSFORMERS

note 1: 19 additional parties each contributed one member
note 2: on 5 October 2021, Interim President Mahamat Idriss DEBY appointed 93 members to the interim National Transitional Council (NTC); 30% of the NTC members were retained from parties previously represented in the National Assembly

International organization participation: ACP, AfDB, AU, BDEAC, CEMAC, EITI (compliant country), FAO, FZ, G-77, IAEA, IBRD, ICAO, ICCt, ICRM, IDA, IDB, IFAD, IFC, IFRCS, ILO, IMF, Interpol, IOC, IOM, IPU, ITSO, ITU, ITUC (NGOs), LCBC, MIGA, MNJTF, NAM, OIC, OIF, OPCW, UN, UNCTAD, UNESCO, UNIDO, UNOCI, UNOOSA, UNWTO, UPU, WCO, WHO, WIPO, WMO, WTO

Diplomatic representation in the US: *chief of mission:* Ambassador KITOKO GATA Ngoulou (since 30 June 2023)
chancery: 2401 Massachusetts Avenue NW, Washington, DC 20008
telephone: [1] (202) 652-1312
FAX: [1] (202) 578-0431
email address and website:
info@chadembassy.us
https://chadembassy.us/

Diplomatic representation from the US: *chief of mission:* Ambassador Alexander LASKARIS (since 19 August 2022)
embassy: Rond-Point Chagoua, B.P. 413, N'Djamena
mailing address: 2410 N'Djamena Place, Washington DC 20521-2410
telephone: [235] 6885-1065
FAX: [235] 2253-9102
email address and website:
NdjamenaACS@state.gov
https://td.usembassy.gov/

Flag description: three equal vertical bands of blue (hoist side), gold, and red; the flag combines the blue and red French (former colonial) colors with the red and yellow (gold) of the Pan-African colors; blue symbolizes the sky, hope, and the south of the country, which is relatively well-watered; gold represents the sun, as well as the desert in the north of the country; red stands for progress, unity, and sacrifice
note: almost identical to the flag of Romania but with a darker shade of blue; also similar to the flags of Andorra and Moldova, both of which have a national coat of arms centered in the yellow band; design based on the flag of France

National symbol(s): goat (north), lion (south); national colors: blue, yellow, red

National anthem: *name:* "La Tchadienne" (The Chadian)
lyrics/music: Louis GIDROL and his students/Paul VILLARD
note: adopted 1960

National heritage: *total World Heritage Sites:* 2 (1 natural, 1 mixed)
selected World Heritage Site locales: Lakes of Ounianga (n); Ennedi Massif: Natural and Cultural Landscape (m)

ECONOMY

Economic overview: oil-dependent economy challenged by market fluctuations, regional instability, refugee influx, and climate vulnerability; high levels of extreme poverty and food insecurity; recent growth driven by oil and agricultural recovery; debt-restructuring agreement under G20 Common Framework

Real GDP (purchasing power parity): $32.446 billion (2023 est.)
$31.161 billion (2022 est.)
$30.311 billion (2021 est.)
note: data in 2021 dollars
comparison ranking: 145

Real GDP growth rate: 4.12% (2023 est.)
2.8% (2022 est.)
-1.17% (2021 est.)
note: annual GDP % growth based on constant local currency
comparison ranking: 74

Real GDP per capita: $1,800 (2023 est.)
$1,800 (2022 est.)
$1,800 (2021 est.)
note: data in 2021 dollars
comparison ranking: 209

GDP (official exchange rate): $13.149 billion (2023 est.)
note: data in current dollars at official exchange rate

Inflation rate (consumer prices): 10.84% (2023 est.)
5.79% (2022 est.)
-0.77% (2021 est.)
note: annual % change based on consumer prices
comparison ranking: 183

GDP - composition, by sector of origin: *agriculture:* 25.1% (2023 est.)
industry: 44.4% (2023 est.)
services: 28.7% (2023 est.)
note: figures may not total 100% due to non-allocated consumption not captured in sector-reported data
comparison rankings: services 211; industry 24; agriculture 20

GDP - composition, by end use: *household consumption:* 74.6% (2023 est.)
government consumption: 4.2% (2023 est.)
investment in fixed capital: 25.8% (2023 est.)
exports of goods and services: 43.5% (2023 est.)
imports of goods and services: -48.1% (2023 est.)
note: figures may not total 100% due to rounding or gaps in data collection

Agricultural products: sorghum, groundnuts, millet, cereals, beef, sugarcane, yams, maize, cassava, milk (2022)
note: top ten agricultural products based on tonnage

Industries: oil, cotton textiles, brewing, natron (sodium carbonate), soap, cigarettes, construction materials

Industrial production growth rate: 3.27% (2023 est.)
note: annual % change in industrial value added based on constant local currency
comparison ranking: 102

Labor force: 5.806 million (2023 est.)
note: number of people ages 15 or older who are employed or seeking work
comparison ranking: 75

Unemployment rate: 1.08% (2023 est.)
1.1% (2022 est.)
1.51% (2021 est.)
note: % of labor force seeking employment
comparison ranking: 8

Youth unemployment rate (ages 15-24): *total:* 1.5% (2023 est.)
male: 2.1% (2023 est.)
female: 0.7% (2023 est.)
note: % of labor force ages 15-24 seeking employment
comparison ranking: total 198

Population below poverty line: 42.3% (2018 est.)
note: % of population with income below national poverty line

Gini Index coefficient - distribution of family income: 37.4 (2022 est.)
note: index (0-100) of income distribution; higher values represent greater inequality
comparison ranking: 59

Household income or consumption by percentage share: *lowest 10%:* 2.8% (2022 est.)
highest 10%: 29.6% (2022 est.)
note: % share of income accruing to lowest and highest 10% of population

Remittances: 0% of GDP (2023 est.)
0% of GDP (2022 est.)
0% of GDP (2021 est.)

Budget: *revenues:* $2.29 billion (2020 est.)
expenditures: $2.12 billion (2020 est.)

Public debt: 52.5% of GDP (2017 est.)
comparison ranking: 97

Taxes and other revenues: 13.5% (of GDP) (2017 est.)
comparison ranking: 150

Current account balance: -$558 million (2017 est.)
-$926 million (2016 est.)
comparison ranking: 123

Exports: $6.503 billion (2022 est.)
$4.565 billion (2021 est.)
$2.863 billion (2020 est.)
note: GDP expenditure basis - exports of goods and services in current dollars
comparison ranking: 128

Exports - partners: Germany 25%, China 21%, UAE 20%, Taiwan 12%, France 10% (2022)
note: top five export partners based on percentage share of exports

Exports - commodities: crude petroleum, gold, oil seeds, gum resins, cotton (2022)
note: top five export commodities based on value in dollars

Imports: $5.028 billion (2022 est.)
$5.211 billion (2021 est.)
$4.502 billion (2020 est.)
note: GDP expenditure basis - imports of goods and services in current dollars
comparison ranking: 151

Imports - partners: China 25%, UAE 20%, France 7%, US 7%, Belgium 7% (2022)
note: top five import partners based on percentage share of imports

Imports - commodities: vaccines, jewelry, electric generators, broadcasting equipment, packaged medicine (2022)
note: top five import commodities based on value in dollars

Reserves of foreign exchange and gold: $211.591 million (2021 est.)
$390.675 million (2020 est.)
$310.032 million (2019 est.)
note: holdings of gold (year-end prices)/foreign exchange/special drawing rights in current dollars
comparison ranking: 187

Debt - external: $2.352 billion (2022 est.)
note: present value of external debt in current US dollars
comparison ranking: 69

Exchange rates: Cooperation Financiere en Afrique Centrale francs (XAF) per US dollar -

Exchange rates: 606.57 (2023 est.)
623.76 (2022 est.)
554.531 (2021 est.)
575.586 (2020 est.)
585.911 (2019 est.)

ENERGY

Electricity access: *electrification - total population:* 11.7% (2022 est.)
electrification - urban areas: 46.3%
electrification - rural areas: 1.3%

Electricity: *installed generating capacity:* 90,000 kW (2022 est.)
consumption: 301.523 million kWh (2022 est.)
transmission/distribution losses: 48.261 million kWh (2022 est.)
comparison rankings: transmission/distribution losses 38; consumption 186; installed generating capacity 188

Electricity generation sources: *fossil fuels:* 94.5% of total installed capacity (2022 est.)
wind: 2.6% of total installed capacity (2022 est.)
biomass and waste: 2.9% of total installed capacity (2022 est.)

Petroleum: *total petroleum production:* 124,000 bbl/day (2023 est.)
refined petroleum consumption: 15,000 bbl/day (2022 est.)
crude oil estimated reserves: 1.5 billion barrels (2021 est.)

Carbon dioxide emissions: 2.064 million metric tonnes of CO_2 (2022 est.)
from petroleum and other liquids: 2.064 million metric tonnes of CO_2 (2022 est.)
comparison ranking: total emissions 159

Energy consumption per capita: 1.649 million Btu/person (2022 est.)
comparison ranking: 189

COMMUNICATIONS

Telephones - fixed lines: *total subscriptions:* 5,000 (2022 est.)
subscriptions per 100 inhabitants: (2022 est.) less than 1
comparison ranking: total subscriptions 204

Telephones - mobile cellular: *total subscriptions:* 12.087 million (2022 est.)
subscriptions per 100 inhabitants: 68 (2022 est.)
comparison ranking: total subscriptions 82

Telecommunication systems: *general assessment:* the telecom infrastructure is particularly poor; fixed, mobile and internet is well below African averages; Chad's telecom market offers some potential for investors to develop services given the low starting base; the country's first 3G/LTE mobile license was awarded in April 2014; Chad finally gained access to international fiber bandwidth in 2012 its national backbone infrastructure remains underdeveloped; the World Bank-funded Central African Backbone (CAB) project takes in Chad, while the country is also party to a Trans-Saharan Backbone project which will link a fiber cable to Nigeria and Algeria (2022)
domestic: fixed-line connections less than 1 per 100 persons; mobile-cellular subscribership base of about 60 per 100 persons (2021)
international: country code - 235; satellite earth station - 1 Intelsat (Atlantic Ocean)

Broadcast media: 1 state-owned TV station; 2 privately-owned TV stations; state-owned radio network, Radiodiffusion Nationale Tchadienne (RNT), operates national and regional stations; over 10 private radio stations; some stations rebroadcast programs from international broadcasters (2017)

Internet country code: .td

Internet users: *total:* 3.06 million (2021 est.)
percent of population: 18% (2021 est.)
comparison ranking: total 119

Broadband - fixed subscriptions: *total:* (2020 est.)
subscriptions per 100 inhabitants: (2020 est.)

TRANSPORTATION

National air transport system: *number of registered air carriers:* 2 (2020)
inventory of registered aircraft operated by air carriers: 3

Civil aircraft registration country code prefix: TT

Airports: 42 (2024)
comparison ranking: 96

Pipelines: 582 km oil (2013)

Roadways: *total:* 40,000 km (2018)
note: consists of 25,000 km of national and regional roads and 15,000 km of local roads; 206 km of urban roads are paved
comparison ranking: total 92

Waterways: 12,400 km (2022) (Chari and Logone Rivers are navigable only in wet season) Chari is 11,400 km Legone is 1,000 km
comparison ranking: 12

MILITARY AND SECURITY

Military and security forces: Chadian National Army (Armee Nationale du Tchad, ANT): Land Forces (l'Armee de Terre, AdT), Chadian Air Force (l'Armee de l'Air Tchadienne, AAT), General Direction of the Security Services of State Institutions (Direction Generale des Services de Securite des Institutions de l'Etat, GDSSIE); National Gendarmerie; Ministry of Public Security and Immigration: National Nomadic Guard of Chad (GNNT) (2023)
note 1: the GDSSIE, formerly known as the Republican Guard, is the presidential guard force and is considered to be Chad's elite military unit; it is reportedly a division-sized force with infantry, armor, and special forces/anti-terrorism regiments (known as the Special Anti-Terrorist Group or SATG, aka Division of Special Anti-Terrorist Groups or DGSAT)
note 2: the Chadian National Police are under the Ministry of Public Security and Immigration; border security duties are shared by the Army, Customs (Ministry of Public Security and Immigration), the Gendarmerie, and the GNNT

Military expenditures: 2.9% of GDP (2023 est.)
2.6% of GDP (2022 est.)
2.5% of GDP (2021 est.)
2.9% of GDP (2020 est.)
2% of GDP (2019 est.)
comparison ranking: 36

Military and security service personnel strengths: limited and varied information; estimated to have up to 40,000 active ANT personnel (approximately 30-35,000 Ground Forces, 5,000 GDSSIE, and a few hundred Air Force); approximately 5,000 National Gendarmerie; approximately 3,000 Nomadic Guard (2023)

Military equipment inventories and acquisitions: the ANT is mostly armed with older or secondhand equipment from Belgium, France, Italy, Russia, the former Soviet Union, and Switzerland; in recent years it has received equipment, including donations, from other countries including China, Turkey, and the US (2023)

Military service age and obligation: 20 is the legal minimum age for compulsory military service for men with an 18-36 month service obligation (information varies); women are subject to 12 months of compulsory military or civic service at age 21; 18-35 for voluntary service (18-25 for officer recruits); soldiers released from active duty are in the reserves until the age of 50 (2023)

Military deployments: Chad has committed approximately 1,000-1,500 troops to the Multinational Joint Task Force (MNJTF) against Boko Haram and other terrorist groups operating in the general area of the Lake Chad Basin and along Nigeria's northeast border; national MNJTF troop contingents are deployed within their own territories, although cross-border operations are conducted periodically (2024)

Military - note: the ANT has considerable combat experience against insurgents and terrorist groups; it also has a tradition of deep involvement in domestic politics; over the past decade, the ANT has received substantial foreign military assistance, particularly from France, which maintains a military base in N'Djamena; the ANT's operational focus is on counterterrorism and counterinsurgency operations; it is engaged with the Boko Haram and Islamic State of Iraq and ash-Sham in West Africa terrorist groups in

the Lake Chad Basin area; in addition, the ANT conducts frequent operations against internal anti-government militias and armed dissident groups
a number of rebel groups operate in northern Chad, some from bases in southern Libya, including the FACT (Front pour le Changement et la Concorde au Tchad), the Military Command Council for the Salvation of the Republic le Conseil de Commandement Militaire pour le salut de la République or CCSMR), the Union of Forces for Democracy and Development (le Union des Forces pour la Démocratie et le Développement or UFDD), and the Union of Resistance Forces (le Union des Forces de la Résistance UFR); former Chadian President Idriss DEBY was killed in April 2021 during fighting in the northern part of the country between the FACT and the Chadian Army (2023)

TERRORISM

Terrorist group(s): Boko Haram; Islamic State of Iraq and ash-Sham - West Africa (ISIS-WA)
note: details about the history, aims, leadership, organization, areas of operation, tactics, targets, weapons, size, and sources of support of the group(s) appear(s) in the Terrorism reference guide

TRANSNATIONAL ISSUES

Refugees and internally displaced persons: *refugees (country of origin):* 694,569 (Sudan) (includes refugees since 15 April 2023), 26,692 (Cameroon) (2023); 134,015 (Central African Republic), 21,381 (Nigeria) (2024)
IDPs: 215,918 (majority are in the east) (2023)

Trafficking in persons: tier rating: Tier 2 Watch List — Chad does not fully meet the minimum standards for the elimination of trafficking but is making significant efforts to do so, therefore Chad was upgraded to Tier 2 Watch List; for more details, go to: https:// www.state.gov/reports/2024-trafficking-in-persons-report/chad/

Illicit drugs: NA

CHILE

INTRODUCTION

Background: Indigenous groups inhabited central and southern Chile for several thousand years, living in mixed pastoralist and settled communities. The Inca then ruled the north of the country for nearly a century prior to the arrival of the Spanish in the 16th century. In 1541, the Spanish established the Captaincy General of Chile, which lasted until Chile declared its independence in 1810. The subsequent struggle with the Spanish became tied to other South American independence conflicts, with a decisive victory not being achieved until 1818. In the War of the Pacific (1879-83), Chile defeated Peru and Bolivia to win its current northernmost regions. By the 1880s, the Chilean central government cemented its control over the central and southern regions inhabited by Mapuche Indigenous peoples. Between 1891 and 1973, a series of elected governments succeeded each other until the Marxist government of Salvador ALLENDE was overthrown in 1973 in a military coup led by General Augusto PINOCHET, who ruled until a democratically elected president was inaugurated in 1990. Economic reforms that were maintained consistently since the 1980s contributed to steady growth, reduced poverty rates by over half, and helped secure the country's commitment to democratic and representative government. Chile has increasingly assumed regional and international leadership roles befitting its status as a stable, democratic nation.

GEOGRAPHY

Location: Southern South America, bordering the South Pacific Ocean, between Argentina and Peru

Geographic coordinates: 30 00 S, 71 00 W

Map references: South America

Area: *total:* 756,102 sq km
land: 743,812 sq km
water: 12,290 sq km
note: includes Easter Island (Isla de Pascua) and Isla Sala y Gomez
comparison ranking: total 39

Area - comparative: slightly smaller than twice the size of Montana

Land boundaries: *total:* 7,801 km
border countries (3): Argentina 6,691 km; Bolivia 942 km; Peru 168 km

Coastline: 6,435 km

Maritime claims: *territorial sea:* 12 nm
contiguous zone: 24 nm
exclusive economic zone: 200 nm
continental shelf: 200/350 nm

Climate: temperate; desert in north; Mediterranean in central region; cool and damp in south

Terrain: low coastal mountains, fertile central valley, rugged Andes in east

Elevation: *highest point:* Nevado Ojos del Salado 6,893 m (highest volcano in the world)
lowest point: Pacific Ocean 0 m
mean elevation: 1,871 m

Natural resources: copper, timber, iron ore, nitrates, precious metals, molybdenum, hydropower

Land use: *agricultural land:* 21.1% (2018 est.)
arable land: 1.7% (2018 est.)
permanent crops: 0.6% (2018 est.)
permanent pasture: 18.8% (2018 est.)
forest: 21.9% (2018 est.)
other: 57% (2018 est.)

Irrigated land: 11,100 sq km (2012)

Major lakes (area sq km): *fresh water lake(s):* Lago General Carrera (shared with Argentina) - 2,240 sq km; Lago O'Higgins (shared with Argentina) - 1,010 sq km; Lago Llanquihue - 800 sq km; Lago Fagnano (shared with Argentina) - 590 sq km

Population distribution: 90% of the population is located in the middle third of the country around the capital of Santiago; the far north (anchored by the Atacama Desert) and the extreme south are relatively underpopulated

Natural hazards: severe earthquakes; active volcanism; tsunamis
volcanism: significant volcanic activity due to more than three-dozen active volcanoes along the Andes Mountains; Lascar (5,592 m), which last erupted in 2007, is the most active volcano in the northern Chilean Andes; Llaima (3,125 m) in central Chile, which last erupted in 2009, is another of the country's most active; Chaiten's 2008 eruption forced major evacuations; other notable historically active volcanoes include Cerro Hudson, Calbuco, Copahue, Guallatiri, Llullaillaco, Nevados de Chillan, Puyehue, San Pedro, and Villarrica; see note 2 under "Geography - note"

Geography - note: *note 1:* the longest north-south trending country in the world, extending across 39 degrees of latitude; strategic location relative to sea lanes between the Atlantic and Pacific Oceans (Strait of Magellan, Beagle Channel, Drake Passage)
note 2: Chile is one of the countries along the Ring of Fire, a belt of active volcanoes and earthquake epicenters bordering the Pacific Ocean; up to 90% of

the world's earthquakes and some 75% of the world's volcanoes occur within the Ring of Fire
note 3: the Atacama Desert – the driest desert in the world – spreads across the northern part of the country; Ojos del Salado (6,893 m) in the Atacama Desert is the highest active volcano in the world, Chile's tallest mountain, and the second highest in the Western Hemisphere and the Southern Hemisphere – its small crater lake (at 6,390 m) is the world's highest lake

PEOPLE AND SOCIETY

Population: *total:* 18,664,652
male: 9,169,736
female: 9,494,916 (2024 est.)
comparison rankings: female 67; male 67; total 67

Nationality: *noun:* Chilean(s)
adjective: Chilean

Ethnic groups: White and non-Indigenous 88.9%, Mapuche 9.1%, Aymara 0.7%, other Indigenous groups 1% (includes Rapa Nui, Likan Antai, Quechua, Colla, Diaguita, Kawesqar, Yagan or Yamana), unspecified 0.3% (2012 est.)

Languages: Spanish 99.5% (official), English 10.2%, Indigenous 1% (includes Mapudungun, Aymara, Quechua, Rapa Nui), other 2.3%, unspecified 0.2% (2012 est.)
major-language sample(s):
La Libreta Informativa del Mundo, la fuente indispensable de información básica. (Spanish)
note: shares sum to more than 100% because some respondents gave more than one answer on the census

Religions: Roman Catholic 42%, Evangelical 14%, other 6%, none 37% (2021 est.)

Demographic profile: Chile is in the advanced stages of demographic transition and is becoming an aging society - with fertility below replacement level, low mortality rates, and life expectancy on par with developed countries. Nevertheless, with its dependency ratio nearing its low point, Chile could benefit from its favorable age structure. It will need to keep its large working-age population productively employed, while preparing to provide for the needs of its growing proportion of elderly people, especially as women - the traditional caregivers - increasingly enter the workforce. Over the last two decades, Chile has made great strides in reducing its poverty rate, which is now lower than most Latin American countries. However, its severe income inequality ranks as the worst among members of the Organization for Economic Cooperation and Development. Unequal access to quality education perpetuates this uneven income distribution.
Chile has historically been a country of emigration but has slowly become more attractive to immigrants since transitioning to democracy in 1990 and improving its economic stability (other regional destinations have concurrently experienced deteriorating economic and political conditions). Most of Chile's small but growing foreign-born population consists of transplants from other Latin American countries, especially Peru.

Age structure: *0-14 years:* 19.2% (male 1,822,908/female 1,751,528)
15-64 years: 67.3% (male 6,274,620/female 6,278,467)
65 years and over: 13.6% (2024 est.) (male 1,072,208/female 1,464,921)

Dependency ratios: *total dependency ratio:* 45.2
youth dependency ratio: 26.8
elderly dependency ratio: 18.4
potential support ratio: 5.4 (2021 est.)

Median age: *total:* 36.9 years (2024 est.)
male: 35.8 years
female: 38.2 years
comparison ranking: total 85

Population growth rate: 0.61% (2024 est.)
comparison ranking: 136

Birth rate: 12.4 births/1,000 population (2024 est.)
comparison ranking: 140

Death rate: 6.6 deaths/1,000 population (2024 est.)
comparison ranking: 133

Net migration rate: 0.3 migrant(s)/1,000 population (2024 est.)
comparison ranking: 74

Population distribution: 90% of the population is located in the middle third of the country around the capital of Santiago; the far north (anchored by the Atacama Desert) and the extreme south are relatively underpopulated

Urbanization: *urban population:* 88% of total population (2023)
rate of urbanization: 0.78% annual rate of change (2020-25 est.)

Major urban areas - population: 6.903 million SANTIAGO (capital), 1.009 million Valparaiso, 912,000 Concepcion (2023)

Sex ratio: *at birth:* 1.04 male(s)/female
0-14 years: 1.04 male(s)/female
15-64 years: 1 male(s)/female
65 years and over: 0.73 male(s)/female
total population: 0.97 male(s)/female (2024 est.)

Maternal mortality ratio: 15 deaths/100,000 live births (2020 est.)
comparison ranking: 136

Infant mortality rate: *total:* 6.3 deaths/1,000 live births (2024 est.)
male: 6.9 deaths/1,000 live births
female: 5.7 deaths/1,000 live births
comparison ranking: total 166

Life expectancy at birth: *total population:* 80.3 years (2024 est.)
male: 77.3 years
female: 83.3 years
comparison ranking: total population 55

Total fertility rate: 1.75 children born/woman (2024 est.)
comparison ranking: 148

Gross reproduction rate: 0.85 (2024 est.)

Contraceptive prevalence rate: 76.3% (2015/16)

Drinking water source: *improved: urban:* 100% of population
rural: 100% of population
total: 100% of population

Current health expenditure: 9.8% of GDP (2020)

Physician density: 2.84 physicians/1,000 population (2020)

Hospital bed density: 2.1 beds/1,000 population (2018)

Sanitation facility access: *improved: urban:* 100% of population
rural: 100% of population
total: 100% of population

Obesity - adult prevalence rate: 28% (2016)
comparison ranking: 32

Alcohol consumption per capita: *total:* 7.8 liters of pure alcohol (2019 est.)
beer: 2.76 liters of pure alcohol (2019 est.)
wine: 2.61 liters of pure alcohol (2019 est.)
spirits: 2.43 liters of pure alcohol (2019 est.)
other alcohols: 0 liters of pure alcohol (2019 est.)
comparison ranking: total 47

Tobacco use: *total:* 29.2% (2020 est.)
male: 31.6% (2020 est.)
female: 26.8% (2020 est.)
comparison ranking: total 34

Children under the age of 5 years underweight: 0.5% (2014)
comparison ranking: 122

Currently married women (ages 15-49): 46.3% (2023 est.)

Education expenditures: 5.6% of GDP (2019 est.)
comparison ranking: 53

Literacy: *definition:* age 15 and over can read and write
total population: 97%
male: 97.1%
female: 97% (2021)

School life expectancy (primary to tertiary education): *total:* 17 years
male: 16 years
female: 17 years (2020)

ENVIRONMENT

Environment - current issues: air pollution from industrial and vehicle emissions; water pollution from raw sewage; noise pollution; improper garbage disposal; soil degradation; widespread deforestation and mining threaten the environment; wildlife conservation

Environment - international agreements: *party to:* Antarctic-Environmental Protection, Antarctic-Marine Living Resources, Antarctic Seals, Antarctic Treaty, Biodiversity, Climate Change, Climate Change-Kyoto Protocol, Climate Change-Paris Agreement, Comprehensive Nuclear Test Ban, Desertification, Endangered Species, Environmental Modification, Hazardous Wastes, Law of the Sea, Marine Dumping-London Convention, Marine Dumping-London Protocol, Nuclear Test Ban, Ozone Layer Protection, Ship Pollution, Wetlands, Whaling
signed, but not ratified: none of the selected agreements

Climate: temperate; desert in north; Mediterranean in central region; cool and damp in south

Urbanization: *urban population:* 88% of total population (2023)
rate of urbanization: 0.78% annual rate of change (2020-25 est.)

Revenue from forest resources: 0.49% of GDP (2018 est.)
comparison ranking: 67

Revenue from coal: 0.01% of GDP (2018 est.)
comparison ranking: 46

Air pollutants: *particulate matter emissions:* 20.49 micrograms per cubic meter (2019 est.)
carbon dioxide emissions: 85.82 megatons (2016 est.)
methane emissions: 15.97 megatons (2020 est.)

Waste and recycling: *municipal solid waste generated annually:* 6.517 million tons (2009 est.)
municipal solid waste recycled annually: 24,113 tons (2009 est.)

percent of municipal solid waste recycled: 0.4% (2009 est.)

Major lakes (area sq km): *fresh water lake(s):* Lago General Carrera (shared with Argentina) - 2,240 sq km; Lago O'Higgins (shared with Argentina) - 1,010 sq km; Lago Llanquihue - 800 sq km; Lago Fagnano (shared with Argentina) - 590 sq km

Total water withdrawal: *municipal:* 1.29 billion cubic meters (2020 est.)
industrial: 1.66 billion cubic meters (2020 est.)
agricultural: 29.42 billion cubic meters (2020 est.)

Total renewable water resources: 923.1 billion cubic meters (2020 est.)

Geoparks: *total global geoparks and regional networks:* 1
global geoparks and regional networks: Kutralkura (2023)

GOVERNMENT

Country name: *conventional long form:* Republic of Chile
conventional short form: Chile
local long form: República de Chile
local short form: Chile
etymology: derivation of the name is unclear, but it may come from the Mapuche word "chilli" meaning "limit of the earth" or from the Quechua "chiri" meaning "cold"

Government type: presidential republic

Capital: *name:* Santiago; note - Valparaiso is the seat of the national legislature
geographic coordinates: 33 27 S, 70 40 W
time difference: UTC-3 (2 hours ahead of Washington, DC, during Standard Time)
daylight saving time: +1hr, begins second Sunday in August; ends second Sunday in May; note - Punta Arenas observes DST throughout the year
time zone note: Chile has three time zones: the continental portion at UTC-3; the southern Magallanes region, which does not use daylight savings time and remains at UTC-3 for the summer months; and Easter Island at UTC-5
etymology: Santiago is named after the biblical figure Saint James (ca. A.D. 3-44), patron saint of Spain, but especially revered in Galicia; "Santiago" derives from the local Galician evolution of the Vulgar Latin "Sanctu Iacobu"; Valparaiso derives from the Spanish "Valle Paraiso" meaning "Paradise Valley"

Administrative divisions: 16 regions (regiones, singular - region); Aysen, Antofagasta, Araucania, Arica y Parinacota, Atacama, Biobio, Coquimbo, Libertador General Bernardo O'Higgins, Los Lagos, Los Rios, Magallanes y de la Antartica Chilena (Magallanes and Chilean Antarctica), Maule, Nuble, Region Metropolitana (Santiago), Tarapaca, Valparaiso
note: the US does not recognize any claims to Antarctica

Independence: 18 September 1810 (from Spain)

National holiday: Independence Day, 18 September (1810)

Legal system: civil law system influenced by several West European civil legal systems; judicial review of legislative acts by the Constitutional Tribunal

Constitution: *history:* many previous; latest adopted 11 September 1980, effective 11 March 1981; in September 2022 and again in December 2023, referendums presented for a new constitution were both defeated, and the September 1980 constitution remains in force
amendments: proposed by members of either house of the National Congress or by the president of the republic; passage requires at least four-sevenths majority vote of the membership in both houses and approval by the president; passage of amendments to constitutional articles, such as the republican form of government, basic rights and freedoms, the Constitutional Tribunal, electoral justice, the Council of National Security, or the constitutional amendment process, requires at least four-sevenths majority vote by both houses of Congress and approval by the president; the president can opt to hold a referendum when Congress and the president disagree on an amendment; amended many times, last in 2022

International law organization participation: has not submitted an ICJ jurisdiction declaration; accepts ICCt jurisdiction

Citizenship: *citizenship by birth:* yes
citizenship by descent only: yes
dual citizenship recognized: yes
residency requirement for naturalization: 5 years

Suffrage: 18 years of age; universal

Executive branch: *chief of state:* President Gabriel BORIC (since 11 March 2022)
head of government: President Gabriel BORIC (since 11 March 2022)
cabinet: Cabinet appointed by the president
elections/appointments: president directly elected by absolute majority popular vote in 2 rounds if needed for a single 4-year term; election last held on 21 November 2021 with a runoff held on 19 December 2021 (next to be held on 23 November 2025 with runoff if needed on 20 December)
election results:
2021: Gabriel BORIC elected president in second round; percent of vote in first round - Jose Antonio KAST (FSC) 27.9%; Gabriel BORIC (AD) 25.8%; Franco PARISI (PDG) 12.8%; Sebastian SICHEL (ChP+) 12.8%; Yasna PROVOSTE (New Social Pact) 11.6%; other 9.1%; percent of vote in second round - Gabriel BORIC 55.9%; Jose Antonio KAST 44.1%
2017: Sebastian PINERA Echenique elected president in second round; percent of vote in first round - Sebastian PINERA Echenique (independent) 36.6%; Alejandro GUILLIER (independent) 22.7%; Beatriz SANCHEZ (independent) 20.3%; Jose Antonio KAST (independent) 7.9%; Carolina GOIC (PDC) 5.9%; Marco ENRIQUEZ-OMINAMI (PRO) 5.7%; other 0.9%; percent of vote in second round - Sebastian PINERA Echenique 54.6%, Alejandro GUILLIER 45.4%
note: the president is both chief of state and head of government

Legislative branch: *description:* bicameral National Congress or Congreso Nacional consists of:
Senate or Senado (50 seats); members directly elected in multi-seat constituencies by open party-list proportional representation vote to serve 8-year terms with one-half of the membership renewed every 4 years)
Chamber of Deputies or Camara de Diputados (155 seats; members directly elected in multi-seat constituencies by open party-list proportional representation vote to serve 4-year terms)
elections: Senate - last held on 21 November 2021 (next to be held on 23 November 2025) Chamber of Deputies - last held on 21 November 2021 (next to be held on 23 November 2025)
election results: Senate - percent of vote by party/coalition - NA; seats by party/coalition - ChP+ 12 (RN 5, UDI 5, EVOPOLI 2), NPS 8 (PS 4, PPD 2, PDC 2), AD 4 (PCCh 2, FREVS 2), PLR 1, independent 2; composition - men 37, women 13, percentage women 26%
Chamber of Deputies - percent of vote by party/coalition - NA; seats by party/coalition - ChP+ 53 (RN 25, UDI 23, EVOPOLI 4, PRI 1), AD 37 (PCCh 12, CS 9, RD 8, Commons 6, FREVS 2), NPS 37 (PS 13, PDC 8, PPD 7, PL 4, PRSD 4, CIU 1), FSC 15 (PLR 14, PCC 1), PDG 6, PH 3, PEV 2, IU 1, independent 1; composition - men 100, women 55, percentage women 35.5%; total National Congress percentage women 33.2% as of January 2024
note: Senate seats by party/coalition as of May 2022 - ChP+ 24 (RN 12, UDI 9, EVOPOLI 3), NPS 18 (PS 7, PPD 6, PDC 5), AD 6 (PCCh 2, FREVS 2, RD 2), PLR 1, independent 1

Judicial branch: *highest court(s):* Supreme Court or Corte Suprema (consists of a court president and 20 members or ministros); Constitutional Court (consists of 10 members and is independent of the rest of the judiciary); Elections Qualifying Court (consists of 5 members)
judge selection and term of office: Supreme Court president and judges (ministers) appointed by the president of the republic and ratified by the Senate from lists of candidates provided by the court itself; judges appointed for life with mandatory retirement at age 70; Constitutional Court members appointed - 3 by the Supreme Court, 3 by the president of the republic, 2 by the Chamber of Deputies, and 2 by the Senate; members serve 9-year terms with partial membership replacement every 3 years (the court reviews constitutionality of legislation); Elections Qualifying Court members appointed by lottery - 1 by the former president or vice president of the Senate and 1 by the former president or vice president of the Chamber of Deputies, 2 by the Supreme Court, and 1 by the Appellate Court of Valparaiso; members appointed for 4-year terms
subordinate courts: Courts of Appeal; oral criminal tribunals; military tribunals; local police courts; specialized tribunals and courts in matters such as family, labor, customs, taxes, and electoral affairs

Political parties: Approve Dignity (Apruebo Dignidad) coalition or AD (included PC, FA, and FREVS); note - dissolved 2023 Broad Front Coalition (Frente Amplio) or FA (includes RD, CS, and Comunes)
Chile We Can Do More (Chile Podemos Más) or ChP+ (coalition includes EVOPOLI, PRI, RN, UDI)
Christian Democratic Party or PDC
Common Sense Party or Sc
Commons (Comunes)
Communist Party of Chile or PCCh
Democratic Revolution or RD
Democrats or PD
Equality Party or PI
Green Ecological Party or PEV (dissolved 7 February 2022)
Green Popular Alliance or AVP
Humanist Action Party or PAH
Humanist Party or PH
Independent Democratic Union or UDI
Liberal Party (Partido Liberal de Chile) or PL
National Renewal or RN
New Social Pact or NPS (includes PDC, PL, PPD, PRSD, PS)

Party for Democracy or PPD
Party of the People or PDG
Political Evolution or EVOPOLI
Popular Party or PP
Progressive Homeland Party or PRO
Radical Party or PR
Republican Party or PLR
Social Christian Party or PSC
Social Convergence or CS
Social Green Regionalist Federation or FREVS
Socialist Party or PS
Yellow Movement for Chile or AMAR

International organization participation: APEC, BIS, CAN (associate), CD, CELAC, FAO, G-15, G-77, IADB, IAEA, IBRD, ICAO, ICC (national committees), ICCt, ICRM, IDA, IFAD, IFC, IFRCS, IHO, ILO, IMF, IMO, IMSO, Interpol, IOC, IOM, IPU, ISO, ITSO, ITU, ITUC (NGOs), LAES, LAIA, Mercosur (associate), MIGA, MINUSTAH, NAM, OAS, OECD (enhanced engagement), OPANAL, OPCW, Pacific Alliance, PCA, PROSUR, SICA (observer), UN, UNASUR, UNCTAD, UNESCO, UNFICYP, UNHCR, UNIDO, Union Latina, UNMOGIP, UNTSO, UNWTO, UPU, WCO, WFTU (NGOs), WHO, WIPO, WMO, WTO

Diplomatic representation in the US: *chief of mission:* Ambassador Juan Gabriel VALDES Soublette (since 7 June 2022)
chancery: 1732 Massachusetts Avenue NW, Washington, DC 20036
telephone: [1] (202) 785-1746
FAX: [1] (202) 887-5579
email address and website:
echile.eeuu@minrel.gob.cl
https://chile.gob.cl/estados-unidos/en/
consulate(s) general: Chicago, Houston, Los Angeles, Miami, New York, San Francisco

Diplomatic representation from the US: *chief of mission:* Ambassador Bernadette M. MEEHAN (since 30 September 2022)
embassy: Avenida Andres Bello 2800, Las Condes, Santiago
mailing address: 3460 Santiago Place, Washington DC 20521-3460
telephone: [56] (2) 2330-3000
FAX: [56] (2) 2330-3710
email address and website:
SantiagoUSA@state.gov
https://cl.usembassy.gov/

Flag description: two equal horizontal bands of white (top) and red; a blue square the same height as the white band at the hoist-side end of the white band; the square bears a white five-pointed star in the center representing a guide to progress and honor; blue symbolizes the sky, white is for the snow-covered Andes, and red represents the blood spilled to achieve independence
note: design influenced by the US flag

National symbol(s): huemul (mountain deer), Andean condor; national colors: red, white, blue

National anthem: *name:* "Himno Nacional de Chile" (National Anthem of Chile)
lyrics/music: Eusebio LILLO Robles and Bernardo DE VERA y Pintado/Ramon CARNICER y Battle
note: music adopted 1828, original lyrics adopted 1818, adapted lyrics adopted 1847; under Augusto PINOCHET's military rule, a verse glorifying the army was added; however, as a protest, some citizens refused to sing this verse; it was removed when democracy was restored in 1990

National heritage: *total World Heritage Sites:* 7 (all cultural)
selected World Heritage Site locales: Rapa Nui National Park; Churches of Chiloe; Historic Valparaiso; Humberstone and Santa Laura Saltpeter Works; Sewell Mining Town; Qhapaq Ñan/Andean Road System; Chinchorro archeological sites

ECONOMY

Economic overview: export-driven economy; leading copper producer; though hit by COVID-19, fairly quick rebound from increased liquidity and rapid vaccine rollouts; decreasing poverty but still lingering inequality; public debt rising but still manageable; recent political violence has had negative economic consequences

Real GDP (purchasing power parity): $579.201 billion (2023 est.)
$577.937 billion (2022 est.)
$566.279 billion (2021 est.)
note: data in 2021 dollars
comparison ranking: 44

Real GDP growth rate: 0.22% (2023 est.)
2.06% (2022 est.)
11.33% (2021 est.)
note: annual GDP % growth based on constant local currency
comparison ranking: 184

Real GDP per capita: $29,500 (2023 est.)
$29,500 (2022 est.)
$29,100 (2021 est.)
note: data in 2021 dollars
comparison ranking: 79

GDP (official exchange rate): $335.533 billion (2023 est.)
note: data in current dollars at official exchange rate

Inflation rate (consumer prices): 7.58% (2023 est.)
11.64% (2022 est.)
4.52% (2021 est.)
note: annual % change based on consumer prices
comparison ranking: 148

Credit ratings: Fitch rating: A- (2020)

Moody's rating: A1 (2018)

Standard & Poors rating: A+ (2017)
note: The year refers to the year in which the current credit rating was first obtained.

GDP - composition, by sector of origin: *agriculture:* 3.5% (2023 est.)
industry: 29.7% (2023 est.)
services: 56.9% (2023 est.)
note: figures may not total 100% due to non-allocated consumption not captured in sector-reported data
comparison rankings: services 108; industry 68; agriculture 133

GDP - composition, by end use: *household consumption:* 60.6% (2023 est.)
government consumption: 15.1% (2023 est.)
investment in fixed capital: 23.8% (2023 est.)
investment in inventories: -0.9% (2023 est.)
exports of goods and services: 31.1% (2023 est.)
imports of goods and services: -29.8% (2023 est.)
note: figures may not total 100% due to rounding or gaps in data collection

Agricultural products: grapes, milk, apples, wheat, potatoes, chicken, tomatoes, sugar beets, maize, oats (2022)
note: top ten agricultural products based on tonnage

Industries: copper, lithium, other minerals, foodstuffs, fish processing, iron and steel, wood and wood products, transport equipment, cement, textiles

Industrial production growth rate: 1.56% (2023 est.)
note: annual % change in industrial value added based on constant local currency
comparison ranking: 126

Labor force: 9.848 million (2023 est.)
note: number of people ages 15 or older who are employed or seeking work
comparison ranking: 56

Unemployment rate: 9.04% (2023 est.)
8.3% (2022 est.)
9.33% (2021 est.)
note: % of labor force seeking employment
comparison ranking: 156

Youth unemployment rate (ages 15-24): *total:* 22% (2023 est.)
male: 20.2% (2023 est.)
female: 24.5% (2023 est.)
note: % of labor force ages 15-24 seeking employment
comparison ranking: total 56

Population below poverty line: 10.8% (2020 est.)
note: % of population with income below national poverty line

Gini Index coefficient - distribution of family income: 43 (2022 est.)
note: index (0-100) of income distribution; higher values represent greater inequality
comparison ranking: 30

Average household expenditures: *on food:* 18% of household expenditures (2022 est.)
on alcohol and tobacco: 3.3% of household expenditures (2022 est.)

Household income or consumption by percentage share: *lowest 10%:* 2.3% (2022 est.)
highest 10%: 34.5% (2022 est.)
note: % share of income accruing to lowest and highest 10% of population

Remittances: 0.02% of GDP (2023 est.)
0.02% of GDP (2022 est.)
0.02% of GDP (2021 est.)
note: personal transfers and compensation between resident and non-resident individuals/households/entities

Budget: *revenues:* $78.577 billion (2022 est.)
expenditures: $72.673 billion (2022 est.)
note: central government revenues (excluding grants) and expenses converted to US dollars at average official exchange rate for year indicated

Public debt: 23.6% of GDP (2017 est.)
comparison ranking: 178

Taxes and other revenues: 21.27% (of GDP) (2022 est.)
note: central government tax revenue as a % of GDP
comparison ranking: 77

Current account balance: -$11.899 billion (2023 est.)
-$26.162 billion (2022 est.)
-$22.962 billion (2021 est.)
note: balance of payments - net trade and primary/secondary income in current dollars
comparison ranking: 196

Exports: $104.349 billion (2023 est.)
$107.071 billion (2022 est.)
$100.448 billion (2021 est.)
note: balance of payments - exports of goods and services in current dollars
comparison ranking: 48

Exports - partners: China 39%, US 14%, Japan 8%, South Korea 6%, Brazil 5% (2022)
note: top five export partners based on percentage share of exports

Exports - commodities: copper ore, refined copper, carbonates, fish, raw copper (2022)
note: top five export commodities based on value in dollars

Imports: $99.808 billion (2023 est.)
$118.941 billion (2022 est.)
$102.637 billion (2021 est.)
note: balance of payments - imports of goods and services in current dollars
comparison ranking: 47

Imports - partners: China 26%, US 22%, Brazil 10%, Argentina 5%, Germany 3% (2022)
note: top five import partners based on percentage share of imports

Imports - commodities: refined petroleum, cars, crude petroleum, garments, trucks (2022)
note: top five import commodities based on value in dollars

Reserves of foreign exchange and gold: $46.377 billion (2023 est.)
$39.102 billion (2022 est.)
$51.252 billion (2021 est.)
note: holdings of gold (year-end prices)/foreign exchange/special drawing rights in current dollars
comparison ranking: 47

Exchange rates: Chilean pesos (CLP) per US dollar -

Exchange rates: 840.067 (2023 est.)
873.314 (2022 est.)
758.955 (2021 est.)
792.727 (2020 est.)
702.897 (2019 est.)

ENERGY

Electricity access: *electrification - total population:* 100% (2022 est.)

Electricity: *installed generating capacity:* 35.598 million kW (2022 est.)
consumption: 86.628 billion kWh (2022 est.)
transmission/distribution losses: 4.313 billion kWh (2022 est.)
comparison rankings: transmission/distribution losses 156; consumption 37; installed generating capacity 34

Electricity generation sources: *fossil fuels:* 43.4% of total installed capacity (2022 est.)
solar: 15.3% of total installed capacity (2022 est.)
wind: 10.3% of total installed capacity (2022 est.)
hydroelectricity: 25.3% of total installed capacity (2022 est.)
geothermal: 0.5% of total installed capacity (2022 est.)
biomass and waste: 5.1% of total installed capacity (2022 est.)

Coal: *production:* 499,000 metric tons (2022 est.)
consumption: 8.637 million metric tons (2022 est.)
exports: 23,000 metric tons (2022 est.)
imports: 8.09 million metric tons (2022 est.)
proven reserves: 1.181 billion metric tons (2022 est.)

Petroleum: *total petroleum production:* 11,000 bbl/day (2023 est.)
refined petroleum consumption: 405,000 bbl/day (2023 est.)
crude oil estimated reserves: 150 million barrels (2021 est.)

Natural gas: *production:* 1.2 billion cubic meters (2022 est.)
consumption: 6.916 billion cubic meters (2022 est.)
exports: 159.558 million cubic meters (2018 est.)
imports: 5.137 billion cubic meters (2022 est.)
proven reserves: 97.976 billion cubic meters (2021 est.)

Carbon dioxide emissions: 79.689 million metric tonnes of CO2 (2022 est.)
from coal and metallurgical coke: 15.94 million metric tonnes of CO2 (2022 est.)
from petroleum and other liquids: 50.15 million metric tonnes of CO2 (2022 est.)
from consumed natural gas: 13.599 million metric tonnes of CO2 (2022 est.)
comparison ranking: total emissions 47

Energy consumption per capita: 69.194 million Btu/person (2022 est.)
comparison ranking: 72

COMMUNICATIONS

Telephones - fixed lines: *total subscriptions:* 2.217 million (2022 est.)
subscriptions per 100 inhabitants: 11 (2022 est.)
comparison ranking: total subscriptions 51

Telephones - mobile cellular: *total subscriptions:* 26.415 million (2022 est.)
subscriptions per 100 inhabitants: 135 (2022 est.)
comparison ranking: total subscriptions 50

Telecommunication systems: *general assessment:* the market for fixed and mobile telephony is highly competitive and rapidly evolving; the mobile rate is among the highest in South America; LTE infrastructure is extensive and 5G spectrum auctions which took place in February 2021 prompted deployment of 5G networks, following extensive trials held by the MNOs; fixed broadband is relatively high for the region, with services among the fastest and least expensive in Latin America; government initiatives such as the National Fiber Optic project and Fibra Óptica Austral are providing high-capacity connectivity across the country and will further increase fixed-line broadband; there is a strong focus on fiber broadband, with the number of fiber subscribers having increased 61.7% in 2020, year-on-year; technological improvements have allowed operators to provide a variety of services via their networks, giving rise to a number of bundled packages at competitive prices, including access to video on demand services which in turn is increasing fixed-line broadband; traditional fixed- line teledensity continues to fall as consumers switch to mobile networks and to fixed broadband for voice and data connectivity; more than 8,300 schools receive free broadband as part of the 'Connectivity for Education 2030' project (2021)
domestic: number of fixed-line connections 13 per 100, mobile-cellular usage continues to increase, reaching 136 telephones per 100 persons (2021)
international: country code - 56; landing points for the Pan-Am, Prat, SAm-1, American Movil-Telxius West Coast Cable, FOS Quellon-Chacabuco, Fibra Optical Austral, SAC and Curie submarine cables providing links to the US, Caribbean and to Central and South America; satellite earth stations - 2 Intelsat (Atlantic Ocean) (2019)

Broadcast media: national and local terrestrial TV channels, coupled with extensive cable TV networks; the state-owned Television Nacional de Chile (TVN) network is self-financed through commercial advertising revenues and is not under direct government control; large number of privately owned TV stations; about 250 radio stations

Internet country code: .cl

Internet users: *total:* 17.1 million (2021 est.)
percent of population: 90% (2021 est.)
comparison ranking: total 46

Broadband - fixed subscriptions: *total:* 3,763,826 (2020 est.)
subscriptions per 100 inhabitants: 20 (2020 est.)
comparison ranking: total 41

TRANSPORTATION

National air transport system: *number of registered air carriers:* 9 (2020)
inventory of registered aircraft operated by air carriers: 173
annual passenger traffic on registered air carriers: 19,517,185 (2018)
annual freight traffic on registered air carriers: 1,226,440,000 (2018) mt-km

Civil aircraft registration country code prefix: CC

Airports: 374 (2024)
comparison ranking: 18

Heliports: 114 (2024)

Pipelines: 3,160 km gas, 781 km liquid petroleum gas, 985 km oil, 722 km refined products (2013)

Railways: *total:* 7,281.5 km (2014)
narrow gauge: 3,853.5 km (2014) 1.000-m gauge
broad gauge: 3,428 km (2014) 1.676-m gauge (1,691 km electrified)
comparison ranking: total 30

Roadways: *total:* 77,801 km (2016)
comparison ranking: total 64

Merchant marine: *total:* 249 (2023)
by type: bulk carrier 3, container ship 5, general cargo 66, oil tanker 14, other 161
comparison ranking: total 64

Ports: *total ports:* 39 (2024)
large: 0
medium: 2
small: 10
very small: 27
ports with oil terminals: 25
key ports: Antofagasta, Bahia de Valdivia, Bahia de Valparaiso, Coronel, Iquique, Mejillones, Puerto Montt, Puerto San Antonio, Rada de Arica, Rada Punta Arenas, Talcahuano, Tocopilla

MILITARY AND SECURITY

Military and security forces: Armed Forces of Chile (Fuerzas Armadas de Chile): Chilean Army (Ejército de Chile), Chilean Navy (Armada de Chile, includes Marine Corps and Maritime Territory and Merchant Marine Directorate or Directemar), Chilean Air Force (Fuerza Aerea de Chile, FACh) (2024)
note 1: the Directemar is the country's coast guard
note 2: the National Police Force (Carabineros de Chile) are responsible to both the Ministry of Defense and the Ministry of the Interior and Public Security

Military expenditures: 1.5% of GDP (2023 est.)
1.6% of GDP (2022 est.)
2% of GDP (2021 est.)
2% of GDP (2020 est.)
1.9% of GDP (2019 est.)
comparison ranking: 91

Military and security service personnel strengths: approximately 80,000 active armed forces personnel (45,000 Army; 25,000 Navy; 10,000 Air Force); approximately 50,000 Carabineros (2023)

Military equipment inventories and acquisitions: the Chilean military inventory is comprised of a wide mix of mostly Western equipment and some domestically produced systems; in recent years, it has received military hardware from a variety of countries, including Australia, Germany, New Zealand, the UK, and the US; Chile's defense industry has capabilities in military aircraft, ships, and vehicles (2023)

Military service age and obligation: 18-45 years of age for voluntary military service for men; 17-24 for women; selective compulsory service (there are usually enough volunteers to make compulsory service unnecessary); service obligation is a minimum of 12 months for Army and 22 months for Navy and Air Force (2023)
note: as of 2021, women comprised approximately 18% of the armed forces

Military - note: the Chilean military's primary responsibility is territorial defense and ensuring the country's sovereignty; it also assists with disaster and humanitarian relief and some internal security duties such as border security or maintaining public order if required; a key focus in recent years has been assisting with securing the border area with Bolivia and Peru; it trains regularly and participates in bilateral and multinational training exercises, as well as international peacekeeping operations
Chile and Argentina have a joint peacekeeping force known as the Combined Southern Cross Peacekeeping Force (FPC), designed to be made available to the UN; the FPC is made up of air, ground, and naval components, as well as a combined logistics support unit
the Chilean Army was founded in 1810, but traces its origins back to the Army of the Kingdom of Chile, which was established by the Spanish Crown in the early 1600s; Chile's military aviation was inaugurated in 1913 with the creation of a military aviation school; the Navy traces its origins to 1817; it was first led by a British officer and the first ships were largely crewed by American, British, and Irish sailors; by the 1880s, the Chilean Navy was one of the most powerful in the Americas, and included the world's first protected cruiser (a ship with an armored deck to protect vital machine spaces) (2024)

SPACE

Space agency/agencies: the Chilean Space Agency was established in 2001 and dissolved in 2014, at which time the space program became part of the Ministry of Defense; the Ministry of Science also participates in Chile's space program (2024)

Space program overview: has a space program with a considerable history and largely focused on the acquisition and operation of satellites; operates foreign-built satellites and satellite ground stations; building small remote sensing (RS) satellites; researching and developing additional capabilities and technologies associated with the production of satellites and satellite subsystems; is a world leader in astronomy and astrophysics (Chile's Atacama Desert, where the skies are exceptionally clear and dry for more than 300 days a year, is home to more than a dozen astronomical observatories including the Cerro Tololo Inter-American Observatory, the Las Campanas Observatory, and the European Southern Observatory); Chile is also home to several astronomy institutes; has established relations with space agencies and industries of Canada, China, France, India, Israel, Mexico, Russia, the UK, and the US (2024)
note: further details about the key activities, programs, and milestones of the country's space program, as well as government spending estimates on the space sector, appear in the Space Programs reference guide

TRANSNATIONAL ISSUES

Refugees and internally displaced persons: *refugees (country of origin):* 444,423 (Venezuela) (economic and political crisis; includes Venezuelans who have claimed asylum or have received alternative legal stay) (2023)

Illicit drugs: transshipment country for cocaine destined for Europe and the region; some money laundering activity, especially through the Iquique Free Trade Zone; imported precursors passed on to Bolivia; domestic cocaine consumption is rising, making Chile a significant consumer of cocaine

CHINA

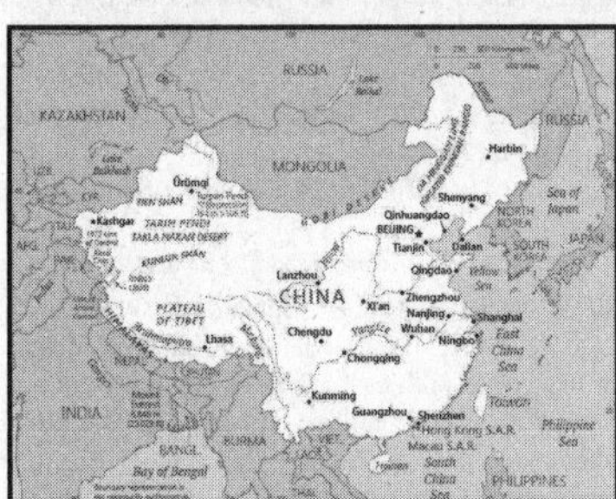

INTRODUCTION

Background: China's historical civilization dates to at least the 13th century B.C., first under the Shang (to 1046 B.C.) and then the Zhou (1046-221 B.C.) dynasties. The imperial era of China began in 221 B.C. under the Qin Dynasty and lasted until the fall of the Qing Dynasty in 1912. During this period, China alternated between periods of unity and disunity under a succession of imperial dynasties. In the 19th century, the Qing Dynasty suffered heavily from overextension by territorial conquest, insolvency, civil war, imperialism, military defeats, and foreign expropriation of ports and infrastructure. It collapsed following the Revolution of 1911, and China became a republic under SUN Yat-sen of the Kuomintang (KMT or Nationalist) Party. However, the republic was beset by division, warlordism, and continued foreign intervention. In the late 1920s, a civil war erupted between the ruling KMT-controlled government, led by CHIANG Kai-shek, and the Chinese Communist Party (CCP). Japan occupied much of northeastern China in the early 1930s, and then launched a full-scale invasion of the country in 1937. The resulting eight years of warfare devastated the country and cost up to 20 million Chinese lives by the time of Japan's defeat in 1945. The Nationalist-Communist civil war continued with renewed intensity after the end of World War II and culminated with a CCP victory in 1949, under the leadership of MAO Zedong.

MAO and the CCP established an autocratic socialist system that, while ensuring the PRC's sovereignty, imposed strict controls over everyday life and launched agricultural, economic, political, and social policies – such as the Great Leap Forward (1958-1962) and the Cultural Revolution (1966-1976) – that cost the lives of millions of people. MAO died in 1976. Beginning in 1978, leaders DENG Xiaoping, JIANG Zemin, and hU Jintao focused on market-oriented economic development and opening up the country to foreign trade, while maintaining the rule of the CCP. Since the change, China has been among the world's fastest growing economies, with real gross domestic product averaging over 9% growth annually through 2021, lifting an estimated 800 million people out of poverty and dramatically improving overall living standards. By 2011, the PRC's economy was the second largest in the world. Current leader XI Jinping has continued these policies but has also maintained tight political controls. Over the past decade, China has increased its global outreach, including military deployments, participation in international organizations, and a global connectivity plan in 2013 called the "Belt and Road Initiative" (BRI). Many nations have signed on to BRI agreements to attract PRC investment, but others have expressed concerns about such issues as the opaque nature of the projects, financing, and potentially unsustainable debt obligations. XI Jinping assumed the positions of General Secretary of the Chinese Communist Party and Chairman of the Central Military Commission in 2012 and President in 2013. In 2018, the PRC's National People's Congress passed an amendment abolishing presidential term limits, which allowed XI to gain a third five-year term in 2023.

GEOGRAPHY

Location: Eastern Asia, bordering the East China Sea, Korea Bay, Yellow Sea, and South China Sea, between North Korea and Vietnam

Geographic coordinates: 35 00 N, 105 00 E

Map references: Asia

Area: *total:* 9,596,960 sq km
land: 9,326,410 sq km
water: 270,550 sq km
comparison ranking: total 5

Area - comparative: slightly smaller than the US

Land boundaries: *total:* 22,457 km
border countries (14): Afghanistan 91 km; Bhutan 477 km; Burma 2,129 km; India 2,659 km; Kazakhstan 1,765 km; North Korea 1,352 km;

Kyrgyzstan 1,063 km; Laos 475 km; Mongolia 4,630 km; Nepal 1,389 km; Pakistan 438 km; Russia (northeast) 4,133 km and Russia (northwest) 46 km; Tajikistan 477 km; Vietnam 1,297 km

Coastline: 14,500 km

Maritime claims: *territorial sea:* 12 nm
contiguous zone: 24 nm
exclusive economic zone: 200 nm
continental shelf: 200 nm or to the edge of the continental margin

Climate: extremely diverse; tropical in south to subarctic in north

Terrain: mostly mountains, high plateaus, deserts in west; plains, deltas, and hills in east

Elevation: *highest point:* Mount Everest (highest peak in Asia and highest point on earth above sea level) 8,849 m
lowest point: Turpan Pendi (Turfan Depression) -154 m
mean elevation: 1,840 m

Natural resources: coal, iron ore, helium, petroleum, natural gas, arsenic, bismuth, cobalt, cadmium, ferrosilicon, gallium, germanium, hafnium, indium, lithium, mercury, tantalum, tellurium, tin, titanium, tungsten, antimony, manganese, magnesium, molybdenum, selenium, strontium, vanadium, magnetite, aluminum, lead, zinc, rare earth elements, uranium, hydropower potential (world's largest), arable land

Land use: *agricultural land:* 54.7% (2018 est.)
arable land: 11.3% (2018 est.)
permanent crops: 1.6% (2018 est.)
permanent pasture: 41.8% (2018 est.)
forest: 22.3% (2018 est.)
other: 23% (2018 est.)

Irrigated land: 690,070 sq km (2012)

Major lakes (area sq km): *fresh water lake(s):* Dongting Hu - 3,100 sq km; Poyang Hu - 3,350 sq km; Hongze Hu - 2,700 sq km; Tai Hu - 2,210 sq km; Hulun Nur - 1,590
salt water lake(s): Quinghai Hu - 4,460 sq km; Nam Co - 2,500 sq km; Siling Co - 1,860 sq km; Tangra Yumco - 1,400 sq km; Bosten Hu 1,380 sq km

Major rivers (by length in km): Yangtze - 6,300 km; Huang He - 5,464 km; Amur river source (shared with Mongolia and Russia [m]) - 4,444 km; Lancang Jiang (Mekong) river source (shared with Burma, Laos, Thailand, Cambodia, and Vietnam [m]) - 4,350 km; Yarlung Zangbo Jiang (Brahmaputra) river source (shared with India and Bangladesh [m]) - 3,969 km; Yin-tu Ho (Indus) river source (shared with India and Pakistan [m]) - 3,610 km; Nu Jiang (Salween) river source (shared with Thailand and Burma [m]) - 3,060 km; Irrawaddy river source (shared with Burma [m]) - 2,809 km; Zhu Jiang (Pearl) (shared with Vietnam [s]) - 2,200 km; Yuan Jiang (Red river) source (shared with Vietnam [m]) - 1,149 km
note – [s] after country name indicates river source; [m] after country name indicates river mouth

Major watersheds (area sq km): Pacific Ocean drainage: Amur (1,929,955 sq km), Huang He (944,970 sq km), Mekong (805,604 sq km), Yangtze (1,722,193 sq km)

Indian Ocean drainage: Brahmaputra (651,335 sq km), Ganges (1,016,124 sq km), Indus (1,081,718 sq km), Irrawaddy (413,710 sq km), Salween (271,914 sq km)

Arctic Ocean drainage: Ob (2,972,493 sq km)

Internal (endorheic basin) drainage: Tarim Basin (1,152,448 sq km), Amu Darya (534,739 sq km), Syr Darya (782,617 sq km), Lake Balkash (510,015 sq km)

Major aquifers: North China Aquifer System (Huang Huai Hai Plain), Song-Liao Plain, Tarim Basin

Population distribution: overwhelming majority of the population is found in the eastern half of the country; the west, with its vast mountainous and desert areas, remains sparsely populated; though ranked first in the world in total population, overall density is less than that of many other countries in Asia and Europe; high population density is found along the Yangtze and Yellow River valleys, the Xi Jiang River delta, the Sichuan Basin (around Chengdu), in and around Beijing, and the industrial area around Shenyang

Natural hazards: frequent typhoons (about five per year along southern and eastern coasts); damaging floods; tsunamis; earthquakes; droughts; land subsidence
volcanism: China contains some historically active volcanoes including Changbaishan (also known as Baitoushan, Baegdu, or P'aektu-san), Hainan Dao, and Kunlun although most have been relatively inactive in recent centuries

Geography - note: *note 1:* world's fourth largest country (after Russia, Canada, and US) and largest country situated entirely in Asia; Mount Everest on the border with Nepal is the world's tallest peak above sea level
note 2: the largest cave chamber in the world is the Miao Room, in the Gebihe cave system at China's Ziyun Getu He Chuandong National Park, which encloses some 10.78 million cu m (380.7 million cu ft) of volume; the world's largest sinkhole is the Xiaoxhai Tiankeng sinkhole in Chongqing Municipality, which is 660 m deep, with a volume of 130 million cu m
note 3: China appears to have been the center of domestication for two of the world's leading cereal crops: millet in the north along the Yellow River and rice in the south along the lower or middle Yangtze River

PEOPLE AND SOCIETY

Population: *total:* 1,416,043,270
male: 722,201,504
female: 693,841,766 (2024 est.)
comparison rankings: female 1; male 2; total 1

Nationality: *noun:* Chinese (singular and plural)
adjective: Chinese

Ethnic groups: Han Chinese 91.1%, ethnic minorities 8.9% (includes Zhang, Hui, Manchu, Uighur, Miao, Yi, Tujia, Tibetan, Mongol, Dong, Buyei, Yao, Bai, Korean, Hani, Li, Kazakh, Dai, and other nationalities) (2021 est.)
note: the PRC officially recognizes 56 ethnic groups

Languages: Standard Chinese or Mandarin (official; Putonghua, based on the Beijing dialect), Yue (Cantonese), Wu (Shanghainese), Minbei (Fuzhou), Minnan (Hokkien-Taiwanese), Xiang, Gan, Hakka dialects, minority languages; note - Zhuang is official in Guangxi Zhuang, Yue is official in Guangdong, Mongolian is official in Nei Mongol, Uyghur is official in Xinjiang Uygur, Kyrgyz is official in Xinjiang Uyghur, and Tibetan is official in Xizang (Tibet)
major-language sample(s):
世界概況 一 不可缺少的基本消息來源 (Standard Chinese)

Religions: folk religion 21.9%, Buddhist 18.2%, Christian 5.1%, Muslim 1.8%, Hindu < 0.1%, Jewish < 0.1%, other 0.7% (includes Daoist (Taoist)), unaffiliated 52.1% (2021 est.)
note: officially atheist

Age structure: *0-14 years:* 16.3% (male 122,644,111/female 107,926,176)
15-64 years: 69.3% (male 505,412,555/female 476,599,793)
65 years and over: 14.4% (2024 est.) (male 94,144,838/female 109,315,797)

Dependency ratios: *total dependency ratio:* 44.5
youth dependency ratio: 25.5
elderly dependency ratio: 19
potential support ratio: 5.3 (2021 est.)
note: data do not include Hong Kong, Macau, and Taiwan

Median age: *total:* 40.2 years (2024 est.)
male: 39 years
female: 41.5 years
comparison ranking: total 61

Population growth rate: 0.23% (2024 est.)
comparison ranking: 172

Birth rate: 10.2 births/1,000 population (2024 est.)
comparison ranking: 183

Death rate: 7.7 deaths/1,000 population (2024 est.)
comparison ranking: 95

Net migration rate: -0.1 migrant(s)/1,000 population (2024 est.)
comparison ranking: 100

Population distribution: overwhelming majority of the population is found in the eastern half of the country; the west, with its vast mountainous and desert areas, remains sparsely populated; though ranked first in the world in total population, overall density is less than that of many other countries in Asia and Europe; high population density is found along the Yangtze and Yellow River valleys, the Xi Jiang River delta, the Sichuan Basin (around Chengdu), in and around Beijing, and the industrial area around Shenyang

Urbanization: *urban population:* 64.6% of total population (2023)
rate of urbanization: 1.78% annual rate of change (2020-25 est.)
note: data do not include Hong Kong and Macau

Major urban areas - population: 29.211 million Shanghai, 21.766 million BEIJING (capital), 17.341 million Chongqing, 14.284 million Guangzhou, 14.239 million Tianjin, 13.073 million Shenzhen (2023)

Sex ratio: *at birth:* 1.09 male(s)/female
0-14 years: 1.14 male(s)/female
15-64 years: 1.06 male(s)/female
65 years and over: 0.86 male(s)/female
total population: 1.04 male(s)/female (2024 est.)

Maternal mortality ratio: 23 deaths/100,000 live births (2020 est.)
comparison ranking: 117

Infant mortality rate: *total:* 6.2 deaths/1,000 live births (2024 est.)
male: 6.7 deaths/1,000 live births
female: 5.7 deaths/1,000 live births
comparison ranking: total 167

Life expectancy at birth: *total population:* 78.7 years (2024 est.)
male: 76 years
female: 81.7 years
comparison ranking: total population 75

Total fertility rate: 1.55 children born/woman (2024 est.)

comparison ranking: 193

Gross reproduction rate: 0.74 (2024 est.)

Contraceptive prevalence rate: 84.5% (2017)

Drinking water source: *improved: urban:* 97.3% of population
rural: 91.5% of population
total: 95.1% of population
unimproved: urban: 2.7% of population
rural: 8.5% of population
total: 4.9% of population (2020 est.)

Current health expenditure: 5.6% of GDP (2020)

Physician density: 2.23 physicians/1,000 population (2019)

Hospital bed density: 4.3 beds/1,000 population (2017)

Sanitation facility access: *improved: urban:* 97.6% of population
rural: 90.6% of population
total: 94.9% of population
unimproved: urban: 2.4% of population
rural: 9.4% of population
total: 5.1% of population (2020 est.)

Obesity - adult prevalence rate: 6.2% (2016)
comparison ranking: 169

Alcohol consumption per capita: *total:* 4.48 liters of pure alcohol (2019 est.)
beer: 1.66 liters of pure alcohol (2019 est.)
wine: 0.18 liters of pure alcohol (2019 est.)
spirits: 2.63 liters of pure alcohol (2019 est.)
other alcohols: 0 liters of pure alcohol (2019 est.)
comparison ranking: total 89

Tobacco use: *total:* 25.6% (2020 est.)
male: 49.4% (2020 est.)
female: 1.7% (2020 est.)
comparison ranking: total 44

Children under the age of 5 years underweight: 2.4% (2013)
comparison ranking: 100

Currently married women (ages 15-49): 75.9% (2023 est.)

Child marriage: *women married by age 15:* 0.1%
women married by age 18: 2.8%
men married by age 18: 0.7% (2020 est.)

Education expenditures: 3.6% of GDP (2020 est.)
comparison ranking: 133

Literacy: *definition:* age 15 and over can read and write
total population: 96.8%
male: 98.5%
female: 95.2% (2018)

School life expectancy (primary to tertiary education): *total:* 14 years
male: 14 years
female: 14 years (2015)

People - note: in October 2015, the Chinese Government announced that it would change its rules to allow all couples to have two children, loosening a 1979 mandate that restricted many couples to one child; the new policy was implemented on 1 January 2016 to address China's rapidly aging population and future economic needs

ENVIRONMENT

Environment - current issues: air pollution (greenhouse gases, sulfur dioxide particulates) from reliance on coal produces acid rain; China is the world's largest single emitter of carbon dioxide from the burning of fossil fuels; water shortages, particularly in the north; water pollution from untreated wastes; coastal destruction due to land reclamation, industrial development, and aquaculture; deforestation and habitat destruction; poor land management leads to soil erosion, landslides, floods, droughts, dust storms, and desertification; trade in endangered species

Environment - international agreements: *party to:* Antarctic-Environmental Protection, Antarctic-Marine Living Resources, Antarctic Treaty, Biodiversity, Climate Change, Climate Change-Kyoto Protocol, Climate Change-Paris Agreement, Desertification, Endangered Species, Environmental Modification, Hazardous Wastes, Law of the Sea, Marine Dumping-London Convention, Marine Dumping- London Protocol, Ozone Layer Protection, Ship Pollution, Tropical Timber 2006, Wetlands, Whaling
signed, but not ratified: Comprehensive Nuclear Test Ban

Climate: extremely diverse; tropical in south to subarctic in north

Urbanization: *urban population:* 64.6% of total population (2023)
rate of urbanization: 1.78% annual rate of change (2020-25 est.)
note: data do not include Hong Kong and Macau

Revenue from forest resources: 0.08% of GDP (2018 est.)
comparison ranking: 117

Revenue from coal: 0.57% of GDP (2018 est.)
comparison ranking: 9

Air pollutants: *particulate matter emissions:* 38.15 micrograms per cubic meter (2019 est.)
carbon dioxide emissions: 9,893.04 megatons (2016 est.)
methane emissions: 1,490.24 megatons (2020 est.)

Waste and recycling: *municipal solid waste generated annually:* 210 million tons (2015 est.)

Major lakes (area sq km): *fresh water lake(s):* Dongting Hu - 3,100 sq km; Poyang Hu - 3,350 sq km; Hongze Hu - 2,700 sq km; Tai Hu - 2,210 sq km; Hulun Nur - 1,590
salt water lake(s): Quinghai Hu - 4,460 sq km; Nam Co - 2,500 sq km; Siling Co - 1,860 sq km; Tangra Yumco - 1,400 sq km; Bosten Hu 1,380 sq km

Major rivers (by length in km): Yangtze - 6,300 km; Huang He - 5,464 km; Amur river source (shared with Mongolia and Russia [m]) - 4,444 km; Lancang Jiang (Mekong) river source (shared with Burma, Laos, Thailand, Cambodia, and Vietnam [m]) - 4,350 km; Yarlung Zangbo Jiang (Brahmaputra) river source (shared with India and Bangladesh [m]) - 3,969 km; Yin-tu Ho (Indus) river source (shared with India and Pakistan [m]) - 3,610 km; Nu Jiang (Salween) river source (shared with Thailand and Burma [m]) - 3,060 km; Irrawaddy river source (shared with Burma [m]) - 2,809 km; Zhu Jiang (Pearl) (shared with Vietnam [s]) - 2,200 km; Yuan Jiang (Red river) source (shared with Vietnam [m]) - 1,149 km
note – [s] after country name indicates river source; [m] after country name indicates river mouth

Major watersheds (area sq km): Pacific Ocean drainage: Amur (1,929,955 sq km), Huang He (944,970 sq km), Mekong (805,604 sq km), Yangtze (1,722,193 sq km)

Indian Ocean drainage: Brahmaputra (651,335 sq km), Ganges (1,016,124 sq km), Indus (1,081,718 sq km), Irrawaddy (413,710 sq km), Salween (271,914 sq km)

Arctic Ocean drainage: Ob (2,972,493 sq km)

Internal (endorheic basin) drainage: Tarim Basin (1,152,448 sq km), Amu Darya (534,739 sq km), Syr Darya (782,617 sq km), Lake Balkash (510,015 sq km)

Major aquifers: North China Aquifer System (Huang Huai Hai Plain), Song-Liao Plain, Tarim Basin

Total water withdrawal: *municipal:* 117.01 billion cubic meters (2020 est.)
industrial: 103.04 billion cubic meters (2020 est.)
agricultural: 361.24 billion cubic meters (2020 est.)

Total renewable water resources: 2.84 trillion cubic meters (2020 est.)

Geoparks: *total global geoparks and regional networks:* 47 (2024)
global geoparks and regional networks: Alxa; Arxan; Dali-Cangshan; Danxiashan; Dunhuang; Enshi Grand Canyon- Tenglongdong; Fangshan; Funiushan; Guangwushan-Noushuihe; Hexigten; Hong Kong; Huanggang Dabieshan; Huangshan; Jingpohu; Jiuhuashan; Keketuohai; Leiqiong; Leye Fengshan; Linxia; Longhushan; Longyan; Lushan; Mount Changbaishan; Mount Kunlun; Ningde; Qinling Zhongnanshan; Sanqingshan; Shennongjia; Shilin; Songshan; Taining; Taishan; Tianzhushan; Wangwushan-Daimeishan; Wudalianchi; Wugongshan; Xiangxi; Xingwen; Yingyi; Yandangshan; Yanqing; Yimengshan; Yuntaishan; Zhangjlajle; Zhangye; Zhijingdong Cave; Zigong (2024)

GOVERNMENT

Country name: *conventional long form:* People's Republic of China
conventional short form: China
local long form: Zhonghua Renmin Gongheguo
local short form: Zhongguo
abbreviation: PRC
etymology: English name derives from the Qin (Chin) rulers of the 3rd century B.C., who comprised the first imperial dynasty of ancient China; the Chinese name Zhongguo translates as "Central Nation" or "Middle Kingdom"

Government type: communist party-led state

Capital: *name:* Beijing
geographic coordinates: 39 55 N, 116 23 E
time difference: UTC+8 (13 hours ahead of Washington, DC, during Standard Time)
time zone note: China is the largest country (in terms of area) with just one time zone; before 1949 it was divided into five
etymology: the Chinese meaning is "Northern Capital"

Administrative divisions: 23 provinces (sheng, singular and plural), 5 autonomous regions (zizhiqu, singular and plural), 4 municipalities (shi, singular and plural), and two special administrative regions (tebie xingzhengqu, singular and plural)
provinces: Anhui, Fujian, Gansu, Guangdong, Guizhou, Hainan, Hebei, Heilongjiang, Henan, Hubei, Hunan, Jiangsu, Jiangxi, Jilin, Liaoning, Qinghai, Shaanxi, Shandong, Shanxi, Sichuan, Yunnan, Zhejiang; (see note on Taiwan)
autonomous regions: Guangxi, Nei Mongol (Inner Mongolia), Ningxia, Xinjiang Uyghur, Xizang (Tibet)
municipalities: Beijing, Chongqing, Shanghai, Tianjin
special administrative regions: Hong Kong, Macau

note: China considers Taiwan its 23rd province; see separate entries for the special administrative regions of Hong Kong and Macau

Independence: *1 October 1949 (People's Republic of China established); notable earlier dates:* 221 B.C. (unification under the Qin Dynasty); 1 January 1912 (Qing Dynasty replaced by the Republic of China)

National holiday: National Day (anniversary of the founding of the People's Republic of China), 1 October (1949)

Legal system: civil law influenced by Soviet and continental European civil law systems; legislature retains power to interpret statutes; note - on 28 May 2020, the National People's Congress adopted the PRC Civil Code, which codifies personal relations and property relations

Constitution: *history:* several previous; latest promulgated 4 December 1982
amendments: proposed by the Standing Committee of the National People's Congress or supported by more than one fifth of the National People's Congress membership; passage requires more than two-thirds majority vote of the Congress membership; amended several times, last in 2018

International law organization participation: has not submitted an ICJ jurisdiction declaration; non-party state to the ICCt

Citizenship: *citizenship by birth:* no
citizenship by descent only: least one parent must be a citizen of China
dual citizenship recognized: no
residency requirement for naturalization: while naturalization is theoretically possible, in practical terms it is extremely difficult; residency is required but not specified

Suffrage: 18 years of age; universal

Executive branch: *chief of state:* President XI Jinping (since 14 March 2013)
head of government: Premier LI Qiang (since 11 March 2023)
cabinet: State Council appointed by National People's Congress
elections/appointments: president and vice president indirectly elected by National People's Congress; election last held on 10 March 2023 (next to be held in March 2028); premier nominated by president, confirmed by National People's Congress
election results:
2023: XI Jinping reelected president; National People's Congress vote - 2,952 (unanimously); HAN Zheng elected vice president with 2,952 votes
2018: XI Jinping reelected president; National People's Congress vote - 2,970 (unanimously); WANG Qishan elected vice president with 2,969 votes
note: ultimate authority rests with the Communist Party Central Committee's 25-member Political Bureau (Politburo) and its seven-member Standing Committee; XI Jinping holds the three most powerful positions as party general secretary, state president, and chairman of the Central Military Commission

Legislative branch: *description:* unicameral National People's Congress (NPC) or Quanguo Renmin Daibiao Dahui (maximum of 3,000 seats; members indirectly elected by municipal, regional, and provincial people's congresses, and the People's Liberation Army; members serve 5-year terms)
elections: the 14th NPC convened on 5 March 2023; the 15th NPC will convene in March 2028
election results: percent of vote - NA; seats by party - NA; the 14th NPC consists of 2,977 delegates; 2,187 men, 790 women, percentage women 26.5%
note: in practice, only members of the Chinese Communist Party (CCP), its 8 allied independent parties, and CCP-approved independent candidates are elected

Judicial branch: *highest court(s):* Supreme People's Court (consists of over 340 judges, including the chief justice and 13 grand justices organized into a civil committee and tribunals for civil, economic, administrative, complaint and appeal, and communication and transportation cases)
judge selection and term of office: chief justice appointed by the People's National Congress (NPC); limited to 2 consecutive 5-year-terms; other justices and judges nominated by the chief justice and appointed by the Standing Committee of the NPC; term of other justices and judges determined by the NPC
subordinate courts: Higher People's Courts; Intermediate People's Courts; District and County People's Courts; Autonomous Region People's Courts; International Commercial Courts; Special People's Courts for military, maritime, transportation, and forestry issues

Political parties: Chinese Communist Party or CCP
note: China has 8 nominally independent small parties controlled by the CCP

International organization participation: ADB, AfDB (nonregional member), APEC, Arctic Council (observer), ARF, ASEAN (dialogue partner), BIS, BRICS, CDB, CICA, EAS, FAO, FATF, G-20, G-24 (observer), G-5, G-77, IADB, IAEA, IBRD, ICAO, ICC (national committees), ICRM, IDA, IFAD, IFC, IFRCS, IHO, ILO, IMF, IMO, IMSO, Interpol, IOC, IOM (observer), IPU, ISO, ITSO, ITU, LAIA (observer), MIGA, MINURSO, MONUSCO, NAM (observer), NSG, OAS (observer), OPCW, Pacific Alliance (observer), PCA, PIF (partner), SAARC (observer), SCO, SICA (observer), UN, UNAMID, UNCTAD, UNESCO, UNFICYP, UNHCR, UNHRC, UNIDO, UNIFIL, UNISFA, UNMIL, UNMISS, UNOCI, UNOOSA, UN Security Council (permanent), UNTSO, UNWTO, UPU, WCO, WHO, WIPO, WMO, WTO, ZC

Diplomatic representation in the US: *chief of mission:* Ambassador XIE Feng (since 30 June 2023)
chancery: 3505 International Place NW, Washington, DC 20008
telephone: [1] (202) 495-2266
FAX: [1] (202) 495-2138
email address and website:
chinaemppress_us@mfa.gov.cn
http://www.china-embassy.org/eng/
consulate(s) general: Chicago, Los Angeles, New York, San Francisco; note - the US ordered closure of the Houston consulate in late July 2020

Diplomatic representation from the US: *chief of mission:* Ambassador Nicholas BURNS (since 2 April 2022)
embassy: 55 Anjialou Road, Chaoyang District, Beijing 100600
mailing address: 7300 Beijing Place, Washington DC 20521-7300
telephone: [86] (10) 8531-3000
FAX: [86] (10) 8531-4200
email address and website:
BeijingACS@state.gov
https://china.usembassy-china.org.cn/
consulate(s) general: Guangzhou, Shanghai, Shenyang, Wuhan; note - the Chinese Government ordered closure of the US consulate in Chengdu in late July 2020

Flag description: red with a large yellow five-pointed star and four smaller yellow five-pointed stars (arranged in a vertical arc toward the middle of the flag) in the upper hoist-side corner; the color red represents revolution, while the stars symbolize the four social classes - the working class, the peasantry, the urban petty bourgeoisie, and the national bourgeoisie (capitalists) - united under the Communist Party of China

National symbol(s): dragon, giant panda; national colors: red, yellow

National anthem: *name:* "Yiyongjun Jinxingqu" (The March of the Volunteers)
lyrics/music: TIAN Han/NIE Er
note: adopted 1949; the anthem, though banned during the Cultural Revolution, is more commonly known as "Zhongguo Guoge" (Chinese National Song); it was originally the theme song to the 1935 Chinese movie, "Sons and Daughters in a Time of Storm"

National heritage: *total World Heritage Sites:* 57 (39 cultural, 14 natural, 4 mixed)
selected World Heritage Site locales: Imperial Palaces of the Ming and Qing Dynasties (c); Mausoleum of the First Qin Emperor (c); The Great Wall (c); Summer Palace (c); Jiuzhaigou Valley (n); Potala Palace (c); Ancient Pingyao (c); Historic Macau (c); Dengfeng (c); Grand Canal (c); Mount Huangshan (m)

Government - note: in 2018, the Beijing established an investigatory National Supervisory Commission to oversee all state employees

ECONOMY

Economic overview: one of the world's top two economies; sustained growth due to export relations, its manufacturing sector, and low-wage workers; only major economy to avoid COVID-19 economic decline; recovery efforts slowing due to longstanding poverty imbalances and other institutional issues; state-sponsored economic controls

Real GDP (purchasing power parity): $31.227 trillion (2023 est.)
$29.683 trillion (2022 est.)
$28.822 trillion (2021 est.)
note: data in 2021 dollars
comparison ranking: 1

Real GDP growth rate: 5.2% (2023 est.)
2.99% (2022 est.)
8.45% (2021 est.)
note: annual GDP % growth based on constant local currency
comparison ranking: 46

Real GDP per capita: $22,100 (2023 est.)
$21,000 (2022 est.)
$20,400 (2021 est.)
note: data in 2021 dollars
comparison ranking: 97

GDP (official exchange rate): $17.795 trillion (2023 est.)
note: data in current dollars at official exchange rate

Inflation rate (consumer prices): 0.23% (2023 est.)
1.97% (2022 est.)
0.98% (2021 est.)
note: annual % change based on consumer prices

comparison ranking: 8

Credit ratings: Fitch rating: A+ (2007)

Moody's rating: A1 (2017)

Standard & Poors rating: A+ (2017)
note: The year refers to the year in which the current credit rating was first obtained.

GDP - composition, by sector of origin: *agriculture:* 7.1% (2023 est.)
industry: 38.3% (2023 est.)
services: 54.6% (2023 est.)
note: figures may not total 100% due to non-allocated consumption not captured in sector-reported data
comparison rankings: services 121; industry 33; agriculture 99

GDP - composition, by end use: *household consumption:* 37.4% (2022 est.)
government consumption: 16.1% (2022 est.)
investment in fixed capital: 41.9% (2022 est.)
investment in inventories: 1.2% (2022 est.)
exports of goods and services: 19.7% (2023 est.)
imports of goods and services: -17.6% (2023 est.)
note: figures may not total 100% due to rounding or gaps in data collection

Agricultural products: maize, rice, vegetables, wheat, sugarcane, potatoes, cucumbers/gherkins, tomatoes, watermelons, pork (2022)
note: top ten agricultural products based on tonnage

Industries: world leader in gross value of industrial output; mining and ore processing, iron, steel, aluminum, and other metals, coal; machine building; armaments; textiles and apparel; petroleum; cement; chemicals; fertilizer; consumer products (including footwear, toys, and electronics); food processing; transportation equipment, including automobiles, railcars and locomotives, ships, aircraft; telecommunications equipment, commercial space launch vehicles, satellites

Industrial production growth rate: 3.58% (2023 est.)
note: annual % change in industrial value added based on constant local currency
comparison ranking: 91

Labor force: 779.246 million (2023 est.)
note: number of people ages 15 or older who are employed or seeking work
comparison ranking: 1

Unemployment rate: 4.67% (2023 est.)
4.98% (2022 est.)
4.55% (2021 est.)
note: % of labor force seeking employment
comparison ranking: 89

Youth unemployment rate (ages 15-24): *total:* 15.7% (2023 est.)
male: 16.9% (2023 est.)
female: 14.2% (2023 est.)
note: % of labor force ages 15-24 seeking employment
comparison ranking: total 93

Population below poverty line: 0% (2020 est.)
note: % of population with income below national poverty line

Gini Index coefficient - distribution of family income: 37.1 (2020 est.)
note: index (0-100) of income distribution; higher values represent greater inequality
comparison ranking: 61

Average household expenditures: *on food:* 20.1% of household expenditures (2022 est.)
on alcohol and tobacco: 3% of household expenditures (2022 est.)

Household income or consumption by percentage share: *lowest 10%:* 3.1% (2020 est.)
highest 10%: 29.4% (2020 est.)
note: % share of income accruing to lowest and highest 10% of population

Remittances: 0.28% of GDP (2023 est.)
0.15% of GDP (2022 est.)
0.13% of GDP (2021 est.)
note: personal transfers and compensation between resident and non-resident individuals/households/entities

Budget: *revenues:* $2.684 trillion (2022 est.) note: central government revenues (excluding grants) converted to US dollars at average official exchange rate for year indicated
expenditures: $4.893 trillion (2019 est.)

Public debt: 47% of GDP (2017 est.)
note: official data; data cover both central and local government debt, including debt officially recognized by China's National Audit Office report in 2011; data exclude policy bank bonds, Ministry of Railway debt, and China Asset Management Company debt
comparison ranking: 114

Taxes and other revenues: 7.7% (of GDP) (2022 est.)
note: central government tax revenue as a % of GDP
comparison ranking: 191

Current account balance: $252.987 billion (2023 est.)
$443.374 billion (2022 est.)
$352.886 billion (2021 est.)
note: balance of payments - net trade and primary/secondary income in current dollars
comparison ranking: 2

Exports: $3.511 trillion (2023 est.)
$3.719 trillion (2022 est.)
$3.555 trillion (2021 est.)
note: balance of payments - exports of goods and services in current dollars
comparison ranking: 1

Exports - partners: US 15%, Hong Kong 7%, Japan 5%, Germany 4%, South Korea 4% (2022)
note: top five export partners based on percentage share of exports

Exports - commodities: broadcasting equipment, integrated circuits, computers, garments, machine parts (2022)
note: top five export commodities based on value in dollars

Imports: $3.125 trillion (2023 est.)
$3.142 trillion (2022 est.)
$3.094 trillion (2021 est.)
note: balance of payments - imports of goods and services in current dollars
comparison ranking: 2

Imports - partners: US 7%, South Korea 7%, Japan 6%, Australia 6%, China 6% (2022)
note: top five import partners based on percentage share of imports

Imports - commodities: crude petroleum, integrated circuits, iron ore, natural gas, gold (2022)
note: top five import commodities based on value in dollars

Reserves of foreign exchange and gold: $3.45 trillion (2023 est.)
$3.307 trillion (2022 est.)
$3.428 trillion (2021 est.)
note: holdings of gold (year-end prices)/foreign exchange/special drawing rights in current dollars
comparison ranking: 1

Debt - external: $408.967 billion (2022 est.)
note: present value of external debt in current US dollars
comparison ranking: 1

Exchange rates: Renminbi yuan (RMB) per US dollar -

Exchange rates: 7.084 (2023 est.)
6.737 (2022 est.)
6.449 (2021 est.)
6.901 (2020 est.)
6.908 (2019 est.)

ENERGY

Electricity access: *electrification - total population:* 100% (2022 est.)

Electricity: *installed generating capacity:* 2.594 billion kW (2022 est.)
consumption: 8.54 trillion kWh (2022 est.)
exports: 20.176 billion kWh (2022 est.)
imports: 5.87 billion kWh (2022 est.)
transmission/distribution losses: 327.874 billion kWh (2022 est.)
comparison rankings: transmission/distribution losses 211; imports 44; exports 14; consumption 1; installed generating capacity 1

Electricity generation sources: *fossil fuels:* 64.9% of total installed capacity (2022 est.)
nuclear: 4.7% of total installed capacity (2022 est.)
solar: 4.7% of total installed capacity (2022 est.)
wind: 8.5% of total installed capacity (2022 est.)
hydroelectricity: 15.1% of total installed capacity (2022 est.)
biomass and waste: 2.1% of total installed capacity (2022 est.)

Nuclear energy: Number of operational nuclear reactors: 56 (2023)

Number of nuclear reactors under construction: 25 (2023)

Net capacity of operational nuclear reactors: 54.15GW (2023 est.)

Percent of total electricity production: 4.9% (2023 est.)

Coal: *production:* 4.827 billion metric tons (2022 est.)
consumption: 5.313 billion metric tons (2022 est.)
exports: 12.925 million metric tons (2022 est.)
imports: 313.937 million metric tons (2022 est.)
proven reserves: 143.197 billion metric tons (2022 est.)

Petroleum: *total petroleum production:* 4.984 million bbl/day (2023 est.)
refined petroleum consumption: 15.148 million bbl/day (2022 est.)
crude oil estimated reserves: 26.023 billion barrels (2021 est.)

Natural gas: *production:* 225.341 billion cubic meters (2022 est.)
consumption: 366.16 billion cubic meters (2022 est.)
exports: 5.617 billion cubic meters (2022 est.)
imports: 142.784 billion cubic meters (2022 est.)
proven reserves: 6.654 trillion cubic meters (2021 est.)

Carbon dioxide emissions: 13.506 billion metric tonnes of CO_2 (2022 est.)
from coal and metallurgical coke: 11.059 billion metric tonnes of CO_2 (2022 est.)

from petroleum and other liquids: 1.729 billion metric tonnes of CO_2 (2022 est.)
from consumed natural gas: 716.939 million metric tonnes of CO_2 (2022 est.)
comparison ranking: total emissions 1

Energy consumption per capita: 122.004 million Btu/person (2022 est.)
comparison ranking: 34

COMMUNICATIONS

Telephones - fixed lines: *total subscriptions:* 179.414 million (2022 est.)
subscriptions per 100 inhabitants: 13 (2022 est.)
comparison ranking: total subscriptions 1

Telephones - mobile cellular: *total subscriptions:* 1.781 billion (2022 est.)
subscriptions per 100 inhabitants: 125 (2022 est.)
comparison ranking: total subscriptions 1

Telecommunication systems: *general assessment:* China has the largest Internet market in the world with almost all subscribers accessing Internet through mobile devices; market is driven through government-allied investment; fast-developing data center market; government aims to provide universal and affordable broadband coverage through market competition and private investment in state-controlled enterprises; 3G and LTE subscribers will migrate to 5G aiming for 2 million 5G base stations by the end of 2022; government strengthens IoT policies to boost economic growth; China is pushing development of smart cities beyond Beijing; Beijing residents carry virtual card integrating identity, social security, health, and education documents; government controls gateways to global Internet through censorship, surveillance, and shutdowns; major exporter of broadcasting equipment worldwide (2022)
domestic: nearly 13 per 100 fixed line and 122 per 100 mobile-cellular (2021)
international: country code - 86; landing points for the RJCN, EAC-C2C, TPE, APCN-2, APG, NCP, TEA, SeaMeWe-3, SJC2, Taiwan Strait Express-1, AAE-1, APCN-2, AAG, FEA, FLAG and TSE submarine cables providing connectivity to Asia, the Middle East, Europe, and the US; satellite earth stations - 7 (5 Intelsat - 4 Pacific Ocean and 1 Indian Ocean; 1 Intersputnik - Indian Ocean region; and 1 Inmarsat - Pacific and Indian Ocean regions) (2019)

Broadcast media: all broadcast media are owned by, or affiliated with, the Chinese Communisty Party (CCP) or a government agency; no privately owned TV or radio stations; state-run Chinese Central TV, provincial, and municipal stations offer more than 2,000 channels; the Central Propaganda Department as well as local (provincial, municipal) sends directives to all domestic media outlets to guide its reporting with the government maintaining authority to approve all programming; foreign-made TV programs must be approved/censored prior to broadcast; increasingly, PRC nationals turn to online platforms (Bilibili, Tencent Video, iQiyi, etc) to access PRC and international films and television shows. Video platforms have to abide by regulations issued by the Cyberspace Administration of China (CAC), which align with censorship policies from CCP propaganda authorities. (2022)

Internet country code: .cn

Internet users: *total:* 1.022 billion (2021 est.)
percent of population: 73% (2021 est.)
comparison ranking: total 1

Broadband - fixed subscriptions: *total:* 483,549,500 (2020 est.)
subscriptions per 100 inhabitants: 34 (2020 est.)
comparison ranking: total 1

TRANSPORTATION

National air transport system: *number of registered air carriers:* 56 (2020)
inventory of registered aircraft operated by air carriers: 2,890
annual passenger traffic on registered air carriers: 436,183,969 (2018)
annual freight traffic on registered air carriers: 611,439,830 (2018) mt-km

Civil aircraft registration country code prefix: B

Airports: 531 (2024)
comparison ranking: 15

Heliports: 104 (2024)

Pipelines: 76,000 km gas, 30,400 km crude oil, 27,700 km refined petroleum products, 797,000 km water (2018)

Railways: *total:* 150,000 km (2021) 1.435-m gauge (100,000 km electrified); 104,0000 traditional, 40,000 high-speed
comparison ranking: total 2

Roadways: *total:* 5.2 million km (2020)
paved: 4.578 million km (2020) (includes 168000 km of expressways)
unpaved: 622,000 km (2017)
comparison ranking: total 3

Waterways: 27,700 km (2020) (navigable waterways)
comparison ranking: 6

Merchant marine: *total:* 8,314 (2023)
by type: bulk carrier 1,831, container ship 419, general cargo 1,392, oil tanker 1,196, other 3,476
comparison ranking: total 2

Ports: *total ports:* 66 (2024)
large: 5
medium: 9
small: 25
very small: 27
ports with oil terminals: 48
key ports: Chaozhou, Dalian, Fang-Cheng, Guangzhou, Hankow, Lon Shui Terminal, Qingdao Gang, Qinhuangdao, Shanghai, Shekou, Tianjin Xin Gang, Weihai, Wenzhou, Xiamen

Transportation - note: seven of the world's ten largest container ports are in China

MILITARY AND SECURITY

Military and security forces: People's Liberation Army (PLA): Ground Forces, Navy (PLAN, includes naval aviation), Navy Marine Corps (PLANMC), Air Force (PLAAF, includes airborne forces), Rocket Force (strategic missile force), Aerospace Force, Cyberspace Force, Information Support Force, Joint Logistics Support Force, People's Armed Police (PAP, includes Coast Guard, Border Defense Force, Internal Security Forces); PLA Reserve Force (2024)
note 1: the PAP is a paramilitary police component of China's armed forces that is under the dual authority of the Central Committee of the Communist Party and the Central Military Commission and charged with internal security, law enforcement, counterterrorism, and maritime rights protection
note 2: in 2018, the Coast Guard was moved from the State Oceanic Administration to the PAP; in 2013, China merged four of its five major maritime law enforcement agencies – the China Marine Surveillance (CMS), Maritime Police, Fishery Law Enforcement (FLE), and Anti-Smuggling Police – into a unified coast guard

Military expenditures: 1.5% of GDP (2023 est.)
1.5% of GDP (2022 est.)
1.5% of GDP (2021 est.)
1.7% of GDP (2020 est.)
1.7% of GDP (2019 est.)
comparison ranking: 90

Military and security service personnel strengths: approximately 2 million active-duty troops (approximately 1 million Ground; 250,000 Navy/Marines; 350-400,000 Air Force; 120,000 Rocket Forces; 150-175,000 Strategic Support Forces); estimated 600-650,000 People's Armed Police (2023)

Military equipment inventories and acquisitions: the PLA has a mix of some older and an increasing amount of modern, largely domestically produced systems; Russia has been the top supplier of foreign military equipment in recent years; China has one of the world's largest defense-industrial sectors and is capable of producing advanced weapons systems across all military domains (2024)
note: the PLA is in the midst of a decades-long modernization effort; in 2017, President XI set three developmental goals for the force - becoming a mechanized force with increased information and strategic capabilities by 2020, a fully modernized force by 2035, and a world-class military by mid-century

Military service age and obligation: 18-22 years of age for men for selective compulsory military service, with a 2-year service obligation; women 18-19 years of age who are high school graduates and meet requirements for specific military jobs are subject to conscription (2024)
note: the PLA's conscription system functions as a levy; the PLA establishes the number of enlistees needed, which produces quotas for the provinces; each province provides a set number of soldiers or sailors; if the number of volunteers fails to meet quotas, the local governments may compel individuals to enter military service

Military deployments: 400 Lebanon (UNIFIL); 1,030 South Sudan (UNMISS); 150 Sudan/South Sudan (UNISFA); up to 2,000 Djibouti (2024)

Military - note: established in 1927, the PLA is the military arm of the ruling Chinese Communist Party (CCP), which oversees the PLA through its Central Military Commission; the Central Military Commission (CMC) is China's top military decision making body
the PLA is the world's largest military; its primary responsibility is external security but it also has some domestic security duties; China's stated defense policy includes safeguarding sovereignty, security, and development interests while emphasizing a greater global role for the PLA; the PLA conducts air, counterspace, cyber, electronic warfare, joint, land, maritime, missile, nuclear, and space operations; it trains regularly, including multinational and multiservice exercises, deploys overseas, and participates in international peacekeeping missions
the PRC's internal security forces consist primarily of the Ministry of Public Security (MPS), the Ministry of State Security (MSS), the People's Armed Police (PAP), and the militia; the PLA support the internal security forces as necessary:
–the MPS controls the civilian national police, which serves as the first-line force for public order; its primary mission is domestic law enforcement

and maintaining order, including anti-rioting and anti-terrorism
–the MSS is the PRC's main civilian intelligence and counterintelligence service
–the PAP is a paramilitary component (or adjunct) of the PLA; its primary missions include internal security, maintaining public order, maritime security, and assisting the PLA in times of war; it is under the command of the CMC; the China Coast Guard (CCG) administratively falls under the PAP; the CCG has a variety of missions, such as maritime sovereignty enforcement, surveillance, resource protection, anti-smuggling, and general law enforcement; it is the largest maritime law enforcement fleet in the world
–the militia is an armed reserve of civilians which serves as an auxiliary and reserve force for the PLA upon mobilization, although it is distinct from the PLA's reserve forces; militia units are organized around towns, villages, urban sub-districts, and enterprises, and vary widely in composition and mission; they have dual civilian-military command structures; a key component of the militia are the local maritime forces, commonly referred to as the People's Armed Forces Maritime Militia (PAFMM); the PAFMM consists of mariners (and their vessels) who receive training, equipment, and other forms of support from the Navy and CCG (although the PAFMM remains separate from both) to perform tasks such as maritime patrolling, surveillance and reconnaissance, emergency/disaster response, transportation, search and rescue, and auxiliary tasks in support of naval operations in wartime; the PAFMM's tasks are often conducted in conjunction or coordination with the Navy and the CCG; it has been used to assert Beijing's maritime claims in the Sea of Japan and South China Sea (2023)

SPACE

Space agency/agencies: China National Space Administration (CNSA; established in 1993); Administration for Science, Technology, and Industry for National Defense (SASTIND; subordinate to the Ministry of Industry and Information Technology); People's Liberation Army (PLA) Aerospace Force (in 2024, the PLA created the Aerospace Force from the former Strategic Support Force, which had included the Space Systems Department and the China Manned Space Engineering Office or CMSEO) (2024)

Space launch site(s): Jiuquan Launch Center (Inner Mongolia), Xichang Launch Center (Sichuan), Wenchang Launch Center (Hainan; Wenchang includes a commercial launch pad, the Hainan Commercial Space Launch Site, which was scheduled to be completed in 2024), Taiyuan Launch Center (Shanxi), Eastern Spaceport (Shandong; a coastal spaceport designed to facilitate maritime launches); note - China also has a ship capable of conducting space launches (2024)

Space program overview: has a large, comprehensive, and ambitious space program and is considered one of the World's leading space powers; capable of manufacturing and operating the full spectrum of space launch vehicles (SLVs) and spacecraft, including human crewed, satellite launchers, lunar/inter-planetary/asteroid probes, satellites (communications, remote sensing, navigational, scientific, etc.), space stations, and re-usable space transportation systems, such as orbital space planes/ shuttles; trains astronauts (taikonauts); researches and develops a range of other space-related capabilities, including advanced telecommunications, optics, spacecraft components, satellite payloads, etc.; participates in international space programs, such as the Square Kilometer Array Project radio telescope project and co-leads (with Australian and Japan) the Global Earth Observation System of Systems; has signed space cooperation agreements with more than 30 countries, including Brazil, Canada, France, and Russia, as well as the European Space Agency (note – the US NASA is barred by a 2011 law from cooperating with the Chinese bilaterally in space unless approved by the US Congress; the US also objected to China's participation in the International Space Station program); has a space industry dominated by two state-owned aerospace enterprises but since announcing in 2014 that it would allow private investment into the traditionally state-dominated space industry has developed a substantial commercial space sector, including space launch services (2024)
note: further details about the key activities, programs, and milestones of the country's space program, as well as government spending estimates on the space sector, appear in the Space Programs reference guide

TRANSNATIONAL ISSUES

Refugees and internally displaced persons: *refugees (country of origin):* 303,107 (Vietnam), undetermined (North Korea) (mid-year 2021)
IDPs: undetermined (2021)

Trafficking in persons: tier rating: Tier 3 — China does not fully meet the minimum standards for elimination of trafficking and is not making significant efforts to do so, therefore, China remained on Tier 3; for more details, go to: https://www.state.gov/reports/2024-trafficking-in-persons-report/china/

Illicit drugs: a major source of precursor chemicals for narcotics such as fentanyl and methamphetamine, new psychoactive substances (NPS), and synthetic drugs; is a destination and transit country for methamphetamine and heroin produced in South east and Southwest Asia; China remains a major source of precursor chemicals sold in North America via the internet and shipped to overseas customers; domestic use of synthetic drugs is prevalent; chemical alterations of drugs circumvent laws and hamper efforts to stem the flow of these
(2021)

CHRISTMAS ISLAND

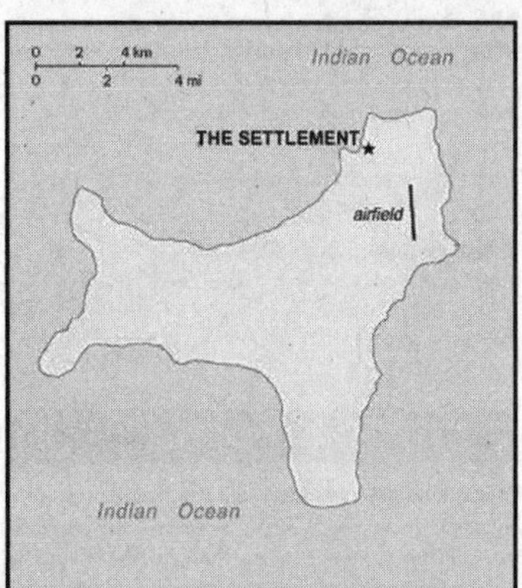

INTRODUCTION

Background: Although Europeans sighted Christmas Island in 1615, it was named for the day of its rediscovery in 1643. Steep cliffs and dense jungle hampered attempts to explore the island over the next two centuries. The discovery of phosphate on the island in 1887 led to the UK annexing it the following year. In 1898, 200 Chinese indentured servants were brought in to work the mines, along with Malays, Sikhs, and a small number of Europeans. The UK administered Christmas Island from Singapore. Japan invaded the island in 1942, but islanders sabotaged Japanese mining operations, making the mines relatively unproductive. After World War II, Australia and New Zealand bought the company mining the phosphate, and in 1958, the UK transferred sovereignty from Singapore to Australia in exchange for $20 million to compensate for the loss of future phosphate income. In 1980, Australia set up the Christmas Island National Park and expanded its boundaries throughout the 1980s until it covered more than 60% of the island's territory. The phosphate mine was closed in 1987 because of environmental concerns, and Australia has rejected several efforts to reopen it.

In the 1980s, boats of asylum seekers started landing on Christmas Island, and the migrants claimed refugee status because they were on Australian territory. In 2001, Australia declared Christmas Island to be outside the Australian migration zone and built an immigration detention center on the island. Completed in 2008, the controversial detention center was closed in 2018 but then reopened in 2019. In 2020, the center served as a coronavirus quarantine facility for Australian citizens evacuated from China.

GEOGRAPHY

Location: Southeastern Asia, island in the Indian Ocean, south of Indonesia

Geographic coordinates: 10 30 S, 105 40 E

Map references: Southeast Asia

Area: *total:* 135 sq km
land: 135 sq km
water: 0 sq km
comparison ranking: total 222

Area - comparative: about three-quarters the size of Washington, DC

Land boundaries: *total:* 0 km

Coastline: 138.9 km

Maritime claims: *territorial sea:* 12 nm
contiguous zone: 12 nm
exclusive fishing zone: 200 nm

Climate: tropical with a wet season (December to April) and dry season; heat and humidity moderated by trade winds

Terrain: steep cliffs along coast rise abruptly to central plateau

Elevation: *highest point:* Murray Hill 361 m
lowest point: Indian Ocean 0 m

Natural resources: phosphate, beaches

Land use: *agricultural land:* 0% (2018 est.)
other: 100% (2018 est.)

Irrigated land: NA

Population distribution: majority of the population lives on the northern tip of the island

Natural hazards: the narrow fringing reef surrounding the island can be a maritime hazard

Geography - note: located along major sea lanes of the Indian Ocean

PEOPLE AND SOCIETY

Population: *total:* 1,692
male: 1,007
female: 685 (2021 est.)
comparison rankings: female 228; male 228; total 232

Nationality: *noun:* Christmas Islander(s)
adjective: Christmas Island

Ethnic groups: Chinese 70%, European 20%, Malay 10% (2001)
note: no indigenous population

Languages: English (official) 27.6%, Mandarin 17.2%, Malay 17.1%, Cantonese 3.9%, Min Nan 1.6%, Tagalog 1%, other 4.5%, unspecified 27.1% (2016 est.)
note: data represent language spoken at home

Religions: Muslim 19.4%, Buddhist 18.3%, Roman Catholic 8.8%, Protestant 6.5% (includes Anglican 3.6%, Uniting Church 1.2%, other 1.7%), other Christian 3.3%, other 0.6%, none 15.3%, unspecified 27.7% (2016 est.)

Age structure: *0-14 years:* 16.6%
15-64 years: 70.4%
65 years and over: 13% (2021)

Median age: *total:* 38 years (2021 est.)
comparison ranking: total 78

Population growth rate: 1.11% (2014 est.)
comparison ranking: 84

Population distribution: majority of the population lives on the northern tip of the island

ENVIRONMENT

Environment - current issues: loss of rainforest; impact of phosphate mining

Climate: tropical with a wet season (December to April) and dry season; heat and humidity moderated by trade winds

GOVERNMENT

Country name: *conventional long form:* Territory of Christmas Island
conventional short form: Christmas Island
etymology: named by English Captain William MYNORS for the day of its rediscovery, Christmas Day (25 December 1643); the island had been sighted by Europeans as early as 1615

Government type: non-self-governing overseas territory of Australia

Dependency status: non-self-governing territory of Australia; administered from Canberra by the Department of Infrastructure, Transport, Cities & Regional Development

Capital: *name:* The Settlement (Flying Fish Cove)
geographic coordinates: 10 25 S, 105 43 E
time difference: UTC+7 (12 hours ahead of Washington, DC, during Standard Time)
etymology: self-descriptive name for the main locus of population

Administrative divisions: none (territory of Australia)

Independence: none (territory of Australia)

National holiday: Australia Day (commemorates the arrival of the First Fleet of Australian settlers), 26 January (1788)

Legal system: legal system is under the authority of the governor general of Australia and Australian law

Constitution: *history:* 1 October 1958 (Christmas Island Act 1958)
amendments: amended many times, last in 2020

Citizenship: see Australia

Suffrage: 18 years of age

Executive branch: *chief of state:* King CHARLES III (since 8 September 2022); represented by Governor-General of the Commonwealth of Australia General David HURLEY (since 1 July 2019)
head of government: Administrator Ms. Farzian ZAINAL (since 11 May 2023)
cabinet: NA
elections/appointments: the monarchy is hereditary; governor general appointed by the monarch on the recommendation of the Australian prime minister; administrator appointed by the governor-general of Australia for a 2- year term and represents the monarch and Australia

Legislative branch: *description:* unicameral Christmas Island Shire Council (9 seats; members directly elected by simple majority vote to serve 4-year terms)
elections: held every 2 years with half the members standing for election; last held in October 2023 (next to be held in October 2025)
election results: percent of vote - NA; seats by party - independent 9; composition as of January 2024 - men 8, women 1, percentage women 13%

Judicial branch: *highest court(s):* under the terms of the Territorial Law Reform Act 1992, Western Australia provides court services as needed for the island, including the Supreme Court and subordinate courts (District Court, Magistrate Court, Family Court, Children's Court, and Coroners' Court)

Political parties: none

International organization participation: none

Diplomatic representation in the US: none (territory of Australia)

Diplomatic representation from the US: *embassy:* none (territory of Australia)

Flag description: territorial flag; divided diagonally from upper hoist to lower fly; the upper triangle is green with a yellow image of the Golden Bosun Bird superimposed; the lower triangle is blue with the Southern Cross constellation, representing Australia, superimposed; a centered yellow disk displays a green map of the island
note: the flag of Australia is used for official purposes

National symbol(s): golden bosun bird

National anthem: *note:* as a territory of Australia, "Advance Australia Fair" remains official as the national anthem, while "God Save the King" serves as the royal anthem (see Australia)

ECONOMY

Economic overview: high-income Australian territorial economy; development through government services and phosphate mining; operates Australia's Immigration Detention Centre; increasing tourism and government investments; sustained environmental protections

Industries: tourism, phosphate extraction (near depletion)

Exports - partners: NZ 25%, Indonesia 18%, Singapore 12%, Australia 9%, Ireland 8% (2022)
note: top five export partners based on percentage share of exports

Exports - commodities: phosphates, fertilizers, chemical analysis instruments, electrical transformers, measuring instruments (2022)
note: top five export commodities based on value in dollars

Imports - partners: Australia 93%, US 3%, Malaysia 2%, Singapore 1%, Fiji 0% (2022)
note: top five import partners based on percentage share of imports

Imports - commodities: refined petroleum, cars, iron structures, air conditioners, paintings (2022)
note: top five import commodities based on value in dollars

Exchange rates: Australian dollars (AUD) per US dollar -

Exchange rates: 1.505 (2023 est.)
1.442 (2022 est.)
1.331 (2021 est.)
1.453 (2020 est.)
1.439 (2019 est.)

COMMUNICATIONS

Telecommunication systems: *general assessment:* internet access on Christmas Island is provided by satellite; improvements through the Regional Connectivity Program to the macro and small cell mobile sites will provide new and improved mobile, voice and data connectivity for residents and visitors; the upgrade will also support local businesses and community facilities, enabling increased residential

access to essential services such as telehealth and education (2022)
domestic: improvements to Christmas Island include an upgrade to the macro cell base stations and deploy a new macro cell base station at the airport (2022)
international: international code - 61 8; ASC submarine cable to Singapore and Australia; satellite earth station - 1 (Intelsat provides telephone and telex service) (2019)

Broadcast media: 1 community radio station; satellite broadcasts of several Australian radio and TV stations (2017)

Internet country code: .cx

Internet users: *total:* 1,139 (2021 est.)
percent of population: 78.6% (2021 est.)
comparison ranking: total 229

TRANSPORTATION

Airports: 1 (2024)
comparison ranking: 229

Railways: *total:* 18 km (2017)
standard gauge: 18 km (2017) 1.435-m (not in operation)
note: the 18-km Christmas Island Phosphate Company Railway between Flying Fish Cove and South Point was decommissioned in 1987; some tracks and scrap remain in place
comparison ranking: total 135

Roadways: *total:* 142 km
*paved:*32 km
*unpaved:*110 km (2011)
comparison ranking: total 212

Ports: *total ports:* 1 (2024)
large: 0
medium: 1
small: 0
very small: 0
ports with oil terminals: 0
key ports: Flying Fish Cove

MILITARY AND SECURITY

Military - note: defense is the responsibility of Australia

CLIPPERTON ISLAND

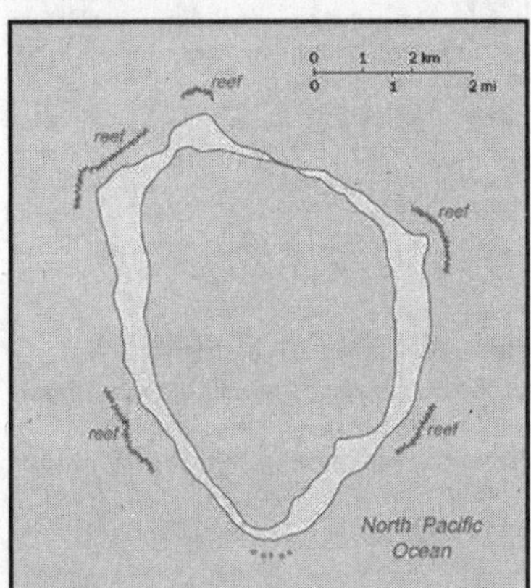

INTRODUCTION

Background: This isolated atoll was named for John CLIPPERTON, an English pirate who was rumored to have made it his hideout early in the 18th century. Annexed by France in 1855 and claimed by the US, it was seized by Mexico in 1897. Arbitration eventually awarded the island to France in 1931, which took possession in 1935.

GEOGRAPHY

Location: Middle America, atoll in the North Pacific Ocean, 1,120 km southwest of Mexico

Geographic coordinates: 10 17 N, 109 13 W

Map references: Political Map of the World

Area: *total:* 6 sq km
land: 6 sq km
water: 0 sq km
comparison ranking: total 245

Area - comparative: about 12 times the size of The Mall in Washington, DC

Land boundaries: *total:* 0 km

Coastline: 11.1 km

Maritime claims: *territorial sea:* 12 nm
exclusive economic zone: 200 nm

Climate: tropical; humid, average temperature 20-32 degrees Celsius, wet season (May to October)

Terrain: coral atoll

Elevation: *highest point:* Rocher Clipperton 29 m
lowest point: Pacific Ocean 0 m

Natural resources: fish

Land use: *agricultural land:* 0% (2018 est.)
forest: 0% (2018 est.)
other: 100% (2018 est.)

Natural hazards: subject to tropical storms and hurricanes from May to October

Geography - note: the atoll reef is approximately 12 km (7.5 mi) in circumference; an attempt to colonize the atoll in the early 20th century ended in disaster and was abandoned in 1917

PEOPLE AND SOCIETY

Population: *total:* uninhabited

ENVIRONMENT

Environment - current issues: no natural resources, guano deposits depleted; the ring-shaped atoll encloses a stagnant fresh-water lagoon

Climate: tropical; humid, average temperature 20-32 degrees Celsius, wet season (May to October)

GOVERNMENT

Country name: *conventional long form:* none
conventional short form: Clipperton Island
local long form: none
local short form: Ile Clipperton
former: sometimes referred to as Ile de la Passion or Atoll Clipperton
etymology: named after an 18th-century English pirate who supposedly used the island as a base

Dependency status: possession of France; administered directly by the Minister of Overseas France

Legal system: the laws of France apply

Flag description: the flag of France is used

MILITARY AND SECURITY

Military - note: defense is the responsibility of France

COCOS (KEELING) ISLANDS

INTRODUCTION

Background: British sea captain William KEELING discovered the Cocos (Keeling) Islands in 1609, and they were named for their coconut trees in 1622. Some maps began referring to them as the Keeling Islands in 1703. In 1825, Scottish trader John CLUNIES-ROSS was trying to get to Christmas Island but was blown off course and landed on Cocos (Keeling) Islands. The next year, a British trader hired CLUNIES-ROSS's brother to bring slaves and a harem of Malay women to create the first permanent settlement on the island. By the 1830s, the Clunies-Ross family had firmly established themselves as the leaders of the islands, and they ruled Cocos (Keeling) Islands in a feudal style until 1978.

The UK annexed the islands in 1857 and administered them from Ceylon after 1878 and from Singapore after 1886. The Cocos (Keeling) Islands hosted a cable relaying station and was attacked by the Germans in World War I. The Japanese similarly attacked the islands in World War II. The UK transferred the islands to Australia in 1955, when they were officially named the Cocos (Keeling) Islands, and in 1978, Australia bought all the land held by the Clunies-Ross family, ending their control of the islands. In a referendum in 1984, most islanders voted

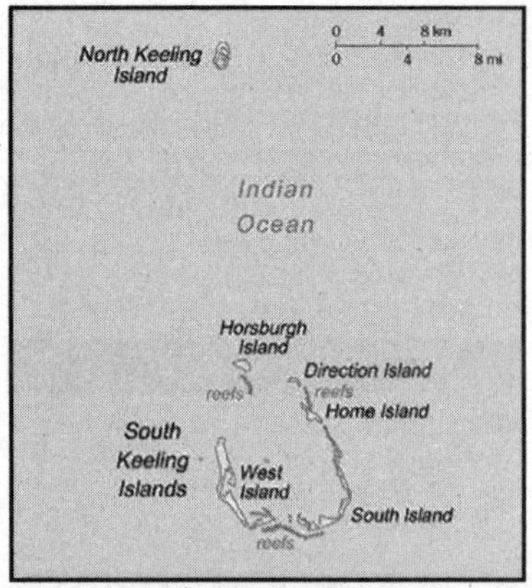

to integrate with Australia, and Western Australian laws have applied on the islands since 1992.

GEOGRAPHY

Location: Southeastern Asia, group of islands in the Indian Ocean, southwest of Indonesia, about halfway between Australia and Sri Lanka

Geographic coordinates: 12 30 S, 96 50 E

Map references: Southeast Asia

Area: *total:* 14 sq km
land: 14 sq km
water: 0 sq km
note: includes the two main islands of West Island and Home Island
comparison ranking: total 239

Area - comparative: about 24 times the size of The Mall in Washington, DC

Land boundaries: *total:* 0 km

Coastline: 26 km

Maritime claims: *territorial sea:* 12 nm
exclusive fishing zone: 200 nm

Climate: tropical with high humidity, moderated by the southeast trade winds for about nine months of the year

Terrain: flat, low-lying coral atolls

Elevation: *highest point:* South Point on South Island 9 m
lowest point: Indian Ocean 0 m

Natural resources: fish

Land use: *agricultural land:* 0% (2018 est.)
forest: 0% (2018 est.)
other: 100% (2018 est.)

Irrigated land: NA

Population distribution: only Home Island and West Island are populated

Natural hazards: cyclone season is October to April

Geography - note: *note:* there are 27 coral islands in the group; apart from North Keeling Island, which lies 30 km north of the main group, the islands form a horseshoe-shaped atoll surrounding a lagoon; North Keeling Island was declared a national park in 1995 and is administered by Parks Australia; the population on the two inhabited islands generally is split between the ethnic Europeans on West Island and the ethnic Malays on Home Island; the islands are thickly covered with coconut palms and other vegetation

PEOPLE AND SOCIETY

Population: *total:* 593
male: 301
female: 292 (2021 est.)
comparison rankings: female 229; male 229; total 236

Nationality: *noun:* Cocos Islander(s)
adjective: Cocos Islander

Ethnic groups: Europeans, Cocos Malays

Languages: Malay (Cocos dialect) 68.8%, English 22.3%, unspecified 8.9%; note - data represent language spoken at home (2016 est.)
major-language sample(s):
Buku Fakta Dunia, sumber yang diperlukan untuk maklumat asas. (Malay)

Religions: Muslim (predominantly Sunni) 75%, Anglican 3.5%, Roman Catholic 2.2%, none 12.9%, unspecified 6.3% (2016 est.)

Age structure: *0-14 years:* 21.2%
15-64 years: 61.5%
65 years and over: 17.3% (2021)

Median age: *total:* 40 years (2021 est.)
comparison ranking: total 62

Death rate: 8.89 deaths/1,000 population (2021 est.)
comparison ranking: 66

Population distribution: only Home Island and West Island are populated

ENVIRONMENT

Environment - current issues: freshwater resources are limited to rainwater accumulations in natural underground reservoirs; illegal fishing a concern

Climate: tropical with high humidity, moderated by the southeast trade winds for about nine months of the year

GOVERNMENT

Country name: *conventional long form:* Territory of Cocos (Keeling) Islands
conventional short form: Cocos (Keeling) Islands
etymology: the name refers to the abundant coconut trees on the islands and to English Captain William KEELING, the first European to sight the islands in 1609

Government type: non-self-governing overseas territory of Australia

Dependency status: non-self governing territory of Australia; administered from Canberra by the Department of Infrastructure, Transport, Cities & Regional Development

Capital: *name:* West Island
geographic coordinates: 12 10 S, 96 50 E
time difference: UTC+6.5 (11.5 hours ahead of Washington, DC, during Standard Time)

Administrative divisions: none (territory of Australia)

Independence: none (territory of Australia)

National holiday: Australia Day (commemorates the arrival of the First Fleet of Australian settlers), 26 January (1788)

Legal system: common law based on the Australian model

Constitution: *history:* 23 November 1955 (Cocos (Keeling) Islands Act 1955)
amendments: amended many times, last in 2020

Citizenship: see Australia

Suffrage: 18 years of age

Executive branch: *chief of state:* King CHARLES III (since 8 September 2022); represented by Governor-General of the Commonwealth of Australia General David HURLEY (since 1 July 2019)
head of government: Administrator Farzian ZAINAL (since 11 May 2023)
cabinet: NA
elections/appointments: the monarchy is hereditary; governor general appointed by the monarch on the recommendation of the Australian prime minister; administrator appointed by the governor-general for a 2-year term and represents the monarch and Australia

Legislative branch: *description:* unicameral Cocos (Keeling) Islands Shire Council (7 seats; members directly elected by simple majority vote to serve 4-year terms with 4 members renewed every 2 years)
elections: last held on 21 October 2023 (next to be held in October 2025)
election results: percent of vote by party - NA; seats by party - NA; composition - men 6, women 1, percent of women 16.7%

Judicial branch: *highest court(s):* under the terms of the Territorial Law Reform Act 1992, Western Australia provides court services as needed for the island including the Supreme Court and subordinate courts (District Court, Magistrate Court, Family Court, Children's Court, and Coroners' Court)

Political parties: none

International organization participation: none

Diplomatic representation in the US: none (territory of Australia)

Diplomatic representation from the US: *embassy:* none (territory of Australia)

Flag description: the flag of Australia is used

National anthem: *note:* as a territory of Australia, "Advance Australia Fair" remains official as the national anthem, while "God Save the King" serves as the royal anthem (see Australia)

ECONOMY

Agricultural products: vegetables, bananas, pawpaws, coconuts

Industries: copra products, tourism

Exports - partners: US 45%, UK 12%, France 7%, Canada 6%, Poland 5% (2022)
note: top five export partners based on percentage share of exports

Exports - commodities: integrated circuits, vaccines and cultures, furniture, carbon batteries, rubber gloves (2021)

Imports - partners: Australia 75%, US 18%, Netherlands 2%, UK 2%, Turkey 1% (2022)
note: top five import partners based on percentage share of imports

Imports - commodities: gold, x-ray equipment, cars, prefabricated buildings, packaged medicines (2019)

Exchange rates: Australian dollars (AUD) per US dollar -

Exchange rates: 1.505 (2023 est.)
1.442 (2022 est.)
1.331 (2021 est.)
1.453 (2020 est.)
1.439 (2019 est.)

COMMUNICATIONS

Telecommunication systems: *general assessment:* telephone service is part of the Australian network; an operational local mobile-cellular network available; wireless Internet connectivity available
domestic: local area code - 08
international: international code - 61 8; telephone, telex, and facsimile communications with Australia and elsewhere via satellite; satellite earth station - 1 (Intelsat)

Broadcast media: 1 local radio station staffed by community volunteers; satellite broadcasts of several Australian radio and TV stations available (2017)

Internet country code: .cc

Internet users: *total:* 80 (2021 est.)
percent of population: 13.4% (2021 est.)
comparison ranking: total 233

TRANSPORTATION

Airports: 1 (2024)
comparison ranking: 218

Roadways: *total:* 22 km
*paved:*10 km
*unpaved:*12 km (2007)
comparison ranking: total 223

MILITARY AND SECURITY

Military - note: defense is the responsibility of Australia

COLOMBIA

INTRODUCTION

Background: Colombia was one of three countries that emerged after the dissolution of Gran Colombia in 1830 – the others are Ecuador and Venezuela. A decades-long conflict among government forces, paramilitaries, and antigovernment insurgent groups heavily funded by the drug trade – principally the Revolutionary Armed Forces of Colombia (FARC) – escalated during the 1990s. In the wake of the paramilitary demobilization in the 2000s, new criminal groups arose that included some former paramilitaries. After four years of formal peace negotiations, the Colombian Government signed a final accord with the FARC in 2016 that called for its members to demobilize, disarm, and reincorporate into society and politics. The accord also committed the Colombian Government to create three new institutions to form a 'comprehensive system for truth, justice, reparation, and non-repetition,' including a truth commission, a special unit to coordinate the search for those who disappeared during the conflict, and a 'Special Jurisdiction for Peace' to administer justice for conflict-related crimes. Despite decades of internal conflict and drug-trade-related security challenges, Colombia maintains relatively strong and independent democratic institutions characterized by peaceful, transparent elections and the protection of civil liberties.

GEOGRAPHY

Location: Northern South America, bordering the Caribbean Sea, between Panama and Venezuela, and bordering the North Pacific Ocean, between Ecuador and Panama

Geographic coordinates: 4 00 N, 72 00 W

Map references: South America

Area: *total:* 1,138,910 sq km
land: 1,038,700 sq km
water: 100,210 sq km
note: includes Isla de Malpelo, Roncador Cay, and Serrana Bank
comparison ranking: total 27

Area - comparative: slightly less than twice the size of Texas

Land boundaries: *total:* 6,672 km
border countries (5): Brazil 1,790 km; Ecuador 708 km; Panama 339 km; Peru 1,494 km; Venezuela 2,341 km

Coastline: 3,208 km (Caribbean Sea 1,760 km, North Pacific Ocean 1,448 km)

Maritime claims: *territorial sea:* 12 nm
exclusive economic zone: 200 nm
continental shelf: 200-m depth or to the depth of exploitation

Climate: tropical along coast and eastern plains; cooler in highlands

Terrain: flat coastal lowlands, central highlands, high Andes Mountains, eastern lowland plains (Llanos)

Elevation: *highest point:* Pico Cristobal Colon 5,730 m
lowest point: Pacific Ocean 0 m
mean elevation: 593 m

Natural resources: petroleum, natural gas, coal, iron ore, nickel, gold, copper, emeralds, hydropower

Land use: *agricultural land:* 37.5% (2018 est.)
arable land: 1.4% (2018 est.)
permanent crops: 1.6% (2018 est.)
permanent pasture: 34.5% (2018 est.)
forest: 54.4% (2018 est.)
other: 8.1% (2018 est.)

Irrigated land: 10,900 sq km (2012)

Major rivers (by length in km): Rio Negro river source (shared with Venezuela and Brazil [m]) - 2,250 km; Orinoco (shared with Venezuela [s]) - 2,101 km
note – [s] after country name indicates river source; [m] after country name indicates river mouth

Major watersheds (area sq km): Atlantic Ocean drainage: Amazon (6,145,186 sq km), Orinoco (953,675 sq km)

Major aquifers: Amazon Basin

Population distribution: the majority of people live in the north and west where agricultural opportunities and natural resources are found; the vast grasslands of the llanos to the south and east, which make up approximately 60% of the country, are sparsely populated

Natural hazards: highlands subject to volcanic eruptions; occasional earthquakes; periodic droughts
volcanism: Galeras (4,276 m) is one of Colombia's most active volcanoes, having erupted in 2009 and 2010 causing major evacuations; it has been deemed a Decade Volcano by the International Association of Volcanology and Chemistry of the Earth's Interior, worthy of study due to its explosive history and close proximity to human populations; Nevado del Ruiz (5,321 m), 129 km (80 mi) west of Bogota, erupted in 1985 producing lahars (mudflows) that killed 23,000 people; the volcano last erupted in 1991; additionally, after 500 years of dormancy, Nevado del Huila reawakened in 2007 and has experienced frequent eruptions since then; other historically active volcanoes include Cumbal, Dona Juana, Nevado del Tolima, and Purace

Geography - note: only South American country with coastlines on both the North Pacific Ocean and Caribbean Sea

PEOPLE AND SOCIETY

Population: *total:* 49,588,357
male: 24,206,371
female: 25,381,986 (2024 est.)
comparison rankings: female 29; male 30; total 30

Nationality: *noun:* Colombian(s)
adjective: Colombian

Ethnic groups: Mestizo and White 87.6%, Afro-Colombian (includes Mulatto, Raizal, and Palenquero) 6.8%, Indigenous 4.3%, unspecified 1.4% (2018 est.)

Languages: Spanish (official) 98.9%, indigenous 1%, Portuguese 0.1%; 65 indigenous languages exist (2023 est.)
major-language sample(s):
La Libreta Informativa del Mundo, la fuente indispensable de información básica. (Spanish)

Religions: Roman Catholic 63.6%, Protestant 17.2% (Evangelical 16.7%, Adventist 0.3%, other Protestant 0.2%), Jehovah's Witness 0.6%, Church of Jesus Christ 0.1%, other 0.3%, believer, 0.2%. agnostic 1%, atheist 1%, none 14.2%, unspecified 1.8% (2023 est.)

Demographic profile: Colombia is in the midst of a demographic transition resulting from steady declines in its fertility, mortality, and population growth rates. The birth rate has fallen from more than 6 children per woman in the 1960s to just below replacement level today as a result of increased literacy, family planning services, and urbanization. However, income inequality is among the worst in the world, and almost one-third of the population lives below the poverty line.

Colombia experiences significant legal and illegal economic emigration and refugee outflows. Large-scale labor emigration dates to the 1960s; the United States and, until recently, Venezuela have been the main host countries. Emigration to Spain picked up in the 1990s because of its economic growth, but this flow has since diminished because of Spain's ailing economy and high unemployment. Venezuela's political and economic crisis since 2015 has prompted many Colombians to return home.

Forced displacement continues to be prevalent because of violence among guerrillas, paramilitary groups, and Colombian security forces. Afro-Colombian and indigenous populations are disproportionately affected. Even with the Colombian Government's December 2016 peace agreement with the Revolutionary Armed Forces of Colombia (FARC), the risk of displacement remains as other rebel groups fill the void left by the FARC. As of April 2023, almost 6.9 million people were internally displaced in Colombia. This estimate may undercount actual numbers because many internally displaced persons are not registered. Historically, Colombia also has one of the world's highest levels of forced disappearances. The Colombian Truth Commission estimated than nearly 122,000 people were the victims of forced disappearances during the countries five-decade-long armed conflict—including human rights activists, trade unionists, Afro-Colombians, indigenous people, and farmers in rural conflict zones.

Because of political violence and economic problems, Colombia received limited numbers of immigrants during the 19th and 20th centuries, mostly from the Middle East, Europe, and Japan. More recently, growth in the oil, mining, and manufacturing sectors has attracted increased labor migration; the primary source countries are Venezuela, the US, Mexico, and Argentina. Colombia has also become a transit area for illegal migrants from Africa, Asia, and the Caribbean – especially Haiti and Cuba – who are en route to the US or Canada. Between 2016 and October 2022, Colombia was host to the largest number of Venezuelan refugees and migrants, totaling almost 2.9 million. Ecuadorian migrants also go to Colombia, most of them attempting to transit the dense and dangerous jungles of the Darien Gap to enter Panama and head onward to the US.

Age structure: *0-14 years:* 22.3% (male 5,643,995/female 5,394,147)
15-64 years: 66.5% (male 16,127,377/female 16,859,161)
65 years and over: 11.2% (2024 est.) (male 2,434,999/female 3,128,678)

Dependency ratios: *total dependency ratio:* 43.5
youth dependency ratio: 31
elderly dependency ratio: 12.5
potential support ratio: 8 (2021 est.)

Median age: *total:* 32.7 years (2024 est.)
male: 31.5 years
female: 34 years
comparison ranking: total 114

Population growth rate: 0.48% (2024 est.)
comparison ranking: 152

Birth rate: 14.9 births/1,000 population (2024 est.)
comparison ranking: 112

Death rate: 8 deaths/1,000 population (2024 est.)
comparison ranking: 91

Net migration rate: -2.1 migrant(s)/1,000 population (2024 est.)
comparison ranking: 168

Population distribution: the majority of people live in the north and west where agricultural opportunities and natural resources are found; the vast grasslands of the llanos to the south and east, which make up approximately 60% of the country, are sparsely populated

Urbanization: *urban population:* 82.4% of total population (2023)
rate of urbanization: 1.01% annual rate of change (2020-25 est.)

Major urban areas - population: 11.508 million BOGOTA (capital), 4.102 million Medellin, 2.864 million Cali, 2.349 million Barranquilla, 1.381 million Bucaramanga, 1.088 million Cartagena (2023)

Sex ratio: *at birth:* 1.05 male(s)/female
0-14 years: 1.05 male(s)/female
15-64 years: 0.96 male(s)/female
65 years and over: 0.78 male(s)/female
total population: 0.95 male(s)/female (2024 est.)

Mother's mean age at first birth: 21.7 years (2015 est.)
note: data represents median age at first birth among women 25-49

Maternal mortality ratio: 75 deaths/100,000 live births (2020 est.)
comparison ranking: 80

Infant mortality rate: *total:* 11.7 deaths/1,000 live births (2024 est.)
male: 13.1 deaths/1,000 live births
female: 10.2 deaths/1,000 live births
comparison ranking: total 114

Life expectancy at birth: *total population:* 74.9 years (2024 est.)
male: 71.3 years
female: 78.7 years
comparison ranking: total population 134

Total fertility rate: 1.94 children born/woman (2024 est.)
comparison ranking: 114

Gross reproduction rate: 0.95 (2024 est.)

Contraceptive prevalence rate: 81% (2015/16)

Drinking water source: *improved: urban:* 100% of population
rural: 87.5% of population
total: 97.7% of population
unimproved: urban: 0% of population
rural: 12.5% of population
total: 2.3% of population (2020 est.)

Current health expenditure: 9% of GDP (2020)

Physician density: 2.33 physicians/1,000 population (2020)

Hospital bed density: 1.7 beds/1,000 population (2018)

Sanitation facility access: *improved: urban:* 99.1% of population
rural: 87.7% of population
total: 97% of population
unimproved: urban: 0.9% of population
rural: 12.3% of population
total: 3% of population (2020 est.)

Obesity - adult prevalence rate: 22.3% (2016)
comparison ranking: 78

Alcohol consumption per capita: *total:* 4.09 liters of pure alcohol (2019 est.)
beer: 3.09 liters of pure alcohol (2019 est.)
wine: 0.06 liters of pure alcohol (2019 est.)
spirits: 0.92 liters of pure alcohol (2019 est.)
other alcohols: 0.02 liters of pure alcohol (2019 est.)
comparison ranking: total 93

Tobacco use: *total:* 8.5% (2020 est.)
male: 12.4% (2020 est.)
female: 4.6% (2020 est.)
comparison ranking: total 143

Children under the age of 5 years underweight: 3.7% (2015/16)
comparison ranking: 81

Currently married women (ages 15-49): 55.3% (2023 est.)

Education expenditures: 4.9% of GDP (2020 est.)
comparison ranking: 81

Literacy: *definition:* age 15 and over can read and write
total population: 95.6%
male: 95.4%
female: 95.9% (2020)

School life expectancy (primary to tertiary education): *total:* 14 years
male: 14 years
female: 15 years (2020)

ENVIRONMENT

Environment - current issues: deforestation resulting from timber exploitation in the jungles of the Amazon and the region of Chocó; illicit drug crops grown by peasants in the national parks; soil erosion; soil and water quality damage from overuse of pesticides; air pollution, especially in Bogota, from vehicle emissions

Environment - international agreements: *party to:* Antarctic-Environmental Protection, Antarctic Treaty, Biodiversity, Climate Change, Climate Change-Kyoto Protocol, Climate Change-Paris Agreement, Comprehensive Nuclear Test Ban, Desertification, Endangered Species, Hazardous Wastes, Marine Life Conservation, Nuclear Test Ban, Ozone Layer Protection, Ship Pollution, Tropical Timber 2006, Wetlands, Whaling
signed, but not ratified: Law of the Sea

Climate: tropical along coast and eastern plains; cooler in highlands

Urbanization: *urban population:* 82.4% of total population (2023)
rate of urbanization: 1.01% annual rate of change (2020-25 est.)

Revenue from forest resources: 0.1% of GDP (2018 est.)
comparison ranking: 110

Revenue from coal: 0.75% of GDP (2018 est.)
comparison ranking: 8

Air pollutants: *particulate matter emissions:* 14.04 micrograms per cubic meter (2019 est.)
carbon dioxide emissions: 97.81 megatons (2016 est.)
methane emissions: 81.52 megatons (2020 est.)

Waste and recycling: *municipal solid waste generated annually:* 12,150,120 tons (2011 est.)
municipal solid waste recycled annually: 2,089,821 tons (2013 est.)
percent of municipal solid waste recycled: 17.2% (2013 est.)

Major rivers (by length in km): Rio Negro river source (shared with Venezuela and Brazil [m]) - 2,250 km; Orinoco (shared with Venezuela [s]) - 2,101 km
note – [s] after country name indicates river source; [m] after country name indicates river mouth

Major watersheds (area sq km): Atlantic Ocean drainage: Amazon (6,145,186 sq km), Orinoco (953,675 sq km)

Major aquifers: Amazon Basin

Total water withdrawal: *municipal:* 3.72 billion cubic meters (2020 est.)
industrial: 360 million cubic meters (2020 est.)
agricultural: 25.04 billion cubic meters (2020 est.)

Total renewable water resources: 2.36 trillion cubic meters (2020 est.)

GOVERNMENT

Country name: *conventional long form:* Republic of Colombia
conventional short form: Colombia
local long form: República de Colombia
local short form: Colombia
etymology: the country is named after explorer Christopher COLUMBUS

Government type: presidential republic

Capital: *name:* Bogotá
geographic coordinates: 4 36 N, 74 05 W
time difference: UTC-5 (same time as Washington, DC, during Standard Time)
etymology: originally referred to as "Bacata," meaning "enclosure outside of the farm fields," by the indigenous Muisca

Administrative divisions: 32 departments (departamentos, singular - departamento) and 1 capital district* (distrito capital); Amazonas, Antioquia, Arauca, Atlantico, Bogota*, Bolivar, Boyaca, Caldas, Caqueta, Casanare, Cauca, Cesar, Choco, Cordoba, Cundinamarca, Guainia, Guaviare, Huila, La Guajira, Magdalena, Meta, Narino, Norte de Santander, Putumayo, Quindio, Risaralda, Archipielago de San Andres, Providencia y Santa Catalina (colloquially San Andres y Providencia), Santander, Sucre, Tolima, Valle del Cauca, Vaupes, Vichada

Independence: 20 July 1810 (from Spain)

National holiday: Independence Day, 20 July (1810)

Legal system: civil law system influenced by the Spanish and French civil codes

Constitution: *history:* several previous; latest promulgated 4 July 1991
amendments: proposed by the government, by Congress, by a constituent assembly, or by public petition; passage requires a majority vote by Congress in each of two consecutive sessions; passage of amendments to constitutional articles on citizen rights, guarantees, and duties also require approval in a referendum by over one half of voters and participation of over one fourth of citizens registered to vote; amended many times, last in 2020

International law organization participation: has not submitted an ICJ jurisdiction declaration; accepts ICCt jurisdiction

Citizenship: *citizenship by birth:* no
citizenship by descent only: least one parent must be a citizen or permanent resident of Colombia
dual citizenship recognized: yes
residency requirement for naturalization: 5 years

Suffrage: 18 years of age; universal

Executive branch: *chief of state:* President Gustavo Francisco PETRO Urrego (since 7 August 2022)
head of government: President Gustavo Francisco PETRO Urrego (since 7 August 2022)
cabinet: Cabinet appointed by the president
elections/appointments: president directly elected by absolute majority vote in 2 rounds if needed for a single 4-year term; election last held on 29 May 2022 with a runoff held on 19 June 2022 (next to be held on 31 May 2026); note - political reform in 2015 eliminated presidential reelection
election results:
2022: Gustavo Francisco PETRO Urrego elected president in second round; percent of vote in first round - Gustavo Francisco PETRO Urrego (PHxC) 40.3%, Rodolfo HERNÁNDEZ Suárez (LIGA) 28.2%, Federico GUTIÉRREZ Zuluaga (Team for Colombia / CREEMOS) 23.9%, other 7.6%; percent of vote in second round - Gustavo Francisco PETRO Urrego 50.4%, Rodolfo HERNÁNDEZ Suarez 47.3%, blank 2.3%
2018: Iván DUQUE Márquez elected president in second round; percent of vote - Iván DUQUE Márquez (CD) 54%, Gustavo Francisco PETRO Urrego (Humane Colombia) 41.8%, other/blank/invalid 4.2%
note: the president is both chief of state and head of government

Legislative branch: *description:* bicameral Congress or Congreso consists of:
Senate or Senado (108 seats; 100 members elected in a single nationwide constituency by party-list proportional representation vote, 2 members elected in a special nationwide constituency for indigenous communities, 5 members of the Commons political party, formerly the People's Alternative Revolutionary Force (FARC), for 2 legislative terms only: 2018-2022 and 2022-2026 as per the 2016 peace accord, and 1 seat reserved for the runner-up presidential candidate in the recent election; all members serve 4-year terms)
Chamber of Representatives or Camara de Representantes (188 seats; 162 members elected in multi-seat constituencies by party-list proportional representation vote, 2 members elected in a special nationwide constituency for Afro-Colombians, 1 member elected by Colombians residing abroad, 1 member elected in a special nationwide constituency for the indigenous communities, 5 members of the Commons political party for two legislative terms only: 2018-2022 and 2022-2026 as per the 2016 peace accord, 16 seats for rural conflict victims for two legislative terms only: 2022-2026 and 2026-2030, and 1 seat reserved for the runner-up vice presidential candidate in the recent election; all members serve 4-year terms)
elections: Senate - last held on 13 March 2022 (next to be held in March 2026)
Chamber of Representatives - last held on 13 March 2022 (next to be held in March 2026)
election results: Senate - percent of vote by party/coalition - PHxC 16.9%, PC 13.1%, PL 12.4%, Green Alliance and Center Hope Coalition 11.5%, CD 11.4%, CR 9.4%, U Party 8.8%, MIRA–Colombia Free and Just Coalition 3.4%, other 13.1%; seats by party/coalition - PHxC- 20, PC 15, PL 14, Green Alliance and Center Hope Coalition 13, CD 13, CR 11, U Party 10, MIRA–Colombia Free and Just Coalition 4; composition - men 73, women 33, percentage women 31.1%
Chamber of Representatives - percent of vote by party/coalition- PHxC 17.6%, PL 14%, PC 12.4%, CD 10.2% U Party 8.6%, CR 7.9%, Green Alliance 6.5%, others 22.4%; seats by party/coalition - PL 32, PHxC 27, CP 25, CD 16, CR 16, U Party 15, Green Alliance and Center Hope Coalition 11, others 24; composition - men 133, women 54, percentage women 28.9%; total Congress percentage women 29.7%

Judicial branch: *highest court(s):* Supreme Court of Justice or Corte Suprema de Justicia (consists of the Civil-Agrarian and Labor Chambers each with 7 judges, and the Penal Chamber with 9 judges); Constitutional Court (consists of 9 magistrates); Council of State (consists of 27 judges); Superior Judiciary Council (consists of 13 magistrates)
judge selection and term of office: Supreme Court judges appointed by the Supreme Court members from candidates submitted by the Superior Judiciary Council; judges elected for individual 8-year terms; Constitutional Court magistrates - nominated by the president, by the Supreme Court, and elected by the Senate; judges elected for individual 8-year terms; Council of State members appointed by the State Council plenary from lists nominated by the Superior Judiciary Council
subordinate courts: Superior Tribunals (appellate courts for each of the judicial districts); regional courts; civil municipal courts; Superior Military Tribunal; first instance administrative courts

Political parties: Alternative Democratic Pole or PDA
Citizens Option (Opcion Ciudadana) or OC (formerly known as the National Integration Party or PIN)
The Commons (formerly People's Alternative Revolutionary Force or FARC)
Conservative Party or PC
Democratic Center Party or CD
Fair and Free Colombia (Colombia Justa Libres)
Green Alliance
Historic Pact for Colombia or PHxC (coalition composed of several left-leaning political parties and social movements)
Humane Colombia
Independent Movement of Absolute Renovation or MIRA
League of Anti-Corruption Rulers or LIGA
Liberal Party or PL
People's Alternative Revolutionary Force or FARC
Radical Change or CR
Team for Colombia - also known as the Experience Coalition or Coalition of the Regions (coalition composed of center-right and right-wing parties)
Union Party for the People or U Party
We Believe Colombia or CREEMOS
note: Colombia has numerous smaller political parties and movements

International organization participation: ACS, BCIE, BIS, CABEI, CAN, Caricom (observer), CD, CDB, CELAC, EITI (candidate country), FAO, G-3, G-24, G-77, IADB, IAEA, IBRD, ICAO, ICC (national committees), ICCt, ICRM, IDA, IFAD, IFC, IFRCS, IHO, ILO, IMF, IMO, IMSO, Interpol, IOC, IOM, IPU, ISO, ITSO, ITU, ITUC (NGOs), LAES, LAIA, Mercosur (associate), MIGA, NAM, OAS, OPANAL, OPCW, Pacific Alliance, PCA, PROSUR, UN, UNASUR, UNCTAD, UNESCO, UNHCR, UNIDO, Union Latina, UNOOSA, UNWTO, UPU, WCO, WFTU (NGOs), WHO, WIPO, WMO, WTO

Diplomatic representation in the US: *chief of mission:* Ambassador Daniel GARCÍA-PEÑA JARAMILLO (since 18 September 2024)
chancery: 1724 Massachusetts Avenue NW, Washington, DC 20036
telephone: [1] (202) 387-8338
FAX: [1] (202) 232-8643
email address and website:
eestadosunidos@cancilleria.gov.co
https://www.colombiaemb.org/
consulate(s) general: Atlanta, Boston, Chicago, Houston, Los Angeles, Miami, New York, Newark (NJ), Orlando, San Francisco, San Juan (Puerto Rico)

Diplomatic representation from the US: *chief of mission:* Ambassador (vacant); Chargé d'Affaires Francisco L. PALMIERI (since 1 June 2022)
embassy: Carrera 45, No. 24B-27, Bogota
mailing address: 3030 Bogota Place, Washington DC 20521-3030
telephone: [57] (601) 275-2000
FAX: [57] (601) 275-4600
email address and website:
ACSBogota@state.gov
https://co.usembassy.gov/

Flag description: *three horizontal bands of yellow (top, double-width), blue, and red; the flag retains the three main colors of the banner of Gran Colombia, the short-lived South American republic that broke up in 1830; various interpretations of the colors exist and include:* yellow for the gold in Colombia's land, blue for the seas on its shores, and red for the blood spilled in attaining freedom; alternatively, the colors have been described as representing more elemental concepts such as sovereignty and justice (yellow), loyalty and vigilance (blue), and valor and generosity (red); or simply the principles of liberty, equality, and fraternity
note: similar to the flag of Ecuador, which is longer and bears the Ecuadorian coat of arms superimposed in the center

National symbol(s): Andean condor; national colors: yellow, blue, red

National anthem: *name:* "Himno Nacional de la Republica de Colombia" (National Anthem of the Republic of Colombia)
lyrics/music: Rafael NUNEZ/Oreste SINDICI
note: adopted 1920; the anthem was created from an inspirational poem written by President Rafael NUNEZ

National heritage: *total World Heritage Sites:* 9 (6 cultural, 2 natural, 1 mixed)
selected World Heritage Site locales: Chiribiquete National Park (m); Coffee Cultural Landscape of Colombia (c); Historic Center of Santa Cruz de Mompox (c); Los Katíos National Park (n); Malpelo Fauna and Flora Sanctuary (n); Tierradentro National Archeological Park (c); San Agustín Archaeological Park (c); Colonial Cartagena (c); Qhapaq Ñan/ Andean Road System (c)

ECONOMY

Economic overview: prior to COVID-19, one of the most consistent growth economies; declining poverty; large stimulus package has mitigated economic fallout, but delayed key infrastructure investments; successful inflation management; sound flexible exchange rate regime; domestic economy suffers from lack of trade integration and infrastructure

Real GDP (purchasing power parity): $978.024 billion (2023 est.)
$972.073 billion (2022 est.)
$906.034 billion (2021 est.)
note: data in 2021 dollars
comparison ranking: 32

Real GDP growth rate: 0.61% (2023 est.)
7.29% (2022 est.)
10.8% (2021 est.)
note: annual GDP % growth based on constant local currency
comparison ranking: 177

Real GDP per capita: $18,800 (2023 est.)
$18,700 (2022 est.)
$17,600 (2021 est.)
note: data in 2021 dollars
comparison ranking: 104

GDP (official exchange rate): $363.54 billion (2023 est.)
note: data in current dollars at official exchange rate

Inflation rate (consumer prices): 11.74% (2023 est.)
10.18% (2022 est.)
3.5% (2021 est.)
note: annual % change based on consumer prices
comparison ranking: 187

Credit ratings: Fitch rating: BBB- (2020)

Moody's rating: Baa2 (2014)

Standard & Poors rating: BBB- (2017)
note: The year refers to the year in which the current credit rating was first obtained.

GDP - composition, by sector of origin: *agriculture:* 8.7% (2023 est.)
industry: 24.5% (2023 est.)
services: 56.9% (2023 est.)
note: figures may not total 100% due to non-allocated consumption not captured in sector-reported data comparison rankings: services 107; industry 104; agriculture 85

GDP - composition, by end use: *household consumption:* 77.5% (2023 est.)
government consumption: 14.6% (2023 est.)
investment in fixed capital: 17.6% (2023 est.)
investment in inventories: -4.8% (2023 est.)
exports of goods and services: 17.8% (2023 est.)
imports of goods and services: -22.7% (2023 est.)
note: figures may not total 100% due to rounding or gaps in data collection

Agricultural products: sugarcane, oil palm fruit, milk, rice, potatoes, bananas, plantains, maize, chicken, avocados (2022)
note: top ten agricultural products based on tonnage

Industries: textiles, food processing, oil, clothing and footwear, beverages, chemicals, cement; gold, coal, emeralds

Industrial production growth rate: -1.95% (2023 est.)
note: annual % change in industrial value added based on constant local currency
comparison ranking: 180

Labor force: 26.003 million (2023 est.)
note: number of people ages 15 or older who are employed or seeking work
comparison ranking: 25

Unemployment rate: 9.57% (2023 est.)
10.55% (2022 est.)
13.9% (2021 est.)
note: % of labor force seeking employment
comparison ranking: 162

Youth unemployment rate (ages 15-24): *total:* 19.3% (2023 est.)
male: 16.1% (2023 est.)
female: 23.7% (2023 est.)
note: % of labor force ages 15-24 seeking employment
comparison ranking: total 66

Population below poverty line: 36.6% (2022 est.)
note: % of population with income below national poverty line

Gini Index coefficient - distribution of family income: 54.8 (2022 est.)
note: index (0-100) of income distribution; higher values represent greater inequality
comparison ranking: 3

Average household expenditures: *on food:* 18.5% of household expenditures (2022 est.)
on alcohol and tobacco: 3.5% of household expenditures (2022 est.)

Household income or consumption by percentage share: *lowest 10%:* 1% (2022 est.)
highest 10%: 43.5% (2022 est.)
note: % share of income accruing to lowest and highest 10% of population

Remittances: 2.78% of GDP (2023 est.)
2.74% of GDP (2022 est.)
2.7% of GDP (2021 est.)
note: personal transfers and compensation between resident and non-resident individuals/households/entities

Budget: *revenues:* $98.462 billion (2022 est.)
expenditures: $113.035 billion (2022 est.)
note: central government revenues (excluding grants) and expenses converted to US dollars at average official exchange rate for year indicated

Public debt: 70.14% of GDP (2022 est.)
note: central government debt as a % of GDP
comparison ranking: 57

Taxes and other revenues: 15.28% (of GDP) (2022 est.)
note: central government tax revenue as a % of GDP
comparison ranking: 136

Current account balance: -$9.715 billion (2023 est.)
-$21.367 billion (2022 est.)
-$17.956 billion (2021 est.)
note: balance of payments - net trade and primary/secondary income in current dollars
comparison ranking: 193

Exports: $67.762 billion (2023 est.)
$73.06 billion (2022 est.)
$50.907 billion (2021 est.)
note: balance of payments - exports of goods and services in current dollars
comparison ranking: 57

Exports - partners: US 26%, Panama 10%, Netherlands 6%, India 4%, Brazil 4% (2022)
note: top five export partners based on percentage share of exports

Exports - commodities: crude petroleum, coal, coffee, refined petroleum, gold (2022)
note: top five export commodities based on value in dollars

Imports: $75.983 billion (2023 est.)
$89.649 billion (2022 est.)
$70.914 billion (2021 est.)
note: balance of payments - imports of goods and services in current dollars
comparison ranking: 52

Imports - partners: US 26%, China 25%, Brazil 7%, Mexico 5%, Germany 3% (2022)
note: top five import partners based on percentage share of imports

Imports - commodities: refined petroleum, cars, broadcasting equipment, corn, packaged medicine (2022)
note: top five import commodities based on value in dollars

Reserves of foreign exchange and gold: $59.041 billion (2023 est.)
$56.704 billion (2022 est.)
$58.019 billion (2021 est.)
note: holdings of gold (year-end prices)/foreign exchange/special drawing rights in current dollars
comparison ranking: 40

Debt - external: $97.915 billion (2022 est.)
note: present value of external debt in current US dollars
comparison ranking: 7

Exchange rates: Colombian pesos (COP) per US dollar -

Exchange rates: 4,325.955 (2023 est.)
4,256.194 (2022 est.)
3,744.244 (2021 est.)
3,693.276 (2020 est.)
3,281.622 (2019 est.)

ENERGY

Electricity access: *electrification - total population:* 100% (2022 est.)

Electricity: *installed generating capacity:* 18.896 million kW (2022 est.)
consumption: 80.936 billion kWh (2022 est.)
exports: 48.176 million kWh (2022 est.)
imports: 479 million kWh (2022 est.)
transmission/distribution losses: 4.69 billion kWh (2022 est.)
comparison rankings: transmission/distribution losses 161; imports 93; exports 91; consumption 38; installed generating capacity 52

Electricity generation sources: *fossil fuels:* 28.1% of total installed capacity (2022 est.)
solar: 0.4% of total installed capacity (2022 est.)
wind: 0.1% of total installed capacity (2022 est.)
hydroelectricity: 68.9% of total installed capacity (2022 est.)
biomass and waste: 2.6% of total installed capacity (2022 est.)

Coal: *production:* 58.747 million metric tons (2022 est.)
consumption: 7.88 million metric tons (2022 est.)
exports: 60.923 million metric tons (2022 est.)
imports: 800 metric tons (2022 est.)
proven reserves: 4.554 billion metric tons (2022 est.)

Petroleum: *total petroleum production:* 800,000 bbl/day (2023 est.)
refined petroleum consumption: 320,000 bbl/day (2022 est.)
crude oil estimated reserves: 2.036 billion barrels (2021 est.)

Natural gas: *production:* 11.29 billion cubic meters (2022 est.)
consumption: 11.451 billion cubic meters (2022 est.)
imports: 161.491 million cubic meters (2022 est.)
proven reserves: 87.782 billion cubic meters (2021 est.)

Carbon dioxide emissions: 70.163 million metric tonnes of CO2 (2022 est.)
from coal and metallurgical coke: 6.507 million metric tonnes of CO2 (2022 est.)
from petroleum and other liquids: 43.723 million metric tonnes of CO2 (2022 est.)
from consumed natural gas: 19.932 million metric tonnes of CO2 (2022 est.)
comparison ranking: total emissions 49

Energy consumption per capita: 25.8 million Btu/person (2022 est.)
comparison ranking: 121

COMMUNICATIONS

Telephones - fixed lines: *total subscriptions:* 7.588 million (2022 est.)
subscriptions per 100 inhabitants: 15 (2022 est.)
comparison ranking: total subscriptions 22

Telephones - mobile cellular: *total subscriptions:* 80.812 million (2022 est.)
subscriptions per 100 inhabitants: 156 (2022 est.)
comparison ranking: total subscriptions 21

Telecommunication systems: *general assessment:* the telecom sector had a solid year thanks to positive performances in the fixed-line broadband, mobile broadband, and mobile voice and data markets; the fixed-line penetration remained stable by the end of 2020, though began to increase into 2021 as a result of the particular demands on households resulting from government measures associated with addressing the pandemic; the mobile market reached a penetration rate of 136% (an increase of over three percentage points on 2019) and managed to keep the same upward growth trajectory that it has sustained over the last ten years; the fixed-line broadband market also expanded, with the number of subscribers increasing 11.4%, and with revenue increasing 9.9% thanks to increased data usage as many customers were forced to work or study from home during the year; the mobile broadband market was the standout performer in 2020, with a 13% increase in the number of subscribers year-on-year, the penetration rate is relatively low compared to other Latin American countries; most significant of all was the surge in mobile broadband traffic a 51% increase over the previous year (2022)
domestic: fixed-line connections stand at about 15 per 100 persons; mobile cellular telephone subscribership is 150 per 100 persons (2021)
international: country code - 57; landing points for the SAC, Maya-1, SAIT, ACROS, AMX-1, CFX-1, PCCS, Deep Blue Cable, Globe Net, PAN-AM, SAm-1 submarine cable systems providing links to the US, parts of the Caribbean, and Central and South America; satellite earth stations - 10 (6 Intelsat, 1 Inmarsat, 3 fully digitalized international switching centers) (2019)

Broadcast media: combination of state-owned and privately owned broadcast media provide service; more than 500 radio stations and many national, regional, and local TV stations (2019)

Internet country code: .co

Internet users: *total:* 37.96 million (2021 est.)
percent of population: 73% (2021 est.)
comparison ranking: total 26

Broadband - fixed subscriptions: *total:* 7,764,772 (2020 est.)
subscriptions per 100 inhabitants: 15 (2020 est.)
comparison ranking: total 28

TRANSPORTATION

National air transport system: *number of registered air carriers:* 12 (2020)
inventory of registered aircraft operated by air carriers: 157
annual passenger traffic on registered air carriers: 33,704,037 (2018)
annual freight traffic on registered air carriers: 1,349,450,000 (2018) mt-km

Civil aircraft registration country code prefix: HJ, HK

Airports: 662 (2024)
comparison ranking: 11

Heliports: 55 (2024)

Pipelines: 4,991 km gas, 6,796 km oil, 3,429 km refined products (2013)

Railways: *total:* 2,141 km (2019)
standard gauge: 150 km (2019) 1.435-m gauge
narrow gauge: 1,991 km (2019) 0.914-m gauge
comparison ranking: total 71

Roadways: *total:* 206,102 km (2022)
comparison ranking: total 25

Waterways: 24,725 km (2019) (18,225 km navigable; the most important waterway, the River Magdalena, of which 1,092 km is navigable, is dredged regularly to ensure safe passage of cargo vessels and container barges)
comparison ranking: 7

Merchant marine: *total:* 153 (2023)
by type: general cargo 28, oil tanker 13, other 112
comparison ranking: total 74

Ports: *total ports:* 14 (2024)
large: 0
medium: 2
small: 8
very small: 3
size unknown: 1
ports with oil terminals: 10
key ports: Barranquilla, Buenaventura, Cartagena, Covenas, El Bosque, Mamonal, Pozos Colorados, Puerto Bolivar, Puerto Prodeco, Santa Marta

MILITARY AND SECURITY

Military and security forces: Military Forces of Colombia (Fuerzas Militares de Colombia): National Army (Ejercito Nacional), Republic of Colombia Navy (Armada Republica de Colombia, ARC; includes Coast Guard and marines), Colombian Air Force (Fuerza Aerea de Colombia, FAC); Colombian National Police (PNC) (2024)
note: the PNC is a civilian force that is under the jurisdiction of the Ministry of Defense

Military expenditures: 2.9% of GDP (2023 est.)
3% of GDP (2022 est.)
3% of GDP (2021 est.)
3% of GDP (2020 est.)
3.1% of GDP (2019 est.)
comparison ranking: 37

Military and security service personnel strengths: information varies; approximately 265,000 active troops (200,000 Army; 50,000 Navy, including about 20,000 marines; 15,000 Air Force); approximately 175,000 National Police (2023)

Military equipment inventories and acquisitions: the military's inventory includes a wide mix of equipment from a variety of suppliers, including Canada, Germany, Israel, South Korea, and especially the US; Colombia's defense industry is active in producing air, land, and naval platforms (2024)

Military service age and obligation: 18-24 years of age for compulsory (men) and voluntary (men and women) military service; conscript service obligation is 18 months or 12 months for those with a college degree; conscripted soldiers reportedly include regular soldiers (conscripts without a high school degree), drafted high school graduates (bachilleres), and rural (campesino) soldiers who serve in their home regions (2024)
note: the Colombian military first incorporated women in 1976 in administrative positions; women were incorporated as non-commissioned officers in 1983 and officers in 2009; as of 2023, about 6,000 women served in the uniformed military while more than 30,000 served in the National Police

Military deployments: 275 Egypt (MFO) (2024)

Military - note: the Colombian military is responsible for defending and maintaining the country's independence, national sovereignty, and territorial integrity but also has a considerable internal security role, which includes protecting the civilian population, as well as private and state-owned assets, and ensuring a secure environment; the military's primary focus is the conduct of operations against domestic illegal armed groups, including drug traffickers, several factions of the former Revolutionary Armed Forces of Colombia (FARC) terrorist group, and the insurgent/terrorist group National Liberation Army (ELN); these operations are challenged by difficult topography and long and porous land borders
the Colombian Government signed a peace agreement with the FARC in 2016, but some former members (known as dissidents) have returned to fighting (note - these dissident groups include the US-designated foreign terrorist groups Revolutionary Armed Forces of Colombia - People's Army or FARC-EP and Segunda Marquetalia); since 2017, the Colombian Government has had periodic cease-fire and peace discussions with ELN and the FARC dissidents, including a 6-month cease-fire with the ELN in 2023-2024
the military is also focused on the security challenges posed by its neighbor, Venezuela, where instability has attracted narcotics traffickers, and both the ELN and FARC dissidents operate openly; Colombia shares a 1,370-mile (2,200 km) border with Venezuela; ELN and FARC insurgents have also used neighboring Ecuador to rest, resupply, and shelter
Colombia has close security ties with the US, including joint training, military assistance, and designation in 2022 as a Major Non-NATO Ally, which provides foreign partners with certain benefits in the areas of defense, trade, and security cooperation; it also has close ties with some regional neighbors, such as Argentina, Chile, and Peru; Colombian military and security forces have training programs with their counterparts from a variety of countries, mostly those from Mexico, Central America, and the Caribbean (2024)

SPACE

Space agency/agencies: Colombian Space Commission (Comision Colombiana Del Espacio, CCE; established 2006); Air and Space Operations Command (Colombian military); note – the Colombian Space Agency (Agencia Espacial Del Colombia, AEC) is a private, non-profit agency established in 2017 (2024)

Space program overview: has a small program focused on acquiring satellites, particularly remote sensing (RS) satellites; operates satellites and produces nanosatellites; researches other space technologies, including telecommunications, satellite navigation, and astronautics; has relations with a variety of foreign space agencies or commercial space industries, including those of Denmark, India, Russia, Sweden, the US, and some members of the Latin American and Caribbean Space Agency (ALCE) (2024)
note: further details about the key activities, programs, and milestones of the country's space program, as well as government spending estimates on the space sector, appear in the Space Programs reference guide

TERRORISM

Terrorist group(s): National Liberation Army (ELN); Revolutionary Armed Forces of Colombia - People's Army (FARC-EP); Segunda Marquetalia
note: details about the history, aims, leadership, organization, areas of operation, tactics, targets, weapons, size, and sources of support of the group(s) appear(s) in the Terrorism reference guide

TRANSNATIONAL ISSUES

Refugees and internally displaced persons:
refugees (country of origin): 2,875,743 (Venezuela) (economic and political crisis; includes Venezuelans who have claimed asylum, are recognized as refugees, or received alternative legal stay) (2023)
IDPs: 6,863,334 (conflict between government and illegal armed groups and drug traffickers since 1985) (2023)
stateless persons: 11 (2022)

Illicit drugs: Colombia is the world's top cocaine producer and exporter; is a source of heroin and marijuana; coca cultivation estimated at 234,000 hectares (ha) in 2021; pure cocaine production decreased to 972 metric tons in 2021; a major source of precursor or essential chemicals used in the production of illicit narcotics

COMOROS

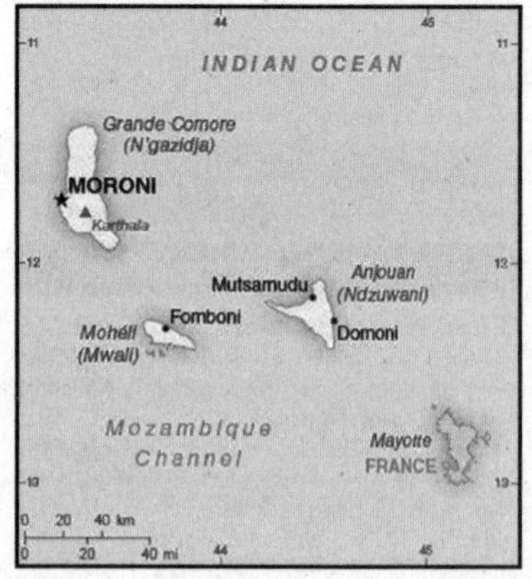

INTRODUCTION

Background: For centuries prior to colonization in the 19th century, the Comoros archipelago in the Indian Ocean served as a key node in maritime trade networks that connected the Middle East, India, and eastern African regions. Composed of the islands of Anjouan, Mayotte, Moheli, and Grande Comore, Comoros spent most of the 20th century as a colonial outpost until it declared independence from France on 6 July 1975. Residents of Mayotte, however, voted to remain in France, and the French Government has since classified it as a French Overseas Department.

Since independence, Comoros has weathered approximately 20 successful and attempted coups, mostly between 1975 and 2000, resulting in prolonged political instability and stunted economic development. In 2002, President AZALI Assoumani became the first elected president following the completion of the Fomboni Accords, in which the islands of Grande Comore, Anjouan, and Moheli agreed to rotate the presidency among the islands every five years. This powersharing agreement also included provisions allowing each island to maintain its local government. In 2007, Mohamed BACAR effected Anjouan's de-facto secession from the Union of the Comoros, refusing to step down when Comoros' other islands held legitimate elections. The African Union (AU) initially attempted to resolve the political crisis with sanctions and a naval blockade of Anjouan, but in 2008, the AU and Comoran soldiers seized the island. The island's inhabitants generally welcomed the move. In 2011, Ikililou DHOININE won the presidency in peaceful elections widely deemed to be free and fair. In closely contested elections in 2016, AZALI won a second term, when the rotating presidency returned to Grande Comore. In 2018, a referendum – which the opposition parties boycotted – approved a new constitution that extended presidential term limits and abolished the requirement for the presidency to rotate between the three main islands. AZALI formed a new government later that year, and he subsequently ran and was reelected in 2019. AZALI was reelected again in January 2024 in an election that the opposition disputed but the Supreme Court validated.

GEOGRAPHY

Location: Southern Africa, group of islands at the northern mouth of the Mozambique Channel, about two-thirds of the way between northern Madagascar and northern Mozambique

Geographic coordinates: 12 10 S, 44 15 E

Map references: Africa

Area: *total:* 2,235 sq km
land: 2,235 sq km
water: 0 sq km
comparison ranking: total 179

Area - comparative: slightly more than 12 times the size of Washington, DC

Land boundaries: *total:* 0 km

Coastline: 340 km

Maritime claims: *territorial sea:* 12 nm
exclusive economic zone: 200 nm

Climate: tropical marine; rainy season (November to May)

Terrain: volcanic islands, interiors vary from steep mountains to low hills

Elevation: *highest point:* Karthala 2,360 m
lowest point: Indian Ocean 0 m

Natural resources: fish

Land use: *agricultural land:* 84.4% (2018 est.)
arable land: 46.7% (2018 est.)
permanent crops: 29.6% (2018 est.)
permanent pasture: 8.1% (2018 est.)
forest: 1.4% (2018 est.)
other: 14.2% (2018 est.)

Irrigated land: 1.3 sq km (2012)

Population distribution: the capital city of Maroni, located on the western side of the island of Grande Comore, is the country's largest city; however, of the three islands that comprise Comoros, it is Anjouan that is the most densely populated as shown in this population distribution map

Natural hazards: cyclones possible during rainy season (December to April); volcanic activity on Grand Comore
volcanism: Karthala (2,361 m) on Grand Comore Island last erupted in 2007; a 2005 eruption forced thousands of people to be evacuated and produced a large ash cloud

Geography - note: important location at northern end of Mozambique Channel; the only Arab League country that lies entirely in the Southern Hemisphere

PEOPLE AND SOCIETY

Population: *total:* 900,141
male: 435,758
female: 464,383 (2024 est.)
comparison rankings: female 164; male 165; total 164

Nationality: *noun:* Comoran(s)
adjective: Comoran

Ethnic groups: Antalote, Cafre, Makoa, Oimatsaha, Sakalava

Languages: Arabic (official), French (official), Shikomoro (official; similar to Swahili), Comorian

Religions: Muslim 98.1% (overwhelmingly Sunni Muslim, small Shia Muslim and Ahmadiyya Muslim populations), ethnic religionist 1.1%, Christian 0.6%, other 0.3% (2020 est.)
note: Sunni Islam is the state religion

Demographic profile: Comoros' population is a melange of Arabs, Persians, Indonesians, Africans, and Indians, and the much smaller number of Europeans that settled on the islands between the 8th and 19th centuries, when they served as a regional trade hub. The Arab and Persian influence is most evident in the islands' overwhelmingly Muslim majority – about 98% of Comorans are Sunni Muslims. The country is densely populated, averaging nearly 350 people per square mile, although this varies widely among the islands, with Anjouan being the most densely populated.
Given the large share of land dedicated to agriculture and Comoros' growing population, habitable land is becoming increasingly crowded. The combination of increasing population pressure on limited land and resources, widespread poverty, and poor job prospects motivates thousands of Comorans each year to attempt to illegally migrate using small fishing boats to the neighboring island of Mayotte, which is a French territory. The majority of legal Comoran migration to France came after Comoros' independence from France in 1975, with the flow peaking in the mid-1980s.
At least 150,000 to 200,000 people of Comoran citizenship or descent live abroad, mainly in France, where they have gone seeking a better quality of life, job opportunities, higher education (Comoros has no universities), advanced health care, and to finance elaborate traditional wedding ceremonies (aada). Remittances from the diaspora are an economic mainstay, in 2013 representing approximately 25% of Comoros' GDP and significantly more than the value of its exports of goods and services (only 15% of GDP). Grand Comore, Comoros' most populous island, is both the primary source of emigrants and the main recipient of remittances. Most remittances are spent on private consumption, but this often goes toward luxury goods and the aada and does not contribute to economic development or poverty reduction. Although the majority of the diaspora is now French-born with more distant ties to Comoros, it is unclear whether they will sustain the current level of remittances.

Age structure: *0-14 years:* 32.6% (male 146,480/female 146,626)
15-64 years: 62.8% (male 271,139/female 294,231)
65 years and over: 4.6% (2024 est.) (male 18,139/female 23,526)

Dependency ratios: *total dependency ratio:* 74.1
youth dependency ratio: 66.6
elderly dependency ratio: 7.5
potential support ratio: 13.3 (2021 est.)

Median age: *total:* 22.7 years (2024 est.)
male: 22.1 years
female: 23.3 years
comparison ranking: total 183

Population growth rate: 1.3% (2024 est.)
comparison ranking: 73

Birth rate: 21.6 births/1,000 population (2024 est.)
comparison ranking: 58

Death rate: 6.4 deaths/1,000 population (2024 est.)
comparison ranking: 140

Net migration rate: -2.2 migrant(s)/1,000 population (2024 est.)
comparison ranking: 170

Population distribution: the capital city of Maroni, located on the western side of the island of Grande Comore, is the country's largest city; however, of the three islands that comprise Comoros, it is Anjouan that is the most densely populated as shown in this population distribution map

Urbanization: *urban population:* 30.1% of total population (2023)
rate of urbanization: 2.97% annual rate of change (2020-25 est.)

Major urban areas - population: 62,000 MORONI (capital) (2018)

Sex ratio: *at birth:* 1.03 male(s)/female
0-14 years: 1 male(s)/female
15-64 years: 0.92 male(s)/female
65 years and over: 0.77 male(s)/female
total population: 0.94 male(s)/female (2024 est.)

Mother's mean age at first birth: 23 years (2012 est.)
note: data represents median age at first birth among women 25-49

Maternal mortality ratio: 217 deaths/100,000 live births (2020 est.)
comparison ranking: 43

Infant mortality rate: *total:* 54.9 deaths/1,000 live births (2024 est.)
male: 64.9 deaths/1,000 live births
female: 44.7 deaths/1,000 live births
comparison ranking: total 14

Life expectancy at birth: *total population:* 67.8 years (2024 est.)
male: 65.5 years
female: 70.2 years
comparison ranking: total population 193

Total fertility rate: 2.61 children born/woman (2024 est.)
comparison ranking: 65

Gross reproduction rate: 1.28 (2024 est.)

Contraceptive prevalence rate: 19.4% (2012)

Drinking water source: *improved: urban:* 97.4% of population
rural: 88.5% of population
total: 91% of population
unimproved: urban: 2.6% of population
rural: 11.5% of population
total: 8.9% of population (2017 est.)

Current health expenditure: 5.4% of GDP (2020)

Physician density: 0.26 physicians/1,000 population (2018)

Sanitation facility access: *improved: urban:* 62.4% of population
rural: 43.6% of population
total: 49% of population
unimproved: urban: 37.6% of population
rural: 56.4% of population
total: 51% of population (2017 est.)

Obesity - adult prevalence rate: 7.8% (2016)
comparison ranking: 157

Alcohol consumption per capita: *total:* 0.18 liters of pure alcohol (2019 est.)
beer: 0.04 liters of pure alcohol (2019 est.)
wine: 0.07 liters of pure alcohol (2019 est.)
spirits: 0.07 liters of pure alcohol (2019 est.)
other alcohols: 0 liters of pure alcohol (2019 est.)

comparison ranking: total 173

Tobacco use: *total:* 20.3% (2020 est.)
male: 29.5% (2020 est.)
female: 11.1% (2020 est.)
comparison ranking: total 83

Currently married women (ages 15-49): 61.2% (2023 est.)

Education expenditures: 2.6% of GDP (2015 est.)
comparison ranking: 174

Literacy: *definition:* age 15 and over can read and write
total population: 62%
male: 67%
female: 56.9% (2021)

School life expectancy (primary to tertiary education): *total:* 11 years
male: 11 years
female: 11 years (2014)

ENVIRONMENT

Environment - current issues: deforestation; soil degradation and erosion results from forest loss and from crop cultivation on slopes without proper terracing; marine biodiversity affected as soil erosion leads to the silting of coral reefs

Environment - international agreements: *party to:* Biodiversity, Climate Change, Climate Change-Kyoto Protocol, Climate Change-Paris Agreement, Comprehensive Nuclear Test Ban, Desertification, Endangered Species, Hazardous Wastes, Law of the Sea, Ozone Layer Protection, Ship Pollution, Wetlands
signed, but not ratified: none of the selected agreements

Climate: tropical marine; rainy season (November to May)

Urbanization: *urban population:* 30.1% of total population (2023)
rate of urbanization: 2.97% annual rate of change (2020-25 est.)

Revenue from forest resources: 1.39% of GDP (2018 est.)
comparison ranking: 46

Revenue from coal: 0% of GDP (2018 est.)
comparison ranking: 182

Air pollutants: *particulate matter emissions:* 14.37 micrograms per cubic meter (2019 est.)
carbon dioxide emissions: 0.2 megatons (2016 est.)
methane emissions: 0.19 megatons (2020 est.)

Waste and recycling: *municipal solid waste generated annually:* 91,013 tons (2015 est.)

Total water withdrawal: *municipal:* 4.8 million cubic meters (2017 est.)
industrial: 500,000 cubic meters (2017 est.)
agricultural: 4.7 million cubic meters (2017 est.)

Total renewable water resources: 1.2 billion cubic meters (2020 est.)

GOVERNMENT

Country name: *conventional long form:* Union of the Comoros
conventional short form: Comoros
local long form: Udzima wa Komori (Comorian)/Union des Comores (French)/Al Ittihad al Qumuri (Arabic)
local short form: Komori (Comorian)/Les Comores (French)/Juzur al Qamar (Arabic)
former: Comorian State, Federal Islamic Republic of the Comoros
etymology: name derives from the Arabic designation "Juzur al Qamar" meaning "Islands of the Moon"

Government type: federal presidential republic

Capital: *name:* Moroni
geographic coordinates: 11 42 S, 43 14 E
time difference: UTC+3 (8 hours ahead of Washington, DC, during Standard Time)
etymology: Moroni derives from "mroni," which means "at the river" in Shingazidja, the Comorian language spoken on Grande Comore (N'gazidja)

Administrative divisions: 3 islands; Anjouan (Ndzuwani), Grande Comore (N'gazidja), Moheli (Mwali)

Independence: 6 July 1975 (from France)

National holiday: Independence Day, 6 July (1975)

Legal system: mixed legal system of Islamic religious law, the French civil code of 1975, and customary law

Constitution: *history:* previous 1996, 2001; newest adopted 30 July 2018
amendments: proposed by the president of the union or supported by at least one third of the Assembly of the Union membership; adoption requires approval by at least three-quarters majority of the total Assembly membership or approval in a referendum
note: a referendum held on 30 July 2018 - boycotted by the opposition - overwhelmingly approved a new constitution that allows for 2 consecutive 5-year presidential terms while retaining the rotating presidency within the islands

International law organization participation: has not submitted an ICJ jurisdiction declaration; accepts ICCt jurisdiction

Citizenship: *citizenship by birth:* no
citizenship by descent only: at least one parent must be a citizen of the Comoros
dual citizenship recognized: no
residency requirement for naturalization: 10 years

Suffrage: 18 years of age; universal

Executive branch: *chief of state:* President AZALI Assoumani (since 26 May 2016)
head of government: President AZALI Assoumani (since 26 May 2016)
cabinet: Council of Ministers appointed by the president
elections/appointments: president directly elected by absolute majority vote in 2 rounds if needed for a 5-year term; election last held on 14 January 2024 (next to be held in 2029)
election results:
2024: AZALI Assoumani reelected president in first round - AZALI Assoumani (CRC) 63%, SALIM ISSA Abdallah (PJ) 20.3%, DAOUDOU Abdallah Mohamed (Orange Party) 5.9%, Bourhane HAMIDOU (independent) 5.1%
2019: AZALI Assoumani elected president in first round - AZALI Assoumani (CRC) 60.8%, Ahamada MAHAMOUDOU (PJ) 14.6%, Mouigni Baraka Said SOILIHI (independent) 5.6%, other 19%
note: the president is both chief of state and head of government

Legislative branch: *description:* unicameral Assembly of the Union (24 members directly elected by absolute majority vote in 2 rounds if needed; members serve 5-year terms)
elections: last held on 19 January 2020 with a runoff on 23 February 2020 (next to be held in 2025)
election results: percent of vote by party in first round - CRC 60.9%, Orange Party 4.3%, independent 30.8%, other 4%; seats by party in the first round - CRC 16, Orange Party 1, independent 2; percent of vote by party in the second round - CRC 54.1%, Orange Party 18.9%, independent 26.1%, other 1%; seats by party in the second round - CRC 4, Orange Party 1; composition - men 20, women 4, percentage women 16.7%; note - main opposition parties boycotted election;
note: opposition parties, which had demanded "transparent, free, and democratic" elections, boycotted the 2020 elections

Judicial branch: *highest court(s):* Supreme Court or Cour Supreme (consists of 7 judges)
judge selection and term of office: Supreme Court judges - selection and term of office NA
subordinate courts: Court of Appeals (in Moroni); Tribunal de premiere instance; island village (community) courts; religious courts

Political parties: Convention for the Renewal of the Comoros or CRC
Juwa Party (Parti Juwa) or PJ
Orange Party (2020)

International organization participation: ACP, AfDB, AMF, AOSIS, AU, CAEU (candidates), COMESA, FAO, FZ, G-77, IBRD, ICAO, ICCt, ICRM, IDA, IDB, IFAD, IFC, IFRCS, ILO, IMF, IMO, IMSO, InOC, Interpol, IOC, IOM, ITSO, ITU, ITUC (NGOs), LAS, MIGA, NAM, OIC, OIF, OPCW, UN, UNCTAD, UNESCO, UNIDO, UPU, WCO, WHO, WIPO, WMO, WTO (observer)

Diplomatic representation in the US: *chief of mission:* Ambassador Issimail CHANFI (since 23 December 2020); note - also Permanent Representative to the UN
chancery: Permanent Mission to the UN, 866 United Nations Plaza, Suite 495, New York, NY 10017
telephone: [1] (212) 750-1637
FAX: [1] (212) 750-1657
email address and website:
comoros@un.int
https://www. un.int/comoros/

Diplomatic representation from the US: *embassy:* the US does not have an embassy in Comoros; the US Ambassador to Madagascar is accredited to Comoros

Flag description: four equal horizontal bands of yellow (top), white, red, and blue, with a green isosceles triangle based on the hoist; centered within the triangle is a vertical white crescent moon with the convex side facing the hoist and four white, five-pointed stars placed vertically in a line between the points of the crescent; the horizontal bands and the four stars represent the four main islands of the archipelago - Mwali, N'gazidja, Ndzuwani, and Mahore (Mayotte - department of France, but claimed by Comoros)
note: the crescent, stars, and color green are traditional symbols of Islam

National symbol(s): four five-pointed stars and crescent moon; national colors: green, white

National anthem: *name:* "Udzima wa ya Masiwa" (The Union of the Great Islands)
lyrics/music: Said Hachim SIDI ABDEREMANE/Said Hachim SIDI ABDEREMANE and Kamildine ABDALLAH
note: adopted 1978

ECONOMY

Economic overview: small trade-based island economy; declining remittances; new structural and fiscal reforms; adverse cyclone and COVID-19 impacts; manageable debts; fragile liquidity environment; large foreign direct investment; state-owned enterprises suffering

Real GDP (purchasing power parity): $2.961 billion (2023 est.)
$2.883 billion (2022 est.)
$2.816 billion (2021 est.)
note: data in 2021 dollars
comparison ranking: 196

Real GDP growth rate: 2.7% (2023 est.)
2.39% (2022 est.)
2.11% (2021 est.)
note: annual GDP % growth based on constant local currency
comparison ranking: 117

Real GDP per capita: $3,500 (2023 est.)
$3,400 (2022 est.)
$3,400 (2021 est.)
note: data in 2021 dollars
comparison ranking: 191

GDP (official exchange rate): $1.352 billion (2023 est.)
note: data in current dollars at official exchange rate

Inflation rate (consumer prices): 1% (2017 est.)
1.8% (2016 est.)
note: annual % change based on consumer prices
comparison ranking: 18

GDP - composition, by sector of origin: *agriculture:* 37.2% (2023 est.)
industry: 9% (2023 est.)
services: 49.6% (2023 est.)
note: figures may not total 100% due to non-allocated consumption not captured in sector-reported data
comparison rankings: services 150; industry 199; agriculture 4

GDP - composition, by end use: *household consumption:* 100.1% (2023 est.)
government consumption: 9.3% (2023 est.)
investment in fixed capital: 12.7% (2023 est.)
exports of goods and services: 13% (2023 est.)
imports of goods and services: -35% (2023 est.)
note: figures may not total 100% due to rounding or gaps in data collection

Agricultural products: coconuts, bananas, cassava, yams, maize, taro, milk, tomatoes, sweet potatoes, pulses (2022)
note: top ten agricultural products based on tonnage

Industries: fishing, tourism, perfume distillation

Industrial production growth rate: 0% (2023 est.)
note: annual % change in industrial value added based on constant local currency
comparison ranking: 153

Labor force: 234,000 (2023 est.)
note: number of people ages 15 or older who are employed or seeking work
comparison ranking: 176

Unemployment rate: 5.8% (2023 est.)
5.85% (2022 est.)
5.86% (2021 est.)
note: % of labor force seeking employment
comparison ranking: 115

Youth unemployment rate (ages 15-24): *total:* 10.9% (2023 est.)
male: 9.9% (2023 est.)
female: 12.2% (2023 est.)
note: % of labor force ages 15-24 seeking employment
comparison ranking: total 122

Gini Index coefficient - distribution of family income: 45.3 (2014 est.)
note: index (0-100) of income distribution; higher values represent greater inequality
comparison ranking: 20

Household income or consumption by percentage share: *lowest 10%:* 1.6% (2014 est.)
highest 10%: 33.7% (2014 est.)
note: % share of income accruing to lowest and highest 10% of population

Remittances: 20.77% of GDP (2023 est.)
22.68% of GDP (2022 est.)
22.22% of GDP (2021 est.)
note: personal transfers and compensation between resident and non-resident individuals/households/entities

Budget: *revenues:* $223 million (2018 est.)
expenditures: $228 million (2018 est.)

Public debt: 32.4% of GDP (2017 est.)
comparison ranking: 163

Taxes and other revenues: 25.3% (of GDP) (2017 est.)
comparison ranking: 43

Current account balance: -$6.614 million (2022 est.)
-$4.076 million (2021 est.)
-$22.048 million (2020 est.)
note: balance of payments - net trade and primary/secondary income in current dollars
comparison ranking: 84

Exports: $165.347 million (2022 est.)
$128.331 million (2021 est.)
$68.937 million (2020 est.)
note: balance of payments - exports of goods and services in current dollars
comparison ranking: 207

Exports - partners: Turkey 23%, India 19%, UAE 9%, US 9%, Indonesia 8% (2022)
note: top five export partners based on percentage share of exports

Exports - commodities: cloves, ships, vanilla, essential oils, scrap iron (2022)
note: top five export commodities based on value in dollars

Imports: $479.94 million (2022 est.)
$415.965 million (2021 est.)
$343.608 million (2020 est.)
note: balance of payments - imports of goods and services in current dollars
comparison ranking: 205

Imports - partners: UAE 25%, China 19%, India 12%, France 8%, Tanzania 7% (2022)
note: top five import partners based on percentage share of imports

Imports - commodities: rice, refined petroleum, poultry, water, synthetic fabric (2022)
note: top five import commodities based on value in dollars

Reserves of foreign exchange and gold: $324.561 million (2023 est.)
$283.746 million (2022 est.)
$329.672 million (2021 est.)
note: holdings of gold (year-end prices)/foreign exchange/special drawing rights in current dollars
comparison ranking: 179

Debt - external: $233.947 million (2022 est.)
note: present value of external debt in current US dollars
comparison ranking: 99

Exchange rates: Comoran francs (KMF) per US dollar -

Exchange rates: 454.991 (2023 est.)
467.184 (2022 est.)
415.956 (2021 est.)
430.721 (2020 est.)
439.463 (2019 est.)

ENERGY

Electricity access: *electrification - total population:* 89.9% (2022 est.)
electrification - urban areas: 100%
electrification - rural areas: 82.9%

Electricity: *installed generating capacity:* 4.036 million kW (2022 est.)
consumption: 113.052 million kWh (2022 est.)
transmission/distribution losses: 22.1 million kWh (2022 est.)
comparison rankings: transmission/distribution losses 26; consumption 198; installed generating capacity 99

Electricity generation sources: *fossil fuels:* 100% of total installed capacity (2022 est.)

Coal: *imports:* 2,000 metric tons (2022 est.)

Petroleum: *refined petroleum consumption:* 3,000 bbl/day (2022 est.)

Carbon dioxide emissions: 372,000 metric tonnes of CO_2 (2022 est.)
from petroleum and other liquids: 372,000 metric tonnes of CO_2 (2022 est.)
comparison ranking: total emissions 192

Energy consumption per capita: 6.223 million Btu/person (2022 est.)
comparison ranking: 164

COMMUNICATIONS

Telephones - fixed lines: *total subscriptions:* 7,000 (2022 est.)
subscriptions per 100 inhabitants: (2022 est.) less than 1
comparison ranking: total subscriptions 198

Telephones - mobile cellular: *total subscriptions:* 839,000 (2022 est.)
subscriptions per 100 inhabitants: 100 (2022 est.)
comparison ranking: total subscriptions 168

Telecommunication systems: *general assessment:* Comoros launched a special program for the construction of a wireless network to inter connect the 3 islands of the archipelago; telephone service limited to the islands' few towns (2020)
domestic: fixed-line connections less than 1 per 100 persons; mobile-cellular usage about 104 per 100 persons (2021)
international: country code - 269; landing point for the EASSy, Comoros Domestic Cable System, Avassa, and FLY-LION3 fiber-optic submarine cable system connecting East Africa with Europe; HF radiotelephone communications to Madagascar and Reunion (2019)

Broadcast media: national state-owned TV station and a TV station run by Anjouan regional government; national state-owned radio; regional governments on the islands of Grande Comore and Anjouan each operate a radio station; a few independent and small community radio stations operate on the islands of Grande Comore and Moheli, and these two islands have access to Mayotte Radio and French TV

Internet country code: .km

Internet users: *total:* 221,400 (2021 est.)
percent of population: 27% (2021 est.)
comparison ranking: total 179

Broadband - fixed subscriptions: *total:* 1,066 (2020 est.)
subscriptions per 100 inhabitants: 0.1 (2020 est.)
comparison ranking: total 201

TRANSPORTATION

National air transport system: *number of registered air carriers:* 2 (2020)
inventory of registered aircraft operated by air carriers: 9

Civil aircraft registration country code prefix: D6

Airports: 3 (2024)
comparison ranking: 191

Roadways: *total:* 849 km
*paved:*673 km
*unpaved:*207 km (2019)
comparison ranking: total 189

Merchant marine: *total:* 273 (2023)
by type: bulk carrier 17, container ship 7, general cargo 125, oil tanker 36, other 88
comparison ranking: total 58

Ports: *total ports:* 4 (2024)
large: 0
medium: 0
small: 0
very small: 4
ports with oil terminals: 3
key ports: Dzaoudzi, Fomboni, Moroni, Moutsamoudu

MILITARY AND SECURITY

Military and security forces: National Army for Development (l'Armee Nationale de Developpement, AND): Comoran Defense Force (Force Comorienne de Defense or FCD; includes Comoran National Gendarmerie); Ministry of Interior: Coast Guard, Federal Police, National Directorate of Territorial Safety (2024)
note 1: when the Gendarmerie serves as the judicial police, it reports to the Minister of Justice; the Gendarmerie also has an intervention platoon that may act under the authority of the interior minister
note 2: the National Directorate of Territorial Safety oversees customs and immigration
note 3: the FCD is also known as the Comoran Security Force

Military and security service personnel strengths: estimated 600 Defense Force personnel; estimated 500 Federal Police (2023)

Military equipment inventories and acquisitions: the defense forces are lightly armed with a mix of mostly older equipment originating from several countries, including France, Italy, Russia, and the US (2023)

Military service age and obligation: 18 years of age for 2-year voluntary military service for men and women; no conscription (2021)

Military - note: the focus for the security forces is search and rescue operations and maintaining internal security; a defense treaty with France provides naval resources for the protection of territorial waters, training of Comoran military personnel, and air surveillance; France maintains a small maritime base and a Foreign Legion contingent on neighboring Mayotte (2024)

CONGO, DEMOCRATIC REPUBLIC OF THE

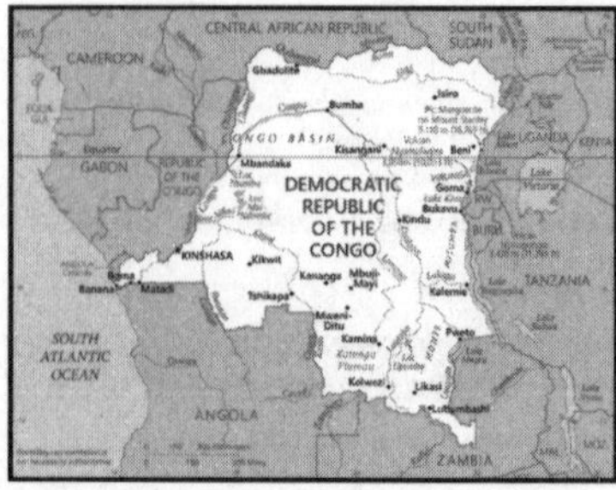

INTRODUCTION

Background: Bantu, Sudanic, and other migrants from West and Northeastern Africa arrived in the Congo River Basin between 2000 B.C. and A.D. 500. The territory that is now the Democratic Republic of the Congo is extremely diverse, with more than 200 ethnic groups that trace their histories to many communal organizations and kingdoms. The Kingdom of Kongo, for example, ruled the area around the mouth of the Congo River from the 14th to 19th centuries. Meanwhile, the Kingdoms of Luba and Lunda, located to the south and east, were also notable political groupings in the territory and ruled from the 16th and 17th centuries to the 19th century. European prospectors in the Congo Basin invaded and splintered these kingdoms in the late 1800's, sponsored by King LEOPOLD II of Belgium, and the kingdoms were eventually forced to grant Leopold the rights to the Congo territory as his private property. During this period, known as the Congo Free State, the king's private colonial military forced the local population to produce rubber. From 1885 to 1908, millions of Congolese people died as a result of disease, inhumane treatment, and exploitation. International condemnation finally forced LEOPOLD to cede the land to the state of Belgium, creating the Belgian Congo.

The Republic of the Congo gained its independence from Belgium in 1960, but its early years were marred by instability. Col. Joseph MOBUTU seized power and declared himself president in a 1965 coup. He subsequently changed his name to MOBUTU Sese Seko and the country's name to Zaire. MOBUTU retained his position for 32 years, using sham elections and brute force. In 1994, a massive inflow of refugees from conflict in neighboring Rwanda and Burundi sparked ethnic strife and civil war. A rebellion backed by Rwanda and Uganda and fronted by Laurent KABILA toppled the MOBUTU regime in 1997. KABILA renamed the country the Democratic Republic of the Congo (DRC). In 1998, another insurrection – again backed by Rwanda and Uganda – challenged the KABILA regime, but troops from Angola, Chad, Namibia, Sudan, and Zimbabwe helped quell the uprising.

In 2001, KABILA was assassinated, and his son, Joseph KABILA, was named head of state. In 2002, the new president negotiated the withdrawal of Rwandan forces occupying the eastern DRC; the remaining warring parties subsequently signed the Pretoria Accord to end the fighting and establish a government of national unity. KABILA was elected as president in 2006 and 2011. The DRC constitution barred him from running for a third term, so in 2016, the DRC Government delayed national elections for two years. This fueled significant civil and political unrest, with sporadic street protests and exacerbation of tensions in the eastern DRC regions.

The results of the 2018 elections were disputed, but opposition candidate Felix TSHISEKEDI, son of long-time opposition leader Etienne TSHISEKEDI, was announced as the election winner. This was the first transfer of power to an opposition candidate without significant violence or a coup since 1960. In December 2023, the DRC held its fourth electoral cycle since independence; TSHISEKEDI was proclaimed the winner despite some allegations of fraud, with his Sacred Union alliance retaining a large parliamentary majority.

The DRC continues to experience violence – particularly in the East – perpetrated by more than 100 armed groups active in the region, including the March 23 (M23) rebel group, the ISIS-affiliated Allied Democratic Forces (ADF, or ISIS-DRC), the Democratic Forces for the Liberation of Rwanda (FDLR), and assorted local militias known as Mai Mai militias. The UN Organization Stabilization Mission in the DRC (MONUSCO) has operated in the region since 1999 and is the largest and most expensive UN peacekeeping mission in the world.

GEOGRAPHY

Location: Central Africa, northeast of Angola

Geographic coordinates: 0 00 N, 25 00 E

Map references: Africa

Area: *total:* 2,344,858 sq km
land: 2,267,048 sq km
water: 77,810 sq km
comparison ranking: total 12

Area - comparative: slightly less than one-fourth the size of the US

Land boundaries: *total:* 11,027 km
border countries (9): Angola 2,646 km (of which 225 km is the boundary of Angola's discontiguous Cabinda Province); Burundi 236 km; Central African Republic 1,747 km; Republic of the Congo 1,775 km; Rwanda 221 km; South Sudan 714 km; Tanzania 479 km; Uganda 877 km; Zambia 2,332 km

Coastline: 37 km

Maritime claims: *territorial sea:* 12 nm

exclusive economic zone: since 2011, the DRC has had a Common Interest Zone agreement with Angola for the mutual development of off-shore resources

Climate: tropical; hot and humid in equatorial river basin; cooler and drier in southern highlands; cooler and wetter in eastern highlands; north of Equator - wet season (April to October), dry season (December to February); south of Equator - wet season (November to March), dry season (April to October)

Terrain: vast central basin is a low-lying plateau; mountains in east

Elevation: *highest point:* Pic Marguerite on Mont Ngaliema (Mount Stanley) 5,110 m
lowest point: Atlantic Ocean 0 m
mean elevation: 726 m

Natural resources: cobalt, copper, niobium, tantalum, petroleum, industrial and gem diamonds, gold, silver, zinc, manganese, tin, uranium, coal, hydropower, timber
note 1: coltan, the industrial name for a columbite–tantalite mineral from which niobium and tantalum are extracted, is mainly artisanal and small-scale; tantalum, tin, tungsten, and gold extracted from central Africa are considered "conflict minerals" and as such are subject to international monitoring
note 2: the DROC is the World's leading producer of cobalt, accounting for as much as 70% of the World's supply; between 20-30% of this cobalt is produced in artisanal and small-scale mining operations

Land use: *agricultural land:* 11.4% (2018 est.)
arable land: 3.1% (2018 est.)
permanent crops: 0.3% (2018 est.)
permanent pasture: 8% (2018 est.)
forest: 67.9% (2018 est.)
other: 20.7% (2018 est.)

Irrigated land: 110 sq km (2012)

Major lakes (area sq km): *fresh water lake(s):* Lake Tanganyika (shared with Burundi, Tanzania, and Zambia) - 32,000 sq km; Lake Albert (shared with Uganda) - 5,590 sq km; Lake Mweru (shared with Zambia) - 4,350 sq km; Lac Mai-Ndombe - 2,300 sq km; Lake Kivu (shared with Rwanda) - 2,220 sq km; Lake Edward (shared with Uganda) - 2,150 sq km; Lac Tumba - 500 sq km; Lac Upemba - 530 sq km

Major rivers (by length in km): Zaïre (Congo) river mouth (shared with Zambia [s], Angola, and Republic of Congo) - 4,700 km; Ubangi river mouth (shared with Central African Republic [s] and Republic of Congo) - 2,270 km note – [s] after country name indicates river source; [m] after country name indicates river mouth

Major watersheds (area sq km):Atlantic Ocean drainage: Congo (3,730,881 sq km), *(Mediterranean Sea)* Nile (3,254,853 sq km)

Indian Ocean drainage: Zambezi (1,332,412 sq km)

Major aquifers: Congo Basin

Population distribution: urban clusters are spread throughout the country, particularly in the northeast along the border with Uganda, Rwanda, and Burundi; the largest city is the capital, Kinshasha, located in the west along the Congo River; the south is least densely populated as shown in this population distribution map

Natural hazards: periodic droughts in south; Congo River floods (seasonal); active volcanoes in the east along the Great Rift Valley
volcanism: Nyiragongo (3,470 m), which erupted in 2002 and is experiencing ongoing activity, poses a major threat to the city of Goma, home to a quarter million people; the volcano produces unusually fast-moving lava, known to travel up to 100 km /hr; Nyiragongo has been deemed a Decade Volcano by the International Association of Volcanology and Chemistry of the Earth's Interior, worthy of study due to its explosive history and close proximity to human populations; its neighbor, Nyamuragira, which erupted in 2010, is Africa's most active volcano; Visoke is the only other historically active volcano

Geography - note: *note 1:* second largest country in Africa (after Algeria) and largest country in Sub-Saharan Africa; straddles the equator; dense tropical rain forest in central river basin and eastern highlands; the narrow strip of land that controls the lower Congo River is the DRC's only outlet to the South Atlantic Ocean
note 2: because of its speed, cataracts, rapids, and turbulence the Congo River, most of which flows through the DRC, has never been accurately measured along much of its length; nonetheless, it is conceded to be the deepest river in the world; estimates of its greatest depth vary between 220 and 250 meters

PEOPLE AND SOCIETY

Population: *total:* 115,403,027
male: 57,688,160
female: 57,714,867 (2024 est.)
comparison rankings: female 14; male 14; total 14

Nationality: *noun:* Congolese (singular and plural)
adjective: Congolese or Congo

Ethnic groups: more than 200 African ethnic groups of which the majority are Bantu; the four largest groups - Mongo, Luba, Kongo (all Bantu), and the Mangbetu-Azande (Hamitic) - make up about 45% of the population

Languages: French (official), Lingala (a trade language), Kingwana (a dialect of Kiswahili or Swahili), Kikongo, Tshiluba
major-language sample(s):
Buku oyo ya bosembo ya Mokili Mobimba Ezali na Makanisi ya Liboso Mpenza. (Lingala)

Religions: Christian 93/1% (Roman Catholic 29.9%, Protestant 26.7%, other Christian 36.5%), Kimbanguist 2.8%, Muslim 1.3%, other (includes syncretic sects and indigenous beliefs) 1.2%, none 1.3%, unspecified 0.2% (2014 est.)

Demographic profile: Despite a wealth of fertile soil, hydroelectric power potential, and mineral resources, the Democratic Republic of the Congo (DRC) struggles with many socioeconomic problems, including high infant and maternal mortality rates, malnutrition, poor vaccination coverage, lack of access to improved water sources and sanitation, and frequent and early fertility. Ongoing conflict, mismanagement of resources, and a lack of investment have resulted in food insecurity; almost 25% of children under the age of 5 were malnourished as of 2018. The overall coverage of basic public services – education, health, sanitation, and potable water – is very limited and piecemeal, with substantial regional and rural/urban disparities. Fertility remains high at more than 5 children per woman and is likely to remain high because of the low use of contraception and the cultural preference for larger families.

The DRC is a source and host country for refugees. Between 2012 and 2014, more than 119,000 Congolese refugees returned from the Republic of Congo to the relative stability of northwest DRC, but more than 1 million Congolese refugees and asylum seekers were hosted by neighboring countries as of December 2022. In addition, an estimated 5.5 million Congolese were internally displaced as of October 2022, the vast majority fleeing violence between rebel group and Congolese armed forces. Thousands of refugees have come to the DRC from neighboring countries, including Rwanda, the Central African Republic, South Sudan, and Burundi.

Age structure: *0-14 years:* 45.7% (male 26,584,268/ female 26,208,891)
15-64 years: 51.8% (male 29,845,450/female 29,884,958)
65 years and over: 2.5% (2024 est.) (male 1,258,442/ female 1,621,018)

Dependency ratios: *total dependency ratio:* 98
youth dependency ratio: 92.1
elderly dependency ratio: 5.9
potential support ratio: 17.1 (2021 est.)

Median age: *total:* 16.9 years (2024 est.)
male: 16.7 years
female: 17 years
comparison ranking: total 224

Population growth rate: 3.11% (2024 est.)
comparison ranking: 7

Birth rate: 39.2 births/1,000 population (2024 est.)
comparison ranking: 6

Death rate: 7.6 deaths/1,000 population (2024 est.)
comparison ranking: 98

Net migration rate: -0.6 migrant(s)/1,000 population (2024 est.)
comparison ranking: 127

Population distribution: urban clusters are spread throughout the country, particularly in the northeast along the border with Uganda, Rwanda, and Burundi; the largest city is the capital, Kinshasha, located in the west along the Congo River; the south is least densely populated as shown in this population distribution map

Urbanization: *urban population:* 47.4% of total population (2023)
rate of urbanization: 4.33% annual rate of change (2020-25 est.)

Major urban areas - population: 16.316 million KINSHASA (capital), 2.892 million Mbuji-Mayi, 2.812 million Lubumbashi, 1.664 million Kananga, 1.423 million Kisangani, 1.249 million Bukavu (2023)

Sex ratio: *at birth:* 1.03 male(s)/female
0-14 years: 1.01 male(s)/female
15-64 years: 1 male(s)/female
65 years and over: 0.78 male(s)/female
total population: 1 male(s)/female (2024 est.)

Mother's mean age at first birth: 19.9 years (2013/14 est.)
note: data represents median age at first birth among women 20-49

Maternal mortality ratio: 547 deaths/100,000 live births (2020 est.)
comparison ranking: 11

Infant mortality rate: *total:* 57.4 deaths/1,000 live births (2024 est.)
male: 62.9 deaths/1,000 live births
female: 51.9 deaths/1,000 live births
comparison ranking: total 11

Life expectancy at birth: *total population:* 62.6 years (2024 est.)
male: 60.7 years
female: 64.6 years

comparison ranking: total population 215

Total fertility rate: 5.49 children born/woman (2024 est.)
comparison ranking: 3

Gross reproduction rate: 2.7 (2024 est.)

Contraceptive prevalence rate: 28.1% (2017/18)

Drinking water source: *improved: urban:* 88.8% of population
rural: 34.7% of population
total: 59.4% of population
unimproved: urban: 11.2% of population
rural: 65.3% of population
total: 40.6% of population (2020 est.)

Current health expenditure: 4.1% of GDP (2020)

Physician density: 0.38 physicians/1,000 population (2018)

Sanitation facility access: *improved: urban:* 53.4% of population
rural: 20.5% of population
total: 35.5% of population
unimproved: urban: 46.6% of population
rural: 79.5% of population
total: 64.5% of population (2020 est.)

Obesity - adult prevalence rate: 6.7% (2016)
comparison ranking: 164

Alcohol consumption per capita: *total:* 0.56 liters of pure alcohol (2019 est.)
beer: 0.5 liters of pure alcohol (2019 est.)
wine: 0.01 liters of pure alcohol (2019 est.)
spirits: 0.05 liters of pure alcohol (2019 est.)
other alcohols: 0 liters of pure alcohol (2019 est.)
comparison ranking: total 161

Tobacco use: *total:* 12.8% (2020 est.)
male: 22.7% (2020 est.)
female: 2.9% (2020 est.)
comparison ranking: total 118

Children under the age of 5 years underweight: 23.1% (2017/18)
comparison ranking: 7

Currently married women (ages 15-49): 55.3% (2023 est.)

Child marriage: *women married by age 15:* 8.4%
women married by age 18: 29.1%
men married by age 18: 5.6% (2018 est.)

Education expenditures: 2.7% of GDP (2021 est.)
comparison ranking: 171

Literacy: *definition:* age 15 and over can read and write French, Lingala, Kingwana, or Tshiluba
total population: 80%
male: 89.5%
female: 70.8% (2021)

School life expectancy (primary to tertiary education): *total:* 11 years
male: 10 years
female: 9 years (2013)

ENVIRONMENT

Environment - current issues: poaching threatens wildlife populations; water pollution; deforestation (forests endangered by fires set to clear the land for agricultural purposes; forests also used as a source of fuel); soil erosion; mining (diamonds, gold, coltan - a mineral used in creating capacitors for electronic devices) causing environmental damage

Environment - international agreements: *party to:* Biodiversity, Climate Change, Climate Change-Kyoto Protocol, Climate Change-Paris Agreement, Comprehensive Nuclear Test Ban, Desertification, Endangered Species, Hazardous Wastes, Law of the Sea, Marine Dumping-London Convention, Nuclear Test Ban, Ozone Layer Protection, Tropical Timber 2006, Wetlands
signed, but not ratified: Environmental Modification

Climate: tropical; hot and humid in equatorial river basin; cooler and drier in southern highlands; cooler and wetter in eastern highlands; north of Equator - wet season (April to October), dry season (December to February); south of Equator - wet season (November to March), dry season (April to October)

Urbanization: *urban population:* 47.4% of total population (2023)
rate of urbanization: 4.33% annual rate of change (2020-25 est.)

Food insecurity: *widespread lack of access: due to internal conflict in eastern regions and high food prices* - according to an October 2022 analysis, 24.5 million people were projected to experience acute food insecurity between January and June 2023; this is due to the intensification of the conflict in the northeastern provinces, which, among other factors, has prevented completion of the harvests and likely will reduce food availability in the months to come (2023)

Revenue from forest resources: 8.72% of GDP (2018 est.)
comparison ranking: 6

Revenue from coal: 0% of GDP (2018 est.)
comparison ranking: 90

Air pollutants: *particulate matter emissions:* 31.58 micrograms per cubic meter (2019 est.)
carbon dioxide emissions: 2.02 megatons (2016 est.)
methane emissions: 61.24 megatons (2020 est.)

Waste and recycling: *municipal solid waste generated annually:* 14,385,226 tons (2016 est.)
municipal solid waste recycled annually: 704,876 tons (2005 est.)
percent of municipal solid waste recycled: 4.9% (2005 est.)

Major lakes (area sq km): *fresh water lake(s):* Lake Tanganyika (shared with Burundi, Tanzania, and Zambia) - 32,000 sq km; Lake Albert (shared with Uganda) - 5,590 sq km; Lake Mweru (shared with Zambia) - 4,350 sq km; Lac Mai-Ndombe - 2,300 sq km; Lake Kivu (shared with Rwanda) - 2,220 sq km; Lake Edward (shared with Uganda) - 2,150 sq km; Lac Tumba - 500 sq km; Lac Upemba - 530 sq km

Major rivers (by length in km): Zaïre (Congo) river mouth (shared with Zambia [s], Angola, and Republic of Congo) - 4,700 km; Ubangi river mouth (shared with Central African Republic [s] and Republic of Congo) - 2,270 km note – [s] after country name indicates river source; [m] after country name indicates river mouth

Major watersheds (area sq km):Atlantic Ocean drainage: Congo (3,730,881 sq km), *(Mediterranean Sea)* Nile (3,254,853 sq km)

Indian Ocean drainage: Zambezi (1,332,412 sq km)

Major aquifers: Congo Basin

Total water withdrawal: *municipal:* 460 million cubic meters (2020 est.)
industrial: 150 million cubic meters (2020 est.)
agricultural: 70 million cubic meters (2020 est.)

Total renewable water resources: 1.29 trillion cubic meters (2020 est.)

GOVERNMENT

Country name: *conventional long form:* Democratic Republic of the Congo
conventional short form: DRC
local long form: République démocratique du Congo
local short form: RDC
former: Congo Free State, Belgian Congo, Congo/Leopoldville, Congo/Kinshasa, Zaire
abbreviation: DRC (or DROC)
etymology: named for the Congo River, most of which lies within the DRC; the river name derives from Kongo, a Bantu kingdom that occupied its mouth and whose name stems from its people the Bakongo, meaning "hunters"

Government type: semi-presidential republic

Capital: *name:* Kinshasa
geographic coordinates: 4 19 S, 15 18 E
time difference: UTC+1 (6 hours ahead of Washington, DC, during Standard Time)
time zone note: the DRC has two time zones
etymology: founded as a trading post in 1881 and named Leopoldville in honor of King LEOPOLD II of the Belgians, who controlled the Congo Free State, the vast central African territory that became the Democratic Republic of the Congo in 1960; in 1966, Leopoldville was renamed Kinshasa, after a village of that name that once stood near the site

Administrative divisions: 26 provinces (provinces, singular - province); Bas-Uele (Lower Uele), Equateur, Haut-Katanga (Upper Katanga), Haut-Lomami (Upper Lomami), Haut-Uele (Upper Uele), Ituri, Kasai, Kasai-Central, Kasai-Oriental (East Kasai), Kinshasa, Kongo Central, Kwango, Kwilu, Lomami, Lualaba, Mai-Ndombe, Maniema, Mongala, Nord-Kivu (North Kivu), Nord- Ubangi (North Ubangi), Sankuru, Sud-Kivu (South Kivu), Sud-Ubangi (South Ubangi), Tanganyika, Tshopo, Tshuapa

Independence: 30 June 1960 (from Belgium)

National holiday: Independence Day, 30 June (1960)

Legal system: civil law system primarily based on Belgian law, but also customary and tribal law

Constitution: *history:* several previous; latest adopted 13 May 2005, approved by referendum 18-19 December 2005, promulgated 18 February 2006
amendments: proposed by the president of the republic, by the government, by either house of Parliament, or by public petition; agreement on the substance of a proposed bill requires absolute majority vote in both houses; passage requires a referendum only if both houses in joint meeting fail to achieve three-fifths majority vote; constitutional articles, including the form of government, universal suffrage, judicial independence, political pluralism, and personal freedoms, cannot be amended; amended 2011

International law organization participation: accepts compulsory ICJ jurisdiction with reservations; accepts ICCt jurisdiction

Citizenship: *citizenship by birth:* no
citizenship by descent only: at least one parent must be a citizen of the Democratic Republic of the Congo
dual citizenship recognized: no
residency requirement for naturalization: 5 years

Suffrage: 18 years of age; universal and compulsory

Executive branch: *chief of state:* President Felix TSHISEKEDI (since 20 January 2024)
head of government: Prime Minister Judith SUMINWA Tuluka (since 29 May 2024)

cabinet: Ministers of State appointed by the president
elections/appointments: president directly elected by simple majority vote for a 5-year term (eligible for a second term); election last held on 20 December 2023 (next to be held on 20 December 2028); prime minister appointed by the president
election results:
2023: Felix TSHISEKEDI reelected president; percent of vote - Felix TSHISEKEDI (UDPS) 73.3%, Moise KATUMBI (Ensemble) 18.8%, Martin FAYULU (ECIDE) 5.3%, other 2.6%
2018: Felix TSHISEKEDI elected president; percent of vote - Felix TSHISEKEDI (UDPS) 38.6%, Martin FAYULU (Lamuka coalition) 34.8%, Emmanuel Ramazani SHADARY (PPRD) 23.9%, other 2.7%; note - election marred by serious voting irregularities

Legislative branch: *description:* bicameral Parliament or Parlement consists of:
Senate (109 seats; 109 members to include 108 indirectly elected by provincial assemblies by proportional representation vote to serve 5-year terms and a former president, appointed for life)
National Assembly (500 seats; 439 members directly elected in multi-seat constituencies by proportional representation vote and 61 directly elected in single-seat constituencies by simple majority vote; members serve 5-year terms)
elections: Senate - last held on 29 April 2024 (next to be held 29 April 2029)
National Assembly - last held on 20 December 2023 (next to be held in December 2028)
election results: Senate - percent of vote by party - NA; seats by party - UDPS 15, AFDC-A 6, AB 5, A24 4, AACPG 4, MLC 4, A/VK2018 3, ANB 3, Ensemble 3, 2ATDC 2, A/A-UNC 2, AA/C 2, AAAP 2, AVC-A 2, FPAV 2. A/B50 1, A1 1, A3A 1, AAAD 1, AAeC 1, ACP-A 1, AN 1, APCF 1, ARDEV-A 1, ART&A 1, ATVA 1, AV 1, CDER 1, CFC 1, MSL 1, independent 26; composition- men 84, women 16, percentage women 15.8%
National Assembly - percent of vote by party- NA; seats by party - PPRD 62, UDPS 41, PPPD 29, MSR 27, MLC 22, PALU 19, UNC 17, ARC 16, AFDC 15, ECT 11, RRC 11, other 214 (includes numerous political parties that won 10 or fewer seats and 2 constituencies where voting was halted), independent 16; composition - men 415, women 62, percent of women 13%; total Parliament percentage women 13.5%

Judicial branch: *highest court(s):* Court of Cassation or Cour de Cassation (consists of 26 justices and organized into legislative and judiciary sections); Constitutional Court (consists of 9 judges)
judge selection and term of office: Court of Cassation judges nominated by the Judicial Service Council, an independent body of public prosecutors and selected judges of the lower courts; judge tenure NA; Constitutional Court judges - 3 nominated by the president, 3 by the Judicial Service Council, and 3 by the legislature; judges appointed by the president to serve 9-year non-renewable terms with one-third of the membership renewed every 3 years
subordinate courts: State Security Court; Court of Appeals (organized into administrative and judiciary sections); Tribunal de Grande; magistrates' courts; customary courts

Political parties: Christian Democrat Party or PDC
Congolese Rally for Democracy or RCD
Convention of Christian Democrats or CDC
Engagement for Citizenship and Development or ECIDE
Forces of Renewal or FR
Movement for the Liberation of the Congo or MLC
Nouvel Elan
Our Congo or CNB ("Congo Na Biso")
People's Party for Reconstruction and Democracy or PPRD
Social Movement for Renewal or MSR
Together for Change ("Ensemble")
Unified Lumumbist Party or PALU
Union for the Congolese Nation or UNC
Union for Democracy and Social Progress or UDPS

International organization participation: ACP, AfDB, AU, CEMAC, CEPGL, COMESA, EITI (compliant country), FAO, G-24, G-77, IAEA, IBRD, ICAO, ICC (NGOs), ICCt, ICRM, IDA, IFAD, IFC, IFRCS, IHO, ILO, IMF, IMO, Interpol, IOC, IOM, IPU, ISO, ITSO, ITU, ITUC (NGOs), LCBC (observer), MIGA, NAM, OIF, OPCW, PCA, SADC, UN, UNCTAD, UNESCO, UNHCR, UNIDO, UNWTO, UPU, WCO, WFTU (NGOs), WHO, WIPO, WMO, WTO

Diplomatic representation in the US: *chief of mission:* Ambassador (vacant); Chargé d'Affaires Michael SHAKU YUMI (since 1 August 2024)
chancery: 1100 Connecticut Avenue NW, Suite 725, Washington DC 20036
telephone: [1] (202) 234-7690
FAX: [1] (202) 234-2609
email address and website:
ambassade@ambardcusa.org
https://www.ambardcusa.org/
representative office: New York

Diplomatic representation from the US: *chief of mission:* Ambassador Lucy TAMLYN (since 6 February 2023)
embassy: 310 Avenue des Aviateurs, Kinshasa, Gombe
mailing address: 2220 Kinshasa Place, Washington DC 20521-2220
telephone: [243] 081 556-0151
FAX: [243] 81 556-0175
email address and website:
ACSKinshasa@state.gov
https://cd.usembassy.gov/

Flag description: sky blue field divided diagonally from the lower hoist corner to upper fly corner by a red stripe bordered by two narrow yellow stripes; a yellow, five-pointed star appears in the upper hoist corner; blue represents peace and hope, red the blood of the country's martyrs, and yellow the country's wealth and prosperity; the star symbolizes unity and the brilliant future for the country

National symbol(s): leopard; national colors: sky blue, red, yellow

National anthem: *name:* "Debout Congolaise" (Arise Congolese)
lyrics/music: Joseph LUTUMBA/Simon-Pierre BOKA di Mpasi Londi
note: adopted 1960; replaced when the country was known as Zaire; but readopted in 1997

National heritage: *total World Heritage Sites:* 5 (all natural)
selected World Heritage Site locales: Garamba National Park; Kahuzi-Biega National Park; Okapi Wildlife Reserve; Salonga National Park; Virunga National Park

ECONOMY

Economic overview: very poor, large, natural resource-rich sub-Saharan country; possesses the world's second largest rainforest; increasing Chinese extractive sector trade; massive decrease in government investments; increasing current account deficit and public debts

Real GDP (purchasing power parity): $154.012 billion (2023 est.)
$141.867 billion (2022 est.)
$130.244 billion (2021 est.)
note: data in 2021 dollars
comparison ranking: 82

Real GDP growth rate: 8.56% (2023 est.)
8.92% (2022 est.)
6.2% (2021 est.)
note: annual GDP % growth based on constant local currency
comparison ranking: 8

Real GDP per capita: $1,500 (2023 est.)
$1,400 (2022 est.)
$1,400 (2021 est.)
note: data in 2021 dollars
comparison ranking: 219

GDP (official exchange rate): $66.383 billion (2023 est.)
note: data in current dollars at official exchange rate

Inflation rate (consumer prices): 41.5% (2017 est.)
2.89% (2016 est.)
0.74% (2015 est.)
note: annual % change based on consumer prices
comparison ranking: 212

Credit ratings: Moody's rating: Caa1 (2019)

Standard & Poors rating: CCC+ (2017)
note: The year refers to the year in which the current credit rating was first obtained.

GDP - composition, by sector of origin: *agriculture:* 17.4% (2023 est.)
industry: 46.5% (2023 est.)
services: 33.5% (2023 est.)
note: figures may not total 100% due to non-allocated consumption not captured in sector-reported data
comparison rankings: services 206; industry 19; agriculture 46

GDP - composition, by end use: *household consumption:* 62.7% (2023 est.)
government consumption: 7.9% (2023 est.)
investment in fixed capital: 31.7% (2023 est.)
investment in inventories: 0.4% (2023 est.)
exports of goods and services: 44.2% (2023 est.)
imports of goods and services: -47% (2023 est.)
note: figures may not total 100% due to rounding or gaps in data collection

Agricultural products: cassava, plantains, sugarcane, oil palm fruit, maize, rice, root vegetables, bananas, sweet potatoes, groundnuts (2022)
note: top ten agricultural products based on tonnage

Industries: mining (copper, cobalt, gold, diamonds, coltan, zinc, tin, tungsten), mineral processing, consumer products (textiles, plastics, footwear, cigarettes), metal products, processed foods and beverages, timber, cement, commercial ship repair

Industrial production growth rate: 14.56% (2023 est.)
note: annual % change in industrial value added based on constant local currency
comparison ranking: 5

Labor force: 35.983 million (2023 est.)
note: number of people ages 15 or older who are employed or seeking work
comparison ranking: 17

Unemployment rate: 4.54% (2023 est.)

4.59% (2022 est.)
5.27% (2021 est.)
note: % of labor force seeking employment
comparison ranking: 88

Youth unemployment rate (ages 15-24): *total:* 8.6% (2023 est.)
male: 10.9% (2023 est.)
female: 6.7% (2023 est.)
note: % of labor force ages 15-24 seeking employment
comparison ranking: total 147

Population below poverty line: 63% (2014 est.)

Gini Index coefficient - distribution of family income: 44.7 (2020 est.)
comparison ranking: 23

Household income or consumption by percentage share: *lowest 10%:* 2.1% (2020 est.)
highest 10%: 35.8% (2020 est.)

Remittances: 2.05% of GDP (2023 est.)
2.05% of GDP (2022 est.)
2.44% of GDP (2021 est.)
note: personal transfers and compensation between resident and non-resident individuals/households/entities

Budget: *revenues:* $7.524 billion (2021 est.)
expenditures: $5.109 billion (2021 est.)
note: central government revenues and expenses (excluding grants/extrabudgetary units/social security funds) converted to US dollars at average official exchange rate for year indicated

Public debt: 15.99% of GDP (2022 est.)
comparison ranking: 193

Taxes and other revenues: 11.41% (of GDP) (2022 est.)
comparison ranking: 171

Current account balance: -$587.407 million (2021 est.)
-$1.052 billion (2020 est.)
-$1.693 billion (2019 est.)
note: balance of payments - net trade and primary/secondary income in current dollars
comparison ranking: 124

Exports: $22.354 billion (2021 est.)
$13.932 billion (2020 est.)
$15.173 billion (2019 est.)
note: balance of payments - exports of goods and services in current dollars
comparison ranking: 87

Exports - partners: China 55%, Singapore 5%, UAE 5%, Hong Kong 4%, Tanzania 4% (2022)
note: top five export partners based on percentage share of exports

Exports - commodities: refined copper, cobalt, copper ore, raw copper, crude petroleum (2022)
note: top five export commodities based on value in dollars

Imports: $22.193 billion (2021 est.)
$14.557 billion (2020 est.)
$16.892 billion (2019 est.)
note: balance of payments - imports of goods and services in current dollars
comparison ranking: 94

Imports - partners: China 33%, Zambia 10%, South Africa 10%, UAE 5%, India 4% (2022)
note: top five import partners based on percentage share of imports

Imports - commodities: refined petroleum, sulfur, plastic products, trucks, stone processing machines (2022)
note: top five import commodities based on value in dollars

Reserves of foreign exchange and gold: $3.467 billion (2021 est.)
$747.655 million (2020 est.)
$1.194 billion (2019 est.)
note: holdings of gold (year-end prices)/foreign exchange/special drawing rights in current dollars
comparison ranking: 109

Debt - external: $5.383 billion (2022 est.)
note: present value of external debt in current US dollars
comparison ranking: 52

Exchange rates: Congolese francs (CDF) per US dollar -

Exchange rates: 1,989.391 (2021 est.)
1,851.122 (2020 est.)
1,647.76 (2019 est.)
1,622.524 (2018 est.)
1,464.418 (2017 est.)

ENERGY

Electricity access: *electrification - total population:* 21.5% (2022 est.)
electrification - urban areas: 45.3%
electrification - rural areas: 1%

Electricity: *installed generating capacity:* 2.904 million kW (2022 est.)
consumption: 11.252 billion kWh (2022 est.)
exports: 62 million kWh (2022 est.)
imports: 1.476 billion kWh (2022 est.)
transmission/distribution losses: 1.201 billion kWh (2022 est.)
comparison rankings: transmission/distribution losses 105; imports 69; exports 90; consumption 97; installed generating capacity 109

Electricity generation sources: *solar:* 0.1% of total installed capacity (2022 est.)
hydroelectricity: 99.7% of total installed capacity (2022 est.)
biomass and waste: 0.3% of total installed capacity (2022 est.)

Coal: *consumption:* 23,000 metric tons (2022 est.)
exports: (2022 est.) less than 1 metric ton
imports: 23,000 metric tons (2022 est.)
proven reserves: 987.999 million metric tons (2022 est.)

Petroleum: *total petroleum production:* 19,000 bbl/day (2023 est.)
refined petroleum consumption: 26,000 bbl/day (2022 est.)
crude oil estimated reserves: 180 million barrels (2021 est.)

Natural gas: *production:* 380,000 cubic meters (2019 est.)
consumption: 380,000 cubic meters (2019 est.)
proven reserves: 991.09 million cubic meters (2021 est.)

Carbon dioxide emissions: 3.86 million metric tonnes of CO2 (2022 est.)
from coal and metallurgical coke: 53,000 metric tonnes of CO2 (2022 est.)
from petroleum and other liquids: 3.807 million metric tonnes of CO2 (2022 est.)
from consumed natural gas: 1,000 metric tonnes of CO2 (2019 est.)
comparison ranking: total emissions 143

Energy consumption per capita: 970,000 Btu/person (2022 est.)
comparison ranking: 192

COMMUNICATIONS

Telephones - fixed lines: *total subscriptions:* 0 (2021 est.) less than 1
subscriptions per 100 inhabitants: (2021 est.) less than 1
comparison ranking: total subscriptions 224

Telephones - mobile cellular: *total subscriptions:* 49.844 million (2022 est.)
subscriptions per 100 inhabitants: 50 (2022 est.)
comparison ranking: total subscriptions 33

Telecommunication systems: *general assessment:* the telecom system remains one of the least developed in the region; the government can only loosely regulate the sector; the investment made in infrastructure is derived from donor countries or from the efforts of foreign (particularly Chinese) companies and banks; efforts have been made to improve the regulation of the telecom sector; the limited fixed-line infrastructure has become the principal providers of basic telecom services; the development of the DRC's internet and broadband market has been held back by the poorly developed national and international infrastructure; the country was finally connected to international bandwidth through the WACS submarine cable in 2013; breakages in the WACS cable have exposed the vulnerability of international bandwidth, which is still limited; the Equiano submarine cable, and has also completed a 5,000km cable running through the DRC to link to cable systems landing in countries facing the Atlantic and Indian Oceans; the first commercial LTE networks were launched in May 2018 soon after LTE licenses were issued; mobile operators are keen to develop mobile data services, capitalizing on the growth of smartphones usage; there has been some progress with updating technologies, most of the GSM network has been upgraded to 3G by 2021 (2022)
domestic: inadequate fixed-line infrastructure with fixed-line connections less than 1 per 100 persons; mobile-cellular subscriptions over 49 per 100 persons (2021)
international: country code - 243; ACE and WACS submarine cables to West and South Africa and Europe; satellite earth station - 1 Intelsat (Atlantic Ocean) (2019)

Broadcast media: state-owned TV broadcast station with near national coverage; more than a dozen privately owned TV stations - 2 with near national coverage; 2 state-owned radio stations are supplemented by more than 100 private radio stations; transmissions of at least 2 international broadcasters are available

Internet country code: .cd

Internet users: *total:* 21,102,720 (2021 est.)
percent of population: 23.2% (2021 est.)
comparison ranking: total 42

Broadband - fixed subscriptions: *total:* 31,000 (2020 est.)
subscriptions per 100 inhabitants: 0.03 (2020 est.)
comparison ranking: total 153

TRANSPORTATION

National air transport system: *number of registered air carriers:* 8 (2020)

inventory of registered aircraft operated by air carriers: 13
annual passenger traffic on registered air carriers: 932,043 (2018)
annual freight traffic on registered air carriers: 890,000 (2018) mt-km

Civil aircraft registration country code prefix: 9Q

Airports: 272 (2024)
comparison ranking: 25

Heliports: 1 (2024)

Pipelines: 62 km gas, 77 km oil, 756 km refined products (2013)

Railways: *total:* 4,007 km (2014)
narrow gauge: 3,882 km (2014) 1.067-m gauge (858 km electrified)
125 1.000-mm gauge
comparison ranking: total 47

Roadways: *total:* 152,373 km
paved: 3,047 km
unpaved: 149,326 km
urban: 7,400 km
non-urban: 144,973 km (2015)
comparison ranking: total 34

Waterways: 15,000 km (2011) (including the Congo River, its tributaries, and unconnected lakes)
comparison ranking: 9

Merchant marine: *total:* 24 (2023)
by type: general cargo 5, oil tanker 2, other 17
comparison ranking: total 143

Ports: *total ports:* 3 (2024)
large: 0
medium: 0
small: 2
very small: 1
ports with oil terminals: 2
key ports: Banana, Boma, Matadi

MILITARY AND SECURITY

Military and security forces: Armed Forces of the Democratic Republic of the Congo (Forces d'Armees de la Republique Democratique du Congo, FARDC): Land Forces, National Navy (La Marine Nationale), Congolese Air Force (Force Aerienne Congolaise, FAC); Republican Guard

Ministry of Interior: Congolese National Police (2024)

note: the Republican Guard is a division-size element with armored and infantry units; it is regarded as the country's most capable unit and is under the direct control of the president

Military expenditures: 1.2% of GDP (2023 est.)
0.7% of GDP (2022 est.)
0.7% of GDP (2021 est.)
0.7% of GDP (2020 est.)
0.9% of GDP (2019 est.)
comparison ranking: 113

Military and security service personnel strengths: estimates vary; up to 140,000 active troops, including approximately 10,000 Republican Guard (2023)

Military equipment inventories and acquisitions: the FARDC is equipped mostly with Soviet-era and older French weapons and equipment; in 2024, the DRC signed an agreement with China for the provision of military equipment (2024)

Military service age and obligation: 18-45 years of age for voluntary military service for men and women; 18-45 years of age for compulsory military service for men; it is unclear how much conscription is used (2023)
note: in eastern Congo, fighters from armed groups, including some associated with government security forces, have been accused of forced recruitment of child soldiers

Military - note: the FARDC's primary focus is internal security and conducting operations against rebels and other illegal armed groups (IOGs); while it is large on paper, the FARDC is widely assessed to suffer from insufficient training, low equipment readiness, poor morale and leadership, ill-discipline, and widespread corruption; it was created out of the armed factions of the Congo wars that ended in 2003, incorporating various militia, paramilitary, and rebel formations; the DRC's most effective military force, the Republican Guard, is overseen by the office of the presidency rather than the FARDC and focuses largely on protecting the president and government institutions and enforcing internal security
the FARDC is actively conducting operations against a variety of IOGs operating in the DRC, particularly in the eastern provinces of Ituri, North Kivu, and South Kivu, where more than 15 significant and cohesive IOGs operate; there is also IOG-related violence in Maniema, Kasai, Kasai Central, and Tanganyika provinces; some estimates place over 100 IOGs operating in the country, including organized militias, such as the Nduma Defense of Congo-Renewal (NDC-R), which controls a large portion of North Kivu; Mai Mai groups (local militias that operate variously as self-defense networks and criminal rackets); and foreign-origin groups seeking safe haven and resources, such as the Ugandan-origin Allied Democratic Forces (ADF; aka Islamic State of Iraq and ash-Sham in the DRC), the Democratic Forces for the Liberation of Rwanda (FDLR), multiple groups originating from Burundi, the Lords Resistance Army (LRA), and the March 23 Movement (aka M23 or Congolese Revolutionary Army), which the DRC has accused Rwanda of backing; the FARDC has been accused of collaborating with some IOGs, such as the NDC-R
the UN Organization Stabilization Mission in the Democratic Republic of the Congo (MONUSCO) has operated in the central and eastern parts of the country since 1999; as of 2023, MONUSCO had around 14,000 personnel assigned, but it was drawing down its forces towards a complete withdrawal at the request of the DRC Government; MONUSCO includes a Force Intervention Brigade (FIB; three infantry battalions, plus artillery and special forces), the first ever UN peacekeeping force specifically tasked to carry out targeted offensive operations to neutralize and disarm groups considered a threat to state authority and civilian security (2024)

TERRORISM

Terrorist group(s): Islamic State of Iraq and ash-Sham – Democratic Republic of the Congo (ISIS-DRC)
note: details about the history, aims, leadership, organization, areas of operation, tactics, targets, weapons, size, and sources of support of the group(s) appear(s) in the Terrorism reference guide

TRANSNATIONAL ISSUES

Refugees and internally displaced persons: *refugees (country of origin):* 208,328 (Rwanda), 53,297 (South Sudan) (refugees and asylum seekers), 49,836 (Burundi) (2023); 212,211 (Central African Republic) (2024)
IDPs: 6.38 million (fighting between government forces and rebels since mid-1990s; conflict in Kasai region since 2016) (2023)

Illicit drugs: country of origin of methamphetamine destined for overseas markets;

CONGO, REPUBLIC OF THE

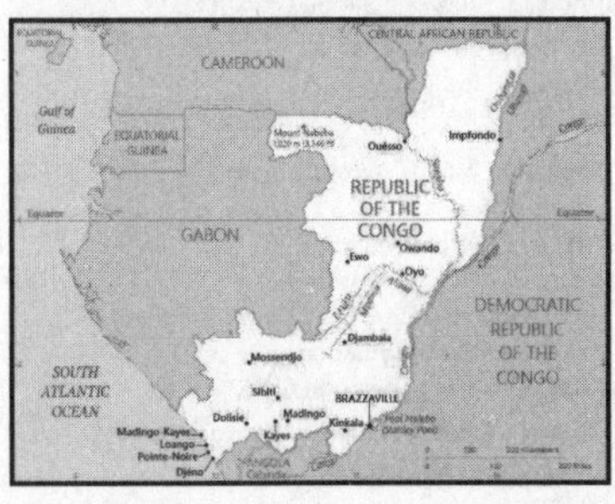

INTRODUCTION

Background: Upon independence in 1960, the former French region of Middle Congo became the Republic of the Congo. From 1968 to 1992, the country was named the People's Republic of the Congo. A quarter-century of experimentation with Marxism was abandoned in 1990, and a democratically elected government took office in 1992, at which time the country reverted to "the Republic of the Congo" name. A two-year civil war that ended in 1999 restored to power former President Denis SASSOU-Nguesso, who had ruled from 1979 to 1992. A new constitution adopted three years later provided for a multiparty system and a seven-year presidential term, and the next elections retained SASSOU-Nguesso. After a year of renewed fighting, SASSOU-Nguesso and southern-based rebel groups agreed to a final peace accord in 2003. SASSOU-Nguesso was reelected in 2009 and, after passing a constitutional referendum allowing him to run for additional terms, was reelected again in 2016 and 2021. The Republic of the Congo is one of Africa's largest petroleum producers.

GEOGRAPHY

Location: Central Africa, bordering the South Atlantic Ocean, between Angola and Gabon

Geographic coordinates: 1 00 S, 15 00 E

Map references: Africa

Area: *total:* 342,000 sq km
land: 341,500 sq km
water: 500 sq km
comparison ranking: total 65

Area - comparative: slightly smaller than Montana; about twice the size of Florida

Land boundaries: *total:* 5,554 km
border countries (5): Angola 231 km; Cameroon 494 km; Central African Republic 487 km; Democratic Republic of the Congo 1,775 km; Gabon 2,567 km

Coastline: 169 km

Maritime claims: *territorial sea:* 12 nm
contiguous zone: 24 nm
exclusive economic zone: 200 nm

Climate: tropical; rainy season (March to June); dry season (June to October); persistent high temperatures and humidity; particularly enervating climate astride the Equator

Terrain coastal plain, southern basin, central plateau, northern basin

Elevation: *highest point:* Mont Nabeba 1,020 m
lowest point: Atlantic Ocean 0 m
mean elevation: 430 m

Natural resources: petroleum, timber, potash, lead, zinc, uranium, copper, phosphates, gold, magnesium, natural gas, hydropower

Land use: *agricultural land:* 31.1% (2018 est.)
arable land: 1.6% (2018 est.)
permanent crops: 0.2% (2018 est.)
permanent pasture: 29.3% (2018 est.)
forest: 65.6% (2018 est.)
other: 3.3% (2018 est.)

Irrigated land: 20 sq km (2012)

Major rivers (by length in km): Oubangui (Ubangi) (shared with Central African Republic [s] and Democratic Republic of Congo [m]) - 2,270 km
note – [s] after country name indicates river source; [m] after country name indicates river mouth

Major watersheds (area sq km): Atlantic Ocean drainage: Congo (3,730,881 sq km)

Major aquifers: Congo Basin

Population distribution: the population is primarily located in the south, in and around the capital of Brazzaville as shown in this population distribution map

Natural hazards: seasonal flooding

Geography - note: about 70% of the population lives in Brazzaville, Pointe-Noire, or along the railroad between them

PEOPLE AND SOCIETY

Population: *total:* 6,097,665
male: 3,045,973
female: 3,051,692 (2024 est.)
comparison rankings: female 113; male 112; total 113

Nationality: *noun:* Congolese (singular and plural)
adjective: Congolese or Congo

Ethnic groups: Kongo (Bakongo) 40.5%, Teke 16.9%, Mbochi 13.1%, foreigner 8.2%, Sangha 5.6%, Mbere/Mbeti/Kele 4.4%, Punu 4.3%, Pygmy 1.6%, Oubanguiens 1.6%, Duma 1.5%, Makaa 1.3%, other and unspecified 1% (2014-15 est.)

Languages: French (official), French Lingala and Monokutuba (trade languages), many local languages and dialects (of which Kikongo is the most widespread)
major-language sample(s):
Buku oyo ya bosembo ya Mokili Mobimba Ezali na Makanisi ya Liboso Mpenza. (Lingala)

Religions: Roman Catholic 33.1%, Awakening Churches/Christian Revival 22.3%, Protestant 19.9%, Salutiste 2.2%, Muslim 1.6%, Kimbanguiste 1.5%, other 8.1%, none 11.3% (2007 est.)

Demographic profile: The Republic of the Congo is one of the most urbanized countries in Africa, with nearly 70% of Congolese living in urban areas. The population is concentrated in the southwest of the country, mainly in the capital Brazzaville, Pointe-Noire, and along the railway line that connects the two. The tropical jungles in the north of the country are sparsely populated. Most Congolese are Bantu, and most belong to one of four main ethnic groups, the Kongo, Teke, Mbochi, and Sangha, which consist of over 70 subgroups.

The Republic of Congo is in the early stages of a demographic transition, whereby a population shifts from high fertility and mortality rates to low fertility and mortality rates associated with industrialized societies. Its total fertility rate (TFR), the average number of children born per woman, remains high at 4.4 as of 2022. While its TFR has steadily decreased, the progress slowed beginning in about 1995. The slowdown in fertility reduction has delayed the demographic transition and Congo's potential to reap a demographic dividend, the economic boost that can occur when the share of the working-age population is larger than the dependent age groups.

The TFR differs significantly between urban and rural areas – 3.7 in urban areas versus 6.5 in rural areas. The TFR also varies among regions. The urban regions of Brazzaville and Pointe-Noire have much lower TFRs than other regions, which are predominantly or completely rural. The gap between desired fertility and actual fertility is also greatest in rural areas. Rural families may have more children to contribute to agricultural production and/or due to a lack of information about and access to contraception. Urban families may prefer to have fewer children because raising them is more expensive and balancing work and childcare may be more difficult. The number of births among teenage girls, the frequency of giving birth before the age of fifteen, and a lack of education are the most likely reasons for higher TFRs in rural areas. Although 90% of school-age children are enrolled in primary school, repetition and dropout rates are high and the quality of education is poor. Congolese women with no or little education start having children earlier and have more children in total than those with at least some secondary education.

Age structure: *0-14 years:* 37.8% (male 1,162,298/female 1,143,668)
15-64 years: 57.8% (male 1,770,337/female 1,756,925)
65 years and over: 4.3% (2024 est.) (male 113,338/female 151,099)

Dependency ratios: *total dependency ratio:* 78.8
youth dependency ratio: 74
elderly dependency ratio: 4.8
potential support ratio: 20.9 (2021 est.)

Median age: *total:* 20.7 years (2024 est.)
male: 20.5 years
female: 20.9 years
comparison ranking: total 200

Population growth rate: 2.38% (2024 est.)
comparison ranking: 23

Birth rate: 28.7 births/1,000 population (2024 est.)
comparison ranking: 30

Death rate: 4.8 deaths/1,000 population (2024 est.)
comparison ranking: 203

Net migration rate: -0.1 migrant(s)/1,000 population (2024 est.)
comparison ranking: 97

Population distribution: the population is primarily located in the south, in and around the capital of Brazzaville as shown in this population distribution map

Urbanization: *urban population:* 69.2% of total population (2023)
rate of urbanization: 3.19% annual rate of change (2020-25 est.)

Major urban areas - population: 2.638 million BRAZZAVILLE (capital), 1.336 million Pointe-Noire (2023)

Sex ratio: *at birth:* 1.03 male(s)/female
0-14 years: 1.02 male(s)/female
15-64 years: 1.01 male(s)/female
65 years and over: 0.75 male(s)/female
total population: 1 male(s)/female (2024 est.)

Mother's mean age at first birth: 19.6 years (2011/12 est.)
note: data represents median age at first birth among women 20-49

Maternal mortality ratio: 282 deaths/100,000 live births (2020 est.)
comparison ranking: 30

Infant mortality rate: *total:* 30.6 deaths/1,000 live births (2024 est.)
male: 33.5 deaths/1,000 live births
female: 27.7 deaths/1,000 live births
comparison ranking: total 48

Life expectancy at birth: *total population:* 72.9 years (2024 est.)
male: 71.5 years
female: 74.3 years
comparison ranking: total population 156

Total fertility rate: 3.79 children born/woman (2024 est.)
comparison ranking: 29

Gross reproduction rate: 1.87 (2024 est.)

Contraceptive prevalence rate: 30.1% (2014/15)

Drinking water source: *improved:* *urban:* 97.5% of population
rural: 56.4% of population
total: 84.2% of population
unimproved: *urban:* 2.5% of population
rural: 43.6% of population
total: 15.8% of population (2020 est.)

Current health expenditure: 4.5% of GDP (2020)

Physician density: 0.1 physicians/1,000 population (2018)

Sanitation facility access: *improved:* *urban:* 73.4% of population
rural: 15.1% of population
total: 54.7% of population
unimproved: *urban:* 26.6% of population
rural: 84.9% of population
total: 45.3% of population (2020 est.)

Obesity - adult prevalence rate: 9.6% (2016)
comparison ranking: 143

Alcohol consumption per capita: *total:* 5.74 liters of pure alcohol (2019 est.)

beer: 5.11 liters of pure alcohol (2019 est.)
wine: 0.1 liters of pure alcohol (2019 est.)
spirits: 0.52 liters of pure alcohol (2019 est.)
other alcohols: 0.01 liters of pure alcohol (2019 est.)
comparison ranking: total 75

Tobacco use: *total:* 14.5% (2020 est.)
male: 26.8% (2020 est.)
female: 2.1% (2020 est.)
comparison ranking: total 105

Children under the age of 5 years underweight: 12.3% (2014/15)
comparison ranking: 42

Currently married women (ages 15-49): 51.8% (2023 est.)

Child marriage: *women married by age 15:* 8.4%
women married by age 18: 29.1%
men married by age 18: 5.6% (2018 est.)

Education expenditures: 4.5% of GDP (2020 est.)
comparison ranking: 102

Literacy: *definition:* age 15 and over can read and write
total population: 80.6%
male: 85.9%
female: 75.4% (2021)

School life expectancy (primary to tertiary education): *total:* 11 years
male: 11 years
female: 11 years (2012)

ENVIRONMENT

Environment - current issues: air pollution from vehicle emissions; water pollution from raw sewage; tap water is not potable; deforestation; wildlife protection

Environment - international agreements: *party to:* Biodiversity, Climate Change, Climate Change-Kyoto Protocol, Climate Change-Paris Agreement, Desertification, Endangered Species, Hazardous Wastes, Law of the Sea, Marine Dumping-London Protocol, Ozone Layer Protection, Ship Pollution, Tropical Timber 2006, Wetlands
signed, but not ratified: none of the selected agreements

Climate: tropical; rainy season (March to June); dry season (June to October); persistent high temperatures and humidity; particularly enervating climate astride the Equator

Urbanization: *urban population:* 69.2% of total population (2023)
rate of urbanization: 3.19% annual rate of change (2020-25 est.)

Food insecurity: *severe localized food insecurity: due to floods* - above average rainfall amounts since November 2022 triggered flooding in December 2022 and January 2023 in central and northern parts of the country, displacing people; according to damage assessment reports, about 165,000 people have been affected in 23 districts in the departments of Cuvette, Likouala, Plateaux and Sangha (2023)

Revenue from forest resources: 3.17% of GDP (2018 est.)
comparison ranking: 23

Revenue from coal: 0% of GDP (2018 est.)
comparison ranking: 70

Air pollutants: *particulate matter emissions:* 29.48 micrograms per cubic meter (2019 est.)
carbon dioxide emissions: 3.28 megatons (2016 est.)
methane emissions: 2.24 megatons (2020 est.)

Waste and recycling: *municipal solid waste generated annually:* 451,200 tons (1993 est.)
municipal solid waste recycled annually: 118,214 tons (2005 est.)
percent of municipal solid waste recycled: 26.2% (2005 est.)

Major rivers (by length in km): Oubangui (Ubangi) (shared with Central African Republic [s] and Democratic Republic of Congo [m]) - 2,270 km
note – [s] after country name indicates river source; [m] after country name indicates river mouth

Major watersheds (area sq km): Atlantic Ocean drainage: Congo (3,730,881 sq km)

Major aquifers: Congo Basin

Total water withdrawal: *municipal:* 60 million cubic meters (2020 est.)
industrial: 20 million cubic meters (2020 est.)
agricultural: 4 million cubic meters (2017 est.)

Total renewable water resources: 832 billion cubic meters (2020 est.)

GOVERNMENT

Country name: *conventional long form:* Republic of the Congo
conventional short form: Congo (Brazzaville)
local long form: République du Congo
local short form: Congo
former: French Congo, Middle Congo, People's Republic of the Congo, Congo/Brazzaville
etymology: named for the Congo River, which makes up much of the country's eastern border; the river name derives from Kongo, a Bantu kingdom that occupied its mouth at the time of Portuguese discovery in the late 15th century and whose name stems from its people the Bakongo, meaning "hunters"

Government type: presidential republic

Capital: *name:* Brazzaville
geographic coordinates: 4 15 S, 15 17 E
time difference: UTC+1 (6 hours ahead of Washington, DC, during Standard Time)
etymology: named after the Italian-born French explorer and humanitarian, Pierre Savorgnan de BRAZZA (1852-1905), who promoted French colonial interests in central Africa and worked against slavery and the abuse of African laborers

Administrative divisions: 12 departments (departments, singular - department); Bouenza, Brazzaville, Cuvette, Cuvette-Ouest, Kouilou, Lekoumou, Likouala, Niari, Plateaux, Pointe-Noire, Pool, Sangha

Independence: 15 August 1960 (from France)

National holiday: Independence Day, 15 August (1960)

Legal system: mixed legal system of French civil law and customary law

Constitution: *history:* several previous; latest approved by referendum 25 October 2015
amendments: proposed by the president of the republic or by Parliament; passage of presidential proposals requires Supreme Court review followed by approval in a referendum; such proposals may also be submitted directly to Parliament, in which case passage requires at least three-quarters majority vote of both houses in joint session; proposals by Parliament require three-fourths majority vote of both houses in joint session; constitutional articles including those affecting the country's territory, republican form of government, and secularity of the state are not amendable

International law organization participation: has not submitted an ICJ jurisdiction declaration; accepts ICCt jurisdiction

Citizenship: *citizenship by birth:* no
citizenship by descent only: at least one parent must be a citizen of the Republic of the Congo
dual citizenship recognized: no
residency requirement for naturalization: 10 years

Suffrage: 18 years of age; universal

Executive branch: *chief of state:* President Denis SASSOU-Nguesso (since 1997)
head of government: Prime Minister Anatole Collinet MAKOSSO (since 12 May 2021)
cabinet: Council of Ministers appointed by the president
elections/appointments: president directly elected by absolute majority popular vote in 2 rounds if needed for a 5-year term (eligible for 2 additional terms); election last held on 21 March 2021 (next to be held on 21 March 2026)
election results:
2021: Denis SASSOU-Nguesso reelected president in the first round; percent of vote - Denis SASSOU-Nguesso (PCT) 88.4%, Guy Price Parfait KOLELAS (MCDDI) 8.0%, other 3.6%
2016: Denis SASSOU-Nguesso reelected president in the first round; percent of vote - Denis SASSOU-Nguesso (PCT) 60.4%, Guy Price Parfait KOLELAS (MCDDI) 15.1%, Jean-Marie MOKOKO (independent) 13.9%, Pascal Tsaty MABIALA (UPADS) 4.4%, other 6.2%

Legislative branch: *description:* bicameral Parliament consists of:
Senate (72 seats; members indirectly elected by local, district, and regional councils by simple majority vote to serve 6- year terms) note- the Senate is renewed in its entirety following a constitutional reform implemented in 2015 ending the renewal by half
National Assembly (151 seats; members directly elected in single-seat constituencies by absolute majority popular vote in 2 rounds if needed; members serve 5-year terms)
elections: Senate - last held on 20 August 2023 (next to be held 31 August 2029)
National Assembly - last held on 10 and 31 July 2022 (next to be held in July 2027)
election results: Senate - percent of vote by party - NA; seats by party - PCT 52, Independents 7, RDPS 3, MAR 2, Club 2002 PUR 2, PRL 1, UDLC 1, MCDDI 1, LCEM 1, UPADS 1, RC 1; composition - men 49, women 23, percentage women 34.7%
National Assembly - percent of vote by party - NA; seats by party - PCT 112, UPADS 7, UDH-YUKI 7, MAR 4, RLP 2, CLUB 2002 2, DRR 2, RDPS 2, PAC 1, MSD 1, MDP 1, CPR 1, PPRD 1, CR 1, MCDDI 1, independent 6; composition - men 129, women 22, percentage women 14.6%; total Parliament percentage women 20.2%

Judicial branch: *highest court(s):* Supreme Court or Cour Supreme (consists of NA judges); Constitutional Court (consists of 9 members); note - a High Court of Justice, outside the judicial authority, tries cases involving treason by the President of the Republic
judge selection and term of office: Supreme Court judges elected by Parliament and serve until age 65; Constitutional Court members appointed by the president of the republic - 3 directly by the president and 6 nominated by Parliament; members appointed

for renewable 9-year terms with one-third of the membership renewed every 3 years
subordinate courts: Court of Audit and Budgetary Discipline; courts of appeal; regional and district courts; employment tribunals; juvenile courts

Political parties: Alliance of the Presidential Majority or AMP
Action Movement for Renewal or MAR
Citizen's Rally or RC
Congolese Labour Party or PCT
Congolese Movement for Democracy and Integral Development or MCDDI
Congo on the Move or LCEM
Movement for Unity, Solidarity, and Work or MUST
Pan-African Union for Social Development or UPADS
Club 2002-Party for the Unity and the Republic or Club 2002
Patriotic Union for Democracy and Progress or UPDP
Perspectives and Realities Club or CPR
Rally for Democracy and Social Progress or RDPS
Republican and Liberal Party or PRL
Union of Democratic Forces or UDF
Union for Democracy and Republic or UDR
Union of Humanist Democrats or UDH-YUKI
Union for the Republic or UR

International organization participation: ACP, AfDB, AU, BDEAC, CEMAC, EITI (compliant country), FAO, FZ, G-77, IAEA, IBRD, ICAO, ICCt, ICRM, IDA, IFAD, IFC, IFRCS, ILO, IMF, IMO, Interpol, IOC, IOM, IPU, ISO (correspondent), ITSO, ITU, ITUC (NGOs), LCBC (observer), MIGA, NAM, OIF, OPCW, UN, UNCTAD, UNESCO, UNHCR, UNIDO, UNWTO, UPU, WCO, WFTU (NGOs), WHO, WIPO, WMO, WTO

Diplomatic representation in the US: *chief of mission:* Ambassador Serge MOMBOULI (since 31 July 2001)
chancery: 1720 16th Street NW, Washington, DC 20009
telephone: [1] (202) 726-5500
FAX: [1] (202) 726-1860
email address and website:
info@ambacongo-us.org
http://www.ambacongo-us.org/en-us/home.aspx

Diplomatic representation from the US: *chief of mission:* Ambassador Eugene S. YOUNG (since 30 March 2022)
embassy: 70-83 Section D, Boulevard Denis Sassou N'Guesso, Brazzaville
mailing address: 2090 Brazzaville Place, Washington DC 20521-2090
telephone: [242] 06 612-2000, [242] 05 387-9700
email address and website:
BrazzavilleACS@state.gov
https://cg.usembassy.gov/

Flag description: divided diagonally from the lower hoist side by a yellow band; the upper triangle (hoist side) is green and the lower triangle is red; green symbolizes agriculture and forests, yellow the friendship and nobility of the people, red is unexplained but has been associated with the struggle for independence
note: uses the popular Pan-African colors of Ethiopia

National symbol(s): lion, elephant; national colors: green, yellow, red

National anthem: *name:* "La Congolaise" (The Congolese)
lyrics/music: Jacques TONDRA and Georges KIBANGHI/Jean ROYER and Joseph SPADILIERE
note: originally adopted 1959, restored 1991

National heritage: *total World Heritage Sites:* 2 (natural)
selected World Heritage Site locales: Sangha Trinational Forest; Forest Massif of Odzala-Kokoua

ECONOMY

Economic overview: primarily an oil- and natural resources-based economy; recovery from mid-2010s oil devaluation has been slow and curtailed by COVID-19; extreme poverty increasing, particularly in southern rural regions; attempting to implement recommended CEMAC reforms; increasing likelihood of debt default

Real GDP (purchasing power parity): $38.163 billion (2023 est.)
$37.448 billion (2022 est.)
$36.904 billion (2021 est.)
note: data in 2021 dollars
comparison ranking: 140

Real GDP growth rate: 1.91% (2023 est.)
1.48% (2022 est.)
1.02% (2021 est.)
note: annual GDP % growth based on constant local currency
comparison ranking: 143

Real GDP per capita: $6,200 (2023 est.)
$6,300 (2022 est.)
$6,300 (2021 est.)
note: data in 2021 dollars
comparison ranking: 167

GDP (official exchange rate): $15.321 billion (2023 est.)
note: data in current dollars at official exchange rate

Inflation rate (consumer prices): 4.3% (2023 est.)
3.04% (2022 est.)
1.72% (2021 est.)
note: annual % change based on consumer prices
comparison ranking: 91

Credit ratings: Fitch rating: CCC (2019)

Moody's rating: Caa2 (2018)

Standard & Poors rating: CCC+ (2020)
note: The year refers to the year in which the current credit rating was first obtained.

GDP - composition, by sector of origin: *agriculture:* 9% (2023 est.)
industry: 45.2% (2023 est.)
services: 40.4% (2023 est.)
note: figures may not total 100% due to non-allocated consumption not captured in sector-reported data
comparison rankings: services 191; industry 21; agriculture 82

GDP - composition, by end use: *household consumption:* 44.1% (2023 est.)
government consumption: 13.1% (2023 est.)
investment in fixed capital: 24.9% (2023 est.)
investment in inventories: 0.3% (2023 est.)
exports of goods and services: 56.9% (2023 est.)
imports of goods and services: -39.3% (2023 est.)
note: figures may not total 100% due to rounding or gaps in data collection

Agricultural products: cassava, sugarcane, oil palm fruit, bananas, plantains, root vegetables, game meat, vegetables, mangoes/guavas, fruits (2022)
note: top ten agricultural products based on tonnage

Industries: petroleum extraction, cement, lumber, brewing, sugar, palm oil, soap, flour, cigarettes

Industrial production growth rate: 0.75% (2023 est.)
note: annual % change in industrial value added based on constant local currency
comparison ranking: 143

Labor force: 2.461 million (2023 est.)
note: number of people ages 15 or older who are employed or seeking work
comparison ranking: 120

Unemployment rate: 20.05% (2023 est.)
20.26% (2022 est.)
22.08% (2021 est.)
note: % of labor force seeking employment
comparison ranking: 200

Youth unemployment rate (ages 15-24): *total:* 41.2% (2023 est.)
male: 42.4% (2023 est.)
female: 40.1% (2023 est.)
note: % of labor force ages 15-24 seeking employment
comparison ranking: total 9

Remittances: 0.02% of GDP (2023 est.)
0.02% of GDP (2022 est.)
0.3% of GDP (2021 est.)
note: personal transfers and compensation between resident and non-resident individuals/households/entities

Budget: *revenues:* $2.393 billion (2020 est.)
expenditures: $2.409 billion (2020 est.)
note: central government revenues (excluding grants) and expenses converted to US dollars at average official exchange rate for year indicated

Public debt: 130.8% of GDP (2017 est.)
comparison ranking: 9

Taxes and other revenues: 6.51% (of GDP) (2021 est.)
note: central government tax revenue as a % of GDP
comparison ranking: 199

Current account balance: $1.716 billion (2021 est.)
$1.441 billion (2020 est.)
$1.632 billion (2019 est.)
note: balance of payments - net trade and primary/secondary income in current dollars
comparison ranking: 48

Exports: $7.752 billion (2021 est.)
$4.67 billion (2020 est.)
$7.855 billion (2019 est.)
note: balance of payments - exports of goods and services in current dollars
comparison ranking: 125

Exports - partners: China 39%, India 20%, UAE 15%, Italy 5%, Vietnam 4% (2022)
note: top five export partners based on percentage share of exports

Exports - commodities: crude petroleum, refined copper, wood, tin ores, rare earth ores (2022)
note: top five export commodities based on value in dollars

Imports: $4.487 billion (2021 est.)
$3.279 billion (2020 est.)
$4.945 billion (2019 est.)
note: balance of payments - imports of goods and services in current dollars
comparison ranking: 154

Imports - partners: China 26%, France 9%, UAE 6%, Belgium 6%, India 5% (2022)
note: top five import partners based on percentage share of imports

Imports - commodities: poultry, garments, vaccines, ships, fish (2022)

note: top five import commodities based on value in dollars

Reserves of foreign exchange and gold: $715.391 million (2023 est.)
$835.649 million (2022 est.)
$828.56 million (2021 est.)
note: holdings of gold (year-end prices)/foreign exchange/special drawing rights in current dollars
comparison ranking: 166

Debt - external: $6.482 billion (2022 est.)
note: present value of external debt in current US dollars
comparison ranking: 45

Exchange rates: Cooperation Financiere en Afrique Centrale francs (XAF) per US dollar -

Exchange rates: 606.57 (2023 est.)
623.76 (2022 est.)
554.531 (2021 est.)
575.586 (2020 est.)
585.911 (2019 est.)

ENERGY

Electricity access: *electrification - total population:* 50.6% (2022 est.)
electrification - urban areas: 67.5%
electrification - rural areas: 12.4%

Electricity: *installed generating capacity:* 842,000 kW (2022 est.)
consumption: 2.174 billion kWh (2022 est.)
exports: 25.21 million kWh (2022 est.)
imports: 22 million kWh (2022 est.)
transmission/distribution losses: 1.823 billion kWh (2022 est.)
comparison rankings: transmission/distribution losses 124; imports 121; exports 93; consumption 147; installed generating capacity 138

Electricity generation sources: *fossil fuels:* 77.5% of total installed capacity (2022 est.)
hydroelectricity: 22.5% of total installed capacity (2022 est.)

Coal: *imports:* 1 metric tons (2022 est.)

Petroleum: *total petroleum production:* 267,000 bbl/day (2023 est.)
refined petroleum consumption: 12,000 bbl/day (2022 est.)
crude oil estimated reserves: 2.882 billion barrels (2021 est.)

Natural gas: *production:* 423 million cubic meters (2022 est.)
consumption: 423 million cubic meters (2022 est.)
proven reserves: 283.99 billion cubic meters (2021 est.)

Carbon dioxide emissions: 2.542 million metric tonnes of CO2 (2022 est.)
from petroleum and other liquids: 1.712 million metric tonnes of CO2 (2022 est.)
from consumed natural gas: 830,000 metric tonnes of CO2 (2022 est.)
comparison ranking: total emissions 152

Energy consumption per capita: 7.238 million Btu/person (2022 est.)
comparison ranking: 159

COMMUNICATIONS

Telephones - fixed lines: *total subscriptions:* 17,000 (2020 est.)
subscriptions per 100 inhabitants: (2020 est.) less than 1
comparison ranking: total subscriptions 177

Telephones - mobile cellular: *total subscriptions:* 5.648 million (2021 est.)
subscriptions per 100 inhabitants: 97 (2021 est.)
comparison ranking: total subscriptions 122

Telecommunication systems: *general assessment:* suffering from economic challenges of stimulating recovery and reducing poverty; primary network consists of broadband through fiber link to the West Africa Cable System; key exchanges are in Brazzaville, Pointe- Noire, and Dolisie; intercity lines frequently out of order; youth are seeking the Internet more than their parents and often gain access through cyber cafes; only the most affluent have Internet access in their homes; fiber network project with aims to connect north and south regions; DRC operator added fiber link between Brazzaville and Kinshasa (2024)
domestic: fixed-line infrastructure inadequate, providing less than 1 fixed-line connection per 100 persons; mobilecellular 97 per 100 persons (2021)
international: country code - 242; WACS submarine cables to Europe and Western and South Africa; satellite earth station - 1 Intelsat (Atlantic Ocean) (2019)

Broadcast media: 1 state-owned TV and 3 state-owned radio stations; several privately owned TV and radio stations; satellite TV service is available; rebroadcasts of several international broadcasters are available

Internet country code: .cg

Internet users: *total:* 1,794,390 (2021 est.)
percent of population: 32.1% (2021 est.)
comparison ranking: total 137

Broadband - fixed subscriptions: *total:* 1,000 (2020 est.)
subscriptions per 100 inhabitants: 0.02 (2020 est.)
comparison ranking: total 204

TRANSPORTATION

National air transport system: *number of registered air carriers:* 3 (2020)
inventory of registered aircraft operated by air carriers: 12
annual passenger traffic on registered air carriers: 333,899 (2018)
annual freight traffic on registered air carriers: 4.6 million (2018) mt-km

Civil aircraft registration country code prefix: TN

Airports: 56 (2024)
comparison ranking: 81

Pipelines: 232 km gas, 4 km liquid petroleum gas, 982 km oil (2013)

Railways: *total:* 510 km (2014)
narrow gauge: 510 km (2014) 1.067-m gauge
comparison ranking: total 111

Roadways: *total:* 23,324 km
paved: 3,111 km
unpaved: 20,213 km (2017)
note: road network in Congo is composed of 23,324 km of which 17,000 km are classified as national, departmental, and routes of local interest: 6,324 km are non-classified routes
comparison ranking: total 111

Waterways: 1,120 km (2011) (commercially navigable on Congo and Oubangui Rivers above Brazzaville; there are many ferries across the river to Kinshasa; the Congo south of Brazzaville-Kinshasa to the coast is not navigable because of rapids, necessitating a rail connection to Pointe-Noire; other rivers are used for local traffic only)
comparison ranking: 65

Merchant marine: *total:* 11 (2023)
by type: oil tanker 1, other 10
comparison ranking: total 159

Ports: *total ports:* 5 (2024)
large: 0
medium: 0
small: 1
very small: 4
ports with oil terminals: 4
key ports: Djeno Terminal, Dussafu Terminal, N'kossa Terminal, Pointe Noire, Yombo Terminal

MILITARY AND SECURITY

Military and security forces: Congolese Armed Forces (Forces Armees Congolaises, FAC): Army, Navy, Congolese Air Force, National Gendarmerie

Ministry of Interior: National Police (2024)
note: the National Gendarmerie (GN) is a paramilitary force with domestic law enforcement and security responsibilities; it is under the Ministry of Defense, but also reports to the Ministry of Interior; the GN nominally includes the Republican Guard (GR), which is responsible for presidential security and has a separate command structure

Military expenditures: 2% of GDP (2023 est.)
1.8% of GDP (2022 est.)
2.5% of GDP (2021 est.)
3.2% of GDP (2020 est.)
2.3% of GDP (2019 est.)
comparison ranking: 71

Military and security service personnel strengths: approximately 14,000 active-duty troops (including about 4,000 Gendarmerie) (2023)

Military equipment inventories and acquisitions: the FAC has mostly Soviet-era armaments, with a small mix of Chinese, French, and South African equipment (2024)

Military service age and obligation: 18 years of age for voluntary military service for men and women; conscription ended in 1969 (2022)

Military deployments: has about 190 mostly police personnel deployed to the Central African Republic (MINUSCA) (2024)

Military - note: the FAC's primary focus is internal security; it is organized into approximately nine military zones; the Army's primary combat forces are an infantry brigade and a Republican Guard force
since its creation in 1961, the FAC has had a turbulent history; it has been sidelined by some national leaders in favor of personal militias, endured an internal rebellion (1996), and clashed with various rebel groups and political or ethnic militias (1993-1996, 2002-2005, 2017); during the 1997-1999 civil war, the military generally split along ethnic lines, with most northern officers supporting eventual winner SASSOU-Nguesso, and most southerners backing the rebels; others joined ethnic-based factions loyal to regional warlords; forces backing SASSOU-Nguesso were supported by Angolan troops and received some French assistance; the FAC also has undergone at least three reorganizations that included the incorporation of former rebel combatants and various ethnic and political militias; in recent years, France has provided some advice and

training, and a military cooperation agreement was signed with Russia in 2019 (2024)

TRANSNATIONAL ISSUES

Refugees and internally displaced persons: *refugees (country of origin):* 33,593 (Central African Republic), 29,785 (Democratic Republic of the Congo) (refugees and asylum seekers) (2024)
IDPs: 27,000 (multiple civil wars since 1992) (2022)

Trafficking in persons: tier rating: Tier 2 Watch List — the government did not demonstrate overall increasing efforts to eliminate trafficking compared with the previous reporting period, therefore the Republic of the Congo remained on Tier 2 Watch List for the second consecutive year; for more details, go to: https://www.state.gov/reports/2024-trafficking-in-persons-report/ republic-of-the-congo/

COOK ISLANDS

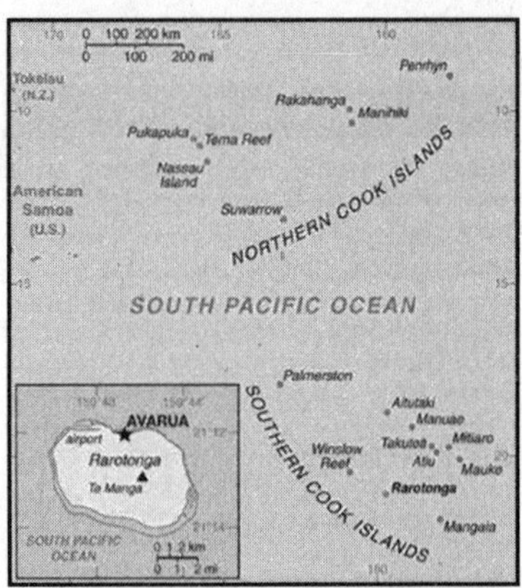

INTRODUCTION

Background: Polynesians from Tahiti were probably the first people to settle Rarotonga – the largest of the Cook Islands – around A.D. 900. Over time, Samoans and Tongans also settled in Rarotonga, and Rarotongans voyaged to the northern Cook Islands, settling Manihiki and Rakahanga. Pukapuka and Penrhyn in the northern Cook Islands were settled directly from Samoa. Prior to European contact, there was considerable travel and trade between inhabitants of the different islands and atolls, but they were not united in a single political entity. Spanish navigators were the first Europeans to spot the northern Cook Islands in 1595, followed by the first landing in 1606, but no further European contact occurred until the 1760s. In 1773, British explorer James COOK spotted Manuae in the southern Cook Islands, and Russian mapmakers named the islands after COOK in the 1820s.

Fearing France would militarily occupy the islands as it did in Tahiti, Rarotongans asked the UK for protectorate status in the 1840s and 1860s, a request the UK ignored. In 1888, Queen MAKEA TAKAU of Rarotonga formally petitioned for protectorate status, to which the UK reluctantly agreed. In 1901, the UK placed Rarotonga and the rest of the islands in the New Zealand Colony, and in 1915, the Cook Islands Act organized the islands into one political entity. It remained a protectorate until 1965, when New Zealand granted the Cook Islands self-governing status. The Cook Islands has a great deal of local autonomy and is an independent member of international organizations, but it is in free association with New Zealand, which is responsible for its defense and foreign affairs. In September 2023, the US recognized the Cook Islands as a sovereign and independent state.

GEOGRAPHY

Location: Oceania, group of islands in the South Pacific Ocean, about halfway between Hawaii and New Zealand

Geographic coordinates: 21 14 S, 159 46 W

Map references: Oceania

Area: *total:* 236 sq km
land: 236 sq km
water: 0 sq km
comparison ranking: total 215

Area - comparative: 1.3 times the size of Washington, DC

Land boundaries: *total:* 0 km

Coastline: 120 km

Maritime claims: *territorial sea:* 12 nm
exclusive economic zone: 200 nm
continental shelf: 200 nm or to the edge of the continental margin

Climate: tropical oceanic; moderated by trade winds; a dry season from April to November and a more humid season from December to March

Terrain: low coral atolls in north; volcanic, hilly islands in south

Elevation: *highest point:* Te Manga 652 m
lowest point: Pacific Ocean 0 m

Natural resources: coconuts (copra)

Land use: *agricultural land:* 8.4% (2018 est.)
arable land: 4.2% (2018 est.)
permanent crops: 4.2% (2018 est.)
permanent pasture: 0% (2018 est.)
forest: 64.6% (2018 est.)
other: 27% (2018 est.)

Irrigated land: NA

Population distribution: most of the population is found on the island of Rarotonga

Natural hazards: tropical cyclones (November to March)

Geography - note: the northern Cook Islands are seven low-lying, sparsely populated, coral atolls; the southern Cook Islands, where most of the population lives, consist of eight elevated, fertile, volcanic isles, including the largest, Rarotonga, at 67 sq km

PEOPLE AND SOCIETY

Population: *total:* 7,761
male: 3,980
female: 3,781 (2024 est.)
comparison rankings: female 224; male 223; total 224

Nationality: *noun:* Cook Islander(s)
adjective: Cook Islander

Ethnic groups: Cook Island Maori 77.4%, part Cook Island Maori 8.3%, Fijian 3.6%, New Zealand Maori/European 3.4%, Filipino 2.9%, other Pacific Islands 1.8%, other 2.6% (2021 est.)

Languages: English (official) 86.4%, Cook Islands Maori (Rarotongan) (official) 76.2%, other 8.3% (2011 est.)
note: shares sum to more than 100% because some respondents gave more than one answer on the census

Religions: Protestant 55% (Cook Islands Christian Church 43.1%, Seventh Day Adventist 8.3%, Assemblies of God 3.6%), Roman Catholic 16.7%, Church of Jesus Christ 3.9%, Jehovah's Witness 2.2%, Apostolic Church 2.1%, other 4.5%, none/unspecified 15.6% (2021 est.)

Age structure: *0-14 years:* 18.2% (male 738/female 671)
15-64 years: 65.9% (male 2,634/female 2,479)
65 years and over: 16% (2024 est.) (male 608/female 631)

Dependency ratios: *total dependency ratio:* 53.8
youth dependency ratio: 36.4
elderly dependency ratio: 17.4
potential support ratio: 5.8 (2021)

Median age: *total:* 41.1 years (2024 est.)
male: 40.7 years
female: 41.4 years
comparison ranking: total 53

Population growth rate: -2.24% (2024 est.)
comparison ranking: 236

Birth rate: 12.1 births/1,000 population (2024 est.)
comparison ranking: 147

Death rate: 9.4 deaths/1,000 population (2024 est.)
comparison ranking: 48

Net migration rate: -25.1 migrant(s)/1,000 population (2024 est.)
comparison ranking: 230

Population distribution: most of the population is found on the island of Rarotonga

Urbanization: *urban population:* 76.2% of total population (2023)
rate of urbanization: 0.52% annual rate of change (2020-25 est.)

Sex ratio: *at birth:* 1.04 male(s)/female
0-14 years: 1.1 male(s)/female
15-64 years: 1.06 male(s)/female
65 years and over: 0.96 male(s)/female
total population: 1.05 male(s)/female (2024 est.)

Infant mortality rate: *total:* 15.1 deaths/1,000 live births (2024 est.)
male: 19 deaths/1,000 live births
female: 11.1 deaths/1,000 live births
comparison ranking: total 95

Life expectancy at birth: *total population:* 77.6 years (2024 est.)
male: 74.8 years
female: 80.6 years
comparison ranking: total population 88

Total fertility rate: 2.02 children born/woman (2024 est.)
comparison ranking: 104

Gross reproduction rate: 0.99 (2024 est.)

Drinking water source: *improved:*
total: 100% of population

Current health expenditure: 3.2% of GDP (2020)

Physician density: 1.41 physicians/1,000 population (2014)

Sanitation facility access: *improved:*
total: 99.1% of population
unimproved:
total: 0.9% of population (2020 est.)

Obesity - adult prevalence rate: 55.9% (2016)
comparison ranking: 2

Alcohol consumption per capita: *total:* 12.97 liters of pure alcohol (2019 est.)
beer: 3.62 liters of pure alcohol (2019 est.)
wine: 2.28 liters of pure alcohol (2019 est.)
spirits: 7.07 liters of pure alcohol (2019 est.)
other alcohols: 0 liters of pure alcohol (2019 est.)
comparison ranking: total 1

Tobacco use: *total:* 24% (2020 est.)
male: 27.7% (2020 est.)
female: 20.3% (2020 est.)
comparison ranking: total 60

Currently married women (ages 15-49): 42.6% (2023 est.)

Education expenditures: 4.6% of GDP (2021 est.)
comparison ranking: 92

School life expectancy (primary to tertiary education): *total:* 15 years
male: 15 years
female: 14 years (2012)

ENVIRONMENT

Environment - current issues: limited land presents solid and liquid waste disposal problems; soil destruction and deforestation; environmental degradation due to indiscriminate use of pesticides; improper disposal of pollutants; overfishing and destructive fishing practices; over dredging of lagoons and coral rubble beds; unregulated building

Environment - international agreements: *party to:* Antarctic-Marine Living Resources, Biodiversity, Climate Change, Climate Change-Kyoto Protocol, Climate Change-Paris Agreement, Comprehensive Nuclear Test Ban, Desertification, Hazardous Wastes, Law of the Sea, Ozone Layer Protection, Ship Pollution
signed, but not ratified: none of the selected agreements

Climate: tropical oceanic; moderated by trade winds; a dry season from April to November and a more humid season from December to March

Urbanization: *urban population:* 76.2% of total population (2023)
rate of urbanization: 0.52% annual rate of change (2020-25 est.)

Air pollutants: *particulate matter emissions:* 7.8 micrograms per cubic meter (2019 est.)

Total renewable water resources: 0 cubic meters (2017 est.)

GOVERNMENT

Country name: *conventional long form:* none
conventional short form: Cook Islands
former: Hervey Islands
etymology: named after Captain James COOK, the British explorer who visited the islands in 1773 and 1777

Government type: parliamentary democracy

Dependency status: self-governing in free association with New Zealand; Cook Islands is fully responsible for internal affairs; New Zealand retains responsibility for external affairs and defense in consultation with the Cook Islands

Capital: *name:* Avarua
geographic coordinates: 21 12 S, 159 46 W
time difference: UTC-10 (5 hours behind Washington, DC, during Standard Time)
etymology: translates as "two harbors" in Maori

Administrative divisions: none

Independence: 4 August 1965 (Cook Islands became self-governing state in free association with New Zealand)

National holiday: Constitution Day, the first Monday in August (1965)

Legal system: common law similar to New Zealand common law

Constitution: *history:* 4 August 1965 (Cook Islands Constitution Act 1964)
amendments: proposed by Parliament; passage requires at least two-thirds majority vote by the Parliament membership in each of several readings and assent of the chief of state's representative; passage of amendments relating to the chief of state also requires two-thirds majority approval in a referendum; amended many times, last in 2004

International law organization participation: has not submitted an ICJ jurisdiction declaration (New Zealand normally retains responsibility for external affairs); accepts ICCt jurisdiction

Suffrage: 18 years of age; universal

Executive branch: *chief of state:* King CHARLES III (since 8 September 2022); represented by Sir Tom J. MARSTERS (since 9 August 2013); New Zealand High Commissioner Catherine GRAHAM (since 8 September 2024)
head of government: Prime Minister Mark BROWN (since 1 October 2020)
cabinet: Cabinet chosen by the prime minister
elections/appointments: the monarchy is hereditary; UK representative appointed by the monarch; New Zealand high commissioner appointed by the New Zealand Government; following legislative elections, the leader of the majority party or majority coalition usually becomes prime minister

Legislative branch: *description:* unicameral Parliament, formerly the Legislative Assembly (24 seats; members directly elected in single-seat constituencies by simple majority vote to serve 4-year terms)
elections: last held on 1 August 2022 (next to be held by 2026)
election results: percent of vote by party - CIP 44%, Demo 26.9%, Cook Islands United Party 26.9%, OCI 2.7%, other 0.2% independent 7.3%; seats by party - CIP 12, Demo 5, Cook Islands United Party 3, OCI 1, independent 3; composition - men 18, women 6, percentage women 25%
note: the House of Ariki, a 24-member parliamentary body of traditional leaders appointed by the King's representative, serves as a consultative body to the Parliament

Judicial branch: *highest court(s):* Court of Appeal (consists of the chief justice and 3 judges of the High Court); High Court (consists of the chief justice and at least 4 judges and organized into civil, criminal, and land divisions); note - appeals beyond the Cook Islands Court of Appeal are heard by the Judicial Committee of the Privy Council (in London)
judge selection and term of office: High Court chief justice appointed by the Queen's Representative on the advice of the Executive Council tendered by the prime minister; other judges appointed by the Queen's Representative, on the advice of the Executive Council tendered by the chief justice, High Court chief justice, and the minister of justice; chief justice and judges appointed for 3-year renewable terms
subordinate courts: justices of the peace

Political parties: Cook Islands Party or CIP
Cook Islands United Party
Democratic Party or Demo
One Cook Islands Movement or OCI

International organization participation: ACP, ADB, AOSIS, FAO, ICAO, ICCt, ICRM, IFAD, IFRCS, IMO, IMSO, IOC, ITUC (NGOs), OPCW, PIF, Sparteca, SPC, UNESCO, UPU, WHO, WMO

Diplomatic representation in the US: none (self-governing in free association with New Zealand)

Diplomatic representation from the US: *embassy:* none (self-governing in free association with New Zealand)
note: on 25 September 2023, the US officially established diplomatic relations with Cook Islands

Flag description: blue with the flag of the UK in the upper hoist-side quadrant and a large circle of 15 white five-pointed stars (one for every island) centered in the outer half of the flag

National symbol(s): a circle of 15, five-pointed, white stars on a blue field, Tiare maori (Gardenia taitensis) flower; national colors: green, white

National anthem: *name:* "Te Atua Mou E" (To God Almighty)
lyrics/music: Tepaeru Te RITO/Thomas DAVIS
note: adopted 1982; as prime minister, Sir Thomas DAVIS composed the anthem; his wife, a tribal chief, wrote the lyrics

ECONOMY

Economic overview: high-income self-governing New Zealand territorial economy; tourism-based activity but diversifying; severely curtailed by COVID-19 pandemic; copra and tropical fruit exporter; Asian Development Bank aid recipient

Real GDP (purchasing power parity): $266 million (2022 est.)
$257 million (2021 est.)
$287 million (2020 est.)
note: data are in 2015 dollars
comparison ranking: 218

Real GDP growth rate: 10.5% (2022 est.)
-24.5% (2021 est.)
-5.2% (2020 est.)
comparison ranking: 5

Real GDP per capita: $15,600 (2022 est.)

$15,100 (2021 est.)
$16,800 (2020 est.)
note: data are in 2015 dollars
comparison ranking: 122

GDP (official exchange rate): $336 million (2022 est.)

Agricultural products: coconuts, vegetables, papayas, pork, sweet potatoes, tomatoes, fruits, mangoes/guavas, watermelons, eggs (2022)
note: top ten agricultural products based on tonnage

Industries: fishing, fruit processing, tourism, clothing, handicrafts

Budget: *revenues:* $113.674 million (2022 est.)
expenditures: $129.088 million (2022 est.)
note: central government revenues and expenses (excluding grants/extrabudgetary units/social security funds) converted to US dollars at average official exchange rate for year indicated

Exports: $31.4 million (2021 est.)
note: Data are in current year dollars and do not include illicit exports or re-exports.
comparison ranking: 214

Exports - partners: Japan 42%, France 27%, Thailand 12%, US 4%, Italy 3% (2022)
note: top five export partners based on percentage share of exports

Exports - commodities: fish, ships, surveying equipment, sports equipment, garments (2022)
note: top five export commodities based on value in dollars

Imports: $215 million (2021 est.)
comparison ranking: 212

Imports - partners: NZ 51%, Italy 18%, Fiji 11%, China 7%, Australia 3% (2022)
note: top five import partners based on percentage share of imports

Imports - commodities: refined petroleum, ships, cars, plastic products, other foods (2022)
note: top five import commodities based on value in dollars

Exchange rates: New Zealand dollars (NZD) per US dollar -

Exchange rates: 1.628 (2023 est.)
1.577 (2022 est.)
1.414 (2021 est.)
1.542 (2020 est.)
1.518 (2019 est.)

ENERGY

Electricity: *installed generating capacity:* 17,000 kW (2022 est.)
consumption: 37.5 million kWh (2022 est.)
transmission/distribution losses: 3.2 million kWh (2022 est.)
comparison rankings: transmission/distribution losses 7; consumption 205; installed generating capacity 206

Electricity generation sources: *fossil fuels:* 60.9% of total installed capacity (2022 est.)
solar: 39.1% of total installed capacity (2022 est.)

Coal: *imports:* 1.3 metric tons (2022 est.)

Petroleum: *refined petroleum consumption:* 600 bbl/day (2022 est.)

Carbon dioxide emissions: 87,000 metric tonnes of CO2 (2022 est.)
from petroleum and other liquids: 87,000 metric tonnes of CO2 (2022 est.)
comparison ranking: total emissions 209

COMMUNICATIONS

Telephones - fixed lines: *total subscriptions:* 7,000 (2021 est.)
subscriptions per 100 inhabitants: 41 (2021 est.)
comparison ranking: total subscriptions 193

Telephones - mobile cellular: *total subscriptions:* 17,000 (2021 est.)
subscriptions per 100 inhabitants: 100 (2021 est.)
comparison ranking: total subscriptions 217

Telecommunication systems: *general assessment:* demand for mobile broadband is increasing due to mobile services being the primary and most widespread source for Internet access across the region; Telecom Cook Islands offers international direct dialing, Internet, email, and fax; individual islands are connected by a combination of satellite earth stations, microwave systems, and VHF and HF radiotelephone (2020)
domestic: service is provided by small exchanges connected to subscribers by open-wire, cable, and fiber-optic cable; nearly 41 per 100 fixed-line and about 100 per 100 mobile-cellular (2021)
international: country code - 682; the Manatua submarine cable to surrounding islands of Niue, Samoa, French Polynesia and other Cook Islands, the topography of the South Pacific region has made Internet connectivity a serious issue for many of the remote islands; submarine fiber-optic networks are expensive to build and maintain; satellite earth station - 1 Intelsat (Pacific Ocean) (2019)

Broadcast media: 1 privately owned TV station broadcasts from Rarotonga providing a mix of local news and overseas-sourced programs (2019)

Internet country code: .ck

Internet users: *total:* 11,382 (2021 est.)
percent of population: 64.8% (2021 est.)
comparison ranking: total 217

Broadband - fixed subscriptions: *total:* 2,700 (2018 est.)
subscriptions per 100 inhabitants: 15 (2018 est.)
comparison ranking: total 195

TRANSPORTATION

National air transport system: *number of registered air carriers:* 1 (2020)
inventory of registered aircraft operated by air carriers: 6

Civil aircraft registration country code prefix: E5

Airports: 10 (2024)
comparison ranking: 161

Roadways: *total:* 295 km
*paved:*207 km
*unpaved:*88 km (2018)
comparison ranking: total 204

Merchant marine: *total:* 190 (2023)
by type: bulk carrier 19, general cargo 44, oil tanker 58, other 69
comparison ranking: total 70

Ports: *total ports:* 1 (2024)
large: 0
medium: 0
small: 0
very small: 1
ports with oil terminals: 1
key ports: Avatiu

MILITARY AND SECURITY

Military and security forces: no regular military forces; Cook Islands Police Service

Military - note: defense is the responsibility of New Zealand in consultation with the Cook Islands and at its request
the Cook Islands have a "shiprider" agreement with the US, which allows local maritime law enforcement officers to embark on US Coast Guard (USCG) and US Navy (USN) vessels, including to board and search vessels suspected of violating laws or regulations within its designated exclusive economic zone (EEZ) or on the high seas; "shiprider" agreements also enable USCG personnel and USN vessels with embarked USCG law enforcement personnel to work with host nations to protect critical regional resources (2024)

CORAL SEA ISLANDS

INTRODUCTION

Background: The widely scattered Coral Sea Islands were first charted in 1803, but they were too small to host permanent human habitation. The 1870s and 1880s saw attempts at guano mining, but these were soon abandoned. The islands became an Australian territory in 1969, and the boundaries were extended in 1997. A small meteorological staff has operated on the Willis Islets since 1921, and several other islands host unmanned weather stations, beacons, and lighthouses. Much of the territory lies within national marine nature reserves.

GEOGRAPHY

Location: Oceania, islands in the Coral Sea, northeast of Australia

Geographic coordinates: 18 00 S, 152 00 E

Map references: Oceania

Area: *total:* 3 sq km less than
land: 3 sq km less than
water: 0 sq km
note: includes numerous small islands and reefs scattered over a sea area of about 780,000 sq km (300,000 sq mi) with the Willis Islets the most important
comparison ranking: total 252

Area - comparative: about four times the size of the National Mall in Washington, DC

Land boundaries: *total:* 0 km

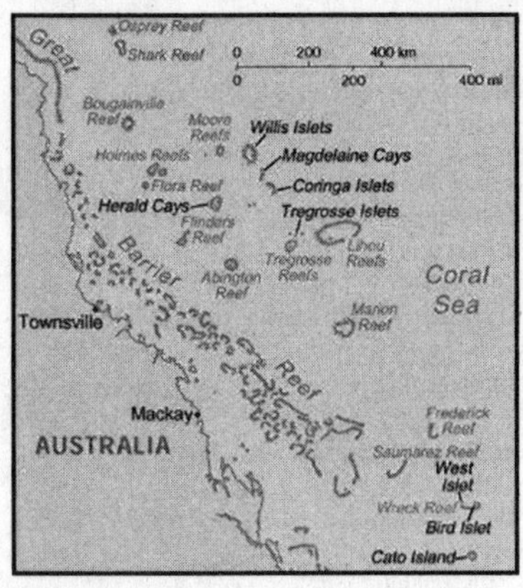

Coastline: 3,095 km

Maritime claims: *territorial sea:* 3 nm
exclusive fishing zone: 200 nm

Climate: tropical

Terrain: sand and coral reefs and islands (cays)

Elevation: *highest point:* unnamed location on Cato Island 9 m
lowest point: Pacific Ocean 0 m

Natural resources: fish

Land use: *agricultural land:* 0% (2018 est.)
other: 100% (2018 est.)

Natural hazards: occasional tropical cyclones

Geography - note: important nesting area for birds and turtles

PEOPLE AND SOCIETY

Population: *total:* no indigenous inhabitants (2021)
note: a staff of four operates the meteorological station on Willis Island

ENVIRONMENT

Environment - current issues: no permanent freshwater resources; damaging activities include coral mining, destructive fishing practices (overfishing, blast fishing)

Climate: tropical

GOVERNMENT

Country name: *conventional long form:* Coral Sea Islands Territory
conventional short form: Coral Sea Islands
etymology: self-descriptive name to reflect the islands' position in the Coral Sea off the northeastern coast of Australia

Dependency status: territory of Australia; administered from Canberra by the Department of Regional Australia, Local Government, Arts and Sport

Legal system: the common law legal system of Australia applies where applicable

Citizenship: see Australia

Diplomatic representation in the US: none (territory of Australia)

Diplomatic representation from the US: *embassy:* none (territory of Australia)

Flag description: the flag of Australia is used

COMMUNICATIONS

Communications - note: automatic weather stations on many of the isles and reefs relay data to the mainland

MILITARY AND SECURITY

Military - note: defense is the responsibility of Australia

COSTA RICA

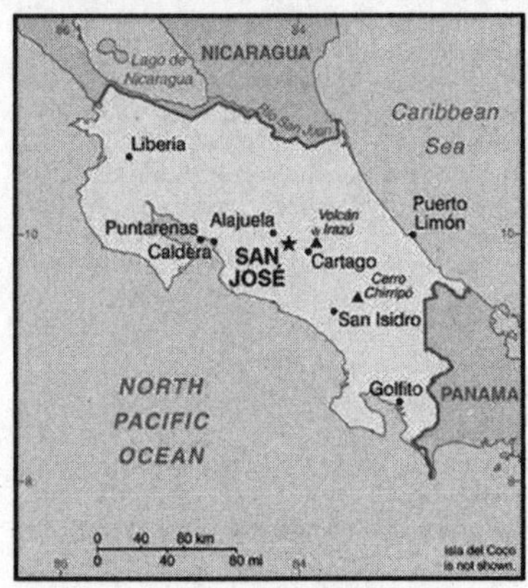

INTRODUCTION

Background: Although explored by the Spanish early in the 16th century, initial attempts at colonizing Costa Rica proved unsuccessful due to a combination of factors, including disease from mosquito-infested swamps, brutal heat, resistance from Indigenous populations, and pirate raids. It was not until 1563 that a permanent settlement of Cartago was established in the cooler, fertile central highlands. The area remained a colony for some two-and-a-half centuries. In 1821, Costa Rica was one of several Central American provinces that jointly declared independence from Spain. Two years later it joined the United Provinces of Central America, but this federation disintegrated in 1838, at which time Costa Rica proclaimed its sovereignty and independence.

Since the late 19th century, only two brief periods of violence have marred the country's democratic development. General Federico TINOCO Granados led a coup in 1917, but the threat of US intervention pushed him to resign in 1919. In 1948, landowner Jose FIGUERES Ferrer raised his own army and rebelled against the government. The brief civil war ended with an agreement to allow FIGUERES to remain in power for 18 months, then step down in favor of the previously elected Otilio ULATE. FIGUERES was later elected twice in his own right, in 1953 and 1970.

Costa Rica experienced destabilizing waves of refugees from Central American civil wars in the 1970s and 1980s, but peace in the region has since helped the economy rebound. Although it still maintains a large agricultural sector, Costa Rica has expanded its economy to include strong technology and tourism industries.

GEOGRAPHY

Location: Central America, bordering both the Caribbean Sea and the North Pacific Ocean, between Nicaragua and Panama

Geographic coordinates: 10 00 N, 84 00 W

Map references: Central America and the Caribbean

Area: *total:* 51,100 sq km
land: 51,060 sq km
water: 40 sq km
note: includes Isla del Coco
comparison ranking: total 129

Area - comparative: slightly smaller than West Virginia

Land boundaries: *total:* 661 km
border countries (2): Nicaragua 313 km; Panama 348 km

Coastline: 1,290 km

Maritime claims: *territorial sea:* 12 nm
exclusive economic zone: 200 nm
continental shelf: 200 nm

Climate: tropical and subtropical; dry season (December to April); rainy season (May to November); cooler in highlands

Terrain: coastal plains separated by rugged mountains including over 100 volcanic cones, of which several are major active volcanoes

Elevation: *highest point:* Cerro Chirripo 3,819 m
lowest point: Pacific Ocean 0 m
mean elevation: 746 m

Natural resources: hydropower

Land use: *agricultural land:* 37.1% (2018 est.)
arable land: 4.9% (2018 est.)
permanent crops: 6.7% (2018 est.)
permanent pasture: 25.5% (2018 est.)
forest: 51.5% (2018 est.)
other: 11.4% (2018 est.)

Irrigated land: 1,015 sq km (2012)

Population distribution: roughly half of the nation's population resides in urban areas; the capital of San Jose is the largest city and home to approximately one-fifth of the population

Natural hazards: occasional earthquakes, hurricanes along Atlantic coast; frequent flooding of lowlands at onset of rainy season and landslides; active volcanoes
volcanism: Arenal (1,670 m), which erupted in 2010, is the most active volcano in Costa Rica; a 1968 eruption destroyed the town of Tabacon; Irazu (3,432 m), situated just east of San Jose, has the

potential to spew ash over the capital city as it did between 1963 and 1965; other historically active volcanoes include Miravalles, Poas, Rincon de la Vieja, and Turrialba

Geography - note: four volcanoes, two of them active, rise near the capital of San Jose in the center of the country; one of the volcanoes, Irazu, erupted destructively in 1963-65

PEOPLE AND SOCIETY

Population: *total:* 5,265,575
male: 2,635,481
female: 2,630,094 (2024 est.)
comparison rankings: female 124; male 123; total 123

Nationality: *noun:* Costa Rican(s)
adjective: Costa Rican

Ethnic groups: White or Mestizo 83.6%, Mulatto 6.7%, Indigenous 2.4%, Black or African descent 1.1%, other 1.1%, none 2.9%, unspecified 2.2% (2011 est.)

Languages: Spanish (official), English
major-language sample(s):
La Libreta Informativa del Mundo, la fuente indispensable de información básica. (Spanish)

Religions: Roman Catholic 47.5%, Evangelical and Pentecostal 19.8%, Jehovah's Witness 1.4%, other Protestant 1.2%, other 3.1%, none 27% (2021 est.)

Demographic profile: Costa Rica's political stability, high standard of living, and well-developed social benefits system set it apart from its Central American neighbors. Through the government's sustained social spending - almost 20% of GDP annually - Costa Rica has made tremendous progress toward achieving its goal of providing universal access to education, healthcare, clean water, sanitation, and electricity. Since the 1970s, expansion of these services has led to a rapid decline in infant mortality, an increase in life expectancy at birth, and a sharp decrease in the birth rate. The average number of children born per women has fallen from about 7 in the 1960s to 3.5 in the early 1980s to below replacement level today. Costa Rica's poverty rate is lower than in most Latin American countries, but it has stalled at around 20% for almost two decades.
Costa Rica is a popular regional immigration destination because of its job opportunities and social programs. Almost 9% of the population is foreign-born, with Nicaraguans comprising nearly three-quarters of the foreign population. Many Nicaraguans who perform unskilled seasonal labor enter Costa Rica illegally or overstay their visas, which continues to be a source of tension. Less than 3% of Costa Rica's population lives abroad. The overwhelming majority of expatriates have settled in the United States after completing a university degree or in order to work in a highly skilled field.

Age structure: *0-14 years:* 18.8% (male 506,041/female 482,481)
15-64 years: 70.2% (male 1,862,872/female 1,832,024)
65 years and over: 11.1% (2024 est.) (male 266,568/female 315,589)

Dependency ratios: *total dependency ratio:* 45.1
youth dependency ratio: 29.8
elderly dependency ratio: 15.3
potential support ratio: 6.5 (2021 est.)

Median age: *total:* 35.5 years (2024 est.)
male: 34.9 years
female: 36.1 years
comparison ranking: total 96

Population growth rate: 0.74% (2024 est.)
comparison ranking: 119

Birth rate: 10.8 births/1,000 population (2024 est.)
comparison ranking: 171

Death rate: 5.3 deaths/1,000 population (2024 est.)
comparison ranking: 188

Net migration rate: 1.9 migrant(s)/1,000 population (2024 est.)
comparison ranking: 52

Population distribution: roughly half of the nation's population resides in urban areas; the capital of San Jose is the largest city and home to approximately one-fifth of the population

Urbanization: *urban population:* 82.6% of total population (2023)
rate of urbanization: 1.5% annual rate of change (2020-25 est.)

Major urban areas - population: 1.462 million SAN JOSE (capital) (2023)

Sex ratio: *at birth:* 1.05 male(s)/female
0-14 years: 1.05 male(s)/female
15-64 years: 1.02 male(s)/female
65 years and over: 0.84 male(s)/female
total population: 1 male(s)/female (2024 est.)

Maternal mortality ratio: 22 deaths/100,000 live births (2020 est.)
comparison ranking: 118

Infant mortality rate: *total:* 6.7 deaths/1,000 live births (2024 est.)
male: 7 deaths/1,000 live births
female: 6.3 deaths/1,000 live births
comparison ranking: total 158

Life expectancy at birth: *total population:* 80.3 years (2024 est.)
male: 77.7 years
female: 82.9 years
comparison ranking: total population 54

Total fertility rate: 1.43 children born/woman (2024 est.)
comparison ranking: 210

Gross reproduction rate: 0.7 (2024 est.)

Contraceptive prevalence rate: 70.9% (2018)

Drinking water source: *improved:* *urban:* 100% of population
rural: 100% of population
total: 100% of population

Current health expenditure: 7.9% of GDP (2020)

Physician density: 3.3 physicians/1,000 population (2020)

Hospital bed density: 1.1 beds/1,000 population (2019)

Sanitation facility access: *improved:* *urban:* 99% of population
rural: 97.1% of population
total: 98.7% of population
unimproved: *urban:* 1% of population
rural: 2.9% of population
total: 1.3% of population (2020 est.)

Obesity - adult prevalence rate: 25.7% (2016)
comparison ranking: 48

Alcohol consumption per capita: *total:* 3.07 liters of pure alcohol (2019 est.)
beer: 2.17 liters of pure alcohol (2019 est.)
wine: 0.15 liters of pure alcohol (2019 est.)
spirits: 0.36 liters of pure alcohol (2019 est.)
other alcohols: 0.39 liters of pure alcohol (2019 est.)
comparison ranking: total 113

Tobacco use: *total:* 8.8% (2020 est.)
male: 12.9% (2020 est.)
female: 4.6% (2020 est.)
comparison ranking: total 140

Children under the age of 5 years underweight: 2.9% (2018)
comparison ranking: 91

Currently married women (ages 15-49): 48.4% (2023 est.)

Child marriage: *women married by age 15:* 2%
women married by age 18: 17.1% (2018 est.)

Education expenditures: 6.7% of GDP (2020 est.)
comparison ranking: 26

Literacy: *definition:* age 15 and over can read and write
total population: 98%
male: 98%
female: 98.1% (2021)

School life expectancy (primary to tertiary education): *total:* 17 years
male: 16 years
female: 17 years (2019)

ENVIRONMENT

Environment - current issues: deforestation and land use change, largely a result of the clearing of land for cattle ranching and agriculture; soil erosion; coastal marine pollution; fisheries protection; solid waste management; air pollution

Environment - international agreements: *party to:* Biodiversity, Climate Change, Climate Change-Kyoto Protocol, Climate Change-Paris Agreement, Comprehensive Nuclear Test Ban, Desertification, Endangered Species, Environmental Modification, Hazardous Wastes, Law of the Sea, Marine Dumping-London Convention, Nuclear Test Ban, Ozone Layer Protection, Tropical Timber 2006, Wetlands, Whaling
signed, but not ratified: Marine Life Conservation

Climate: tropical and subtropical; dry season (December to April); rainy season (May to November); cooler in highlands

Urbanization: *urban population:* 82.6% of total population (2023)
rate of urbanization: 1.5% annual rate of change (2020-25 est.)

Revenue from forest resources: 0.82% of GDP (2018 est.)
comparison ranking: 58

Revenue from coal: 0% of GDP (2018 est.)
comparison ranking: 152

Air pollutants: *particulate matter emissions:* 14.7 micrograms per cubic meter (2019 est.)
carbon dioxide emissions: 8.02 megatons (2016 est.)
methane emissions: 5.61 megatons (2020 est.)

Waste and recycling: *municipal solid waste generated annually:* 1.46 million tons (2014 est.)
municipal solid waste recycled annually: 18,396 tons (2014 est.)
percent of municipal solid waste recycled: 1.3% (2014 est.)

Total water withdrawal: *municipal:* 830 million cubic meters (2020 est.)
industrial: 230 million cubic meters (2020 est.)
agricultural: 2.08 billion cubic meters (2020 est.)

Total renewable water resources: 113 billion cubic meters (2020 est.)

GOVERNMENT

Country name: *conventional long form:* Republic of Costa Rica
conventional short form: Costa Rica
local long form: República de Costa Rica
local short form: Costa Rica
etymology: the name means "rich coast" in Spanish and was first applied in the early colonial period of the 16th century

Government type: presidential republic

Capital: *name:* San José
geographic coordinates: 9 56 N, 84 05 W
time difference: UTC-6 (1 hour behind Washington, DC, during Standard Time)
etymology: named in honor of Saint Joseph

Administrative divisions: 7 provinces (provincias, singular - provincia); Alajuela, Cartago, Guanacaste, Heredia, Limon, Puntarenas, San Jose

Independence: 15 September 1821 (from Spain)

National holiday: Independence Day, 15 September (1821)

Legal system: civil law system based on Spanish civil code; judicial review of legislative acts in the Supreme Court

Constitution: *history:* many previous; latest effective 8 November 1949
amendments: proposals require the signatures of at least 10 Legislative Assembly members or petition of at least 5% of qualified voters; consideration of proposals requires two-thirds majority approval in each of three readings by the Assembly, followed by preparation of the proposal as a legislative bill and its approval by simple majority of the Assembly; passage requires at least two-thirds majority vote of the Assembly membership; a referendum is required only if approved by at least two thirds of the Assembly; amended many times, last in 2020

International law organization participation: accepts compulsory ICJ jurisdiction; accepts ICCt jurisdiction

Citizenship: *citizenship by birth:* yes
citizenship by descent only: yes
dual citizenship recognized: yes
residency requirement for naturalization: 7 years

Suffrage: 18 years of age; universal and compulsory

Executive branch: *chief of state:* President Rodrigo CHAVES Robles (since 8 May 2022)
head of government: President Rodrigo CHAVES Robles (since 8 May 2022)
cabinet: Cabinet selected by the president
elections/appointments: president and vice presidents directly elected on the same ballot by modified majority popular vote (40% threshold) for a 4-year term (eligible for non-consecutive terms); election last held on 6 February 2022 with a runoff on 3 April 2022 (next to be held in February 2026 with a runoff in April 2026)
election results:
2022: Rodrigo CHAVES Robles elected president in second round; percent of vote in first round - Jose Maria FIGUERES Olsen (PLN) 27.3%, Rodrigo CHAVES Robles (PPSD) 16.8%, Fabricio ALVARADO Munoz (PNR) 14.9%, Eliecer FEINZAIG Mintz (PLP) 12.4%, Lineth SABORIO Chaverri (PUSC) 12.4%, Jose Maria VILLALTA Florez-Estrada 8.7% (PFA), other 7.5%; percent of vote in second round - Rodrigo CHAVES Robles (PPSD) 52.8%, Jose Maria FIGUERES Olsen (PLN) 47.2%
2018: Carlos ALVARADO Quesada elected president in second round; percent of vote in first round - Fabricio ALVARADO Munoz (PRN) 25%; Carlos ALVARADO Quesada (PAC) 21.6%; Antonio ALVAREZ (PLN) 18.6%; Rodolfo PIZA (PUSC) 16%; Juan Diego CASTRO (PIN) 9.5%; Rodolfo HERNANDEZ (PRSC) 4.9%, other 4.4%; percent of vote in second round - Carlos ALVARADO Quesada (PAC) 60.7%; Fabricio ALVARADO Munoz (PRN) 39.3%
note: the president is both chief of state and head of government

Legislative branch: *description:* unicameral Legislative Assembly or Asamblea Legislativa (57 seats; members directly elected in multi-seat constituencies - corresponding to the country's 7 provinces - by closed party-list proportional representation vote; members serve 4-year terms)
elections: last held on 6 February 2022 (next to be held in February 2026)
election results: percent of vote by party - PLN 24.8%, PPSD 15%, PUSC 11.4%, PNR 10.1%, PLP 9.1%, 8.3%, other 21.3%; seats by party - PLN 19, PPSD 10, PUSC 9, PNR 7, PLP 6, PFA 6; composition - men 30, women 27, percentage women 47.4%

Judicial branch: *highest court(s):* Supreme Court of Justice (consists of 22 judges organized into 3 cassation chambers each with 5 judges and the Constitutional Chamber with 7 judges)
judge selection and term of office: Supreme Court of Justice judges elected by the National Assembly for 8-year terms with renewal decided by the National Assembly
subordinate courts: appellate courts; trial courts; first instance and justice of the peace courts; Superior Electoral Tribunal

Political parties: Accessibility Without Exclusion or PASE
Broad Front (Frente Amplio) or PFA
Citizen Action Party or PAC
Costa Rican Renewal Party or PRC
Here Costa Rica Commands Party or ACRM
Liberal Progressive Party or PLP
Libertarian Movement Party or ML
National Integration Party or PIN
National Liberation Party or PLN
National Restoration Party or PRN
New Generation or PNG
New Republic Party or PNR
Social Christian Republican Party or PRSC
Social Christian Unity Party or PUSC of UNIDAD
Social Democratic Progress Party or PPSD

International organization participation: ACS, BCIE, CACM, CD, CELAC, FAO, G-77, IADB, IAEA, IBRD, ICAO, ICC (national committees), ICCt, ICRM, IDA, IFAD, IFC, IFRCS, ILO, IMF, IMO, IMSO, Interpol, IOC, IOM, IPU, ISO, ITSO, ITU, ITUC (NGOs), LAES, LAIA (observer), MIGA, NAM (observer), OAS, OIF (observer), OPANAL, OPCW, Pacific Alliance (observer), PCA, SICA, UN, UNCTAD, UNESCO, UNHCR, UNIDO, Union Latina, UNOOSA, UNWTO, UPU, WCO, WFTU (NGOs), WHO, WIPO, WMO, WTO

Diplomatic representation in the US: *chief of mission:* Ambassador Catalina CRESPO SANCHO (since 19 April 2023)
chancery: 2114 S Street NW, Washington, DC 20008
telephone: [1] (202) 499-2980
FAX: [1] (202) 265-4795
email address and website:
embcr-us@rree.go.cr
http://www.costarica-embassy.org/index.php?q=node/21
consulate(s) general: Atlanta, Houston, Los Angeles, Miami, New York, Washington DC

Diplomatic representation from the US: *chief of mission:* Ambassador Cynthia A. TELLES (since 11 March 2022)
embassy: Calle 98 Via 104, Pavas, San Jose
mailing address: 3180 St. George's Place, Washington DC 20521-3180
telephone: [506] 2519-2000
FAX: [506] 2519-2305
email address and website:
acssanjose@state.gov
https://cr.usembassy.gov/

Flag description: five horizontal bands of blue (top), white, red (double width), white, and blue, with the coat of arms in a white elliptical disk placed toward the hoist side of the red band; Costa Rica retained the earlier blue-white-blue flag of Central America until 1848 when, in response to revolutionary activity in Europe, it was decided to incorporate the French colors into the national flag and a central red stripe was added; today the blue color is said to stand for the sky, opportunity, and perseverance, white denotes peace, happiness, and wisdom, while red represents the blood shed for freedom, as well as the generosity and vibrancy of the people
note: somewhat resembles the flag of North Korea; similar to the flag of Thailand but with the blue and red colors reversed

National symbol(s): yiguirro (clay-colored robin); national colors: blue, white, red

National anthem: *name:* "Himno Nacional de Costa Rica" (National Anthem of Costa Rica)
lyrics/music: Jose Maria ZELEDON Brenes/Manuel Maria GUTIERREZ
note: adopted 1949; the anthem's music was originally written for an 1853 welcome ceremony for diplomatic missions from the US and UK; the lyrics were added in 1903

National heritage: *total World Heritage Sites:* 4 (1 cultural, 3 natural)
selected World Heritage Site locales: Guanacaste Conservation Area (n); Cocos Island National Park (n); Precolumbian Stone Spheres (c); La Amistad International Park (n)

ECONOMY

Economic overview: trade-based upper middle-income economy; green economy leader, having reversed deforestation; investing in blue economy infrastructure; declining poverty until hard impacts of COVID-19; lingering inequality and growing government debts have prompted a liquidity crisis

Real GDP (purchasing power parity): $134.238 billion (2023 est.)
$127.71 billion (2022 est.)
$122.15 billion (2021 est.)
note: data in 2021 dollars
comparison ranking: 90

Real GDP growth rate: 5.11% (2023 est.)
4.55% (2022 est.)
7.94% (2021 est.)

note: annual GDP % growth based on constant local currency
comparison ranking: 50

Real GDP per capita: $25,800 (2023 est.)
$24,700 (2022 est.)
$23,700 (2021 est.)
note: data in 2021 dollars
comparison ranking: 87

GDP (official exchange rate): $86.498 billion (2023 est.)
note: data in current dollars at official exchange rate

Inflation rate (consumer prices): 0.53% (2023 est.)
8.27% (2022 est.)
1.73% (2021 est.)
note: annual % change based on consumer prices
comparison ranking: 13

Credit ratings: Fitch rating: B (2020)

Moody's rating: B2 (2020)

Standard & Poors rating: B (2020)
note: The year refers to the year in which the current credit rating was first obtained.

GDP - composition, by sector of origin: *agriculture:* 3.8% (2023 est.)
industry: 20.5% (2023 est.)
services: 68% (2023 est.)
note: figures may not total 100% due to non-allocated consumption not captured in sector-reported data
comparison rankings: services 45; industry 134; agriculture 132

GDP - composition, by end use: *household consumption:* 65.4% (2023 est.)
government consumption: 14.9% (2023 est.)
investment in fixed capital: 16.2% (2023 est.)
investment in inventories: -0.8% (2023 est.)
exports of goods and services: 37.3% (2023 est.)
imports of goods and services: -33% (2023 est.)
note: figures may not total 100% due to rounding or gaps in data collection

Agricultural products: sugarcane, pineapples, bananas, milk, oil palm fruit, fruits, oranges, chicken, cassava, rice (2022)
note: top ten agricultural products based on tonnage

Industries: medical equipment, food processing, textiles and clothing, construction materials, fertilizer, plastic products

Industrial production growth rate: 8.35% (2023 est.)
note: annual % change in industrial value added based on constant local currency
comparison ranking: 27

Labor force: 2.408 million (2023 est.)
note: number of people ages 15 or older who are employed or seeking work
comparison ranking: 121

Unemployment rate: 8.3% (2023 est.)
11.33% (2022 est.)
15.14% (2021 est.)
note: % of labor force seeking employment
comparison ranking: 149

Youth unemployment rate (ages 15-24): *total:* 24.1% (2023 est.)
male: 21% (2023 est.)
female: 28.3% (2023 est.)
note: % of labor force ages 15-24 seeking employment
comparison ranking: total 47

Population below poverty line: 25.5% (2022 est.)
note: % of population with income below national poverty line

Gini Index coefficient - distribution of family income: 47.2 (2022 est.)
note: index (0-100) of income distribution; higher values represent greater inequality
comparison ranking: 16

Average household expenditures: *on food:* 31.1% of household expenditures (2022 est.)
on alcohol and tobacco: 0.7% of household expenditures (2022 est.)

Household income or consumption by percentage share: *lowest 10%:* 1.7% (2022 est.)
highest 10%: 35.7% (2022 est.)
note: % share of income accruing to lowest and highest 10% of population

Remittances: 0.73% of GDP (2023 est.)
0.9% of GDP (2022 est.)
0.91% of GDP (2021 est.)
note: personal transfers and compensation between resident and non-resident individuals/households/entities

Budget: *revenues:* $20.224 billion (2022 est.)
expenditures: $19.799 billion (2022 est.)
note: central government revenues (excluding grants) and expenses converted to US dollars at average official exchange rate for year indicated

Public debt: 71.11% of GDP (2022 est.)
comparison ranking: 53

Taxes and other revenues: 14.35% (of GDP) (2022 est.)
note: central government tax revenue as a % of GDP
comparison ranking: 146

Current account balance: -$844.64 million (2023 est.)
-$2.235 billion (2022 est.)
-$2.061 billion (2021 est.)
note: balance of payments - net trade and primary/secondary income in current dollars
comparison ranking: 136

Exports: $33.699 billion (2023 est.)
$29.404 billion (2022 est.)
$23.609 billion (2021 est.)
note: balance of payments - exports of goods and services in current dollars
comparison ranking: 77

Exports - partners: US 40%, Netherlands 7%, Guatemala 5%, Belgium 5%, Nicaragua 3% (2022)
note: top five export partners based on percentage share of exports

Exports - commodities: medical instruments, orthopedic appliances, bananas, tropical fruits, other foods (2022)
note: top five export commodities based on value in dollars

Imports: $28.441 billion (2023 est.)
$27.07 billion (2022 est.)
$21.94 billion (2021 est.)
note: balance of payments - imports of goods and services in current dollars
comparison ranking: 83

Imports - partners: US 39%, China 14%, Mexico 5%, Guatemala 3%, Brazil 3% (2022)
note: top five import partners based on percentage share of imports

Imports - commodities: refined petroleum, plastic products, medical instruments, cars, broadcasting equipment (2022)
note: top five import commodities based on value in dollars

Reserves of foreign exchange and gold: $13.225 billion (2023 est.)
$8.554 billion (2022 est.)
$6.921 billion (2021 est.)
note: holdings of gold (year-end prices)/foreign exchange/special drawing rights in current dollars
comparison ranking: 79

Debt - external: $12.877 billion (2022 est.)
note: present value of external debt in current US dollars
comparison ranking: 32

Exchange rates: Costa Rican colones (CRC) per US dollar -

Exchange rates: 544.051 (2023 est.)
647.136 (2022 est.)
620.785 (2021 est.)
584.901 (2020 est.)
587.295 (2019 est.)

ENERGY

Electricity access: *electrification - total population:* 100% (2022 est.)

Electricity: *installed generating capacity:* 3.692 million kW (2022 est.)
consumption: 10.619 billion kWh (2022 est.)
exports: 773.979 million kWh (2022 est.)
imports: 54.231 million kWh (2022 est.)
transmission/distribution losses: 1.14 billion kWh (2022 est.)
comparison rankings: transmission/distribution losses 104; imports 114; exports 70; consumption 100; installed generating capacity 104

Electricity generation sources: *solar:* 0.6% of total installed capacity (2022 est.)
wind: 11% of total installed capacity (2022 est.)
hydroelectricity: 75% of total installed capacity (2022 est.)
geothermal: 11.9% of total installed capacity (2022 est.)
biomass and waste: 1.5% of total installed capacity (2022 est.)

Coal: *consumption:* 30,000 metric tons (2022 est.)
exports: (2022 est.) less than 1 metric ton
imports: 500 metric tons (2022 est.)

Petroleum: *total petroleum production:* 400 bbl/day (2023 est.)
refined petroleum consumption: 62,000 bbl/day (2022 est.)

Carbon dioxide emissions: 7.966 million metric tonnes of CO2 (2022 est.)
from coal and metallurgical coke: 74,000 metric tonnes of CO2 (2022 est.)
from petroleum and other liquids: 7.892 million metric tonnes of CO2 (2022 est.)
comparison ranking: total emissions 119

Energy consumption per capita: 31.43 million Btu/person (2022 est.)
comparison ranking: 112

COMMUNICATIONS

Telephones - fixed lines: *total subscriptions:* 492,000 (2022 est.)
subscriptions per 100 inhabitants: 9 (2022 est.)
comparison ranking: total subscriptions 92

Telephones - mobile cellular: *total subscriptions:* 7.876 million (2022 est.)
subscriptions per 100 inhabitants: 152 (2022 est.)
comparison ranking: total subscriptions 103

Telecommunication systems: *general assessment:* the fixed broadband market is one of the few parts of Costa Rica's telecom sector to experience solid growth in recent years, both in size and revenue; the country's fiber network expanded by 56% in 2020, reaching about 176,200km; fixed-line broadband traffic volume also increased by more than 30%, year-on-year; other areas of the market have proven relatively lack luster, with slow or even negative growth; some of this can be attributed to the economic and social impacts of the pandemic, but the fixed-line and mobile sectors have both been struggling to produce decent results since well before the start of the crisis; the rollout of 5G network infrastructure in Costa Rica is unlikely to occur to any scale before 2023, but this may be one of the few remaining areas of opportunity open to investors outside of fixed-line internet and pay TV services (2021)
domestic: roughly 11 per 100 fixed-line and 152 per 100 mobile-cellular (2021)
international: country code - 506; landing points for the ARCOS-1, MAYA-1, and the PAC submarine cables that provide links to South and Central America, parts of the Caribbean, and the US; connected to Central American Microwave System; satellite earth stations - 2 Intelsat (Atlantic Ocean) (2019)

Broadcast media: over two dozen privately owned TV stations and 1 publicly owned TV station nationwide; cable network services are widely available; more than 100 privately owned radio stations and a public radio network (2022)

Internet country code: .cr

Internet users: *total:* 4.316 million (2021 est.)
percent of population: 83% (2021 est.)
comparison ranking: total 106

Broadband - fixed subscriptions: *total:* 992,725 (2020 est.)
subscriptions per 100 inhabitants: 20 (2020 est.)
comparison ranking: total 74

TRANSPORTATION

National air transport system: *number of registered air carriers:* 1 (2020)
inventory of registered aircraft operated by air carriers: 39
annual passenger traffic on registered air carriers: 1,948,546 (2018)
annual freight traffic on registered air carriers: 11.13 million (2018) mt-km

Civil aircraft registration country code prefix: TI

Airports: 129 (2024)
comparison ranking: 41

Heliports: 8 (2024)

Pipelines: 662 km refined products (2013)

Railways: *total:* 278 km (2014)
narrow gauge: 278 km (2014) 1.067-m gauge
note: the entire rail network fell into disrepair and out of use at the end of the 20th century; since 2005, certain sections of rail have been rehabilitated
comparison ranking: total 124

Roadways: *total:* 5,035 km (2017)
comparison ranking: total 150

Waterways: 730 km (2011) (seasonally navigable by small craft)
comparison ranking: 80

Merchant marine: *total:* 11 (2023)
by type: other 11
comparison ranking: total 157

Ports: *total ports:* 6 (2024)
large: 0
medium: 0
small: 1
very small: 5
ports with oil terminals: 4
key ports: Golfito, Puerto Caldera, Puerto Limon, Puerto Moin, Puerto Quepos, Puntarenas

MILITARY AND SECURITY

Military and security forces: no regular military forces; Ministry of Public Security: National Police (Fuerza Pública), Air Surveillance Service (Servicio de Vigilancia Aérea), National Coast Guard Service (Servicio Nacional de Guardacostas), Drug Control Police (Policía Control de Drogas), Border Police (Policia de Fronteras), Professional Migration Police (Policía Profesional de Migración); Ministry of Presidency: Directorate of Intelligence and Security (DIS), Special Intervention Unit (UEI) (2024)
note: Costa Rica's armed forces were constitutionally abolished in 1949

Military expenditures: 0.6% of GDP (2023 est.)
0.6% of GDP (2022 est.)
0.7% of GDP (2021 est.)
0.7% of GDP (2020 est.)
0.7% of GDP (2019 est.)
comparison ranking: 153

Military and security service personnel strengths: 15-17,000 Ministry of Public Security personnel (2024)

Military equipment inventories and acquisitions: the National Police are lightly armed although small special units are trained and equipped for tactical operations; the US has provided equipment and support to forces such the National Coast Guard, including secondhand US vessels and aircraft (2024)

Military - note: Costa Rica relies on specialized paramilitary units within the Ministry of Public Security (MPS) for internal security missions and countering transnational threats such as narcotics smuggling and organized crime, as well as for participating in regional security operations and exercises; MPS forces have received advisory and training support from both Colombia and the US; since 2012, the US has also provided some military equipment, including aircraft and patrol boats (2024)

SPACE

Space agency/agencies: Costa Rican Space Agency (ACE; established 2021); ACE is a non-state, public entity subject to guidelines issued by the Ministry of Science, Technology, and Telecommunications (2023)

Space program overview: has a small, recently established program focused on promoting the use of space to develop the country's economy and industry, including acquiring and utilizing satellites; has built a remote sensing (RS) cube satellite; has relations with the space agencies and commercial space industries of the US, members of the European Space Agency, and members of the Latin American and Caribbean Space Agency (2024)
note: further details about the key activities, programs, and milestones of the country's space program, as well as government spending estimates on the space sector, appear in the Space Programs reference guide

TRANSNATIONAL ISSUES

Refugees and internally displaced persons: *refugees (country of origin):* 29,405 (Venezuela) (economic and political crisis; includes Venezuelans who have claimed asylum, are recognized as refugees, or received alternative legal stay) (2023)
stateless persons: 192 (2022)

Illicit drugs: Costa Rica remains a significant transshipment point for cocaine enroute to the United States from South America; a key transit point in international narcotics trafficking; transit and warehousing hub for illicit drug trafficking; growing domestic drug consumption problem; a major source of precursor or essential chemicals used in the production of illicit narcotics

COTE D'IVOIRE

INTRODUCTION

Background: Various small kingdoms ruled the area of Cote d'Ivoire between the 15th and 19th centuries, when European explorers arrived and then began to expand their presence. In 1844, France established a protectorate. During this period, many of these kingdoms and tribes fought to maintain their cultural identities – some well into the 20th century. For example, the Sanwi kingdom – originally founded in the 17th century – tried to break away from Cote d'Ivoire and establish an independent state in 1969.

Cote d'Ivoire achieved independence from France in 1960 but has maintained close ties. Foreign investment and the export and production of cocoa drove economic growth that led Cote d'Ivoire to become one of the most prosperous states in West Africa. Then in 1999, a military coup overthrew the government, and a year later, junta leader Robert GUEI held rigged elections and declared himself the winner. Popular protests forced him to step aside, and Laurent GBAGBO was elected. Ivoirian dissidents and members of the military launched a failed coup in 2002 that developed into a civil war. In 2003, a cease-fire resulted in rebels holding the north, the government holding the south, and peacekeeping forces occupying a buffer zone in the middle. In 2007, President GBAGBO and former rebel leader Guillaume SORO signed an agreement in which SORO joined GBAGBO's government as prime minister. The two agreed to reunite the country by

dismantling the buffer zone, integrating rebel forces into the national armed forces, and holding elections.

In 2010, Alassane Dramane OUATTARA won the presidential election, but GBAGBO refused to hand over power, resulting in five months of violent conflict. Armed OUATTARA supporters and UN and French troops eventually forced GBAGBO to step down in 2011. OUATTARA won a second term in 2015 and a controversial third term in 2020 – despite the two-term limit in the Ivoirian constitution – in an election boycotted by the opposition. Through political compromise with OUATTARA, the opposition participated peacefully in 2021 legislative elections and won a substantial minority of seats. Also in 2021, the International Criminal Court in The Hague ruled on a final acquittal for GBAGBO, who was on trial for crimes against humanity, paving the way for GBAGBO's return to Abidjan the same year. GBAGBO has publicly met with OUATTARA since his return as a demonstration of political reconciliation.

GEOGRAPHY

Location: Western Africa, bordering the North Atlantic Ocean, between Ghana and Liberia

Geographic coordinates: 8 00 N, 5 00 W

Map references: Africa

Area: *total:* 322,463 sq km
land: 318,003 sq km
water: 4,460 sq km
comparison ranking: total 70

Area - comparative: slightly larger than New Mexico

Land boundaries: *total:* 3,458 km
border countries (5): Burkina Faso 545 km; Ghana 720 km; Guinea 816 km; Liberia 778 km; Mali 599 km

Coastline: 515 km

Maritime claims: *territorial sea:* 12 nm
exclusive economic zone: 200 nm
continental shelf: 200 nm

Climate: tropical along coast, semiarid in far north; three seasons - warm and dry (November to March), hot and dry (March to May), hot and wet (June to October)

Terrain: mostly flat to undulating plains; mountains in northwest

Elevation: *highest point:* Monts Nimba 1,752 m
lowest point: Gulf of Guinea 0 m
mean elevation: 250 m

Natural resources: petroleum, natural gas, diamonds, manganese, iron ore, cobalt, bauxite, copper, gold, nickel, tantalum, silica sand, clay, cocoa beans, coffee, palm oil, hydropower

Land use: *agricultural land:* 64.8% (2018 est.)
arable land: 9.1% (2018 est.)
permanent crops: 14.2% (2018 est.)
permanent pasture: 41.5% (2018 est.)
forest: 32.7% (2018 est.)
other: 2.5% (2018 est.)

Irrigated land: 730 sq km (2012)

Major lakes (area sq km): *salt water lake(s):* Lagune Aby - 780 sq km

Major watersheds (area sq km): Atlantic Ocean drainage: Niger (2,261,741 sq km), Volta (410,991 sq km)

Population distribution: the population is primarily located in the forested south, with the highest concentration of people residing in and around the cities on the Atlantic coast; most of the northern savanna remains sparsely populated with higher concentrations located along transportation corridors as shown in this population distribution map

Natural hazards: coast has heavy surf and no natural harbors; during the rainy season torrential flooding is possible

Geography - note: most of the inhabitants live along the sandy coastal region; apart from the capital area, the forested interior is sparsely populated

PEOPLE AND SOCIETY

Population: *total:* 29,981,758
male: 15,040,032
female: 14,941,726 (2024 est.)
comparison rankings: female 52; male 52; total 52

Nationality: *noun:* Ivoirian(s)
adjective: Ivoirian

Ethnic groups: Akan 38%, Voltaique or Gur 22%, Northern Mande 22%, Kru 9.1%, Southern Mande 8.6%, other 0.3% (2021 est.)

Languages: French (official), 60 native dialects of which Dioula is the most widely spoken
major-language sample(s):
The World Factbook, une source indispensable d'informations de base. (French)

Religions: Muslim 42.9%, Catholic 17.2%, Evangelical 11.8%, Methodist 1.7%, other Christian 3.2%, animist 3.6%, other religion 0.5%, none 19.1% (2014 est.)
note: the majority of foreign migrant workers are Muslim (72.7%) and Christian (17.7%)

Demographic profile: Cote d'Ivoire's population is likely to continue growing for the foreseeable future because almost 60% of the populace is younger than 25 as of 2020, the total fertility rate is holding steady at about 3.5 children per woman, and contraceptive use is under 30%. The country will need to improve education, health care, and gender equality in order to turn its large and growing youth cohort into human capital. Even prior to 2010 unrest that shuttered schools for months, access to education was poor, especially for women. The lack of educational attainment contributes to Cote d'Ivoire's high rates of unskilled labor, adolescent pregnancy, and HIV/AIDS prevalence.

Following its independence in 1960, Cote d'Ivoire's stability and the blossoming of its labor-intensive cocoa and coffee industries in the southwest made it an attractive destination for migrants from other parts of the country and its neighbors, particularly Burkina Faso. The HOUPHOUET-BOIGNY administration continued the French colonial policy of encouraging labor immigration by offering liberal land ownership laws. Foreigners from West Africa, Europe (mainly France), and Lebanon composed about 25% of the population by 1998.

Ongoing economic decline since the 1980s and the power struggle after HOUPHOUET-BOIGNY's death in 1993 ushered in the politics of "Ivoirite," institutionalizing an Ivoirian identity that further marginalized northern Ivoirians and scapegoated immigrants. The hostile Muslim north-Christian south divide snowballed into a 2002 civil war, pushing tens of thousands of foreign migrants, Liberian refugees, and Ivoirians to flee to war-torn Liberia or other regional countries and more than a million people to be internally displaced. Subsequently, violence following the contested 2010 presidential election prompted some 250,000 people to seek refuge in Liberia and other neighboring countries and again internally displaced as many as a million people. By July 2012, the majority had returned home, but ongoing inter-communal tension and armed conflict continue to force people from their homes.

Age structure: *0-14 years:* 36.1% (male 5,437,108/female 5,390,782)
15-64 years: 60.9% (male 9,200,957/female 9,060,748)
65 years and over: 3% (2024 est.) (male 401,967/female 490,196)

Dependency ratios: *total dependency ratio:* 79.2
youth dependency ratio: 74.9
elderly dependency ratio: 4.3
potential support ratio: 19.3 (2021 est.)

Median age: *total:* 21.2 years (2024 est.)
male: 21.2 years
female: 21.2 years
comparison ranking: total 195

Population growth rate: 2.13% (2024 est.)
comparison ranking: 36

Birth rate: 27.5 births/1,000 population (2024 est.)
comparison ranking: 35

Death rate: 7.3 deaths/1,000 population (2024 est.)
comparison ranking: 109

Net migration rate: 1.1 migrant(s)/1,000 population (2024 est.)
comparison ranking: 62

Population distribution: the population is primarily located in the forested south, with the highest concentration of people residing in and around the cities on the Atlantic coast; most of the northern savanna remains sparsely populated with higher concentrations located along transportation corridors as shown in this population distribution map

Urbanization: *urban population:* 53.1% of total population (2023)
rate of urbanization: 3.38% annual rate of change (2020-25 est.)

Major urban areas - population: 231,000 YAMOUSSOUKRO (capital) (2018), 5.686 million ABIDJAN (seat of government) (2023)

Sex ratio: *at birth:* 1.03 male(s)/female
0-14 years: 1.01 male(s)/female
15-64 years: 1.02 male(s)/female
65 years and over: 0.82 male(s)/female
total population: 1.01 male(s)/female (2024 est.)

Mother's mean age at first birth: 19.6 years (2011/12 est.)
note: data represents median age at first birth among women 20-49

Maternal mortality ratio: 480 deaths/100,000 live births (2020 est.)
comparison ranking: 15

Infant mortality rate: *total:* 52.5 deaths/1,000 live births (2024 est.)
male: 59.5 deaths/1,000 live births
female: 45.2 deaths/1,000 live births
comparison ranking: total 17

Life expectancy at birth: *total population:* 63.2 years (2024 est.)
male: 60.9 years
female: 65.4 years
comparison ranking: total population 212

Total fertility rate: 3.4 children born/woman (2024 est.)
comparison ranking: 39

Gross reproduction rate: 1.67 (2024 est.)

Contraceptive prevalence rate: 27.8% (2020)

Drinking water source: *improved: urban:* 89.9% of population
rural: 69.1% of population
total: 79.8% of population
unimproved: urban: 10.1% of population
rural: 30.9% of population
total: 20.2% of population (2020 est.)

Current health expenditure: 3.3% of GDP (2020)

Physician density: 0.16 physicians/1,000 population (2019)

Sanitation facility access: *improved: urban:* 77.8% of population
rural: 35% of population
total: 57.1% of population
unimproved: urban: 22.2% of population
rural: 65% of population
total: 42.9% of population (2020 est.)

Obesity - adult prevalence rate: 10.3% (2016)
comparison ranking: 139

Alcohol consumption per capita: *total:* 1.7 liters of pure alcohol (2019 est.)
beer: 1.13 liters of pure alcohol (2019 est.)
wine: 0.33 liters of pure alcohol (2019 est.)
spirits: 0.2 liters of pure alcohol (2019 est.)
other alcohols: 0.04 liters of pure alcohol (2019 est.)
comparison ranking: total 133

Tobacco use: *total:* 9.4% (2020 est.)
male: 17.9% (2020 est.)
female: 0.9% (2020 est.)
comparison ranking: total 136

Children under the age of 5 years underweight: 12.8% (2016)
comparison ranking: 40

Currently married women (ages 15-49): 60.3% (2023 est.)

Child marriage: *women married by age 15:* 7%
women married by age 18: 27%
men married by age 18: 3.5% (2016 est.)

Education expenditures: 3.4% of GDP (2020 est.)
comparison ranking: 144

Literacy: *definition:* age 15 and over can read and write
total population: 89.9%
male: 93.1%
female: 86.7% (2019)

School life expectancy (primary to tertiary education): *total:* 11 years
male: 11 years
female: 10 years (2020)

ENVIRONMENT

Environment - current issues: deforestation (most of the country's forests - once the largest in West Africa - have been heavily logged); water pollution from sewage, and from industrial, mining, and agricultural effluents

Environment - international agreements: *party to:* Biodiversity, Climate Change, Climate Change-Kyoto Protocol, Climate Change-Paris Agreement, Comprehensive Nuclear Test Ban, Desertification, Endangered Species, Hazardous Wastes, Law of the Sea, Marine Dumping-London Convention, Nuclear Test Ban, Ozone Layer Protection, Ship Pollution, Tropical Timber 2006, Wetlands, Whaling
signed, but not ratified: none of the selected agreements

Climate: tropical along coast, semiarid in far north; three seasons - warm and dry (November to March), hot and dry (March to May), hot and wet (June to October)

Urbanization: *urban population:* 53.1% of total population (2023)
rate of urbanization: 3.38% annual rate of change (2020-25 est.)

Revenue from forest resources: 2.04% of GDP (2016 est.)
comparison ranking: 34

Revenue from coal: 0% of GDP (2018 est.)
comparison ranking: 166

Air pollutants: *particulate matter emissions:* 40.41 micrograms per cubic meter (2019 est.)
carbon dioxide emissions: 9.67 megatons (2016 est.)
methane emissions: 10.3 megatons (2020 est.)

Waste and recycling: *municipal solid waste generated annually:* 4,440,814 tons (2010 est.)
municipal solid waste recycled annually: 133,224 tons (2005 est.)
percent of municipal solid waste recycled: 3% (2005 est.)

Major lakes (area sq km): *salt water lake(s):* Lagune Aby - 780 sq km

Major watersheds (area sq km): Atlantic Ocean drainage: Niger (2,261,741 sq km), Volta (410,991 sq km)

Total water withdrawal: *municipal:* 320 million cubic meters (2020 est.)
industrial: 240 million cubic meters (2020 est.)
agricultural: 600 million cubic meters (2020 est.)

Total renewable water resources: 84.14 billion cubic meters (2020 est.)

GOVERNMENT

Country name: *conventional long form:* Republic of Côte d'Ivoire
conventional short form: Côte d'Ivoire
local long form: République de Côte d'Ivoire
local short form: Cote d'Ivoire
former: Ivory Coast
etymology: name reflects the intense ivory trade that took place in the region from the 15th to 17th centuries
note: pronounced coat-div-whar

Government type: presidential republic

Capital: *name:* Yamoussoukro (legislative capital), Abidjan (administrative capital); note - although Yamoussoukro has been the official capital since 1983, Abidjan remains the administrative capital as well as the officially designated economic capital; the US, like other countries, maintains its Embassy in Abidjan
geographic coordinates: 6 49 N, 5 16 W
time difference: UTC 0 (5 hours ahead of Washington, DC, during Standard Time)
etymology: Yamoussoukro is named after Queen YAMOUSSOU, who ruled in the village of N'Gokro in 1929 at the time of French colonization; the village was renamed Yamoussoukro, the suffix "-kro" meaning "town" in the native Baoule language; Abidjan's name supposedly comes from a misunderstanding; tradition states that an old man carrying branches met a European explorer who asked for the name of the nearest village; the man, not understanding and terrified by this unexpected encounter, fled shouting "min-chan m'bidjan," which in the Ebrie language means: "I return from cutting leaves"; the explorer, thinking that his question had been answered, recorded the name of the locale as Abidjan; a different version has the first colonists asking native women the name of the place and getting a similar response

Administrative divisions: 12 districts and 2 autonomous districts*; Abidjan*, Bas-Sassandra, Comoe, Denguele, Goh-Djiboua, Lacs, Lagunes, Montagnes, Sassandra-Marahoue, Savanes, Vallee du Bandama, Woroba, Yamoussoukro*, Zanzan

Independence: 7 August 1960 (from France)

National holiday: Independence Day, 7 August (1960)

Legal system: civil law system based on the French civil code; judicial review of legislation held in the Constitutional Chamber of the Supreme Court

Constitution: *history:* previous 1960, 2000; latest draft completed 24 September 2016, approved by the National Assembly 11 October 2016, approved by referendum 30 October 2016, promulgated 8 November 2016
amendments: proposed by the president of the republic or by Parliament; consideration of drafts or proposals requires an absolute majority vote by the parliamentary membership; passage of amendments affecting presidential elections, presidential term of office and vacancies, and amendment procedures requires approval by absolute majority in a referendum; passage of other proposals by the president requires at least four-fifths majority vote by Parliament; constitutional articles on the sovereignty of the state and its republican and secular form of government cannot be amended; amended 2020

International law organization participation: accepts compulsory ICJ jurisdiction with reservations; accepts ICCt jurisdiction

Citizenship: *citizenship by birth:* no
citizenship by descent only: at least one parent must be a citizen of Cote d'Ivoire
dual citizenship recognized: no
residency requirement for naturalization: 5 years

Suffrage: 18 years of age; universal

Executive branch: *chief of state:* President Alassane Dramane OUATTARA (since 4 December 2010)
head of government: Prime Minister Robert BREUGRE MAMBE (since 17 October 2023)

cabinet: Council of Ministers appointed by the president
elections/appointments: president directly elected by absolute majority popular vote in 2 rounds if needed for a single renewable 5-year term; election last held on 31 October 2020 (next to be held in 2025); vice president elected on same ballot as president; prime minister appointed by the president; note – because President OUATTARA promulgated the new constitution in 2016, he has claimed that the clock is reset on term limits, allowing him to run for up to two additional terms
election results:
2020: Alassane OUATTARA reelected president; percent of vote - Alassane OUATTARA (RDR) 94.3%, Kouadio Konan BERTIN (PDCI-RDA) 2.0%, other 3.7%
2015: Alassane OUATTARA reelected president; percent of vote - Alassane OUATTARA (RDR) 83.7%, Pascal Affi N'GUESSAN (FPI) 9.3%, Konan Bertin KOUADIO (independent) 3.9%, other 3.1%

Legislative branch: *description:* bicameral Parliament consists of:
Senate or Senat (99 seats; 66 members indirectly elected by the National Assembly and members of municipal, autonomous districts, and regional councils, and 33 members appointed by the president; members serve 5-year terms) National Assembly (255 seats - 254 for 2021-2026 term; members directly elected in single- and multi-seat constituencies by simple majority vote to serve 5-year terms)
elections: Senate - last held on 16 September 2023 (next to be held in September 2028)
National Assembly - last held on 6 March 2021 (next to be held on 31 March 2026)
election results: Senate - percent by party/coalition NA; seats by party/coalition - RHDP 56, PDCI-RDA 6, independent 2, vacant 2; composition - men 73, women 24, percentage women 15.6% (2 seats vacant); note - 33 members appointed - RHDP 25, independent 8
National Assembly - percent of vote by party/coalition - RHDP 49.2%, PDCI-RRA-EDS 16.5%, DPIC 6%, TTB 2.1%, IPF 2%, other 24.2%; seats by party/coalition - RHDP, 137, PDCI-RRA-EDS 50, DPIC 23, EDS 8, TTB 8, IPF 2, independent 26, vacant 1; composition - men 220, women 34, percentage women 13.4%; note - total Parliament percentage women 16.5%

Judicial branch: *highest court(s):* Supreme Court or Cour Supreme (organized into Judicial, Audit, Constitutional, and Administrative Chambers; consists of the court president, 3 vice presidents for the Judicial, Audit, and Administrative chambers, and 9 associate justices or magistrates)
judge selection and term of office: judges nominated by the Superior Council of the Magistrature, a 7-member body consisting of the national president (chairman), 3 "bench" judges, and 3 public prosecutors; judges appointed for life
subordinate courts: Courts of Appeal (organized into civil, criminal, and social chambers); first instance courts; peace courts

Political parties: African Peoples' Party-Cote d'Ivoire or PPA-CI
Democratic Party of Cote d'Ivoire or PDCI
Ivorian Popular Front or FPI
Liberty and Democracy for the Republic or LIDER
Movement of the Future Forces or MFA
Pan-African Congress for People's Justice and Equality or COJEP
Rally of Houphouetists for Democracy and Peace or RHDP
Rally of the Republicans or RDR
Together for Democracy and Sovereignty or EDS
Together to Build (UDPCI, FPI,and allies)
Union for Cote d'Ivoire or UPCI
Union for Democracy and Peace in Cote d'Ivoire or UDPCI

International organization participation: ACP, AfDB, AU, ECOWAS, EITI (compliant country), Entente, FAO, FZ, G-24, G-77, IAEA, IBRD, ICAO, ICC, ICCt, ICRM, IDA, IDB, IFAD, IFC, IFRCS, ILO, IMF, IMO, Interpol, IOC, IOM, IPU, ISO, ITSO, ITU, ITUC (NGOs), MIGA, MINUSCA, MONUSCO, NAM, OIC, OIF, OPCW, UN, UNCTAD, UNESCO, UNHCR, UNHRC, UNIDO, UNMISS, Union Latina, UNWTO, UPU, WADB (regional), WAEMU, WCO, WFTU (NGOs), WHO, WIPO, WMO, WTO

Diplomatic representation in the US: *chief of mission:* Ambassador Ibrahima TOURE (since 13 January 2022)
chancery: 2424 Massachusetts Avenue NW, Washington, DC 20008
telephone: [1] (202) 797-0300
FAX: [1] (202) 204-3967
email address and website:
info@ambacidc.org
Ambassade de Cote D'ivoire aux USA (ambaciusa.org)

Diplomatic representation from the US: *chief of mission:* Ambassador Jessica Davis BA (since 2 March 2023)
embassy: B.P. 730 Abidjan Cidex 03
mailing address: 2010 Abidjan Place, Washington DC 20521-2010
telephone: [225] 27-22-49-40-00
FAX: [225] 27-22-49-43-23
email address and website:
AbjAmCit@state.gov
https://ci.usembassy.gov/

Flag description: three equal vertical bands of orange (hoist side), white, and green; orange symbolizes the land (savannah) of the north and fertility, white stands for peace and unity, green represents the forests of the south and the hope for a bright future
note: similar to the flag of Ireland, which is longer and has the colors reversed - green (hoist side), white, and orange; also similar to the flag of Italy, which is green (hoist side), white, and red; design was based on the flag of France

National symbol(s): elephant; national colors: orange, white, green

National anthem: *name:* "L'Abidjanaise" (Song of Abidjan)
lyrics/music: Mathieu EKRA, Joachim BONY, and Pierre Marie COTY/Pierre Marie COTY and Pierre Michel PANGO
note: adopted 1960; although the nation's capital city moved from Abidjan to Yamoussoukro in 1983, the anthem still owes its name to the former capital

National heritage: *total World Heritage Sites:* 5 (2 cultural, 3 natural)
selected World Heritage Site locales: Comoé National Park (n); Historic Grand-Bassam (c); Mount Nimba Strict Nature Reserve (n); Sudanese-style Mosques (c); Taï National Park (n)

ECONOMY

Economic overview: one of West Africa's most influential, stable, and rapidly developing economies; poverty declines in urban but increases in rural areas; strong construction sector and increasingly diverse economic portfolio; increasing but manageable public debt; large labor force in agriculture

Real GDP (purchasing power parity): $202.758 billion (2023 est.)
$190.319 billion (2022 est.)
$179.178 billion (2021 est.)
note: data in 2021 dollars
comparison ranking: 77

Real GDP growth rate: 6.54% (2023 est.)
6.22% (2022 est.)
7.06% (2021 est.)
note: annual GDP % growth based on constant local currency
comparison ranking: 24

Real GDP per capita: $7,000 (2023 est.)
$6,800 (2022 est.)
$6,500 (2021 est.)
note: data in 2021 dollars
comparison ranking: 159

GDP (official exchange rate): $78.789 billion (2023 est.)
note: data in current dollars at official exchange rate

Inflation rate (consumer prices): 4.39% (2023 est.)
5.28% (2022 est.)
4.09% (2021 est.)
note: annual % change based on consumer prices
comparison ranking: 93

Credit ratings: Fitch rating: B+ (2015)

Moody's rating: Ba3 (2015)
note: The year refers to the year in which the current credit rating was first obtained.

GDP - composition, by sector of origin: *agriculture:* 14.4% (2023 est.)
industry: 24.5% (2023 est.)
services: 54.3% (2023 est.)
note: figures may not total 100% due to non-allocated consumption not captured in sector-reported data comparison rankings: services 122; industry 103; agriculture 59

GDP - composition, by end use: *household consumption:* 67.7% (2023 est.)
government consumption: 10.3% (2023 est.)
investment in fixed capital: 25.5% (2023 est.)
investment in inventories: 0.3% (2023 est.)
exports of goods and services: 22.9% (2023 est.)
imports of goods and services: -26.6% (2023 est.)
note: figures may not total 100% due to rounding or gaps in data collection

Agricultural products: yams, cassava, oil palm fruit, cocoa beans, sugarcane, plantains, rice, rubber, maize, cashews (2022)
note: top ten agricultural products based on tonnage

Industries: foodstuffs, beverages; wood products, oil refining, gold mining, truck and bus assembly, textiles, fertilizer, building materials, electricity

Industrial production growth rate: 9.06% (2023 est.)
note: annual % change in industrial value added based on constant local currency
comparison ranking: 21

Labor force: 10.954 million (2023 est.)

note: number of people ages 15 or older who are employed or seeking work
comparison ranking: 53

Unemployment rate: 2.4% (2023 est.)
2.43% (2022 est.)
2.59% (2021 est.)
note: % of labor force seeking employment
comparison ranking: 28

Youth unemployment rate (ages 15-24): *total:* 4% (2023 est.)
male: 3.3% (2023 est.)
female: 4.9% (2023 est.)
note: % of labor force ages 15-24 seeking employment
comparison ranking: total 184

Population below poverty line: 37.5% (2021 est.)
note: % of population with income below national poverty line

Gini Index coefficient - distribution of family income: 35.3 (2021 est.)
note: index (0-100) of income distribution; higher values represent greater inequality
comparison ranking: 74

Average household expenditures: *on food:* 38.2% of household expenditures (2022 est.)
on alcohol and tobacco: 3.2% of household expenditures (2022 est.)

Household income or consumption by percentage share: *lowest 10%:* 3.1% (2021 est.)
highest 10%: 27.8% (2021 est.)
note: % share of income accruing to lowest and highest 10% of population

Remittances: 0.57% of GDP (2023 est.)
1.48% of GDP (2022 est.)
0.6% of GDP (2021 est.)
note: personal transfers and compensation between resident and non-resident individuals/households/entities

Budget: *revenues:* $9.755 billion (2022 est.)
expenditures: $13.255 billion (2022 est.)
note: central government revenues (excluding grants) and expenses converted to US dollars at average official exchange rate for year indicated

Public debt: 47% of GDP (2017 est.)
comparison ranking: 115

Taxes and other revenues: 11.94% (of GDP) (2022 est.)
note: central government tax revenue as a % of GDP
comparison ranking: 166

Current account balance: -$5.394 billion (2022 est.)
-$2.874 billion (2021 est.)
-$1.974 billion (2020 est.)
note: balance of payments - net trade and primary/secondary income in current dollars
comparison ranking: 184

Exports: $17.211 billion (2022 est.)
$16.23 billion (2021 est.)
$13.232 billion (2020 est.)
note: balance of payments - exports of goods and services in current dollars
comparison ranking: 97

Exports - partners: Switzerland 9%, Mali 8%, Netherlands 8%, US 6%, France 5% (2022)
note: top five export partners based on percentage share of exports

Exports - commodities: cocoa beans, gold, rubber, refined petroleum, cocoa paste (2022)
note: top five export commodities based on value in dollars

Imports: $19.948 billion (2022 est.)
$16.191 billion (2021 est.)
$12.66 billion (2020 est.)
note: balance of payments - imports of goods and services in current dollars
comparison ranking: 96

Imports - partners: China 18%, Nigeria 11%, France 8%, India 5%, Belgium 4% (2022)
note: top five import partners based on percentage share of imports

Imports - commodities: crude petroleum, refined petroleum, ships, rice, fish (2022)
note: top five import commodities based on value in dollars

Reserves of foreign exchange and gold: $6.257 billion (31 December 2017 est.)
$4.935 billion (31 December 2016 est.)
comparison ranking: 93

Debt - external: $23.623 billion (2022 est.)
note: present value of external debt in current US dollars
comparison ranking: 22

Exchange rates: Communaute Financiere Africaine francs (XOF) per US dollar -

Exchange rates: 606.57 (2023 est.)
623.76 (2022 est.)
554.531 (2021 est.)
575.586 (2020 est.)
585.911 (2019 est.)

ENERGY

Electricity access: *electrification - total population:* 70.4% (2022 est.)
electrification - urban areas: 95%
electrification - rural areas: 45.3%

Electricity: *installed generating capacity:* 2.282 million kW (2022 est.)
consumption: 8.744 billion kWh (2022 est.)
exports: 901.596 million kWh (2022 est.)
imports: 297 million kWh (2022 est.)
transmission/distribution losses: 1.778 billion kWh (2022 est.)
comparison rankings: transmission/distribution losses 120; imports 102; exports 69; consumption 112; installed generating capacity 119

Electricity generation sources: *fossil fuels:* 68.9% of total installed capacity (2022 est.)
solar: 0.2% of total installed capacity (2022 est.)
hydroelectricity: 30.1% of total installed capacity (2022 est.)
biomass and waste: 0.7% of total installed capacity (2022 est.)

Coal: *imports:* 500 metric tons (2022 est.)

Petroleum: *total petroleum production:* 29,000 bbl/day (2023 est.)
refined petroleum consumption: 60,000 bbl/day (2022 est.)
crude oil estimated reserves: 100 million barrels (2021 est.)

Natural gas: *production:* 2.635 billion cubic meters (2022 est.)
consumption: 2.635 billion cubic meters (2022 est.)
proven reserves: 28.317 billion cubic meters (2021 est.)

Carbon dioxide emissions: 12.733 million metric tonnes of CO_2 (2022 est.)
from coal and metallurgical coke: 1,000 metric tonnes of CO_2 (2022 est.)
from petroleum and other liquids: 7.79 million metric tonnes of CO_2 (2022 est.)
from consumed natural gas: 4.942 million metric tonnes of CO_2 (2022 est.)
comparison ranking: total emissions 101

Energy consumption per capita: 7.733 million Btu/person (2022 est.)
comparison ranking: 157

COMMUNICATIONS

Telephones - fixed lines: *total subscriptions:* 263,000 (2022 est.)
subscriptions per 100 inhabitants: (2022 est.) less than 1
comparison ranking: total subscriptions 113

Telephones - mobile cellular: *total subscriptions:* 49.006 million (2022 est.)
subscriptions per 100 inhabitants: 174 (2022 est.)
comparison ranking: total subscriptions 36

Telecommunication systems: *general assessment:* in recent years the government of Ivory Coast has helped develop a competitive telecom sector focused on the provision of converged services, thus allowing operators to offer fixed-line and mobile services under a universal services license regime; the fixed internet and broadband sectors remain underdeveloped; this is a legacy of poor international connectivity, which resulted in high wholesale prices, limited bandwidth, and a lack of access for alternative operators to international infrastructure; these limitations were addressed following the landing of a second cable in November 2011; Orange Group has also launched its 20,000km Djoliba cable system, reaching across eight countries in the region, while the 2Africa submarine cable is being developed by a consortium of companies; with a landing station providing connectivity to Côte d'Ivoire, the system is expected to be completed in late 2023 (2022)
domestic: 1 per 100 fixed-line teledensity; mobile subscriptions are 162 per 100 persons (2021)
international: country code - 225; landing point for the SAT-3/WASC, ACE, MainOne, and WACS fiber-optic submarine cable that provides connectivity to Europe and South and West Africa; satellite earth stations - 2 Intelsat (1 Atlantic Ocean and 1 Indian Ocean) (2019)

Broadcast media: state-controlled Radiodiffusion Television Ivoirieinne (RTI) is made up of 2 radio stations (Radio Cote d'Ivoire and Frequence2) and 2 television stations (RTI1 and RTI2), with nationwide coverage, broadcasts mainly in French; after 2011 post-electoral crisis, President OUATTARA's administration reopened RTI Bouake', the broadcaster's office in Cote d'Ivoire's 2nd largest city, where facilities were destroyed during the 2002 rebellion; Cote d'Ivoire is also home to 178 proximity radio stations, 16 religious radio stations, 5 commercial radio stations, and 5 international radios stations, according to the Haute Autorite' de la Communication Audiovisuelle (HACA); govt now runs radio UNOCIFM, a radio station previously owned by the UN Operation in Cote d'Ivoire; in Dec 2016, the govt announced 4 companies had been granted licenses to operate -Live TV, Optimum Media Cote d'Ivoire, the Audiovisual Company of Cote d'Ivoire

(Sedaci), and Sorano-CI, out of the 4 companies only one has started operating (2019)

Internet country code: .ci

Internet users: *total:* 12.15 million (2021 est.)
percent of population: 45% (2021 est.)
comparison ranking: total 55

Broadband - fixed subscriptions: *total:* 260,097 (2020 est.)
subscriptions per 100 inhabitants: 1 (2020 est.)
comparison ranking: total 110

TRANSPORTATION

National air transport system: *number of registered air carriers:* 1 (2020)
inventory of registered aircraft operated by air carriers: 10
annual passenger traffic on registered air carriers: 779,482 (2018)
annual freight traffic on registered air carriers: 5.8 million (2018) mt-km

Civil aircraft registration country code prefix: TU

Airports: 29 (2024)
comparison ranking: 121

Heliports: 1 (2024)

Pipelines: 101 km condensate, 256 km gas, 118 km oil, 5 km oil/gas/water, 7 km water (2013)

Railways: *total:* 660 km (2008)
narrow gauge: 660 km (2008) 1.000-m gauge
note: an additional 622 km of this railroad extends into Burkina Faso
comparison ranking: total 103

Roadways: *total:* 81,996 km
paved: 6,502 km
unpaved: 75,494 km (2007)
note: includes intercity and urban roads; another 20,000 km of dirt roads are in poor condition and 150,000 km of dirt roads are impassable
comparison ranking: total 62

Waterways: 980 km (2011) (navigable rivers, canals, and numerous coastal lagoons)
comparison ranking: 72

Merchant marine: *total:* 25 (2023)
by type: oil tanker 2, other 23
comparison ranking: total 140

Ports: *total ports:* 5 (2024)
large: 1
medium: 0 small: 0
very small: 4
ports with oil terminals: 5
key ports: Abidjan, Baobab Marine Terminal, Espoir Marine Terminal, Port Bouet, San Pedro

MILITARY AND SECURITY

Military and security forces: Armed Forces of Cote d'Ivoire (Forces Armees de Cote d'Ivoire, FACI; aka Republican Forces of Ivory Coast, FRCI): Army (Land Force), National Navy, Air Force, Special Forces; National Gendarmerie (under the Ministry of Defense)

Ministry of Security and Civil Protection: National Police, Coordination Center for Operational Decisions (a mix of police, gendarmerie, and FACI personnel for assisting police in providing security in some large cities), Directorate of Territorial Surveillance (2024)
note: the National Gendarmerie is a military force established to ensure public safety, maintain order, enforce laws, and protect institutions, people, and property; it is organized into "legions" and has both territorial and mobile units; the Mobile Gendarmerie is responsible for maintaining and restoring order and is considered the backbone of the country's domestic security; the Territorial Gendarmerie is responsible for the administrative, judicial, and military police; the Gendarmerie also has separate specialized units for security, intervention (counterterrorism, hostage rescue, etc), VIP protection, and surveillance; the Directorate of Territorial Surveillance is responsible for countering internal threats

Military expenditures: 0.9% of GDP (2023 est.)
0.9% of GDP (2022 est.)
1.1% of GDP (2021 est.)
1.1% of GDP (2020 est.)
1.1% of GDP (2019 est.)
comparison ranking: 135

Military and security service personnel strengths: approximately 25,000 active troops (23,000 Army, including about 2,000 Special Forces; 1,000 Navy; 1,000 Air Force); 5-10,000 Gendarmerie (2023)

Military equipment inventories and acquisitions: the inventory of the FACI consists mostly of older or second-hand equipment, typically of French or Soviet-era origin; Cote d'Ivoire was under a partial UN arms embargo from 2004 to 2016; in recent years it has received some new and second-hand equipment from a variety of suppliers, including Bulgaria, China, France, South Africa, and Turkey (2024)

Military service age and obligation: 18-26 years of age for compulsory and voluntary military service for men and women; conscription is reportedly not enforced (2023)

Military deployments: 180 Central African Republic (MINUSCA) (2024)

Military - note: the military (FACI) was established in 1960 from home defense units the French colonial government began standing up in 1950; the FACI has mutinied several times since the late 1990s, most recently in 2017, and has had a large role in the country's political turmoil; it is responsible for external defense but also has a considerable internal role supporting the National Gendarmerie and other internal security forces; the operational focus of the FACI is the threat posed by Islamic militants associated with the al-Qa'ida in the Islamic Maghreb (AQIM) terrorist group operating across the border in Burkina Faso and Mali; AQIM militants conducted significant attacks in the country in 2016 and 2020; Côte d'Ivoire since 2016 has stepped up border security and completed building a joint counter-terrorism training center with France near Abidjan in 2020
Cote d'Ivoire has close security ties with France, which maintains a military presence; the UN had a 9,000-strong peacekeeping force in Cote d'Ivoire (UNOCI) from 2004 until 2017 (2024)

SPACE

Space agency/agencies: announced in 2021 that it was in the process of establishing a national space agency (space issues currently managed by the Ministry of Scientific Research) (2024)

Space program overview: has as small, nascent program focused on acquiring a remote sensing (RS) satellite for purposes detecting illegal gold mining, facilitating access to drinking water, mapping deforestation, and national security issues (2024)
note: further details about the key activities, programs, and milestones of the country's space program, as well as government spending estimates on the space sector, appear in the Space Programs reference guide

TERRORISM

Terrorist group(s): al-Qa'ida in the Islamic Maghreb (AQIM); Jama'at Nusrat al Islam wal Muslimeen (JNIM)
note: details about the history, aims, leadership, organization, areas of operation, tactics, targets, weapons, size, and sources of support of the group(s) appear(s) in the Terrorism reference guide

TRANSNATIONAL ISSUES

Refugees and internally displaced persons: IDPs: 302,000 (post-election conflict in 2010-11, as well as civil war from 2002-04; land disputes; most pronounced in western and southwestern regions) (2022)
stateless persons: 930,578 (2022); note - many Ivoirians lack documentation proving their nationality, which prevent them from accessing education and healthcare; birth on Ivorian soil does not automatically result in citizenship; disputes over citizenship and the associated rights of the large population descended from migrants from neighboring countries is an ongoing source of tension and contributed to the country's 2002 civil war; some observers believe the government's mass naturalizations of thousands of people over the last couple of years is intended to boost its electoral support base; the government in October 2013 acceded to international conventions on statelessness and in August 2013 reformed its nationality law, key steps to clarify the nationality of thousands of residents; since the adoption of the Abidjan Declaration to eradicate statelessness in West Africa in February 2015, 6,400 people have received nationality papers in Cote d'Ivoire; in September 2020, Cote d'Ivoire adopted Africa's first statelessness determination procedure to regularize the status of stateless people

Illicit drugs: illicit producer of cannabis, mostly for local consumption; utility as a narcotic transshipment point to Europe reduced by ongoing political instability; while rampant corruption and inadequate supervision leave the banking system vulnerable to money laundering, the lack of a developed financial system limits the country's utility as a major money-laundering center

CROATIA

INTRODUCTION

Background: The lands that today comprise Croatia were part of the Austro-Hungarian Empire until the end of World War I. In 1918, the Croats, Serbs, and Slovenes formed a kingdom known after 1929 as Yugoslavia. Following World War II, Yugoslavia became a federal independent communist state consisting of six socialist republics, including Croatia, under the strong hand of Josip Broz, aka TITO. Although Croatia declared its independence from Yugoslavia in 1991, it took four years of sporadic, but often bitter, fighting before Yugoslav forces were cleared from Croatian lands, along with a majority of Croatia's ethnic Serb population. Under UN supervision, the last Serb-held enclave in eastern Slavonia was returned to Croatia in 1998. The country joined NATO in 2009 and the EU in 2013. In January 2023, Croatia further integrated into the EU by joining the Eurozone and the Schengen Area.

GEOGRAPHY

Location: Southeastern Europe, bordering the Adriatic Sea, between Bosnia and Herzegovina and Slovenia

Geographic coordinates: 45 10 N, 15 30 E

Map references: Europe

Area: *total:* 56,594 sq km
land: 55,974 sq km
water: 620 sq km
comparison ranking: total 127

Area - comparative: slightly smaller than West Virginia

Land boundaries: *total:* 2,237 km
border countries (5): Bosnia and Herzegovina 956 km; Hungary 348 km; Montenegro 19 km; Serbia 314 km; Slovenia 600 km

Coastline: 5,835 km (mainland 1,777 km, islands 4,058 km)

Maritime claims: *territorial sea:* 12 nm
continental shelf: 200-m depth or to the depth of exploitation

Climate: Mediterranean and continental; continental climate predominant with hot summers and cold winters; mild winters, dry summers along coast

Terrain: geographically diverse; flat plains along Hungarian border, low mountains and highlands near Adriatic coastline and islands

Elevation: *highest point:* Dinara 1,831 m
lowest point: Adriatic Sea 0 m
mean elevation: 331 m

Natural resources: oil, some coal, bauxite, low-grade iron ore, calcium, gypsum, natural asphalt, silica, mica, clays, salt, hydropower

Land use: *agricultural land:* 23.7% (2018 est.)
arable land: 16% (2018 est.)
permanent crops: 1.5% (2018 est.)
permanent pasture: 6.2% (2018 est.)
forest: 34.4% (2018 est.)
other: 41.9% (2018 est.)

Irrigated land: 171 sq km (2020)

Major rivers (by length in km): Dunav (Danube) (shared with Germany [s], Austria, Slovakia, Hungary, Serbia, Bulgaria, Ukraine, Moldova, and Romania [m]) - 2,888 km
note – [s] after country name indicates river source; [m] after country name indicates river mouth

Major watersheds (area sq km): Atlantic Ocean drainage: *(Black Sea)* Danube (795,656 sq km)

Population distribution: more of the population lives in the northern half of the country, with approximately a quarter of the populace residing in and around the capital of Zagreb; many of the islands are sparsely populated

Natural hazards: destructive earthquakes

Geography - note: controls most land routes from Western Europe to Aegean Sea and Turkish Straits; most Adriatic Sea islands lie off the coast of Croatia – some 1,200 islands, islets, ridges, and rocks

PEOPLE AND SOCIETY

Population: *total:* 4,150,116
male: 2,003,431
female: 2,146,685 (2024 est.)
comparison rankings: female 129; male 130; total 129

Nationality: *noun:* Croat(s), Croatian(s)
adjective: Croatian
note: the French designation of "Croate" to Croatian mercenaries in the 17th century eventually became "Cravate" and later came to be applied to the soldiers' scarves - the cravat; Croatia celebrates Cravat Day every 18 October

Ethnic groups: Croat 91.6%, Serb 3.2%, other 3.9% (including Bosniak, Romani, Albanian, Italian, and Hungarian), unspecified 1.3% (2021 est.)

Languages: Croatian (official) 95.2%, Serbian 1.2%, other 3.1% (including Bosnian, Romani, Albanian, and Italian) unspecified 0.5% (2021 est.)
major-language sample(s):
Knjiga svjetskih cinjenica, nužan izvor osnovnih informacija. (Croatian)

Religions: Roman Catholic 79%, Orthodox 3.3%, Protestant 0.3%, other Christian 4.8%, Muslim 1.3%, other 1.1%, agnostic 1.7%, none or atheist 4.7%, unspecified 3.9% (2021 est.)

Age structure: *0-14 years:* 13.8% (male 296,527/female 278,236)
15-64 years: 63.1% (male 1,307,814/female 1,309,394)
65 years and over: 23.1% (2024 est.) (male 399,090/female 559,055)

Dependency ratios: *total dependency ratio:* 56.5
youth dependency ratio: 22.1
elderly dependency ratio: 34.4
potential support ratio: 2.9 (2021 est.)

Median age: *total:* 45.1 years (2024 est.)
male: 43.2 years
female: 47 years
comparison ranking: total 20

Population growth rate: -0.46% (2024 est.)
comparison ranking: 220

Birth rate: 8.5 births/1,000 population (2024 est.)
comparison ranking: 205

Death rate: 13.1 deaths/1,000 population (2024 est.)
comparison ranking: 13

Net migration rate: 0 migrant(s)/1,000 population (2024 est.)
comparison ranking: 86

Population distribution: more of the population lives in the northern half of the country, with approximately a quarter of the populace residing in and around the capital of Zagreb; many of the islands are sparsely populated

Urbanization: *urban population:* 58.6% of total population (2023)
rate of urbanization: 0.05% annual rate of change (2020-25 est.)

Major urban areas - population: 684,000 ZAGREB (capital) (2023)

Sex ratio: *at birth:* 1.06 male(s)/female
0-14 years: 1.07 male(s)/female
15-64 years: 1 male(s)/female
65 years and over: 0.71 male(s)/female
total population: 0.93 male(s)/female (2024 est.)

Mother's mean age at first birth: 29 years (2020 est.)

Maternal mortality ratio: 5 deaths/100,000 live births (2020 est.)
comparison ranking: 169

Infant mortality rate: *total:* 8.4 deaths/1,000 live births (2024 est.)
male: 8.2 deaths/1,000 live births
female: 8.7 deaths/1,000 live births
comparison ranking: total 143

Life expectancy at birth: *total population:* 77.7 years (2024 est.)
male: 74.6 years
female: 81 years
comparison ranking: total population 86

Total fertility rate: 1.46 children born/woman (2024 est.)
comparison ranking: 206

Gross reproduction rate: 0.71 (2024 est.)

Drinking water source: *improved:*
total: 100% of population
unimproved:

Current health expenditure: 7.8% of GDP (2020)

Physician density: 3.47 physicians/1,000 population (2019)

Hospital bed density: 5.5 beds/1,000 population (2017)

Sanitation facility access: *improved: urban:* 99.5% of population
rural: 98.4% of population
total: 99% of population
unimproved: urban: 0.5% of population
rural: 1.6% of population
total: 1% of population (2020 est.)

Obesity - adult prevalence rate: 24.4% (2016)
comparison ranking: 59

Alcohol consumption per capita: *total:* 9.64 liters of pure alcohol (2019 est.)
beer: 4.75 liters of pure alcohol (2019 est.)
wine: 3.52 liters of pure alcohol (2019 est.)
spirits: 1.37 liters of pure alcohol (2019 est.)
other alcohols: 0.36 liters of pure alcohol (2019 est.)
comparison ranking: total 25

Tobacco use: *total:* 36.9% (2020 est.)
male: 37.6% (2020 est.)
female: 36.1% (2020 est.)
comparison ranking: total 11

Currently married women (ages 15-49): 50.8% (2023 est.)

Education expenditures: 5.5% of GDP (2020 est.)
comparison ranking: 60

Literacy: *definition:* age 15 and over can read and write
total population: 99.4%
male: 99.7%
female: 99.2% (2021)

School life expectancy (primary to tertiary education): *total:* 15 years
male: 14 years
female: 16 years (2020)

ENVIRONMENT

Environment - current issues: air pollution improving but still a concern in urban settings and in emissions arriving from neighboring countries; surface water pollution in the Danube River Basin

Environment - international agreements: *party to:* Air Pollution, Air Pollution-Heavy Metals, Air Pollution-Multi-effect Protocol, Air Pollution-Nitrogen Oxides, Air Pollution-Persistent Organic Pollutants, Air Pollution-Sulphur 94, Air Pollution-Volatile Organic Compounds, Biodiversity, Climate Change, Climate Change-Kyoto Protocol, Climate Change-Paris Agreement, Comprehensive Nuclear Test Ban, Desertification, Endangered Species, Hazardous Wastes, Law of the Sea, Marine Dumping-London Convention, Nuclear Test Ban, Ozone Layer Protection, Ship Pollution, Tropical Timber 2006, Wetlands, Whaling
signed, but not ratified: none of the selected agreements

Climate: Mediterranean and continental; continental climate predominant with hot summers and cold winters; mild winters, dry summers along coast

Urbanization: *urban population:* 58.6% of total population (2023)
rate of urbanization: 0.05% annual rate of change (2020-25 est.)

Revenue from forest resources: 0.26% of GDP (2018 est.)
comparison ranking: 87

Revenue from coal: 0% of GDP (2018 est.)
comparison ranking: 129

Air pollutants: *particulate matter emissions:* 15.29 micrograms per cubic meter (2019 est.)
carbon dioxide emissions: 17.49 megatons (2016 est.)
methane emissions: 3.98 megatons (2020 est.)

Waste and recycling: *municipal solid waste generated annually:* 1.654 million tons (2015 est.)
municipal solid waste recycled annually: 269,933 tons (2015 est.)
percent of municipal solid waste recycled: 16.3% (2015 est.)

Major rivers (by length in km): Dunav (Danube) (shared with Germany [s], Austria, Slovakia, Hungary, Serbia, Bulgaria, Ukraine, Moldova, and Romania [m]) - 2,888 km
note – [s] after country name indicates river source; [m] after country name indicates river mouth

Major watersheds (area sq km): Atlantic Ocean drainage: *(Black Sea)* Danube (795,656 sq km)

Total water withdrawal: *municipal:* 460 million cubic meters (2020 est.)
industrial: 700 million cubic meters (2020 est.)
agricultural: 80 million cubic meters (2020 est.)

Total renewable water resources: 105.5 billion cubic meters (2020 est.)

Geoparks: *total global geoparks and regional networks:* 3 (2024)
global geoparks and regional networks: Biokovo-Imotski Lakes; Papuk; Vis Archipelago (2024)

GOVERNMENT

Country name: *conventional long form:* Republic of Croatia
conventional short form: Croatia
local long form: Republika Hrvatska
local short form: Hrvatska
former: People's Republic of Croatia, Socialist Republic of Croatia
etymology: name derives from the Croats, a Slavic tribe who migrated to the Balkans in the 7th century A.D.

Government type: parliamentary republic

Capital: *name:* Zagreb
geographic coordinates: 45 48 N, 16 00 E
time difference: UTC+1 (6 hours ahead of Washington, DC, during Standard Time)
daylight saving time: +1hr, begins last Sunday in March; ends last Sunday in October
etymology: the name seems to be related to "digging"; archeologists suggest that the original settlement was established beyond a water-filled hole or *graba* and that the name derives from this; *za* in Slavic means "beyond"; the overall meaning may be "beyond the trench (fault, channel, ditch)"

Administrative divisions: 20 counties (zupanije, zupanija - singular) and 1 city* (grad - singular) with special county status; Bjelovarsko-Bilogorska (Bjelovar-Bilogora), Brodsko-Posavska (Brod-Posavina), Dubrovacko-Neretvanska (Dubrovnik-Neretva), Istarska (Istria), Karlovacka (Karlovac), Koprivnicko-Krizevacka (Koprivnica-Krizevci), Krapinsko-Zagorska (Krapina-Zagorje), Licko-Senjska (Lika-Senj), Medimurska (Medimurje), Osjecko-Baranjska (Osijek-Baranja), Pozesko-Slavonska (Pozega- Slavonia), Primorsko-Goranska (Primorje-Gorski Kotar), Sibensko-Kninska (Sibenik-Knin), Sisacko-Moslavacka (Sisak- Moslavina), Splitsko-Dalmatinska (Split-Dalmatia), Varazdinska (Varazdin), Viroviticko-Podravska (Virovitica-Podravina), Vukovarsko-Srijemska (Vukovar-Syrmia), Zadarska (Zadar), Zagreb*, Zagrebacka (Zagreb county)

Independence: *25 June 1991 (from Yugoslavia); note - 25 June 1991 was the day the Croatian parliament voted for independence; following a three-month moratorium to allow the European Community to solve the Yugoslav crisis peacefully, parliament adopted a decision on 8 October 1991 to sever constitutional relations with Yugoslavia; notable earlier dates:* ca. 925 (Kingdom of Croatia established); 1 December 1918 (Kingdom of Serbs, Croats, and Slovenes (Yugoslavia) established)

National holiday: Statehood Day (National Day), 30 May (1990); note - marks the day in 1990 that the first modern multi-party Croatian parliament convened

Legal system: civil law system influenced by legal heritage of Austria-Hungary; note - Croatian law was fully harmonized with the European Community acquis as of the June 2010 completion of EU accession negotiations

Constitution: *history:* several previous; latest adopted 22 December 1990
amendments: proposed by at least one fifth of the Assembly membership, by the president of the republic, by the Government of Croatia, or through petition by at least 10% of the total electorate; proceedings to amend require majority vote by the Assembly; passage requires two-thirds majority vote by the Assembly; passage by petition requires a majority vote in a referendum and promulgation by the Assembly; amended several times, last in 2014

International law organization participation: has not submitted an ICJ jurisdiction declaration; accepts ICCt jurisdiction

Citizenship: *citizenship by birth:* no
citizenship by descent only: at least one parent must be a citizen of Croatia
dual citizenship recognized: yes
residency requirement for naturalization: 5 years

Suffrage: 18 years of age; universal

Executive branch: *chief of state:* President Zoran MILANOVIC (since 18 February 2020)
head of government: Prime Minister Andrej PLENKOVIC (since 19 October 2016)
cabinet: Council of Ministers named by the prime minister and approved by the Assembly
elections/appointments: president directly elected by absolute majority popular vote in 2 rounds if needed for a 5-year term (eligible for a second term); election last held on 22 December 2019 with a runoff on 5 January 2020 (next to be held in 2024); the leader of the majority party or majority coalition usually appointed prime minister by the president and approved by the Assembly
election results:
2019: Zoran MILANOVIC elected president in second round; percent of vote in second round - Zoran MILANOVIC (SDP) 52.7%, Kolinda GRABAR-KITAROVIC (HDZ) 47.3%
2015: Kolinda GRABAR-KITAROVIC elected president in second round; percent of vote in second round - Kolinda GRABAR-KITAROVIC (HDZ) 50.7%, Ivo JOSIPOVIC (Forward Croatia Progressive Alliance) 49.3%

Legislative branch: *description:* unicameral Assembly or Hrvatski Sabor (151 seats; 140 members

in 10 multi-seat constituencies and 3 members in a single constituency for Croatian diaspora directly elected by proportional representation vote using the D'Hondt method with a 5% threshold; an additional 8 members elected from a nationwide constituency by simple majority by voters belonging to minorities recognized by Croatia; the Serb minority elects 3 Assembly members, the Hungarian and Italian minorities elect 1 each, the Czech and Slovak minorities elect 1 jointly, and all other minorities elect 2; all members serve 4-year terms
elections: last election held on 17 April 2024 (next to be held by April 2028)
election results: percent of vote by party/coalition - HDZ-led coalition 40.4%, SDP 27.8%, DP 9.3%, MOST 7.3%, We Can! 6.6%, SDSS 2.0%, Independents 1.3%, NPS 1.3%, IDS 1.3%, Bosniaks Together 0.7%, DZMH 0.7%, Focus 0.7%, SRRH 0.7%; seats by party/coalition - HDZ-led coalition 61, SDP 42, DP 14, MOST 11, We Can! 10, SDSS 3, Independents 2, NPS 2, IDS 2, Bosniaks Together 1, DZMH 1, Focus 1, SRRH 1; composition - men 101, women 50, percent of women 33%
note: of the 151 seats, 140 members come from 10 multi-seat constituencies, with 3 members in a constituency for Croatian diaspora; voters belonging to recognized minorities elect an additional 8 members from a nationwide constituency: the Serb minority elects 3 members, the Hungarian and Italian minorities elect 1 each, the Czech and Slovak minorities elect 1 jointly, and all other minorities elect 2

Judicial branch: *highest court(s):* Supreme Court (consists of the court president and vice president, 25 civil department justices, and 16 criminal department justices)
judge selection and term of office: president of Supreme Court nominated by the president of Croatia and elected by the Sabor for a 4-year term; other Supreme Court justices appointed by the National Judicial Council; all judges serve until age 70
subordinate courts: Administrative Court; county, municipal, and specialized courts; note - there is an 11-member Constitutional Court with jurisdiction limited to constitutional issues but is outside of the judicial system

Political parties: Bosniaks Together
The Bridge or MOST (formerly the Bridge of Independent Lists)
Croatia Romani Union Kali Sara (SRRH)
Croatian Democratic Union or HDZ
Democratic Union of Hungarians in Croatia (DZMH)
Focus or Fokus
Homeland Movement or DP (also known as Miroslav Škoro Homeland Movement or DPMS)
Independent Democratic Serb Party or SDSS
Independent Platform of the North (NPS)
Istrian Democratic Assembly or IDS
Social Democratic Party of Croatia or SDP
We Can! or Mozemo!

International organization participation: AIIB, Australia Group, BIS, BSEC (observer), CD, CE, CEI, EAPC, EBRD, ECB, EMU, EU, FAO, G-11, IADB, IAEA, IBRD, ICAO, ICC (national committees), ICCt, ICRM, IDA, IFAD, IFC, IFRCS, IHO, ILO, IMF, IMO, IMSO, Interpol, IOC, IOM, IPU, ISO, ITSO, ITU, ITUC (NGOs), MIGA, MINURSO, NAM (observer), NATO, NSG, OAS (observer), OIF (observer), OPCW, OSCE, PCA, Schengen Convention, SELEC, UN, UNCTAD, UNESCO, UNFICYP, UNHCR, UNIDO, UNIFIL, UNMIL, UNMOGIP, UNWTO, UPU, Wassenaar Arrangement, WCO, WHO, WIPO, WMO, WTO, ZC

Diplomatic representation in the US: *chief of mission:* Ambassador Pjer ŠIMUNOVIĆ (since 8 September 2017)
chancery: 2343 Massachusetts Avenue NW, Washington, DC 20008
telephone: [1] (202) 588-5899
FAX: [1] (202) 588-8937
email address and website:
washington@mvep.hr
https://mvep.gov.hr/embassy-114969/114969
consulate(s) general: Chicago, Los Angeles, New York, Seattle (WA)
consulate(s): Anchorage (AL), Houston, Kansas City (MO),Minneapolis/St. Paul (MN), New Orleans, Pittsburgh (PA)

Diplomatic representation from the US: *chief of mission:* Ambassador Nathalie RAYES (since 25 January 2024)
embassy: Ulica Thomasa Jeffersona 2, 10010 Zagreb
mailing address: 5080 Zagreb Place, Washington DC 20521-5080
telephone: [385] (1) 661-2200
FAX: [385] (1) 665-8933
email address and website:
ZagrebACS@state.gov
https://hr.usembassy.gov/

Flag description: *three equal horizontal bands of red (top), white, and blue - the Pan-Slav colors - superimposed by the Croatian coat of arms; the coat of arms consists of one main shield (a checkerboard of 13 red and 12 silver (white) fields) surmounted by five smaller shields that form a crown over the main shield; the five small shields represent five historic regions (from left to right):* Croatia, Dubrovnik, Dalmatia, Istria, and Slavonia
note: the Pan-Slav colors were inspired by the 19th-century flag of Russia

National symbol(s): red-white checkerboard; national colors: red, white, blue

National anthem: *name:* "Lijepa nasa domovino" (Our Beautiful Homeland)
lyrics/music: Antun MIHANOVIC/Josip RUNJANIN
note: adopted in 1972 while still part of Yugoslavia; "Lijepa nasa domovino," whose lyrics were written in 1835, served as an unofficial anthem beginning in 1891

National heritage: *total World Heritage Sites:* 10 (8 cultural, 2 natural)
selected World Heritage Site locales: Plitvice Lakes National Park (n); Historic Split (c); Old City of Dubrovnik (c); Euphrasian Basilica; Historic Trogir (c); Šibenik Cathedral (c); Stari Grad Plain (c); Zadar and Fort St. Nikola Venetian Defense Works (c); Primeval Beech Forests (n); Stećci Medieval Tombstones Graveyards (c)

ECONOMY

Economic overview: tourism-based economy that was one of the hardest hit by COVID-19 economic disruptions; newest euro user since 2023, helping recover from a 6-year recession; public debt increases due to COVID-19 and stimulus packages; weak exports; continuing emigration; new liquefied natural gas import terminal

Real GDP (purchasing power parity): $159.305 billion (2023 est.)
$154.574 billion (2022 est.)
$144.425 billion (2021 est.)
note: data in 2021 dollars
comparison ranking: 81

Real GDP growth rate: 3.06% (2023 est.)
7.03% (2022 est.)
13.04% (2021 est.)
note: annual GDP % growth based on constant local currency
comparison ranking: 107

Real GDP per capita: $41,300 (2023 est.)
$40,100 (2022 est.)
$37,200 (2021 est.)
note: data in 2021 dollars
comparison ranking: 59

GDP (official exchange rate): $82.689 billion (2023 est.)
note: data in current dollars at official exchange rate

Inflation rate (consumer prices): 7.94% (2023 est.)
10.78% (2022 est.)
2.55% (2021 est.)
note: annual % change based on consumer prices
comparison ranking: 154

Credit ratings: Fitch rating: BBB- (2019)

Moody's rating: Ba1 (2020)

Standard & Poors rating: BBB- (2019)
note: The year refers to the year in which the current credit rating was first obtained.

GDP - composition, by sector of origin: *agriculture:* 3% (2023 est.)
industry: 18.8% (2023 est.)
services: 61.2% (2023 est.)
note: figures may not total 100% due to non-allocated consumption not captured in sector-reported data
comparison rankings: services 79; industry 145; agriculture 140

GDP - composition, by end use: *household consumption:* 58% (2023 est.)
government consumption: 21.1% (2023 est.)
investment in fixed capital: 19.4% (2023 est.)
investment in inventories: 2.6% (2023 est.)
exports of goods and services: 54% (2023 est.)
imports of goods and services: -55.9% (2023 est.)
note: figures may not total 100% due to rounding or gaps in data collection

Agricultural products: maize, wheat, maize, sugar beets, milk, barley, soybeans, sunflower seeds, grapes, pork (2022)
note: top ten agricultural products based on tonnage

Industries: chemicals and plastics, machine tools, fabricated metal, electronics, pig iron and rolled steel products, aluminum, paper, wood products, construction materials, textiles, shipbuilding, petroleum and petroleum refining, food and beverages, tourism

Industrial production growth rate: -0.47% (2023 est.)
note: annual % change in industrial value added based on constant local currency
comparison ranking: 160

Labor force: 1.744 million (2023 est.)
note: number of people ages 15 or older who are employed or seeking work
comparison ranking: 132

Unemployment rate: 6.06% (2023 est.)
6.96% (2022 est.)
7.61% (2021 est.)
note: % of labor force seeking employment

comparison ranking: 123

Youth unemployment rate (ages 15-24): *total:* 19.2% (2023 est.)
male: 17.3% (2023 est.)
female: 22.3% (2023 est.)
note: % of labor force ages 15-24 seeking employment
comparison ranking: total 67

Population below poverty line: 18% (2021 est.)
note: % of population with income below national poverty line

Gini Index coefficient - distribution of family income: 28.9 (2021 est.)
note: index (0-100) of income distribution; higher values represent greater inequality
comparison ranking: 131

Average household expenditures: *on food:* 19.3% of household expenditures (2022 est.)
on alcohol and tobacco: 7.7% of household expenditures (2022 est.)

Household income or consumption by percentage share: *lowest 10%:* 3.1% (2021 est.)
highest 10%: 22.3% (2021 est.)
note: % share of income accruing to lowest and highest 10% of population

Remittances: 6.89% of GDP (2023 est.)
7.51% of GDP (2022 est.)
7.23% of GDP (2021 est.)
note: personal transfers and compensation between resident and non-resident individuals/households/entities

Budget: *revenues:* $3.678 billion (2022 est.)
expenditures: $3.662 billion (2022 est.)
note: central government revenues (excluding grants) and expenses converted to US dollars at average official exchange rate for year indicated

Public debt: 82.08% of GDP (2022 est.)
note: central government debt as a % of GDP
comparison ranking: 38

Taxes and other revenues: 21.41% (of GDP) (2022 est.)
note: central government tax revenue as a % of GDP
comparison ranking: 72

Current account balance: $956.968 million (2023 est.)
-$2.336 billion (2022 est.)
$651.685 million (2021 est.)
note: balance of payments - net trade and primary/secondary income in current dollars
comparison ranking: 57

Exports: $44.969 billion (2023 est.)
$41.903 billion (2022 est.)
$34.367 billion (2021 est.)
note: balance of payments - exports of goods and services in current dollars
comparison ranking: 69

Exports - partners: Italy 13%, Slovenia 11%, Germany 11%, Hungary 10%, Bosnia and Herzegovina 9% (2022)
note: top five export partners based on percentage share of exports

Exports - commodities: refined petroleum, electricity, natural gas, garments, wood (2022)
note: top five export commodities based on value in dollars

Imports: $46.571 billion (2023 est.)
$46.664 billion (2022 est.)
$36.256 billion (2021 est.)
note: balance of payments - imports of goods and services in current dollars
comparison ranking: 70

Imports - partners: Italy 14%, Germany 12%, Slovenia 11%, Hungary 7%, US 7% (2022)
note: top five import partners based on percentage share of imports

Imports - commodities: natural gas, refined petroleum, electricity, garments, cars (2022)
note: top five import commodities based on value in dollars

Reserves of foreign exchange and gold: $3.176 billion (2023 est.)
$29.726 billion (2022 est.)
$28.309 billion (2021 est.)
note: holdings of gold (year-end prices)/foreign exchange/special drawing rights in current dollars
comparison ranking: 62

Exchange rates: euros (EUR) per US dollar -

Exchange rates: 0.925 (2023 est.)
0.95 (2022 est.)
0.845 (2021 est.)
0.876 (2020 est.)
0.893 (2019 est.)
note: Croatia used the kuna prior to conversion to the euro on 1 January 2023. During the transition period the exchange rate was fixed at 7.53450 kuna to 1 euro.

ENERGY

Electricity access: *electrification - total population:* 100% (2022 est.)

Electricity: *installed generating capacity:* 5.417 million kW (2022 est.)
consumption: 17.111 billion kWh (2022 est.)
exports: 7.226 billion kWh (2022 est.)
imports: 11.92 billion kWh (2022 est.)
transmission/distribution losses: 1.729 billion kWh (2022 est.)
comparison rankings: transmission/distribution losses 118; imports 23; exports 30; consumption 80; installed generating capacity 86

Electricity generation sources: *fossil fuels:* 36.4% of total installed capacity (2022 est.)
solar: 1.1% of total installed capacity (2022 est.)
wind: 16.2% of total installed capacity (2022 est.)
hydroelectricity: 38.3% of total installed capacity (2022 est.)
geothermal: 0.4% of total installed capacity (2022 est.)
biomass and waste: 7.5% of total installed capacity (2022 est.)

Coal: *consumption:* 702,000 metric tons (2022 est.)
exports: 1,000 metric tons (2022 est.)
imports: 702,000 metric tons (2022 est.)

Petroleum: *total petroleum production:* 11,000 bbl/day (2023 est.)
refined petroleum consumption: 70,000 bbl/day (2022 est.)
crude oil estimated reserves: 71 million barrels (2021 est.)

Natural gas: *production:* 741.456 million cubic meters (2022 est.)
consumption: 2.502 billion cubic meters (2022 est.)
exports: 1.038 billion cubic meters (2022 est.)
imports: 3.006 billion cubic meters (2022 est.)
proven reserves: 24.919 billion cubic meters (2021 est.)

Carbon dioxide emissions: 15.944 million metric tonnes of CO_2 (2022 est.)
from coal and metallurgical coke: 1.563 million metric tonnes of CO_2 (2022 est.)
from petroleum and other liquids: 9.474 million metric tonnes of CO_2 (2022 est.)
from consumed natural gas: 4.907 million metric tonnes of CO_2 (2022 est.)
comparison ranking: total emissions 94

Energy consumption per capita: 78.371 million Btu/person (2022 est.)
comparison ranking: 65

COMMUNICATIONS

Telephones - fixed lines: *total subscriptions:* 1.235 million (2022 est.)
subscriptions per 100 inhabitants: 31 (2022 est.)
comparison ranking: total subscriptions 66

Telephones - mobile cellular: *total subscriptions:* 4.48 million (2022 est.)
subscriptions per 100 inhabitants: 111 (2022 est.)
comparison ranking: total subscriptions 129

Telecommunication systems: *general assessment:* the mobile market is served by three MNOs, supplemented by a number of MVNOs; the network operators have focused on improving ARPU by encouraging prepaid subscribers to migrate to postpaid plans, and on developing revenue from mobile data services; 5G services are widely available, though the sector will only show its full potential later in 2021 following the award of licenses in several bands; this will contribute towards the government's national broadband plan to 2027, which is tied to the EC's two allied projects aimed at providing gigabit connectivity by the end of 2025; the broadband sector benefits from effective competition between the DSL and cable platforms, while there are also numerous fiber deployments in urban areas; the number of FttP subscribers broached 134,000 in March 2021. (2021)
domestic: fixed-line teledensity 31 per 100 persons; mobile-cellular telephone subscriptions are 108 per 100 (2021)
international: country code - 385; the ADRIA-1 submarine cable provides connectivity to Albania and Greece; digital international service is provided through the main switch in Zagreb; Croatia participates in the Trans-Asia-Europe fiberoptic project, which consists of 2 fiber-optic trunk connections with Slovenia and a fiber-optic trunk line from Rijeka to Split and Dubrovnik (2019)

Broadcast media: the national state-owned public broadcaster, Croatian Radiotelevision, operates 4 terrestrial TV networks, a satellite channel that rebroadcasts programs for Croatians living abroad, and 6 regional TV centers; 2 private broadcasters operate national terrestrial networks; 29 privately owned regional TV stations; multi-channel cable and satellite TV subscription services are available; state-owned public broadcaster operates 4 national radio networks and 23 regional radio stations; 2 privately owned national radio networks and 117 local radio stations (2019)

Internet country code: .hr

Internet users: *total:* 3.321 million (2021 est.)
percent of population: 81% (2021 est.)
comparison ranking: total 115

Broadband - fixed subscriptions: *total:* 1,030,973 (2020 est.)
subscriptions per 100 inhabitants: 25 (2020 est.)
comparison ranking: total 73

TRANSPORTATION

National air transport system: *number of registered air carriers:* 2 (2020)
inventory of registered aircraft operated by air carriers: 18
annual passenger traffic on registered air carriers: 2,093,577 (2018)
annual freight traffic on registered air carriers: 530,000 (2018) mt-km

Civil aircraft registration country code prefix: 9A

Airports: 40 (2024)
comparison ranking: 101

Heliports: 4 (2024)

Pipelines: 2,410 km gas, 610 km oil (2011)

Railways: *total:* 2,617 km (2020) 980 km electrified
comparison ranking: total 63

Roadways: *total:* 26,958 km (2022)
comparison ranking: total 103

Waterways: 4,714 km (2022) Danube 2,859 km, Sava 562 km, Drava 505 km, Neretva 20 km, Bosut 151 km, Kupa 296 km, Mura 53 km, Korana 134 km, Lonja 134 km
comparison ranking: 25

Merchant marine: *total:* 384 (2023)
by type: bulk carrier 10, general cargo 32, oil tanker 14, other 328
comparison ranking: total 50

Ports: *total ports:* 16 (2024)
large: 2
medium: 0
small: 6
very small: 8
ports with oil terminals: 8
key ports: Bakar, Dubrovnik, Omisalj, Rijeka Luka, Rovinj, Sibenik, Split, Zadar

MILITARY AND SECURITY

Military and security forces: Armed Forces of the Republic of Croatia (Oruzane Snage Republike Hrvatske, OSRH): Ground Forces (Hrvatska Kopnena Vojska, HKoV), Naval Forces (Hrvatska Ratna Mornarica, HRM; includes Coast Guard), Air Force (Hrvatsko Ratno Zrakoplovstvo, HRZ) (2024)
note: the Ministry of the Interior is responsible for internal security, including law enforcement (Croatia Police) and border security

Military expenditures: 1.8% of GDP (2024 est.)
1.8% of GDP (2023)
1.8% of GDP (2022)
2% of GDP (2021)
1.7% of GDP (2020)
comparison ranking: 77

Military and security service personnel strengths: approximately 14,000 active-duty personnel (10,000 Army; 1,500 Navy; 1,500 Air force; 1,000 joint/other) (2024)

Military equipment inventories and acquisitions: the military's inventory is a mix of Soviet-era equipment and a growing amount of more modern, NATO-compatible weapon systems from Western suppliers, including France, Germany, and the US (2024)

Military service age and obligation: 18-27 years of age for voluntary military service; conscription abolished in 2008 but slated to be reinstated in January 2025 (2024)
note: as of 2024, women comprised about 14% of the military's full-time personnel

Military deployments: 150 Kosovo (KFOR/NATO); 175 Lithuania (NATO; Croatia also has a few hundred personnel participating in several other EU, NATO, and UN missions (2024)

Military - note: the Armed Forces of Croatia (OSRH) are responsible for the defense of Croatia's sovereignty and territory, contributing to international humanitarian, peacekeeping, and security missions, and providing assistance to civil authorities for such missions as responding to disasters, search and rescue, anti-terrorism, and internal security in times of crisis if called upon by the prime minister or the president; Croatia joined NATO in 2009, and the OSRH participates in NATO missions, including its peacekeeping force in Kosovo and the Enhanced Forward Presence mission in Eastern Europe; it also contributes to EU and UN missions; the OSRH trains regularly with NATO and regional partners
the OSRH was established in 1991 from the Croatian National Guard during the Croatian War of Independence (1991-95); during the war, the ground forces grew to as many as 60 brigades and dozens of independent battalions, and a single military offensive against Serbian forces in 1995 included some 100,000 Croatian troops; in 2000, Croatia initiated an effort to modernize and reform the OSRH into a small, professional military capable of meeting the challenges of NATO membership (2024)

TRANSNATIONAL ISSUES

Refugees and internally displaced persons: *refugees (country of origin):* 24,525 (Ukraine) (as of 29 February 2024)
stateless persons: 2,889 (2022)
note: 843,010 estimated refugee and migrant arrivals (January 2015-September 2023)

Illicit drugs: drug trafficking groups are major players in the procurement and transportation of large quantities of cocaine destined for European markets

CUBA

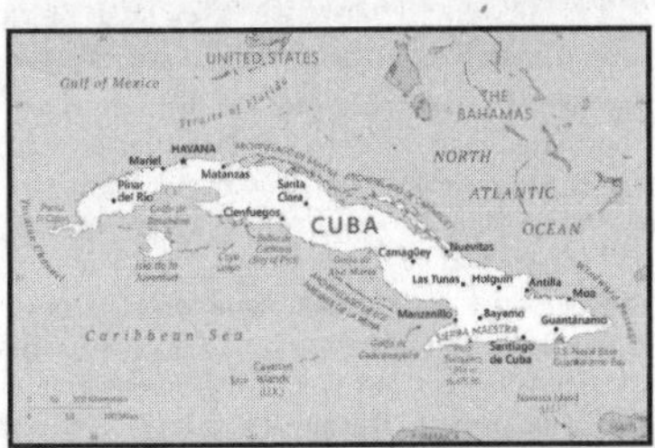

INTRODUCTION

Background: The native Amerindian population of Cuba began to decline after the arrival of Christopher COLUMBUS in 1492, as the country was developed as a Spanish colony during the next several centuries. Large numbers of African slaves were imported to work the coffee and sugar plantations, and Havana became the launching point for the annual treasure fleets bound for Spain from Mexico and Peru. Spanish rule eventually provoked an independence movement, and occasional rebellions were harshly suppressed. US intervention during the Spanish-American War in 1898 assisted the Cubans in overthrowing Spanish rule. The Treaty of Paris established Cuban independence from Spain in 1898, and after three-and-a-half years of subsequent US military rule, Cuba became an independent republic in 1902.

Cuba then experienced a string of governments mostly dominated by the military and corrupt politicians. Fidel CASTRO led a rebel army to victory in 1959; his authoritarian rule held the subsequent regime together for nearly five decades. He handed off the presidency to his younger brother Raul CASTRO in 2008. Cuba's communist revolution, with Soviet support, was exported throughout Latin America and Africa during the 1960s, 1970s, and 1980s. Miguel DIAZ-CANEL Bermudez, hand-picked by Raul CASTRO to succeed him, was approved as president by the National Assembly and took office in 2018. DIAZ-CANEL was appointed First Secretary of the Communist Party in 2021 after the retirement of Raul CASTRO and continues to serve as both president and first secretary.

Cuba traditionally and consistently portrays the US embargo, in place since 1961, as the source of its socioeconomic difficulties. As a result of efforts begun in 2014 to reestablish diplomatic relations, the US and Cuba reopened embassies in their respective countries in 2015. The embargo remains in place, however, and the relationship between the US and Cuba remains tense. Illicit migration of Cuban nationals to the US via maritime and overland routes has been a longstanding challenge. In 2017, the US and Cuba signed a Joint Statement ending the so-called "wet-foot, dry-foot" policy, by which Cuban nationals who reached US soil were permitted to stay. Irregular Cuban maritime migration has dropped significantly since 2016, when migrant interdictions at sea topped 5,000, but land border crossings continue.

GEOGRAPHY

Location: Caribbean, island between the Caribbean Sea and the North Atlantic Ocean, 150 km south of Key West, Florida

Geographic coordinates: 21 30 N, 80 00 W

Map references: Central America and the Caribbean

Area: *total:* 110,860 sq km
land: 109,820 sq km
water: 1,040 sq km
comparison ranking: total 106

Area - comparative: slightly smaller than Pennsylvania

Land boundaries: *total:* 28.5 km

border countries (1): US Naval Base at Guantanamo Bay 28.5 km
note: Guantanamo Naval Base is leased by the US and remains part of Cuba

Coastline: 3,735 km

Maritime claims: *territorial sea:* 12 nm
contiguous zone: 24 nm
exclusive economic zone: 200 nm

Climate: tropical; moderated by trade winds; dry season (November to April); rainy season (May to October)

Terrain: mostly flat to rolling plains, with rugged hills and mountains in the southeast

Elevation: *highest point:* Pico Turquino 1,974 m
lowest point: Caribbean Sea 0 m
mean elevation: 108 m

Natural resources: cobalt, nickel, iron ore, chromium, copper, salt, timber, silica, petroleum, arable land

Land use: *agricultural land:* 60.3% (2018 est.)
arable land: 33.8% (2018 est.)
permanent crops: 3.6% (2018 est.)
permanent pasture: 22.9% (2018 est.)
forest: 27.3% (2018 est.)
other: 12.4% (2018 est.)

Irrigated land: 8,700 sq km (2012)

Population distribution: large population clusters found throughout the country, the more significant ones being in the larger towns and cities, particularly the capital of Havana

Natural hazards: the east coast is subject to hurricanes from August to November (in general, the country averages about one hurricane every other year); droughts are common

Geography - note: largest country in Caribbean and westernmost island of the Greater Antilles

PEOPLE AND SOCIETY

Population: *total:* 10,966,038
male: 5,441,507
female: 5,524,531 (2024 est.)
comparison rankings: female 84; male 87; total 85

Nationality: *noun:* Cuban(s)
adjective: Cuban

Ethnic groups: White 64.1%, Mulatto or mixed 26.6%, Black 9.3% (2012 est.)
note: data represent racial self-identification from Cuba's 2012 national census

Languages: Spanish (official)
major-language sample(s):
La Libreta Informativa del Mundo, la fuente indispensable de información básica. (Spanish)

Religions: Christian 58.9%, folk religion 17.6%, Buddhist <1%, Hindu <1%, Jewish <1%, Muslim <1%, other <1%, none 23.2% (2020 est.)
note: folk religions include religions of African origin, spiritualism, and others intermingled with Catholicism or Protestantism; data is estimative because no authoritative source on religious affiliation exists for Cuba

Age structure: *0-14 years:* 16.3% (male 918,066/female 866,578)
15-64 years: 66.5% (male 3,670,531/female 3,623,658)
65 years and over: 17.2% (2024 est.) (male 852,910/female 1,034,295)

Dependency ratios: *total dependency ratio:* 45.9
youth dependency ratio: 23.1
elderly dependency ratio: 22.9
potential support ratio: 4.4 (2021 est.)

Median age: *total:* 42.6 years (2024 est.)
male: 41 years
female: 44.4 years
comparison ranking: total 42

Population growth rate: -0.17% (2024 est.)
comparison ranking: 209

Birth rate: 9.9 births/1,000 population (2024 est.)
comparison ranking: 188

Death rate: 9.5 deaths/1,000 population (2024 est.)
comparison ranking: 45

Net migration rate: -2.1 migrant(s)/1,000 population (2024 est.)
comparison ranking: 169

Population distribution: large population clusters found throughout the country, the more significant ones being in the larger towns and cities, particularly the capital of Havana

Urbanization: *urban population:* 77.5% of total population (2023)
rate of urbanization: 0.19% annual rate of change (2020-25 est.)

Major urban areas - population: 2.149 million HAVANA (capital) (2023)

Sex ratio: *at birth:* 1.06 male(s)/female
0-14 years: 1.06 male(s)/female
15-64 years: 1.01 male(s)/female
65 years and over: 0.82 male(s)/female
total population: 0.99 male(s)/female (2024 est.)

Maternal mortality ratio: 39 deaths/100,000 live births (2020 est.)
comparison ranking: 105

Infant mortality rate: *total:* 4 deaths/1,000 live births (2024 est.)
male: 4.5 deaths/1,000 live births
female: 3.5 deaths/1,000 live births
comparison ranking: total 187

Life expectancy at birth: *total population:* 80.1 years (2024 est.)
male: 77.8 years
female: 82.6 years
comparison ranking: total population 58

Total fertility rate: 1.71 children born/woman (2024 est.)
comparison ranking: 162

Gross reproduction rate: 0.83 (2024 est.)

Contraceptive prevalence rate: 69% (2019)

Drinking water source: *improved: urban:* 98.9% of population
rural: 97% of population
total: 98.5% of population
unimproved: urban: 1.1% of population
rural: 3% of population
total: 1.5% of population (2020 est.)

Current health expenditure: 12.5% of GDP (2020)

Physician density: 8.42 physicians/1,000 population (2018)

Hospital bed density: 5.3 beds/1,000 population (2017)

Sanitation facility access: *improved: urban:* 94.8% of population
rural: 87% of population
total: 93% of population
unimproved: urban: 5.2% of population
rural: 13% of population
total: 7% of population (2017 est.)

Obesity - adult prevalence rate: 24.6% (2016)
comparison ranking: 56

Alcohol consumption per capita: *total:* 4.7 liters of pure alcohol (2019 est.)
beer: 1.77 liters of pure alcohol (2019 est.)
wine: 0.23 liters of pure alcohol (2019 est.)
spirits: 2.69 liters of pure alcohol (2019 est.)
other alcohols: 0.01 liters of pure alcohol (2019 est.)
comparison ranking: total 85

Tobacco use: *total:* 17.9% (2020 est.)
male: 25.5% (2020 est.)
female: 10.3% (2020 est.)
comparison ranking: total 92

Children under the age of 5 years underweight: 2.4% (2019)
comparison ranking: 99

Currently married women (ages 15-49): 58% (2023 est.)

Child marriage: *women married by age 15:* 4.8%
women married by age 18: 29.4%
men married by age 18: 5.9% (2019 est.)

Literacy: *definition:* age 15 and over can read and write
total population: 99.7%
male: 99.6%
female: 99.7% (2021)

School life expectancy (primary to tertiary education): *total:* 14 years
male: 13 years
female: 15 years (2021)

People - note: illicit emigration is a continuing problem; Cubans attempt to depart the island and enter the US using homemade rafts, alien smugglers, direct flights, or falsified visas; Cubans also use non-maritime routes to enter the US including direct flights to Miami and overland via the southwest border; the number of Cubans migrating to the US surged after the announcement of normalization of US-Cuban relations in late December 2014 but has decreased since the end of the so-called "wet-foot, dry-foot" policy on 12 January 2017

ENVIRONMENT

Environment - current issues: soil degradation and desertification (brought on by poor farming techniques and natural disasters) are the main environmental problems; biodiversity loss; deforestation; air and water pollution

Environment - international agreements: *party to:* Antarctic Treaty, Biodiversity, Climate Change, Climate Change-Kyoto Protocol, Climate Change-Paris Agreement, Comprehensive Nuclear Test Ban, Desertification, Endangered Species, Environmental Modification, Hazardous Wastes, Law of the Sea, Marine Dumping-London Convention, Ozone Layer Protection, Ship Pollution, Wetlands
signed, but not ratified: Marine Life Conservation

Climate: tropical; moderated by trade winds; dry season (November to April); rainy season (May to October)

Urbanization: *urban population:* 77.5% of total population (2023)
rate of urbanization: 0.19% annual rate of change (2020-25 est.)

Revenue from forest resources: 0.06% of GDP (2018 est.)
comparison ranking: 125

Revenue from coal: 0% of GDP (2018 est.)
comparison ranking: 60

Air pollutants: *particulate matter emissions:* 13.32 micrograms per cubic meter (2019 est.)
carbon dioxide emissions: 28.28 megatons (2016 est.)
methane emissions: 9.3 megatons (2020 est.)

Waste and recycling: *municipal solid waste generated annually:* 2,692,692 tons (2007 est.)
municipal solid waste recycled annually: 255,536 tons (2015 est.)
percent of municipal solid waste recycled: 9.5% (2015 est.)

Total water withdrawal: *municipal:* 1.7 billion cubic meters (2020 est.)
industrial: 740 million cubic meters (2020 est.)
agricultural: 4.52 billion cubic meters (2020 est.)

Total renewable water resources: 38.12 billion cubic meters (2020 est.)

GOVERNMENT

Country name: *conventional long form:* Republic of Cuba
conventional short form: Cuba
local long form: República de Cuba
local short form: Cuba
etymology: name derives from the Taino Indian designation for the island "coabana" meaning "great place"

Government type: communist state

Capital: *name:* Havana
geographic coordinates: 23 07 N, 82 21 W
time difference: UTC-5 (same time as Washington, DC, during Standard Time)
daylight saving time: +1hr, begins second Sunday in March; ends first Sunday in November; note - Cuba has been known to alter the schedule of DST on short notice in an attempt to conserve electricity for lighting
etymology: the sites of Spanish colonial cities often retained their original Taino names; Habana, the Spanish name for the city, may be based on the name of a local Taino chief, HABAGUANEX

Administrative divisions: 15 provinces (provincias, singular - provincia) and 1 special municipality* (municipio especial); Artemisa, Camaguey, Ciego de Avila, Cienfuegos, Granma, Guantanamo, Holguin, Isla de la Juventud*, La Habana (Havana), Las Tunas, Matanzas, Mayabeque, Pinar del Rio, Sancti Spiritus, Santiago de Cuba, Villa Clara

Independence: 20 May 1902 (from Spain 10 December 1898; administered by the US from 1898 to 1902); not acknowledged by the Cuban Government as a day of independence

National holiday: Triumph of the Revolution (Liberation Day), 1 January (1959)

Legal system: civil law system based on Spanish civil code

Constitution: *history:* several previous; latest drafted 14 July 2018, approved by the National Assembly 22 December 2018, approved by referendum 24 February 2019
amendments: proposed by the National Assembly of People's Power; passage requires approval of at least two-thirds majority of the National Assembly membership; amendments to constitutional articles on the authorities of the National Assembly, Council of State, or any rights and duties in the constitution also require approval in a referendum; constitutional articles on the Cuban political, social, and economic system cannot be amended

International law organization participation: has not submitted an ICJ jurisdiction declaration; non-party state to the ICCt

Citizenship: *citizenship by birth:* yes
citizenship by descent only: yes
dual citizenship recognized: no
residency requirement for naturalization: unknown

Suffrage: 16 years of age; universal

Executive branch: *chief of state:* President Miguel DIAZ-CANEL Bermudez (since 19 April 2018)
head of government: Prime Minister Manuel MARRERO Cruz (since 21 December 2019)
cabinet: Council of Ministers proposed by the president and appointed by the National Assembly
elections/appointments: president and vice president indirectly elected by the National Assembly for a 5-year term (eligible for a second term); election last held on 19 April 2023 (next to be held in 2028)
election results:
2023: Miguel DIAZ-CANEL Bermudez (PCC) reelected president; percent of National Assembly vote - 97.7%; Salvador Antonio VALDES Mesa (PCC) reelected vice president; percent of National Assembly vote - 93.4%
2018: Miguel DIAZ-CANEL Bermudez (PCC) elected president; percent of National Assembly vote - 98.8%; Salvador Antonio VALDES Mesa (PCC) elected vice president; percent of National Assembly vote - 98.1%
note - on 19 April 2018, DIAZ-CANEL succeeded Raul CASTRO as president of the Councils of State and Ministers; on 10 October 2019 he was elected to the newly created position of President of the Republic, which replaced the position of President of the Councils of State and Ministers

Legislative branch: *description:* unicameral National Assembly of People's Power or Asámblea Nacional del Poder Popular (474 seats; (470 seats filled in 2023); members directly elected by absolute majority vote; members serve 5-year terms); note 1 - the National Candidature Commission submits a slate of approved candidates; to be elected, candidates must receive more than 50% of valid votes otherwise the seat remains vacant or the Council of State can declare another election
elections: last held on 26 March 2023 (next to be held in early 2028)
election results: Cuba's Communist Party is the only legal party, and officially sanctioned candidates run unopposed; composition- men 208, women 262, percent of women 55.7%
note: the National Candidature Commission submits a slate of approved candidates; to be elected, candidates must receive more than 50% of valid votes, otherwise the seat remains vacant or the Council of State can declare another election

Judicial branch: *highest court(s):* People's Supreme Court (consists of court president, vice president, 41 professional justices, and NA lay judges); organization includes the State Council, criminal, civil, administrative, labor, crimes against the state, and military courts)
judge selection and term of office: professional judges elected by the National Assembly are not subject to a specific term; lay judges nominated by workplace collectives and neighborhood associations and elected by municipal or provincial assemblies; lay judges appointed for 5-year terms and serve up to 30 days per year
subordinate courts: People's Provincial Courts; People's Regional Courts; People's Courts

Political parties: Cuban Communist Party or PCC

International organization participation: ACP, ACS, ALBA, AOSIS, CABEI, CELAC, EAEU (observer), FAO, G-77, IAEA, ICAO, ICC (national committees), ICRM, IFAD, IFRCS, IHO, ILO, IMO, IMSO, Interpol, IOC, IOM (observer), IPU, ISO, ITSO, ITU, LAES, LAIA, NAM, OAS (excluded from formal participation since 1962), OPANAL, OPCW, PCA, Petrocaribe, PIF (partner), UN, UNCTAD, UNESCO, UNHRC, UNIDO, Union Latina, UNOOSA, UNWTO, UPU, WCO, WFTU (NGOs), WHO, WIPO, WMO, WTO

Diplomatic representation in the US: *chief of mission:* Ambassador (vacant); Chargé d'Affaires Lianys TORRES RIVERA (since 14 January 2021)
chancery: 2630 16th Street NW, Washington, DC 20009
telephone: [1] (202) 797-8515
FAX: [1] (202) 797-8521
email address and website:
recepcion@usadc.embacuba.cu
https://misiones.cubaminrex.cu/en/usa/embassy-cuba-usa

Diplomatic representation from the US: *chief of mission:* Ambassador (vacant); Chargé d'Affaires Benjamin G. ZIFF (since 14 July 2022)
embassy: Calzada between L & M Streets, Vedado, Havana
mailing address: 3200 Havana Place, Washington DC 20521-3200
telephone: [53] (7) 839-4100
FAX: [53] (7) 839-4247
email address and website:
acshavana@state.gov
https://cu.usembassy.gov/

Flag description: *five equal horizontal bands of blue (top, center, and bottom) alternating with white; a red equilateral triangle based on the hoist side bears a white, five-pointed star in the center; the blue bands refer to the three old divisions of the island:* central, occidental, and oriental; the white bands describe the purity of the independence ideal; the triangle symbolizes liberty, equality, and fraternity, while the red color stands for the blood shed in the independence struggle; the white star, called La Estrella Solitaria (the Lone Star) lights the way to freedom and was taken from the flag of Texas
note: design similar to the Puerto Rican flag, with the colors of the bands and triangle reversed

National symbol(s): royal palm; national colors: red, white, blue

National anthem: *name:* "La Bayamesa" (The Bayamo Song)
lyrics/music: Pedro FIGUEREDO
note: adopted 1940; Pedro FIGUEREDO first performed "La Bayamesa" in 1868 during the Ten Years War against the Spanish; a leading figure in the uprising, FIGUEREDO was captured in 1870 and executed by a firing squad; just prior to the fusillade he is reputed to have shouted, "Morir por la Patria es vivir" (To die for the country is to live), a line from the anthem

National heritage: *total World Heritage Sites:* 9 (7 cultural, 2 natural)
selected World Heritage Site locales: Old Havana (c); Trinidad and the Valley de los Ingenios (c); San

Pedro de la Roca Castle (c); Desembarco del Granma National Park (n); Viñales Valley (c); Archaeological Landscape of the First Coffee Plantations (c); Alejandro de Humboldt National Park (n); Historic Cienfuegos (c); Historic Camagüey (c)

ECONOMY

Economic overview: still largely state-run planned economy, although privatization increasing under new constitution; widespread protests due to lack of basic necessities and electricity; massive foreign investment increases recently; known tobacco exporter; unique oil-for-doctors relationship with Venezuela; widespread corruption

Real GDP (purchasing power parity): $137 billion (2017 est.)
$134.8 billion (2016 est.)
$134.2 billion (2015 est.)
note: data are in 2016 dollars
comparison ranking: 87

Real GDP growth rate: 1.77% (2022 est.)
1.25% (2021 est.)
-10.95% (2020 est.)
note: annual GDP % growth based on constant local currency
comparison ranking: 147

Real GDP per capita: $12,300 (2016 est.)
$12,200 (2015 est.)
$12,100 (2014 est.)
note: data are in 2016 US dollars
comparison ranking: 138

GDP (official exchange rate): $107.352 billion (2020 est.)
note: data in current dollars at official exchange rate

Inflation rate (consumer prices): 5.5% (2017 est.)
4.5% (2016 est.)
comparison ranking: 115

Credit ratings: Moody's rating: Caa2 (2014)
note: The year refers to the year in which the current credit rating was first obtained.

GDP - composition, by sector of origin: *agriculture:* 0.8% (2022 est.)
industry: 23.8% (2022 est.)
services: 74.6% (2022 est.)
note: figures may not total 100% due to non-allocated consumption not captured in sector-reported data
comparison rankings: services 24; industry 110; agriculture 191

GDP - composition, by end use: *household consumption:* 59.6% (2022 est.)
government consumption: 32.5% (2022 est.)
investment in fixed capital: 11.5% (2022 est.)
investment in inventories: 5.1% (2022 est.)
exports of goods and services: 40% (2022 est.)
imports of goods and services: -48.8% (2022 est.)
note: figures may not total 100% due to rounding or gaps in data collection

Agricultural products: sugarcane, cassava, plantains, vegetables, mangoes/guavas, milk, pumpkins/squash, tomatoes, sweet potatoes, bananas (2022)
note: top ten agricultural products based on tonnage

Industries: petroleum, nickel, cobalt, pharmaceuticals, tobacco, construction, steel, cement, agricultural machinery, sugar

Industrial production growth rate: -6.73% (2022 est.)
note: annual % change in industrial value added based on constant local currency
comparison ranking: 203

Labor force: 5.317 million (2023 est.)
note: number of people ages 15 or older who are employed or seeking work
comparison ranking: 81

Unemployment rate: 1.16% (2023 est.)
1.25% (2022 est.)
1.37% (2021 est.)
note: % of labor force seeking employment
comparison ranking: 10

Youth unemployment rate (ages 15-24): *total:* 3% (2023 est.)
male: 3.3% (2023 est.)
female: 2.5% (2023 est.)
note: % of labor force ages 15-24 seeking employment
comparison ranking: total 194

Budget: *revenues:* $54.52 billion (2017 est.)
expenditures: $64.64 billion (2017 est.)

Public debt: 47.7% of GDP (2017 est.)
comparison ranking: 112

Taxes and other revenues: 58.1% (of GDP) (2017 est.)
comparison ranking: 3

Current account balance: $985.4 million (2017 est.)
$2.008 billion (2016 est.)
comparison ranking: 55

Exports: $8.769 billion (2020 est.)
$12.632 billion (2019 est.)
$14.53 billion (2018 est.)
note: GDP expenditure basis - exports of goods and services in current dollars
comparison ranking: 121

Exports - partners: China 40%, Spain 13%, Germany 5%, Portugal 4%, Switzerland 4% (2022)
note: top five export partners based on percentage share of exports

Exports - commodities: tobacco, nickel, zinc ore, liquor, raw sugar (2022)
note: top five export commodities based on value in dollars

Imports: $8.067 billion (2020 est.)
$10.971 billion (2019 est.)
$12.567 billion (2018 est.)
note: GDP expenditure basis - imports of goods and services in current dollars
comparison ranking: 130

Imports - partners: Spain 23%, China 12%, US 10%, Brazil 8%, Netherlands 6% (2022)
note: top five import partners based on percentage share of imports

Imports - commodities: poultry, wheat, milk, plastic products, soybean oil (2022)
note: top five import commodities based on value in dollars

Reserves of foreign exchange and gold: $11.35 billion (31 December 2017 est.)
$12.3 billion (31 December 2016 est.)
comparison ranking: 74

Exchange rates: Cuban pesos (CUP) per US dollar -

Exchange rates: 24 (2023 est.)
24 (2022 est.)
24 (2021 est.)
1 (2020 est.)
1 (2019 est.)
note: official exchange rate of 24 Cuban pesos per US dollar effective 1 January 2021

ENERGY

Electricity access: *electrification - total population:* 100% (2022 est.)

Electricity: *installed generating capacity:* 7.667 million kW (2022 est.)
consumption: 14.559 billion kWh (2022 est.)
transmission/distribution losses: 3.688 billion kWh (2022 est.)
comparison rankings: transmission/distribution losses 151; consumption 86; installed generating capacity 75

Electricity generation sources: *fossil fuels:* 95.4% of total installed capacity (2022 est.)
solar: 1.5% of total installed capacity (2022 est.)
wind: 0.1% of total installed capacity (2022 est.)
hydroelectricity: 0.7% of total installed capacity (2022 est.)
biomass and waste: 2.4% of total installed capacity (2022 est.)

Coal: *consumption:* 2,000 metric tons (2022 est.)
imports: 4,000 metric tons (2022 est.)

Petroleum: *total petroleum production:* 34,000 bbl/day (2023 est.)
refined petroleum consumption: 165,000 bbl/day (2022 est.)
crude oil estimated reserves: 124 million barrels (2021 est.)

Natural gas: *production:* 659.434 million cubic meters (2022 est.)
consumption: 659.434 million cubic meters (2022 est.)
proven reserves: 70.792 billion cubic meters (2021 est.)

Carbon dioxide emissions: 21.693 million metric tonnes of CO_2 (2022 est.)
from coal and metallurgical coke: 7,000 metric tonnes of CO_2 (2022 est.)
from petroleum and other liquids: 20.46 million metric tonnes of CO_2 (2022 est.)
from consumed natural gas: 1.226 million metric tonnes of CO_2 (2022 est.)
comparison ranking: total emissions 83

Energy consumption per capita: 32.255 million Btu/person (2022 est.)
comparison ranking: 111

COMMUNICATIONS

Telephones - fixed lines: *total subscriptions:* 1.574 million (2022 est.)
subscriptions per 100 inhabitants: 14 (2022 est.)
comparison ranking: total subscriptions 59

Telephones - mobile cellular: *total subscriptions:* 7.6 million (2022 est.)
subscriptions per 100 inhabitants: 68 (2022 est.)
comparison ranking: total subscriptions 106

Telecommunication systems: *general assessment:* internet availability has increased substantially over the past few years, only about 70 percent of Cubans have Internet access; 69 percent (7.6 million) have acces to cell phone service, 68 percent have internet access through their cell phone; in 2021 the Cuban Government passed a decree that strengthened its authority to censor Internet and telephonic communications; state control of the telecom sector hinders development; Cuba has the lowest mobile phone and Internet subscription rates in the region; fixed-line density is also very low; thaw of US-Cuba relations encouraged access to services,

such as Wi-Fi hot spots; access to websites and mobile applications is controlled and censored; DSL and Internet are available in Havana, though costs are too high for most Cubans and access can be turned off by the government; international investment and agreement to improve internet access through cost-free and direct connection between networks (2021)
domestic: fixed-line density remains low at a little over 14 per 100 inhabitants; mobile-cellular service has expanded to about 63 per 100 persons (2021)
international: country code - 53; the ALBA-1, GTMO-1, and GTMO-PR fiber-optic submarine cables link Cuba, Jamaica, and Venezuela; satellite earth station - 1 Intersputnik (Atlantic Ocean region) (2019)

Broadcast media: *government owns and controls all broadcast media:* eight national TV channels (Cubavision, Cubavision Plus, Tele Rebelde, Multivision, Educational Channel 1 and 2, Canal Clave, Canal Habana), two international channels (Cubavision Internacional and Canal Caribe), multiple regional TV stations, 7 national radio networks, and multiple regional stations; the Cuban Government beams over the Radio-TV Marti signal; although private ownership of electronic media is prohibited, several online independent news sites exist; those that are not openly critical of the government are often tolerated; the others are blocked by the government; there are no independent TV channels, but several outlets have created strong audiovisual content (El Toque, for example); a community of young Youtubers is also growing, mostly with channels about sports, technology and fashion; Christian denominations are creating original video content to distribute via social media (2023)

Internet country code: .cu

Internet users: *total:* 7.81 million (2021 est.)
percent of population: 71% (2021 est.)
note: private citizens are prohibited from buying computers or accessing the Internet without special authorization; foreigners may access the Internet in large hotels but are subject to firewalls; some Cubans buy illegal passwords on the black market or take advantage of public outlets to access limited email and the government-controlled "intranet"; issues relating to COVID-19 impact research into internet adoption, so actual internet user figures may be different than published numbers suggest
comparison ranking: total 77

Broadband - fixed subscriptions: *total:* 231,654 (2020 est.)
subscriptions per 100 inhabitants: 2 (2020 est.)
comparison ranking: total 115

TRANSPORTATION

National air transport system: *number of registered air carriers:* 4 (2020)
inventory of registered aircraft operated by air carriers: 18
annual passenger traffic on registered air carriers: 560,754 (2018)
annual freight traffic on registered air carriers: 17.76 million (2018) mt-km

Civil aircraft registration country code prefix: CU

Airports: 123 (2024)
comparison ranking: 42

Heliports: 4 (2024)

Pipelines: 41 km gas, 230 km oil (2013)

Railways: *total:* 8,367 km (2017)
standard gauge: 8,195 km (2017) 1.435-m gauge (124 km electrified)
narrow gauge: 172 km (2017) 1.000-m gauge
note: As of 2013, 70 km of standard gauge and 12 km of narrow gauge track were not for public use
comparison ranking: total 26

Roadways: *total:* 60,000 km (2015)
paved: 20,000 km (2001)
unpaved: 40,000 km (2001)
comparison ranking: total 79

Waterways: 240 km (2011) (almost all navigable inland waterways are near the mouths of rivers)
comparison ranking: 103

Merchant marine: *total:* 65 (2023)
by type: general cargo 13, oil tanker 10, other 42
comparison ranking: total 111

Ports: *total ports:* 34 (2024)
large: 6
medium: 3
small: 10
very small: 6
size unknown: 9
ports with oil terminals: 14
key ports: Antilla, Bahai de la Habana, Bahia de Sagua de Tanamo, Cabanas, Casilda, Cienfuegos, Nuevitas Bay, Puerto Guantanamo, Santiago de Cuba

MILITARY AND SECURITY

Military and security forces: Revolutionary Armed Forces (Fuerzas Armadas Revolucionarias, FAR): Revolutionary Army (Ejercito Revolucionario, ER), Revolutionary Navy (Marina de Guerra Revolucionaria, MGR, includes Marine Corps), Revolutionary Air and Air Defense Forces (Defensas Anti-Aereas y Fuerza Aerea Revolucionaria, DAAFAR); Paramilitary forces: Youth Labor Army (Ejercito Juvenil del Trabajo, EJT), Territorial Militia Troops (Milicia de Tropas de Territoriales, MTT), Civil Defense Force

Ministry of Interior: Border Guards, State Security, National Revolutionary Police (2023)

Military expenditures: 4.2% of GDP (2020 est.)
3.2% of GDP (2019 est.)
2.9% of GDP (2018 est.)
2.9% of GDP (2017 est.)
3.1% of GDP (2016 est.)
comparison ranking: 14

Military and security service personnel strengths: limited available information; estimated 50,000 active personnel, including approximately 40,000 Army (2023)

Military equipment inventories and acquisitions: the military's inventory is comprised of Russian and Soviet-era equipment (2024)

Military service age and obligation: 17-28 years of age for compulsory (men) and voluntary (men and women) military service; conscripts serve for 24 months (2024)

Military - note: the Revolutionary Armed Forces (FAR) are a central pillar of the Cuban regime and viewed as the guardian of the Cuban revolution; the FAR has a large role in the country's politics and economy; many senior government posts are held by military officers, and a FAR-controlled umbrella enterprise known as the Armed Forces Business Group (Grupo de Administración Empresarial or GAESA) has interests in banking and finance, construction, import/export, ports, real estate, retail, shipping, transportation, and tourism
the FAR is largely focused on protecting territorial integrity and the state, and perceives the US as its primary threat; the fall of the Soviet Union in 1991 and the subsequent end of Soviet military aid had far-reaching consequences for the FAR, transforming it from one of the largest and most capable militaries in the region, as well as one that was heavily involved in foreign missions during the Cold War, particularly in Africa, into a much smaller, home-based and defensive force with limited capabilities and armed with Soviet-era weapons and equipment (2023)

TRANSNATIONAL ISSUES

Trafficking in persons: tier rating: Tier 3 — Cuba does not fully meet the minimum standards for the elimination of trafficking and is not making significant efforts to do so, therefore, Cuba remained on Tier 3; for more details, go to: https://www.state.gov/reports/2024-trafficking-in-persons-report/cuba/

Illicit drugs: Cuba is not a major consumer, producer, or transshipment point for illicit drugs; domestic production and consumption curbed by aggressive policing; prescription drug abuse remains low

CURACAO

INTRODUCTION

Background: The original Arawak Indian settlers who arrived on Curacao from South America in about A.D. 1000 were largely enslaved by the Spanish early in the 16th century and forcibly relocated to other colonies where labor was needed. The Dutch seized Curacao from the Spanish in 1634. Once the center of the Caribbean slave trade, Curacao was hard hit economically when the Dutch abolished slavery in 1863. Its prosperity (and that of neighboring Aruba) was restored in the early 20th century with the construction of the Isla Refineria to service the newly discovered Venezuelan oilfields. In 1954, Curacao and several other Dutch Caribbean colonies were reorganized as the Netherlands Antilles, part of the Kingdom of the Netherlands. In referenda in 2005 and 2009, the citizens of Curacao voted to become a self-governing country within the Kingdom of the Netherlands. The change in status became effective

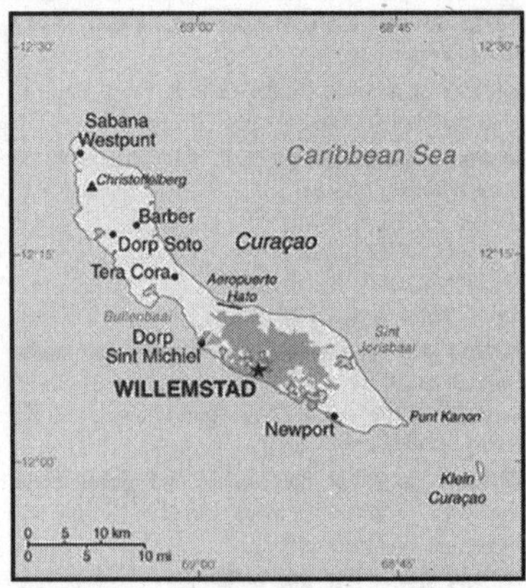

in 2010 with the dissolution of the Netherlands Antilles.

GEOGRAPHY

Location: Caribbean, an island in the Caribbean Sea, 55 km off the coast of Venezuela

Geographic coordinates: 12 10 N, 69 00 W

Map references: Central America and the Caribbean

Area: *total:* 444 sq km
land: 444 sq km
water: 0 sq km
comparison ranking: total 199

Area - comparative: more than twice the size of Washington, DC

Land boundaries: 0

Coastline: 364 km

Maritime claims: *territorial sea:* 12 nm
exclusive economic zone: 200 nm

Climate: tropical marine climate, ameliorated by northeast trade winds, results in mild temperatures; semiarid with average rainfall of 60 cm/ year

Terrain: generally low, hilly terrain

Elevation: *highest point:* Mt. Christoffel 372 m
lowest point: Caribbean Sea 0 m

Natural resources: calcium phosphates, protected harbors, hot springs

Land use: *agricultural land:* 10% (2018 est.)
arable land: 10% (2018)
other: 90% (2018 est.)

Irrigated land: NA

Population distribution: largest concentration on the island is Willemstad; smaller settlements near the coast can be found throughout the island, particularly in the northwest

Natural hazards: Curacao is south of the Caribbean hurricane belt and is rarely threatened

Geography - note: Curacao is a part of the Windward Islands (southern) group in the Lesser Antilles

PEOPLE AND SOCIETY

Population: *total:* 153,289
male: 73,755
female: 79,534 (2024 est.)
comparison rankings: female 187; male 187; total 187

Nationality: *noun:* Curacaoan
adjective: Curacaoan; Dutch

Ethnic groups: Curacaoan 75.4%, Dutch 6%, Dominican 3.6%, Colombian 3%, Bonairean, Sint Eustatian, Saban 1.5%, Haitian 1.2%, Surinamese 1.2%, Venezuelan 1.1%, Aruban 1.1%, other 5%, unspecified 0.9% (2011 est.)

Languages: Papiamento (official) (a creole language that is a mixture of Portuguese, Spanish, Dutch, English, and, to a lesser extent, French, as well as elements of African languages and the language of the Arawak) 80%, Dutch (official) 8.8%, Spanish 5.6%, English (official) 3.1%, other 2.3%, unspecified 0.3% (2011 est.)
note: data represent most spoken language in household

Religions: Roman Catholic 72.8%, Pentecostal 6.6%, Protestant 3.2%, Adventist 3%, Jehovah's Witness 2%, Evangelical 1.9%, other 3.8%, none 6%, unspecified 0.6% (2011 est.)

Age structure: *0-14 years:* 19.2% (male 15,069/ female 14,337)
15-64 years: 62.3% (male 47,258/female 48,217)
65 years and over: 18.5% (2024 est.) (male 11,428/ female 16,980)

Dependency ratios: *total dependency ratio:* 47
youth dependency ratio: 25.6
elderly dependency ratio: 21.4
potential support ratio: 4.7 (2021 est.)

Median age: *total:* 37.8 years (2024 est.)
male: 35.5 years
female: 40.2 years
comparison ranking: total 81

Population growth rate: 0.28% (2024 est.)
comparison ranking: 168

Birth rate: 12.9 births/1,000 population (2024 est.)
comparison ranking: 135

Death rate: 8.9 deaths/1,000 population (2024 est.)
comparison ranking: 64

Net migration rate: -1.3 migrant(s)/1,000 population (2024 est.)
comparison ranking: 152

Population distribution: largest concentration on the island is Willemstad; smaller settlements near the coast can be found throughout the island, particularly in the northwest

Urbanization: *urban population:* 89% of total population (2023)
rate of urbanization: 0.57% annual rate of change (2020-25 est.)

Major urban areas - population: 144,000 WILLEMSTAD (capital) (2018)

Sex ratio: *at birth:* 1.05 male(s)/female
0-14 years: 1.05 male(s)/female
15-64 years: 0.98 male(s)/female
65 years and over: 0.67 male(s)/female
total population: 0.93 male(s)/female (2024 est.)

Infant mortality rate: *total:* 7.5 deaths/1,000 live births (2024 est.)
male: 8.3 deaths/1,000 live births
female: 6.7 deaths/1,000 live births
comparison ranking: total 152

Life expectancy at birth: *total population:* 79.9 years (2024 est.)
male: 77.6 years
female: 82.3 years
comparison ranking: total population 59

Total fertility rate: 1.96 children born/woman (2024 est.)
comparison ranking: 111

Gross reproduction rate: 0.96 (2024 est.)

Contraceptive prevalence rate: NA

Drinking water source: *improved: total:* 100% of population
unimproved: total: 0% of population (2017)

Sanitation facility access: *improved: total:* 100% of population
unimproved: total: 0% of population (2017)

Currently married women (ages 15-49): 49.7% (2023 est.)

Education expenditures: 7.4% of GDP (2020 est.)
comparison ranking: 16

School life expectancy (primary to tertiary education): *total:* 17 years
male: 18 years
female: 18 years (2013)

ENVIRONMENT

Environment - current issues: problems in waste management that threaten environmental sustainability on the island include pollution of marine areas from domestic sewage, inadequate sewage treatment facilities, industrial effluents and agricultural runoff, the mismanagement of toxic substances, and ineffective regulations; the refinery in Sint Anna Bay, at the eastern edge of Willemstad's large natural harbor, processes heavy crude oil from Venezuela; it has caused significant environmental damage to the surrounding area because of neglect and a lack of strict environmental controls; the release of noxious fumes and potentially hazardous particles causes schools downwind to regularly close

Climate: tropical marine climate, ameliorated by northeast trade winds, results in mild temperatures; semiarid with average rainfall of 60 cm/ year

Urbanization: *urban population:* 89% of total population (2023)
rate of urbanization: 0.57% annual rate of change (2020-25 est.)

Revenue from forest resources: 0% of GDP (2018 est.)
comparison ranking: 182

Revenue from coal: 0% of GDP (2018 est.)
comparison ranking: 116

Air pollutants: *carbon dioxide emissions:* 5.39 megatons (2016 est.)

Waste and recycling: *municipal solid waste generated annually:* 24,704 tons (2013 est.)
municipal solid waste recycled annually: 494 tons (2013 est.)
percent of municipal solid waste recycled: 2% (2013 est.)

Total renewable water resources: NA

GOVERNMENT

Country name: *conventional long form:* Country of Curacao
conventional short form: Curacao
local long form: Land Curacao (Dutch)/ Pais Korsou (Papiamento)
local short form: Curacao (Dutch)/ Korsou (Papiamento)
former: Netherlands Antilles; Curacao and Dependencies
etymology: the most plausible name derivation is that the island was designated Isla de la Curacion

(Spanish meaning "Island of the Cure" or "Island of Healing") or Ilha da Curacao (Portuguese meaning the same) to reflect the locale's function as a recovery stop for sick crewmen

Government type: parliamentary democracy

Dependency status: constituent country within the Kingdom of the Netherlands; full autonomy in internal affairs granted in 2010; Dutch Government responsible for defense and foreign affairs

Capital: *name:* Willemstad
geographic coordinates: 12 06 N, 68 55 W
time difference: UTC-4 (1 hour ahead of Washington, DC, during Standard Time)
etymology: named after Prince WILLIAM II of Orange (1626-1650), who served as stadtholder (Dutch head of state) from 1647 to 1650, shortly after the the Dutch captured Curacao from the Spanish in 1634

Administrative divisions: none (part of the Kingdom of the Netherlands)
note: Curacao is one of four constituent countries of the Kingdom of the Netherlands; the other three are the Netherlands, Aruba, and Sint Maarten

Independence: none (part of the Kingdom of the Netherlands)

National holiday: King's Day (birthday of King WILLEM-ALEXANDER), 27 April (1967); note - King's or Queen's Day are observed on the ruling monarch's birthday; celebrated on 26 April if 27 April is a Sunday

Legal system: based on Dutch civil law

Constitution: *history:* previous 1947, 1955; latest adopted 5 September 2010, entered into force 10 October 2010 (regulates governance of Curacao but is subordinate to the Charter for the Kingdom of the Netherlands); note - in October 2010, with the dissolution of the Netherlands Antilles, Curacao became a semi-autonomous entity within the Kingdom of the Netherlands

Citizenship: see the Netherlands

Suffrage: 18 years of age; universal

Executive branch: *chief of state:* King WILLEM-ALEXANDER of the Netherlands (since 30 April 2013); represented by Governor Lucille A. GEORGE-WOUT (since 4 November 2013)
head of government: Prime Minister Gilmar PISAS (since 14 June 2021)
cabinet: Cabinet sworn-in by the governor
elections/appointments: the monarch is hereditary; governor appointed by the monarch; following legislative elections, the leader of the majority party usually elected prime minister by the Parliament of Curacao; last election held on 19 March 2021 (next to be held in 2025)

Legislative branch: *description:* unicameral Parliament of Curacao (21 seats; members directly elected by party-list proportional representation vote to serve 4-year terms)
elections: last held on 19 March 2021 (next to be held in 2025)
election results: percent of vote by party - MFK 27.8%, PAR 13.9%, PNP 12.5%, MAN 6.4%, KEM 5.4%, TPK 5.2%; seats by party - MFK 9, PAR 4, PNP 4, MAN 2, KEM 1, TPK 1; composition - men 15, women 6, percent of women 28.6%

Judicial branch: *highest court(s):* Joint Court of Justice of Aruba, Curacao, Sint Maarten, and of Bonaire, Sint Eustatius and Saba or "Joint Court of Justice" (sits as a 3-judge panel); final appeals heard by the Supreme Court, in The Hague, Netherlands
judge selection and term of office: Joint Court judges appointed by the monarch for life
subordinate courts: first instance courts, appeals court; specialized courts

Political parties: Korsou di Nos Tur or KdnT
Korsou Esun Miho or KEM
Movementu Futuro Korsou or MFK
Movementu Progresivo or MP
Movishon Antia Nobo or MAN
Partido Antia Restruktura or PAR
Partido Inovashon Nashonal or PIN
Partido Nashonal di Pueblo or PNP
Pueblo Soberano or PS
Trabou pa Kòrsou or TPK
Un Korsou Hustu

International organization participation: ACS (associate), Caricom (observer), FATF, ILO, ITU, UNESCO (associate), UPU

Diplomatic representation in the US: none (represented by the Kingdom of the Netherlands)

Diplomatic representation from the US: *chief of mission:* Consul General Margy BOND (since 20 January 2022); note - also accredited to Aruba and Sint Maarten
embassy: P.O. Box 158, J.B. Gorsiraweg 1
mailing address: 3160 Curacao Place, Washington DC 20521-3160
telephone: [599] (9) 461-3066
FAX: [599] (9) 461-6489
email address and website:
ACSCuracao@state.gov
https://cw.usconsulate.gov/

Flag description: *on a blue field a horizontal yellow band somewhat below the center divides the flag into proportions of 5:1:2;* two five-pointed white stars - the smaller above and to the left of the larger - appear in the canton; the blue of the upper and lower sections symbolizes the sky and sea respectively; yellow represents the sun; the stars symbolize Curacao and its uninhabited smaller sister island of Klein Curacao; the five star points signify the five continents from which Curacao's people derive

National symbol(s): laraha (citrus tree); national colors: blue, yellow, white

National anthem: *name:* "Himmo di Korsou" (Anthem of Curacao)
lyrics/music: Guillermo ROSARIO, Mae HENRIQUEZ, Enrique MULLER, Betty DORAN/ Frater Candidus NOWENS, Errol "El Toro" COLINA
note: adapted 1978; the lyrics, originally written in 1899, were rewritten in 1978 to make them less colonial in nature

National heritage: *total World Heritage Sites:* 1 (cultural); note - excerpted from the Netherlands entry
selected World Heritage Site locales: Historic Willemstad

ECONOMY

Economic overview: high-income island economy; developed infrastructure; tourism and financial services-based economy; investing in information technology incentives; oil refineries service Venezuela and China; unique COVID-19 stimulus support applied to government debts rather than household support

Real GDP (purchasing power parity): $4.137 billion (2022 est.)
$3.834 billion (2021 est.)
$3.68 billion (2020 est.)
note: data in 2021 dollars
comparison ranking: 190

Real GDP growth rate: 7.9% (2022 est.)
4.2% (2021 est.)
-18.04% (2020 est.)
note: annual GDP % growth based on constant local currency
comparison ranking: 14

Real GDP per capita: $27,600 (2022 est.)
$25,200 (2021 est.)
$23,700 (2020 est.)
note: data in 2021 dollars
comparison ranking: 84

GDP (official exchange rate): $3.074 billion (2022 est.)
note: data in current dollars at official exchange rate

Inflation rate (consumer prices): 2.62% (2019 est.)
2.58% (2018 est.)
1.59% (2017 est.)
note: annual % change based on consumer prices
comparison ranking: 55

GDP - composition, by sector of origin: *agriculture:* 0.3% (2022 est.)
industry: 11.2% (2022 est.)
services: 73.4% (2022 est.)
note: figures may not total 100% due to non-allocated consumption not captured in sector-reported data
comparison rankings: services 27; industry 186; agriculture 202

GDP - composition, by end use: *household consumption:* 73.2% (2018 est.)
government consumption: 14.5% (2018 est.)
investment in fixed capital: 34% (2018 est.)
investment in inventories: 7% (2018 est.)
exports of goods and services: 63.2% (2018 est.)
imports of goods and services: -92% (2018 est.)
note: figures may not total 100% due to rounding or gaps in data collection

Agricultural products: aloe, sorghum, peanuts, vegetables, tropical fruit

Industries: tourism, petroleum refining, petroleum transshipment, light manufacturing, financial and business services

Industrial production growth rate: 4.3% (2014 est.)
note: annual % change in industrial value added based on constant local currency
comparison ranking: 59

Youth unemployment rate (ages 15-24): *total:* 42.2% (2020 est.)
male: 38.1%
female: 47.1%
comparison ranking: total 8

Remittances: 5.16% of GDP (2022 est.)
5.18% of GDP (2021 est.)
5.22% of GDP (2020 est.)
note: personal transfers and compensation between resident and non-resident individuals/households/ entities

Current account balance: -$877.284 million (2022 est.)
-$507.018 million (2021 est.)
-$688.805 million (2020 est.)
note: balance of payments - net trade and primary/ secondary income in current dollars

comparison ranking: 139

Exports: $2.049 billion (2022 est.)
$1.373 billion (2021 est.)
$1.014 billion (2020 est.)
note: balance of payments - exports of goods and services in current dollars
comparison ranking: 166

Exports - partners: US 17%, Costa Rica 16%, India 9%, Netherlands 7%, Guatemala 7% (2022)
note: top five export partners based on percentage share of exports

Exports - commodities: refined petroleum, petroleum coke, fish, coal tar oil, scrap iron (2022)
note: top five export commodities based on value in dollars

Imports: $2.904 billion (2022 est.)
$1.919 billion (2021 est.)
$1.709 billion (2020 est.)
note: balance of payments - imports of goods and services in current dollars
comparison ranking: 164

Imports - partners: US 35%, Netherlands 22%, China 7%, Ecuador 5%, Philippines 3% (2022)
note: top five import partners based on percentage share of imports

Imports - commodities: refined petroleum, cars, garments, integrated circuits, packaged medicine (2022)
note: top five import commodities based on value in dollars

Exchange rates: Netherlands Antillean guilders (ANG) per US dollar -

Exchange rates: 1.79 (2023 est.)
1.79 (2022 est.)
1.79 (2021 est.)
1.79 (2020 est.)
1.79 (2019 est.)

ENERGY

Electricity access: *electrification - total population:* 100% (2022 est.)

COMMUNICATIONS

Telephones - fixed lines: *total subscriptions:* 53,000 (2021 est.)
subscriptions per 100 inhabitants: 28 (2021 est.)
comparison ranking: total subscriptions 153

Telephones - mobile cellular: *total subscriptions:* 168,000 (2021 est.)
subscriptions per 100 inhabitants: 88 (2021 est.)
comparison ranking: total subscriptions 187

Telecommunication systems: *general assessment:* fully automatic modern telecommunications system; telecom sector across the Caribbean region continues to be one of the growth areas; given the lack of economic diversity in the region, with a high dependence on tourism and activities such as fisheries and offshore financial services the telecom sector contributes greatly to the GDP (2020)
domestic: roughly 28 per 100 users for fixed-line and 88 per 100 users for cellular-mobile (2021)
international: country code - +599, PCCS submarine cable system to US, Caribbean and Central and South America (2019)

Broadcast media: government-run TeleCuracao operates a TV station and a radio station; 2 other privately owned TV stations and several privately owned radio stations (2019)

Internet country code: .cw

Internet users: *total:* 111,956 (2021 est.)
percent of population: 68.1% (2021 est.)
comparison ranking: total 186

Broadband - fixed subscriptions: *total:* 55,000 (2020 est.)
subscriptions per 100 inhabitants: 34 (2020 est.)
comparison ranking: total 141

TRANSPORTATION

National air transport system: *number of registered air carriers:* 2 (2020)
inventory of registered aircraft operated by air carriers: 11

Civil aircraft registration country code prefix: PJ

Airports: 1 (2024)
comparison ranking: 221

Roadways: *total:* 550 km
comparison ranking: total 194

Merchant marine: *total:* 57 (2023)
by type: general cargo 5, oil tanker 1, other 51
comparison ranking: total 116

Ports: *total ports:* 4 (2024)
large: 0
medium: 2
small: 1
very small: 1
ports with oil terminals: 3
key ports: Bullenbaai, Caracasbaai, Sint Michelsbaai, Willemstad

MILITARY AND SECURITY

Military and security forces: no regular military forces; Curacao Militia (CURMIL); Police Department for local law enforcement, supported by the Royal Netherlands Marechaussee (Gendarmerie), the Dutch Caribbean Police Force (Korps Politie Caribisch Nederland, KPCN), and the Dutch Caribbean Coast Guard (DCCG or Kustwacht Caribisch Gebied (KWCARIB)) (2024)

Military - note: defense is the responsibility of the Kingdom of the Netherlands; the Dutch Government controls foreign and defense policy; the Dutch Caribbean Coast Guard (DCCG) provides maritime security (2024)

TRANSNATIONAL ISSUES

Refugees and internally displaced persons: *refugees (country of origin):* 14,000 (Venezuela) (2022)

Trafficking in persons: tier rating: Tier 2 Watch List — Curaçao does not fully meet the minimum standards for the elimination of trafficking but is making significant efforts to do so, therefore Curaçao was upgraded to Tier 2 Watch List; for more details, go to: https://www.state.gov/reports/2024-trafficking-in-persons-report/curacao/

Illicit drugs: northbound transshipment points for cocaine from Colombia and Venezuela; cocaine is transported to the United States, other Caribbean islands, Africa, and Europe

CYPRUS

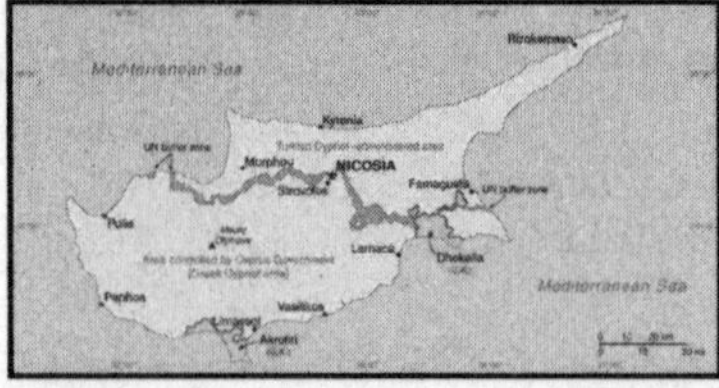

INTRODUCTION

Background: A former British colony, Cyprus became independent in 1960 after years of resistance to British rule. Tensions between the Greek Cypriot majority and Turkish Cypriot minority came to a head in December 1963, when violence broke out in the capital of Nicosia. Despite the deployment of UN peacekeepers in 1964, sporadic intercommunal violence continued and forced most Turkish Cypriots into enclaves throughout the island. In 1974, a Greek Government-sponsored attempt to overthrow the elected president of Cyprus was met by military intervention from Turkey, which soon controlled more than a third of the island. In 1983, the Turkish Cypriot administered area declared itself the "Turkish Republic of Northern Cyprus" (TRNC), but it is recognized only by Turkey. A UN-mediated agreement to reunite Cyprus, the Annan Plan, failed to win approval from both communities in 2004. The most recent round of reunification negotiations was suspended in 2017 after failure to achieve a breakthrough.

The entire island joined the EU in 2004, although the EU acquis – the body of common rights and obligations – applies only to the areas under the internationally recognized government and is suspended in the TRNC. However, individual Turkish Cypriots able to document their eligibility for Republic of Cyprus citizenship have the same legal rights accorded to citizens of other EU states.

GEOGRAPHY

Location: Middle East, island in the Mediterranean Sea, south of Turkey; note - Cyprus views itself as part of Europe; geopolitically, it can be classified as falling within Europe, the Middle East, or both

Geographic coordinates: 35 00 N, 33 00 E

Map references: Middle East

Area: *total:* 9,251 sq km (of which 3,355 sq km are in north Cyprus)

land: 9,241 sq km
water: 10 sq km
comparison ranking: total 169

Area - comparative: about 0.6 times the size of Connecticut

Land boundaries: *total:* 156 km
border sovereign base areas: Akrotiri 48 km; Dhekelia 108 km

Coastline: 648 km

Maritime claims: *territorial sea:* 12 nm
contiguous zone: 24 nm
continental shelf: 200-m depth or to the depth of exploitation

Climate: temperate; Mediterranean with hot, dry summers and cool winters

Terrain: central plain with mountains to north and south; scattered but significant plains along southern coast

Elevation: *highest point:* Mount Olympus 1,951 m
lowest point: Mediterranean Sea 0 m
mean elevation: 91 m

Natural resources: copper, pyrites, asbestos, gypsum, timber, salt, marble, clay earth pigment

Land use: *agricultural land:* 13.4% (2018 est.)
arable land: 9.8% (2018 est.)
permanent crops: 3.2% (2018 est.)
permanent pasture: 0.4% (2018 est.)
forest: 18.8% (2018 est.)
other: 67.8% (2018 est.)

Irrigated land: 268 sq km (2020)

Population distribution: *population concentrated in central Nicosia and in the major cities of the south:* Paphos, Limassol, and Larnaca

Natural hazards: moderate earthquake activity; droughts

Geography - note: the third largest island in the Mediterranean Sea (after Sicily and Sardinia); several small Cypriot enclaves exist within the Dhekelia Sovereign Base Area

PEOPLE AND SOCIETY

Population: *total:* 1,320,525
male: 675,196
female: 645,329 (2024 est.)
comparison rankings: female 157; male 158; total 158

Nationality: *noun:* Cypriot(s)
adjective: Cypriot

Ethnic groups: Greek 98.8%, other 1% (includes Maronite, Armenian, Turkish-Cypriot), unspecified 0.2% (2011 est.)
note: data represent only the Greek-Cypriot citizens in the Republic of Cyprus

Languages: Greek (official) 80.9%, Turkish (official) 0.2%, English 4.1%, Romanian 2.9%, Russian 2.5%, Bulgarian 2.2%, Arabic 1.2%, Filipino 1.1%, other 4.3%, unspecified 0.6% (2011 est.)
major-language sample(s):
Το Παγκόσμιο Βιβλίο Δεδομένων, η απαραίτητη πηΥή βασικών πληροφοριών. (Greek)
note: data represent only the Republic of Cyprus

Religions: Eastern Orthodox Christian 89.1%, Roman Catholic 2.9%, Protestant/Anglican 2%, Muslim 1.8%, Buddhist 1%, other (includes Maronite Catholic, Armenian Apostolic, Hindu) 1.4%, unknown 1.1%, none/atheist 0.6% (2011 est.)
note: data represent only the government-controlled area of Cyprus

Age structure: *0-14 years:* 15.6% (male 105,533/female 100,099)
15-64 years: 70% (male 486,569/female 437,651)
65 years and over: 14.4% (2024 est.) (male 83,094/female 107,579)

Dependency ratios: *total dependency ratio:* 43.8
youth dependency ratio: 23
elderly dependency ratio: 20.8
potential support ratio: 4.8 (2021 est.)
note: data represent the whole country

Median age: *total:* 39.5 years (2024 est.)
male: 38.2 years
female: 41 years
comparison ranking: total 67

Population growth rate: 0.95% (2024 est.)
comparison ranking: 95

Birth rate: 10.2 births/1,000 population (2024 est.)
comparison ranking: 182

Death rate: 7 deaths/1,000 population (2024 est.)
comparison ranking: 123

Net migration rate: 6.3 migrant(s)/1,000 population (2024 est.)
comparison ranking: 13

Population distribution: *population concentrated in central Nicosia and in the major cities of the south:* Paphos, Limassol, and Larnaca

Urbanization: *urban population:* 67% of total population (2023)
rate of urbanization: 0.76% annual rate of change (2020-25 est.)

Major urban areas - population: 269,000 NICOSIA (capital) (2018)

Sex ratio: *at birth:* 1.05 male(s)/female
0-14 years: 1.05 male(s)/female
15-64 years: 1.11 male(s)/female
65 years and over: 0.77 male(s)/female
total population: 1.05 male(s)/female (2024 est.)

Mother's mean age at first birth: 30 years (2020 est.)
note: data represents only government-controlled areas

Maternal mortality ratio: 68 deaths/100,000 live births (2020 est.)
comparison ranking: 89

Infant mortality rate: *total:* 8.1 deaths/1,000 live births (2024 est.)
male: 9.7 deaths/1,000 live births
female: 6.4 deaths/1,000 live births
comparison ranking: total 144

Life expectancy at birth: *total population:* 80.2 years (2024 est.)
male: 77.4 years
female: 83.1 years
comparison ranking: total population 56

Total fertility rate: 1.49 children born/woman (2024 est.)
comparison ranking: 203

Gross reproduction rate: 0.73 (2024 est.)

Contraceptive prevalence rate: NA

Drinking water source: *improved: urban:* 99.7% of population
rural: 99.8% of population
total: 99.8% of population
unimproved: urban: 0.3% of population
rural: 0.2% of population
total: 0.2% of population (2020 est.)

Current health expenditure: 8.1% of GDP (2020)

Physician density: 3.14 physicians/1,000 population (2019)

Hospital bed density: 3.4 beds/1,000 population (2017)

Sanitation facility access: *improved: urban:* 99.7% of population
rural: 98.8% of population
total: 99.4% of population
unimproved: urban: 0.3% of population
rural: 1.2% of population
total: 0.6% of population (2020 est.)

Obesity - adult prevalence rate: 21.8% (2016)
comparison ranking: 84

Alcohol consumption per capita: *total:* 9.59 liters of pure alcohol (2019 est.)
beer: 2.85 liters of pure alcohol (2019 est.)
wine: 2.72 liters of pure alcohol (2019 est.)
spirits: 4.02 liters of pure alcohol (2019 est.)
other alcohols: 0 liters of pure alcohol (2019 est.)
comparison ranking: total 26

Tobacco use: *total:* 35.1% (2020 est.)
male: 47% (2020 est.)
female: 23.2% (2020 est.)
comparison ranking: total 14

Children under the age of 5 years underweight: NA

Currently married women (ages 15-49): 54.5% (2023 est.)

Education expenditures: 6.1% of GDP (2020 est.)
comparison ranking: 39

Literacy: *definition:* age 15 and over can read and write
total population: 99.4%
male: 99.6%
female: 99.2% (2021)

School life expectancy (primary to tertiary education): *total:* 16 years
male: 16 years
female: 16 years (2020)

People - note: demographic data for Cyprus represent the population of the government-controlled area and the area administered by Turkish Cypriots, unless otherwise indicated

ENVIRONMENT

Environment - current issues: water resource problems (no natural reservoir catchments, seasonal disparity in rainfall, sea water intrusion to island's largest aquifer, increased salination in the north); water pollution from sewage, industrial wastes, and pesticides; coastal degradation; erosion; loss of wildlife habitats from urbanization

Environment - international agreements: *party to:* Air Pollution, Air Pollution-Heavy Metals, Air Pollution-Multi-effect Protocol, Air Pollution-Nitrogen Oxides, Air Pollution-Persistent Organic Pollutants, Air Pollution-Sulphur 94, Biodiversity, Climate Change, Climate Change-Kyoto Protocol, Climate Change-Paris Agreement, Comprehensive Nuclear Test Ban, Desertification, Endangered Species, Environmental Modification, Hazardous Wastes, Law of the Sea, Marine Dumping-London Convention, Nuclear Test Ban, Ozone Layer Protection, Ship Pollution, Tropical Timber 2006, Wetlands, Whaling
signed, but not ratified: none of the selected agreements

Climate: temperate; Mediterranean with hot, dry summers and cool winters

Urbanization: *urban population:* 67% of total population (2023)
rate of urbanization: 0.76% annual rate of change (2020-25 est.)

Revenue from forest resources: 0% of GDP (2018 est.)
comparison ranking: 194

Revenue from coal: 0% of GDP (2018 est.)
comparison ranking: 147

Air pollutants: *particulate matter emissions:* 14.52 micrograms per cubic meter (2019 est.)
carbon dioxide emissions: 6.63 megatons (2016 est.)
methane emissions: 0.86 megatons (2020 est.)

Waste and recycling: *municipal solid waste generated annually:* 541,000 tons (2015 est.)
municipal solid waste recycled annually: 72,007 tons (2015 est.)
percent of municipal solid waste recycled: 13.3% (2015 est.)

Total water withdrawal: *municipal:* 100 million cubic meters (2020 est.)
industrial: 20 million cubic meters (2020 est.)
agricultural: 170 million cubic meters (2020 est.)

Total renewable water resources: 780 million cubic meters (2020 est.)

Geoparks: *total global geoparks and regional networks:* 1
global geoparks and regional networks: Troodos (2023)

GOVERNMENT

Country name: *conventional long form:* Republic of Cyprus
conventional short form: Cyprus
local long form: Kypriaki Dimokratia (Greek)/ Kibris Cumhuriyeti (Turkish)
local short form: Kypros (Greek)/ Kibris (Turkish)
etymology: the derivation of the name "Cyprus" is unknown, but the extensive mining of copper metal on the island in antiquity gave rise to the Latin word "cuprum" for copper
note: the Turkish Cypriot community, which administers the northern part of the island, refers to itself as the "Turkish Republic of Northern Cyprus" or "TRNC" ("Kuzey Kibris Turk Cumhuriyeti" or "KKTC")

Government type: Republic of Cyprus - presidential republic; self-declared "Turkish Republic of Northern Cyprus" (TRNC) - parliamentary republic with enhanced presidency
note: a separation of the two main ethnic communities inhabiting the island began following the outbreak of communal strife in 1963; this separation was further solidified when a Greek military-junta-supported coup attempt prompted the Turkish military intervention in July 1974 that gave the Turkish Cypriots de facto control in the north; Greek Cypriots control the only internationally recognized government on the island; on 15 November 1983, then Turkish Cypriot "President" Rauf DENKTAS declared independence and the formation of the "TRNC," which is recognized only by Turkey

Capital: *name:* Nicosia (Lefkosia/Lefkosa)
geographic coordinates: 35 10 N, 33 22 E
time difference: UTC+2 (7 hours ahead of Washington, DC, during Standard Time)
daylight saving time: +1hr, begins last Sunday in March; ends last Sunday in October
etymology: a mispronunciation of the city's Greek name Lefkosia and its Turkish name Lefkosa, both of which mean "White City"; the Greek name may derive from the Greek phrase "leuke ousia" ("white estate")

Administrative divisions: 6 districts; Ammochostos (Famagusta; all but a small part located in the Turkish Cypriot community), Keryneia (Kyrenia; the only district located entirely in the Turkish Cypriot community), Larnaka (Larnaca; with a small part located in the Turkish Cypriot community), Lefkosia (Nicosia; a small part administered by Turkish Cypriots), Lemesos (Limassol), Pafos (Paphos); note - the 5 "districts" of the "Turkish Republic of Northern Cyprus" are Gazimagusa (Famagusta), Girne (Kyrenia), Guzelyurt (Morphou), Iskele (Trikomo), Lefkosa (Nicosia)

Independence: 16 August 1960 (from the UK); note - Turkish Cypriots proclaimed self-rule on 13 February 1975 and independence in 1983, but these proclamations are recognized only by Turkey

National holiday: Independence Day, 1 October (1960); note - Turkish Cypriots celebrate 15 November (1983) as "Republic Day"

Legal system: mixed legal system of English common law and civil law with European law supremacy

Constitution: *history:* ratified 16 August 1960; note - in 1963, the constitution was partly suspended as Turkish Cypriots withdrew from the government; Turkish-held territory in 1983 was declared the "Turkish Republic of Northern Cyprus" ("TRNC"); in 1985, the "TRNC" approved its own constitution
amendments: constitution of the Republic of Cyprus - proposed by the House of Representatives; passage requires at least two-thirds majority vote of the total membership of the "Greek Community" and the "Turkish Community"; however, all seats of Turkish Cypriot members have remained vacant since 1964; amended many times, last in 2020;
constitution of the "Turkish Republic of Northern Cyprus" - proposed by at least 10 members of the "Assembly of the Republic"; passage requires at least two-thirds majority vote of the total Assembly membership and approval by referendum; amended 2014

International law organization participation: accepts compulsory ICJ jurisdiction with reservations; accepts ICCt jurisdiction

Citizenship: *citizenship by birth:* no
citizenship by descent only: at least one parent must be a citizen of Cyprus
dual citizenship recognized: yes
residency requirement for naturalization: 7 years

Suffrage: 18 years of age; universal

Executive branch: *chief of state:* President Nikos CHRISTODOULIDIS (since 28 February 2023)
head of government: President Nikos CHRISTODOULIDIS (since 28 February 2023)
cabinet: Council of Ministers appointed by the president; note - under the 1960 constitution, 3 of the ministerial posts reserved for Turkish Cypriots, appointed by the vice president; positions currently filled by Greek Cypriots
elections/appointments: president directly elected by absolute majority popular vote in 2 rounds if needed for a 5-year term (limited to 2 consecutive terms); election last held on held 5 February 2023 with a runoff on 12 February 2023 (next to be held in 2028)
election results:
2023: Nikos CHRISTODOULIDIS elected president in second round; percent of vote in first round - Nikos CHRISTODOULIDIS (independent) 32%, Andreas MAVROGIANNIS (independent) 29.6%, Averof NEOFYTOU (DISY) 26.1%, Christos CHRISTOU (ELAM) 6%, other 6.3%; percent of vote in second round - Nikos CHRISTODOULIDS 52%, Andreas MAVROGIANNIS 48%
2018: Nikos ANASTASIADIS reelected president in second round; percent of vote in first round - Nikos ANASTASIADIS (DISY) 35.5%, Stavros MALAS (AKEL) 30.2%, Nicolas PAPADOPOULOS (DIKO) 25.7%, other 8.6%; percent of vote in second round - Nikos ANASTASIADIS 56%, Stavros MALAS 44%
note: vice presidency reserved for a Turkish Cypriot, but the post has been vacant since 1974 because Turkish Cypriots do not participate in the Republic of Cyprus Government

Legislative branch: *description:* area under government control: unicameral House of Representatives or Vouli Antiprosopon (80 seats; 56 assigned to Greek Cypriots, 24 to Turkish Cypriots, but only those assigned to Greek Cypriots are filled; members directly elected by both proportional representation and preferential vote; members serve 5-year terms; note - 3 seats each are reserved for the Latin, Maronite, and Armenian religious groups;
area administered by Turkish Cypriots: unicameral "Assembly of the Republic" or Cumhuriyet Meclisi (50 seats; members directly elected in multi-seat constituencies by proportional representation vote using a hybrid d'Hondt method with voter preference for individual candidates
elections: area under government control; last held on 30 May 2021 (next to be held in 2026); area administered by Turkish Cypriots: last held on 23 January 2022 (next to be held in 2027)
election results:
area under government control: House of Representatives - percent of vote by party/coalition - DISY 27.8%, AKEL 22.3%, DIKO 11.3%, ELAM 6.8%, EDEK-SP 6.7%, DIPA 6.1%, Movement of Ecologists - Citizens' Cooperation 4.4%, other 14.6%; seats by party/coalition - DISY 17, AKEL 15, DIKO 9, ELAM 4, EDEK-SP 4, DIPA 4, Movement of Ecologists - Citizens' Cooperation 3; composition - men 48, women 8, percent of women 14.3%
area administered by Turkish Cypriots - "Assembly of the Republic" - percent of vote by party - UBP 39.5%, CTP 32%, DP 7.4%, HP 6.7%, YDP 6.4%, other 8%; seats by party - UBP 24, CTP 18, DP 3, HP 3, YDP 2; composition NA
note: the area of Cyprus that Turkish Cypriots administer has a separate unicameral Assembly of the Republic, or Cumhuriyet Meclisi (50 seats); members are directly elected in multi-seat constituencies by proportional representation vote

Judicial branch: *highest court(s):* Supreme Court of Cyprus (consists of 13 judges, including the court president); note - the highest court in the "TRNC" is the "Supreme Court" (consists of 8 "judges," including the "court president")
judge selection and term of office: Republic of Cyprus Supreme Court judges appointed by the president of the republic upon the recommendation of the Supreme Court judges; judges can serve until age 68; "TRNC Supreme Court" judges appointed by the "Supreme Council of Judicature," a 12-member body of judges, the attorney general, appointees by the president of the "TRNC," and by the "Legislative

Assembly," and members elected by the bar association; judge tenure NA
subordinate courts: Republic of Cyprus district courts; Assize Courts; Administrative Court; specialized courts for issues relating to family, industrial disputes, the military, and rent control; "TRNC Assize Courts"; "district and family courts"

Political parties: *area under government control:*
Democratic Front or DIPA
Democratic Party or DIKO
Democratic Rally or DISY
Movement of Ecologists - Citizens' Alliance
Movement of Social Democrats EDEK
National Popular Front or ELAM
Progressive Party of the Working People or AKEL (Communist Party)
Solidarity Movement
area administered by Turkish Cypriots:
Communal Democracy Party or TDP
Communal Liberation Party - New Forces or TKP-YG
Cyprus Socialist Party or KSP
Democratic Party or DP
National Democratic Party or NDP
National Unity Party or UBP
New Cyprus Party or YKP
People's Party or HP
Rebirth Party or YDP
Republican Turkish Party or CTP
United Cyprus Party or BKP

International organization participation: Australia Group, C, CD, CE, EBRD, ECB, EIB, EMU, EU, FAO, IAEA, IBRD, ICAO, ICC (national committees), ICCt, ICRM, IDA, IFAD, IFC, IFRCS, IHO, ILO, IMF, IMO, IMSO, Interpol, IOC, IOM, IPU, ISO, ITSO, ITU, ITUC (NGOs), MIGA, NAM, NSG, OAS (observer), OIF, OPCW, OSCE, PCA, UN, UNCTAD, UNESCO, UNHCR, UNIDO, UNIFIL, UNWTO, UPU, WCO, WFTU (NGOs), WHO, WIPO, WMO, WTO

Diplomatic representation in the US: *chief of mission:* Ambassador Evangelos SAVVA (since 15 September 2023)
chancery: 2211 R Street NW, Washington, DC 20008
telephone: [1] (202) 462-5772
FAX: [1] (202) 483-6710
email address and website:
info@cyprusembassy.net
https://www.cyprusembassy.net/
consulate(s) general: New York
honorary consulate(s): Atlanta, Chicago, Houston, Kirkland (WA), Los Angeles, New Orleans, San Francisco

Diplomatic representation from the US: *chief of mission:* Ambassador Julie D. FISHER (since 21 February 2023)
embassy: Metochiou and Ploutarchou Street, 2407, Engomi, Nicosia
mailing address: 5450 Nicosia Place, Washington DC 20521-5450
telephone: [357] (22) 393939
FAX: [357] (22) 780944
email address and website:
ACSNicosia@state.gov
https://cy.usembassy.gov/

Flag description: centered on a white field is a copper-colored silhouette of the island (the island has long been famous for its copper deposits) above two olive-green-colored, crossed olive branches; the branches symbolize the hope for peace and reconciliation between the Greek and Turkish communities
note: one of only two national flags that uses a map as a design element; the flag of Kosovo is the other
note: the "Turkish Republic of Northern Cyprus" flag retains the white field of the Cyprus national flag but displays narrow horizontal red stripes positioned a small distance from the top and bottom edges between which are centered a red crescent and a red five-pointed star; the banner is modeled after the Turkish national flag but with the colors reversed

National symbol(s): Cypriot mouflon (wild sheep), white dove; national colors: blue, white

National anthem: *name:* "Ymnos eis tin Eleftherian" (Hymn to Liberty)
lyrics/music: Dionysios SOLOMOS/Nikolaos MANTZAROS
note: adopted 1960; Cyprus adopted the Greek national anthem as its own; the Turkish Cypriot community in Cyprus uses the anthem of Turkey

National heritage: *total World Heritage Sites:* 3 (all cultural)
selected World Heritage Site locales: Paphos; Painted Churches in the Troodos Region; Choirokoitia

ECONOMY

Economic overview: services-based, high-income EU island economy; heavy tourism; sustained growth between recovery of national banking system and COVID-19 trade restrictions; high living standards; a known financial hub, its stock exchange functions as an investment bridge between EU-and EEU-member countries
note: Even though the whole of the island is part of the EU, implementation of the EU "acquis communautaire» has been suspended in the area administered by Turkish Cypriots, known locally as the Turkish Republic of Northern Cyprus, until political conditions permit the reunification of the island. Its market-based economy is roughly one-fifth the size of its southern neighbor and is likewise dominated by the service sector with a large portion of the population employed by the government. Manufacturing is limited mainly to food and beverages, furniture and fixtures, construction materials, metal and non-metal products, textiles and clothing. Little trade exists with the Republic of Cyprus outside of construction, historically relying heavily upon Turkey for financial aid, defense, telecommunications, utilities, and postal services. The Turkish Lira is the preferred currency, though foreign currencies are widely accepted in business transactions.

Real GDP (purchasing power parity): $46.976 billion (2023 est.)
$45.845 billion (2022 est.)
$43.637 billion (2021 est.)
note: data in 2021 dollars
comparison ranking: 128

Real GDP growth rate: 2.47% (2023 est.)
5.06% (2022 est.)
9.91% (2021 est.)
note: annual GDP % growth based on constant local currency
comparison ranking: 127

Real GDP per capita: $50,600 (2023 est.)
$50,200 (2022 est.)
$48,500 (2021 est.)
note: data in 2021 dollars
comparison ranking: 40

GDP (official exchange rate): $32.23 billion (2023 est.)
note: data in current dollars at official exchange rate

Inflation rate (consumer prices): 3.54% (2023 est.)
8.4% (2022 est.)
2.45% (2021 est.)
note: annual % change based on consumer prices
comparison ranking: 68

Credit ratings: Fitch rating: BBB- (2018)

Moody's rating: Ba2 (2018)

Standard & Poors rating: BBB- (2018)
note: The year refers to the year in which the current credit rating was first obtained.

GDP - composition, by sector of origin: *agriculture:* 1.6% (2023 est.)
industry: 12.2% (2023 est.)
services: 74% (2023 est.)
note: figures may not total 100% due to non-allocated consumption not captured in sector-reported data
comparison rankings: services 26; industry 179; agriculture 171

GDP - composition, by end use: *household consumption:* 59.9% (2023 est.)
government consumption: 19.1% (2023 est.)
investment in fixed capital: 22.1% (2023 est.)
investment in inventories: -0.2% (2023 est.)
exports of goods and services: 89.4% (2023 est.)
imports of goods and services: -90.3% (2023 est.)
note: figures may not total 100% due to rounding or gaps in data collection

Agricultural products: milk, potatoes, sheep milk, pork, goat milk, wheat, chicken, barley, grapes, olives (2022)
note: top ten agricultural products based on tonnage

Industries: tourism, food and beverage processing, cement and gypsum, ship repair and refurbishment, textiles, light chemicals, metal products, wood, paper, stone and clay products
note: area administered by Turkish Cypriots - foodstuffs, textiles, clothing, ship repair, clay, gypsum, copper, furniture

Industrial production growth rate: 3.16% (2023 est.)
note: annual % change in industrial value added based on constant local currency
comparison ranking: 106

Labor force: 693,000 (2023 est.)
note: number of people ages 15 or older who are employed or seeking work
comparison ranking: 155

Unemployment rate: 5.96% (2023 est.)
6.81% (2022 est.)
7.51% (2021 est.)
note: % of labor force seeking employment
comparison ranking: 120

Youth unemployment rate (ages 15-24): *total:* 17.5% (2023 est.)
male: 19.6% (2023 est.)
female: 15.1% (2023 est.)
note: % of labor force ages 15-24 seeking employment
comparison ranking: total 80

Population below poverty line: 13.9% (2021 est.)
note: % of population with income below national poverty line

Gini Index coefficient - distribution of family income: 31.3 (2021 est.)
note: index (0-100) of income distribution; higher values represent greater inequality
comparison ranking: 117

Household income or consumption by percentage share: *lowest 10%:* 3.5% (2021 est.)
highest 10%: 25.7% (2021 est.)
note: % share of income accruing to lowest and highest 10% of population

Remittances: 1.86% of GDP (2023 est.)
1.79% of GDP (2022 est.)
2.13% of GDP (2021 est.)
note: personal transfers and compensation between resident and non-resident individuals/households/entities

Budget: *revenues:* $11.644 billion (2022 est.)
expenditures: $10.765 billion (2022 est.)
note: central government revenues (excluding grants) and expenses converted to US dollars at average official exchange rate for year indicated

Public debt: 97.5% of GDP (2017 est.)
note: data cover general government debt and include debt instruments issued (or owned) by government entities other than the treasury; the data include treasury debt held by foreign entities; the data exclude debt issued by subnational entities, as well as intragovernmental debt; intragovernmental debt consists of treasury borrowings from surpluses in the social funds, such as for retirement, medical care, and unemployment
comparison ranking: 22

Taxes and other revenues: 24.71% (of GDP) (2022 est.)
note: central government tax revenue as a % of GDP
comparison ranking: 50

Current account balance: -$3.886 billion (2023 est.)
-$2.357 billion (2022 est.)
-$1.812 billion (2021 est.)
note: balance of payments - net trade and primary/secondary income in current dollars
comparison ranking: 172

Exports: $28.808 billion (2023 est.)
$27.72 billion (2022 est.)
$26.303 billion (2021 est.)
note: balance of payments - exports of goods and services in current dollars
comparison ranking: 80

Exports - partners: Hong Kong 10%, Greece 10%, Lebanon 7%, UK 6%, Liberia 5% (2022)
note: top five export partners based on percentage share of exports

Exports - commodities: ships, refined petroleum, packaged medicine, cheese, scented mixtures (2022)
note: top five export commodities based on value in dollars

Imports: $29.091 billion (2023 est.)
$27.658 billion (2022 est.)
$25.164 billion (2021 est.)
note: balance of payments - imports of goods and services in current dollars
comparison ranking: 82

Imports - partners: Greece 19%, Turkey 12%, Italy 9%, China 9%, Israel 5% (2022)
note: top five import partners based on percentage share of imports

Imports - commodities: refined petroleum, ships, cars, packaged medicine, garments (2022)
note: top five import commodities based on value in dollars

Reserves of foreign exchange and gold: $1.789 billion (2023 est.)
$1.671 billion (2022 est.)
$1.611 billion (2021 est.)
note: holdings of gold (year-end prices)/foreign exchange/special drawing rights in current dollars
comparison ranking: 139

Debt - external: (2019)

Exchange rates: euros (EUR) per US dollar -

Exchange rates: 0.925 (2023 est.)
0.95 (2022 est.)
0.845 (2021 est.)
0.876 (2020 est.)
0.893 (2019 est.)

ENERGY

Electricity access: *electrification - total population:* 100% (2022 est.)

Electricity: *installed generating capacity:* 2.145 million kW (2022 est.)
consumption: 5.024 billion kWh (2022 est.)
transmission/distribution losses: 236.617 million kWh (2022 est.)
comparison rankings: transmission/distribution losses 68; consumption 131; installed generating capacity 121

Electricity generation sources: *fossil fuels:* 83.3% of total installed capacity (2022 est.)
solar: 11.5% of total installed capacity (2022 est.)
wind: 4.3% of total installed capacity (2022 est.)
biomass and waste: 1% of total installed capacity (2022 est.)

Coal: *consumption:* 53,000 metric tons (2022 est.)
exports: 71.6 metric tons (2022 est.)
imports: 78,000 metric tons (2022 est.)

Petroleum: *refined petroleum consumption:* 45,000 bbl/day (2022 est.)

Carbon dioxide emissions: 6.713 million metric tonnes of CO2 (2022 est.)
from coal and metallurgical coke: 118,000 metric tonnes of CO2 (2022 est.)
from petroleum and other liquids: 6.595 million metric tonnes of CO2 (2022 est.)
comparison ranking: total emissions 129

Energy consumption per capita: 106.317 million Btu/person (2022 est.)
comparison ranking: 46

COMMUNICATIONS

Telephones - fixed lines: *total subscriptions:* 297,000 (2022 est.)
subscriptions per 100 inhabitants: 34 (2021 est.)
comparison ranking: total subscriptions 109

Telephones - mobile cellular: *total subscriptions:* 1.392 million (2022 est.)
subscriptions per 100 inhabitants: 149 (2021 est.)
comparison ranking: total subscriptions 160

Telecommunication systems: *general assessment:* Cyprus suffered from the effects of the pandemic in 2020 and 2021, when the tourism sector was essentially closed; during 2022, there were adverse effects caused by Russia's invasion of Ukraine, which has resulted in a dramatic drop in the number of Russian tourists entering the country; the mobile market is served by four mobile network operators; the number of mobile subscribers fell in 2020, largely the result of subscribers scaling back on multiple SIM cards as an economic measure; the broadband market continues to develop steadily, providing the country with one of the highest broadband penetration rates in the region; DSL remains the dominant access platform, accounting for about two-thirds of fixed broadband connections; although fiber infrastructure in Cyprus is minimal (supported by the government and regulator) to extend an FttP service to about 200,000 premises; as a result, the number of dSl subscribers is set to fall steadily in coming years as customers are migrated to the fiber platform (2023)
domestic: fixed-line about 34 per 100 and about 149 per 100 for mobile-cellular teledensity (2021)
international: country code - 357 (area administered by Turkish Cypriots uses the country code of Turkey - 90); a number of submarine cables, including the SEA-ME-WE-3, CADmOs, MedNautilus Submarine System, POSEIDON, TE North/TGN-Eurasia/SEACOM/Alexandros/Medes, UGARIT, Aphrodite2, Hawk, Lev Submarine System, and Tamares combine to provide connectivity to Europe, the Middle East, Africa, Asia, Australia, and Southeast Asia; Turcyos-1 and Turcyos-2 submarine cable in Turkish North Cyprus link to Turkey; tropospheric scatter; satellite earth stations - 8 (3 Intelsat - 1 Atlantic Ocean and 2 Indian Ocean, 2 Eutelsat, 2 Intersputnik, and 1 Arabsat) (2019)

Broadcast media: mixture of state and privately run TV and radio services; the public broadcaster operates 2 TV channels and 4 radio stations; 6 private TV broadcasters, satellite and cable TV services including telecasts from Greece and Turkey, and a number of private radio stations are available; in areas administered by Turkish Cypriots, there are 2 public TV stations, 4 public radio stations, and 7 privately owned TV and 21 radio broadcast stations plus 6 radio and 4 TV channels of local universities, plus 1 radio station of military, security forces and 1 radio station of civil defense cooperation, as well as relay stations from Turkey (2019)

Internet country code: .cy

Internet users: *total:* 809,900 (2021 est.)
percent of population: 91% (2021 est.)
comparison ranking: total 154

Broadband - fixed subscriptions: *total:* 332,080 (2020 est.)
subscriptions per 100 inhabitants: 37 (2020 est.)
comparison ranking: total 103

TRANSPORTATION

National air transport system: *number of registered air carriers:* 2 (2020)
inventory of registered aircraft operated by air carriers: 6
annual passenger traffic on registered air carriers: 401,408 (2018)
annual freight traffic on registered air carriers: 20,000 (2018) mt-km

Civil aircraft registration country code prefix: 5B

Airports: 13 (2024)
comparison ranking: 152

Heliports: 69 (2024)

Roadways: *total:* 13,027 km (2022)

Turkish Cypriot control: 7,000 km (2011)
comparison ranking: total 128

Merchant marine: *total:* 1,005 (2023)
by type: bulk carrier 243, container ship 154, general cargo 211, oil tanker 47, other 350
comparison ranking: total 23

Ports: *total ports:* 6 (2024)
large: 0
medium: 0
small: 3
very small: 3

ports with oil terminals: 4
key ports: Dhekelia, Famagusta, Kyrenia, Larnaca, Limassol, Xeros

MILITARY AND SECURITY

Military and security forces: Republic of Cyprus: Cypriot National Guard (Ethniki Froura, EF; includes Army Land Forces, Naval Command, Air Command) (2024)

Military expenditures: 1.8% of GDP (2023 est.)
1.8% of GDP (2022)
1.8% of GDP (2021)
1.8% of GDP (2020)
1.6% of GDP (2019)
comparison ranking: 79

Military and security service personnel strengths: approximately 15,000 total active-duty personnel (2023)

Military equipment inventories and acquisitions: the military's inventory includes a large quantity of Russian and Soviet-era weapons and equipment along with a smaller mix of mostly older Brazilian, European, Israeli, and US armaments; in 2023, Cyprus announced a 5-year modernization program to replace its Russian-made weapon systems with modern equipment from the West; the country had been under an arms embargo by the US since 1987 but the embargo was lifted in 2022 with conditions that require certifying each year (2024)

Military service age and obligation: Cypriot National Guard (CNG): 18-50 years of age for compulsory military service for all Greek Cypriot males; 17 years of age for voluntary service; 14-month service obligation (2023)
note: the CNG accepts all foreign nationals of at least partial Cypriot descent under age 32 as volunteers; dual citizenship Cypriot origin citizens, who were born in Cyprus or abroad, have the obligation to serve in the CNG on repatriation, regardless of whether or not they possess a foreign citizenship; a person is considered as having Cypriot origin where a grandparent or parent was/is a Cypriot citizen

Military - note: established in 1964, the National Guard (EF) is responsible for ensuring Cyprus's territorial integrity and sovereignty; its primary focus is Turkey, which invaded Cyprus in 1974 and maintains a large military presence in the unrecognized Turkish Republic of Northern Cyprus; the majority of the force is deployed along the "Green Line" that separates the Greek Cypriots from the Turkish Cypriots; the EF also participates in some internal missions, such as providing assistance during natural disasters; Greece is its main security partner and maintains about 1,000 troops on Cyprus; the EF has conducted training exercises with other militaries including France, Israel, and the US; since Cyprus joined the EU in 2004, the EF has actively participated in the EU's Common Security and Defense Policy and has sent small numbers of personnel to some EU and missions; Cyprus is also part of the Organization for Security and Cooperation in Europe (2024)

TERRORISM

Terrorist group(s): Islamic State of Iraq and ash-Sham (ISIS)
note: details about the history, aims, leadership, organization, areas of operation, tactics, targets, weapons, size, and sources of support of the group(s) appear(s) in the Terrorism reference guide

TRANSNATIONAL ISSUES

Refugees and internally displaced persons: *refugees (country of origin):* 10,869 (Syria) (mid-year 2022); 17,270 (Ukraine) (as of 11 February 2024)
IDPs: 246,000 (both Turkish and Greek Cypriots; many displaced since 1974) (2022)
stateless persons: 74 (2022)
note: 55,098 estimated refugee and migrant arrivals (January 2015-August 2023)

Illicit drugs: the ROC financial system is vulnerable to money laundering by domestic and foreign criminals; proceeds generated by illicit activity abroad pose a greater threat; primary sources of illicit proceeds are investment fraud, corruption, advance fee fraud, tax evasion, illegal drugs, and tobacco smuggling. Additionally, cybercrime, especially phishing, e-mail hacking, and ransomware use, continues to increase. Criminals have reportedly used ROC banks to launder proceeds, particularly from Russian and Ukrainian illicit activity.

CZECHIA

INTRODUCTION

Background: At the close of World War I, the Czechs and Slovaks of the former Austro-Hungarian Empire merged to form Czechoslovakia, a parliamentarian democracy. During the interwar years, having rejected a federal system, the new country's predominantly Czech leaders were frequently preoccupied with meeting the increasingly strident demands of other ethnic minorities within the republic, most notably the Slovaks, the Sudeten Germans, and the Ruthenians (Ukrainians). On the eve of World War II, Nazi Germany occupied the territory that today comprises Czechia, and Slovakia became an independent state allied with Germany. After the war, a reunited but truncated Czechoslovakia (less Ruthenia) fell within the Soviet sphere of influence when the pro-Soviet Communist party staged a coup in February 1948. In 1968, an invasion by fellow Warsaw Pact troops ended the efforts of the country's leaders to liberalize communist rule and create "socialism with a human face," ushering in a period of repression known as "normalization." The peaceful "Velvet Revolution" swept the Communist Party from power at the end of 1989 and inaugurated a return to democratic rule and a market economy. On 1 January 1993, the country underwent a nonviolent "velvet divorce" into its two national components, the Czech Republic and Slovakia. The Czech Republic joined NATO in 1999 and the European Union in 2004. The country formally added the short-form name Czechia in 2016, while also continuing to use the full form name, the Czech Republic.

GEOGRAPHY

Location: Central Europe, between Germany, Poland, Slovakia, and Austria

Geographic coordinates: 49 45 N, 15 30 E

Map references: Europe

Area: *total:* 78,867 sq km
land: 77,247 sq km
water: 1,620 sq km
comparison ranking: total 116

Area - comparative: about two-thirds the size of Pennsylvania; slightly smaller than South Carolina

Land boundaries: *total:* 2,046 km
border countries (4): Austria 402 km; Germany 704 km; Poland 699 km; Slovakia 241 km

Coastline: 0 km (landlocked)

Maritime claims: none (landlocked)

Climate: temperate; cool summers; cold, cloudy, humid winters

Terrain: Bohemia in the west consists of rolling plains, hills, and plateaus surrounded by low mountains; Moravia in the east consists of very hilly country

Elevation: *highest point:* Snezka 1,602 m
lowest point: Labe (Elbe) River 115 m
mean elevation: 433 m

Natural resources: hard coal, soft coal, kaolin, clay, graphite, timber, arable land

Land use: *agricultural land:* 54.8% (2018 est.)
arable land: 41% (2018 est.)
permanent crops: 1% (2018 est.)
permanent pasture: 12.8% (2018 est.)
forest: 34.4% (2018 est.)
other: 10.8% (2018 est.)

Irrigated land: 220 sq km (2020)

Major rivers (by length in km): Labe (Elbe) river source (shared with Germany [m]) - 1,252 km
note – [s] after country name indicates river source; [m] after country name indicates river mouth

Major watersheds (area sq km): Atlantic Ocean drainage: *(Black Sea)* Danube (795,656 sq km)

Population distribution: a fairly even distribution throughout most of the country, but the northern and eastern regions tend to have larger urban concentrations

Natural hazards: flooding

Geography - note: *note 1:* landlocked; strategically located astride some of oldest and most significant land routes in Europe; Moravian Gate is a traditional military corridor between the North European Plain and the Danube in central Europe
note 2: the Hranice Abyss in Czechia is the world's deepest surveyed underwater cave at 404 m (1,325 ft); its survey is not complete, and it could end up being some 800-1,200 m deep

PEOPLE AND SOCIETY

Population: *total:* 10,837,890
male: 5,335,737
female: 5,502,153 (2024 est.)
comparison rankings: female 85; male 88; total 86

Nationality: *noun:* Czech(s)
adjective: Czech

Ethnic groups: Czech 57.3%, Moravian 3.4%, other 7.7%, unspecified 31.6% (2021 est.)
note: includes only persons with one ethnicity

Languages: Czech (official) 88.4%, Slovak 1.5%, other 2.6%, unspecified 7.2% (2021 est.)
major-language sample(s):
World Factbook, nepostradatelný zdroj základních informací. (Czech)
note: includes only persons with one mother tongue

Religions: Roman Catholic 7%, other believers belonging to a church or religious society 6% (includes Evangelical United Brethren Church and Czechoslovak Hussite Church), believers unaffiliated with a religious society 9.1%, none 47.8%, unspecified 30.1% (2021 est.)

Age structure: *0-14 years:* 15.7% (male 871,303/female 826,896)
15-64 years: 63.8% (male 3,542,298/female 3,373,127)
65 years and over: 20.5% (2024 est.) (male 922,136/female 1,302,130)

Dependency ratios: *total dependency ratio:* 57.4
youth dependency ratio: 25.2
elderly dependency ratio: 32.2
potential support ratio: 3.1 (2021 est.)

Median age: *total:* 44.2 years (2024 est.)
male: 42.7 years
female: 45.7 years
comparison ranking: total 31

Population growth rate: 0.04% (2024 est.)
comparison ranking: 190

Birth rate: 9.8 births/1,000 population (2024 est.)
comparison ranking: 190

Death rate: 12 deaths/1,000 population (2024 est.)
comparison ranking: 17

Net migration rate: 2.7 migrant(s)/1,000 population (2024 est.)
comparison ranking: 40

Population distribution: a fairly even distribution throughout most of the country, but the northern and eastern regions tend to have larger urban concentrations

Urbanization: *urban population:* 74.6% of total population (2023)
rate of urbanization: 0.2% annual rate of change (2020-25 est.)

Major urban areas - population: 1.323 million PRAGUE (capital) (2023)

Sex ratio: *at birth:* 1.05 male(s)/female
0-14 years: 1.05 male(s)/female
15-64 years: 1.05 male(s)/female
65 years and over: 0.71 male(s)/female
total population: 0.97 male(s)/female (2024 est.)

Mother's mean age at first birth: 28.5 years (2020 est.)

Maternal mortality ratio: 3 deaths/100,000 live births (2020 est.)
comparison ranking: 182

Infant mortality rate: *total:* 2.6 deaths/1,000 live births (2024 est.)
male: 2.7 deaths/1,000 live births
female: 2.4 deaths/1,000 live births
comparison ranking: total 214

Life expectancy at birth: *total population:* 78.6 years (2024 est.)
male: 75.6 years
female: 81.8 years
comparison ranking: total population 76

Total fertility rate: 1.73 children born/woman (2024 est.)
comparison ranking: 154

Gross reproduction rate: 0.85 (2024 est.)

Drinking water source: *improved: urban:* 99.9% of population
rural: 99.8% of population
total: 99.9% of population
unimproved: urban: 0.1% of population
rural: 0.2% of population
total: 0.1% of population (2020 est.)

Current health expenditure: 9.2% of GDP (2020)

Physician density: 4.15 physicians/1,000 population (2020)

Hospital bed density: 6.6 beds/1,000 population (2018)

Sanitation facility access: *improved: urban:* 100% of population
rural: 100% of population
total: 100% of population

Obesity - adult prevalence rate: 26% (2016)
comparison ranking: 46

Alcohol consumption per capita: *total:* 12.73 liters of pure alcohol (2019 est.)
beer: 6.77 liters of pure alcohol (2019 est.)
wine: 2.73 liters of pure alcohol (2019 est.)
spirits: 3.24 liters of pure alcohol (2019 est.)
other alcohols: 0 liters of pure alcohol (2019 est.)
comparison ranking: total 3

Tobacco use: *total:* 30.7% (2020 est.)
male: 35% (2020 est.)
female: 26.4% (2020 est.)
comparison ranking: total 29

Currently married women (ages 15-49): 48.4% (2023 est.)

Education expenditures: 5.1% of GDP (2020 est.)
comparison ranking: 71

Literacy: *definition:* NA
total population: 99%
male: 99%
female: 99% (2011)

School life expectancy (primary to tertiary education): *total:* 16 years
male: 16 years
female: 17 years (2020)

ENVIRONMENT

Environment - current issues: air and water pollution in areas of northwest Bohemia and in northern Moravia around Ostrava present health risks; acid rain damaging forests; land pollution caused by industry, mining, and agriculture

Environment - international agreements: *party to:* Air Pollution, Air Pollution-Heavy Metals, Air Pollution-Multi-effect Protocol, Air Pollution-Nitrogen Oxides, Air Pollution-Persistent Organic Pollutants, Air Pollution-Sulphur 85, Air Pollution-Sulphur 94, Air Pollution-Volatile Organic Compounds, Antarctic-Environmental Protection, Antarctic Treaty, Biodiversity, Climate Change, Climate Change-Kyoto Protocol, Climate Change-Paris Agreement, Comprehensive Nuclear Test Ban, Desertification, Endangered Species, Environmental Modification, Hazardous Wastes, Law of the Sea, Nuclear Test Ban, Ozone Layer Protection, Ship Pollution, Tropical Timber 2006, Wetlands, Whaling
signed, but not ratified: none of the selected agreements

Climate: temperate; cool summers; cold, cloudy, humid winters

Urbanization: *urban population:* 74.6% of total population (2023)
rate of urbanization: 0.2% annual rate of change (2020-25 est.)

Revenue from forest resources: 0.17% of GDP (2017 est.)
comparison ranking: 97

Revenue from coal: 0.14% of GDP (2018 est.)
comparison ranking: 23

Air pollutants: *particulate matter emissions:* 14.34 micrograms per cubic meter (2019 est.)
carbon dioxide emissions: 102.22 megatons (2016 est.)
methane emissions: 13.11 megatons (2020 est.)

Waste and recycling: *municipal solid waste generated annually:* 3.337 million tons (2015 est.)
municipal solid waste recycled annually: 850,935 tons (2015 est.)
percent of municipal solid waste recycled: 25.5% (2015 est.)

Major rivers (by length in km): Labe (Elbe) river source (shared with Germany [m]) - 1,252 km
note – [s] after country name indicates river source; [m] after country name indicates river mouth

Major watersheds (area sq km): Atlantic Ocean drainage: *(Black Sea)* Danube (795,656 sq km)

Total water withdrawal: *municipal:* 630 million cubic meters (2020 est.)
industrial: 700 million cubic meters (2020 est.)
agricultural: 40 million cubic meters (2020 est.)

Total renewable water resources: 13.5 billion cubic meters (2020 est.)

Geoparks: *total global geoparks and regional networks:* 1
global geoparks and regional networks: Bohemian Paradise (2023)

GOVERNMENT

Country name: *conventional long form:* Czech Republic
conventional short form: Czechia
local long form: Ceska republika
local short form: Cesko
etymology: name derives from the Czechs, a West Slavic tribe who rose to prominence in the late 9th century A.D.; the country officially adopted the English short-form name of Czechia on 1 July 2016

Government type: parliamentary republic

Capital: *name:* Prague
geographic coordinates: 50 05 N, 14 28 E
time difference: UTC+1 (6 hours ahead of Washington, DC, during Standard Time)
daylight saving time: +1hr, begins last Sunday in March; ends last Sunday in October
etymology: the name may derive from an old Slavic root "praga" or "prah", meaning "ford", and refer to the city's origin at a crossing point of the Vltava (Moldau) River

Administrative divisions: 13 regions (kraje, singular - kraj) and 1 capital city* (hlavni mesto); Jihocesky (South Bohemia), Jihomoravsky (South Moravia), Karlovarsky (Karlovy Vary), Kralovehradecky (Hradec Kralove), Liberecky (Liberec), Moravskoslezsky (Moravia-Silesia), Olomoucky (Olomouc), Pardubicky (Pardubice), Plzensky (Pilsen), Praha (Prague)*, Stredocesky (Central Bohemia), Ustecky (Usti), Vysocina (Highlands), Zlinsky (Zlin)

Independence: 1 January 1993 (Czechoslovakia split into the Czech Republic and Slovakia); note - although 1 January is the day the Czech Republic came into being, the Czechs commemorate 28 October 1918, the day the former Czechoslovakia declared its independence from the Austro-Hungarian Empire, as their independence day

National holiday: Czechoslovak Founding Day, 28 October (1918)

Legal system: new civil code enacted in 2014, replacing civil code of 1964 - based on former Austro-Hungarian civil codes and socialist theory - and reintroducing former Czech legal terminology

Constitution: *history:* previous 1960; latest ratified 16 December 1992, effective 1 January 1993
amendments: passage requires at least three-fifths concurrence of members present in both houses of Parliament; amended several times, last in 2021

International law organization participation: has not submitted an ICJ jurisdiction declaration; accepts ICCt jurisdiction

Citizenship: *citizenship by birth:* no
citizenship by descent only: at least one parent must be a citizen of Czechia
dual citizenship recognized: no
residency requirement for naturalization: 5 years

Suffrage: 18 years of age; universal

Executive branch: *chief of state:* President Petr PAVEL (since 9 March 2023)
head of government: Prime Minister Petr FIALA (since 17 December 2021)
cabinet: Cabinet appointed by the president on the recommendation of the prime minister
elections/appointments: president directly elected by absolute majority popular vote in 2 rounds if needed for a 5-year term (limited to 2 consecutive terms); elections last held on 13 to 14 January 2023 with a second round held from 27 to 28 January 2023; next election to be by January 2028; prime minister appointed by the president for a 4-year term
election results:
2023: Petr PAVEL elected in the second round; percent of vote in the first round - Petr PAVEL (independent) 35.4%, Andrej BABIS (ANO) 35%, Danuse NERUDOVA (Mayors and Independents) 13.9%, Pavel FISCHER (independent) 6.8%; percent of vote in the second round - Petr PAVEL 58.3%, Andrej BABIS 41.6%
2018: Milos ZEMAN reelected president in the second round; percent of vote - Milos ZEMAN (SPO) 51.4%, Jiri DRAHOS (independent) 48.6%

Legislative branch: *description:* bicameral Parliament or Parlament consists of:
Senate or Senat (81 seats; members directly elected in single-seat constituencies by absolute majority vote in 2 rounds if needed; members serve 6-year terms with one-third of the membership renewed every 2 years)
Chamber of Deputies or Poslanecka Snemovna (200 seats; members directly elected in 14 multi-seat constituencies by proportional representation vote with a 5% threshold required to fill a seat; members serve 4-year terms)
elections: Senate - last held on 20 to 21 September 2024 with a runoff from 27 to 28 September 2024 (next to be held in September 2026)
Chamber of Deputies - last held on 8 to 9 October 2021 (next to be held by October 2025)
election results: Senate - percent of vote - NA; - seats by party/coalition - NA
Chamber of Deputies - percent of vote by party/coalition – SPOLU 27.8%, ANO 27.1%, Pirates and STAN 15.6%, SPD 9.6%, other 19.9%; seats by party/coalition - ANO 72, SPOLU 71, Pirates and STAN 37, SPD 20; composition - men 148, women 52, percent of women 26%; note - total Parliament percent of women 23.8%

Judicial branch: *highest court(s):* Supreme Court (organized into Civil Law and Commercial Division, and Criminal Division each with a court chief justice, vice justice, and several judges); Constitutional Court (consists of 15 justices); Supreme Administrative Court (consists of 36 judges, including the court president and vice president, and organized into 6-, 7-, and 9-member chambers)
judge selection and term of office: Supreme Court judges proposed by the Chamber of Deputies and appointed by the president; judges appointed for life; Constitutional Court judges appointed by the president and confirmed by the Senate; judges appointed for 10-year, renewable terms; Supreme Administrative Court judges selected by the president of the Court; unlimited terms
subordinate courts: High Court; regional and district courts

Political parties: Action of Dissatisfied Citizens or ANO (*Akce nespokojených občanů*)
Christian and Democratic Union - Czechoslovak People's Party or *KDU-ČSL*
Civic Democratic Party or ODS
Communist Party of Bohemia and Moravia or KSČM
Czech Pirate Party or Piráti
ForMOST or ProMOST
Freedom and Direct Democracy or SPD
Independents or NEZ
Mayors and Independents or STAN
Mayors for the Liberec Region or SLK
Ostravak
Přísaha
Senator 21 or SEN 21
Social Democracy SOCDEM
Svobodni
Tradition Responsibility Prosperity 09 or TOP 09
Tábor 2020 or T2020
United Democrats - Association of Independents or SD-SN

International organization participation: Australia Group, BIS, BSEC (observer), CD, CE, CEI, CERN, EAPC, EBRD, ECB, EIB, ESA, EU, FAO, IAEA, IBRD, ICAO, ICC (national committees), ICCt, ICRM, IDA, IEA, IFC, IFRCS, ILO, IMF, IMO, IMSO, Interpol, IOC, IOM, IPU, ISO, ITSO, ITU, ITUC (NGOs), MIGA, MONUSCO, NATO, NEA, NSG, OAS (observer), OECD, OIF (observer), OPCW, OSCE, PCA, Schengen Convention, SELEC, UN, UNCTAD, UNESCO, UNHCR, UNIDO, UNOOSA, UNWTO, UPU, Wassenaar Arrangement, WCO, WFTU (NGOs), WHO, WIPO, WMO, WTO, ZC

Diplomatic representation in the US: *chief of mission:* Ambassador Miloslav STASEK (since 16 September 2022)
chancery: 3900 Spring of Freedom Street NW, Washington, DC 20008-3803
telephone: [1] (202) 274-9100
FAX: [1] (202) 966-8540
email address and website:
washington@embassy.mzv.cz
https://www. mzv. cz/washington/
consulate(s) general: Chicago, Los Angeles, New York

Diplomatic representation from the US: *chief of mission:* Ambassador Bijan SABET (since 15 February 2023)
embassy: Trziste 15, 118 01 Praha 1 - Mala Strana
mailing address: 5630 Prague Place, Washington DC 20521-5630
telephone: [420] 257-022-000
FAX: [420] 257-022-809
email address and website:
ACSPrg@state.gov
https://cz.usembassy.gov/

Flag description: two equal horizontal bands of white (top) and red with a blue isosceles triangle based on the hoist side
note: combines the white and red colors of Bohemia with blue from the arms of Moravia; is identical to the flag of the former Czechoslovakia

National symbol(s): silver (or white), double-tailed, rampant lion; national colors: white, red, blue

National anthem: *name:* "Kde domov muj?" (Where is My Home?)
lyrics/music: Josef Kajetan TYL/Frantisek Jan SKROUP
note: adopted 1993; the anthem was originally written as incidental music to the play "Fidlovacka" (1834), it soon became very popular as an unofficial anthem of the Czech nation; its first verse served as the official Czechoslovak anthem beginning in 1918, while the second verse (Slovak) was dropped after the split of Czechoslovakia in 1993

National heritage: *total World Heritage Sites:* 17 (16 cultural, 1 natural)
selected World Heritage Site locales: Historic Prague (c); Historic Telč (c); Historic Český Krumlov (c); Lednice-Valtice Cultural Landscape (c); Historic Kutná Hora (c); Holy Trinity Column, Olomouc (c);

Karlovy Vary Spa (c); Zatec and the Landscape of Saaz Hops; Žatec and the Landscape of Saaz Hops (n)

ECONOMY

Economic overview: high-income, diversified EU economy; manufacturing-oriented exporter led by automotive industry; growth stalled by inflation and energy supply disruption; business-friendly regulatory frameworks; tight labor market with low unemployment; seeking reforms to support decarbonization and improve energy efficiency

Real GDP (purchasing power parity): $519.007 billion (2023 est.)
$520.629 billion (2022 est.)
$508.67 billion (2021 est.)
note: data in 2021 dollars
comparison ranking: 47

Real GDP growth rate: -0.31% (2023 est.)
2.35% (2022 est.)
3.55% (2021 est.)
note: annual GDP % growth based on constant local currency
comparison ranking: 193

Real GDP per capita: $47,700 (2023 est.)
$48,800 (2022 est.)
$48,400 (2021 est.)
note: data in 2021 dollars
comparison ranking: 48

GDP (official exchange rate): $330.858 billion (2023 est.)
note: data in current dollars at official exchange rate

Inflation rate (consumer prices): 10.66% (2023 est.)
15.1% (2022 est.)
3.84% (2021 est.)
note: annual % change based on consumer prices
comparison ranking: 181

Credit ratings: Fitch rating: AA- (2018)

Moody's rating: Aa3 (2019)

Standard & Poors rating: AA- (2011)
note: The year refers to the year in which the current credit rating was first obtained.

GDP - composition, by sector of origin: *agriculture:* 1.6% (2023 est.)
industry: 30.2% (2023 est.)
services: 59.8% (2023 est.)
note: figures may not total 100% due to non-allocated consumption not captured in sector-reported data
comparison rankings: services 86; industry 66; agriculture 169

GDP - composition, by end use: *household consumption:* 45.6% (2023 est.)
government consumption: 20.4% (2023 est.)
investment in fixed capital: 27% (2023 est.)
investment in inventories: 1.9% (2023 est.)
exports of goods and services: 72% (2023 est.)
imports of goods and services: -66.9% (2023 est.)
note: figures may not total 100% due to rounding or gaps in data collection

Agricultural products: wheat, sugar beets, milk, barley, rapeseed, potatoes, maize, pork, triticale, oats (2022)
note: top ten agricultural products based on tonnage

Industries: motor vehicles, metallurgy, machinery and equipment, glass, armaments

Industrial production growth rate: -0.44% (2023 est.)
note: annual % change in industrial value added based on constant local currency
comparison ranking: 159

Labor force: 5.502 million (2023 est.)
note: number of people ages 15 or older who are employed or seeking work
comparison ranking: 77

Unemployment rate: 2.59% (2023 est.)
2.22% (2022 est.)
2.8% (2021 est.)
note: % of labor force seeking employment
comparison ranking: 30

Youth unemployment rate (ages 15-24): *total:* 8.3% (2023 est.)
male: 7.8% (2023 est.)
female: 9% (2023 est.)
note: % of labor force ages 15-24 seeking employment
comparison ranking: total 148

Population below poverty line: 10.2% (2021 est.)
note: % of population with income below national poverty line

Gini Index coefficient - distribution of family income: 26.2 (2021 est.)
note: index (0-100) of income distribution; higher values represent greater inequality
comparison ranking: 144

Average household expenditures: *on food:* 16.4% of household expenditures (2022 est.)
on alcohol and tobacco: 8.2% of household expenditures (2022 est.)

Household income or consumption by percentage share: *lowest 10%:* 3.9% (2021 est.)
highest 10%: 22.2% (2021 est.)
note: % share of income accruing to lowest and highest 10% of population

Remittances: 1.27% of GDP (2023 est.)
1.43% of GDP (2022 est.)
1.56% of GDP (2021 est.)
note: personal transfers and compensation between resident and non-resident individuals/households/entities

Budget: *revenues:* $94.01 billion (2022 est.)
expenditures: $103.959 billion (2022 est.)
note: central government revenues (excluding grants) and expenses converted to US dollars at average official exchange rate for year indicated

Public debt: 34.7% of GDP (2017 est.)
comparison ranking: 156

Taxes and other revenues: 13.13% (of GDP) (2022 est.)
note: central government tax revenue as a % of GDP
comparison ranking: 154

Current account balance: $1.281 billion (2023 est.)
-$17.366 billion (2022 est.)
-$7.686 billion (2021 est.)
note: balance of payments - net trade and primary/secondary income in current dollars
comparison ranking: 52

Exports: $236.688 billion (2023 est.)
$217.731 billion (2022 est.)
$205.626 billion (2021 est.)
note: balance of payments - exports of goods and services in current dollars
comparison ranking: 34

Exports - partners: Germany 32%, Slovakia 8%, Poland 7%, France 5%, Austria 5% (2022)
note: top five export partners based on percentage share of exports

Exports - commodities: cars, vehicle parts/accessories, broadcasting equipment, computers, plastic products (2022)
note: top five export commodities based on value in dollars

Imports: $219.393 billion (2023 est.)
$218.002 billion (2022 est.)
$197.515 billion (2021 est.)
note: balance of payments - imports of goods and services in current dollars
comparison ranking: 34

Imports - partners: Germany 24%, China 13%, Poland 10%, Slovakia 6%, Russia 4% (2022)
note: top five import partners based on percentage share of imports

Imports - commodities: broadcasting equipment, vehicle parts/accessories, natural gas, machine parts, plastic products (2022)
note: top five import commodities based on value in dollars

Reserves of foreign exchange and gold: $148.379 billion (2023 est.)
$139.981 billion (2022 est.)
$173.618 billion (2021 est.)
note: holdings of gold (year-end prices)/foreign exchange/special drawing rights in current dollars
comparison ranking: 19

Debt - external: (2019)

Exchange rates: koruny (CZK) per US dollar -

Exchange rates: 22.198 (2023 est.)
23.357 (2022 est.)
21.678 (2021 est.)
23.21 (2020 est.)
22.932 (2019 est.)

ENERGY

Electricity access: *electrification - total population:* 100% (2022 est.)

Electricity: *installed generating capacity:* 21.914 million kW (2022 est.)
consumption: 62.077 billion kWh (2022 est.)
exports: 30.255 billion kWh (2022 est.)
imports: 16.726 billion kWh (2022 est.)
transmission/distribution losses: 3.414 billion kWh (2022 est.)
comparison rankings: transmission/distribution losses 146; imports 13; exports 6; consumption 47; installed generating capacity 47

Electricity generation sources: *fossil fuels:* 48.4% of total installed capacity (2022 est.)
nuclear: 39.3% of total installed capacity (2022 est.)
solar: 3.1% of total installed capacity (2022 est.)
wind: 0.8% of total installed capacity (2022 est.)
hydroelectricity: 2.2% of total installed capacity (2022 est.)
biomass and waste: 6.2% of total installed capacity (2022 est.)

Nuclear energy: Number of operational nuclear reactors: 6 (2023)

Net capacity of operational nuclear reactors: 3.93GW (2023 est.)

Percent of total electricity production: 40% (2023 est.)

Coal: *production:* 37.423 million metric tons (2022 est.)
consumption: 40.239 million metric tons (2022 est.)
exports: 2.575 million metric tons (2022 est.)
imports: 4.516 million metric tons (2022 est.)

proven reserves: 3.595 billion metric tons (2022 est.)

Petroleum: *total petroleum production:* 4,000 bbl/day (2023 est.)
refined petroleum consumption: 211,000 bbl/day (2023 est.)
crude oil estimated reserves: 15 million barrels (2021 est.)

Natural gas: *production:* 224.725 million cubic meters (2022 est.)
consumption: 7.602 billion cubic meters (2022 est.)
imports: 8.608 billion cubic meters (2022 est.)
proven reserves: 3.964 billion cubic meters (2021 est.)

Carbon dioxide emissions: 91.213 million metric tonnes of CO2 (2022 est.)
from coal and metallurgical coke: 51.306 million metric tonnes of CO2 (2022 est.)
from petroleum and other liquids: 25.255 million metric tonnes of CO2 (2022 est.)
from consumed natural gas: 14.652 million metric tonnes of CO2 (2022 est.)
comparison ranking: total emissions 44

Energy consumption per capita: 149.874 million Btu/person (2022 est.)
comparison ranking: 28

COMMUNICATIONS

Telephones - fixed lines: *total subscriptions:* 1.214 million (2022 est.)
subscriptions per 100 inhabitants: 12 (2022 est.)
comparison ranking: total subscriptions 68

Telephones - mobile cellular: *total subscriptions:* 13.475 million (2022 est.)
subscriptions per 100 inhabitants: 128 (2022 est.)
comparison ranking: total subscriptions 78

Telecommunication systems: *general assessment:* telcos in the Czech Republic have become multi-service providers, offering a full range of fixed and mobile services; this has enabled the Mobile Network Operators (MNOs) to expand the reach of their 5G networks while they have been closing down 3G networks and repurposing the internet for 5G and long-term evolution (LTE) use
(2024)
domestic: roughly 12 fixed-telephone subscriptions per 100 inhabitants and mobile telephone usage of 128 per 100 inhabitants (2022)
international: country code - 420; satellite earth stations - 6 (2 Intersputnik - Atlantic and Indian Ocean regions, 1 Intelsat, 1 Eutelsat, 1 Inmarsat, 1 Globalstar) (2019)

Broadcast media: 22 TV stations operate nationally, with 17 of them in private hands; publicly operated Czech Television has 5 national channels; throughout the country, there are some 350 TV channels in operation, many through cable, satellite, and IPTV subscription services; 63 radio broadcasters are registered, operating over 80 radio stations, including 7 multiregional radio stations or networks; publicly operated broadcaster Czech Radio operates 4 national, 14 regional, and 4 Internet stations; both Czech Radio and Czech Television are partially financed through a license fee (2019)

Internet country code: .cz

Internet users: *total:* 9.13 million (2021 est.)
percent of population: 83% (2021 est.)
comparison ranking: total 64

Broadband - fixed subscriptions: *total:* 3,845,426 (2020 est.)
subscriptions per 100 inhabitants: 36 (2020 est.)
comparison ranking: total 39

TRANSPORTATION

National air transport system: *number of registered air carriers:* 4 (2020)
inventory of registered aircraft operated by air carriers: 48
annual passenger traffic on registered air carriers: 5,727,200 (2018)
annual freight traffic on registered air carriers: 25.23 million (2018) mt-km

Civil aircraft registration country code prefix: OK

Airports: 243 (2024)
comparison ranking: 28

Heliports: 82 (2024)

Pipelines: 7,160 km gas, 675 km oil, 94 km refined products (2016)

Railways: *total:* 9,548 km (2020) 3,242 km electrified
comparison ranking: total 24

Roadways: *total:* 129,418 km (2022)
comparison ranking: total 40

Waterways: 664 km (2010) (principally on Elbe, Vltava, Oder, and other navigable rivers, lakes, and canals)
comparison ranking: 84

MILITARY AND SECURITY

Military and security forces: Czech Armed Forces: Land Forces, Air Forces, Cyber Forces, Special Forces (2024)

Military expenditures: 2.1% of GDP (2024 est.)
1.5% of GDP (2023)
1.3% of GDP (2022)
1.4% of GDP (2021)
1.3% of GDP (2020)
comparison ranking: 63

Military and security service personnel strengths: approximately 29,000 active personnel (23,000 Army; 6,000 Air Force) (2024)

Military equipment inventories and acquisitions: the Czech military has a mix of Soviet-era and more modern equipment, mostly of Western European origin from such suppliers as Austria, Germany, and Spain; Czechia has a considerable domestic defense industry; during the Cold War, Czechoslovakia was a major producer of tanks, armored personnel carriers, military trucks, and trainer aircraft (2024)
note: in 2019, Czechia announced a modernization plan to acquire more Western equipment that was compliant with NATO standards, including aircraft and armored vehicles.

Military service age and obligation: 18-28 years of age for voluntary military service for men and women; conscription abolished 2004 (2024)
note: as of 2023, women comprised nearly 14% of the military's full-time personnel

Military deployments: up to 130 Lithuania (NATO); 130 Slovakia (NATO) (2024)

Military - note: the Czech military is responsible for national and territorial defense, assisting civil authorities during natural disasters or other emergencies, boosting border security alongside the police, participating in international peacekeeping operations, and supporting its collective security commitments to the EU and NATO, both of which Czechia considers pillars of its national security strategy; Czechia is a member of the Organization for Security and Cooperation in Europe, contributes to UN peacekeeping operations, and actively participates in EU military and security missions under the EU Common Security and Defense Policy; the Czech military has been an active member of NATO since the country joined in 2009 and participates in a variety of NATO's collective defense missions, including contributing to the Enhanced Forward Presence in Eastern Europe, Baltic Air Policing operations, rapid response forces, and operations in Kosovo; it also exercises regularly with NATO partners and maintains close bilateral ties to a number of militaries particularly partner members of the Visegrad Group (Hungary, Poland, and Slovakia) and Germany
the military has commands for its land, air, cyber/information operations, and territorial forces, as well as a joint operations command and a special forces directorate; the Territorial Command is responsible for the active reserves and regional military commands that align with each of Czechia's 13 regions and the capital, Prague (2024)

TRANSNATIONAL ISSUES

Refugees and internally displaced persons: *refugees (country of origin):* 381,400 (Ukraine) (as of 31 January 2024)
stateless persons: 1,625 (2022)

Illicit drugs: main country of origin of methamphetamine in European markets; manufacture of methamphetamine continues to be mostly based on pseudoephedrine from Poland or Turkey

DENMARK

INTRODUCTION

Background: Once the seat of Viking raiders and later a major north European power, Denmark has evolved into a modern, prosperous nation that is part of the general political and economic integration of Europe. It joined NATO in 1949 and the EEC (now the EU) in 1973. The country has opted out of certain elements of the EU's Maastricht Treaty, including the European Economic and Monetary Union and justice and home affairs issues. a 2022 referendum resulted in the removal of Denmark's 30-year opt-out on defense issues, now allowing Denmark to participate fully in the EU's Common Security and Defense Policy.

GEOGRAPHY

Location: Northern Europe, bordering the Baltic Sea and the North Sea, on a peninsula north of Germany (Jutland); also includes several major islands (Sjaelland, Fyn, and Bornholm)

Geographic coordinates: 56 00 N, 10 00 E

Map references: Europe

Area: *total:* 43,094 sq km
land: 42,434 sq km
water: 660 sq km
note: includes the island of Bornholm in the Baltic Sea and the rest of metropolitan Denmark (the Jutland Peninsula, and the major islands of Sjaelland and Fyn) but excludes the Faroe Islands and Greenland
comparison ranking: total 133

Area - comparative: slightly less than twice the size of Massachusetts; about two-thirds the size of West Virginia

Land boundaries: *total:* 141 km
border countries: Germany 140 km; Canada 1.3 km

Coastline: 7,314 km

Maritime claims: *territorial sea:* 12 nm
contiguous zone: 24 nm
exclusive economic zone: 200 nm
continental shelf: 200-m depth or to the depth of exploitation

Climate: temperate; humid and overcast; mild, windy winters and cool summers

Terrain: low and flat to gently rolling plains

Elevation: *highest point:* Store Mollehoj 171 m
lowest point: Lammefjord -7 m
mean elevation: 34 m

Natural resources: petroleum, natural gas, fish, arable land, salt, limestone, chalk, stone, gravel and sand

Land use: *agricultural land:* 63.4% (2018 est.)
arable land: 58.9% (2018 est.)
permanent crops: 0.1% (2018 est.)
permanent pasture: 4.4% (2018 est.)
forest: 12.9% (2018 est.)
other: 23.7% (2018 est.)

Irrigated land: 2,360 sq km (2020)

Population distribution: with excellent access to the North Sea, Skagerrak, Kattegat, and the Baltic Sea, population centers tend to be along coastal areas, particularly in Copenhagen and the eastern side of the country's mainland

Natural hazards: flooding is a threat in some areas of the country (e.g., parts of Jutland, along the southern coast of the island of Lolland) that are protected from the sea by a system of dikes

Geography - note: composed of the Jutland Peninsula and a group of more than 400 islands (Danish Archipelago); controls Danish Straits (Skagerrak and Kattegat) linking Baltic and North Seas; about one-quarter of the population lives in greater Copenhagen

PEOPLE AND SOCIETY

Population: *total:* 5,973,136
male: 2,975,261
female: 2,997,875 (2024 est.)
comparison rankings: female 115; male 115; total 115

Nationality: *noun:* Dane(s)
adjective: Danish

Ethnic groups: Danish (includes Greenlandic (who are predominantly Inuit) and Faroese) 84.2%, Turkish 1.1%, other 14.7% (largest groups are Polish, Romanian, Syrian, Ukrainian, German, and Iraqi) (2023 est.)
note: data represent population by country of origin

Languages: Danish, Faroese, Greenlandic (an Inuit dialect), German (small minority); note - English is the predominant second language
major-language sample(s):
Verdens Faktabog, den uundværlig kilde til grundlæggende oplysninger. (Danish)

Religions: Evangelical Lutheran (official) 71.4%, Muslim 4.3%, other/none/unspecified (denominations include Roman Catholic, Jehovah's Witness, Serbian Orthodox Christian, Jewish, Baptist, Buddhist, Church of Jesus Christ, Pentecostal, and nondenominational Christian) 24.3% (2024 est.)

Demographic profile: Modern immigration to Denmark began in the 1960s and 1970s, although immigration, primarily from the Nordic countries and Western Europe, has earlier roots. Dutch migrants came in the 16th century and Germans in the 18th, in both cases to work in agriculture. Between the late 19th century and World War I, Denmark absorbed unskilled Polish, German, and Swedish labor migrants in significant numbers, sometimes at the request of the Danish Government. Between the two World Wars, Denmark received many Eastern European, Jewish, and German migrants. It wasn't until after World War II, that refugees began seeking sanctuary in Demark, including a large number of German refugees and later Hungarians, Czechs, and Polish Jews. Denmark also imported foreign labor during the 1960s, mainly from Turkey, the former Yugoslavia, and Pakistan. Although the "guest worker" program was halted in 1973, immigrants continued to arrive to be reunited with family members who were already in Denmark as refugees or as guest workers. Non-European refugees came from Chile, Uganda, and Vietnam. In the 1990s, Denmark began receiving migrants and refugees from new places, including Russia, Hungary, Bosnia, Iran, Iraq, and Lebanon. Despite raising more restrictions on immigration, in the 2000s, Denmark continued to receive asylum seekers, particularly from Afghanistan, Iraq, Somalia, and the former Yugoslavia, as well as labor migrants from new EU member states.
In more recent years, Denmark has severely limited its refugee intake, aiming to accept as few refugees outside of the UN resettlement program as possible. In the mid-2010s, Denmark passed legislation enabling it to withdraw temporary protective status as soon as conditions in the home country, as determined by Denmark, have improved. This policy has lead Denmark, to deem Damascus and other areas in Syria safe for return, making it the only country in Europe to do so. Consequently, some Syrian refugees have had their residency status revoked, and they are detained in deportation centers because Denmark does not have diplomatic relations with Syria and, therefore, cannot send them back. Copenhagen hopes its stricter policies will discourage asylum seekers, particularly those from non-Western countries.

Age structure: *0-14 years:* 16.2% (male 496,793/female 471,018)
15-64 years: 62.9% (male 1,903,315/female 1,856,615)
65 years and over: 20.8% (2024 est.) (male 575,153/female 670,242)

Dependency ratios: *total dependency ratio:* 57.3
youth dependency ratio: 25.4
elderly dependency ratio: 31.9
potential support ratio: 3.1 (2021 est.)

Median age: *total:* 42.2 years (2024 est.)
male: 41 years
female: 43.4 years
comparison ranking: total 45

Population growth rate: 0.44% (2024 est.)
comparison ranking: 155

Birth rate: 11.3 births/1,000 population (2024 est.)
comparison ranking: 160

Death rate: 9.6 deaths/1,000 population (2024 est.)
comparison ranking: 41

Net migration rate: 2.7 migrant(s)/1,000 population (2024 est.)
comparison ranking: 41

Population distribution: with excellent access to the North Sea, Skagerrak, Kattegat, and the Baltic Sea, population centers tend to be along coastal areas, particularly in Copenhagen and the eastern side of the country's mainland

Urbanization: *urban population:* 88.5% of total population (2023)
rate of urbanization: 0.54% annual rate of change (2020-25 est.)

Major urban areas - population: 1.381 million COPENHAGEN (capital) (2023)

Sex ratio: *at birth:* 1.07 male(s)/female
0-14 years: 1.05 male(s)/female
15-64 years: 1.03 male(s)/female
65 years and over: 0.86 male(s)/female
total population: 0.99 male(s)/female (2024 est.)

Mother's mean age at first birth: 29.8 years (2020 est.)

Maternal mortality ratio: 5 deaths/100,000 live births (2020 est.)
comparison ranking: 167

Infant mortality rate: *total:* 3 deaths/1,000 live births (2024 est.)
male: 3.4 deaths/1,000 live births
female: 2.5 deaths/1,000 live births
comparison ranking: total 210

Life expectancy at birth: *total population:* 82.1 years (2024 est.)
male: 80.2 years
female: 84.1 years
comparison ranking: total population 35

Total fertility rate: 1.77 children born/woman (2024 est.)
comparison ranking: 144

Gross reproduction rate: 0.86 (2024 est.)

Drinking water source: *improved: urban:* 100% of population
rural: 100% of population
total: 100% of population

Current health expenditure: 10.5% of GDP (2020)

Physician density: 4.23 physicians/1,000 population (2018)

Hospital bed density: 2.6 beds/1,000 population (2019)

Sanitation facility access: *improved: urban:* 100% of population
rural: 100% of population
total: 100% of population

Obesity - adult prevalence rate: 19.7% (2016)
comparison ranking: 109

Alcohol consumption per capita: *total:* 9.16 liters of pure alcohol (2019 est.)
beer: 3.42 liters of pure alcohol (2019 est.)
wine: 4.08 liters of pure alcohol (2019 est.)
spirits: 1.66 liters of pure alcohol (2019 est.)
other alcohols: 0 liters of pure alcohol (2019 est.)
comparison ranking: total 33

Tobacco use: *total:* 17.5% (2020 est.)
male: 17.8% (2020 est.)
female: 17.1% (2020 est.)
comparison ranking: total 97

Currently married women (ages 15-49): 59.6% (2023 est.)

Child marriage: *women married by age 18:* 0.7% (2021 est.)

Education expenditures: 6.4% of GDP (2020 est.)
comparison ranking: 32

School life expectancy (primary to tertiary education): *total:* 19 years
male: 18 years
female: 19 years (2020)

ENVIRONMENT

Environment - current issues: air pollution, principally from vehicle and power plant emissions; nitrogen and phosphorus pollution of the North Sea; drinking and surface water becoming polluted from animal wastes and pesticides; much of country's household and industrial waste is recycled

Environment - international agreements: *party to:* Air Pollution, Air Pollution-Heavy Metals, Air Pollution-Multi-effect Protocol, Air Pollution-Nitrogen Oxides, Air Pollution-Persistent Organic Pollutants, Air Pollution-Sulphur 85, Air Pollution-Sulphur 94, Air Pollution-Volatile Organic Compounds, Antarctic Treaty, Biodiversity, Climate Change, Climate Change-Kyoto Protocol, Climate Change-Paris Agreement, Comprehensive Nuclear Test Ban, Desertification, Endangered Species, Environmental Modification, Hazardous Wastes, Law of the Sea, Marine Dumping-London Convention, Marine Dumping-London Protocol, Marine Life Conservation, Nuclear Test Ban, Ozone Layer Protection, Ship Pollution, Tropical Timber 2006, Wetlands, Whaling
signed, but not ratified: Antarctic-Environmental Protection

Climate: temperate; humid and overcast; mild, windy winters and cool summers

Urbanization: *urban population:* 88.5% of total population (2023)
rate of urbanization: 0.54% annual rate of change (2020-25 est.)

Revenue from forest resources: 0.02% of GDP (2018 est.)
comparison ranking: 140

Revenue from coal: 0% of GDP (2018 est.)
comparison ranking: 108

Air pollutants: *particulate matter emissions:* 9.66 micrograms per cubic meter (2019 est.)
carbon dioxide emissions: 31.79 megatons (2016 est.)
methane emissions: 6.54 megatons (2020 est.)

Waste and recycling: *municipal solid waste generated annually:* 4.485 million tons (2015 est.)
municipal solid waste recycled annually: 1,223,060 tons (2015 est.)
percent of municipal solid waste recycled: 27.3% (2015 est.)

Total water withdrawal: *municipal:* 400 million cubic meters (2020 est.)
industrial: 50 million cubic meters (2020 est.)
agricultural: 530 million cubic meters (2020 est.)

Total renewable water resources: 6 billion cubic meters (2020 est.)

Geoparks: *total global geoparks and regional networks:* 3 (2024)
global geoparks and regional networks: Odsherred; South Fyn Archipelago; Vestjylland (2024)

GOVERNMENT

Country name: *conventional long form:* Kingdom of Denmark
conventional short form: Denmark
local long form: Kongeriget Danmark
local short form: Danmark
etymology: the name derives from the words "Dane(s)" and "mark"; the latter referring to a march (borderland) or forest

Government type: parliamentary constitutional monarchy

Capital: *name:* Copenhagen
geographic coordinates: 55 40 N, 12 35 E
time difference: UTC+1 (6 hours ahead of Washington, DC, during Standard Time)
daylight saving time: +1hr, begins last Sunday in March; ends last Sunday in October; note - applies to continental Denmark only, not to its North Atlantic components
etymology: name derives from the city's Danish appellation Kobenhavn, meaning "Merchant's Harbor"

Administrative divisions: metropolitan Denmark - 5 regions (regioner, singular - region); Hovedstaden (Capital), Midtjylland (Central Jutland), Nordjylland (North Jutland), Sjaelland (Zealand), Syddanmark (Southern Denmark)

Independence: ca. 965 (unified and Christianized under Harald I GORMSSON); 5 June 1849 (became a parliamentary constitutional monarchy)

National holiday: Constitution Day, 5 June (1849); note - closest equivalent to a national holiday

Legal system: civil law; judicial review of legislative acts

Constitution: *history:* several previous; latest adopted 5 June 1953
amendments: proposed by the Folketing (Parliament) with consent of the government; passage requires approval by the next Folketing following a general election, approval by simple majority vote of at least 40% of voters in a referendum, and assent of the chief of state; changed several times, last in 2009 (Danish Act of Succession)

International law organization participation: accepts compulsory ICJ jurisdiction with reservations; accepts ICCt jurisdiction

Citizenship: *citizenship by birth:* no
citizenship by descent only: at least one parent must be a citizen of Denmark
dual citizenship recognized: yes
residency requirement for naturalization: 7 years

Suffrage: 18 years of age; universal

Executive branch: *chief of state:* King FREDERIK X (since 14 January 2024)
head of government: Prime Minister Mette FREDERIKSEN (since 27 June 2019)
cabinet: Council of State appointed by the monarch
elections/appointments: the monarchy is hereditary; following legislative elections, the leader of the majority party or majority coalition usually appointed prime minister by the monarch
note: Queen MARGRETHE II abdicated on 14 January 2024, the first Danish monarch to voluntarily abdicate since King ERIC III in 1146

Legislative branch: *description:* unicameral People's Assembly or Folketing (179 seats, including 2 each representing Greenland and the Faroe Islands; members directly elected in multi-seat constituencies by party-list proportional representation vote; members serve 4-year terms unless the Folketing is dissolved earlier)
elections: last held on 1 November 2022 (next to be held by 31 October 2026)
election results: percent of vote by party - SDP 27.5%, V 13.3%, M 9.3%, SF 8.3%, E 8.1%, LA 8.1%, C 5.5%, EL 5.1%, SLP 3.8%, AP 3.3%, NB 3.3%, DF 2.6%; seats by party - SDP 50, V 23, M 16, SF 15, E 14, LA 14, C 10, EL 9, SLP 7, AP 6, NB 6, DF 5; composition - men 98, women 81, percentage women 45.3%

Judicial branch: *highest court(s):* Supreme Court (consists of the court president and 18 judges)

judge selection and term of office: judges appointed by the monarch upon the recommendation of the Minister of Justice, with the advice of the Judicial Appointments Council, a 6-member independent body of judges and lawyers; judges appointed for life with retirement at age 70
subordinate courts: Special Court of Indictment and Revision; 2 High Courts; Maritime and Commercial Court; county courts

Political parties: The Alternative or AP
Conservative People's Party or DKF or C
Danish People's Party or DF or O
Denmark Democrats or E
Green Left or SF or F (formerly Socialist People's Party or SF or F)
Liberal Alliance or LA or I
Liberal Party (Venstre) or V
Moderates or M
New Right Party or NB or D
Red-Green Alliance (Unity List) or EL
Social Democrats or SDP or A
Social Liberal Party or SLP or B

International organization participation: ADB (nonregional member), AfDB (nonregional member), Arctic Council, Australia Group, BIS, CBSS, CD, CE, CERN, EAPC, EBRD, ECB, EIB, EITI (implementing country), ESA, EU, FAO, FATF, G-9, IADB, IAEA, IBRD, ICAO, ICC (national committees), ICCt, ICRM, IDA, IEA, IFAD, IFC, IFRCS, IGAD (partners), IHO, ILO, IMF, IMO, IMSO, Interpol, IOC, IOM, IPU, ISO, ITSO, ITU, ITUC (NGOs), MIGA, NATO, NC, NEA, NIB, NSG, OAS (observer), OECD, OPCW, OSCE, Paris Club, PCA, Schengen Convention, UN, UNCTAD, UNESCO, UNHCR, UNIDO, UNMIL, UNMISS, UNOOSA, UNRWA, UNTSO, UPU, Wassenaar Arrangement, WCO, WHO, WIPO, WMO, WTO, ZC

Diplomatic representation in the US: *chief of mission:* Ambassador Jesper Møller SØRENSEN (since 15 September 2023)
chancery: 3200 Whitehaven Street NW, Washington, DC 20008
telephone: [1] (202) 234-4300
FAX: [1] (202) 328-1470
email address and website:
wasamb@um.dk
https://usa.um.dk/en
consulate(s) general: Chicago, Houston, New York, Silicon Valley (CA)

Diplomatic representation from the US: *chief of mission:* Ambassador Alan LEVENTHAL (since 1 July 2022)
embassy: Dag Hammarskjolds Alle 24, 2100 Kobenhavn 0
mailing address: 5280 Copenhagen Place, Washington DC 20521-5280
telephone: [45] 33-41-71-00
FAX: [45] 35-43-02-23
email address and website:
CopenhagenACS@state.gov
https://dk.usembassy.gov/

Flag description: red with a white cross that extends to the edges of the flag; the vertical part of the cross is shifted to the hoist side; the banner is referred to as the Dannebrog (Danish flag) and is one of the oldest national flags in the world; traditions as to the origin of the flag design vary, but the best known is a legend that the banner fell from the sky during an early-13th century battle; caught up by the Danish king before it ever touched the earth, this heavenly talisman inspired the royal army to victory; in actuality, the flag may derive from a crusade banner or ensign
note: the shifted cross design element was subsequently adopted by the other Nordic countries of Finland, Iceland, Norway, and Sweden, as well as by the Faroe Islands

National symbol(s): lion, mute swan; national colors: red, white

National anthem: *name:* "Der er et yndigt land" (There is a Lovely Country); "Kong Christian" (King Christian)
lyrics/music: Adam Gottlob OEHLENSCHLAGER/ Hans Ernst KROYER; Johannes EWALD/unknown
note: Denmark has two national anthems with equal status; "Der er et yndigt land," adopted 1844, is a national anthem, while "Kong Christian," adopted 1780, serves as both a national and royal anthem; "Kong Christian" is also known as "Kong Christian stod ved hojen mast" (King Christian Stood by the Lofty Mast) and "Kongesangen" (The King's Anthem); within Denmark, the royal anthem is played only when royalty is present and is usually followed by the national anthem; when royalty is not present, only the national anthem is performed; outside Denmark, the royal anthem is played, unless the national anthem is requested

National heritage: *total World Heritage Sites:* 11 (8 cultural, 3 natural); note - includes three sites in Greenland
selected World Heritage Site locales: Denmark: Mounds, Runic Stones, and Church at Jelling (c); Roskilde Cathedral (c); Kronborg Castle (c); Wadden Sea (n); Stevns Klint (n); Christiansfeld, Moravian Church Settlement (c); Par force hunting landscape, North Zealand (c); Greenland: Ilulissat Icefjord (n); Kujataa, Norse and Inuit Farming (c); Aasivissuit–Nipisat, Inuit Hunting Ground (c); Viking-Age Ring Fortresses (c)

ECONOMY

Economic overview: high-income, EU member, trade-oriented Nordic economy; growth driven by pharmaceuticals, energy and services; large share of employment in public sector; fixed exchange rate pegged to euro; strong fiscal position; tight labor market addressed by migrant workers and higher average retirement age

Real GDP (purchasing power parity): $428.385 billion (2023 est.)
$420.44 billion (2022 est.)
$409.262 billion (2021 est.)
note: data in 2021 dollars
comparison ranking: 53

Real GDP growth rate: 1.89% (2023 est.)
2.73% (2022 est.)
6.84% (2021 est.)
note: annual GDP % growth based on constant local currency
comparison ranking: 144

Real GDP per capita: $72,000 (2023 est.)
$71,200 (2022 est.)
$69,900 (2021 est.)
note: data in 2021 dollars
comparison ranking: 15

GDP (official exchange rate): $404.199 billion (2023 est.)
note: data in current dollars at official exchange rate

Inflation rate (consumer prices): 3.31% (2023 est.)
7.7% (2022 est.)
1.85% (2021 est.)
note: annual % change based on consumer prices
comparison ranking: 64

Credit ratings: Fitch rating: AAA (2003)

Moody's rating: Aaa (1999)

Standard & Poors rating: AAA (2001)
note: The year refers to the year in which the current credit rating was first obtained.

GDP - composition, by sector of origin: *agriculture:* 1% (2023 est.)
industry: 21.5% (2023 est.)
services: 66.1% (2023 est.)
note: figures may not total 100% due to non-allocated consumption not captured in sector-reported data
comparison rankings: services 54; industry 125; agriculture 183

GDP - composition, by end use: *household consumption:* 45.8% (2023 est.)
government consumption: 22.6% (2023 est.)
investment in fixed capital: 21.8% (2023 est.)
investment in inventories: 0.2% (2023 est.)
exports of goods and services: 69% (2023 est.)
imports of goods and services: -59.4% (2023 est.)
note: figures may not total 100% due to rounding or gaps in data collection

Agricultural products: milk, wheat, barley, potatoes, sugar beets, pork, rapeseed, rye, oats, chicken (2022)
note: top ten agricultural products based on tonnage

Industries: wind turbines, pharmaceuticals, medical equipment, shipbuilding and refurbishment, iron, steel, nonferrous metals, chemicals, food processing, machinery and transportation equipment, textiles and clothing, electronics, construction, furniture and other wood products

Industrial production growth rate: 7.92% (2023 est.)
note: annual % change in industrial value added based on constant local currency
comparison ranking: 30

Labor force: 3.18 million (2023 est.)
note: number of people ages 15 or older who are employed or seeking work
comparison ranking: 104

Unemployment rate: 5.14% (2023 est.)
4.43% (2022 est.)
5.04% (2021 est.)
note: % of labor force seeking employment
comparison ranking: 97

Youth unemployment rate (ages 15-24): *total:* 11.7% (2023 est.)
male: 12% (2023 est.)
female: 11.3% (2023 est.)
note: % of labor force ages 15-24 seeking employment
comparison ranking: total 116

Population below poverty line: 12.4% (2021 est.)
note: % of population with income below national poverty line

Gini Index coefficient - distribution of family income: 28.3 (2021 est.)
note: index (0-100) of income distribution; higher values represent greater inequality
comparison ranking: 136

Average household expenditures: *on food:* 11.7% of household expenditures (2022 est.)
on alcohol and tobacco: 4% of household expenditures (2022 est.)

Household income or consumption by percentage share: *lowest 10%:* 3.7% (2021 est.)
highest 10%: 23.8% (2021 est.)
note: % share of income accruing to lowest and highest 10% of population

Remittances: 0.35% of GDP (2023 est.)
0.31% of GDP (2022 est.)
0.35% of GDP (2021 est.)
note: personal transfers and compensation between resident and non-resident individuals/households/entities

Budget: *revenues:* $145.764 billion (2022 est.)
expenditures: $130.785 billion (2022 est.)
note: central government revenues (excluding grants) and expenses converted to US dollars at average official exchange rate for year indicated

Public debt: 35.3% of GDP (2017 est.)
note: data cover general government debt and include debt instruments issued (or owned) by government entities other than the treasury; the data include treasury debt held by foreign entities; the data include debt issued by subnational entities, as well as intra-governmental debt; intragovernmental debt consists of treasury borrowings from surpluses in the social funds, such as for retirement, medical care, and unemployment; debt instruments for the social funds are not sold at public auctions
comparison ranking: 152

Taxes and other revenues: 30.56% (of GDP) (2022 est.)
note: central government tax revenue as a % of GDP
comparison ranking: 23

Current account balance: $44.195 billion (2023 est.)
$53.067 billion (2022 est.)
$36.94 billion (2021 est.)
note: balance of payments - net trade and primary/secondary income in current dollars
comparison ranking: 13

Exports: $278.917 billion (2023 est.)
$279.939 billion (2022 est.)
$237.861 billion (2021 est.)
note: balance of payments - exports of goods and services in current dollars
comparison ranking: 33

Exports - partners: Germany 15%, US 11%, Sweden 10%, Netherlands 6%, Norway 5% (2022)
note: top five export partners based on percentage share of exports

Exports - commodities: packaged medicine, garments, fish, electricity, refined petroleum (2022)
note: top five export commodities based on value in dollars

Imports: $240.269 billion (2023 est.)
$235.68 billion (2022 est.)
$210.716 billion (2021 est.)
note: balance of payments - imports of goods and services in current dollars
comparison ranking: 33

Imports - partners: Germany 20%, Sweden 12%, China 9%, Netherlands 8%, Norway 5% (2022)
note: top five import partners based on percentage share of imports

Imports - commodities: garments, cars, refined petroleum, electricity, packaged medicine (2022)
note: top five import commodities based on value in dollars

Reserves of foreign exchange and gold: $109.371 billion (2023 est.)
$96.073 billion (2022 est.)
$82.236 billion (2021 est.)
note: holdings of gold (year-end prices)/foreign exchange/special drawing rights in current dollars
comparison ranking: 36

Exchange rates: Danish kroner (DKK) per US dollar -

Exchange rates: 6.89 (2023 est.)
7.076 (2022 est.)
6.287 (2021 est.)
6.542 (2020 est.)
6.669 (2019 est.)

ENERGY

Electricity access: *electrification - total population:* 100% (2022 est.)

Electricity: *installed generating capacity:* 19.503 million kW (2022 est.)
consumption: 33.167 billion kWh (2022 est.)
exports: 17.392 billion kWh (2022 est.)
imports: 18.797 billion kWh (2022 est.)
transmission/distribution losses: 1.965 billion kWh (2022 est.)
comparison rankings: transmission/distribution losses 126; imports 10; exports 17; consumption 64; installed generating capacity 50

Electricity generation sources: *fossil fuels:* 11.2% of total installed capacity (2022 est.)
solar: 6.3% of total installed capacity (2022 est.)
wind: 56.4% of total installed capacity (2022 est.)
biomass and waste: 26.1% of total installed capacity (2022 est.)

Coal: *consumption:* 1.788 million metric tons (2022 est.)
exports: 826,000 metric tons (2022 est.)
imports: 1.89 million metric tons (2022 est.)

Petroleum: *total petroleum production:* 63,000 bbl/day (2023 est.)
refined petroleum consumption: 152,000 bbl/day (2023 est.)
crude oil estimated reserves: 441 million barrels (2021 est.)

Natural gas: *production:* 1.879 billion cubic meters (2022 est.)
consumption: 2.208 billion cubic meters (2022 est.)
exports: 2.041 billion cubic meters (2022 est.)
imports: 2.582 billion cubic meters (2022 est.)
proven reserves: 29.534 billion cubic meters (2021 est.)

Carbon dioxide emissions: 30.308 million metric tonnes of CO2 (2022 est.)
from coal and metallurgical coke: 3.973 million metric tonnes of CO2 (2022 est.)
from petroleum and other liquids: 21.706 million metric tonnes of CO2 (2022 est.)
from consumed natural gas: 4.628 million metric tonnes of CO2 (2022 est.)
comparison ranking: total emissions 74

Energy consumption per capita: 100.26 million Btu/person (2022 est.)
comparison ranking: 51

COMMUNICATIONS

Telephones - fixed lines: *total subscriptions:* 712,000 (2022 est.)
subscriptions per 100 inhabitants: 12 (2022 est.)
comparison ranking: total subscriptions 81

Telephones - mobile cellular: *total subscriptions:* 7.444 million (2022 est.)
subscriptions per 100 inhabitants: 127 (2022 est.)
comparison ranking: total subscriptions 109

Telecommunication systems: *general assessment:* Denmark has one of the highest broadband subscription rates globally, with a near universal availability of super-fast connections; extensive cable and DSL infrastructure has been supported by a progressive regulatory regime which has encouraged operator access to both copper and fiber networks; fiber networks have a fastgrowing footprint, while a number of community and metropolitan schemes have supplemented their own commitments to build out fiber nationally; a number of wholesale fiber schemes have also added to the wider availability of fiber broadband; the reach of LTE infrastructure is comprehensive, while the Mobile Network Operators by mid-2021 had also provided about 90% population coverage with 5G; services based on 5G were initially launched using trial 3.5GHz licenses; the multi-spectrum auction held in April 2021 has enabled them to improve the resilience and capacity of 5G; all MNOs are engaged in closing down their 3G networks and repurposing spectrum for LTE and 5G use (2021)
domestic: fixed-line roughly 12 per 100 and about 124 per 100 for mobile-cellular subscriptions (2021)
international: country code - 45; landing points for the NSC, COBRAcable, CANTAT-3, DANICE, Havfrue/AEC-2, TAT-14m Denmark-Norway-5 & 6, Skagenfiber West & East, GC1, GC2, GC3, GC-KPN, Kattegat 1 & 2 & 3, Energinet Lyngsa-Laeso, Energinet Laeso-Varberg, Fehmarn Balt, Baltica, German-Denmark 2 & 3, Ronne-Rodvig, Denmark- Sweden 15 & 16 & 17 & 18, IP-Only Denmark-Sweden, Scandinavian South, Scandinavian Ring North, Danica North, 34 series of fiber-optic submarine cables link Denmark with Canada, Faroe Islands, Germany, Iceland, Netherlands, Norway, Poland, Russia, Sweden, US, and UK; satellite earth stations - 18 (6 Intelsat, 10 Eutelsat, 1 Orion, 1 Inmarsat (Blaavand-Atlantic-East)); note - the Nordic countries (Denmark, Finland, Iceland, Norway, and Sweden) share the Danish earth station and the Eik, Norway, station for worldwide Inmarsat access (2019)

Broadcast media: strong public-sector TV presence with state-owned Danmarks Radio (DR) operating 6 channels and publicly owned TV2 operating roughly a half-dozen channels; broadcasts of privately owned stations are available via satellite and cable feed; DR operates 4 nationwide FM radio stations, 10 digital audio broadcasting stations, and 14 web-based radio stations; 140 commercial and 187 community (non-commercial) radio stations (2019)

Internet country code: .dk

Internet users: *total:* 5.841 million (2021 est.)
percent of population: 99% (2021 est.)
comparison ranking: total 82

Broadband - fixed subscriptions: *total:* 2,590,282 (2020 est.)
subscriptions per 100 inhabitants: 45 (2020 est.)
comparison ranking: total 51

TRANSPORTATION

National air transport system: *number of registered air carriers:* 10 (2020)

inventory of registered aircraft operated by air carriers: 76
annual passenger traffic on registered air carriers: 582,011 (2015)
annual freight traffic on registered air carriers: mt-km

Civil aircraft registration country code prefix: OY

Airports: 99 (2024)
comparison ranking: 54

Heliports: 25 (2024)

Pipelines: 1,536 km gas, 330 km oil (2015)

Railways: *total:* 2,682 km (2020) 876 km electrified
comparison ranking: total 61

Roadways: *total:* 73,591 km (2022)
comparison ranking: total 68

Waterways: 400 km (2010)
comparison ranking: 97

Merchant marine: *total:* 715 (2023)
by type: bulk carrier 15, container ship 132, general cargo 69, oil tanker 107, other 392
comparison ranking: total 33

Ports: *total ports:* 69 (2024)
large: 1
medium: 2
small: 30
very small: 36
ports with oil terminals: 33
key ports: Abenra, Alborg, Arhus, Assens, Augustenborg, Bandholm, Esbjerg, Faborg, Fredericia, Frederikshavn, Haderslev, Holstebro-Stuer, Kalundborg, Kobenhavn, Kolding, Korsor, Marstal, Middelfart, Naestved, Nakskov, Nyborg, Nykobing, Odense, Randers, Ronne, Rudkobing, Sakskobing, Skagen Havn, Sonderborg, Stubbekobing, Studstrup, Svendborg, Vejle

MILITARY AND SECURITY

Military and security forces: Danish Armed Forces (Forsvaret): Royal Danish Army, Royal Danish Navy, Royal Danish Air Force, Danish Home Guard (Reserves) (2024)

Military expenditures: 2.4% of GDP (2024 est.)
2% of GDP (2023)
1.4% of GDP (2022)
1.3% of GDP (2021)
1.4% of GDP (2020)
comparison ranking: 49

Military and security service personnel strengths: approximately 17,000 active-duty personnel (10,000 Army; 3,500 Navy; 3,500 Air Force) (2024)

Military equipment inventories and acquisitions: the Danish military inventory is comprised of a mix of modern European, US, and domestically produced equipment; the US has been the largest supplier of military equipment to Denmark in recent years; the Danish defense industry is active in the production of naval vessels, defense electronics, and subcomponents of larger weapons systems, such as the US F-35 fighter aircraft (2023)

Military service age and obligation: 18 years of age for compulsory and voluntary military service; conscripts serve an initial training period that varies from 4 to 12 months depending on specialization; former conscripts are assigned to mobilization units; women eligible to volunteer for military service; in addition to full time employment, the Danish military offers reserve contracts in all three branches (2023)
note 1: women have been able serve in all military occupations, including combat arms, since 1988; as of 2022, they made up about 9% of the military's full-time personnel; in 2024, Denmark announced that it would extend military conscription to women in 2026
note 2: Denmark has had compulsory military service since 1849; conscripts are chosen by lottery; conscientious objectors can choose to instead serve 6 months in a non-military position, for example in Beredskabsstyrelsen (dealing with non-military disasters like fires, flood, pollution, etc.) or overseas foreign aid work
note 3: foreigners who have lived in Denmark for at least one year or in another EU country for six years may apply to join the armed forces, provided they are fluent in Danish

Military deployments: approximately 800 Latvia (NATO); Denmark contributes small numbers of air, ground, and naval forces to a variety of other NATO and international missions (2024)

Military - note: the Danish Armed Forces (Forsvaret) have a variety of missions, including enforcing the country's sovereignty, monitoring Danish waters and airspace, search and rescue, environmental protection, host nation support for alliance partners, international peacekeeping, fulfilling Denmark's commitments to NATO, and providing assistance to the police for border control, guard tasks, air surveillance, and during national disasters and other emergencies
NATO has been a cornerstone of Danish security and defense police since it joined in 1949 as one of the organization's original members under the North Atlantic Treaty (also known as the Washington Treaty); the Forsvaret regularly exercises with NATO allies and participates in a number of NATO missions, including its Enhanced Forward Presence in Eastern Europe, air policing in the Baltics, naval operations in the Baltic Sea and North Atlantic, and an advisory mission in Iraq; the Forsvaret leads NATO's Multinational Division – North (inaugurated 2019), a headquarters based in Latvia that supports the defense planning of Estonia, Latvia, and Lithuania, and the coordination of regional military activities, including NATO's forward deployed forces; it also takes part in other international missions for Europe and the UN ranging from peacekeeping in Africa to protecting Europe's external borders by patrolling the Mediterranean Sea in support of the European Border and Coast Guard Agency; Denmark is a member of the EU and voted to join the EU's Common Defense and Security Policy in a June 2022 referendum; the Forsvaret cooperates closely with the militaries of other Nordic countries through the Nordic Defense Cooperation (NORDEFCO; established 2009), which consists of Denmark, Finland, Iceland, Norway, and Sweden in such areas as armaments, training and exercises, and operations; it also has a joint composite special operations command with Belgium and the Netherlands
the Defense Command is Denmark's overall military command authority for land, air, and naval operations, although the Army, Air Force, and Navy also have their own individual service commands; an Arctic Command protects the sovereignty of Denmark in the Arctic region, including the Faroe Islands and Greenland, and conducts maritime pollution prevention, environmental monitoring, fishery inspections, search and rescue, and hydrographical surveys, plus support to governmental science missions; there is also a joint service Special Operations Command, which includes the Sirius Dog Sled Patrol, an elite unit that patrols the most remote parts of northeast Greenland (2024)

SPACE

Space agency/agencies: no formal space agency; the Ministry of Higher Education and Science has responsibility for coordinating Danish space activities managing international cooperation; the Danish Space Research Institute (Dansk Rumforskningsinstitut (DRKI) was the country's space agency from 1966-2005; DTU Space, National Space Institute, is Denmark's national space institute (2024)

Space program overview: a member of the European Space Agency (ESA) and fully integrated within its structure; participates in ESA programs, particularly those linked to human spaceflight and satellite-based remote sensing activities, as well as technology programs involving telecommunications and navigation; independently builds and operates satellites, particularly those with meteorological, science, technology, and signal/traffic monitoring capabilities; conducts research and development of such technologies as measurement and instrumentation systems, microwaves, remote sensing, electromagnetic systems, astrophysics, geomagnetism, etc.; in addition to cooperating with the eSa and EU, as well as bi-laterally with member states, it has relations with the space agencies and industries of Canada, India, Japan, and the US (2024)
note: further details about the key activities, programs, and milestones of the country's space program, as well as government spending estimates on the space sector, appear in the Space Programs reference guide

TERRORISM

Terrorist group(s): Islamic State of Iraq and ash-Sham (ISIS); Islamic Revolutionary Guard Corps/Qods Force
note: details about the history, aims, leadership, organization, areas of operation, tactics, targets, weapons, size, and sources of support of the group(s) appear(s) in the Terrorism reference guide

TRANSNATIONAL ISSUES

Refugees and internally displaced persons: *refugees (country of origin):* 19,424 (Syria), 5,885 (Eritrea) (mid-year 2022); 37,530 (Ukraine) (as of 3 March 2024)
stateless persons: 11,644 (2022)

DJIBOUTI

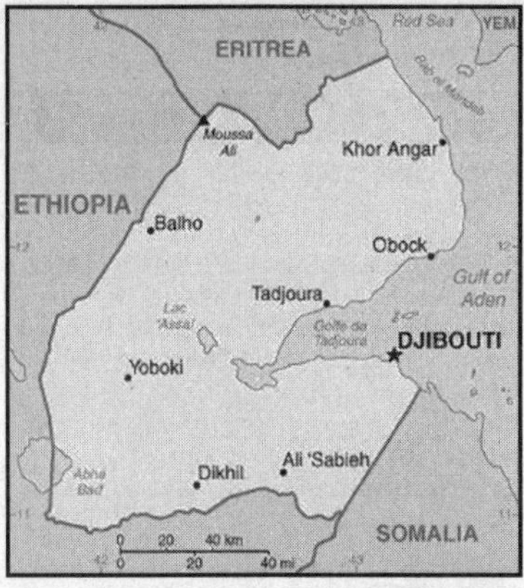

INTRODUCTION

Background: Present-day Djibouti was the site of the medieval Ifat and Adal Sultanates. In the late 19th century, the Afar sultans signed treaties with the French that allowed the latter to establish the colony of French Somaliland in 1862. The French signed additional treaties with the ethnic Somali in 1885.

Tension between the ethnic Afar and Somali populations increased over time, as the ethnic Somalis perceived that the French unfairly favored the Afar and gave them disproportionate influence in local governance. In 1958, the French held a referendum that provided residents of French Somaliland the option to either continue their association with France or to join neighboring Somalia as it established its independence. Ethnic Somali protested the vote, because French colonial leaders did not recognize many Somali as residents, which gave the Afar outsized influence in the decision to uphold ties with France. After a second referendum in 1967, the French changed the territory's name to the French Territory of the Afars and the Issas, in part to underscore their relationship with the ethnic Afar and downplay the significance of the ethnic Somalis. A final referendum in 1977 established Djibouti as an independent nation and granted ethnic Somalis Djiboutian nationality, formally resetting the balance of power between the majority ethnic Somalis and minority ethnic Afar residents. Upon independence, the country was named after its capital city of Djibouti. Hassan Gouled APTIDON, an ethnic Somali leader, installed an authoritarian one-party state and served as president until 1999. Unrest between the Afar minority and Somali majority culminated in a civil war during the 1990s that ended in 2001 with a peace accord between Afar rebels and the Somali Issa-dominated government. In 1999, Djibouti's first multiparty presidential election resulted in the election of Ismail Omar GUELLEH as president; he was reelected to a second term in 2005 and extended his tenure in office via a constitutional amendment, which allowed him to serve his third and fourth terms, and to begin a fifth term in 2021.

Djibouti occupies a strategic geographic location at the intersection of the Red Sea and the Gulf of Aden. Its ports handle 95% of Ethiopia's trade. Djibouti's ports also service transshipments between Europe, the Middle East, and Asia. The government has longstanding ties to France, which maintains a military presence in the country, as do the US, Japan, Italy, Germany, Spain, and China.

GEOGRAPHY

Location: Eastern Africa, bordering the Gulf of Aden and the Red Sea, between Eritrea and Somalia

Geographic coordinates: 11 30 N, 43 00 E

Map references: Africa

Area: *total:* 23,200 sq km
land: 23,180 sq km
water: 20 sq km
comparison ranking: total 150

Area - comparative: slightly smaller than New Jersey

Land boundaries: *total:* 528 km
border countries (3): Eritrea 125 km; Ethiopia 342 km; Somalia 61 km

Coastline: 314 km

Maritime claims: *territorial sea:* 12 nm
contiguous zone: 24 nm
exclusive economic zone: 200 nm

Climate: desert; torrid, dry

Terrain: coastal plain and plateau separated by central mountains

Elevation: *highest point:* Moussa Ali 2,021 m
lowest point: Lac Assal -155 m
mean elevation: 430 m

Natural resources: potential geothermal power, gold, clay, granite, limestone, marble, salt, diatomite, gypsum, pumice, petroleum

Land use: *agricultural land:* 73.4% (2018 est.)
arable land: 0.1% (2018 est.)
permanent crops: 0% (2018 est.)
permanent pasture: 73.3% (2018 est.)
forest: 0.2% (2018 est.)
other: 26.4% (2018 est.)

Irrigated land: 10 sq km (2012)

Major lakes (area sq km): *salt water lake(s):* Abhe Bad/Abhe Bid Hayk (shared with Ethiopia) - 780 sq km

Population distribution: most densely populated areas are in the east; the largest city is Djibouti, with a population over 600,000; no other city in the country has a total population over 50,000 as shown in this population distribution map

Natural hazards: earthquakes; droughts; occasional cyclonic disturbances from the Indian Ocean bring heavy rains and flash floods
volcanism: experiences limited volcanic activity; Ardoukoba (298 m) last erupted in 1978; Manda-Inakir, located along the Ethiopian border, is also historically active

Geography - note: strategic location near world's busiest shipping lanes and close to Arabian oilfields; terminus of rail traffic into Ethiopia; mostly wasteland; Lac Assal (Lake Assal) is the lowest point in Africa and the saltiest lake in the world

PEOPLE AND SOCIETY

Population: *total:* 994,974
male: 450,796
female: 544,178 (2024 est.)
comparison rankings: female 162; male 164; total 162

Nationality: *noun:* Djiboutian(s)
adjective: Djiboutian

Ethnic groups: Somali 60%, Afar 35%, other 5% (mostly Yemeni Arab, also French, Ethiopian, and Italian)

Languages: French (official), Arabic (official), Somali, Afar

Religions: Sunni Muslim 94% (nearly all Djiboutians), other 6% (mainly foreign-born residents - Shia Muslim, Christian, Hindu, Jewish, Baha'i, and atheist)

Demographic profile: Djibouti is a poor, predominantly urban country, characterized by high rates of illiteracy, unemployment, and childhood malnutrition. Approximately 70% of the population lives in cities and towns (predominantly in the capital, Djibouti). The rural population subsists primarily on nomadic herding. Prone to droughts and floods, the country has few natural resources and must import more than 80% of its food from neighboring countries or Europe. Health care, particularly outside the capital, is limited by poor infrastructure, shortages of equipment and supplies, and a lack of qualified personnel. More than a third of health care recipients are migrants because the services are still better than those available in their neighboring home countries. The nearly universal practice of female genital cutting reflects Djibouti's lack of gender equality and is a major contributor to obstetrical complications and its high rates of maternal and infant mortality. A 1995 law prohibiting the practice has never been enforced. Because of its political stability and its strategic location at the confluence of East Africa and the Gulf States along the Gulf of Aden and the Red Sea, Djibouti is a key transit point for migrants and asylum seekers heading for the Gulf States and beyond. Each year some 100,000 people, mainly Ethiopians and some Somalis, journey through Djibouti, usually to the port of Obock, to attempt a dangerous sea crossing to Yemen. However, with the escalation of the ongoing Yemen conflict, Yemenis began fleeing to Djibouti in March 2015, with almost 20,000 arriving by August 2017. Most Yemenis remain unregistered and head for Djibouti City rather than seeking asylum at one of Djibouti's three spartan refugee camps. Djibouti has been hosting refugees and asylum seekers, predominantly Somalis and lesser numbers of Ethiopians and Eritreans, at camps for 20 years, despite lacking potable water, food shortages, and unemployment.

Age structure: *0-14 years:* 28.4% (male 141,829/female 140,696)
15-64 years: 67.4% (male 290,654/female 379,778)
65 years and over: 4.2% (2024 est.) (male 18,313/female 23,704)

Dependency ratios: *total dependency ratio:* 50.6
youth dependency ratio: 47.5
elderly dependency ratio: 6.9

potential support ratio: 14.4 (2021 est.)
Median age: *total:* 26.3 years (2024 est.)
male: 24.4 years
female: 27.9 years
comparison ranking: total 164
Population growth rate: 1.89% (2024 est.)
comparison ranking: 45
Birth rate: 21.8 births/1,000 population (2024 est.)
comparison ranking: 56
Death rate: 7 deaths/1,000 population (2024 est.)
comparison ranking: 120
Net migration rate: 4.2 migrant(s)/1,000 population (2024 est.)
comparison ranking: 23
Population distribution: most densely populated areas are in the east; the largest city is Djibouti, with a population over 600,000; no other city in the country has a total population over 50,000 as shown in this population distribution map
Urbanization: *urban population:* 78.6% of total population (2023)
rate of urbanization: 1.56% annual rate of change (2020-25 est.)
Major urban areas - population: 600,000 DJIBOUTI (capital) (2023)
Sex ratio: *at birth:* 1.03 male(s)/female
0-14 years: 1.01 male(s)/female
15-64 years: 0.77 male(s)/female
65 years and over: 0.77 male(s)/female
total population: 0.83 male(s)/female (2024 est.)
Maternal mortality ratio: 234 deaths/100,000 live births (2020 est.)
comparison ranking: 39
Infant mortality rate: *total:* 45.2 deaths/1,000 live births (2024 est.)
male: 52.1 deaths/1,000 live births
female: 38 deaths/1,000 live births
comparison ranking: total 25
Life expectancy at birth: *total population:* 65.9 years (2024 est.)
male: 63.4 years
female: 68.5 years
comparison ranking: total population 202
Total fertility rate: 2.11 children born/woman (2024 est.)
comparison ranking: 94
Gross reproduction rate: 1.04 (2024 est.)
Contraceptive prevalence rate: 19% (2012)
Drinking water source: *improved:* *urban:* 99.7% of population
rural: 59.3% of population
total: 90.8% of population
unimproved: *urban:* 0.3% of population
rural: 40.7% of population
total: 9.2% of population (2020 est.)
Current health expenditure: 2% of GDP (2020)
Physician density: 0.22 physicians/1,000 population (2014)
Hospital bed density: 1.4 beds/1,000 population (2017)
Sanitation facility access: *improved:* *urban:* 87.7% of population
rural: 24.2% of population
total: 73.8% of population
unimproved: *urban:* 12.3% of population
rural: 75.8% of population
total: 26.2% of population (2020 est.)
Obesity - adult prevalence rate: 13.5% (2016)
comparison ranking: 131
Alcohol consumption per capita: *total:* 0.21 liters of pure alcohol (2019 est.)
beer: 0.05 liters of pure alcohol (2019 est.)
wine: 0.02 liters of pure alcohol (2019 est.)
spirits: 0.14 liters of pure alcohol (2019 est.)
other alcohols: 0 liters of pure alcohol (2019 est.)
comparison ranking: total 172
Children under the age of 5 years underweight: 16.2% (2019)
comparison ranking: 31
Currently married women (ages 15-49): 50.6% (2023 est.)
Child marriage: *women married by age 15:* 1.4%
women married by age 18: 6.5% (2019 est.)
Education expenditures: 3.6% of GDP (2018 est.)
comparison ranking: 136
School life expectancy (primary to tertiary education): *total:* 7 years
male: 7 years
female: 7 years (2011)

ENVIRONMENT

Environment - current issues: inadequate supplies of potable water; water pollution; limited arable land; deforestation (forests threatened by agriculture and the use of wood for fuel); desertification; endangered species
Environment - international agreements: *party to:* Biodiversity, Climate Change, Climate Change-Kyoto Protocol, Climate Change-Paris Agreement, Comprehensive Nuclear Test Ban, Desertification, Endangered Species, Hazardous Wastes, Law of the Sea, Ozone Layer Protection, Ship Pollution, Wetlands
signed, but not ratified: none of the selected agreements
Climate: desert; torrid, dry
Urbanization: *urban population:* 78.6% of total population (2023)
rate of urbanization: 1.56% annual rate of change (2020-25 est.)
Food insecurity: *widespread lack of access: due to unfavorable weather and high food prices* - about 250,000 people were estimated to have faced acute food insecurity between March and June 2023, mainly due to the lingering impact of a prolonged and severe drought between late 2020 and early 2023, and high food prices (2023)
Revenue from forest resources: 0.26% of GDP (2018 est.)
comparison ranking: 85
Revenue from coal: 0% of GDP (2018 est.)
comparison ranking: 62
Air pollutants: *particulate matter emissions:* 19.98 micrograms per cubic meter (2019 est.)
carbon dioxide emissions: 0.62 megatons (2016 est.)
methane emissions: 0.52 megatons (2020 est.)
Waste and recycling: *municipal solid waste generated annually:* 114,997 tons (2002 est.)
Major lakes (area sq km): *salt water lake(s):* Abhe Bad/Abhe Bid Hayk (shared with Ethiopia) - 780 sq km
Total water withdrawal: *municipal:* 20 million cubic meters (2020 est.)
industrial: 0 cubic meters (2017 est.)
agricultural: 3 million cubic meters (2017 est.)
Total renewable water resources: 300 million cubic meters (2020 est.)

GOVERNMENT

Country name: *conventional long form:* Republic of Djibouti
conventional short form: Djibouti
local long form: République de Djibouti (French)/ Jumhuriyat Jibuti (Arabic)
local short form: Djibouti (French)/ Jibuti (Arabic)
former: French Somaliland, French Territory of the Afars and Issas
etymology: the country name derives from the capital city of Djibouti
Government type: presidential republic
Capital: *name:* Djibouti
geographic coordinates: 11 35 N, 43 09 E
time difference: UTC+3 (8 hours ahead of Washington, DC, during Standard Time)
etymology: the origin of the name is disputed; multiple descriptions, possibilities, and theories have been proposed
Administrative divisions: 6 districts (cercles, singular - cercle); Ali Sabieh, Arta, Dikhil, Djibouti, Obock, Tadjourah
Independence: 27 June 1977 (from France)
National holiday: Independence Day, 27 June (1977)
Legal system: mixed legal system based primarily on the French civil code (as it existed in 1997), Islamic religious law (in matters of family law and successions), and customary law
Constitution: *history:* approved by referendum 4 September 1992
amendments: proposed by the president of the republic or by the National Assembly; Assembly consideration of proposals requires assent of at least one third of the membership; passage requires a simple majority vote by the Assembly and approval by simple majority vote in a referendum; the president can opt to bypass a referendum if adopted by at least two-thirds majority vote of the Assembly; constitutional articles on the sovereignty of Djibouti, its republican form of government, and its pluralist form of democracy cannot be amended; amended 2006, 2008, 2010
International law organization participation: accepts compulsory ICJ jurisdiction with reservations; accepts ICCt jurisdiction
Citizenship: *citizenship by birth:* no
citizenship by descent only: the mother must be a citizen of Djibouti
dual citizenship recognized: no
residency requirement for naturalization: 10 years
Suffrage: 18 years of age; universal
Executive branch: *chief of state:* President Ismail Omar GUELLEH (since 8 May 1999)
head of government: Prime Minister Abdoulkader Kamil MOHAMED (since 1 April 2013)
cabinet: Council of Ministers appointed by the prime minister
elections/appointments: president directly elected by absolute majority popular vote in 2 rounds if needed for a 5-year term; election last held on 9 April

2021 (next to be held in April 2026); prime minister appointed by the president
election results:
2021: Ismail Omar GUELLEH reelected president for a fifth term; percent of vote - Ismail Omar GUELLEH (RPP) 97.4%, Zakaria Ismael FARAH (MDEND) 2.7%
2016: Ismail Omar GUELLEH reelected president for a fourth term; percent of vote - Ismail Omar GUELLEH (RPP) 87%, Omar Elmi KHAIREH (CDU) 7.3%, other 5.6%

Legislative branch: *description:* unicameral National Assembly or Assemblée Nationale, formerly the Chamber of Deputies (65 seats; members directly elected in multi-seat constituencies by party-list proportional representation vote using the D'Hondt method; members serve 5-year terms)
elections: last held on 24 February 2023 (next to be held in February 2028)
election results: percent of vote by party - UMP 93.6%, UDJ 6.3%; seats by party - UMP 58, UDJ 7; composition - men 48, women 17, percentage women 26.2%
note: most opposition parties boycotted the 2023 polls, stating the elections were "not free, not transparent, and not democratic"

Judicial branch: *highest court(s):* Supreme Court or Cour Supreme (consists of NA magistrates); Constitutional Council (consists of 6 magistrates)
judge selection and term of office: Supreme Court magistrates appointed by the president with the advice of the Superior Council of the Magistracy (CSM), a 10-member body consisting of 4 judges, 3 members (non-parliamentarians and judges) appointed by the president, and 3 appointed by the National Assembly president or speaker; magistrates appointed for life with retirement at age 65; Constitutional Council magistrate appointments - 2 by the president of the republic, 2 by the president of the National Assembly, and 2 by the CSM; magistrates appointed for 8-year, nonrenewable terms
subordinate courts: High Court of Appeal; Courts of First Instance; customary courts; State Court (replaced sharia courts in 2003)

Political parties: Front for Restoration of Unity and Democracy (Front pour la Restauration de l'Unite Democratique) or FRUD
National Democratic Party or PND
People's Rally for Progress or RPP
Peoples Social Democratic Party or PPSD
Union for Democracy and Justice or UDJ
Union for the Presidential Majority coalition or UMP
Union of Reform Partisans or UPR

International organization participation: ACP, AfDB, AFESD, AMF, ATMIS, AU, CAEU (candidates), COMESA, FAO, G-77, IBRD, ICAO, ICCt, ICRM, IDA, IDB, IFAD, IFC, IFRCS, IGAD, ILO, IMF, IMO, Interpol, IOC, IOM, IPU, ITU, ITUC (NGOs), LAS, MIGA, MINURSO, NAM, OIC, OIF, OPCW, UN, UNCTAD, UNESCO, UNHCR, UNIDO, UNWTO, UPU, WCO, WFTU (NGOs), WHO, WIPO, WMO, WTO

Diplomatic representation in the US: *chief of mission:* Ambassador Mohamed Siad DOUALEH (28 January 2016)
chancery: 1156 15th Street NW, Suite 515, Washington, DC 20005
telephone: [1] (202) 331-0270
FAX: [1] (202) 331-0302
email address and website:
info@djiboutiembassyus.org
https://www.djiboutiembassyus.org/

Diplomatic representation from the US: *chief of mission:* Ambassador (vacant); Chargé d'Affaires Christopher SNIPES (since October 2023)
embassy: Lot 350-B Haramouss, B.P. 185
mailing address: 2150 Djibouti Place, Washington DC 20521-2150
telephone: [253] 21-45-30-00
FAX: [253] 21-45-31-29
email address and website:
DjiboutiACS@state.gov
https://dj.usembassy.gov/

Flag description: two equal horizontal bands of light blue (top) and light green with a white isosceles triangle based on the hoist side bearing a red five-pointed star in the center; blue stands for sea and sky and the Issa Somali people; green symbolizes earth and the Afar people; white represents peace; the red star recalls the struggle for independence and stands for unity

National symbol(s): red star; national colors: light blue, green, white, red

National anthem: *name:* "Jabuuti" (Djibouti)
lyrics/music: Aden ELMI/Abdi ROBLEH
note: adopted 1977

ECONOMY

Economic overview: food import-dependent Horn of Africa economy driven by various national military bases and port-based trade; fairly resilient from COVID-19 disruptions; major re-exporter; increasing Ethiopian and Chinese trade relations; investing in infrastructure

Real GDP (purchasing power parity): $7.38 billion (2023 est.)
$6.918 billion (2022 est.)
$6.669 billion (2021 est.)
note: data in 2021 dollars
comparison ranking: 172

Real GDP growth rate: 6.68% (2023 est.)
3.73% (2022 est.)
4.52% (2021 est.)
note: annual GDP % growth based on constant local currency
comparison ranking: 23

Real GDP per capita: $6,500 (2023 est.)
$6,200 (2022 est.)
$6,000 (2021 est.)
note: data in 2021 dollars
comparison ranking: 164

GDP (official exchange rate): $4.099 billion (2023 est.)
note: data in current dollars at official exchange rate

Inflation rate (consumer prices): 1.5% (2023 est.)
5.18% (2022 est.)
1.18% (2021 est.)
note: annual % change based on consumer prices
comparison ranking: 31

GDP - composition, by sector of origin: *agriculture:* 1.8% (2023 est.)
industry: 15.3% (2023 est.)
services: 76.9% (2023 est.)
note: figures may not total 100% due to non-allocated consumption not captured in sector-reported data
comparison rankings: services 21; industry 169; agriculture 163

GDP - composition, by end use: *household consumption:* 60.6% (2023 est.)
government consumption: 14.5% (2023 est.)
investment in fixed capital: 29.4% (2023 est.)
exports of goods and services: 169.1% (2023 est.)
imports of goods and services: -173.6% (2023 est.)
note: figures may not total 100% due to rounding or gaps in data collection

Agricultural products: vegetables, beans, milk, beef, camel milk, lemons/limes, goat meat, lamb/mutton, tomatoes, beef offal (2022)
note: top ten agricultural products based on tonnage

Industries: construction, agricultural processing, shipping

Industrial production growth rate: 10% (2023 est.)
note: annual % change in industrial value added based on constant local currency
comparison ranking: 17

Labor force: 256,000 (2023 est.)
note: number of people ages 15 or older who are employed or seeking work
comparison ranking: 172

Unemployment rate: 26.26% (2023 est.)
26.37% (2022 est.)
27.55% (2021 est.)
note: % of labor force seeking employment
comparison ranking: 206

Youth unemployment rate (ages 15-24): *total:* 76.5% (2023 est.)
male: 75.4% (2023 est.)
female: 78.1% (2023 est.)
note: % of labor force ages 15-24 seeking employment
comparison ranking: total 1

Population below poverty line: 21.1% (2017 est.)
note: % of population with income below national poverty line

Gini Index coefficient - distribution of family income: 41.6 (2017 est.)
note: index (0-100) of income distribution; higher values represent greater inequality
comparison ranking: 35

Household income or consumption by percentage share: *lowest 10%:* 1.9% (2017 est.)
highest 10%: 32.3% (2017 est.)
note: % share of income accruing to lowest and highest 10% of population

Remittances: 1.41% of GDP (2023 est.)
1.54% of GDP (2022 est.)
2.35% of GDP (2021 est.)
note: personal transfers and compensation between resident and non-resident individuals/households/entities

Budget: *revenues:* $725 million (2019 est.)
expenditures: $754 million (2019 est.)

Public debt: 31.8% of GDP (2017 est.)
comparison ranking: 164

Taxes and other revenues: 35.3% (of GDP) (2017 est.)
comparison ranking: 15

Current account balance: $656.207 million (2022 est.)
-$225.106 million (2021 est.)
$366.358 million (2020 est.)
note: balance of payments - net trade and primary/secondary income in current dollars

comparison ranking: 59

Exports: $5.674 billion (2022 est.)
$5.16 billion (2021 est.)
$3.695 billion (2020 est.)
note: balance of payments - exports of goods and services in current dollars
comparison ranking: 137

Exports - partners: Ethiopia 61%, China 17%, India 7%, Jordan 2%, Central African Republic 1% (2022)
note: top five export partners based on percentage share of exports

Exports - commodities: palm oil, chlorides, seed oils, flax yarn, cattle (2022)
note: top five export commodities based on value in dollars

Imports: $5.096 billion (2022 est.)
$5.483 billion (2021 est.)
$3.425 billion (2020 est.)
note: balance of payments - imports of goods and services in current dollars
comparison ranking: 150

Imports - partners: China 38%, UAE 20%, India 10%, Morocco 6%, Turkey 6% (2022)
note: top five import partners based on percentage share of imports

Imports - commodities: refined petroleum, palm oil, fertilizers, cars, raw sugar (2022)
note: top five import commodities based on value in dollars

Reserves of foreign exchange and gold: $502.034 million (2023 est.)
$589.437 million (2022 est.)
$588.418 million (2021 est.)
note: holdings of gold (year-end prices)/foreign exchange/special drawing rights in current dollars
comparison ranking: 162

Debt - external: $2.331 billion (2022 est.)
note: present value of external debt in current US dollars
comparison ranking: 70

Exchange rates: Djiboutian francs (DJF) per US dollar -

Exchange rates: 177.721 (2023 est.)
177.721 (2022 est.)
177.721 (2021 est.)
177.721 (2020 est.)
177.721 (2019 est.)

ENERGY

Electricity access: *electrification - total population:* 65% (2022 est.)
electrification - urban areas: 72.8%
electrification - rural areas: 36.6%

Electricity: *installed generating capacity:* 150,000 kW (2022 est.)
consumption: 516.233 million kWh (2022 est.)
imports: 512 million kWh (2022 est.)
transmission/distribution losses: 128.74 million kWh (2022 est.)
comparison rankings: transmission/distribution losses 54; imports 90; consumption 174; installed generating capacity 179

Electricity generation sources: *fossil fuels:* 99.1% of total installed capacity (2022 est.)
solar: 0.9% of total installed capacity (2022 est.)

Coal: *exports:* 8 metric tons (2022 est.)
imports: 1,000 metric tons (2022 est.)

Petroleum: *refined petroleum consumption:* 4,000 bbl/day (2022 est.)

Carbon dioxide emissions: 660,000 metric tonnes of CO2 (2022 est.)
from petroleum and other liquids: 660,000 metric tonnes of CO2 (2022 est.)
comparison ranking: total emissions 183

Energy consumption per capita: 9.559 million Btu/person (2022 est.)
comparison ranking: 152

COMMUNICATIONS

Telephones - fixed lines: *total subscriptions:* 28,000 (2022 est.)
subscriptions per 100 inhabitants: 2 (2022 est.)
comparison ranking: total subscriptions 167

Telephones - mobile cellular: *total subscriptions:* 519,000 (2022 est.)
subscriptions per 100 inhabitants: 46 (2022 est.)
comparison ranking: total subscriptions 174

Telecommunication systems: *general assessment:* Djibouti remains one of the last bastions where the national telco has a monopoly on telecom services, including fixed lines, mobile, internet, and broadband with the exception of broad band fiber; despite the country benefiting from its location as a hub for international submarine cables, prices for telecom services remain relatively high, and out of reach for a number of customers, weighing on market advancement; the Djibouti government is aiming to sell a minority stake in the incumbent telco (retaining some control of decisions) while securing the financial backing and the management acumen of a foreign operator; this is part of a larger plan to modernize the country's economy more generally; the state expects to conduct a sale of up to 40% of the company to an international investor (2023)
domestic: about 2 per 100 fixed-line teledensity and nearly 44 per 100 mobile-cellular (2021)
international: country code - 253; landing points for the SEA-ME-WE-3 & 5, EASSy, Aden-Djibouti, Africa-1, DARE-1, EIG, MENA, Bridge International, PEACE Cable, and SEACOM fiber-optic submarine cable systems providing links to Asia, the Middle East, Europe, Southeast Asia, Australia and Africa; satellite earth stations - 2 (1 Intelsat - Indian Ocean and 1 Arabsat) (2019)

Broadcast media: state-owned Radiodiffusion-Television de Djibouti operates the sole terrestrial TV station, as well as the only 2 domestic radio networks; no private TV or radio stations; transmissions of several international broadcasters are available (2019)

Internet country code: .dj

Internet users: *total:* 759,000 (2021 est.)
percent of population: 69% (2021 est.)
comparison ranking: total 157

Broadband - fixed subscriptions: *total:* 25,053 (2020 est.)
subscriptions per 100 inhabitants: 3 (2020 est.)
comparison ranking: total 159

TRANSPORTATION

National air transport system: *number of registered air carriers:* 2 (2020)
inventory of registered aircraft operated by air carriers: 4

Civil aircraft registration country code prefix: J2

Airports: 10 (2024)
comparison ranking: 159

Heliports: 6 (2024)

Railways: *total:* 97 km (2017) (Djibouti segment of the 756 km Addis Ababa-Djibouti railway)
standard gauge: 97 km (2017) 1.435-m gauge
comparison ranking: total 128

Roadways: *total:* 2,893 km (2013)
comparison ranking: total 165

Merchant marine: *total:* 40 (2023)
by type: bulk carrier 1, container ship 1, general cargo 4, oil tanker 13, other 21
comparison ranking: total 126

Ports: *total ports:* 2 (2024)
large: 0
medium: 0
small: 2
very small: 0
ports with oil terminals: 2
key ports: Djibouti, Doraleh

MILITARY AND SECURITY

Military and security forces: Djibouti Armed Forces (Forces Armées Djiboutiennes or FAD): Army, Navy, Air Force; Djibouti Coast Guard

Ministry of Interior: National Police (2024)
note: the National Police is responsible for security within Djibouti City and has primary control over immigration and customs procedures for all land border-crossing points, while the National Gendarmerie, which reports to the Ministry of Defense, is responsible for all security outside of Djibouti City, as well as for protecting critical infrastructure within the city, such as the international airport

Military expenditures: 3.5% of GDP (2019 est.)
3.5% of GDP (2018 est.)
3.3% of GDP (2017 est.)
2.7% of GDP (2016 est.)
2.5% of GDP (2015 est.)
comparison ranking: 24

Military and security service personnel strengths: approximately 10,000 active-duty military personnel; approximately 2,000 Gendarmerie (2023)

Military equipment inventories and acquisitions: the FAD's inventory includes mostly older French and Soviet-era weapons systems, although in recent years it has received limited amounts of more modern, but largely secondhand equipment from a variety of other countries, including China, the Netherlands, and the US (2023)

Military service age and obligation: 18 years of age for voluntary military service for men and women; 16-25 years of age for voluntary military training; no conscription (2023)

Military deployments: approximately 950 Somalia (ATMIS; note - ATMIS troop contingents are drawing down towards a final exit in December 2024); Djibouti has about 200 police deployed to the Central African Republic under MINUSCA (2024)

Military - note: Djibouti's military forces are largely focused on border, coastal, and internal security duties, such as counterterrorism; China, France, Italy, Japan, and the US maintain bases in Djibouti for regional military missions, including counterterrorism, counter-piracy, crisis response, and security assistance (note – France has multiple bases and hosts troop contingents from Germany and Spain); the EU and NATO also maintain a presence to support multinational naval counter-piracy operations and maritime training efforts (2023)

TERRORISM

Terrorist group(s): al-Shabaab
note: details about the history, aims, leadership, organization, areas of operation, tactics, targets, weapons, size, and sources of support of the group(s) appear(s) in the Terrorism reference guide

TRANSNATIONAL ISSUES

Refugees and internally displaced persons: *refugees (country of origin):* 6,518 (Yemen) (mid-year 2022); 13,467 (Somalia) (2024)

Trafficking in persons: tier rating: Tier 3 — Djibouti does not fully meet the minimum standards for the elimination of trafficking and is not making significant efforts to do so; therefore, Djibouti remained on Tier 3; for more details, go to: https://www.state.gov/reports/2024-trafficking-in-persons-report/djibouti/

DOMINICA

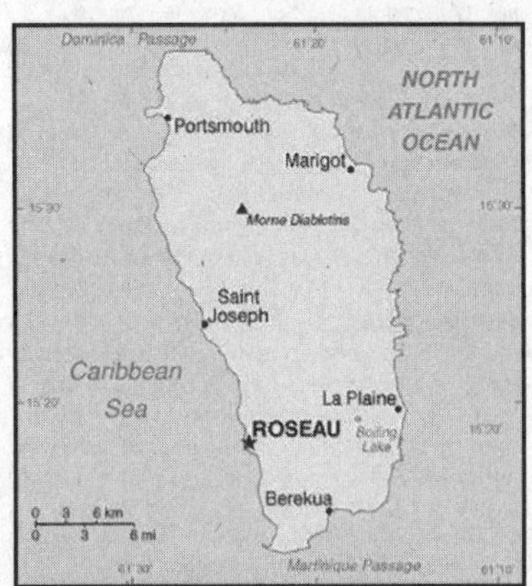

INTRODUCTION

Background: Dominica was the last of the Caribbean islands to be colonized by Europeans, due chiefly to the fierce resistance of the native Caribs. France ceded possession to Britain in 1763, and Dominica became a British colony in 1805. Slavery ended in 1833, and in 1835, the first three men of African descent were elected to the legislative assembly of Dominica. In 1871, Dominica became first part of the British Leeward Islands and then the British Windward Islands until 1958. In 1967, Dominica became an associated state of the UK, formally taking responsibility for its internal affairs, and the country gained its independence in 1978. In 1980, Dominica's fortunes improved when Mary Eugenia CHARLES – the first female prime minister in the Caribbean – replaced a corrupt and tyrannical administration, and she served for the next 15 years. In 2017, Hurricane Maria passed over the island, causing extensive damage to structures, roads, communications, and the power supply, and largely destroying critical agricultural areas.

GEOGRAPHY

Location: Caribbean, island between the Caribbean Sea and the North Atlantic Ocean, about halfway between Puerto Rico and Trinidad and Tobago

Geographic coordinates: 15 25 N, 61 20 W

Map references: Central America and the Caribbean

Area: *total:* 751 sq km
land: 751 sq km
water: NEGL
comparison ranking: total 188

Area - comparative: slightly more than four times the size of Washington, DC

Land boundaries: *total:* 0 km

Coastline: 148 km

Maritime claims: *territorial sea:* 12 nm
contiguous zone: 24 nm
exclusive economic zone: 200 nm

Climate: tropical; moderated by northeast trade winds; heavy rainfall

Terrain: rugged mountains of volcanic origin

Elevation: *highest point:* Morne Diablotins 1,447 m
lowest point: Caribbean Sea 0 m

Natural resources: timber, hydropower, arable land

Land use: *agricultural land:* 34.7% (2018 est.)
arable land: 8% (2018 est.)
permanent crops: 24% (2018 est.)
permanent pasture: 2.7% (2018 est.)
forest: 59.2% (2018 est.)
other: 6.1% (2018 est.)

Irrigated land: NA

Population distribution: population is mosly clustered along the coast, with roughly a third living in the parish of St. George, in or around the capital of Roseau; the volcanic interior is sparsely populated

Natural hazards: flash floods are a constant threat; destructive hurricanes can be expected during the late summer months
volcanism: Dominica was the last island to be formed in the Caribbean some 26 million years ago, it lies in the middle of the volcanic island arc of the Lesser Antilles that extends from the island of Saba in the north to Grenada in the south; of the 16 volcanoes that make up this arc, five are located on Dominica, more than any other island in the Caribbean: Morne aux Diables (861 m), Morne Diablotins (1,430 m), Morne Trois Pitons (1,387 m), Watt Mountain (1,224 m), which last erupted in 1997, and Morne Plat Pays (940 m); the two best known volcanic features on Dominica, the Valley of Desolation and the Boiling Lake thermal areas, lie on the flanks of Watt Mountain and both are popular tourist destinations

Geography - note: known as "The Nature Island of the Caribbean" due to its spectacular, lush, and varied flora and fauna, which are protected by an extensive natural park system; the most mountainous of the Lesser Antilles, its volcanic peaks are cones of lava craters and include Boiling Lake, the second-largest thermally active lake in the world

PEOPLE AND SOCIETY

Population: *total:* 74,661
male: 37,753
female: 36,908 (2024 est.)
comparison rankings: female 202; male 201; total 201

Nationality: *noun:* Dominican(s)
adjective: Dominican

Ethnic groups: African descent 84.5%, mixed 9%, Indigenous 3.8%, other 2.1%, unspecified 0.6% (2011 est.)

Languages: English (official), French patois

Religions: Roman Catholic 52.7%, Protestant 29.7% (includes Seventh Day Adventist 6.7%, Pentecostal 6.1%, Baptist 5.2%, Christian Union Church 3.9%, Methodist 2.6%, Gospel Mission 2.1%, other Protestant 3.1%), Jehovah's Witness 1.3%, Rastafarian 1.1%, other 4.3%, none 9.4%, unspecified 1.4% (2011 est.)

Age structure: *0-14 years:* 20.7% (male 7,891/female 7,530)
15-64 years: 65.6% (male 25,000/female 24,009)
65 years and over: 13.7% (2024 est.) (male 4,862/female 5,369)

Dependency ratios: *total dependency ratio:* 41.2
youth dependency ratio: 28
elderly dependency ratio: 13.2
potential support ratio: 7.6 (2021)

Median age: *total:* 37 years (2024 est.)
male: 36.5 years
female: 37.6 years
comparison ranking: total 84

Population growth rate: -0.01% (2024 est.)
comparison ranking: 196

Birth rate: 13.3 births/1,000 population (2024 est.)
comparison ranking: 129

Death rate: 8.1 deaths/1,000 population (2024 est.)
comparison ranking: 87

Net migration rate: -5.3 migrant(s)/1,000 population (2024 est.)
comparison ranking: 205

Population distribution: population is mosly clustered along the coast, with roughly a third living in the parish of St. George, in or around the capital of Roseau; the volcanic interior is sparsely populated

Urbanization: *urban population:* 72% of total population (2023)
rate of urbanization: 0.84% annual rate of change (2020-25 est.)

Major urban areas - population: 15,000 ROSEAU (capital) (2018)

Sex ratio: *at birth:* 1.05 male(s)/female
0-14 years: 1.05 male(s)/female
15-64 years: 1.04 male(s)/female
65 years and over: 0.91 male(s)/female
total population: 1.02 male(s)/female (2024 est.)

Infant mortality rate: *total:* 10.7 deaths/1,000 live births (2024 est.)
male: 14.5 deaths/1,000 live births
female: 6.8 deaths/1,000 live births
comparison ranking: total 127

Life expectancy at birth: *total population:* 78.7 years (2024 est.)
male: 75.8 years
female: 81.8 years
comparison ranking: total population 74

Total fertility rate: 2.01 children born/woman (2024 est.)
comparison ranking: 106

Gross reproduction rate: 0.98 (2024 est.)

Drinking water source: *improved: urban:* 95.7% of population
unimproved: urban: 4.3% of population

Current health expenditure: 5.7% of GDP (2020)

Physician density: 1.1 physicians/1,000 population (2018)

Hospital bed density: 3.8 beds/1,000 population

Obesity - adult prevalence rate: 27.9% (2016)
comparison ranking: 34

Alcohol consumption per capita: *total:* 6.32 liters of pure alcohol (2019 est.)
beer: 1.64 liters of pure alcohol (2019 est.)
wine: 0.29 liters of pure alcohol (2019 est.)
spirits: 4.39 liters of pure alcohol (2019 est.)
other alcohols: 0 liters of pure alcohol (2019 est.)
comparison ranking: total 67

Currently married women (ages 15-49): 40.3% (2023 est.)

Education expenditures: 5.5% of GDP (2021 est.)
comparison ranking: 57

People - note: 3,000-3,500 Kalinago (Carib) still living on Dominica are the only pre-Columbian population remaining in the Caribbean; only 70-100 may be "pure" Kalinago because of years of integration into the broader population

ENVIRONMENT

Environment - current issues: water shortages a continuing concern; pollution from agrochemicals and from untreated sewage; forests endangered by the expansion of farming; soil erosion; pollution of the coastal zone by agricultural and industrial chemicals, and untreated sewage

Environment - international agreements: *party to:* Biodiversity, Climate Change, Climate Change-Kyoto Protocol, Climate Change-Paris Agreement, Desertification, Endangered Species, Environmental Modification, Hazardous Wastes, Law of the Sea, Ozone Layer Protection, Ship Pollution, Whaling
signed, but not ratified: none of the selected agreements

Climate: tropical; moderated by northeast trade winds; heavy rainfall

Urbanization: *urban population:* 72% of total population (2023)
rate of urbanization: 0.84% annual rate of change (2020-25 est.)

Revenue from forest resources: 0.03% of GDP (2018 est.)
comparison ranking: 135

Revenue from coal: 0% of GDP (2018 est.)
comparison ranking: 162

Air pollutants: *particulate matter emissions:* 8.22 micrograms per cubic meter (2019 est.)
carbon dioxide emissions: 0.18 megatons (2016 est.)
methane emissions: 0.04 megatons (2020 est.)

Waste and recycling: *municipal solid waste generated annually:* 13,176 tons (2013 est.)

Total water withdrawal: *municipal:* 20 million cubic meters (2020 est.)
industrial: 0 cubic meters (2017 est.)
agricultural: 1 million cubic meters (2017 est.)

Total renewable water resources: 200 million cubic meters (2020 est.)

GOVERNMENT

Country name: *conventional long form:* Commonwealth of Dominica
conventional short form: Dominica
etymology: the island was named by explorer Christopher COLUMBUS for the day of the week on which he spotted it, Sunday ("Domingo" in Latin), 3 November 1493

Government type: parliamentary republic

Capital: *name:* Roseau
geographic coordinates: 15 18 N, 61 24 W
time difference: UTC-4 (1 hour ahead of Washington, DC, during Standard Time)
etymology: the name is French for "reed"; the first settlement was named after the river reeds that grew in the area

Administrative divisions: 10 parishes; Saint Andrew, Saint David, Saint George, Saint John, Saint Joseph, Saint Luke, Saint Mark, Saint Patrick, Saint Paul, Saint Peter

Independence: 3 November 1978 (from the UK)

National holiday: Independence Day, 3 November (1978)

Legal system: common law based on the English model

Constitution: *history:* previous 1967 (preindependence); latest presented 25 July 1978, entered into force 3 November 1978
amendments: proposed by the House of Assembly; passage of amendments to constitutional sections such as fundamental rights and freedoms, the government structure, and constitutional amendment procedures requires approval by three fourths of the Assembly membership in the final reading of the amendment bill, approval by simple majority in a referendum, and assent of the president; amended several times, last in 2015

International law organization participation: accepts compulsory ICJ jurisdiction; accepts ICCt jurisdiction

Citizenship: *citizenship by birth:* yes
citizenship by descent only: yes
dual citizenship recognized: yes
residency requirement for naturalization: 5 years

Suffrage: 18 years of age; universal

Executive branch: *chief of state:* President Sylvanie BURTON (since 2 October 2023)
head of government: Prime Minister Roosevelt SKERRIT (since 8 January 2004)
cabinet: Cabinet appointed by the president on the advice of the prime minister
elections/appointments: president nominated by the prime minister and leader of the opposition party and elected by the House of Assembly for a 5-year term (eligible for a second term); election last held on 27 September 2023 (next to be held in October 2028); prime minister appointed by the president
election results:
2023: parliament elects Sylvanie BURTON (DLP) with 20 votes for and five against
2018: Charles A. SAVARIN (DLP) reelected president unopposed

Legislative branch: *description:* unicameral House of Assembly (32 seats; 21 representatives directly elected in single-seat constituencies by simple majority vote, 9 senators appointed by the president - 5 on the advice of the prime minister, and 4 on the advice of the leader of the opposition party, plus 2 ex-officio members - the house speaker and the attorney general; members serve 5-year terms)
elections: last held on 6 December 2022 (next to be held in 2027); note - tradition dictates that the election is held within 5 years of the last election, but technically it is 5 years from the first seating of parliament plus a 90-day grace period
election results: percent of vote by party - DLP 82.3%, independent 16.9%; (elected) seats by party - DLP 19, independent 2; composition - men 20, women 12, percent of women 37.5%

Judicial branch: *highest court(s):* the Eastern Caribbean Supreme Court (ECSC) is the superior court of the Organization of Eastern Caribbean States; the ECSC - headquartered on St. Lucia - consists of the Court of Appeal - headed by the chief justice and 4 judges - and the High Court with 18 judges; the Court of Appeal is itinerant, traveling to member states on a schedule to hear appeals from the High Court and subordinate courts; High Court judges reside in the member states, with 2 in Dominica; note - in 2015, Dominica acceded to the Caribbean Court of Justice as final court of appeal, replacing that of the Judicial Committee of the Privy Council, in London
judge selection and term of office: chief justice of Eastern Caribbean Supreme Court appointed by the Her Majesty, Queen ELIZABETH II; other justices and judges appointed by the Judicial and Legal Services Commission, an independent body of judicial officials; Court of Appeal justices appointed for life with mandatory retirement at age 65; High Court judges appointed for life with mandatory retirement at age 62
subordinate courts: Court of Summary Jurisdiction; magistrates' courts

Political parties: Dominica Freedom Party or DFP
Dominica Labor Party or DLP
Dominica United Workers Party or UWP

International organization participation: ACP, ACS, AOSIS, C, Caricom, CD, CDB, CELAC, Commonwealth of Nations, ECCU, FAO, G-77, IAEA, IBRD, ICCt, ICRM, IDA, IFAD, IFC, IFRCS, ILO, IMF, IMO, Interpol, IOC, ISO (correspondent), ITU, ITUC (NGOs), MIGA, NAM, OAS, OECS, OIF, OPANAL, OPCW, Petrocaribe, UN, UNCTAD, UNESCO, UNIDO, UPU, WFTU, WHO, WIPO, WMO, WTO

Diplomatic representation in the US: *chief of mission:* Ambassador Steve FERROL (since 15 September 2023)
chancery: 3216 New Mexico Ave NW Washington, DC 20016
telephone: [1] (202) 364-6781
FAX: [1] (202) 364-6791
email address and website:
embdomdc@gmail.com
consulate(s) general: New York

Diplomatic representation from the US: *embassy:* the US does not have an embassy in Dominica; the US Ambassador to Barbados is accredited to Dominica

Flag description: green with a centered cross of three equal bands - the vertical part is yellow (hoist side), black, and white and the horizontal part is yellow (top), black, and white; superimposed in the center of the cross is a red disk bearing a Sisserou parrot, unique to Dominica, encircled by 10 green, five-pointed stars edged in yellow; the 10 stars represent the 10 administrative divisions (parishes); green symbolizes the island's lush vegetation; the triple-colored cross represents the Christian Trinity; the yellow color denotes sunshine, the main agricultural products (citrus and bananas), and the native Carib Indians; black is for the rich soil and the African heritage of most citizens; white signifies rivers, waterfalls, and the purity of aspirations; the red disc stands for social justice

National symbol(s): Sisserou parrot, Carib Wood flower; national colors: green, yellow, black, white, red

National anthem: *name:* "Isle of Beauty"
lyrics/music: Wilfred Oscar Morgan POND/Lemuel McPherson CHRISTIAN
note: adopted 1967

National heritage: *total World Heritage Sites:* 1 (natural)
selected World Heritage Site locales: Pitons Management Area

ECONOMY

Economic overview: highly agrarian OECS island economy; ECCU-member state; large banana exporter; improved oversight of its citizenship-by-investment program; emerging ecotourism, information and communications, and education industries

Real GDP (purchasing power parity): $1.159 billion (2023 est.)
$1.106 billion (2022 est.)
$1.048 billion (2021 est.)
note: data in 2021 dollars
comparison ranking: 208

Real GDP growth rate: 4.71% (2023 est.)
5.58% (2022 est.)
6.89% (2021 est.)
note: annual GDP % growth based on constant local currency
comparison ranking: 62

Real GDP per capita: $15,900 (2023 est.)
$15,200 (2022 est.)
$14,500 (2021 est.)
note: data in 2021 dollars
comparison ranking: 117

GDP (official exchange rate): $653.993 million (2023 est.)
note: data in current dollars at official exchange rate

Inflation rate (consumer prices): 3.48% (2023 est.)
7.78% (2022 est.)
1.48% (2021 est.)
note: annual % change based on consumer prices
comparison ranking: 66

GDP - composition, by sector of origin: *agriculture:* 14.8% (2023 est.)
industry: 12.2% (2023 est.)
services: 58.5% (2023 est.)
note: figures may not total 100% due to non-allocated consumption not captured in sector-reported data
comparison rankings: services 96; industry 178; agriculture 57

GDP - composition, by end use: *household consumption:* 87.7% (2018 est.)
government consumption: 27.4% (2018 est.)
investment in fixed capital: 32.7% (2018 est.)
exports of goods and services: 29.2% (2018 est.)
imports of goods and services: -77.8% (2018 est.)
note: figures may not total 100% due to rounding or gaps in data collection

Agricultural products: taro, grapefruits, yams, bananas, plantains, coconuts, milk, yautia, oranges, sugarcane (2022)
note: top ten agricultural products based on tonnage

Industries: soap, coconut oil, tourism, copra, furniture, cement blocks, shoes

Industrial production growth rate: 5.01% (2023 est.)
note: annual % change in industrial value added based on constant local currency
comparison ranking: 50

Remittances: 9.05% of GDP (2023 est.)
6.22% of GDP (2022 est.)
7.24% of GDP (2021 est.)
note: personal transfers and compensation between resident and non-resident individuals/households/entities

Budget: *revenues:* $233.831 million (2017 est.)
expenditures: $164.673 million (2017 est.)
note: central government revenues and expenses (excluding grants/extrabudgetary units/social security funds) converted to US dollars at average official exchange rate for year indicated

Public debt: 82.7% of GDP (2017 est.)
comparison ranking: 34

Taxes and other revenues: 40.9% (of GDP) (2017 est.)
comparison ranking: 9

Current account balance: -$221.939 million (2023 est.)
-$162.036 million (2022 est.)
-$182.647 million (2021 est.)
note: balance of payments - net trade and primary/secondary income in current dollars
comparison ranking: 111

Exports: $185.062 million (2023 est.)
$174.041 million (2022 est.)
$117.709 million (2021 est.)
note: balance of payments - exports of goods and services in current dollars
comparison ranking: 205

Exports - partners: Bahamas, The 12%, Guyana 8%, Antigua and Barbuda 7%, Dominican Republic 7%, Barbados 6% (2022)
note: top five export partners based on percentage share of exports

Exports - commodities: power equipment, soap, raw iron bars, natural gas, tropical fruits (2022)
note: top five export commodities based on value in dollars

Imports: $414.13 million (2023 est.)
$350.982 million (2022 est.)
$313.729 million (2021 est.)
note: balance of payments - imports of goods and services in current dollars
comparison ranking: 206

Imports - partners: US 51%, China 9%, Indonesia 4%, Trinidad and Tobago 4%, Italy 3% (2022)
note: top five import partners based on percentage share of imports

Imports - commodities: refined petroleum, natural gas, crude petroleum, plastic products, cars (2022)
note: top five import commodities based on value in dollars

Reserves of foreign exchange and gold: $183.53 million (2023 est.)
$204.343 million (2022 est.)
$190.843 million (2021 est.)
note: holdings of gold (year-end prices)/foreign exchange/special drawing rights in current dollars
comparison ranking: 185

Debt - external: $282.847 million (2022 est.)
note: present value of external debt in current US dollars
comparison ranking: 95

Exchange rates: East Caribbean dollars (XCD) per US dollar -

Exchange rates: 2.7 (2023 est.)
2.7 (2022 est.)
2.7 (2021 est.)
2.7 (2020 est.)
2.7 (2019 est.)

ENERGY

Electricity access: *electrification - total population:* 100% (2022 est.)

Electricity: *installed generating capacity:* 42,000 kW (2022 est.)
consumption: 162.827 million kWh (2022 est.)
transmission/distribution losses: 8 million kWh (2022 est.)
comparison rankings: transmission/distribution losses 14; consumption 192; installed generating capacity 197

Electricity generation sources: *fossil fuels:* 75.9% of total installed capacity (2022 est.)
solar: 0.1% of total installed capacity (2022 est.)
wind: 0.6% of total installed capacity (2022 est.)
hydroelectricity: 23.4% of total installed capacity (2022 est.)

Petroleum: *refined petroleum consumption:* 1,000 bbl/day (2022 est.)

Carbon dioxide emissions: 175,000 metric tonnes of CO2 (2022 est.)
from petroleum and other liquids: 175,000 metric tonnes of CO2 (2022 est.)
comparison ranking: total emissions 205

Energy consumption per capita: 35.086 million Btu/person (2022 est.)
comparison ranking: 107

COMMUNICATIONS

Telephones - fixed lines: *total subscriptions:* 7,000 (2021 est.)
subscriptions per 100 inhabitants: 10 (2021 est.)
comparison ranking: total subscriptions 196

Telephones - mobile cellular: *total subscriptions:* 62,000 (2021 est.)
subscriptions per 100 inhabitants: 86 (2021 est.)
comparison ranking: total subscriptions 204

Telecommunication systems: *general assessment:* the telecom sector has seen a decline in subscriber numbers (particularly for prepaid mobile services the mainstay of short term visitors) and revenue; fixed and mobile broadband services are two areas that have benefited from the crisis as employees and students have resorted to working from home; one area of the telecom market that is not prepared for growth

is 5G mobile; governments, regulators, and even the mobile network operators have shown that they have not been investing in 5G opportunities at the present time; network expansion and enhancements remain concentrated around improving LTE coverage (2021)
domestic: 10 fixed-line connections per 100 persons; mobile-cellular subscriptions are about 86 per 100 persons (2021)
international: country code - 1-767; landing points for the ECFS and the Southern Caribbean Fiber submarine cables providing connectivity to other islands in the eastern Caribbean extending from the British Virgin Islands to Trinidad and to the US; microwave radio relay and SHF radiotelephone links to Martinique and Guadeloupe; VHF and UHF radiotelephone links to Saint Lucia (2019)

Broadcast media: no terrestrial TV service available; subscription cable TV provider offers some locally produced programming plus channels from the US, Latin America, and the Caribbean; state-operated radio broadcasts on 6 stations; privately owned radio broadcasts on about 15 stations (2019)

Internet country code: .dm

Internet users: *total:* 58,320 (2021 est.)
percent of population: 81% (2021 est.)
comparison ranking: total 198

Broadband - fixed subscriptions: *total:* 16,000 (2020 est.)
subscriptions per 100 inhabitants: 22 (2020 est.)
comparison ranking: total 172

TRANSPORTATION

Civil aircraft registration country code prefix: J7

Airports: 2 (2024)
comparison ranking: 202

Roadways: *total:* 1,512 km
paved: 762 km
*unpaved:*750 km (2018)
comparison ranking: total 176

Merchant marine: *total:* 77 (2023)
by type: general cargo 26, oil tanker 10, other 41
comparison ranking: total 101

Ports: *total ports:* 2 (2024)
large: 0
medium: 0
small: 0
very small: 2
ports with oil terminals: 1
key ports: Portsmouth, Roseau

MILITARY AND SECURITY

Military and security forces: no regular military forces; Commonwealth of Dominica Police Force (includes Coast Guard) under the Ministry of Justice, Immigration, and National Security (2024)

Military - note: Dominica has been a member of the Caribbean Regional Security System (RSS) since its creation in 1982; RSS signatories (Antigua and Barbuda, Barbados, Grenada, Guyana, St. Kitts and Nevis, St. Lucia, and St. Vincent and the Grenadines) agreed to prepare contingency plans and assist one another, on request, in national emergencies, prevention of smuggling, search and rescue, immigration control, fishery protection, customs and excise control, maritime policing duties, protection of off-shore installations, pollution control, national and other disasters, and threats to national security (2024)

TRANSNATIONAL ISSUES

Illicit drugs: a transit point for cocaine and marijuana destined for North America, Europe, and elsewhere in the Caribbean; some local demand for cocaine and some use of synthetic drugs

DOMINICAN REPUBLIC

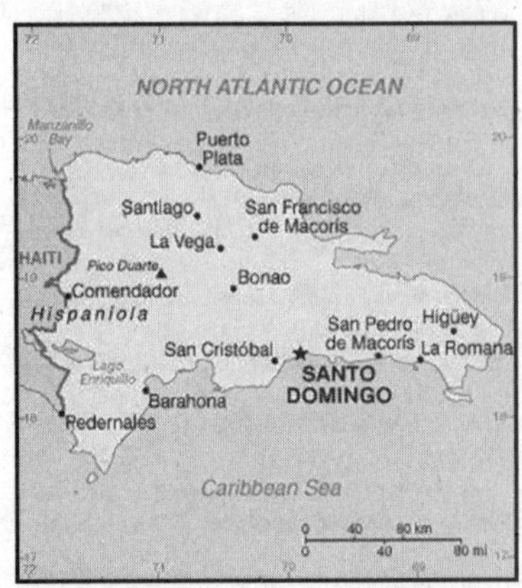

INTRODUCTION

Background: The Taino – indigenous inhabitants of Hispaniola prior to the arrival of Europeans – divided the island now known as the Dominican Republic and Haiti into five chiefdoms and territories. Christopher COLUMBUS explored and claimed the island on his first voyage in 1492; it became a springboard for Spanish conquest of the Caribbean and the American mainland. In 1697, Spain recognized French dominion over the western third of the island, which in 1804 became Haiti. The remainder of the island, by then known as Santo Domingo, sought to gain its own independence in 1821, but the Haitians conquered and ruled it for 22 years; it finally attained independence as the Dominican Republic in 1844. In 1861, the Dominicans voluntarily returned to the Spanish Empire, but two years later, they launched a war that restored independence in 1865.

A legacy of unsettled and mostly non-representative rule followed, capped by the dictatorship of Rafael Leonidas TRUJILLO from 1930 to 1961. Juan BOSCH was elected president in 1962 but was deposed in a military coup in 1963. In 1965, the US led an intervention in the midst of a civil war sparked by an uprising to restore BOSCH. In 1966, Joaquin BALAGUER defeated BOSCH in the presidential election. BALAGUER maintained a tight grip on power for most of the next 30 years, until international reaction to flawed elections forced him to curtail his term in 1996. Since then, regular competitive elections have been held.

GEOGRAPHY

Location: Caribbean, eastern two-thirds of the island of Hispaniola, between the Caribbean Sea and the North Atlantic Ocean, east of Haiti

Geographic coordinates: 19 00 N, 70 40 W

Map references: Central America and the Caribbean

Area: *total:* 48,670 sq km
land: 48,320 sq km
water: 350 sq km
comparison ranking: total 131

Area - comparative: slightly more than twice the size of New Jersey

Land boundaries: *total:* 376 km
border countries (1): Haiti 376 km

Coastline: 1,288 km

Maritime claims: *territorial sea:* 12 nm
contiguous zone: 24 nm
exclusive economic zone: 200 nm
continental shelf: 200 nm or to the edge of the continental margin
measured from claimed archipelagic straight baselines

Climate: tropical maritime; little seasonal temperature variation; seasonal variation in rainfall

Terrain: rugged highlands and mountains interspersed with fertile valleys

Elevation: *highest point:* Pico Duarte 3,098 m
lowest point: Lago Enriquillo -46 m
mean elevation: 424 m

Natural resources: nickel, bauxite, gold, silver, arable land

Land use: *agricultural land:* 51.5% (2018 est.)
arable land: 16.6% (2018 est.)
permanent crops: 10.1% (2018 est.)
permanent pasture: 24.8% (2018 est.)
forest: 40.8% (2018 est.)
other: 7.7% (2018 est.)

Irrigated land: 2,980 sq km (2018)

Major lakes (area sq km): *salt water lake(s):* Lago de Enriquillo - 500 sq km

Population distribution: coastal development is significant, especially in the southern coastal plains and the Cibao Valley, where population density is highest; smaller population clusters exist in the interior mountains (Cordillera Central)

Natural hazards: lies in the middle of the hurricane belt and subject to severe storms from June to October; occasional flooding; periodic droughts

Geography - note: shares island of Hispaniola with Haiti (eastern two-thirds makes up the Dominican Republic, western one-third is Haiti); the second largest country in the Antilles (after Cuba); geographically diverse with the Caribbean's tallest mountain, Pico Duarte, and lowest elevation and largest lake, Lago Enriquillo

PEOPLE AND SOCIETY

Population: *total:* 10,815,857
male: 5,465,776
female: 5,350,081 (2024 est.)
comparison rankings: female 87; male 86; total 87

Nationality: *noun:* Dominican(s)
adjective: Dominican

Ethnic groups: mixed 70.4% (Mestizo/Indio 58%, Mulatto 12.4%), Black 15.8%, White 13.5%, other 0.3% (2014 est.)
note: respondents self-identified their race; the term "indio" in the Dominican Republic is not associated with people of indigenous ancestry but people of mixed ancestry or skin color between light and dark

Languages: Spanish (official)
major-language sample(s):
La Libreta Informativa del Mundo, la fuente indispensable de información básica. (Spanish)

Religions: Evangelical 50.2%, Roman Catholic 30.1%, none 18.5%, unspecified 1.2% (2023 est.)

Age structure: *0-14 years:* 25.5% (male 1,402,847/female 1,358,833)
15-64 years: 66.9% (male 3,667,584/female 3,563,848)
65 years and over: 7.6% (2024 est.) (male 395,345/female 427,400)

Dependency ratios: *total dependency ratio:* 53.8
youth dependency ratio: 42.2
elderly dependency ratio: 11.6
potential support ratio: 8.6 (2021 est.)

Median age: *total:* 29.2 years (2024 est.)
male: 29.1 years
female: 29.4 years
comparison ranking: total 145

Population growth rate: 0.76% (2024 est.)
comparison ranking: 115

Birth rate: 17.3 births/1,000 population (2024 est.)
comparison ranking: 87

Death rate: 7.1 deaths/1,000 population (2024 est.)
comparison ranking: 118

Net migration rate: -2.7 migrant(s)/1,000 population (2024 est.)
comparison ranking: 175

Population distribution: coastal development is significant, especially in the southern coastal plains and the Cibao Valley, where population density is highest; smaller population clusters exist in the interior mountains (Cordillera Central)

Urbanization: *urban population:* 84.4% of total population (2023)
rate of urbanization: 1.64% annual rate of change (2020-25 est.)

Major urban areas - population: 3.524 million SANTO DOMINGO (capital) (2023)

Sex ratio: *at birth:* 1.04 male(s)/female
0-14 years: 1.03 male(s)/female
15-64 years: 1.03 male(s)/female
65 years and over: 0.93 male(s)/female
total population: 1.02 male(s)/female (2024 est.)

Mother's mean age at first birth: 20.9 years (2013 est.)
note: data represents median age at first birth among women 25-49

Maternal mortality ratio: 107 deaths/100,000 live births (2020 est.)
comparison ranking: 67

Infant mortality rate: *total:* 21.7 deaths/1,000 live births (2024 est.)
male: 24.3 deaths/1,000 live births
female: 19 deaths/1,000 live births
comparison ranking: total 74

Life expectancy at birth: *total population:* 72.6 years (2024 est.)
male: 71 years
female: 74.3 years
comparison ranking: total population 160

Total fertility rate: 2.15 children born/woman (2024 est.)
comparison ranking: 92

Gross reproduction rate: 1.06 (2024 est.)

Contraceptive prevalence rate: 62.8% (2019)

Drinking water source: *improved: urban:* 98.3% of population
rural: 91.7% of population
total: 97.2% of population
unimproved: urban: 1.7% of population
rural: 8.3% of population
total: 2.8% of population (2020 est.)

Current health expenditure: 4.9% of GDP (2020)

Physician density: 1.45 physicians/1,000 population (2019)

Hospital bed density: 1.6 beds/1,000 population (2017)

Sanitation facility access: *improved: urban:* 97.4% of population
rural: 91.3% of population
total: 96.3% of population
unimproved: urban: 2.6% of population
rural: 8.7% of population
total: 3.7% of population (2020 est.)

Obesity - adult prevalence rate: 27.6% (2016)
comparison ranking: 37

Alcohol consumption per capita: *total:* 5.56 liters of pure alcohol (2019 est.)
beer: 3.15 liters of pure alcohol (2019 est.)
wine: 0.17 liters of pure alcohol (2019 est.)
spirits: 2.18 liters of pure alcohol (2019 est.)
other alcohols: 0.06 liters of pure alcohol (2019 est.)
comparison ranking: total 78

Tobacco use: *total:* 10.6% (2020 est.)
male: 14.6% (2020 est.)
female: 6.5% (2020 est.)
comparison ranking: total 135

Children under the age of 5 years underweight: 3% (2019)
comparison ranking: 89

Currently married women (ages 15-49): 52.1% (2023 est.)

Child marriage: *women married by age 15:* 9.4%
women married by age 18: 31.5% (2019 est.)

Education expenditures: 4.6% of GDP (2020 est.)
comparison ranking: 93

Literacy: *definition:* age 15 and over can read and write
total population: 95.5%
male: 95.4%
female: 95.6% (2022)

School life expectancy (primary to tertiary education): *total:* 14 years
male: 13 years
female: 15 years (2017)

ENVIRONMENT

Environment - current issues: water shortages; soil eroding into the sea damages coral reefs; deforestation

Environment - international agreements: *party to:* Biodiversity, Climate Change, Climate Change-Kyoto Protocol, Climate Change-Paris Agreement, Comprehensive Nuclear Test Ban, Desertification, Endangered Species, Hazardous Wastes, Law of the Sea, Marine Dumping-London Convention, Marine Life Conservation, Nuclear Test Ban, Ozone Layer Protection, Ship Pollution, Wetlands, Whaling
signed, but not ratified: none of the selected agreements

Climate: tropical maritime; little seasonal temperature variation; seasonal variation in rainfall

Urbanization: *urban population:* 84.4% of total population (2023)
rate of urbanization: 1.64% annual rate of change (2020-25 est.)

Revenue from forest resources: 0.03% of GDP (2018 est.)
comparison ranking: 133

Revenue from coal: 0% of GDP (2018 est.)
comparison ranking: 176

Air pollutants: *particulate matter emissions:* 7.59 micrograms per cubic meter (2019 est.)
carbon dioxide emissions: 25.26 megatons (2016 est.)
methane emissions: 8.1 megatons (2020 est.)

Waste and recycling: *municipal solid waste generated annually:* 4,063,910 tons (2015 est.)
municipal solid waste recycled annually: 333,241 tons (2015 est.)
percent of municipal solid waste recycled: 8.2% (2015 est.)

Major lakes (area sq km): *salt water lake(s):* Lago de Enriquillo - 500 sq km

Total water withdrawal: *municipal:* 860 million cubic meters (2020 est.)
industrial: 660 million cubic meters (2020 est.)
agricultural: 7.56 billion cubic meters (2020 est.)

Total renewable water resources: 23.5 billion cubic meters (2020 est.)

GOVERNMENT

Country name: *conventional long form:* Dominican Republic
conventional short form: The Dominican
local long form: República Dominicana
local short form: La Dominicana
former: Santo Domingo (the capital city's name formerly applied to the entire country)
etymology: the country name derives from the capital city of Santo Domingo (Saint Dominic)

Government type: presidential republic

Capital: *name:* Santo Domingo
geographic coordinates: 18 28 N, 69 54 W
time difference: UTC-4 (1 hour ahead of Washington, DC, during Standard Time)
etymology: named after Saint Dominic de GUZMAN (1170-1221), founder of the Dominican Order

Administrative divisions: 10 regions (regiones, singular - region); Cibao Nordeste, Cibao Noroeste, Cibao Norte, Cibao Sur, El Valle, Enriquillo, Higuamo, Ozama, Valdesia, Yuma

Independence: 27 February 1844 (from Haiti)

National holiday: Independence Day, 27 February (1844)

Legal system: civil law system based on the French civil code; Criminal Procedures Code modified in 2004 to include important elements of an accusatory system

Constitution: *history:* many previous (38 total); latest proclaimed 13 June 2015
amendments: proposed by a special session of the National Congress called the National Revisory Assembly; passage requires at least two-thirds majority approval by at least one half of those present in both houses of the Assembly; passage of amendments to constitutional articles, such as fundamental rights and guarantees, territorial composition, nationality, or the procedures for constitutional reform, also requires approval in a referendum

International law organization participation: accepts compulsory ICJ jurisdiction; accepts ICCt jurisdiction

Citizenship: *citizenship by birth:* no
citizenship by descent only: at least one parent must be a citizen of the Dominican Republic
dual citizenship recognized: yes
residency requirement for naturalization: 2 years

Suffrage: 18 years of age; universal and compulsory; married persons regardless of age can vote; note - members of the armed forces and national police by law cannot vote

Executive branch: *chief of state:* President Luis Rodolfo ABINADER Corona (since 16 August 2020)
head of government: President Luis Rodolfo ABINADER Corona (since 16 August 2020)
cabinet: Cabinet nominated by the president
elections/appointments: president and vice president directly elected on the same ballot by absolute vote in 2 rounds if needed for a 4-year term (eligible for a maximum of two consecutive terms); election last held on 19 May 2024 (next to be held on 21 May 2028)
election results:
2024: Luis Rodolfo ABINADER Corona reelected president; percent of vote - Luis Rodolfo ABINADER Corona (PRM) 57.5%, Leonel Antonio FERNÁNDEZ Reyna (FP) 28.8%, Abel MARTÍNEZ (PLD) 10.4%, other 3.3%
2020: Luis Rodolfo ABINADER Corona elected president in first round; percent of vote - Luis Rodolfo ABINADER Corona (PRM) 52.5%, Gonzalo CASTILLO Terrero (PLD) 37.5%, Leonel Antonio FERNÁNDEZ Reyna (FP) 8.9%, other 1.1%
note: the president is both chief of state and head of government

Legislative branch: *description:* bicameral National Congress or Congreso Nacional consists of:
Senate or Senado (32 seats; 26 members directly elected in single-seat constituencies by simple majority vote, and 6 members indirectly elected based upon province-wide party plurality votes for its candidates to the Chamber of Deputies; all members serve 4-year terms; note - in 2019, the Central Election Commission changed the electoral system for seats in 26 constituencies to simple majority vote but retained indirect election for the remaining 6 constituencies; previously, all 32 members were indirectly elected; the change had been challenged by the ruling and opposition parties)
House of Representatives or Camara de Diputados (190 seats; 178 members directly elected in multi-seat constituencies by closed party-list proportional representation vote using the D'Hondt method, 5 members in a nationwide constituency, and 7 diaspora members directly elected by simple majority vote; members serve 4-year terms)
elections: Senate - last held on 19 May 2024 (next to be held on 21 May 2028)
House of Representatives - last held on 19 May 2024 (next to be held on 21 May 2028)
election results: Senate - percent of vote by party - NA; seats by party - PRM 24, FP 3, APD 1, PPG 1, PRI 1, PRL 1, PRSC 1; composition - men NA, women NA, percentage women NA%
House of Representatives - percent of vote by party - NA; seats by party - PRM 142, FP 28, PLD 13, PRSC 2, other 5; composition - men NA, women NA, percentage women NA%; total National Congress percent of women NA%

Judicial branch: *highest court(s):* Supreme Court of Justice or Suprema Corte de Justicia (consists of a minimum of 16 magistrates); Constitutional Court or Tribunal Constitucional (consists of 13 judges); note - the Constitutional Court was established in 2010 by constitutional amendment
judge selection and term of office: Supreme Court and Constitutional Court judges appointed by the National Council of the Judiciary comprised of the president, the leaders of both chambers of congress, the president of the Supreme Court, and a non-governing party congressional representative; Supreme Court judges appointed for 7-year terms; Constitutional Court judges appointed for 9-year terms
subordinate courts: courts of appeal; courts of first instance; justices of the peace; special courts for juvenile, labor, and land cases; Contentious Administrative Court for cases filed against the government

Political parties: Alliance for Democracy or APD
Broad Front (Frente Amplio)
Country Alliance or AP
Dominican Liberation Party or PLD
Dominican Revolutionary Party or PRD
Dominicans For Change or DXC
Independent Revolutionary Party or PRI
Institutional Social Democratic Bloc or BIS
Liberal Reformist Party or PRL (formerly the Liberal Party of the Dominican Republic or PLRD)
Modern Revolutionary Party or PRM
National Progressive Front or FNP
People's First Party or PPG
People's Force or FP
Social Christian Reformist Party or PRSC

International organization participation: ACP, ACS, AOSIS, BCIE, Caricom (observer), CD, CELAC, FAO, G-77, IADB, IAEA, IBRD, ICAO, ICC (national committees), ICCt, ICRM, IDA, IFAD, IFC, IFRCS, IHO, ILO, IMF, IMO, Interpol, IOC, IOM, IPU, ISO (correspondent), ITSO, ITU, ITUC (NGOs), LAES, LAIA, MIGA, MINUSMA, NAM, OAS, OIF (observer), OPANAL, OPCW, Pacific Alliance (observer), PCA, Petrocaribe, SICA (associated member), UN, UNCTAD, UNESCO, UNHRC, UNIDO, Union Latina, UNOOSA, UNWTO, UPU, WCO, WFTU (NGOs), WHO, WIPO, WMO, WTO

Diplomatic representation in the US: *chief of mission:* Ambassador Sonia GUZMÁN DE HERNÁNDEZ (since 18 January 2021)
chancery: 1715 22nd Street NW, Washington, DC 20008
telephone: [1] (202) 332-6280
FAX: [1] (202) 265-8057
email address and website:
embassy@drembassyusa.org
http://drembassyusa.org/
consulate(s) general: Boston, Chicago, Houston, Los Angelos, Miami, New Jersey, New Orleans, New York, Orlando, Philadelphia

Diplomatic representation from the US: *chief of mission:* Ambassador (vacant); Chargé d'Affaires Patricia AGUILERA (since 1 October 2023)
embassy: Av. Republica de Colombia #57, Santo Domingo
mailing address: 3470 Santo Domingo Place, Washington DC 20521-3470
telephone: (809) 567-7775
email address and website:
SDOAmericans@state.gov
https://do.usembassy.gov/

Flag description: a centered white cross that extends to the edges divides the flag into four rectangles - the top ones are ultramarine blue (hoist side) and vermilion red, and the bottom ones are vermilion red (hoist side) and ultramarine blue; a small coat of arms featuring a shield supported by a laurel branch (left) and a palm branch (right) is at the center of the cross; above the shield a blue ribbon displays the motto, DIOS, PATRIA, LIBERTAD (God, Fatherland, Liberty), and below the shield, REPUBLICA DOMINICANA appears on a red ribbon; in the shield a bible is opened to a verse that reads "Y la verdad nos hara libre" (And the truth shall set you free); blue stands for liberty, white for salvation, and red for the blood of heroes

National symbol(s): palmchat (bird); national colors: red, white, blue

National anthem: *name:* "Himno Nacional" (National Anthem)
lyrics/music: Emilio PRUD'HOMME/Jose REYES
note: adopted 1934; also known as "Quisqueyanos valientes" (Valient Sons of Quisqueye); the anthem never refers to the people as Dominican but rather calls them "Quisqueyanos," a reference to the indigenous name of the island

National heritage: *total World Heritage Sites:* 1 (cultural)
selected World Heritage Site locales: Colonial City of Santo Domingo

ECONOMY

Economic overview: surging middle-income tourism, construction, mining, and telecommunications OECS economy; major foreign US direct investment and free-trade zones; developing local financial markets; improving debt management; declining poverty

Real GDP (purchasing power parity): $261.616 billion (2023 est.)
$255.582 billion (2022 est.)
$243.74 billion (2021 est.)
note: data in 2021 dollars
comparison ranking: 66

Real GDP growth rate: 2.36% (2023 est.)
4.86% (2022 est.)
12.27% (2021 est.)
note: annual GDP % growth based on constant local currency
comparison ranking: 129

Real GDP per capita: $23,100 (2023 est.)
$22,800 (2022 est.)

$21,900 (2021 est.)
note: data in 2021 dollars
comparison ranking: 91

GDP (official exchange rate): $121.444 billion (2023 est.)
note: data in current dollars at official exchange rate

Inflation rate (consumer prices): 4.79% (2023 est.)
8.81% (2022 est.)
8.24% (2021 est.)
note: annual % change based on consumer prices
comparison ranking: 100

Credit ratings: Fitch rating: BB- (2016)

Moody's rating: Ba3 (2017)

Standard & Poors rating: BB- (2015)
note: The year refers to the year in which the current credit rating was first obtained.

GDP - composition, by sector of origin: *agriculture:* 6.4% (2023 est.)
industry: 31.1% (2023 est.)
services: 56% (2023 est.)
note: figures may not total 100% due to non-allocated consumption not captured in sector-reported data
comparison rankings: services 114; industry 60; agriculture 102

GDP - composition, by end use: *household consumption:* 64.7% (2023 est.)
government consumption: 11.3% (2023 est.)
investment in fixed capital: 32.2% (2023 est.)
investment in inventories: -0.9% (2023 est.)
exports of goods and services: 21.1% (2023 est.)
imports of goods and services: -28.5% (2023 est.)
note: figures may not total 100% due to rounding or gaps in data collection

Agricultural products: sugarcane, bananas, papayas, plantains, rice, milk, avocados, watermelons, vegetables, pineapples (2022)
note: top ten agricultural products based on tonnage

Industries: tourism, sugar processing, gold mining, textiles, cement, tobacco, electrical components, medical devices

Industrial production growth rate: -0.07% (2023 est.)
note: annual % change in industrial value added based on constant local currency
comparison ranking: 155

Labor force: 5.302 million (2023 est.)
note: number of people ages 15 or older who are employed or seeking work
comparison ranking: 82

Unemployment rate: 5.56% (2023 est.)
5.5% (2022 est.)
7.7% (2021 est.)
note: % of labor force seeking employment
comparison ranking: 108

Youth unemployment rate (ages 15-24): *total:* 11.8% (2023 est.)
male: 9.5% (2023 est.)
female: 15.4% (2023 est.)
note: % of labor force ages 15-24 seeking employment
comparison ranking: total 115

Population below poverty line: 23.9% (2021 est.)
note: % of population with income below national poverty line

Gini Index coefficient - distribution of family income: 37 (2022 est.)
note: index (0-100) of income distribution; higher values represent greater inequality
comparison ranking: 62

Average household expenditures: *on food:* 26.6% of household expenditures (2022 est.)
on alcohol and tobacco: 3.8% of household expenditures (2022 est.)

Household income or consumption by percentage share: *lowest 10%:* 2.6% (2022 est.)
highest 10%: 28.3% (2022 est.)
note: % share of income accruing to lowest and highest 10% of population

Remittances: 8.65% of GDP (2023 est.)
9.05% of GDP (2022 est.)
11.4% of GDP (2021 est.)
note: personal transfers and compensation between resident and non-resident individuals/households/entities

Budget: *revenues:* $18.303 billion (2022 est.)
expenditures: $20.072 billion (2022 est.)
note: central government revenues (excluding grants) and expenses converted to US dollars at average official exchange rate for year indicated

Public debt: 37.2% of GDP (2017 est.)
comparison ranking: 140

Taxes and other revenues: 13.82% (of GDP) (2022 est.)
note: central government tax revenue as a % of GDP
comparison ranking: 149

Current account balance: -$4.376 billion (2023 est.)
-$6.549 billion (2022 est.)
-$2.685 billion (2021 est.)
note: balance of payments - net trade and primary/secondary income in current dollars
comparison ranking: 178

Exports: $25.843 billion (2023 est.)
$25.169 billion (2022 est.)
$20.601 billion (2021 est.)
note: balance of payments - exports of goods and services in current dollars
comparison ranking: 83

Exports - partners: US 50%, Switzerland 8%, Haiti 7%, China 3%, India 3% (2022)
note: top five export partners based on percentage share of exports

Exports - commodities: medical instruments, gold, tobacco, power equipment, garments (2022)
note: top five export commodities based on value in dollars

Imports: $34.455 billion (2023 est.)
$36.838 billion (2022 est.)
$28.69 billion (2021 est.)
note: balance of payments - imports of goods and services in current dollars
comparison ranking: 74

Imports - partners: US 44%, China 15%, Brazil 4%, Colombia 3%, Spain 3% (2022)
note: top five import partners based on percentage share of imports

Imports - commodities: refined petroleum, natural gas, cars, plastic products, crude petroleum (2022)
note: top five import commodities based on value in dollars

Reserves of foreign exchange and gold: $15.547 billion (2023 est.)
$14.523 billion (2022 est.)
$13.125 billion (2021 est.)
note: holdings of gold (year-end prices)/foreign exchange/special drawing rights in current dollars
comparison ranking: 80

Exchange rates: Dominican pesos (DOP) per US dollar -

Exchange rates: 56.158 (2023 est.)
55.141 (2022 est.)
57.221 (2021 est.)
56.525 (2020 est.)
51.295 (2019 est.)

ENERGY

Electricity access: *electrification - total population:* 98.1% (2022 est.)
electrification - urban areas: 98.8%
electrification - rural areas: 95%

Electricity: *installed generating capacity:* 5.573 million kW (2022 est.)
consumption: 19.087 billion kWh (2022 est.)
transmission/distribution losses: 2.448 billion kWh (2022 est.)
comparison rankings: transmission/distribution losses 130; consumption 75; installed generating capacity 84

Electricity generation sources: *fossil fuels:* 85.8% of total installed capacity (2022 est.)
solar: 2.6% of total installed capacity (2022 est.)
wind: 6.1% of total installed capacity (2022 est.)
hydroelectricity: 4.6% of total installed capacity (2022 est.)
biomass and waste: 0.8% of total installed capacity (2022 est.)

Coal: *consumption:* 2.188 million metric tons (2022 est.)
exports: 5.9 metric tons (2022 est.)
imports: 2.188 million metric tons (2022 est.)

Petroleum: *refined petroleum consumption:* 134,000 bbl/day (2022 est.)

Natural gas: *consumption:* 2.44 billion cubic meters (2022 est.)
exports: 96.479 million cubic meters (2022 est.)
imports: 2.537 billion cubic meters (2022 est.)

Carbon dioxide emissions: 27.132 million metric tonnes of CO2 (2022 est.)
from coal and metallurgical coke: 4.941 million metric tonnes of CO2 (2022 est.)
from petroleum and other liquids: 17.403 million metric tonnes of CO2 (2022 est.)
from consumed natural gas: 4.788 million metric tonnes of CO2 (2022 est.)
comparison ranking: total emissions 75

Energy consumption per capita: 36.656 million Btu/person (2022 est.)
comparison ranking: 104

COMMUNICATIONS

Telephones - fixed lines: *total subscriptions:* 1.144 million (2022 est.)
subscriptions per 100 inhabitants: 10 (2022 est.)
comparison ranking: total subscriptions 70

Telephones - mobile cellular: *total subscriptions:* 10.15 million (2022 est.)
subscriptions per 100 inhabitants: 90 (2022 est.)
comparison ranking: total subscriptions 94

Telecommunication systems: *general assessment:* the Dominican Republic's telecom sector continued its solid form throughout 2020 and into 2021, shrugging off the economic turmoil unleashed by the Covid-19 pandemic to maintain a decade-long run of low but positive growth across all areas of the market; the Dominican Republic remains behind most of its counterparts in the Latin American region, especially in terms of fixed-line network coverage;

mobile subscriptions are on par with the regional average, but at subscription levels of around 88% there is still ample opportunity for growth; in terms of growth, the standout winner was once again the mobile broadband segment; the market is expected to see close to 8% growth in 2021, building further on the gains it already made in 2020 when lock downs and work-from-home rules encouraged many people to find ways to upgrade their internet access and performance; the limited coverage of fixed-line broadband networks makes mobile the first, if not only, choice for most people in the country (2021)
domestic: fixed-line teledensity is about 10 per 100 persons; mobile cellular subscriptions 88 per 100 persons (2021)
international: country code - 1-809; 1-829; 1-849; landing point for the ARCOS-1, Antillas 1, AMX-1, SAm-1, East-West, Deep Blue Cable and the Fibralink submarine cables that provide links to South and Central America, parts of the Caribbean, and US; satellite earth station - 1 Intelsat (Atlantic Ocean) (2019)

Broadcast media: combination of state-owned and privately owned broadcast media; 1 state-owned TV network and a number of private TV networks; networks operate repeaters to extend signals throughout country; combination of state-owned and privately owned radio stations with more than 300 radio stations operating (2019)

Internet country code: .do

Internet users: *total:* 9.35 million (2021 est.)
percent of population: 85% (2021 est.)
comparison ranking: total 62

Broadband - fixed subscriptions: *total:* 1,031,858 (2020 est.)
subscriptions per 100 inhabitants: 10 (2020 est.)
comparison ranking: total 72

TRANSPORTATION

National air transport system: *number of registered air carriers:* 1 (2020)
inventory of registered aircraft operated by air carriers: 6

Civil aircraft registration country code prefix: HI

Airports: 32 (2024)
comparison ranking: 116

Heliports: 4 (2024)

Pipelines: 27 km gas, 103 km oil (2013)

Railways: *total:* 496 km (2014)
standard gauge: 354 km (2014) 1.435-m gauge
narrow gauge: 142 km (2014) 0.762-m gauge
comparison ranking: total 113

Roadways: *total:* 19,705 km
paved: 9,872 km
unpaved: 9,833 km (2002)
comparison ranking: total 115

Merchant marine: *total:* 40 (2023)
by type: container ship 1, general cargo 2, oil tanker 1, other 36
comparison ranking: total 124

Ports: *total ports:* 17 (2024)
large: 0
medium: 2
small: 7
very small: 6
size unknown: 2
ports with oil terminals: 7
key ports: Andres (Andres Lng Terminal), Las Calderas, Puerto de Haina, Puerto Plata, Punta Nizao Oil Terminal, San Pedro de Macoris, Santa Barbara de Samana, Santa Cruz de Barahona, Santo Domingo

MILITARY AND SECURITY

Military and security forces: Armed Forces of the Dominican Republic: Army of the Dominican Republic (Ejercito de la República Dominicana, ERD), Navy (Armada de República Dominicana or ARD; includes naval infantry), Dominican Air Force (Fuerza Aerea de la República Dominicana, FARD) (2024)
note 1: in addition to the three main branches of the military, the Ministry of Defense directs the Airport Security Authority and Civil Aviation (CESAC), Port Security Authority (CESEP), the Tourist Security Corps (CESTUR), and Border Security Corps (CESFRONT); these specialized corps are joint forces, made up of personnel from all military branches in addition to civilian personnel; these forces may also assist in overall citizen security working together with the National Police, which is under the Ministry of Interior

Military expenditures: 0.6% of GDP (2023 est.)
0.7% of GDP (2022 est.)
0.7% of GDP (2021 est.)
0.8% of GDP (2020 est.)
0.7% of GDP (2019 est.)
comparison ranking: 150

Military and security service personnel strengths: information varies; approximately 60,000 active personnel (30,000 Army; 13,000 Navy; 17,000 Air Force); approximately 35,000 National Police (2023)

Military equipment inventories and acquisitions: the military's equipment inventory comes largely from the US, with smaller quantities from such suppliers as Brazil and Spain (2024)

Military service age and obligation: 16-23 years of age for voluntary military service for men and women (ages vary slightly according to the military service; under 18 admitted with permission of parents); recruits must have completed primary school and be Dominican Republic citizens (2024)
note: as of 2023, women made up approximately 18% of the active duty military

Military - note: the military is responsible for defending the independence, integrity, and sovereignty of the Dominican Republic; it also has an internal security role, which includes assisting with airport, border, port, tourism, and urban security, supporting the police in maintaining or restoring public order, countering transnational crime, and providing disaster or emergency relief/management; a key area of focus is securing the country's 217-mile (350-kilometer) long border with Haiti; the Army in recent years, for example, has assigned three of its six infantry brigades and some 10-12,000 troops to assist with security along the Haitian border; these forces complement the personnel of the Border Security Corps permanently deployed along the border; the Air Force and Navy also provide support to the Haitian border mission; the Army has a brigade dedicated to managing and providing relief during natural disasters; the military also contributes personnel to the National Drug Control Directorate, and both the Air Force and Navy devote assets to detecting and interdicting narcotics trafficking; the Navy conducts regular bilateral maritime interdiction exercises with the US Navy (2024)

TRANSNATIONAL ISSUES

Refugees and internally displaced persons: *refugees (country of origin):* 121,141 (Venezuela) (economic and political crisis; includes Venezuelans who have claimed asylum or have received alternative legal stay) (2023)
stateless persons: 133,770 (2016); note - a September 2013 Constitutional Court ruling revoked the citizenship of those born after 1929 to immigrants without proper documentation, even though the constitution at the time automatically granted citizenship to children born in the Dominican Republic and the 2010 constitution provides that constitutional provisions cannot be applied retroactively; the decision overwhelmingly affected people of Haitian descent whose relatives had come to the Dominican Republic since the 1890s as a cheap source of labor for sugar plantations; a May 2014 law passed by the Dominican Congress regularizes the status of those with birth certificates but will require those without them to prove they were born in the Dominican Republic and to apply for naturalization; the government has issued documents to thousands of individuals who may claim citizenship under this law, but no official estimate has been released

Trafficking in persons: tier rating: Tier 2 Watch List — the government did not demonstrate overall increasing efforts to eliminate trafficking compared with the previous reporting period, therefore the Dominican Republic remained on Tier 2 Watch List for the second consecutive year; for more details, go to: https://www.state.gov/reports/2024-trafficking-in-persons-report/ dominican-republic/

Illicit drugs: major transshipment point for cocaine shipments to the United States and Europe in the Caribbean; some drugs are consumed locally.

ECUADOR

INTRODUCTION

Background: What is now Ecuador formed part of the northern Inca Empire until the Spanish conquest in 1533. Quito – the traditional name for the area – became a seat of Spanish colonial government in 1563 and part of the Viceroyalty of New Granada in 1717. The territories of the Viceroyalty – New Granada (Colombia), Venezuela, and Quito – gained their independence between 1819 and 1822 and formed a federation known as Gran Colombia. When Quito withdrew to become an independent republic in 1830, the traditional name was changed to the "Republic of the Equator." Between 1904 and 1942, Ecuador lost territories in a series of conflicts with its neighbors. A border war with Peru that flared in 1995 was resolved in 1999. Although Ecuador has had nearly 50 years of civilian governance, the period has been marked by political instability.

GEOGRAPHY

Location: Western South America, bordering the Pacific Ocean at the Equator, between Colombia and Peru

Geographic coordinates: 2 00 S, 77 30 W

Map references: South America

Area: *total:* 283,561 sq km
land: 276,841 sq km
water: 6,720 sq km
note: includes Galapagos Islands
comparison ranking: total 75

Area - comparative: slightly smaller than Nevada

Land boundaries: *total:* 2,237 km
border countries (2): Colombia 708 km; Peru 1529 km

Coastline: 2,237 km

Maritime claims: *territorial sea:* 12 nm
exclusive economic zone: 200 nm
continental shelf: 200 nm
note: Ecuador has declared its right to extend its continental shelf to 350 nm measured from the baselines of the Galapagos Archipelago

Climate: tropical along coast, becoming cooler inland at higher elevations; tropical in Amazonian jungle lowlands

Terrain: coastal plain (costa), inter-Andean central highlands (sierra), and flat to rolling eastern jungle (oriente)

Elevation: *highest point:* Chimborazo 6,267
lowest point: Pacific Ocean 0 m
mean elevation: 1,117 m
note: because the earth is not a perfect sphere and has an equatorial bulge, the highest point on the planet farthest from its center is Mount Chimborazo not Mount Everest, which is merely the highest peak above sea level

Natural resources: petroleum, fish, timber, hydropower

Land use: *agricultural land:* 29.7% (2018 est.)
arable land: 4.7% (2018 est.)
permanent crops: 5.6% (2018 est.)
permanent pasture: 19.4% (2018 est.)
forest: 38.9% (2018 est.)
other: 31.4% (2018 est.)

Irrigated land: 10,000 sq km (2020)

Major watersheds (area sq km): Atlantic Ocean drainage: Amazon (6,145,186 sq km)

Population distribution: nearly half of the population is concentrated in the interior in the Andean intermontane basins and valleys, with large concentrations also found along the western coastal strip; the rainforests of the east remain sparsely populated

Natural hazards: frequent earthquakes; landslides; volcanic activity; floods; periodic droughts
volcanism: volcanic activity concentrated along the Andes Mountains; Sangay (5,230 m), which erupted in 2010, is mainland Ecuador's most active volcano; other historically active volcanoes in the Andes include Antisana, Cayambe, Chacana, Cotopaxi, Guagua Pichincha, Reventador, Sumaco, and Tungurahua; Fernandina (1,476 m), a shield volcano that last erupted in 2009, is the most active of the many Galapagos volcanoes; other historically active Galapagos volcanoes include Wolf, Sierra Negra, Cerro Azul, Pinta, Marchena, and Santiago

Geography - note: *note 1:* Cotopaxi in Andes is highest active volcano in world
note 2: genetic research indicates that the cherry-sized tomato originated in Ecuador without any human domestication; later domestication in Mexico transformed the plant into the large modern tomato; archeological research indicates that the cacao tree, whose seeds are used to make chocolate and which was long thought to have originated in Mesoamerica, was first domesticated in the upper Amazon region of northwest South America – present-day Ecuador –about 3,300 B.C.

PEOPLE AND SOCIETY

Population: *total:* 18,309,984
male: 9,023,170
female: 9,286,814 (2024 est.)
comparison rankings: female 69; male 69; total 68

Nationality: *noun:* Ecuadorian(s)
adjective: Ecuadorian

Ethnic groups: Mestizo (mixed Indigenous and White) 77.5%, Montubio 7.7%, Indigenous 7.7%, White 2.2%, Afroecuadorian 2%, Mulatto 1.4%, Black 1.3%, other 0.1% (2022 est.)

Languages: Spanish (Castilian; official) 98.6%, indigenous 3.9% (Quechua 3.2%, other indigenous 0.7%), foreign 2.8%, other 0.6% (includes Ecuadorian sign language) (2022 est.)
major-language sample(s):
La Libreta Informativa del Mundo, la fuente indispensable de información básica. (Spanish)
The World Factbook, the indispensable source for basic information.
note 1: shares sum to more than 100% because some respondents gave more than one answer on the census
note 2: Quechua and Shuar are official languages of intercultural relations; other indigenous languages are in official use by indigenous peoples in the areas they inhabit

Religions: Roman Catholic 68.2%, Protestant 19% (Evangelical 18.3%, Adventist 0.6%, other Protestant 0.2%), Jehovah's Witness 1.4%, other 2.3%, none 8.2% don't know/no response 1% (2023 est.)

Demographic profile: Ecuador's high poverty and income inequality most affect indigenous, mixed race, and rural populations. The government has increased its social spending to ameliorate these problems, but critics question the efficiency and implementation of its national development plan. Nevertheless, the conditional cash transfer program, which requires participants' children to attend school and have medical check-ups, has helped improve educational attainment and health care among poor children. Ecuador's total fertility rate – the average number of children born per woman – is just below replacement level as of 2023, but its population is continuing to grow.

Ecuador continues to be both a country of emigration and immigration. The first large-scale emigration of largely undocumented Ecuadorians occurred between 1980 and 2000, when an economic crisis drove Ecuadorians from southern provinces to New York City, where they had connections from the earlier Panama hat trade. Emigration from all parts of Ecuador in the late 1990s was caused by another economic downturn, political instability, and a currency crisis. Spain was the logical destination because of its shared language and the wide availability of low-skilled, informal jobs at a time when increased border surveillance made illegal migration to the US difficult. Ecuador became Spain's second largest immigrant source country. The bulk of Ecuadorian emigration, however, occurred between 2000 and 2007, largely to the US, Spain, and Italy. Emigration has again surged since 2017, as economic problems, high unemployment, poverty, and violence have lead thousands of Ecuadorian migrants and refugees to head to the US.

As of 2021, Ecuadorians were the fourth-highest nationality coming into contact with US Customs and Border Protection at the US-Mexico border. Most Ecuadorian migrants and refugees traverse the dangerous Darien Gap between Colombia and Panama to reach Mexico. Although Mexico reinstated a visa requirement in September 2021, Ecuadorians continue to enter Mexico illegally and then travel to the US or Canada. Some wind up staying in Mexico if their journeys north fail. Emigrants represent 8-10% of Ecuador's population, as of 2021. Ecuador hosts one of the region's largest refugee populations. From 2000-2005, Colombians arrived in growing numbers to escape armed conflict, and they have continued to immigrate to Ecuador steadily. Between 2008, when Ecuador lifted visa requirements for all countries, and 2016, immigrants entered from Haiti, Cuba, and other continents. The influx of Venezuelans began in 2017, and, as of May 2022, Ecuador was home to the third-largest community of Venezuelan migrants and refugees in the world at over half a million. Immigrants and refugees account for 3-5% of the Ecuador's population, as of 2021.

Age structure: *0-14 years:* 26.8% (male 2,505,729/female 2,395,198)
15-64 years: 64.1% (male 5,771,234/female 5,972,938)
65 years and over: 9.1% (2024 est.) (male 746,207/female 918,678)

Dependency ratios: *total dependency ratio:* 50.9
youth dependency ratio: 39.4
elderly dependency ratio: 11.5
potential support ratio: 8.7 (2021 est.)

Median age: *total:* 28 years (2024 est.)
male: 27 years
female: 28.9 years
comparison ranking: total 153

Population growth rate: 0.94% (2024 est.)
comparison ranking: 99

Birth rate: 17.7 births/1,000 population (2024 est.)
comparison ranking: 83

Death rate: 7.2 deaths/1,000 population (2024 est.)
comparison ranking: 113

Net migration rate: -1.1 migrant(s)/1,000 population (2024 est.)
comparison ranking: 150

Population distribution: nearly half of the population is concentrated in the interior in the Andean intermontane basins and valleys, with large concentrations also found along the western coastal strip; the rainforests of the east remain sparsely populated

Urbanization: *urban population:* 64.8% of total population (2023)
rate of urbanization: 1.62% annual rate of change (2020-25 est.)

Major urban areas - population: 3.142 million Guayaquil, 1.957 million QUITO (capital) (2023)

Sex ratio: *at birth:* 1.05 male(s)/female
0-14 years: 1.05 male(s)/female
15-64 years: 0.97 male(s)/female
65 years and over: 0.81 male(s)/female
total population: 0.97 male(s)/female (2024 est.)

Maternal mortality ratio: 66 deaths/100,000 live births (2020 est.)
comparison ranking: 90

Infant mortality rate: *total:* 11.2 deaths/1,000 live births (2024 est.)
male: 12.2 deaths/1,000 live births
female: 10.2 deaths/1,000 live births
comparison ranking: total 121

Life expectancy at birth: *total population:* 74.9 years (2024 est.)
male: 69.7 years
female: 80.4 years
comparison ranking: total population 135

Total fertility rate: 2.21 children born/woman (2024 est.)
comparison ranking: 83

Gross reproduction rate: 1.08 (2024 est.)

Contraceptive prevalence rate: 77.9% (2018/19)
note: percent of women aged 15-50

Drinking water source: *improved: urban:* 100% of population
rural: 87.1% of population
total: 95.4% of population
unimproved: urban: 0% of population
rural: 12.9% of population
total: 4.6% of population (2020 est.)

Current health expenditure: 8.5% of GDP (2020)

Physician density: 2.22 physicians/1,000 population (2017)

Hospital bed density: 1.4 beds/1,000 population (2016)

Sanitation facility access: *improved: urban:* 100% of population
rural: 96.9% of population
total: 98.9% of population
unimproved: urban: 0% of population
rural: 3.1% of population
total: 1.1% of population (2020 est.)

Obesity - adult prevalence rate: 19.9% (2016)
comparison ranking: 106

Alcohol consumption per capita: *total:* 3.05 liters of pure alcohol (2019 est.)
beer: 2.32 liters of pure alcohol (2019 est.)
wine: 0.09 liters of pure alcohol (2019 est.)
spirits: 0.61 liters of pure alcohol (2019 est.)
other alcohols: 0.03 liters of pure alcohol (2019 est.)
comparison ranking: total 114

Tobacco use: *total:* 11.3% (2020 est.)
male: 18.4% (2020 est.)
female: 4.2% (2020 est.)
comparison ranking: total 128

Children under the age of 5 years underweight: 5.2% (2018/19)
comparison ranking: 73

Currently married women (ages 15-49): 55.1% (2023 est.)

Child marriage: *women married by age 15:* 3.8%
women married by age 18: 22.2% (2018 est.)

Education expenditures: 3.7% of GDP (2021 est.)
comparison ranking: 128

Literacy: *definition:* age 15 and over can read and write
total population: 93.9%
male: 94.9%
female: 93.1% (2022)

School life expectancy (primary to tertiary education): *total:* 15 years
male: 14 years
female: 15 years (2020)

ENVIRONMENT

Environment - current issues: deforestation; soil erosion; desertification; water pollution; pollution from oil production wastes in ecologically sensitive areas of the Amazon Basin and Galapagos Islands

Environment - international agreements: *party to:* Antarctic-Environmental Protection, Antarctic Treaty, Biodiversity, Climate Change, Climate Change-Kyoto Protocol, Climate Change-Paris Agreement, Comprehensive Nuclear Test Ban, Desertification, Endangered Species, Hazardous Wastes, Law of the Sea, Nuclear Test Ban, Ozone Layer Protection, Ship Pollution, Tropical Timber 2006, Wetlands, Whaling
signed, but not ratified: none of the selected agreements

Climate: tropical along coast, becoming cooler inland at higher elevations; tropical in Amazonian jungle lowlands

Urbanization: *urban population:* 64.8% of total population (2023)
rate of urbanization: 1.62% annual rate of change (2020-25 est.)

Revenue from forest resources: 0.27% of GDP (2018 est.)
comparison ranking: 83

Revenue from coal: 0% of GDP (2018 est.)
comparison ranking: 61

Air pollutants: *particulate matter emissions:* 16.55 micrograms per cubic meter (2019 est.)
carbon dioxide emissions: 41.15 megatons (2016 est.)
methane emissions: 23.51 megatons (2020 est.)

Waste and recycling: *municipal solid waste generated annually:* 5,297,211 tons (2015 est.)
municipal solid waste recycled annually: 683,340 tons (2015 est.)
percent of municipal solid waste recycled: 12.9% (2015 est.)

Major watersheds (area sq km): Atlantic Ocean drainage: Amazon (6,145,186 sq km)

Total water withdrawal: *municipal:* 1.29 billion cubic meters (2020 est.)
industrial: 550 million cubic meters (2020 est.)
agricultural: 8.8 billion cubic meters (2020 est.)

Total renewable water resources: 442.4 billion cubic meters (2020 est.)

Geoparks: *total global geoparks and regional networks:* 1
global geoparks and regional networks: Imbabura (2023)

GOVERNMENT

Country name: *conventional long form:* Republic of Ecuador
conventional short form: Ecuador
local long form: República del Ecuador
local short form: Ecuador
etymology: the country's position on the globe, straddling the Equator, accounts for its Spanish name

Government type: presidential republic

Capital: *name:* Quito
geographic coordinates: 0 13 S, 78 30 W
time difference: UTC-5 (same time as Washington, DC, during Standard Time)
time zone note: Ecuador has two time zones, including the Galapagos Islands (UTC-6)
etymology: named after the Quitu, a Pre-Columbian indigenous people credited with founding the city; the name is also a combination of two Tsafiki words: quitso (meaning "center" or "half") + *to* or *tu* ("the world"); the combination roughly translates as "center of the world" and reflects the fact that native peoples recognized that at the two annual equinoxes, the overhead sun in that area (only about 20 km (12 mi) north of the equator) did not display any shade and thus must be in the middle of the world

Administrative divisions: 24 provinces (provincias, singular - provincia); Azuay, Bolivar, Canar, Carchi, Chimborazo, Cotopaxi, El Oro, Esmeraldas, Galapagos, Guayas, Imbabura, Loja, Los Rios, Manabi, Morona Santiago, Napo, Orellana, Pastaza, Pichincha, Santa Elena, Santo Domingo de los Tsachilas, Sucumbios, Tungurahua, Zamora Chinchipe

Independence: 24 May 1822 (from Spain)

National holiday: Independence Day (independence of Quito), 10 August (1809)

Legal system: civil law based on the Chilean civil code with modifications; traditional law in indigenous communities

Constitution: *history:* many previous; latest approved 20 October 2008
amendments: proposed by the president of the republic through a referendum, by public petition of at least 1% of registered voters, or by agreement of at least one-third membership of the National Assembly; passage requires two separate readings a year apart and approval by at least two-thirds majority vote of the Assembly, and approval by absolute majority in a referendum; amendments such as changes to the structure of the state, constraints on personal rights and guarantees, or constitutional amendment procedures are not allowed; amended 2011, 2015, 2018, 2024

International law organization participation: has not submitted an ICJ jurisdiction declaration; accepts ICCt jurisdiction

Citizenship: *citizenship by birth:* yes
citizenship by descent only: yes
dual citizenship recognized: no
residency requirement for naturalization: 3 years

Suffrage: 18-65 years of age; universal and compulsory; 16-18, over 65, and other eligible voters, voluntary

Executive branch: *chief of state:* President Daniel NOBOA Azin (since 23 November 2023)
head of government: President Daniel NOBOA Azin (since 23 November 2023)
cabinet: Cabinet appointed by the president
elections/appointments: president and vice president directly elected on the same ballot by absolute majority popular vote in 2 rounds if needed for a 4-year term (eligible for a second term); election last held on 20 August 2023 with a runoff on 15 October 2023 (next to be held on 28 February 2025); note – on 18 May 2023, Ecuador's National Electoral Council announced that the legislative and presidential elections—originally scheduled for February 2025—would be held on 20 August 2023 with a runoff on 15 October 2023 after former president Guillermo LASSO dissolved the National Assembly by decree on 17 May 2023; though eligible for a second term, LASSO announced that he would not run in the 2023 election; President Daniel NOBOA Azin will serve out the remainder of the current presidential term (2021–2025)
election results:
2023: Daniel NOBOA Azin elected president; percent of vote in the second round - Luisa GONZÁLEZ Alcivar (MRC) 33.6%, Daniel NOBOA Azin (ADN) 23.5%, Christian Gustavo ZURITA Ron (Construye) 16.4%, Jan Tomislav TOPIĆ Feraud (Por Un País Sin Miedo) 14.7%, Otto Ramón SONNENHOLZNER Sper (Avanza) 7.1% other 4.7%; percent of vote in the second round - Daniel NOBOA Azin 51.8%, Luisa GONZÁLEZ Alcivar 48.2%
2021: Guillermo LASSO Mendoza elected president; percent of vote in the first round - Andres ARAUZ (UNES) 32.7%, Guillermo LASSO Mendoza (CREO) 19.7%, Yaku PEREZ Guartambel (MUPP) 19.4%, Xavier HERVAS Mora (ID) 15.7%, other 12.5%; percent of vote in the second round - Guillermo LASSO Mendoza (CREO) 52.5%, Andres ARAUZ (UNES) 47.5%
note: the president is both chief of state and head of government

Legislative branch: *description:* unicameral National Assembly or Asamblea Nacional (137 seats; 116 members directly elected in single-seat constituencies by simple majority vote, 15 members directly elected in a single nationwide constituency by open-list proportional representation vote, and 6 directly elected in multi-seat constituencies for Ecuadorians living abroad by simple majority vote; members serve 4-year terms); note - all Assembly members have alternates from the same party who cast votes when a primary member is absent, resigns, or is removed from office
elections: last held on 20 August 2023 (next to be held on 28 February 2025); note – on 18 May 2023, Ecuador's National Electoral Council announced that the legislative and presidential elections - originally scheduled for February 2025 - would be held on 20 August 2023 after President Guillermo LASSO dissolved the National Assembly by decree on 17 May 2023; a return to a regular election cycle will occur in February 2025
election results: percent of vote by party - RC5 38%, Construye 20.4%, ADN 10.2%, PSC 10.2%, Actuemos 5.8%, MUPP 2.9%, other 12.4%; seats by party - RC5 52, Construye 28, ADN 14, PSC 14, Actuemos 8, MUPP 4, other 17; composition - men 78, women 59, percentage women 43.1%; note - defections by National Assembly members are commonplace, resulting in frequent changes in the numbers of seats held by the various parties
note: all Assembly members have alternates from the same party who cast votes when a primary member is absent, resigns, or is removed from office

Judicial branch: *highest court(s):* National Court of Justice or Corte Nacional de Justicia (consists of 21 judges, including the chief justice and organized into 5 specialized chambers); Constitutional Court or Corte Constitucional (consists of the court president and 8 judges)
judge selection and term of office: candidates for the National Court of Justice evaluated and appointed justices by the Judicial Council, a 9-member independent body of law professionals; justices elected for 9-year, non-renewable terms, with one-third of the membership renewed every 3 years; candidates for the Constitutional Court evaluated and appointed judges by a 6-member independent body of law professionals; judges appointed for 4-year renewable terms
subordinate courts: provincial courts (one for each province except Galapagos); fiscal, criminal, and administrative tribunals; Election Dispute Settlement Courts; cantonal courts

Political parties: Actuemos Ecuador or Actuemos
AMIGO movement, Independent Mobilizing Action Generating Opportunities (Movimiento AMIGO (Acción Movilizadora Independiente Generando Oportunidades)) or AM16O
Avanza Party or AVANZA
Central Democratic Movement or CD
Citizen Revolution Movement or MRC or RC5
Creating Opportunities Movement or CREO
Democratic Left or ID
Democracy Yes Movement (Movimiento Democracia Si)
For A Country Without Fear (Por Un País Sin Miedo) (an alliance including PSC, CD, and PSP)
Green Movement (Movimiento Verde)
Movimiento Construye or Construye
National Democratic Action (Acción Democrática Nacional) or ADN
Pachakutik Plurinational Unity Movement or MUPP
Patriotic Society Party or PSP
People, Equality, and Democracy Party (Partido Pueblo, Igualdad y Democracia) or PID
Popular Unity Party (Partido Unidad Popular) or UP
Revolutionary and Democratic Ethical Green Movement (Movimiento Verde Ético Revolucionario y Democrático) or MOVER
Social Christian Party or PSC
Socialist Party
Society United for More Action or SUMA
Total Renovation Movement (Movimiento Renovacion Total) or RETO

International organization participation: CAN, CD, CELAC, FAO, G-11, G-77, IADB, IAEA, IBRD, ICAO, ICC (national committees), ICCt, ICRM, IDA, IFAD, IFC, IFRCS, IHO, ILO, IMF, IMO, Interpol, IOC, IOM, IPU, ISO, ITSO, ITU, ITUC (NGOs), LAES, LAIA, Mercosur (associate), MIGA, MINUSTAH, NAM, OAS, OPANAL, OPCW, OPEC, Pacific Alliance (observer), PCA, PROSUR, SICA (observer), UN, UNCTAD, UNESCO, UNHCR, UNIDO, Union Latina, UNISFA, UNMIL, UNMISS, UNOCI, UNWTO, UPU, WCO, WFTU (NGOs), WHO, WIPO, WMO, WTO

Diplomatic representation in the US: *chief of mission:* Ambassador Cristian ESPINOSA Cañizares (since 18 September 2024)
chancery: 2535 15th Street NW, Washington, DC 20009
telephone: [1] (202) 234-7200
FAX: [1] (202) 333-2893
email address and website:
eecuusanotifications@mmrree.gob.ec
Contact – Washington (cancilleria.gob.ec)
consulate(s) general: Atlanta, Chicago, Houston, Los Angeles, Miami, Minneapolis (MN), New Haven (CT), New York, Newark (NJ), Phoenix, San Juan (PR)

Diplomatic representation from the US: *chief of mission:* Ambassador Michael J. FITZPATRICK (since 3 July 2019)
embassy: E12-170 Avenida Avigiras y Avenida Eloy Alfaro, Quito
mailing address: 3420 Quito Place, Washington DC 20521-3420
telephone: [593] (2) 398-5000
email address and website:
ACSQuito@state.gov
https://ec.usembassy.gov/
consulate(s) general: Guayaquil

Flag description: three horizontal bands of yellow (top, double width), blue, and red with the coat of arms superimposed at the center of the flag; the flag retains the three main colors of the banner of Gran Colombia, the South American republic that broke up in 1830; the yellow color represents sunshine, grain, and mineral wealth, blue the sky, sea,

and rivers, and red the blood of patriots spilled in the struggle for freedom and justice
note: similar to the flag of Colombia, which is shorter and does not bear a coat of arms

National symbol(s): Andean condor; national colors: yellow, blue, red

National anthem: *name:* "Salve, Oh Patria!" (We Salute You, Our Homeland)
lyrics/music: Juan Leon MERA/Antonio NEUMANE
note: adopted 1948; Juan Leon MERA wrote the lyrics in 1865; only the chorus and second verse are sung

National heritage: *total World Heritage Sites:* 5 (3 cultural, 2 natural)
selected World Heritage Site locales: Historic Quito (c); Galápagos Islands (n); Historic Cuenca (c); Qhapaq Ñan/ Andean Road System (c); Sangay National Park (n)

ECONOMY Economic overview

highly informal South American economy; USD currency user; major banana exporter; hard hit by COVID-19; macroeconomic fragility from oil dependency; successful debt restructuring; China funding budget deficits; social unrest hampering economic activity

Real GDP (purchasing power parity): $260.213 billion (2023 est.)
$254.226 billion (2022 est.)
$239.415 billion (2021 est.)
note: data in 2021 dollars
comparison ranking: 67

Real GDP growth rate: 2.36% (2023 est.)
6.19% (2022 est.)
9.82% (2021 est.)
note: annual GDP % growth based on constant local currency
comparison ranking: 130

Real GDP per capita: $14,300 (2023 est.)
$14,100 (2022 est.)
$13,500 (2021 est.)
note: data in 2021 dollars
comparison ranking: 127

GDP (official exchange rate): $118.845 billion (2023 est.)
note: data in current dollars at official exchange rate

Inflation rate (consumer prices): 2.22% (2023 est.)
3.47% (2022 est.)
0.13% (2021 est.)
note: annual % change based on consumer prices
comparison ranking: 44

Credit ratings: Fitch rating: B- (2020)

Moody's rating: Caa3 (2020)

Standard & Poors rating: B- (2020)
note: The year refers to the year in which the current credit rating was first obtained.

GDP - composition, by sector of origin: *agriculture:* 7.7% (2023 est.)
industry: 26.9% (2023 est.)
services: 59.7% (2023 est.)
note: figures may not total 100% due to non-allocated consumption not captured in sector-reported data comparison rankings: services 89; industry 85; agriculture 95

GDP - composition, by end use: *household consumption:* 64.3% (2023 est.)
government consumption: 13.9% (2023 est.)
investment in fixed capital: 19.7% (2023 est.)
investment in inventories: 1.8% (2023 est.)
exports of goods and services: 29.1% (2023 est.)
imports of goods and services: -28.8% (2023 est.)
note: figures may not total 100% due to rounding or gaps in data collection

Agricultural products: sugarcane, bananas, oil palm fruit, milk, maize, rice, plantains, chicken, cocoa beans, pineapples (2022)
note: top ten agricultural products based on tonnage

Industries: petroleum, food processing, textiles, wood products, chemicals

Industrial production growth rate: -0.75% (2023 est.)
note: annual % change in industrial value added based on constant local currency
comparison ranking: 163

Labor force: 8.893 million (2023 est.)
note: number of people ages 15 or older who are employed or seeking work
comparison ranking: 61

Unemployment rate: 3.37% (2023 est.)
3.76% (2022 est.)
4.55% (2021 est.)
note: % of labor force seeking employment
comparison ranking: 56

Youth unemployment rate (ages 15-24): *total:* 7.2% (2023 est.)
male: 5.9% (2023 est.)
female: 9.4% (2023 est.)
note: % of labor force ages 15-24 seeking employment
comparison ranking: total 157

Population below poverty line: 25.2% (2022 est.)
note: % of population with income below national poverty line

Gini Index coefficient - distribution of family income: 45.5 (2022 est.)
note: index (0-100) of income distribution; higher values represent greater inequality
comparison ranking: 19

Average household expenditures: *on food:* 26.4% of household expenditures (2022 est.)
on alcohol and tobacco: 0.8% of household expenditures (2022 est.)

Household income or consumption by percentage share: *lowest 10%:* 1.7% (2022 est.)
highest 10%: 34.3% (2022 est.)
note: % share of income accruing to lowest and highest 10% of population

Remittances: 4.33% of GDP (2023 est.)
4.07% of GDP (2022 est.)
4.07% of GDP (2021 est.)
note: personal transfers and compensation between resident and non-resident individuals/households/entities

Budget: *revenues:* $35.962 billion (2022 est.)
expenditures: $35.347 billion (2022 est.)
note: central government revenues (excluding grants) and expenses converted to US dollars at average official exchange rate for year indicated

Public debt: 45.4% of GDP (2017 est.)
comparison ranking: 120

Taxes and other revenues: 13.04% (of GDP) (2022 est.)
note: central government tax revenue as a % of GDP
comparison ranking: 155

Current account balance: $2.291 billion (2023 est.)
$2.133 billion (2022 est.)
$3.098 billion (2021 est.)
note: balance of payments - net trade and primary/secondary income in current dollars
comparison ranking: 46

Exports: $34.64 billion (2023 est.)
$35.943 billion (2022 est.)
$29.037 billion (2021 est.)
note: balance of payments - exports of goods and services in current dollars
comparison ranking: 76

Exports - partners: US 27%, China 17%, Panama 14%, Chile 4%, Colombia 3% (2022)
note: top five export partners based on percentage share of exports

Exports - commodities: crude petroleum, shellfish, bananas, fish, refined petroleum (2022)
note: top five export commodities based on value in dollars

Imports: $34.447 billion (2023 est.)
$36.051 billion (2022 est.)
$28.128 billion (2021 est.)
note: balance of payments - imports of goods and services in current dollars
comparison ranking: 75

Imports - partners: US 26%, China 23%, Colombia 6%, Peru 4%, Brazil 4% (2022)
note: top five import partners based on percentage share of imports

Imports - commodities: refined petroleum, coal tar oil, cars, natural gas, soybean meal (2022)
note: top five import commodities based on value in dollars

Reserves of foreign exchange and gold: $4.442 billion (2023 est.)
$8.459 billion (2022 est.)
$7.912 billion (2021 est.)
note: holdings of gold (year-end prices)/foreign exchange/special drawing rights in current dollars
comparison ranking: 116

Debt - external: $39.129 billion (2022 est.)
note: present value of external debt in current US dollars
comparison ranking: 14

Exchange rates: the US dollar became Ecuador's currency in 2001

ENERGY

Electricity access: *electrification - total population:* 100% (2022 est.)

Electricity: *installed generating capacity:* 8.377 million kW (2022 est.)
consumption: 27.702 billion kWh (2022 est.)
exports: 524 million kWh (2022 est.)
imports: 363.8 million kWh (2022 est.)
transmission/distribution losses: 4.783 billion kWh (2022 est.)
comparison rankings: transmission/distribution losses 163; imports 98; exports 75; consumption 68; installed generating capacity 70

Electricity generation sources: *fossil fuels:* 19% of total installed capacity (2022 est.)
solar: 0.1% of total installed capacity (2022 est.)
wind: 0.2% of total installed capacity (2022 est.)
hydroelectricity: 79.3% of total installed capacity (2022 est.)
biomass and waste: 1.3% of total installed capacity (2022 est.)

Coal: *consumption:* 21,000 metric tons (2022 est.)
exports: 100 metric tons (2022 est.)
imports: 21,000 metric tons (2022 est.)
proven reserves: 24 million metric tons (2022 est.)

Petroleum: *total petroleum production:* 480,000 bbl/day (2023 est.)
refined petroleum consumption: 225,000 bbl/day (2022 est.)
crude oil estimated reserves: 8.273 billion barrels (2021 est.)

Natural gas: *production:* 309.778 million cubic meters (2022 est.)
consumption: 309.778 million cubic meters (2022 est.)
proven reserves: 10.902 billion cubic meters (2021 est.)

Carbon dioxide emissions: 31.306 million metric tonnes of CO2 (2022 est.)
from coal and metallurgical coke: 56,000 metric tonnes of CO2 (2022 est.)
from petroleum and other liquids: 30.637 million metric tonnes of CO2 (2022 est.)
from consumed natural gas: 613,000 metric tonnes of CO2 (2022 est.)
comparison ranking: total emissions 73

Energy consumption per capita: 30.111 million Btu/person (2022 est.)
comparison ranking: 116

COMMUNICATIONS

Telephones - fixed lines: *total subscriptions:* 1.644 million (2022 est.)
subscriptions per 100 inhabitants: 9 (2022 est.)
comparison ranking: total subscriptions 57

Telephones - mobile cellular: *total subscriptions:* 17.491 million (2022 est.)
subscriptions per 100 inhabitants: 97 (2022 est.)
comparison ranking: total subscriptions 67

Telecommunication systems: *general assessment:* Ecuador has a small telecom market dominated by the mobile sector; the evolution of the market has been influenced by the poor fixed-line infrastructure, which has stymied the development of fixed-line broadband services; to some extent poor infrastructure has been the result of topographical challenges which have rendered the cost of deploying networks to remote and mountainous areas prohibitive; although Ecuador has several fixed-line operators and a large number of ISPs, the state-owned incumbent leads the fixed-line market, and thus also the fixed broadband market; thus far the MVNO sector has been slow to develop, partly because the incumbent operators also have their low-cost brands and thus there is little business case for new market entrants; the government is keen to advance and improve teledensity; from 2022, additional revenue will be earmarked for programs aimed at expanding the reach of internet and mobile services in rural areas of the country; Ecuador lacks a national 5G roadmap; the mobile operators have conducted several 5G pilots, but no progress has been made on allocation spectrum for 5G, or on developing strategies to encourage investment in the sector (2022)
domestic: according to 2021 statistics from the Ministry of Telecommunications and Information Society, 50 percent of Ecuadorian homes do not have access to fixed internet; fixed-line teledensity is about 10 per 100 persons; mobilecellular service with a subscribership of nearly 94 per 100 persons (2021)
international: country code - 593; landing points for the SPSC (Mistral Submarine Cable), Panamerican Cable System (PAN-AM), Pacific Caribbean Cable System (PCCS), America Movil-Telxius West Coast Cable and SAm-1 submarine (SAm-1) cables that provide links to South and Central America, and extending onward to the Caribbean and the US; satellite earth station - 1 Intelsat (Atlantic Ocean) (2019)

Broadcast media: *the Communication Council, an official entity, carried out a media registry in Ecuador in December 2020. It registered 956 media outlets, 89% are private, 5% are public and 6% belong to small communities. The government controls most of the 44 public media, this includes national media and multiple local radio stations. In addition, of the 956 registered media, 58% are radio and 18% print. Two provinces have the largest number of media outlets:* Guayas has 172 media outlets and Pichincha has 130 media outlets. (2020) so also sent to the National Assembly a new regulation proposal that is still under discussion. (2022)

Internet country code: .ec

Internet users: *total:* 13.68 million (2021 est.)
percent of population: 76% (2021 est.)
according to 2021 statistics from Ecuador's Ministry of Telecommunications and Information Society, 50% of homes do not have access to fixed internet
comparison ranking: total 52

Broadband - fixed subscriptions: *total:* 2,371,297 (2020 est.)
subscriptions per 100 inhabitants: 13 (2020 est.)
comparison ranking: total 55

TRANSPORTATION

National air transport system: *number of registered air carriers:* 7 (2020)
inventory of registered aircraft operated by air carriers: 35
annual passenger traffic on registered air carriers: 5,365,261 (2018)
annual freight traffic on registered air carriers: 64.2 million (2018) mt-km

Civil aircraft registration country code prefix: HC

Airports: 310 (2024)
comparison ranking: 22

Heliports: 28 (2024)

Pipelines: 485 km extra heavy crude, 123 km gas, 2,131 km oil, 1,526 km refined products (2017)

Railways: *total:* 965 km (2022)
narrow gauge: 965 km (2022) 1.067-m gauge
note: passenger service limited to certain sections of track, mostly for tourist trains
comparison ranking: total 90

Roadways: *total:* 43,950 km
paved: 8,895 km
unpaved: 35,055 km (2022)
comparison ranking: total 89

Waterways: 1,500 km (2012) (most inaccessible)
comparison ranking: 55

Merchant marine: *total:* 154 (2023)
by type: container ship 1, general cargo 8, oil tanker 28, other 117
comparison ranking: total 73

Ports: *total ports:* 6 (2024)
large: 0
medium: 0
small: 2
very small: 4
ports with oil terminals: 5
key ports: Esmeraldas, Guayaquil, La Libertad, Manta, Puerto Bolivar, Puerto Maritimo de Guayaquil

MILITARY AND SECURITY

Military and security forces: Ecuadorian Armed Forces: the Ecuadorian Army (Ejército Ecuatoriano), Ecuadorian Navy (Armada del Ecuador, Fuerza Naval del Ecuador, FNE; includes naval infantry, naval aviation, coast guard), Ecuadorian Air Force (Fuerza Aerea Ecuatoriana, FAE) (2024)
note: the National Police of Ecuador (Policía Nacional del Ecuador) is under the Ministry of Government/Interior

Military expenditures: 2% of GDP (2023 est.)
2% of GDP (2022 est.)
2% of GDP (2021 est.)
2.3% of GDP (2020 est.)
2.2% of GDP (2019 est.)
comparison ranking: 74

Military and security service personnel strengths: approximately 40,000 active military personnel (25,000 Army; 9,000 Navy; 6,000 Air Force) (2023)

Military equipment inventories and acquisitions: the military's inventory includes a diverse mix of older and smaller quantities of more modern equipment derived from a variety of sources such as Brazil, China, France, Italy, Germany, Russia/Soviet-Union, Spain, Turkey, the UK, and the US (2024)

Military service age and obligation: 18-22 years of age for selective conscript military service for men, although conscription was suspended in 2008; 18 years of age for voluntary military service for men and women; 12-month service obligation (2023)
note: in 2022, women made up an estimated 3-4% of the military

Military - note: the military is responsible for preserving Ecuador's national sovereignty and defending the integrity of the state; it also has some domestic security responsibilities and may complement police operations in maintaining public order if required; the military shares responsibility for border enforcement with the National Police; it participates in bilateral and multinational training exercises and has sent troops on UN peacekeeping missions; the military has defense ties to regional countries, such as Chile, Colombia, and Peru, and security ties with the US have been revived in recent years
border conflicts with Peru dominated the military's focus until the late 1990s and border security remains a priority, but in more recent years, security challenges have included counterinsurgency and counternarcotics operations, particularly in the northern border area where violence and other criminal activity related to terrorism, insurgency, and narco-trafficking in Colombia, as well as refugees from Venezuela, have spilled over the border; the military has established a joint service task force for counterinsurgency and counternarcotics operations and boosted troop deployments along those borders; other missions include countering illegal mining, smuggling, and maritime piracy; since 2012, the Ecuadorian Government has expanded the military's role in general public security and domestic crime operations, in part due to rising violence, police corruption, and police ineffectiveness
the Joint Command of the Armed Forces (El Comando Conjunto de las Fuerzas Armadas or CCFFAA) is the military's highest body for planning, preparation, and strategic conduct of military

operations; the chief of the CCFFAA is appointed by the president; the military is deployed throughout the country in five joint service operational commands or task forces; it also has a cyber defense command the military has had a large role in Ecuador's political history; it ruled the country from 1963-1966 and 1972-1979, and supported a dictatorship in 1970-1972; during the 1980s, the military remained loyal to the civilian government, but civilian-military relations were at times tenuous, and the military had considerable autonomy from civilian oversight; it was involved in coup attempts in 2000 and 2010 (2024)

SPACE

Space agency/agencies: Ecuadorian Civilian Space Agency (EXA; a civilian independent research and development institution in charge of the administration and execution of Ecuador's space program, established 2007); Ecuadorian Space Institute (established 2012, disbanded 2018) (2024)

Space program overview: has a small program focused on acquiring or manufacturing satellites; builds scientific satellites; conducts research and develops some space-related technologies; has established relations with the space agencies and industries of China and Russia, as well as the Latin American and Caribbean Space Agency (ALCE) and its member states (2024)
note: further details about the key activities, programs, and milestones of the country's space program, as well as government spending estimates on the space sector, appear in the Space Programs reference guide

TRANSNATIONAL ISSUES

Refugees and internally displaced persons: *refugees (country of origin):* 65,854 (Colombia) (refugees and asylum seekers) (2021); 474,945 (Venezuela) (economic and political crisis; includes Venezuelans who have claimed asylum, are recognized as refugees, or have received alternative legal stay) (2023)

Illicit drugs: Ecuador is a major transit country for cocaine destined for the United States and other international destinations; criminal groups traffic cocaine precursor chemicals for drug gangs; not a major drug producing country; a major source of precursor or essential chemicals used in the production of illicit narcotics

EGYPT

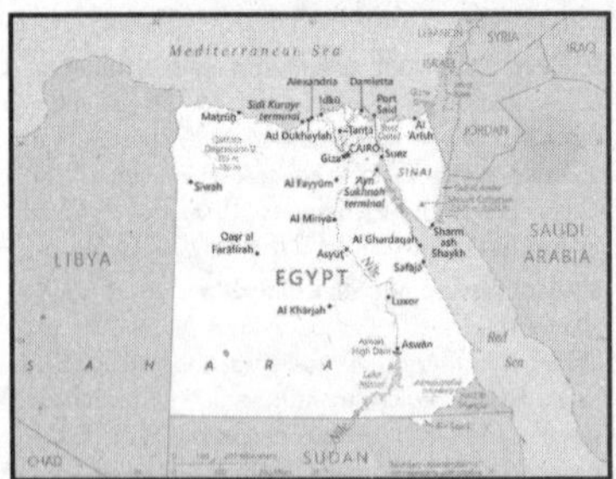

INTRODUCTION

Background: The regularity and richness of the annual Nile River flood, coupled with semi-isolation provided by deserts to the east and west, allowed for the development of one of the world's great civilizations in Egypt. A unified kingdom arose circa 3200 B.C., and a series of dynasties ruled in Egypt for the next three millennia. The last native dynasty fell to the Persians in 341 B.C., who in turn were replaced by the Greeks, Romans, and Byzantines. Arab conquerors introduced Islam and the Arabic language in the 7th century and ruled for the next six centuries. The Mamluks, a local military caste, took control around 1250 and continued to govern after the Ottoman Turks conquered Egypt in 1517.

Completion of the Suez Canal in 1869 elevated Egypt as an important world transportation hub. Ostensibly to protect its investments, Britain seized control of Egypt's government in 1882, but the country's nominal allegiance to the Ottoman Empire continued until 1914. Egypt gained partial independence from the UK in 1922 and full sovereignty in 1952. British forces evacuated the Suez Canal Zone in 1956. The completion of the Aswan High Dam in 1971 and the resultant Lake Nasser have reaffirmed the time-honored place of the Nile River in the agriculture and ecology of Egypt. A rapidly growing population (the largest in the Arab world), limited arable land, and dependence on the Nile all continue to overtax resources and stress society. The government has struggled to meet the demands of Egypt's fast-growing population as it implements large-scale infrastructure projects, energy cooperation, and foreign direct investment appeals.

Inspired by the 2010 Tunisian revolution, Egyptian opposition groups led demonstrations and labor strikes countrywide, culminating in President Hosni MUBARAK's ouster in 2011. Egypt's military assumed national leadership until a new legislature was in place in early 2012; later that same year, Muslim Brotherhood candidate Mohamed MORSI won the presidential election. Following protests throughout the spring of 2013 against MORSI's government and the Muslim Brotherhood, the Egyptian Armed Forces intervened and removed MORSI from power in July 2013 and replaced him with interim president Adly MANSOUR. Simultaneously, the government began enacting laws to limit freedoms of assembly and expression. In 2014, voters approved a new constitution by referendum and then elected former defense minister Abdel Fattah EL-SISI president. EL-SISI was reelected to a second four-year term in 2018 and a

GEOGRAPHY

Location: Northern Africa, bordering the Mediterranean Sea, between Libya and the Gaza Strip, and the Red Sea north of Sudan, and includes the Asian Sinai Peninsula

Geographic coordinates: 27 00 N, 30 00 E

Map references: Africa

Area: *total:* 1,001,450 sq km
land: 995,450 sq km
water: 6,000 sq km
comparison ranking: total 31

Area - comparative: more than eight times the size of Ohio; slightly more than three times the size of New Mexico

Land boundaries: *total:* 2,612 km
border countries (4): Gaza Strip 13 km; Israel 208 km; Libya 1,115 km; Sudan 1,276 km

Coastline: 2,450 km

Maritime claims: *territorial sea:* 12 nm
contiguous zone: 24 nm
exclusive economic zone: 200 nm or the equidistant median line with Cyprus
continental shelf: 200 nm

Climate: desert; hot, dry summers with moderate winters

Terrain: vast desert plateau interrupted by Nile valley and delta

Elevation: *highest point:* Mount Catherine 2,629 m
lowest point: Qattara Depression -133 m
mean elevation: 321 m

Natural resources: petroleum, natural gas, iron ore, phosphates, manganese, limestone, gypsum, talc, asbestos, lead, rare earth elements, zinc

Land use: *agricultural land:* 3.6% (2018 est.)
arable land: 2.8% (2018 est.)
permanent crops: 0.8% (2018 est.)
permanent pasture: 0% (2018 est.)
forest: 0.1% (2018 est.)
other: 96.3% (2018 est.)

Irrigated land: 36,500 sq km (2012)

Major lakes (area sq km): *salt water lake(s):* Lake Manzala - 1,360 sq km
note - largest of Nile Delta lakes

Major rivers (by length in km): An Nīl (Nile) river mouth (shared with Rwanda [s], Tanzania, Uganda, South Sudan, and Sudan) - 6,650 km
note – [s] after country name indicates river source; [m] after country name indicates river mouth

Major watersheds (area sq km): Atlantic Ocean drainage: *(Mediterranean Sea)* Nile (3,254,853 sq km)

Major aquifers: Nubian Aquifer System

Population distribution: approximately 95% of the population lives within 20 km of the Nile River and its delta; vast areas of the country remain sparsely populated or uninhabited as shown in this population distribution map

Natural hazards: periodic droughts; frequent earthquakes; flash floods; landslides; hot, driving windstorms called khamsin occur in spring; dust storms; sandstorms

Geography - note: *note:* controls Sinai Peninsula, the only land bridge between Africa and remainder of Eastern Hemisphere; controls Suez Canal, a sea link between Indian Ocean and Mediterranean Sea; size, and juxtaposition to Israel, establish its major role in Middle Eastern geopolitics; dependence on upstream neighbors; dominance of Nile basin issues

PEOPLE AND SOCIETY

Population: *total:* 111,247,248
male: 57,142,484
female: 54,104,764 (2024 est.)
comparison rankings: female 15; male 15; total 15

Nationality: *noun:* Egyptian(s)
adjective: Egyptian

Ethnic groups: Egyptian 99.7%, other 0.3% (2006 est.)
note: data represent respondents by nationality

Languages: Arabic (official); English and French widely understood by educated classes
major-language sample(s):
كتاب حقائق العالم، أفضل مصدر للمعلومات الأساسية (Arabic)

Religions: Muslim (predominantly Sunni) 90%, Christian (majority Coptic Orthodox, other Christians include Armenian Apostolic, Catholic, Maronite, Orthodox, and Anglican) 10%

Demographic profile: Egypt is the most populous country in the Arab world and the third-most-populous country in Africa, behind Nigeria and Ethiopia. Most of the country is desert, so about 95% of the population is concentrated in a narrow strip of fertile land along the Nile River, which represents only about 5% of Egypt's land area. Egypt's rapid population growth – 46% between 1994 and 2014 – stresses limited natural resources, jobs, housing, sanitation, education, and health care.

Although the country's total fertility rate (TFR) fell from roughly 5.5 children per woman in 1980 to just over 3 in the late 1990s, largely as a result of state-sponsored family planning programs, the population growth rate dropped more modestly because of decreased mortality rates and longer life expectancies. During the last decade, Egypt's TFR decline stalled for several years and then reversed, reaching 3.6 in 2011, and is under 3 as of 2022. Contraceptive use has held steady at about 60%, while preferences for larger families and early marriage may have strengthened in the wake of the recent 2011 revolution. The large cohort of women of or nearing childbearing age will sustain high population growth for the foreseeable future (an effect called population momentum).

Nevertheless, post-MUBARAK governments have not made curbing population growth a priority. To increase contraceptive use and to prevent further overpopulation will require greater government commitment and substantial social change, including encouraging smaller families and better educating and empowering women. Currently, literacy, educational attainment, and labor force participation rates are much lower for women than men. In addition, the prevalence of violence against women, the lack of female political representation, and the perpetuation of the nearly universal practice of female genital cutting continue to keep women from playing a more significant role in Egypt's public sphere.

Population pressure, poverty, high unemployment, and the fragmentation of inherited land holdings have historically motivated Egyptians, primarily young men, to migrate internally from rural and smaller urban areas in the Nile Delta region and the poorer rural south to Cairo, Alexandria, and other urban centers in the north, while a much smaller number migrated to the Red Sea and Sinai areas. Waves of forced internal migration also resulted from the 1967 Arab-Israeli War and the floods caused by the completion of the Aswan High Dam in 1970. Limited numbers of students and professionals emigrated temporarily prior to the early 1970s, when economic problems and high unemployment pushed the Egyptian Government to lift restrictions on labor migration. At the same time, high oil revenues enabled Saudi Arabia, Iraq, and other Gulf states, as well as Libya and Jordan, to fund development projects, creating a demand for unskilled labor (mainly in construction), which attracted tens of thousands of young Egyptian men.

Between 1970 and 1974 alone, Egyptian migrants in the Gulf countries increased from approximately 70,000 to 370,000. Egyptian officials encouraged legal labor migration both to alleviate unemployment and to generate remittance income (remittances continue to be one of Egypt's largest sources of foreign currency and GDP). During the mid-1980s, however, depressed oil prices resulting from the Iran-Iraq War, decreased demand for low-skilled labor, competition from less costly South Asian workers, and efforts to replace foreign workers with locals significantly reduced Egyptian migration to the Gulf States. The number of Egyptian migrants dropped from a peak of almost 3.3 million in 1983 to about 2.2 million at the start of the 1990s, but numbers gradually recovered.

In the 2000s, Egypt began facilitating more labor migration through bilateral agreements, notably with Arab countries and Italy, but illegal migration to Europe through overstayed visas or maritime human smuggling via Libya also rose. The Egyptian Government estimated there were 6.5 million Egyptian migrants in 2009, with roughly 75% being temporary migrants in other Arab countries (Libya, Saudi Arabia, Jordan, Kuwait, and the United Arab Emirates) and 25% being predominantly permanent migrants in the West (US, UK, Italy, France, and Canada).

During the 2000s, Egypt became an increasingly important transit and destination country for economic migrants and asylum seekers, including Palestinians, East Africans, and South Asians and, more recently, Iraqis and Syrians. Egypt draws many refugees because of its resettlement programs with the West; Cairo has one of the largest urban refugee populations in the world. Many East African migrants are interned or live in temporary encampments along the Egypt-Israel border, and some have been shot and killed by Egyptian border guards.

Age structure: *0-14 years:* 33.8% (male 19,349,395/female 18,243,571)
15-64 years: 60.6% (male 34,646,369/female 32,792,151)
65 years and over: 5.6% (2024 est.) (male 3,146,720/female 3,069,042)

Dependency ratios: *total dependency ratio:* 60.8
youth dependency ratio: 53.2
elderly dependency ratio: 7.7
potential support ratio: 13 (2021 est.)

Median age: *total:* 24.4 years (2024 est.)
male: 24.3 years
female: 24.4 years
comparison ranking: total 177

Population growth rate: 1.49% (2024 est.)
comparison ranking: 65

Birth rate: 19.5 births/1,000 population (2024 est.)
comparison ranking: 73

Death rate: 4.3 deaths/1,000 population (2024 est.)
comparison ranking: 212

Net migration rate: -0.3 migrant(s)/1,000 population (2024 est.)
comparison ranking: 115

Population distribution: approximately 95% of the population lives within 20 km of the Nile River and its delta; vast areas of the country remain sparsely populated or uninhabited as shown in this population distribution map

Urbanization: *urban population:* 43.1% of total population (2023)
rate of urbanization: 1.9% annual rate of change (2020-25 est.)

Major urban areas - population: 22.183 million CAIRO (capital), 5.588 million Alexandria, 778,000 Bur Sa'id (2023)

Sex ratio: *at birth:* 1.06 male(s)/female
0-14 years: 1.06 male(s)/female
15-64 years: 1.06 male(s)/female
65 years and over: 1.03 male(s)/female
total population: 1.06 male(s)/female (2024 est.)

Mother's mean age at first birth: 22.6 years (2014 est.)
note: data represents median age at first birth among women 25-49

Maternal mortality ratio: 17 deaths/100,000 live births (2020 est.)
comparison ranking: 129

Infant mortality rate: *total:* 16.8 deaths/1,000 live births (2024 est.)
male: 17.8 deaths/1,000 live births
female: 15.9 deaths/1,000 live births
comparison ranking: total 88

Life expectancy at birth: *total population:* 75 years (2024 est.)
male: 73.8 years
female: 76.2 years
comparison ranking: total population 132

Total fertility rate: 2.65 children born/woman (2024 est.)
comparison ranking: 63

Gross reproduction rate: 1.28 (2024 est.)

Contraceptive prevalence rate: 58.5% (2014)

Drinking water source: *improved: urban:* 99.7% of population
rural: 99.7% of population
total: 99.7% of population
unimproved: urban: 0.3% of population
rural: 0.3% of population
total: 0.3% of population (2020 est.)

Current health expenditure: 4.4% of GDP (2020)

Physician density: 0.75 physicians/1,000 population (2019)

Hospital bed density: 1.4 beds/1,000 population (2017)

Sanitation facility access: *improved: urban:* 99.9% of population
rural: 98.2% of population
total: 98.9% of population
unimproved: urban: 0.1% of population
rural: 1.8% of population
total: 1.1% of population (2020 est.)

Obesity - adult prevalence rate: 32% (2016)
comparison ranking: 19

Alcohol consumption per capita: *total:* 0.14 liters of pure alcohol (2019 est.)
beer: 0.09 liters of pure alcohol (2019 est.)
wine: 0.01 liters of pure alcohol (2019 est.)
spirits: 0.04 liters of pure alcohol (2019 est.)
other alcohols: 0 liters of pure alcohol (2019 est.)
comparison ranking: total 175

Tobacco use: *total:* 24.3% (2020 est.)

male: 48.1% (2020 est.)
female: 0.4% (2020 est.)
comparison ranking: total 54

Children under the age of 5 years underweight: 7% (2014)
comparison ranking: 66

Currently married women (ages 15-49): 71.1% (2023 est.)

Education expenditures: 2.5% of GDP (2020 est.)
comparison ranking: 175

Literacy: *definition:* age 15 and over can read and write
total population: 73.1%
male: 78.8%
female: 67.4% (2021)

School life expectancy (primary to tertiary education): *total:* 14 years
male: 14 years
female: 14 years (2018)

ENVIRONMENT

Environment - current issues: agricultural land being lost to urbanization and windblown sands; increasing soil salination below Aswan High Dam; desertification; oil pollution threatening coral reefs, beaches, and marine habitats; other water pollution from agricultural pesticides, raw sewage, and industrial effluents; limited natural freshwater resources away from the Nile, which is the only perennial water source; rapid growth in population overstraining the Nile and natural resources

Environment - international agreements: *party to:* Biodiversity, Climate Change, Climate Change-Kyoto Protocol, Climate Change-Paris Agreement, Desertification, Endangered Species, Environmental Modification, Hazardous Wastes, Law of the Sea, Marine Dumping-London Convention, Marine Dumping-London Protocol, Nuclear Test Ban, Ozone Layer Protection, Ship Pollution, Wetlands
signed, but not ratified: Comprehensive Nuclear Test Ban

Climate: desert; hot, dry summers with moderate winters

Urbanization: *urban population:* 43.1% of total population (2023)
rate of urbanization: 1.9% annual rate of change (2020-25 est.)

Revenue from forest resources: 0.15% of GDP (2018 est.)
comparison ranking: 101

Air pollutants: *particulate matter emissions:* 63.16 micrograms per cubic meter (2019 est.)
carbon dioxide emissions: 238.56 megatons (2016 est.)
methane emissions: 59.68 megatons (2020 est.)

Waste and recycling: *municipal solid waste generated annually:* 21 million tons (2012 est.)
municipal solid waste recycled annually: 2.625 million tons (2013 est.)
percent of municipal solid waste recycled: 12.5% (2013 est.)

Major lakes (area sq km): *salt water lake(s):* Lake Manzala - 1,360 sq km
note - largest of Nile Delta lakes

Major rivers (by length in km): An Nīl (Nile) river mouth (shared with Rwanda [s], Tanzania, Uganda, South Sudan, and Sudan) - 6,650 km note – [s] after country name indicates river source; [m] after country name indicates river mouth

Major watersheds (area sq km): Atlantic Ocean drainage: *(Mediterranean Sea)* Nile (3,254,853 sq km)

Major aquifers: Nubian Aquifer System

Total water withdrawal: *municipal:* 10.75 billion cubic meters (2020 est.)
industrial: 5.4 billion cubic meters (2020 est.)
agricultural: 61.35 billion cubic meters (2020 est.)

Total renewable water resources: 57.5 billion cubic meters (2020 est.)

GOVERNMENT

Country name: *conventional long form:* Arab Republic of Egypt
conventional short form: Egypt
local long form: Jumhuriyat Misr al-Arabiyah
local short form: Misr
former: United Arab Republic (short-lived unification with Syria)
etymology: the English name "Egypt" derives from the ancient Greek name for the country "Aigyptos"; the Arabic name "Misr" can be traced to the ancient Akkadian "misru" meaning border or frontier

Government type: presidential republic

Capital: *name:* Cairo
geographic coordinates: 30 03 N, 31 15 E
time difference: UTC+2 (7 hours ahead of Washington, DC, during Standard Time)
daylight saving time: +1hr, begins last Friday in April; ends last Thursday in October
etymology: from the Arabic "al-Qahira," meaning "the victorious"

Administrative divisions: 27 governorates (muhafazat, singular - muhafazat); Ad Daqahliyah, Al Bahr al Ahmar (Red Sea), Al Buhayrah, Al Fayyum, Al Gharbiyah, Al Iskandariyah (Alexandria), Al Isma'iliyah (Ismailia), Al Jizah (Giza), Al Minufiyah, Al Minya, Al Qahirah (Cairo), Al Qalyubiyah, Al Uqsur (Luxor), Al Wadi al Jadid (New Valley), As Suways (Suez), Ash Sharqiyah, Aswan, Asyut, Bani Suwayf, Bur Sa'id (Port Said), Dumyat (Damietta), Janub Sina' (South Sinai), Kafr ash Shaykh, Matruh, Qina, Shamal Sina' (North Sinai), Suhaj

Independence: 28 February 1922 (from UK protectorate status; the military-led revolution that began on 23 July 1952 led to a republic being declared on 18 June 1953 and all British troops withdrawn on 18 June 1956); note - it was ca. 3200 B.C. that the Two Lands of Upper (southern) and Lower (northern) Egypt were first united politically

National holiday: Revolution Day, 23 July (1952)

Legal system: mixed legal system based on Napoleonic civil and penal law, Islamic religious law, and vestiges of colonial-era laws; judicial review of the constitutionality of laws by the Supreme Constitutional Court

Constitution: *history:* several previous; latest approved by a constitutional committee in December 2013, approved by referendum held on 14-15 January 2014, ratified by interim president on 19 January 2014
amendments: proposed by the president of the republic or by one fifth of the House of Representatives members; a decision to accept the proposal requires majority vote by House members; passage of amendment requires a two-thirds majority vote by House members and passage by majority vote in a referendum; articles of reelection of the president and principles of freedom are not amendable unless the amendment "brings more guarantees;" amended 2019

International law organization participation: accepts compulsory ICJ jurisdiction with reservations; non-party state to the ICCt

Citizenship: *citizenship by birth:* no
citizenship by descent only: if the father was born in Egypt
dual citizenship recognized: only with prior permission from the government
residency requirement for naturalization: 10 years

Suffrage: 18 years of age; universal and compulsory

Executive branch: *chief of state:* President Abdel Fattah EL-SISI (since 8 June 2014)
head of government: Prime Minister Mostafa MADBOULY (since 7 June 2018)
cabinet: Cabinet ministers nominated by the executive branch and approved by the House of Representatives
elections/appointments: president elected by absolute majority popular vote in 2 rounds if needed for a 6-year term (eligible for 3 consecutive terms); election last held on 10 to 12 December 2023; next to held in 2029); prime minister appointed by the president, approved by the House of Representatives
election results:
2023: Abdel Fattah EL-SISI reelected president in first round; percent of valid votes cast - Abdel Fattah EL-SISI (independent) 89.6%, Hazam OMAR (Republican People's Party) 4.5%, Farid ZAHRAN (Egyptian Social Democratic Party 4%, Abdel-Samad YAMAMA 1.9%
2018: Abdelfattah ELSISI reelected president in first round; percent of valid votes cast - Abdelfattah ELSISI (independent) 97.1%, Moussa Mostafa MOUSSA (El Ghad Party) 2.9%; note - more than 7% of ballots cast were deemed invalid

Legislative branch: *description:* bicameral Parliament consists of:
Senate or Majlis Al-Shiyoukh (300 seats; 100 members directly elected in single seat constituencies, 100 directly elected by closed party-list vote, and 100 appointed by the president; note - the upper house, previously the Shura Council, was eliminated in the 2014 constitution, reestablished as the Senate, following passage in a 2019 constitutional referendum and approved by the House of Representatives in June 2020
House of Representatives or Majlis Al-Nowaab (596 seats; 448 members directly elected by individual candidacy system, 120 members - with quotas for women, youth, Christians and workers - elected in party-list constituencies by simple majority popular vote, and 28 members appointed by the president; members of both houses serve 5-year terms
elections: Senate - first round held on 11-12 August 2020 (9-10 August for diaspora); second round held on 8-9 September (6-7 September for diaspora) (next to be held in 2025)
House of Representatives - last held 24-25 October and 7-8 November 2020) (next to be held in 2025)
election results: Senate - percent of vote by party - NA; seats by party - Nation's Future Party 100, independent 100; composition - men 258, women 41, percent of women 13.7%
House of Representatives - percent of vote by party - NA; seats by party - Nation's Future Party 316, Republican People's Party 50, New Wafd Party 26,

Homeland Defenders Party 23, Modern Egypt Party 11, Reform and Development Party 9, Al-Nour Party 7, Egyptian Conference Party 7, Egyptian Freedom Party 7, Egyptian Social Democratic Party 7, Tagammu 6, Justice Party 2, Etradet Geel Party 1, independent 124; composition - men 428, women 164, percent of women 27.5%; total Parliament percent of women 23%

Judicial branch: *highest court(s):* Supreme Constitutional Court (SCC) (consists of the court president and 10 justices); the SCC serves as the final court of arbitration on the constitutionality of laws and conflicts between lower courts regarding jurisdiction and rulings; Court of Cassation (CC) (consists of the court president and 550 judges organized in circuits with cases heard by panels of 5 judges); the CC is the highest appeals body for civil and criminal cases, also known as "ordinary justices"; Supreme Administrative Court (SAC) (consists of the court president and NA judges and organized in circuits with cases heard by panels of 5 judges); the SAC is the highest court of the State Council
judge selection and term of office: under the 2014 constitution, all judges and justices selected and appointed by the Supreme Judiciary Council and approved as a formality by the president of the Republic; judges appointed for life; under the 2019 amendments, the president has the power to appoint heads of judiciary authorities and courts, the prosecutor general, and the head of the Supreme Constitutional Court
subordinate courts: Courts of Appeal; Courts of First Instance; courts of limited jurisdiction; Family Court (established in 2004)

Political parties: Al-Nour
Arab Democratic Nasserist Party
Congress Party
Conservative Party
Democratic Peace Party
Egyptian National Movement Party
Egyptian Social Democratic Party
El Ghad Party
El Serh El Masry el Hor
Eradet Geel Party
Free Egyptians Party
Freedom Party
Justice Party
Homeland's Protector Party
Modern Egypt Party
My Homeland Egypt Party
Nation's Future Party (Mostaqbal Watan)
National Progressive Unionist (Tagammu) Party
Reform and Development Party
Republican People's Party
Revolutionary Guards Party
Wafd Party

International organization participation: ABEDA, AfDB, AFESD, AMF, AU, BRICS, BSEC (observer), CAEU, CD, CICA, COMESA, D-8, EBRD, FAO, G-15, G-24, G-77, IAEA, IBRD, ICAO, ICC (national committees), ICRM, IDA, IDB, IFAD, IFC, IFRCS, IHO, ILO, IMF, IMO, IMSO, Interpol, IOC, IOM, IPU, ISO, ITSO, ITU, LAS, LCBC (observer), MIGA, MINURSO, MONUSCO, NAM, OAPEC, OAS (observer), OIC, OIF, OSCE (partner), PCA, UN, UNAMID, UNCTAD, UNESCO, UNHCR, UNIDO, UNISFA, UNMISS, UNOCI, UNOOSA, UNRWA, UNWTO, UPU, WCO, WFTU (NGOs), WHO, WIPO, WMO, WTO

Diplomatic representation in the US: *chief of mission:* Ambassador Motaz Mounir ZAHRAN (since 17 September 2020)
chancery: 3521 International Court NW, Washington, DC 20008
telephone: [1] (202) 895-5400
FAX: (202) 244-4319
email address and website:
embassy@egyptembassy.net
https://www.egyptembassy.net/
consulate(s) general: Chicago, Houston, Los Angeles, New York

Diplomatic representation from the US: *chief of mission:* Ambassador Herro MUSTAFA GARG (since 15 November 2023)
embassy: 5 Tawfik Diab St., Garden City, Cairo
mailing address: 7700 Cairo Place, Washington DC 20512-7700
telephone: [20-2] 2797-3300
FAX: [20-2] 2797-3200
email address and website:
ConsularCairoACS@state.gov
https://eg.usembassy.gov/
consulate(s) general: Alexandria

Flag description: three equal horizontal bands of red (top), white, and black; the national emblem (a gold Eagle of Saladin facing the hoist side with a shield superimposed on its chest above a scroll bearing the name of the country in Arabic) centered in the white band; the band colors derive from the Arab Liberation flag and represent oppression (black), overcome through bloody struggle (red), to be replaced by a bright future (white)
note: similar to the flag of Syria, which has two green stars in the white band; Iraq, which has an Arabic inscription centered in the white band; and Yemen, which has a plain white band

National symbol(s): golden eagle, white lotus; national colors: red, white, black

National anthem: *name:* "Bilady, Bilady, Bilady" (My Homeland, My Homeland, My Homeland)
lyrics/music: Younis-al QADI/Sayed DARWISH
note: adopted 1979; the current anthem, less militaristic than the previous one, was created after the signing of the 1979 peace treaty with Israel; Sayed DARWISH, commonly considered the father of modern Egyptian music, composed the anthem

National heritage: *total World Heritage Sites:* 7 (6 cultural, 1 natural)
selected World Heritage Site locales: Memphis and its Necropolis (c); Ancient Thebes with its Necropolis (c); Nubian Monuments (c); Saint Catherine Area (c); Abu Mena (c); Historic Cairo (c); Wadi Al-Hitan (Whale Valley) (n)

ECONOMY

Economic overview: Africa's second-largest economy; 2030 Vision to diversify markets and energy infrastructure; improving fiscal, external, and current accounts; underperforming private sector; poor labor force participation; expanded credit access

Real GDP (purchasing power parity): $1.912 trillion (2023 est.)
$1.842 trillion (2022 est.)
$1.729 trillion (2021 est.)
note: data in 2021 dollars
comparison ranking: 17

Real GDP growth rate: 3.76% (2023 est.)
6.59% (2022 est.)
3.29% (2021 est.)
note: annual GDP % growth based on constant local currency
comparison ranking: 84

Real GDP per capita: $17,000 (2023 est.)
$16,600 (2022 est.)
$15,800 (2021 est.)
note: data in 2021 dollars
comparison ranking: 112

GDP (official exchange rate): $395.926 billion (2023 est.)
note: data in current dollars at official exchange rate

Inflation rate (consumer prices): 33.88% (2023 est.)
13.9% (2022 est.)
5.21% (2021 est.)
note: annual % change based on consumer prices
comparison ranking: 209

Credit ratings: Fitch rating: B+ (2019)

Moody's rating: B2 (2019)

Standard & Poors rating: B (2018)
note: The year refers to the year in which the current credit rating was first obtained.

GDP - composition, by sector of origin: *agriculture:* 10.6% (2023 est.)
industry: 32.7% (2023 est.)
services: 51.6% (2023 est.)
note: figures may not total 100% due to non-allocated consumption not captured in sector-reported data comparison rankings: services 134; industry 50; agriculture 73

GDP - composition, by end use: *household consumption:* 82.6% (2023 est.)
government consumption: 6.8% (2023 est.)
investment in fixed capital: 15.2% (2022 est.)
investment in inventories: -2.3% (2023 est.)
exports of goods and services: 19.1% (2023 est.)
imports of goods and services: -21.3% (2023 est.)
note: figures may not total 100% due to rounding or gaps in data collection

Agricultural products: sugarcane, sugar beets, wheat, maize, tomatoes, potatoes, rice, milk, onions, oranges (2022)
note: top ten agricultural products based on tonnage

Industries: textiles, food processing, tourism, chemicals, pharmaceuticals, hydrocarbons, construction, cement, metals, light manufactures

Industrial production growth rate: -0.57% (2023 est.)
note: annual % change in industrial value added based on constant local currency
comparison ranking: 162

Labor force: 33.431 million (2023 est.)
note: number of people ages 15 or older who are employed or seeking work
comparison ranking: 20

Unemployment rate: 7.31% (2023 est.)
7.34% (2022 est.)
7.44% (2021 est.)
note: % of labor force seeking employment
comparison ranking: 139

Youth unemployment rate (ages 15-24): *total:* 19% (2023 est.)
male: 12.6% (2023 est.)
female: 49.2% (2023 est.)
note: % of labor force ages 15-24 seeking employment
comparison ranking: total 69

Population below poverty line: 29.7% (2019 est.)
note: % of population with income below national poverty line

Gini Index coefficient - distribution of family income: 31.9 (2019 est.)
note: index (0-100) of income distribution; higher values represent greater inequality
comparison ranking: 109

Average household expenditures: *on food:* 37.1% of household expenditures (2022 est.)
on alcohol and tobacco: 4.6% of household expenditures (2022 est.)

Household income or consumption by percentage share: *lowest 10%:* 3.8% (2019 est.)
highest 10%: 27.5% (2019 est.)
note: % share of income accruing to lowest and highest 10% of population

Remittances: 6.11% of GDP (2023 est.)
5.94% of GDP (2022 est.)
7.41% of GDP (2021 est.)
note: personal transfers and compensation between resident and non-resident individuals/households/entities

Budget: *revenues:* $69.999 billion (2015 est.)
expenditures: $96.057 billion (2015 est.)
note: central government revenues (excluding grants) and expenses converted to US dollars at average official exchange rate for year indicated

Public debt: 103% of GDP (2017 est.)
note: data cover central government debt and include debt instruments issued (or owned) by government entities other than the treasury; the data include treasury debt held by foreign entities; the data include debt issued by subnational entities, as well as intragovernmental debt; intragovernmental debt consists of treasury borrowings from surpluses in the social funds, such as for retirement, medical care, and unemployment; debt instruments for the social funds are sold at public auctions
comparison ranking: 18

Taxes and other revenues: 12.52% (of GDP) (2015 est.)
note: central government tax revenue as a % of GDP
comparison ranking: 159

Current account balance: -$10.537 billion (2022 est.)
-$18.611 billion (2021 est.)
-$14.236 billion (2020 est.)
note: balance of payments - net trade and primary/secondary income in current dollars
comparison ranking: 194

Exports: $76.295 billion (2022 est.)
$58.339 billion (2021 est.)
$40.102 billion (2020 est.)
note: balance of payments - exports of goods and services in current dollars
comparison ranking: 54

Exports - partners: Turkey 8%, Italy 6%, US 6%, Spain 6%, India 5% (2022)
note: top five export partners based on percentage share of exports

Exports - commodities: natural gas, fertilizers, garments, refined petroleum, crude petroleum (2022)
note: top five export commodities based on value in dollars

Imports: $97.144 billion (2022 est.)
$94.039 billion (2021 est.)
$72.482 billion (2020 est.)
note: balance of payments - imports of goods and services in current dollars
comparison ranking: 48

Imports - partners: China 17%, US 7%, Saudi Arabia 7%, UAE 6%, Turkey 5% (2022)
note: top five import partners based on percentage share of imports

Imports - commodities: refined petroleum, wheat, crude petroleum, natural gas, plastics (2022)
note: top five import commodities based on value in dollars

Reserves of foreign exchange and gold: $33.07 billion (2023 est.)
$32.144 billion (2022 est.)
$39.824 billion (2021 est.)
note: holdings of gold (year-end prices)/foreign exchange/special drawing rights in current dollars
comparison ranking: 43

Debt - external: $97.5 billion (2022 est.)
note: present value of external debt in current US dollars
comparison ranking: 8

Exchange rates: Egyptian pounds (EGP) per US dollar -

Exchange rates: 30.626 (2023 est.)
19.16 (2022 est.)
15.645 (2021 est.)
15.759 (2020 est.)
16.771 (2019 est.)

ENERGY

Electricity access: *electrification - total population:* 100% (2022 est.)

Electricity: *installed generating capacity:* 59.248 million kW (2022 est.)
consumption: 176.719 billion kWh (2022 est.)
exports: 1.61 billion kWh (2022 est.)
imports: 176 million kWh (2022 est.)
transmission/distribution losses: 37.615 billion kWh (2022 est.)
comparison rankings: transmission/distribution losses 201; imports 107; exports 61; consumption 25; installed generating capacity 23

Electricity generation sources: *fossil fuels:* 88.5% of total installed capacity (2022 est.)
solar: 2.1% of total installed capacity (2022 est.)
wind: 2.9% of total installed capacity (2022 est.)
hydroelectricity: 6.2% of total installed capacity (2022 est.)
biomass and waste: 0.2% of total installed capacity (2022 est.)

Nuclear energy: Number of nuclear reactors under construction: 4 (2023)

Coal: *production:* 289,000 metric tons (2022 est.)
consumption: 3.083 million metric tons (2022 est.)
exports: 92.8 metric tons (2022 est.)
imports: 2.733 million metric tons (2022 est.)
proven reserves: 182 million metric tons (2022 est.)

Petroleum: *total petroleum production:* 667,000 bbl/day (2023 est.)
refined petroleum consumption: 851,000 bbl/day (2022 est.)
crude oil estimated reserves: 3.3 billion barrels (2021 est.)

Natural gas: *production:* 64.817 billion cubic meters (2022 est.)
consumption: 60.089 billion cubic meters (2022 est.)
exports: 9.28 billion cubic meters (2022 est.)
imports: 6.648 billion cubic meters (2022 est.)
proven reserves: 1.784 trillion cubic meters (2021 est.)

Carbon dioxide emissions: 240.225 million metric tonnes of CO_2 (2022 est.)
from coal and metallurgical coke: 6.77 million metric tonnes of CO_2 (2022 est.)
from petroleum and other liquids: 115.575 million metric tonnes of CO_2 (2022 est.)
from consumed natural gas: 117.879 million metric tonnes of CO_2 (2022 est.)
comparison ranking: total emissions 29

Energy consumption per capita: 36.463 million Btu/person (2022 est.)
comparison ranking: 105

COMMUNICATIONS

Telephones - fixed lines: *total subscriptions:* 11.6 million (2022 est.)
subscriptions per 100 inhabitants: 10 (2022 est.)
comparison ranking: total subscriptions 15

Telephones - mobile cellular: *total subscriptions:* 103.45 million (2022 est.)
subscriptions per 100 inhabitants: 93 (2022 est.)
comparison ranking: total subscriptions 17

Telecommunication systems: *general assessment:* Egypt's large telecom market is supported by a population of about 109 million and benefits from effective competition in most sectors; a liberal regulatory regime allows for unified licenses which permit operators to offer fixed-line as well as mobile services; in recent years the government has developed a number of digital migration projects aimed at increasing average broadband speeds, delivering fiber broadband to about 60% of the population, developing an in-house satellite program, and creating a knowledge-based economy through the greater adoption of ICTs; the New Administrative Capital being built is only one of more than a dozen smart city projects, which together are stimulating investment in 5G and fiber broadband, as well as the adoption of IoT and AI solutions; the country endeavors to be a significant ICT hub in the North Africa and Middle East regions; Egypt's mature mobile market has one of the highest subscription rates in Africa; progress in the adoption of mobile data services has been hampered by the lack of sufficient spectrum; the regulator in September 2020 made available 60MHz in the 2.6GHz band, though the spectrum was not allocated until late 2021; the additional spectrum will go far to enabling the MNOs to improve the quality of mobile broadband services offered; further 5G trials are to be held later in 2022, focused on the New Administrative Capital; the international cable infrastructure remains an important asset for Egypt, which benefits from its geographical position; Telecom Egypt has become one of the largest concerns in this segment, being a participating member in numerous cable systems; in mid-2021 the telco announced plans to build the Hybrid African Ring Path system, connecting a number of landlocked countries in Africa with Italy, France, and Portugal; the system will partly use the company's existing terrestrial and sub sea cable networks (2022)
domestic: fixed-line roughly 10 per 100, mobile-cellular 95 per 100 (2021)
international: country code - 20; landing points for Aletar, Africa-1, FEA, Hawk, IMEWE, and the SEA-ME-WE-3 & 4 submarine cable networks linking to Asia, Africa, the Middle East, and Australia ; satellite earth stations - 4 (2 Intelsat - Atlantic Ocean and Indian Ocean, 1 Arabsat, and 1 Inmarsat);

tropospheric scatter to Sudan; microwave radio relay to Israel; a participant in Medarabtel (2019)

Broadcast media: mix of state-run and private broadcast media; state-run TV operates 2 national and 6 regional terrestrial networks, as well as a few satellite channels; dozens of private satellite channels and a large number of Arabic satellite channels are available for free; some limited satellite services are also available via subscription; state-run radio operates about 30 stations belonging to 8 networks; privately-owned radio includes 8 major stations, 4 of which belong to 1 network (2019)

Internet country code: .eg

Internet users: *total:* 79.2 million (2021 est.)
percent of population: 72% (2021 est.)
comparison ranking: total 10

Broadband - fixed subscriptions: *total:* 9,349,469 (2020 est.)
subscriptions per 100 inhabitants: 9 (2020 est.)
comparison ranking: total 22

Communications - note: one of the largest and most famous libraries in the ancient world was the Great Library of Alexandria in Egypt (founded about 295 B.C., it may have survived in some form into the 5th century A.D.); seeking to resurrect the great center of learning and communication, the Egyptian Government in 2002 inaugurated the Bibliotheca Alexandrina, an Egyptian National Library on the site of the original Great Library, which commemorates the original archive and also serves as a center of cultural and scientific excellence

TRANSPORTATION

National air transport system: *number of registered air carriers:* 14 (2020)
inventory of registered aircraft operated by air carriers: 101
annual passenger traffic on registered air carriers: 12,340,832 (2018)
annual freight traffic on registered air carriers: 437.63 million (2018) mt-km

Civil aircraft registration country code prefix: SU

Airports: 73 (2024)
comparison ranking: 69

Heliports: 56 (2024)

Pipelines: 486 km condensate, 74 km condensate/ gas, 7,986 km gas, 957 km liquid petroleum gas, 5,225 km oil, 37 km oil/gas/ water, 895 km refined products, 65 km water (2013)

Railways: *total:* 5,085 km (2014)
standard gauge: 5,085 km (2014) 1.435-m gauge (62 km electrified)
comparison ranking: total 38

Roadways: *total:* 65,050 km
paved: 48,000 km
unpaved: 17,050 km (2019)
comparison ranking: total 75

Waterways: 3,500 km (2018) (includes the Nile River, Lake Nasser, Alexandria-Cairo Waterway, and numerous smaller canals in Nile Delta; the Suez Canal (193.5 km including approaches) is navigable by oceangoing vessels drawing up to 17.68 m)
comparison ranking: 31

Merchant marine: *total:* 441 (2023)
by type: bulk carrier 14, container ship 6, general cargo 23, oil tanker 42, other 356
comparison ranking: total 45

Ports: *total ports:* 31 (2024)
large: 5
medium: 1
small: 8
very small: 16
size unknown: 1
ports with oil terminals: 17
key ports: Ain Sukhna Terminal, Al Iskandariyh (Alexandria), As Suways, Bur Sa'id, Damietta, Ras Shukhier

MILITARY AND SECURITY

Military and security forces: Egyptian Armed Forces (EAF): Army (includes Republican Guard), Navy (includes Coast Guard), Air Force, Air Defense Forces, Border Guard Forces; Interior Ministry: Public Security Sector Police, the Central Security Force, National Security Agency (2024)
note 1: the Public Security Sector Police are responsible for law enforcement nationwide; the Central Security Force protects infrastructure and is responsible for crowd control; the National Security Agency is responsible for internal security threats and counterterrorism along with other security services
note 2: in addition to its external defense duties, the EAF also has a mandate to assist police in protecting vital infrastructure during a state of emergency; military personnel were granted full arrest authority in 2011 but normally only use this authority during states of emergency and "periods of significant turmoil"

Military expenditures: 1% of GDP (2023 est.)
1.2% of GDP (2022 est.)
1.3% of GDP (2021 est.)
1.3% of GDP (2020 est.)
1.3% of GDP (2019 est.)
comparison ranking: 131

Military and security service personnel strengths: information varies; approximately 450,000 active-duty personnel (325,000 Army; 18,000 Navy; 30,000 Air Force; 75,000 Air Defense Command); approximately 300,000 Central Security Forces personnel (2023)

Military equipment inventories and acquisitions: the EAF's inventory is comprised of a mix of domestically produced, Soviet-era, and more modern, particularly Western, weapons systems; in recent years, the EAF has embarked on an equipment modernization program with significant purchases from foreign suppliers; major suppliers have included China, France, Germany, Italy, Russia, and the US; Egypt has an established defense industry that produces a range of products from small arms to armored vehicles and naval vessels; it also has licensed and co-production agreements with several countries, including Germany and the US (2024)

Military service age and obligation: voluntary enlistment possible from age 16 for men and 17 for women; 18-30 years of age for conscript service for men; service obligation 14-36 months, followed by a 9-year reserve obligation; active service length depends on education; high school drop-outs serve for the full 36 months, while college graduates serve for lesser periods of time, depending on their education level (2023)
note: conscripts make up a considerable portion of the military and the Central Security Force

Military deployments: 1,000 (plus nearly 200 police) Central African Republic (MINUSCA); also has about 350 police deployed to the Democratic Republic of the Congo under MONUSCO (2024)

Military - note: the Egyptian Armed Forces (EAF) are responsible for external defense but also have an internal role assisting police and paramilitary security forces during emergencies and in anti-terrorism operations; the EAF also participates in foreign peacekeeping and other security missions, as well as both bilateral and multinational exercises; the military has considerable political power and independence; it has long had a crucial role in Egypt's politics and has a large stake in the civilian economy, including running banks, businesses, gas stations, shipping lines, and utilities, and producing consumer and industrial goods, importing commodities, and building and managing infrastructure projects, such as bridges, roads, hospitals, and housing
the EAF is the largest and one of the best equipped militaries in the region; key areas of concern for the EAF include Islamist militant groups operating out of the Sinai Peninsula, regional challenges such as ongoing conflicts and instability, and maritime security; since 2011, the EAF has been conducting operations alongside other security forces in the North Sinai governorate against several militant groups, particularly the Islamic State of Iraq and ash-Sham (ISIS); over the past decade, it has deployed large numbers of troops along Egypt's border with Libya, provided air support to the Saudi-led coalition's intervention in Yemen, and most recently boosted its presence on the border with Gaza in response to the HAMAS-Israel conflict; the Navy in recent years has sought to modernize and expand its capabilities and profile in the Eastern Mediterranean and Red Sea, including the acquisition of helicopter carriers, modern frigates, and attack submarines; in 2020, the EAF inaugurated a large joint service military base on the Red Sea to secure the country's southern coasts, protect economic investments and natural resources, and confront security challenges in the Red Sea region
Egypt is a major security partner of the US and one of the largest recipients of US military aid in the region; it also has Major Non-NATO Ally status with the US, a designation under US law that provides foreign partners with certain benefits in the areas of defense trade and security cooperation
the Multinational Force & Observers (MFO) has operated in the Sinai since 1982 as a peacekeeping and monitoring force to supervise the implementation of the security provisions of the 1979 Egyptian-Israeli Treaty of Peace; the MFO is an independent international organization, created by agreement between Egypt and Israel; it is composed of about 1,150 troops from 13 countries; Colombia, Fiji, and the US are the leading providers of troops to the MFO (2024)

SPACE

Space agency/agencies: Egyptian Space Agency (EgSA; public economic authority established 2019); National Authority for Remote Sensing and Space Science (NARSS; formed in 1994 from the Remote Sensing Center, which was established in 1971) (2024)

Space program overview: has a growing program with a focus on developing the capabilities to manufacture satellites and associated support infrastructure; seeks to become a regional space power; operates satellites; builds satellites jointly with foreign

partners but developing localized satellite manufacturing capabilities; acquiring through technology transfers and domestic development programs other space-related technologies, including those related to communications, Earth imaging/ remote sensing (RS), and satellite payloads and components; cooperating on space-related issues with a variety of foreign governments and commercial space companies, including those of Belarus, Canada, China, the European Space Agency and its member states (particularly France, Germany, Italy), Ghana, India, Japan, Kazakhstan, Kenya, Nigeria, Russia, South Africa, Sudan, Uganda, Ukraine, the UAE, and the US; also a member of the Arab Space Coordination Group, established by the UAE in 2019; has a commercial space sector that focuses on satellite communications, satellite design and production, RS, and space applications (2024)
note: further details about the key activities, programs, and milestones of the country's space program, as well as government spending estimates on the space sector, appear in the Space Programs reference guide

TERRORISM

Terrorist group(s): Army of Islam; Islamic State of Iraq and ash-Sham – Sinai Province (ISIS-SP); al-Qa'ida
note: details about the history, aims, leadership, organization, areas of operation, tactics, targets, weapons, size, and sources of support of the group(s) appear(s) in the Terrorism reference guide

TRANSNATIONAL ISSUES

Refugees and internally displaced persons: *refugees (country of origin):* 70,021 (West Bank and Gaza Strip) (mid-year 2022); 52,446 (Sudan) (refugees and asylum seekers), 20,970 (South Sudan) (refugees and asylum seekers), 21,105 (Eritrea) (refugees and asylum seekers), 15,585 (Ethiopia) (refugees and asylum seekers), 10,025 (Yemen) (refugees and asylum seekers), 6,815 (Iraq) (refugees and asylum seekers), 6,802 (Somalia) (refugees and asylum seekers) (2022); 464,827 (Sudan) (refugees since 15 April 2023), 156,159 (Syria) (2024)
stateless persons: 10 (2022)

Illicit drugs: major source of precursor chemicals used in the production of illicit narcotics

EL SALVADOR

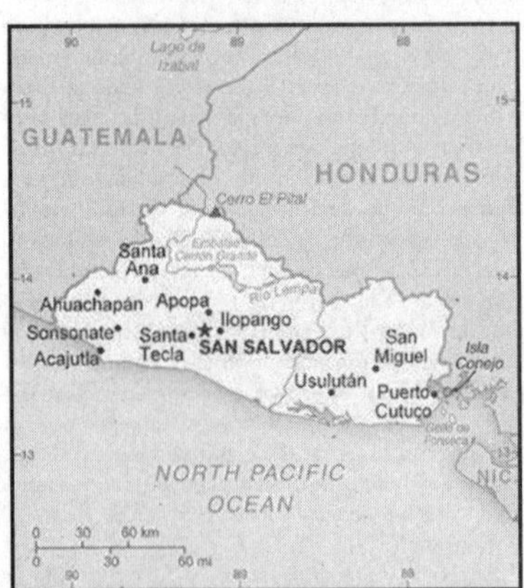

INTRODUCTION

Background: El Salvador achieved independence from Spain in 1821 and from the Central American Federation in 1839. A 12-year civil war, which cost about 75,000 lives, was brought to a close in 1992 when the government and leftist rebels signed a treaty that provided for military and political reforms. El Salvador is beset by one of the world's highest homicide rates and pervasive criminal gangs.

GEOGRAPHY

Location: Central America, bordering the North Pacific Ocean, between Guatemala and Honduras

Geographic coordinates: 13 50 N, 88 55 W

Map references: Central America and the Caribbean

Area: *total:* 21,041 sq km
land: 20,721 sq km
water: 320 sq km
comparison ranking: total 153

Area - comparative: about the same size as New Jersey

Land boundaries: *total:* 590 km
border countries (2): Guatemala 199 km; Honduras 391 km

Coastline: 307 km

Maritime claims: *territorial sea:* 12 nm
contiguous zone: 24 nm
exclusive economic zone: 200 nm

Climate: tropical; rainy season (May to October); dry season (November to April); tropical on coast; temperate in uplands

Terrain: mostly mountains with narrow coastal belt and central plateau

Elevation: *highest point:* Cerro El Pital 2,730 m
lowest point: Pacific Ocean 0 m
mean elevation: 442 m

Natural resources: hydropower, geothermal power, petroleum, arable land

Land use: *agricultural land:* 74.7% (2018 est.)
arable land: 33.1% (2018 est.)
permanent crops: 10.9% (2018 est.)
permanent pasture: 30.7% (2018 est.)
forest: 13.6% (2018 est.)
other: 11.7% (2018 est.)

Irrigated land: 274 sq km (2020)

Population distribution: athough it is the smallest country in land area in Central America, El Salvador has a population that is 18 times larger than Belize; at least 20% of the population lives abroad; high population density country-wide, with particular concentration around the capital of San Salvador

Natural hazards: known as the Land of Volcanoes; frequent and sometimes destructive earthquakes and volcanic activity; extremely susceptible to hurricanes
volcanism: significant volcanic activity; San Salvador (1,893 m), which last erupted in 1917, has the potential to cause major harm to the country's capital, which lies just below the volcano's slopes; San Miguel (2,130 m), which last erupted in 2002, is one of the most active volcanoes in the country; other historically active volcanoes include Conchaguita, Ilopango, Izalco, and Santa Ana

Geography - note: smallest Central American country and only one without a coastline on the Caribbean Sea

PEOPLE AND SOCIETY

Population: *total:* 6,628,702
male: 3,172,244
female: 3,456,458 (2024 est.)
comparison rankings: female 107; male 110; total 110

Nationality: *noun:* Salvadoran(s)
adjective: Salvadoran

Ethnic groups: Mestizo 86.3%, White 12.7%, Indigenous 0.2% (includes Lenca, Kakawira, Nahua-Pipil), Black 0.1%, other 0.6% (2007 est.)

Languages: Spanish (official), Nawat (among some indigenous)
major-language sample(s):
La Libreta Informativa del Mundo, la fuente indispensable de información básica. (Spanish)

Religions: Roman Catholic 43.9%, Protestant 39.6% (Evangelical - unspecified 38.2%, Evangelical - Methodist 1.3%, Evangelical - Baptist 0.1%), none 16.3%, unspecified 0.2% (2023 est.)

Demographic profile: El Salvador is the smallest and most densely populated country in Central America. It is well into its demographic transition, experiencing slower population growth, a decline in its number of youths, and the gradual aging of its population. The increased use of family planning has substantially lowered El Salvador's fertility rate, from approximately 6 children per woman in the 1970s to replacement level today. A 2008 national family planning survey showed that female sterilization remained the most common contraception method in El Salvador - its sterilization rate is among the highest in Latin America and the Caribbean - but that the use of injectable contraceptives is growing. Fertility differences between rich and poor and urban and rural women are narrowing.

Salvadorans fled during the 1979 to 1992 civil war mainly to the United States but also to Canada and to neighboring Mexico, Guatemala, Honduras, Nicaragua, and Costa Rica. Emigration to the United States increased again in the 1990s and 2000s as a result of deteriorating economic conditions, natural disasters (Hurricane Mitch in 1998 and earthquakes in 2001), and family reunification. At least 20% of El Salvador's population lives abroad. The remittances they send home account for close to 20% of GDP, are the second largest source of external income after exports, and have helped reduce poverty.

Age structure: *0-14 years:* 25.3% (male 855,841/ female 818,642)

15-64 years: 66.3% (male 2,077,745/female 2,317,416)
65 years and over: 8.4% (2024 est.) (male 238,658/female 320,400)

Dependency ratios: *total dependency ratio:* 51.3
youth dependency ratio: 39
elderly dependency ratio: 12.3
potential support ratio: 8.1 (2021 est.)

Median age: *total:* 29.7 years (2024 est.)
male: 28.2 years
female: 31.2 years
comparison ranking: total 143

Population growth rate: 0.34% (2024 est.)
comparison ranking: 163

Birth rate: 17.1 births/1,000 population (2024 est.)
comparison ranking: 90

Death rate: 5.9 deaths/1,000 population (2024 est.)
comparison ranking: 161

Net migration rate: -7.7 migrant(s)/1,000 population (2024 est.)
comparison ranking: 219

Population distribution: athough it is the smallest country in land area in Central America, El Salvador has a population that is 18 times larger than Belize; at least 20% of the population lives abroad; high population density country-wide, with particular concentration around the capital of San Salvador

Urbanization: *urban population:* 75.4% of total population (2023)
rate of urbanization: 1.33% annual rate of change (2020-25 est.)

Major urban areas - population: 1.116 million SAN SALVADOR (capital) (2023)

Sex ratio: *at birth:* 1.05 male(s)/female
0-14 years: 1.05 male(s)/female
15-64 years: 0.9 male(s)/female
65 years and over: 0.74 male(s)/female
total population: 0.92 male(s)/female (2024 est.)

Mother's mean age at first birth: 20.8 years (2008 est.)
note: data represents median age at first birth among women 25-29

Maternal mortality ratio: 43 deaths/100,000 live births (2020 est.)
comparison ranking: 100

Infant mortality rate: *total:* 11.7 deaths/1,000 live births (2024 est.)
male: 13.3 deaths/1,000 live births
female: 10 deaths/1,000 live births
comparison ranking: total 112

Life expectancy at birth: *total population:* 75.9 years (2024 est.)
male: 72.4 years
female: 79.5 years
comparison ranking: total population 121

Total fertility rate: 2.02 children born/woman (2024 est.)
comparison ranking: 105

Gross reproduction rate: 0.98 (2024 est.)

Contraceptive prevalence rate: 71.9% (2014)

Drinking water source: *improved: urban:* 99.6% of population
rural: 94.2% of population
total: 98.2% of population
unimproved: urban: 0.4% of population
rural: 5.8% of population
total: 1.8% of population (2020 est.)

Current health expenditure: 9.9% of GDP (2020)

Physician density: 2.87 physicians/1,000 population (2018)

Hospital bed density: 1.2 beds/1,000 population (2017)

Sanitation facility access: *improved: urban:* 100% of population
rural: 97.1% of population
total: 99.2% of population
unimproved: urban: 0% of population
rural: 2.9% of population
total: 0.8% of population (2020 est.)

Obesity - adult prevalence rate: 24.6% (2016)
comparison ranking: 57

Alcohol consumption per capita: *total:* 2.94 liters of pure alcohol (2019 est.)
beer: 1.5 liters of pure alcohol (2019 est.)
wine: 0.06 liters of pure alcohol (2019 est.)
spirits: 1.37 liters of pure alcohol (2019 est.)
other alcohols: 0 liters of pure alcohol (2019 est.)
comparison ranking: total 116

Tobacco use: *total:* 7.9% (2020 est.)
male: 14.1% (2020 est.)
female: 1.7% (2020 est.)
comparison ranking: total 151

Children under the age of 5 years underweight: 5% (2014)
comparison ranking: 74

Currently married women (ages 15-49): 55% (2023 est.)

Child marriage: *women married by age 15:* 4.3%
women married by age 18: 19.7% (2021 est.)

Education expenditures: 4.1% of GDP (2020 est.)
comparison ranking: 111

Literacy: *definition:* age 15 and over can read and write
total population: 89.1%
male: 91.3%
female: 87.3% (2019)

School life expectancy (primary to tertiary education): *total:* 12 years
male: 12 years
female: 12 years (2018)

ENVIRONMENT

Environment - current issues: deforestation; soil erosion; water pollution; contamination of soils from disposal of toxic wastes

Environment - international agreements: *party to:* Biodiversity, Climate Change, Climate Change-Kyoto Protocol, Climate Change-Paris Agreement, Comprehensive Nuclear Test Ban, Desertification, Endangered Species, Hazardous Wastes, Nuclear Test Ban, Ozone Layer Protection, Ship Pollution, Wetlands
signed, but not ratified: Law of the Sea

Climate: tropical; rainy season (May to October); dry season (November to April); tropical on coast; temperate in uplands

Urbanization: *urban population:* 75.4% of total population (2023)
rate of urbanization: 1.33% annual rate of change (2020-25 est.)

Revenue from forest resources: 0.6% of GDP (2018 est.)
comparison ranking: 62

Revenue from coal: 0% of GDP (2018 est.)
comparison ranking: 158

Air pollutants: *particulate matter emissions:* 22.15 micrograms per cubic meter (2019 est.)
carbon dioxide emissions: 7.17 megatons (2016 est.)
methane emissions: 4.71 megatons (2020 est.)

Waste and recycling: *municipal solid waste generated annually:* 1,648,996 tons (2010 est.)

Total water withdrawal: *municipal:* 470 million cubic meters (2020 est.)
industrial: 210 million cubic meters (2020 est.)
agricultural: 1.43 billion cubic meters (2020 est.)

Total renewable water resources: 26.27 billion cubic meters (2020 est.)

GOVERNMENT

Country name: *conventional long form:* Republic of El Salvador
conventional short form: El Salvador
local long form: República de El Salvador
local short form: El Salvador
etymology: name is an abbreviation of the original Spanish conquistador designation for the area "Provincia de Nuestro Senor Jesus Cristo, el Salvador del Mundo" (Province of Our Lord Jesus Christ, the Saviour of the World), which became simply "El Salvador" (The Savior)

Government type: presidential republic

Capital: *name:* San Salvador
geographic coordinates: 13 42 N, 89 12 W
time difference: UTC-6 (1 hour behind Washington, DC, during Standard Time)
etymology: Spanish for "Holy Savior" (referring to Jesus Christ)

Administrative divisions: 14 departments (departamentos, singular - departamento); Ahuachapan, Cabanas, Chalatenango, Cuscatlan, La Libertad, La Paz, La Union, Morazan, San Miguel, San Salvador, San Vicente, Santa Ana, Sonsonate, Usulutan

Independence: 15 September 1821 (from Spain)

National holiday: Independence Day, 15 September (1821)

Legal system: civil law system with minor common law influence; judicial review of legislative acts in the Supreme Court

Constitution: *history:* many previous; latest drafted 16 December 1983, enacted 23 December 1983
amendments: proposals require agreement by absolute majority of the Legislative Assembly membership; passage requires at least two-thirds majority vote of the Assembly; constitutional articles on basic principles, and citizen rights and freedoms cannot be amended; amended 2003, 2009, 2014

International law organization participation: has not submitted an ICJ jurisdiction declaration; non-party state to the ICCt

Citizenship: *citizenship by birth:* yes
citizenship by descent only: yes
dual citizenship recognized: yes
residency requirement for naturalization: 5 years

Suffrage: 18 years of age; universal

Executive branch: *chief of state:* President Nayib Armando BUKELE Ortez (since 1 June 2019)
head of government: President Nayib Armando BUKELE Ortez (since 1 June 2019)
cabinet: Council of Ministers selected by the president

elections/appointments: president and vice president directly elected on the same ballot by absolute majority popular vote in 2 rounds if needed for a single 5-year term; election last held on 4 February 2024 (next to be held in 2029)
election results:
2024: Nayib Armando BUKELE Ortez reelected president - Nayib Armando BUKELE Ortez (Nuevas Ideas) 84.7%, Manuel FLORES (FMLN) 6.4%, Joel SANCHEZ (ARENA) 5.6%, Luis PARADA (NT) 2%, other 1.3%
2019: Nayib Armando BUKELE Ortez elected president - Nayib Armando BUKELE Ortez (GANA) 53.1%, Carlos CALLEJA Hakker (ARENA) 31.7%, Hugo MARTINEZ (FMLN) 14.4%, other 0.8%
note: the president is both chief of state and head of government

Legislative branch: *description:* unicameral Legislative Assembly or Asamblea Legislativa (84 seats; members directly elected in multi-seat constituencies and a single nationwide constituency by open-list proportional representation vote to serve 3-year terms)
elections: last held on 28 February 2021 (next to be held in 2024)
election results: percent of vote by party - NI 66.5%, ARENA 12.2%, FMLN 6.9%, GANA 5.3%, PCN 4.1%, other 5%; seats by party - NI 56, ARENA 14, GANA 5, FMLN 4, other 5; composition - men 61, women 23, percent of women 27.4%

Judicial branch: *highest court(s):* Supreme Court or Corte Suprema de Justicia (consists of 15 judges, including its president, and 15 substitute judges organized into Constitutional, Civil, Penal, and Administrative Conflict Chambers)
judge selection and term of office: judges elected by the Legislative Assembly on the recommendation of both the National Council of the Judicature, an independent body elected by the Legislative Assembly, and the Bar Association; judges elected for 9-year terms, with renewal of one-third of membership every 3 years; consecutive reelection is allowed
subordinate courts: Appellate Courts; Courts of First Instance; Courts of Peace

Political parties: Christian Democratic Party or PDC
Farabundo Marti National Liberation Front or FMLN
Great Alliance for National Unity or GANA
National Coalition Party or PCN
Nationalist Republican Alliance or ARENA
New Ideas (Nuevas Ideas) or NI
Our Time (Nuestro Tiempo) or NT
Vamos or V

International organization participation: ACS, BCIE, CACM, CD, CELAC, FAO, G-11, G-77, IADB, IAEA, IBRD, ICAO, ICC (national committees), ICRM, IDA, IFAD, IFC, IFRCS, ILO, IMF, IMO, Interpol, IOC, IOM, IPU, ISO (correspondent), ITSO, ITU, ITUC (NGOs), LAES, LAIA (observer), MIGA, MINURSO, MINUSTAH, NAM (observer), OAS, OPANAL, OPCW, Pacific Alliance (observer), PCA, Petrocaribe, SICA, UN, UNCTAD, UNESCO, UNIDO, UNIFIL, Union Latina, UNISFA, UNMISS, UNOCI, UNOOSA, UNWTO, UPU, WCO, WFTU (NGOs), WHO, WIPO, WMO, WTO

Diplomatic representation in the US: *chief of mission:* Ambassador Carmen Milena MAYORGA VALERA (since 23 December 2020)
chancery: 1400 16th Street NW, Suite 100, Washington, DC 20036
telephone: [1] (202) 595-7500
FAX: [1] (202) 232-3763
email address and website:
infoEEUU@rree.gob.sv
consulate(s) general: Aurora (CO), Boston, Charlotte (NC), Chicago, Dallas, Doral (FL), Duluth (GA), El Paso (TX), Elizabeth (NJ), Fresno (CA), Houston, Las Vegas (NV), Laredo (TX), Long Island (NY), Los Angeles, McAllen (TX), New York, Omaha (NE), San Bernardino (CA), San Francisco, Salt Lake City, Seattle, Silver Spring (MD), Springdale (AR), St. Paul (MN), Tucson (AZ), Woodbridge (VA)

Diplomatic representation from the US: *chief of mission:* Ambassador William H. DUNCAN (since 24 January 2023)
embassy: Final Boulevard Santa Elena, Antiguo Cuscatlan, La Libertad, San Salvador
mailing address: 3450 San Salvador Place, Washington, DC 20521-3450
telephone: [503] 2501-2999
FAX: [503] 2501-2150
email address and website:
ACSSanSal@state.gov
https://sv.usembassy.gov/

Flag description: three equal horizontal bands of cobalt blue (top), white, and cobalt blue with the national coat of arms centered in the white band; the coat of arms features a round emblem encircled by the words REPUBLICA DE EL SALVADOR EN LA AMERICA CENTRAL; the banner is based on the former blue-white-blue flag of the Federal Republic of Central America; the blue bands symbolize the Pacific Ocean and the Caribbean Sea, while the white band represents the land between the two bodies of water, as well as peace and prosperity
note: similar to the flag of Nicaragua, which has a different coat of arms centered in the white band; also similar to the flag of Honduras, which has five blue stars arranged in an X pattern centered in the white band

National symbol(s): turquoise-browed motmot (bird); national colors: blue, white National anthem *name:* "Himno Nacional de El Salvador" (National Anthem of El Salvador)
lyrics/music: Juan Jose CANAS/Juan ABERLE
note: officially adopted 1953, in use since 1879; at 4:20 minutes, the anthem of El Salvador is one of the world's longest

National heritage: *total World Heritage Sites:* 1 (cultural)
selected World Heritage Site locales: Joya de Cerén Archaeological Site

ECONOMY

Economic overview: growth-challenged Central American economy buttressed via remittances; dense labor force; fairly aggressive COVID-19 stimulus plan; new and lower banking reserve requirements; earthquake, tropical storm, and crime disruptions; widespread corruption

Real GDP (purchasing power parity): $71.957 billion (2023 est.)
$69.516 billion (2022 est.)
$67.623 billion (2021 est.)
note: data in 2021 dollars
comparison ranking: 107

Real GDP growth rate: 3.51% (2023 est.)
2.8% (2022 est.)
11.9% (2021 est.)
note: annual GDP % growth based on constant local currency
comparison ranking: 90

Real GDP per capita: $11,300 (2023 est.)
$11,000 (2022 est.)
$10,700 (2021 est.)
note: data in 2021 dollars
comparison ranking: 142

GDP (official exchange rate): $34.016 billion (2023 est.)
note: data in current dollars at official exchange rate

Inflation rate (consumer prices): 4.05% (2023 est.)
7.2% (2022 est.)
3.47% (2021 est.)
note: annual % change based on consumer prices
comparison ranking: 82

Credit ratings: Fitch rating: B- (2017)
Moody's rating: B3 (2018)
Standard & Poors rating: B- (2018)
note: The year refers to the year in which the current credit rating was first obtained.

GDP - composition, by sector of origin: *agriculture:* 4.6% (2023 est.)
industry: 25% (2023 est.)
services: 59.8% (2023 est.)
note: figures may not total 100% due to non-allocated consumption not captured in sector-reported data comparison rankings: services 87; industry 97; agriculture 121

GDP - composition, by end use: *household consumption:* 81.4% (2023 est.)
government consumption: 18% (2023 est.)
investment in fixed capital: 22% (2023 est.)
investment in inventories: -2.7% (2023 est.)
exports of goods and services: 31.1% (2023 est.)
imports of goods and services: -49.8% (2023 est.)
note: figures may not total 100% due to rounding or gaps in data collection

Agricultural products: sugarcane, maize, milk, chicken, beans, sorghum, coconuts, oranges, eggs, yautia (2022)
note: top ten agricultural products based on tonnage

Industries: food processing, beverages, petroleum, chemicals, fertilizer, textiles, furniture, light metals Industrial production growth rate
4.12% (2023 est.)
note: annual % change in industrial value added based on constant local currency
comparison ranking: 75

Labor force: 2.87 million (2023 est.)
note: number of people ages 15 or older who are employed or seeking work
comparison ranking: 114

Unemployment rate: 2.76% (2023 est.)
3% (2022 est.)
4.33% (2021 est.)
note: % of labor force seeking employment
comparison ranking: 36

Youth unemployment rate (ages 15-24): *total:* 7.2% (2023 est.)
male: 5.3% (2023 est.)
female: 10.8% (2023 est.)
note: % of labor force ages 15-24 seeking employment
comparison ranking: total 156

Population below poverty line: 26.6% (2022 est.)
note: % of population with income below national poverty line

Gini Index coefficient - distribution of family income: 38.8 (2022 est.)

note: index (0-100) of income distribution; higher values represent greater inequality
comparison ranking: 48

Average household expenditures: *on food:* 26.5% of household expenditures (2022 est.)
on alcohol and tobacco: 0.5% of household expenditures (2022 est.)

Household income or consumption by percentage share: *lowest 10%:* 1.9% (2022 est.)
highest 10%: 28.7% (2022 est.)
note: % share of income accruing to lowest and highest 10% of population

Remittances: 23.94% of GDP (2023 est.)
24.05% of GDP (2022 est.)
25.74% of GDP (2021 est.)
note: personal transfers and compensation between resident and non-resident individuals/households/entities

Budget: *revenues:* $9.359 billion (2023 est.)
expenditures: $9.371 billion (2023 est.)
note: central government revenues (excluding grants) and expenses converted to US dollars at average official exchange rate for year indicated

Public debt: 66.47% of GDP (2021 est.)
note: central government debt as a % of GDP
comparison ranking: 62

Taxes and other revenues: 19.69% (of GDP) (2021 est.)
note: central government tax revenue as a % of GDP
comparison ranking: 86

Current account balance: -$465.688 million (2023 est.)
-$2.182 billion (2022 est.)
-$1.25 billion (2021 est.)
note: balance of payments - net trade and primary/secondary income in current dollars
comparison ranking: 120

Exports: $10.629 billion (2023 est.)
$10.164 billion (2022 est.)
$8.351 billion (2021 est.)
note: balance of payments - exports of goods and services in current dollars
comparison ranking: 114

Exports - partners: US 38%, Guatemala 16%, Honduras 16%, Nicaragua 7%, Costa Rica 4% (2022)
note: top five export partners based on percentage share of exports

Exports - commodities: garments, plastic products, electrical capacitors, fabric, raw sugar (2022)
note: top five export commodities based on value in dollars

Imports: $17.032 billion (2023 est.)
$18.184 billion (2022 est.)
$15.483 billion (2021 est.)
note: balance of payments - imports of goods and services in current dollars
comparison ranking: 103

Imports - partners: US 30%, China 16%, Guatemala 12%, Mexico 8%, Honduras 6% (2022)
note: top five import partners based on percentage share of imports

Imports - commodities: refined petroleum, garments, natural gas, plastic products, plastics (2022)
note: top five import commodities based on value in dollars

Reserves of foreign exchange and gold: $3.426 billion (2021 est.)
$3.083 billion (2020 est.)
$4.446 billion (2019 est.)
note: holdings of gold (year-end prices)/foreign exchange/special drawing rights in current dollars
comparison ranking: 110

Debt - external: $11.276 billion (2022 est.)
note: present value of external debt in current US dollars
comparison ranking: 36

Exchange rates: the US dollar is used as a medium of exchange and circulates freely in the economy

ENERGY

Electricity access: *electrification - total population:* 100% (2022 est.)

Electricity: *installed generating capacity:* 2.853 million kW (2022 est.)
consumption: 6.666 billion kWh (2022 est.)
exports: 85.75 million kWh (2022 est.)
imports: 1.351 billion kWh (2022 est.)
transmission/distribution losses: 953.156 million kWh (2022 est.)
comparison rankings: transmission/distribution losses 96; imports 72; exports 89; consumption 120; installed generating capacity 111

Electricity generation sources: *fossil fuels:* 9.1% of total installed capacity (2022 est.)
solar: 16.2% of total installed capacity (2022 est.)
hydroelectricity: 35.6% of total installed capacity (2022 est.)
geothermal: 24.8% of total installed capacity (2022 est.)
biomass and waste: 14.3% of total installed capacity (2022 est.)

Coal: *consumption:* 500 metric tons (2022 est.)
imports: 2,000 metric tons (2022 est.)

Petroleum: *total petroleum production:* 3 bbl/day (2023 est.)
refined petroleum consumption: 58,000 bbl/day (2022 est.)

Natural gas: *consumption:* 226.472 million cubic meters (2022 est.)
imports: 226.472 million cubic meters (2022 est.)

Carbon dioxide emissions: 8.256 million metric tonnes of CO2 (2022 est.)
from coal and metallurgical coke: 1,000 metric tonnes of CO2 (2022 est.)
from petroleum and other liquids: 7.814 million metric tonnes of CO2 (2022 est.)
from consumed natural gas: 441,000 metric tonnes of CO2 (2022 est.)
comparison ranking: total emissions 116

Energy consumption per capita: 23.672 million Btu/person (2022 est.)
comparison ranking: 128

COMMUNICATIONS

Telephones - fixed lines: *total subscriptions:* 863,000 (2022 est.)
subscriptions per 100 inhabitants: 14 (2022 est.)
comparison ranking: total subscriptions 74

Telephones - mobile cellular: *total subscriptions:* 11.509 million (2022 est.)
subscriptions per 100 inhabitants: 182 (2022 est.)
comparison ranking: total subscriptions 87

Telecommunication systems: *general assessment:* El Salvador is the smallest country in central America geographically, it has the fourth largest economy in the region; the country's telecom sector has been restricted by poor infrastructure and unequal income distribution; there have been organizational delays which have slowed the development of telecom services; El Salvador's fixed-line teledensity is substantially lower than the Latin American and Caribbean average; there has been a significant drop in the number of fixed lines since 2010, particularly in 2017, largely due to the substitution for mobile-only alternatives; about 94% of all telephony lines in the country are on mobile networks; mobile subscriptions are remarkably high considering El Salvador's economic indicators, being about a third higher than average for Latin America and the Caribbean; the country was one of the last in the region to provide LTE services, mainly due to the inadequate provision of suitable spectrum; the multi-spectrum auction conducted at the end of 2019 has allowed MNOs to improve the reach and quality of their service offerings; El Salvador's telecom legislation is one of the more liberal in Latin America, encouraging competition in most areas and permitting foreign investment; there are no regulations which promote wholesale broadband; the only effective cross-platform competition in the broadband market comes from the few cable operators; there has been some market consolidation in recent years (2021)
domestic: fixed-line services, roughly 14 per 100, mobile-cellular competition now at 175 subscribers per 100 inhabitants (2021)
international: country code - 503; satellite earth station - 1 Intelsat (Atlantic Ocean); connected to Central American Microwave System (2019)

Broadcast media: multiple privately owned national terrestrial TV networks, supplemented by cable TV networks that carry international channels; hundreds of commercial radio broadcast stations and two known government-owned radio broadcast station; transition to digital transmission to begin in 2018 along with adaptation of the Japanese-Brazilian Digital Standard (ISDB-T) (2022)

Internet country code: .sv

Internet users: *total:* 3.969 million (2021 est.)
percent of population: 63% (2021 est.)
comparison ranking: total 110

Broadband - fixed subscriptions: *total:* 586,000 (2020 est.)
subscriptions per 100 inhabitants: 9 (2020 est.)
comparison ranking: total 87

TRANSPORTATION

National air transport system: *number of registered air carriers:* 1 (2020)
inventory of registered aircraft operated by air carriers: 13
annual passenger traffic on registered air carriers: 2,545,105 (2018)
annual freight traffic on registered air carriers: 10.73 million (2018) mt-km

Civil aircraft registration country code prefix: YS

Airports: 27 (2024)
comparison ranking: 125

Railways: *total:* 12.5 km (2014)
narrow gauge: 12.5 km (2014) 0.914-mm gauge
comparison ranking: total 136

Roadways: *total:* 9,012 km
paved: 5,341 km
unpaved: 3,671 km (2017)
comparison ranking: total 139

Waterways: 422 km (2022) (Rio Lempa River is partially navigable by small craft)
comparison ranking: 96

Merchant marine: *total:* 5 (2023)
by type: other 5
comparison ranking: total 169

Ports: *total ports:* 3 (2024)
large: 0
medium: 0
small: 0
very small: 3
ports with oil terminals: 3
key ports: Acajutla, Acajutla Offshore Terminal, La Union

MILITARY AND SECURITY

Military and security forces: *the Armed Force of El Salvador (La Fuerza Armada de El Salvador, FAES):* Army of El Salvador (Ejercito de El Salvador, ES), Navy of El Salvador (Fuerza Naval de El Salvador, FNES), Salvadoran Air Force (Fuerza Aerea Salvadorena, FAS) (2024)
note: the National Civil Police (Policia Nacional Civil, PNC) are under the Ministry of Justice and Public Safety; in 2016, El Salvador created a combined Army commando and PNC unit to combat criminal gang violence

Military expenditures: 1.2% of GDP (2023 est.)
1.2% of GDP (2022 est.)
1.2% of GDP (2021 est.)
1.2% of GDP (2020 est.)
1.2% of GDP (2019 est.)
comparison ranking: 114

Military and security service personnel strengths: approximately 25,000 active military personnel (21,000 Army; 2,000 Navy; 2,000 Air Force) (2023)

Military equipment inventories and acquisitions: the FAES is lightly armed with an inventory of mostly older imported arms and equipment, largely from the US (2023)

Military service age and obligation: 18-30 years of age for selective compulsory military service; 16-22 years of age for voluntary military service for men and women; service obligation is 12 months, with 11 months for officers and non-commissioned officers (2023)

Military - note: the Armed Force of El Salvador (FAES) is responsible for defending national sovereignty and ensuring territorial integrity but also has considerable domestic security responsibilities; while the National Civil Police (PNC) is responsible for maintaining public security, the country's constitution allows the president to use the FAES "in exceptional circumstances" to maintain internal peace and public security; in 2016, the government created a special 1,000-strong joint unit of Army commandos and police to fight criminal gangs; more military personnel were devoted to internal security beginning in 2019 when President BUKELE signed a decree authorizing military involvement in police duties to combat rising gang violence, organized crime, and narcotics trafficking, as well as assisting with border security; since the decree, a considerable portion of the Army has been deployed in support of the PNC; in multiple cases since 2022, for example, as many as 8,000 troops have been deployed alongside thousands of police on single operations against criminal gang members
the FAES exercises with regional partners and the US, in such areas as internal security and disaster relief operations; it has deployed small numbers of personnel on UN peacekeeping missions and in support of military operations in Iraq (2003-2009)
the military led the country for much of the 20th century; from 1980 to 1992, it fought a bloody civil war against guerrillas from the Farabundo Martí National Liberation Front or FMLN, the paramilitary arm of the Democratic Revolutionary Front (Frente Democrático Revolucionario), a coalition of left-wing dissident political groups backed by Cuba and the Soviet Union; the FAES received considerable US support during the conflict; significant human rights violations occurred during the war and approximately 75,000 Salvadorans, mostly civilians, were killed (2023)

TRANSNATIONAL ISSUES

Refugees and internally displaced persons: **IDPs:** 52,000 (2022)

Illicit drugs: a transit country for illicit drugs destined for the United States; a major source of precursor or essential chemicals used in the production of illicit narcotics

EQUATORIAL GUINEA

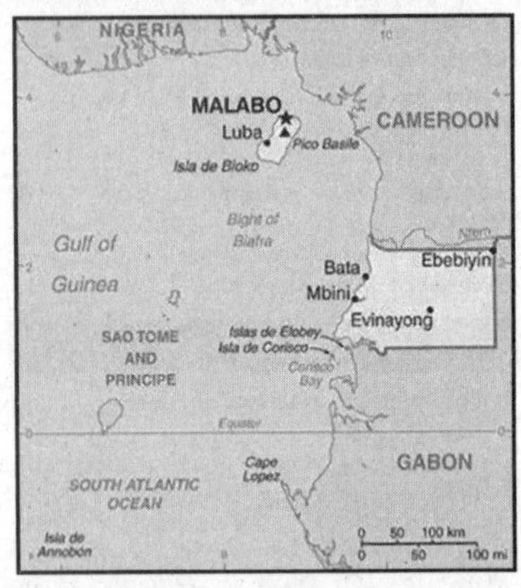

INTRODUCTION

Background: Equatorial Guinea consists of a continental territory and five inhabited islands; it is one of the smallest countries by area and population in Africa. The mainland region was most likely predominantly inhabited by Pygmy ethnic groups prior to the migration of various Bantu-speaking ethnic groups around the second millennium BC. The island of Bioko, the largest of Equatorial Guinea's five inhabited islands and the location of the country's capital of Malabo, has been occupied since at least 1000 B.C. In the early 1470s, Portuguese explorers landed on Bioko Island, and Portugal soon after established control of the island and other areas of modern Equatorial Guinea. In 1778, Portugal ceded its colonial hold over present-day Equatorial Guinea to Spain in the Treaty of El Pardo. The borders of modern-day Equatorial Guinea would evolve between 1778 and 1968 as the area remained under European colonial rule.

In 1968, Equatorial Guinea was granted independence from Spain and elected Francisco MACIAS NGUEMA as its first president. MACIAS consolidated power soon after his election and ruled brutally for over a decade. Under his regime, Equatorial Guinea experienced mass suppression, purges, and killings. Some estimates indicate that a third of the population either went into exile or was killed under MACIAS' rule. In 1979, present-day President OBIANG Nguema Mbasogo, then a senior military officer, deposed MACIAS in a violent coup. OBIANG has ruled since and has been elected in non-competitive contests several times, most recently in 2022. The president exerts near-total control over the political system.

Equatorial Guinea experienced rapid economic growth in the early years of the 21st century due to the discovery of large offshore oil reserves in 1996. Production peaked in 2004 and has declined since. The country's economic windfall from oil production resulted in massive increases in government revenue, a significant portion of which was earmarked for infrastructure development. Systemic corruption, however, has hindered socio-economic development, and the population has seen only limited improvements to living standards. Equatorial Guinea continues to seek to diversify its economy, increase foreign investment, and assume a greater role in regional and international affairs.

GEOGRAPHY

Location: Central Africa, bordering the Bight of Biafra, between Cameroon and Gabon

Geographic coordinates: 2 00 N, 10 00 E

Map references: Africa

Area: *total:* 28,051 sq km
land: 28,051 sq km
water: 0 sq km
comparison ranking: total 145

Area - comparative: slightly smaller than Maryland

Land boundaries: *total:* 528 km
border countries (2): Cameroon 183 km; Gabon 345 km

Coastline: 296 km

Maritime claims: *territorial sea:* 12 nm
exclusive economic zone: 200 nm

Climate: tropical; always hot, humid

Terrain: coastal plains rise to interior hills; islands are volcanic

Elevation: *highest point:* Pico Basile 3,008 m
lowest point: Atlantic Ocean 0 m
mean elevation: 577 m

Natural resources: petroleum, natural gas, timber, gold, bauxite, diamonds, tantalum, sand and gravel, clay

Land use: *agricultural land:* 10.1% (2018 est.)
arable land: 4.3% (2018 est.)
permanent crops: 2.1% (2018 est.)
permanent pasture: 3.7% (2018 est.)
forest: 57.5% (2018 est.)
other: 32.4% (2018 est.)

Irrigated land: NA

Population distribution: only two large cities over 30,000 people (Bata on the mainland, and the capital Malabo on the island of Bioko); small communities are scattered throughout the mainland and the five inhabited islands as shown in this population distribution map

Natural hazards: violent windstorms; flash floods
volcanism: Santa Isabel (3,007 m), which last erupted in 1923, is the country's only historically active volcano; Santa Isabel, along with two dormant volcanoes, form Bioko Island in the Gulf of Guinea

Geography - note: insular and continental regions widely separated; despite its name, no part of the Equator passes through Equatorial Guinea; the mainland part of the country is located just north of the Equator

PEOPLE AND SOCIETY

Population: *total:* 1,795,834
male: 962,385
female: 833,449 (2024 est.)
comparison rankings: female 153; male 153; total 154

Nationality: *noun:* Equatorial Guinean(s) or Equatoguinean(s)
adjective: Equatorial Guinean or Equatoguinean

Ethnic groups: Fang 78.1%, Bubi 9.4%, Ndowe 2.8%, Nanguedambo 2.7%, Bisio 0.9%, foreigner 5.3%, other 0.7%, unspecified 0.2% (2011 est.)

Languages: Spanish (official) 67.6%, other (includes Fang, Bubi, Portuguese (official), French (official), Fa d'Ambo spoken in Annobon) 32.4% (1994 est.)
major-language sample(s):
La Libreta Informativa del Mundo, la fuente indispensable de información básica. (Spanish)

Religions: Roman Catholic 88%, Protestant 5%, Muslim 2%, other 5% (animist, Baha'i, Jewish) (2015 est.)

Demographic profile: Equatorial Guinea is one of the smallest and least populated countries in continental Africa and is the only independent African country where Spanish is an official language. Despite a boom in oil production in the 1990s, authoritarianism, corruption, and resource mismanagement have concentrated the benefits among a small elite. These practices have perpetuated income inequality and unbalanced development, such as low public spending on education and health care. Unemployment remains problematic because the oil-dominated economy employs a small labor force dependent on skilled foreign workers. The agricultural sector, Equatorial Guinea's main employer, continues to deteriorate because of a lack of investment and the migration of rural workers to urban areas. About two-thirds of the population lives below the poverty line as of 2020.
Equatorial Guinea's large and growing youth population – about 60% are under the age of 25 as of 2022 – is particularly affected because job creation in the non-oil sectors is limited, and young people often do not have the skills needed in the labor market. Equatorial Guinean children frequently enter school late, have poor attendance, and have high dropout rates. Thousands of Equatorial Guineans fled across the border to Gabon in the 1970s to escape the dictatorship of Francisco MACIAS NGUEMA; smaller numbers have followed in the decades since. Continued inequitable economic growth and high youth unemployment increases the likelihood of ethnic and regional violence.

Age structure: *0-14 years:* 35.6% (male 330,636/female 309,528)
15-64 years: 59.4% (male 585,139/female 481,121)
65 years and over: 5% (2024 est.) (male 46,610/female 42,800)

Dependency ratios: *total dependency ratio:* 72.2
youth dependency ratio: 66.7
elderly dependency ratio: 5.4
potential support ratio: 18.5 (2021 est.)

Median age: *total:* 22.1 years (2024 est.)
male: 22.7 years
female: 21.5 years
comparison ranking: total 186

Population growth rate: 3.23% (2024 est.)
comparison ranking: 5

Birth rate: 29 births/1,000 population (2024 est.)
comparison ranking: 28

Death rate: 8.9 deaths/1,000 population (2024 est.)
comparison ranking: 61

Net migration rate: 12.1 migrant(s)/1,000 population (2024 est.)
comparison ranking: 6

Population distribution: only two large cities over 30,000 people (Bata on the mainland, and the capital Malabo on the island of Bioko); small communities are scattered throughout the mainland and the five inhabited islands as shown in this population distribution map

Urbanization: *urban population:* 74.4% of total population (2023)
rate of urbanization: 3.62% annual rate of change (2020-25 est.)

Major urban areas - population: 297,000 MALABO (capital) (2018)

Sex ratio: *at birth:* 1.03 male(s)/female
0-14 years: 1.07 male(s)/female
15-64 years: 1.22 male(s)/female
65 years and over: 1.09 male(s)/female
total population: 1.16 male(s)/female (2024 est.)

Maternal mortality ratio: 212 deaths/100,000 live births (2020 est.)
comparison ranking: 45

Infant mortality rate: *total:* 77.4 deaths/1,000 live births (2024 est.)
male: 83.3 deaths/1,000 live births
female: 71.3 deaths/1,000 live births
comparison ranking: total 4

Life expectancy at birth: *total population:* 63.9 years (2024 est.)
male: 61.6 years
female: 66.2 years
comparison ranking: total population 210

Total fertility rate: 4.12 children born/woman (2024 est.)
comparison ranking: 21

Gross reproduction rate: 2.03 (2024 est.)

Contraceptive prevalence rate: NA

Drinking water source: *improved: urban:* 81.7% of population
rural: 32.1% of population
total: 67.6% of population
unimproved: urban: 18.3% of population
rural: 67.9% of population
total: 32.4% of population (2017 est.)

Current health expenditure: 3.8% of GDP (2020)

Physician density: 0.4 physicians/1,000 population (2017)

Sanitation facility access: *improved: urban:* 81.2% of population
rural: 63.4% of population
total: 76.2% of population
unimproved: urban: 18.8% of population
rural: 36.6% of population
total: 23.8% of population (2020 est.)

Obesity - adult prevalence rate: 8% (2016)
comparison ranking: 156

Alcohol consumption per capita: *total:* 6.11 liters of pure alcohol (2019 est.)
beer: 3.83 liters of pure alcohol (2019 est.)
wine: 1.24 liters of pure alcohol (2019 est.)
spirits: 0.99 liters of pure alcohol (2019 est.)
other alcohols: 0.05 liters of pure alcohol (2019 est.)
comparison ranking: total 69

Currently married women (ages 15-49): 60.2% (2023 est.)

Education expenditures: NA

Literacy: *definition:* age 15 and over can read and write
total population: 95.3%
male: 97.4%
female: 93% (2015)

ENVIRONMENT

Environment - current issues: deforestation (forests are threatened by agricultural expansion, fires, and grazing); desertification; water pollution (tap water is non-potable); wildlife preservation

Environment - international agreements: *party to:* Biodiversity, Climate Change, Climate Change-Kyoto Protocol, Climate Change-Paris Agreement, Desertification, Endangered Species, Hazardous Wastes, Law of the Sea, Marine Dumping-London Convention, Nuclear Test Ban, Ozone Layer Protection, Ship Pollution, Wetlands
signed, but not ratified: Comprehensive Nuclear Test Ban

Climate: tropical; always hot, humid

Urbanization: *urban population:* 74.4% of total population (2023)
rate of urbanization: 3.62% annual rate of change (2020-25 est.)

Revenue from forest resources: 1.52% of GDP (2018 est.)
comparison ranking: 42

Revenue from coal: 0% of GDP (2018 est.)
comparison ranking: 135

Air pollutants: *particulate matter emissions:* 25.67 micrograms per cubic meter (2019 est.)
carbon dioxide emissions: 5.65 megatons (2016 est.)
methane emissions: 11.21 megatons (2020 est.)

Waste and recycling: *municipal solid waste generated annually:* 198,443 tons (2016 est.)

Total water withdrawal: *municipal:* 20 million cubic meters (2020 est.)

industrial: 3 million cubic meters (2017 est.)
agricultural: 1 million cubic meters (2017 est.)

Total renewable water resources: 26 billion cubic meters (2020 est.)

GOVERNMENT

Country name: *conventional long form:* Republic of Equatorial Guinea
conventional short form: Equatorial Guinea
local long form: Republica de Guinea Ecuatorial (Spanish)/ République de Guinée équatoriale (French)
local short form: Guinea Ecuatorial (Spanish)/ Guinée équatoriale (French)
former: Spanish Guinea
etymology: the country is named for the Guinea region of West Africa that lies along the Gulf of Guinea and stretches north to the Sahel; the "equatorial" refers to the fact that the country lies just north of the Equator

Government type: presidential republic

Capital: *name:* Malabo; note - Malabo is on the island of Bioko; some months of the year, the government operates out of Bata on the mainland region.
geographic coordinates: 3 45 N, 8 47 E
time difference: UTC+1 (6 hours ahead of Washington, DC, during Standard Time)
etymology: named after King MALABO (Malabo Lopelo Melaka) (1837–1937), the last king of the Bubi, the ethnic group indigenous to the island of Bioko

Administrative divisions: 8 provinces (provincias, singular - provincia); Annobon, Bioko Norte, Bioko Sur, Centro Sur, Djibloho, Kie-Ntem, Litoral, Wele-Nzas

Independence: 12 October 1968 (from Spain)

National holiday: Independence Day, 12 October (1968)

Legal system: mixed system of civil and customary law

Constitution: *history:* previous 1968, 1973, 1982; approved by referendum 17 November 1991
amendments: proposed by the president of the republic or supported by three fourths of the membership in either house of the National Assembly; passage requires three-fourths majority vote by both houses of the Assembly and approval in a referendum if requested by the president; amended several times, last in 2012

International law organization participation: accepts compulsory ICJ jurisdiction; accepts ICCt jurisdiction

Citizenship: *citizenship by birth:* no
citizenship by descent only: at least one parent must be a citizen of Equatorial Guinea
dual citizenship recognized: no
residency requirement for naturalization: 10 years

Suffrage: 18 years of age; universal

Executive branch: *chief of state:* President OBIANG Nguema Mbasogo (since 3 August 1979)
head of government: Prime Minister Manuela ROKA Botey (since 1 February 2023)
cabinet: Council of Ministers appointed by the president and overseen by the prime minister
elections/appointments: president directly elected by simple majority popular vote for a 7-year term (eligible for a second term); election last held on 20 November 2022 (next to be held in 2029); prime minister and deputy prime ministers appointed by the president; President OBIANG Nguema Mbasogo since 3 August 1979 when he seized power in a military coup)
election results:
2022: OBIANG Nguema Mbasogo reelected president; percent of vote - OBIANG Nguema Mbasogo (PDGE) 95%, other 6.1%
2016: OBIANG Nguema Mbasogo reelected president; percent of vote - OBIANG Nguema Mbasogo (PDGE) 93.5%, other 6.5%

Legislative branch: *description:* bicameral National Assembly or Asemblea Nacional consists of:
Senate or Senado (70 seats statutory, 74 seats for current term; 55 members directly elected in multi-seat constituencies by closed party-list proportional representation vote, 15 appointed by the president, and 4 ex-officio)
Chamber of Deputies or Camara de los Diputados (100 seats; members directly elected in multi-seat constituencies by closed party-list proportional representation vote to serve 5-year terms)
elections: Senate - last held on 19 January 2023 (next to be held in 2028)
Chamber of Deputies - last held on 19 January 2023 (next to be held in 2028)
election results: Senate - percent of vote by party - NA; (elected) seats by party - PDGE 55; composition - men 60, women 20, percentage women 25% (includes 15 appointed and 2 ex-officio members)
Chamber of Deputies - percent of vote by party - NA; seats by party - PDGE 100; composition - men 68, women 32, percentage women 32%; total National Assembly percentage women 28.9%

Judicial branch: *highest court(s):* Supreme Court of Justice (consists of the President of the Supreme Court and nine judges organized into civil, criminal, commercial, labor, administrative, and customary sections); Constitutional Court (consists of the court president and 4 members)
judge selection and term of office: Supreme Court judges appointed by the president for five-year terms; Constitutional Court members appointed by the president, 2 of whom are nominated by the Chamber of Deputies; note - judges subject to dismissal by the president at any time
subordinate courts: Court of Guarantees; military courts; Courts of Appeal; first instance tribunals; district and county tribunals

Political parties: Center Right Union or UCD
Convergence Party for Social Democracy or CPDS
Democratic Party for Equatorial Guinea or PDGE
Liberal Democratic Convention or CLD
Liberal Party or PL
National Congress of Equatorial Guinea (CNGE)
National Democratic Party (PNDGE)
National Democratic Union or UDENA
National Union for Democracy PUNDGE
Popular Action of Equatorial Guinea or APGE
Popular Union or UP
Progressive Democratic Alliance or ADP
Social and Popular Convergence Party or CSDP
Social Democratic Coalition Party (PCSD)
Social Democratic Party of Equatorial Guinea or PSDGE
Social Democratic Union or UDS
Socialist Party of Equatorial Guinea

International organization participation: ACP, AfDB, AU, BDEAC, CEMAC, CPLP, FAO, Francophonie, FZ, G-77, IBRD, ICAO, ICRM, IDA, IFAD, IFC, IFRCS, ILO, IMF, IMO, Interpol, IOC, IPU, ITSO, ITU, MIGA, NAM, OAS (observer), OIF, OPCW, UN, UNCTAD, UNESCO, UNIDO, UNWTO, UPU, WHO, WIPO, WTO (observer)

Diplomatic representation in the US: *chief of mission:* Ambassador Dr. Crisantos OBAMA ONDO (since 27 February 2024)
chancery: 2020 16th Street NW, Washington, DC 20009
telephone: [1] (202) 518-5700
FAX: [1] (202) 518-5252
email address and website:
info@egembassydc.com
https://www.egembassydc.com/
consulate(s) general: Houston

Diplomatic representation from the US: *chief of mission:* Ambassador David R. GILMOUR (since 24 May 2022)
embassy: Malabo II Highway (between the Headquarters of Sonagas and the offices of the United Nations), Malabo
mailing address: 2320 Malabo Place, Washington, DC 20521-2520
telephone: [240] 333 09-57-41
email address and website:
Malaboconsular@state.gov
https://gq.usembassy.gov/

Flag description: three equal horizontal bands of green (top), white, and red, with a blue isosceles triangle based on the hoist side and the coat of arms centered in the white band; the coat of arms has six yellow six-pointed stars (representing the mainland and five offshore islands) above a gray shield bearing a silk-cotton tree and below which is a scroll with the motto UNIDAD, PAZ, JUSTICIA (Unity, Peace, Justice); green symbolizes the jungle and natural resources, blue represents the sea that connects the mainland to the islands, white stands for peace, and red recalls the fight for independence

National symbol(s): silk cotton tree; national colors: green, white, red, blue

National anthem: *name:* "Caminemos pisando la senda" (Let Us Tread the Path)
lyrics/music: Atanasio Ndongo MIYONO/Atanasio Ndongo MIYONO or Ramiro Sanchez LOPEZ (disputed)
note: adopted 1968

ECONOMY

Economic overview: growing CEMAC economy and new OPEC member; large oil and gas reserves; targeting economic diversification and poverty reduction; still recovering from CEMAC crisis; improving public financial management; persistent poverty; hard-hit by COVID-19

Real GDP (purchasing power parity): $28.938 billion (2023 est.)
$30.685 billion (2022 est.)
$29.585 billion (2021 est.)
note: data in 2021 dollars
comparison ranking: 150

Real GDP growth rate: -5.69% (2023 est.)
3.72% (2022 est.)
0.86% (2021 est.)
note: annual GDP % growth based on constant local currency
comparison ranking: 215

Real GDP per capita: $16,900 (2023 est.)
$18,300 (2022 est.)
$18,100 (2021 est.)

note: data in 2021 dollars
comparison ranking: 113

GDP (official exchange rate): $12.117 billion (2023 est.)
note: data in current dollars at official exchange rate

Inflation rate (consumer prices): 4.79% (2022 est.)
-0.1% (2021 est.)
4.77% (2020 est.)
note: annual % change based on consumer prices
comparison ranking: 101

GDP - composition, by sector of origin: *agriculture:* 2.9% (2023 est.)
industry: 51.2% (2023 est.)
services: 44.9% (2023 est.)
note: figures may not total 100% due to non-allocated consumption not captured in sector-reported data comparison rankings: services 170; industry 12; agriculture 142

GDP - composition, by end use: *household consumption:* 54.7% (2023 est.)
government consumption: 26% (2023 est.)
investment in fixed capital: 10.8% (2023 est.)
investment in inventories: 0.1% (2019 est.)
exports of goods and services: 47.8% (2023 est.)
imports of goods and services: -39.3% (2023 est.)
note: figures may not total 100% due to rounding or gaps in data collection

Agricultural products: sweet potatoes, cassava, plantains, oil palm fruit, root vegetables, bananas, coconuts, coffee, cocoa beans, chicken (2022)
note: top ten agricultural products based on tonnage

Industries: petroleum, natural gas, sawmilling

Industrial production growth rate: -11.87% (2023 est.)
note: annual % change in industrial value added based on constant local currency
comparison ranking: 214

Labor force: 593,000 (2023 est.)
note: number of people ages 15 or older who are employed or seeking work
comparison ranking: 158

Unemployment rate: 8.67% (2023 est.)
8.75% (2022 est.)
9.19% (2021 est.)
note: % of labor force seeking employment
comparison ranking: 152

Youth unemployment rate (ages 15-24): *total:* 16.4% (2023 est.)
male: 15.1% (2023 est.)
female: 17.8% (2023 est.)
note: % of labor force ages 15-24 seeking employment
comparison ranking: total 87

Remittances: 0% of GDP (2019 est.)
0% of GDP (2018 est.)
0% of GDP (2017 est.)

Budget: *revenues:* $3.62 billion (2022 est.)
expenditures: $1.512 billion (2022 est.)
note: central government revenues and expenses (excluding grants/extrabudgetary units/social security funds) converted to US dollars at average official exchange rate for year indicated

Public debt: 37.4% of GDP (2017 est.)
comparison ranking: 139

Taxes and other revenues: 6.69% (of GDP) (2022 est.)
note: central government tax revenue as a % of GDP
comparison ranking: 198

Current account balance: -$738 million (2017 est.)
-$1.457 billion (2016 est.)
comparison ranking: 129

Exports: $6.231 billion (2022 est.)
$5.851 billion (2021 est.)
$4.041 billion (2020 est.)
note: GDP expenditure basis - exports of goods and services in current dollars
comparison ranking: 130

Exports - partners: Zambia 21%, Spain 15%, China 15%, India 10%, Italy 6% (2022)
note: top five export partners based on percentage share of exports

Exports - commodities: crude petroleum, natural gas, fertilizers, packaged medicine, cars (2022)
note: top five export commodities based on value in dollars

Imports: $4.297 billion (2022 est.)
$4.351 billion (2021 est.)
$3.669 billion (2020 est.)
note: GDP expenditure basis - imports of goods and services in current dollars
comparison ranking: 155

Imports - partners: Zambia 38%, China 14%, Spain 10%, Nigeria 7%, US 4% (2022)
note: top five import partners based on percentage share of imports

Imports - commodities: ships, refined copper, iron alloys, raw copper, poultry (2022)
note: top five import commodities based on value in dollars

Reserves of foreign exchange and gold: $1.538 billion (2023 est.)
$1.458 billion (2022 est.)
$44.271 million (2021 est.)
note: holdings of gold (year-end prices)/foreign exchange/special drawing rights in current dollars
comparison ranking: 192

Exchange rates: Cooperation Financiere en Afrique Centrale francs (XAF) per US dollar -

Exchange rates: 606.57 (2023 est.)
623.76 (2022 est.)
554.531 (2021 est.)
575.586 (2020 est.)
585.911 (2019 est.)

ENERGY

Electricity access: *electrification - total population:* 67% (2022 est.)
electrification - urban areas: 89.8%
electrification - rural areas: 1.4%

Electricity: *installed generating capacity:* 349,000 kW (2022 est.)
consumption: 1.326 billion kWh (2022 est.)
transmission/distribution losses: 147.498 million kWh (2022 est.)
comparison rankings: transmission/distribution losses 57; consumption 157; installed generating capacity 161

Electricity generation sources: *fossil fuels:* 67.1% of total installed capacity (2022 est.)
hydroelectricity: 32.9% of total installed capacity (2022 est.)

Coal: *imports:* 17.1 metric tons (2022 est.)

Petroleum: *total petroleum production:* 98,000 bbl/day (2023 est.)
refined petroleum consumption: 6,000 bbl/day (2022 est.)
crude oil estimated reserves: 1.1 billion barrels (2021 est.)

Natural gas: *production:* 6.75 billion cubic meters (2022 est.)
consumption: 1.504 billion cubic meters (2022 est.)
exports: 4.964 billion cubic meters (2022 est.)
proven reserves: 139.007 billion cubic meters (2021 est.)

Carbon dioxide emissions: 3.806 million metric tonnes of CO_2 (2022 est.)
from petroleum and other liquids: 855,000 metric tonnes of CO_2 (2022 est.)
from consumed natural gas: 2.951 million metric tonnes of CO_2 (2022 est.)
comparison ranking: total emissions 145

Energy consumption per capita: 41.487 million Btu/person (2022 est.)
comparison ranking: 100

COMMUNICATIONS

Telephones - fixed lines: *total subscriptions:* 11,000 (2022 est.)
subscriptions per 100 inhabitants: (2022 est.) less than 1
comparison ranking: total subscriptions 185

Telephones - mobile cellular: *total subscriptions:* 893,000 (2022 est.)
subscriptions per 100 inhabitants: 53 (2022 est.)
comparison ranking: total subscriptions 165

Telecommunication systems: *general assessment:* the telecom service is forecasted to register a growth of more than 6% during the period of 2022-2026; mobile data is the largest contributor to total service revenue in 2021, followed by mobile voice, fixed broadband, mobile messaging, and fixed voice; the launch of the international submarine cable ACE, which connects 13 West African countries with Europe, will improve international capacity, bringing opportunities to data center providers; 4G network expansion and 4G service promotion will allow consumers and businesses to leverage 4G services (2022)
domestic: fixed-line density is less than 1 per 100 persons and mobile-cellular subscribership is roughly 39 per 100 (2021)
international: country code - 240; landing points for the ACE, Ceiba-1, and Ceiba-2 submarine cables providing communication from Bata and Malabo, Equatorial Guinea to numerous Western African and European countries; satellite earth station - 1 Intelsat (Indian Ocean) (2019)

Broadcast media: the state maintains control of broadcast media with domestic broadcast media limited to 1 state-owned TV station, 1 private TV station owned by the president's eldest son (who is the Vice President), 1 state-owned radio station, and 1 private radio station owned by the president's eldest son; satellite TV service is available; transmissions of multiple international broadcasters are generally accessible (2019)

Internet country code: .gq

Internet users: *total:* 864,000 (2021 est.)
percent of population: 54% (2021 est.)
comparison ranking: total 152

Broadband - fixed subscriptions: *total:* 1,000 (2020 est.)
subscriptions per 100 inhabitants: 0.1 (2020 est.)
comparison ranking: total 202

TRANSPORTATION

National air transport system: *number of registered air carriers:* 6 (2020)
inventory of registered aircraft operated by air carriers: 15
annual passenger traffic on registered air carriers: 466,435 (2018)
annual freight traffic on registered air carriers: 350,000 (2018) mt-km

Civil aircraft registration country code prefix: 3C

Airports: 7 (2024)
comparison ranking: 171

Pipelines: 42 km condensate, 5 km condensate/gas, 79 km gas, 71 km oil (2013)

Roadways: *total:* 2,880 km (2017)
comparison ranking: total 166

Merchant marine: *total:* 53 (2023)
by type: bulk carrier 1, general cargo 16, oil tanker 7, other 29
comparison ranking: total 118

Ports: *total ports:* 7 (2024)
large: 0
medium: 0
small: 1
very small: 6
ports with oil terminals: 6
key ports: Bata, Ceiba Terminal, Cogo, Luba, Malabo, Punta Europa Terminal, Serpentina Terminal

MILITARY AND SECURITY

Military and security forces: Equatorial Guinea Armed Forces (Fuerzas Armadas de Guinea Ecuatorial, FAGE): Equatorial Guinea National Guard (Guardia Nacional de Guinea Ecuatorial, GNGE (Army)), Navy, Air Force; Gendarmerie (Guardia Civil) (2024)
note: police report to the Ministry of National Security, while gendarmes report to the Ministry of National Defense; police generally are responsible for maintaining law and order in the cities, while gendarmes are responsible for security outside cities and for special events

Military expenditures: 1.6% of GDP (2023 est.)
1.1% of GDP (2022 est.)
1.3% of GDP (2021 est.)
1.5% of GDP (2020 est.)
1.5% of GDP (2019 est.)
comparison ranking: 86

Military and security service personnel strengths: approximately 1,500 active-duty troops; approximately 500 Gendarmerie (2023)

Military equipment inventories and acquisitions: the FAGE is armed with mostly older (typically Soviet-era) and second-hand weapons systems; in recent years, it has sought to modernize its naval inventory with purchases of vessels from several countries, including Bulgaria and Israel; China and Russia have also supplied some equipment to the FAGE (2024)

Military service age and obligation: 18 years of age for selective compulsory military service, although conscription is rare in practice; 24-month service obligation (2023)

Military - note: the Armed Forces of Equatorial Guinea (FAGE) are responsible for defending the territory and sovereignty of the country; it also has some internal security duties, including fulfilling some police functions in border areas, sensitive sites, and high-traffic areas; the FAGE's National Guard (Army) is a small force with a few infantry battalions; over the past decade, the country has made considerable investments in naval capabilities to protect its oil installations and combat piracy and crime in the Gulf of Guinea; while the Navy is small, its inventory includes a light frigate and a corvette, as well as several off-shore patrol vessels; the Air Force has a handful of operational combat aircraft and ground attack-capable helicopters (2023)

TRANSNATIONAL ISSUES

Trafficking in persons: tier rating: Tier 2 Watch List—Equatorial Guinea does not fully meet the minimum standards for the elimination of trafficking, but it is making significant efforts to do so and was upgraded to Tier 2 Watch List; for more details, go to: https://www.state.gov/reports/2024-trafficking-in-persons-report/equatorial-guinea/

ERITREA

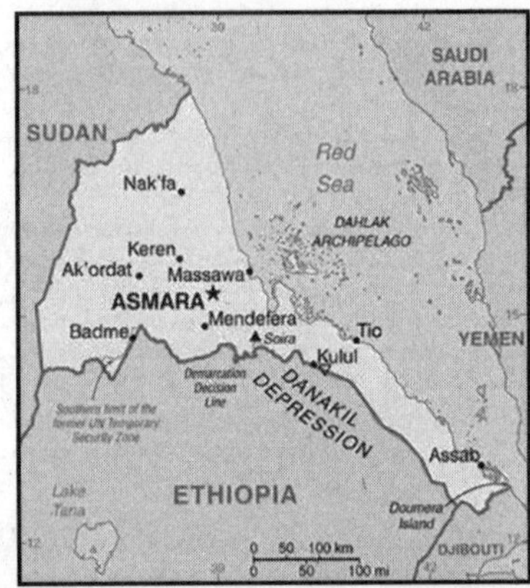

INTRODUCTION

Background: Eritrea won independence from Italian colonial control in 1941, but the UN only established it as an autonomous region within the Ethiopian federation in 1952, after a decade of British administrative control. Ethiopia's full annexation of Eritrea as a province 10 years later sparked a violent 30-year conflict for independence that ended in 1991 with Eritrean fighters defeating government forces. Eritreans overwhelmingly approved independence in a 1993 referendum. ISAIAS Afwerki has been Eritrea's only president since independence; his rule, particularly since 2001, has been characterized by highly autocratic and repressive actions. His government has created a highly militarized society by instituting an unpopular program of mandatory conscription into national service – divided between military and civilian service – of indefinite length.

A two-and-a-half-year border war with Ethiopia that erupted in 1998 ended under UN auspices in 2000. Ethiopia rejected a subsequent 2007 Eritrea-Ethiopia Boundary Commission (EEBC) demarcation. More than a decade of a tense "no peace, no war" stalemate ended in 2018 when the newly elected Ethiopian prime minister accepted the EEBC's 2007 ruling, and the two countries signed declarations of peace and friendship. Eritrean leaders then engaged in intensive diplomacy around the Horn of Africa, bolstering regional peace, security, and cooperation, as well as brokering rapprochements between governments and opposition groups. In 2018, the UN Security Council lifted an arms embargo that had been imposed on Eritrea since 2009, after the UN Somalia-Eritrea Monitoring Group reported they had not found evidence of Eritrean support in recent years for al-Shabaab. The country's rapprochement with Ethiopia led to a resumption of economic ties, but the level of air transport, trade, and tourism have remained roughly the same since late 2020.

The Eritrean economy remains agriculture-dependent, and the country is still one of Africa's poorest nations. Eritrea faced new international condemnation and US sanctions in mid-2021 for its participation in the war in Ethiopia's Tigray Regional State, where Eritrean forces were found to have committed war crimes and crimes against humanity. As most Eritrean troops were departing northern Ethiopia in January 2023, ISAIAS began a series of diplomatic engagements aimed at bolstering Eritrea's foreign partnerships and regional influence. Despite the country's improved relations with its neighbors, ISAIAS has not let up on repression, and conscription and militarization continue.

GEOGRAPHY

Location: Eastern Africa, bordering the Red Sea, between Djibouti and Sudan

Geographic coordinates: 15 00 N, 39 00 E

Map references: Africa

Area: *total:* 117,600 sq km
land: 101,000 sq km
water: 16,600 sq km
comparison ranking: total 101

Area - comparative: *slightly smaller than Pennsylvania Area comparison map:*

Land boundaries: *total:* 1,840 km
border countries (3): Djibouti 125 km; Ethiopia 1,033 km; Sudan 682 km

Coastline: 2,234 km (mainland on Red Sea 1,151 km, islands in Red Sea 1,083 km)

Maritime claims: *territorial sea:* 12 nm

Climate: hot, dry desert strip along Red Sea coast; cooler and wetter in the central highlands (up to 61 cm of rainfall annually, heaviest June to September); semiarid in western hills and lowlands

Terrain: dominated by extension of Ethiopian north-south trending highlands, descending on the east to a coastal desert plain, on the northwest to hilly terrain and on the southwest to flat-to-rolling plains

Elevation: *highest point:* Soira 3,018 m
lowest point: near Kulul within the Danakil Depression -75 m
mean elevation: 853 m

Natural resources: gold, potash, zinc, copper, salt, possibly oil and natural gas, fish

Land use: *agricultural land:* 75.1% (2018 est.)
arable land: 6.8% (2018 est.)
permanent crops: 0% (2018 est.)
permanent pasture: 68.3% (2018 est.)
forest: 15.1% (2018 est.)
other: 9.8% (2018 est.)

Irrigated land: 210 sq km (2012)

Population distribution: density is highest in the center of the country in and around the cities of Asmara (capital) and Keren; smaller settlements exist in the north and south as shown in this population distribution map

Natural hazards: frequent droughts, rare earthquakes and volcanoes; locust swarms
volcanism: Dubbi (1,625 m), which last erupted in 1861, was the country's only historically active volcano until Nabro (2,218 m) came to life on 12 June 2011

Geography - note: strategic geopolitical position along world's busiest shipping lanes; Eritrea retained the entire coastline of Ethiopia along the Red Sea upon de jure independence from Ethiopia on 24 May 1993

PEOPLE AND SOCIETY

Population: *total:* 6,343,956
male: 3,122,433
female: 3,221,523 (2024 est.)
comparison rankings: female 110; male 111; total 111

Nationality: *noun:* Eritrean(s)
adjective: Eritrean

Ethnic groups: Tigrinya 50%, Tigre 30%, Saho 4%, Afar 4%, Kunama 4%, Bilen 3%, Hedareb/Beja 2%, Nara 2%, Rashaida 1% (2021 est.)
note: data represent Eritrea's nine recognized ethnic groups

Languages: Tigrinya (official), Arabic (official), English (official), Tigre, Kunama, Afar, other Cushitic languages

Religions: Eritrean Orthodox, Roman Catholic, Evangelical Lutheran, Sunni Muslim

Demographic profile: Eritrea is a persistently poor country that has made progress in some socioeconomic categories but not in others. Education and human capital formation are national priorities for facilitating economic development and eradicating poverty. To this end, Eritrea has made great strides in improving adult literacy – doubling the literacy rate over the last 20 years – in large part because of its successful adult education programs. The overall literacy rate was estimated to be more than 75% in 2018; more work needs to be done to raise female literacy and school attendance among nomadic and rural communities. Subsistence farming fails to meet the needs of Eritrea's growing population because of repeated droughts, dwindling arable land, overgrazing, soil erosion, and a shortage of farmers due to conscription and displacement. The government's emphasis on spending on defense over agriculture and its lack of foreign exchange to import food also contribute to food insecurity.
Eritrea has been a leading refugee source country since at least the 1960s, when its 30-year war for independence from Ethiopia began. Since gaining independence in 1993, Eritreans have continued migrating to Sudan, Ethiopia, Yemen, Egypt, or Israel because of a lack of basic human rights or political freedom, educational and job opportunities, or to seek asylum because of militarization. Eritrea's large diaspora has been a source of vital remittances, funding its war for independence and providing 30% of the country's GDP annually since it became independent.
In the last few years, Eritreans have increasingly been trafficked and held hostage by Bedouins in the Sinai Desert, where they are victims of organ harvesting, rape, extortion, and torture. Some Eritrean trafficking victims are kidnapped after being smuggled to Sudan or Ethiopia, while others are kidnapped from within or around refugee camps or crossing Eritrea's borders. Eritreans composed approximately 90% of the conservatively estimated 25,000-30,000 victims of Sinai trafficking from 2009-2013, according to a 2013 consultancy firm report.

Age structure: *0-14 years:* 35.7% (male 1,138,382/female 1,123,925)
15-64 years: 60.3% (male 1,882,547/female 1,944,266)
65 years and over: 4% (2024 est.) (male 101,504/female 153,332)

Dependency ratios: *total dependency ratio:* 77.9
youth dependency ratio: 70.8
elderly dependency ratio: 7.1
potential support ratio: 14 (2021 est.)

Median age: *total:* 21.3 years (2024 est.)
male: 20.8 years
female: 21.8 years
comparison ranking: total 192

Population growth rate: 1.12% (2024 est.)
comparison ranking: 82

Birth rate: 26.3 births/1,000 population (2024 est.)
comparison ranking: 41

Death rate: 6.5 deaths/1,000 population (2024 est.)
comparison ranking: 139

Net migration rate: -8.7 migrant(s)/1,000 population (2024 est.)
comparison ranking: 220

Population distribution: density is highest in the center of the country in and around the cities of Asmara (capital) and Keren; smaller settlements exist in the north and south as shown in this population distribution map

Urbanization: *urban population:* 43.3% of total population (2023)
rate of urbanization: 3.67% annual rate of change (2020-25 est.)

Major urban areas - population: 1.073 million ASMARA (capital) (2023)

Sex ratio: *at birth:* 1.03 male(s)/female
0-14 years: 1.01 male(s)/female
15-64 years: 0.97 male(s)/female
65 years and over: 0.66 male(s)/female
total population: 0.97 male(s)/female (2024 est.)

Mother's mean age at first birth: 21.3 years (2010 est.)
note: data represents median age at first birth among women 25-29

Maternal mortality ratio: 322 deaths/100,000 live births (2020 est.)
comparison ranking: 28

Infant mortality rate: *total:* 39.8 deaths/1,000 live births (2024 est.)
male: 46.6 deaths/1,000 live births
female: 32.8 deaths/1,000 live births
comparison ranking: total 29

Life expectancy at birth: *total population:* 67.5 years (2024 est.)
male: 64.9 years
female: 70.2 years
comparison ranking: total population 197

Total fertility rate: 3.43 children born/woman (2024 est.)
comparison ranking: 37

Gross reproduction rate: 1.69 (2024 est.)

Drinking water source: *improved: urban:* 73.2% of population
rural: 53.3% of population
total: 57.8% of population
unimproved: urban: 26.8% of population
rural: 46.7% of population
total: 42.2% of population (2015 est.)

Current health expenditure: 4.1% of GDP (2020)

Physician density: 0.08 physicians/1,000 population (2020)

Hospital bed density: 0.7 beds/1,000 population (2011)

Sanitation facility access: *improved: urban:* 44.5% of population
rural: 7.3% of population
total: 15.7% of population
unimproved: urban: 55.5% of population
rural: 92.7% of population
total: 84.3% of population (2017 est.)

Obesity - adult prevalence rate: 5% (2016)
comparison ranking: 183

Alcohol consumption per capita: *total:* 0.93 liters of pure alcohol (2019 est.)
beer: 0.42 liters of pure alcohol (2019 est.)
wine: 0 liters of pure alcohol (2019 est.)
spirits: 0 liters of pure alcohol (2019 est.)
other alcohols: 0.51 liters of pure alcohol (2019 est.)
comparison ranking: total 153

Tobacco use: *total:* 7.5% (2020 est.)
male: 14.7% (2020 est.)
female: 0.2% (2020 est.)
comparison ranking: total 153

Children under the age of 5 years underweight: NA

Currently married women (ages 15-49): 52.3% (2023 est.)

Literacy: *definition:* age 15 and over can read and write
total population: 76.6%
male: 84.4%
female: 68.9% (2018)

School life expectancy (primary to tertiary education): *total:* 8 years
male: 8 years
female: 7 years (2015)

ENVIRONMENT

Environment - current issues: deforestation; desertification; soil erosion; overgrazing

Environment - international agreements: *party to:* Biodiversity, Climate Change, Climate

Change-Kyoto Protocol, Comprehensive Nuclear Test Ban, Desertification, Endangered Species, Hazardous Wastes, Ozone Layer Protection, Whaling
signed, but not ratified: Climate Change-Paris Agreement

Climate: hot, dry desert strip along Red Sea coast; cooler and wetter in the central highlands (up to 61 cm of rainfall annually, heaviest June to September); semiarid in western hills and lowlands

Urbanization: *urban population:* 43.3% of total population (2023)
rate of urbanization: 3.67% annual rate of change (2020-25 est.)

Air pollutants: *particulate matter emissions:* 22.74 micrograms per cubic meter (2019 est.)
carbon dioxide emissions: 0.71 megatons (2016 est.)
methane emissions: 4.48 megatons (2020 est.)

Waste and recycling: *municipal solid waste generated annually:* 726,957 tons (2011 est.)

Total water withdrawal: *municipal:* 30 million cubic meters (2020 est.)
industrial: 1 million cubic meters (2017 est.)
agricultural: 550 million cubic meters (2020 est.)

Total renewable water resources: 7.32 billion cubic meters (2020 est.)

GOVERNMENT

Country name: *conventional long form:* State of Eritrea
conventional short form: Eritrea
local long form: Hagere Ertra
local short form: Ertra
former: Eritrea Autonomous Region in Ethiopia
etymology: the country name derives from the ancient Greek appellation "Erythra Thalassa" meaning Red Sea, which is the major water body bordering the country

Government type: presidential republic

Capital: *name:* Asmara
geographic coordinates: 15 20 N, 38 56 E
time difference: UTC+3 (8 hours ahead of Washington, DC, during Standard Time)
etymology: the name means "they [women] made them unite," which according to Tigrinya oral tradition refers to the women of the four clans in the Asmara area who persuaded their menfolk to unite and defeat their common enemy; the name has also been translated as "live in peace"

Administrative divisions: 6 regions (zobatat, singular - zoba); 'Anseba, Debub (South), Debubawi K'eyyih Bahri (Southern Red Sea), Gash-Barka, Ma'ikel (Central), Semienawi K'eyyih Bahri (Northern Red Sea)

Independence: 24 May 1993 (from Ethiopia)

National holiday: Independence Day, 24 May (1991)

Legal system: mixed legal system of civil, customary, and Islamic religious law

Constitution: *history:* ratified by the Constituent Assembly 23 May 1997 (never implemented)
amendments: proposed by the president of Eritrea or by assent of at least one half of the National Assembly membership; passage requires at least an initial three-quarters majority vote by the Assembly and, after one year, final passage by at least four-fifths majority vote by the Assembly

International law organization participation: has not submitted an ICJ jurisdiction declaration; non-party state to the ICCt

Citizenship: *citizenship by birth:* no
citizenship by descent only: at least one parent must be a citizen of Eritrea
dual citizenship recognized: no
residency requirement for naturalization: 20 years

Suffrage: 18 years of age; universal

Executive branch: *chief of state:* President ISAIAS Afwerki (since 24 May 1993)
head of government: President ISAIAS Afwerki (since 8 June 1993)
cabinet: State Council appointed by the president
elections/appointments: president indirectly elected by the National Assembly for a 5-year term (eligible for a second term), according to the constitution; the only election held was on 24 May 1993, following independence from Ethiopia (next postponed indefinitely)
election results:
1993: ISAIAS Afwerki elected president by the transitional National Assembly; percent of National Assembly vote - ISAIAS Afwerki (PFDJ) 95%, other 5%
note: the president is both chief of state and head of government and is head of the State Council and National Assembly

Legislative branch: *description:* National Assembly (Hagerawi Baito) (seats - NA; members to be directly elected to serve 5-year terms)
elections: NA
election results: NA
note: in 1997, after the new constitution was adopted, the government formed a Transitional National Assembly to serve as the country's legislative body until countrywide elections to form a National Assembly could be held; the constitution stipulates that once past the transition stage, all National Assembly members will be elected by secret ballot of all eligible voters; National Assembly elections scheduled for December 2001 were postponed indefinitely due to the war with Ethiopia; as of 2024, no sitting legislative body exists

Judicial branch: *highest court(s):* High Court (consists of 20 judges and organized into civil, commercial, criminal, labor, administrative, and customary sections)
judge selection and term of office: High Court judges appointed by the president
subordinate courts: regional/zonal courts; community courts; special courts; sharia courts (for issues dealing with Muslim marriage, inheritance, and family); military courts

Political parties: People's Front for Democracy and Justice or PFDJ (the only party recognized by the government)

International organization participation: ACP, AfDB, AU, COMESA, FAO, G-77, IAEA, IBRD, ICAO, ICC (NGOs), IDA, IFAD, IFC, IFRCS (observer), IGAD, ILO, IMF, IMO, Interpol, IOC, ISO (correspondent), ITU, ITUC (NGOs), LAS (observer), MIGA, NAM, OPCW, PCA, UN, UNCTAD, UNESCO, UNHRC, UNIDO, UNWTO, UPU, WCO, WFTU (NGOs), WHO, WIPO, WMO

Diplomatic representation in the US: *chief of mission:* Ambassador (vacant); Chargé d'Affaires Berhane Gebrehiwet SOLOMON (since 15 March 2011)
chancery: 1708 New Hampshire Avenue NW, Washington, DC 20009
telephone: [1] (202) 319-1991
FAX: [1] (202) 319-1304
email address and website:
embassyeritrea@embassyeritrea.org
https://us.embassyeritrea.org/

Diplomatic representation from the US: *chief of mission:* Ambassador (vacant); Chargé d'Affaires Leslie FRERIKSEN (since 18 July 2022)
embassy: 179 Alaa Street, Asmara
mailing address: 7170 Asmara Place, Washington DC 20521-7170
telephone: [291] (1) 12-00-04
FAX: [291] (1) 12-75-84
email address and website:
consularasmara@state.gov
https://er.usembassy.gov/

Flag description: red isosceles triangle (based on the hoist side) dividing the flag into two right triangles; the upper triangle is green, the lower one is blue; a gold wreath encircling a gold olive branch is centered on the hoist side of the red triangle; green stands for the country's agriculture economy, red signifies the blood shed in the fight for freedom, and blue symbolizes the bounty of the sea; the wreath-olive branch symbol is similar to that on the first flag of Eritrea from 1952; the shape of the red triangle broadly mimics the shape of the country
note: one of several flags where a prominent component of the design reflects the shape of the country; other such flags are those of Bosnia and Herzegovina, Brazil, and Vanuatu

National symbol(s): camel; national colors: green, red, blue

National anthem: *name:* "Ertra, Ertra, Ertra" (Eritrea, Eritrea, Eritrea)
lyrics/music: SOLOMON Tsehaye Beraki/ Isaac Abraham MEHAREZGI and ARON Tekle Tesfatsion
note: adopted 1993; upon independence from Ethiopia

National heritage: *total World Heritage Sites:* 1 (cultural)
selected World Heritage Site locales: Asmara: A Modernist African City

ECONOMY

Economic overview: largely agrarian economy with a significant mining sector; substantial fiscal surplus due to tight controls; high and vulnerable debts; increased Ethiopian trade and shared port usage decreasing prices; financial and economic data integrity challenges

Real GDP (purchasing power parity): $9.702 billion (2017 est.)
$8.953 billion (2016 est.)
$8.791 billion (2015 est.)
note: data are in 2017 dollars
comparison ranking: 168

Real GDP growth rate: 5% (2017 est.)
1.9% (2016 est.)
2.6% (2015 est.)
comparison ranking: 56

Real GDP per capita: $1,600 (2017 est.)
$1,500 (2016 est.)
$1,500 (2015 est.)
note: data are in 2017 dollars
comparison ranking: 216

GDP (official exchange rate): $5.813 billion (2017 est.)

Inflation rate (consumer prices): 9% (2017 est.)
9% (2016 est.)

comparison ranking: 166

GDP - composition, by sector of origin: *agriculture:* 11.7% (2017 est.)
industry: 29.6% (2017 est.)
services: 58.7% (2017 est.)
comparison rankings: services 95; industry 69; agriculture 68

GDP - composition, by end use: *household consumption:* 80.9% (2017 est.)
government consumption: 24.3% (2017 est.)
investment in fixed capital: 6.4% (2017 est.)
investment in inventories: 0.1% (2017 est.)
exports of goods and services: 10.9% (2017 est.)
imports of goods and services: -22.5% (2017 est.)

Agricultural products: sorghum, milk, barley, vegetables, root vegetables, cereals, pulses, millet, wheat, beef (2022)
note: top ten agricultural products based on tonnage

Industries: food processing, beverages, clothing and textiles, light manufacturing, salt, cement
Industrial production growth rate
4.3% (2014 est.)
note: annual % change in industrial value added based on constant local currency
comparison ranking: 71

Labor force: 1.8 million (2023 est.)
note: number of people ages 15 or older who are employed or seeking work
comparison ranking: 129

Unemployment rate: 5.87% (2023 est.)
5.94% (2022 est.)
6.34% (2021 est.)
note: % of labor force seeking employment
comparison ranking: 117

Youth unemployment rate (ages 15-24): *total:* 10% (2023 est.)
male: 8.9% (2023 est.)
female: 11.3% (2023 est.)
note: % of labor force ages 15-24 seeking employment
comparison ranking: total 135

Budget: *revenues:* $633 million (2018 est.)
expenditures: $549 million (2018 est.)

Public debt: 131.2% of GDP (2017 est.)
comparison ranking: 8

Taxes and other revenues: 34.9% (of GDP) (2017 est.)
comparison ranking: 17

Current account balance: -$137 million (2017 est.)
-$105 million (2016 est.)
comparison ranking: 100

Exports: $624.3 million (2017 est.)
$485.4 million (2016 est.)
comparison ranking: 189

Exports - partners: China 52%, UAE 33%, South Korea 9%, Japan 2%, Madagascar 2% (2022)
note: top five export partners based on percentage share of exports

Exports - commodities: zinc ore, gold, copper ore, wheat, garments (2022)
note: top five export commodities based on value in dollars

Imports: $1.127 billion (2017 est.)
$1.048 billion (2016 est.)
comparison ranking: 191

Imports - partners: China 34%, UAE 26%, Turkey 12%, US 7%, India 4% (2022)
note: top five import partners based on percentage share of imports

Imports - commodities: ships, sorghum, wheat, construction vehicles, other foods (2022)
note: top five import commodities based on value in dollars

Reserves of foreign exchange and gold: $191.694 million (2019 est.)
$163.034 million (2018 est.)
$143.412 million (2017 est.)
note: holdings of gold (year-end prices)/foreign exchange/special drawing rights in current dollars
comparison ranking: 181

Debt - external: $471.009 million (2022 est.)
note: present value of external debt in current US dollars
comparison ranking: 90

Exchange rates: nakfa (ERN) per US dollar -

Exchange rates: 15.075 (2023 est.)
15.075 (2022 est.)
15.075 (2021 est.)
15.075 (2020 est.)
15.075 (2019 est.)

ENERGY

Electricity access: *electrification - total population:* 55.4% (2022 est.)
electrification - urban areas: 75.5%
electrification - rural areas: 36%

Electricity: *installed generating capacity:* 219,000 kW (2022 est.)
consumption: 337.42 million kWh (2022 est.)
transmission/distribution losses: 50.261 million kWh (2022 est.)
comparison rankings: transmission/distribution losses 40; consumption 183; installed generating capacity 170

Electricity generation sources: *fossil fuels:* 96.3% of total installed capacity (2022 est.)
solar: 3.2% of total installed capacity (2022 est.)
wind: 0.5% of total installed capacity (2022 est.)

Petroleum: *refined petroleum consumption:* 4,000 bbl/day (2022 est.)

Carbon dioxide emissions: 671,000 metric tonnes of CO2 (2022 est.)
from petroleum and other liquids: 671,000 metric tonnes of CO2 (2022 est.)
comparison ranking: total emissions 182

Energy consumption per capita: 2.53 million Btu/person (2022 est.)
comparison ranking: 181

COMMUNICATIONS

Telephones - fixed lines: *total subscriptions:* 66,000 (2021 est.)
subscriptions per 100 inhabitants: 2 (2021 est.)
comparison ranking: total subscriptions 148

Telephones - mobile cellular: *total subscriptions:* 1.801 million (2021 est.)
subscriptions per 100 inhabitants: 50 (2021 est.)
comparison ranking: total subscriptions 154

Telecommunication systems: *general assessment:* Eritrea's telecom sector operates under a state-owned monopoly for fixed and mobile services; as a result of such restrictions on competition, the country has the least developed telecommunications market in Africa; mobile penetration stands at only about 20%, while fixed-line internet use barely registers; this is exacerbated by the very low use of computers, with only about 4% of households having a computer, and most of these being in the capital, Asmara; the 3G network continues to rollout which provides basic internet access to a limited number of Eritreans who can afford the expensive services; investment in telecom infrastructure is still required to improve the quality of services; the government has embarked on a work program to do exactly that, specifically aimed at extending services to remote areas, improving the quality of services, and ensuring that more telecoms infrastructure is supported by solar power to compensate for the poor state of the electricity network (2022)
domestic: fixed-line subscribership is less than 2 per 100 persons and mobile-cellular is just over 50 per 100 (2021)
international: country code - 291 (2019)

Broadcast media: government controls broadcast media with private ownership prohibited; 1 state-owned TV station; 2 state-owned radio networks; purchases of satellite dishes and subscriptions to international broadcast media are permitted (2023)

Internet country code: .er

Internet users: *total:* 792,000 (2021 est.)
percent of population: 22% (2021 est.)
comparison ranking: total 156

Broadband - fixed subscriptions: *total:* 5,000 (2020 est.)
subscriptions per 100 inhabitants: 0.1 (2020 est.)
comparison ranking: total 189

TRANSPORTATION

National air transport system: *number of registered air carriers:* 1 (2020)
inventory of registered aircraft operated by air carriers: 1
annual passenger traffic on registered air carriers: 102,729 (2018)

Civil aircraft registration country code prefix: E3

Airports: 10 (2024)
comparison ranking: 160

Railways: *total:* 306 km (2018)
narrow gauge: 306 km (2018) 0.950-m gauge
comparison ranking: total 122

Roadways: *total:* 16,000 km (2018)
paved: 1,600 km (2000)
unpaved: 14,400 km (2000)
comparison ranking: total 120

Merchant marine: *total:* 9 (2023)
by type: general cargo 4, oil tanker 1, other 4
comparison ranking: total 161

Ports: *total ports:* 2 (2024)
large: 0
medium: 0
small: 2
very small: 0
ports with oil terminals: 2
key ports: Assab, Mitsiwa Harbor

MILITARY AND SECURITY

Military and security forces: Eritrean Defense Forces (EDF): Eritrean Ground Forces, Eritrean Navy, Eritrean Air Force (includes Air Defense Force); People's Militia (aka People's Army or Hizbawi Serawit) (2023)
note: police are responsible for maintaining internal security, but the government sometimes used the armed forces, reserves, demobilized soldiers, or civilian militia to meet domestic as well as external

security requirements; the armed forces have authority to arrest and detain civilians

Military expenditures: 10% of GDP (2019 est.)
10.2% of GDP (2018 est.)
10.3% of GDP (2017 est.)
10.4% of GDP (2016 est.)
10.6% of GDP (2015 est.)
comparison ranking: 1

Military and security service personnel strengths: limited available information; estimated 150,000-200,000 personnel (2023)

Military equipment inventories and acquisitions: the EDF inventory is comprised primarily of older Russian and Soviet-era systems; Eritrea was under a UN arms embargo from 2009 to 2018; from the 1990s to 2008, Russia was the leading supplier of arms to Eritrea, and in recent years, Eritrea has expressed interest in purchasing additional Russian equipment (2023)

Military service age and obligation: Eritrea mandates military service for all citizens between the ages of 18 and 40; 18-month conscript service obligation, which includes 4-6 months of military training and 12 months of military or other national service (military service is most common); in practice, military and national service is often extended indefinitely; citizens up to the age of 55 eligible for recall during mobilization (2023)

Military - note: the military's primary responsibilities are external defense, border security, and providing the regime a vehicle for national cohesion; the Army is the dominant service; it is a large, conscript-based force and estimated to have more than 20 infantry divisions, including some that are mechanized, as well as a division of commandos/special forces since the country's independence in 1991, the Eritrean military has participated in numerous conflicts, including the Hanish Island Crisis with Yemen (1995), the First Congo War (1996-1997), the Second Sudanese Civil War (1996-1998), the Eritrea-Ethiopia War (1998-2000), the Djiboutian-Eritrean border conflict (2008), and the Tigray conflict in Ethiopia (2020-2022); during the Tigray conflict, the Eritrean Defense Forces were accused of widespread human rights abuses (2023)

TRANSNATIONAL ISSUES

Trafficking in persons: tier rating: Tier 3 — Eritrea does not fully meet the minimum standards for the elimination of trafficking and is not making significant efforts to do so, therefore Eritrea remained on Tier 3; for more details, go to: https://www.state.gov/reports/2024-trafficking-in-persons-report/eritrea/

ESTONIA

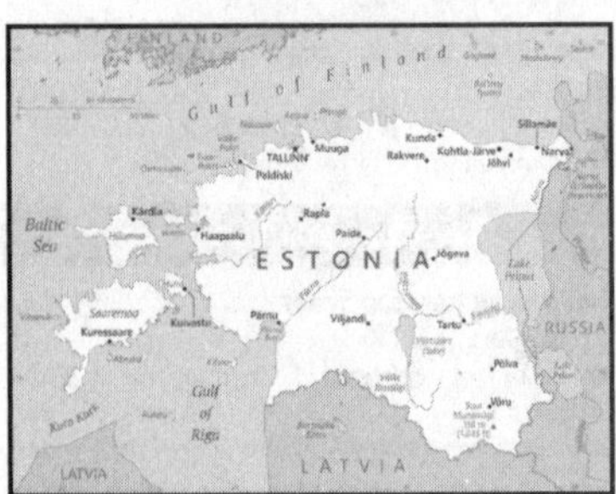

INTRODUCTION

Background: After centuries of Danish, Swedish, German, and Russian rule, Estonia attained independence in 1918. Forcibly incorporated into the USSR in 1940 – an action never recognized by the US and many other countries – it regained its freedom in 1991 with the collapse of the Soviet Union. Since the last Russian troops left in 1994, Estonia has been free to promote economic and political ties with the West. It joined both NATO and the EU in 2004, formally joined the OECD in 2010, and adopted the euro as its official currency in 2011.

GEOGRAPHY

Location: Eastern Europe, bordering the Baltic Sea and Gulf of Finland, between Latvia and Russia

Geographic coordinates: 59 00 N, 26 00 E

Map references: Europe

Area: *total:* 45,228 sq km
land: 42,388 sq km
water: 2,840 sq km
note: includes 1,520 islands in the Baltic Sea
comparison ranking: total 132

Area - comparative: about twice the size of New Jersey

Land boundaries: *total:* 657 km
border countries (2): Latvia 333 km; Russia 324 km

Coastline: 3,794 km

Maritime claims: *territorial sea:* 12 nm
exclusive economic zone: limits as agreed to by Estonia, Finland, Latvia, Sweden, and Russia

Climate: maritime; wet, moderate winters, cool summers

Terrain: marshy, lowlands; flat in the north, hilly in the south

Elevation: *highest point:* Suur Munamagi 318 m
lowest point: Baltic Sea 0 m
mean elevation: 61 m

Natural resources: oil shale, peat, rare earth elements, phosphorite, clay, limestone, sand, dolomite, arable land, sea mud

Land use: *agricultural land:* 22.2% (2018 est.)
arable land: 14.9% (2018 est.)
permanent crops: 0.1% (2018 est.)
permanent pasture: 7.2% (2018 est.)
forest: 52.1% (2018 est.)
other: 25.7% (2018 est.)

Irrigated land: 20 sq km (2016)

Major lakes (area sq km): *fresh water lake(s):* Lake Peipus - 4,300 sq km (shared with Russia); Lake Võrtsjärv - 270 sq km

Population distribution: a fairly even distribution throughout most of the country, with urban areas attracting larger and denser populations

Natural hazards: sometimes flooding occurs in the spring

Geography - note: the mainland terrain is flat, boggy, and partly wooded; offshore lie more than 1,500 islands

PEOPLE AND SOCIETY

Population: *total:* 1,193,791
male: 563,079
female: 630,712 (2024 est.)
comparison rankings: female 158; male 160; total 160

Nationality: *noun:* Estonian(s)
adjective: Estonian

Ethnic groups: Estonian 69.1%, Russian 23.7%, Ukrainian 2.1%, other 4.6%, unspecified 0.5% (2021 est.)

Languages: Estonian (official) 67.2%, Russian 28.5%, other 3.7%, unspecified 0.6% (2021est.)

Religions: Orthodox 16.5%, Protestant 9.2% (Lutheran 7.7%, other Protestant 1.5%), other 3% (includes Roman Catholic, Muslim, Jehovah's Witness, Pentecostal, Buddhist, and Taara Believer), none 58.4%, unspecified 12.9% (2021 est.)

Age structure: *0-14 years:* 15.2% (male 92,980/female 88,753)
15-64 years: 62.2% (male 373,989/female 368,113)
65 years and over: 22.6% (2024 est.) (male 96,110/female 173,846)

Dependency ratios: *total dependency ratio:* 58.3
youth dependency ratio: 26.1
elderly dependency ratio: 32.3
potential support ratio: 3.1 (2021 est.)

Median age: *total:* 45 years (2024 est.)
male: 41.9 years
female: 48.2 years
comparison ranking: total 22

Population growth rate: -0.76% (2024 est.)
comparison ranking: 228

Birth rate: 8.2 births/1,000 population (2024 est.)
comparison ranking: 212

Death rate: 13.2 deaths/1,000 population (2024 est.)
comparison ranking: 12

Net migration rate: -2.7 migrant(s)/1,000 population (2024 est.)
comparison ranking: 174

Population distribution: a fairly even distribution throughout most of the country, with urban areas attracting larger and denser populations

Urbanization: *urban population:* 69.8% of total population (2023)
rate of urbanization: -0.03% annual rate of change (2020-25 est.)

Major urban areas - population: 454,000 TALLINN (capital) (2023)

Sex ratio: *at birth:* 1.05 male(s)/female
0-14 years: 1.05 male(s)/female

15-64 years: 1.02 male(s)/female
65 years and over: 0.55 male(s)/female
total population: 0.89 male(s)/female (2024 est.)

Mother's mean age at first birth: 28.2 years (2020 est.)

Maternal mortality ratio: 5 deaths/100,000 live births (2020 est.)
comparison ranking: 164

Infant mortality rate: *total:* 3.3 deaths/1,000 live births (2024 est.)
male: 3.2 deaths/1,000 live births
female: 3.4 deaths/1,000 live births
comparison ranking: total 196

Life expectancy at birth: *total population:* 78.4 years (2024 est.)
male: 73.8 years
female: 83.2 years
comparison ranking: total population 79

Total fertility rate: 1.62 children born/woman (2024 est.)
comparison ranking: 178

Gross reproduction rate: 0.79 (2024 est.)

Contraceptive prevalence rate: NA

Drinking water source: *improved: urban:* 100% of population
rural: NA
total: 99.6% of population

Current health expenditure: 7.8% of GDP (2020)

Physician density: 3.47 physicians/1,000 population (2019)

Hospital bed density: 4.6 beds/1,000 population (2018)

Sanitation facility access: *improved: urban:* 99.8% of population
rural: 100% of population
total: 99.8% of population
unimproved: urban: 0.2% of population
rural: 0% of population
total: 0.2% of population (2020 est.)

Obesity - adult prevalence rate: 21.2% (2016)
comparison ranking: 93

Alcohol consumption per capita: *total:* 11.65 liters of pure alcohol (2019 est.)
beer: 4 liters of pure alcohol (2019 est.)
wine: 1.92 liters of pure alcohol (2019 est.)
spirits: 4.6 liters of pure alcohol (2019 est.)
other alcohols: 1.13 liters of pure alcohol (2019 est.)
comparison ranking: total 7

Tobacco use: *total:* 29.7% (2020 est.)
male: 36.3% (2020 est.)
female: 23% (2020 est.)
comparison ranking: total 32

Children under the age of 5 years underweight: 0.4% (2013/15)
comparison ranking: 126

Currently married women (ages 15-49): 52.3% (2023 est.)

Education expenditures: 6.6% of GDP (2020 est.)
comparison ranking: 29

Literacy: *definition:* age 15 and over can read and write
total population: 99.9%
male: 99.9%
female: 99.9% (2021)

School life expectancy (primary to tertiary education): *total:* 16 years
male: 15 years
female: 17 years (2020)

ENVIRONMENT

Environment - current issues: air polluted with sulfur dioxide from oil-shale burning power plants in northeast; however, the amounts of pollutants emitted into the air have fallen dramatically and the pollution load of wastewater at purification plants has decreased substantially due to improved technology and environmental monitoring; Estonia has more than 1,400 natural and manmade lakes, the smaller of which in agricultural areas need to be monitored; coastal seawater is polluted in certain locations

Environment - international agreements: *party to:* Air Pollution, Air Pollution-Heavy Metals, Air Pollution-Nitrogen Oxides, Air Pollution-Persistent Organic Pollutants, Air Pollution-Sulphur 85, Air Pollution-Volatile Organic Compounds, Antarctic Treaty, Biodiversity, Climate Change, Climate Change-Kyoto Protocol, Climate Change-Paris Agreement, Comprehensive Nuclear Test Ban, Desertification, Endangered Species, Environmental Modification, Hazardous Wastes, Law of the Sea, Marine Dumping-London Protocol, Ozone Layer Protection, Ship Pollution, Tropical Timber 2006, Wetlands, Whaling
signed, but not ratified: none of the selected agreements

Climate: maritime; wet, moderate winters, cool summers

Urbanization: *urban population:* 69.8% of total population (2023)
rate of urbanization: -0.03% annual rate of change (2020-25 est.)

Revenue from forest resources: 0.85% of GDP (2018 est.)
comparison ranking: 56

Revenue from coal: 0% of GDP (2018 est.)
comparison ranking: 156

Air pollutants: *particulate matter emissions:* 6.35 micrograms per cubic meter (2019 est.)
carbon dioxide emissions: 16.59 megatons (2016 est.)
methane emissions: 0.99 megatons (2020 est.)

Waste and recycling: *municipal solid waste generated annually:* 473,000 tons (2015 est.)
municipal solid waste recycled annually: 117,020 tons (2015 est.)
percent of municipal solid waste recycled: 24.7% (2015 est.)

Major lakes (area sq km): *fresh water lake(s):* Lake Peipus - 4,300 sq km (shared with Russia); Lake Võrtsjärv - 270 sq km

Total water withdrawal: *municipal:* 60 million cubic meters (2020 est.)
industrial: 790 million cubic meters (2020 est.)
agricultural: 4.5 million cubic meters (2017 est.)

Total renewable water resources: 12.81 billion cubic meters (2020 est.)

GOVERNMENT

Country name: *conventional long form:* Republic of Estonia
conventional short form: Estonia
local long form: Eesti Vabariik
local short form: Eesti
former: Estonian Soviet Socialist Republic (while occupied by the USSR)
etymology: the country name may derive from the Aesti, an ancient people who lived along the eastern Baltic Sea in the first centuries A.D.

Government type: parliamentary republic

Capital: *name:* Tallinn
geographic coordinates: 59 26 N, 24 43 E
time difference: UTC+2 (7 hours ahead of Washington, DC, during Standard Time)
daylight saving time: +1hr, begins last Sunday in March; ends last Sunday in October
etymology: the Estonian name is generally believed to be derived from "Taani-linn" (originally meaning "Danish castle", now "Danish town") after a stronghold built in the area by the Danes; it could also have come from "tali-linn" ("winter castle" or "winter town") or "talu-linn" ("home castle" or "home town")

Administrative divisions: 15 urban municipalities (linnad, singular - linn), 64 rural municipalities (vallad, singular vald)
urban municipalities: Haapsalu, Keila, Kohtla-Jarve, Loksa, Maardu, Narva, Narva-Joesuu, Paide, Parnu, Rakvere, Sillamae, Tallinn, Tartu, Viljandi, Voru
rural municipalities: Alutaguse, Anija, Antsla, Elva, Haademeeste, Haljala, Harku, Hiiumaa, Jarva, Joelahtme, Jogeva, Johvi, Kadrina, Kambja, Kanepi, Kastre, Kehtna, Kihnu, Kiili, Kohila, Kose, Kuusalu, Laane-Harju, Laane-Nigula, Laaneranna, Luganuse, Luunja, Marjamaa, Muhu, Mulgi, Mustvee, Noo, Otepaa, Peipsiaare, Pohja-Parnumaa, Pohja- Sakala, Poltsamaa, Polva, Raasiku, Rae, Rakvere, Räpina, Rapla, Rouge, Ruhnu, Saarde, Saaremaa, Saku, Saue, Setomaa, Tapa, Tartu, Toila, Tori, Torva, Turi, Vaike-Maarja, Valga, Viimsi, Viljandi, Vinni, Viru-Nigula, Vormsi, Voru

Independence: 24 February 1918 (from Soviet Russia); 20 August 1991 (declared from the Soviet Union); 6 September 1991 (recognized by the Soviet Union)

National holiday: Independence Day, 24 February (1918); note - 24 February 1918 was the date Estonia declared its independence from Soviet Russia and established its statehood; 20 August 1991 was the date it declared its independence from the Soviet Union restoring its statehood

Legal system: civil law system

Constitution: *history:* several previous; latest adopted 28 June 1992, entered into force 3 July 1992
amendments: proposed by at least one-fifth of Parliament members or by the president of the republic; passage requires three readings of the proposed amendment and a simple majority vote in two successive memberships of Parliament; passage of amendments to the "General Provisions" and "Amendment of the Constitution" chapters requires at least three-fifths majority vote by Parliament to conduct a referendum and majority vote in a referendum; amended several times, last in 2015

International law organization participation: accepts compulsory ICJ jurisdiction with reservations; accepts ICCt jurisdiction

Citizenship: *citizenship by birth:* no
citizenship by descent only: at least one parent must be a citizen of Estonia
dual citizenship recognized: no
residency requirement for naturalization: 5 years

Suffrage: 18 years of age; universal; age 16 for local elections

Executive branch: *chief of state:* President Alar KARIS (since 11 October 2021)
head of government: Prime Minister Kaja KALLAS (since 26 January 2021)
cabinet: Cabinet appointed by the prime minister, approved by Parliament
elections/appointments: president indirectly elected by Parliament for a 5-year term (eligible for a second term); if a candidate does not secure two thirds of the votes after 3 rounds of balloting, then an electoral college consisting of Parliament members and local council members elects the president, choosing between the 2 candidates with the highest number of votes; if a president is still not elected, the process begins again; election last held on 30 to 31 August 2021 (next to be held in 2026); prime minister nominated by the president and approved by Parliament
election results:
2021: Alar KARIS (independent) elected president; won second round of voting in parliament with 72 of 101 votes
2016: Kersti KALJULAID elected president; won sixth round of voting in parliament with 81 of 98 votes (17 ballots blank); KALJULAID sworn in on 10 October 2016 - first female head of state of Estonia
note - Prime Minister Kaja KALLAS resigned on 15 July 2024 but will continue as acting prime minister until the new government is sworn in

Legislative branch: *description:* unicameral Parliament or Riigikogu (101 seats; members are elected at general elections for a term of four years.)
elections: last held on 5 March 2023; next elections 7 March 2027
election results: percent of vote by party - Reform 31.2%, EKRE 16.1%, Center 15.3%, E200 13.3%, SDE 9.3%, Pro Patria 8.2%, Left 2.4%, Right 2.3%, Greens 1.0%; seats by party - Reform 37, EKRE 17, Center 16, E200 14, SDE 9, Pro Patria 8; composition - men 71, women 30, percent of women 29.7%

Judicial branch: *highest court(s):* Supreme Court (consists of 19 justices, including the chief justice, and organized into civil, criminal, administrative, and constitutional review chambers)
judge selection and term of office: the chief justice is proposed by the president of the republic and appointed by the Riigikogu; other justices proposed by the chief justice and appointed by the Riigikogu; justices appointed for life
subordinate courts: circuit (appellate) courts; administrative, county, city, and specialized courts

Political parties: Conservative People's Party (Konservatiivne Rahvaerakond) or EKRE
Estonia 200 or E200
Estonia Centre Party of (Keskerakond) or KE
Estonian Free Party or VAP
Estonian Greens or EER
Estonian Nationalists and Conservatives or ERK
Estonian Reform Party (Reformierakond) or RE
Estonian United Left Party or EÜVP
Fatherland or I
Pro Patria (Isamaa)
The Right or PP
Social Democratic Party or SDE

International organization participation: Australia Group, BA, BIS, CBSS, CD, CE, EAPC, EBRD, ECB, EIB, EMU, ESA (cooperating state), EU, FAO, IAEA, IBRD, ICAO, ICC (national committees), ICCt, ICRM, IDA, IEA, IFAD, IFC, IFRCS, IHO, ILO, IMF, IMO, Interpol, IOC, IOM, IPU, ISO, ITSO, ITU, ITUC (NGOs), MIGA, NATO, NIB, NSG, OAS (observer), OECD, OIF (observer), OPCW, OSCE, PCA, Schengen Convention, UN, UNCTAD, UNESCO, UNHCR, UNTSO, UPU, Wassenaar Arrangement, WCO, WHO, WIPO, WMO, WTO

Diplomatic representation in the US: *chief of mission:* Ambassador Kristjan PRIKK (since 7 July 2021)
chancery: 2131 Massachusetts Ave, NW Washington, DC, 20008
telephone: [1] (202) 588-0101
FAX: [1] (202) 588-0108
email address and website:
Embassy.Washington@mfa.ee
https://washington.mfa.ee/
consulate(s) general: New York, San Francisco

Diplomatic representation from the US: *chief of mission:* Ambassador George P. KENT (since 21 February 2023)
embassy: Kentmanni 20, 15099 Tallinn
mailing address: 4530 Tallinn Place, Washington DC 20521-4530
telephone: [372] 668-8100
FAX: [372] 668-8265
email address and website:
acstallinn@state.gov
https://ee.usembassy.gov/

Flag description: three equal horizontal bands of blue (top), black, and white; various interpretations are linked to the flag colors; blue represents faith, loyalty, and devotion, while also reminiscent of the sky, sea, and lakes of the country; black symbolizes the soil of the country and the dark past and suffering endured by the Estonian people; white refers to the striving towards enlightenment and virtue, and is the color of birch bark and snow, as well as summer nights illuminated by the midnight sun

National symbol(s): barn swallow, cornflower; national colors: blue, black, white

National anthem: *name:* "Mu isamaa, mu onn ja room" (My Native Land, My Pride and Joy)
lyrics/music: Johann Voldemar JANNSEN/Fredrik PACIUS
note: adopted 1920, though banned between 1940 and 1990 under Soviet occupation; the anthem, used in Estonia since 1869, shares the same melody as Finland's but has different lyrics

National heritage: *total World Heritage Sites:* 2 (both cultural)
selected World Heritage Site locales: Historic Center (Old Town) of Tallinn; Struve Geodetic Arc

ECONOMY

Economic overview: advanced, service-based EU and eurozone economy; economic downturn due to inflation, trade, and energy impacts of Ukraine war; decline in intra-EU trade; low public debt relative to EU members; recovery depends on improving private investment and productivity rates

Real GDP (purchasing power parity): $57.377 billion (2023 est.)
$59.155 billion (2022 est.)
$59.429 billion (2021 est.)
note: data in 2021 dollars
comparison ranking: 117

Real GDP growth rate: -3.01% (2023 est.)
-0.46% (2022 est.)
7.25% (2021 est.)
note: annual GDP % growth based on constant local currency
comparison ranking: 210

Real GDP per capita: $42,000 (2023 est.)
$43,900 (2022 est.)
$44,700 (2021 est.)
note: data in 2021 dollars
comparison ranking: 57

GDP (official exchange rate): $40.745 billion (2023 est.)
note: data in current dollars at official exchange rate

Inflation rate (consumer prices): 9.16% (2023 est.)
19.4% (2022 est.)
4.65% (2021 est.)
note: annual % change based on consumer prices
comparison ranking: 168

Credit ratings: Fitch rating: AA- (2018)

Moody's rating: A1 (2002)

Standard & Poors rating: AA- (2011)
note: The year refers to the year in which the current credit rating was first obtained.

GDP - composition, by sector of origin: *agriculture:* 2.2% (2023 est.)
industry: 22.3% (2023 est.)
services: 63.8% (2023 est.)
note: figures may not total 100% due to non-allocated consumption not captured in sector-reported data comparison rankings: services 64; industry 123; agriculture 153

GDP - composition, by end use: *household consumption:* 53% (2023 est.)
government consumption: 20.9% (2023 est.)
investment in fixed capital: 26.6% (2023 est.)
investment in inventories: 0.1% (2023 est.)
exports of goods and services: 78.4% (2023 est.)
imports of goods and services: -77.8% (2023 est.)
note: figures may not total 100% due to rounding or gaps in data collection

Agricultural products: wheat, milk, barley, rapeseed, oats, peas, potatoes, rye, pork, beans (2022)
note: top ten agricultural products based on tonnage

Industries: food, engineering, electronics, wood and wood products, textiles; information technology, telecommunications

Industrial production growth rate: -9.7% (2023 est.)
note: annual % change in industrial value added based on constant local currency
comparison ranking: 208

Labor force: 752,000 (2023 est.)
note: number of people ages 15 or older who are employed or seeking work
comparison ranking: 153

Unemployment rate: 6.35% (2023 est.)
5.57% (2022 est.)
6.18% (2021 est.)
note: % of labor force seeking employment
comparison ranking: 129

Youth unemployment rate (ages 15-24): *total:* 17.1% (2023 est.)
male: 18.2% (2023 est.)
female: 16% (2023 est.)
note: % of labor force ages 15-24 seeking employment
comparison ranking: total 82

Population below poverty line: 22.5% (2022 est.)
note: % of population with income below national poverty line

Gini Index coefficient - distribution of family income: 31.8 (2021 est.)
note: index (0-100) of income distribution; higher values represent greater inequality

comparison ranking: 110

Average household expenditures: *on food:* 18.7% of household expenditures (2022 est.)
on alcohol and tobacco: 7.8% of household expenditures (2022 est.)

Household income or consumption by percentage share: *lowest 10%:* 3.1% (2021 est.)
highest 10%: 24.3% (2021 est.)
note: % share of income accruing to lowest and highest 10% of population

Remittances: 1.2% of GDP (2023 est.)
1.24% of GDP (2022 est.)
1.6% of GDP (2021 est.)
note: personal transfers and compensation between resident and non-resident individuals/households/entities

Budget: *revenues:* $13.907 billion (2022 est.)
expenditures: $13.505 billion (2022 est.)
note: central government revenues (excluding grants) and expenses converted to US dollars at average official exchange rate for year indicated

Public debt: 25.2% of GDP (2022 est.)
note: central government debt as a % of GDP
comparison ranking: 175

Taxes and other revenues: 21.01% (of GDP) (2022 est.)
note: central government tax revenue as a % of GDP
comparison ranking: 80

Current account balance: -$848.528 million (2023 est.)
-$1.231 billion (2022 est.)
-$1.002 billion (2021 est.)
note: balance of payments - net trade and primary/secondary income in current dollars
comparison ranking: 137

Exports: $31.939 billion (2023 est.)
$32.461 billion (2022 est.)
$29.522 billion (2021 est.)
note: balance of payments - exports of goods and services in current dollars
comparison ranking: 79

Exports - partners: Finland 13%, Latvia 12%, Sweden 8%, Lithuania 7%, Russia 6% (2022)
note: top five export partners based on percentage share of exports

Exports - commodities: electricity, broadcasting equipment, refined petroleum, wood, coal tar oil (2022)
note: top five export commodities based on value in dollars

Imports: $31.701 billion (2023 est.)
$32.671 billion (2022 est.)
$29.937 billion (2021 est.)
note: balance of payments - imports of goods and services in current dollars
comparison ranking: 78

Imports - partners: Finland 13%, Germany 10%, Lithuania 8%, Latvia 8%, Russia 8% (2022)
note: top five import partners based on percentage share of imports

Imports - commodities: refined petroleum, cars, electricity, natural gas, coal tar oil (2022)
note: top five import commodities based on value in dollars

Reserves of foreign exchange and gold: $2.593 billion (2023 est.)
$2.217 billion (2022 est.)
$2.371 billion (2021 est.)
note: holdings of gold (year-end prices)/foreign exchange/special drawing rights in current dollars
comparison ranking: 132

Exchange rates: euros (EUR) per US dollar -

Exchange rates: 0.925 (2023 est.)
0.95 (2022 est.)
0.845 (2021 est.)
0.876 (2020 est.)
0.893 (2019 est.)

ENERGY

Electricity access: *electrification - total population:* 100% (2022 est.)

Electricity: *installed generating capacity:* 2.871 million kW (2022 est.)
consumption: 7.476 billion kWh (2022 est.)
exports: 6.173 billion kWh (2022 est.)
imports: 7.182 billion kWh (2022 est.)
transmission/distribution losses: 532 million kWh (2022 est.)
comparison rankings: transmission/distribution losses 81; imports 35; exports 34; consumption 115; installed generating capacity 110

Electricity generation sources: *fossil fuels:* 63.5% of total installed capacity (2022 est.)
solar: 5.1% of total installed capacity (2022 est.)
wind: 9.6% of total installed capacity (2022 est.)
hydroelectricity: 0.2% of total installed capacity (2022 est.)
biomass and waste: 21.7% of total installed capacity (2022 est.)

Coal: *consumption:* 3,000 metric tons (2022 est.)
exports: 18.5 metric tons (2022 est.)
imports: 2,000 metric tons (2022 est.)

Petroleum: *total petroleum production:* 24,000 bbl/day (2023 est.)
refined petroleum consumption: 28,000 bbl/day (2023 est.)

Natural gas: *consumption:* 354.912 million cubic meters (2022 est.)
exports: 706.983 million cubic meters (2022 est.)
imports: 1.255 billion cubic meters (2022 est.)

Carbon dioxide emissions: 5.16 million metric tonnes of CO2 (2022 est.)
from coal and metallurgical coke: 7,000 metric tonnes of CO2 (2022 est.)
from petroleum and other liquids: 4.466 million metric tonnes of CO2 (2022 est.)
from consumed natural gas: 688,000 metric tonnes of CO2 (2022 est.)
comparison ranking: total emissions 132

Energy consumption per capita: 73.259 million Btu/person (2022 est.)
comparison ranking: 69

COMMUNICATIONS

Telephones - fixed lines: *total subscriptions:* 266,000 (2022 est.)
subscriptions per 100 inhabitants: 20 (2022 est.)
comparison ranking: total subscriptions 112

Telephones - mobile cellular: *total subscriptions:* 2.056 million (2022 est.)
subscriptions per 100 inhabitants: 155 (2022 est.)
comparison ranking: total subscriptions 150

Telecommunication systems: *general assessment:* investment in Estonia's telecom market has been focused on fixed-line infrastructure upgrades, and the deployment of 5G services; fixed broadband subscribers are gradually migrating from digital subscriber lines (DSL) to fiber, with the legacy copper being replaced; the Mobile Network Operators (MNOs) have comprehensive long-term evolution (LTE) infrastructure in place, and have in recent years channeled investment to 5G; several 5G trials have been undertaken in recent years, though commercial service launches have been restricted by the lack of available internet services
(2024)
domestic: 20 per 100 for fixed-line subscribership and approximately 155 per 100 for mobile-cellular (2022)
international: country code - 372; landing points for the EE-S-1, EESF-3, Baltic Sea Submarine Cable, FEC and EESF-2 fiber-optic submarine cables to other Estonia points, Finland, and Sweden; 2 international switches are located in Tallinn (2019)

Broadcast media: the publicly owned broadcaster, Eesti Rahvusringhaaling (ERR), operates 3 TV channels and 5 radio networks; growing number of private commercial radio stations broadcasting nationally, regionally, and locally; fully transitioned to digital television in 2010; national private TV channels expanding service; a range of channels are aimed at Russian-speaking viewers; in 2016, there were 42 on-demand services available in Estonia, including 19 pay TVOD and SVOD services; roughly 85% of households accessed digital television services

Internet country code: .ee

Internet users: *total:* 1.183 million (2021 est.)
percent of population: 91% (2021 est.)
comparison ranking: total 147

Broadband - fixed subscriptions: *total:* 415,610 (2020 est.)
subscriptions per 100 inhabitants: 31 (2020 est.)
comparison ranking: total 96

TRANSPORTATION

National air transport system: *number of registered air carriers:* 3 (2020)
inventory of registered aircraft operated by air carriers: 14
annual passenger traffic on registered air carriers: 31,981 (2018)

Civil aircraft registration country code prefix: ES

Airports: 26 (2024)
comparison ranking: 128

Heliports: 2 (2024)

Pipelines: 2,360 km gas (2016)

Railways: *total:* 1,441 km (2020) 225 km electrified
comparison ranking: total 83

Roadways: *total:* 89,382 km (2022)
comparison ranking: total 57

Waterways: 335 km (2011) (320 km are navigable year-round)
comparison ranking: 100

Merchant marine: *total:* 72 (2023)
by type: general cargo 3, oil tanker 3, other 66
comparison ranking: total 108

Ports: *total ports:* 20 (2024)
large: 4
medium: 1
small: 4
very small: 11
ports with oil terminals: 5
key ports: Muuga - Port of Tallin, Paldiski Lounasadam, Paljassaare, Sillamae, Vanasadam - Port of Tallinn

MILITARY AND SECURITY

Military and security forces: Estonian Defense Forces: Land Forces, Navy, Air Force, Estonian Defense League

Ministry of Interior: Police and Border Guard Board, Internal Security Service (2024)

Military expenditures: 3.4% of GDP (2024 est.)
2.9% of GDP (2023)
2.2% of GDP (2022)
2% of GDP (2021)
2.3% of GDP (2020)
comparison ranking: 26

Military and security service personnel strengths: approximately 7,500 active-duty personnel; approximately 15,000 Defense League (2024)
note: the Estonian Defense Forces rely largely on reservists who have completed compulsory conscription in the previous 10 years to fill out its active duty and Territorial Defense units during a crisis; there are more than 40,000 trained reservists and approximately 230,000 Estonians are enrolled in the mobilization registry

Military equipment inventories and acquisitions: the Estonian military has a mix of weapons and equipment from western European suppliers, as well as Israel, South Korea, Turkey, and the US (2024)

Military service age and obligation: 18-27 for compulsory military or governmental service for men; conscript service requirement 8-11 months depending on education; non-commissioned officers, reserve officers, and specialists serve 11 months; women can volunteer, and as of 2018 could serve in any military branch (2024)
note 1: conscripts comprise approximately 3,000-3,300 of the Estonian military's 7,000 active-duty personnel and serve in all branches, except for the Air Force; after conscript service, reservists are called up for training every 5 years; Estonia has had conscription since 1991
note 2: in 2021, women comprised about 10% of the full-time professional military force; the Defense League includes a Women's Voluntary Defense Organization of more than 3,000 members

Military - note: the Estonian military is a compact force that relies heavily on conscripts and reservists and the support of its NATO allies; Estonia's defense policy aims to guarantee the country's independence and sovereignty, protect its territorial integrity, including waters and airspace, and preserve constitutional order; Estonia's main defense goals are developing and maintaining a credible deterrent to outside aggression and ensuring the Estonian Defense Forces (EDF) can fulfill their commitments to NATO and interoperate with the armed forces of NATO and EU member states; the EDF's primary external focus is Russia; since Russia's full-scale invasion of Ukraine in 2022, Estonia has boosted defense spending, sent arms to Ukraine, and sought to boost the EDF's capabilities in such areas as air defense, artillery, personnel readiness, and surveillance
Estonia has been a member of NATO since 2004 and is fully integrated within the NATO structure; since 2017, Estonia has hosted a UK-led multinational NATO ground force battlegroup as part of the Alliance's Enhanced Forward Presence initiative; as the EDF Air Force does not have any combat aircraft, NATO has provided airspace protection for Estonia since 2004 through its Baltic Air Policing mission; NATO member countries that possess air combat capabilities voluntarily contribute to the mission on four-month rotations; NATO fighter aircraft have been hosted at Estonia's Ämari Air Base since 2014; Estonia also hosts a NATO cyber security center; it cooperates closely with the EU on defense issues through the EU Common Security and Defense Policy and is a member of the UK-led Joint Expeditionary Force, a pool of high-readiness military forces from 10 Baltic and Scandinavian countries designed to respond to a wide range of contingencies in the North Atlantic, Baltic Sea, and High North regions; Estonia also has close defense ties with its Baltic neighbors and has bilateral military agreements with a number of European countries, as well as Canada and the US
(2024)

TRANSNATIONAL ISSUES

Refugees and internally displaced persons: *refugees (country of origin):* 38,020 (Ukraine) (as of 2 March 2024)
stateless persons: 70,604 (2022); note - following independence in 1991, automatic citizenship was restricted to those who were Estonian citizens prior to the 1940 Soviet occupation and their descendants; thousands of ethnic Russians remained stateless when forced to choose between passing Estonian language and citizenship tests or applying for Russian citizenship; one reason for demurring on Estonian citizenship was to retain the right of visa-free travel to Russia; stateless residents can vote in local elections but not general elections; stateless parents who have been lawful residents of Estonia for at least five years can apply for citizenship for their children before they turn 15 years old

Illicit drugs: producer of synthetic drugs; important transshipment zone for cannabis, cocaine, opiates, and synthetic drugs since joining the European Union and the Schengen Accord; potential money laundering related to organized crime and drug trafficking is a concern, as is possible use of the gambling sector to launder funds; major use of opiates and ecstasy

ESWATINI

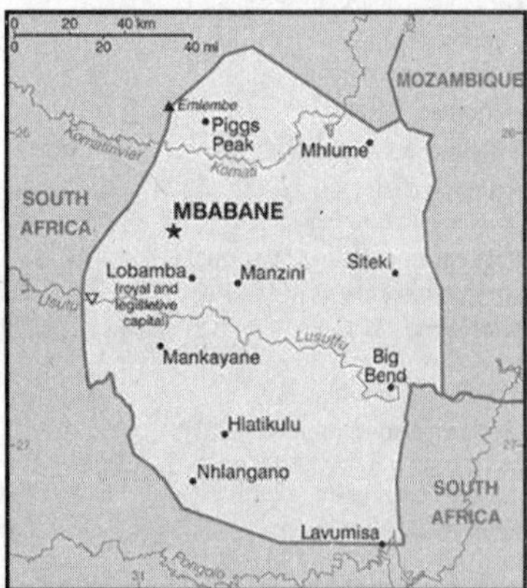

INTRODUCTION

Background: A Swazi kingdom was founded in the mid-18th century and ruled by a series of kings, including MSWATI II, a 19th century ruler whose name was adopted for the country and its predominant ethnic group. European countries defined the kingdom's modern borders during the late-19th century, and Swaziland (as it became known) was administered as a UK high commission territory from 1903 until its independence in 1968. A new constitution that came into effect in 2005 included provisions for a more independent parliament and judiciary, but the legal status of political parties remains unclear, and the kingdom is still considered an absolute monarchy. King MSWATI III renamed the country from Swaziland to Eswatini in 2018 to reflect the name most commonly used by its citizens.

In 2021, MSWATI III used security forces to suppress prodemocracy protests. A national dialogue and reconciliation process agreed to in the wake of violence has not materialized. In November 2023, King MSWATI III appointed a new prime minister following peaceful national elections. Despite its classification as a lower-middle income country, Eswatini suffers from severe poverty, corruption, and high unemployment. Eswatini has the world's highest HIV/AIDS prevalence rate, although recent years have shown marked declines in new infections. Eswatini is the only country in Africa that recognizes Taiwan.

GEOGRAPHY

Location: Southern Africa, between Mozambique and South Africa

Geographic coordinates: 26 30 S, 31 30 E

Map references: Africa

Area: *total:* 17,364 sq km
land: 17,204 sq km
water: 160 sq km
comparison ranking: total 158

Area - comparative: slightly smaller than New Jersey

Land boundaries: *total:* 546 km
border countries (2): Mozambique 108 km; South Africa 438 km

Coastline: 0 km (landlocked)

Maritime claims: none (landlocked)

Climate: varies from tropical to near temperate

Terrain: mostly mountains and hills; some moderately sloping plains

Elevation: *highest point:* Emlembe 1,862 m
lowest point: Great Usutu River 21 m
mean elevation: 305 m

Natural resources: asbestos, coal, clay, cassiterite, hydropower, forests, small gold and diamond deposits, quarry stone, and talc

Land use: *agricultural land:* 68.3% (2018 est.)
arable land: 9.8% (2018 est.)
permanent crops: 0.8% (2018 est.)
permanent pasture: 57.7% (2018 est.)
forest: 31.7% (2018 est.)
other: 0% (2018 est.)

Irrigated land: 500 sq km (2012)

Population distribution: because of its mountainous terrain, the population distribution is uneven throughout the country, concentrating primarily in valleys and plains as shown in this population distribution map

Natural hazards: drought

Geography - note: landlocked; almost completely surrounded by South Africa

PEOPLE AND SOCIETY

Population: *total:* 1,138,089
male: 538,600
female: 599,489 (2024 est.)
comparison rankings: female 160; male 161; total 161

Nationality: *noun:* liSwati (singular), emaSwati (plural); note - former term, Swazi(s), still used among English speakers
adjective: Swati; note - former term, Swazi, still used among English speakers

Ethnic groups: predominantly Swazi; smaller populations of other African ethnic groups, including the Zulu, as well as people of European ancestry

Languages: English (official, used for government business), siSwati (official)

Religions: Christian 90% (Zionist - a blend of Christianity and traditional African religions - 40%, Roman Catholic 20%, other Christian 30% - includes Anglican, Methodist, Church of Jesus Christ, Jehovah's Witness), Muslim 2%, other 8% (includes Baha'i, Buddhist, Hindu, indigenous, Jewish) (2015 est.)

Demographic profile: Eswatini, a small, predominantly rural, landlocked country surrounded by South Africa and Mozambique, suffers from severe poverty and the world's highest HIV/AIDS prevalence rate. A weak and deteriorating economy, high unemployment, rapid population growth, and an uneven distribution of resources all combine to worsen already persistent poverty and food insecurity, especially in rural areas. Erratic weather (frequent droughts and intermittent heavy rains and flooding), overuse of small plots, the overgrazing of cattle, and outdated agricultural practices reduce crop yields and further degrade the environment, exacerbating Eswatini's poverty and subsistence problems. Eswatini's extremely high HIV/AIDS prevalence rate – nearly 28% of adults have the disease – compounds these issues. Agricultural production has declined due to HIV/AIDS, as the illness causes households to lose manpower and to sell livestock and other assets to pay for medicine and funerals.

Swazis, mainly men from the country's rural south, have been migrating to South Africa to work in coal, and later gold, mines since the late 19th century. Although the number of miners abroad has never been high in absolute terms because of Eswatini's small population, the outflow has had important social and economic repercussions. The peak of mining employment in South Africa occurred during the 1980s. Cross-border movement has accelerated since the 1990s, as increasing unemployment has pushed more Swazis to look for work in South Africa (creating a "brain drain" in the health and educational sectors); southern Swazi men have continued to pursue mining, although the industry has downsized. Women now make up an increasing share of migrants and dominate cross-border trading in handicrafts, using the proceeds to purchase goods back in Eswatini. Much of today's migration, however, is not work-related but focuses on visits to family and friends, tourism, and shopping.

Age structure: *0-14 years:* 31.6% (male 180,328/female 179,840)
15-64 years: 64.3% (male 341,298/female 390,884)
65 years and over: 4% (2024 est.) (male 16,974/female 28,765)

Dependency ratios: *total dependency ratio:* 64
youth dependency ratio: 57.4
elderly dependency ratio: 6.5
potential support ratio: 15.3 (2021 est.)

Median age: *total:* 24.6 years (2024 est.)
male: 23.4 years
female: 25.8 years
comparison ranking: total 175

Population growth rate: 0.7% (2024 est.)
comparison ranking: 127

Birth rate: 22.3 births/1,000 population (2024 est.)
comparison ranking: 51

Death rate: 9.4 deaths/1,000 population (2024 est.)
comparison ranking: 49

Net migration rate: -6 migrant(s)/1,000 population (2024 est.)
comparison ranking: 209

Population distribution: because of its mountainous terrain, the population distribution is uneven throughout the country, concentrating primarily in valleys and plains as shown in this population distribution map

Urbanization: *urban population:* 24.8% of total population (2023)
rate of urbanization: 2.42% annual rate of change (2020-25 est.)

Major urban areas - population: 68,000 MBABANE (capital) (2018)

Sex ratio: *at birth:* 1.03 male(s)/female
0-14 years: 1 male(s)/female
15-64 years: 0.87 male(s)/female
65 years and over: 0.59 male(s)/female
total population: 0.9 male(s)/female (2024 est.)

Maternal mortality ratio: 437 deaths/100,000 live births (2017 est.)
comparison ranking: 22

Infant mortality rate: *total:* 36.7 deaths/1,000 live births (2024 est.)
male: 40.7 deaths/1,000 live births
female: 32.5 deaths/1,000 live births
comparison ranking: total 33

Life expectancy at birth: *total population:* 60.7 years (2024 est.)
male: 58.7 years
female: 62.8 years
comparison ranking: total population 219

Total fertility rate: 2.37 children born/woman (2024 est.)
comparison ranking: 73

Gross reproduction rate: 1.17 (2024 est.)

Contraceptive prevalence rate: 66.1% (2014)

Drinking water source: *improved: urban:* 97.5% of population
rural: 74.8% of population
total: 80.3% of population
unimproved: urban: 2.5% of population
rural: 25.2% of population
total: 19.7% of population (2020 est.)

Current health expenditure: 6.5% of GDP (2020)

Physician density: 0.14 physicians/1,000 population (2020)

Hospital bed density: 2.1 beds/1,000 population (2011)

Sanitation facility access: *improved: urban:* 92.3% of population
rural: 83.9% of population
total: 85.9% of population
unimproved: urban: 7.7% of population
rural: 16.1% of population
total: 14.1% of population (2020 est.)

Obesity - adult prevalence rate: 16.5% (2016)
comparison ranking: 124

Alcohol consumption per capita: *total:* 7.68 liters of pure alcohol (2019 est.)
beer: 2.45 liters of pure alcohol (2019 est.)
wine: 0.06 liters of pure alcohol (2019 est.)
spirits: 0 liters of pure alcohol (2019 est.)
other alcohols: 5.17 liters of pure alcohol (2019 est.)
comparison ranking: total 50

Tobacco use: *total:* 9.2% (2020 est.)
male: 16.5% (2020 est.)
female: 1.8% (2020 est.)
comparison ranking: total 138

Children under the age of 5 years underweight: 5.8% (2014)
comparison ranking: 70

Currently married women (ages 15-49): 37.1% (2023 est.)

Education expenditures: 5% of GDP (2021 est.)
comparison ranking: 75

Literacy: *definition:* age 15 and over can read and write
total population: 88.4%
male: 88.3%
female: 88.5% (2018)

School life expectancy (primary to tertiary education): *total:* 13 years
male: 13 years
female: 12 years (2013)

ENVIRONMENT

Environment - current issues: limited supplies of potable water; wildlife populations being depleted because of excessive hunting; population growth, deforestation, and overgrazing lead to soil erosion and soil degradation

Environment - international agreements: *party to:* Biodiversity, Climate Change, Climate Change-Kyoto Protocol, Climate Change-Paris Agreement, Comprehensive Nuclear Test Ban, Desertification, Endangered Species, Hazardous Wastes, Law of the Sea, Nuclear Test Ban, Ozone Layer Protection, Wetlands
signed, but not ratified: none of the selected agreements

Climate: varies from tropical to near temperate

Urbanization: *urban population:* 24.8% of total population (2023)
rate of urbanization: 2.42% annual rate of change (2020-25 est.)

Food insecurity: *severe localized food insecurity: due to higher staple food prices* - the price of maize meal, the key food staple, increased in the first five months of 2022 and, as of May 2022, were 3 percent higher on a yearly basis; wheat flour prices were also at record highs in May 2022; this mainly reflects the elevated global prices and the country's high dependence on imported wheat to satisfy national consumption needs (2022)

Revenue from forest resources: 2.25% of GDP (2018 est.)
comparison ranking: 30

Revenue from coal: 0.1% of GDP (2018 est.)
comparison ranking: 26

Air pollutants: *particulate matter emissions:* 15.07 micrograms per cubic meter (2019 est.)
carbon dioxide emissions: 1.16 megatons (2016 est.)
methane emissions: 1.9 megatons (2020 est.)

Waste and recycling: *municipal solid waste generated annually:* 218,199 tons (2016 est.)

Total water withdrawal: *municipal:* 40 million cubic meters (2020 est.)
industrial: 20 million cubic meters (2020 est.)
agricultural: 1.01 billion cubic meters (2020 est.)

Total renewable water resources: 4.51 billion cubic meters (2020 est.)

GOVERNMENT

Country name: *conventional long form:* Kingdom of Eswatini
conventional short form: Eswatini
local long form: Umbuso weSwatini
local short form: eSwatini
former: Swaziland
etymology: the country name derives from 19th century King MSWATI II, under whose rule Swati territory was expanded and unified
note: pronounced ay-swatini or eh-swatini

Government type: absolute monarchy

Capital: *name:* Mbabane (administrative capital); Lobamba (royal and legislative capital)
geographic coordinates: 26 19 S, 31 08 E
time difference: UTC+2 (7 hours ahead of Washington, DC, during Standard Time)
etymology: named after a Swati chief, Mbabane KUNENE, who lived in the area at the onset of British settlement

Administrative divisions: 4 regions; Hhohho, Lubombo, Manzini, Shiselweni

Independence: 6 September 1968 (from the UK)

National holiday: Independence Day (Somhlolo Day), 6 September (1968)

Legal system: mixed legal system of civil, common, and customary law

Constitution: *history:* previous 1968, 1978; latest signed by the king 26 July 2005, effective 8 February 2006
amendments: proposed at a joint sitting of both houses of Parliament; passage requires majority vote by both houses and/or majority vote in a referendum, and assent of the king; passage of amendments affecting "specially entrenched" constitutional provisions requires at least three-fourths majority vote by both houses, passage by simple majority vote in a referendum, and assent of the king; passage of "entrenched" provisions requires at least two-thirds majority vote of both houses, passage in a referendum, and assent of the king

International law organization participation: accepts compulsory ICJ jurisdiction with reservations; non-party state to the ICCt

Citizenship: *citizenship by birth:* no
citizenship by descent only: both parents must be citizens of Eswatini
dual citizenship recognized: no
residency requirement for naturalization: 5 years

Suffrage: 18 years of age

Executive branch: *chief of state:* King MSWATI III (since 25 April 1986)
head of government: Prime Minister Russell DLAMINI (since 6 November 2023)
cabinet: Cabinet recommended by the prime minister, confirmed by the monarch; at least one-half of the cabinet membership must be appointed from among elected members of the House of Assembly
elections/appointments: the monarchy is hereditary; prime minister appointed by the monarch from among members of the House of Assembly

Legislative branch: *description:* bicameral Parliament or Libandla consists of:
Senate (30 seats; 20 members appointed by the monarch and 10 indirectly elected by simple majority vote by the House of Assembly; members serve 5-year terms)
House of Assembly (70 seats statutory, current 69; 59 members directly elected in single-seat constituencies or tinkhundla by absolute majority vote in 2 rounds if needed, 10 members appointed by the monarch, 4 women, one each representing each region, elected by the members if representation of elected women is less than 30%, and 1 ex-officio member - the attorney general; members serve 5-year terms)
elections: Senate - last election held on 12 October 2023 , senate fully constituted on November 5 when monarch appointed remaining 20 senators; (next to be held in 2028)
House of Assembly - last held on 29 September 2023 (next to be held in 2028)
election results: Senate - percent of seats by party - NA; seats by party - NA; composition - men 16, women 14, percentage women 46.7%
House of Assembly - percent of vote by party - NA; seats by party - independent 59; composition - men 58, women 16, percent of women 17.14%; total Parliament percentage women 28.8%

Judicial branch: *highest court(s):* Supreme Court (consists of the chief justice and at least 4 justices) and the High Court (consists of the chief justice - ex officio - and 4 justices); note - the Supreme Court has jurisdiction in all constitutional matters
judge selection and term of office: justices of the Supreme Court and High Court appointed by the monarch on the advice of the Judicial Service Commission (JSC), a judicial advisory body consisting of the Supreme Court Chief Justice, 4 members appointed by the monarch, and the chairman of the Civil Service Commission; justices of both courts eligible for retirement at age 65 with mandatory retirement at age 75
subordinate courts: magistrates' courts; National Swazi Courts for administering customary/traditional laws (jurisdiction restricted to customary law for Swazi citizens)

Political parties: *political parties exist but conditions for their operations, particularly in elections, are undefined, legally unclear, or culturally restricted; the following are considered political associations:*
African United Democratic Party or AUDP
Ngwane National Liberatory Congress or NNLC
People's United Democratic Movement or PUDEMO
Swazi Democratic Party or SWADEPA

International organization participation: ACP, AfDB, AU, C, COMESA, FAO, G-77, IAEA, IBRD, ICAO, ICRM, IDA, IFAD, IFC, IFRCS, ILO, IMF, IMO, Interpol, IOC, IOM, ISO (correspondent), ITSO, ITU, ITUC (NGOs), MIGA, NAM, OPCW, PCA, SACU, SADC, UN, UNCTAD, UNESCO, UNIDO, UNWTO, UPU, WCO, WHO, WIPO, WMO, WTO

Diplomatic representation in the US: *chief of mission:* Ambassador Kennedy Fitzgerald GROENING (7 June 2022)
chancery: 1712 New Hampshire Avenue NW, Washington, DC 20009
telephone: [1] (202) 234-5002
FAX: [1] (202) 234-8254
email address and website:
swaziland@compuserve.com

Diplomatic representation from the US: *chief of mission:* Ambassador (vacant) Chargé d'Affaires Caitlin PIPER (since 27 October 2023)
embassy: Corner of MR 103 and Cultural Center Drive, Ezulwini, P.O. Box D202, The Gables, H106
mailing address: 2350 Mbabane Place, Washington DC 20521-2350
telephone: (268) 2417-9000
FAX: [268] 2416-3344
email address and website:
ConsularMbabane@state.gov
Homepage - U.S. Embassy in Eswatini (usembassy.gov)

Flag description: three horizontal bands of blue (top), red (triple width), and blue; the red band is edged in yellow; centered in the red band is a large black and white shield covering two spears and a staff decorated with feather tassels, all placed horizontally; blue stands for peace and stability, red represents past struggles, and yellow the mineral resources of the country; the shield, spears, and staff symbolize protection from the country's enemies, while the black and white of the shield are meant to portray black and white people living in peaceful coexistence

National symbol(s): lion, elephant; national colors: blue, yellow, red

National anthem: *name:* "Nkulunkulu Mnikati wetibusiso temaSwati" (Oh God, Bestower of the Blessings of the Swazi)
lyrics/music: Andrease Enoke Fanyana SIMELANE/David Kenneth RYCROFT
note: adopted 1968; uses elements of both ethnic Swazi and Western music styles

ECONOMY

Economic overview: landlocked southern African economy; South African trade dependent and currency pegging; CMA and SACU member state; COVID-19 economic slowdown; growing utilities inflation; persistent poverty and unemployment; HIV/AIDS labor force disruptions

Real GDP (purchasing power parity): $12.814 billion (2023 est.)

$12.222 billion (2022 est.)
$12.164 billion (2021 est.)
note: data in 2021 dollars
comparison ranking: 161

Real GDP growth rate: 4.84% (2023 est.)
0.48% (2022 est.)
10.68% (2021 est.)
note: annual GDP % growth based on constant local currency
comparison ranking: 60

Real GDP per capita: $10,600 (2023 est.)
$10,200 (2022 est.)
$10,200 (2021 est.)
note: data in 2021 dollars
comparison ranking: 145

GDP (official exchange rate): $4.598 billion (2023 est.)
note: data in current dollars at official exchange rate

Inflation rate (consumer prices): 2.6% (2019 est.)
4.82% (2018 est.)
6.22% (2017 est.)
note: annual % change based on consumer prices
comparison ranking: 54

Credit ratings: Moody's rating: B3 (2020)
note: The year refers to the year in which the current credit rating was first obtained.

GDP - composition, by sector of origin: *agriculture:* 8.1% (2023 est.)
industry: 33.5% (2023 est.)
services: 53.5% (2023 est.)
note: figures may not total 100% due to non-allocated consumption not captured in sector-reported data comparison rankings: services 126; industry 47; agriculture 90

GDP - composition, by end use: *household consumption:* 61.7% (2022 est.)
government consumption: 17.6% (2022 est.)
investment in fixed capital: 11.8% (2022 est.)
exports of goods and services: 43.8% (2022 est.)
imports of goods and services: -47.6% (2022 est.)
note: figures may not total 100% due to rounding or gaps in data collection

Agricultural products: sugarcane, maize, root vegetables, grapefruits, oranges, milk, pineapples, bananas, beef, potatoes (2022)
note: top ten agricultural products based on tonnage

Industries: soft drink concentrates, coal, forestry, sugar processing, textiles, and apparel

Industrial production growth rate: 1.53% (2023 est.)
note: annual % change in industrial value added based on constant local currency comparison ranking: 129

Labor force: 405,000 (2023 est.)
note: number of people ages 15 or older who are employed or seeking work comparison ranking: 163

Unemployment rate: 37.64% (2023 est.)
37.85% (2022 est.)
35.71% (2021 est.)
note: % of labor force seeking employment
comparison ranking: 209

Youth unemployment rate (ages 15-24): *total:* 65% (2023 est.)
male: 62.4% (2023 est.)
female: 67.5% (2023 est.)
note: % of labor force ages 15-24 seeking employment
comparison ranking: total 2

Population below poverty line: 58.9% (2016 est.)
note: % of population with income below national poverty line

Gini Index coefficient - distribution of family income: 54.6 (2016 est.)
note: index (0-100) of income distribution; higher values represent greater inequality comparison ranking: 4

Household income or consumption by percentage share: *lowest 10%:* 1.4% (2016 est.)
highest 10%: 42.7% (2016 est.)
note: % share of income accruing to lowest and highest 10% of population

Remittances: 2.62% of GDP (2023 est.)
2.64% of GDP (2022 est.)
2.72% of GDP (2021 est.)
note: personal transfers and compensation between resident and non-resident individuals/households/entities

Budget: *revenues:* $1.217 billion (2021 est.)
expenditures: $1.183 billion (2021 est.)
note: central government revenues and expenses (excluding grants/extrabudgetary units/social security funds) converted to US dollars at average official exchange rate for year indicated

Public debt: 35.4% of GDP (2021 est.)
comparison ranking: 150

Taxes and other revenues: 24.13% (of GDP) (2021 est.)
comparison ranking: 53

Current account balance: -$140.972 million (2022 est.)
$125.318 million (2021 est.)
$270.942 million (2020 est.)
note: balance of payments - net trade and primary/secondary income in current dollars
comparison ranking: 101

Exports: $2.095 billion (2022 est.)
$2.132 billion (2021 est.)
$1.808 billion (2020 est.)
note: balance of payments - exports of goods and services in current dollars
comparison ranking: 165

Exports - partners: South Africa 66%, Kenya 5%, Nigeria 3%, Democratic Republic of the Congo 3%, Mozambique 3% (2022)
note: top five export partners based on percentage share of exports

Exports - commodities: scented mixtures, raw sugar, garments, industrial acids/oils/alcohols, wood (2022)
note: top five export commodities based on value in dollars

Imports: $2.288 billion (2022 est.)
$2.173 billion (2021 est.)
$1.686 billion (2020 est.)
note: balance of payments - imports of goods and services in current dollars
comparison ranking: 171

Imports - partners: South Africa 76%, China 4%, US 3%, Mozambique 3%, Mauritania 3% (2022)
note: top five import partners based on percentage share of imports

Imports - commodities: refined petroleum, gold, plastic products, electricity, garments (2022)
note: top five import commodities based on value in dollars

Reserves of foreign exchange and gold: $479.261 million (2023 est.)
$452.352 million (2022 est.)
$572.282 million (2021 est.)
note: holdings of gold (year-end prices)/foreign exchange/special drawing rights in current dollars
comparison ranking: 165

Debt - external: $758.868 million (2022 est.)
note: present value of external debt in current US dollars
comparison ranking: 85

Exchange rates: emalangeni per US dollar -

Exchange rates: 18.454 (2023 est.)
16.362 (2022 est.)
14.783 (2021 est.)
16.47 (2020 est.)
14.452 (2019 est.)

ENERGY

Electricity access: *electrification - total population:* 82.3% (2022 est.)
electrification - urban areas: 86.1%
electrification - rural areas: 81.6%

Electricity: *installed generating capacity:* 287,000 kW (2022 est.)
consumption: 1.344 billion kWh (2022 est.)
imports: 914.13 million kWh (2022 est.)
transmission/distribution losses: 155.872 million kWh (2022 est.)
comparison rankings: transmission/distribution losses 60; imports 80; consumption 156; installed generating capacity 166

Electricity generation sources: *fossil fuels:* 7.1% of total installed capacity (2022 est.)
solar: 0.2% of total installed capacity (2022 est.)
hydroelectricity: 51.2% of total installed capacity (2022 est.)
biomass and waste: 41.5% of total installed capacity (2022 est.)

Coal: *production:* 219,000 metric tons (2022 est.)
consumption: 124,000 metric tons (2022 est.)
exports: 5,000 metric tons (2022 est.)
imports: 147,000 metric tons (2022 est.)
proven reserves: 4.644 billion metric tons (2022 est.)

Petroleum: *refined petroleum consumption:* 6,000 bbl/day (2022 est.)

Carbon dioxide emissions: 1.151 million metric tonnes of CO2 (2022 est.)
from coal and metallurgical coke: 264,000 metric tonnes of CO2 (2022 est.)
from petroleum and other liquids: 887,000 metric tonnes of CO2 (2022 est.)
comparison ranking: total emissions 171

Energy consumption per capita: 17.642 million Btu/person (2022 est.)
comparison ranking: 133

COMMUNICATIONS

Telephones - fixed lines: *total subscriptions:* 38,000 (2022 est.)
subscriptions per 100 inhabitants: 3 (2022 est.)
comparison ranking: total subscriptions 161

Telephones - mobile cellular: *total subscriptions:* 1.468 million (2022 est.)
subscriptions per 100 inhabitants: 122 (2022 est.)
comparison ranking: total subscriptions 159

Telecommunication systems: *general assessment:* Eswatini was one of the last countries in the world to open up its telecom market to competition; until 2011 the state-owned Eswatini Posts and Telecommunications also acted as the industry regulator and had a stake in the country's sole mobile

network; a new independent regulatory authority was established in late 2013 and has since embarked on significant changes to the sector; mobile market subscriptions have been affected by the common use among subscribers when they use SIM cards from different networks in order to access cheaper on-net calls; subscriber growth has slowed in recent years, but was expected to have reached 8% in 2021, as people adapted to the changing needs for connectivity caused by the pandemic; the internet sector has been open to competition with a small number of licensed ISPs; DSL services were introduced in 2008, development of the sector has been hampered by the limited fixed-line infrastructure and by a lack of competition in the access and backbone networks; Eswatini is landlocked and so depends on neighboring countries for international bandwidth; this has meant that access pricing is relatively high, and market subscriptions remains relatively low; prices have fallen recently in line with greater bandwidth availability resulting from several new submarine cable systems which have reached the region in recent years; in September 2020 a terrestrial cable linked Mozambique with Eswatini and South Africa (2022)
domestic: fixed-line stands at nearly 4 per 100 and mobile-cellular teledensity roughly 120 telephones per 100 persons (2021)
international: country code - 268; satellite earth station - 1 Intelsat (Atlantic Ocean)

Broadcast media: 1 state-owned TV station; satellite dishes are able to access South African providers; state-owned radio network with 3 channels; 1 private radio station (2019)

Internet country code: .sz

Internet users: *total:* 708,000 (2021 est.)
percent of population: 59% (2021 est.)
comparison ranking: total 160

Broadband - fixed subscriptions: *total:* 12,000 (2020 est.)
subscriptions per 100 inhabitants: 1 (2020 est.)
comparison ranking: total 178

TRANSPORTATION

Civil aircraft registration country code prefix: 3DC

Airports: 16 (2024)
comparison ranking: 146

Railways: *total:* 301 km (2014)
narrow gauge: 301 km (2014) 1.067-m gauge
comparison ranking: total 123

Roadways: *total:* 4,594 km
paved: 1,500 km
unpaved: 3,000 km (2022)
comparison ranking: total 152

MILITARY AND SECURITY

Military and security forces: Umbutfo Eswatini Defense Force (UEDF): Army (includes a small air wing); the Royal Eswatini Police Service (REPS) (2024)

Military expenditures: 1.6% of GDP (2023 est.)
1.6% of GDP (2022 est.)
1.7% of GDP (2021 est.)
1.8% of GDP (2020 est.)
1.9% of GDP (2019 est.)
comparison ranking: 81

Military and security service personnel strengths: approximately 3,000 active-duty personnel (2023)

Military equipment inventories and acquisitions: the UEDF has a light and small inventory of mostly older equipment originating from Europe, South Africa, and the US (2023)

Military service age and obligation: 18-35 years of age for voluntary military service for men and women; no conscription (2023)

Military - note: the UEDF's primary mission is external security but it also has domestic security responsibilities, including protecting members of the royal family; the king is the UEDF commander in chief and holds the position of minister of defense, although the UEDF reports to the Army commander and principal undersecretary of defense for day-to-day operations; the Royal Eswatini Police Service (REPS) is responsible for maintaining internal security as well as migration and border crossing enforcement; it is under the prime minister, although the king is the force's titular commissioner in chief; the UEDF was originally created in 1973 as the Royal Swaziland Defense Force (2023)

ETHIOPIA

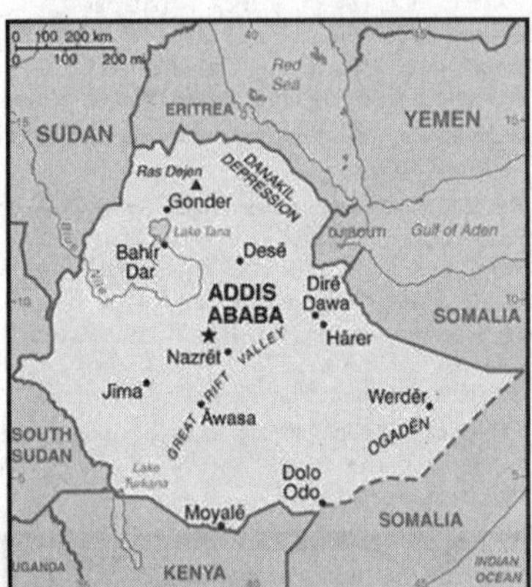

INTRODUCTION

Background: The area that is modern-day Ethiopia is rich in cultural and religious diversity with more than 80 ethnic groups. The oldest hominid yet found comes from Ethiopia, and Ethiopia was the second country to officially adopt Christianity in the 4th century A.D. A series of monarchies ruled the area that is now Ethiopia from 980 B.C. to 1855, when the Amhara kingdoms of northern Ethiopia united in an empire under Tewodros II. Many Ethiopians still speak reverently about the Battle of Adwa in 1896, when they defeated Italian forces and won their freedom from colonial rule.

Emperor Haile SELASSIE became an internationally renowned figure in 1935, when he unsuccessfully appealed to the League of Nations to prevent Italy from occupying Ethiopia from 1936 to 1941. SELASSIE survived an attempted coup in 1960, annexed modern-day Eritrea in 1962, and played a leading role in establishing the Organization of African Unity in 1963. However, in 1974, a military junta called the Derg deposed him and established a socialist state. Torn by bloody coups, uprisings, drought, and massive displacement, the Derg regime was toppled in 1991 by a coalition of opposing forces, the Ethiopian People's Revolutionary Democratic Front (EPRDF). The EPRDF became an ethno-federalist political coalition that ruled Ethiopia from 1991 until its dissolution in 2019. Ethiopia adopted its constitution in 1994 and held its first multiparty elections in 1995.

A two-and-a-half-year border war with Eritrea in the late 1990s ended with a peace treaty in 2000. Ethiopia subsequently rejected the 2007 Eritrea-Ethiopia Boundary Commission demarcation. This resulted in more than a decade of a tense "no peace, no war" stalemate between the two countries. In 2012, longtime Prime Minister MELES Zenawi died in office and was replaced by his Deputy Prime Minister HAILEMARIAM Desalegn, marking the first peaceful transition of power in decades. Following a wave of popular dissent and anti-government protest that began in 2015, HAILEMARIAM resigned in 2018, and ABIY Ahmed Ali took office the same year as Ethiopia's first ethnic Oromo prime minister. In 2018, ABIY promoted a rapprochement between Ethiopia and Eritrea that was marked with a peace agreement and a reopening of their shared border. In 2019, Ethiopia's nearly 30-year ethnic-based ruling coalition, the EPRDF, merged into a single unity party called the Prosperity Party; however, the lead coalition party, the Tigray People's Liberation Front (TPLF), declined to join. In 2020, a military conflict erupted between forces aligned with the TPLF and the Ethiopian military. The conflict – which was marked by atrocities committed by all parties – ended in 2022 with a cessation of hostilities agreement between the TPLF and the Ethiopian Government. However, Ethiopia continues to experience ethnic-based violence as other groups – including the Oromo Liberation Army (OLA) and Amhara militia Fano – seek concessions from the Ethiopian Government.

GEOGRAPHY

Location: Eastern Africa, west of Somalia

Geographic coordinates: 8 00 N, 38 00 E

Map references: Africa

Area: *total:* 1,104,300 sq km
land: 1,096,570 sq km
water: 7,730 sq km
note: area numbers are approximate since a large portion of the Ethiopia-Somalia border is undefined
comparison ranking: total 28

Area - comparative: slightly less than twice the size of Texas

Land boundaries: *total:* 5,925 km
border countries (6): Djibouti 342 km; Eritrea 1,033 km; Kenya 867 km; Somalia 1,640 km; South Sudan 1,299 km; Sudan 744 km

Coastline: 0 km (landlocked)

Maritime claims: none (landlocked)

Climate: tropical monsoon with wide topographic-induced variation

Terrain: high plateau with central mountain range divided by Great Rift Valley

Elevation: *highest point:* Ras Dejen 4,550 m
lowest point: Danakil Depression -125 m
mean elevation: 1,330 m

Natural resources: small reserves of gold, platinum, copper, potash, natural gas, hydropower

Land use: *agricultural land:* 36.3% (2018 est.)
arable land: 15.2% (2018 est.)
permanent crops: 1.1% (2018 est.)
permanent pasture: 20% (2018 est.)
forest: 12.2% (2018 est.)
other: 51.5% (2018 est.)

Irrigated land: 1,813 sq km (2020)

Major lakes (area sq km): *fresh water lake(s):* Lake Tana - 3,600 sq km; Abaya Hayk - 1,160 sq km; Ch'amo Hayk - 550 sq km
salt water lake(s): Lake Turkana (shared with Kenya) - 6,400 sq km; Abhe Bid Hayk/Abhe Bad (shared with Djibouti) - 780 sq km;

Major rivers (by length in km): Blue Nile river source (shared with Sudan [m]) - 1,600 km
note – [s] after country name indicates river source; [m] after country name indicates river mouth

Major watersheds (area sq km): Atlantic Ocean drainage: *(Mediterranean Sea)* Nile (3,254,853 sq km)

Major aquifers: Ogaden-Juba Basin, Sudd Basin (Umm Ruwaba Aquifer)

Population distribution: highest density is found in the highlands of the north and middle areas of the country, particularly around the centrally located capital city of Addis Ababa; the far east and southeast are sparsely populated as shown in this population distribution map

Natural hazards: geologically active Great Rift Valley susceptible to earthquakes, volcanic eruptions; frequent droughts
volcanism: volcanic activity in the Great Rift Valley; Erta Ale (613 m), which has caused frequent lava flows in recent years, is the country's most active volcano; Dabbahu became active in 2005, forcing evacuations; other historically active volcanoes include Alayta, Dalaffilla, Dallol, Dama Ali, Fentale, Kone, Manda Hararo, and Manda-Inakir

Geography - note: *note 1:* landlocked – entire coastline along the Red Sea was lost with the de jure independence of Eritrea on 24 May 1993; Ethiopia is, therefore, the most populous landlocked country in the world; the Blue Nile, the chief headstream of the Nile by water volume, rises in T'ana Hayk (Lake Tana) in northwest Ethiopia
note 2: three major crops may have originated in Ethiopia: coffee (almost certainly), grain sorghum, and castor bean

PEOPLE AND SOCIETY

Population: *total:* 118,550,298
male: 59,062,093
female: 59,488,205 (2024 est.)
comparison rankings: female 12; male 13; total 12

Nationality: *noun:* Ethiopian(s)
adjective: Ethiopian

Ethnic groups: Oromo 35.8%, Amhara 24.1%, Somali 7.2%, Tigray 5.7%, Sidama 4.1%, Guragie 2.6%, Welaita 2.3%, Afar 2.2%, Silte 1.3%, Kefficho 1.2%, other 13.5% (2022 est.)

Languages: Oromo (official regional working language) 33.8%, Amharic (official national language) 29.3%, Somali (official regional working language) 6.2%, Tigrigna (Tigrinya) (official regional working language) 5.9%, Sidamo 4%, Wolaytta 2.2%, Gurage 2%, Afar (official regional working language) 1.7%, Hadiyya 1.7%, Gamo 1.5%, Gedeo 1.3%, Opuuo 1.2%, Kafa 1.1%, other 8.1%, English (2007 est.)
major-language sample(s):
Kitaaba Addunyaa Waan Qabataamaatiif - Kan Madda Odeeffannoo bu'uraawaatiif baay'ee barbaachisaa ta'e. (Oromo)
የአለም እውነታ መጽሐፍ፣ ለመሠረታዊ መረጃ አጅግ አስፈላጊ የሆነ ምንጭ:: (Amharic)

Religions: Ethiopian Orthodox 43.8%, Muslim 31.3%, Protestant 22.8%, Catholic 0.7%, traditional 0.6%, other 0.8% (2016 est.)

Demographic profile: Ethiopia is a predominantly agricultural country – nearly 80% of the population lives in rural areas – that is in the early stages of demographic transition. Infant, child, and maternal mortality have fallen sharply over the past decade, but the total fertility rate has declined more slowly and the population continues to grow. The rising age of marriage and the increasing proportion of women remaining single have contributed to fertility reduction. While the use of modern contraceptive methods among married women has increased significantly from 6 percent in 2000 to 27 percent in 2012, the overall rate is still quite low.
Ethiopia's rapid population growth is putting increasing pressure on land resources, expanding environmental degradation, and raising vulnerability to food shortages. With about 40 percent of the population below the age of 15 and a fertility rate of 4 children per woman (and even higher in rural areas), Ethiopia will have to make further progress in meeting its family planning needs if it is to achieve the age structure necessary for reaping a demographic dividend in the coming decades.
Poverty, drought, political repression, and forced government resettlement have driven Ethiopia's internal and external migration since the 1960s. Before the 1974 revolution, only small numbers of the Ethiopian elite went abroad to study and then returned home, but under the brutal Derg regime thousands fled the country, primarily as refugees. Between 1982 and 1991 there was a new wave of migration to the West for family reunification. Since the defeat of the Derg in 1991, Ethiopians have migrated to escape violence among some of the country's myriad ethnic groups or to pursue economic opportunities. Internal and international trafficking of women and children for domestic work and prostitution is a growing problem.

Age structure: *0-14 years:* 38.7% (male 23,092,496/female 22,765,882)
15-64 years: 58% (male 34,175,328/female 34,536,238)
65 years and over: 3.4% (2024 est.) (male 1,794,269/female 2,186,085)

Dependency ratios: *total dependency ratio:* 75.7
youth dependency ratio: 70.2
elderly dependency ratio: 5.5
potential support ratio: 18.1 (2021 est.)

Median age: *total:* 20.4 years (2024 est.)
male: 20.2 years
female: 20.7 years
comparison ranking: total 203

Population growth rate: 2.37% (2024 est.)
comparison ranking: 26

Birth rate: 29.6 births/1,000 population (2024 est.)
comparison ranking: 27

Death rate: 5.8 deaths/1,000 population (2024 est.)
comparison ranking: 164

Net migration rate: -0.1 migrant(s)/1,000 population (2024 est.)
comparison ranking: 96

Population distribution: highest density is found in the highlands of the north and middle areas of the country, particularly around the centrally located capital city of Addis Ababa; the far east and southeast are sparsely populated as shown in this population distribution map

Urbanization: *urban population:* 23.2% of total population (2023)
rate of urbanization: 4.4% annual rate of change (2020-25 est.)

Major urban areas - population: 5.461 million ADDIS ABABA (capital) (2023)

Sex ratio: *at birth:* 1.03 male(s)/female
0-14 years: 1.01 male(s)/female
15-64 years: 0.99 male(s)/female
65 years and over: 0.82 male(s)/female
total population: 0.99 male(s)/female (2024 est.)

Mother's mean age at first birth: 19.3 years (2019 est.)
note: data represents median age at first birth among women 20-49

Maternal mortality ratio: 267 deaths/100,000 live births (2020 est.)
comparison ranking: 32

Infant mortality rate: *total:* 32.6 deaths/1,000 live births (2024 est.)
male: 37.4 deaths/1,000 live births
female: 27.6 deaths/1,000 live births
comparison ranking: total 40

Life expectancy at birth: *total population:* 67.7 years (2024 est.)
male: 65.4 years
female: 70 years
comparison ranking: total population 196

Total fertility rate: 3.84 children born/woman (2024 est.)
comparison ranking: 27

Gross reproduction rate: 1.89 (2024 est.)

Contraceptive prevalence rate: 37.7% (2020)

Drinking water source: *improved: urban:* 98.5% of population
rural: 70.2% of population
total: 76.4% of population
unimproved: urban: 1.5% of population
rural: 29.8% of population
total: 23.6% of population (2020 est.)

Current health expenditure: 3.5% of GDP (2020)

Physician density: 0.11 physicians/1,000 population (2020)

Hospital bed density: 0.3 beds/1,000 population (2016)

Sanitation facility access: *improved: urban:* 52.5% of population

rural: 8.1% of population
total: 17.7% of population
unimproved: urban: 47.5% of population
rural: 91.9% of population
total: 82.3% of population (2020 est.)

Obesity - adult prevalence rate: 4.5% (2016)
comparison ranking: 185

Alcohol consumption per capita: *total:* 1.16 liters of pure alcohol (2019 est.)
beer: 0.92 liters of pure alcohol (2019 est.)
wine: 0 liters of pure alcohol (2019 est.)
spirits: 0.2 liters of pure alcohol (2019 est.)
other alcohols: 0.03 liters of pure alcohol (2019 est.)
comparison ranking: total 149

Tobacco use: *total:* 5.1% (2020 est.)
male: 8.8% (2020 est.)
female: 1.3% (2020 est.)
comparison ranking: total 161

Children under the age of 5 years underweight: 21.1% (2019)
comparison ranking: 12

Currently married women (ages 15-49): 67.5% (2023 est.)

Child marriage: *women married by age 15:* 14.1%
women married by age 18: 40.3%
men married by age 18: 5% (2016 est.)

Education expenditures: 4.5% of GDP (2019 est.)
comparison ranking: 101

Literacy: *definition:* age 15 and over can read and write
total population: 51.8%
male: 57.2%
female: 44.4% (2017)

School life expectancy (primary to tertiary education): *total:* 9 years
male: 8 years
female: 8 years (2012)

ENVIRONMENT

Environment - current issues: deforestation; overgrazing; soil erosion; desertification; loss of biodiversity; water shortages in some areas from water-intensive farming and poor management; industrial pollution and pesticides contribute to air, water, and soil pollution

Environment - international agreements: *party to:* Biodiversity, Climate Change, Climate Change-Kyoto Protocol, Climate Change-Paris Agreement, Comprehensive Nuclear Test Ban, Desertification, Endangered Species, Hazardous Wastes, Ozone Layer Protection
signed, but not ratified: Environmental Modification, Law of the Sea, Nuclear Test Ban

Climate: tropical monsoon with wide topographic-induced variation

Urbanization: *urban population:* 23.2% of total population (2023)
rate of urbanization: 4.4% annual rate of change (2020-25 est.)

Food insecurity: *widespread lack of access:* due to conflict in Tigray Region, drought conditions in southeastern areas, high food prices - The difficult and worsening food security situation is the result of multiple shocks affecting food availability and access including: the conflict in northern Tigray Region and in adjacent areas of Amhara and Afar regions, which began in November 2020; in Tigray region alone, 5.3 million people are estimated to be severely food insecure; the failure of the March-May 2022 "Gu-Genna" rains in southern pastoral areas of southern Oromiya Region and southern Somali Region, exacerbated drought conditions prevailing since late 2020, causing severe crop and livestock losses; severe macroeconomic challenges including insufficient foreign currency reserves and the continuous depreciation of the national currency, as a result, inflation is at very high levels, with the year-on-year food inflation rate estimated at 35.5 percent in July, one the highest of the last decade; these difficulties are exacerbated by the ripple effects of the Ukraine war, which triggered hikes in international prices of wheat, fuel, and fertilizers (2023)

Revenue from forest resources: 5.81% of GDP (2018 est.)
comparison ranking: 11

Revenue from coal: 0% of GDP (2018 est.)
comparison ranking: 118

Air pollutants: *particulate matter emissions:* 21.8 micrograms per cubic meter (2019 est.)
carbon dioxide emissions: 14.87 megatons (2016 est.)
methane emissions: 114.21 megatons (2020 est.)

Waste and recycling: *municipal solid waste generated annually:* 6,532,787 tons (2015 est.)

Major lakes (area sq km): *fresh water lake(s):* Lake Tana - 3,600 sq km; Abaya Hayk - 1,160 sq km; Ch'amo Hayk - 550 sq km
salt water lake(s): Lake Turkana (shared with Kenya) - 6,400 sq km; Abhe Bid Hayk/Abhe Bad (shared with Djibouti) - 780 sq km;

Major rivers (by length in km): Blue Nile river source (shared with Sudan [m]) - 1,600 km
note – [s] after country name indicates river source; [m] after country name indicates river mouth

Major watersheds (area sq km): Atlantic Ocean drainage: *(Mediterranean Sea)* Nile (3,254,853 sq km)

Major aquifers: Ogaden-Juba Basin, Sudd Basin (Umm Ruwaba Aquifer)

Total water withdrawal: *municipal:* 810 million cubic meters (2020 est.)
industrial: 50 million cubic meters (2020 est.)
agricultural: 9.69 billion cubic meters (2020 est.)

Total renewable water resources: 122 billion cubic meters (2020 est.)

GOVERNMENT

Country name: *conventional long form:* Federal Democratic Republic of Ethiopia
conventional short form: Ethiopia
local long form: YeItyop'iya Federalawi Demokrasiyawi Ripeblik
local short form: Ityop'iya
former: Abyssinia, Italian East Africa
abbreviation: FDRE
etymology: the country name derives from the Greek word "Aethiopia," which in classical times referred to lands south of Egypt in the Upper Nile region

Government type: federal parliamentary republic

Capital: *name:* Addis Ababa
geographic coordinates: 9 02 N, 38 42 E
time difference: UTC+3 (8 hours ahead of Washington, DC, during Standard Time)
etymology: the name in Amharic means "new flower" and was bestowed on the city in 1889, three years after its founding

Administrative divisions: 12 ethnically based regional states (kililoch, singular - kilil) and 2 chartered cities* (astedader akabibiwach, singular - astedader akabibi); Adis Abeba* (Addis Ababa), Afar, Amara (Amhara), Binshangul Gumuz, Dire Dawa*, Gambela Hizboch (Gambela), Hareri Hizb (Harari), Oromia, Sidama, Sumale, Tigray, YeDebub Biheroch Bihereseboch na Hizboch (Southern Nations, Nationalities and Peoples), YeDebub M'irab Ityop'iya Hizboch (Southwest Ethiopia Peoples), Southern Ethiopia Peoples

Independence: oldest independent country in Africa and one of the oldest in the world - at least 2,000 years (may be traced to the Aksumite Kingdom, which coalesced in the first century B.C.)

National holiday: Derg Downfall Day (defeat of MENGISTU regime), 28 May (1991)

Legal system: civil law system

Constitution: *history:* several previous; latest drafted June 1994, adopted 8 December 1994, entered into force 21 August 1995
amendments: proposals submitted for discussion require two-thirds majority approval in either house of Parliament or majority approval of one-third of the State Councils; passage of amendments other than constitutional articles on fundamental rights and freedoms and the initiation and amendment of the constitution requires two-thirds majority vote in a joint session of Parliament and majority vote by two thirds of the State Councils; passage of amendments affecting rights and freedoms and amendment procedures requires two-thirds majority vote in each house of Parliament and majority vote by all the State Councils

International law organization participation: has not submitted an ICJ jurisdiction declaration; non-party state to the ICCt

Citizenship: *citizenship by birth:* no
citizenship by descent only: at least one parent must be a citizen of Ethiopia
dual citizenship recognized: no
residency requirement for naturalization: 4 years

Suffrage: 18 years of age; universal

Executive branch: *chief of state:* President TAYE Atske Selassie (since 7 October 2024)
head of government: Prime Minister ABIY Ahmed Ali (since April 2018)
cabinet: Council of Ministers selected by the prime minister and approved by the House of People's Representatives
elections/appointments: president indirectly elected by both chambers of Parliament for a 6-year term (eligible for a second term); election held on 21 June 2021 and 30 September 2021 (the scheduled 29 August 2020 election was postponed by Prime Minister ABIY due to the COVID-19 pandemic); prime minister designated by the majority party following legislative elections
election results:
2021: SAHLE-WORK Zewde reelected president during joint session of Parliament, vote - 659 (unanimous); ABIY confirmed Prime Minister by House of Peoples' Representatives (4 October 2021)
2018: SAHLE-WORK Zewde elected president during joint session of Parliament, vote - 659 (unanimous); note - snap election held on 25 October 2018 due to resignation of President MULATA Teshome

note: SAHLE-WORK Zewde is the first female elected head of state in Ethiopia

Legislative branch: *description:* bicameral Parliament consists of:
House of Federation or Yefedereshein Mikir Bete (153 seats maximum; 144 seats current; members indirectly elected by state assemblies to serve 5-year terms)
House of People's Representatives or Yehizb Tewokayoch Mekir Bete (547 seats maximum; 470 seats current; members directly elected in single-seat constituencies by simple majority vote; 22 seats reserved for minorities; all members serve 5-year terms)
elections: House of Federation - last held 4 October 2021 (next expected in October 2026)
House of People's Representatives - last held in two parts on 21 June 2021 and 30 September 2021 (next expected in June 2026)
election results: House of Federation - percent of vote by party/coalition - NA; seats by party/coalition - NA; composition - men 102, women 43, percentage women 29.7%
House of Representatives - percent of vote by party/coalition - NA; seats by party/coalition - Prosperity Party 454, NAMA 5, EZEMA 4, Gedeo People's Democratic organization 2, Kucha People Democratic Party 1, independent 4; composition - men 275, women 195, percentage women 41.3%; note - total Parliament percentage women 38.9%
note: the House of Federation is responsible for interpreting the constitution and federal-regional issues, and the House of People's Representatives is responsible for passing legislation

Judicial branch: *highest court(s):* Federal Supreme Court (consists of 11 judges); note - the House of Federation has jurisdiction for all constitutional issues
judge selection and term of office: president and vice president of Federal Supreme Court recommended by the prime minister and appointed by the House of People's Representatives; other Supreme Court judges nominated by the Federal Judicial Administrative Council (a 10-member body chaired by the president of the Federal Supreme Court) and appointed by the House of People's Representatives; judges serve until retirement at age 60
subordinate courts: federal high courts and federal courts of first instance; state court systems (mirror structure of federal system); sharia courts and customary and traditional courts

Political parties: Ethiopian Citizens for Social Justice and Democracy or EZEMA
Gedeo People's Democratic Party
Independent
Kucha People Democratic Party
National Movement of Amhara or NAMA
Prosperity Party or PP

International organization participation: ACP, AfDB, ATMIS, AU, BRICS, COMESA, EITI, FAO, G-24, G-77, IAEA, IBRD, ICAO, ICRM, IDA, IFAD, IFC, IFRCS, IGAD, ILO, IMF, IMO, Interpol, IOC, IOM, IPU, ISO, ITSO, ITU, ITUC (NGOs), MIGA, NAM, OPCW, PCA, UN, UNCTAD, UNESCO, UNHCR, UNIDO, UNMISS, UNOOSA, UNWTO, UPU, WCO, WFTU (NGOs), WHO, WIPO, WMO, WTO (accession candidate)

Diplomatic representation in the US: *chief of mission:* Ambassador (vacant); Chargé d'Affaires Aster Mamo ANA (since 31 July 2024)
chancery: 3506 International Drive NW, Washington, DC 20008
telephone: [1] (202) 364-1200
FAX: [1] (202) 587-0195
email address and website:
ethiopia@ethiopianembassy.org
https://ethiopianembassy.org/
consulate(s) general: Los Angeles, St. Paul (MN)

Diplomatic representation from the US: *chief of mission:* Ambassador Ervin MASSINGA (since 4 October 2023)
embassy: Entoto Street, P.O. Box 1014, Addis Ababa
mailing address: 2030 Addis Ababa Place, Washington DC 20521-2030
telephone: [251] 111-30-60-00
FAX: [251] 111-24-24-01
email address and website:
AddisACS@state.gov
https://et.usembassy.gov/

Flag description: three equal horizontal bands of green (top), yellow, and red, with a yellow pentagram and single yellow rays emanating from the angles between the points on a light blue disk centered on the three bands; green represents hope and the fertility of the land, yellow symbolizes justice and harmony, while red stands for sacrifice and heroism in the defense of the land; the blue of the disk symbolizes peace and the pentagram represents the unity and equality of the nationalities and peoples of Ethiopia
note: Ethiopia is the oldest independent country in Africa, and the three main colors of her flag (adopted ca. 1895) were so often appropriated by other African countries upon independence that they became known as the Pan-African colors; the emblem in the center of the current flag was added in 1996

National symbol(s): Abyssinian lion (traditional), yellow pentagram with five rays of light on a blue field (promoted by current government); national colors: green, yellow, red

National anthem: *name:* "Whedefit Gesgeshi Woud Enat Ethiopia" (March Forward, Dear Mother Ethiopia)
lyrics/music: DEREJE Melaku Mengesha/ SOLOMON Lulu
note: adopted 1992

National heritage: *total World Heritage Sites:* 11 (9 cultural, 2 natural)
selected World Heritage Site locales: Rock-Hewn Churches, Lalibela (c); Simien National Park (n); Fasil Ghebbi, Gondar Region (c); Axum (c); Lower Valley of the Awash (c); Lower Valley of the Omo (c); Tiya (c); Harar Jugol, the Fortified Historic Town (c); Konso Cultural Landscape (c); Gedeo Cultural Landscape (c)

ECONOMY

Economic overview: growing Horn of Africa construction- and services-based economy; port access via Djibouti and Eritrea; widespread but declining poverty; COVID-19, locust invasion, and Tigray crisis disruptions; public investment increases; second largest African labor force

Real GDP (purchasing power parity): $354.604 billion (2023 est.)
$332.968 billion (2022 est.)
$316.145 billion (2021 est.)
note: data in 2021 dollars
comparison ranking: 56

Real GDP growth rate: 6.5% (2023 est.)
5.32% (2022 est.)
5.64% (2021 est.)
note: annual GDP % growth based on constant local currency
comparison ranking: 25

Real GDP per capita: $2,800 (2023 est.)
$2,700 (2022 est.)
$2,600 (2021 est.)
note: data in 2021 dollars
comparison ranking: 198

GDP (official exchange rate): $163.698 billion (2023 est.)
note: data in current dollars at official exchange rate

Inflation rate (consumer prices): 30.22% (2023 est.)
33.89% (2022 est.)
26.84% (2021 est.)
note: annual % change based on consumer prices
comparison ranking: 206

Credit ratings: Fitch rating: B (2014)
Moody's rating: B2 (2020)
Standard & Poors rating: B (2014)
note: The year refers to the year in which the current credit rating was first obtained.

GDP - composition, by sector of origin: *agriculture:* 35.8% (2023 est.)
industry: 24.5% (2023 est.)
services: 37% (2023 est.)
note: figures may not total 100% due to non-allocated consumption not captured in sector-reported data comparison rankings: services 202; industry 102; agriculture 6

GDP - composition, by end use: *household consumption:* 78.9% (2023 est.)
government consumption: 6.3% (2023 est.)
investment in fixed capital: 22.2% (2023 est.)
exports of goods and services: 6.6% (2023 est.)
imports of goods and services: -14% (2023 est.)
note: figures may not total 100% due to rounding or gaps in data collection

Agricultural products: maize, wheat, cereals, sorghum, milk, barley, taro, potatoes, millet, beans (2022)
note: top ten agricultural products based on tonnage

Industries: food processing, beverages, textiles, leather, garments, chemicals, metals processing, cement

Industrial production growth rate: 6.93% (2023 est.)
note: annual % change in industrial value added based on constant local currency
comparison ranking: 34

Labor force: 61.664 million (2023 est.)
note: number of people ages 15 or older who are employed or seeking work
comparison ranking: 11

Unemployment rate: 3.5% (2023 est.)
3.49% (2022 est.)
3.94% (2021 est.)
note: % of labor force seeking employment
comparison ranking: 60

Youth unemployment rate (ages 15-24): *total:* 5.6% (2023 est.)
male: 4% (2023 est.)
female: 7.4% (2023 est.)
note: % of labor force ages 15-24 seeking employment
comparison ranking: total 172

Population below poverty line: 23.5% (2015 est.)
note: % of population with income below national poverty line

Gini Index coefficient - distribution of family income: 35 (2015 est.)
note: index (0-100) of income distribution; higher values represent greater inequality
comparison ranking: 77

Average household expenditures: *on food:* 39.7% of household expenditures (2022 est.)
on alcohol and tobacco: 3.1% of household expenditures (2022 est.)

Household income or consumption by percentage share: *lowest 10%:* 2.9% (2015 est.)
highest 10%: 28.5% (2015 est.)
note: % share of income accruing to lowest and highest 10% of population

Remittances: 0.36% of GDP (2023 est.)
0.4% of GDP (2022 est.)
0.4% of GDP (2021 est.)
note: personal transfers and compensation between resident and non-resident individuals/households/entities

Budget: *revenues:* $7.009 billion (2022 est.)
expenditures: $8.83 billion (2022 est.)
note: central government revenues and expenses (excluding grants/extrabudgetary units/social security funds) converted to US dollars at average official exchange rate for year indicated

Public debt: 31.45% of GDP (2019 est.)
note: central government debt as a % of GDP
comparison ranking: 166

Taxes and other revenues: 4.51% (of GDP) (2022 est.)
note: central government tax revenue as a % of GDP
comparison ranking: 202

Current account balance: -$4.788 billion (2023 est.)
-$5.16 billion (2022 est.)
-$4.507 billion (2021 est.)
note: balance of payments - net trade and primary/secondary income in current dollars
comparison ranking: 181

Exports: $10.865 billion (2023 est.)
$10.971 billion (2022 est.)
$9.496 billion (2021 est.)
note: balance of payments - exports of goods and services in current dollars
comparison ranking: 112

Exports - partners: UAE 17%, US 13%, Germany 6%, Saudi Arabia 6%, Somalia 6% (2022)
note: top five export partners based on percentage share of exports

Exports - commodities: coffee, gold, garments, cut flowers, vegetables (2022)
note: top five export commodities based on value in dollars

Imports: $22.951 billion (2023 est.)
$24.187 billion (2022 est.)
$20.859 billion (2021 est.)
note: balance of payments - imports of goods and services in current dollars
comparison ranking: 92

Imports - partners: China 24%, US 9%, India 8%, UAE 6%, UK 4% (2022)
note: top five import partners based on percentage share of imports

Imports - commodities: wheat, refined petroleum, fertilizers, vaccines, palm oil (2022)
note: top five import commodities based on value in dollars

Reserves of foreign exchange and gold: $3.046 billion (2020 est.)
$2.993 billion (2019 est.)
$3.987 billion (2018 est.)
note: holdings of gold (year-end prices)/foreign exchange/special drawing rights in current dollars
comparison ranking: 115

Debt - external: $21.522 billion (2022 est.)
note: present value of external debt in current US dollars
comparison ranking: 25

Exchange rates: birr (ETB) per US dollar -

Exchange rates: 54.601 (2023 est.)
51.756 (2022 est.)
43.734 (2021 est.)
34.927 (2020 est.)
29.07 (2019 est.)

ENERGY

Electricity access: *electrification - total population:* 55% (2022 est.)
electrification - urban areas: 94%
electrification - rural areas: 43%

Electricity: *installed generating capacity:* 5.73 million kW (2022 est.)
consumption: 10.596 billion kWh (2022 est.)
exports: 1.665 billion kWh (2022 est.)
transmission/distribution losses: 3.154 billion kWh (2022 est.)
comparison rankings: transmission/distribution losses 142; exports 59; consumption 101; installed generating capacity 83

Electricity generation sources: *solar:* 0.2% of total installed capacity (2022 est.)
wind: 3.8% of total installed capacity (2022 est.)
hydroelectricity: 95.7% of total installed capacity (2022 est.)
biomass and waste: 0.2% of total installed capacity (2022 est.)

Coal: *production:* 8,000 metric tons (2022 est.)
consumption: 660,000 metric tons (2022 est.)
exports: 1,000 metric tons (2022 est.)
imports: 666,000 metric tons (2022 est.)

Petroleum: *refined petroleum consumption:* 110,000 bbl/day (2022 est.)
crude oil estimated reserves: 428,000 barrels (2021 est.)

Natural gas: *proven reserves:* 24.919 billion cubic meters (2021 est.)

Carbon dioxide emissions: 17.232 million metric tonnes of CO_2 (2022 est.)
from coal and metallurgical coke: 1.38 million metric tonnes of CO_2 (2022 est.)
from petroleum and other liquids: 15.852 million metric tonnes of CO_2 (2022 est.)
comparison ranking: total emissions 92

Energy consumption per capita: 2.34 million Btu/person (2022 est.)
comparison ranking: 183

COMMUNICATIONS

Telephones - fixed lines: *total subscriptions:* 862,000 (2022 est.)
subscriptions per 100 inhabitants: (2022 est.) less than 1
comparison ranking: total subscriptions 75

Telephones - mobile cellular: *total subscriptions:* 69.123 million (2022 est.)
subscriptions per 100 inhabitants: 56 (2022 est.)
comparison ranking: total subscriptions 25

Telecommunication systems: *general assessment:* Ethio telecom is the major provider, but no longer has a complete monopoly on all telecom services; a consortium led by Kenyan Safaricom launched service in October 2022; the World Bank in early 2021 provided a $200 million loan to help develop the country's digital transformation, while the government has embarked on its 2020-2030 program as well as its Digital Ethiopia 2025 strategy, both aimed at making better use of digital technologies to promote socioeconomic development (2023)
domestic: fixed-line subscriptions less than 1 per 100 while mobile-cellular stands at a little over 54 per 100 people (2021)
international: country code - 251; open-wire to Sudan and Djibouti; microwave radio relay to Kenya and Djibouti; 2 domestic satellites provide the national trunk service; satellite earth stations - 3 Intelsat (1 Atlantic Ocean and 2 Pacific Ocean) (2016)

Broadcast media: 10 public/state broadcasters; 9 public/state radio stations; 13 commercial FM radio stations; 18 commercial TV stations; 45 community radio stations; 5 community TV stations (2023)

Internet country code: .et

Internet users: *total:* 20.4 million (2021 est.)
percent of population: 17% (2021 est.)
comparison ranking: total 44

Broadband - fixed subscriptions: *total:* 212,000 (2020 est.)
subscriptions per 100 inhabitants: 0.2 (2020 est.)
comparison ranking: total 118

TRANSPORTATION

National air transport system: *number of registered air carriers:* 1 (2020)
inventory of registered aircraft operated by air carriers: 75
annual passenger traffic on registered air carriers: 11,501,244 (2018)
annual freight traffic on registered air carriers: 2,089,280,000 (2018) mt-km

Civil aircraft registration country code prefix: ET

Airports: 57 (2024)
comparison ranking: 79

Heliports: 1 (2024)

Railways: *total:* 659 km (2017) (Ethiopian segment of the 756 km Addis Ababa-Djibouti railroad)
standard gauge: 659 km (2017) 1.435-m gauge
note: electric railway with redundant power supplies; under joint control of Djibouti and Ethiopia and managed by a Chinese contractor
comparison ranking: total 104

Roadways: *total:* 180,000 km (2023)
comparison ranking: total 30

Merchant marine: *total:* 12 (2023)
by type: general cargo 10, oil tanker 2
comparison ranking: total 156

MILITARY AND SECURITY

Military and security forces: Ethiopian National Defense Force (ENDF): Ground Forces (Army), Ethiopian Air Force (Ye Ityopya Ayer Hayl, ETAF) (2024)
note 1: national and regional police forces are responsible for law enforcement and maintenance of order, with the ENDF sometimes providing internal

security support; the Ethiopian Federal Police (EFP) report to the Prime Minister's Office

note 2: the regional governments control regional security forces, including "special" paramilitary forces, which generally operate independently from the federal government and in some cases operate as regional defense forces maintaining national borders; in April 2023, the federal government ordered the integration of these regional special forces into the EFP or ENDF; in some cases, the regional governments have maintained former members of the special forces for "crowd control/Adma Bitena" as a separate unit within their security structures; local militias also operate across the country in loose and varying coordination with regional security and police forces, the ENDF, and the EFP

note 3: in 2020 the Ethiopian Government announced it had re-established a navy, which had been disbanded in 1996; in March 2019, Ethiopia signed a defense cooperation agreement with France which stipulated that France would support the establishment of an Ethiopian navy

note 4: in 2018, Ethiopia established a Republican Guard military unit as a separate command operationally under the Office of the Prime Minister and administratively accountable to the Ministry of Defense; it is responsible for protecting senior officials and government institutions and conducting some military operations

Military expenditures: 1% of GDP (2023 est.)
1.7% of GDP (2022 est.)
0.5% of GDP (2021 est.)
0.5% of GDP (2020 est.)
0.6% of GDP (2019 est.)
comparison ranking: 128

Military and security service personnel strengths: information varies; prior to the 2020-2022 Tigray conflict, approximately 150,000 active-duty troops (2023)

Military equipment inventories and acquisitions: the ENDF's inventory has traditionally been comprised mostly of Russian and Soviet-era equipment; it suffered considerable equipment losses during the 2020-2022 Tigray conflict; in recent years, Ethiopia has diversified its arms sources to include weapons from China, Israel, Turkey, Ukraine, and the UAE; Ethiopia has a modest industrial defense base centered on small arms and production of armored vehicles (2024)

Military service age and obligation: 18-22 years of age for voluntary military service (although the military may, when necessary, recruit a person more than 22 years old); no compulsory military service, but the military can conduct callups when necessary and compliance is compulsory (2023)

Military deployments: as many as 10,000 troops in Somalia (approximately 3,000 for ATMIS; the remainder under a bilateral agreement with the Somali Government; note - foreign troop contingents in Somalia under ATMIS are drawing down towards a final departure in December 2024); 1,500 South Sudan (UNMISS) (2024)

Military - note: the ENDF has been one of sub-Saharan Africa's largest, most experienced, and best equipped militaries, but it suffered heavy casualties and equipment losses during the 2020-2022 Tigray conflict; the ENDF is focused on both external threats emanating from its neighbors and internal threats from multiple internal armed groups; since 1998, the ENDF has engaged in several conventional and counterinsurgency operations, including border wars with Eritrea (1998-2000) and Somalia (2006-2008) and internal conflicts with the Tigray regional state (2020-2022), several insurgent groups and ethnic militias (including the ethno-nationalist Amhara Fano), and the al-Shabaab terrorist group

as of 2024, the ENDF was conducting counterinsurgency operations against anti-government militants in several states, including in Oromya (Oromia) against the Oromo Liberation Army (OLA), an insurgent group that claims to be fighting for greater autonomy for the Oromo, Ethiopia's largest ethnic group; in 2022, militants from the Somalia-based al-Shabaab terrorist group launched an incursion into Ethiopia's Somali (Sumale) regional state, attacking villages and security forces; the Ethiopian Government claimed that regional security forces killed hundreds of al-Shabaab fighters and subsequently deployed additional ENDF troops into Somalia's Gedo region to prevent further incursions (2024)

SPACE

Space agency/agencies: Ethiopian Space Science and Geospatial Institute (ESSGI; formed in 2022 from the joining of the Ethiopian Space Science and Technology Institute or ESSTI and the Ethiopian Geospatial Information Institute or EGII) (2024)

Space program overview: has a small space program with a focus on acquiring and operating satellites, as well as research and astronomy; jointly builds satellites with foreign partners and operates and exploits remote sensing (RS) satellites; developing the ability to manufacture satellites and their associated payloads; involved in astronomy and in the construction of space observatories; cooperates on space-related issues with a variety of countries, including China, France, India, Russia, and multiple African countries, particularly Kenya, Rwanda, Sudan, Tanzania, and Uganda; shares RS data with neighboring countries (2024)

note: further details about the key activities, programs, and milestones of the country's space program, as well as government spending estimates on the space sector, appear in the Space Programs reference guide

TERRORISM

Terrorist group(s): al-Shabaab; Islamic Revolutionary Guard Corps (IRGC)/Qods Force

note: details about the history, aims, leadership, organization, areas of operation, tactics, targets, weapons, size, and sources of support of the group(s) appear(s) in the Terrorism reference guide

TRANSNATIONAL ISSUES

Refugees and internally displaced persons: *refugees (country of origin):* 167,391 (Eritrea) (2023); 420,502 (South Sudan), 314,976 (Somalia), 111,778 (Sudan) (refugees since 15 April 2023) (2024)

IDPs: 4.385 million (includes conflict- and climate-induced IDPs, excluding unverified estimates from the Amhara region; border war with Eritrea from 1998-2000; ethnic clashes; and ongoing fighting between the Ethiopian military and separatist rebel groups in the Somali and Oromia regions; natural disasters; intercommunal violence; most IDPs live in Sumale state) (2023)

Illicit drugs: transit hub for heroin originating in Southwest and Southeast Asia and destined for Europe, as well as cocaine destined for markets in southern Africa; cultivates qat (khat) for local use and regional export, principally to Djibouti and Somalia (legal in all three countries); the lack of a well-developed financial system limits the country's utility as a money laundering center

EUROPEAN UNION

INTRODUCTION

Preliminary statement: The European Union's (EU) evolution is unprecedented in history, transforming from a regional economic agreement among six neighboring states in 1951 to today's hybrid intergovernmental and supranational organization of 27 countries across the European continent. For such a large number of nation-states to cede some of their sovereignty to an overarching entity is unique. Dynastic unions for territorial consolidation were long the norm in Europe, although country-level unions were sometimes arranged, such as the Polish-Lithuanian Commonwealth and the Austro-Hungarian Empire.

Although the EU is not a federation in the strict sense, it is far more than a free-trade association such as ASEAN or Mercosur, and it has certain attributes associated with independent nations: its own flag, currency (for some members), and law-making abilities, as well as diplomatic representation and a common foreign and security policy in its dealings with external partners.

For these reasons, The World Factbook includes basic information on the EU as a separate entity.

Background: In the aftermath and devastation of the two World Wars, a number of far-sighted European leaders in the late 1940s sought to respond to the overwhelming desire for peace and reconciliation on the continent. In 1950, French Foreign Minister Robert SCHUMAN proposed pooling the production of coal and steel in Western Europe, which would bring France and West Germany together and be open to other countries as well. The following year, the European Coal and Steel Community (ECSC) was set up when six members –Belgium, France, West Germany, Italy, Luxembourg, and the Netherlands – signed the Treaty of Paris.

Within a few years, the ECSC was so successful that member states decided to further integrate their economies. In 1957, envisioning an "ever closer union," the Treaties of Rome created the European Economic Community (EEC) and the European Atomic Energy Community (Euratom), which eliminated trade barriers among the six member states to create a common market. In 1967, the institutions of all three communities were formally merged into the European Community (EC), creating a single Commission, a single Council of Ministers, and a legislative body known today as the European Parliament. Members of the European Parliament were initially selected by national parliaments, but direct elections began in 1979 and have been held every five years since.

In 1973, the first enlargement of the EC added Denmark, Ireland, and the UK. The 1980s saw further membership expansion, with Greece joining in 1981 and Spain and Portugal in 1986. The 1992 Treaty of Maastricht laid the basis for further cooperation in foreign and defense policy and judicial and internal affairs, as well as the creation of an economic and monetary union – including a common currency. The Maastricht Treaty created the European Union (EU), at the time standing alongside the EC. In 1995, Austria, Finland, and Sweden joined the EU/EC, raising the total number of member states to 15. On 1 January 1999, the new euro currency was launched in world markets and became the unit of exchange for all EU member states except Denmark, Sweden, and the UK. In 2002, citizens of the 12 participating member states began using euro banknotes and coins.

In an effort to ensure that the EU could function efficiently with an expanded membership, the Treaty of Nice in 2000 set forth rules to streamline the size and procedures of the EU's institutions. An effort to establish a "Constitution for Europe," growing out of a Convention held in 2002-2003, foundered when it was rejected in referenda in France and the Netherlands in 2005. A subsequent effort in 2007 incorporated many features of the rejected draft Constitutional Treaty, while also making a number of substantive as well as symbolic changes. The new treaty, referred to as the Treaty of Lisbon, sought to amend existing treaties rather than replace them. The treaty was approved at a conference of member states, and after all member states ratified, the Lisbon Treaty came into force on 1 December 2009, at which point the EU officially replaced and succeeded the EC.

Ten new countries joined the EU in 2004 – Cyprus, the Czech Republic, Estonia, Hungary, Latvia, Lithuania, Malta, Poland, Slovakia, and Slovenia. Bulgaria and Romania joined in 2007 and Croatia in 2013. UK citizens on 23 June 2016 narrowly voted to leave the EU; the formal exit, widely known as "Brexit," took place on 31 January 2020. The EU and the UK negotiated a withdrawal agreement that included a status quo transition period through December 2020, when the follow-on EU-UK Trade and Cooperation Agreement was concluded. Current EU membership stands at 27. Eight of the newer member states – Croatia, Cyprus, Estonia, Latvia, Lithuania, Malta, Slovakia, and Slovenia – have now adopted the euro, bringing total euro-zone membership to 20.

GEOGRAPHY

Location: Europe between the North Atlantic Ocean in the west and Russia, Belarus, and Ukraine to the east

Map references: Europe

Area: *total:* 4,236,351 sq km
rank by area (sq km):
1. France (includes five overseas regions) 643,801
2. Spain 505,370
3. Sweden 450,295
4. Germany 357,022
5. Finland 338,145
6. Poland 312,685
7. Italy 301,340
8. Romania 238,391
9. Greece 131,957
10. Bulgaria 110,879
11. Hungary 93,028
12. Portugal 92,090
13. Austria 83,871
14. Czechia 78,867
15. Ireland 70,273
16. Lithuania 65,300
17. Latvia 64,589
18. Croatia 56,594
19. Slovakia 49,035
20. Estonia 45,228
21. Denmark 43,094
22. Netherlands 41,543
23. Belgium 30,528
24. Slovenia 20,273
25. Cyprus 9,251
26. Luxembourg 2,586
27. Malta 316

Area - comparative: less than one half the size of the United States

Land boundaries: *total:* 13,770 km
border countries: Albania 212 km; Andorra 118 km; Belarus 1,176 km; Bosnia and Herzegovina 956 km; Holy See 3 km; Liechtenstein 34 km; North Macedonia 396 km; Moldova 683 km; Monaco 6 km; Montenegro 19 km; Norway 2,375 km; Russia 2,435 km; San Marino 37 km; Serbia 1,353 km; Switzerland 1,729 km; Turkey 415 km; United Kingdom 499 km; Ukraine 1,324 km
note: data for European continent only

Coastline: 53,563.9 km

Climate: cold temperate; potentially subarctic in the north to temperate; mild wet winters; hot dry summers in the south

Terrain: fairly flat along Baltic and Atlantic coasts; mountainous in the central and southern areas

Elevation: *highest point:* Mont Blanc, France 4,810 m
lowest point: Zuidplaspolder, Netherlands -7 m

Natural resources: iron ore, natural gas, petroleum, coal, copper, lead, zinc, bauxite, uranium, potash, salt, hydropower, arable land, timber, fish

Irrigated land: 154,539.82 sq km (2011 est.)

Population distribution: population distribution varies considerably from country to country but tends to follow a pattern of coastal and river settlement, with urban agglomerations forming large hubs facilitating large scale housing, industry, and commerce; the area in and around the Netherlands, Belgium, and Luxembourg (known collectively as Benelux), is the most densely populated area in the EU

Natural hazards: flooding along coasts; avalanches in mountainous area; earthquakes in the south; volcanic eruptions in Italy; periodic droughts in Spain; ice floes in the Baltic Sea region

PEOPLE AND SOCIETY

Population: *total:* 451,815,312
male: 220,631,332
female: 231,183,980 (2024 est.)

Languages: Bulgarian, Croatian, Czech, Danish, Dutch, English, Estonian, Finnish, French, German, Greek, Hungarian, Irish, Italian, Latvian, Lithuanian, Maltese, Polish, Portuguese, Romanian, Slovak, Slovene, Spanish, Swedish
note: only the 24 official languages are listed; German, the major language of Germany and Austria, is the most widely spoken mother tongue - about 16% of the EU population; English is the most widely spoken foreign language - about 29% of the EU population is conversant with it; English is an official language in Ireland and Malta and thus remained an official EU language after the UK left the bloc (2020)

Religions: Roman Catholic 41%, Orthodox 10%, Protestant 9%, other Christian 4%, Muslim 2%, other 4% (includes Jewish, Sikh, Buddhist, Hindu), atheist 10%, non-believer/agnostic 17%, unspecified 3% (2019 est.)

Age structure: *0-14 years:* 14.5% (male 33,606,273/female 31,985,118)
15-64 years: 63.5% (male 143,874,460/female 143,104,994)
65 years and over: 22% (2024 est.) (male 43,150,599/female 56,093,868)

Dependency ratios: *total dependency ratio:* NA
youth dependency ratio: NA
elderly dependency ratio: NA
potential support ratio: NA

Median age: *total:* 44 years (2020)
male: 42.6 years
female: 45.5 years

Population growth rate: 0.1% (2021 est.)

Birth rate: 8.9 births/1,000 population (2024 est.)

Death rate: 11.2 deaths/1,000 population (2024 est.)

Net migration rate: -2.85 migrant(s)/1,000 population

Population distribution: population distribution varies considerably from country to country but tends to follow a pattern of coastal and river settlement, with urban agglomerations forming large hubs facilitating large scale housing, industry, and commerce; the area in and around the Netherlands, Belgium, and Luxembourg (known collectively as Benelux), is the most densely populated area in the EU

Sex ratio: *at birth:* 1.05 male(s)/female
0-14 years: 1.05 male(s)/female
15-64 years: 1.01 male(s)/female
65 years and over: 0.77 male(s)/female
total population: 0.95 male(s)/female (2024 est.)

Infant mortality rate: *total:* 3.4 deaths/1,000 live births (2024 est.)

Life expectancy at birth: *total population:* 77.63 years (2021)
male: 72.98 years
female: 82.51 years

Total fertility rate: 1.54 children born/woman (2024 est.)

Gross reproduction rate: 0.75 (2024 est.)

Education expenditures: 5% of GDP (2020 est.)

ENVIRONMENT

Environment - current issues: various forms of air, soil, and water pollution; see individual country entries

Environment - international agreements: *party to:* Air Pollution, Air Pollution-Heavy Metals, Air Pollution-Multi-effect Protocol, Air Pollution-Nitrogen Oxides, Air Pollution-Persistent Organic Pollutants, Air Pollution-Sulphur 94, Antarctic-Marine Living Resources, Biodiversity, Climate Change, Climate Change-Kyoto Protocol, Climate Change-Paris Agreement, Desertification, Endangered Species, Hazardous Wastes, Law of the Sea, Ozone Layer Protection, Tropical Timber 2006
signed, but not ratified: Air Pollution-Volatile Organic Compounds

Climate: cold temperate; potentially subarctic in the north to temperate; mild wet winters; hot dry summers in the south

Revenue from forest resources: 0.05% of GDP (2018 est.)

Revenue from coal: 0.02% of GDP (2018 est.)

Air pollutants: *carbon dioxide emissions:* 2,881.62 megatons (2016 est.)

Total renewable water resources: 1.7 trillion cubic meters (2019)

GOVERNMENT

Union name: *conventional long form:* European Union
abbreviation: EU

Political structure: a hybrid and unique intergovernmental and supranational organization

Capital: *name:* Brussels (Belgium), Strasbourg (France), Luxembourg, Frankfurt (Germany); note - the European Council, a gathering of member-state heads of state and/or government, and the Council of the European Union, a gathering of member-state cabinet ministers, meet in Brussels, Belgium, except for Council of the EU meetings held in Luxembourg in April, June, and October; the European Parliament meets in Brussels and Strasbourg, France, and has administrative offices in Luxembourg; the Court of Justice of the European Union is located in Luxembourg; and the European Central Bank is located in Frankfurt, Germany
geographic coordinates: (Brussels) 50 50 N, 4 20 E
time difference: UTC+1 (6 hours ahead of Washington, DC, during Standard Time)
daylight saving time: +1hr, begins last Sunday in March; ends last Sunday in October
time zone note: the 27 European Union member states spread across three time zones; a proposal has been put forward to do away with daylight savings time in all EU member states

Member states: 27 countries: Austria, Belgium, Bulgaria, Croatia, Cyprus, Czechia, Denmark, Estonia, Finland, France, Germany, Greece, Hungary, Ireland, Italy, Latvia, Lithuania, Luxembourg, Malta, Netherlands, Poland, Portugal, Romania, Slovakia, Slovenia, Spain, Sweden; note - 9 candidate countries: Albania, Bosnia and Herzegovina, Georgia, Moldova, Montenegro, North Macedonia, Serbia, Turkey, Ukraine
there are 13 overseas countries and territories (OCTs) (1 with Denmark, 6 with France [French Polynesia, French Southern and Antarctic Lands, New Caledonia, Saint Barthelemy, Saint Pierre and Miquelon, Wallis and Futuna], and 6 with the Netherlands [Aruba, Bonaire, Curacao, Saba, Sint Eustatius, Sint Maarten]), all are part of the Overseas Countries and Territories Association (OCTA)
note: there are non-European OCTs having special relations with Denmark, France, and the Netherlands (list is annexed to the Treaty on the Functioning of the European Union), that are associated with the EU to promote their economic and social development; member states apply to their trade with OCTs the same treatment as they accord each other pursuant to the treaties; OCT nationals are in principle EU citizens, but these countries are neither part of the EU, nor subject to the EU

Independence: 7 February 1992 (Maastricht Treaty signed establishing the European Union); 1 November 1993 (Maastricht Treaty entered into force)
note: the Treaties of Rome, signed on 25 March 1957 and subsequently entered into force on 1 January 1958, created the European Economic Community and the European Atomic Energy Community; a series of subsequent treaties have been adopted to increase efficiency and transparency, to prepare for new member states, and to introduce new areas of cooperation - such as a single currency; the Treaty of Lisbon, signed on 13 December 2007 and entered into force on 1 December 2009 is the most recent of these treaties and is intended to make the EU more democratic, more efficient, and better able to address global problems with one voice

National holiday: Europe Day (also known as Schuman Day), 9 May (1950); note - the day in 1950 that Robert SCHUMAN proposed the creation of what became the European Coal and Steel Community, the progenitor of today's European Union, with the aim of achieving a united Europe

Legal system: unique supranational system of laws in which, according to an interpretive declaration of member-state governments appended to the Treaty of Lisbon, "the Treaties and the law adopted by the Union on the basis of the Treaties have primacy over the law of Member States" under conditions laid down in the case law of the Court of Justice; key principles of EU jurisprudence include universal rights as guaranteed by the Charter of Fundamental Rights and as resulting from constitutional traditions common to the EU's 27 member states; EU law is divided into 'primary' and 'secondary' legislation; primary legislation is derived from the consolidated versions of the Treaty on European Union and the Treaty on the Functioning of the European Union and are the basis for all EU action; secondary legislation - which includes directives, regulations, and decisions - is derived from the principles and objectives set out in the treaties

Constitution: *history:* none; note - the EU legal order relies primarily on two consolidated texts encompassing all provisions as amended from a series of past treaties: the Treaty on European Union (TEU) and the Treaty on the Functioning of the EU (TFEU); The TEU as modified by the 2009 Lisbon Treaty states in Article 1 that "the HIGH CONTRACTING PARTIES establish among themselves a EUROPEAN UNION ... on which the Member States confer competences to attain objectives they have in common"; Article 1 of the TEU states further that the EU is "founded on the present Treaty and on the Treaty on the Functioning of the European Union (hereinafter referred to as 'the Treaties')," both possessing the same legal value; Article 6 of the TEU provides that a separately adopted Charter of Fundamental Rights of the European Union "shall have the same legal value as the Treaties"
amendments: European Union treaties can be amended in several ways: 1) Ordinary Revision Procedure (for key amendments to the treaties); initiated by an EU member state, by the European Parliament, or by the European Commission; following adoption of the proposal by the European Council, a convention is formed of national government representatives to review the proposal and a conference of government representatives subsequently reviews the proposal; passage requires ratification by all EU member states; 2) Simplified Revision Procedure (for amendment of EU internal policies and actions); passage of a proposal requires unanimous European Council vote following European Council consultation with the European Commission, the European Parliament, and the European Central Bank (if the amendment concerns monetary matters) and requires ratification by all EU member states; 3) Passerelle Clause (allows the alteration of a legislative procedure without a formal amendment of the treaties); 4) Flexibility Clause (permits the EU to decide in subject areas where EU competences have not been explicitly granted in the Treaties but are necessary to the attainment of the objectives set out in the Treaty); note - the Treaty of Lisbon (signed in December 2007 and effective in December 2009) amended the two treaties that formed the EU - the Maastricht Treaty (1992), also known as the TEU, and the Treaty of Rome (1957), known in updated form as the TFEU

Suffrage: 18 years of age (16 years in Austria); universal; voting for the European Parliament is permitted in each member state

Executive branch: *under the EU treaties there are three distinct institutions, each of which conducts functions that may be regarded as executive in nature:*
European Council - brings together member-state heads of state or government, along with the president of the European Commission, and meets at least four times a year; its aim is to provide the impetus for the development of the Union and to issue general policy guidance; the Treaty of Lisbon established the position of "permanent" (full-time) president of the European Council; leaders of the EU member states appoint the president for a 2 1/2 year term, renewable once; the president's responsibilities include chairing European Council meetings and providing policy and organizational continuity; the current president is Charles MICHEL (Belgium), since 1 December

2019, who succeeded Donald TUSK (Poland; 2014 - 2019)
Council of the European Union - consists of gatherings of member-state officials, ranging from working-level diplomats to cabinet ministers in a given policy field, such as foreign affairs, agriculture, or economy; it conducts policymaking and coordinating functions as well as legislative functions; representatives from one member state chair meetings of the Council of the EU, based on a 6-month rotating presidency except for the meetings of EU Foreign Ministers in the Foreign Affairs Council that are chaired by the High Representative for Foreign Affairs and Security Policy
European Commission - headed by a College of Commissioners comprised of 27 members (one from each member state) including the president; each commissioner is responsible for one or more policy areas; the Commission has the sole right to initiate EU legislation (except for foreign and security/ defense policy), and is also responsible for promoting the general interest of the EU, acting as "guardian of the Treaties" by monitoring the application of EU law, implementing/ executing the EU budget, managing programs, negotiating on the EU's behalf in policy areas where the member states have conferred sole competency, such as trade, and ensuring the Union's external representation in some policy areas; its current president is Ursula VON DER LEYEN (Germany) elected on 16 July 2019 (took office on 1 December 2019); the president of the European Commission is nominated by the European Council and confirmed by the European Parliament; the Commission president allocates specific responsibilities among the members of the College (appointed by common accord of the member-state governments in consultation with the president-elect); the European Parliament confirms the entire Commission for a 5-year term.
note: for external representation and foreign policy making, member-state leaders appointed Joseph BORRELL (Spain) as the High Representative of the Union for Foreign Affairs and Security Policy; BORRELL took office on 1 December 2019, succeeding Federica MOGHERINI (Italy (2014 - 2019); the High Representative's concurrent appointment as Vice President of the European Commission was meant to bring more coherence to the EU's foreign policy (including policies managed by the Commission that are particularly relevant for EU external relations, such as trade, humanitarian aid and crisis management, neighborhood policy and enlargement, as well as between member-state capitals and the EU); the High Representative helps develop and implement the EU's Common Foreign and Security Policy and Common Security and Defense Policy components, chairs the Council of the EU's meetings of member-state foreign ministers, called the Foreign Affairs Council, represents and acts for the Union in many international contexts, and oversees the European External Action Service, the diplomatic corps of the EU, established on 1 December 2010

Legislative branch: *description:* two legislative bodies consisting of the Council of the European Union (27 seats; ministers representing the 27 member states) and the European Parliament (720 seats; seats allocated among member states roughly in proportion to population size; members elected by proportional representation to serve 5-year terms); note - the European Parliament President, Roberta METSOLA, was elected in January 2022 and reelected in July 2024 by a majority of fellow members of the European Parliament (MEPs) and represents the Parliament within the EU and internationally; the Council of the EU and the MEPs share responsibilities for adopting the bulk of EU legislation; the two bodies must come to agreement for a commission proposal to become law, after negotiations in which they reconcile differences in each body's text of the proposal, except in the area of Common Foreign and Security Policy, which is governed by consensus of the EU member-state governments)
elections: last held on 6-9 June 2024 (next to be held in June 2029)
election results: European Parliament percent of vote - NA; seats by party - EPP 188, S&D 136, PfE 84, ECR 78, Renew 77, Greens/EFA 53, GUE-NGL 46, ESN 25, non-attached 12, other 21; composition - men 424, women 281, percentage women 39.8%

Judicial branch: *highest court(s):* Court of Justice of the European Union, which includes the Court of Justice (informally known as the European Court of Justice or ECJ) and the General Court (consists of 27 judges, one drawn from each member state); the ECJ includes 11 Advocates General while the General Court can include additional judges; both the ECJ and the General Court may sit in a "Grand Chamber" of 15 judges in special cases but usually in chambers of 3 to 5 judges
judge selection and term of office: judges appointed by the common consent of the member states to serve 6-year renewable terms
note: the ECJ is the supreme judicial authority of the EU; it ensures that EU law is interpreted and applied uniformly throughout the EU, resolves disputes among EU institutions and member states, and reviews issues and opinions regarding questions of EU law referred by member state courts

Political parties: The Left or GUE/NGL
European Conservatives and Reformists or ECR
Greens/European Free Alliance or Greens/EFA
European People's Party or EPP
Europe of Sovereign Nations or ESN
Patriots for Europe or PfE
Progressive Alliance of Socialists and Democrats or S&D
Renew Europe or Renew (formerly Alliance of Liberals and Democrats for Europe or ALDE)

International organization participation: ARF, ASEAN (dialogue member), Australian Group, BIS, BSEC (observer), CBSS, CERN, EBRD, FAO, FATF, G-7, G-10, G-20, IDA, IEA, IGAD (partners), LAIA (observer), NSG (observer), OAS (observer), OECD, PIF (partner), SAARC (observer), SICA (observer), UN (observer), UNRWA (observer), WCO, WTO, ZC (observer)

Diplomatic representation in the US: *chief of mission:* Ambassador Jovita NELIUPŠIENĖ, Head of Delegation (since 27 February 2024)
chancery: 2175 K Street NW, Washington, DC 20037
telephone: [1] (202) 862-9500
FAX: [1] (202) 429-1766
email address and website:
delegation-usa-info@eeas.europa.eu
Delegation of the European Union to the United States of America | EEAS (europa.eu)

Diplomatic representation from the US: *chief of mission:* Ambassador Mark GITENSTEIN (since 24 January 2022)
embassy: Zinnerstraat - 13 - Rue Zinner, B-1000 Brussels
mailing address: use embassy street address
telephone: [32] (2) 811-4100
email address and website:
https://useu.usmission.gov/

Flag description: a blue field with 12 five-pointed gold stars arranged in a circle in the center; blue represents the sky of the Western world, the stars are the peoples of Europe in a circle, a symbol of unity; the number of stars is fixed

National symbol(s): a circle of 12, five-pointed, golden yellow stars on a blue field; union colors: blue, yellow

National anthem: *name:* "Ode to Joy"
lyrics/music: no lyrics/Ludwig VAN BEETHOVEN, arranged by Herbert VON KARAJAN
note: official EU anthem since 1985; the anthem is meant to represent all of Europe rather than just the organization, conveying ideas of peace, freedom, and unity

ECONOMY

Real GDP (purchasing power parity): $24.177 trillion (2023 est.)
$24.05 trillion (2022 est.)
$23.216 trillion (2021 est.)
note: data in 2021 dollars

Real GDP growth rate: 0.45% (2023 est.)
3.48% (2022 est.)
6.01% (2021 est.)
note: annual GDP % growth based on constant local currency

Real GDP per capita: $53,800 (2023 est.)
$53,800 (2022 est.)
$51,900 (2021 est.)
note: data in 2021 dollars

GDP (official exchange rate): $18.349 trillion (2023 est.)
note: data in current dollars at official exchange rate

Inflation rate (consumer prices): 6.3% (2023 est.)
8.83% (2022 est.)
2.55% (2021 est.)
note: annual % change based on consumer prices

Credit ratings: Fitch rating: AAA (2010)

Moody's rating: Aaa (2014)

Standard & Poors rating: AA (2016)
note: The year refers to the year in which the current credit rating was first obtained.

GDP - composition, by sector of origin: *agriculture:* 1.7% (2023 est.)
industry: 23.7% (2023 est.)
services: 65% (2023 est.)
note: figures may not total 100% due to non-allocated consumption not captured in sector-reported data

GDP - composition, by end use: *household consumption:* 52.3% (2023 est.)
government consumption: 21.1% (2023 est.)
investment in fixed capital: 22.2% (2023 est.)
investment in inventories: 0.7% (2023 est.)
exports of goods and services: 52.7% (2023 est.)
imports of goods and services: -49% (2023 est.)

note: figures may not total 100% due to rounding or gaps in data collection

Agricultural products: milk, wheat, sugar beets, maize, barley, potatoes, grapes, pork, rapeseed, tomatoes (2022)
note: top ten agricultural products based on tonnage for all EU member states

Industries: *among the world's largest and most technologically advanced regions, the EU industrial base includes:* ferrous and non-ferrous metal production and processing, metal products, petroleum, coal, cement, chemicals, pharmaceuticals, aerospace, rail transportation equipment, passenger and commercial vehicles, construction equipment, industrial equipment, shipbuilding, electrical power equipment, machine tools and automated manufacturing systems, electronics and telecommunications equipment, fishing, food and beverages, furniture, paper, textiles

Industrial production growth rate: -1.01% (2023 est.)
note: annual % change in industrial value added based on constant local currency

Labor force: 221.858 million (2023 est.)
note: number of people ages 15 or older who are employed or seeking work

Unemployment rate: 6.02% (2023 est.)
6.15% (2022 est.)
7.02% (2021 est.)
note: % of labor force seeking employment

Youth unemployment rate (ages 15-24): *total:* 16.1% (2023 est.)
male: 16.4% (2023 est.)
female: 16% (2023 est.)
note: % of labor force ages 15-24 seeking employment

Gini Index coefficient - distribution of family income: 30.8 (2016 est.)

Household income or consumption by percentage share: *lowest 10%:* 2.8%
highest 10%: 23.8% (2016 est.)

Remittances: 0.77% of GDP (2023 est.)
0.79% of GDP (2022 est.)
0.77% of GDP (2021 est.)
note: personal transfers and compensation between resident and non-resident individuals/households/entities

Public debt: 86.8% of GDP (2014)

Taxes and other revenues: 19.94% (of GDP) (2022 est.)
note: central government tax revenue as a % of GDP

Current account balance: $404.9 billion (2017 est.)
$359.7 billion (2016 est.)

Exports: $9.712 trillion (2023 est.)
$9.478 trillion (2022 est.)
$8.789 trillion (2021 est.)
note: balance of payments - exports of goods and services in current dollars

Exports - partners: US 20%, UK 12%, China 9%, Switzerland 7%, Turkey 4% (2022)
note: top five non-EU export partners based on percentage share of external exports; does not include internal trade among EU member states

Exports - commodities: cars, packaged medicine, refined petroleum, vaccines, vehicle parts/accessories (2022)
note: top five export commodities based on value in dollars; includes both exports to external partners and internal trade among EU member states

Imports: $9.004 trillion (2023 est.)
$9.143 trillion (2022 est.)
$8.103 trillion (2021 est.)
note: balance of payments - imports of goods and services in current dollars

Imports - partners: China 20%, US 11%, UK 8%, Norway 6%, Russia 6% (2022)
note: top five non-EU import partners based on percentage share of external imports; does not include internal trade among EU member states

Imports - commodities: natural gas, crude petroleum, cars, refined petroleum, garments (2022)
note: top five import commodities based on value in dollars; includes both imports from external partners and internal
trade among EU member states

Reserves of foreign exchange and gold: $740.9 billion (31 December 2014 est.)
note: data are for the European Central Bank

Exchange rates: euros (EUR) per US dollar -

Exchange rates: 0.925 (2023 est.)
0.95 (2022 est.)
0.845 (2021 est.)
0.876 (2020 est.)
0.893 (2019 est.)

ENERGY

Electricity access: *electrification - total population:* 100% (2022 est.)

Carbon dioxide emissions: 3.475 billion metric tonnes of CO2 (2015 est.)

COMMUNICATIONS

Telephones - fixed lines: *total subscriptions:* 155.005 million (2022 est.)
subscriptions per 100 inhabitants: 36 (2022 est.)

Telephones - mobile cellular: *total subscriptions:* 552.316 million (2022 est.)
subscriptions per 100 inhabitants: 124 (2022 est.)

Telecommunication systems: note - see individual country entries of member states

Internet country code: .eu; note - see country entries of member states for individual country codes

Internet users: *total:* 389,063,826 (2021 est.)
percent of population: 87% (2021 est.)

Broadband - fixed subscriptions: *total:* 163,772,540 (2020 est.)
subscriptions per 100 inhabitants: 37 (2020 est.)

TRANSPORTATION

National air transport system: *annual passenger traffic on registered air carriers:* 636,860,155 (2018)
annual freight traffic on registered air carriers: 31,730,660,000 (2018)

Airports: 4,585 (2024)

Heliports: 1,755 (2024)

Railways: *total:* 4,894,173 km (2019)

Roadways: *total:* 4,894,173 km (2019) 4,894,173

Waterways: 42,000 km (2017) 42,000 km

MILITARY AND SECURITY

Military and security forces: *the EU's Common Security and Defense Policy (CSDP) provides the civilian, military, and political structures for EU crisis management and security issues; the highest bodies are:*
the Political and Security Committee (PSC), which meets at the ambassadorial level as a preparatory body for the Council of the EU; it assists with defining policies and preparing a crisis response
the European Union Military Committee (EUMC) is the EU's highest military body; it is composed of the chiefs of defense (CHODs) of the Member States, who are regularly represented by their permanent Military Representatives; the EUMC provides the PSC with advice and recommendations on all military matters within the EU
the Committee for Civilian Aspects of Crisis Management (CIVCOM) provides advice and recommendations to the PSC in parallel with the EUMC on civilian aspects of crisis management
the Politico-Military Group (PMG) provides advice and recommendations to the PSC on political aspects of EU military and civil-military issues, including concepts, capabilities and operations and missions, and monitors implementation
other bodies set up under the CSDP include the Security and Defense Policy Directorate (SECDEFPOL), the Integrated approach for Security and Peace Directorate (ISP), the EU Military Staff (EUMS), the Civilian Planning and Conduct Capability (CPCC), the Military Planning and Conduct Capability (MPCC), the European Defense Agency, the European Security and Defense College (ESDC), the EU Institute for Security Studies, and the EU Satellite Center (2024)
note 1: Frontex is the European Border and Coast Guard Agency that supports EU Member States and Schengen-associated countries in the management of the EU's external borders and the fight against cross-border crime; it has a standing corps of uniformed border guard officers directly employed by Frontex as staff members and regularly deployed to border guarding missions, plus thousands of other officers seconded by EU member states
note 2: in 2017, the EU set up the Permanent Structured Cooperation on Defense (PESCO), a mechanism for deepening defense cooperation amongst member states through binding commitments and collaborative programs on a variety of military-related capabilities such as cyber, maritime surveillance, medical support, operational readiness, procurement, and training; similar efforts to promote collaboration and cooperation that same year amongst members included the Military Planning and Conduct Capability (MPCC), the Coordinated Annual Review on Defense (CARD), and the European Defense Fund (EDF)

Military expenditures: 1.8% of GDP (2023 est.)
1.6% of GDP (2022 est.)
1.6% of GDP (2021 est.)
1.6% of GDP (2020 est.)
1.4% of GDP (2019 est.)
note 1: the European Defense Fund (EDF) has a budget of approximately $8 billion for 2021-2027; about $2.7 billion is devoted to funding collaborative defense research while about $5.3 billion is allocated for collaborative capability development projects that complement national contributions; the EDF identifies critical defense domains that it will support
note 2: NATO is resourced through the direct and indirect contributions of its members; NATO's common funds are direct contributions to collective budgets, capabilities and programs, which equate to

only 0.3% of total NATO defense spending (approximately $3.3 billion for 2023) to develop capabilities and run NATO, its military commands, capabilities, and infrastructure; NATO's 2014 Defense Investment Pledge called for NATO members to meet the 2% of GDP guideline for defense spending and the 20% of annual defense expenditure on major new equipment by 2024
note 3: average spending for all NATO countries in 2023 was 2.5% of GDP in 2023 and 2.7% of GDP in 2024

Military and security service personnel strengths: the 27 EU countries have a cumulative total of approximately 1.34 million active-duty troops; the largest EU country military forces belong to France, Germany, and Italy (2023)
note: the combined forces of NATO have approximately 3.3 million active duty personnel

Military deployments: since 2003, the EU has launched more than 30 civilian and military crisis-management, advisory, and training missions in Africa, Asia, Europe, and the Middle East, as well as counter-piracy operations off the coast of Somalia and a naval operation in the Mediterranean to disrupt human smuggling and trafficking networks and prevent the loss of life at sea (2024)
note: in response to the 2022 Russian invasion of Ukraine, the EU announced that it would develop a rapid deployment force consisting of up to 5,000 troops by 2025

Military - note: the EU partners with the North Atlantic Treaty Organization (NATO); NATO is an alliance of 32 countries from North America and Europe; its role is to safeguard the security of its member countries by political and military means; NATO conducts crisis management and peacekeeping missions; member countries that participate in the military aspect of the Alliance contribute forces and equipment, which remain under national command and control until a time when they are required by NATO for a specific purpose (i.e., conflict or crisis, peacekeeping); NATO, however, does possess some common capabilities owned and operated by the Alliance, such as some early warning radar aircraft; relations between NATO and the EU were institutionalized in the early 2000s, building on steps taken during the 1990s to promote greater European responsibility in defense matters; cooperation and coordination covers a broad array of issues, including crisis management, defense and political consultations, civil preparedness, capacity building, military capabilities, maritime security, planning, cyber defense, countering hybrid threats, information sharing, logistics, defense industry, counterterrorism, etc.; since Russia's invasion of Ukraine in February 2022, the EU and NATO have intensified their work and cooperation; NATO and the EU have 23 member countries in common
there are no permanent standing EU forces, but Europe has a variety of multinational military organizations that may be deployed through the EU, in a NATO environment, upon the mandate of the participating countries, or upon the mandate of other international organizations, such as the UN or OSCE including:
EU Battlegroups (BGs) are rapid reaction multinational army units that form a key part of the EU's capacity to respond to crises and conflicts; their deployment is subject to a unanimous decision by the European Council; BGs typically consists of 1,500-2,000 troops organized around an infantry battalion depending on the mission; the troops and equipment are drawn from EU member states and under the direction of a lead nation; two BGs are always on standby for a period of six months; the BGs were declared operational in 2007 but have never been used operationally due to political and financial obstacles
the **European Corps (Eurocorps)** is an independent multinational land force corps headquarters composed of personnel from six framework nations and five associated nations; the corps has no standing operational units; during a crisis, units would be drawn from participating states, and the corps would be placed at the service of the EU and NATO; Eurocorps was established in 1992 by France and Germany; Belgium (1993), Spain (1994), and Luxembourg (1996) joined over the next few years; Poland joined in 2022; Greece and Turkey (since 2002), Italy, Romania, and Austria (since 2009, 2016, and 2021 respectively) participate as associated nations; Eurocorps is headquartered in France
the **European Gendarmerie Force (EURGENDFOR)** is an operational, pre-organized, and rapidly deployable European gendarmerie/police force; it is not established at the EU level, but is capable of performing police tasks, including law enforcement, stability operations, and training in support of the EU, the UN, OSCE, NATO, and other international organizations or ad hoc coalitions; member state gendarmeries include those of France, Italy, the Netherlands, Poland, Portugal, Romania, and Spain; the Lithuanian Public Security Service is a partner, while Turkey's Gendarmerie is an observer force
the **European Medical Corps (EMC)** was set up in the aftermath of the Ebola crisis in West Africa in 2014 to enable the deployment of teams and equipment from EU member states to provide medical assistance and public health expertise in response to emergencies inside and outside the EU; as of 2024, 12 European states had committed teams and equipment to the EMC
the **European Medical Command (EMC)** was formed to provide a standing EU medical capability, increase medical operational readiness, and improve interoperability amongst the participating EU members; it operates closely with the NATO Framework Nations Concept's Multinational Medical Coordination Center (MMCC) under a single administrative and infrastructural framework (MMCC/EMC); the EMC was declared operational in May 2022
the **European Air Transport Command (EATC)** is a single multinational command for more than 150 military air mobility assets from seven member states, including transport, air-to-air refueling, and aeromedical evacuation; the EATC headquarters is located in the Netherlands, but the air assets remain located at member national air bases; the EATC was established in 2010
the **European Air Group (EAG)** is an independent organization formed by the air forces of its seven member nations (Belgium, France, Germany, Italy, Netherlands, Spain, and the UK) that is focused on improving interoperability between the air forces of EAG members and its 14 partner and associate nations; it was established in the late 1990s and is headquartered in the UK
the **European Maritime Force (EUROMARFOR or EMF)** is a four-nation (France, Italy, Portugal, and Spain), non-standing naval force with the ability to carry out naval, air, and amphibious operations; EUROMARFOR was formed in 1995 to conduct missions such as crisis response, humanitarian missions, peacekeeping, peace enforcement, and sea control; it can deploy under EU, NATO, or UN mandate, but also as long as the four partner nations agree
the **Combined Joint Expeditionary Force (CJEF)** is a deployable, combined France-UK military force of up to 10,000 personnel for use in a wide range of crisis scenarios, up to and including high intensity combat operations; the CJEF has no standing forces but would be available at short notice for French-UK bilateral, NATO, EU, UN, or other operations; it was established in 2010 and declared operational in 2020
the **1st German/Netherlands (Dutch) Corps** is a combined army corps headquarters that has the ability to conduct operations under the command and control of Germany and the Netherlands, NATO, or the EU; in peacetime, approximately 1,100 Dutch and German soldiers are assigned, but during a crisis up to 80,000 troops may be assigned; it was formed in 1995 and is headquartered in Germany
the **Lithuanian-Polish-Ukrainian Brigade (LITPOLUKRBRIG)** is comprised of an international staff, three battalions, and specialized units; units affiliated with the multinational brigade remain within the structures of the armed forces of their respective countries until the brigade is activated for participation in an international operation; it was formed in 2014 and is headquartered in Poland
in 2022, the EU approved a new defense strategy (Strategic Compass) designed to increase the bloc's capacity to act, including setting up a **Rapid Deployment Capacity (EU RDC)** consisting of up to 5,000 troops by 2025 (2024)

SPACE

Space agency/agencies: the only EU agency dedicated to space is the EU Agency for the Space Program (EUSPA; established in 2021); the EUSPA originated with the Galileo Joint Undertaking (GJU) set up in 2002 by the European Community (EC) and the European Space Agency (ESA) to manage the development phase of Europe's Galileo satellite navigation program; the GJU's responsibilities were assumed by the European Global Navigation Satellite System Supervisory Authority (GSA) in 2007
the ESA (established 1975 from the European Launcher Development Organization and the European Space Research Organization, which were established in the early 1960s) is an independent organization although it maintains close ties with the EU through an ESA/EC Framework Agreement; the ESA and EC share a joint European Strategy for Space and have together developed a European Space Policy
the ESA has 22 member states; the national bodies responsible for space in these countries sit on ESA's governing Council: Austria, Belgium, Czechia, Denmark, Estonia, Finland, France, Germany, Greece, Hungary, Ireland, Italy, Luxembourg, the Netherlands, Norway, Poland, Portugal, Romania, Spain, Sweden, Switzerland, and the UK; Canada also sits on the Council and takes part in some projects under a Cooperation Agreement; Latvia, Lithuania, Slovakia, and Slovenia are Associate Members; Bulgaria, Croatia, Cyprus, and Malta have cooperation agreements with ESA; ESA has established formal cooperation with all member states of the EU that are not ESA members (2024)

Space launch site(s): ESA's spaceport is located in Kourou, French Guiana; Europe also has or is developing commercial space ports in Italy, Norway, Sweden, and the UK, as well as maritime launch capabilities with a logistics base in Germany (2024)

Space program overview: the EUSPA's mission is to provide a link between European users and space technologies and capabilities, including remote sensing (RS), satellite navigation, and telecommunications; it is responsible for the operational management of the European Geostationary Navigation Overlay Service (EGNOS) and Galileo satellite navigation programs; the EU has a space strategy, which includes encouraging investment in and the use of space services and data, fostering competition and innovation, developing space technologies, and reinforcing Europe's autonomy in accessing space
the ESA is a comprehensive space agency and active across all areas of the space sector outside of launching humans into space, including producing and operating satellites with a full spectrum of capabilities (communications, multipurpose, navigational, RS, science/technology), satellite launch vehicles (SLVs), space launches, human space flight (has an astronaut training program), space transportation/automated transfer vehicles, re-usable spacecraft, space station modules, spacecraft components, robotic space labs, lunar/planetary surface rovers, interplanetary space probes and exploration, space telescopes, research, science, technology development, etc.; ESA also participates in international space programs such as the International Space Station and works closely with Europe's commercial space industry; it also cooperates with a broad range of space agencies and industries of non-member countries, including China, Japan, Russia, and the US; many of its programs are conducted jointly, particularly with the US space program
Europe has a large and advanced commercial space sector capable of developing and producing a full range of capabilities and technologies; a key focus for both the ESA and EUSPA is encouraging the European commercial space sector; Europe is a global leader in satellite-based communications and hosts the headquarters of three of the world's major satellite communications companies (2024)
note: further details about the key activities, programs, and milestones of the country's space program, as well as government spending estimates on the space sector, appear in the Space Programs reference guide

TERRORISM

Terrorist group(s): see individual EU member states

FALKLAND ISLANDS (ISLAS MALVINAS)

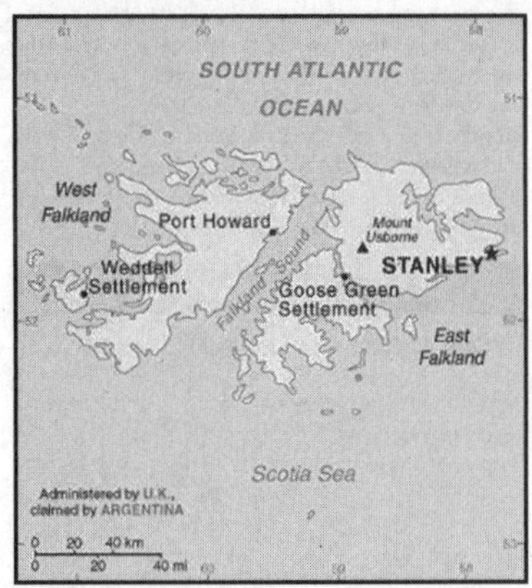

INTRODUCTION

Background: Although first sighted by an English navigator in 1592, the first landing (English) did not occur until almost a century later in 1690, and the first settlement (French) was not established until 1764. The colony was turned over to Spain two years later, and the islands have since been the subject of a territorial dispute, first between Britain and Spain, then between Britain and Argentina. The UK asserted its claim to the islands by establishing a naval garrison there in 1833. Argentina invaded the islands in 1982. The British responded with an expeditionary force and after fierce fighting forced an Argentine surrender on 14 June 1982. With hostilities ended and Argentine forces withdrawn, UK administration resumed. In response to renewed calls from Argentina for Britain to relinquish control of the islands, a referendum was held in 2013 that resulted in 99.8% of the population voting to remain a part of the UK.

GEOGRAPHY

Location: Southern South America, islands in the South Atlantic Ocean, about 500 km east of southern Argentina

Geographic coordinates: 51 45 S, 59 00 W

Map references: South America

Area: *total:* 12,173 sq km
land: 12,173 sq km
water: 0 sq km
note: includes the two main islands of East and West Falkland and about 200 small islands
comparison ranking: total 163

Area - comparative: slightly smaller than Connecticut

Land boundaries: *total:* 0 km

Coastline: 1,288 km

Maritime claims: *territorial sea:* 12 nm
continental shelf: 200 nm
exclusive fishing zone: 200 nm

Climate: cold marine; strong westerly winds, cloudy, humid; rain occurs on more than half of days in year; average annual rainfall is 60 cm in Stanley; occasional snow all year, except in January and February, but typically does not accumulate

Terrain: rocky, hilly, mountainous with some boggy, undulating plains

Elevation: *highest point:* Mount Usborne 705 m
lowest point: Atlantic Ocean 0 m

Natural resources: fish, squid, wildlife, calcified seaweed, sphagnum moss

Land use: *agricultural land:* 92.4% (2018 est.)
arable land: 0% (2018 est.)
permanent crops: 0% (2018 est.)
permanent pasture: 92.4% (2018 est.)
forest: 0% (2018 est.)
other: 7.6% (2018 est.)

Irrigated land: NA

Population distribution: a very small population, with most residents living in and around Stanley

Natural hazards: strong winds persist throughout the year

Geography - note: deeply indented coast provides good natural harbors; short growing season

PEOPLE AND SOCIETY

Population: *total:* 3,662 (2021 est.)
note: data include all persons usually resident in the islands at the time of the 2021 census
comparison ranking: total 228

Nationality: *noun:* Falkland Islander(s)
adjective: Falkland Island

Ethnic groups: Falkland Islander 48.3%, British 23.1%, St. Helenian 7.5%, Chilean 4.6%, mixed 6%, other 8.5%, unspecified 2% (2016 est.)
note: data represent population by national identity

Languages: English 89%, Spanish 7.7%, other 3.3% (2006 est.)

Religions: Christian 57.1%, other 1.6%, none 35.4%, unspecified 6% (2016 est.)

Dependency ratios: *total dependency ratio:* 39.8
youth dependency ratio: 24.8
elderly dependency ratio: 14.9
potential support ratio: 6.7 (2021)

Population growth rate: 0.01% (2014 est.)
comparison ranking: 193

Birth rate: 10.9 births/1,000 population (2012 est.)
comparison ranking: 166

Death rate: 4.9 deaths/1,000 population (2012 est.)
comparison ranking: 201

Population distribution: a very small population, with most residents living in and around Stanley

Urbanization: *urban population:* 79.7% of total population (2023)
rate of urbanization: 0.53% annual rate of change (2020-25 est.)

Major urban areas - population: 2,000 STANLEY (capital) (2018)

Sex ratio: *total population:* 1.12 male(s)/female (2016 est.)

Life expectancy at birth: *total population:* (2017 est.) 77.9
male: 75.6
female: 79.6

Drinking water source: *improved: urban:* 100% of population
rural: 78.2% of population
total: 95.3% of population
unimproved: urban: 0% of population
rural: 21.8% of population
total: 4.7% of population (2020)

Sanitation facility access: *improved: urban:* 100% of population
rural: 100% of population
total: 100% of population
unimproved: urban: 0% of population
rural: 0% of population
total: 0% of population (2020)

Currently married women (ages 15-49): 44.8% (2023 est.)

ENVIRONMENT

Environment - current issues: overfishing by unlicensed vessels is a problem; reindeer - introduced to the islands in 2001 from South Georgia - are part of a farming effort to produce specialty meat and diversify the islands' economy; this is the only commercial reindeer herd in the world unaffected by the 1986 Chornobyl disaster; grazing threatens important habitats including tussac grass and its ecosystem with penguins and sea lions; soil erosion from fires

Climate: cold marine; strong westerly winds, cloudy, humid; rain occurs on more than half of days in year; average annual rainfall is 60 cm in Stanley; occasional snow all year, except in January and February, but typically does not accumulate

Urbanization: *urban population:* 79.7% of total population (2023)
rate of urbanization: 0.53% annual rate of change (2020-25 est.)

GOVERNMENT

Country name: *conventional long form:* none
conventional short form: Falkland Islands (Islas Malvinas)
etymology: the archipelago takes its name from the Falkland Sound, the strait separating the two main islands; the channel itself was named after the Viscount of FALKLAND, who sponsored an expedition to the islands in 1690; the Spanish name for the archipelago derives from the French "Iles Malouines," meaning Islands of Malo, the name applied to the islands by French explorer Louis-Antoine de BOUGAINVILLE in 1764 after the port of Saint-Malo

Government type: parliamentary democracy (Legislative Assembly); self-governing overseas territory of the UK

Dependency status: overseas territory of the UK; also claimed by Argentina

Capital: *name:* Stanley
geographic coordinates: 51 42 S, 57 51 W
time difference: UTC-4 (1 hour ahead of Washington, DC, during Standard Time)
etymology: named after Edward SMITH-STANLEY (1799-1869), the 14th Earl of Derby, a British statesman and threetime prime minister of the UK who never visited the islands

Administrative divisions: none (administered by the UK; claimed by Argentina)

Independence: none (overseas territory of the UK; also claimed by Argentina)

National holiday: Liberation Day, 14 June (1982)

Legal system: English common law and local statutes

Constitution: *history:* previous 1985; latest entered into force 1 January 2009 (The Falkland Islands Constitution Order 2008)

Citizenship: see United Kingdom

Suffrage: 18 years of age; universal

Executive branch: *chief of state:* King CHARLES III (since 8 September 2022); represented by Governor Alison BLAKE (since 23 July 2022)
head of government: Chief Executive Andy KEELING (since April 2021)
cabinet: Executive Council elected by the Legislative Council
elections/appointments: the monarchy is hereditary; governor appointed by the monarch; chief executive appointed by the governor

Legislative branch: *description:* unicameral Legislative Assembly, formerly the Legislative Council (10 seats; 5 members directly elected from the Stanley constituency and 3 members from the Camp constituency, both by simple majority vote, 2 appointed non-voting ex-officio members - the chief executive, appointed by the governor, and the financial secretary; the attorney general and Commander British Forces South Atlantic Islands are also invited to attend; members serve 4-year terms)
elections: last held on 4 November 2021 (next to be held in November 2025)
election results: percent of vote - NA; seats - independent 8; composition of elected members - men 6, women 2, percentage women 25% (does not include speaker)

Judicial branch: *highest court(s):* Court of Appeal (consists of the court president, the chief justice as an ex officio non-resident member, and 2 justices of appeal); Supreme Court (consists of the chief justice); note - appeals beyond the Court of Appeal are referred to the Judicial Committee of the Privy Council (in London)
judge selection and term of office: chief justice, court of appeal president, and justices appointed by the governor; tenure specified in each justice's instrument of appointment
subordinate courts: Magistrate's Court (senior magistrate presides over civil and criminal divisions); Court of Summary Jurisdiction

Political parties: none; all independents

International organization participation: UPU

Diplomatic representation in the US: none (administered by the UK; claimed by Argentina)

Diplomatic representation from the US: *embassy:* none (administered by the UK; claimed by Argentina)

Flag description: blue with the flag of the UK in the upper hoist-side quadrant and the Falkland Island coat of arms centered on the outer half of the flag; the coat of arms contains a white ram (sheep raising was once the major economic activity) above the sailing ship Desire (whose crew discovered the islands) with a scroll at the bottom bearing the motto DESIRE THE RIGHT

National symbol(s): ram

National anthem: *name:* "Song of the Falklands"
lyrics/music: Christopher LANHAM
note: adopted 1930s; the song is the local unofficial anthem; as a territory of the United Kingdom, "God Save the King" is official (see United Kingdom)

ECONOMY

Economic overview: British South American territorial economy; longstanding fishing industry; surging tourism prior to COVID-19 and Brexit; recent offshore hydrocarbon discoveries threaten ecotourism industries; no central bank and must have British approval on currency shifts

Real GDP (purchasing power parity): $206.4 million (2015 est.)
$164.5 million (2014 est.)
comparison ranking: 220

Real GDP growth rate: 25.5% (2015 est.)
-1.8% (2014 est.)
comparison ranking: 3

Real GDP per capita: $70,800 (2015 est.)
$63,000 (2014 est.)
comparison ranking: 17

GDP (official exchange rate): $206.4 million (2015 est.)

Inflation rate (consumer prices): 1.4% (2014 est.)
comparison ranking: 26

GDP - composition, by sector of origin: *agriculture:* 41% (2015 est.)
industry: 20.6% (2015 est.)
services: 38.4% (2015 est.)
comparison rankings: services 200; industry 133; agriculture 3

Agricultural products: fodder and vegetable crops; venison, sheep, dairy products; fish, squid

Industries: fish and wool processing; tourism

Labor force: 1,850 (2016 est.)
comparison ranking: 206

Unemployment rate: 1% (2016 est.)
comparison ranking: 6

Gini Index coefficient - distribution of family income: 36 (2015)
comparison ranking: 70

Public debt: 0% of GDP (2015 est.)
comparison ranking: 206

Exports: $257.3 million (2015 est.)
comparison ranking: 200

Exports - partners: Spain 70%, Morocco 9%, US 8%, Namibia 5%, Germany 2% (2022)
note: top five export partners based on percentage share of exports

Exports - commodities: shellfish, fish, wool, sheep and goat meat, surveying equipment (2022)
note: top five export commodities based on value in dollars

Imports - partners: UK 73%, Spain 24%, Netherlands 1%, Ireland 0%, Switzerland 0% (2022)
note: top five import partners based on percentage share of imports

Imports - commodities: refined petroleum, prefabricated buildings, aircraft, plastic products, iron structures (2022)
note: top five import commodities based on value in dollars

Exchange rates: Falkland pounds (FKP) per US dollar -

Exchange rates: 0.805 (2023 est.)
0.811 (2022 est.)
0.727 (2021)
0.78 (2020 est.)
0.783 (2019 est.)

ENERGY

Electricity: *installed generating capacity:* 10,000 kW (2022 est.)
consumption: 19.957 million kWh (2022 est.)
transmission/distribution losses: 900,000 kWh (2022 est.)
comparison rankings: transmission/distribution losses 3; consumption 208; installed generating capacity 208

Electricity generation sources: *fossil fuels:* 67.9% of total installed capacity (2022 est.)
wind: 32.1% of total installed capacity (2022 est.)

Petroleum: *refined petroleum consumption:* 300 bbl/day (2022 est.)

Carbon dioxide emissions: 38,000 metric tonnes of CO_2 (2022 est.)
from petroleum and other liquids: 38,000 metric tonnes of CO_2 (2022 est.)
comparison ranking: total emissions 213

Energy consumption per capita: (2019 est.)

COMMUNICATIONS

Telephones - fixed lines: *total subscriptions:* 2,000 (2021 est.)
subscriptions per 100 inhabitants: 53 (2021 est.)
comparison ranking: total subscriptions 218

Telephones - mobile cellular: *total subscriptions:* 6,000 (2021 est.)
subscriptions per 100 inhabitants: 160 (2021 est.)
comparison ranking: total subscriptions 221

Telecommunication systems: *general assessment:* the replacement of the rural internet and phone system was delayed due to COVID; upgrades started at the end of 2019, this included the replacement of all Multi Service Access Nodes (MSANs), the technology used to connect larger settlements; in early 2020 a new system to replace the WiMAX system (the technology used to connect smaller settlements and households) had been delayed as well due to COVID-19; once the equipment is received it will be installed in the largest base stations on East Falklands: Malo, Bombilla, and Mt Pleasant peak
"We also have MSAN equipment and radio links due to arrive towards the end of this month, and these and will be installed at Chartres, New Island, Sea Lion Island, Onion Range, Sand Bay, and Mare Harbour enabling us to migrate additional customers from the existing WiMAX network and also releasing equipment for spares." (2020)
domestic: fixed-line subscriptions approximately 53 per 100, 160 per 100 for mobile-cellular (2021)
international: country code - 500; satellite earth station - 1 Intelsat (Atlantic Ocean) with links through London to other countries (2015)

Broadcast media: TV service provided by a multi-channel service provider; radio services provided by the public broadcaster, Falkland Islands Radio Service, broadcasting on both AM and FM frequencies, and by the British Forces Broadcasting Service (BFBS) (2007)

Internet country code: .fk

Internet users: *total:* 3,762 (2021 est.)

percent of population: 99% (2021 est.)
comparison ranking: total 225

Broadband - fixed subscriptions: *total:* 1,000 (2020 est.)
subscriptions per 100 inhabitants: 33 (2020 est.)
comparison ranking: total 208

TRANSPORTATION

National air transport system: *number of registered air carriers:* 1 (2020)
inventory of registered aircraft operated by air carriers: 5

Civil aircraft registration country code prefix: VP-F

Airports: 34 (2024)
comparison ranking: 113

Roadways: *total:* 440 km
paved: 50 km
unpaved: 390 km (2008)
comparison ranking: total 198

Merchant marine: *total:* 2 (2023)
by type: general cargo 1, other 1
comparison ranking: total 180

Ports: *total ports:* 1 (2024)
large: 0
medium: 1
small: 0
very small: 0
ports with oil terminals: 1
key ports: Stanley

MILITARY AND SECURITY

Military and security forces: no regular military forces

Military - note: defense is the responsibility of the UK, which maintains a military presence on the islands

FAROE ISLANDS

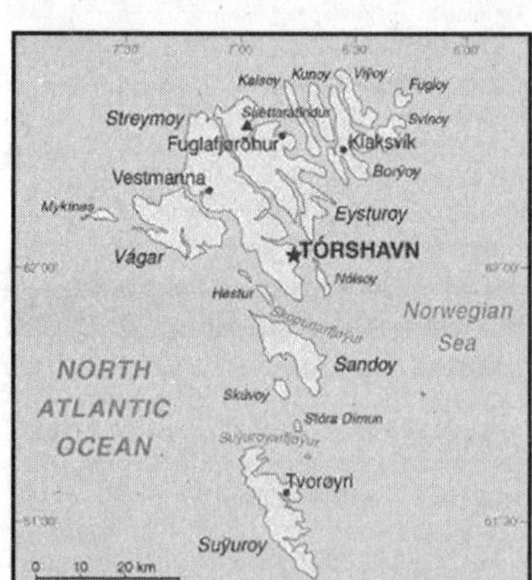

INTRODUCTION

Background: The Faroe Islands were already populated by about A.D. 500, but whether the original settlers were Celtic or early Norse (or someone else) has yet to be determined. Viking settlers arrived on the islands in the 9th century, and the islands served as an important stepping stone for medieval Viking exploration of the North Atlantic. The islands have been connected politically to Denmark since the 14th century, and today the Faroe Islands are a self-governing dependency of Denmark. The Home Rule Act of 1948 granted a high degree of self-government to the Faroese, who have autonomy over most internal affairs and external trade, while Denmark is responsible for justice, defense, and some foreign affairs. The Faroe Islands are not part of the European Union.

GEOGRAPHY

Location: Northern Europe, island group between the Norwegian Sea and the North Atlantic Ocean, about halfway between Iceland and Norway

Geographic coordinates: 62 00 N, 7 00 W

Map references: Europe

Area: *total:* 1,393 sq km
land: 1,393 sq km
water: 0 sq km (some lakes and streams)
comparison ranking: total 182

Area - comparative: eight times the size of Washington, DC

Land boundaries: *total:* 0 km

Coastline: 1,117 km

Maritime claims: *territorial sea:* 12 nm
continental shelf: 200 nm or agreed boundaries or median line
exclusive fishing zone: 200 nm or agreed boundaries or median line

Climate: mild winters, cool summers; usually overcast; foggy, windy

Terrain: rugged, rocky, some low peaks; cliffs along most of coast

Elevation: *highest point:* Slaettaratindur 882 m
lowest point: Atlantic Ocean 0 m

Natural resources: fish, whales, hydropower, possible oil and gas

Land use: *agricultural land:* 2.1% (2018 est.)
arable land: 2.1% (2018 est.)
permanent crops: 0% (2018 est.)
permanent pasture: 0% (2018 est.)
forest: 0.1% (2018 est.)
other: 97.8% (2018 est.)

Population distribution: the island of Streymoy is by far the most populous with over 40% of the population; it has approximately twice as many inhabitants as Eysturoy, the second most populous island; seven of the inhabited islands have fewer than 100 people

Natural hazards: strong winds and heavy rains can occur throughout the year

Geography - note: archipelago of 17 inhabited islands and one uninhabited island, and a few uninhabited islets; strategically located along important sea lanes in northeastern Atlantic; precipitous terrain limits habitation to small coastal lowlands

PEOPLE AND SOCIETY

Population: *total:* 52,933
male: 27,400
female: 25,533 (2024 est.)
comparison rankings: female 208; male 208; total 208

Nationality: *noun:* Faroese (singular and plural)
adjective: Faroese

Ethnic groups: Faroese 83.8% (Scandinavian and Anglo-Saxon descent), Danish 8.3%, Filipino 1.2%, other Nordic 0.9%, other 4.5% (includes Polish and Romanian) (2024 est.)
note: data represent respondents by country of birth

Languages: Faroese 93.8% (derived from Old Norse), Danish 3.2%, other 3% (2011 est.)
note: data represent population by primary language

Religions: Christian 87% (predominantly Evangelical Lutheran), other 0.9%, none 3.7%, unspecified 8.9% (2011 est.)

Age structure: *0-14 years:* 20% (male 5,489/female 5,122)
15-64 years: 61.5% (male 17,188/female 15,346)
65 years and over: 18.5% (2024 est.) (male 4,723/female 5,065)

Dependency ratios: *total dependency ratio:* 62.8
youth dependency ratio: 33.6
elderly dependency ratio: 29.1
potential support ratio: 3.4 (2021)

Median age: *total:* 36.8 years (2024 est.)
male: 36.9 years
female: 36.8 years
comparison ranking: total 86

Population growth rate: 0.63% (2024 est.)
comparison ranking: 135

Birth rate: 14.9 births/1,000 population (2024 est.)
comparison ranking: 114

Death rate: 8.6 deaths/1,000 population (2024 est.)
comparison ranking: 70

Net migration rate: 0 migrant(s)/1,000 population (2024 est.)
comparison ranking: 93

Population distribution: the island of Streymoy is by far the most populous with over 40% of the population; it has approximately twice as many inhabitants as Eysturoy, the second most populous island; seven of the inhabited islands have fewer than 100 people

Urbanization: *urban population:* 43% of total population (2023)
rate of urbanization: 0.89% annual rate of change (2020-25 est.)

Major urban areas - population: 21,000 TORSHAVN (capital) (2018)

Sex ratio: *at birth:* 1.07 male(s)/female
0-14 years: 1.07 male(s)/female
15-64 years: 1.12 male(s)/female
65 years and over: 0.93 male(s)/female
total population: 1.07 male(s)/female (2024 est.)

Infant mortality rate: *total:* 5.7 deaths/1,000 live births (2024 est.)
male: 6.3 deaths/1,000 live births
female: 5.1 deaths/1,000 live births
comparison ranking: total 171

Life expectancy at birth: *total population:* 81.7 years (2024 est.)
male: 79.2 years
female: 84.4 years
comparison ranking: total population 42

Total fertility rate: 2.27 children born/woman (2024 est.)
comparison ranking: 79

Gross reproduction rate: 1.09 (2024 est.)

Drinking water source: *improved:*
total: 100% of population

Physician density: 2.62 physicians/1,000 population (2016)

Hospital bed density: 4.2 beds/1,000 population (2016)

Currently married women (ages 15-49): 34.8% (2023 est.)

Education expenditures: 7.6% of GDP (2019 est.)
comparison ranking: 14

ENVIRONMENT

Environment - current issues: coastal erosion, landslides and rockfalls, flash flooding, wind storms; oil spills

Climate: mild winters, cool summers; usually overcast; foggy, windy

Urbanization: *urban population:* 43% of total population (2023)
rate of urbanization: 0.89% annual rate of change (2020-25 est.)

Revenue from forest resources: 0% of GDP (2017 est.)
comparison ranking: 201

Air pollutants: *carbon dioxide emissions:* 0.63 megatons (2016 est.)

Waste and recycling: *municipal solid waste generated annually:* 61,000 tons (2014 est.)
municipal solid waste recycled annually: 40,870 tons (2012 est.)
percent of municipal solid waste recycled: 67% (2012 est.)

Total renewable water resources: 0 cubic meters (2017 est.)

GOVERNMENT

Country name: *conventional long form:* none
conventional short form: Faroe Islands
local long form: none
local short form: Foroyar
etymology: the archipelago's name may derive from the Old Norse word "faer," meaning sheep

Government type: parliamentary democracy (Faroese Parliament); part of the Kingdom of Denmark

Dependency status: part of the Kingdom of Denmark; self-governing overseas administrative division of Denmark since 1948

Capital: *name:* Torshavn
geographic coordinates: 62 00 N, 6 46 W
time difference: UTC 0 (5 hours ahead of Washington, DC, during Standard Time)
daylight saving time: +1hr, begins last Sunday in March; ends last Sunday in October
etymology: the meaning in Danish is "Thor's harbor"

Administrative divisions: part of the Kingdom of Denmark; self-governing overseas administrative division of Denmark; there are 29 first-order municipalities (kommunur, singular - kommuna) Eidhi, Eystur, Famjin, Fuglafjordhur, Fugloy, Hov, Husavik, Hvalba, Hvannasund, Klaksvik, Kunoy, Kvivik, Nes, Porkeri, Runavik, Sandur, Sjovar, Skalavik, Skopun, Skuvoy, Sorvagur, Sumba, Sunda, Torshavn, Tvoroyri, Vagar, Vagur, Vestmanna, Vidhareidhi

Independence: none (part of the Kingdom of Denmark; self-governing overseas administrative division of Denmark)

National holiday: Olaifest (Olavsoka) (commemorates the death in battle of King OLAF II of Norway, later St. OLAF), 29 July (1030)

Legal system: the laws of Denmark apply where applicable

Constitution: *history:* 5 June 1953 (Danish Constitution), 23 March 1948 (Home Rule Act), and 24 June 2005 (Takeover Act) serve as the Faroe Islands' constitutional position in the Unity of the Realm
amendments: see entry for Denmark

Citizenship: see Denmark

Suffrage: 18 years of age; universal

Executive branch: *chief of state:* King FREDERIK X of Denmark (since 14 January 2024), represented by High Commissioner Lene Moyell JOHANSEN, chief administrative officer (since 15 May 2017) (2024)
head of government: Prime Minister Aksel V. JOHANNESEN (since 22 December 2022)
cabinet: Landsstyri appointed by the prime minister
elections/appointments: the monarchy is hereditary; high commissioner appointed by the monarch; following legislative elections, the leader of the majority party or majority coalition usually elected prime minister by the Faroese Parliament; election last held on 8 December 2022 (next to be held in 2026)

Legislative branch: *description:* unicameral Faroese Parliament or Logting (33 seats; members directly elected in a single nationwide constituency by proportional representation vote; members serve 4-year terms) the Faroe Islands elect 2 members to the Danish Parliament to serve 4-year terms
elections: Faroese Parliament - last held on 8 December 2022 (next to be held in 2026)
Faroese seats in the Danish Parliament last held on 31 October 2022 (next to be held no later than 31 October 2026)
election results: Faroese Parliament percent of vote by party - JF 26.6%, B 20%, A 18.9%, E 17.7%, F 7.5%, H 6.6%, seats by party - JF 9, B 7, A 6, E 6, F 3, H 2; composition - men 24, women 9; percentage women 27.3%
Faroese seats in Danish Parliament - percent of vote by party - NA; seats by party - JF 1, B 1; composition - men 2, women 0; percentage women 0%

Judicial branch: *highest court(s):* Faroese Court or Raett (Rett - Danish) decides both civil and criminal cases; the Court is part of the Danish legal system
subordinate courts: Court of the First Instance or Tribunal de Premiere Instance; Court of Administrative Law or Tribunal Administratif; Mixed Commercial Court; Land Court

Political parties: Center Party or H (Midflokkurin)
People's Party or A (Folkaflokkurin)
Progress Party or F (Framsokn)
Republic or E (Tjodveldi) (formerly the Republican Party)
Self-Government Party or D (Sjalvstyri or Sjalvstyrisflokkurin)
Social Democratic Party or JF (Javnadarflokkurin) or JF
Union Party or B (Sambandsflokkurin)

International organization participation: Arctic Council, IMO (associate), NC, NIB, UNESCO (associate), UPU

Diplomatic representation in the US: none (self-governing overseas administrative division of Denmark)

Diplomatic representation from the US: *embassy:* none (self-governing overseas administrative division of Denmark)

Flag description: white with a red cross outlined in blue extending to the edges of the flag; the vertical part of the cross is shifted toward the hoist side in the style of the Dannebrog (Danish flag); referred to as Merkid, meaning "the banner" or "the mark," the flag resembles those of neighboring Iceland and Norway, and uses the same three colors - but in a different sequence; white represents the clear Faroese sky, as well as the foam of the waves; red and blue are traditional Faroese colors
note: the blue on the flag is a lighter blue (azure) than that found on the flags of Iceland or Norway

National symbol(s): ram; national colors: red, white, blue

National anthem: *name:* "Mitt alfagra land" (My Fairest Land)
lyrics/music: Simun av SKAROI/Peter ALBERG
note: adopted 1948; the anthem is also known as "Tu alfagra land mitt" (Thou Fairest Land of Mine); as a self-governing overseas administrative division of Denmark, the Faroe Islands are permitted their own national anthem

ECONOMY

Economic overview: high-income Danish territorial economy; party neither to the EU nor the Schengen Area; associate Nordic Council member; very low unemployment; unique foreign ownership allowance in fishing industry; known salmon exporter; growing IT industries

Real GDP (purchasing power parity): $3.798 billion (2022 est.)
$3.603 billion (2021 est.)
$3.407 billion (2020 est.)
note: data in 2021 dollars
comparison ranking: 193

Real GDP growth rate: 5.4% (2022 est.)
5.76% (2021 est.)
-1.93% (2020 est.)
note: annual GDP % growth based on constant local currency
comparison ranking: 39

Real GDP per capita: $71,500 (2022 est.)
$68,100 (2021 est.)
$65,000 (2020 est.)
note: data in 2021 dollars
comparison ranking: 16

GDP (official exchange rate): $3.556 billion (2022 est.)
note: data in current dollars at official exchange rate

Inflation rate (consumer prices): -0.3% (2016)
-1.7% (2015)

comparison ranking: 4

GDP - composition, by sector of origin: *agriculture:* 18.7% (2022 est.)
industry: 18.1% (2022 est.)
services: 52.3% (2022 est.)
note: figures may not total 100% due to non-allocated consumption not captured in sector-reported data
comparison rankings: services 130; industry 152; agriculture 41

GDP - composition, by end use: *household consumption:* 41.4% (2022 est.)
government consumption: 27.4% (2022 est.)
investment in fixed capital: 31.4% (2022 est.)
exports of goods and services: 62.4% (2022 est.)
imports of goods and services: -62.5% (2022 est.)
note: figures may not total 100% due to rounding or gaps in data collection

Agricultural products: milk, potatoes, lamb/mutton, sheepskins, sheep offal, beef, sheep fat, beef offal, cattle hides, beef suet (2022)
note: top ten agricultural products based on tonnage

Industries: fishing, fish processing, tourism, small ship repair and refurbishment, handicrafts

Industrial production growth rate: 4.3% (2014 est.)
note: annual % change in industrial value added based on constant local currency
comparison ranking: 70

Labor force: 27,540 (2017 est.)
comparison ranking: 198

Unemployment rate: 2.2% (2017 est.)
3.4% (2016 est.)
comparison ranking: 23

Population below poverty line: 10% (2015 est.)

Remittances: 4.45% of GDP (2022 est.)
4.33% of GDP (2021 est.)
4.86% of GDP (2020 est.)
note: personal transfers and compensation between resident and non-resident individuals/households/entities

Public debt: 35% of GDP (2014 est.)
comparison ranking: 155

Taxes and other revenues: 30.2% (of GDP) (2014 est.)
comparison ranking: 24

Exports: $2.219 billion (2022 est.)
$1.923 billion (2021 est.)
$1.552 billion (2020 est.)
note: GDP expenditure basis - exports of goods and services in current dollars
comparison ranking: 163

Exports - partners: Russia 26.4%, UK 14.1%, Germany 8.4%, China 7.9%, Spain 6.8%, Denmark 6.2%, US 4.7%, Poland 4.4%, Norway 4.1% (2017)

Exports - commodities: fish and fish products (2021)

Imports: $2.223 billion (2022 est.)
$1.906 billion (2021 est.)
$1.597 billion (2020 est.)
note: GDP expenditure basis - imports of goods and services in current dollars
comparison ranking: 174

Imports - partners: Denmark 33%, China 10.7%, Germany 7.6%, Poland 6.8%, Norway 6.7%, Ireland 5%, Chile 4.3% (2017)

Imports - commodities: goods for household consumption, machinery and transport equipment, fuels, raw materials and semi-manufactures, cars

Exchange rates: Danish kroner (DKK) per US dollar -

Exchange rates: 6.89 (2023 est.)
7.076 (2022 est.)
6.287 (2021 est.)
6.542 (2020 est.)
6.669 (2019 est.)

ENERGY

Electricity access: *electrification - total population:* 100% (2022 est.)
electrification - urban areas: 99.9%
electrification - rural areas: 100%

Electricity: *installed generating capacity:* 178,000 kW (2022 est.)
consumption: 394.337 million kWh (2022 est.)
transmission/distribution losses: 25.063 million kWh (2022 est.)
comparison rankings: transmission/distribution losses 28; consumption 180; installed generating capacity 175

Electricity generation sources: *fossil fuels:* 62.6% of total installed capacity (2022 est.)
wind: 11.2% of total installed capacity (2022 est.)
hydroelectricity: 26.2% of total installed capacity (2022 est.)

Coal: *imports:* (2022 est.) less than 1 metric ton

Petroleum: *refined petroleum consumption:* 5,000 bbl/day (2022 est.)

Carbon dioxide emissions: 825,000 metric tonnes of CO_2 (2022 est.)
from petroleum and other liquids: 825,000 metric tonnes of CO_2 (2022 est.)
comparison ranking: total emissions 174

Energy consumption per capita: (2019)

COMMUNICATIONS

Telephones - fixed lines: *total subscriptions:* 15,000 (2021 est.)
subscriptions per 100 inhabitants: 29 (2021 est.)
comparison ranking: total subscriptions 181

Telephones - mobile cellular: *total subscriptions:* 59,000 (2021 est.)
subscriptions per 100 inhabitants: 112 (2021 est.)
comparison ranking: total subscriptions 205

Telecommunication systems: *general assessment:* the Faroe Islands have a highly developed communication network, which covers the whole country; from telecommunication and mobile phones to the internet and media, the Faroe Islands are at the forefront of modern communications technology; working within the special geographic circumstances of the Faroe Islands; companies have become world experts in providing digital communication solutions to remote and sparsely populated areas (2022)
domestic: 29 per 100 teledensity for fixed-line and nearly 110 per 100 for mobile-cellular (2021)
international: country code - 298; landing points for the SHEFA-2, FARICE-1, and CANTAT-3 fiber-optic submarine cables from the Faroe Islands, to Denmark, Germany, UK and Iceland; satellite earth stations - 1 Orion; (2019)

Broadcast media: 1 publicly owned TV station; the Faroese telecommunications company distributes local and international channels through its digital terrestrial network; publicly owned radio station supplemented by 3 privately owned stations broadcasting over multiple frequencies

Internet country code: .fo

Internet users: *total:* 51,728 (2021 est.)
percent of population: 97.6% (2021 est.)
comparison ranking: total 201

Broadband - fixed subscriptions: *total:* 18,443 (2020 est.)
subscriptions per 100 inhabitants: 38 (2020 est.)
comparison ranking: total 169

TRANSPORTATION

National air transport system: *number of registered air carriers:* 1 (2020) (registered in Denmark)
inventory of registered aircraft operated by air carriers: 3 (registered in Denmark)

Civil aircraft registration country code prefix: OY-H

Airports: 1 (2024)
comparison ranking: 228

Heliports: 12 (2024)

Roadways: *total:* 960 km
paved: 500 km
unpaved: 460 km (2017)
note: those islands not connected by roads (bridges or tunnels) are connected by seven different ferry links operated by the nationally owned company SSL; 28 km of tunnels
comparison ranking: total 188

Merchant marine: *total:* 91 (2023)
by type: container ships 6, general cargo 45, other 40
comparison ranking: total 95

Ports: *total ports:* 9 (2024)
large: 0
medium: 0
small: 0
very small: 9
ports with oil terminals: 5
key ports: Fuglafjordur, Klaksvik, Kongshavn, Runavik, Sorvagur, Torshavn, Tvoroyri, Vagur, Vestmanna

MILITARY AND SECURITY

Military and security forces: no regular military forces or conscription

Military - note: the Government of Denmark has responsibility for defense; as such, the Danish military's Joint Arctic Command in Nuuk, Greenland is responsible for coordinating the defense of the Faroe Islands; the Joint Arctic Command has a contact element in the capital of Torshavn

FIJI

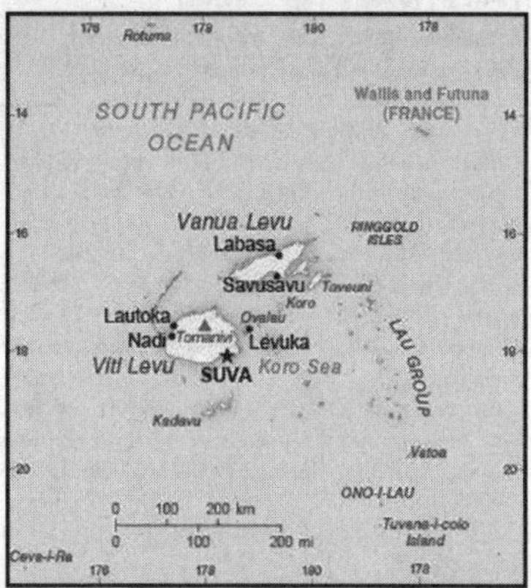

INTRODUCTION

Background: Austronesians settled Fiji around 1000 B.C., followed by successive waves of Melanesians starting around the first century A.D. Fijians traded with Polynesian groups in Samoa and Tonga, and by about 900, much of Fiji was in the Tu'i Tongan Empire's sphere of influence. The Tongan influence declined significantly by 1200, while Melanesian seafarers continued to periodically arrive in Fiji, further mixing Melanesian and Polynesian cultural traditions. The first European spotted Fiji in 1643 and by the 1800s, European merchants, missionaries, traders, and whalers frequented the islands. Rival kings and chiefs competed for power, at times aided by Europeans, and in 1865, Seru Epenisa CAKOBAU united many groups into the Confederacy of Independent Kingdoms of Viti. The arrangement proved weak, however, and in 1871 CAKOBAU formed the Kingdom of Fiji in an attempt to centralize power. Fearing a hostile takeover by a foreign power as the kingdom's economy began to falter, CAKOBAU ceded Fiji to the UK in 1874.

The first British governor set up a plantation-style economy and brought in more than 60,000 Indians as indentured laborers, most of whom chose to stay in Fiji rather than return to India when their contracts expired. In the early 1900s, society was divided along ethnic lines, with iTaukei (indigenous Fijians), Europeans, and Indo-Fijians living in separate areas and maintaining their own languages and traditions. ITaukei fears of an Indo-Fijian takeover of government delayed independence through the 1960s; Fiji achieved independence in 1970 with agreements to allocate parliamentary seats by ethnic groups. After two coups in 1987, a new constitution in 1990 cemented iTaukei control of politics, leading thousands of Indo-Fijians to leave. A reformed constitution in 1997 was more equitable and led to the election of an Indo-Fijian prime minister in 1999, who was ousted in a coup the following year. In 2005, the new prime minister put forward a bill that would grant pardons to the coup perpetrators, leading Josaia Voreqe "Frank" BAINIMARAMA to launch a coup in 2006. BAINIMARAMA appointed himself prime minister in 2007 and retained the position after elections in 2014 and 2018 that international observers deemed credible. BAINIMARAMA's party lost control of the prime minister position after elections in 2022 with former opposition leader Sitiveni Ligamamada RABUKA winning the office by a narrow margin.

GEOGRAPHY

Location: Oceania, island group in the South Pacific Ocean, about two-thirds of the way from Hawaii to New Zealand

Geographic coordinates: 18 00 S, 175 00 E

Map references: Oceania

Area: *total:* 18,274 sq km
land: 18,274 sq km
water: 0 sq km
comparison ranking: total 156

Area - comparative: slightly smaller than New Jersey

Land boundaries: *total:* 0 km

Coastline: 1,129 km

Maritime claims: *territorial sea:* 12 nm
contiguous zone: 24 nm
exclusive economic zone: 200 nm
continental shelf: 200-m depth or to the depth of exploitation
measured from claimed archipelagic straight baselines

Climate: tropical marine; only slight seasonal temperature variation

Terrain: mostly mountains of volcanic origin

Elevation: *highest point:* Tomanivi 1,324 m
lowest point: Pacific Ocean 0 m

Natural resources: timber, fish, gold, copper, offshore oil potential, hydropower

Land use: *agricultural land:* 23.3% (2018 est.)
arable land: 9% (2018 est.)
permanent crops: 4.7% (2018 est.)
permanent pasture: 9.6% (2018 est.)
forest: 55.7% (2018 est.)
other: 21% (2018 est.)

Irrigated land: 40 sq km (2012)

Population distribution: approximately 70% of the population lives on the island of Viti Levu; roughly half of the population lives in urban areas

Natural hazards: cyclonic storms can occur from November to January

Geography - note: consists of 332 islands, approximately 110 of which are inhabited, and more than 500 islets

PEOPLE AND SOCIETY

Population: *total:* 951,611
male: 482,304
female: 469,307 (2024 est.)
comparison rankings: female 163; male 162; total 163

Nationality: *noun:* Fijian(s)
adjective: Fijian

Ethnic groups: iTaukei 56.8% (predominantly Melanesian with a Polynesian admixture), Indo-Fijian 37.5%, Rotuman 1.2%, other 4.5% (European, part European, other Pacific Islanders, Chinese) (2007 est.)
note: a 2010 law replaces 'Fijian' with 'iTaukei' when referring to the original and native settlers of Fiji

Languages: English (official), iTaukei (official), Fiji Hindi (official)

Religions: Protestant 45% (Methodist 34.6%, Assembly of God 5.7%, Seventh Day Adventist 3.9%, and Anglican 0.8%), Hindu 27.9%, other Christian 10.4%, Roman Catholic 9.1%, Muslim 6.3%, Sikh 0.3%, other 0.3%, none 0.8% (2007 est.)

Age structure: *0-14 years:* 24.7% (male 119,910/female 114,904)
15-64 years: 66.4% (male 323,339/female 308,921)
65 years and over: 8.9% (2024 est.) (male 39,055/female 45,482)

Dependency ratios: *total dependency ratio:* 53
youth dependency ratio: 44.2
elderly dependency ratio: 8.7
potential support ratio: 11.4 (2021 est.)

Median age: *total:* 31.6 years (2024 est.)
male: 31.4 years
female: 31.8 years
comparison ranking: total 124

Population growth rate: 0.4% (2024 est.)
comparison ranking: 157

Birth rate: 15.9 births/1,000 population (2024 est.)
comparison ranking: 99

Death rate: 6.5 deaths/1,000 population (2024 est.)
comparison ranking: 135

Net migration rate: -5.5 migrant(s)/1,000 population (2024 est.)
comparison ranking: 206

Population distribution: approximately 70% of the population lives on the island of Viti Levu; roughly half of the population lives in urban areas

Urbanization: *urban population:* 58.7% of total population (2023)
rate of urbanization: 1.37% annual rate of change (2020-25 est.)

Major urban areas - population: 178,000 SUVA (capital) (2018)

Sex ratio: *at birth:* 1.05 male(s)/female
0-14 years: 1.04 male(s)/female
15-64 years: 1.05 male(s)/female
65 years and over: 0.86 male(s)/female
total population: 1.03 male(s)/female (2024 est.)

Maternal mortality ratio: 38 deaths/100,000 live births (2020 est.)
comparison ranking: 107

Infant mortality rate: *total:* 9.7 deaths/1,000 live births (2024 est.)
male: 11.1 deaths/1,000 live births
female: 8.1 deaths/1,000 live births
comparison ranking: total 133

Life expectancy at birth: *total population:* 74.8 years (2024 est.)
male: 72.2 years
female: 77.6 years
comparison ranking: total population 136

Total fertility rate: 2.21 children born/woman (2024 est.)
comparison ranking: 84

Gross reproduction rate: 1.08 (2024 est.)

Contraceptive prevalence rate: 35.5% (2021)

Drinking water source: *improved: urban:* 98.2% of population
rural: 89.1% of population
total: 94.3% of population
unimproved: urban: 1.8% of population
rural: 10.9% of population
total: 5.7% of population (2020 est.)

Current health expenditure: 3.8% of GDP (2020)

Physician density: 0.86 physicians/1,000 population (2015)

Hospital bed density: 2 beds/1,000 population (2016)

Sanitation facility access: *improved: urban:* 100% of population
rural: 100% of population
total: 100% of population

Obesity - adult prevalence rate: 30.2% (2016)
comparison ranking: 24

Alcohol consumption per capita: *total:* 2.71 liters of pure alcohol (2019 est.)
beer: 1.64 liters of pure alcohol (2019 est.)
wine: 0.29 liters of pure alcohol (2019 est.)
spirits: 0.79 liters of pure alcohol (2019 est.)
other alcohols: 0 liters of pure alcohol (2019 est.)
comparison ranking: total 120

Tobacco use: *total:* 23.1% (2020 est.)
male: 35.6% (2020 est.)
female: 10.5% (2020 est.)
comparison ranking: total 65

Children under the age of 5 years underweight: 4.6% (2021) NA
comparison ranking: 77

Currently married women (ages 15-49): 58.8% (2023 est.)

Child marriage: *women married by age 15:* 0.2%
women married by age 18: 4%
men married by age 18: 1.7% (2021 est.)

Education expenditures: 5.7% of GDP (2020 est.)
comparison ranking: 51

Literacy: *total population:* 99.1%
male: 99.1%
female: 99.1% (2018)

ENVIRONMENT

Environment - current issues: the widespread practice of waste incineration is a major contributor to air pollution in the country, as are vehicle emissions in urban areas; deforestation and soil erosion are significant problems; a contributory factor to erosion is clearing of land by bush burning, a widespread practice that threatens biodiversity

Environment - international agreements: *party to:* Biodiversity, Climate Change, Climate Change-Kyoto Protocol, Climate Change-Paris Agreement, Comprehensive Nuclear Test Ban, Desertification, Endangered Species, Law of the Sea, Marine Life Conservation, Nuclear Test Ban, Ozone Layer Protection, Ship Pollution, Tropical Timber 2006, Wetlands
signed, but not ratified: none of the selected agreements

Climate: tropical marine; only slight seasonal temperature variation

Urbanization: *urban population:* 58.7% of total population (2023)
rate of urbanization: 1.37% annual rate of change (2020-25 est.)

Revenue from forest resources: 0.59% of GDP (2018 est.)
comparison ranking: 63

Revenue from coal: 0% of GDP (2018 est.)
comparison ranking: 185

Air pollutants: *particulate matter emissions:* 7.36 micrograms per cubic meter (2019 est.)
carbon dioxide emissions: 2.05 megatons (2016 est.)
methane emissions: 0.95 megatons (2020 est.)

Waste and recycling: *municipal solid waste generated annually:* 189,390 tons (2011 est.)
municipal solid waste recycled annually: 10,322 tons (2013 est.)
percent of municipal solid waste recycled: 5.5% (2013 est.)

Total water withdrawal: *municipal:* 30 million cubic meters (2020 est.)
industrial: 10 million cubic meters (2020 est.)
agricultural: 50 million cubic meters (2020 est.)

Total renewable water resources: 28.55 billion cubic meters (2020 est.)

GOVERNMENT

Country name: *conventional long form:* Republic of Fiji
conventional short form: Fiji
local long form: Republic of Fiji (English)/ Matanitu ko Viti (Fijian)
local short form: Fiji (English)/ Viti (Fijian)
etymology: the Fijians called their home Viti, but the neighboring Tongans called it Fisi, and in the Anglicized spelling of the Tongan pronunciation - promulgated by explorer Captain James COOK - the designation became Fiji

Government type: parliamentary republic

Capital: *name:* Suva (on Viti Levu)
geographic coordinates: 18 08 S, 178 25 E
time difference: UTC+12 (17 hours ahead of Washington, DC, during Standard Time)
etymology: the name means "little hill" in the native Fijian (iTaukei) language and refers to a mound where a temple once stood

Administrative divisions: 14 provinces and 1 dependency*; Ba, Bua, Cakaudrove, Kadavu, Lau, Lomaiviti, Macuata, Nadroga and Navosa, Naitasiri, Namosi, Ra, Rewa, Rotuma*, Serua, Tailevu

Independence: 10 October 1970 (from the UK)

National holiday: Fiji (Independence) Day, 10 October (1970)

Legal system: common law system based on the English model

Constitution: *history:* several previous; latest signed into law 6 September 2013
amendments: proposed as a bill by Parliament and supported by at least three quarters of its members, followed by referral to the president and then to the Electoral Commission, which conducts a referendum; passage requires approval by at least three-quarters of registered voters and assent by the president

International law organization participation: has not submitted an ICJ jurisdiction declaration; accepts ICCt jurisdiction

Citizenship: *citizenship by birth:* no
citizenship by descent only: at least one parent must be a citizen of Fiji
dual citizenship recognized: yes
residency requirement for naturalization: at least 5 years residency out of the 10 years preceding application

Suffrage: 18 years of age; universal

Executive branch: *chief of state:* President Ratu Wiliame KATONIVERE (since 12 November 2021)
head of government: Prime Minister Sitiveni Ligamamada RABUKA (since 24 December 2022)
cabinet: Cabinet appointed by the prime minister from among members of Parliament and is responsible to Parliament
elections/appointments: president elected by Parliament for a 3-year term (eligible for a second term); election last held on 22 October 2021 (next to be held in 2024); prime minister endorsed by the president
election results: 2021: Ratu Wiliame KATONIVERE elected president; Wiliame KATONIVERE (People's Alliance) 28 votes, Teimumu KEPA (SODELPA) 23 votes
2018: Jioji Konousi KONROTE reelected president (unopposed)

Legislative branch: *description:* unicameral Parliament (55 seats; members directly elected in a nationwide, multi-seat constituency by open-list proportional representation vote with a 5% electoral threshold; members serve 4-year terms)
elections: last held on 14 December 2022 (next to be held in 2026)
election results: percent of vote by party - FijiFirst 42.5%, People's Alliance 35.8%, NFP 8.9%, SODELPA 5.1%, other 7.7%; seats by party - FijiFirst 26, People's Alliance 21, NFP 5, SODELPA 3; composition - men 50, women 5, percentage women 9.1%

Judicial branch: *highest court(s):* Supreme Court (consists of the chief justice, all justices of the Court of Appeal, and judges appointed specifically as Supreme Court judges); Court of Appeal (consists of the court president, all puisne judges of the High Court, and judges specifically appointed to the Court of Appeal); High Court (chaired by the chief justice and includes a minimum of 10 puisne judges; High Court organized into civil, criminal, family, employment, and tax divisions)
judge selection and term of office: chief justice appointed by the president of Fiji on the advice of the prime minister following consultation with the parliamentary leader of the opposition; judges of the Supreme Court, the president of the Court of Appeal, the justices of the Court of Appeal, and puisne judges of the High Court appointed by the president of Fiji upon the nomination of the Judicial Service Commission after consulting with the cabinet minister and the committee of the House of Representatives responsible for the administration of justice; the chief justice, Supreme Court judges and justices of Appeal generally required to retire at age 70, but this requirement may be waived for one or more sessions of the court; puisne judges appointed for not less than 4 years nor more than 7 years, with mandatory retirement at age 65
subordinate courts: Magistrates' Court (organized into civil, criminal, juvenile, and small claims divisions)

Political parties: Fiji First
Fiji Labor Party or FLP
Freedom Alliance (formerly Fiji United Freedom Party or FUFP)
National Federation Party or NFP
People's Alliance
Peoples Democratic Party or PDP

Social Democratic Liberal Party or SODELPA
Unity Fiji

International organization participation: ACP, ADB, AOSIS, C, CP, FAO, G-77, IAEA, IBRD, ICAO, ICCt, ICRM, IDA, IFAD, IFC, IFRCS, IHO, ILO, IMF, IMO, Interpol, IOC, IOM, ISO, ITSO, ITU, ITUC (NGOs), MIGA, OPCW, PCA, PIF, Sparteca (suspended), SPC, UN, UNCTAD, UNDOF, UNESCO, UNIDO, UNISFA, UNMISS, UNWTO, UPU, WCO, WFTU (NGOs), WHO, WIPO, WMO, WTO

Diplomatic representation in the US: *chief of mission:* Ambassador Ilisoni VUIDREKETI (since 17 June 2024)
chancery: 1707 L Street NW, Suite 200, Washington, DC 20036
telephone: [1] (917) 208-4560
FAX: [1] (202) 466-8325
email address and website:
info@FijiEmbassyDC.com
https://www.fijiembassydc.com/

Diplomatic representation from the US: *chief of mission:* Ambassador Marie DAMOUR (since 24 November 2022); note - also accredited to Kiribati, Nauru, Tonga, and Tuvalu
embassy: 158 Princes Road, Tamavua, Suva
mailing address: 4290 Suva Place, Washington DC 20521-4290
telephone: [679] 331-4466
FAX: [679] 330-2267
email address and website:
SuvaACS@state.gov
https://fj.usembassy.gov/

Flag description: light blue with the flag of the UK in the upper hoist-side quadrant and the Fijian shield centered on the outer half of the flag; the blue symbolizes the Pacific Ocean and the Union Jack reflects the links with Great Britain; the shield - taken from Fiji's coat of arms - depicts a yellow lion, holding a coconut pod between its paws, above a white field quartered by the cross of Saint George; the four quarters depict stalks of sugarcane, a palm tree, a banana bunch, and a white dove of peace

National symbol(s): Fijian canoe; national color: light blue

National anthem: *name:* "God Bless Fiji"
lyrics/music: Michael Francis Alexander PRESCOTT/C. Austin MILES (adapted by Michael Francis Alexander PRESCOTT)
note: adopted 1970; known in Fijian as "Meda Dau Doka" (Let Us Show Pride); adapted from the hymn, "Dwelling in Beulah Land," the anthem's English lyrics are generally sung, although they differ in meaning from the official Fijian lyrics

National heritage: *total World Heritage Sites:* 1 (cultural)
selected World Heritage Site locales: Levuka Historical Port Town

ECONOMY

Economic overview: upper-middle income, tourism-based Pacific island economy; susceptible to ocean rises; key energy and infrastructure investments; post-pandemic tourism resurgence; improved debt standing; limited workforce

Real GDP (purchasing power parity): $12.699 billion (2023 est.)
$11.756 billion (2022 est.)
$9.795 billion (2021 est.)
note: data in 2021 dollars
comparison ranking: 162

Real GDP growth rate: 8.03% (2023 est.)
20.02% (2022 est.)
-4.88% (2021 est.)
note: annual GDP % growth based on constant local currency
comparison ranking: 12

Real GDP per capita: $13,600 (2023 est.)
$12,600 (2022 est.)
$10,600 (2021 est.)
note: data in 2021 dollars
comparison ranking: 131

GDP (official exchange rate): $5.495 billion (2023 est.)
note: data in current dollars at official exchange rate

Inflation rate (consumer prices): 4.52% (2022 est.)
0.16% (2021 est.)
-2.6% (2020 est.)
note: annual % change based on consumer prices
comparison ranking: 95

Credit ratings: Moody's rating: Ba3 (2017)
Standard & Poors rating: BB- (2019)
note: The year refers to the year in which the current credit rating was first obtained.

GDP - composition, by sector of origin: *agriculture:* 8.3% (2023 est.)
industry: 16.1% (2023 est.)
services: 52.9% (2023 est.)
note: figures may not total 100% due to non-allocated consumption not captured in sector-reported data
comparison rankings: services 128; industry 166; agriculture 89

GDP - composition, by end use: *household consumption:* 67.5% (2023 est.)
government consumption: 20.6% (2023 est.)
investment in fixed capital: 17.6% (2023 est.)
investment in inventories: -4.8% (2023 est.)
exports of goods and services: 55.2% (2023 est.)
imports of goods and services: -65.8% (2023 est.)
note: figures may not total 100% due to rounding or gaps in data collection

Agricultural products: sugarcane, cassava, taro, chicken, vegetables, coconuts, ginger, rice, milk, sweet potatoes (2022)
note: top ten agricultural products based on tonnage

Industries: tourism, sugar processing, clothing, copra, gold, silver, lumber

Industrial production growth rate: 15.32% (2023 est.)
note: annual % change in industrial value added based on constant local currency
comparison ranking: 4

Labor force: 391,000 (2023 est.)
note: number of people ages 15 or older who are employed or seeking work
comparison ranking: 164

Unemployment rate: 4.33% (2023 est.)
4.48% (2022 est.)
4.68% (2021 est.)
note: % of labor force seeking employment
comparison ranking: 84

Youth unemployment rate (ages 15-24): *total:* 15.2% (2023 est.)
male: 11.7% (2023 est.)
female: 22.1% (2023 est.)
note: % of labor force ages 15-24 seeking employment
comparison ranking: total 94

Population below poverty line: 24.1% (2019 est.)
note: % of population with income below national poverty line

Gini Index coefficient - distribution of family income: 30.7 (2019 est.)
note: index (0-100) of income distribution; higher values represent greater inequality
comparison ranking: 119

Household income or consumption by percentage share: *lowest 10%:* 3.5% (2019 est.)
highest 10%: 24.2% (2019 est.)
note: % share of income accruing to lowest and highest 10% of population

Remittances: 9.1% of GDP (2023 est.)
9.21% of GDP (2022 est.)
9.14% of GDP (2021 est.)
note: personal transfers and compensation between resident and non-resident individuals/households/entities

Budget: *revenues:* $1.019 billion (2021 est.)
expenditures: $1.488 billion (2021 est.)
note: central government revenues and expenses (excluding grants/extrabudgetary units/social security funds) converted to US dollars at average official exchange rate for year indicated

Public debt: 48.9% of GDP (2017 est.)
comparison ranking: 109

Taxes and other revenues: 15.87% (of GDP) (2021 est.)
note: central government tax revenue as a % of GDP
comparison ranking: 131

Current account balance: -$865.665 million (2022 est.)
-$686.577 million (2021 est.)
-$614.13 million (2020 est.)
note: balance of payments - net trade and primary/secondary income in current dollars
comparison ranking: 138

Exports: $2.376 billion (2022 est.)
$1.171 billion (2021 est.)
$1.23 billion (2020 est.)
note: balance of payments - exports of goods and services in current dollars
comparison ranking: 159

Exports - partners: US 39%, Australia 11%, Tonga 5%, NZ 5%, China 4% (2022)
note: top five export partners based on percentage share of exports

Exports - commodities: water, fish, refined petroleum, wood, garments (2022)
note: top five export commodities based on value in dollars

Imports: $3.434 billion (2022 est.)
$2.344 billion (2021 est.)
$1.977 billion (2020 est.)
note: balance of payments - imports of goods and services in current dollars
comparison ranking: 162

Imports - partners: Singapore 23%, China 16%, Australia 13%, NZ 11%, South Korea 8% (2022)
note: top five import partners based on percentage share of imports

Imports - commodities: refined petroleum, plastic products, plastics, wheat, garments (2022)
note: top five import commodities based on value in dollars

Reserves of foreign exchange and gold: $1.548 billion (2023 est.)
$1.557 billion (2022 est.)
$1.518 billion (2021 est.)

note: holdings of gold (year-end prices)/foreign exchange/special drawing rights in current dollars
comparison ranking: 138

Debt - external: $1.235 billion (2022 est.)
note: present value of external debt in current US dollars
comparison ranking: 79

Exchange rates: Fijian dollars (FJD) per US dollar -

Exchange rates: 2.25 (2023 est.)
2.201 (2022 est.)
2.071 (2021 est.)
2.169 (2020 est.)
2.16 (2019 est.)

ENERGY

Electricity access: *electrification - total population:* 92% (2022 est.)
electrification - urban areas: 97.6%
electrification - rural areas: 86.8%

Electricity: *installed generating capacity:* 413,000 kW (2022 est.)
consumption: 936.309 million kWh (2022 est.)
transmission/distribution losses: 101.775 million kWh (2022 est.)
comparison rankings: transmission/distribution losses 48; consumption 160; installed generating capacity 156

Electricity generation sources: *fossil fuels:* 40.2% of total installed capacity (2022 est.)
solar: 1.3% of total installed capacity (2022 est.)
wind: 0.3% of total installed capacity (2022 est.)
hydroelectricity: 54.6% of total installed capacity (2022 est.)
biomass and waste: 3.6% of total installed capacity (2022 est.)

Coal: *consumption:* 2.1 metric tons (2022 est.)
imports: 2.1 metric tons (2022 est.)

Petroleum: *refined petroleum consumption:* 9,000 bbl/day (2022 est.)

Carbon dioxide emissions: 1.248 million metric tonnes of CO2 (2022 est.)
from petroleum and other liquids: 1.248 million metric tonnes of CO2 (2022 est.)
comparison ranking: total emissions 167

Energy consumption per capita: 21.041 million Btu/person (2022 est.)
comparison ranking: 129

COMMUNICATIONS

Telephones - fixed lines: *total subscriptions:* 49,000 (2021 est.)
subscriptions per 100 inhabitants: 5 (2021 est.)
comparison ranking: total subscriptions 155

Telephones - mobile cellular: *total subscriptions:* 992,000 (2021 est.)
subscriptions per 100 inhabitants: 107 (2021 est.)
comparison ranking: total subscriptions 163

Telecommunication systems: *general assessment:* Fiji is the leading market to watch in terms of both LTE and 5G development in the region; the market boasts relatively sophisticated, advanced digital infrastructure, with telcos' heavy investment resulting in the country having the highest mobile and internet subscriptions in the Pacific Islands region; LTE, LTE-A, and fiber technologies have received the most investment by the Fijian mobile operators, LTE now accounts for the largest share of connections in the mobile segment; concentrating on the more highly populated areas, the operators are preparing for the next growth area of high-speed data; they also have 5G in mind, and are preparing their networks to be 5G-ready, anticipating an easier migration to the technology based on the relatively high LTE subscription rate; Fiji presents a challenging geographic environment for infrastructure development due to its population being spread across more than 100 islands; the majority of Fijians live on the two main islands of Viti Levu and Vanua Levu; in July 2018, the two islands were linked by the Savusavu submarine cable system, which provides a more secure link in times of emergency weather events such as the regular tropical cyclones that often cause massive destruction to the area, including destroying essential infrastructure such as electricity and telecommunications equipment; notably, the December 2021 eruption of the Hunga Tonga–Hunga Ha'apai submarine volcano in Tonga damaged the Tonga Cable which connects Fiji, and Tonga blocking the latter off from internet services; cable theft and damage of critical communications infrastructure has also become a concern in Fiji, prompting authorities to establish a joint task force to tackle the issue (2022)
domestic: fixed-line nearly 5 per 100 persons and mobile-cellular teledensity roughly 110 per 100 persons (2021)
international: country code - 679; landing points for the ICN1, SCCN, Southern Cross NEXT, Tonga Cable and Tui- Samoa submarine cable links to US, NZ, Australia and Pacific islands of Fiji, Vanuatu, Kiribati, Samoa, Tokelau, Tonga, Fallis & Futuna, and American Samoa; satellite earth stations - 2 Inmarsat (Pacific Ocean) (2019)

Broadcast media: Fiji TV, a publicly traded company, operates a free-to-air channel; Digicel Fiji operates the Sky Fiji and Sky Pacific multichannel pay-TV services; state-owned commercial company, Fiji Broadcasting Corporation, Ltd, operates 6 radio stations - 2 public broadcasters and 4 commercial broadcasters with multiple repeaters; 5 radio stations with repeaters operated by Communications Fiji, Ltd; transmissions of multiple international broadcasters are available

Internet country code: .fj

Internet users: *total:* 809,600 (2021 est.)
percent of population: 88% (2021 est.)
comparison ranking: total 155

Broadband - fixed subscriptions: *total:* 23,062 (2020 est.)
subscriptions per 100 inhabitants: 3 (2020 est.)
comparison ranking: total 162

TRANSPORTATION

National air transport system: *number of registered air carriers:* 2 (2020)
inventory of registered aircraft operated by air carriers: 16
annual passenger traffic on registered air carriers: 1,670,216 (2018)
annual freight traffic on registered air carriers: 106.83 million (2018) mt-km

Civil aircraft registration country code prefix: DQ

Airports: 26 (2024)
comparison ranking: 127

Heliports: 2 (2024)

Railways: *total:* 597 km (2008)
narrow gauge: 597 km (2008) 0.600-m gauge
note: belongs to the government-owned Fiji Sugar Corporation; used to haul sugarcane during the harvest season, which runs from May to December
comparison ranking: total 108

Roadways: *total:* 7,500 km (2023)
comparison ranking: total 143

Waterways: 203 km (2012) (122 km are navigable by motorized craft and 200-metric-ton barges)
comparison ranking: 107

Merchant marine: *total:* 74 (2023)
by type: general cargo 21, oil tanker 4, other 49
comparison ranking: total 105

Ports: *total ports:* 5 (2024)
large: 0
medium: 0
small: 2
very small: 3
ports with oil terminals: 4
key ports: Lautoka Harbor, Levuka, Malai, Savusavu Bay, Suva Harbor

MILITARY AND SECURITY

Military and security forces: Republic of Fiji Military Force (RFMF): Land Force Command, Maritime Command (2024)
note: the RFMF is subordinate to the president as the commander-in-chief, while the Fiji Police Force reports to the Ministry of Defense, National Security, and Policing

Military expenditures: 1.1% of GDP (2023 est.)
1.2% of GDP (2022 est.)
1.5% of GDP (2021 est.)
1.4% of GDP (2020 est.)
1.6% of GDP (2019 est.)
comparison ranking: 120

Military and security service personnel strengths: approximately 4,000 active personnel (2023)

Military equipment inventories and acquisitions: the RFMF is lightly armed and equipped; Australia has provided patrol boats and a few armored personnel carriers; it also provides logistical support for RFMF regional or UN operations; in recent years, China has provided construction equipment and military vehicles (2024)

Military service age and obligation: 18-25 years of age for voluntary military service for men and women; mandatory retirement at age 55 (2023)

Military deployments: 170 Egypt (MFO); 160 Iraq (UNAMI); 150 Golan Heights (UNDOF) (2024)

Military - note: established in 1920, the RFMF is a small and lightly-armed force with a history of intervening in the country's politics, including coups in 1987 and 2006, and a mutiny in 2000, and it continues to have significant political power; the RFMF is responsible for external security but can be assigned some domestic security responsibilities in specific circumstances; it also has a tradition of participating in UN peacekeeping operations, having sent troops on nearly 20 such missions since first deploying personnel to South Lebanon in 1978; these deployments have offered experience and a source of financial support; the RFMF has an infantry regiment and a small naval element comprised of patrol boats
Fiji has a "shiprider" agreement with the US, which allows local maritime law enforcement officers to embark on US Coast Guard (USCG) and US Navy (USN) vessels, including to board and search vessels

suspected of violating laws or regulations within Fiji's designated exclusive economic zone (EEZ) or on the high seas; "shiprider" agreements also enable USCG personnel and USN vessels with embarked USCG law enforcement personnel to work with host nations to protect critical regional resources (2024)

TRANSNATIONAL ISSUES

Trafficking in persons: tier rating: Tier 2 Watch List — the government did not demonstrate overall increasing efforts to eliminate trafficking compared with the previous reporting period, therefore Fiji was downgraded to Tier 2 Watch List; for more details, go to: https://www.state.gov/reports/2024-trafficking-in-persons-report/fiji/

FINLAND

INTRODUCTION

Background: Finland was a province and then a grand duchy under Sweden from the 12th to the 19th centuries and an autonomous grand duchy of Russia after 1809. It gained complete independence in 1917. During World War II, Finland successfully defended its independence through cooperation with Germany and resisted subsequent invasions by the Soviet Union, albeit with some loss of territory. During the next half-century, Finland transformed from a farm/forest economy to a diversified modern industrial economy; per-capita income is among the highest in Western Europe. A member of the EU since 1995, Finland was the only Nordic state to join the euro single currency at its initiation in January 1999. In the 21st century, the key features of Finland's modern welfare state are high-quality education, promotion of equality, and a national social welfare system, although the system is currently facing the challenges of an aging population and the fluctuations of an export-driven economy. Following Russia's invasion of Ukraine in 2022, Finland opted to join NATO; it became the organization's 31st member in April 2023.

GEOGRAPHY

Location: Northern Europe, bordering the Baltic Sea, Gulf of Bothnia, and Gulf of Finland, between Sweden and Russia

Geographic coordinates: 64 00 N, 26 00 E

Map references: Europe

Area: *total:* 338,145 sq km
land: 303,815 sq km
water: 34,330 sq km
comparison ranking: total 66

Area - comparative: slightly more than two times the size of Georgia; slightly smaller than Montana

Land boundaries: *total:* 2,563 km
border countries (3): Norway 709 km; Sweden 545 km; Russia 1,309 km

Coastline: 1,250 km

Maritime claims: *territorial sea:* 12 nm (in the Gulf of Finland - 3 nm)
contiguous zone: 24 nm
continental shelf: 200 m depth or to the depth of exploitation
exclusive fishing zone: 12 nm; extends to continental shelf boundary with Sweden, Estonia, and Russia

Climate: cold temperate; potentially subarctic but comparatively mild because of moderating influence of the North Atlantic Current, Baltic Sea, and more than 60,000 lakes

Terrain: mostly low, flat to rolling plains interspersed with lakes and low hills

Elevation: *highest point:* Halti (alternatively Haltia, Haltitunturi, Haltiatunturi) 1,328 m
lowest point: Baltic Sea 0 m
mean elevation: 164 m

Natural resources: timber, iron ore, copper, lead, zinc, chromite, nickel, gold, silver, limestone

Land use: *agricultural land:* 7.5% (2018 est.)
arable land: 7.4% (2018 est.)
permanent crops: 0% (2018 est.)
permanent pasture: 0.1% (2018 est.)
forest: 72.9% (2018 est.)
other: 19.6% (2018 est.)

Irrigated land: 80 sq km (2015)

Major lakes (area sq km): *fresh water lake(s):* Saimaa - 1,760 sq km; Paijanne - 1,090 sq km; Inarijarvi - 1,000 sq km; Oulujarvi - 900 sq km; Pielinen - 850 sq km

Population distribution: the vast majority of people are found in the south; the northern interior areas remain sparsely populated

Natural hazards: severe winters in the north

Geography - note: long boundary with Russia; Helsinki is northernmost national capital on European continent; population concentrated on small southwestern coastal plain

PEOPLE AND SOCIETY

Population: *total:* 5,626,414
male: 2,773,656
female: 2,852,758 (2024 est.)
comparison rankings: female 118; male 119; total 118

Nationality: *noun:* Finn(s)
adjective: Finnish

Ethnic groups: Finnish, Swedish, Russian, Estonian, Romani, Sami
note: 90.9% of the population has a Finnish background (2022 est.)

Languages: Finnish (official) 85.9%, Swedish (official) 5.2%, Russian 1.7%, other 7.2% (2022 est.)
major-language sample(s):
World Factbook, korvaamaton perustietolähde. (Finnish)

Religions: Lutheran 66.6%, Greek Orthodox 1.1%, other 1.7%, none 30.6% (2022 est.)

Demographic profile: Finland has a relatively high fertility rate for Europe at about 1.75 children per woman in 2023. Finnish women have high labor force participation rates, and their educational attainment is higher than that of Finnish men. Finland's family policy, like other Nordic countries, puts an emphasis on reconciling work and family life. Both parents can stay at home with an earnings-based allowance until the baby is about 11 months old. Finland also has a publicly subsidized childcare system. Alternatively, parents can choose to take care of a small child through home care leave with a flat allowance rate. These benefits have encouraged fathers to do a greater share of housework and childcare, although women still perform the lion's share of domestic work. In other instances, women have reduced the burden of household work by outsourcing domestic chores, rather than men taking on more of the responsibilities. Finland has high family size ideals compared to other European countries, and childlessness and one-child families are not favored. The proportion of couples having at least three children has been growing since the 1970s.

Finland has historically been a country of emigration. In the 20th century, Finns emigrated largely in two waves. Before World War II, the majority of Finns went to North America, and after World War II most went to Sweden, where industrialization was generating much-needed jobs that offered higher salaries and a better standard of living. In the 1980s and early 1990s, Finnish returnees (mainly from Sweden) began to outnumber Finnish emigrants. Also arriving in Finland between April 1990 and 2010, were Ingrian Finns – descendants of ethnic Finns who settled near St. Petersburg, Russia, in the 17th century – who immigrated to Finland under the Right of Return Law. In addition, the country has absorbed immigrants from Russia, Estonia, the former Yugoslavia, and Sweden for a variety of reasons, most commonly for marriage and family reunification. Finland has also accepted refugees and asylum seekers from Somalia, Iraq, China, and Thailand.

Age structure: *0-14 years:* 16.2% (male 464,939/ female 444,585)
15-64 years: 60.3% (male 1,725,072/female 1,668,604)
65 years and over: 23.5% (2024 est.) (male 583,645/ female 739,569)

Dependency ratios: *total dependency ratio:* 62.1
youth dependency ratio: 25
elderly dependency ratio: 37.1
potential support ratio: 2.7 (2021 est.)

Median age: *total:* 43.3 years (2024 est.)
male: 41.8 years
female: 44.9 years
comparison ranking: total 36

Population growth rate: 0.2% (2024 est.)
comparison ranking: 178

Birth rate: 10.2 births/1,000 population (2024 est.)
comparison ranking: 184

Death rate: 10.4 deaths/1,000 population (2024 est.)
comparison ranking: 30

Net migration rate: 2.2 migrant(s)/1,000 population (2024 est.)
comparison ranking: 47

Population distribution: the vast majority of people are found in the south; the northern interior areas remain sparsely populated

Urbanization: *urban population:* 85.8% of total population (2023)
rate of urbanization: 0.42% annual rate of change (2020-25 est.)

Major urban areas - population: 1.338 million HELSINKI (capital) (2023)

Sex ratio: *at birth:* 1.05 male(s)/female
0-14 years: 1.05 male(s)/female
15-64 years: 1.03 male(s)/female
65 years and over: 0.79 male(s)/female
total population: 0.97 male(s)/female (2024 est.)

Mother's mean age at first birth: 29.5 years (2020 est.)

Maternal mortality ratio: 8 deaths/100,000 live births (2020 est.)
comparison ranking: 152

Infant mortality rate: *total:* 2.1 deaths/1,000 live births (2024 est.)
male: 2.3 deaths/1,000 live births
female: 1.9 deaths/1,000 live births
comparison ranking: total 221

Life expectancy at birth: *total population:* 82.2 years (2024 est.)
male: 79.3 years
female: 85.2 years
comparison ranking: total population 31

Total fertility rate: 1.74 children born/woman (2024 est.)
comparison ranking: 150

Gross reproduction rate: 0.85 (2024 est.)

Contraceptive prevalence rate: 85.5% (2015)
note: percent of women aged 18-49

Drinking water source: *improved: urban:* 100% of population
rural: 100% of population
total: 100% of population

Current health expenditure: 9.6% of GDP (2020)

Physician density: 4.64 physicians/1,000 population (2018)

Hospital bed density: 3.6 beds/1,000 population (2018)

Sanitation facility access: *improved: urban:* 100% of population
rural: 100% of population
total: 100% of population

Obesity - adult prevalence rate: 22.2% (2016)
comparison ranking: 80

Alcohol consumption per capita: *total:* 8.23 liters of pure alcohol (2019 est.)
beer: 3.76 liters of pure alcohol (2019 est.)
wine: 1.59 liters of pure alcohol (2019 est.)
spirits: 1.96 liters of pure alcohol (2019 est.)
other alcohols: 0.91 liters of pure alcohol (2019 est.)
comparison ranking: total 41

Tobacco use: *total:* 21.6% (2020 est.)
male: 26.9% (2020 est.)
female: 16.3% (2020 est.)
comparison ranking: total 75

Currently married women (ages 15-49): 57.2% (2023 est.)

Child marriage: *women married by age 18:* 0.1% (2017 est.)

Education expenditures: 5.9% of GDP (2020 est.)
comparison ranking: 46

School life expectancy (primary to tertiary education): *total:* 19 years
male: 18 years
female: 20 years (2020)

ENVIRONMENT

Environment - current issues: limited air pollution in urban centers; some water pollution from industrial wastes, agricultural chemicals; habitat loss threatens wildlife populations

Environment - international agreements: *party to:* Air Pollution, Air Pollution-Heavy Metals, Air Pollution-Multi-effect Protocol, Air Pollution-Nitrogen Oxides, Air Pollution-Persistent Organic Pollutants, Air Pollution-Sulphur 85, Air Pollution-Sulphur 94, Air Pollution-Volatile Organic Compounds, Antarctic-Environmental Protection, Antarctic-Marine Living Resources, Antarctic Treaty, Biodiversity, Climate Change, Climate Change-Kyoto Protocol, Climate Change-Paris Agreement, Comprehensive Nuclear Test Ban, Desertification, Endangered Species, Environmental Modification, Hazardous Wastes, Law of the Sea, Marine Dumping-London Convention, Marine Dumping-London Protocol, Marine Life Conservation, Nuclear Test Ban, Ozone Layer Protection, Ship Pollution, Tropical Timber 2006, Wetlands, Whaling
signed, but not ratified: none of the selected agreements

Climate: cold temperate; potentially subarctic but comparatively mild because of moderating influence of the North Atlantic Current, Baltic Sea, and more than 60,000 lakes

Urbanization: *urban population:* 85.8% of total population (2023)
rate of urbanization: 0.42% annual rate of change (2020-25 est.)

Revenue from forest resources: 0.36% of GDP (2018 est.)
comparison ranking: 74

Revenue from coal: 0% of GDP (2018 est.)
comparison ranking: 93

Air pollutants: *particulate matter emissions:* 5.47 micrograms per cubic meter (2019 est.)
carbon dioxide emissions: 45.87 megatons (2016 est.)
methane emissions: 4.46 megatons (2020 est.)

Waste and recycling: *municipal solid waste generated annually:* 2.738 million tons (2015 est.)
municipal solid waste recycled annually: 769,926 tons (2015 est.)
percent of municipal solid waste recycled: 28.1% (2015 est.)

Major lakes (area sq km): *fresh water lake(s):* Saimaa - 1,760 sq km; Paijanne - 1,090 sq km; Inarijarvi - 1,000 sq km; Oulujarvi - 900 sq km; Pielinen - 850 sq km

Total water withdrawal: *municipal:* 1 billion cubic meters (2020 est.)
industrial: 2 billion cubic meters (2020 est.)
agricultural: 500 million cubic meters (2020 est.)

Total renewable water resources: 110 billion cubic meters (2020 est.)

Geoparks: *total global geoparks and regional networks:* 4 (2024)
global geoparks and regional networks: Impact Crater Lake - Lappajarvi; Rokua; Lauhanvuori-Haemeenkangas; Saimaa; Salpausselka (2024)

GOVERNMENT

Country name: *conventional long form:* Republic of Finland
conventional short form: Finland
local long form: Suomen tasavalta (Finnish)/ Republiken Finland (Swedish)
local short form: Suomi (Finnish)/ Finland (Swedish)
etymology: name may derive from the ancient Fenni peoples who are first described as living in northeastern Europe in the first centuries A.D.

Government type: parliamentary republic

Capital: *name:* Helsinki
geographic coordinates: 60 10 N, 24 56 E
time difference: UTC+2 (7 hours ahead of Washington, DC, during Standard Time)
daylight saving time: +1hr, begins last Sunday in March; ends last Sunday in October
etymology: the name may derive from the Swedish *helsing*, an archaic name for "neck" (*hals*), and which may refer to a narrowing of the Vantaa River that flows into the Gulf of Finland at Helsinki; *fors* refers to "rapids," so *helsing fors* meaning becomes "the narrows' rapids"

Administrative divisions: 19 regions (maakunnat, singular - maakunta (Finnish); landskapen, singular - landskapet (Swedish)); Aland (Swedish), Ahvenanmaa (Finnish); Etela-Karjala (Finnish), Sodra Karelen (Swedish) [South Karelia]; Etela-Pohjanmaa (Finnish), Sodra Osterbotten (Swedish)

[South Ostrobothnia]; Etela-Savo (Finnish), Sodra Savolax (Swedish) [South Savo]; Kanta-Hame (Finnish), Egentliga Tavastland (Swedish); Kainuu (Finnish), Kajanaland (Swedish); Keski-Pohjanmaa (Finnish), Mellersta Osterbotten (Swedish) [Central Ostrobothnia]; Keski-Suomi (Finnish), Mellersta Finland (Swedish) [Central Finland]; Kymenlaakso (Finnish), Kymmenedalen (Swedish); Lappi (Finnish), Lappland (Swedish); Paijat-Hame (Finnish), Paijanne-Tavastland (Swedish); Pirkanmaa (Finnish), Birkaland (Swedish) [Tampere]; Pohjanmaa (Finnish), Osterbotten (Swedish) [Ostrobothnia]; Pohjois-Karjala (Finnish), Norra Karelen (Swedish) [North Karelia]; Pohjois-Pohjanmaa (Finnish), Norra Osterbotten (Swedish) [North Ostrobothnia]; Pohjois-Savo (Finnish), Norra Savolax (Swedish) [North Savo]; Satakunta (Finnish and Swedish); Uusimaa (Finnish), Nyland (Swedish) [Newland]; Varsinais-Suomi (Finnish), Egentliga Finland (Swedish) [Southwest Finland]

Independence: 6 December 1917 (from Russia)

National holiday: Independence Day, 6 December (1917)

Legal system: civil law system based on the Swedish model

Constitution: *history:* previous 1906, 1919; latest drafted 17 June 1997, approved by Parliament 11 June 1999, entered into force 1 March 2000
amendments: proposed by Parliament; passage normally requires simple majority vote in two readings in the first parliamentary session and at least two-thirds majority vote in a single reading by the newly elected Parliament; proposals declared "urgent" by five-sixths of Parliament members can be passed by at least two-thirds majority vote in the first parliamentary session only; amended several times, last in 2018

International law organization participation: accepts compulsory ICJ jurisdiction with reservations; accepts ICCt jurisdiction

Citizenship: *citizenship by birth:* no
citizenship by descent only: at least one parent must be a citizen of Finland
dual citizenship recognized: yes
residency requirement for naturalization: 6 years

Suffrage: 18 years of age; universal

Executive branch: *chief of state:* President Alexander STUBB (since 1 March 2024)
head of government: Prime Minister Petteri ORPO (since 20 June 2023)
cabinet: Council of State or Valtioneuvosto appointed by the president, responsible to Parliament
elections/appointments: president directly elected by absolute majority popular vote in 2 rounds if needed for a 6-year term (eligible for a second term); first round held on 28 January 2024 with a runoff on 11 February 2024 (next to be held by 28 January 2030); prime minister appointed by Parliament
election results:
2024: Alexander STUBB elected in the second round; percent of vote in the first round - Alexander STUBB (KoK) 27.2%, Pekka HAAVISTO (Vihr) 25.8%, Jussi HALLA-AHO (PS) 19.0%, Olli REHN (Kesk) 15.3%; percent of vote in second round - STUBB 51.6%, HAAVISTO 48.4%
2018: Sauli NIINISTO reelected president; percent of vote - Sauli NIINISTO (independent) 62.7%, Pekka HAAVISTO (Vihr) 12.4%, Laura HUHTASAARI (PS) 6.9%, Paavo VAYRYNEN (independent) 6.2%, Matti VANHANEN (Kesk) 4.1%, other 7.7%

Legislative branch: *description:* unicameral Parliament or Eduskunta (200 seats; 199 members directly elected in single- and multi-seat constituencies by proportional representation vote and 1 member in the province of Aland directly elected by simple majority vote; members serve 4-year terms)
elections: last held on 2 April 2023 (next to be held on 30 April 2027)
election results: percent of vote by party/coalition - Kok 24%, PS 23%, SDP 21.5%. Center Party 11.5%, Vihr 6.5%, Vas 5.5%, SFP 4.5%, KD 2.5%, Aland 0.5%; Movement Now 0.5%; seats by party/coalition - Kok 48, PS 46, SDP 43, Center Party 23, Vihr 13, Vas 11, SFP 9, KD 5; Aland 1; Movement Now 1; composition - men 108, women 92, percentage women 46%

Judicial branch: *highest court(s):* Supreme Court or Korkein Oikeus (consists of the court president and 18 judges); Supreme Administrative Court (consists of 21 judges, including the court president and organized into 3 chambers); note - Finland has a dual judicial system - courts with civil and criminal jurisdiction and administrative courts with jurisdiction for litigation between individuals and administrative organs of the state and communities
judge selection and term of office: Supreme Court and Supreme Administrative Court judges appointed by the president of the republic; judges serve until mandatory retirement at age 68
subordinate courts: 6 Courts of Appeal; 8 regional administrative courts; 27 district courts; special courts for issues relating to markets, labor, insurance, impeachment, land, tenancy, and water rights

Political parties: Aland Coalition (a coalition of several political parties on the Aland Islands)
Center Party or Kesk
Christian Democrats or KD
Finns Party or PS
Green League or Vihr
Left Alliance or Vas
Movement Now or Liike Nyt
National Coalition Party or Kok
Social Democratic Party or SDP
Swedish People's Party or RKP or SFP

International organization participation: ADB (nonregional member), AfDB (nonregional member), Arctic Council, Australia Group, BIS, CBSS, CD, CE, CERN, EAPC, EBRD, ECB, EIB, EITI (implementing country), EMU, ESA, EU, FAO, FATF, G-9, IADB, IAEA, IBRD, ICAO, ICC (national committees), ICCt, ICRM, IDA, IEA, IFAD, IFC, IFRCS, IHO, ILO, IMF, IMO, IMSO, Interpol, IOC, IOM, IPU, ISO, ITSO, ITU, ITUC (NGOs), MIGA, NATO, NC, NEA, NIB, NSG, OAS (observer), OECD, OPCW, OSCE, Pacific Alliance (observer), Paris Club, PCA, PFP, Schengen Convention, UN, UNCTAD, UNESCO, UNHCR, UNHRC, UNIDO, UNIFIL, UNMIL, UNMOGIP, UNOOSA, UNRWA, UNSOM, UNTSO, UPU, Wassenaar Arrangement, WCO, WFTU (NGOs), WHO, WIPO, WMO, WTO, ZC

Diplomatic representation in the US: *chief of mission:* Ambassador Leena-Kaisa MIKKOLA (since 18 September 2024)
chancery: 3301 Massachusetts Avenue NW, Washington, DC 20008
telephone: [1] (202) 298-5800
FAX: [1] (202) 298-6030
email address and website:
sanomat.WAS@gov.fi
https://finlandabroad.fi/web/usa/mission
consulate(s) general: Los Angeles, New York

Diplomatic representation from the US: *chief of mission:* Ambassador Douglas HICKEY (since 11 May 2022)
embassy: Itainen Puistotie 14 B, 00140 Helsinki
mailing address: 5310 Helsinki Place, Washington DC 20521-5310
telephone: [358] (9) 616-250
FAX: [358] (9) 174-681
email address and website:
HelsinkiACS@state.gov
https://fi.usembassy.gov/

Flag description: white with a blue cross extending to the edges of the flag; the vertical part of the cross is shifted to the hoist side in the style of the Dannebrog (Danish flag); the blue represents the thousands of lakes scattered across the country, while the white is for the snow that covers the land in winter

National symbol(s): lion; national colors: blue, white

National anthem: *name:* "Maamme" (Our Land)
lyrics/music: Johan Ludvig RUNEBERG/Fredrik PACIUS
note: in use since 1848; although never officially adopted by law, the anthem has been popular since it was first sung by a student group in 1848; Estonia's anthem uses the same melody as that of Finland

National heritage: *total World Heritage Sites:* 7 (6 cultural, 1 natural)
selected World Heritage Site locales: Fortress of Suomenlinna (c); Old Rauma (c); Petäjävesi Old Church (c); Verla Groundwood and Board Mill (c); Bronze Age Burial Site of Sammallahdenmäki (c); High Coast / Kvarken Archipelago (n); Struve Geodetic Arc (c)

ECONOMY

Economic overview: high-income, export-based EU and eurozone economy; major timber, metals, engineering, telecom, and electronics industries; emerging from recession triggered by inflation, weak consumer and export demand, and lower private investment; labor market reform plan to address structural rigidities

Real GDP (purchasing power parity): $321.126 billion (2023 est.)
$324.486 billion (2022 est.)
$320.209 billion (2021 est.)
note: data in 2021 dollars
comparison ranking: 58

Real GDP growth rate: -1.04% (2023 est.)
1.34% (2022 est.)
2.84% (2021 est.)
note: annual GDP % growth based on constant local currency
comparison ranking: 200

Real GDP per capita: $57,500 (2023 est.)
$58,400 (2022 est.)
$57,800 (2021 est.)
note: data in 2021 dollars
comparison ranking: 31

GDP (official exchange rate): $300.187 billion (2023 est.)
note: data in current dollars at official exchange rate

Inflation rate (consumer prices): 6.25% (2023 est.)
7.12% (2022 est.)
2.19% (2021 est.)
note: annual % change based on consumer prices

comparison ranking: 132

Credit ratings: Fitch rating: AA+ (2016)

Moody's rating: Aa1 (2016)

Standard & Poors rating: AA+ (2014)
note: The year refers to the year in which the current credit rating was first obtained.

GDP - composition, by sector of origin: *agriculture:* 2.5% (2023 est.)
industry: 24.5% (2023 est.)
services: 60.7% (2023 est.)
note: figures may not total 100% due to non-allocated consumption not captured in sector-reported data
comparison rankings: services 81; industry 101; agriculture 147

GDP - composition, by end use: *household consumption:* 52.5% (2023 est.)
government consumption: 25.2% (2023 est.)
investment in fixed capital: 23.4% (2023 est.)
investment in inventories: -0.7% (2023 est.)
exports of goods and services: 41% (2023 est.)
imports of goods and services: -41.4% (2023 est.)
note: figures may not total 100% due to rounding or gaps in data collection

Agricultural products: milk, barley, oats, wheat, potatoes, sugar beets, pork, chicken, peas, beef (2022)
note: top ten agricultural products based on tonnage

Industries: metals and metal products, electronics, machinery and scientific instruments, shipbuilding, pulp and paper, foodstuffs, chemicals, textiles, clothing

Industrial production growth rate: -2.72% (2023 est.)
note: annual % change in industrial value added based on constant local currency
comparison ranking: 189

Labor force: 2.88 million (2023 est.)
note: number of people ages 15 or older who are employed or seeking work
comparison ranking: 113

Unemployment rate: 7.16% (2023 est.)
6.72% (2022 est.)
7.61% (2021 est.)
note: % of labor force seeking employment
comparison ranking: 138

Youth unemployment rate (ages 15-24): *total:* 15.9% (2023 est.)
male: 16.4% (2023 est.)
female: 15.5% (2023 est.)
note: % of labor force ages 15-24 seeking employment
comparison ranking: total 90

Population below poverty line: 12.2% (2022 est.)
note: % of population with income below national poverty line

Gini Index coefficient - distribution of family income: 27.7 (2021 est.)
note: index (0-100) of income distribution; higher values represent greater inequality
comparison ranking: 139

Average household expenditures: *on food:* 11.9% of household expenditures (2022 est.)
on alcohol and tobacco: 5.1% of household expenditures (2022 est.)

Household income or consumption by percentage share: *lowest 10%:* 3.8% (2021 est.)
highest 10%: 22.9% (2021 est.)
note: % share of income accruing to lowest and highest 10% of population

Remittances: 0.23% of GDP (2023 est.)
0.23% of GDP (2022 est.)
0.23% of GDP (2021 est.)
note: personal transfers and compensation between resident and non-resident individuals/households/entities

Budget: *revenues:* $105.182 billion (2022 est.)
expenditures: $106.991 billion (2022 est.)
note: central government revenues (excluding grants) and expenses converted to US dollars at average official exchange rate for year indicated

Public debt: 61.3% of GDP (2017 est.)
note: data cover general government debt and include debt instruments issued (or owned) by government entities other than the treasury; the data include treasury debt held by foreign entities; the data include debt issued by subnational entities, as well as intragovernmental debt; intragovernmental debt consists of treasury borrowings from surpluses in the social funds, such as for retirement, medical care, and unemployment; debt instruments for the social funds are not sold at public auctions
comparison ranking: 78

Taxes and other revenues: 21.08% (of GDP) (2022 est.)
note: central government tax revenue as a % of GDP
comparison ranking: 79

Current account balance: -$4.364 billion (2023 est.)
-$7.074 billion (2022 est.)
$1.222 billion (2021 est.)
note: balance of payments - net trade and primary/secondary income in current dollars
comparison ranking: 177

Exports: $122.953 billion (2023 est.)
$127.706 billion (2022 est.)
$116.762 billion (2021 est.)
note: balance of payments - exports of goods and services in current dollars
comparison ranking: 44

Exports - partners: Germany 11%, US 10%, Sweden 10%, Netherlands 7%, China 5% (2022)
note: top five export partners based on percentage share of exports

Exports - commodities: paper, refined petroleum, steel, wood pulp, wood (2022)
note: top five export commodities based on value in dollars

Imports: $124.221 billion (2023 est.)
$134.575 billion (2022 est.)
$116.72 billion (2021 est.)
note: balance of payments - imports of goods and services in current dollars
comparison ranking: 42

Imports - partners: Sweden 15%, Germany 14%, China 8%, Norway 7%, Netherlands 6% (2022)
note: top five import partners based on percentage share of imports

Imports - commodities: crude petroleum, refined petroleum, cars, garments, electricity (2022)
note: top five import commodities based on value in dollars

Reserves of foreign exchange and gold: $16.929 billion (2023 est.)
$16.036 billion (2022 est.)
$16.744 billion (2021 est.)
note: holdings of gold (year-end prices)/foreign exchange/special drawing rights in current dollars
comparison ranking: 73

Exchange rates: euros (EUR) per US dollar -

Exchange rates: 0.925 (2023 est.)
0.95 (2022 est.)
0.845 (2021 est.)
0.876 (2020 est.)
0.893 (2019 est.)

ENERGY

Electricity access: *electrification - total population:* 100% (2022 est.)

Electricity: *installed generating capacity:* 24.784 million kW (2022 est.)
consumption: 80.082 billion kWh (2022 est.)
exports: 6.896 billion kWh (2022 est.)
imports: 19.825 billion kWh (2022 est.)
transmission/distribution losses: 3.009 billion kWh (2022 est.)
comparison rankings: transmission/distribution losses 140; imports 9; exports 32; consumption 39; installed generating capacity 41

Electricity generation sources: *fossil fuels:* 9.9% of total installed capacity (2022 est.)
nuclear: 34.5% of total installed capacity (2022 est.)
solar: 0.4% of total installed capacity (2022 est.)
wind: 17% of total installed capacity (2022 est.)
hydroelectricity: 19.2% of total installed capacity (2022 est.)
biomass and waste: 19% of total installed capacity (2022 est.)

Nuclear energy: Number of operational nuclear reactors: 5 (2023)

Net capacity of operational nuclear reactors: 4.93GW (2023 est.)

Percent of total electricity production: 42% (2023 est.)

Coal: *production:* 808,000 metric tons (2022 est.)
consumption: 4.141 million metric tons (2022 est.)
exports: 37,000 metric tons (2022 est.)
imports: 4.068 million metric tons (2022 est.)

Petroleum: *total petroleum production:* 8,000 bbl/day (2023 est.)
refined petroleum consumption: 175,000 bbl/day (2023 est.)

Natural gas: *consumption:* 1.157 billion cubic meters (2022 est.)
exports: 106.77 million cubic meters (2022 est.)
imports: 1.372 billion cubic meters (2022 est.)

Carbon dioxide emissions: 36.006 million metric tonnes of CO2 (2022 est.)
from coal and metallurgical coke: 8.577 million metric tonnes of CO2 (2022 est.)
from petroleum and other liquids: 25.198 million metric tonnes of CO2 (2022 est.)
from consumed natural gas: 2.231 million metric tonnes of CO2 (2022 est.)
comparison ranking: total emissions 67

Energy consumption per capita: 181.313 million Btu/person (2022 est.)
comparison ranking: 21

COMMUNICATIONS

Telephones - fixed lines: *total subscriptions:* 186,000 (2022 est.)
subscriptions per 100 inhabitants: 3 (2022 est.)
comparison ranking: total subscriptions 120

Telephones - mobile cellular: *total subscriptions:* 7.13 million (2022 est.)
subscriptions per 100 inhabitants: 129 (2022 est.)
comparison ranking: total subscriptions 111

Telecommunication systems: *general assessment:* Finland's telecom market is among the more progressive in Europe, with operators having been at the forefront in deploying technologies and with the regulator being among the first to auction spectrum for 5G use; these efforts have been supported by the government which is working towards its target of providing a broadband service of at least 100Mb/s by 2025; 5G services were available to more than 40% of the population by early 2021, and take-up among subscribers has been strong although most will remain with LTE in the short term; the country enjoys one of the highest broadband and mobile subscription rates in the region, with customers able to make use of the latest iterations of technologies including DOCSIS3.1, LTE-A, 5G, and GPON fiber infrastructure; Finland has emerged as one of the pioneers in 5G; the auction of spectrum in the 700MHz and 3.5GHh bands has enabled network operators to extend the availability of LTE services nationally and to prepare for 5G services; Spectrum in the 2.5GHz band was auctioned in mid-2020 and has since enabled the MNOs to widen their 5G footprint considerably; there is an ongoing shift away from DSL to fiber and mobile networks (2021)
domestic: fixed-line 4 per 100 subscriptions and nearly 129 per 100 mobile-cellular (2021)
international: country code - 358; landing points for Botnia, BCS North-1 & 2, SFL, SFS-4, C-Lion1, Eastern Lights, Baltic Sea Submarine Cable, FEC, and EESF-2 & 3 submarine cables that provide links to many Finland points, Estonia, Sweden, Germany, and Russia; satellite earth stations - access to Intelsat transmission service via a Swedish satellite earth station, 1 Inmarsat (Atlantic and Indian Ocean regions); note - Finland shares the Inmarsat earth station with the other Nordic countries (Denmark, Iceland, Norway, and Sweden) (2019)

Broadcast media: a mix of 3 publicly operated TV stations and numerous privately owned TV stations; several free and special-interest pay-TV channels; cable and satellite multi-channel subscription services are available; all TV signals are broadcast digitally; Internet television, such as Netflix and others, is available; public broadcasting maintains a network of 13 national and 25 regional radio stations; a large number of private radio broadcasters and access to Internet radio

Internet country code: .fi
note - Aland Islands assigned .ax

Internet users: *total:* 5.115 million (2021 est.)
percent of population: 93% (2021 est.)
comparison ranking: total 92

Broadband - fixed subscriptions: *total:* 1.846 million (2020 est.)
subscriptions per 100 inhabitants: 33 (2020 est.)
comparison ranking: total 59

TRANSPORTATION

National air transport system: *number of registered air carriers:* 3 (2020)
inventory of registered aircraft operated by air carriers: 77
annual passenger traffic on registered air carriers: 13,364,839 (2018)
annual freight traffic on registered air carriers: 957.64 million (2018) mt-km

Civil aircraft registration country code prefix: OH

Airports: 98 (2024)
comparison ranking: 55

Heliports: 15 (2024)

Pipelines: 1,288 km gas transmission pipes, 1,976 km distribution pipes (2016)

Railways: *total:* 5,918 km (2020) 3,349 km electrified
comparison ranking: total 33

Roadways: *total:* 108,637 km (2019)
private and forest roads: 350,000 km (2012)
urban: 26,000 km (2012)
comparison ranking: total 47

Waterways: 8,000 km (2013) (includes Saimaa Canal system of 3,577 km; southern part leased from Russia; water transport used frequently in the summer and widely replaced with sledges on the ice in winter; there are 187,888 lakes in Finland that cover 31,500 km); Finland also maintains 8,200 km of coastal fairways
comparison ranking: 19

Merchant marine: *total:* 282 (2023)
by type: bulk carrier 9, general cargo 75, oil tanker 4, other 194
comparison ranking: total 57

Ports: *total ports:* 37 (2024)
large: 5
medium: 7
small: 11
very small: 14
ports with oil terminals: 21
key ports: Helsinki, Kaskinen, Kokkola, Kotka, Kristinestad, Mantyluoto, Oulu, Pietarsaari, Pori, Rauma, Turku, Vaasa

MILITARY AND SECURITY

Military and security forces: Finnish Defense Forces (FDF; Puolustusvoimat): Army (Maavoimat), Navy (Merivoimat), Air Force (Ilmavoimat) (2024)
note: the Border Guard (Rajavartiolaitos) and National Police are under the Ministry of the Interior; the Border Guard becomes part of the FDF in wartime

Military expenditures: 2.4% of GDP (2024 est.)
2.5% of GDP (2023)
2% of GDP (2022)
1.9% of GDP (2021)
1.5% of GDP (2020)
comparison ranking: 48

Military and security service personnel strengths: approximately 31,000 active-duty personnel (23,000 Army; 5,000 Navy; 3,000 Air Force) (2024)
note: active-duty figures include about 21,000 conscripts carrying out their obligated military service (approximately 17,000 Army; 3,500 Navy; 1,000 Air Force)

Military equipment inventories and acquisitions: the military's inventory consists of a wide mix of modern US, European, Israeli, South Korean, and domestically produced weapons systems; the Finnish defense industry produces a variety of military equipment, including wheeled armored vehicles and naval vessels; Finland also cooperates with other European countries and the US in the joint production of arms (2024)

Military service age and obligation: at age 18, all Finnish men are obligated to serve 5.5-12 months of service within a branch of the military or the Border Guard (length of service depends on the type of duty); women 18-29 may volunteer for service; there is also an option to perform non-military service which lasts for 8.5 or 11.5 months; after completing their initial conscript obligation, individuals enter the reserves and remain eligible for mobilization until the age of 50 for rank-and-file and 60 for noncommissioned and commissioned officers (2024)
note 1: Finland has had conscription since 1951; each year, the military inducts and trains approximately 21,000 conscripts; women have served on a voluntary basis since 1995, and as of 2022 made up about 19% of the military's fulltime personnel

Military deployments: 165 Lebanon (UNIFIL) (2024)

Military - note: the Finnish Defense Forces (FDF) are focused primarily on territorial defense, which is based on having a large, trained reserve force created by general conscription; active-duty FDF units absorb and train more than 20,000 conscripts annually; the resulting pool of trained reservists gives the FDF a wartime strength of approximately 280,000 and a total reserve of some 900,000 citizens with military service; other FDF responsibilities include support to international peacekeeping operations and some domestic security duties, such as assisting the National Police in maintaining law and order in crises
the FDF is also focused on fulfilling its new commitment to NATO; following Russia's full-scale invasion of Ukraine in 2022, Finland reassessed its security policy situation and applied for NATO membership, gaining entry in April 2023; as a member of the Alliance, Finland is part of NATO's collective defense and is covered by the security guarantees enshrined in Article 5 of the North Atlantic Treaty (also known as the Washington Treaty); Finland had been part of NATO's Partnership for Peace program since 1994, and the FDF exercised with some NATO members and participated in NATO-led military missions in the Balkans, Afghanistan, and Iraq; in 2024, it joined NATO's Air Policing mission in Eastern Europe
Finland is a signatory of the EU's Common Security and Defense Policy and actively participates in EU crisis management missions and operations; the FDF also cooperates closely with the militaries of other Nordic countries through the Nordic Defense Cooperation structure (NORDEFCO; established 2009), which consists of Denmark, Finland, Iceland, Norway, and Sweden and involves cooperation in such areas as armaments, education, human resources, training and exercises, and operations; Sweden, the UK, and the US are close bi-lateral defense partners; in 2022, Finland signed a mutual security agreement with the UK, and since 2014 has been part of the UK-led Joint Expeditionary Force, a pool of high-readiness military forces from 10 Baltic and Scandinavian countries designed to respond to a wide range of contingencies in the North Atlantic, Baltic Sea, and High North regions (2024)

TRANSNATIONAL ISSUES

Refugees and internally displaced persons: *refugees (country of origin):* 9,175 (Iraq) (mid-year 2022); 66,195 (Ukraine) (as of 29 February 2024)
stateless persons: 3,546 (2022)

FRANCE

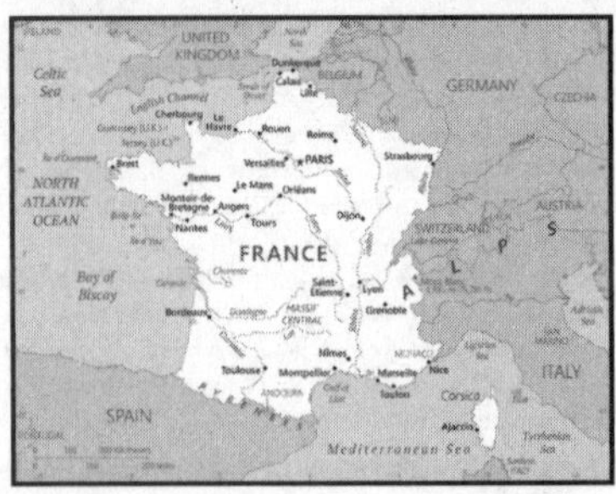

INTRODUCTION

Background: France today is one of the most modern countries in the world and is a leader among European nations. It plays an influential global role as a permanent member of the United Nations Security Council, NATO, the G-7, the G-20, the EU, and other multilateral organizations. France rejoined NATO's integrated military command structure in 2009, reversing then President Charles DE GAULLE's 1966 decision to withdraw French forces from NATO. Since 1958, it has constructed a hybrid presidential-parliamentary governing system resistant to the instabilities experienced in earlier, more purely parliamentary administrations. In recent decades, its reconciliation and cooperation with Germany have proved central to the economic integration of Europe, including the introduction of a common currency, the euro, in January 1999. In the early 21st century, five French overseas entities – French Guiana, Guadeloupe, Martinique, Mayotte, and Reunion – became French regions and were made part of France proper.

GEOGRAPHY

Location: *metropolitan France:* Western Europe, bordering the Bay of Biscay and English Channel, between Belgium and Spain, southeast of the UK; bordering the Mediterranean Sea, between Italy and Spain;

French Guiana: Northern South America, bordering the North Atlantic Ocean, between Brazil and Suriname;

Guadeloupe: Caribbean, islands between the Caribbean Sea and the North Atlantic Ocean, southeast of Puerto Rico;

Martinique: Caribbean, island between the Caribbean Sea and North Atlantic Ocean, north of Trinidad and Tobago;

Mayotte: Southern Indian Ocean, island in the Mozambique Channel, about halfway between northern Madagascar and northern Mozambique;

Reunion: Southern Africa, island in the Indian Ocean, east of Madagascar

Geographic coordinates: *metropolitan France:* 46 00 N, 2 00 E;

French Guiana: 4 00 N, 53 00 W;

Guadeloupe: 16 15 N, 61 35 W;

Martinique: 14 40 N, 61 00 W;

Mayotte: 12 50 S, 45 10 E;

Reunion: 21 06 S, 55 36 E

Map references: *metropolitan France:* Europe;

French Guiana: South America;

Guadeloupe: Central America and the Caribbean;

Martinique: Central America and the Caribbean;

Mayotte: Africa;

Reunion: World

Area: *total:* 643,801 sq km ; 551,500 sq km (metropolitan France)
land: 640,427 sq km ; 549,970 sq km (metropolitan France)
water: 3,374 sq km ; 1,530 sq km (metropolitan France)
note: the first numbers include the overseas regions of French Guiana, Guadeloupe, Martinique, Mayotte, and Reunion
comparison ranking: total 45

Area - comparative: slightly more than four times the size of Georgia; slightly less than the size of Texas

Land boundaries: *total:* 3,956 km
border countries (8): Andorra 55 km; Belgium 556 km; Germany 418 km; Italy 476 km; Luxembourg 69 km; Monaco 6 km; Spain 646 km; Switzerland 525 km
metropolitan France - total: 2751 km

French Guiana - total: 1205 km

Coastline: 4,853 km
metropolitan France: 3,427 km

Maritime claims: *territorial sea:* 12 nm
contiguous zone: 24 nm
exclusive economic zone: 200 nm (does not apply to the Mediterranean Sea)
continental shelf: 200m depth or to the depth of exploitation

Climate: *metropolitan France:* generally cool winters and mild summers, but mild winters and hot summers along the Mediterranean; occasional strong, cold, dry, north-to-northwesterly wind known as the mistral

French Guiana: tropical; hot, humid; little seasonal temperature variation

Guadeloupe and Martinique: subtropical tempered by trade winds; moderately high humidity; rainy season (June to October); vulnerable to devastating cyclones (hurricanes) every eight years on average

Mayotte: tropical; marine; hot, humid, rainy season during northeastern monsoon (November to May); dry season is cooler (May to November)

Reunion: tropical, but temperature moderates with elevation; cool and dry (May to November), hot and rainy (November to April)

Terrain: *metropolitan France:* mostly flat plains or gently rolling hills in north and west; remainder is mountainous, especially Pyrenees in south, Alps in east;

French Guiana: low-lying coastal plains rising to hills and small mountains;

Guadeloupe: Basse-Terre is volcanic in origin with interior mountains; Grande-Terre is low limestone formation; most of the seven other islands are volcanic in origin;

Martinique: mountainous with indented coastline; dormant volcano;

Mayotte: generally undulating, with deep ravines and ancient volcanic peaks;

Reunion: mostly rugged and mountainous; fertile lowlands along coast

Elevation: *highest point:* Mont Blanc 4,810
lowest point: Rhone River delta -2 m
mean elevation: 375 m
note: to assess the possible effects of climate change on the ice and snow cap of Mont Blanc, its surface and peak have been extensively measured in recent years; these new peak measurements have exceeded the traditional height of 4,807 m and have varied between 4,808 m and 4,811 m; the actual rock summit is 4,792 m and is 40 m away from the ice-covered summit

Natural resources: *metropolitan France:* coal, iron ore, bauxite, zinc, uranium, antimony, arsenic, potash, feldspar, fluorspar, gypsum, timber, arable land, fish; French Guiana: gold deposits, petroleum, kaolin, niobium, tantalum, clay

Land use: *agricultural land:* 52.7% (2018 est.)
arable land: 33.4% (2018 est.)
permanent crops: 1.8% (2018 est.)
permanent pasture: 17.5% (2018 est.)
forest: 29.2% (2018 est.)
other: 18.1% (2018 est.)

Irrigated land: 14,236 sq km (2020)

Major lakes (area sq km): *fresh water lake(s):* Lake Geneva (shared with Switzerland) - 580 sq km

Major rivers (by length in km): Rhin (Rhine) (shared with Switzerland [s], Germany, and Netherlands [m]) - 1,233 km; Loire - 1,012 km
note – [s] after country name indicates river source; [m] after country name indicates river mouth

Major watersheds (area sq km): Atlantic Ocean drainage: Loire (115,282 sq km), Seine (78,919 sq km), Rhine-Maas (198,735 sq km), *(Adriatic Sea)* Po (76,997 sq km), *(Mediterranean Sea)* Rhone (100,543 sq km)

Major aquifers: Paris Basin

Population distribution: much of the population is concentrated in the north and southeast; although there are many urban agglomerations throughout the country, Paris is by far the largest city, with Lyon ranked a distant second

Natural hazards: *metropolitan France:* flooding; avalanches; midwinter windstorms; drought; forest fires in south near the Mediterranean;
overseas departments: hurricanes (cyclones); flooding;
volcanism: Montagne Pelee (1,394 m) on the island of Martinique in the Caribbean is the most active volcano of the Lesser Antilles arc, it last erupted in 1932; a catastrophic eruption in May 1902 destroyed the city of St. Pierre, killing an estimated 30,000 people; La Soufriere (1,467 m) on the island of Guadeloupe in the Caribbean last erupted from July 1976 to March 1977; these volcanoes are part of the volcanic island arc of the Lesser Antilles that extends from Saba in the north to Grenada in the south

Geography - note: largest West European nation; most major French rivers – the Meuse, Seine, Loire, Charente, Dordogne, and Garonne –flow northward or westward into the Atlantic Ocean, only the Rhone flows southward into the Mediterranean Sea

PEOPLE AND SOCIETY

Population: *total:* 68,374,591
male: 33,557,094
female: 34,817,497 (2024 est.)
comparison rankings: female 21; male 23; total 22

Nationality: *noun:* Frenchman(men), Frenchwoman(women)
adjective: French

Ethnic groups: Celtic and Latin with Teutonic, Slavic, North African (Algerian, Moroccan, Tunisian), Indochinese, Basque minorities
note: overseas departments: Black, White, Mulatto, East Indian, Chinese, Indigenous

Languages: French (official) 100%, declining regional dialects and languages (Provencal, Breton, Alsatian, Corsican, Catalan, Basque, Flemish, Occitan, Picard)
major-language sample(s):
The World Factbook, une source indispensable d'informations de base. (French)
note: overseas departments - French, Creole patois, Mahorian (a Swahili dialect)

Religions: Roman Catholic 47%, Muslim 4%, Protestant 2%, Buddhist 2%, Orthodox 1%, Jewish 1%, other 1%, none 33%, unspecified 9% (2021 est.)
note: France maintains a tradition of secularism and has not officially collected data on religious affiliation since the 1872 national census, which complicates assessments of France's religious composition; an 1872 law prohibiting state authorities from collecting data on individuals' ethnicity or religious beliefs was reaffirmed by a 1978 law emphasizing the prohibition of the collection or exploitation of personal data revealing an individual's race, ethnicity, or political, philosophical, or religious opinions; a 1905 law codified France's separation of church and state

Age structure: *0-14 years:* 17.3% (male 6,060,087/female 5,792,805)
15-64 years: 60.7% (male 20,875,861/female 20,615,847)
65 years and over: 22% (2024 est.) (male 6,621,146/female 8,408,845)

Dependency ratios: *total dependency ratio:* 63.1
youth dependency ratio: 28.3
elderly dependency ratio: 34.8
potential support ratio: 2.9 (2021 est.)

Median age: *total:* 42.6 years (2024 est.)
male: 41 years
female: 44.2 years
comparison ranking: total 41

Population growth rate: 0.2% (2024 est.)
comparison ranking: 177

Birth rate: 10.9 births/1,000 population (2024 est.)
comparison ranking: 164

Death rate: 10 deaths/1,000 population (2024 est.)
comparison ranking: 35

Net migration rate: 1.1 migrant(s)/1,000 population (2024 est.)
comparison ranking: 65

Population distribution: much of the population is concentrated in the north and southeast; although there are many urban agglomerations throughout the country, Paris is by far the largest city, with Lyon ranked a distant second

Urbanization: *urban population:* 81.8% of total population (2023)
rate of urbanization: 0.67% annual rate of change (2020-25 est.)

Major urban areas - population: 11.208 million PARIS (capital), 1.761 million Lyon, 1.628 million Marseille-Aix-en-Provence, 1.079 million Lille, 1.060 million Toulouse, 1.000 million Bordeaux (2023)

Sex ratio: *at birth:* 1.05 male(s)/female
0-14 years: 1.05 male(s)/female
15-64 years: 1.01 male(s)/female
65 years and over: 0.79 male(s)/female
total population: 0.96 male(s)/female (2024 est.)

Mother's mean age at first birth: 28.9 years (2020 est.)

Maternal mortality ratio: 8 deaths/100,000 live births (2020 est.)
comparison ranking: 150

Infant mortality rate: *total:* 3.1 deaths/1,000 live births (2024 est.)
male: 3.4 deaths/1,000 live births
female: 2.8 deaths/1,000 live births
comparison ranking: total 204

Life expectancy at birth: *total population:* 82.6 years (2024 est.)
male: 79.8 years
female: 85.5 years
comparison ranking: total population 25

Total fertility rate: 1.9 children born/woman (2024 est.)
comparison ranking: 121

Gross reproduction rate: 0.93 (2024 est.)

Drinking water source: *improved: urban:* 100% of population
rural: 100% of population
total: 100% of population

Current health expenditure: 12.2% of GDP (2020)

Physician density: 3.27 physicians/1,000 population (2019)

Hospital bed density: 5.9 beds/1,000 population (2018)

Sanitation facility access: *improved: urban:* 100% of population
rural: 100% of population
total: 100% of population

Obesity - adult prevalence rate: 21.6% (2016)
comparison ranking: 87

Alcohol consumption per capita: *total:* 11.44 liters of pure alcohol (2019 est.)
beer: 2.52 liters of pure alcohol (2019 est.)
wine: 6.44 liters of pure alcohol (2019 est.)
spirits: 2.3 liters of pure alcohol (2019 est.)
other alcohols: 0.18 liters of pure alcohol (2019 est.)
comparison ranking: total 8

Tobacco use: *total:* 33.4% (2020 est.)
male: 34.9% (2020 est.)
female: 31.9% (2020 est.)
comparison ranking: total 19

Children under the age of 5 years underweight: NA

Currently married women (ages 15-49): 54.8% (2023 est.)

Education expenditures: 5.5% of GDP (2020 est.)
comparison ranking: 56

School life expectancy (primary to tertiary education): *total:* 16 years
male: 16 years
female: 16 years (2020)

ENVIRONMENT

Environment - current issues: some forest damage from acid rain; air pollution from industrial and vehicle emissions; water pollution from urban wastes, agricultural runoff

Environment - international agreements: *party to:* Air Pollution, Air Pollution-Heavy Metals, Air Pollution-Multi-effect Protocol, Air Pollution-Nitrogen Oxides, Air Pollution-Persistent Organic Pollutants, Air Pollution-Sulphur 85, Air Pollution-Sulphur 94, Air Pollution-Volatile Organic Compounds, Antarctic-Environmental Protection, Antarctic-Marine Living Resources, Antarctic Seals, Antarctic Treaty, Biodiversity, Climate Change, Climate Change-Kyoto Protocol, Climate Change-Paris Agreement, Comprehensive Nuclear Test Ban, Desertification, Endangered Species, Hazardous Wastes, Law of the Sea, Marine Dumping-London Convention, Marine Dumping-London Protocol, Marine Life Conservation, Ozone Layer Protection, Ship Pollution, Tropical Timber 2006, Wetlands, Whaling
signed, but not ratified: none of the selected agreements

Climate: *metropolitan France:* generally cool winters and mild summers, but mild winters and hot summers along the Mediterranean; occasional strong, cold, dry, north-to-northwesterly wind known as the mistral

French Guiana: tropical; hot, humid; little seasonal temperature variation

Guadeloupe and Martinique: subtropical tempered by trade winds; moderately high humidity; rainy season (June to October); vulnerable to devastating cyclones (hurricanes) every eight years on average

Mayotte: tropical; marine; hot, humid, rainy season during northeastern monsoon (November to May); dry season is cooler (May to November)

Reunion: tropical, but temperature moderates with elevation; cool and dry (May to November), hot and rainy (November to April)

Urbanization: *urban population:* 81.8% of total population (2023)
rate of urbanization: 0.67% annual rate of change (2020-25 est.)

Revenue from forest resources: 0.03% of GDP (2018 est.)
comparison ranking: 136

Revenue from coal: 0% of GDP (2018 est.)
comparison ranking: 184

Air pollutants: *particulate matter emissions:* 10.46 micrograms per cubic meter (2019 est.)
methane emissions: 55.99 megatons (2020 est.)

Waste and recycling: *municipal solid waste generated annually:* 33.399 million tons (2015 est.)
municipal solid waste recycled annually: 7,434,617 tons (2015 est.)
percent of municipal solid waste recycled: 22.3% (2015 est.)

Major lakes (area sq km): *fresh water lake(s):* Lake Geneva (shared with Switzerland) - 580 sq km

Major rivers (by length in km): Rhin (Rhine) (shared with Switzerland [s], Germany, and Netherlands [m]) - 1,233 km; Loire - 1,012 km
note – [s] after country name indicates river source; [m] after country name indicates river mouth

Major watersheds (area sq km): Atlantic Ocean drainage: Loire (115,282 sq km), Seine (78,919 sq km), Rhine-Maas (198,735 sq km), *(Adriatic Sea)* Po (76,997 sq km), *(Mediterranean Sea)* Rhone (100,543 sq km)

Major aquifers: Paris Basin

Total water withdrawal: *municipal:* 5.31 billion cubic meters (2020 est.)
industrial: 17.78 billion cubic meters (2020 est.)
agricultural: 3.18 billion cubic meters (2020 est.)

Total renewable water resources: 211 billion cubic meters (2020 est.)

Geoparks: *total global geoparks and regional networks:* 9 (2024)
global geoparks and regional networks: Armorique; Beaujolais; Causses du Quersey; Chablais; Haute-Provence; Luberon; Massif des Bauges; Monts d'Ardèche; Normandie-Maine (2024)

GOVERNMENT

Country name: *conventional long form:* French Republic
conventional short form: France
local long form: République française
local short form: France
etymology: name derives from the Latin "Francia" meaning "Land of the Franks"; the Franks were a group of Germanic tribes located along the middle and lower Rhine River in the 3rd century A.D. who merged with Gallic-Roman populations in succeeding centuries and to whom they passed on their name

Government type: semi-presidential republic

Capital: *name:* Paris
geographic coordinates: 48 52 N, 2 20 E
time difference: UTC+1 (6 hours ahead of Washington, DC, during Standard Time)
daylight saving time: +1hr, begins last Sunday in March; ends last Sunday in October
time zone note: applies to metropolitan France only; for its overseas regions the time difference is UTC-4 for Guadeloupe and Martinique, UTC-3 for French Guiana, UTC+3 for Mayotte, and UTC+4 for Reunion
etymology: name derives from the Parisii, a Celtic tribe that inhabited the area from the 3rd century B.C., but who were conquered by the Romans in the 1st century B.C.; the Celtic settlement became the Roman town of Lutetia Parisiorum (Lutetia of the Parisii); over subsequent centuries it became Parisium and then just Paris

Administrative divisions: 18 regions (regions, singular - region); Auvergne-Rhone-Alpes, Bourgogne-Franche-Comte (Burgundy-Free County), Bretagne (Brittany), Centre-Val de Loire (Center-Loire Valley), Corse (Corsica), Grand Est (Grand East), Guadeloupe, Guyane (French Guiana), Hauts-de-France (Upper France), Ile-de-France, Martinique, Mayotte, Normandie (Normandy), Nouvelle-Aquitaine (New Aquitaine), Occitanie (Occitania), Pays de la Loire (Lands of the Loire), Provence-Alpes-Cote d'Azur, Reunion
note: France is divided into 13 metropolitan regions (including the "collectivity" of Corse or Corsica) and 5 overseas regions (French Guiana, Guadeloupe, Martinique, Mayotte, and Reunion) and is subdivided into 96 metropolitan departments and 5 overseas departments (which are the same as the overseas regions)

Dependent areas: Clipperton Island, French Polynesia, French Southern and Antarctic Lands, New Caledonia, Saint Barthelemy, Saint Martin, Saint Pierre and Miquelon, Wallis and Futuna (8)
note: the US Government does not recognize claims to Antarctica; New Caledonia has been considered a "sui generis" collectivity of France since 1998, a unique status falling between that of an independent country and a French overseas department

Independence: *no official date of independence:* 486 (Frankish tribes unified under Merovingian kingship); 10 August 843 (Western Francia established from the division of the Carolingian Empire); 14 July 1789 (French monarchy overthrown); 22 September 1792 (First French Republic founded); 4 October 1958 (Fifth French Republic established)

National holiday: Fête de la Fédération, 14 July (1790); note - often incorrectly referred to as Bastille Day, the celebration commemorates the holiday held on the first anniversary of the storming of the Bastille (on 14 July 1789) and the establishment of a constitutional monarchy; other names for the holiday are *la Fête nationale* (National Holiday) and *le Quatorze Juillet* (14th of July)

Legal system: civil law; review of administrative but not legislative acts

Constitution: *history:* many previous; latest effective 4 October 1958
amendments: proposed by the president of the republic (upon recommendation of the prime minister and Parliament) or by Parliament; proposals submitted by Parliament members require passage by both houses followed by approval in a referendum; passage of proposals submitted by the government can bypass a referendum if submitted by the president to Parliament and passed by at least three-fifths majority vote by Parliament's National Assembly; amended many times, last in 2008

International law organization participation: has not submitted an ICJ jurisdiction declaration; accepts ICCt jurisdiction

Citizenship: *citizenship by birth:* no
citizenship by descent only: at least one parent must be a citizen of France
dual citizenship recognized: yes
residency requirement for naturalization: 5 years

Suffrage: 18 years of age; universal

Executive branch: *chief of state:* President Emmanuel MACRON (since 14 May 2017)
head of government: Prime Minister Michel BARNIER (since 5 September 2024)
cabinet: Council of Ministers appointed by the president at the suggestion of the prime minister
elections/appointments: president directly elected by absolute majority popular vote in 2 rounds if needed for a 5-year term (eligible for a second term); election last held on 10 April 2022 with a runoff held on 24 April 2022 (next to be held in April 2027); prime minister appointed by the president
election results:
2022: Emmanuel MACRON reelected in second round; percent of vote in first round - Emmanuel MACRON (LREM) 27.8%, Marine LE PEN (RN) 23.2%, Jean-Luc MELENCHON (LFI) 22%, Eric ZEMMOUR (Reconquete) 7.1%, Valerie PECRESSE (LR) 4.8%, Yannick JADOT (EELV) 4.6%, other 10.6%; percent of vote in second round - MACRON 58.5%, LE PEN 41.5%
2017: Emmanuel MACRON elected president in second round; percent of vote in first round - Emmanuel MACRON (EM) 24%, Marine LE PEN (FN) 21.3%, Francois FILLON (LR) 20%, Jean-Luc MELENCHON (FI) 19.6%, Benoit HAMON (PS) 6.4%, other 8.7%; percent of vote in second round - MACRON 66.1%, LE PEN 33.9%
note - Gabriel ATTAL, who initially took office as prime minister on 9 January 2024, resigned on 16 July 2024 following the parliamentary elections and is serving as prime minister in a caretaker status until a new prime minister is sworn into office

Legislative branch: *description:* bicameral Parliament or Parlement consists of:
Senate or Sénat (348 seats - 328 for metropolitan France and overseas departments and regions of Guadeloupe, Martinique, French Guiana, Reunion, and Mayotte, 2 for New Caledonia, 2 for French Polynesia, 1 for Saint-Pierre and Miquelon, 1 for Saint-Barthelemy, 1 for Saint-Martin, 1 for Wallis and Futuna, and 12 for French nationals abroad; members indirectly elected by departmental electoral colleges using absolute majority vote in 2 rounds if needed for departments with 1-3 members, and proportional representation vote in departments with 4 or more members; members serve 6-year terms with one-half of the membership renewed every 3 years)
National Assembly or Assemblée Nationale (577 seats - 556 for metropolitan France, 10 for overseas departments, and 11 for citizens abroad; members directly elected by absolute majority vote in 2 rounds if needed to serve 5-year terms)
elections: Senate - last held on 24 September 2023 (next to be held by 30 September 2026) National Assembly - last held on 30 June and 7 July 2024 (next to be held on 30 June 2029)
election results: Senate - percent of vote by party - NA; seats by political caucus (party or group of parties) LR 139, SER 69, UC 51, RDPI 21, CRCE 17, LIRT 17, EST 16, RDSE 14; composition - men 222, women 126, percentage women 36.2%.
National Assembly - percent of vote by party/coalition in the first round - RN 29.26%, NPF 28.06%, ENS 20.04%, LR 6.57%, UXD 3.96%, other 12.11%; seats by party/coalition in the first round - RN 37, NPF 32, ENS 2, LR 1, UXD 1, other 3; percent of vote in the second round - RN 32.05%, NPF 25.68, ENS 23.14% LR 5.41%, UXD 5.0%, other 8.72%, seats by party/coalition in the second round - NPF 146, ENS 148, RN 88, LR 38, UXD 16, other 65; composition - men 369, women 208, percentage women 36%

Judicial branch: *highest court(s):* Court of Cassation or Cour de Cassation (consists of the court president, 6 divisional presiding judges, 120 trial judges, and 70 deputy judges organized into 6 divisions - 3 civil, 1 commercial, 1 labor, and 1 criminal); Constitutional Council (consists of 9 members)
judge selection and term of office: Court of Cassation judges appointed by the president of the republic from nominations from the High Council of the Judiciary, presided over by the Court of Cassation and 15 appointed members; judges appointed for life; Constitutional Council members - 3 appointed by the president of the republic and 3 each by the National Assembly and Senate presidents; members serve 9-year, non-renewable terms with one-third of the membership renewed every 3 years
subordinate courts: appellate courts or Cour d'Appel; regional courts or Tribunal de Grande Instance; first instance courts or Tribunal d'instance; administrative courts
note: in April 2021, the French Government submitted a bill on judicial reform to Parliament

Political parties: Citizen and Republican Movement or MRC
Debout la France or DLF
Democratic Movement or MoDem
Ensemble or ENS (electoral coalition including RE, MoDem, Horizons, PRV, UDI)
The Ecologists - the Greens or EELV
French Communist Party or PCF
Horizons
La France Insoumise or FI
Liberties, Independents, Overseas and Territories or LIOT
Movement of Progressives or MDP
National Rally or RN (formerly National Front or FN)
New Democrats or LND (formerly Ecology Democracy Solidarity or EDS)
New Popular Front or NFP (electoral coalition including FI, EELV, PS, PCF)
Radical Party of the Left or PRV
Reconquete or REC
Renaissance or RE
Résistons!
Socialist Party or PS
The Republicans or LR
Union of Democrats and Independents or UDI
Union of Far Right or UXD (electoral coalition of LR, RN)

International organization participation: ADB (nonregional member), AfDB (nonregional member), Arctic Council (observer), Australia Group, BDEAC, BIS, BSEC (observer), CBSS (observer), CE, CERN, EAPC, EBRD, ECB, EIB, EITI (implementing country), EMU, ESA, EU, FAO, FATF, FZ, G-5, G-7, G-8, G-10, G-20, IADB, IAEA, IBRD, ICAO, ICC (national committees), ICCt, ICRM, IDA, IEA, IFAD, IFC, IFRCS, IGAD (partners), IHO, ILO, IMF, IMO, IMSO, InOC, Interpol, IOC, IOM, IPU, ISO, ITSO, ITU, ITUC (NGOs), MIGA, MINURSO, MINUSTAH, MONUSCO, NATO, NEA, NSG, OAS (observer), OECD, OIF, OPCW, OSCE, Pacific Alliance (observer), Paris Club, PCA, PIF (partner), Schengen Convention, SELEC (observer), SPC, UN, UNCTAD, UNESCO, UNHCR, UNHRC, UNIDO, UNIFIL, Union Latina, UNMIL, UNOCI, UNOOSA, UNRWA, UN Security Council (permanent), UNTSO, UNWTO, UPU, Wassenaar Arrangement, WCO, WFTU (NGOs), WHO, WIPO, WMO, WTO, ZC

Diplomatic representation in the US: *chief of mission:* Ambassador Laurent BILI (since 19 April 2023)
chancery: 4101 Reservoir Road NW, Washington, DC 20007
telephone: [1] (202) 944-6000
FAX: [1] (202) 944-6166
email address and website:
info@ambafrance-us.org
https://franceintheus.org/
consulate(s) general: Atlanta, Boston, Chicago, Houston, Los Angeles, Miami, New Orleans, New York, San Francisco

Diplomatic representation from the US: *chief of mission:* Ambassador Denise Campbell BAUER (since 5 February 2022); note - also accredited to Monaco
embassy: 2 avenue Gabriel, 75008 Paris
mailing address: 9200 Paris Place, Washington DC 20521-9200
telephone: [33] (1) 43-12-22-22, [33] (1) 42-66-97-83
FAX: [33] (1) 42-66-97-83
email address and website:
Citizeninfo@state.gov
https://fr.usembassy.gov/
consulate(s) general: Marseille, Strasbourg
consulate(s): Bordeaux, Lyon, Rennes

Flag description: three equal vertical bands of blue (hoist side), white, and red; known as the "Le drapeau tricolore" (French Tricolor), the origin of the flag dates to 1790 and the French Revolution when the "ancient French color" of white was combined with the blue and red colors of the Parisian militia; the official flag for all French dependent areas
note: for the first four years, 1790-94, the order of colors was reversed, red-white-blue, instead of the current blue-white-red; the design and/or colors are similar to a number of other flags, including those of Belgium, Chad, Cote d'Ivoire, Ireland, Italy, Luxembourg, and Netherlands

National symbol(s): Gallic rooster, fleur-de-lis, Marianne (female personification of the country); national colors: blue, white, red

National anthem: *name:* "La Marseillaise" (The Song of Marseille)
lyrics/music: Claude-Joseph ROUGET de Lisle
note: adopted 1795, restored 1870; originally known as "Chant de Guerre pour l'Armee du Rhin" (War Song for the Army of the Rhine), the National Guard of Marseille made the song famous by singing it while marching into Paris in 1792 during the French Revolutionary Wars

National heritage: *total World Heritage Sites:* 53 (45 cultural, 7 natural, 1 mixed); note - includes one site in New Caledonia and one site in French Polynesia
selected World Heritage Site locales: Chartres Cathedral (c); Palace and Park of Versailles (c); Prehistoric Sites and Decorated Caves of the Vézère Valley (c); Pyrénées - Mont Perdu (m); Cistercian Abbey of Fontenay (c); Paris, Banks of the Seine (c); The Loire Valley between Sully-sur-Loire and Chalonnes (c); Pont du Gard (Roman Aqueduct) (c); Amiens Cathedral (c); Palace and Park of Fontainebleau (c); Historic Fortified City of Carcassonne (c); Gulf of Porto: Calanche of Piana, Gulf of Girolata, Scandola Reserve (n)

ECONOMY

Economic overview: high-income, advanced and diversified EU economy and euro user; strong tourism, aircraft manufacturing, pharmaceuticals, and industrial sectors; high public debt; ongoing pension reform efforts; transitioning to a green economy via "France 2030" strategy

Real GDP (purchasing power parity): $3.764 trillion (2023 est.)
$3.738 trillion (2022 est.)
$3.648 trillion (2021 est.)
note: data in 2021 dollars
comparison ranking: 9

Real GDP growth rate: 0.7% (2023 est.)
2.45% (2022 est.)
6.44% (2021 est.)
note: annual GDP % growth based on constant local currency
comparison ranking: 174

Real GDP per capita: $55,200 (2023 est.)
$55,000 (2022 est.)
$53,800 (2021 est.)
note: data in 2021 dollars
comparison ranking: 35

GDP (official exchange rate): $3.031 trillion (2023 est.)
note: data in current dollars at official exchange rate

Inflation rate (consumer prices): 4.88% (2023 est.)
5.22% (2022 est.)
1.64% (2021 est.)
note: annual % change based on consumer prices
comparison ranking: 104

Credit ratings: Fitch rating: AA (2014)
Moody's rating: Aa2 (2015)
Standard & Poors rating: AA (2013)
note: The year refers to the year in which the current credit rating was first obtained.

GDP - composition, by sector of origin: *agriculture:* 1.9% (2023 est.)
industry: 18.7% (2023 est.)
services: 69.2% (2023 est.)
note: figures may not total 100% due to non-allocated consumption not captured in sector-reported data
comparison rankings: services 41; industry 146; agriculture 157

GDP - composition, by end use: *household consumption:* 53.7% (2023 est.)
government consumption: 23.3% (2023 est.)
investment in fixed capital: 24.8% (2023 est.)
investment in inventories: 0.4% (2023 est.)
exports of goods and services: 32.7% (2023 est.)
imports of goods and services: -34.9% (2023 est.)
note: figures may not total 100% due to rounding or gaps in data collection

Agricultural products: wheat, sugar beets, milk, barley, maize, potatoes, grapes, rapeseed, pork, sunflower seeds (2022)
note: top ten agricultural products based on tonnage

Industries: machinery, chemicals, automobiles, metallurgy, aircraft, electronics, textiles, food processing, tourism

Industrial production growth rate: 0.74% (2023 est.)
note: annual % change in industrial value added based on constant local currency
comparison ranking: 144

Labor force: 31.825 million (2023 est.)
note: number of people ages 15 or older who are employed or seeking work
comparison ranking: 21

Unemployment rate: 7.32% (2023 est.)
7.31% (2022 est.)
7.87% (2021 est.)
note: % of labor force seeking employment
comparison ranking: 140

Youth unemployment rate (ages 15-24): *total:* 17.1% (2023 est.)
male: 18.1% (2023 est.)
female: 16% (2023 est.)
note: % of labor force ages 15-24 seeking employment
comparison ranking: total 83

Population below poverty line: 15.6% (2021 est.)
note: % of population with income below national poverty line

Gini Index coefficient - distribution of family income: 31.5 (2021 est.)
note: index (0-100) of income distribution; higher values represent greater inequality
comparison ranking: 113

Average household expenditures: *on food:* 13.6% of household expenditures (2022 est.)

on alcohol and tobacco: 4.1% of household expenditures (2022 est.)

Household income or consumption by percentage share: *lowest 10%:* 2.9% (2021 est.)
highest 10%: 24.9% (2021 est.)
note: % share of income accruing to lowest and highest 10% of population

Remittances: 1.15% of GDP (2023 est.)
1.22% of GDP (2022 est.)
1.11% of GDP (2021 est.)
note: personal transfers and compensation between resident and non-resident individuals/households/entities

Budget: *revenues:* $1.229 trillion (2022 est.)
expenditures: $1.362 trillion (2022 est.)
note: central government revenues (excluding grants) and expenses converted to US dollars at average official exchange rate for year indicated

Public debt: 98.66% of GDP (2022 est.)
note: central government debt as a % of GDP
comparison ranking: 21

Taxes and other revenues: 24.62% (of GDP) (2022 est.)
note: central government tax revenue as a % of GDP
comparison ranking: 52

Current account balance: -$22.792 billion (2023 est.)
-$56.672 billion (2022 est.)
$9.868 billion (2021 est.)
note: balance of payments - net trade and primary/secondary income in current dollars
comparison ranking: 201

Exports: $1.052 trillion (2023 est.)
$1.013 trillion (2022 est.)
$925.551 billion (2021 est.)
note: balance of payments - exports of goods and services in current dollars
comparison ranking: 5

Exports - partners: Germany 13%, Italy 9%, US 8%, Belgium 8%, Spain 8% (2022)
note: top five export partners based on percentage share of exports

Exports - commodities: aircraft, packaged medicine, cars, natural gas, vehicle parts/accessories (2022)
note: top five export commodities based on value in dollars

Imports: $1.099 trillion (2023 est.)
$1.103 trillion (2022 est.)
$963.999 billion (2021 est.)
note: balance of payments - imports of goods and services in current dollars
comparison ranking: 5

Imports - partners: Germany 15%, Belgium 9%, Spain 8%, Italy 8%, Netherlands 8% (2022)
note: top five import partners based on percentage share of imports

Imports - commodities: natural gas, cars, refined petroleum, crude petroleum, garments (2022)
note: top five import commodities based on value in dollars

Reserves of foreign exchange and gold: $240.792 billion (2023 est.)
$242.416 billion (2022 est.)
$244.28 billion (2021 est.)
note: holdings of gold (year-end prices)/foreign exchange/special drawing rights in current dollars
comparison ranking: 15

Exchange rates: euros (EUR) per US dollar -

Exchange rates: 0.925 (2023 est.)
0.95 (2022 est.)
0.845 (2021 est.)
0.876 (2020 est.)
0.893 (2019 est.)

ENERGY

Electricity access: *electrification - total population:* 100% (2022 est.)

Electricity: *installed generating capacity:* 148.914 million kW (2022 est.)
consumption: 425.994 billion kWh (2022 est.)
exports: 37.329 billion kWh (2022 est.)
imports: 53.255 billion kWh (2022 est.)
transmission/distribution losses: 36.223 billion kWh (2022 est.)
comparison rankings: transmission/distribution losses 200; imports 2; exports 4; consumption 10; installed generating capacity 9

Electricity generation sources: *fossil fuels:* 12.1% of total installed capacity (2022 est.)
nuclear: 62.5% of total installed capacity (2022 est.)
solar: 4.5% of total installed capacity (2022 est.)
wind: 8.5% of total installed capacity (2022 est.)
hydroelectricity: 9.5% of total installed capacity (2022 est.)
tide and wave: 0.1% of total installed capacity (2022 est.)
biomass and waste: 2.7% of total installed capacity (2022 est.)

Nuclear energy: Number of operational nuclear reactors: 56 (2023)

Number of nuclear reactors under construction: 1 (2023)

Net capacity of operational nuclear reactors: 61.37GW (2023 est.)

Percent of total electricity production: 64.8% (2023 est.)

Number of nuclear reactors permanently shut down: 14 (2023)

Coal: *production:* 2.419 million metric tons (2022 est.)
consumption: 12.985 million metric tons (2022 est.)
exports: 120,000 metric tons (2022 est.)
imports: 10.181 million metric tons (2022 est.)
proven reserves: 160 million metric tons (2022 est.)

Petroleum: *total petroleum production:* 80,000 bbl/day (2023 est.)
refined petroleum consumption: 1.554 million bbl/day (2023 est.)
crude oil estimated reserves: 61.719 million barrels (2021 est.)

Natural gas: *production:* 20.132 million cubic meters (2022 est.)
consumption: 37.001 billion cubic meters (2022 est.)
exports: 15.25 billion cubic meters (2022 est.)
imports: 56.281 billion cubic meters (2022 est.)
proven reserves: 7.787 billion cubic meters (2021 est.)

Carbon dioxide emissions: 311.904 million metric tonnes of CO2 (2022 est.)
from coal and metallurgical coke: 27.266 million metric tonnes of CO2 (2022 est.)
from petroleum and other liquids: 207.798 million metric tonnes of CO2 (2022 est.)
from consumed natural gas: 76.84 million metric tonnes of CO2 (2022 est.)
comparison ranking: total emissions 19

Energy consumption per capita: 121.928 million Btu/person (2022 est.)
comparison ranking: 35

COMMUNICATIONS

Telephones - fixed lines: *total subscriptions:* 37.74 million (2022 est.)
subscriptions per 100 inhabitants: 58 (2022 est.)
comparison ranking: total subscriptions 5

Telephones - mobile cellular: *total subscriptions:* 76.807 million (2022 est.)
subscriptions per 100 inhabitants: 119 (2022 est.)
comparison ranking: total subscriptions 24

Telecommunication systems: *general assessment:* France's telecom market is one of the largest in Europe; there is a multi-year Engage 2025 plan which is focused on growth in the developing markets, and on the greater use of artificial intelligence and data; there are many MVNOs in the market; LTE networks provide near universal coverage, and carry about 95% of mobile data traffic; operators have launched 5G services, and these have been supported by the late-2020 auction of spectrum in the 3.5GHz range; France's fixed broadband market is increasingly focused on fiber, which accounted for 71% of all fixed lines at the beginning of 2021; growth in the fiber sector has been stimulated by households securing faster data packages during the pandemic; the number of DSL lines has fallen sharply as customers migrate to fiber infrastructure (2021)
domestic: nearly 59 per 100 persons for fixed-line and over 110 per 100 for mobile-cellular subscriptions (2021)
international: country code - 33; landing points for Circe South, TAT-14, INGRID, FLAG Atlantic-1, Apollo, HUGO, IFC-1, ACE, SeaMeWe-3 & 4, Dunant, Africa-1, AAE-1, Atlas Offshore, Hawk, IMEWE, Med Cable, PEACE Cable, and TE North/TGN-Eurasia/SEACOM/Alexandros/Medex submarine cables providing links throughout Europe, Asia, Australia, the Middle East, Southeast Asia, Africa and US; satellite earth stations - more than 3 (2 Intelsat (with total of 5 antennas - 2 for Indian Ocean and 3 for Atlantic Ocean), NA Eutelsat, 1 Inmarsat - Atlantic Ocean region); HF radiotelephone communications with more than 20 countries (2019)
overseas departments: country codes: French Guiana - 594; landing points for Ella Link, Kanawa, Americas II to South America, Europe, Caribbean and US; Guadeloupe - 590; landing points for GCN, Southern Caribbean Fiber, and ECFS around the Caribbean and US; Martinique - 596; landing points for Americas II, ECFS, and Southern Caribbean Fiber to South America, US and around the Caribbean; Mayotte - 262; landing points for FLY-LION3 and LION2 to East Africa and East African Islands in Indian Ocean; Reunion - 262; landing points for SAFE, METISS, and LION submarine cables to Asia, South and East Africa, Southeast Asia and nearby Indian Ocean Island countries of Mauritius, and Madagascar (2019)

Broadcast media: a mix of both publicly operated and privately owned TV stations; state-owned France television stations operate 4 networks, one of which is a network of regional stations, and has part-interest in several thematic cable/satellite channels and international channels; a large number of privately owned regional and local TV stations; multi-channel satellite and cable services provide a large number of channels; public broadcaster Radio France operates 7 national networks, a series of regional networks, and operates services for overseas territories and foreign audiences; Radio France Internationale, under the Ministry of Foreign Affairs, is a leading international broadcaster; a large number of commercial FM stations, with many of them consolidating into commercial networks

Internet country code: metropolitan France - .fr; French Guiana - .gf; Guadeloupe - .gp; Martinique - .mq; Mayotte - .yt; Reunion - .re

Internet users: *total:* 55.9 million (2021 est.)
percent of population: 86% (2021 est.)
comparison ranking: total 19

Broadband - fixed subscriptions: *total:* 30.627 million (2020 est.)
subscriptions per 100 inhabitants: 47 (2020 est.)
comparison ranking: total 7

TRANSPORTATION

National air transport system: *number of registered air carriers:* 19 (2020)
inventory of registered aircraft operated by air carriers: 553
annual passenger traffic on registered air carriers: 70,188,028 (2018)
annual freight traffic on registered air carriers: 4,443,790,000 (2018) mt-km

Civil aircraft registration country code prefix: F

Airports: 689 (2024)
note: Includes 27 airports in French overseas departments (French Guiana, Guadeloupe, Martinique, Mayotte, Reunion)
comparison ranking: 10

Heliports: 290 (2024)

Pipelines: 15,322 km gas, 2,939 km oil, 5,084 km refined products (2013)

Railways: *total:* 27,860 km (2020) 16,660 km electrified
narrow gauge: -5 km
comparison ranking: total 10

Roadways: *total:* 1,090,059 km (2022)
comparison ranking: total 7

Waterways: *metropolitan France:* 8,501 km (1,621 km navigable by craft up to 3,000 metric tons) (2010)

Merchant marine: *total:* 553 (2023)
by type: container ship 32, general cargo 48, oil tanker 25, other 448
note: includes Monaco
comparison ranking: total 41

Ports: *total ports:* 66 (2024)
large: 6
medium: 12
small: 22
very small: 26
ports with oil terminals: 31
key ports: Bayonne, Bordeaux, Boulogne-sur-Mer, Dunkerque Port Est, Dunkerque Port Ouest, La Pallice, La Rochelle, Les Sables d'Olonne, Lorient, Montoir, Nantes, Le Havre, Rouen, Rade de Brest, Rade de Cherbourg, Rochefort, St. Nazaire, Toulon

Transportation - note: begun in 1988 and completed in 1994, the Channel Tunnel (nicknamed the Chunnel) is a 50.5-km (31.4-mi) rail tunnel beneath the English Channel at the Strait of Dover that runs from Folkestone, Kent, England to Coquelles, Pas-de-Calais in northern France; it is the only fixed link between the island of Great Britain and mainland Europe

MILITARY AND SECURITY

Military and security forces: French Armed Forces (Forces Armées Françaises): Army (l'Armee de Terre; includes Foreign Legion), Navy (Marine Nationale), Air and Space Force (l'Armee de l'Air et de l'Espace); includes Air Defense), National Guard (Reserves), National Gendarmerie (2024)
note: under the direction of the Ministry of the Interior, the civilian National Police and the National Gendarmerie maintain internal security; the National Gendarmerie is a paramilitary police force that is a branch of the Armed Forces and therefore part of the Ministry of Defense but under the jurisdiction of the Ministry of the Interior; it also has additional duties to the Ministry of Justice; the Gendarmerie includes the National Gendarmerie Intervention Group (Groupe d'intervention de la Gendarmerie Nationale or GIGN), an elite national-level tactical police unit set up in 1973 in response to the 1972 Munich massacre

Military expenditures: 2.1% of GDP (2024 est.)
1.9% of GDP (2023)
1.9% of GDP (2022)
1.9% of GDP (2021)
2% of GDP (2020)
comparison ranking: 65

Military and security service personnel strengths: approximately 205,000 active-duty troops (120,000 Army; 35,000 Navy; 40,000 Air Force; 10,000 other, such as joint staffs, administration, logistics, procurement, medical service, etc.); approximately 100,000 National Gendarmerie; approximately 75,000 National Guard (2024)

Military equipment inventories and acquisitions: the French military's inventory consists mostly of domestically produced weapons systems, including some jointly produced with other European countries; there is a smaller mix of armaments from other Western countries, particularly the US; France has a large and sophisticated defense industry capable of manufacturing the full spectrum of air, land, and naval military weapons systems (2024)
note: two major future acquisition programs for the French military included the Franco-German-Spanish Future Combat Air System, or FCAS (known in France as the système combat aérien du futur, or SCAF) and a next-generation tank development project with Germany known as the Main Ground Combat System, or MGCS

Military service age and obligation: generally 17-30 years of age for both men and women with some variations by service, position, and enlisted versus officer; basic service contract is for 12 months; no conscription (abolished 2001) (2024)
note 1: in 2023, women comprised more than 16% of the uniformed armed forces
note 2: French citizens can also volunteer for the Voluntary Military Service (VMS), which allows unemployed youth aged 18-25 to learn a trade or gain work experience while receiving basic military training and sports activities; French citizens may also join the military operational reserve up to age 72
note 3: men between the ages of 17.5 and 39.5 years of age, of any nationality, may join the French Foreign Legion; those volunteers selected for service sign five-year contracts

Military deployments: France typically has up to 30,000 total air, ground, and naval forces deployed on permanent or temporary foreign missions; up to 10,000 are permanently deployed, including Djibouti (1,400); French Guyana (2,000); French Polynesia (900); French West Indies (1,000); Reunion Island (1,700); West Africa (1,600; Cote d'Ivoire, Gabon, Senegal), and the UAE (700)
other non-permanent deployments include operations in Chad (1,000), NATO missions in Europe (2,000), the Middle East (850), and various EU (500) and UN (over 700, mostly in Lebanon under UNIFIL) missions (2024)

Military - note: the French military has a global footprint and a wide range of missions and responsibilities; it operates under France's overall defense and national security strategy, currently defined through the five major strategic functions of anticipation, prevention, deterrence, protection, and intervention; the military's responsibilities include protecting French territory, population, and interests, and fulfilling France's commitments to NATO, European security, and international peacekeeping operations under the UN; it is the largest military in the EU and has a leading role in the EU security framework, as well as in NATO; in recent years, it has actively participated in coalition peacekeeping and other security operations in regions such as Africa, the Middle East, and the Balkans, often in a lead role; the military regularly conducts large-scale exercises and participates in a variety of bi-lateral and multinational exercises; it also has a domestic security mission, including providing enhanced security at sensitive sites and large events and support during national crises or disasters, such as fighting forest fires; in recent years, defense responsibilities have expanded to include cyber and space domains
in 2010, France and the UK signed a declaration on defense and security cooperation that included greater military interoperability and a Combined Joint Expeditionary Force (CJEF), a deployable, combined Anglo-French military force for use in a wide range of crisis scenarios, up to and including high intensity combat operations; the CJEF has no standing forces, but would be available at short notice for French-UK bilateral, NATO, EU, UN, or other operations; combined training exercises began in 2011, and as of 2020, the CJEF was assessed as having full operating capacity with the ability to rapidly deploy over 10,000 personnel capable of high intensity operations, peacekeeping, disaster relief, and humanitarian assistance
the French Foreign Legion, established in 1831, is a military force that is open to foreign recruits willing to serve in the French military for service in France and abroad; the Foreign Legion is an integrated part of the French Army and is comprised of approximately 8,000 personnel; its combat units are a mix of armored cavalry and airborne, light, mechanized, and motorized infantry regiments (2024)

SPACE

Space agency/agencies: National Center for Space Studies (Centre National D'études Spatiales, CNES; established 1961); established a military Space Command (Le Commandement de l'Espace, CDE) under the Air and Space Force, 2020 (2024)

Space launch site(s): Guiana Space Center (Kourou, French Guiana; also serves as the spaceport for the ESA); note – prior to the completion of the Guiana

Space Center in 1969, France launched rockets from Algeria (2024)

Space program overview: has one of Europe's largest space programs and is a key member of the European Space Agency (ESA), as well as one of its largest contributors; has independent capabilities in all areas of space categories except for autonomous manned space flight; can build, launch, and operate a range of space/satellite launch vehicles (SLVs) and spacecraft, including exploratory probes and a full spectrum of satellites; trained astronauts until training mission shifted to ESA in 2001; develops a wide range of space-related technologies; hosts the ESA headquarters; participates in international space programs such as the Square Kilometer Array Project (world's largest radio telescope) and International Space Station (ISS); cooperates with a broad range of space agencies and commercial space companies, including those of China, Egypt, individual ESA and EU member countries, India, Indonesia, Israel, Japan, Mexico, Russia, the UAE, the US, and several African countries; has a large commercial space sector involved in such areas as satellite construction and payloads, launch capabilities, and a range of other space-related capabilities and technologies (2024)
note: further details about the key activities, programs, and milestones of the country's space program, as well as government spending estimates on the space sector, appear in the Space Programs reference guide

TERRORISM

Terrorist group(s): Islamic Revolutionary Guard Corps/Qods Force; Islamic State of Iraq and ash-Sham (ISIS); al-Qa'ida
note: details about the history, aims, leadership, organization, areas of operation, tactics, targets, weapons, size, and sources of support of the group(s) appear(s) in the Terrorism reference guide

TRANSNATIONAL ISSUES

Refugees and internally displaced persons: *refugees (country of origin):* 55,681 (Afghanistan), 39,091 (Syria), 33,834 (Sri Lanka), 33,148 (Russia), 31,935 (Democratic Republic of the Congo), 24,223 (Sudan), 21,225 (Guinea), 18,008 (Serbia and Kosovo), 17,032 (Turkey), 13,974 (Iraq), 12,286 (Cote d'Ivoire), 11,489 (Eritrea), 11,012 (Cambodia), 10,543 (China), 10,236 (Albania), 10,210 (Somalia), 8,858 (Bangladesh), 8,124 (Mauritania), 8,101 (Mali), 7,991 (Vietnam), 6,913 (Bosnia and Herzegovina), 6,910 (Haiti), 6,808 (Angola), 6,498 (Laos), 6,417 (Armenia), 6,111 (Nigeria), 5,896 (Georgia) (mid-year 2022); 69,462 (Ukraine) (as of 31 January 2024)
stateless persons: 3,633 (2022)

Illicit drugs: *metropolitan France:* transshipment point for South American cocaine, Southwest Asian heroin, and European synthetics;

French Guiana: small amount of marijuana grown for local consumption; minor transshipment point to Europe;

Martinique: transshipment point for cocaine and marijuana bound for the US and Europe

FRENCH POLYNESIA

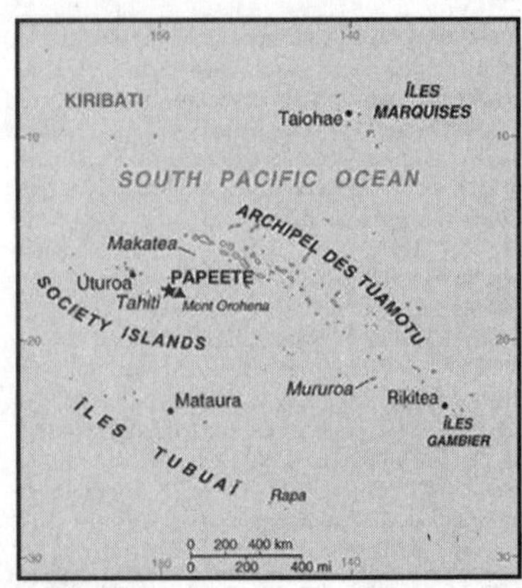

INTRODUCTION

Background: French Polynesia consists of five archipelagos – the Austral Islands, the Gambier Islands, the Marquesas Islands, the Society Islands, and the Tuamotu Archipelago. The Marquesas were first settled around 200 B.C. and the Society Islands around A.D. 300. Raiatea in the Society Islands became a center for religion and culture. Exploration of the other islands emanated from Raiatea, and by 1000, there were small permanent settlements in all the island groups. Ferdinand MAGELLAN was the first European to see the islands of French Polynesia in 1520. In 1767, British explorer Samuel WALLIS was the first European to visit Tahiti, followed by French navigator Louis Antoine de BOUGAINVILLE in 1768 and British explorer James COOK in 1769. King POMARE I united Tahiti and surrounding islands into the Kingdom of Tahiti in 1788. Protestant missionaries arrived in 1797, and POMARE I's successor converted in the 1810s, along with most Tahitians. In the 1830s, Queen POMARE IV refused to allow French Catholic missionaries to operate, leading France to declare a protectorate over Tahiti and fight the French-Tahitian War of the 1840s in an attempt to annex the islands.

In 1880, King POMARE V ceded Tahiti and its possessions to France, changing its status into a colony. France then claimed the Gambier Islands and Tuamotu Archipelago and by 1901 had incorporated all five island groups into its establishments in Oceania. A Tahitian nationalist movement formed in 1940, leading France to grant French citizenship to the islanders in 1946 and change it to an overseas territory. In 1957, the islands' name was changed to French Polynesia, and the following year, 64% of voters chose to stay part of France when they approved a new constitution. Uninhabited Mururoa Atoll was established as a French nuclear test site in 1962, and tests were conducted between 1966 and 1992 (underground beginning in 1975). France also conducted tests at Fangataufa Atoll, including its last nuclear test in 1996.

France granted French Polynesia partial internal autonomy in 1977 and expanded autonomy in 1984. French Polynesia was converted into an overseas collectivity in 2003 and renamed an overseas territory in 2004. Pro-independence politicians won a surprise majority in local elections that same year, but in subsequent elections, they have been relegated to a vocal minority. In 2013, French Polynesia was relisted on the UN List of Non-Self-Governing Territories.

GEOGRAPHY

Location: Oceania, five archipelagoes (Archipel des Tuamotu, Iles Gambier, Iles Marquises, Iles Tubuai, Society Islands) in the South Pacific Ocean about halfway between South America and Australia

Geographic coordinates: 15 00 S, 140 00 W

Map references: Oceania

Area: *total:* 4,167 sq km (118 islands and atolls; 67 are inhabited)
land: 3,827 sq km
water: 340 sq km
comparison ranking: total 174

Area - comparative: slightly less than one-third the size of Connecticut

Land boundaries: *total:* 0 km

Coastline: 2,525 km

Maritime claims: *territorial sea:* 12 nm
exclusive economic zone: 200 nm

Climate: tropical, but moderate

Terrain: mixture of rugged high islands and low islands with reefs

Elevation: *highest point:* Mont Orohena 2,241 m
lowest point: Pacific Ocean 0 m

Natural resources: timber, fish, cobalt, hydropower

Land use: *agricultural land:* 12.5% (2018 est.)
arable land: 0.7% (2018 est.)
permanent crops: 6.3% (2018 est.)
permanent pasture: 5.5% (2018 est.)
forest: 43.7% (2018 est.)
other: 43.8% (2018 est.)

Irrigated land: 10 sq km (2012)

Population distribution: the majority of the population lives in the Society Islands, one of five archipelagos that includes the most populous island - Tahiti - with approximately 70% of the nation's population

Natural hazards: occasional cyclonic storms in January

Geography - note: *includes five archipelagoes:* four volcanic (Iles Gambier, Iles Marquises, Iles Tubuai, Society Islands) and one coral (Archipel des Tuamotu); the Tuamotu Archipelago forms the largest group of atolls in the world – 78 in total, 48 inhabited; Makatea in the Tuamotu Archipelago is one of the three great phosphate rock islands in the Pacific Ocean – the others are Banaba (Ocean Island) in Kiribati and Nauru

PEOPLE AND SOCIETY

Population: *total:* 303,540
male: 155,138
female: 148,402 (2024 est.)
comparison rankings: female 182; male 180; total 182

Nationality: *noun:* French Polynesian(s)
adjective: French Polynesian

Ethnic groups: Polynesian 78%, Chinese 12%, local French 6%, metropolitan French 4%

Languages: French (official) 73.5%, Tahitian 20.1%, Marquesan 2.6%, Austral languages 1.2%, Paumotu 1%, other 1.6% (2017 est.)
major-language sample(s):
The World Factbook, une source indispensable d'informations de base. (French)

Religions: Protestant 54%, Roman Catholic 30%, other 10%, no religion 6%

Age structure: *0-14 years:* 20.3% (male 31,659/female 30,006)
15-64 years: 68.7% (male 107,162/female 101,228)
65 years and over: 11% (2024 est.) (male 16,317/female 17,168)

Dependency ratios: *total dependency ratio:* 45.6
youth dependency ratio: 31.6
elderly dependency ratio: 14
potential support ratio: 7.1 (2021 est.)

Median age: *total:* 35.3 years (2024 est.)
male: 35 years
female: 35.6 years
comparison ranking: total 98

Population growth rate: 0.66% (2024 est.)
comparison ranking: 133

Birth rate: 13 births/1,000 population (2024 est.)
comparison ranking: 134

Death rate: 5.8 deaths/1,000 population (2024 est.)
comparison ranking: 167

Net migration rate: -0.6 migrant(s)/1,000 population (2024 est.)
comparison ranking: 126

Population distribution: the majority of the population lives in the Society Islands, one of five archipelagos that includes the most populous island - Tahiti - with approximately 70% of the nation's population

Urbanization: *urban population:* 62.3% of total population (2023)
rate of urbanization: 0.65% annual rate of change (2020-25 est.)

Major urban areas - population: 136,000 PAPEETE (capital) (2018)

Sex ratio: *at birth:* 1.05 male(s)/female
0-14 years: 1.06 male(s)/female
15-64 years: 1.06 male(s)/female
65 years and over: 0.95 male(s)/female
total population: 1.05 male(s)/female (2024 est.)

Infant mortality rate: *total:* 4.3 deaths/1,000 live births (2024 est.)
male: 5.2 deaths/1,000 live births
female: 3.4 deaths/1,000 live births
comparison ranking: total 184

Life expectancy at birth: *total population:* 78.9 years (2024 est.)
male: 76.6 years
female: 81.3 years
comparison ranking: total population 69

Total fertility rate: 1.79 children born/woman (2024 est.)
comparison ranking: 143

Gross reproduction rate: 0.87 (2024 est.)

Drinking water source: *improved:*
total: 100% of population

Sanitation facility access: *improved:*
total: 97% of population

Currently married women (ages 15-49): 27.2% (2023 est.)

ENVIRONMENT

Environment - current issues: sea level rise; extreme weather events (cyclones, storms, and tsunamis producing floods, landslides, erosion, and reef damage); droughts; fresh water scarcity

Climate: tropical, but moderate

Urbanization: *urban population:* 62.3% of total population (2023)
rate of urbanization: 0.65% annual rate of change (2020-25 est.)

Air pollutants: *carbon dioxide emissions:* 0.77 megatons (2016 est.)

Waste and recycling: *municipal solid waste generated annually:* 147,000 tons (2013 est.)
municipal solid waste recycled annually: 57,330 tons (2013 est.)
percent of municipal solid waste recycled: 39% (2013 est.)

GOVERNMENT

Country name: *conventional long form:* Overseas Lands of French Polynesia
conventional short form: French Polynesia
local long form: Pays d'outre-mer de la Polynésie française
local short form: Polynesie Francaise
former: Establishments in Oceania, French Establishments in Oceania
etymology: the term "Polynesia" is an 18th-century construct composed of two Greek words, "poly" (many) and "nesoi" (islands), and refers to the more than 1,000 islands scattered over the central and southern Pacific Ocean

Government type: parliamentary democracy (Assembly of French Polynesia); an overseas collectivity of France

Dependency status: overseas country of France; note - overseas territory of France from 1946-2003; overseas collectivity of France since 2003, though it is often referred to as an overseas country due to its degree of autonomy

Capital: *name:* Papeete (located on Tahiti)
geographic coordinates: 17 32 S, 149 34 W
time difference: UTC-10 (5 hours behind Washington, DC, during Standard Time)
etymology: the name means "water basket" and refers to the fact that the islanders originally used calabashes enclosed in baskets to fetch water at a spring in the area

Administrative divisions: *5 administrative subdivisions (subdivisions administratives, singular - subdivision administrative):* Iles Australes (Austral Islands), Iles du Vent (Windward Islands), Iles Marquises (Marquesas Islands), Iles Sous-le-Vent (Leeward Islands), Iles Tuamotu-Gambier; note - the Leeward Islands and the Windward Islands together make up the Society Islands (Iles de la Societe)

Independence: none (overseas land of France)

National holiday: Fête de la Fédération, 14 July (1790); note - the local holiday is Internal Autonomy Day, 29 June (1880)

Legal system: the laws of France, where applicable, apply

Constitution: *history:* 4 October 1958 (French Constitution)
amendments: French constitution amendment procedures apply

Citizenship: see France

Suffrage: 18 years of age; universal

Executive branch: *chief of state:* President Emmanuel MACRON (since 14 May 2017), represented by High Commissioner of the Republic Eric SPITZ (since 23 September 2022)
head of government: President of French Polynesia Moetai BROTHERSON (since 12 May 2023)
cabinet: Council of Ministers approved by the Assembly from a list of its members submitted by the president
elections/appointments: French president directly elected by absolute majority popular vote in 2 rounds if needed for a 5-year term (eligible for a second term); high commissioner appointed by the French president on the advice of the French Ministry of Interior; French Polynesia president indirectly elected by Assembly of French Polynesia for a 5-year term (no term limits)

Legislative branch: *description:* unicameral Assembly of French Polynesia or Assemblée de la Polynésie française (57 seats; elections held in 2 rounds; in the second round, 38 members directly elected in multi-seat constituencies by a closed-list proportional representation vote; the party receiving the most votes gets an additional 19 seats; members serve 5-year terms; French Polynesia indirectly elects 2 senators to the French Senate via an electoral college by absolute majority vote for 6-year terms with one-half the membership renewed every 3 years and directly elects 3 deputies to the French National Assembly by absolute majority vote in 2 rounds if needed for 5-year terms
elections: Assembly of French Polynesia - last held on 16 and 30 April 2023 (next to be held in 2028)
French Senate - last held on 24 September 2023 (next to be held on 30 September 2026)
French National Assembly - last held in 2 rounds on 12 and 19 June 2022 (next to be held in 2027)
election results: Assembly of French Polynesia - percent of vote by party - People's Servant Party 66.7%; List of the People 26.3%, I Love Polynesia 5.3%, Rally of Mahoi People 1.8%; seats by party - People's Servant People 38; List of the People 15, I Love Polynesia 3, Rally of the Mahoi People 1, composition - men 29, women 28, percentage women 49.1%
French Senate - percent of vote by party - NA; seats by party - Popular Rally 1, People's Servant Party 1; composition - NA
French National Assembly - percent of vote by party - NA; seats by party - People's Servant Party 3; composition - NA

Judicial branch: *highest court(s):* Court of Appeal or Cour d'Appel (composition NA); note - appeals beyond the French Polynesia Court of Appeal are heard by the Court of Cassation (in Paris)

judge selection and term of office: judges assigned from France normally for 3 years
subordinate courts: Court of the First Instance or Tribunal de Premiere Instance; Court of Administrative Law or Tribunal Administratif

Political parties: I Love Polynesia (A here la Porinetia)
List of the People (Tapura Huiraatira)
People's Servant Party (Tavini Huiraatira)
Rally of the Maohi People (Amuitahira'a o te Nuna'a Maohi) (formerly known as Popular Rally (Tahoeraa Huiraatira))

International organization participation: ITUC (NGOs), PIF, SPC, UPU, WMO

Diplomatic representation in the US: none (overseas lands of France)

Diplomatic representation from the US: *embassy:* none (overseas lands of France)

Flag description: *two red horizontal bands encase a wide white band in a 1:2:1* ratio; centered on the white band is a disk with a blue and white wave pattern depicting the sea on the lower half and a gold and white ray pattern depicting the sun on the upper half; a Polynesian canoe rides on the wave pattern; the canoe has a crew of five represented by five stars that symbolize the five island groups; red and white are traditional Polynesian colors
note: identical to the red-white-red flag of Tahiti, the largest and most populous of the islands in French Polynesia, but which has no emblem in the white band; the flag of France is used for official occasions

National symbol(s): outrigger canoe, Tahitian gardenia (Gardenia taitensis) flower; national colors: red, white

National anthem: *name:* "Ia Ora 'O Tahiti Nui" (Long Live Tahiti Nui)
lyrics/music: Maeva BOUGES, Irmine TEHEI, Angele TEROROTUA, Johanna NOUVEAU, Patrick AMARU, Louis MAMATUI, and Jean-Pierre CELESTIN (the compositional group created both the lyrics and music)
note: adopted 1993; serves as a local anthem; as a territory of France, "La Marseillaise" is official (see France)

National heritage: *total World Heritage Sites:* 1 (cultural); note - excerpted from the France entry
selected World Heritage Site locales: Taputapuātea

Government - note: under certain acts of France, French Polynesia has acquired autonomy in all areas except those relating to police, monetary policy, tertiary education, immigration, and defense and foreign affairs; the duties of its president are fashioned after those of the French prime minister

ECONOMY

Economic overview: small, territorial-island tourism-based economy; large French financing; lower EU import duties; Pacific Islands Forum member; fairly resilient from COVID-19; oil-dependent infrastructure

Real GDP (purchasing power parity): $5.65 billion (2021 est.)
$5.52 billion (2020 est.)
$5.94 billion (2019 est.)
note: data are in 2015 dollars
comparison ranking: 179

Real GDP growth rate: 4.47% (2022 est.)
2.09% (2021 est.)
-7.05% (2020 est.)
note: annual GDP % growth based on constant local currency
comparison ranking: 69

Real GDP per capita: $18,600 (2021 est.)
$18,300 (2020 est.)
$19,800 (2019 est.)
note: data are in 2015 dollars
comparison ranking: 106

GDP (official exchange rate): $5.815 billion (2022 est.)
note: data in current dollars at official exchange rate

Inflation rate (consumer prices): 0% (2015 est.)
0.3% (2014 est.)
comparison ranking: 5

GDP - composition, by sector of origin: *agriculture:* 2.3% (2019 est.)
industry: 10.7% (2019 est.)
services: 76.2% (2019 est.)
note: figures may not total 100% due to non-allocated consumption not captured in sector-reported data
comparison rankings: services 23; industry 188; agriculture 152

GDP - composition, by end use: *household consumption:* 71.5% (2022 est.)
government consumption: 31.7% (2022 est.)
investment in fixed capital: 21.8% (2022 est.)
exports of goods and services: 21.1% (2022 est.)
imports of goods and services: -46.1% (2022 est.)
note: figures may not total 100% due to rounding or gaps in data collection

Agricultural products: coconuts, fruits, root vegetables, pineapples, eggs, cassava, sugarcane, tropical fruits, watermelons, tomatoes (2022)
note: top ten agricultural products based on tonnage

Industries: tourism, pearls, agricultural processing, handicrafts, phosphates

Industrial production growth rate: 4.3% (2014 est.)
note: annual % change in industrial value added based on constant local currency
comparison ranking: 56

Labor force: 137,000 (2023 est.)
note: number of people ages 15 or older who are employed or seeking work
comparison ranking: 181

Unemployment rate: 11.72% (2023 est.)
11.91% (2022 est.)
12.49% (2021 est.)
note: % of labor force seeking employment
comparison ranking: 176

Youth unemployment rate (ages 15-24): *total:* 37.3% (2023 est.)
male: 33.8% (2023 est.)
female: 42% (2023 est.)
note: % of labor force ages 15-24 seeking employment
comparison ranking: total 13

Remittances: 10% of GDP (2022 est.)
9.46% of GDP (2021 est.)
10.04% of GDP (2020 est.)
note: personal transfers and compensation between resident and non-resident individuals/households/entities

Current account balance: $411.963 million (2016 est.)
$291.182 million (2015 est.)
$264.32 million (2014 est.)
note: balance of payments - net trade and primary/secondary income in current dollars
comparison ranking: 65

Exports: $162 million (2021 est.)
$94.4 million (2020 est.)
$184 million (2019 est.)
note: balance of payments - exports of goods and services in current dollars
comparison ranking: 208

Exports - partners: France 18%, US 18%, Hong Kong 18%, Japan 13%, Netherlands 9% (2022)
note: top five export partners based on percentage share of exports

Exports - commodities: pearls, fish, aircraft parts, coconut oil, electrical power accessories (2022)
note: top five export commodities based on value in dollars

Imports: $1.66 billion (2021 est.)
$1.75 billion (2020 est.)
$2.24 billion (2019 est.)
note: balance of payments - imports of goods and services in current dollars
comparison ranking: 182

Imports - partners: France 30%, China 13%, US 9%, South Korea 6%, NZ 6% (2022)
note: top five import partners based on percentage share of imports

Imports - commodities: refined petroleum, cars, packaged medicine, beef, plastic products (2022)
note: top five import commodities based on value in dollars

Exchange rates: Comptoirs Francais du Pacifique francs (XPF) per US dollar -

Exchange rates: 110.347 (2023 est.)
113.474 (2022 est.)
100.88 (2021 est.)
104.711 (2020 est.)
106.589 (2019 est.)

ENERGY

Electricity access: *electrification - total population:* 100% (2022 est.)

Electricity: *installed generating capacity:* 280,000 kW (2022 est.)
consumption: 653.978 million kWh (2022 est.)
transmission/distribution losses: 42.663 million kWh (2022 est.)
comparison rankings: transmission/distribution losses 36; consumption 167; installed generating capacity 168

Electricity generation sources: *fossil fuels:* 67.5% of total installed capacity (2022 est.)
solar: 6.7% of total installed capacity (2022 est.)
hydroelectricity: 25.8% of total installed capacity (2022 est.)

Coal: *imports:* (2022 est.) less than 1 metric ton

Petroleum: *refined petroleum consumption:* 6,000 bbl/day (2022 est.)

Carbon dioxide emissions: 929,000 metric tonnes of CO_2 (2022 est.)
from petroleum and other liquids: 929,000 metric tonnes of CO_2 (2022 est.)
comparison ranking: total emissions 172

Energy consumption per capita: (2019)

COMMUNICATIONS

Telephones - fixed lines: *total subscriptions:* 139,000 (2022 est.)
subscriptions per 100 inhabitants: 45 (2022 est.)

comparison ranking: total subscriptions 128

Telephones - mobile cellular: *total subscriptions:* 328,000 (2022 est.)
subscriptions per 100 inhabitants: 107 (2022 est.)
comparison ranking: total subscriptions 178

Telecommunication systems: *general assessment:* French Polynesia has one of the most advanced telecoms infrastructures in the Pacific Islands region; the remoteness of the territory with its scattering of 130 islands and atolls has made connectivity vital for its inhabitants; the first submarine cable was deployed in 2010 and since then additional cables have been connected to the islands, vastly improving French Polynesia's international connectivity; an additional domestic submarine cable, the Natitua Sud, will connect more remote islands by the end of 2022; French Polynesia is also a hub for satellite communications in the region; a considerable number of consumers access FttP-based services; with the first data center in French Polynesia on the cards, the quality and price of broadband services is expected to improve as content will be able to be cached locally, reducing costs for consumers; for 2022, fixed broadband subscriptions reached an estimated 22%; about 43% of the territory's mobile connections are on 3G networks, while LTE accounts for 12%; by 2025, LTE is expected to account for more than half of all connections; it is also estimated that 77% of mobile subscribers will have smart phones by 2025 (2022)
domestic: fixed-line subscriptions nearly 36 per 100 persons and mobile-cellular density is roughly 106 per 100 persons (2021)
international: country code - 689; landing points for the NATITUA, Manatua, and Honotua submarine cables to other French Polynesian Islands, Cook Islands, Niue, Samoa and US; satellite earth station - 1 Intelsat (Pacific Ocean) (2019)

Broadcast media: French public overseas broadcaster Reseau Outre-Mer provides 2 TV channels and 1 radio station; 1 government-owned TV station; a small number of privately owned radio stations (2019)

Internet country code: .pf

Internet users: *total:* 218,100 (2021 est.)
percent of population: 72.7% (2021 est.)
comparison ranking: total 180

Broadband - fixed subscriptions: *total:* 64,000 (2020 est.)
subscriptions per 100 inhabitants: 23 (2020 est.)
comparison ranking: total 138

TRANSPORTATION

National air transport system: *number of registered air carriers:* 2 (2020) (registered in France)
inventory of registered aircraft operated by air carriers: 19 (registered in France)

Civil aircraft registration country code prefix: F-OH

Airports: 54 (2024)
comparison ranking: 84

Roadways: *total:* 2,590 km
paved: 1,735 km
unpaved: 855 km (1999)
comparison ranking: total 170

Merchant marine: *total:* 24 (2023)
by type: general cargo 14
comparison ranking: total 145

Ports: *total ports:* 6 (2024)
large: 0
medium: 0
small: 1
very small: 5
ports with oil terminals: 1
key ports: Atuona, Baie Taiohae, Papeete, Port Rikitea, Uturoa, Vaitape

MILITARY AND SECURITY

Military and security forces: no regular military forces

Military - note: defense is the responsibility of France; France maintains forces (about 900 troops) in French Polynesia

FRENCH SOUTHERN AND ANTARCTIC LANDS

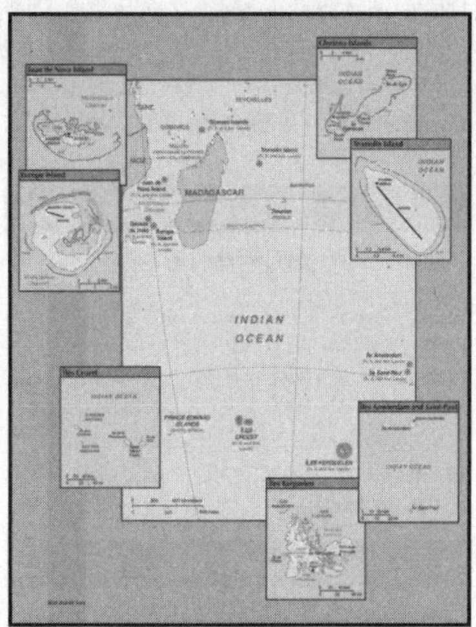

INTRODUCTION

Background: In 2007, the Iles Eparses became an integral part of the French Southern and Antarctic Lands (TAAF). The Southern Lands are now divided into five administrative districts, two of which are archipelagos, the Iles Crozet and Iles Kerguelen; the third is a district composed of two volcanic islands, Ile Saint-Paul and Ile Amsterdam; the fourth, Iles Eparses, consists of five scattered tropical islands around Madagascar. They contain no permanent inhabitants and are visited only by researchers studying the native fauna, scientists at the various scientific stations, fishermen, and military personnel. The fifth district is the Antarctic portion, which consists of "Adelie Land," a thin slice of the Antarctic continent discovered and claimed by the French in 1840.

Ile Amsterdam: Discovered but not named in 1522 by the Spanish, the island subsequently received the appellation of Nieuw Amsterdam from a Dutchman; it was claimed by France in 1843. A short-lived attempt at cattle farming began in 1871. A French meteorological station established on the island in 1949 is still in use.

Ile Saint Paul: Claimed by France since 1893, the island was a fishing industry center from 1843 to 1914. In 1928, a spiny lobster cannery was established, but when the company went bankrupt in 1931, seven workers were abandoned. Only two survived until 1934 when rescue finally arrived.

Iles Crozet: A large archipelago formed from the Crozet Plateau, Iles Crozet is divided into two main groups: L'Occidental (the West), which includes Ile aux Cochons, Ilots des Apotres, Ile des Pingouins, and the reefs Brisants de l'Heroine; and L'Oriental (the East), which includes Ile d'Est and Ile de la Possession, the largest island of the Crozets. Discovered and claimed by France in 1772, the islands were used for seal hunting and as a base for whaling. Originally administered as a dependency of Madagascar, they became part of the TAAF in 1955.

Iles Kerguelen: This island group, discovered in 1772, consists of one large island (Ile Kerguelen) and about 300 smaller islands. A permanent group of 50 to 100 scientists resides at the main base at Port-aux-Francais.

Adelie Land: The only non-insular district of the TAAF is the Antarctic claim known as "Adelie Land." The US Government does not recognize it as a French dependency.

Bassas da India: A French possession since 1897, this atoll is a volcanic rock surrounded by reefs and is awash at high tide.

Europa Island: This heavily wooded island has been a French possession since 1897; it is the site of a small military garrison that staffs a weather station.

Glorioso Islands: A French possession since 1892, the Glorioso Islands are composed of two lushly vegetated coral islands (Ile Glorieuse and Ile du Lys) and three rock islets. A military garrison operates a weather and radio station on Ile Glorieuse.

Juan de Nova Island: Named after a famous 15th-century Spanish navigator and explorer, the island has been a French possession since 1897. It has been exploited for its guano and phosphate. Presently a small military garrison oversees a meteorological station.

Tromelin Island: First explored by the French in 1776, the island came under the jurisdiction of Reunion in 1814. At present, it serves as a sea turtle sanctuary and is the site of an important meteorological station.

GEOGRAPHY

Location: southeast and east of Africa, islands in the southern Indian Ocean, some near Madagascar and others about equidistant between Africa, Antarctica, and Australia; note - French Southern and Antarctic Lands include Ile Amsterdam, Ile Saint-Paul, Iles Crozet, Iles Kerguelen, Bassas da India, Europa Island, Glorioso Islands, Juan de Nova Island, and

Tromelin Island in the southern Indian Ocean, along with the French-claimed sector of Antarctica, "Adelie Land"; the US does not recognize the French claim to "Adelie Land"

Geographic coordinates: Ile Amsterdam (Ile Amsterdam et Ile Saint-Paul): 37 50 S, 77 32 E;

Ile Saint-Paul (Ile Amsterdam et Ile Saint-Paul): 38 72 S, 77 53 E;

Iles Crozet: 46 25 S, 51 00 E;

Iles Kerguelen: 49 15 S, 69 35 E;

Bassas da India (Iles Eparses): 21 30 S, 39 50 E;

Europa Island (Iles Eparses): 22 20 S, 40 22 E;

Glorioso Islands (Iles Eparses): 11 30 S, 47 20 E;

Juan de Nova Island (Iles Eparses): 17 03 S, 42 45 E;

Tromelin Island (Iles Eparses): 15 52 S, 54 25 E

Map references: Antarctic RegionAfrica

Area: Ile Amsterdam (Ile Amsterdam et Ile Saint-Paul): total - 55 sq km; land - 55 sq km; water - 0 sq km

Ile Saint-Paul (Ile Amsterdam et Ile Saint-Paul): total - 7 sq km; land - 7 sq km; water - 0 sq km

Iles Crozet: total - 352 sq km; land - 352 sq km; water - 0 sq km

Iles Kerguelen: total - 7,215 sq km; land - 7,215 sq km; water - 0 sq km

Bassas da India (Iles Eparses): total - 80 sq km; land - 0.2 sq km; water - 79.8 sq km (lagoon)

Europa Island (Iles Eparses): total - 28 sq km; land - 28 sq km; water - 0 sq km

Glorioso Islands (Iles Eparses): total - 5 sq km; land - 5 sq km; water - 0 sq km

Juan de Nova Island (Iles Eparses): total - 4.4 sq km; land - 4.4 sq km; water - 0 sq km

Tromelin Island (Iles Eparses): total - 1 sq km; land - 1 sq km; water - 0 sq km
note: excludes "Adelie Land" claim of about 500,000 sq km in Antarctica that is not recognized by the US

Area - comparative: Ile Amsterdam (Ile Amsterdam et Ile Saint-Paul): less than one-half the size of Washington, DC;

Ile Saint-Paul (Ile Amsterdam et Ile Saint-Paul): more than 10 times the size of the National Mall in Washington, DC;

Iles Crozet: about twice the size of Washington, DC;

Iles Kerguelen: slightly larger than Delaware;

Bassas da India (Iles Eparses): land area about one-third the size of the National Mall in Washington, DC;

Europa Island (Iles Eparses): about one-sixth the size of Washington, DC;

Glorioso Islands (Iles Eparses): about eight times the size of the National Mall in Washington, DC;

Juan de Nova Island (Iles Eparses): about seven times the size of the National Mall in Washington, DC;

Tromelin Island (Iles Eparses): about 1.7 times the size of the National Mall in Washington, DC

Land boundaries: *total:* 0 km

Coastline: Ile Amsterdam (Ile Amsterdam et Ile Saint-Paul): 28 km

Ile Saint-Paul (Ile Amsterdam et Ile Saint-Paul): Iles Kerguelen: 2,800 km

Bassas da India (Iles Eparses): 35.2 km

Europa Island (Iles Eparses): 22.2 km

Glorioso Islands (Iles Eparses): 35.2 km

Juan de Nova Island (Iles Eparses): 24.1 km

Tromelin Island (Iles Eparses): 3.7 km

Maritime claims: *territorial sea:* 12 nm
exclusive economic zone: 200 nm from Iles Kerguelen and Iles Eparses (does not include the rest of French Southern and Antarctic Lands); Juan de Nova Island and Tromelin Island claim a continental shelf of 200-m depth or to the depth of exploitation

Climate: Ile Amsterdam et Ile Saint-Paul: oceanic with persistent westerly winds and high humidity;

Iles Crozet: windy, cold, wet, and cloudy;

Iles Kerguelen: oceanic, cold, overcast, windy;

Iles Eparses: tropical

Terrain: Ile Amsterdam (Ile Amsterdam et Ile Saint-Paul): a volcanic island with steep coastal cliffs; the center floor of the volcano is a large plateau;

Ile Saint-Paul (Ile Amsterdam et Ile Saint-Paul): triangular in shape, the island is the top of a volcano, rocky with steep cliffs on the eastern side; has active thermal springs;

Iles Crozet: a large archipelago formed from the Crozet Plateau is divided into two groups of islands;

Iles Kerguelen: the interior of the large island of Ile Kerguelen is composed of high mountains, hills, valleys, and plains with peninsulas stretching off its coasts;

Bassas da India (Iles Eparses): atoll, awash at high tide; shallow (15 m) lagoon;

Europa Island, Glorioso Islands, Juan de Nova Island: low, flat, and sandy;

Tromelin Island (Iles Eparses): low, flat, sandy; likely volcanic seamount

Elevation: *highest point:* Mont de la Dives on Ile Amsterdam (Ile Amsterdam et Ile Saint- Paul) 867 m
lowest point: Indian Ocean 0 m
highest points throughout the French Southern and Antarctic Lands: unnamed location on Ile Saint-Paul (Ile Amsterdam et Ile Saint-Paul) 272 m; Pic Marion-Dufresne in Iles Crozet 1090 m; Mont Ross in Iles Kerguelen 1850 m; unnamed location on Bassas de India (Iles Eparses) 2.4 m;24 unnamed location on Europa Island (Iles Eparses) 24 m; unnamed location on Glorioso Islands (Iles Eparses) 12 m; unnamed location on Juan de Nova Island (Iles Eparses) 10 m; unnamed location on Tromelin Island (Iles Eparses) 7 m

Natural resources: fish, crayfish, note, Glorioso Islands and Tromelin Island (Iles Eparses) have guano, phosphates, and coconuts
note: in the 1950's and 1960's, several species of trout were introduced to Iles Kerguelen of which two, brown trout and brook trout, survived to establish wild populations; reindeer were also introduced to Iles Kerguelen in 1956 as a source of fresh meat for whaling crews – the herd today, one of two in the Southern Hemisphere, is estimated to number around 4,000

Natural hazards: Ile Amsterdam and Ile Saint-Paul are inactive volcanoes; Iles Eparses subject to periodic cyclones; Bassas da India is a maritime hazard since it is under water for a period of three hours prior to and following the high tide and surrounded by reefs
volcanism: Reunion Island - Piton de la Fournaise (2,632 m), which has erupted many times in recent years including 2010, 2015, and 2017, is one of the world's most active volcanoes; although rare, eruptions outside the volcano's caldera could threaten nearby cities

Geography - note: islands' component is widely scattered across remote locations in the southern Indian Ocean

Bassas da India (Iles Eparses): atoll is a circular reef atop a long-extinct, submerged volcano;

Europa Island and Juan de Nova Island (Iles Eparses): wildlife sanctuary for seabirds and sea turtles;

Glorioso Island (Iles Eparses): islands and rocks are surrounded by an extensive reef system;

Tromelin Island (Iles Eparses): climatologically important location for forecasting cyclones in the western Indian Ocean; wildlife sanctuary (seabirds, tortoises)

PEOPLE AND SOCIETY

Population: *total:* no indigenous inhabitants

Ile Amsterdam (Ile Amsterdam et Ile Saint-Paul): uninhabited but has a meteorological station

Ile Saint-Paul (Ile Amsterdam et Ile Saint-Paul): uninhabited but is frequently visited by fishermen and has a scientific research cabin for short stays

Iles Crozet: uninhabited except for 18 to 30 people staffing the Alfred Faure research station on Ile del la Possession

Iles Kerguelen: 50 to 100 scientists are located at the main base at Port-aux-Francais on Ile Kerguelen

Bassas da India (Iles Eparses): uninhabitable

Europa Island, Glorioso Islands, Juan de Nova Island (Iles Eparses): a small French military garrison and a few meteorologists on each possession; visited by scientists

Tromelin Island (Iles Eparses): uninhabited, visited by scientists

ENVIRONMENT

Environment - current issues: introduction of foreign species on Iles Crozet has caused severe damage to the original ecosystem; overfishing of Patagonian toothfish around Iles Crozet and Iles Kerguelen

Climate: Ile Amsterdam et Ile Saint-Paul: oceanic with persistent westerly winds and high humidity;

Iles Crozet: windy, cold, wet, and cloudy;

Iles Kerguelen: oceanic, cold, overcast, windy;

Iles Eparses: tropical

GOVERNMENT

Country name: *conventional long form:* Territory of the French Southern and Antarctic Lands
conventional short form: French Southern and Antarctic Lands
local long form: Terres australes et antarctiques françaises
local short form: Terres Australes et Antarctiques Francaises
abbreviation: TAAF
etymology: self-descriptive name specifying the territories' affiliation and location in the Southern Hemisphere

Dependency status: overseas territory of France since 1955

Administrative divisions: none (overseas territory of France); there are no first-order administrative divisions as defined by the US Government, but there are 5 administrative districts named Iles Crozet, Iles Eparses, Iles Kerguelen, Ile Saint-Paul et Ile Amsterdam; the fifth district is the "Adelie Land" claim in Antarctica that is not recognized by the US

Legal system: the laws of France, where applicable, apply

Citizenship: see France

Executive branch: *chief of state:* President Emmanuel MACRON (since 14 May 2017), represented by Prefect Florence JEANBLANC-RISLER (since 5 October 2022)

International organization participation: UPU

Diplomatic representation in the US: none (overseas territory of France)

Diplomatic representation from the US: *embassy:* none (overseas territory of France)

Flag description: the flag of France is used

National anthem: *note:* as a territory of France, "La Marseillaise" is official (see France)

ECONOMY

Economic overview: very small, fishing-based, domestic economic activity; military base servicing

Exports - partners: France 80%, Singapore 5%, Belgium 5%, Poland 3%, Czechia 2% (2022)
note: top five export partners based on percentage share of exports

Exports - commodities: fish, shellfish, measuring instruments, aluminum products, trunks and cases (2022)
note: top five export commodities based on value in dollars

Imports - partners: France 23%, US 13%, Netherlands 12%, Poland 11%, Germany 9% (2022)
note: top five import partners based on percentage share of imports

Imports - commodities: refined petroleum, surveying equipment, gas turbines, tractors, trucks (2022)
note: top five import commodities based on value in dollars

COMMUNICATIONS

Internet country code: .tf

Communications - note: has one or more meteorological stations on each possession

TRANSPORTATION

Airports: 4 (2024)
comparison ranking: 182

Heliports: 3 (2024)

Merchant marine: *total:* 2 (2023)
by type: other 2
comparison ranking: total 179

MILITARY AND SECURITY

Military - note: defense is the responsibility of France; the French military maintains a Foreign Legion detachment on Mayotte to maintain France's presence in the region and support French forces operating in the southern zone of the Indian Ocean and the east coast of Africa; the detachment regularly deploys to the outlying Glorioso Islands

GABON

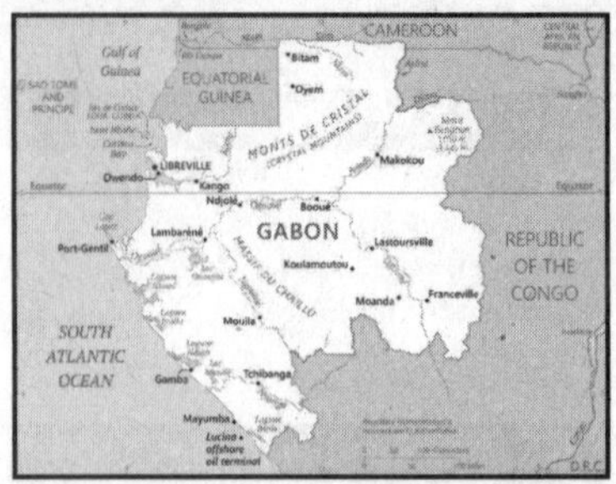

INTRODUCTION

Background: Gabon, a sparsely populated country known for its dense rainforests and vast petroleum reserves, is one of the most prosperous and stable countries in central Africa. Approximately 40 ethnic groups are represented, the largest of which is the Fang, a group that covers the northern third of Gabon and expands north into Equatorial Guinea and Cameroon. From about the early 1300s, various kingdoms emerged in present-day Gabon and the surrounding area, including the Kingdoms of Loango and Orungu. Because most early Bantu languages spoken in these kingdoms did not have a written form, much of Gabon's early history was lost over time. Portuguese traders who arrived in the mid-1400s gave the area its name of Gabon. At that time, indigenous trade networks began to engage with European traders, exchanging goods such as ivory and wood. For a century beginning in the 1760s, trade came to focus mostly on enslaved people. While many groups in Gabon participated in the slave trade, the Fang were a notable exception. As the slave trade declined in the late 1800s, France colonized the country and directed a widespread extraction of Gabonese resources. Anti-colonial rhetoric by Gabon's educated elites increased significantly in the early 1900s, but no widespread rebellion materialized. French decolonization after World War II led to the country's independence in 1960.

Within a year of independence, the government changed from a parliamentary to a presidential system, and Leon M'BA won the first presidential election in 1961. El Hadj Omar BONGO Ondimba was M'BA's vice president and assumed the presidency after M'BA's death in 1967. BONGO went on to dominate the country's political scene for four decades (1967-2009). In 1968, he declared Gabon a single-party state and created the still-dominant Parti Democratique Gabonais (PDG). In the early 1990s, he reintroduced a multiparty system under a new constitution in response to growing political opposition. He was reelected by wide margins in 1995, 1998, 2002, and 2005 against a divided opposition and amidst allegations of fraud. After BONGO's death in 2009, a new election brought his son, Ali BONGO Ondimba, to power, and he was reelected in 2016. He won a third term in the August 2023 election but was overthrown in a military coup a few days later. Gen. Brice OLIGUI Nguema led a military group called the Committee for the Transition and Restoration of Institutions that arrested BONGO, canceled the election results, and dissolved state institutions. In September 2023, OLIGUI was sworn in as transitional president of Gabon.

GEOGRAPHY

Location: Central Africa, bordering the Atlantic Ocean at the Equator, between Republic of the Congo and Equatorial Guinea

Geographic coordinates: 1 00 S, 11 45 E

Map references: Africa

Area: *total:* 267,667 sq km
land: 257,667 sq km
water: 10,000 sq km
comparison ranking: total 78

Area - comparative: slightly smaller than Colorado

Land boundaries: *total:* 3,261 km
border countries (3): Cameroon 349 km; Republic of the Congo 2,567 km; Equatorial Guinea 345 km

Coastline: 885 km

Maritime claims: *territorial sea:* 12 nm
contiguous zone: 24 nm
exclusive economic zone: 200 nm

Climate: tropical; always hot, humid

Terrain: narrow coastal plain; hilly interior; savanna in east and south

Elevation: *highest point:* Mont Bengoue 1,050 m
lowest point: Atlantic Ocean 0 m
mean elevation: 377 m

Natural resources: petroleum, natural gas, diamond, niobium, manganese, uranium, gold, timber, iron ore, hydropower

Land use: *agricultural land:* 19% (2018 est.)
arable land: 1.2% (2018 est.)
permanent crops: 0.6% (2018 est.)
permanent pasture: 17.2% (2018 est.)
forest: 81% (2018 est.)
other: 0% (2018 est.)

Irrigated land: 40 sq km (2012)

Major watersheds (area sq km): Atlantic Ocean drainage: Congo (3,730,881 sq km)

Major aquifers: Congo Basin

Population distribution: the relatively small population is spread in pockets throughout the country; the largest urban center is the capital of Libreville, located along the Atlantic coast in the northwest as shown in this population distribution map

Natural hazards: none

Geography - note: a small population and oil and mineral reserves have helped Gabon become one of Africa's wealthier countries; in general, these circumstances have allowed the country to maintain and conserve its pristine rain forest and rich biodiversity

PEOPLE AND SOCIETY

Population: *total:* 2,455,105
male: 1,270,023
female: 1,185,082 (2024 est.)
comparison rankings: female 145; male 143; total 145

Nationality: *noun:* Gabonese (singular and plural)
adjective: Gabonese

Ethnic groups: Fang 23.5%, Shira-Punu'Vii 20.6%, Nzabi-Duma 11.2%, Mbede-Teke 5.6%, Myene 4.4%, Kota-Kele 4.3%, Okande- Tsogho 1.6%, other 12.6%, foreigner 16.2% (2021 est.)

Languages: French (official), Fang, Myene, Nzebi, Bapounou/Eschira, Bandjabi

Religions: Protestant 46.4% (Revival Church 37%, other Protestant 9.4%), Roman Catholic 29.8%, other Christian 4%, Muslim 10.8%, traditional/animist 1.1%, other 0.9%, none 7% (2019-21 est.)

Demographic profile: Gabon's oil revenues have given it one of the highest per capita income levels in Sub-Saharan Africa, but the wealth is not evenly distributed and poverty is widespread. Unemployment is especially prevalent among the large youth population; more than 60% of the population is under the age of 25 as of 2020. With a fertility rate still averaging more than 3 children per woman, the youth population will continue to grow and further strain the mismatch between Gabon's supply of jobs and the skills of its labor force.
Gabon has been a magnet to migrants from neighboring countries since the 1960s because of the discovery of oil, as well as the country's political stability and timber, mineral, and natural gas resources. Nonetheless, income inequality and high unemployment have created slums in Libreville full of migrant workers from Senegal, Nigeria, Cameroon, Benin, Togo, and elsewhere in West Africa. In 2011, Gabon declared an end to refugee status for 9,500 remaining Congolese nationals to whom it had granted asylum during the Republic of the Congo's civil war between 1997 and 2003. About 5,400 of these refugees received permits to reside in Gabon.

Age structure: *0-14 years:* 34.6% (male 429,133/female 421,120)
15-64 years: 61.1% (male 787,480/female 711,913)
65 years and over: 4.3% (2024 est.) (male 53,410/female 52,049)

Dependency ratios: *total dependency ratio:* 67.6
youth dependency ratio: 61
elderly dependency ratio: 6.5
potential support ratio: 15.3 (2021 est.)

Median age: *total:* 22 years (2024 est.)
male: 22.5 years
female: 21.5 years
comparison ranking: total 187

Population growth rate: 2.37% (2024 est.)
comparison ranking: 25

Birth rate: 25.7 births/1,000 population (2024 est.)
comparison ranking: 43

Death rate: 5.5 deaths/1,000 population (2024 est.)
comparison ranking: 181

Net migration rate: 3.5 migrant(s)/1,000 population (2024 est.)
comparison ranking: 31

Population distribution: the relatively small population is spread in pockets throughout the country; the largest urban center is the capital of Libreville, located along the Atlantic coast in the northwest as shown in this population distribution map

Urbanization: *urban population:* 91% of total population (2023)
rate of urbanization: 2.27% annual rate of change (2020-25 est.)

Major urban areas - population: 870,000 LIBREVILLE (capital) (2023)

Sex ratio: *at birth:* 1.03 male(s)/female
0-14 years: 1.02 male(s)/female
15-64 years: 1.11 male(s)/female
65 years and over: 1.03 male(s)/female
total population: 1.07 male(s)/female (2024 est.)

Mother's mean age at first birth: 19.6 years (2012 est.)
note: data represents median age at first birth among women 20-49

Maternal mortality ratio: 227 deaths/100,000 live births (2020 est.)
comparison ranking: 40

Infant mortality rate: *total:* 26.9 deaths/1,000 live births (2024 est.)
male: 29.7 deaths/1,000 live births
female: 24 deaths/1,000 live births
comparison ranking: total 57

Life expectancy at birth: *total population:* 70.4 years (2024 est.)
male: 68.6 years
female: 72.1 years
comparison ranking: total population 175

Total fertility rate: 3.21 children born/woman (2024 est.)
comparison ranking: 43

Gross reproduction rate: 1.58 (2024 est.)

Contraceptive prevalence rate: 31.1% (2012)

Drinking water source: *improved: urban:* 97.2% of population
rural: 55.3% of population
total: 93.1% of population
unimproved: urban: 2.8% of population
rural: 44.7% of population
total: 6.9% of population (2020 est.)

Current health expenditure: 3.4% of GDP (2020)

Physician density: 0.65 physicians/1,000 population (2018)

Hospital bed density: 6.3 beds/1,000 population

Sanitation facility access: *improved: urban:* 81.3% of population
rural: 55.1% of population
total: 78.7% of population
unimproved: urban: 18.7% of population
rural: 44.9% of population
total: 21.3% of population (2020 est.)

Obesity - adult prevalence rate: 15% (2016)
comparison ranking: 127

Alcohol consumption per capita: *total:* 6.47 liters of pure alcohol (2019 est.)
beer: 5.31 liters of pure alcohol (2019 est.)
wine: 0.62 liters of pure alcohol (2019 est.)
spirits: 0.5 liters of pure alcohol (2019 est.)
other alcohols: 0.04 liters of pure alcohol (2019 est.)
comparison ranking: total 64

Children under the age of 5 years underweight: 6.4% (2019/20)
comparison ranking: 69

Currently married women (ages 15-49): 49.7% (2023 est.)

Education expenditures: 3.2% of GDP (2020 est.)
comparison ranking: 150

Literacy: *definition:* age 15 and over can read and write
total population: 85.5%
male: 86.2%
female: 84.7% (2021)

ENVIRONMENT

Environment - current issues: deforestation (the forests that cover three-quarters of the country are threatened by excessive logging); burgeoning population exacerbating disposal of solid waste; oil industry contributing to water pollution; wildlife poaching

Environment - international agreements: *party to:* Biodiversity, Climate Change, Climate Change-Kyoto Protocol, Climate Change-Paris Agreement, Comprehensive Nuclear Test Ban, Desertification, Endangered Species, Hazardous Wastes, Law of the Sea, Marine Dumping-London Convention, Nuclear Test Ban, Ozone Layer Protection, Ship Pollution, Tropical Timber 2006, Wetlands, Whaling
signed, but not ratified: none of the selected agreements

Climate: tropical; always hot, humid

Urbanization: *urban population:* 91% of total population (2023)
rate of urbanization: 2.27% annual rate of change (2020-25 est.)

Revenue from forest resources: 2.6% of GDP (2018 est.)
comparison ranking: 26

Revenue from coal: 0% of GDP (2018 est.)
comparison ranking: 68

Air pollutants: *particulate matter emissions:* 26.29 micrograms per cubic meter (2019 est.)
carbon dioxide emissions: 5.32 megatons (2016 est.)
methane emissions: 1.13 megatons (2020 est.)

Waste and recycling: *municipal solid waste generated annually:* 238,102 tons (1995 est.)

Major watersheds (area sq km): Atlantic Ocean drainage: Congo (3,730,881 sq km)

Major aquifers: Congo Basin

Total water withdrawal: *municipal:* 80 million cubic meters (2020 est.)
industrial: 10 million cubic meters (2020 est.)
agricultural: 40 million cubic meters (2020 est.)

Total renewable water resources: 166 billion cubic meters (2020 est.)

GOVERNMENT

Country name: *conventional long form:* Gabonese Republic
conventional short form: Gabon
local long form: République Gabonaise
local short form: Gabon
etymology: name originates from the Portuguese word "gabao" meaning "cloak," which is roughly the shape that the early explorers gave to the estuary of the Komo River by the capital of Libreville

Government type: presidential republic

Capital: *name:* Libreville
geographic coordinates: 0 23 N, 9 27 E
time difference: UTC+1 (6 hours ahead of Washington, DC, during Standard Time)
etymology: original site settled by freed slaves and the name means "free town" in French; named in imitation of Freetown, the capital of Sierra Leone

Administrative divisions: 9 provinces; Estuaire, Haut-Ogooue, Moyen-Ogooue, Ngounie, Nyanga, Ogooue-Ivindo, Ogooue-Lolo, Ogooue- Maritime, Woleu-Ntem

Independence: 17 August 1960 (from France)

National holiday: Independence Day, 17 August (1960)

Legal system: mixed legal system of French civil law and customary law

Constitution: *history:* previous 1961; latest drafted May 1990, adopted 15 March 1991, promulgated 26 March 1991
amendments: proposed by the president of the republic, by the Council of Ministers, or by one third of either house of Parliament; passage requires Constitutional Court evaluation, at least two-thirds majority vote of two thirds of the Parliament membership convened in joint session, and approval in a referendum; constitutional articles on Gabon's democratic form of government cannot be amended; amended several times, last in 2023 (presidential term reduced to 5 years and election reduced to a single vote)

International law organization participation: has not submitted an ICJ jurisdiction declaration; accepts ICCt jurisdiction

Citizenship: *citizenship by birth:* no
citizenship by descent only: at least one parent must be a citizen of Gabon
dual citizenship recognized: no
residency requirement for naturalization: 10 years

Suffrage: 18 years of age; universal

Executive branch: *chief of state:* Transitional President Gen. Brice OLIGUI Nguema (since 4 September 2023)
head of government: Prime Minister Raymond NDONG SIMA (since 7 September 2023)
cabinet: formerly the Council of Ministers, appointed by the prime minister in consultation with the president
elections/appointments: formerly, the president directly elected by plurality vote for a 5-year term (no term limits); election last held on 26 August 2023; prime minister appointed by the president; note - in August 2023, Gen. Brice OLIGUI Nguema led a military group called Committee for the Transition and Restoration of Institutions in a coup in which President Ali BONGO Ondimba was arrested and detained, election results were canceled, and state institutions were dissolved; in September 2023, OLIGUI was sworn in as transitional president; a general election is planned for August 2025
election results:
2016: Ali BONGO Ondimba reelected president; percent of vote - Ali BONGO Ondimba (PDG) 49.8%, Jean PING (UFC) 48.2%, other 2.0%
2009: Ali BONGO Ondimba elected president; percent of vote - Ali BONGO Ondimba (PDG) 41.7%, Andre MBA OBAME (independent) 25.9%, Pierre MAMBOUNDOU (UPG) 25.2%, Zacharie MYBOTO (UGDD) 3.9%, other 3.3%

Legislative branch: **description:** Transitional Parliament (formerly the bicameral Parliament) consists of:
Senate (70 seats; members appointed by Transitional president; member term NA)
National Assembly (98 seats; members appointed by the Transitional president; member term NA)
note - all members represent legally recognized political parties or leading political figures, civil society, and defense and security forces
elections: on 11 September 2023, Transitional President Gen. Brice OLIGUI Nguema appointed 168 members to the Transitional Parliament; elections for a permanent legislature reportedly to follow

2-year transition; note - the military government announced on 13 November 2023 that presidential and legislative elections will be held in August 2025
election results: all members of the Transitional Parliament appointed by the Transitional president

Judicial branch: *highest court(s):* Supreme Court (consists of 4 permanent specialized supreme courts - Supreme Court or Cour de Cassation, Administrative Supreme Court or Conseil d'Etat, Accounting Supreme Court or Cour des Comptes, Constitutional Court or Cour Constitutionnelle, and the non-permanent Court of State Security, initiated only for cases of high treason by the president and criminal activity by executive branch officials)
judge selection and term of office: appointment and tenure of Supreme, Administrative, Accounting, and State Security courts NA; Constitutional Court judges appointed - 3 by the national president, 3 by the president of the Senate, and 3 by the president of the National Assembly; judges serve single renewable 7-year terms
subordinate courts: Courts of Appeal; county courts; military courts

Political parties: Gabonese Democratic Party or PDG
Restoration of Republican Values or RV
The Democrats or LD
Paul Mba Abessole

International organization participation: ACP, AfDB, AU (suspended), BDEAC, CEMAC, FAO, FZ, G-24, G-77, IAEA, IBRD, ICAO, ICCt, ICRM, IDA, IDB, IFAD, IFC, IFRCS, ILO, IMF, IMO, IMSO, Interpol, IOC, IOM, IPU, ISO, ITSO, ITU, ITUC (NGOs), MIGA, MINUSCA, NAM, OIC, OIF, OPCW, UN, UNCTAD, UNESCO, UNIDO, UNWTO, UPU, WCO, WHO, WIPO, WMO, WTO

Diplomatic representation in the US: *chief of mission:* Ambassador Noël Nelson MESSONE (12 December 2022)
chancery: 2034 20th Street NW, Suite 200, Washington, DC 20009
telephone: [1] (202) 797-1000
FAX: [1] (301) 332-0668
email address and website:
info@gaboneembassyusa.org
https://gabonembassyusa.org/en/
consulate(s) general: New York

Diplomatic representation from the US: *chief of mission:* Ambassador Vernelle Trim FITZPATRICK (since 26 January 2024); note - also accredited to Sao Tome and Principe
embassy: Sabliere, B.P. 4000, Libreville
mailing address: 2270 Libreville Place, Washington, DC 20521-2270
telephone: [241] 011-45-71-00
FAX: [241] 011-45-71-05
email address and website:
ACSLibreville@state.gov
https://ga.usembassy.gov/

Flag description: three equal horizontal bands of green (top), yellow, and blue; green represents the country's forests and natural resources, gold represents the equator (which transects Gabon) as well as the sun, blue represents the sea

National symbol(s): black panther; national colors: green, yellow, blue

On Gabon's coat of arms, panthers representing vigilance and courage support a shield with a ship and an okoume tree, which is a symbol of the timber trade. The ribbon below the shield has the national motto in French, "Union, Travail, Justice" ("Union, Work, Justice"); the ribbon above the shield has the Latin phrase "Uniti Progrediemur" ("We shall go forward united"): National anthem: name: "La Concorde" (The Concorde)
lyrics/music: Georges Aleka DAMAS
note: adopted 1960

National heritage: *total World Heritage Sites:* 2 (1 natural, 1 mixed)
selected World Heritage Site locales: Ecosystem and Relict Cultural Landscape of Lopé-Okanda (m); Ivindo National Park (n)

ECONOMY

Economic overview: natural-resource-rich, upper-middle-income, Central African economy; significant reliance on oil and mineral exports; highly urbanized population; high levels of poverty and unemployment; uncertainty on institutional and development reform progress following 2023 military coup

Real GDP (purchasing power parity): $48.201 billion (2023 est.)
$47.134 billion (2022 est.)
$45.776 billion (2021 est.)
note: data in 2021 dollars
comparison ranking: 127

Real GDP growth rate: 2.26% (2023 est.)
2.97% (2022 est.)
1.47% (2021 est.)
note: annual GDP % growth based on constant local currency
comparison ranking: 131

Real GDP per capita: $19,800 (2023 est.)
$19,700 (2022 est.)
$19,600 (2021 est.)
note: data in 2021 dollars
comparison ranking: 102

GDP (official exchange rate): $20.516 billion (2023 est.)
note: data in current dollars at official exchange rate

Inflation rate (consumer prices): 3.63% (2023 est.)
4.23% (2022 est.)
1.09% (2021 est.)
note: annual % change based on consumer prices
comparison ranking: 71

Credit ratings: Fitch rating: CCC (2020)

Moody's rating: Caa1 (2018)

Standard & Poors rating: N/A (2016)
note: The year refers to the year in which the current credit rating was first obtained.

GDP - composition, by sector of origin: *agriculture:* 5.8% (2023 est.)
industry: 52.9% (2023 est.)
services: 36.4% (2023 est.)
note: figures may not total 100% due to non-allocated consumption not captured in sector-reported data
comparison rankings: services 203; industry 10; agriculture 108

GDP - composition, by end use: *household consumption:* 32.3% (2023 est.)
government consumption: 11.6% (2023 est.)
investment in fixed capital: 17.1% (2023 est.)
exports of goods and services: 56.7% (2023 est.)
imports of goods and services: -17.4% (2023 est.)
note: figures may not total 100% due to rounding or gaps in data collection

Agricultural products: plantains, cassava, sugarcane, yams, taro, vegetables, maize, groundnuts, game meat, rubber (2022)
note: top ten agricultural products based on tonnage

Industries: petroleum extraction and refining; manganese, gold; chemicals, ship repair, food and beverages, textiles, lumbering and plywood, cement

Industrial production growth rate: 3.5% (2023 est.)
note: annual % change in industrial value added based on constant local currency
comparison ranking: 96

Labor force: 763,000 (2023 est.)
note: number of people ages 15 or older who are employed or seeking work
comparison ranking: 152

Unemployment rate: 20.36% (2023 est.)
20.5% (2022 est.)
21.23% (2021 est.)
note: % of labor force seeking employment
comparison ranking: 201

Youth unemployment rate (ages 15-24): *total:* 36.5% (2023 est.)
male: 31.7% (2023 est.)
female: 42.9% (2023 est.)
note: % of labor force ages 15-24 seeking employment
comparison ranking: total 15

Population below poverty line: 33.4% (2017 est.)
note: % of population with income below national poverty line

Gini Index coefficient - distribution of family income: 38 (2017 est.)
note: index (0-100) of income distribution; higher values represent greater inequality
comparison ranking: 54

Household income or consumption by percentage share: *lowest 10%:* 2.2% (2017 est.)
highest 10%: 27.7% (2017 est.)
note: % share of income accruing to lowest and highest 10% of population

Remittances: 0.09% of GDP (2023 est.)
0.09% of GDP (2022 est.)
0.09% of GDP (2021 est.)
note: personal transfers and compensation between resident and non-resident individuals/households/entities

Budget: *revenues:* $2.939 billion (2021 est.)
expenditures: $2.732 billion (2021 est.)
note: central government revenues and expenses (excluding grants/extrabudgetary units/social security funds) converted to US dollars at average official exchange rate for year indicated

Public debt: 62.7% of GDP (2017 est.)
comparison ranking: 72

Taxes and other revenues: 9.13% (of GDP) (2021 est.)
note: central government tax revenue as a % of GDP
comparison ranking: 184

Current account balance: $140.996 million (2015 est.)
$1.112 billion (2014 est.)
$1.463 billion (2013 est.)
note: balance of payments - net trade and primary/secondary income in current dollars
comparison ranking: 70

Exports: $12.935 billion (2022 est.)
$11.229 billion (2021 est.)
$7.275 billion (2020 est.)
note: GDP expenditure basis - exports of goods and services in current dollars

comparison ranking: 104

Exports - partners: China 43%, South Korea 8%, Italy 7%, India 7%, Indonesia 5% (2022)
note: top five export partners based on percentage share of exports

Exports - commodities: crude petroleum, manganese ore, wood, veneer sheets, refined petroleum (2022)
note: top five export commodities based on value in dollars

Imports: $3.499 billion (2022 est.)
$3.353 billion (2021 est.)
$3.454 billion (2020 est.)
note: GDP expenditure basis - imports of goods and services in current dollars
comparison ranking: 161

Imports - partners: China 22%, France 21%, UAE 5%, US 5%, Belgium 4% (2022)
note: top five import partners based on percentage share of imports

Imports - commodities: poultry, plastic products, iron pipes, fish, excavation machinery (2022)
note: top five import commodities based on value in dollars

Reserves of foreign exchange and gold: $1.372 billion (2019 est.)
$1.321 billion (2018 est.)
$965.054 million (2017 est.)
note: holdings of gold (year-end prices)/foreign exchange/special drawing rights in current dollars
comparison ranking: 134

Debt - external: $6.06 billion (2022 est.)
note: present value of external debt in current US dollars
comparison ranking: 48

Exchange rates: Cooperation Financiere en Afrique Centrale francs (XAF) per US dollar -

Exchange rates: 606.57 (2023 est.)
623.76 (2022 est.)
554.531 (2021 est.)
575.586 (2020 est.)
585.911 (2019 est.)

ENERGY

Electricity access: *electrification - total population:* 93.5% (2022 est.)
electrification - urban areas: 98.5%
electrification - rural areas: 29%

Electricity: *installed generating capacity:* 784,000 kW (2022 est.)
consumption: 2.497 billion kWh (2022 est.)
imports: 544.035 million kWh (2022 est.)
transmission/distribution losses: 433.104 million kWh (2022 est.)
comparison rankings: transmission/distribution losses 77; imports 89; consumption 144; installed generating capacity 140

Electricity generation sources: *fossil fuels:* 58.1% of total installed capacity (2022 est.)
solar: 0.1% of total installed capacity (2022 est.)
hydroelectricity: 41.4% of total installed capacity (2022 est.)
biomass and waste: 0.5% of total installed capacity (2022 est.)

Coal: *imports:* 82,000 metric tons (2022 est.)

Petroleum: *total petroleum production:* 204,000 bbl/day (2023 est.)
refined petroleum consumption: 16,000 bbl/day (2022 est.)
crude oil estimated reserves: 2 billion barrels (2021 est.)

Natural gas: *production:* 463 million cubic meters (2022 est.)
consumption: 463 million cubic meters (2022 est.)
proven reserves: 25.995 billion cubic meters (2021 est.)

Carbon dioxide emissions: 3.47 million metric tonnes of CO2 (2022 est.)
from coal and metallurgical coke: 251,000 metric tonnes of CO2 (2022 est.)
from petroleum and other liquids: 2.311 million metric tonnes of CO2 (2022 est.)
from consumed natural gas: 908,000 metric tonnes of CO2 (2022 est.)
comparison ranking: total emissions 148

Energy consumption per capita: 23.955 million Btu/person (2022 est.)
comparison ranking: 127

COMMUNICATIONS

Telephones - fixed lines: *total subscriptions:* 43,000 (2022 est.)
subscriptions per 100 inhabitants: 2 (2022 est.)
comparison ranking: total subscriptions 160

Telephones - mobile cellular: *total subscriptions:* 2.995 million (2022 est.)
subscriptions per 100 inhabitants: 125 (2022 est.)
comparison ranking: total subscriptions 141

Telecommunication systems: *general assessment:* the telecom market was liberalized in 1999 when the government awarded three mobile telephony licenses and two ISP licenses and established an independent regulatory authority; in contrast with the mobile market, Gabon's fixed-line and internet sectors have remained underdeveloped due to a lack of competition and high prices; the country has sufficient international bandwidth on the SAT-3/WASC/SAFE submarine cable; the arrival of the ACE submarine cable, combined with progressing work on the CAB cable, has increased back haul capacity supporting mobile data traffic (2022)
domestic: fixed-line 1 per 100 subscriptions; mobile cellular subscriptions are 134 per 100 persons (2021)
international: country code - 241; landing points for the SAT-3/WASC, ACE and Libreville-Port Gentil Cable fiber-optic submarine cable that provides connectivity to Europe and West Africa; satellite earth stations - 3 Intelsat (Atlantic Ocean) (2019)

Broadcast media: state owns and operates 2 TV stations and 2 radio broadcast stations; a few private radio and TV stations; transmissions of at least 2 international broadcasters are accessible; satellite service subscriptions are available

Internet country code: .ga

Internet users: *total:* 1.656 million (2021 est.)
percent of population: 72% (2021 est.)
comparison ranking: total 142

Broadband - fixed subscriptions: *total:* 44,607 (2020 est.)
subscriptions per 100 inhabitants: 2 (2020 est.)
comparison ranking: total 144

TRANSPORTATION

National air transport system: *number of registered air carriers:* 3 (2020)
inventory of registered aircraft operated by air carriers: 8

Civil aircraft registration country code prefix: TR

Airports: 40 (2024)
comparison ranking: 102

Pipelines: 807 km gas, 1,639 km oil, 3 km water (2013)

Railways: *total:* 649 km (2014)
standard gauge: 649 km (2014) 1.435-m gauge
comparison ranking: total 105

Roadways: *total:* 14,300 km
paved: 900 km
unpaved: 13,400 km (2001)
comparison ranking: total 127

Waterways: 1,600 km (2010) (310 km on Ogooue River)
comparison ranking: 51

Merchant marine: *total:* 87 (2023)
by type: bulk carrier 1, general cargo 19, oil tanker 30, other 37
comparison ranking: total 96

Ports: *total ports:* 9 (2024)
large: 0
medium: 2
small: 2
very small: 5
ports with oil terminals: 7
key ports: Libreville, Oguendjo Terminal, Port Gentil, Port Owendo

MILITARY AND SECURITY

Military and security forces: Gabonese Armed Forces (Force Armées Gabonaise or FAG; aka Gabonese Defense and Security Forces or Forces de Défense et de Sécurité Gabonaises): Army (Armée de Terre, AT), Navy (Marine Nationale, MN), Air Force (l'Armée de l'Air, AA), Light Aviation (L'Aviation Légère des Armées, ALA), Fire Brigade (du Corps des Sapeurs-Pompiers); National Gendarmerie (Gendarmerie Gabonaise, GENA); Republican Guard (Garde Républicaine,GEN GR); Military Health Service (Service de Santé Militaire, SSM); Military Engineering (Génie Militaire) (2024)
note 1: the National Police Forces, under the Ministry of Interior, and the National Gendarmerie (GENA), under the Ministry of Defense, are responsible for law enforcement and public security; elements of the armed forces and the Republican Guard, an elite unit that protects the president under his direct authority, sometimes perform internal security functions
note 2: the GENA is organized into regionally-based "legions," mobile forces, a national parks security unit, and a special intervention group

Military expenditures: 1.3% of GDP (2023 est.)
1.3% of GDP (2022 est.)
1.7% of GDP (2021 est.)
1.8% of GDP (2020 est.)
1.6% of GDP (2019 est.)
comparison ranking: 110

Military and security service personnel strengths: approximately 6,500 active-duty troops including the Republican Guard and Gendarmerie (2023)

Military equipment inventories and acquisitions: the Gabonese military has a mix of older and more modern weapons and equipment from a variety of suppliers including Brazil, China, France, Germany, Russia/former Soviet Union, and South Africa (2024)

Military service age and obligation: 18-26 years of age for voluntary military service; no conscription (2023)

Military - note: the Gabonese military is a small and lightly armed force that is responsible for both external and internal security; in August 2023, it seized control of the government in a coup; some members of the military attempted a failed coup in 2019 (2024)

SPACE

Space agency/agencies: Gabonese Studies and Space Observations Agency (Agence Gabonaise d'Etudes et d'Observations Spatiales or AGEOS; established 2015) (2024)

Space program overview: has a small space program focused on the acquisition, processing, analysis, and furnishing of data from foreign remote sensing (RS) satellites for environmental management, mapping, natural resources, land use planning, and maritime surveillance, as well as research and innovation; has relationships with Brazil, China, the European Space Agency (ESA) and its member states (particularly France), Kenya, Niger, Rwanda, South Africa, and the US; shares RS data with neighboring countries (2024)
note: further details about the key activities, programs, and milestones of the country's space program, as well as government spending estimates on the space sector, appear in the Space Programs reference guide

TRANSNATIONAL ISSUES

Trafficking in persons: tier rating: Tier 2 Watch List — Gabon does not fully meet the minimum standards for the elimination of trafficking, but the government has devoted sufficient resources to a written plan that, if implemented, would constitute significant efforts to meet the minimum standards; therefore, Gabon was granted a waiver per the Trafficking Victims Protection Act from an otherwise required downgrade to Tier 3 and remained on Tier 2 Watch List for the third consecutive year; for more details, go to: https://www.state.gov/reports/2024-trafficking-in-persons-report/gabon/

GAMBIA, THE

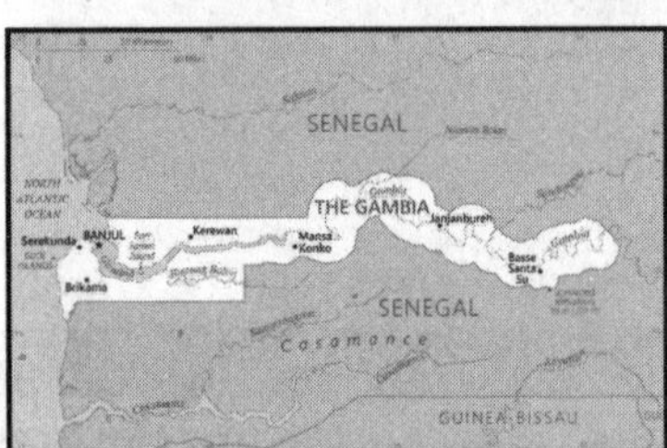

INTRODUCTION

Background: In the 10th century, Muslim merchants established some of The Gambia's earliest large settlements as trans-Saharan trade hubs. These settlements eventually grew into major export centers sending slaves, gold, and ivory across the Sahara. Between the 16th and 17th centuries, European colonial powers began establishing trade with The Gambia. In 1664, the United Kingdom established a colony in The Gambia focused on exporting enslaved people across the Atlantic. During the roughly 300 years of the trans-Atlantic slave trade, the UK and other European powers may have exported as many as 3 million people from The Gambia.

The Gambia gained its independence from the UK in 1965. Geographically surrounded by Senegal, it formed the short-lived confederation of Senegambia between 1982 and 1989. In 1994, Yahya JAMMEH led a military coup overthrowing the president and banning political activity. He subsequently won every presidential election until 2016, when he lost to Adama BARROW, who headed an opposition coalition during free and fair elections. BARROW won reelection in 2021. The Gambia is the only member of the Economic Community of West African States that does not have presidential term limits. Since the 2016 election, The Gambia and the US have enjoyed improved relations. US assistance to the country has supported democracy-strengthening activities, capacity building, economic development, and security sector education and training programs.

GEOGRAPHY

Location: Western Africa, bordering the North Atlantic Ocean and Senegal

Geographic coordinates: 13 28 N, 16 34 W

Map references: Africa

Area: *total:* 11,300 sq km
land: 10,120 sq km
water: 1,180 sq km
comparison ranking: total 165

Area - comparative: slightly less than twice the size of Delaware

Land boundaries: *total:* 749 km
border countries (1): Senegal 749 km

Coastline: 80 km

Maritime claims: *territorial sea:* 12 nm
contiguous zone: 18 nm
continental shelf: extent not specified
exclusive fishing zone: 200 nm

Climate: tropical; hot, rainy season (June to November); cooler, dry season (November to May)

Terrain: flood plain of the Gambia River flanked by some low hills

Elevation: *highest point:* unnamed elevation 63 m; 3 km southeast of the town of Sabi
lowest point: Atlantic Ocean 0 m
mean elevation: 34 m

Natural resources: fish, clay, silica sand, titanium (rutile and ilmenite), tin, zircon

Land use: *agricultural land:* 56.1% (2018 est.)
arable land: 41% (2018 est.)
permanent crops: 0.5% (2018 est.)
permanent pasture: 14.6% (2018 est.)
forest: 43.9% (2018 est.)
other: 0% (2018 est.)

Irrigated land: 50 sq km (2012)

Major rivers (by length in km): Gambia river mouth (shared with Senegal and Guinea [s]) - 1,094 km
note – [s] after country name indicates river source; [m] after country name indicates river mouth

Major aquifers: Senegalo-Mauritanian Basin

Population distribution: settlements are found scattered along the Gambia River; the largest communities, including the capital of Banjul, and the country's largest city, Serekunda, are found at the mouth of the Gambia River along the Atlantic coast as shown in this population distribution map

Natural hazards: droughts

Geography - note: almost an enclave of Senegal; smallest country on the African mainland

PEOPLE AND SOCIETY

Population: *total:* 2,523,327
male: 1,250,490
female: 1,272,837 (2024 est.)
comparison rankings: female 144; male 144; total 144

Nationality: *noun:* Gambian(s)
adjective: Gambian

Ethnic groups: Mandinka/Jahanka 33.3%, Fulani/Tukulur/Lorobo 18.2%, Wolof 12.9%, Jola/Karoninka 11%, Serahuleh 7.2%, Serer 3.5%, other 4%, non-Gambian 9.9% (2019-20 est.)

Languages: English (official), Mandinka, Wolof, Fula, other indigenous vernaculars

Religions: Muslim 96.4%, Christian 3.5%, other or none 0.1% (2019-20 est.)

Demographic profile: The Gambia's youthful age structure – approximately 55% of the population is under the age of 25 as of 2021 – is likely to persist because the country's total fertility rate remains strong at nearly 4 children per woman. The overall literacy rate is around 50%, and is significantly lower for women than for men. At least 70% of the populace are farmers who are reliant on rain-fed agriculture and cannot afford improved seeds and fertilizers. Crop failures caused by droughts between 2011 and 2013 increased poverty, food shortages, and malnutrition.
The Gambia is a source country for migrants and a transit and destination country for migrants and refugees. Since the 1980s, economic deterioration, drought, and high unemployment, especially among youths, have driven both domestic migration (largely urban) and migration abroad (legal and illegal). Emigrants are largely skilled workers, including doctors and nurses, and provide a significant amount of remittances. The top receiving countries for Gambian emigrants are Spain, the US, Nigeria, Senegal, and the UK. While the Gambia and Spain do not share historic, cultural, or trade ties, rural Gambians have migrated to Spain in large numbers because of its proximity and the availability of jobs in its underground economy (this flow slowed following the onset of Spain's late 2007 economic crisis).
The Gambia's role as a host country to refugees is a result of wars in several of its neighboring West African countries. Since 2006, refugees from the Casamance conflict in Senegal have replaced their pattern of flight and return with permanent

settlement in The Gambia, often moving in with relatives along the Senegal-Gambia border. The strain of providing for about 7,400 Casamance refugees increased poverty among Gambian villagers. The number of refugees decreased to around 3,500 by 2022.

Age structure: *0-14 years:* 38.2% (male 486,472/ female 477,309)
15-64 years: 58.1% (male 723,360/female 743,127)
65 years and over: 3.7% (2024 est.) (male 40,658/ female 52,401)

Dependency ratios: *total dependency ratio:* 85
youth dependency ratio: 80.5
elderly dependency ratio: 4.5
potential support ratio: 22.2 (2021 est.)

Median age: *total:* 20.2 years (2024 est.)
male: 19.8 years
female: 20.6 years
comparison ranking: total 205

Population growth rate: 2.16% (2024 est.)
comparison ranking: 34

Birth rate: 27.3 births/1,000 population (2024 est.)
comparison ranking: 36

Death rate: 5.6 deaths/1,000 population (2024 est.)
comparison ranking: 177

Net migration rate: 0 migrant(s)/1,000 population (2024 est.)
comparison ranking: 80

Population distribution: settlements are found scattered along the Gambia River; the largest communities, including the capital of Banjul, and the country's largest city, Serekunda, are found at the mouth of the Gambia River along the Atlantic coast as shown in this population distribution map

Urbanization: *urban population:* 64.5% of total population (2023)
rate of urbanization: 3.75% annual rate of change (2020-25 est.)

Major urban areas - population: 481,000 BANJUL (capital) (2023)
note: includes the local government areas of Banjul and Kanifing

Sex ratio: *at birth:* 1.03 male(s)/female
0-14 years: 1.02 male(s)/female
15-64 years: 0.97 male(s)/female
65 years and over: 0.78 male(s)/female
total population: 0.98 male(s)/female (2024 est.)

Mother's mean age at first birth: 20.7 years (2019/20 est.)
note: data represents median age at first birth among women 25-49

Maternal mortality ratio: 458 deaths/100,000 live births (2020 est.)
comparison ranking: 17

Infant mortality rate: *total:* 35.7 deaths/1,000 live births (2024 est.)
male: 39.1 deaths/1,000 live births
female: 32.2 deaths/1,000 live births
comparison ranking: total 35

Life expectancy at birth: *total population:* 68.4 years (2024 est.)
male: 66.7 years
female: 70.1 years
comparison ranking: total population 189

Total fertility rate: 3.52 children born/woman (2024 est.)
comparison ranking: 33

Gross reproduction rate: 1.74 (2024 est.)

Contraceptive prevalence rate: 18.9% (2019/20)

Drinking water source: *improved: urban:* 91.8% of population
rural: 85.7% of population
total: 89.5% of population
unimproved: urban: 8.2% of population
rural: 14.3% of population
total: 10.5% of population (2020 est.)

Current health expenditure: 2.6% of GDP (2020)

Physician density: 0.08 physicians/1,000 population (2020)

Hospital bed density: 1.1 beds/1,000 population (2011)

Sanitation facility access: *improved: urban:* 75.8% of population
rural: 33.6% of population
total: 60% of population
unimproved: urban: 24.2% of population
rural: 66.4% of population
total: 40% of population (2020 est.)

Obesity - adult prevalence rate: 10.3% (2016)
comparison ranking: 138

Alcohol consumption per capita: *total:* 2.67 liters of pure alcohol (2019 est.)
beer: 0.21 liters of pure alcohol (2019 est.)
wine: 0 liters of pure alcohol (2019 est.)
spirits: 0.02 liters of pure alcohol (2019 est.)
other alcohols: 2.44 liters of pure alcohol (2019 est.)
comparison ranking: total 121

Tobacco use: *total:* 11.1% (2020 est.)
male: 21.4% (2020 est.)
female: 0.8% (2020 est.)
comparison ranking: total 130

Children under the age of 5 years underweight: 11.6% (2019/20)
comparison ranking: 50

Currently married women (ages 15-49): 60.9% (2023 est.)

Child marriage: *women married by age 15:* 5.6%
women married by age 18: 23.1%
men married by age 18: 0.2% (2020 est.)

Education expenditures: 2.8% of GDP (2020 est.)
comparison ranking: 166

Literacy: *definition:* age 15 and over can read and write
total population: 58.1%
male: 65.2%
female: 51.2% (2021)

ENVIRONMENT

Environment - current issues: deforestation due to slash-and-burn agriculture; desertification; water pollution; water-borne diseases

Environment - international agreements: *party to:* Biodiversity, Climate Change, Climate Change-Kyoto Protocol, Climate Change-Paris Agreement, Desertification, Endangered Species, Hazardous Wastes, Law of the Sea, Nuclear Test Ban, Ozone Layer Protection, Ship Pollution, Wetlands, Whaling
signed, but not ratified: Comprehensive Nuclear Test Ban

Climate: tropical; hot, rainy season (June to November); cooler, dry season (November to May)

Urbanization: *urban population:* 64.5% of total population (2023)
rate of urbanization: 3.75% annual rate of change (2020-25 est.)

Revenue from forest resources: 2.47% of GDP (2018 est.)
comparison ranking: 28

Revenue from coal: 0% of GDP (2018 est.)
comparison ranking: 53

Air pollutants: *particulate matter emissions:* 39.1 micrograms per cubic meter (2019 est.)
carbon dioxide emissions: 0.53 megatons (2016 est.)
methane emissions: 1.96 megatons (2020 est.)

Waste and recycling: *municipal solid waste generated annually:* 193,441 tons (2002 est.)

Major rivers (by length in km): Gambia river mouth (shared with Senegal and Guinea [s]) - 1,094 km
note – [s] after country name indicates river source; [m] after country name indicates river mouth

Major aquifers: Senegalo-Mauritanian Basin

Total water withdrawal: *municipal:* 40 million cubic meters (2020 est.)
industrial: 20 million cubic meters (2020 est.)
agricultural: 40 million cubic meters (2020 est.)

Total renewable water resources: 8 billion cubic meters (2020 est.)

GOVERNMENT

Country name: *conventional long form:* Republic of The Gambia
conventional short form: The Gambia
etymology: named for the Gambia River that flows through the heart of the country

Government type: presidential republic

Capital: *name:* Banjul
geographic coordinates: 13 27 N, 16 34 W
time difference: UTC 0 (5 hours ahead of Washington, DC, during Standard Time)
etymology: Banjul is located on Saint Mary's Island at the mouth of the Gambia River; the Mandinka used to gather fibrous plants on the island for the manufacture of ropes; "bang julo" is Mandinka for "rope fiber"; mispronunciation over time caused the term became the word Banjul

Administrative divisions: 5 regions, 1 city*, and 1 municipality**; Banjul*, Central River, Kanifing**, Lower River, North Bank, Upper River, West Coast

Independence: 18 February 1965 (from the UK)

National holiday: Independence Day, 18 February (1965)

Legal system: mixed legal system of English common law, Islamic law, and customary law

Constitution: *history:* previous 1965 (Independence Act), 1970; latest adopted 8 April 1996, approved by referendum 8 August 1996, effective 16 January 1997; note - in early 2018, the "Constitutional Review Commission," was established to draft and assist in instituting a new constitution; a second draft completed in March 2020 was rejected by the National Assembly in September; the president announced in January 2022 government plans to draft a new constitution
amendments: proposed by the National Assembly; passage requires at least three-fourths majority vote by the Assembly membership in each of several readings and approval by the president of the republic; a referendum is required for amendments affecting national sovereignty, fundamental rights and freedoms, government structures and authorities, taxation, and public funding; passage by referendum requires participation of at least 50% of eligible

voters and approval by at least 75% of votes cast; amended 2001, 2004, 2018

International law organization participation: accepts compulsory ICJ jurisdiction with reservations; accepts ICCt jurisdiction

Citizenship: *citizenship by birth:* yes
citizenship by descent only: yes
dual citizenship recognized: no
residency requirement for naturalization: 5 years

Suffrage: 18 years of age; universal

Executive branch: *chief of state:* President Adama BARROW (since 19 January 2022)
head of government: Vice President Mohammed JALLOW (since 23 February 2024)
cabinet: Cabinet appointed by the president
elections/appointments: president directly elected by simple majority popular vote for a 5-year term (no term limits); election last held on 4 December 2021 (next to be held in 2026); vice president appointed by the president
election results:
2021: Adama BARROW reelected president; percent of vote - Adama BARROW (NPP) 53.2%, Ousainou DARBOE (UDP) 27.7%, Mamma KANDEH (GDC) 12.3%, other 6.8%
2016: Adama BARROW elected president; percent of vote - Adama BARROW (Coalition 2016) 43.3%, Yahya JAMMEH (APRC) 39.6%, Mamma KANDEH (GDC) 17.1%

Legislative branch: *description:* unicameral National Assembly (58 seats; 53 members directly elected in single-seat constituencies by simple majority vote and 5 appointed by the president; members serve 5-year terms)
elections: last held on 9 April 2022 (next to be held in 2027)
election results: percent of vote by party - NPP 33.9%, UDP 28.3%, independent 22.6%, NRP 7.5%, PDOIS 3.7%, APRL 3.7%; seats by party - NPP 18, UDP 15, independent 12, NRP 4, APRL 2, PDOIS 2; composition - men 53, women 5, percentage women 8.6%

Judicial branch: *highest court(s):* Supreme Court of The Gambia (consists of the chief justice and 6 justices; court sessions held with 5 justices)
judge selection and term of office: justices appointed by the president after consultation with the Judicial Service Commission, a 6-member independent body of high-level judicial officials, a presidential appointee, and a National Assembly appointee; justices appointed for life or until mandatory retirement at age 75
subordinate courts: Court of Appeal; High Court; Special Criminal Court; Khadis or Muslim courts; district tribunals; magistrates courts; cadi courts

Political parties: Alliance for Patriotic Reorientation and Construction or APRC
Gambia Democratic Congress or GDC
Gambia Moral Congress or GMC
National People's Party or NPP
People's Progressive Party or PPP
United Democratic Party or UDP

International organization participation: ACP, AfDB, AU, ECOWAS, FAO, G-77, IBRD, ICAO, ICCt, ICRM, IDA, IDB, IFAD, IFC, IFRCS, ILO, IMF, IMO, Interpol, IOC, IOM, IPU, ISO (correspondent), ITSO, ITU, ITUC (NGOs), MIGA, NAM, OIC, OPCW, UN, UNAMID, UNCTAD, UNESCO, UNHRC, UNIDO, UNISFA, UNMIL, UNOCI, UNWTO, UPU, WCO, WFTU (NGOs), WHO, WIPO, WMO, WTO

Diplomatic representation in the US: *chief of mission:* Ambassador Momodou Lamin BAH (12 December 2022)
chancery: 5630 16th Street NW, Washington, DC 20011
telephone: [1] (202) 785-1399
FAX: [1] (202) 785-1430
email address and website:
info@gambiaembassydc.us
https://www.gambiaembassydc.us/home

Diplomatic representation from the US: *chief of mission:* Ambassador Sharon L. CROMER (since 18 March 2022)
embassy: Kairaba Avenue, Fajara, P.M.B. 19, Banjul
mailing address: 2070 Banjul Place, Washington DC 20521-2070
telephone: [220] 439-2856
FAX: [220] 439-2475
email address and website:
ConsularBanjul@state.gov
https://gm.usembassy.gov/

Flag description: three equal horizontal bands of red (top), blue with white edges, and green; red stands for the sun and the savannah, blue represents the Gambia River, and green symbolizes forests and agriculture; the white stripes denote unity and peace

National symbol(s): lion; national colors: red, blue, green, white

National anthem: *name:* "For The Gambia, Our Homeland"
lyrics/music: Virginia Julie HOWE/adapted by Jeremy Frederick HOWE
note: adopted 1965; the music is an adaptation of the traditional Mandinka song "Foday Kaba Dumbuya"

National heritage: *total World Heritage Sites:* 2 (both cultural)
selected World Heritage Site locales: Kunta Kinteh Island and Related Sites; Stone Circles of Senegambia

ECONOMY

Economic overview: low-income West African economy; agriculture-dominant; high poverty rate; heightened inflation; dependent on foreign assistance and remittances; structural reforms conditioned by IMF Extended Credit Facility program

Real GDP (purchasing power parity): $7.905 billion (2023 est.)
$7.508 billion (2022 est.)
$7.156 billion (2021 est.)
note: data in 2021 dollars
comparison ranking: 170

Real GDP growth rate: 5.3% (2023 est.)
4.92% (2022 est.)
5.26% (2021 est.)
note: annual GDP % growth based on constant local currency
comparison ranking: 42

Real GDP per capita: $2,900 (2023 est.)
$2,800 (2022 est.)
$2,700 (2021 est.)
note: data in 2021 dollars
comparison ranking: 196

GDP (official exchange rate): $2.34 billion (2023 est.)
note: data in current dollars at official exchange rate

Inflation rate (consumer prices): 16.97% (2023 est.)
11.51% (2022 est.)
7.37% (2021 est.)
note: annual % change based on consumer prices
comparison ranking: 195

GDP - composition, by sector of origin: *agriculture:* 24.6% (2023 est.)
industry: 15.2% (2023 est.)
services: 51.5% (2023 est.)
note: figures may not total 100% due to non-allocated consumption not captured in sector-reported data
comparison rankings: services 136; industry 170; agriculture 21

GDP - composition, by end use: *household consumption:* 81.6% (2023 est.)
government consumption: 8.8% (2023 est.)
investment in fixed capital: 39.3% (2023 est.)
exports of goods and services: 5.4% (2023 est.)
imports of goods and services: -35.1% (2023 est.)
note: figures may not total 100% due to rounding or gaps in data collection

Agricultural products: groundnuts, milk, rice, millet, oil palm fruit, maize, vegetables, cassava, fruits, sorghum (2022)
note: top ten agricultural products based on tonnage

Industries: peanuts, fish, hides, tourism, beverages, agricultural machinery assembly, woodworking, metalworking, clothing

Industrial production growth rate: 6.5% (2023 est.)
note: annual % change in industrial value added based on constant local currency
comparison ranking: 38

Labor force: 969,000 (2023 est.)
note: number of people ages 15 or older who are employed or seeking work
comparison ranking: 149

Unemployment rate: 6.48% (2023 est.)
6.08% (2022 est.)
6.21% (2021 est.)
note: % of labor force seeking employment
comparison ranking: 131

Youth unemployment rate (ages 15-24): *total:* 10.6% (2023 est.)
male: 10.9% (2023 est.)
female: 10.4% (2023 est.)
note: % of labor force ages 15-24 seeking employment
comparison ranking: total 130

Population below poverty line: 53.4% (2020 est.)
note: % of population with income below national poverty line

Gini Index coefficient - distribution of family income: 38.8 (2020 est.)
note: index (0-100) of income distribution; higher values represent greater inequality
comparison ranking: 50

Household income or consumption by percentage share: *lowest 10%:* 2.6% (2020 est.)
highest 10%: 30.6% (2020 est.)
note: % share of income accruing to lowest and highest 10% of population

Remittances: 26.82% of GDP (2023 est.)
23.07% of GDP (2022 est.)
27.16% of GDP (2021 est.)
note: personal transfers and compensation between resident and non-resident individuals/households/entities

Budget: *revenues:* $308.887 million (2018 est.)
expenditures: $221.137 million (2018 est.)

note: central government revenues and expenses (excluding grants/extrabudgetary units/social security funds) converted to US dollars at average official exchange rate for year indicated

Public debt: 88% of GDP (2017 est.)
comparison ranking: 28

Taxes and other revenues: 20.3% (of GDP) (2017 est.)
comparison ranking: 83

Current account balance: -$90.251 million (2022 est.)
-$86.877 million (2021 est.)
-$86.553 million (2020 est.)
note: balance of payments - net trade and primary/secondary income in current dollars
comparison ranking: 94

Exports: $267.377 million (2022 est.)
$142.652 million (2021 est.)
$175.682 million (2020 est.)
note: balance of payments - exports of goods and services in current dollars
comparison ranking: 199

Exports - partners: India 31%, China 23%, Italy 7%, Chile 7%, Portugal 5% (2022)
note: top five export partners based on percentage share of exports

Exports - commodities: coconuts/Brazil nuts/cashews, wood, shellfish, scrap iron, fish oil (2022)
note: top five export commodities based on value in dollars

Imports: $829.516 million (2022 est.)
$726.23 million (2021 est.)
$690.979 million (2020 est.)
note: balance of payments - imports of goods and services in current dollars
comparison ranking: 195

Imports - partners: China 31%, Senegal 12%, India 8%, Brazil 8%, US 5% (2022)
note: top five import partners based on percentage share of imports

Imports - commodities: cotton fabric, rice, raw sugar, poultry, palm oil (2022)
note: top five import commodities based on value in dollars

Reserves of foreign exchange and gold: $577.028 million (2023 est.)
$568.244 million (2022 est.)
$652.671 million (2021 est.)
note: holdings of gold (year-end prices)/foreign exchange/special drawing rights in current dollars
comparison ranking: 175

Debt - external: $696.707 million (2022 est.)
note: present value of external debt in current US dollars
comparison ranking: 86

Exchange rates: dalasis (GMD) per US dollar -

Exchange rates: 61.096 (2023 est.)
54.923 (2022 est.)
51.484 (2021 est.)
51.502 (2020 est.)
50.062 (2019 est.)

ENERGY

Electricity access: *electrification - total population:* 65.4% (2022 est.)
electrification - urban areas: 82.8%
electrification - rural areas: 31.2%

Electricity: *installed generating capacity:* 140,000 kW (2022 est.)
consumption: 405.405 million kWh (2022 est.)
transmission/distribution losses: 104.176 million kWh (2022 est.)
comparison rankings: transmission/distribution losses 50; consumption 179; installed generating capacity 180

Electricity generation sources: *fossil fuels:* 99.4% of total installed capacity (2022 est.)
solar: 0.6% of total installed capacity (2022 est.)

Petroleum: *refined petroleum consumption:* 3,000 bbl/day (2022 est.)

Carbon dioxide emissions: 524,000 metric tonnes of CO_2 (2022 est.)
from petroleum and other liquids: 524,000 metric tonnes of CO_2 (2022 est.)
comparison ranking: total emissions 189

Energy consumption per capita: 2.651 million Btu/person (2022 est.)
comparison ranking: 179

COMMUNICATIONS

Telephones - fixed lines: *total subscriptions:* 60,000 (2021 est.)
subscriptions per 100 inhabitants: 2 (2021 est.)
comparison ranking: total subscriptions 150

Telephones - mobile cellular: *total subscriptions:* 2.678 million (2021 est.)
subscriptions per 100 inhabitants: 101 (2021 est.)
comparison ranking: total subscriptions 144

Telecommunication systems: *general assessment:* Gambia's telecom market has five mobile networks providing effective competition; mobile subscriptions are well above the African average, itself a testament to the poor condition of the fixed-line infrastructure and the lack of availability of fixed services in many rural areas of the country; there are only four licensed ISPs, which are small networks serving local areas, and so competition is minimal; their limited services are complemented by the fixed-wireless offerings of three of the MNOs; the government has embarked on a National Broadband Network program aimed at closing the digital divide affecting many parts of the country; despite efforts to improve internet connectivity, the country ranks among the lowest globally in terms of digital readiness. (2022)
domestic: fixed-line subscriptions are 2 per 100 and mobile-cellular teledensity nearly 110 per 100 persons (2021)
international: country code - 220; landing point for the ACE submarine cable to West Africa and Europe; microwave radio relay links to Senegal and Guinea-Bissau; satellite earth station - 1 Intelsat (Atlantic Ocean) (2019)

Broadcast media: 1 state-run TV-channel; one privately-owned TV-station; 1 Online TV-station; three state-owned radio station and 31 privately owned radio stations; eight community radio stations; transmissions of multiple international broadcasters are available, some via shortwave radio; cable and satellite TV subscription services are obtainable in some parts of the country
(2019)

Internet country code: .gm

Internet users: *total:* 858,000 (2021 est.)
percent of population: 33% (2021 est.)
comparison ranking: total 153

Broadband - fixed subscriptions: *total:* 5,000 (2020 est.)
subscriptions per 100 inhabitants: 0.2 (2020 est.)
comparison ranking: total 187

TRANSPORTATION

National air transport system: *number of registered air carriers:* 2 (2020)
inventory of registered aircraft operated by air carriers: 6
annual passenger traffic on registered air carriers: 53,735 (2018)

Civil aircraft registration country code prefix: C5

Airports: 1 (2024)
comparison ranking: 222

Roadways: *total:* 2,977 km
paved: 518 km
unpaved: 2,459 km (2011)
comparison ranking: total 162

Waterways: 390 km (2010) (on River Gambia; small oceangoing vessels can reach 190 km)
comparison ranking: 98

Merchant marine: *total:* 15 (2023)
by type: general cargo 5, other 10
comparison ranking: total 151

Ports: *total ports:* 1 (2024)
large: 0
medium: 0
small: 0
very small: 1
ports with oil terminals: 1
key ports: Banjul

MILITARY AND SECURITY

Military and security forces: Gambian Armed Forces (GAF; aka Armed Forces of the Gambia): the Gambian National Army (GNA), Gambia Navy, Gambia Air Force, Republican National Guard (RNG)

Ministry of Interior: Gambia Police Force (GPF) (2024)
note: the RNG is responsible for VIP protection, riot control, and presidential security, while the GPF maintains internal security

Military expenditures: 0.6% of GDP (2023 est.)
0.7% of GDP (2022 est.)
0.8% of GDP (2021 est.)
0.8% of GDP (2020 est.)
0.8% of GDP (2019 est.)
comparison ranking: 155

Military and security service personnel strengths: estimated 3,000 military personnel (2023)

Military equipment inventories and acquisitions: the military of Gambia has a limited inventory of mostly older or donated equipment originating from several suppliers, including China, Turkey, the UK, and the US (2023)

Military service age and obligation: 18-25 years of age for male and female voluntary military service (18-22 for officers); no conscription; service obligation six months (2024)

Military - note: the Gambian security forces have a history of involvement in domestic politics, including multiple coups attempts and mutinies, with the latest being an attempted coup in 2022; since 2017, Gambia's security sector has been undergoing reforms as part of a national reconstruction effort to recover from the 22 years of Yahya JAMMEH's autocratic rule under which the security forces were severely under-resourced in terms of finances and equipment and were largely directed towards regime protection and suppressing dissent; international partners, including member states of the EU, particularly France and Germany, as well as Turkey and the US have provided support to military and police reforms; several members of the Economic Community of West African States (ECOWAS) have also provided security forces for stability, plus assistance and training through the ECOWAS Mission in the Gambia (ECOMIG); as of 2023, ECOMIG continued to provide about 1,000 military and gendarmerie personnel from Ghana, Nigeria, and Senegal

the GAF is a small and lightly armed force responsible for external defense, providing maritime security, countering human trafficking, and aiding civil authorities in emergencies and natural disaster relief; it also engages in activities such as engineering, education, health, and agriculture for domestic socio-economic development; the GAF participates in peacekeeping missions, and since its first deployments in the 1990s, has been involved in more than 10 UN peacekeeping missions while contributing about 4,000 total troops

the GAF traces its origins to the Gambia Regiment of the British Army; established in 1901, the Gambia Regiment was part of the West African Frontier Force (WAFF, later Royal West African Frontier Force or RWAFF) and served in both World Wars, including the British 1944-45 military campaign in Burma; the Gambia Regiment was disbanded in 1958 and replaced by the Field Force, a police paramilitary unit; the Field Force was responsible for The Gambia's security until the establishment of the GAF in 1985; in addition, a defense agreement signed in 1965 between The Gambia and Senegal provided mutual assistance in the face of an external threat; from 1981-1989, The Gambia and Senegal formed a Confederal Army that was made up of troops from both countries (2023)

TRANSNATIONAL ISSUES

Refugees and internally displaced persons: IDPs: 5,600 (2022)

GAZA STRIP

INTRODUCTION

Background: The Gaza Strip has been under the de facto governing authority of the Islamic Resistance Movement (HAMAS) since 2007 and has faced years of conflict, poverty, and humanitarian crises. Inhabited since at least the 15th century B.C., the Gaza Strip area has been dominated by many different peoples and empires throughout its history; it was incorporated into the Ottoman Empire in the early 16th century. The Gaza Strip fell to British forces during World War I, becoming a part of the British Mandate of Palestine. Following the 1948 Arab-Israeli War, Egypt administered the newly formed Gaza Strip; Israel captured it in the Six-Day War in 1967. Under a series of agreements known as the Oslo Accords signed between 1993 and 1999, Israel transferred to the newly-created Palestinian Authority (PA) security and civilian responsibility for many Palestinian-populated areas of the Gaza Strip, as well as the West Bank.

In 2000, a violent intifada or uprising began in response to perceived Israeli provocations, and in 2001, negotiations to determine the permanent status of the West Bank, East Jerusalem, and Gaza Strip stalled. Subsequent attempts to re-start negotiations have not resulted in progress toward determining final status and resolving the Israeli-Palestinian conflict. Israel in 2005 unilaterally withdrew all of its settlers and soldiers and dismantled its military facilities in the Gaza Strip, but it continues to control the Gaza Strip's land borders, maritime territorial waters, cyberspace, telecommunications, and airspace. In 2006, HAMAS won a majority in the Palestinian Legislative Council election. Fatah, the dominant Palestinian political faction in the West Bank, and HAMAS failed to maintain a unity government, leading to violent clashes between their respective supporters and HAMAS's violent seizure of all PA military and governmental institutions in the Gaza Strip in 2007. Since HAMAS's takeover, Israel and Egypt have enforced tight restrictions on movement and access of goods and individuals into and out of the territory. Fatah and HAMAS have since negotiated a series of agreements aimed at restoring political unity between the Gaza Strip and the West Bank but have struggled to enact them.

Palestinian militants in the Gaza Strip and the Israel Defense Forces periodically exchange projectiles and air strikes, respectively, threatening broader conflict. In 2021, HAMAS launched rockets into Israel, sparking an 11-day conflict that also involved other Gaza-based militant groups. Egypt, Qatar, and the UN Special Coordinator for the Middle East Peace Process negotiated ceasefires, averting a broader conflict. Since 2018, HAMAS has coordinated demonstrations along the Gaza-Israel security fence. HAMAS has also stood by while other militant groups, such as Palestinian Islamic Jihad, fought brief conflicts with Israel, most recently in August 2022 and May 2023.

On 7 October 2023, HAMAS militants inside the Gaza Strip launched a combined unguided rocket and ground attack into Israel. The attack began with a barrage of more than 3,000 rockets fired toward Israel from Gaza, and included thousands of terrorists infiltrating Israel by land, sea, and air via paragliders. Militants attacked military bases, clashed with security forces mostly in southern Israel, and simultaneously infiltrated civilian communities. During the attack, terrorists carried out massacres and murdered civilians, including torture, acts of abuse and rape, a massacre at the Supernova music festival near Kibbutz Re'im, as well as kidnapping approximately 240 civilians, including men, women, children, and soldiers. These attacks were followed soon after by Israeli Defense Forces (IDF) air strikes inside Gaza. The next day, Israeli Prime Minister NETANYAHU formally declared war on Gaza. The IDF on 28 October launched a large-scale ground assault inside Gaza that is ongoing as of April 2024.

GEOGRAPHY

Location: Middle East, bordering the Mediterranean Sea, between Egypt and Israel

Geographic coordinates: 31 25 N, 34 20 E

Map references: Middle East

Area: *total:* 360 sq km
land: 360 sq km
water: 0 sq km
comparison ranking: total 206

Area - comparative: slightly more than twice the size of Washington, DC

Land boundaries: *total:* 72 km
border countries (2): Egypt 13 km; Israel 59 km

Coastline: 40 km

Maritime claims: *see entry for Israel note:* effective 3 January 2009, the Gaza maritime area is closed to all maritime traffic and is under blockade imposed by Israeli Navy until further notice

Climate: temperate, mild winters, dry and warm to hot summers

Terrain: flat to rolling, sand- and dune-covered coastal plain

Elevation: *highest point:* Abu 'Awdah (Joz Abu 'Awdah) 105 m
lowest point: Mediterranean Sea 0 m

Natural resources: arable land, natural gas

Irrigated land: (2013) 151 sq km; note - includes the West Bank

Population distribution: population concentrated in major cities, particularly Gaza City in the north

Natural hazards: droughts

Geography - note: once a strategic strip of land along Mideast-North African trade routes that has experienced an incredibly turbulent history

PEOPLE AND SOCIETY

Population: *total:* 2,141,643
male: 1,086,340
female: 1,055,303 (2024 est.)
comparison rankings: female 149; male 148; total 148

Nationality: *noun:* NA
adjective: NA

Ethnic groups: Palestinian Arab

Languages: Arabic, Hebrew (spoken by many Palestinians), English (widely understood)
major-language sample(s):
يمكن الاستغناء عنه للمعلومات الأساسية
كتاب حقائق العالم، المصدر الذي لا
(Arabic)

Religions: Muslim 98.0 - 99.0% (predominantly Sunni), Christian <1.0%, other, unaffiliated, unspecified <1.0% (2012 est.)
note: Israel dismantled its settlements in September 2005; Gaza has had no Jewish population since then

Age structure: *0-14 years:* 38.8% (male 427,450/female 404,288)
15-64 years: 58.3% (male 627,235/female 620,903)
65 years and over: 2.9% (2024 est.) (male 31,655/female 30,112)

Dependency ratios: *total dependency ratio:* 74.3
youth dependency ratio: 68.2
elderly dependency ratio: 6.1
potential support ratio: 16.5 (2021 est.)
note: data represent Gaza Strip and the West Bank

Median age: *total:* 19.5 years (2024 est.)
male: 19.3 years
female: 19.8 years
comparison ranking: total 208

Population growth rate: 2.02% (2024 est.)
comparison ranking: 40

Birth rate: 26.8 births/1,000 population (2024 est.)
comparison ranking: 38

Death rate: 2.9 deaths/1,000 population (2024 est.)
comparison ranking: 225

Net migration rate: -3.7 migrant(s)/1,000 population (2024 est.)
comparison ranking: 190

Population distribution: population concentrated in major cities, particularly Gaza City in the north

Urbanization: *urban population:* 77.6% of total population (2023)
rate of urbanization: 2.85% annual rate of change (2020-25 est.)
note: data represent Gaza Strip and the West Bank

Major urban areas - population: 778,000 Gaza (2023)

Sex ratio: *at birth:* 1.06 male(s)/female
0-14 years: 1.06 male(s)/female
15-64 years: 1.01 male(s)/female
65 years and over: 1.05 male(s)/female
total population: 1.03 male(s)/female (2024 est.)

Maternal mortality ratio: 20 deaths/100,000 live births (2020 est.)
note: data represent Gaza Strip and the West Bank
comparison ranking: 126

Infant mortality rate: *total:* 15.1 deaths/1,000 live births (2024 est.)
male: 16.3 deaths/1,000 live births
female: 13.8 deaths/1,000 live births
comparison ranking: total 91

Life expectancy at birth: *total population:* 75.5 years (2024 est.)
male: 73.7 years
female: 77.4 years
comparison ranking: total population 126

Total fertility rate: 3.26 children born/woman (2024 est.)
comparison ranking: 42

Gross reproduction rate: 1.58 (2024 est.)

Contraceptive prevalence rate: 57.3% (2019/20)
note: includes Gaza Strip and West Bank

Drinking water source: *improved: urban:* 98.9% of population
rural: 99% of population
total: 98.9% of population
unimproved: urban: 1.1% of population
rural: 1% of population
total: 1.1% of population (2020 est.)
note: includes Gaza Strip and the West Bank

Current health expenditure: NA

Physician density: 2.71 physicians/1,000 population (2020)

Hospital bed density: 1.3 beds/1,000 population (2019)

Sanitation facility access: *improved: urban:* 99.9% of population
rural: 98.6% of population
total: 99.6% of population
unimproved: urban: 0.1% of population
rural: 1.4% of population
total: 0.4% of population (2020 est.)
note: note includes Gaza Strip and the West Bank

Children under the age of 5 years underweight: 2.1% (2019/20)
note: estimate is for Gaza Strip and the West Bank
comparison ranking: 102

Currently married women (ages 15-49): 62.4% (2023 est.)
note: data includes Gaza and the West Bank

Child marriage: *women married by age 15:* 0.7%
women married by age 18: 13.4% (2020 est.)
note: includes both the Gaza Strip and the West Bank

Education expenditures: 5.3% of GDP (2018 est.)
note: includes Gaza Strip and the West Bank
comparison ranking: 66

Literacy: *definition:* age 15 and over can read and write
total population: 97.5%
male: 98.8%
female: 96.2% (2020)
note: estimates are for Gaza Strip and the West Bank

School life expectancy (primary to tertiary education): *total:* 13 years
male: 12 years
female: 14 years (2021)
note: data represent Gaza Strip and the West Bank

ENVIRONMENT

Environment - current issues: soil degradation; desertification; water pollution from chemicals and pesticides; salination of fresh water; improper sewage treatment; water-borne disease; depletion and contamination of underground water resources

Climate: temperate, mild winters, dry and warm to hot summers

Urbanization: *urban population:* 77.6% of total population (2023)
rate of urbanization: 2.85% annual rate of change (2020-25 est.)
note: data represent Gaza Strip and the West Bank

Revenue from forest resources: 0% of GDP (2018 est.)
comparison ranking: 197

Air pollutants: *particulate matter emissions:* 30.82 micrograms per cubic meter (2019 est.)
carbon dioxide emissions: 3.23 megatons (2016 est.)
note: data represent combined total from the Gaza Strip and the West Bank.

Waste and recycling: *municipal solid waste generated annually:* 1.387 million tons (2016 est.)
municipal solid waste recycled annually: 6,935 tons (2013 est.)
percent of municipal solid waste recycled: 0.5% (2013 est.)
note: data represent combined total from the Gaza Strip and the West Bank.

Total water withdrawal: *municipal:* 181.2 million cubic meters (2017 est.)
industrial: 32 million cubic meters (2017 est.)
agricultural: 162 million cubic meters (2017 est.)
note: data represent combined total from the Gaza Strip and the West Bank.

Total renewable water resources: 840 million cubic meters (2020 est.)
note: data represent combined total from the Gaza Strip and the West Bank.

GOVERNMENT

Country name: *conventional long form:* none
conventional short form: Gaza, Gaza Strip
local long form: none
local short form: Qita' Ghazzah
etymology: named for the largest city in the enclave, Gaza, whose settlement can be traced back to at least the 15th century B.C. (as "Ghazzat")

ECONOMY

Real GDP (purchasing power parity): $27.418 billion (2023 est.)
$29.016 billion (2022 est.)
$27.878 billion (2021 est.)
note: data in 2021 dollars; entry includes West Bank and Gaza Strip
comparison ranking: 152

Real GDP growth rate: -5.51% (2023 est.)
4.08% (2022 est.)
7.01% (2021 est.)
note: annual GDP % growth based on constant local currency; entry includes West Bank and Gaza Strip
comparison ranking: 214

Real GDP per capita: $5,300 (2023 est.)
$5,800 (2022 est.)
$5,700 (2021 est.)
note: data in 2021 dollars; entry includes West Bank and Gaza Strip
comparison ranking: 174

GDP (official exchange rate): $17.396 billion (2023 est.)
note: data in current dollars at official exchange rate; entry includes West Bank and Gaza Strip

Inflation rate (consumer prices): 5.87% (2023 est.)
3.74% (2022 est.)
1.24% (2021 est.)
note: annual % change based on consumer prices; entry includes West Bank and Gaza Strip
comparison ranking: 123

GDP - composition, by sector of origin: *agriculture:* 5.7% (2022 est.)

industry: 17.4% (2022 est.)
services: 58.3% (2022 est.)
note: figures may not total 100% due to non-allocated consumption not captured in sector-reported data
comparison rankings: services 100; industry 155; agriculture 110

GDP - composition, by end use: *household consumption:* 101.6% (2023 est.)
government consumption: 20.2% (2023 est.)
investment in fixed capital: 24.8% (2023 est.)
investment in inventories: 1.5% (2023 est.)
exports of goods and services: 19.6% (2023 est.)
imports of goods and services: -66.9% (2023 est.)
note: figures may not total 100% due to rounding or gaps in data collection

Agricultural products: tomatoes, milk, cucumbers/gherkins, olives, potatoes, sheep milk, eggplants, pumpkins/squash, grapes, chicken (2022)
note: top ten agricultural products based on tonnage

Industries: textiles, food processing, furniture

Industrial production growth rate: -8.57% (2023 est.)
note: annual % change in industrial value added based on constant local currency; entry includes West Bank and Gaza Strip
comparison ranking: 206

Labor force: 1.389 million (2022 est.)
note: number of people ages 15 or older who are employed or seeking work; entry includes West Bank and Gaza Strip
comparison ranking: 137

Unemployment rate: 24.42% (2022 est.)
26.39% (2021 est.)
25.9% (2020 est.)
note: % of labor force seeking employment; entry includes West Bank and Gaza Strip
comparison ranking: 205

Youth unemployment rate (ages 15-24): *total:* 36% (2022 est.)
male: 31.6% (2022 est.)
female: 56.7% (2022 est.)
note: % of labor force ages 15-24 seeking employment
comparison ranking: total 17

Population below poverty line: 29.2% (2016 est.)
note: % of population with income below national poverty line; entry includes West Bank and Gaza Strip

Gini Index coefficient - distribution of family income: 33.7 (2016 est.)
note: index (0-100) of income distribution; higher values represent greater inequality; entry includes West Bank and Gaza Strip
comparison ranking: 95

Household income or consumption by percentage share: *lowest 10%:* 2.9% (2016 est.)
highest 10%: 25.2% (2016 est.)
note: % share of income accruing to lowest and highest 10% of population; entry includes West Bank and Gaza Strip

Remittances: 21.84% of GDP (2023 est.)
21.13% of GDP (2022 est.)
20.77% of GDP (2021 est.)
note: personal transfers and compensation between resident and non-resident individuals/households/entities; entry includes West Bank and Gaza Strip

Budget: *revenues:* $3.803 billion (2020 est.)
expenditures: $5.002 billion (2020 est.)
see entry for the West Bank

Taxes and other revenues: 21.47% (of GDP) (2021 est.)
note: central government tax revenue as a % of GDP; entry includes West Bank and Gaza Strip
comparison ranking: 70

Current account balance: -$2.037 billion (2022 est.)
-$1.778 billion (2021 est.)
-$1.903 billion (2020 est.)
note: balance of payments - net trade and primary/secondary income in current dollars; entry includes West Bank and Gaza Strip
comparison ranking: 159

Exports: $3.533 billion (2022 est.)
$3.14 billion (2021 est.)
$2.385 billion (2020 est.)
note: balance of payments - exports of goods and services in current dollars; entry includes West Bank and Gaza Strip
comparison ranking: 151

Exports - partners: Israel 81%, Jordan 10%, UAE 2%, US 1%, Turkey 1% (2022)
note: top five export partners based on percentage share of exports; entry includes the West Bank and the Gaza Strip

Exports - commodities: building stone, scrap iron, plastic products, furniture, seats (2022)
note: top five export commodities based on value in dollars; entry includes the West Bank and the Gaza Strip

Imports: $12.257 billion (2022 est.)
$10.094 billion (2021 est.)
$8.065 billion (2020 est.)
note: balance of payments - imports of goods and services in current dollars; entry includes West Bank and Gaza Strip
comparison ranking: 113

Imports - partners: Israel 57%, Turkey 6%, Egypt 6%, Jordan 4%, China 4% (2022)
note: top five import partners based on percentage share of imports; entry includes the West Bank and the Gaza Strip

Imports - commodities: refined petroleum, electricity, animal food, cars, cement (2022)
note: top five import commodities based on value in dollars; entry includes the West Bank and the Gaza Strip

Reserves of foreign exchange and gold: $1.323 billion (2023 est.)
$896.9 million (2022 est.)
$872.541 million (2021 est.)
note: holdings of gold (year-end prices)/foreign exchange/special drawing rights in current dollars; entry includes West Bank and Gaza Strip
comparison ranking: 151

Exchange rates: see entry for the West Bank

ENERGY

Electricity access: *electrification - total population:* 100% (2022 est.)
note: includes the West Bank and the Gaza Strip

Electricity: *installed generating capacity:* 352,000 kW (2022 est.)
consumption: 6.746 billion kWh (2022 est.)
imports: 6.7 billion kWh (2022 est.)
transmission/distribution losses: 880.312 million kWh (2022 est.)
note: includes the West Bank and the Gaza Strip
comparison rankings: transmission/distribution losses 93; imports 39; consumption 119; installed generating capacity 160

Electricity generation sources: *fossil fuels:* 77.5% of total installed capacity (2022 est.)
solar: 22.4% of total installed capacity (2022 est.)
note: includes the West Bank and the Gaza Strip

Coal: *exports:* (2022 est.) less than 1 metric ton
note: includes the West Bank and the Gaza Strip

Petroleum: *refined petroleum consumption:* 29,000 bbl/day (2022 est.)
note: includes the West Bank and the Gaza Strip

Carbon dioxide emissions: 3.942 million metric tonnes of CO_2 (2022 est.)
from petroleum and other liquids: 3.942 million metric tonnes of CO_2 (2022 est.)
note: includes the West Bank and the Gaza Strip
comparison ranking: total emissions 141

Energy consumption per capita: 15.201 million Btu/person (2022 est.)
note: includes the West Bank and the Gaza Strip
comparison ranking: 139

COMMUNICATIONS

Telephones - fixed lines: *total subscriptions:* 458,000 (2022 est.)
subscriptions per 100 inhabitants: 9 (2021 est.)
note: entry includes the West Bank and the Gaza Strip
comparison ranking: total subscriptions 97

Telephones - mobile cellular: *total subscriptions:* 4.388 million (2022 est.)
subscriptions per 100 inhabitants: 78 (2021 est.)
note: entry includes the West Bank and the Gaza Strip
comparison ranking: total subscriptions 131

Telecommunication systems: *general assessment:* Israel, which controls Palestinian frequencies and telecom infrastructure, limits mobile internet speeds in the Palestinian territories to levels that are significantly lower than in Israel and Jewish West Bank settlements; the World Bank urged Israel to let Palestinian cellular companies set up more advanced networks, and to ease restrictions on the import of equipment needed to build and operate them; Israel is rolling out fifth generation technology for its citizens, while the West Bank operates on 3G and Gaza, 2G; Israeli mobile operators don't officially service Palestinian areas, but many Palestinians use the faster Israeli networks with SIM cards; the Times of Israel reported in November that Israel tentatively agreed to let Palestinian operators launch 4G services (2022)
domestic: fixed-line 9 per 100 and mobile-cellular 28 per 100 (includes West Bank) (2021)
international: country code 970 or 972 (2018)

Broadcast media: 1 TV station and about 10 radio stations; satellite TV accessible

Internet country code: .ps; note - IANA has designated .ps for the Gaza Strip, same as the West Bank

Internet users: *total:* 3,602,452 (2020 est.)
percent of population: 75% (2020 est.)
note: includes the West Bank
comparison ranking: total 114

Broadband - fixed subscriptions: *total:* 376,911 (2020 est.)
subscriptions per 100 inhabitants: 7 (2020 est.)
note: includes the West Bank

comparison ranking: total 100

TRANSPORTATION

Roadways: *note:* see entry for the West Bank

MILITARY AND SECURITY

Military and security forces: HAMAS maintains security forces inside Gaza in addition to its military wing, the 'Izz al-Din al-Qassam Brigades; the military wing ostensibly reports to the HAMAS Political Bureau but operates with considerable autonomy; there are several other militant groups operating in the Gaza Strip, most notably the Al-Quds Brigades of Palestinian Islamic Jihad, which are usually but not always beholden to HAMAS's authority (2024)

Military expenditures: not available

Military and security service personnel strengths: the military wing of HAMAS has an estimated 20-25,000 fighters (2023)

Military equipment inventories and acquisitions: the military wing is armed with light weapons, including an inventory of rocket, anti-tank, anti-aircraft, indirect fire (typically mortars), and armed UAV capabilities; HAMAS acquires its weapons through smuggling or local construction and receives significant military support from Iran (2024)

Military - note: since seizing control of the Gaza Strip in 2007, the terrorist group HAMAS has had repeated clashes with Israel, including armed conflicts in 2008-09, 2012, 2014, 2021, and 2023-24; the Palestine Islamic Jihad (PIJ) terrorist group also operates in the Gaza Strip and has cooperated with HAMAS (2024)

TERRORISM

Terrorist group(s): Army of Islam; Abdallah Azzam Brigades; al-Aqsa Martyrs Brigade; HAMAS; Islamic Revolutionary Guard Corps/Qods Force; Islamic State of Iraq and ash-Sham - Sinai Province (ISIS-SP); Mujahidin Shura Council in the Environs of Jerusalem; Palestine Islamic Jihad (PIJ); Palestine Liberation Front; Popular Front for the Liberation of Palestine (PFLP); PFLP-General Command
note: details about the history, aims, leadership, organization, areas of operation, tactics, targets, weapons, size, and sources of support of the group(s) appear(s) in the Terrorism reference guide

TRANSNATIONAL ISSUES

Refugees and internally displaced persons: *refugees (country of origin):* 1.6 million (Palestinian refugees) (2022)
IDPs: 1.7 million or approximately 75% of the population (as of 26 January 2024, since HAMAS's attack on Israel on 7 October 2023)
1.6 million (includes persons displaced within the Gaza Strip due to the intensification of the Israeli-Palestinian conflict between June 2014 and 7 October 2023 and other Palestinian IDPs in the Gaza Strip and West Bank who fled as long ago as 1967, although confirmed cumulative data do not go back beyond 2006) (2022)

GEORGIA

INTRODUCTION

Background: The region of present-day Georgia once contained the ancient kingdoms of Colchis (known as Egrisi locally) and Kartli-Iberia. The area came under Roman influence in the first centuries A.D., and Christianity became the state religion in the 330s. Persian, Arab, and Turk domination was followed by a Georgian golden age (11th-13th centuries) that was cut short when the Mongols invaded in 1236. Subsequently, the Ottoman and Persian empires competed for influence in the region. Georgia was absorbed into the Russian Empire in the 19th century. Independent for three years (1918-1921) following the Russian revolution, it was forcibly incorporated into the USSR in 1921 and regained its independence when the Soviet Union dissolved in 1991.

In 2003, mounting public discontent over rampant corruption, ineffective government services, and a government attempt to manipulate parliamentary elections touched off widespread protests that led to the resignation of Eduard SHEVARDNADZE, who had been president since 1995. In the aftermath of this "Rose Revolution," new elections in 2004 swept Mikheil SAAKASHVILI and his United National Movement (UNM) party into power. SAAKASHVILI made progress on market reforms and governance, but he faced accusations of abuse of office. Progress was further complicated when Russian support for the separatist regions of Abkhazia and South Ossetia led to a five-day conflict between Russia and Georgia in August 2008, which included Russia invading large portions of Georgian territory. Russia initially pledged to pull back from most Georgian territory but then unilaterally recognized the independence of Abkhazia and South Ossetia, and Russian military forces have remained in those regions.

Billionaire Bidzina IVANISHVILI's unexpected entry into politics in 2011 brought the divided opposition together under his Georgian Dream coalition, which won a majority of seats in the 2012 parliamentary elections and removed UNM from power. Conceding defeat, SAAKASHVILI named IVANISHVILI as prime minister and left the country after his presidential term ended in 2013. IVANISHVILI voluntarily resigned from office after the presidential succession, and in the years since, the prime minister position has seen frequent turnover. In 2021, SAAKASHVILI returned to Georgia, where he was immediately arrested to serve six years in prison on outstanding abuse-of-office convictions.

Popular support for integration with the West is high in Georgia. Joining the EU and NATO are among the country's top foreign policy goals, and Georgia applied for EU membership in 2022, becoming a candidate country in December 2023. Georgia and the EU have a Deep and Comprehensive Free Trade Agreement, and since 2017, Georgian citizens have been able to travel to the Schengen area without a visa.

GEOGRAPHY

Location: Southwestern Asia, bordering the Black Sea, between Turkey and Russia, with a sliver of land north of the Caucasus extending into Europe; note - Georgia views itself as part of Europe; geopolitically, it can be classified as falling within Europe, the Middle East, or both

Geographic coordinates: 42 00 N, 43 30 E

Map references: Asia

Area: *total:* 69,700 sq km
land: 69,700 sq km
water: 0 sq km
note: approximately 12,560 sq km, or about 18% of Georgia's area, is Russian occupied; the seized area includes all of Abkhazia and the breakaway region of South Ossetia, which consists of the northern part of Shida Kartli, eastern slivers of the Imereti region and Racha-Lechkhumi and Kvemo Svaneti, and part of western Mtskheta-Mtianeti
comparison ranking: total 121

Area - comparative: slightly smaller than South Carolina; slightly larger than West Virginia

Land boundaries: *total:* 1,814 km
border countries (4): Armenia 219 km; Azerbaijan 428 km; Russia 894 km; Turkey 273 km

Coastline: 310 km

Maritime claims: *territorial sea:* 12 nm
exclusive economic zone: 200 nm

Climate: warm and pleasant; Mediterranean-like on Black Sea coast

Terrain: largely mountainous with Great Caucasus Mountains in the north and Lesser Caucasus Mountains in the south; Kolkhet'is Dablobi (Kolkhida Lowland) opens to the Black Sea in the west; Mtkvari River Basin in the east; fertile soils in river valley flood plains and foothills of Kolkhida Lowland

Elevation: *highest point:* Mt'a Shkhara 5,193 m
lowest point: Black Sea 0 m
mean elevation: 1,432 m

Natural resources: timber, hydropower, manganese deposits, iron ore, copper, minor coal and oil deposits; coastal climate and soils allow for important tea and citrus growth

Land use: *agricultural land:* 35.5% (2018 est.)
arable land: 5.8% (2018 est.)
permanent crops: 1.8% (2018 est.)
permanent pasture: 27.9% (2018 est.)
forest: 39.4% (2018 est.)

other: 25.1% (2018 est.)

Irrigated land: 4,330 sq km (2012)

Population distribution: settlement concentrated in the central valley, particularly in the capital city of Tbilisi in the east; smaller urban agglomerations dot the Black Sea coast, with Bat'umi being the largest

Natural hazards: earthquakes

Geography - note: *note 1:* strategically located east of the Black Sea; Georgia controls much of the Caucasus Mountains and the routes through them
note 2: the world's four deepest caves are all in Georgia, including two that are the only known caves on earth deeper than 2,000 m: Krubera Cave at -2,197 m (-7,208 ft; reached in 2012) and Veryovkina Cave at -2,212 (-7,257 ft; reached in 2018)

PEOPLE AND SOCIETY

Population: *total:* 4,900,961
male: 2,343,068
female: 2,557,893 (2024 est.)
comparison rankings: female 126; male 126; total 126

Nationality: *noun:* Georgian(s)
adjective: Georgian

Ethnic groups: Georgian 86.8%, Azeri 6.3%, Armenian 4.5%, other 2.3% (includes Russian, Ossetian, Yazidi, Ukrainian, Kist, Greek) (2014 est.)

Languages: Georgian (official) 87.6%, Azeri 6.2%, Armenian 3.9%, Russian 1.2%, other 1% (including Abkhaz, the official language in Abkhazia) (2014 est.)
major-language sample(s):
მსოფლიო ფაქტების წიგნი, ძირითადი ინფორმაციის აუცილებელი წყარო.
(Georgian)

Religions: Eastern Orthodox Christian (official) 83.4%, Muslim 10.7%, Armenian Apostolic Christian 2.9%, other 1.2% (includes Roman Catholic Christian, Jehovah's Witness, Yazidi, Protestant Christian, Jewish), none 0.5%, unspecified/no answer 1.2% (2014 est.)

Demographic profile: Analyzing population trends in Georgia since independence in 1991 has proven difficult due to a lack of reliable demographic statistics. Censuses were fairly accurately and regularly updated through a vital statistics system during Georgia's period of Soviet rule, but from independence until about 2010, the system broke down as a result of institutional and economic change, social unrest, and large-scale outmigration. The 2002 census is believed to have significantly overestimated the size of Georgia's population, in part because respondents continued to include relatives living abroad as part of their household count. The 2014 census indicates that Georgia's population is decreasing and aging. Census data shows that the median age increased from 34.5 years in 2002 to 37.7 years in 2014. The working-age population (ages 15-65 years) was fairly high in 2002 and rose between 2005 and 2011. Nonetheless, Georgia did not reap economic benefits from this age structure, since the working-age population increase seems to have stimulated labor outmigration to Russia, Ukraine, and other neighboring countries.

Since the Russian invasion of Ukraine in 2022, Georgia has seen its economy grow to its highest level in years due to the influx of Russian businesses, information and communications technology specialists, and money transfers. This growth may only be temporary and conditions could still easily change depending on future events. Meanwhile, the Russian inflow is also a source of concern, as some Georgians fear it could prompt Putin to target their country next. In addition, Ukrainian refugees use Georgia not just as a transit country but also as a destination. Some 25,000 Ukrainians remain in the country as of November 2022; they pose an additional strain on resources in Georgia, which has a significant population of its own displaced citizens – from the 2008 Russian occupation of Abkhazia and South Ossetia – who continue to need government support.

Age structure: *0-14 years:* 20.6% (male 520,091/female 489,882)
15-64 years: 62.7% (male 1,500,036/female 1,572,637)
65 years and over: 16.7% (2024 est.) (male 322,941/female 495,374)

Dependency ratios: *total dependency ratio:* 55.4
youth dependency ratio: 32.8
elderly dependency ratio: 22.6
potential support ratio: 4.4 (2021 est.)

Median age: *total:* 38.3 years (2024 est.)
male: 35.9 years
female: 40.6 years
comparison ranking: total 75

Population growth rate: -0.5% (2024 est.)
comparison ranking: 222

Birth rate: 12 births/1,000 population (2024 est.)
comparison ranking: 148

Death rate: 13.3 deaths/1,000 population (2024 est.)
comparison ranking: 11

Net migration rate: -3.8 migrant(s)/1,000 population (2024 est.)
comparison ranking: 193

Population distribution: settlement concentrated in the central valley, particularly in the capital city of Tbilisi in the east; smaller urban agglomerations dot the Black Sea coast, with Bat'umi being the largest

Urbanization: *urban population:* 60.7% of total population (2023)
rate of urbanization: 0.35% annual rate of change (2020-25 est.)
note: data include Abkhazia and South Ossetia

Major urban areas - population: 1.082 million TBILISI (capital) (2023)

Sex ratio: *at birth:* 1.07 male(s)/female
0-14 years: 1.06 male(s)/female
15-64 years: 0.95 male(s)/female
65 years and over: 0.65 male(s)/female
total population: 0.92 male(s)/female (2024 est.)

Mother's mean age at first birth: 25.9 years (2019 est.)
note: data does not cover Abkhazia and South Ossetia

Maternal mortality ratio: 28 deaths/100,000 live births (2020 est.)
comparison ranking: 114

Infant mortality rate: *total:* 21.7 deaths/1,000 live births (2024 est.)
male: 23.6 deaths/1,000 live births
female: 19.7 deaths/1,000 live births
comparison ranking: total 72

Life expectancy at birth: *total population:* 72.8 years (2024 est.)
male: 68.7 years
female: 77.2 years
comparison ranking: total population 158

Total fertility rate: 1.95 children born/woman (2024 est.)
comparison ranking: 112

Gross reproduction rate: 0.94 (2024 est.)

Contraceptive prevalence rate: 40.6% (2018)

Drinking water source: *improved: urban:* 99.4% of population
rural: 94.3% of population
total: 97.3% of population
unimproved: urban: 0.6% of population
rural: 5.7% of population
total: 2.7% of population (2020 est.)

Current health expenditure: 7.6% of GDP (2020)

Physician density: 5.11 physicians/1,000 population (2020)

Hospital bed density: 2.9 beds/1,000 population (2014)

Sanitation facility access: *improved: urban:* 96.3% of population
rural: 72.7% of population
total: 86.7% of population
unimproved: urban: 3.7% of population
rural: 27.3% of population
total: 13.3% of population (2020 est.)

Obesity - adult prevalence rate: 21.7% (2016)
comparison ranking: 85

Alcohol consumption per capita: *total:* 7.45 liters of pure alcohol (2019 est.)
beer: 1.71 liters of pure alcohol (2019 est.)
wine: 3.19 liters of pure alcohol (2019 est.)
spirits: 2.52 liters of pure alcohol (2019 est.)
other alcohols: 0.02 liters of pure alcohol (2019 est.)
comparison ranking: total 53

Tobacco use: *total:* 31.7% (2020 est.)
male: 56.3% (2020 est.)
female: 7.1% (2020 est.)
comparison ranking: total 24

Children under the age of 5 years underweight: 2.1% (2018)
comparison ranking: 104

Currently married women (ages 15-49): 67.1% (2023 est.)

Child marriage: *women married by age 15:* 0.3%
women married by age 18: 13.9%
men married by age 18: 0.5% (2018 est.)

Education expenditures: 3.6% of GDP (2021 est.)
comparison ranking: 135

Literacy: *definition:* age 15 and over can read and write
total population: 99.6%
male: 99.7%
female: 99,5% (2019)

School life expectancy (primary to tertiary education): *total:* 16 years
male: 16 years
female: 16 years (2021)

ENVIRONMENT

Environment - current issues: air pollution, particularly in Rust'avi; heavy water pollution of Mtkvari River and the Black Sea; inadequate supplies of potable water; soil pollution from toxic chemicals;

land and forest degradation; biodiversity loss; waste management

Environment - international agreements: *party to:* Air Pollution, Biodiversity, Climate Change, Climate Change-Kyoto Protocol, Climate Change-Paris Agreement, Comprehensive Nuclear Test Ban, Desertification, Endangered Species, Hazardous Wastes, Law of the Sea, Marine Dumping-London Protocol, Ozone Layer Protection, Ship Pollution, Wetlands
signed, but not ratified: none of the selected agreements

Climate: warm and pleasant; Mediterranean-like on Black Sea coast

Urbanization: *urban population:* 60.7% of total population (2023)
rate of urbanization: 0.35% annual rate of change (2020-25 est.)
note: data include Abkhazia and South Ossetia

Revenue from forest resources: 0.07% of GDP (2018 est.)
comparison ranking: 122

Revenue from coal: 0.01% of GDP (2018 est.)
comparison ranking: 52

Air pollutants: *particulate matter emissions:* 19.06 micrograms per cubic meter (2019 est.)
carbon dioxide emissions: 10.13 megatons (2016 est.)
methane emissions: 6.05 megatons (2020 est.)

Waste and recycling: *municipal solid waste generated annually:* 800,000 tons (2015 est.)

Total water withdrawal: *municipal:* 610 million cubic meters (2020 est.)
industrial: 340 million cubic meters (2020 est.)
agricultural: 710 million cubic meters (2020 est.)

Total renewable water resources: 63.33 billion cubic meters (2020 est.)

GOVERNMENT

Country name: *conventional long form:* none
conventional short form: Georgia
local long form: Republic of Georgia
local short form: Sak'art'velo
former: Georgian Soviet Socialist Republic
etymology: the Western name may derive from the Persian designation "gurgan" meaning "Land of the Wolves"; the native name "Sak'art'velo" means "Land of the Kartvelians" and refers to the core central Georgian region of Kartli

Government type: semi-presidential republic

Capital: *name:* Tbilisi
geographic coordinates: 41 41 N, 44 50 E
time difference: UTC+4 (9 hours ahead of Washington, DC, during Standard Time)
etymology: the name in Georgian means "warm place," referring to the numerous sulfuric hot springs in the area

Administrative divisions: 9 regions (mkharebi, singular - mkhare), 1 city (kalaki), and 2 autonomous republics (avtomnoy respubliki, singular - avtom respublika)
regions: Guria, Imereti, Kakheti, Kvemo Kartli, Mtskheta Mtianeti, Racha-Lechkhumi and Kvemo Svaneti, Samegrelo and Zemo Svaneti, Samtskhe-Javakheti, Shida Kartli; note - the breakaway region of South Ossetia consists of the northern part of Shida Kartli, eastern slivers of the Imereti region and Racha-Lechkhumi and Kvemo Svaneti, and part of western Mtskheta-Mtianeti
city: Tbilisi
autonomous republics: Abkhazia or Ap'khazet'is Avtonomiuri Respublika (Sokhumi), Ajaria or Acharis Avtonomiuri Respublika (Bat'umi)
note 1: the administrative centers of the two autonomous republics are shown in parentheses
note 2: the United States recognizes the breakaway regions of Abkhazia and South Ossetia to be part of Georgia

Independence: 9 *April 1991 (from the Soviet Union); notable earlier date:* A.D. 1008 (Georgia unified under King BAGRAT III)

National holiday: Independence Day, 26 May (1918); note - 26 May 1918 was the date of independence from Soviet Russia, 9 April 1991 was the date of independence from the Soviet Union

Legal system: civil law system

Constitution: *history:* previous 1921, 1978 (based on 1977 Soviet Union constitution); latest approved 24 August 1995, effective 17 October 1995
amendments: proposed as a draft law supported by more than one half of the Parliament membership or by petition of at least 200,000 voters; passage requires support by at least three fourths of the Parliament membership in two successive sessions three months apart and the signature and promulgation by the president of Georgia; amended several times, last in 2020 (legislative electoral system revised)

International law organization participation: accepts compulsory ICJ jurisdiction; accepts ICCt jurisdiction

Citizenship: *citizenship by birth:* no
citizenship by descent only: at least one parent must be a citizen of Georgia
dual citizenship recognized: no
residency requirement for naturalization: 10 years

Suffrage: 18 years of age; universal

Executive branch: *chief of state:* President Salome ZOURABICHVILI (since 16 December 2018)
head of government: Prime Minister Irakli KOBAKHIDZE (since 8 February 2024)
cabinet: Cabinet of Ministers
elections/appointments: president directly elected by absolute majority popular vote in 2 rounds if needed for a 5-year term (eligible for a second term); election last held on 28 November 2018 (next to be held in 2024); prime minister nominated by Parliament, appointed by the president; note - 2017 constitutional amendments made the 2018 election the last where the president was directly elected; future presidents will be elected by a 300-member College of Electors; in light of these changes, ZOURABICHVILI was allowed a six-year term
election results:
2024: Irakli KOBAKHIDZE approved as prime minister by Parliamentary vote 84-10
2018: Salome ZOURABICHVILI elected president in second round; percent of vote in second round - Salome ZOURABICHVILI (independent, backed by Georgian Dream) 59.5%, Grigol VASHADZE (UNM) 40.5%; Irakli GARIBASHVILI approved as prime minister by Parliamentary vote 89-2; note-resigned on January 29, 2024
note: Irakli GARIBASHVILI resigned on 29 January 2024 to prepare for general elections in October 2024

Legislative branch: *description:* unicameral Parliament or Sakartvelos Parlamenti (150 seats statutory, 140 as of October 2024); 120 members directly elected in a single nationwide constituency by closed, party-list proportional representation vote and 30 directly elected in single-seat constituencies by at least 50% majority vote, with a runoff if needed; no party earning less than 40% of total votes may claim a majority; members serve 4-year terms)
elections: last held on 26 October 2024
election results: percent of vote by party - Georgian Dream 53.9%, the Coalition for Change 11%, Unity-National Movement 10.2%, Strong Georgia 8.8%, Gakharia for Georgia 7.8%; seats by party - Georgian Dream 89, Coalition for Change 19, Unity-National Movement 16, Strong Georgia 14, Gakharia for Georgia 12

Judicial branch: *highest court(s):* Supreme Court (consists of 28 judges organized into several specialized judicial chambers; number of judges determined by the president of Georgia); Constitutional Court (consists of 9 judges); note - the Abkhazian and Ajarian Autonomous republics each have a supreme court and a hierarchy of lower courts
judge selection and term of office: Supreme Court judges nominated by the High Council of Justice (a 14-member body consisting of the Supreme Court chairperson, common court judges, and appointees of the president of Georgia) and appointed by Parliament; judges appointed for life; Constitutional Court judges appointed 3 each by the president, by Parliament, and by the Supreme Court judges; judges appointed for 10- year terms
subordinate courts: Courts of Appeal; regional (town) and district courts

Political parties: Citizens
European Socialists
For Georgia
Georgian Dream
Girchi
Law and Justice
Lelo for Georgia
National Democratic Party
People's Power
Progress and Freedom
Republican Party
State for the People
Strategy Aghmashenebeli
United National Movement or UNM
Victorious Georgia

International organization participation: ADB, BSEC, CD, CE, CPLP (associate), EAPC, EBRD, FAO, G-11, GCTU, GUAM, IAEA, IBRD, ICAO, ICC (national committees), ICCt, ICRM, IDA, IFAD, IFC, IFRCS, ILO, IMF, IMO, Interpol, IOC, IOM, IPU, ISO (correspondent), ITSO, ITU, ITUC (NGOs), MIGA, OAS (observer), OIF (observer), OPCW, OSCE, PFP, SELEC (observer), UN, UNCTAD, UNESCO, UNIDO, UNWTO, UPU, WCO, WHO, WIPO, WMO, WTO

Diplomatic representation in the US: *chief of mission:* Ambassador David ZALKALIANI (since 7 June 2022)
chancery: 1824 R Street NW, Washington, DC 20009
telephone: [1] (202) 387-2390
FAX: [1] (202) 387-0864
email address and website:
embgeo.usa@mfa.gov.ge
https://georgiaembassyusa.org/contact/
consulate(s) general: New York, San Francisco

Diplomatic representation from the US: *chief of mission:* Ambassador Robin L. DUNNIGAN (since 12 October 2023)

embassy: 29 Georgian-American Friendship Avenue, Didi Dighomi, Tbilisi, 0131
mailing address: 7060 Tbilisi Place, Washington, DC 20521-7060
telephone: [995] (32) 227-70-00
FAX: [995] (32) 253-23-10
email address and website:
askconsultbilisi@state.gov
https://ge.usembassy.gov/

Flag description: white rectangle with a central red cross extending to all four sides of the flag; each of the four quadrants displays a small red bolnur-katskhuri cross; sometimes referred to as the Five-Cross Flag; although adopted as the official Georgian flag in 2004, the five-cross design is based on a 14th century banner of the Kingdom of Georgia

National symbol(s): Saint George, lion; national colors: red, white

National anthem: *name:* "Tavisupleba" (Liberty)
lyrics/music: Davit MAGRADSE/ Zakaria PALIASHVILI (adapted by Joseb KETSCHAKMADSE)
note: adopted 2004; after the Rose Revolution, a new anthem with music based on the operas "Abesalom da Eteri" and "Daisi" was adopted

National heritage: *total World Heritage Sites:* 4 (3 cultural, 1 natural)
selected World Heritage Site locales: Gelati Monastery (c); Historical Monuments of Mtskheta (c); Upper Svaneti (c); Colchic Rainforests and Wetlands (n)

ECONOMY

Economic overview: main economic activities include cultivation of agricultural products, such as grapes, citrus fruits, and hazelnuts; mining of manganese, copper, and gold; producing alcoholic and nonalcoholic beverages

Real GDP (purchasing power parity): $83.656 billion (2023 est.)
$77.838 billion (2022 est.)
$70.151 billion (2021 est.)
note: data in 2021 dollars
comparison ranking: 102

Real GDP growth rate: 7.47% (2023 est.)
10.96% (2022 est.)
10.64% (2021 est.)
note: annual GDP % growth based on constant local currency
comparison ranking: 18

Real GDP per capita: $22,200 (2023 est.)
$21,000 (2022 est.)
$18,900 (2021 est.)
note: data in 2021 dollars
comparison ranking: 96

GDP (official exchange rate): $30.536 billion (2023 est.)
note: data in current dollars at official exchange rate

Inflation rate (consumer prices): 2.49% (2023 est.)
11.9% (2022 est.)
9.57% (2021 est.)
note: annual % change based on consumer prices
comparison ranking: 51

Credit ratings: Fitch rating: BB (2019)

Moody's rating: Ba2 (2017)

Standard & Poors rating: BB (2019)
note: The year refers to the year in which the current credit rating was first obtained.

GDP - composition, by sector of origin: *agriculture:* 6% (2023 est.)
industry: 19% (2023 est.)
services: 61.7% (2023 est.)
note: figures may not total 100% due to non-allocated consumption not captured in sector-reported data
comparison rankings: services 77; industry 143; agriculture 107

GDP - composition, by end use: *household consumption:* 68.9% (2023 est.)
government consumption: 12.7% (2023 est.)
investment in fixed capital: 21.5% (2023 est.)
investment in inventories: 4.5% (2023 est.)
exports of goods and services: 49.4% (2023 est.)
imports of goods and services: -56.9% (2023 est.)
note: figures may not total 100% due to rounding or gaps in data collection

Agricultural products: milk, grapes, potatoes, wheat, maize, apples, watermelons, barley, tangerines/mandarins, tomatoes (2022)
note: top ten agricultural products based on tonnage

Industries: steel, machine tools, electrical appliances, mining (manganese, copper, gold), chemicals, wood products, wine

Industrial production growth rate: 6.15% (2023 est.)
note: annual % change in industrial value added based on constant local currency
comparison ranking: 39

Labor force: 1.853 million (2023 est.)
note: number of people ages 15 or older who are employed or seeking work
comparison ranking: 128

Unemployment rate: 11.62% (2023 est.)
11.66% (2022 est.)
11.79% (2021 est.)
note: % of labor force seeking employment
comparison ranking: 175

Youth unemployment rate (ages 15-24): *total:* 30.2% (2023 est.)
male: 28.7% (2023 est.)
female: 32.7% (2023 est.)
note: % of labor force ages 15-24 seeking employment
comparison ranking: total 24

Population below poverty line: 15.6% (2022 est.)
note: % of population with income below national poverty line

Gini Index coefficient - distribution of family income: 34.2 (2021 est.)
note: index (0-100) of income distribution; higher values represent greater inequality
comparison ranking: 86

Average household expenditures: *on food:* 32.1% of household expenditures (2022 est.)
on alcohol and tobacco: 3.4% of household expenditures (2022 est.)

Household income or consumption by percentage share: *lowest 10%:* 2.7% (2021 est.)
highest 10%: 26.2% (2021 est.)
note: % share of income accruing to lowest and highest 10% of population

Remittances: 14.74% of GDP (2023 est.)
15.42% of GDP (2022 est.)
14.02% of GDP (2021 est.)
note: personal transfers and compensation between resident and non-resident individuals/households/entities

Budget: *revenues:* $6.712 billion (2022 est.)
expenditures: $6.23 billion (2022 est.)
note: central government revenues (excluding grants) and expenses converted to US dollars at average official exchange rate for year indicated

Public debt: 42.97% of GDP (2022 est.)
note: central government debt as a % of GDP
comparison ranking: 125

Taxes and other revenues: 22.9% (of GDP) (2022 est.)
note: central government tax revenue as a % of GDP
comparison ranking: 63

Current account balance: -$1.326 billion (2023 est.)
-$1.12 billion (2022 est.)
-$1.943 billion (2021 est.)
note: balance of payments - net trade and primary/secondary income in current dollars
comparison ranking: 145

Exports: $15.161 billion (2023 est.)
$13.24 billion (2022 est.)
$8.086 billion (2021 est.)
note: balance of payments - exports of goods and services in current dollars
comparison ranking: 99

Exports - partners: China 11%, Azerbaijan 10%, Russia 9%, Armenia 8%, Bulgaria 7% (2022)
note: top five export partners based on percentage share of exports

Exports - commodities: copper ore, cars, fertilizers, iron alloys, wine (2022)
note: top five export commodities based on value in dollars

Imports: $17.791 billion (2023 est.)
$15.665 billion (2022 est.)
$11.151 billion (2021 est.)
note: balance of payments - imports of goods and services in current dollars
comparison ranking: 102

Imports - partners: Turkey 17%, Russia 12%, China 8%, US 8%, Germany 5% (2022)
note: top five import partners based on percentage share of imports

Imports - commodities: cars, refined petroleum, natural gas, packaged medicine, copper ore (2022)
note: top five import commodities based on value in dollars

Reserves of foreign exchange and gold: $5.002 billion (2023 est.)
$4.886 billion (2022 est.)
$4.271 billion (2021 est.)
note: holdings of gold (year-end prices)/foreign exchange/special drawing rights in current dollars
comparison ranking: 108

Debt - external: $6.976 billion (2022 est.)
note: present value of external debt in current US dollars
comparison ranking: 44

Exchange rates: laris (GEL) per US dollar -

Exchange rates: 2.628 (2023 est.)
2.916 (2022 est.)
3.222 (2021 est.)
3.109 (2020 est.)
2.818 (2019 est.)

ENERGY

Electricity access: *electrification - total population:* 100% (2022 est.)

Electricity: *installed generating capacity:* 4.128 million kW (2022 est.)
consumption: 13.902 billion kWh (2022 est.)

exports: 4.131 billion kWh (2022 est.)
imports: 4.693 billion kWh (2022 est.)
transmission/distribution losses: 905.421 million kWh (2022 est.)
comparison rankings: transmission/distribution losses 94; imports 47; exports 42; consumption 88; installed generating capacity 97

Electricity generation sources: *fossil fuels:* 23.8% of total installed capacity (2022 est.)
wind: 0.6% of total installed capacity (2022 est.)
hydroelectricity: 75.6% of total installed capacity (2022 est.)

Coal: *production:* 256,000 metric tons (2022 est.)
consumption: 516,000 metric tons (2022 est.)
exports: 100 metric tons (2022 est.)
imports: 241,000 metric tons (2022 est.)
proven reserves: 900.999 million metric tons (2022 est.)

Petroleum: *total petroleum production:* 300 bbl/day (2023 est.)
refined petroleum consumption: 32,000 bbl/day (2022 est.)
crude oil estimated reserves: 35 million barrels (2021 est.)

Natural gas: *production:* 8.76 million cubic meters (2022 est.)
consumption: 2.796 billion cubic meters (2022 est.)
imports: 2.787 billion cubic meters (2022 est.)
proven reserves: 8.495 billion cubic meters (2021 est.)

Carbon dioxide emissions: 10.958 million metric tonnes of CO2 (2022 est.)
from coal and metallurgical coke: 1.157 million metric tonnes of CO2 (2022 est.)
from petroleum and other liquids: 4.34 million metric tonnes of CO2 (2022 est.)
from consumed natural gas: 5.46 million metric tonnes of CO2 (2022 est.)
comparison ranking: total emissions 104

Energy consumption per capita: 58.044 million Btu/person (2022 est.)
comparison ranking: 84

COMMUNICATIONS

Telephones - fixed lines: *total subscriptions:* 301,000 (2022 est.)
subscriptions per 100 inhabitants: 8 (2022 est.)
comparison ranking: total subscriptions 106

Telephones - mobile cellular: *total subscriptions:* 5.844 million (2022 est.)
subscriptions per 100 inhabitants: 156 (2022 est.)
comparison ranking: total subscriptions 120

Telecommunication systems: *general assessment:* the telecom sector has been attempting for many years to overcome the decades of under-investment in its fixed-line infrastructure during the Soviet era; concerted efforts to privatize state-owned enterprises and open up the telecom market have been mostly successful, with a large number of operators now competing in both the fixed-line and the mobile segments; Georgia's government moved fast following the collapse of the Soviet Union to liberalize the country's telecom market; this resulted in a relatively high number of operators competing in the under-developed fixed-line segment as well as in the emerging mobile market; the mobile and mobile broadband segments have both demonstrated solid growth in 2021; this upturn follows a significant contraction in subscriber numbers as well as revenue during 2020 due to the Covid-19 crisis; funding has continued to flow into mobile ventures, with the Mobile Network Operators (MNOs) preparing for 5G
(2024)
domestic: fixed-line subscriptions 8 per 100, mobile-cellular tele density roughly 156 per 100 persons (2022)
international: country code - 995; landing points for the Georgia-Russia, Diamond Link Global, and Caucasus Cable System fiber-optic submarine cable that provides connectivity to Russia, Romania and Bulgaria; international service is available by microwave, landline, and satellite through the Moscow switch; international electronic mail and telex service are available (2019)

Broadcast media: The Tbilisi-based Georgian Public Broadcaster (GPB) includes Channel 1, Channel 2, and the Batumi-based Adjara TV, and the State Budget funds all three; there are also a number of independent commercial television broadcasters, such as Imedi, Rustavi 2, Pirveli TV, Maestro, Kavkasia, Georgian Dream Studios (GDS), Obiektivi, Mtavari Arkhi, and a small Russian language operator TOK TV; Tabula and Post TV are web-based television outlets; all of these broadcasters and web-based television outlets, except GDS, carry the news; the Georgian Orthodox Church also operates a satellitebased television station called Unanimity; there are 26 regional television broadcasters across Georgia that are members of the Georgian Association of Regional Broadcasters and/or the Alliance of Georgian Broadcasters; the broadcaster organizations seek to strengthen the regional media's capacities and distribution of regional products: a nationwide digital switchover occurred in 2015; there are several dozen private radio stations; GPB operates 2 radio stations (2019)

Internet country code: .ge

Internet users: *total:* 2.888 million (2021 est.)
percent of population: 76% (2021 est.)
comparison ranking: total 123

Broadband - fixed subscriptions: *total:* 986,809 (2021 est.)
subscriptions per 100 inhabitants: 25 (2021 est.)
comparison ranking: total 75

TRANSPORTATION

National air transport system: *number of registered air carriers:* 4 (2020)
inventory of registered aircraft operated by air carriers: 12
annual passenger traffic on registered air carriers: 516,034 (2018)
annual freight traffic on registered air carriers: 750,000 (2018) mt-km

Civil aircraft registration country code prefix: 4L

Airports: 19 (2024)
comparison ranking: 137

Heliports: 4 (2024)

Pipelines: 1,596 km gas, 1,175 km oil (2013)

Railways: *total:* 1,363 km (2014)
narrow gauge: 37 km (2014) 0.912-m gauge (37 km electrified)
broad gauge: 1,326 km (2014) 1.520-m gauge (1,251 km electrified)
comparison ranking: total 84

Roadways: *total:* 40,044 km (2021)
comparison ranking: total 91

Merchant marine: *total:* 26 (2023)
by type: general cargo 3, other 23
comparison ranking: total 139

Ports: *total ports:* 3 (2024)
large: 0
medium: 0
small: 1
very small: 2
ports with oil terminals: 2
key ports: Batumi, Sokhumi, Supsa Marine Terminal

MILITARY AND SECURITY

Military and security forces: Georgian Defense Forces (GDF; aka Defense Forces of Georgia or DFG): Ground Forces, Air Force, National Guard, Special Operations Forces, National Guard; Ministry of Internal Affairs: Border Police, Coast Guard (includes Georgian naval forces, which were merged with the Coast Guard in 2009) (2024)
note: the Ministry of Internal Affairs also has forces for protecting strategic infrastructure and conducting special operations

Military expenditures: 1.7% of GDP (2023 est.)
1.7% of GDP (2022 est.)
1.7% of GDP (2021 est.)
1.8% of GDP (2020 est.)
1.8% of GDP (2019 est.)
comparison ranking: 80

Military and security service personnel strengths: estimates vary; approximately 30,000 troops, including active National Guard forces (2023)
note: in December 2020, the Parliament of Georgia adopted a resolution determining that the Georgian Defense Forces would have a maximum peacetime strength of 37,000 troops

Military equipment inventories and acquisitions: the majority of the military's inventory consists of Soviet-era weapons and equipment, although in recent years it has received armaments from a number of European countries, as well as the US (2023)

Military service age and obligation: 18-27 years of age for voluntary military service for men and women; conscription was abolished in 2016, but reinstated in 2017 for men 18-27 years of age; conscript service obligation is 12 months (2024)
note 1: approximately 6-7,000 individuals are called up annually for conscription for service; conscripts serve in the Defense Forces, the Ministry of Internal Affairs, or the Ministry of Corrections
note 2: as of 2022, women made up about 8% of the military's full-time personnel

Military - note: the Defense Forces of Georgia (DFG) are responsible for protecting the independence, sovereignty, and territorial integrity of the country; the DFG also provides units for multinational military operations abroad and supports the Border Police in border protection and civil authorities in counter-terrorist operations, if requested; it is focused primarily on Russia, which maintains military bases and troops in occupied Abkhazia and South Ossetia; a five-day conflict with Russian forces in 2008 resulted in the defeat and expulsion of Georgian forces from the breakaway regions
Georgia is not a member of NATO but has had a relationship with the Alliance since 1992 and declared its aspiration to join in 2002; the military is working to make itself more compatible with NATO and has participated in multinational exercises and security operations abroad with NATO, such as Afghanistan, where it was one of the top non-NATO contributors,

and Kosovo; the DFG has also contributed troops to EU and UN missions (2024)

TRANSNATIONAL ISSUES

Refugees and internally displaced persons: *refugees (country of origin):* 26,660 (Ukraine) (as of 30 December 2023)

IDPs: 308,000 (displaced in the 1990s as a result of armed conflict in the breakaway republics of Abkhazia and South Ossetia; displaced in 2008 by fighting between Georgia and Russia over South Ossetia) (2022)
stateless persons: 530 (2022)

Illicit drugs: a transit country for opiates produced in Asia trafficked into Ukraine or Moldova via the Black Sea for other European destinations; not a major corridor for synthetic drug smuggling operations; domestic synthetic market for ecstasy/MDMA, amphetamines, and cannabis with ecstasy laced with fentanyl the drug of choice

GERMANY

INTRODUCTION

Background: As Europe's largest economy and second most-populous nation (after Russia), Germany is a key member of the continent's economic, political, and defense organizations. European power struggles immersed Germany in two devastating world wars in the first half of the 20th century and left the country occupied by the victorious Allied powers of the US, UK, France, and the Soviet Union in 1945. With the advent of the Cold War, two German states were formed in 1949: the western Federal Republic of Germany (FRG) and the eastern German Democratic Republic (GDR). The democratic FRG embedded itself in key western economic and security organizations, including the EC (now the EU) and NATO, while the communist GDR was on the front line of the Soviet-led Warsaw Pact. The decline of the Soviet Union and the end of the Cold War allowed German reunification to occur in 1990. Since then, Germany has expended considerable funds to bring eastern productivity and wages up to western standards. In January 1999, Germany and 10 other EU countries introduced a common European exchange currency, the euro.

GEOGRAPHY

Location: Central Europe, bordering the Baltic Sea and the North Sea, between the Netherlands and Poland, south of Denmark

Geographic coordinates: 51 00 N, 9 00 E

Map references: Europe

Area: *total:* 357,022 sq km
land: 348,672 sq km
water: 8,350 sq km
comparison ranking: total 64

Area - comparative: three times the size of Pennsylvania; slightly smaller than Montana

Land boundaries: *total:* 3,694 km
border countries (9): Austria 801 km; Belgium 133 km; Czechia 704 km; Denmark 140 km; France 418 km; Luxembourg 128 km; Netherlands 575 km; Poland 447 km; Switzerland 348 km

Coastline: 2,389 km

Maritime claims: *territorial sea:* 12 nm
exclusive economic zone: 200 nm
continental shelf: 200-m depth or to the depth of exploitation

Climate: temperate and marine; cool, cloudy, wet winters and summers; occasional warm mountain (foehn) wind

Terrain: lowlands in north, uplands in center, Bavarian Alps in south

Elevation: *highest point:* Zugspitze 2,963 m
lowest point: Neuendorf bei Wilster -3.5 m
mean elevation: 263 m

Natural resources: coal, lignite, natural gas, iron ore, copper, nickel, uranium, potash, salt, construction materials, timber, arable land

Land use: *agricultural land:* 48% (2018 est.)
arable land: 34.1% (2018 est.)
permanent crops: 0.6% (2018 est.)
permanent pasture: 13.3% (2018 est.)
forest: 31.8% (2018 est.)
other: 20.2% (2018 est.)

Irrigated land: 5,056 sq km (2020)

Major lakes (area sq km): *fresh water lake(s):* Lake Constance (shared with Switzerland and Austria) - 540 sq km
salt water lake(s): Stettiner Haff/Zalew Szczecinski (shared with Poland) - 900 sq km

Major rivers (by length in km): Donau (Danube) river source (shared with Austria, Slovakia, Hungary, Croatia, Serbia, Bulgaria, Ukraine, Moldova, and Romania [m]) - 2,888 km; Elbe river mouth (shared with Czechia [s]) - 1,252 km; Rhein (Rhine) (shared with Switzerland [s], France, and Netherlands [m]) - 1,233 km
note – [s] after country name indicates river source; [m] after country name indicates river mouth

Major watersheds (area sq km): Atlantic Ocean drainage: Rhine-Maas (198,735 sq km), *(Black Sea)* Danube (795,656 sq km)

Population distribution: second most populous country in Europe; a fairly even distribution throughout most of the country, with urban areas attracting larger and denser populations, particularly in the far western part of the industrial state of North Rhine- Westphalia

Natural hazards: flooding

Geography - note: strategic location on North European Plain and along the entrance to the Baltic Sea; most major rivers in Germany – the Rhine, Weser, Oder, Elbe – flow northward; the Danube, which originates in the Black Forest, flows eastward

PEOPLE AND SOCIETY

Population: *total:* 84,119,100
male: 41,572,702
female: 42,546,398 (2024 est.)
comparison rankings: female 18; male 19; total 19

Nationality: *noun:* German(s)
adjective: German

Ethnic groups: German 85.4%, Turkish 1.8%, Ukrainian 1.4%, Syrian 1.1%, Romanian 1%, Poland 1%, other/stateless/unspecified 8.3% (2022 est.)
note: data represent population by nationality

Languages: German (official); note - Danish, Frisian, Sorbian, and Romani are official minority languages; Low German, Danish, North Frisian, Sater Frisian, Lower Sorbian, Upper Sorbian, and Romani are recognized as regional languages
major-language sample(s):
Das World Factbook, die unverzichtbare Quelle für grundlegende Informationen. (German)

Religions: Roman Catholic 24.8%, Protestant 22.6%, Muslim 3.7%, other 5.1%, none 43.8% (2022 est.)

Age structure: *0-14 years:* 13.8% (male 5,925,800/ female 5,688,603)
15-64 years: 62.5% (male 26,705,657/female 25,875,865)
65 years and over: 23.7% (2024 est.) (male 8,941,245/female 10,981,930)

Dependency ratios: *total dependency ratio:* 56.4
youth dependency ratio: 21.7
elderly dependency ratio: 34.7
potential support ratio: 2.9 (2021 est.)

Median age: *total:* 46.8 years (2024 est.)
male: 45.5 years
female: 48.3 years
comparison ranking: total 9

Population growth rate: -0.12% (2024 est.)
comparison ranking: 206

Birth rate: 8.9 births/1,000 population (2024 est.)
comparison ranking: 200

Death rate: 12 deaths/1,000 population (2024 est.)
comparison ranking: 15

Net migration rate: 1.8 migrant(s)/1,000 population (2024 est.)
comparison ranking: 53

Population distribution: second most populous country in Europe; a fairly even distribution throughout most of the country, with urban areas attracting larger and denser populations, particularly in the far western part of the industrial state of North Rhine- Westphalia

Urbanization: *urban population:* 77.8% of total population (2023)
rate of urbanization: 0.13% annual rate of change (2020-25 est.)

Major urban areas - population: 3.574 million BERLIN (capital), 1.788 million Hamburg, 1.576 million Munich, 1.144 million Cologne, 796,000 Frankfurt (2023)

Sex ratio: *at birth:* 1.05 male(s)/female
0-14 years: 1.04 male(s)/female
15-64 years: 1.03 male(s)/female
65 years and over: 0.81 male(s)/female
total population: 0.98 male(s)/female (2024 est.)

Mother's mean age at first birth: 29.9 years (2020 est.)

Maternal mortality ratio: 4 deaths/100,000 live births (2020 est.)
comparison ranking: 175

Infant mortality rate: *total:* 3.1 deaths/1,000 live births (2024 est.)
male: 3.5 deaths/1,000 live births
female: 2.7 deaths/1,000 live births
comparison ranking: total 206

Life expectancy at birth: *total population:* 81.9 years (2024 est.)
male: 79.6 years
female: 84.4 years
comparison ranking: total population 38

Total fertility rate: 1.58 children born/woman (2024 est.)
comparison ranking: 190

Gross reproduction rate: 0.77 (2024 est.)

Contraceptive prevalence rate: 67% (2018)
note: percent of women aged 18-49

Drinking water source: *improved: urban:* 100% of population
rural: 100% of population
total: 100% of population

Current health expenditure: 12.8% of GDP (2020)

Physician density: 4.44 physicians/1,000 population (2020)

Hospital bed density: 8 beds/1,000 population (2017)

Sanitation facility access: *improved: urban:* 100% of population
rural: 100% of population
total: 100% of population

Obesity - adult prevalence rate: 22.3% (2016)
comparison ranking: 79

Alcohol consumption per capita: *total:* 10.56 liters of pure alcohol (2019 est.)
beer: 5.57 liters of pure alcohol (2019 est.)
wine: 3.02 liters of pure alcohol (2019 est.)
spirits: 1.97 liters of pure alcohol (2019 est.)
other alcohols: 0 liters of pure alcohol (2019 est.)
comparison ranking: total 19

Tobacco use: *total:* 22% (2020 est.)
male: 24.1% (2020 est.)
female: 19.9% (2020 est.)
comparison ranking: total 74

Children under the age of 5 years underweight: 0.5% (2014/17)
comparison ranking: 121

Currently married women (ages 15-49): 54.4% (2023 est.)

Education expenditures: 4.7% of GDP (2020 est.)
comparison ranking: 89

Literacy: *total population:* NA
male: NA
female: NA

School life expectancy (primary to tertiary education): *total:* 17 years
male: 17 years
female: 17 years (2020)

ENVIRONMENT

Environment - current issues: emissions from coal-burning utilities and industries contribute to air pollution; acid rain, resulting from sulfur dioxide emissions, is damaging forests; pollution in the Baltic Sea from raw sewage and industrial effluents from rivers in eastern Germany; hazardous waste disposal; government established a mechanism for ending the use of nuclear power by 2022; government working to meet EU commitment to identify nature preservation areas in line with the EU's Flora, Fauna, and Habitat directive

Environment - international agreements: *party to:* Air Pollution, Air Pollution-Heavy Metals, Air Pollution-Multi-effect Protocol, Air Pollution-Nitrogen Oxides, Air Pollution-Persistent Organic Pollutants, Air Pollution-Sulphur 85, Air Pollution-Sulphur 94, Air Pollution-Volatile Organic Compounds, Antarctic-Environmental Protection, Antarctic-Marine Living Resources, Antarctic Seals, Antarctic Treaty, Biodiversity, Climate Change, Climate Change-Kyoto Protocol, Climate Change-Paris Agreement, Comprehensive Nuclear Test Ban, Desertification, Endangered Species, Environmental Modification, Hazardous Wastes, Law of the Sea, Marine Dumping-London Convention, Marine Dumping-London Protocol, Nuclear Test Ban, Ozone Layer Protection, Ship Pollution, Tropical Timber 2006, Wetlands, Whaling
signed, but not ratified: none of the selected agreements

Climate: temperate and marine; cool, cloudy, wet winters and summers; occasional warm mountain (foehn) wind

Urbanization: *urban population:* 77.8% of total population (2023)
rate of urbanization: 0.13% annual rate of change (2020-25 est.)

Revenue from forest resources: 0.03% of GDP (2018 est.)
comparison ranking: 137

Revenue from coal: 0.02% of GDP (2018 est.)
comparison ranking: 44

Air pollutants: *particulate matter emissions:* 10.73 micrograms per cubic meter (2019 est.)
carbon dioxide emissions: 727.97 megatons (2016 est.)
methane emissions: 49.92 megatons (2020 est.)

Waste and recycling: *municipal solid waste generated annually:* 51.046 million tons (2015 est.)
municipal solid waste recycled annually: 24,415,302 tons (2015 est.)
percent of municipal solid waste recycled: 47.8% (2015 est.)

Major lakes (area sq km): *fresh water lake(s):* Lake Constance (shared with Switzerland and Austria) - 540 sq km
salt water lake(s): Stettiner Haff/Zalew Szczecinski (shared with Poland) - 900 sq km

Major rivers (by length in km): Donau (Danube) river source (shared with Austria, Slovakia, Hungary, Croatia, Serbia, Bulgaria, Ukraine, Moldova, and Romania [m]) - 2,888 km; Elbe river mouth (shared with Czechia [s]) - 1,252 km; Rhein (Rhine) (shared with Switzerland [s], France, and Netherlands [m]) - 1,233 km
note – [s] after country name indicates river source; [m] after country name indicates river mouth

Major watersheds (area sq km): Atlantic Ocean drainage: Rhine-Maas (198,735 sq km), *(Black Sea)* Danube (795,656 sq km)

Total water withdrawal: *municipal:* 10.4 billion cubic meters (2020 est.)
industrial: 17.68 billion cubic meters (2020 est.)
agricultural: 400 million cubic meters (2020 est.)

Total renewable water resources: 154 billion cubic meters (2020 est.)

Geoparks: *total global geoparks and regional networks:* 8
global geoparks and regional networks: Bergstraße-Odenwald ; Harz, Braunschweiger Land; Swabian Alb; TERRA.vita; Vulkaneifel; Thuringia Inselsberg -Drei Gleichen; Muskauer Faltenbogen / Luk Muzakowa (includes Poland); Ries (2023)

GOVERNMENT

Country name: *conventional long form:* Federal Republic of Germany
conventional short form: Germany
local long form: Bundesrepublik Deutschland
local short form: Deutschland
former: German Reich
etymology: the Gauls (Celts) of Western Europe may have referred to the newly arriving Germanic tribes who settled in neighboring areas east of the Rhine during the first centuries B.C. as 'Germani,' a term the Romans adopted as 'Germania'; the native designation 'Deutsch' comes from the Old High German 'diutisc' meaning 'of the people'

Government type: federal parliamentary republic

Capital: *name:* Berlin
geographic coordinates: 52 31 N, 13 24 E
time difference: UTC+1 (6 hours ahead of Washington, DC, during Standard Time)
daylight saving time: +1hr, begins last Sunday in March; ends last Sunday in October
etymology: the origin of the name is unclear but may be related to the old West Slavic (Polabian) word 'berl' or 'birl,' meaning 'swamp'

Administrative divisions: 16 states (Laender, singular - Land); Baden-Wuerttemberg, Bayern (Bavaria), Berlin, Brandenburg, Bremen, Hamburg, Hessen (Hesse), Mecklenburg-Vorpommern (Mecklenburg-Western Pomerania), Niedersachsen (Lower Saxony), Nordrhein-Westfalen (North Rhine-Westphalia), Rheinland-Pfalz (Rhineland-Palatinate), Saarland, Sachsen (Saxony), Sachsen-Anhalt (Saxony-Anhalt), Schleswig-Holstein, Thueringen (Thuringia); note - Bayern, Sachsen, and Thueringen refer to themselves as free states (Freistaaten, singular - Freistaat), while Bremen calls itself a Free Hanseatic City (Freie Hansestadt) and Hamburg considers itself a Free and Hanseatic City (Freie und Hansestadt)

Independence: *18 January 1871 (establishment of the German Empire); divided into four zones of occupation (UK, US, USSR, and France) in 1945 following World War II; Federal Republic of*

Germany (FRG or West Germany) proclaimed on 23 May 1949 and included the former UK, US, and French zones; German Democratic Republic (GDR or East Germany) proclaimed on 7 October 1949 and included the former USSR zone; West Germany and East Germany unified on 3 October 1990; all four powers formally relinquished rights on 15 March 1991; notable earlier dates: 10 August 843 (Eastern Francia established from the division of the Carolingian Empire); 2 February 962 (crowning of OTTO I, recognized as the first Holy Roman Emperor)

National holiday: German Unity Day, 3 October (1990)

Legal system: civil law system

Constitution: *history:* previous 1919 (Weimar Constitution); latest drafted 10-23 August 1948, approved 12 May 1949, promulgated 23 May 1949, entered into force 24 May 1949
amendments: proposed by Parliament; passage and enactment into law require two-thirds majority vote by both the Bundesrat (upper house) and the Bundestag (lower house) of Parliament; articles including those on basic human rights and freedoms cannot be amended; amended many times, last in 2020; note - in early 2021, the German federal government introduced a bill to incorporate children's rights into the constitution

International law organization participation: accepts compulsory ICJ jurisdiction with reservations; accepts ICCt jurisdiction

Citizenship: *citizenship by birth:* no
citizenship by descent only: at least one parent must be a German citizen or a resident alien who has lived in Germany at least 8 years
dual citizenship recognized: yes, but requires prior permission from government
residency requirement for naturalization: 8 years

Suffrage: 18 years of age; universal; age 16 for some state and municipal elections

Executive branch: *chief of state:* President Frank-Walter STEINMEIER (since 19 March 2017)
head of government: Chancellor Olaf SCHOLZ (since 8 December 2021)
cabinet: Cabinet or Bundesminister (Federal Ministers) recommended by the chancellor, appointed by the president
elections/appointments: president indirectly elected by a Federal Convention consisting of all members of the Federal Parliament (Bundestag) and an equivalent number of delegates indirectly elected by the state parliaments; president serves a 5-year term (eligible for a second term); election last held on 13 February 2022 (next to be held in February 2027); following the most recent Federal Parliament election, the party or coalition with the most representatives usually elects the chancellor who is appointed by the president to serve a renewable 4-year term; Federal Parliament vote for chancellor last held on 8 December 2021 (next to be held after the Bundestag election in 2025)
election results:
2022: Frank-Walter STEINMEIER reelected president; Federal Convention vote count - Frank-Walter STEINMEIER (SPD) 1,045, Max OTTE (CDU) 140, Gerhard TRABERT (The Left) 96, Stefanie GEBAUER (Free Voters) 58, abstentions 86
2021: Olaf SCHOLZ (SPD) elected chancellor; Federal Parliament vote - 395 to 303
2017: Frank-Walter STEINMEIER elected president; Federal Convention vote count - Frank-Walter STEINMEIER (SPD) 931, Christopher Butterwegge (independent) 128, abstentions 103

Legislative branch: *description:* bicameral Parliament or Parlament consists of:
Federal Council or Bundesrat (69 seats statutory, 71 current; members appointed by each of the 16 state governments) Federal Diet or Bundestag (736 seats statutory, 736 for the 2021-25 term - total seats can vary each electoral term; currently includes 4 seats for independent members; approximately one-half of members directly elected in multi-seat constituencies by proportional representation vote and approximately one-half directly elected in single-seat constituencies by simple majority vote; members' terms depend upon the states they represent)
elections: Bundesrat - none; determined by the composition of the state-level governments; the composition of the Bundesrat has the potential to change any time one of the 16 states holds an election
Bundestag - last held on 26 September 2021 (next to be held by September 2025); almost all postwar German governments have been coalitions
election results: Bundesrat - composition - men 43, women 26, percentage women 37.7%
Bundestag - percent of vote by party - SPD 28%, CDU/CSU 26.8%, Alliance '90/Greens 16%, FDP 12.5%, AfD 11%, The Left 5.3%, other .04%; seats by party - SPD 206, CDU/CSU 197, Alliance '90/Greens 118, FDP 92, AfD 81, The Left 39, other 3; composition - men 476, women 260, percentage women 34.9%; note - total Parliament percentage women 35.5%
note: due to Germany's recognition of the concepts of 'overhang' (when a party's share of the nationwide votes would entitle it to fewer seats than the number of individual constituency seats won in an election under Germany's mixed member proportional system) and 'leveling' (whereby additional seats are elected to supplement the members directly elected by each constituency in order to ensure that each party's share of the total seats is roughly proportional to the party's overall shares of votes at the national level), the 20th Bundestag is the largest to date

Judicial branch: *highest court(s):* Federal Court of Justice (court consists of 127 judges, including the court president, vice presidents, presiding judges, other judges and organized into 25 Senates subdivided into 12 civil panels, 5 criminal panels, and 8 special panels); Federal Constitutional Court or Bundesverfassungsgericht (consists of 2 Senates each subdivided into 3 chambers, each with a chairman and 8 members)
judge selection and term of office: Federal Court of Justice judges selected by the Judges Election Committee, which consists of the Secretaries of Justice from each of the 16 federated states and 16 members appointed by the Federal Parliament; judges appointed by the president; judges serve until mandatory retirement at age 65; Federal Constitutional Court judges - one-half elected by the House of Representatives and one-half by the Senate; judges appointed for 12- year terms with mandatory retirement at age 68
subordinate courts: Federal Administrative Court; Federal Finance Court; Federal Labor Court; Federal Social Court; each of the 16 federated states or Land has its own constitutional court and a hierarchy of ordinary (civil, criminal, family) and specialized (administrative, finance, labor, social) courts; two English-speaking commercial courts opened in late 2020 in the state of Baden-Wuerttemberg - English-speaking Stuttgart Commercial Court and English-speaking Mannheim Commercial Court

Political parties: Alliance '90/Greens
Alternative for Germany or AfD
Christian Democratic Union or CDU
Christian Social Union or CSU
Free Democratic Party or FDP
Free Voters
The Left or Die Linke
Social Democratic Party or SPD

International organization participation: ADB (nonregional member), AfDB (nonregional member), Arctic Council (observer), Australia Group, BIS, BSEC (observer), CBSS, CD, CDB, CE, CERN, EAPC, EBRD, ECB, EIB, EITI (implementing country), EMU, ESA, EU, FAO, FATF, G-5, G-7, G-8, G-10, G-20, IADB, IAEA, IBRD, ICAO, ICC (national committees), ICCt, ICRM, IDA, IEA, IFAD, IFC, IFRCS, IGAD (partners), IHO, ILO, IMF, IMO, IMSO, Interpol, IOC, IOM, IPU, ISO, ITSO, ITU, ITUC (NGOs), MIGA, MINURSO, NATO, NEA, NSG, OAS (observer), OECD, OPCW, OSCE, Pacific Alliance (observer), Paris Club, PCA, Schengen Convention, SELEC (observer), SICA (observer), UN, UNAMID, UNCTAD, UNESCO, UNHCR, UNHRC, UNIDO, UNIFIL, UNMISS, UNOOSA, UNRWA, UNSOM, UNWTO, UPU, Wassenaar Arrangement, WCO, WHO, WIPO, WMO, WTO, ZC

Diplomatic representation in the US: *chief of mission:* Ambassador Andreas MICHAELIS (since 15 September 2023)
chancery: 4645 Reservoir Road NW, Washington, DC 20007
telephone: [1] (202) 298-4000
FAX: [1] (202) 298-4261
email address and website:
info@washington.diplo.de
https://www.germany.info/us-en
consulate(s) general: Atlanta, Boston, Chicago, Houston, Los Angeles, Miami, New York, San Francisco

Diplomatic representation from the US: *chief of mission:* Ambassador (vacant); Chargé d'Affaires Alan MELTZER (since July 2024)
embassy: Pariser Platz 2, 10117 Berlin
Clayallee 170, 14191 Berlin (administrative services)
mailing address: 5090 Berlin Place, Washington DC 20521-5090
telephone: [49] (30) 8305-0
FAX: [49] (30) 8305-1215
email address and website:
BerlinPCO@state.gov
https://de.usembassy.gov/
consulate(s) general: Dusseldorf, Frankfurt am Main, Hamburg, Leipzig, Munich

Flag description: three equal horizontal bands of black (top), red, and gold; these colors have played an important role in German history and can be traced back to the medieval banner of the Holy Roman Emperor - a black eagle with red claws and beak on a gold field

National symbol(s): eagle; national colors: black, red, yellow

National anthem: *name:* 'Das Lied der Deutschen' (Song of the Germans)
lyrics/music: August Heinrich HOFFMANN VON FALLERSLEBEN/Franz Joseph HAYDN

note: adopted 1922; the anthem, also known as 'Deutschlandlied' (Song of Germany), was originally adopted for its connection to the March 1848 liberal revolution; following appropriation by the Nazis of the first verse, specifically the phrase, 'Deutschland, Deutschland ueber alles' (Germany, Germany above all) to promote nationalism, it was banned after 1945; in 1952, its third verse was adopted by West Germany as its national anthem; in 1990, it became the national anthem for the reunited Germany

National heritage: *total World Heritage Sites:* 52 (49 cultural, 3 natural)
selected World Heritage Site locales: Museumsinsel (Museum Island), Berlin (c); Palaces and Parks of Potsdam and Berlin (c); Speyer Cathedral (c); Upper Middle Rhine Valley (c); Aachen Cathedral (c); Bauhaus and its Sites in Weimar, Dessau, and Bernau (c); Caves and Ice Age Art in the Swabian Jura (c); Mines of Rammelsberg, Historic Town of Goslar, and Upper Harz Water Management System (c); Roman Monuments, Cathedral of St. Peter, and Church of Our Lady in Trier (c); Hanseatic City of Lübeck (c); Old Town of Regensburg (c); Messel Pit Fossil Site (n)

ECONOMY

Economic overview: leading diversified, export-driven, core EU and eurozone economy; key automotive, chemical, engineering, finance, and green energy industries; growth stalled by energy crisis; tight labor market with falling working-age population; fiscal rebalancing with phaseout of energy price supports

Real GDP (purchasing power parity): $5.23 trillion (2023 est.)
$5.246 trillion (2022 est.)
$5.153 trillion (2021 est.)
note: data in 2021 dollars
comparison ranking: 6

Real GDP growth rate: -0.3% (2023 est.)
1.81% (2022 est.)
3.16% (2021 est.)
note: annual GDP % growth based on constant local currency
comparison ranking: 192

Real GDP per capita: $61,900 (2023 est.)
$62,600 (2022 est.)
$61,900 (2021 est.)
note: data in 2021 dollars
comparison ranking: 27

GDP (official exchange rate): $4.456 trillion (2023 est.)
note: data in current dollars at official exchange rate

Inflation rate (consumer prices): 5.95% (2023 est.)
6.87% (2022 est.)
3.07% (2021 est.)
note: annual % change based on consumer prices
comparison ranking: 127

Credit ratings: Fitch rating: AAA (1994)

Moody's rating: Aaa (1986)

Standard & Poors rating: AAA (1983)
note: The year refers to the year in which the current credit rating was first obtained. Credit ratings prior to 1989 refer to West Germany.

GDP - composition, by sector of origin: *agriculture:* 0.7% (2023 est.)
industry: 28.1% (2023 est.)
services: 62.6% (2023 est.)
note: figures may not total 100% due to non-allocated consumption not captured in sector-reported data
comparison rankings: services 70; industry 78; agriculture 195

GDP - composition, by end use: *household consumption:* 50.7% (2023 est.)
government consumption: 21.6% (2023 est.)
investment in fixed capital: 21.9% (2023 est.)
investment in inventories: 1.6% (2023 est.)
exports of goods and services: 47.1% (2023 est.)
imports of goods and services: -43% (2023 est.)
note: figures may not total 100% due to rounding or gaps in data collection

Agricultural products: milk, sugar beets, wheat, barley, potatoes, pork, rapeseed, maize, rye, triticale (2022)
note: top ten agricultural products based on tonnage

Industries: iron, steel, coal, cement, chemicals, machinery, vehicles, machine tools, electronics, automobiles, food and beverages, shipbuilding, textiles

Industrial production growth rate: -1.59% (2023 est.)
note: annual % change in industrial value added based on constant local currency
comparison ranking: 176

Labor force: 44.784 million (2023 est.)
note: number of people ages 15 or older who are employed or seeking work
comparison ranking: 15

Unemployment rate: 3.05% (2023 est.)
3.14% (2022 est.)
3.64% (2021 est.)
note: % of labor force seeking employment
comparison ranking: 47

Youth unemployment rate (ages 15-24): *total:* 6% (2023 est.)
male: 6.7% (2023 est.)
female: 5.1% (2023 est.)
note: % of labor force ages 15-24 seeking employment
comparison ranking: total 168

Population below poverty line: 14.8% (2021 est.)
note: % of population with income below national poverty line

Gini Index coefficient - distribution of family income: 31.7 (2019 est.)
note: index (0-100) of income distribution; higher values represent greater inequality
comparison ranking: 111

Average household expenditures: *on food:* 11.8% of household expenditures (2022 est.)
on alcohol and tobacco: 3.5% of household expenditures (2022 est.)

Household income or consumption by percentage share: *lowest 10%:* 3.1% (2019 est.)
highest 10%: 25.2% (2019 est.)
note: % share of income accruing to lowest and highest 10% of population

Remittances: 0.46% of GDP (2023 est.)
0.47% of GDP (2022 est.)
0.46% of GDP (2021 est.)
note: personal transfers and compensation between resident and non-resident individuals/households/entities

Budget: *revenues:* $1.19 trillion (2022 est.)
expenditures: $1.31 trillion (2022 est.)
note: central government revenues (excluding grants) and expenses converted to US dollars at average official exchange rate for year indicated

Public debt: 63.9% of GDP (2017 est.)
note: general government gross debt is defined in the Maastricht Treaty as consolidated general government gross debt at nominal value, outstanding at the end of the year in the following categories of government liabilities (as defined in ESA95): currency and deposits (AF.2), securities other than shares excluding financial derivatives (AF.3, excluding AF.34), and loans (AF.4); the general government sector comprises the sub-sectors of central government, state government, local government and social security funds; the series are presented as a percentage of GDP and in millions of euros; GDP used as a denominator is the gross domestic product at current market prices; data expressed in national currency are converted into euro using end-of-year exchange rates provided by the European Central Bank
comparison ranking: 66

Taxes and other revenues: 11.23% (of GDP) (2022 est.)
note: central government tax revenue as a % of GDP
comparison ranking: 173

Current account balance: $262.723 billion (2023 est.)
$174.831 billion (2022 est.)
$312.08 billion (2021 est.)
note: balance of payments - net trade and primary/secondary income in current dollars
comparison ranking: 1

Exports: $2.104 trillion (2023 est.)
$2.092 trillion (2022 est.)
$2.034 trillion (2021 est.)
note: balance of payments - exports of goods and services in current dollars
comparison ranking: 3

Exports - partners: US 10%, France 7%, China 7%, Netherlands 7%, Italy 6% (2022)
note: top five export partners based on percentage share of exports

Exports - commodities: cars, packaged medicine, vehicle parts/accessories, vaccines, plastic products (2022)
note: top five export commodities based on value in dollars

Imports: $1.927 trillion (2023 est.)
$1.997 trillion (2022 est.)
$1.798 trillion (2021 est.)
note: balance of payments - imports of goods and services in current dollars
comparison ranking: 3

Imports - partners: China 10%, Netherlands 9%, Poland 6%, Belgium 6%, Italy 5% (2022)
note: top five import partners based on percentage share of imports

Imports - commodities: natural gas, cars, garments, vehicle parts/accessories, crude petroleum (2022)
note: top five import commodities based on value in dollars

Reserves of foreign exchange and gold: $322.7 billion (2023 est.)
$293.914 billion (2022 est.)
$295.736 billion (2021 est.)
note: holdings of gold (year-end prices)/foreign exchange/special drawing rights in current dollars
comparison ranking: 14

Exchange rates: euros (EUR) per US dollar -

Exchange rates: 0.925 (2023 est.)
0.95 (2022 est.)

0.845 (2021 est.)
0.876 (2020 est.)
0.893 (2019 est.)

ENERGY

Electricity access: *electrification - total population:* 100% (2022 est.)

Electricity: *installed generating capacity:* 261.086 million kW (2022 est.)
consumption: 507.248 billion kWh (2022 est.)
exports: 76.291 billion kWh (2022 est.)
imports: 49.269 billion kWh (2022 est.)
transmission/distribution losses: 26.49 billion kWh (2022 est.)
comparison rankings: transmission/distribution losses 195; imports 3; exports 1; consumption 9; installed generating capacity 6

Electricity generation sources: *fossil fuels:* 48.9% of total installed capacity (2022 est.)
nuclear: 5.7% of total installed capacity (2022 est.)
solar: 10.3% of total installed capacity (2022 est.)
wind: 22.1% of total installed capacity (2022 est.)
hydroelectricity: 2.5% of total installed capacity (2022 est.)
biomass and waste: 10.5% of total installed capacity (2022 est.)

Nuclear energy: Percent of total electricity production: 1.4% (2023 est.)

Number of nuclear reactors permanently shut down: 33 (2023)

Coal: *production:* 138.981 million metric tons (2022 est.)
consumption: 186.725 million metric tons (2022 est.)
exports: 2.248 million metric tons (2022 est.)
imports: 44.851 million metric tons (2022 est.)
proven reserves: 35.9 billion metric tons (2022 est.)

Petroleum: *total petroleum production:* 131,000 bbl/day (2023 est.)
refined petroleum consumption: 2.052 million bbl/day (2023 est.)
crude oil estimated reserves: 115.2 million barrels (2021 est.)

Natural gas: *production:* 4.824 billion cubic meters (2022 est.)
consumption: 77.516 billion cubic meters (2022 est.)
imports: 83.926 billion cubic meters (2022 est.)
proven reserves: 23.39 billion cubic meters (2021 est.)

Carbon dioxide emissions: 668.292 million metric tonnes of CO_2 (2022 est.)
from coal and metallurgical coke: 227.546 million metric tonnes of CO_2 (2022 est.)
from petroleum and other liquids: 291.027 million metric tonnes of CO_2 (2022 est.)
from consumed natural gas: 149.719 million metric tonnes of CO_2 (2022 est.)
comparison ranking: total emissions 8

Energy consumption per capita: 132.263 million Btu/person (2022 est.)
comparison ranking: 31

COMMUNICATIONS

Telephones - fixed lines: *total subscriptions:* 38.58 million (2022 est.)
subscriptions per 100 inhabitants: 46 (2022 est.)
comparison ranking: total subscriptions 4

Telephones - mobile cellular: *total subscriptions:* 104.4 million (2022 est.)
subscriptions per 100 inhabitants: 125 (2022 est.)
comparison ranking: total subscriptions 16

Telecommunication systems: *general assessment:* with one of Europe's largest telecom markets, Germany hosts a number of significant operators which offer effective competition in the mobile and broadband sectors; the German mobile market is driven by mobile data, with the number of mobile broadband subscribers having increased rapidly in recent years; with LTE now effectively universally available, considerable progress has recently been made in building out 5G networks (2022)
domestic: 46 per 100 for fixed-line and 128 per 100 for mobile-cellular subscriptions (2021)
international: country code - 49; landing points for SeaMeWe-3, TAT-14, AC-1, CONTACT-3, Fehmarn Balt, C-Lion1, GC1, GlobalConnect-KPN, and Germany-Denmark 2 & 3 - submarine cables to Europe, Africa, the Middle East, Asia, Southeast Asia and Australia; as well as earth stations in the Inmarsat, Intelsat, Eutelsat, and Intersputnik satellite systems (2019)

Broadcast media: a mixture of publicly operated and privately owned TV and radio stations; 70 national and regional public broadcasters compete with nearly 400 privately owned national and regional TV stations; more than 90% of households have cable or satellite TV; hundreds of radio stations including multiple national radio networks, regional radio networks, and a large number of local radio stations

Internet country code: .de

Internet users: *total:* 75.53 million (2021 est.)
percent of population: 91% (2021 est.)
comparison ranking: total 11

Broadband - fixed subscriptions: *total:* 36,215,303 (2020 est.)
subscriptions per 100 inhabitants: 43 (2020 est.)
comparison ranking: total 5

TRANSPORTATION

National air transport system: *number of registered air carriers:* 20 (2020)
inventory of registered aircraft operated by air carriers: 1,113
annual passenger traffic on registered air carriers: 109,796,202 (2018)
annual freight traffic on registered air carriers: 7,969,860,000 (2018) mt-km

Civil aircraft registration country code prefix: D

Airports: 838 (2024)
comparison ranking: 8

Heliports: 388 (2024)

Pipelines: 37 km condensate, 26,985 km gas, 2,400 km oil, 4,479 km refined products, 8 km water (2013)

Railways: *total:* 39,379 km (2020) 20,942 km electrified
15 km 0.900-mm gauge, 24 km 0.750-mm gauge (2015)
comparison ranking: total 6

Roadways: *total:* 830,000 km 830,000 km
paved: 830,000 km (2022) (includes 13,155 km of expressways)
note: includes local roads
comparison ranking: total 10

Waterways: 7,300 km (2022) (Rhine River carries most goods; Main-Danube Canal links North Sea and Black Sea)
comparison ranking: 20

Merchant marine: *total:* 595 (2023)
by type: bulk carrier 1, container ship 69, general cargo 82, oil tanker 32, other 411
comparison ranking: total 38

Ports: *total ports:* 35 (2024)
large: 5
medium: 4
small: 11
very small: 15
ports with oil terminals: 12
key ports: Brake, Bremen, Bremerhaven, Cuxhaven, Emden, Hamburg, Kiel, Lubeck, Rostock

MILITARY AND SECURITY

Military and security forces: Federal Armed Forces (Bundeswehr): Army (Heer), Navy (Deutsche Marine, includes naval air arm), Air Force (Luftwaffe, includes air defense), Joint Support and Enabling Service (Streitkraeftebasis, SKB), Central Medical Service (Zentraler Sanitaetsdienst, ZSanDstBw), Cyber and Information Space Command (Kommando Cyber und Informationsraum, Kdo CIR) (2024)
note: responsibility for internal and border security is shared by the police forces of the 16 states, the Federal Criminal Police Office, and the Federal Police; the states' police forces report to their respective interior ministries while the Federal Police forces report to the Federal Ministry of the Interior

Military expenditures: 2.1% of GDP (2024 est.)
1.7% of GDP (2023)
1.5% of GDP (2022)
1.5% of GDP (2021)
1.5% of GDP (2020)
comparison ranking: 66

Military and security service personnel strengths: approximately 185,000 active-duty armed forces personnel (62,000 Army; 16,000 Navy; 27,000 Air Force; 20,000 Medical Service, 14,000 Cyber and Information Space Command; 45,000 other, including central staff, support, logistics, etc.) (2024)

Military equipment inventories and acquisitions: the inventory of Federal Armed Forces is comprised of weapons systems produced domestically or jointly with other European countries and Western imports, particularly from the US; Germany's defense industry is capable of manufacturing the full spectrum of air, land, and naval military weapons systems, and Germany is one of the world's leading arms exporters; it also participates in joint defense production projects with the US and European partners (2024)

Military service age and obligation: 17-23 years of age for voluntary military service for men and women (must have completed compulsory full-time education and have German citizenship); conscription ended July 2011; service obligation 7-23 months or 12 years; in July 2020, the government launched a new voluntary conscript initiative focused on homeland security tasks; volunteers serve for 7 months plus 5 months as reservists over a 6 year period (2024)
note: women have been eligible for voluntary service in all military branches and positions since 2001 and accounted for about 12% of the active-duty German military in 2023

Military deployments: 100 Estonia; up to 500 Iraq (NATO); Lebanon 170 (UNIFIL); up to 1,700

Lithuania (NATO); 100 Romania (NATO); 280 Slovakia (NATO) (2024)
note: the German military has over 2,000 ground forces, plus air and naval contingents deployed on some 18 foreign missions

Military - note: the Bundeswehr's core mission is the defense of Germany and its NATO partners; it has a wide range of peacetime duties, including crisis management, cyber security, deterrence, homeland security, humanitarian and disaster relief, and international peacekeeping and stability operations; as a key member of NATO and the EU, the Bundeswehr typically operates in a coalition environment, and its capabilities are largely based on NATO and EU planning goals and needs; it has participated in a range of NATO and EU missions in Europe, Africa, and Asia, as well as global maritime operations; the Bundeswehr has close bilateral defense ties with a number of EU countries, including the Czechia, France, the Netherlands, and Romania, as well as the UK and the US; it also contributes forces to UN peacekeeping missions
the Bundeswehr was established in 1955; at the height of the Cold War in the 1980s, it had nearly 600,000 personnel, over 7,000 tanks, and 1,000 combat aircraft; in addition, over 400,000 soldiers from other NATO countries—including about 200,000 US military personnel—were stationed in West Germany; in the years following the collapse of the Soviet Union and the end of the Cold War, the Bundeswehr shrank by more than 60% in size (over 90% in tanks and about 80% in aircraft), while funding fell from nearly 3% of GDP and over 4% of government spending in the mid-1980s to 1.2% and 1.6% respectively; by the 2010s, the Bundeswehr's ability to fulfill its regional security commitments had deteriorated; the Russian annexation of Crimea in 2014 and full-scale assault on Ukraine in 2022 led to renewed emphasis on Germany's leadership role in European defense and NATO and efforts to boost funding for the Bundeswehr to improve readiness, modernize, and expand (2024)

SPACE

Space agency/agencies: German Aerospace Center (Deutsches Zentrum für Luft- und Raumfahrt, DLR; established 1997); predecessor organization, German Test and Research Institute for Aviation and Space Flight, was established in 1969; note – the Federal Republic of Germany was allowed to research space flight after gaining sovereignty in 1955 (2024)

Space launch site(s): establishing a commercial ship-based launch pad 350 kms (217 miles) off the German coast in the remotest corner of its exclusive economic zone; each launch is to be supervised by a control ship and a multifunctional mission control center in Bremen, Germany; the launch ship will be based out of Bremerhaven (2024)

Space program overview: has one of Europe's largest space programs; is a key member of the European Space Agency (ESA) and one of its largest contributors; builds and operates satellites, satellite/space launch vehicles (SLVs), space probes, unmanned orbiters, and reusable space planes; conducts research and develops a range of other space-related capabilities technologies, including satellite payloads (cameras, remote sensing, communications, optics, sensors, etc.), rockets and rocket propulsion, propulsion assisted landing technologies, and aeronautics; participates in ESA's astronaut training program and human space flight operations and hosts the European Astronaut Center; participates in other international space programs, such as the International Space Station (ISS); hosts the mission control centers for the ISS and the ESA, as well as the European Organization for the Exploitation of Meteorological Satellites (EUMETSAT); in addition to ESA/EU and their member states, has ties to a range of foreign space programs, including those of China, Japan, Russia, and the US; has a robust commercial space industry sector that develops a broad range of space capabilities, including satellite launchers, and cooperates closely with DLR, ESA, and other international commercial entities and government agencies (2024)
note: further details about the key activities, programs, and milestones of the country's space program, as well as government spending estimates on the space sector, appear in the Space Programs reference guide

TERRORISM

Terrorist group(s): Islamic Revolutionary Guard Corps/Qods Force; Islamic State of Iraq and ash-Sham (ISIS); al-Qa'ida
note: details about the history, aims, leadership, organization, areas of operation, tactics, targets, weapons, size, and sources of support of the group(s) appear(s) in the Terrorism reference guide

TRANSNATIONAL ISSUES

Refugees and internally displaced persons: *refugees (country of origin):* 664,238 (Syria), 183,631 (Afghanistan), 151,254 (Iraq), 64,496 (Eritrea), 47,658 (Iran), 38,755 (Turkey), 32,155 (Somalia), 13,334 (Russia), 12,155 (Nigeria), 9,250 (Pakistan), 6,257 (Serbia and Kosovo), 6,912 (Ethiopia), 5,532 (Azerbaijan) (mid-year 2022); 1,139,690 (Ukraine) (as of 3 February 2024)
stateless persons: 28,941 (2022)

Illicit drugs: maritime transshipment point for cocaine heading for European drug; a major source of precursor or essential chemicals used in the production of illicit narcotics

GHANA

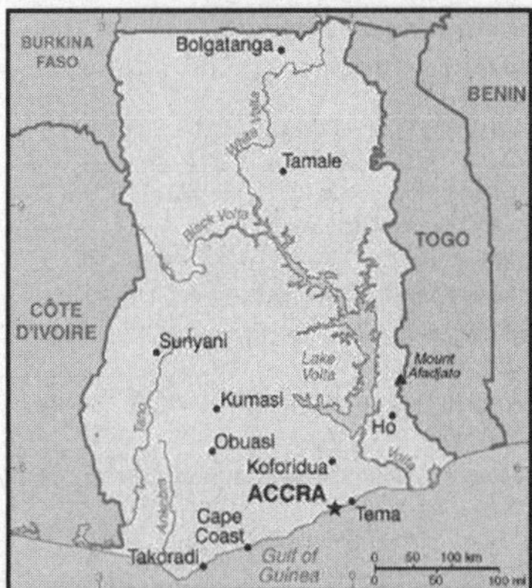

INTRODUCTION

Background: Ghana is a multiethnic country rich in natural resources and is one of the most stable and democratic countries in West Africa. Ghana has been inhabited for at least several thousand years, but little is known about its early inhabitants. By the 12th century, the gold trade started to boom in Bono (Bonoman) state in what is today southern Ghana, and it became the genesis of the Akan people's power and wealth in the region. Beginning in the 15th century, the Portuguese, followed by other European powers, arrived and competed for trading rights. Numerous kingdoms and empires emerged in the area, among the most powerful were the Kingdom of Dagbon in the north and the Asante (Ashanti) Empire in the south. By the mid-18th century, Asante was a highly organized state with immense wealth; it provided enslaved people for the Atlantic slave trade, and in return received firearms that facilitated its territorial expansion. The Asante resisted increasing British influence in the coastal areas, engaging in a series of wars during the 19th century before ultimately falling under British control. Formed from the merger of the British colony of the Gold Coast and the Togoland trust territory, Ghana in 1957 became the first Sub-Saharan country in colonial Africa to gain its independence, with Kwame NKRUMAH as its first leader.

Ghana endured a series of coups before Lt. Jerry RAWLINGS took power in 1981 and banned political parties. After approving a new constitution and restoring multiparty politics in 1992, RAWLINGS won presidential elections in 1992 and 1996 but was constitutionally prevented from running for a third term in 2000. John KUFUOR of the opposition New Patriotic Party (NPP) succeeded him and was reelected in 2004. John Atta MILLS of the National Democratic Congress won the 2008 presidential election and took over as head of state. MILLS died in 2012 and was constitutionally succeeded by his vice president, John Dramani MAHAMA, who subsequently won the 2012 presidential election. In 2016, Nana Addo Dankwa AKUFO-ADDO of the NPP defeated MAHAMA, marking the third time that Ghana's presidency had changed parties since the return to democracy. AKUFO-ADDO was reelected in 2020. In recent years, Ghana has taken an active role in promoting regional stability and is highly integrated in international affairs.

GEOGRAPHY

Location: Western Africa, bordering the Gulf of Guinea, between Cote d'Ivoire and Togo

Geographic coordinates: 8 00 N, 2 00 W

Map references: Africa

Area: *total:* 238,533 sq km
land: 227,533 sq km
water: 11,000 sq km
comparison ranking: total 82

Area - comparative: slightly smaller than Oregon

Land boundaries: *total:* 2,420 km
border countries (3): Burkina Faso 602 km; Cote d'Ivoire 720 km; Togo 1098 km

Coastline: 539 km

Maritime claims: *territorial sea:* 12 nm
contiguous zone: 24 nm
exclusive economic zone: 200 nm
continental shelf: 200 nm

Climate: tropical; warm and comparatively dry along southeast coast; hot and humid in southwest; hot and dry in north

Terrain: mostly low plains with dissected plateau in south-central area

Elevation: *highest point:* Mount Afadjato 885 m
lowest point: Atlantic Ocean 0 m
mean elevation: 190 m

Natural resources: gold, timber, industrial diamonds, bauxite, manganese, fish, rubber, hydropower, petroleum, silver, salt, limestone

Land use: *agricultural land:* 69.1% (2018 est.)
arable land: 20.7% (2018 est.)
permanent crops: 11.9% (2018 est.)
permanent pasture: 36.5% (2018 est.)
forest: 21.2% (2018 est.)
other: 9.7% (2018 est.)

Irrigated land: 360 sq km (2013)

Major rivers (by length in km): Volta river mouth (shared with Burkina Faso [s]) - 1,600 km
note – [s] after country name indicates river source; [m] after country name indicates river mouth

Major watersheds (area sq km): Atlantic Ocean drainage: Volta (410,991 sq km)

Population distribution: population is concentrated in the southern half of the country, with the highest concentrations being on or near the Atlantic coast as shown in this population distribution map

Natural hazards: dry, dusty, northeastern harmattan winds from January to March; droughts

Geography - note: Lake Volta is the world's largest artificial lake (manmade reservoir) by surface area (8,482 sq km; 3,275 sq mi); the lake was created following the completion of the Akosombo Dam in 1965, which holds back the White Volta and Black Volta Rivers

PEOPLE AND SOCIETY

Population: *total:* 34,589,092
male: 16,902,073
female: 17,687,019 (2024 est.)
comparison rankings: female 43; male 45; total 44

Nationality: *noun:* Ghanaian(s)
adjective: Ghanaian

Ethnic groups: Akan 45.7%, Mole-Dagbani 18.5%, Ewe 12.8%, Ga-Dangme 7.1%, Gurma 6.4%, Guan 3.2%, Grusi 2.7%, Mande 2%, other 1.6% (2021 est.)

Languages: Asante 16%, Ewe 14%, Fante 11.6%, Boron (Brong) 4.9%, Dagomba 4.4%, Dangme 4.2%, Dagarte (Dagaba) 3.9%, Kokomba 3.5%, Akyem 3.2%, Ga 3.1%, other 31.2% (2010 est.)
note: English is the official language

Religions: Christian 71.3% (Pentecostal/Charismatic 31.6%, Protestant 17.4%, Catholic 10%, other 12.3%), Muslim 19.9%, traditionalist 3.2%, other 4.5%, none 1.1% (2021 est.)

Demographic profile: Ghana has a young age structure, with approximately 56% of the population under the age of 25 as of 2020. Its total fertility rate fell significantly during the 1980s and 1990s but has stalled at around four children per woman for the last few years. Fertility remains higher in the northern region than the Greater Accra region. On average, desired fertility has remained stable for several years; urban dwellers want fewer children than rural residents. Increased life expectancy, due to better health care, nutrition, and hygiene, and reduced fertility have increased Ghana's share of elderly persons; Ghana's proportion of persons aged 60+ is among the highest in Sub-Saharan Africa. Poverty has declined in Ghana, but it remains pervasive in the northern region, which is susceptible to droughts and floods and has less access to transportation infrastructure, markets, fertile farming land, and industrial centers. The northern region also has lower school enrollment, higher illiteracy, and fewer opportunities for women.

Ghana was a country of immigration in the early years after its 1957 independence, attracting labor migrants largely from Nigeria and other neighboring countries to mine minerals and harvest cocoa – immigrants composed about 12% of Ghana's population in 1960. In the late 1960s, worsening economic and social conditions discouraged immigration, and hundreds of thousands of immigrants, mostly Nigerians, were expelled.

During the 1970s, severe drought and an economic downturn transformed Ghana into a country of emigration; neighboring Cote d'Ivoire was the initial destination. Later, hundreds of thousands of Ghanaians migrated to Nigeria to work in its booming oil industry, but most were deported in 1983 and 1985 as oil prices plummeted. Many Ghanaians then turned to more distant destinations, including other parts of Africa, Europe, and North America, but the majority continued to migrate within West Africa. Since the 1990s, increased emigration of skilled Ghanaians, especially to the US and the UK, drained the country of its health care and education professionals. Internally, poverty and other developmental disparities continue to drive Ghanaians from the north to the south, particularly to its urban centers.

Age structure: *0-14 years:* 37.4% (male 6,527,386/female 6,400,245)
15-64 years: 58.2% (male 9,690,498/female 10,444,197)
65 years and over: 4.4% (2024 est.) (male 684,189/female 842,577)

Dependency ratios: *total dependency ratio:* 68.7
youth dependency ratio: 62.9
elderly dependency ratio: 5.9
potential support ratio: 17 (2021 est.)

Median age: *total:* 21.4 years (2024 est.)
male: 20.6 years
female: 22.3 years
comparison ranking: total 191

Population growth rate: 2.15% (2024 est.)
comparison ranking: 35

Birth rate: 27.6 births/1,000 population (2024 est.)
comparison ranking: 33

Death rate: 5.9 deaths/1,000 population (2024 est.)
comparison ranking: 162

Net migration rate: -0.2 migrant(s)/1,000 population (2024 est.)
comparison ranking: 107

Population distribution: population is concentrated in the southern half of the country, with the highest concentrations being on or near the Atlantic coast as shown in this population distribution map

Urbanization: *urban population:* 59.2% of total population (2023)
rate of urbanization: 3.06% annual rate of change (2020-25 est.)

Major urban areas - population: 3.768 million Kumasi, 2.660 million ACCRA (capital), 1.078 million Sekondi Takoradi (2023)

Sex ratio: *at birth:* 1.03 male(s)/female
0-14 years: 1.02 male(s)/female
15-64 years: 0.93 male(s)/female
65 years and over: 0.81 male(s)/female
total population: 0.96 male(s)/female (2024 est.)

Mother's mean age at first birth: 22.1 years (2022 est.)
note: data represents median age at first birth among women 25-49

Maternal mortality ratio: 263 deaths/100,000 live births (2020 est.)
comparison ranking: 34

Infant mortality rate: *total:* 31.2 deaths/1,000 live births (2024 est.)
male: 34.5 deaths/1,000 live births
female: 27.8 deaths/1,000 live births
comparison ranking: total 46

Life expectancy at birth: *total population:* 70.1 years (2024 est.)
male: 68.4 years
female: 71.8 years
comparison ranking: total population 180

Total fertility rate: 3.56 children born/woman (2024 est.)
comparison ranking: 32

Gross reproduction rate: 1.75 (2024 est.)

Contraceptive prevalence rate: 27.2% (2017/18)

Drinking water source: *improved: urban:* 98.7% of population
rural: 83.8% of population
total: 92.4% of population
unimproved: urban: 1.3% of population
rural: 16.2% of population
total: 7.6% of population (2020 est.)

Current health expenditure: 4% of GDP (2020)

Physician density: 0.17 physicians/1,000 population (2020)

Hospital bed density: 0.9 beds/1,000 population (2011)

Sanitation facility access: *improved: urban:* 84.8% of population
rural: 52.8% of population
total: 71.1% of population
unimproved: urban: 15.2% of population
rural: 47.2% of population
total: 28.9% of population (2020 est.)

Obesity - adult prevalence rate: 10.9% (2016)
comparison ranking: 136

Alcohol consumption per capita: *total:* 1.59 liters of pure alcohol (2019 est.)
beer: 0.53 liters of pure alcohol (2019 est.)
wine: 0.05 liters of pure alcohol (2019 est.)
spirits: 0.39 liters of pure alcohol (2019 est.)
other alcohols: 0.61 liters of pure alcohol (2019 est.)
comparison ranking: total 137

Tobacco use: *total:* 3.5% (2020 est.)
male: 6.6% (2020 est.)
female: 0.3% (2020 est.)
comparison ranking: total 164

Children under the age of 5 years underweight: 12.6% (2017/18)
comparison ranking: 41

Currently married women (ages 15-49): 54.3% (2023 est.)

Child marriage: *women married by age 15:* 5%
women married by age 18: 19.3%
men married by age 18: 3.9% (2018 est.)

Education expenditures: 3.9% of GDP (2018 est.)
comparison ranking: 121

Literacy: *definition:* age 15 and over can read and write
total population: 79%
male: 83.5%
female: 74.5% (2018)

School life expectancy (primary to tertiary education): *total:* 12 years
male: 12 years
female: 12 years (2020)

ENVIRONMENT

Environment - current issues: recurrent drought in north severely affects agricultural activities; deforestation; overgrazing; soil erosion; poaching and habitat destruction threaten wildlife populations; water pollution; inadequate supplies of potable water

Environment - international agreements: *party to:* Biodiversity, Climate Change, Climate Change-Kyoto Protocol, Climate Change-Paris Agreement, Comprehensive Nuclear Test Ban, Desertification, Endangered Species, Environmental Modification, Hazardous Wastes, Law of the Sea, Marine Dumping-London Protocol, Nuclear Test Ban, Ozone Layer Protection, Ship Pollution, Tropical Timber 2006, Wetlands, Whaling
signed, but not ratified: Marine Life Conservation

Climate: tropical; warm and comparatively dry along southeast coast; hot and humid in southwest; hot and dry in north

Urbanization: *urban population:* 59.2% of total population (2023)
rate of urbanization: 3.06% annual rate of change (2020-25 est.)

Revenue from forest resources: 3.51% of GDP (2018 est.)
comparison ranking: 21

Revenue from coal: 0% of GDP (2018 est.)
comparison ranking: 139

Air pollutants: *particulate matter emissions:* 46.04 micrograms per cubic meter (2019 est.)
carbon dioxide emissions: 16.67 megatons (2016 est.)
methane emissions: 22.75 megatons (2020 est.)

Waste and recycling: *municipal solid waste generated annually:* 3,538,275 tons (2005 est.)

Major rivers (by length in km): Volta river mouth (shared with Burkina Faso [s]) - 1,600 km
note – [s] after country name indicates river source; [m] after country name indicates river mouth

Major watersheds (area sq km): Atlantic Ocean drainage: Volta (410,991 sq km)

Total water withdrawal: *municipal:* 300 million cubic meters (2020 est.)
industrial: 100 million cubic meters (2020 est.)
agricultural: 1.07 billion cubic meters (2020 est.)

Total renewable water resources: 56.2 billion cubic meters (2020 est.)

GOVERNMENT

Country name: *conventional long form:* Republic of Ghana
conventional short form: Ghana
former: Gold Coast
etymology: named for the medieval West African kingdom of the same name but whose location was actually further north than the modern country

Government type: presidential republic

Capital: *name:* Accra
geographic coordinates: 5 33 N, 0 13 W
time difference: UTC 0 (5 hours ahead of Washington, DC, during Standard Time)
etymology: the name derives from the Akan word "nkran" meaning "ants," and refers to the numerous anthills in the area around the capital

Administrative divisions: 16 regions; Ahafo, Ashanti, Bono, Bono East, Central, Eastern, Greater Accra, North East, Northern, Oti, Savannah, Upper East, Upper West, Volta, Western, Western North

Independence: 6 March 1957 (from the UK)

National holiday: Independence Day, 6 March (1957)

Legal system: mixed system of English common law and customary law

Constitution: *history:* several previous; latest drafted 31 March 1992, approved and promulgated 28 April 1992, entered into force 7 January 1993
amendments: proposed by Parliament; consideration requires prior referral to the Council of State, a body of prominent citizens who advise the president of the republic; passage of amendments to "entrenched" constitutional articles (including those on national sovereignty, fundamental rights and freedoms, the structure and authorities of the branches of government, and amendment procedures) requires approval in a referendum by at least 40% participation of eligible voters and at least 75% of votes cast, followed by at least two-thirds majority vote in Parliament, and assent of the president; amendments to non-entrenched articles do not require referenda; amended 1996

International law organization participation: has not submitted an ICJ jurisdiction declaration; accepts ICCt jurisdiction

Citizenship: *citizenship by birth:* no
citizenship by descent only: at least one parent or grandparent must be a citizen of Ghana
dual citizenship recognized: yes
residency requirement for naturalization: 5 years

Suffrage: 18 years of age; universal

Executive branch: *chief of state:* President Nana Addo Dankwa AKUFO-ADDO (since 7 January 2017)
head of government: President Nana Addo Dankwa AKUFO-ADDO (since 7 January 2017)
cabinet: Council of Ministers; nominated by the president, approved by Parliament
elections/appointments: president and vice president directly elected on the same ballot by absolute majority popular vote in 2 rounds if needed for a 4-year term (eligible for a second term); election last held on 7 December 2020 (next to be held on 7 December 2024); the president is both chief of state and head of government
election results:
2020: Nana Addo Dankwa AKUFO-ADDO reelected president in the first round; percent of vote - Nana Addo Dankwa AKUFO-ADDO (NPP) 51.3%, John Dramani MAHAMA (NDC) 47.4%, other 1.3%
2016: Nana Addo Dankwa AKUFO-ADDO elected president in the first round; percent of vote - Nana Addo Dankwa AKUFO-ADDO (NPP) 53.7%, John Dramani MAHAMA (NDC) 44.5%, other 1.8% (2020)

Legislative branch: *description:* unicameral Parliament (275 seats; members directly elected in single-seat constituencies by simple majority vote to serve 4-year terms)
elections: last held on 7 December 2020 (next to be held in December 2024)
election results: percent of vote by party - NPP 50.4%, NDC 46.2%, independent 2.3%, other 1.1%; seats by party- NPP 137, NDC 137, independent 1; composition- men 235, women 40, percentage women 14.6%

Judicial branch: *highest court(s):* Supreme Court (consists of the chief justice and 13 justices)
judge selection and term of office: chief justice appointed by the president in consultation with the Council of State (a small advisory body of prominent citizens) and with the approval of Parliament; other justices appointed by the president upon the advice of the Judicial Council (an 18-member independent body of judicial, military and police officials, and presidential nominees) and on the advice of the Council of State; justices can retire at age 60, with compulsory retirement at age 70
subordinate courts: Court of Appeal; High Court; Circuit Court; District Court; regional tribunals

Political parties: All Peoples Congress or APC
Convention People's Party or CPP
Ghana Freedom Party or GFP
Ghana Union Movement or GUM
Great Consolidated Popular Party or GCPP
Liberal Party of Ghana or LPG
National Democratic Congress or NDC
National Democratic Party or NDP
New Patriotic Party or NPP
People's National Convention or PNC
Progressive People's Party or PPP
United Front Party or UFP
United Progressive Party or UPP

International organization participation: ACP, AfDB, ATMIS, AU, C, ECOWAS, EITI (compliant country), FAO, G-24, G-77, IAEA, IBRD, ICAO, ICC (national committees), ICCt, ICRM, IDA, IFAD, IFC, IFRCS, ILO, IMF, IMO, IMSO, Interpol, IOC, IOM, IPU, ISO, ITSO, ITU, ITUC (NGOs), MIGA, MINURSO, MONUSCO, NAM, OAS (observer), OIF, OPCW, UN, UNAMID, UNCTAD, UNESCO, UNHCR, UNHRC, UNIDO, UNIFIL, UNISFA, UNMIL, UNMISS, UNOCI, UNOOSA, UNSOM, UNWTO, UPU, WCO, WFTU (NGOs), WHO, WIPO, WMO, WTO

Diplomatic representation in the US: *chief of mission:* Ambassador Alima MAHAMA (since 7 July 2021)
chancery: 3512 International Drive NW, Washington, DC 20008
telephone: [1] (202) 686-4520
FAX: [1] (202) 686-4527
email address and website:
info@ghanaembassydc.org
https://ghanaembassydc.org/
consulate(s) general: New York

Diplomatic representation from the US: *chief of mission:* Ambassador Virginia E. PALMER (since 16 June 2022)
embassy: No. 24, Fourth Circular Road, Cantonments, Accra, P.O. Box 2288, Accra
mailing address: 2020 Accra Place, Washington DC 20521-2020
telephone: [233] (0) 30-274-1000
email address and website:
ACSAccra@state.gov
https://gh.usembassy.gov/

Flag description: three equal horizontal bands of red (top), yellow, and green, with a large black five-pointed star centered in the yellow band; red symbolizes the blood shed for independence, yellow represents the country's mineral wealth, while green stands for its forests and natural wealth; the black star is said to be the lodestar of African freedom
note: uses the popular Pan-African colors of Ethiopia; similar to the flag of Bolivia, which has a coat of arms centered in the yellow band

National symbol(s): black star, golden eagle; national colors: red, yellow, green, black

National anthem: *name:* "God Bless Our Homeland Ghana"
lyrics/music: unknown/Philip GBEHO
note: music adopted 1957, lyrics adopted 1966; the lyrics were changed twice, in 1960 when a republic was declared and after a 1966 coup

National heritage: *total World Heritage Sites:* 2 (both cultural)
selected World Heritage Site locales: Forts and Castles, Volta, Greater Accra, Central and Western Regions; Asante Traditional Buildings

ECONOMY

Economic overview: West African lower-middle income economy; major gold, oil and cocoa exporter; macroeconomic challenges following nearly four decades of sustained growth; recent progress in debt restructuring, fiscal reforms, financial stability, and curbing runaway inflation under 2023-26 IMF credit facility program

Real GDP (purchasing power parity): $229.639 billion (2023 est.)
$223.07 billion (2022 est.)
$214.867 billion (2021 est.)
note: data in 2021 dollars
comparison ranking: 71

Real GDP growth rate: 2.94% (2023 est.)
3.82% (2022 est.)
5.08% (2021 est.)
note: annual GDP % growth based on constant local currency
comparison ranking: 111

Real GDP per capita: $6,700 (2023 est.)
$6,700 (2022 est.)
$6,500 (2021 est.)
note: data in 2021 dollars
comparison ranking: 161

GDP (official exchange rate): $76.37 billion (2023 est.)
note: data in current dollars at official exchange rate

Inflation rate (consumer prices): 38.11% (2023 est.)
31.26% (2022 est.)
9.97% (2021 est.)
note: annual % change based on consumer prices
comparison ranking: 211

Credit ratings: Fitch rating: B (2013)

Moody's rating: B3 (2015)

Standard & Poors rating: B- (2020)
note: The year refers to the year in which the current credit rating was first obtained.

GDP - composition, by sector of origin: *agriculture:* 21.1% (2023 est.)
industry: 29.5% (2023 est.)
services: 42.5% (2023 est.)
note: figures may not total 100% due to non-allocated consumption not captured in sector-reported data
comparison rankings: services 182; industry 71; agriculture 37

GDP - composition, by end use: *household consumption:* 84.2% (2023 est.)
government consumption: 5.9% (2023 est.)
investment in fixed capital: 10.7% (2023 est.)
investment in inventories: 0.2% (2023 est.)
exports of goods and services: 34% (2023 est.)
imports of goods and services: -35% (2023 est.)
note: figures may not total 100% due to rounding or gaps in data collection

Agricultural products: cassava, yams, plantains, maize, oil palm fruit, taro, rice, cocoa beans, oranges, pineapples (2022)
note: top ten agricultural products based on tonnage

Industries: mining, lumbering, light manufacturing, aluminum smelting, food processing, cement, small commercial ship building, petroleum

Industrial production growth rate: -1.22% (2023 est.)
note: annual % change in industrial value added based on constant local currency
comparison ranking: 170

Labor force: 14.887 million (2023 est.)
note: number of people ages 15 or older who are employed or seeking work
comparison ranking: 43

Unemployment rate: 3.08% (2023 est.)
3.08% (2022 est.)
3.34% (2021 est.)
note: % of labor force seeking employment
comparison ranking: 51

Youth unemployment rate (ages 15-24): *total:* 5.5% (2023 est.)
male: 5.6% (2023 est.)
female: 5.4% (2023 est.)
note: % of labor force ages 15-24 seeking employment
comparison ranking: total 175

Population below poverty line: 23.4% (2016 est.)
note: % of population with income below national poverty line

Gini Index coefficient - distribution of family income: 43.5 (2016 est.)
note: index (0-100) of income distribution; higher values represent greater inequality
comparison ranking: 29

Average household expenditures: *on food:* 38.3% of household expenditures (2022 est.)
on alcohol and tobacco: 0.6% of household expenditures (2022 est.)

Household income or consumption by percentage share: *lowest 10%:* 1.6% (2016 est.)
highest 10%: 32.2% (2016 est.)
note: % share of income accruing to lowest and highest 10% of population

Remittances: 6.41% of GDP (2023 est.)
6.24% of GDP (2022 est.)
5.24% of GDP (2021 est.)
note: personal transfers and compensation between resident and non-resident individuals/households/entities

Budget: *revenues:* $11.684 billion (2022 est.)
expenditures: $16.842 billion (2022 est.)
note: central government revenues and expenses (excluding grants/extrabudgetary units/social security funds) converted to US dollars at average official exchange rate for year indicated

Public debt: 71.8% of GDP (2017 est.)
comparison ranking: 51

Taxes and other revenues: 12.3% (of GDP) (2022 est.)
note: central government tax revenue as a % of GDP
comparison ranking: 160

Current account balance: -$1.517 billion (2022 est.)
-$2.541 billion (2021 est.)
-$2.134 billion (2020 est.)
note: balance of payments - net trade and primary/secondary income in current dollars
comparison ranking: 151

Exports: $25.744 billion (2022 est.)
$23.901 billion (2021 est.)
$22.077 billion (2020 est.)
note: balance of payments - exports of goods and services in current dollars
comparison ranking: 84

Exports - partners: UAE 24%, Switzerland 17%, US 14%, India 10%, China 10% (2022)
note: top five export partners based on percentage share of exports

Exports - commodities: gold, crude petroleum, cocoa beans, coconuts/Brazil nuts/cashews, cocoa paste (2022)
note: top five export commodities based on value in dollars

Imports: $26.329 billion (2022 est.)
$25.967 billion (2021 est.)
$24.545 billion (2020 est.)
note: balance of payments - imports of goods and services in current dollars
comparison ranking: 84

Imports - partners: China 41%, Netherlands 7%, India 5%, US 5%, Cote d'Ivoire 4% (2022)
note: top five import partners based on percentage share of imports

Imports - commodities: refined petroleum, plastic products, garments, coated flat-rolled iron, ships (2022)
note: top five import commodities based on value in dollars

Reserves of foreign exchange and gold: $3.624 billion (2023 est.)
$5.205 billion (2022 est.)
$9.917 billion (2021 est.)
note: holdings of gold (year-end prices)/foreign exchange/special drawing rights in current dollars

comparison ranking: 107

Exchange rates: cedis (GHC) per US dollar -

Exchange rates: 11.02 (2023 est.)
8.272 (2022 est.)
5.806 (2021 est.)
5.596 (2020 est.)
5.217 (2019 est.)

ENERGY

Electricity access: *electrification - total population:* 85.1% (2022 est.)
electrification - urban areas: 95%
electrification - rural areas: 71.6%

Electricity: *installed generating capacity:* 5.444 million kW (2022 est.)
consumption: 19.142 billion kWh (2022 est.)
exports: 1.787 billion kWh (2022 est.)
imports: 48.461 million kWh (2022 est.)
transmission/distribution losses: 1.619 billion kWh (2022 est.)
comparison rankings: transmission/distribution losses 116; imports 115; exports 58; consumption 74; installed generating capacity 85

Electricity generation sources: *fossil fuels:* 66% of total installed capacity (2022 est.)
solar: 0.6% of total installed capacity (2022 est.)
hydroelectricity: 33.3% of total installed capacity (2022 est.)
biomass and waste: 0.1% of total installed capacity (2022 est.)

Coal: *consumption:* 85,000 metric tons (2022 est.)
exports: 9 metric tons (2022 est.)
imports: 85,000 metric tons (2022 est.)

Petroleum: *total petroleum production:* 174,000 bbl/day (2023 est.)
refined petroleum consumption: 110,000 bbl/day (2022 est.)
crude oil estimated reserves: 660 million barrels (2021 est.)

Natural gas: *production:* 3.192 billion cubic meters (2022 est.)
consumption: 3.912 billion cubic meters (2022 est.)
imports: 539.629 million cubic meters (2022 est.)
proven reserves: 22.653 billion cubic meters (2021 est.)

Carbon dioxide emissions: 22.882 million metric tonnes of CO2 (2022 est.)
from coal and metallurgical coke: 172,000 metric tonnes of CO2 (2022 est.)
from petroleum and other liquids: 15.035 million metric tonnes of CO2 (2022 est.)
from consumed natural gas: 7.675 million metric tonnes of CO2 (2022 est.)
comparison ranking: total emissions 81

Energy consumption per capita: 11.416 million Btu/person (2022 est.)
comparison ranking: 147

COMMUNICATIONS

Telephones - fixed lines: *total subscriptions:* 330,000 (2022 est.)
subscriptions per 100 inhabitants: (2022 est.) less than 1
comparison ranking: total subscriptions 103

Telephones - mobile cellular: *total subscriptions:* 40.045 million (2022 est.)
subscriptions per 100 inhabitants: 120 (2022 est.)
comparison ranking: total subscriptions 41

Telecommunication systems: *general assessment:* challenged by unreliable electricity and shortage of skilled labor, Ghana seeks to extend telecom services nationally; investment in fiber infrastructure and off-grid solutions provide data coverage to over 23 million people; launch of LTE has improved mobile data services, including m-commerce and banking; moderately competitive Internet market, most through mobile networks; international submarine cables, and terrestrial cables have improved Internet capacity; LTE services are widely available; the relatively high cost of 5G-compatible devices also inhibits most subscribers from migrating from 3G and LTE platforms (2022)
domestic: fixed-line data less than 1 per 100 subscriptions; mobile-cellular subscriptions 123 per 100 persons (2021)
international: country code - 233; landing points for the SAT-3/WASC, MainOne, ACE, WACS and GLO-1 fiber-optic submarine cables that provide connectivity to South and West Africa, and Europe; satellite earth stations - 4 Intelsat (Atlantic Ocean); microwave radio relay link to Panaftel system connects Ghana to its neighbors; GhanaSat-1 nanosatellite launched in 2017 (2017)

Broadcast media: state-owned TV station, 2 state-owned radio networks; several privately owned TV stations and a large number of privately owned radio stations; transmissions of multiple international broadcasters are accessible; several cable and satellite TV subscription services are obtainable

Internet country code: .gh

Internet users: *total:* 22.44 million (2021 est.)
percent of population: 68% (2021 est.)
comparison ranking: total 39

Broadband - fixed subscriptions: *total:* 78,371 (2020 est.)
subscriptions per 100 inhabitants: 0.3 (2020 est.)
comparison ranking: total 132

TRANSPORTATION

National air transport system: *number of registered air carriers:* 3 (2020)
inventory of registered aircraft operated by air carriers: 21
annual passenger traffic on registered air carriers: 467,438 (2018)

Civil aircraft registration country code prefix: 9G

Airports: 11 (2024)
comparison ranking: 156

Heliports: 7 (2024)

Pipelines: 681.3 km gas, 11.4 km oil, 435 km refined products (2022)

Railways: *total:* 947 km (2022)
narrow gauge: 947 km (2022) 1.067-m gauge
comparison ranking: total 92

Roadways: *total:* 65,725 km
paved: 14,948 km
unpaved: 50,777 km (2021)
urban: 28,480 km 27% total paved 73% total unpaved
comparison ranking: total 74

Waterways: 1,293 km (2011) (168 km for launches and lighters on Volta, Ankobra, and Tano Rivers; 1,125 km of arterial and feeder waterways on Lake Volta)
comparison ranking: 60

Merchant marine: *total:* 52 (2023)
by type: general cargo 8, oil tanker 3, other 41
comparison ranking: total 119

Ports: *total ports:* 4 (2024)
large: 0
medium: 1
small: 1
very small: 2
ports with oil terminals: 3
key ports: Saltpond, Sekondi, Takoradi, Tema

MILITARY AND SECURITY

Military and security forces: Ghana Armed Forces (GAF): Army, Navy, Air Force (2024)
note: the Ghana Police Service is under the Ministry of the Interior

Military expenditures: 0.4% of GDP (2023 est.)
0.4% of GDP (2022 est.)
0.5% of GDP (2021 est.)
0.4% of GDP (2020 est.)
0.4% of GDP (2019 est.)
comparison ranking: 162

Military and security service personnel strengths: approximately 16,000 active personnel (12,000 Army; 2,000 Navy; 2,000 Air Force) (2024)

Military equipment inventories and acquisitions: the military's inventory is a mix of older and some newer Chinese, Russian, and Western equipment, including US, which has donated items such as patrol boats; the government in recent years has committed to an increase in funding for equipment acquisitions, including armor, mechanized, and special forces capabilities for the Army, light attack aircraft for the Air Force, and more modern coastal patrol vessels for the Navy (2024)

Military service age and obligation: 18-27 years of age for voluntary military service, with basic education certificate; no conscription (2024)
note: as of 2024, women comprised approximately 15% of the military; Ghanaian women first began serving in the late 1950s

Military deployments: 875 Lebanon (UNIFIL); 725 (plus about 275 police) South Sudan (UNMISS); 670 Sudan (UNISFA) (2024)
note: since sending a contingent of troops to the Congo in 1960, the military has been a regular contributor to African-and UN-sponsored peacekeeping missions

Military - note: the military's primary missions are border defense, assisting with internal security, peacekeeping, and protecting the country's territorial waters, particularly its offshore oil and gas infrastructure; it has benefited from cooperation with foreign partners, such as the UK and the US, and experience gained from participation in multiple international peacekeeping missions
in 2022, Ghana began beefing up its military presence in the north of the country against threats from the terrorist organization Jama'at Nasr al-Islam wal Muslimin (JNIM), a coalition of al-Qa'ida linked militant groups, which has conducted attacks in the neighboring countries of Burkina Faso, Cote d'Ivoire, and Togo; Ghana's northern frontier with Burkina Faso is also an area with well-established smuggling routes, porous borders, and illegal gold mining; Ghana has also made efforts to increase its naval capabilities to protect its maritime claims and counter threats such as piracy
the military traces its origins to the Gold Coast Constabulary that was established in 1879 and

renamed the Gold Coast Regiment in 1901; the Gold Coast Regiment was part of the West African Frontier Force, a multi-regiment unit formed by the British colonial office in 1900 to garrison Britain's West African colonies, which went on to serve in both World Wars; following Ghana's independence in 1957, the Gold Coast Regiment formed the basis for the new Ghanaian Army (2024)

SPACE

Space agency/agencies: Ghana Space Science and Technology Center (GSSTC; established 2011); note – the GSSTC is eventually slated to become the Ghana Space Agency (2024)

Space program overview: has a small, nascent space program focused on research in space sciences and exploiting remote sensing (RS) technology for natural resource management, weather forecasting, agriculture, and national security issues; relies on foreign imagery for analysis but seeks to develop its own RS satellite capabilities; one of Africa's leaders in satellite dish research; trains aerospace scientists and engineers; has established relations on space-related issues with China, Japan, and South Africa; cooperating with Egypt, Kenya, Nigeria, Sudan, and Uganda to establish a joint satellite to monitor climate changes in the African continent; partner of the Square Kilometer Array (SKA) international astronomy initiative (2024)
note: further details about the key activities, programs, and milestones of the country's space program, as well as government spending estimates on the space sector, appear in the Space Programs reference guide

TRANSNATIONAL ISSUES

Illicit drugs: Ghana is a transit and destination point for illicit drugs trafficked from Asia and South America to other African countries, Europe, and to a lesser extent North America; not a significant source for drugs entering the United States; limited local consumption of controlled pharmaceuticals, cocaine, and heroin from Asia and South America; cannabis cultivated and produced in large quantities in most rural areas of Ghana

GIBRALTAR

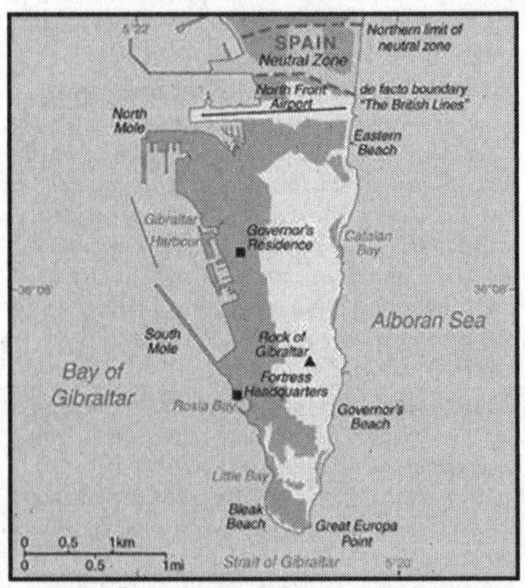

INTRODUCTION

Background: Spain reluctantly ceded the strategically important Gibraltar to Great Britain in the 1713 Treaty of Utrecht, and the British garrison at Gibraltar was formally declared a colony in 1830. In a referendum held in 1967, Gibraltarians voted overwhelmingly to remain a British dependency. After the UK granted Gibraltar autonomy in 1969, Spain closed the border and severed all communication links. Between 1997 and 2002, the UK and Spain held a series of talks on establishing temporary joint sovereignty over Gibraltar. In response to these talks, the Gibraltar Government called a referendum in 2002 in which the majority of citizens voted overwhelmingly against sharing sovereignty with Spain. Since 2004, Spain, the UK, and Gibraltar have held tripartite talks to resolve problems that affect the local population, and work continues on cooperation agreements in areas such as taxation and financial services, communications and maritime security, legal and customs services, environmental protection, and education and visa services. A new noncolonial constitution came into force in 2007, and the European Court of First Instance recognized Gibraltar's right to regulate its own tax regime in 2008. The UK retains responsibility for defense, foreign relations, internal security, and financial stability.

Spain and the UK continue to spar over the territory. In 2009, for example, a dispute over Gibraltar's claim to territorial waters extending out three miles gave rise to periodic non-violent maritime confrontations between Spanish and UK naval patrols. Spain renewed its demands for an eventual return of Gibraltar to Spanish control after the UK's 2016 vote to leave the EU, but London has dismissed any connection between the vote and its sovereignty over Gibraltar.

GEOGRAPHY

Location: Southwestern Europe, bordering the Strait of Gibraltar, which links the Mediterranean Sea and the North Atlantic Ocean, on the southern coast of Spain

Geographic coordinates: 36 08 N, 5 21 W

Map references: Europe

Area: *total:* 7 sq km
land: 6.5 sq km
water: 0 sq km
comparison ranking: total 244

Area - comparative: more than 10 times the size of The National Mall in Washington, D.C.

Land boundaries: *total:* 1.2 km
border countries (1): Spain 1.2 km

Coastline: 12 km

Maritime claims: *territorial sea:* 3 nm

Climate: Mediterranean with mild winters and warm summers

Terrain: a narrow coastal lowland borders the Rock of Gibraltar

Elevation: *highest point:* Rock of Gibraltar 426 m
lowest point: Mediterranean Sea 0 m

Natural resources: none

Land use: *agricultural land:* 0% (2011 est.)
other: 100% (2018 est.)

Irrigated land: NA

Natural hazards: occasional droughts; no streams or large bodies of water on the peninsula (all potable water comes from desalination)

Geography - note: *note 1:* strategic location on Strait of Gibraltar that links the North Atlantic Ocean and Mediterranean Sea
note 2: one of only two British territories where traffic drives on the right, the other being the island of Diego Garcia in the British Indian Ocean Territory

PEOPLE AND SOCIETY

Population: *total:* 29,683
male: 14,919
female: 14,764 (2024 est.)
comparison rankings: female 217; male 217; total 217

Nationality: *noun:* Gibraltarian(s)
adjective: Gibraltar

Ethnic groups: Gibraltarian 79%, other British 13.2%, Spanish 2.1%, Moroccan 1.6%, other EU 2.4%, other 1.6% (2012 est.)
note: data represent population by nationality

Languages: English (used in schools and for official purposes), Spanish, Italian, Portuguese

Religions: Roman Catholic 72.1%, Church of England 7.7%, other Christian 3.8%, Muslim 3.6%, Jewish 2.4%, Hindu 2%, other 1.1%, none 7.1%, unspecified 0.1% (2012 est.)

Age structure: *0-14 years:* 20% (male 3,045/female 2,895)
15-64 years: 62.5% (male 9,383/female 9,179)
65 years and over: 17.5% (2024 est.) (male 2,491/female 2,690)

Dependency ratios: *total dependency ratio:* 60.1
youth dependency ratio: 27.4
elderly dependency ratio: 32.7
potential support ratio: 3.1 (2021)

Median age: *total:* 36.8 years (2024 est.)
male: 36.2 years
female: 37.5 years
comparison ranking: total 88

Population growth rate: 0.17% (2024 est.)
comparison ranking: 179

Birth rate: 13.7 births/1,000 population (2024 est.)
comparison ranking: 124

Death rate: 8.7 deaths/1,000 population (2024 est.)
comparison ranking: 69

Net migration rate: -3.2 migrant(s)/1,000 population (2024 est.)
comparison ranking: 186

Urbanization: *urban population:* 100% of total population (2023)
rate of urbanization: 0.45% annual rate of change (2015-20 est.)

Major urban areas - population: 35,000 GIBRALTAR (capital) (2018)

Sex ratio: *at birth:* 1.05 male(s)/female
0-14 years: 1.05 male(s)/female
15-64 years: 1.02 male(s)/female
65 years and over: 0.93 male(s)/female
total population: 1.01 male(s)/female (2024 est.)

Infant mortality rate: *total:* 6 deaths/1,000 live births (2024 est.)
male: 6.8 deaths/1,000 live births
female: 5.2 deaths/1,000 live births
comparison ranking: total 169

Life expectancy at birth: *total population:* 80.9 years (2024 est.)
male: 78.1 years
female: 83.8 years
comparison ranking: total population 48

Total fertility rate: 1.89 children born/woman (2024 est.)
comparison ranking: 123

Gross reproduction rate: 0.92 (2024 est.)

Drinking water source: *improved: urban:* 100% of population
rural: NA
total: 100% of population

Sanitation facility access: *improved: urban:* 100% of population
rural: NA
total: 100% of population

Currently married women (ages 15-49): 40.7% (2023 est.)

Education expenditures: NA

Literacy: *total population:* NA
male: NA
female: NA

ENVIRONMENT

Environment - current issues: *limited natural freshwater resources:* more than 90% of drinking water supplied by desalination, the remainder from stored rainwater; a separate supply of saltwater used for sanitary services

Climate: Mediterranean with mild winters and warm summers

Urbanization: *urban population:* 100% of total population (2023)
rate of urbanization: 0.45% annual rate of change (2015-20 est.)

Air pollutants: *carbon dioxide emissions:* 0.63 megatons (2016 est.)

Waste and recycling: *municipal solid waste generated annually:* 16,954 tons (2012 est.)

GOVERNMENT

Country name: *conventional long form:* none
conventional short form: Gibraltar
etymology: from the Spanish derivation of the Arabic "Jabal Tariq," which means "Mountain of Tariq" and which refers to the Rock of Gibraltar

Government type: parliamentary democracy (Parliament); self-governing overseas territory of the UK

Dependency status: overseas territory of the UK

Capital: *name:* Gibraltar
geographic coordinates: 36 08 N, 5 21 W
time difference: UTC+1 (6 hours ahead of Washington, DC, during Standard Time)
daylight saving time: +1hr, begins last Sunday in March; ends last Sunday in October
etymology: from the Spanish derivation of the Arabic "Jabal Tariq," which means "Mountain of Tariq" and which refers to the Rock of Gibraltar

Administrative divisions: none (overseas territory of the UK)

Independence: none (overseas territory of the UK)

National holiday: National Day, 10 September (1967); note - day of the national referendum to decide whether to remain with the UK or join Spain

Legal system: the laws of the UK, where applicable, apply

Constitution: *history:* previous 1969; latest passed by referendum 30 November 2006, entered into effect 14 December 2006, entered into force 2 January 2007
amendments: proposed by Parliament and requires prior consent of the British monarch (through the Secretary of State); passage requires at least three-fourths majority vote in Parliament followed by simple majority vote in a referendum; note – only sections 1 through 15 in Chapter 1 (Protection of Fundamental Rights and Freedoms) can be amended by Parliament

Citizenship: see United Kingdom

Suffrage: 18 years of age; universal; and British citizens with six months residence or more

Executive branch: *chief of state:* King CHARLES III (since 8 September 2022); represented by Governor Sir David STEEL (since 11 June 2020)
head of government: Chief Minister Fabian PICARDO (since 9 December 2011)
cabinet: Council of Ministers appointed from among the 17 elected members of Parliament by the governor in consultation with the chief minister
elections/appointments: the monarchy is hereditary; governor appointed by the monarch; following legislative elections, the leader of the majority party or majority coalition usually appointed chief minister by the governor

Legislative branch: *description:* unicameral Parliament (18 seats; 17 members directly elected in a single nationwide constituency by majority vote and 1 appointed by Parliament as speaker; members serve 4-year terms)
elections: last held on 12 October 2023 (next to be held by October 2027)
election results: percent of vote by party - GSLP-Liberal Alliance 49.9%, GSD 48% independent 2.1%; seats by party - GLSP-Liberal Alliance 9 (GSLP 7, LPG 2), GSD 8; composition including Parliament speaker - men 13, women 5, percentage women 38.5%

Judicial branch: *highest court(s):* Court of Appeal (consists of at least 3 judges, including the court president); Supreme Court of Gibraltar (consists of the chief justice and 3 judges); note - appeals beyond the Court of Appeal are heard by the Judicial Committee of the Privy Council (in London)
judge selection and term of office: Court of Appeal and Supreme Court judges appointed by the governor upon the advice of the Judicial Service Commission, a 7-member body of judges and appointees of the governor; tenure of the Court of Appeal president based on terms of appointment; Supreme Court chief justice and judges normally appointed until retirement at age 67 but tenure can be extended 3 years
subordinate courts: Court of First Instance; Magistrates' Court; specialized tribunals for issues relating to social security, taxes, and employment

Political parties: Gibraltar Liberal Party or Liberal Party of Gibraltar or LPG
Gibraltar Social Democrats or GSD
Gibraltar Socialist Labor Party or GSLP
GSLP-Liberal Alliance
Together Gibraltar or TG

International organization participation: ICC (NGOs), Interpol (subbureau), UPU

Diplomatic representation in the US: none (overseas territory of the UK)

Diplomatic representation from the US: *embassy:* none (overseas territory of the UK)

Flag description: two horizontal bands of white (top, double width) and red with a three-towered red castle in the center of the white band; hanging from the castle gate is a gold key centered in the red band; the design is that of Gibraltar's coat of arms granted on 10 July 1502 by King Ferdinand and Queen Isabella of Spain; the castle symbolizes Gibraltar as a fortress, while the key represents Gibraltar's strategic importance - the key to the Mediterranean

National symbol(s): Barbary macaque; national colors: red, white, yellow

National anthem: *name:* "Gibraltar Anthem"
lyrics/music: Peter EMBERLEY
note: adopted 1994; serves as a local anthem; as an overseas territory of the United Kingdom, "God Save the King" is official (see United Kingdom)

ECONOMY

Economic overview: British territorial high-income economy; Brexit caused significant economic disruption to longstanding financial services, shipping, and tourism industries; ongoing negotiations to rejoin EU Schengen Area; independent taxation authority

Real GDP (purchasing power parity): $2.044 billion (2014 est.)
note: data are in 2014 dollars
comparison ranking: 199

Real GDP per capita: $61,700 (2014 est.)
(2008)
(2007)
comparison ranking: 28

GDP (official exchange rate): $2.044 billion (2014 est.)

Agricultural products: none

Industries: tourism, banking and finance, ship repairing, tobacco

Industrial production growth rate: 4.3% (2014 est.)
note: annual % change in industrial value added based on constant local currency
comparison ranking: 73

Labor force: 24,420 (2014 est.)
comparison ranking: 200

Unemployment rate: 1% (2016 est.)
comparison ranking: 7

Exports: $202.3 million (2014 est.)
comparison ranking: 202

Exports - partners: Ireland 20%, India 18%, Brazil 12%, Netherlands 10%, South Korea 8% (2022)
note: top five export partners based on percentage share of exports

Exports - commodities: refined petroleum, crude petroleum, ships, cars, natural gas (2022)
note: top five export commodities based on value in dollars

Imports - partners: Spain 19%, Italy 17%, Greece 11%, Nigeria 10%, UK 6% (2022)
note: top five import partners based on percentage share of imports

Imports - commodities: refined petroleum, crude petroleum, coal tar oil, ships, cars (2022)
note: top five import commodities based on value in dollars

Exchange rates: Gibraltar pounds (GIP) per US dollar -

Exchange rates: 0.805 (2023 est.)
0.811 (2022 est.)
0.727 (2021 est.)
0.78 (2020 est.)
0.783 (2019 est.)

ENERGY

Electricity access: *electrification - total population:* 100% (2022 est.)

Electricity: *installed generating capacity:* 43,000 kW (2022 est.)
consumption: 244.5 million kWh (2022 est.)
transmission/distribution losses: 7 million kWh (2022 est.)
comparison rankings: transmission/distribution losses 13; consumption 188; installed generating capacity 196

Electricity generation sources: *fossil fuels:* 100% of total installed capacity (2022 est.)

Petroleum: *refined petroleum consumption:* 84,000 bbl/day (2022 est.)

Natural gas: *consumption:* 75.781 million cubic meters (2022 est.)
imports: 75.781 million cubic meters (2022 est.)

Carbon dioxide emissions: 14.297 million metric tonnes of CO2 (2022 est.)
from petroleum and other liquids: 14.149 million metric tonnes of CO2 (2022 est.)
from consumed natural gas: 148,000 metric tonnes of CO2 (2022 est.)
comparison ranking: total emissions 97

Energy consumption per capita: (2019 est.)

COMMUNICATIONS

Telephones - fixed lines: *total subscriptions:* 17,000 (2022 est.)
subscriptions per 100 inhabitants: 53 (2022 est.)
comparison ranking: total subscriptions 178

Telephones - mobile cellular: *total subscriptions:* 37,000 (2022 est.)
subscriptions per 100 inhabitants: 112 (2022 est.)
comparison ranking: total subscriptions 211

Telecommunication systems: *general assessment:* Gibraltar's population is urban-based, served by a digital telephone exchange supported by a fiber optic and copper infrastructure; near universal mobile and Internet use (2019)
domestic: 53 per 100 fixed-line and 100 per 100 mobile-cellular (2021)
international: country code - 350; landing point for the EIG to Europe, Asia, Africa and the Middle East via submarine cables; radiotelephone; microwave radio relay; satellite earth station - 1 Intelsat (Atlantic Ocean) (2019)

Broadcast media: Gibraltar Broadcasting Corporation (GBC) provides TV and radio broadcasting services via 1 TV station and 4 radio stations; British Forces Broadcasting Service (BFBS) operates 1 radio station; broadcasts from Spanish radio and TV stations are accessible

Internet country code: .gi

Internet users: *total:* 31,152 (2021 est.)
percent of population: 94.4% (2021 est.)
comparison ranking: total 209

Broadband - fixed subscriptions: *total:* 21,009 (2020 est.)
subscriptions per 100 inhabitants: 62 (2020 est.)
comparison ranking: total 164

TRANSPORTATION

Civil aircraft registration country code prefix: VP-G

Airports: 1 (2024)
comparison ranking: 216

Roadways: *total:* 29 km
paved: 29 km (2007)
comparison ranking: total 222

Merchant marine: *total:* 129 (2023)
by type: bulk carrier 8, container ship 5, general cargo 31, oil tanker 16, other 69
comparison ranking: total 78

Ports: *total ports:* 1 (2024)
large: 0
medium: 1
small: 0
very small: 0
ports with oil terminals: 1
key ports: Europa Point

MILITARY AND SECURITY

Military and security forces: Royal Gibraltar Regiment (2024)

Military and security service personnel strengths: the Royal Gibraltar Regiment has more than 400 personnel (2023)

Military - note: defense is the responsibility of the UK

GREECE

INTRODUCTION

Background: Greece won independence from the Ottoman Empire in 1830 and became a kingdom. During the second half of the 19th century and the first half of the 20th century, it gradually added neighboring islands and territories, most with Greekspeaking populations. In World War II, Greece was first invaded by Italy (1940) and subsequently occupied by Germany (1941-44); fighting endured in a protracted civil war between supporters of the king and other anti-communist and communist rebels. The communists were defeated in 1949, and Greece joined NATO in 1952. In 1967, a military coup forced the king to flee the country. The ensuing military dictatorship collapsed in 1974, and Greece abolished the monarchy to become a parliamentary republic.

In 1981, Greece joined the EC (now the EU); it became the 12th member of the European Economic and Monetary Union in 2001. From 2009 until 2019, Greece suffered a severe economic crisis due to nearly a decade of chronic overspending and structural rigidities. Beginning in 2010, Greece entered three bailout agreements – the first two with the European Commission, the European Central Bank, and the IMF; and the third in 2015 with the European Stability Mechanism – worth in total about $300 billion. The Greek Government formally exited the third bailout in 2018, and Greece's economy has since improved significantly. In 2022, the country finalized its early repayment to the IMF and graduated on schedule from the EU's enhanced surveillance framework.

GEOGRAPHY

Location: Southern Europe, bordering the Aegean Sea, Ionian Sea, and the Mediterranean Sea, between Albania and Turkey

Geographic coordinates: 39 00 N, 22 00 E

Map references: Europe

Area: *total:* 131,957 sq km
land: 130,647 sq km
water: 1,310 sq km
comparison ranking: total 97

Area - comparative: slightly smaller than Alabama

Land boundaries: *total:* 1,110 km
border countries (4): Albania 212 km; Bulgaria 472 km; North Macedonia 234 km; Turkey 192 km

Coastline: 13,676 km

Maritime claims: *territorial sea:* 6 nm
continental shelf: 200-m depth or to the depth of exploitation

Climate: temperate; mild, wet winters; hot, dry summers

Terrain: mountainous with ranges extending into the sea as peninsulas or chains of islands

Elevation: *highest point:* Mount Olympus 2,917
lowest point: Mediterranean Sea 0 m
mean elevation: 498 m
note: Mount Olympus actually has 52 peaks but its highest point, Mytikas (meaning "nose"), rises to 2,917 meters; in Greek mythology, Olympus' Mytikas peak was the home of the Greek gods

Natural resources: lignite, petroleum, iron ore, bauxite, lead, zinc, nickel, magnesite, marble, salt, hydropower potential

Land use: *agricultural land:* 63.4% (2018 est.)
arable land: 19.7% (2018 est.)
permanent crops: 8.9% (2018 est.)
permanent pasture: 34.8% (2018 est.)
forest: 30.5% (2018 est.)
other: 6.1% (2018 est.)

Irrigated land: 11,853 sq km (2019)

Population distribution: one-third of the population lives in and around metropolitan Athens; the remainder of the country has moderate population density mixed with sizeable urban clusters

Natural hazards: severe earthquakes
volcanism: Santorini (367 m) has been deemed a Decade Volcano by the International Association of Volcanology and Chemistry of the Earth's Interior, worthy of study due to its explosive history and close proximity to human populations; although there have been very few eruptions in recent centuries, Methana and Nisyros in the Aegean are classified as historically active

Geography - note: strategic location dominating the Aegean Sea and southern approach to Turkish Straits; a peninsular country, possessing an archipelago of about 2,000 islands

PEOPLE AND SOCIETY

Population: *total:* 10,461,091
male: 5,117,862
female: 5,343,229 (2024 est.)
comparison rankings: female 88; male 92; total 90

Nationality: *noun:* Greek(s)
adjective: Greek

Ethnic groups: Greek 91.6%, Albanian 4.4%, other 4% (2011 est.)
note: data represent citizenship; Greece does not collect data on ethnicity

Languages: Greek (official) 99%, other (includes English and French) 1%
major-language sample(s):
Παγκόσμιο Βιβλίο Δεδομένων, η απαραίτητη πηγή βασικών πληροφοριών. (Greek)

Religions: Greek Orthodox 81-90%, Muslim 2%, other 3%, none 4-15%, unspecified 1% (2015 est.)

Age structure: *0-14 years:* 13.8% (male 742,131/female 699,079)
15-64 years: 62.6% (male 3,278,906/female 3,267,140)
65 years and over: 23.6% (2024 est.) (male 1,096,825/female 1,377,010)

Dependency ratios: *total dependency ratio:* 57.7
youth dependency ratio: 22.2
elderly dependency ratio: 35.5
potential support ratio: 2.8 (2021 est.)

Median age: *total:* 46.5 years (2024 est.)
male: 44.6 years
female: 48.3 years
comparison ranking: total 10

Population growth rate: -0.35% (2024 est.)
comparison ranking: 215

Birth rate: 7.4 births/1,000 population (2024 est.)
comparison ranking: 219

Death rate: 12 deaths/1,000 population (2024 est.)
comparison ranking: 16

Net migration rate: 1.1 migrant(s)/1,000 population (2024 est.)
comparison ranking: 63

Population distribution: one-third of the population lives in and around metropolitan Athens; the remainder of the country has moderate population density mixed with sizeable urban clusters

Urbanization: *urban population:* 80.7% of total population (2023)
rate of urbanization: 0.11% annual rate of change (2020-25 est.)

Major urban areas - population: 3.154 million ATHENS (capital), 815,000 Thessaloniki (2023)

Sex ratio: *at birth:* 1.07 male(s)/female
0-14 years: 1.06 male(s)/female
15-64 years: 1 male(s)/female
65 years and over: 0.8 male(s)/female
total population: 0.96 male(s)/female (2024 est.)

Mother's mean age at first birth: 30.7 years (2020 est.)

Maternal mortality ratio: 8 deaths/100,000 live births (2020 est.)
comparison ranking: 149

Infant mortality rate: *total:* 3.4 deaths/1,000 live births (2024 est.)
male: 3.8 deaths/1,000 live births
female: 3 deaths/1,000 live births
comparison ranking: total 195

Life expectancy at birth: *total population:* 81.9 years (2024 est.)
male: 79.4 years
female: 84.6 years
comparison ranking: total population 40

Total fertility rate: 1.41 children born/woman (2024 est.)
comparison ranking: 211

Gross reproduction rate: 0.68 (2024 est.)

Drinking water source: *improved: urban:* 100% of population
rural: 100% of population
total: 100% of population

Current health expenditure: 9.5% of GDP (2020)

Physician density: 6.31 physicians/1,000 population (2019)

Hospital bed density: 4.2 beds/1,000 population (2018)

Sanitation facility access: *improved: urban:* 100% of population
rural: 100% of population
total: 100% of population

Obesity - adult prevalence rate: 24.9% (2016)
comparison ranking: 54

Alcohol consumption per capita: *total:* 6.33 liters of pure alcohol (2019 est.)
beer: 2.13 liters of pure alcohol (2019 est.)
wine: 2.66 liters of pure alcohol (2019 est.)
spirits: 1.45 liters of pure alcohol (2019 est.)
other alcohols: 0.08 liters of pure alcohol (2019 est.)
comparison ranking: total 66

Tobacco use: *total:* 33.5% (2020 est.)
male: 36.5% (2020 est.)
female: 30.5% (2020 est.)
comparison ranking: total 18

Currently married women (ages 15-49): 54.1% (2023 est.)

Education expenditures: 4.4% of GDP (2020 est.)
comparison ranking: 103

Literacy: *definition:* age 15 and over can read and write
total population: 97.9%
male: 98.5%
female: 97.4% (2018)

School life expectancy (primary to tertiary education): *total:* 20 years
male: 20 years
female: 20 years (2020)

ENVIRONMENT

Environment - current issues: air pollution; air emissions from transport and electricity power stations; water pollution; degradation of coastal zones; loss of biodiversity in terrestrial and marine ecosystems; increasing municipal and industrial waste

Environment - international agreements: *party to:* Air Pollution, Air Pollution-Nitrogen Oxides, Air Pollution-Sulphur 94, Antarctic-Environmental Protection, Antarctic-Marine Living Resources, Antarctic Treaty, Biodiversity, Climate Change, Climate Change-Kyoto Protocol, Climate Change-Paris Agreement, Comprehensive Nuclear Test Ban, Desertification, Endangered Species, Environmental Modification, Hazardous Wastes, Law of the Sea, Marine Dumping-London Convention, Nuclear Test Ban, Ozone Layer Protection, Ship Pollution, Tropical Timber 2006, Wetlands
signed, but not ratified: Air Pollution-Heavy Metals, Air Pollution-Multi-effect Protocol, Air Pollution-Persistent Organic Pollutants, Air Pollution-Volatile Organic Compounds

Climate: temperate; mild, wet winters; hot, dry summers

Urbanization: *urban population:* 80.7% of total population (2023)
rate of urbanization: 0.11% annual rate of change (2020-25 est.)

Revenue from forest resources: 0.01% of GDP (2018 est.)
comparison ranking: 149

Revenue from coal: 0.04% of GDP (2018 est.)
comparison ranking: 32

Air pollutants: *particulate matter emissions:* 14.62 micrograms per cubic meter (2019 est.)
carbon dioxide emissions: 62.43 megatons (2016 est.)
methane emissions: 9.8 megatons (2020 est.)

Waste and recycling: *municipal solid waste generated annually:* 5,477,424 tons (2014 est.)
municipal solid waste recycled annually: 1,040,711 tons (2014 est.)
percent of municipal solid waste recycled: 19% (2014 est.)

Total water withdrawal: *municipal:* 1.69 billion cubic meters (2020 est.)
industrial: 330 million cubic meters (2020 est.)
agricultural: 8.11 billion cubic meters (2020 est.)

Total renewable water resources: 68.4 billion cubic meters (2020 est.)

Geoparks: *total global geoparks and regional networks:* 9 (2024)
global geoparks and regional networks: Chelmos Vouraikos; Grevena - Kozani; Kefalonia-Ithaca; Lavreotiki; Lesvos Island; Meteora Pyli; Psiloritis; Sitia; Vikos - Aoos (2024)

GOVERNMENT

Country name: *conventional long form:* Hellenic Republic
conventional short form: Greece
local long form: Elliniki Dimokratia
local short form: Ellas or Ellada
former: Hellenic State, Kingdom of Greece
etymology: the English name derives from the Roman (Latin) designation "Graecia," meaning "Land of the Greeks"; the Greeks call their country "Hellas" or "Ellada"

Government type: parliamentary republic

Capital: *name:* Athens
geographic coordinates: 37 59 N, 23 44 E
time difference: UTC+2 (7 hours ahead of Washington, DC, during Standard Time)
daylight saving time: +1hr, begins last Sunday in March; ends last Sunday in October
etymology: Athens is the oldest European capital city; according to tradition, the city is named after Athena, the Greek goddess of wisdom; in actuality, the appellation probably derives from a lost name in a pre-Hellenic language

Administrative divisions: 13 regions (perifereies, singular - perifereia) and 1 autonomous monastic state* (aftonomi monastiki politeia); Agion Oros* (Mount Athos), Anatoliki Makedonia kai Thraki (East Macedonia and Thrace), Attiki (Attica), Dytiki Ellada (West Greece), Dytiki Makedonia (West Macedonia), Ionia Nisia (Ionian Islands), Ipeiros (Epirus), Kentriki Makedonia (Central Macedonia), Kriti (Crete), Notio Aigaio (South Aegean), Peloponnisos (Peloponnese), Sterea Ellada (Central Greece), Thessalia (Thessaly), Voreio Aigaio (North Aegean)

Independence: 3 February 1830 (from the Ottoman Empire); note - 25 March 1821, outbreak of the national revolt against the Ottomans; 3 February 1830, signing of the London Protocol recognizing Greek independence by Great Britain, France, and Russia

National holiday: Independence Day, 25 March (1821)

Legal system: civil legal system based on Roman law

Constitution: *history:* many previous; latest entered into force 11 June 1975
amendments: proposed by at least 50 members of Parliament and agreed by three-fifths majority vote in two separate ballots at least 30 days apart; passage requires absolute majority vote by the next elected Parliament; entry into force finalized through a "special parliamentary resolution"; articles on human rights and freedoms and the form of government cannot be amended; amended 1986, 2001, 2008, 2019

International law organization participation: accepts compulsory ICJ jurisdiction with reservations; accepts ICCt jurisdiction

Citizenship: *citizenship by birth:* no
citizenship by descent only: at least one parent must be a citizen of Greece
dual citizenship recognized: yes
residency requirement for naturalization: 10 years

Suffrage: 17 years of age; universal and compulsory

Executive branch: *chief of state:* President Ekaterini SAKELLAROPOULOU (since 13 March 2020)
head of government: Prime Minister Kyriakos MITSOTAKIS (since 26 June 2023)
cabinet: Cabinet appointed by the president on the recommendation of the prime minister
elections/appointments: president elected by Hellenic Parliament for a 5-year term (eligible for a second term); election last held on 22 January 2020 (next to be held by February 2025); president appoints as prime minister the leader of the majority party or coalition in the Hellenic Parliament
election results:
2020: Katerina SAKELLAROPOULOU (independent) elected president by Parliament - 261 of 300 votes; note - SAKELLAROPOULOU is Greece's first woman president
2015: Prokopis PAVLOPOULOS (ND) elected president by Parliament - 233 of 300 votes

Legislative branch: *description:* unicameral Hellenic Parliament or Vouli ton Ellinon (300 seats; 280 members in multi-seat and single-seat constituencies and 15 members - including 3 seats for Greek diaspora - in a single nationwide constituency directly elected by open party-list proportional representation vote; members serve up to 4 years); note - only parties surpassing a 3% threshold are entitled to parliamentary seats; parties need 10 seats to become formal parliamentary groups but can retain that status if the party participated in the last election and received the minimum 3% threshold
elections: last held on 25 June 2023 (next to be held in 2027)
election results: percent of vote by party - ND 40.6%, SYRIZA-PS 17.8%, PASOK-KINAL 11.9%, KKE 7.7%, Spartans 4.6%, Greek Solution 4.4%, NIKI 3.7%, Course of Freedom 3.2%, other 6.1%; seats by party - ND 158, SYRIZA-PS 48, PASOK-KINAL 32, KKE 20, Spartans 12, Greek Solution 12, NIKI 10, Course of Freedom 8; composition - men 231, women 69, percentage women 23%

Judicial branch: *highest court(s):* Supreme Civil and Criminal Court or Areios Pagos (consists of 56 judges, including the court presidents); Council of State (supreme administrative court) (consists of the president, 7 vice presidents, 42 privy councilors, 48 associate councilors and 50 reporting judges, organized into six 5- and 7-member chambers; Court of Audit (government audit and enforcement) consists of the president, 5 vice presidents, 20 councilors, and 90 associate and reporting judges
judge selection and term of office: Supreme Court judges appointed by presidential decree on the advice of the Supreme Judicial Council (SJC), which includes the president of the Supreme Court, other judges, and the prosecutor of the Supreme Court; judges appointed for life following a 2-year probationary period; Council of State president appointed by the Greek Cabinet to serve a 4-year term; other judge appointments and tenure NA; Court of Audit president appointed by decree of the president of the republic on the advice of the SJC; court president serves a 4-year term or until age 67; tenure of vice presidents, councilors, and judges NA
subordinate courts: Courts of Appeal and Courts of First Instance (district courts)

Political parties: Coalition of the Radical Left-Progressive Alliance or SYRIZA-PS
Communist Party of Greece or KKE
Course of Freedom
Democratic Patriotic Movement-Victory or NIKI
Greek Solution
New Democracy or ND
PASOK - Movement for Change or PASOK-KINAL
Spartans

International organization participation: Australia Group, BIS, BSEC, CD, CE, CERN, EAPC, EBRD, ECB, EIB, EMU, ESA, EU, FAO, FATF, IAEA, IBRD, ICAO, ICC (national committees), ICCt, ICRM, IDA, IEA, IFAD, IFC, IFRCS, IGAD (partners), IHO, ILO, IMF, IMO, IMSO, Interpol, IOC, IOM, IPU, ISO, ITSO, ITU, ITUC (NGOs), MIGA, NATO, NEA, NSG, OAS (observer), OECD, OIF, OPCW, OSCE, PCA, Schengen Convention, SELEC, UN, UNCTAD, UNESCO, UNHCR, UNIDO, UNIFIL, UNWTO, UPU, Wassenaar Arrangement, WCO, WFTU (NGOs), WHO, WIPO, WMO, WTO, ZC

Diplomatic representation in the US: *chief of mission:* Ambassador Ekaterini NASSIKA (since 27 February 2024)
chancery: 2217 Massachusetts Avenue NW, Washington, DC 20008
telephone: [1] (202) 939-1300
FAX: [1] (202) 939-1324
email address and website:
gremb.was@mfa.gr
https://www.mfa.gr/usa/en/the-embassy/
consulate(s) general: Boston, Chicago, Los Angeles, New York, Tampa (FL), San Francisco
consulate(s): Atlanta, Houston

Diplomatic representation from the US: *chief of mission:* Ambassador George James TSUNIS (since 10 May 2022)
embassy: 91 Vasillisis Sophias Avenue, 10160 Athens
mailing address: 7100 Athens Place, Washington DC 20521-7100
telephone: [30] (210) 721-2951
FAX: [30] (210) 724-5313
email address and website:
athensamericancitizenservices@state.gov
https://gr.usembassy.gov/
consulate(s) general: Thessaloniki

Flag description: nine equal horizontal stripes of blue alternating with white; a blue square bearing a white cross appears in the upper hoist-side corner; the cross symbolizes Greek Orthodoxy, the established religion of the country; there is no agreed upon meaning for the nine stripes or for the colors
note: Greek legislation states that the flag colors are cyan and white, but cyan can mean "blue" in Greek,

so the exact shade of blue has never been set and has varied from a light to a dark blue over time; in general, the hue of blue normally encountered is a form of azure

National symbol(s): Greek cross (white cross on blue field, arms equal length); national colors: blue, white

National anthem: *name:* "Ymnos eis tin Eleftherian" (Hymn to Liberty)
lyrics/music: Dionysios SOLOMOS/Nikolaos MANTZAROS
note: adopted 1864; the anthem is based on a 158-stanza poem by the same name, which was inspired by the Greek Revolution of 1821 against the Ottomans (only the first two stanzas are used); Cyprus also uses "Hymn to Liberty" as its anthem

National heritage: *total World Heritage Sites:* 19 (17 cultural, 2 mixed)
selected World Heritage Site locales: Acropolis, Athens (c); Archaeological site of Delphi (c); Meteora (m); Medieval City of Rhodes (c); Archaeological site of Olympia (c); Archaeological site of Mycenae and Tiryns (c); Old Town of Corfu (c); Mount Athos (m); Delos (c); Archaeological Site of Philippi (c)

ECONOMY

Economic overview: developed EU and eurozone economy; strong post-COVID growth driven by tourism, shipping industry, exports, and foreign investment supported by EU cohesion funds; public debt remains high despite recent budget surplus; challenges from negative household savings, high unemployment, corruption, and competitiveness gaps

Real GDP (purchasing power parity): $375.78 billion (2023 est.)
$368.37 billion (2022 est.)
$348.977 billion (2021 est.)
note: data in 2021 dollars
comparison ranking: 55

Real GDP growth rate: 2.01% (2023 est.)
5.56% (2022 est.)
8.38% (2021 est.)
note: annual GDP % growth based on constant local currency
comparison ranking: 138

Real GDP per capita: $36,300 (2023 est.)
$35,300 (2022 est.)
$33,000 (2021 est.)
note: data in 2021 dollars
comparison ranking: 66

GDP (official exchange rate): $238.206 billion (2023 est.)
note: data in current dollars at official exchange rate

Inflation rate (consumer prices): 3.46% (2023 est.)
9.65% (2022 est.)
1.22% (2021 est.)
note: annual % change based on consumer prices
comparison ranking: 65

Credit ratings: Fitch rating: BB (2020)

Moody's rating: Ba3 (2020)

Standard & Poors rating: BB- (2019)
note: The year refers to the year in which the current credit rating was first obtained.

GDP - composition, by sector of origin: *agriculture:* 3.8% (2023 est.)
industry: 15.7% (2023 est.)
services: 67.6% (2023 est.)
note: figures may not total 100% due to non-allocated consumption not captured in sector-reported data
comparison rankings: services 49; industry 168; agriculture 131

GDP - composition, by end use: *household consumption:* 68.4% (2023 est.)
government consumption: 19.7% (2023 est.)
investment in fixed capital: 13.9% (2023 est.)
investment in inventories: 2.9% (2023 est.)
exports of goods and services: 44.9% (2023 est.)
imports of goods and services: -49.8% (2023 est.)
note: figures may not total 100% due to rounding or gaps in data collection

Agricultural products: maize, wheat, sheep milk, peaches/nectarines, oranges, grapes, tomatoes, milk, watermelons, potatoes (2022)
note: top ten agricultural products based on tonnage

Industries: tourism, food and tobacco processing, textiles, chemicals, metal products; mining, petroleum

Industrial production growth rate: 1.68% (2023 est.)
note: annual % change in industrial value added based on constant local currency
comparison ranking: 121

Labor force: 4.645 million (2023 est.)
note: number of people ages 15 or older who are employed or seeking work
comparison ranking: 92

Unemployment rate: 11% (2023 est.)
12.43% (2022 est.)
14.66% (2021 est.)
note: % of labor force seeking employment
comparison ranking: 169

Youth unemployment rate (ages 15-24): *total:* 26.6% (2023 est.)
male: 24.3% (2023 est.)
female: 29.5% (2023 est.)
note: % of labor force ages 15-24 seeking employment
comparison ranking: total 35

Population below poverty line: 18.8% (2021 est.)
note: % of population with income below national poverty line

Gini Index coefficient - distribution of family income: 32.9 (2021 est.)
note: index (0-100) of income distribution; higher values represent greater inequality
comparison ranking: 101

Average household expenditures: *on food:* 18.8% of household expenditures (2022 est.)
on alcohol and tobacco: 5% of household expenditures (2022 est.)

Household income or consumption by percentage share: *lowest 10%:* 2.6% (2021 est.)
highest 10%: 24.8% (2021 est.)
note: % share of income accruing to lowest and highest 10% of population

Remittances: 0.22% of GDP (2023 est.)
0.28% of GDP (2022 est.)
0.32% of GDP (2021 est.)
note: personal transfers and compensation between resident and non-resident individuals/households/entities

Budget: *revenues:* $105.353 billion (2022 est.)
expenditures: $110.844 billion (2022 est.)
note: central government revenues (excluding grants) and expenses converted to US dollars at average official exchange rate for year indicated

Public debt: 203.29% of GDP (2022 est.)
note: central government debt as a % of GDP
comparison ranking: 2

Taxes and other revenues: 27.81% (of GDP) (2022 est.)
note: central government tax revenue as a % of GDP
comparison ranking: 29

Current account balance: -$15.056 billion (2023 est.)
-$22.623 billion (2022 est.)
-$13.858 billion (2021 est.)
note: balance of payments - net trade and primary/secondary income in current dollars
comparison ranking: 198

Exports: $106.65 billion (2023 est.)
$106.189 billion (2022 est.)
$87.521 billion (2021 est.)
note: balance of payments - exports of goods and services in current dollars
comparison ranking: 47

Exports - partners: Italy 10%, Bulgaria 7%, Germany 6%, Cyprus 5%, Turkey 5% (2022)
note: top five export partners based on percentage share of exports

Exports - commodities: refined petroleum, packaged medicine, aluminum, natural gas, plastic products (2022)
note: top five export commodities based on value in dollars

Imports: $117.922 billion (2023 est.)
$127.82 billion (2022 est.)
$103.532 billion (2021 est.)
note: balance of payments - imports of goods and services in current dollars
comparison ranking: 45

Imports - partners: China 12%, Germany 9%, Russia 9%, Italy 7%, Iraq 7% (2022)
note: top five import partners based on percentage share of imports

Imports - commodities: crude petroleum, natural gas, refined petroleum, garments, packaged medicine (2022)
note: top five import commodities based on value in dollars

Reserves of foreign exchange and gold: $13.608 billion (2023 est.)
$12.061 billion (2022 est.)
$14.447 billion (2021 est.)
note: holdings of gold (year-end prices)/foreign exchange/special drawing rights in current dollars
comparison ranking: 82

Exchange rates: euros (EUR) per US dollar -

Exchange rates: 0.925 (2023 est.)
0.95 (2022 est.)
0.845 (2021 est.)
0.876 (2020 est.)
0.893 (2019 est.)

ENERGY

Electricity access: *electrification - total population:* 100% (2022 est.)

Electricity: *installed generating capacity:* 22.336 million kW (2022 est.)
consumption: 47.283 billion kWh (2022 est.)
exports: 4.303 billion kWh (2022 est.)
imports: 7.751 billion kWh (2022 est.)
transmission/distribution losses: 5.344 billion kWh (2022 est.)
comparison rankings: transmission/distribution losses 166; imports 34; exports 41; consumption 55; installed generating capacity 45

Electricity generation sources: *fossil fuels:* 53.4% of total installed capacity (2022 est.)
solar: 14.5% of total installed capacity (2022 est.)
wind: 22.1% of total installed capacity (2022 est.)
hydroelectricity: 8.9% of total installed capacity (2022 est.)
biomass and waste: 1% of total installed capacity (2022 est.)

Coal: *production:* 13.703 million metric tons (2022 est.)
consumption: 13.988 million metric tons (2022 est.)
exports: 362,000 metric tons (2022 est.)
imports: 71,000 metric tons (2022 est.)
proven reserves: 2.876 billion metric tons (2022 est.)

Petroleum: *total petroleum production:* 5,000 bbl/day (2023 est.)
refined petroleum consumption: 303,000 bbl/day (2023 est.)
crude oil estimated reserves: 10 million barrels (2021 est.)

Natural gas: *production:* 3.284 million cubic meters (2021 est.)
consumption: 5.173 billion cubic meters (2022 est.)
exports: 10.647 billion cubic meters (2022 est.)
imports: 15.946 billion cubic meters (2022 est.)
proven reserves: 991.09 million cubic meters (2021 est.)

Carbon dioxide emissions: 62.142 million metric tonnes of CO2 (2022 est.)
from coal and metallurgical coke: 6.449 million metric tonnes of CO2 (2022 est.)
from petroleum and other liquids: 45.457 million metric tonnes of CO2 (2022 est.)
from consumed natural gas: 10.236 million metric tonnes of CO2 (2022 est.)
comparison ranking: total emissions 53

Energy consumption per capita: 94.151 million Btu/person (2022 est.)
comparison ranking: 56

COMMUNICATIONS

Telephones - fixed lines: *total subscriptions:* 4.907 million (2022 est.)
subscriptions per 100 inhabitants: 47 (2022 est.)
comparison ranking: total subscriptions 29

Telephones - mobile cellular: *total subscriptions:* 11.326 million (2022 est.)
subscriptions per 100 inhabitants: 109 (2022 est.)
comparison ranking: total subscriptions 88

Telecommunication systems: *general assessment:* Greece's telecom market is susceptible to the country's volatile economy, and, as a result, revenue among the key networks has been variable; broadband subscriptions in Greece are developing steadily; the main networks are concentrating investment on fiber-based next generation networks, enabling them to reach the European broadband targets for 2025; their work is also supported by government ultra-fast broadband projects, largely funded by the EC and aimed at delivering a service of at least 100Mb/s to under served areas; Greece's well-developed mobile market is dominated by the three MNOs; Networks continue to invest in LTE infrastructure and technologies to provide networks capable of meeting customer demand for data services; after extensive trials of 5G, the MNOs were able to launch commercial services in early 2021 following the December 2020 allocation of frequencies in a range of bands; the rapid rollout of 5G encouraged the shut down of the 3G network (a process expected to be completed by the end of 2021) and reallocate for LTE and 5G. (2023)
domestic: 47 per 100 subscribers for fixed-line and 110 per 100 for mobile-cellular (2021)
international: country code - 30; landing points for the SEA-ME-WE-3, Adria-1, Italy-Greece 1, OTEGLOBE, MedNautilus Submarine System, Aphrodite 2, AAE-1 and Silphium optical telecommunications submarine cable that provides links to Europe, the Middle East, Africa, Southeast Asia, Asia and Australia; tropospheric scatter; satellite earth stations - 4 (2 Intelsat - 1 Atlantic Ocean and 1 Indian Ocean, 1 Eutelsat, and 1 Inmarsat - Indian Ocean region) (2019)

Broadcast media: broadcast media dominated by the private sector; roughly 150 private TV channels, about 10 of which broadcast nationwide; 1 government-owned terrestrial TV channel with national coverage; 3 privately owned satellite channels; multi-channel satellite and cable TV services available; upwards of 1,500 radio stations, all of them privately owned; government-owned broadcaster has 2 national radio stations

Internet country code: .gr

Internet users: *total:* 7.8 million (2021 est.)
percent of population: 78% (2021 est.)
comparison ranking: total 78

Broadband - fixed subscriptions: *total:* 4,257,026 (2020 est.)
subscriptions per 100 inhabitants: 41 (2020 est.)
comparison ranking: total 35

TRANSPORTATION

National air transport system: *number of registered air carriers:* 11 (2020)
inventory of registered aircraft operated by air carriers: 97
annual passenger traffic on registered air carriers: 15,125,933 (2018)
annual freight traffic on registered air carriers: 21.91 million (2018) mt-km

Civil aircraft registration country code prefix: SX

Airports: 81 (2024)
comparison ranking: 66

Heliports: 51 (2024)

Pipelines: 1,466 km gas, 94 km oil (2013)

Railways: *total:* 2,345 km (2020) 731 km electrified
comparison ranking: total 67

Roadways: *total:* 117,000 km (2018)
comparison ranking: total 43

Waterways: 6 km (2012) (the 6-km-long Corinth Canal crosses the Isthmus of Corinth; it shortens a sea voyage by 325 km)
comparison ranking: 117

Merchant marine: *total:* 1,215 (2023)
by type: bulk carrier 132, container ship 4, general cargo 79, oil tanker 299, other 701
comparison ranking: total 20

Ports: *total ports:* 57 (2024)
large: 1
medium: 7
small: 7
very small: 42
ports with oil terminals: 13
key ports: Alexandroupoli, Iraklion, Kerkira, Ormos Aliveriou, Piraievs, Soudha, Thessaloniki, Volos

MILITARY AND SECURITY

Military and security forces: Hellenic Armed Forces: Hellenic Army (Ellinikos Stratos, ES; includes National Guard), Hellenic Navy (Elliniko Polemiko Navtiko, EPN), Hellenic Air Force (Elliniki Polemiki Aeroporia, EPA; includes air defense) (2024)
note 1: the police (under the Ministry of Citizen Protection) and the armed forces (Ministry of National Defense) share law enforcement duties in certain border areas; the Greek Coast Guard is under the Ministry of Shipping Affairs and Island Policy
note 2: the National Guard was established in 1982 as an official part of the Army to help protect Greece and provide reinforcements and support to the Army in peacetime and in times of mobilization and war; members undergo weekly training run by the Army, which also provides weapons and ammunition

Military expenditures: 3.1% of GDP (2024 est.)
3.1% of GDP (2023)
3.9% of GDP (2022)
3.7% of GDP (2021)
2.9% of GDP (2020)
comparison ranking: 31

Military and security service personnel strengths: approximately 115,000 active-duty personnel (80,000 Army; 15,000 Navy; 20,000 Air Force); approximately 35,000 National Guard (2024)

Military equipment inventories and acquisitions: the military's inventory consists of a mix of imported weapons from Europe and the US, as well as a limited number of domestically produced systems; in recent years, France, Germany, and the US have been major suppliers; Greece's defense industry is capable of producing a range of military hardware, including naval vessels and associated subsystems (2024)
note: Greece is in the midst of a military modernization program which includes acquisitions of fighter aircraft and naval ships from France and armored vehicles and tanks from Germany; it has also boosted purchases of US equipment, including fighter aircraft upgrades, helicopters, and naval patrol craft

Military service age and obligation: 19-45 years of age for compulsory military service for men; 12-month obligation for all services (note - as an exception, the duration of the full military service is 9 instead of 12 months if conscripts, after the initial training, serve the entire remaining time in certain areas of the eastern borders, in Cyprus, or in certain military units); 18 years of age for voluntary military service for men and women (2023)
note 1: compulsory service applies to any individual whom the Greek authorities consider to be Greek, regardless of whether the individual considers himself Greek, has a foreign citizenship and passport, or was born or lives outside of Greece; Greek citizens living permanently outside of Greece have the right to postpone their conscription; they are permanently exempted from their military obligations when they reach the age of 45 years old
note 2: as of 2023, women comprised nearly 17% of the military's full-time personnel

Military deployments: approximately 1,000 Cyprus; 110 Kosovo (NATO); 120 Lebanon (UNIFIL) (2024)

Military - note: the Hellenic Armed Forces (HAF) are responsible for protecting Greece's independence, sovereignty, and territorial integrity; the HAF also maintains a presence on Cyprus (the Hellenic Force in Cyprus or ELDYK) to assist and support the

Cypriot National Guard; as a member of the EU, NATO, and other international organizations, the HAF participates in multinational peacekeeping and other security missions abroad, taking a particular interest in missions occurring in the near regions, such as the Balkans, the Mediterranean and Aegean seas, the Middle East, and North Africa; areas of focus for the HAF include instability in the Balkans, territorial disputes with Turkey, and support to European security through the EU and NATO

Greece's NATO membership is a key component of its security; it became a NATO member in 1952 and occupies a strategic location in the Eastern Mediterranean on NATO's southern flank; Greece is host to several NATO facilities, including the Deployable Corps Greece (NDC-GR) headquarters in Thessaloniki, the Combined Air Operations Center in Larissa, the Multinational Peace Support Operations Training Center in Kilkis, the Multinational Sealift Coordination Center in Athens, and the Naval Base, Maritime Interdiction Operational Training Centre, and NATO Missile Firing Installation at Souda, Crete (2024)

SPACE

Space agency/agencies: Hellenic Space Center (HSC; aka Hellenic Space Agency; established 2018) (2024)

Space program overview: has a relatively new and growing space program focused on building and operating satellites; also researches and develops technologies in a variety of other space sectors, including such areas as remote sensing (RS), telecommunications, defense, environmental studies, and agricultural development; has a national space strategy; as a member of the European Space Agency (ESA), it contributes to, participates in, and benefits from ESA capabilities and programs; cooperates with space agencies and commercial space sectors of ESA and EU member states, as well as the US; has a robust commercial space sector that researches, develops, and produces a variety of space technologies and capabilities, including satellite components, electronics, sensors, and communications (2024)
note: further details about the key activities, programs, and milestones of the country's space program, as well as government spending estimates on the space sector, appear in the Space Programs reference guide

TERRORISM

Terrorist group(s): Islamic State of Iraq and ash-Sham (ISIS); Revolutionary Struggle; Revolutionary People's Liberation Party/Front (DHKP/C)
note: details about the history, aims, leadership, organization, areas of operation, tactics, targets, weapons, size, and sources of support of the group(s) appear(s) in the Terrorism reference guide

TRANSNATIONAL ISSUES

Refugees and internally displaced persons: *refugees (country of origin):* 41,594 (Syria), 33,549 (Afghanistan), 14,228 (Iraq), 6,366 (West Bank and Gaza) (midyear 2022); 27,365 (Ukraine) (as of 31 December 2023)
stateless persons: 4,488 (2022)
note: 1,289,013 estimated refugee and migrant arrivals (January 2015-March 2024)

Illicit drugs: a gateway to Europe for traffickers smuggling cannabis products and heroin from the Middle East and Southwest Asia to the West and precursor chemicals to the East; some South American cocaine transits or is consumed in Greece; money laundering related to drug trafficking and organized crime

GREENLAND

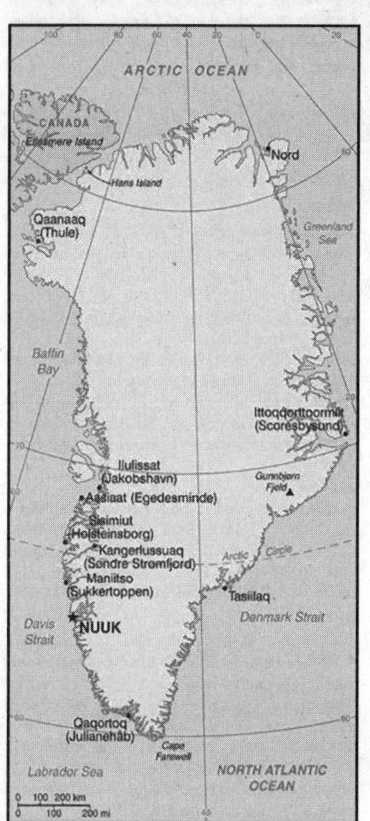

INTRODUCTION

Background: Greenland, the world's largest island, is about 80% ice capped. The Inuit came to Greenland from North America in a series of migrations that stretched from 2500 BC to the11th century. Vikings reached the island in the 10th century from Iceland; Danish colonization began in the 18th century, and Greenland became part of the Kingdom of Denmark in 1953. It joined the European Community (now the EU) with Denmark in 1973 but withdrew in 1985 over a dispute centered on stringent fishing quotas. Greenland remains a member of the EU's Overseas Countries and Territories Association. The Danish parliament granted Greenland home rule in 1979; the law went into effect the following year. Greenland voted in favor of self-government in 2008 and acquired greater responsibility for internal affairs when the Act on Greenland Self-Government was signed into law in 2009. The Kingdom of Denmark, however, continues to exercise control over several policy areas on behalf of Greenland, including foreign affairs, security, and financial policy, in consultation with Greenland's Self-Rule Government.

GEOGRAPHY

Location: Northern North America, island between the Arctic Ocean and the North Atlantic Ocean, northeast of Canada

Geographic coordinates: 72 00 N, 40 00 W

Map references: Arctic Region

Area: *total:* 2,166,086 sq km
land: 2,166,086 sq km (approximately 1,710,000 sq km ice-covered)
comparison ranking: total 13

Area - comparative: slightly more than three times the size of Texas

Land boundaries: *total:* 0 km

Coastline: 44,087 km

Maritime claims: *territorial sea:* 3 nm
continental shelf: 200 nm or agreed boundaries or median line
exclusive fishing zone: 200 nm or agreed boundaries or median line

Climate: arctic to subarctic; cool summers, cold winters

Terrain: flat to gradually sloping icecap covers all but a narrow, mountainous, barren, rocky coast

Elevation: *highest point:* Gunnbjorn Fjeld 3,694 m
lowest point: Atlantic Ocean 0 m
mean elevation: 1,792 m

Natural resources: coal, iron ore, lead, zinc, molybdenum, diamonds, gold, platinum, niobium, tantalite, uranium, fish, seals, whales, hydropower, possible oil and gas

Land use: *agricultural land:* 0.6% (2018 est.)
arable land: 0% (2018 est.)
permanent crops: 0% (2018 est.)
permanent pasture: 0.6% (2018 est.)
forest: 0% (2018 est.)
other: 99.4% (2018 est.)

Irrigated land: NA

Population distribution: settlement concentrated on the southwest shoreline, with limited settlements scattered along the remaining coast; interior is uninhabited

Natural hazards: continuous permafrost over northern two-thirds of the island

Geography - note: dominates North Atlantic Ocean between North America and Europe; sparse population confined to small settlements along coast; close to one-quarter of the population lives in the capital, Nuuk; world's second largest ice sheet after that of

Antarctica covering an area of 1.71 million sq km (660,000 sq mi) or about 79% of the island, and containing 2.85 million cu km (684 thousand cu mi) of ice (this is almost 7% of all of the world's fresh water); if all this ice were converted to liquid water, one estimate is that it would be sufficient to raise the height of the world's oceans by 7.2 m (24 ft)

PEOPLE AND SOCIETY

Population: *total:* 57,751
male: 29,843
female: 27,908 (2024 est.)
comparison rankings: female 206; male 206; total 206

Nationality: *noun:* Greenlander(s)
adjective: Greenlandic

Ethnic groups: Greenlandic 88.1%, Danish 7.1%, Filipino 1.6%, other Nordic peoples 0.9%, and other 2.3% (2024 est.)
note: data represent population by country of birth

Languages: Greenlandic, Danish, English
note: West Greenlandic or Kalaallisut is the official language; Tunumiisut (East Greenlandic) and Inuktun (Polar Inuit Greenlandic) are considered dialects of Kalaallisut and spoken by about 10% of Greenlanders

Religions: Evangelical Lutheran, traditional Inuit spiritual beliefs

Age structure: *0-14 years:* 20.4% (male 5,964/female 5,798)
15-64 years: 67.1% (male 20,050/female 18,711)
65 years and over: 12.5% (2024 est.) (male 3,829/female 3,399)

Dependency ratios: *total dependency ratio:* 43.6
youth dependency ratio: 30
elderly dependency ratio: 13.6
potential support ratio: 7.4 (2021)

Median age: *total:* 35.3 years (2024 est.)
male: 35.9 years
female: 34.7 years
comparison ranking: total 100

Population growth rate: -0.05% (2024 est.)
comparison ranking: 200

Birth rate: 13.5 births/1,000 population (2024 est.)
comparison ranking: 126

Death rate: deaths/1,000 population (2024 est.)
comparison ranking: 51

Net migration rate: -4.9 migrant(s)/1,000 population (2024 est.)
comparison ranking: 202

Population distribution: settlement concentrated on the southwest shoreline, with limited settlements scattered along the remaining coast; interior is uninhabited

Urbanization: *urban population:* 87.9% of total population (2023)
rate of urbanization: 0.41% annual rate of change (2020-25 est.)

Major urban areas - population: 18,000 NUUK (capital) (2018)

Sex ratio: *at birth:* 1.05 male(s)/female
0-14 years: 1.03 male(s)/female
15-64 years: 1.07 male(s)/female
65 years and over: 1.13 male(s)/female
total population: 1.07 male(s)/female (2024 est.)

Infant mortality rate: *total:* 8.5 deaths/1,000 live births (2024 est.)
male: 9.9 deaths/1,000 live births
female: 6.9 deaths/1,000 live births
comparison ranking: total 142

Life expectancy at birth: *total population:* 74.5 years (2024 est.)
male: 71.8 years
female: 77.3 years
comparison ranking: total population 141

Total fertility rate: 1.88 children born/woman (2024 est.)
comparison ranking: 124

Gross reproduction rate: 0.92 (2024 est.)

Contraceptive prevalence rate: NA

Drinking water source: *improved: urban:* 100% of population
rural: 100% of population
total: 100% of population

Physician density: 1.87 physicians/1,000 population (2016)

Hospital bed density: 14 beds/1,000 population (2016)

Sanitation facility access: *improved: urban:* 100% of population
rural: 100% of population
total: 100% of population

Currently married women (ages 15-49): 39.4% (2023 est.)

Education expenditures: 10.2% of GDP (2019 est.)
comparison ranking: 4

Literacy: *definition:* age 15 and over can read and write
total population: 100%
male: 100%
female: 100% (2015)

ENVIRONMENT

Environment - current issues: especially vulnerable to climate change and disruption of the Arctic environment; preservation of the Inuit traditional way of life, including whaling and seal hunting

Climate: arctic to subarctic; cool summers, cold winters

Urbanization: *urban population:* 87.9% of total population (2023)
rate of urbanization: 0.41% annual rate of change (2020-25 est.)

Revenue from forest resources: 0% of GDP (2018 est.)
comparison ranking: 198

Revenue from coal: 0% of GDP (2018 est.)
comparison ranking: 89

Air pollutants: *carbon dioxide emissions:* 0.51 megatons (2016 est.)

Waste and recycling: *municipal solid waste generated annually:* 50,000 tons (2010 est.)

GOVERNMENT

Country name: *conventional long form:* none
conventional short form: Greenland
local long form: none
local short form: Kalaallit Nunaat
etymology: named by Norwegian adventurer Erik THORVALDSSON (Erik the Red) in A.D. 985 in order to entice settlers to the island

Government type: parliamentary democracy (Parliament of Greenland or Inatsisartut)

Dependency status: part of the Kingdom of Denmark; self-governing overseas administrative division of Denmark since 1979

Capital: *name:* Nuuk
geographic coordinates: 64 11 N, 51 45 W
time difference: UTC-2 (3 hours ahead of Washington, DC, during Standard Time)
daylight saving time: +1hr, begins last Sunday in March; ends last Sunday in October
time zone note: Greenland has four time zones
etymology: "nuuk" is the Inuit word for "cape" and refers to the city's position at the end of the Nuup Kangerlua fjord

Administrative divisions: 5 municipalities (kommuner, singular kommune); Avannaata, Kujalleq, Qeqertalik, Qeqqata, Sermersooq
note: Northeast Greenland National Park (Kalaallit Nunaanni Nuna Eqqissisimatitaq) and the Pituffik Space Base (formerly known as Thule Air Base) in northwest Greenland are two unincorporated areas; the national park's 972,000 sq km - about 46% of the island - makes it the largest national park in the world and also the most northerly

Independence: none (extensive self-rule as part of the Kingdom of Denmark; foreign affairs is the responsibility of Denmark, but Greenland actively participates in international agreements relating to Greenland)

National holiday: National Day, June 21; note - marks the summer solstice and the longest day of the year in the Northern Hemisphere

Legal system: the laws of Denmark apply where applicable and Greenlandic law applies to other areas

Constitution: *history:* previous 1953 (Greenland established as a constituency in the Danish constitution), 1979 (Greenland Home Rule Act); latest 21 June 2009 (Greenland Self-Government Act)

Citizenship: see Denmark

Suffrage: 18 years of age; universal

Executive branch: *chief of state:* King FREDERIK X of Denmark (since 14 January 2024), represented by High Commissioner Julie Praest WILCHE (since May 2022) (2024)
head of government: Premier Mute B. EGEDE (since 23 April 2021)
cabinet: Self-rule Government (Naalakkersuisut) elected by the Parliament (Inatsisartut)
elections/appointments: the monarchy is hereditary; high commissioner appointed by the monarch; premier indirectly elected by Parliament for a 4-year term
election results:
2021: Mute B. EGEDE elected premier; Parliament vote - Mute B. EGEDE (Inuit Ataqatigiit) unanimous
2014: Kim KIELSEN elected premier; Parliament vote - Kim KIELSEN (S) 27.2%, Sara OLSVIG (IA) 25.5%, Randi Vestergaard EVALDSEN (D) 19.5%, other 27.8%

Legislative branch: *description:* unicameral Parliament or Inatsisartut (31 seats; members directly elected in multi-seat constituencies by party-list proportional representation vote - by the d'Hondt method - to serve 4-year terms)
Greenland elects 2 members to the Danish Parliament to serve 4-year terms
elections: Greenland Parliament - last held on 6 April 2021 (next to be held in 2025)
election results: Greenland Parliament - percent of vote by party - IA 38.7%, S 32.2%, N 12.9%, D 9.7%,

A 6.5%; seats by party - IA 12, S 10, N 4, D 3, A 2; composition as of May 2024 - men 20, women 11, percentage women 35%
Greenland members in Danish Parliament - percent of vote by party - NA; seats by party - IA 1, S 1; composition - 2 women

Judicial branch: *highest court(s):* High Court of Greenland (consists of the presiding professional judge and 2 lay assessors); note - appeals beyond the High Court of Greenland can be heard by the Supreme Court (in Copenhagen)
judge selection and term of office: judges appointed by the monarch upon the recommendation of the Judicial Appointments Council, a 6-member independent body of judges and lawyers; judges appointed for life with retirement at age 70
subordinate courts: Court of Greenland; 18 district or magistrates' courts

Political parties: Democrats Party (Demokraatit) or D
Fellowship Party (Atassut) or A
Forward Party (Siumut) or S
Inuit Community (Inuit Ataqatigiit) or IA
Signpost Party (Naleraq) or N (formerly Partii Naleraq)

International organization participation: Arctic Council, ICC, NC, NIB, UPU

Diplomatic representation in the US: *chief of mission:* Kenneth HØEGH, Head of Representation (since 1 August 2021)
chancery: 3200 Whitehaven Street, NW
Washington, DC 20008
telephone: [1] (202) 234-4300
FAX: [1] (202) 328-1470
email address and website:
washington@nanoq.gl
All Greenlandic Representations I GrÃ¸nlands ReprÃ¦sentation (grl-rep.dk);
https://naalakkersuisut.gl/en/Naalakkersuisut/Groenlands-repraesentation-Washington

Note: Greenland also has offices in the Danish consulates in Chicago and New York

Diplomatic representation from the US: *chief of mission:* Consul Monica BLAND (since July 2023)
embassy: Aalisartut Aqqutaa 47
Nuuk 3900
Greenland
telephone: (+299) 384100
email address and website:
USConsulateNuuk@state.gov
Homepage - U.S. Embassy & Consulate in the Kingdom of Denmark (usembassy.gov)

Flag description: two equal horizontal bands of white (top) and red with a large disk slightly to the hoist side of center - the top half of the disk is red, the bottom half is white; the design represents the sun reflecting off a field of ice; the colors are the same as those of the Danish flag and symbolize Greenland's links to the Kingdom of Denmark

National symbol(s): polar bear; national colors: red, white

National anthem: *name:* "Nunarput utoqqarsuanngoravit" (Our Country, Who's Become So Old also translated as You Our Ancient Land)
lyrics/music: Henrik LUND/Jonathan PETERSEN
note: adopted 1916; the government also recognizes "Nuna asiilasooq" as a secondary anthem

National heritage: *total World Heritage Sites:* 3 (2 cultural, 1 natural); note - excerpted from the Denmark entry
selected World Heritage Site locales: Ilulissat Icefjord (n); Kujataa, Norse and Inuit Farming (c); Aasivissuit–Nipisat, Inuit Hunting Ground (c)

ECONOMY

Economic overview: large self-governing Danish territorial economy; preferential EU market access; high-income economy; dependent on Danish financial support, even for whaling and sealing industries; growing tourism; hydropower-fueled but environmentally fragile economy

Real GDP (purchasing power parity): $3.857 billion (2021 est.)
$3.808 billion (2020 est.)
$3.801 billion (2019 est.)
note: data in 2021 dollars
comparison ranking: 192

Real GDP growth rate: 1.29% (2021 est.)
0.19% (2020 est.)
2.83% (2019 est.)
note: annual GDP % growth based on constant local currency
comparison ranking: 159

Real GDP per capita: $68,100 (2021 est.)
$67,600 (2020 est.)
$67,600 (2019 est.)
note: data in 2021 dollars
comparison ranking: 19

GDP (official exchange rate): $3.236 billion (2021 est.)
note: data in current dollars at official exchange rate

Inflation rate (consumer prices): 0.3% (January 2017 est.)
1.2% (January 2016 est.)
comparison ranking: 9

GDP - composition, by sector of origin: *agriculture:* 17.5% (2021 est.)
industry: 16.1% (2021 est.)
services: 62.7% (2021 est.)
note: figures may not total 100% due to non-allocated consumption not captured in sector-reported data
comparison rankings: services 69; industry 165; agriculture 45

GDP - composition, by end use: *household consumption:* 35.8% (2021 est.)
government consumption: 45.1% (2021 est.)
investment in fixed capital: 33.3% (2021 est.)
exports of goods and services: 35.4% (2021 est.)
imports of goods and services: -49.7% (2021 est.)
note: figures may not total 100% due to rounding or gaps in data collection

Agricultural products: sheep, cattle, reindeer, fish, shellfish

Industries: fish processing (mainly shrimp and Greenland halibut), anorthosite and ruby mining, handicrafts, hides and skins, small shipyards

Industrial production growth rate: -10.63% (2021 est.)
note: annual % change in industrial value added based on constant local currency
comparison ranking: 210

Labor force: 26,840 (2015 est.)
comparison ranking: 199

Unemployment rate: 9.1% (2015 est.)
10.3% (2014 est.)
comparison ranking: 158

Population below poverty line: 16.2% (2015 est.)

Gini Index coefficient - distribution of family income: 33.9 (2015 est.)
comparison ranking: 90

Budget: *revenues:* $1.719 billion (2016 est.)
expenditures: $1.594 billion (2016 est.)

Public debt: 13% of GDP (2015 est.)
comparison ranking: 195

Taxes and other revenues: 77.4% (of GDP) (2016 est.)
comparison ranking: 1

Exports: $1.147 billion (2021 est.)
$1.108 billion (2020 est.)
$1.23 billion (2019 est.)
note: GDP expenditure basis - exports of goods and services in current dollars
comparison ranking: 179

Exports - partners: Denmark 49%, China 24%, UK 6%, Japan 5%, Taiwan 3% (2022)
note: top five export partners based on percentage share of exports

Exports - commodities: fish, shellfish, processed crustaceans, precious stones, animal products (2022)
note: top five export commodities based on value in dollars

Imports: $1.609 billion (2021 est.)
$1.441 billion (2020 est.)
$1.533 billion (2019 est.)
note: GDP expenditure basis - imports of goods and services in current dollars
comparison ranking: 183

Imports - partners: Denmark 56%, Sweden 22%, France 10%, Iceland 3%, Canada 3% (2022)
note: top five import partners based on percentage share of imports

Imports - commodities: refined petroleum, aircraft, garments, construction vehicles, plastic products (2022)
note: top five import commodities based on value in dollars

Exchange rates: Danish kroner (DKK) per US dollar -

Exchange rates: 6.89 (2023 est.)
7.076 (2022 est.)
6.287 (2021 est.)
6.542 (2020 est.)
6.669 (2019 est.)

ENERGY

Electricity access: *electrification - total population:* 100% (2022 est.)

Electricity: *installed generating capacity:* 188,000 kW (2022 est.)
consumption: 558.48 million kWh (2022 est.)
transmission/distribution losses: 10 million kWh (2022 est.)
comparison rankings: transmission/distribution losses 16; consumption 173; installed generating capacity 174

Electricity generation sources: *fossil fuels:* 23.4% of total installed capacity (2022 est.)
hydroelectricity: 76.2% of total installed capacity (2022 est.)
biomass and waste: 0.4% of total installed capacity (2022 est.)

Coal: *imports:* 2 metric tons (2022 est.)
proven reserves: 383 million metric tons (2022 est.)

Petroleum: *refined petroleum consumption:* 4,000 bbl/day (2022 est.)

Carbon dioxide emissions: 562,000 metric tonnes of CO2 (2022 est.)
from petroleum and other liquids: 562,000 metric tonnes of CO2 (2022 est.)
comparison ranking: total emissions 188

COMMUNICATIONS

Telephones - fixed lines: *total subscriptions:* 6,000 (2020 est.)
subscriptions per 100 inhabitants: 11 (2020 est.)
comparison ranking: total subscriptions 199

Telephones - mobile cellular: *total subscriptions:* 67,000 (2021 est.)
subscriptions per 100 inhabitants: 118 (2021 est.)
comparison ranking: total subscriptions 201

Telecommunication systems: *general assessment:* adequate domestic and international service provided by satellite, cables, and microwave radio relay; the fundamental telecommunications infrastructure consists of a digital radio link from Nanortalik in south Greenland to Uummannaq in north Greenland; satellites cover north and east Greenland for domestic and foreign telecommunications; a marine cable connects south and west Greenland to the rest of the world, extending from Nuuk and Qaqortoq to Canada and Iceland; a contract has been awarded to build a 5G network in Greenland, initially covering three towns, with 10 towns, including Greenland's capital Nuuk to follow (2022)
domestic: nearly 11 per 100 for fixed-line subscriptions and 118 per 100 for mobile-cellular (2021)
international: country code - 299; landing points for Greenland Connect, Greenland Connect North, Nunavut Undersea Fiber System submarine cables to Greenland, Iceland, and Canada; satellite earth stations - 15 (12 Intelsat, 1 Eutelsat, 2 Americom GE-2 (all Atlantic Ocean)) (2019)

Broadcast media: the Greenland Broadcasting Company provides public radio and TV services throughout the island with a broadcast station and a series of repeaters; a few private local TV and radio stations; Danish public radio rebroadcasts are available (2019)

Internet country code: .gl

Internet users: *total:* 38,920 (2021 est.)
percent of population: 69.5% (2021 est.)
comparison ranking: total 204

Broadband - fixed subscriptions: *total:* 15,649 (2020 est.)
subscriptions per 100 inhabitants: 28 (2020 est.)
comparison ranking: total 173

TRANSPORTATION

National air transport system: *number of registered air carriers:* 1 (2020) (registered in Denmark)
inventory of registered aircraft operated by air carriers: 8 (registered in Denmark)

Civil aircraft registration country code prefix: OY-H

Airports: 25 (2024)
comparison ranking: 129

Heliports: 55 (2024)

Roadways: *note:* although there are short roads in towns, there are no roads between towns; inter-urban transport is either by sea or by air

Merchant marine: *total:* 10 (2023)
by type: other 10
comparison ranking: total 160

Ports: *total ports:* 23 (2024)
large: 0
medium: 0
small: 7
very small: 10
size unknown: 6
ports with oil terminals: 5
key ports: Aasiaat, Ilulissat (Jakobshavn), Kusanartoq, Nuuk, Paamuit (Frederikshab), Qeqertarsuaq, Sisimiut

MILITARY AND SECURITY

Military and security forces: no regular military forces

Military - note: the Danish military's Joint Arctic Command in Nuuk is responsible for coordinating Denmark's defense of Greenland

GRENADA

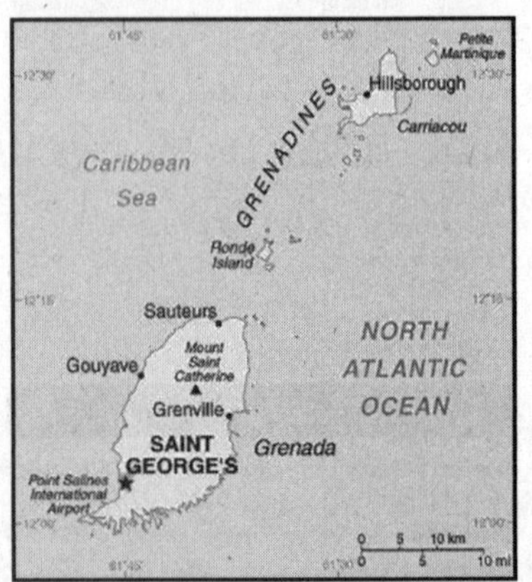

INTRODUCTION

Background: The indigenous Carib people inhabited Grenada when Christopher COLUMBUS landed on the island in 1498, but it remained uncolonized for more than a century. The French settled Grenada in the 17th century, established sugar estates, and imported large numbers of African slaves. Britain took the island in 1762 and vigorously expanded sugar production. In the 19th century, cacao eventually surpassed sugar as the main export crop; in the 20th century, nutmeg became the leading export. In 1967, Britain gave Grenada autonomy over its internal affairs. Full independence was attained in 1974, making Grenada one of the smallest independent countries in the Western Hemisphere. In 1979, a leftist New Jewel Movement seized power under Maurice BISHOP, ushering in the Grenada Revolution. On 19 October 1983, factions within the revolutionary government overthrew and killed BISHOP and members of his party. Six days later, US forces and those of six other Caribbean nations intervened, quickly capturing the ringleaders and their hundreds of Cuban advisers. Rule of law was restored, and democratic elections were reinstituted the following year and have continued since.

GEOGRAPHY

Location: Caribbean, island between the Caribbean Sea and Atlantic Ocean, north of Trinidad and Tobago

Geographic coordinates: 12 07 N, 61 40 W

Map references: Central America and the Caribbean

Area: *total:* 344 sq km
land: 344 sq km
water: 0 sq km
comparison ranking: total 207

Area - comparative: twice the size of Washington, DC

Land boundaries: *total:* 0 km

Coastline: 121 km

Maritime claims: *territorial sea:* 12 nm
exclusive economic zone: 200 nm

Climate: tropical; tempered by northeast trade winds

Terrain: volcanic in origin with central mountains

Elevation: *highest point:* Mount Saint Catherine 840 m
lowest point: Caribbean Sea 0 m

Natural resources: timber, tropical fruit

Land use: *agricultural land:* 32.3% (2018 est.)
arable land: 8.8% (2018 est.)
permanent crops: 20.6% (2018 est.)
permanent pasture: 2.9% (2018 est.)
forest: 50% (2018 est.)
other: 17.7% (2018 est.)

Irrigated land: 20 sq km (2012)

Population distribution: approximately one-third of the population is found in the capital of St. George's; the island's population is concentrated along the coast

Natural hazards: lies on edge of hurricane belt; hurricane season lasts from June to November
volcanism: Mount Saint Catherine (840 m) lies on the island of Grenada; Kick 'em Jenny, an active submarine volcano (seamount) on the Caribbean Sea floor, lies about 8 km north of the island of Grenada; these two volcanoes are at the southern end of the volcanic island arc of the Lesser Antilles that extends up to the Netherlands dependency of Saba in the north

Geography - note: the administration of the islands of the Grenadines group is divided between Saint Vincent and the Grenadines and Grenada

PEOPLE AND SOCIETY

Population: *total:* 114,621
male: 58,168
female: 56,453 (2024 est.)
comparison rankings: female 190; male 189; total 190

Nationality: *noun:* Grenadian(s)
adjective: Grenadian

Ethnic groups: African descent 82.4%, mixed 13.3%, East Indian 2.2%, other 1.3%, unspecified 0.9% (2011 est.)

Languages: English (official), French patois

Religions: Protestant 49.2% (includes Pentecostal 17.2%, Seventh Day Adventist 13.2%, Anglican 8.5%, Baptist 3.2%, Church of God 2.4%, Evangelical 1.9%, Methodist 1.6%, other 1.2%), Roman Catholic 36%, Jehovah's Witness 1.2%, Rastafarian 1.2%, other 5.5%, none 5.7%, unspecified 1.3% (2011 est.)

Age structure: *0-14 years:* 21.9% (male 13,095/female 12,003)
15-64 years: 65.3% (male 38,129/female 36,726)
65 years and over: 12.8% (2024 est.) (male 6,944/female 7,724)

Dependency ratios: *total dependency ratio:* 51.3
youth dependency ratio: 36.4
elderly dependency ratio: 14.9
potential support ratio: 6.7 (2021 est.)

Median age: *total:* 35.4 years (2024 est.)
male: 35.2 years
female: 35.7 years
comparison ranking: total 97

Population growth rate: 0.27% (2024 est.)
comparison ranking: 169

Birth rate: 13.3 births/1,000 population (2024 est.)
comparison ranking: 128

Death rate: 8.4 deaths/1,000 population (2024 est.)
comparison ranking: 76

Net migration rate: -2.2 migrant(s)/1,000 population (2024 est.)
comparison ranking: 171

Population distribution: approximately one-third of the population is found in the capital of St. George's; the island's population is concentrated along the coast

Urbanization: *urban population:* 37.1% of total population (2023)
rate of urbanization: 0.86% annual rate of change (2020-25 est.)

Major urban areas - population: 39,000 SAINT GEORGE'S (capital) (2018)

Sex ratio: *at birth:* 1.1 male(s)/female
0-14 years: 1.09 male(s)/female
15-64 years: 1.04 male(s)/female
65 years and over: 0.9 male(s)/female
total population: 1.03 male(s)/female (2024 est.)

Maternal mortality ratio: 21 deaths/100,000 live births (2020 est.)
comparison ranking: 121

Infant mortality rate: *total:* 9 deaths/1,000 live births (2024 est.)
male: 8.6 deaths/1,000 live births
female: 9.5 deaths/1,000 live births
comparison ranking: total 139

Life expectancy at birth: *total population:* 76.3 years (2024 est.)
male: 73.7 years
female: 79.1 years
comparison ranking: total population 112

Total fertility rate: 1.9 children born/woman (2024 est.)
comparison ranking: 118

Gross reproduction rate: 0.91 (2024 est.)

Drinking water source: *improved: total:* 96.8% of population
unimproved: total: 3.2% of population (2017 est.)

Current health expenditure: 5.8% of GDP (2020)

Physician density: 1.44 physicians/1,000 population (2018)

Hospital bed density: 3.6 beds/1,000 population (2017)

Sanitation facility access: *improved:*
total: 93.7% of population
unimproved:
total: 6.3% of population (2020 est.)

Obesity - adult prevalence rate: 21.3% (2016)
comparison ranking: 91

Alcohol consumption per capita: *total:* 8.62 liters of pure alcohol (2019 est.)
beer: 3.54 liters of pure alcohol (2019 est.)
wine: 0.56 liters of pure alcohol (2019 est.)
spirits: 4.21 liters of pure alcohol (2019 est.)
other alcohols: 0.31 liters of pure alcohol (2019 est.)
comparison ranking: total 37

Currently married women (ages 15-49): 41.3% (2023 est.)

Education expenditures: 3.6% of GDP (2018 est.)
comparison ranking: 140

Literacy: *definition:* age 15 and over can read and write
total population: 98.6%
male: 98.6%
female: 98.6% (2014 est.)

School life expectancy (primary to tertiary education): *total:* 19 years
male: 18 years
female: 19 years (2018)

ENVIRONMENT

Environment - current issues: deforestation causing habitat destruction and species loss; coastal erosion and contamination; pollution and sedimentation; inadequate solid waste management

Environment - international agreements: *party to:* Biodiversity, Climate Change, Climate Change-Kyoto Protocol, Climate Change-Paris Agreement, Comprehensive Nuclear Test Ban, Desertification, Endangered Species, Law of the Sea, Ozone Layer Protection, Ship Pollution, Wetlands, Whaling
signed, but not ratified: none of the selected agreements

Climate: tropical; tempered by northeast trade winds

Urbanization: *urban population:* 37.1% of total population (2023)
rate of urbanization: 0.86% annual rate of change (2020-25 est.)

Revenue from forest resources: 0% of GDP (2018 est.)
comparison ranking: 161

Revenue from coal: 0% of GDP (2018 est.)
comparison ranking: 74

Air pollutants: *particulate matter emissions:* 10.08 micrograms per cubic meter (2019 est.)
carbon dioxide emissions: 0.27 megatons (2016 est.)
methane emissions: 2.04 megatons (2020 est.)

Waste and recycling: *municipal solid waste generated annually:* 29,536 tons (2012 est.)

Total water withdrawal: *municipal:* 10 million cubic meters (2020 est.)
industrial: 0 cubic meters (2017 est.)
agricultural: 2.1 million cubic meters (2017 est.)

Total renewable water resources: 200 million cubic meters (2020 est.)

GOVERNMENT

Country name: *conventional long form:* none
conventional short form: Grenada
etymology: derivation of the name remains obscure; some sources attribute the designation to Spanish influence (most likely named for the Spanish city of Granada), with subsequent French and English interpretations resulting in the present-day Grenada; in Spanish "granada" means "pomegranate"

Government type: parliamentary democracy under a constitutional monarchy; a Commonwealth realm

Capital: *name:* Saint George's
geographic coordinates: 12 03 N, 61 45 W
time difference: UTC-4 (1 hour ahead of Washington, DC, during Standard Time)
etymology: the 1763 Treaty of Paris transferred possession of Grenada from France to Great Britain; the new administration renamed Ville de Fort Royal (Fort Royal Town) to Saint George's Town, after the patron saint of England; eventually the name became simply Saint George's

Administrative divisions: 6 parishes and 1 dependency*; Carriacou and Petite Martinique*, Saint Andrew, Saint David, Saint George, Saint John, Saint Mark, Saint Patrick

Independence: 7 February 1974 (from the UK)

National holiday: Independence Day, 7 February (1974)

Legal system: common law based on English model

Constitution: *history:* previous 1967; latest presented 19 December 1973, effective 7 February 1974, suspended 1979 following a revolution but restored in 1983
amendments: proposed by either house of Parliament; passage requires two-thirds majority vote by the membership in both houses and assent of the governor general; passage of amendments to constitutional sections, such as personal rights and freedoms, the structure, authorities, and procedures of the branches of government, the delimitation of electoral constituencies, or the procedure for amending the constitution, also requires two-thirds majority approval in a referendum; amended 1991, 1992

International law organization participation: has not submitted an ICJ jurisdiction declaration; accepts ICCt jurisdiction

Citizenship: *citizenship by birth:* yes
citizenship by descent only: yes
dual citizenship recognized: yes
residency requirement for naturalization: 7 years for persons from a non-Caribbean state and 4 years for a person from a Caribbean state

Suffrage: 18 years of age; universal

Executive branch: *chief of state:* King CHARLES III (since 8 September 2022); represented by Governor General Cecile LA GRENADE (since 7 May 2013)
head of government: Prime Minister Dickon MITCHELL (since 24 June 2022)
cabinet: Cabinet appointed by the governor general on the advice of the prime minister
elections/appointments: the monarchy is hereditary; governor general appointed by the monarch; following legislative elections, the leader of the majority party or majority coalition usually appointed prime minister by the governor general

Legislative branch: *description:* bicameral Parliament consists of:
Senate (13 seats; members appointed by the governor general - 10 on the advice of the prime minister and 3 on the advice of the leader of the opposition party; members serve 5-year terms)
House of Representatives (15 seats; members directly elected in single-seat constituencies by simple majority vote to serve 5-year terms)
elections: Senate - last appointments on 3 August 2022 (next to be held no later than 2027)
House of Representatives - last held on 23 June 2022 (next to be held no later than 2027)
election results: Senate - percent by party - NA; seats by party - NDC 7, NNP 3, independent 3; composition - men 11, women 5, percentage women 31.3%
House of Representatives - percent of vote by party - NDC 51.8%; NNP 47.8%; other 0.4%; seats by party - NDC 9; NNP 6; composition - men 9, women 4, percentage women 30.8%; note - total Parliament percentage women 31%

Judicial branch: *highest court(s):* regionally, the Eastern Caribbean Supreme Court (ECSC) is the superior court of the Organization of Eastern Caribbean States; the ECSC - headquartered on St. Lucia - consists of the Court of Appeal - headed by the chief justice and 4 judges - and the High Court with 18 judges; the Court of Appeal is itinerant, traveling to member states on a schedule to hear appeals from the High Court and subordinate courts; High Court judges reside in the member states, with 2 in Grenada; appeals beyond the ECSC in civil and criminal matters are heard by the Judicial Committee of the Privy Council (in London)
judge selection and term of office: chief justice of Eastern Caribbean Supreme Court appointed by Her Majesty, Queen ELIZABETH II; other justices and judges appointed by the Judicial and Legal Services Commission, and independent body of judicial officials; Court of Appeal justices appointed for life with mandatory retirement at age 65; High Court judges appointed for life with mandatory retirement at age 62
subordinate courts: magistrates' courts; Court of Magisterial Appeals

Political parties: National Democratic Congress or NDC
New National Party or NNP

International organization participation: ACP, ACS, AOSIS, CARIFORUM, CARIBCAN, Caricom, CBI, CDB, CELAC, CSME, ECCU, EPA, FAO, G-77, IBRD, ICAO, ICCt (signatory), ICRM, IDA, IFAD, IFC, IFRCS, ILO, IMF, IMO, Interpol, IOC, ITU, ITUC, LAES, MIGA, NAM, OAS, OECS, OPANAL, OPCW, Petrocaribe, UN, UNCTAD, UNESCO, UNIDO, UPU, WHO, WIPO, WTO

Diplomatic representation in the US: *chief of mission:* Ambassador Tarlie FRANCIS (since 15 September 2023)
chancery: 1701 New Hampshire Avenue NW, Washington, DC 20009
telephone: [1] (202) 265-2561
FAX: [1] (202) 265-2468
email address and website:
embassy@grenadaembassyusa.org
https://grenadaembassyusa.org/
consulate(s) general: Miami, New York

Diplomatic representation from the US: *chief of mission:* the US does not have an official embassy in Grenada; the US Ambassador to Barbados, Ambassador Richard F. NYHUS, is accredited to Grenada
embassy: Lance-aux-Epines, Saint George's
mailing address: 3180 Grenada Place, Washington DC 20521-3180
telephone: [1] (473) 444-1173
FAX: [1] (473) 444-4820
email address and website:
StgeorgesACS@state.gov
https://bb.usembassy.gov/embassy/grenada/

Flag description: a rectangle divided diagonally into yellow triangles (top and bottom) and green triangles (hoist side and outer side), with a red border around the flag; there are seven yellow, five-pointed stars with three centered in the top red border, three centered in the bottom red border, and one on a red disk superimposed at the center of the flag; there is also a symbolic nutmeg pod on the hoist-side triangle (Grenada is a leading nutmeg producer); the seven stars stand for the seven administrative divisions, with the central star denoting the capital, St. George's; yellow represents the sun and the warmth of the people, green stands for vegetation and agriculture, and red symbolizes harmony, unity, and courage

National symbol(s): Grenada dove, bougainvillea flower; national colors: red, yellow, green

National anthem: *name:* "Hail Grenada"
lyrics/music: Irva Merle BAPTISTE/Louis Arnold MASANTO
note: adopted 1974; as a Commonwealth country, in addition to the national anthem, "God Save the King" serves as the royal anthem (see United Kingdom)

ECONOMY

Economic overview: small OECS service-based economy; large tourism, construction, transportation, and education sectors; major spice exporter; shrinking but still high public debt; vulnerable to hurricanes; emerging blue economy incentives

Real GDP (purchasing power parity): $2.008 billion (2023 est.)
$1.916 billion (2022 est.)
$1.785 billion (2021 est.)
note: data in 2021 dollars
comparison ranking: 201

Real GDP growth rate: 4.81% (2023 est.)
7.32% (2022 est.)
4.69% (2021 est.)
note: annual GDP % growth based on constant local currency
comparison ranking: 61

Real GDP per capita: $15,900 (2023 est.)
$15,300 (2022 est.)
$14,300 (2021 est.)
note: data in 2021 dollars
comparison ranking: 118

GDP (official exchange rate): $1.32 billion (2023 est.)
note: data in current dollars at official exchange rate

Inflation rate (consumer prices): 2.7% (2023 est.)
2.58% (2022 est.)
1.22% (2021 est.)
note: annual % change based on consumer prices
comparison ranking: 56

Credit ratings: Standard & Poors rating: SD (2013)
note: The year refers to the year in which the current credit rating was first obtained.

GDP - composition, by sector of origin: *agriculture:* 3.3% (2023 est.)
industry: 14.9% (2023 est.)
services: 64.3% (2023 est.)
note: figures may not total 100% due to non-allocated consumption not captured in sector-reported data
comparison rankings: services 61; industry 172; agriculture 136

GDP - composition, by end use: *household consumption:* 63% (2017 est.)
government consumption: 12% (2017 est.)
investment in fixed capital: 20% (2017 est.)
investment in inventories: -0.1% (2017 est.)
exports of goods and services: 60% (2017 est.)
imports of goods and services: -55% (2017 est.)

Agricultural products: coconuts, sugarcane, eggs, bananas, vegetables, fruits, plantains, root vegetables, grapefruits, avocados (2022)
note: top ten agricultural products based on tonnage

Industries: food and beverages, textiles, light assembly operations, tourism, construction, education, call-center operations

Industrial production growth rate: -4.07% (2023 est.)
note: annual % change in industrial value added based on constant local currency
comparison ranking: 196

Labor force: 55,270 (2017 est.)
comparison ranking: 189

Unemployment rate: 24% (2017 est.)
28.2% (2016 est.)
comparison ranking: 203

Population below poverty line: 25% (2018 est.)

Gini Index coefficient - distribution of family income: 43.8 (2018 est.)
comparison ranking: 26

Household income or consumption by percentage share: *lowest 10%:* 2.1% (2018 est.)
highest 10%: 33.7% (2018 est.)

Remittances: 3.74% of GDP (2023 est.)
5.74% of GDP (2022 est.)
5.53% of GDP (2021 est.)
note: personal transfers and compensation between resident and non-resident individuals/households/entities

Budget: *revenues:* $288.404 million (2017 est.)
expenditures: $222.475 million (2017 est.)
note: central government revenues and expenses (excluding grants/extrabudgetary units/social security funds) converted to US dollars at average official exchange rate for year indicated

Public debt: 70.4% of GDP (2017 est.)
comparison ranking: 55

Taxes and other revenues: 25.8% (of GDP) (2017 est.)
comparison ranking: 41

Current account balance: -$184.237 million (2023 est.)
-$135.727 million (2022 est.)
-$162.344 million (2021 est.)
note: balance of payments - net trade and primary/secondary income in current dollars
comparison ranking: 109

Exports: $899.153 million (2023 est.)
$712.263 million (2022 est.)
$537.898 million (2021 est.)
note: balance of payments - exports of goods and services in current dollars
comparison ranking: 183

Exports - partners: US 33%, Antigua and Barbuda 10%, India 4%, Saint Vincent and the Grenadines 4%, France 3% (2022)
note: top five export partners based on percentage share of exports

Exports - commodities: nutmeg/cardamom, frozen fruits and nuts, fish, other fruits, toilet paper (2022)
note: top five export commodities based on value in dollars

Imports: $1.021 billion (2023 est.)
$791.232 million (2022 est.)
$621.896 million (2021 est.)
note: balance of payments - imports of goods and services in current dollars
comparison ranking: 192

Imports - partners: US 37%, Trinidad and Tobago 11%, Cayman Islands 11%, China 5%, UK 3% (2022)
note: top five import partners based on percentage share of imports

Imports - commodities: refined petroleum, poultry, plastic products, wheat, cars (2022)
note: top five import commodities based on value in dollars

Reserves of foreign exchange and gold: $404.13 million (2023 est.)
$371.767 million (2022 est.)
$348.259 million (2021 est.)
note: holdings of gold (year-end prices)/foreign exchange/special drawing rights in current dollars
comparison ranking: 176

Debt - external: $458.369 million (2022 est.)
note: present value of external debt in current US dollars
comparison ranking: 91

Exchange rates: East Caribbean dollars (XCD) per US dollar -

Exchange rates: 2.7 (2023 est.)
2.7 (2022 est.)
2.7 (2021 est.)
2.7 (2020 est.)
2.7 (2019 est.)

ENERGY

Electricity access: *electrification - total population:* 94.2% (2022 est.)

Electricity: *installed generating capacity:* 56,000 kW (2022 est.)
consumption: 224.749 million kWh (2022 est.)
transmission/distribution losses: 15.877 million kWh (2022 est.)
comparison rankings: transmission/distribution losses 23; consumption 189; installed generating capacity 191

Electricity generation sources: *fossil fuels:* 97.8% of total installed capacity (2022 est.)
solar: 2.2% of total installed capacity (2022 est.)
wind: 0.1% of total installed capacity (2022 est.)

Coal: *exports:* (2022 est.) less than 1 metric ton
imports: 0.7 metric tons (2022 est.)

Petroleum: *refined petroleum consumption:* 2,000 bbl/day (2022 est.)

Carbon dioxide emissions: 364,000 metric tonnes of CO2 (2022 est.)
from petroleum and other liquids: 364,000 metric tonnes of CO2 (2022 est.)
comparison ranking: total emissions 193

Energy consumption per capita: 40.666 million Btu/person (2022 est.)
comparison ranking: 101

COMMUNICATIONS

Telephones - fixed lines: *total subscriptions:* 26,000 (2021 est.)
subscriptions per 100 inhabitants: 21 (2021 est.)
comparison ranking: total subscriptions 169

Telephones - mobile cellular: *total subscriptions:* 101,000 (2021 est.)
subscriptions per 100 inhabitants: 81 (2021 est.)
comparison ranking: total subscriptions 193

Telecommunication systems: *general assessment:* the telecom sector has seen a decline in subscriber numbers (particularly for prepaid mobile services the mainstay of short term visitors) and revenue; fixed and mobile broadband services are two areas that have benefited from the crisis as employees and students have resorted to working from home; one area of the telecom market that is not prepared for growth is 5G mobile; governments, regulators, and even the mobile network operators have shown that they have not been investing in 5G opportunities at the present time; network expansion and enhancements remain concentrated around improving LTE coverage (2021)
domestic: 21 per 100 for fixed-line and 81 per 100 for mobile-cellular (2021)
international: country code - 1-473; landing points for the ECFS, Southern Caribbean Fiber and CARCIP submarine cables with links to 13 Caribbean islands extending from the British Virgin Islands to Trinidad & Tobago including Puerto Rico and Barbados; SHF radiotelephone links to Trinidad and Tobago and Saint Vincent; VHF and UHF radio links to Trinidad (2019)

Broadcast media: multiple publicly and privately owned television and radio stations; Grenada Information Service (GIS) is government-owned and provides television and radio services; the Grenada Broadcasting Network, jointly owned by the government and the Caribbean Communications Network of Trinidad and Tobago, operates a TV station and 2 radio stations; Meaningful Television (MTV) broadcasts island-wide and is part of a locally-owned media house, Moving Target Company, that also includes an FM radio station and a weekly newspaper; multi-channel cable TV subscription service is provided by Columbus Communications Grenada (FLOW GRENADA) and is available island wide; approximately 25 private radio stations also broadcast throughout the country (2019)

Internet country code: .gd

Internet users: *total:* 93,600 (2021 est.)
percent of population: 78% (2021 est.)
comparison ranking: total 189

Broadband - fixed subscriptions: *total:* 32,000 (2020 est.)
subscriptions per 100 inhabitants: 28 (2020 est.)
comparison ranking: total 150

TRANSPORTATION

Civil aircraft registration country code prefix: J3

Airports: 2 (2024)
comparison ranking: 204

Roadways: *total:* 1,127 km
paved: 902 km
unpaved: 225 km (2017)
comparison ranking: total 184

Merchant marine: *total:* 6 (2023)
by type: general cargo 3, other 3
comparison ranking: total 166

Ports: *total ports:* 1 (2024)
large: 0
medium: 0
small: 1
very small: 0
ports with oil terminals: 1
key ports: St. George's

MILITARY AND SECURITY

Military and security forces: no regular military forces; the Royal Grenada Police Force (under the Ministry of National Security) includes a Coast Guard and a paramilitary Special Services Unit (2024)

Military - note: Grenada joined the Caribbean Regional Security System (RSS) in 1985; RSS signatories (Antigua and Barbuda, Barbados, Dominica, Guyana, Saint Kitts and Nevis, Saint Lucia, and Saint Vincent and the Grenadines) agreed to prepare contingency plans and assist one another, on request, in national emergencies, prevention of smuggling, search and rescue, immigration control, fishery protection, customs and excise control, maritime policing duties, protection of offshore installations, pollution control, national and other disasters, and threats to national security (2024)

TRANSNATIONAL ISSUES

Illicit drugs: a transit point for cocaine and marijuana destined for North America, Europe, and elsewhere in the Caribbean; some local demand for cocaine and some use of synthetic drugs

GUAM

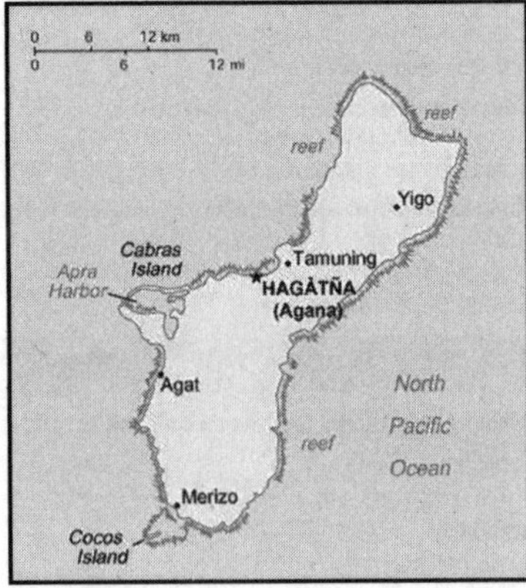

INTRODUCTION

Background: Guam was settled by Austronesian people around 1500 B.C. These people became the indigenous Chamorro and were influenced by later migrations, including the Micronesians in the first millennium A.D., and island Southeast Asians around 900. Society was stratified, with higher classes living along the coast and lower classes living inland. Spanish explorer Ferdinand MAGELLAN was the first European to see Guam in 1521, and Spain claimed the island in 1565 because it served as a refueling stop for ships between Mexico and the Philippines. Spain formally colonized Guam in 1668. Spain's brutal repression of the Chamorro, along with new diseases and intermittent warfare, reduced the indigenous population from more than 100,000 to less than 5,000 by the 1700s. Spain tried to repopulate the island by forcing people from nearby islands to settle on Guam and preventing them from escaping.

Guam became a hub for whalers and traders in the western Pacific in the early 1800s. During the 1898 Spanish-American War, the US Navy occupied Guam and set up a military administration. The US Navy opposed local control of government despite repeated petitions from the Chamorro. Japan invaded Guam in 1941 and instituted a repressive regime. During the US recapture of Guam in 1944, the island's two largest villages were destroyed. After World War II, political pressure from local Chamorro leaders led to Guam being established as an unincorporated organized US territory in 1950, with US citizenship granted to all Chamorro. In a referendum in 1982, more than 75% of voters chose closer relations with the US over independence, although no change in status was made because of disagreements on the future right of Chamorro self-determination. The US military holds about 29% of Guam's land and stations several thousand troops on the island. The installations are some of the most strategically important US bases in the Pacific; they also constitute the island's most important source of income and economic stability.

GEOGRAPHY

Location: Oceania, island in the North Pacific Ocean, about three-quarters of the way from Hawaii to the Philippines

Geographic coordinates: 13 28 N, 144 47 E

Map references: Oceania

Area: *total:* 544 sq km
land: 544 sq km
water: 0 sq km
comparison ranking: total 194

Area - comparative: three times the size of Washington, DC

Land boundaries: *total:* 0 km

Coastline: 125.5 km

Maritime claims: *territorial sea:* 12 nm
exclusive economic zone: 200 nm

Climate: tropical marine; generally warm and humid, moderated by northeast trade winds; dry season (January to June), rainy season (July to December); little seasonal temperature variation

Terrain: volcanic origin, surrounded by coral reefs; relatively flat coralline limestone plateau (source of most fresh water), with steep coastal cliffs and narrow coastal plains in north, low hills in center, mountains in south

Elevation: *highest point:* Mount Lamlam 406 m
lowest point: Pacific Ocean 0 m

Natural resources: aquatic wildlife (supporting tourism), fishing (largely undeveloped)

Land use: *agricultural land:* 33.4% (2018 est.)
arable land: 1.9% (2018 est.)
permanent crops: 16.7% (2018 est.)
permanent pasture: 14.8% (2018 est.)
forest: 47.9% (2018 est.)
other: 18.7% (2018 est.)

Irrigated land: 2 sq km (2012)

Population distribution: no large cities exist on the island, though large villages (municipalities) attract much of the population; the largest of these is Dededo

Natural hazards: frequent squalls during rainy season; relatively rare but potentially destructive typhoons (June to December)

Geography - note: largest and southernmost island in the Mariana Islands archipelago and the largest island in Micronesia; strategic location in western North Pacific Ocean

PEOPLE AND SOCIETY

Population: *total:* 169,532
male: 87,345
female: 82,187 (2024 est.)
comparison rankings: female 186; male 185; total 185

Nationality: *noun:* Guamanian(s) (US citizens)
adjective: Guamanian

Ethnic groups: Native Hawaiian and other Pacific Islander 46.1% (Chamorro 32.8%, Chuukese 6.7%, Palauan 1.4%, Pohnpeian 1.4%, Yapese 1%, other Native Hawaiian and other Pacific Islander 2.8%), Asian 35.5% (Filipino 29.1%, Korean 2.2%, Japanese 1.4%, Chinese (except Taiwanese) 1.3%, other Asian 1.5%), White 6.8%, African descent or African-American 0.9%, Indigenous 0.1%, other 0.6%, mixed 10% (2020 est.)

Languages: English 43.3%, Filipino 24.9%, Chamorro 16%, other Pacific Island languages 9.4%, Asian languages 6.5% (2020 est.)

Religions: Christian (predominantly Roman Catholic) 94.2%, folk religions 1.5%, Buddhist 1.1%, other 1.6%, unaffiliated 1.7% (2020 est.)

Age structure: *0-14 years:* 26.4% (male 23,139/female 21,632)
15-64 years: 62.7% (male 55,591/female 50,741)
65 years and over: 10.9% (2024 est.) (male 8,615/female 9,814)

Dependency ratios: *total dependency ratio:* 60.7
youth dependency ratio: 42.3
elderly dependency ratio: 18.4
potential support ratio: 5.4 (2021 est.)

Median age: *total:* 30.3 years (2024 est.)
male: 29.6 years
female: 31.1 years
comparison ranking: total 137

Population growth rate: 0.11% (2024 est.)
comparison ranking: 184

Birth rate: 18.1 births/1,000 population (2024 est.)
comparison ranking: 78

Death rate: 6.1 deaths/1,000 population (2024 est.)
comparison ranking: 150

Net migration rate: -10.9 migrant(s)/1,000 population (2024 est.)
comparison ranking: 224

Population distribution: no large cities exist on the island, though large villages (municipalities) attract much of the population; the largest of these is Dededo

Urbanization: *urban population:* 95.2% of total population (2022)
rate of urbanization: 0.84% annual rate of change (2020-25 est.)

Major urban areas - population: 147,000 HAGATNA (capital) (2018)

Sex ratio: *at birth:* 1.07 male(s)/female
0-14 years: 1.07 male(s)/female
15-64 years: 1.1 male(s)/female
65 years and over: 0.88 male(s)/female
total population: 1.06 male(s)/female (2024 est.)

Infant mortality rate: *total:* 10.9 deaths/1,000 live births (2024 est.)
male: 11 deaths/1,000 live births
female: 10.9 deaths/1,000 live births
comparison ranking: total 124

Life expectancy at birth: *total population:* 78 years (2024 est.)
male: 75.6 years
female: 80.5 years
comparison ranking: total population 83

Total fertility rate: children born/woman (2024 est.)
comparison ranking: 59

Gross reproduction rate: (2024 est.)

Drinking water source: *improved:*

total: 99.7% of population
unimproved:
total: 0.3% of population (2020 est.)

Sanitation facility access: *improved: urban:* 89.8% of population (2015 est.)
rural: 89.8% of population (2015 est.)
total: 89.8% of population (2015 est.)
unimproved: urban: 10.2% of population (2015 est.)
rural: 10.2% of population (2015 est.)
total: 10.2% of population (2015 est.)

Currently married women (ages 15-49): 37% (2023 est.)

ENVIRONMENT

Environment - current issues: fresh water scarcity; reef damage; inadequate sewage treatment; extermination of native bird populations by the rapid proliferation of the brown tree snake, an exotic, invasive species

Climate: tropical marine; generally warm and humid, moderated by northeast trade winds; dry season (January to June), rainy season (July to December); little seasonal temperature variation

Urbanization: *urban population:* 95.2% of total population (2022)
rate of urbanization: 0.84% annual rate of change (2020-25 est.)

Revenue from forest resources: 0% of GDP (2018 est.)
comparison ranking: 200

Revenue from coal: 0% of GDP (2018 est.)
comparison ranking: 102

Waste and recycling: *municipal solid waste generated annually:* 141,500 tons (2012 est.)
municipal solid waste recycled annually: 25,258 tons (2011 est.)
percent of municipal solid waste recycled: 17.9% (2011 est.)

GOVERNMENT

Country name: *conventional long form:* none
conventional short form: Guam
local long form: none
local short form: Guahan
abbreviation: GU
etymology: the native Chamorro name for the island "Guahan" (meaning "we have" or "ours") was changed to Guam in the 1898 Treaty of Paris, whereby Spain relinquished Guam, Cuba, Puerto Rico, and the Philippines to the US

Government type: unincorporated organized territory of the US with local self-government; republican form of territorial government with separate executive, legislative, and judicial branches

Dependency status: unincorporated organized territory of the US with policy relations between Guam and the Federal Government under the jurisdiction of the Office of Insular Affairs, US Department of the Interior, Washington, DC

Capital: *name:* Hagatna (Agana)
geographic coordinates: 13 28 N, 144 44 E
time difference: UTC+10 (15 hours ahead of Washington, DC, during Standard Time)
etymology: the name is derived from the Chamoru word "haga," meaning "blood", and may refer to the bloodlines of the various families that established the original settlement

Administrative divisions: none (territory of the US)

Independence: none (territory of the US)

National holiday: Discovery Day (or Magellan Day), first Monday in March (1521)

Legal system: common law modeled on US system; US federal laws apply

Constitution: *history:* effective 1 July 1950 (Guam Act of 1950 serves as a constitution)
amendments: amended many times, last in 2015

Citizenship: see United States

Suffrage: 18 years of age; universal; note - Guamanians are US citizens but do not vote in US presidential elections

Executive branch: *chief of state:* President Joseph R. BIDEN Jr. (since 20 January 2021)
head of government: Governor Lourdes LEON GUERRERO (since 7 January 2019)
cabinet: Cabinet appointed by the governor with the consent of the Legislature
elections/appointments: president and vice president indirectly elected on the same ballot by an Electoral College of 'electors' chosen from each state to serve a 4-year term (eligible for a second term); under the US Constitution, residents of unincorporated territories, such as Guam, do not vote in elections for US president and vice president; however, they may vote in Democratic and Republican presidential primary elections; governor and lieutenant governor elected on the same ballot by absolute majority vote in 2 rounds if needed for a 4-year term (eligible for 2 consecutive terms); gubernatorial election last held on 8 November 2022 (next to be held in November 2026)
election results:
2022: Lourdes LEON GUERRERO reelected governor; percent of vote - Lourdes LEON GUERRERO (Democratic Party) 55%, Felix CAMACHO (Republican Party) 44%; Josh TENORIO (Democratic Party) elected lieutenant governor
2018: Lourdes LEON GUERRERO elected governor; percent of vote - Lourdes LEON GUERRERO (Democratic Party) 50.7%, Ray TENORIO (Republican Party) 26.4%; Josh TENORIO (Democratic Party) elected lieutenant governor

Legislative branch: *description:* unicameral Legislature of Guam or Liheslaturan Guahan (15 seats; members elected in a single countrywide constituency by simple majority vote to serve 2-year terms)
Guam directly elects 1 member by simple majority vote to serve a 2-year term as the delegate to the US House of Representatives; note - the delegate can vote when serving on a committee and when the House meets as the Committee of the Whole House, but not when legislation is submitted for a "full floor" House vote
elections: Guam Legislature - last held on 8 November 2022 (next to be held on 5 November 2024)
delegate to the US House of Representatives - last held on 8 November 2022 (next to be held on 5 November 2024)
election results: Guam Legislature - percent of vote by party - NA; seats by party - Democratic Party 9, Republican Party 6; composition - men 9, women 6, percent of women 40%
Guam delegate to the US House of Representatives - Democratic Party 1 (man)

Judicial branch: *highest court(s):* Supreme Court of Guam (consists of 3 justices); note - appeals beyond the Supreme Court of Guam are referred to the US Supreme Court
judge selection and term of office: justices appointed by the governor and confirmed by the Guam legislature; justices appointed for life subject to retention election every 10 years
subordinate courts: Superior Court of Guam - includes several divisions; US Federal District Court for the District of Guam (a US territorial court; appeals beyond this court are heard before the US Court of Appeals for the Ninth Circuit)

Political parties: Democratic Party
Republican Party

International organization participation: AOSIS (observer), IOC, PIF (observer), SPC, UPU

Diplomatic representation in the US: none (territory of the US)

Diplomatic representation from the US: *embassy:* none (territory of the US)

Flag description: territorial flag is dark blue with a narrow red border on all four sides; centered is a red-bordered, pointed, vertical ellipse containing a beach scene, a proa or outrigger canoe with sail, and a palm tree with the word GUAM superimposed in bold red letters; the proa is sailing in Agana Bay with the promontory of Puntan Dos Amantes, near the capital, in the background; the shape of the central emblem is that of a Chamorro sling stone, used as a weapon for defense or hunting; blue represents the sea and red the blood shed in the struggle against oppression
note: the US flag is the national flag

National symbol(s): coconut tree; national colors: deep blue, red

National anthem: *name:* "Fanohge Chamoru" (Stand Ye Guamanians)
lyrics/music: Ramon Manalisay SABLAN [English], Lagrimas UNTALAN [Chamoru]/Ramon Manalisay SABLAN
note: adopted 1919; the local anthem is also known as "Guam Hymn"; as a territory of the United States, "The StarSpangled Banner," which generally follows the playing of "Stand Ye Guamanians," is official (see United States)

ECONOMY

Economic overview: small Pacific island US territorial economy; upper income, tourism-based economy; hard-hit by COVID-19 disruptions; relaunched many industries via vaccination tourism; domestic economy relies on multiple military bases; environmentally fragile economy

Real GDP (purchasing power parity): $5.793 billion (2016 est.)
$5.697 billion (2015 est.)
$5.531 billion (2014 est.)
comparison ranking: 178

Real GDP growth rate: 5.1% (2022 est.)

2.06% (2021 est.)
-10.52% (2020 est.)
note: annual GDP % growth based on constant local currency
comparison ranking: 52

Real GDP per capita: $35,600 (2016 est.)
$35,200 (2015 est.)
$34,400 (2014 est.)
comparison ranking: 69

GDP (official exchange rate): $6.91 billion (2022 est.)
note: data in current dollars at official exchange rate

Inflation rate (consumer prices): 1% (2017 est.)
0% (2016 est.)
comparison ranking: 19

GDP - composition, by end use: *household consumption:* 59.9% (2022 est.)
government consumption: 55% (2016 est.)
investment in fixed capital: 20.6% (2016 est.)
exports of goods and services: 7.9% (2022 est.)
imports of goods and services: -64% (2022 est.)
note: figures may not total 100% due to rounding or gaps in data collection

Agricultural products: fruits, copra, vegetables; eggs, pork, poultry, beef

Industries: national defense, tourism, construction, transshipment services, concrete products, printing and publishing, food processing, textiles

Industrial production growth rate: 4.3% (2014 est.)
note: annual % change in industrial value added based on constant local currency
comparison ranking: 68

Labor force: 80,000 (2023 est.)
note: number of people ages 15 or older who are employed or seeking work
comparison ranking: 186

Unemployment rate: 5.42% (2023 est.)
5.53% (2022 est.)
6% (2021 est.)
note: % of labor force seeking employment
comparison ranking: 104

Youth unemployment rate (ages 15-24): *total:* 12.9% (2023 est.)
male: 12.6% (2023 est.)
female: 13.2% (2023 est.)
note: % of labor force ages 15-24 seeking employment
comparison ranking: total 107

Average household expenditures: *on food:* 34.6% of household expenditures (2021 est.)
on alcohol and tobacco: 1.3% of household expenditures (2021 est.)

Budget: *revenues:* $1.24 billion (2016 est.)
expenditures: $1.299 billion (2016 est.)

Public debt: 22.1% of GDP (2016 est.)
comparison ranking: 181

Taxes and other revenues: 21.4% (of GDP) (2016 est.)
comparison ranking: 74

Exports: $186 million (2021 est.)
$371 million (2020 est.)
$1.403 billion (2019 est.)
note: GDP expenditure basis - exports of goods and services in current dollars
comparison ranking: 204

Exports - partners: Singapore 30%, Taiwan 20%, South Korea 14%, Philippines 12%, Hong Kong 8% (2022)
note: top five export partners based on percentage share of exports

Exports - commodities: refined petroleum, scrap iron, scrap copper, trunks and cases, aircraft parts (2022)
note: top five export commodities based on value in dollars

Imports: $3.667 billion (2021 est.)
$3.383 billion (2020 est.)
$3.552 billion (2019 est.)
note: GDP expenditure basis - imports of goods and services in current dollars
comparison ranking: 160

Imports - partners: South Korea 37%, Singapore 35%, Japan 12%, Taiwan 3%, Hong Kong 3% (2022)
note: top five import partners based on percentage share of imports

Imports - commodities: refined petroleum, cars, raw iron bars, electric generating sets, trunks and cases (2022)
note: top five import commodities based on value in dollars

Exchange rates: the US dollar is used

ENERGY

Electricity access: *electrification - total population:* 100% (2022 est.)

Electricity: *installed generating capacity:* 525,000 kW (2022 est.)
consumption: 1.662 billion kWh (2022 est.)
transmission/distribution losses: 90.023 million kWh (2022 est.)
comparison rankings: transmission/distribution losses 45; consumption 151; installed generating capacity 151

Electricity generation sources: *fossil fuels:* 94.9% of total installed capacity (2022 est.)
solar: 5.1% of total installed capacity (2022 est.)
wind: 0.1% of total installed capacity (2022 est.)

Petroleum: *refined petroleum consumption:* 12,000 bbl/day (2022 est.)
crude oil estimated reserves: Data represented includes both Guam and Northern Mariana Islands

Carbon dioxide emissions: 1.83 million metric tonnes of CO2 (2022 est.)
from petroleum and other liquids: 1.83 million metric tonnes of CO2 (2022 est.)
comparison ranking: total emissions 161

Energy consumption per capita: 150.555 million Btu/person (2019 est.)
comparison ranking: 27

COMMUNICATIONS

Telephones - fixed lines: *total subscriptions:* 70,000 (2021 est.)
subscriptions per 100 inhabitants: 41 (2021 est.)
comparison ranking: total subscriptions 146

Telephones - mobile cellular: *total subscriptions:* 98,000 (2009 est.)
subscriptions per 100 inhabitants: 62 (2009 est.)
comparison ranking: total subscriptions 195

Telecommunication systems: *general assessment:* Guam's telecommunications companies provide important services that allow other businesses on island to operate; Guam plays a larger, and growing role, in global telecommunications infrastructure, the submarine fiber optic cables that land on Guam benefit island residents and the local economy; in the Asia-Pacific region the demand for 4G, 5G, and broadband access is rapidly increasing; the 11 submarine cables that currently land on Guam, connecting the U.S. to the Asia-Pacific region, are some of the more than 400 cables that are the backbone of global telecommunications, providing nearly all of the world's internet and phone service; as of January 2024, one of the world's most dominant companies will be landing two new subsea cables on Guam; in May 2024 a global arm of a leading telecommunications and technology company, announced its plans to develop a regional network hub in Guam by establishing a new dedicated point-of-presence (PoP) in Piti at the carrier-neutral GNC iX data center; this PoP will serve growing connectivity demand in the region and will be a key connection point for new cable systems including the Echo cable and central Pacific Connect cable that are being constructed to provide additional low latency network reliability and redundancy throughout Asia and between Asia, Australia, and the U.S. (2021)
domestic: fixed-line subscriptions 41 per 100 and 62 per 100 mobile-cellular subscriptions in 2004 (2021)
international: country code - 1-671; major landing points for Atisa, HANTRU1, HK-G, JGA-N, JGA-S, PIPE-1, SEA-US, SxS, Tata TGN-Pacific, AJC, GOKI, AAG, AJC and Mariana-Guam Cable submarine cables between Asia, Australia, and the US (Guam is a transpacific communications hub for major carriers linking the US and Asia); satellite earth stations - 2 Intelsat (Pacific Ocean) (2019)

Broadcast media: about a dozen TV channels, including digital channels; multi-channel cable TV services are available; roughly 20 radio stations

Internet country code: .gu

Internet users: *total:* 136,850 (2021 est.)
percent of population: 80.5% (2021 est.)
comparison ranking: total 184

Broadband - fixed subscriptions: *total:* 3,000 (2020 est.)
subscriptions per 100 inhabitants: 2 (2020 est.)
comparison ranking: total 193

TRANSPORTATION

Civil aircraft registration country code prefix: N

Airports: 3 (2024)
comparison ranking: 185

Heliports: 2 (2024)

Roadways: *total:* 1,045 km (2008)
comparison ranking: total 186

Merchant marine: *total:* 3 (2023)
by type: other 3
comparison ranking: total 173

Ports: *total ports:* 1 (2024)
large: 0
medium: 1
small: 0
very small: 0
ports with oil terminals: 1
key ports: Apra Harbor

MILITARY AND SECURITY

Military and security forces: Guam Police Department (GPD); Guam (US) National Guard

Military - note: defense is the responsibility of the US; the US military maintains over 6,000 personnel on Guam, including an air base, an air wing, and a naval installation command (2024)

GUATEMALA

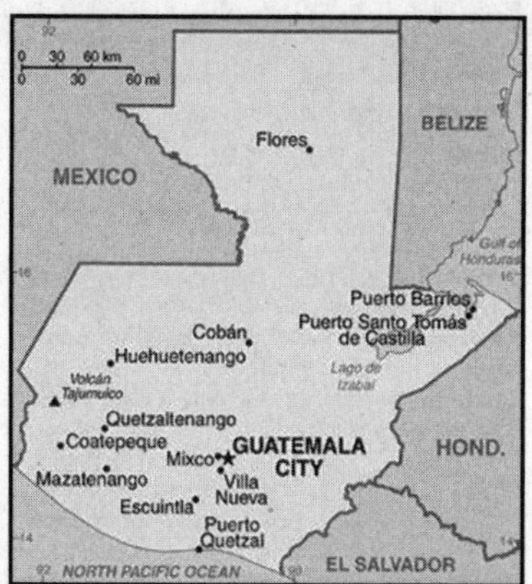

INTRODUCTION

Background: The Maya civilization flourished in Guatemala and surrounding regions during the first millennium A.D. After almost three centuries as a Spanish colony, Guatemala won its independence in 1821. During the second half of the 20th century, it experienced a variety of military and civilian governments, as well as a 36-year guerrilla war. In 1996, the government signed a peace agreement formally ending the internal conflict.

GEOGRAPHY

Location: Central America, bordering the North Pacific Ocean, between El Salvador and Mexico, and bordering the Gulf of Honduras (Caribbean Sea) between Honduras and Belize

Geographic coordinates: 15 30 N, 90 15 W

Map references: Central America and the Caribbean

Area: *total:* 108,889 sq km
land: 107,159 sq km
water: 1,730 sq km
comparison ranking: total 107

Area - comparative: slightly smaller than Pennsylvania

Land boundaries: *total:* 1,667 km
border countries (4): Belize 266 km; El Salvador 199 km; Honduras 244 km; Mexico 958 km

Coastline: 400 km

Maritime claims: *territorial sea:* 12 nm
exclusive economic zone: 200 nm
continental shelf: 200-m depth or to the depth of exploitation

Climate: tropical; hot, humid in lowlands; cooler in highlands

Terrain: *two east-west trending mountain chains divide the country into three regions:* the mountainous highlands, the Pacific coast south of mountains, and the vast northern Peten lowlands

Elevation: *highest point:* Volcan Tajumulco (highest point in Central America) 4,220 m
lowest point: Pacific Ocean 0 m
mean elevation: 759 m

Natural resources: petroleum, nickel, rare woods, fish, chicle, hydropower

Land use: *agricultural land:* 41.2% (2018 est.)
arable land: 14.2% (2018 est.)
permanent crops: 8.8% (2018 est.)
permanent pasture: 18.2% (2018 est.)
forest: 33.6% (2018 est.)
other: 25.2% (2018 est.)

Irrigated land: 3,375 sq km (2012)

Major lakes (area sq km): *fresh water lake(s):* Lago de Izabal - 590 sq km

Population distribution: the vast majority of the populace resides in the southern half of the country, particularly in the mountainous regions; more than half of the population lives in rural areas

Natural hazards: numerous volcanoes in mountains, with occasional violent earthquakes; Caribbean coast extremely susceptible to hurricanes and other tropical storms
volcanism: significant volcanic activity in the Sierra Madre range; Santa Maria (3,772 m) has been deemed a Decade Volcano by the International Association of Volcanology and Chemistry of the Earth's Interior, worthy of study due to its explosive history and close proximity to human populations; Pacaya (2,552 m), which erupted in May 2010 causing an ashfall on Guatemala City and prompting evacuations, is one of the country's most active volcanoes with frequent eruptions since 1965; other historically active volcanoes include Acatenango, Almolonga, Atitlan, Fuego, and Tacana; see note 2 under "Geography - note"

Geography - note: *note 1:* despite having both eastern and western coastlines (Caribbean Sea and Pacific Ocean respectively), there are no natural harbors on the west coast
note 2: Guatemala is one of the countries along the Ring of Fire, a belt of active volcanoes and earthquake epicenters bordering the Pacific Ocean; up to 90% of the world's earthquakes and some 75% of the world's volcanoes occur within the Ring of Fire

PEOPLE AND SOCIETY

Population: *total:* 18,255,216
male: 9,050,684
female: 9,204,532 (2024 est.)
comparison rankings: female 70; male 68; total 69

Nationality: *noun:* Guatemalan(s)
adjective: Guatemalan

Ethnic groups: Mestizo (mixed Indigenous-Spanish - in local Spanish called Ladino) 56%, Maya 41.7%, Xinca (Indigenous, non-Maya) 1.8%, African descent 0.2%, Garifuna (mixed West and Central African, Island Carib, and Arawak) 0.1%, foreign 0.2% (2018 est.)

Languages: Spanish (official) 69.9%, Maya languages 29.7% (Q'eqchi' 8.3%, K'iche 7.8%, Mam 4.4%, Kaqchikel 3%, Q'anjob'al 1.2%, Poqomchi' 1%, other 4%), other 0.4% (includes Xinca and Garifuna) (2018 est.)
major-language sample(s):
La Libreta Informativa del Mundo, la fuente indispensable de información básica. (Spanish)
note: the 2003 Law of National Languages officially recognized 23 indigenous languages, including 21 Maya languages, Xinca, and Garifuna

Religions: Evangelical 45.7%, Roman Catholic 42.4%, none 11%, unspecified 0.9% (2023 est.)

Demographic profile: Guatemala is a predominantly poor country that struggles in several areas of health and development, including infant, child, and maternal mortality, malnutrition, literacy, and contraceptive awareness and use. The country's large indigenous population is disproportionately affected. Guatemala is the most populous country in Central America and has the highest fertility rate in Latin America. It also has the highest population growth rate in Latin America, which is likely to continue because of its large reproductive-age population and high birth rate. Almost half of Guatemala's population is under age 19, making it the youngest population in Latin America. Guatemala's total fertility rate has slowly declined during the last few decades due in part to limited government-funded health programs. However, the birth rate is still more close to three children per woman and is markedly higher among its rural and indigenous populations.
Guatemalans have a history of emigrating legally and illegally to Mexico, the United States, and Canada because of a lack of economic opportunity, political instability, and natural disasters. Emigration, primarily to the United States, escalated during the 1960 to 1996 civil war and accelerated after a peace agreement was signed. Thousands of Guatemalans who fled to Mexico returned after the war, but labor migration to southern Mexico continues.

Age structure: *0-14 years:* 31.5% (male 2,925,079/female 2,819,927)
15-64 years: 63.2% (male 5,688,500/female 5,839,958)
65 years and over: 5.4% (2024 est.) (male 437,105/female 544,647)

Dependency ratios: *total dependency ratio:* 60.9
youth dependency ratio: 53
elderly dependency ratio: 7.9
potential support ratio: 12.7 (2021 est.)

Median age: *total:* 24.8 years (2024 est.)
male: 24.2 years
female: 25.4 years
comparison ranking: total 174

Population growth rate: 1.49% (2024 est.)
comparison ranking: 64

Birth rate: 21.4 births/1,000 population (2024 est.)
comparison ranking: 59

Death rate: 4.9 deaths/1,000 population (2024 est.)
comparison ranking: 200

Net migration rate: -1.6 migrant(s)/1,000 population (2024 est.)
comparison ranking: 161

Population distribution: the vast majority of the populace resides in the southern half of the country, particularly in the mountainous regions; more than half of the population lives in rural areas

Urbanization: *urban population:* 53.1% of total population (2023)
rate of urbanization: 2.59% annual rate of change (2020-25 est.)

Major urban areas - population: 3.095 million GUATEMALA CITY (capital) (2023)

Sex ratio: *at birth:* 1.05 male(s)/female
0-14 years: 1.04 male(s)/female
15-64 years: 0.97 male(s)/female
65 years and over: 0.8 male(s)/female
total population: 0.98 male(s)/female (2024 est.)

Mother's mean age at first birth: 20.6 years (2014/15 est.)
note: data represents median age at first birth among women 25-49

Maternal mortality ratio: 96 deaths/100,000 live births (2020 est.)
comparison ranking: 70

Infant mortality rate: *total:* 25 deaths/1,000 live births (2024 est.)
male: 28.1 deaths/1,000 live births
female: 21.7 deaths/1,000 live births
comparison ranking: total 59

Life expectancy at birth: *total population:* 73.5 years (2024 est.)
male: 71.5 years
female: 75.6 years
comparison ranking: total population 149

Total fertility rate: 2.52 children born/woman (2024 est.)
comparison ranking: 70

Gross reproduction rate: 1.23 (2024 est.)

Contraceptive prevalence rate: 60.6% (2014/15)

Drinking water source: *improved: urban:* 97.9% of population
rural: 92.2% of population
total: 95% of population
unimproved: urban: 2.1% of population
rural: 8% of population
total: 5% of population (2020 est.)

Current health expenditure: 6.5% of GDP (2020)

Physician density: 1.24 physicians/1,000 population (2020)

Hospital bed density: 0.4 beds/1,000 population (2017)

Sanitation facility access: *improved: urban:* 90.4% of population
rural: 66.3% of population
total: 78.8% of population
unimproved: urban: 9.6% of population
rural: 33.7% of population
total: 21.2% of population (2020 est.)

Obesity - adult prevalence rate: 21.2% (2016)
comparison ranking: 92

Alcohol consumption per capita: *total:* 1.63 liters of pure alcohol (2019 est.)
beer: 0.9 liters of pure alcohol (2019 est.)
wine: 0.05 liters of pure alcohol (2019 est.)
spirits: 0.68 liters of pure alcohol (2019 est.)
other alcohols: 0.01 liters of pure alcohol (2019 est.)
comparison ranking: total 135

Tobacco use: *total:* 10.9% (2020 est.)
male: 20.1% (2020 est.)
female: 1.6% (2020 est.)
comparison ranking: total 131

Children under the age of 5 years underweight: 14.4% (2021/22)
comparison ranking: 36

Currently married women (ages 15-49): 57.2% (2023 est.)

Education expenditures: 3.1 % of GDP (2021 est.)
comparison ranking: 158

Literacy: *definition:* age 15 and over can read and write
total population: 83.3%
male: 87.7%
female: 79.3% (2021)

School life expectancy (primary to tertiary education): *total:* 11 years
male: 11 years
female: 10 years (2019)

ENVIRONMENT

Environment - current issues: deforestation in the Peten rainforest; soil erosion; water pollution

Environment - international agreements: *party to:* Antarctic Treaty, Biodiversity, Climate Change, Climate Change-Kyoto Protocol, Climate Change-Paris Agreement, Comprehensive Nuclear Test Ban, Desertification, Endangered Species, Environmental Modification, Hazardous Wastes, Law of the Sea, Marine Dumping-London Convention, Marine Dumping-London Protocol, Nuclear Test Ban, Ozone Layer Protection, Ship Pollution, Tropical Timber 2006, Wetlands
signed, but not ratified: none of the selected agreements

Climate: tropical; hot, humid in lowlands; cooler in highlands

Urbanization: *urban population:* 53.1% of total population (2023)
rate of urbanization: 2.59% annual rate of change (2020-25 est.)

Revenue from forest resources: 0.78% of GDP (2018 est.)
comparison ranking: 59

Revenue from coal: 0% of GDP (2018 est.)
comparison ranking: 91

Air pollutants: *particulate matter emissions:* 20.75 micrograms per cubic meter (2019 est.)
carbon dioxide emissions: 16.78 megatons (2016 est.)
methane emissions: 10.7 megatons (2020 est.)

Waste and recycling: *municipal solid waste generated annually:* 2,756,741 tons (2015 est.)

Major lakes (area sq km): *fresh water lake(s):* Lago de Izabal - 590 sq km

Total water withdrawal: *municipal:* 840 million cubic meters (2020 est.)
industrial: 600 million cubic meters (2020 est.)
agricultural: 1.89 billion cubic meters (2020 est.)

Total renewable water resources: 127.91 billion cubic meters (2020 est.)

GOVERNMENT

Country name: *conventional long form:* Republic of Guatemala
conventional short form: Guatemala
local long form: República de Guatemala
local short form: Guatemala
etymology: the Spanish conquistadors used many native Americans as allies in their conquest of Guatemala; the site of their first capital (established in 1524), a former Maya settlement, was called "Quauhtemallan" by their Nahuatl-speaking Mexican allies, a name that means "land of trees" or "forested land", but which the Spanish pronounced "Guatemala"; the Spanish applied that name to a re-founded capital city three years later and eventually it became the name of the country

Government type: presidential republic

Capital: *name:* Guatemala City
geographic coordinates: 14 37 N, 90 31 W
time difference: UTC-6 (1 hour behind Washington, DC, during Standard Time)
etymology: the Spanish conquistadors used many native Americans as allies in their conquest of Guatemala; the site of their first capital (established in 1524), a former Maya settlement, was called "Quauhtemallan" by their Nahuatl-speaking Mexican allies, a name that means "land of trees" or "forested land", but which the Spanish pronounced "Guatemala"; the Spanish applied that name to a re-founded capital city three years later and eventually it became the name of the country

Administrative divisions: 22 departments (departamentos, singular - departamento); Alta Verapaz, Baja Verapaz, Chimaltenango, Chiquimula, El Progreso, Escuintla, Guatemala, Huehuetenango, Izabal, Jalapa, Jutiapa, Peten, Quetzaltenango, Quiche, Retalhuleu, Sacatepequez, San Marcos, Santa Rosa, Solola, Suchitepequez, Totonicapan, Zacapa

Independence: 15 September 1821 (from Spain)

National holiday: Independence Day, 15 September (1821)

Legal system: civil law system; judicial review of legislative acts

Constitution: *history:* several previous; latest adopted 31 May 1985, effective 14 January 1986; suspended and reinstated in 1994
amendments: proposed by the president of the republic, by agreement of 10 or more deputies of Congress, by the Constitutional Court, or by public petition of at least 5,000 citizens; passage requires at least two-thirds majority vote by the Congress membership and approval by public referendum, referred to as "popular consultation"; constitutional articles such as national sovereignty, the republican form of government, limitations on those seeking the presidency, or presidential tenure cannot be amended; amended 1993

International law organization participation: has not submitted an ICJ jurisdiction declaration; accepts ICCt jurisdiction

Citizenship: *citizenship by birth:* yes
citizenship by descent only: yes
dual citizenship recognized: yes
residency requirement for naturalization: 5 years with no absences of six consecutive months or longer or absences totaling more than a year

Suffrage: 18 years of age; universal; note - active duty members of the armed forces and police by law cannot vote and are restricted to their barracks on election day

Executive branch: *chief of state:* President Bernardo ARÉVALO de León (since 15 January 2024)
head of government: President Bernardo ARÉVALO de León (since 15 January 2024)
cabinet: Council of Ministers appointed by the president
elections/appointments: president and vice president directly elected on the same ballot by absolute

majority popular vote in 2 rounds if needed for a 4-year term (not eligible for consecutive terms); election last held on 25 June 2023 with a runoff on 20 August 2023 (next to be held in June 2027)
election results:
2023: Bernardo ARÉVALO de León elected president in second round; percent of vote in first round - Sandra TORRES (UNE) 21%; Bernardo ARÉVALO de León (SEMILLA) 15.6%, Manuel CONDE Orellana (VAMOS) 10.4%; Armando CASTILLO Alvarado (VIVA) 9.6%, other 43.4%; percent of vote in second round - Bernardo ARÉVALO de León 60.9%, Sandra TORRES 39.1%
2019: Alejandro GIAMMATTEI elected president; percent of vote in first round - Sandra TORRES (UNE) 25.5%, Alejandro GIAMMATTEI (VAMOS) 14%, Edmond MULET (PHG) 11.2%, Thelma CABRERA (MLP) 10.4%, Roberto ARZU (PAN-PODEMOS) 6.1%, other 32.8%; percent of vote in second round - Alejandro GIAMMATTEI 58%, Sandra TORRES 42%
note: the president is both chief of state and head of government

Legislative branch: *description:* unicameral Congress of the Republic or Congreso de la Republica (160 seats; 128 members directly elected in multi-seat constituencies in the country's 22 departments and 32 directly elected in a single nationwide constituency by closed party-list proportional representation vote, using the D'Hondt method; members serve 4-year terms)
elections: last held on 25 June 2023 (next to be held in June 2027)
election results: percent of vote by party - NA; seats by party - VAMOS 39, UNE 28, SEMILLA 23, CABAL 18, Valor-Unionist 12, VIVA 11, TODOS 6, VOS 4, BIEN 4, CREO 3, PPN 3, Victoria 3, Blue 2, Elephant 2, Change 1, Winaq- URNG 1; composition - men 128, women 32, percentage women 20%

Judicial branch: *highest court(s):* Supreme Court of Justice or Corte Suprema de Justicia (consists of 13 magistrates, including the court president and organized into 3 chambers); note - the court president also supervises trial judges countrywide; note - the Constitutional Court or Corte de Constitucionalidad of Guatemala resides outside the country's judicial system; its sole purpose is the interpretation of the constitution and to see that the laws and regulations are not superior to the constitution (consists of 5 titular magistrates and 5 substitute magistrates)
judge selection and term of office: Supreme Court magistrates elected by the Congress of the Republic from candidates proposed by the Postulation Committee, an independent body of deans of the country's university law schools, representatives of the country's law associations, and representatives of the Courts of Appeal; magistrates elected for concurrent, renewable 5-year terms; Constitutional Court judges - 1 elected by the Congress of the Republic, 1 by the Supreme Court, 1 by the president of the republic, 1 by the (public) University of San Carlos, and 1 by the Assembly of the College of Attorneys and Notaries; judges elected for renewable, consecutive 5-year terms; the presidency of the court rotates among the magistrates for a single 1-year term
subordinate courts: Appellate Courts of Accounts, Contentious Administrative Tribunal, courts of appeal, first instance courts, child and adolescence courts, minor or peace courts

Political parties: Bienestar Nacional or BIEN
Blue Party (Partido Azul) or Blue

CABAL

Cambio
Citizen Prosperity or PC
Commitment, Renewal, and Order or CREO
Elephant Community (Comunidad Elefante) or Elephant
Everyone Together for Guatemala or TODOS
Guatemalan National Revolutionary Unity or URNG-MAIZ or URNG
Humanist Party of Guatemala or PHG
Movement for the Liberation of Peoples or MLP
Movimiento Semilla or SEMILLA
National Advancement Party or PAN
National Convergence Front or FCN-NACION
National Unity for Hope or UNE
Nationalist Change Union or UCN (dissolved 16 December 2021)
Nosotros or PPN

PODEMOS

Political Movement Winaq or Winaq

TODOS

Value or VALOR
Vamos por una Guatemala Diferente or VAMOS
Victory or VICTORIA
Vision with Values or VIVA
Will, Opportunity and Solidarity (Voluntad, Oportunidad y Solidaridad) or VOS

International organization participation: ACS, BCIE, CACM, CD, CELAC, EITI (compliant country), FAO, G-24, G-77, IADB, IAEA, IBRD, ICAO, ICC (national committees), ICCt (signatory), ICRM, IDA, IFAD, IFC, IFRCS, IHO, ILO, IMF, IMO, Interpol, IOC, IOM, IPU, ISO (correspondent), ITSO, ITU, ITUC (NGOs), LAES, LAIA (observer), MIGA, MINUSTAH, MONUSCO, NAM, OAS, OPANAL, OPCW, Pacific Alliance (observer), PCA, Petrocaribe, SICA, UN, UNCTAD, UNESCO, UNHCR, UNIDO, UNIFIL, Union Latina, UNISFA, UNITAR, UNMISS, UNOCI, UNOOSA, UNWTO, UPU, WCO, WFTU (NGOs), WHO, WIPO, WMO, WTO

Diplomatic representation in the US: *chief of mission:* Ambassador Hugo Eduardo BETETA (since 17 June 2024)
chancery: 2220 R Street NW, Washington, DC 20008
telephone: [1] (202) 745-4953
FAX: [1] (202) 745-1908
email address and website:
embestadosunidos@minex.gob.gt
https://estadosunidos.minex.gob.gt/home/home.aspx
consulate(s) general: Atlanta, Chicago, Columbus (OH), Denver, Houston, Los Angeles, Miami, Nashville (TN), New York, Oklahoma City, Omaha (NE), Philadelphia, Phoenix, Providence (RI), Raleigh (NC), Rockville (MD), San Francisco, Seattle
consulate(s): Dallas, Del Rio (TX), Lake Worth (FL), McAllen (TX), Riverhead (NY), San Bernardino (CA), Tucson (AZ)

Diplomatic representation from the US: *chief of mission:* Ambassador Tobin BRADLEY (since 12 February 2024)
embassy: Avenida Reforma 7-01, Zone 10, Guatemala City
mailing address: 3190 Guatemala Place, Washington DC 20521-3190
telephone: [502] 2326-4000
FAX: [502] 2326-4654
email address and website:
AmCitsGuatemala@state.gov
https://gt.usembassy.gov/

Flag description: three equal vertical bands of light blue (hoist side), white, and light blue, with the coat of arms centered in the white band; the coat of arms includes a green and red quetzal (the national bird) representing liberty and a scroll bearing the inscription LIBERTAD 15 DE SEPTIEMBRE DE 1821 (the original date of independence from Spain) - all superimposed on a pair of crossed rifles signifying Guatemala's willingness to defend itself and a pair of crossed swords representing honor - and framed by a laurel wreath symbolizing victory; the blue bands represent the Pacific Ocean and Caribbean Sea; the white band denotes peace and purity
note: one of only two national flags featuring a firearm, the other is Mozambique

National symbol(s): quetzal (bird); national colors: blue, white

National anthem: *name:* "Himno Nacional de Guatemala" (National Anthem of Guatemala)
lyrics/music: Jose Joaquin PALMA/Rafael Alvarez OVALLE
note: adopted 1897, modified lyrics adopted 1934; Cuban poet Jose Joaquin PALMA anonymously submitted lyrics to a public contest calling for a national anthem; his authorship was not discovered until 1911

National heritage: *total World Heritage Sites:* 4 (3 cultural, 1 mixed)
selected World Heritage Site locales: Antigua Guatemala (c); Tikal National Park (m); Archaeological Park and Ruins of Quirigua (c); National Archaeological Park Tak'alik Ab'aj (c)

ECONOMY

Economic overview: developing Central American economy; steady economic growth fueled by remittances; high poverty and income inequality; limited government services, lack of employment opportunities, and frequent natural disasters impede human development efforts and drive emigration

Real GDP (purchasing power parity): $223.183 billion (2023 est.)
$215.668 billion (2022 est.)
$207.138 billion (2021 est.)
note: data in 2021 dollars
comparison ranking: 72

Real GDP growth rate: 3.48% (2023 est.)
4.12% (2022 est.)
8% (2021 est.)
note: annual GDP % growth based on constant local currency
comparison ranking: 92

Real GDP per capita: $12,700 (2023 est.)
$12,400 (2022 est.)
$12,100 (2021 est.)
note: data in 2021 dollars
comparison ranking: 135

GDP (official exchange rate): $102.05 billion (2023 est.)
note: data in current dollars at official exchange rate

Inflation rate (consumer prices): 6.21% (2023 est.)
6.89% (2022 est.)
4.26% (2021 est.)
note: annual % change based on consumer prices
comparison ranking: 131

Credit ratings: Fitch rating: BB- (2020)

Moody's rating: Ba1 (2010)

Standard & Poors rating: BB- (2017)
note: The year refers to the year in which the current credit rating was first obtained.

GDP - composition, by sector of origin: *agriculture:* 9.2% (2023 est.)
industry: 22.2% (2023 est.)
services: 62.4% (2023 est.)
note: figures may not total 100% due to non-allocated consumption not captured in sector-reported data
comparison rankings: services 71; industry 124; agriculture 81

GDP - composition, by end use: *household consumption:* 87.8% (2023 est.)
government consumption: 11.6% (2023 est.)
investment in fixed capital: 16.6% (2023 est.)
investment in inventories: -0.2% (2023 est.)
exports of goods and services: 17.2% (2023 est.)
imports of goods and services: -32.9% (2023 est.)
note: figures may not total 100% due to rounding or gaps in data collection

Agricultural products: sugarcane, bananas, oil palm fruit, maize, cantaloupes/melons, potatoes, milk, tomatoes, chicken, pineapples (2022)
note: top ten agricultural products based on tonnage

Industries: sugar, textiles and clothing, furniture, chemicals, petroleum, metals, rubber, tourism

Industrial production growth rate: 1.91% (2023 est.)
note: annual % change in industrial value added based on constant local currency
comparison ranking: 118

Labor force: 7.258 million (2023 est.)
note: number of people ages 15 or older who are employed or seeking work
comparison ranking: 67

Unemployment rate: 2.71% (2023 est.)
3.05% (2022 est.)
2.17% (2021 est.)
note: % of labor force seeking employment
comparison ranking: 34

Youth unemployment rate (ages 15-24): *total:* 5.9% (2023 est.)
male: 4.1% (2023 est.)
female: 9.6% (2023 est.)
note: % of labor force ages 15-24 seeking employment
comparison ranking: total 169

Population below poverty line: 59.3% (2014 est.)
note: % of population with income below national poverty line

Gini Index coefficient - distribution of family income: 48.3 (2014 est.)
note: index (0-100) of income distribution; higher values represent greater inequality
comparison ranking: 14

Average household expenditures: *on food:* 34.4% of household expenditures (2022 est.)
on alcohol and tobacco: 1.3% of household expenditures (2022 est.)

Household income or consumption by percentage share: *lowest 10%:* 1.7% (2014 est.)
highest 10%: 38.1% (2014 est.)
note: % share of income accruing to lowest and highest 10% of population

Remittances: 19.46% of GDP (2023 est.)
19.16% of GDP (2022 est.)
17.9% of GDP (2021 est.)
note: personal transfers and compensation between resident and non-resident individuals/households/entities

Budget: *revenues:* $15.09 billion (2022 est.)
expenditures: $15.376 billion (2022 est.)
note: central government revenues (excluding grants) and expenses converted to US dollars at average official exchange rate for year indicated

Public debt: 31.56% of GDP (2020 est.)
note: central government debt as a % of GDP
comparison ranking: 165

Taxes and other revenues: 11.9% (of GDP) (2022 est.)
note: central government tax revenue as a % of GDP
comparison ranking: 167

Current account balance: $3.281 billion (2023 est.)
$1.197 billion (2022 est.)
$1.89 billion (2021 est.)
note: balance of payments - net trade and primary/secondary income in current dollars
comparison ranking: 41

Exports: $17.308 billion (2023 est.)
$18.141 billion (2022 est.)
$15.246 billion (2021 est.)
note: balance of payments - exports of goods and services in current dollars
comparison ranking: 95

Exports - partners: US 32%, El Salvador 12%, Honduras 10%, Nicaragua 6%, Mexico 4% (2022)
note: top five export partners based on percentage share of exports

Exports - commodities: garments, coffee, bananas, palm oil, raw sugar (2022)
note: top five export commodities based on value in dollars

Imports: $33.041 billion (2023 est.)
$33.939 billion (2022 est.)
$27.343 billion (2021 est.)
note: balance of payments - imports of goods and services in current dollars
comparison ranking: 76

Imports - partners: US 34%, China 18%, Mexico 9%, El Salvador 4%, Costa Rica 3% (2022)
note: top five import partners based on percentage share of imports

Imports - commodities: refined petroleum, video displays, paper, plastic products, cars (2022)
note: top five import commodities based on value in dollars

Reserves of foreign exchange and gold: $21.311 billion (2023 est.)
$20.415 billion (2022 est.)
$20.935 billion (2021 est.)
note: holdings of gold (year-end prices)/foreign exchange/special drawing rights in current dollars
comparison ranking: 71

Debt - external: $10.336 billion (2022 est.)
note: present value of external debt in current US dollars
comparison ranking: 37

Exchange rates: quetzales (GTQ) per US dollar -

Exchange rates: 7.832 (2023 est.)
7.748 (2022 est.)
7.734 (2021 est.)
7.722 (2020 est.)
7.697 (2019 est.)

ENERGY

Electricity access: *electrification - total population:* 99.1% (2022 est.)
electrification - urban areas: 97.7%
electrification - rural areas: 98.2%

Electricity: *installed generating capacity:* 5.21 million kW (2022 est.)
consumption: 11.387 billion kWh (2022 est.)
exports: 1.116 billion kWh (2022 est.)
imports: 1.141 billion kWh (2022 est.)
transmission/distribution losses: 1.781 billion kWh (2022 est.)
comparison rankings: transmission/distribution losses 121; imports 74; exports 67; consumption 96; installed generating capacity 88

Electricity generation sources: *fossil fuels:* 32.6% of total installed capacity (2022 est.)
solar: 1.8% of total installed capacity (2022 est.)
wind: 2.6% of total installed capacity (2022 est.)
hydroelectricity: 38.6% of total installed capacity (2022 est.)
geothermal: 2.5% of total installed capacity (2022 est.)
biomass and waste: 22% of total installed capacity (2022 est.)

Coal: *consumption:* 1.296 million metric tons (2022 est.)
exports: 15.3 metric tons (2022 est.)
imports: 1.304 million metric tons (2022 est.)

Petroleum: *total petroleum production:* 6,000 bbl/day (2023 est.)
refined petroleum consumption: 115,000 bbl/day (2022 est.)
crude oil estimated reserves: 86.11 million barrels (2021 est.)

Natural gas: *production:* 3.276 million cubic meters (2022 est.)
consumption: 2.986 million cubic meters (2022 est.)

Carbon dioxide emissions: 18.056 million metric tonnes of CO_2 (2022 est.)
from coal and metallurgical coke: 2.941 million metric tonnes of CO_2 (2022 est.)
from petroleum and other liquids: 15.109 million metric tonnes of CO_2 (2022 est.)
from consumed natural gas: 6,000 metric tonnes of CO_2 (2022 est.)
comparison ranking: total emissions 89

Energy consumption per capita: 16.807 million Btu/person (2022 est.)
comparison ranking: 134

COMMUNICATIONS

Telephones - fixed lines: *total subscriptions:* 1.918 million (2022 est.)
subscriptions per 100 inhabitants: 11 (2022 est.)

comparison ranking: total subscriptions 52

Telephones - mobile cellular: *total subscriptions:* 20.553 million (2022 est.)
subscriptions per 100 inhabitants: 115 (2022 est.)
comparison ranking: total subscriptions 62

Telecommunication systems: *general assessment:* Guatemala's telecom infrastructure has suffered from years of under investment from state and provincial government; the poor state of fixed-line infrastructure has led to Guatemala having one of the lowest fixed-line teledensities in the region; in many rural regions of the country there is no fixed-line access available, and so mobile services are adopted by necessity; private investment has been supported by government and regulatory efforts, resulting in a steady growth in the number of fixed lines which has supported growth in the fixed broadband segment; delays in launching LTE services left the country lagging behind in the development of mobile broadband and the benefits which it can bring to the country's social and economic growth; two new submarine cables are due for completion by 2022; improved international connectivity should drive further uptake of both fixed and mobile broadband services; intense competition among the networks has helped to improve services and lower prices for end-users; given the commercial impetus of networks, insufficient government financial investment has resulted in many regional areas remaining with poor or non-existent services; the country benefits from one of the most open regulatory frameworks, with all telecom sectors having been open to competition since 1996; mobile subscriptions are on par with the regional average, though the slower growth in the mobile subscriber base suggests a level of market saturation, with the emphasis among networks being on generating revenue via mobile data services (2021)
domestic: fixed-line teledensity roughly 13 per 100 persons; fixed-line investments are concentrating on improving rural connectivity; mobile-cellular teledensity about 126 per 100 persons (2021)
international: country code - 502; landing points for the ARCOS, AMX-1, American Movil-Texius West Coast Cable and the SAm-1 fiber-optic submarine cable system that, together, provide connectivity to South and Central America, parts of the Caribbean, and the US; connected to Central American Microwave System; satellite earth station - 1 Intelsat (Atlantic Ocean) (2019)

Broadcast media: 4 privately owned national terrestrial TV channels dominate TV broadcasting; multi-channel satellite and cable services are available; 1 government-owned radio station and hundreds of privately owned radio stations (2019)

Internet country code: .gt

Internet users: *total:* 9.18 million (2021 est.)
percent of population: 51% (2021 est.)
comparison ranking: total 63

Broadband - fixed subscriptions: *total:* 612,000 (2020 est.)
subscriptions per 100 inhabitants: 3 (2020 est.)
comparison ranking: total 86

TRANSPORTATION

National air transport system: *number of registered air carriers:* 3 (2020)
inventory of registered aircraft operated by air carriers: 5
annual passenger traffic on registered air carriers: 145,795 (2018)
annual freight traffic on registered air carriers: 110,000 (2018) mt-km

Civil aircraft registration country code prefix: TG

Airports: 58 (2024)
comparison ranking: 78

Heliports: 2 (2024)

Pipelines: 480 km oil (2013)

Railways: *total:* 800 km (2018)
narrow gauge: 800 km (2018) 0.914-m gauge
note: despite the existence of a railway network, all rail service was suspended in 2007 and no passenger or freight train currently runs in the country (2018)
comparison ranking: total 96

Roadways: *total:* 17,440 km
paved: 7,420 km
unpaved: 9,440 km (2022)
comparison ranking: total 118

Waterways: 990 km (2012) (260 km navigable year round; additional 730 km navigable during high-water season)
comparison ranking: 71

Merchant marine: *total:* 9 (2023)
by type: oil tanker 1, other 8
comparison ranking: total 162

Ports: *total ports:* 3 (2024)
large: 0
medium: 0
small: 2
very small: 1
ports with oil terminals: 2
key ports: Puerto Barrios, Puerto Quetzal, Santo Tomas de Castilla

MILITARY AND SECURITY

Military and security forces: Army of Guatemala (Ejercito de Guatemala; aka Armed Forces of Guatemala or Fuerzas Armadas de Guatemala): Land Forces (Fuerzas de Tierra), Naval Forces (Fuerzas de Mar), and Air Force (Fuerza de Aire) (2024)
note: the National Civil Police (Policia Nacional Civil or PNC) are under the Ministry of Government (Interior)

Military expenditures: 0.4% of GDP (2023 est.)
0.4% of GDP (2022 est.)
0.4% of GDP (2021 est.)
0.4% of GDP (2020 est.)
0.4% of GDP (2019 est.)
comparison ranking: 161

Military and security service personnel strengths: information varies; approximately 20,000 active military personnel (18,000 Land Forces; 1,000 Naval Forces; 1,000 Air Forces); approximately 30,000 National Civil Police (2023)

Military equipment inventories and acquisitions: the military is lightly armed with an inventory mostly comprised of older US equipment; in recent years, Guatemala has received small amounts of equipment from several countries, including Colombia, Spain, and the US (2024)

Military service age and obligation: all male citizens 18-50 are eligible for military service; most of the force is volunteer; a selective draft system is employed, resulting in a small portion of 17-21 year-olds being conscripted; conscript service obligation varies from 12-24 months; women may volunteer (2023)

Military deployments: 190 Democratic Republic of the Congo (MONUSCO) (2024)

Military - note: the military is responsible for maintaining sovereignty, territorial integrity, and the honor of Guatemala, but has long focused on internal security; since the 2000s, the Guatemalan Government has used the military to support the National Civil Police in internal security operations (as permitted by the constitution) to combat organized crime, gang violence, and narco-trafficking; in recent years however, the military has sought to place more focus on other missions such as border security and traditional military operations; it has also created new brigades for cybersecurity (2024) and responding to national emergencies/providing humanitarian assistance (2023); it participates in UN missions on a small scale and has a peacekeeping operations training command that offers training to regional countries; the military has security ties with regional partners such as Brazil, Colombia, El Salvador, and Honduras; cooperation with El Salvador and Honduras has included a combined police-military anti-gang task force to patrol border areas; it also has ties with the US, including joint training exercises and material assistance
the military held power during most of Guatemala's 36-year civil war (1960-1996) and conducted a campaign of widespread violence and repression, particularly against the country's majority indigenous population; more than 200,000 people were estimated to have been killed or disappeared during the conflict (2024)

TRANSNATIONAL ISSUES

Refugees and internally displaced persons: IDPs: 242,000 (more than three decades of internal conflict that ended in 1996 displaced mainly the indigenous Maya population and rural peasants; ongoing drug cartel and gang violence) (2022)

Illicit drugs: a major transit country for illegal drugs; illicit cultivation of opium poppies, marijuana, and coca plants in rural areas; a major source of precursor or essential chemicals used in the production of illicit narcotics

GUERNSEY

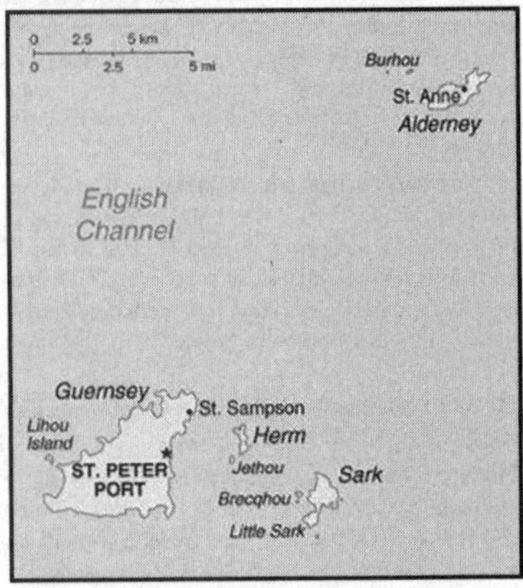

INTRODUCTION

Background: Guernsey and the other Channel Islands represent the last remnants of the medieval Duchy of Normandy, which held sway in both France and England. The islands were the only British soil that Germany occupied in World War II. The Bailiwick of Guernsey consists of the main island of Guernsey and a number of smaller islands, including Alderney, Sark, Herm, Jethou, Brecqhou, and Lihou. The Bailiwick is a self-governing British Crown dependency that is not part of the UK. However, the UK Government is constitutionally responsible for its defense and international representation.

GEOGRAPHY

Location: Western Europe, islands in the English Channel, northwest of France

Geographic coordinates: 49 28 N, 2 35 W

Map references: Europe

Area: *total:* 78 sq km
land: 78 sq km
water: 0 sq km
note: includes Alderney, Guernsey, Herm, Sark, and some other smaller islands
comparison ranking: total 226

Area - comparative: about one-half the size of Washington, DC

Land boundaries: *total:* 0 km

Coastline: 50 km

Maritime claims: *territorial sea:* 12 nm
exclusive fishing zone: 12 nm

Climate: temperate with mild winters and cool summers; about 50% of days are overcast

Terrain: mostly flat with low hills in southwest

Elevation: *highest point:* Le Moulin on Sark 114 m
lowest point: English Channel 0 m

Natural resources: cropland

Irrigated land: NA

Natural hazards: very large tidal variation and fast currents can make local waters dangerous

Geography - note: large, deepwater harbor at Saint Peter Port

PEOPLE AND SOCIETY

Population: *total:* 67,787
male: 33,712
female: 34,075 (2024 est.)
comparison rankings: female 204; male 203; total 203

Nationality: *noun:* Channel Islander(s)
adjective: Channel Islander

Ethnic groups: Guernsey 53.5%, UK and Ireland 23.8%, Portugal 2.1%, Latvia 1.4%, other Europe 2.7%, other Crown Dependencies 0.7%, other 5.3%, unspecified 10.5% (2022 est.)
note: data represent population by country of birth; the native population is of British and Norman-French descent

Languages: English, French, Norman-French dialect spoken in country districts

Religions: Protestant (Anglican, Presbyterian, Baptist, Congregational, Methodist), Roman Catholic

Age structure: *0-14 years:* 14.3% (male 4,999/female 4,717)
15-64 years: 64.1% (male 21,937/female 21,547)
65 years and over: 21.5% (2024 est.) (male 6,776/female 7,811)
2023 population pyramid:

Dependency ratios: *total dependency ratio:* 48.6
youth dependency ratio: 23.9
elderly dependency ratio: 24.6
potential support ratio: 4.1 (2021 est.)
note: data represent Guernsey and Jersey

Median age: *total:* 45 years (2024 est.)
male: 43.8 years
female: 46.2 years
comparison ranking: total 23

Population growth rate: 0.21% (2024 est.)
comparison ranking: 176

Birth rate: 9.7 births/1,000 population (2024 est.)
comparison ranking: 192

Death rate: 9.2 deaths/1,000 population (2024 est.)
comparison ranking: 54

Net migration rate: 1.6 migrant(s)/1,000 population (2024 est.)
comparison ranking: 55

Urbanization: *urban population:* 31.2% of total population (2023)
rate of urbanization: 0.68% annual rate of change (2020-25 est.)
note: data include Guernsey and Jersey

Major urban areas - population: 16,000 SAINT PETER PORT (capital) (2018)

Sex ratio: *at birth:* 1.05 male(s)/female
0-14 years: 1.06 male(s)/female
15-64 years: 1.02 male(s)/female
65 years and over: 0.87 male(s)/female
total population: 0.99 male(s)/female (2024 est.)

Infant mortality rate: *total:* 3.3 deaths/1,000 live births (2024 est.)
male: 3.7 deaths/1,000 live births
female: 2.7 deaths/1,000 live births
comparison ranking: total 197

Life expectancy at birth: *total population:* 83.6 years (2024 est.)
male: 80.9 years
female: 86.4 years
comparison ranking: total population 11

Total fertility rate: 1.59 children born/woman (2024 est.)
comparison ranking: 188

Gross reproduction rate: 0.77 (2024 est.)

Drinking water source: *improved: total:* 94.2% of population
unimproved: total: 5.9% of population (2017 est.)
note: includes data for Jersey

Sanitation facility access: *improved:*
total: 98% of population
unimproved:
total: 1.2% of population (2017)
note: data represent Guernsey and Jersey

ENVIRONMENT

Environment - current issues: coastal erosion, coastal flooding; declining biodiversity due to land abandonment and succession to scrub or woodland

Climate: temperate with mild winters and cool summers; about 50% of days are overcast

Urbanization: *urban population:* 31.2% of total population (2023)
rate of urbanization: 0.68% annual rate of change (2020-25 est.)
note: data include Guernsey and Jersey

Waste and recycling: *municipal solid waste generated annually:* 178,933 tons (2016 est.)
municipal solid waste recycled annually: 50,871 tons (2016 est.)
percent of municipal solid waste recycled: 28.4% (2016 est.)
note: data include combined totals for Guernsey and Jersey.

GOVERNMENT

Country name: *conventional long form:* Bailiwick of Guernsey
conventional short form: Guernsey
former: Norman Isles
etymology: the name is of Old Norse origin, but the meaning of the root "Guern(s)" is uncertain; the "-ey" ending means "island"

Government type: parliamentary democracy (States of Deliberation)

Dependency status: British crown dependency

Capital: *name:* Saint Peter Port
geographic coordinates: 49 27 N, 2 32 W
time difference: UTC 0 (5 hours ahead of Washington, DC, during Standard Time)
daylight saving time: +1hr, begins last Sunday in March; ends last Sunday in October
etymology: Saint Peter Port is the name of the town and its surrounding parish; the "port" distinguishes this parish from that of Saint Peter on the other side of the island

Administrative divisions: *none (British Crown dependency); there are no first-order administrative divisions as defined by the US Government, but there are 10 parishes:* Castel, Forest, Saint Andrew, Saint Martin, Saint Peter Port,

Saint Pierre du Bois, Saint Sampson, Saint Saviour, Torteval, Vale
note: two additional parishes for Guernsey are sometimes listed - Saint Anne on the island of Alderney and Saint Peter on the island of Sark - but they are generally not included in the enumeration of parishes

Independence: none (British Crown dependency)

National holiday: Liberation Day, 9 May (1945)

Legal system: customary legal system based on Norman customary law; includes elements of the French civil code and English common law

Constitution: *history:* unwritten; includes royal charters, statutes, and common law and practice
amendments: new laws or changes to existing laws are initiated by the States of Deliberation; passage requires majority vote; many laws have been passed; in 2019, 60 laws were passed

Citizenship: see United Kingdom

Suffrage: 16 years of age; universal

Executive branch: *chief of state:* King CHARLES III (since 8 September 2022); represented by Lieutenant-Governor Richard CRIPWELL (since 15 February 2022)
head of government: Chief Minister Lyndon TROTT (since 13 December 2023)
cabinet: none
elections/appointments: the monarchy is hereditary; lieutenant governor and bailiff appointed by the monarch; chief minister, who is the president of the Policy and Resources Committee indirectly elected by the States of Deliberation for a 4-year term; last held on 7 October 2020 (next to be held in 2024)
election results:
2020: Peter FERBRACHE (independent) elected president of the Policy and Resources Committee and chief minister: percent of States of Guernsey vote - 57.5%
2016: Gavin ST. PIER (independent) elected president of the Policy and Resources Committee and chief minister
note: the chief minister is the president of the Policy and Resources Committee and is the de facto head of government; the Policy and Resources Committee, elected by the States of Deliberation, functions as the executive; the 5 members all have equal voting rights

Legislative branch: *description:* unicameral States of Deliberation (40 seats; 38 People's Deputies and 2 representatives of the States of Alderney; members directly elected by majority vote to serve 4-year terms); note - non-voting members include the bailiff (presiding officer), attorney-general, and solicitor-general
elections: last held on 7 October 2020 (next to be held in June 2025)
election results: percent of vote - GPI 24.0%, GP 10%, APG 3.4%, independent 62.6%; seats - GPI 10, GP 6, independent 22, States of Alderney 2; composition - men 32, women 8, percentage women 20%

Judicial branch: *highest court(s):* Guernsey Court of Appeal (consists of the Bailiff of Guernsey, who is the ex-officio president of the Guernsey Court of Appeal, and at least 12 judges); Royal Court (organized into 3 divisions - Full Court sits with 1 judge and 7 to 12 jurats acting as judges of fact, Ordinary Court sits with 1 judge and normally 3 jurats, and Matrimonial Causes Division sits with 1 judge and 4 jurats); note - appeals beyond Guernsey courts are heard by the Judicial Committee of the Privy Council (in London)
judge selection and term of office: Royal Court Bailiff, Deputy Bailiff, and Court of Appeal justices appointed by the British Crown and hold office at Her Majesty's pleasure; jurats elected by the States of Election, a body chaired by the Bailiff and a number of jurats
subordinate courts: Court of Alderney; Court of the Seneschal of Sark; Magistrates' Court (includes Juvenile Court); Contracts Court; Ecclesiastical Court; Court of Chief Pleas

Political parties: Alliance Party Guernsey or APG
Guernsey Partnership of Independents or GPI
Guernsey Party or GP

International organization participation: UPU

Diplomatic representation in the US: none (British crown dependency)

Diplomatic representation from the US: *embassy:* none (British crown dependency)

Flag description: white with the red cross of Saint George (patron saint of England) extending to the edges of the flag and a yellow equal-armed cross of William the Conqueror superimposed on the Saint George cross; the red cross represents the old ties with England and the fact that Guernsey is a British Crown dependency; the gold cross is a replica of the one used by William the Conqueror at the Battle of Hastings in 1066

National symbol(s): Guernsey cow, donkey; national colors: red, white, yellow

National anthem: *name:* "Sarnia Cherie" (Guernsey Dear)
lyrics/music: George DEIGHTON/Domencio SANTANGELO
note: adopted 1911; serves as a local anthem; as a British crown dependency, "God Save the King" is official (see United Kingdom)

ECONOMY

Economic overview: high-income English Channel island economy; strong financial sector but stressed due to COVID-19 disruptions; manufacturing, tourism, and construction industries suffered but expected to recover; stable inflation; maintains independent taxation authority

Real GDP (purchasing power parity): $3.465 billion (2015 est.)
$3.451 billion (2014 est.)
note: data are in 2015 dollars
comparison ranking: 195

Real GDP growth rate: 7.81% (2022 est.)
15.46% (2021 est.)
-8.47% (2020 est.)
note: annual GDP % growth based on constant local currency; entry includes Jersey and Guernsey
comparison ranking: 15

Real GDP per capita: $52,500 (2014 est.)
comparison ranking: 38

GDP (official exchange rate): $11.228 billion (2022 est.)
note: data in current dollars at official exchange rate; entry includes Jersey and Guernsey

GDP - composition, by sector of origin: *agriculture:* 0.8% (2022 est.)
industry: 8.4% (2022 est.)
services: 92% (2022 est.)
note: figures may not total 100% due to non-allocated consumption not captured in sector-reported data
comparison rankings: services 3; industry 203; agriculture 189

Agricultural products: tomatoes, greenhouse flowers, sweet peppers, eggplant, fruit; Guernsey cattle

Industries: tourism, banking

Industrial production growth rate: 1.64% (2022 est.)
note: annual % change in industrial value added based on constant local currency; entry includes Jersey and Guernsey
comparison ranking: 122

Labor force: 86,000 (2023 est.)
note: number of people ages 15 or older who are employed or seeking work;entry includes Jersey and Guernsey
comparison ranking: 184

Unemployment rate: 5.98% (2023 est.)
5.91% (2022 est.)
6.61% (2021 est.)
note: % of labor force seeking employment; entry includes Jersey and Guernsey
comparison ranking: 122

Youth unemployment rate (ages 15-24): *total:* 13.5% (2023 est.)
male: 13.7% (2023 est.)
female: 13.2% (2023 est.)
note: % of labor force ages 15-24 seeking employment
comparison ranking: total 105

Exports - partners: almost entirely United Kingdom (2022)

Exports - commodities: aircraft, photo lab equipment, clocks, ships, paintings, scientific instruments (2022)

Imports - partners: almost entirely United Kingdom (2022)

Imports - commodities: ships, aircraft, refined petroleum, mineral manufactures, beverages (2022)

Exchange rates: Guernsey pound per US dollar

Exchange rates: 0.805 (2023 est.)
0.811 (2022 est.)
0.727 (2021 est.)
0.78 (2020 est.)
0.783 (2019 est.)

ENERGY

Electricity access: *electrification - total population:* 100% (2022 est.)
note: includes Guernsey and Jersey

COMMUNICATIONS

Telephones - fixed lines: *total subscriptions:* 33,930 (2021 est.)
subscriptions per 100 inhabitants: 53 (2021 est.)
comparison ranking: total subscriptions 165

Telephones - mobile cellular: *total subscriptions:* 71,485 (2021 est.)
subscriptions per 100 inhabitants: 112 (2021 est.)
comparison ranking: total subscriptions 197

Telecommunication systems: *general assessment:* fixed network broadband services are those delivered over physical copper connections, fiber connections and fixed wireless communications links (e.g. WiMax); they do not include services delivered over 2G, 3G and 4G mobile networks (2021)
domestic: fixed-line 53 per 100 and mobile-cellular 112 per 100 persons (2021)
international: country code - 44; landing points for Guernsey-Jersey, HUGO, INGRID, Channel Islands -9 Liberty and UK-Channel Islands-7 submarine cable to UK and France (2019)

Broadcast media: multiple UK terrestrial TV broadcasts are received via a transmitter in Jersey with relays in Jersey, Guernsey, and Alderney; satellite packages are available; BBC Radio Guernsey and 1 other radio station operating

Internet country code: .gg

Internet users: *total:* 55,069 (2021 est.)
percent of population: 86.6% (2021 est.)
comparison ranking: total 200

Broadband - fixed subscriptions: *total:* 25,336 (2020 est.)
subscriptions per 100 inhabitants: 40 (2020 est.)
comparison ranking: total 158

TRANSPORTATION

National air transport system: *number of registered air carriers:* 1 (2020) (registered in UK)
inventory of registered aircraft operated by air carriers: 9 (registered in UK)

Civil aircraft registration country code prefix: 2

Airports: 2 (2024)
comparison ranking: 207

Roadways: *total:* 260 km (2017)
comparison ranking: total 206

Ports: *total ports:* 3 (2024)
large: 0
medium: 0
small: 1
very small: 2
ports with oil terminals: 2
key ports: Alderney Harbour, Saint Peter Port, Saint Sampson

MILITARY AND SECURITY

Military - note: defense is the responsibility of the UK

TRANSNATIONAL ISSUES

Illicit drugs: NA

GUINEA

INTRODUCTION

Background: Guinea's deep Muslim heritage arrived via the neighboring Almoravid Empire in the 11th century. Following Almoravid decline, Guinea existed on the fringe of several African kingdoms, all competing for regional dominance. In the 13th century, the Mali Empire took control of Guinea and encouraged its already growing Muslim faith. After the fall of the West African empires, various smaller kingdoms controlled Guinea. In the 18th century, Fulani Muslims established an Islamic state in central Guinea that provided one of the earliest examples of a written constitution and alternating leadership. European traders first arrived in the 16th century, and the French secured colonial rule in the 19th century.

In 1958, Guinea achieved independence from France. Sekou TOURE became Guinea's first post-independence president; he established a dictatorial regime and ruled until his death in 1984, after which General Lansana CONTE staged a coup and seized the government. He too established an authoritarian regime and manipulated presidential elections until his death in 2008, when Captain Moussa Dadis CAMARA led a military coup, seized power, and suspended the constitution. In 2009, CAMARA was wounded in an assassination attempt and was exiled to Burkina Faso. In 2010 and 2013 respectively, the country held its first free and fair presidential and legislative elections. Alpha CONDE won the 2010 and 2015 presidential elections, and his first cabinet was the first all-civilian government in Guinean history. CONDE won a third term in 2020 after a constitutional change to term limits. In 2021, Col Mamady DOUMBOUYA led another successful military coup, establishing the National Committee for Reconciliation and Development (CNRD), suspending the constitution, and dissolving the government and the legislature. DOUMBOUYA was sworn in as transition president and appointed Mohamed BEAVOGUI as transition prime minister. The National Transition Council (CNT), which acts as the legislative body for the transition, was formed in 2022 and consists of appointed members representing a broad swath of Guinean society.

GEOGRAPHY

Location: Western Africa, bordering the North Atlantic Ocean, between Guinea-Bissau and Sierra Leone

Geographic coordinates: 11 00 N, 10 00 W

Map references: Africa

Area: *total:* 245,857 sq km
land: 245,717 sq km
water: 140 sq km
comparison ranking: total 79

Area - comparative: slightly smaller than Oregon; slightly larger than twice the size of Pennsylvania

Land boundaries: *total:* 4,046 km
border countries (6): Cote d'Ivoire 816 km; Guinea-Bissau 421 km; Liberia 590 km; Mali 1062 km; Senegal 363 km; Sierra Leone 794 km

Coastline: 320 km

Maritime claims: *territorial sea:* 12 nm
exclusive economic zone: 200 nm

Climate: generally hot and humid; monsoonal-type rainy season (June to November) with southwesterly winds; dry season (December to May) with northeasterly harmattan winds

Terrain: generally flat coastal plain, hilly to mountainous interior

Elevation: *highest point:* Mont Nimba 1,752 m
lowest point: Atlantic Ocean 0 m
mean elevation: 472 m

Natural resources: bauxite, iron ore, diamonds, gold, uranium, hydropower, fish, salt

Land use: *agricultural land:* 58.1% (2018 est.)
arable land: 11.8% (2018 est.)
permanent crops: 2.8% (2018 est.)
permanent pasture: 43.5% (2018 est.)
forest: 26.5% (2018 est.)
other: 15.4% (2018 est.)

Irrigated land: 950 sq km (2012)

Major rivers (by length in km): Niger river source (shared with Mali, and Nigeria [m]) - 4,200 km; Gambie (Gambia) river source (shared with Senegal and The Gambia [m]) - 1,094 km
note – [s] after country name indicates river source; [m] after country name indicates river mouth

Major watersheds (area sq km): Atlantic Ocean drainage: Niger (2,261,741 sq km), Senegal (456,397 sq km)

Population distribution: areas of highest density are in the west and south; interior is sparsely populated as shown in this population distribution map

Natural hazards: hot, dry, dusty harmattan haze may reduce visibility during dry season

Geography - note: the Niger and its important tributary the Milo River have their sources in the Guinean highlands

PEOPLE AND SOCIETY

Population: *total:* 13,986,179
male: 6,985,606
female: 7,000,573 (2024 est.)
comparison rankings: female 75; male 75; total 75

Nationality: *noun:* Guinean(s)
adjective: Guinean

Ethnic groups: Fulani (Peuhl) 33.4%, Malinke 29.4%, Susu 21.2%, Guerze 7.8%, Kissi 6.2%, Toma 1.6%, other/foreign 0.4% (2018 est.)

Languages: French (official), Pular, Maninka, Susu, other native languages
note: about 40 languages are spoken; each ethnic group has its own language

Religions: Muslim 85.2%, Christian 13.4%, animist 0.2%, none 1.2% (2018 est.)

Demographic profile: Guinea's strong population growth is a result of declining mortality rates and sustained elevated fertility. The population growth rate was somewhat tempered in the 2000s because of a period of net outmigration. Although life expectancy and mortality rates have improved over the last two decades, the nearly universal practice of female genital cutting continues to contribute to high infant and maternal mortality rates. Guinea's total fertility remains high at about 5 children per woman as of 2022 because of the ongoing preference for larger families, low contraceptive usage and availability, a lack of educational attainment and empowerment among women, and poverty. A lack of literacy and vocational training programs limit job prospects for youths, but even those with university degrees often have no option but to work in the informal sector. About 60% of the country's large youth population is unemployed.

Tensions and refugees have spilled over Guinea's borders with Sierra Leone, Liberia, and Cote d'Ivoire. During the 1990s Guinea harbored as many as half a million refugees from Sierra Leone and Liberia, more refugees than any other African country for much of that decade. About half sought refuge in the volatile "Parrot's Beak" region of southwest Guinea, a wedge of land jutting into Sierra Leone near the Liberian border. Many were relocated within Guinea in the early 2000s because the area suffered repeated crossborder attacks from various government and rebel forces, as well as anti-refugee violence.

Age structure: *0-14 years:* 40.9% (male 2,884,146/female 2,835,794)
15-64 years: 55.1% (male 3,846,852/female 3,856,366)
65 years and over: 4% (2024 est.) (male 254,608/female 308,413)

Dependency ratios: *total dependency ratio:* 82.4
youth dependency ratio: 76.3
elderly dependency ratio: 6.1
potential support ratio: 16.3 (2021 est.)

Median age: *total:* 19.4 years (2024 est.)
male: 19.2 years
female: 19.6 years
comparison ranking: total 209

Population growth rate: 2.74% (2024 est.)
comparison ranking: 12

Birth rate: 35.3 births/1,000 population (2024 est.)
comparison ranking: 12

Death rate: 7.8 deaths/1,000 population (2024 est.)
comparison ranking: 92

Net migration rate: 0 migrant(s)/1,000 population (2024 est.)
comparison ranking: 89

Population distribution: areas of highest density are in the west and south; interior is sparsely populated as shown in this population distribution map

Urbanization: *urban population:* 38.1% of total population (2023)
rate of urbanization: 3.64% annual rate of change (2020-25 est.)

Major urban areas - population: 2.111 million CONAKRY (capital) (2023)

Sex ratio: *at birth:* 1.03 male(s)/female
0-14 years: 1.02 male(s)/female
15-64 years: 1 male(s)/female
65 years and over: 0.83 male(s)/female
total population: 1 male(s)/female (2024 est.)

Mother's mean age at first birth: 19.9 years (2018 est.)
note: data represents median age at first birth among women 20-49

Maternal mortality ratio: 553 deaths/100,000 live births (2020 est.)
comparison ranking: 10

Infant mortality rate: *total:* 47 deaths/1,000 live births (2024 est.)
male: 51.6 deaths/1,000 live births
female: 42.3 deaths/1,000 live births
comparison ranking: total 21

Life expectancy at birth: *total population:* 64.6 years (2024 est.)
male: 62.7 years
female: 66.6 years
comparison ranking: total population 206

Total fertility rate: 4.78 children born/woman (2024 est.)
comparison ranking: 11

Gross reproduction rate: 2.36 (2024 est.)

Contraceptive prevalence rate: 10.9% (2018)

Drinking water source: *improved: urban:* 99.5% of population
rural: 76.9% of population
total: 85.2% of population
unimproved: urban: 0.5% of population
rural: 23.1% of population
total: 14.8% of population (2020 est.)

Current health expenditure: 4% of GDP (2020)

Physician density: 0.23 physicians/1,000 population (2018)

Hospital bed density: 0.3 beds/1,000 population (2011)

Sanitation facility access: *improved: urban:* 90.9% of population
rural: 38.7% of population
total: 58% of population
unimproved: urban: 9.1% of population
rural: 61.3% of population
total: 42% of population (2020 est.)

Obesity - adult prevalence rate: 7.7% (2016)
comparison ranking: 158

Alcohol consumption per capita: *total:* 0.33 liters of pure alcohol (2019 est.)
beer: 0.29 liters of pure alcohol (2019 est.)
wine: 0.01 liters of pure alcohol (2019 est.)
spirits: 0.03 liters of pure alcohol (2019 est.)
other alcohols: 0 liters of pure alcohol (2019 est.)
comparison ranking: total 168

Children under the age of 5 years underweight: 16.3% (2018)
comparison ranking: 30

Currently married women (ages 15-49): 68.7% (2023 est.)

Child marriage: *women married by age 15:* 17%
women married by age 18: 46.5%
men married by age 18: 1.9% (2018 est.)

Education expenditures: 2.2% of GDP (2020 est.)
comparison ranking: 181

Literacy: *definition:* age 15 and over can read and write
total population: 45.3%
male: 61.2%
female: 31.3% (2021)

School life expectancy (primary to tertiary education): *total:* 9 years
male: 10 years
female: 8 years (2014)

ENVIRONMENT

Environment - current issues: deforestation; inadequate potable water; desertification; soil contamination and erosion; overfishing, overpopulation in forest region; poor mining practices lead to environmental damage; water pollution; improper waste disposal

Environment - international agreements: *party to:* Biodiversity, Climate Change, Climate Change-Kyoto Protocol, Climate Change-Paris Agreement, Comprehensive Nuclear Test Ban, Desertification, Endangered Species, Hazardous Wastes, Law of the Sea, Ozone Layer Protection, Ship Pollution, Wetlands, Whaling
signed, but not ratified: none of the selected agreements

Climate: generally hot and humid; monsoonal-type rainy season (June to November) with southwesterly winds; dry season (December to May) with northeasterly harmattan winds

Urbanization: *urban population:* 38.1% of total population (2023)
rate of urbanization: 3.64% annual rate of change (2020-25 est.)

Food insecurity: *severe localized food insecurity: due to reduced incomes* - about 1.22 million people are projected to be in need of food assistance between June and August 2022, primarily due to food access constraints on account of the economic effects of the COVID-19 pandemic (2022)

Revenue from forest resources: 4.81% of GDP (2018 est.)
comparison ranking: 12

Revenue from coal: 0% of GDP (2018 est.)
comparison ranking: 114

Air pollutants: *particulate matter emissions:* 37.57 micrograms per cubic meter (2019 est.)
carbon dioxide emissions: 3 megatons (2016 est.)
methane emissions: 11.13 megatons (2020 est.)

Waste and recycling: *municipal solid waste generated annually:* 596,911 tons (1996 est.)
municipal solid waste recycled annually: 29,846 tons (2005 est.)
percent of municipal solid waste recycled: 5% (2005 est.)

Major rivers (by length in km): Niger river source (shared with Mali, and Nigeria [m]) - 4,200 km; Gambie (Gambia) river source (shared with Senegal and The Gambia [m]) - 1,094 km
note – [s] after country name indicates river source; [m] after country name indicates river mouth

Major watersheds (area sq km): Atlantic Ocean drainage: Niger (2,261,741 sq km), Senegal (456,397 sq km)

Total water withdrawal: *municipal:* 230 million cubic meters (2020 est.)
industrial: 60 million cubic meters (2020 est.)
agricultural: 600 million cubic meters (2020 est.)

Total renewable water resources: 226 billion cubic meters (2020 est.)

GOVERNMENT

Country name: *conventional long form:* Republic of Guinea
conventional short form: Guinea
local long form: République de Guinée
local short form: Guinée
former: French Guinea
etymology: the country is named after the Guinea region of West Africa that lies along the Gulf of Guinea and stretches north to the Sahel

Government type: presidential republic

Capital: *name:* Conakry
geographic coordinates: 9 30 N, 13 42 W
time difference: UTC 0 (5 hours ahead of Washington, DC, during Standard Time)
etymology: according to tradition, the name derives from the fusion of the name Cona, a Baga wine and cheese producer who lived on Tombo Island (the original site of the present-day capital), and the word nakiri, which in Susu means "the other bank" or "the other side"; supposedly, Baga's palm grove produced the best wine on the island and people traveling to sample his vintage, would say: "I am going to Cona, on the other bank (*Cona-nakiri*)," which over time became Conakry

Administrative divisions: 7 regions administrative (administrative regions) and 1 gouvenorat (gover-norate)*; Boke, Conakry*, Faranah, Kankan, Kindia, Labe, Mamou, N'Zerekore

Independence: 2 October 1958 (from France)

National holiday: Independence Day, 2 October (1958)

Legal system: civil law system based on the French model

Constitution: *history:* previous 1958, 1990; 2010 and a referendum in 2020, which was suspended on 5 September 2021 via a coup d'etat; on 27 September, the Transitional Charter was released, which supersedes the constitution until a new constitution is promulgated
amendments: proposed by the National Assembly or by the president of the republic; consideration of proposals requires approval by simple majority vote by the Assembly; passage requires approval in refer-endum; the president can opt to submit amendments directly to the Assembly, in which case approval requires at least two-thirds majority vote; revised in 2020

International law organization participation: accepts compulsory ICJ jurisdiction with reservations; accepts ICCt jurisdiction

Citizenship: *citizenship by birth:* no
citizenship by descent only: at least one parent must be a citizen of Guinea
dual citizenship recognized: no
residency requirement for naturalization: na

Suffrage: 18 years of age; universal

Executive branch: *chief of state:* President Col. Mamady DOUMBOUYA (since 1 October 2021)
head of government: Prime Minister Mamadou Oury BAH (since 27 February 2024)
cabinet: formerly the Council of Ministers appointed by the president; note - on 5 September 2021, the military arrested and detained the president, sus-pended the constitution, and dissolved the govern-ment and legislature
elections/appointments: formerly, the president was directly elected by absolute majority popular vote in 2 rounds if needed for a 5-year term (eligible for a second term) and the prime minister appointed by the president; election last held on 18 October 2020; note - a new election timetable has not been announced by the transitional government; note - on 5 September 2021, Col. Mamady DOUMBOUYA led a military coup in which President CONDE was arrested and detained, the constitution suspended, and the government and People's National Assembly dissolved; on 1 October 2021, DOUMBOUYA was sworn in as transitional president
election results:
2020: Alpha CONDE reelected president in the first round; percent of vote - Alpha CONDE (RPG) 59.5%, Cellou Dalein DIALLO (UFDG) 33.5%, other 7%
2015: Alpha CONDE reelected president in the first round; percent of vote - Alpha CONDE (RPG) 57.8%, Cellou Dalein DIALLO (UFDG) 31.4%, other 10.8%

Legislative branch: *description:* formerly the People's National Assembly; note - on 5 September 2021, Col. Mamady DOUMBOUYA led a military coup in which President CONDE was arrested and detained, the constitution suspended, and the government and People's National Assembly dissolved; on 22 January 2022, an 81-member Transitional National Council was installed; on 19 February 2024 Guinea's military leaders dissolved the government
elections: 81 members to the Transitional National Council were appointed by the transitional presi-dent Col. Mamady DOUMBOUYA on 22 January 2022; elections for a permanent legislature had not been announced as of late January 2022; on 19 February 2024 Guinea's military leaders dissolved the government
election results: 81 members of the National Transitional Council appointed on 22 January 2022 by the transitional president; the members represent all of the country's socio-professional organizations and political parties

Judicial branch: *highest court(s):* Supreme Court or Cour Supreme (organized into Administrative Chamber and Civil, Penal, and Social Chamber; court consists of the first president, 2 chamber presidents, 10 councilors, the solicitor general, and NA deputies); Constitutional Court - suspended on 5 September 2021
judge selection and term of office: Supreme Court first president appointed by the national president after consultation with the National Assembly; other members appointed by presidential decree; members serve 9-year terms until age 65
subordinate courts: Court of Appeal or Cour d'Ap-pel; High Court of Justice or Cour d'Assises; Court of Account (Court of Auditors); Courts of First Instance (Tribunal de Premiere Instance); labor court; military tribunal; justices of the peace; specialized courts

Political parties: African Congress for Democracy and Renewal or CADRE
Alliance for National Renewal or ARN
Alliance for National Renewal or ARENA
Bloc Liberal or BL
Citizen Generation or GECI
Citizen Party for the Defense of Collective Interests or PCDIC
Democratic Alliance for Renewal or ADR
Democratic National Movement or MND
Democratic Union for Renewal and Progress or UDRP
Democratic Union of Guinea or UDG
Democratic People's Movement of Guinea or MPDG
Democratic Workers' Party of Guinea or PDTG
Front for the National Alliance or FAN
Generation for Reconciliation Union and Prosperity or GRUP
Guinea for Democracy and Balance or GDE
Guinean Party for Peaceful Coexistence and Development or PGCD
Guinean Party for Solidarity and Democracy or PGSD
Guinean Union for Democracy and Development or UGDD
Guinean Rally for Development or RGD
Guinean Rally for Unity and Development or RGUD
Guinean Renaissance Party or PGR
Modern Guinea
Movement for Solidarity and Development or MSD
National Committee for Reconciliation and Development
National Front for Development or FND
National Union for Prosperity or UNP
National Party for Hope and Development or PEDN
New Democratic Forces or NFD
New Generation for the Republic or NGR
New Guinea or NG
New Political Generation or NGP
Party for Progress and Change or PPC
Party of Citizen Action through Labor or PACT
Party of Democrats for Hope or PADES
Party of Freedom and Progress or PLP
Party of Hope for National Development or PEDN
Rally for Renaissance and Development or RRD
Rally for the Guinean People or RPG
Rally for the Integrated Development of Guinea or RDIG
Rally for the Republic or RPR
Union of Democratic Forces of Guinea or UFDG
Union for Progress and Renewal or UPR
Union for the Defense of Republican Interests or UDIR
Union for the Progress of Guinea or UPG
Union of Democratic Forces or UFD a or UFDG
Union of Democrats for the Renaissance of Guinea or UDRG
Union of Republican Forces or UFR
Unity and Progress Party or PUP

International organization participation: ACP, AfDB, EITI (compliant country), FAO, G-77, IBRD, ICAO, ICCt, ICRM, IDA, IDB, IFAD, IFC, IFRCS, ILO, IMF, IMO, Interpol, IOC, IOM, IPU, ISO (cor-respondent), ITSO, ITU, ITUC (NGOs), MIGA, MINURSO, MONUSCO, NAM, OIC, OIF, OPCW, UN, UNCTAD, UNESCO, UNHCR, UNIDO, UNISFA, UNMISS, UNOCI, UNWTO, UPU, WCO, WFTU (NGOs), WHO, WIPO, WMO, WTO

Diplomatic representation in the US: *chief of mission:* Ambassador Fatoumata KABA (since 19 April 2023)
chancery: 2112 Leroy Place NW, Washington, DC 20008
telephone: [1] (202) 986-4300
FAX: [1] (202) 986-3800
email address and website:
http://guineaembassyusa.org/en/welcome-to-the-embassy-of-guinea-washington-usa/
consulate(s): Los Angelos

Diplomatic representation from the US: *chief of mission:* Ambassador Troy Damian FITRELL (since January 2022)
embassy: Transversale No. 2, Centre Administratif de Koloma, Commune de Ratoma, Conakry
mailing address: 2110 Conakry Place, Washington DC 20521-2110
telephone: [224] 65-10-40-00
FAX: [224] 65-10-42-97
email address and website:
ConakryACS@state.gov
https://gn.usembassy.gov/

Flag description: three equal vertical bands of red (hoist side), yellow, and green; red represents the people's sacrifice for liberation and work; yellow stands for the sun, for the riches of the earth, and

for justice; green symbolizes the country's vegetation and unity
note: uses the popular Pan-African colors of Ethiopia; the colors from left to right are the reverse of those on the flags of neighboring Mali and Senegal

National symbol(s): elephant; national colors: red, yellow, green

National anthem: *name:* "Liberte" (Liberty)
lyrics/music: unknown/Fodeba KEITA
note: adopted 1958

National heritage: *total World Heritage Sites:* 1 (natural)
selected World Heritage Site locales: Mount Nimba Strict Nature Reserve

ECONOMY

Economic overview: growing but primarily agrarian West African economy; major mining sector; improving fiscal and debt balances prior to COVID-19; economy increasingly vulnerable to climate change; slow infrastructure improvements; gender wealth and human capital gaps

Real GDP (purchasing power parity): $56.655 billion (2023 est.)
$52.918 billion (2022 est.)
$50.543 billion (2021 est.)
note: data in 2021 dollars
comparison ranking: 120

Real GDP growth rate: 7.06% (2023 est.)
4.7% (2022 est.)
3.9% (2021 est.)
note: annual GDP % growth based on constant local currency
comparison ranking: 20

Real GDP per capita: $4,000 (2023 est.)
$3,800 (2022 est.)
$3,700 (2021 est.)
note: data in 2021 dollars
comparison ranking: 185

GDP (official exchange rate): $23.612 billion (2023 est.)
note: data in current dollars at official exchange rate

Inflation rate (consumer prices): 7.8% (2023 est.)
10.49% (2022 est.)
12.6% (2021 est.)
note: annual % change based on consumer prices
comparison ranking: 151

GDP - composition, by sector of origin: *agriculture:* 28.2% (2023 est.)
industry: 31.3% (2023 est.)
services: 31.9% (2023 est.)
note: figures may not total 100% due to non-allocated consumption not captured in sector-reported data
comparison rankings: services 208; industry 59; agriculture 13

GDP - composition, by end use: *household consumption:* 52% (2023 est.)
government consumption: 12.3% (2023 est.)
investment in fixed capital: 23.6% (2023 est.)
exports of goods and services: 39.2% (2023 est.)
imports of goods and services: -29.8% (2023 est.)
note: figures may not total 100% due to rounding or gaps in data collection

Agricultural products: cassava, rice, groundnuts, oil palm fruit, maize, fonio, plantains, potatoes, sweet potatoes, yams (2022)
note: top ten agricultural products based on tonnage

Industries: bauxite, gold, diamonds, iron ore; light manufacturing, agricultural processing

Industrial production growth rate: 11.47% (2023 est.)
note: annual % change in industrial value added based on constant local currency
comparison ranking: 11

Labor force: 4.401 million (2023 est.)
note: number of people ages 15 or older who are employed or seeking work
comparison ranking: 96

Unemployment rate: 5.3% (2023 est.)
5.33% (2022 est.)
5.77% (2021 est.)
note: % of labor force seeking employment
comparison ranking: 102

Youth unemployment rate (ages 15-24): *total:* 7.3% (2023 est.)
male: 6.3% (2023 est.)
female: 8.2% (2023 est.)
note: % of labor force ages 15-24 seeking employment
comparison ranking: total 155

Population below poverty line: 43.7% (2018 est.)
note: % of population with income below national poverty line

Gini Index coefficient - distribution of family income: 29.6 (2018 est.)
note: index (0-100) of income distribution; higher values represent greater inequality
comparison ranking: 125

Household income or consumption by percentage share: *lowest 10%:* 3.5% (2018 est.)
highest 10%: 23.1% (2018 est.)
note: % share of income accruing to lowest and highest 10% of population

Remittances: 2.36% of GDP (2023 est.)
2.51% of GDP (2022 est.)
2.14% of GDP (2021 est.)
note: personal transfers and compensation between resident and non-resident individuals/households/entities

Budget: *revenues:* $1.949 billion (2019 est.)
expenditures: $2.014 billion (2019 est.)

Public debt: 37.9% of GDP (2017 est.)
comparison ranking: 137

Taxes and other revenues: 16.6% (of GDP) (2017 est.)
comparison ranking: 120

Current account balance: $3.35 billion (2022 est.)
$4.639 billion (2021 est.)
$2.685 billion (2020 est.)
note: balance of payments - net trade and primary/secondary income in current dollars
comparison ranking: 40

Exports: $8.898 billion (2022 est.)
$10.266 billion (2021 est.)
$8.996 billion (2020 est.)
note: balance of payments - exports of goods and services in current dollars
comparison ranking: 120

Exports - partners: China 37%, India 27%, UAE 25%, Switzerland 3%, Spain 2% (2022)
note: top five export partners based on percentage share of exports

Exports - commodities: gold, aluminum ore, coconuts/Brazil nuts/cashews, cocoa beans, fish (2022)
note: top five export commodities based on value in dollars

Imports: $5.749 billion (2022 est.)
$5.353 billion (2021 est.)
$6.314 billion (2020 est.)
note: balance of payments - imports of goods and services in current dollars
comparison ranking: 146

Imports - partners: China 37%, India 10%, Netherlands 8%, UAE 4%, Belgium 4% (2022)
note: top five import partners based on percentage share of imports

Imports - commodities: refined petroleum, rice, garments, plastic products, wheat (2022)
note: top five import commodities based on value in dollars

Reserves of foreign exchange and gold: $1.499 billion (2020 est.)
$1.379 billion (2019 est.)
$1.242 billion (2018 est.)
note: holdings of gold (year-end prices)/foreign exchange/special drawing rights in current dollars
comparison ranking: 128

Debt - external: $3.329 billion (2022 est.)
note: present value of external debt in current US dollars
comparison ranking: 63

Exchange rates: Guinean francs (GNF) per US dollar -

Exchange rates: 9,565.082 (2020 est.)
9,183.876 (2019 est.)
9,011.134 (2018 est.)
9,088.319 (2017 est.)
8,967.927 (2016 est.)

ENERGY

Electricity access: *electrification - total population:* 47.7% (2022 est.)
electrification - urban areas: 91%
electrification - rural areas: 21.3%

Electricity: *installed generating capacity:* 1.191 million kW (2022 est.)
consumption: 2.625 billion kWh (2022 est.)
transmission/distribution losses: 418.8 million kWh (2022 est.)
comparison rankings: transmission/distribution losses 75; consumption 143; installed generating capacity 133

Electricity generation sources: *fossil fuels:* 33.6% of total installed capacity (2022 est.)
solar: 0.7% of total installed capacity (2022 est.)
hydroelectricity: 65.7% of total installed capacity (2022 est.)

Coal: *imports:* 2,000 metric tons (2022 est.)

Petroleum: *refined petroleum consumption:* 30,000 bbl/day (2022 est.)

Carbon dioxide emissions: 4.502 million metric tonnes of CO_2 (2022 est.)
from coal and metallurgical coke: 5,000 metric tonnes of CO_2 (2022 est.)
from petroleum and other liquids: 4.497 million metric tonnes of CO_2 (2022 est.)
comparison ranking: total emissions 137

Energy consumption per capita: 4.891 million Btu/person (2022 est.)
comparison ranking: 170

COMMUNICATIONS

Telephones - fixed lines: *total subscriptions:* 0 (2021 est.)

subscriptions per 100 inhabitants: (2021 est.) less than 1
comparison ranking: total subscriptions 222

Telephones - mobile cellular: *total subscriptions:* 13.795 million (2021 est.)
subscriptions per 100 inhabitants: 102 (2021 est.)
comparison ranking: total subscriptions 76

Telecommunication systems: *general assessment:* the number of mobile subscribers grew strongly while revenue also increased steadily; fixed broadband services are still very limited and expensive, though there have been some positive developments in recent years; the landing of the first international submarine cable in 2012, and the setting up of an IXP in mid-2013, increased the bandwidth available to the ISPs, and helped reduce the cost of internet services for end-users; a National Backbone Network was completed in mid-2020, connecting administrative centers across the country; almost all internet connections are made via mobile networks; GSM services account for a dwindling proportion of connections, in line with the greater reach of services based on 3G and LTE (2022)
domestic: fixed-line teledensity is less than 1 per 100 persons; mobile-cellular subscribership is just over 105 per 100 persons (2020)
international: country code - 224; ACE submarine cable connecting Guinea with 20 landing points in Western and South Africa and Europe; satellite earth station - 1 Intelsat (Atlantic Ocean (2019)

Broadcast media: Government maintains control over broadcast media; single state-run TV station; state-run radio broadcast station also operates several stations in rural areas; a dozen private television stations; a steadily increasing number of privately owned radio stations, nearly all in Conakry, and about a dozen community radio stations; foreign TV programming available via satellite and cable subscription services
(2022)

Internet country code: .gn

Internet users: *total:* 4.9 million (2021 est.)
percent of population: 35% (2021 est.)
comparison ranking: total 94

Broadband - fixed subscriptions: *total:* 1,000 (2020 est.)
subscriptions per 100 inhabitants: 0.01 (2020 est.)
comparison ranking: total 203

TRANSPORTATION

Civil aircraft registration country code prefix: 3X

Airports: 16 (2024)
comparison ranking: 147

Heliports: 1 (2024)

Railways: *total:* 1,086 km (2017)
standard gauge: 279 km (2017) 1.435-m gauge
narrow gauge: 807 km (2017) 1.000-m gauge
comparison ranking: total 88

Roadways: *total:* 44,301 km
paved: 3,346 km
unpaved: 40,955 km (2018)
comparison ranking: total 88

Waterways: 1,300 km (2011) (navigable by shallow-draft native craft in the northern part of the Niger River system)
comparison ranking: 58

Merchant marine: *total:* 2 (2023)
by type: other 2
comparison ranking: total 175

Ports: *total ports:* 4 (2024)
large: 0
medium: 1
small: 0
very small: 3
ports with oil terminals: 2
key ports: Benti, Conakry, Kamsar, Victoria

MILITARY AND SECURITY

Military and security forces: Guinean (or National) Armed Forces (Forces Armées Guinéennes): Army, Guinean Navy (Armee de Mer or Marine Guineenne), Guinean Air Force (Force Aerienne de Guinee), Presidential Security Battalion (Battailon Autonome de la Sécurité Presidentielle, BASP), National Gendarmerie (2023)
note: the National Gendarmerie is overseen by the Ministry of Defense, while the National Police is under the Ministry of Security; the Gendarmerie and National Police share responsibility for internal security, but only the Gendarmerie can arrest police or military officials

Military expenditures: 2.2% of GDP (2023 est.)
1.8% of GDP (2022 est.)
1.5% of GDP (2021 est.)
1.4% of GDP (2020 est.)
1.6% of GDP (2019 est.)
comparison ranking: 53

Military and security service personnel strengths: approximately 12,000 active personnel, including about 1,500 Gendarmerie (2023)

Military equipment inventories and acquisitions: the inventory of the Guinean military consists largely of aging and outdated (mostly Soviet-era) equipment; in recent years, it has received small amounts of equipment from China, France, and South Africa (2023)

Military service age and obligation: 18 years of age for voluntary and selective conscripted service; 9-12 months of service (2023)

Military - note: the Guinean military is a small and lightly armed force that is responsible for territorial defense, but also has some domestic security responsibilities and has historically been involved in suppressing public protests; the military has undergone some attempts at reform since 2010, but in 2021 the Army's special forces led a military overthrow of the government (2024)

TRANSNATIONAL ISSUES

Illicit drugs: NA

GUINEA-BISSAU

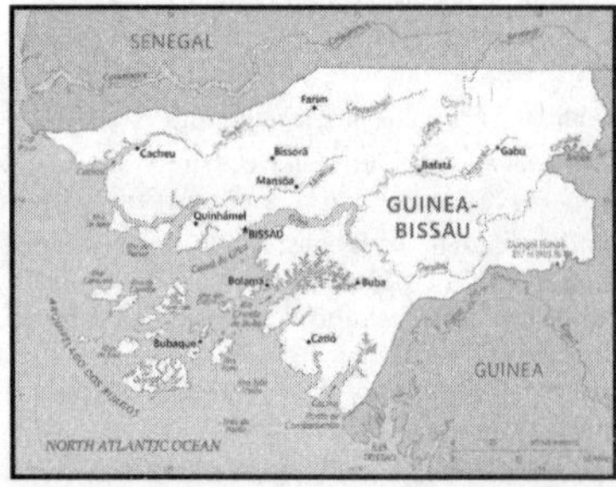

INTRODUCTION

Background: For much of its history, Guinea-Bissau was under the control of the Mali Empire and the Kaabu Kingdom. In the 16th century, Portugal began establishing trading posts along Guinea-Bissau's shoreline. Initially, the Portuguese were restricted to the coastline and islands. However, the slave and gold trades were lucrative to local African leaders, and the Portuguese were slowly able to expand their power and influence inland. Starting in the 18th century, the Mali Empire and Kingdom of Kaabu slowly disintegrated into smaller local entities. By the 19th century, Portugal had fully incorporated Guinea-Bissau into its empire.

Since gaining independence in 1974, Guinea-Bissau has experienced considerable political and military upheaval. In 1980, a military coup established General Joao Bernardo 'Nino' VIEIRA as president. VIEIRA's regime suppressed political opposition and purged political rivals. Several coup attempts through the 1980s and early 1990s failed to unseat him, but a military mutiny and civil war in 1999 led to VIEIRA's ouster. In 2000, a transitional government turned over power to opposition leader Kumba YALA. In 2003, a bloodless military coup overthrew YALA and installed businessman Henrique ROSA as interim president. In 2005, VIEIRA was reelected, pledging to pursue economic development and national reconciliation; he was assassinated in 2009. Malam Bacai SANHA was then elected president, but he passed away in 2012 from a long-term illness. A military coup blocked the second round of the election to replace him, but after mediation from the Economic Community of Western African States, a civilian transitional government assumed power. In 2014, Jose Mario VAZ was elected president in a free and fair election, and in 2019, he became the first president in Guinea-Bissau's history to complete a full term. Umaro Sissoco EMBALO was elected president in 2019, but he did not take office until 2020 because of a prolonged challenge to the election results.

GEOGRAPHY

Location: Western Africa, bordering the North Atlantic Ocean, between Guinea and Senegal

Geographic coordinates: 12 00 N, 15 00 W

Map references: Africa

Area: *total:* 36,125 sq km
land: 28,120 sq km
water: 8,005 sq km
comparison ranking: total 137

Area - comparative: slightly less than three times the size of Connecticut

Land boundaries: *total:* 762 km
border countries (2): Guinea 421 km; Senegal 341 km

Coastline: 350 km

Maritime claims: *territorial sea:* 12 nm
exclusive economic zone: 200 nm

Climate: tropical; generally hot and humid; monsoonal-type rainy season (June to November) with southwesterly winds; dry season (December to May) with northeasterly harmattan winds

Terrain: mostly low-lying coastal plain with a deeply indented estuarine coastline rising to savanna in east; numerous off-shore islands including the Arquipelago Dos Bijagos consisting of 18 main islands and many small islets

Elevation: *highest point:* Dongol Ronde 277 m
lowest point: Atlantic Ocean 0 m
mean elevation: 70 m

Natural resources: fish, timber, phosphates, bauxite, clay, granite, limestone, unexploited deposits of petroleum

Land use: *agricultural land:* 44.8% (2018 est.)
arable land: 8.2% (2018 est.)
permanent crops: 6.9% (2018 est.)
permanent pasture: 29.7% (2018 est.)
forest: 55.2% (2018 est.)
other: 0% (2018 est.)

Irrigated land: 250 sq km (2012)

Major aquifers: Senegalo-Mauritanian Basin

Population distribution: approximately one-fifth of the population lives in the capital city of Bissau along the Atlantic coast; the remainder is distributed among the eight other, mainly rural, regions as shown in this population distribution map

Natural hazards: hot, dry, dusty harmattan haze may reduce visibility during dry season; brush fires

Geography - note: this small country is swampy along its western coast and low-lying inland

PEOPLE AND SOCIETY

Population: *total:* 2,132,325
male: 1,042,910
female: 1,089,415 (2024 est.)
comparison rankings: female 147; male 151; total 150

Nationality: *noun:* Bissau-Guinean(s)
adjective: Bissau-Guinean

Ethnic groups: Balanta 30%, Fulani 30%, Manjaco 14%, Mandinga 13%, Papel 7%, unspecified smaller ethnic groups 6% (2015 est.)

Languages: Portuguese-based Creole, Portuguese (official; largely used as a second or third language), Pular (a Fula language), Mandingo

Religions: Muslim 46.1%, folk religions 30.6%, Christian 18.9%, other or unaffiliated 4.4% (2020 est.)

Demographic profile: Guinea-Bissau's young and growing population is sustained by high fertility; approximately 60% of the population is under the age of 25 as of 2020. Its large reproductive-age population and total fertility rate of more than 4 children per woman offsets the country's high infant and maternal mortality rates. The latter is among the world's highest because of the prevalence of early childbearing, a lack of birth spacing, the high percentage of births outside of health care facilities, and a shortage of medicines and supplies.
Guinea-Bissau's history of political instability, a civil war, and several coups (the latest in 2012) have resulted in a fragile state with a weak economy, high unemployment, rampant corruption, widespread poverty, and thriving drug and child trafficking. With the country lacking educational infrastructure, school funding and materials, and qualified teachers, and with the cultural emphasis placed on religious education, parents frequently send boys to study in residential Koranic schools (daaras) in Senegal and The Gambia. They often are extremely deprived and are forced into street begging or agricultural work by marabouts (Muslim religious teachers), who enrich themselves at the expense of the children. Boys who leave their marabouts often end up on the streets of Dakar or other large Senegalese towns and are vulnerable to even worse abuse.
Some young men lacking in education and job prospects become involved in the flourishing international drug trade. Local drug use and associated violent crime are growing.

Age structure: *0-14 years:* 42.3% (male 453,513/female 448,514)
15-64 years: 54.6% (male 561,868/female 602,280)
65 years and over: 3.1% (2024 est.) (male 27,529/female 38,621)

Dependency ratios: *total dependency ratio:* 76.6
youth dependency ratio: 71.6
elderly dependency ratio: 5
potential support ratio: 20.1 (2021 est.)

Median age: *total:* 18.4 years (2024 est.)
male: 17.8 years
female: 18.9 years
comparison ranking: total 221

Population growth rate: 2.54% (2024 est.)
comparison ranking: 18

Birth rate: 36 births/1,000 population (2024 est.)
comparison ranking: 11

Death rate: 7.2 deaths/1,000 population (2024 est.)
comparison ranking: 114

Net migration rate: -3.5 migrant(s)/1,000 population (2024 est.)
comparison ranking: 188

Population distribution: approximately one-fifth of the population lives in the capital city of Bissau along the Atlantic coast; the remainder is distributed among the eight other, mainly rural, regions as shown in this population distribution map

Urbanization: *urban population:* 45.5% of total population (2023)
rate of urbanization: 3.22% annual rate of change (2020-25 est.)

Major urban areas - population: 664,000 BISSAU (capital) (2023)

Sex ratio: *at birth:* 1.03 male(s)/female
0-14 years: 1.01 male(s)/female
15-64 years: 0.93 male(s)/female
65 years and over: 0.71 male(s)/female
total population: 0.96 male(s)/female (2024 est.)

Maternal mortality ratio: 725 deaths/100,000 live births (2020 est.)
comparison ranking: 5

Infant mortality rate: *total:* 46.4 deaths/1,000 live births (2024 est.)
male: 52 deaths/1,000 live births
female: 40.6 deaths/1,000 live births
comparison ranking: total 22

Life expectancy at birth: *total population:* 64.5 years (2024 est.)
male: 62.2 years
female: 66.8 years
comparison ranking: total population 207

Total fertility rate: 4.62 children born/woman (2024 est.)
comparison ranking: 13

Gross reproduction rate: 2.28 (2024 est.)

Contraceptive prevalence rate: 20.6% (2018/19)

Drinking water source: *improved: urban:* 90.6% of population
rural: 59.1% of population
total: 73.1% of population
unimproved: urban: 9.4% of population
rural: 40.9% of population
total: 26.9% of population (2020 est.)

Current health expenditure: 8.4% of GDP (2020)

Physician density: 0.2 physicians/1,000 population (2020)

Sanitation facility access: *improved: urban:* 62.4% of population
rural: 7.6% of population
total: 31.8% of population
unimproved: urban: 37.6% of population
rural: 92.4% of population
total: 68.2% of population (2020 est.)

Obesity - adult prevalence rate: 9.5% (2016)
comparison ranking: 144

Alcohol consumption per capita: *total:* 3.21 liters of pure alcohol (2019 est.)
beer: 0.41 liters of pure alcohol (2019 est.)
wine: 0.98 liters of pure alcohol (2019 est.)
spirits: 0.54 liters of pure alcohol (2019 est.)
other alcohols: 1.28 liters of pure alcohol (2019 est.)
comparison ranking: total 108

Tobacco use: *total:* 9% (2020 est.)
male: 17% (2020 est.)
female: 0.9% (2020 est.)
comparison ranking: total 139

Children under the age of 5 years underweight: 18.8% (2019)
comparison ranking: 22

Currently married women (ages 15-49): 56.7% (2023 est.)

Child marriage: *women married by age 15:* 8.1%
women married by age 18: 25.7%
men married by age 18: 2.2% (2019 est.)

Education expenditures: 2.7% of GDP (2020 est.)
comparison ranking: 168

Literacy: *definition:* age 15 and over can read and write
total population: 52.9%
male: 67%
female: 39.9% (2021)

ENVIRONMENT

Environment - current issues: deforestation (rampant felling of trees for timber and agricultural purposes); soil erosion; overgrazing; overfishing

Environment - international agreements: *party to:* Biodiversity, Climate Change, Climate

Change-Kyoto Protocol, Climate Change-Paris Agreement, Comprehensive Nuclear Test Ban, Desertification, Endangered Species, Hazardous Wastes, Law of the Sea, Nuclear Test Ban, Ozone Layer Protection, Ship Pollution, Wetlands, Whaling
signed, but not ratified: none of the selected agreements

Climate: tropical; generally hot and humid; monsoonal-type rainy season (June to November) with southwesterly winds; dry season (December to May) with northeasterly harmattan winds

Urbanization: *urban population:* 45.5% of total population (2023)
rate of urbanization: 3.22% annual rate of change (2020-25 est.)

Revenue from forest resources: 9.24% of GDP (2018 est.)
comparison ranking: 4

Revenue from coal: 0% of GDP (2018 est.)
comparison ranking: 179

Air pollutants: *particulate matter emissions:* 34.85 micrograms per cubic meter (2019 est.)
carbon dioxide emissions: 0.29 megatons (2016 est.)
methane emissions: 1.46 megatons (2020 est.)

Waste and recycling: *municipal solid waste generated annually:* 289,514 tons (2015 est.)

Major aquifers: Senegalo-Mauritanian Basin

Total water withdrawal: *municipal:* 30 million cubic meters (2020 est.)
industrial: 10 million cubic meters (2020 est.)
agricultural: 140 million cubic meters (2020 est.)

Total renewable water resources: 31.4 billion cubic meters (2020 est.)

GOVERNMENT

Country name: *conventional long form:* Republic of Guinea-Bissau
conventional short form: Guinea-Bissau
local long form: Republica da Guine-Bissau
local short form: Guine-Bissau
former: Portuguese Guinea
etymology: the country is named after the Guinea region of West Africa that lies along the Gulf of Guinea and stretches north to the Sahel; "Bissau," the name of the capital city, distinguishes the country from neighboring Guinea

Government type: semi-presidential republic

Capital: *name:* Bissau
geographic coordinates: 11 51 N, 15 35 W
time difference: UTC 0 (5 hours ahead of Washington, DC, during Standard Time)
etymology: the meaning of Bissau is uncertain, it might be an alternative name for the Papel people who live in the area of the city of Bissau

Administrative divisions: 9 regions (regioes, singular - regiao); Bafata, Biombo, Bissau, Bolama/Bijagos, Cacheu, Gabu, Oio, Quinara, Tombali

Independence: 24 September 1973 (declared); 10 September 1974 (from Portugal)

National holiday: Independence Day, 24 September (1973)

Legal system: mixed legal system of civil law, which incorporated Portuguese law at independence and influenced by Economic Community of West African States (ECOWAS), West African Economic and Monetary Union (UEMOA), African Francophone Public Law, and customary law

Constitution: *history:* promulgated 16 May 1984; note - constitution suspended following military coup April 2012, restored 2014; note - in May 2020, President EMBALO established a commission to draft a revised constitution
amendments: proposed by the National People's Assembly if supported by at least one third of its members, by the Council of State (a presidential consultant body), or by the government; passage requires approval by at least two-thirds majority vote of the Assembly; constitutional articles on the republican and secular form of government and national sovereignty cannot be amended; amended 1991, 1993, 1996

International law organization participation: accepts compulsory ICJ jurisdiction; non-party state to the ICCt

Citizenship: *citizenship by birth:* yes
citizenship by descent only: yes
dual citizenship recognized: no
residency requirement for naturalization: 5 years

Suffrage: 18 years of age; universal

Executive branch: *chief of state:* President Umaro Sissoco EMBALO (since 27 February 2020)
head of government: Prime Minister Rui Duarte DE BARROS (since 20 December 2023)
cabinet: Cabinet nominated by the prime minister, appointed by the president
elections/appointments: president directly elected by absolute majority popular vote in 2 rounds if needed for up to 2 consecutive 5-year terms; election last held on 24 November 2019 with a runoff on 29 December 2019 (next to be held in 2024); prime minister appointed by the president after consultation with party leaders in the National People's Assembly; note - the president cannot apply for a third consecutive term; note - President EMBALO was declared winner of the 29 December 2019 runoff presidential election by the electoral commission; in late February 2020, EMBALO inaugurated himself with only military leadership present, even though the Supreme Court of Justice had yet to rule on an electoral litigation appeal lodged by his political rival Domingos Simoes PEREIRA
election results:
2019: Umaro Sissoco EMBALO elected president in second round; percent of vote in first round - Domingos Simoes PEREIRA (PAIGC) 40.1%, Umaro Sissoco EMBALO (Madem G15) 27.7%, Nuno Gomez NABIAM (APU-PDGB) 13.2%, Jose Mario VAZ (independent) 12.4%, other 6.6%; percent of vote in second round - Umaro Sissoco EMBALO 53.6%, Domingos Simoes PEREIRA 46.5%
2014: Jose Mario VAZ elected president in second round; percent of vote in first round - Jose Mario VAZ (PAIGC) 41%, Nuno Gomez NABIAM (independent) 25.1%, other 33.9%; percent of vote in second round - Jose Mario VAZ 61.9%, Nuno Gomez NABIAM 38.1% (2019)

Legislative branch: *description:* unicameral National People's Assembly or Assembleia Nacional Popular (102 seats; 100 members directly elected in 27 multi-seat constituencies by closed party-list proportional representation vote and 2 elected in single-seat constituencies for citizens living abroad (Africa 1, Europe 1); all members serve 4-year terms)
elections: last held on 4 June 2023 (next to be held on 30 June 2027); note - on 4 December 2023 the president dissolved the parliament with new elections to be held at a future date
election results: percent of vote by party - PAIGC 39.4%, Madem G-15 21.1%, PRS 14.9%, other 12.5%; seats by party - PAIGC 54, Madem G-15 29, PRS- 12, other 7; composition - men 92, women 10, percentage women 9.8%

Judicial branch: *highest court(s):* Supreme Court or Supremo Tribunal de Justica (consists of 9 judges and organized into Civil, Criminal, and Social and Administrative Disputes Chambers); note - the Supreme Court has both appellate and constitutional jurisdiction
judge selection and term of office: judges nominated by the Higher Council of the Magistrate, a major government organ responsible for judge appointments, dismissals, and judiciary discipline; judges appointed by the president for life
subordinate courts: Appeals Court; regional (first instance) courts; military court

Political parties: African Party for the Independence of Guinea and Cabo Verde or PAIGC
Democratic Convergence Party or PCD
Movement for Democratic Alternation Group of 15 or MADEM-G15
National People's Assembly – Democratic Party of Guinea Bissau or APU-PDGB
New Democracy Party or PND
Party for Social Renewal or PRS
Republican Party for Independence and Development or PRID
Union for Change or UM

International organization participation: ACP, AfDB, AOSIS, AU, CPLP, ECOWAS, FAO, FZ, G-77, IBRD, ICAO, ICRM, IDA, IDB, IFAD, IFC, IFRCS, ILO, IMF, IMO, Interpol, IOC, IOM, IPU, ITSO, ITU, ITUC (NGOs), MIGA, MINUSMA, NAM, OIC, OIF, OPCW, UN, UNCTAD, UNESCO, UNIDO, UNWTO, UPU, WADB (regional), WAEMU, WCO, WFTU (NGOs), WHO, WIPO, WMO, WTO

Diplomatic representation in the US: *chief of mission:* Ambassador Maria Da Conceição NOBRE CABRAL (since 18 September 2024)
chancery: 918 16th Street, NW (Mezzanine Suite) Washington DC 20006
telephone: [1] (202) 872-4222
FAX: [1] (202) 872-4226

Diplomatic representation from the US: *chief of mission:* Ambassador Michael RAYNOR (since 20 April 2022)
mailing address: 2080 Bissau Place, Washington DC 20521-2080
email address and website:
dakarACS@state.gov
https://gw.usmission.gov/

Flag description: two equal horizontal bands of yellow (top) and green with a vertical red band on the hoist side; there is a black five-pointed star centered in the red band; yellow symbolizes the sun; green denotes hope; red represents blood shed during the struggle for independence; the black star stands for African unity
note: uses the popular Pan-African colors of Ethiopia; the flag design was heavily influenced by the Ghanaian flag

National symbol(s): black star; national colors: red, yellow, green, black

National anthem: *name:* "Esta e a Nossa Patria Bem Amada" (This Is Our Beloved Country)
lyrics/music: Amilcar Lopes CABRAL/XIAO He

note: adopted 1974; a delegation from then Portuguese Guinea visited China in 1963 and heard music by XIAO He; Amilcar Lopes CABRAL, the leader of Guinea-Bissau's independence movement, asked the composer to create a piece that would inspire his people to struggle for independence

ECONOMY

Economic overview: extremely poor West African economy; ethnically diverse labor force; increasing government expenditures; slight inflation due to food supply disruptions; major cashew exporter; systemic banking instabilities and corruption; vulnerable to oil price shocks

Real GDP (purchasing power parity): $5.099 billion (2023 est.)
$4.892 billion (2022 est.)
$4.694 billion (2021 est.)
note: data in 2021 dollars
comparison ranking: 184

Real GDP growth rate: 4.25% (2023 est.)
4.2% (2022 est.)
6.4% (2021 est.)
note: annual GDP % growth based on constant local currency
comparison ranking: 71

Real GDP per capita: $2,400 (2023 est.)
$2,300 (2022 est.)
$2,300 (2021 est.)
note: data in 2021 dollars
comparison ranking: 207

GDP (official exchange rate): $1.966 billion (2023 est.)
note: data in current dollars at official exchange rate

Inflation rate (consumer prices): 9.39% (2022 est.)
2.24% (2021 est.)
1.14% (2020 est.)
note: annual % change based on consumer prices
comparison ranking: 172

GDP - composition, by sector of origin: *agriculture:* 33.7% (2023 est.)
industry: 16.1% (2023 est.)
services: 45.1% (2023 est.)
note: figures may not total 100% due to non-allocated consumption not captured in sector-reported data
comparison rankings: services 166; industry 164; agriculture 10

GDP - composition, by end use: *household consumption:* 66.6% (2023 est.)
government consumption: 19% (2023 est.)
investment in fixed capital: 23.8% (2023 est.)
investment in inventories: 0.2% (2023 est.)
exports of goods and services: 17.9% (2023 est.)
imports of goods and services: -28.3% (2023 est.)
note: figures may not total 100% due to rounding or gaps in data collection

Agricultural products: rice, groundnuts, cashews, root vegetables, oil palm fruit, plantains, cassava, vegetables, sweet potatoes, coconuts (2022)
note: top ten agricultural products based on tonnage

Industries: agricultural products processing, beer, soft drinks

Industrial production growth rate: 4% (2023 est.)
note: annual % change in industrial value added based on constant local currency
comparison ranking: 78

Labor force: 726,000 (2023 est.)
note: number of people ages 15 or older who are employed or seeking work
comparison ranking: 154

Unemployment rate: 3.18% (2023 est.)
3.2% (2022 est.)
3.63% (2021 est.)
note: % of labor force seeking employment
comparison ranking: 54

Youth unemployment rate (ages 15-24): *total:* 4% (2023 est.)
male: 3.9% (2023 est.)
female: 4.2% (2023 est.)
note: % of labor force ages 15-24 seeking employment
comparison ranking: total 185

Population below poverty line: 47.7% (2018 est.)
note: % of population with income below national poverty line

Gini Index coefficient - distribution of family income: 33.4 (2021 est.)
note: index (0-100) of income distribution; higher values represent greater inequality
comparison ranking: 98

Household income or consumption by percentage share: *lowest 10%:* 3.4% (2021 est.)
highest 10%: 26.1% (2021 est.)
note: % share of income accruing to lowest and highest 10% of population

Remittances: 9.38% of GDP (2023 est.)
12.02% of GDP (2022 est.)
11.95% of GDP (2021 est.)
note: personal transfers and compensation between resident and non-resident individuals/households/entities

Budget: *revenues:* $220.219 million (2019 est.)
expenditures: $210.858 million (2019 est.)
note: central government revenues and expenses (excluding grants/extrabudgetary units/social security funds) converted to US dollars at average official exchange rate for year indicated

Public debt: 53.9% of GDP (2017 est.)
comparison ranking: 91

Taxes and other revenues: 9.16% (of GDP) (2019 est.)
note: central government tax revenue as a % of GDP
comparison ranking: 183

Current account balance: -$146.64 million (2022 est.)
-$14.128 million (2021 est.)
-$38.683 million (2020 est.)
note: balance of payments - net trade and primary/secondary income in current dollars
comparison ranking: 104

Exports: $280.065 million (2022 est.)
$334.904 million (2021 est.)
$232.536 million (2020 est.)
note: balance of payments - exports of goods and services in current dollars
comparison ranking: 198

Exports - partners: India 92%, Cote d'Ivoire 2%, Togo 2%, Netherlands 1%, South Korea 1% (2022)
note: top five export partners based on percentage share of exports

Exports - commodities: coconuts/Brazil nuts/cashews, fish, fish oil, palm oil, dried fruits (2022)
note: top five export commodities based on value in dollars

Imports: $577.899 million (2022 est.)
$518.162 million (2021 est.)
$439.386 million (2020 est.)
note: balance of payments - imports of goods and services in current dollars
comparison ranking: 200

Imports - partners: Portugal 34%, Senegal 22%, China 14%, Netherlands 6%, Spain 3% (2022)
note: top five import partners based on percentage share of imports

Imports - commodities: refined petroleum, steel, rice, flavored water, beer (2022)
note: top five import commodities based on value in dollars

Reserves of foreign exchange and gold: $356.4 million (31 December 2017 est.)
$349.4 million (31 December 2016 est.)
comparison ranking: 170

Debt - external: $808.187 million (2022 est.)
note: present value of external debt in current US dollars
comparison ranking: 84

Exchange rates: Communaute Financiere Africaine francs (XOF) per US dollar -

Exchange rates: 606.57 (2023 est.)
623.76 (2022 est.)
554.531 (2021 est.)
575.586 (2020 est.)
585.911 (2019 est.)

ENERGY

Electricity access: *electrification - total population:* 37.4% (2022 est.)
electrification - urban areas: 61%
electrification - rural areas: 15.8%

Electricity: *installed generating capacity:* 28,000 kW (2022 est.)
consumption: 78.87 million kWh (2022 est.)
transmission/distribution losses: 6 million kWh (2022 est.)
comparison rankings: transmission/distribution losses 12; consumption 201; installed generating capacity 203

Electricity generation sources: *fossil fuels:* 97.6% of total installed capacity (2022 est.)
solar: 2.4% of total installed capacity (2022 est.)

Petroleum: *refined petroleum consumption:* 2,000 bbl/day (2022 est.)

Carbon dioxide emissions: 362,000 metric tonnes of CO_2 (2022 est.)
from petroleum and other liquids: 362,000 metric tonnes of CO_2 (2022 est.)
comparison ranking: total emissions 194

Energy consumption per capita: 2.372 million Btu/person (2022 est.)
comparison ranking: 182

COMMUNICATIONS

Telephones - fixed lines: *total subscriptions:* 4,800 (2009 est.)
subscriptions per 100 inhabitants: (2018 est.) less than 1
comparison ranking: total subscriptions 205

Telephones - mobile cellular: *total subscriptions:* 2.652 million (2022 est.)
subscriptions per 100 inhabitants: 126 (2022 est.)
comparison ranking: total subscriptions 146

Telecommunication systems: *general assessment:* small system including a combination of microwave radio relay, open-wire lines, radiotelephone,

and mobile cellular communications; 2 mobile network operators; one of the poorest countries in the world and this is reflected in the country's telecommunications development; radio is the most important source of information for the public (2020)
domestic: fixed-line teledensity less than 1 per 100 persons; mobile cellular teledensity is just over 109 per 100 persons (2021)
international: country code - 245; ACE submarine cable connecting Guinea-Bissau with 20 landing points in Western and South Africa and Europe (2019)

Broadcast media: 1 state-owned TV station, Televisao da Guine-Bissau (TGB) and a second station, Radio e Televisao de Portugal (RTP) Africa, is operated by Portuguese public broadcaster (RTP); 1 state-owned radio station, several private radio stations, and some community radio stations; multiple international broadcasters are available (2019)

Internet country code: .gw

Internet users: *total:* 735,000 (2021 est.)
percent of population: 35% (2021 est.)
comparison ranking: total 159

Broadband - fixed subscriptions: *total:* 2,383 (2020 est.)
subscriptions per 100 inhabitants: 0.1 (2020 est.)
comparison ranking: total 198

TRANSPORTATION

Civil aircraft registration country code prefix: J5

Airports: 7 (2024)
comparison ranking: 170

Roadways: *total:* 4,400 km
paved: 453 km
unpaved: 3,947 km (2016)
comparison ranking: total 153

Waterways: 1,367 km (2022) major rivers Geba-550km, Corubal 560 km, Cacheu 257 km (rivers are partially navigable; many inlets and creeks provide shallow-water access to much of interior)
comparison ranking: 56

Merchant marine: *total:* 20 (2023)
by type: bulk carrier 3, general cargo 12, other 5
comparison ranking: total 147

Ports: *total ports:* 2 (2024)
large: 0
medium: 0
small: 0
very small: 2
ports with oil terminals: 1
key ports: Bissau, Rio Cacheu

MILITARY AND SECURITY

Military and security forces: People's Revolutionary Armed Force (Forcas Armadas Revolucionarias do Povo or FARP): Army, Navy, Air Force

Ministry of Internal Administration: National Guard (a gendarmerie force), Public Order Police, Border Police, Rapid Intervention Police, Maritime Police (2024)
note: the Public Order Police is responsible for maintaining law and order, while the Judicial Police, under the Ministry of Justice, has primary responsibility for investigating drug trafficking, terrorism, and other transnational crimes

Military expenditures: 1.4% of GDP (2023 est.)
1.6% of GDP (2022 est.)
1.8% of GDP (2021 est.)
1.7% of GDP (2020 est.)
1.9% of GDP (2019 est.)
comparison ranking: 98

Military and security service personnel strengths: approximately 4,000 active troops, including a few hundred air and naval personnel (2023)

Military equipment inventories and acquisitions: the FARP is outfitted mostly with Soviet-era equipment (2023)

Military service age and obligation: 18-25 years of age for selective compulsory military service for men and women (Air Force service is voluntary); 16 years of age or younger, with parental consent, for voluntary service (2023)

Military - note: the FARP is focused on external security, but also has some internal security duties, and it has been influential in the country's politics since independence was gained in 1974, having staged at least nine coup attempts as well as several mutinies; FARP members were suspected of coup plotting as recently as 2021, and it put down an attempted coup in 2022, while the National Guard attempted a coup in December 2023; since the 2000s, the FARP has undergone various attempts at defense and security sector reforms with limited success under the auspices of the African Union, the EU, the Economic Community of West Africa (ECOWAS), and the UN from 2012-2020, ECOWAS deployed a security force to Guinea-Bissau to manage the post-coup transition, including protecting key political figures and public buildings, restoring civil institutions, and re-establishing the rule of law; at the height of the deployment, the force, known as the ECOWAS Mission in Guinea-Bissau (ECOMIB), deployed nearly 700 military and police personnel from Burkina Faso, Nigeria, and Senegal; as of 2024, ECOMIB remained in Guinea-Bissau (2024)

TRANSNATIONAL ISSUES

Refugees and internally displaced persons: *refugees (country of origin):* 7,757 (Senegal) (2022)

Trafficking in persons: tier rating: Tier 2 Watch List — The Government of Guinea-Bissau does not fully meet the minimum standards for the elimination of trafficking but is making significant efforts to do so, therefore Guinea-Bissau was upgraded to Tier 2 Watch List; for more details, go to: https://www.state.gov/reports/2024-trafficking-in-persons-report/guinea-bissau/

Illicit drugs: important transit country for South American cocaine en route to Europe; enabling environment for trafficker operations due to pervasive corruption; archipelago-like geography near the capital facilitates drug smuggling

GUYANA

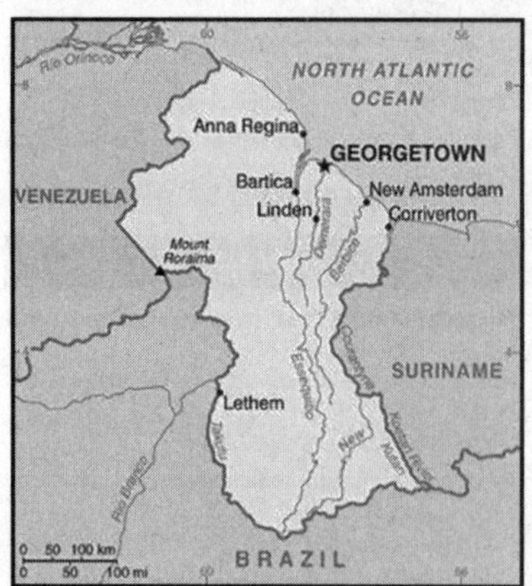

INTRODUCTION

Background: Originally a Dutch colony in the 17th century, by 1815 Guyana had become a British possession. The abolition of slavery led to former slaves settling urban areas and indentured servants being imported from India to work the sugar plantations. The resulting ethnocultural divide has persisted and has led to turbulent politics. Guyana achieved independence from the UK in 1966, and since then primarily socialist-oriented governments have ruled the country.

In 1992, Cheddi JAGAN was elected president in what is considered the country's first free and fair election since independence. After his death five years later, his wife, Janet JAGAN, became president but resigned in 1999 due to poor health. Her successor, Bharrat JAGDEO, was elected in 2001 and again in 2006. Donald RAMOTAR won in 2011, but early elections held in 2015 resulted in the first change in governing party, and David GRANGER took office. After a 2018 no-confidence vote against the GRANGER government, the administration ignored a constitutional requirement to hold elections and remained in place until the 2020 elections, when Irfaan ALI became president.

The discovery of massive offshore oil reserves in 2015 has been Guyana's primary economic and political focus, with many hoping the reserves will transform one of the poorest countries in the region. Guyana is the only English-speaking country in South America and shares cultural and historical bonds with the Anglophone Caribbean.

GEOGRAPHY

Location: Northern South America, bordering the North Atlantic Ocean, between Suriname and Venezuela

Geographic coordinates: 5 00 N, 59 00 W

Map references: South America

Area: *total:* 214,969 sq km
land: 196,849 sq km
water: 18,120 sq km
comparison ranking: total 85

Area - comparative: slightly smaller than Idaho; almost twice the size of Tennessee

Land boundaries: *total:* 2,933 km
border countries (3): Brazil 1,308 km; Suriname 836 km; Venezuela 789 km

Coastline: 459 km

Maritime claims: *territorial sea:* 12 nm
exclusive economic zone: 200 nm
continental shelf: 200 nm or to the outer edge of the continental margin

Climate: tropical; hot, humid, moderated by northeast trade winds; two rainy seasons (May to August, November to January)

Terrain: mostly rolling highlands; low coastal plain; savanna in south

Elevation: *highest point:* Laberintos del Norte on Mount Roraima 2,775 m
lowest point: Atlantic Ocean 0 m
mean elevation: 207 m

Natural resources: bauxite, gold, diamonds, hardwood timber, shrimp, fish

Land use: *agricultural land:* 8.4% (2018 est.)
arable land: 2.1% (2018 est.)
permanent crops: 0.1% (2018 est.)
permanent pasture: 6.2% (2018 est.)
forest: 77.4% (2018 est.)
other: 14.2% (2018 est.)

Irrigated land: 1,430 sq km (2012)

Major watersheds (area sq km): Atlantic Ocean drainage: Amazon (6,145,186 sq km), Orinoco (953,675 sq km)

Population distribution: population is heavily concentrated in the northeast in and around Georgetown, with noteable concentrations along the Berbice River to the east; the remainder of the country is sparsely populated

Natural hazards: flash flood threat during rainy seasons

Geography - note: the third-smallest country in South America after Suriname and Uruguay; substantial portions of its western and eastern territories are claimed by Venezuela and Suriname respectively; contains some of the largest unspoiled rainforests on the continent

PEOPLE AND SOCIETY

Population: *total:* 794,099
male: 405,244
female: 388,855 (2024 est.)
comparison rankings: female 166; male 166; total 166

Nationality: *noun:* Guyanese (singular and plural)
adjective: Guyanese

Ethnic groups: East Indian 39.8%, African descent 29.3%, mixed 19.9%, Indigenous 10.5%, other 0.5% (includes Portuguese, Chinese, White) (2012 est.)

Languages: English (official), Guyanese Creole, Amerindian languages (including Caribbean and Arawak languages), Indian languages (including Caribbean Hindustani, a dialect of Hindi), Chinese (2014 est.)

Religions: Protestant 34.8% (Pentecostal 22.8%, Seventh Day Adventist 5.4%, Anglican 5.2%, Methodist 1.4%), Hindu 24.8%, other Christian 20.8%, Roman Catholic 7.1%, Muslim 6.8%, Jehovah's Witness 1.3%, Rastafarian 0.5%, other 0.9%, none 3.1% (2012 est.)

Demographic profile: Guyana is the only English-speaking country in South America and shares cultural and historical bonds with the Anglophone Caribbean. Guyana's two largest ethnic groups are the Afro-Guyanese (descendants of African slaves) and the Indo-Guyanese (descendants of Indian indentured laborers), which together comprise about three quarters of Guyana's population. Tensions periodically have boiled over between the two groups, which back ethnically based political parties and vote along ethnic lines. Poverty reduction has stagnated since the late 1990s. About one-third of the Guyanese population lives below the poverty line; indigenous people are disproportionately affected. Although Guyana's literacy rate is reported to be among the highest in the Western Hemisphere, the level of functional literacy is considerably lower, which has been attributed to poor education quality, teacher training, and infrastructure.

Guyana's emigration rate is among the highest in the world - more than 55% of its citizens reside abroad - and it is one of the largest recipients of remittances relative to GDP among Latin American and Caribbean counties. Although remittances are a vital source of income for most citizens, the pervasive emigration of skilled workers deprives Guyana of professionals in healthcare and other key sectors. More than 80% of Guyanese nationals with tertiary level educations have emigrated. Brain drain and the concentration of limited medical resources in Georgetown hamper Guyana's ability to meet the health needs of its predominantly rural population. Guyana has one of the highest HIV prevalence rates in the region and continues to rely on international support for its HIV treatment and prevention programs.

Age structure: *0-14 years:* 23.5% (male 95,223/female 91,272)
15-64 years: 68.4% (male 281,669/female 261,261)
65 years and over: 8.1% (2024 est.) (male 28,352/female 36,322)

Dependency ratios: *total dependency ratio:* 53.6
youth dependency ratio: 44.1
elderly dependency ratio: 9.5
potential support ratio: 10.6 (2021 est.)

Median age: *total:* 28.3 years (2024 est.)
male: 28.2 years
female: 28.4 years
comparison ranking: total 150

Population growth rate: 0.32% (2024 est.)
comparison ranking: 164

Birth rate: 16.7 births/1,000 population (2024 est.)
comparison ranking: 95

Death rate: 7 deaths/1,000 population (2024 est.)
comparison ranking: 122

Net migration rate: -6.6 migrant(s)/1,000 population (2024 est.)
comparison ranking: 214

Population distribution: population is heavily concentrated in the northeast in and around Georgetown, with noteable concentrations along the Berbice River to the east; the remainder of the country is sparsely populated

Urbanization: *urban population:* 27.2% of total population (2023)
rate of urbanization: 1.01% annual rate of change (2020-25 est.)

Major urban areas - population: 110,000 GEORGETOWN (capital) (2018)

Sex ratio: *at birth:* 1.05 male(s)/female
0-14 years: 1.04 male(s)/female
15-64 years: 1.08 male(s)/female
65 years and over: 0.78 male(s)/female
total population: 1.04 male(s)/female (2024 est.)

Mother's mean age at first birth: 20.8 years (2009 est.)
note: data represents median age at first birth among women 25-29

Maternal mortality ratio: 112 deaths/100,000 live births (2020 est.)
comparison ranking: 65

Infant mortality rate: *total:* 21.1 deaths/1,000 live births (2024 est.)
male: 23.9 deaths/1,000 live births
female: 18.3 deaths/1,000 live births
comparison ranking: total 75

Life expectancy at birth: *total population:* 72.4 years (2024 est.)
male: 70.6 years
female: 74.3 years
comparison ranking: total population 163

Total fertility rate: 2.05 children born/woman (2024 est.)
comparison ranking: 99

Gross reproduction rate: 1 (2024 est.)

Contraceptive prevalence rate: 29.9% (2019/20)

Drinking water source: *improved:* *urban:* 100% of population
rural: 95.6% of population
total: 96.8% of population
unimproved: *urban:* 0% of population
rural: 4.4% of population
total: 3.2% of population (2020 est.)

Current health expenditure: 5.5% of GDP (2020)

Physician density: 1.42 physicians/1,000 population (2020)

Hospital bed density: 1.7 beds/1,000 population (2016)

Sanitation facility access: *improved:* *urban:* 97.8% of population
rural: 95.4% of population
total: 96% of population
unimproved: *urban:* 2.2% of population
rural: 4.6% of population
total: 4% of population (2020 est.)

Obesity - adult prevalence rate: 20.2% (2016)
comparison ranking: 102

Alcohol consumption per capita: *total:* 5.11 liters of pure alcohol (2019 est.)
beer: 2.75 liters of pure alcohol (2019 est.)
wine: 0.04 liters of pure alcohol (2019 est.)
spirits: 2.3 liters of pure alcohol (2019 est.)
other alcohols: 0.02 liters of pure alcohol (2019 est.)
comparison ranking: total 83

Tobacco use: *total:* 12.1% (2020 est.)
male: 21.7% (2020 est.)

female: 2.4% (2020 est.)
comparison ranking: total 121

Children under the age of 5 years underweight: 9.4% (2019)
comparison ranking: 59

Currently married women (ages 15-49): 62.6% (2023 est.)

Education expenditures: 4.5% of GDP (2018 est.)
comparison ranking: 98

Literacy: *definition:* age 15 and over has ever attended school
total population: 88.8%
male: 89.3%
female: 88.4% (2021)

School life expectancy (primary to tertiary education): *total:* 11 years
male: 11 years
female: 12 years (2012)

ENVIRONMENT

Environment - current issues: water pollution from sewage and agricultural and industrial chemicals; deforestation

Environment - international agreements: *party to:* Biodiversity, Climate Change, Climate Change-Kyoto Protocol, Climate Change-Paris Agreement, Comprehensive Nuclear Test Ban, Desertification, Endangered Species, Hazardous Wastes, Law of the Sea, Marine Dumping-London Protocol, Ozone Layer Protection, Ship Pollution, Tropical Timber 2006
signed, but not ratified: none of the selected agreements

Climate: tropical; hot, humid, moderated by northeast trade winds; two rainy seasons (May to August, November to January)

Urbanization: *urban population:* 27.2% of total population (2023)
rate of urbanization: 1.01% annual rate of change (2020-25 est.)

Revenue from forest resources: 4.56% of GDP (2018 est.)
comparison ranking: 13

Revenue from coal: 0% of GDP (2018 est.)
comparison ranking: 175

Air pollutants: *particulate matter emissions:* 11.11 micrograms per cubic meter (2019 est.)
carbon dioxide emissions: 2.38 megatons (2016 est.)
methane emissions: 1.81 megatons (2020 est.)

Waste and recycling: *municipal solid waste generated annually:* 179,252 tons (2010 est.)
municipal solid waste recycled annually: 968 tons (2010 est.)
percent of municipal solid waste recycled: 0.5% (2010 est.)

Major watersheds (area sq km): Atlantic Ocean drainage: Amazon (6,145,186 sq km), Orinoco (953,675 sq km)

Total water withdrawal: *municipal:* 60 million cubic meters (2020 est.)
industrial: 20 million cubic meters (2020 est.)
agricultural: 1.36 billion cubic meters (2020 est.)

Total renewable water resources: 271 billion cubic meters (2020 est.)

GOVERNMENT

Country name: *conventional long form:* Cooperative Republic of Guyana
conventional short form: Guyana
former: British Guiana
etymology: the name is derived from Guiana, the original name for the region that included British Guiana, Dutch Guiana, and French Guiana; ultimately the word is derived from an indigenous Amerindian language and means "Land of Many Waters" (referring to the area's multitude of rivers and streams)

Government type: parliamentary republic

Capital: *name:* Georgetown
geographic coordinates: 6 48 N, 58 09 W
time difference: UTC-4 (1 hour ahead of Washington, DC, during Standard Time)
etymology: when the British took possession of the town from the Dutch in 1812, they renamed it Georgetown in honor of King GEORGE III (1738-1820)

Administrative divisions: 10 regions; Barima-Waini, Cuyuni-Mazaruni, Demerara-Mahaica, East Berbice-Corentyne, Essequibo Islands-West Demerara, Mahaica-Berbice, Pomeroon-Supenaam, Potaro-Siparuni, Upper Demerara-Berbice, Upper Takutu-Upper Essequibo

Independence: 26 May 1966 (from the UK)

National holiday: Republic Day, 23 February (1970)

Legal system: common law system, based on the English model, with some Roman-Dutch civil law influence

Constitution: *history:* several previous; latest promulgated 6 October 1980
amendments: proposed by the National Assembly; passage of amendments affecting constitutional articles, such as national sovereignty, government structure and powers, and constitutional amendment procedures, requires approval by the Assembly membership, approval in a referendum, and assent of the president; other amendments only require Assembly approval; amended many times, last in 2016

International law organization participation: has not submitted an ICJ jurisdiction declaration; accepts ICCt jurisdiction

Citizenship: *citizenship by birth:* yes
citizenship by descent only: yes
dual citizenship recognized: no
residency requirement for naturalization: na

Suffrage: 18 years of age; universal

Executive branch: *chief of state:* President Mohammed Irfaan ALI (since 2 August 2020)
head of government: President Mohammed Irfaan ALI (since 2 August 2020)
cabinet: Cabinet of Ministers appointed by the president, responsible to the National Assembly
elections/appointments: the predesignated candidate of the winning party in the last National Assembly election becomes president for a 5-year term (no term limits); election last held on 2 March 2020 (next to be held in 2025); prime minister appointed by the president
election results:
2020: Mohammed Irfaan ALI (PPP/C) designated president by the majority party in the National Assembly
2015: David GRANGER (APNU-AFC) designated president by the majority party in the National Assembly
note: the president is both chief of state and head of government

Legislative branch: *description:* unicameral National Assembly (70 seats; 40 members directly elected in single-seat, nationwide constituencies, 25 directly elected in multi-seat constituencies – all by closed-list proportional representation vote, 2 nonelected ministers, 2 non-elected parliamentary secretaries, and the speaker; members serve 5-year terms)
elections: ast held on 2 March 2020 (next to be held in 2025)
election results: percent of vote by party - PPP/C 50.69%, APNU-AFC 47.34%, LJP 0.58%, ANUG 0.5%, TNM 0.05%, other 0.84%; seats by party - PPP/C 33, APNU-AFC 31, LJP-ANUG-TNM 1; composition - men 43, women 28, percentage women 39.4%; note - the initial results were declared invalid and a partial recount was conducted from 6 May to 8 June 2020, in which PPP/C was declared the winner

Judicial branch: *highest court(s):* Supreme Court of Judicature (consists of the Court of Appeal with a chief justice and 3 justices, and the High Court with a chief justice and 10 justices organized into 3- or 5-judge panels); note - in 2009, Guyana acceded to the Caribbean Court of Justice as the final court of appeal in civil and criminal cases, replacing that of the Judicial Committee of the Privy Council (in London)
judge selection and term of office: Court of Appeal and High Court chief justices appointed by the president; other judges of both courts appointed by the Judicial Service Commission, a body appointed by the president; judges appointed for life with retirement at age 65
subordinate courts: Land Court; magistrates' courts

Political parties: A New and United Guyana or ANUG
A Partnership for National Unity or APNU
Alliance for Change or AFC
Justice for All Party
Liberty and Justice Party or LJP
National Independent Party or NIP
People's Progressive Party/Civic or PPP/C
The New Movement or TNM
The United Force or TUF
United Republican Party or URP

International organization participation: ACP, ACS, AOSIS, C, Caricom, CD, CDB, CELAC, FAO, G-77, IADB, IBRD, ICAO, ICCt, ICRM, IDA, IFAD, IFC, IFRCS, ILO, IMF, IMO, Interpol, IOC, IOM, ISO (correspondent), ITU, LAES, MIGA, NAM, OAS, OIC, OPANAL, OPCW, PCA, Petrocaribe, PROSUR, UN, UNASUR, UNCTAD, UNESCO, UNIDO, UPU, WCO, WFTU (NGOs), WHO, WIPO, WMO, WTO

Diplomatic representation in the US: *chief of mission:* Ambassador Samuel Archibald HINDS (since 7 July 2021)
chancery: 2490 Tracy Place NW, Washington, DC 20008
telephone: [1] (202) 265-6900
FAX: [1] (202) 232-1297
email address and website:
guyanaembassydc@verizon.net
http://www.guyanaembassydc.org/
consulate(s) general: New York

Diplomatic representation from the US: *chief of mission:* Ambassador Nicole THERIOT (since 14 October 2023)
embassy: 100 Young and Duke Streets, Kingston, Georgetown
mailing address: 3170 Georgetown Place, Washington DC 20521-3170
telephone: [592] 225-4900 through 4909
FAX: [592] 225-8497
email address and website:
acsgeorge@state.gov
https://gy.usembassy.gov/

Flag description: green with a red isosceles triangle (based on the hoist side) superimposed on a long, yellow arrowhead; there is a narrow, black border between the red and yellow, and a narrow, white border between the yellow and the green; green represents forest and foliage; yellow stands for mineral resources and a bright future; white symbolizes Guyana's rivers; red signifies zeal and the sacrifice of the people; black indicates perseverance; also referred to by its nickname The Golden Arrowhead

National symbol(s): Canje pheasant (hoatzin), jaguar, Victoria Regia water lily; national colors: red, yellow, green, black, white

National anthem: *name:* "Dear Land of Guyana, of Rivers and Plains"
lyrics/music: Archibald Leonard LUKERL/Robert Cyril Gladstone POTTER
note: adopted 1966

ECONOMY

Economic overview: small, hydrocarbon-driven South American export economy; major forest coverage being leveraged in carbon credit offsets to encourage preservation; strengthening financial sector; large bauxite and gold resources

Real GDP (purchasing power parity): $40.539 billion (2023 est.)
$30.476 billion (2022 est.)
$18.647 billion (2021 est.)
note: data in 2021 dollars
comparison ranking: 137

Real GDP growth rate: 33.02% (2023 est.)
63.44% (2022 est.)
20.01% (2021 est.)
note: annual GDP % growth based on constant local currency
comparison ranking: 2

Real GDP per capita: $49,800 (2023 est.)
$37,700 (2022 est.)
$23,200 (2021 est.)
note: data in 2021 dollars
comparison ranking: 42

GDP (official exchange rate): $16.786 billion (2023 est.)
note: data in current dollars at official exchange rate

Inflation rate (consumer prices): 2.82% (2023 est.)
6.12% (2022 est.)
5.03% (2021 est.)
note: annual % change based on consumer prices
comparison ranking: 58

GDP - composition, by sector of origin: *agriculture:* 10% (2022 est.)
industry: 67.8% (2022 est.)
services: 19.3% (2022 est.)
note: figures may not total 100% due to non-allocated consumption not captured in sector-reported data
comparison rankings: services 214; industry 2; agriculture 77

GDP - composition, by end use: *household consumption:* 71.1% (2017 est.)
government consumption: 18.2% (2017 est.)
investment in fixed capital: 25.4% (2017 est.)
exports of goods and services: 47.8% (2017 est.)
imports of goods and services: -63% (2017 est.)

Agricultural products: sugarcane, rice, plantains, papayas, cassava, pumpkins/squash, chicken, milk, eggplants, ginger (2022)
note: top ten agricultural products based on tonnage

Industries: bauxite, sugar, rice milling, timber, textiles, gold mining

Industrial production growth rate: 98.53% (2022 est.)
note: annual % change in industrial value added based on constant local currency
comparison ranking: 1

Labor force: 295,000 (2023 est.)
note: number of people ages 15 or older who are employed or seeking work
comparison ranking: 168

Unemployment rate: 12.43% (2023 est.)
12.42% (2022 est.)
14.93% (2021 est.)
note: % of labor force seeking employment
comparison ranking: 182

Youth unemployment rate (ages 15-24): *total:* 25.9% (2023 est.)
male: 21.5% (2023 est.)
female: 32.4% (2023 est.)
note: % of labor force ages 15-24 seeking employment
comparison ranking: total 40

Remittances: 3.27% of GDP (2023 est.)
3.57% of GDP (2022 est.)
6.81% of GDP (2021 est.)
note: personal transfers and compensation between resident and non-resident individuals/households/entities

Budget: *revenues:* $1.333 billion (2019 est.)
expenditures: $1.467 billion (2019 est.)

Public debt: 52.2% of GDP (2017 est.)
comparison ranking: 98

Taxes and other revenues: 28.1% (of GDP) (2017 est.)
comparison ranking: 28

Current account balance: -$254.121 million (2022 est.)
-$2.503 billion (2021 est.)
-$396.533 million (2020 est.)
note: balance of payments - net trade and primary/secondary income in current dollars
comparison ranking: 114

Exports: $11.536 billion (2022 est.)
$4.64 billion (2021 est.)
$2.799 billion (2020 est.)
note: balance of payments - exports of goods and services in current dollars
comparison ranking: 111

Exports - partners: Panama 32%, Netherlands 15%, US 13%, UAE 6%, Italy 6% (2022)
note: top five export partners based on percentage share of exports

Exports - commodities: crude petroleum, gold, rice, aluminum ore, liquor (2022)
note: top five export commodities based on value in dollars

Imports: $7.067 billion (2022 est.)
$6.611 billion (2021 est.)
$3.756 billion (2020 est.)
note: balance of payments - imports of goods and services in current dollars
comparison ranking: 135

Imports - partners: US 28%, China 14%, Brazil 7%, Trinidad and Tobago 7%, Suriname 4% (2022)
note: top five import partners based on percentage share of imports

Imports - commodities: refined petroleum, valves, iron pipes, construction vehicles, cars (2022)
note: top five import commodities based on value in dollars

Reserves of foreign exchange and gold: $895.275 million (2023 est.)
$917.877 million (2022 est.)
$790.785 million (2021 est.)
note: holdings of gold (year-end prices)/foreign exchange/special drawing rights in current dollars
comparison ranking: 158

Debt - external: $1.631 billion (2022 est.)
note: present value of external debt in current US dollars
comparison ranking: 75

Exchange rates: Guyanese dollars (GYD) per US dollar -

Exchange rates: 208.5 (2023 est.)
208.5 (2022 est.)
208.5 (2021 est.)
208.5 (2020 est.)
208.5 (2019 est.)

ENERGY

Electricity access: *electrification - total population:* 93% (2022 est.)
electrification - urban areas: 98%
electrification - rural areas: 91.6%

Electricity: *installed generating capacity:* 385,000 kW (2022 est.)
consumption: 904.608 million kWh (2022 est.)
transmission/distribution losses: 233.463 million kWh (2022 est.)
comparison rankings: transmission/distribution losses 67; consumption 161; installed generating capacity 157

Electricity generation sources: *fossil fuels:* 98.1% of total installed capacity (2022 est.)
solar: 1.1% of total installed capacity (2022 est.)
biomass and waste: 0.7% of total installed capacity (2022 est.)

Coal: *imports:* (2022 est.) less than 1 metric ton

Petroleum: *total petroleum production:* 391,000 bbl/day (2023 est.)
refined petroleum consumption: 16,000 bbl/day (2022 est.)

Natural gas: *consumption:* 3.981 million cubic meters (2022 est.)
imports: 3.981 million cubic meters (2022 est.)

Carbon dioxide emissions: 2.499 million metric tonnes of CO_2 (2022 est.)

from petroleum and other liquids: 2.491 million metric tonnes of CO_2 (2022 est.)
from consumed natural gas: 8,000 metric tonnes of CO_2 (2022 est.)
comparison ranking: total emissions 153

Energy consumption per capita: 42.797 million Btu/person (2022 est.)
comparison ranking: 99

COMMUNICATIONS

Telephones - fixed lines: *total subscriptions:* 125,000 (2021 est.)
subscriptions per 100 inhabitants: 16 (2021 est.)
comparison ranking: total subscriptions 129

Telephones - mobile cellular: *total subscriptions:* 856,000 (2021 est.)
subscriptions per 100 inhabitants: 106 (2021 est.)
comparison ranking: total subscriptions 167

Telecommunication systems: *general assessment:* after many years of delays and legal challenges, the 2016 Telecommunications Act was brought into force in October 2020 by the newly elected government of the People's Party Progressive (PPP); the Telecommunications Act sets out a framework for enabling competition across all segments of the telecommunications sector in Guyana; the mobile market has been open to competition since 2001; the Telecommunications Act presents the country with the potential to benefit from a more level playing field that may attract new players, but nevertheless Guyana's relatively small size and low GDP may restrict it from reaching its full potential for some more years to come (2021)
domestic: fixed-line teledensity is about 16 per 100 persons; mobile-cellular teledensity about 110 per 100 persons (2021)
international: country code - 592; landing point for the SG-SCS submarine cable to Suriname, and the Caribbean; satellite earth station - 1 Intelsat (Atlantic Ocean) (2019)

Broadcast media: government-dominated broadcast media; the National Communications Network (NCN) TV is state-owned; a few private TV stations relay satellite services; the state owns and operates 2 radio stations broadcasting on multiple frequencies capable of reaching the entire country; government limits on licensing of new private radio stations has constrained competition in broadcast media

Internet country code: .gy

Internet users: *total:* 680,000 (2021 est.)
percent of population: 85% (2021 est.)
comparison ranking: total 161

Broadband - fixed subscriptions: *total:* 95,000 (2020 est.)
subscriptions per 100 inhabitants: 12 (2020 est.)
comparison ranking: total 128

TRANSPORTATION

Civil aircraft registration country code prefix: 8R

Airports: 51 (2024)
comparison ranking: 86

Roadways: *total:* 3,995 km
paved: 799 km
unpaved: 3,196 km (2019)
comparison ranking: total 157

Waterways: 330 km (2012) (the Berbice, Demerara, and Essequibo Rivers are navigable by oceangoing vessels for 150 km, 100 km, and 80 km respectively)
comparison ranking: 101

Merchant marine: *total:* 80 (2023)
by type: general cargo 45, oil tanker 10, other 25
comparison ranking: total 99

Ports: *total ports:* 3 (2024)
large: 0
medium: 1
small: 0
very small: 2
ports with oil terminals: 3
key ports: Georgetown, Linden, New Amsterdam

MILITARY AND SECURITY

Military and security forces: the Guyana Defense Force (GDF) is a unified force with ground, air, and coast guard components, as well as the Guyana National Reserve (2024)
note: the Guyana Police Force under the Ministry of Home Affairs is responsible for internal security

Military expenditures: 0.6% of GDP (2023 est.)
0.6% of GDP (2022 est.)
1% of GDP (2021 est.)
1.2% of GDP (2020 est.)
1.3% of GDP (2019 est.)
comparison ranking: 152

Military and security service personnel strengths: approximately 3,500 active-duty military personnel (2024)

Military equipment inventories and acquisitions: the military has a limited inventory comprised mostly of older or second-hand platforms from a variety of foreign suppliers, including Brazil, China, the former Soviet Union, the UK, and the US (2024)

Military service age and obligation: 18-25 years of age or older for voluntary military service; no conscription (2024)

Military - note: the Guyana Defense Force (GDF) was established in 1965; its primary missions are defense of the country, including border security, assisting civil authorities with law and order as needed, and contributing to Guyana's economic development; key areas of concern include disaster response, illegal fishing, narcotics trafficking, piracy, porous borders, and threats from Venezuela over disputed territory; the GDF participates in both bilateral and multinational exercises and has relationships with Brazil, China, France, the UK, and the US; the GDF's ground force officers are trained at the British Royal Military Academy at Sandhurst, while coast guard officers receive training at the British Royal Naval College
Guyana joined the Caribbean Regional Security System (RSS) in 2022; RSS signatories (Antigua and Barbuda, Barbados, Dominica, Grenada, Saint Kitts and Nevis, Saint Lucia, and Saint Vincent and the Grenadines) agreed to prepare contingency plans and assist one another, on request, in national emergencies, prevention of smuggling, search and rescue, immigration control, fishery protection, customs and excise control, maritime policing duties, protection of offshore installations, pollution control, national and other disasters, and threats to national security (2024)

TRANSNATIONAL ISSUES

Refugees and internally displaced persons: *refugees (country of origin):* 21,676 (Venezuela) (economic and political crisis; includes Venezuelans who have claimed asylum, are recognized as refugees, or received alternative legal stay) (2023)

Illicit drugs: a transit country for cocaine destined for the United States, Canada, the Caribbean, Europe, and West Africa; growing domestic marijuana cultivation and consumption

HAITI

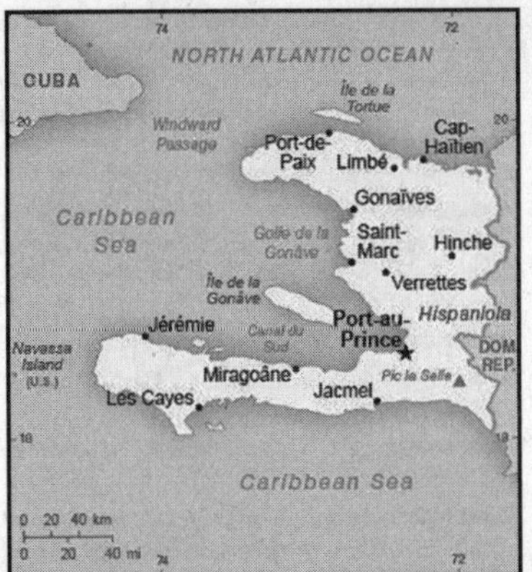

INTRODUCTION

Background: The native Taino – who inhabited the island of Hispaniola when Christopher COLUMBUS first landed in 1492 – were virtually wiped out by Spanish settlers within 25 years. In the early 17th century, the French established a presence on Hispaniola. In 1697, Spain ceded to the French the western third of the island, which later became Haiti. The French colony, based on forestry and sugar-related industries, became one of the wealthiest in the Caribbean but relied heavily on the forced labor of enslaved Africans and environmentally degrading practices. In the late 18th century, Toussaint L'OUVERTURE led a revolution of Haiti's nearly half a million slaves that ended France's rule on the island. After a prolonged struggle, and under the leadership of Jean-Jacques DESSALINES, Haiti became the first country in the world led by former slaves after declaring its independence in 1804, but it was forced to pay an indemnity of 100 million francs (equivalent to $22 billion USD in March 2023) to France for more than a century and was shunned by other countries for nearly 40 years. In 1862, the US officially recognized Haiti, but foreign economic influence and internal political instability induced the US to occupy Haiti from 1915 to 1934.

Francois "Papa Doc" DUVALIER and then his son Jean-Claude "Baby Doc" DUVALIER led repressive and corrupt regimes that ruled Haiti in 1957-1971 and 1971-1986, respectively. Jean-Bertrand ARISTIDE was Haiti's first democratically elected president in 1991 and was elected a second time in 2000, but coups interrupted his first term after only a few months and ended his second term in 2004. President Jovenel MOÏSE was assassinated in 2021, leading the country further into an extra-constitutional governance structure and contributing to the country's growing fragility. The Government of Haiti then installed Ariel HENRY – whom President MOÏSE had nominated shortly before his death – as prime minister.

On 29 February 2024, a significant escalation of gang violence occurred on the 20th anniversary of ARISTIDE's second overthrow, after the announcement that HENRY would not hold elections until August 2025. HENRY's return from an overseas trip was diverted to Puerto Rico when the airport closed due to gang violence. With control of much of the capital, Port-au-Prince, gang leaders called for the ouster of HENRY'S government. By mid-March, Haiti's continued violence, HENRY'S inability to return to the country, and increasing pressure from the international community led HENRY to pledge to resign. On 25 April 2024, HENRY formally submitted his resignation as a nine-member Transitional Presidential Council assumed control, tasked with returning stability to the country and preparing elections. Since January 2023, Haiti has had no sitting elected officials.

The country has long been plagued by natural disasters. In 2010, a major 7.0 magnitude earthquake struck Haiti with an epicenter about 25 km (15 mi) west of the capital, Port-au-Prince. An estimated 300,000 people were killed, and some 1.5 million left homeless. The earthquake was assessed as the worst in this region in 200 years. A 7.2 magnitude earthquake hit Haiti's southern peninsula in 2021, causing well over 2,000 deaths; an estimated 500,000 required emergency humanitarian aid. Haiti is the poorest country in the Western Hemisphere, as well as one of the most unequal in wealth distribution.

GEOGRAPHY

Location: Caribbean, western one-third of the island of Hispaniola, between the Caribbean Sea and the North Atlantic Ocean, west of the Dominican Republic

Geographic coordinates: 19 00 N, 72 25 W

Map references: Central America and the Caribbean

Area: *total:* 27,750 sq km
land: 27,560 sq km
water: 190 sq km
comparison ranking: total 147

Area - comparative: slightly smaller than Maryland

Land boundaries: *total:* 376 km
border countries (1): Dominican Republic 376 km

Coastline: 1,771 km

Maritime claims: *territorial sea:* 12 nm
contiguous zone: 24 nm
exclusive economic zone: 200 nm
continental shelf: to depth of exploitation

Climate: tropical; semiarid where mountains in east cut off trade winds

Terrain: mostly rough and mountainous

Elevation: *highest point:* Pic la Selle 2,674 m
lowest point: Caribbean Sea 0 m
mean elevation: 470 m

Natural resources: bauxite, copper, calcium carbonate, gold, marble, hydropower, arable land

Land use: *agricultural land:* 66.4% (2018 est.)
arable land: 38.5% (2018 est.)
permanent crops: 10.2% (2018 est.)
permanent pasture: 17.7% (2018 est.)
forest: 3.6% (2018 est.)
other: 30% (2018 est.)

Irrigated land: 800 sq km (2013)

Population distribution: fairly even distribution; largest concentrations located near coastal areas

Natural hazards: lies in the middle of the hurricane belt and subject to severe storms from June to October; occasional flooding and earthquakes; periodic droughts

Geography - note: shares island of Hispaniola with Dominican Republic (western one-third is Haiti, eastern two-thirds is the Dominican Republic); it is the most mountainous nation in the Caribbean

PEOPLE AND SOCIETY

Population: *total:* 11,753,943
male: 5,792,443
female: 5,961,500 (2024 est.)
comparison rankings: female 83; male 85; total 83

Nationality: *noun:* Haitian(s)
adjective: Haitian

Ethnic groups: Black 95%, mixed and White 5%

Languages: French (official), Creole (official)
major-language sample(s): The World Factbook, une source indispensable d'informations de base. (French)
The World Factbook, sous endispansab pou enfomasyon debaz. (Haitian Creole)

Religions: Catholic 55%, Protestant 29%, Vodou 2.1%, other 4.6%, none 10% (2018 est.)
note: 50-80% of Haitians incorporate some elements of Vodou culture or practice in addition to another religion, most often Roman Catholicism; Vodou was recognized as an official religion in 2003

Age structure: *0-14 years:* 30.5% (male 1,790,061/female 1,794,210)
15-64 years: 65.3% (male 3,787,782/female 3,887,791)
65 years and over: 4.2% (2024 est.) (male 214,600/female 279,499)

Dependency ratios: *total dependency ratio:* 58.3
youth dependency ratio: 51.2
elderly dependency ratio: 7.1
potential support ratio: 14.1 (2021 est.)

Median age: *total:* 25 years (2024 est.)
male: 24.7 years
female: 25.3 years
comparison ranking: total 173

Population growth rate: 1.23% (2024 est.)
comparison ranking: 77

Birth rate: 21.2 births/1,000 population (2024 est.)
comparison ranking: 60

Death rate: 7.3 deaths/1,000 population (2024 est.)
comparison ranking: 111

Net migration rate: -1.6 migrant(s)/1,000 population (2024 est.)
comparison ranking: 160

Population distribution: fairly even distribution; largest concentrations located near coastal areas

Urbanization: *urban population:* 59.7% of total population (2023)
rate of urbanization: 2.47% annual rate of change (2020-25 est.)

Major urban areas - population: 2.987 million PORT-AU-PRINCE (capital) (2023)

Sex ratio: *at birth:* 1.01 male(s)/female
0-14 years: 1 male(s)/female
15-64 years: 0.97 male(s)/female

65 years and over: 0.77 male(s)/female
total population: 0.97 male(s)/female (2024 est.)

Mother's mean age at first birth: 22.4 years (2016/7 est.)
note: data represents median age at first birth among women 25-49

Maternal mortality ratio: 350 deaths/100,000 live births (2020 est.)
comparison ranking: 27

Infant mortality rate: *total:* 36.8 deaths/1,000 live births (2024 est.)
male: 40.2 deaths/1,000 live births
female: 33.5 deaths/1,000 live births
comparison ranking: total 32

Life expectancy at birth: *total population:* 65.6 years (2024 est.)
male: 63.8 years
female: 67.4 years
comparison ranking: total population 205

Total fertility rate: 2.44 children born/woman (2024 est.)
comparison ranking: 72

Gross reproduction rate: 1.21 (2024 est.)

Contraceptive prevalence rate: 34.3% (2016/17)

Drinking water source: *improved: urban:* 91.9% of population
rural: 56.1% of population
total: 76.5% of population
unimproved: urban: 8.1% of population
rural: 43.9% of population
total: 23.5% of population (2020 est.)

Current health expenditure: 3.3% of GDP (2020)

Physician density: 0.23 physicians/1,000 population (2018)

Hospital bed density: 0.7 beds/1,000 population (2013)

Sanitation facility access: *improved: urban:* 82.9% of population
rural: 42.6% of population
total: 65.6% of population
unimproved: urban: 17.1% of population
rural: 57.4% of population
total: 34.4% of population (2020 est.)

Obesity - adult prevalence rate: 22.7% (2016)
comparison ranking: 72

Alcohol consumption per capita: *total:* 2.85 liters of pure alcohol (2019 est.)
beer: 0.55 liters of pure alcohol (2019 est.)
wine: 0.03 liters of pure alcohol (2019 est.)
spirits: 2.26 liters of pure alcohol (2019 est.)
other alcohols: 0 liters of pure alcohol (2019 est.)
comparison ranking: total 118

Tobacco use: *total:* 7.7% (2020 est.)
male: 12.2% (2020 est.)
female: 3.1% (2020 est.)
comparison ranking: total 152

Children under the age of 5 years underweight: 9.5% (2016/17)
comparison ranking: 58

Currently married women (ages 15-49): 51.4% (2023 est.)

Child marriage: *women married by age 15:* 2.1%
women married by age 18: 14.9%
men married by age 18: 1.6% (2017 est.)

Education expenditures: 1.4% of GDP (2020 est.)
comparison ranking: 192

Literacy: *definition:* age 15 and over can read and write
total population: 61.7%
male: 65.3%
female: 58.3% (2016)

ENVIRONMENT

Environment - current issues: extensive deforestation (much of the remaining forested land is being cleared for agriculture and used as fuel); soil erosion; overpopulation leads to inadequate supplies of potable water and a lack of sanitation; natural disasters

Environment - international agreements: *party to:* Biodiversity, Climate Change, Climate Change-Kyoto Protocol, Climate Change-Paris Agreement, Desertification, Hazardous Wastes, Law of the Sea, Marine Dumping-London Convention, Marine Life Conservation, Ozone Layer Protection
signed, but not ratified: Nuclear Test Ban

Climate: tropical; semiarid where mountains in east cut off trade winds

Urbanization: *urban population:* 59.7% of total population (2023)
rate of urbanization: 2.47% annual rate of change (2020-25 est.)

Food insecurity: *severe localized food insecurity: due to high food prices, natural disasters, and worsening civil insecurity* - about 4.9 million people are estimated to face severe acute food insecurity and were in need of urgent food assistance between March and June 2023; the high levels of food insecurity are the result of sustained economic downturn, reducing domestic food production, elevated food prices, fuel shortage and frequent natural disasters; the situation is exacerbated by worsening insecurity, which has limited access to essential services, including markets, caused population displacements and hampered delivery of humanitarian assistance (2023)

Revenue from forest resources: 0.68% of GDP (2018 est.)
comparison ranking: 60

Revenue from coal: 0% of GDP (2018 est.)
comparison ranking: 78

Air pollutants: *particulate matter emissions:* 9.69 micrograms per cubic meter (2019 est.)
carbon dioxide emissions: 2.98 megatons (2016 est.)
methane emissions: 6.12 megatons (2020 est.)

Waste and recycling: *municipal solid waste generated annually:* 2,309,852 tons (2015 est.)

Total water withdrawal: *municipal:* 190 million cubic meters (2020 est.)
industrial: 50 million cubic meters (2020 est.)
agricultural: 1.21 billion cubic meters (2020 est.)

Total renewable water resources: 14.02 billion cubic meters (2020 est.)

GOVERNMENT

Country name: *conventional long form:* Republic of Haiti
conventional short form: Haiti
local long form: République d'Haïti (French)/ Repiblik d Ayiti (Haitian Creole)
local short form: Haïti (French)/ Ayiti (Haitian Creole)
etymology: the native Taino name means "Land of High Mountains" and was originally applied to the entire island of Hispaniola

Government type: semi-presidential republic

Capital: *name:* Port-au-Prince
geographic coordinates: 18 32 N, 72 20 W
time difference: UTC-5 (same time as Washington, DC, during Standard Time)
daylight saving time: +1hr, begins second Sunday in March; ends first Sunday in November
etymology: according to tradition, in 1706, a Captain de Saint-Andre named the bay and its surrounding area after his ship Le Prince; the name of the town that grew there means, "the Port of The Prince"

Administrative divisions: 10 departments (departements, singular - departement); Artibonite, Centre, Grand'Anse, Nippes, Nord, Nord-Est, Nord- Ouest, Ouest, Sud, Sud-Est

Independence: 1 January 1804 (from France)

National holiday: Independence Day, 1 January (1804)

Legal system: civil law system strongly influenced by Napoleonic Code

Constitution: *history:* many previous; latest adopted 10 March 1987, with substantial revisions in June 2012; note – the constitution is commonly referred to as the "amended 1987 constitution"
amendments: proposed by the executive branch or by either the Senate or the Chamber of Deputies; consideration of proposed amendments requires support by at least two-thirds majority of both houses; passage requires at least two-thirds majority of the membership present and at least two-thirds majority of the votes cast; approved amendments enter into force after installation of the next president of the republic; constitutional articles on the democratic and republican form of government cannot be amended; amended many times, last in 2012

International law organization participation: accepts compulsory ICJ jurisdiction; non-party state to the ICCt

Citizenship: *citizenship by birth:* no
citizenship by descent only: at least one parent must be a native-born citizen of Haiti
dual citizenship recognized: yes
residency requirement for naturalization: 5 years

Suffrage: 18 years of age; universal

Executive branch: *chief of state:* President (vacant)
head of government: Prime Minister Garry CONILLE (since 3 June 2024)
cabinet: Cabinet chosen by the prime minister in consultation with the president; parliament must ratify the Cabinet and Prime Minister's governing policy
elections/appointments: president directly elected by absolute majority popular vote in 2 rounds if needed for a 5-year term (eligible for a single non-consecutive term); last election was 20 November 2016; new elections were delayed in 2022 and 2023 and have not been scheduled by the transitional presidential council
election results:
2016: Jovenel MOÏSE elected president in first round; percent of vote - Jovenel MOÏSE (PHTK) 55.6%, Jude CELESTIN (LAPEH) 19.6%, Jean-Charles MOÏSE (PPD) 11%, Maryse NARCISSE (FL) 9%; other 4.8%
2011: Michel MARTELLY elected president in second round; percent of vote in second round - Michel MARTELLY (Peasant's Response) 68%, Mirlande MANIGAT (RDNP) 32%
note: former Prime Minister Ariel HENRY, who had assumed executive responsibilities following the assassination of President MOÏSE on 7 July 2021, resigned on 24 April 2024; a nine-member

Presidential Transitional Council, equipped with presidential powers, was sworn in on 25 April 2024 and will remain in place until 7 February 2026

Legislative branch: *description:* bicameral National Assembly or the Assemblée nationale consists of:
Senate or le Sénat de la République (30 seats; 0 filled as of January 2023); members directly elected in multi-seat constituencies by absolute majority vote in 2 rounds if needed; members serve 6-year terms (2-term limit) with one-third of the membership renewed every 2 years)
Chamber of Deputies or Chambre des députés (119 seats; 0 filled as of January 2023; members directly elected in single-seat constituencies by absolute majority vote in 2 rounds if needed; members serve 4-year terms; no term limits); note - when the 2 chambers meet collectively it is known as the National Assembly or L'Assemblée nationale and is convened for specific purposes spelled out in the constitution
elections: Senate - last held on 20 November 2016 with a runoff on 29 January 2017 (next originally scheduled for 27 October 2019 but postponed until political and civil society actors agree to a consensual process)
Chamber of Deputies - last held on 9 August 2015 with runoff on 25 October 2015 and 20 November 2016 (next originally scheduled for 27 October 2019 but postponed until political and civil society actors agree to a consensual process)
election results: Senate - percent of vote by party - NA; seats by party - NA; composition - NA
Chamber of Deputies - percent of vote by party - NA; seats by party - NA; composition - NA
note: the Senate and Chamber of Deputies as of January 2023 were not functional

Judicial branch: *highest court(s):* Supreme Court or Cour de cassation (currently 11 of 12 judges as prescribed by the constitution, 8 of whom were appointed in March 2023); note - Haiti is a member of the Caribbean Court of Justice; Constitutional Court, called for in the 1987 constitution but not yet established; High Court of Justice, for trying high government officials - currently not functional
judge selection and term of office: judges appointed by the president from candidate lists submitted by the Senate of the National Assembly; note - Article 174 of Haiti's constitution states that judges of the Supreme Court are appointed for 10 years, whereas Article 177 states that judges of the Supreme Court are appointed for life
subordinate courts: Courts of Appeal; Courts of First Instance; magistrate's courts; land, labor, and children's courts
note: the Superior Council of the Judiciary or Conseil Superieur du Pouvoir Judiciaire is a 9-member body charged with the administration and oversight of the judicial branch of government

Political parties: Alternative League for Haitian Progress and Emancipation (Ligue Alternative pour le Progres et l'Emancipation Haitienne) or LAPEH
Christian Movement for a New Haiti or MCNH or Mochrenha
Christian National Movement for the Reconstruction of Haiti or UNCRH
Combat of Peasant Workers to Liberate Haiti (Konbit Travaye Peyizan Pou Libere Ayiti) or Kontra Pep La
Convention for Democratic Unity or KID
Cooperative Action to Rebuild Haiti or KONBA
December 16 Platform or Platfom 16 Desanm
Democratic Alliance Party or ALYANS (coalition includes KID and PPRH)
Democratic Centers' National Council or CONACED
Democratic and Popular Sector (Secteur Democratique et Populaire) or SDP
Democratic Unity Convention (Konvansyon Inite Demokratik) or KID
Dessalinian Patriotic and Popular Movement or MOPOD
Effort and Solidarity to Create an Alternative for the People or ESKAMP
Fanmi Lavalas or FL
Forward (En Avant)
Fusion of Haitian Social Democrats (Fusion Des Sociaux-Démocrates Haïtiens) or FHSD
G18 Policy Platform (Plateforme Politique G18)
Haiti in Action (Ayiti An Aksyon Haiti's Action) or AAA
Haitian Tet Kale Party (Parti Haitien Tet Kale) or PHTK
Independent Movement for National Reconciliation or MIRN
Lavni Organization or LAVNI
Lod Demokratik
Love Haiti (Renmen Ayiti) or RA
MTV Ayiti
National Consortium of Haitian Political Parties (Consortium National des Partis Politiques Haitiens) or CNPPH
National Shield Network (Reseau Bouclier National)
Organization of the People's Struggle (Oganizasyon Pep Kap Lite) or OPL
Patriotic Unity (Inite Patriyotik) or Inite
Platform Pitit Desalin (Politik Pitit Dessalines) or PPD
Political Party for Us All or Bridge (Pont) or Pou Nou Tout
Popular Patriotic Dessalinien Movement (Mouvement Patriotique Populaire Dessalinien) or MOPOD
Rally of Progressive National Democrats (Rassemblement des Democrates Nationaux Progressistes) or RDNP
Respe (Respect)
Women and Families Political Parties (Defile Pati Politik Fanm Ak Fanmi)

International organization participation: ACP, ACS, AOSIS, Caricom, CD, CDB, CELAC, FAO, G-77, IADB, IAEA, IBRD, ICAO, ICC (NGOs), ICRM, IDA, IFAD, IFC, IFRCS, ILO, IMF, IMO, Interpol, IOC, IOM, IPU, ITSO, ITU, ITUC (NGOs), LAES, MIGA, NAM, OAS, OIF, OPANAL, OPCW, PCA, Petrocaribe, UN, UNCTAD, UNESCO, UNIDO, Union Latina, UNWTO, UPU, WCO, WFTU (NGOs), WHO, WIPO, WMO, WTO

Diplomatic representation in the US: *chief of mission:* Ambassador (vacant); Chargé d'Affaires Louis Harold JOSEPH (since 15 May 2023)
chancery: 2311 Massachusetts Avenue NW, Washington, DC 20008
telephone: [1] (202) 332-4090
FAX: [1] (202) 745-7215
email address and website:
amb.washington@diplomatie.ht
https://www.haiti.org/
consulate(s) general: Atlanta, Boston, Chicago, Miami, Orlando (FL), New York

Diplomatic representation from the US: *chief of mission:* Ambassador-designate Dennis HANKINS (since 14 March 2024); note - as of March 2024, Haiti has no government official to whom the Ambassador-designate can present his credentials
embassy: Tabarre 41, Route de Tabarre, Port-au-Prince
mailing address: 3400 Port-au-Prince Place, Washington, DC 20521-3400
telephone: [011] (509) 2229-8000
FAX: [011] (509) 2229-8027
email address and website:
acspap@state.gov
https://ht.usembassy.gov/

Flag description: two equal horizontal bands of blue (top) and red with a centered white rectangle bearing the coat of arms, which contains a palm tree flanked by flags and two cannons above a scroll bearing the motto L'UNION FAIT LA FORCE (Union Makes Strength); the colors are taken from the French Tricolor and represent the union of blacks and mulattoes

National symbol(s): Hispaniolan trogon (bird), hibiscus flower; national colors: blue, red

National anthem: *name:* "La Dessalinienne" (The Dessalines Song)
lyrics/music: Justin LHERISSON/Nicolas GEFFRARD
note: adopted 1904; named for Jean-Jacques DESSALINES, a leader in the Haitian Revolution and first ruler of an independent Haiti

National heritage: *total World Heritage Sites:* 1 (cultural)
selected World Heritage Site locales: National History Park – Citadel, Sans Souci, Ramiers

ECONOMY

Economic overview: small Caribbean island economy and OECS-member state; extreme poverty and inflation; enormous income inequality; ongoing civil unrest due to recent presidential assassination; US preferential market access; very open to foreign direct investment

Real GDP (purchasing power parity): $34.406 billion (2023 est.)
$35.059 billion (2022 est.)
$35.659 billion (2021 est.)
note: data in 2021 dollars
comparison ranking: 143

Real GDP growth rate: -1.86% (2023 est.)
-1.68% (2022 est.)
-1.8% (2021 est.)
note: annual GDP % growth based on constant local currency
comparison ranking: 205

Real GDP per capita: $2,900 (2023 est.)
$3,000 (2022 est.)
$3,100 (2021 est.)
note: data in 2021 dollars
comparison ranking: 195

GDP (official exchange rate): $19.851 billion (2023 est.)
note: data in current dollars at official exchange rate

Inflation rate (consumer prices): 36.81% (2023 est.)
33.98% (2022 est.)
16.84% (2021 est.)
note: annual % change based on consumer prices
comparison ranking: 210

GDP - composition, by sector of origin: *agriculture:* 18.2% (2023 est.)
industry: 31% (2023 est.)
services: 47.8% (2023 est.)

note: figures may not total 100% due to non-allocated consumption not captured in sector-reported data
comparison rankings: services 156; industry 61; agriculture 43

GDP - composition, by end use: *household consumption:* 100.2% (2023 est.)
government consumption: 6.2% (2023 est.)
investment in fixed capital: 13.9% (2023 est.)
exports of goods and services: 5.3% (2023 est.)
imports of goods and services: -25.5% (2023 est.)
note: figures may not total 100% due to rounding or gaps in data collection

Agricultural products: sugarcane, cassava, mangoes/guavas, plantains, bananas, maize, avocados, tropical fruits, rice, vegetables (2022)
note: top ten agricultural products based on tonnage

Industries: textiles, sugar refining, flour milling, cement, light assembly using imported parts

Industrial production growth rate: -3.82% (2023 est.)
note: annual % change in industrial value added based on constant local currency
comparison ranking: 194

Labor force: 5.238 million (2023 est.)
note: number of people ages 15 or older who are employed or seeking work
comparison ranking: 85

Unemployment rate: 14.62% (2023 est.)
14.72% (2022 est.)
15.25% (2021 est.)
note: % of labor force seeking employment
comparison ranking: 188

Youth unemployment rate (ages 15-24): *total:* 36.8% (2023 est.)
male: 29.1% (2023 est.)
female: 46.6% (2023 est.)
note: % of labor force ages 15-24 seeking employment
comparison ranking: total 14

Gini Index coefficient - distribution of family income: (2012)

Remittances: 21.4% of GDP (2023 est.)
18.75% of GDP (2022 est.)
19.13% of GDP (2021 est.)
note: personal transfers and compensation between resident and non-resident individuals/households/entities

Budget: *revenues:* $1.179 billion (2020 est.)
expenditures: $1.527 billion (2020 est.)

Public debt: 31.1% of GDP (2017 est.)
comparison ranking: 167

Taxes and other revenues: 18.2% (of GDP) (2017 est.)
comparison ranking: 101

Current account balance: -$491.954 million (2022 est.)
$87.656 million (2021 est.)
$51.548 million (2020 est.)
note: balance of payments - net trade and primary/secondary income in current dollars
comparison ranking: 121

Exports: $1.355 billion (2022 est.)
$1.272 billion (2021 est.)
$1.018 billion (2020 est.)
note: balance of payments - exports of goods and services in current dollars
comparison ranking: 175

Exports - partners: US 84%, Canada 4%, Mexico 2%, Thailand 1%, France 1% (2022)
note: top five export partners based on percentage share of exports

Exports - commodities: garments, essential oils, scrap iron, bedding, tropical fruits (2022)
note: top five export commodities based on value in dollars

Imports: $5.451 billion (2022 est.)
$5.048 billion (2021 est.)
$4.177 billion (2020 est.)
note: balance of payments - imports of goods and services in current dollars
comparison ranking: 148

Imports - partners: US 31%, Dominican Republic 26%, China 16%, Indonesia 3%, India 2% (2022)
note: top five import partners based on percentage share of imports

Imports - commodities: refined petroleum, rice, cotton fabric, garments, plastic products (2022)
note: top five import commodities based on value in dollars

Reserves of foreign exchange and gold: $2.368 billion (2022 est.)
$2.734 billion (2021 est.)
$2.59 billion (2020 est.)
note: holdings of gold (year-end prices)/foreign exchange/special drawing rights in current dollars
comparison ranking: 120

Debt - external: $1.645 billion (2022 est.)
note: present value of external debt in current US dollars
comparison ranking: 74

Exchange rates: gourdes (HTG) per US dollar -

Exchange rates: 141.036 (2023 est.)
115.631 (2022 est.)
89.227 (2021 est.)
93.51 (2020 est.)
88.815 (2019 est.)

ENERGY

Electricity access: *electrification - total population:* 49.3% (2022 est.)
electrification - urban areas: 83%
electrification - rural areas: 1.2% (2019 est.)

Electricity: *installed generating capacity:* 471,000 kW (2022 est.)
consumption: 418.367 million kWh (2022 est.)
transmission/distribution losses: 624 million kWh (2022 est.)
comparison rankings: transmission/distribution losses 87; consumption 176; installed generating capacity 153

Electricity generation sources: *fossil fuels:* 85.9% of total installed capacity (2022 est.)
solar: 0.3% of total installed capacity (2022 est.)
hydroelectricity: 13.8% of total installed capacity (2022 est.)

Coal: *imports:* 5.7 metric tons (2022 est.)

Petroleum: *refined petroleum consumption:* 19,000 bbl/day (2022 est.)

Natural gas: *consumption:* 3.256 million cubic meters (2022 est.)
imports: 3.256 million cubic meters (2022 est.)

Carbon dioxide emissions: 2.805 million metric tonnes of CO2 (2022 est.)
from petroleum and other liquids: 2.799 million metric tonnes of CO2 (2022 est.)
from consumed natural gas: 6,000 metric tonnes of CO2 (2022 est.)
comparison ranking: total emissions 150

Energy consumption per capita: 3.403 million Btu/person (2022 est.)
comparison ranking: 176

COMMUNICATIONS

Telephones - fixed lines: *total subscriptions:* 6,000 (2021 est.)
subscriptions per 100 inhabitants: (2021 est.) less than 1
comparison ranking: total subscriptions 202

Telephones - mobile cellular: *total subscriptions:* 7.319 million (2021 est.)
subscriptions per 100 inhabitants: 64 (2021 est.)
comparison ranking: total subscriptions 110

Telecommunication systems: *general assessment:* Haiti is in desperate need of maintaining effective communication services to enable it to keep going through the countless natural disasters, the country's telecoms sector is really only surviving on the back of international goodwill to repair and replace the systems destroyed in the latest upheaval; Haiti's fixed-line infrastructure is now practically non-existent, having been torn apart by Hurricane Matthew in 2016; what aid and additional investment has been forthcoming has been directed towards mobile solutions; over half of the country can afford a mobile handset or the cost of a monthly subscription; and mobile broadband subscriptions is half of that again – an estimated 28% in 2022; international aid continues to flow in to try and help the country's telecoms sector recover – the World Bank has released a further $120 million to go on top of the $60 million grant provided after the last major 7.2 earthquake in August 2021 (2022)
domestic: fixed-line is less than 1 per 100; mobile-cellular teledensity is nearly 64 per 100 persons (2021)
international: country code - 509; landing points for the BDSNi and Fibralink submarine cables to 14 points in the Bahamas and Dominican Republic; satellite earth station - 1 Intelsat (Atlantic Ocean) (2019)

Broadcast media: per 2019 data released by Haitian telecommunications regulator CONATEL (Conseil National des Télécommunications), there are 398 legal sound broadcasting stations on the territory, including about 60 community radio stations, and 7 radio stations on the AM band; the FM band in Haiti is oversaturated by 158 percent; most radio stations broadcast 17 to 19 hours a day; there are 105 television stations operating in Haiti, including 36 TV stations in Port- au- Prince, 41 others in the provinces, and more than 40 radio-television stations; a large number of broadcasting stations operate irregularly and some stations operate with technical parameters that do not comply with established standards, thus causing harmful interference to existing telecommunications systems; VOA Creole Service broadcasts daily on 30 affiliate stations
(2019)

Internet country code: .ht

Internet users: *total:* 4.29 million (2021 est.)
percent of population: 39% (2021 est.)
comparison ranking: total 108

Broadband - fixed subscriptions: *total:* 31,000 (2020 est.)
subscriptions per 100 inhabitants: 0.3 (2020 est.)
comparison ranking: total 152

TRANSPORTATION

National air transport system: *number of registered air carriers:* 1 (2020)
inventory of registered aircraft operated by air carriers: 1

Civil aircraft registration country code prefix: HH

Airports: 17 (2024)
comparison ranking: 145

Heliports: 1 (2024)

Roadways: *total:* 3,875 km (2022)
comparison ranking: total 158

Merchant marine: *total:* 4 (2023)
by type: general cargo 3, other 1
comparison ranking: total 170

Ports: *total ports:* 5 (2024)
large: 0
medium: 1
small: 0
very small: 4
ports with oil terminals: 1
key ports: Cap Haitien, Jacmel, Miragoane, Petit Goave, Port au Prince

MILITARY AND SECURITY

Military and security forces: *the Haitian Armed Forces (FAdH):* Army
Ministry of Justice and Public Security: Haitian National Police (Police Nationale d'Haïti or PNH) (2024)
note: the PNH is responsible for maintaining public security; it includes police, corrections, fire, emergency response, airport security, port security, and coast guard functions; its units include a presidential guard and a paramilitary rapidresponse Motorized Intervention Unit or BIM

Military and security service personnel strengths: up to 2,000 trained military troops (the force is planned to eventually have around 5,000 personnel); estimates for the National Police range from a low of 9,000 to a high of about 13,000 (2023)

Military equipment inventories and acquisitions: in recent years, Canada, Taiwan, the US, and the UAE have provide some equipment to the Haitian security forces, including vehicles (2024)

Military service age and obligation: men and women 18-25 may volunteer for the FAdH (2023)

Military - note: Haiti's military was disbanded in 1995 after it participated in multiple coups and was accused of other political interference and human rights violations; the military was reinstated by former President MOISE in 2017 after the UN ended its peacekeeping operation in Haiti; the reconstituted military established an Army command in 2018 and has received training assistance from Argentina, Colombia, Ecuador, and Mexico; the military's stated mission is to assist with natural disaster relief, border security, and combating transnational crime; in 2023, Prime Minister HENRY called upon the military to assist the National Police (PNH) in combating armed gangs, which have overwhelmed the PNH, killed hundreds of Haitians, and seized control of much of the capital Port-au-Prince since the assassination of President MOISE in 2021; as of 2024, at least 300 criminal groups were operating in Haiti
in 2023, the UN Security Council approved the deployment of a Kenya-led multinational security support mission (MSS) to help bring gang violence under control; the first contingent of MSS personnel from the Kenya National Police Service arrived in mid-2024; the Bahamas, Bangladesh, Barbados, Benin, Chad, and Jamaica have also pledged forces; the mission is slated to have a total of 2,500 personnel (2024)

TRANSNATIONAL ISSUES

Refugees and internally displaced persons: IDPs: 362,551 (violence among armed gangs in primarily in the metropolitan area of Port-au-Prince) (2024)
stateless persons: 2,992 (2018); note - individuals without a nationality who were born in the Dominican Republic prior to January 2010

Trafficking in persons: *tier rating:* Special Category

Illicit drugs: a transit point for cocaine from South America and marijuana from Jamaica en route to the United States; not a producer or large consumer of illicit drugs; some cultivation of cannabis for local consumption

HEARD ISLAND AND MCDONALD ISLANDS

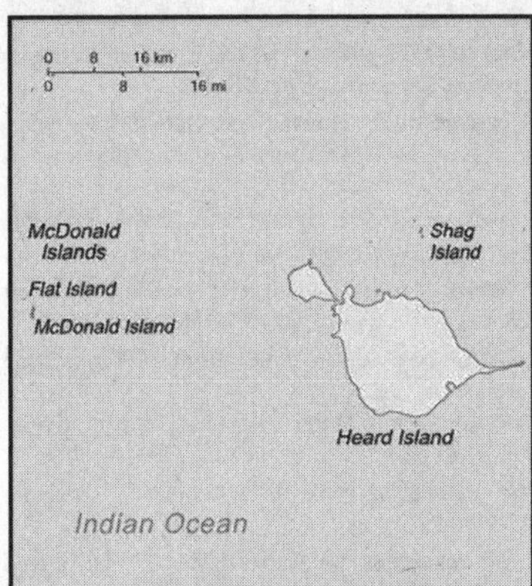

INTRODUCTION

Background: American sailor John HEARD discovered Heard Island in 1853 while fellow American William MCDONALD discovered the McDonald Islands the following year. Starting in 1855, sealers lived on the islands and harvested elephant seal oil; by the time the practice was ended in 1877, most of the islands' seals were killed. The UK formally claimed the islands in 1910, and Australian explorer Douglas MAWSON visited Heard Island in 1929. In 1947, the UK transferred the islands to Australia for its Antarctica research, but Australia closed the research station on Heard Island in 1954 when it opened a new research station on the Antarctic continent. McDonald Island has been an active volcano since it emerged from dormancy in 1992, and the island doubled in size after an eruption in 1996. In 1997, the islands were named a UNESCO World Heritage site. Populated by a large number of bird species, seals, and penguins, the islands are primarily used for research, with limited fishing permitted in the surrounding waters.

GEOGRAPHY

Location: islands in the Indian Ocean, about two-thirds of the way from Madagascar to Antarctica

Geographic coordinates: 53 06 S, 72 31 E

Map references: Antarctic Region

Area: *total:* 412 sq km
land: 412 sq km
water: 0 sq km
comparison ranking: total 202

Area - comparative: slightly more than two times the size of Washington, DC

Land boundaries: *total:* 0 km

Coastline: 101.9 km

Maritime claims: *territorial sea:* 12 nm
exclusive fishing zone: 200 nm

Climate: antarctic

Terrain: Heard Island - 80% ice-covered, bleak and mountainous, dominated by a large massif (Big Ben) and an active volcano (Mawson Peak); McDonald Islands - small and rocky

Elevation: *highest point:* Mawson Peak on Big Ben volcano 2,745 m
lowest point: Indian Ocean 0 m

Natural resources: fish

Land use: *agricultural land:* 0% (2011 est.)
other: 100% (2018 est.)

Natural hazards: Mawson Peak, an active volcano, is on Heard Island

Geography - note: Mawson Peak on Heard Island is the highest Australian mountain (at 2,745 meters, it is taller than Mt. Kosciuszko in Australia proper), and one of only two active volcanoes located in Australian territory, the other being McDonald Island; in 1992, McDonald Island broke its dormancy and began erupting; it has erupted several times since, most recently in 2005

PEOPLE AND SOCIETY

Population: *total:* uninhabited

ENVIRONMENT

Environment - current issues: none; uninhabited and mostly ice covered

Climate: antarctic

Land use: *agricultural land:* 0% (2011 est.)
other: 100% (2018 est.)

GOVERNMENT

Country name: *conventional long form:* Territory of Heard Island and McDonald Islands
conventional short form: Heard Island and McDonald Islands
abbreviation: HIMI
etymology: named after American Captain John HEARD, who sighted the island on 25 November 1853, and American Captain William McDONALD, who discovered the islands on 4 January 1854

Dependency status: territory of Australia; administered from Canberra by the Department of Agriculture, Water and the Environment (Australian Antarctic Division)

Legal system: the laws of Australia apply where applicable

Diplomatic representation in the US: none (territory of Australia)

Diplomatic representation from the US: *embassy:* none (territory of Australia)

Flag description: the flag of Australia is used

National heritage: *total World Heritage Sites:* 1 (natural); note - excerpted from the Australia entry
selected World Heritage Site locales: Heard Island and McDonald Islands

COMMUNICATIONS

Internet country code: .hm

TRANSPORTATION

Heliports: 2 (2024)

MILITARY AND SECURITY

Military - note: defense is the responsibility of Australia

TRANSNATIONAL ISSUES

Illicit drugs: NA

HOLY SEE (VATICAN CITY)

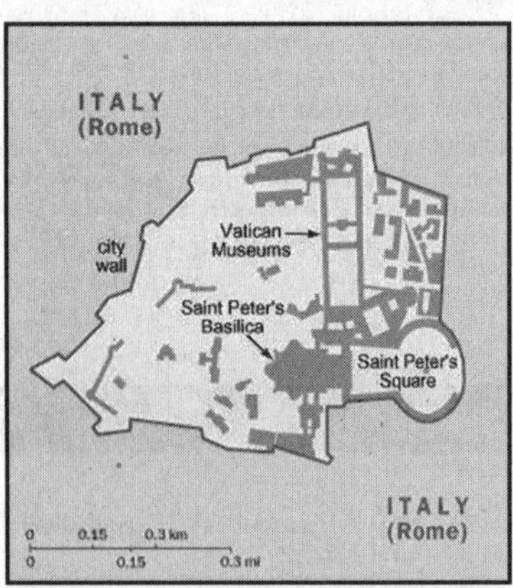

INTRODUCTION

Background: Popes in their secular role ruled portions of the Italian peninsula for more than a thousand years until the mid-19th century, when the newly established Kingdom of Italy seized many of the Papal States. In 1870, the pope's holdings were further circumscribed when Rome itself was annexed. Disputes between Italy and a series of "prisoner" popes were resolved in 1929 by three Lateran Treaties, which established the independent state of Vatican City and granted Roman Catholicism special status in Italy. In 1984, a concordat between the Holy See and Italy modified some of the earlier treaty provisions, including the primacy of Roman Catholicism as the Italian state religion.

Present concerns of the Holy See include religious freedom, threats against minority Christian communities in Africa and the Middle East, the plight of refugees and migrants, climate change and the environment, conflict and war, nuclear weapons, artificial intelligence, sexual misconduct by clergy, humanitarian issues, interreligious dialogue and reconciliation, and the application of church doctrine in an era of rapid change and globalization. About 1.3 billion people worldwide profess Catholicism, the world's largest Christian faith.

GEOGRAPHY

Location: Southern Europe, an enclave of Rome (Italy)

Geographic coordinates: 41 54 N, 12 27 E

Map references: Europe

Area: *total:* 0 sq km
land: 0.44 sq km
water: 0 sq km
comparison ranking: total 256

Area - comparative: about 0.7 times the size of the National Mall in Washington, DC

Land boundaries: *total:* 3.4 km
border countries (1): Italy 3.4 km

Coastline: 0 km (landlocked)

Maritime claims: none (landlocked)

Climate: temperate; mild, rainy winters (September to May) with hot, dry summers (May to September)

Terrain: urban; low hill

Elevation: *highest point:* Vatican Gardens (Vatican Hill) 78 m
lowest point: Saint Peter's Square 19 m

Natural resources: none

Land use: *agricultural land:* 0% (2018 est.)
other: 100% (2018 est.)

Natural hazards: occasional earthquakes

Geography - note: landlocked; an enclave in Rome, Italy; world's smallest state; beyond the territorial boundary of Vatican City, the Lateran Treaty of 1929 grants the Holy See extraterritorial authority over 23 sites in Rome and five outside of Rome, including the Pontifical Palace at Castel Gandolfo (the Pope's summer residence)

PEOPLE AND SOCIETY

Population: *total:* 1,000 (2022 est.)
comparison ranking: total 235

Nationality: *noun:* none
adjective: none

Ethnic groups: Italian, Swiss, Argentinian, and other nationalities from around the world (2017)

Languages: Italian, Latin, French, various other languages
major-language sample(s):
L'Almanacco dei fatti del mondo, l'indispensabile fonte per le informazioni di base. (Italian)

Religions: Roman Catholic

Population growth rate: 0% (2014 est.)
comparison ranking: 194

Urbanization: *urban population:* 100% of total population (2023)
rate of urbanization: 0% annual rate of change (2020-25 est.)

Major urban areas - population: 1,000 VATICAN CITY (capital) (2018)

Drinking water source: *improved:* improved: *total:* 100% of population (2019 est.)

ENVIRONMENT

Environment - current issues: some air pollution from the surrounding city of Rome

Environment - international agreements: *party to:* Comprehensive Nuclear Test Ban, Ozone Layer Protection
signed, but not ratified: Air Pollution, Environmental Modification

Climate: temperate; mild, rainy winters (September to May) with hot, dry summers (May to September)

Urbanization: *urban population:* 100% of total population (2023)
rate of urbanization: 0% annual rate of change (2020-25 est.)

Air pollutants: *methane emissions:* 0 megatons (2020 est.)

Total renewable water resources: 0 cubic meters (2017 est.)

GOVERNMENT

Country name: *conventional long form:* The Holy See (Vatican City State)
conventional short form: Holy See (Vatican City)
local long form: La Santa Sede (Stato della Citta del Vaticano)
local short form: Santa Sede (Citta del Vaticano)
etymology: "holy" comes from the Greek word "hera" meaning "sacred"; "see" comes from the Latin word "sedes" meaning "seat," and refers to the episcopal chair; the term "Vatican" derives from the hill Mons Vaticanus on which the Vatican is located and which

comes from the Latin "vaticinari" (to prophesy), referring to the fortune tellers and soothsayers who frequented the area in Roman times

Government type: ecclesiastical elective monarchy; self-described as an "absolute monarchy"

Capital: *name:* Vatican City
geographic coordinates: 41 54 N, 12 27 E
time difference: UTC+1 (6 hours ahead of Washington, DC, during Standard Time)
daylight saving time: +1hr, begins last Sunday in March; ends last Sunday in October
etymology: the term "Vatican" derives from the hill Mons Vaticanus on which the Vatican is located and which comes from the Latin "vaticinari" (to prophesy), referring to the fortune tellers and soothsayers who frequented the area in Roman times

Administrative divisions: none

Independence: 11 February 1929; note - the three treaties signed with Italy on 11 February 1929 acknowledged, among other things, the full sovereignty of the Holy See and established its territorial extent; however, the origin of the Papal States, which over centuries varied considerably in extent, may be traced back to A.D. 754

National holiday: Election Day of Pope FRANCIS, 13 March (2013)

Legal system: religious legal system based on canon (religious) law

Constitution: *history:* previous 1929, 2000; latest issued by Pope FRANCIS 13 May 2023, effective 7 June 2023 (Fundamental Law of Vatican City State, the main governing document of the Vatican's civil entities); the Roman Curia is the administrative apparatus – the departments and ministries – used by the pontiff in governing the church; note - Pope Francis in October 2013, instituted a 9-member Council of Cardinal Advisers to reform the Roman Curia to include writing a new constitution; in June 2018, Pope Francis approved the Council of Cardinals' first draft of the new apostolic constitution, *Predicate Evangelium* (Preach the Gospel); it became effective 5 June 2022, replacing *Pastor Bonus*, the previous governing document of the Roman Curia
amendments: note - although the Fundamental Law of Vatican City State makes no mention of amendments, Article Four (drafting laws), states that this legislative responsibility resides with the Pontifical Commission for Vatican City State; draft legislation is submitted through the Secretariat of State and considered by the pope

International law organization participation: has not submitted an ICJ jurisdiction declaration; non-party state to the ICCt

Citizenship: *citizenship by birth:* no
citizenship by descent only: no
dual citizenship recognized: no
residency requirement for naturalization: not applicable
note: in the Holy See, citizenship is acquired by law, ex iure, or by adminstrative decision; in the first instance, citizenship is a function of holding office within the Holy See as in the case of cardinals resident in Vatican City or diplomats of the Holy See; in the second instance, citizenship may be requested in a limited set of circumstances for those who reside within Vatican City under papal authorization, as a function of their office or service, or as the spouses and children of current citizens; citizenship is lost once an individual no longer permanently resides in Vatican City, normally reverting to the citizenship previously held

Suffrage: election of the pope is limited to cardinals less than 80 years old

Executive branch: *chief of state:* Pope FRANCIS (since 13 March 2013)
head of government: President of the Pontifical Commission for the State of Vatican City and President of the Governorate of the Vatican City State Fernando VERGEZ ALZAGA (since 1 October 2021)
cabinet: Pontifical Commission for the State of Vatican City appointed by the pope
elections/appointments: pope elected by the College of Cardinals, usually for life or until voluntary resignation; election last held on 13 March 2013 after the resignation of Pope BENEDICT XVI (next to be held after the death or resignation of the current pope); Secretary of State appointed by the pope
election results:
2013: Jorge Mario BERGOGLIO, former Archbishop of Buenos Aires, elected Pope FRANCIS

Legislative branch: *description:* unicameral Pontifical Commission for the State of Vatican City or Pontificia Commissione per lo Stato della Citta del Vaticano; 7 seats appointed by the pope
elections: appointment dates vary
election results: composition - men 6, woman 1

Judicial branch: *highest court(s):* Supreme Court or Supreme Tribunal of the Apostolic Signatura (consists of the cardinal prefect, who serves as ex-officio president of the court, and 2 other cardinals of the Prefect Signatura); note - judicial duties were established by the Motu Proprio, papal directive, of Pope PIUS XII on 1 May 1946; most Vatican City criminal matters are handled by the Republic of Italy courts
judge selection and term of office: cardinal prefect appointed by the pope; the other 2 cardinals of the court appointed by the cardinal prefect on a yearly basis
subordinate courts: Appellate Court of Vatican City; Tribunal of Vatican City

Political parties: none

International organization participation: CE (observer), IAEA, Interpol, IOM, ITSO, ITU, ITUC (NGOs), OAS (observer), OPCW, OSCE, Schengen Convention (de facto member), UN (observer), UNCTAD, UNHCR, UNWTO (observer), UPU, WIPO, WTO (observer)

Diplomatic representation in the US: *chief of mission:* Apostolic Nuncio Cardinal Christophe PIERRE (since 27 June 2016)
chancery: 3339 Massachusetts Avenue NW, Washington, DC 20008
telephone: [1] (202) 333-7121
FAX: [1] (202) 337-4036
email address and website:
nuntiususa@nuntiususa.org
http://www.nuntiususa.org/

Diplomatic representation from the US: *chief of mission:* Ambassador Joe DONNELLY (since 11 April 2022)
embassy: Via Sallustiana, 49, 00187 Rome
mailing address: 5660 Holy See Place, Washington DC 20521-5660
telephone: [39] (06) 4674-1
FAX: [39] (06) 4674-3411
email address and website:
https://va.usembassy.gov/

Flag description: two vertical bands of yellow (hoist side) and white with the arms of the Holy See, consisting of the crossed keys of Saint Peter surmounted by the three-tiered papal tiara, centered in the white band; the yellow color represents the pope's spiritual power, the white his worldly power

National symbol(s): crossed keys beneath a papal tiara; national colors: yellow, white

National anthem: *name:* "Inno e Marcia Pontificale" (Hymn and Pontifical March); often called The Pontifical Hymn
lyrics/music: Raffaello LAVAGNA/Charles-Francois GOUNOD
note: adopted 1950

National heritage: *total World Heritage Sites:* 2 (both cultural)
selected World Heritage Site locales: Historic Center of Rome, the Properties of the Holy See in that City Enjoying Extraterritorial Rights and San Paolo Fuori le Mura; Vatican City

ECONOMY

Economic overview: limited, tourism-based economy; euro user but issues commemorative stamps and coins; solar energy producer; some printing industry to support museums and religious needs

Industries: printing; production of coins, medals, postage stamps; mosaics, staff uniforms; worldwide banking and financial activities

Labor force: 4,822 (2016)
comparison ranking: 203

Exchange rates: euros (EUR) per US dollar -

Exchange rates: 0.925 (2023 est.)
0.95 (2022 est.)
0.845 (2021 est.)
0.876 (2020 est.)
0.893 (2019 est.)
note: while not an EU member state, the Holy See has a 2000 monetary agreement with Italy and the EU to produce limited euro coinage—but not banknotes—that began enforcement in January 2002

ENERGY

Electricity access: *electrification - total population:* 100% (2021)

COMMUNICATIONS

Telecommunication systems: *general assessment:* the Vatican's interior telecommunication system is composed of two strongly integrated sub-systems: fixed infrastructure and mobile infrastructure; it is important to note that the mobile communication system has been designed to be capable of using satellite connections so that it is possible to ensure telecommunication services whenever needed, including wherever the Pope travels; the telephone system operates through an automatic digital exchange (2020)
domestic: the telephone system operates through an automatic digital exchange (2020)
international: country code - 39; uses Italian system

Broadcast media: the Vatican Television Center (CTV) transmits live broadcasts of the Pope's Sunday and Wednesday audiences, as well as the Pope's public celebrations; CTV also produces documentaries; Vatican Radio is the Holy See's official broadcasting service broadcasting via shortwave, AM and FM frequencies, and via satellite and Internet connections; Vatican News website partners with Vatican Radio and provides Catholic news provided by the Vatican (2021)

Internet country code: .va

Internet users: *total:* 383 (2021 est.)
percent of population: 75% (2021 est.)
comparison ranking: total 232

Communications - note: the Vatican Apostolic Library is one of the world's oldest libraries, formally established in 1475, but actually much older; it holds a significant collection of historic texts including 1.1 million printed books and 75,000 codices (manuscript books with handwritten contents); it serves as a research library for history, law, philosophy, science, and theology; the library's collections have been described as "the world's greatest treasure house of the writings at the core of Western tradition"

TRANSPORTATION

Heliports: 1 (2024)

MILITARY AND SECURITY

Military and security forces: the Pontifical Swiss Guard Corps (Corpo della Guardia Svizzera Pontificia) serves as the de facto military force of Vatican City; the Gendarmerie Corps of Vatican City (Corpo della Gendarmeriais) is a police force that helps augment the Pontifical Swiss Guard Corps during the Pope's appearances, as well as providing general security, traffic direction, and investigative duties for the Vatican City State (2024)
note: the Swiss Guard Corps has protected the Pope and his residence since 1506

Military service age and obligation: Pontifical Swiss Guard Corps: 19-30 years of age for voluntary military service; no conscription; must be a single Roman Catholic male with Swiss citizenship who has completed basic training with the Swiss military and can obtain a certificate of good conduct; qualified candidates must apply to serve; the service contract is between 2 and 25 years (2024)

Military - note: defense is the responsibility of Italy

TRANSNATIONAL ISSUES

Illicit drugs: NA

HONDURAS

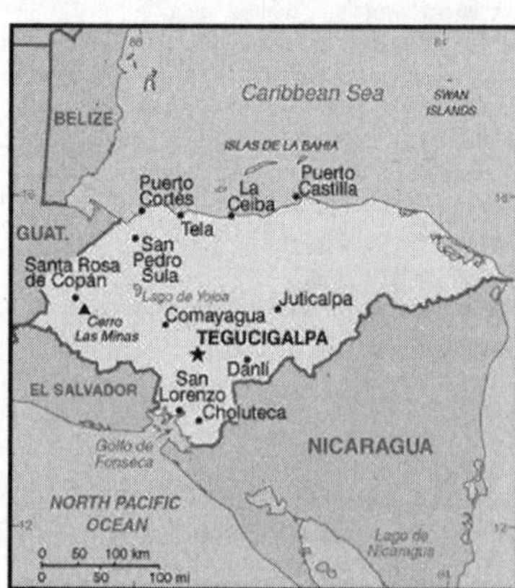

INTRODUCTION

Background: Once part of Spain's vast empire in the New World, Honduras became an independent nation in 1821. After two and a half decades of mostly military rule, a freely elected civilian government came to power in 1982. During the 1980s, Honduras proved a haven for anti-Sandinista contras fighting the Marxist Nicaraguan Government and an ally to Salvadoran Government forces fighting leftist guerrillas. Hurricane Mitch devastated the country in 1998, killing about 5,600 people and causing approximately $2 billion in damage. Since then, the economy has slowly rebounded, despite COVID-19 and severe storm-related setbacks in 2020 and 2021.

GEOGRAPHY

Location: Central America, bordering the Caribbean Sea, between Guatemala and Nicaragua and bordering the Gulf of Fonseca (North Pacific Ocean), between El Salvador and Nicaragua

Geographic coordinates: 15 00 N, 86 30 W

Map references: Central America and the Caribbean

Area: *total:* 112,090 sq km
land: 111,890 sq km
water: 200 sq km
comparison ranking: total 103

Area - comparative: slightly larger than Tennessee

Land boundaries: *total:* 1,575 km
border countries (3): Guatemala 244 km; El Salvador 391 km; Nicaragua 940 km

Coastline: 823 km (Caribbean Sea 669 km, Gulf of Fonseca 163 km)

Maritime claims: *territorial sea:* 12 nm
contiguous zone: 24 nm
exclusive economic zone: 200 nm
continental shelf: natural extension of territory or to 200 nm

Climate: subtropical in lowlands, temperate in mountains

Terrain: mostly mountains in interior, narrow coastal plains

Elevation: *highest point:* Cerro Las Minas 2,870 m
lowest point: Caribbean Sea 0 m
mean elevation: 684 m

Natural resources: timber, gold, silver, copper, lead, zinc, iron ore, antimony, coal, fish, hydropower

Land use: *agricultural land:* 28.8% (2018 est.)
arable land: 9.1% (2018 est.)
permanent crops: 4% (2018 est.)
permanent pasture: 15.7% (2018 est.)
forest: 45.3% (2018 est.)
other: 25.9% (2018 est.)

Irrigated land: 900 sq km (2012)

Major lakes (area sq km): *salt water lake(s):* Laguna de Caratasca - 1,110 sq km

Population distribution: most residents live in the mountainous western half of the country; unlike other Central American nations, Honduras is the only one with an urban population that is distributed between two large centers - the capital of Tegucigalpa and the city of San Pedro Sula; the Rio Ulua valley in the north is the only densely populated lowland area

Natural hazards: frequent, but generally mild, earthquakes; extremely susceptible to damaging hurricanes and floods along the Caribbean coast

Geography - note: has only a short Pacific coast but a long Caribbean shoreline, including the virtually uninhabited eastern Mosquito Coast

PEOPLE AND SOCIETY

Population: *total:* 9,529,188
male: 4,591,247
female: 4,937,941 (2024 est.)
comparison rankings: female 96; male 97; total 96

Nationality: *noun:* Honduran(s)
adjective: Honduran

Ethnic groups: Mestizo (mixed Indigenous and European) 90%, Indigenous 7%, African descent 2%, White 1%

Languages: Spanish (official), Amerindian dialects
major-language sample(s):
La Libreta Informativa del Mundo, la fuente indispensable de información básica. (Spanish)

Religions: Evangelical 55%, Roman Catholic 33.4%, none 10.1%, unspecified 1.5% (2023 est.)

Demographic profile: Honduras is one of the poorest countries in Latin America and has one of the world's highest murder rates. More than half of the population lives in poverty and per capita income is one of the lowest in the region. Poverty rates are higher among rural and indigenous people and in the south, west, and along the eastern border than in the north and central areas where most of Honduras' industries and infrastructure are concentrated. The increased productivity needed to break Honduras' persistent high poverty rate depends, in part, on further improvements in educational attainment. Although primary-school enrollment is near 100%, educational quality is poor, the drop-out rate and grade repetition remain high, and teacher and school accountability is low.
Honduras' population growth rate has slowed since the 1990s and is now 1.2% annually with a birth rate that averages 2.1 children per woman and more among rural, indigenous, and poor women. Honduras' young adult population - ages 15 to 29 - is projected to continue growing rapidly for the next three decades and then stabilize or slowly shrink. Population growth and limited job prospects outside of agriculture will continue to drive emigration. Remittances represent about a fifth of GDP.

Age structure: *0-14 years:* 28.7% (male 1,378,026/female 1,353,238)
15-64 years: 65.7% (male 2,980,393/female 3,282,159)

65 years and over: 5.6% (2024 est.) (male 232,828/ female 302,544)

Dependency ratios: *total dependency ratio:* 53.3
youth dependency ratio: 46.9
elderly dependency ratio: 6.4
potential support ratio: 15.5 (2021 est.)

Median age: *total:* 25.7 years (2024 est.)
male: 24.8 years
female: 26.6 years
comparison ranking: total 168

Population growth rate: 1.29% (2024 est.)
comparison ranking: 74

Birth rate: 19.9 births/1,000 population (2024 est.)
comparison ranking: 68

Death rate: 5.4 deaths/1,000 population (2024 est.)
comparison ranking: 185

Net migration rate: -1.7 migrant(s)/1,000 population (2024 est.)
comparison ranking: 165

Population distribution: most residents live in the mountainous western half of the country; unlike other Central American nations, Honduras is the only one with an urban population that is distributed between two large centers - the capital of Tegucigalpa and the city of San Pedro Sula; the Rio Ulua valley in the north is the only densely populated lowland area

Urbanization: *urban population:* 60.2% of total population (2023)
rate of urbanization: 2.48% annual rate of change (2020-25 est.)

Major urban areas - population: 1.568 million TEGUCIGALPA (capital), 982,000 San Pedro Sula (2023)

Sex ratio: *at birth:* 1.03 male(s)/female
0-14 years: 1.02 male(s)/female
15-64 years: 0.91 male(s)/female
65 years and over: 0.77 male(s)/female
total population: 0.93 male(s)/female (2024 est.)

Mother's mean age at first birth: 20.3 years (2011/12 est.)
note: data represents median age a first birth among women 25-49

Maternal mortality ratio: 72 deaths/100,000 live births (2020 est.)
comparison ranking: 85

Infant mortality rate: *total:* 15.4 deaths/1,000 live births (2024 est.)
male: 17.5 deaths/1,000 live births
comparison ranking: total 90

Life expectancy at birth: *total population:* 73.1 years (2024 est.)
male: 69.6 years
female: 76.8 years
comparison ranking: total population 152

Total fertility rate: 2.33 children born/woman (2024 est.)
comparison ranking: 76

Gross reproduction rate: 1.15 (2024 est.)

Contraceptive prevalence rate: 69.4% (2019)

Drinking water source: *improved: urban:* 100% of population
rural: 90.7% of population
total: 96.1% of population
unimproved: urban: 0% of population
rural: 9.3% of population
total: 3.9% of population (2020 est.)

Current health expenditure: 9% of GDP (2020)

Physician density: 0.5 physicians/1,000 population (2020)

Hospital bed density: 0.6 beds/1,000 population (2017)

Sanitation facility access: *improved: urban:* 96.7% of population
rural: 87.9% of population
total: 93% of population
unimproved: urban: 3.3% of population
rural: 12.1% of population
total: 7% of population (2020 est.)

Obesity - adult prevalence rate: 21.4% (2016)
comparison ranking: 89

Alcohol consumption per capita: *total:* 2.73 liters of pure alcohol (2019 est.)
beer: 1.6 liters of pure alcohol (2019 est.)
wine: 0.04 liters of pure alcohol (2019 est.)
spirits: 1.09 liters of pure alcohol (2019 est.)
other alcohols: 0 liters of pure alcohol (2019 est.)
comparison ranking: total 119

Children under the age of 5 years underweight: 7.1% (2019)
comparison ranking: 65

Currently married women (ages 15-49): % (2023 est.)

Child marriage: *women married by age 15:* 9.2%
women married by age 18: 34%
men married by age 18: 10% (2019 est.)

Education expenditures: 6.4% of GDP (2020 est.)
comparison ranking: 34

Literacy: *definition:* age 15 and over can read and write
total population: 88.5%
male: 88.2%
female: 88.7% (2019)

School life expectancy (primary to tertiary education): *total:* 10 years
male: 10 years
female: 11 years (2019)

ENVIRONMENT

Environment - current issues: urban population expanding; deforestation results from logging and the clearing of land for agricultural purposes; further land degradation and soil erosion hastened by uncontrolled development and improper land use practices such as farming of marginal lands; mining activities polluting Lago de Yojoa (the country's largest source of fresh water), as well as several rivers and streams, with heavy metals

Environment - international agreements: *party to:* Biodiversity, Climate Change, Climate Change-Kyoto Protocol, Climate Change-Paris Agreement, Comprehensive Nuclear Test Ban, Desertification, Endangered Species, Environmental Modification, Hazardous Wastes, Law of the Sea, Marine Dumping-London Convention, Nuclear Test Ban, Ozone Layer Protection, Ship Pollution, Tropical Timber 2006, Wetlands
signed, but not ratified: none of the selected agreements

Climate: subtropical in lowlands, temperate in mountains

Urbanization: *urban population:* 60.2% of total population (2023)
rate of urbanization: 2.48% annual rate of change (2020-25 est.)

Revenue from forest resources: 0.91% of GDP (2018 est.)
comparison ranking: 54

Revenue from coal: 0% of GDP (2018 est.)
comparison ranking: 172

Air pollutants: *particulate matter emissions:* 18.93 micrograms per cubic meter (2019 est.)
carbon dioxide emissions: 9.81 megatons (2016 est.)
methane emissions: 7.72 megatons (2020 est.)

Waste and recycling: *municipal solid waste generated annually:* 2,162,028 tons (2016 est.)

Major lakes (area sq km): *salt water lake(s):* Laguna de Caratasca - 1,110 sq km

Total water withdrawal: *municipal:* 320 million cubic meters (2020 est.)
industrial: 111 million cubic meters (2020 est.)
agricultural: 1.18 billion cubic meters (2020 est.)

Total renewable water resources: 92.16 billion cubic meters (2020 est.)

GOVERNMENT

Country name: *conventional long form:* Republic of Honduras
conventional short form: Honduras
local long form: República de Honduras
local short form: Honduras
etymology: the name means "depths" in Spanish and refers to the deep anchorage in the northern Bay of Trujillo

Government type: presidential republic

Capital: *name:* Tegucigalpa; note - article eight of the Honduran constitution states that the twin cities of Tegucigalpa and Comayaguela, jointly, constitute the capital of the Republic of Honduras; however, virtually all governmental institutions are on the Tegucigalpa side, which in practical terms makes Tegucigalpa the capital
geographic coordinates: 14 06 N, 87 13 W
time difference: UTC-6 (1 hour behind Washington, DC during Standard Time)
etymology: while most sources agree that Tegucigalpa is of Nahuatl derivation, there is no consensus on its original meaning

Administrative divisions: 18 departments (departamentos, singular - departamento); Atlantida, Choluteca, Colon, Comayagua, Copan, Cortes, El Paraiso, Francisco Morazan, Gracias a Dios, Intibuca, Islas de la Bahia, La Paz, Lempira, Ocotepeque, Olancho, Santa Barbara, Valle, Yoro

Independence: 15 September 1821 (from Spain)

National holiday: Independence Day, 15 September (1821)

Legal system: civil law system

Constitution: *history:* several previous; latest approved 11 January 1982, effective 20 January 1982
amendments: proposed by the National Congress with at least two-thirds majority vote of the membership; passage requires at least two-thirds majority vote of Congress in its next annual session; constitutional articles, such as the form of government, national sovereignty, the presidential term, and the procedure for amending the constitution, cannot be amended; amended several times, last in 2021

International law organization participation: accepts compulsory ICJ jurisdiction with reservations; accepts ICCt jurisdiction

Citizenship: *citizenship by birth:* yes
citizenship by descent only: yes

dual citizenship recognized: yes
residency requirement for naturalization: 1 to 3 years

Suffrage: 18 years of age; universal and compulsory

Executive branch: *chief of state:* President Iris Xiomara CASTRO de Zelaya (since 27 January 2022)
head of government: President Iris Xiomara CASTRO de Zelaya (since 27 January 2022)
cabinet: Cabinet appointed by president
elections/appointments: president directly elected by simple majority popular vote for a 4-year term; election last held on 28 November 2021 (next to be held on 30 November 2025); note - in 2015, the Constitutional Chamber of the Honduran Supreme Court struck down the constitutional provisions on presidential term limits
election results:
2021: Iris Xiomara CASTRO de Zelaya elected president; percent of vote - Iris Xiomara CASTRO de Zelaya (LIBRE) 51.1%, Nasry Juan ASFURA Zablah (PNH) 36.9%, Yani Benjamin ROSENTHAL Hidalgo (PL) 10%, other 2%
2017: Juan Orlando HERNANDEZ Alvarado reelected president; percent of vote - Juan Orlando HERNANDEZ Alvarado (PNH) 43%, Salvador NASRALLA (Alianza de Oposicion contra la Dictadura) 41.4%, Luis Orlando ZELAYA Medrano (PL) 14.7%, other 0.9%
note: the president is both chief of state and head of government

Legislative branch: *description:* unicameral National Congress or Congreso Nacional (128 seats; members directly elected in 18 multi-seat constituencies by closed party-list proportional representation vote; members serve 4-year terms)
elections: last held on 28 November 2021 (next to be held on 30 November 2025)
election results: percent of vote by party - LIBRE 39.8%, PNH 31.3%, PL 16.4%, PSH 10.9%, DC 0.8%, PAC 0.8%; seats by party - LIBRE 51, PNH 40, PL 21, PSH 14, DC 1, PAC 1; composition - men 93, women 35, percentage women 27.3%
note: seats by party as of 1 May 2022 - LIBRE 50, PNH 44, PL 22, PSH 10, DC 1, PAC 1

Judicial branch: *highest court(s):* Supreme Court of Justice or Corte Suprema de Justicia (15 principal judges, including the court president, and 6 alternates; court organized into civil, criminal, constitutional, and labor chambers); note - the court has both judicial and constitutional jurisdiction
judge selection and term of office: court president elected by his peers; judges elected by the National Congress from candidates proposed by the Nominating Board, a diverse 7-member group of judicial officials and other government and non-government officials nominated by each of their organizations; judges elected by Congress for renewable, 7-year terms
subordinate courts: courts of appeal; courts of first instance; justices of the peace

Political parties: Anti-Corruption Party or PAC
Christian Democratic Party or DC
Democratic Liberation of Honduras or Liderh
Democratic Unification Party or UD
The Front or El Frente
Honduran Patriotic Alliance or AP
Innovation and Unity Party or PINU
Liberal Party or PL
Liberty and Refoundation Party or LIBRE
National Party of Honduras or PNH
New Route or NR
Opposition Alliance against the Dictatorship or Alianza de Oposicion contra la Dictadura (electoral coalition)
Savior Party of Honduras or PSH
Vamos or Let's Go
We Are All Honduras (Todos Somos Honduras) or TSH

International organization participation: ACS, BCIE, CACM, CD, CELAC, EITI (candidate country), FAO, G-11, G-77, IADB, IAEA, IBRD, ICAO, ICCt, ICRM, IDA, IFAD, IFC, IFRCS, ILO, IMF, IMO, Interpol, IOC (suspended), IOM, IPU, ISO (subscriber), ITSO, ITU, ITUC (NGOs), LAES, LAIA (observer), MIGA, MINURSO, MINUSTAH, NAM, OAS, OPANAL, OPCW, Pacific Alliance (observer), PCA, Petrocaribe, SICA, UN, UNCTAD, UNHRC, UNESCO, UNIDO, Union Latina, UNWTO, UPU, WCO (suspended), WFTU (NGOs), WHO, WIPO, WMO, WTO

Diplomatic representation in the US: *chief of mission:* Ambassador Javier Efrain BU SOTO (since 12 December 2022)
chancery: 1220 19th Street NW, Suite #320, Washington, DC 20036
telephone: [1] (202) 966-7702
FAX: [1] (202) 966-9751
email address and website:
info@wadchn.com
https://hondurasembusa.org/
consulate(s) general: Atlanta, Boston, Charlotte (NC), Chicago, Dallas, Houston, Los Angeles, McAllen (TX), Miami, New Orleans, New York, San Francisco, Seattle

Diplomatic representation from the US: *chief of mission:* Ambassador Laura F. DOGU (since 12 April 2022)
embassy: Avenida La Paz, Tegucigalpa M.D.C.
mailing address: 3480 Tegucigalpa Place, Washington DC 20521-3480
telephone: [504] 2236-9320,
FAX: [504] 2236-9037
email address and website:
usahonduras@state.gov
https://hn.usembassy.gov/

Flag description: *three equal horizontal bands of cerulean blue (top), white, and cerulean blue, with five cerulean, five-pointed stars arranged in an X pattern centered in the white band; the stars represent the members of the former Federal Republic of Central America:* Costa Rica, El Salvador, Guatemala, Honduras, and Nicaragua; the blue bands symbolize the Pacific Ocean and the Caribbean Sea; the white band represents the land between the two bodies of water and the peace and prosperity of its people
note: similar to the flag of El Salvador, which features a round emblem encircled by the words REPUBLICA DE EL SALVADOR EN LA AMERICA CENTRAL centered in the white band; also similar to the flag of Nicaragua, which features a triangle encircled by the words REPUBLICA DE NICARAGUA on top and AMERICA CENTRAL on the bottom, centered in the white band

National symbol(s): scarlet macaw, white-tailed deer; national colors: blue, white

National anthem: *name:* "Himno Nacional de Honduras" (National Anthem of Honduras)
lyrics/music: Augusto Constancio COELLO/Carlos HARTLING
note: adopted 1915; the anthem's seven verses chronicle Honduran history; on official occasions, only the chorus and last verse are sung

National heritage: *total World Heritage Sites:* 2 (1 cultural, 1 natural)
selected World Heritage Site locales: Maya Site of Copan (c); Río Plátano Biosphere Reserve (n)

ECONOMY

Economic overview: second-fastest-growing Central American economy; COVID-19 and two hurricanes crippled activity; high poverty and inequality; declining-but-still-high violent crime disruption; systemic corruption; coffee and banana exporter; enormous remittances

Real GDP (purchasing power parity): $68.854 billion (2023 est.)
$66.473 billion (2022 est.)
$63.828 billion (2021 est.)
note: data in 2021 dollars
comparison ranking: 110

Real GDP growth rate: 3.58% (2023 est.)
4.14% (2022 est.)
12.57% (2021 est.)
note: annual GDP % growth based on constant local currency
comparison ranking: 89

Real GDP per capita: $6,500 (2023 est.)
$6,400 (2022 est.)
$6,200 (2021 est.)
note: data in 2021 dollars
comparison ranking: 163

GDP (official exchange rate): $34.401 billion (2023 est.)
note: data in current dollars at official exchange rate

Inflation rate (consumer prices): 6.66% (2023 est.)
9.09% (2022 est.)
4.48% (2021 est.)
note: annual % change based on consumer prices
comparison ranking: 138

Credit ratings: Moody's rating: B1 (2017)

Standard & Poors rating: BB- (2017)
note: The year refers to the year in which the current credit rating was first obtained.

GDP - composition, by sector of origin: *agriculture:* 12% (2023 est.)
industry: 26% (2023 est.)
services: 57.4% (2023 est.)
note: figures may not total 100% due to non-allocated consumption not captured in sector-reported data
comparison rankings: services 105; industry 89; agriculture 66

GDP - composition, by end use: *household consumption:* 86.4% (2023 est.)
government consumption: 14.4% (2023 est.)
investment in fixed capital: 24.2% (2023 est.)
investment in inventories: -1.1% (2023 est.)
exports of goods and services: 37% (2023 est.)
imports of goods and services: -60.9% (2023 est.)
note: figures may not total 100% due to rounding or gaps in data collection

Agricultural products: sugarcane, oil palm fruit, milk, maize, bananas, coffee, cantaloupes/melons, chicken, oranges, beans (2022)
note: top ten agricultural products based on tonnage

Industries: sugar processing, coffee, woven and knit apparel, wood products, cigars

Industrial production growth rate: -2.04% (2023 est.)
note: annual % change in industrial value added based on constant local currency
comparison ranking: 183

Labor force: 4.676 million (2023 est.)
note: number of people ages 15 or older who are employed or seeking work
comparison ranking: 91

Unemployment rate: 6.06% (2023 est.)
7.04% (2022 est.)
7.94% (2021 est.)
note: % of labor force seeking employment
comparison ranking: 124

Youth unemployment rate (ages 15-24): *total:* 11% (2023 est.)
male: 7.5% (2023 est.)
female: 17% (2023 est.)
note: % of labor force ages 15-24 seeking employment
comparison ranking: total 119

Population below poverty line: 48% (2019 est.)
note: % of population with income below national poverty line

Gini Index coefficient - distribution of family income: 48.2 (2019 est.)
note: index (0-100) of income distribution; higher values represent greater inequality
comparison ranking: 15

Average household expenditures: *on food:* 31.6% of household expenditures (2022 est.)
on alcohol and tobacco: 4.9% of household expenditures (2022 est.)

Household income or consumption by percentage share: *lowest 10%:* 1.2% (2019 est.)
highest 10%: 34.6% (2019 est.)
note: % share of income accruing to lowest and highest 10% of population

Remittances: 25.58% of GDP (2023 est.)
27% of GDP (2022 est.)
25.59% of GDP (2021 est.)
note: personal transfers and compensation between resident and non-resident individuals/households/entities

Budget: *revenues:* $5.333 billion (2020 est.)
expenditures: $5.696 billion (2020 est.)
note: central government revenues (excluding grants) and expenses converted to US dollars at average official exchange rate for year indicated

Public debt: 39.5% of GDP (2017 est.)
comparison ranking: 133

Taxes and other revenues: 15.07% (of GDP) (2020 est.)
note: central government tax revenue as a % of GDP
comparison ranking: 138

Current account balance: -$1.335 billion (2023 est.)
-$2.063 billion (2022 est.)
-$1.538 billion (2021 est.)
note: balance of payments - net trade and primary/secondary income in current dollars
comparison ranking: 146

Exports: $9.701 billion (2023 est.)
$9.403 billion (2022 est.)
$8.052 billion (2021 est.)
note: balance of payments - exports of goods and services in current dollars
comparison ranking: 116

Exports - partners: US 51%, Nicaragua 8%, El Salvador 8%, Guatemala 5%, Germany 4% (2022)
note: top five export partners based on percentage share of exports

Exports - commodities: garments, coffee, insulated wire, palm oil, bananas (2022)
note: top five export commodities based on value in dollars

Imports: $17.861 billion (2023 est.)
$17.943 billion (2022 est.)
$14.869 billion (2021 est.)
note: balance of payments - imports of goods and services in current dollars
comparison ranking: 101

Imports - partners: US 47%, Guatemala 10%, China 10%, El Salvador 7%, Mexico 4% (2022)
note: top five import partners based on percentage share of imports

Imports - commodities: refined petroleum, cotton yarn, garments, synthetic fibers, plastic products (2022)
note: top five import commodities based on value in dollars

Reserves of foreign exchange and gold: $7.543 billion (2023 est.)
$8.41 billion (2022 est.)
$8.667 billion (2021 est.)
note: holdings of gold (year-end prices)/foreign exchange/special drawing rights in current dollars
comparison ranking: 95

Debt - external: $7.611 billion (2022 est.)
note: present value of external debt in current US dollars
comparison ranking: 43

Exchange rates: lempiras (HNL) per US dollar -

Exchange rates: 24.602 (2023 est.)
24.486 (2022 est.)
24.017 (2021 est.)
24.582 (2020 est.)
24.509 (2019 est.)

ENERGY

Electricity access: *electrification - total population:* 94.4% (2022 est.)
electrification - urban areas: 100%
electrification - rural areas: 86.8%

Electricity: *installed generating capacity:* 3.195 million kW (2022 est.)
consumption: 8.789 billion kWh (2022 est.)
exports: 3 million kWh (2022 est.)
imports: 212.156 million kWh (2022 est.)
transmission/distribution losses: 3.424 billion kWh (2022 est.)
comparison rankings: transmission/distribution losses 147; imports 105; exports 99; consumption 111; installed generating capacity 107

Electricity generation sources: *fossil fuels:* 36.9% of total installed capacity (2022 est.)
solar: 9.9% of total installed capacity (2022 est.)
wind: 6.5% of total installed capacity (2022 est.)
hydroelectricity: 33.3% of total installed capacity (2022 est.)
geothermal: 3% of total installed capacity (2022 est.)
biomass and waste: 10.4% of total installed capacity (2022 est.)

Coal: *consumption:* 190,000 metric tons (2022 est.)
imports: 190,000 metric tons (2022 est.)

Petroleum: *total petroleum production:* 20 bbl/day (2023 est.)
refined petroleum consumption: 67,000 bbl/day (2022 est.)

Carbon dioxide emissions: 9.428 million metric tonnes of CO2 (2022 est.)
from coal and metallurgical coke: 429,000 metric tonnes of CO2 (2022 est.)
from petroleum and other liquids: 8.999 million metric tonnes of CO2 (2022 est.)
comparison ranking: total emissions 107

Energy consumption per capita: 16.386 million Btu/person (2022 est.)
comparison ranking: 135

COMMUNICATIONS

Telephones - fixed lines: *total subscriptions:* 414,000 (2022 est.)
subscriptions per 100 inhabitants: 4 (2022 est.)
comparison ranking: total subscriptions 100

Telephones - mobile cellular: *total subscriptions:* 7.937 million (2022 est.)
subscriptions per 100 inhabitants: 76 (2022 est.)
comparison ranking: total subscriptions 102

Telecommunication systems: *general assessment:* Honduras is among the poorest countries in Central America and has long been plagued by an unstable political framework which has rendered telecom sector reform difficult; this has created real difficulties for telcos as well as consumers; fixed-line teledensity, at only 4.9%, is significantly lower than the Latin American and Caribbean average; poor fixed-line infrastructure has been exacerbated by low investment and topographical difficulties which have made investment in rural areas unattractive or uneconomical; the internet has been slow to develop; DSL and cable modem technologies are available but are relatively expensive, while higher speed services are largely restricted to the major urban centers; the demand for broadband is steadily increasing and there has been some investment in network upgrades to fiber-based infrastructure
(2022)
domestic: fixed-line teledensity of 5 per 100; mobile-cellular subscribership is roughly 74 per 100 persons (2021)
international: country code - 504; landing points for both the ARCOS and the MAYA-1 fiber-optic submarine cable systems that together provide connectivity to South and Central America, parts of the Caribbean, and the US; satellite earth stations - 2 Intelsat (Atlantic Ocean); connected to Central American Microwave System (2019)

Broadcast media: multiple privately owned terrestrial TV networks, supplemented by multiple cable TV networks; Radio Honduras is the lone government-owned radio network; roughly 300 privately owned radio stations (2019)

Internet country code: .hn

Internet users: *total:* 4.8 million (2021 est.)
percent of population: 48% (2021 est.)
comparison ranking: total 99

Broadband - fixed subscriptions: *total:* 396,916 (2020)
subscriptions per 100 inhabitants: 4 (2020 est.)
comparison ranking: total 97

TRANSPORTATION

National air transport system: *number of registered air carriers:* 4 (2020)
inventory of registered aircraft operated by air carriers: 26

annual passenger traffic on registered air carriers: 251,149 (2018)
annual freight traffic on registered air carriers: 450,000 (2018) mt-km

Civil aircraft registration country code prefix: HR

Airports: 129 (2024)
comparison ranking: 40

Heliports: 6 (2024)

Railways: *total:* 699 km (2014)
narrow gauge: 164 km (2014) 1.067-m gauge
115 km 1.057-mm gauge
420 km 0.914-mm gauge
comparison ranking: total 100

Roadways: *total:* 14,742 km
paved: 3,367 km
unpaved: 11,375 km (2012) (1,543 km summer only)
note: an additional 8,951 km of non-official roads used by the coffee industry
comparison ranking: total 126

Waterways: 465 km (2012) (most navigable only by small craft)
comparison ranking: 93

Merchant marine: *total:* 489 (2023)
by type: general cargo 233, oil tanker 82, other 174
comparison ranking: total 43

Ports: *total ports:* 8 (2024)
large: 0
medium: 0
small: 1
very small: 7
ports with oil terminals: 3
key ports: Coxen Hole, La Ceiba, Puerto Castilla, Puerto Cortes, Puerto de Hencan, Puerto Este, Tela, Trujillo

MILITARY AND SECURITY

Military and security forces: Honduran Armed Forces (Fuerzas Armadas de Honduras, FFAA): Army (Ejercito), Honduran Naval Forces (Fuerzas Naval Hondurena, FNH; includes marines), Honduran Air Force (Fuerza Aerea Hondurena, FAH), Honduran Military Police of Public Order (Policía Militar del Orden Público or PMOP) (2024)
note 1: the National Police of Honduras (Policía Nacional de Honduras, PNH) are under the Secretariat of Security and responsible for internal security; some larger cities have police forces that operate independently of the national police and report to municipal authorities
note 2: the PMOP supports the PNH against narcotics trafficking and organized crime; it is subordinate to the Secretariat of Defense/FFAA, but conducts operations sanctioned by civilian security officials as well as by military leaders
note 3: the National Interinstitutional Security Force is an interagency command that coordinates the overlapping responsibilities of the HNP, PMOP, and other security organizations such as the National Intelligence Directorate and the Public Ministry (public prosecutor), but exercises coordination, command, and control responsibilities only during interagency operations involving those forces

Military expenditures: 1.5% of GDP (2023 est.)
1.4% of GDP (2022 est.)
1.5% of GDP (2021 est.)
1.6% of GDP (2020 est.)
1.6% of GDP (2019 est.)
comparison ranking: 92

Military and security service personnel strengths: approximately 16,000 active personnel (7,500 Army; 1,500 Navy, including about 1,000 marines; 2,000 Air Force; 5,000 Military Police of Public Order); approximately 18,000 National Police (2023)

Military equipment inventories and acquisitions: the FFAA's inventory is comprised of a mix of older or secondhand and limited amounts of more equipment from a wide mix of suppliers, including Colombia, Germany, Israel, the Netherlands, South Korea, the UK, and the US (2024)

Military service age and obligation: 18-22 years of age for voluntary military service for men and women; 24-36 month service obligation; no conscription (2024)
note: as of 2023, women made up about 9% of the active duty military

Military - note: the Honduran Armed Forces (FFAA) are responsible for maintaining the country's territory, defending its sovereignty, providing emergency/humanitarian assistance, and supporting the National Police (PNH); the FFAA's primary focus is internal and border security, and since 2011 a considerable portion of it has been deployed to support the PNH in combating narcotics trafficking and organized crime; military support to domestic security included the creation of the Military Police of Public Order (PMOP) in 2013 to provide security in areas controlled by street gangs to combat crime and make arrests; the PMOP also has sent personnel to reinforce security operations along the country's border as part of a tri-national security task force with El Salvador and Guatemala
the FFAA has received military equipment, training, humanitarian, and technical assistance from the US military; the US military maintains a joint service task force co-located with the FFAA at Soto Cano Air Base (2024)

TRANSNATIONAL ISSUES

Refugees and internally displaced persons: IDPs: 247,000 (violence, extortion, threats, forced recruitment by urban gangs between 2004 and 2018) (2023)

Illicit drugs: transshipment point for cocaine destined for the United States and precursor chemicals used to produce illicit drugs; some small-scale coca cultivation

HONG KONG

INTRODUCTION

Background: The UK seized Hong Kong in 1841, and China formally ceded it the following year at the end of the First Opium War. The Kowloon Peninsula was added in 1860 at the end of the Second Opium War, and the UK obtained a 99-year lease of the New Territories in 1898. Pursuant to a UK-China agreement in 1984, Hong Kong became the Hong Kong Special Administrative Region (HKSAR) of the People's Republic of China as of 1 July 1997. In this agreement, China promised that, under its "one country, two systems" formula, China's socialist economic and strict political system would not be imposed on Hong Kong and that Hong Kong would enjoy a "high degree of autonomy" in all matters except foreign and defense affairs for the next 50 years.

After the handover, Hong Kong continued to enjoy success as an international financial center. However, growing Chinese political influence and dissatisfaction with the Hong Kong Government in the 2010s became central issues and led to considerable civil unrest, including large-scale pro-democracy demonstrations in 2019 after the HKSAR attempted to revise a local ordinance to allow extraditions to mainland China. In response to the protests, the governments of the HKSAR and China reduced the city's autonomy and placed new restrictions on the rights of Hong Kong residents, moves that were widely criticized as contravening obligations under the Hong Kong Basic Law and the Sino-British Joint Declaration. Democratic lawmakers and political figures were arrested in a widespread crackdown, while others fled abroad. At the same time, dozens of civil society groups and several independent media outlets were closed or disbanded. In 2021, Beijing imposed a more restrictive electoral system, restructuring the Legislative Council (LegCo) and allowing only government-approved candidates to run for office. The changes ensured that virtually all seats in the 2021 LegCo election went to pro-establishment candidates and effectively ended political opposition to Beijing. In 2024, the LegCo passed a new national security law (Article 23 of the Basic Law) further expanding the Hong Kong Government's power to curb dissent.

GEOGRAPHY

Location: Eastern Asia, bordering the South China Sea and China

Geographic coordinates: 22 15 N, 114 10 E

Map references: Southeast Asia

Area: *total:* 1,108 sq km
land: 1,073 sq km
water: 35 sq km
comparison ranking: total 183

Area - comparative: six times the size of Washington, DC

Land boundaries: *total:* 33 km
regional borders (1): China 33 km

Coastline: 733 km

Maritime claims: *territorial sea:* 12 nm

Climate: subtropical monsoon; cool and humid in winter, hot and rainy from spring through summer, warm and sunny in fall

Terrain: hilly to mountainous with steep slopes; lowlands in north

Elevation: *highest point:* Tai Mo Shan 958 m
lowest point: South China Sea 0 m

Natural resources: outstanding deepwater harbor, feldspar

Land use: *agricultural land:* 5% (2018 est.)
arable land: 3.2% (2018 est.)
permanent crops: 0.9% (2018 est.)
permanent pasture: 0.9% (2018 est.)
forest: 0% (2018 est.)
other: 95% (2018 est.)

Irrigated land: 10 sq km (2012)

Population distribution: population fairly evenly distributed

Natural hazards: occasional typhoons

Geography - note: consists of a mainland area (the New Territories) and more than 200 islands

PEOPLE AND SOCIETY

Population: *total:* 7,297,821
male: 3,367,812
female: 3,930,009 (2024 est.)
comparison rankings: female 103; male 106; total 106

Nationality: *noun:* Chinese/Hong Konger
adjective: Chinese/Hong Kong

Ethnic groups: Chinese 91.6%, Filipino 2.7%, Indonesian 1.9%, other 3.7% (2021 est.)

Languages: Cantonese (official) 85.4%, English (official) 4.5%, Putonghua (official) 2.2%, other Chinese dialects 2.8%, other 2%, persons under 5 or mute 3.2% (2021 est.)
major-language sample(s):

世界概況, 必須擁有的基本資料参考书
(Cantonese)
note: data represent population by usual spoken language

Religions: Buddhist or Taoist 27.9%, Protestant 6.7%, Roman Catholic 5.3%, Muslim 4.2%, Hindu 1.4%, Sikh 0.2%, other or none 54.3% (2016 est.)
note: many people practice Confucianism, regardless of their religion or not having a religious affiliation

Age structure: *0-14 years:* 13.2% (male 505,718/ female 459,956)
15-64 years: 64.8% (male 2,123,216/female 2,609,102)
65 years and over: 21.9% (2024 est.) (male 738,878/ female 860,951)

Dependency ratios: *total dependency ratio:* 46.6
youth dependency ratio: 17.8
elderly dependency ratio: 28.7
potential support ratio: 3.5 (2021 est.)

Median age: *total:* 47.2 years (2024 est.)
male: 45.3 years
female: 48.6 years
comparison ranking: total 7

Population growth rate: 0.12% (2024 est.)
comparison ranking: 183

Birth rate: 7.6 births/1,000 population (2024 est.)
comparison ranking: 218

Death rate: 8.1 deaths/1,000 population (2024 est.)
comparison ranking: 89

Net migration rate: 1.6 migrant(s)/1,000 population (2024 est.)
comparison ranking: 54

Population distribution: population fairly evenly distributed

Urbanization: *urban population:* 100% of total population (2023)
rate of urbanization: 0.58% annual rate of change (2020-25 est.)

Major urban areas - population: 7.685 million Hong Kong (2023)

Sex ratio: *at birth:* 1.06 male(s)/female
0-14 years: 1.1 male(s)/female
15-64 years: 0.81 male(s)/female
65 years and over: 0.86 male(s)/female
total population: 0.86 male(s)/female (2024 est.)

Mother's mean age at first birth: 29.8 years (2008 est.)

Infant mortality rate: *total:* 2.5 deaths/1,000 live births (2024 est.)
male: 2.8 deaths/1,000 live births
female: 2.2 deaths/1,000 live births
comparison ranking: total 215

Life expectancy at birth: *total population:* 84 years (2024 est.)
male: 81.3 years
female: 86.8 years
comparison ranking: total population 7

Total fertility rate: 1.24 children born/woman (2024 est.)
comparison ranking: 223

Gross reproduction rate: 0.6 (2024 est.)

Contraceptive prevalence rate: 66.7% (2017)

Drinking water source: *improved: urban:* 100% of population
rural: NA
total: 100% of population

Physician density: 2.04 physicians/1,000 population (2020)

Hospital bed density: 4.9 beds/1,000 population (2020)

Sanitation facility access: *improved: urban:* 96.4% of population
rural: NA
total: 96.4% of population
unimproved: urban: 3.6% of population
rural: NA
total: 3.6% of population (2017)

Currently married women (ages 15-49): 47.7% (2023 est.)

Education expenditures: 4% of GDP (2021 est.)
comparison ranking: 115

School life expectancy (primary to tertiary education): *total:* 17 years
male: 17 years
female: 17 years (2021)

ENVIRONMENT

Environment - current issues: air and water pollution from rapid urbanization; urban waste pollution; industrial pollution

Climate: subtropical monsoon; cool and humid in winter, hot and rainy from spring through summer, warm and sunny in fall

Urbanization: *urban population:* 100% of total population (2023)
rate of urbanization: 0.58% annual rate of change (2020-25 est.)

Revenue from forest resources: 0% of GDP (2018 est.)
comparison ranking: 179

Revenue from coal: 0% of GDP (2018 est.)
comparison ranking: 177

Air pollutants: *carbon dioxide emissions:* 43.64 megatons (2016 est.)

Waste and recycling: *municipal solid waste generated annually:* 5,679,816 tons (2015 est.)
municipal solid waste recycled annually: 1,931,138 tons (2016 est.)
percent of municipal solid waste recycled: 34% (2016 est.)

GOVERNMENT

Country name: *conventional long form:* Hong Kong Special Administrative Region
conventional short form: Hong Kong
local long form: Heung Kong Takpit Hangching Ku (Eitel/Dyer-Ball)
local short form: Heung Kong (Eitel/Dyer-Ball)
abbreviation: HK
etymology: probably an imprecise phonetic rendering of the Cantonese name meaning "fragrant harbor"

Government type: presidential limited democracy; a special administrative region of the People's Republic of China

Dependency status: special administrative region of the People's Republic of China

Administrative divisions: none (special administrative region of the People's Republic of China)

Independence: none (special administrative region of China)

National holiday: National Day (Anniversary of the Founding of the People's Republic of China), 1 October (1949); note - 1 July (1997) is celebrated as Hong Kong Special Administrative Region Establishment Day

Legal system: mixed legal system of common law based on the English model and Chinese customary law (in matters of family and land tenure); PRC imposition of National Security Law incorporates elements of Chinese civil law

Constitution: *history:* several previous (governance documents while under British authority); latest drafted April 1988 to February 1989, approved March 1990, effective 1 July 1997 (Basic Law of the Hong Kong Special Administrative Region of the People's Republic of China serves as the constitution); note - since 1990, China's National People's Congress has interpreted specific articles of the Basic Law
amendments: proposed by the Standing Committee of the National People's Congress (NPC), the People's Republic of China State Council, or the Special Administrative Region of Hong Kong; submittal of proposals to the NPC requires two- thirds majority vote by the Legislative Council of Hong Kong, approval by two thirds of Hong Kong's deputies to the NPC, and approval by the Hong Kong chief executive; final passage requires approval by the NPC

Citizenship: see China

Suffrage: 18 years of age in direct elections for 20 of the 90 Legislative Council seats and all of the seats in 18 district councils; universal for permanent residents living in the territory of Hong Kong for the past 7 years; note - in indirect elections, suffrage is limited to about 220,000 members of functional constituencies for the other 70 legislature seats and a 1,500- member election committee for the chief executive drawn from broad sectoral groupings, central government bodies, municipal organizations, and elected Hong Kong officials

Executive branch: *chief of state:* President of China XI Jinping (since 14 March 2013)
head of government: Chief Executive John LEE Ka-chiu (since 1 July 2022)
cabinet: Executive Council or ExCo appointed by the chief executive
elections/appointments: president indirectly elected by National People's Congress for a 5-year term (eligible for a second term); election last held on 10 March 2023 (next to be held in March 2028); chief executive indirectly elected by the Election Committee and appointed by the PRC Government for a 5-year term (eligible for a second term); election last held on 8 May 2022 (next to be held in 2027)
election results:
2022: John LEE was the only candidate and won with over 99% of the vote by the Election Committee
2017: Carrie LAM elected; Election Committee vote - Carrie LAM (non-partisan) 777, John TSANG (non-partisan) 365, WOO Kwok-hing (non-partisan) 21, 23 ballots rejected (1,186 votes cast)
note: electoral changes that Beijing imposed in March 2021 expanded the Election Committee to 1,500 members

Legislative branch: *description:* unicameral Legislative Council or LegCo (90 seats); 20 members directly elected, 70 indirectly elected; members serve 4-year terms
elections: last held on 19 Dec 2021 (next to be held in 2025)
election results: percent of vote by bloc: pro-Beijing 93.8%, non-establishment 6.2%; seats by association/bloc/party - pro-Beijing 89 (DAB 19, HKFTU 8, BPA 7, NPP 5, LP 4, NTAS 4, HKFEW 2, HKFLU 2, CF 2, RT 1, PP 1, KWND 1, NPHK 1, NCF-1; other/independent 41), non-aligned 1 (Third Side); composition - men 73, women 17, percentage women 18.9%
note 1: all political candidates are evaluated by the Candidate Eligibility Review Committee (CERC), which was established in April 2022; CERC members are all appointed by the chief executive
note 2: Hong Kong's leading pro-democracy political parties boycotted the 2021 election

Judicial branch: *highest court(s):* Court of Final Appeal (consists of the chief justice, 3 permanent judges, and 20 non-permanent judges); note - a sitting bench consists of the chief justice, 3 permanent judges, and 1 non-permanent judge
judge selection and term of office: all judges appointed by the Hong Kong Chief Executive upon the recommendation of the Judicial Officers Recommendation Commission, an independent body consisting of the Secretary for Justice, other judges, and judicial and legal professionals; permanent judges serve until normal retirement at age 65, but term can be extended; non-permanent judges appointed for renewable 3-year terms without age limit
subordinate courts: High Court (consists of the Court of Appeal and Court of First Instance); District Courts (includes Family and Land Courts); magistrates' courts; specialized tribunals

Political parties: Business and Professionals Alliance for Hong Kong or BPA
Civil Force or CF
Democratic Alliance for the Betterment and Progress of Hong Kong or DAB
Federation of Hong Kong and Kowloon Labour Unions or HKFLU
Hong Kong Federation of Education Workers or HKFEW
Hong Kong Federation of Trade Unions or HKFTU
Kowloon West New Dynamic or KWND
Liberal Party or LP
New Century Forum or NCF
New People's Party or NPP
New Prospect for Hong Kong or NPHK
New Territories Association of Societies or NTAS
Professional Power or PP
Roundtable or RT
Third Side or TS
note 1: there is no political party ordinance, so there are no registered political parties; politically active groups register as societies or companies
note 2: by the end of 2021, the leading pro-democracy figures in Hong Kong had been effectively removed from the political arena under the provisions of Beijing's 2021 electoral changes or via charges under the 2020 national security law; in addition, dozens of pro-democracy organizations, including political parties, unions, churches, civil rights groups, and media organizations have disbanded or closed; as of 2023, nearly all politically active groups were pro-Beijing

International organization participation: ADB, APEC, BIS, FATF, ICC (national committees), IHO, IMF, IMO (associate), Interpol (subbureau), IOC, ISO (correspondent), ITUC (NGOs), UNWTO (associate), UPU, WCO, WMO, WTO

Diplomatic representation in the US: *chief of mission:* none (Special Administrative Region of China)

HKETO offices: New York, San Francisco, Washington DC

Note: Hong Kong is a Special Administrative Region of China and does not have a diplomatic presence; the Hong Kong Economic and Trade Office (HKETO) carries out normal liaison activities and communication with the US Government and other US entities; the position of the Hong Kong Commissioner to the US Government of the Hong Kong Special Administrative Region is vacant; address: 1520 18th Street NW, Washington, DC 20036; telephone: [1] (202) 331-8947; FAX: [1] (202) 331-8958; email: hketo@hketowashington.gov.hk; website: https://www.hketowashington.gov.hk/

Diplomatic representation from the US: *chief of mission:* Consul General Gregory MAY (since September 2022); note - also accredited to Macau
embassy: 26 Garden Road, Central, Hong Kong
mailing address: 8000 Hong Kong Place, Washington DC 20521-8000
telephone: [852] 2523-9011
FAX: [852] 2845-1598
email address and website:
acshk@state.gov
https://hk.usconsulate.gov/

Flag description: red with a stylized, white, five-petal Bauhinia flower in the center; each petal contains a small, red, five-pointed star in its middle; the red color is the same as that on the Chinese flag and represents the motherland; the fragrant Bauhinia - developed in Hong Kong the late 19th century - has come to symbolize the region; the five stars echo those on the flag of China

National symbol(s): orchid tree flower; national colors: red, white

National anthem: *note:* as a Special Administrative Region of China, "Yiyongjun Jinxingqu" is the official anthem (see China)

ECONOMY

Economic overview: high-income tourism- and services-based economy; global financial hub; COVID-19 and political protests fueled recent recession; ongoing recovery but lower-skilled unemployment remains high; investing in job-reskilling programs

Real GDP (purchasing power parity): $485.559 billion (2023 est.)
$470.434 billion (2022 est.)
$488.412 billion (2021 est.)
note: data in 2021 dollars
comparison ranking: 50

Real GDP growth rate: 3.22% (2023 est.)
-3.68% (2022 est.)
6.45% (2021 est.)
note: annual GDP % growth based on constant local currency
comparison ranking: 102

Real GDP per capita: $64,400 (2023 est.)
$64,000 (2022 est.)
$65,900 (2021 est.)
note: data in 2021 dollars
comparison ranking: 24

GDP (official exchange rate): $382.055 billion (2023 est.)
note: data in current dollars at official exchange rate

Inflation rate (consumer prices): 2.1% (2023 est.)
1.88% (2022 est.)
1.57% (2021 est.)
note: annual % change based on consumer prices
comparison ranking: 40

Credit ratings: Fitch rating: AA- (2020)

Moody's rating: Aa3 (2020)

Standard & Poors rating: AA+ (2017)
note: The year refers to the year in which the current credit rating was first obtained.

GDP - composition, by sector of origin: *agriculture:* 0.1% (2022 est.)
industry: 6.3% (2022 est.)
services: 91% (2022 est.)
note: figures may not total 100% due to non-allocated consumption not captured in sector-reported data
comparison rankings: services 5; industry 210; agriculture 210

GDP - composition, by end use: *household consumption:* 70.3% (2023 est.)
government consumption: 13.2% (2023 est.)
investment in fixed capital: 16.7% (2023 est.)
investment in inventories: -1% (2023 est.)
exports of goods and services: 176.2% (2023 est.)
imports of goods and services: -175.4% (2023 est.)
note: figures may not total 100% due to rounding or gaps in data collection

Agricultural products: pork, chicken, spinach, vegetables, game meat, pork offal, fruits, onions, lettuce, pork fat (2022)
note: top ten agricultural products based on tonnage

Industries: trading and logistics, financial services, professional services, tourism, cultural and creative, clothing and textiles, shipping, electronics, toys, clocks and watches

Industrial production growth rate: 5.06% (2022 est.)
note: annual % change in industrial value added based on constant local currency
comparison ranking: 48

Labor force: 3.825 million (2023 est.)
note: number of people ages 15 or older who are employed or seeking work
comparison ranking: 97

Unemployment rate: 3.93% (2023 est.)
4.32% (2022 est.)
5.17% (2021 est.)
note: % of labor force seeking employment
comparison ranking: 74

Youth unemployment rate (ages 15-24): *total:* 10.5% (2023 est.)
male: 11.3% (2023 est.)
female: 9.6% (2023 est.)
note: % of labor force ages 15-24 seeking employment
comparison ranking: total 132

Population below poverty line: 19.9% (2016 est.)

Gini Index coefficient - distribution of family income: 53.9 (2016 est.)
comparison ranking: 5

Average household expenditures: *on food:* 11.7% of household expenditures (2022 est.)
on alcohol and tobacco: 0.8% of household expenditures (2022 est.)

Household income or consumption by percentage share: *lowest 10%:* 1.8%
highest 10%: 38.1% (2016)

Remittances: 0.11% of GDP (2023 est.)
0.12% of GDP (2022 est.)
0.12% of GDP (2021 est.)
note: personal transfers and compensation between resident and non-resident individuals/households/entities

Budget: *revenues:* $70.124 billion (2020 est.)
expenditures: $105.849 billion (2020 est.)

Public debt: 0.1% of GDP (2017 est.)
comparison ranking: 205

Taxes and other revenues: 23.2% (of GDP) (2017 est.)
comparison ranking: 60

Current account balance: $35.366 billion (2023 est.)
$36.525 billion (2022 est.)
$43.659 billion (2021 est.)
note: balance of payments - net trade and primary/secondary income in current dollars
comparison ranking: 18

Exports: $673.305 billion (2023 est.)
$697.583 billion (2022 est.)
$752.621 billion (2021 est.)
note: balance of payments - exports of goods and services in current dollars
comparison ranking: 14

Exports - partners: China 21%, India 13%, Netherlands 6%, Switzerland 4%, US 3% (2022)
note: top five export partners based on percentage share of exports

Exports - commodities: gold, integrated circuits, gas turbines, broadcasting equipment, machine parts (2022)
note: top five export commodities based on value in dollars

Imports: $670.085 billion (2023 est.)
$682.881 billion (2022 est.)
$732.087 billion (2021 est.)
note: balance of payments - imports of goods and services in current dollars
comparison ranking: 14

Imports - partners: China 44%, Taiwan 11%, Singapore 8%, South Korea 5%, Japan 4% (2022)
note: top five import partners based on percentage share of imports

Imports - commodities: integrated circuits, broadcasting equipment, machine parts, gold, jewelry (2022)
note: top five import commodities based on value in dollars

Reserves of foreign exchange and gold: $425.553 billion (2023 est.)
$424.025 billion (2022 est.)
$496.856 billion (2021 est.)
note: holdings of gold (year-end prices)/foreign exchange/special drawing rights in current dollars
comparison ranking: 9

Exchange rates: Hong Kong dollars (HKD) per US dollar -

Exchange rates: 7.83 (2023 est.)
7.831 (2022 est.)
7.773 (2021 est.)
7.757 (2020 est.)
7.836 (2019 est.)

ENERGY

Electricity access: *electrification - total population:* 100% (2022 est.)

Electricity: *installed generating capacity:* 13.388 million kW (2022 est.)
consumption: 44.677 billion kWh (2022 est.)
imports: 12.573 billion kWh (2022 est.)
transmission/distribution losses: 3.834 billion kWh (2022 est.)
comparison rankings: transmission/distribution losses 152; imports 21; consumption 56; installed generating capacity 56

Electricity generation sources: *fossil fuels:* 99.4% of total installed capacity (2022 est.)
solar: 0.2% of total installed capacity (2022 est.)
biomass and waste: 0.4% of total installed capacity (2022 est.)

Coal: *consumption:* 6.217 million metric tons (2022 est.)
exports: 800 metric tons (2022 est.)
imports: 5.681 million metric tons (2022 est.)

Petroleum: *total petroleum production:* 96 bbl/day (2023 est.)
refined petroleum consumption: 414,000 bbl/day (2022 est.)

Natural gas: *consumption:* 4.835 billion cubic meters (2022 est.)
imports: 4.835 billion cubic meters (2022 est.)

Carbon dioxide emissions: 87.498 million metric tonnes of CO2 (2022 est.)
from coal and metallurgical coke: 14.039 million metric tonnes of CO2 (2022 est.)
from petroleum and other liquids: 63.975 million metric tonnes of CO2 (2022 est.)
from consumed natural gas: 9.484 million metric tonnes of CO2 (2022 est.)
comparison ranking: total emissions 45

Energy consumption per capita: 167.815 million Btu/person (2022 est.)
comparison ranking: 23

COMMUNICATIONS

Telephones - fixed lines: *total subscriptions:* 3.673 million (2022 est.)
subscriptions per 100 inhabitants: 49 (2022 est.)
comparison ranking: total subscriptions 34

Telephones - mobile cellular: *total subscriptions:* 21.861 million (2022 est.)
subscriptions per 100 inhabitants: 292 (2022 est.)
comparison ranking: total subscriptions 58

Telecommunication systems: *general assessment:* Hong Kong's telecommunications sector continues to stay near the top of world rankings for the industry; it has kept its #1 spot in the Asian region in terms of the maturity of its telecom market – a reflection of the high penetration rates across mobile, mobile broadband, and fixed broadband; even fixed-line teledensity in Hong Kong is impressive at over 50%, although it too has started a gradual decline in keeping with most other telecom markets around the world, as consumers slowly transition over to the mobile platform for all of their communication needs (2022)
domestic: fixed-line is over 51 per 100 and mobile-cellular is 319 subscriptions per 100 (2021)
international: country code - 852; landing points for the AAE-1, AAG, APCN-2, APG, ASE, FEA, FNAL, RNAL, H2HE, SeaMeWe-3, SJC and TGN-IA submarine cables that provide connections to Asia, US, Australia, the Middle East, and Europe; satellite earth stations - 3 Intelsat (1 Pacific Ocean and 2 Indian Ocean); coaxial cable to Guangzhou, China (2022)

Broadcast media: 34 commercial terrestrial TV networks each with multiple stations; multi-channel satellite and cable TV systems available; 3 licensed broadcasters of terrestrial radio, one of which is government funded, operate about 12 radio stations; note - 4 digital radio broadcasters operated in Hong Kong from 2010 to 2017, but all digital radio services were terminated in September 2017 due to weak market demand (2019)

Internet country code: .hk

Internet users: *total:* 6.975 million (2021 est.)

percent of population: 93% (2021 est.)
comparison ranking: total 81

Broadband - fixed subscriptions: *total:* 2,885,586 (2020 est.)
subscriptions per 100 inhabitants: 39 (2020 est.)
comparison ranking: total 47

TRANSPORTATION

National air transport system: *number of registered air carriers:* 12 (2020) (registered in China)
inventory of registered aircraft operated by air carriers: 275 (registered in China)
annual passenger traffic on registered air carriers: 47,101,822 (2018)
annual freight traffic on registered air carriers: 12,676,720,000 (2018) mt-km

Civil aircraft registration country code prefix: B-H

Airports: 3 (2024)
comparison ranking: 196

Heliports: 94 (2024)

Roadways: *total:* 2,193 km
paved: 2,193 km (2021)
comparison ranking: total 173

Merchant marine: *total:* 2,537 (2023)
by type: bulk carrier 1,047, container ship 560, general cargo 144, oil tanker 394, other 392
comparison ranking: total 10

Ports: *total ports:* 1 (2024)
large: 1
medium: 0
small: 0
very small: 0
ports with oil terminals: 1
key ports: Hong Kong

MILITARY AND SECURITY

Military and security forces: no regular indigenous military forces; Hong Kong Police Force (specialized units include the Police Counterterrorism Response Unit, the Explosive Ordnance Disposal Bureau, the Special Duties Unit, the Airport Security Unit, and the VIP Protection Unit) (2024)
note: the Hong Kong garrison of China's People's Liberation Army (PLA) includes elements of the PLA Army, PLA Navy, and PLA Air Force; these forces are under the direct leadership of the Central Military Commission in Beijing and under administrative control of the adjacent Southern Theater Command

Military - note: defense is the responsibility of China

TRANSNATIONAL ISSUES

Trafficking in persons: tier rating: Tier 2 Watch List — the government did not demonstrate overall increasing efforts to eliminate trafficking compared with the previous reporting period, therefore Hong Kong was downgraded to Tier 2 Watch List; for more details, go to: https://www.state.gov/reports/2024-trafficking-in-persons-report/hong-kong/

Illicit drugs: modern banking system provides conduit for money laundering; groups involved in money laundering range from local street organizations to sophisticated international syndicates involved in assorted criminal activities, including drug trafficking; major source of precursor chemicals used in the production of illicit narcotics

HUNGARY

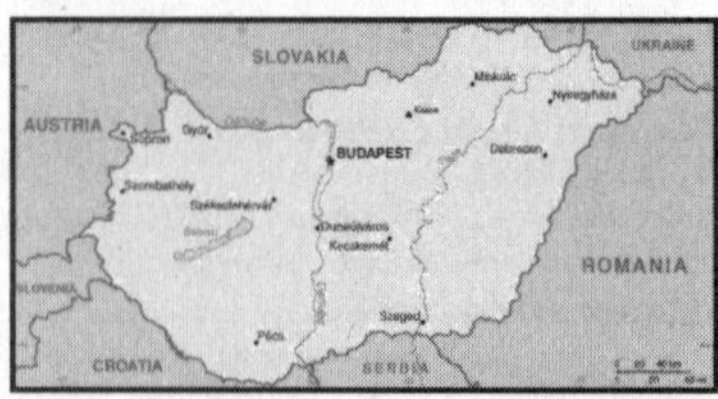

INTRODUCTION

Background: Hungary became a Christian kingdom in A.D. 1000 and for many centuries served as a bulwark against Ottoman Turkish expansion in Europe. The kingdom eventually became part of the Austro-Hungarian Empire, which collapsed during World War I. The country fell under communist rule after World War II. In 1956, Moscow responded to a Hungarian revolt and announcement of its withdrawal from the Warsaw Pact with a massive military intervention. Under the leadership of Janos KADAR in 1968, Hungary began liberalizing its economy, introducing so-called "Goulash Communism." Hungary held its first multiparty elections in 1990 and initiated a free market economy. It joined NATO in 1999 and the EU five years later.

GEOGRAPHY

Location: Central Europe, northwest of Romania

Geographic coordinates: 47 00 N, 20 00 E

Map references: Europe

Area: *total:* 93,028 sq km
land: 89,608 sq km
water: 3,420 sq km
comparison ranking: total 110

Area - comparative: slightly smaller than Virginia; about the same size as Indiana

Land boundaries: *total:* 2,106 km
border countries (7): Austria 321 km; Croatia 348 km; Romania 424 km; Serbia 164 km; Slovakia 627 km; Slovenia 94 km; Ukraine 128 km

Coastline: 0 km (landlocked)

Maritime claims: none (landlocked)

Climate: temperate; cold, cloudy, humid winters; warm summers

Terrain: mostly flat to rolling plains; hills and low mountains on the Slovakian border

Elevation: *highest point:* Kekes 1,014 m
lowest point: Tisza River 78 m
mean elevation: 143 m

Natural resources: bauxite, coal, natural gas, fertile soils, arable land

Land use: *agricultural land:* 58.9% (2018 est.)
arable land: 48.5% (2018 est.)
permanent crops: 2% (2018 est.)
permanent pasture: 8.4% (2018 est.)
forest: 22.5% (2018 est.)
other: 18.6% (2018 est.)

Irrigated land: 1,010 sq km (2019)

Major lakes (area sq km): *fresh water lake(s):* Lake Balaton - 590 sq km

Major rivers (by length in km): Duna (Danube) (shared with Germany [s], Austria, Slovakia, Croatia, Serbia, Bulgaria, Ukraine, Moldova, and Romania [m]) - 2,888 km
note – [s] after country name indicates river source; [m] after country name indicates river mouth

Major watersheds (area sq km): Atlantic Ocean drainage: *(Black Sea)* Danube (795,656 sq km)

Population distribution: a fairly even distribution throughout most of the country, with urban areas attracting larger and denser populations

Geography - note: landlocked; strategic location astride main land routes between Western Europe and Balkan Peninsula as well as between Ukraine and Mediterranean basin; the north-south flowing Duna (Danube) and Tisza Rivers divide the country into three large regions

PEOPLE AND SOCIETY

Population: *total:* 9,855,745
male: 4,812,668
female: 5,043,077 (2024 est.)
comparison rankings: female 94; male 95; total 95

Nationality: *noun:* Hungarian(s)
adjective: Hungarian

Ethnic groups: Hungarian 84.3%, Romani 2.1%, German 1%, other 1.2%, unspecified 13.7% (2022 est.)
note: percentages add up to more than 100% because respondents were able to identify more than one ethnic group; Romani populations are usually underestimated in official statistics and may represent 5–10% of Hungary's population

Languages: Hungarian (official) 98.8%, English 25.3%, German 12.6%, Russian 2.1%, French 1.5%, Romanian 1.4%, other 5.1% (2022 est.)
major-language sample(s):
A World Factbook nélkülözhetetlen forrása az alapvető információknak. (Hungarian)
note: percentages add up to more than 100% because respondents were able to identify more than one spoken language

Religions: Catholic 30.1% (Roman Catholic 27.5%, Greek Catholic 1.7%, other Catholic 0.9%), Calvinist 9.8%, Lutheran 1.8%, other Christian (includes Orthodox) 1.6%, other 0.4%, none 16.1%, no answer 40.1% (2022 est.)

Age structure: *0-14 years:* 14.6% (male 753,955/female 683,943)
15-64 years: 63.9% (male 3,195,761/female 3,104,750)
65 years and over: 21.5% (2024 est.) (male 862,952/female 1,254,384)

Dependency ratios: *total dependency ratio:* 53.8
youth dependency ratio: 22.4
elderly dependency ratio: 31.4
potential support ratio: 3.2 (2021 est.)

Median age: *total:* 44.8 years (2024 est.)
male: 42.8 years
female: 46.7 years
comparison ranking: total 27

Population growth rate: -0.28% (2024 est.)
comparison ranking: 212

Birth rate: 9.1 births/1,000 population (2024 est.)
comparison ranking: 198

Death rate: deaths/1,000 population (2024 est.)
comparison ranking: 6

Net migration rate: 2.5 migrant(s)/1,000 population (2024 est.)
comparison ranking: 44

Population distribution: a fairly even distribution throughout most of the country, with urban areas attracting larger and denser populations

Urbanization: *urban population:* 72.9% of total population (2023)
rate of urbanization: 0.05% annual rate of change (2020-25 est.)

Major urban areas - population: 1.778 million BUDAPEST (capital) (2023)

Sex ratio: *at birth:* 1.06 male(s)/female
0-14 years: 1.1 male(s)/female
15-64 years: 1.03 male(s)/female
65 years and over: 0.69 male(s)/female
total population: 0.95 male(s)/female (2024 est.)

Mother's mean age at first birth: years (2020 est.)

Maternal mortality ratio: 15 deaths/100,000 live births (2020 est.)
comparison ranking: 137

Infant mortality rate: *total:* 4.7 deaths/1,000 live births (2024 est.)
male: 5 deaths/1,000 live births
female: 4.3 deaths/1,000 live births
comparison ranking: total 180

Life expectancy at birth: *total population:* 76 years (2024 est.)
male: 72.9 years
female: 79.3 years
comparison ranking: total population 119

Total fertility rate: 1.6 children born/woman (2024 est.)
comparison ranking: 186

Gross reproduction rate: 0.78 (2024 est.)

Drinking water source: *improved: urban:* 100% of population
rural: 100% of population
total: 100% of population

Current health expenditure: 7.3% of GDP (2020)

Physician density: physicians/1,000 population (2020)

Hospital bed density: 7 beds/1,000 population (2018)

Sanitation facility access: *improved: urban:* 100% of population
rural: 100% of population
total: 100% of population

Obesity - adult prevalence rate: % (2016)
comparison ranking: 42

Alcohol consumption per capita: *total:* 10.79 liters of pure alcohol (2019 est.)
beer: 3.96 liters of pure alcohol (2019 est.)
wine: 3.33 liters of pure alcohol (2019 est.)
spirits: 3.5 liters of pure alcohol (2019 est.)
other alcohols: 0 liters of pure alcohol (2019 est.)
comparison ranking: total 16

Tobacco use: *total:* 31.8% (2020 est.)
male: 35.8% (2020 est.)
female: 27.8% (2020 est.)
comparison ranking: total 22

Children under the age of 5 years underweight: NA

Currently married women (ages 15-49): % (2023 est.)

Education expenditures: 4.8% of GDP (2020 est.)
comparison ranking: 84

Literacy: *definition:* age 15 and over can read and write
total population: 99.1%
male: 99.1%
female: 99.1% (2021)

School life expectancy (primary to tertiary education): *total:* 15 years
male: 15 years
female: 15 years (2020)

ENVIRONMENT

Environment - current issues: air and water pollution are some of Hungary's most serious environmental problems; water quality in the Hungarian part of the Danube has improved but is still plagued by pollutants from industry and large-scale agriculture; soil pollution

Environment - international agreements: *party to:* Air Pollution, Air Pollution-Heavy Metals, Air Pollution-Multi-effect Protocol, Air Pollution-Nitrogen Oxides, Air Pollution-Persistent Organic Pollutants, Air Pollution-Sulphur 85, Air Pollution-Sulphur 94, Air Pollution-Volatile Organic Compounds, Antarctic Treaty, Biodiversity, Climate Change, Climate Change-Kyoto Protocol, Climate Change-Paris Agreement, Comprehensive Nuclear Test Ban, Desertification, Endangered Species, Environmental Modification, Hazardous Wastes, Law of the Sea, Marine Dumping-London Convention, Nuclear Test Ban, Ozone Layer Protection, Ship Pollution, Tropical Timber 2006, Wetlands, Whaling
signed, but not ratified: Antarctic-Environmental Protection

Climate: temperate; cold, cloudy, humid winters; warm summers

Urbanization: *urban population:* 72.9% of total population (2023)
rate of urbanization: 0.05% annual rate of change (2020-25 est.)

Revenue from forest resources: 0.1% of GDP (2018 est.)
comparison ranking: 112

Revenue from coal: 0.01% of GDP (2018 est.)
comparison ranking: 49

Air pollutants: *particulate matter emissions:* 14.24 micrograms per cubic meter (2019 est.)
carbon dioxide emissions: 45.54 megatons (2016 est.)
methane emissions: 7.25 megatons (2020 est.)

Waste and recycling: *municipal solid waste generated annually:* 3.712 million tons (2015 est.)
municipal solid waste recycled annually: 962,893 tons (2015 est.)
percent of municipal solid waste recycled: 25.9% (2015 est.)

Major lakes (area sq km): *fresh water lake(s):* Lake Balaton - 590 sq km

Major rivers (by length in km): Duna (Danube) (shared with Germany [s], Austria, Slovakia, Croatia, Serbia, Bulgaria, Ukraine, Moldova, and Romania [m]) - 2,888 km
note – [s] after country name indicates river source; [m] after country name indicates river mouth

Major watersheds (area sq km): Atlantic Ocean drainage: *(Black Sea)* Danube (795,656 sq km)

Total water withdrawal: *municipal:* 660 million cubic meters (2020 est.)
industrial: 3.45 billion cubic meters (2020 est.)
agricultural: 550 million cubic meters (2020 est.)

Total renewable water resources: 104 billion cubic meters (2020 est.)

Geoparks: *total global geoparks and regional networks:* 4 (2024)
global geoparks and regional networks: Bakony-Balaton; Bukk Region; Hungary; Novohrad-Nógrád (includes Slovakia) (2024)

GOVERNMENT

Country name: *conventional long form:* none
conventional short form: Hungary
local long form: none
local short form: Magyarorszag
former: Kingdom of Hungary, Hungarian People's Republic, Hungarian Soviet Republic, Hungarian Republic
etymology: the Byzantine Greeks refered to the tribes that arrived on the steppes of Eastern Europe in the 9th century as the "Oungroi," a name that was later Latinized to "Ungri" and which became "Hungari"; the name originally meant an "[alliance of] ten tribes"; the Hungarian name "Magyarorszag" means "Country of the Magyars"; the term may derive from the most prominent of the Hungarian tribes, the Megyer

Government type: parliamentary republic

Capital: *name:* Budapest
geographic coordinates: 47 30 N, 19 05 E
time difference: UTC+1 (6 hours ahead of Washington, DC, during Standard Time)
daylight saving time: +1hr, begins last Sunday in March; ends last Sunday in October
etymology: the Hungarian capital city was formed in 1873 from the merger of three cities on opposite banks of the Danube: Buda and Obuda (Old Buda) on the western shore and Pest on the eastern; the origins of the original names are obscure, but according to the second century A.D. geographer, Ptolemy, the settlement that would become Pest was called "Pession" in ancient times; "Buda" may derive from either a Slavic or Turkic personal name

Administrative divisions: 19 counties (megyek, singular - megye), 25 cities with county rights (megyei jogu varosok, singular - megyei jogu varos), and 1 capital city (fovaros)
counties: Bacs-Kiskun, Baranya, Bekes, Borsod-Abauj-Zemplen, Csongrad-Csanad, Fejer, Gyor-Moson-Sopron, Hajdu-Bihar, Heves, Jasz-Nagykun-Szolnok, Komarom-Esztergom, Nograd, Pest, Somogy, Szabolcs-Szatmar-Bereg, Tolna, Vas, Veszprem, Zala
cities with county rights: Baja, Bekescsaba, Debrecen, Dunaujvaros, Eger, Erd, Esztergom, Gyor, Hodmezovasarhely, Kaposvar, Kecskemet, Miskolc, Nagykanizsa, Nyiregyhaza, Pecs, Salgotarjan,

Sopron, Szeged, Szekesfehervar, Szekszard, Szolnok, Szombathely, Tatabanya, Veszprem, Zalaegerszeg
capital city: Budapest

Independence: *16 November 1918 (republic proclaimed); notable earlier dates:* 25 December 1000 (crowning of King STEPHEN I, traditional founding date); 30 March 1867 (Austro-Hungarian dual monarchy established)

National holiday: Saint Stephen's Day, 20 August (1083); note - commemorates his canonization and the transfer of his remains to Buda (now Budapest) in 1083

Legal system: civil legal system influenced by the German model

Constitution: *history:* previous 1949 (heavily amended in 1989 following the collapse of communism); latest approved 18 April 2011, signed 25 April 2011, effective 1 January 2012
amendments: proposed by the president of the republic, by the government, by parliamentary committee, or by Parliament members; passage requires two-thirds majority vote of Parliament members and approval by the president; amended several times, last in 2018

International law organization participation: accepts compulsory ICJ jurisdiction with reservations; accepts ICC jurisdiction

Citizenship: *citizenship by birth:* no
citizenship by descent only: at least one parent must be a citizen of Hungary
dual citizenship recognized: yes
residency requirement for naturalization: 8 years

Suffrage: 18 years of age, 16 if married and marriage is registered in Hungary; universal

Executive branch: *chief of state:* President Tamas SULYOK (since 5 March 2024)
head of government: Prime Minister Viktor ORBAN (since 29 May 2010)
cabinet: Cabinet of Ministers proposed by the prime minister and appointed by the president
elections/appointments: president indirectly elected by the National Assembly with two-thirds majority vote in first round or simple majority vote in second round for a 5-year term (eligible for a second term); election last held on 26 February 2024 (next to be held in spring 2029); prime minister elected by the National Assembly on the recommendation of the president; election last held on 3 April 2022 (next to be held in April or May 2027)
election results:
2024: Tamas SULYOK elected president; National Assembly vote - 134 to 5
2022: Katalin NOVAK (Fidesz) elected president; National Assembly vote - 137 to 51

Legislative branch: *description:* unicameral National Assembly or Orszaggyules (199 seats; 106 members directly elected in single-member constituencies by simple majority vote and 93 members directly elected in a single nationwide constituency by party-list proportional representation vote, using the D'Hondt method; members serve 4-year terms)
elections: last held on 3 April 2022 (next to be held in April 2026)
election results: percent of vote by party list - Fidesz-KDNP 54.1%, United for Hungary 34.5%, Mi Hazank 5.9%, other 5.5%; seats by party list - Fidesz-KDNP 135, United for Hungary 57, Mi Hazank 6, independent 1; composition - men 170, women 29, percentage women 14.6%

Judicial branch: *highest court(s):* Curia or Supreme Judicial Court (consists of the president, vice president, department heads, and has a maximum of 113 judges, and is organized into civil, criminal, and administrative-labor departments; Constitutional Court (consists of 15 judges, including the court president and vice president)
judge selection and term of office: Curia president elected by the National Assembly on the recommendation of the president of the republic; other Curia judges appointed by the president upon the recommendation of the National Judicial Council, a separate 15-member administrative body; judge tenure based on interim evaluations until normal retirement at age 62; Constitutional Court judges, including the president of the court, elected by the National Assembly; court vice president elected by the court itself; members serve 12-year terms with mandatory retirement at age 62
subordinate courts: 5 regional courts of appeal; 19 regional or county courts (including Budapest Metropolitan Court); 20 administrative-labor courts; 111 district or local courts

Political parties: Christian Democratic People's Party or KDNP
Democratic Coalition or DK
Dialogue for Hungary or Párbeszéd
Fidesz-Hungarian Civic Alliance or Fidesz
Hungarian Socialist Party or MSZP
Jobbik - Conservatives or Jobbik
LMP-Hungary's Green Party or LMP
Mi Hazank (Our Homeland Movement) or MHM
Momentum Movement or Momentum
Movement for a Better Hungary or Jobbik
National Self-Government of Germans in Hungary or MNOÖ
On the People's Side or A Nép Pártján
Our Homeland Movement or Mi Hazánk
TISZA – Respect and Freedom Party or TISZA

International organization participation: Australia Group, BIS, CD, CE, CEI, CERN, EAPC, EBRD, ECB, EIB, ESA (cooperating state), EU, FAO, G-9, IAEA, IBRD, ICAO, ICC (national committees), ICCt, ICRM, IDA, IEA, IFAD, IFC, IFRCS, ILO, IMF, IMO, IMSO, Interpol, IOC, IOM, IPU, ISO, ITSO, ITU, ITUC (NGOs), MIGA, MINURSO, NATO, NEA, NSG, OAS (observer), OECD, OIF (observer), OPCW, OSCE, PCA, Schengen Convention, SELEC, UN, UNCTAD, UNESCO, UNFICYP, UNHCR, UNIDO, UNIFIL, UNOOSA, UNWTO, UPU, Wassenaar Arrangement, WCO, WFTU (NGOs), WHO, WIPO, WMO, WTO, ZC

Diplomatic representation in the US: *chief of mission:* Ambassador Szabolcs Ferenc TAKÁCS (since 23 December 2020)
chancery: 1500 Rhode Island Avenue, N.W. Washington, D.C. 20005
telephone: [1] (202) 362-6730
FAX: [1] (202) 966-8135
email address and website:
info.was@mfa.gov.hu
https://washington.mfa.gov.hu/eng
consulate(s) general: Chicago, Los Angeles, New York
consulate(s): Houston, Miami

Diplomatic representation from the US: *chief of mission:* Ambassador David PRESSMAN (since 14 September 2022)
embassy: Szabadsag ter 12, H-1054 Budapest
mailing address: 5270 Budapest Place, US Department of State, Washington, DC 20521-5270
telephone: [36] (1) 475-4400
FAX: [36] (1) 475-4248
email address and website:
acs.budapest@state.gov
https://hu.usembassy.gov/

Flag description: *three equal horizontal bands of red (top), white, and green; the flag dates to the national movement of the 18th and 19th centuries, and fuses the medieval colors of the Hungarian coat of arms with the revolutionary tricolor form of the French flag; folklore attributes virtues to the colors:* red for strength, white for faithfulness, and green for hope; alternatively, the red is seen as being for the blood spilled in defense of the land, white for freedom, and green for the pasturelands that make up so much of the country

National symbol(s): Holy Crown of Hungary (Crown of Saint Stephen); national colors: red, white, green

National anthem: *name:* "Himnusz" (Hymn)
lyrics/music: Ferenc KOLCSEY/Ferenc ERKEL
note: adopted 1844

National heritage: *total World Heritage Sites:* 8 (7 cultural, 1 natural)
selected World Heritage Site locales: Budapest, including the Banks of the Danube, the Buda Castle Quarter, and Andrássy Avenue (c); Old Village of Hollókő and its Surroundings (c); Caves of Aggtelek Karst and Slovak Karst (n); Millenary Benedictine Abbey of Pannonhalma and its Natural Environment (c); Hortobágy National Park - the Puszta (c); Early Christian Necropolis of Pécs (Sopianae) (c); Fertö / Neusiedlersee Cultural Landscape (c); Tokaj Wine Region Historic Cultural Landscape (c)

ECONOMY

Economic overview: high-income EU and OECD economy; tightening fiscal policy in response to budget deficit; delayed EU cohesion fund disbursement due to judicial independence concerns; high inflation and low consumer confidence; seeking alternatives to dependence on Russian natural gas

Real GDP (purchasing power parity): $388.906 billion (2023 est.)
$392.468 billion (2022 est.)
$375.268 billion (2021 est.)
note: data in 2021 dollars
comparison ranking: 54

Real GDP growth rate: -0.91% (2023 est.)
4.58% (2022 est.)
7.06% (2021 est.)
note: annual GDP % growth based on constant local currency
comparison ranking: 199

Real GDP per capita: $40,600 (2023 est.)
$40,700 (2022 est.)
$38,600 (2021 est.)
note: data in 2021 dollars
comparison ranking: 60

GDP (official exchange rate): $212.389 billion (2023 est.)
note: data in current dollars at official exchange rate

Inflation rate (consumer prices): 17.12% (2023 est.)
14.61% (2022 est.)
5.11% (2021 est.)
note: annual % change based on consumer prices
comparison ranking: 196

Credit ratings: Fitch rating: BBB (2019)

Moody's rating: Baa3 (2016)

Standard & Poors rating: BBB (2019)
note: The year refers to the year in which the current credit rating was first obtained.

GDP - composition, by sector of origin: *agriculture:* 4.7% (2023 est.)
industry: 24.3% (2023 est.)
services: 57.6% (2023 est.)
note: figures may not total 100% due to non-allocated consumption not captured in sector-reported data
comparison rankings: services 104; industry 105; agriculture 120

GDP - composition, by end use: *household consumption:* 49.5% (2023 est.)
government consumption: 20% (2023 est.)
investment in fixed capital: 26.3% (2023 est.)
investment in inventories: -1% (2023 est.)
exports of goods and services: 81.2% (2023 est.)
imports of goods and services: -76.1% (2023 est.)
note: figures may not total 100% due to rounding or gaps in data collection

Agricultural products: wheat, maize, milk, barley, sunflower seeds, rapeseed, sugar beets, pork, grapes, apples (2022)
note: top ten agricultural products based on tonnage

Industries: mining, metallurgy, construction materials, processed foods, textiles, chemicals (especially pharmaceuticals), motor vehicles

Industrial production growth rate: -5.16% (2023 est.)
note: annual % change in industrial value added based on constant local currency
comparison ranking: 198

Labor force: 5.006 million (2023 est.)
note: number of people ages 15 or older who are employed or seeking work
comparison ranking: 86

Unemployment rate: 4.13% (2023 est.)
3.61% (2022 est.)
4.05% (2021 est.)
note: % of labor force seeking employment
comparison ranking: 79

Youth unemployment rate (ages 15-24): *total:* 12.8% (2023 est.)
male: 13.5% (2023 est.)
female: 11.8% (2023 est.)
note: % of labor force ages 15-24 seeking employment
comparison ranking: total 108

Population below poverty line: 12.1% (2021 est.)
note: % of population with income below national poverty line

Gini Index coefficient - distribution of family income: 29.2 (2021 est.)
note: index (0-100) of income distribution; higher values represent greater inequality
comparison ranking: 128

Average household expenditures: *on food:* 17.6% of household expenditures (2022 est.)
on alcohol and tobacco: 7.6% of household expenditures (2022 est.)

Household income or consumption by percentage share: *lowest 10%:* 3.5% (2021 est.)
highest 10%: 24.1% (2021 est.)
note: % share of income accruing to lowest and highest 10% of population

Remittances: 1.7% of GDP (2023 est.)
2.2% of GDP (2022 est.)
2.1% of GDP (2021 est.)
note: personal transfers and compensation between resident and non-resident individuals/households/entities

Budget: *revenues:* $69.793 billion (2022 est.)
expenditures: $75.081 billion (2022 est.)
note: central government revenues (excluding grants) and expenses converted to US dollars at average official exchange rate for year indicated

Public debt: 75.53% of GDP (2022 est.)
note: central government debt as a % of GDP
comparison ranking: 45

Taxes and other revenues: 23.43% (of GDP) (2022 est.)
note: central government tax revenue as a % of GDP
comparison ranking: 57

Current account balance: $623.545 million (2023 est.)
-$14.47 billion (2022 est.)
-$7.337 billion (2021 est.)
note: balance of payments - net trade and primary/secondary income in current dollars
comparison ranking: 60

Exports: $172.484 billion (2023 est.)
$160.038 billion (2022 est.)
$145.539 billion (2021 est.)
note: balance of payments - exports of goods and services in current dollars
comparison ranking: 37

Exports - partners: Germany 24%, Italy 6%, Romania 5%, Slovakia 5%, Austria 4% (2022)
note: top five export partners based on percentage share of exports

Exports - commodities: cars, vehicle parts/accessories, electric batteries, packaged medicine, computers (2022)
note: top five export commodities based on value in dollars

Imports: $161.558 billion (2023 est.)
$167.744 billion (2022 est.)
$145.058 billion (2021 est.)
note: balance of payments - imports of goods and services in current dollars
comparison ranking: 35

Imports - partners: Germany 21%, China 7%, Austria 7%, Slovakia 6%, Poland 6% (2022)
note: top five import partners based on percentage share of imports

Imports - commodities: natural gas, vehicle parts/accessories, electricity, cars, plastic products (2022)
note: top five import commodities based on value in dollars

Reserves of foreign exchange and gold: $45.719 billion (2023 est.)
$41.219 billion (2022 est.)
$43.483 billion (2021 est.)
note: holdings of gold (year-end prices)/foreign exchange/special drawing rights in current dollars
comparison ranking: 51

Exchange rates: forints (HUF) per US dollar -

Exchange rates: 353.088 (2023 est.)
372.596 (2022 est.)
303.141 (2021 est.)
307.997 (2020 est.)
290.66 (2019 est.)

ENERGY

Electricity access: *electrification - total population:* 100% (2022 est.)

Electricity: *installed generating capacity:* 11.995 million kW (2022 est.)
consumption: 43.186 billion kWh (2022 est.)
exports: 9.439 billion kWh (2022 est.)
imports: 21.589 billion kWh (2022 est.)
transmission/distribution losses: 2.801 billion kWh (2022 est.)
comparison rankings: transmission/distribution losses 136; imports 8; exports 26; consumption 57; installed generating capacity 60

Electricity generation sources: *fossil fuels:* 33.1% of total installed capacity (2022 est.)
nuclear: 44.2% of total installed capacity (2022 est.)
solar: 13.6% of total installed capacity (2022 est.)
wind: 1.8% of total installed capacity (2022 est.)
hydroelectricity: 0.5% of total installed capacity (2022 est.)
biomass and waste: 6.8% of total installed capacity (2022 est.)

Nuclear energy: Number of operational nuclear reactors: 4 (2023)

Net capacity of operational nuclear reactors: 1.92GW (2023 est.)

Percent of total electricity production: 48.8% (2023 est.)

Coal: *production:* 5.45 million metric tons (2022 est.)
consumption: 6.18 million metric tons (2022 est.)
exports: 132,000 metric tons (2022 est.)
imports: 804,000 metric tons (2022 est.)
proven reserves: 2.909 billion metric tons (2022 est.)

Petroleum: *total petroleum production:* 36,000 bbl/day (2023 est.)
refined petroleum consumption: 175,000 bbl/day (2023 est.)
crude oil estimated reserves: 12.1 million barrels (2021 est.)

Natural gas: *production:* 1.523 billion cubic meters (2022 est.)
consumption: 9.485 billion cubic meters (2022 est.)
imports: 9.314 billion cubic meters (2022 est.)
proven reserves: 3.738 billion cubic meters (2021 est.)

Carbon dioxide emissions: 44.884 million metric tonnes of CO_2 (2022 est.)
from coal and metallurgical coke: 4.915 million metric tonnes of CO_2 (2022 est.)
from petroleum and other liquids: 21.781 million metric tonnes of CO_2 (2022 est.)
from consumed natural gas: 18.187 million metric tonnes of CO_2 (2022 est.)
comparison ranking: total emissions 60

Energy consumption per capita: 102.832 million Btu/person (2022 est.)
comparison ranking: 49

COMMUNICATIONS

Telephones - fixed lines: *total subscriptions:* 2.845 million (2022 est.)
subscriptions per 100 inhabitants: 29 (2022 est.)
comparison ranking: total subscriptions 41

Telephones - mobile cellular: *total subscriptions:* 10.372 million (2022 est.)
subscriptions per 100 inhabitants: 104 (2022 est.)
comparison ranking: total subscriptions 93

Telecommunication systems: *general assessment:* Hungary's telecom infrastructure has been upgraded in recent years following considerable investments

made by telcos as they upgrade their mobile networks to 5G and deploy more fiber; these developments have helped operators to promote converged fixed and mobile service; the number of fixed lines continue to fall as subscribers migrate to the mobile platform for voice and data services; a number of measures aimed at promoting competition in the broadband market encourage investment in technology upgrades; Hungary has the highest fixed broadband penetration rate in Eastern Europe; there remains considerable growth in mobile broadband services delivered via upgraded networks; 5G development is supported by the government, universities, other telcos, and vendors (2024)
domestic: fixed-line connections, with 29 fixed per 100 persons and 104 mobile-cellular subscriptions per 100 (2022)
international: country code - 36; Hungary has fiber-optic cable connections with all neighboring countries; the international switch is in Budapest; satellite earth stations - 2 Intelsat (Atlantic Ocean and Indian Ocean regions), 1 Inmarsat, 1 (very small aperture terminal) VSAT system of ground terminals

Broadcast media: mixed system of state-supported public service broadcast media and private broadcasters; the 5 publicly owned TV channels and the 2 main privately owned TV stations are the major national broadcasters; a large number of special interest channels; highly developed market for satellite and cable TV services with about two-thirds of viewers utilizing their services; 4 state-supported public-service radio networks; a large number of local stations including commercial, public service, nonprofit, and community radio stations; digital transition completed at the end of 2013; government-linked businesses have greatly consolidated ownership in broadcast and print media (2019)

Internet country code: .hu

Internet users: *total:* 8.633 million (2021 est.)
percent of population: 89% (2021 est.)
comparison ranking: total 67

Broadband - fixed subscriptions: *total:* 3,382,136 (2021 est.)
subscriptions per 100 inhabitants: 34.83 (2021 est.)
comparison ranking: total 42

TRANSPORTATION

National air transport system: *number of registered air carriers:* 5 (2020)
inventory of registered aircraft operated by air carriers: 145
annual passenger traffic on registered air carriers: 31,226,848 (2018)

Civil aircraft registration country code prefix: HA

Airports: 109 (2024)
comparison ranking: 49

Heliports: 14 (2024)

Pipelines: 5,874 km gas (high-pressure transmission system), 83,732 km gas (low-pressure distribution network), 850 km oil, 1,200 km refined products (2018)

Railways: *total:* 7,687 km (2020) 3,111 km electrified
comparison ranking: total 28

Roadways: *total:* 216,443 km (2022)
comparison ranking: total 23

Waterways: 1,622 km (2011) (most on Danube River)

comparison ranking: 49

Merchant marine: *total:* 1 (2023)
by type: other 1
comparison ranking: total 187

MILITARY AND SECURITY

Military and security forces: Hungarian Defense Forces (HDF or Magyar Honvédség): the HDF is organized as a joint force under a general staff with commands for land, air, cyber, special operations, territorial defense, and support forces (2024)
note: the National Police are under the Ministry of Interior and responsible for maintaining order nationwide; the Ministry of Interior also has the Counterterrorism Center, a special police force responsible for protecting the president and the prime minister and for preventing, uncovering, and detecting terrorist acts

Military expenditures: 2.1% of GDP (2024 est.)
2.1% of GDP (2023)
1.8% of GDP (2022)
1.7% of GDP (2021)
1.8% of GDP (2020)
comparison ranking: 58

Military and security service personnel strengths: approximately 21,000 active-duty troops (16,000 Army; 5,000 Air Force) (2024)
note: in 2017, Hungary announced plans to increase the number of active soldiers to around 37,000 but did not give a timeline

Military equipment inventories and acquisitions: the HDF has a mix of Soviet-era and more modern, Western equipment from such countries as Germany, France, Sweden, and the US; in 2017, Budapest launched a modernization program known as Zrinyi 2026, which was aimed at replacing its Soviet-era weaponry with modern systems, and increasing Hungary's defense expenditure to 2% of GDP by 2024, in line with NATO spending targets (2024)

Military service age and obligation: 18-25 years of age for voluntary military service; no conscription (abolished 2005); 6-month service obligation (2023)
note: as of 2021, women comprised over 20% of Hungary's full-time military personnel

Military deployments: 150 Bosnia-Herzegovina (EUFOR stabilization force); 150 Iraq (NATO); 410 Kosovo (NATO/KFOR); note - Hungary has small numbers of troops on several UN missions (2024)

Military - note: the Hungarian Defense Forces (HDF) are responsible for ensuring the defense of the country's sovereignty, territorial integrity, and citizens, and fulfilling Hungary's commitments to the EU and NATO, as well as contributing to other international peacekeeping efforts under the UN; the HDF is also responsible for some aspects of domestic security, crisis management, disaster response, and assisting law enforcement forces in border security; Hungary's most recent national security strategy addressed migration as an important security concern, alongside other issues, such as great power competition and cyber security; modernizing the HDF by replacing Soviet-era equipment with Western systems and building up Hungary's defense industrial capacity has been a priority over the past decade
Hungary has been a member of NATO since 1999 and considers the collective defense ensured within the Alliance as a cornerstone of the country's security; NATO membership is complemented by Hungary's ties to the EU under its Common Security and Defense Policy; the HDF has participated in multiple NATO-led security missions, including in Afghanistan, Iraq, and Kosovo, as well as EU-led missions in Bosnia and Herzegovina and Mali; it hosts a NATO battlegroup comprised of troops from Croatia, Hungary, Italy, and the US, and NATO's Multinational Division Center, a headquarters capable of commanding a division-sized force (typically 15-20,000 troops) in a crisis; both organizations were established as a result of Russian aggression against Ukraine; Hungary also hosts NATO's Center of Excellence for Military Medicine; Hungary is a member of the Visegrad Group, a regional platform that brings together Czechia, Hungary, Poland, and Slovakia to discuss cultural, defense, and political cooperation (2024)

SPACE

Space agency/agencies: Hungarian Space Office (HSO; established 1992) (2024)

Space program overview: has a history of involvement in space activities going back to the Soviet era; growing a modern space program focused on acquiring satellites and contributing to the European Space Agency (ESA); has a national space strategy; builds and operates satellites; researches and develops space technologies, including communications, navigation, and subsystems for satellites; has an astronaut corps; in addition to being an ESA member and cooperating with individual ESA and EU member states, particularly France, has relations with a variety of other foreign space agencies and industries, including those of Brazil, Israel, Russia, Singapore, Turkey, the UAE, and the US; national space strategy included the goals of fostering innovation and increasing Hungary's competitiveness in the commercial space sector (2024)
note: further details about the key activities, programs, and milestones of the country's space program, as well as government spending estimates on the space sector, appear in the Space Programs reference guide

TERRORISM

Terrorist group(s): Islamic State of Iraq and ash-Sham (ISIS)
note: details about the history, aims, leadership, organization, areas of operation, tactics, targets, weapons, size, and sources of support of the group(s) appear(s) in the Terrorism reference guide

TRANSNATIONAL ISSUES

Refugees and internally displaced persons: *refugees (country of origin):* 66,135 (Ukraine) (as of 15 April 2024)
stateless persons: 130 (2022)

Illicit drugs: transshipment point for Southwest Asian heroin and cannabis and for South American cocaine destined for Western Europe; limited producer of precursor chemicals, particularly for amphetamine and methamphetamine; efforts to counter money laundering, related to organized crime and drug trafficking are improving but remain vulnerable; significant consumer of ecstasy

ICELAND

INTRODUCTION

Background: Settled by Norwegian and Celtic (Scottish and Irish) immigrants during the late 9th and 10th centuries A.D., Iceland boasts the world's oldest functioning legislative assembly, the Althingi, which was established in 930. Independent for over 300 years, Iceland was subsequently ruled by Norway and Denmark. Fallout from the Askja volcano of 1875 devastated the Icelandic economy and caused widespread famine. Over the next quarter-century, 20% of the island's population emigrated, mostly to Canada and the US. Denmark granted limited home rule in 1874 and complete independence in 1944. The second half of the 20th century saw substantial economic growth driven primarily by the fishing industry. The economy diversified greatly after the country joined the European Economic Area in 1994, but the global financial crisis hit Iceland especially hard in the years after 2008. The economy is now on an upward trajectory, primarily thanks to a tourism and construction boom. Literacy, longevity, and social cohesion are first-rate by world standards.

GEOGRAPHY

Location: Northern Europe, island between the Greenland Sea and the North Atlantic Ocean, northwest of the United Kingdom

Geographic coordinates: 65 00 N, 18 00 W

Map references: Arctic Region

Area: *total:* 103,000 sq km
land: 100,250 sq km
water: 2,750 sq km
comparison ranking: total 108

Area - comparative: slightly smaller than Pennsylvania; about the same size as Kentucky

Land boundaries: *total:* 0 km

Coastline: 4,970 km

Maritime claims: *territorial sea:* 12 nm
exclusive economic zone: 200 nm
continental shelf: 200 nm or to the edge of the continental margin

Climate: temperate; moderated by North Atlantic Current; mild, windy winters; damp, cool summers

Terrain: mostly plateau interspersed with mountain peaks, icefields; coast deeply indented by bays and fiords

Elevation: *highest point:* Hvannadalshnukur (at Vatnajokull Glacier) 2,110 m
lowest point: Atlantic Ocean 0 m
mean elevation: 557 m

Natural resources: fish, hydropower, geothermal power, diatomite

Land use: *agricultural land:* 18.7% (2018 est.)
arable land: 1.2% (2018 est.)
permanent crops: 0% (2018 est.)
permanent pasture: 17.5% (2018 est.)
forest: 0.3% (2018 est.)
other: 81% (2018 est.)

Irrigated land: 0.5 sq km (2020)

Population distribution: Iceland is almost entirely urban with half of the population located in and around the capital of Reykjavik; smaller clusters are primarily found along the coast in the north and west

Natural hazards: earthquakes and volcanic activity
volcanism: Iceland, situated on top of a hotspot, experiences severe volcanic activity; Eyjafjallajokull (1,666 m) erupted in 2010, sending ash high into the atmosphere and seriously disrupting European air traffic; scientists continue to monitor nearby Katla (1,512 m), which has a high probability of eruption in the very near future, potentially disrupting air traffic; Grimsvoetn and Hekla are Iceland's most active volcanoes; other historically active volcanoes include Askja, Bardarbunga, Brennisteinsfjoll, Esjufjoll, Hengill, Krafla, Krisuvik, Kverkfjoll, Oraefajokull, Reykjanes, Torfajokull, and Vestmannaeyjar

Geography - note: strategic location between Greenland and Europe; westernmost European country; Reykjavik is the northernmost national capital in the world; more land covered by glaciers than in all of continental Europe

PEOPLE AND SOCIETY

Population: *total:* 364,036
male: 182,268
female: 181,768 (2024 est.)
comparison rankings: female 178; male 178; total 178

Nationality: *noun:* Icelander(s)
adjective: Icelandic

Ethnic groups: Icelandic 78.7%, Polish 5.8%, Danish 1%, Ukrainian 1%, other 13.5% (2024 est.)
note: data represent population by country of birth

Languages: Icelandic, English, Polish, Nordic languages, German

Religions: Evangelical Lutheran Church of Iceland (official) 58.6% Roman Catholic 3.8%, Independent Congregation of Reykjavik 2.6%, Independent Congregation of Hafnarfjordur 1.9%, pagan worship 1.5%, Icelandic Ethical Humanist Association 1.4%, other (includes Zuist and Pentecostal) or unspecified 18.7%, none 7.7% (2024 est.)

Demographic profile: Iceland is one of the most gender-equal countries in the world. Its welfare policies enable both men and women to balance work and family life. Iceland lagged its Nordic neighbors in introducing new childcare policies, and even when they did in the 1990s, parents still faced a childcare gap between the paid parental leave period and the start of pre-school. The female labor participation rate continued to grow from the 1960s to the 2000s, as women's educational attainment increased. Icelanders are marrying later, if they marry at all, and people are having children later. The interval between births has decreased. Non-marital cohabitation and childbearing outside of marriage are common. Approximately 2 out of 3 children are born out of wedlock, which is among the highest in Europe. Iceland's total fertility rate (TFR) has been fairly stable, hovering around replacement level (2.1 children per woman), for decades – a rate higher even than its Nordic neighbors.

Iceland has fluctuated over time between being a country of net emigration and one of net immigration. Most Icelandic emigrants return to their native country after a few years. From 1960 to 1996, Iceland registered a net outflow, followed by a net inflow until the 2008 banking crisis. During and after the crisis, more Icelanders left the country than immigrated to it. Following the crisis, Iceland returned to being a country of net immigration. In 2017, the country's foreign-born population accounted for 11% of the population and 17% had an immigrant background. The countries of origin have become more diverse over time, with Polish immigrants composing the largest share in 2017. Foreigners acquiring Icelandic citizenship must have a basic comprehension of the Icelandic language. The requirement that new citizens modify or change their names to be more Icelandic was dropped in 1996. The most popular emigration destination was Sweden, followed by Denmark and Norway in 2021.

Age structure: *0-14 years:* 19.8% (male 36,692/female 35,239)
15-64 years: 63.2% (male 116,210/female 113,810)
65 years and over: 17.1% (2024 est.) (male 29,366/female 32,719)

Dependency ratios: *total dependency ratio:* 50.5
youth dependency ratio: 28
elderly dependency ratio: 22.5
potential support ratio: 4.5 (2021 est.)

Median age: *total:* 38 years (2024 est.)
male: 37.4 years
female: 38.6 years
comparison ranking: total 79

Population growth rate: 0.85% (2024 est.)
comparison ranking: 107

Birth rate: 12.6 births/1,000 population (2024 est.)
comparison ranking: 138

Death rate: 6.6 deaths/1,000 population (2024 est.)
comparison ranking: 132

Net migration rate: 2.5 migrant(s)/1,000 population (2024 est.)
comparison ranking: 45

Population distribution: Iceland is almost entirely urban with half of the population located in and around the capital of Reykjavik; smaller clusters are primarily found along the coast in the north and west

Urbanization: *urban population:* 94% of total population (2023)
rate of urbanization: 0.74% annual rate of change (2020-25 est.)

Major urban areas - population: 216,000 REYKJAVIK (capital) (2018)

Sex ratio: *at birth:* 1.05 male(s)/female
0-14 years: 1.04 male(s)/female
15-64 years: 1.02 male(s)/female

65 years and over: 0.9 male(s)/female
total population: 1 male(s)/female (2024 est.)

Mother's mean age at first birth: 28.7 years (2020 est.)

Maternal mortality ratio: 3 deaths/100,000 live births (2020 est.)
comparison ranking: 180

Infant mortality rate: *total:* 1.6 deaths/1,000 live births (2024 est.)
male: 1.8 deaths/1,000 live births
female: 1.4 deaths/1,000 live births
comparison ranking: total 225

Life expectancy at birth: *total population:* 84 years (2024 est.)
male: 81.8 years
female: 86.3 years
comparison ranking: total population 8

Total fertility rate: 1.94 children born/woman (2024 est.)
comparison ranking: 113

Gross reproduction rate: 0.95 (2024 est.)

Drinking water source: *improved: urban:* 100% of population
rural: 100% of population
total: 100% of population

Current health expenditure: 9.6% of GDP (2020)

Physician density: 4.14 physicians/1,000 population (2019)

Hospital bed density: 2.8 beds/1,000 population (2019)

Sanitation facility access: *improved: urban:* 100% of population
rural: 100% of population
total: 100% of population

Obesity - adult prevalence rate: 21.9% (2016)
comparison ranking: 83

Alcohol consumption per capita: *total:* 7.72 liters of pure alcohol (2019 est.)
beer: 4.39 liters of pure alcohol (2019 est.)
wine: 2.11 liters of pure alcohol (2019 est.)
spirits: 1.22 liters of pure alcohol (2019 est.)
other alcohols: 0 liters of pure alcohol (2019 est.)
comparison ranking: total 49

Tobacco use: *total:* 12% (2020 est.)
male: 11.9% (2020 est.)
female: 12% (2020 est.)
comparison ranking: total 122

Currently married women (ages 15-49): % (2023 est.)

Education expenditures: 7.7% of GDP (2020 est.)
comparison ranking: 13

School life expectancy (primary to tertiary education): *total:* 19 years
male: 18 years
female: 21 years (2020)

ENVIRONMENT

Environment - current issues: water pollution from fertilizer runoff

Environment - international agreements: *party to:* Air Pollution, Air Pollution-Persistent Organic Pollutants, Antarctic Treaty, Biodiversity, Climate Change, Climate Change-Kyoto Protocol, Climate Change-Paris Agreement, Comprehensive Nuclear Test Ban, Desertification, Endangered Species, Hazardous Wastes, Law of the Sea, Marine Dumping-London Convention, Marine Dumping- London Protocol, Nuclear Test Ban, Ozone Layer Protection, Ship Pollution, Wetlands, Whaling
signed, but not ratified: Air Pollution-Heavy Metals, Environmental Modification, Marine Life Conservation

Climate: temperate; moderated by North Atlantic Current; mild, windy winters; damp, cool summers

Land use: *agricultural land:* 18.7% (2018 est.)
arable land: 1.2% (2018 est.)
permanent crops: 0% (2018 est.)
permanent pasture: 17.5% (2018 est.)
forest: 0.3% (2018 est.)
other: 81% (2018 est.)

Urbanization: *urban population:* 94% of total population (2023)
rate of urbanization: 0.74% annual rate of change (2020-25 est.)

Revenue from forest resources: 0% of GDP (2018 est.)
comparison ranking: 164

Revenue from coal: 0% of GDP (2018 est.)
comparison ranking: 153

Air pollutants: *particulate matter emissions:* 5.79 micrograms per cubic meter (2019 est.)
carbon dioxide emissions: 2.06 megatons (2016 est.)
methane emissions: 0.59 megatons (2020 est.)

Waste and recycling: *municipal solid waste generated annually:* 525,000 tons (2015 est.)
municipal solid waste recycled annually: 293,003 tons (2013 est.)
percent of municipal solid waste recycled: 55.8% (2013 est.)

Total water withdrawal: *municipal:* 80 million cubic meters (2020 est.)
industrial: 200 million cubic meters (2020 est.)
agricultural: 300,000 cubic meters (2017 est.)

Total renewable water resources: 170 billion cubic meters (2020 est.)

Geoparks: *total global geoparks and regional networks:* 2
global geoparks and regional networks: Katla; Reykjanes (2023)

GOVERNMENT

Country name: *conventional long form:* none
conventional short form: Iceland
local long form: none
local short form: Island
etymology: Floki VILGERDARSON, an early Norse explorer of the island (9th century), applied the name "Land of Ice" after spotting a fjord full of drift ice to the north and spending a bitter winter on the island; he eventually settled on the island, however, after he saw how it greened up in the summer and that it was, in fact, habitable

Government type: unitary parliamentary republic

Capital: *name:* Reykjavik
geographic coordinates: 64 09 N, 21 57 W
time difference: UTC 0 (5 hours ahead of Washington, DC, during Standard Time)
etymology: the name means "smoky bay" in Icelandic and refers to the steamy, smoke-like vapors discharged by hot springs in the area

Administrative divisions: 64 municipalities (sveitarfelog, singular - sveitarfelagidh); Akranes, Akureyri, Arneshreppur, Asahreppur, Blaskogabyggdh, Bolungarvik, Borgarbyggdh, Dalabyggdh, Dalvikurbyggdh, Eyjafjardharsveit, Eyja-og Miklaholtshreppur, Fjallabyggdh, Fjardhabyggdh, Fljotsdalshreppur, Floahreppur, Gardhabaer, Grimsnes-og Grafningshreppur, Grindavikurbaer, Grundarfjardharbaer, Grytubakkahreppur, Hafnarfjordhur, Horgarsveit, Hrunamannahreppur, Hunathing Vestra, Hunabyggdh, Hvalfjardharsveit, Hveragerdhi, Isafjardharbaer, Kaldrananeshreppur, Kjosarhreppur, Kopavogur, Langanesbyggdh, Mosfellsbaer, Mulathing, Myrdalshreppur, Nordhurthing, Rangarthing Eystra, Rangarthing Ytra, Reykholahreppur, Reykjanesbaer, Reykjavik, Seltjarnarnes, Skaftarhreppur, Skagabyggdh, Skagafjordhur, Skeidha-og Gnupverjahreppur, Skorradalshreppur, Snaefellsbaer, Strandabyggdh, Stykkisholmur, Sudhavikurhreppur, Sudhurnesjabaer, Svalbardhsstrandarhreppur, Sveitarfelagidh Arborg, Sveitarfelagidh Hornafjordhur, Sveitarfelagidh Olfus, Sveitarfelagidh Skagastrond, Sveitarfelagidh Vogar, Talknafjardharhreppur, Thingeyjarsveit, Tjorneshreppur, Vestmannaeyjar, Vesturbyggdh, Vopnafjardharhreppur

Independence: 1 December 1918 (became a sovereign state under the Danish Crown); 17 June 1944 (from Denmark; birthday of Jon SIGURDSSON, leader of Iceland's 19th Century independence movement)

National holiday: Independence Day, 17 June (1944)

Legal system: civil law system influenced by the Danish model

Constitution: *history:* several previous; latest ratified 16 June 1944, effective 17 June 1944 (at independence)
amendments: proposed by the Althingi; passage requires approval by the Althingi and by the next elected Althingi, and confirmation by the president of the republic; proposed amendments to Article 62 of the constitution – that the Evangelical Lutheran Church shall be the state church of Iceland – also require passage by referendum; amended many times, last in 2013

International law organization participation: has not submitted an ICJ jurisdiction declaration; accepts ICCt jurisdiction

Citizenship: *citizenship by birth:* no
citizenship by descent only: at least one parent must be a citizen of Iceland
dual citizenship recognized: yes
residency requirement for naturalization: 3 to 7 years

Suffrage: 18 years of age; universal

Executive branch: *chief of state:* President Halla TOMASDOTTIR (since 1 August 2024)
head of government: Prime Minister Bjarni BENEDIKTSSON (since 9 April 2024)
cabinet: Cabinet appointed by the president upon the recommendation of the prime minister
elections/appointments: president directly elected by simple majority popular vote for a 4-year term (no term limits); election last held on 1 June 2024 (next to be held in June 2028); following legislative elections, the leader of the majority party or majority coalition becomes prime minister
election results:
2024: percent of vote - Halla TOMASDOTTIR (independent) 34.1%, Katrin JAKOBSDOTTIR (Left-Green Movement) 25.2%, Halla Hrund LOGADOTTIR (independent) 15.7%, Jon GNARR (Social Democratic Alliance) 10.1%, Baldur PORHALLSSON (independent) 8.4%, other 6.5%

2020: Gudni Thorlacius JOHANNESSON reelected president; percent of vote - Gudni Thorlacius JOHANNESSON (independent) 92.2%, Gudmundur Franklin JONSSON (independent) 7.8%
2016: Gudni Thorlacius JOHANNESSON elected president; Gudni Thorlacius JOHANNESSON (independent) 39.1%, Halla TOMASDOTTIR (independent) 27.9%, Andri Snær MAGNASON (Democracy Movement) 14.3%, David ODDSSON (independent) 13.7%, other 5%

Legislative branch: *description:* unicameral Althingi or Parliament (63 seats; members directly elected in multi-seat constituencies by closed-list proportional representation vote using the D'Hondt method; members serve 4-year terms)
elections: last held on 25 September 2021 (next to be held in 2025)
election results: percent of vote by party - IP 24.4%, PP 17.3%, LGM 12.6%, People's Party 8.9%, Pirate Party 8.6%, SDA 9.9%, Reform Party 8.3%, CP 5.5%; seats by party - IP 16, PP 13, LGM 8, People's Party 6, Pirate Party 6, SDA 6, Reform Party 5, CP 3; composition - men 33, women 30; percentage women 47.6%

Judicial branch: *highest court(s):* Supreme Court or Haestirettur (consists of 7 judges)
judge selection and term of office: judges proposed by Ministry of Interior selection committee and appointed by the president; judges appointed for an indefinite period
subordinate courts: Appellate Court or Landsrettur; 8 district courts; Labor Court

Political parties: Centrist Party (Midflokkurinn) or CP
Independence Party (Sjalfstaedisflokkurinn) or IP
Left-Green Movement (Vinstrihreyfingin-graent frambod) or LGM
People's Party (Flokkur Folksins)
Pirate Party (Piratar)
Progressive Party (Framsoknarflokkurinn) or PP
Reform Party (Vidreisn)
Social Democratic Alliance (Samfylkingin) or SDA

International organization participation: Arctic Council, Australia Group, BIS, CBSS, CD, CE, EAPC, EBRD, EFTA, FAO, FATF, IAEA, IBRD, ICAO, ICC (national committees), ICCt, ICRM, IDA, IFAD, IFC, IFRCS, IHO, ILO, IMF, IMO, IMSO, Interpol, IOC, IOM, IPU, ISO, ITSO, ITU, ITUC (NGOs), MIGA, NATO, NC, NEA, NIB, NSG, OAS (observer), OECD, OPCW, OSCE, PCA, Schengen Convention, UN, UNCTAD, UNESCO, UPU, WCO, WHO, WIPO, WMO, WTO

Diplomatic representation in the US: *chief of mission:* Ambassador Svanhildur Hólm VALSDÓTTIR (since 18 September 2024)
chancery: House of Sweden, 2900 K Street NW, #509, Washington, DC 20007
telephone: [1] (202) 265-6653
FAX: [1] (202) 265-6656
email address and website:
washington@mfa.is
https://www.government.is/diplomatic-missions/embassy-of-iceland-in-washington-d.c/

Diplomatic representation from the US: *chief of mission:* Ambassador Carrin F. PATMAN (since 6 October 2022)
embassy: Engjateigur 7, 105 Reykjavik
mailing address: 5640 Reykjavik Place, Washington, D.C. 20521-5640
telephone: [354] 595-2200
FAX: [354] 562-9118
email address and website:
ReykjavikConsular@state.gov
https://is.usembassy.gov/

Flag description: *blue with a red cross outlined in white extending to the edges of the flag; the vertical part of the cross is shifted to the hoist side in the style of the Dannebrog (Danish flag); the colors represent three of the elements that make up the island:* red is for the island's volcanic fires, white recalls the snow and ice fields of the island, and blue is for the surrounding ocean

National symbol(s): gyrfalcon; national colors: blue, white, red

National anthem: *name:* "Lofsongur" (Song of Praise)
lyrics/music: Matthias JOCHUMSSON/Sveinbjorn SVEINBJORNSSON
note: adopted 1944; also known as "O, Gud vors lands" (O, God of Our Land), the anthem was originally written and performed in 1874

National heritage: *total World Heritage Sites:* 3 (1 cultural, 2 natural)
selected World Heritage Site locales: Thingvellir National Park (c); Surtsey (n); Vatnajökull National Park - Dynamic Nature of Fire and Ice (n)

ECONOMY

Economic overview: high-income north Atlantic island economy; non-EU member but market integration via European Economic Area (EEA); dominant tourism, fishing, and aluminum industries vulnerable to demand swings and volcanic activity; inflation remains above target rate; barriers to foreign business access and economic diversification

Real GDP (purchasing power parity): $26.155 billion (2023 est.)
$25.134 billion (2022 est.)
$23.084 billion (2021 est.)
note: data in 2021 dollars
comparison ranking: 154

Real GDP growth rate: 4.06% (2023 est.)
8.88% (2022 est.)
5.15% (2021 est.)
note: annual GDP % growth based on constant local currency
comparison ranking: 76

Real GDP per capita: $66,500 (2023 est.)
$65,800 (2022 est.)
$62,000 (2021 est.)
note: data in 2021 dollars
comparison ranking: 20

GDP (official exchange rate): $31.02 billion (2023 est.)
note: data in current dollars at official exchange rate

Inflation rate (consumer prices): 8.74% (2023 est.)
8.31% (2022 est.)
4.44% (2021 est.)
note: annual % change based on consumer prices
comparison ranking: 162

Credit ratings: Fitch rating: A (2017)

Moody's rating: A2 (2019)

Standard & Poors rating: A (2017)
note: The year refers to the year in which the current credit rating was first obtained.

GDP - composition, by sector of origin: *agriculture:* 3.9% (2023 est.)
industry: 21% (2023 est.)
services: 64.6% (2023 est.)
note: figures may not total 100% due to non-allocated consumption not captured in sector-reported data
comparison rankings: services 60; industry 129; agriculture 128

GDP - composition, by end use: *household consumption:* 50% (2023 est.)
government consumption: 25.7% (2023 est.)
investment in fixed capital: 23.7% (2023 est.)
investment in inventories: 0.7% (2023 est.)
exports of goods and services: 43.4% (2023 est.)
imports of goods and services: -43.4% (2023 est.)
note: figures may not total 100% due to rounding or gaps in data collection

Agricultural products: milk, chicken, barley, lamb/mutton, potatoes, pork, beef, eggs, other meats, cucumbers/gherkins (2022)
note: top ten agricultural products based on tonnage

Industries: tourism, fish processing; aluminum smelting; geothermal power, hydropower; medical/pharmaceutical products

Industrial production growth rate: 3.24% (2023 est.)
note: annual % change in industrial value added based on constant local currency
comparison ranking: 104

Labor force: 239,000 (2023 est.)
note: number of people ages 15 or older who are employed or seeking work
comparison ranking: 175

Unemployment rate: 3.56% (2023 est.)
3.79% (2022 est.)
6.03% (2021 est.)
note: % of labor force seeking employment
comparison ranking: 62

Youth unemployment rate (ages 15-24): *total:* 9.2% (2023 est.)
male: 10.5% (2023 est.)
female: 7.9% (2023 est.)
note: % of labor force ages 15-24 seeking employment
comparison ranking: total 142

Population below poverty line: 8.8% (2017 est.)
note: % of population with income below national poverty line

Gini Index coefficient - distribution of family income: 26.1 (2017 est.)
note: index (0-100) of income distribution; higher values represent greater inequality
comparison ranking: 145

Household income or consumption by percentage share: *lowest 10%:* 4% (2017 est.)
highest 10%: 22.1% (2017 est.)
note: % share of income accruing to lowest and highest 10% of population

Remittances: 0.66% of GDP (2023 est.)
0.67% of GDP (2022 est.)
0.74% of GDP (2021 est.)
note: personal transfers and compensation between resident and non-resident individuals/households/entities

Budget: *revenues:* $9 billion (2022 est.)
expenditures: $9.498 billion (2022 est.)
note: central government revenues (excluding grants) and expenses converted to US dollars at average official exchange rate for year indicated

Public debt: % of GDP (2022 est.)
note: central government debt as a % of GDP
comparison ranking: 31

Taxes and other revenues: % (of GDP) (2022 est.)
note: central government tax revenue as a % of GDP

comparison ranking: 65

Current account balance: $324.663 million (2023 est.)
-$498.416 million (2022 est.)
-$687.447 million (2021 est.)
note: balance of payments - net trade and primary/secondary income in current dollars
comparison ranking: 66

Exports: $13.49 billion (2023 est.)
$13.109 billion (2022 est.)
$9.606 billion (2021 est.)
note: balance of payments - exports of goods and services in current dollars
comparison ranking: 103

Exports - partners: Netherlands 27%, UK 9%, US 8%, Germany 8%, France 6% (2022)
note: top five export partners based on percentage share of exports

Exports - commodities: fish, aluminum, iron alloys, aluminum wire, animal meal (2022)
note: top five export commodities based on value in dollars

Imports: $13.484 billion (2023 est.)
$13.146 billion (2022 est.)
$10.065 billion (2021 est.)
note: balance of payments - imports of goods and services in current dollars
comparison ranking: 109

Imports - partners: Norway 12%, Netherlands 10%, Denmark 8%, Germany 8%, China 7% (2022)
note: top five import partners based on percentage share of imports

Imports - commodities: refined petroleum, aluminum oxide, cars, carbon-based electronics, aircraft (2022)
note: top five import commodities based on value in dollars

Reserves of foreign exchange and gold: $5.809 billion (2023 est.)
$5.887 billion (2022 est.)
$7.079 billion (2021 est.)
note: holdings of gold (year-end prices)/foreign exchange/special drawing rights in current dollars
comparison ranking: 91

Exchange rates: Icelandic kronur (ISK) per US dollar -

Exchange rates: 137.943 (2023 est.)
135.28 (2022 est.)
126.989 (2021 est.)
135.422 (2020 est.)
122.607 (2019 est.)

ENERGY

Electricity access: *electrification - total population:* 100% (2022 est.)

Electricity: *installed generating capacity:* 3.006 million kW (2022 est.)
consumption: 19.296 billion kWh (2022 est.)
transmission/distribution losses: 568.767 million kWh (2022 est.)
comparison rankings: transmission/distribution losses 82; consumption 73; installed generating capacity 108

Electricity generation sources: *hydroelectricity:* 70.2% of total installed capacity (2022 est.)
geothermal: 29.8% of total installed capacity (2022 est.)

Coal: *consumption:* 188,000 metric tons (2022 est.)
exports: (2022 est.) less than 1 metric ton
imports: 113,000 metric tons (2022 est.)

Petroleum: *refined petroleum consumption:* 18,000 bbl/day (2023 est.)

Carbon dioxide emissions: 3.579 million metric tonnes of CO2 (2022 est.)
from coal and metallurgical coke: 514,000 metric tonnes of CO2 (2022 est.)
from petroleum and other liquids: 3.065 million metric tonnes of CO2 (2022 est.)
comparison ranking: total emissions 147

COMMUNICATIONS

Telephones - fixed lines: *total subscriptions:* 93,000 (2022 est.)
subscriptions per 100 inhabitants: 25 (2022 est.)
comparison ranking: total subscriptions 137

Telephones - mobile cellular: *total subscriptions:* 457,000 (2022 est.)
subscriptions per 100 inhabitants: 123 (2022 est.)
comparison ranking: total subscriptions 176

Telecommunication systems: *general assessment:* Iceland has one of the smallest yet most progressive telecom markets in Europe; the country in 2020 became the top in Europe for fiber penetration; it aims to provide a fixed broadband service of at least 100Mb/s to 99.9% of the population by the end of 2021, an ambitious target by international standards and one which it is likely to achieve given the progress which operators have made in extending the reach of fiber networks; there is effective competition in the mobile and broadband markets, with a number of players having emerged to challenge the dominance of the two leading operators which have interests across the telecom sectors; the telecom market has shown some resilience in recent years following the significant economic downturn a decade ago, supported by continuing investment in mobile and fixed-line broadband infrastructure by operators and well as by the government's Telecommunications Fund which is supporting Next Generation Access networks, particularly in rural areas (2022)
domestic: 27 per 100 for fixed line and nearing 118 per 100 for mobile-cellular subscriptions (2021)
international: country code - 354; landing points for the CANTAT-3, FARICE-1, Greenland Connect and DANICE submarine cable system that provides connectivity to Canada, the Faroe Islands, Greenland, UK, Denmark, and Germany; satellite earth stations - 2 Intelsat (Atlantic Ocean), 1 Inmarsat (Atlantic and Indian Ocean regions); note - Iceland shares the Inmarsat earth station with the other Nordic countries (Denmark, Finland, Norway, and Sweden) (2019)

Broadcast media: state-owned public TV broadcaster (RUV) operates 21 TV channels nationally (RUV and RUV 2, though RUV 2 is used less frequently); RUV broadcasts nationally, every household in Iceland is required to have RUV as it doubles as the emergency broadcast network; RUV also operates stringer offices in the north (Akureyri) and the east (Egilsstadir) but operations are all run out of RUV headquarters in Reykjavik; there are 3 privately owned TV stations; Stod 2 (Channel 2) is owned by Syn, following 365 Media and Vodafone merger, and is headquartered in Reykjavik; Syn also operates 4 sports channels under Stod 2; N4 is the only television station headquartered outside of Reykjavik, in Akureyri, with local programming for the north, south, and east of Iceland; Hringbraut is the newest station and is headquartered in Reykjavik; all of these television stations have nationwide penetration as 100% of households have multi-channel services though digital and/or fiber-optic connections RUV operates 3 radio stations (RAS 1, RAS2, and Rondo) as well as 4 regional stations (but they mostly act as range extenders for RUV radio broadcasts nationwide); there is 1 privately owned radio conglomerate, Syn (4 stations), that broadcasts nationwide, and 3 other radio stations that broadcast to the most densely populated regions of the country. In addition, there are upwards of 20 radio stations that operate regionally (2019)

Internet country code: .is

Internet users: *total:* 370,000 (2021 est.)
percent of population: 100% (2021 est.)
comparison ranking: total 174

Broadband - fixed subscriptions: *total:* 141,816 (2020 est.)
subscriptions per 100 inhabitants: 42 (2020 est.)
comparison ranking: total 124

TRANSPORTATION

National air transport system: *number of registered air carriers:* 6 (2020)
inventory of registered aircraft operated by air carriers: 63
annual passenger traffic on registered air carriers: 7,819,740 (2018)
annual freight traffic on registered air carriers: 163.65 million (2018) mt-km

Civil aircraft registration country code prefix: TF

Airports: 83 (2024)
comparison ranking: 63

Heliports: 1 (2024)

Roadways: *total:* 12,905 km (2021)
comparison ranking: total 129

Merchant marine: *total:* 39 (2023)
by type: general cargo 5, oil tanker 2, other 32
comparison ranking: total 127

Ports: *total ports:* 43 (2024)
large: 0
medium: 2
small: 2
very small: 17
size unknown: 22
ports with oil terminals: 5
key ports: Grundartangi, Reykjavik, Seydhisfjordhur, Vestmannaeyjar

MILITARY AND SECURITY

Military and security forces: no regular military forces; the Icelandic National Police, the nine regional police forces, and the Icelandic Coast Guard fall under the purview of the Ministry of Justice (2024)
note: the Icelandic Coast Guard is responsible for operational defense tasks in Iceland including but not limited to operation of Keflavik Air Base, special security zones, and Iceland's air defense systems

Military equipment inventories and acquisitions: the Icelandic Coast Guard's inventory consists of equipment from mostly European suppliers (2024)

Military - note: Iceland was one of the original 12 countries to sign the North Atlantic Treaty (also known as the Washington Treaty) in 1949; Iceland is the only NATO member that has no standing military force; defense of Iceland remains a NATO commitment and NATO maintains an air policing presence in Icelandic airspace; Iceland participates in international peacekeeping missions with the civilian-manned Icelandic Crisis Response Unit (ICRU)

Iceland cooperates with the militaries of other Nordic countries through the Nordic Defense Cooperation (NORDEFCO), which consists of Denmark, Finland, Iceland, Norway, and Sweden; areas of cooperation include armaments, education, human resources, training and exercises, and operations; NORDEFCO was established in 2009

in 1951, Iceland and the US concluded an agreement to make arrangements regarding the defense of Iceland and for the use of facilities in Iceland to that end; the agreement, along with NATO membership, is one of the two pillars of Iceland's security policy; since 2007 Iceland has concluded cooperation agreements with Canada, Denmark, Norway, and the UK; it also has regular consultations with Germany and France on security and defense (2024)

TRANSNATIONAL ISSUES

Refugees and internally displaced persons: *stateless persons:* 68 (2022)

INDIA

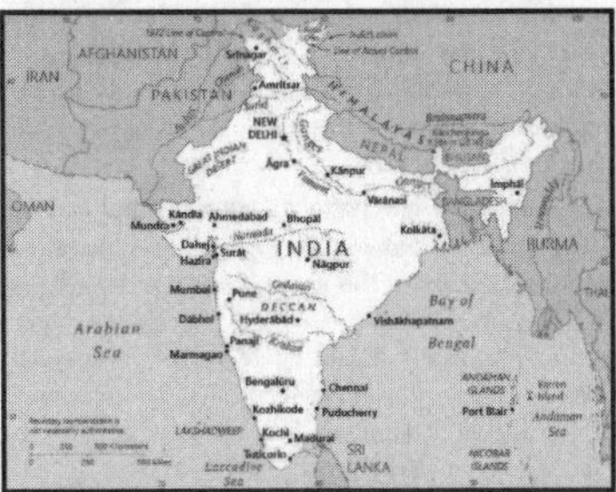

INTRODUCTION

Background: The Indus Valley civilization, one of the world's oldest, flourished during the 3rd and 2nd millennia B.C. and extended into northwestern India. Aryan tribes from the northwest infiltrated the Indian subcontinent about 1500 B.C.; their merger with the earlier Dravidian inhabitants created the classical Indian culture. The Maurya Empire of the 4th and 3rd centuries B.C. – which reached its zenith under ASHOKA – united much of South Asia. The Gupta dynasty (4th to 6th centuries A.D.) ushered in The Golden Age, which saw a flowering of Indian science, art, and culture. Islam spread across the subcontinent over a period of 700 years. In the 10th and 11th centuries, Turks and Afghans invaded India and established the Delhi Sultanate. In the early 16th century, the Emperor BABUR established the Mughal Dynasty, which ruled large sections of India for more than three centuries. European explorers began establishing footholds in India during the 16th century.

By the 19th century, Great Britain had become the dominant political power on the subcontinent, and India was seen as the "Jewel in the Crown" of the British Empire. The British Indian Army played a vital role in both World Wars. Years of nonviolent resistance to British rule, led by Mohandas GANDHI and Jawaharlal NEHRU, eventually resulted in Indian independence in 1947. Large-scale communal violence took place before and after the subcontinent partition into two separate states – India and Pakistan. The neighboring countries have fought three wars since independence, the last of which was in 1971 and resulted in East Pakistan becoming the separate nation of Bangladesh. India's nuclear weapons tests in 1998 emboldened Pakistan to conduct its own tests that same year. In 2008, terrorists originating from Pakistan conducted a series of coordinated attacks in Mumbai, India's financial capital. India's economic growth after economic reforms in 1991, a massive youth population, and a strategic geographic location have contributed to the country's emergence as a regional and global power. However, India still faces pressing problems such as extensive poverty, widespread corruption, and environmental degradation, and its restrictive business climate challenges economic growth expectations.

GEOGRAPHY

Location: Southern Asia, bordering the Arabian Sea and the Bay of Bengal, between Burma and Pakistan

Geographic coordinates: 20 00 N, 77 00 E

Map references: Asia

Area: *total:* 3,287,263 sq km
land: 2,973,193 sq km
water: 314,070 sq km
comparison ranking: total 8

Area - comparative: slightly more than one-third the size of the US

Land boundaries: *total:* 13,888 km
border countries (6): Bangladesh 4,142 km; Bhutan 659 km; Burma 1,468 km; China 2,659 km; Nepal 1,770 km;
Pakistan 3,190 km

Coastline: 7,000 km

Maritime claims: *territorial sea:* 12 nm
contiguous zone: 24 nm
exclusive economic zone: 200 nm
continental shelf: 200 nm or to the edge of the continental margin

Climate: varies from tropical monsoon in south to temperate in north

Terrain: upland plain (Deccan Plateau) in south, flat to rolling plain along the Ganges, deserts in west, Himalayas in north

Elevation: *highest point:* Kanchenjunga 8,586 m
lowest point: Indian Ocean 0 m
mean elevation: 160 m

Natural resources: coal (fourth-largest reserves in the world), antimony, iron ore, lead, manganese, mica, bauxite, rare earth elements, titanium ore, chromite, natural gas, diamonds, petroleum, limestone, arable land

Land use: *agricultural land:* 60.5% (2018 est.)
arable land: 52.8% (2018 est.)
permanent crops: 4.2% (2018 est.)
permanent pasture: 3.5% (2018 est.)
forest: 23.1% (2018 est.)
other: 16.4% (2018 est.)

Irrigated land: 715,539 sq km (2020)

Major lakes (area sq km): *salt water lake(s):* Chilika Lake - 1,170 sq km

Major rivers (by length in km): Brahmaputra (shared with China [s] and Bangladesh [m]) - 3,969 km; Indus (shared with China [s] and Pakistan [m]) - 3,610 km; Ganges river source (shared with Bangladesh [m]) - 2,704 km; Godavari - 1,465 km; Sutlej (shared with China [s] and Pakistan [m]) - 1,372 km; Yamuna - 1,370 km; Narmada - 1,289 km; Chenab river source (shared with Pakistan [m]) - 1,086 km; Ghaghara river mouth (shared with China [s] and Nepal) - 1,080 km

note – [s] after country name indicates river source; [m] after country name indicates river mouth

Major watersheds (area sq km): Indian Ocean drainage: Brahmaputra (651,335 sq km), Ganges (1,016,124 sq km), Indus (1,081,718 sq km), Irrawaddy (413,710 sq km)

Major aquifers: Indus-Ganges-Brahmaputra Basin

Population distribution: with the notable exception of the deserts in the northwest, including the Thar Desert, and the mountain fringe in the north, a very high population density exists throughout most of the country; the core of the population is in the north along the banks of the Ganges, with other river valleys and southern coastal areas also having large population concentrations

Natural hazards: *droughts; flash floods, as well as widespread and destructive flooding from monsoonal rains; severe thunderstorms; earthquakes volcanism:* Barren Island (354 m) in the Andaman Sea has been active in recent years

Geography - note: dominates South Asian subcontinent; near important Indian Ocean trade routes; Kanchenjunga, third tallest mountain in the world, lies on the border with Nepal

PEOPLE AND SOCIETY

Population: *total:* 1,409,128,296
male: 725,784,825
female: 683,343,471 (2024 est.)
comparison rankings: female 2; male 1; total 2

Nationality: *noun:* Indian(s)

adjective: Indian

Ethnic groups: Indo-Aryan 72%, Dravidian 25%, and other 3% (2000)

Languages: Hindi 43.6%, Bengali 8%, Marathi 6.9%, Telugu 6.7%, Tamil 5.7%, Gujarati 4.6%, Urdu 4.2%, Kannada 3.6%, Odia 3.1%, Malayalam 2.9%, Punjabi 2.7%, Assamese 1.3%, Maithili 1.1%, other 5.6%; English is the subsidiary official language but is the most important one for national, political, and commercial communication (2011 est.)
major-language sample(s):

विश्व फेसबुक, आधारभूत जानकारी का एक अपरिहार्य स्रोत

(Hindi)

note 1: there are 22 other recognized languages – Assamese, Bengali, Bodo, Dogri, Gujarati, Hindi, Kannada, Kashmiri, Konkani, Maithili, Malayalam, Manipuri, Marathi, Nepali, Odia, Punjabi, Sanskrit, Santali, Sindhi, Tamil, Telugu, Urdu
note 2: Hindustani is a popular variant of Hindi/Urdu spoken widely throughout northern India but is not an official language

Religions: Hindu 79.8%, Muslim 14.2%, Christian 2.3%, Sikh 1.7%, other and unspecified 2% (2011 est.)

Age structure: *0-14 years:* 24.5% (male 181,115,052/female 163,647,028)
15-64 years: 68.7% (male 500,568,593/female 467,593,781)
65 years and over: 6.8% (2024 est.) (male 44,101,180/female 52,102,662)

Dependency ratios: *total dependency ratio:* 48.1
youth dependency ratio: 38.1
elderly dependency ratio: 10.1
potential support ratio: 9.9 (2021 est.)

Median age: *total:* 29.8 years (2024 est.)
male: 29.1 years
female: 30.5 years
comparison ranking: total 142

Population growth rate: 0.72% (2024 est.)
comparison ranking: 121

Birth rate: 16.2 births/1,000 population (2024 est.)
comparison ranking: 98

Death rate: 9.1 deaths/1,000 population (2024 est.)
comparison ranking: 56

Net migration rate: 0.1 migrant(s)/1,000 population (2024 est.)
comparison ranking: 77

Population distribution: with the notable exception of the deserts in the northwest, including the Thar Desert, and the mountain fringe in the north, a very high population density exists throughout most of the country; the core of the population is in the north along the banks of the Ganges, with other river valleys and southern coastal areas also having large population concentrations

Urbanization: *urban population:* 36.4% of total population (2023)
rate of urbanization: 2.33% annual rate of change (2020-25 est.)

Major urban areas - population: 32.941 million NEW DELHI (capital), 21.297 million Mumbai, 15.333 million Kolkata, 13.608 million Bangalore, 11.776 million Chennai, 10.801 million Hyderabad (2023)

Sex ratio: *at birth:* 1.1 male(s)/female
0-14 years: 1.11 male(s)/female
15-64 years: 1.07 male(s)/female
65 years and over: 0.85 male(s)/female
total population: 1.06 male(s)/female (2024 est.)

Mother's mean age at first birth: 21.2 years (2019/21)
note: data represents median age at first birth among women 25-49

Maternal mortality ratio: 103 deaths/100,000 live births (2020 est.)
comparison ranking: 68

Infant mortality rate: *total:* 30.4 deaths/1,000 live births (2024 est.)
male: 30 deaths/1,000 live births
female: 30.8 deaths/1,000 live births
comparison ranking: total 49

Life expectancy at birth: *total population:* 68.2 years (2024 est.)
male: 66.5 years
female: 70.1 years
comparison ranking: total population 190

Total fertility rate: 2.03 children born/woman (2024 est.)
comparison ranking: 101

Gross reproduction rate: 0.97 (2024 est.)

Contraceptive prevalence rate: 66.7% (2019/20)

Drinking water source: *improved: urban:* 96.9% of population
rural: 94.7% of population
total: 95.5% of population
unimproved: urban: 3.1% of population
rural: 5.3% of population
total: 4.5% of population (2020 est.)

Current health expenditure: 3% of GDP (2020)

Physician density: 0.74 physicians/1,000 population (2020)

Hospital bed density: 0.5 beds/1,000 population (2017)

Sanitation facility access: *improved: urban:* 98.6% of population
rural: 75.2% of population
total: 83.4% of population
unimproved: urban: 1.4% of population
rural: 24.8% of population
total: 16.6% of population (2020 est.)

Obesity - adult prevalence rate: 3.9% (2016)
comparison ranking: 189

Alcohol consumption per capita: *total:* 3.09 liters of pure alcohol (2019 est.)
beer: 0.23 liters of pure alcohol (2019 est.)
wine: 0 liters of pure alcohol (2019 est.)
spirits: 2.85 liters of pure alcohol (2019 est.)
other alcohols: 0 liters of pure alcohol (2019 est.)
comparison ranking: total 111

Tobacco use: *total:* 27.2% (2020 est.)
male: 41.3% (2020 est.)
female: 13% (2020 est.)
comparison ranking: total 40

Children under the age of 5 years underweight: 31.5% (2019/21)
comparison ranking: 5

Currently married women (ages 15-49): 72.6% (2023 est.)

Child marriage: *women married by age 15:* 4.8%
women married by age 18: 23.3%
men married by age 18: 2.6% (2021 est.)

Education expenditures: 4.5% of GDP (2020 est.)
comparison ranking: 100

Literacy: *definition:* age 15 and over can read and write
total population: 74.4%
male: 82.4%
female: 65.8% (2018)

School life expectancy (primary to tertiary education): *total:* 12 years
male: 12 years
female: 12 years (2020)

ENVIRONMENT

Environment - current issues: deforestation; soil erosion; overgrazing; desertification; air pollution from industrial effluents and vehicle emissions; water pollution from raw sewage and runoff of agricultural pesticides; tap water is not potable throughout the country; huge and growing population is overstraining natural resources; preservation and quality of forests; biodiversity loss

Environment - international agreements: *party to:* Antarctic-Environmental Protection, Antarctic-Marine Living Resources, Antarctic Treaty, Biodiversity, Climate Change, Climate Change-Kyoto Protocol, Climate Change-Paris Agreement, Desertification, Endangered Species, Environmental Modification, Hazardous Wastes, Law of the Sea, Nuclear Test Ban, Ozone Layer Protection, Ship Pollution, Tropical Timber 2006, Wetlands, Whaling
signed, but not ratified: none of the selected agreements

Climate: varies from tropical monsoon in south to temperate in north

Urbanization: *urban population:* 36.4% of total population (2023)
rate of urbanization: 2.33% annual rate of change (2020-25 est.)

Revenue from forest resources: 0.14% of GDP (2018 est.)
comparison ranking: 103

Revenue from coal: 1.15% of GDP (2018 est.)
comparison ranking: 4

Air pollutants: *particulate matter emissions:* 50.17 micrograms per cubic meter (2019 est.)
carbon dioxide emissions: 2,407.67 megatons (2016 est.)
methane emissions: 559.11 megatons (2020 est.)

Waste and recycling: *municipal solid waste generated annually:* 168,403,240 tons (2001 est.)
municipal solid waste recycled annually: 8,420,162 tons (2013 est.)
percent of municipal solid waste recycled: 5% (2013 est.)

Major lakes (area sq km): *salt water lake(s):* Chilika Lake - 1,170 sq km

Major rivers (by length in km): Brahmaputra (shared with China [s] and Bangladesh [m]) - 3,969 km; Indus (shared with China [s] and Pakistan [m]) - 3,610 km; Ganges river source (shared with Bangladesh [m]) - 2,704 km; Godavari - 1,465 km; Sutlej (shared with China [s] and Pakistan [m]) - 1,372 km; Yamuna - 1,370 km; Narmada - 1,289 km; Chenab river source (shared with Pakistan [m]) - 1,086 km; Ghaghara river mouth (shared with China [s] and Nepal) - 1,080 km

note – [s] after country name indicates river source; [m] after country name indicates river mouth

Major watersheds (area sq km): Indian Ocean drainage: Brahmaputra (651,335 sq km), Ganges (1,016,124 sq km), Indus (1,081,718 sq km), Irrawaddy (413,710 sq km)

Major aquifers: Indus-Ganges-Brahmaputra Basin

Total water withdrawal: *municipal:* 56 billion cubic meters (2020 est.)
industrial: 17 billion cubic meters (2020 est.)
agricultural: 688 billion cubic meters (2020 est.)

Total renewable water resources: 1.91 trillion cubic meters (2019 est.)

GOVERNMENT

Country name: *conventional long form:* Republic of India
conventional short form: India
local long form: Republic of India (English)/ Bharatiya Ganarajya (Hindi)
local short form: India (English)/ Bharat (Hindi)
etymology: the English name derives from the Indus River; the Indian name "Bharat" may derive from the "Bharatas" tribe mentioned in the Vedas of the second millennium B.C.; the name is also associated with Emperor Bharata, the legendary conqueror of all of India

Government type: federal parliamentary republic

Capital: *name:* New Delhi
geographic coordinates: 28 36 N, 77 12 E
time difference: UTC+5.5 (10.5 hours ahead of Washington, DC, during Standard Time)
etymology: the city's name is associated with various myths and legends; the original name for the city may have been Dhilli or Dhillika; alternatively, the name could be a corruption of the Hindustani words "dehleez" or "dehali" - both terms meaning "threshold" or "gateway" - and indicative of the city as a gateway to the Gangetic Plain; after the British decided to move the capital of their Indian Empire from Calcutta to Delhi in 1911, they created a new governmental district south of the latter designated as New Delhi; the new capital was not formally inaugurated until 1931

Administrative divisions: 28 states and 8 union territories*; Andaman and Nicobar Islands*, Andhra Pradesh, Arunachal Pradesh, Assam, Bihar, Chandigarh*, Chhattisgarh, Dadra and Nagar Haveli and Daman and Diu*, Delhi*, Goa, Gujarat, Haryana, Himachal Pradesh, Jammu and Kashmir*, Jharkhand, Karnataka, Kerala, Ladakh*, Lakshadweep*, Madhya Pradesh, Maharashtra, Manipur, Meghalaya, Mizoram, Nagaland, Odisha, Puducherry*, Punjab, Rajasthan, Sikkim, Tamil Nadu, Telangana, Tripura, Uttar Pradesh, Uttarakhand, West Bengal
note: although its status is that of a union territory, the official name of Delhi is National Capital Territory of Delhi

Independence: 15 August 1947 (from the UK)

National holiday: Republic Day, 26 January (1950)

Legal system: common law system based on the English model; separate personal law codes apply to Muslims, Christians, and Hindus; judicial review of legislative acts

Constitution: *history:* previous 1935 (preindependence); latest draft completed 4 November 1949, adopted 26 November 1949, effective 26 January 1950
amendments: proposed by either the Council of States or the House of the People; passage requires majority participation of the total membership in each house and at least two-thirds majority of voting members of each house, followed by assent of the president of India; proposed amendments to the constitutional amendment procedures also must be ratified by at least one half of the India state legislatures before presidential assent; amended many times, last in 2023

International law organization participation: accepts compulsory ICJ jurisdiction with reservations; non-party state to the ICCt

Citizenship: *citizenship by birth:* no
citizenship by descent only: at least one parent must be a citizen of India
dual citizenship recognized: no
residency requirement for naturalization: 5 years

Suffrage: 18 years of age; universal

Executive branch: *chief of state:* President Droupadi MURMU (since 25 July 2022)
head of government: Prime Minister Narendra MODI (since 26 May 2014)
cabinet: Union Council of Ministers recommended by the prime minister, appointed by the president
elections/appointments: president indirectly elected by an electoral college consisting of elected members of both houses of Parliament for a 5-year term (no term limits); election last held on 18 July 2022 (next to be held in July 2027); vice president indirectly elected by an electoral college consisting of elected members of both houses of Parliament for a 5-year term (no term limits); election last held on 5 August 2022 (next to be held in August 2027); following legislative elections, the prime minister is elected by Lok Sabha members of the majority party
election results:
2022: Droupadi MURMU elected president; percent of electoral college vote - Droupadi MURMU (BJP) 64%, Yashwant SINHA (AITC) 35.9%; Jagdeep DHANKHAR elected vice president; percent of electoral college vote - Jagdeep DHANKHAR (BJP) 74.4%, Margaret ALVA (INC) 25.6%
2017: Ram Nath KOVIND elected president; percent of electoral college vote - Ram Nath KOVIND (BJP) 65.6%, Meira KUMAR (INC) 34.4%; Venkaiah NAIDU elected vice president; percent of electoral college vote - Venkaiah NAIDU (BJP) 67.9%, Gopal-krishna GANDHI 32.1%

Legislative branch: *description:* bicameral Parliament or Sansad consists of:
Council of States or Rajya Sabha (245 seats; 233 members indirectly elected by state and territorial assemblies by proportional representation vote and 12 members appointed by the president; members serve 6-year terms with one-third of the membership renewed every 2 years at various dates)
House of the People or Lok Sabha (545 seats; 543 members directly elected in single-seat constituencies by simple majority vote and 2 appointed by the president; members serve 5-year terms)
elections: Council of States - held by state and territorial assemblies being held from 12 January to 30 June 2024 for expiry of 68 seats
House of the People - last held in 7 phases from 19 April to 1 June 2024 (next to be held in 2027)
election results: Council of States (2022) - percent of vote by party - NA; seats by party - BJP 97, INC 34, AITC 13, DMK 10, other 2, independent 2; composition as of March 2024 - men 206, women 32, percentage women 13.8%
House of the People - percent of vote by party - NA; seats by party - BJP 240, INC 99, SP 37, AITC 29, DMK 22, BJD 12, RJD 4, AAP 3, other 93
seats by party - BJP 303, INC 52, DMK 24, AITC 22, YSRCP 22, SS 18, JDU 16, BJD 12, BSP 10, TRS 9, LJP 6, NCP 5, SP 5, other 35, independent 4, vacant 2; composition as of March 2024 - men 446, women 77, percentage women 14.7%; total Parliament percentage women 14.3%
note: in late September 2023, both Rajya Sabha and Lok Sabha passed a bill that reserves one third of the House seats for women; implementation could begin for the House election in 2029

Judicial branch: *highest court(s):* Supreme Court (consists of 28 judges, including the chief justice)
judge selection and term of office: justices appointed by the president to serve until age 65
subordinate courts: High Courts; District Courts; Labour Court

Political parties: Aam Aadmi Party or AAP
All India Trinamool Congress or AITC
Bahujan Samaj Party or BSP
Bharatiya Janata Party or BJP
Biju Janata Dal or BJD
Communist Party of India-Marxist or CPI(M)
Dravida Munnetra Khazhagam
Indian National Congress or INC
Nationalist Congress Party or NCP
Rashtriya Janata Dal or RJD
Samajwadi Party or SP
Shiromani Akali Dal or SAD
Shiv Sena or SS
Telegana Rashtra Samithi or TRS
Telugu Desam Party or TDP
YSR Congress or YSRCP or YCP

International organization participation: ADB, AfDB (nonregional member), Arctic Council (observer), ARF, ASEAN (dialogue partner), BIMSTEC, BIS, BRICS, C, CD, CERN (observer), CICA, CP, EAS, FAO, FATF, G-15, G-20, G-24, G-5, G-77, IAEA, IBRD, ICAO, ICC (national committees), ICRM, IDA, IFAD, IFC, IFRCS, IHO, ILO, IMF, IMO, IMSO, Interpol, IOC, IOM, IPU, ISO, ITSO, ITU, ITUC (NGOs), LAS (observer), MIGA, MINURSO, MONUSCO, NAM, OAS (observer), OECD, OPCW, Pacific Alliance (observer), PCA, PIF (partner), Quad, SAARC, SACEP, SCO (observer), UN, UNCTAD, UNDOF, UNESCO, UNHCR, UNHRC, UNIDO, UNIFIL, UNISFA, UNITAR, UNMISS, UNOCI, UNSOM, UNWTO, UPU, Wassenaar Arrangement, WCO, WFTU (NGOs), WHO, WIPO, WMO, WTO

Diplomatic representation in the US: *chief of mission:* Ambassador Vinay Mohan KWATRA (since 18 September 2024)
chancery: 2107 Massachusetts Avenue NW, Washington, DC 20008
telephone: [1] (202) 939-7000
FAX: [1] (202) 265-4351
email address and website:
hoc.washington@mea.gov.in
https://www.indianembassyusa.gov.in/
consulate(s) general: Atlanta, Chicago, Houston, New York, San Francisco, Seattle

Diplomatic representation from the US: *chief of mission:* Ambassador Eric M. GARCETTI (since 11 May 2023)
embassy: Shantipath, Chanakyapuri, New Delhi - 110021
mailing address: 9000 New Delhi Place, Washington DC 20521-9000
telephone: [91] (11) 2419-8000
FAX: [91] (11) 2419-0017
email address and website:
acsnd@state.gov
https://in.usembassy.gov/
consulate(s) general: Chennai (Madras), Hyderabad, Kolkata (Calcutta), Mumbai (Bombay)

Flag description: three equal horizontal bands of saffron (subdued orange) (top), white, and green, with a blue chakra (24-spoked wheel) centered in the white band; saffron represents courage, sacrifice, and the spirit of renunciation; white signifies purity and truth; green stands for faith and fertility; the blue chakra symbolizes the wheel of life in movement and death in stagnation
note: similar to the flag of Niger, which has a small orange disk centered in the white band

National symbol(s): the Lion Capital of Ashoka, which depicts four Asiatic lions standing back to back mounted on a circular abacus, is the official emblem; Bengal tiger; lotus flower; national colors: saffron, white, green

National anthem: *name:* "Jana-Gana-Mana" (Thou Art the Ruler of the Minds of All People)
lyrics/music: Rabindranath TAGORE
note: adopted 1950; Rabindranath TAGORE, a Nobel laureate, also wrote Bangladesh's national anthem

National heritage: *total World Heritage Sites:* 42 (34 cultural, 7 natural, 1 mixed)
selected World Heritage Site locales: Taj Mahal (c); Red Fort Complex (c); Ellora Caves (c); Hill Forts of Rajasthan (c); Sundarbans National Park (n); Rock Shelters of Bhimbetka (c); Champaner-Pavagadh Archaeological Park (c); Dholavira: A Harappan City (c); Jaipur (c); Mahabodhi Temple Complex at Bodh Gaya (c); Manas Wildlife Sanctuary (n); Nanda Devi and Valley of Flowers National Parks (n); Khangchendzonga National Park (m)

ECONOMY

Economic overview: largest South Asian economy; still informal domestic economies; COVID-19 reversed both economic growth and poverty reduction; credit access weaknesses contributing to lower private consumption and inflation; new social and infrastructure equity efforts

Real GDP (purchasing power parity): $13.104 trillion (2023 est.)
$12.18 trillion (2022 est.)
$11.384 trillion (2021 est.)
note: data in 2021 dollars
comparison ranking: 3

Real GDP growth rate: 7.58% (2023 est.)
6.99% (2022 est.)
9.69% (2021 est.)
note: annual GDP % growth based on constant local currency
comparison ranking: 17

Real GDP per capita: $9,200 (2023 est.)
$8,600 (2022 est.)
$8,100 (2021 est.)
note: data in 2021 dollars
comparison ranking: 150

GDP (official exchange rate): $3.55 trillion (2023 est.)
note: data in current dollars at official exchange rate

Inflation rate (consumer prices): 5.65% (2023 est.)
6.7% (2022 est.)
5.13% (2021 est.)
note: annual % change based on consumer prices
comparison ranking: 120

Credit ratings: Fitch rating: BBB- (2006)

Moody's rating: Baa3 (2020)

Standard & Poors rating: BBB- (2007)
note: The year refers to the year in which the current credit rating was first obtained.

GDP - composition, by sector of origin: *agriculture:* 16% (2023 est.)
industry: 25% (2023 est.)
services: 49.8% (2023 est.)
note: figures may not total 100% due to non-allocated consumption not captured in sector-reported data
comparison rankings: services 148; industry 96; agriculture 53

GDP - composition, by end use: *household consumption:* 60.3% (2023 est.)
government consumption: 10.5% (2023 est.)
investment in fixed capital: 31.3% (2023 est.)
investment in inventories: 2.4% (2023 est.)
exports of goods and services: 21.9% (2023 est.)
imports of goods and services: -24% (2023 est.)
note: figures may not total 100% due to rounding or gaps in data collection

Agricultural products: sugarcane, rice, milk, wheat, bison milk, potatoes, vegetables, bananas, maize, onions (2022)
note: top ten agricultural products based on tonnage

Industries: textiles, chemicals, food processing, steel, transportation equipment, cement, mining, petroleum, machinery, software, pharmaceuticals

Industrial production growth rate: 9.02% (2023 est.)
note: annual % change in industrial value added based on constant local currency
comparison ranking: 22

Labor force: 593.729 million (2023 est.)
note: number of people ages 15 or older who are employed or seeking work
comparison ranking: 2

Unemployment rate: 4.17% (2023 est.)
4.82% (2022 est.)
6.38% (2021 est.)
note: % of labor force seeking employment
comparison ranking: 81

Youth unemployment rate (ages 15-24): *total:* 15.8% (2023 est.)
male: 15.8% (2023 est.)
female: 15.7% (2023 est.)
note: % of labor force ages 15-24 seeking employment
comparison ranking: total 91

Gini Index coefficient - distribution of family income: 32.8 (2021 est.)
note: index (0-100) of income distribution; higher values represent greater inequality
comparison ranking: 103

Average household expenditures: *on food:* 32% of household expenditures (2022 est.)
on alcohol and tobacco: 2.1% of household expenditures (2022 est.)

Household income or consumption by percentage share: *lowest 10%:* 3.3% (2021 est.)
highest 10%: 25.6% (2021 est.)
note: % share of income accruing to lowest and highest 10% of population

Remittances: 3.52% of GDP (2023 est.)
3.32% of GDP (2022 est.)
2.82% of GDP (2021 est.)
note: personal transfers and compensation between resident and non-resident individuals/households/entities

Budget: *revenues:* $364.86 billion (2018 est.)
expenditures: $432.856 billion (2018 est.)
note: central government revenues and expenses (excluding grants/extrabudgetary units/social security funds) converted to US dollars at average official exchange rate for year indicated

Public debt: 46.52% of GDP (2018 est.)
note: central government debt as a % of GDP
comparison ranking: 119

Taxes and other revenues: 12.02% (of GDP) (2018 est.)
note: central government tax revenue as a % of GDP
comparison ranking: 165

Current account balance: -$32.336 billion (2023 est.)
-$79.051 billion (2022 est.)
-$33.422 billion (2021 est.)
note: balance of payments - net trade and primary/secondary income in current dollars
comparison ranking: 204

Exports: $773.224 billion (2023 est.)
$767.643 billion (2022 est.)
$643.08 billion (2021 est.)
note: balance of payments - exports of goods and services in current dollars
comparison ranking: 10

Exports - partners: US 18%, UAE 7%, Netherlands 4%, China 3%, Bangladesh 3% (2022)
note: top five export partners based on percentage share of exports

Exports - commodities: refined petroleum, diamonds, packaged medicine, garments, jewelry (2022)
note: top five export commodities based on value in dollars

Imports: $859.485 billion (2023 est.)
$902.304 billion (2022 est.)
$717.119 billion (2021 est.)
note: balance of payments - imports of goods and services in current dollars
comparison ranking: 7

Imports - partners: China 15%, UAE 7%, US 7%, Saudi Arabia 6%, Russia 6% (2022)
note: top five import partners based on percentage share of imports

Imports - commodities: crude petroleum, coal, gold, natural gas, diamonds (2022)
note: top five import commodities based on value in dollars

Reserves of foreign exchange and gold: $627.793 billion (2023 est.)
$567.298 billion (2022 est.)
$638.485 billion (2021 est.)

note: holdings of gold (year-end prices)/foreign exchange/special drawing rights in current dollars
comparison ranking: 7

Debt - external: $186.653 billion (2022 est.)
note: present value of external debt in current US dollars
comparison ranking: 3

Exchange rates: Indian rupees (INR) per US dollar -

Exchange rates: 82.599 (2023 est.)
78.604 (2022 est.)
73.918 (2021 est.)
(2020 est.)
70.42 (2019 est.)

ENERGY

Electricity access: *electrification - total population:* 99.2% (2022 est.)
electrification - urban areas: 100%
electrification - rural areas: 99.3%

Electricity: *installed generating capacity:* 487.407 million kW (2022 est.)
consumption: 1.463 trillion kWh (2022 est.)
exports: 9.574 billion kWh (2022 est.)
imports: 9.127 billion kWh (2022 est.)
transmission/distribution losses: 296.958 billion kWh (2022 est.)
comparison rankings: transmission/distribution losses 210; imports 27; exports 24; consumption 3; installed generating capacity 3

Electricity generation sources: *fossil fuels:* 76.1% of total installed capacity (2022 est.)
nuclear: 2.6% of total installed capacity (2022 est.)
solar: 5.2% of total installed capacity (2022 est.)
wind: 4.3% of total installed capacity (2022 est.)
hydroelectricity: 9.9% of total installed capacity (2022 est.)
biomass and waste: 1.9% of total installed capacity (2022 est.)

Nuclear energy: Number of operational nuclear reactors: 20 (2023)

Number of nuclear reactors under construction: 7 (2023)

Net capacity of operational nuclear reactors: 6.92GW (2023 est.)

Percent of total electricity production: 3.1% (2023 est.)

Coal: *production:* 985.671 million metric tons (2022 est.)
consumption: 1.2 billion metric tons (2022 est.)
exports: 1.775 million metric tons (2022 est.)
imports: 215.649 million metric tons (2022 est.)
proven reserves: 111.052 billion metric tons (2022 est.)

Petroleum: *total petroleum production:* 795,000 bbl/day (2023 est.)
refined petroleum consumption: 5.049 million bbl/day (2022 est.)
crude oil estimated reserves: 4.605 billion barrels (2021 est.)

Natural gas: *production:* 33.17 billion cubic meters (2022 est.)
consumption: 58.867 billion cubic meters (2022 est.)
exports: 91.921 million cubic meters (2019 est.)
imports: 27.446 billion cubic meters (2022 est.)
proven reserves: 1.381 trillion cubic meters (2021 est.)

Carbon dioxide emissions: 2.805 billion metric tonnes of CO2 (2022 est.)
from coal and metallurgical coke: 2.067 billion metric tonnes of CO2 (2022 est.)
from petroleum and other liquids: 620.731 million metric tonnes of CO2 (2022 est.)
from consumed natural gas: 117.577 million metric tonnes of CO2 (2022 est.)
comparison ranking: total emissions 3

Energy consumption per capita: 24.793 million Btu/person (2022 est.)
comparison ranking: 124

COMMUNICATIONS

Telephones - fixed lines: *total subscriptions:* 27.45 million (2022 est.)
subscriptions per 100 inhabitants: 2 (2022 est.)
comparison ranking: total subscriptions 8

Telephones - mobile cellular: *total subscriptions:* 1.143 billion (2022 est.)
subscriptions per 100 inhabitants: 81 (2022 est.)
comparison ranking: total subscriptions 2

Telecommunication systems: *general assessment:* India's telecommunications sector has struggled for growth over the last five years; the sector's lackluster performance has been in spite of concerted efforts by the government to bolster the underlying infrastructure in a bid to achieve universal coverage; instead, the country's relatively liberal regulatory environment has encouraged fierce competition and price wars among the operators; State-owned as well as private operators have been forced to seek redress from the government in order to avoid bankruptcy; one particular area of contention has been the billions owed by the operators to the government in the form of Adjusted Gross Revenue (AGR) dues – usage and licensing fees charged by the Department of Telecommunications (DoT) – that have been the subject of long-standing court battles over what should be counted as revenue; the government won that battle in the Supreme Court in 2019, but the financial impairment of that decision has pushed a number of telcos to the brink; add the impact of the Covid-19 crisis in 2020 and 2021 to the mix, and the government had to come to the industry's rescue by introducing a major reform package in September 2021; along with changes to the definition of AGR with regard to non-telecom revenue, the package includes a four-year moratorium on AGR dues and spectrum instalments; the government has also deferred the spectrum auctions for 5G until later in 2022; mobile spectrum in India is already in short supply in terms of providing the necessary capacity to reach universal coverage, but the cash-strapped MNOs may not yet be in a sufficiently strong financial position for which to make the 5G spectrum auction viable (2022)
domestic: fixed-line subscriptions 2 per 100 and mobile-cellular at nearly 82 per 100 (2021)
international: country code - 91; a number of major international submarine cable systems, including SEA-ME-WE-3 & 4, AAE-1, BBG, EIG, FALCON, FEA, GBICS, MENA, IMEWE, SEACOM/ Tata TGN-Eurasia, SAFE, WARF, Bharat Lanka Cable System, IOX, Chennai-Andaman & Nicobar Island Cable, SAEx2, Tata TGN-Tata Indicom and i2icn that provide connectivity to Europe, Africa, Asia, the Middle East, South East Asia, numerous Indian Ocean islands including Australia ; satellite earth stations - 8 Intelsat (Indian Ocean) and 1 Inmarsat; Indian Ocean region (2022)

Broadcast media: Doordarshan, India's public TV network, has a monopoly on terrestrial broadcasting and operates about 20 national, regional, and local services; a large and increasing number of privately owned TV stations are distributed by cable and satellite service providers; in 2020, 130 million households paid for cable and satellite television across India and as of 2018, cable and satellite TV offered over 850 TV channels; government controls AM radio with All India Radio operating domestic and external networks; news broadcasts via radio are limited to the All India Radio Network; since 2000, privately owned FM stations have been permitted and their numbers have increased rapidly (2020)

Internet country code: .in

Internet users: *total:* 644 million (2021 est.)
percent of population: 46% (2021 est.)
comparison ranking: total 2

Broadband - fixed subscriptions: *total:* 22.95 million (2020 est.)
subscriptions per 100 inhabitants: 2 (2020 est.)
comparison ranking: total 9

TRANSPORTATION

National air transport system: *number of registered air carriers:* 14 (2020)
inventory of registered aircraft operated by air carriers: 485
annual passenger traffic on registered air carriers: 164,035,637 (2018)
annual freight traffic on registered air carriers: 2,703,960,000 (2018) mt-km

Civil aircraft registration country code prefix: VT

Airports: 311 (2024)
comparison ranking: 21

Heliports: 276 (2024)

Pipelines: 17,389 km natural gas, 10, 419 km crude oil, 3,544 liquid petroleum gas, 14,729 km refined products (2020) 9 km condensate/gas, 20 km oil/gas/water (2013) (2020)

Railways: *total:* 65,554 km (2014)
narrow gauge: 1,604 km (2014) 1.000-m gauge
broad gauge: 63,950 km (2014) (39, 329 km electrified)
comparison ranking: total 4

Roadways: *total:* 6,371,847 km (2021) note: includes 140,995 km of national highways and expressways, 171.039 km of state highways , and 6,059,813 km of other roads
note: includes 96,214 km of national highways and expressways, 147,800 km of state highways, and 4,455,010 km of other roads
comparison ranking: total 2

Waterways: 14,500 km (2012) (5,200 km on major rivers and 485 km on canals suitable for mechanized vessels)
comparison ranking: 10

Merchant marine: *total:* 1,859 (2023)
by type: bulk carrier 66, container ship 22, general cargo 607, oil tanker 144, other 1020
comparison ranking: total 15

Ports: *total ports:* 56 (2024)
large: 4
medium: 4
small: 13
very small: 30
size unknown: 5
ports with oil terminals: 18
key ports: Calcutta, Chennai (Madras), Jawaharlal Nehru Port (Nhava Shiva), Kattupalli Port, Kochi (Cochin), Mumbai (Bombay), New Mangalore, Vishakhapatnam

MILITARY AND SECURITY

Military and security forces: Indian Armed Forces: Army, Navy, Air Force, Coast Guard; Defense Security Corps

Ministry of Home Affairs: Central Armed Police Forces (includes Assam Rifles, Border Security Force, Central Industrial Security Force, Central Reserve Police Force, Indo-Tibetan Border Police, National Security Guards, Sashastra Seema Bal), Special Protection Group, National Disaster Response Force (NDRF)

Ministry of Railways: Railway Protection Force (2024)
note 1: the Defense Security Corps provides security for Ministry of Defense sites
note 2: the Border Security Force (BSF) is responsible for the Indo-Pakistan and Indo-Bangladesh borders; the Sashastra Seema Bal (SSB or Armed Border Force) guards the Indo-Nepal and Indo-Bhutan borders
note 3: the Central Reserve Police Force (CRPF) includes a Rapid Reaction Force (RAF) for riot control and the Commando Battalion for Resolute Action (COBRA) for counter-insurgency operations
note 4: the Assam Rifles are under the administrative control of the Ministry of Home Affairs, while operational control falls under the Ministry of Defense (specifically the Indian Army)
note 5: the Territorial Army (TA) is a military reserve force composed of part-time volunteers who provide support services to the Indian Army; it is a part of the Regular Army with the role of relieving Regular Army units from static duties and assisting civil authorities with natural calamities and maintaining essential services in emergencies, as well as providing units for the Regular Army as required

Military expenditures: 2.3% of GDP (2023 est.)
2.1% of GDP (2022 est.)
2.2% of GDP (2021 est.)
2.5% of GDP (2020 est.)
2..4% of GDP (2019 est.)
comparison ranking: 50

Military and security service personnel strengths: information varies; approximately 1.5 million active personnel (approximately 1.25 million Army; 65,000 Navy; 140,000 Air Force; 12,000 Coast Guard) (2023)

Military equipment inventories and acquisitions: much of the military's inventory consists of Russian- and Soviet-origin equipment; there is a smaller, but growing mix of Western and domestically produced arms; Russia continues to be the leading provider of arms to India, although in recent years India has increased acquisitions from other suppliers, including France, Israel, and the US; it is one of the world's largest importers of arms; India's defense industry is capable of producing a range of air, land, missile, and naval weapons systems for both domestic use and export; it also produces weapons systems under license (2024)

Military service age and obligation: ages vary by service, but generally 16.5-27 years of age for voluntary military service for men and women; no conscription (2023)
note 1: in 2022, the Indian Government began recruiting men aged 17.5-21 annually to serve on 4-year contracts under a process called the Agnipath scheme; at the end of their tenure, 25% would be retained for longer terms of service, while the remainder would be forced to leave the military, although some of those leaving would be eligible to serve in the Coast Guard, the Merchant Navy, civilian positions in the Ministry of Defense, and in the paramilitary forces of the Ministry of Home Affairs, such as the Central Armed Police Forces and Assam Rifles
note 2: as of 2023, women made up less than 1% of the Army, about 1% of the Air Force, and about 6% of the Navy
note 3: the Indian military accepts citizens of Nepal and Bhutan; descendants of refugees from Tibet who arrived before 1962 and have resided permanently in India; peoples of Indian origin from nations such as Burma, the Democratic Republic of the Congo, Ethiopia, Kenya, Malawi, Pakistan, Sri Lanka, Tanzania, Uganda, and Vietnam with the intention of permanently settling in India; eligible candidates from "friendly foreign nations" may apply to the Armed Forces Medical Services
note 4: the British began to recruit Nepalese citizens (Gurkhas) into the East India Company Army during the Anglo- Nepalese War (1814-1816), and the Gurkhas subsequently were brought into the British Indian Army; following the partition of India in 1947, an agreement between Nepal, India, and Great Britain allowed for the transfer of the 10 regiments from the British Indian Army to the separate British and Indian armies; six regiments of Gurkhas (aka Gorkhas in India) regiments went to the new Indian Army; a seventh regiment was later added

Military deployments: 1,800 Democratic Republic of the Congo (MONUSCO); 200 Golan Heights (UNDOF); 890 Lebanon (UNIFIL); 2,350 South Sudan (UNMISS); 590 Sudan (UNISFA) (2024)
note: India has over 6,000 total military and police personnel deployed on UN missions

Military - note: the Indian military performs a variety of missions; it is primarily focused on China and Pakistan and territorial defense, while secondary missions include regional power projection, UN peacekeeping deployments, humanitarian operations, and support to internal security forces; it has fought in several significant conflicts and counterinsurgency operations since 1947 and regularly conducts large-scale exercises; the military may act internally under the Armed Forces (Special Powers) Act (AFSPA) of 1958, an act of the Indian Parliament that granted special powers to put down separatist movements in "disturbed areas"; the AFSPA of 1958 and a virtually identical law, the Armed Forces (Jammu & Kashmir) Special Powers Act of 1990, have been in force since 1958 in parts of northeast India, and since 1990 in Jammu & Kashmir
the short 1962 Sino-India War left in place one of the World's longest disputed international borders, resulting in occasional standoffs between Indian and Chinese security forces, including lethal clashes in 1975 and 2020; meanwhile, India and Pakistan have fought several conflicts since 1947, including the Indo-Pakistan War of 1965 and the Indo-Pakistan and Bangladesh War of Independence of 1971, as well clashes over the disputed region of Kashmir (the First Kashmir War of 1947 and the 1999 Kargil Conflict); a fragile cease-fire in Kashmir was reached in 2003, revised in 2018, and reaffirmed in 2021, although the Line of Control remains contested, and India has accused Pakistan of backing armed separatists and terrorist organizations in Jammu and Kashmir where Indian forces have conducted counterinsurgency operations since the 1980s; in addition, India and Pakistan have battled over the Siachen Glacier of Kashmir, which was seized by India in 1984 with Pakistan attempting to retake the area at least three times between 1985 and 1995; despite a cease-fire, both sides continue to maintain a permanent military presence there with outposts at altitudes above 20,000 feet (over 6,000 meters) where most casualties are due to extreme weather and the hazards of operating in the high mountain terrain of the world's highest conflict, including avalanches, exposure, and altitude sickness (2024)

SPACE

Space agency/agencies: Indian Space Research Organization (ISRO; established 1969); the ISRO is subordinate to the Department of Space (DOS; established 1972); India's first space organization was the Indian National Committee for Space Research (INCOSPAR; established 1962); Defense Space Agency (DSA; established 2019 to command the space assets of the Army, Navy, and Air Force; the Defense Imagery Processing and Analysis Center, Defense Satellite Control Center, and Defense Space Research Organization were also merged into the DSA); National Space Promotion and Authorization Center (established 2020 to facilitate India's private sector in the country's space program) (2024)

Space launch site(s): Satish Dhawan Space Center (aka Sriharikota Range; located in Andhra Pradesh); Vikram Sarabhai Space Center (Kerala) (2024)

Space program overview: has one of the world's largest space programs; designs, builds, launches, operates, and tracks the full spectrum of satellites, including communications, navigation, remote sensing (RS), and scientific/technology; designs, builds, and launches rockets, space/satellite launch vehicles (SLVs), and lunar/interplanetary probes; launches satellites for foreign partners; developing astronaut corps and human flight capabilities (with assistance from Russia, US); researching and developing additional space-related technologies and capabilities; has space-related agreements with more than 50 countries, including China, France, Germany, Japan, Russia, and the US, as well as the European Space Agency; participates in international space projects such as the Square Kilometer Array (SKA) radio telescope; has a government-owned company under the administrative control of DOS; NewSpace India Limited (NSIL) is the commercial arm of the ISRO with the responsibility of researching and developing space-related technologies and promoting India's growing space industry (2024)
note: further details about the key activities, programs, and milestones of the country's space program, as well as government spending estimates on the space sector, appear in the Space Programs reference guide

TERRORISM

Terrorist group(s): Harakat ul-Mujahidin; Harakat ul-Jihad-i-Islami; Hizbul Mujahideen; Indian Mujahedeen; Islamic State of Iraq and ash-Sham – India; Jaish-e-Mohammed; Lashkar-e Tayyiba; al-Qa'ida; al-Qa'ida in the Indian Subcontinent; Islamic Revolutionary Guard Corps (IRGC)/Qods Force
note: details about the history, aims, leadership, organization, areas of operation, tactics, targets, weapons, size, and sources of support of the group(s) appear(s) in the Terrorism reference guide

TRANSNATIONAL ISSUES

Refugees and internally displaced persons: *refugees (country of origin):* 92,131 (Sri Lanka), 72,315 (Tibet/China), 10,064 (Afghanistan) (mid-year 2022); 78,731 (Burma) (refugees and asylum seekers) (2023)
IDPs: 631,000 (armed conflict and intercommunal violence) (2022)
stateless persons: 20,330 (2022)

Illicit drugs: India is a source, transit, and destination for illicit narcotics and precursor chemicals; drug abuse in India growing, facilitated by illicit narcotics and the availability of over-the-counter medicines; commonly abused substances in India include heroin, cannabis, and cocaine, with growing use of pharmaceutical drugs in recent years including tramadol, opioids, and MDMA (ecstasy) analogues; largest producer of generic drugs in the world which is also used to produce illicit synthetic drugs such as pharmaceutical opioids, methamphetamine, heroin, MDMA, and ketamine

INDIAN OCEAN

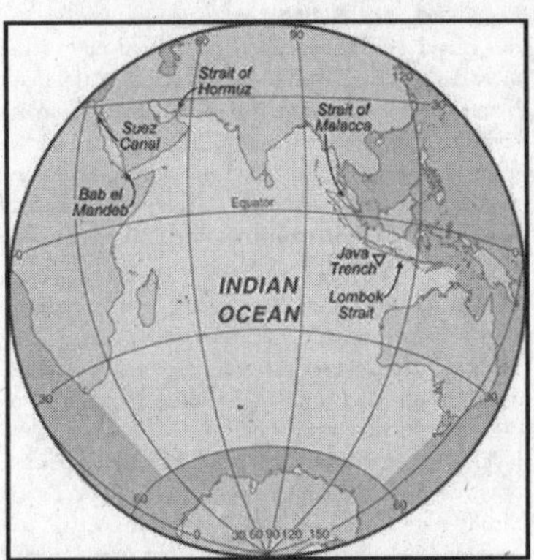

INTRODUCTION

Background: The Indian Ocean is the third largest of the world's five ocean basins (after the Pacific Ocean and Atlantic Ocean, but larger than the Southern Ocean and Arctic Ocean). Four critically important access waterways are the Suez Canal (Egypt), Bab el Mandeb (Djibouti-Yemen), Strait of Hormuz (Iran-Oman), and Strait of Malacca (Indonesia-Malaysia). The International Hydrographic Organization decided in 2000 to delimit a fifth world ocean basin, the Southern Ocean, which removed the portion of the Indian Ocean south of 60 degrees south latitude.

GEOGRAPHY

Location: body of water between Africa, the Southern Ocean, Asia, and Australia

Geographic coordinates: 20 00 S, 80 00 E

Map references: Map of the world oceans

Area: *total:* 70.56 million sq km
note: includes Andaman Sea, Arabian Sea, Bay of Bengal, Great Australian Bight, Gulf of Aden, Gulf of Oman, Mozambique Channel, Persian Gulf, Red Sea, Savu Sea, Strait of Malacca, Timor Sea, and other tributary water bodies

Area - comparative: almost 7 times the size of the US

Coastline: 66,526 km

Climate: northeast monsoon (December to April), southwest monsoon (June to October); tropical cyclones occur during May/June and October/November in the northern Indian Ocean and January/February in the southern Indian Ocean

Ocean volume: *ocean volume:* 264 million cu km
percent of World Ocean total volume: 19.8%

Major ocean currents: the counterclockwise Indian Ocean Gyre comprised of the southward flowing warm Agulhas and East Madagascar Currents in the west, the eastward flowing South Indian Current in the south, the northward flowing cold West Australian Current in the east, and the westward flowing South Equatorial Current in the north; a distinctive annual reversal of surface currents occurs in the northern Indian Ocean; low atmospheric pressure over southwest Asia from hot, rising, summer air results in the southwest monsoon and southwest-to-northeast winds and clockwise currents, while high pressure over northern Asia from cold, falling, winter air results in the northeast monsoon and northeast-to-southwest winds and counterclockwise currents

Elevation: *highest point:* sea level
lowest point: Java Trench -7,192 m unnamed deep
mean depth: -3,741 m
ocean zones: Composed of water and in a fluid state, the oceans are delimited differently than the solid continents. They are divided into three zones based on depth and light level. Sunlight entering the water may travel about 1,000 m into the oceans under the right conditions, but there is rarely any significant light beyond 200 m.
The upper 200 m (656 ft) of oceans is called the euphotic, or "sunlight," zone. This zone contains the vast majority of commercial fisheries and is home to many protected marine mammals and sea turtles. Only a small amount of light penetrates beyond this depth.
The zone between 200 m (656 ft) and 1,000 m (3,280 ft) is usually referred to as the "twilight" zone, but is officially the dysphotic zone. In this zone, the intensity of light rapidly dissipates as depth increases. Such a minuscule amount of light penetrates beyond a depth of 200 m that photosynthesis is no longer possible.
The aphotic, or "midnight," zone exists in depths below 1,000 m (3,280 ft). Sunlight does not penetrate to these depths, and the zone is bathed in darkness.

Natural resources: oil and gas fields, fish, shrimp, sand and gravel aggregates, placer deposits, polymetallic nodules

Natural hazards: occasional icebergs pose navigational hazard in southern reaches

Geography - note: major chokepoints include Bab el Mandeb, Strait of Hormuz, Strait of Malacca, southern access to the Suez Canal, and the Lombok Strait

ENVIRONMENT

Environment - current issues: marine pollution caused by ocean dumping, improper waste disposal, and oil spills; deep sea mining; oil pollution in Arabian Sea, Persian Gulf, and Red Sea; coral reefs threatened due to climate change, direct human pressures, and inadequate governance, awareness, and political will; loss of biodiversity; endangered marine species include the dugong, seals, turtles, and whales

Climate: northeast monsoon (December to April), southwest monsoon (June to October); tropical cyclones occur during May/June and October/November in the northern Indian Ocean and January/February in the southern Indian Ocean

Marine fisheries: *the Indian Ocean fisheries are the third most important in the world, accounting for 15.5%, or 12,220,000 mt of the global catch in 2020; tuna, small pelagic fish, and shrimp are important species in these regions; the Food and Agriculture Organization delineated two fishing regions in the Indian Ocean:*
Eastern Indian Ocean region (Region 57) is the most important and the fifth-largest-producing region in the world with 8.4%, or 6,590,000 mt, of the global catch in 2020; the region encompasses the waters north of 55º South latitude and east of 80º East longitude, including the Bay of Bengal and Andaman Sea, with the major producers including India (2,362,481 mt), Indonesia (1,940,558 mt), Burma (1,114,777 mt), Bangladesh (877,837 mt), and Sri Lanka (373,369 mt); the principal catches include shad, skipjack tuna, mackerel, shrimp, and sardinellas
Western Indian Ocean region (Region 51) is the world's sixth-largest-producing region with more than 7.1% or 5,630,000 mt of the global catch in 2020; this region encompasses the waters north of 40º South latitude and west of 80º East longitude, including the western Indian Ocean, Arabian Sea, Persian Gulf, and Red Sea, as well as the waters along

the east coast of Africa and Madagascar, the south coast of the Arabian Peninsula, and the west coast of India; major producers include India (2,207,125 mt), Oman (580,048 mt), Pakistan (341,730 mt), and Mozambique (274,791 mt); the principal catches include skipjack and yellowfin tuna, mackerel, sardines, shrimp, and cephalopods

Regional fisheries bodies: Indian Ocean Tuna Commission, Commission for the Conservation of Southern Bluefin Tuna, Regional Commission for Fisheries (Persian Gulf/Gulf of Oman), Southeast Asia Fisheries Development Center, Southwest Indian Ocean Fisheries Commission, South Indian Ocean Fisheries Agreement

GOVERNMENT

Country name: *etymology:* named for the country of India, which makes up much of its northern border

INDONESIA

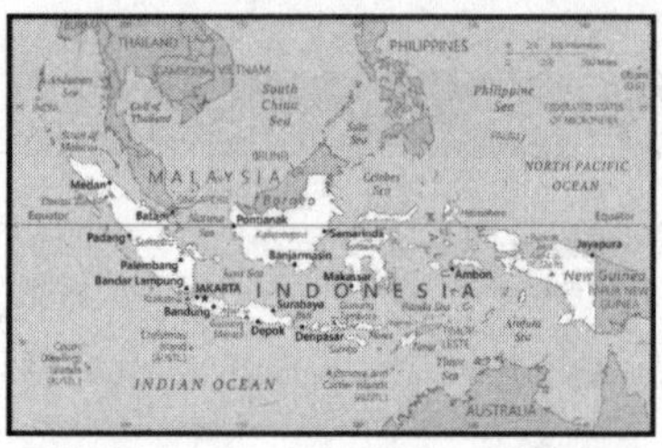

INTRODUCTION

Background: The archipelago was once largely under the control of Buddhist and Hindu rulers. By around the 7th century, a Buddhist kingdom arose on Sumatra and expanded into Java and the Malay Peninsula until it was conquered in the late 13th century by the Hindu Majapahit Empire from Java. Majapahit (1290-1527) united most of modern-day Indonesia and Malaysia. Traders introduced Islam around the 11th century, and the religion was gradually over the next 500 years. The Portuguese conquered parts of Indonesia in the 16th century, but the Dutch ousted them (except in East Timor) and began colonizing the islands in the early 17th century. It would be the early 20th century before Dutch colonial rule was established across the entirety of what would become the boundaries of the modern Indonesian state.

Japan occupied the islands from 1942 to 1945. Indonesia declared its independence shortly before Japan's surrender, but it required four years of sometimes brutal fighting, intermittent negotiations, and UN mediation before the Netherlands agreed to transfer sovereignty in 1949. A period of sometimes unruly parliamentary democracy ended in 1957 when President SOEKARNO declared martial law and instituted "Guided Democracy." After an abortive coup in 1965 by alleged communist sympathizers, SOEKARNO was gradually eased from power. From 1967 until 1998, President SUHARTO ruled Indonesia with his "New Order" government. After street protests toppled SUHARTO in 1998, free and fair legislative elections took place in 1999 while the country's first direct presidential election occurred in 2004. Indonesia has since become a robust democracy, holding four direct presidential elections, each considered by international observers to have been largely free and fair.

Indonesia is now the world's third-most-populous democracy and the world's largest Muslim-majority nation. It has had strong economic growth since overcoming the Asian financial crisis of the late 1990s. By the 2020s, it had the largest economy in Southeast Asia, and its economy ranked in the world's top 10 in terms of purchasing power parity. It has also made considerable gains in reducing poverty. Although relations amongst its diverse population–there are more than 300 ethnic groups–have been harmonious in the 2000s, there have been areas of sectarian discontent and violence, as well as instances of religious extremism and terrorism. A political settlement to an armed separatist conflict in Aceh was achieved in 2005, but a separatist group in Papua continued to conduct a low-intensity conflict as of 2024.

GEOGRAPHY

Location: Southeastern Asia, archipelago between the Indian Ocean and the Pacific Ocean

Geographic coordinates: 5 00 S, 120 00 E

Map references: Southeast Asia

Area: *total:* 1,904,569 sq km
land: 1,811,569 sq km
water: 93,000 sq km
comparison ranking: total 16

Area - comparative: slightly less than three times the size of Texas

Land boundaries: *total:* 2,958 km
border countries (3): Malaysia 1,881 km; Papua New Guinea 824 km; Timor-Leste 253 km

Coastline: 54,716 km

Maritime claims: *territorial sea:* 12 nm
exclusive economic zone: 200 nm
measured from claimed archipelagic straight baselines

Climate: tropical; hot, humid; more moderate in highlands

Terrain: mostly coastal lowlands; larger islands have interior mountains

Elevation: *highest point:* Puncak Jaya 4,884 m
lowest point: Indian Ocean 0 m
mean elevation: 367 m

Natural resources: petroleum, tin, natural gas, nickel, timber, bauxite, copper, fertile soils, coal, gold, silver
note: Indonesia is the World's leading producer of nickel with an output of 1.6 million mt in 2022

Land use: *agricultural land:* 31.2% (2018 est.)
arable land: 13% (2018 est.)
permanent crops: 12.1% (2018 est.)
permanent pasture: 6.1% (2018 est.)
forest: 51.7% (2018 est.)
other: 17.1% (2018 est.)

Irrigated land: 67,220 sq km (2012)

Major lakes (area sq km): *fresh water lake(s):* Danau Toba - 1,150 sq km
note - located in the caldera of a super volcano that erupted more than 70,000 years ago; it is the largest volcanic lake in the World

Major rivers (by length in km): Sepik (shared with Papua New Guinea [s]) - 1,126 km; Fly (shared with Papua New Guinea [s]) - 1,050 km
note – [s] after country name indicates river source; [m] after country name indicates river mouth

Population distribution: major concentration on the island of Java, which is considered one of the most densely populated places on earth; of the outer islands (those surrounding Java and Bali), Sumatra contains some of the most significant clusters, particularly in the south near the Selat Sunda, and along the northeastern coast near Medan; the cities of Makasar (Sulawesi), Banjarmasin (Kalimantan) are also heavily populated

Natural hazards: occasional floods; severe droughts; tsunamis; earthquakes; volcanoes; forest fires
volcanism: Indonesia contains the most volcanoes of any country in the world - some 76 are historically active; significant volcanic activity occurs on Java, Sumatra, the Sunda Islands, Halmahera Island, Sulawesi Island, Sangihe Island, and in the Banda Sea; Merapi (2,968 m), Indonesia's most active volcano and in eruption since 2010, has been deemed a Decade Volcano by the International Association of Volcanology and Chemistry of the Earth's Interior, worthy of study due to its explosive history and close proximity to human populations; on 22 December 2018, a large explosion and flank collapse destroyed most of the 338 m high island of Anak Krakatau (Child of Krakatau) and generated a deadly tsunami inundating portions of western Java and southern Sumatra leaving more than 400 dead; other notable historically active volcanoes include Agung, Awu, Karangetang, Krakatau (Krakatoa), Makian, Raung, Sinabung, and Tambora; see note 2 under "Geography - note"

Geography - note: *note 1:* according to Indonesia's National Coordinating Agency for Survey and Mapping, the total number of islands in the archipelago is 13,466, of which 922 are permanently inhabited (Indonesia is the world's largest country comprised solely of islands); the country straddles the equator and occupies a strategic location astride or along major sea lanes from the Indian Ocean to the Pacific Ocean
note 2: Indonesia is one of the countries along the Ring of Fire, a belt of active volcanoes and earthquake epicenters bordering the Pacific Ocean; up to 90% of the world's earthquakes and some 75% of the world's volcanoes occur within the Ring of Fire; 80% of tsunamis, caused by volcanic or seismic events, occur within the "Pacific Ring of Fire"
note 3: despite having the fourth largest population in the world, Indonesia is the most heavily forested region on earth after the Amazon
note 4: two major food crops apparently developed on the island of New Guinea: bananas and sugarcane

PEOPLE AND SOCIETY

Population: *total:* 281,562,465
male: 140,800,047
female: 140,762,418 (2024 est.)
comparison rankings: female 4; male 4; total 4

Nationality: *noun:* Indonesian(s)
adjective: Indonesian

Ethnic groups: Javanese 40.1%, Sundanese 15.5%, Malay 3.7%, Batak 3.6%, Madurese 3%, Betawi 2.9%, Minangkabau 2.7%, Buginese 2.7%, Bantenese 2%, Banjarese 1.7%, Balinese 1.7%, Acehnese 1.4%, Dayak 1.4%, Sasak 1.3%, Chinese 1.2%, other 15% (2010 est.)

Languages: Bahasa Indonesia (official, modified form of Malay), English, Dutch, local dialects (of which the most widely spoken is Javanese); note - more than 700 languages are used in Indonesia
major-language sample(s):
Fakta Dunia, sumber informasi dasar yang sangat diperlukan. (Indonesian)

Religions: Muslim 87.4%, Protestant 7.5%, Roman Catholic 3.1%, Hindu 1.7%, other 0.8% (includes Buddhist and Confucian) (2022 est.)

Demographic profile: Indonesia has the world's fourth-largest population. It is predominantly Muslim and has the largest Muslim population of any country in the world. The population is projected to increase to as much as 320 million by 2045. A government-supported family planning program. The total fertility rate (TFR) – the average number of births per woman – from 5.6 in the mid-1960s to 2.7 in the mid-1990s. The success of the program was also due to the social acceptance of family planning, which received backing from influential Muslim leaders and organizations.
The fertility decline slowed in the late 1990's when responsibility for family planning programs shifted to the district level, where the programs were not prioritized. Since 2012 the national government revitalized the national family planning program, and Indonesia's TFR has slowly decreased to 2.3 in 2020. The government may reach its goal of achieving replacement level fertility – 2.1 children per woman – but the large number of women of childbearing age ensures significant population growth for many years.
Indonesia is a source country for labor migrants, a transit country for asylum seekers, and a destination mainly for highly skilled migrant workers. International labor migration, both legal and illegal, from Indonesia to other parts of Asia (most commonly Malaysia) and the Middle East has taken place for decades because of high unemployment and underemployment, poverty, and low wages domestically. Increasing numbers of migrant workers are drawn to Australia, Canada, New Zealand, and the US. The majority of Indonesian labor migration is temporary and consists predominantly of low-skilled workers, mainly women working as domestics.
Indonesia's strategic location between Asia and Australia and between the Pacific and Indian Oceans – and its relatively easy accessibility via boat – appeal to asylum seekers. It is also an attractive transit location because of its easy entry requirements and the ability to continue on to Australia. Recent asylum seekers have come from Afghanistan, Burma (Rohingyas), Iraq, Somalia, and Sri Lanka. Since 2013, when Australia tightening its immigration policy, thousands of migrants and asylum seekers have been stranded in Indonesia, where they live in precarious conditions and receive only limited support from international organizations. The situation for refugees in Indonesia has also worsened because Australia and the US, which had resettled the majority of refugees in Indonesia, have significantly lowered their intake.

Age structure: *0-14 years:* 23.8% (male 34,247,218/female 32,701,367)
15-64 years: 68.3% (male 96,268,201/female 95,961,293)
65 years and over: 8% (2024 est.) (male 10,284,628/female 12,099,758)

Dependency ratios: *total dependency ratio:* 47.6
youth dependency ratio: 37.6
elderly dependency ratio: 10
potential support ratio: 10 (2021 est.)

Median age: *total:* 31.5 years (2024 est.)
male: 30.8 years
female: 32.3 years
comparison ranking: total 125

Population growth rate: 0.73% (2024 est.)
comparison ranking: 120

Birth rate: 14.8 births/1,000 population (2024 est.)
comparison ranking: 115

Death rate: 6.8 deaths/1,000 population (2024 est.)
comparison ranking: 128

Net migration rate: -0.7 migrant(s)/1,000 population (2024 est.)
comparison ranking: 132

Population distribution: major concentration on the island of Java, which is considered one of the most densely populated places on earth; of the outer islands (those surrounding Java and Bali), Sumatra contains some of the most significant clusters, particularly in the south near the Selat Sunda, and along the northeastern coast near Medan; the cities of Makasar (Sulawesi), Banjarmasin (Kalimantan) are also heavily populated

Urbanization: *urban population:* 58.6% of total population (2023)
rate of urbanization: 1.99% annual rate of change (2020-25 est.)

Major urban areas - population: 11.249 million JAKARTA (capital), 3.729 million Bekasi, 3.044 million Surabaya, 3.041 million Depok, 2.674 million Bandung, 2.514 million Tangerang (2023)

Sex ratio: *at birth:* 1.05 male(s)/female
0-14 years: 1.05 male(s)/female
15-64 years: 1 male(s)/female
65 years and over: 0.85 male(s)/female
total population: 1 male(s)/female (2024 est.)

Mother's mean age at first birth: 22.4 years (2017 est.)
note: data represents median age at first birth among women 25-49

Maternal mortality ratio: 173 deaths/100,000 live births (2020 est.)
comparison ranking: 52

Infant mortality rate: *total:* 18.9 deaths/1,000 live births (2024 est.)
male: 21.3 deaths/1,000 live births
female: 16.4 deaths/1,000 live births
comparison ranking: total 80

Life expectancy at birth: *total population:* 73.6 years (2024 est.)
male: 71.3 years
female: 76 years
comparison ranking: total population 148

Total fertility rate: 1.96 children born/woman (2024 est.)
comparison ranking: 110

Gross reproduction rate: 0.96 (2024 est.)

Contraceptive prevalence rate: 55.5% (2018)

Drinking water source: *improved: urban:* 98.2% of population
rural: 86.8% of population
total: 93.3% of population
unimproved: urban: 1.8% of population
rural: 13.2% of population
total: 6.7% of population (2020 est.)

Current health expenditure: 3.4% of GDP (2020)

Physician density: 0.62 physicians/1,000 population (2020)

Hospital bed density: 1 beds/1,000 population (2017)

Sanitation facility access: *improved: urban:* 97.2% of population
rural: 86.5% of population
total: 92.5% of population
unimproved: urban: 2.8% of population
rural: 13.5% of population
total: 7.5% of population (2020 est.)

Obesity - adult prevalence rate: 6.9% (2016)
comparison ranking: 162

Alcohol consumption per capita: *total:* 0.08 liters of pure alcohol (2019 est.)
beer: 0.06 liters of pure alcohol (2019 est.)
wine: 0.01 liters of pure alcohol (2019 est.)
spirits: 0.02 liters of pure alcohol (2019 est.)
other alcohols: 0 liters of pure alcohol (2019 est.)
comparison ranking: total 178

Tobacco use: *total:* 37.6% (2020 est.)
male: 71.4% (2020 est.)
female: 3.7% (2020 est.)
comparison ranking: total 9

Children under the age of 5 years underweight: 17.7% (2018)
comparison ranking: 26

Currently married women (ages 15-49): 70% (2023 est.)

Child marriage: *women married by age 15:* 2%
women married by age 18: 16.3% (2017 est.)

Education expenditures: 3.5% of GDP (2020 est.)
comparison ranking: 141

Literacy: *definition:* age 15 and over can read and write
total population: 96%
male: 97.4%
female: 94.6% (2020)

School life expectancy (primary to tertiary education): *total:* 14 years
male: 14 years
female: 14 years (2018)

People - note: Indonesia is the fourth most populous nation in the World after China, India, and the United States; more than half of the Indonesian population - roughly 150 million people or 55% - live on the island of Java (about the size of California) making it the most crowded island on earth

ENVIRONMENT

Environment - current issues: large-scale deforestation (much of it illegal) and related wildfires cause heavy smog; over-exploitation of marine resources; environmental problems associated with rapid urbanization and economic development, including air pollution, traffic congestion, garbage management, and reliable water and waste water services; water pollution from industrial wastes, sewage

Environment - international agreements: *party to:* Biodiversity, Climate Change, Climate Change-Kyoto Protocol, Climate Change-Paris Agreement, Comprehensive Nuclear Test Ban, Desertification, Endangered Species, Hazardous Wastes, Law of the Sea, Nuclear Test Ban, Ozone Layer Protection, Ship Pollution, Tropical Timber 2006, Wetlands
signed, but not ratified: Marine Life Conservation

Climate: tropical; hot, humid; more moderate in highlands

Urbanization: *urban population:* 58.6% of total population (2023)
rate of urbanization: 1.99% annual rate of change (2020-25 est.)

Revenue from forest resources: 0.39% of GDP (2018 est.)
comparison ranking: 71

Revenue from coal: 1.06% of GDP (2018 est.)
comparison ranking: 5

Air pollutants: *particulate matter emissions:* 19.34 micrograms per cubic meter (2019 est.)
carbon dioxide emissions: 563.32 megatons (2016 est.)
methane emissions: 244.5 megatons (2020 est.)

Waste and recycling: *municipal solid waste generated annually:* 65.2 million tons (2016 est.)
municipal solid waste recycled annually: 4.564 million tons (2016 est.)
percent of municipal solid waste recycled: 7% (2016 est.)

Major lakes (area sq km): *fresh water lake(s):* Danau Toba - 1,150 sq km
note - located in the caldera of a super volcano that erupted more than 70,000 years ago; it is the largest volcanic lake in the World

Major rivers (by length in km): Sepik (shared with Papua New Guinea [s]) - 1,126 km; Fly (shared with Papua New Guinea [s]) - 1,050 km
note – [s] after country name indicates river source; [m] after country name indicates river mouth

Total water withdrawal: *municipal:* 23.8 billion cubic meters (2020 est.)
industrial: 9.14 billion cubic meters (2020 est.)
agricultural: 189.7 billion cubic meters (2020 est.)

Total renewable water resources: 2.02 trillion cubic meters (2020 est.)

Geoparks: *total global geoparks and regional networks:* 10
global geoparks and regional networks: Batur; Belitong; Ciletuh - Palabuhanratu; Gunung Sewu; Ijen; Maros Pangkep; Merangin Jambi; Raja Ampat; Rinjani-Lombok; Toba Caldera (2023)

GOVERNMENT

Country name: *conventional long form:* Republic of Indonesia
conventional short form: Indonesia
local long form: Republik Indonesia
local short form: Indonesia
former: Netherlands East Indies (Dutch East Indies), Netherlands New Guinea
etymology: the name is an 18th-century construct of two Greek words, "Indos" (India) and "nesoi" (islands), meaning "Indian islands"

Government type: presidential republic

Capital: *name:* Jakarta; note - Indonesian lawmakers on 18 January 2022 approved the relocation of the country's capital from Jakarta to a site on the island of Borneo between Samarinda City and the port city of Balikpapan; Nusantara ("archipelago"), the name of the new capital, is expected to be established in August 2024
geographic coordinates: 6 10 S, 106 49 E
time difference: UTC+7 (12 hours ahead of Washington, DC, during Standard Time)
time zone note: Indonesia has three time zones
etymology: "Jakarta" derives from the Sanscrit "Jayakarta" meaning "victorious city" and refers to a successful defeat and expulsion of the Portuguese in 1527; previously the port had been named "Sunda Kelapa"

Administrative divisions: 35 provinces (provinsi-provinsi, singular - provinsi), 1 autonomous province*, 1 special region** (daerah istimewa), and 1 national capital district*** (daerah khusus ibukota); Aceh*, Bali, Banten, Bengkulu, Gorontalo, Jakarta***, Jambi, Jawa Barat (West Java), Jawa Tengah (Central Java), Jawa Timur (East Java), Kalimantan Barat (West Kalimantan), Kalimantan Selatan (South Kalimantan), Kalimantan Tengah (Central Kalimantan), Kalimantan Timur (East Kalimantan), Kalimantan Utara (North Kalimantan), Kepulauan Bangka Belitung (Bangka Belitung Islands), Kepulauan Riau (Riau Islands), Lampung, Maluku, Maluku Utara (North Maluku), Nusa Tenggara Barat (West Nusa Tenggara), Nusa Tenggara Timur (East Nusa Tenggara), Papua, Papua Barat (West Papua), Papua Barat Daya (Southwest Papua), Papua Pegunungan (Papua Highlands), Papua Selatan (South Papua), Papua Tengah (Central Papua), Riau, Sulawesi Barat (West Sulawesi), Sulawesi Selatan (South Sulawesi), Sulawesi Tengah (Central Sulawesi), Sulawesi Tenggara (Southeast Sulawesi), Sulawesi Utara (North Sulawesi), Sumatera Barat (West Sumatra), Sumatera Selatan (South Sumatra), Sumatera Utara (North Sumatra), Yogyakarta**
note: following the implementation of decentralization beginning on 1 January 2001, regencies and municipalities have become the key administrative units responsible for providing most government services

Independence: 17 August 1945 (declared independence from the Netherlands)

National holiday: Independence Day, 17 August (1945)

Legal system: civil law system based on the Roman-Dutch model and influenced by customary law

Constitution: *history:* drafted July to August 1945, effective 18 August 1945, abrogated by 1949 and 1950 constitutions; 1945 constitution restored 5 July 1959
amendments: proposed by the People's Consultative Assembly, with at least two thirds of its members present; passage requires simple majority vote by the Assembly membership; constitutional articles on the unitary form of the state cannot be amended; amended several times, last in 2002

International law organization participation: has not submitted an ICJ jurisdiction declaration; non-party state to the ICCt

Citizenship: *citizenship by birth:* no
citizenship by descent only: at least one parent must be a citizen of Indonesia
dual citizenship recognized: no
residency requirement for naturalization: 5 continuous years

Suffrage: 17 years of age; universal; married persons regardless of age

Executive branch: *chief of state:* President PRABOWO Subianto Djojohadikusumo (since 20 October 2024)
head of government: President PRABOWO Subianto Djojohadikusumo (since 20 October 2024)
cabinet: Cabinet appointed by the president
elections/appointments: president and vice president directly elected by absolute majority popular vote for a 5-year term (eligible for a second term); election last held on 14 February 2024 (next to be held in 2029)
election results:
2024: PRABOWO Subianto elected president (assumes office 20 October 2024); percent of vote - PRABOWO Subianto (GERINDRA) 58.6%, Anies Rasyid BASWEDAN (Independent) 24.9%, GANJAR Pranowo (PDI-P) 16.5%
2019: Joko WIDODO reelected president; percent of vote - Joko WIDODO (PDI-P) 55.5%, PRABOWO Subianto Djojohadikusumo (GERINDRA) 44.5%
note: the president is both chief of state and head of government

Legislative branch: *description:* bicameral People's Consultative Assembly or Majelis Permusyawaratan Rakyat (MPR) consists of: Regional Representative Council or Dewan Perwakilan Daerah (136 seats; non-partisan members directly elected in multi-seat constituencies - 4 each from the country's 34 electoral districts - by proportional representation vote to serve 5-year terms); note - the Regional Representative Council has no legislative authority
House of Representatives or Dewan Perwakilan Rakyat (580 seats; members directly elected in multi-seat constituencies by single non-transferable vote to serve 5-year terms)
elections: Regional Representative Council - last held on 14 February 2024 (next to be held in 2029)
House of Representatives - last held on 14 February 2024 (next to be held in 2029)
election results: Regional Representative Council - all seats elected on a non-partisan basis; composition - men 102, women 34, percentage women 25%
House of Representatives - percent of vote by party - PDI-P 16.7%, Golkar 15.3%, Gerindra 13.2%, PKB 10.6%, Nasdem 9.7%, PKS 8.4%, PD 7.4%, PAN 7.2%; other 11.5% (10 additional parties received votes); seats by party - PDI-P 110, Golkar 102, Gerindra 86, PKB 68, Nasdem 69, PKS 53, PD 44, PAN 48; composition - men 449, women 126, percentage women 21.9%; total People's Consultative Assembly percentage women NA

Judicial branch: *highest court(s):* Supreme Court or Mahkamah Agung (51 judges divided into 8 chambers); Constitutional Court or Mahkamah Konstitusi (consists of 9 judges)
judge selection and term of office: Supreme Court judges nominated by Judicial Commission, appointed by president with concurrence of parliament; judges serve until retirement at age 65; Constitutional Court judges - 3 nominated by president, 3 by Supreme Court, and 3 by parliament; judges appointed by the president; judges serve until mandatory retirement at age 70
subordinate courts: High Courts of Appeal, district courts, religious courts

Political parties: Democrat Party or PD
Functional Groups Party or GOLKAR

Great Indonesia Movement Party or GERINDRA
Indonesia Democratic Party-Struggle or PDI-P
National Awakening Party or PKB
National Democratic Party or NasDem
National Mandate Party or PAN
Prosperous Justice Party or PKS

International organization participation: ADB, APEC, ARF, ASEAN, BIS, CD, CICA (observer), CP, D-8, EAS, EITI (compliant country), FAO, G-11, G-15, G-20, G-77, IAEA, IBRD, ICAO, ICC (national committees), ICRM, IDA, IDB, IFAD, IFC, IFRCS, IHO, ILO, IMF, IMO, IMSO, Interpol, IOC, IOM (observer), IORA, IPU, ISO, ITSO, ITU, ITUC (NGOs), MIGA, MINURSO, MINUSTAH, MONUSCO, MSG (associate member), NAM, OECD (enhanced engagement), OIC, OPCW, PIF (partner), UN, UNAMID, UNCTAD, UNESCO, UNHRC, UNIDO, UNIFIL, UNISFA, UNMIL, UNOOSA, UNWTO, UPU, WCO, WFTU (NGOs), WHO, WIPO, WMO, WTO

Diplomatic representation in the US: *chief of mission:* Ambassador (vacant); Chargé d'Affaires Ida Bagus Made BIMANTARA (since 30 November 2023)
chancery: 2020 Massachusetts Avenue NW, Washington, DC 20036
telephone: [1] (202) 775-5200
FAX: [1] (202) 775-5236
email address and website:
washington.kbri@kemlu.go.id
Embassy of The Republic of Indonesia, in Washington D.C., The United States of America (kemlu.go.id)
consulate(s) general: Chicago, Houston, Los Angeles, New York, San Francisco

Diplomatic representation from the US: *chief of mission:* Ambassador Kamala Shirin LAKHDHIR (since 8 August 2024)
embassy: Jl. Medan Merdeka Selatan No. 3-5, Jakarta 10110
mailing address: 8200 Jakarta Place, Washington DC 20521-8200
telephone: [62] (21) 5083-1000
FAX: [62] (21) 385-7189
email address and website:
jakartaacs@state.gov
https://id.usembassy.gov/
consulate(s) general: Surabaya
consulate(s): Medan

Flag description: two equal horizontal bands of red (top) and white; the colors derive from the banner of the Majapahit Empire of the 13th-15th centuries; red symbolizes courage, white represents purity
note: similar to the flag of Monaco, which is shorter; also similar to the flag of Poland, which is white (top) and red

National symbol(s): garuda (mythical bird); national colors: red, white

National anthem: *name:* "Indonesia Raya" (Great Indonesia)
lyrics/music: Wage Rudolf SOEPRATMAN
note: adopted 1945

National heritage: *total World Heritage Sites:* 10 (6 cultural, 4 natural)
selected World Heritage Site locales: Borobudur Temple Compounds (c); Komodo National Park (n); Prambanan Temple Compounds (c); Ujung Kulon National Park (n); Sangiran Early Man Site (c); Lorentz National Park (n); Tropical Rainforest Heritage of Sumatra (n); Cultural Landscape of Bali Province (c); Ombilin Coal Mining Heritage of Sawahlunto (c); Cosmological Axis of Yogyakarta and its Historic Landmarks (c)

ECONOMY

Economic overview: one of the fastest growing economies and largest in Southeast Asia; upper middle-income country; human capital and competitiveness phase of its 20-year development plan; COVID-19 reversed poverty reduction trajectory; strengthening financial resilience

Real GDP (purchasing power parity): $3.906 trillion (2023 est.)
$3.718 trillion (2022 est.)
$3.531 trillion (2021 est.)
note: data in 2021 dollars
comparison ranking: 8

Real GDP growth rate: 5.05% (2023 est.)
5.31% (2022 est.)
3.7% (2021 est.)
note: annual GDP % growth based on constant local currency
comparison ranking: 53

Real GDP per capita: $14,100 (2023 est.)
$13,500 (2022 est.)
$12,900 (2021 est.)
note: data in 2021 dollars
comparison ranking: 128

GDP (official exchange rate): $1.371 trillion (2023 est.)
note: data in current dollars at official exchange rate

Inflation rate (consumer prices): 3.67% (2023 est.)
4.21% (2022 est.)
1.56% (2021 est.)
note: annual % change based on consumer prices
comparison ranking: 73

Credit ratings: Fitch rating: BBB (2017)
Moody's rating: Baa2 (2018)
Standard & Poors rating: BBB (2019)
note: The year refers to the year in which the current credit rating was first obtained.

GDP - composition, by sector of origin: *agriculture:* 12.5% (2023 est.)
industry: 40.2% (2023 est.)
services: 42.9% (2023 est.)
note: figures may not total 100% due to non-allocated consumption not captured in sector-reported data
comparison rankings: services 178; industry 29; agriculture 64

GDP - composition, by end use: *household consumption:* 54.4% (2023 est.)
government consumption: 7.4% (2023 est.)
investment in fixed capital: 29.3% (2023 est.)
investment in inventories: 1.2% (2023 est.)
exports of goods and services: 21.7% (2023 est.)
imports of goods and services: -19.6% (2023 est.)
note: figures may not total 100% due to rounding or gaps in data collection

Agricultural products: oil palm fruit, rice, sugarcane, maize, coconuts, cassava, bananas, eggs, mangoes/guavas, chicken (2022)
note: top ten agricultural products based on tonnage

Industries: petroleum and natural gas, textiles, automotive, electrical appliances, apparel, footwear, mining, cement, medical instruments and appliances, handicrafts, chemical fertilizers, plywood, rubber, processed food, jewelry, and tourism

Industrial production growth rate: 5% (2023 est.)
note: annual % change in industrial value added based on constant local currency
comparison ranking: 51

Labor force: 140.931 million (2023 est.)
note: number of people ages 15 or older who are employed or seeking work
comparison ranking: 4

Unemployment rate: 3.42% (2023 est.)
3.46% (2022 est.)
3.83% (2021 est.)
note: % of labor force seeking employment
comparison ranking: 58

Youth unemployment rate (ages 15-24): *total:* 13.9% (2023 est.)
male: 14.2% (2023 est.)
female: 13.6% (2023 est.)
note: % of labor force ages 15-24 seeking employment
comparison ranking: total 98

Population below poverty line: 9.4% (2023 est.)
note: % of population with income below national poverty line

Gini Index coefficient - distribution of family income: 38.3 (2023 est.)
note: index (0-100) of income distribution; higher values represent greater inequality
comparison ranking: 53

Average household expenditures: *on food:* 33.7% of household expenditures (2022 est.)
on alcohol and tobacco: 7.4% of household expenditures (2022 est.)

Household income or consumption by percentage share: *lowest 10%:* 3.1% (2023 est.)
highest 10%: 31.4% (2023 est.)
note: % share of income accruing to lowest and highest 10% of population

Remittances: 1.06% of GDP (2023 est.)
0.99% of GDP (2022 est.)
0.79% of GDP (2021 est.)
note: personal transfers and compensation between resident and non-resident individuals/households/entities

Budget: *revenues:* $130.872 billion (2020 est.)
expenditures: $192.97 billion (2020 est.)

Public debt: % of GDP (2022 est.)
note: central government debt as a % of GDP
comparison ranking: 121

Taxes and other revenues: % (of GDP) (2022 est.)
note: central government tax revenue as a % of GDP
comparison ranking: 169

Current account balance: -$1.88 billion (2023 est.)
$13.215 billion (2022 est.)
$3.511 billion (2021 est.)
note: balance of payments - net trade and primary/secondary income in current dollars
comparison ranking: 156

Exports: $292.79 billion (2023 est.)
$315.746 billion (2022 est.)
$246.787 billion (2021 est.)
note: balance of payments - exports of goods and services in current dollars
comparison ranking: 32

Exports - partners: China 21%, US 10%, Japan 8%, India 8%, Malaysia 5% (2022)
note: top five export partners based on percentage share of exports

Exports - commodities: coal, palm oil, iron alloys, natural gas, steel (2022)

note: top five export commodities based on value in dollars

Imports: $264.426 billion (2023 est.)
$273.031 billion (2022 est.)
$217.579 billion (2021 est.)
note: balance of payments - imports of goods and services in current dollars
comparison ranking: 31

Imports - partners: China 31%, Singapore 10%, Japan 6%, Malaysia 5%, Thailand 5% (2022)
note: top five import partners based on percentage share of imports

Imports - commodities: refined petroleum, crude petroleum, vehicle parts/accessories, natural gas, plastics (2022)
note: top five import commodities based on value in dollars

Reserves of foreign exchange and gold: $146.359 billion (2023 est.)
$137.222 billion (2022 est.)
$144.908 billion (2021 est.)
note: holdings of gold (year-end prices)/foreign exchange/special drawing rights in current dollars
comparison ranking: 20

Exchange rates: Indonesian rupiah (IDR) per US dollar -

Exchange rates: 15,236.885 (2023 est.)
14,849.854 (2022 est.)
14,308.144 (2021 est.)
14,582.203 (2020 est.)
14,147.671 (2019 est.)

ENERGY

Electricity access: *electrification - total population:* 100% (2022 est.)
electrification - urban areas: 100%
electrification - rural areas: 98.2%

Electricity: *installed generating capacity:* 69.706 million kW (2022 est.)
consumption: 312.423 billion kWh (2022 est.)
imports: 972.7 million kWh (2022 est.)
transmission/distribution losses: 25.71 billion kWh (2022 est.)
comparison rankings: transmission/distribution losses 192; imports 77; consumption 13; installed generating capacity 20

Electricity generation sources: *fossil fuels:* 79.9% of total installed capacity (2022 est.)
solar: 0.1% of total installed capacity (2022 est.)
wind: 0.1% of total installed capacity (2022 est.)
hydroelectricity: 8.1% of total installed capacity (2022 est.)
geothermal: 4.9% of total installed capacity (2022 est.)
biomass and waste: 6.8% of total installed capacity (2022 est.)

Coal: *production:* 659.357 million metric tons (2022 est.)
consumption: 202.283 million metric tons (2022 est.)
exports: 469.09 million metric tons (2022 est.)
imports: 12.396 million metric tons (2022 est.)
proven reserves: 34.869 billion metric tons (2022 est.)

Petroleum: *total petroleum production:* 865,000 bbl/day (2023 est.)
refined petroleum consumption: 1.728 million bbl/day (2022 est.)
crude oil estimated reserves: 2.48 billion barrels (2021 est.)

Natural gas: *production:* 57.41 billion cubic meters (2022 est.)
consumption: 36.061 billion cubic meters (2022 est.)
exports: 22.064 billion cubic meters (2022 est.)
imports: 1.027 billion cubic meters (2022 est.)
proven reserves: 1.408 trillion cubic meters (2021 est.)

Carbon dioxide emissions: 684.926 million metric tonnes of CO2 (2022 est.)
from coal and metallurgical coke: 386.828 million metric tonnes of CO2 (2022 est.)
from petroleum and other liquids: 224.45 million metric tonnes of CO2 (2022 est.)
from consumed natural gas: 73.649 million metric tonnes of CO2 (2022 est.)
comparison ranking: total emissions 7

Energy consumption per capita: 33.039 million Btu/person (2022 est.)
comparison ranking: 110

COMMUNICATIONS

Telephones - fixed lines: *total subscriptions:* 8.424 million (2022 est.)
subscriptions per 100 inhabitants: 3 (2022 est.)
comparison ranking: total subscriptions 20

Telephones - mobile cellular: *total subscriptions:* 316.553 million (2022 est.)
subscriptions per 100 inhabitants: 115 (2022 est.)
comparison ranking: total subscriptions 4

Telecommunication systems: *general assessment:* Indonesia faces more than the usual number of obstacles in terms of enabling widespread access to quality telecommunications services for its population of more than 270 million; the geographical challenges have been further compounded by a variety of social, political, and economic problems over the years that have kept the country's wealth distributed very thinly; the fixed-line (fiber) and mobile operators have continued to expand and upgrade their networks across the country; Indonesia's 18,000 islands (many of which, however, are sparsely populated) makes the deployment of fixed-line infrastructure on a broad scale difficult; there has been renewed activity in fiber optic cable, but the bundling of fixed-line telephony with TV and internet services will see the country's teledensity stabilize; mobile subscriptions have reached more than 130% and is projected to exceed 150% by 2026; with 4G LTE universally available, the major mobile companies have been busy launching 5G services in selected areas; the rollout of 5G will be hampered by the lack of availability of suitable frequencies; the 4G had to be reallocated from broadcasting services, and indications are that the same process is going to have to be followed in order to allow the expansion of 5G into its core frequency bands (3.3 to 4.2GHz) (2022)
domestic: fixed-line subscribership roughly 3 per 100 and mobile-cellular 134 per 100 persons (2021)
international: country code - 62; landing points for the SEA-ME-WE-3 & 5, DAMAI, JASUKA, BDM, Dumai-Melaka Cable System, IGG, JIBA, Link 1, 3, 4, & 5, PGASCOM, B3J2, Tanjung Pandam-Sungai Kakap Cable System, JAKABARE, JAYABAYA, INDIGO-West, Matrix Cable System, ASC, SJJK, Jaka2LaDeMa, S-U-B Cable System, JBCS, MKCS, BALOK, Palapa Ring East, West and Middle, SMPCS Packet-1 and 2, LTCS, TSCS, SEA-US and Kamal Domestic Submarine Cable System, 35 submarine cable networks that provide links throughout Asia, the Middle East, Australia, Southeast Asia, Africa and Europe; satellite earth stations - 2 Intelsat (1 Indian Ocean and 1 Pacific Ocean) (2019)

Broadcast media: mixture of about a dozen national TV networks - 1 public broadcaster, the remainder private broadcasters - each with multiple transmitters; more than 100 local TV stations; widespread use of satellite and cable TV systems; public radio broadcaster operates 6 national networks, as well as regional and local stations; overall, more than 700 radio stations with more than 650 privately operated (2019)

Internet country code: .id

Internet users: *total:* 167.4 million (2021 est.)
percent of population: 62% (2021 est.)
comparison ranking: total 5

Broadband - fixed subscriptions: *total:* 11,722,218 (2020 est.)
subscriptions per 100 inhabitants: 4 (2020 est.)
comparison ranking: total 17

TRANSPORTATION

National air transport system: *number of registered air carriers:* 25 (2020)
inventory of registered aircraft operated by air carriers: 611
annual passenger traffic on registered air carriers: 115,154,100 (2018)
annual freight traffic on registered air carriers: 1,131,910,000 (2018) mt-km

Civil aircraft registration country code prefix: PK

Airports: 513 (2024)
comparison ranking: 16

Heliports: 24 (2024)

Pipelines: 1,064 km condensate, 150 km condensate/gas, 11,702 km gas, 119 km liquid petroleum gas, 7,767 km oil, 77 km oil/gas/ water, 728 km refined products, 53 km unknown, 44 km water (2013)

Railways: *total:* 8,159 km (2014)
narrow gauge: 8,159 km (2014) 1.067-m gauge (565 km electrified)
note: 4,816 km operational
comparison ranking: total 27

Roadways: *total:* 496,607 km
paved: 283,102 km
unpaved: 213,505 km (2011)
comparison ranking: total 13

Waterways: 21,579 km (2011)
comparison ranking: 8

Merchant marine: *total:* 11,422 (2023)
by type: bulk carrier 160, container ship 219, general cargo 2,347, oil tanker 714, other 7,982
comparison ranking: total 1

Ports: *total ports:* 123 (2024)
large: 3
medium: 6
small: 18
very small: 96
ports with oil terminals: 79

key ports: Belawan, Cilacap, Dumai, Jakarta, Kasim Terminal, Merak Mas Terminal, Palembang, Surabaya, Ujung Pandang

MILITARY AND SECURITY

Military and security forces: Indonesian National Armed Forces (Tentara Nasional Indonesia, TNI): Army (TNI-Angkatan Darat (TNI-AD)), Navy (TNI-Angkatan Laut (TNI-AL); includes Marine Corps (Korps Marinir or KorMar)), Air Force (TNI-Angkatan Udara (TNI-AU)) (2024)
note 1: in 2014, Indonesia created a Maritime Security Agency (Bakamla) to coordinate the actions of all maritime security agencies, including the Navy, the Indonesian Sea and Coast Guard (Kesatuan Penjagaan Laut dan Pantai, KPLP), the Water Police (Polair), Customs (Bea Cukai), and Ministry of Marine Affairs and Fisheries
note 2: the Indonesian National Police, which reports directly to the president, includes a paramilitary Mobile Brigade Corps (BRIMOB) and Detachment 88 (Densus or Detasemen Khusus 88 Antiteror), a specialized counterterrorism force

Military expenditures: 0.8% of GDP (2023 est.)
0.8% of GDP (2022 est.)
0.8% of GDP (2021 est.)
0.8% of GDP (2020 est.)
0.8% of GDP (2019 est.)
comparison ranking: 137

Military and security service personnel strengths: approximately 400,000 active-duty troops (300,000 Army; 60,000 Navy, including about 20,000 marines; 30,000 Air Force) (2023)

Military equipment inventories and acquisitions: the military's inventory is a wide mix of Chinese, Russian, and Western (including US) equipment; in recent years, major suppliers have included China, France, Germany, the Netherlands, South Korea, and the US; the TNI has been engaged in a modernization program for more than a decade; Indonesia has a growing defense industry fueled by technology transfers and cooperation agreements with several countries; in 2019, the Indonesian Government said that growing its domestic defense industry would be a national priority over the following decade (2024)

Military service age and obligation: 18-45 years of age for voluntary military service for men and women, with selective conscription authorized (men, age 18), but not utilized; 24-month service obligation, with reserve obligation to age 45 (officers) (2024)
note: as of 2023, women comprised about 7% of the Indonesian military

Military deployments: 225 (plus about 140 police) Central African Republic (MINUSCA); 1,025 Democratic Republic of the Congo (MONUSCO); 1,225 Lebanon (UNIFIL) (2024)

Military - note: the military is responsible for external defense, combatting separatism, and responding to natural disasters; in certain conditions it may provide operational support to police, such as for counterterrorism operations, maintaining public order, and addressing communal conflicts; the TNI has undergone reforms since the 1990s to improve its professionalism and limit its involvement in internal politics
the Army is involved in counterinsurgency operations in Papua against the West Papua Liberation Army, the military wing of the Free Papua Organization, which has been fighting a low-level insurgency since Indonesia annexed the former Dutch colony in the 1960s; the Army has also been assisting police in Sulawesi in countering the Mujahideen Indonesia Timur (MIT; aka East Indonesia Mujahideen), a local militant group affiliated with the Islamic State of Iraq and ash-Sham (ISIS)
the Navy is responsible for coastal defense and patrolling Indonesia's territorial waters where it faces such issues as piracy, transnational crime, illegal fishing, and incursions by Chinese vessels; Indonesia is not a formal claimant in the South China Sea, although some of its waters lie within China's "nine-dash line" maritime claims, resulting in some stand offs in recent years; since 2016, the Indonesian military has bolstered its presence on Great Natuna Island (aka Pulau Natuna Besar), the main island of the Middle Natuna Archipelago, which is part of the Riau Islands Province, and held military exercises in the surrounding waters (2024)

SPACE

Space agency/agencies: Indonesian Space Agency (INASA; formed 2022); National Research and Innovation Agency (BRIN; established 2021); Research Organization for Aeronautics and Space (ORPA; formed 2021) (2024)

Space launch site(s): Stasiun Peluncuran Roket rocket launch facility (West Java); building a space launch facility/spaceport on Biak, Papua (estimated completion date is 2025) (2024)

Space program overview: has had a space program since the 1960s that has focused largely on rocket development and the acquisition and operation of satellites; operates satellites; manufactures remote sensing (RS) satellites; has a sounding (research) rocket program geared towards development of an indigenous orbital satellite launch vehicle (SLV) and independent satellite launch capabilities; researching and developing a range of other space-related technologies and capabilities related to satellite payloads, communications, RS, and astronomy; has relations with several foreign space agencies and industries, including those of France, Germany, India, Japan, Russia, and the US (2024)
note: further details about the key activities, programs, and milestones of the country's space program, as well as government spending estimates on the space sector, appear in the Space Programs reference guide

TERRORISM

Terrorist group(s): Islamic State of Iraq and ash-Sham (aka Jemaah Anshorut Daulah); Jemaah Islamiyah
note: details about the history, aims, leadership, organization, areas of operation, tactics, targets, weapons, size, and sources of support of the group(s) appear(s) in the Terrorism reference guide

TRANSNATIONAL ISSUES

Refugees and internally displaced persons: *refugees (country of origin):* 5,684 (Afghanistan) (mid-year 2022)

IDPs: 72,000 (inter-communal, inter-faith, and separatist violence between 1998 and 2004 in Aceh and Papua; religious attacks and land conflicts in 2007 and 2013; most IDPs in Aceh, Maluku, East Nusa Tengarra) (2022)
stateless persons: 866 (2022)

Illicit drugs: major transit point and destination for illicit narcotics; a destination for methamphetamine, ecstasy, and other illicit drugs; methamphetamine production facilities within Indonesia

IRAN

INTRODUCTION

Background: Known as Persia until 1935, Iran became an Islamic republic in 1979 after the ruling monarchy was overthrown and Shah Mohammad Reza PAHLAVI was forced into exile. Conservative clerical forces led by Ayatollah Ruhollah KHOMEINI established a theocratic system of government with ultimate political authority vested in a religious scholar known as the Supreme Leader, who is accountable only to the Assembly of Experts – an elected 88-member body of clerics. US-Iran relations became strained when Iranian students seized the US Embassy in Tehran in November 1979 and held embassy personnel hostage until mid-January 1981. The US cut off diplomatic relations with Iran in April 1980. From 1980 to 1988, Iran fought a bloody, indecisive war with Iraq that eventually expanded into the Persian Gulf and led to clashes between US Navy and Iranian military forces. Iran has been designated a state sponsor of terrorism since 1984.

After the election of reformer Hojjat ol-Eslam Mohammad KHATAMI as president in 1997 and a reformist Majles (legislature) in 2000, a political reform campaign in response to popular dissatisfaction was initiated, but conservative politicians blocked reform measures while increasing repression. Municipal and legislative elections in 2003 and 2004 saw conservatives reestablish control over Iran's elected government institutions, culminating in the 2005 inauguration of hardliner Mahmud AHMADI-NEJAD as president. His reelection in 2009 sparked nationwide protests over allegations of electoral fraud, and the protests persisted until 2011. In 2013, Iranians elected to the presidency centrist cleric Dr. Hasan Fereidun RUHANI, a longtime senior regime member who promised to reform society and foreign policy. In 2019, Tehran's sudden decision to increase the gasoline price sparked nationwide protests, which the regime violently suppressed. Conservatives won the majority in Majles elections in 2020, and hardline cleric Ebrahim RAISI was elected president in 2021, resulting in a conservative monopoly across the regime's elected and unelected institutions.

Iran continues to be subject to a range of international sanctions and export controls because of its involvement in terrorism, weapons proliferation, human rights abuses, and concerns over the nature of its nuclear program. Iran received nuclear-related sanctions relief in exchange for nuclear concessions under the Joint Comprehensive Plan of Action's (JCPOA) Implementation Day beginning in 2016. However, the US reimposed nuclear-related sanctions on Iran after it unilaterally terminated its JCPOA participation in 2018. In October 2023, the EU and the UK also decided to maintain nuclear-proliferation-related measures on Iran, as well as arms and missile embargoes, in response to Iran's non-compliance with its JCPOA commitments.

As president, RAISI has concentrated on deepening Iran's foreign relations with anti-US states – particularly China and Russia – to weather US sanctions and diplomatic pressure, while supporting negotiations to restore a nuclear deal that began in 2021. RAISI contended with nationwide protests that began in September 2022 and persisted for over three months after the death of a Kurdish Iranian woman, Mahsa AMINI, in morality police custody. Young people and women led the protests, and demands focused on regime change.

GEOGRAPHY

Location: Middle East, bordering the Gulf of Oman, the Persian Gulf, and the Caspian Sea, between Iraq and Pakistan

Geographic coordinates: 32 00 N, 53 00 E

Map references: Middle East

Area: *total:* 1,648,195 sq km
land: 1,531,595 sq km
water: 116,600 sq km
comparison ranking: total 19

Area - comparative: almost 2.5 times the size of Texas; slightly smaller than Alaska

Land boundaries: *total:* 5,894 km
border countries (7): Afghanistan 921 km; Armenia 44 km; Azerbaijan 689 km; Iraq 1,599 km; Pakistan 959 km; Turkey 534 km; Turkmenistan 1,148 km

Coastline: *2,440 km - note:* Iran also borders the Caspian Sea (740 km)

Maritime claims: *territorial sea:* 12 nm
contiguous zone: 24 nm
exclusive economic zone: bilateral agreements or median lines in the Persian Gulf
continental shelf: natural prolongation

Climate: mostly arid or semiarid, subtropical along Caspian coast

Terrain: rugged, mountainous rim; high, central basin with deserts, mountains; small, discontinuous plains along both coasts

Elevation: *highest point:* Kuh-e Damavand 5,625 m
lowest point: Caspian Sea -28 m
mean elevation: 1,305 m

Natural resources: petroleum, natural gas, coal, chromium, copper, iron ore, lead, manganese, zinc, sulfur

Land use: *agricultural land:* 30.1% (2018 est.)
arable land: 10.8% (2018 est.)
permanent crops: 1.2% (2018 est.)
permanent pasture: 18.1% (2018 est.)
forest: 6.8% (2018 est.)
other: 63.1% (2018 est.)

Irrigated land: 79,721 sq km (2020)

Major lakes (area sq km): *salt water lake(s):* Caspian Sea (shared with Russia, Azerbaijan, Turkmenistan, and Kazakhstan) - 374,000 sq km; Lake Urmia - 5,200 sq km; Lake Namak - 750 sq km

Major rivers (by length in km): Euphrates (shared with Turkey [s], Syria, and Iraq [m]) - 3,596 km; Tigris (shared with Turkey, Syria, and Iraq [m]) - 1,950 km; Helmand (shared with Afghanistan [s]) - 1,130 km
note – [s] after country name indicates river source; [m] after country name indicates river mouth

Major watersheds (area sq km): Indian Ocean drainage: *(Persian Gulf)* Tigris and Euphrates (918,044 sq km)

Population distribution: population is concentrated in the north, northwest, and west, reflecting the position of the Zagros and Elburz Mountains; the vast dry areas in the center and eastern parts of the country, around the deserts of the Dasht-e Kavir and Dasht-e Lut, have a much lower population density

Natural hazards: periodic droughts, floods; dust storms, sandstorms; earthquakes

Geography - note: strategic location on the Persian Gulf and Strait of Hormuz, which are vital maritime pathways for crude oil transport

PEOPLE AND SOCIETY

Population: *total:* 88,386,937
male: 44,795,539
female: 43,591,398 (2024 est.)
comparison rankings: female 17; male 17; total 17

Nationality: *noun:* Iranian(s)
adjective: Iranian

Ethnic groups: Persian, Azeri, Kurd, Lur, Baloch, Arab, Turkmen, and Turkic tribes

Languages: Persian Farsi (official), Azeri and other Turkic dialects, Kurdish, Gilaki and Mazandarani, Luri, Balochi, Arabic
major-language sample(s):
ی برای کسب اطلاعات کلی جهان
چکیده نامه جهان، منبعی ضرور
(Persian)

Religions: Muslim (official) 98.5%, Christian 0.7%, Baha'i 0.3%, agnostic 0.3%, other (includes Zoroastrian, Jewish, Hindu) 0.2% (2020 est.)

Age structure: *0-14 years:* 23.3% (male 10,512,797/female 10,040,282)
15-64 years: 69.8% (male 31,413,125/female 30,267,241)
65 years and over: 7% (2024 est.) (male 2,869,617/female 3,283,875)

Dependency ratios: *total dependency ratio:* 45.3
youth dependency ratio: 34.6
elderly dependency ratio: 10.7
potential support ratio: 9.3 (2021 est.)

Median age: *total:* 33.8 years (2024 est.)
male: 33.6 years
female: 34.1 years
comparison ranking: total 110

Population growth rate: 0.88% (2024 est.)
comparison ranking: 104

Birth rate: 14.3 births/1,000 population (2024 est.)
comparison ranking: 119

Death rate: 5.3 deaths/1,000 population (2024 est.)
comparison ranking: 187

Net migration rate: -0.3 migrant(s)/1,000 population (2024 est.)
comparison ranking: 113

Population distribution: population is concentrated in the north, northwest, and west, reflecting the position of the Zagros and Elburz Mountains; the vast dry areas in the center and eastern parts of the country, around the deserts of the Dasht-e Kavir and Dasht-e Lut, have a much lower population density

Urbanization: *urban population:* 77.3% of total population (2023)
rate of urbanization: 1.32% annual rate of change (2020-25 est.)

Major urban areas - population: 9.500 million TEHRAN (capital), 3.368 million Mashhad, 2.258 million Esfahan, 1.721 million Shiraz, 1.661 million Tabriz, 1.594 million Karaj (2023)

Sex ratio: *at birth:* 1.05 male(s)/female
0-14 years: 1.05 male(s)/female
15-64 years: 1.04 male(s)/female
65 years and over: 0.87 male(s)/female
total population: 1.03 male(s)/female (2024 est.)

Maternal mortality ratio: 22 deaths/100,000 live births (2020 est.)
comparison ranking: 119

Infant mortality rate: *total:* 14.3 deaths/1,000 live births (2024 est.)
male: 15.4 deaths/1,000 live births
female: 13.2 deaths/1,000 live births
comparison ranking: total 97

Life expectancy at birth: *total population:* 75.6 years (2024 est.)
male: 74.3 years
female: 77.1 years
comparison ranking: total population 125

Total fertility rate: 1.91 children born/woman (2024 est.)
comparison ranking: 117

Gross reproduction rate: 0.93 (2024 est.)

Drinking water source: *improved: urban:* 99.8% of population
rural: 98.1% of population
total: 99.4% of population
unimproved: urban: 0.2% of population
rural: 1.9% of population
total: 0.6% of population (2020 est.)

Current health expenditure: 5.3% of GDP (2020)

Physician density: 1.58 physicians/1,000 population (2018)

Hospital bed density: 1.6 beds/1,000 population (2017)

Sanitation facility access: *improved: urban:* 100% of population
rural: 100% of population
total: 100% of population

Obesity - adult prevalence rate: 25.8% (2016)
comparison ranking: 47

Alcohol consumption per capita: *total:* 0.02 liters of pure alcohol (2019 est.)
beer: 0 liters of pure alcohol (2019 est.)
wine: 0 liters of pure alcohol (2019 est.)
spirits: 0.02 liters of pure alcohol (2019 est.)
other alcohols: 0 liters of pure alcohol (2019 est.)
comparison ranking: total 181

Tobacco use: *total:* 13.6% (2020 est.)
male: 24.1% (2020 est.)
female: 3.1% (2020 est.)
comparison ranking: total 113

Children under the age of 5 years underweight: 4.3% (2017)
comparison ranking: 78

Currently married women (ages 15-49): 70.3% (2023 est.)

Education expenditures: 3.6% of GDP (2020 est.)
comparison ranking: 137

Literacy: *definition:* age 15 and over can read and write
total population: 88.7%
male: 92.4%
female: 88.7% (2021)

School life expectancy (primary to tertiary education): *total:* 15 years
male: 15 years
female: 15 years (2020)

ENVIRONMENT

Environment - current issues: air pollution, especially in urban areas, from vehicle emissions, refinery operations, and industrial effluents; deforestation; overgrazing; desertification; oil pollution in the Persian Gulf; wetland losses from drought; soil degradation (salination); inadequate supplies of potable water; water pollution from raw sewage and industrial waste; urbanization

Environment - international agreements: *party to:* Biodiversity, Climate Change, Climate Change-Kyoto Protocol, Desertification, Endangered Species, Hazardous Wastes, Marine Dumping-London Convention, Marine Dumping-London Protocol, Nuclear Test Ban, Ozone Layer Protection, Ship Pollution, Wetlands
signed, but not ratified: Climate Change-Paris Agreement, Comprehensive Nuclear Test Ban, Environmental Modification, Law of the Sea, Marine Life Conservation

Climate: mostly arid or semiarid, subtropical along Caspian coast

Urbanization: *urban population:* 77.3% of total population (2023)
rate of urbanization: 1.32% annual rate of change (2020-25 est.)

Revenue from forest resources: 0.01% of GDP (2017 est.)
comparison ranking: 152

Revenue from coal: 0.01% of GDP (2017 est.)
comparison ranking: 47

Air pollutants: *particulate matter emissions:* 31.62 micrograms per cubic meter (2019 est.)
carbon dioxide emissions: 661.71 megatons (2016 est.)
methane emissions: 158.71 megatons (2020 est.)

Waste and recycling: *municipal solid waste generated annually:* 17.885 million tons (2017 est.)
municipal solid waste recycled annually: 894,250 tons (2017 est.)
percent of municipal solid waste recycled: 5% (2017 est.)

Major lakes (area sq km): *salt water lake(s):* Caspian Sea (shared with Russia, Azerbaijan, Turkmenistan, and Kazakhstan) - 374,000 sq km; Lake Urmia - 5,200 sq km; Lake Namak - 750 sq km

Major rivers (by length in km): Euphrates (shared with Turkey [s], Syria, and Iraq [m]) - 3,596 km; Tigris (shared with Turkey, Syria, and Iraq [m]) - 1,950 km; Helmand (shared with Afghanistan [s]) - 1,130 km
note – [s] after country name indicates river source; [m] after country name indicates river mouth

Major watersheds (area sq km): Indian Ocean drainage: *(Persian Gulf)* Tigris and Euphrates (918,044 sq km)

Total water withdrawal: *municipal:* 6.2 billion cubic meters (2020 est.)
industrial: 1.1 billion cubic meters (2020 est.)
agricultural: 86 billion cubic meters (2020 est.)

Total renewable water resources: 137.05 billion cubic meters (2020 est.)

Geoparks: *total global geoparks and regional networks:* 3
global geoparks and regional networks: Aras; Qeshm Island; Tabas (2023)

GOVERNMENT

Country name: *conventional long form:* Islamic Republic of Iran
conventional short form: Iran
local long form: Jomhuri-ye Eslami-ye Iran
local short form: Iran
former: Persia
etymology: name derives from the Avestan term "aryanam" meaning "Land of the Noble [Ones]"

Government type: theocratic republic

Capital: *name:* Tehran
geographic coordinates: 35 42 N, 51 25 E
time difference: UTC+3.5 (8.5 hours ahead of Washington, DC)
daylight saving time: does not observe daylight savings time
etymology: various explanations of the city's name have been proffered, but the most plausible states that it derives from the Persian words *tah* meaning "end or bottom" and *ran* meaning "[mountain] slope" to signify "bottom of the mountain slope"; Tehran lies at the bottom slope of the Elburz Mountains

Administrative divisions: 31 provinces (ostanha, singular - ostan); Alborz, Ardabil, Azarbayjan-e Gharbi (West Azerbaijan), Azarbayjan-e Sharqi (East Azerbaijan), Bushehr, Chahar Mahal va Bakhtiari, Esfahan, Fars, Gilan, Golestan, Hamadan, Hormozgan, Ilam, Kerman, Kermanshah, Khorasan-e Jonubi (South Khorasan), Khorasan-e Razavi (Razavi Khorasan), Khorasan-e Shomali (North Khorasan), Khuzestan, Kohgiluyeh va Bowyer Ahmad, Kordestan, Lorestan, Markazi, Mazandaran, Qazvin, Qom, Semnan, Sistan va Baluchestan, Tehran, Yazd, Zanjan

Independence: *1 April 1979 (Islamic Republic of Iran proclaimed); notable earlier dates:* ca. 550 B.C. (Achaemenid (Persian) Empire established); A.D. 1501 (Iran reunified under the Safavid Dynasty); 1794 (beginning of Qajar Dynasty); 12 December 1925 (modern Iran established under the PAHLAVI Dynasty)

National holiday: Republic Day, 1 April (1979)

Legal system: religious legal system based on secular and Islamic law

Constitution: *history:* previous 1906; latest adopted 24 October 1979, effective 3 December 1979
amendments: proposed by the supreme leader – after consultation with the Exigency Council – and submitted as an edict to the "Council for Revision of the Constitution," a body consisting of various executive, legislative, judicial, and academic leaders and members; passage requires absolute majority vote in a referendum and approval of the supreme leader; articles including Iran's political system, its religious basis, and its form of government cannot be amended; amended 1989

International law organization participation: has not submitted an ICJ jurisdiction declaration; non-party state to the ICCt

Citizenship: *citizenship by birth:* no
citizenship by descent only: the father must be a citizen of Iran
dual citizenship recognized: no
residency requirement for naturalization: 5 years

Suffrage: 18 years of age; universal

Executive branch: *chief of state:* Supreme Leader Ali Hoseini-KHAMENEI (since 4 June 1989)
head of government: President Masoud PEZESHKIAN (assumed office on 30 July 2024)
cabinet: Council of Ministers selected by the president with legislative approval; the supreme leader has some control over appointments to several ministries
elections/appointments: supreme leader appointed for life by Assembly of Experts; president directly elected by absolute majority popular vote in 2 rounds if needed for a 4-year term (eligible for a second term and an additional nonconsecutive term); election last held on 28 June 2024 first round (runoff held on 5 July 2024)
election results:
2024: first round results - Masoud PEZESHKIAN (independent) 44.4%, Saeed JALILI (Front of Islamic Revolution Stability) 40.4%, Mohammad Baqer QAKIBAF (Progress and Justice Population of Islamic Iran) 14.3%, other 0.9%; second round results - Masoud PEZESHKIAN elected; Masoud PEZESHKIAN 54.8%, Saeed JALILI 45.2%
2021: Ebrahim RAISI elected president; percent of vote - Ebrahim RAISI (independent) 72.4%, Mohsen REZAI (RFII) 13.8%, Abbdolnaser HEMATI (ECP) 9.8%, Amir-Hosein Qazizadeh-HASHEMI (Islamic Law Party) 4%

Note: presidential election held early due to the death of President Ebrahim RAISI in a helicopter accident in May 2024

Legislative branch: *description:* unicameral Islamic Consultative Assembly or Majles-e Shura-ye Eslami or Majles (290 seats; 285 members directly elected in single- and multi-seat constituencies by multiple non-transferable vote in 2 rounds, 1 seat each for Zoroastrians, Jews, Assyrian and Chaldean Christians, Armenians in the north of the country and Armenians in the south; members serve 4-year

terms); note - all candidates to the Majles must be approved by the Council of Guardians, a 12-member group of which 6 are appointed by the supreme leader and 6 are jurists nominated by the judiciary and elected by the Majles
elections: first round held on 1 March 2024 for 245 seats; second round for 45 remaining seats to be held on 10 May 2024 (next full Majles election to be held in 2028)
election results: percent of vote by coalition in first round - NA; seats by coalition in first round - conservatives and hardliners 200, other 45; composition - NA

Judicial branch: *highest court(s):* Supreme Court (consists of the chief justice and organized into 42 two-bench branches, each with a justice and a judge)
judge selection and term of office: Supreme Court president appointed by the head of the High Judicial Council (HJC), a 5-member body to include the Supreme Court chief justice, the prosecutor general, and 3 clergy, in consultation with judges of the Supreme Court; president appointed for a single, renewable 5-year term; other judges appointed by the HJC; judge tenure NA
subordinate courts: Penal Courts I and II; Islamic Revolutionary Courts; Courts of Peace; Special Clerical Court (functions outside the judicial system and handles cases involving clerics); military courts

Political parties: Combatant Clergy Association (an active political group)
Executives of Construction Party
Front of Islamic Revolutionary Stability
Islamic Coalition Party
Progress and Justice Population of Islamic Iran
Militant Clerics Society (Majma-e Ruhaniyoun-e Mobarez) or MRM
Moderation and Development Party
National Trust Party (Hezb-e E'temad-eMelli) or HEM
Progress and Justice Society
Union of Islamic Iran People's Party (Hezb-e Ettehad-e Iran-e Eslami)

International organization participation: BRICS, CICA, CP, D-8, ECO, FAO, G-15, G-24, G-77, IAEA, IBRD, ICAO, ICC (national committees), ICRM, IDA, IDB, IFAD, IFC, IFRCS, IHO, ILO, IMF, IMO, IMSO, Interpol, IOC, IOM, IPU, ISO, ITSO, ITU, MIGA, NAM, OIC, OPCW, OPEC, PCA, SAARC (observer), SCO (observer), UN, UNAMID, UNCTAD, UNESCO, UNHCR, UNIDO, UNITAR, UNOOSA, UNWTO, UPU, WCO, WFTU (NGOs), WHO, WIPO, WMO, WTO (observer)

Diplomatic representation in the US: none

Note: Iran has an Interests Section in the Pakistani Embassy; address: Iranian Interests Section, Embassy of Pakistan, 1250 23rd Street NW, Washington, DC 20037; telephone: [1] (202) 965-4990; FAX [1] (202) 965-1073; email: requests@daftar.org; info@daftar-washington.com; website: https://daftar.org/

Diplomatic representation from the US: *embassy:* none; the US Interests Section is located in the Embassy of Switzerland; US Foreign Interests Section, Embassy of Switzerland, Pasdaran, Shahid Mousavi Street (Golestan 5th), Corner of Paydarfard Street, No. 55, Tehran

Flag description: three equal horizontal bands of green (top), white, and red; the national emblem (a stylized representation of the word Allah in the shape of a tulip, a symbol of martyrdom) in red is centered in the white band; ALLAH AKBAR (God is Great) in white Arabic script is repeated 11 times along the bottom edge of the green band and 11 times along the top edge of the red band; green is the color of Islam and also represents growth, white symbolizes honesty and peace, red stands for bravery and martyrdom

National symbol(s): lion; national colors: green, white, red

National anthem: *name:* "Soroud-e Melli-ye Jomhouri-ye Eslami-ye Iran" (National Anthem of the Islamic Republic of Iran)
lyrics/music: multiple authors/Hassan RIAHI
note 1: adopted 1990; Iran has had six national anthems; the first, entitled "Salam-e Shah" (Royal Salute) was in use from 1873-1909; next came "Salamati-ye Dowlat-e Elliye-ye Iran" (Salute of the Sublime State of Persia, 1909-1933); it was followed by "Sorud-e melli" (The Imperial Anthem of Iran; 1933-1979), which chronicled the exploits of the Pahlavi Dynasty; "Ey Iran" (Oh Iran) functioned unofficially as the national anthem for a brief period between the ouster of the Shah in 1979 and the early days of the Islamic Republic in 1980; "Payandeh Bada Iran" (Long Live Iran) was used between 1980 and 1990 during the time of Ayatollah KHOMEINI
note 2: a recording of the current Iranian national anthem is unavailable since the US Navy Band does not record anthems for countries from which the US does not anticipate official visits; the US does not have diplomatic relations with Iran

National heritage: *total World Heritage Sites:* 27 (25 cultural, 2 natural)
selected World Heritage Site locales: Persepolis (c); Tchogha Zanbil (c); Bam and its Cultural Landscape (c); Golestan Palace (c); Shushtar Historical Hydraulic System (c); Pasargadae (c); Hyrcanian Forests (n); Tabriz Historic Bazaar Complex (c); Meidan Emam, Esfahan (c); Bisotun (c)

ECONOMY

Economic overview: traditionally state-controlled economy but reforming state-owned financial entities; strong oil/gas, agricultural, and service sectors; recent massive inflation due to exchange rate depreciation, international sanctions, and investor uncertainty; increasing poverty

Real GDP (purchasing power parity): $1.44 trillion (2023 est.)
$1.373 trillion (2022 est.)
$1.323 trillion (2021 est.)
note: data in 2021 dollars
comparison ranking: 22

Real GDP growth rate: 4.95% (2023 est.)
3.78% (2022 est.)
4.72% (2021 est.)
note: annual GDP % growth based on constant local currency
comparison ranking: 58

Real GDP per capita: $16,200 (2023 est.)
$15,500 (2022 est.)
$15,000 (2021 est.)
note: data in 2021 dollars
comparison ranking: 115

GDP (official exchange rate): $401.505 billion (2023 est.)
note: data in current dollars at official exchange rate

Inflation rate (consumer prices): 44.58% (2023 est.)
43.49% (2022 est.)
43.39% (2021 est.)
note: annual % change based on consumer prices
comparison ranking: 213

GDP - composition, by sector of origin: *agriculture:* 13% (2023 est.)
industry: 41.8% (2023 est.)
services: 42.7% (2023 est.)
note: figures may not total 100% due to non-allocated consumption not captured in sector-reported data
comparison rankings: services 180; industry 25; agriculture 62

GDP - composition, by end use: *household consumption:* 47.2% (2023 est.)
government consumption: 13.2% (2023 est.)
investment in fixed capital: 26.9% (2023 est.)
investment in inventories: 9.5% (2023 est.)
exports of goods and services: 28.6% (2023 est.)
imports of goods and services: -26.9% (2023 est.)
note: figures may not total 100% due to rounding or gaps in data collection

Agricultural products: wheat, sugarcane, milk, sugar beets, tomatoes, barley, potatoes, vegetables, oranges, chicken (2022)
note: top ten agricultural products based on tonnage

Industries: petroleum, petrochemicals, gas, fertilizer, caustic soda, textiles, cement and other construction materials, food processing (particularly sugar refining and vegetable oil production), ferrous and nonferrous metal fabrication, armaments

Industrial production growth rate: 8.84% (2023 est.)
note: annual % change in industrial value added based on constant local currency
comparison ranking: 23

Labor force: 29.159 million (2023 est.)
note: number of people ages 15 or older who are employed or seeking work
comparison ranking: 24

Unemployment rate: 9.1% (2023 est.)
9.09% (2022 est.)
9.28% (2021 est.)
note: % of labor force seeking employment
comparison ranking: 157

Youth unemployment rate (ages 15-24): *total:* 22.8% (2023 est.)
male: 20% (2023 est.)
female: 35.5% (2023 est.)
note: % of labor force ages 15-24 seeking employment
comparison ranking: total 51

Gini Index coefficient - distribution of family income: 34.8 (2022 est.)
note: index (0-100) of income distribution; higher values represent greater inequality
comparison ranking: 79

Average household expenditures: *on food:* 28.4% of household expenditures (2022 est.)
on alcohol and tobacco: 0.5% of household expenditures (2022 est.)

Household income or consumption by percentage share: *lowest 10%:* 2.8% (2022 est.)
highest 10%: 26.8% (2022 est.)
note: % share of income accruing to lowest and highest 10% of population

Remittances: 0.55% of GDP (2020 est.)
0.47% of GDP (2019 est.)
0.4% of GDP (2018 est.)

Budget: *revenues:* $60.714 billion (2019 est.)
expenditures: $90.238 billion (2019 est.)

Public debt: 39.5% of GDP (2017 est.)
note: includes publicly guaranteed debt
comparison ranking: 134

Taxes and other revenues: 17.3% (of GDP) (2017 est.)
comparison ranking: 110

Current account balance: $9.491 billion (2017 est.)
$16.28 billion (2016 est.)
comparison ranking: 28

Exports: $110.882 billion (2022 est.)
$82.015 billion (2021 est.)
$46.568 billion (2020 est.)
note: GDP expenditure basis - exports of goods and services in current dollars
comparison ranking: 46

Exports - partners: China 36%, Turkey 20%, Kuwait 6%, Pakistan 5%, India 4% (2022)
note: top five export partners based on percentage share of exports

Exports - commodities: ethylene polymers, refined copper, acyclic alcohols, aluminum, natural gas (2022)
note: top five export commodities based on value in dollars

Imports: $102.47 billion (2022 est.)
$77.33 billion (2021 est.)
$58.461 billion (2020 est.)
note: GDP expenditure basis - imports of goods and services in current dollars
comparison ranking: 46

Imports - partners: China 28%, UAE 19%, Brazil 13%, Turkey 9%, India 6% (2022)
note: top five import partners based on percentage share of imports

Imports - commodities: broadcasting equipment, corn, soybeans, vehicle parts/accessories, rice (2022)
note: top five import commodities based on value in dollars

Reserves of foreign exchange and gold: $120.6 billion (31 December 2017 est.)
$133.7 billion (31 December 2016 est.)
comparison ranking: 23

Debt - external: $269.852 million (2022 est.)
note: present value of external debt in current US dollars
comparison ranking: 97

Exchange rates: Iranian rials (IRR) per US dollar -

Exchange rates: 42,000 (2023 est.)
42,000 (2022 est.)
42,000 (2021 est.)
42,000 (2020 est.)
42,000 (2019 est.)

ENERGY

Electricity access: *electrification - total population:* 100% (2022 est.)

Electricity: *installed generating capacity:* 80.74 million kW (2022 est.)
consumption: 315.843 billion kWh (2022 est.)
exports: 9.47 billion kWh (2022 est.)
imports: 2.273 billion kWh (2022 est.)
transmission/distribution losses: 37.65 billion kWh (2022 est.)
comparison rankings: transmission/distribution losses 202; imports 58; exports 25; consumption 12; installed generating capacity 18

Electricity generation sources: *fossil fuels:* 93.5% of total installed capacity (2022 est.)
nuclear: 1.7% of total installed capacity (2022 est.)
solar: 0.2% of total installed capacity (2022 est.)
wind: 0.2% of total installed capacity (2022 est.)
hydroelectricity: 4.4% of total installed capacity (2022 est.)

Nuclear energy: Number of operational nuclear reactors: 1 (2023)

Number of nuclear reactors under construction: 1 (2023)

Net capacity of operational nuclear reactors: 0.92GW (2023 est.)

Percent of total electricity production: 1.7% (2023 est.)

Coal: *production:* 2.791 million metric tons (2022 est.)
consumption: 3.531 million metric tons (2022 est.)
exports: 261,000 metric tons (2022 est.)
imports: 852,000 metric tons (2022 est.)
proven reserves: 1.203 billion metric tons (2022 est.)

Petroleum: *total petroleum production:* 3.985 million bbl/day (2023 est.)
refined petroleum consumption: 2.136 million bbl/day (2022 est.)
crude oil estimated reserves: 208.6 billion barrels (2021 est.)

Natural gas: *production:* 263.28 billion cubic meters (2022 est.)
consumption: 244.89 billion cubic meters (2022 est.)
exports: 19.251 billion cubic meters (2022 est.)
imports: 2.788 billion cubic meters (2022 est.)
proven reserves: 33.987 trillion cubic meters (2021 est.)

Carbon dioxide emissions: 750.453 million metric tonnes of CO2 (2022 est.)
from coal and metallurgical coke: 6.714 million metric tonnes of CO2 (2022 est.)
from petroleum and other liquids: 259.198 million metric tonnes of CO2 (2022 est.)
from consumed natural gas: 484.541 million metric tonnes of CO2 (2022 est.)
comparison ranking: total emissions 6

Energy consumption per capita: 152.479 million Btu/person (2022 est.)
comparison ranking: 25

COMMUNICATIONS

Telephones - fixed lines: *total subscriptions:* 29.342 million (2022 est.)
subscriptions per 100 inhabitants: 33 (2022 est.)
comparison ranking: total subscriptions 7

Telephones - mobile cellular: *total subscriptions:* 145.668 million (2022 est.)
subscriptions per 100 inhabitants: 165 (2022 est.)
comparison ranking: total subscriptions 12

Telecommunication systems: *general assessment:* Iran's telecom infrastructure has suffered from sanctions in recent years, which prevented the import of equipment and devices and encouraged widespread smuggling, with a consequent loss of tax revenue; to address this, the government introduced a device registration scheme, and bolstered the capacity for domestically manufactured mobile phones; companies have invested in broadening the reach of their LTE networks, which has increased network capacity and improved the quality of mobile broadband services; the country is also looking to 5G; the sector is still limited by low frequency bands; the government is addressing this with plans to reallocate the 3.5GHz band for 5G use; Iran is keen to grow its digital economy; Iran offers significant opportunities for growth in the telecoms sector; the country has one of the largest populations in the Middle East, and there is a high proportion of youthful, tech savvy users having considerable demand for both fixed and mobile telecom services; companies are offering national roaming to improve services in rural areas (2022)
domestic: approximately 33 per 100 for fixed-line and 155 per 100 for mobile-cellular subscriptions (2021)
international: country code - 98; landing points for Kuwait-Iran, GBICS & MENA, FALCON, OMRAN/3PEG Cable System, POI and UAE-Iran submarine fiber-optic cable to the Middle East, Africa and India; (TAE) fiber-optic line runs from Azerbaijan through the northern portion of Iran to Turkmenistan with expansion to Georgia and Azerbaijan; HF radio and microwave radio relay to Turkey, Azerbaijan, Pakistan, Afghanistan, Turkmenistan, Syria, Kuwait, Tajikistan, and Uzbekistan; satellite earth stations - 13 (9 Intelsat and 4 Inmarsat) (2019)

Broadcast media: state-run broadcast media with no private, independent broadcasters; Islamic Republic of Iran Broadcasting (IRIB), the state-run TV broadcaster, operates more than 60 television channels, more than 50 radio stations, and dozens of newspapers and websites; about 20 foreign Persian-language TV stations broadcasting on satellite TV are capable of being seen in Iran; satellite dishes are illegal and, while their use is subjectively tolerated, authorities confiscate satellite dishes from time to time; most major international broadcasters transmit to Iran (2023)

Internet country code: .ir

Internet users: *total:* 69.52 million (2021 est.)
percent of population: 79% (2021 est.)
comparison ranking: total 13

Broadband - fixed subscriptions: *total:* 9,564,195 (2020 est.)
subscriptions per 100 inhabitants: 11 (2020 est.)
comparison ranking: total 21

TRANSPORTATION

National air transport system: *number of registered air carriers:* 22 (2020)
inventory of registered aircraft operated by air carriers: 237
annual passenger traffic on registered air carriers: 25,604,871 (2018)
annual freight traffic on registered air carriers: 290.74 million (2018) mt-km

Civil aircraft registration country code prefix: EP

Airports: 173 (2024)
comparison ranking: 33

Heliports: 89 (2024)

Pipelines: 7 km condensate, 973 km condensate/gas, 20,794 km gas, 570 km liquid petroleum gas, 8,625 km oil, 7,937 km refined products (2013)

Railways: *total:* 8,483.5 km (2014)
standard gauge: 8,389.5 km (2014) 1.435-m gauge (189.5 km electrified)
broad gauge: 94 km (2014) 1.676-m gauge
comparison ranking: total 25

Roadways: *total:* 223,485 km
paved: 195,618 km
unpaved: 27,867 km (2016)
comparison ranking: total 21

Waterways: 850 km (2012) (on Karun River; some navigation on Lake Urmia)
comparison ranking: 76

Merchant marine: *total:* 965 (2023)
by type: bulk carrier 32, container ship 28, general cargo 398, oil tanker 86, other 421
comparison ranking: total 24

Ports: *total ports:* 18 (2024)
large: 0
medium: 4
small: 6
very small: 8
ports with oil terminals: 13
key ports: Abadan, Bandar Abbas, Bushehr, Khorramshahr

MILITARY AND SECURITY

Military and security forces: *the military forces of Iran are divided between the Islamic Republic of Iran Regular Forces (Artesh) and the Islamic Revolutionary Guard Corps (Sepah):*

Islamic Republic of Iran Regular Forces or Islamic Republic of Iran Army (Artesh): Ground Forces, Navy (includes marines), Air Force, Air Defense Forces

Islamic Revolutionary Guard Corps (IRGC or Sepah): Ground Forces, Navy (includes marines), Aerospace Force (controls strategic missile force), Qods Force (aka Quds Force; special operations), Cyber Electronic Command, Basij Paramilitary Forces

Ministry of Interior: Law Enforcement Command
Ministry of Intelligence and Security (2024)
note 1: the Artesh Navy operates Iran's larger warships and operates in the Gulf of Oman, the Caspian Sea, and deep waters in the region and beyond; the IRGC Navy has responsibility for the closer-in waters of the Persian Gulf and Strait of Hormuz
note 2: the Basij is a volunteer paramilitary group under the IRGC with local organizations across the country, which sometimes acts as an auxiliary law enforcement unit for the IRGC; it is formally known as the Organization for the Mobilization of the Oppressed and also known as the Popular Mobilization Army
note 3: the Ministry of Intelligence and Security and law enforcement forces under the Interior Ministry, which report to the president, and the IRGC, which reports to the supreme leader, share responsibility for law enforcement and maintaining order
note 4: the Law Enforcement Command (FARAJA) is the uniformed police of Iran and includes branches for public security, traffic control, anti-narcotics, special forces (riot control, counterterrorism, hostage rescue, etc), intelligence, and criminal investigations; it has responsibility for border security (Border Guard Command)

Military expenditures: 2.1% of GDP (2023 est.)
2.5% of GDP (2022 est.)
2.3% of GDP (2021 est.)
2.1% of GDP (2020 est.)
2.5% of GDP (2019 est.)
comparison ranking: 62

Military and security service personnel strengths: information varies; up to 600,000 active armed forces personnel; approximately 400,000 Islamic Republic of Iran Regular Forces (350,000 Ground Forces; 18,000 Navy; 40,000 Air Force/Air Defense Forces); approximately 150-190,000 Islamic Revolutionary Guard Corps (100-150,000 Ground Forces; 20,000 Navy; 15,000 Aerospace Force; 5-15,000 Qods Force); estimated 90,000 active Basij Paramilitary Forces (2023)

Military equipment inventories and acquisitions: the Iranian military's inventory includes a mix of domestically produced and mostly older foreign equipment largely of Chinese, Russian, Soviet, and US origin (US equipment acquired prior to the Islamic Revolution in 1979); it also has some military equipment from North Korea, including midget submarines and ballistic missiles; in recent years, Iran has received some newer equipment from Russia; Iran has a defense industry with the capacity to develop, produce, support, and sustain air, land, missile, and naval weapons programs (2024)

Military service age and obligation: military service is compulsory for all Iranian men 18-19 to approximately age 40; 16 for voluntary military service (may be as low as 15 for the Basij); conscript military service obligation is up to 24 months, depending on the location of service (soldiers serving in places of high security risk and deprived areas serve shorter terms); women exempted from military service (2023)
note: conscripts serve in the Artesh, IRGC, and Law Enforcement, while Navy and Air/Air Defense Force personnel are primarily volunteers

Military deployments: continues to maintain a military presence in Syria reportedly of a few thousand personnel, mostly of special operations and IRGC forces (2024)
note: Iran has recruited, trained, and funded thousands of Syrian and foreign fighters to support the ASAD regime during the Syrian civil war

Military - note: the Islamic Revolutionary Guard Corps (IRGC) was formed in May 1979 in the immediate aftermath of Shah Mohammad Reza PAHLAVI's fall, as leftists, nationalists, and Islamists jockeyed for power; while the interim prime minister controlled the government and state institutions, such as the Army, followers of Ayatollah Ruhollah KHOMEINI organized counterweights, including the IRGC, to protect the Islamic revolution; the IRGC's command structure bypassed the elected president and went directly to KHOMEINI; the IRGC played a critical role in helping KHOMEINI consolidate power in the aftermath of the 1979 revolution, and it ensured that KHOMEINI's Islamic revolutionary vision prevailed against domestic challenges from nationalists and leftist factions in the scramble for control after the Shah's departure
the Iran-Iraq War (1980–88) transformed the IRGC into more of a conventional fighting force with its own ground, air, naval, and special forces, plus control over Iran's strategic missile and rocket forces; today, the IRGC is a highly institutionalized and parallel military force to Iran's regular armed forces (Artesh); it is heavily involved in internal security and has significant influence in the political and economic spheres of Iranian society, as well as Iran's foreign policy; on the economic front, it owns factories and corporations and subsidiaries in banking, infrastructure, housing, airlines, tourism and other sectors; its special operations forces, known as the Qods/Quds Force, specialize in foreign missions and have provided advice, funding, guidance, material support, training, and weapons to militants in countries such as Afghanistan, Iraq, Syria, and Yemen, as well as extremist groups, including HAMAS, Hizballah, Kata'ib Hizballah, and Palestine Islamic Jihad; the Qods Force also conducts intelligence and reconnaissance operations; note - both the IRGC and the Qods Force have been designated as foreign terrorist organizations by the US
the Supreme Council for National Security (SCNS) is the senior-most body for formulating Iran's foreign and security policy; it is formally chaired by the president, who also appoints the SCNS secretary; its members include the speaker of the Majles, the head of the judiciary, the chief of the Armed Forces General Staff (chief of defense or CHOD), the commanders of the Artesh (regular forces) and IRGC, and the ministers of defense, foreign affairs, interior, and intelligence; the SCNS reports to the supreme leader; the supreme leader is the commander-in-chief of the armed forces
the Iranian Armed Forces are divided between the regular forces (Artesh) and the IRGC; the Artesh primarily focuses on defending Iran's borders and territorial waters from external threats, while the IRGC has a broader mission to defend the Iranian revolution from any foreign or domestic threat; in 1989, Iran established the Armed Forces General Staff to coordinate military action across both the Artesh and the IRGC; Iran also has a joint military headquarters, the Khatam ol-Anbia Central Headquarters, to command the Artesh and IRGC in wartime (2024)

SPACE

Space agency/agencies: Iranian Space Agency (ISA; created in 2003 from merging the activities of the Iranian Remote Sensing Center and some of the activities of the Telecommunications Company of Iran); Iran Space Research Center (established, 2000); Ministry of Defense and Armed Forces Logistics; Aerospace Industries Organization (AIO; under the Ministry of Defense); Islamic Revolutionary Guard Corps (IRGC) Space Command (formed in 2020) (2024)

Space launch site(s): Imam Khomeini Space Center (aka Semnan Space Center; Semnan province); Shahroud Space Center (IGRC military base; Semnan Province); Qom Space Center (Qom Province); inaugurated its first space monitoring center located near Delijan (Markazi Province) in 2013 (2024)

Space program overview: has an ambitious civil and military space program focused on acquiring and operating satellites and developing indigenous satellite/space launch vehicles (SLV); designs, builds, and operates satellites, including communications, remote sensing (RS), and scientific; manufactures and operates SLVs; researching and developing other space-related capabilities and technologies in such areas as telecommunications, RS, navigation, and space situational awareness; UN Security Council and other international sanctions against Iran's weapons of mass destruction program have severely limited Iran's cooperation with foreign space agencies and commercial space industries; in recent years, however, it has cooperated with North Korea and Russia on space issues; Iran has also had relations with regional and international space organizations, such as the Asia-Pacific Space Cooperation Organization and the International Telecommunications Satellite Organization; it was a founding member of the UN Committee on the Peaceful Uses of Outer Space (COPUOS) established in 1958 (2024)
note: further details about the key activities, programs, and milestones of the country's space program, as well as government spending estimates on the space sector, appear in the Space Programs reference guide

TERRORISM

Terrorist group(s): Islamic Revolutionary Guard Corps (IRGC)/Qods Force; Islamic State of Iraq and ash-Sham (ISIS); Jaysh al Adl (Jundallah); Kurdistan Workers' Party (PKK); al-Qa'ida
note: details about the history, aims, leadership, organization, areas of operation, tactics, targets, weapons, size, and sources of support of the group(s) appear(s) in the Terrorism reference guide

TRANSNATIONAL ISSUES

Refugees and internally displaced persons: *refugees (country of origin):* 500,000 undocumented Afghans, 750,000 Afghan refugee card holders, 12,000 Iraqi refugee card holders (2022)
stateless persons: 34 (mid-year 2021)

Trafficking in persons: tier rating: Tier 3 — Iran does not fully meet the minimum standards for the elimination of trafficking and is not making significant efforts to do so, therefore, Iran remained on Tier 3; for more details, go to: https://www.state.gov/reports/2024- trafficking-in-persons-report/iran/

Illicit drugs: significant transit and destination country for opiates and cannabis products mainly from Afghanistan and Pakistan; produces and consumes methamphetamine and traffics it to international markets; one of the primary transshipment routes for Southwest Asian heroin to Europe; opium and cannabis most widely used drugs domestically along with increase in crystal methamphetamine

IRAQ

INTRODUCTION

Background: Formerly part of the Ottoman Empire, Iraq was occupied by the United Kingdom during World War I and was declared a League of Nations mandate under UK administration in 1920. Iraq attained its independence as a kingdom in 1932. It was proclaimed a republic in 1958 after a coup overthrew the monarchy, but in actuality, a series of strongmen ruled the country until 2003. The last was SADDAM Hussein, from 1979 to 2003. Territorial disputes with Iran led to an inconclusive and costly war from 1980 to 1988. In 1990, Iraq seized Kuwait but was expelled by US-led UN coalition forces during the two-month-long Gulf War of 1991. After Iraq's expulsion, the UN Security Council (UNSC) required Iraq to scrap all weapons of mass destruction and long-range missiles and to allow UN verification inspections. Continued Iraqi noncompliance with UNSC resolutions led to the Second Gulf War in 2003, when US-led forces ousted the SADDAM regime.

In 2005, Iraqis approved a constitution in a national referendum and elected a 275-member Council of Representatives (COR). The COR approved most of the cabinet ministers, marking the transition to Iraq's first constitutional government in nearly a half-century. Iraq's constitution also established the Kurdistan Regional Government (KRG), a semi-autonomous region that administers the governorates of Erbil, Dahuk, and As Sulaymaniyah. Iraq has held four national legislative elections since 2006, most recently in 2021. The COR approved Mohammad Shia' al-SUDANI as prime minister in 2022. Iraq has repeatedly postponed elections for provincial councils – last held in 2013 – and since 2019, the prime minister has had the authority to appoint governors rather than provincial councils.

Between 2014 and 2017, Iraq fought a military campaign against the Islamic State of Iraq and ash-Sham (ISIS) to recapture territory the group seized in 2014. In 2017, then-Prime Minister Haydar al-ABADI publicly declared victory against ISIS, although military operations against the group continue in rural areas. Also in 2017, Baghdad forcefully seized disputed territories across central and northern Iraq from the KRG, after a non-binding Kurdish independence referendum.

GEOGRAPHY

Location: Middle East, bordering the Persian Gulf, between Iran and Kuwait

Geographic coordinates: 33 00 N, 44 00 E

Map references: Middle East

Area: *total:* 438,317 sq km
land: 437,367 sq km
water: 950 sq km
comparison ranking: total 60

Area - comparative: slightly more than three times the size of New York state

Land boundaries: *total:* 3,809 km
border countries (6): Iran 1,599 km; Jordan 179 km; Kuwait 254 km; Saudi Arabia 811 km; Syria 599 km; Turkey 367 km

Coastline: 58 km

Maritime claims: *territorial sea:* 12 nm
continental shelf: not specified

Climate: mostly desert; mild to cool winters with dry, hot, cloudless summers; northern mountainous regions along Iranian and Turkish borders experience cold winters with occasionally heavy snows that melt in early spring, sometimes causing extensive flooding in central and southern Iraq

Terrain: mostly broad plains; reedy marshes along Iranian border in south with large flooded areas; mountains along borders with Iran and Turkey

Elevation: *highest point:* Cheekha Dar (Kurdish for "Black Tent") 3,611 m
lowest point: Persian Gulf 0 m
mean elevation: 312 m

Natural resources: petroleum, natural gas, phosphates, sulfur

Land use: *agricultural land:* 18.1% (2018 est.)
arable land: 8.4% (2018 est.)
permanent crops: 0.5% (2018 est.)
permanent pasture: 9.2% (2018 est.)
forest: 1.9% (2018 est.)
other: 80% (2018 est.)

Irrigated land: 35,250 sq km (2012)

Major lakes (area sq km): *fresh water lake(s):* Lake Hammar - 1,940 sq km

Major rivers (by length in km): Euphrates river mouth (shared with Turkey[s], Syria, and Iran) - 3,596 km; Tigris river mouth (shared with Turkey[s], Syria, and Iran) - 1,950 km; the Tigris and Euphrates join to form the Shatt al Arab
note – [s] after country name indicates river source; [m] after country name indicates river mouth

Major watersheds (area sq km): Indian Ocean drainage: *(Persian Gulf)* Tigris and Euphrates (918,044 sq km)

Major aquifers: Arabian Aquifer System

Population distribution: population is concentrated in the north, center, and eastern parts of the country, with many of the larger urban agglomerations found along extensive parts of the Tigris and Euphrates Rivers; much of the western and southern areas are either lightly populated or uninhabited

Natural hazards: dust storms; sandstorms; floods

Geography - note: strategic location on Shatt al Arab waterway and at the head of the Persian Gulf

PEOPLE AND SOCIETY

Population: *total:* 42,083,436
male: 21,193,356
female: 20,890,080 (2024 est.)
comparison rankings: female 35; male 35; total 35

Nationality: *noun:* Iraqi(s)
adjective: Iraqi

Ethnic groups: Arab 75-80%, Kurdish 15-20%, other 5% (includes Turkmen, Yezidi, Shabak, Kaka'i, Bedouin, Romani, Assyrian, Circassian, Sabaean-Mandaean, Persian)
note: data is a 1987 government estimate; no more recent reliable numbers are available

Languages: Arabic (official), Kurdish (official); Turkmen (a Turkish dialect) and Syriac (Neo-Aramaic) are recognized as official languages where native speakers of these languages are present
major-language sample(s):
كتاب حقائق العالم، أحسن مصدر للمعلومات الأساسية
(Arabic)

راستیەکانی جیهان، باشترین سەرچاوەیە بۆ زانیارییە بنەڕەتییەکان (Kurdish)

Religions: Muslim (official) 95-98% (Shia 61-64%, Sunni 29-34%), Christian 1% (includes Catholic, Orthodox, Protestant, Assyrian Church of the East), other 1-4% (2015 est.)
note: the last census in Iraq was in 1997; while there has been voluntary relocation of many Christian families to northern Iraq, the overall Christian population has decreased at least 50% and perhaps as much as 90% since 2003, according to US Embassy estimates, with many fleeing to Syria, Jordan, and Lebanon

Age structure: *0-14 years:* 34.6% (male 7,447,266/female 7,130,883)
15-64 years: 61.7% (male 13,064,516/female 12,907,702)
65 years and over: 3.6% (2024 est.) (male 681,574/female 851,495)

Dependency ratios: *total dependency ratio:* 71
youth dependency ratio: 65.2
elderly dependency ratio: 5.8
potential support ratio: 17.1 (2021 est.)

Median age: *total:* 22.4 years (2024 est.)
male: 22 years
female: 22.7 years
comparison ranking: total 184

Population growth rate: 1.99% (2024 est.)
comparison ranking: 41

Birth rate: 23.7 births/1,000 population (2024 est.)
comparison ranking: 48

Death rate: 3.9 deaths/1,000 population (2024 est.)
comparison ranking: 217

Net migration rate: 0 migrant(s)/1,000 population (2024 est.)
comparison ranking: 84

Population distribution: population is concentrated in the north, center, and eastern parts of the country, with many of the larger urban agglomerations found along extensive parts of the Tigris and Euphrates Rivers; much of the western and southern areas are either lightly populated or uninhabited

Urbanization: *urban population:* 71.6% of total population (2023)
rate of urbanization: 2.91% annual rate of change (2020-25 est.)

Major urban areas - population: 7.711 million BAGHDAD (capital), 1.792 million Mosul, 1.448 million Basra, 1.075 million Kirkuk, 958,000 Najaf, 897,000 Erbil (2023)

Sex ratio: *at birth:* 1.05 male(s)/female
0-14 years: 1.04 male(s)/female
15-64 years: 1.01 male(s)/female
65 years and over: 0.8 male(s)/female
total population: 1.02 male(s)/female (2024 est.)

Maternal mortality ratio: 76 deaths/100,000 live births (2020 est.)
comparison ranking: 78

Infant mortality rate: *total:* 18.7 deaths/1,000 live births (2024 est.)
male: 20.4 deaths/1,000 live births
female: 17 deaths/1,000 live births
comparison ranking: total 81

Life expectancy at birth: *total population:* 73.7 years (2024 est.)
male: 71.9 years
female: 75.7 years
comparison ranking: total population 146

Total fertility rate: 3.1 children born/woman (2024 est.)
comparison ranking: 47

Gross reproduction rate: 1.51 (2024 est.)

Contraceptive prevalence rate: 52.8% (2018)

Drinking water source: *improved: urban:* 100% of population
rural: 97.4% of population
total: 99.3% of population
unimproved: urban: 0% of population
rural: 2.6% of population
total: 0.7% of population (2020 est.)

Current health expenditure: 5.1% of GDP (2020)

Physician density: 0.97 physicians/1,000 population (2020)

Hospital bed density: 1.3 beds/1,000 population (2017)

Sanitation facility access: *improved: urban:* 100% of population
rural: 100% of population
total: 100% of population

Obesity - adult prevalence rate: 30.4% (2016)
comparison ranking: 23

Alcohol consumption per capita: *total:* 0.16 liters of pure alcohol (2019 est.)
beer: 0.11 liters of pure alcohol (2019 est.)
wine: 0 liters of pure alcohol (2019 est.)
spirits: 0.04 liters of pure alcohol (2019 est.)
other alcohols: 0 liters of pure alcohol (2019 est.)
comparison ranking: total 174

Tobacco use: *total:* 18.5% (2020 est.)
male: 35.1% (2020 est.)
female: 1.8% (2020 est.)
comparison ranking: total 91

Children under the age of 5 years underweight: 3.9% (2018)
comparison ranking: 80

Currently married women (ages 15-49): 65.5% (2023 est.)

Child marriage: *women married by age 15:* 7.2%
women married by age 18: 27.9% (2018 est.)

Education expenditures: 4.7% of GDP (2016)
comparison ranking: 87

Literacy: *definition:* age 15 and over can read and write
total population: 85.6%
male: 91.2%
female: 79.9% (2017)

ENVIRONMENT

Environment - current issues: government water control projects drained most of the inhabited marsh areas east of An Nasiriyah by drying up or diverting the feeder streams and rivers; a once sizable population of Marsh Arabs, who inhabited these areas for thousands of years, has been displaced; furthermore, the destruction of the natural habitat poses serious threats to the area's wildlife populations; inadequate supplies of potable water; soil degradation (salination) and erosion; desertification; military and industrial infrastructure has released heavy metals and other hazardous substances into the air, soil, and groundwater; major sources of environmental damage are effluents from oil refineries, factory and sewage discharges into rivers, fertilizer and chemical contamination of the soil, and industrial air pollution in urban areas

Environment - international agreements: *party to:* Biodiversity, Climate Change, Climate Change-Kyoto Protocol, Comprehensive Nuclear Test Ban, Desertification, Endangered Species, Hazardous Wastes, Law of the Sea, Nuclear Test Ban, Ozone Layer Protection, Ship Pollution, Wetlands
signed, but not ratified: Climate Change-Paris Agreement, Environmental Modification

Climate: mostly desert; mild to cool winters with dry, hot, cloudless summers; northern mountainous regions along Iranian and Turkish borders experience cold winters with occasionally heavy snows that melt in early spring, sometimes causing extensive flooding in central and southern Iraq

Urbanization: *urban population:* 71.6% of total population (2023)
rate of urbanization: 2.91% annual rate of change (2020-25 est.)

Food insecurity: *severe localized food insecurity: due to civil conflict and economic slowdown* - the 2022 Humanitarian Needs Overview identified 2.5 million people in need of humanitarian assistance, of which 960,000 have acute humanitarian needs; while the number of people in need remained similar to the previous year, the severity of those needs increased, largely due to the impact of the COVID-19 pandemic on top of an existing humanitarian crisis, leading to a 35% increase in the number of people in acute need; more than half of these are concentrated in the governorates of Nineveh and Anbar; the number of severely food insecure people is estimated at about 435,000, while 731,000 are vulnerable to food insecurity (2022)

Revenue from forest resources: 0% of GDP (2018 est.)
comparison ranking: 188

Revenue from coal: 0% of GDP (2018 est.)
comparison ranking: 136

Air pollutants: *particulate matter emissions:* 39.29 micrograms per cubic meter (2019 est.)
carbon dioxide emissions: 190.06 megatons (2016 est.)
methane emissions: 17.44 megatons (2020 est.)

Waste and recycling: *municipal solid waste generated annually:* 13.14 million tons (2015 est.)

Major lakes (area sq km): *fresh water lake(s):* Lake Hammar - 1,940 sq km

Major rivers (by length in km): Euphrates river mouth (shared with Turkey[s], Syria, and Iran) - 3,596 km; Tigris river mouth (shared with Turkey[s], Syria, and Iran) - 1,950 km; the Tigris and Euphrates join to form the Shatt al Arab
note – [s] after country name indicates river source; [m] after country name indicates river mouth

Major watersheds (area sq km): Indian Ocean drainage: *(Persian Gulf)* Tigris and Euphrates (918,044 sq km)

Major aquifers: Arabian Aquifer System

Total water withdrawal: *municipal:* 6.9 billion cubic meters (2020 est.)
industrial: 5.49 billion cubic meters (2020 est.)
agricultural: 44.23 billion cubic meters (2020 est.)

Total renewable water resources: 89.86 billion cubic meters (2020 est.)

GOVERNMENT

Country name: *conventional long form:* Republic of Iraq

conventional short form: Iraq
local long form: Jumhuriyat al-Iraq/Komar-i Eraq
local short form: Al Iraq/Eraq
former: Mesopotamia, Mandatory Iraq, Hashemite Kingdom of Iraq
etymology: the name probably derives from "Uruk" (Biblical "Erech"), the ancient Sumerian and Babylonian city on the Euphrates River

Government type: federal parliamentary republic

Capital: *name:* Baghdad
geographic coordinates: 33 20 N, 44 24 E
time difference: UTC+3 (8 hours ahead of Washington, DC, during Standard Time)
etymology: although the origin of the name is disputed, it likely has compound Persian roots with *bagh* and *dad* meaning "god" and "given" respectively to create the meaning of "bestowed by God"

Administrative divisions: 18 governorates (muhafazat, singular - muhafazah (Arabic); parezgakan, singular - parezga (Kurdish)); 'Al Anbar; Al Basrah; Al Muthanna; Al Qadisiyah (Ad Diwaniyah); An Najaf; Arbil (Erbil) (Arabic), Hewler (Kurdish); As Sulaymaniyah (Arabic), Slemani (Kurdish); Babil; Baghdad; Dahuk (Arabic), Dihok (Kurdish); Dhi Qar; Diyala; Karbala'; Kirkuk; Maysan; Ninawa; Salah ad Din; Wasit
note: Iraq's Kurdistan Regional Government administers Arbil, Dahuk, and As Sulaymaniyah (as Hewler, Dihok, and Slemani respectively)

Independence: 3 October 1932 (from League of Nations mandate under British administration); note - on 28 June 2004 the Coalition Provisional Authority transferred sovereignty to the Iraqi Interim Government

National holiday: Independence Day, 3 October (1932); Republic Day, 14 July (1958)

Legal system: mixed legal system of civil and Islamic law

Constitution: *history:* several previous; latest adopted by referendum 15 October 2005
amendments: proposed by the president of the republic and the Council of Minsters collectively, or by one fifth of the Council of Representatives members; passage requires at least two-thirds majority vote by the Council of Representatives, approval by referendum, and ratification by the president; passage of amendments to articles on citizen rights and liberties requires two-thirds majority vote of Council of Representatives members after two successive electoral terms, approval in a referendum, and ratification by the president

International law organization participation: has not submitted an ICJ jurisdiction declaration; non-party state to the ICCt

Citizenship: *citizenship by birth:* no
citizenship by descent only: at least one parent must be a citizen of Iraq
dual citizenship recognized: yes
residency requirement for naturalization: 10 years

Suffrage: 18 years of age; universal

Executive branch: *chief of state:* President Latif RASHID (since 13 October 2022)
head of government: Prime Minister Mohammed Shia al-SUDANI (since 27 October 2022)
cabinet: Council of Ministers proposed by the prime minister, approved by Council of Representatives (COR)
elections/appointments: president indirectly elected by COR to serve a 4-year term (eligible for a second term); COR parliamentary election for president last held on 13 October 2022 (next to be held NA)
election results:
2022: Latif RASHID elected president in second round; COR vote in first round - Latif RASHID (PUK) 157, Barham SALIH (PUK) 99; COR vote in second round - Latif RASHID 167, Barham SALIH 99; Mohammed Shia' al-SUDANI approved as prime minister
2018: Barham SALIH elected president in second round; COR vote in first round - Barham SALIH (PUK) 165, Fuad HUSAYN (KDP) 90; COR vote in second round - Barham SALIH 219, Fuad HUSAYN 22; Adil ABD AL-MAHDI approved as prime minister

Legislative branch: *description:* unicameral Council of Representatives of Iraq (COR) or Majlis an-Nuwwab al-Iraqiyy (329 seats; 320 members directly elected in 83 multi-seat constituencies by single nontransferable vote, 9 seats elected by religious minorities - 5 by Christians, 1 each by Sabaean-Mandaeans, Yazidis, Shabaks andFayli Kurds, and 25% of seats allocated to women; members serve 4-year terms)
elections: last held on 10 October 2021 (next to be held in 2025)
election results: percent of vote by party/coalition - NA; seats by party/coalition - Taqadum 47, State of Law Coalition 43, Al Fatah Alliance 37, Kurdistan Democratic Party 31, Kurdistan Coalition 18, Azm Alliance 16, Imtidad 16, State Forces Alliance 11, Ishraqat Kanun 10, New Generation Movement 9, National Contract Party 8, Tasmim Alliance 7, Babiliyun Movement 3, other 73; composition - men 234, women 95, percentage women 29.2%; note - seat counts reflect updated numbers following the 12 June 2022 Sadrist Trend withdrawal from government formation, and its 73 seats were reallocated to other parties

Judicial branch: *highest court(s):* Federal Supreme Court or FSC (consists of 9 judges); note - court jurisdiction limited to constitutional issues, application of federal laws, ratification of election results for the COR, judicial competency disputes, and disputes between regions or governorates and the central government; Court of Cassation (consists of a court president, 5 vice presidents, and at least 24 judges)
judge selection and term of office: Federal Supreme Court (FSC) judges nominated by the High Judicial Council (HJC) president, the FSC chief justice, the public prosecutor's office chief, and the head of the Judicial Oversight Commission; FSC members required to retire at age 72; Court of Cassation judges appointed by the HJC and confirmed by the Council of Representatives to serve until retirement, nominally at age 63, but can be extended to age 66 by the HJC
subordinate courts: Courts of Appeal (governorate level); civil courts, including first instance, personal status, labor, and customs; criminal courts including felony, misdemeanor, investigative, major crimes, juvenile, and traffic courts

Political parties: Al Fatah Alliance
Azm Alliance
Babiliyun Movement
Imtidad
Ishraqat Konun
Kurdistan Democratic Party
National Contract Party
New Generation Movement
Patriotic Union of Kurdistan
Sadrist Bloc
State Forces Alliance
State of Law Coalition
Taqadum
Tasmim Alliance

International organization participation: ABEDA, AFESD, AIIB, AMF, CAEU, CICA, EITI (compliant country), FAO, G-77, IAEA, IBRD, ICAO, ICRM, IDA, IDB, IFAD, IFC, IFRCS, ILO, IMF, IMO, IMSO, Interpol, IOC, IPU, ISO, ITSO, ITU, LAS, MIGA, NAM, OAPEC, OIC, OPCW, OPEC, PCA, UN, UNCTAD, UNESCO, UNIDO, UNWTO, UPU, WCO, WFTU (NGOs), WHO, WIPO, WMO, WTO (observer)

Diplomatic representation in the US: *chief of mission:* Ambassador Nazar Issa Abdulhadi AL-KHIRULLAH (since 30 June 2023)
chancery: 1801 P Street NW, Washington, DC 20036
telephone: [1] (202) 483-7500
FAX: [1] (202) 462-8815
email address and website:
washington@scrdiraq.gov.iq
https://www.iraqiembassy.us/
consulate(s) general: Detroit, Los Angeles

Diplomatic representation from the US: *chief of mission:* Ambassador Alina L. ROMANOWSKI (since 2 June 2022)
embassy: Al-Kindi Street, International Zone, Baghdad; note - consulate in Al Basrah closed as of 28 September 2018
mailing address: 6060 Baghdad Place, Washington DC 20521-6060
telephone: 0760-030-3000
email address and website:
BaghdadACS@state.gov
https://iq.usembassy.gov/

Flag description: three equal horizontal bands of red (top), white, and black; the Takbir (Arabic expression meaning "God is great") in green Arabic script is centered in the white band; the band colors derive from the Arab Liberation flag and represent oppression (black), overcome through bloody struggle (red), to be replaced by a bright future (white); the Council of Representatives approved this flag in 2008 as a compromise replacement for the Ba'thist SADDAM-era flag
note: similar to the flag of Syria, which has two stars but no script; Yemen, which has a plain white band; and that of Egypt, which has a golden Eagle of Saladin centered in the white band

National symbol(s): golden eagle; national colors: red, white, black

National anthem: *name:* "Mawtini" (My Homeland)
lyrics/music: Ibrahim TOUQAN/Mohammad FLAYFEL
note: adopted 2004; following the ouster of SADDAM Husayn, Iraq adopted "Mawtini," a popular folk song throughout the Arab world; also serves as an unofficial anthem of the Palestinian people

National heritage: *total World Heritage Sites:* 6 (5 cultural, 1 mixed)
selected World Heritage Site locales: Ashur (Qal'at Sherqat) (c); Babylon (c); Erbil Citadel (c); Hatra (c); Samarra Archaeological City (c); The Ahwar (Marshland) of Southern Iraq: Refuge of Biodiversity and the Relict Landscape of the Mesopotamian Cities (m)

ECONOMY

Economic overview: highly oil-dependent Middle Eastern economy; fiscal sustainability subject to fluctuation in oil prices; rising public confidence in economic conditions; import-dependent for most sectors; persistent challenges of corruption, informal markets, banking access, and political fragility

Real GDP (purchasing power parity): $572.939 billion (2023 est.)
$590.267 billion (2022 est.)
$548.372 billion (2021 est.)
note: data in 2021 dollars
comparison ranking: 45

Real GDP growth rate: -2.94% (2023 est.)
7.64% (2022 est.)
1.5% (2021 est.)
note: annual GDP % growth based on constant local currency
comparison ranking: 209

Real GDP per capita: $12,600 (2023 est.)
$13,300 (2022 est.)
$12,600 (2021 est.)
note: data in 2021 dollars
comparison ranking: 136

GDP (official exchange rate): $250.843 billion (2023 est.)
note: data in current dollars at official exchange rate

Inflation rate (consumer prices): 4.99% (2022 est.)
6.04% (2021 est.)
0.57% (2020 est.)
note: annual % change based on consumer prices
comparison ranking: 107

Credit ratings: Fitch rating: B- (2015)

Moody's rating: Caa1 (2017)

Standard & Poors rating: B- (2015)
note: The year refers to the year in which the current credit rating was first obtained.

GDP - composition, by sector of origin: *agriculture:* 2.8% (2023 est.)
industry: 55.6% (2023 est.)
services: 42.3% (2023 est.)
note: figures may not total 100% due to non-allocated consumption not captured in sector-reported data
comparison rankings: services 185; industry 8; agriculture 144

GDP - composition, by end use: *household consumption:* 40.3% (2021 est.)
government consumption: 17.7% (2021 est.)
investment in fixed capital: 10.1% (2021 est.)
investment in inventories: 11.3% (2021 est.)
exports of goods and services: 37.3% (2021 est.)
imports of goods and services: -24.2% (2021 est.)
note: figures may not total 100% due to rounding or gaps in data collection

Agricultural products: wheat, dates, tomatoes, maize, watermelons, grapes, potatoes, milk, cucumbers/gherkins, eggplants (2022)
note: top ten agricultural products based on tonnage

Industries: petroleum, chemicals, textiles, leather, construction materials, food processing, fertilizer, metal fabrication/processing

Industrial production growth rate: -6.34% (2023 est.)
note: annual % change in industrial value added based on constant local currency
comparison ranking: 202

Labor force: 11.812 million (2023 est.)
note: number of people ages 15 or older who are employed or seeking work
comparison ranking: 50

Unemployment rate: 15.53% (2023 est.)
15.59% (2022 est.)
16.17% (2021 est.)
note: % of labor force seeking employment
comparison ranking: 192

Youth unemployment rate (ages 15-24): *total:* 32.2% (2023 est.)
male: 27.8% (2023 est.)
female: 62% (2023 est.)
note: % of labor force ages 15-24 seeking employment
comparison ranking: total 22

Population below poverty line: 23% (2014 est.)

Gini Index coefficient - distribution of family income: (2012 est.)

Average household expenditures: *on food:* 28.8% of household expenditures (2022 est.)
on alcohol and tobacco: 4.3% of household expenditures (2022 est.)

Remittances: 0.35% of GDP (2023 est.)
0.38% of GDP (2022 est.)
0.4% of GDP (2021 est.)
note: personal transfers and compensation between resident and non-resident individuals/households/entities

Budget: *revenues:* $90.204 billion (2019 est.)
expenditures: $64.512 billion (2019 est.)
note: central government revenues and expenses (excluding grants/extrabudgetary units/social security funds) converted to US dollars at average official exchange rate for year indicated

Public debt: 27.44% of GDP (2018 est.)
note: central government debt as a % of GDP
comparison ranking: 173

Taxes and other revenues: 1.34% (of GDP) (2019 est.)
note: central government tax revenue as a % of GDP
comparison ranking: 206

Current account balance: $58.01 billion (2022 est.)
$24.565 billion (2021 est.)
-$6.306 billion (2020 est.)
note: balance of payments - net trade and primary/secondary income in current dollars
comparison ranking: 9

Exports: $127.079 billion (2022 est.)
$78.261 billion (2021 est.)
$50.666 billion (2020 est.)
note: balance of payments - exports of goods and services in current dollars
comparison ranking: 42

Exports - partners: India 32%, China 28%, US 8%, South Korea 7%, Greece 5% (2022)
note: top five export partners based on percentage share of exports

Exports - commodities: crude petroleum, refined petroleum, gold, petroleum coke, natural gas (2022)
note: top five export commodities based on value in dollars

Imports: $69.162 billion (2022 est.)
$50.707 billion (2021 est.)
$54.865 billion (2020 est.)
note: balance of payments - imports of goods and services in current dollars
comparison ranking: 58

Imports - partners: UAE 32%, China 21%, Turkey 20%, India 4%, South Korea 2% (2022)
note: top five import partners based on percentage share of imports

Imports - commodities: refined petroleum, broadcasting equipment, cars, jewelry, garments (2022)
note: top five import commodities based on value in dollars

Reserves of foreign exchange and gold: $112.233 billion (2023 est.)
$97.009 billion (2022 est.)
$64.231 billion (2021 est.)
note: holdings of gold (year-end prices)/foreign exchange/special drawing rights in current dollars
comparison ranking: 34

Debt - external: $15.065 billion (2022 est.)
note: present value of external debt in current US dollars
comparison ranking: 30

Exchange rates: Iraqi dinars (IQD) per US dollar -

Exchange rates: 1,312.5 (2023 est.)
1,450 (2022 est.)
1,450 (2021 est.)
1,192 (2020 est.)
1,182 (2019 est.)

ENERGY

Electricity access: *electrification - total population:* 100% (2022 est.)

Electricity: *installed generating capacity:* 31.339 million kW (2022 est.)
consumption: 65.908 billion kWh (2022 est.)
imports: 3.534 billion kWh (2022 est.)
transmission/distribution losses: 71.17 billion kWh (2022 est.)
comparison rankings: transmission/distribution losses 206; imports 53; consumption 44; installed generating capacity 36

Electricity generation sources: *fossil fuels:* 98% of total installed capacity (2022 est.)
hydroelectricity: 2% of total installed capacity (2022 est.)

Coal: *imports:* 3,000 metric tons (2022 est.)

Petroleum: *total petroleum production:* 4.437 million bbl/day (2023 est.)
refined petroleum consumption: 918,000 bbl/day (2022 est.)
crude oil estimated reserves: 145.019 billion barrels (2021 est.)

Natural gas: *production:* 9.86 billion cubic meters (2022 est.)
consumption: 19.298 billion cubic meters (2022 est.)
imports: 9.438 billion cubic meters (2022 est.)
proven reserves: 3.729 trillion cubic meters (2021 est.)

Carbon dioxide emissions: 156.892 million metric tonnes of CO_2 (2022 est.)
from coal and metallurgical coke: 6,000 metric tonnes of CO_2 (2022 est.)
from petroleum and other liquids: 119.027 million metric tonnes of CO_2 (2022 est.)
from consumed natural gas: 37.858 million metric tonnes of CO_2 (2022 est.)
comparison ranking: total emissions 33

Energy consumption per capita: 57.702 million Btu/person (2022 est.)
comparison ranking: 85

COMMUNICATIONS

Telephones - fixed lines: *total subscriptions:* 2.392 million (2022 est.)
subscriptions per 100 inhabitants: 5 (2022 est.)
comparison ranking: total subscriptions 47

Telephones - mobile cellular: *total subscriptions:* 43.688 million (2022 est.)
subscriptions per 100 inhabitants: 98 (2022 est.)
comparison ranking: total subscriptions 39

Telecommunication systems: *general assessment:* civil stability has made it easier for mobile and fixed-line operators to rebuild telecom services and infrastructure damaged during previous periods of violence; the government extended the licenses held by the MNOs for an additional three years to compensate for the chaos and destruction caused between 2014 and 2017 when Islamic State controlled many areas of the country; the companies have struggled to develop LTE services; most services are still based on GSM and 3G, except in Iraq's Kurdistan region where LTE is more widely available (2022)
domestic: about 7 per 100 for fixed-line and 86 per 100 for mobile-cellular subscriptions (2021)
international: country code - 964; landing points for FALCON, and GBICS/MENA submarine cables providing connections to the Middle East, Africa and India; satellite earth stations - 4 (2 Intelsat - 1 Atlantic Ocean and 1 Indian Ocean, 1 Intersputnik - Atlantic Ocean region, and 1 Arabsat (inoperative)); local microwave radio relay connects border regions to Jordan, Kuwait, Syria, and Turkey (2019)

Broadcast media: the number of private radio and TV stations has increased rapidly since 2003; government-owned TV and radio stations are operated by the publicly funded Iraqi Media Network; private broadcast media are mostly linked to political, ethnic, or religious groups; satellite TV is available to an estimated 70% of viewers and many of the broadcasters are based abroad; transmissions of multiple international radio broadcasters are accessible (2019)

Internet country code: .iq

Internet users: *total:* 21.56 million (2021 est.)
percent of population: 49% (2021 est.)
comparison ranking: total 41

Broadband - fixed subscriptions: *total:* 6,254,099 (2020 est.)
subscriptions per 100 inhabitants: 16 (2020 est.)
comparison ranking: total 30

TRANSPORTATION

National air transport system: *number of registered air carriers:* 4 (2020)
inventory of registered aircraft operated by air carriers: 34
annual passenger traffic on registered air carriers: 2,075,065 (2018)
annual freight traffic on registered air carriers: 16.2 million (2018) mt-km

Civil aircraft registration country code prefix: YI

Airports: 71 (2024)
comparison ranking: 71

Heliports: 10 (2024)

Pipelines: 2,455 km gas, 913 km liquid petroleum gas, 5,432 km oil, 1,637 km refined products (2013)

Railways: *total:* 2,272 km (2014)
standard gauge: 2,272 km (2014) 1.435-m gauge
comparison ranking: total 68

Roadways: *total:* 58,592 km (2021)
comparison ranking: total 81

Waterways: 5,279 km (2012) (the Euphrates River (2,815 km), Tigris River (1,899 km), and Third River (565 km) are the principal waterways)
comparison ranking: 24

Merchant marine: *total:* 74 (2023)
by type: general cargo 1, oil tanker 6, other 67
comparison ranking: total 103

Ports: *total ports:* 6 (2024)
large: 0
medium: 1
small: 1
very small: 4
ports with oil terminals: 3
key ports: Al Basrah, Al-Basra Oil Terminal, Khawr Al Amaya, Khawr Al Zubair, Umm Qasr

MILITARY AND SECURITY

Military and security forces: Ministry of Defense: Iraqi Army, Army Aviation Command, Iraqi Navy, Iraqi Air Force, Iraqi Air Defense Command, Special Forces Command, Special Security Division

National-Level Security Forces: Iraqi Counterterrorism Service (CTS; reports to the Prime Minister), Prime Minister's Special Forces (Security) Division, Presidential Brigades

Ministry of Interior: Federal Police Forces Command, Border Guard Forces Command, Federal Intelligence and Investigations Agency, Emergency Response Division, Facilities Protection Directorate, and Provincial Police

Ministry of Oil: Energy Police Directorate

Popular Mobilization Committee (PMC): Popular Mobilization Forces (PMF), Tribal Mobilization Forces (TMF); the PMF and TMF are a collection of more than 50 militias of widely varied sizes and political interests
the federal constitution provides the Kurdistan Regional Government (KRG) the right to maintain its own military/militia (peshmerga) and security forces, but the two main Kurdish political parties, the Kurdistan Democratic Party (KDP) and the Patriotic Union of Kurdistan (PUK), each maintain their own forces and participate in the staffing of the joint KDP-PUK Regional Guard Brigades:
KRG Ministry of **Peshmerga:** Unit (or Division) 70 Forces and Counter Terrorism Group (CTG) of the PUK; Unit (or Division) 80 Forces and Counterterrorism Directorate (CTD) of the KDP; Regional Guard Brigades
KRG Ministry of **Interior:** both the KDP and PUK maintain separate police, emergency response, and internal security/ intelligence (Asayish) services under nominal Ministry of Interior control (2024)
note: the Iraqi military and associated forces are collectively known as the Iraqi Security Forces (ISF)

Military expenditures: 3% of GDP (2023 est.)
2.1% of GDP (2022 est.)
3.7% of GDP (2021 est.)
4.1% of GDP (2020 est.)
3.8% of GDP (2019 est.)
comparison ranking: 33

Military and security service personnel strengths: information varies; approximately 200,000 personnel under the Ministry of Defense (190,000 Army/ Aviation Command/ Special Forces; 5,000 Navy; 5,000 Air/Air Defense Forces); approximately 20-25,000 National-Level Security Forces; estimated 200,000+ Popular Mobilization Forces

Ministry of Peshmerga: approximately 150,000 (45-50,000 Regional Guard Brigades; 40-45,000 Unit 70 Forces; 65-70,000 Unit 80 Forces) (2023)

Military equipment inventories and acquisitions: the Iraqi military's inventory includes a mix of equipment from a wide variety of sources, including China, several European countries, South Africa, South Korea, Russia, and the US (2024)

Military service age and obligation: 18-40 years of age for voluntary military service; no conscription (2023)
note: service in the armed forces was mandatory in Iraq from 1935 up until 2003; in 2021, the Iraqi cabinet approved a draft law to reinstate compulsory military service and referred the proposed law to the Iraqi parliament; as of 2023, the proposed law had been shelved

Military - note: the Iraqi security forces (ISF) are primarily focused on internal security duties; they are actively conducting counterinsurgency and counterterrorism operations against the Islamic State of Iraq and ash-Sham (ISIS) terrorist group, particularly in northern and western Iraq; the Counter Terrorism Service (CTS), which is comprised of three special forces brigades, is the ISF's principal operational unit against ISIS
Kurdish Security Forces (KSF, aka Peshmerga) also conduct operations against ISIS; the KSF are recognized as a legitimate Iraqi military force under the country's constitution and have operated jointly with the Iraqi military against ISIS militants, but largely operate outside of Iraqi military command structure; since 2021, the ISF and the KSF have conducted joint counter-ISIS operations in an area known as the Kurdish Coordination Line (KCL), a swath of disputed territory in northern Iraq claimed by both the Kurdistan Regional Government and the central Iraqi Government; the KSF/ Peshmerga report to the Kurdistan Regional Government or Kurdistan Democratic Party and Patriotic Union of Kurdistan parties instead of the Iraqi Ministry of Defense
Popular Mobilization Commission and Affiliated Forces (PMF or PMC), also known as Popular Mobilization Units (PMU, or al-Hashd al-Sha'abi in Arabic), tribal militia units have fought alongside the Iraqi military against ISIS since 2014, but the majority of these forces continue to largely ignore the 2016 Law of the Popular Mobilization Authority, which mandated that armed militias must be regulated in a fashion similar to Iraq's other security forces and act under the Iraqi Government's direct control; the Iraqi Government funds the PMF, and the prime minister legally commands it, but many of the militia units take orders from associated political parties and/or other government officials, including some with ties to the Iranian Revolutionary Guard Corps (IRGC) and some that have been designated as terrorist organizations by the US; the PMF/PMU is an umbrella organization comprised of many different militias, the majority of which are **Shia:**
–Shia militias backed by Iran; they are considered the most active and capable, and include such groups as the Badr Organization (Saraya al-Sala), Asaib Ahl al-Haq, and Kataib Hizballah
–Shia militias affiliated with Shia political parties, but not aligned with Iran, such as the Peace Brigades (Saray al-Salam)

–Shia militias not connected with political parties, but affiliated with the Najaf-based Grand Ayatollah Ali al-SISTANI (Iraq's supreme Shia cleric), such as the Hawza militias
–other PMF/PMU militias include Sunni Tribal Mobilization militias, or Hashd al-Asha'iri; some of these militias take orders from the ISF and local authorities while others respond to orders from the larger Shia PMU militias; still other militias include Yazidi and Christian militias and the Turkmen brigades; the links of these forces to the PMU are not always clear-cut and may be loosely based on financial, legal, or political incentives
two international military task forces operate in Iraq to assist the country's security forces at the request of the Iraqi Government; in October 2018, NATO established an advisory, training and capacity-building mission for the Iraqi military known as the NATO Mission Iraq (NMI); in December 2021, a US-led task force that leads the defeat ISIS mission in Iraq, Combined Joint Task Force – Operation Inherent Resolve (CJTF-OIR), transitioned from a combat role to an advise, assist, and enable role (2024)

TERRORISM

Terrorist group(s): Ansar al-Islam; Asa'ib Ahl al-Haq; Islamic Revolutionary Guard Corps (IRGC)/Qods Force; Islamic State of Iraq and ash-Sham (ISIS); Jaysh Rijal al-Tariq al-Naqshabandi; Kata'ib Hizballah; Kurdistan Workers' Party (PKK)
note: details about the history, aims, leadership, organization, areas of operation, tactics, targets, weapons, size, and sources of support of the group(s) appear(s) in the Terrorism reference guide

TRANSNATIONAL ISSUES

Refugees and internally displaced persons: *refugees (country of origin):* 7,864 (West Bank and Gaza Strip) (mid-year 2022); 273,258 (Syria), 8,575 (Iran), 8,091 (Turkey) (2023)
IDPs: 1.142 million (displacement in central and northern Iraq since January 2014) (2023)
stateless persons: 47,253 (2022); note - in the 1970s and 1980s under SADDAM Husayn's regime, thousands of Iraq's Faili Kurds, followers of Shia Islam, were stripped of their Iraqi citizenship, had their property seized by the government, and many were deported; some Faili Kurds had their citizenship reinstated under the 2006 Iraqi Nationality Law, but others lack the documentation to prove their Iraqi origins; some Palestinian refugees persecuted by the SADDAM regime remain stateless

IRELAND

INTRODUCTION

Background: Celtic tribes arrived in Ireland between 600 and 150 B.C. Norse invasions that began in the late 8th century finally ended when King Brian BORU defeated the Danes in 1014. Norman invasions began in the 12th century and set off more than seven centuries of Anglo- Irish struggle marked by fierce rebellions and harsh repressions. The Irish famine of the mid-19th century caused an almost 25-percent decline in the island's population through starvation, disease, and emigration. The population of the island continued to fall until the 1960s, but over the last 50 years, Ireland's high birthrate has made it demographically one of the youngest populations in the EU.

The modern Irish state traces its origins to the failed 1916 Easter Monday Uprising that galvanized nationalist sentiment. The ensuing guerrilla war led to independence from the UK in 1921 with the signing of the Anglo-Irish Treaty and the creation of the Irish Free State. The treaty was deeply controversial in Ireland, in part because it helped solidify the country's partition, with six of the 32 counties remaining in the UK as Northern Ireland. The split between pro-Treaty and anti-Treaty partisans led to the Irish Civil War (1922-23). The traditionally dominant political parties in Ireland, Fine Gael and Fianna Fail, are de facto descendants of the opposing sides of the treaty debate. Ireland declared itself a republic in 1949 and formally left the British Dominion.

Beginning in the 1960s, deep sectarian divides between the Catholic and Protestant populations and systemic discrimination in Northern Ireland erupted into years of violence known as the Troubles. In 1998, the governments of Ireland and the UK, along with most political parties in Northern Ireland, reached the Belfast/Good Friday Agreement with the support of the US. This agreement helped end the Troubles and initiated a new phase of cooperation between the Irish and British Governments.

Ireland was neutral in World War II and continues its policy of military neutrality. Ireland joined the European Community in 1973 and the euro-zone currency union in 1999. The economic boom years of the Celtic Tiger (1995-2007) saw rapid economic growth that came to an abrupt end in 2008 with the meltdown of the Irish banking system. As a small, open economy, Ireland has excelled at courting foreign direct investment, especially from US multi-nationals, which has helped the economy recover from the financial crisis and insulated it somewhat from the economic shocks of the COVID-19 pandemic.

GEOGRAPHY

Location: Western Europe, occupying five-sixths of the island of Ireland in the North Atlantic Ocean, west of Great Britain

Geographic coordinates: 53 00 N, 8 00 W

Map references: Europe

Area: *total:* 70,273 sq km
land: 68,883 sq km
water: 1,390 sq km
comparison ranking: total 120

Area - comparative: slightly larger than West Virginia

Land boundaries: *total:* 490 km
border countries: UK 499 km

Coastline: 1,448 km

Maritime claims: *territorial sea:* 12 nm
exclusive fishing zone: 200 nm

Climate: temperate maritime; modified by North Atlantic Current; mild winters, cool summers; consistently humid; overcast about half the time

Terrain: mostly flat to rolling interior plain surrounded by rugged hills and low mountains; sea cliffs on west coast Elevation
highest point: Carrauntoohil 1,041 m
lowest point: Atlantic Ocean 0 m
mean elevation: 118 m

Natural resources: natural gas, peat, copper, lead, zinc, silver, barite, gypsum, limestone, dolomite

Land use: *agricultural land:* 66.1% (2018 est.)
arable land: 15.4% (2018 est.)
permanent crops: 0% (2018 est.)
permanent pasture: 50.7% (2018 est.)
forest: 10.9% (2018 est.)
other: 23% (2018 est.)

Irrigated land: 0 sq km (2022)

Population distribution: population distribution is weighted to the eastern side of the island, with the largest concentration being in and around Dublin; populations in the west are small due to mountainous land, poorer soil, lack of good transport routes, and fewer job opportunities

Natural hazards: rare extreme weather events

Geography - note: strategic location on major air and sea routes between North America and northern Europe; over 40% of the population resides within 100 km of Dublin

PEOPLE AND SOCIETY

Population: *total:* 5,233,461
male: 2,590,542
female: 2,642,919 (2024 est.)
comparison rankings: female 123; male 124; total 124

Nationality: *noun:* Irishman(men), Irishwoman(women), Irish (collective plural)
adjective: Irish

Ethnic groups: Irish 76.6%, Irish travelers 0.6%, other White 9.9%, Asian 3.3%, Black 1.5%, other (includes Arab, Roma, and persons of mixed backgrounds) 2%, unspecified 2.6% (2022 est.)

Languages: English (official, the language generally used), Irish (Gaelic or Gaeilge) (official, spoken by approximately 37.7% of the population)

Religions: Roman Catholic 69.2% (includes lapsed), Protestant 3.7% (Church of Ireland/England/Anglican/Episcopalian 2.5%, other Protestant 1.2%), Orthodox 2%, other Christian 0.9%, Muslim 1.6%, other 1.4%, agnostic/atheist 0.1%, none 14.5%, unspecified 6.7% (2022 est.)

Age structure: *0-14 years:* 18.6% (male 498,124/female 477,848)
15-64 years: 65.5% (male 1,701,680/female 1,728,041)
65 years and over: 15.8% (2024 est.) (male 390,738/female 437,030)

Dependency ratios: *total dependency ratio:* 53.2
youth dependency ratio: 30.5
elderly dependency ratio: 22.7
potential support ratio: 4.4 (2021 est.)

Median age: *total:* 40.2 years (2024 est.)
male: 39.7 years
female: 40.6 years
comparison ranking: total 60

Population growth rate: 0.93% (2024 est.)
comparison ranking: 100

Birth rate: 11.1 births/1,000 population (2024 est.)
comparison ranking: 163

Death rate: 7.4 deaths/1,000 population (2024 est.)
comparison ranking: 104

Net migration rate: 5.6 migrant(s)/1,000 population (2024 est.)
comparison ranking: 17

Population distribution: population distribution is weighted to the eastern side of the island, with the largest concentration being in and around Dublin; populations in the west are small due to mountainous land, poorer soil, lack of good transport routes, and fewer job opportunities

Urbanization: *urban population:* 64.5% of total population (2023)
rate of urbanization: 1.15% annual rate of change (2020-25 est.)

Major urban areas - population: 1.270 million DUBLIN (capital) (2023)

Sex ratio: *at birth:* 1.06 male(s)/female
0-14 years: 1.04 male(s)/female
15-64 years: 0.98 male(s)/female
65 years and over: 0.89 male(s)/female
total population: 0.98 male(s)/female (2024 est.)

Mother's mean age at first birth: 30.9 years (2020 est.)

Maternal mortality ratio: 5 deaths/100,000 live births (2020 est.)
comparison ranking: 163

Infant mortality rate: *total:* 3.3 deaths/1,000 live births (2024 est.)
male: 3.2 deaths/1,000 live births
female: 3.3 deaths/1,000 live births
comparison ranking: total 198

Life expectancy at birth: *total population:* 82 years (2024 est.)
male: 80.3 years
female: 83.9 years
comparison ranking: total population 36

Total fertility rate: 1.72 children born/woman (2024 est.)
comparison ranking: 158

Gross reproduction rate: 0.84 (2024 est.)

Contraceptive prevalence rate: NA

Drinking water source: *improved: urban:* 97% of population
rural: 98.1% of population
total: 97.4% of population
unimproved: urban: 3% of population
rural: 1.9% of population
total: 2.6% of population (2020 est.)

Current health expenditure: 7.1% of GDP (2020)

Physician density: 3.49 physicians/1,000 population (2020)

Hospital bed density: 3 beds/1,000 population (2018)

Sanitation facility access: *improved: urban:* 97.8% of population
rural: 99.1% of population
total: 98.3% of population
unimproved: urban: 2.2% of population
rural: 0.9% of population
total: 1.7% of population (2020 est.)

Obesity - adult prevalence rate: 25.3% (2016)
comparison ranking: 51

Alcohol consumption per capita: *total:* 10.91 liters of pure alcohol (2019 est.)
beer: 4.92 liters of pure alcohol (2019 est.)
wine: 2.88 liters of pure alcohol (2019 est.)
spirits: 2.29 liters of pure alcohol (2019 est.)
other alcohols: 0.82 liters of pure alcohol (2019 est.)
comparison ranking: total 15

Tobacco use: *total:* 20.8% (2020 est.)
male: 22.5% (2020 est.)
female: 19% (2020 est.)
comparison ranking: total 81

Currently married women (ages 15-49): 52.1% (2023 est.)

Education expenditures: 3.1% of GDP (2020 est.)
comparison ranking: 156

School life expectancy (primary to tertiary education): *total:* 19 years
male: 18 years
female: 19 years (2020)

ENVIRONMENT

Environment - current issues: water pollution, especially of lakes, from agricultural runoff; acid rain kills plants, destroys soil fertility, and contributes to deforestation

Environment - international agreements: *party to:* Air Pollution, Air Pollution-Nitrogen Oxides, Air Pollution-Persistent Organic Pollutants, Air Pollution-Sulphur 94, Biodiversity, Climate Change, Climate Change-Kyoto Protocol, Climate Change-Paris Agreement, Comprehensive Nuclear Test Ban, Desertification, Endangered Species, Environmental Modification, Hazardous Wastes, Law of the Sea, Marine Dumping-London Convention, Marine Dumping-London Protocol, Nuclear Test Ban, Ozone Layer Protection, Ship Pollution, Tropical Timber 2006, Wetlands, Whaling
signed, but not ratified: Air Pollution-Heavy Metals, Air Pollution-Multi-effect Protocol, Marine Life Conservation

Climate: temperate maritime; modified by North Atlantic Current; mild winters, cool summers; consistently humid; overcast about half the time

Urbanization: *urban population:* 64.5% of total population (2023)
rate of urbanization: 1.15% annual rate of change (2020-25 est.)

Revenue from forest resources: 0.01% of GDP (2018 est.)
comparison ranking: 157

Revenue from coal: 0% of GDP (2018 est.)
comparison ranking: 128

Air pollutants: *particulate matter emissions:* 8.2 micrograms per cubic meter (2019 est.)
carbon dioxide emissions: 37.71 megatons (2016 est.)
methane emissions: 13.67 megatons (2020 est.)

Waste and recycling: *municipal solid waste generated annually:* 2,692,537 tons (2012 est.)
municipal solid waste recycled annually: 888,537 tons (2012 est.)
percent of municipal solid waste recycled: 33% (2012 est.)

Total water withdrawal: *municipal:* 990 million cubic meters (2020 est.)
industrial: 520 million cubic meters (2020 est.)
agricultural: 40 million cubic meters (2020 est.)

Total renewable water resources: 52 billion cubic meters (2020 est.)

Geoparks: *total global geoparks and regional networks:* 3
global geoparks and regional networks: Burren & Cliffs of Moher; Copper Coast; Marble Arch Caves (includes United Kingdom) (2023)

GOVERNMENT

Country name: *conventional long form:* none
conventional short form: Ireland
local long form: none
local short form: Eire
etymology: the modern Irish name "Eire" evolved from the Gaelic "Eriu," the name of the matron goddess of Ireland (goddess of the land); the names "Ireland" in English and "Eire" in Irish are direct translations of each other

Government type: parliamentary republic

Capital: *name:* Dublin
geographic coordinates: 53 19 N, 6 14 W
time difference: UTC 0 (5 hours ahead of Washington, DC, during Standard Time)
daylight saving time: +1hr, begins last Sunday in March; ends last Sunday in October
etymology: derived from Irish *dubh* and *lind* meaning respectively "black, dark" and "pool" and which referred to the dark tidal pool where the River Poddle entered the River Liffey; today the area is the site of the castle gardens behind Dublin Castle

Administrative divisions: 28 counties and 3 cities*; Carlow, Cavan, Clare, Cork, Cork*, Donegal, Dublin*, Dun Laoghaire-Rathdown, Fingal, Galway, Galway*, Kerry, Kildare, Kilkenny, Laois, Leitrim, Limerick, Longford, Louth, Mayo, Meath, Monaghan, Offaly, Roscommon, Sligo, South Dublin, Tipperary, Waterford, Westmeath, Wexford, Wicklow

Independence: 6 December 1921 (from the UK by the Anglo-Irish Treaty, which ended British rule);

6 December 1922 (Irish Free State established); 18 April 1949 (Republic of Ireland Act enabled)

National holiday: Saint Patrick's Day, 17 March; note - marks the traditional death date of Saint Patrick, patron saint of Ireland, during the latter half of the fifth century A.D. (most commonly cited years are c. 461 and c. 493); although Saint Patrick's feast day was celebrated in Ireland as early as the ninth century, it only became an official public holiday in Ireland in 1903

Legal system: common law system based on the English model but substantially modified by customary law; judicial review of legislative acts by Supreme Court

Constitution: *history:* previous 1922; latest drafted 14 June 1937, adopted by plebiscite 1 July 1937, effective 29 December 1937
amendments: proposed as bills by Parliament; passage requires majority vote by both the Senate and House of Representatives, majority vote in a referendum, and presidential signature; amended many times, last in 2019

International law organization participation: accepts compulsory ICJ jurisdiction with reservations; accepts ICCt jurisdiction

Citizenship: *citizenship by birth:* no, unless a parent of a child born in Ireland has been legally resident in Ireland for at least three of the four years prior to the birth of the child
citizenship by descent only: yes
dual citizenship recognized: yes
residency requirement for naturalization: 4 of the previous 8 years

Suffrage: 18 years of age; universal

Executive branch: *chief of state:* President Michael D. HIGGINS (since 11 November 2011)
head of government: Taoiseach (Prime Minister) Simon HARRIS (since 9 April 2024)
cabinet: Cabinet nominated by the prime minister, appointed by the president, approved by the Dali Eireann (lower house of Parliament)
elections/appointments: president directly elected by majority popular vote for a 7-year term (eligible for a second term); election last held on 26 October 2018 (next to be held no later than November 2025); taoiseach (prime minister) nominated by the House of Representatives (Dail Eireann), appointed by the president
election results:
2024: Simon HARRIS is elected taoiseach by parliament, 88 votes to 69, and is appointed taoiseach by the president
2018: Michael D. HIGGINS reelected president in first round; percent of vote in first round - Michael D. HIGGINS (independent) 55.8%, Peter CASEY (independent) 23.3%, Sean GALLAGHER (independent) 6.4%, Liadh NI RIADA (Sinn Fein) 6.4%, Joan FREEMAN (independent) 6%, Gavin DUFFY (independent) 2.2%
2011: Michael D. HIGGINS elected president in second round; percent of vote in first round - Michael D. HIGGINS (Labor) 39.6%, Sean GALLAGHER (independent) 28.5%, Martin McGuinness (Sinn Féin) 13.7%, Gay Mitchell (Fine Gael) 6.4%, David Norris (independent) 6.2%, Mary DAVIS (independent) 2.7%; percent of vote in second round - Michael D. HIGGINS 56.8%, Sean GALLAGHER 35.5%
note: Taoiseach Leo VARADKAR resigned from the ruling party on 20 March 2024 but remained as the caretaker taoiseach until a successor was appointed on 9 April 2024

Legislative branch: *description:* bicameral Parliament or Oireachtas consists of:
Senate or Seanad Eireann (60 seats; 49 members indirectly elected from 5 vocational panels of nominees by an electoral college, 11 appointed by the prime minister
House of Representatives or Dail Eireann (160 seats; members directly elected in multi-seat constituencies by proportional representation vote; all Parliament members serve 5-year terms)
elections: Senate - last held early on 21-30 May 2020 (next to be held in March 2025)
House of Representatives - last held on 8 February 2020 (next to be held no later than March 2025)
election results: Senate - percent of vote by party - Fianna Fail 35%, Fine Gael 26.7%, Green Party 6.7%, Labor Party 6.7%, Sinn Fein 6.7%, other 1.6%, independent 16.7%; seats by party - Fianna Fail 21, Fine Gael 16, Green Party 4, Labor Party 4, Sinn Fein 4, other 1, independent 10; composition - men 36, women 24, percentage women 40%
House of Representatives - percent of vote by party - Fianna Fail 23.8%, Sinn Fein 23.1%, Fine Gael 21.9%, Green Party 7.5%, other 11.8%, independent 11.9%; seats by party - Fianna Fail 38, Sinn Fein 37, Fine Gael 35, Green Party 12, Labor Party 6, Social Democrats 6, PBPS 5, other 2, independent 19; composition - men 123, women 37, percentage women 23.1%; total Parliament percentage women 27.7%

Judicial branch: *highest court(s):* Supreme Court of Ireland (consists of the chief justice, 9 judges, 2 ex-officio members - the presidents of the High Court and Court of Appeal - and organized in 3-, 5-, or 7-judge panels, depending on the importance or complexity of an issue of law)
judge selection and term of office: judges nominated by the prime minister and Cabinet and appointed by the president; chief justice serves in the position for 7 years; judges can serve until age 70
subordinate courts: High Court, Court of Appeal; circuit and district courts; criminal courts

Political parties: Aontu
Solidarity-People Before Profit or PBPS
Fianna Fail
Fine Gael
Green Party
Human Dignity Alliance
Labor (Labour) Party
Right to Change or RTC
Sinn Fein
Social Democrats
Socialist Party
The Workers' Party

International organization participation: ADB (nonregional member), Australia Group, BIS, CD, CE, EAPC, EBRD, ECB, EIB, EMU, ESA, EU, FAO, FATF, IAEA, IBRD, ICAO, ICC (national committees), ICCt, ICRM, IDA, IEA, IFAD, IFC, IFRCS, IGAD (partners), IHO, ILO, IMF, IMO, Interpol, IOC, IOM, IPU, ISO, ITSO, ITU, ITUC (NGOs), MIGA, MINURSO, MONUSCO, NEA, NSG, OAS (observer), OECD, OPCW, OSCE, Paris Club, PCA, PFP, UN, UNCTAD, UNDOF, UNESCO, UNHCR, UNIDO, UNIFIL, UNOCI, UNRWA, UNTSO, UPU, Wassenaar Arrangement, WCO, WHO, WIPO, WMO, WTO, ZC

Diplomatic representation in the US: *chief of mission:* Ambassador Geraldine BYRNE NASON (since 16 September 2022)
chancery: 2234 Massachusetts Avenue NW, Washington, DC 20008
telephone: [1] (202) 462-3939
FAX: [1] (202) 232-5993
email address and website:
https://www.ireland.ie/en/usa/washington/
consulate(s) general: Atlanta, Austin (TX), Boston, Chicago, Los Angeles, Miami, New York, San Francisco

Diplomatic representation from the US: *chief of mission:* Ambassador Claire D. CRONIN (since 10 February 2022)
embassy: 42 Elgin Road, Ballsbridge, Dublin 4
mailing address: 5290 Dublin Place, Washington DC 20521-5290
telephone: [353] (1) 668-8777
FAX: [353] (1) 688-8056
email address and website:
ACSDublin@state.gov
https://ie.usembassy.gov/

Flag description: three equal vertical bands of green (hoist side), white, and orange; officially the flag colors have no meaning, but a common interpretation is that the green represents the Irish nationalist (Gaelic) tradition of Ireland; orange represents the Orange tradition (minority supporters of William of Orange); white symbolizes peace (or a lasting truce) between the green and the orange
note: similar to the flag of Cote d'Ivoire, which is shorter and has the colors reversed - orange (hoist side), white, and green; also similar to the flag of Italy, which is shorter and has colors of green (hoist side), white, and red

National symbol(s): harp, shamrock (trefoil); national colors: blue, green

National anthem: *name:* "Amhran na bhFiann" (The Soldier's Song)
lyrics/music: Peadar KEARNEY [English], Liam O RINN [Irish]/Patrick HEENEY and Peadar KEARNEY
note: adopted 1926; instead of "Amhran na bhFiann," the song "Ireland's Call" is often used at athletic events where citizens of Ireland and Northern Ireland compete as a unified team

National heritage: *total World Heritage Sites:* 2 (both cultural)
selected World Heritage Site locales: Brú na Bóinne - Archaeological Ensemble of the Bend of the Boyne; Sceilg Mhichfl

ECONOMY

Economic overview: strong, export-based EU economy; multinational-business-friendly environment known for resilience, even amid COVID-19 disruptions; real wage growth beyond other OECD members; high livings standards; strong social equity and cohesion; aging labor force

Real GDP (purchasing power parity): $608.463 billion (2023 est.)
$628.57 billion (2022 est.)
$574.387 billion (2021 est.)
note: data in 2021 dollars
comparison ranking: 42

Real GDP growth rate: -3.2% (2023 est.)
9.43% (2022 est.)
15.13% (2021 est.)
note: annual GDP % growth based on constant local currency
comparison ranking: 211

Real GDP per capita: $115,600 (2023 est.)
$122,600 (2022 est.)
$114,100 (2021 est.)
note: data in 2021 dollars
comparison ranking: 4

GDP (official exchange rate): $545.629 billion (2023 est.)
note: data in current dollars at official exchange rate

Inflation rate (consumer prices): 6.3% (2023 est.)
7.83% (2022 est.)
2.34% (2021 est.)
note: annual % change based on consumer prices
comparison ranking: 133

Credit ratings: Fitch rating: A+ (2017)

Moody's rating: A2 (2017)

Standard & Poors rating: AA- (2019)
note: The year refers to the year in which the current credit rating was first obtained.

GDP - composition, by sector of origin: *agriculture:* 0.9% (2023 est.)
industry: 37.6% (2023 est.)
services: 56.6% (2023 est.)
note: figures may not total 100% due to non-allocated consumption not captured in sector-reported data
comparison rankings: services 109; industry 37; agriculture 186

GDP - composition, by end use: *household consumption:* 27% (2023 est.)
government consumption: 12.3% (2023 est.)
investment in fixed capital: 23.4% (2023 est.)
investment in inventories: 3.2% (2023 est.)
exports of goods and services: 134.1% (2023 est.)
imports of goods and services: -100.6% (2023 est.)
note: figures may not total 100% due to rounding or gaps in data collection

Agricultural products: milk, barley, wheat, beef, potatoes, pork, oats, chicken, rapeseed, lamb/mutton (2022)
note: top ten agricultural products based on tonnage

Industries: pharmaceuticals, chemicals, computer hardware and software, food products, beverages and brewing; medical devices

Industrial production growth rate: -10.79% (2023 est.)
note: annual % change in industrial value added based on constant local currency
comparison ranking: 211

Labor force: 2.766 million (2023 est.)
note: number of people ages 15 or older who are employed or seeking work
comparison ranking: 116

Unemployment rate: 4.34% (2023 est.)
4.48% (2022 est.)
6.19% (2021 est.)
note: % of labor force seeking employment
comparison ranking: 85

Youth unemployment rate (ages 15-24): *total:* 10.5% (2023 est.)
male: 10.5% (2023 est.)
female: 10.6% (2023 est.)
note: % of labor force ages 15-24 seeking employment
comparison ranking: total 131

Population below poverty line: 14% (2021 est.)
note: % of population with income below national poverty line

Gini Index coefficient - distribution of family income: 30.1 (2021 est.)
note: index (0-100) of income distribution; higher values represent greater inequality
comparison ranking: 122

Average household expenditures: *on food:* 8.2% of household expenditures (2022 est.)
on alcohol and tobacco: 5.6% of household expenditures (2022 est.)

Household income or consumption by percentage share: *lowest 10%:* 3.6% (2021 est.)
highest 10%: 24.8% (2021 est.)
note: % share of income accruing to lowest and highest 10% of population

Remittances: 0.08% of GDP (2023 est.)
0.08% of GDP (2022 est.)
0.04% of GDP (2021 est.)
note: personal transfers and compensation between resident and non-resident individuals/households/entities

Budget: *revenues:* $118.278 billion (2022 est.)
expenditures: $105.516 billion (2022 est.)
note: central government revenues (excluding grants) and expenses converted to US dollars at average official exchange rate for year indicated

Public debt: 46.71% of GDP (2022 est.)
note: central government debt as a % of GDP
comparison ranking: 117

Taxes and other revenues: 17.27% (of GDP) (2022 est.)
note: central government tax revenue as a % of GDP
comparison ranking: 112

Current account balance: $53.997 billion (2023 est.)
$57.807 billion (2022 est.)
$70.909 billion (2021 est.)
note: balance of payments - net trade and primary/secondary income in current dollars
comparison ranking: 10

Exports: $731.814 billion (2023 est.)
$729.135 billion (2022 est.)
$685.814 billion (2021 est.)
note: balance of payments - exports of goods and services in current dollars
comparison ranking: 12

Exports - partners: US 30%, Germany 12%, UK 8%, Belgium 7%, China 7% (2022)
note: top five export partners based on percentage share of exports

Exports - commodities: vaccines, packaged medicine, nitrogen compounds, integrated circuits, scented mixtures (2022)
note: top five export commodities based on value in dollars

Imports: $548.827 billion (2023 est.)
$516.084 billion (2022 est.)
$479.284 billion (2021 est.)
note: balance of payments - imports of goods and services in current dollars
comparison ranking: 17

Imports - partners: UK 26%, US 16%, Germany 9%, China 6%, Netherlands 6% (2022)
note: top five import partners based on percentage share of imports

Imports - commodities: aircraft, nitrogen compounds, refined petroleum, natural gas, vaccines (2022)
note: top five import commodities based on value in dollars

Reserves of foreign exchange and gold: $12.905 billion (2023 est.)
$13.039 billion (2022 est.)
$13.247 billion (2021 est.)
note: holdings of gold (year-end prices)/foreign exchange/special drawing rights in current dollars
comparison ranking: 96

Exchange rates: euros (EUR) per US dollar -

Exchange rates: 0.925 (2023 est.)
0.95 (2022 est.)
0.845 (2021 est.)
0.876 (2020 est.)
0.893 (2019 est.)

ENERGY

Electricity access: *electrification - total population:* 100% (2022 est.)

Electricity: *installed generating capacity:* 11.53 million kW (2022 est.)
consumption: 30.736 billion kWh (2022 est.)
exports: 1.342 billion kWh (2022 est.)
imports: 1.552 billion kWh (2022 est.)
transmission/distribution losses: 2.455 billion kWh (2022 est.)
comparison rankings: transmission/distribution losses 131; imports 65; exports 64; consumption 66; installed generating capacity 62

Electricity generation sources: *fossil fuels:* 58.2% of total installed capacity (2022 est.)
solar: 0.3% of total installed capacity (2022 est.)
wind: 35.9% of total installed capacity (2022 est.)
hydroelectricity: 1.5% of total installed capacity (2022 est.)
biomass and waste: 4.1% of total installed capacity (2022 est.)

Coal: *consumption:* 1.322 million metric tons (2022 est.)
exports: 96,000 metric tons (2022 est.)
imports: 1.335 million metric tons (2022 est.)
proven reserves: 40 million metric tons (2022 est.)

Petroleum: *total petroleum production:* 600 bbl/day (2023 est.)
refined petroleum consumption: 156,000 bbl/day (2023 est.)

Natural gas: *production:* 1.447 billion cubic meters (2022 est.)
consumption: 5.28 billion cubic meters (2022 est.)
imports: 3.836 billion cubic meters (2022 est.)
proven reserves: 9.911 billion cubic meters (2021 est.)

Carbon dioxide emissions: 35.957 million metric tonnes of CO2 (2022 est.)
from coal and metallurgical coke: 2.973 million metric tonnes of CO2 (2022 est.)
from petroleum and other liquids: 22.441 million metric tonnes of CO2 (2022 est.)
from consumed natural gas: 10.543 million metric tonnes of CO2 (2022 est.)
comparison ranking: total emissions 68

Energy consumption per capita: 118.037 million Btu/person (2022 est.)
comparison ranking: 37

COMMUNICATIONS

Telephones - fixed lines: *total subscriptions:* 1.498 million (2022 est.)
subscriptions per 100 inhabitants: 30 (2022 est.)
comparison ranking: total subscriptions 60

Telephones - mobile cellular: *total subscriptions:* 5.69 million (2022 est.)
subscriptions per 100 inhabitants: 113 (2022 est.)
comparison ranking: total subscriptions 121

Telecommunication systems: *general assessment:* Ireland's telecom market has rebounded from a long period in which fiscal constraints inhibited investment in the sector; significant infrastructure projects are underway, including the NBN which aims to deliver a fiberbased service of at least 150Mb/s nationally by the end of 2022; the renewed optimism has been seen in company investment in extending fiber-based networks providing 1Gb/s services; the mobile sector is preparing for a multifrequency availability later in 2021 which will greatly increase the amount of frequencies available, and provide a boost for 5G services; the MNOs are rapidly expanding the reach of 5G (2021)
domestic: fixed-line 32 per 100 and mobile-cellular 108 per 100 subscriptions. (2021)
international: country code - 353; landing point for the AEConnect -1, Celtic-Norse, Havfrue/AEC-2, GTT Express, Celtic, ESAT-1, IFC-1, Solas, Pan European Crossing, ESAT-2, CeltixConnect -1 & 2, GTT Atlantic, Sirius South, Emerald Bridge Fibres and Geo Eirgrid submarine cable with links to the US, Canada, Norway, Isle of Man and UK; satellite earth stations - 81 (2019)

Broadcast media: publicly owned broadcaster Radio Telefis Eireann (RTE) operates 4 TV stations; commercial TV stations are available; about 75% of households utilize multi-channel satellite and TV services that provide access to a wide range of stations; RTE operates 4 national radio stations and has launched digital audio broadcasts on several stations; a number of commercial broadcast stations operate at the national, regional, and local levels (2019)

Internet country code: .ie

Internet users: *total:* 4.75 million (2021 est.)
percent of population: 95% (2021 est.)
comparison ranking: total 101

Broadband - fixed subscriptions: *total:* 1,516,473 (2020 est.)
subscriptions per 100 inhabitants: 31 (2020 est.)
comparison ranking: total 65

TRANSPORTATION

National air transport system: *number of registered air carriers:* 9 (2020)
inventory of registered aircraft operated by air carriers: 450
annual passenger traffic on registered air carriers: 1.676 million (2018)
annual freight traffic on registered air carriers: 168.71 million (2018) mt-km

Civil aircraft registration country code prefix: EI

Airports: 100 (2024)
comparison ranking: 53

Heliports: 5 (2024)

Pipelines: 2,427 km gas (2017)

Railways: *total:* 1,688 km (2020) 53 km electrified
comparison ranking: total 78

Roadways: *total:* 102,227 km (2022)
comparison ranking: total 48

Waterways: 956 km (2010) (pleasure craft only)
comparison ranking: 73

Merchant marine: *total:* 94 (2023)
by type: bulk carrier 12, general cargo 32, oil tanker 1, other 49
comparison ranking: total 93

Ports: *total ports:* 21 (2024)
large: 1
medium: 3
small: 3
very small: 14
ports with oil terminals: 8
key ports: Cobh, Cork, Dublin, Foynes

MILITARY AND SECURITY

Military and security forces: Irish Defense Forces (Oglaigh na h-Eireannn): Army, Air Corps, Naval Service, Reserve Defense Forces (2024)
note: An Garda Siochana (or Garda) is the national police force and maintains internal security under the auspices of the Department of Justice

Military expenditures: 0.2% of GDP (2023 est.)
0.3% of GDP (2022)
0.3% of GDP (2021)
0.3% of GDP (2020)
0.3% of GDP (2019)
comparison ranking: 165

Military and security service personnel strengths: approximately 7,500 active-duty personnel (authorized establishment of 9,500) (2024)

Military equipment inventories and acquisitions: the Irish Defense Forces have a small inventory of imported weapons systems from a variety of mostly European countries, particularly the UK (2024)

Military service age and obligation: 18 years of age for men and women for voluntary military service; 12-year service (5 active, 7 reserves) (2024)
note 1: as of 2024, women made up about 7.5% of the military's full-time personnel
note 2: the Defense Forces are open to refugees under the Refugee Act of 1996 and nationals of the European Economic Area, which include EU member states, Iceland, Liechtenstein, and Norway

Military deployments: 130 Golan Heights (UNDOF); 325 Lebanon (UNIFIL) (2024)

Military - note: Ireland has a long-standing policy of military neutrality; however, it participates in multinational peacekeeping and humanitarian operations, as well as crisis management; Ireland is a signatory of the EU's Common Security and Defense Policy and has committed a battalion of troops to the EU's Rapid Reaction Force; Ireland is not a member of NATO but has a relationship with it going back to 1997, when it deployed personnel in support of the NATO-led peacekeeping operation in Bosnia and Herzegovina; Ireland joined NATO's Partnership for Peace program in 1999; it has been active in UN peacekeeping operations since the 1950s
the Irish Defense Forces trace their origins back to the Irish Volunteers, a unit established in 1913 which took part in the 1916 Easter Rising and the Irish War of Independence (1919-1921) (2024)

TERRORISM

Terrorist group(s): Continuity Irish Republican Army; New Irish Republican Army; Islamic State of Iraq and ash-Sham (ISIS)
note: details about the history, aims, leadership, organization, areas of operation, tactics, targets, weapons, size, and sources of support of the group(s) appear(s) in the Terrorism reference guide

TRANSNATIONAL ISSUES

Refugees and internally displaced persons: *refugees (country of origin):* 105,210 (Ukraine) (as of 8 March 2024)
stateless persons: 7 (2022)

Illicit drugs: transshipment point for and consumer of hashish from North Africa to the UK and Netherlands and of European-produced synthetic drugs; increasing consumption of South American cocaine; minor transshipment point for heroin and cocaine destined for Western Europe; despite recent legislation, narcotics-related money laundering - using bureaux de change, trusts, and shell companies involving the offshore financial community - remains a concern

ISLE OF MAN

INTRODUCTION

Background: The Isle of Man was part of the Norwegian Kingdom of the Hebrides until the 13th century, when it was ceded to Scotland. The isle came under English lordship in the 14th century before being purchased by the British Government in 1765. Current concerns include reviving the almost extinct Manx Gaelic language. The Isle of Man is a British Crown dependency, which makes it a self-governing possession of the British Crown that is not part of the UK. The UK Government, however, remains constitutionally responsible for its defense and international representation.

GEOGRAPHY

Location: Western Europe, island in the Irish Sea, between Great Britain and Ireland

Geographic coordinates: 54 15 N, 4 30 W

Map references: Europe

Area: *total:* 572 sq km

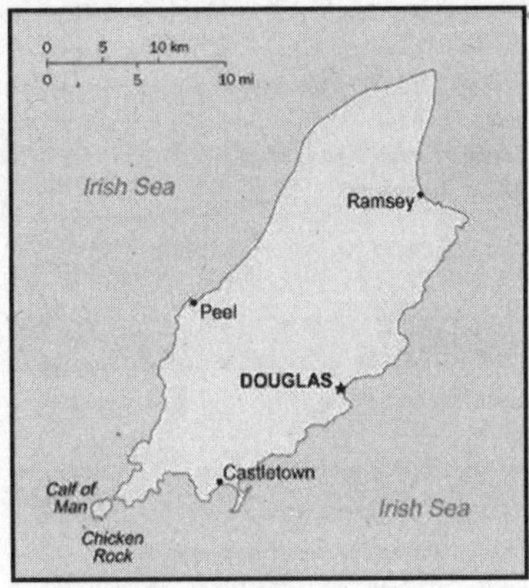

land: 572 sq km
water: 0 sq km
comparison ranking: total 193

Area - comparative: slightly more than three times the size of Washington, DC

Land boundaries: *total:* 0 km

Coastline: 160 km

Maritime claims: *territorial sea:* 12 nm
exclusive fishing zone: 12 nm

Climate: temperate; cool summers and mild winters; overcast about a third of the time

Terrain: hills in north and south bisected by central valley

Elevation: *highest point:* Snaefell 621 m
lowest point: Irish Sea 0 m

Natural resources: none

Land use: *agricultural land:* 74.7% (2018 est.)
arable land: 43.8% (2018 est.)
permanent crops: 0% (2018 est.)
permanent pasture: 30.9% (2018 est.)
forest: 6.1% (2018 est.)
other: 19.2% (2018 est.)

Irrigated land: 0 sq km (2022)

Population distribution: most people concentrated in cities and large towns of which Douglas, in the southeast, is the largest

Natural hazards: occasional high winds and rough seas

Geography - note: one small islet, the Calf of Man, lies to the southwest and is a bird sanctuary

PEOPLE AND SOCIETY

Population: *total:* 92,269
male: 46,331
female: 45,938 (2024 est.)
comparison rankings: female 198; male 198; total 198

Nationality: *noun:* Manxman (men), Manxwoman (women)
adjective: Manx

Ethnic groups: White 94.7%, Asian 3.1%, Mixed 1%, Black 0.6%, other 0.4% (2021 est.)
note: data represent population by nationality

Languages: English, Manx Gaelic (about 2% of the population has some knowledge)

Religions: Christian 54.7%, Muslim 0.5%, Buddhist 0.5%, Hindu 0.4%, Jewish 0.2%, none 43.8% (2021 est.)

Age structure: *0-14 years:* 16% (male 7,701/female 7,100)
15-64 years: 61.9% (male 29,035/female 28,044)
65 years and over: 22.1% (2024 est.) (male 9,595/female 10,794)

Dependency ratios: *total dependency ratio:* 58.6
youth dependency ratio: 23.6
elderly dependency ratio: 34.9
potential support ratio: 2.9 (2021)

Median age: *total:* 44.9 years (2024 est.)
male: 43.7 years
female: 46.1 years
comparison ranking: total 26

Population growth rate: 0.45% (2024 est.)
comparison ranking: 153

Birth rate: 10.4 births/1,000 population (2024 est.)
comparison ranking: 178

Death rate: 10.2 deaths/1,000 population (2024 est.)
comparison ranking: 34

Net migration rate: 4.3 migrant(s)/1,000 population (2024 est.)
comparison ranking: 22

Population distribution: most people concentrated in cities and large towns of which Douglas, in the southeast, is the largest

Urbanization: *urban population:* 53.5% of total population (2023)
rate of urbanization: 0.97% annual rate of change (2020-25 est.)

Major urban areas - population: 27,000 DOUGLAS (capital) (2018)

Sex ratio: *at birth:* 1.08 male(s)/female
0-14 years: 1.08 male(s)/female
15-64 years: 1.04 male(s)/female
65 years and over: 0.89 male(s)/female
total population: 1.01 male(s)/female (2024 est.)

Infant mortality rate: *total:* 4.1 deaths/1,000 live births (2024 est.)
male: 4.4 deaths/1,000 live births
female: 3.7 deaths/1,000 live births
comparison ranking: total 186

Life expectancy at birth: *total population:* 82.5 years (2024 est.)
male: 80.7 years
female: 84.4 years
comparison ranking: total population 28

Total fertility rate: 1.88 children born/woman (2024 est.)
comparison ranking: 127

Gross reproduction rate: 0.9 (2024 est.)

Contraceptive prevalence rate: NA

Drinking water source: *improved:*
total: 99.1% of population
unimproved:
total: 0.9% of population (2020)

ENVIRONMENT

Environment - current issues: air pollution, marine pollution; waste disposal (both household and industrial)

Climate: temperate; cool summers and mild winters; overcast about a third of the time

Urbanization: *urban population:* 53.5% of total population (2023)
rate of urbanization: 0.97% annual rate of change (2020-25 est.)

Revenue from forest resources: 0% of GDP (2017 est.)
comparison ranking: 181

Waste and recycling: *municipal solid waste generated annually:* 50,551 tons (2011 est.)
municipal solid waste recycled annually: 25,276 tons (2011 est.)
percent of municipal solid waste recycled: 50% (2011 est.)

GOVERNMENT

Country name: *conventional long form:* none
conventional short form: Isle of Man
abbreviation: I.O.M.
etymology: the name "man" may be derived from the Celtic word for "mountain"

Government type: parliamentary democracy (Tynwald)

Dependency status: British crown dependency

Capital: *name:* Douglas
geographic coordinates: 54 09 N, 4 29 W
time difference: UTC 0 (5 hours ahead of Washington, DC, during Standard Time)
daylight saving time: +1hr, begins last Sunday in March; ends last Sunday in October
etymology: name derives from the Dhoo and Glass Rivers, which flow through the valley in which the town is located and which in Manx mean the "dark" and the "light" rivers respectively

Administrative divisions: none; there are no first-order administrative divisions as defined by the US Government, but there are 24 local authorities each with its own elections

Independence: none (British Crown dependency)

National holiday: Tynwald Day, 5 July (1417); date Tynwald Day was first recorded

Legal system: the laws of the UK apply where applicable and include Manx statutes

Constitution: *history:* development of the Isle of Man constitution dates to at least the 14th century
amendments: proposed as a bill in the House of Keys, by the "Government," by a "Member of the House," or through petition to the House or Legislative Council; passage normally requires three separate readings and approval of at least 13 House members; following both House and Council agreement, assent is required by the lieutenant governor on behalf of the Crown; the constitution has been expanded and amended many times, last in 2020

Citizenship: see United Kingdom

Suffrage: 16 years of age; universal

Executive branch: *chief of state:* Lord of Mann King CHARLES III (since 8 September 2022); represented by Lieutenant Governor Sir John LORIMER (since 29 September 2021)
head of government: Chief Minister Alfred CANNAN (since 12 October 2021)
cabinet: Council of Ministers appointed by the lieutenant governor
elections/appointments: the monarchy is hereditary; lieutenant governor appointed by the monarch; chief minister indirectly elected by the Tynwald for a

5-year term (eligible for second term); election last held on 23 September 2021 (next to be held in 2026)
election results:
2021: Alfred CANNAN (independent) elected chief minister; Tynwald House of Keys vote - 21 of 24
2016: Howard QUAYLE elected chief minister; Tynwald House of Keys vote - 21 of 33

Legislative branch: *description:* bicameral Tynwald or the High Court of Tynwald consists of:
Legislative Council (11 seats; includes the President of Tynwald, 2 ex-officio (non-voting) members - the Lord Bishop of Sodor and Man and the attorney general - and 8 members indirectly elected by the House of Keys with renewal of 4 members every 2 years; elected members serve 4-year terms)
House of Keys (24 seats; 2 members each from 12 constituencies directly elected by simple majority vote to serve 5-year terms)
elections: Legislative Council - last held 14 March 2023 (next to be held by March 2028)
House of Keys - last held on 23 September 2021 (next to be held on 24 September 2026)
election results:
Legislative Council - composition - men 6, women 4, vacant 1; percentage women 36.4%
House of Keys - percent of vote by party - Liberal Vannin 5.3%, Manx Labour Party 5.1%, Green Party 3.3% independent 86.3%; seats by party - independent 21; Manx Labour Party 2, Liberal Vannin 1; composition – men 14, women 10, percentage women 41.7%; total Tynwald percentage women 40%

Judicial branch: *highest court(s):* Isle of Man High Court of Justice (consists of 3 permanent judges or "deemsters" and 1 judge of appeal; organized into the Staff of Government Division or Court of Appeal and the Civil Division); the Court of General Gaol Delivery is not formally part of the High Court but is administered as though part of the High Court and deals with serious criminal cases; note - appeals beyond the Court of Appeal are referred to the Judicial Committee of the Privy Council (in London)
judge selection and term of office: deemsters appointed by the Lord Chancellor of England on the nomination of the lieutenant governor; deemsters can serve until age 70
subordinate courts: High Court; Court of Summary Gaol Delivery; Summary Courts; Magistrate's Court; specialized courts

Political parties: Green Party
Liberal Vannin Party or LVP
Manx Labor Party
Mec Vannin (sometimes referred to as the Manx Nationalist Party)
note: most members sit as independents

International organization participation: UPU

Diplomatic representation in the US: none (British crown dependency)

Diplomatic representation from the US: *embassy:* none (British crown dependency)

Flag description: red with the Three Legs of Man emblem (triskelion), in the center; the three legs are joined at the thigh and bent at the knee; in order to have the toes pointing clockwise on both sides of the flag, a two-sided emblem is used; the flag is based on the coat of arms of the last recognized Norse King of Mann, MAGNUS III (r. 1252-65); the triskelion has its roots in an early Celtic sun symbol

National symbol(s): triskelion (a motif of three legs); national colors: red, white

National anthem: *name:* "Arrane Ashoonagh dy Vannin" (O Land of Our Birth)
lyrics/music: William Henry GILL [English], John J. KNEEN [Manx]/traditional
note: adopted 2003, in use since 1907; serves as a local anthem; as a British Crown dependency, "God Save the King" is official (see United Kingdom) and is played when the sovereign, members of the royal family, or the lieutenant governor are present

ECONOMY

Economic overview: high-income British island economy; known financial services and tourism industries; taxation incentives for technology and financial firms to operate; historic fishing and agriculture industries are declining; major online gambling and film industry locale

Real GDP (purchasing power parity): $6.792 billion (2015 est.)
$7.428 billion (2014 est.)
note: data are in 2014 dollars
comparison ranking: 173

Real GDP growth rate: 3.84% (2021 est.)
-8.84% (2020 est.)
0.25% (2019 est.)
note: annual GDP % growth based on constant local currency
comparison ranking: 83

Real GDP per capita: $84,600 (2014 est.)
comparison ranking: 9

GDP (official exchange rate): $7.931 billion (2021 est.)
note: data in current dollars at official exchange rate

Inflation rate (consumer prices): 4.1% (2017 est.)
1% (2016 est.)
comparison ranking: 85

Credit ratings: Moody's rating: Aa3 (2020)

Standard & Poors rating: N/A
note: The year refers to the year in which the current credit rating was first obtained.

GDP - composition, by sector of origin: *agriculture:* 0.3% (2021 est.)
industry: 9.4% (2021 est.)
services: 91.8% (2021 est.)
note: figures may not total 100% due to non-allocated consumption not captured in sector-reported data
comparison rankings: services 4; industry 198; agriculture 204

Agricultural products: cereals, vegetables; cattle, sheep, pigs, poultry

Industries: financial services, light manufacturing, tourism

Industrial production growth rate: 9.95% (2021 est.)
note: annual % change in industrial value added based on constant local currency
comparison ranking: 18

Unemployment rate: 1.1% (2017 est.)
comparison ranking: 9

Exports - partners: almost entirely United Kingdom (2022)

Exports - commodities: crude petroleum, artwork, vegetables, fruits, whiskies (2022)

Imports - partners: almost entirely United Kingdom (2022)

Imports - commodities: ships, delivery trucks (2022)

Exchange rates: Manx pounds (IMP) per US dollar -

Exchange rates: 0.805 (2023 est.)
0.811 (2022 est.)
0.727 (2021 est.)
0.78 (2020 est.)
0.783 (2019 est.)

ENERGY

Electricity access: *electrification - total population:* 100% (2022 est.)

COMMUNICATIONS

Telecommunication systems: *general assessment:* the Isle of Man has an extensive communications infrastructure consisting of telephone cables, submarine cables, and an array of television and mobile phone transmitters and towers (2022)
domestic: landline, telefax, mobile cellular telephone system
international: country code - 44; fiber-optic cable, microwave radio relay, satellite earth station, submarine cable

Broadcast media: national public radio broadcasts over 3 FM stations and 1 AM station; 2 commercial broadcasters operating with 1 having multiple FM stations; receives radio and TV services via relays from British TV and radio broadcasters

Internet country code: .im

TRANSPORTATION

Civil aircraft registration country code prefix: M

Airports: 4 (2024)
comparison ranking: 180

Heliports: 1 (2024)

Railways: *total:* 63 km (2008)
narrow gauge: 6 km (2008) 1.076-m gauge (6 km electrified)
57 0.914-mm gauge (29 km electrified) note: primarily summer tourist attractions
comparison ranking: total 131

Roadways: *total:* 1,107 km (2022)
paved: 1,107 km
comparison ranking: total 185

Merchant marine: *total:* 269 (2023)
by type: bulk carrier 102, container ship 6, general cargo 27, oil tanker 56, other 78
comparison ranking: total 62

Ports: *total ports:* 2 (2024)
large: 0
medium: 0
small: 2
very small: 0
ports with oil terminals: 1
key ports: Douglas, Ramsey

MILITARY AND SECURITY

Military - note: defense is the responsibility of the UK

ISRAEL

INTRODUCTION

Background: Israel has become a regional economic and military powerhouse, leveraging its prosperous high-tech sector, large defense industry, and concerns about Iran to foster partnerships around the world. The State of Israel was established in 1948. The UN General Assembly proposed in 1947 partitioning the British Mandate for Palestine into an Arab and Jewish state. The Jews accepted the proposal, but the local Arabs and the Arab states rejected the UN plan and launched a war. The Arabs were subsequently defeated in the 1947-1949 war that followed the UN proposal and the British withdrawal. Israel joined the UN in 1949 and saw rapid population growth, primarily due to Jewish refugee migration from Europe and the Middle East. Israel and its Arab neighbors fought wars in 1956, 1967, and 1973, and Israel signed peace treaties with Egypt in 1979 and Jordan in 1994. Israel took control of the West Bank, the eastern part of Jerusalem, the Gaza Strip, the Sinai Peninsula, and the Golan Heights in the course of the 1967 war. It ceded the Sinai back to Egypt in the 1979-1982 period but has continued to administer the other territories through military authorities. Israel and Palestinian officials signed interim agreements in the 1990s that created a period of Palestinian self-rule in parts of the West Bank and Gaza. Israel withdrew from Gaza in 2005. The most recent formal efforts between Israel and the Palestinian Authority to negotiate final status issues occurred in 2013 and 2014, and the US continues its efforts to advance peace. Israel signed the US-brokered normalization agreements (the Abraham Accords) with Bahrain, the UAE, and Morocco in 2020 and reached an agreement with Sudan in 2021. Immigration to Israel continues, with more than 44,000 estimated new immigrants, mostly Jewish, in the first 11 months of 2023.

Former Prime Minister Benjamin NETANYAHU returned to office in 2022, continuing his dominance of Israel's political landscape at the head of Israel's most rightwing and religious government. NETANYAHU previously served as premier from 1996 to 1999 and from 2009 to 2021, becoming Israel's longest serving prime minister.

On 7 October 2023, HAMAS militants launched a combined unguided rocket and ground terrorist attack from Gaza into southern Israel. The same day Israel's Air Force launched air strikes inside Gaza and initiated a sustained air campaign against HAMAS targets across the Gaza Strip. The following day, NETANYAHU formally declared war on HAMAS, and on 28 October, the Israel Defense Forces launched a large-scale ground assault inside Gaza.

The Israeli economy has undergone a dramatic transformation in the last 30 years, led by cutting-edge high-tech sectors. Offshore gas discoveries in the Mediterranean place Israel at the center of a potential regional natural gas market. In 2022, a US-brokered agreement between Israel and Lebanon established their maritime boundary, allowing Israel to begin production on additional gas fields in the Mediterranean. However, Israel's economic development has been uneven. Structural issues such as low labor-force participation among religious and minority populations, low workforce productivity, high costs for housing and consumer staples, and high income inequality concern both economists and the general population. The current war with Hamas disrupted Israel's solid economic fundamentals, but it is not likely to have long-term structural implications for the economy.

GEOGRAPHY

Location: Middle East, bordering the Mediterranean Sea, between Egypt and Lebanon

Geographic coordinates: 31 30 N, 34 45 E

Map references: Middle East

Area: *total:* 21,937 sq km
land: 21,497 sq km
water: 440 sq km
comparison ranking: total 152

Area - comparative: slightly larger than New Jersey

Land boundaries: *total:* 1,068 km
border countries (6): Egypt 208 km; Gaza Strip 59 km; Jordan 327 km (20 km are within the Dead Sea); Lebanon 81 km; Syria 83 km; West Bank 330 km

Coastline: 273 km

Maritime claims: *territorial sea:* 12 nm
continental shelf: to depth of exploitation

Climate: temperate; hot and dry in southern and eastern desert areas

Terrain: Negev desert in the south; low coastal plain; central mountains; Jordan Rift Valley

Elevation: *highest point:* Mitspe Shlagim 2,224 m; note - this is the highest named point, the actual highest point is an unnamed dome slightly to the west of Mitspe Shlagim at 2,236 m; both points are on the northeastern border of Israel, along the southern end of the Anti-Lebanon mountain range
lowest point: Dead Sea -431 m
mean elevation: 508 m

Natural resources: timber, potash, copper ore, natural gas, phosphate rock, magnesium bromide, clays, sand

Land use: *agricultural land:* 23.8% (2018 est.)
arable land: 13.7% (2018 est.)
permanent crops: 3.8% (2018 est.)
permanent pasture: 6.3% (2018 est.)
forest: 7.1% (2018 est.)
other: 69.1% (2018 est.)

Irrigated land: 2,159 sq km (2020)

Major lakes (area sq km): *salt water lake(s):* Dead Sea (shared with Jordan and West Bank) - 1,020 sq km
note - endorheic hypersaline lake; 9.6 times saltier than the ocean; lake shore is 431 meters below sea level

Population distribution: population concentrated in and around Tel-Aviv, as well as around the Sea of Galilee; the south remains sparsely populated with the exception of the shore of the Gulf of Aqaba

Natural hazards: sandstorms may occur during spring and summer; droughts; periodic earthquakes

Geography - note: *note 1:* Lake Tiberias (Sea of Galilee) is an important freshwater source; the Dead Sea is the second saltiest body of water in the world (after Lake Assal in Djibouti)
note 2: the Malham Cave in Mount Sodom is the world's longest salt cave at 10 km (6 mi); its survey is not complete, and its length will undoubtedly increase; Mount Sodom is actually a hill some 220 m (722 ft) high that is 80% salt (multiple salt layers covered by a veneer of rock)

PEOPLE AND SOCIETY

Population: *total:* 9,402,617
male: 4,731,275
female: 4,671,342 (2024 est.)
note: approximately 236,600 Israeli settlers live in East Jerusalem (2021); following the March 2019 US recognition of the Golan Heights as being part of Israel, *The World Factbook* no longer includes Israeli settler population of the Golan Heights (estimated at 23,400 in 2019) in its overall Israeli settler total
comparison rankings: female 97; male 96; total 98

Nationality: *noun:* Israeli(s)
adjective: Israeli

Ethnic groups: Jewish 73.5% (of which Israel-born 79.7%, Europe/America/Oceania-born 14.3%, Africa-born 3.9%, Asia-born 2.1%), Arab 21.1%, other 5.4% (2022 est.)

Languages: Hebrew (official), Arabic (special status under Israeli law), English (most commonly used foreign language)
major-language sample(s):
העולם, המקור החיוני למידע בסיסי
ספר עובדות
(Hebrew)

Religions: Jewish 73.5%, Muslim 18.1%, Christian 1.9%, Druze 1.6%, other 4.9% (2022 est.)

Age structure: *0-14 years:* 27.5% (male 1,320,629/female 1,260,977)
15-64 years: 60.3% (male 2,885,485/female 2,781,777)
65 years and over: 12.3% (2024 est.) (male 525,161/female 628,588)

Dependency ratios: *total dependency ratio:* 66.9
youth dependency ratio: 47
elderly dependency ratio: 19.9
potential support ratio: 5 (2021 est.)

Median age: *total:* 30.1 years (2024 est.)
male: 29.6 years
female: 30.7 years
comparison ranking: total 140

Population growth rate: 1.58% (2024 est.)
comparison ranking: 59

Birth rate: 19.1 births/1,000 population (2024 est.)
comparison ranking: 74

Death rate: 5.2 deaths/1,000 population (2024 est.)
comparison ranking: 189

Net migration rate: 1.9 migrant(s)/1,000 population (2024 est.)
comparison ranking: 51

Population distribution: population concentrated in and around Tel-Aviv, as well as around the Sea of Galilee; the south remains sparsely populated with the exception of the shore of the Gulf of Aqaba

Urbanization: *urban population:* 92.9% of total population (2023)
rate of urbanization: 1.51% annual rate of change (2020-25 est.)

Major urban areas - population: 4.421 million Tel Aviv-Yafo, 1.174 million Haifa, 970,000 JERUSALEM (capital) (2023)

Sex ratio: *at birth:* 1.05 male(s)/female
0-14 years: 1.05 male(s)/female
15-64 years: 1.04 male(s)/female
65 years and over: 0.84 male(s)/female
total population: 1.01 male(s)/female (2024 est.)

Mother's mean age at first birth: 27.7 years (2019 est.)

Maternal mortality ratio: 3 deaths/100,000 live births (2020 est.)
comparison ranking: 178

Infant mortality rate: *total:* 2.8 deaths/1,000 live births (2024 est.)
male: 3.3 deaths/1,000 live births
female: 2.3 deaths/1,000 live births
comparison ranking: total 213

Life expectancy at birth: *total population:* 83.1 years (2024 est.)
male: 81.1 years
female: 85.1 years
comparison ranking: total population 16

Total fertility rate: 2.92 children born/woman (2024 est.)
comparison ranking: 50

Gross reproduction rate: 1.42 (2024 est.)

Drinking water source: *improved: urban:* 100% of population
rural: 100% of population
total: 100% of population

Current health expenditure: 8.3% of GDP (2020)

Physician density: 3.63 physicians/1,000 population (2020)

Hospital bed density: 3 beds/1,000 population (2018)

Sanitation facility access: *improved: urban:* 100% of population
rural: 99.3% of population
total: 99.9% of population
unimproved: urban: 0% of population
rural: 0.7% of population
total: 0.1% of population (2020 est.)

Obesity - adult prevalence rate: 26.1% (2016)
comparison ranking: 45

Alcohol consumption per capita: *total:* 3.07 liters of pure alcohol (2019 est.)
beer: 1.78 liters of pure alcohol (2019 est.)
wine: 0.08 liters of pure alcohol (2019 est.)
spirits: 1.16 liters of pure alcohol (2019 est.)
other alcohols: 0.04 liters of pure alcohol (2019 est.)
comparison ranking: total 112

Tobacco use: *total:* 21.2% (2020 est.)
male: 28.9% (2020 est.)
female: 13.5% (2020 est.)
comparison ranking: total 77

Currently married women (ages 15-49): 51.7% (2023 est.)

Education expenditures: 7.1% of GDP (2020 est.)
comparison ranking: 19

Literacy: *definition:* age 15 and over can read and write
total population: 97.8%
male: 98.7%
female: 96.8% (2011)

School life expectancy (primary to tertiary education): *total:* 16 years
male: 15 years
female: 17 years (2020)

ENVIRONMENT

Environment - current issues: limited arable land and restricted natural freshwater resources; desertification; air pollution from industrial and vehicle emissions; groundwater pollution from industrial and domestic waste, chemical fertilizers, and pesticides

Environment - international agreements: *party to:* Biodiversity, Climate Change, Climate Change-Kyoto Protocol, Climate Change-Paris Agreement, Desertification, Endangered Species, Hazardous Wastes, Nuclear Test Ban, Ozone Layer Protection, Ship Pollution, Wetlands, Whaling
signed, but not ratified: Comprehensive Nuclear Test Ban, Marine Life Conservation

Climate: temperate; hot and dry in southern and eastern desert areas

Urbanization: *urban population:* 92.9% of total population (2023)
rate of urbanization: 1.51% annual rate of change (2020-25 est.)

Revenue from forest resources: 0% of GDP (2018 est.)
comparison ranking: 175

Revenue from coal: 0% of GDP (2018 est.)
comparison ranking: 170

Air pollutants: *particulate matter emissions:* 19.47 micrograms per cubic meter (2019 est.)
carbon dioxide emissions: 65.17 megatons (2016 est.)
methane emissions: 13.02 megatons (2020 est.)

Waste and recycling: *municipal solid waste generated annually:* 5.4 million tons (2015 est.)
municipal solid waste recycled annually: 1.35 million tons (2017 est.)
percent of municipal solid waste recycled: 25% (2017 est.)

Major lakes (area sq km): *salt water lake(s):* Dead Sea (shared with Jordan and West Bank) - 1,020 sq km
note - endorheic hypersaline lake; 9.6 times saltier than the ocean; lake shore is 431 meters below sea level

Total water withdrawal: *municipal:* 1 billion cubic meters (2020 est.)
industrial: 100 million cubic meters (2020 est.)
agricultural: 1.2 billion cubic meters (2020 est.)

Total renewable water resources: 1.78 billion cubic meters (2020 est.)

GOVERNMENT

Country name: *conventional long form:* State of Israel
conventional short form: Israel
local long form: Medinat Yisra'el
local short form: Yisra'el
former: Mandatory Palestine
etymology: named after the ancient Kingdom of Israel; according to Biblical tradition, the Jewish patriarch Jacob received the name "Israel" ("He who struggles with God") after he wrestled an entire night with an angel of the Lord; Jacob's 12 sons became the ancestors of the Israelites, also known as the Twelve Tribes of Israel, who formed the Kingdom of Israel

Government type: parliamentary democracy

Capital: *name:* Jerusalem; note - the US recognized Jerusalem as Israel's capital in December 2017 without taking a position on the specific boundaries of Israeli sovereignty
geographic coordinates: 31 46 N, 35 14 E
time difference: UTC+2 (7 hours ahead of Washington, DC, during Standard Time)
daylight saving time: +1hr, Friday before the last Sunday in March; ends the last Sunday in October
etymology: Jerusalem's settlement may date back to 2800 B.C.; it is named Urushalim in Egyptian texts of the 14th century B.C.; *uru-shalim* likely means "foundation of [by] the god Shalim", and derives from Hebrew/Semitic *yry*, "to found or lay a cornerstone", and *Shalim*, the Canaanite god of dusk and the nether world; Shalim was associated with sunset and peace and the name is based on the same S-L-M root from which Semitic words for "peace" are derived (Salam or Shalom in modern Arabic and Hebrew); this confluence has thus led to naming interpretations such as "The City of Peace" or "The Abode of Peace"

Administrative divisions: 6 districts (mehozot, singular - mehoz); Central, Haifa, Jerusalem, Northern, Southern, Tel Aviv

Independence: 14 May 1948 (following League of Nations mandate under British administration)

National holiday: Independence Day, 14 May (1948); note - Israel declared independence on 14 May 1948, but the Jewish calendar is lunar and the holiday may occur in April or May

Legal system: mixed legal system of English common law, British Mandate regulations, and Jewish, Christian, and Muslim religious laws

Constitution: *history:* no formal constitution; some functions of a constitution are filled by the Declaration of Establishment (1948), the Basic Laws, and the Law of Return (as amended)
amendments: proposed by Government of Israel ministers or by the Knesset; passage requires a majority vote of Knesset members and subject to Supreme Court judicial review; 11 of the 13 Basic Laws have been amended at least once, latest in 2020 (Basic Law: the Knesset)

International law organization participation: has not submitted an ICJ jurisdiction declaration; withdrew acceptance of ICCt jurisdiction in 2002

Citizenship: *citizenship by birth:* no
citizenship by descent only: at least one parent must be a citizen of Israel
dual citizenship recognized: yes, but naturalized citizens are not allowed to maintain dual citizenship
residency requirement for naturalization: 3 out of the 5 years preceding the application for naturalization
note: Israeli law (Law of Return, 5 July 1950) provides for the granting of citizenship to any Jew - defined as a person being born to a Jewish mother or having converted to Judaism while renouncing any other religion - who immigrates to and expresses a desire to settle in Israel on the basis of the Right of aliyah; the 1970 amendment of this act extended the right to family members including the spouse of a Jew, any child or grandchild, and the spouses of children and grandchildren

Suffrage: 18 years of age; universal; 17 years of age for municipal elections

Executive branch: *chief of state:* President Isaac HERZOG (since 7 July 2021)
head of government: Prime Minister Benyamin NETANYAHU (since 29 December 2022)
cabinet: Cabinet selected by prime minister and approved by the Knesset
elections/appointments: president indirectly elected by the Knesset for a single 7-year term; election last held on 2 June 2021 (next to be held in June 2028); following legislative elections, the president, in consultation with party leaders, tasks a Knesset member (usually the member of the largest party) with forming a new government
election results:
2021: Isaac HERZOG elected president; Knesset vote in first round - Isaac HERZOG (independent) 87, Miriam PERETZ (independent) 26, invalid/blank 7
2014: Reuven RIVLIN elected president in second round; Knesset vote - Reuven RIVLIN (Likud) 63, Meir SHEETRIT (The Movement) 53, other/invalid 4

Legislative branch: *description:* unicameral Knesset (120 seats; members directly elected in a single nationwide constituency by closed party-list proportional representation vote, with a 3.25% vote threshold to gain representation; members serve 4-year terms)
elections: last held on 1 November 2022 (next to be held in November 2026)
election results: percent by party - Likud 23.4%, Yesh Atid 17.8%, Religious Zionism (electoral alliance of Religious Zionist Party, Jewish Power, and Noam) 10.8%, National Unity 9.1%, Shas 8.2%, UTJ 5.9%, Yisrael Beiteinu 4.5%, United Arab List 4.1%, Hadash-Ta'al 3.8%, Labor 3.7%, Meretz 3.2%, other 1.6%; seats by party - Likud 32, Yesh Atid 24, Religious Zionism (electoral alliance of Religious Zionist Party, Jewish Power, and Noam) 14, National Unity 12, Shas 11, UTJ 7, Yisrael Beiteinu 6, Hadash-Ta'al 5, United Arab List 5, Labor 4; composition - men 90, women 30, percentage women 25%; note - following the 1 November 2022 election, the Religious Zionism Alliance split into its three constituent parties in the Knesset: Religious Zionism 7 seats, Jewish Power (Otzma Yehudit) 6, and Noam 1

Judicial branch: *highest court(s):* Supreme Court (consists of the president, deputy president, 13 justices, and 2 registrars) and normally sits in panels of 3 justices; in special cases, the panel is expanded with an uneven number of justices
judge selection and term of office: judges selected by the 9-member Judicial Selection Committee, consisting of the Minister of Justice (chair), the president of the Supreme Court, two other Supreme Court justices, 1 other Cabinet minister, 2 Knesset members, and 2 representatives of the Israel Bar Association; judges can serve up to mandatory retirement at age 70
subordinate courts: district and magistrate courts; national and regional labor courts; family and juvenile courts; special and Rabbinical courts

Political parties: Balad
Blue and White
Hadash
Jewish Power (Otzma Yehudit)
Labor Party or HaAvoda
Likud
Meretz
National Unity (alliance includes Blue and White and New Hope)
New Hope
Noam
Religious Zionism (election alliance of Religious Zionist Party, Jewish Power (Otzma Yehudit), and Noam) Religious Zionist Party
Shas
Ta'al
United Arab List
United Torah Judaism or UTJ (alliance includes Agudat Israel and Degel HaTorah)
Yesh Atid
Yisrael Beiteinu

International organization participation: BIS, BSEC (observer), CE (observer), CERN, CICA, EBRD, FAO, IADB, IAEA, IBRD, ICAO, ICC (national committees), ICRM, IDA, IFAD, IFC, IFRCS, ILO, IMF, IMO, IMSO, Interpol, IOC, IOM, IPU, ISO, ITSO, ITU, ITUC (NGOs), MIGA, OAS (observer), OECD, OPCW (signatory), OSCE (partner), Pacific Alliance (observer), Paris Club, PCA, SELEC (observer), UN, UNCTAD, UNESCO, UNHCR, UNIDO, UNWTO, UPU, WCO, WHO, WIPO, WMO, WTO

Diplomatic representation in the US: *chief of mission:* Ambassador Michael HERZOG (since 1 December 2021)
chancery: 3514 International Drive NW, Washington, DC 20008
telephone: [1] (202) 364-5500
FAX: [1] (202) 364-5607
email address and website:
consular@washington.mfa.gov.il
https://embassies.gov.il/washington/Pages/default.aspx
consulate(s) general: Atlanta, Boston, Chicago, Houston, Los Angeles, Miami, New York, San Francisco

Diplomatic representation from the US: *chief of mission:* Ambassador Jacob J. LEW (since 5 November 2023)
embassy: 14 David Flusser Street, Jerusalem, 9378322
mailing address: 6350 Jerusalem Place, Washington DC 20521-6350
telephone: [972] (2) 630-4000
FAX: [972] (2) 630-4070
email address and website:
JerusalemACS@state.gov
https://il.usembassy.gov/
branch office(s): Tel Aviv
note: on 14 May 2018, the US Embassy relocated to Jerusalem from Tel Aviv; on 4 March 2019, Consulate General Jerusalem merged into US Embassy Jerusalem to form a single diplomatic mission

Flag description: white with a blue hexagram (six-pointed linear star) known as the Magen David (Star of David or Shield of David) centered between two equal horizontal blue bands near the top and bottom edges of the flag; the basic design resembles a traditional Jewish prayer shawl (tallit), which is white with blue stripes; the hexagram as a Jewish symbol dates back to medieval times
note: the Israeli flag proclamation states that the flag colors are sky blue and white, but the exact shade of blue has never been set and can vary from a light to a dark blue

National symbol(s): Star of David (Magen David), menorah (seven-branched lampstand); national colors: blue, white

National anthem: *name:* "Hatikvah" (The Hope)
lyrics/music: Naftali Herz IMBER/traditional, arranged by Samuel COHEN
note: adopted 2004, unofficial since 1948; used as the anthem of the Zionist movement since 1897; the 1888 arrangement by Samuel COHEN is thought to be based on the Romanian folk song "Carul cu boi" (The Ox Driven Cart)

National heritage: *total World Heritage Sites:* 9 (all cultural)
selected World Heritage Site locales: Masada; Old City of Acre; White City of Tel-Aviv - the Modern Movement; Biblical Tels - Megiddo, Hazor, Beer Sheba; Incense Route - Desert Cities in the Negev; Bahá'i Holy Places; Sites of Human Evolution at Mount Carmel; Caves of Maresha and Bet-Guvrin; Necropolis of Bet She'arim

ECONOMY

Economic overview: high-income, technology- and industrial-based economy; economic contraction and fiscal deficits resulting from war in Gaza; labor force stabilizing following military reservist mobilization; high-tech industry remains resilient while construction and tourism among hardest-hit sectors

Real GDP (purchasing power parity): $471.03 billion (2023 est.)
$461.808 billion (2022 est.)
$432.271 billion (2021 est.)
note: data in 2021 dollars
comparison ranking: 51

Real GDP growth rate: 2% (2023 est.)
6.83% (2022 est.)
8.61% (2021 est.)

note: annual GDP % growth based on constant local currency
comparison ranking: 139

Real GDP per capita: $48,300 (2023 est.)
$48,300 (2022 est.)
$46,100 (2021 est.)
note: data in 2021 dollars
comparison ranking: 45

GDP (official exchange rate): $509.901 billion (2023 est.)
note: data in current dollars at official exchange rate

Inflation rate (consumer prices): 4.23% (2023 est.)
4.39% (2022 est.)
1.51% (2021 est.)
note: annual % change based on consumer prices
comparison ranking: 88

Credit ratings: Fitch rating: A+ (2016)

Moody's rating: A1 (2008)

Standard & Poors rating: AA- (2018)
note: the year refers to the year in which the current credit rating was first obtained.

GDP - composition, by sector of origin: *agriculture:* 1.3% (2021 est.)
industry: 17.2% (2021 est.)
services: 72.4% (2021 est.)
note: figures may not total 100% due to non-allocated consumption not captured in sector-reported data
comparison rankings: services 30; industry 159; agriculture 177

GDP - composition, by end use: *household consumption:* 48.2% (2023 est.)
government consumption: 22.4% (2023 est.)
investment in fixed capital: 24% (2023 est.)
investment in inventories: 1.7% (2023 est.)
exports of goods and services: 30.9% (2023 est.)
imports of goods and services: -27.1% (2023 est.)
note: figures may not total 100% due to rounding or gaps in data collection

Agricultural products: milk, chicken, potatoes, tomatoes, avocados, bananas, grapefruits, eggs, tangerines/mandarins, carrots/turnips (2022)
note: top ten agricultural products based on tonnage

Industries: high-technology products (including aviation, communications, computer-aided design and manufactures, medical electronics, fiber optics), wood and paper products, potash and phosphates, food, beverages, and tobacco, caustic soda, cement, pharmaceuticals, construction, metal products, chemical products, plastics, cut diamonds, textiles, footwear

Industrial production growth rate: 6.05% (2021 est.)
note: annual % change in industrial value added based on constant local currency
comparison ranking: 42

Labor force: 4.554 million (2023 est.)
note: number of people ages 15 or older who are employed or seeking work
comparison ranking: 93

Unemployment rate: 3.39% (2023 est.)
3.7% (2022 est.)
4.81% (2021 est.)
note: % of labor force seeking employment
comparison ranking: 57

Youth unemployment rate (ages 15-24): *total:* 6% (2023 est.)
male: 6.1% (2023 est.)
female: 5.9% (2023 est.)
note: % of labor force ages 15-24 seeking employment
comparison ranking: total 167

Population below poverty line: 22% (2014 est.)
note: Israel's poverty line is $7.30 per person per day

Gini Index coefficient - distribution of family income: 37.9 (2021 est.)
note: index (0-100) of income distribution; higher values represent greater inequality
comparison ranking: 56

Average household expenditures: *on food:* 16% of household expenditures (2022 est.)
on alcohol and tobacco: 2.8% of household expenditures (2022 est.)

Household income or consumption by percentage share: *lowest 10%:* 1.9% (2021 est.)
highest 10%: 27.1% (2021 est.)
note: % share of income accruing to lowest and highest 10% of population

Remittances: 0.19% of GDP (2023 est.)
0.24% of GDP (2022 est.)
0.25% of GDP (2021 est.)
note: personal transfers and compensation between resident and non-resident individuals/households/entities

Budget: *revenues:* $180.935 billion (2022 est.)
expenditures: $184.823 billion (2022 est.)
note: central government revenues (excluding grants) and expenses converted to US dollars at average official exchange rate for year indicated

Public debt: 72.6% of GDP (2020 est.)
comparison ranking: 50

Taxes and other revenues: 25.01% (of GDP) (2022 est.)
note: central government tax revenue as a % of GDP
comparison ranking: 47

Current account balance: $25.089 billion (2023 est.)
$20.34 billion (2022 est.)
$19.095 billion (2021 est.)
note: balance of payments - net trade and primary/secondary income in current dollars
comparison ranking: 22

Exports: $156.165 billion (2023 est.)
$166.227 billion (2022 est.)
$143.505 billion (2021 est.)
note: balance of payments - exports of goods and services in current dollars
comparison ranking: 38

Exports - partners: US 25%, China 7%, West Bank/Gaza Strip 6%, Ireland 5%, UK 4% (2022)
note: top five export partners based on percentage share of exports

Exports - commodities: diamonds, integrated circuits, refined petroleum, fertilizers, medical instruments (2022)
note: top five export commodities based on value in dollars

Imports: $137.567 billion (2023 est.)
$150.804 billion (2022 est.)
$125.948 billion (2021 est.)
note: balance of payments - imports of goods and services in current dollars
comparison ranking: 40

Imports - partners: China 14%, US 11%, Turkey 7%, Germany 6%, India 5% (2022)
note: top five import partners based on percentage share of imports

Imports - commodities: diamonds, cars, crude petroleum, refined petroleum, garments (2022)
note: top five import commodities based on value in dollars

Reserves of foreign exchange and gold: $204.661 billion (2023 est.)
$194.231 billion (2022 est.)
$212.934 billion (2021 est.)
note: holdings of gold (year-end prices)/foreign exchange/special drawing rights in current dollars
comparison ranking: 22

Exchange rates: new Israeli shekels (ILS) per US dollar -

Exchange rates: 3.667 (2023 est.)
3.36 (2022 est.)
3.23 (2021 est.)
3.442 (2020 est.)
3.565 (2019 est.)

ENERGY

Electricity access: *electrification - total population:* 100% (2022 est.)

Electricity: *installed generating capacity:* 22.207 million kW (2022 est.)
consumption: 65.442 billion kWh (2022 est.)
exports: 6.916 billion kWh (2022 est.)
transmission/distribution losses: 3.557 billion kWh (2022 est.)
comparison rankings: transmission/distribution losses 148; exports 31; consumption 45; installed generating capacity 46

Electricity generation sources: *fossil fuels:* 90.1% of total installed capacity (2022 est.)
solar: 9.7% of total installed capacity (2022 est.)
wind: 0.2% of total installed capacity (2022 est.)

Coal: *consumption:* 6.476 million metric tons (2022 est.)
exports: 8.9 metric tons (2022 est.)
imports: 6.561 million metric tons (2022 est.)

Petroleum: *total petroleum production:* 15,000 bbl/day (2023 est.)
refined petroleum consumption: 230,000 bbl/day (2023 est.)
crude oil estimated reserves: 12.73 million barrels (2021 est.)

Natural gas: *production:* 22.886 billion cubic meters (2022 est.)
consumption: 11.51 billion cubic meters (2022 est.)
exports: 9.578 billion cubic meters (2022 est.)
imports: 59.369 million cubic meters (2022 est.)
proven reserves: 176.018 billion cubic meters (2021 est.)

Carbon dioxide emissions: 64.871 million metric tonnes of CO_2 (2022 est.)
from coal and metallurgical coke: 14.043 million metric tonnes of CO_2 (2022 est.)
from petroleum and other liquids: 28.858 million metric tonnes of CO_2 (2022 est.)
from consumed natural gas: 21.97 million metric tonnes of CO_2 (2022 est.)
comparison ranking: total emissions 51

Energy consumption per capita: 113.455 million Btu/person (2022 est.)
comparison ranking: 43

COMMUNICATIONS

Telephones - fixed lines: *total subscriptions:* 3.574 million (2022 est.)
subscriptions per 100 inhabitants: 40 (2022 est.)
comparison ranking: total subscriptions 35

Telephones - mobile cellular: *total subscriptions:* 13.758 million (2022 est.)
subscriptions per 100 inhabitants: 152 (2022 est.)
comparison ranking: total subscriptions 77

Telecommunication systems: *general assessment:* Israel's developed economy largely revolves around high technology products and services, primarily used in the medical, biotechnology, agricultural, materials, and military industries; the country also attracts investment in its cyber-security industry, and has established itself as a hub for thousands of start-up companies; to underpin these developments, Israel has developed a robust telecoms sector; household broadband subscriptions is high, with a focus on fiber-network deployment; LTE services are almost universally available, while the August 2020 multi-frequency bands also enabled the MNOs to provide services based on 5G; 5G will be supported by moves to close down GSM and 3G networks in stages through to the end of 2025, with the physical assets and frequencies to be repurposed for LTE and 5G use (2023)
domestic: fixed-line nearly 39 per 100 and nearly 140 per 100 for mobile-cellular subscriptions (2021)
international: country code - 972; landing points for the MedNautilus Submarine System, Tameres North, Jonah and Lev Submarine System, submarine cables that provide links to Europe, Cyprus, and parts of the Middle East; satellite earth stations - 3 Intelsat (2 Atlantic Ocean and 1 Indian Ocean) (2019)

Broadcast media: the Israel Broadcasting Corporation (est 2015) broadcasts on 3 channels, two in Hebrew and the other in Arabic; multi-channel satellite and cable TV packages provide access to foreign channels; the Israeli Broadcasting Corporation broadcasts on 8 radio networks with multiple repeaters and Israel Defense Forces Radio broadcasts over multiple stations; about 15 privately owned radio stations; overall more than 100 stations and repeater stations (2019)

Internet country code: .il

Internet users: *total:* 8.01 million (2021 est.)
percent of population: 90% (2021 est.)
comparison ranking: total 75

Broadband - fixed subscriptions: *total:* 2,602,079 (2020 est.)
subscriptions per 100 inhabitants: 30 (2020 est.)
comparison ranking: total 50

TRANSPORTATION

National air transport system: *number of registered air carriers:* 6 (2020)
inventory of registered aircraft operated by air carriers: 64
annual passenger traffic on registered air carriers: 7,404,373 (2018)
annual freight traffic on registered air carriers: 994.54 million (2018) mt-km

Civil aircraft registration country code prefix: 4X

Airports: 37 (2024)
comparison ranking: 107

Heliports: 11 (2024)

Pipelines: 763 km gas, 442 km oil, 261 km refined products (2013)

Railways: *total:* 1,497 km (2021) (2019)
standard gauge: 1,497 km (2021) 1.435-m gauge
comparison ranking: total 82

Roadways: *total:* 20,391 km
paved: 20,391 km (2021) (includes 449 km of expressways)
comparison ranking: total 114

Merchant marine: *total:* 41 (2023)
by type: container ship 4, general cargo 1, oil tanker 4, other 32
comparison ranking: total 123

Ports: *total ports:* 5 (2024)
large: 0
medium: 1
small: 2
very small: 2
ports with oil terminals: 4
key ports: Ashdod, Ashqelon, Elat, Hadera, Haifa

MILITARY AND SECURITY

Military and security forces: Israel Defense Forces (IDF): Ground Forces, Israel Naval Force (IN, includes commandos), Israel Air Force (IAF, includes air defense) (2024)
note 1: the national police, including the border police and the immigration police, are under the authority of the Ministry of Public Security
note 2: the Israeli Security Agency (ISA) is charged with combating terrorism and espionage in Israel and the West Bank and Gaza Strip; it is under the authority of the Prime Minister; ISA forces operating in the West Bank fall under the IDF for operations and operational debriefing

Military expenditures: 4.5% of GDP (2023 est.)
4.5% of GDP (2022 est.)
5% of GDP (2021 est.)
5% of GDP (2020 est.)
5.2% of GDP (2019 est.)
comparison ranking: 13

Military and security service personnel strengths: approximately 170,000 active-duty personnel (130,000 Ground Forces; 10,000 Naval; 30,000 Air Force) (2023)

Military equipment inventories and acquisitions: the majority of the IDF's inventory is comprised of weapons that are domestically produced or imported from Europe and the US; the US has been the leading supplier of arms in recent years; Israel has a broad defense industrial base that can develop, produce, support, and sustain a wide variety of weapons systems for both domestic use and export, particularly armored vehicles, unmanned aerial systems, air defense, and guided missiles (2024)

Military service age and obligation: 18 years of age for compulsory military service; 17 years of age for voluntary military service; Jews and Druze can be conscripted; Christians, Circassians, and Muslims may volunteer; both sexes are obligated to military service; conscript service obligation is 32 months for enlisted men and about 24 months for enlisted women (varies based on military occupation); officers serve 48 months; Air Force pilots commit to 9 years of service; reserve obligation to age 41-51 (men), age 24 (women) (2024)
note: the IDF recruits foreign Jews and non-Jews with a minimum of one Jewish grandparent, as well as converts to Judaism; each year the IDF brings in about 800-1,000 foreign recruits from around the world

Military - note: the IDF is responsible for external defense but also has some domestic security responsibilities; its primary operational focuses include the threat posed by Iran, instability in Syria, and terrorist organizations, including HAMAS, Hizballah, the Islamic State of Iraq and ash-Sham (ISIS), and Palestine Islamic Jihad (PIJ); it has considerable experience in conventional and unconventional warfare; since the country's founding in 1948, the IDF has been in conflicts against one or more of its Arab neighbors in 1948-49, 1956, 1967, 1967-70 ("War of Attrition"), 1973, 1982, and 2006; it bombed nuclear sites in Iraq in 1981 and Syria in 2007, and since the outbreak of the Syrian civil war in 2011, has conducted numerous air strikes in Syria against Iranian, Iranian-backed militia, Hizballah, and Syrian Government targets; over the same period, the IDF has carried out strikes against Hizballah in Lebanon in response to attacks on Israeli territory; the IDF has conducted numerous operations against HAMAS and PIJ, which operate out of the Gaza Strip and have launched dozens of rocket attacks against Israel; HAMAS and Israel fought an 11-day conflict in 2021, which ended in an informal truce, although sporadic clashes continued; in October 2023, HAMAS conducted a surprise ground assault from Gaza into Israel, supported by rockets and armed drones, killing more than 1,000 Israelis and foreigners living in Israel; the attack resulted in an IDF ground invasion of Gaza where fighting continued into 2024
since its creation from armed Jewish militias during the First Arab-Israeli War in 1948-49, the IDF, particularly the Ground Force, has been guided by a requirement to rapidly mobilize and defend the country's territory from numerically superior neighboring countries; the active-duty military is backed up by a large force of trained reserves–approximately 300-400,000 personnel–that can be mobilized rapidly
Israel's primary security partner is the US; consistent with a 10-year (2019-2028) Memorandum of Understanding, the US annually provides over $3 billion in military financing and cooperative military programs, such as missile defense; the US also provides Israel access to US-produced military weapons systems including advanced fighter aircraft; Israel has Major Non-NATO Ally status with the US, a designation under US law that provides foreign partners with certain benefits in the areas of defense trade and security cooperation
the United Nations Disengagement Observer Force (UNDOF) has operated in the Golan between Israel and Syria since 1974 to monitor the ceasefire following the 1973 Arab-Israeli War and supervise the areas of separation between the two countries; UNDOF consists of about 1,000 military personnel (2024)

SPACE

Space agency/agencies: Israel Space Agency (ISA; established 1983 under the Ministry of Science and Technology; origins go back to the creation of a National Committee for Space Research, established 1960); Ministry of Defense Space Department (2024)

Space launch site(s): Palmachim Airbase (Central district) (2024)

Space program overview: has an ambitious space program and one of the most advanced in the region; designs, builds, and operates communications, remote sensing (RS), and scientific satellites; designs, builds, and operates sounding (research) rockets and orbital satellite/space launch vehicles (SLVs); launches satellites on domestic and foreign rockets; researches and develops a range of other space-related capabilities with a focus on lightweight and miniaturized technologies, including small satellites with high resolution RS imaging and communications capabilities; has relations with a variety of

foreign space agencies and space industries, including those of Canada, the European Space Agency (and individual member states, such as France, Germany, and Italy), India, Japan, Mexico, and the US; has a substantial commercial space sector, including state-owned enterprises, in areas such as launchers, propulsion, satellite manufacturing, particularly micro- and nano-satellites, payloads and applications, RS, communications, and ground stations (2024)
note: further details about the key activities, programs, and milestones of the country's space program, as well as government spending estimates on the space sector, appear in the Space Programs reference guide

TERRORISM

Terrorist group(s): Islamic State of Iraq and ash-Sham (ISIS); Popular Front for the Liberation of Palestine; Palestinian Islamic Jihad; HAMAS
note: details about the history, aims, leadership, organization, areas of operation, tactics, targets, weapons, size, and sources of support of the group(s) appear(s) in the Terrorism reference guide

TRANSNATIONAL ISSUES

Refugees and internally displaced persons: *refugees (country of origin):* 12,181 (Eritrea), 5,061 (Ukraine) (2019)
stateless persons: 35 (2022)

Illicit drugs: increasingly concerned about ecstasy, cocaine, and heroin abuse; drugs arrive in country from Lebanon and, increasingly, from Jordan; money-laundering center

ITALY

INTRODUCTION

Background: Italy became a nation-state in 1861 when the regional states of the peninsula, along with Sardinia and Sicily, were united under King Victor EMMANUEL II. An era of parliamentary government came to a close in the early 1920s when Benito MUSSOLINI established a Fascist dictatorship. His alliance with Nazi Germany led to Italy's defeat in World War II. A democratic republic replaced the monarchy in 1946, and economic revival followed. Italy is a charter member of NATO, as well as the European Economic Community (EEC) and its successors, the EC and the EU. It has been at the forefront of European economic and political unification, joining the Economic and Monetary Union in 1999. Persistent problems include sluggish economic growth, high youth and female unemployment, organized crime, corruption, and economic disparities between southern Italy and the more prosperous north.

GEOGRAPHY

Location: Southern Europe, a peninsula extending into the central Mediterranean Sea, northeast of Tunisia

Geographic coordinates: 42 50 N, 12 50 E

Map references: Europe

Area: *total:* 301,340 sq km
land: 294,140 sq km
water: 7,200 sq km
note: includes Sardinia and Sicily
comparison ranking: total 73

Area - comparative: almost twice the size of Georgia; slightly larger than Arizona

Land boundaries: *total:* 1,836.4 km
border countries (6): Austria 404 km; France 476 km; Holy See (Vatican City) 3.4 km; San Marino 37 km; Slovenia 218 km; Switzerland 698 km

Coastline: 7,600 km

Maritime claims: *territorial sea:* 12 nm
continental shelf: 200-m depth or to the depth of exploitation

Climate: predominantly Mediterranean; alpine in far north; hot, dry in south

Terrain: mostly rugged and mountainous; some plains, coastal lowlands

Elevation: *highest point:* Mont Blanc (Monte Bianco) de Courmayeur (a secondary peak of Mont Blanc) 4,748 m
lowest point: Mediterranean Sea 0 m
mean elevation: 538 m

Natural resources: coal, antimony, mercury, zinc, potash, marble, barite, asbestos, pumice, fluorspar, feldspar, pyrite (sulfur), natural gas and crude oil reserves, fish, arable land

Land use: *agricultural land:* 47.1% (2018 est.)
arable land: 22.8% (2018 est.)
permanent crops: 8.6% (2018 est.)
permanent pasture: 15.7% (2018 est.)
forest: 31.4% (2018 est.)
other: 21.5% (2018 est.)

Irrigated land: 26,010 sq km (2013)

Major watersheds (area sq km): Atlantic Ocean drainage: Rhine-Maas (198,735 sq km), *(Black Sea)* Danube (795,656 sq km), *(Adriatic Sea)* Po (76,997 sq km), *(Mediterranean Sea)* Rhone (100,543 sq km)

Population distribution: despite a distinctive pattern with an industrial north and an agrarian south, a fairly even population distribution exists throughout most of the country, with coastal areas, the Po River Valley, and urban centers (particularly Milan, Rome, and Naples), attracting larger and denser populations

Natural hazards: regional risks include landslides, mudflows, avalanches, earthquakes, volcanic eruptions, flooding; land subsidence in Venice
volcanism: significant volcanic activity; Etna (3,330 m), which is in eruption as of 2013, is Europe's most active volcano; flank eruptions pose a threat to nearby Sicilian villages; Etna, along with the famous Vesuvius, which remains a threat to the millions of nearby residents in the Bay of Naples area, have both been deemed Decade Volcanoes by the International Association of Volcanology and Chemistry of the Earth's Interior, worthy of study due to their explosive history and close proximity to human populations; Stromboli, on its namesake island, has also been continuously active with moderate volcanic activity; other historically active volcanoes include Campi Flegrei, Ischia, Larderello, Pantelleria, Vulcano, and Vulsini

Geography - note: strategic location dominating central Mediterranean as well as southern sea and air approaches to Western Europe

PEOPLE AND SOCIETY

Population: *total:* 60,964,931
male: 29,414,065
female: 31,550,866 (2024 est.)
comparison rankings: female 24; male 25; total 24

Nationality: *noun:* Italian(s)
adjective: Italian

Ethnic groups: Italian (includes small clusters of German-, French-, and Slovene-Italians in the north, Albanian-Italians, Croat-Italians, and Greek-Italians in the south)

Languages: Italian (official), German (parts of Trentino-Alto Adige region are predominantly German-speaking), French (small French-speaking minority in Valle d'Aosta region), Slovene (Slovene-speaking minority in the Trieste-Gorizia area), Croatian (in Molise)
major-language sample(s):
L'Almanacco dei fatti del mondo, l'indispensabile fonte per le informazioni di base. (Italian)

Religions: Christian 80.8% (overwhelmingly Roman Catholic with very small groups of Jehovah's Witnesses and Protestants), Muslim 4.9%, unaffiliated 13.4%, other 0.9% (2020 est.)

Age structure: *0-14 years:* 11.9% (male 3,699,167/female 3,531,734)
15-64 years: 64.5% (male 19,378,160/female 19,958,137)
65 years and over: 23.6% (2024 est.) (male 6,336,738/female 8,060,995)

Dependency ratios: *total dependency ratio:* 57.1
youth dependency ratio: 19.9
elderly dependency ratio: 37.2
potential support ratio: 2.7 (2021 est.)

Median age: *total:* 48.4 years (2024 est.)

male: 47.4 years
female: 49.4 years
comparison ranking: total 5

Population growth rate: -0.08% (2024 est.)
comparison ranking: 201

Birth rate: 7.1 births/1,000 population (2024 est.)
comparison ranking: 222

Death rate: 11.2 deaths/1,000 population (2024 est.)
comparison ranking: 22

Net migration rate: 3.4 migrant(s)/1,000 population (2024 est.)
comparison ranking: 33

Population distribution: despite a distinctive pattern with an industrial north and an agrarian south, a fairly even population distribution exists throughout most of the country, with coastal areas, the Po River Valley, and urban centers (particularly Milan, Rome, and Naples), attracting larger and denser populations

Urbanization: *urban population:* 72% of total population (2023)
rate of urbanization: 0.27% annual rate of change (2020-25 est.)

Major urban areas - population: 4.316 million ROME (capital), 3.155 million Milan, 2.179 million Naples, 1.802 million Turin, 913,000 Bergamo, 850,000 Palermo (2023)

Sex ratio: *at birth:* 1.06 male(s)/female
0-14 years: 1.05 male(s)/female
15-64 years: 0.97 male(s)/female
65 years and over: 0.79 male(s)/female
total population: 0.93 male(s)/female (2024 est.)

Mother's mean age at first birth: 31.4 years (2020 est.)

Maternal mortality ratio: 5 deaths/100,000 live births (2020 est.)
comparison ranking: 165

Infant mortality rate: *total:* 3.1 deaths/1,000 live births (2024 est.)
male: 3.2 deaths/1,000 live births
female: 2.9 deaths/1,000 live births
comparison ranking: total 207

Life expectancy at birth: *total population:* 83 years (2024 est.)
male: 80.7 years
female: 85.5 years
comparison ranking: total population 19

Total fertility rate: 1.26 children born/woman (2024 est.)
comparison ranking: 219

Gross reproduction rate: 0.61 (2024 est.)

Contraceptive prevalence rate: 65.1% (2013)
note: percent of women aged 18-49

Drinking water source: *improved:*
total: 99.9% of population
unimproved:
total: 0.1% of population (2020 est.)

Current health expenditure: 9.6% of GDP (2020)

Physician density: 3.95 physicians/1,000 population (2020)

Hospital bed density: 3.1 beds/1,000 population (2018)

Sanitation facility access: *improved: urban:* 100% of population
rural: 100% of population
total: 100% of population

Obesity - adult prevalence rate: 19.9% (2016)
comparison ranking: 108

Alcohol consumption per capita: *total:* 7.65 liters of pure alcohol (2019 est.)
beer: 1.99 liters of pure alcohol (2019 est.)
wine: 4.83 liters of pure alcohol (2019 est.)
spirits: 0.83 liters of pure alcohol (2019 est.)
other alcohols: 0 liters of pure alcohol (2019 est.)
comparison ranking: total 51

Tobacco use: *total:* 23.1% (2020 est.)
male: 26.6% (2020 est.)
female: 19.5% (2020 est.)
comparison ranking: total 64

Children under the age of 5 years underweight: NA

Currently married women (ages 15-49): 52.5% (2023 est.)

Education expenditures: 4.3% of GDP (2020 est.)
comparison ranking: 106

Literacy: *definition:* age 15 and over can read and write
total population: 99.2%
male: 99.4%
female: 99% (2018)

School life expectancy (primary to tertiary education): *total:* 16 years
male: 16 years
female: 17 years (2020)

ENVIRONMENT

Environment - current issues: air pollution from industrial emissions such as sulfur dioxide; coastal and inland rivers polluted from industrial and agricultural effluents; acid rain damaging lakes; inadequate industrial waste treatment and disposal facilities

Environment - international agreements: *party to:* Air Pollution, Air Pollution-Nitrogen Oxides, Air Pollution-Persistent Organic Pollutants, Air Pollution-Sulphur 85, Air Pollution-Sulphur 94, Air Pollution-Volatile Organic Compounds, Antarctic-Environmental Protection, Antarctic-Marine Living Resources, Antarctic Seals, Antarctic Treaty, Biodiversity, Climate Change, Climate Change-Kyoto Protocol, Climate Change-Paris Agreement, Comprehensive Nuclear Test Ban, Desertification, Endangered Species, Environmental Modification, Hazardous Wastes, Law of the Sea, Marine Dumping-London Convention, Marine Dumping-London Protocol, Nuclear Test Ban, Ozone Layer Protection, Ship Pollution, Tropical Timber 2006, Wetlands, Whaling
signed, but not ratified: Air Pollution-Heavy Metals, Air Pollution-Multi-effect Protocol

Climate: predominantly Mediterranean; alpine in far north; hot, dry in south

Urbanization: *urban population:* 72% of total population (2023)
rate of urbanization: 0.27% annual rate of change (2020-25 est.)

Revenue from forest resources: 0.01% of GDP (2018 est.)
comparison ranking: 150

Revenue from coal: 0% of GDP (2018 est.)
comparison ranking: 85

Air pollutants: *particulate matter emissions:* 14.22 micrograms per cubic meter (2019 est.)
methane emissions: 41.3 megatons (2020 est.)

Waste and recycling: *municipal solid waste generated annually:* 29.524 million tons (2015 est.)
municipal solid waste recycled annually: 7,646,716 tons (2015 est.)
percent of municipal solid waste recycled: 25.9% (2015 est.)

Major watersheds (area sq km): **Atlantic Ocean drainage:** Rhine-Maas (198,735 sq km), *(Black Sea)* Danube (795,656 sq km), *(Adriatic Sea)* Po (76,997 sq km), *(Mediterranean Sea)* Rhone (100,543 sq km)

Total water withdrawal: *municipal:* 9.19 billion cubic meters (2020 est.)
industrial: 7.7 billion cubic meters (2020 est.)
agricultural: 17 billion cubic meters (2020 est.)

Total renewable water resources: 191.3 billion cubic meters (2020 est.)

Geoparks: *total global geoparks and regional networks:* 11
global geoparks and regional networks: Adamello-Brenta; Alpi Apuane; Aspromonte; Beigua; Cilento, Vallo di Diano e Alburni; Madonie; Maiella; Pollino; Rocca di Cerere; Sesia Val Grande; Tuscan Mining Park (2023)

GOVERNMENT

Country name: *conventional long form:* Italian Republic
conventional short form: Italy
local long form: Repubblica Italiana
local short form: Italia
former: Kingdom of Italy
etymology: derivation is unclear, but the Latin "Italia" may come from the Oscan "Viteliu" meaning "[Land] of Young Cattle" (the bull was a symbol of southern Italic tribes)

Government type: parliamentary republic

Capital: *name:* Rome
geographic coordinates: 41 54 N, 12 29 E
time difference: UTC+1 (6 hours ahead of Washington, DC, during Standard Time)
daylight saving time: +1hr, begins last Sunday in March; ends last Sunday in October
etymology: by tradition, named after Romulus, one of the legendary founders of the city and its first king

Administrative divisions: 15 regions (regioni, singular - regione) and 5 autonomous regions (regioni autonome, singular - regione autonoma)
regions: Abruzzo, Basilicata, Calabria, Campania, Emilia-Romagna, Lazio (Latium), Liguria, Lombardia, Marche, Molise, Piemonte (Piedmont), Puglia (Apulia), Toscana (Tuscany), Umbria, Veneto
autonomous regions: Friuli Venezia Giulia, Sardegna (Sardinia), Sicilia (Sicily), Trentino-Alto Adige (Trentino-South Tyrol) or Trentino-Suedtirol (German), Valle d'Aosta (Aosta Valley) or Vallee d'Aoste (French)

Independence: 17 March 1861 (Kingdom of Italy proclaimed; Italy was not finally unified until 1871)

National holiday: Republic Day, 2 June (1946)

Legal system: civil law system; judicial review of legislation under certain conditions in Constitutional Court

Constitution: *history:* previous 1848 (originally for the Kingdom of Sardinia and adopted by the Kingdom of Italy in 1861); latest enacted 22 December 1947, adopted 27 December 1947, entered into force 1 January 1948
amendments: proposed by both houses of Parliament; passage requires two successive debates and approval by absolute majority of each house on the second vote; a referendum is only required when

requested by one fifth of the members of either house, by voter petition, or by 5 Regional Councils (elected legislative assemblies of the 15 first-level administrative regions and 5 autonomous regions of Italy); referendum not required if an amendment has been approved by a two-thirds majority in each house in the second vote; amended many times, last in 2020; note - in June 2024, the Senate approved in its first vote an amendment calling for the direct election of the prime minister; subsequent votes by both the Senate and House of Deputies is required for passage; lacking approval by Parliament, approval is required by constitutional referendum

International law organization participation: accepts compulsory ICJ jurisdiction with reservations; accepts ICCt jurisdiction

Citizenship: *citizenship by birth:* no
citizenship by descent only: at least one parent must be a citizen of Italy
dual citizenship recognized: yes
residency requirement for naturalization: 4 years for EU nationals, 5 years for refugees and specified exceptions, 10 years for all others

Suffrage: 18 years of age; universal except in senatorial elections, where minimum age is 25

Executive branch: *chief of state:* President Sergio MATTARELLA (since 3 February 2015)
head of government: Prime Minister Giorgia MELONI (since 22 October 2022); the prime minister's official title is President of the Council of Ministers
cabinet: Council of Ministers proposed by the prime minister, known officially as the President of the Council of Ministers and locally as the Premier; nominated by the president
elections/appointments: president indirectly elected by an electoral college consisting of both houses of Parliament and 58 regional representatives for a 7-year term (no term limits); election last held on 24-29 January 2022 (eight rounds) (next to be held in 2029); prime minister appointed by the president, confirmed by parliament
election results:
2022: Sergio MATTARELLA (independent) reelected president; electoral college vote count in eighth round - 759 out of 1,009 (505 vote threshold)
2015: Sergio MATTARELLA (independent) elected president; electoral college vote count in fourth round - 665 out of 995 (505 vote threshold)

Legislative branch: *description:* bicameral Parliament or Parlamento consists of:
Senate or Senato della Repubblica (205 seats; 122 members in multi-seat constituencies directly elected by proportional representation vote, 74 members in single-seat constituencies directly elected by plurality vote, 4 members in multi-seat constituencies abroad directly elected by proportional representation vote, and 5 members appointed by the president of Italy; all members serve 5-year terms)
Chamber of Deputies or Camera dei Deputati (400 seats; 245 members directly elected in multi-seat constituencies by proportional representation vote; 147 members directly elected in single-seat constituencies by plurality vote and 8 members in multi-seat constituencies abroad directly elected by proportional representation vote; members serve 5-year terms)
elections: Senate - last held on 25 September 2022 (next to be held no later than December 2027)
Chamber of Deputies - last held on 25 September 2022; note - snap elections were called when Prime Minister DRAGHI resigned and the parliament was dissolved on 21 July 2022 (next to be held on 30 September 2027)
election results: Senate - percent of vote by party/coalition - NA; seats by party/coalition - center-right coalition 113 (FdI 65, Lega 30, FI 18), center-left coalition 43 (PD 40, AVS 3), M5S 28, Action-Italia Viva 9, SVP 2, MAIE 1, ScN 1; composition - men 131, women 74, percentage women 36.1%
Chamber of Deputies - percent of vote by party - NA; seats by party - center-right coalition 230 (FdI 119, Lega 66, FI 45), center-left coalition 83 (PD 69, AVS 12, +EU 2), M5S 52, Action-Italia Viva 21, SVP 3, MAIE 1, ScN 1; composition - men 271, women 129, percentage women 32.3%; total Parliament percentage women 33.6%

Judicial branch: *highest court(s):* Supreme Court of Cassation or Corte Suprema di Cassazione (consists of the first president (chief justice), deputy president, 54 justices presiding over 6 civil and 7 criminal divisions, and 288 judges; an additional 30 judges of lower courts serve as supporting judges; cases normally heard by 5-judge panels; more complex cases heard by 9-judge panels); Constitutional Court or Corte Costituzionale (consists of the court president and 14 judges)
judge selection and term of office: Supreme Court judges appointed by the High Council of the Judiciary, headed by the president of the republic; judges may serve for life; Constitutional Court judges - 5 appointed by the president, 5 elected by Parliament, 5 elected by select higher courts; judges serve up to 9 years
subordinate courts: various lower civil and criminal courts (primary and secondary tribunals and courts of appeal)

Political parties: Action-Italia Viva
Associative Movement of Italians Abroad or MAIE
Brothers of Italy or FdI
Democratic Party or PD
Five Star Movement or M5S
Forza Italia or FI
Free and Equal (Liberi e Uguali) or LeU
Greens and Left Alliance or AVS
Italexit
League or Lega
More Europe or +EU
Popular Union or PU
South calls North or ScN
South Tyrolean Peoples Party or SVP
other minor parties

International organization participation: ADB (nonregional member), AfDB (nonregional member), Arctic Council (observer), Australia Group, BIS, BSEC (observer), CBSS (observer), CD, CDB, CE, CEI, CERN, EAPC, EBRD, ECB, EIB, EITI (implementing country), EMU, ESA, EU, FAO, FATF, G-7, G-8, G-10, G-20, IADB, IAEA, IBRD, ICAO, ICC (national committees), ICCt, ICRM, IDA, IEA, IFAD, IFC, IFRCS, IGAD (partners), IHO, ILO, IMF, IMO, IMSO, Interpol, IOC, IOM, IPU, ISO, ITSO, ITU, ITUC (NGOs), LAIA (observer), MIGA, MINURSO, NATO, NEA, NSG, OAS (observer), OECD, OPCW, OSCE, Pacific Alliance (observer), Paris Club, PCA, PIF (partner), Schengen Convention, SELEC (observer), SICA (observer), UN, UNCTAD, UNESCO, UNHCR, UNIDO, UNIFIL, Union Latina, UNMOGIP, UNOOSA, UNRWA, UNTSO, UNWTO, UPU, Wassenaar Arrangement, WCO, WHO, WIPO, WMO, WTO, ZC

Diplomatic representation in the US: *chief of mission:* Ambassador Mariangela ZAPPIA (since 15 September 2021)
chancery: 3000 Whitehaven Street NW, Washington, DC 20008
telephone: [1] (202) 612-4400
FAX: [1] (202) 518-2154
email address and website:
washington.ambasciata@esteri.it
https://ambwashingtondc.esteri.it/ambasciata_washington/en/
consulate(s) general: Boston, Chicago, Houston, Miami, New York, Los Angeles, Philadelphia, San Francisco
consulate(s): Detroit

Diplomatic representation from the US: *chief of mission:* Ambassador Jack MARKELL (since September 2023); note - also accredited to San Marino
embassy: via Vittorio Veneto 121, 00187 Roma
mailing address: 9500 Rome Place, Washington DC 20521-9500
telephone: [39] 06-46741
FAX: [39] 06-4674-2244
email address and website:
uscitizenrome@state.gov
https://it.usembassy.gov/
consulate(s) general: Florence, Milan, Naples

Flag description: three equal vertical bands of green (hoist side), white, and red; design inspired by the French flag brought to Italy by Napoleon in 1797; colors are those of Milan (red and white) combined with the green uniform color of the Milanese civic guard
note: similar to the flag of Mexico, which is longer, uses darker shades of green and red, and has its coat of arms centered on the white band; Ireland, which is longer and is green (hoist side), white, and orange; also similar to the flag of the Cote d'Ivoire, which has the colors reversed - orange (hoist side), white, and green

National symbol(s): white, five-pointed star (Stella d'Italia); national colors: red, white, green

National anthem: *name:* "Il Canto degli Italiani" (The Song of the Italians)
lyrics/music: Goffredo MAMELI/Michele NOVARO
note: adopted 1946; the anthem, originally written in 1847, is also known as "L'Inno di Mameli" (Mameli's Hymn), and "Fratelli D'Italia" (Brothers of Italy)

National heritage: *total World Heritage Sites:* 59 (53 cultural, 6 natural)
selected World Heritage Site locales: Historic Center of Rome (c); Archaeological Areas of Pompeii, Herculaneum, and Torre Annunziata (c); Venice and its Lagoon (c); Historic Center of Florence (c); Piazza del Duomo, Pisa (c); Historic Centre of Naples (c); Portovenere, Cinque Terre, and the Islands (c); Villa d'Este, Tivoli (c); Mount Etna (n); Rock Drawings in Valcamonica (c); Historic Siena (c)

ECONOMY

Economic overview: core EU economy; strong services, manufacturing, and tourism sectors; sustained recovery in post-COVID inflationary environment; high public debt levels; increasing poverty levels particularly in poorer south; strong exports to EU and US partners

Real GDP (purchasing power parity): $3.097 trillion (2023 est.)
$3.068 trillion (2022 est.)
$2.951 trillion (2021 est.)
note: data in 2021 dollars
comparison ranking: 11

Real GDP growth rate: 0.92% (2023 est.)
3.99% (2022 est.)
8.31% (2021 est.)
note: annual GDP % growth based on constant local currency
comparison ranking: 166

Real GDP per capita: $52,700 (2023 est.)
$52,100 (2022 est.)
$49,900 (2021 est.)
note: data in 2021 dollars
comparison ranking: 37

GDP (official exchange rate): $2.255 trillion (2023 est.)
note: data in current dollars at official exchange rate

Inflation rate (consumer prices): 5.62% (2023 est.)
8.2% (2022 est.)
1.87% (2021 est.)
note: annual % change based on consumer prices
comparison ranking: 119

Credit ratings: Fitch rating: BBB- (2020)

Moody's rating: Baa3 (2018)

Standard & Poors rating: BBB (2017)
note: The year refers to the year in which the current credit rating was first obtained.

GDP - composition, by sector of origin: *agriculture:* 1.9% (2023 est.)
industry: 23.1% (2023 est.)
services: 64.9% (2023 est.)
note: figures may not total 100% due to non-allocated consumption not captured in sector-reported data
comparison rankings: services 58; industry 114; agriculture 160

GDP - composition, by end use: *household consumption:* 59.6% (2023 est.)
government consumption: 18.1% (2023 est.)
investment in fixed capital: 21.2% (2023 est.)
investment in inventories: -0.3% (2023 est.)
exports of goods and services: 35.1% (2023 est.)
imports of goods and services: -33.7% (2023 est.)
note: figures may not total 100% due to rounding or gaps in data collection

Agricultural products: milk, grapes, wheat, tomatoes, maize, apples, olives, oranges, potatoes, pork (2022)
note: top ten agricultural products based on tonnage

Industries: tourism, machinery, iron and steel, chemicals, food processing, textiles, motor vehicles, clothing, footwear, ceramics

Industrial production growth rate: -0.02% (2023 est.)
note: annual % change in industrial value added based on constant local currency
comparison ranking: 154

Labor force: 25.669 million (2023 est.)
note: number of people ages 15 or older who are employed or seeking work
comparison ranking: 26

Unemployment rate: 7.62% (2023 est.)
8.07% (2022 est.)
9.5% (2021 est.)
note: % of labor force seeking employment
comparison ranking: 142

Youth unemployment rate (ages 15-24): *total:* 22.7% (2023 est.)
male: 21.2% (2023 est.)
female: 25.2% (2023 est.)
note: % of labor force ages 15-24 seeking employment
comparison ranking: total 52

Population below poverty line: 20.1% (2021 est.)
note: % of population with income below national poverty line

Gini Index coefficient - distribution of family income: 34.8 (2021 est.)
note: index (0-100) of income distribution; higher values represent greater inequality
comparison ranking: 80

Average household expenditures: *on food:* 14.6% of household expenditures (2022 est.)
on alcohol and tobacco: 4.2% of household expenditures (2022 est.)

Household income or consumption by percentage share: *lowest 10%:* 2.3% (2021 est.)
highest 10%: 26.2% (2021 est.)
note: % share of income accruing to lowest and highest 10% of population

Remittances: 0.47% of GDP (2023 est.)
0.51% of GDP (2022 est.)
0.49% of GDP (2021 est.)
note: personal transfers and compensation between resident and non-resident individuals/households/entities

Budget: *revenues:* $857.336 billion (2022 est.)
expenditures: $1.015 trillion (2022 est.)
note: central government revenues (excluding grants) and expenses converted to US dollars at average official exchange rate for year indicated

Public debt: 131.8% of GDP (2017 est.)
note: Italy reports its data on public debt according to guidelines set out in the Maastricht Treaty; general government gross debt is defined in the Maastricht Treaty as consolidated general government gross debt at nominal value, outstanding at the end of the year, in the following categories of government liabilities (as defined in ESA95): currency and deposits (AF.2), securities other than shares excluding financial derivatives (AF.3, excluding AF.34), and loans (AF.4); the general government sector comprises central, state, and local government and social security funds
comparison ranking: 7

Taxes and other revenues: 24.92% (of GDP) (2022 est.)
note: central government tax revenue as a % of GDP
comparison ranking: 48

Current account balance: $11.552 billion (2023 est.)
-$32.783 billion (2022 est.)
$51.549 billion (2021 est.)
note: balance of payments - net trade and primary/secondary income in current dollars
comparison ranking: 27

Exports: $793.589 billion (2023 est.)
$752.864 billion (2022 est.)
$691.428 billion (2021 est.)
note: balance of payments - exports of goods and services in current dollars
comparison ranking: 9

Exports - partners: Germany 12%, US 11%, France 10%, Spain 5%, UK 4% (2022)
note: top five export partners based on percentage share of exports

Exports - commodities: packaged medicine, refined petroleum, garments, cars, vehicle parts/accessories (2022)
note: top five export commodities based on value in dollars

Imports: $756.154 billion (2023 est.)
$785.549 billion (2022 est.)
$644.93 billion (2021 est.)
note: balance of payments - imports of goods and services in current dollars
comparison ranking: 10

Imports - partners: Germany 14%, France 8%, China 8%, Netherlands 5%, Spain 5% (2022)
note: top five import partners based on percentage share of imports

Imports - commodities: natural gas, crude petroleum, cars, packaged medicine, garments (2022)
note: top five import commodities based on value in dollars

Reserves of foreign exchange and gold: $247.396 billion (2023 est.)
$224.581 billion (2022 est.)
$227.478 billion (2021 est.)
note: holdings of gold (year-end prices)/foreign exchange/special drawing rights in current dollars
comparison ranking: 17

Exchange rates: euros (EUR) per US dollar -

Exchange rates: 0.925 (2023 est.)
0.95 (2022 est.)
0.845 (2021 est.)
0.876 (2020 est.)
0.893 (2019 est.)

ENERGY

Electricity access: *electrification - total population:* 100% (2022 est.)

Electricity: *installed generating capacity:* 123.327 million kW (2022 est.)
consumption: 298.32 billion kWh (2022 est.)
exports: 4.419 billion kWh (2022 est.)
imports: 47.402 billion kWh (2022 est.)
transmission/distribution losses: 18.827 billion kWh (2022 est.)
comparison rankings: transmission/distribution losses 188; imports 4; exports 40; consumption 14; installed generating capacity 11

Electricity generation sources: *fossil fuels:* 63.7% of total installed capacity (2022 est.)
solar: 9.9% of total installed capacity (2022 est.)
wind: 7.5% of total installed capacity (2022 est.)
hydroelectricity: 10% of total installed capacity (2022 est.)
geothermal: 2% of total installed capacity (2022 est.)
biomass and waste: 7% of total installed capacity (2022 est.)

Nuclear energy: Number of nuclear reactors permanently shut down: 4 (2023)

Coal: *production:* 1.618 million metric tons (2022 est.)
consumption: 13.127 million metric tons (2022 est.)
exports: 294,000 metric tons (2022 est.)
imports: 12.462 million metric tons (2022 est.)
proven reserves: 609.999 million metric tons (2022 est.)

Petroleum: *total petroleum production:* 116,000 bbl/day (2023 est.)
refined petroleum consumption: 1.246 million bbl/day (2023 est.)
crude oil estimated reserves: 497.934 million barrels (2021 est.)

Natural gas: *production:* 3.117 billion cubic meters (2022 est.)
consumption: 68.735 billion cubic meters (2022 est.)
exports: 4.594 billion cubic meters (2022 est.)
imports: 72.579 billion cubic meters (2022 est.)
proven reserves: 45.76 billion cubic meters (2021 est.)

Carbon dioxide emissions: 316.578 million metric tonnes of CO2 (2022 est.)
from coal and metallurgical coke: 27.291 million metric tonnes of CO2 (2022 est.)
from petroleum and other liquids: 157.6 million metric tonnes of CO2 (2022 est.)
from consumed natural gas: 131.687 million metric tonnes of CO2 (2022 est.)
comparison ranking: total emissions 18

Energy consumption per capita: 98.458 million Btu/person (2022 est.)
comparison ranking: 54

COMMUNICATIONS

Telephones - fixed lines: *total subscriptions:* 19.982 million (2022 est.)
subscriptions per 100 inhabitants: 34 (2022 est.)
comparison ranking: total subscriptions 13

Telephones - mobile cellular: *total subscriptions:* 78.503 million (2022 est.)
subscriptions per 100 inhabitants: 133 (2022 est.)
comparison ranking: total subscriptions 22

Telecommunication systems: *general assessment:* Italy's large telecom market has one of the most progressive fiber sectors in Europe, with regulatory measures encouraging network sharing; regulatory measures have also been introduced to facilitate access to next generation networks (NGNs), and a number of deals have been brokered which enable the main telcoms to provide bundled services to large numbers of the population; Italy's vibrant mobile market has one of the highest subscription rates in Europe, though the number of subscribers has fallen in recent years as customers respond to attractive off-net pricing which has reduced the financial benefit of having SIM cards from different providers; network companies were among the first in Europe to trial services based on 5G; the high cost also encouraged the regulator in early 2021 to consider extending the licenses by an additional six years (2021)
domestic: 34 per 100 for fixed-line and nearly 132 per 100 for mobile-cellular subscriptions (2021)
international: country code - 39; landing points for Italy-Monaco, Italy-Libya, Italy-Malta, Italy-Greece-1, Italy-Croatia, BlueMed, Janna, FEA, SeaMeWe-3 & 4 & 5, Trapani-Kelibia, Columbus-III, Didon, GO-1, HANNIBAL System, MENA, Bridge International, Malta-Italy Interconnector, Melita1, IMEWE, VMSCS, AAE-1, and OTEGLOBE, submarine cables that provide links to Asia, the Middle East, Europe, North Africa, Southeast Asia, Australia and US; satellite earth stations - 3 Intelsat (with a total of 5 antennas - 3 for Atlantic Ocean and 2 for Indian Ocean) (2019)

Broadcast media: two Italian media giants dominate with 3 national terrestrial stations and privately owned companies with 3 national terrestrial stations; a large number of private stations, a satellite TV network; 3 AM/FM nationwide radio stations; about 1,300 commercial radio stations

Internet country code: .it

Internet users: *total:* 44.25 million (2021 est.)
percent of population: 75% (2021 est.)
comparison ranking: total 22

Broadband - fixed subscriptions: *total:* 18,128,787 (2020 est.)
subscriptions per 100 inhabitants: 30 (2020 est.)
comparison ranking: total 12

TRANSPORTATION

National air transport system: *number of registered air carriers:* 9 (2020)
inventory of registered aircraft operated by air carriers: 180
annual passenger traffic on registered air carriers: 27,630,435 (2018)
annual freight traffic on registered air carriers: 1.418 billion (2018) mt-km

Civil aircraft registration country code prefix: I

Airports: 636 (2024)
comparison ranking: 12

Heliports: 155 (2024)

Pipelines: 20,223 km gas, 1,393 km oil, 1,574 km refined products (2013)

Railways: *total:* 18,475 km (2020) 12,936 km electrified
1289.3 0.950-mm gauge (151.3 km electrified)
comparison ranking: total 15

Roadways: *total:* 228,863 km (2021)
comparison ranking: total 19

Waterways: 2,400 km (2012) (used for commercial traffic; of limited overall value compared to road and rail)
comparison ranking: 38

Merchant marine: *total:* 1,276 (2023)
by type: bulk carrier 17, container ship 6, general cargo 109, oil tanker 95, other 1,049
comparison ranking: total 18

Ports: *total ports:* 123 (2024)
large: 12
medium: 11
small: 71
very small: 28
size unknown: 1
ports with oil terminals: 33
key ports: Brindisi, Civitavecchia, Genova, Gioia Tauro, La Spezia, Livorno, Messina, Napoli, Porto di Lido-Venezia, Siracusa, Taranto, Trieste

MILITARY AND SECURITY

Military and security forces: Italian Armed Forces (Forze Armate Italiane): Army (Esercito Italiano, EI), Navy (Marina Militare Italiana, MMI; includes aviation, marines), Italian Air Force (Aeronautica Militare Italiana, AMI); Carabinieri Corps (Arma dei Carabinieri, CC) (2024)
note 1: the National Police and Carabinieri (gendarmerie or military police) maintain internal security; the National Police reports to the Ministry of Interior while the Carabinieri reports to the Ministry of Defense but is also under the coordination of the Ministry of Interior; the Carabinieri is primarily a domestic police force organized along military lines, with some overseas responsibilities
note 2: the Financial Guard (Guardia di Finanza) under the Ministry of Economy and Finance is a force with military status and nationwide remit for financial crime investigations, including narcotics trafficking, smuggling, and illegal immigration

Military expenditures: 1.5% of GDP (2024 est.)
1.5% of GDP (2023)
1.5% of GDP (2022)
1.5% of GDP (2021)
1.6% of GDP (2020)
comparison ranking: 95

Military and security service personnel strengths: approximately 170,000 active personnel (100,000 Army; 30,000 Navy; 40,000 Air Force); approximately 108,000 Carabinieri (2024)

Military equipment inventories and acquisitions: the military's inventory includes a mix of domestically manufactured, imported, and jointly produced weapons systems, mostly from Europe and the US; in recent years, the US has been the lead supplier of military hardware to Italy; the Italian defense industry is capable of producing equipment across all the military domains with particular strengths in aircraft, armored vehicles, and naval vessels; it also participates in joint development and production of advanced weapons systems with other European countries and the US (2024)

Military service age and obligation: 17-25 years of age for voluntary military service for men and women (some variations on age depending on the military branch); voluntary service is a minimum of 12 months with the option to extend in the Armed Forces or compete for positions in the Military Corps of the Italian Red Cross, the State Police, the Carabinieri, the Guardia di Finanza, the Penitentiary Police, or the National Fire Brigade; recruits can also volunteer for 4 years military service; conscription abolished 2004 (2024)
note: women serve in all military branches; as of 2023, women made up about 8% of the military's full-time personnel

Military deployments: 120 Djibouti; approximately 750 Bulgaria (NATO); approximately 650 Middle East (NATO, European Assistance Mission Iraq); 250 Hungary (NATO; up to 1,500 Kosovo (NATO/KFOR); 250 Latvia (NATO); 1,325 Lebanon (UNIFIL); 200 Libya; 350 Niger; 250 Romania (NATO); 150 Somalia (EUTM) (2024)
note 1: Italy has about 11,500 total air, ground, and naval forces deployed on foreign missions
note 2: since 1960, Italy has committed more than 60,000 troops to UN missions, and it hosts a training center in Vicenza for police personnel destined for peacekeeping missions

Military - note: the Italian military is responsible for Italy's national defense and security and fulfilling the country's commitments to the EU, NATO, and the UN; it also has some domestic security duties; for example, the Army has provided troops for guarding public buildings and for more than a decade several thousand Army and Carabinieri personnel have been deployed domestically to support the National Police as part of a government effort to curb crime in various Italian cities
Italy has been an active member of NATO since its founding in 1948, and the Alliance is a cornerstone of Rome's national security strategy; it is a strong supporter of European/EU defense cooperation and integration; Italy is a frequent participant in EU, NATO, UN, and other multinational military, security, and humanitarian operations; key areas of emphasis for Italy's security policy and multinational cooperation are NATO/Europe's eastern and southern flanks, including the Mediterranean Sea, East and North Africa, and the Middle East and its adjacent waters

Italy is one of NATO's leading contributors of military forces and participates in such missions as NATO's Air Policing in the Baltics, the Enhanced Forward Presence in Eastern Europe, and maritime patrols in the Mediterranean and beyond; it hosts NATO's Joint Force Command in Naples and a NATO Rapid Deployable Corps headquarters in Milan, as well as the headquarters for the EU's Mediterranean naval operations force in Rome; in addition, Italy has close defense ties with the US and hosts several US military air, army, and naval bases and facilities (2024)

SPACE

Space agency/agencies: Italian Space Agency (L'Agenzia Spaziale Italiana or ASI; established 1988); Joint Space Operations Command (Comando Interforze delle Operazioni Spaziali or COS; established 2020) (2024)

Space launch site(s): the Broglio (aka San Marco, Malindi) Space Center, located near Malindi, Kenya, served from 1967 to 1988 as an Italian and international satellite launch facility; in 2020, Kenya concluded a new deal with Italy to conduct rocket launches from the site again in the future; in 2018, the Italian Government designated the Taranto-Grottaglie Airport as a future spaceport and signed framework agreements with commercial space companies that could lead to suborbital and orbital launches from what would be called the Grottaglie Spaceport (2024)

Space program overview: has one of the largest space programs in Europe; is a key member of the European Space Agency (ESA) and one of its largest contributors; designs, builds, launches, and operates communications, remote sensing (RS), and scientific satellites; designs and manufacturers sounding (research) rockets and orbital satellite launch vehicles (SLVs); hosts the ESA Center for Earth Observation; has astronaut cadre in the ESA astronaut corps; researches, develops, and builds a range of other space-related technologies and participates in a wide array of international programs with astronauts, cargo containers, construction, expertise, modules, scientific experiments, and technology; outside of the ESA/EU and their individual member states, has cooperated with a variety of foreign space agencies and industries, including those of Argentina, Brazil, Canada, China, Israel, Japan, Kenya, Mexico, Russia, South Korea, Thailand, the UAE, and the US; participates in international space projects such as the International Space Station (ISS); has a considerable commercial space industrial sector encompassing a wide range of capabilities, including manufacturing satellites, satellite payloads, launch vehicles, propulsion systems, cargo containers, and their sub-components (2024)

note: further details about the key activities, programs, and milestones of the country's space program, as well as government spending estimates on the space sector, appear in the Space Programs reference guide

TERRORISM

Terrorist group(s): Islamic State of Iraq and ash-Sham (ISIS)
note: details about the history, aims, leadership, organization, areas of operation, tactics, targets, weapons, size, and sources of support of the group(s) appear(s) in the Terrorism reference guide

TRANSNATIONAL ISSUES

Refugees and internally displaced persons: *refugees (country of origin):* 21,441 (Nigeria), 17,706 (Afghanistan), 17,619 (Pakistan), 11,193 (Mali), 8,405 (Somalia), 6,324 (Gambia), 5,768 (Bangladesh), 5,463 (Iraq) (mid-year 2022); 169,165 (Ukraine) (as of 23 February 2024)
stateless persons: 3,000 (2022)
note: 861,413 estimated refugee and migrant arrivals (January 2015-March 2024)

Illicit drugs: important gateway for drug trafficking; organized crime groups allied with Colombian and Spanish groups trafficking cocaine to Europe

J

JAMAICA

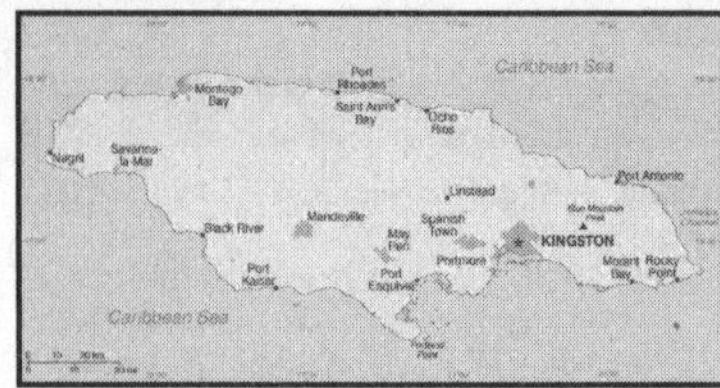

INTRODUCTION

Background: Europeans first saw Jamaica when Christopher COLUMBUS arrived in 1494, and the Spanish settled the island early in the 16th century. The Native Taino, who had inhabited Jamaica for centuries, were gradually exterminated and replaced with African slaves. England seized the island in 1655 and established a plantation economy based on sugar, cocoa, and coffee. The abolition of slavery in 1834 freed a quarter-million slaves, many of whom became small farmers. Jamaica gradually increased its independence from Britain. In 1958, it joined other British Caribbean colonies in forming the Federation of the West Indies. Jamaica withdrew from the Federation in 1961 and gained full independence in 1962. Deteriorating economic conditions during the 1970s led to recurring violence as rival gangs affiliated with the major political parties evolved into powerful organized crime networks involved in international drug smuggling and money laundering. Violent crime, drug trafficking, corruption, and poverty pose significant challenges to the government today. Nonetheless, many rural and resort areas remain relatively safe and contribute substantially to the economy.

GEOGRAPHY

Location: Caribbean, island in the Caribbean Sea, south of Cuba

Geographic coordinates: 18 15 N, 77 30 W

Map references: Central America and the Caribbean

Area: *total:* 10,991 sq km
land: 10,831 sq km
water: 160 sq km
comparison ranking: total 166

Area - comparative: about half the size of New Jersey; slightly smaller than Connecticut

Land boundaries: *total:* 0 km

Coastline: 1,022 km

Maritime claims: *territorial sea:* 12 nm
contiguous zone: 24 nm
exclusive economic zone: 200 nm
continental shelf: 200 nm or to edge of the continental margin
measured from claimed archipelagic straight baselines

Climate: tropical; hot, humid; temperate interior

Terrain: mostly mountains, with narrow, discontinuous coastal plain

Elevation: *highest point:* Blue Mountain Peak 2,256 m
lowest point: Caribbean Sea 0 m
mean elevation: 18 m

Natural resources: bauxite, alumina, gypsum, limestone

Land use: *agricultural land:* 41.4% (2018 est.)
arable land: 11.1% (2018 est.)
permanent crops: 9.2% (2018 est.)
permanent pasture: 21.1% (2018 est.)
forest: 31.1% (2018 est.)
other: 27.5% (2018 est.)

Irrigated land: 250 sq km (2012)

Population distribution: population density is high throughout, but increases in and around Kingston, Montego Bay, and Port Esquivel

Natural hazards: hurricanes (especially July to November)

Geography - note: third largest island in the Caribbean (after Cuba and Hispaniola); strategic location between Cayman Trench and Jamaica Channel, the main sea lanes for the Panama Canal

PEOPLE AND SOCIETY

Population: *total:* 2,823,713
male: 1,397,495
female: 1,426,218 (2024 est.)
comparison rankings: female 140; male 141; total 140

Nationality: *noun:* Jamaican(s)
adjective: Jamaican

Ethnic groups: Black 92.1%, mixed 6.1%, East Indian 0.8%, other 0.4%, unspecified 0.7% (2011 est.)

Languages: English, Jamaican patois

Religions: Protestant 64.8% (includes Seventh Day Adventist 12.0%, Pentecostal 11.0%, Other Church of God 9.2%, New Testament Church of God 7.2%, Baptist 6.7%, Church of God in Jamaica 4.8%, Church of God of Prophecy 4.5%, Anglican 2.8%, United Church 2.1%, Methodist 1.6%, Revived 1.4%, Brethren 0.9%, and Moravian 0.7%), Roman Catholic 2.2%, Jehovah's Witness 1.9%, Rastafarian 1.1%, other 6.5%, none 21.3%, unspecified 2.3% (2011 est.)

Age structure: *0-14 years:* 23.8% (male 342,691/female 329,773)
15-64 years: 65.7% (male 914,364/female 941,816)
65 years and over: 10.4% (2024 est.) (male 140,440/female 154,629)

Dependency ratios: *total dependency ratio:* 38
youth dependency ratio: 28
elderly dependency ratio: 13.4
potential support ratio: 7.4 (2021 est.)

Median age: *total:* 30.9 years (2024 est.)
male: 30.1 years
female: 31.7 years
comparison ranking: total 130

Population growth rate: 0.1% (2024 est.)
comparison ranking: 185

Birth rate: 15.6 births/1,000 population (2024 est.)
comparison ranking: 105

Death rate: 7.5 deaths/1,000 population (2024 est.)
comparison ranking: 100

Net migration rate: -7.1 migrant(s)/1,000 population (2024 est.)
comparison ranking: 217

Population distribution: population density is high throughout, but increases in and around Kingston, Montego Bay, and Port Esquivel

Urbanization: *urban population:* 57.4% of total population (2023)
rate of urbanization: 0.79% annual rate of change (2020-25 est.)

Major urban areas - population: 597,000 KINGSTON (capital) (2023)

Sex ratio: *at birth:* 1.05 male(s)/female
0-14 years: 1.04 male(s)/female
15-64 years: 0.97 male(s)/female
65 years and over: 0.91 male(s)/female
total population: 0.98 male(s)/female (2024 est.)

Mother's mean age at first birth: 21.2 years (2008 est.)
note: data represents median age at first birth among women 25-29

Maternal mortality ratio: 99 deaths/100,000 live births (2020 est.)
comparison ranking: 69

Infant mortality rate: *total:* 10.7 deaths/1,000 live births (2024 est.)
male: 11.9 deaths/1,000 live births
female: 9.4 deaths/1,000 live births
comparison ranking: total 129

Life expectancy at birth: *total population:* 76.3 years (2024 est.)
male: 74.5 years
female: 78.1 years
comparison ranking: total population 111

Total fertility rate: 2.05 children born/woman (2024 est.)
comparison ranking: 98

Gross reproduction rate: 1 (2024 est.)

Drinking water source: *improved: urban:* 98.3% of population
rural: 93.9% of population
total: 96.4% of population
unimproved: urban: 1.7% of population
rural: 6.1% of population
total: 3.6% of population (2020 est.)

Current health expenditure: 6.6% of GDP (2020)

Physician density: 0.53 physicians/1,000 population (2018)

Hospital bed density: 1.7 beds/1,000 population (2017)

Sanitation facility access: *improved: urban:* 98.6% of population
rural: 99.4% of population
total: 98.9% of population
unimproved: urban: 1.4% of population
rural: 0.6% of population
total: 1.1% of population (2020 est.)

Obesity - adult prevalence rate: 24.7% (2016)
comparison ranking: 55

Alcohol consumption per capita: *total:* 3.46 liters of pure alcohol (2019 est.)
beer: 1.19 liters of pure alcohol (2019 est.)
wine: 0.25 liters of pure alcohol (2019 est.)
spirits: 1.66 liters of pure alcohol (2019 est.)
other alcohols: 0.35 liters of pure alcohol (2019 est.)
comparison ranking: total 104

Tobacco use: *total:* 9.4% (2020 est.)

male: 15% (2020 est.)
female: 3.8% (2020 est.)
comparison ranking: total 137

Children under the age of 5 years underweight: 2.5% (2018/19)
comparison ranking: 96

Currently married women (ages 15-49): 32.7% (2023 est.)

Education expenditures: 6% of GDP (2021 est.)
comparison ranking: 43

Literacy: *definition:* age 15 and over has ever attended school
total population: 88.7%
male: 84%
female: 93.1% (2015)

School life expectancy (primary to tertiary education): *total:* 12 years
male: 11 years
female: 13 years (2015)

ENVIRONMENT

Environment - current issues: heavy rates of deforestation; coastal waters polluted by industrial waste, sewage, and oil spills; damage to coral reefs; air pollution in Kingston from vehicle emissions; land erosion

Environment - international agreements: *party to:* Biodiversity, Climate Change, Climate Change-Kyoto Protocol, Climate Change-Paris Agreement, Comprehensive Nuclear Test Ban, Desertification, Endangered Species, Hazardous Wastes, Law of the Sea, Marine Dumping-London Convention, Marine Life Conservation, Nuclear Test Ban, Ozone Layer Protection, Ship Pollution, Wetlands
signed, but not ratified: none of the selected agreements

Climate: tropical; hot, humid; temperate interior

Urbanization: *urban population:* 57.4% of total population (2023)
rate of urbanization: 0.79% annual rate of change (2020-25 est.)

Revenue from forest resources: 0.15% of GDP (2018 est.)
comparison ranking: 102

Revenue from coal: 0% of GDP (2018 est.)
comparison ranking: 94

Air pollutants: *particulate matter emissions:* 14.83 micrograms per cubic meter (2019 est.)
carbon dioxide emissions: 8.23 megatons (2016 est.)
methane emissions: 1.08 megatons (2020 est.)

Waste and recycling: *municipal solid waste generated annually:* 1,051,695 tons (2016 est.)

Total water withdrawal: *municipal:* 140 million cubic meters (2020 est.)
industrial: 1.1 billion cubic meters (2020 est.)
agricultural: 110 million cubic meters (2020 est.)

Total renewable water resources: 10.82 billion cubic meters (2020 est.)

GOVERNMENT

Country name: *conventional long form:* none
conventional short form: Jamaica
etymology: from the native Taino word "haymaca" meaning "Land of Wood and Water" or possibly "Land of Springs"

Government type: parliamentary democracy (Parliament) under a constitutional monarchy; a Commonwealth realm

Capital: *name:* Kingston
geographic coordinates: 18 00 N, 76 48 W
time difference: UTC-5 (same time as Washington, DC, during Standard Time)
etymology: the name is a blending of the words "king's" and "town"; the English king at the time of the city's founding in 1692 was WILLIAM III (r. 1689-1702)

Administrative divisions: 14 parishes; Clarendon, Hanover, Kingston, Manchester, Portland, Saint Andrew, Saint Ann, Saint Catherine, Saint Elizabeth, Saint James, Saint Mary, Saint Thomas, Trelawny, Westmoreland
note: for local government purposes, Kingston and Saint Andrew were amalgamated in 1923 into the present single corporate body known as the Kingston and Saint Andrew Corporation

Independence: 6 August 1962 (from the UK)

National holiday: Independence Day, 6 August (1962)

Legal system: common law system based on the English model

Constitution: *history:* several previous (preindependence); latest drafted 1961-62, submitted to British Parliament 24 July 1962, entered into force 6 August 1962 (at independence)
amendments: proposed by Parliament; passage of amendments to "non-entrenched" constitutional sections, such as lowering the voting age, requires majority vote by the Parliament membership; passage of amendments to "entrenched" sections, such as fundamental rights and freedoms, requires two-thirds majority vote of Parliament; passage of amendments to "specially entrenched" sections such as the dissolution of Parliament or the executive authority of the monarch requires two-thirds approval by Parliament and approval in a referendum; amended many times, last in 2017; note - in mid-July 2024, Jamaica's Constitutional Reform Committee submitted its report on recommendations for reform of the constitution and awaiting debate in Parliament

International law organization participation: has not submitted an ICJ jurisdiction declaration; non-party state to the ICCt

Citizenship: *citizenship by birth:* yes
citizenship by descent only: yes
dual citizenship recognized: yes
residency requirement for naturalization: 4 out of the previous 5 years

Suffrage: 18 years of age; universal

Executive branch: *chief of state:* King CHARLES III (since 8 September 2022); represented by Governor General Sir Patrick L. ALLEN (since 26 February 2009)
head of government: Prime Minister Andrew HOLNESS (since 3 March 2016)
cabinet: Cabinet appointed by the governor general on the advice of the prime minister
elections/appointments: the monarchy is hereditary; governor general appointed by the monarch on the recommendation of the prime minister; following legislative elections, the leader of the majority party or majority coalition in the House of Representatives is appointed prime minister by the governor general
note: the Jamaican Government, in May 2023, announced plans to hold a referendum in 2024 to determine whether or not to remain in the Commonwealth or become a republic

Legislative branch: *description:* bicameral Parliament consists of:
Senate (21 seats; 13 members appointed by the governor general on the advice of the prime minister and 8 members appointed by the governor general on the advice of the opposition party leader; members serve 5-year terms (no term limits) or until Parliament is dissolved)
House of Representatives (63 seats; members directly elected in single-seat constituencies by simple majority vote to serve 5-year terms (no term limits) or until Parliament is dissolved)
elections: Senate - last full slate of appointments early on 3 September 2020 (next full slate in 2025)
House of Representatives - last held on 3 September 2020 (next to be held in 2025)
election results: Senate - percent by party - NA; seats by party - NA; composition - men 13, women 8, percentage women 38.1%
House of Representatives - percent of vote by party - JLP 57%, PNP 42.8%, independent 0.2%; seats by party - JLP 48, PNP 15; composition - men 45, women 14; percentage women 23.7%; note - total Parliament percentage women 27.5%

Judicial branch: *highest court(s):* Court of Appeal (consists of president of the court and a minimum of 4 judges); Supreme Court (40 judges organized in specialized divisions); note - appeals beyond Jamaica's highest courts are referred to the Judicial Committee of the Privy Council (in London) rather than to the Caribbean Court of Justice (the appellate court for member states of the Caribbean Community)
judge selection and term of office: chief justice of the Supreme Court and president of the Court of Appeal appointed by the governor-general on the advice of the prime minister; other judges of both courts appointed by the governorgeneral on the advice of the Judicial Service Commission; judges of both courts serve till age 70
subordinate courts: resident magistrate courts, district courts, and petty sessions courts

Political parties: Jamaica Labor Party or JLP
Jamaica Progressive Party or JPP
People's National Party or PNP
United Independents' Congress or UIC

International organization participation: ACP, ACS, AOSIS, C, Caricom, CDB, CELAC, FAO, G-15, G-77, IADB, IAEA, IBRD, ICAO, ICC (NGOs), ICRM, IDA, IFAD, IFC, IFRCS, IHO, ILO, IMF, IMO, Interpol, IOC, IOM, ISO, ITSO, ITU, LAES, MIGA, NAM, OAS, OPANAL, OPCW, Petrocaribe, UN, UNCTAD, UNESCO, UNIDO, UNITAR, UNWTO, UPU, WCO, WFTU (NGOs), WHO, WIPO, WMO, WTO

Diplomatic representation in the US: *chief of mission:* Ambassador Audrey Patrice MARKS (since 18 January 2017)
chancery: 1520 New Hampshire Avenue NW, Washington, DC 20036
telephone: [1] (202) 452-0660
FAX: [1] (202) 452-0036
email address and website:
contactus@jamaicaembassy.org
Jamaican Embassy (embassyofjamaica.org)
consulate(s) general: Miami, New York

Diplomatic representation from the US: *chief of mission:* Ambassador N. Nickolas PERRY (since 13 May 2022)
embassy: 142 Old Hope Road, Kingston 6
mailing address: 3210 Kingston Place, Washington DC 20521-3210
telephone: (876) 702-6000
FAX: (876) 702-6348

email address and website:
KingstonACS@state.gov
https://jm.usembassy.gov/

Flag description: diagonal yellow cross divides the flag into four triangles - green (top and bottom) and black (hoist side and fly side); green represents hope, vegetation, and agriculture, black reflects hardships overcome and to be faced, and yellow recalls golden sunshine and the island's natural resources

National symbol(s): green-and-black streamertail (bird), Guaiacum officinale (Guaiacwood); national colors: green, yellow, black

National anthem: *name:* "Jamaica, Land We Love"
lyrics/music: Hugh Braham SHERLOCK/Robert Charles LIGHTBOURNE
note: adopted 1962

National heritage: *total World Heritage Sites:* 1 (mixed)
selected World Heritage Site locales: Blue and John Crow Mountains

ECONOMY

Economic overview: upper middle-income Caribbean island economy; ongoing debt restructuring; hurricane-vulnerable economy; high crime, youth unemployment, and poverty; susceptible to commodity shocks from ongoing Russia invasion of Ukraine

Real GDP (purchasing power parity): $29.225 billion (2023 est.)
$28.596 billion (2022 est.)
$27.177 billion (2021 est.)
note: data in 2021 dollars
comparison ranking: 149

Real GDP growth rate: 2.2% (2023 est.)
5.22% (2022 est.)
4.6% (2021 est.)
note: annual GDP % growth based on constant local currency
comparison ranking: 134

Real GDP per capita: $10,300 (2023 est.)
$10,100 (2022 est.)
$9,600 (2021 est.)
note: data in 2021 dollars
comparison ranking: 146

GDP (official exchange rate): $19.423 billion (2023 est.)
note: data in current dollars at official exchange rate

Inflation rate (consumer prices): 6.47% (2023 est.)
10.35% (2022 est.)
5.86% (2021 est.)
note: annual % change based on consumer prices
comparison ranking: 137

Credit ratings: Fitch rating: B+ (2019)
Moody's rating: B2 (2019)
Standard & Poors rating: B+ (2019)
note: The year refers to the year in which the current credit rating was first obtained.

GDP - composition, by sector of origin: *agriculture:* 9% (2023 est.)
industry: 18.6% (2023 est.)
services: 60.1% (2023 est.)
note: figures may not total 100% due to non-allocated consumption not captured in sector-reported data
comparison rankings: services 83; industry 149; agriculture 83

GDP - composition, by end use: *household consumption:* 76.2% (2019 est.)
government consumption: 13.6% (2019 est.)
investment in fixed capital: 24.1% (2019 est.)
investment in inventories: 0.2% (2019 est.)
exports of goods and services: 38% (2019 est.)
imports of goods and services: -52.1% (2019 est.)
note: figures may not total 100% due to rounding or gaps in data collection

Agricultural products: sugarcane, yams, goat milk, chicken, coconuts, oranges, bananas, pumpkins/squash, plantains, sweet potatoes (2022)
note: top ten agricultural products based on tonnage

Industries: agriculture, mining, manufacture, construction, financial and insurance services, tourism, telecommunications

Industrial production growth rate: 4.98% (2023 est.)
note: annual % change in industrial value added based on constant local currency
comparison ranking: 52

Labor force: 1.559 million (2023 est.)
note: number of people ages 15 or older who are employed or seeking work
comparison ranking: 133

Unemployment rate: 4.42% (2023 est.)
4.08% (2022 est.)
5.19% (2021 est.)
note: % of labor force seeking employment
comparison ranking: 86

Youth unemployment rate (ages 15-24): *total:* 13.8% (2023 est.)
male: 13.1% (2023 est.)
female: 14.9% (2023 est.)
note: % of labor force ages 15-24 seeking employment
comparison ranking: total 101

Population below poverty line: 17.1% (2016 est.)

Gini Index coefficient - distribution of family income: 40.2 (2021 est.)
comparison ranking: 44

Household income or consumption by percentage share: *lowest 10%:* 2.2% (2021 est.)
highest 10%: 29.9% (2021 est.)

Remittances: 19.1% of GDP (2023 est.)
21.57% of GDP (2022 est.)
25.29% of GDP (2021 est.)
note: personal transfers and compensation between resident and non-resident individuals/households/entities

Budget: *revenues:* $4.041 billion (2020 est.)
expenditures: $4.12 billion (2020 est.)
note: central government revenues and expenses (excluding grants/extrabudgetary units/social security funds) converted to US dollars at average official exchange rate for year indicated

Public debt: 106.28% of GDP (2020 est.)
note: central government debt as a % of GDP
comparison ranking: 17

Taxes and other revenues: 25.71% (of GDP) (2020 est.)
note: central government tax revenue as a % of GDP
comparison ranking: 42

Current account balance: -$129.756 million (2022 est.)
$149.262 million (2021 est.)
-$156.91 million (2020 est.)
note: balance of payments - net trade and primary/secondary income in current dollars
comparison ranking: 98

Exports: $6.424 billion (2022 est.)
$4.401 billion (2021 est.)
$3.249 billion (2020 est.)
note: balance of payments - exports of goods and services in current dollars
comparison ranking: 129

Exports - partners: US 57%, Russia 5%, Canada 4%, UK 4%, Iceland 2% (2022)
note: top five export partners based on percentage share of exports

Exports - commodities: refined petroleum, natural gas, aluminum oxide, liquor, aluminum ore (2022)
note: top five export commodities based on value in dollars

Imports: $9.726 billion (2022 est.)
$7.405 billion (2021 est.)
$5.913 billion (2020 est.)
note: balance of payments - imports of goods and services in current dollars
comparison ranking: 127

Imports - partners: US 36%, China 12%, Trinidad and Tobago 6%, Brazil 5%, Turkey 4% (2022)
note: top five import partners based on percentage share of imports

Imports - commodities: refined petroleum, crude petroleum, natural gas, cars, plastic products (2022)
note: top five import commodities based on value in dollars

Reserves of foreign exchange and gold: $4.869 billion (2023 est.)
$4.52 billion (2022 est.)
$4.838 billion (2021 est.)
note: holdings of gold (year-end prices)/foreign exchange/special drawing rights in current dollars
comparison ranking: 106

Debt - external: $9.148 billion (2022 est.)
note: present value of external debt in current US dollars
comparison ranking: 41

Exchange rates: Jamaican dollars (JMD) per US dollar -

Exchange rates: 154.159 (2023 est.)
153.427 (2022 est.)
150.79 (2021 est.)
142.403 (2020 est.)
133.312 (2019 est.)

ENERGY

Electricity access: *electrification - total population:* 100% (2022 est.)

Electricity: *installed generating capacity:* 1.222 million kW (2022 est.)
consumption: 3.367 billion kWh (2022 est.)
transmission/distribution losses: 1.212 billion kWh (2022 est.)
comparison rankings: transmission/distribution losses 106; consumption 138; installed generating capacity 132

Electricity generation sources: *fossil fuels:* 86.6% of total installed capacity (2022 est.)
solar: 3% of total installed capacity (2022 est.)
wind: 6.1% of total installed capacity (2022 est.)
hydroelectricity: 3.1% of total installed capacity (2022 est.)
biomass and waste: 1.2% of total installed capacity (2022 est.)

Coal: *consumption:* 65,000 metric tons (2022 est.)
exports: 100 metric tons (2022 est.)
imports: 65,000 metric tons (2022 est.)

Petroleum: *total petroleum production:* 3,000 bbl/day (2023 est.)
refined petroleum consumption: 49,000 bbl/day (2022 est.)

Natural gas: *consumption:* 664.834 million cubic meters (2022 est.)
imports: 664.834 million cubic meters (2022 est.)

Carbon dioxide emissions: 8.86 million metric tonnes of CO2 (2022 est.)
from coal and metallurgical coke: 147,000 metric tonnes of CO2 (2022 est.)
from petroleum and other liquids: 7.411 million metric tonnes of CO2 (2022 est.)
from consumed natural gas: 1.302 million metric tonnes of CO2 (2022 est.)
comparison ranking: total emissions 110

Energy consumption per capita: 46.586 million Btu/person (2022 est.)
comparison ranking: 97

COMMUNICATIONS

Telephones - fixed lines: *total subscriptions:* 447,000 (2022 est.)
subscriptions per 100 inhabitants: 16 (2022 est.)
comparison ranking: total subscriptions 98

Telephones - mobile cellular: *total subscriptions:* 3.003 million (2022 est.)
subscriptions per 100 inhabitants: 106 (2022 est.)
comparison ranking: total subscriptions 140

Telecommunication systems: *general assessment:* Jamaica's telecom sector has for many years been propped up by the mobile sector, which accounts for the vast majority of internet connections and voice lines; it also accounts for just over half of telecom sector revenue; in December 2020, the government announced the rollout of a national broadband network costing up to $237 million; the funding will be spent on improving connectivity in under served areas, improving access to education, and deploying networks to public locations such as hospitals, municipal institutions, and police stations; to aid in this national broadband effort, the government received a donation of 650km of fiber cabling from local cable TV providers and the two main toll road operators; to encourage the use of digital channels as the country deals with the Covid-19 pandemic (2021)
domestic: fixed-line subscriptions nearly 17 per 100, cellular-mobile roughly 103 per 100 subscriptions (2021)
international: country code - 1-876 and 1-658; landing points for the ALBA-1, CFX-1, Fibralink, East-West, and Cayman-Jamaican Fiber System submarine cables providing connections to South America, parts of the Caribbean, Central America and the US; satellite earth stations - 2 Intelsat (Atlantic Ocean) (2019)

Broadcast media: 3 free-to-air TV stations, subscription cable services, and roughly 30 radio stations (2019)

Internet country code: .jm

Internet users: *total:* 2.296 million (2021 est.)
percent of population: 82% (2021 est.)
comparison ranking: total 131

Broadband - fixed subscriptions: *total:* 385,603 (2020 est.)
subscriptions per 100 inhabitants: 13 (2020 est.)
comparison ranking: total 99

TRANSPORTATION

National air transport system: *number of registered air carriers:* 0 (2020)

Civil aircraft registration country code prefix: 6Y

Airports: 20 (2024)
comparison ranking: 135

Heliports: 2 (2024)

Roadways: *total:* 25,595 km (2017)
comparison ranking: total 105

Merchant marine: *total:* 40 (2023)
by type: bulk carrier 1, general cargo 11, oil tanker 1, other 27
comparison ranking: total 125

Ports: *total ports:* 11 (2024)
large: 0
medium: 1
small: 2
very small: 8
ports with oil terminals: 5
key ports: Falmouth, Kingston, Lucea, Montego Bay, Ocho Rios, Port Antonio, Port Esquivel, Port Kaiser, Rio Bueno, Rocky Point, Savannah la Mar

MILITARY AND SECURITY

Military and security forces: Jamaica Defense Force (JDF): Ground Forces (Jamaica Regiment), Air Wing, Coast Guard; Jamaica Constabulary Force (JCF); Jamaica National Service Corps (JNSC) (2024)
note 1: the Coast Guard and Air Wing are operationally combined under the joint Military-Air-Cyber Command, along with the Military Cyber Corps, Special Activities Regiment, Support Brigade, and Military Intelligence Unit
note 2: the JCF is the country's police force; it has primary responsibility for internal security and has units for community policing, special response, intelligence gathering, and internal affairs; both it and the JDF are under the Ministry of National Security
note 3: the JNSC is a third category of service that military recruits can join as a preparatory phase for future careers; JNSC soldiers receive basic military, vocational, and life skills training; upon completion of 12 months of service, soldiers can continue on with the JDF or the JDF reserves or seek opportunities in other public sector entities such as the JCF, the Department of Correctional Services, the Jamaica Fire Brigade, the Jamaica Customs Agency, or the Passport Immigration and Citizenship Agency

Military expenditures: 1.2% of GDP (2023 est.)
1.3% of GDP (2022 est.)
1.4% of GDP (2021 est.)
1.7% of GDP (2020 est.)
1.6% of GDP (2019 est.)
comparison ranking: 116

Military and security service personnel strengths: approximately 5,000 personnel (2023)

Military equipment inventories and acquisitions: the JDF is lightly armed with a limited inventory featuring equipment mostly from Australia, Canada, Japan, the Netherlands, the UK, and the US (2024)

Military service age and obligation: 18-23 for voluntary military service (17 with parental consent) for men and women; 18-28 for the reserves; no conscription; since 2017, the JDF's standard mode of recruitment is to enroll recruits ages 18-23 through the Jamaica National Service Corps (JNSC), which has a service requirement of 12 months (2024)
note: as of 2022, women made up about 20% of the JDF's uniformed personnel

Military - note: in addition to its responsibility of defending against external aggression, the JDF's primary missions are border, internal, and maritime security, including support to police operations in combating crime and violence; other missions include search and rescue, disaster response, humanitarian assistance, and peacekeeping; it has arrest authority and partners with the Jamaica Constabulary Force (JCF); both the JDF and JCF are under the Ministry of National Security, which directs policy for the security forces; the JDF participates in bilateral and multinational training exercises, including with the militaries of Canada, the UK, the US, and other Caribbean nations
while Jamaica had a militia force as early as the 1660s, the JDF was constituted in 1962 from the West India Regiment (WIR), a British colonial regiment which dates back to 1795 (2024)

TRANSNATIONAL ISSUES

Illicit drugs: Jamaica is the largest Caribbean source of marijuana and a transit point for cocaine trafficked from South America to North America and other international markets; criminal gangs in Jamaica, Haiti, and Central America use marijuana for currency to obtain guns or other contraband from criminal entities in Haiti and Central America

JAN MAYEN

INTRODUCTION

Background: This desolate, mountainous island in the Arctic Ocean was named after a Dutch whaling captain who indisputably discovered it in 1614 (earlier claims are inconclusive). Visited only occasionally by seal hunters and trappers over the centuries, the island came under Norwegian sovereignty in 1929. The long dormant Beerenberg volcano, the northernmost active volcano on earth, resumed activity in 1970, and the most recent eruption occurred in 1985.

GEOGRAPHY

Location: Northern Europe, island between the Greenland Sea and the Norwegian Sea, northeast of Iceland

Geographic coordinates: 71 00 N, 8 00 W

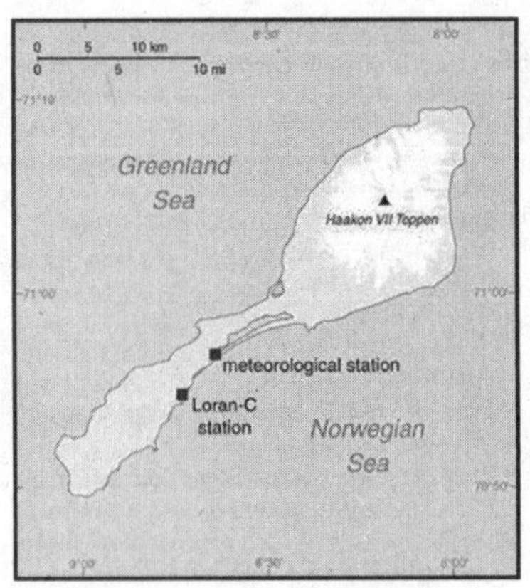

Map references: Arctic Region

Area: *total:* 377 sq km
land: 377 sq km
water: 0 sq km
comparison ranking: total 205

Area - comparative: slightly more than twice the size of Washington, DC

Land boundaries: *total:* 0 km

Coastline: 124.1 km

Maritime claims: *territorial sea:* 12 nm
contiguous zone: 24 nm
exclusive economic zone: 200 nm
continental shelf: 200-m depth or to the depth of exploitation

Climate: arctic maritime with frequent storms and persistent fog

Terrain: volcanic island, partly covered by glaciers

Elevation: *highest point:* Haakon VII Toppen on Beerenberg 2,277
lowest point: Norwegian Sea 0 m
note: Beerenberg volcano has numerous peaks; the highest point on the volcano rim is named Haakon VII Toppen, after Norway's first king following the reestablishment of Norwegian independence in 1905

Natural resources: none

Land use: *agricultural land:* 0% (2011 est.)
other: 100% (2018 est.)

Irrigated land: 0 sq km (2022)

Natural hazards: dominated by the volcano Beerenberg
volcanism: Beerenberg (2,227 m) is Norway's only active volcano; volcanic activity resumed in 1970; the most recent eruption occurred in 1985

Geography - note: *barren volcanic spoon-shaped island with some moss and grass flora; island consists of two parts:* a larger northeast Nord-Jan (the spoon "bowl") and the smaller Sor-Jan (the "handle"), linked by a 2.5 km-wide isthmus (the "stem") with two large lakes, Sorlaguna (South Lagoon) and Nordlaguna (North Lagoon)

PEOPLE AND SOCIETY

Population: *total:* no indigenous inhabitants
note: military personnel operate the the weather and coastal services radio station

ENVIRONMENT

Environment - current issues: pollutants transported from southerly latitudes by winds, ocean currents, and rivers accumulate in the food chains of native animals; climate change

Climate: arctic maritime with frequent storms and persistent fog

GOVERNMENT

Country name: *conventional long form:* none
conventional short form: Jan Mayen
etymology: named after Dutch Captain Jan Jacobszoon MAY, one of the first explorers to reach the island in 1614

Dependency status: territory of Norway; since August 1994, administered from Oslo through the county governor (fylkesmann) of Nordland; however, authority has been delegated to a station commander of the Norwegian Defense Communication Service; in 2010, Norway designated the majority of Jan Mayen as a nature reserve

Legal system: the laws of Norway apply where applicable

Flag description: the flag of Norway is used

COMMUNICATIONS

Broadcast media: a coastal radio station has been remotely operated since 1994

MILITARY AND SECURITY

Military - note: defense is the responsibility of Norway

JAPAN

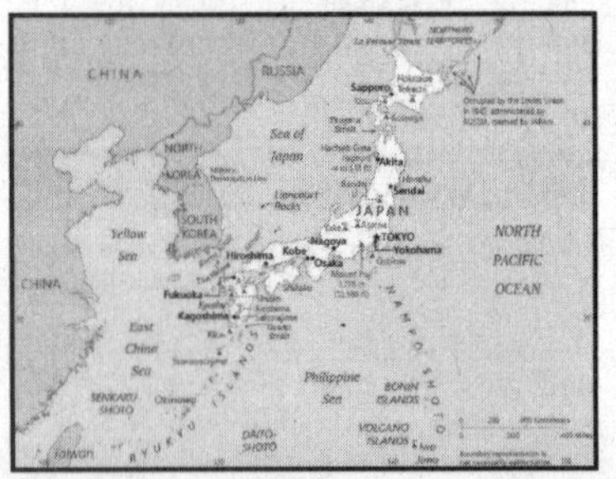

INTRODUCTION

Background: In 1603, after decades of civil warfare, the Tokugawa shogunate (a military-led, dynastic government) ushered in a long period of relative political stability and isolation from foreign influence. For more than two centuries, this policy enabled Japan to enjoy a flowering of its indigenous culture. Japan opened its ports after signing the Treaty of Kanagawa with the US in 1854 and began to intensively modernize and industrialize. During the late 19th and early 20th centuries, Japan became a regional power that was able to defeat the forces of both China and Russia. It occupied Korea, Formosa (Taiwan), and southern Sakhalin Island. In 1931-32, Japan occupied Manchuria, and in 1937, it launched a full-scale invasion of China. Japan attacked US forces at Pearl Harbor, Hawaii, in 1941, triggering America's entry into World War II, and Japan soon occupied much of East and Southeast Asia. After its defeat in World War II, the country recovered to become an economic power and a US ally.

While the emperor retains his throne as a symbol of national unity, elected politicians hold the decision-making power. After three decades of unprecedented growth, Japan's economy experienced a major slowdown starting in the 1990s, but the country remains an economic power. In 2011, Japan's strongest-ever earthquake and an accompanying tsunami devastated the northeast part of Honshu, killed thousands, and damaged several nuclear power plants. ABE Shinzo was reelected as prime minister in 2012, and he embarked on ambitious economic and security reforms to improve Japan's economy and bolster the country's international standing. In 2019, ABE became Japan's longest-serving post-war prime minister; he resigned in 2020 and was succeeded by SUGA Yoshihide. KISHIDA Fumio became prime minister in 2021.

GEOGRAPHY

Location: Eastern Asia, island chain between the North Pacific Ocean and the Sea of Japan, east of the Korean Peninsula

Geographic coordinates: 36 00 N, 138 00 E

Map references: Asia

Area: *total:* 377,915 sq km
land: 364,485 sq km
water: 13,430 sq km
note: includes Bonin Islands (Ogasawara-gunto), Daito-shoto, Minami-jima, Okino-tori-shima, Ryukyu Islands (Nansei-shoto), and Volcano Islands (Kazan-retto)
comparison ranking: total 63

Area - comparative: slightly smaller than California

Land boundaries: *total:* 0 km

Coastline: 29,751 km

Maritime claims: *territorial sea:* 12 nm; between 3 nm and 12 nm in the international straits - La Perouse or Soya, Tsugaru, Osumi, and the Korea and Tsushima Straits
contiguous zone: 24 nm
exclusive economic zone: 200 nm

Climate: varies from tropical in south to cool temperate in north

Terrain: mostly rugged and mountainous

Elevation: *highest point:* Mount Fuji 3,776 m
lowest point: Hachiro-gata -4 m
mean elevation: 438 m

Natural resources: negligible mineral resources, fish
note: with virtually no natural energy resources, Japan is almost totally dependent on imported sources of energy

Land use: *agricultural land:* 12.5% (2018 est.)
arable land: 11.7% (2018 est.)
permanent crops: 0.8% (2018 est.)
permanent pasture: 0% (2018 est.)
forest: 68.5% (2018 est.)
other: 19% (2018 est.)

Irrigated land: 15,730 sq km (2014)

Major lakes (area sq km): *fresh water lake(s):* Biwa-ko 688 sq km

Population distribution: all primary and secondary regions of high population density lie on the coast; one-third of the population resides in and around Tokyo on the central plain (Kanto Plain)

Natural hazards: many dormant and some active volcanoes; about 1,500 seismic occurrences (mostly tremors but occasional severe earthquakes) every year; tsunamis; typhoons
volcanism: both Unzen (1,500 m) and Sakura-jima (1,117 m), which lies near the densely populated city of Kagoshima, have been deemed Decade Volcanoes by the International Association of Volcanology and Chemistry of the Earth's Interior, worthy of study due to their explosive history and close proximity to human populations; other notable historically active volcanoes include Asama, Honshu Island's most active volcano, Aso, Bandai, Fuji, Iwo-Jima, Kikai, Kirishima, Komaga-take, Oshima, Suwanosejima, Tokachi, Yake-dake, and Usu; see note 2 under "Geography - note"

Geography - note: *note 1:* strategic location in northeast Asia; composed of four main islands (the "Home Islands") – Hokkaido, Honshu (the largest, most populous, and site of Tokyo, the capital), Shikoku, and Kyushu
note 2: a 2023 Geospatial Information Authority of Japan survey technically detected 100,000 islands and islets, but only the 14,125 islands with a circumference of at least 100 m (330 ft) were officially counted; only about 260 of the islands are inhabited
note 3: Japan annually records the most earthquakes in the world; it is one of the countries along the Ring of Fire, a belt of active volcanoes and earthquake epicenters bordering the Pacific Ocean; up to 90% of the world's earthquakes and some 75% of the world's volcanoes occur within the Ring of Fire

PEOPLE AND SOCIETY

Population: *total:* 123,201,945
male: 59,875,269
female: 63,326,676 (2024 est.)
comparison rankings: female 11; male 11; total 11

Nationality: *noun:* Japanese (singular and plural)
adjective: Japanese

Ethnic groups: Japanese 97.5%, Chinese 0.6%, Vietnam 0.4%, South Korean 0.3%, other 1.2% (includes Filipino, Brazilian, Nepalese, Indonesian, American, and Taiwanese) (2022 est.)
note: data represent population by nationality; up to 230,000 Brazilians of Japanese origin migrated to Japan in the 1990s to work in industries; some have returned to Brazil

Languages: Japanese
major-language sample(s):
必要不可欠な基本情報の源、ワールド・ファクトブック
(Japanese)

Religions: Shintoism 48.6%, Buddhism 46.4%, Christianity 1.1%, other 4% (2021 est.)
note: total adherents among persons claiming a religious affiliation

Age structure: *0-14 years:* 12.1% (male 7,701,196/female 7,239,389)
15-64 years: 58.4% (male 36,197,840/female 35,777,966)
65 years and over: 29.5% (2024 est.) (male 15,976,233/female 20,309,321)

Dependency ratios: *total dependency ratio:* 71.1
youth dependency ratio: 20.1
elderly dependency ratio: 51
potential support ratio: 2 (2021 est.)

Median age: *total:* 49.9 years (2024 est.)
male: 48.3 years
female: 51.3 years
comparison ranking: total 3

Population growth rate: -0.43% (2024 est.)
comparison ranking: 218

Birth rate: 6.9 births/1,000 population (2024 est.)
comparison ranking: 225

Death rate: 11.9 deaths/1,000 population (2024 est.)
comparison ranking: 18

Net migration rate: 0.7 migrant(s)/1,000 population (2024 est.)
comparison ranking: 70

Population distribution: all primary and secondary regions of high population density lie on the coast; one-third of the population resides in and around Tokyo on the central plain (Kanto Plain)

Urbanization: *urban population:* 92% of total population (2023)
rate of urbanization: -0.25% annual rate of change (2020-25 est.)

Major urban areas - population: 37.194 million TOKYO (capital), 19.013 million Osaka, 9.569 million Nagoya, 5.490 million Kitakyushu-Fukuoka, 2.937 million Shizuoka-Hamamatsu, 2.666 million Sapporo (2023)

Sex ratio: *at birth:* 1.06 male(s)/female
0-14 years: 1.06 male(s)/female
15-64 years: 1.01 male(s)/female
65 years and over: 0.79 male(s)/female
total population: 0.95 male(s)/female (2024 est.)

Mother's mean age at first birth: 30.7 years (2018 est.)

Maternal mortality ratio: 4 deaths/100,000 live births (2020 est.)
comparison ranking: 173

Infant mortality rate: *total:* 1.9 deaths/1,000 live births (2024 est.)
male: 2 deaths/1,000 live births
female: 1.7 deaths/1,000 live births
comparison ranking: total 222

Life expectancy at birth: *total population:* 85.2 years (2024 est.)
male: 82.3 years
female: 88.2 years
comparison ranking: total population 4

Total fertility rate: 1.4 children born/woman (2024 est.)
comparison ranking: 212

Gross reproduction rate: 0.68 (2024 est.)

Contraceptive prevalence rate: 39.8% (2015)
note: percent of women aged 20-49

Drinking water source: *improved:*
total: 99.1% of population
unimproved:
total: 0.1% of population (2020 est.)

Current health expenditure: 10.9% of GDP (2020)

Physician density: 2.48 physicians/1,000 population (2018)

Hospital bed density: 13 beds/1,000 population (2018)

Sanitation facility access: *improved:*
total: 99.9% of population
unimproved:
total: 0.1% of population (2020 est.)

Obesity - adult prevalence rate: 4.3% (2016)
comparison ranking: 186

Alcohol consumption per capita: *total:* 8.36 liters of pure alcohol (2019 est.)
beer: 1.35 liters of pure alcohol (2019 est.)
wine: 0.29 liters of pure alcohol (2019 est.)
spirits: 1.63 liters of pure alcohol (2019 est.)
other alcohols: 5.09 liters of pure alcohol (2019 est.)
comparison ranking: total 39

Tobacco use: *total:* 20.1% (2020 est.)
male: 30.1% (2020 est.)
female: 10% (2020 est.)
comparison ranking: total 89

Currently married women (ages 15-49): 46.8% (2023 est.)

Education expenditures: 3.4% of GDP (2020 est.)
comparison ranking: 142

School life expectancy (primary to tertiary education): *total:* 15 years
male: 15 years
female: 15 years (2019)

ENVIRONMENT

Environment - current issues: air pollution from power plant emissions results in acid rain; acidification of lakes and reservoirs degrading water quality and threatening aquatic life; Japan is one of the largest consumers of fish and tropical timber, contributing to the depletion of these resources in Asia and elsewhere; following the 2011 Fukushima nuclear disaster, Japan originally planned to phase out nuclear power, but it has now implemented a new policy of seeking to restart nuclear power plants that meet strict new safety standards; waste management is an ongoing issue; Japanese municipal facilities used to burn high volumes of trash, but air pollution issues forced the government to adopt an aggressive recycling policy

Environment - international agreements: *party to:* Antarctic-Environmental Protection, Antarctic-Marine Living Resources, Antarctic Seals, Antarctic Treaty, Biodiversity, Climate Change, Climate

Change-Kyoto Protocol, Climate Change-Paris Agreement, Comprehensive Nuclear Test Ban, Desertification, Endangered Species, Environmental Modification, Hazardous Wastes, Law of the Sea, Marine Dumping-London Convention, Marine Dumping-London Protocol, Nuclear Test Ban, Ozone Layer Protection, Ship Pollution, Tropical Timber 2006, Wetlands
signed, but not ratified: none of the selected agreements

Climate: varies from tropical in south to cool temperate in north

Urbanization: *urban population:* 92% of total population (2023)
rate of urbanization: -0.25% annual rate of change (2020-25 est.)

Revenue from forest resources: 0.02% of GDP (2018 est.)
comparison ranking: 138

Revenue from coal: 0% of GDP (2018 est.)
comparison ranking: 137

Air pollutants: *particulate matter emissions:* 10.84 micrograms per cubic meter (2019 est.)
carbon dioxide emissions: 1,135.89 megatons (2016 est.)
methane emissions: 29.99 megatons (2020 est.)

Waste and recycling: *municipal solid waste generated annually:* 43.981 million tons (2015 est.)
municipal solid waste recycled annually: 2,155,069 tons (2015 est.)
percent of municipal solid waste recycled: 4.9% (2015 est.)

Major lakes (area sq km): *fresh water lake(s):* Biwa-ko 688 sq km

Total water withdrawal: *municipal:* 14.8 billion cubic meters (2020 est.)
industrial: 10.3 billion cubic meters (2020 est.)
agricultural: 53.3 billion cubic meters (2020 est.)

Total renewable water resources: 430 billion cubic meters (2020 est.)

Geoparks: *total global geoparks and regional networks:* 10
global geoparks and regional networks: Aso UNESCO; Hakusan Tedorigawa; Itoigawa; Izu Peninsula; Mt. Apoi; Muroto; Oki Islands; San'in Kaigan; Toya - Usu; Unzen (2023)

GOVERNMENT

Country name: *conventional long form:* none
conventional short form: Japan
local long form: Nihon-koku/Nippon-koku
local short form: Nihon/Nippon
etymology: the English word for Japan comes via the Chinese name for the country "Cipangu"; both Nihon and Nippon mean "where the sun originates" and are frequently translated as "Land of the Rising Sun"

Government type: parliamentary constitutional monarchy

Capital: *name:* Tokyo
geographic coordinates: 35 41 N, 139 45 E
time difference: UTC+9 (14 hours ahead of Washington, DC, during Standard Time)
etymology: originally known as Edo, meaning "estuary" in Japanese, the name was changed to Tokyo, meaning "eastern capital," in 1868

Administrative divisions: 47 prefectures; Aichi, Akita, Aomori, Chiba, Ehime, Fukui, Fukuoka, Fukushima, Gifu, Gunma, Hiroshima, Hokkaido, Hyogo, Ibaraki, Ishikawa, Iwate, Kagawa, Kagoshima, Kanagawa, Kochi, Kumamoto, Kyoto, Mie, Miyagi, Miyazaki, Nagano, Nagasaki, Nara, Niigata, Oita, Okayama, Okinawa, Osaka, Saga, Saitama, Shiga, Shimane, Shizuoka, Tochigi, Tokushima, Tokyo, Tottori, Toyama, Wakayama, Yamagata, Yamaguchi, Yamanashi

Independence: *3 May 1947 (current constitution adopted as amendment to Meiji Constitution); notable earlier dates:* 11 February 660 B.C. (mythological date of the founding of the nation by Emperor JIMMU); 29 November 1890 (Meiji Constitution provides for constitutional monarchy)

National holiday: Birthday of Emperor NARUHITO, 23 February (1960); note - celebrates the birthday of the current emperor

Legal system: civil law system based on German model; system also reflects Anglo-American influence and Japanese traditions; judicial review of legislative acts in the Supreme Court

Constitution: *history:* previous 1890; latest approved 6 October 1946, adopted 3 November 1946, effective 3 May 1947
amendments: proposed by the Diet; passage requires approval by at least two-thirds majority of both houses of the Diet and approval by majority in a referendum; note - the constitution has not been amended since its enactment in 1947

International law organization participation: accepts compulsory ICJ jurisdiction with reservations; accepts ICCt jurisdiction

Citizenship: *citizenship by birth:* no
citizenship by descent only: at least one parent must be a citizen of Japan
dual citizenship recognized: no
residency requirement for naturalization: 5 years

Suffrage: 18 years of age; universal

Executive branch: *chief of state:* Emperor NARUHITO (since 1 May 2019)
head of government: Prime Minister Shigeru ISHIBA (since 1 October 2024)
cabinet: Cabinet appointed by the prime minister
elections/appointments: the monarchy is hereditary; the leader of the majority party or majority coalition in the House of Representatives usually becomes prime minister
election results: 2024: Shigeru ISHIBA (LDP) elected prime minister on 27 September 2024; upper house vote - 143 of 242 votes; lower house vote - 291 of 461 votes (note - ISHIBA resigned as prime minister on 11 November 2024 following parliamentary elections but was re-elected over Yoshihiko NODA (CDP) in the second round of voting in the lower house, 221-160)
2021: Fumio KISHIDA reelected prime minister on 10 November 2021; upper house vote - Fumio KISHIDA (LDP) 141, Yukio EDANO (CDP) 60; lower house vote - Fumio KISHIDA 297, Yukio EDANO 108

Legislative branch: *description:* bicameral National Diet or Kokkai consists of:
House of Councilors or Sangi-in (248 seats; 148 members directly elected in multi-seat districts by simple majority vote and 100 directly elected in a single national constituency by proportional representation vote; members serve 6-year terms with half the membership renewed every 3 years)
House of Representatives or Shuugi-in (465 seats; 289 members directly elected in single-seat districts by simple majority vote and 176 directly elected in multi-seat districts by party-list proportional representation vote; members serve up to 4-year terms)
elections: House of Councillors - last held on 10 July 2022 (next to be held in July 2025)
House of Representatives - last held on 27 October 2024 (next to be held by October 2025)
election results: House of Councillors - percent of vote by party - NA; seats by party/grouping as of January 2024 - LDP 116, CDP-SDP 40, Komeito 27, JCP 11, Ishin 21, DPP 11, Reiwa 5, OW 2, NHK 2, independent 12; composition - men 182, women 66; percentage women 26.6%
House of Representatives - percent of vote by party - LDP 26.7%, CDP 21.2%, Ishin 9.4%, DPP 11.3%, Komeito 10.9%, Reiwa 7%, JCP 6.2%, Sanseito Party 3.4%, CPJ 2.1%; seats by party as of October 2024 - LDP 191, CDP 148, Ishin 38, DPP 28, Komeito 24, Reiwa 9, JCP 8, Sanseito Party 3, CPJ 3, SDP 1, Independents 12 ; composition - men 392 men, women 73; percentage women 15.7%

Judicial branch: *highest court(s):* Supreme Court or Saiko saibansho (consists of the chief justice and 14 associate justices); note - the Supreme Court has jurisdiction in constitutional issues
judge selection and term of office: Supreme Court chief justice designated by the Cabinet and appointed by the monarch; associate justices appointed by the Cabinet and confirmed by the monarch; all justices are reviewed in a popular referendum at the first general election of the House of Representatives following each judge's appointment and every 10 years afterward
subordinate courts: 8 High Courts (Koto-saiban-sho), each with a Family Court (Katei-saiban-sho); 50 District Courts (Chiho saibansho), with 203 additional branches; 438 Summary Courts (Kani saibansho)

Political parties: Conservative Party of Japan or CPJ
Constitutional Democratic Party of Japan or CDP
Democratic Party for the People or DPFP or DPP
Japan Communist Party or JCP
Japan Innovation Party or Nippon Ishin no kai or Ishin
Komeito or Komei
Liberal Democratic Party or LDP
Okinawa Social Mass Party or Okinawa Whirlwind or OW
Party to Protect the People from NHK or NHK
Reiwa Shinsengumi
Sanseito Party
Social Democratic Party or SDP

International organization participation: ADB, AfDB (nonregional member), APEC, Arctic Council (observer), ARF, ASEAN (dialogue partner), Australia Group, BIS, CD, CE (observer), CERN (observer), CICA (observer), CP, CPLP (associate), EAS, EBRD, EITI (implementing country), FAO, FATF, G-5, G-7, G-8, G-10, G-20, IADB, IAEA, IBRD, ICAO, ICC (national committees), ICCt, ICRM, IDA, IEA, IFAD, IFC, IFRCS, IGAD (partners), IHO, ILO, IMF, IMO, IMSO, Interpol, IOC, IOM, IPU, ISO, ITSO, ITU, ITUC (NGOs), LAIA (observer), MIGA, NEA, NSG, OAS (observer), OECD, OPCW, OSCE (partner), Pacific Alliance (observer), Paris Club, PCA, PIF (partner), Quad, SAARC (observer), SELEC (observer), SICA (observer), UN, UNCTAD, UNESCO, UNHCR, UNHRC, UNIDO, UNMISS, UNOOSA, UNRWA, UNWTO, UPU, Wassenaar Arrangement, WCO, WFTU (NGOs), WHO, WIPO, WMO, WTO, ZC

Diplomatic representation in the US: *chief of mission:* Ambassador YAMADA Shigeo (since 27 February 2024)
chancery: 2520 Massachusetts Avenue NW, Washington, DC 20008
telephone: [1] (202) 238-6700
FAX: [1] (202) 328-2187
email address and website:
emb-consulate.dc@ws.mofa.go.jp
https://www.us.emb-japan.go.jp/itprtop_en/index.html
consulate(s) general: Chicago
consulate(s): Anchorage (AK), Atlanta, Boston, Denver (CO), Detroit (MI), Hagatna (Guam), Honolulu, Houston, Los Angeles, Miami, Nashville (TN), New York, Portland (OR), San Francisco, Saipan (Northern Mariana Islands), Seattle (WA)

Diplomatic representation from the US: *chief of mission:* Ambassador Rahm EMANUEL (since 25 March 2022)
embassy: 1-10-5 Akasaka, Minato-ku, Tokyo 107-8420
mailing address: 9800 Tokyo Place, Washington DC 20521-9800
telephone: [81] (03) 3224-5000
FAX: [81] (03) 3224-5856
email address and website:
TokyoACS@state.gov
https://jp.usembassy.gov/
consulate(s) general: Naha (Okinawa), Osaka-Kobe, Sapporo
consulate(s): Fukuoka, Nagoya

Flag description: white with a large red disk (representing the sun without rays) in the center

National symbol(s): red sun disc, chrysanthemum; national colors: red, white

National anthem: *name:* "Kimigayo" (The Emperor's Reign)
lyrics/music: unknown/Hiromori HAYASHI
note: adopted 1999; unofficial national anthem since 1883; oldest anthem lyrics in the world, dating to the 10th century or earlier; there is some opposition to the anthem because of its association with militarism and worship of the emperor

National heritage: *total World Heritage Sites:* 25 (20 cultural, 5 natural)
selected World Heritage Site locales: Buddhist Monuments in the Horyu-ji Area (c); Historic Monuments of Ancient Nara (c); Himeji-jo (c); Shiretoko (n); Mozu-Furuichi Kofun Group: Mounded Tombs of Ancient Japan (c); Iwami Ginzan Silver Mine and its Cultural Landscape (c); Jomon Prehistoric Sites in Northern Japan (c); Yakushima (n); Historic Monuments of Ancient Kyoto (c); Hiroshima Peace Memorial (Genbaku Dome) (c)

ECONOMY

Economic overview: fourth-largest economy; trade-oriented and highly diversified; high public debt levels; real wage declines in inflationary environment; sustained near-zero central bank rates coupled with depreciation of yen; strong rebound in tourism

Real GDP (purchasing power parity): $5.761 trillion (2023 est.)
$5.652 trillion (2022 est.)
$5.599 trillion (2021 est.)
note: data in 2021 dollars
comparison ranking: 5

Real GDP growth rate: 1.92% (2023 est.)
0.95% (2022 est.)
2.56% (2021 est.)
note: annual GDP % growth based on constant local currency
comparison ranking: 142

Real GDP per capita: $46,300 (2023 est.)
$45,200 (2022 est.)
$44,500 (2021 est.)
note: data in 2021 dollars
comparison ranking: 51

GDP (official exchange rate): $4.213 trillion (2023 est.)
note: data in current dollars at official exchange rate

Inflation rate (consumer prices): 3.27% (2023 est.)
2.5% (2022 est.)
-0.23% (2021 est.)
note: annual % change based on consumer prices
comparison ranking: 63

Credit ratings: Fitch rating: A (2015)

Moody's rating: A1 (2014)

Standard & Poors rating: A+ (2015)
note: The year refers to the year in which the current credit rating was first obtained.

GDP - composition, by sector of origin: *agriculture:* 1% (2022 est.)
industry: 26.9% (2022 est.)
services: 71.4% (2022 est.)
note: figures may not total 100% due to non-allocated consumption not captured in sector-reported data
comparison rankings: services 34; industry 84; agriculture 182

GDP - composition, by end use: *household consumption:* 55.6% (2022 est.)
government consumption: 21.6% (2022 est.)
investment in fixed capital: 26% (2022 est.)
investment in inventories: 0.6% (2022 est.)
exports of goods and services: 21.5% (2022 est.)
imports of goods and services: -25.3% (2022 est.)
note: figures may not total 100% due to rounding or gaps in data collection

Agricultural products: rice, milk, sugar beets, vegetables, eggs, chicken, potatoes, cabbages, sugarcane, pork (2022)
note: top ten agricultural products based on tonnage

Industries: motor vehicles, electronic equipment, machine tools, steel and nonferrous metals, ships, chemicals, textiles, processed foods

Industrial production growth rate: -1.25% (2022 est.)
note: annual % change in industrial value added based on constant local currency
comparison ranking: 171

Labor force: 69.349 million (2023 est.)
note: number of people ages 15 or older who are employed or seeking work
comparison ranking: 10

Unemployment rate: 2.58% (2023 est.)
2.6% (2022 est.)
2.83% (2021 est.)
note: % of labor force seeking employment
comparison ranking: 29

Youth unemployment rate (ages 15-24): *total:* 4.1% (2023 est.)
male: 4.5% (2023 est.)
female: 3.7% (2023 est.)
note: % of labor force ages 15-24 seeking employment
comparison ranking: total 182

Average household expenditures: *on food:* 16.3% of household expenditures (2022 est.)
on alcohol and tobacco: 2.7% of household expenditures (2022 est.)

Remittances: 0.13% of GDP (2023 est.)
0.13% of GDP (2022 est.)
0.11% of GDP (2021 est.)
note: personal transfers and compensation between resident and non-resident individuals/households/entities

Budget: *revenues:* $661.986 billion (2022 est.)
expenditures: $892.184 billion (2022 est.)
note: central government revenues and expenses (excluding grants and social security funds) converted to US dollars at average official exchange rate for year indicated

Public debt: 216.21% of GDP (2022 est.)
note: central government debt as a % of GDP
comparison ranking: 1

Taxes and other revenues: 35.2% (of GDP) (2017 est.)
comparison ranking: 16

Current account balance: $150.691 billion (2023 est.)
$90.277 billion (2022 est.)
$196.525 billion (2021 est.)
note: balance of payments - net trade and primary/secondary income in current dollars
comparison ranking: 3

Exports: $920.737 billion (2023 est.)
$922.813 billion (2022 est.)
$920.639 billion (2021 est.)
note: balance of payments - exports of goods and services in current dollars
comparison ranking: 7

Exports - partners: US 19%, China 19%, South Korea 7%, Taiwan 7%, Thailand 4% (2022)
note: top five export partners based on percentage share of exports

Exports - commodities: cars, machinery, integrated circuits, vehicle parts/accessories, refined petroleum (2022)
note: top five export commodities based on value in dollars

Imports: $989.843 billion (2023 est.)
$1.081 trillion (2022 est.)
$942.45 billion (2021 est.)
note: balance of payments - imports of goods and services in current dollars
comparison ranking: 6

Imports - partners: China 22%, Australia 10%, US 10%, UAE 5%, Saudi Arabia 4% (2022)
note: top five import partners based on percentage share of imports

Imports - commodities: crude petroleum, natural gas, coal, integrated circuits, garments (2022)
note: top five import commodities based on value in dollars

Reserves of foreign exchange and gold: $1.295 trillion (2023 est.)
$1.228 trillion (2022 est.)
$1.406 trillion (2021 est.)
note: holdings of gold (year-end prices)/foreign exchange/special drawing rights in current dollars
comparison ranking: 2

Exchange rates: yen (JPY) per US dollar -

Exchange rates: 140.491 (2023 est.)
131.498 (2022 est.)
109.754 (2021 est.)

106.775 (2020 est.)
109.01 (2019 est.)

ENERGY

Electricity access: *electrification - total population:* 100% (2022 est.)

Electricity: *installed generating capacity:* 349.94 million kW (2022 est.)
consumption: 939.314 billion kWh (2022 est.)
transmission/distribution losses: 52.053 billion kWh (2022 est.)
comparison rankings: transmission/distribution losses 205; consumption 5; installed generating capacity 4

Electricity generation sources: *fossil fuels:* 71.7% of total installed capacity (2022 est.)
nuclear: 5.2% of total installed capacity (2022 est.)
solar: 9.4% of total installed capacity (2022 est.)
wind: 1% of total installed capacity (2022 est.)
hydroelectricity: 6.8% of total installed capacity (2022 est.)
geothermal: 0.3% of total installed capacity (2022 est.)
biomass and waste: 5.6% of total installed capacity (2022 est.)

Nuclear energy: Number of operational nuclear reactors: 12 (2023)

Number of nuclear reactors under construction: 2 (2023)

Net capacity of operational nuclear reactors: 11.05GW (2023 est.)

Percent of total electricity production: 5.5% (2023 est.)

Number of nuclear reactors permanently shut down: 27 (2023)

Coal: *production:* 29.141 million metric tons (2022 est.)
consumption: 216.332 million metric tons (2022 est.)
exports: 917,000 metric tons (2022 est.)
imports: 191.092 million metric tons (2022 est.)
proven reserves: 350 million metric tons (2022 est.)

Petroleum: *total petroleum production:* 8,000 bbl/day (2023 est.)
refined petroleum consumption: 3.289 million bbl/day (2023 est.)
crude oil estimated reserves: 44.115 million barrels (2021 est.)

Natural gas: *production:* 2.22 billion cubic meters (2022 est.)
consumption: 92.843 billion cubic meters (2022 est.)
exports: 271.607 million cubic meters (2022 est.)
imports: 92.567 billion cubic meters (2022 est.)
proven reserves: 20.898 billion cubic meters (2021 est.)

Carbon dioxide emissions: 1.049 billion metric tonnes of CO_2 (2022 est.)
from coal and metallurgical coke: 442.647 million metric tonnes of CO_2 (2022 est.)
from petroleum and other liquids: 406.998 million metric tonnes of CO_2 (2022 est.)
from consumed natural gas: 199.783 million metric tonnes of CO_2 (2022 est.)
comparison ranking: total emissions 5

Energy consumption per capita: 136.122 million Btu/person (2022 est.)
comparison ranking: 30

COMMUNICATIONS

Telephones - fixed lines: *total subscriptions:* 60.721 million (2022 est.)
subscriptions per 100 inhabitants: 49 (2022 est.)
comparison ranking: total subscriptions 3

Telephones - mobile cellular: *total subscriptions:* 207.648 million (2022 est.)
subscriptions per 100 inhabitants: 168 (2022 est.)
comparison ranking: total subscriptions 8

Telecommunication systems: *general assessment:* Japan has one of the best developed telecom markets globally, the fixed-line segment remains stagnant and the focus for growth is in the mobile sector; the MNOs have shifted their investment from LTE to 5G, and growth in 5G showed early promise although there have been recent setbacks; these have partly been attributed to the economic difficulties, the impact of restrictions imposed during the pandemic, and unfavorable investment climate (not helped by the delay of the Tokyo Olympics from 2020 to 2021), and to restrictions in the supply of 5G-enabled devices; the fixed broadband market is dominated by fiber, with a strong cable platform also evident; fiber will continue to increase its share of the fixed broadband market, largely at the expense of DSL; the mobile market is dominated by three MNOs, mobile broadband subscriber growth is expected to be relatively low over the next five years, partly due to the high existing subscriptions though growth has been stimulated by measures which have encouraged people to school and work from home; there has also been a boost in accessing entertainment via mobile devices since 2020 (2021)
domestic: 49 per 100 for fixed-line and 161 per 100 for mobile-cellular subscriptions (2021)
international: country code - 81; numerous submarine cables with landing points for HSCS, JIH, RJCN, APCN-2, JUS, EAC-C2C, PC-1, Tata TGN-Pacific, FLAG North Asia Loop/REACH North Asia Loop, APCN-2, FASTER, SJC, SJC2, Unity/EAC-Pacific, JGA-N, APG, ASE, AJC, JUPITER, MOC, Okinawa Cellular Cable, KJCN, GOKI, KJCN, and SeaMeWE-3, submarine cables provide links throughout Asia, Australia, the Middle East, Europe, Southeast Asia, Africa and US; satellite earth stations - 7 Intelsat (Pacific and Indian Oceans), 1 Intersputnik (Indian Ocean region), 2 Inmarsat (Pacific and Indian Ocean regions), and 8 SkyPerfect JSAT (2019)

Broadcast media: a mixture of public and commercial broadcast TV and radio stations; 5 national terrestrial TV networks including 1 public broadcaster; the large number of radio and TV stations available provide a wide range of choices; satellite and cable services provide access to international channels (2023)

Internet country code: .jp

Internet users: *total:* 99.6 million (2021 est.)
percent of population: 83% (2021 est.)
comparison ranking: total 8

Broadband - fixed subscriptions: *total:* 44,000,791 (2020 est.)
subscriptions per 100 inhabitants: 35 (2020 est.)
comparison ranking: total 3

TRANSPORTATION

National air transport system: *number of registered air carriers:* 22 (2020)
inventory of registered aircraft operated by air carriers: 673
annual passenger traffic on registered air carriers: 126,387,527 (2018)
annual freight traffic on registered air carriers: 9,420,660,000 (2018) mt-km

Civil aircraft registration country code prefix: JA

Airports: 279 (2024)
comparison ranking: 24

Heliports: 2,839 (2024)

Pipelines: 4,456 km gas, 174 km oil, 104 km oil/gas/water (2013)

Railways: *total:* 27,311 km (2015)
standard gauge: 4,800 km (2015) 1.435-m gauge (4,800 km electrified)
narrow gauge: 124 km (2015) 1.372-m gauge (124 km electrified)
dual gauge: 132 km (2015) 1.435-1.067-m gauge (132 km electrified)
22,207 km 1.067-mm gauge (15,430 km electrified)
48 km 0.762-m gauge (48 km electrified)
comparison ranking: total 11

Roadways: *total:* 1,218,772 km
paved: 992,835 km (includes 8,428 km of expressways)
unpaved: 225,937 km (2015)
comparison ranking: total 6

Waterways: 1,770 km (2010) (seagoing vessels use inland seas)
comparison ranking: 46

Merchant marine: *total:* 5,229 (2023)
by type: bulk carrier 166, container ship 49, general cargo 1,893, oil tanker 666, other 2,455
comparison ranking: total 4

Ports: *total ports:* 163 (2024)
large: 11
medium: 26
small: 54
very small: 71
size unknown: 1
ports with oil terminals: 99
key ports: Kawasaki Ko, Kobe, Mikawa, Nagasaki, Nagoya Ko, Onomichi-Itozaki, Osaka, Tokyo Ko, Wakamatsu Ko, Wakayama-Shimotsu Ko, Yokohama Ko

MILITARY AND SECURITY

Military and security forces: Japan Self-Defense Force (JSDF): Ground Self-Defense Force (Rikujou Jieitai, GSDF; includes aviation), Maritime Self-Defense Force (Kaijou Jieitai, MSDF; includes naval aviation), Air Self-Defense Force (Koukuu Jieitai, ASDF) (2024)
note: the Coast Guard is under the Ministry of Land, Infrastructure, Transport and Tourism; it is barred by law from operating as a military force, but in times of conflict Article 80 of the 1954 Self-Defense Forces Act permits the transfer of control of the coast guard to the Ministry of Defense with Cabinet approval

Military expenditures: 1.4% of GDP (2024 est.)
1.2% of GDP (2023)
1.1% of GDP (2022)
1% of GDP (2021)

1% of GDP (2020)
note: the Japanese Government in 2022 pledged to increase defense expenditures to 2% of GDP in line with NATO standards by March 2028; if the planned increase occurs, Japan would have the world's third largest defense budget
comparison ranking: 101

Military and security service personnel strengths: approximately 230-240,000 active personnel (145-150,000 Ground; 40-45,000 Maritime; 40-45,000 Air); 14,000 Coast Guard (2023)

Military equipment inventories and acquisitions: the JSDF is equipped with a mix of imported and domestically produced equipment; Japan has a robust defense industry and is capable of producing a wide range of air, ground, and naval weapons systems; the majority of its weapons imports are from the US and some domestically produced weapons are US-origin and manufactured under license (2024)

Military service age and obligation: 18-32 years of age for voluntary military service for men and women; no conscription (2024)
note: as of 2023, women made up about 9% of the military's full-time personnel

Military deployments: approximately 200 Djibouti (2024)

Military - note: the Japan Self-Defense Force's (JSDF) primary concerns are perceived threats posed by China and North Korea; it has a range of missions, including territorial defense, monitoring the country's air and maritime spaces, countering piracy and terrorism, and conducting humanitarian operations; it exercises regularly with the US military and increasingly with other regional countries, such as Australia
Japan's alliance with the US (signed in 1951) is one of the cornerstones of the country's security, as well as a large component of the US security role in Asia; approximately 55,000 US troops and other military assets, including aircraft and naval ships, are stationed in Japan and have exclusive use of more than 80 bases and facilities; in exchange for their use, the US guarantees Japan's security; the Japanese Government provides about $2 billion per year to offset the cost of stationing US forces in Japan; in addition, it pays compensation to localities hosting US troops, rent for bases, and costs for new facilities to support the US presence; Japan also has Major Non-NATO Ally (MNNA) status with the US, a designation under US law that provides foreign partners with certain benefits in the areas of defense trade and security cooperation Japan was disarmed after its defeat in World War II; shortly after the Korean War began in 1950, US occupation forces in Japan created a 75,000-member lightly armed force called the National Police Reserve; the JSDF was founded in 1954; Article 9 of Japan's 1947 constitution renounced the use of force as a means of settling international disputes; however, Japan has interpreted Article 9 to mean that it can maintain a military for national defense purposes and, since 1991, has allowed the JSDF to participate in noncombat roles overseas in a number of UN peacekeeping missions and in the US-led coalition in Iraq; in 2014-2015, the Japanese Government reinterpreted the constitution as allowing for "collective self-defense," described as the use of force on others' behalf if Japan's security was threatened; in 2022, the government released three security policy documents that labeled China as an "unprecedented strategic challenge," declared Japan's intention to develop "counterstrike" capabilities, including cruise missiles and armed drones, and outlined plans to increase Japan's security-related expenditures to 2% of its national gross domestic product (GDP), in line with NATO standards (post-war Japan generally has limited defense spending to 1% of its GDP) (2024)

SPACE

Space agency/agencies: Japan Aerospace Exploration Agency (JAXA; established in 2003) (2024)

Space launch site(s): Tanegashima Space Center/ Yoshinobu Launch Complex (Kagoshima), Uchinoura Space Center (Kagoshima), Noshiro Testing Center (Akita) (2024)

Space program overview: has one of the world's largest and most advanced space programs with independent capabilities in all areas of space categories except for autonomous manned space flight; designs, builds, launches, and operates the full spectrum of satellites, including communications, remote sensing (RS), astronomical observation, scientific, and navigational/ positional; designs, builds, and independently launches satellite/space launch vehicles (SLVs) and other spacecraft, including interplanetary and Lunar probes, space station modules and space labs, and space transportation systems; has a wide range of research and development programs, including reusable SLVs, space-based astronomy, spacecraft components, robotics, solar sails, radio waves, and space plasma; has an astronaut training program; participates in international space programs, including the International Space Station (ISS), leading the Asia-Pacific Regional Space Agency Forum, and co-leading the Global Earth Observation System of Systems; cooperates with a variety of foreign space agencies and industries, including those of Canada, the European Space Agency (ESA) and its individual member states, India, Russia, the UAE, the US, and a range of other countries and space agencies throughout Africa, Europe, and the Asia-Pacific regions; has a substantial commercial space industry that develops an array of space-related capabilities and technologies, including satellites, satellite payloads and subcomponents, and SLVs; in recent years, the Japanese Government has encouraged and supported the development of space startup companies (2024)
note: further details about the key activities, programs, and milestones of the country's space program, as well as government spending estimates on the space sector, appear in the Space Programs reference guide

TRANSNATIONAL ISSUES

Refugees and internally displaced persons: *stateless persons:* 531 (2022)

JERSEY

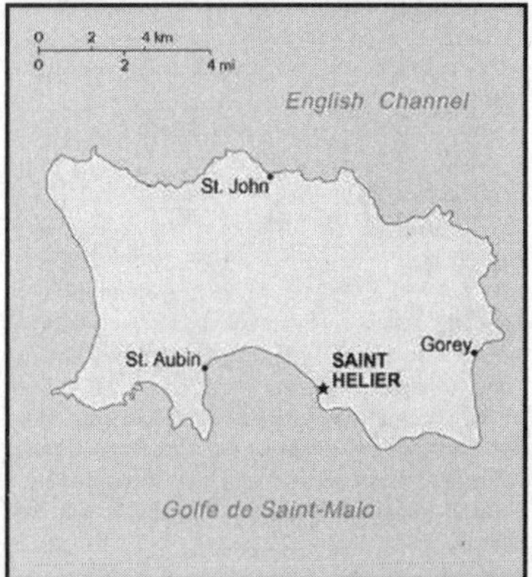

INTRODUCTION

Background: Jersey and the other Channel Islands represent the last remnants of the medieval Duchy of Normandy that held sway in both France and England. These islands were the only British soil that Germany occupied in World War II. The Bailiwick of Jersey is a British Crown dependency, which means that it is not part of the UK but is rather a self-governing possession of the British Crown. However, the UK Government is constitutionally responsible for its defense and international representation.

GEOGRAPHY

Location: Western Europe, island in the English Channel, northwest of France

Geographic coordinates: 49 15 N, 2 10 W

Map references: Europe

Area: *total:* 116 sq km
land: 116 sq km
water: 0 sq km
comparison ranking: total 223

Area - comparative: about two-thirds the size of Washington, DC

Land boundaries: *total:* 0 km

Coastline: 70 km

Maritime claims: *territorial sea:* 12 nm
exclusive fishing zone: 12 nm

Climate: temperate; mild winters and cool summers

Terrain: gently rolling plain with low, rugged hills along north coast

Elevation: *highest point:* Les Platons 136 m
lowest point: English Channel 0 m

Natural resources: arable land

Land use: *agricultural land:* 66% (2018 est.)

arable land: 66% (2018 est.)
permanent crops: 0% (2018 est.)
permanent pasture: 0% (2018 est.)
forest: 0% (2018 est.)
other: 34% (2018 est.)

Irrigated land: NA

Population distribution: fairly even distribution; no notable trends

Natural hazards: very large tidal variation can be hazardous to navigation

Geography - note: largest and southernmost of Channel Islands; about 30% of population concentrated in Saint Helier

PEOPLE AND SOCIETY

Population: *total:* 103,387
male: 51,028
female: 52,359 (2024 est.)
comparison rankings: female 193; male 193; total 193

Nationality: *noun:* Channel Islander(s)
adjective: Channel Islander

Ethnic groups: Jersey 44.4%, British 30.5%, Portuguese/Madeiran 9.4%, Polish 3%, Irish 2.1%, other 10.6% (2021 est.)

Languages: English (official) 94.5%, Portuguese 4.6%, other 0.9% (includes French (official) and Jerriais) (2001 est.)
note: data represent main spoken language; the traditional language of Jersey is Jerriais or Jersey French (a Norman language), which was spoken by fewer than 3,000 people as of 2001; two thirds of Jerriais speakers are aged 60 and over

Religions: Christian 85.2%, Baha'i 0.3%, Hindu 0.1%, Jewish 0.1%, Muslim 0.1%, atheist 1.1%, agnostic 13.1% (2020 est.)

Age structure: *0-14 years:* 17% (male 9,082/female 8,530)
15-64 years: 64.6% (male 33,840/female 32,989)
65 years and over: 18.3% (2024 est.) (male 8,106/ female 10,840)

Dependency ratios: *total dependency ratio:* 44.5
youth dependency ratio: 21.3
elderly dependency ratio: 23.2
potential support ratio: 4.3 (2021 est.)
note: data represent Guernsey and Jersey

Median age: *total:* 38.2 years (2024 est.)
male: 37 years
female: 39.7 years
comparison ranking: total 76

Population growth rate: 0.56% (2024 est.)
comparison ranking: 146

Birth rate: 12.2 births/1,000 population (2024 est.)
comparison ranking: 143

Death rate: 7.8 deaths/1,000 population (2024 est.)
comparison ranking: 93

Net migration rate: 1.2 migrant(s)/1,000 population (2024 est.)
comparison ranking: 61

Population distribution: fairly even distribution; no notable trends

Urbanization: *urban population:* 31.2% of total population (2023)
rate of urbanization: 0.68% annual rate of change (2020-25 est.)
note: data include Guernsey and Jersey

Major urban areas - population: 34,000 SAINT HELIER (capital) (2018)

Sex ratio: *at birth:* 1.06 male(s)/female
0-14 years: 1.06 male(s)/female
15-64 years: 1.03 male(s)/female
65 years and over: 0.75 male(s)/female
total population: 0.98 male(s)/female (2024 est.)

Infant mortality rate: *total:* 3.7 deaths/1,000 live births (2024 est.)
male: 4.2 deaths/1,000 live births
female: 3.3 deaths/1,000 live births
comparison ranking: total 192

Life expectancy at birth: *total population:* 83 years (2024 est.)
male: 80.6 years
female: 85.7 years
comparison ranking: total population 17

Total fertility rate: 1.66 children born/woman (2024 est.)
comparison ranking: 170

Gross reproduction rate: 0.81 (2024 est.)

Drinking water source: *improved: total:* 94.2% of population
unimproved: total: 5.9% of population (2017 est.)
note: includes data for Guernsey

Sanitation facility access: *improved:*
total: 98.5% of population
unimproved:
total: 1.5% of population (2017)

ENVIRONMENT

Environment - current issues: habitat and species depletion due to human encroachment; water pollution; improper solid waste disposal

Climate: temperate; mild winters and cool summers

Urbanization: *urban population:* 31.2% of total population (2023)
rate of urbanization: 0.68% annual rate of change (2020-25 est.)
note: data include Guernsey and Jersey

Waste and recycling: *municipal solid waste generated annually:* 178,933 tons (2016 est.)
municipal solid waste recycled annually: 50,871 tons (2016 est.)
percent of municipal solid waste recycled: 28.4% (2016 est.)
note: data include combined totals for Guernsey and Jersey.

GOVERNMENT

Country name: *conventional long form:* Bailiwick of Jersey
conventional short form: Jersey
former: Norman Isles
etymology: the name is of Old Norse origin, but the meaning of the root "Jer(s)" is uncertain; the "-ey" ending means "island"

Government type: parliamentary democracy (Assembly of the States of Jersey)

Dependency status: British crown dependency

Capital: *name:* Saint Helier
geographic coordinates: 49 11 N, 2 06 W
time difference: UTC 0 (5 hours ahead of Washington, DC, during Standard Time)
daylight saving time: +1hr, begins last Sunday in March; ends last Sunday in October
etymology: named after Saint HELIER, the patron saint of Jersey, who was reputedly martyred on the island in A.D. 555

Administrative divisions: none (British crown dependency); there are no first-order administrative divisions as defined by the US Government, but there are 12 parishes; Grouville, Saint Brelade, Saint Clement, Saint Helier, Saint John, Saint Lawrence, Saint Martin, Saint Mary, Saint Ouen, Saint Peter, Saint Saviour, Trinity

Independence: none (British Crown dependency)

National holiday: Liberation Day, 9 May (1945)

Legal system: the laws of the UK apply where applicable; includes local statutes

Constitution: *history:* unwritten; partly statutes, partly common law and practice
amendments: proposed by a government minister to the Assembly of the States of Jersey, by an Assembly member, or by an elected parish head; passage requires several Assembly readings, a majority vote by the Assembly, review by the UK Ministry of Justice, and approval of the British monarch (Royal Assent)

Citizenship: see United Kingdom

Suffrage: 16 years of age; universal

Executive branch: *chief of state:* King CHARLES III (since 8 September 2022); represented by Lieutenant Governor Jerry KYD (since 8 October 2022)
head of government: Chief Minister Lyndon FARNHAM (since 25 January 2024); Bailiff Timothy Le COCQ (since 17 October 2019)
cabinet: Council of Ministers appointed individually by the states
elections/appointments: the monarchy is hereditary; Council of Ministers, including the chief minister, indirectly elected by the Assembly of States; lieutenant governor and bailiff appointed by the monarch

Legislative branch: *description:* unicameral Assembly of the States of Jersey (49 elected members; 8 senators to serve 4-year terms, and 29 deputies and 12 connetables, or heads of parishes, to serve 4-year terms; 5 non-voting members appointed by the monarch include the bailiff, lieutenant governor, dean of Jersey, attorney general, and the solicitor general)
elections: last held on 22 June 2022 (next to be held in 2026)
election results: percent of vote by party - BW 66.8%, RJ 12.3%, JA 2.0%, PP 2%, JLC 4.1%; seats by party - BW 35, RJ 10, JLC 2, JA 1, PP 1; composition - men 28, women 21, percentage women 42.9%

Judicial branch: *highest court(s):* Jersey Court of Appeal (consists of the bailiff, deputy bailiff, and 12 judges); Royal Court (consists of the bailiff, deputy bailiff, 6 commissioners and lay people referred to as jurats, and is organized into Heritage, Family, Probate, and Samedi Divisions); appeals beyond the Court of Appeal are heard by the Judicial Committee of the Privy Council (in London)

judge selection and term of office: Jersey Court of Appeal bailiffs and judges appointed by the Crown upon the advice of the Secretary of State for Justice; bailiffs and judges appointed for "extent of good behavior;" Royal Court bailiffs appointed by the Crown upon the advice of the Secretary of State for Justice; commissioners appointed by the bailiff; jurats appointed by the Electoral College; bailiffs and commissioners appointed for "extent of good behavior;" jurats appointed until retirement at age 72
subordinate courts: Magistrate's Court; Youth Court; Petty Debts Court; Parish Hall Enquiries (a process of preliminary investigation into youth and minor adult offenses to determine need for presentation before a court)

Political parties: Better Way or BW (group of independent candidates)
Jersey Alliance or JA
Jersey Liberal Conservatives or JLC
Progress Party or PP
Reform Jersey or RJ
note: most deputies sit as independents

International organization participation: UPU

Diplomatic representation in the US: none (British Crown dependency)

Diplomatic representation from the US: *embassy:* none (British Crown dependency)

Flag description: white with a diagonal red cross extending to the corners of the flag; in the upper quadrant, surmounted by a yellow crown, a red shield with three lions in yellow; according to tradition, the ships of Jersey - in an attempt to differentiate themselves from English ships flying the horizontal cross of St. George - rotated the cross to the "X" (saltire) configuration; because this arrangement still resembled the Irish cross of St. Patrick, the yellow Plantagenet crown and Jersey coat of arms were added

National symbol(s): Jersey cow; national colors: red, white

National anthem: *name:* "Isle de Siez Nous" (Island Home)
lyrics/music: Gerard LE FEUVRE
note: adopted 2008; serves as a local anthem; as a British Crown dependency, "God Save the King" is official (see United Kingdom)

ECONOMY

Economic overview: British territorial island economy; strong offshore banking and finance sectors; low asset taxation; strong tourism sector prior to COVID-19 and Brexit; one of the most expensive places to live; minimal welfare system; historical cider industry

Real GDP (purchasing power parity): $5.569 billion (2016 est.)
$5.514 billion (2015 est.)
$4.98 billion (2014 est.)
note: data are in 2015 dollars
comparison ranking: 180

Real GDP growth rate: 7.81% (2022 est.)
15.46% (2021 est.)
-8.47% (2020 est.)
note: annual GDP % growth based on constant local currency; entry includes Jersey and Guernsey
comparison ranking: 16

Real GDP per capita: $56,600 (2016 est.)
$49,500 (2015 est.)
comparison ranking: 33

GDP (official exchange rate): $11.228 billion (2022 est.)
note: data in current dollars at official exchange rate; entry includes Jersey and Guernsey

GDP - composition, by sector of origin: *agriculture:* 0.8% (2022 est.)
industry: 8.4% (2022 est.)
services: 92% (2022 est.)
note: figures may not total 100% due to non-allocated consumption not captured in sector-reported data
comparison rankings: services 2; industry 202; agriculture 187

Agricultural products: potatoes, cauliflower, tomatoes; beef, dairy products

Industries: tourism, banking and finance, dairy, electronics

Industrial production growth rate: 1.64% (2022 est.)
note: annual % change in industrial value added based on constant local currency; entry includes Jersey and Guernsey
comparison ranking: 123

Labor force: 86,000 (2023 est.)
note: number of people ages 15 or older who are employed or seeking work;entry includes Jersey and Guernsey
comparison ranking: 185

Unemployment rate: 5.98% (2023 est.)
5.91% (2022 est.)
6.61% (2021 est.)
note: % of labor force seeking employment; entry includes Jersey and Guernsey
comparison ranking: 121

Youth unemployment rate (ages 15-24): *total:* 13.5% (2023 est.)
male: 13.7% (2023 est.)
female: 13.2% (2023 est.)
note: % of labor force ages 15-24 seeking employment
comparison ranking: total 103

Gini Index coefficient - distribution of family income: 0.3 (2014 est.)
comparison ranking: 153

Exports - partners: almost entirely United Kingdom (2022)

Exports - commodities: refined petroleum, beverages, ships, jewelry, artwork (2022)

Imports - partners: almost entirely United Kingdom (2022)

Imports - commodities: artwork, ships, vegetables, fruits, jewelry (2022)

Exchange rates: Jersey pounds (JEP) per US dollar

Exchange rates: 0.805 (2023 est.)
0.811 (2022 est.)
0.727 (2021 est.)
0.78 (2020 est.)
0.783 (2019 est.)

ENERGY

Electricity access: *electrification - total population:* 100% (2022 est.)
note: includes Guernsey and Jersey

Carbon dioxide emissions: 450,000 metric tonnes of CO2 (2012 est.)
comparison ranking: total emissions 190

COMMUNICATIONS

Telephones - fixed lines: *total subscriptions:* 48,122 (2021 est.)
subscriptions per 100 inhabitants: 47 (2021 est.)
comparison ranking: total subscriptions 156

Telephones - mobile cellular: *total subscriptions:* 124,083 (2021 est.)
subscriptions per 100 inhabitants: 120 (2021 est.)
comparison ranking: total subscriptions 190

Telecommunication systems: *general assessment:* the telecommunication services comprise of Internet, telephone, broadcasting and postal services, which allow islanders to contact people and receive information; Internet connectivity to the rest of the world is provided by undersea cables linked to Guernsey, the UK and France; (2021)
domestic: fixed-line 47 per 100 and mobile-cellular 120 per 100 subscriptions (2021)
international: country code - 44; landing points for the INGRID, UK-Channel Islands-8, and Guernsey-Jersey-4, submarine cable connectivity to Guernsey, the UK, and France (2019)

Broadcast media: multiple UK terrestrial TV broadcasts are received via a transmitter in Jersey; satellite packages available; BBC Radio Jersey and 1 other radio station operating

Internet country code: .je

Internet users: *total:* 96,038 (2021 est.)
percent of population: 93% (2021 est.)
comparison ranking: total 188

Broadband - fixed subscriptions: *total:* 39,699 (2020 est.)
subscriptions per 100 inhabitants: 37 (2020 est.)
comparison ranking: total 145

TRANSPORTATION

National air transport system: *number of registered air carriers:* 1 (2020) (registered in UK)
inventory of registered aircraft operated by air carriers: 4 (registered in UK)

Airports: 1 (2024)
comparison ranking: 233

Roadways: *total:* 576 km (2010)
comparison ranking: total 193

Ports: *total ports:* 1 (2024)
large: 0
medium: 0
small: 1
very small: 0
ports with oil terminals: 1
key ports: Saint Helier Harbour

MILITARY AND SECURITY

Military - note: defense is the responsibility of the UK

JORDAN

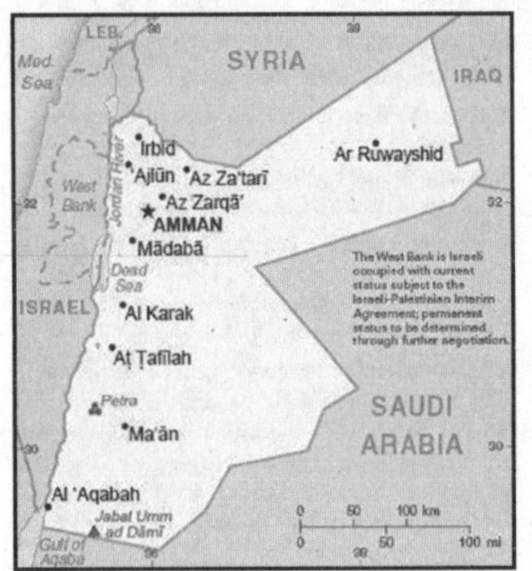

INTRODUCTION

Background: After World War I and the dissolution of the Ottoman Empire, the League of Nations awarded Britain the mandate to govern much of the Middle East. In 1921, Britain demarcated from Palestine a semi-autonomous region of Transjordan and recognized ABDALLAH I from the Hashemite family as the country's first leader. The Hashemites also controlled the Hijaz, or the western coastal area of modern-day Saudi Arabia, until 1925, when IBN SAUD and Wahhabi tribes pushed them out. The country gained its independence in 1946 and thereafter became the Hashemite Kingdom of Jordan.

The country has had four kings. Long-time ruler King HUSSEIN (r. 1953-99) successfully navigated competing pressures from the major powers (US, UK, and Soviet Union), various Arab states, Israel, and Palestinian militants, the latter of which led to a brief civil war in 1970 that is known as "Black September" and ended in King HUSSEIN ousting the militants.

Jordan's borders have changed since it gained independence. In 1948, Jordan took control of the West Bank and East Jerusalem in the first Arab-Israeli War, eventually annexing those territories in 1950 and granting its new Palestinian residents Jordanian citizenship. In 1967, Jordan lost the West Bank and East Jerusalem to Israel in the Six-Day War but retained administrative claims to the West Bank until 1988, when King HUSSEIN permanently relinquished Jordanian claims to the West Bank in favor of the Palestine Liberation Organization (PLO). King HUSSEIN signed a peace treaty with Israel in 1994, after Israel and the PLO signed the Oslo Accords in 1993.

Jordanian kings continue to claim custodianship of the Muslim holy sites in Jerusalem by virtue of their Hashemite heritage as descendants of the Prophet Mohammad and agreements with Israel and Jerusalem-based religious and Palestinian leaders. After Israel captured East Jerusalem in the 1967 War, it authorized the Jordanian-controlled Islamic Trust, or Waqf, to continue administering the Al Haram ash Sharif/Temple Mount holy compound, and the Jordan-Israel peace treaty reaffirmed Jordan's "special role" in administering the Muslim holy shrines in Jerusalem. Jordanian kings claim custodianship of the Christian sites in Jerusalem on the basis of the 7th-century Pact of Omar, when the Muslim leader, after conquering Jerusalem, agreed to permit Christian worship.

King HUSSEIN died in 1999 and was succeeded by his eldest son and current King ABDALLAH II. In 2009, ABDALLAH II designated his son HUSSEIN as the Crown Prince. During his reign, ABDALLAH II has contended with a series of challenges, including the Arab Spring influx of refugees from neighboring states, the COVID-19 pandemic, the effects of the war in Ukraine, a perennially weak economy, and the Israel-HAMAS conflict that began in October 2023.

GEOGRAPHY

Location: Middle East, northwest of Saudi Arabia, between Israel (to the west) and Iraq

Geographic coordinates: 31 00 N, 36 00 E

Map references: Middle East

Area: *total:* 89,342 sq km
land: 88,802 sq km
water: 540 sq km
comparison ranking: total 112

Area - comparative: about three-quarters the size of Pennsylvania; slightly smaller than Indiana

Land boundaries: *total:* 1,744 km
border countries (5): Iraq 179 km; Israel 307 km; Saudi Arabia 731 km; Syria 379 km; West Bank 148 km

Coastline: 26 km

Maritime claims: *territorial sea:* 3 nm

Climate: mostly arid desert; rainy season in west (November to April)

Terrain: mostly arid desert plateau; a great north-south geological rift along the west of the country is the dominant topographical feature and includes the Jordan River Valley, the Dead Sea, and the Jordanian Highlands

Elevation: *highest point:* Jabal Umm ad Dami 1,854 m
lowest point: Dead Sea -431 m
mean elevation: 812 m

Natural resources: phosphates, potash, shale oil

Land use: *agricultural land:* 11.4% (2018 est.)
arable land: 2% (2018 est.)
permanent crops: 1% (2018 est.)
permanent pasture: 8.4% (2018 est.)
forest: 1.1% (2018 est.)
other: 87.5% (2018 est.)

Irrigated land: 833 sq km (2020)

Major lakes (area sq km): *salt water lake(s):* Dead Sea (shared with Israel and West Bank) - 1,020 sq km
note - endorheic hypersaline lake; 9.6 times saltier than the ocean; lake shore is 431 meters below sea level

Major watersheds (area sq km): Indian Ocean drainage: *(Persian Gulf)* Tigris and Euphrates (918,044 sq km)

Major aquifers: Arabian Aquifer System

Population distribution: population heavily concentrated in the west, and particularly the northwest, in and around the capital of Amman; a sizeable, but smaller population is located in the southwest along the shore of the Gulf of Aqaba

Natural hazards: droughts; periodic earthquakes; flash floods

Geography - note: strategic location at the head of the Gulf of Aqaba and as the Arab country that shares the longest border with Israel and the occupied West Bank; the Dead Sea, the lowest point in Asia and the second saltiest body of water in the world (after Lac Assal in Djibouti), lies on Jordan's western border with Israel and the West Bank; Jordan is almost landlocked but does have a 26 km southwestern coastline with a single port, Al 'Aqabah (Aqaba)

PEOPLE AND SOCIETY

Population: *total:* 11,174,024
male: 5,844,979
female: 5,329,045 (2024 est.)
note: increased estimate reflects revised assumptions about the net migration rate due to the increased flow of Syrian refugees
comparison rankings: female 89; male 84; total 84

Nationality: *noun:* Jordanian(s)
adjective: Jordanian

Ethnic groups: Jordanian 69.3%, Syrian 13.3%, Palestinian 6.7%, Egyptian 6.7%, Iraqi 1.4%, other 2.6% (2015 est.)
note: data represent population by self-identified nationality in national census

Languages: Arabic (official), English (widely understood among upper and middle classes)
major-language sample(s):
يمكن الاستغناء عنه للمعلومات الأساسية
كتاب حقائق العالم، المصدر الذي لا
(Arabic)

Religions: Muslim 97.1% (official; predominantly Sunni), Christian 2.1% (majority Greek Orthodox, but some Greek and Roman Catholics, Syrian Orthodox, Coptic Orthodox, Armenian Orthodox, and Protestant denominations), Buddhist 0.4%, Hindu 0.1%, Jewish <0.1%, folk <0.1%, other <0.1%, unaffiliated <0.1% (2020 est.)

Age structure: *0-14 years:* 30.9% (male 1,771,840/female 1,678,178)
15-64 years: 64.9% (male 3,844,575/female 3,409,164)
65 years and over: 4.2% (2024 est.) (male 228,564/female 241,703)

Dependency ratios: *total dependency ratio:* 57.1
youth dependency ratio: 51.2
elderly dependency ratio: 5.8
potential support ratio: 17.1 (2021 est.)

Median age: *total:* 25 years (2024 est.)
male: 25.5 years
female: 24.4 years
comparison ranking: total 172

Population growth rate: 0.78% (2024 est.)
comparison ranking: 114

Birth rate: 22.2 births/1,000 population (2024 est.)
comparison ranking: 52

Death rate: 3.5 deaths/1,000 population (2024 est.)
comparison ranking: 222

Net migration rate: -10.9 migrant(s)/1,000 population (2024 est.)
comparison ranking: 223

Population distribution: population heavily concentrated in the west, and particularly the northwest, in and around the capital of Amman; a sizeable, but smaller population is located in the southwest along the shore of the Gulf of Aqaba

Urbanization: *urban population:* 92% of total population (2023)
rate of urbanization: 0.98% annual rate of change (2020-25 est.)

Major urban areas - population: 2.232 million AMMAN (capital) (2023)

Sex ratio: *at birth:* 1.06 male(s)/female
0-14 years: 1.06 male(s)/female
15-64 years: 1.13 male(s)/female
65 years and over: 0.95 male(s)/female
total population: 1.1 male(s)/female (2024 est.)

Mother's mean age at first birth: 24.6 years (2017/18 est.)
note: data represents median age at first birth among women 25-49

Maternal mortality ratio: 41 deaths/100,000 live births (2020 est.)
comparison ranking: 103

Infant mortality rate: *total:* 13.2 deaths/1,000 live births (2024 est.)
male: 14.3 deaths/1,000 live births
female: 12.1 deaths/1,000 live births
comparison ranking: total 106

Life expectancy at birth: *total population:* 76.5 years (2024 est.)
male: 75 years
female: 78.1 years
comparison ranking: total population 109

Total fertility rate: 2.87 children born/woman (2024 est.)
comparison ranking: 52

Gross reproduction rate: 1.39 (2024 est.)

Contraceptive prevalence rate: 51.8% (2017/18)

Drinking water source: *improved: urban:* 99.2% of population
rural: 97.9% of population
total: 99.1% of population
unimproved: urban: 0.8% of population
rural: 2.1% of population
total: 0.9% of population (2020 est.)

Current health expenditure: 7.5% of GDP (2020)

Physician density: 2.66 physicians/1,000 population (2019)

Hospital bed density: 1.5 beds/1,000 population (2017)

Sanitation facility access: *improved: urban:* 98.8% of population
rural: 97.8% of population
total: 98.7% of population
unimproved: urban: 1.2% of population
rural: 2.2% of population
total: 1.3% of population (2020 est.)

Obesity - adult prevalence rate: 35.5% (2016)
comparison ranking: 13

Alcohol consumption per capita: *total:* 0.25 liters of pure alcohol (2019 est.)
beer: 0.06 liters of pure alcohol (2019 est.)
wine: 0 liters of pure alcohol (2019 est.)
spirits: 0.19 liters of pure alcohol (2019 est.)
other alcohols: 0 liters of pure alcohol (2019 est.)
comparison ranking: total 171

Tobacco use: *total:* 34.8% (2020 est.)
male: 56.8% (2020 est.)
female: 12.8% (2020 est.)
comparison ranking: total 16

Children under the age of 5 years underweight: 2.7% (2019)
comparison ranking: 94

Currently married women (ages 15-49): 55.6% (2023 est.)

Child marriage: *women married by age 15:* 1.5%
women married by age 18: 9.7%
men married by age 18: 0.1% (2018 est.)

Education expenditures: 3.2% of GDP (2021 est.)
comparison ranking: 151

Literacy: *definition:* age 15 and over can read and write
total population: 98.4%
male: 98.7%
female: 98.4% (2021)

School life expectancy (primary to tertiary education): *total:* 11 years
male: 10 years
female: 11 years (2020)

ENVIRONMENT

Environment - current issues: limited natural freshwater resources; declining water table; salinity; deforestation; overgrazing; soil erosion; desertification; biodiversity and ecosystem damage/loss

Environment - international agreements: *party to:* Biodiversity, Climate Change, Climate Change-Kyoto Protocol, Climate Change-Paris Agreement, Comprehensive Nuclear Test Ban, Desertification, Endangered Species, Hazardous Wastes, Law of the Sea, Marine Dumping-London Convention, Nuclear Test Ban, Ozone Layer Protection, Ship Pollution, Wetlands
signed, but not ratified: none of the selected agreements

Climate: mostly arid desert; rainy season in west (November to April)

Urbanization: *urban population:* 92% of total population (2023)
rate of urbanization: 0.98% annual rate of change (2020-25 est.)

Revenue from forest resources: 0.02% of GDP (2018 est.)
comparison ranking: 142

Revenue from coal: 0% of GDP (2018 est.)
comparison ranking: 149

Air pollutants: *particulate matter emissions:* 25.87 micrograms per cubic meter (2019 est.)
carbon dioxide emissions: 25.11 megatons (2016 est.)
methane emissions: 6.04 megatons (2020 est.)

Waste and recycling: *municipal solid waste generated annually:* 2,529,997 tons (2013 est.)
municipal solid waste recycled annually: 177,100 tons (2014 est.)
percent of municipal solid waste recycled: 7% (2014 est.)

Major lakes (area sq km): *salt water lake(s):* Dead Sea (shared with Israel and West Bank) - 1,020 sq km
note - endorheic hypersaline lake; 9.6 times saltier than the ocean; lake shore is 431 meters below sea level

Major watersheds (area sq km): Indian Ocean drainage: *(Persian Gulf)* Tigris and Euphrates (918,044 sq km)

Major aquifers: Arabian Aquifer System

Total water withdrawal: *municipal:* 500 million cubic meters (2020 est.)
industrial: 40 million cubic meters (2020 est.)
agricultural: 570 million cubic meters (2020 est.)

Total renewable water resources: 940 million cubic meters (2020 est.)

GOVERNMENT

Country name: *conventional long form:* Hashemite Kingdom of Jordan
conventional short form: Jordan
local long form: Al Mamlakah al Urduniyah al Hashimiyah
local short form: Al Urdun
former: Transjordan
etymology: named for the Jordan River, which makes up part of Jordan's northwest border

Government type: parliamentary constitutional monarchy

Capital: *name:* Amman
geographic coordinates: 31 57 N, 35 56 E
time difference: UTC+3 (8 hours ahead of Washington, DC, during Standard Time)
etymology: in the 13th century B.C., the Ammonites named their main city "Rabbath Ammon"; "rabbath" designated "capital," so the name meant "The Capital of [the] Ammon[ites]"; over time, the "Rabbath" came to be dropped and the city became known simply as "Ammon" and then "Amman"

Administrative divisions: 12 governorates (muhafazat, singular - muhafazah); 'Ajlun, Al 'Aqabah, Al Balqa', Al Karak, Al Mafraq, Al 'Asimah (Amman), At Tafilah, Az Zarqa', Irbid, Jarash, Ma'an, Madaba

Independence: 25 May 1946 (from League of Nations mandate under British administration)

National holiday: Independence Day, 25 May (1946)

Legal system: mixed system developed from codes instituted by the Ottoman Empire (based on French law), British common law, and Islamic law

Constitution: *history:* previous 1928 (preindependence); latest initially adopted 28 November 1947, revised and ratified 1 January 1952
amendments: constitutional amendments require at least a two-thirds majority vote of both the Senate and the House and ratification by the king; amended several times, last in 2022

International law organization participation: has not submitted an ICJ jurisdiction declaration; accepts ICCt jurisdiction

Citizenship: *citizenship by birth:* no
citizenship by descent only: the father must be a citizen of Jordan
dual citizenship recognized: yes
residency requirement for naturalization: 15 years

Suffrage: 18 years of age; universal

Executive branch: *chief of state:* King ABDALLAH II (since 7 February 1999)
head of government: Prime Minister Jafar HASSAN (since 15 September 2024)
cabinet: Cabinet appointed by the monarch in consultation with the prime minister
elections/appointments: prime minister appointed by the monarch

Legislative branch: *description:* bicameral National Assembly or Majlis al-'Umma consists of:
Senate or the House of Notables or Majlis al-Ayan (65 seats; members appointed by the monarch to serve 4-year terms)
Chamber of Deputies or Majlis al-Nuwaab (138 seats; 97 members directly elected in multi-seat constituencies by openlist proportional representation vote; of these, 12 seats reserved for Christian, Circassian, and Chechen minorities, and 18 reserved for women; the remaining 41 members directly elected from a single national constituency by closed partylist proportional representation vote; of these, 2 seats reserved for Christians and 1 each for members of the Chechen and Circassian minorities; party candidate lists must include at least 1 woman among the first 3 candidates and 1 among the next 3 candidates; all members serve 4-year terms)
elections: Senate - last appointments on 27 Sep 2020 (next appointments by November 2024)
Chamber of Deputies - last held on 10 September 2024 (next to be held in 2028)
election results: Senate - composition - men 55, women 10, percent of women 15.4%
House of Representatives - percentage by party - NA; seats by party - Islamic Action Front 31, Mithaq 21, Irada 19, and Taqadum 8, other (includes seats reserved for women, minorities)
note: in 2022, a new electoral law - effective for the anticipated 2024 election - will increase the total number of Chamber of Deputies' seats to 138 from 130; 97 members to be directly elected from multi-seat geographic districts by open list proportional representation vote, with over 7 percent of total votes needed to gain a seat, and 41 members to be directly elected from a single national district by closed party-list proportional representation vote, with over a 2.5 percent of total votes needed to gain a seat

Judicial branch: *highest court(s):* Court of Cassation or Supreme Court (consists of 15 members, including the chief justice); Constitutional Court (consists of 9 members)
judge selection and term of office: Supreme Court chief justice appointed by the king; other judges nominated by the Judicial Council, an 11-member judicial policymaking body consisting of high-level judicial officials and judges, and approved by the king; judge tenure not limited; Constitutional Court members appointed by the king for 6-year nonrenewable terms with one-third of the membership renewed every 2 years
subordinate courts: Courts of Appeal; Great Felonies Court; religious courts; military courts; juvenile courts; Land Settlement Courts; Income Tax Court; Higher Administrative Court; Customs Court; special courts including the State Security Court

Political parties: 'Azem
Blessed Land Party
Building and Labor Coalition
Eradah Party
Growth Party
Islamic Action Front or IAF
Jordanian al-Ansar Party
Jordanian al-Ghad Party
Jordanian Arab Socialist Ba'ath Party or JASBP
Jordanian Civil Democratic Party
Jordanian Communist Party or JCP
Jordanian Equality Party
Jordanian Democratic People's Party or HASD
Jordanian Democratic Popular Unity Party or JDPUP/Wihda
Jordanian Democratic Unionist Party
Jordanian Flame Party
Jordanian Future and Life Party
Jordanian Model Party
Jordanian National Integration Party
Jordanian National Loyalty Party
Jordanian Reform and Renewal Party or Hassad
Jordanian Shura Party
Jordanian Social Democratic Party or JSDP
Justice and Reform Party or JRP
Labor Party
National Charter Party
National Coalition Party
National Constitutional Party
National Current Party or NCP
National Islamic Party
National Union
Nationalist Movement Party or Hsq
New Path Party
Progress Party

International organization participation: ABEDA, AFESD, AMF, CAEU, CD, CICA, EBRD, FAO, G-11, G-77, IAEA, IBRD, ICAO, ICC, ICCt, ICRM, IDA, IDB, IFAD, IFC, IFRCS, ILO, IMF, IMO, IMSO, Interpol, IOC, IOM, IPU, ISO, ITSO, ITU, ITUC (NGOs), LAS, MIGA, MINUSTAH, MONUSCO, NAM, NATO (partner), OIC, OPCW, OSCE (partner), PCA, UN, UNAMID, UNCTAD, UNESCO, UNHCR, UNIDO, UNISFA, UNMIL, UNMISS, UNOCI, UNOOSA, UNRWA, UNWTO, UPU, WCO, WFTU (NGOs), WHO, WIPO, WMO, WTO

Diplomatic representation in the US: *chief of mission:* Ambassador Dina Khalil Tawfiq KAWAR (since 27 June 2016)
chancery: 3504 International Drive NW, Washington, DC 20008
telephone: [1] (202) 966-2664
FAX: [1] (202) 966-3110
email address and website:
hkjconsular@jordanembassyus.org
http://www.jordanembassyus.org/

Diplomatic representation from the US: *chief of mission:* Ambassador Yael LEMPERT (since 3 September 2023)
embassy: Abdoun, Al-Umawyeen St., Amman
mailing address: 6050 Amman Place, Washington DC 20521-6050
telephone: [962] (6) 590-6000
FAX: [962] (6) 592-0163
email address and website:
Amman-ACS@state.gov
https://jo.usembassy.gov/

Flag description: three equal horizontal bands of black (top), representing the Abbassid Caliphate, white, representing the Ummayyad Caliphate, and green, representing the Fatimid Caliphate; a red isosceles triangle on the hoist side, representing the Great Arab Revolt of 1916, and bearing a small white seven-pointed star symbolizing the seven verses of the opening Sura (Al-Fatiha) of the Holy Koran; the seven points on the star represent faith in One God, humanity, national spirit, humility, social justice, virtue, and aspirations; design is based on the Arab Revolt flag of World War I

National symbol(s): eagle; national colors: black, white, green, red

National anthem: *name:* "As-salam al-malaki al-urdoni" (Long Live the King of Jordan)
lyrics/music: Abdul-Mone'm al-RIFAI'/Abdul-Qader al-TANEER
note: adopted 1946; the shortened version of the anthem is used most commonly, while the full version is reserved for special occasions

National heritage: *total World Heritage Sites:* 6 (5 cultural, 1 mixed)
selected World Heritage Site locales: Petra (c); Quseir Amra (c); Um er-Rasas (Kastrom Mefa'a) (c); Wadi Rum Protected Area (m); Baptism Site "Bethany Beyond the Jordan" (Al-Maghtas) (c); As-Salt - The Place of Tolerance and Urban Hospitality (c)

ECONOMY

Economic overview: low growth, upper middle-income Middle Eastern economy; high debt and unemployment, especially for youth and women; key US foreign assistance recipient; natural resource-poor and import-reliant

Real GDP (purchasing power parity): $106.806 billion (2023 est.)
$104.084 billion (2022 est.)
$101.617 billion (2021 est.)
note: data in 2021 dollars
comparison ranking: 95

Real GDP growth rate: 2.62% (2023 est.)
2.43% (2022 est.)
3.66% (2021 est.)
note: annual GDP % growth based on constant local currency
comparison ranking: 121

Real GDP per capita: $9,400 (2023 est.)
$9,200 (2022 est.)
$9,100 (2021 est.)
note: data in 2021 dollars
comparison ranking: 149

GDP (official exchange rate): $50.814 billion (2023 est.)
note: data in current dollars at official exchange rate

Inflation rate (consumer prices): 2.08% (2023 est.)
4.23% (2022 est.)
1.35% (2021 est.)
note: annual % change based on consumer prices
comparison ranking: 39

Credit ratings: Fitch rating: BB- (2019)

Moody's rating: B1 (2013)

Standard & Poors rating: B+ (2017)
note: The year refers to the year in which the current credit rating was first obtained.

GDP - composition, by sector of origin: *agriculture:* 4.8% (2023 est.)
industry: 24.1% (2023 est.)
services: 60.6% (2023 est.)
note: figures may not total 100% due to non-allocated consumption not captured in sector-reported data
comparison rankings: services 82; industry 106; agriculture 119

GDP - composition, by end use: *household consumption:* 78.9% (2021 est.)
government consumption: 15.8% (2021 est.)
investment in fixed capital: 22.2% (2021 est.)
investment in inventories: 3% (2021 est.)
exports of goods and services: 30.3% (2021 est.)
imports of goods and services: -50.2% (2021 est.)
note: figures may not total 100% due to rounding or gaps in data collection

Agricultural products: tomatoes, milk, chicken, potatoes, cucumbers/gherkins, olives, watermelons,

peaches/nectarines, sheep milk, chilies/ peppers (2022)
note: top ten agricultural products based on tonnage

Industries: tourism, information technology, clothing, fertilizer, potash, phosphate mining, pharmaceuticals, petroleum refining, cement, inorganic chemicals, light manufacturing

Industrial production growth rate: 3.28% (2023 est.)
note: annual % change in industrial value added based on constant local currency
comparison ranking: 100

Labor force: 3.063 million (2023 est.)
note: number of people ages 15 or older who are employed or seeking work
comparison ranking: 110

Unemployment rate: 17.94% (2023 est.)
18.2% (2022 est.)
19.84% (2021 est.)
note: % of labor force seeking employment
comparison ranking: 195

Youth unemployment rate (ages 15-24): *total:* 40.8% (2023 est.)
male: 39.3% (2023 est.)
female: 47.1% (2023 est.)
note: % of labor force ages 15-24 seeking employment
comparison ranking: total 10

Population below poverty line: 15.7% (2018 est.)
note: % of population with income below national poverty line

Average household expenditures: *on food:* 26.1% of household expenditures (2022 est.)
on alcohol and tobacco: 4.5% of household expenditures (2022 est.)

Remittances: 9.72% of GDP (2023 est.)
10.1% of GDP (2022 est.)
10.96% of GDP (2021 est.)
note: personal transfers and compensation between resident and non-resident individuals/households/entities

Budget: *revenues:* $16.073 billion (2018 est.)
expenditures: $14.464 billion (2018 est.)
note: central government revenues (excluding grants) and expenses converted to US dollars at average official exchange rate for year indicated

Public debt: 101.14% of GDP (2022 est.)
note: central government debt as a % of GDP
comparison ranking: 19

Taxes and other revenues: 17.51% (of GDP) (2022 est.)
note: central government tax revenue as a % of GDP
comparison ranking: 106

Current account balance: -$4.159 billion (2022 est.)
-$3.718 billion (2021 est.)
-$2.505 billion (2020 est.)
note: balance of payments - net trade and primary/secondary income in current dollars
comparison ranking: 174

Exports: $20.335 billion (2022 est.)
$13.87 billion (2021 est.)
$10.444 billion (2020 est.)
note: balance of payments - exports of goods and services in current dollars
comparison ranking: 91

Exports - partners: US 20%, India 14%, Saudi Arabia 7%, China 6%, Iraq 6% (2022)
note: top five export partners based on percentage share of exports

Exports - commodities: fertilizers, garments, phosphates, jewelry, phosphoric acid (2022)
note: top five export commodities based on value in dollars

Imports: $29.955 billion (2022 est.)
$23.321 billion (2021 est.)
$18.424 billion (2020 est.)
note: balance of payments - imports of goods and services in current dollars
comparison ranking: 79

Imports - partners: China 17%, UAE 12%, Saudi Arabia 12%, India 6%, US 4% (2022)
note: top five import partners based on percentage share of imports

Imports - commodities: refined petroleum, cars, gold, crude petroleum, jewelry (2022)
note: top five import commodities based on value in dollars

Reserves of foreign exchange and gold: $15.56 billion (31 December 2017 est.)
$15.543 billion (2016 est.)
$16.572 billion (2015 est.)
note: holdings of gold (year-end prices)/foreign exchange/special drawing rights in current dollars
comparison ranking: 69

Debt - external: $16.293 billion (2022 est.)
note: present value of external debt in current US dollars
comparison ranking: 28

Exchange rates: Jordanian dinars (JOD) per US dollar -

Exchange rates: 0.71 (2023 est.)
0.71 (2022 est.)
0.71 (2021 est.)
0.71 (2020 est.)
0.71 (2019 est.)

ENERGY

Electricity access: *electrification - total population:* 100% (2022 est.)
electrification - urban areas: 100%
electrification - rural areas: 98.9%

Electricity: *installed generating capacity:* 6.805 million kW (2022 est.)
consumption: 19.679 billion kWh (2022 est.)
exports: 177.332 million kWh (2022 est.)
imports: 389.867 million kWh (2022 est.)
transmission/distribution losses: 2.4 billion kWh (2022 est.)
comparison rankings: transmission/distribution losses 129; imports 97; exports 86; consumption 72; installed generating capacity 79

Electricity generation sources: *fossil fuels:* 77.1% of total installed capacity (2022 est.)
solar: 15.4% of total installed capacity (2022 est.)
wind: 7.4% of total installed capacity (2022 est.)
hydroelectricity: 0.1% of total installed capacity (2022 est.)

Coal: *consumption:* 479,000 metric tons (2022 est.)
exports: (2022 est.) less than 1 metric ton
imports: 297,000 metric tons (2022 est.)

Petroleum: *total petroleum production:* 20 bbl/day (2023 est.)
refined petroleum consumption: 97,000 bbl/day (2022 est.)
crude oil estimated reserves: 1 million barrels (2021 est.)

Natural gas: *production:* 187.262 million cubic meters (2022 est.)
consumption: 4.382 billion cubic meters (2022 est.)
exports: 375.998 million cubic meters (2018 est.)
imports: 4.255 billion cubic meters (2022 est.)
proven reserves: 6.031 billion cubic meters (2021 est.)

Carbon dioxide emissions: 21.261 million metric tonnes of CO_2 (2022 est.)
from coal and metallurgical coke: 1.124 million metric tonnes of CO_2 (2022 est.)
from petroleum and other liquids: 13.256 million metric tonnes of CO_2 (2022 est.)
from consumed natural gas: 6.881 million metric tonnes of CO_2 (2022 est.)
comparison ranking: total emissions 85

Energy consumption per capita: 30.906 million Btu/person (2022 est.)
comparison ranking: 113

COMMUNICATIONS

Telephones - fixed lines: *total subscriptions:* 466,000 (2022 est.)
subscriptions per 100 inhabitants: 4 (2022 est.)
comparison ranking: total subscriptions 94

Telephones - mobile cellular: *total subscriptions:* 7.626 million (2022 est.)
subscriptions per 100 inhabitants: 68 (2022 est.)
comparison ranking: total subscriptions 105

Telecommunication systems: *general assessment:* Jordan's government has focused on the use of ICT in a range of sectors, aimed at transforming the relatively small economy through the use of digital services; this policy has helped the country rise in the league tables for digital connectivity and internet readiness, and it has also attracted investment from foreign companies; during the ongoing global pandemic, the start-up sector has been further encouraged to develop solutions to combat the crisis, while other efforts have facilitated e-government services and encouraged businesses to adapt to new methods of working through their own digital transformation; these developments have been supported by the highly developed mobile sector, led by three major regional players which have near-comprehensive LTE network coverage (2022)
domestic: fixed-line stands at nearly 4 per 100 persons and mobile cellular subscriptions at 65 per 100 persons (2021)
international: country code - 962; landing point for the FEA and Taba-Aqaba submarine cable networks providing connectivity to Europe, the Middle East, Southeast Asia and Asia; satellite earth stations - 33 (3 Intelsat, 1 Arabsat, and 29 land and maritime Inmarsat terminals (2019)

Broadcast media: radio and TV dominated by the government-owned Jordan Radio and Television Corporation (JRTV) that operates a main network, a sports network, a film network, and a satellite channel; first independent TV broadcaster aired in 2007; international satellite TV and Israeli and Syrian TV broadcasts are available; roughly 30 radio stations with JRTV operating the main government-owned station; transmissions of multiple international radio broadcasters are available

Internet country code: .jo

Internet users: *total:* 9.13 million (2021 est.)
percent of population: 83% (2021 est.)
comparison ranking: total 65

Broadband - fixed subscriptions: *total:* 630,545 (2020 est.)
subscriptions per 100 inhabitants: 6 (2020 est.)
comparison ranking: total 85

TRANSPORTATION

National air transport system: *number of registered air carriers:* 4 (2020)
inventory of registered aircraft operated by air carriers: 54
annual passenger traffic on registered air carriers: 3,383,805 (2018)
annual freight traffic on registered air carriers: 175.84 million (2018) mt-km

Civil aircraft registration country code prefix: JY

Airports: 17 (2024)
comparison ranking: 144

Heliports: 6 (2024)

Pipelines: 473 km gas, 49 km oil (2013)

Railways: *total:* 509 km (2020)
narrow gauge: 509 km (2014) 1.050-m gauge
comparison ranking: total 112

Roadways: *total:* 7,203 km
paved: 7,203 km (2011)
comparison ranking: total 144

Merchant marine: *total:* 34 (2023)
by type: general cargo 5, other 29
comparison ranking: total 131

Ports: *total ports:* 1 (2024)
large: 0
medium: 0
small: 0
very small: 1
ports with oil terminals: 1
key ports: Al Aqabah

MILITARY AND SECURITY

Military and security forces: Jordanian Armed Forces (JAF): Royal Jordanian Army (includes Special Operations Forces, Border Guards, Royal Guard), Royal Jordanian Air Force, Royal Jordanian Navy

Ministry of Interior: Public Security Directorate (includes national police, the Gendarmerie, and the Civil Defense Directorate) (2024)
note: the JAF report administratively to the minister of defense and have a support role for internal security; the prime minister serves as defense minister, but there is no separate ministry of defense

Military expenditures: 4.5% of GDP (2023 est.)
4.8% of GDP (2022 est.)
5% of GDP (2021 est.)
5% of GDP (2020 est.)
5.6% of GDP (2019 est.)
comparison ranking: 11

Military and security service personnel strengths: approximately 100,000 active-duty armed forces personnel (85,000 Army; 14,000 Air Force; 1,000 Navy); approximately 15,000 Gendarmerie Forces (2023)

Military equipment inventories and acquisitions: the JAF inventory is comprised of a wide mix of imported equipment, much of it older or secondhand, from China, Europe, some Gulf States, Russia, and the US (2024)

Military service age and obligation: 17 years of age for voluntary military service for men and women); initial service term is 24 months, with option to reenlist for up to 18 years; conscription was abolished in 1991, but in 2020 Jordan announced the reinstatement of compulsory military service for jobless men aged between 25 and 29 with 12 months of service, made up of 3 months of military training and 9 months of professional and technical training; in 2019, Jordan announced a voluntary 4-month National Military Service program for men and women aged between 18-25 years who have been unemployed for at least 6 months; service would include 1 month for military training with the remaining 3 months dedicated to vocational training in the sectors of construction and tourism (2023)
note: women comprised about 3% of the military as of 2023

Military deployments: Jordan has about 200 police deployed to the MONUSCO mission in the Democratic Republic of the Congo (2024)

Military - note: the JAF traces its origins back to the Arab Legion, which was formed under the British protectorate of Transjordan in the 1920s; it is responsible for territorial defense and border security and has a supporting role for internal security; the JAF participates in both bilateral and multinational exercises, UN peacekeeping missions, and has taken part in regional military operations alongside international forces in Afghanistan, Syria, and Yemen
the JAF's primary concerns include terrorist and criminal threats emanating from its borders with Syria and Iraq, as well as the ongoing Israel-Hamas war in Gaza and conflicts in southern Lebanon/northern Israel and the Red Sea; the terrorist group Hizballah and Iranian-backed militia forces operate in southwestern Syria near Jordan's border while fighters from the Islamic State of Iraq and ash-Sham (ISIS) terrorist group continue to operate in both Iraq and Syria; ISIS fighters have included Jordanian nationals, some of whom have returned to Jordan; individuals and groups sympathetic to Palestinian causes have planned and conducted terrorist attacks in Jordan
the US is a key security partner, and Jordan is one of the largest recipients of US military aid in the region; it cooperates with the US on a number of issues, including border and maritime security, arms transfers, cybersecurity, and counterterrorism; Jordan has Major Non-NATO Ally status with the US, a designation under US law that provides foreign partners with certain benefits in the areas of defense trade and security cooperation (2024)

TERRORISM

Terrorist group(s): Islamic State of Iraq and ash-Sham (ISIS)
note: details about the history, aims, leadership, organization, areas of operation, tactics, targets, weapons, size, and sources of support of the group(s) appear(s) in the Terrorism reference guide

TRANSNATIONAL ISSUES

Refugees and internally displaced persons: *refugees (country of origin):* 2.4 million (Palestinian refugees) (2020); 12,866 (Yemen), 6,013 Sudan (2021); 33,951 (Iraq) (mid-year 2022) (2022); 638,760 (Syria) (2024)
stateless persons: 64 (2022)

Illicit drugs: primarily a transshipment country for amphetamine tablets originating in Lebanon and Syria and destined for Saudi Arabia, Israel, and Gulf countries; the government is increasingly concerned about domestic consumption of illicit drugs

KAZAKHSTAN

INTRODUCTION

Background: Ethnic Kazakhs derive from a mix of Turkic nomadic tribes that migrated to the region in the 15th century. The Russian Empire conquered the Kazakh steppe in the 18th and 19th centuries, and Kazakhstan became a Soviet Republic in 1925. Forced agricultural collectivization led to repression and starvation, resulting in more than a million deaths in the early 1930s. During the 1950s and 1960s, the agricultural "Virgin Lands" program generated an influx of settlers – mostly ethnic Russians, but also other nationalities – and by the time of Kazakhstan's independence in 1991, ethnic Kazakhs were a minority. However, non-Muslim ethnic minorities departed Kazakhstan in large numbers from the mid-1990s through the mid-2000s, and a national program has repatriated about a million ethnic Kazakhs (from Uzbekistan, Tajikistan, Mongolia, and the Xinjiang region of China) to Kazakhstan. As a result of this shift, the ethnic Kazakh share of the population now exceeds two-thirds.

Kazakhstan's economy is the largest in Central Asia, mainly due to the country's vast natural resources. Current issues include diversifying the economy, attracting foreign direct investment, enhancing Kazakhstan's economic competitiveness, and strengthening economic relations with neighboring states and foreign powers.

GEOGRAPHY

Location: Central Asia, northwest of China; a small portion west of the Ural (Oral) River in easternmost Europe

Geographic coordinates: 48 00 N, 68 00 E

Map references: Asia

Area: *total:* 2,724,900 sq km
land: 2,699,700 sq km
water: 25,200 sq km
comparison ranking: total 10

Area - comparative: slightly less than four times the size of Texas

Land boundaries: *total:* 13,364 km
border countries (5): China 1,765 km; Kyrgyzstan 1,212 km; Russia 7,644 km; Turkmenistan 413 km; Uzbekistan 2,330 km

Coastline: 0 km (landlocked); note - Kazakhstan borders the Aral Sea, now split into two bodies of water (1,070 km), and the Caspian Sea (1,894 km)

Maritime claims: none (landlocked)

Climate: continental, cold winters and hot summers, arid and semiarid

Terrain: vast flat steppe extending from the Volga in the west to the Altai Mountains in the east and from the plains of western Siberia in the north to oases and deserts of Central Asia in the south

Elevation: *highest point:* Pik Khan-Tengri 7,010 m
note - the northern most 7,000 meter peak in the World
lowest point: Qauyndy Oyysy -132 m
mean elevation: 387 m

Natural resources: major deposits of petroleum, natural gas, coal, iron ore, manganese, chrome ore, nickel, cobalt, copper, molybdenum, lead, zinc, bauxite, gold, uranium

Land use: *agricultural land:* 77.4% (2018 est.)
arable land: 8.9% (2018 est.)
permanent crops: 0% (2018 est.)
permanent pasture: 68.5% (2018 est.)
forest: 1.2% (2018 est.)
other: 21.4% (2018 est.)

Irrigated land: 18,099 sq km (2020)

Major lakes (area sq km): *fresh water lake(s):* Ozero Balkhash - 22,000 sq km; Ozero Zaysan - 1,800 sq km
salt water lake(s): Caspian Sea (shared with Iran, Azerbaijan, Turkmenistan, and Russia) - 374,000 sq km; Aral Sea (north) - 3,300 sq km; Ozero Alakol - 2,650 sq km; Ozero Teniz 1,590 sq km; Ozero Seletytenzi - 780 sq km; Ozero Sasykkol - 740 sq km

Major rivers (by length in km): Syr Darya river mouth (shared with Kyrgyzstan [s], Uzbekistan, and Tajikistan) - 3,078 km
note – [s] after country name indicates river source; [m] after country name indicates river mouth

Major watersheds (area sq km): Internal (endorheic basin) drainage: Tarim Basin (1,152,448 sq km), Amu Darya (534,739 sq km), Syr Darya (782,617 sq km), Lake Balkash (510,015 sq km)

Population distribution: most of the country displays a low population density, particularly the interior; population clusters appear in urban agglomerations in the far northern and southern portions of the country

Natural hazards: earthquakes in the south; mudslides around Almaty

Geography - note: world's largest landlocked country and one of only two landlocked countries in the world that extends into two continents (the other is Azerbaijan); Russia leases approximately 6,000 sq km of territory enclosing the Baikonur Cosmodrome; in 2004, Kazakhstan and Russia extended the lease to 2050

PEOPLE AND SOCIETY

Population: *total:* 20,260,006
male: 9,817,172
female: 10,442,834 (2024 est.)
comparison rankings: female 63; male 64; total 64

Nationality: *noun:* Kazakhstani(s)
adjective: Kazakhstani

Ethnic groups: Kazakh 71%, Russian 14.9%, Uzbek 3.3%, Ukrainian 1.9%, Uyghurs 1.5%, German 1.1%, Tatar 1.1%, other 4.9%, unspecified 0.3% (2023 est.)

Languages: Kazakh (official, Qazaq) 80.1%, Russian 83.7%, English 35.1% (2021 est.)
major-language sample(s):
Әлемдік деректер кітабы, негізгі ақпараттың таптырмайтын көзі. (Kazakh)
Книга фактов о мире – незаменимый источник базовой информации. (Russian)
note: percentages are based on population that understands the spoken language

Religions: Muslim 69.3%, Christian 17.2% (Orthodox 17%, other 0.2%), Buddhism 0.1%, other 0.1%, non-believers 2.3%, unspecified 11% (2021 est.)

Demographic profile: Nearly 40% of Kazakhstan's population is under the age of 25. Like many former Soviet states, Kazakhstan's total fertility rate (TFR) – the average number of births per woman – decreased after independence amidst economic problems and fell below replacement level, 2.1. However, in the late 2000s, as the economy improved and incomes rose, Kazakhstan experienced a small baby boom and TFR reached 2.5. TFR has since fallen and is now just over 2.1. Mortality rates are also decreasing and life expectancy is rising, signs that Kazakhstan's demographic transition is progressing.
Kazakhstan has a diverse population consisting of Asian ethnic groups (predominantly Kazakhs, as well as Uzbeks, Uighurs, and Tatars) and ethnic Europeans (mainly Russians but also Ukrainians and Germans). Approximately two thirds of Kazakhstan's population today is Kazakh. During the mid-20th century, as Kazakhstan industrialized, waves of ethnic Russians and deportees from other parts of the Soviet Union arrived. Eventually, the ethnic Russian population outnumbered the Kazakhs. In the 1990s, following Kazakhstan's independence, Russian and other ethnic Europeans began emigrating, while some ethnic Kazakhs (referred to as Oralmans) returned to their homeland from neighboring countries, China, and Mongolia. As a result, the country's ethnic make-up changed, and a Kazakh majority was reestablished.
In recent years, Kazakhstan has shifted from being mainly a migrant-sending country to a migrant-receiving country. Due to its oil-driven economic boom, Kazakhstan has become a more popular destination. The country needs highly skilled workers in the industrial, business, and education sectors and low-skilled labor in agriculture, markets, services, and construction. Kazakhstan is increasingly reliant on migrant workers, primarily from Kyrgyzstan, Tajikistan, and Uzbekistan, to fill its labor shortage. At the same time, highly skilled Kazakhs continue to emigrate, mostly to Russia, seeking higher salaries or further education.

Age structure: *0-14 years:* 27.6% (male 2,883,200/ female 2,712,772)
15-64 years: 62.8% (male 6,233,881/female 6,486,019)
65 years and over: 9.6% (2024 est.) (male 700,091/ female 1,244,043)

Dependency ratios: *total dependency ratio:* 60
youth dependency ratio: 47.2
elderly dependency ratio: 12.7
potential support ratio: 7.9 (2021 est.)

Median age: *total:* 31.9 years (2024 est.)

male: 30 years
female: 33.8 years
comparison ranking: total 121

Population growth rate: 0.86% (2024 est.)
comparison ranking: 106

Birth rate: 17.2 births/1,000 population (2024 est.)
comparison ranking: 89

Death rate: 8.1 deaths/1,000 population (2024 est.)
comparison ranking: 84

Net migration rate: -0.4 migrant(s)/1,000 population (2024 est.)
comparison ranking: 117

Population distribution: most of the country displays a low population density, particularly the interior; population clusters appear in urban agglomerations in the far northern and southern portions of the country

Urbanization: *urban population:* 58.2% of total population (2023)
rate of urbanization: 1.19% annual rate of change (2020-25 est.)

Major urban areas - population: 1.987 million Almaty, 1.291 million NUR-SULTAN (capital), 1.155 million Shimkent (2023)

Sex ratio: *at birth:* 1.07 male(s)/female
0-14 years: 1.06 male(s)/female
15-64 years: 0.96 male(s)/female
65 years and over: 0.56 male(s)/female
total population: 0.94 male(s)/female (2024 est.)

Mother's mean age at first birth: 28.9 years (2019 est.)

Maternal mortality ratio: 13 deaths/100,000 live births (2020 est.)
comparison ranking: 139

Infant mortality rate: *total:* 8 deaths/1,000 live births (2024 est.)
male: 8.9 deaths/1,000 live births
female: 7 deaths/1,000 live births
comparison ranking: total 146

Life expectancy at birth: *total population:* 73.3 years (2024 est.)
male: 69 years
female: 77.9 years
comparison ranking: total population 151

Total fertility rate: 2.58 children born/woman (2024 est.)
comparison ranking: 66

Gross reproduction rate: 1.25 (2024 est.)

Contraceptive prevalence rate: 53% (2018)
note: percent of women aged 18-49

Drinking water source: *improved: urban:* 100% of population
rural: 93.8% of population
total: 97.4% of population
unimproved: urban: 0% of population
rural: 6.2% of population
total: 2.6% of population (2020 est.)

Current health expenditure: 3.8% of GDP (2020)

Physician density: 3.98 physicians/1,000 population (2020)

Hospital bed density: 6.1 beds/1,000 population (2014)

Sanitation facility access: *improved: urban:* 99.9% of population
rural: 99.9% of population
total: 99.9% of population
unimproved: urban: 0.1% of population
rural: 0.1% of population
total: 0.1% of population (2020 est.)

Obesity - adult prevalence rate: 21% (2016)
comparison ranking: 94

Alcohol consumption per capita: *total:* 3.73 liters of pure alcohol (2019 est.)
beer: 2.52 liters of pure alcohol (2019 est.)
wine: 0.16 liters of pure alcohol (2019 est.)
spirits: 1.05 liters of pure alcohol (2019 est.)
other alcohols: 0 liters of pure alcohol (2019 est.)
comparison ranking: total 100

Tobacco use: *total:* 23.2% (2020 est.)
male: 39.6% (2020 est.)
female: 6.7% (2020 est.)
comparison ranking: total 63

Children under the age of 5 years underweight: 2% (2015)
comparison ranking: 105

Currently married women (ages 15-49): 61.8% (2023 est.)

Education expenditures: 4.5% of GDP (2020 est.)
comparison ranking: 97

Literacy: *definition:* age 15 and over can read and write
total population: 99.8%
male: 99.8%
female: 99.7% (2018)

School life expectancy (primary to tertiary education): *total:* 16 years
male: 15 years
female: 16 years (2020)

ENVIRONMENT

Environment - current issues: radioactive or toxic chemical sites associated with former defense industries and test ranges scattered throughout the country pose health risks for humans and animals; industrial pollution is severe in some cities; because the two main rivers that flowed into the Aral Sea have been diverted for irrigation, it is drying up and leaving behind a harmful layer of chemical pesticides and natural salts; these substances are then picked up by the wind and blown into noxious dust storms; pollution in the Caspian Sea; desertification; soil pollution from overuse of agricultural chemicals and salination from poor infrastructure and wasteful irrigation practices

Environment - international agreements: *party to:* Air Pollution, Antarctic Treaty, Biodiversity, Climate Change, Climate Change-Kyoto Protocol, Climate Change-Paris Agreement, Comprehensive Nuclear Test Ban, Desertification, Endangered Species, Environmental Modification, Hazardous Wastes, Ozone Layer Protection, Ship Pollution, Wetlands
signed, but not ratified: none of the selected agreements

Climate: continental, cold winters and hot summers, arid and semiarid

Urbanization: *urban population:* 58.2% of total population (2023)
rate of urbanization: 1.19% annual rate of change (2020-25 est.)

Revenue from forest resources: 0% of GDP (2018 est.)
comparison ranking: 162

Revenue from coal: 0.99% of GDP (2018 est.)
comparison ranking: 6

Air pollutants: *particulate matter emissions:* 26.5 micrograms per cubic meter (2019 est.)
carbon dioxide emissions: 247.21 megatons (2016 est.)
methane emissions: 45.03 megatons (2020 est.)

Waste and recycling: *municipal solid waste generated annually:* 4,659,740 tons (2012 est.)
municipal solid waste recycled annually: 136,064 tons (2012 est.)
percent of municipal solid waste recycled: 2.9% (2012 est.)

Major lakes (area sq km): *fresh water lake(s):* Ozero Balkhash - 22,000 sq km; Ozero Zaysan - 1,800 sq km
salt water lake(s): Caspian Sea (shared with Iran, Azerbaijan, Turkmenistan, and Russia) - 374,000 sq km; Aral Sea (north) - 3,300 sq km; Ozero Alakol - 2,650 sq km; Ozero Teniz 1,590 sq km; Ozero Seletytenzi - 780 sq km; Ozero Sasykkol - 740 sq km

Major rivers (by length in km): Syr Darya river mouth (shared with Kyrgyzstan [s], Uzbekistan, and Tajikistan) - 3,078 km
note – [s] after country name indicates river source; [m] after country name indicates river mouth

Major watersheds (area sq km): Internal (endorheic basin) drainage: Tarim Basin (1,152,448 sq km), Amu Darya (534,739 sq km), Syr Darya (782,617 sq km), Lake Balkash (510,015 sq km)

Total water withdrawal: *municipal:* 4.62 billion cubic meters (2020 est.)
industrial: 4.54 billion cubic meters (2020 est.)
agricultural: 15.4 billion cubic meters (2020 est.)

Total renewable water resources: 108.41 billion cubic meters (2020 est.)

GOVERNMENT

Country name: *conventional long form:* Republic of Kazakhstan
conventional short form: Kazakhstan
local long form: Qazaqstan Respublikasy
local short form: Qazaqstan
former: Kazakh Soviet Socialist Republic
etymology: the name "Kazakh" may derive from the Turkic word "kaz" meaning "to wander," recalling the Kazakh's nomadic lifestyle; the Persian suffix "-stan" means "place of" or "country," so the word Kazakhstan literally means "Land of the Wanderers"

Government type: presidential republic

Capital: *name:* Astana
geographic coordinates: 51 10 N, 71 25 E
time difference: UTC+5 (10 hours ahead of Washington, DC, during Standard Time)
time zone note: On 1 March 2024, Kazakhstan moved from two time zones to using one time zone
etymology: the name means "capital city" in Kazakh
note: on 17 September 2022, Kazakhstan changed the name of its capital city from Nur-Sultan back to Astana; this was not the first time the city had its name changed; founded in 1830 as Akmoly, it became Akmolinsk in 1832, Tselinograd in 1961, Akmola (Aqmola) in 1992, Astana in 1998, and Nur-Sultan in 2019; the latest name change occurred just three and a half years after the city was renamed to honor a long-serving (28-year) former president, who subsequently fell out of favor

Administrative divisions: 17 provinces (oblystar, singular - oblys) and 4 cities* (qalalar, singular - qala); Abay (Semey), Almaty (Qonaev), Almaty*, Aqmola (Kokshetau), Aqtobe, Astana*, Atyrau, Batys Qazaqstan [West Kazakhstan] (Oral), Bayqongyr*,

Mangghystau (Aqtau), Pavlodar, Qaraghandy, Qostanay, Qyzylorda, Shyghys Qazaqstan [East Kazakhstan] (Oskemen), Shymkent*, Soltustik Qazaqstan [North Kazakhstan] (Petropavl), Turkistan, Ulytau (Zhezqazghan), Zhambyl (Taraz), Zhetisu (Taldyqorghan)
note: administrative divisions have the same names as their administrative centers (exceptions have the administrative center name following in parentheses); in 1995, the Governments of Kazakhstan and Russia entered into an agreement whereby Russia would lease for a period of 20 years an area of 6,000 sq km enclosing the Baikonur space launch facilities and the city of Bayqongyr (Baikonur, formerly Leninsk); in 2004, a new agreement extended the lease to 2050

Independence: 16 December 1991 (from the Soviet Union)

National holiday: Independence Day, 16 December (1991)

Legal system: civil law system influenced by Roman-Germanic law and by the theory and practice of the Russian Federation

Constitution: *history:* previous 1937, 1978 (preindependence), 1993; latest approved by referendum 30 August 1995, effective 5 September 1995
amendments: introduced by a referendum initiated by the president of the republic, on the recommendation of Parliament, or by the government; the president has the option of submitting draft amendments to Parliament or directly to a referendum; passage of amendments by Parliament requires four-fifths majority vote of both houses and the signature of the president; passage by referendum requires absolute majority vote by more than one half of the voters in at least two thirds of the oblasts, major cities, and the capital, followed by the signature of the president; amended several times, last in 2022

International law organization participation: has not submitted an ICJ jurisdiction declaration; non-party state to the ICCt

Citizenship: *citizenship by birth:* no
citizenship by descent only: at least one parent must be a citizen of Kazakhstan
dual citizenship recognized: no
residency requirement for naturalization: 5 years

Suffrage: 18 years of age; universal

Executive branch: *chief of state:* President Kasym-Zhomart TOKAYEV (since 20 March 2019)
head of government: Prime Minister Olzhas BEKTENOV (since 6 February 2024)
cabinet: the president appoints ministers based on the prime minister's recommendations; the president has veto power over all appointments and independently appoints the ministers of defense, internal affairs, and foreign affairs
elections/appointments: president directly elected by simple majority popular vote for a single 7-year term (prior to September 2022, the president of Kazakhstan could serve up to two 5-year terms; legislation passed in September 2022 reduced the maximum number of terms to one 7-year term); election last held on 20 November 2022 (next to be held in 2029); prime minister and deputy prime ministers appointed by the president, approved by the Mazhilis
election results:
2024: Olzhas BEKTENOV elected as prime minister; 69-0 in parliament
2022: Kasym-Zhomart TOKAYEV reelected president; percent of vote - Kassym-Jomart TOKAYEV (Amanat) 81.3%, Zhiguli DAYRABAEV (Auyl) 3.4%, Qaraqat or Karakat ÄBDEN (KÄQŪA) 2.6%, Meyram KAZHYKEN (Amanat) 2.5%, Nurlan AUYESBAYEV (NSDP) 2.2%, Saltanat TURSYNBEKOVA (QA-DJ) 2.1%, other 5.8%
2019: Kasym-Zhomart TOKAYEV elected president; percent of vote - Kasym-Zhomart TOKAYEV (Amanat) 71%, Amirzhan KOSANOV (Ult Tagdyry) 16.2%, Daniya YESPAYEVA (Ak Zhol) 5.1%, other 7.7%
note: Prime Minister Alikhan SMAILOV resigned on 5 February 2024

Legislative branch: *description:* bicameral Parliament of the Republic of Kazakhstan consists of:
Senate (50 seats); 40 members indirectly elected by 2-round majority vote by the oblast-level assemblies and 10 members appointed by decree of the president; members serve 6-year terms, with one-half of the membership renewed every 3 years)
Mazhilis (98 seats; 69 members directly elected in a single national constituency by party list proportional representation vote (5% minimum threshold to gain seats) and 29 directly elected in single-seat constituencies to serve 5-year terms
elections: Senate - last held on 14 January 2023 (next to be held in 2026)
Mazhilis - last held on 19 March 2023 (next to be held in March 2028)
election results: Senate - percent of vote by party - NA; seats by party - NA; composition - men 39, women 11, percentage women 22%
Mazhilis - percent of vote by party - Nur Otan 53.9%, Auvl 10.9%, Respublica 8.6%, Ak Zhol 8.4%, QHP 6.8%, NSDP 5.2%, Baytak 2.3%, Against all 3.9%; percent of vote by party (single-mandate districts) - Nur Otan 75.9%, independent 24%; seats by party - Nur Otan 62, Auvl 8, Respublica 6, Ak Zhol 6, QHP 5, NSDP 4, independent 7; composition - men 79, women 19, percentage women 18.4%; note - total Parliament percentage women 20.9%

Judicial branch: *highest court(s):* Supreme Court of the Republic (consists of 44 members); Constitutional Council (consists of the chairperson and 6 members)
judge selection and term of office: Supreme Court judges proposed by the president of the republic on recommendation of the Supreme Judicial Council and confirmed by the Senate; judges normally serve until age 65 but can be extended to age 70; Constitutional Council - the president of the republic, the Senate chairperson, and the Mazhilis chairperson each appoints 2 members for a 6-year term; chairperson of the Constitutional Council appointed by the president for a 6-year term
subordinate courts: regional and local courts

Political parties: Ak Zhol Democratic Party or Ak Zhol
Amanat Party (formerly Nur Otan (Radiant Fatherland))
Auyl People's Democratic Patriotic Party or Auyl
Baytak (Boundless) Party
National Social Democratic Party or NSDP
People's Democratic (Patriotic) Party or Auyl or AHDPP
People's Party of Kazakhstan or PPK
Respublica

International organization participation: ADB, CICA, CIS, CSTO, EAEU, EAPC, EBRD, ECO, EITI (compliant country), FAO, GCTU, IAEA, IBRD, ICAO, ICC (NGOs), ICRM, IDA, IDB, IFAD, IFC, IFRCS, ILO, IMF, IMO, Interpol, IOC, IOM, IPU, ISO, ITSO, ITU, MIGA, MINURSO, NAM (observer), NSG, OAS (observer), OIC, OPCW, OSCE, PFP, SCO, UN, UNCTAD, UNESCO, UNHRC, UNIDO, UN Security Council (temporary), UNWTO, UPU, WCO, WFTU (NGOs), WHO, WIPO, WMO, WTO, ZC

Diplomatic representation in the US: *chief of mission:* Ambassador Yerzhan ASHIKBAYEV (since 7 July 2021)
chancery: 1401 16th Street NW, Washington, DC 20036
telephone: [1] (202) 232-5488
FAX: [1] (202) 232-5845
email address and website:
washington@mfa.kz
https://www.gov.kz/memleket/entities/mfa-washington?lang=en
consulate(s) general: New York, San Francisco

Diplomatic representation from the US: *chief of mission:* Ambassador Daniel N. ROSENBLUM (since 14 November 2022)
embassy: Rakhymzhan Koshkarbayev Avenue, No. 3, Astana 010010
mailing address: 2230 Astana Place, Washington DC 20521-2230
telephone: [7] (7172) 70-21-00
FAX: [7] (7172) 54-09-14
email address and website:
USAKZ@state.gov
https://kz.usembassy.gov/
consulate(s) general: Almaty

Flag description: a gold sun with 32 rays above a soaring golden steppe eagle, both centered on a sky blue background; the hoist side displays a national ornamental pattern "koshkar-muiz" (the horns of the ram) in gold; the blue color is of religious significance to the Turkic peoples of the country, and so symbolizes cultural and ethnic unity; it also represents the endless sky as well as water; the sun, a source of life and energy, exemplifies wealth and plenitude; the sun's rays are shaped like grain, which is the basis of abundance and prosperity; the eagle has appeared on the flags of Kazakh tribes for centuries and represents freedom, power, and the flight to the future

National symbol(s): golden eagle; national colors: blue, yellow

National anthem: *name:* "Menin Qazaqstanim" (My Kazakhstan)
lyrics/music: Zhumeken NAZHIMEDENOV and Nursultan NAZARBAYEV/Shamshi KALDAYAKOV
note: adopted 2006; President Nursultan NAZARBAYEV played a role in revising the lyrics

National heritage: *total World Heritage Sites:* 6 (3 cultural, 3 natural)
selected World Heritage Site locales: Mausoleum of Khoja Ahmed Yasawi (c); Petroglyphs at Tanbaly (c); Saryarka - Steppe and Lakes of Northern Kazakhstan (n); Silk Roads: the Chang'an-Tianshan Corridor (c); Western Tien-Shan (n); Cold Winter Deserts of Turan (n)

ECONOMY

Economic overview: oil and gas giant, with growing international investment; domestic economy hit hard by COVID-19 disruptions; reforming civil society and improving business confidence; legacy state controls and Russian influence inhibit growth and autonomy

Real GDP (purchasing power parity): $705.52 billion (2023 est.)
$671.285 billion (2022 est.)
$650.47 billion (2021 est.)
note: data in 2021 dollars
comparison ranking: 39

Real GDP growth rate: 5.1% (2023 est.)
3.2% (2022 est.)
4.3% (2021 est.)
note: annual GDP % growth based on constant local currency
comparison ranking: 51

Real GDP per capita: $35,500 (2023 est.)
$34,200 (2022 est.)
$33,900 (2021 est.)
note: data in 2021 dollars
comparison ranking: 70

GDP (official exchange rate): $261.421 billion (2023 est.)
note: data in current dollars at official exchange rate

Inflation rate (consumer prices): 14.72% (2023 est.)
15.03% (2022 est.)
8.04% (2021 est.)
note: annual % change based on consumer prices
comparison ranking: 193

Credit ratings: Fitch rating: BBB (2016)

Moody's rating: Baa3 (2016)

Standard & Poors rating: BBB- (2016)
note: The year refers to the year in which the current credit rating was first obtained.

GDP - composition, by sector of origin: *agriculture:* 4.3% (2023 est.)
industry: 32% (2023 est.)
services: 56% (2023 est.)
note: figures may not total 100% due to non-allocated consumption not captured in sector-reported data
comparison rankings: services 115; industry 55; agriculture 123

GDP - composition, by end use: *household consumption:* 49% (2022 est.)
government consumption: 11.3% (2022 est.)
investment in fixed capital: 21.4% (2022 est.)
investment in inventories: 2.8% (2022 est.)
exports of goods and services: 41.8% (2022 est.)
imports of goods and services: -26.3% (2022 est.)
note: figures may not total 100% due to rounding or gaps in data collection

Agricultural products: wheat, milk, potatoes, barley, watermelons, sunflower seeds, cantaloupes/melons, onions, maize, linseed (2022)
note: top ten agricultural products based on tonnage

Industries: oil, coal, iron ore, manganese, chromite, lead, zinc, copper, titanium, bauxite, gold, silver, phosphates, sulfur, uranium, iron and steel; tractors and other agricultural machinery, electric motors, construction materials

Industrial production growth rate: 7.36% (2023 est.)
note: annual % change in industrial value added based on constant local currency
comparison ranking: 31

Labor force: 9.587 million (2023 est.)
note: number of people ages 15 or older who are employed or seeking work
comparison ranking: 57

Unemployment rate: 4.85% (2023 est.)
4.86% (2022 est.)
5.56% (2021 est.)
note: % of labor force seeking employment
comparison ranking: 92

Youth unemployment rate (ages 15-24): *total:* 3.8% (2023 est.)
male: 2.9% (2023 est.)
female: 5% (2023 est.)
note: % of labor force ages 15-24 seeking employment
comparison ranking: total 187

Population below poverty line: 5.2% (2022 est.)
note: % of population with income below national poverty line

Gini Index coefficient - distribution of family income: 29.2 (2021 est.)
note: index (0-100) of income distribution; higher values represent greater inequality
comparison ranking: 129

Average household expenditures: *on food:* 49.1% of household expenditures (2022 est.)
on alcohol and tobacco: 2.4% of household expenditures (2022 est.)

Household income or consumption by percentage share: *lowest 10%:* 4.3% (2021 est.)
highest 10%: 24.8% (2021 est.)
note: % share of income accruing to lowest and highest 10% of population

Remittances: 0.17% of GDP (2023 est.)
0.21% of GDP (2022 est.)
0.16% of GDP (2021 est.)
note: personal transfers and compensation between resident and non-resident individuals/households/entities

Budget: *revenues:* $39.879 billion (2022 est.)
expenditures: $36.451 billion (2022 est.)
note: central government revenues (excluding grants) and expenses converted to US dollars at average official exchange rate for year indicated

Public debt: 22.41% of GDP (2021 est.)
note: central government debt as a % of GDP
comparison ranking: 180

Taxes and other revenues: 9.45% (of GDP) (2021 est.)
note: central government tax revenue as a % of GDP
comparison ranking: 181

Current account balance: -$8.658 billion (2023 est.)
$7.054 billion (2022 est.)
-$2.673 billion (2021 est.)
note: balance of payments - net trade and primary/secondary income in current dollars
comparison ranking: 191

Exports: $90.167 billion (2023 est.)
$93.598 billion (2022 est.)
$71.726 billion (2021 est.)
note: balance of payments - exports of goods and services in current dollars
comparison ranking: 51

Exports - partners: China 14%, Italy 13%, Russia 9%, UK 8%, Netherlands 6% (2022)
note: top five export partners based on percentage share of exports

Exports - commodities: crude petroleum, gold, refined copper, iron alloys, radioactive chemicals (2022)
note: top five export commodities based on value in dollars

Imports: $71.811 billion (2023 est.)
$60.151 billion (2022 est.)
$49.597 billion (2021 est.)
note: balance of payments - imports of goods and services in current dollars
comparison ranking: 57

Imports - partners: Russia 29%, China 28%, Germany 5%, South Korea 4%, Turkey 3% (2022)
note: top five import partners based on percentage share of imports

Imports - commodities: garments, cars, broadcasting equipment, plastic products, packaged medicine (2022)
note: top five import commodities based on value in dollars

Reserves of foreign exchange and gold: $35.965 billion (2023 est.)
$35.076 billion (2022 est.)
$34.378 billion (2021 est.)
note: holdings of gold (year-end prices)/foreign exchange/special drawing rights in current dollars
comparison ranking: 54

Debt - external: $22.643 billion (2022 est.)
note: present value of external debt in current US dollars
comparison ranking: 23

Exchange rates: tenge (KZT) per US dollar -

Exchange rates: 456.165 (2023 est.)
460.165 (2022 est.)
425.908 (2021 est.)
412.953 (2020 est.)
382.747 (2019 est.)

ENERGY

Electricity access: *electrification - total population:* 100% (2022 est.)

Electricity: *installed generating capacity:* 26.033 million kW (2022 est.)
consumption: 108.34 billion kWh (2022 est.)
exports: 2.726 billion kWh (2022 est.)
imports: 1.902 billion kWh (2022 est.)
transmission/distribution losses: 9.758 billion kWh (2022 est.)
comparison rankings: transmission/distribution losses 178; imports 60; exports 50; consumption 33; installed generating capacity 40

Electricity generation sources: *fossil fuels:* 89% of total installed capacity (2022 est.)
solar: 1.4% of total installed capacity (2022 est.)
wind: 1.5% of total installed capacity (2022 est.)
hydroelectricity: 8% of total installed capacity (2022 est.)

Nuclear energy: Number of nuclear reactors permanently shut down: 1 (2023)

Coal: *production:* 118.195 million metric tons (2022 est.)
consumption: 84.852 million metric tons (2022 est.)
exports: 37.309 million metric tons (2022 est.)
imports: 31,000 metric tons (2022 est.)
proven reserves: 25.605 billion metric tons (2022 est.)

Petroleum: *total petroleum production:* 1.955 million bbl/day (2023 est.)
refined petroleum consumption: 288,000 bbl/day (2022 est.)
crude oil estimated reserves: 30 billion barrels (2021 est.)

Natural gas: *production:* 27.011 billion cubic meters (2022 est.)
consumption: 22.623 billion cubic meters (2022 est.)

exports: 7.77 billion cubic meters (2022 est.)
imports: 2.181 billion cubic meters (2022 est.)
proven reserves: 2.407 trillion cubic meters (2021 est.)

Carbon dioxide emissions: 265.46 million metric tonnes of CO2 (2022 est.)
from coal and metallurgical coke: 185.014 million metric tonnes of CO2 (2022 est.)
from petroleum and other liquids: 36.066 million metric tonnes of CO2 (2022 est.)
from consumed natural gas: 44.38 million metric tonnes of CO2 (2022 est.)
comparison ranking: total emissions 26

Energy consumption per capita: 176.085 million Btu/person (2022 est.)
comparison ranking: 22

COMMUNICATIONS

Telephones - fixed lines: *total subscriptions:* 2.888 million (2022 est.)
subscriptions per 100 inhabitants: 15 (2022 est.)
comparison ranking: total subscriptions 40

Telephones - mobile cellular: *total subscriptions:* 25.299 million (2022 est.)
subscriptions per 100 inhabitants: 130 (2022 est.)
comparison ranking: total subscriptions 52

Telecommunication systems: *general assessment:* Kazakhstan has one of the most developed telecommunications sectors in the region; this is especially true of the mobile segment, where the country has the second fastest average mobile data rates in Central Asia after Azerbaijan; the competing Mobile Network Operators (MNOs) have built extensive Long Term Evolution (LTE) networks: about 76% of mobile subscribers were on LTE as of March 2024, while the company's LTE network provided 89% geographic coverage; this widespread network coverage, as well as the development of 5G networks, has been encouraged by the government with the second stage of its Digital Kazakhstan program, by which most settlements across the country will be furnished with mobile internet connectivity; the remaining rural villages will be covered by satellite services; at the turn of the century, Kazakhstan had a relatively high fixed-line tele density thanks to efforts to invest in the fixed-line infrastructure and in next-generation networks; the gobal demand for traditional voice services are decreasing as customers are increasingly attracted to the flexibility of the mobile platform for voice as well as data services
(2024)
domestic: fixed telephone subscriptions are 15 per 100 persons; mobile-cellular subscriber base 130 per 100 persons (2022)
international: country code - 7; international traffic with other former Soviet republics and China carried by landline and microwave radio relay and with other countries by satellite and by the TAE fiber-optic cable; satellite earth stations - 2 Intelsat

Broadcast media: the state owns nearly all radio and TV transmission facilities and operates national TV and radio networks; there are 96 TV channels, many of which are owned by the government, and 4 state-run radio stations; some former state-owned media outlets have been privatized; households with satellite dishes have access to foreign media; a small number of commercial radio stations operate along with state-run radio stations; recent legislation requires all media outlets to register with the government and all TV providers to broadcast in digital format by 2018; broadcasts reach some 99% of the population as well as neighboring countries (2018)

Internet country code: .kz

Internet users: *total:* 17.29 million (2021 est.)
percent of population: 91% (2021 est.)
comparison ranking: total 45

Broadband - fixed subscriptions: *total:* 2,620,400 (2020 est.)
subscriptions per 100 inhabitants: 14 (2020 est.)
comparison ranking: total 48

TRANSPORTATION

National air transport system: *number of registered air carriers:* 12 (2020)
inventory of registered aircraft operated by air carriers: 84
annual passenger traffic on registered air carriers: 7,143,797 (2018)
annual freight traffic on registered air carriers: 50.22 million (2018) mt-km

Civil aircraft registration country code prefix: UP

Airports: 132 (2024)
comparison ranking: 38

Heliports: 30 (2024)

Pipelines: 658 km condensate, 15,429 km gas (2020), 8,020 km oil (2020), 1,095 km refined products, 1,975 km water (2017) (2020)

Railways: *total:* 16,636 km (2021)
broad gauge: 16,636 km (2021) 1.520-m gauge (4,237 km electrified)
comparison ranking: total 17

Roadways: *total:* 96,167 km
paved: 83,813 km
unpaved: 12,354 km (2021)
comparison ranking: total 52

Waterways: 43,983 km (2020) (on the Ertis (Irtysh) River (80%) and Syr Darya (Syrdariya) River)
comparison ranking: 4

Merchant marine: *total:* 122 (2023)
by type: general cargo 3, oil tanker 7, other 112
comparison ranking: total 82

MILITARY AND SECURITY

Military and security forces: Armed Forces of the Republic of Kazakhstan: Land Forces, Naval Forces, Air and Air Defense Forces

Ministry of Internal Affairs: National Police, National Guard

Committee for National Security (KNB): Border Guard Service (2024)
note: the National Guard is a gendarmerie type force administered by the Ministry of Internal Affairs, but also serves the Ministry of Defense; it is responsible for fighting crime, maintaining public order, and ensuring public safety; other duties include anti-terrorism operations, guarding prisons, riot control, and territorial defense in time of war

Military expenditures: 0.8% of GDP (2023 est.)
0.7% of GDP (2022 est.)
1% of GDP (2021 est.)
1.1% of GDP (2020 est.)
1.1% of GDP (2019 est.)
comparison ranking: 141

Military and security service personnel strengths: information varies; approximately 40,000 active-duty personnel (25,000 Land Forces; 3,000 Naval Forces; 12,000 Air and Air Defense Forces); approximately 30,000 National Guard (2023)

Military equipment inventories and acquisitions: the Kazakh military's inventory is comprised of mostly Russian and Soviet-era equipment; in recent years, other suppliers have included China, France, Israel, South Korea, and Turkey; Kazakhstan has a defense industry capable of assembling or producing such items as naval vessels, combat vehicles, helicopters, and radar systems (2024)

Military service age and obligation: all men 18-27 are required to serve in the military for 12-24 months; women may volunteer (2023)
note: as of 2022, more than 10,000 women served in the Armed Forces and the National Guard

Military - note: the military's principal responsibilities are territorial defense while the National Police, National Guard, Committee for National Security, and Border Service have primary responsibility for internal security, although the military may provide assistance as required; the military also participates in humanitarian and peacekeeping operations; in 2008, Kazakhstan opened up Central Asia's first peacekeeper training center for military personnel of Kazakhstan, NATO, and other partners
in 2022, Kazakhstan initiated a wide-ranging effort to enhance the country's security sector, including organizational changes such as establishing new National Guard units, enhancing existing ones, and forming a special operations force, spending increases for equipment acquisitions, a new doctrine with renewed emphasis on defense of the border, and reforms to improve professionalism in the military
Kazakhstan has been a member of the Collective Security Treaty Organization (CSTO) since 1994 and has obligated troops to CSTO's rapid reaction force; it also has a relationship with NATO focused on democratic, institutional, and defense reforms; relations with NATO started in 1992, and Kazakhstan joined NATO's Partnership for Peace program in 1995; Kazakhstan's armed forces were formed in 1992 following the breakup of the Soviet Union and the disbandment of the Soviet Turkestan Military District whose forces formed the core of the new Kazakh military (2023)

SPACE

Space agency/agencies: National Space Agency of the Republic of Kazakhstan (KazCosmos; established 2007) (2024)

Space launch site(s): Baikonur Cosmodrome/Space Center (Baikonur) (2024)
note 1: the Baikonur cosmodrome and the surrounding area are leased and administered by Russia until 2050 for approximately $115 million/year; the cosmodrome was originally built by the Soviet Union in the mid-1950s and is the site of the World's first successful satellite launch (Sputnik) in 1957; it is also the largest space launch facility in the World, comprising 15 launch pads for space launch vehicles, four launch pads for testing intercontinental ballistic missiles, more than 10 assembly and test facilities, and other infrastructure
note 2: in 2018, Kazakhstan and Russia agreed that Kazakhstan would build, maintain, and operate a new space launch facility (Baiterek) at the Baikonur space center (estimated to be ready for operations in 2025)

Space program overview: has an active and ambitious space program that originated with the former Soviet Union; focused on the acquisition and operation of

satellites; builds (with foreign assistance) and operates communications, remote sensing (RS), and scientific satellites; building space infrastructure, such as launch and testing facilities, ground stations, and rocket manufacturing; has an astronaut (cosmonaut) program; has relations with a variety of foreign space agencies and industries, including those of China, France, Germany, India, Israel, Italy, Japan, Russia, Saudi Arabia, Sweden, Thailand, Turkey, Ukraine, UAE, and the UK; has state-owned and private companies that assist in the development and building of the country's space program, including satellites, satellite payloads, and associated capabilities; they also work closely with foreign commercial entities (2024)
note: further details about the key activities, programs, and milestones of the country's space program, as well as government spending estimates on the space sector, appear in the Space Programs reference guide

TRANSNATIONAL ISSUES

Refugees and internally displaced persons: *stateless persons:* 7,558 (2022)

Illicit drugs: part of the "Northern Route," land drug trafficking route from Afghanistan to Russia and Europe; domestic manufacturing of synthetics increasing and domestic drug use trends to synthetic drugs outpacing heroin and cannabis;

KENYA

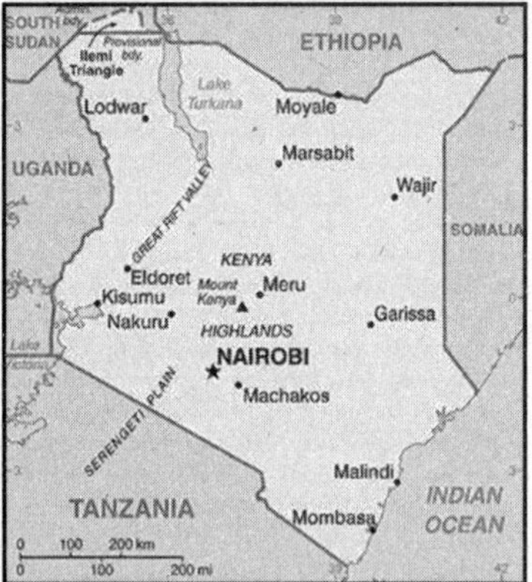

INTRODUCTION

Background: Trade centers such as Mombasa have existed along the Kenyan and Tanzanian coastlines, known as the Land of Zanj, since at least the 2nd century. These centers traded with the outside world, including China, India, Indonesia, the Middle East, North Africa, and Persia. By around the 9th century, the mix of Africans, Arabs, and Persians who lived and traded there became known as Swahili ("people of the coast") with a distinct language (KiSwahili) and culture. The Portuguese arrived in the 1490s and, using Mombasa as a base, sought to monopolize trade in the Indian Ocean. The Portuguese were pushed out in the late 1600s by the combined forces of Oman and Pate, an island off the coast. In 1890, Germany and the UK divided up the region, with the UK taking the north and the Germans the south, including present-day Tanzania, Burundi, and Rwanda. In 1895, the British established the East Africa Protectorate, which in 1920 was converted into a colony, and named Kenya after its highest mountain. Numerous political disputes between the colony and the UK led to the violent Mau Mau Uprising, which began in 1952, and the eventual declaration of independence in 1963.

Jomo KENYATTA, the founding president and an icon of the liberation struggle, led Kenya from independence in 1963 until his death in 1978, when Vice President Daniel Arap MOI took power in a constitutional succession. The country was a de facto one-party state from 1969 until 1982, after which time the ruling Kenya African National Union (KANU) changed the constitution to make itself the sole legal political party. MOI gave in to internal and external pressure for political liberalization in 1991, but the ethnically fractured opposition failed to dislodge KANU from power in elections in 1992 and 1997, which were marred by violence and fraud. MOI stepped down in 2002 after fair and peaceful elections. Mwai KIBAKI, running as the candidate of the multiethnic, united opposition group, the National Rainbow Coalition (NARC), defeated KANU candidate Uhuru KENYATTA, the son of the founding president, and assumed the presidency following a campaign centered on an anticorruption platform.

Opposition candidate Raila ODINGA challenged KIBAKI's reelection in 2007 on the grounds of widespread vote rigging, leading to two months of ethnic violence that caused more than 1,100 deaths and displaced hundreds of thousands. African Union-sponsored mediation resulted in a power-sharing accord that brought ODINGA into the government as prime minister and outlined a reform agenda. In 2010, Kenyans overwhelmingly voted to adopt a new constitution that eliminated the prime minister, introduced additional checks and balances to executive power, and devolved power and resources to 47 newly created counties. Uhuru KENYATTA won the first presidential election under the new constitution in 2013. He won a second and final term in office in 2017 after a contentious repeat election. In 2022, William RUTO won a close presidential election; he assumed the office the following month after the Kenyan Supreme Court upheld the victory.

GEOGRAPHY

Location: Eastern Africa, bordering the Indian Ocean, between Somalia and Tanzania

Geographic coordinates: 1 00 N, 38 00 E

Map references: Africa

Area: *total:* 580,367 sq km
land: 569,140 sq km
water: 11,227 sq km
comparison ranking: total 51

Area - comparative: five times the size of Ohio; slightly more than twice the size of Nevada

Land boundaries: *total:* 3,457 km
border countries (5): Ethiopia 867 km; Somalia 684 km; South Sudan 317 km; Tanzania 775 km; Uganda 814 km

Coastline: 536 km

Maritime claims: *territorial sea:* 12 nm
exclusive economic zone: 200 nm
continental shelf: 200-m depth or to the depth of exploitation

Climate: varies from tropical along coast to arid in interior

Terrain: low plains rise to central highlands bisected by Great Rift Valley; fertile plateau in west

Elevation: *highest point:* Mount Kenya 5,199 m
lowest point: Indian Ocean 0 m
mean elevation: 762 m

Natural resources: limestone, soda ash, salt, gemstones, fluorspar, zinc, diatomite, gypsum, wildlife, hydropower

Land use: *agricultural land:* 48.1% (2018 est.)
arable land: 9.8% (2018 est.)
permanent crops: 0.9% (2018 est.)
permanent pasture: 37.4% (2018 est.)
forest: 6.1% (2018 est.)
other: 45.8% (2018 est.)

Irrigated land: 1,030 sq km (2012)

Major lakes (area sq km): *fresh water lake(s):* Lake Victoria (shared with Tanzania and Uganda) - 62,940 sq km
salt water lake(s): Lake Turkana (shared with Ethiopia) - 6,400 sq km

Major watersheds (area sq km): Atlantic Ocean drainage: *(Mediterranean Sea)* Nile (3,254,853 sq km)

Major aquifers: Ogaden-Juba Basin

Population distribution: population heavily concentrated in the west along the shore of Lake Victoria; other areas of high density include the capital of Nairobi, and in the southeast along the Indian Ocean coast as shown in this population distribution map

Natural hazards: recurring drought; flooding during rainy seasons
volcanism: limited volcanic activity; the Barrier (1,032 m) last erupted in 1921; South Island is the only other historically active volcano

Geography - note: *the Kenyan Highlands comprise one of the most successful agricultural production regions in Africa; glaciers are found on Mount Kenya, Africa's second highest peak; unique physiography supports abundant and varied wildlife of scientific and economic value; Lake Victoria, the world's largest tropical lake and the second largest fresh water lake, is shared among three countries:* Kenya, Tanzania, and Uganda

PEOPLE AND SOCIETY

Population: *total:* 58,246,378
male: 29,091,800
female: 29,154,578 (2024 est.)
comparison rankings: female 26; male 26; total 26

Nationality: *noun:* Kenyan(s)
adjective: Kenyan

Ethnic groups: Kikuyu 17.1%, Luhya 14.3%, Kalenjin 13.4%, Luo 10.7%, Kamba 9.8%, Somali 5.8%, Kisii 5.7%, Mijikenda 5.2%, Meru 4.2%, Maasai 2.5%, Turkana 2.1%, non-Kenyan 1%, other 8.2% (2019 est.)

Languages: English (official), Kiswahili (official), numerous indigenous languages
major-language sample(s):
The World Factbook, the indispensable source for basic information. (English)
The World Factbook, Chanzo cha Lazima Kuhusu Habari ya Msingi. (Kiswahili)

Religions: Christian 85.5% (Protestant 33.4%, Catholic 20.6%, Evangelical 20.4%, African Instituted Churches 7%, other Christian 4.1%), Muslim 10.9%, other 1.8%, none 1.6%, don't know/no answer 0.2% (2019 est.)

Demographic profile: Kenya has experienced dramatic population growth since the mid-20th century as a result of its high birth rate and its declining mortality rate. Almost 40% of Kenyans are under the age of 15 as of 2020 because of sustained high fertility, early marriage and childbearing, and an unmet need for family planning. Kenya's persistent rapid population growth strains the labor market, social services, arable land, and natural resources. Although Kenya in 1967 was the first Sub-Saharan country to launch a nationwide family planning program, progress in reducing the birth rate has largely stalled since the late 1990s, when the government decreased its support for family planning to focus on the HIV epidemic. Government commitment and international technical support spurred Kenyan contraceptive use, decreasing the fertility rate (children per woman) from about 8 in the late 1970s to less than 5 children twenty years later, but it has plateaued at about 3 children as of 2022.
Kenya is a source of emigrants and a host country for refugees. In the 1960s and 1970s, Kenyans pursued higher education in the UK because of colonial ties, but as British immigration rules tightened, the US, the then Soviet Union, and Canada became attractive study destinations. Kenya's stagnant economy and political problems during the 1980s and 1990s led to an outpouring of Kenyan students and professionals seeking permanent opportunities in the West and southern Africa. Nevertheless, Kenya's relative stability since its independence in 1963 has attracted hundreds of thousands of refugees escaping violent conflicts in neighboring countries; Kenya was sheltering nearly 280,000 Somali refugees as of 2022.

Age structure: *0-14 years:* 35.8% (male 10,464,384/female 10,366,997)
15-64 years: 60.9% (male 17,731,068/female 17,723,012)
65 years and over: 3.4% (2024 est.) (male 896,348/female 1,064,569)

Dependency ratios: *total dependency ratio:* 70.2
youth dependency ratio: 65.3
elderly dependency ratio: 4.8
potential support ratio: 20.7 (2021 est.)

Median age: *total:* 21.2 years (2024 est.)
male: 21.1 years
female: 21.4 years
comparison ranking: total 196

Population growth rate: 2.06% (2024 est.)
comparison ranking: 38

Birth rate: 25.6 births/1,000 population (2024 est.)
comparison ranking: 44

Death rate: 4.9 deaths/1,000 population (2024 est.)
comparison ranking: 199

Net migration rate: -0.2 migrant(s)/1,000 population (2024 est.)
comparison ranking: 102

Population distribution: population heavily concentrated in the west along the shore of Lake Victoria; other areas of high density include the capital of Nairobi, and in the southeast along the Indian Ocean coast as shown in this population distribution map

Urbanization: *urban population:* 29.5% of total population (2023)
rate of urbanization: 4.09% annual rate of change (2020-25 est.)

Major urban areas - population: 5.325 million NAIROBI (capital), 1.440 million Mombassa (2023)

Sex ratio: *at birth:* 1.02 male(s)/female
0-14 years: 1.01 male(s)/female
15-64 years: 1 male(s)/female
65 years and over: 0.84 male(s)/female
total population: 1 male(s)/female (2024 est.)

Mother's mean age at first birth: 20.3 years (2014 est.)
note: data represents median age at first birth among women 25-49

Maternal mortality ratio: 530 deaths/100,000 live births (2020 est.)
comparison ranking: 12

Infant mortality rate: *total:* 26.1 deaths/1,000 live births (2024 est.)
male: 29 deaths/1,000 live births
female: 23.1 deaths/1,000 live births
comparison ranking: total 58

Life expectancy at birth: *total population:* 70.4 years (2024 est.)
male: 68.6 years
female: 72.2 years
comparison ranking: total population 176

Total fertility rate: 3.16 children born/woman (2024 est.)
comparison ranking: 45

Gross reproduction rate: 1.56 (2024 est.)

Contraceptive prevalence rate: 64.6% (2020)

Drinking water source: *improved: urban:* 91.3% of population
rural: 63.3% of population
total: 71.2% of population
unimproved: urban: 8.7% of population
rural: 36.7% of population
total: 28.8% of population (2020 est.)

Current health expenditure: 4.3% of GDP (2020)

Physician density: 0.16 physicians/1,000 population (2018)

Sanitation facility access: *improved: urban:* 84% of population
rural: 48.1% of population
total: 58.2% of population
unimproved: urban: 16% of population
rural: 51.9% of population
total: 41.8% of population (2020 est.)

Obesity - adult prevalence rate: 7.1% (2016)
comparison ranking: 161

Alcohol consumption per capita: *total:* 1.68 liters of pure alcohol (2019 est.)
beer: 0.81 liters of pure alcohol (2019 est.)
wine: 0.04 liters of pure alcohol (2019 est.)
spirits: 0.81 liters of pure alcohol (2019 est.)
other alcohols: 0.03 liters of pure alcohol (2019 est.)
comparison ranking: total 134

Tobacco use: *total:* 11.1% (2020 est.)
male: 19.5% (2020 est.)
female: 2.7% (2020 est.)
comparison ranking: total 129

Children under the age of 5 years underweight: 10.1% (2022)
comparison ranking: 56

Currently married women (ages 15-49): 56.8% (2023 est.)

Education expenditures: 4.8% of GDP (2021 est.)
comparison ranking: 83

Literacy: *definition:* age 15 and over can read and write
total population: 82.6%
male: 85.5%
female: 79.8% (2021)

ENVIRONMENT

Environment - current issues: water pollution from urban and industrial wastes; water shortage and degraded water quality from increased use of pesticides and fertilizers; flooding; water hyacinth infestation in Lake Victoria; deforestation; soil erosion; desertification; poaching

Environment - international agreements: *party to:* Biodiversity, Climate Change, Climate Change-Kyoto Protocol, Climate Change-Paris Agreement, Comprehensive Nuclear Test Ban, Desertification, Endangered Species, Hazardous Wastes, Law of the Sea, Marine Dumping-London Convention, Marine Dumping-London Protocol, Marine Life Conservation, Nuclear Test Ban, Ozone Layer Protection, Ship Pollution, Wetlands, Whaling
signed, but not ratified: none of the selected agreements

Climate: varies from tropical along coast to arid in interior

Urbanization: *urban population:* 29.5% of total population (2023)
rate of urbanization: 4.09% annual rate of change (2020-25 est.)

Food insecurity: *exceptional shortfall in aggregate food production/supplies: due to drought conditions* - about 4.4 million people were projected to be severely acutely food insecure between October and December 2022 reflecting consecutive poor rainy seasons since late 2020 that affected crop and livestock production; prices of maize are at high levels across the country due to reduced availabilities and high fuel prices inflating production and transportation costs (2023)

Revenue from forest resources: 1.3% of GDP (2018 est.)
comparison ranking: 47

Revenue from coal: 0% of GDP (2018 est.)
comparison ranking: 142

Air pollutants: *particulate matter emissions:* 12.52 micrograms per cubic meter (2019 est.)
carbon dioxide emissions: 17.91 megatons (2016 est.)
methane emissions: 37.65 megatons (2020 est.)

Waste and recycling: *municipal solid waste generated annually:* 5,595,099 tons (2010 est.)
municipal solid waste recycled annually: 447,608 tons (2009 est.)

percent of municipal solid waste recycled: 8% (2009 est.)

Major lakes (area sq km): *fresh water lake(s):* Lake Victoria (shared with Tanzania and Uganda) - 62,940 sq km
salt water lake(s): Lake Turkana (shared with Ethiopia) - 6,400 sq km

Major watersheds (area sq km): Atlantic Ocean drainage: *(Mediterranean Sea)* Nile (3,254,853 sq km)

Major aquifers: Ogaden-Juba Basin

Total water withdrawal: *municipal:* 500 million cubic meters (2020 est.)
industrial: 300 million cubic meters (2020 est.)
agricultural: 3.23 billion cubic meters (2020 est.)

Total renewable water resources: 30.7 billion cubic meters (2020 est.)

GOVERNMENT

Country name: *conventional long form:* Republic of Kenya
conventional short form: Kenya
local long form: Republic of Kenya (English)/ Jamhuri ya Kenya (Swahili)
local short form: Kenya
former: British East Africa
etymology: named for Mount Kenya; the meaning of the name is unclear but may derive from the Kikuyu, Embu, and Kamba words "kirinyaga," "kirenyaa," and "kiinyaa" - all of which mean "God's resting place"

Government type: presidential republic

Capital: *name:* Nairobi
geographic coordinates: 1 17 S, 36 49 E
time difference: UTC+3 (8 hours ahead of Washington, DC, during Standard Time)
etymology: the name derives from the Maasai expression meaning "cool waters" and refers to a cold water stream that flowed through the area in the late 19th century

Administrative divisions: 47 counties; Baringo, Bomet, Bungoma, Busia, Elgeyo/Marakwet, Embu, Garissa, Homa Bay, Isiolo, Kajiado, Kakamega, Kericho, Kiambu, Kilifi, Kirinyaga, Kisii, Kisumu, Kitui, Kwale, Laikipia, Lamu, Machakos, Makueni, Mandera, Marsabit, Meru, Migori, Mombasa, Murang'a, Nairobi City, Nakuru, Nandi, Narok, Nyamira, Nyandarua, Nyeri, Samburu, Siaya, Taita/ Taveta, Tana River, Tharaka-Nithi, Trans Nzoia, Turkana, Uasin Gishu, Vihiga, Wajir, West Pokot

Independence: 12 December 1963 (from the UK)

National holiday: Jamhuri Day (Independence Day), 12 December (1963); note - Madaraka Day, 1 June (1963) marks the day Kenya attained internal self-rule

Legal system: mixed legal system of English common law, Islamic law, and customary law; judicial review in the new Supreme Court established by the new constitution

Constitution: *history:* current constitution passed by referendum on 4 August 2010
amendments: amendments can be proposed by either house of Parliament or by petition of at least one million eligible voters; passage of amendments by Parliament requires approval by at least two-thirds majority vote of both houses in each of two readings, approval in a referendum by majority of votes cast by at least 20% of eligible voters in at least one half of Kenya's counties, and approval by the president; passage of amendments introduced by petition requires approval by a majority of county assemblies, approval by majority vote of both houses, and approval by the president

International law organization participation: accepts compulsory ICJ jurisdiction with reservations; accepts ICCt jurisdiction

Citizenship: *citizenship by birth:* no
citizenship by descent only: at least one parent must be a citizen of Kenya
dual citizenship recognized: yes
residency requirement for naturalization: 4 out of the previous 7 years

Suffrage: 18 years of age; universal

Executive branch: *chief of state:* President William RUTO (since 13 September 2022)
head of government: President William RUTO (since 13 September 2022)
cabinet: Cabinet appointed by the president, subject to confirmation by the National Assembly
elections/appointments: president and deputy president directly elected on the same ballot by majority vote nationwide and at least 25% of the votes cast in at least 24 of the 47 counties; failure to meet these thresholds requires a runoff between the top two candidates; election last held on 9 August 2022 (next to be held on 10 August 2027)
election results:
2022: William RUTO elected president in first round; percent of vote - William RUTO (UDA) 50.5%, Raila ODINGA (ODM) 48.9%, other 0.6%
2017: Uhuru KENYATTA reelected president; percent of vote - Uhuru KENYATTA (JP) 98.3%, Raila ODINGA (ODM) 1%, other 0.7%; note - Kenya held a previous presidential election on 8 August 2017, but Kenya's Supreme Court on 1 September 2017 nullified the results, citing irregularities; the political opposition boycotted the October vote
note: the president is both chief of state and head of government

Legislative branch: *description:* bicameral Parliament consists of:
Senate (68 seats; 47 members directly elected in single-seat constituencies by simple majority vote and 20 directly elected by proportional representation vote - 16 women, 2 representing youth, 2 representing the disabled, and one Senate speaker; members serve 5-year terms)
National Assembly (350 seats; 290 members directly elected in single-seat constituencies by simple majority vote, 47 women in single-seat constituencies elected by simple majority vote, and 12 members nominated by the National Assembly - 6 representing youth and 6 representing the disabled, and one Assembly speaker; members serve 5-year terms)
elections: Senate - last held on 9 August 2022 (next to be held on 10 August 2027)
National Assembly - last held on 9 August 2022 (next to be held on 10 August 2027)
election results: Senate - percent of vote by party/coalition - NA; seats by party/coalition - Kenya Kwanza 33, Azimio La Umoja 32, independent 2, other 1; composition - men 46, women 21, percentage women is 31.3%
National Assembly - percent of vote by party/coalition - NA; seats by party/coalition - Kenya Kwanza alliance 176, Azimio La Umoja alliance 161, independent 12, other 1; composition - men 267, women 81, percentage women 24.6%

Judicial branch: *highest court(s):* Supreme Court (consists of chief and deputy chief justices and 5 judges)
judge selection and term of office: chief and deputy chief justices nominated by Judicial Service Commission (JSC) and appointed by the president with approval of the National Assembly; other judges nominated by the JSC and appointed by president; chief justice serves a nonrenewable 10-year term or until age 70, whichever comes first; other judges serve until age 70
subordinate courts: High Court; Court of Appeal; military courts; magistrates' courts; religious courts

Political parties: Azimio La Umoja–One Kenya Coalition Party
Amani National Congress or ANC
Chama Cha Kazi or CCK
Democratic Action Party or DAP-K
Democratic Party or DP
Forum for the Restoration of Democracy–Kenya or FORD-Kenya
Grand Dream Development Party or GDDP
Jubilee Party or JP
Kenya African National Union or KANU
Kenya Kwanza coalition
Kenya Union Party or KUP
Maendeleo Chap Chap Party or MCC
Movement for Democracy and Growth or MDG
National Agenda Party or NAP-K
National Ordinary People Empowerment Union or NOPEU
Orange Democratic Movement or ODM
Pamoja African Alliance or PAA]
The Service Party or TSP
United Democratic Alliance or UDA
United Democratic Movement or UDM
United Democratic Party or UDP
United Party of Independent Alliance or UPIA
United Progressive Alliance or UPA
Wiper Democratic Movement-Kenya or WDM-K

International organization participation: ACP, AfDB, ATMIS, AU, C, CD, COMESA, EAC, EADB, FAO, G-15, G-77, IAEA, IBRD, ICAO, ICCT, ICRM, IDA, IFAD, IFC, IFRCS, IGAD, ILO, IMF, IMO, IMSO, Interpol, IOC, IOM, IPU, ISO, ITSO, ITU, ITUC (NGOs), MIGA, MONUSCO, NAM, OPCW, PCA, UN, UNAMID, UNCTAD, UNESCO, UNHCR, UNIDO, UNIFIL, UNISFA, UNMIL, UNMISS, UNOOSA, UNSOM, UNWTO, UPU, WCO, WHO, WMO, WTO

Diplomatic representation in the US: *chief of mission:* Ambassador David Kipkorir Kiplagat KERICH (since 18 September 2024)
chancery: 2249 R St NW, Washington, DC 20008
telephone: [1] (202) 387-6101
FAX: [1] (202) 462-3829
email address and website:
information@kenyaembassydc.org
https://kenyaembassydc.org/#
consulate(s): New York

Diplomatic representation from the US: *chief of mission:* Ambassador Margaret "Meg" WHITMAN (since 5 August 2022)
embassy: P.O. Box 606 Village Market, 00621 Nairobi
mailing address: 8900 Nairobi Place, Washington, DC 20521-8900
telephone: [254] (20) 363-6000
FAX: [254] (20) 363-6157
email address and website:

kenya_acs@state.gov
https://ke.usembassy.gov/

Flag description: three equal horizontal bands of black (top), red, and green; the red band is edged in white; a large Maasai warrior's shield covering crossed spears is superimposed at the center; black symbolizes the majority population, red the blood shed in the struggle for freedom, green stands for natural wealth, and white for peace; the shield and crossed spears symbolize the defense of freedom

National symbol(s): lion; national colors: black, red, green, white

National anthem: *name:* "Ee Mungu Nguvu Yetu" (Oh God of All Creation)
lyrics/music: Graham HYSLOP, Thomas KALUME, Peter KIBUKOSYA, Washington OMONDI, and George W. SENOGA-ZAKE/traditional, adapted by Graham HYSLOP, Thomas KALUME, Peter KIBUKOSYA, Washington OMONDI, and George W. SENOGA-ZAKE
note: adopted 1963; based on a traditional Kenyan folk song

National heritage: *total World Heritage Sites:* 7 (4 cultural, 3 natural)
selected World Heritage Site locales: Lake Turkana National Parks (n); Mount Kenya National Park (n); Lamu Old Town (c); Sacred Mijikenda Kaya Forests (c); Fort Jesus, Mombasa (c); Kenya Lake System in the Great Rift Valley (n); Thimlich Ohinga Archaeological Site (c)

ECONOMY

Economic overview: fast growing, third largest Sub-Saharan economy; strong agriculture sector with emerging services and tourism industries; IMF program to address current account and debt service challenges; business-friendly policies foster infrastructure investment, digital innovation and public-private partnerships; vulnerable to climate change-induced droughts

Real GDP (purchasing power parity): $314.063 billion (2023 est.)
$297.9 billion (2022 est.)
$284.129 billion (2021 est.)
note: data in 2021 dollars
comparison ranking: 60

Real GDP growth rate: 5.43% (2023 est.)
4.85% (2022 est.)
7.59% (2021 est.)
note: annual GDP % growth based on constant local currency
comparison ranking: 38

Real GDP per capita: $5,700 (2023 est.)
$5,500 (2022 est.)
$5,400 (2021 est.)
note: data in 2021 dollars
comparison ranking: 170

GDP (official exchange rate): $107.441 billion (2023 est.)
note: data in current dollars at official exchange rate

Inflation rate (consumer prices): 7.67% (2023 est.)
7.66% (2022 est.)
6.11% (2021 est.)
note: annual % change based on consumer prices
comparison ranking: 149

Credit ratings: Fitch rating: B+ (2007)

Moody's rating: B2 (2018)

Standard & Poors rating: B+ (2010)
note: The year refers to the year in which the current credit rating was first obtained.

GDP - composition, by sector of origin: *agriculture:* 21.3% (2023 est.)
industry: 17.1% (2023 est.)
services: 55.5% (2023 est.)
note: figures may not total 100% due to non-allocated consumption not captured in sector-reported data comparison rankings: services 116; industry 160; agriculture 33

GDP - composition, by end use: *household consumption:* 77% (2023 est.)
government consumption: 12.3% (2023 est.)
investment in fixed capital: 17.7% (2023 est.)
investment in inventories: 0.4% (2023 est.)
exports of goods and services: 11.8% (2023 est.)
imports of goods and services: -20.6% (2023 est.)
note: figures may not total 100% due to rounding or gaps in data collection

Agricultural products: sugarcane, milk, maize, tea, bananas, potatoes, cabbages, camel milk, cassava, mangoes/guavas (2022)
note: top ten agricultural products based on tonnage

Industries: agriculture, transportation, services, manufacturing, construction, telecommunications, tourism, retail

Industrial production growth rate: 2.2% (2023 est.)
note: annual % change in industrial value added based on constant local currency
comparison ranking: 114

Labor force: 25.502 million (2023 est.)
note: number of people ages 15 or older who are employed or seeking work
comparison ranking: 27

Unemployment rate: 5.68% (2023 est.)
5.81% (2022 est.)
5.69% (2021 est.)
note: % of labor force seeking employment
comparison ranking: 113

Youth unemployment rate (ages 15-24): *total:* 12.2% (2023 est.)
male: 8.1% (2023 est.)
female: 16.3% (2023 est.)
note: % of labor force ages 15-24 seeking employment
comparison ranking: total 113

Population below poverty line: 36.1% (2015 est.)
note: % of population with income below national poverty line

Gini Index coefficient - distribution of family income: 38.7 (2021 est.)
note: index (0-100) of income distribution; higher values represent greater inequality
comparison ranking: 51

Average household expenditures: *on food:* 56.7% of household expenditures (2022 est.)
on alcohol and tobacco: 3.7% of household expenditures (2022 est.)

Household income or consumption by percentage share: *lowest 10%:* 2.9% (2021 est.)
highest 10%: 31.8% (2021 est.)
note: % share of income accruing to lowest and highest 10% of population

Remittances: 3.92% of GDP (2023 est.)
3.58% of GDP (2022 est.)
3.44% of GDP (2021 est.)
note: personal transfers and compensation between resident and non-resident individuals/households/entities

Budget: *revenues:* $20.202 billion (2023 est.)
expenditures: $29.933 billion (2023 est.)
note: central government revenues (excluding grants) and expenses converted to US dollars at average official exchange rate for year indicated

Public debt: 54.2% of GDP (2017 est.)
comparison ranking: 90

Taxes and other revenues: 13.26% (of GDP) (2021 est.)
note: central government tax revenue as a % of GDP
comparison ranking: 153

Current account balance: -$5.766 billion (2022 est.)
-$5.744 billion (2021 est.)
-$4.792 billion (2020 est.)
note: balance of payments - net trade and primary/secondary income in current dollars
comparison ranking: 187

Exports: $13.859 billion (2022 est.)
$11.825 billion (2021 est.)
$9.709 billion (2020 est.)
note: balance of payments - exports of goods and services in current dollars
comparison ranking: 102

Exports - partners: US 10%, Uganda 9%, Pakistan 7%, Netherlands 7%, Rwanda 6% (2022)
note: top five export partners based on percentage share of exports

Exports - commodities: tea, cut flowers, garments, coffee, titanium ore (2022)
note: top five export commodities based on value in dollars

Imports: $24.406 billion (2022 est.)
$21.853 billion (2021 est.)
$17.717 billion (2020 est.)
note: balance of payments - imports of goods and services in current dollars
comparison ranking: 87

Imports - partners: China 26%, UAE 14%, India 11%, Malaysia 4%, Saudi Arabia 4% (2022)
note: top five import partners based on percentage share of imports

Imports - commodities: refined petroleum, palm oil, garments, wheat, plastics (2022)
note: top five import commodities based on value in dollars

Reserves of foreign exchange and gold: $7.342 billion (2023 est.)
$7.969 billion (2022 est.)
$9.491 billion (2021 est.)
note: holdings of gold (year-end prices)/foreign exchange/special drawing rights in current dollars
comparison ranking: 78

Debt - external: $31.029 billion (2022 est.)
note: present value of external debt in current US dollars
comparison ranking: 21

Exchange rates: Kenyan shillings (KES) per US dollar -

Exchange rates: 139.846 (2023 est.)
117.866 (2022 est.)
109.638 (2021 est.)
106.451 (2020 est.)
101.991 (2019 est.)

ENERGY

Electricity access: *electrification - total population:* 76% (2022 est.)

electrification - urban areas: 98%
electrification - rural areas: 65.6%

Electricity: *installed generating capacity:* 3.746 million kW (2022 est.)
consumption: 9.622 billion kWh (2022 est.)
exports: 18 million kWh (2022 est.)
imports: 221.841 million kWh (2022 est.)
transmission/distribution losses: 2.947 billion kWh (2022 est.)
comparison rankings: transmission/distribution losses 138; imports 104; exports 96; consumption 105; installed generating capacity 103

Electricity generation sources: *fossil fuels:* 8% of total installed capacity (2022 est.)
solar: 3.1% of total installed capacity (2022 est.)
wind: 17.3% of total installed capacity (2022 est.)
hydroelectricity: 24.6% of total installed capacity (2022 est.)
geothermal: 44.6% of total installed capacity (2022 est.)
biomass and waste: 2.3% of total installed capacity (2022 est.)

Coal: *consumption:* 1.168 million metric tons (2022 est.)
exports: (2022 est.) less than 1 metric ton
imports: 1.168 million metric tons (2022 est.)

Petroleum: *refined petroleum consumption:* 119,000 bbl/day (2022 est.)

Carbon dioxide emissions: 19.471 million metric tonnes of CO2 (2022 est.)
from coal and metallurgical coke: 2.638 million metric tonnes of CO2 (2022 est.)
from petroleum and other liquids: 16.833 million metric tonnes of CO2 (2022 est.)
comparison ranking: total emissions 88

Energy consumption per capita: 5.692 million Btu/person (2022 est.)
comparison ranking: 168

COMMUNICATIONS

Telephones - fixed lines: *total subscriptions:* 63,000 (2022 est.)
subscriptions per 100 inhabitants: (2022 est.) less than 1
comparison ranking: total subscriptions 149

Telephones - mobile cellular: *total subscriptions:* 65.737 million (2022 est.)
subscriptions per 100 inhabitants: 122 (2022 est.)
comparison ranking: total subscriptions 26

Telecommunication systems: *general assessment:* Kenya's telecom market continues to undergo considerable changes in the wake of increased competition, improved international connectivity, and rapid developments in the mobile market; the country is directly connected to a number of submarine cables, and with Mombasa through a terrestrial network, the country serves as a key junction for onward connectivity to the Arabian states and the Far East; numerous competitors are rolling out national and metropolitan backbone networks and wireless access networks to deliver services to population centers across the country; several fiber infrastructure sharing agreements have been forged, and as a result the number of fiber broadband connections has increased sharply in recent years; much of the progress in the broadband segment is due to the government's revised national broadband strategy, which has been updated with goals through to 2030, and which are largely dependent on mobile broadband platforms based on LTE and 5G (2022)
domestic: fixed-line subscriptions stand at less than 1 per 100 persons; mobile-cellular subscriptions at 123 per 100 persons (2021)
international: country code - 254; landing point for the EASSy, TEAMS, LION2, DARE1, PEACE Cable, and SEACOM fiber-optic submarine cable systems covering East, North and South Africa, Europe, the Middle East, and Asia; satellite earth stations - 4 Intelsat; launched first micro satellites in 2018 (2019)

Broadcast media: about a half-dozen large-scale privately owned media companies with TV and radio stations, as well as a state-owned TV broadcaster, provide service nationwide; satellite and cable TV subscription services available; state-owned radio broadcaster operates 2 national radio channels and provides regional and local radio services in multiple languages; many private radio stations broadcast on a national level along with over 100 private and non-profit regional stations broadcasting in local languages; TV transmissions of all major international broadcasters available, mostly via paid subscriptions; direct radio frequency modulation transmissions available for several foreign government-owned broadcasters (2019)

Internet country code: .ke

Internet users: *total:* 15.37 million (2021 est.)
percent of population: 29% (2021 est.)
comparison ranking: total 50

Broadband - fixed subscriptions: *total:* 674,191 (2020 est.)
subscriptions per 100 inhabitants: 1 (2020 est.)
comparison ranking: total 82

TRANSPORTATION

National air transport system: *number of registered air carriers:* 25 (2020)
inventory of registered aircraft operated by air carriers: 188
annual passenger traffic on registered air carriers: 5,935,831 (2018)
annual freight traffic on registered air carriers: 294.97 million (2018) mt-km

Civil aircraft registration country code prefix: 5Y

Airports: 370 (2024)
comparison ranking: 19

Pipelines: 4 km oil, 1,432 km refined products (2018)

Railways: *total:* 3,819 km (2018)
standard gauge: 485 km (2018) 1.435-m gauge
narrow gauge: 3,334 km (2018) 1.000-m gauge
comparison ranking: total 51

Roadways: *total:* 161,451 km
paved: 18,603 km
unpaved: 157,596 km (2023)
comparison ranking: total 32

Waterways: (2011) none specifically; the only significant inland waterway is the part of Lake Victoria within the boundaries of Kenya; Kisumu is the main port and has ferry connections to Uganda and Tanzania

Merchant marine: *total:* 26 (2023)
by type: oil tanker 4, other 22
comparison ranking: total 138

Ports: *total ports:* 4 (2024)
large: 0
medium: 1
small: 2
very small: 1
ports with oil terminals: 1
key ports: Kilifi, Lamu, Malindi, Mombasa

MILITARY AND SECURITY

Military and security forces: Kenya Defense Forces (KDF): Kenya Army, Kenya Navy, Kenya Air Force (2024)
note 1: the National Police Service maintains internal security and reports to the Ministry of Interior and Coordination of National Government; it includes a paramilitary General Service Unit and Rapid Deployment Unit, as well as a Border Police Unit
note 2: the Kenya Coast Guard Service (established 2018) is under the Ministry of Interior but led by a military officer and comprised of personnel from the military, as well as the National Police Service, intelligence services, and other government agencies

Military expenditures: 1% of GDP (2023 est.)
1.1% of GDP (2022 est.)
1.2% of GDP (2021 est.)
1.2% of GDP (2020 est.)
1.2% of GDP (2019 est.)
comparison ranking: 122

Military and security service personnel strengths: approximately 24,000 personnel (20,000 Army; 1,500 Navy; 2,500 Air Force) (2023)

Military equipment inventories and acquisitions: the KDF's inventory is a mix of older, donated/secondhand, and some modern weapon systems from a variety of sources; major suppliers have included China, France, South Africa, Turkey, the UK, and the US; in late 2023, the Kenyan Government unveiled a five-year spending plan to procure upgraded military equipment, including aerial surveillance drones, tactical vehicles, and air defense systems (2024)

Military service age and obligation: no conscription; 18-26 years of age for voluntary service for men and women (under 18 with parental consent; upper limit 30 years of age for specialists, tradesmen, or women with a diploma; 39 years of age for chaplains/imams); 9-year service obligation (7 years for Kenyan Navy) and subsequent 3-year re-enlistments; applicants must be Kenyan citizens (2024)

Military deployments: 400 Democratic Republic of the Congo (MONUSCO); more than 3,000 troops deployed in Somalia under ATMIS (note - ATMIS troop contingents are drawing down towards a final exit in December 2024) (2024)

Military - note: the KDF's chief security concerns and missions include protecting the country's sovereignty and territory, regional disputes, the threat posed by the al-Shabaab terrorist group based in neighboring Somalia, maritime crime and piracy, and assisting civil authorities in responding to emergency, disaster, or political unrest as requested; it has conducted operations in neighboring Somalia since 2011 and taken part in numerous regional peacekeeping and security missions; the KDF is a leading member of the Africa Standby Force; it participates in multinational exercises, and has ties to a variety of foreign militaries, including those of France, the UK, and the US
Kenyan military forces intervened in Somalia in October 2011 to combat the al-Shabaab terrorist group, which had conducted numerous cross-border attacks into Kenya; in November 2011, the UN and the African Union invited Kenya to incorporate its

forces into the African Union Mission in Somalia (AMISOM); Kenyan forces were formally integrated into AMISOM (now the AU Transition Mission in Somalia or ATMIS) in February 2012
the Kenya Military Forces were created following independence in 1963; the current KDF was established and its composition laid out in the 2010 constitution; it is governed by the Kenya Defense Forces Act of 2012; the Army traces its origins back to the Kings African Rifles (KAR), a British colonial regiment raised from Britain's East Africa possessions from 1902 until independence in the 1960s; the KAR conducted both military and internal security functions within the colonial territories, and served outside the territories during both World Wars (2024)

SPACE

Space agency/agencies: Kenya Space Agency (KSA; established, 2017) (2024)

Space launch site(s): Luigi Broglio Space Center (aka Malindi Space Center, Malindi Station, San Marco Satellite Launching and Tracking Station; Kilifi County; over 20 sounding rockets and nine satellites launched from the site, 1967-1989); in 2020, Kenya concluded a new deal with Italy to conduct rocket launches from the site again in the future (2024)

Space program overview: has a national space strategy focused on acquiring and applying space technologies and applications for agriculture, communications, disaster and resource management, security, urban planning, and weather monitoring; jointly develops and builds nanosatellites with foreign partners; operates satellites; researching and developing satellite payloads and imagery data analysis capabilities; has cooperated on space issues with China, Japan, India, Italy, and the US, as well as a variety African partners, including Egypt and South Africa; developing a satellite imagery/geospatial analysis and data sharing portal that contains 17 years of satellite imagery for other African countries, including Ghana, Senegal, Sierra Leone, and Tanzania; cooperating with Egypt, Ethiopia, Ghana, Nigeria, Sudan, and Uganda to establish a joint remote sensing (RS) satellite to monitor climate changes on the African continent (African Development Satellite program) (2024)
note: further details about the key activities, programs, and milestones of the country's space program, as well as government spending estimates on the space sector, appear in the Space Programs reference guide

TERRORISM

Terrorist group(s): al-Shabaab; Islamic Revolutionary Guard Corps (IRGC)/Qods Force
note: details about the history, aims, leadership, organization, areas of operation, tactics, targets, weapons, size, and sources of support of the group(s) appear(s) in the Terrorism reference guide

TRANSNATIONAL ISSUES

Refugees and internally displaced persons: *refugees (country of origin):* 21,847 (Ethiopia), 5,756 (Sudan) (2023); 298,117 (Somalia), 176,776 (South Sudan), 59,384 (Democratic Republic of the Congo), 8,701 (Burundi) (2024)
IDPs: 30,000 (election-related violence, intercommunal violence, resource conflicts, al-Shabaab attacks in 2017 and 2018) (2022)
stateless persons: 16,779 (2022); note - the stateless population consists of Nubians, Kenyan Somalis, and coastal Arabs; the Nubians are descendants of Sudanese soldiers recruited by the British to fight for them in East Africa more than a century ago; Nubians did not receive Kenyan citizenship when the country became independent in 1963; only recently have Nubians become a formally recognized tribe and had less trouble obtaining national IDs; Galjeel and other Somalis who have lived in Kenya for decades are included with more recent Somali refugees and denied ID cards

Illicit drugs: a transit country for illicit drugs and precursor chemicals; domestic drug consumption of cannabis and miraa (khat) is growing; heroin enters Kenya via Tanzania and in shipments across the Indian Ocean from Southwest Asia mostly destined for international markets, principally Europe; cocaine enters Kenya primarily via transshipment through Ethiopia

KIRIBATI

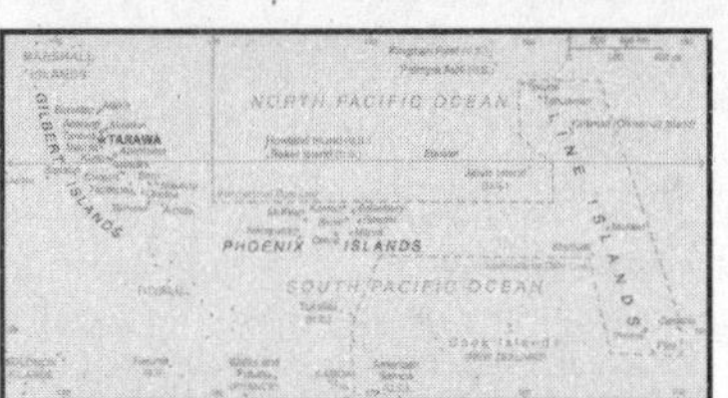

INTRODUCTION

Background: Kiribati is made up of three distinct island groups – the Gilbert Islands, the Line Islands, and the Phoenix Islands. The first Austronesian voyagers arrived in the Gilbert Islands as early as 3000 B.C., but these islands were not widely settled until about A.D. 200 by Micronesians. Around 1300, Samoans and Tongans invaded the southern Gilbert Islands, then known as Tungaru, bringing Polynesian cultural elements with them. Later arrivals of Fijians brought Melanesian elements to the Gilbert Islands, and extensive intermarriage between the Micronesian, Polynesian, and Melanesian people led to the creation of what would become Gilbertese cultural traditions by the time Europeans spotted the islands in the 1600s. The Phoenix Islands and Line Islands were both visited by various Melanesian and Polynesian peoples, but their isolation and lack of natural resources meant that long-term settlements were not possible. Both island groups were uninhabited by the time of European contact.

Kiribati experienced sustained European contact by the 1760s; all three island groups were named and charted by 1826. American whaling ships frequently passed through the islands, and the UK declared a protectorate over the Gilbert and nearby Ellice Islands in 1892, in an attempt to block growing US influence. Phosphate-rich Banaba Island was annexed to the protectorate in 1900. In 1916, the protectorate became a colony, and some Line Islands were added in 1916 and 1919, with the final ones added in 1972. The Phoenix Islands were added to the colony in 1937, and the UK agreed to share jurisdiction of some with the US because of their strategic location for aviation. During World War II, the islands were occupied by Japanese forces but were ejected by US amphibious assaults. The Ellice Islands became its own colony in 1974 and was renamed Tuvalu for "eight standing together" in 1975. The Gilbert Islands became fully selfgoverning in 1977 and independent in 1979 under the new name of Kiribati, the Gilbertese spelling of Gilberts. The US relinquished all claims to the sparsely inhabited Phoenix and Line Islands in a 1979 treaty of friendship.

In 2012, Kiribati purchased a 22 sq km (8.5 sq mi) plot of land in Fiji for potential eventual resettlement of its population because of climate change, and in 2014 Fijian Prime Minister Voreqe BAINIMARAMA said residents of Kiribati would be welcome to relocate to Fiji if their country is swamped by rising sea levels.

GEOGRAPHY

Location: Oceania, group of 32 coral atolls and one raised coral island in the Pacific Ocean, straddling the Equator; the capital Tarawa is about halfway between Hawaii and Australia

Geographic coordinates: 1 25 N, 173 00 E

Map references: Oceania

Area: *total:* 811 sq km
land: 811 sq km
water: 0 sq km
note: includes three island groups - Gilbert Islands, Line Islands, and Phoenix Islands - dispersed over about 3.5 million sq km (1.35 million sq mi)
comparison ranking: total 186

Area - comparative: four times the size of Washington, DC

Land boundaries: *total:* 0 km

Coastline: 1,143 km

Maritime claims: *territorial sea:* 12 nm
exclusive economic zone: 200 nm

Climate: tropical; marine, hot and humid, moderated by trade winds

Terrain: mostly low-lying coral atolls surrounded by extensive reefs

Elevation: *highest point:* unnamed elevation on Banaba 81 m
lowest point: Pacific Ocean 0 m
mean elevation: 2 m

Natural resources: phosphate (production discontinued in 1979), coconuts (copra), fish

Land use: *agricultural land:* 42% (2018 est.)
arable land: 2.5% (2018 est.)
permanent crops: 39.5% (2018 est.)
permanent pasture: 0% (2018 est.)
forest: 15% (2018 est.)
other: 43% (2018 est.)

Irrigated land: 0 sq km (2022)

Population distribution: consists of three achipelagos spread out over an area roughly the size of India; the eastern Line Islands and central Phoenix Islands are sparsely populated, but the western Gilbert Islands are some of the most densely settled places on earth, with the main island of South Tarawa boasting a population density similar to Tokyo or Hong Kong

Natural hazards: typhoons can occur any time, but usually November to March; occasional tornadoes; low level of some of the islands make them sensitive to changes in sea level

Geography - note: 21 of the 33 islands are inhabited; Banaba (Ocean Island) in Kiribati is one of the three great phosphate rock islands in the Pacific Ocean – the others are Makatea in French Polynesia, and Nauru; Kiribati is the only country in the world to fall into all four hemispheres (northern, southern, eastern, and western)

PEOPLE AND SOCIETY

Population: *total:* 116,545
male: 56,364
female: 60,181 (2024 est.)
comparison rankings: female 189; male 190; total 189

Nationality: *noun:* I-Kiribati (singular and plural)
adjective: Kiribati

Ethnic groups: I-Kiribati 95.78%, I-Kiribati/mixed 3.8%, Tuvaluan 0.2%, other 1.7% (2020 est.)

Languages: Gilbertese, English (official)

Religions: Roman Catholic 58.9%, Kiribati Uniting Church 21.2%, Kiribati Protestant Church 8.4%, Church of Jesus Christ 5.6%, Seventh Day Adventist 2.1%, Baha'i 2.1%, other 1.7% (2020 est.)

Age structure: *0-14 years:* 26.8% (male 15,895/female 15,304)
15-64 years: 67.9% (male 38,046/female 41,059)
65 years and over: 5.4% (2024 est.) (male 2,423/female 3,818)

Dependency ratios: *total dependency ratio:* 66.4
youth dependency ratio: 60.2
elderly dependency ratio: 6.2
potential support ratio: 16.1 (2021 est.)

Median age: *total:* 27.3 years (2024 est.)
male: 26.4 years
female: 28.2 years
comparison ranking: total 160

Population growth rate: 1% (2024 est.)
comparison ranking: 91

Birth rate: 19.7 births/1,000 population (2024 est.)
comparison ranking: 70

Death rate: 6.9 deaths/1,000 population (2024 est.)
comparison ranking: 125

Net migration rate: -2.8 migrant(s)/1,000 population (2024 est.)
comparison ranking: 176

Population distribution: consists of three achipelagos spread out over an area roughly the size of India; the eastern Line Islands and central Phoenix Islands are sparsely populated, but the western Gilbert Islands are some of the most densely settled places on earth, with the main island of South Tarawa boasting a population density similar to Tokyo or Hong Kong

Urbanization: *urban population:* 57.8% of total population (2023)
rate of urbanization: 2.77% annual rate of change (2020-25 est.)

Major urban areas - population: 64,000 TARAWA (capital) (2018)

Sex ratio: *at birth:* 1.05 male(s)/female
0-14 years: 1.04 male(s)/female
15-64 years: 0.93 male(s)/female
65 years and over: 0.63 male(s)/female
total population: 0.94 male(s)/female (2024 est.)

Mother's mean age at first birth: 23.1 years (2009 est.)
note: data represents median age at first birth among women 25-29

Maternal mortality ratio: 76 deaths/100,000 live births (2020 est.)
comparison ranking: 79

Infant mortality rate: *total:* 31.5 deaths/1,000 live births (2024 est.)
male: 33.5 deaths/1,000 live births
female: 29.4 deaths/1,000 live births
comparison ranking: total 45

Life expectancy at birth: *total population:* 68.5 years (2024 est.)
male: 65.9 years
female: 71.3 years
comparison ranking: total population 188

Total fertility rate: 2.15 children born/woman (2024 est.)
comparison ranking: 91

Gross reproduction rate: 1.05 (2024 est.)

Contraceptive prevalence rate: 33.5% (2018/19)

Drinking water source: *improved: urban:* 97.2% of population
rural: 63.1% of population
total: 82% of population
unimproved: urban: 2.8% of population
rural: 36.9% of population
total: 18% of population (2020 est.)

Current health expenditure: 11.6% of GDP (2020)

Physician density: 0.2 physicians/1,000 population (2013)

Hospital bed density: 1.9 beds/1,000 population (2016)

Sanitation facility access: *improved: urban:* 75.4% of population
rural: 45.4% of population
total: 62.1% of population
unimproved: urban: 24.6% of population
rural: 54.6% of population
total: 37.9% of population (2020 est.)

Obesity - adult prevalence rate: 46% (2016)
comparison ranking: 9

Alcohol consumption per capita: *total:* 0.43 liters of pure alcohol (2019 est.)
beer: 0.26 liters of pure alcohol (2019 est.)
wine: 0 liters of pure alcohol (2019 est.)
spirits: 0.17 liters of pure alcohol (2019 est.)
other alcohols: 0 liters of pure alcohol (2019 est.)
comparison ranking: total 165

Tobacco use: *total:* 40.6% (2020 est.)
male: 53.9% (2020 est.)
female: 27.3% (2020 est.)
comparison ranking: total 3

Children under the age of 5 years underweight: 6.9% (2018/19)
comparison ranking: 67

Currently married women (ages 15-49): 67.6% (2023 est.)

Child marriage: *women married by age 15:* 2.4%
women married by age 18: 18.4%
men married by age 18: 8.6% (2019 est.)

Education expenditures: 12.4% of GDP (2019 est.)
comparison ranking: 3

ENVIRONMENT

Environment - current issues: heavy pollution in lagoon of south Tarawa atoll due to overcrowding mixed with traditional practices such as lagoon latrines and open-pit dumping; ground water at risk; potential for water shortages, disease; coastal erosion

Environment - international agreements: *party to:* Biodiversity, Climate Change, Climate Change-Kyoto Protocol, Climate Change-Paris Agreement, Comprehensive Nuclear Test Ban, Desertification, Hazardous Wastes, Law of the Sea, Marine Dumping-London Convention, Ozone Layer Protection, Ship Pollution, Wetlands, Whaling
signed, but not ratified: none of the selected agreements

Climate: tropical; marine, hot and humid, moderated by trade winds

Urbanization: *urban population:* 57.8% of total population (2023)
rate of urbanization: 2.77% annual rate of change (2020-25 est.)

Revenue from forest resources: 0.04% of GDP (2018 est.)
comparison ranking: 131

Revenue from coal: 0% of GDP (2018 est.)
comparison ranking: 169

Air pollutants: *particulate matter emissions:* 7.62 micrograms per cubic meter (2019 est.)
carbon dioxide emissions: 0.07 megatons (2016 est.)
methane emissions: 0.02 megatons (2020 est.)

Waste and recycling: *municipal solid waste generated annually:* 35,724 tons (2016 est.)

Total renewable water resources: 0 cubic meters (2017 est.)

GOVERNMENT

Country name: *conventional long form:* Republic of Kiribati
conventional short form: Kiribati
local long form: Republic of Kiribati
local short form: Kiribati
former: Gilbert Islands
etymology: the name is the local pronunciation of "Gilberts," the former designation of the islands; originally named after explorer Thomas GILBERT, who mapped many of the islands in 1788
note: pronounced keer-ree-bahss

Government type: presidential republic

Capital: *name:* Tarawa

geographic coordinates: 1 21 N, 173 02 E
time difference: UTC+12 (17 hours ahead of Washington, DC, during Standard Time)
time zone note: Kiribati has three time zones: the Gilbert Islands group at UTC+12, the Phoenix Islands at UTC+13, and the Line Islands at UTC+14
etymology: in Kiribati creation mythology, "tarawa" was what the spider Nareau named the land to distinguish it from "karawa" (the sky) and "marawa" (the ocean)

Administrative divisions: *3 geographical units:* Gilbert Islands, Line Islands, Phoenix Islands; note - there are no first-order administrative divisions, but there are 6 districts (Banaba, Central Gilberts, Line Islands, Northern Gilberts, Southern Gilberts, Tarawa) and 21 island councils - one for each of the inhabited islands (Abaiang, Abemama, Aranuka, Arorae, Banaba, Beru, Butaritari, Kanton, Kiritimati, Kuria, Maiana, Makin, Marakei, Nikunau, Nonouti, Onotoa, Tabiteuea, Tabuaeran, Tamana, Tarawa, Teraina)

Independence: 12 July 1979 (from the UK)

National holiday: Independence Day, 12 July (1979)

Legal system: English common law supplemented by customary law

Constitution: *history:* The Gilbert and Ellice Islands Order in Council 1915, The Gilbert Islands Order in Council 1975 (preindependence); latest promulgated 12 July 1979 (at independence)
amendments: proposed by the House of Assembly; passage requires two-thirds majority vote by the Assembly membership; passage of amendments affecting the constitutional section on amendment procedures and parts of the constitutional chapter on citizenship requires deferral of the proposal to the next Assembly meeting where approval is required by at least two-thirds majority vote of the Assembly membership and support of the nominated or elected Banaban member of the Assembly; amendments affecting the protection of fundamental rights and freedoms also requires approval by at least two-thirds majority in a referendum; amended several times, last in 2018

International law organization participation: has not submitted an ICJ jurisdiction declaration; non-party state to the ICCt

Citizenship: *citizenship by birth:* no
citizenship by descent only: at least one parent must be a native-born citizen of Kiribati
dual citizenship recognized: no
residency requirement for naturalization: 7 years

Suffrage: 18 years of age; universal

Executive branch: *chief of state:* President Taneti MAAMAU (since 11 March 2016)
head of government: President Taneti MAAMAU (since 11 March 2016)
cabinet: Cabinet appointed by the president from among House of Assembly members
elections/appointments: president directly elected by simple majority popular vote following nomination of candidates from among House of Assembly members for a 4-year term (eligible for 2 additional terms); election last held on 22 June 2020 (next to be held in 2024); vice president appointed by the president
election results: 2020:Taneti MAAMAU reelected president; percent of vote - Taneti MAAMAU (TKB) 59.3%, Banuera BERINA (BKM) 40.7%
note: the president is both chief of state and head of government

Legislative branch: *description:* unicameral House of Assembly or Maneaba Ni Maungatabu (45 seats; 44 members directly elected in single- and multi-seat constituencies by absolute majority vote in two rounds if needed, and 1 member appointed by the Rabi Council of Leaders - representing Banaba Island; members serve 4-year terms)
elections: first round held on 14 August 2024; second round held on 19 August 2024 (next to be held in 2028)
election results: percent of vote by party - NA; seats by party - 33 TKP, 8 BKM, 4 Independents; composition - 40 men, 5 women; percentage women 11% (as of September 2024)

Judicial branch: *highest court(s):* High Court (consists of a chief justice and other judges as prescribed by the president); note - the High Court has jurisdiction on constitutional issues
judge selection and term of office: chief justice appointed by the president on the advice of the cabinet in consultation with the Public Service Commission (PSC); other judges appointed by the president on the advice of the chief justice along with the PSC
subordinate courts: Court of Appeal; magistrates' courts

Political parties: Boutokaan Kiribati Moa Party (Supporting Kiribati First) or BKM
Tobwaan Kiribati Party (Embracing Kiribati) or TKP

International organization participation: ABEDA, ACP, ADB, AOSIS, C, FAO, IBRD, ICAO, ICRM, IDA, IFAD, IFC, IFRCS, ILO, IMF, IMO, IOC, ITU, ITUC (NGOs), OPCW, PIF, Sparteca, SPC, UN, UNCTAD, UNDP, UNESCO, UPU, WHO, WIPO, WMO

Diplomatic representation in the US: *chief of mission:* Ambassador Teburoro TITO (since 24 January 2018); note - also Permanent Representative to the UN
chancery: 685 Third Avenue, Suite 1109, New York, NY 10017
telephone: [1] (212) 867-3310
FAX: [1] (212) 867-3320
email address and website:
Kimission.newyork@mfa.gov.ki

Diplomatic representation from the US: *chief of mission:* Ambassador Marie DAMOUR (since 6 December 2022); note - Ambassador DAMOUR is based in the US Embassy in the Republic of Fiji and is accredited to Kiribati as well as Nauru, Tonga, and Tuvalu

Note: the US does not have an embassy in Kiribati but has announced its intention to open an embassy

Flag description: the upper half is red with a yellow frigatebird flying over a yellow rising sun, and the lower half is blue with three horizontal wavy white stripes to represent the Pacific ocean; the white stripes represent the three island groups - the Gilbert, Line, and Phoenix Islands; the 17 rays of the sun represent the 16 Gilbert Islands and Banaba (formerly Ocean Island); the frigatebird symbolizes authority and freedom

National symbol(s): frigatebird; national colors: red, white, blue, yellow

National anthem: *name:* "Teirake kaini Kiribati" (Stand Up, Kiribati)
lyrics/music: Urium Tamuera IOTEBA
note: adopted 1979

National heritage: *total World Heritage Sites:* 1 (natural)
selected World Heritage Site locales: Phoenix Islands Protected Area

ECONOMY

Economic overview: lower-middle income, Pacific island economy; environmentally fragile; sizable remittances; key phosphate mining fund; tourism and fishing industries; public sector-dominated economy; recent withdrawal from Pacific Islands Forum; ongoing constitutional crisis

Real GDP (purchasing power parity): $423.828 million (2023 est.)
$406.41 million (2022 est.)
$391.315 million (2021 est.)
note: data in 2021 dollars
comparison ranking: 215

Real GDP growth rate: 4.29% (2023 est.)
3.86% (2022 est.)
8.71% (2021 est.)
note: annual GDP % growth based on constant local currency
comparison ranking: 70

Real GDP per capita: $3,200 (2023 est.)
$3,100 (2022 est.)
$3,000 (2021 est.)
note: data in 2021 dollars
comparison ranking: 192

GDP (official exchange rate): $279.034 million (2023 est.)
note: data in current dollars at official exchange rate

Inflation rate (consumer prices): 2.05% (2021 est.)
2.55% (2020 est.)
-1.81% (2019 est.)
note: annual % change based on consumer prices
comparison ranking: 37

GDP - composition, by sector of origin: *agriculture:* 23% (2016 est.)
industry: 7% (2016 est.)
services: 70% (2016 est.)
comparison rankings: services 37; industry 207; agriculture 25

GDP - composition, by end use: *exports of goods and services:* 7.4% (2023 est.)
imports of goods and services: -92.5% (2023 est.)
note: figures may not total 100% due to rounding or gaps in data collection

Agricultural products: coconuts, bananas, vegetables, taro, tropical fruits, pork, chicken, nuts, eggs, pork offal (2022)
note: top ten agricultural products based on tonnage

Industries: fishing, handicrafts

Industrial production growth rate: 21.11% (2021 est.)
note: annual % change in industrial value added based on constant local currency
comparison ranking: 2

Youth unemployment rate (ages 15-24): *total:* 22.5% (2019 est.)
male: 21.2%
female: 24.6%
comparison ranking: total 54

Population below poverty line: 21.9% (2020 est.)
note: % of population with income below national poverty line

Gini Index coefficient - distribution of family income: 27.8 (2019 est.)
note: index (0-100) of income distribution; higher values represent greater inequality
comparison ranking: 138

Household income or consumption by percentage share: *lowest 10%:* 4% (2019 est.)
highest 10%: 22.9% (2019 est.)
note: % share of income accruing to lowest and highest 10% of population

Remittances: 5.38% of GDP (2023 est.)
10.48% of GDP (2022 est.)
4.62% of GDP (2021 est.)
note: personal transfers and compensation between resident and non-resident individuals/households/entities

Budget: *revenues:* $213.334 million (2022 est.)
expenditures: $221.12 million (2022 est.)
note: central government revenues (excluding grants) and expenses converted to US dollars at average official exchange rate for year indicated

Public debt: 26.3% of GDP (2017 est.)
comparison ranking: 174

Taxes and other revenues: 20.22% (of GDP) (2022 est.)
note: central government tax revenue as a % of GDP
comparison ranking: 84

Current account balance: -$6.46 million (2022 est.)
$20.251 million (2021 est.)
$71.279 million (2020 est.)
note: balance of payments - net trade and primary/secondary income in current dollars
comparison ranking: 83

Exports: $19.677 million (2022 est.)
$10.754 million (2021 est.)
$21.228 million (2020 est.)
note: balance of payments - exports of goods and services in current dollars
comparison ranking: 217

Exports - partners: Thailand 55%, Philippines 15%, Japan 10%, Indonesia 8%, South Korea 4% (2022)
note: top five export partners based on percentage share of exports

Exports - commodities: fish, ships, coconut oil, copra, raw sugar (2022)
note: top five export commodities based on value in dollars

Imports: $254.438 million (2022 est.)
$201.984 million (2021 est.)
$148.77 million (2020 est.)
note: balance of payments - imports of goods and services in current dollars
comparison ranking: 209

Imports - partners: Taiwan 25%, China 22%, Fiji 13%, Australia 9%, South Korea 7% (2022)
note: top five import partners based on percentage share of imports

Imports - commodities: ships, refined petroleum, rice, twine and rope, prepared meat (2022)
note: top five import commodities based on value in dollars

Exchange rates: Australian dollars (AUD) per US dollar -

Exchange rates: 1.505 (2023 est.)
1.442 (2022 est.)
1.331 (2021 est.)
1.453 (2020 est.)
1.439 (2019 est.)
note: the Australian dollar circulates as legal tender

ENERGY

Electricity access: *electrification - total population:* 94.4% (2022 est.)
electrification - urban areas: 86%
electrification - rural areas: 94.3% (2020 est.)

Electricity: *installed generating capacity:* 11,000 kW (2022 est.)
consumption: 26.225 million kWh (2022 est.)
transmission/distribution losses: 5 million kWh (2022 est.)
comparison rankings: transmission/distribution losses 9; consumption 207; installed generating capacity 207

Electricity generation sources: *fossil fuels:* 84.5% of total installed capacity (2022 est.)
solar: 15.5% of total installed capacity (2022 est.)

Petroleum: *refined petroleum consumption:* 500 bbl/day (2022 est.)

Carbon dioxide emissions: 78,000 metric tonnes of CO_2 (2022 est.)
from petroleum and other liquids: 78,000 metric tonnes of CO_2 (2022 est.)
comparison ranking: total emissions 210

Energy consumption per capita: 8.403 million Btu/person (2022 est.)
comparison ranking: 155

COMMUNICATIONS

Telephones - fixed lines: *total subscriptions:* 0 (2022 est.)
subscriptions per 100 inhabitants: (2022 est.) less than 1
comparison ranking: total subscriptions 223

Telephones - mobile cellular: *total subscriptions:* 64,000 (2022 est.)
subscriptions per 100 inhabitants: 49 (2022 est.)
comparison ranking: total subscriptions 202

Telecommunication systems: *general assessment:* generally good national and international service; wireline service available on Tarawa and Kiritimati (Christmas Island); connections to outer islands by HF/VHF radiotelephone; recently formed (mobile network operator) MNO is implementing the first phase of improvements with 3G and 4G upgrades on some islands; islands are connected to each other and the rest of the world via satellite; launch of Kacific-1 in December 2019 will improve telecommunication for Kiribati (2020)
domestic: fixed-line less than 1 per 100 and mobile-cellular approximately 42 per 100 subscriptions (2021)
international: country code - 686; landing point for the Southern Cross NEXT submarine cable system from Australia, 7 Pacific Ocean island countries to the US; satellite earth station - 1 Intelsat (Pacific Ocean) (2019)

Broadcast media: multi-channel TV packages provide access to Australian and US stations; 1 government-operated radio station broadcasts on AM, FM, and shortwave (2017)

Internet country code: .ki

Internet users: *total:* 70,200 (2021 est.)
percent of population: 54% (2021 est.)
comparison ranking: total 195

Broadband - fixed subscriptions: *total:* 185 (2020 est.)
subscriptions per 100 inhabitants: 0.2 (2020 est.)
comparison ranking: total 213

TRANSPORTATION

National air transport system: *number of registered air carriers:* 2 (2020)
inventory of registered aircraft operated by air carriers: 8
annual passenger traffic on registered air carriers: 66,567 (2018)

Civil aircraft registration country code prefix: T3

Airports: 21 (2024)
comparison ranking: 132

Roadways: *total:* 670 km (2017)
comparison ranking: total 192

Waterways: 5 km (2012) (small network of canals in Line Islands)
comparison ranking: 118

Merchant marine: *total:* 74 (2023)
by type: bulk carrier 2, general cargo 24, oil tanker 11, other 37
comparison ranking: total 104

Ports: *total ports:* 3 (2024)
large: 0
medium: 0
small: 0
very small: 3
ports with oil terminals: 0
key ports: Canton Island, English Harbor, Tarawa Atoll

MILITARY AND SECURITY

Military and security forces: no regular military forces; Kiribati Police and Prison Service (Ministry of Justice) (2024)

Military - note: Australia, NZ, and the US have provided security assistance; Kiribati has a "ship rider" agreement with the US, which allows local maritime law enforcement officers to embark on US Coast Guard (USCG) and US Navy (USN) vessels, including to board and search vessels suspected of violating laws or regulations within Kiribati's designated exclusive economic zone (EEZ) or on the high seas; ship rider agreements also enable USCG personnel and USN vessels with embarked USCG law enforcement personnel to work with host nations to protect critical regional resources (2024)

KOREA, NORTH

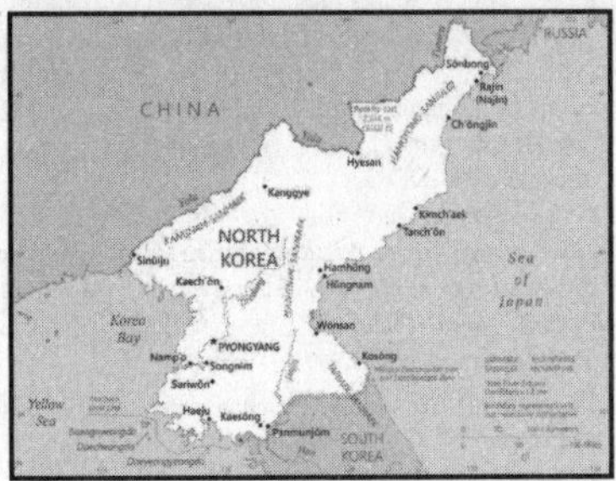

INTRODUCTION

Background: The first recorded kingdom (Choson) on the Korean Peninsula dates from approximately 2300 B.C. Over the subsequent centuries, three main kingdoms – Kogoryo, Paekche, and Silla – were established on the Peninsula. By the 5th century A.D., Kogoryo emerged as the most powerful, with control over much of the Peninsula and part of Manchuria (modern-day northeast China). However, Silla allied with the Chinese to create the first unified Korean state in 688. Following the collapse of Silla in the 9th century, Korea was unified under the Koryo (Goryeo; 918-1392) and the Chosen (Joseon; 1392-1910) dynasties. Korea became the object of intense imperialistic rivalry among the Chinese (its traditional benefactor), Japanese, and Russian empires in the latter half of the 19th and early 20th centuries. After the Sino-Japanese War (1894-95) and the Russo-Japanese War (1904-05), Korea was occupied by Imperial Japan. In 1910, Japan formally annexed the entire peninsula. After World War II, the northern half came under Soviet-sponsored communist control.

In 1948, North Korea (formally known as the Democratic People's Republic of Korea or DPRK) was founded under President KIM Il Sung, who consolidated power and cemented autocratic one-party rule under the Korean Worker's Party (KWP). North Korea failed to conquer UN-backed South Korea (formally the Republic of Korea or ROK) during the Korean War (1950-53), after which a demilitarized zone separated the two Koreas. KIM's authoritarian rule included tight control over North Korean citizens and the demonization of the Us as the central threat to North Korea's political and social system. In addition, he molded the country's economic, military, and political policies around the core objective of unifying Korea under Pyongyang's control. North Korea also declared a central ideology of *juche* ("self-reliance") as a check against outside influence, while continuing to rely heavily on China and the Soviet Union for economic support. KIM Il Sung's son, KIM Jong Il, was officially designated as his father's successor in 1980, and he assumed a growing political and managerial role until the elder KIM's death in 1994. Under KIM Jong Il's reign, North Korea continued developing nuclear weapons and ballistic missiles. KIM Jong Un was publicly unveiled as his father's successor in 2010. Following KIM Jong Il's death in 2011, KIM Jong Un quickly assumed power and has since occupied the regime's highest political and military posts.

After the end of Soviet aid in 1991, North Korea faced serious economic setbacks that exacerbated decades of economic mismanagement and resource misallocation. Since the mid-1990s, North Korea has faced chronic food shortages and economic stagnation. In recent years, the North's domestic agricultural production has improved but still falls far short of producing sufficient food for its population. Starting in 2002, North Korea began to tolerate semi-private markets but has made few other efforts to meet its goal of improving the overall standard of living. New economic development plans in the 2010s failed to meet government-mandated goals for key industrial sectors, food production, or overall economic performance. At the onset of the COVID-19 pandemic in 2020, North Korea instituted a nationwide lockdown that severely restricted its economy and international engagement. Since then, KIM has repeatedly expressed concerns with the regime's economic failures and food problems, but in 2021, he vowed to continue "self-reliant" policies and has reinvigorated his pursuit of greater regime control of the economy.

As of 2024, despite slowly renewing cross-border trade with China, North Korea remained one of the world's most isolated countries and one of Asia's poorest. In 2024, Pyongyang announced it was ending all economic cooperation with South Korea. The move followed earlier proclamations that it was scrapping a 2018 military pact with South Korea to de-escalate tensions along their militarized border, abandoning the country's decades-long pursuit of peaceful unification with South Korea, and designating the South as North Korea's "principal enemy."

GEOGRAPHY

Location: Eastern Asia, northern half of the Korean Peninsula bordering the Korea Bay and the Sea of Japan, between China and South Korea

Geographic coordinates: 40 00 N, 127 00 E

Map references: Asia

Area: *total:* 120,538 sq km
land: 120,408 sq km
water: 130 sq km
comparison ranking: total 99

Area - comparative: slightly larger than Virginia; slightly smaller than Mississippi

Land boundaries: *total:* 1,607 km
border countries (3): China 1,352 km; South Korea 237 km; Russia 18 km

Coastline: 2,495 km

Maritime claims: *territorial sea:* 12 nm
exclusive economic zone: 200 nm
note: military boundary line 50 nm in the Sea of Japan and the exclusive economic zone limit in the Yellow Sea where all foreign vessels and aircraft without permission are banned

Climate: temperate, with rainfall concentrated in summer; long, bitter winters

Terrain: mostly hills and mountains separated by deep, narrow valleys; wide coastal plains in west, discontinuous in east

Elevation: *highest point:* Paektu-san 2,744 m
lowest point: Sea of Japan 0 m
mean elevation: 600 m

Natural resources: coal, iron ore, limestone, magnesite, graphite, copper, zinc, lead, precious metals, hydropower

Land use: *agricultural land:* 21.8% (2018 est.)
arable land: 19.5% (2018 est.)
permanent crops: 1.9% (2018 est.)
permanent pasture: 0.4% (2018 est.)
forest: 46% (2018 est.)
other: 32.2% (2018 est.)

Irrigated land: 14,600 sq km (2012)

Population distribution: population concentrated in the plains and lowlands; least populated regions are the mountainous provinces adjacent to the Chinese border; largest concentrations are in the western provinces, particularly the municipal district of Pyongyang, and around Hungnam and Wonsan in the east

Natural hazards: late spring droughts often followed by severe flooding; occasional typhoons during the early fall
volcanism: P'aektu-san (2,744 m) (also known as Baitoushan, Baegdu, or Changbaishan), on the Chinese border, is considered historically active

Geography - note: strategic location bordering China, South Korea, and Russia; mountainous interior is isolated and sparsely populated

PEOPLE AND SOCIETY

Population: *total:* 26,298,666
male: 12,828,269
female: 13,470,397 (2024 est.)
comparison rankings: female 54; male 56; total 56

Nationality: *noun:* Korean(s)
adjective: Korean

Ethnic groups: racially homogeneous; there is a small Chinese community and a few ethnic Japanese

Languages: Korean
major-language sample(s):
월드 팩트북, 필수적인 기본 정보 제공처
(Korean)

Religions: traditionally Buddhist and Confucian, some Christian and syncretic Chondogyo (Religion of the Heavenly Way)
note: autonomous religious activities now almost nonexistent; government-sponsored religious groups exist to provide illusion of religious freedom

Age structure: *0-14 years:* 19.9% (male 2,673,822/female 2,548,775)
15-64 years: 68.9% (male 9,054,771/female 9,066,447)
65 years and over: 11.2% (2024 est.) (male 1,099,676/female 1,855,175)

Dependency ratios: *total dependency ratio:* 43.5
youth dependency ratio: 27.2
elderly dependency ratio: 16.3
potential support ratio: 6.1 (2021 est.)

Median age: *total:* 35.9 years (2024 est.)
male: 34.5 years
female: 37.4 years

comparison ranking: total 94

Population growth rate: 0.4% (2024 est.)
comparison ranking: 158

Birth rate: 13.2 births/1,000 population (2024 est.)
comparison ranking: 130

Death rate: 9.2 deaths/1,000 population (2024 est.)
comparison ranking: 55

Net migration rate: 0 migrant(s)/1,000 population (2024 est.)
comparison ranking: 91

Population distribution: population concentrated in the plains and lowlands; least populated regions are the mountainous provinces adjacent to the Chinese border; largest concentrations are in the western provinces, particularly the municipal district of Pyongyang, and around Hungnam and Wonsan in the east

Urbanization: *urban population:* 63.2% of total population (2023)
rate of urbanization: 0.85% annual rate of change (2020-25 est.)

Major urban areas - population: 3.158 million PYONGYANG (capital) (2023)

Sex ratio: *at birth:* 1.06 male(s)/female
0-14 years: 1.05 male(s)/female
15-64 years: 1 male(s)/female
65 years and over: 0.59 male(s)/female
total population: 0.95 male(s)/female (2024 est.)

Maternal mortality ratio: 107 deaths/100,000 live births (2020 est.)
comparison ranking: 66

Infant mortality rate: *total:* 15.4 deaths/1,000 live births (2024 est.)
male: 16.9 deaths/1,000 live births
female: 13.8 deaths/1,000 live births
comparison ranking: total 89

Life expectancy at birth: *total population:* 73.5 years (2024 est.)
male: 70.2 years
female: 77 years
comparison ranking: total population 150

Total fertility rate: 1.81 children born/woman (2024 est.)
comparison ranking: 138

Gross reproduction rate: 0.88 (2024 est.)

Contraceptive prevalence rate: 70.2% (2017)

Drinking water source: *improved: urban:* 97.8% of population
rural: 89.1% of population
total: 94.5% of population
unimproved: urban: 2.2% of population
rural: 10.9% of population
total: 5.5% of population (2020 est.)

Physician density: 3.68 physicians/1,000 population (2017)

Sanitation facility access: *improved: urban:* 92.7% of population
rural: 73.1% of population
total: 85.3% of population
unimproved: urban: 7.3% of population
rural: 26.9% of population
total: 14.7% of population (2020 est.)

Obesity - adult prevalence rate: 6.8% (2016)
comparison ranking: 163

Alcohol consumption per capita: *total:* 3.61 liters of pure alcohol (2019 est.)
beer: 0.12 liters of pure alcohol (2019 est.)
wine: 0 liters of pure alcohol (2019 est.)
spirits: 3.48 liters of pure alcohol (2019 est.)
other alcohols: 0 liters of pure alcohol (2019 est.)
comparison ranking: total 102

Tobacco use: *total:* 17.4% (2020 est.)
male: 34.8% (2020 est.)
female: 0% (2020 est.)
comparison ranking: total 98

Children under the age of 5 years underweight: 9.3% (2017)
comparison ranking: 60

Currently married women (ages 15-49): 69.7% (2023 est.)

Child marriage: *women married by age 18:* 0.1% (2017 est.)

Literacy: *definition:* age 15 and over can read and write
total population: 100%
male: 100%
female: 100% (2015)

School life expectancy (primary to tertiary education): *total:* 11 years
male: 11 years
female: 11 years (2015)

ENVIRONMENT

Environment - current issues: water pollution; inadequate supplies of potable water; waterborne disease; deforestation; soil erosion and degradation

Environment - international agreements: *party to:* Antarctic Treaty, Biodiversity, Climate Change, Climate Change-Kyoto Protocol, Climate Change-Paris Agreement, Desertification, Environmental Modification, Hazardous Wastes, Ozone Layer Protection, Ship Pollution, Wetlands
signed, but not ratified: Antarctic-Environmental Protection, Law of the Sea

Climate: temperate, with rainfall concentrated in summer; long, bitter winters

Urbanization: *urban population:* 63.2% of total population (2023)
rate of urbanization: 0.85% annual rate of change (2020-25 est.)

Food insecurity: *widespread lack of access: due to low food consumption levels, poor dietary diversity, and economic downturn* - a large portion of the population suffers from low levels of food consumption and very poor dietary diversity; the economic constraints, particularly resulting from the global impact of the COVID-19 pandemic, have increased the population's vulnerability to food insecurity; the food gap is estimated at about 860,000 mt, equivalent to approximately 2-3 months of food use, if this gap is not adequately covered through commercial imports and/or food aid, households could experience a harsh lean period (2022)

Air pollutants: *particulate matter emissions:* 41.46 micrograms per cubic meter (2019 est.)
carbon dioxide emissions: 28.28 megatons (2016 est.)
methane emissions: 18.68 megatons (2020 est.)

Total water withdrawal: *municipal:* 900 million cubic meters (2020 est.)
industrial: 1.15 billion cubic meters (2020 est.)
agricultural: 6.61 billion cubic meters (2020 est.)

Total renewable water resources: 77.15 billion cubic meters (2020 est.)

GOVERNMENT

Country name: *conventional long form:* Democratic People's Republic of Korea
conventional short form: North Korea
local long form: Choson-minjujuui-inmin-konghwaguk
local short form: Choson
abbreviation: DPRK
etymology: derived from the Chinese name for Goryeo, which was the Korean dynasty that united the peninsula in the 10th century A.D.; the North Korean name "Choson" means "[Land of the] Morning Calm"

Government type: dictatorship, single-party communist state

Capital: *name:* Pyongyang
geographic coordinates: 39 01 N, 125 45 E
time difference: UTC+9 (14 hours ahead of Washington, DC, during Standard Time)
time zone note: on 5 May 2018, North Korea reverted to UTC+9, the same time zone as South Korea
etymology: the name translates as "flat land" in Korean

Administrative divisions: 9 provinces (do, singular and plural) and 4 special administration cities (si, singular and plural)
provinces: Chagang, Hambuk (North Hamgyong), Hamnam (South Hamgyong), Hwangbuk (North Hwanghae), Hwangnam (South Hwanghae), Kangwon, P'yongbuk (North Pyongan), P'yongnam (South Pyongan), Ryanggang
special administration cities: Kaesong, Nampo, P'yongyang, Rason
note: P'yongyang is identified as a directly controlled city, while Kaesong, Nampo, and Rason are designated as special cities

Independence: 15 August 1945 (from Japan)

National holiday: Founding of the Democratic People's Republic of Korea (DPRK), 9 September (1948)

Legal system: civil law system based on the Prussian model; system influenced by Japanese traditions and Communist legal theory

Constitution: *history:* previous 1948, 1972; latest adopted 1998 (during KIM Jong-il era)
amendments: proposed by the Supreme People's Assembly (SPA); passage requires more than two-thirds majority vote of the total SPA membership; revised several times, last in 2023

International law organization participation: has not submitted an ICJ jurisdiction declaration; non-party state to the ICCt

Citizenship: *citizenship by birth:* no
citizenship by descent only: at least one parent must be a citizen of North Korea
dual citizenship recognized: no
residency requirement for naturalization: unknown

Suffrage: 17 years of age; universal and compulsory

Executive branch: *chief of state:* State Affairs Commission President KIM Jong Un (since 17 December 2011)
head of government: Supreme People's Assembly President CHOE Ryong Hae (since 11 April 2019)
cabinet: Cabinet or Naegak members appointed by the Supreme People's Assembly except the Minister of People's Armed Forces

elections/appointments: chief of state and premier indirectly elected by the Supreme People's Assembly; election last held on 10 March 2019 (next to be held in March 2024)
election results:
2019: KIM Jong Un reelected unopposed
note 1: KIM Jong Un's titles include general secretary of the Workers' Party of Korea (KWP), chairman of the KWP Central Military Commission, president of the State Affairs Commission, and supreme commander of the Korean People's Army
note 2: within the North Korean system, KIM Jong Un's role as chief of state is secondary to his role as general secretary of the Korean Workers' Party; chief of state is used to engage with non-communist countries such as the US; North Korea revised its constitution in 2019 to define "the Chairman of the State Affairs Commission" as "the supreme leader who represents the state"; functions as the commander-in-chief and chief executive; the specific titles associated with this office have changed multiple times under KIM's tenure, however, KIM Jong Un has been supreme leader since his father's death in 2011
note 3: the head of government functions as the technical head of state and performs related duties, such as receiving ambassadors' credentials

Legislative branch: *description:* unicameral Supreme People's Assembly (SPA) or Ch'oego Inmin Hoeui (687 seats; members directly elected by majority vote in 2 rounds if needed to serve 5-year terms)
elections: last held on 10 March 2019 (next to be held in 2024)
election results: percent of vote by party - NA; seats by party - KWP 607, KSDP 50, Chondoist Chongu Party 22, General Association of Korean Residents in Japan (Chongryon) 5, religious associations 3; ruling party approves a list of candidates who are elected without opposition; composition as of February 2024 - men 566, women 121, percentage women 17.6%
note: the SPA functions as a rubberstamp legislature; the Korean Workers' Party selects all candidates

Judicial branch: *highest court(s):* Supreme Court or Central Court (consists of one judge and 2 "People's Assessors" or, for some cases, 3 judges)
judge selection and term of office: judges elected by the Supreme People's Assembly for 5-year terms
subordinate courts: lower provincial courts as determined by the Supreme People's Assembly

Political parties: *major parties:*
Korean Workers' Party or KWP (formally known as Workers' Party of Korea)
General Association of Korean Residents in Japan (Chongryon; under KWP control)
minor parties:
Chondoist Chongu Party (under KWP control)
Social Democratic Party or KSDP (under KWP control)

International organization participation: ARF, FAO, G-77, ICAO, ICRM, IFAD, IFRCS, IHO, IMO, IMSO, IOC, IPU, ISO, ITSO, ITU, NAM, UN, UNCTAD, UNESCO, UNIDO, UNWTO, UPU, WFTU (NGOs), WHO, WIPO, WMO

Diplomatic representation in the US: none

Note: North Korea has a Permanent Mission to the UN in New York

Diplomatic representation from the US: *embassy:* none; the Swedish Embassy in Pyongyang represents the US as consular protecting power

Flag description: three horizontal bands of blue (top), red (triple width), and blue; the red band is edged in white; on the hoist side of the red band is a white disk with a red five-pointed star; the broad red band symbolizes revolutionary traditions; the narrow white bands stand for purity, strength, and dignity; the blue bands signify sovereignty, peace, and friendship; the red star represents socialism

National symbol(s): red star, chollima (winged horse); national colors: red, white, blue

National anthem: *name:* "Aegukka" (Patriotic Song)
lyrics/music: PAK Se Yong/KIM Won Gyun
note: adopted 1947; both North Korea's and South Korea's anthems share the same name and have a vaguely similar melody but have different lyrics; the North Korean anthem is also known as "Ach'imun pinnara" (Let Morning Shine)

National heritage: *total World Heritage Sites:* 2 (both cultural)
selected World Heritage Site locales: Koguryo Tombs Complex; Historic Monuments and Sites in Kaesong

ECONOMY

Economic overview: one of the last centrally planned economies; hard hit by COVID-19, crop failures, international sanctions, and isolationist policies; declining growth and trade, and heavily reliant on China; poor exchange rate stability; economic data integrity issues

Real GDP (purchasing power parity): $40 billion (2015 est.)
note: data are in 2015 dollars
North Korea does not publish reliable National Income Accounts data; the data shown are derived from purchasing power parity (PPP) GDP estimates that were made by Angus MADDISON in a study conducted for the OECD; his figure for 1999 was extrapolated to 2015 using estimated real growth rates for North Korea's GDP and an inflation factor based on the US GDP deflator; the results were rounded to the nearest $10 billion.
comparison ranking: 138

Real GDP growth rate: -1.1% (2015 est.)
1% (2014 est.)
comparison ranking: 202

Real GDP per capita: $1,700 (2015 est.)
$1,800 (2014 est.)
note: data are in 2015 US dollars
comparison ranking: 211

GDP (official exchange rate): $28 billion (2013 est.)

GDP - composition, by sector of origin: *agriculture:* 22.5% (2017 est.)
industry: 47.6% (2017 est.)
services: 29.9% (2017 est.)
comparison rankings: services 209; industry 15; agriculture 29

GDP - composition, by end use: *exports of goods and services:* 5.9% (2016 est.)
imports of goods and services: -11.1% (2016 est.)

Agricultural products: maize, rice, vegetables, apples, cabbages, fruits, sweet potatoes, potatoes, beans, soybeans (2022)
note: top ten agricultural products based on tonnage

Industries: military products; machine building, electric power, chemicals; mining (coal, iron ore, limestone, magnesite, graphite, copper, zinc, lead, and precious metals), metallurgy; textiles, food processing; tourism

Industrial production growth rate: 4.3% (2014 est.)
note: annual % change in industrial value added based on constant local currency
comparison ranking: 65

Labor force: 15.837 million (2023 est.)
note: number of people ages 15 or older who are employed or seeking work
comparison ranking: 39

Unemployment rate: 3% (2023 est.)
2.97% (2022 est.)
3.13% (2021 est.)
note: % of labor force seeking employment
comparison ranking: 45

Youth unemployment rate (ages 15-24): *total:* 7.1% (2023 est.)
male: 6.3% (2023 est.)
female: 7.8% (2023 est.)
note: % of labor force ages 15-24 seeking employment
comparison ranking: total 158

Exports: $222 million (2018)
$4.582 billion (2017 est.)
$2.908 billion (2015 est.)
comparison ranking: 201

Exports - partners: China 53%, Senegal 11%, Nigeria 6%, Poland 4%, Netherlands 3% (2022)
note: top five export partners based on percentage share of exports

Exports - commodities: tungsten ore, refined petroleum, iron alloys, electricity, molybdenum ore (2022)
note: top five export commodities based on value in dollars

Imports: $2.32 billion (2018 est.)
$3.86 billion (2016 est.)
comparison ranking: 170

Imports - partners: China 98%, Zimbabwe 0%, Netherlands 0%, India 0%, Colombia 0% (2022)
note: top five import partners based on percentage share of imports

Imports - commodities: plastic products, tobacco, soybean oil, rubber tires, packaged medicine (2022)
note: top five import commodities based on value in dollars

Exchange rates: North Korean won (KPW) per US dollar (average market rate)

Exchange rates: 135 (2017 est.)
130 (2016 est.)
130 (2015 est.)

ENERGY

Electricity access: *electrification - total population:* 54.7% (2022 est.)

Electricity: *installed generating capacity:* 8.277 million kW (2022 est.)
consumption: 18.24 billion kWh (2022 est.)
transmission/distribution losses: 4.033 billion kWh (2022 est.)
comparison rankings: transmission/distribution losses 154; consumption 77; installed generating capacity 71

Electricity generation sources: *fossil fuels:* 42.1% of total installed capacity (2022 est.)
solar: 0.3% of total installed capacity (2022 est.)
hydroelectricity: 57.6% of total installed capacity (2022 est.)

Coal: *production:* 21.747 million metric tons (2022 est.)
consumption: 21.747 million metric tons (2022 est.)
proven reserves: 10.6 billion metric tons (2022 est.)

Petroleum: *refined petroleum consumption:* 17,000 bbl/day (2022 est.)

Carbon dioxide emissions: 61.605 million metric tonnes of CO2 (2022 est.)
from coal and metallurgical coke: 58.987 million metric tonnes of CO2 (2022 est.)
from petroleum and other liquids: 2.617 million metric tonnes of CO2 (2022 est.)
comparison ranking: total emissions 54

Energy consumption per capita: 25.876 million Btu/person (2022 est.)
comparison ranking: 120

COMMUNICATIONS

Telephones - fixed lines: *total subscriptions:* 1.18 million (2021 est.)
subscriptions per 100 inhabitants: 5 (2021 est.)
comparison ranking: total subscriptions 69

Telephones - mobile cellular: *total subscriptions:* 6 million (2021 est.)
subscriptions per 100 inhabitants: 23 (2021 est.)
comparison ranking: total subscriptions 118

Telecommunication systems: *general assessment:* despite years of isolationism, economic underachievement, and international sanctions, North Korea has improved its telecommunications infrastructure in the last decade; Inconsistent electric power supply and likely difficulties procuring new hardware, however, present enduring obstacles to building reliable high-speed telecom networks; mobile phone use is estimated to have increased to nearly 25% of the polulation as of 2018, yet the high cost of ownership makes mobile communications inaccessible to North Koreans of lower socioeconomic status; strict regime censorship and monitoring of telecom systems in North Korea restricts users from legally contacting anyone outside the country or accessing the global Internet; for those citizens living close to China, it has been possible to illegally obtain Chinese handsets and SIM cards, and to connect to towers located just across the border; while this offers access to the outside world and at much lower prices than the state-controlled offerings, the risks are high including steep fines and the possibility of jail time; North Korea has been effective in building an IT sector and a nascent digital economy on the back of a concerted effort to grow a sizeable, well-trained IT workforce; but even here, its capabilities have been directed more towards nefarious activities such as cyber crime and hacking into foreign countries' computer and financial systems; North Korea's determination to maintain ideological control of its populace by isolating itself from the rest of the world will probably lead to tighter controls on communications inside and outside of the country (2023)
domestic: fixed-lines are approximately 5 per 100 and mobile-cellular 23 per 100 persons (2021)
international: country code - 850; satellite earth stations - 2 (1 Intelsat - Indian Ocean, 1 Russian - Indian Ocean region); other international connections through Moscow and Beijing

Broadcast media: no independent media; radios and TVs are pre-tuned to government stations; 4 government-owned TV stations; the Korean Workers' Party owns and operates the Korean Central Broadcasting Station, and the state-run Voice of Korea operates an external broadcast service; the government prohibits listening to and jams foreign broadcasts (2019)

Internet country code: .kp

TRANSPORTATION

National air transport system number of registered air carriers: 1 (2020)
inventory of registered aircraft operated by air carriers: 4
annual passenger traffic on registered air carriers: 103,560 (2018)
annual freight traffic on registered air carriers: 250,000 (2018) mt-km

Civil aircraft registration country code prefix: P

Airports: 83 (2024)
comparison ranking: 61

Heliports: 8 (2024)

Pipelines: 6 km oil (2013)

Railways: *total:* 7,435 km (2014)
standard gauge: 7,435 km (2014) 1.435-m gauge (5,400 km electrified)
note: figures are approximate; some narrow-gauge railway also exists
comparison ranking: total 29

Roadways: *total:* 25,554 km
paved: 724 km
unpaved: 24,830 km (2006)
comparison ranking: total 106

Waterways: 2,250 km (2011) (most navigable only by small craft)
comparison ranking: 40

Merchant marine: *total:* 264 (2023)
by type: bulk carrier 10, container ship 5, general cargo 191, oil tanker 29, other 29 comparison ranking: total 63

Ports: *total ports:* 10 (2024)
large: 0
medium: 0
small: 7
very small: 3
ports with oil terminals: 0
key ports: Ch'ongjin, Haeju Hang, Hungnam, Najin, Nampo, Senbong, Wonsan

MILITARY AND SECURITY

Military and security forces: Korean People's Army (KPA): KPA Ground Forces, KPA Navy, KPA Air Force and Air Defense Forces, KPA Strategic Forces (missile forces), KPA Special Forces (special operations forces); Security Guard Command (aka Bodyguard Command); Military Security Command

Ministry of Social Security (formerly Ministry of Public Security): Border Guard General Bureau, civil security forces; Ministry of State Security: internal security, investigations (2024)
note 1: North Korea employs a systematic and intentional overlap of powers and responsibilities among its multiple internal security organizations to prevent any potential subordinate consolidation of power and assure that each unit provided a check and balance on the other
note 2: Kim Jong Un is the KPA supreme commander, while operational control of the armed forces resides in the General Staff Department (GSD), which reports directly to Kim; the GSD maintains overall control of all military forces and is charged with turning Kim's directives into operational military orders; the Ministry of National Defense (MND) is responsible for administrative control of the military and external relations with foreign militaries
note 3: the Security Guard Command protects the Kim family, other senior leadership figures, and government facilities
note 4: the North also has a large paramilitary/militia force organized into the Worker Peasant Red Guard and Red Youth Guard; these organizations are present at all levels of government (province, county, ward) and are under the control of the Korean Workers' Party in peacetime, but revert to KPA control in crisis or war; they are often mobilized for domestic projects, such as road building and agricultural support

Military expenditures: defense spending is a regime priority; between 2010 and 2020, military expenditures accounted for an estimated 20-30% of North Korea's GDP annually; spending estimates ranged from $7 billion to $11 billion annually; in 2023, North Korea announced that it would spend nearly 16% of state expenditures on defense; North Korea in the 2010s and 2020s has increasingly relied on illicit activities — including cybercrime — to generate revenue for its weapons of mass destruction and ballistic missile programs to evade US and UN sanctions

Military and security service personnel strengths: information varies; estimated 1-1.2 million active-duty troops; estimated 200,000 internal security forces (2023)

Military equipment inventories and acquisitions: the KPA is equipped with older weapon systems originally acquired from the former Soviet Union, Russia, and China, and some domestically produced equipment; North Korea produces a diverse array of military hardware, including small arms, munitions, light armored vehicles, tanks, naval vessels and submarines, and some advanced weapons systems, such as cruise and ballistic missiles; most are copies or upgrades of older foreign supplied equipment (2024)
note: since 2006, the UN Security Council has passed nearly a dozen resolutions sanctioning North Korea for developing nuclear weapons and related activities, starting with Resolution 1718, which condemned the North's first nuclear test and placed sanctions on the supply of heavy weaponry (including tanks, armored combat vehicles, large caliber artillery, combat aircraft, attack helicopters, warships, and missiles and missile launchers), missile technology and material, and select luxury goods; additional resolutions have expanded to include all arms, including small arms and light weapons; the US and other countries have also imposed unilateral sanctions

Military service age and obligation: 17 years of age for compulsory military service for men and women; service obligation varies from 5-13 years; reportedly up to 10 years (7 for women) for those serving in combat units and 13 years (7 for women) for specialized combat units, such as missile forces (2024)
note: the bulk of the KPA is made up of conscripts; as many as 20% of North Korean males between the ages of 16 and 54 are in the military at a given time and possibly up to 30 percent of males between the ages of 18 and 27, not counting the reserves or paramilitary units; women comprise about 20% of the military by some estimates

Military deployments: approximately 10,000 Russia (2024)

Military - note: North Korea is one of the most militarized countries in the World, and the Korean People's Army (KPA) is one of the World's largest military forces; founded in 1948, the KPA's primary

responsibilities are national defense and protection of the Kim regime; it also provides considerable support to domestic economic projects such as agriculture production and infrastructure construction; North Korea views the US as its primary external security threat
in addition to the invasion of South Korea and the subsequent Korean War (1950-53), North Korea from the 1960s to the 1980s launched a considerable number of limited military and subversive actions against South Korea using special forces and terrorist tactics; including aggressive skirmishes along the DMZ, overt attempts to assassinate South Korean leaders, kidnappings, the bombing of an airliner, and a failed effort in 1968 to foment an insurrection and conduct a guerrilla war in the South with more than 100 seaborne commandos; from the 1990s until 2010, the North lost two submarines and a semi-submersible boat attempting to insert infiltrators into the South (1996, 1998) and provoked several engagements in the Northwest Islands area along the disputed Northern Limit Line (NLL), including naval skirmishes between patrol boats in 1999 and 2002, the torpedoing and sinking of a South Korean Navy corvette in 2010, and the bombardment of a South Korean military installation on Yeonpyeong Island, also in 2010; since 2010, further minor incidents continue to occur periodically along the DMZ, where both the KPA and the South Korean military maintain large numbers of troops; in late 2023 and early 2024, the Kim regime abandoned decades of official policy and declared that South Korea was not inhabited by "fellow countrymen" but a separate and "hostile" state that the North would "subjugate" if war broke out
North Korea also has a history of provocative regional military actions and posturing that are of major concern to the international community, including: proliferation of military-related items; ballistic and cruise missile development and testing; weapons of mass destruction (WMD) programs including tests of nuclear devices in 2006, 2009, 2013, 2016, and 2017; and large conventional armed forces; despite high-level efforts to ease tensions during the 2018-19 timeframe, including summits with the leaders of China, South Korea, and the US, North Korea has continued developing its WMD programs and, in recent years, issued statements condemning the US and vowing to further strengthen its military capabilities, including long range missiles and nuclear weapons (2024)

SPACE

Space agency/agencies: National Aerospace Development Administration (NADA; established 2013); predecessor organization, Korean Committee of Space Technology (KCST; established 1980s); State Space Development Bureau; Academy of Defense Science; Ministry of People's Armed Forces (2024)

Space launch site(s): Sohae Satellite Launching Station (aka Tongch'ang-dong Space Launch Center; North Pyongan province); Tonghae Satellite Launching Ground (North Hamgyong province) (2024)

Space program overview: North Korea's leader has emphasized the development of space capabilities, particularly space launch vehicles (SLVs) and remote sensing (RS) satellites; manufactures small satellites; manufactures and launches rockets/SLVs; note – the SLV program is closely related to North Korea's development of intercontinental ballistic missiles (2024)
note: further details about the key activities, programs, and milestones of the country's space program, as well as government spending estimates on the space sector, appear in the Space Programs reference guide

TRANSNATIONAL ISSUES

Refugees and internally displaced persons: IDPs: undetermined (2021)

Trafficking in persons: tier rating: Tier 3 — the government of North Korea does not fully meet the minimum standards for the elimination of trafficking and is not making significant efforts to do so, therefore, North Korea remained on Tier 3; for more details, go to: https://www.state.gov/reports/2024-trafficking-in-persons-report/north-korea/

Illicit drugs: at present there is insufficient information to determine the current level of involvement of government officials in the production or trafficking of illicit drugs, but for years, from the 1970s into the 2000s, citizens of North Korea , many of them diplomatic employees of the government, were apprehended abroad while trafficking in narcotics; police investigations in Taiwan, Japan and Australia during that period have linked North Korea to large illicit shipments of heroin and methamphetamine

KOREA, SOUTH

INTRODUCTION

Background: The first recorded kingdom (Choson) on the Korean Peninsula dates from approximately 2300 B.C. Over the subsequent centuries, three main kingdoms – Kogoryo, Baekche, and Silla – were established on the Peninsula. By the 5th century A.D., Kogoryo emerged as the most powerful, with control over much of the Peninsula and part of Manchuria (modern-day northeast China). However, Silla allied with the Chinese to create the first unified Korean state in 688. Following the collapse of Silla in the 9th century, Korea was unified under the Koryo (Goryeo; 918-1392) and the Chosen (Joseon; 1392-1910) dynasties.

Korea became the object of intense imperialistic rivalry among the Chinese (its traditional benefactor), Japanese, and Russian empires in the latter half of the 19th and early 20th centuries. After the Sino-Japanese War (1894-95) and the Russo-Japanese War (1904-1905), Korea was occupied by Imperial Japan. In 1910, Japan formally annexed the entire Peninsula. Korea regained its independence after Japan's surrender to the US and its allies in 1945. A US-supported democratic government (Republic of Korea, ROK) was set up in the southern half of the Korean Peninsula, while a communist-style government backed by the Soviet Union was installed in the north (North Korea; aka Democratic People's Republic of Korea, DPRK). During the Korean War (1950-53), US troops and UN forces fought alongside ROK soldiers to defend South Korea from a North Korean invasion supported by communist China and the Soviet Union. After the 1953 armistice, the two Koreas were separated by a demilitarized zone.

Syngman RHEE led the country as its first president from 1948 to 1960. PARK Chung-hee took over leadership of the country in a 1961 coup. During his controversial rule (1961-79), South Korea achieved rapid economic growth, with per capita income rising to roughly 17 times the level of North Korea by 1979. PARK was assassinated in 1979, and subsequent years were marked by political turmoil and continued military rule as the country's pro-democracy movement grew. South Korea held its first free presidential election under a revised democratic constitution in 1987, with former South Korean Army general ROH Tae-woo winning a close race. In 1993, KIM Young-sam became the first civilian president of South Korea's new democratic era. President KIM Dae-jung (1998-2003) won the Nobel Peace Prize in 2000 for his contributions to South Korean democracy and his "Sunshine Policy" of engagement with North Korea. President PARK Geun-hye, daughter of former South Korean President PARK Chung-hee, took office in 2013 as South Korea's first female leader. In 2016, the National Assembly passed an impeachment motion against PARK over her alleged involvement in a corruption and influence-peddling scandal, triggering an early presidential election in 2017 won by MOON Jae-in. In 2022, longtime prosecutor and political newcomer YOON Suk Yeol won the presidency by the slimmest margin in South Korean history.

Discord and tensions with North Korea, punctuated by North Korean military provocations, missile launches, and nuclear tests, have permeated inter-Korean relations for years. Relations remained strained, despite a period of respite in 2018-2019 ushered in by North Korea's participation in the 2018 Winter

Olympic and Paralympic Games in South Korea and high-level diplomatic meetings, including historic US-North Korea summits. In 2024, Pyongyang announced it was ending all economic cooperation with South Korea, a move that followed earlier proclamations that it was scrapping a 2018 military pact to de-escalate tensions along their militarized border, abandoning the country's decades-long pursuit of peaceful unification with South Korea, and designating the South as North Korea's "principal enemy."

GEOGRAPHY

Location: Eastern Asia, southern half of the Korean Peninsula bordering the Sea of Japan and the Yellow Sea

Geographic coordinates: 37 00 N, 127 30 E

Map references: Asia

Area: *total:* 99,720 sq km
land: 96,920 sq km
water: 2,800 sq km
comparison ranking: total 109

Area - comparative: slightly smaller than Pennsylvania; slightly larger than Indiana

Land boundaries: *total:* 237 km
border countries (1): North Korea 237 km

Coastline: 2,413 km

Maritime claims: *territorial sea:* 12 nm; between 3 nm and 12 nm in the Korea Strait
contiguous zone: 24 nm
exclusive economic zone: 200 nm
continental shelf: not specified

Climate: temperate, with rainfall heavier in summer than winter; cold winters

Terrain: mostly hills and mountains; wide coastal plains in west and south

Elevation: *highest point:* Halla-san 1,950 m
lowest point: Sea of Japan 0 m
mean elevation: 282 m

Natural resources: coal, tungsten, graphite, molybdenum, lead, hydropower potential

Land use: *agricultural land:* 18.1% (2018 est.)
arable land: 15.3% (2018 est.)
permanent crops: 2.2% (2018 est.)
permanent pasture: 0.6% (2018 est.)
forest: 63.9% (2018 est.)
other: 18% (2018 est.)

Irrigated land: 7,780 sq km (2012)

Population distribution: with approximately 70% of the country considered mountainous, the country's population is primarily concentrated in the lowland areas, where density is quite high; Gyeonggi Province in the northwest, which surrounds the capital of Seoul and contains the port of Incheon, is the most densely populated province; Gangwon in the northeast is the least populated

Natural hazards: occasional typhoons bring high winds and floods; low-level seismic activity common in southwest
volcanism: Halla (1,950 m) is considered historically active although it has not erupted in many centuries

Geography - note: strategic location on Korea Strait; about 3,000 mostly small and uninhabited islands lie off the western and southern coasts

PEOPLE AND SOCIETY

Population: *total:* 52,081,799
male: 26,119,111
female: 25,962,688 (2024 est.)
comparison rankings: female 28; male 28; total 28

Nationality: *noun:* Korean(s)
adjective: Korean

Ethnic groups: homogeneous

Languages: Korean, English
major-language sample(s):

월드 팩트북, 필수적인 기본 정보 제공처
(Korean)

Religions: Protestant 17%, Buddhist 16%, Catholic 6%, none 60% (2021 est.)
note: many people also carry on at least some Confucian traditions and practices

Age structure: *0-14 years:* 11.3% (male 3,024,508/female 2,873,523)
15-64 years: 69.4% (male 18,653,915/female 17,465,817)
65 years and over: 19.3% (2024 est.) (male 4,440,688/female 5,623,348)

Dependency ratios: *total dependency ratio:* 39.9
youth dependency ratio: 16.6
elderly dependency ratio: 23.3
potential support ratio: 4.3 (2021 est.)

Median age: *total:* 45.5 years (2024 est.)
male: 44 years
female: 47.3 years
comparison ranking: total 15

Population growth rate: 0.21% (2024 est.)
comparison ranking: 175

Birth rate: 7 births/1,000 population (2024 est.)
comparison ranking: 223

Death rate: 7.4 deaths/1,000 population (2024 est.)
comparison ranking: 105

Net migration rate: 2.6 migrant(s)/1,000 population (2024 est.)
comparison ranking: 43

Population distribution: with approximately 70% of the country considered mountainous, the country's population is primarily concentrated in the lowland areas, where density is quite high; Gyeonggi Province in the northwest, which surrounds the capital of Seoul and contains the port of Incheon, is the most densely populated province; Gangwon in the northeast is the least populated

Urbanization: *urban population:* 81.5% of total population (2023)
rate of urbanization: 0.31% annual rate of change (2020-25 est.)

Major urban areas - population: 9.988 million SEOUL (capital), 3.472 million Busan, 2.849 million Incheon, 2.181 million Daegu (Taegu), 1.577 million Daejon (Taejon), 1.529 million Gwangju (Kwangju) (2023)

Sex ratio: *at birth:* 1.05 male(s)/female
0-14 years: 1.05 male(s)/female
15-64 years: 1.07 male(s)/female
65 years and over: 0.79 male(s)/female
total population: 1.01 male(s)/female (2024 est.)

Mother's mean age at first birth: 32.2 years (2019 est.)

Maternal mortality ratio: 8 deaths/100,000 live births (2020 est.)
comparison ranking: 153

Infant mortality rate: *total:* 2.8 deaths/1,000 live births (2024 est.)
male: 3 deaths/1,000 live births
female: 2.6 deaths/1,000 live births
comparison ranking: total 212

Life expectancy at birth: *total population:* 83.4 years (2024 est.)
male: 80.3 years
female: 86.6 years
comparison ranking: total population 15

Total fertility rate: 1.12 children born/woman (2024 est.)
comparison ranking: 226

Gross reproduction rate: 0.55 (2024 est.)

Contraceptive prevalence rate: 82.3% (2018)
note: percent of women aged 20-49

Drinking water source: *improved:*
total: 99.9% of population
unimproved:
total: 0.1% of population (2020 est.)

Current health expenditure: 8.4% of GDP (2020)

Physician density: 2.48 physicians/1,000 population (2019)

Hospital bed density: 12.4 beds/1,000 population (2018)

Sanitation facility access: *total:* 99.9% of population
unimproved:
total: 0.1% of population (2020 est.)

Obesity - adult prevalence rate: 4.7% (2016)
comparison ranking: 184

Alcohol consumption per capita: *total:* 7.74 liters of pure alcohol (2019 est.)
beer: 1.72 liters of pure alcohol (2019 est.)
wine: 0.15 liters of pure alcohol (2019 est.)
spirits: 0.22 liters of pure alcohol (2019 est.)
other alcohols: 5.66 liters of pure alcohol (2019 est.)
comparison ranking: total 48

Tobacco use: *total:* 20.8% (2020 est.)
male: 35.7% (2020 est.)
female: 5.9% (2020 est.)
comparison ranking: total 82

Children under the age of 5 years underweight: 0.9% (2019/21)
comparison ranking: 118

Currently married women (ages 15-49): 52.9% (2023 est.)

Education expenditures: 4.7% of GDP (2019 est.)
comparison ranking: 90

Literacy: *total population:* 98.8%
male: 99.2%
female: 98.4%

School life expectancy (primary to tertiary education): *total:* 17 years
male: 17 years
female: 16 years (2020)

ENVIRONMENT

Environment - current issues: air pollution in large cities; acid rain; water pollution from the discharge of sewage and industrial effluents; drift net fishing; solid waste disposal; transboundary air pollution from China

Environment - international agreements: *party to:* Antarctic-Environmental Protection, Antarctic-Marine Living Resources, Antarctic Treaty, Biodiversity, Climate Change, Climate Change-Kyoto Protocol, Climate Change-Paris Agreement, Comprehensive Nuclear Test Ban, Desertification, Endangered Species, Environmental Modification,

Hazardous Wastes, Law of the Sea, Marine Dumping-London Convention, Marine Dumping-London Protocol, Nuclear Test Ban, Ozone Layer Protection, Ship Pollution, Tropical Timber 2006, Wetlands, Whaling
signed, but not ratified: none of the selected agreements

Climate: temperate, with rainfall heavier in summer than winter; cold winters

Urbanization: *urban population:* 81.5% of total population (2023)
rate of urbanization: 0.31% annual rate of change (2020-25 est.)

Revenue from forest resources: 0.01% of GDP (2018 est.)
comparison ranking: 148

Revenue from coal: 0% of GDP (2018 est.)
comparison ranking: 148

Air pollutants: *particulate matter emissions:* 24.04 micrograms per cubic meter (2019 est.)
carbon dioxide emissions: 620.3 megatons (2016 est.)
methane emissions: 30.28 megatons (2020 est.)

Waste and recycling: *municipal solid waste generated annually:* 18,218,975 tons (2014 est.)
municipal solid waste recycled annually: 10,567,006 tons (2014 est.)
percent of municipal solid waste recycled: 58% (2014 est.)

Total water withdrawal: *municipal:* 6.672 billion cubic meters (2020 est.)
industrial: 4.45 billion cubic meters (2020 est.)
agricultural: 15.96 billion cubic meters (2020 est.)

Total renewable water resources: 69.7 billion cubic meters (2020 est.)

Geoparks: *total global geoparks and regional networks:* 5
global geoparks and regional networks: Cheongsong; Hantangang; Jeju Island; Jeonbuk West Coast; Mudeungsan (2023)

GOVERNMENT

Country name: *conventional long form:* Republic of Korea
conventional short form: South Korea
local long form: Taehan-min'guk
local short form: Han'guk
abbreviation: ROK
etymology: derived from the Chinese name for Goryeo, which was the Korean dynasty that united the peninsula in the 10th century A.D.; the South Korean name "Han'guk" derives from the long form, "Taehan-min'guk," which is itself a derivation from "Daehan-je'guk," which means "the Great Empire of the Han"; "Han" refers to the "Sam'han" or the "Three Han Kingdoms" (Goguryeo, Baekje, and Silla from the Three Kingdoms Era, 1st-7th centuries A.D.)

Government type: presidential republic

Capital: *name:* Seoul; note - Sejong, located some 120 km (75 mi) south of Seoul, serves as an administrative capital for segments of the South Korean Government
geographic coordinates: 37 33 N, 126 59 E
time difference: UTC+9 (14 hours ahead of Washington, DC, during Standard Time)
etymology: the name originates from the Korean word meaning "capital city" and which is believed to be derived from Seorabeol, the name of the capital of the ancient Korean Kingdom of Silla

Administrative divisions: 9 provinces (do, singular and plural), 6 metropolitan cities (gwangyeoksi, singular and plural), 1 special city (teugbyeolsi), and 1 special self-governing city (teukbyeoljachisi)
provinces: Chungcheongbuk-do (North Chungcheong), Chungcheongnam-do (South Chungcheong), Gangwon-do, Gyeongsangbuk-do (North Gyeongsang), Gyeonggi-do, Gyeongsangnam-do (South Gyeongsang), Jeju-do (Jeju), Jeollabuk-do (North Jeolla), Jeollanam-do (South Jeolla)
metropolitan cities: Busan (Pusan), Daegu (Taegu), Daejeon (Taejon), Gwangju (Kwangju), Incheon (Inch'on), Ulsan
special city: Seoul
special self-governing city: Sejong

Independence: 15 August 1945 (from Japan)

National holiday: Liberation Day, 15 August (1945)

Legal system: mixed legal system combining European civil law, Anglo-American law, and Chinese classical thought

Constitution: *history:* several previous; latest passed by National Assembly 12 October 1987, approved in referendum 28 October 1987, effective 25 February 1988
amendments: proposed by the president or by majority support of the National Assembly membership; passage requires at least two-thirds majority vote by the Assembly membership, approval in a referendum by more than one half of the votes by more than one half of eligible voters, and promulgation by the president; amended several times, last in 1987

International law organization participation: has not submitted an ICJ jurisdiction declaration; accepts ICCt jurisdiction

Citizenship: *citizenship by birth:* no
citizenship by descent only: at least one parent must be a citizen of South Korea
dual citizenship recognized: no
residency requirement for naturalization: 5 years

Suffrage: 18 years of age; universal; note - the voting age was lowered from 19 to 18 beginning with the 2020 national election

Executive branch: *chief of state:* President YOON Suk Yeol (since 10 May 2022)
head of government: President YOON Suk Yeol (since 10 May 2022)
cabinet: State Council appointed by the president on the prime minister's recommendation
elections/appointments: president directly elected by simple majority popular vote for a single 5-year term; election last held on 9 March 2022 (next to be held in March 2027); prime minister appointed by president with consent of the National Assembly
election results:
2022: YOON Suk-yeol elected president; YOON Suk-yeol (PPP) 48.6%, LEE Jae-myung (DP) 47.8%; other 3.6%
2017: MOON Jae-in elected president; MOON Jae-in (DP) 41.1%, HONG Joon-pyo (Liberty Korea Party) 24%, AHN Cheol-soo (PP) 21.4%, YOO Seung-min (Bareun Party) 6.8%, SIM Sang-jung (Justice Party) 6.2%
note: the president is both chief of state and head of government; Prime Minister HAN Duck-soo (since 21 May 2022) serves as the principal executive assistant to the president, similar to the role of a vice president

Legislative branch: *description:* unicameral National Assembly or Gukhoe (300 seats; 253 members directly elected in single-seat constituencies by simple majority vote and 47 directly elected in a single national constituency by proportional representation vote; members serve 4-year terms)
elections: last held on 10 April 2024 (next to be held in April 2028)
election results: percent of vote by party/coalition (constituency) - Democratic Alliance 52.3%, PPP 45.7%, others 2%; percent of vote by party/coalition (proportional) - PPP 36.7%, Democratic Alliance 26.7%, Rebuilding Korea Party 24.3%, New Reform Party 3.6%, New Future Party 1.7%, others 7%; seats by party - Democratic Alliance 176 (DPK 169), PPP 108, Rebuilding Korea Party 12, New Reform Party 3, New Future Party 1; composition - men 240, women 60, percentage women 20%

Judicial branch: *highest court(s):* Supreme Court (consists of a chief justice and 13 justices); Constitutional Court (consists of a court head and 8 justices)
judge selection and term of office: Supreme Court chief justice appointed by the president with the consent of the National Assembly; other justices appointed by the president upon the recommendation of the chief justice and consent of the National Assembly; position of the chief justice is a 6-year nonrenewable term; other justices serve 6-year renewable terms; Constitutional Court justices appointed - 3 by the president, 3 by the National Assembly, and 3 by the Supreme Court chief justice; court head serves until retirement at age 70, while other justices serve 6-year renewable terms with mandatory retirement at age 65
subordinate courts: High Courts; District Courts; Branch Courts (organized under the District Courts); specialized courts for family and administrative issues

Political parties: Basic Income Party
Democratic Party of Korea or DPK
New Future Party
New Reform Party
Open Democratic Party or ODP
People Power Party or PPP
Progressive Party or Jinbo Party
Rebuilding Korea Party
Social Democratic Party
note: the Democratic Alliance Coalition consists of the DPK and the smaller Basic Income, Jinbo, Open Democratic, and Social Democratic parties, as well as two independents; for the 2024 election, the Basic Income Party, the ODP, and the Social Democratic Party formed the New Progressive Alliance

International organization participation: ADB, AfDB (nonregional member), APEC, Arctic Council (observer), ARF, ASEAN (dialogue partner), Australia Group, BIS, CABEI, CD, CICA, CP, EAS, EBRD, FAO, FATF, G-20, IADB, IAEA, IBRD, ICAO, ICC (national committees), ICCt, ICRM, IDA, IEA, IFAD, IFC, IFRCS, IHO, ILO, IMF, IMO, IMSO, Interpol, IOC, IOM, IPU, ISO, ITSO, ITU, ITUC (NGOs), LAIA (observer), MIGA, MINURSO, MINUSTAH, NEA, NSG, OAS (observer), OECD, OPCW, OSCE (partner), Pacific Alliance (observer), Paris Club (associate), PCA, PIF (partner), SAARC (observer), SICA (observer), UN, UNAMID, UNCTAD, UNESCO, UNHCR, UNHRC, UNIDO, UNIFIL, UNISFA, UNMIL, UNMISS, UNMOGIP, UNOCI, UNOOSA, UNWTO, UPU, Wassenaar Arrangement, WCO, WHO, WIPO, WMO, WTO, ZC

Diplomatic representation in the US: *chief of mission:* Ambassador CHO Hyundong (since 19 April 2023)
chancery: 2450 Massachusetts Avenue NW, Washington, DC 20008
telephone: [1] (202) 939-5600
FAX: [1] (202) 797-0595
email address and website:
generalusa@mofa.go.kr
https://overseas.mofa.go.kr/us-en/index.do
consulate(s) general: Anchorage (AK), Atlanta, Boston, Chicago, Dallas, Hagatna (Guam), Honolulu, Houston, Los Angeles, New York, San Francisco, Seattle, Philadelphia

Diplomatic representation from the US: *chief of mission:* Ambassador Philip S. GOLDBERG (since 29 July 2022)
embassy: 188 Sejong-daero, Jongno-gu, Seoul
mailing address: 9600 Seoul Place, Washington, DC 20521-9600
telephone: [82] (2) 397-4114
FAX: [82] (2) 397-4101
email address and website:
seoulinfoACS@state.gov
https://kr.usembassy.gov/
consulate(s): Busan

Flag description: white with a red (top) and blue yin-yang symbol in the center; there is a different black trigram from the ancient I Ching (Book of Changes) in each corner of the white field; the South Korean national flag is called Taegukki; white is a traditional Korean color and represents peace and purity; the blue section represents the negative cosmic forces of the yin, while the red symbolizes the opposite positive forces of the yang; each trigram (kwae) denotes one of the four universal elements, which together express the principle of movement and harmony

National symbol(s): taegeuk (yin yang symbol), Hibiscus syriacus (Rose of Sharon), Siberian tiger; national colors: red, white, blue, black

National anthem: *name:* "Aegukga" (Patriotic Song)
lyrics/music: YUN Ch'i-Ho or AN Ch'ang-Ho/ AHN Eaktay
note: adopted 1948, well-known by 1910; both North Korea's and South Korea's anthems share the same name and have a vaguely similar melody but have different lyrics

National heritage: *total World Heritage Sites:* 16 (14 cultural, 2 natural)
selected World Heritage Site locales: Jeju Volcanic Island and Lava Tubes (n); Changdeokgung Palace Complex (c); Jongmyo Shrine (c); Seokguram Grotto and Bulguksa Temple (c); Gochang, Hwasun, and Ganghwa Dolmen Sites (c); Gyeongju Historic Areas (c); Namhansanseong (c); Baekje Historic Areas (c); Sansa, Buddhist Mountain Monasteries in Korea (c); Royal Tombs of the Joseon Dynasty (c)

ECONOMY

Economic overview: strong export- and technology-oriented East Asian economy; manufacturing led by semiconductor and automotive industries; aging workforce; increased restraint in fiscal policy while maintaining industry support initiatives

Real GDP (purchasing power parity): $2.615 trillion (2023 est.)
$2.58 trillion (2022 est.)
$2.515 trillion (2021 est.)
note: data in 2021 dollars
comparison ranking: 14

Real GDP growth rate: 1.36% (2023 est.)
2.61% (2022 est.)
4.3% (2021 est.)
note: annual GDP % growth based on constant local currency
comparison ranking: 156

Real GDP per capita: $50,600 (2023 est.)
$49,900 (2022 est.)
$48,600 (2021 est.)
note: data in 2021 dollars
comparison ranking: 41

GDP (official exchange rate): $1.713 trillion (2023 est.)
note: data in current dollars at official exchange rate

Inflation rate (consumer prices): 3.59% (2023 est.)
5.09% (2022 est.)
2.5% (2021 est.)
note: annual % change based on consumer prices
comparison ranking: 70

Credit ratings: Fitch rating: AA- (2012)

Moody's rating: Aa2 (2015)

Standard & Poors rating: AA (2016)
note: The year refers to the year in which the current credit rating was first obtained.

GDP - composition, by sector of origin: *agriculture:* 1.6% (2023 est.)
industry: 31.6% (2023 est.)
services: 58.4% (2023 est.)
note: figures may not total 100% due to non-allocated consumption not captured in sector-reported data
comparison rankings: services 98; industry 58; agriculture 168

GDP - composition, by end use: *household consumption:* 48.9% (2023 est.)
government consumption: 18.9% (2023 est.)
investment in fixed capital: 32.2% (2023 est.)
exports of goods and services: 44% (2023 est.)
imports of goods and services: -43.9% (2023 est.)
note: figures may not total 100% due to rounding or gaps in data collection

Agricultural products: rice, vegetables, cabbages, milk, pork, onions, chicken, eggs, tangerines/mandarins, potatoes (2022)
note: top ten agricultural products based on tonnage

Industries: electronics, telecommunications, automobile production, chemicals, shipbuilding, steel

Industrial production growth rate: 1.14% (2023 est.)
note: annual % change in industrial value added based on constant local currency
comparison ranking: 137

Labor force: 29.611 million (2023 est.)
note: number of people ages 15 or older who are employed or seeking work
comparison ranking: 23

Unemployment rate: 2.64% (2023 est.)
2.86% (2022 est.)
3.64% (2021 est.)
note: % of labor force seeking employment
comparison ranking: 32

Youth unemployment rate (ages 15-24): *total:* 5.4% (2023 est.)
male: 5.4% (2023 est.)
female: 5.4% (2023 est.)
note: % of labor force ages 15-24 seeking employment
comparison ranking: total 176

Population below poverty line: 14.4% (2016 est.)

Gini Index coefficient - distribution of family income: 31.4 (2016 est.)
note: index (0-100) of income distribution; higher values represent greater inequality
comparison ranking: 116

Average household expenditures: *on food:* 12.1% of household expenditures (2022 est.)
on alcohol and tobacco: 1.8% of household expenditures (2022 est.)

Household income or consumption by percentage share: *lowest 10%:* 2.8% (2016 est.)
highest 10%: 24% (2016 est.)
note: % share of income accruing to lowest and highest 10% of population

Remittances: 0.45% of GDP (2023 est.)
0.47% of GDP (2022 est.)
0.43% of GDP (2021 est.)
note: personal transfers and compensation between resident and non-resident individuals/households/ entities

Budget: *revenues:* $542.275 billion (2022 est.)
expenditures: $563.156 billion (2022 est.)
note: central government revenues (excluding grants) and expenses converted to US dollars at average official exchange rate for year indicated

Public debt: 51.18% of GDP (2022 est.)
note: central government debt as a % of GDP
comparison ranking: 102

Taxes and other revenues: 18.44% (of GDP) (2022 est.)
note: central government tax revenue as a % of GDP
comparison ranking: 98

Current account balance: $35.488 billion (2023 est.)
$25.829 billion (2022 est.)
$85.228 billion (2021 est.)
note: balance of payments - net trade and primary/ secondary income in current dollars
comparison ranking: 17

Exports: $769.534 billion (2023 est.)
$825.961 billion (2022 est.)
$769.424 billion (2021 est.)
note: balance of payments - exports of goods and services in current dollars
comparison ranking: 11

Exports - partners: China 21%, US 16%, Vietnam 9%, Japan 4%, Hong Kong 4% (2022)
note: top five export partners based on percentage share of exports

Exports - commodities: integrated circuits, refined petroleum, cars, broadcasting equipment, ships (2022)
note: top five export commodities based on value in dollars

Imports: $761.102 billion (2023 est.)
$817.594 billion (2022 est.)
$698.98 billion (2021 est.)
note: balance of payments - imports of goods and services in current dollars
comparison ranking: 9

Imports - partners: China 23%, US 11%, Japan 8%, Australia 6%, Saudi Arabia 5% (2022)
note: top five import partners based on percentage share of imports

Imports - commodities: crude petroleum, integrated circuits, natural gas, coal, refined petroleum (2022)
note: top five import commodities based on value in dollars

Reserves of foreign exchange and gold: $420.93 billion (2023 est.)

$423.366 billion (2022 est.)
$463.281 billion (2021 est.)
note: holdings of gold (year-end prices)/foreign exchange/special drawing rights in current dollars
comparison ranking: 10

Exchange rates: South Korean won (KRW) per US dollar -

Exchange rates: 1,305.663 (2023 est.)
1,291.447 (2022 est.)
1,143.952 (2021 est.)
1,180.266 (2020 est.)
1,165.358 (2019 est.)

ENERGY

Electricity access: *electrification - total population:* 100% (2022 est.)

Electricity: *installed generating capacity:* 146.539 million kW (2022 est.)
consumption: 586.766 billion kWh (2022 est.)
transmission/distribution losses: 19.994 billion kWh (2022 est.)
comparison rankings: transmission/distribution losses 189; consumption 6; installed generating capacity 10

Electricity generation sources: *fossil fuels:* 65.1% of total installed capacity (2022 est.)
nuclear: 27.6% of total installed capacity (2022 est.)
solar: 4.6% of total installed capacity (2022 est.)
wind: 0.6% of total installed capacity (2022 est.)
hydroelectricity: 0.4% of total installed capacity (2022 est.)
tide and wave: 0.1% of total installed capacity (2022 est.)
biomass and waste: 1.7% of total installed capacity (2022 est.)

Nuclear energy: Number of operational nuclear reactors: 26 (2023)

Number of nuclear reactors under construction: 2 (2023)

Net capacity of operational nuclear reactors: 25.83GW (2023 est.)

Percent of total electricity production: 31.5% (2023 est.)

Number of nuclear reactors permanently shut down: 2 (2023)

Coal: *production:* 15.595 million metric tons (2022 est.)
consumption: 136.413 million metric tons (2022 est.)
exports: 29,000 metric tons (2022 est.)
imports: 121.272 million metric tons (2022 est.)
proven reserves: 326 million metric tons (2022 est.)

Petroleum: *total petroleum production:* 38,000 bbl/day (2023 est.)
refined petroleum consumption: 2.452 million bbl/day (2023 est.)

Natural gas: *production:* 55.127 million cubic meters (2021 est.)
consumption: 59.48 billion cubic meters (2022 est.)
exports: 93.639 million cubic meters (2022 est.)
imports: 62.622 billion cubic meters (2022 est.)
proven reserves: 7.079 billion cubic meters (2021 est.)

Carbon dioxide emissions: 643.456 million metric tonnes of CO_2 (2022 est.)
from coal and metallurgical coke: 268.556 million metric tonnes of CO_2 (2022 est.)
from petroleum and other liquids: 250.135 million metric tonnes of CO_2 (2022 est.)
from consumed natural gas: 124.765 million metric tonnes of CO_2 (2022 est.)
comparison ranking: total emissions 9

Energy consumption per capita: 235.518 million Btu/person (2022 est.)
comparison ranking: 13

COMMUNICATIONS

Telephones - fixed lines: *total subscriptions:* 22.81 million (2022 est.)
subscriptions per 100 inhabitants: 44 (2022 est.)
comparison ranking: total subscriptions 12

Telephones - mobile cellular: *total subscriptions:* 76.992 million (2022 est.)
subscriptions per 100 inhabitants: 149 (2022 est.)
comparison ranking: total subscriptions 23

Telecommunication systems: *general assessment:* South Korea is second only to Hong Kong in the world rankings of telecom market maturity; it is also on the leading edge of the latest telecom technology developments, including around 6G; with its highly urbanized, tech-savvy population, South Korea also enjoys very high communication levels across all segments – fixed-line telephony (44% at the start of 2022), fixed broadband (46%), mobile voice and data (144%), and mobile broadband (120%); the performance of the mobile sector is on a par with other developed markets around the region, but it's the wire line segment that allows South Korea to stand out from the crowd; this is partly a reflection of the large proportion of its population who live in apartment buildings (around 60%), making fiber and apartment LAN connections relatively easy and cost-effective to deploy; the government's Ultra Broadband convergence Network (UBcN) had aimed to reach 50% adoption by the end of 2022, but that target may be a few more years away; fixed-line teledensity is also at a very high level compared to most of the rest of the world, but it has been on a sharp decline from a rate of 60% ten years ago; on the mobile front, users have enthusiastically migrated from one generation of mobile platform to the next as each iteration becomes available; there also doesn't appear to be any great concern about there being a lack of demand for 5G in South Korea (when the country is already well supported by 4G networks), with 30% of all subscribers having already made the switch; part of the reason behind the rapid transition may be the subsidized handsets on offer from each of the MNOs and the MVNOs (2022)
domestic: fixed-line approximately 45 per 100 and mobile-cellular services 141 per 100 persons; rapid assimilation of a full range of telecommunications technologies leading to a boom in e-commerce (2021)
international: country code - 82; landing points for EAC-C2C, FEA, SeaMeWe-3, TPE, APCN-2, APG, FLAG North Asia Loop/REACH North Asia Loop, KJCN, NCP, and SJC2 submarine cables providing links throughout Asia, Australia, the Middle East, Africa, Europe, Southeast Asia and US; satellite earth stations - 66 (2019)

Broadcast media: multiple national TV networks with 2 of the 3 largest networks publicly operated; the largest privately owned network, Seoul Broadcasting Service (SBS), has ties with other commercial TV networks; cable and satellite TV subscription services available; publicly operated radio broadcast networks and many privately owned radio broadcasting networks, each with multiple affiliates, and independent local stations

Internet country code: .kr

Internet users: *total:* 50.96 million (2021 est.)
percent of population: 98% (2021 est.)
comparison ranking: total 20

Broadband - fixed subscriptions: *total:* 22,327,182 (2020 est.)
subscriptions per 100 inhabitants: 44 (2020 est.)
comparison ranking: total 10

TRANSPORTATION

National air transport system: *number of registered air carriers:* 14 (2020)
inventory of registered aircraft operated by air carriers: 424
annual passenger traffic on registered air carriers: 88,157,579 (2018)
annual freight traffic on registered air carriers: 11,929,560,000 (2018) mt-km

Civil aircraft registration country code prefix: HL

Airports: 89 (2024)
comparison ranking: 58

Heliports: 1,275 (2024)

Pipelines: 3,790 km gas, 16 km oil, 889 km refined products (2018)

Railways: *total:* 3,979 km (2016)
standard gauge: 3,979 km (2016) 1.435-m gauge (2,727 km electrified)
comparison ranking: total 48

Roadways: *total:* 100,428 km
paved: 92,795 km (includes 4,193 km of expressways)
unpaved: 7,633 km (2016)
comparison ranking: total 49

Waterways: 1,600 km (2011) (most navigable only by small craft)
comparison ranking: 52

Merchant marine: *total:* 2,149 (2023)
by type: bulk carrier 93, container ship 115, general cargo 362, oil tanker 219, other 1,360 comparison ranking: total 12

Ports: *total ports:* 15 (2024)
large: 2
medium: 5
small: 4
very small: 4
ports with oil terminals: 10
key ports: Busan, Gwangyang Hang, Inchon, Masan, Mokpo, Pyeongtaek Hang, Ulsan

MILITARY AND SECURITY

Military and security forces: Armed Forces of the Republic of Korea: Republic of Korea Army (ROKA), Republic of Korea Navy (ROKN, includes Marine Corps, ROKMC), Republic of Korea Air Force (ROKAF)

Ministry of Maritime Affairs and Fisheries: Korea Coast Guard; Ministry of Interior and Safety: Korean National Police Agency (2023)
note 1: the military reserves include Mobilization Reserve Forces (First Combat Forces) and Homeland Defense Forces (Regional Combat Forces)

Military expenditures: 2.7% of GDP (2023 est.)
2.6% of GDP (2022)
2.6% of GDP (2021)
2.6% of GDP (2020)

2.7% of GDP (2019)
comparison ranking: 41

Military and security service personnel strengths: approximately 500,000 active-duty personnel (365,000 Army; 70,000 Navy, including about 30,000 Marines; 65,000 Air Force) (2023)

Military equipment inventories and acquisitions: the South Korean military is equipped with a mix of domestically produced and imported weapons systems; South Korea has a robust defense industry and production includes armored fighting vehicles, artillery, aircraft, naval ships, and missiles; its weapons are designed to be compatible with US and NATO systems; in recent years the top foreign weapons supplier has been the US, and some domestically produced systems are built under US license (2024)

Military service age and obligation: 18-35 years of age for compulsory military service for all men; minimum conscript service obligation varies by service - 18 months (Army, Marines, auxiliary police), 20 months (Navy, conscripted firefighters), 21 months (Air Force, social service), 36 months for alternative service; 18-29 years of age for voluntary military service for men and women (2024)
note 1: women, in service since 1950, are able to serve in all branches and as of 2024 more than 15,000 served in the armed forces
note 2: the military brings on over 200,000 conscripts each year

Military deployments: 250 Lebanon (UNIFIL); 275 South Sudan (UNMISS); 170 United Arab Emirates; note - since 2009, South Korea has kept a naval flotilla with approximately 300 personnel in the waters off of the Horn of Africa and the Arabian Peninsula (2024)

Military - note: the South Korean military is primarily focused on the threat from North Korea; it also deploys abroad for multinational missions, including peacekeeping and other security operations
South Korea's primary defense partner is the US, and the 1953 US-South Korea Mutual Defense Treaty is a cornerstone of the country's national security; the Treaty committed the US to provide assistance in the event of an attack and gave the US permission to station land, air, and sea forces in and about the territory of South Korea as determined by mutual agreement; the US maintains approximately 28,000 military personnel in the country and conducts bilateral exercises with the South Korean military; South Korea has Major Non-NATO Ally (MNNA) status with the US, a designation under US law that provides foreign partners with certain benefits in the areas of defense trade and security cooperation; the South Korean military has assisted the US in conflicts in Afghanistan (5,000 troops; 2001-2014), Iraq (20,000 troops; 2003-2008), and Vietnam (325,000 troops; 1964-1973)
in 2016, South Korea concluded an agreement with the EU for participation in EU Common Security and Defense Policy (CSDP) missions and operations, such as the EU Naval Force Somalia – Operation Atalanta, which protects maritime shipping and conducts counter-piracy operations off the coast of East Africa
South Korea has been engaged with NATO through dialogue and security cooperation since 2005 and is considered by NATO to be a global partner; in 2022, South Korea established its Mission to NATO to further institutionalize its cooperative relationship; it has participated in NATO-led missions and exercises, including in Afghanistan as part of the NATO-led International Security Assistance Force, 2010-2013; it has also cooperated with NATO in countering the threat of piracy in the Gulf of Aden by providing naval vessels as escorts
in addition to the invasion of South Korea and the subsequent Korean War (1950-53), North Korea from the 1960s to the 1980s launched a considerable number of limited military and subversive actions against South Korea using special forces and terrorist tactics; including aggressive skirmishes along the DMZ, overt attempts to assassinate South Korean leaders, kidnappings, the bombing of an airliner, and a failed effort in 1968 to foment an insurrection and conduct a guerrilla war in the South with more than 100 seaborne commandos; from the 1990s until 2010, the North lost two submarines and a semi-submersible boat attempting to insert infiltrators into the South (1996, 1998) and provoked several engagements in the Northwest Islands area along the disputed Northern Limit Line (NLL), including naval skirmishes between patrol boats in 1999 and 2002, the torpedoing and sinking of a South Korean corvette, the *Cheonan*, in 2010, and the bombardment of a South Korean Marine Corps installation on Yeonpyeong Island, also in 2010; since 2010, further minor incidents continue to occur periodically along the DMZ, where both the North and the South Korean militaries maintain large numbers of troops; ; in late 2023 and early 2024, the Kim regime abandoned decades of official policy and declared that South Korea was not inhabited by "fellow countrymen" but a separate and "hostile" state that the North would "subjugate" if war broke out (2024)

SPACE

Space agency/agencies: Korea AeroSpace Administration (KASA; established 2024); Korea Aerospace Research Institute (KARI; established 1989 and previously acted as South Korea's space agency); Korea Advanced Institute of Science and Technology (KAIST); Korean Astronomy and Space Science Institute (KASI; funded by the South Korean Government) (2024)
note 1: the South Korean space program works closely with the Agency for Defense Development (ADD), a national agency for research and development in defense technology established in 1970
note 2: in January 2022, the South Korean military announced the formation of a space branch under its Joint Chiefs of Staff to coordinate the development of space and space-enabled capabilities across the Army, Navy and Air Force

Space launch site(s): Naro Space Center (South Jeolla province) (2024)

Space program overview: has a growing and ambitious space program focused on developing satellites, satellite/space launch vehicles (SLVs), and interplanetary probes; has a national space strategy; manufacturers and operates satellites, including those with communications, remote sensing (RS), scientific, and multipurpose capabilities; manufactures and launches SLVs; developing interplanetary space vehicles, including orbital probes and landers; participates in international space programs and has relations with an array of foreign space agencies and industries, including those of Australia, the European Space Agency (ESA) and its member states (particularly France, Germany, Italy, Spain, UK), India, Israel, Japan, Peru, Russia, UAE, and especially the US; has a robust and growing commercial space industry that works closely with government space program in the development of satellites and space launch capabilities; the South Korean Government has said it aims to capture 10% of the global space market by 2045 (2024)
note: further details about the key activities, programs, and milestones of the country's space program, as well as government spending estimates on the space sector, appear in the Space Programs reference guide

TRANSNATIONAL ISSUES

Refugees and internally displaced persons: *stateless persons:* 202 (2022)

Illicit drugs: precursor chemicals used for illicit drugs, such as acetic anhydride, pseudoephedrine, and ephedrine, imported from the United States, Japan, India, and China and then either resold within South Korea or smuggled into other countries

KOSOVO

INTRODUCTION

Background: The Ottoman Empire took control of Kosovo in 1389 after defeating Serbian forces. Large numbers of Turks and Albanians moved to the region, and by the end of the 19th century, Albanians had replaced Serbs as the majority ethnic group in Kosovo. Serbia reacquired control of Kosovo during the First Balkan War of 1912, and after World War II, Kosovo became an autonomous province of Serbia in the Socialist Federal Republic of Yugoslavia (SFRY). Increasing Albanian nationalism in the 1980s led to riots and calls for Kosovo's independence, but in 1989, Belgrade – which has in turn served as the capital of Serbia and Yugoslavia – revoked Kosovo's autonomous status. When the SFRY broke up in 1991, Kosovo Albanian leaders organized an independence referendum, and Belgrade's repressive response led to an insurgency. Kosovo remained part of Serbia, which joined with Montenegro to declare a new Federal Republic of Yugoslavia (FRY) in 1992.

In 1998, Belgrade launched a brutal counterinsurgency campaign, with some 800,000 ethnic Albanians expelled from their homes in Kosovo. After international mediation failed, a NATO military operation began in March 1999 and forced Belgrade to withdraw its forces from Kosovo.

UN Security Council Resolution 1244 (1999) placed Kosovo under the temporary control of the UN Interim Administration Mission in Kosovo (UNMIK). Negotiations in 2006-07 ended without agreement between Serbia and Kosovo, though the UN issued a comprehensive report that endorsed independence. On 17 February 2008, the Kosovo Assembly declared Kosovo independent.

Serbia continues to reject Kosovo's independence, but the two countries began EU-facilitated discussions in 2013 to normalize relations, which resulted in several agreements. Additional agreements were reached in 2015 and 2023, but implementation remains incomplete. In 2022, Kosovo formally applied for membership in the EU, which is contingent on fulfillment of accession criteria, and the Council of Europe. Kosovo is also seeking UN and NATO memberships.

GEOGRAPHY

Location: Southeastern Europe, between Serbia and Macedonia

Geographic coordinates: 42 35 N, 21 00 E

Map references: Europe

Area: *total:* 10,887 sq km
land: 10,887 sq km
water: 0 sq km
comparison ranking: total 167

Area - comparative: slightly larger than Delaware

Land boundaries: *total:* 714 km
border countries (4): Albania 112 km; North Macedonia 160 km; Montenegro 76 km; Serbia 366 km

Coastline: 0 km (landlocked)

Maritime claims: none (landlocked)

Climate: influenced by continental air masses resulting in relatively cold winters with heavy snowfall and hot, dry summers and autumns; Mediterranean and alpine influences create regional variation; maximum rainfall between October and December

Terrain: flat fluvial basin at an elevation of 400-700 m above sea level surrounded by several high mountain ranges with elevations of 2,000 to 2,500 m

Elevation: *highest point:* Gjeravica/Deravica 2,656 m
lowest point: Drini i Bardhe/Beli Drim (located on the border with Albania) 297 m
mean elevation: 450 m

Natural resources: nickel, lead, zinc, magnesium, lignite, kaolin, chrome, bauxite

Land use: *agricultural land:* 52.8% (2018 est.)
arable land: 27.4% (2018 est.)
permanent crops: 1.9% (2018 est.)
permanent pasture: 23.5% (2018 est.)
forest: 41.7% (2018 est.)
other: 5.5% (2018 est.)

Irrigated land: NA

Major watersheds (area sq km): Atlantic Ocean drainage: *(Black Sea)* Danube (795,656 sq km)

Population distribution: population clusters exist throughout the country, the largest being in the east in and around the capital of Pristina

Geography - note: *the 41-km long Nerodimka River divides into two branches, each of which flows into a different sea:* the northern branch flows into the Sitnica River, which via the Ibar, Morava, and Danube Rivers ultimately flows into the Black Sea; the southern branch flows via the Lepenac and Vardar Rivers into the Aegean Sea

PEOPLE AND SOCIETY

Population: *total:* 1,977,093
male: 1,017,992
female: 959,101 (2024 est.)
comparison rankings: female 152; male 152; total 152

Nationality: *noun:* Kosovan
adjective: Kosovan
note: Kosovo, a neutral term, is sometimes also used as a noun or adjective as in Kosovo Albanian, Kosovo Serb, Kosovo minority, or Kosovo citizen

Ethnic groups: Albanians 92.9%, Bosniaks 1.6%, Serbs 1.5%, Turk 1.1%, Ashkali 0.9%, Egyptian 0.7%, Gorani 0.6%, Romani 0.5%, other/unspecified 0.2% (2011 est.)
note: these estimates may under-represent Serb, Romani, and some other ethnic minorities because they are based on the 2011 Kosovo national census, which excluded northern Kosovo (a largely Serb-inhabited region) and was partially boycotted by Serb and Romani communities in southern Kosovo

Languages: Albanian (official) 94.5%, Bosnian 1.7%, Serbian (official) 1.6%, Turkish 1.1%, other 0.9% (includes Romani), unspecified 0.1% (2011 est.)
major-language sample(s): Libri i fakteve boterore, burimi i pazevendesueshem per informacione elementare (Albanian)
Knjiga svetskih činjenica, neophodan izvor osnovnih informacija. (Serbian)
note: these estimates may under-represent Serb, Romani, and other ethnic minority languages because they are based on the 2011 Kosovo national census, which excluded northern Kosovo (a largely Serb-inhabited region) and was partially boycotted by Serb and Romani communities in southern Kosovo

Religions: Muslim 95.6%, Roman Catholic 2.2%, Orthodox 1.5%, other 0.1%, none 0.1%, unspecified 0.6% (2011 est.)
note: these estimates may under-represent Serb, Romani, and some other ethnic minorities because they are based on the 2011 Kosovo national census, which excluded northern Kosovo (a largely Serb-inhabited region) and was partially boycotted by Serb and Romani communities in southern Kosovo

Age structure: *0-14 years:* 22.7% (male 233,010/female 216,304)
15-64 years: 68.9% (male 712,403/female 649,932)
65 years and over: 8.4% (2024 est.) (male 72,579/female 92,865)

Dependency ratios: *total dependency ratio:* 46.9
youth dependency ratio: 32.3
elderly dependency ratio: 14.6
potential support ratio: 6.9 (2021)

Median age: *total:* 32 years (2024 est.)
male: 31.7 years
female: 32.4 years
comparison ranking: total 119

Population growth rate: 0.68% (2024 est.)
comparison ranking: 130

Birth rate: 14.4 births/1,000 population (2024 est.)
comparison ranking: 117

Death rate: 7.2 deaths/1,000 population (2024 est.)
comparison ranking: 112

Net migration rate: -0.4 migrant(s)/1,000 population (2024 est.)
comparison ranking: 119

Population distribution: population clusters exist throughout the country, the largest being in the east in and around the capital of Pristina

Major urban areas - population: 218,782 PRISTINA (capital) (2020)

Sex ratio: *at birth:* 1.08 male(s)/female
0-14 years: 1.08 male(s)/female
15-64 years: 1.1 male(s)/female
65 years and over: 0.78 male(s)/female
total population: 1.06 male(s)/female (2024 est.)

Infant mortality rate: *total:* 22.9 deaths/1,000 live births (2024 est.)
male: 24.2 deaths/1,000 live births
female: 21.5 deaths/1,000 live births
comparison ranking: total 66

Life expectancy at birth: *total population:* 73.1 years (2024 est.)
male: 71 years
female: 75.5 years
comparison ranking: total population 153

Total fertility rate: 1.87 children born/woman (2024 est.)
comparison ranking: 129

Gross reproduction rate: 0.9 (2024 est.)

ENVIRONMENT

Environment - current issues: air pollution (pollution from power plants and nearby lignite mines take a toll on people's health); water scarcity and pollution; land degradation

Climate: influenced by continental air masses resulting in relatively cold winters with heavy snowfall and hot, dry summers and autumns; Mediterranean and alpine influences create regional variation; maximum rainfall between October and December

Revenue from forest resources: 0% of GDP (2018 est.)
comparison ranking: 165

Revenue from coal: 0.31% of GDP (2018 est.)
comparison ranking: 18

Air pollutants: *carbon dioxide emissions:* 8.94 megatons (2016 est.)
methane emissions: 0.54 megatons (2020 est.)

Waste and recycling: *municipal solid waste generated annually:* 319,000 tons (2015 est.)

Major watersheds (area sq km): Atlantic Ocean drainage: *(Black Sea)* Danube (795,656 sq km)

GOVERNMENT

Country name: *conventional long form:* Republic of Kosovo
conventional short form: Kosovo
local long form: Republika e Kosoves (Albanian)/ Republika Kosovo (Serbian)
local short form: Kosove (Albanian)/ Kosovo (Serbian)
etymology: name derives from the Serbian "kos" meaning "blackbird," an ellipsis (linguistic omission) for "kosove polje" or "field of the blackbirds"

Government type: parliamentary republic

Capital: *name:* Pristina (Prishtine, Prishtina)
geographic coordinates: 42 40 N, 21 10 E
time difference: UTC+1 (6 hours ahead of Washington, DC, during Standard Time)
daylight saving time: +1hr, begins last Sunday in March; ends last Sunday in October
etymology: the name may derive from a Proto-Slavic word reconstructed as "pryshchina," meaning "spring (of water)"

Administrative divisions: 38 municipalities (komunat, singular - komuna (Albanian); opstine, singular - opstina (Serbian)); Decan (Decani), Dragash (Dragas), Ferizaj (Urosevac), Fushe Kosove (Kosovo Polje), Gjakove (Dakovica), Gjilan (Gnjilane), Gllogovc (Glogovac), Gracanice (Gracanica), Hani i Elezit (Deneral Jankovic), Istog (Istok), Junik, Kacanik, Kamenice (Kamenica), Kline (Klina), Kllokot (Klokot), Leposaviq (Leposavic), Lipjan (Lipljan), Malisheve (Malisevo), Mamushe (Mamusa), Mitrovice e Jugut (Juzna Mitrovica) [South Mitrovica], Mitrovice e Veriut (Severna Mitrovica) [North Mitrovica], Novoberde (Novo Brdo), Obiliq (Obilic), Partesh (Partes), Peje (Pec), Podujeve (Podujevo), Prishtine (Pristina), Prizren, Rahovec (Orahovac), Ranillug (Ranilug), Shterpce (Strpce), Shtime (Stimlje), Skenderaj (Srbica), Suhareke (Suva Reka), Viti (Vitina), Vushtrri (Vucitrn), Zubin Potok, Zvecan

Independence: 17 February 2008 (from Serbia)

National holiday: Independence Day, 17 February (2008)

Legal system: civil law system; note - the European Union Rule of Law Mission (EULEX) retained limited executive powers within the Kosovo judiciary for complex cases from 2008 to 2018

Constitution: *history:* previous 1974, 1990; latest (postindependence) draft finalized 2 April 2008, signed 7 April 2008, ratified 9 April 2008, entered into force 15 June 2008; note - amendment 24, passed by the Assembly in August 2015, established the Kosovo Relocated Specialist Institution, referred to as the Kosovo Specialist Chamber or "Specialist Court," to try war crimes, crimes against humanity, and other crimes under Kosovo law committed during and immediately after the Kosovo War (1998-2000)
amendments: proposed by the government, by the president of the republic, or by one fourth of Assembly deputies; passage requires two-thirds majority vote of the Assembly, including two-thirds majority vote of deputies representing non-majority communities, followed by a favorable Constitutional Court assessment; amended several times, last in 2020

International law organization participation: has not submitted an ICJ jurisdiction declaration; non-party state to the ICCt

Citizenship: *citizenship by birth:* no
citizenship by descent only: at least one parent must be a citizen of Kosovo
dual citizenship recognized: yes
residency requirement for naturalization: 5 years

Suffrage: 18 years of age; universal

Executive branch: *chief of state:* President Vjosa OSMANI-Sadriu (since 4 April 2021)
head of government: Prime Minister Albin KURTI (since 22 March 2021)
cabinet: Cabinet elected by the Assembly
elections/appointments: president indirectly elected by at least two-thirds majority vote of the Assembly for a 5-year term; if a candidate does not attain a two-thirds threshold in the first two ballots, the candidate winning a simple majority vote in the third ballot is elected (eligible for a second term); election last held on 3 to 4 April 2021 (next to be held in 2026); prime minister indirectly elected by the Assembly
election results:
2021: Vjosa OSMANI-Sadriu elected president in third ballot; Assembly vote - Vjosa OSMANI-Sadriu (Guxo!) 71 votes; Albin KURTI (LVV) elected prime minister; Assembly vote - 67 for, 30 against
2017: Ramush HARADINAJ (AAK) elected prime minister; Assembly vote - 61 for, 1 abstention, 0 against (opposition boycott)
2016: Hashim THACI elected president in third ballot; Assembly vote - Hashim THACI (PDK) 71 votes

Legislative branch: *description:* unicameral Assembly or Kuvendi i Kosoves/Skupstina Kosova (120 seats; 100 members directly elected by open-list proportional representation vote with 20 seats reserved for ethnic minorities - 10 for Serbs and 10 for other ethnic minorities; members serve 4-year terms)
elections: last held on 14 February 2021 (next to be held in 2025)
election results: percent of vote by party - LVV 50%, PDK 16.9%, LDK 12.7%, AAK 7.1%, Serb List 5.1%, other 8.2%; seats by party - LVV 58, PDK 19, LDK 15, Serb List 10, AAK 8, other 10; composition - men 79, women 41, percentage women 34.2%

Judicial branch: *highest court(s):* Supreme Court (consists of the court president and 18 judges and organized into Appeals Panel of the Kosovo Property Agency and Special Chamber); Constitutional Court (consists of the court president, vice president, and 7 judges)
judge selection and term of office: Supreme Court judges nominated by the Kosovo Judicial Council, a 13-member independent body staffed by judges and lay members, and also responsible for overall administration of Kosovo's judicial system; judges appointed by the president of the Republic of Kosovo; judges appointed until mandatory retirement age; Constitutional Court judges nominated by the Kosovo Assembly and appointed by the president of the republic to serve single, 9-year terms
subordinate courts: Court of Appeals (organized into 4 departments: General, Serious Crime, Commercial Matters, and Administrative Matters); Basic Court (located in 7 municipalities, each with several branches)
note: in August 2015, the Kosovo Assembly approved a constitutional amendment that established the Kosovo Relocated Specialist Judicial Institution, also referred to as the Kosovo Specialist Chambers or "Special Court"; the court, located at the Hague in the Netherlands, began operating in late 2016 and has jurisdiction to try crimes against humanity, war crimes, and other crimes under Kosovo law that occurred in the 1998-2000 period

Political parties: Alliance for the Future of Kosovo or AAK
Ashkali Party for Integration or PAI
Civic Initiative for Freedom, Justice, and Survival
Democratic League of Kosovo or LDK
Democratic Party of Kosovo or PDK
New Democratic Initiative of Kosovo or IRDK
New Democratic Party or NDS
Progressive Movement of Kosovar Roma or LPRK
Romani Initiative
Self-Determination Movement (Lëvizja Vetevendosje or Vetevendosie) or LVV or VV
Serb List or SL
Social Democratic Union or SDU
Turkish Democratic Party of Kosovo or KDTP
Unique Gorani Party or JGP
Vakat Coalition or VAKAT

International organization participation: FIFA, IBRD, IDA, IFC, IMF, IOC, ITUC (NGOs), MIGA, OIF (observer)

Diplomatic representation in the US: *chief of mission:* Ambassador Ilir DUGOLLI (since 13 January 2022)
chancery: 3612 Massachusetts Ave NW, Washington, D.C. 20007
telephone: [1] (202) 450-2130
FAX: [1] (202) 735-0609
email address and website:
embassy.usa@rks-gov.net
U.S. Embassies of the Republic of Kosovo (ambasadat.net)
consulate(s) general: New York
consulate(s): Des Moines (IA)

Diplomatic representation from the US: *chief of mission:* Ambassador Jeffrey M. HOVENIER (since 10 January 2022)
embassy: Arberia/Dragodan, Rr. 4 KORRIKU Nr. 25, Pristina
mailing address: 9520 Pristina Place, Washington DC 20521-9520
telephone: [383] 38-59-59-3000
FAX: [383] 38-604-890
email address and website:
PristinaACS@state.gov
https://xk.usembassy.gov/

Flag description: *centered on a dark blue field is a gold-colored silhouette of Kosovo surmounted by six white, five-pointed stars arrayed in a slight arc; each star represents one of the major ethnic groups of Kosovo:* Albanians, Serbs, Turks, Gorani, Roma, and Bosniaks
note: one of only two national flags that uses a map as a design element; the flag of Cyprus is the other

National symbol(s): six, five-pointed, white stars; national colors: blue, gold, white

National anthem: *name:* Europe
lyrics/music: no lyrics/Mendi MENGJIQI
note: adopted 2008; Kosovo chose to exclude lyrics in its anthem so as not to offend the country's minority ethnic groups

National heritage: *total World Heritage Sites:* 1 (cultural)
selected World Heritage Site locales: Medieval Monuments in Kosovo

ECONOMY

Economic overview: small-but-growing European economy; non-EU member but unilateral euro user; very high unemployment, especially youth; vulnerable reliance on diaspora tourism services, curtailed by COVID-19 disruptions; unclear public loan portfolio health

Real GDP (purchasing power parity): $23.794 billion (2023 est.)
$23.025 billion (2022 est.)
$22.08 billion (2021 est.)
note: data in 2021 dollars
comparison ranking: 156

Real GDP growth rate: 3.34% (2023 est.)
4.28% (2022 est.)
10.75% (2021 est.)
note: annual GDP % growth based on constant local currency
comparison ranking: 99

Real GDP per capita: $13,500 (2023 est.)
$13,000 (2022 est.)
$12,400 (2021 est.)
note: data in 2021 dollars
comparison ranking: 132

GDP (official exchange rate): $10.438 billion (2023 est.)
note: data in current dollars at official exchange rate

Inflation rate (consumer prices): 4.94% (2023 est.)
11.58% (2022 est.)
3.35% (2021 est.)
note: annual % change based on consumer prices
comparison ranking: 105

GDP - composition, by sector of origin: *agriculture:* 7.8% (2023 est.)
industry: 26.3% (2023 est.)
services: 46% (2023 est.)
note: figures may not total 100% due to non-allocated consumption not captured in sector-reported data
comparison rankings: services 165; industry 87; agriculture 92

GDP - composition, by end use: *household consumption:* 83.9% (2023 est.)
government consumption: 12.5% (2023 est.)
investment in fixed capital: 31.6% (2023 est.)
investment in inventories: 2.7% (2023 est.)
exports of goods and services: 39.7% (2023 est.)
imports of goods and services: -70.5% (2023 est.)
note: figures may not total 100% due to rounding or gaps in data collection

Agricultural products: wheat, corn, berries, potatoes, peppers, fruit; dairy, livestock; fish

Industries: mineral mining, construction materials, base metals, leather, machinery, appliances, foodstuffs and beverages, textiles

Industrial production growth rate: 1.56% (2023 est.)
note: annual % change in industrial value added based on constant local currency
comparison ranking: 127

Labor force: 500,300 (2017 est.)
note: includes those estimated to be employed in the gray economy
comparison ranking: 160

Unemployment rate: 30.5% (2017 est.)
27.5% (2016 est.)
note: Kosovo has a large informal sector that may not be reflected in these data
comparison ranking: 208

Youth unemployment rate (ages 15-24): *total:* 48.8% (2020 est.)
male: 44.9%
female: 57.3%
comparison ranking: total 5

Population below poverty line: 17.6% (2015 est.)
note: % of population with income below national poverty line

Gini Index coefficient - distribution of family income: 29 (2017 est.)
note: index (0-100) of income distribution; higher values represent greater inequality
comparison ranking: 130

Household income or consumption by percentage share: *lowest 10%:* 3.8% (2017 est.)
highest 10%: 24.6% (2017 est.)
note: % share of income accruing to lowest and highest 10% of population

Remittances: 18.2% of GDP (2023 est.)
17.24% of GDP (2022 est.)
18.01% of GDP (2021 est.)
note: personal transfers and compensation between resident and non-resident individuals/households/entities

Budget: *revenues:* $1.951 billion (2020 est.)
expenditures: $2.547 billion (2020 est.)

Public debt: 21.2% of GDP (2017 est.)
comparison ranking: 183

Taxes and other revenues: 29% (of GDP) (2017 est.)
comparison ranking: 26

Current account balance: -$794.765 million (2023 est.)
-$983.283 million (2022 est.)
-$818.351 million (2021 est.)
note: balance of payments - net trade and primary/secondary income in current dollars
comparison ranking: 131

Exports: $4.155 billion (2023 est.)
$3.579 billion (2022 est.)
$3.138 billion (2021 est.)
note: balance of payments - exports of goods and services in current dollars
comparison ranking: 143

Exports - partners: United States 16%, Albania 15%, North Macedonia 12%, Germany 8%, Italy 8% (2021)

Exports - commodities: mattress materials, iron alloys, metal piping, scrap iron, building plastics, mineral water, seating (2021)

Imports: $7.362 billion (2023 est.)
$6.661 billion (2022 est.)
$6.128 billion (2021 est.)
note: balance of payments - imports of goods and services in current dollars
comparison ranking: 134

Imports - partners: Germany 13%, Turkey 13%, China 10%, Serbia 7%, Italy 6% (2021)

Imports - commodities: refined petroleum, cars, iron rods, electricity, cigars, packaged medicines (2021)

Reserves of foreign exchange and gold: $1.245 billion (2023 est.)
$1.248 billion (2022 est.)
$1.244 billion (2021 est.)
note: holdings of gold (year-end prices)/foreign exchange/special drawing rights in current dollars
comparison ranking: 143

Exchange rates: euros (EUR) per US dollar -

Exchange rates: 0.925 (2023 est.)
0.951 (2022 est.)
0.845 (2021 est.)
0.877 (2020 est.)
0.893 (2019 est.)
note: Kosovo, which is neither an EU member state nor a party to a formal EU monetary agreement, uses the euro as its de facto currency

ENERGY

Electricity: *installed generating capacity:* 1.547 million kW (2022 est.)
consumption: 6.487 billion kWh (2022 est.)
exports: 3.139 billion kWh (2022 est.)
imports: 3.687 billion kWh (2022 est.)
transmission/distribution losses: 1.05 billion kWh (2022 est.)
comparison rankings: transmission/distribution losses 98; imports 51; exports 45; consumption 122; installed generating capacity 129

Electricity generation sources: *fossil fuels:* 90.8% of total installed capacity (2022 est.)
solar: 0.2% of total installed capacity (2022 est.)
wind: 5.2% of total installed capacity (2022 est.)
hydroelectricity: 3.8% of total installed capacity (2022 est.)

Coal: *production:* 9.074 million metric tons (2022 est.)
consumption: 8.927 million metric tons (2022 est.)
exports: 127,000 metric tons (2022 est.)
imports: 12,000 metric tons (2022 est.)
proven reserves: 1.564 billion metric tons (2022 est.)

Petroleum: *refined petroleum consumption:* 15,000 bbl/day (2022 est.)

Carbon dioxide emissions: 8.619 million metric tonnes of CO_2 (2022 est.)
from coal and metallurgical coke: 6.427 million metric tonnes of CO_2 (2022 est.)
from petroleum and other liquids: 2.192 million metric tonnes of CO_2 (2022 est.)
comparison ranking: total emissions 112

Energy consumption per capita: 57.072 million Btu/person (2022 est.)
comparison ranking: 88

COMMUNICATIONS

Telephones - fixed lines: *total subscriptions:* 383,763 (2022 est.)
subscriptions per 100 inhabitants: 25 (2022 est.)
comparison ranking: total subscriptions 101

Telephones - mobile cellular: *total subscriptions:* 1,777,859 (2022 est.)
subscriptions per 100 inhabitants: 98 (2022 est.)
comparison ranking: total subscriptions 155

Telecommunication systems: *general assessment:* Kosovo has benefited from financial and regulatory assistance as part of the EU pre-accession process; the telecom sector has been liberalized, and legislation has aligned the sector with the EU's revised regulatory framework; infrastructure development includes WiMax and other municipal wireless internet services; digitalization of TV broadcasting;

network upgrades include a 5G roll-out in the coming years (2022)
domestic: fixed-line roughly 25 per 100 and mobile-cellular 98 per 100 persons (2022)
international: country code - 383

Internet country code: .xk; note - assigned as a temporary code under UN Security Council resolution 1244/99

Internet users: *total:* 1,756,300 (2021 est.)
percent of population: 91% (2021 est.)
comparison ranking: total 139

TRANSPORTATION

National air transport system: *number of registered air carriers:* 0 (2020)

Civil aircraft registration country code prefix: Z6

Airports: 4 (2024)
comparison ranking: 178

Heliports: 6 (2024)

Railways: *total:* 437 km (2020)
comparison ranking: total 116

Roadways: *total:* 2,248 km (2022)
comparison ranking: total 172

MILITARY AND SECURITY

Military and security forces: Kosovo Security Force (KSF; Forca e Sigurisë së Kosovës or FSK): Land Force, National Guard (2024)
note: the Kosovo Police are under the Ministry of Internal Affairs

Military expenditures: 1.3% of GDP (2023 est.)
1.1% of GDP (2022 est.)
1.1% of GDP (2021 est.)
1% of GDP (2020 est.)
0.8% of GDP (2019 est.)
comparison ranking: 111

Military and security service personnel strengths: approximately 3,300 KSF personnel, including about 800 reserves (2024)

Military equipment inventories and acquisitions: the KSF is equipped with small arms and light vehicles and has relied on limited amounts of donated equipment from several countries, particularly Turkey and the US (2024)

Military service age and obligation: any citizen of Kosovo over the age of 18 is eligible to serve in the Kosovo Security Force; upper age for enlisting is 30 for officers, 25 for other ranks, although these may be waived for recruits with key skills considered essential for the KSF
(2024)

Military - note: the Kosovo Security Force (KSF) was established in 2009 as a small (1,500 personnel), lightly armed disaster response force; the NATO-led Kosovo Force (KFOR) was charged with assisting in the development of the KSF and bringing it up to standards designated by NATO; the KSF was certified as fully operational by the North Atlantic Council in 2013, indicating the then 2,200-strong KSF was entirely capable of performing the tasks assigned under its mandate, which included non-military security functions that were not appropriate for the police, plus missions such as search and rescue, explosive ordnance disposal, control and clearance of hazardous materials, firefighting, and other humanitarian assistance tasks
in 2019, Kosovo approved legislation that began a process to transition the KSF by 2028 into a professional military (the Kosovo Armed Forces) led by a General Staff and comprised of a Land Force, a National Guard, a Logistics Command, and a Doctrine and Training Command; it would have a strength of up to 5,000 with about 3,000 reserves; at the same time, the KSF's mission was expanded to include traditional military functions, such as territorial defense and international peacekeeping; the KSF's first international mission was the deployment of a small force to Kuwait in 2021
the NATO-led KFOR has operated in the country as a peace support force since 1999; in addition to assisting in the development of the KSF, KFOR is responsible for providing a safe and secure environment and ensuring freedom of movement for all citizens; as of 2024, it numbered about 4,400 troops from 28 countries; Kosovo regards the US as a key ally and security guarantor, and the US has provided considerable support to the KSF, including equipment and training (2024)

TERRORISM

Terrorist group(s): Islamic State of Iraq and ash-Sham (ISIS)
note: details about the history, aims, leadership, organization, areas of operation, tactics, targets, weapons, size, and sources of support of the group(s) appear(s) in the Terrorism reference guide

TRANSNATIONAL ISSUES

Disputes - international: *note:* NATO-led Kosovo Force peacekeepers deployed under UN Security Council Resolution 1244 continue to ensure a safe and secure environment and freedom of movement for all Kosovo citizens; in September 2023, KFOR deployed additional forces in the north of Kosovo and increased patrols along the border with Serbia after Kosovo- Serb paramilitaries attacked Kosovo police near the town of Banjska; some of Kosovo's ethnic Serb minority, most of whom live in the northern regions, view themselves as part of Serbia, and Serbian municipalities along the northern border have challenged the final status of Kosovo-Serbia boundary; some protests have turned violent

Refugees and internally displaced persons: IDPs: 16,000 (primarily ethnic Serbs displaced during the 1998-1999 war fearing reprisals from the majority ethnic- Albanian population; a smaller number of ethnic Serbs, Roma, Ashkali, and Egyptians fled their homes in 2004 as a result of violence) (2022)
note: 9,011 estimated refugee and migrant arrivals (January 2015-August 2023)

KUWAIT

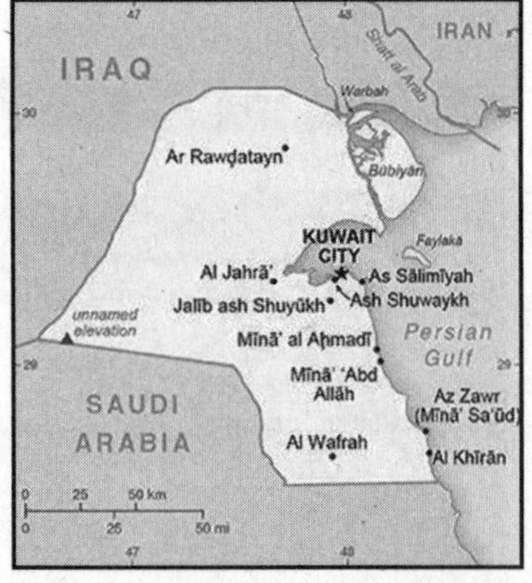

INTRODUCTION

Background: Kuwait has been ruled by the AL-SABAH dynasty since the 18th century. The threat of Ottoman invasion in 1899 prompted Amir Mubarak AL-SABAH to seek protection from Britain, ceding foreign and defense responsibility to Britain until 1961, when the country attained its independence. Iraq attacked and overran Kuwait in 1990. After several weeks of aerial bombardment, a US-led UN coalition began a ground assault in 1991 that liberated Kuwait in four days. In 1992, the Amir reconstituted the parliament that he had dissolved in 1986. Amid the 2010-11 uprisings and protests across the Arab world, stateless Arabs known as Bidoon staged small protests demanding citizenship, jobs, and other benefits available to Kuwaiti nationals. Other demographic groups, notably Islamists and Kuwaitis from tribal backgrounds, soon joined the growing protest movements, which culminated with the resignation of the prime minister amid allegations of corruption. Demonstrations renewed in 2012 in response to a decree amending the electoral law that lessened the voting power of the tribal blocs.

An opposition coalition of Sunni Islamists, tribal populists, and some liberals largely boycotted legislative elections in 2012 and 2013, which ushered in a legislature more amenable to the government's agenda. Faced with the prospect of painful subsidy cuts, oppositionists and independents actively participated in the 2016 election, winning nearly half the seats, but the opposition became increasingly factionalized. Between 2006 and his death in 2020, the Amir dissolved the National Assembly on seven occasions and shuffled the cabinet over a dozen times, usually citing political stagnation and gridlock between the legislature and the government.

The current Amir, who assumed his role in 2020, launched a "National Dialogue" in 2021 meant to resolve political gridlock. As part of this initiative, the Amir pardoned several opposition figures who had been living in exile, and they returned to Kuwait. Legislative challenges remain, and the cabinet has been reshuffled six times since 2020.

GEOGRAPHY

Location: Middle East, bordering the Persian Gulf, between Iraq and Saudi Arabia

Geographic coordinates: 29 30 N, 45 45 E

Map references: Middle East

Area: *total:* 17,818 sq km
land: 17,818 sq km
water: 0 sq km
comparison ranking: total 157

Area - comparative: slightly smaller than New Jersey

Land boundaries: *total:* 475 km
border countries (2): Iraq 254 km; Saudi Arabia 221 km

Coastline: 499 km

Maritime claims: *territorial sea:* 12 nm

Climate: dry desert; intensely hot summers; short, cool winters

Terrain: flat to slightly undulating desert plain

Elevation: *highest point:* 3.6 km W. of Al-Salmi Border Post 300 m
lowest point: Persian Gulf 0 m
mean elevation: 108 m

Natural resources: petroleum, fish, shrimp, natural gas

Land use: *agricultural land:* 8.5% (2018 est.)
arable land: 0.6% (2018 est.)
permanent crops: 0.3% (2018 est.)
permanent pasture: 7.6% (2018 est.)
forest: 0.4% (2018 est.)
other: 91.1% (2018 est.)

Irrigated land: 100 sq km (2015)

Major watersheds (area sq km): Indian Ocean drainage: *(Persian Gulf)* Tigris and Euphrates (918,044 sq km)

Major aquifers: Arabian Aquifer System

Population distribution: densest settlement is along the Persian Gulf, particularly in Kuwait City and on Bubiyan Island; significant population threads extend south and west along highways that radiate from the capital, particularly in the southern half of the country

Natural hazards: sudden cloudbursts are common from October to April and bring heavy rain, which can damage roads and houses; sandstorms and dust storms occur throughout the year but are most common between March and August

Geography - note: strategic location at head of Persian Gulf

PEOPLE AND SOCIETY

Population: *total:* 3,138,355
male: 1,810,542
female: 1,327,813 (2024 est.)
comparison rankings: female 142; male 133; total 136

Nationality: *noun:* Kuwaiti(s)
adjective: Kuwaiti

Ethnic groups: Kuwaiti 30.4%, other Arab 27.4%, Asian 40.3%, African 1%, other 0.9% (includes European, North American, South American, and Australian) (2018 est.)

Languages: Arabic (official), English widely spoken
major-language sample(s):
يمكن الاستغناء عنه للمعلومات الأساسية
كتاب حقائق العالم، المصدر الذى لا
(Arabic)

Religions: Muslim (official) 74.6%, Christian 18.2%, other and unspecified 7.2% (2013 est.)
note: data represent the total population; about 72% of the population consists of immigrants

Age structure: *0-14 years:* 23% (male 376,415/female 346,190)
15-64 years: 73.4% (male 1,386,349/female 917,465)
65 years and over: 3.6% (2024 est.) (male 47,778/female 64,158)

Dependency ratios: *total dependency ratio:* 34.4
youth dependency ratio: 28.4
elderly dependency ratio: 6
potential support ratio: 24.9 (2021 est.)

Median age: *total:* 30.3 years (2024 est.)
male: 31.1 years
female: 28.9 years
comparison ranking: total 138

Population growth rate: 1.1% (2024 est.)
comparison ranking: 85

Birth rate: 17.5 births/1,000 population (2024 est.)
comparison ranking: 85

Death rate: 2.3 deaths/1,000 population (2024 est.)
comparison ranking: 227

Net migration rate: -4.2 migrant(s)/1,000 population (2024 est.)
comparison ranking: 196

Population distribution: densest settlement is along the Persian Gulf, particularly in Kuwait City and on Bubiyan Island; significant population threads extend south and west along highways that radiate from the capital, particularly in the southern half of the country

Urbanization: *urban population:* 100% of total population (2023)
rate of urbanization: 1.35% annual rate of change (2020-25 est.)

Major urban areas - population: 3.298 million KUWAIT (capital) (2023)

Sex ratio: *at birth:* 1.05 male(s)/female
0-14 years: 1.09 male(s)/female
15-64 years: 1.51 male(s)/female
65 years and over: 0.74 male(s)/female
total population: 1.36 male(s)/female (2024 est.)

Maternal mortality ratio: 7 deaths/100,000 live births (2020 est.)
comparison ranking: 155

Infant mortality rate: *total:* 7.2 deaths/1,000 live births (2024 est.)
male: 7.4 deaths/1,000 live births
female: 6.9 deaths/1,000 live births
comparison ranking: total 155

Life expectancy at birth: *total population:* 79.6 years (2024 est.)
male: 78.1 years
female: 81.1 years
comparison ranking: total population 63

Total fertility rate: 2.21 children born/woman (2024 est.)
comparison ranking: 82

Gross reproduction rate: 1.08 (2024 est.)

Drinking water source: *improved:*
total: 100% of population
unimproved:
total: 0% of population (2020 est.)

Current health expenditure: 6.3% of GDP (2020)

Physician density: 2.34 physicians/1,000 population (2020)

Hospital bed density: 2 beds/1,000 population (2017)

Sanitation facility access: *improved:*
total: 100% of population
unimproved:
total: 0% of population (2020 est.)

Obesity - adult prevalence rate: 37.9% (2016)
comparison ranking: 11

Alcohol consumption per capita: *total:* 0 liters of pure alcohol (2019 est.)
beer: 0 liters of pure alcohol (2019 est.)
wine: 0 liters of pure alcohol (2019 est.)
spirits: 0 liters of pure alcohol (2019 est.)
other alcohols: 0 liters of pure alcohol (2019 est.)
comparison ranking: total 189

Tobacco use: *total:* 17.9% (2020 est.)
male: 33.5% (2020 est.)
female: 2.2% (2020 est.)
comparison ranking: total 93

Children under the age of 5 years underweight: 2.5% (2020)
comparison ranking: 98

Currently married women (ages 15-49): 59.6% (2023 est.)

Education expenditures: 6.6% of GDP (2020 est.)
comparison ranking: 30

Literacy: *definition:* age 15 and over can read and write
total population: 96.5%
male: 97.1%
female: 95.4% (2020)

School life expectancy (primary to tertiary education): *total:* 15 years
male: 13 years
female: 16 years (2015)

ENVIRONMENT

Environment - current issues: limited natural freshwater resources; some of world's largest and most sophisticated desalination facilities provide much of the water; air and water pollution; desertification; loss of biodiversity

Environment - international agreements: *party to:* Biodiversity, Climate Change, Climate Change-Kyoto Protocol, Climate Change-Paris Agreement, Comprehensive Nuclear Test Ban, Desertification, Endangered Species, Environmental Modification,

Hazardous Wastes, Law of the Sea, Nuclear Test Ban, Ozone Layer Protection, Ship Pollution, Wetlands
signed, but not ratified: Marine Dumping-London Convention

Climate: dry desert; intensely hot summers; short, cool winters

Urbanization: *urban population:* 100% of total population (2023)
rate of urbanization: 1.35% annual rate of change (2020-25 est.)

Revenue from forest resources: 0% of GDP (2018 est.)
comparison ranking: 195

Revenue from coal: 0% of GDP (2018 est.)
comparison ranking: 138

Air pollutants: *particulate matter emissions:* 64.08 micrograms per cubic meter (2019 est.)
carbon dioxide emissions: 98.73 megatons (2016 est.)
methane emissions: 6.21 megatons (2020 est.)

Waste and recycling: *municipal solid waste generated annually:* 1.75 million tons (2010 est.)

Major watersheds (area sq km): Indian Ocean drainage: *(Persian Gulf)* Tigris and Euphrates (918,044 sq km)

Major aquifers: Arabian Aquifer System

Total water withdrawal: *municipal:* 450 million cubic meters (2020 est.)
industrial: 20 million cubic meters (2020 est.)
agricultural: 780 million cubic meters (2020 est.)

Total renewable water resources: 20 million cubic meters (2020 est.)

GOVERNMENT

Country name: *conventional long form:* State of Kuwait
conventional short form: Kuwait
local long form: Dawlat al Kuwayt
local short form: Al Kuwayt
etymology: the name derives from the capital city, which is from Arabic "al-Kuwayt" a diminutive of "kut" meaning "fortress," possibly a reference to a small castle built on the current location of Kuwait City by the Beni Khaled tribe in the 17th century

Government type: constitutional monarchy (emirate)

Capital: *name:* Kuwait City
geographic coordinates: 29 22 N, 47 58 E
time difference: UTC+3 (8 hours ahead of Washington, DC, during Standard Time)
etymology: the name derives from Arabic "al-Kuwayt" a diminutive of "kut" meaning "fortress," possibly a reference to a small castle built on the current location of Kuwait City by the Beni Khaled tribe in the 17th century

Administrative divisions: 6 governorates (muhafazat, singular - muhafazah); Al Ahmadi, Al 'Asimah, Al Farwaniyah, Al Jahra', Hawalli, Mubarak al Kabir

Independence: 19 June 1961 (from the UK)

National holiday: National Day, 25 February (1950)

Legal system: mixed legal system consisting of English common law, French civil law, and Islamic sharia law

Constitution: *history:* approved and promulgated 11 November 1962; suspended 1976 to 1981 (4 articles); 1986 to 1991; May to July 1999
amendments: proposed by the amir or supported by at least one third of the National Assembly; passage requires two-thirds consent of the Assembly membership and promulgation by the amir; constitutional articles on the initiation, approval, and promulgation of general legislation cannot be amended

Note: on 10 May 2024, Amir Sheikh MISHAL al-Ahmad al-Sabah dissolved the National Assembly and suspended several articles of the constitution for up to four years

International law organization participation: has not submitted an ICJ jurisdiction declaration; non-party state to the ICCt

Citizenship: *citizenship by birth:* no
citizenship by descent only: at least one parent must be a citizen of Kuwait
dual citizenship recognized: no
residency requirement for naturalization: not specified

Suffrage: 21 years of age and at least 20-year citizenship

Executive branch: *chief of state:* Amir MISHAL al-Ahmad al-Jabir al-Sabah (since 16 December 2023)
head of government: Prime Minister AHMAD ABDULLAH Al-Ahmad al Sabah (since 15 May 2024)
cabinet: Council of Ministers appointed by the prime minister, approved by the amir
elections/appointments: amir chosen from within the ruling family, confirmed by the National Assembly; prime minister appointed by the amir

Legislative branch: *description:* unicameral National Assembly or Majlis al-Umma (65 seats; 50 members directly elected from 5 multi-seat constituencies by simple majority vote and 15 ex-officio members (cabinet ministers) appointed by the amir; members serve 4-year terms)
elections: last held on 4 April 2024 (next to be held in 2028)
election results: 50 nonpartisan candidates, including 29 opposition candidates; composition - men 63, women 2, percent women 3.1%

Note: on 10 May 2024, Amir Sheikh MISHAL al-Ahmad al-Sabah dissolved the National Assembly, and some powers held by the National Assembly are assumed by the government

Judicial branch: *highest court(s):* Constitutional Court (consists of 5 judges); Supreme Court or Court of Cassation (organized into several circuits, each with 5 judges)
judge selection and term of office: all Kuwaiti judges appointed by the Amir upon recommendation of the Supreme Judicial Council, a consultative body comprised of Kuwaiti judges and Ministry of Justice officials
subordinate courts: High Court of Appeal; Court of First Instance; Summary Court

Political parties: none; the government does not recognize any political parties or allow their formation, although no formal law bans political parties

International organization participation: ABEDA, AfDB (nonregional member), AFESD, AMF, BDEAC, CAEU, CD, FAO, G-77, GCC, IAEA, IBRD, ICAO, ICC (national committees), ICRM, IDA, IDB, IFAD, IFC, IFRCS, IHO, ILO, IMF, IMO, IMSO, Interpol, IOC, IPU, ISO, ITSO, ITU, ITUC (NGOs), LAS, MIGA, NAM, OAPEC, OIC, OPCW, OPEC, Paris Club (associate), PCA, UN, UNCTAD, UNESCO, UNHRC, UNIDO, UNOOSA, UNRWA, UN Security Council (temporary), UNWTO, UPU, WCO, WFTU (NGOs), WHO, WIPO, WMO, WTO

Diplomatic representation in the US: *chief of mission:* Ambassador AL-ZAIN Sabah Naser Saud Al-Sabah (since 19 April 2023)
chancery: 2940 Tilden Street NW, Washington, DC 20008
telephone: [1] (202) 966-0702
FAX: [1] (202) 966-8468
email address and website:
info@kuwaitembassy.us
https://www.kuwaitembassy.us/
consulate(s) general: Beverly Hills (CA), New York

Diplomatic representation from the US: *chief of mission:* Ambassador (vacant); Chargé d'Affaires James HOLTSNIDER (since July 2021)
embassy: P.O. Box 77, Safat 13001
mailing address: 6200 Kuwait Place, Washington DC 20521-6200
telephone: [00] (965) 2259-1001
FAX: [00] (965) 2538-0282
email address and website:
KuwaitACS@state.gov
https://kw.usembassy.gov/

Flag description: three equal horizontal bands of green (top), white, and red with a black trapezoid based on the hoist side; colors and design are based on the Arab Revolt flag of World War I; green represents fertile fields, white stands for purity, red denotes blood on Kuwaiti swords, black signifies the defeat of the enemy

National symbol(s): golden falcon; national colors: green, white, red, black

National anthem: *name:* "Al-Nasheed Al-Watani" (National Anthem)
lyrics/music: Ahmad MUSHARI al-Adwani/ Ibrahim Nasir al-SOULA
note: adopted 1978; the anthem is only used on formal occasions

ECONOMY

Economic overview: small, high-income, oil-based Middle East economy; renewable energy proponent; regional finance and investment leader; maintains oldest sovereign wealth fund; emerging space and tourism industries; mid-way through 25-year development program

Real GDP (purchasing power parity): $219.06 billion (2023 est.)
$224.057 billion (2022 est.)
$211.099 billion (2021 est.)
note: data in 2021 dollars
comparison ranking: 73

Real GDP growth rate: -2.23% (2023 est.)
6.14% (2022 est.)
1.7% (2021 est.)
note: annual GDP % growth based on constant local currency
comparison ranking: 207

Real GDP per capita: $50,800 (2023 est.)
$52,500 (2022 est.)
$49,700 (2021 est.)
note: data in 2021 dollars
comparison ranking: 39

GDP (official exchange rate): $161.772 billion (2023 est.)
note: data in current dollars at official exchange rate

Inflation rate (consumer prices): 3.64% (2023 est.)
3.98% (2022 est.)

3.42% (2021 est.)
note: annual % change based on consumer prices
comparison ranking: 72

Credit ratings: Fitch rating: AA (2008)

Moody's rating: A1 (2020)

Standard & Poors rating: AA- (2020)
note: The year refers to the year in which the current credit rating was first obtained.

GDP - composition, by sector of origin: *agriculture:* 0.4% (2022 est.)
industry: 67% (2022 est.)
services: 43.6% (2022 est.)
note: figures may not total 100% due to non-allocated consumption not captured in sector-reported data
comparison rankings: services 175; industry 3; agriculture 201

GDP - composition, by end use: *household consumption:* 40.6% (2019 est.)
government consumption: 24.8% (2019 est.)
investment in fixed capital: 24.6% (2019 est.)
exports of goods and services: 52.3% (2019 est.)
imports of goods and services: -44.1% (2019 est.)
note: figures may not total 100% due to rounding or gaps in data collection

Agricultural products: tomatoes, dates, cucumbers/gherkins, eggs, milk, chicken, lamb/mutton, vegetables, potatoes, eggplants (2022)
note: top ten agricultural products based on tonnage

Industries: petroleum, petrochemicals, cement, shipbuilding and repair, water desalination, food processing, construction materials

Industrial production growth rate: 8.05% (2022 est.)
note: annual % change in industrial value added based on constant local currency
comparison ranking: 29

Labor force: 2.463 million (2023 est.)
note: number of people ages 15 or older who are employed or seeking work
comparison ranking: 119

Unemployment rate: 2.08% (2023 est.)
2.12% (2022 est.)
3% (2021 est.)
note: % of labor force seeking employment
comparison ranking: 22

Youth unemployment rate (ages 15-24): *total:* 15% (2023 est.)
male: 9.1% (2023 est.)
female: 29% (2023 est.)
note: % of labor force ages 15-24 seeking employment
comparison ranking: total 95

Average household expenditures: *on food:* 19.2% of household expenditures (2022 est.)
on alcohol and tobacco: 0.1% of household expenditures (2022 est.)

Remittances: 0.01% of GDP (2023 est.)
0.01% of GDP (2022 est.)
0.57% of GDP (2021 est.)
note: personal transfers and compensation between resident and non-resident individuals/households/entities

Budget: *revenues:* $44.254 billion (2015 est.)
expenditures: $59.584 billion (2015 est.)
note: central government revenues and expenses (excluding grants and social security funds) converted to US dollars at average official exchange rate for year indicated

Public debt: 20.6% of GDP (2017 est.)
comparison ranking: 184

Taxes and other revenues: 41.8% (of GDP) (2017 est.)
comparison ranking: 8

Current account balance: $51.396 billion (2023 est.)
$63.078 billion (2022 est.)
$34.943 billion (2021 est.)
note: balance of payments - net trade and primary/secondary income in current dollars
comparison ranking: 11

Exports: $95.476 billion (2023 est.)
$110.923 billion (2022 est.)
$77.121 billion (2021 est.)
note: balance of payments - exports of goods and services in current dollars
comparison ranking: 50

Exports - partners: China 24%, India 15%, South Korea 11%, Japan 9%, Taiwan 7% (2022)
note: top five export partners based on percentage share of exports

Exports - commodities: crude petroleum, refined petroleum, hydrocarbons, natural gas, acyclic alcohols (2022)
note: top five export commodities based on value in dollars

Imports: $63.43 billion (2023 est.)
$55.909 billion (2022 est.)
$48.954 billion (2021 est.)
note: balance of payments - imports of goods and services in current dollars
comparison ranking: 60

Imports - partners: UAE 20%, China 16%, Saudi Arabia 9%, US 7%, Japan 4% (2022)
note: top five import partners based on percentage share of imports

Imports - commodities: cars, gold, jewelry, garments, packaged medicine (2022)
note: top five import commodities based on value in dollars

Reserves of foreign exchange and gold: $52.619 billion (2023 est.)
$52.462 billion (2022 est.)
$49.525 billion (2021 est.)
note: holdings of gold (year-end prices)/foreign exchange/special drawing rights in current dollars
comparison ranking: 44

Debt - external: (2017)

Exchange rates: Kuwaiti dinars (KD) per US dollar -

Exchange rates: 0.307 (2023 est.)
0.306 (2022 est.)
0.302 (2021 est.)
0.306 (2020 est.)
0.304 (2019 est.)

ENERGY

Electricity access: *electrification - total population:* 100% (2022 est.)

Electricity: *installed generating capacity:* 20.25 million kW (2022 est.)
consumption: 78.703 billion kWh (2022 est.)
transmission/distribution losses: 7.727 billion kWh (2022 est.)
comparison rankings: transmission/distribution losses 173; consumption 41; installed generating capacity 49

Electricity generation sources: *fossil fuels:* 99.8% of total installed capacity (2022 est.)
solar: 0.2% of total installed capacity (2022 est.)

Coal: *consumption:* 145,000 metric tons (2022 est.)
imports: 77,000 metric tons (2022 est.)

Petroleum: *total petroleum production:* 2.91 million bbl/day (2023 est.)
refined petroleum consumption: 372,000 bbl/day (2022 est.)
crude oil estimated reserves: 101.5 billion barrels (2021 est.)

Natural gas: *production:* 19.285 billion cubic meters (2022 est.)
consumption: 26.083 billion cubic meters (2022 est.)
imports: 7.988 billion cubic meters (2022 est.)
proven reserves: 1.784 trillion cubic meters (2021 est.)

Carbon dioxide emissions: 100.596 million metric tonnes of CO2 (2022 est.)
from coal and metallurgical coke: 337,000 metric tonnes of CO2 (2022 est.)
from petroleum and other liquids: 49.09 million metric tonnes of CO2 (2022 est.)
from consumed natural gas: 51.169 million metric tonnes of CO2 (2022 est.)
comparison ranking: total emissions 41

Energy consumption per capita: 402.03 million Btu/person (2022 est.)
comparison ranking: 6

COMMUNICATIONS

Telephones - fixed lines: *total subscriptions:* 573,000 (2022 est.)
subscriptions per 100 inhabitants: 13 (2022 est.)
comparison ranking: total subscriptions 85

Telephones - mobile cellular: *total subscriptions:* 7.726 million (2022 est.)
subscriptions per 100 inhabitants: 181 (2022 est.)
comparison ranking: total subscriptions 104

Telecommunication systems: *general assessment:* Kuwait's telecom infrastructure is well developed, with a focus on mobile infrastructure and services; the telecom sector is important to the country's economy, and this will become more pronounced in coming years as the economy is purposefully transitioned away from a dependence on oil and gas to one which is increasingly knowledge-based and focused on ICT and related services; the MNOs have focused investment on 5G networks, which support and promote the growth of data traffic; this in turn has been a catalyst for revenue growth in recent quarters; while Kuwait's mobile sector shows considerable progress; the country's fixed broadband system is the lowest in the region; the government has stepped up efforts to build up fixed broadband networks, and ultimately this sector offers a potential future growth opportunity; improvements to the fixed broadband infrastructure will help develop sectors such as e-commerce, along with smart infrastructure developments, and tech start-ups (2022)
domestic: fixed-line subscriptions are nearly 13 per 100 and mobile-cellular stands at nearly 163 per 100 subscriptions (2021)
international: country code - 965; landing points for the FOG, GBICS, MENA, Kuwait-Iran, and FALCON submarine cables linking Africa, the Middle East, and Asia; microwave radio relay to Saudi Arabia; satellite earth stations - 6 (3 Intelsat - 1 Atlantic Ocean and 2 Indian Ocean, 1 Inmarsat - Atlantic Ocean, and 2 Arabsat) (2019)

Broadcast media: state-owned TV broadcaster. operates 4 networks and a satellite channel; several private TV broadcasters have emerged; satellite TV available and pan-Arab TV stations are especially popular; state-owned Radio Kuwait broadcasts on a number of channels in Arabic and English; first private radio station emerged in 2005; transmissions of at least 2 international radio broadcasters are available (2019)

Internet country code: .kw

Internet users: *total:* 4.3 million (2021 est.)
percent of population: 100% (2021 est.)
comparison ranking: total 107

Broadband - fixed subscriptions: *total:* 73,948 (2020 est.)
subscriptions per 100 inhabitants: 2 (2020 est.)
comparison ranking: total 133

TRANSPORTATION

National air transport system: *number of registered air carriers:* 2 (2020)
inventory of registered aircraft operated by air carriers: 44
annual passenger traffic on registered air carriers: 6,464,847 (2018)
annual freight traffic on registered air carriers: 392.36 million (2018) mt-km

Civil aircraft registration country code prefix: 9K

Airports: 6 (2024)
comparison ranking: 174

Heliports: 20 (2024)

Pipelines: 261 km gas, 540 km oil, 57 km refined products (2013)

Roadways: *total:* 5,749 km (201)
paved: 4,887 km
*unpaved:*862 km (2018)
comparison ranking: total 148

Merchant marine: *total:* 176 (2023)
by type: general cargo 15, oil tanker 28, other 133
comparison ranking: total 72

Ports: *total ports:* 6 (2024)
large: 0
medium: 2
small: 1
very small: 3
ports with oil terminals: 4
key ports: Al Kuwayt, Doha Harbor, Mina Abd Allah, Mina Al Ahmadi, Mina Ash Shuaybah, Mina Az Zawr

MILITARY AND SECURITY

Military and security forces: Kuwait Armed Forces (KAF): Kuwait Land Forces (KLF), Kuwait Navy, Kuwait Air Force (Al-Quwwat al-Jawwiya al- Kuwaitiya; includes Kuwait Air Defense Force, KADF), 25th Commando Brigade, and the Kuwait Emiri Guard Authority; Kuwait National Guard (KNG) (2024)
note 1: the Emiri Guard Authority and the 25th Commando Brigade exercise independent command authority within the KAF, although activities such as training and equipment procurement are often coordinated with the other services; the 25th Commando Brigade is Kuwait's leading special forces unit; the Emiri Guard Authority (aka Emiri Guard Brigade) is responsible for protecting Kuwait's heads of state
note 2: the National Guard reports directly to the prime minister and the amir and possesses an independent command structure, equipment inventory, and logistics corps separate from the Ministry of Defense, the regular armed services, and the Ministry of Interior; it is responsible for protecting critical infrastructure and providing support for the Ministries of Interior and Defense as required
note 3: the police, Kuwait State Security, and Coast Guard are under the Ministry of Interior

Military expenditures: 5% of GDP (2023 est.)
4.5% of GDP (2022 est.)
6.8% of GDP (2021 est.)
6.3% of GDP (2020 est.)
5.6% of GDP (2019 est.)
comparison ranking: 10

Military and security service personnel strengths: approximately 17,000 active-duty armed forces personnel (12,500 Army, including the Amiri Guard and 25th Commando Brigade; 2,000 Navy; 2,500 Air Force); approximately 7,000 National Guard (2023)

Military equipment inventories and acquisitions: the military's inventory consists of weapons from a wide variety of sources, including Western Europe, Russia, and particularly the US (2024)

Military service age and obligation: 18-55 years of age for voluntary military service; Kuwait reintroduced 12-month mandatory service for men aged 18-35 in May 2017 after having suspended conscription in 2001; mandatory service is divided in two phases – 4 months for training and 8 months for military service; women were allowed to volunteer in 2021 (2023)
note: the National Guard is restricted to citizens, but in 2018, the Army began allowing non-Kuwaitis to join on contract or as non-commissioned officers; that same year, it also began allowing stateless people (Bidoon) to join

Military - note: the Kuwaiti Armed Forces (KAF) are responsible for external defense; the independent National Guard is responsible for protecting critical infrastructure and providing support for the Ministries of Interior and Defense as required, including supporting the KAF Land Forces during a conflict; the National Guard and the Ministry of Interior are the Kuwaiti Government's lead counterterrorism organizations; Kuwait's primary security concerns are potential threats emanating from Iran, including regional militias loyal to Iran, and Islamist terrorist groups
the KAF participates in bilateral and multilateral exercises, as well as a limited number of multinational security operations such as maritime patrols in the Persian Gulf; it also provided a few fighter aircraft to the Saudi-led coalition in Yemen in 2015; the KAF is part of the military arm of the Gulf Cooperation Council
Kuwait's key security partner since the 1991 Gulf War has been the US; the US maintains thousands of military personnel as well as logistics and training facilities in Kuwait as part of a 1991 Defense Cooperation Agreement and a 2013 Acquisition and Cross-Servicing Agreement; the KAF conducts bilateral exercises with the US military and would look to US assistance in the event of an external attack; Kuwait has Major Non-NATO Ally status with the US, a designation under US law that provides foreign partners with certain benefits in the areas of defense trade and security cooperation (2024)

TRANSNATIONAL ISSUES

Refugees and internally displaced persons: *stateless persons:* 92,000 (2022); note - Kuwait's 1959 Nationality Law defined citizens as persons who settled in the country before 1920 and who had maintained normal residence since then; one-third of the population, descendants of Bedouin tribes, missed the window of opportunity to register for nationality rights after Kuwait became independent in 1961 and were classified as bidun (meaning "without"); since the 1980s Kuwait's bidun have progressively lost their rights, including opportunities for employment and education, amid official claims that they are nationals of other countries who have destroyed their identification documents in hopes of gaining Kuwaiti citizenship; Kuwaiti authorities have delayed processing citizenship applications and labeled biduns as "illegal residents," denying them access to civil documentation, such as birth and marriage certificates

Trafficking in persons: tier rating: Tier 2 Watch List — Kuwait does not fully meet the minimum standards for the elimination of trafficking, but the government has devoted sufficient resources to a written plan that, if implemented, would constitute significant efforts to meet the minimum standards; therefore, Kuwait was granted a waiver per the Trafficking Victims Protection Act from an otherwise required downgrade to Tier 3 and remained on Tier 2 Watch List for the third consecutive year; for more details, go to: https://www.state.gov/reports/2024-trafficking-in-persons-report/kuwait/

KYRGYZSTAN

INTRODUCTION

Background: Kyrgyzstan is a Central Asian country of incredible natural beauty and proud nomadic traditions. The Russian Empire annexed most of the territory of present-day Kyrgyzstan in 1876. The Kyrgyz staged a major revolt against the Tsarist Empire in 1916, during which almost one-sixth of the Kyrgyz population was killed. Kyrgyzstan became a Soviet republic in 1926 and achieved independence in 1991 when the USSR dissolved. Nationwide demonstrations in 2005 and 2010 resulted in the ouster of the country's first two presidents, Askar AKAEV and Kurmanbek BAKIEV. Almazbek ATAMBAEV was sworn in as president in 2011. In 2017, ATAMBAEV became the first Kyrgyzstani president to serve a full term and respect constitutional term limits, voluntarily stepping down at the end of his mandate. Former prime minister and ruling Social-Democratic Party of Kyrgyzstan member Sooronbay JEENBEKOV replaced him after winning the 2017

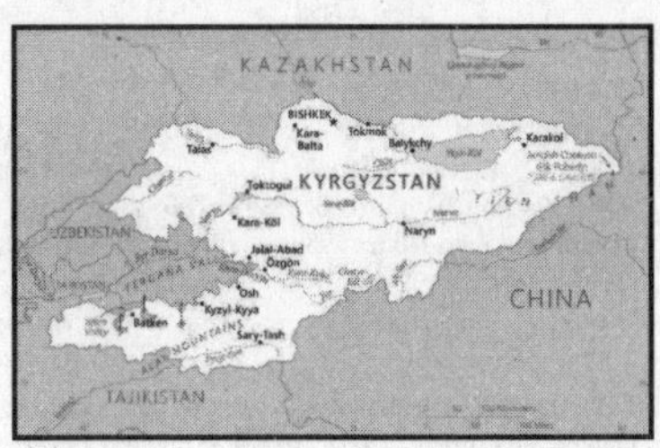

presidential election, which was the most competitive in the country's history despite reported cases of vote buying and abuse of public resources.

In 2020, protests against parliamentary election results spread across Kyrgyzstan, leading to JEENBEKOV's resignation and catapulting previously imprisoned Sadyr JAPAROV to acting president. In 2021, Kyrgyzstanis formally elected JAPAROV as president and approved a referendum to move Kyrgyzstan from a parliamentary to a presidential system. In 2021, Kyrgyzstanis voted in favor of constitutional changes that consolidated power in the presidency. Pro-government parties won a majority in the 2021 legislative elections. Continuing concerns for Kyrgyzstan include the trajectory of democratization, endemic corruption, tense regional relations, vulnerabilities due to climate change, border security vulnerabilities, and potential terrorist threats.

GEOGRAPHY

Location: Central Asia, west of China, south of Kazakhstan

Geographic coordinates: 41 00 N, 75 00 E

Map references: Asia

Area: *total:* 199,951 sq km
land: 191,801 sq km
water: 8,150 sq km
comparison ranking: total 87

Area - comparative: slightly smaller than South Dakota

Land boundaries: *total:* 4,573 km
border countries (4): China 1,063 km; Kazakhstan 1,212 km; Tajikistan 984 km; Uzbekistan 1,314 km

Coastline: 0 km (landlocked)

Maritime claims: none (landlocked)

Climate: dry continental to polar in high Tien Shan Mountains; subtropical in southwest (Fergana Valley); temperate in northern foothill zone

Terrain: peaks of the Tien Shan mountain range and associated valleys and basins encompass the entire country

Elevation: *highest point:* Jengish Chokusu (Pik Pobedy) 7,439 m
lowest point: Kara-Daryya (Karadar'ya) 132 m
mean elevation: 2,988 m

Natural resources: abundant hydropower; gold, rare earth metals; locally exploitable coal, oil, and natural gas; other deposits of nepheline, mercury, bismuth, lead, and zinc

Land use: *agricultural land:* 55.4% (2018 est.)
arable land: 6.7% (2018 est.)
permanent crops: 0.4% (2018 est.)
permanent pasture: 48.3% (2018 est.)
forest: 5.1% (2018 est.)
other: 39.5% (2018 est.)

Irrigated land: 10,043 sq km (2020)

Major lakes (area sq km): *salt water lake(s):* Ozero Issyk-Kul 6,240 sq km
note - second largest saline lake after the Caspian Sea; second highest mountain lake after Lake Titicaca; it is an endorheic mountain basin; although surrounded by snow capped mountains it never freezes

Major rivers (by length in km): Syr Darya river source (shared with Tajikistan, Uzbekistan, and Kazakhstan [m]) - 3,078 km
note – [s] after country name indicates river source; [m] after country name indicates river mouth

Major watersheds (area sq km): Internal (endorheic basin) drainage: Tarim Basin (1,152,448 sq km), *(Aral Sea basin)* Amu Darya (534,739 sq km), Syr Darya (782,617 sq km)

Population distribution: the vast majority of Kyrgyzstanis live in rural areas; densest population settlement is to the north in and around the capital, Bishkek, followed by Osh in the west; the least densely populated area is the east, southeast in the Tien Shan mountains

Natural hazards: major flooding during snow melt; prone to earthquakes

Geography - note: landlocked; entirely mountainous, dominated by the Tien Shan range; 94% of the country is 1,000 m above sea level with an average elevation of 2,750 m; many tall peaks, glaciers, and high-altitude lakes

PEOPLE AND SOCIETY

Population: *total:* 6,172,101
male: 3,021,318
female: 3,150,783 (2024 est.)
comparison rankings: female 112; male 113; total 112

Nationality: *noun:* Kyrgyzstani(s)
adjective: Kyrgyzstani

Ethnic groups: Kyrgyz 73.8%, Uzbek 14.8%, Russian 5.1%, Dungan 1.1%, other 5.2% (includes Uyghur, Tajik, Turk, Kazakh, Tatar, Ukrainian, Korean, German) (2021 est.)

Languages: Kyrgyz (state language) 71.4%, Uzbek 14.4%, Russian (official language) 9%, other 5.2% (2009 est.)
major-language sample(s):
Дүйнөлүк фактылар китеби, негизги маалыматтын маанилүү булагы.
(Kyrgyz)

Religions: Muslim 90% (majority Sunni), Christian 7% (Russian Orthodox 3%), other 3% (includes Jewish, Buddhist, Baha'i) (2017 est.)

Demographic profile: Kyrgyzstan is a sparsely populated country whose population is unevenly distributed. More than 50% of the population lives in or around the two cities of Bishkek and Osh and their surrounding districts, which together account for about 12% of the country's area. Kyrgyzstan's population continues to grow rapidly owing to its high fertility rate and the traditional preference for larger families, a low mortality rate, a growing share of women of reproductive age, and measures to support families with children. The country has a youthful age structure; over 45% of the population is under the age of 25 as of 2022. Nevertheless, Kyrgyzstan is transitioning from an agricultural society with high fertility and mortality rates to an industrial society with lower fertility and mortality rates.

As part of the USSR, Kyrgyzstan's rapid population growth was not problematic because its needs were redistributed among the Soviet States. As an independent state, however, population growth became burdensome. International labor migration continues to serve as a safety valve that decreases pressure on the labor market and resources (healthcare, education, and pensions), while also reducing poverty through much-needed remittances. The main destinations for labor migrants are Russia and Kazakhstan, where wages are higher; almost a third of Kyrgyzstan's working-age population migrates to Russia alone. Outmigration was most pronounced in the 1990s, after the collapse of the USSR, when ethnic Russians, Ukrainians, and Germans left Kyrgyzstan, changing the proportion of ethnic Kyrgyz in the country from barely 50% in 1992 to almost three-quarters today. While Kyrgyzstan is a net emigration country, it does receive immigrants. The majority of immigrants are from the Commonwealth of Independent States – particularly Kazakhstan, Russia, and Uzbekistan – but more recent arrivals also include persons from China, Turkey, and Turkmenistan. Chinese immigrants work primarily in construction and gold mining, while Turkish immigrants mainly work in construction, trade, education, and services. Border areas between Kyrgyzstan, Tajikistan, and Uzbekistan experience irregular migration, but many of these migrants plan to move on to Europe.

Age structure: *0-14 years:* 29.1% (male 922,086/female 873,245)
15-64 years: 64% (male 1,935,200/female 2,013,733)
65 years and over: 6.9% (2024 est.) (male 164,032/female 263,805)

Dependency ratios: *total dependency ratio:* 63.5
youth dependency ratio: 56.4
elderly dependency ratio: 7.2
potential support ratio: 13.9 (2021 est.)

Median age: *total:* 28.3 years (2024 est.)
male: 26.9 years
female: 29.8 years
comparison ranking: total 151

Population growth rate: 0.79% (2024 est.)
comparison ranking: 111

Birth rate: 18.7 births/1,000 population (2024 est.)
comparison ranking: 76

Death rate: 6 deaths/1,000 population (2024 est.)
comparison ranking: 152

Net migration rate: -4.8 migrant(s)/1,000 population (2024 est.)
comparison ranking: 200

Population distribution: the vast majority of Kyrgyzstanis live in rural areas; densest population settlement is to the north in and around the capital, Bishkek, followed by Osh in the west; the least densely populated area is the east, southeast in the Tien Shan mountains

Urbanization: *urban population:* 37.8% of total population (2023)
rate of urbanization: 2.05% annual rate of change (2020-25 est.)

Major urban areas - population: 1.105 million BISHKEK (capital) (2023)

Sex ratio: *at birth:* 1.07 male(s)/female
0-14 years: 1.06 male(s)/female
15-64 years: 0.96 male(s)/female
65 years and over: 0.62 male(s)/female
total population: 0.96 male(s)/female (2024 est.)

Mother's mean age at first birth: 22.6 years (2019 est.)

Maternal mortality ratio: 50 deaths/100,000 live births (2020 est.)
comparison ranking: 97

Infant mortality rate: *total:* 24.5 deaths/1,000 live births (2024 est.)
male: 28.6 deaths/1,000 live births
female: 20.2 deaths/1,000 live births
comparison ranking: total 61

Life expectancy at birth: *total population:* 72.9 years (2024 est.)
male: 68.9 years
female: 77.2 years
comparison ranking: total population 157

Total fertility rate: 2.45 children born/woman (2024 est.)
comparison ranking: 71

Gross reproduction rate: 1.19 (2024 est.)

Contraceptive prevalence rate: 39.4% (2018)

Drinking water source: *improved: urban:* 100% of population
rural: 89.9% of population
total: 93.6% of population
unimproved: urban: 0% of population
rural: 10.1% of population
total: 6.4% of population (2020 est.)

Current health expenditure: 5.3% of GDP (2020)

Physician density: 2.21 physicians/1,000 population (2014)

Hospital bed density: 4.4 beds/1,000 population (2014)

Sanitation facility access: *improved: urban:* 100% of population
rural: 100% of population
total: 100% of population

Obesity - adult prevalence rate: 16.6% (2016)
comparison ranking: 122

Alcohol consumption per capita: *total:* 4.02 liters of pure alcohol (2019 est.)
beer: 0.43 liters of pure alcohol (2019 est.)
wine: 0.23 liters of pure alcohol (2019 est.)
spirits: 3.35 liters of pure alcohol (2019 est.)
other alcohols: 0 liters of pure alcohol (2019 est.)
comparison ranking: total 96

Tobacco use: *total:* 25.4% (2020 est.)
male: 48% (2020 est.)
female: 2.8% (2020 est.)
comparison ranking: total 48

Children under the age of 5 years underweight: 1.8% (2018)
comparison ranking: 110

Currently married women (ages 15-49): 66.2% (2023 est.)

Child marriage: *women married by age 15:* 0.3%
women married by age 18: 12.9% (2018 est.)

Education expenditures: 6.2% of GDP (2020 est.)
comparison ranking: 37

Literacy: *definition:* age 15 and over can read and write
total population: 99.6%
male: 99.7%
female: 99.5% (2018)

School life expectancy (primary to tertiary education): *total:* 14 years
male: 13 years
female: 14 years (2021)

ENVIRONMENT

Environment - current issues: water pollution; many people get their water directly from contaminated streams and wells; as a result, water-borne diseases are prevalent; increasing soil salinity from faulty irrigation practices; air pollution due to rapid increase of traffic

Environment - international agreements: *party to:* Air Pollution, Biodiversity, Climate Change, Climate Change-Kyoto Protocol, Climate Change-Paris Agreement, Comprehensive Nuclear Test Ban, Desertification, Endangered Species, Environmental Modification, Hazardous Wastes, Ozone Layer Protection, Wetlands
signed, but not ratified: none of the selected agreements

Climate: dry continental to polar in high Tien Shan Mountains; subtropical in southwest (Fergana Valley); temperate in northern foothill zone

Urbanization: *urban population:* 37.8% of total population (2023)
rate of urbanization: 2.05% annual rate of change (2020-25 est.)

Revenue from forest resources: 0.01% of GDP (2018 est.)
comparison ranking: 146

Revenue from coal: 0.21% of GDP (2018 est.)
comparison ranking: 21

Air pollutants: *particulate matter emissions:* 37.58 micrograms per cubic meter (2019 est.)
carbon dioxide emissions: 9.79 megatons (2016 est.)
methane emissions: 4.47 megatons (2020 est.)

Waste and recycling: *municipal solid waste generated annually:* 1,113,300 tons (2015 est.)

Major lakes (area sq km): *salt water lake(s):* Ozero Issyk-Kul 6,240 sq km
note - second largest saline lake after the Caspian Sea; second highest mountain lake after Lake Titicaca; it is an endorheic mountain basin; although surrounded by snow capped mountains it never freezes

Major rivers (by length in km): Syr Darya river source (shared with Tajikistan, Uzbekistan, and Kazakhstan [m]) - 3,078 km
note – [s] after country name indicates river source; [m] after country name indicates river mouth

Major watersheds (area sq km): Internal (endorheic basin) drainage: Tarim Basin (1,152,448 sq km), *(Aral Sea basin)* Amu Darya (534,739 sq km), Syr Darya (782,617 sq km)

Total water withdrawal: *municipal:* 220 million cubic meters (2020 est.)
industrial: 340 million cubic meters (2020 est.)
agricultural: 7.1 billion cubic meters (2020 est.)

Total renewable water resources: 23.62 billion cubic meters (2020 est.)

GOVERNMENT

Country name: *conventional long form:* Kyrgyz Republic
conventional short form: Kyrgyzstan
local long form: Kyrgyz Respublikasy
local short form: Kyrgyzstan
etymology: a combination of the Turkic words "kyrg" (forty) and "-yz" (tribes) with the Persian suffix "-stan" (country) creating the meaning "Land of the Forty Tribes"; the name refers to the 40 clans united by the mythic Kyrgyz hero, MANAS

Government type: parliamentary republic

Capital: *name:* Bishkek
geographic coordinates: 42 52 N, 74 36 E
time difference: UTC+6 (11 hours ahead of Washington, DC, during Standard Time)
etymology: founded in 1868 as a Russian settlement on the site of a previously destroyed fortress named "Pishpek"; the name was retained and overtime became "Bishkek"

Administrative divisions: 7 provinces (oblustar, singular - oblus) and 2 cities* (shaarlar, singular - shaar); Batken Oblusu, Bishkek Shaary*, Chuy Oblusu (Bishkek), Jalal-Abad Oblusu, Naryn Oblusu, Osh Oblusu, Osh Shaary*, Talas Oblusu, Ysyk-Kol Oblusu (Karakol)
note: administrative divisions have the same names as their administrative centers (exceptions have the administrative center name following in parentheses)

Independence: 31 August 1991 (from the Soviet Union)

National holiday: Independence Day, 31 August (1991)

Legal system: civil law system, which includes features of French civil law and Russian Federation laws

Constitution: *history:* previous 1993, 2007, 2010; latest approved by referendum in April 2021 that transitioned Kyrgyzstan from a parliamentary to a presidential system, and implemented changes that allow the president to serve for two 5-year terms rather than one 6-year term, reduced the number of seats in Kyrgyzstan's legislature from 120 to 90, and established a Kurultay - a public advisory council
amendments: proposed as a draft law by the majority of the Supreme Council membership or by petition of 300,000 voters; passage requires at least two-thirds majority vote of the Council membership in each of at least three readings of the draft two months apart; the draft may be submitted to a referendum if approved by two thirds of the Council membership; adoption requires the signature of the president

International law organization participation: has not submitted an ICJ jurisdiction declaration; non-party state to the ICCt

Citizenship: *citizenship by birth:* no
citizenship by descent only: at least one parent must be a citizen of Kyrgyzstan
dual citizenship recognized: yes, but only if a mutual treaty on dual citizenship is in force
residency requirement for naturalization: 5 years

Suffrage: 18 years of age; universal

Executive branch: *chief of state:* President Sadyr JAPAROV (since 28 January 2021)
head of government: President Sadyr JAPAROV (since 28 January 2021)
cabinet: Cabinet of Ministers appointed by the president
elections/appointments: president directly elected by absolute majority popular vote in 2 rounds if needed for a five-year term (eligible for a second term); election last held on 10 January 2021 (next to be held in 2027)
election results:
2021: Sadyr JAPAROV elected president in first round; percent of vote - Sadyr JAPAROV (Mekenchil) 79.2%, Adakhan MADUMAROV (United Kyrgyzstan) 6.8%, other 14%
2017: Sooronbay JEENBEKOV elected president; Sooronbay JEENBEKOV (Social Democratic Party of Kyrgyzstan) 54.7%, Omurbek BABANOV

(independent) 33.8%, Adakhan MADUMAROV (United Kyrgyzstan) 6.6%, other 4.9%
note: the president is both chief of state and head of government

Legislative branch: *description:* unicameral Supreme Council or Jogorku Kenesh (90 seats statutory, current 88; 54 seats allocated for proportional division among political party lists from the national vote and 36 seats allocated for candidates running in single-seat constituencies; members serve 5-year terms; parties must receive 5% of the vote to win seats in the Council)
elections: last held on 28 November 2021 (next to be held in 2026)
election results: percent of vote by party - AJK 17.3%, Ishenim 15%, Yntymak 12.1%, Alyans 9.2%, Butun Kyrgyzstan 7.8%, Yiman Nuru 6.8%, other 30%; seats by party - AJK 15, Ishenim 12, Yntymak 9, Alyns 7, Butun Kyrgyzstan 6, Yiman Nuru 5, other 36; composition - men 70, women 19, percentage women 21.1%

Judicial branch: *highest court(s):* Supreme Court (consists of 25 judges); Constitutional Chamber of the Supreme Court (consists of the chairperson, deputy chairperson, and 9 judges)
judge selection and term of office: Supreme Court and Constitutional Court judges appointed by the Supreme Council on the recommendation of the president; Supreme Court judges serve for 10 years, Constitutional Court judges serve for 15 years; mandatory retirement at age 70 for judges of both courts
subordinate courts: Higher Court of Arbitration; oblast (provincial) and city courts

Political parties: Afghan's Party
Alliance
Ata-Jurt Kyrgyzstan (Fatherland) or AJK
Cohesion
Ishenim (Trust)
Light of Faith
Mekenchil or the "Patriotic" Political Party
Social Democrats or SDK
United Kyrgyzstan
Yntymak (Unity)

International organization participation: ADB, CICA, CIS, CSTO, EAEU, EAPC, EBRD, ECO, EITI (compliant country), FAO, GCTU, IAEA, IBRD, ICAO, ICC (NGOs), ICRM, IDA, IDB, IFAD, IFC, IFRCS, ILO, IMF, Interpol, IOC, IOM, IPU, ISO (correspondent), ITSO, ITU, MIGA, NAM (observer), OIC, OPCW, OSCE, PCA, PFP, SCO, UN, UNAMID, UNCTAD, UNESCO, UNIDO, UNISFA, UNMIL, UNMISS, UNWTO, UPU, WCO, WFTU (NGOs), WHO, WIPO, WMO, WTO

Diplomatic representation in the US: *chief of mission:* Ambassador (vacant); (since 26 October 2024)
chancery: 2360 Massachusetts Avenue NW, Washington, DC 20008
telephone: [1] (202) 449-9822
FAX: [1] (202) 449-8275
email address and website:
kgembassy.usa@mfa.gov.kg
Embassy of the Kyrgyz Republic in the USA and Canada (mfa.gov.kg)

Diplomatic representation from the US: *chief of mission:* Ambassador Lesslie VIGUERIE (since 29 December 2022)
embassy: 171 Prospect Mira, Bishkek 720016
mailing address: 7040 Bishkek Place, Washington DC 20521-7040
telephone: [996] (312) 597-000
FAX: [996] (312) 597-744
email address and website:
ConsularBishkek@state.gov
https://kg.usembassy.gov/

Flag description: red field with a yellow sun in the center having 40 rays representing the 40 Kyrgyz tribes; on the obverse side the rays run counterclockwise, on the reverse, clockwise; in the center of the sun is a red ring crossed by two sets of three lines, a stylized representation of a "tunduk" - the crown of a traditional Kyrgyz yurt; red symbolizes bravery and valor, the sun evinces peace and wealth

National symbol(s): white falcon; national colors: red, yellow

National anthem: *name:* "Kyrgyz Respublikasynyn Mamlekettik Gimni" (National Anthem of the Kyrgyz Republic)
lyrics/music: Djamil SADYKOV and Eshmambet KULUEV/Nasyr DAVLESOV and Kalyi MOLDOBASANOV
note: adopted 1992

National heritage: *total World Heritage Sites:* 3 (2 cultural, 1 natural)
selected World Heritage Site locales: Sulaiman-Too Sacred Mountain (c); Silk Roads: the Chang'an-Tianshan Corridor (c); Western Tien Shan (n)

ECONOMY

Economic overview: landlocked, lower-middle-income Central Asian economy; natural resource rich; growing hydroelectricity and tourism; high remittances; corruption limits investment; COVID-19 and political turmoil hurt GDP, limited public revenues, and increased spending

Real GDP (purchasing power parity): $45.461 billion (2023 est.)
$42.826 billion (2022 est.)
$39.302 billion (2021 est.)
note: data in 2021 dollars
comparison ranking: 131

Real GDP growth rate: 6.15% (2023 est.)
8.97% (2022 est.)
5.51% (2021 est.)
note: annual GDP % growth based on constant local currency
comparison ranking: 30

Real GDP per capita: $6,400 (2023 est.)
$6,100 (2022 est.)
$5,800 (2021 est.)
note: data in 2021 dollars
comparison ranking: 165

GDP (official exchange rate): $13.988 billion (2023 est.)
note: data in current dollars at official exchange rate

Inflation rate (consumer prices): 10.75% (2023 est.)
13.92% (2022 est.)
11.91% (2021 est.)
note: annual % change based on consumer prices
comparison ranking: 182

Credit ratings: Moody's rating: B2 (2015)

Standard & Poors rating: NR (2016)
note: The year refers to the year in which the current credit rating was first obtained.

GDP - composition, by sector of origin: *agriculture:* 9.7% (2023 est.)
industry: 22.6% (2023 est.)
services: 50.8% (2023 est.)
note: figures may not total 100% due to non-allocated consumption not captured in sector-reported data comparison rankings: services 143; industry 118; agriculture 78

GDP - composition, by end use: *household consumption:* 88.7% (2022 est.)
government consumption: 16.8% (2022 est.)
investment in fixed capital: 21.5% (2022 est.)
investment in inventories: 14.2% (2022 est.)
exports of goods and services: 29.9% (2022 est.)
imports of goods and services: -87.4% (2022 est.)
note: figures may not total 100% due to rounding or gaps in data collection

Agricultural products: milk, potatoes, maize, wheat, barley, sugar beets, tomatoes, onions, watermelons, carrots/turnips (2022)
note: top ten agricultural products based on tonnage

Industries: small machinery, textiles, food processing, cement, shoes, lumber, refrigerators, furniture, electric motors, gold, rare earth metals

Industrial production growth rate: 4.93% (2023 est.)
note: annual % change in industrial value added based on constant local currency
comparison ranking: 53

Labor force: 3.069 million (2023 est.)
note: number of people ages 15 or older who are employed or seeking work
comparison ranking: 108

Unemployment rate: 4.04% (2023 est.)
4.06% (2022 est.)
4.1% (2021 est.)
note: % of labor force seeking employment
comparison ranking: 75

Youth unemployment rate (ages 15-24): *total:* 8.2% (2023 est.)
male: 7.6% (2023 est.)
female: 9.2% (2023 est.)
note: % of labor force ages 15-24 seeking employment
comparison ranking: total 150

Population below poverty line: 33.3% (2021 est.)
note: % of population with income below national poverty line

Gini Index coefficient - distribution of family income: 28.8 (2021 est.)
note: index (0-100) of income distribution; higher values represent greater inequality
comparison ranking: 132

Household income or consumption by percentage share: *lowest 10%:* 4.1% (2021 est.)
highest 10%: 24.2% (2021 est.)
note: % share of income accruing to lowest and highest 10% of population

Remittances: 18.59% of GDP (2023 est.)
26.58% of GDP (2022 est.)
32.56% of GDP (2021 est.)
note: personal transfers and compensation between resident and non-resident individuals/households/entities

Budget: *revenues:* $3.859 billion (2022 est.)
expenditures: $2.892 billion (2022 est.)
note: central government revenues (excluding grants) and expenses converted to US dollars at average official exchange rate for year indicated

Public debt: 47.09% of GDP (2022 est.)
note: central government debt as a % of GDP
comparison ranking: 113

Taxes and other revenues: 19.54% (of GDP) (2022 est.)
note: central government tax revenue as a % of GDP

comparison ranking: 89

Current account balance: -$5.18 billion (2022 est.)
-$737.696 million (2021 est.)
$374.257 million (2020 est.)
note: balance of payments - net trade and primary/secondary income in current dollars
comparison ranking: 182

Exports: $3.628 billion (2022 est.)
$3.292 billion (2021 est.)
$2.435 billion (2020 est.)
note: balance of payments - exports of goods and services in current dollars
comparison ranking: 149

Exports - partners: Russia 43%, Kazakhstan 18%, Uzbekistan 10%, Turkey 6%, UAE 4% (2022)
note: top five export partners based on percentage share of exports

Exports - commodities: garments, refined petroleum, gold, precious metal ore, dried legumes (2022)
note: top five export commodities based on value in dollars

Imports: $10.655 billion (2022 est.)
$5.928 billion (2021 est.)
$4.051 billion (2020 est.)
note: balance of payments - imports of goods and services in current dollars
comparison ranking: 119

Imports - partners: China 64%, Russia 10%, Uzbekistan 4%, Turkey 4%, Kazakhstan 4% (2022)
note: top five import partners based on percentage share of imports

Imports - commodities: garments, footwear, refined petroleum, cars, fabric (2022)
note: top five import commodities based on value in dollars

Reserves of foreign exchange and gold: $3.237 billion (2023 est.)
$2.799 billion (2022 est.)
$2.983 billion (2021 est.)
note: holdings of gold (year-end prices)/foreign exchange/special drawing rights in current dollars
comparison ranking: 118

Debt - external: $3.457 billion (2022 est.)
note: present value of external debt in current US dollars
comparison ranking: 61

Exchange rates: soms (KGS) per US dollar -

Exchange rates: 87.856 (2023 est.)
84.116 (2022 est.)
84.641 (2021 est.)
77.346 (2020 est.)
69.789 (2019 est.)

ENERGY

Electricity access: *electrification - total population:* 99.7% (2022 est.)
electrification - urban areas: 100%
electrification - rural areas: 99.6%

Electricity: *installed generating capacity:* 4.408 million kW (2022 est.)
consumption: 13.465 billion kWh (2022 est.)
exports: 457 million kWh (2022 est.)
imports: 2.806 billion kWh (2022 est.)
transmission/distribution losses: 2.738 billion kWh (2022 est.)
comparison rankings: transmission/distribution losses 135; imports 56; exports 78; consumption 89; installed generating capacity 93

Electricity generation sources: *fossil fuels:* 14.1% of total installed capacity (2022 est.)
hydroelectricity: 85.9% of total installed capacity (2022 est.)

Coal: *production:* 3.637 million metric tons (2022 est.)
consumption: 3.352 million metric tons (2022 est.)
exports: 1.321 million metric tons (2022 est.)
imports: 738,000 metric tons (2022 est.)
proven reserves: 28.499 billion metric tons (2022 est.)

Petroleum: *total petroleum production:* 6,000 bbl/day (2023 est.)
refined petroleum consumption: 31,000 bbl/day (2022 est.)
crude oil estimated reserves: 40 million barrels (2021 est.)

Natural gas: *production:* 31.026 million cubic meters (2022 est.)
consumption: 438 million cubic meters (2022 est.)
imports: 406.974 million cubic meters (2022 est.)
proven reserves: 5.663 billion cubic meters (2021 est.)

Carbon dioxide emissions: 10.197 million metric tonnes of CO2 (2022 est.)
from coal and metallurgical coke: 5.066 million metric tonnes of CO2 (2022 est.)
from petroleum and other liquids: 4.272 million metric tonnes of CO2 (2022 est.)
from consumed natural gas: 859,000 metric tonnes of CO2 (2022 est.)
comparison ranking: total emissions 106

Energy consumption per capita: 26.992 million Btu/person (2022 est.)
comparison ranking: 119

COMMUNICATIONS

Telephones - fixed lines: *total subscriptions:* 299,000 (2021 est.)
subscriptions per 100 inhabitants: 5 (2021 est.)
comparison ranking: total subscriptions 107

Telephones - mobile cellular: *total subscriptions:* 8.511 million (2021 est.)
subscriptions per 100 inhabitants: 130 (2021 est.)
comparison ranking: total subscriptions 99

Telecommunication systems: *general assessment:* the country's telecom sector (specifically the mobile segment) has been able to prosper; Kyrgyzstan has opened up its telecom market to competition; the mobile market has achieved high levels of penetration (140% in 2021) along with a fairly competitive operating environment with four major players; mobile broadband has come along strongly, reaching over 125% penetration in 2019 before falling back slightly during the COVID-19 crisis; slow-to-moderate growth is expected for both segments in coming years, supported by the anticipated rollout of 5G services which began testing in 2022 with a pilot service in 2023 which has been delayed into 2024 (2024)
domestic: fixed-line subscriptions 5 per 100; mobile-cellular subscribership up to over 130 per 100 persons (2022)
international: country code - 996; connections with other CIS (Commonwealth of Independent States, 9 members post-Soviet Republics in EU) countries by landline or microwave radio relay and with other countries by leased connections with Moscow international gateway switch and by satellite; satellite earth stations - 2 (1 Intersputnik, 1 Intelsat) (2019)

Broadcast media: state-funded public TV broadcaster NTRK has nationwide coverage; also operates Ala-Too 24 news channel which broadcasts 24/7 and 4 other educational, cultural, and sports channels; ELTR is a state-owned TV station with national reach; the switchover to digital TV in 2017 resulted in private TV station growth; approximately 20 stations are struggling to increase their own Kyrgyz-language content up to 60% of airtime, as required by law, instead of rebroadcasting primarily programs from Russian channels or airing unlicensed movies and music; several Russian TV stations also broadcast; state-funded radio stations and about 10 significant private radio stations also exist (2023)

Internet country code: .kg

Internet users: *total:* 5.07 million (2021 est.)
percent of population: 78% (2021 est.)
comparison ranking: total 93

Broadband - fixed subscriptions: *total:* 289,000 (2020 est.)
subscriptions per 100 inhabitants: 4 (2020 est.)
comparison ranking: total 109

TRANSPORTATION

National air transport system: *number of registered air carriers:* 5 (2020)
inventory of registered aircraft operated by air carriers: 17
annual passenger traffic on registered air carriers: 709,198 (2018)

Civil aircraft registration country code prefix: EX

Airports: 28 (2024)
comparison ranking: 122

Heliports: 1 (2024)

Pipelines: 4,195 km gas (2022), 16 km oil (2022) (2022)

Railways: *total:* 424 km (2022)
broad gauge: 424 km (2018) 1.520-m gauge
comparison ranking: total 118

Roadways: *total:* 34,000 km (2022)
paved: 22,600 km (2020)
unpaved: 7,700 km (2020)
comparison ranking: total 96

Waterways: 576 km (2022)
comparison ranking: 89

MILITARY AND SECURITY

Military and security forces: Armed Forces of the Kyrgyz Republic: Land Forces, Air Defense Forces, National Guard; Internal Troops; State Committee for National Security (GKNB): State Border Service (2024)

Military expenditures: 1.5% of GDP (2022 est.)
1.7% of GDP (2021 est.)
1.8% of GDP (2020 est.)
2.3% of GDP (2019 est.)
2.3% of GDP (2018 est.)
comparison ranking: 96

Military and security service personnel strengths: approximately 15,000 active-duty troops (9,000 Land Forces; 3,000 Air Force/Air Defense; 3,000 National Guard) (2023)

Military equipment inventories and acquisitions: the Kyrgyz military inventory is comprised of mostly older Russian and Soviet-era equipment; Russia continues to be the leading supplier of armaments, although in recent years Kyrgyzstan has procured weapons systems from several other countries, including Belarus, Germany, and Turkey (2023)

Military service age and obligation: 18-27 years of age for compulsory or voluntary service for men in the Armed Forces or Interior Ministry; 12-month service obligation (9 months for university graduates), with optional fee-based 3-year service in the call-up mobilization reserve; women may volunteer at age 19; 16-17 years of age for military cadets, who cannot take part in military operations (2023)

Military - note: Kyrgyzstan has been a member of the Collective Security Treaty Organization (CSTO) since 1994 and contributes troops to CSTO's rapid reaction force; it also started a relationship with NATO in 1992 and joined NATO's Partnership for Peace program in 1994

the Kyrgyz military's primary responsibility is defense of the country's sovereignty and territory, although it also has some internal security duties; elements of the military were called out in 2020 to respond to post-election demonstrations for example, and the National Guard's missions include counterterrorism, responding to emergencies, and the protection of government facilities; the military also participates in UN and CSTO peacekeeping missions; border disputes with Tajikistan and Uzbekistan, as well as the threat posed by militant Islamic groups, have been particular areas of concern for both the military and internal security forces; the military's closest security partner is Russia, which provides training and material assistance, and maintains a presence in the country, including an airbase; the military also conducts training with other regional countries such as India, traditionally with a focus on counterterrorism

the Kyrgyz military was formed in 1992 from Soviet Army units then based in Kyrgyzstan following the dissolution of the USSR (2023)

TERRORISM

Terrorist group(s): US-designated foreign terrorist groups such as the Islamic Jihad Union, the Islamic Movement of Uzbekistan, and the Islamic State of Iraq and ash-Sham-Khorasan Province have operated in the area where the Uzbek, Kyrgyz, and Tajik borders converge and ill-defined and porous borders allow for the relatively free movement of people and illicit goods

TRANSNATIONAL ISSUES

Refugees and internally displaced persons: *stateless persons:* 482 (2022)

Trafficking in persons: tier rating: Tier 2 Watch List — the government did not demonstrate overall increasing efforts to eliminate trafficking compared with the previous reporting period, therefore Kyrgyzstan was downgraded to Tier 2 Watch List; for more details, go to: https://www.state.gov/reports/2024-trafficking-in-persons-report/kyrgyzstan/

Illicit drugs: a prime transit route and transshipment route for illegal drugs transiting north from Afghanistan to Russia and Europe; illicit drugs are primarily smuggled into the country from Tajikistan

LAOS

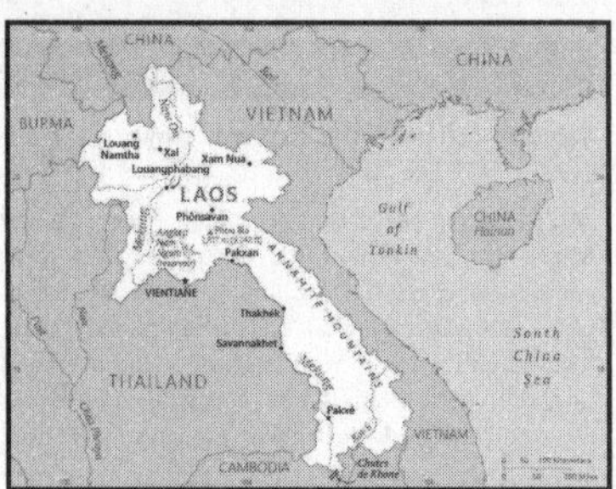

INTRODUCTION

Background: Modern-day Laos has its roots in the ancient Lao kingdom of Lan Xang, established in the 14th century under King FA NGUM. For 300 years, Lan Xang had influence reaching into present-day Cambodia and Thailand, as well as over all of what is now Laos. After centuries of gradual decline, Laos came under the domination of Siam (Thailand) from the late 18th century until the late 19th century, when it became part of French Indochina. The Franco-Siamese Treaty of 1907 defined the current Lao border with Thailand. Following more than 15 years of civil war, the communist Pathet Lao took control of the government in 1975, ending a six-century-old monarchy and instituting a one party–the Lao People's Revolutionary Party–communist state. A gradual, limited return to private enterprise and the liberalization of foreign investment laws began in the late 1980s. Laos became a member of ASEAN in 1997 and the WTO in 2013.

In the 2010s, the country benefited from direct foreign investment, particularly in the natural resource and industry sectors. Construction of a number of large hydropower dams and expanding mining activities have also boosted the economy. Laos has retained its official commitment to communism and maintains close ties with its two communist neighbors, Vietnam and China, both of which continue to exert substantial political and economic influence on the country. China, for example, provided 70% of the funding for a $5.9 billion, 400-km railway line between the Chinese border and the capital Vientiane, which opened for operations in 2021. Laos financed the remaining 30% with loans from China. At the same time, Laos has expanded its economic reliance on the West and other Asian countries, such as Japan, Malaysia, Singapore, Taiwan, and Thailand. Nevertheless, despite steady economic growth for more than a decade, it remains one of Asia's poorest countries.

GEOGRAPHY

Location: Southeastern Asia, northeast of Thailand, west of Vietnam

Geographic coordinates: 18 00 N, 105 00 E

Map references: Southeast Asia

Area: *total:* 236,800 sq km
land: 230,800 sq km
water: 6,000 sq km
comparison ranking: total 84

Area - comparative: about twice the size of Pennsylvania; slightly larger than Utah

Land boundaries: *total:* 5,274 km
border countries (5): Burma 238 km; Cambodia 555 km; China 475 km; Thailand 1,845 km; Vietnam 2,161 km

Coastline: 0 km (landlocked)

Maritime claims: none (landlocked)

Climate: tropical monsoon; rainy season (May to November); dry season (December to April)

Terrain: mostly rugged mountains; some plains and plateaus

Elevation: *highest point:* Phu Bia 2,817 m
lowest point: Mekong River 70 m
mean elevation: 710 m

Natural resources: timber, hydropower, gypsum, tin, gold, gemstones

Land use: *agricultural land:* 10.6% (2018 est.)
arable land: 6.2% (2018 est.)
permanent crops: 0.7% (2018 est.)
permanent pasture: 3.7% (2018 est.)
forest: 67.9% (2018 est.)
other: 21.5% (2018 est.)

Irrigated land: 4,409 sq km (2020)

Major rivers (by length in km): Mènam Khong (Mekong) (shared with China [s], Burma, Thailand, Cambodia, and Vietnam [m]) - 4,350 km
note – [s] after country name indicates river source; [m] after country name indicates river mouth

Major watersheds (area sq km): Pacific Ocean drainage: Mekong (805,604 sq km)

Population distribution: most densely populated area is in and around the capital city of Vientiane; large communities are primarily found along the Mekong River along the southwestern border; overall density is considered one of the lowest in Southeast Asia

Natural hazards: floods, droughts

Geography - note: landlocked; most of the country is mountainous and thickly forested; the Mekong River forms a large part of the western boundary with Thailand

PEOPLE AND SOCIETY

Population: *total:* 7,953,556
male: 3,966,320
female: 3,987,236 (2024 est.)
comparison rankings: female 102; male 103; total 103

Nationality: *noun:* Lao(s) or Laotian(s)
adjective: Lao or Laotian

Ethnic groups: Lao 53.2%, Khmou 11%, Hmong 9.2%, Phouthay 3.4%, Tai 3.1%, Makong 2.5%, Katong 2.2%, Lue 2%, Akha 1.8%, other 11.6% (2015 est.)
note: the Laos Government officially recognizes 49 ethnic groups, but the total number of ethnic groups is estimated to be well over 200

Languages: Lao (official), French, English, various ethnic languages
major-language sample(s):
ແຫລ່ງທີ່ຂາດບໍ່ໄດ້ສໍາລັບຂໍ້ມູນຕົ້ນຕໍ”
(Lao)

Religions: Buddhist 64.7%, Christian 1.7%, none 31.4%, other/not stated 2.1% (2015 est.)

Demographic profile: Laos is a predominantly rural country with a youthful population – almost 55% of the population is under the age of 25. Its progress on health and development issues has been uneven geographically, among ethnic groups, and socioeconomically. Laos has made headway in poverty reduction, with the poverty rate almost halving from 46% in 1992/93 to 22% in 2012/13. Nevertheless, pronounced rural-urban disparities persist, and income inequality is rising. Poverty most affects populations in rural and highland areas, particularly ethnic minority groups.

The total fertility rate (TFR) has decreased markedly from around 6 births per woman on average in 1990 to approximately 2.8 in 2016, but it is still one of the highest in Southeast Asia. TFR is higher in rural and remote areas, among ethnic minority groups, the less-educated, and the poor; it is lower in urban areas and among the more educated and those with higher incomes. Although Laos' mortality rates have improved substantially over the last few decades, the maternal mortality rate and childhood malnutrition remain at high levels. As fertility and mortality rates continue to decline, the proportion of Laos' working-age population will increase, and its share of dependents will shrink. The age structure shift will provide Laos with the potential to realize a demographic dividend during the next few decades, if it can improve educational access and quality and gainfully employ its growing working-age population in productive sectors. Currently, Laos primary school enrollment is nearly universal, but the drop-out rate remains problematic. Secondary school enrollment has also increased but remains low, especially for girls.

Laos has historically been a country of emigration and internal displacement due to conflict and a weak economy. The Laos civil war (1953 – 1975) mainly caused internal displacement (numbering in the hundreds of thousands). Following the end of the Vietnam War in 1975, indigenous people in remote, war-struck areas were resettled and more than 300,000 people fled to Thailand to escape the communist regime that took power. The majority of those who sought refuge in Thailand ultimately were resettled in the US (mainly Hmong who fought with US forces), and lesser numbers went to France, Canada, and Australia.

The Laos Government carried out resettlement programs between the mid-1980s and mid-1990s to relocate ethnic minority groups from the rural northern highlands to development areas in the lowlands ostensibly to alleviate poverty, make basic services more accessible, eliminate slash-and-burn agriculture and opium production, integrate ethnic minorities, and control rebel groups (including Hmong insurgents). For many, however, resettlement has exacerbated poverty, led to the loss of livelihoods, and increased food insecurity and mortality rates. As the resettlement programs started to wane in the second half of the 1990s, migration from the northern highlands to urban centers – chiefly the capital Vientiane – to pursue better jobs in the growing manufacturing and service sectors became the main type of relocation. Migration of villagers from the south seeking work in neighboring Thailand also increased. Thailand is the main international migration destination for Laotians because of the greater availability of jobs and higher pay than at home; nearly a million Laotian migrants were estimated to live in Thailand as of 2015.

Age structure: *0-14 years:* 30.1% (male 1,214,429/female 1,181,845)
15-64 years: 65% (male 2,573,668/female 2,599,957)
65 years and over: 4.8% (2024 est.) (male 178,223/female 205,434)

Dependency ratios: *total dependency ratio:* 54.7
youth dependency ratio: 48
elderly dependency ratio: 6.7
potential support ratio: 14.8 (2021 est.)

Median age: *total:* 25.4 years (2024 est.)
male: 25 years
female: 25.7 years
comparison ranking: total 170

Population growth rate: 1.26% (2024 est.)
comparison ranking: 75

Birth rate: 19.8 births/1,000 population (2024 est.)
comparison ranking: 69

Death rate: 6.2 deaths/1,000 population (2024 est.)
comparison ranking: 147

Net migration rate: -1 migrant(s)/1,000 population (2024 est.)
comparison ranking: 145

Population distribution: most densely populated area is in and around the capital city of Vientiane; large communities are primarily found along the Mekong River along the southwestern border; overall density is considered one of the lowest in Southeast Asia

Urbanization: *urban population:* 38.2% of total population (2023)
rate of urbanization: 2.99% annual rate of change (2020-25 est.)

Major urban areas - population: 721,000 VIENTIANE (capital) (2023)

Sex ratio: *at birth:* 1.04 male(s)/female
0-14 years: 1.03 male(s)/female
15-64 years: 0.99 male(s)/female
65 years and over: 0.87 male(s)/female
total population: 1 male(s)/female (2024 est.)

Maternal mortality ratio: 126 deaths/100,000 live births (2020 est.)
comparison ranking: 60

Infant mortality rate: *total:* 35.4 deaths/1,000 live births (2024 est.)
male: 39.1 deaths/1,000 live births
female: 31.6 deaths/1,000 live births
comparison ranking: total 38

Life expectancy at birth: *total population:* 69 years (2024 est.)
male: 67.4 years
female: 70.7 years
comparison ranking: total population 183

Total fertility rate: 2.24 children born/woman (2024 est.)
comparison ranking: 81

Gross reproduction rate: 1.1 (2024 est.)

Contraceptive prevalence rate: 54.1% (2017)

Drinking water source: *improved: urban:* 97.1% of population
rural: 84.1% of population
total: 88.8% of population
unimproved: urban: 2.9% of population
rural: 15.9% of population
total: 11.2% of population (2020 est.)

Current health expenditure: 2.7% of GDP (2020)

Physician density: 0.35 physicians/1,000 population (2020)

Hospital bed density: 1.5 beds/1,000 population (2012)

Sanitation facility access: *improved: urban:* 100% of population
rural: 72% of population
total: 82.2% of population
unimproved: urban: 0% of population
rural: 28% of population
total: 17.8% of population (2020 est.)

Obesity - adult prevalence rate: 5.3% (2016)
comparison ranking: 179

Alcohol consumption per capita: *total:* 8.15 liters of pure alcohol (2019 est.)
beer: 3.62 liters of pure alcohol (2019 est.)
wine: 0.07 liters of pure alcohol (2019 est.)
spirits: 4.46 liters of pure alcohol (2019 est.)
other alcohols: 0 liters of pure alcohol (2019 est.)
comparison ranking: total 42

Tobacco use: *total:* 31.8% (2020 est.)
male: 53.3% (2020 est.)
female: 10.3% (2020 est.)
comparison ranking: total 21

Children under the age of 5 years underweight: 21.1% (2017)
comparison ranking: 13

Currently married women (ages 15-49): 60.1% (2023 est.)

Child marriage: *women married by age 15:* 7.1%
women married by age 18: 32.7%
men married by age 18: 10.8% (2017 est.)

Education expenditures: 2.3% of GDP (2020 est.)
comparison ranking: 179

Literacy: *definition:* age 15 and over can read and write
total population: 87.1%
male: 91.4%
female: 81.4% (2021)

School life expectancy (primary to tertiary education): *total:* 10 years
male: 10 years
female: 10 years (2020)

ENVIRONMENT

Environment - current issues: unexploded ordnance; deforestation; soil erosion; loss of biodiversity; water pollution, most of the population does not have access to potable water

Environment - international agreements: *party to:* Biodiversity, Climate Change, Climate Change-Kyoto Protocol, Climate Change-Paris Agreement, Comprehensive Nuclear Test Ban, Desertification, Endangered Species, Environmental Modification, Hazardous Wastes, Law of the Sea, Nuclear Test Ban, Ozone Layer Protection, Wetlands, Whaling
signed, but not ratified: none of the selected agreements

Climate: tropical monsoon; rainy season (May to November); dry season (December to April)

Urbanization: *urban population:* 38.2% of total population (2023)
rate of urbanization: 2.99% annual rate of change (2020-25 est.)

Revenue from forest resources: 1.48% of GDP (2018 est.)
comparison ranking: 44

Air pollutants: *particulate matter emissions:* 21.15 micrograms per cubic meter (2019 est.)
carbon dioxide emissions: 17.76 megatons (2016 est.)
methane emissions: 9 megatons (2020 est.)

Waste and recycling: *municipal solid waste generated annually:* 351,900 tons (2015 est.)
municipal solid waste recycled annually: 35,190 tons (2015 est.)
percent of municipal solid waste recycled: 10% (2015 est.)

Major rivers (by length in km): Mènam Khong (Mekong) (shared with China [s], Burma, Thailand, Cambodia, and Vietnam [m]) - 4,350 km
note – [s] after country name indicates river source; [m] after country name indicates river mouth

Major watersheds (area sq km): Pacific Ocean drainage: Mekong (805,604 sq km)

Total water withdrawal: *municipal:* 130 million cubic meters (2020 est.)
industrial: 170 million cubic meters (2020 est.)
agricultural: 7.05 billion cubic meters (2020 est.)

Total renewable water resources: 333.5 billion cubic meters (2020 est.)

GOVERNMENT

Country name: *conventional long form:* Lao People's Democratic Republic
conventional short form: Laos
local long form: Sathalanalat Paxathipatai Paxaxon Lao
local short form: Mueang Lao (unofficial)
abbreviation: Lao PDR
etymology: name means "Land of the Lao [people]"

Government type: communist party-led state

Capital: *name:* Vientiane (Viangchan)
geographic coordinates: 17 58 N, 102 36 E
time difference: UTC+7 (12 hours ahead of Washington, DC, during Standard Time)
etymology: the meaning in Pali, a Buddhist liturgical language, is "city of sandalwood"

Administrative divisions: 17 provinces (khoueng, singular and plural) and 1 prefecture* (kampheng nakhon); Attapu, Bokeo, Bolikhamxay, Champasak, Houaphanh, Khammouan, Louangnamtha, Louangphabang (Luang Prabang), Oudomxai, Phongsali, Salavan, Savannakhet, Viangchan (Vientiane)*, Viangchan, Xaignabouli, Xaisomboun, Xekong, Xiangkhouang

Independence: 19 July 1949 (from France by the Franco-Lao General Convention); 22 October 1953 (Franco-Lao Treaty recognizes full independence)

National holiday: Republic Day (National Day), 2 December (1975)

Legal system: civil law system similar in form to the French system

Constitution: *history:* previous 1947 (preindependence); latest promulgated 13-15 August 1991
amendments: proposed by the National Assembly; passage requires at least two-thirds majority vote of the Assembly membership and promulgation by the president of the republic; amended 2003, 2015

International law organization participation: has not submitted an ICJ jurisdiction declaration; non-party state to the ICCt

Citizenship: *citizenship by birth:* no
citizenship by descent only: at least one parent must be a citizen of Laos
dual citizenship recognized: no
residency requirement for naturalization: 10 years

Suffrage: 18 years of age; universal

Executive branch: *chief of state:* President THONGLOUN Sisoulith (since 22 March 2021)
head of government: Prime Minister SONEXAY (also spelled SONXAI) Siphandon (since 30 December 2022)
cabinet: Council of Ministers appointed by the president and approved by the National Assembly
elections/appointments: president and vice president indirectly elected by the National Assembly for a 5-year term (no term limits); election last held on 22 March 2021 (next to be held in March 2026); prime minister nominated by the president, elected by the National Assembly for a 5-year term
election results:
2021: THONGLOUN Sisoulith (LPRP) elected president; National Assembly vote - 161-1; PHANKHAM Viphavanh (LPRP) elected prime minister; National Assembly vote - 158-3
2016: BOUNNHANG Vorachit (LPRP) elected president; percent of National Assembly vote - NA; THONGLOUN Sisoulith (LPRP) elected prime minister; percent of National Assembly vote - NA

Legislative branch: *description:* unicameral National Assembly or Sapha Heng Xat (164 seats; members directly elected in multi-seat constituencies by simple majority vote from candidate lists provided by the Lao People's Revolutionary Party; members serve 5-year terms)
elections: last held on 21 February 2021 (next to be held in 2026)
election results: percent of vote by party - NA; seats by party - LPRP 158, independent 6; composition - men 128, women 36, percentage women 22%

Judicial branch: *highest court(s):* People's Supreme Court (consists of the court president and organized into criminal, civil, administrative, commercial, family, and juvenile chambers, each with a vice president and several judges)
judge selection and term of office: president of People's Supreme Court appointed by the National Assembly upon the recommendation of the president of the republic for a 5-year term; vice presidents of the People's Supreme Court appointed by the president of the republic upon the recommendation of the National Assembly; appointment of chamber judges NA; tenure of court vice presidents and chamber judges NA
subordinate courts: appellate courts; provincial, municipal, district, and military courts

Political parties: Lao People's Revolutionary Party or LPRP
note: other parties proscribed

International organization participation: ADB, ARF, ASEAN, CP, EAS, FAO, G-77, IAEA, IBRD, ICAO, ICRM, IDA, IFAD, IFC, IFRCS, ILO, IMF, Interpol, IOC, IPU, ISO (subscriber), ITU, MIGA, NAM, OIF, OPCW, PCA, UN, UNCTAD, UNESCO, UNIDO, UNWTO, UPU, WCO, WFTU (NGOs), WHO, WIPO, WMO, WTO

Diplomatic representation in the US: *chief of mission:* Ambassador Sisavath INPHACHANH (since 7 June 2022)
chancery: 2222 S Street NW, Washington, DC 20008
telephone: [1] (202) 332-6416
FAX: [1] (202) 332-4923
email address and website:
embasslao@gmail.com
https://laoembassy.com/

Diplomatic representation from the US: *chief of mission:* Ambassador Heather VARIAVA (since 5 February 2024)
embassy: Ban Somvang Tai, Thadeua Road, Km 9, Hatsayfong District, Vientiane
mailing address: 4350 Vientiane Place, Washington DC 20521-4350
telephone: [856] 21-48-7000
FAX: [856] 21-48-7040
email address and website:
CONSLAO@state.gov
https://la.usembassy.gov/

Flag description: three horizontal bands of red (top), blue (double width), and red with a large white disk centered in the blue band; the red bands recall the blood shed for liberation; the blue band represents the Mekong River and prosperity; the white disk symbolizes the full moon against the Mekong River, but also signifies the unity of the people under the Lao People's Revolutionary Party, as well as the country's bright future

National symbol(s): elephant; national colors: red, white, blue

National anthem: *name:* "Pheng Xat Lao" (Hymn of the Lao People)
lyrics/music: SISANA Sisane/THONGDY Sounthonevichit
note: music adopted 1945, lyrics adopted 1975; the anthem's lyrics were changed following the 1975 Communist revolution that overthrew the monarchy

National heritage: *total World Heritage Sites:* 3 (all cultural)
selected World Heritage Site locales: Town of Luangphrabang; Vat Phou and Associated Ancient Settlements; Megalithic Jar Sites in Xiengkhuang - Plain of Jars

ECONOMY

Economic overview: lower middle-income, socialist Southeast Asian economy; one of the fastest growing economies; declining but still high poverty; natural resource rich; new anticorruption efforts; already high and growing public debt; service sector hit hard by COVID-19

Real GDP (purchasing power parity): $64.173 billion (2023 est.)
$61.856 billion (2022 est.)
$60.225 billion (2021 est.)
note: data in 2021 dollars
comparison ranking: 112

Real GDP growth rate: 3.75% (2023 est.)
2.71% (2022 est.)
2.53% (2021 est.)
note: annual GDP % growth based on constant local currency
comparison ranking: 85

Real GDP per capita: $8,400 (2023 est.)
$8,200 (2022 est.)
$8,100 (2021 est.)
note: data in 2021 dollars
comparison ranking: 153

GDP (official exchange rate): $15.843 billion (2023 est.)
note: data in current dollars at official exchange rate

Inflation rate (consumer prices): 31.23% (2023 est.)
22.96% (2022 est.)
3.76% (2021 est.)
note: annual % change based on consumer prices
comparison ranking: 208

Credit ratings: Fitch rating: CCC (2020)

Moody's rating: Caa2 (2020)
note: the year refers to the year in which the current credit rating was first obtained.

GDP - composition, by sector of origin: *agriculture:* 16.1% (2023 est.)
industry: 30.5% (2023 est.)
services: 44% (2023 est.)
note: figures may not total 100% due to non-allocated consumption not captured in sector-reported data
comparison rankings: services 174; industry 65; agriculture 52

GDP - composition, by end use: *household consumption:* 65.7% (2016 est.)
government consumption: 14% (2016 est.)
investment in fixed capital: 29% (2016 est.)
exports of goods and services: 33.2% (2016 est.)
imports of goods and services: -41.9% (2016 est.)
note: figures may not total 100% due to rounding or gaps in data collection

Agricultural products: cassava, root vegetables, rice, sugarcane, vegetables, bananas, maize, rubber, coffee, watermelons (2022)
note: top ten agricultural products based on tonnage

Industries: mining (copper, tin, gold, gypsum); timber, electric power, agricultural processing, rubber, construction, garments, cement, tourism

Industrial production growth rate: 2.61% (2023 est.)
note: annual % change in industrial value added based on constant local currency
comparison ranking: 111

Labor force: 3.174 million (2023 est.)
note: number of people ages 15 or older who are employed or seeking work
comparison ranking: 105

Unemployment rate: 1.18% (2023 est.)
1.21% (2022 est.)
2% (2021 est.)
note: % of labor force seeking employment
comparison ranking: 12

Youth unemployment rate (ages 15-24): *total:* 2.2% (2023 est.)
male: 2.3% (2023 est.)
female: 2.1% (2023 est.)
note: % of labor force ages 15-24 seeking employment
comparison ranking: total 196

Population below poverty line: 18.3% (2018 est.)
note: % of population with income below national poverty line

Gini Index coefficient - distribution of family income: 38.8 (2018 est.)
note: index (0-100) of income distribution; higher values represent greater inequality
comparison ranking: 49

Average household expenditures: *on food:* 50.5% of household expenditures (2022 est.)
on alcohol and tobacco: 10.8% of household expenditures (2022 est.)

Household income or consumption by percentage share: *lowest 10%:* 3% (2018 est.)
highest 10%: 31.2% (2018 est.)
note: % share of income accruing to lowest and highest 10% of population

Remittances: 1.42% of GDP (2023 est.)
1.55% of GDP (2022 est.)
1.17% of GDP (2021 est.)
note: personal transfers and compensation between resident and non-resident individuals/households/entities

Budget: *revenues:* $2.288 billion (2022 est.)
expenditures: $1.596 billion (2022 est.)
note: central government revenues and expenses (excluding grants/extrabudgetary units/social security funds) converted to US dollars at average official exchange rate for year indicated

Public debt: 63.6% of GDP (2017 est.)
comparison ranking: 69

Taxes and other revenues: 12.11% (of GDP) (2022 est.)
comparison ranking: 163

Current account balance: -$10.954 million (2022 est.)
$446.505 million (2021 est.)
-$230.973 million (2020 est.)
note: balance of payments - net trade and primary/secondary income in current dollars
comparison ranking: 85

Exports: $8.604 billion (2022 est.)
$7.82 billion (2021 est.)
$6.461 billion (2020 est.)
note: balance of payments - exports of goods and services in current dollars
comparison ranking: 123

Exports - partners: Thailand 35%, China 29%, Vietnam 10%, Australia 4%, US 3% (2022)
note: top five export partners based on percentage share of exports

Exports - commodities: electricity, gold, rubber, fertilizers, paper (2022)
note: top five export commodities based on value in dollars

Imports: $7.772 billion (2022 est.)
$6.527 billion (2021 est.)
$5.816 billion (2020 est.)
note: balance of payments - imports of goods and services in current dollars
comparison ranking: 133

Imports - partners: Thailand 56%, China 26%, Vietnam 8%, Malaysia 3%, Singapore 1% (2022)
note: top five import partners based on percentage share of imports

Imports - commodities: refined petroleum, gold, electrical machinery, raw sugar, plastic products (2022)
note: top five import commodities based on value in dollars

Reserves of foreign exchange and gold: $1.77 billion (2023 est.)
$1.576 billion (2022 est.)
$1.951 billion (2021 est.)
note: holdings of gold (year-end prices)/foreign exchange/special drawing rights in current dollars
comparison ranking: 136

Exchange rates: kips (LAK) per US dollar -

Exchange rates: 17,688.874 (2023 est.)
14,035.227 (2022 est.)
9,697.916 (2021 est.)
9,045.788 (2020 est.)
8,679.409 (2019 est.)

ENERGY

Electricity access: *electrification - total population:* 100% (2022 est.)

Electricity: *installed generating capacity:* 12.222 million kW (2022 est.)
consumption: 8.829 billion kWh (2022 est.)
exports: 35.113 billion kWh (2022 est.)
imports: 1.365 billion kWh (2022 est.)
transmission/distribution losses: 3.376 billion kWh (2022 est.)
comparison rankings: transmission/distribution losses 144; imports 71; exports 5; consumption 110; installed generating capacity 58

Electricity generation sources: *fossil fuels:* 27% of total installed capacity (2022 est.)
solar: 0.1% of total installed capacity (2022 est.)
hydroelectricity: 72.7% of total installed capacity (2022 est.)
biomass and waste: 0.2% of total installed capacity (2022 est.)

Coal: *production:* 14.845 million metric tons (2022 est.)
consumption: 13.691 million metric tons (2022 est.)
exports: 845,000 metric tons (2022 est.)
imports: 6,000 metric tons (2022 est.)
proven reserves: 62 million metric tons (2022 est.)

Petroleum: *refined petroleum consumption:* 24,000 bbl/day (2022 est.)

Carbon dioxide emissions: 20.151 million metric tonnes of CO2 (2022 est.)
from coal and metallurgical coke: 16.499 million metric tonnes of CO2 (2022 est.)
from petroleum and other liquids: 3.652 million metric tonnes of CO2 (2022 est.)
comparison ranking: total emissions 86

Energy consumption per capita: 29.176 million Btu/person (2022 est.)
comparison ranking: 117

COMMUNICATIONS

Telephones - fixed lines: *total subscriptions:* 1.3 million (2021 est.)
subscriptions per 100 inhabitants: 18 (2021 est.)
comparison ranking: total subscriptions 62

Telephones - mobile cellular: *total subscriptions:* 4.823 million (2021 est.)
subscriptions per 100 inhabitants: 65 (2021 est.)
comparison ranking: total subscriptions 125

Telecommunication systems: *general assessment:* Laos joined the World Trade Organization (WTO) in 2013; one of the conditions of admittance was to establish an independent regulator for its telecom sector within two years; the government had committed to do so by February 2015 as part of the accession agreement; there still has been no sign of any firm plans being made to create an independent regulatory body; the Ministry of Technology and Communications retains the primary role in regulating the country's telecom market; with the government also having a financial stake (in part or in whole) in every one of the major fixed-line and mobile operators, the MPT's position and decision-making is far from what could be considered independent; sufficient returns on investment cannot be guaranteed with such strict pricing controls as well as the potential for political interference; fixed-line and mobile penetration levels have, as a result, remained much lower than what's seen in neighboring South East Asian markets; there are signs of growth in the mobile broadband segment as LTE network coverage slowly widens and, more recently, the country's first 5G services start to come on stream; residents in the capital will at least be able to enjoy high-speed services in the near future, while the rest of the country waits patiently to catch up with the rest of the world. (2022)
domestic: fixed-line nearly 18 per 100 and 65 per 100 for mobile-cellular subscriptions (2021)
international: country code - 856; satellite earth station - 1 Intersputnik (Indian Ocean region) and a second to be developed by China

Broadcast media: 6 TV stations operating out of Vientiane - 3 government-operated and the others commercial; 17 provincial stations operating with nearly all programming relayed via satellite from the government-operated stations in Vientiane; Chinese and Vietnamese programming relayed via satellite from Lao National TV; broadcasts available from stations in Thailand and Vietnam in border areas; multi-channel satellite and cable TV systems provide access to a wide range of foreign stations; state-controlled radio with state-operated Lao National Radio (LNR) broadcasting on 5 frequencies - 1 AM, 1 SW, and 3 FM; LNR's AM and FM programs are relayed via satellite constituting a large part of the programming schedules of the provincial radio stations; Thai radio broadcasts available in border areas and transmissions of multiple international broadcasters are also accessible

Internet country code: .la

Internet users: *total:* 4.588 million (2021 est.)
percent of population: 62% (2021 est.)
comparison ranking: total 103

Broadband - fixed subscriptions: *total:* 128,000 (2020 est.)
subscriptions per 100 inhabitants: 2 (2020 est.)
comparison ranking: total 126

TRANSPORTATION

National air transport system: *number of registered air carriers:* 1 (2020)
inventory of registered aircraft operated by air carriers: 12
annual passenger traffic on registered air carriers: 1,251,961 (2018)
annual freight traffic on registered air carriers: 1.53 million (2018) mt-km

Civil aircraft registration country code prefix: RDPL

Airports: 18 (2024)
comparison ranking: 142

Pipelines: 540 km refined products (2013)

Railways: *total:* 422 km (2023)
standard gauge: 422 km (2023) 1.435-m gauge (422 km overhead electrification)
comparison ranking: total 120

Roadways: *total:* 59,647 km
paved: 13,718 km
unpaved: 45,929 km (2024)
comparison ranking: total 80

Waterways: 4,600 km (2012) (primarily on the Mekong River and its tributaries; 2,900 additional km are intermittently navigable by craft drawing less than 0.5 m)
comparison ranking: 26

Merchant marine: *total:* 1 (2023)
by type: general cargo 1
comparison ranking: total 184

MILITARY AND SECURITY

Military and security forces: Lao People's Armed Forces (LPAF): Lao People's Army (LPA, includes Riverine Force), Lao People's Air Force (LPAF), Self-Defense Militia Forces (2024)
note: the Ministry of Public Security maintains internal security and is responsible for law enforcement; it oversees local, traffic, immigration, and security police, village police auxiliaries, and other armed police units

Military expenditures: 0.2% of GDP (2019 est.)
0.2% of GDP (2018 est.)
0.2% of GDP (2017 est.)
0.2% of GDP (2016 est.)
0.2% of GDP (2015 est.)
comparison ranking: 166

Military and security service personnel strengths: limited and varied information; estimated 30,000 active-duty troops (26,000 Army; 4,000 Air Force) (2023)

Military equipment inventories and acquisitions: the LPAF is armed with Chinese, Russian, and Soviet-era equipment and weapons (2024)

Military service age and obligation: 18 years of age for compulsory or voluntary military service; minimum 18-month service obligation (2023)

Military - note: the LPAF's primary missions are border and internal security, including counterinsurgency and counterterrorism; China, Russia, and Vietnam are the country's closest security partners (2023)

TRANSNATIONAL ISSUES

Trafficking in persons: tier rating: Tier 2 Watch List — the government did not demonstrate overall increasing efforts to eliminate trafficking compared with the previous reporting period, therefore Laos was downgraded to Tier 2 Watch List; for more details, go to: https://www.state.gov/reports/2024-trafficking-in-persons-report/laos/

Illicit drugs: Laos remains a key transit route for drug trafficking and the movement of precursor chemicals; opium produced is typically smuggled out of the country and refined elsewhere and not trafficked in significant quantities to the United States

LATVIA

INTRODUCTION

Background: Several eastern Baltic tribes merged in medieval times to form the ethnic core of the Latvian people (ca. 8th-12th centuries A.D.). The region subsequently came under the control of Germans, Poles, Swedes, and finally Russians. A Latvian republic emerged following World War I, but the USSR annexed it in 1940 – an action never recognized by the US and many other countries. Latvia reestablished its independence in 1991 after the breakup of the Soviet Union. Although the last Russian troops left in 1994, the status of the Russian minority (some 25% of the population) remains of concern to Moscow. Latvia joined both NATO and the EU in 2004; it joined the euro zone in 2014 and the OECD in 2016.

GEOGRAPHY

Location: Eastern Europe, bordering the Baltic Sea, between Estonia and Lithuania

Geographic coordinates: 57 00 N, 25 00 E

Map references: Europe

Area: *total:* 64,589 sq km
land: 62,249 sq km
water: 2,340 sq km
comparison ranking: total 124

Area - comparative: slightly larger than West Virginia

Land boundaries: *total:* 1,370 km
border countries (4): Belarus 161 km; Estonia 333 km; Lithuania 544 km; Russia 332 km

Coastline: 498 km

Maritime claims: *territorial sea:* 12 nm
exclusive economic zone: limits as agreed to by Estonia, Finland, Latvia, Sweden, and Russia
continental shelf: 200 m depth or to the depth of exploitation

Climate: maritime; wet, moderate winters

Terrain: low plain

Elevation: *highest point:* Gaizina Kalns 312 m
lowest point: Baltic Sea 0 m
mean elevation: 87 m

Natural resources: peat, limestone, dolomite, amber, hydropower, timber, arable land

Land use: *agricultural land:* 29.2% (2018 est.)
arable land: 18.6% (2018 est.)
permanent crops: 0.1% (2018 est.)
permanent pasture: 10.5% (2018 est.)
forest: 54.1% (2018 est.)
other: 16.7% (2018 est.)

Irrigated land: 6 sq km (2016)
note: land in Latvia is often too wet and in need of drainage not irrigation; approximately 16,000 sq km or 85% of agricultural land has been improved by drainage

Population distribution: largest concentration of people is found in and around the port and capital city of Riga; small agglomerations are scattered throughout the country

Natural hazards: large percentage of agricultural fields can become waterlogged and require drainage

Geography - note: most of the country is composed of fertile low-lying plains with some hills in the east

PEOPLE AND SOCIETY

Population: *total:* 1,801,246
male: 836,982
female: 964,264 (2024 est.)
comparison rankings: female 151; male 155; total 153

Nationality: *noun:* Latvian(s)
adjective: Latvian

Ethnic groups: Latvian 62.7%, Russian 24.5%, Belarusian 3.1%, Ukrainian 2.2%, Polish 2%, Lithuanian 1.1%, other 1.8%, unspecified 2.6% (2021 est.)

Languages: Latvian (official) 56.3%, Russian 33.8%, other 0.6% (includes Polish, Ukrainian, and Belarusian), unspecified 9.4% (2011 est.)
major-language sample(s):
World Factbook, neaizstājams avots pamata informāciju. (Latvian)
note: data represent language usually spoken at home

Religions: Lutheran 36.2%, Roman Catholic 19.5%, Orthodox 19.1%, other Christian 1.6%, other 0.1%, unspecified/none 23.5% (2017 est.)

Age structure: *0-14 years:* 14.7% (male 136,482/female 128,492)
15-64 years: 63% (male 562,754/female 572,850)
65 years and over: 22.2% (2024 est.) (male 137,746/female 262,922)

Dependency ratios: *total dependency ratio:* 59.3
youth dependency ratio: 24.9
elderly dependency ratio: 34.4
potential support ratio: 2.9 (2021 est.)

Median age: *total:* 45.5 years (2024 est.)
male: 41.6 years
female: 49.2 years
comparison ranking: total 17

Population growth rate: -1.14% (2024 est.)
comparison ranking: 232

Birth rate: 8.3 births/1,000 population (2024 est.)
comparison ranking: 211

Death rate: 14.7 deaths/1,000 population (2024 est.)
comparison ranking: 4

Net migration rate: -4.9 migrant(s)/1,000 population (2024 est.)
comparison ranking: 201

Population distribution: largest concentration of people is found in and around the port and capital city of Riga; small agglomerations are scattered throughout the country

Urbanization: *urban population:* 68.7% of total population (2023)
rate of urbanization: -0.68% annual rate of change (2020-25 est.)

Major urban areas - population: 621,000 RIGA (capital) (2023)

Sex ratio: *at birth:* 1.05 male(s)/female

0-14 years: 1.06 male(s)/female
15-64 years: 0.98 male(s)/female
65 years and over: 0.52 male(s)/female
total population: 0.87 male(s)/female (2024 est.)

Mother's mean age at first birth: 27.3 years (2020 est.)

Maternal mortality ratio: 18 deaths/100,000 live births (2020 est.)
comparison ranking: 128

Infant mortality rate: *total:* 4.7 deaths/1,000 live births (2024 est.)
male: 5.1 deaths/1,000 live births
female: 4.3 deaths/1,000 live births
comparison ranking: total 179

Life expectancy at birth: *total population:* 76.4 years (2024 est.)
male: 72 years
female: 81 years
comparison ranking: total population 110

Total fertility rate: 1.55 children born/woman (2024 est.)
comparison ranking: 192

Gross reproduction rate: 0.76 (2024 est.)

Drinking water source: *improved: urban:* 99.9% of population
rural: 98.6% of population
total: 99.5% of population
unimproved: urban: 0.1% of population
rural: 1.4% of population
total: 0.5% of population (2020 est.)

Current health expenditure: 7.5% of GDP (2020)

Physician density: 3.4 physicians/1,000 population (2020)

Hospital bed density: 5.5 beds/1,000 population (2018)

Sanitation facility access: *improved: urban:* 98.9% of population
rural: 85.3% of population
total: 94.6% of population
unimproved: urban: 1.1% of population
rural: 14.7% of population
total: 5.4% of population (2020 est.)

Obesity - adult prevalence rate: 23.6% (2016)
comparison ranking: 65

Alcohol consumption per capita: *total:* 12.9 liters of pure alcohol (2019 est.)
beer: 4.9 liters of pure alcohol (2019 est.)
wine: 1.7 liters of pure alcohol (2019 est.)
spirits: 5.3 liters of pure alcohol (2019 est.)
other alcohols: 1 liters of pure alcohol (2019 est.)
comparison ranking: total 2

Tobacco use: *total:* 37% (2020 est.)
male: 50.3% (2020 est.)
female: 23.7% (2020 est.)
comparison ranking: total 10

Children under the age of 5 years underweight: 21.1% (2020/21) NA
comparison ranking: 14

Currently married women (ages 15-49): 49.1% (2023 est.)

Education expenditures: 6% of GDP (2020 est.)
comparison ranking: 44

Literacy: *definition:* age 15 and over can read and write
total population: 99.9%
male: 99.9%
female: 99.9% (2021)

School life expectancy (primary to tertiary education): *total:* 16 years
male: 16 years
female: 17 years (2020)

ENVIRONMENT

Environment - current issues: while land, water, and air pollution are evident, Latvia's environment has benefited from a shift to service industries after the country regained independence; improvements have occurred in drinking water quality, sewage treatment, household and hazardous waste management, as well as reduction of air pollution; concerns include nature protection and the management of water resources and the protection of the Baltic Sea

Environment - international agreements: *party to:* Air Pollution, Air Pollution-Heavy Metals, Air Pollution-Multi-effect Protocol, Air Pollution-Persistent Organic Pollutants, Biodiversity, Climate Change, Climate Change-Kyoto Protocol, Climate Change-Paris Agreement, Comprehensive Nuclear Test Ban, Desertification, Endangered Species, Hazardous Wastes, Law of the Sea, Ozone Layer Protection, Ship Pollution, Tropical Timber 2006, Wetlands
signed, but not ratified: none of the selected agreements

Climate: maritime; wet, moderate winters

Urbanization: *urban population:* 68.7% of total population (2023)
rate of urbanization: -0.68% annual rate of change (2020-25 est.)

Revenue from forest resources: 0.85% of GDP (2018 est.)
comparison ranking: 55

Revenue from coal: 0% of GDP (2018 est.)
comparison ranking: 134

Air pollutants: *particulate matter emissions:* 12.02 micrograms per cubic meter (2019 est.)
carbon dioxide emissions: 7 megatons (2016 est.)
methane emissions: 1.85 megatons (2020 est.)

Waste and recycling: *municipal solid waste generated annually:* 857,000 tons (2015 est.)
municipal solid waste recycled annually: 181,941 tons (2015 est.)
percent of municipal solid waste recycled: 21.2% (2015 est.)

Total water withdrawal: *municipal:* 90 million cubic meters (2020 est.)
industrial: 40 million cubic meters (2020 est.)
agricultural: 60 million cubic meters (2020 est.)

Total renewable water resources: 34.94 billion cubic meters (2020 est.)

GOVERNMENT

Country name: *conventional long form:* Republic of Latvia
conventional short form: Latvia
local long form: Latvijas Republika
local short form: Latvija
former: Latvian Soviet Socialist Republic (while occupied by the USSR)
etymology: the name "Latvia" originates from the ancient Latgalians, one of four eastern Baltic tribes that formed the ethnic core of the Latvian people (ca. 8th-12th centuries A.D.)

Government type: parliamentary republic

Capital: *name:* Riga
geographic coordinates: 56 57 N, 24 06 E
time difference: UTC+2 (7 hours ahead of Washington, DC, during Standard Time)
daylight saving time: +1hr, begins last Sunday in March; ends last Sunday in October
etymology: of the several theories explaining the name's origin, the one relating to the city's role in Baltic and North Sea commerce is the most probable; the name is likely related to the Latvian word "rija," meaning "warehouse," where the 'j' became a 'g' under the heavy German influence in the city from the late Middle Ages to the early 20th century

Administrative divisions: 36 municipalities (novadi, singular - novads) and 7 state cities (valstspilsetu pasvaldibas, singular valstspilsetas pasvaldiba)
municipalities: Adazi, Aizkraukle, Aluksne, Augsdaugava, Balvi, Bauska, Cesis, Dienvidkurzeme, Dobele, Gulbene, Jekabpils, Jelgava, Kekava, Kraslava, Kuldiga, Limbazi, Livani, Ludza, Madona, Marupe, Ogre, Olaine, Preili, Rezekne, Ropazi, Salaspils, Saldus, Saulkrasti, Sigulda, Smiltene, Talsi, Tukums, Valka, Valmiera, Varaklani, Ventspils
cities: Daugavpils, Jelgava, Jurmala, Liepaja, Rezekne, Riga, Ventspils

Independence: 18 November 1918 (from Soviet Russia); 4 May 1990 (declared from the Soviet Union); 6 September 1991 (recognized by the Soviet Union)

National holiday: Independence Day (Republic of Latvia Proclamation Day), 18 November (1918); note - 18 November 1918 was the date Latvia established its statehood and its concomitant independence from Soviet Russia; 4 May 1990 was the date it declared the restoration of Latvian statehood and its concomitant independence from the Soviet Union

Legal system: civil law system with traces of socialist legal traditions and practices

Constitution: *history:* several previous (pre-1991 independence); note - following the restoration of independence in 1991, parts of the 1922 constitution were reintroduced 4 May 1990 and fully reintroduced 6 July 1993
amendments: proposed by two thirds of Parliament members or by petition of one tenth of qualified voters submitted through the president; passage requires at least two-thirds majority vote of Parliament in each of three readings; amendment of constitutional articles, including national sovereignty, language, the parliamentary electoral system, and constitutional amendment procedures, requires passage in a referendum by majority vote of at least one half of the electorate; amended several times, last in 2019

International law organization participation: has not submitted an ICJ jurisdiction declaration; accepts ICCt jurisdiction

Citizenship: *citizenship by birth:* no
citizenship by descent only: at least one parent must be a citizen of Latvia
dual citizenship recognized: no
residency requirement for naturalization: 5 years

Suffrage: 18 years of age; universal

Executive branch: *chief of state:* President Edgars RINKEVICS (since 8 July 2023)
head of government: Prime Minister Evika SILINA (since 15 September 2023)
cabinet: Cabinet of Ministers nominated by the prime minister, appointed by Parliament
elections/appointments: president indirectly elected by Parliament for a 4-year term (eligible for a second term); election last held on 31 May 2023 (next to

be held in 2027); prime minister appointed by the president, confirmed by Parliament
election results:
2023: Edgars RINKEVICS elected president in the third round; Parliament vote - Edgars RINKEVICS (Unity Party) 52, Uldis Pīlēns (independent) 25; Evika SILINA confirmed as prime minister 53-39
2019: Egils LEVITS elected president; Parliament vote - Egils LEVITS (independent) 61, Didzis SMITS (KPV LV) 24, Juris JANSONS (independent) 8; Krisjanis KARINS confirmed as prime minister 61-39
note: on 15 September 2023, Parliament voted 53-39 to approve Prime Minister Evika SILINA

Legislative branch: *description:* unicameral Parliament or Saeima (100 seats; members directly elected in multi-seat constituencies by party-list proportional representation vote; members serve 4-year terms)
elections: last held on 1 October 2022 (next to be held no later than 3 October 2026)
election results: percent of vote by party - JV 19.2%, ZZS 12.6%, AS 11.1%, NA 9.4%, S! 6.9%, LPV 6.3%, PRO 6.2%; seats by party - JV 26, ZZS 16, AS 15, NA 13, S! 11, LPV 9, PRO 10; composition- men 68, women 32, percentage women 32%

Judicial branch: *highest court(s):* Supreme Court (consists of the Senate with 36 judges); Constitutional Court (consists of 7 judges)
judge selection and term of office: Supreme Court judges nominated by chief justice and confirmed by the Saeima; judges serve until age 70, but term can be extended 2 years; Constitutional Court judges - 3 nominated by Saeima members, 2 by Cabinet ministers, and 2 by plenum of Supreme Court; all judges confirmed by Saeima majority vote; Constitutional Court president and vice president serve in their positions for 3 years; all judges serve 10-year terms; mandatory retirement at age 70
subordinate courts: district (city) and regional courts

Political parties: Development/For! or AP!
For Stability or S!
For Latvia's Development LA
Harmony or S
Honor to Serve Riga! or GKR
Latvia First LPV
Latvian Green Party or LZP
National Alliance or NA
New Unity or JV
People, Land, Statehood TZV
Social Democratic Party "Harmony" or S
The Progressives or PRO
Union of Greens and Farmers or ZZS
United List or AS
We for Talsi and Municipality or MTuN

International organization participation: Australia Group, BA, BIS, CBSS, CD, CE, EAPC, EBRD, ECB, EIB, EMU, ESA (cooperating state), EU, FAO, IAEA, IBRD, ICAO, ICC (NGOs), ICCt, ICRM, IDA, IFC, IFRCS, IHO, ILO, IMF, IMO, IMSO, Interpol, IOC, IOM, IPU, ISO (correspondent), ITU, ITUC (NGOs), MIGA, NATO, NIB, NSG, OAS (observer), OIF (observer), OPCW, OSCE, PCA, Schengen Convention, UN, UNCTAD, UNESCO, UNHCR, UNWTO, UPU, Wassenaar Arrangement, WCO, WHO, WIPO, WMO, WTO

Diplomatic representation in the US: *chief of mission:* Ambassador Elita KUZMA (since 18 September 2024)
chancery: 2306 Massachusetts Avenue NW, Washington, DC 20008
telephone: [1] (202) 328-2840
FAX: [1] (202) 328-2860
email address and website:
embassy.usa@mfa.gov.lv
https://www2.mfa.gov.lv/en/usa

Diplomatic representation from the US: *chief of mission:* Ambassador Christopher ROBINSON (since 21 February 2023)
embassy: 1 Samnera Velsa Street (former Remtes), Riga LV-1510
mailing address: 4520 Riga Place, Washington DC 20521-4520
telephone: [371] 6710-7000
FAX: [371] 6710-7050
email address and website:
askconsular-riga@state.gov
https://lv.usembassy.gov/

Flag description: three horizontal bands of maroon (top), white (half-width), and maroon; the flag is one of the older banners in the world; a medieval chronicle mentions a red standard with a white stripe being used by Latvian tribes in about 1280

National symbol(s): white wagtail (bird); national colors: maroon, white

National anthem; *name:* "Dievs, sveti Latviju!" (God Bless Latvia)
lyrics/music: Karlis BAUMANIS
note: adopted 1920, restored 1990; first performed in 1873 while Latvia was a part of Russia; banned during the Soviet occupation from 1940 to 1990

National heritage: *total World Heritage Sites:* 3 (all cultural)
selected World Heritage Site locales: Historic Center of Riga; Struve Geodetic Arc; Old town of Kuldīga

ECONOMY

Economic overview: high-income EU and eurozone member; economic contraction triggered by export decline and energy shocks; recovery driven by easing inflation, wage growth, and investments supported by EU funds; challenges from skilled labor shortages, capital market access, large informal sector, and green and digital transitions

Real GDP (purchasing power parity): $71.154 billion (2023 est.)
$71.355 billion (2022 est.)
$69.308 billion (2021 est.)
note: data in 2021 dollars
comparison ranking: 109

Real GDP growth rate: -0.28% (2023 est.)
2.95% (2022 est.)
6.73% (2021 est.)
note: annual GDP % growth based on constant local currency
comparison ranking: 191

Real GDP per capita: $37,800 (2023 est.)
$38,000 (2022 est.)
$36,800 (2021 est.)
note: data in 2021 dollars
comparison ranking: 65

GDP (official exchange rate): $43.627 billion (2023 est.)
note: data in current dollars at official exchange rate

Inflation rate (consumer prices): 8.94% (2023 est.)
17.31% (2022 est.)
3.28% (2021 est.)
note: annual % change based on consumer prices
comparison ranking: 165

Credit ratings: Fitch rating: A- (2014)
Moody's rating: A3 (2015)
Standard & Poors rating: A+ (2020)
note: The year refers to the year in which the current credit rating was first obtained.

GDP - composition, by sector of origin: *agriculture:* 4.2% (2023 est.)
industry: 20.9% (2023 est.)
services: 63.1% (2023 est.)
note: figures may not total 100% due to non-allocated consumption not captured in sector-reported data
comparison rankings: services 65; industry 130; agriculture 126

GDP - composition, by end use: *household consumption:* 61.1% (2023 est.)
government consumption: 19.7% (2023 est.)
investment in fixed capital: 24.1% (2023 est.)
investment in inventories: -1.1% (2023 est.)
exports of goods and services: 64.1% (2023 est.)
imports of goods and services: -67.9% (2023 est.)
note: figures may not total 100% due to rounding or gaps in data collection

Agricultural products: wheat, milk, rapeseed, barley, oats, potatoes, rye, beans, peas, pork (2022)
note: top ten agricultural products based on tonnage

Industries: processed foods, processed wood products, textiles, processed metals, pharmaceuticals, railroad cars, synthetic fibers, electronics

Industrial production growth rate: 0.71% (2023 est.)
note: annual % change in industrial value added based on constant local currency
comparison ranking: 147

Labor force: 978,000 (2023 est.)
note: number of people ages 15 or older who are employed or seeking work
comparison ranking: 148

Unemployment rate: 6.53% (2023 est.)
6.82% (2022 est.)
7.51% (2021 est.)
note: % of labor force seeking employment
comparison ranking: 133

Youth unemployment rate (ages 15-24): *total:* 12.5% (2023 est.)
male: 14.2% (2023 est.)
female: 10.3% (2023 est.)
note: % of labor force ages 15-24 seeking employment
comparison ranking: total 112

Population below poverty line: 22.5% (2022 est.)
note: % of population with income below national poverty line

Gini Index coefficient - distribution of family income: 34.3 (2021 est.)
note: index (0-100) of income distribution; higher values represent greater inequality
comparison ranking: 85

Average household expenditures: *on food:* 19.1% of household expenditures (2022 est.)
on alcohol and tobacco: 7.4% of household expenditures (2022 est.)

Household income or consumption by percentage share: *lowest 10%:* 2.6% (2021 est.)
highest 10%: 26.2% (2021 est.)
note: % share of income accruing to lowest and highest 10% of population

Remittances: 2.82% of GDP (2023 est.)

3.2% of GDP (2022 est.)
3.34% of GDP (2021 est.)
note: personal transfers and compensation between resident and non-resident individuals/households/entities

Budget: *revenues:* $12.075 billion (2022 est.)
expenditures: $13.672 billion (2022 est.)
note: central government revenues (excluding grants) and expenses converted to US dollars at average official exchange rate for year indicated

Public debt: 36.3% of GDP (2017 est.)
note: data cover general government debt, and includes debt instruments issued (or owned) by government entities, including sub-sectors of central government, state government, local government, and social security funds
comparison ranking: 145

Taxes and other revenues: 22.79% (of GDP) (2022 est.)
note: central government tax revenue as a % of GDP
comparison ranking: 64

Current account balance: -$1.752 billion (2023 est.)
-$1.937 billion (2022 est.)
-$1.579 billion (2021 est.)
note: balance of payments - net trade and primary/secondary income in current dollars
comparison ranking: 153

Exports: $27.947 billion (2023 est.)
$29.374 billion (2022 est.)
$25.43 billion (2021 est.)
note: balance of payments - exports of goods and services in current dollars
comparison ranking: 81

Exports - partners: Lithuania 18%, Estonia 10%, Germany 6%, Russia 6%, Sweden 5% (2022)
note: top five export partners based on percentage share of exports

Exports - commodities: wood, wheat, natural gas, electricity, broadcasting equipment (2022)
note: top five export commodities based on value in dollars

Imports: $29.626 billion (2023 est.)
$31.213 billion (2022 est.)
$26.681 billion (2021 est.)
note: balance of payments - imports of goods and services in current dollars
comparison ranking: 80

Imports - partners: Lithuania 22%, Estonia 10%, Germany 9%, Poland 9%, Russia 6% (2022)
note: top five import partners based on percentage share of imports

Imports - commodities: natural gas, refined petroleum, electricity, cars, packaged medicine (2022)
note: top five import commodities based on value in dollars

Reserves of foreign exchange and gold: $4.957 billion (2023 est.)
$4.46 billion (2022 est.)
$5.491 billion (2021 est.)
note: holdings of gold (year-end prices)/foreign exchange/special drawing rights in current dollars
comparison ranking: 100

Exchange rates: euros (EUR) per US dollar -

Exchange rates: 0.925 (2023 est.)
0.95 (2022 est.)
0.845 (2021 est.)
0.876 (2020 est.)
0.893 (2019 est.)

ENERGY

Electricity access: *electrification - total population:* 100% (2022 est.)

Electricity: *installed generating capacity:* 3.233 million kW (2022 est.)
consumption: 5.982 billion kWh (2022 est.)
exports: 2.997 billion kWh (2022 est.)
imports: 5.307 billion kWh (2022 est.)
transmission/distribution losses: 374.152 million kWh (2022 est.)
comparison rankings: transmission/distribution losses 74; imports 45; exports 49; consumption 126; installed generating capacity 105

Electricity generation sources: *fossil fuels:* 27.5% of total installed capacity (2022 est.)
solar: 0.2% of total installed capacity (2022 est.)
wind: 4.8% of total installed capacity (2022 est.)
hydroelectricity: 67.5% of total installed capacity (2022 est.)

Coal: *consumption:* 20,000 metric tons (2022 est.)
exports: 55,000 metric tons (2022 est.)
imports: 146,000 metric tons (2022 est.)

Petroleum: *total petroleum production:* 2,000 bbl/day (2023 est.)
refined petroleum consumption: 35,000 bbl/day (2023 est.)

Natural gas: *consumption:* 828.214 million cubic meters (2022 est.)
imports: 801.356 million cubic meters (2022 est.)

Carbon dioxide emissions: 6.458 million metric tonnes of CO2 (2022 est.)
from coal and metallurgical coke: 42,000 metric tonnes of CO2 (2022 est.)
from petroleum and other liquids: 4.809 million metric tonnes of CO2 (2022 est.)
from consumed natural gas: 1.606 million metric tonnes of CO2 (2022 est.)
comparison ranking: total emissions 130

Energy consumption per capita: 64.272 million Btu/person (2022 est.)
comparison ranking: 76

COMMUNICATIONS

Telephones - fixed lines: *total subscriptions:* 174,000 (2022 est.)
subscriptions per 100 inhabitants: 9 (2022 est.)
comparison ranking: total subscriptions 122

Telephones - mobile cellular: *total subscriptions:* 2.167 million (2022 est.)
subscriptions per 100 inhabitants: 117 (2022 est.)
comparison ranking: total subscriptions 147

Telecommunication systems: *general assessment:* the telecom market continues to benefit from investment and from regulatory measures aimed at developing 5G and fiber-based infrastructure; the mobile market is dominated by three operators and there is effective competition between them, with the smallest among them having almost a quarter of the market by subscribers; these multi-service operators have focused investment on fiber networks and on expanding the reach of 5G; mobile network capacity has been improved since 2022 following the auction of spectrum in the 700MHz and 1.5GHz bands; operators have entered into agreements with neighboring Estonia and Lithuania to coordinate the use of spectrum for 5G in border areas, improving coverage to end-users without interference; in the fixed-line broadband sector, the country is ranked among the highest in Europe for fiber coverage; it has the second highest rural FttP coverage after Denmark; with this infrastructure in place, the country has also developed a sophisticated digital economy, with e-commerce and e-government services widely available (2024)
domestic: fixed-line 9 per 100 and mobile-cellular nearly 117 per 100 subscriptions (2022)
international: country code - 371; the Latvian network is now connected via fiber-optic cable to Estonia, Finland, and Sweden

Broadcast media: several national and regional commercial TV stations are foreign-owned, 2 national TV stations are publicly owned; system supplemented by privately owned regional and local TV stations; cable and satellite multi-channel TV services with domestic and foreign broadcasts available; publicly owned broadcaster operates 4 radio networks with dozens of stations throughout the country; dozens of private broadcasters also operate radio stations

Internet country code: .lv

Internet users: *total:* 1.729 million (2021 est.)
percent of population: 91% (2021 est.)
comparison ranking: total 141

Broadband - fixed subscriptions: *total:* 490,569 (2020 est.)
subscriptions per 100 inhabitants: 26 (2020 est.)
comparison ranking: total 92

TRANSPORTATION

National air transport system: *number of registered air carriers:* 3 (2020)
inventory of registered aircraft operated by air carriers: 53
annual passenger traffic on registered air carriers: 4,058,762 (2018)
annual freight traffic on registered air carriers: 4.01 million (2018) mt-km

Civil aircraft registration country code prefix: YL

Airports: 56 (2024)
comparison ranking: 80

Heliports: 5 (2024)

Pipelines: 1,213 km gas, 417 km refined products (2018)

Railways: *total:* 2,216 km (2020) 257 km electrified
comparison ranking: total 69

Roadways: *total:* 57,972 km (2022)
comparison ranking: total 83

Waterways: 300 km (2010) (navigable year-round)
comparison ranking: 102

Merchant marine: *total:* 83 (2023)
by type: container ship 2, general cargo 30, oil tanker 10, other 41
comparison ranking: total 97

Ports: *total ports:* 5 (2024)
large: 1
medium: 2
small: 0
very small: 2
ports with oil terminals: 3
key ports: Lielupe, Liepaja, Riga, Salacgriva, Ventspils

MILITARY AND SECURITY

Military and security forces: National Armed Forces (Nacionalie Brunotie Speki or NBS): Land Forces (Latvijas Sauszemes Speki), Naval Force (Latvijas

Juras Speki, includes Coast Guard (Latvijas Kara Flote)), Air Force (Latvijas Gaisa Speki), National Guard (aka Land Guard or Zemessardze) (2024)
note: the National Armed Forces (including the National Guard), the Defense Intelligence and Security Service, and the Constitution Protection Bureau are subordinate to the Ministry of Defense; the State Police, State Border Guards, and State Security Service are under the Ministry of Interior; the State Border Guard may become part of the armed forces during an emergency

Military expenditures: 3.2% of GDP (2024 est.)
2.4% of GDP (2023)
2.1% of GDP (2022)
2.1% of GDP (2021)
2.2% of GDP (2020)
comparison ranking: 29

Military and security service personnel strengths: approximately 8,000 active military forces; approximately 10,000 National Guard (2024)

Military equipment inventories and acquisitions: the Latvian military's inventory consists of a mix of European and US weapons and equipment (2024)

Military service age and obligation: 18 years of age for voluntary military service for men and women; 12 months mandatory military service for men 18-27 years of age (2024)
note 1: conscription was reintroduced in 2024
note 2: as of 2024, women comprised about 16.5% of the military's full-time personnel

Military deployments: 135 Kosovo (KFOR/NATO) (2024)

Military - note: the National Armed Forces are responsible for the defense of the country's sovereignty and territory; they also have some domestic security responsibilities, including coast guard functions, search and rescue, humanitarian assistance, and providing support to other internal security services, including the State Border Service, the State Police, and the State Security Service; the Military Police provides protection to the president and other government officials, foreign dignitaries, and key facilities; for external defense, Latvia's primary security focus is Russia
in 2004, Latvia joined NATO and the EU, which it depends on to play a decisive role in Latvia's security policy; the Latvian military has participated in NATO and EU missions abroad and regularly conducts training and exercises with NATO and EU partner forces
Latvia also hosts NATO partner forces; since 2017, it has hosted a Canadian-led multinational NATO ground force battlegroup as part of the Alliance's Enhanced Forward Presence initiative; in addition, Latvia hosts a NATO-led divisional headquarters (Multinational Division North; activated 2020), which coordinates training and preparation activities of its respective subordinate NATO battlegroups in Estonia and Latvia
the Air Force has no combat aircraft; NATO has provided air protection for Latvia since 2004 through its Baltics Air Policing mission; NATO member countries that possess air combat capabilities voluntarily contribute to the mission on four-month rotations
Latvia is a member of the UK-led Joint Expeditionary Force, a pool of high-readiness military forces from 10 Baltic and Scandinavian countries designed to respond to a wide range of contingencies in the North Atlantic, Baltic Sea, and High North regions (2024)

TRANSNATIONAL ISSUES

Refugees and internally displaced persons: *refugees (country of origin):* 47,615 (Ukraine) (as of 6 March 2024)
stateless persons: 195,354 (2022); note - individuals who were Latvian citizens prior to the 1940 Soviet occupation and their descendants were recognized as Latvian citizens when the country's independence was restored in 1991; citizens of the former Soviet Union residing in Latvia who have neither Latvian nor other citizenship are considered non-citizens (officially there is no statelessness in Latvia) and are entitled to non-citizen passports; children born after Latvian independence to stateless parents are entitled to Latvian citizenship upon their parents' request; non-citizens cannot vote or hold certain government jobs and are exempt from military service but can travel visa-free in the EU under the Schengen accord like Latvian citizens; non-citizens can obtain naturalization if they have been permanent residents of Latvia for at least five years, pass tests in Latvian language and history, and know the words of the Latvian national anthem

Illicit drugs: transshipment and destination point for cocaine, synthetic drugs, opiates, and cannabis from Southwest Asia, Western Europe, Latin America, and neighboring Baltic countries; despite improved legislation, vulnerable to money laundering due to nascent enforcement capabilities and comparatively weak regulation of offshore companies and the gaming industry; CIS organized crime (including counterfeiting, corruption, extortion, stolen cars, and prostitution) accounts for most laundered proceeds

LEBANON

INTRODUCTION

Background: As a result of its location at the crossroads of three continents, the area that is modern-day Lebanon is rich in cultural and religious diversity. This region was subject to various foreign conquerors for much of its history, including the Romans, Arabs, and Ottomans. Following World War I, France acquired a mandate over the northern portion of the former Ottoman Empire province of Syria. From it the French demarcated the region of Lebanon in 1920, and it gained independence in 1943. Lebanon subsequently experienced periods of political turmoil interspersed with prosperity built on its position as a regional center for finance and trade.

The country's 1975-90 civil war, which resulted in an estimated 120,000 fatalities, was followed by years of social and political instability, and sectarianism remains a key element of Lebanese political life. The Israeli defense forces, which occupied parts of Lebanon during the civil war, did not completely withdraw until 2000. Neighboring Syria influenced Lebanon's foreign and domestic policies while its military occupied Lebanon from 1976 until 2005, but its influence diminished significantly after 2005. Over 1.5 million Syrian refugees fled to Lebanon after the start of the Syrian conflict in 2011. Hizballah – a major Lebanese political party, militia, and US-designated foreign terrorist organization – and Israel continued attacks and counterattacks against each other after Syria's withdrawal and fought a brief war in 2006. After HAMAS attacked Israel on 7 October 2023, the intensity and frequency of these cross-border attacks increased substantially into a cycle of hostilities, mostly limited to the border areas as of January 2024. Lebanon's borders with Syria and Israel remain unresolved.

Lebanon's prosperity has significantly diminished since the beginning of the country's economic crisis in 2019, which has crippled its economy, shut down its previously lucrative banking sector, reduced the value of its currency, and caused many Lebanese to emigrate in search of better prospects.

GEOGRAPHY

Location: Middle East, bordering the Mediterranean Sea, between Israel and Syria

Geographic coordinates: 33 50 N, 35 50 E

Map references: Middle East

Area: *total:* 10,400 sq km
land: 10,230 sq km
water: 170 sq km
comparison ranking: total 168

Area - comparative: about one-third the size of Maryland

Land boundaries: *total:* 484 km
border countries (2): Israel 81 km; Syria 403 km

Coastline: 225 km

Maritime claims: *territorial sea:* 12 nm

Climate: Mediterranean; mild to cool, wet winters with hot, dry summers; the Lebanon Mountains experience heavy winter snows

Terrain: narrow coastal plain; El Beqaa (Bekaa Valley) separates Lebanon and Anti-Lebanon Mountains

Elevation: *highest point:* Qornet es Saouda 3,088 m
lowest point: Mediterranean Sea 0 m
mean elevation: 1,250 m

Natural resources: limestone, iron ore, salt, water-surplus state in a water-deficit region, arable land

Land use: *agricultural land:* 63.3% (2018 est.)
arable land: 11.9% (2018 est.)
permanent crops: 12.3% (2018 est.)
permanent pasture: 39.1% (2018 est.)
forest: 13.4% (2018 est.)
other: 23.3% (2018 est.)

Irrigated land: 1,040 sq km (2012)

Population distribution: the majority of the people live on or near the Mediterranean coast, and of these most live in and around the capital, Beirut; favorable growing conditions in the Bekaa Valley, on the southeastern side of the Lebanon Mountains, have attracted farmers and thus the area exhibits a smaller population density

Natural hazards: earthquakes; dust storms, sandstorms

Geography - note: smallest country in continental Asia; Nahr el Litani is the only major river in Near East not crossing an international boundary; rugged terrain historically helped isolate, protect, and develop numerous factional groups based on religion, clan, and ethnicity

PEOPLE AND SOCIETY

Population: *total:* 5,364,482
male: 2,678,543
female: 2,685,939 (2024 est.)
comparison rankings: female 122; male 122; total 122

Nationality: *noun:* Lebanese (singular and plural)
adjective: Lebanese

Ethnic groups: Arab 95%, Armenian 4%, other 1%
note: many Christian Lebanese do not identify as Arab but rather as descendants of the ancient Canaanites and prefer to be called Phoenicians

Languages: Arabic (official), French, English, Armenian
major-language sample(s):
يمكن الاستغناء عنه للمعلومات الأساسية
كتاب حقائق العالم، المصدر الذي لا
(Arabic)
The World Factbook, une source indispensable d'informations de base. (French)

Religions: Muslim 67.8% (31.9% Sunni, 31.2% Shia, smaller percentages of Alawites and Ismailis), Christian 32.4% (Maronite Catholics are the largest Christian group), Druze 4.5%, very small numbers of Jews, Baha'is, Buddhists, and Hindus (2020 est.)
note: data represent the religious affiliation of the citizen population (data do not include Lebanon's sizable Syrian and Palestinian refugee populations); 18 religious sects recognized

Age structure: *0-14 years:* 18.9% (male 519,352/female 495,591)
15-64 years: 71.6% (male 1,939,311/female 1,900,574)
65 years and over: 9.5% (2024 est.) (male 219,880/female 289,774)

Dependency ratios: *total dependency ratio:* 59.3
youth dependency ratio: 44
elderly dependency ratio: 15.3
potential support ratio: 6.5 (2021 est.)

Median age: *total:* 36.3 years (2024 est.)
male: 35.6 years
female: 36.9 years
comparison ranking: total 90

Population growth rate: 0.61% (2024 est.)
comparison ranking: 137

Birth rate: 12.6 births/1,000 population (2024 est.)
comparison ranking: 139

Death rate: 5.6 deaths/1,000 population (2024 est.)
comparison ranking: 176

Net migration rate: -0.9 migrant(s)/1,000 population (2024 est.)
comparison ranking: 141

Population distribution: the majority of the people live on or near the Mediterranean coast, and of these most live in and around the capital, Beirut; favorable growing conditions in the Bekaa Valley, on the southeastern side of the Lebanon Mountains, have attracted farmers and thus the area exhibits a smaller population density

Urbanization: *urban population:* 89.4% of total population (2023)
rate of urbanization: -1.23% annual rate of change (2020-25 est.)

Major urban areas - population: 2.421 million BEIRUT (capital) (2023)

Sex ratio: *at birth:* 1.05 male(s)/female
0-14 years: 1.05 male(s)/female
15-64 years: 1.02 male(s)/female
65 years and over: 0.76 male(s)/female
total population: 1 male(s)/female (2024 est.)

Maternal mortality ratio: 21 deaths/100,000 live births (2020 est.)
comparison ranking: 123

Infant mortality rate: *total:* 6.7 deaths/1,000 live births (2024 est.)
male: 7.3 deaths/1,000 live births
female: 6.2 deaths/1,000 live births
comparison ranking: total 159

Life expectancy at birth: *total population:* 79.2 years (2024 est.)
male: 77.8 years
female: 80.7 years
comparison ranking: total population 67

Total fertility rate: 1.71 children born/woman (2024 est.)
comparison ranking: 159

Gross reproduction rate: 0.83 (2024 est.)

Drinking water source: *improved:*
total: 100% of population

Current health expenditure: 8% of GDP (2020)

Physician density: 2.21 physicians/1,000 population (2019)

Hospital bed density: 2.7 beds/1,000 population (2017)

Sanitation facility access: *improved:*
total: 100% of population

Obesity - adult prevalence rate: 32% (2016)
comparison ranking: 18

Alcohol consumption per capita: *total:* 1.14 liters of pure alcohol (2019 est.)
beer: 0.38 liters of pure alcohol (2019 est.)
wine: 0.21 liters of pure alcohol (2019 est.)
spirits: 0.53 liters of pure alcohol (2019 est.)
other alcohols: 0.02 liters of pure alcohol (2019 est.)
comparison ranking: total 150

Tobacco use: *total:* 38.2% (2020 est.)
male: 47.5% (2020 est.)
female: 28.9% (2020 est.)
comparison ranking: total 8

Children under the age of 5 years underweight: 3.4% (2021) NA
comparison ranking: 85

Currently married women (ages 15-49): 51.4% (2023 est.)

Child marriage: *women married by age 15:* 1.4%
women married by age 18: 6% (2016 est.)

Education expenditures: 1.7% of GDP (2020 est.)
comparison ranking: 190

Literacy: *definition:* age 15 and over can read and write
total population: 95.1%
male: 96.9%
female: 93.3% (2018)

School life expectancy (primary to tertiary education): *total:* 11 years
male: 12 years
female: 11 years (2014)

ENVIRONMENT

Environment - current issues: deforestation; soil deterioration, erosion; desertification; species loss; air pollution in Beirut from vehicular traffic and the burning of industrial wastes; pollution of coastal waters from raw sewage and oil spills; waste-water management

Environment - international agreements: *party to:* Biodiversity, Climate Change, Climate Change-Kyoto Protocol, Climate Change-Paris Agreement, Comprehensive Nuclear Test Ban, Desertification, Endangered Species, Hazardous Wastes, Law of the Sea, Nuclear Test Ban, Ozone Layer Protection, Ship Pollution, Wetlands
signed, but not ratified: Environmental Modification, Marine Life Conservation

Climate: Mediterranean; mild to cool, wet winters with hot, dry summers; the Lebanon Mountains experience heavy winter snows

Urbanization: *urban population:* 89.4% of total population (2023)
rate of urbanization: -1.23% annual rate of change (2020-25 est.)

Food insecurity: *widespread lack of access: due to the ongoing financial and economic crisis* - in September 2021, the United Nations estimated that, taking into account multiple factors other than income, such as access to health, education and public utilities, 82% of the population lives in multidimensional poverty in 2021, up from 42% in 2019 (2022)

Revenue from forest resources: 0% of GDP (2018 est.)
comparison ranking: 185

Revenue from coal: 0% of GDP (2018 est.)
comparison ranking: 130

Air pollutants: *particulate matter emissions:* 24.23 micrograms per cubic meter (2019 est.)
carbon dioxide emissions: 24.8 megatons (2016 est.)
methane emissions: 3.37 megatons (2020 est.)

Waste and recycling: *municipal solid waste generated annually:* 2.04 million tons (2014 est.)

municipal solid waste recycled annually: 163,200 tons (2014 est.)
percent of municipal solid waste recycled: 8% (2014 est.)

Total water withdrawal: *municipal:* 240 million cubic meters (2020 est.)
industrial: 900 million cubic meters (2020 est.)
agricultural: 700 million cubic meters (2020 est.)

Total renewable water resources: 4.5 billion cubic meters (2020 est.)

GOVERNMENT

Country name: *conventional long form:* Lebanese Republic
conventional short form: Lebanon
local long form: Al Jumhuriyah al Lubnaniyah
local short form: Lubnan
former: Greater Lebanon
etymology: derives from the Semitic root "lbn" meaning "white" and refers to snow-capped Mount Lebanon

Government type: parliamentary democratic republic

Capital: *name:* Beirut
geographic coordinates: 33 52 N, 35 30 E
time difference: UTC+2 (7 hours ahead of Washington, DC, during Standard Time)
daylight saving time: +1hr, begins last Sunday in March; ends last Sunday in October
etymology: derived from the Canaanite or Phoenician word "ber'ot," meaning "the wells" or "fountain," which referred to the site's accessible water table

Administrative divisions: 8 governorates (mohafazat, singular - mohafazah); Aakkar, Baalbek-Hermel, Beqaa (Bekaa), Beyrouth (Beirut), Liban- Nord (North Lebanon), Liban-Sud (South Lebanon), Mont-Liban (Mount Lebanon), Nabatiye

Independence: 22 November 1943 (from League of Nations mandate under French administration)

National holiday: Independence Day, 22 November (1943)

Legal system: mixed legal system of civil law based on the French civil code, Ottoman legal tradition, and religious laws covering personal status, marriage, divorce, and other family relations of the Jewish, Islamic, and Christian communities

Constitution: *history:* drafted 15 May 1926, adopted 23 May 1926
amendments: proposed by the president of the republic and introduced as a government bill to the National Assembly or proposed by at least 10 members of the Assembly and agreed upon by two thirds of its members; if proposed by the National Assembly, review and approval by two-thirds majority of the Cabinet is required; if approved, the proposal is next submitted to the Cabinet for drafting as an amendment; Cabinet approval requires at least two-thirds majority, followed by submission to the National Assembly for discussion and vote; passage requires at least two-thirds majority vote of a required two-thirds quorum of the Assembly membership and promulgation by the president; amended several times, last in 2004

International law organization participation: has not submitted an ICJ jurisdiction declaration; non-party state to the ICCt

Citizenship: *citizenship by birth:* no
citizenship by descent only: the father must be a citizen of Lebanon
dual citizenship recognized: yes
residency requirement for naturalization: unknown

Suffrage: 21 years of age; authorized for all men and women regardless of religion; excludes persons convicted of felonies and other crimes or those imprisoned; excludes all military and security service personnel regardless of rank

Executive branch: *chief of state:* president (vacant)
head of government: Caretaker Prime Minister Najib MIQATI (since 20 September 2021)
cabinet: Cabinet chosen by the prime minister in consultation with the president and Parliament
elections/appointments: president indirectly elected by a qualified majority of two-thirds of Parliament members in the first round and if needed a two-thirds quorum of members by simple majority vote in a second round for a 6-year term (eligible for non-consecutive terms); last held on 31 October 2016; prime minister appointed by the president in consultation with Parliament
election results:
2023: on 14 June 2023, Parliament failed in its twelfth attempt to elect a president; note - the Hezbollah bloc withdrew following the first round of voting and a second round was not possible since Parliament lacked the required 86-member quorum for a second round of voting
2016: Michel AWN elected president in second round; Parliament vote - Michel AWN (FPM) 83; the president was finally elected in its 46th attempt on 31 October 2016

Legislative branch: *description:* unicameral House of Representatives or Majlis al-Nuwab in Arabic, Chambre des députés in French (128 seats; members directly elected in multi-member constituencies by open-list proportional representation vote, apportioned evenly between Christians and Muslims; members serve 4-year terms)
elections: last held on 15 May 2022 (next to be held in May 2026)
election results: percent of vote by party/coalition – NA; seats by party/coalition – FPM 16, LF 14, Amal Movement 13, Hezbollah 13, PSP 9, Kata'ib Party 4, other 30, independent 29; composition - men 120, women 8, percentage women 6.3%; note - a dozen of the elected deputies are from groups pushing for reform with origins in the recent protest movements against the established elite and have formed a group called the "Forces of Change"
note: Lebanon's constitution states the Lebanese Parliament cannot conduct regular business until it elects a president when the position is vacant

Judicial branch: *highest court(s):* Court of Cassation or Supreme Court (organized into 8 chambers, each with a presiding judge and 2 associate judges); Constitutional Council (consists of 10 members)
judge selection and term of office: Court of Cassation judges appointed by Supreme Judicial Council, a 10-member body headed by the chief justice, and includes other judicial officials; judge tenure NA; Constitutional Council members appointed - 5 by the Council of Ministers and 5 by parliament; members serve 5-year terms
subordinate courts: Courts of Appeal; Courts of First Instance; specialized tribunals, religious courts; military courts

Political parties: Al-Ahbash (Association of Islamic Charitable Projects) or AICP
Amal Movement ("Hope Movement")
Azm Movement
Ba'th Arab Socialist Party of Lebanon
Free Patriotic Movement or FPM
Future Movement Bloc or FM (resigned from politics in January 2022)
Hizballah
Islamic Action Front or IAF
Kata'ib Party
Lebanese Democratic Party
Lebanese Forces or LF
Marada Movement
Progressive Socialist Party or PSP
Social Democrat Hunshaqian Party
Syrian Social Nationalist Party or SSNP
Tashnaq or Armenian Revolutionary Federation

International organization participation: ABEDA, AFESD, AMF, CAEU, FAO, G-24, G-77, IAEA, IBRD, ICAO, ICC (national committees), ICRM, IDA, IDB, IFAD, IFC, IFRCS, ILO, IMF, IMO, IMSO, Interpol, IOC, IPU, ISO, ITSO, ITU, LAS, MIGA, NAM, OAS (observer), OIC, OIF, OPCW, PCA, UN, UNCTAD, UNESCO, UNHCR, UNIDO, UNRWA, UNWTO, UPU, WCO, WFTU (NGOs), WHO, WIPO, WMO, WTO (observer)

Diplomatic representation in the US: *chief of mission:* Ambassador (vacant); Chargé d'Affaires Waël HACHEM, Counselor (since 15 March 2021)
chancery: 2560 28th Street NW, Washington, DC 20008
telephone: [1] (202) 939-6300
FAX: [1] (202) 939-6324
email address and website:
info@lebanonembassyus.org
http://www.lebanonembassyus.org/
consulate(s) general: Detroit, New York, Los Angeles

Diplomatic representation from the US: *chief of mission:* Ambassador-designate Lisa A. JOHNSON (since 11 January 2024)
embassy: Awkar facing the Municipality
P.O. Box 70-840 Antelias, Beirut
mailing address: 6070 Beirut Place, Washington DC 20521-6070
telephone: [961] (04) 543-600
FAX: [961] (4) 544-019
email address and website:
BeirutACS@state.gov
https://lb.usembassy.gov/

Flag description: three horizontal bands consisting of red (top), white (middle, double width), and red (bottom) with a green cedar tree centered in the white band; the red bands symbolize blood shed for liberation, the white band denotes peace, the snow of the mountains, and purity; the green cedar tree is the symbol of Lebanon and represents eternity, steadiness, happiness, and prosperity

National symbol(s): cedar tree; national colors: red, white, green

National anthem: *name:* "Kulluna lil-watan" (All Of Us, For Our Country!)
lyrics/music: Rachid NAKHLE/Wadih SABRA
note: adopted 1927; chosen following a nationwide competition

National heritage: *total World Heritage Sites:* 6 (all cultural)
selected World Heritage Site locales: Anjar; Baalbek; Byblos; Tyre; Ouadi Qadisha (the Holy Valley) and the Forest of the Cedars of God (Horsh Arz el-Rab); Rachid Karami International Fair-Tripoli

ECONOMY

Economic overview: upper middle-income Middle Eastern economy; economic activity hurt by economic depression, COVID-19, and port explosion; hyperinflation and sharp poverty increases; banks have ceased lending; new financing facility helping with recovery

Real GDP (purchasing power parity): $65.818 billion (2023 est.)
$65.917 billion (2022 est.)
$66.329 billion (2021 est.)
note: data in 2021 dollars
comparison ranking: 111

Real GDP growth rate: -0.15% (2023 est.)
-0.62% (2022 est.)
-7% (2021 est.)
note: annual GDP % growth based on constant local currency
comparison ranking: 189

Real GDP per capita: $12,300 (2023 est.)
$12,000 (2022 est.)
$11,900 (2021 est.)
note: data in 2021 dollars
comparison ranking: 139

GDP (official exchange rate): $17.937 billion (2023 est.)
note: data in current dollars at official exchange rate

Inflation rate (consumer prices): 221.34% (2023 est.)
171.21% (2022 est.)
154.76% (2021 est.)
note: annual % change based on consumer prices
comparison ranking: 219

Credit ratings: Fitch rating: RD (2020)

Moody's rating: C (2020)

Standard & Poors rating: D (2020)
note: The year refers to the year in which the current credit rating was first obtained.

GDP - composition, by sector of origin: *agriculture:* 1.1% (2023 est.)
industry: 2.4% (2023 est.)
services: 47.7% (2023 est.)
note: figures may not total 100% due to non-allocated consumption not captured in sector-reported data
comparison rankings: services 160; industry 216; agriculture 180

GDP - composition, by end use: *household consumption:* 129.7% (2023 est.)
government consumption: 5.8% (2023 est.)
investment in fixed capital: 0.9% (2023 est.)
exports of goods and services: 46.1% (2023 est.)
imports of goods and services: -82.4% (2023 est.)
note: figures may not total 100% due to rounding or gaps in data collection

Agricultural products: potatoes, milk, tomatoes, apples, oranges, olives, cucumbers/gherkins, chicken, lemons/limes, wheat (2022)
note: top ten agricultural products based on tonnage

Industries: banking, tourism, real estate and construction, food processing, wine, jewelry, cement, textiles, mineral and chemical products, wood and furniture products, oil refining, metal fabricating

Industrial production growth rate: 0.74% (2023 est.)
note: annual % change in industrial value added based on constant local currency
comparison ranking: 145

Labor force: 1.771 million (2023 est.)
note: number of people ages 15 or older who are employed or seeking work
comparison ranking: 131

Unemployment rate: 11.57% (2023 est.)
11.6% (2022 est.)
12.62% (2021 est.)
note: % of labor force seeking employment
comparison ranking: 173

Youth unemployment rate (ages 15-24): *total:* 23.7% (2023 est.)
male: 24.6% (2023 est.)
female: 22% (2023 est.)
note: % of labor force ages 15-24 seeking employment
comparison ranking: total 49

Average household expenditures: *on food:* 20.7% of household expenditures (2022 est.)
on alcohol and tobacco: 1.1% of household expenditures (2022 est.)

Remittances: 35.51% of GDP (2023 est.)
30.66% of GDP (2022 est.)
27.47% of GDP (2021 est.)
note: personal transfers and compensation between resident and non-resident individuals/households/entities

Budget: *revenues:* $12.73 billion (2021 est.)
expenditures: $11.356 billion (2021 est.)
note: central government revenues and expenses (excluding grants/extrabudgetary units/social security funds) converted to US dollars at average official exchange rate for year indicated

Public debt: 146.8% of GDP (2017 est.)
note: data cover central government debt and exclude debt instruments issued (or owned) by government entities other than the treasury; the data include treasury debt held by foreign entities; the data include debt issued by subnational entities, as well as intragovernmental debt; intragovernmental debt consists of treasury borrowings from surpluses in the social funds, such as for retirement, medical care, and unemployment
comparison ranking: 4

Taxes and other revenues: 5.68% (of GDP) (2021 est.)
note: central government tax revenue as a % of GDP
comparison ranking: 201

Current account balance: -$5.643 billion (2023 est.)
-$7.265 billion (2022 est.)
-$4.556 billion (2021 est.)
note: balance of payments - net trade and primary/secondary income in current dollars
comparison ranking: 185

Exports: $11.77 billion (2023 est.)
$12.445 billion (2022 est.)
$9.684 billion (2021 est.)
note: balance of payments - exports of goods and services in current dollars
comparison ranking: 109

Exports - partners: UAE 22%, Syria 8%, Egypt 5%, US 5%, Turkey 4% (2022)
note: top five export partners based on percentage share of exports

Exports - commodities: diamonds, plastics, jewelry, gold, scrap iron (2022)
note: top five export commodities based on value in dollars

Imports: $23.313 billion (2023 est.)
$24.536 billion (2022 est.)
$17.667 billion (2021 est.)
note: balance of payments - imports of goods and services in current dollars
comparison ranking: 90

Imports - partners: China 14%, Turkey 13%, Greece 9%, UAE 7%, Italy 5% (2022)
note: top five import partners based on percentage share of imports

Imports - commodities: refined petroleum, cars, gold, broadcasting equipment, diamonds (2022)
note: top five import commodities based on value in dollars

Reserves of foreign exchange and gold: $32.513 billion (2022 est.)
$35.239 billion (2021 est.)
$42.44 billion (2020 est.)
note: holdings of gold (year-end prices)/foreign exchange/special drawing rights in current dollars
comparison ranking: 41

Debt - external: $38.856 billion (2022 est.)
note: present value of external debt in current US dollars
comparison ranking: 15

Exchange rates: Lebanese pounds (LBP) per US dollar -

Exchange rates: 1,507.5 (2022 est.)
1,507.5 (2021 est.)
1,507.5 (2020 est.)
1,507.5 (2019 est.)
1,507.5 (2018 est.)

ENERGY

Electricity access: *electrification - total population:* 100% (2022 est.)

Electricity: *installed generating capacity:* 4.141 million kW (2022 est.)
consumption: 9.166 billion kWh (2022 est.)
imports: 448.671 million kWh (2022 est.)
transmission/distribution losses: 1.328 billion kWh (2022 est.)
comparison rankings: transmission/distribution losses 112; imports 94; consumption 107; installed generating capacity 96

Electricity generation sources: *fossil fuels:* 90.6% of total installed capacity (2022 est.)
solar: 3% of total installed capacity (2022 est.)
wind: 0.1% of total installed capacity (2022 est.)
hydroelectricity: 6% of total installed capacity (2022 est.)
biomass and waste: 0.3% of total installed capacity (2022 est.)

Coal: *consumption:* 207,000 metric tons (2022 est.)
exports: 47.1 metric tons (2022 est.)
imports: 197,000 metric tons (2022 est.)

Petroleum: *refined petroleum consumption:* 174,000 bbl/day (2022 est.)

Carbon dioxide emissions: 26.594 million metric tonnes of CO_2 (2022 est.)
from coal and metallurgical coke: 456,000 metric tonnes of CO_2 (2022 est.)
from petroleum and other liquids: 26.137 million metric tonnes of CO_2 (2022 est.)
comparison ranking: total emissions 76

Energy consumption per capita: 67.466 million Btu/person (2022 est.)
comparison ranking: 75

COMMUNICATIONS

Telephones - fixed lines: *total subscriptions:* 875,000 (2021 est.)
subscriptions per 100 inhabitants: 16 (2021 est.)
comparison ranking: total subscriptions 73

Telephones - mobile cellular: *total subscriptions:* 4.288 million (2021 est.)
subscriptions per 100 inhabitants: 77 (2021 est.)
comparison ranking: total subscriptions 133

Telecommunication systems: *general assessment:* Lebanon's economic crisis has had a dire effect on the country's telecom services; although some progress has been made with developing 5G, the poor economic conditions have contributed to an erratic electricity supply and a lack of fuel to maintain generators; this has meant that internet services to areas of the country are not available on a regular basis, frustrating all those who depend on stable connectivity, and stalling business growth; adding to the difficulties is the political crisis; the cabinet went into caretaker status after the National Assembly election in May 2022 meaning it can only engage in routine decision making; there is little confidence on the ground that sectarian-based political horse-trading will give way to responsible governing to improve the lot of the stressed populace (2023)
domestic: fixed-line is 16 per 100 and 77 per 100 for mobile-cellular subscriptions (2021)
international: country code - 961; landing points for the IMEWE, BERYTAR AND CADMOS submarine cable links to Europe, Africa, the Middle East and Asia; satellite earth stations - 2 Intelsat (1 Indian Ocean and 1 Atlantic Ocean) (2019)

Broadcast media: 7 TV stations, 1 of which is state owned; more than 30 radio stations, 1 of which is state owned; satellite and cable TV services available; transmissions of at least 2 international broadcasters are accessible through partner stations (2019)

Internet country code: .lb

Internet users: *total:* 4.872 million (2021 est.)
percent of population: 87% (2021 est.)
comparison ranking: total 96

Broadband - fixed subscriptions: *total:* 432,070 (2020 est.)
subscriptions per 100 inhabitants: 6 (2020 est.)
comparison ranking: total 94

TRANSPORTATION

National air transport system: *number of registered air carriers:* 1 (2020)
inventory of registered aircraft operated by air carriers: 21
annual passenger traffic on registered air carriers: 2,981,937 (2018)
annual freight traffic on registered air carriers: 56.57 million (2018) mt-km

Civil aircraft registration country code prefix: OD

Airports: 8 (2024)
comparison ranking: 168

Heliports: 3 (2024)

Pipelines: 88 km gas (2013)

Railways: *total:* 401 km (2017)
standard gauge: 319 km (2017) 1.435-m gauge
narrow gauge: 82 km (2017) 1.050-m gauge
note: rail system is still unusable due to damage sustained from fighting in the 1980s and in 2006
comparison ranking: total 121

Roadways: *total:* 21,705 km (2017)
comparison ranking: total 112

Merchant marine: *total:* 51 (2023)
by type: bulk carrier 2, container ship 1, general cargo 30, oil tanker 1, other 17
comparison ranking: total 120

Ports: *total ports:* 5 (2024)
large: 1
medium: 1
small: 0
very small: 3
ports with oil terminals: 3
key ports: Bayrut, Sayda, Selaata, Sidon/zahrani Terminal, Tarabulus

MILITARY AND SECURITY

Military and security forces: Lebanese Armed Forces (LAF): Army Command (includes Presidential Guard Brigade, Land Border Regiments), Naval Forces, Air Forces

Ministry of Interior: Internal Security Forces Directorate (law enforcement; includes Mobile Gendarmerie), Directorate for General Security (DGS; border control, some domestic security duties); Parliamentary Police Force (2024)
note 1: the commander of the LAF is also the head of the Army; the LAF patrols external borders, while official border checkpoints are under the authority of Directorate for General Security
note 2: the Parliamentary Police Force reports to the speaker of parliament and has responsibility for protecting parliament premises and the speaker's residence; both the Internal Security Forces and the Lebanese Armed Forces provide units to the Parliamentary Police Force

Military expenditures: 3.2% of GDP (2021 est.)
3% of GDP (2020 est.)
4.7% of GDP (2019 est.)
5.1% of GDP (2018 est.)
4.6% of GDP (2017 est.)
comparison ranking: 28

Military and security service personnel strengths: approximately 73,000 active troops (70,000 Army; 1,500 Navy; 1,500 Air Force) (2024)

Military equipment inventories and acquisitions: the LAF inventory includes a wide mix of mostly older equipment from a diverse array of countries; in recent years, the US has been the leading supplier of armaments to Lebanon; the country's economic crisis has severely limited military procurement (2024)

Military service age and obligation: 17-25 years of age for men and women for voluntary military service; no conscription (2024)
note: women were allowed to volunteer for military service in the 1980s; as of 2023, they comprised about 5% of the active duty military

Military - note: the primary responsibilities of the Lebanese Armed Forces (LAF) are defense against external attack, border security, protecting the country's territorial waters, and assisting with internal security and development projects; on Lebanon's eastern and northern borders with Syria, the LAF has conducted operations to prevent or eliminate infiltrations of militants linked to the Islamic State of Iraq and ash-Sham (ISIS) and al-Qa'ida terrorist groups since the start of the Syrian civil war in 2011; in the south, its focus is on maintaining stability along its volatile land border with Israel where the LAF and the Israel Defense Forces (IDF) are separated by the "Blue Line," a demarcation line established by the UN in 2000 following the withdrawal of the IDF, which had occupied southern Lebanon since invading in 1982; since the line's establishment, the LAF and IDF have had periodic clashes, and IDF aircraft have routinely entered Lebanese air space
the Iranian-backed terrorist group Hizballah is based in south Lebanon where it has significant influence and acts as a militia alongside the LAF; it has launched periodic cross-border attacks on Israel and threatened additional attacks, while the IDF has conducted air strikes on Hizballah positions and in 2006 launched a ground invasion into southern Lebanon to suppress the group; following the terrorist group HAMAS's attack on Israel from Gaza in October 2023 and subsequent Israeli invasion of Gaza, Hizballah has sought to demonstrate solidarity with HAMAS by launching barrages of missiles, rockets, and armed drones into northern Israel; these attacks continued into 2024 and have been countered by numerous strikes from Israel on Hizballah targets in Lebanon
the LAF's domestic security responsibilities include countering narcotics trafficking and smuggling, managing protests, conducting search and rescue, and intervening to prevent violence between rival political factions; in recent years, the military has faced a financial crisis as government debt and national economic difficulties have undercut its ability to train and fully pay and supply personnel, which has sparked domestic and international fears that the armed forces may disintegrate; the UN, as well as individual countries such as France and the US have provided financial assistance
the UN Interim Force In Lebanon (UNIFIL) has operated in the country since 1978, originally under UNSCRs 425 and 426 to confirm Israeli withdrawal from Lebanon, restore international peace and security, and assist the Lebanese Government in restoring its effective authority in the area; following the July-August 2006 war, the UN Security Council adopted resolution 1701 enhancing UNIFIL and deciding that in addition to the original mandate, it would, among other things, monitor the cessation of hostilities, support the LAF as they deployed throughout the south of Lebanon, and provide assistance for humanitarian access for civilians and the return of displaced persons; UNIFIL has approximately 9,500 military personnel deployed in the country and includes a maritime task force (2024)

TERRORISM

Terrorist group(s): Abdallah Azzam Brigades; al-Aqsa Martyrs Brigade; Asbat al-Ansar; HAMAS; Hizballah; Islamic Revolutionary Guard Corps/Qods Force; Islamic State of Iraq and ash-Sham (ISIS); al-Nusrah Front (Hay'at Tahrir al- Sham); Palestine Liberation Front; Popular Front for the Liberation of Palestine (PFLP); PFLP-General Command
note: details about the history, aims, leadership, organization, areas of operation, tactics, targets, weapons, size, and sources of support of the group(s) appear(s) in the Terrorism reference guide

TRANSNATIONAL ISSUES

Refugees and internally displaced persons: *refugees (country of origin):* 487,000 (Palestinian refugees) (2022); 784,884 (Syria) (2023)
IDPs: 7,000 (2020)

stateless persons: undetermined (2016); note - tens of thousands of persons are stateless in Lebanon, including many Palestinian refugees and their descendants, Syrian Kurds denaturalized in Syria in 1962, children born to Lebanese women married to foreign or stateless men; most babies born to Syrian refugees, and Lebanese children whose births are unregistered

Trafficking in persons: tier rating: Tier 2 Watch List — the government did not demonstrate overall increasing efforts to eliminate trafficking compared to the previous reporting period, therefore Lebanon remained on Tier 2 Watch List for a second consecutive year; for more details, go to: https://www.state.gov/reports/2024-trafficking-in-persons-report/lebanon/

Illicit drugs: source country for amphetamine tablets destined for Saudi Arabia, Qatar, United Arab Emirates, Libya and Sudan; source for captagon

LESOTHO

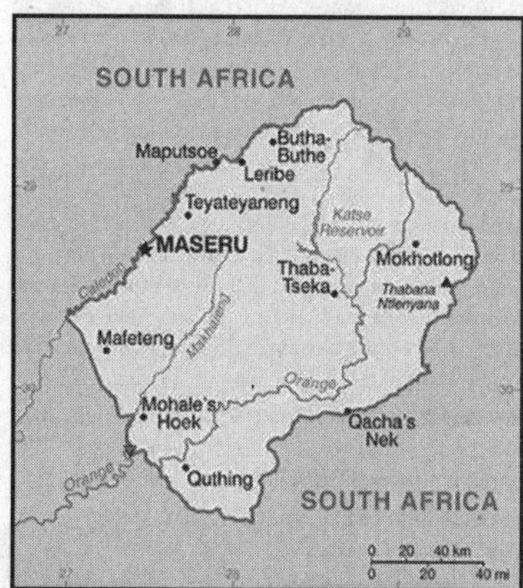

INTRODUCTION

Background: Paramount chief MOSHOESHOE I consolidated what would become Basutoland in the early 19th century and made himself king in 1822. Continuing encroachments by Dutch settlers from the neighboring Orange Free State caused the king to enter into an 1868 agreement with the UK that made Basutoland first a British protectorate and, after 1884, a crown colony. After gaining independence in 1966, the country was renamed the Kingdom of Lesotho. The Basotho National Party ruled the country during its first two decades. King MOSHOESHOE II was exiled in 1990, returned to Lesotho in 1992, was reinstated in 1995, and was then succeeded by his son, King LETSIE III, in 1996. Constitutional government was restored in 1993 after seven years of military rule.

In 1998, violent protests and a military mutiny following a contentious election prompted a brief but bloody intervention by South African and Batswana military forces under the aegis of the Southern African Development Community (SADC). Subsequent constitutional reforms restored relative political stability. Peaceful parliamentary elections were held in 2002, but the National Assembly elections in 2007 were hotly contested, and aggrieved parties disputed how seats were awarded. In 2012, competitive elections saw Prime Minister Motsoahae Thomas THABANE form a coalition government – the first in the country's history – that ousted the 14-year incumbent, Pakalitha MOSISILI, who peacefully transferred power the following month. MOSISILI returned to power in snap elections in 2015 after the collapse of THABANE's coalition government and an alleged attempted military coup. In 2017, THABANE returned to become prime minister but stepped down in 2020 after being implicated in his estranged wife's murder. He was succeeded by Moseketsi MAJORO. In 2022, Ntsokoane Samuel MATEKANE was inaugurated as prime minister and head of a three-party coalition.

GEOGRAPHY

Location: Southern Africa, an enclave of South Africa

Geographic coordinates: 29 30 S, 28 30 E

Map references: Africa

Area: *total:* 30,355 sq km
land: 30,355 sq km
water: 0 sq km
comparison ranking: total 141

Area - comparative: slightly smaller than Maryland

Land boundaries: *total:* 1,106 km
border countries (1): South Africa 1,106 km

Coastline: 0 km (landlocked)

Maritime claims: none (landlocked)

Climate: temperate; cool to cold, dry winters; hot, wet summers

Terrain: mostly highland with plateaus, hills, and mountains

Elevation: *highest point:* Thabana Ntlenyana 3,482 m
lowest point: junction of the Orange and Makhaleng Rivers 1,400 m
mean elevation: 2,161 m

Natural resources: water, agricultural and grazing land, diamonds, sand, clay, building stone

Land use: *agricultural land:* 76.1% (2018 est.)
arable land: 10.1% (2018 est.)
permanent crops: 0.1% (2018 est.)
permanent pasture: 65.9% (2018 est.)
forest: 1.5% (2018 est.)
other: 22.4% (2018 est.)

Irrigated land: 12 sq km (2013)

Major rivers (by length in km): Orange river source (shared with South Africa and Namibia [m]) - 2,092 km
note – [s] after country name indicates river source; [m] after country name indicates river mouth

Major watersheds (area sq km): Atlantic Ocean drainage: Orange (941,351 sq km)

Population distribution: relatively higher population density in the western half of the nation, with the capital of Maseru, and the smaller cities of Mafeteng, Teyateyaneng, and Leribe attracting the most people as shown in this population distribution map

Natural hazards: periodic droughts

Geography - note: landlocked, an enclave of (completely surrounded by) South Africa; mountainous, more than 80% of the country is 1,800 m above sea level

PEOPLE AND SOCIETY

Population: *total:* 2,227,548
male: 1,101,959
female: 1,125,589 (2024 est.)
comparison rankings: female 146; male 147; total 147

Nationality: *noun:* Mosotho (singular), Basotho (plural)
adjective: Basotho

Ethnic groups: Sotho 99.7%, other 0.3% (includes Kwena, Nguni (Hlubi and Phuthi), Zulu)

Languages: Sesotho (official), English (official), Phuthi, Xhosa, Zulu

Religions: Protestant 47.8% (Pentecostal 23.1%, Lesotho Evangelical 17.3%, Anglican 7.4%), Roman Catholic 39.3%, other Christian 9.1%, non-Christian 1.4%, none 2.3% (2014 est.)

Demographic profile: Lesotho faces great socioeconomic challenges. Almost half of its population lives below the poverty line as of 2017, and the country's HIV/AIDS prevalence rate is the second highest in the world as of 2021. In addition, Lesotho is a small, mountainous, landlocked country with little arable land, leaving its population vulnerable to food shortages and reliant on remittances. Lesotho's persistently high infant, child, and maternal mortality rates have been increasing during the last decade, according to the last two Demographic and Health Surveys. Despite these significant shortcomings, Lesotho has made good progress in education; it is on-track to achieve universal primary education and has one of the highest adult literacy rates in Africa.

Lesotho's migration history is linked to its unique geography; it is surrounded by South Africa with which it shares linguistic and cultural traits. Lesotho at one time had more of its workforce employed outside its borders than any other country. Today remittances equal about 20% of its GDP. With few job options at home, a high rate of poverty, and higher wages available across the border, labor migration to South Africa replaced agriculture as the prevailing Basotho source of income decades ago. The majority of Basotho migrants were single men contracted to work as gold miners in South Africa. However, migration trends changed in the 1990s, and fewer men found mining jobs in South Africa because of declining gold prices, stricter immigration policies, and a preference for South African workers.

Although men still dominate cross-border labor migration, more women are working in South Africa, mostly as domestics, because they are widows or their husbands are unemployed. Internal rural-urban flows have also become more frequent, with more women migrating within the country to take up jobs in the garment industry or moving to care for loved ones with HIV/AIDS. Lesotho's small population of immigrants is increasingly composed of Taiwanese and Chinese migrants who are involved in the textile industry and small retail businesses.

Age structure: *0-14 years:* 32% (male 358,137/female 353,618)
15-64 years: 62.7% (male 699,197/female 696,626)
65 years and over: 5.4% (2024 est.) (male 44,625/female 75,345)

Dependency ratios: *total dependency ratio:* 62.1
youth dependency ratio: 55.3
elderly dependency ratio: 6.8
potential support ratio: 14.7 (2021 est.)

Median age: *total:* 23.9 years (2024 est.)
male: 23.4 years
female: 24.3 years
comparison ranking: total 179

Population growth rate: 0.76% (2024 est.)
comparison ranking: 116

Birth rate: 22.9 births/1,000 population (2024 est.)
comparison ranking: 50

Death rate: 10.8 deaths/1,000 population (2024 est.)
comparison ranking: 28

Net migration rate: -4.5 migrant(s)/1,000 population (2024 est.)
comparison ranking: 199

Population distribution: relatively higher population density in the western half of the nation, with the capital of Maseru, and the smaller cities of Mafeteng, Teyateyaneng, and Leribe attracting the most people as shown in this population distribution map

Urbanization: *urban population:* 30.4% of total population (2023)
rate of urbanization: 2.77% annual rate of change (2020-25 est.)

Major urban areas - population: 202,000 MASERU (capital) (2018)

Sex ratio: *at birth:* 1.03 male(s)/female
0-14 years: 1.01 male(s)/female
15-64 years: 1 male(s)/female
65 years and over: 0.59 male(s)/female
total population: 0.98 male(s)/female (2024 est.)

Mother's mean age at first birth: 20.9 years (2014 est.)
note: data represents median age at first birth among women 25-49

Maternal mortality ratio: 566 deaths/100,000 live births (2020 est.)
comparison ranking: 9

Infant mortality rate: *total:* 45.7 deaths/1,000 live births (2024 est.)
male: 51 deaths/1,000 live births
female: 40.2 deaths/1,000 live births
comparison ranking: total 24

Life expectancy at birth: *total population:* 60.2 years (2024 est.)
male: 58.1 years
female: 62.3 years
comparison ranking: total population 221

Total fertility rate: 2.85 children born/woman (2024 est.)
comparison ranking: 53

Gross reproduction rate: 1.4 (2024 est.)

Contraceptive prevalence rate: 64.9% (2018)

Drinking water source: *improved: urban:* 95.7% of population
rural: 77.2% of population
total: 82.6% of population
unimproved: urban: 4.3% of population
rural: 22.8% of population
total: 17.4% of population (2020 est.)

Current health expenditure: 11.8% of GDP (2020)

Physician density: 0.47 physicians/1,000 population (2018)

Sanitation facility access: *improved: urban:* 93.6% of population
rural: 62.4% of population
total: 71.4% of population
unimproved: urban: 6.4% of population
rural: 37.6% of population
total: 28.6% of population (2020 est.)

Obesity - adult prevalence rate: 16.6% (2016)
comparison ranking: 121

Alcohol consumption per capita: *total:* 3.56 liters of pure alcohol (2019 est.)
beer: 1.98 liters of pure alcohol (2019 est.)
wine: 0.44 liters of pure alcohol (2019 est.)
spirits: 0.31 liters of pure alcohol (2019 est.)
other alcohols: 0.82 liters of pure alcohol (2019 est.)
comparison ranking: total 103

Tobacco use: *total:* 24.3% (2020 est.)
male: 43.1% (2020 est.)
female: 5.4% (2020 est.)
comparison ranking: total 55

Children under the age of 5 years underweight: 10.5% (2018)
comparison ranking: 55

Currently married women (ages 15-49): 53.7% (2023 est.)

Child marriage: *women married by age 15:* 1%
women married by age 18: 16.4%
men married by age 18: 1.9% (2018 est.)

Education expenditures: 8.7% of GDP (2021 est.)
comparison ranking: 11

Literacy: *definition:* age 15 and over can read and write
total population: 81%
male: 72.9%
female: 88.8% (2021)

School life expectancy (primary to tertiary education): *total:* 12 years
male: 12 years
female: 13 years (2017)

ENVIRONMENT

Environment - current issues: population pressure forcing settlement in marginal areas results in overgrazing, severe soil erosion, and soil exhaustion; desertification; Highlands Water Project controls, stores, and redirects water to South Africa

Environment - international agreements: *party to:* Biodiversity, Climate Change, Climate Change-Kyoto Protocol, Climate Change-Paris Agreement, Comprehensive Nuclear Test Ban, Desertification, Endangered Species, Hazardous Wastes, Law of the Sea, Marine Life Conservation, Ozone Layer Protection, Wetlands
signed, but not ratified: none of the selected agreements

Climate: temperate; cool to cold, dry winters; hot, wet summers

Urbanization: *urban population:* 30.4% of total population (2023)
rate of urbanization: 2.77% annual rate of change (2020-25 est.)

Food insecurity: *severe localized food insecurity: due to poor harvests and increased food prices* - according to the latest national food security assessment, 22% of the rural population are expected to face acute food insecurity between October 2022 and March 2023, compared to 15% between July and September 2022; the forecasted proportion translates into 320,000 people in rural areas, while an additional 201,000 people in urban areas are foreseen to also need assistance; the foreseen increase of acute food insecurity levels is primarily due to the reduced harvest, high food prices in basic food and non-food commodities and a slow recovery of households' income reflecting a downturn in economic growth; harvesting of the 2022 main-season summer cereal crops, mostly maize and sorghum, is complete; production of maize, the main cereal staple, is about one-third of the average, while the sorghum output is almost negligible; the poor harvest was primarily due to torrential rainfalls during January and February 2022, which caused localized flooding and resulted in crop losses (2022)

Revenue from forest resources: 3.34% of GDP (2018 est.)
comparison ranking: 22

Revenue from coal: 0% of GDP (2018 est.)
comparison ranking: 96

Air pollutants: *particulate matter emissions:* 17.6 micrograms per cubic meter (2019 est.)
carbon dioxide emissions: 2.51 megatons (2016 est.)
methane emissions: 2.56 megatons (2020 est.)

Waste and recycling: *municipal solid waste generated annually:* 73,457 tons (2006 est.)

Major rivers (by length in km): Orange river source (shared with South Africa and Namibia [m]) - 2,092 km
note – [s] after country name indicates river source; [m] after country name indicates river mouth

Major watersheds (area sq km): Atlantic Ocean drainage: Orange (941,351 sq km)

Total water withdrawal: *municipal:* 20 million cubic meters (2020 est.)
industrial: 20 million cubic meters (2020 est.)
agricultural: 3.8 million cubic meters (2017 est.)

Total renewable water resources: 3.02 billion cubic meters (2020 est.)

GOVERNMENT

Country name: *conventional long form:* Kingdom of Lesotho
conventional short form: Lesotho
local long form: Kingdom of Lesotho
local short form: Lesotho
former: Basutoland
etymology: the name translates as "Land of the Sesotho Speakers"

Government type: parliamentary constitutional monarchy

Capital: *name:* Maseru
geographic coordinates: 29 19 S, 27 29 E
time difference: UTC+2 (7 hours ahead of Washington, DC, during Standard Time)
etymology: in the Sesotho language the name means "[place of] red sandstones"

Administrative divisions: 10 districts; Berea, Butha-Buthe, Leribe, Mafeteng, Maseru, Mohale's Hoek, Mokhotlong, Qacha's Nek, Quthing, Thaba-Tseka

Independence: 4 October 1966 (from the UK)

National holiday: Independence Day, 4 October (1966)

Legal system: mixed legal system of English common law and Roman-Dutch law; judicial review of legislative acts in High Court and Court of Appeal

Constitution: *history:* previous 1959, 1967; latest adopted 2 April 1993 (effectively restoring the 1967 version)
amendments: proposed by Parliament; passage of amendments affecting constitutional provisions, including fundamental rights and freedoms, sovereignty of the kingdom, the office of the king, and powers of Parliament, requires a majority vote by the National Assembly, approval by the Senate, approval in a referendum by a majority of qualified voters, and assent of the king; passage of amendments other than those specified provisions requires at least a two-thirds majority vote in both houses of Parliament; amended several times, last in 2011

International law organization participation: accepts compulsory ICJ jurisdiction with reservations; accepts ICCt jurisdiction

Citizenship: *citizenship by birth:* yes
citizenship by descent only: yes
dual citizenship recognized: no
residency requirement for naturalization: 5 years

Suffrage: 18 years of age; universal

Executive branch: *chief of state:* King LETSIE III (since 7 February 1996)
head of government: Prime Minister Ntsokoane Samuel MATEKANE (28 October 2022)
cabinet: consists of the prime minister, appointed by the King on the advice of the Council of State, the deputy prime minister, and 18 other ministers; the prime minister is the leader of the majority party or majority coalition in the National Assembly
elections/appointments: the monarchy is hereditary, but under the terms of the constitution that came into effect after the March 1993 election, the monarch is a "living symbol of national unity" with no executive or legislative powers; under traditional law, the College of Chiefs has the power to depose the monarch, to determine next in line of succession, or to serve as regent in the event that a successor is not of mature age
note - King LETSIE III formerly occupied the throne from November 1990 to February 1995 while his father was in exile

Legislative branch: *description:* bicameral Parliament consists of:
Senate (33 seats; 22 principal chiefs and 11 other senators nominated by the king with the advice of the Council of State, a 13-member body of key government and non-government officials; members serve 5-year terms)
National Assembly (120 seats; 80 members directly elected in single-seat constituencies by simple majority vote and 40 elected through proportional representation; members serve 5-year terms)
elections: Senate - last appointed by the king in November 2022 (next to be appointed 2028)
National Assembly - last held on 7 October 2022 (next to be held in February 2028)
election results: Senate - percent of votes by party - NA, seats by party - NA; composition - men 25, women 8, percentage women 24.2%
National Assembly - percent of votes by party - RFP 38.9%, DC 24.7%, ABC 7.1%, BAP 5.4%, AD 4.0%, MEC 3.2%, LCD 2.3%, SR 2.1%, BNP 1.4%, PFD 0.9%, BCM 0.8%, MPS 0.8%, MIP 0.7%; seats by party - RFP 56, DC 29, ABC 8, BAP 6, AD 5, MEC 4, LCD 3, SR 2, BNP 1, PFD 1, BCM 1, MPS 1, NIP 1, HOPE 1, TBD 1; composition - men 90, women 30, percentage 25%; note - total Parliament percentage women 24.8%

Judicial branch: *highest court(s):* Court of Appeal (consists of the court president, such number of justices of appeal as set by Parliament, and the Chief Justice and the puisne judges of the High Court ex officio); High Court (consists of the chief justice and such number of puisne judges as set by Parliament); note - both the Court of Appeal and the High Court have jurisdiction in constitutional issues
judge selection and term of office: Court of Appeal president and High Court chief justice appointed by the monarch on the advice of the prime minister; puisne judges appointed by the monarch on advice of the Judicial Service Commission, an independent body of judicial officers and officials designated by the monarch; judges of both courts can serve until age 75
subordinate courts: Magistrate Courts; customary or traditional courts; military courts

Political parties: All Basotho Convention or ABC
Alliance of Democrats or AD
Basotho Action Party or BAP
Basotho National Party or BNP
Democratic Congress or DC
Democratic Party of Lesotho or DPL
Lesotho People's Congress or LPC
Movement of Economic Change or MEC
National Independent Party or NIP
Popular Front for Democracy of PFD
Reformed Congress of Lesotho or RCL

International organization participation: ACP, AfDB, AU, C, CD, FAO, G-77, IAEA, IBRD, ICAO, ICCt, ICRM, IDA, IFAD, IFC, IFRCS, ILO, IMF, Interpol, IOC, IOM, IPU, ISO (correspondent), ITU, MIGA, NAM, OPCW, SACU, SADC, UN, UNCTAD, UNESCO, UNHCR, UNIDO, UNWTO, UPU, WCO, WFTU (NGOs), WHO, WIPO, WMO, WTO

Diplomatic representation in the US: *chief of mission:* Ambassador Tumisang MOSOTHO (since 16 September 2022)
chancery: 2511 Massachusetts Avenue NW, Washington, DC 20008
telephone: [1] (202) 797-5533
FAX: [1] (202) 234-6815
email address and website:
lesothoembassy@verizon.net
https://www.gov.ls/

Diplomatic representation from the US: *chief of mission:* Ambassador Maria E. BREWER (since 10 March 2022)
embassy: 254 Kingsway Avenue, Maseru
mailing address: 2340 Maseru Place, Washington DC 20521-2340
telephone: [266] 22312666
FAX: [266] 22310116
email address and website:
USConsularMaseru@state.gov
https://ls.usembassy.gov/

Flag description: *three horizontal stripes of blue (top), white, and green in the proportions of 3:4:3;* the colors represent rain, peace, and prosperity respectively; centered in the white stripe is a black mokorotlo, a traditional Basotho straw hat and national symbol; the redesigned flag was unfurled in October 2006 to celebrate 40 years of independence

National symbol(s): mokorotio (Basotho hat); national colors: blue, white, green, black

National anthem: *name:* "Lesotho fatse la bo ntat'a rona" (Lesotho, Land of Our Fathers)
lyrics/music: Francois COILLARD/Ferdinand-Samuel LAUR
note: adopted 1967; music derives from an 1823 Swiss songbook

National heritage: *total World Heritage Sites:* 1 (mixed)
selected World Heritage Site locales: Maloti-Drakensberg Park

ECONOMY

Economic overview: lower middle-income economy surrounded by South Africa; environmentally fragile and politically unstable; key infrastructure and renewable energy investments; dire poverty; urban job and income losses due to COVID-19; systemic corruption

Real GDP (purchasing power parity): $5.868 billion (2023 est.)
$5.816 billion (2022 est.)
$5.742 billion (2021 est.)
note: data in 2021 dollars
comparison ranking: 176

Real GDP growth rate: 0.9% (2023 est.)
1.29% (2022 est.)
1.85% (2021 est.)
note: annual GDP % growth based on constant local currency
comparison ranking: 167

Real GDP per capita: $2,500 (2023 est.)
$2,500 (2022 est.)
$2,500 (2021 est.)
note: data in 2021 dollars
comparison ranking: 203

GDP (official exchange rate): $2.046 billion (2023 est.)
note: data in current dollars at official exchange rate

Inflation rate (consumer prices): 6.34% (2023 est.)
8.27% (2022 est.)
6.05% (2021 est.)
note: annual % change based on consumer prices
comparison ranking: 134

Credit ratings: Fitch rating: B (2019)
note: The year refers to the year in which the current credit rating was first obtained.

GDP - composition, by sector of origin: *agriculture:* 6.3% (2023 est.)
industry: 29.5% (2023 est.)
services: 51.4% (2023 est.)
note: figures may not total 100% due to non-allocated consumption not captured in sector-reported data
comparison rankings: services 137; industry 70; agriculture 103

GDP - composition, by end use: *household consumption:* 88.7% (2022 est.)
government consumption: 34.2% (2022 est.)
investment in fixed capital: 28% (2022 est.)
investment in inventories: 0.3% (2022 est.)
exports of goods and services: 47.2% (2022 est.)
imports of goods and services: -98.5% (2022 est.)
note: figures may not total 100% due to rounding or gaps in data collection

Agricultural products: milk, potatoes, maize, vegetables, fruits, beans, wheat, game meat, sorghum, wool (2022)
note: top ten agricultural products based on tonnage

Industries: food, beverages, textiles, apparel assembly, handicrafts, construction, tourism

Industrial production growth rate: -0.33% (2023 est.)
note: annual % change in industrial value added based on constant local currency
comparison ranking: 157

Labor force: 1.004 million (2023 est.)
note: number of people ages 15 or older who are employed or seeking work
comparison ranking: 146

Unemployment rate: 16.46% (2023 est.)
16.67% (2022 est.)
18.13% (2021 est.)
note: % of labor force seeking employment
comparison ranking: 193

Youth unemployment rate (ages 15-24): *total:* 24.8% (2023 est.)
male: 17.5% (2023 est.)
female: 34.8% (2023 est.)
note: % of labor force ages 15-24 seeking employment
comparison ranking: total 45

Population below poverty line: 49.7% (2017 est.)
note: % of population with income below national poverty line

Gini Index coefficient - distribution of family income: 44.9 (2017 est.)
note: index (0-100) of income distribution; higher values represent greater inequality
comparison ranking: 22

Household income or consumption by percentage share: *lowest 10%:* 1.7% (2017 est.)
highest 10%: 32.9% (2017 est.)
note: % share of income accruing to lowest and highest 10% of population

Remittances: 24.12% of GDP (2023 est.)
23.29% of GDP (2022 est.)
19.71% of GDP (2021 est.)
note: personal transfers and compensation between resident and non-resident individuals/households/entities

Budget: *revenues:* $1.13 billion (2022 est.)
expenditures: $947.517 million (2022 est.)
note: central government revenues and expenses (excluding grants/extrabudgetary units/social security funds) converted to US dollars at average official exchange rate for year indicated

Public debt: 2.99% of GDP (2020 est.)
note: central government debt as a % of GDP
comparison ranking: 203

Taxes and other revenues: 31.31% (of GDP) (2022 est.)
note: central government tax revenue as a % of GDP
comparison ranking: 20

Current account balance: -$117.501 million (2023 est.)
-$264.265 million (2022 est.)
-$194.1 million (2021 est.)
note: balance of payments - net trade and primary/secondary income in current dollars
comparison ranking: 96

Exports: $886.278 million (2023 est.)
$1.07 billion (2022 est.)
$1.082 billion (2021 est.)
note: balance of payments - exports of goods and services in current dollars
comparison ranking: 184

Exports - partners: South Africa 37%, US 28%, Belgium 19%, UAE 6%, UK 3% (2022)
note: top five export partners based on percentage share of exports

Exports - commodities: garments, diamonds, water, wool, power equipment (2022)
note: top five export commodities based on value in dollars

Imports: $2.058 billion (2023 est.)
$2.244 billion (2022 est.)
$2.222 billion (2021 est.)
note: balance of payments - imports of goods and services in current dollars
comparison ranking: 177

Imports - partners: South Africa 77%, China 6%, Taiwan 5%, Zimbabwe 4%, India 2% (2022)
note: top five import partners based on percentage share of imports

Imports - commodities: refined petroleum, fabric, cotton, garments, electricity (2022)
note: top five import commodities based on value in dollars

Reserves of foreign exchange and gold: $774.095 million (2019 est.)
$728.528 million (2018 est.)
$657.668 million (2017 est.)
note: holdings of gold (year-end prices)/foreign exchange/special drawing rights in current dollars
comparison ranking: 145

Debt - external: $830.976 million (2022 est.)
note: present value of external debt in current US dollars
comparison ranking: 83

Exchange rates: maloti (LSL) per US dollar -

Exchange rates: 18.45 (2023 est.)
16.356 (2022 est.)
14.779 (2021 est.)
16.459 (2020 est.)
14.448 (2019 est.)

ENERGY

Electricity access: *electrification - total population:* 50% (2022 est.)
electrification - urban areas: 83.6%
electrification - rural areas: 37.7%

Electricity: *installed generating capacity:* 75,000 kW (2022 est.)
consumption: 828.817 million kWh (2022 est.)
imports: 429.639 million kWh (2022 est.)
transmission/distribution losses: 102.88 million kWh (2022 est.)
comparison rankings: transmission/distribution losses 49; imports 95; consumption 163; installed generating capacity 189

Electricity generation sources: *fossil fuels:* 0.1% of total installed capacity (2022 est.)
solar: 0.3% of total installed capacity (2022 est.)
hydroelectricity: 99.6% of total installed capacity (2022 est.)

Coal: *imports:* 23,000 metric tons (2022 est.)

Petroleum: *refined petroleum consumption:* 5,000 bbl/day (2022 est.)

Carbon dioxide emissions: 752,000 metric tonnes of CO_2 (2022 est.)
from petroleum and other liquids: 752,000 metric tonnes of CO_2 (2022 est.)
comparison ranking: total emissions 178

Energy consumption per capita: 5.975 million Btu/person (2022 est.)
comparison ranking: 166

COMMUNICATIONS

Telephones - fixed lines: *total subscriptions:* 7,000 (2022 est.)
subscriptions per 100 inhabitants: (2022 est.) less than 1
comparison ranking: total subscriptions 194

Telephones - mobile cellular: *total subscriptions:* 1.557 million (2022 est.)
subscriptions per 100 inhabitants: 68 (2022 est.)
comparison ranking: total subscriptions 157

Telecommunication systems: *general assessment:* until late 2020, Lesotho's telecom regulator maintained a market duopoly which is focused on fixed-line services; competition was insufficient to promote effective price reductions for consumers, while the regulator had no mechanisms in place to monitor the telcos to ensure quality of service and fair pricing for consumers; the small size of the country's population provided little incentive for new players to enter the market; a positive outcome for consumers was the deployment in early 2021 of a service to monitor traffic and billing; this ended the practice whereby the regulator was dependent on telcos submitting data about their performance, billing, and other matters; the regulator has also turned its attention to addressing multiple SIM ownership and stemming incidences of crimes committed using unregistered SIMs; in May 2022, it instructed the country's Mobile Network Operators to begin registering SIM cards on their networks from the following month; fixed-wireless 5G trials began in early 2019 (2022)
domestic: fixed-line is less than 1 per 100 subscriptions; mobile-cellular service subscribership is 80 per 100 persons (2021)
international: country code - 266; Internet accessibility has improved with several submarine fiber optic cables that land on African east and west coasts, but the country's land locked position makes access prices expensive; satellite earth station - 1 Intelsat (Atlantic Ocean) (2019)

Broadcast media: 1 state-owned TV station and 2 state-owned radio stations; most private broadcast media transmitters are connected to government radio signal towers; satellite TV subscription service available; transmissions of multiple international broadcasters obtainable (2019)

Internet country code: .ls

Internet users: *total:* 1.104 million (2021 est.)
percent of population: 48% (2021 est.)
comparison ranking: total 148

Broadband - fixed subscriptions: *total:* 5,060 (2020 est.)
subscriptions per 100 inhabitants: 0.2 (2020 est.)
comparison ranking: total 185

TRANSPORTATION

Civil aircraft registration country code prefix: 7P

Airports: 33 (2024)
comparison ranking: 115

Roadways: *total:* 6,906 km
paved: 1,799 km
unpaved: 5,107 km (2022)
comparison ranking: total 146

MILITARY AND SECURITY

Military and security forces: Lesotho Defense Force (LDF): Army (includes Air Wing) (2024)
note: the Lesotho Mounted Police Service is responsible for internal security and reports to the Minister of Local Government, Chieftainship, Home Affairs and Police

Military expenditures: 1.5% of GDP (2023 est.)
1.6% of GDP (2022 est.)
1.5% of GDP (2021 est.)
1.6% of GDP (2020 est.)
1.8% of GDP (2019 est.)
comparison ranking: 88

Military and security service personnel strengths: approximately 2,000 personnel (2023)

Military equipment inventories and acquisitions: the LDF has a small inventory of mostly older, obsolescent, or second-hand weapons and equipment from a variety of countries (2023)

Military service age and obligation: 18-30 years of age for voluntary military service for both men and women (women can serve in combat arms); no conscription (2024)

Military - note: Lesotho's declared policy for its military is the maintenance of the country's sovereignty and the preservation of internal security; in practice, external security is guaranteed by South Africa; the LDF is a small force comprised of about a half dozen infantry companies; it began in 1964 as the Police Mobile Unit (PMU); the PMU was designated as the Lesotho Paramilitary Force in 1980 and became the Royal Lesotho Defense Force in 1986; it was renamed the Lesotho Defense Force in 1993 (2024)

LIBERIA

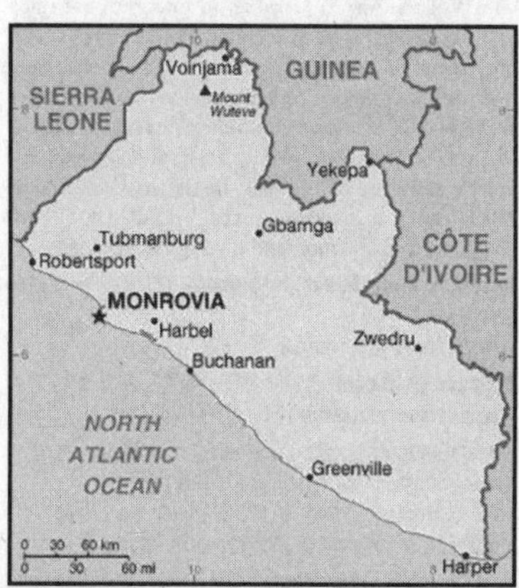

INTRODUCTION

Background: With 28 ethnic groups and languages, Liberia is one of the most ethnically diverse countries in the world. For hundreds of years, the Mali and Songhai Empires claimed most of Liberia. Beginning in the 15th century, European traders began establishing outposts along the Liberian coast. Unlike its neighbors, however, Liberia did not fall under European colonial rule. In the early 19th century, the US began sending freed enslaved people and other people of color to Liberia to establish settlements. In 1847, these settlers declared independence from the US, writing their own constitution and establishing Africa's first republic.

Early in Liberia's history, tensions arose between the Americo-Liberian settlers and the indigenous population. In 1980, Samuel DOE, who was from the indigenous population, led a military coup and ushered in a decade of authoritarian rule. In 1989, Charles TAYLOR launched a rebellion that led to a prolonged civil war in which DOE was killed. A period of relative peace in 1997 permitted an election that brought TAYLOR to power. In 2000, fighting resumed. A 2003 peace agreement ended the war and prompted TAYLOR's resignation. He was later convicted by the UN-backed Special Court for Sierra Leone in The Hague for his involvement in Sierra Leone's civil war.

In 2005, Ellen JOHNSON SIRLEAF became president after two years of transitional governments; she was the first female head of state in Africa. In 2011, JOHNSON SIRLEAF won reelection but struggled to rebuild Liberia's economy – particularly after the 2014-15 Ebola epidemic – and to reconcile a nation still recovering from 14 years of fighting. In 2017, former soccer star George WEAH won the presidential runoff election, marking the first successful transfer of power from one democratically elected government to another since the end of Liberia's civil wars. Like his predecessor, WEAH struggled to improve the country's economy. In 2023, former Vice President Joseph BOAKAI was elected president, edging out WEAH by a thin margin, the first time since 1927 that an incumbent was not re-elected after one term.

GEOGRAPHY

Location: Western Africa, bordering the North Atlantic Ocean, between Cote d'Ivoire and Sierra Leone

Geographic coordinates: 6 30 N, 9 30 W

Map references: Africa

Area: *total:* 111,369 sq km
land: 96,320 sq km
water: 15,049 sq km
comparison ranking: total 104

Area - comparative: slightly larger than Virginia

Land boundaries: *total:* 1,667 km
border countries (3): Guinea 590 km; Cote d'Ivoire 778 km; Sierra Leone 299 km

Coastline: 579 km

Maritime claims: *territorial sea:* 12 nm
contiguous zone: 24 nm
exclusive economic zone: 200 nm
continental shelf: 200 nm

Climate: tropical; hot, humid; dry winters with hot days and cool to cold nights; wet, cloudy summers with frequent heavy showers

Terrain: mostly flat to rolling coastal plains rising to rolling plateau and low mountains in northeast

Elevation: *highest point:* Mount Wuteve 1,447 m
lowest point: Atlantic Ocean 0 m
mean elevation: 243 m

Natural resources: iron ore, timber, diamonds, gold, hydropower

Land use: *agricultural land:* 28.1% (2018 est.)
arable land: 5.2% (2018 est.)
permanent crops: 2.1% (2018 est.)
permanent pasture: 20.8% (2018 est.)
forest: 44.6% (2018 est.)
other: 27.3% (2018 est.)

Irrigated land: 30 sq km (2012)

Population distribution: more than half of the population lives in urban areas, with approximately one-third living within an 80-km radius of Monrovia as shown in this population distribution map

Natural hazards: dust-laden harmattan winds blow from the Sahara (December to March)

Geography - note: facing the Atlantic Ocean, the coastline is characterized by lagoons, mangrove swamps, and river-deposited sandbars; the inland grassy plateau supports limited agriculture

PEOPLE AND SOCIETY

Population: *total:* 5,437,249
male: 2,711,324
female: 2,725,925 (2024 est.)
comparison rankings: female 121; male 120; total 121

Nationality: *noun:* Liberian(s)
adjective: Liberian

Ethnic groups: Kpelle 20.2%, Bassa 13.6%, Grebo 9.9%, Gio 7.9%, Mano 7.2%, Kru 5.5%, Lorma 4.8%, Krahn 4.5%, Kissi, 4.3%, Mandingo 4.2%, Vai 3.8%, Gola 3.8%, Gbandi 2.9%, Mende 1.7%, Sapo 1%, Belle 0.7%, Dey 0.3%, other Liberian ethnic group 0.4%, other African 3%, non-African 0.2% (2022 est.)

Languages: English 20% (official) and 27 indigenous languages, including Liberian English variants

Religions: Christian 84.9%, Muslim 12%, Traditional 0.5%, other 0.1%, none 2.6% (2022 est.)

Demographic profile: Liberia's high fertility rate of nearly 5 children per woman and large youth cohort – more than 60% of the population is under the age of 25 as of 2020 – will sustain a high dependency ratio for many years to come. Significant progress has been made in preventing child deaths, despite a lack of health care workers and infrastructure. Infant and child mortality have dropped nearly 70% since 1990; the annual reduction rate of about 5.4% is the highest in Africa.
Nevertheless, Liberia's high maternal mortality rate remains among the world's worst; it reflects a high unmet need for family planning services, frequency of early childbearing, lack of quality obstetric care, high adolescent fertility, and a low proportion of births attended by a medical professional. Female mortality is also increased by the prevalence of female genital

cutting (FGC), which is practiced by 10 of Liberia's 16 tribes and affects more than two-thirds of women and girls. FGC is an initiation ritual performed in rural bush schools, which teach traditional beliefs on marriage and motherhood and are an obstacle to formal classroom education for Liberian girls.
Liberia has been both a source and a destination for refugees. During Liberia's 14-year civil war (1989-2003), more than 250,000 people became refugees and another half million were internally displaced. Between 2004 and the cessation of refugee status for Liberians in June 2012, the UNHCR helped more than 155,000 Liberians to voluntarily repatriate, while others returned home on their own. Some Liberian refugees spent more than two decades living in other West African countries. Between 2011 and 2022, more than 300,000 Ivoirian refugees in Liberia have been repatriated; as of year-end 2022, less than 2,300 Ivoirian refugees were still living in Liberia.

Age structure: *0-14 years:* 38.9% (male 1,064,100/female 1,052,556)
15-64 years: 57.9% (male 1,566,263/female 1,579,835)
65 years and over: 3.2% (2024 est.) (male 80,961/female 93,534)

Dependency ratios: *total dependency ratio:* 79.7
youth dependency ratio: 73.7
elderly dependency ratio: 6
potential support ratio: 16.7 (2021 est.)

Median age: *total:* 19.9 years (2024 est.)
male: 19.8 years
female: 20 years
comparison ranking: total 207

Population growth rate: 2.32% (2024 est.)
comparison ranking: 28

Birth rate: 32.4 births/1,000 population (2024 est.)
comparison ranking: 20

Death rate: 8.3 deaths/1,000 population (2024 est.)
comparison ranking: 79

Net migration rate: -0.8 migrant(s)/1,000 population (2024 est.)
comparison ranking: 139

Population distribution: more than half of the population lives in urban areas, with approximately one-third living within an 80-km radius of Monrovia as shown in this population distribution map

Urbanization: *urban population:* 53.6% of total population (2023)
rate of urbanization: 3.41% annual rate of change (2015-20 est.)

Major urban areas - population: 1.678 million MONROVIA (capital) (2023)

Sex ratio: *at birth:* 1.03 male(s)/female
0-14 years: 1.01 male(s)/female
15-64 years: 0.99 male(s)/female
65 years and over: 0.87 male(s)/female
total population: 1 male(s)/female (2024 est.)

Mother's mean age at first birth: 19.1 years (2019/20 est.)
note: data represents median age at first birth among women 25-49

Maternal mortality ratio: 652 deaths/100,000 live births (2020 est.)
comparison ranking: 6

Infant mortality rate: *total:* 55.7 deaths/1,000 live births (2024 est.)
male: 61 deaths/1,000 live births
female: 50.2 deaths/1,000 live births
comparison ranking: total 12

Life expectancy at birth: *total population:* 61.6 years (2024 est.)
male: 59.9 years
female: 63.3 years
comparison ranking: total population 217

Total fertility rate: 3.93 children born/woman (2024 est.)
comparison ranking: 26

Gross reproduction rate: 1.94 (2024 est.)

Contraceptive prevalence rate: 24.9% (2019/20)

Drinking water source: *improved: urban:* 96.2% of population
rural: 70.6% of population
total: 84% of population
unimproved: urban: 3.8% of population
rural: 29.4% of population
total: 16% of population (2020 est.)

Current health expenditure: 9.5% of GDP (2020)

Physician density: 0.05 physicians/1,000 population (2018)

Sanitation facility access: *improved: urban:* 68% of population
rural: 25.2% of population
total: 47.5% of population
unimproved: urban: 32% of population
rural: 74.8% of population
total: 52.5% of population (2020 est.)

Obesity - adult prevalence rate: 9.9% (2016)
comparison ranking: 141

Alcohol consumption per capita: *total:* 3.12 liters of pure alcohol (2019 est.)
beer: 0.38 liters of pure alcohol (2019 est.)
wine: 0.44 liters of pure alcohol (2019 est.)
spirits: 2.28 liters of pure alcohol (2019 est.)
other alcohols: 0.02 liters of pure alcohol (2019 est.)
comparison ranking: total 109

Tobacco use: *total:* 8.2% (2020 est.)
male: 14.3% (2020 est.)
female: 2% (2020 est.)
comparison ranking: total 148

Children under the age of 5 years underweight: 10.9% (2019/20)
comparison ranking: 54

Currently married women (ages 15-49): 48.7% (2023 est.)

Child marriage: *women married by age 15:* 5.8% NA
women married by age 18: 24.9% NA
men married by age 18: 8.4% (2020 est.)

Education expenditures: 2.7% of GDP (2021 est.)
comparison ranking: 170

Literacy: *definition:* age 15 and over can read and write
total population: 48.3%
male: 62.7%
female: 34.1% (2017)

ENVIRONMENT

Environment - current issues: tropical rain forest deforestation; soil erosion; loss of biodiversity; hunting of endangered species for bushmeat; pollution of coastal waters from oil residue and raw sewage; pollution of rivers from industrial run-off; burning and dumping of household waste

Environment - international agreements: *party to:* Biodiversity, Climate Change, Climate Change-Kyoto Protocol, Climate Change-Paris Agreement, Comprehensive Nuclear Test Ban, Desertification, Endangered Species, Hazardous Wastes, Law of the Sea, Nuclear Test Ban, Ozone Layer Protection, Ship Pollution, Tropical Timber 2006, Wetlands, Whaling
signed, but not ratified: Environmental Modification, Marine Life Conservation

Climate: tropical; hot, humid; dry winters with hot days and cool to cold nights; wet, cloudy summers with frequent heavy showers

Urbanization: *urban population:* 53.6% of total population (2023)
rate of urbanization: 3.41% annual rate of change (2015-20 est.)

Food insecurity: *severe localized food insecurity: due to high food prices and economic downturn* - levels of acute food insecurity are expected to increase in 2023 associated with high food prices due to high international commodity prices and elevated transportation costs, exacerbated by the unfolding effects of the war in Ukraine on international trade and commodity prices; food availability and access are likely to remain limited by high food prices and below-average imports; an expected further slowdown in economic domestic growth in 2023 is likely to compound food insecurity conditions for the most vulnerable households; in the June to August 2023 lean season period, over 531,000 people are projected to face acute food insecurity (2023)

Revenue from forest resources: 13.27% of GDP (2018 est.)
comparison ranking: 2

Revenue from coal: 0% of GDP (2018 est.)
comparison ranking: 151

Air pollutants: *particulate matter emissions:* 35.8 micrograms per cubic meter (2019 est.)
carbon dioxide emissions: 1.39 megatons (2016 est.)
methane emissions: 6.56 megatons (2020 est.)

Waste and recycling: *municipal solid waste generated annually:* 564,467 tons (2007 est.)

Total water withdrawal: *municipal:* 80 million cubic meters (2020 est.)
industrial: 50 million cubic meters (2020 est.)
agricultural: 10 million cubic meters (2020 est.)

Total renewable water resources: 232 billion cubic meters (2020 est.)

GOVERNMENT

Country name: *conventional long form:* Republic of Liberia
conventional short form: Liberia
etymology: name derives from the Latin word "liber" meaning "free"; so named because the nation was created as a homeland for liberated African-American slaves

Government type: presidential republic

Capital: *name:* Monrovia
geographic coordinates: 6 18 N, 10 48 W
time difference: UTC 0 (5 hours ahead of Washington, DC, during Standard Time)
etymology: named after James MONROE (1758-1831), the fifth president of the United States and supporter of the colonization of Liberia by freed slaves; one of two national capitals named for a US president, the other is Washington, D.C.

Administrative divisions: 15 counties; Bomi, Bong, Gbarpolu, Grand Bassa, Grand Cape Mount, Grand Gedeh, Grand Kru, Lofa, Margibi, Maryland, Montserrado, Nimba, River Cess, River Gee, Sinoe

Independence: 26 July 1847

National holiday: Independence Day, 26 July (1847)

Legal system: mixed legal system of common law, based on Anglo-American law, and customary law

Constitution: *history:* previous 1847 (at independence); latest drafted 19 October 1983, revision adopted by referendum 3 July 1984, effective 6 January 1986
amendments: proposed by agreement of at least two thirds of both National Assembly houses or by petition of at least 10,000 citizens; passage requires at least two-thirds majority approval of both houses and approval in a referendum by at least two-thirds majority of registered voters; amended 2011, 2020

International law organization participation: accepts compulsory ICJ jurisdiction with reservations; accepts ICCt jurisdiction

Citizenship: *citizenship by birth:* no
citizenship by descent only: at least one parent must be a citizen of Liberia
dual citizenship recognized: no
residency requirement for naturalization: 2 years

Suffrage: 18 years of age; universal

Executive branch: *chief of state:* President Joseph BOAKAI (since 22 January 2024)
head of government: President Joseph BOAKAI (since 22 January 2024)
cabinet: Cabinet appointed by the president, confirmed by the Senate
elections/appointments: president directly elected by absolute majority popular vote in 2 rounds if needed for a 6-year term (eligible for a second term); election last held on 10 October 2023 with a runoff on 14 November 2023 (next to be held in October 2029) note - the president is both chief of state and head of government
election results:
2023: Joseph BOAKAI elected president in second round; percent of vote in first round - George WEAH (CDC) 43.8%, Joseph BOAKAI (UP) 43.4%, Edward APPLETON (GDM) 2.2%, Lusinee KAMARA (ALCOP) 2%, Alexander B. CUMMINGS, Jr. (CPP) 1.6%, Tiawan Saye GONGLOE (LPP) 1.4%, other 5.6%; percentage of vote in second round - Joseph BOAKAI 50.6%, George WEAH 49.4%
2017: George WEAH elected president in second round; percent of vote in first round - George WEAH (Coalition for Democratic Change) 38.4%, Joseph BOAKAI (UP) 28.8%, Charles BRUMSKINE (LP) 9.6%, Prince JOHNSON (MDR) 8.2%, Alexander B. CUMMINGS (ANC) 7.2%, other 7.8%; percentage of vote in second round - George WEAH 61.5%, Joseph BOAKAI 38.5%

Legislative branch: *description:* bicameral National Assembly consists of:
The Liberian Senate (30 seats; members directly elected in 15 2-seat districts by simple majority vote to serve 9-year staggered terms; each district elects 1 senator and elects the second senator 3 years later, followed by a 6-year hiatus, after which the first Senate seat is up for election)
House of Representatives (73 seats; members directly elected in single-seat districts by simple majority vote to serve 6- year terms; eligible for a second term)
elections: Senate - general election held on 10 October 2023 with half the seats up for election (next to be held in October 2029)
House of Representatives - last held on 10 October 2023 (next to be held in October 2029)
election results: Senate - percent of vote by party/coalition - CDC 34.3%, UP 12.0%, MDR 7.1%, LRP 1.5%, independent 24.3%; seats by party/coalition - CDC 6, UP 1, MDR 1, LRP 1, independent 6; composition- men 27, women 3, percentage women 10%
House of Representatives - percent of vote by party/coalition - CDC 22.1%, UP 13.1%, CPP 7.6%, MDR 2.8%, PUP 4.3%, ALP 2.5%, LINU 2.3%, MPC 1.0%, NDC 1.0%, VOLT 0.8%, LRP 0.8%, Independent 25.7%; seats by party/ coalition - CDC 25, UP 11, CPP 6, MDR 4, PUP 2, ALP 1, LINU 1, MPC 1, NDC 1, VOLT 1 LRP 1, independent 19; composition- men 65, women 8, percentage women 11%; total Parliament percentage women 10.6%

Judicial branch: *highest court(s):* Supreme Court (consists of a chief justice and 4 associate justices); note - the Supreme Court has jurisdiction for all constitutional cases
judge selection and term of office: chief justice and associate justices appointed by the president of Liberia with consent of the Senate; judges can serve until age 70
subordinate courts: judicial circuit courts; special courts, including criminal, civil, labor, traffic; magistrate and traditional or customary courts

Political parties: All Liberian Party or ALP
Alliance for Peace and Democracy or APD
Alternative National Congress or ANC
Coalition for Democratic Change (includes CDC, NPP, and LPDP)
Collaborating Political Parties or CPP (coalition includes ANC, LP; CPP dissolved in April 2024)
Congress for Democratic Change or CDC
Liberia Destiny Party or LDP
Liberia National Union or LINU
Liberia Transformation Party or LTP
Liberian People Democratic Party or LPDP
Liberian People's Party or LPP
Liberian Restoration Party or LRP
Liberty Party or LP
Movement for Democracy and Reconstruction or MDR
Movement for Economic Empowerment
Movement for Progressive Change or MPC
National Democratic Coalition or NDC
National Democratic Party of Liberia or NDPL
National Patriotic Party or NPP
National Reformist Party or NRP
National Union for Democratic Progress or NUDP
People's Unification Party or PUP
Unity Party or UP
United People's Party
Victory for Change Party or VCP

International organization participation: ACP, AfDB, AU, ECOWAS, EITI (compliant country), FAO, G-77, IAEA, IBRD, ICAO, ICC (NGOs), ICCt, ICRM, IDA, IFAD, IFC, IFRCS, ILO, IMF, IMO, IMSO, Interpol, IOC, IOM, ISO (correspondent), ITU, ITUC (NGOs), MIGA, NAM, OPCW, UN, UNCTAD, UNESCO, UNIDO, UNISFA, UNWTO, UPU, WCO, WFTU (NGOs), WHO, WIPO, WMO, WTO

Diplomatic representation in the US: *chief of mission:* Ambassador Jeff Gongoer DOWANA, Sr. (since 12 December 2022)
chancery: 5201 16th Street NW, Washington, DC 20011
telephone: [1] (202) 723-0437
FAX: [1] (202) 723-0436
email address and website:
info@liberianembassyus.org
http://www.liberianembassyus.org/
consulate(s) general: New York

Diplomatic representation from the US: *chief of mission:* Ambassador (vacant) Chargé d'Affaires Catherine RODRIGUEZ (since 11 August 2023)
embassy: 502 Benson Street, Monrovia
mailing address: 8800 Monrovia Place, Washington DC 20521-8800
telephone: [231] 77-677-7000
FAX: [231] 77-677-7370
email address and website:
ACSMonrovia@state.gov
https://lr.usembassy.gov/

Flag description: 11 equal horizontal stripes of red (top and bottom) alternating with white; a white five-pointed star appears on a blue square in the upper hoist-side corner; the stripes symbolize the signatories of the Liberian Declaration of Independence; the blue square represents the African mainland, and the star represents the freedom granted to the ex-slaves; according to the constitution, the blue color signifies liberty, justice, and fidelity, the white color purity, cleanliness, and guilelessness, and the red color steadfastness, valor, and fervor
note: the design is based on the US flag

National symbol(s): white star; national colors: red, white, blue

National anthem: *name:* "All Hail, Liberia Hail!"
lyrics/music: Daniel Bashiel WARNER/Olmstead LUCA
note: lyrics adopted 1847, music adopted 1860; the anthem's author later became the third president of Liberia

ECONOMY

Economic overview: low-income West African economy; food scarcity, especially in rural areas; high poverty and inflation; bad recession prior to COVID-19 due to Ebola crisis; growing government debt; longest continuously operated rubber plantation; large informal economy

Real GDP (purchasing power parity): $8.884 billion (2023 est.)
$8.484 billion (2022 est.)
$8.095 billion (2021 est.)
note: data in 2021 dollars
comparison ranking: 169

Real GDP growth rate: 4.71% (2023 est.)
4.81% (2022 est.)
4.99% (2021 est.)
note: annual GDP % growth based on constant local currency
comparison ranking: 64

Real GDP per capita: $1,600 (2023 est.)
$1,600 (2022 est.)
$1,600 (2021 est.)
note: data in 2021 dollars
comparison ranking: 214

GDP (official exchange rate): $4.332 billion (2023 est.)
note: data in current dollars at official exchange rate

Inflation rate (consumer prices): 23.56% (2018 est.)
12.42% (2017 est.)
8.83% (2016 est.)
note: annual % change based on consumer prices
comparison ranking: 199

GDP - composition, by sector of origin: *agriculture:* 34.9% (2023 est.)
industry: 22.9% (2023 est.)
services: 38.5% (2023 est.)

note: figures may not total 100% due to non-allocated consumption not captured in sector-reported data
comparison rankings: services 198; industry 115; agriculture 7

GDP - composition, by end use: *household consumption:* 128.8% (2016 est.)
government consumption: 16.7% (2016 est.)
investment in fixed capital: 19.5% (2016 est.)
investment in inventories: 6.7% (2016 est.)
exports of goods and services: 17.5% (2016 est.)
imports of goods and services: -89.2% (2016 est.)

Agricultural products: cassava, rice, sugarcane, oil palm fruit, bananas, rubber, vegetables, plantains, taro, maize (2022)
note: top ten agricultural products based on tonnage

Industries: mining (iron ore and gold), rubber processing, palm oil processing, diamonds

Industrial production growth rate: 13.86% (2023 est.)
note: annual % change in industrial value added based on constant local currency
comparison ranking: 6

Labor force: 2.499 million (2023 est.)
note: number of people ages 15 or older who are employed or seeking work
comparison ranking: 118

Unemployment rate: 2.94% (2023 est.)
2.99% (2022 est.)
3.79% (2021 est.)
note: % of labor force seeking employment
comparison ranking: 43

Youth unemployment rate (ages 15-24): *total:* 2.3% (2023 est.)
male: 2.4% (2023 est.)
female: 2.2% (2023 est.)
note: % of labor force ages 15-24 seeking employment
comparison ranking: total 195

Population below poverty line: 50.9% (2016 est.)
note: % of population with income below national poverty line

Gini Index coefficient - distribution of family income: 35.3 (2016 est.)
note: index (0-100) of income distribution; higher values represent greater inequality
comparison ranking: 75

Household income or consumption by percentage share: *lowest 10%:* 2.9% (2016 est.)
highest 10%: 27.1% (2016 est.)
note: % share of income accruing to lowest and highest 10% of population

Remittances: 18.47% of GDP (2023 est.)
17.24% of GDP (2022 est.)
15.11% of GDP (2021 est.)
note: personal transfers and compensation between resident and non-resident individuals/households/entities

Budget: *revenues:* $5 million (2019 est.)
expenditures: $6 million (2019 est.)

Public debt: 34.4% of GDP (2017 est.)
comparison ranking: 158

Current account balance: $64.806 million (2022 est.)
-$101.746 million (2021 est.)
-$274.971 million (2020 est.)
note: balance of payments - net trade and primary/secondary income in current dollars
comparison ranking: 76

Exports: $1.22 billion (2022 est.)
$1.041 billion (2021 est.)
$731.658 million (2020 est.)
note: balance of payments - exports of goods and services in current dollars
comparison ranking: 176

Exports - partners: Switzerland 28%, France 8%, Germany 8%, UK 8%, Poland 6% (2022)
note: top five export partners based on percentage share of exports

Exports - commodities: gold, ships, iron ore, rubber, refined petroleum (2022)
note: top five export commodities based on value in dollars

Imports: $1.961 billion (2022 est.)
$1.739 billion (2021 est.)
$1.371 billion (2020 est.)
note: balance of payments - imports of goods and services in current dollars
comparison ranking: 179

Imports - partners: China 42%, South Korea 23%, Japan 15%, Germany 5%, Brazil 3% (2022)
note: top five import partners based on percentage share of imports

Imports - commodities: ships, refined petroleum, additive manufacturing machines, centrifuges, rice (2022)
note: top five import commodities based on value in dollars

Reserves of foreign exchange and gold: $599.66 million (2022 est.)
$700.829 million (2021 est.)
$340.966 million (2020 est.)
note: holdings of gold (year-end prices)/foreign exchange/special drawing rights in current dollars
comparison ranking: 171

Debt - external: $835.846 million (2022 est.)
note: present value of external debt in current US dollars
comparison ranking: 82

Exchange rates: Liberian dollars (LRD) per US dollar -

Exchange rates: 152.934 (2022 est.)
166.154 (2021 est.)
191.518 (2020 est.)
186.43 (2019 est.)
144.056 (2018 est.)

ENERGY

Electricity access: *electrification - total population:* 31.8% (2022 est.)
electrification - urban areas: 53.7%
electrification - rural areas: 14.9%

Electricity: *installed generating capacity:* 197,000 kW (2022 est.)
consumption: 615.96 million kWh (2022 est.)
transmission/distribution losses: 179.222 million kWh (2022 est.)
comparison rankings: transmission/distribution losses 62; consumption 169; installed generating capacity 173

Electricity generation sources: *fossil fuels:* 32.8% of total installed capacity (2022 est.)
solar: 0.5% of total installed capacity (2022 est.)
hydroelectricity: 66.7% of total installed capacity (2022 est.)

Coal: *imports:* 78,000 metric tons (2022 est.)

Petroleum: *refined petroleum consumption:* 4,000 bbl/day (2022 est.)

Carbon dioxide emissions: 620,000 metric tonnes of CO_2 (2022 est.)
from petroleum and other liquids: 620,000 metric tonnes of CO_2 (2022 est.)
comparison ranking: total emissions 185

Energy consumption per capita: 1.971 million Btu/person (2022 est.)
comparison ranking: 186

COMMUNICATIONS

Telephones - fixed lines: *total subscriptions:* 6,000 (2021 est.)
subscriptions per 100 inhabitants: (2021 est.) less than 1
comparison ranking: total subscriptions 201

Telephones - mobile cellular: *total subscriptions:* 1.653 million (2021 est.)
subscriptions per 100 inhabitants: 32 (2021 est.)
comparison ranking: total subscriptions 156

Telecommunication systems: *general assessment:* Liberia has a telecom market which is mainly based on mobile networks; this is due to the civil war which destroyed much of the fixed-line infrastructure; to facilitate LTC Mobile's market entry, the government in January 2022 set in train amendments to telecom legislation; internet services are available from a number of wireless ISPs as well as the mobile operators; the high cost and limited bandwidth of connections means that internet access is expensive and rates are very low; additional bandwidth is available from an international submarine cable but considerable investment is still needed in domestic fixed-line infrastructure before end-users can make full use of the cable (2022)
domestic: fixed-line less than 1 per 100; mobile-cellular subscriptions are 32 per 100 persons (2021)
international: country code - 231; landing point for the ACE submarine cable linking 20 West African countries and Europe; satellite earth station - 1 Intelsat (Atlantic Ocean) (2019)

Broadcast media: 8 private and 1 government-owned TV station; satellite TV service available; 1 state-owned radio station; approximately 20 independent radio stations broadcasting in Monrovia, with approximately 80 more local stations operating in other areas; transmissions of 4 international (including the British Broadcasting Corporation and Radio France Internationale) broadcasters are available (2019)

Internet country code: .lr

Internet users: *total:* 1.768 million (2021 est.)
percent of population: 34% (2021 est.)
comparison ranking: total 138

Broadband - fixed subscriptions: *total:* 13,000 (2020 est.)
subscriptions per 100 inhabitants: 0.3 (2020 est.)
comparison ranking: total 175

TRANSPORTATION

Civil aircraft registration country code prefix: A8

Airports: 19 (2024)
comparison ranking: 138

Pipelines: 4 km oil (2013)

Railways: *total:* 429 km (2008)
standard gauge: 345 km (2008) 1.435-m gauge
narrow gauge: 84 km (2008) 1.067-m gauge

note: most sections of the railways inoperable due to damage sustained during the civil wars from 1980 to 2003, but many are being rebuilt
comparison ranking: total 117

Roadways: *total:* 10,600 km
paved: 657 km
unpaved: 9,943 km (2021)
comparison ranking: total 135

Merchant marine: *total:* 4,821 (2023)
by type: bulk carrier 1,895, container ship 1,013, general cargo 170, oil tanker 1,038, other 705
comparison ranking: total 5

Ports: *total ports:* 4 (2024)
large: 0
medium: 0
small: 1
very small: 3
ports with oil terminals: 3
key ports: Buchanan, Cape Palmas, Greenville, Monrovia

MILITARY AND SECURITY

Military and security forces: **Armed Forces of Liberia (AFL):** Army, Liberian Coast Guard, Air Wing; Ministry of Justice: Liberia National Police, Liberia Drug Enforcement Agency (2024)
note: the AFL Air Wing was previously disbanded in 2005 and has been under redevelopment since 2019; the Liberian National Police and the Liberian Drug Enforcement Agency are under the Ministry of Justice

Military expenditures: 0.8% of GDP (2022 est.)
0.7% of GDP (2021 est.)
0.5% of GDP (2020 est.)
0.6% of GDP (2019 est.)
0.5% of GDP (2018 est.)
comparison ranking: 142

Military and security service personnel strengths: approximately 2,000 active personnel (2023)

Military equipment inventories and acquisitions: the military has a limited inventory; in recent years, it has received small quantities of equipment, including donations, from countries such as China and the US (2024)

Military service age and obligation: 18-35 years of age for men and women for voluntary military service; no conscription (2024)

Military - note: the AFL is responsible for external defense and also has some domestic security responsibilities if called upon, such as humanitarian assistance during natural disasters and support to law enforcement; it is a small, lightly equipped force comprised of two combat infantry battalions and supporting units; the infantry battalions were rebuilt with US assistance in 2007-2008 from the restructured AFL following the end of the second civil war in 2003 when military and police forces were disbanded and approximately 100,000 military, police, and rebel combatants were disarmed
the first militia unit established for defense of the Liberia colony was raised in 1832; the AFL traces its origins to the 1908 establishment of the Liberia Frontier Force, which became the Liberian National Guard in 1965; the AFL was established in 1970
the UN Mission in Liberia (UNMIL) was established in 2003 as a peacekeeping force; at its height, UNMIL was comprised of about 15,000 personnel, including more than 3,000 troops absorbed from the Economic Community of West African States (ECOWAS) peacekeeping mission; Liberian forces reassumed full control of the country's security in June of 2016, and the UNMIL mission was ended in 2018 (2024)

TRANSNATIONAL ISSUES

Trafficking in persons: tier rating: Tier 2 Watch List — the government did not demonstrate overall increasing efforts to eliminate trafficking compared with the previous reporting period, therefore Liberia was downgraded to Tier 2 Watch List; for more details, go to: https://www.state.gov/reports/2024-trafficking-in-persons-report/liberia/

Illicit drugs: not a significant transit country for illicit narcotics bound for the United States or Europe; not a key producer of illicit drugs; proximity to major drug transit routes contribute to trafficking cocaine and heroin, to and through Liberia and other West African countries; local drug use involves locally grown cannabis, heroin (mostly smoked), cocaine (snorted), and more recently kush (Cannabis Indic's type flower), mixed with different substances including heroin or synthetic DMT

LIBYA

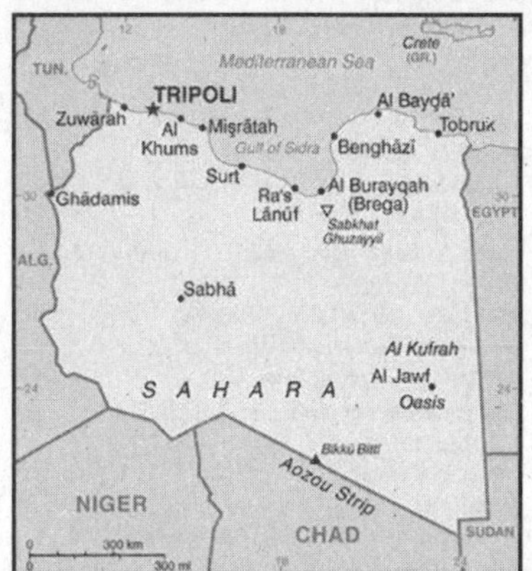

INTRODUCTION

Background: Berbers have inhabited central north Africa since ancient times, but Phoenicians, Greeks, Carthaginians, Persians, Egyptians, Romans, and Vandals have all settled and ruled the region. In the 7th century, Islam spread through the area. In the mid-16th century, Ottoman rule began; the Italians supplanted the Ottoman Turks in the area around Tripoli in 1911 and held it until 1943, when they were defeated in World War II. Libya then came under UN administration and achieved independence in 1951. Col. Muammar al- QADHAFI assumed leadership with a military coup in 1969 and began to espouse a political system that combined socialism and Islam. During the 1970s, QADHAFI used oil revenues to promote his ideology outside Libya, supporting subversive and terrorist activities that included the downing of two airliners – one over Scotland and another in Northern Africa – and a discotheque bombing in Berlin. UN sanctions in 1992 isolated QADHAFI politically and economically; the sanctions were lifted in 2003 when Libya accepted responsibility for the bombings and agreed to claimant compensation. QADHAFI also agreed to end Libya's program to develop weapons of mass destruction, and he made significant strides in normalizing relations with Western nations.

Unrest that began in several Middle Eastern and North African countries in 2010 erupted in Libyan cities in 2011. QADHAFI's brutal crackdown on protesters spawned an eight-month civil war that saw the emergence of a National Transitional Council (NTC), UN authorization of air and naval intervention by the international community, and the toppling of the QADHAFI regime. In 2012, the NTC handed power to an elected parliament, the General National Congress (GNC), which was replaced two years later with the House of Representatives (HoR). In 2015, the UN brokered the Libyan Political Agreement (LPA) among a broad array of political parties and social groups, establishing an interim executive body. However, hardliners continued to oppose and hamper the LPA implementation, leaving Libya with eastern and western-based rival governments. In 2018, the international community supported a recalibrated plan that aimed to break the political deadlock with a National Conference in 2019. These plans, however, were derailed when the easternbased, self-described Libyan National Army (LNA) launched an offensive to seize Tripoli. The LNA offensive collapsed in 2020, and a subsequent UN-sponsored cease-fire helped formalize the pause in fighting between rival camps.

In 2021, the UN-facilitated Libyan Political Dialogue Forum selected a new prime minister for an interim government – the Government of National Unity (GNU) – and a new presidential council charged with preparing for elections and uniting the country's state institutions. The HoR approved the GNU and its cabinet the same year, providing Libya with its first unified government since 2014, but the parliament then postponed the planned presidential election to an undetermined date in the future. In 2022, the HoR voted to replace GNU interim Prime Minister, Abdul Hamid DUBAYBAH, with another government led by Fathi BASHaGha. GNU allegations of an illegitimate HoR vote allowed DUBAYBAH to remain in office and rebuff BASHAGHA's attempts to seat his government in Tripoli. In 2023, the HoR voted to replace BASHAGHA with Osma HAMAD. Special Representative of the UN Security-General for Libya, Abdoulaye BATHILY, is leading international efforts to persuade key Libyan political actors to resolve the core issues impeding elections.

GEOGRAPHY

Location: Northern Africa, bordering the Mediterranean Sea, between Egypt, Tunisia, and Algeria

Geographic coordinates: 25 00 N, 17 00 E

Map references: Africa

Area: *total:* 1,759,540 sq km
land: 1,759,540 sq km
water: 0 sq km
comparison ranking: total 18

Area - comparative: about 2.5 times the size of Texas; slightly larger than Alaska

Land boundaries: *total:* 4,339 km
border countries (6): Algeria 989 km; Chad 1,050 km; Egypt 1,115 km; Niger 342 km; Sudan 382 km; Tunisia 461 km

Coastline: 1,770 km

Maritime claims: *territorial sea:* 12 nm
exclusive fishing zone: 62 nm
note: Gulf of Sidra closing line - 32 degrees, 30 minutes north

Climate: Mediterranean along coast; dry, extreme desert interior

Terrain: mostly barren, flat to undulating plains, plateaus, depressions

Elevation: *highest point:* Bikku Bitti 2,267 m
lowest point: Sabkhat Ghuzayyil -47 m
mean elevation: 423 m

Natural resources: petroleum, natural gas, gypsum

Land use: *agricultural land:* 8.8% (2018 est.)
arable land: 1% (2018 est.)
permanent crops: 0.2% (2018 est.)
permanent pasture: 7.6% (2018 est.)
forest: 0.1% (2018 est.)
other: 91.1% (2018 est.)

Irrigated land: 4,700 sq km (2012)

Major watersheds (area sq km): Internal (endorheic basin) drainage: Lake Chad (2,497,738 sq km)

Major aquifers: Nubian Aquifer System, North Western Sahara Aquifer System, Murzuk-Djado Basin

Population distribution: well over 90% of the population lives along the Mediterranean coast in and between Tripoli to the west and Al Bayda to the east; the interior remains vastly underpopulated due to the Sahara and lack of surface water as shown in this population distribution map

Natural hazards: hot, dry, dust-laden ghibli is a southern wind lasting one to four days in spring and fall; dust storms, sandstorms

Geography - note: *note 1:* more than 90% of the country is desert or semidesert
note 2: the volcano Waw an Namus lies in south central Libya in the middle of the Sahara; the caldera is an oasis – the name means "oasis of mosquitoes" – containing several small lakes surrounded by vegetation and hosting various insects and a large diversity of birds

PEOPLE AND SOCIETY

Population: *total:* 7,361,263
male: 3,747,364
female: 3,613,899 (2024 est.)
note: immigrants make up just over 12% of the total population, according to UN data (2019)
comparison rankings: female 105; male 105; total 105

Nationality: *noun:* Libyan(s)
adjective: Libyan

Ethnic groups: Amazigh and Arab 97%, other 3% (includes Egyptian, Greek, Indian, Italian, Maltese, Pakistani, Tunisian, and Turkish)

Languages: Arabic (official), Italian, English (all widely understood in the major cities); Tamazight (Nafusi, Ghadamis, Suknah, Awjilah, Tamasheq)
major-language sample(s):
يمكن الاستغناء عنه للمعلومات الأساسية
كتاب حقائق العالم، المصدر الذي لا
(Arabic)

Religions: Muslim (official; virtually all Sunni) 96.6%, Christian 2.7%, Buddhist <1%, Hindu <1%, Jewish <1%, folk religion <1%, other <1%, unaffiliated <1% (2020 est.)
note: non-Sunni Muslims include native Ibadhi Muslims (<1% of the population) and foreign Muslims

Demographic profile: Despite continuing unrest, Libya remains a destination country for economic migrants. It is also a hub for transit migration to Europe because of its proximity to southern Europe and its lax border controls. Labor migrants have been drawn to Libya since the development of its oil sector in the 1960s. Until the latter part of the 1990s, most migrants to Libya were Arab (primarily Egyptians and Sudanese). However, international isolation stemming from Libya's involvement in international terrorism and a perceived lack of support from Arab countries led QADHAFI in 1998 to adopt a decade-long pan-African policy that enabled large numbers of Sub-Saharan migrants to enter Libya without visas to work in the construction and agricultural industries. Although Sub-Saharan Africans provided a cheap labor source, they were poorly treated and were subjected to periodic mass expulsions.

By the mid-2000s, domestic animosity toward African migrants and a desire to reintegrate into the international community motivated QADHAFI to impose entry visas on Arab and African immigrants and to agree to joint maritime patrols and migrant repatriations with Italy, the main recipient of illegal migrants departing Libya. As his regime neared collapse in 2011, QADHAFI reversed his policy of cooperating with Italy to curb illegal migration and sent boats loaded with migrants and asylum seekers to strain European resources. Libya's 2011 revolution decreased immigration drastically and prompted nearly 800,000 migrants to flee to third countries, mainly Tunisia and Egypt, or to their countries of origin. The inflow of migrants declined in 2012 but returned to normal levels by 2013, despite continued hostility toward Sub-Saharan Africans and a less-inviting job market.

While Libya is not an appealing destination for migrants, since 2014, transiting migrants – primarily from East and West Africa – continue to exploit its political instability and weak border controls and use it as a primary departure area to migrate across the central Mediterranean to Europe in growing numbers. In addition, approximately 135,000 people were displaced internally as of August 2022 by fighting between armed groups in eastern and western Libya and, to a lesser extent, by inter-tribal clashes in the country's south.

Age structure: *0-14 years:* 32.3% (male 1,211,087/female 1,165,648)
15-64 years: 63.2% (male 2,385,152/female 2,263,780)
65 years and over: 4.6% (2024 est.) (male 151,125/female 184,471)

Dependency ratios: *total dependency ratio:* 50.8
youth dependency ratio: 43.5
elderly dependency ratio: 7.3
potential support ratio: 13.8 (2021 est.)

Median age: *total:* 26.2 years (2024 est.)
male: 26.3 years
female: 26.2 years
comparison ranking: total 165

Population growth rate: 1.44% (2024 est.)
comparison ranking: 68

Birth rate: 20.3 births/1,000 population (2024 est.)
comparison ranking: 65

Death rate: 3.5 deaths/1,000 population (2024 est.)
comparison ranking: 221

Net migration rate: -2.5 migrant(s)/1,000 population (2024 est.)
comparison ranking: 172

Population distribution: well over 90% of the population lives along the Mediterranean coast in and between Tripoli to the west and Al Bayda to the east; the interior remains vastly underpopulated due to the Sahara and lack of surface water as shown in this population distribution map

Urbanization: *urban population:* 81.6% of total population (2023)
rate of urbanization: 1.45% annual rate of change (2020-25 est.)

Major urban areas - population: 1.183 million TRIPOLI (capital), 984,000 Misratah, 859,000 Benghazi (2023)

Sex ratio: *at birth:* 1.05 male(s)/female
0-14 years: 1.04 male(s)/female
15-64 years: 1.05 male(s)/female
65 years and over: 0.82 male(s)/female
total population: 1.04 male(s)/female (2024 est.)

Maternal mortality ratio: 72 deaths/100,000 live births (2020 est.)
comparison ranking: 84

Infant mortality rate: *total:* 10.7 deaths/1,000 live births (2024 est.)
male: 12.1 deaths/1,000 live births
female: 9.3 deaths/1,000 live births
comparison ranking: total 128

Life expectancy at birth: *total population:* 77.7 years (2024 est.)
male: 75.5 years
female: 80 years
comparison ranking: total population 87

Total fertility rate: 3 children born/woman (2024 est.)
comparison ranking: 48

Gross reproduction rate: 1.46 (2024 est.)

Contraceptive prevalence rate: 27.7% (2014)

Drinking water source: *improved:*
total: 99.9% of population
unimproved:
total: 0.1% of population (2020 est.)

Physician density: 2.09 physicians/1,000 population (2017)

Hospital bed density: 3.2 beds/1,000 population (2017)

Sanitation facility access: *improved:*

total: 99.3% of population
unimproved:
total: 0.7% of population (2020 est.)

Obesity - adult prevalence rate: 32.5% (2016)
comparison ranking: 16

Alcohol consumption per capita: *total:* 0.01 liters of pure alcohol (2019 est.)
beer: 0 liters of pure alcohol (2019 est.)
wine: 0.01 liters of pure alcohol (2019 est.)
spirits: 0 liters of pure alcohol (2019 est.)
other alcohols: 0 liters of pure alcohol (2019 est.)
comparison ranking: total 184

Children under the age of 5 years underweight: 11.7% (2014)
comparison ranking: 48

Currently married women (ages 15-49): 59.2% (2023 est.)

Literacy: *definition:* age 15 and over can read and write
total population: 91%
male: 96.7%
female: 85.6% (2015)

ENVIRONMENT

Environment - current issues: desertification; limited natural freshwater resources; the Great Manmade River Project, the largest water development scheme in the world, brings water from large aquifers under the Sahara to coastal cities; water pollution is a significant problem; the combined impact of sewage, oil byproducts, and industrial waste threatens Libya's coast and the Mediterranean Sea

Environment - international agreements: *party to:* Biodiversity, Climate Change, Climate Change-Kyoto Protocol, Comprehensive Nuclear Test Ban, Desertification, Endangered Species, Hazardous Wastes, Marine Dumping-London Convention, Nuclear Test Ban, Ozone Layer Protection, Ship Pollution, Wetlands
signed, but not ratified: Climate Change-Paris Agreement, Law of the Sea

Climate: Mediterranean along coast; dry, extreme desert interior

Urbanization: *urban population:* 81.6% of total population (2023)
rate of urbanization: 1.45% annual rate of change (2020-25 est.)

Food insecurity: *severe localized food insecurity: due to civil insecurity, economic and political instability, and high food prices* - an estimated 800,000 people, 10% of the population, need humanitarian assistance, of which 500,000 require food assistance; the country relies heavily on imports (up to 90%) to cover its cereal consumption requirements (mostly wheat for human consumption and barley for feed); between 2016 and 2020, the country sourced over 30% of its wheat imports from Ukraine, and 20% from the Russian Federation; almost 65% of total maize imports of 650,000 mt, and 50% of total barley imports of 1 million mt originated from Ukraine, making the Libya vulnerable to disruptions in shipments from the Black Sea region (2022)

Revenue from forest resources: 0.06% of GDP (2018 est.)
comparison ranking: 124

Revenue from coal: 0% of GDP (2018 est.)
comparison ranking: 97

Air pollutants: *particulate matter emissions:* 29.84 micrograms per cubic meter (2019 est.)
carbon dioxide emissions: 50.56 megatons (2016 est.)
methane emissions: 45.76 megatons (2020 est.)

Waste and recycling: *municipal solid waste generated annually:* 2,147,596 tons (2011 est.)

Major watersheds (area sq km): Internal (endorheic basin) drainage: Lake Chad (2,497,738 sq km)

Major aquifers: Nubian Aquifer System, North Western Sahara Aquifer System, Murzuk-Djado Basin

Total water withdrawal: *municipal:* 700 million cubic meters (2020 est.)
industrial: 280 million cubic meters (2020 est.)
agricultural: 4.85 billion cubic meters (2020 est.)

Total renewable water resources: 700 million cubic meters (2020 est.)

GOVERNMENT

Country name: *conventional long form:* State of Libya
conventional short form: Libya
local long form: Dawlat Libiya
local short form: Libiya
etymology: name derives from the Libu, an ancient Libyan tribe first mentioned in texts from the 13th century B.C.

Government type: in transition

Capital: *name:* Tripoli (Tarabulus)
geographic coordinates: 32 53 N, 13 10 E
time difference: UTC+2 (7 hours ahead of Washington, DC, during Standard Time)
etymology: originally founded by the Phoenicians as Oea in the 7th century B.C., the city changed rulers many times over the successive centuries; by the beginning of the 3rd century A.D. the region around the city was referred to as Regio Tripolitana by the Romans, meaning "region of the three cities" - namely Oea (i.e., modern Tripoli), Sabratha (to the west), and Leptis Magna (to the east); over time, the shortened name of "Tripoli" came to refer to just Oea, which derives from the Greek words *tria* and *polis* meaning "three cities"

Administrative divisions: 22 governorates (muhafazah, singular - muhafazat); Al Butnan, Al Jabal al Akhdar, Al Jabal al Gharbi, Al Jafarah, Al Jufrah, Al Kufrah, Al Marj, Al Marqab, Al Wahat, An Nuqat al Khams, Az Zawiyah, Banghazi (Benghazi), Darnah, Ghat, Misratah, Murzuq, Nalut, Sabha, Surt, Tarabulus (Tripoli), Wadi al Hayat, Wadi ash Shati

Independence: 24 December 1951 (from UN trusteeship)

National holiday: Liberation Day, 23 October (2011)

Legal system: Libya's post-revolution legal system is in flux and driven by state and non-state entities

Constitution: *history:* previous 1951, 1977; in July 2017, the Constitutional Assembly completed and approved a draft of a new permanent constitution; in September 2018, the House of Representatives passed a constitutional referendum law in a session with contested reports of the quorum needed to pass the vote and submitted it to the High National Elections Commission in December to begin preparations for a constitutional referendum
amendments: note - in early March 2023, the High Council of State voted for a constitutional amendment to provide a groundwork for elections

International law organization participation: has not submitted an ICJ jurisdiction declaration; non-party state to the ICCt

Citizenship: *citizenship by birth:* no
citizenship by descent only: at least one parent or grandparent must be a citizen of Libya
dual citizenship recognized: no
residency requirement for naturalization: varies from 3 to 5 years

Suffrage: 18 years of age, universal

Executive branch: *chief of state:* President, Presidential Council, Mohammed Al MENFI (since 5 February 2021)
head of government: GNU Interim Prime Minister Abdul Hamid DUBAYBAH (since 5 February 2021)
elections/appointments:
Libya's first direct presidential election, scheduled for 24 December 2021, was not held; no new date has been set for elections

Legislative branch: *description:* unicameral House of Representatives (Majlis Al Nuwab) or HoR (200 seats including 32 reserved for women; members directly elected by majority vote; member term NA); note - the High State Council serves as an advisory group for the HoR
elections: last held on 25 June 2014
election results: percent of vote by party - NA; seats by party - NA; note - only 188 of the 200 seats were filled in the June 2014 election because of boycotts and lack of security at some polling stations; some elected members of the House of Representatives also boycotted the election

Judicial branch: *highest court(s):* Libya's judicial system consists of a supreme court, central high courts (in Tripoli, Benghazi, and Sabha), and a series of lower courts; the judicial system is factious given the ongoing tension between Libya's eastern and western regions; since 2011, Libyan political factions and armed groups have targeted judges and courthouses

Political parties: NA

International organization participation: ABEDA, AfDB, AFESD, AMF, AMU, AU, BDEAC, CAEU, COMESA, FAO, G-77, IAEA, IBRD, ICAO, ICC (NGOs), ICRM, IDA, IDB, IFAD, IFC, IFRCS, ILO, IMF, IMO, IMSO, Interpol, IOC, IOM, IPU, ISO, ITSO, ITU, LAS, LCBC, MIGA, NAM, OAPEC, OIC, OPCW, OPEC, PCA, UN, UNCTAD, UNESCO, UNHRC, UNIDO, UNSMIL, UNWTO, UPU, WCO, WFTU (NGOs), WHO, WIPO, WMO, WTO (observer)

Diplomatic representation in the US: *chief of mission:* Ambassador (vacant); Chargé d'Affaires Fadil S M OMAR (since 17 July 2023)
chancery: 1460 Dahlia Street NW, Washington, DC 20012
telephone: [1] (202) 944-9601
FAX: [1] (202) 944-9606
email address and website:
info@embassyoflibyadc.com
https://www.embassyoflibyadc.org/

Diplomatic representation from the US: *chief of mission:* Ambassador (vacant); Chargé d'Affaires Jeremy BERNDT (since 14 October 2023)
embassy: US Embassy Tripoli operations suspended in 2014
mailing address: 8850 Tripoli Place, Washington, DC 20521-8850
telephone: [216] 71-107-000
email address and website:

Webmaster_Libya@state.gov
https://ly.usembassy.gov/
note: the US Embassy in Tripoli closed in July 2014 due to Libyan civil unrest; embassy staff and operations currently are located at US Embassy Tunis, Tunisia

Flag description: *three horizontal bands of red (top), black (double width), and green with a white crescent and star centered on the black stripe; the National Transitional Council reintroduced this flag design of the former Kingdom of Libya (1951-1969) on 27 February 2011; it replaced the former all-green banner promulgated by the QADHAFI regime in 1977; the colors represent the three major regions of the country:* red stands for Fezzan, black symbolizes Cyrenaica, and green denotes Tripolitania; the crescent and star represent Islam, the main religion of the country

National symbol(s): star and crescent, hawk; national colors: red, black, green

National anthem: *name:* "Libya, Libya, Libya"
lyrics/music: Al Bashir AL AREBI/Mohamad Abdel WAHAB
note: also known as "Ya Beladi" or "Oh, My Country!"; adopted 1951; readopted 2011 with some modification to the lyrics; during the QADHAFI years between 1969 and 2011, the anthem was "Allahu Akbar," (God is Great) a marching song of the Egyptian Army in the 1956 Suez War

National heritage: *total World Heritage Sites:* 5 (all cultural)
selected World Heritage Site locales: Archaeological Site of Cyrene; Archaeological Site of Leptis Magna, Archaeological Site of Sabratha; Rock-Art Sites of Tadrart Acacus; Old Town of Ghadamès

ECONOMY

Economic overview: upper middle-income, fossil fuel-based North African economy; 31% economic contraction due to COVID-19 and 2020 oil blockade; reduced government spending; central bank had to devalue currency; public wages are over 60% of expenditures

Real GDP (purchasing power parity): $121.951 billion (2023 est.)
$124.026 billion (2022 est.)
$122.39 billion (2021 est.)
note: data in 2021 dollars
comparison ranking: 92

Real GDP growth rate: -1.67% (2023 est.)
1.34% (2022 est.)
153.49% (2021 est.)
note: annual GDP % growth based on constant local currency
comparison ranking: 204

Real GDP per capita: $17,700 (2023 est.)
$18,200 (2022 est.)
$18,200 (2021 est.)
note: data in 2021 dollars
comparison ranking: 109

GDP (official exchange rate): $50.492 billion (2023 est.)
note: data in current dollars at official exchange rate

Inflation rate (consumer prices): 2.37% (2023 est.)
4.51% (2022 est.)
2.87% (2021 est.)
note: annual % change based on consumer prices
comparison ranking: 49

GDP - composition, by sector of origin: *agriculture:* 1.6% (2023 est.)
industry: 85% (2023 est.)
services: 46.6% (2023 est.)
note: figures may not total 100% due to non-allocated consumption not captured in sector-reported data
comparison rankings: services 163; industry 1; agriculture 173

GDP - composition, by end use: *household consumption:* 26.1% (2023 est.)
government consumption: 31.8% (2023 est.)
investment in fixed capital: 16.1% (2018 est.)
investment in inventories: -1.4% (2023 est.)
exports of goods and services: 68.6% (2023 est.)
imports of goods and services: -41.3% (2023 est.)
note: figures may not total 100% due to rounding or gaps in data collection

Agricultural products: potatoes, watermelons, tomatoes, onions, dates, milk, olives, chicken, wheat, vegetables (2022)
note: top ten agricultural products based on tonnage

Industries: petroleum, petrochemicals, aluminum, iron and steel, food processing, textiles, handicrafts, cement

Industrial production growth rate: 12.54% (2023 est.)
note: annual % change in industrial value added based on constant local currency
comparison ranking: 9

Labor force: 2.398 million (2023 est.)
note: number of people ages 15 or older who are employed or seeking work
comparison ranking: 122

Unemployment rate: 18.74% (2023 est.)
19.32% (2022 est.)
19.6% (2021 est.)
note: % of labor force seeking employment
comparison ranking: 197

Youth unemployment rate (ages 15-24): *total:* 49.4% (2023 est.)
male: 41.2% (2023 est.)
female: 68% (2023 est.)
note: % of labor force ages 15-24 seeking employment
comparison ranking: total 3

Remittances: 0% of GDP (2022 est.)
0% of GDP (2021 est.)
0% of GDP (2020 est.)
note: personal transfers and compensation between resident and non-resident individuals/households/entities

Budget: *revenues:* $28.005 billion (2019 est.)
expenditures: $37.475 billion (2019 est.)

Public debt: 4.7% of GDP (2017 est.)
comparison ranking: 200

Taxes and other revenues: 51.6% (of GDP) (2017 est.)
comparison ranking: 4

Current account balance: $5.675 billion (2021 est.)
-$4.78 billion (2020 est.)
$4.817 billion (2019 est.)
note: balance of payments - net trade and primary/secondary income in current dollars
comparison ranking: 32

Exports: $32.38 billion (2021 est.)
$9.537 billion (2020 est.)
$29.326 billion (2019 est.)
note: balance of payments - exports of goods and services in current dollars
comparison ranking: 78

Exports - partners: Italy 26%, Spain 10%, Germany 9%, China 7%, France 6% (2022)
note: top five export partners based on percentage share of exports

Exports - commodities: crude petroleum, natural gas, gold, refined petroleum, scrap iron (2022)
note: top five export commodities based on value in dollars

Imports: $25.406 billion (2021 est.)
$14.334 billion (2020 est.)
$25.368 billion (2019 est.)
note: balance of payments - imports of goods and services in current dollars
comparison ranking: 85

Imports - partners: Turkey 15%, China 12%, Italy 12%, Greece 10%, UAE 7% (2022)
note: top five import partners based on percentage share of imports

Imports - commodities: refined petroleum, cars, garments, broadcasting equipment, tobacco (2022)
note: top five import commodities based on value in dollars

Reserves of foreign exchange and gold: $92.427 billion (2023 est.)
$86.683 billion (2022 est.)
$82.262 billion (2021 est.)
note: holdings of gold (year-end prices)/foreign exchange/special drawing rights in current dollars
comparison ranking: 29

Exchange rates: Libyan dinars (LYD) per US dollar -

Exchange rates: 4.813 (2023 est.)
4.813 (2022 est.)
4.514 (2021 est.)
1.389 (2020 est.)
1.398 (2019 est.)

ENERGY

Electricity access: *electrification - total population:* 70% (2022 est.)
electrification - urban areas: 100%

Electricity: *installed generating capacity:* 10.517 million kW (2022 est.)
consumption: 24.674 billion kWh (2022 est.)
imports: 847.216 million kWh (2022 est.)
transmission/distribution losses: 6.457 billion kWh (2022 est.)
comparison rankings: transmission/distribution losses 169; imports 83; consumption 70; installed generating capacity 65

Electricity generation sources: *fossil fuels:* 100% of total installed capacity (2022 est.)

Coal: *imports:* 300 metric tons (2022 est.)

Petroleum: *total petroleum production:* 1.245 million bbl/day (2023 est.)
refined petroleum consumption: 230,000 bbl/day (2022 est.)
crude oil estimated reserves: 48.363 billion barrels (2021 est.)

Natural gas: *production:* 11.832 billion cubic meters (2022 est.)
consumption: 9.212 billion cubic meters (2022 est.)
exports: 2.62 billion cubic meters (2022 est.)
proven reserves: 1.505 trillion cubic meters (2021 est.)

Carbon dioxide emissions: 49.751 million metric tonnes of CO_2 (2022 est.)
from petroleum and other liquids: 31.68 million metric tonnes of CO_2 (2022 est.)

from consumed natural gas: 18.072 million metric tonnes of CO_2 (2022 est.)
comparison ranking: total emissions 57

Energy consumption per capita: 117.609 million Btu/person (2022 est.)
comparison ranking: 38

COMMUNICATIONS

Telephones - fixed lines: *total subscriptions:* 1.218 million (2022 est.)
subscriptions per 100 inhabitants: 18 (2022 est.)
comparison ranking: total subscriptions 67

Telephones - mobile cellular: *total subscriptions:* 13.94 million (2022 est.)
subscriptions per 100 inhabitants: 205 (2022 est.)
comparison ranking: total subscriptions 74

Telecommunication systems: *general assessment:* political and security instability in Libya has disrupted its telecom sector; much of its infrastructure remains superior to that in most other African countries; rival operators fight for control; investment in fiber backbone and upgrades to international cables; limited LTE and 5G service; some satellite broadband; in 2021 Libya signed deals and projects with US firms to upgrade portions of its infrastructure, increasing the diversity of its telecommunications networks (2022)
domestic: nearly 23 per 100 fixed-line and over 43 per 100 mobile-cellular subscriptions; service generally adequate (2021)
international: country code - 218; landing points for LFON, EIG, Italy-Libya, Silphium and Tobrok-Emasaed submarine cable system connecting Europe, Africa, the Middle East and Asia; satellite earth stations - 4 Intelsat, Arabsat, and Intersputnik; microwave radio relay to Tunisia and Egypt; tropospheric scatter to Greece; participant in Medarabtel (2019)

Broadcast media: state-funded and private TV stations; some provinces operate local TV stations; pan-Arab satellite TV stations are available; state-funded radio (2019)

Internet country code: .ly

Internet users: *total:* 3,095,400 (2021 est.)
percent of population: 46.2% (2021 est.)
comparison ranking: total 117

Broadband - fixed subscriptions: *total:* 332,000 (2020 est.)
subscriptions per 100 inhabitants: 5 (2020 est.)
comparison ranking: total 104

TRANSPORTATION

National air transport system: *number of registered air carriers:* 9 (2020)
inventory of registered aircraft operated by air carriers: 55
annual passenger traffic on registered air carriers: 927,153 (2018)

Civil aircraft registration country code prefix: 5A

Airports: 66 (2024)
comparison ranking: 73

Pipelines: 882 km condensate, 3,743 km gas, 7,005 km oil (2013)

Roadways: *total:* 34,000 km (2021)
comparison ranking: total 95

Merchant marine: *total:* 96 (2023)
by type: general cargo 2, oil tanker 13, other 81
comparison ranking: total 91

Ports: *total ports:* 14 (2024)
large: 0
medium: 2
small: 3
very small: 9
ports with oil terminals: 10
key ports: Al Burayqah, Az Zawiya, Banghazi, Mersa Tobruq, Mina Tarabulus (Tripoli)

MILITARY AND SECURITY

Military and security forces: the Tripoli-based Government of National Unity (GNU) has access to various ground, air, and naval/coast guard forces comprised of a mix of formations and equipment from the QADHAFI regime, semi-regular and nominally integrated units, tribal armed groups/militias, civilian volunteers, and foreign private military contractors and mercenaries; the GNU has a Ministry of Defense, but has limited control over its security forces
the self-styled Libyan National Army (LNA), under de facto LNA commander Khalifa HAFTER, also includes various ground, air, and naval forces comprised of semi-regular military personnel, militias, and foreign private military contractors and mercenaries; the LNA operates independently from the GNU and exerts influence throughout eastern, central, and southern Libya; some of the armed groups nominally under the LNA operate under their own command structures and engage in their own operations (2024)
note 1: the Stabilization Support Apparatus (SSA) is a state-funded militia established in January 2021 by the GNA; it is tasked with securing government buildings and officials, participating in combat operations, apprehending those suspected of national security crimes, and cooperating with other security bodies; other forces operating in western Libya include the Misrata Counter Terrorism Force, Special Deterrence Forces (aka Radaa), 444 Brigade, 111 Brigade, Nawasi Brigade, and the Joint Operations Force
note 2: the national police force under the Ministry of Interior oversees internal security (with support from military forces under the Ministry of Defense), but much of Libya's security-related police work generally falls to informal armed groups, which receive government salaries but lack formal training, supervision, or consistent accountability

Military expenditures: not available

Military and security service personnel strengths: estimates not available

Military equipment inventories and acquisitions: both the forces aligned with the GNU and the LNA are largely equipped with weapons of Russian or Soviet origin; in recent years, Turkey has the been the primary supplier of arms to the GNU, while the LNA has received quantities from Russia and the United Arab Emirates (2024)
note: Libya is under a UN-imposed arms embargo

Military service age and obligation: not available

Military - note: the western-based GNU and the eastern-based LNA forces are separated by a fortified line of control running roughly from the coastal city of Sirte south to the vicinity of Al Jufra and Brak; Turkey has provided support to the GNU forces, including military trainers, ammunition, weapons, and aerial drones; Russia, the United Arab Emirates, and Egypt have been the main supporters of the LNA; both the LNA and the GNU forces have incorporated foreign fighters into their ranks (2024)

TERRORISM

Terrorist group(s): Ansar al-Sharia groups; Islamic State of Iraq and ash-Sham - Libya (ISIS-L); al-Mulathamun Battalion (al-Mourabitoun); al-Qa'ida in the Islamic Maghreb (AQIM)
note: details about the history, aims, leadership, organization, areas of operation, tactics, targets, weapons, size, and sources of support of the group(s) appear(s) in the Terrorism reference guide

TRANSNATIONAL ISSUES

Refugees and internally displaced persons: *refugees (country of origin):* 11,623 (Syria) (refugees and asylum seekers), 8,302 (Eritrea) (2023); 6,293 (Sudan) (refugees and asylum seekers) (2024)
IDPs: 125,802 (conflict between pro-QADHAFI and anti-QADHAFI forces in 2011; post-QADHAFI tribal clashes 2014) (2023)

LIECHTENSTEIN

INTRODUCTION

Background: The Principality of Liechtenstein was established within the Holy Roman Empire in 1719. Occupied by both French and Russian troops during the Napoleonic Wars, it became a sovereign state in 1806 and joined the German Confederation in 1815. Liechtenstein became fully independent in 1866 when the Confederation dissolved. Until the end of World War I, it was closely tied to Austria, but the economic devastation caused by that conflict forced Liechtenstein to enter into a customs and monetary union with Switzerland. Since World War II (in which Liechtenstein remained neutral), the country's low taxes have spurred outstanding economic growth. In 2000, shortcomings in banking regulatory oversight resulted in concerns about the use of financial institutions for money laundering. However, Liechtenstein implemented anti-money laundering legislation and a Mutual Legal Assistance Treaty with the US that went into effect in 2003.

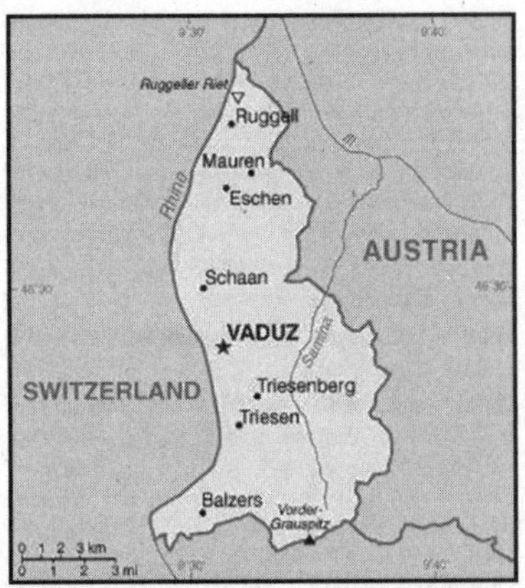

GEOGRAPHY

Location: Central Europe, between Austria and Switzerland

Geographic coordinates: 47 16 N, 9 32 E

Map references: Europe

Area: *total:* 160 sq km
land: 160 sq km
water: 0 sq km
comparison ranking: total 219

Area - comparative: about 0.9 times the size of Washington, DC

Land boundaries: *total:* 75 km
border countries (2): Austria 34 km; Switzerland 41 km

Coastline: 0 km (doubly landlocked)

Maritime claims: none (landlocked)

Climate: continental; cold, cloudy winters with frequent snow or rain; cool to moderately warm, cloudy, humid summers

Terrain: mostly mountainous (Alps) with Rhine Valley in western third

Elevation: *highest point:* Vorder-Grauspitz 2,599 m
lowest point: Ruggeller Riet 430 m

Natural resources: hydroelectric potential, arable land

Land use: *agricultural land:* 37.6% (2018 est.)
arable land: 18.8% (2018 est.)
permanent crops: 0% (2018 est.)
permanent pasture: 18.8% (2018 est.)
forest: 43.1% (2018 est.)
other: 19.3% (2018 est.)

Irrigated land: 0 sq km (2012)

Major watersheds (area sq km): Atlantic Ocean drainage: Rhine-Maas (198,735 sq km)

Population distribution: most of the population is found in the western half of the country along the Rhine River

Natural hazards: avalanches, landslides

Geography - note: along with Uzbekistan, one of only two doubly landlocked countries in the world; variety of microclimatic variations based on elevation

PEOPLE AND SOCIETY

Population: *total:* 40,272
male: 20,072
female: 20,200 (2024 est.)
comparison rankings: female 213; male 212; total 212

Nationality: *noun:* Liechtensteiner(s)
adjective: Liechtenstein

Ethnic groups: Liechtensteiner 65.6%, Swiss 9.6%, Austrian 5.8%, German 4.5%, Italian 3.1%, other 11.4% (2021 est.)
note: data represent population by nationality

Languages: German 91.5% (official, Alemannic is the main dialect), Italian 1.5%, Turkish 1.3%, Portuguese 1.1%, other 4.6% (2015 est.)
major-language sample(s):
Das World Factbook, die unverzichtbare Quelle für grundlegende Informationen. (German)

Religions: Roman Catholic (official) 73.4%, Protestant Reformed 6.3%, Muslim 5.9%, Christian Orthodox 1.3%, Lutheran 1.2%, other Protestant 0.7%, other Christian 0.3%, other 0.8%, none 7%, unspecified 3.3% (2015 est.)

Age structure: *0-14 years:* 15.3% (male 3,412/female 2,732)
15-64 years: 63.9% (male 12,814/female 12,921)
65 years and over: 20.8% (2024 est.) (male 3,846/female 4,547)

Dependency ratios: *total dependency ratio:* 50.2
youth dependency ratio: 21.8
elderly dependency ratio: 28.3
potential support ratio: 3.5 (2021)

Median age: *total:* 44.2 years (2024 est.)
male: 42.4 years
female: 46.1 years
comparison ranking: total 30

Population growth rate: 0.69% (2024 est.)
comparison ranking: 129

Birth rate: 10.3 births/1,000 population (2024 est.)
comparison ranking: 180

Death rate: 8.2 deaths/1,000 population (2024 est.)
comparison ranking: 81

Net migration rate: 4.7 migrant(s)/1,000 population (2024 est.)
comparison ranking: 20

Population distribution: most of the population is found in the western half of the country along the Rhine River

Urbanization: *urban population:* 14.6% of total population (2023)
rate of urbanization: 1.15% annual rate of change (2020-25 est.)

Major urban areas - population: 5,000 VADUZ (capital) (2018)

Sex ratio: *at birth:* 1.26 male(s)/female
0-14 years: 1.25 male(s)/female
15-64 years: 0.99 male(s)/female
65 years and over: 0.85 male(s)/female
total population: 0.99 male(s)/female (2024 est.)

Mother's mean age at first birth: 31.3 years (2017)

Infant mortality rate: *total:* 3.9 deaths/1,000 live births (2024 est.)
male: 4.3 deaths/1,000 live births
female: 3.5 deaths/1,000 live births
comparison ranking: total 189

Life expectancy at birth: *total population:* 83 years (2024 est.)
male: 80.7 years
female: 85.8 years
comparison ranking: total population 20

Total fertility rate: 1.69 children born/woman (2024 est.)
comparison ranking: 168

Gross reproduction rate: 0.75 (2024 est.)

Drinking water source: *improved:*
total: 100% of population
unimproved:
total: 0% of population (2020)

Sanitation facility access: *improved:*
total: 100% of population

Currently married women (ages 15-49): 65.2% (2023 est.)

Education expenditures: 2.6% of GDP (2011 est.)
comparison ranking: 173

School life expectancy (primary to tertiary education): *total:* 15 years
male: 16 years
female: 14 years (2020)

ENVIRONMENT

Environment - current issues: some air pollution generated locally, some carried over from surrounding countries

Environment - international agreements: *party to:* Air Pollution, Air Pollution-Heavy Metals, Air Pollution-Nitrogen Oxides, Air Pollution-Persistent Organic Pollutants, Air Pollution-Sulphur 85, Air Pollution-Sulphur 94, Air Pollution-Volatile Organic Compounds, Biodiversity, Climate Change, Climate Change-Kyoto Protocol, Climate Change-Paris Agreement, Comprehensive Nuclear Test Ban, Desertification, Endangered Species, Hazardous Wastes, Ozone Layer Protection, Wetlands
signed, but not ratified: Air Pollution-Multi-effect Protocol, Law of the Sea

Climate: continental; cold, cloudy winters with frequent snow or rain; cool to moderately warm, cloudy, humid summers

Urbanization: *urban population:* 14.6% of total population (2023)
rate of urbanization: 1.15% annual rate of change (2020-25 est.)

Revenue from forest resources: 0% of GDP (2017 est.)
comparison ranking: 184

Air pollutants: *carbon dioxide emissions:* 0.05 megatons (2016 est.)
methane emissions: 0.02 megatons (2020 est.)

Waste and recycling: *municipal solid waste generated annually:* 32,382 tons (2015 est.)
municipal solid waste recycled annually: 20,919 tons (2015 est.)
percent of municipal solid waste recycled: 64.6% (2015 est.)

Major watersheds (area sq km): Atlantic Ocean drainage: Rhine-Maas (198,735 sq km)

Total water withdrawal: *municipal:* 10 million cubic meters (2020 est.)

Total renewable water resources: 0 cubic meters (2017 est.)

GOVERNMENT

Country name: *conventional long form:* Principality of Liechtenstein
conventional short form: Liechtenstein
local long form: Fuerstentum Liechtenstein
local short form: Liechtenstein

etymology: named after the Liechtenstein dynasty that purchased and united the counties of Schellenburg and Vaduz and that was allowed by the Holy Roman Emperor in 1719 to rename the new property after their family; the name in German means "light (bright) stone"

Government type: constitutional monarchy

Capital: *name:* Vaduz
geographic coordinates: 47 08 N, 9 31 E
time difference: UTC+1 (6 hours ahead of Washington, DC, during Standard Time)
daylight saving time: +1hr, begins last Sunday in March; ends last Sunday in October
etymology: may be a conflation from the Latin *vallis* (valley) and the High German *diutisk* (meaning "German") to produce *Valdutsch* ("German valley"), which over time simplified and came to refer specifically to Vaduz, the town

Administrative divisions: 11 communes (Gemeinden, singular - Gemeinde); Balzers, Eschen, Gamprin, Mauren, Planken, Ruggell, Schaan, Schellenberg, Triesen, Triesenberg, Vaduz

Independence: 23 January 1719 (Principality of Liechtenstein established); 12 July 1806 (independence from the Holy Roman Empire); 24 August 1866 (independence from the German Confederation)

National holiday: National Day, 15 August (1940); note - a National Day was originally established in 1940 to combine celebrations for the Feast of the Assumption (15 August) with those honoring the birthday of former Prince FRANZ JOSEF II (1906-1989) whose birth fell on 16 August; after the prince's death, National Day became the official national holiday by law in 1990

Legal system: civil law system influenced by Swiss, Austrian, and German law

Constitution: *history:* previous 1862; latest adopted 5 October 1921
amendments: proposed by Parliament, by the reigning prince (in the form of "Government" proposals), by petition of at least 1,500 qualified voters, or by at least four communes; passage requires unanimous approval of Parliament members in one sitting or three-quarters majority vote in two successive sittings; referendum required only if petitioned by at least 1,500 voters or by at least four communes; passage by referendum requires absolute majority of votes cast; amended many times, last in 2023

International law organization participation: accepts compulsory ICJ jurisdiction with reservations; accepts ICCt jurisdiction

Citizenship: *citizenship by birth:* no
citizenship by descent only: the father must be a citizen of Liechtenstein; in the case of a child born out of wedlock, the mother must be a citizen
dual citizenship recognized: no
residency requirement for naturalization: 5 years

Suffrage: 18 years of age; universal

Executive branch: *chief of state:* Prince HANS-ADAM II (since 13 November 1989, assumed executive powers on 26 August 1984)
head of government: Prime Minister Daniel RISCH (since 25 March 2021)
cabinet: Cabinet elected by the Parliament, confirmed by the monarch
elections/appointments: the monarchy is hereditary; following legislative elections, the leader of the majority party in Parliament usually appointed the head of government by the monarch, and the leader of the largest minority party in Parliament usually appointed the deputy head of government by the monarch if there is a coalition government
note: the prince's successor is Heir Apparent and Regent of Liechtenstein Prince ALOIS (son of the monarch, born 11 June 1968); on 15 August 2004, HANS-ADAM II transferred the official duties of the ruling prince to ALOIS, but Prince HANS-ADAM II retains status of chief of state

Legislative branch: *description:* unicameral Parliament or Landtag (25 seats; members directly elected in 2 multi-seat constituencies by open-list proportional representation vote to serve 4-year terms)
elections: last held on 7 February 2021 (next to be held on 7 February 2025)
election results: percent of vote by party - FBP 40%, VU 40%, FL 12%, DpL 8%; seats by party - FBP 10, VU 10, FL 3, DpL 2; composition - men 18, women 7, percentage women 28%

Judicial branch: *highest court(s):* Supreme Court or Supreme Court or Fürstlicher Oberster Gerichtshof (consists of 5 judges and 5 substitutes); Constitutional Court or Staatsgerichtshof (consists of 5 judges, and 5 alternates)
judge selection and term of office: judges of both courts elected by the Landtag and appointed by the monarch; Supreme Court judges serve 4-year renewable terms; Constitutional Court judges appointed for renewable 5-year terms
subordinate courts: Court of Appeal (second instance), Regional Court (first instance), Administrative Court, Tribunal Court, district courts

Political parties: Democrats for Liechtenstein (Demokraten pro Liechtenstein) or DpL
Fatherland Union (Vaterlaendische Union) or VU
Progressive Citizens' Party (Fortschrittliche Buergerpartei) or FBP
The Free List (Die Freie Liste) or FL
The Independents (Die Unabhaengigen) or DU

International organization participation: CD, CE, EBRD, EFTA, IAEA, ICCt, ICRM, IFRCS, Interpol, IOC, IPU, ITSO, ITU, ITUC (NGOs), OAS (observer), OPCW, OSCE, PCA, Schengen Convention, UN, UNCTAD, UPU, WIPO, WTO

Diplomatic representation in the US: *chief of mission:* Ambassador Georg SPARBER (since 1 December 2021)
chancery: 2900 K Street NW, Suite 602B, Washington, DC 20007
telephone: [1] (202) 331-0590
FAX: [1] (202) 331-3221
email address and website:
washington@llv.li
https://www.liechtensteinusa.org/

Diplomatic representation from the US: *embassy:* the US does not have an embassy in Liechtenstein; the US Ambassador to Switzerland is accredited to Liechtenstein

Flag description: two equal horizontal bands of blue (top) and red with a gold crown on the hoist side of the blue band; the colors may derive from the blue and red livery design used in the principality's household in the 18th century; the prince's crown was introduced in 1937 to distinguish the flag from that of Haiti

National symbol(s): princely hat (crown); national colors: blue, red

National anthem: *name:* „Oben am jungen Rhein" (High Above the Young Rhine)
lyrics/music: Jakob Joseph JAUCH/Josef FROMMELT
note: adopted 1850, revised 1963; uses the tune of "God Save the King"

ECONOMY

Economic overview: high-income European economy; Schengen Area participant; key European financial leader; integrated with Swiss economy and franc currency user; one of the highest GDP per capita countries; relies on US and Eurozone markets for exports

Real GDP (purchasing power parity): $4.978 billion (2014 est.)
comparison ranking: 185

GDP (official exchange rate): $7.365 billion (2022 est.)
note: data in current dollars at official exchange rate

Inflation rate (consumer prices): -0.4% (2016 est.)
comparison ranking: 3

Credit ratings: Standard & Poors rating: AAA (1996)
note: The year refers to the year in which the current credit rating was first obtained.

GDP - composition, by sector of origin: *agriculture:* 0.2% (2021 est.)
industry: 40.2% (2021 est.)
services: 55.4% (2021 est.)
note: figures may not total 100% due to non-allocated consumption not captured in sector-reported data
comparison rankings: services 117; industry 28; agriculture 207

Agricultural products: wheat, barley, corn, potatoes; livestock, dairy products

Industries: electronics, metal manufacturing, dental products, ceramics, pharmaceuticals, food products, precision instruments, tourism, optical instruments

Industrial production growth rate: 4.3% (2014 est.)
note: annual % change in industrial value added based on constant local currency
comparison ranking: 66

Labor force: 38,520 (2015 est.)
note: 51% of the labor force in Liechtenstein commute daily from Austria, Switzerland, and Germany
comparison ranking: 195

Unemployment rate: 2.4% (2015)
2.4% (2014)
comparison ranking: 27

Exports: $3.217 billion (2015 est.)
$3.774 billion (2014 est.)
note: trade data exclude trade with Switzerland
comparison ranking: 154

Exports - commodities: small specialty machinery, connectors for audio and video, parts for motor vehicles, dental products, hardware, prepared foodstuffs, electronic equipment, optical products

Imports: $2.23 billion (2014 est.)
note: trade data exclude trade with Switzerland
comparison ranking: 173

Imports - commodities: agricultural products, raw materials, energy products, machinery, metal goods, textiles, foodstuffs, motor vehicles

Exchange rates: Swiss francs (CHF) per US dollar -

Exchange rates: 0.898 (2023 est.)
0.955 (2022 est.)
0.914 (2021 est.)
0.939 (2020 est.)
0.994 (2019 est.)

ENERGY

Electricity access: *electrification - total population:* 100% (2022 est.)

COMMUNICATIONS

Telephones - fixed lines: *total subscriptions:* 11,000 (2022 est.)
subscriptions per 100 inhabitants: 28 (2022 est.)
comparison ranking: total subscriptions 188

Telephones - mobile cellular: *total subscriptions:* 50,000 (2022 est.)
subscriptions per 100 inhabitants: 126 (2022 est.)
comparison ranking: total subscriptions 207

Telecommunication systems: *general assessment:* possesses a number of modern communications systems, some of which are shared with the neighboring country of Switzerland (2022)
domestic: fixed-line roughly 30 per 100 and mobile-cellular services 126 per 100 (2021)
international: country code - 423; linked to Swiss networks by cable and microwave radio relay

Broadcast media: relies on foreign terrestrial and satellite broadcasters for most broadcast media services; first Liechtenstein-based TV station established August 2008; Radio Liechtenstein operates multiple radio stations; a Swiss-based broadcaster operates one radio station in Liechtenstein

Internet country code: .li

Internet users: *total:* 37,440 (2021 est.)
percent of population: 96% (2021 est.)
comparison ranking: total 206

Broadband - fixed subscriptions: *total:* 18,050 (2020 est.)
subscriptions per 100 inhabitants: 47 (2020 est.)
comparison ranking: total 170

TRANSPORTATION

Civil aircraft registration country code prefix: HB

Heliports: 2 (2024)

Pipelines: 434.5 km gas (2018)

Railways: *total:* 9 km (2018)
standard gauge: 9 km (2018) 1.435-m gauge (electrified)
note: belongs to the Austrian Railway System connecting Austria and Switzerland
comparison ranking: total 137

Roadways: *total:* 420 km (2022)
comparison ranking: total 200

Waterways: 28 km (2010)
comparison ranking: 116

Merchant marine: *total:* 17 (2023)
by type: bulk carrier 14, general cargo 1, other 2 (includes Switzerland)
comparison ranking: total 150

MILITARY AND SECURITY

Military and security forces: no regular military forces; the National Police maintain internal security and report to the Department of Civil Defense

TRANSNATIONAL ISSUES

Illicit drugs: has strengthened money laundering controls, but money laundering remains a concern due to Liechtenstein's sophisticated offshore financial services sector

LITHUANIA

INTRODUCTION

Background: Lithuanian lands were united under MINDAUGAS in 1236; over the next century, Lithuania extended its territory through alliances and conquest to include most of present-day Belarus and Ukraine. By the end of the 14th century, Lithuania was the largest state in Europe. An alliance with Poland in 1386 led the two countries into a union through a common ruler. In 1569, Lithuania and Poland formally united into a single dual state, the Polish-Lithuanian Commonwealth. This entity survived until 1795 when surrounding countries partitioned its remnants. Lithuania regained its independence after World War I, but the USSR annexed it in 1940 – an action never recognized by the US and many other countries. In 1990, Lithuania became the first of the Soviet republics to declare its independence, but Moscow did not recognize this proclamation until 1991. The last Russian troops withdrew in 1993. Lithuania subsequently restructured its economy for integration into West European institutions; it joined both NATO and the EU in 2004. In 2015, Lithuania joined the euro zone, and it joined the Organization for Economic Cooperation and Development in 2018.

GEOGRAPHY

Location: Eastern Europe, bordering the Baltic Sea, between Latvia and Russia, west of Belarus

Geographic coordinates: 56 00 N, 24 00 E

Map references: Europe

Area: *total:* 65,300 sq km
land: 62,680 sq km
water: 2,620 sq km
comparison ranking: total 123

Area - comparative: slightly larger than West Virginia

Land boundaries: *total:* 1,545 km
border countries (4): Belarus 640 km; Latvia 544 km; Poland 100 km; Russia (Kaliningrad) 261 km

Coastline: 90 km

Maritime claims: *territorial sea:* 12 nm

Climate: transitional, between maritime and continental; wet, moderate winters and summers

Terrain: lowland, many scattered small lakes, fertile soil

Elevation: *highest point:* Aukstojas 294 m
lowest point: Baltic Sea 0 m
mean elevation: 110 m

Natural resources: peat, arable land, amber

Land use: *agricultural land:* 44.8% (2018 est.)
arable land: 34.9% (2018 est.)
permanent crops: 0.5% (2018 est.)
permanent pasture: 9.4% (2018 est.)
forest: 34.6% (2018 est.)
other: 20.6% (2018 est.)

Irrigated land: 16 sq km (2013)

Major lakes (area sq km): *salt water lake(s):* Curonian Lagoon (shared with Russia) - 1,620 sq km

Population distribution: fairly even population distribution throughout the country, but somewhat greater concentrations in the southern cities of Vilnius and Kaunas, and the western port of Klaipeda

Natural hazards: occasional floods, droughts

Geography - note: fertile central plains are separated by hilly uplands that are ancient glacial deposits

PEOPLE AND SOCIETY

Population: *total:* 2,628,186
male: 1,214,994
female: 1,413,192 (2024 est.)
comparison rankings: female 141; male 145; total 142

Nationality: *noun:* Lithuanian(s)
adjective: Lithuanian

Ethnic groups: Lithuanian 84.6%, Polish 6.5%, Russian 5%, Belarusian 1%, other 1.1%, unspecified 1.8% (2021 est.)

Languages: Lithuanian (official) 85.3%, Russian 6.8%, Polish 5.1%, other 1.1%, two mother tongues 1.7% (2021 est.)
major-language sample(s):
Pasaulio enciklopedija – naudingas bendrosios informacijos šaltinis. (Lithuanian)

Religions: Roman Catholic 74.2%, Russian Orthodox 3.7%, Old Believer 0.6%, Evangelical Lutheran 0.6%, Evangelical Reformist 0.2%, other (including Sunni Muslim, Jewish, Greek Catholic, and Karaite) 0.9%, none 6.1%, unspecified 13.7% (2021 est.)

Age structure: *0-14 years:* 15.2% (male 205,154/female 194,386)
15-64 years: 62.6% (male 808,435/female 837,908)
65 years and over: 22.2% (2024 est.) (male 201,405/female 380,898)

Dependency ratios: *total dependency ratio:* 55.7

youth dependency ratio: 23.6
elderly dependency ratio: 32.1
potential support ratio: 3.1 (2021 est.)

Median age: *total:* 45.1 years (2024 est.)
male: 40.9 years
female: 49.2 years
comparison ranking: total 18

Population growth rate: -1.05% (2024 est.)
comparison ranking: 231

Birth rate: 8.9 births/1,000 population (2024 est.)
comparison ranking: 201

Death rate: 15.2 deaths/1,000 population (2024 est.)
comparison ranking: 2

Net migration rate: -4.1 migrant(s)/1,000 population (2024 est.)
comparison ranking: 195

Population distribution: fairly even population distribution throughout the country, but somewhat greater concentrations in the southern cities of Vilnius and Kaunas, and the western port of Klaipeda

Urbanization: *urban population:* 68.7% of total population (2023)
rate of urbanization: -0.12% annual rate of change (2020-25 est.)

Major urban areas - population: 541,000 VILNIUS (capital) (2023)

Sex ratio: *at birth:* 1.06 male(s)/female
0-14 years: 1.06 male(s)/female
15-64 years: 0.96 male(s)/female
65 years and over: 0.53 male(s)/female
total population: 0.86 male(s)/female (2024 est.)

Mother's mean age at first birth: 28.2 years (2020 est.)

Maternal mortality ratio: 9 deaths/100,000 live births (2020 est.)
comparison ranking: 146

Infant mortality rate: *total:* 3.6 deaths/1,000 live births (2024 est.)
male: 4 deaths/1,000 live births
female: 3.1 deaths/1,000 live births
comparison ranking: total 193

Life expectancy at birth: *total population:* 76.1 years (2024 est.)
male: 70.8 years
female: 81.7 years
comparison ranking: total population 117

Total fertility rate: 1.62 children born/woman (2024 est.)
comparison ranking: 179

Gross reproduction rate: 0.79 (2024 est.)

Contraceptive prevalence rate: NA

Drinking water source: *improved: urban:* 100% of population
rural: 93.8% of population
total: 98% of population
unimproved: urban: 0% of population
rural: 6.2% of population
total: 2% of population (2020 est.)

Current health expenditure: 7.5% of GDP (2020)

Physician density: 5.08 physicians/1,000 population (2020)

Hospital bed density: 6.4 beds/1,000 population (2018)

Sanitation facility access: *improved: urban:* 99.5% of population
rural: 88.7% of population
total: 96% of population
unimproved: urban: 0.5% of population
rural: 11.3% of population
total: 4% of population (2020 est.)

Obesity - adult prevalence rate: 26.3% (2016)
comparison ranking: 43

Alcohol consumption per capita: *total:* 11.93 liters of pure alcohol (2019 est.)
beer: 4.61 liters of pure alcohol (2019 est.)
wine: 0.88 liters of pure alcohol (2019 est.)
spirits: 4.96 liters of pure alcohol (2019 est.)
other alcohols: 1.48 liters of pure alcohol (2019 est.)
comparison ranking: total 4

Tobacco use: *total:* 32% (2020 est.)
male: 42.1% (2020 est.)
female: 21.8% (2020 est.)
comparison ranking: total 20

Children under the age of 5 years underweight: 2.5% (2021)
comparison ranking: 97

Currently married women (ages 15-49): 53.4% (2023 est.)

Child marriage: *women married by age 18:* 0.3% (2021 est.)

Education expenditures: 4% of GDP (2019 est.)
comparison ranking: 116

Literacy: *definition:* age 15 and over can read and write
total population: 99.8%
male: 99.8%
female: 99.8% (2021)

School life expectancy (primary to tertiary education): *total:* 16 years
male: 16 years
female: 17 years (2020)

ENVIRONMENT

Environment - current issues: water pollution; air pollution; deforestation; threatened animal and plant species; chemicals and waste materials released into the environment contaminate soil and groundwater; soil degradation and erosion

Environment - international agreements: *party to:* Air Pollution, Air Pollution-Heavy Metals, Air Pollution-Multi-effect Protocol, Air Pollution-Nitrogen Oxides, Air Pollution-Persistent Organic Pollutants, Air Pollution-Sulphur 85, Air Pollution-Sulphur 94, Air Pollution-Volatile Organic Compounds, Biodiversity, Climate Change, Climate Change-Kyoto Protocol, Climate Change-Paris Agreement, Comprehensive Nuclear Test Ban, Desertification, Endangered Species, Environmental Modification, Hazardous Wastes, Law of the Sea, Ozone Layer Protection, Ship Pollution, Tropical Timber 2006, Wetlands, Whaling
signed, but not ratified: none of the selected agreements

Climate: transitional, between maritime and continental; wet, moderate winters and summers

Urbanization: *urban population:* 68.7% of total population (2023)
rate of urbanization: -0.12% annual rate of change (2020-25 est.)

Revenue from forest resources: 0.31% of GDP (2018 est.)
comparison ranking: 80

Revenue from coal: 0% of GDP (2018 est.)
comparison ranking: 141

Air pollutants: *particulate matter emissions:* 10.37 micrograms per cubic meter (2019 est.)
carbon dioxide emissions: 12.96 megatons (2016 est.)
methane emissions: 3.15 megatons (2020 est.)

Waste and recycling: *municipal solid waste generated annually:* 1.3 million tons (2015 est.)
municipal solid waste recycled annually: 297,960 tons (2015 est.)
percent of municipal solid waste recycled: 22.9% (2015 est.)

Major lakes (area sq km): *salt water lake(s):* Curonian Lagoon (shared with Russia) - 1,620 sq km

Total water withdrawal: *municipal:* 140 million cubic meters (2020 est.)
industrial: 60 million cubic meters (2020 est.)
agricultural: 60 million cubic meters (2020 est.)

Total renewable water resources: 24.5 billion cubic meters (2020 est.)

GOVERNMENT

Country name: *conventional long form:* Republic of Lithuania
conventional short form: Lithuania
local long form: Lietuvos Respublika
local short form: Lietuva
former: Lithuanian Soviet Socialist Republic (while occupied by the USSR)
etymology: meaning of the name "Lietuva" remains unclear and is debated by scholars; it may derive from the Lietava, a stream in east central Lithuania

Government type: semi-presidential republic

Capital: *name:* Vilnius
geographic coordinates: 54 41 N, 25 19 E
time difference: UTC+2 (7 hours ahead of Washington, DC, during Standard Time)
daylight saving time: +1hr, begins last Sunday in March; ends last Sunday in October
etymology: named after the Vilnia River, which flows into the Neris River at Vilnius; the river name derives from the Lithuanian word "vilnis" meaning "a surge"

Administrative divisions: 60 municipalities (savivaldybe, singular - savivaldybe); Akmene, Alytaus Miestas, Alytus, Anksciai, Birstonas, Birzai, Druskininkai, Elektrenai, Ignalina, Jonava, Joniskis, Jurbarkas, Kaisiadorys, Kalvarija, Kauno Miestas, Kaunas, Kazlu Rudos, Kedainiai, Kelme, Klaipedos Miestas, Klaipeda, Kretinga, Kupiskis, Lazdijai, Marijampole, Mazeikiai, Moletai, Neringa, Pagegiai, Pakruojis, Palangos Miestas, Panevezio Miestas, Panevezys, Pasvalys, Plunge, Prienai, Radviliskis, Raseiniai, Rietavas, Rokiskis, Sakiai, Salcininkai, Siauliu Miestas, Siauliai, Silale, Silute, Sirvintos, Skuodas, Svencionys, Taurage, Telsiai, Trakai, Ukmerge, Utena, Varena, Vilkaviskis, Vilniaus Miestas, Vilnius, Visaginas, Zarasai

Independence: *16 February 1918 (from Soviet Russia and Germany); 11 March 1990 (declared from the Soviet Union); 6 September 1991 (recognized by the Soviet Union); notable earlier dates:* 6 July 1253 (coronation of MINDAUGAS, traditional founding date); 1 July 1569 (Polish-Lithuanian Commonwealth created)

National holiday: Independence Day (or National Day), 16 February (1918); note - 16 February 1918 was the date Lithuania established its statehood and its concomitant independence from Soviet Russia and Germany; 11 March 1990 was the date it declared the restoration of Lithuanian statehood and its concomitant independence from the Soviet Union

Legal system: civil law system; legislative acts can be appealed to the Constitutional Court

Constitution: *history:* several previous; latest adopted by referendum 25 October 1992, entered into force 2 November 1992
amendments: proposed by at least one fourth of all Parliament members or by petition of at least 300,000 voters; passage requires two-thirds majority vote of Parliament in each of two readings three months apart and a presidential signature; amendments to constitutional articles on national sovereignty and constitutional amendment procedure also require three-fourths voter approval in a referendum; amended many times, last in 2022

International law organization participation: accepts compulsory ICJ jurisdiction with reservations; accepts ICCt jurisdiction

Citizenship: *citizenship by birth:* no
citizenship by descent only: at least one parent must be a citizen of Lithuania
dual citizenship recognized: no
residency requirement for naturalization: 10 years

Suffrage: 18 years of age; universal

Executive branch: *chief of state:* President Gitanas NAUSEDA (since 12 July 2019)
head of government: Prime Minister Ingrida SIMONYTE (since 24 November 2020)
cabinet: Council of Ministers nominated by the prime minister, appointed by the president, approved by Parliament
elections/appointments: president directly elected by absolute majority popular vote in 2 rounds if needed for a 5-year term (eligible for a second term); first round of the election held on 12 May 204 (runoff to be held on 12 May 2024); prime minister appointed by the president, approved by Parliament
election results:
2024: Gitanas NAUSEDA elected president in the second round; percent of vote -Gitanas NAUSEDA (independent) 74.6%, Ingrida SIMONYTE (independent) 24.4%
2019: Gitanas NAUSEDA elected president in second round; percent of vote - Gitanas NAUSEDA (independent) 66.7%, Ingrida SIMONYTE (independent) 33.3%

Legislative branch: *description:* unicameral Parliament or Seimas (141 seats; 71 members directly elected in single-seat constituencies by absolute majority vote and 70 directly elected in a single nationwide constituency by proportional representation vote; members serve 4-year terms)
elections: last held on 13 October 2024 first round (next to be held on 27 October 2024 - second round)
election results: preliminary first-round results percent of vote by party - LSDP 19.4%, TS-LKD 18%, NA 15%, DSVL 9.2%, LRLS 7.7%, LVZS 7%, LLRA-KSS 6%; seats by party - LSDP 20, TS-LKD 18, NA 15, DSVL 8, LRLS 8, LVZS 6, LLRA-KSS 2, Independents 1

Judicial branch: *highest court(s):* Supreme Court (consists of 37 judges); Constitutional Court (consists of 9 judges)
judge selection and term of office: Supreme Court judges nominated by the president and appointed by the Seimas; judges serve 5-year renewable terms; Constitutional Court judges appointed by the Seimas from nominations - 3 each by the president of the republic, the Seimas speaker, and the Supreme Court president; judges serve 9-year, nonrenewable terms; one-third of membership reconstituted every 3 years
subordinate courts: Court of Appeals; district and local courts

Political parties: Dawn of Nemunas or NA
Electoral Action of Poles in Lithuania or LLRA–KŠS
Freedom and Justice Party or LT (formerly Lithuanian Freedom Union (Liberals))
Freedom Party or LP
Homeland Union-Lithuanian Christian Democrats or TS-LKD
Labour Party or DP
Lithuanian Center Party or LCP
Lithuanian Christian Democracy Party or LKDP
Lithuanian Farmers and Greens Union or LVZS
Lithuanian Green Party or LZP
Liberals' Movement or LRLS
Lithuanian List or LL
Lithuanian Regions Party or LRP
Social Democratic Party of Lithuania or LSDP
Union of Democrats for Lithuania or DSVL

International organization participation: Australia Group, BA, BIS, CBSS, CD, CE, EAPC, EBRD, ECB, EIB, EU, FAO, IAEA, IBRD, ICAO, ICC (national committees), ICCt, ICRM, IDA, IFC, IFRCS, ILO, IMF, IMO, Interpol, IOC, IOM, IPU, ISO, ITU, ITUC (NGOs), MIGA, NATO, NIB, NSG, OAS (observer), OECD, OIF (observer), OPCW, OSCE, PCA, Schengen Convention, UN, UNCTAD, UNESCO, UNHRC, UNIDO, UNWTO, UPU, Wassenaar Arrangement, WCO, WHO, WIPO, WMO, WTO

Diplomatic representation in the US: *chief of mission:* Ambassador Audra PLEPYTE (since 7 July 2021)
chancery: 2622 16th Street NW, Washington, DC 20009
telephone: [1] (202) 234-5860
FAX: [1] (202) 328-0466
email address and website:
info@usa.mfa.lt
https://usa. mfa. lt/usa/en/
consulate(s) general: Chicago, Los Angeles, New York

Diplomatic representation from the US: *chief of mission:* Ambassador Kara C. McDONALD (since 26 January 2024)
embassy: Akmenu gatve 6, Vilnius, LT-03106
mailing address: 4510 Vilnius Place, Washington DC 20521-4510
telephone: [370] (5) 266-5500
FAX: [370] (5) 266-5510
email address and website:
consec@state.gov
https://lt.usembassy.gov/

Flag description: three equal horizontal bands of yellow (top), green, and red; yellow symbolizes golden fields, as well as the sun, light, and goodness; green represents the forests of the countryside, in addition to nature, freedom, and hope; red stands for courage and the blood spilled in defense of the homeland

National symbol(s): mounted knight known as Vytis (the Chaser), white stork; national colors: yellow, green, red

National anthem: *name:* "Tautiska giesme" (The National Song)
lyrics/music: Vincas KUDIRKA
note: adopted 1918, restored 1990; written in 1898 while Lithuania was a part of Russia; banned during the Soviet occupation from 1940 to 1990

National heritage: *total World Heritage Sites:* 5 (all cultural)
selected World Heritage Site locales: Vilnius Historic Center; Curonian Spit; Kernavė Archaeological Site; Struve Geodetic Arc; Modernist Kaunas: Architecture of Optimism, 1919-1939

ECONOMY

Economic overview: high-income EU and eurozone member, largest Baltic economy; growth stalled due to Ukraine war impact on energy, exports, and fiscal spending for defense and refugee support; rebound supported by EU fund-driven investments and reduced inflation; structural challenges include pension reform, labor market inefficiencies, health care, and education spending

Real GDP (purchasing power parity): $132.712 billion (2023 est.)
$133.159 billion (2022 est.)
$129.987 billion (2021 est.)
note: data in 2021 dollars
comparison ranking: 91

Real GDP growth rate: -0.34% (2023 est.)
2.44% (2022 est.)
6.28% (2021 est.)
note: annual GDP % growth based on constant local currency
comparison ranking: 194

Real GDP per capita: $46,200 (2023 est.)
$47,000 (2022 est.)
$46,400 (2021 est.)
note: data in 2021 dollars
comparison ranking: 53

GDP (official exchange rate): $77.836 billion (2023 est.)
note: data in current dollars at official exchange rate

Inflation rate (consumer prices): 9.12% (2023 est.)
19.71% (2022 est.)
4.68% (2021 est.)
note: annual % change based on consumer prices
comparison ranking: 167

Credit ratings: Fitch rating: A (2020)

Moody's rating: A3 (2015)

Standard & Poors rating: A+ (2020)
note: The year refers to the year in which the current credit rating was first obtained.

GDP - composition, by sector of origin: *agriculture:* 3% (2023 est.)
industry: 24.1% (2023 est.)
services: 63.1% (2023 est.)
note: figures may not total 100% due to non-allocated consumption not captured in sector-reported data
comparison rankings: services 66; industry 107; agriculture 137

GDP - composition, by end use: *household consumption:* 58.8% (2023 est.)
government consumption: 17.7% (2023 est.)
investment in fixed capital: 23.3% (2023 est.)
investment in inventories: -3.6% (2023 est.)
exports of goods and services: 78.5% (2023 est.)
imports of goods and services: -74.7% (2023 est.)
note: figures may not total 100% due to rounding or gaps in data collection

Agricultural products: wheat, milk, rapeseed, sugar beets, barley, potatoes, beans, triticale, oats, peas (2022)
note: top ten agricultural products based on tonnage

Industries: metal-cutting machine tools, electric motors, televisions, refrigerators and freezers, petroleum refining, shipbuilding (small ships), furniture, textiles, food processing, fertilizer, agricultural machinery, optical equipment, lasers, electronic components, computers, amber jewelry, information technology, video game development, app/software development, biotechnology

Industrial production growth rate: -2.17% (2023 est.)
note: annual % change in industrial value added based on constant local currency
comparison ranking: 184

Labor force: 1.51 million (2023 est.)
note: number of people ages 15 or older who are employed or seeking work
comparison ranking: 134

Unemployment rate: 6.96% (2023 est.)
5.96% (2022 est.)
7.11% (2021 est.)
note: % of labor force seeking employment
comparison ranking: 135

Youth unemployment rate (ages 15-24): *total:* 13.9% (2023 est.)
male: 16.3% (2023 est.)
female: 11.3% (2023 est.)
note: % of labor force ages 15-24 seeking employment
comparison ranking: total 99

Population below poverty line: 20.9% (2021 est.)
note: % of population with income below national poverty line

Gini Index coefficient - distribution of family income: 36.7 (2021 est.)
note: index (0-100) of income distribution; higher values represent greater inequality
comparison ranking: 66

Average household expenditures: *on food:* 19.8% of household expenditures (2022 est.)
on alcohol and tobacco: 5.8% of household expenditures (2022 est.)

Household income or consumption by percentage share: *lowest 10%:* 2.6% (2021 est.)
highest 10%: 29.1% (2021 est.)
note: % share of income accruing to lowest and highest 10% of population

Remittances: 1.25% of GDP (2023 est.)
1.04% of GDP (2022 est.)
1.16% of GDP (2021 est.)
note: personal transfers and compensation between resident and non-resident individuals/households/entities

Budget: *revenues:* $24.347 billion (2022 est.)
expenditures: $24.219 billion (2022 est.)
note: central government revenues (excluding grants) and expenses converted to US dollars at average official exchange rate for year indicated

Public debt: 36.05% of GDP (2022 est.)
note: central government debt as a % of GDP
comparison ranking: 147

Taxes and other revenues: 21.1% (of GDP) (2022 est.)
note: central government tax revenue as a % of GDP
comparison ranking: 78

Current account balance: $1.506 billion (2023 est.)
-$3.874 billion (2022 est.)
$766.788 million (2021 est.)
note: balance of payments - net trade and primary/secondary income in current dollars
comparison ranking: 50

Exports: $61.101 billion (2023 est.)
$61.444 billion (2022 est.)
$53.397 billion (2021 est.)
note: balance of payments - exports of goods and services in current dollars
comparison ranking: 59

Exports - partners: Latvia 13%, Poland 8%, Germany 8%, Russia 6%, US 6% (2022)
note: top five export partners based on percentage share of exports

Exports - commodities: refined petroleum, furniture, plastic products, natural gas, wheat (2022)
note: top five export commodities based on value in dollars

Imports: $58.104 billion (2023 est.)
$62.853 billion (2022 est.)
$50.377 billion (2021 est.)
note: balance of payments - imports of goods and services in current dollars
comparison ranking: 63

Imports - partners: Poland 12%, Germany 11%, Latvia 8%, US 6%, Russia 5% (2022)
note: top five import partners based on percentage share of imports

Imports - commodities: crude petroleum, natural gas, electricity, cars, plastic products (2022)
note: top five import commodities based on value in dollars

Reserves of foreign exchange and gold: $6.168 billion (2023 est.)
$5.365 billion (2022 est.)
$5.58 billion (2021 est.)
note: holdings of gold (year-end prices)/foreign exchange/special drawing rights in current dollars
comparison ranking: 98

Exchange rates: euros (EUR) per US dollar -

Exchange rates: 0.925 (2023 est.)
0.95 (2022 est.)
0.845 (2021 est.)
0.876 (2020 est.)
0.893 (2019 est.)

ENERGY

Electricity access: *electrification - total population:* 100% (2022 est.)

Electricity: *installed generating capacity:* 4.258 million kW (2022 est.)
consumption: 11.227 billion kWh (2022 est.)
exports: 2.652 billion kWh (2022 est.)
imports: 11.22 billion kWh (2022 est.)
transmission/distribution losses: 855.476 million kWh (2022 est.)
comparison rankings: transmission/distribution losses 91; imports 24; exports 51; consumption 98; installed generating capacity 95

Electricity generation sources: *fossil fuels:* 28.1% of total installed capacity (2022 est.)
solar: 4.7% of total installed capacity (2022 est.)
wind: 42.8% of total installed capacity (2022 est.)
hydroelectricity: 6.6% of total installed capacity (2022 est.)
biomass and waste: 17.8% of total installed capacity (2022 est.)

Nuclear energy: Number of nuclear reactors permanently shut down: 2 (2023)

Coal: *consumption:* 263,000 metric tons (2022 est.)
exports: 154,000 metric tons (2022 est.)
imports: 496,000 metric tons (2022 est.)

Petroleum: *total petroleum production:* 4,000 bbl/day (2023 est.)
refined petroleum consumption: 68,000 bbl/day (2023 est.)
crude oil estimated reserves: 12 million barrels (2021 est.)

Natural gas: *consumption:* 1.601 billion cubic meters (2022 est.)
exports: 1.921 billion cubic meters (2022 est.)
imports: 3.53 billion cubic meters (2022 est.)

Carbon dioxide emissions: 12.803 million metric tonnes of CO2 (2022 est.)
from coal and metallurgical coke: 586,000 metric tonnes of CO2 (2022 est.)
from petroleum and other liquids: 9.115 million metric tonnes of CO2 (2022 est.)
from consumed natural gas: 3.102 million metric tonnes of CO2 (2022 est.)
comparison ranking: total emissions 100

Energy consumption per capita: 85.201 million Btu/person (2022 est.)
comparison ranking: 63

COMMUNICATIONS

Telephones - fixed lines: *total subscriptions:* 250,000 (2022 est.)
subscriptions per 100 inhabitants: 9 (2022 est.)
comparison ranking: total subscriptions 117

Telephones - mobile cellular: *total subscriptions:* 3.826 million (2022 est.)
subscriptions per 100 inhabitants: 139 (2022 est.)
comparison ranking: total subscriptions 136

Telecommunication systems: *general assessment:* Lithuania's small telecoms market is among the more advanced in Europe, particularly given the universal access to long-term evolution (LTE) infrastructure and the extensive fiber footprint; Operator investment has been focused on fiber broadband and mobile network upgrades; Fiber is now by far the dominant fixed broadband platform, with the number of Digital Subscriber Line (DSL) and cable connections in steady decline; LTE services are available nationally, operators have made steady investments in 5G (2024)
domestic: nearly 9 per 100 for fixed-line subscriptions; mobile-cellular subscriptions at 139 per 100 persons (2022)
international: country code - 370; landing points for the BCS East, BCS East-West Interlink and NordBalt connecting Lithuania to Sweden, and Latvia ; further transmission by satellite; landline connections to Latvia and Poland (2019)

Broadcast media: public broadcaster operates 3 channels with the third channel - a satellite channel - introduced in 2007; various privately owned commercial TV broadcasters operate national and multiple regional channels; many privately owned local TV stations; multi-channel cable and satellite TV services available; publicly owned broadcaster operates 3 radio networks; many privately owned commercial broadcasters, with repeater stations in various regions throughout the country

Internet country code: .lt

Internet users: *total:* 2.436 million (2021 est.)
percent of population: 87% (2021 est.)
comparison ranking: total 130

Broadband - fixed subscriptions: *total:* 796,814 (2020 est.)
subscriptions per 100 inhabitants: 29 (2020 est.)
comparison ranking: total 77

TRANSPORTATION

National air transport system: *number of registered air carriers:* 3 (2020)
inventory of registered aircraft operated by air carriers: 50
annual passenger traffic on registered air carriers: 26,031 (2018)

Civil aircraft registration country code prefix: LY

Airports: 65 (2024)
comparison ranking: 74

Heliports: 2 (2024)

Pipelines: 1,921 km gas, 121 km refined products (2013)

Railways: *total:* 1,911 km (2020) 152 km electrified
comparison ranking: total 74

Roadways: *total:* 83,821 km (2022)
comparison ranking: total 60

Waterways: 441 km (2007) (navigable year-round)
comparison ranking: 95

Merchant marine: *total:* 59 (2023)
by type: container ship 3, general cargo 19, oil tanker 2, other 35
comparison ranking: total 114

Ports: *total ports:* 2 (2024)
large: 0
medium: 1
small: 0
very small: 1
ports with oil terminals: 2
key ports: Butinge Oil Terminal, Klaipeda

MILITARY AND SECURITY

Military and security forces: Lithuanian Armed Forces (Lietuvos Ginkluotosios Pajegos): Land Forces (Sausumos Pajegos), Naval Forces (Karines Juru Pajegos), Air Forces (Karines Oro Pajegos), Special Operations Forces (Specialiuju Operaciju Pajegos); National Defense Volunteer Forces (Krašto Apsaugos Savanorių Pajegos or KASP); National Riflemen's Union (Lietuvos šaulių sąjunga) (2024)
note 1: the National Rifleman's Union is a civilian paramilitary organization supported by the Lithuanian Government that cooperates with the military but is not part of it; however, in a state of war, its armed formations would fall under the armed forces
note 2: the Lithuanian Police and State Border Guard Service are under the Ministry of Interior; in wartime, the State Border Guard Service becomes part of the armed forces

Military expenditures: 2.9% of GDP (2024 est.)
2.8% of GDP (2023)
2.5% of GDP (2022)
2% of GDP (2021)
2.1% of GDP (2020)
comparison ranking: 38

Military and security service personnel strengths: approximately 18,000 active-duty personnel (14,000 Army, including about 5,000 active National Defense Voluntary Forces); 500 Navy; 1,000 Air Force; 2,500 other, including special operations forces, logistics support, training, etc) (2024)

Military equipment inventories and acquisitions: the military's inventory is a mix of mostly European and US weapons and equipment (2024)

Military service age and obligation: 19-26 years of age for conscripted military service for men; 9-month service obligation; in 2015, Lithuania reinstated conscription after having converted to a professional military in 2008; 18-38 for voluntary service for men and women (2024)
note 1: Lithuania conscripts up to 4,000 males each year; conscripts are selected using an automated lottery system
note 2: as of 2020, women comprised about 12% of the military's full-time personnel

Military deployments: *note:* contributes about 350-550 troops to the Lithuania, Poland, and Ukraine joint military brigade (LITPOLUKRBRIG), which was established in 2014; the brigade is headquartered in Poland and is comprised of an international staff, three battalions, and specialized units; units affiliated with the multinational brigade remain within the structures of the armed forces of their respective countries until the brigade is activated for participation in an international operation

Military - note: the Lithuanian Armed Forces are responsible for the defense of the country's interests, sovereignty, and territory, fulfilling Lithuania's commitments to NATO and European security, and contributing to UN international peacekeeping efforts; Russia is Lithuania's primary security focus, which has only increased since the Russian seizure of Crimea in 2014 and subsequent full-scale attack on Ukraine in 2022; Lithuania has been a member of NATO since 2004 and is reliant on the Alliance as the country's security guarantor; it is actively engaged in both NATO and EU security, as well as bilaterally with allies such as the other Baltic States, Germany, Poland, the UK, Ukraine, and the US; the Lithuanian military has participated in NATO and EU missions abroad and regularly conducts training and exercises with NATO and EU partner forces; it hosts NATO forces, is a member of the UK-led Joint Expeditionary Force, and contributes troops to a multinational brigade with Poland and Ukraine; Lithuania participated in its first UN peacekeeping mission in 1994
since 2017, Lithuania has hosted a German-led multinational NATO ground force battlegroup as part of the Alliance's Enhanced Forward Presence initiative; NATO has also provided air protection for Lithuania since 2004 through its Baltic Air Policing mission; NATO member countries that possess air combat capabilities voluntarily contribute to the mission on four-month rotations; NATO fighter aircraft are hosted at Lithuania's Šiauliai Air Base (2024)

TRANSNATIONAL ISSUES

Refugees and internally displaced persons: *refugees (country of origin):* 41,490 (Ukraine) (as of 11 March 2024)
stateless persons: 2,720 (2022)

Illicit drugs: source country for amphetamine tablets

LUXEMBOURG

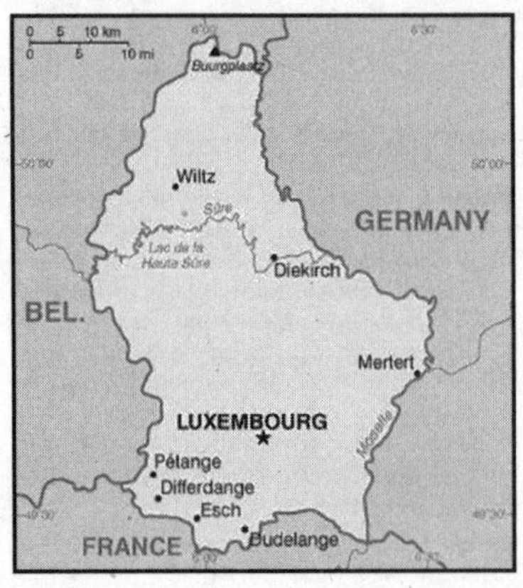

INTRODUCTION

Background: Founded in 963, Luxembourg became a grand duchy in 1815 and a constituent part of the Kingdom of the Netherlands after the Congress of Vienna. When Belgium declared independence from the Netherlands in 1839, Luxembourg lost more than half of its territory to Belgium but gained a larger measure of autonomy within the Kingdom of the Netherlands. Luxembourg gained full independence in 1867 by promising to remain permanently neutral. Overrun by Germany in both world wars, its neutrality ended in 1948 when it entered into the Benelux Customs Union and joined NATO the following year. In 1957, Luxembourg became one of the six founding countries of the EEC (later the EU), and in 1999 it joined the euro currency zone.

GEOGRAPHY

Location: Western Europe, between France and Germany

Geographic coordinates: 49 45 N, 6 10 E

Map references: Europe

Area: *total:* 2,586 sq km
land: 2,586 sq km
water: 0 sq km
comparison ranking: total 178

Area - comparative: slightly smaller than Rhode Island; about half the size of Delaware

Land boundaries: *total:* 327 km
border countries (3): Belgium 130 km; France 69 km; Germany 128 km

Coastline: 0 km (landlocked)

Maritime claims: none (landlocked)

Climate: modified continental with mild winters, cool summers

Terrain: mostly gently rolling uplands with broad, shallow valleys; uplands to slightly mountainous in the north; steep slope down to Moselle flood plain in the southeast

Elevation: *highest point:* Buurgplaatz 559 m
lowest point: Moselle River 133 m
mean elevation: 325 m

Natural resources: iron ore (no longer exploited), arable land

Land use: *agricultural land:* 50.7% (2018 est.)
arable land: 24% (2018 est.)
permanent crops: 0.6% (2018 est.)
permanent pasture: 26.1% (2018 est.)
forest: 33.5% (2018 est.)
other: 15.8% (2018 est.)

Irrigated land: 0 sq km (2012)

Major watersheds (area sq km): Atlantic Ocean drainage: Rhine-Maas (198,735 sq km)

Population distribution: most people live in the south, on or near the border with France

Natural hazards: occasional flooding

Geography - note: landlocked; the only grand duchy in the world

PEOPLE AND SOCIETY

Population: *total:* 671,254
male: 338,702
female: 332,552 (2024 est.)
comparison rankings: female 169; male 168; total 168

Nationality: *noun:* Luxembourger(s)
adjective: Luxembourg

Ethnic groups: Luxembourger 52.9%, Portuguese 14.5%, French 7.6%, Italian 3.7%, Belgian 3%, German 2%, Spanish 1.3%, Romania 1%, other 14% (2022 est.)
note: data represent population by nationality

Languages: Luxembourgish (official administrative, judicial, and national language) 48.9%, Portuguese 15.4%, French (official administrative, judicial, and legislative language) 14.9%, Italian 3.6%, English 3.6%, German (official administrative and judicial language) 2.9%, other 10.8% (2021 est.)

Religions: Christian (predominantly Roman Catholic) 70.6%, Muslim 2.3%, other (includes Buddhist, folk religions, Hindu, Jewish) 0.4%, unaffiliated 26.7% (2020 est.)

Age structure: *0-14 years:* 16.7% (male 57,921/female 54,484)
15-64 years: 67.1% (male 231,214/female 219,497)
65 years and over: 16.1% (2024 est.) (male 49,567/female 58,571)

Dependency ratios: *total dependency ratio:* 44.2
youth dependency ratio: 23
elderly dependency ratio: 21.3
potential support ratio: 4.7 (2021 est.)

Median age: *total:* 39.9 years (2024 est.)
male: 39.4 years
female: 40.4 years
comparison ranking: total 64

Population growth rate: 1.52% (2024 est.)
comparison ranking: 63

Birth rate: 11.6 births/1,000 population (2024 est.)
comparison ranking: 155

Death rate: 7.1 deaths/1,000 population (2024 est.)
comparison ranking: 116

Net migration rate: 10.8 migrant(s)/1,000 population (2024 est.)
comparison ranking: 8

Population distribution: most people live in the south, on or near the border with France

Urbanization: *urban population:* 92.1% of total population (2023)
rate of urbanization: 1.43% annual rate of change (2020-25 est.)

Major urban areas - population: 120,000 LUXEMBOURG (capital) (2018)

Sex ratio: *at birth:* 1.06 male(s)/female
0-14 years: 1.06 male(s)/female
15-64 years: 1.05 male(s)/female
65 years and over: 0.85 male(s)/female
total population: 1.02 male(s)/female (2024 est.)

Mother's mean age at first birth: 31 years (2020 est.)

Maternal mortality ratio: 6 deaths/100,000 live births (2020 est.)
comparison ranking: 159

Infant mortality rate: *total:* 3.2 deaths/1,000 live births (2024 est.)
male: 3.6 deaths/1,000 live births
female: 2.8 deaths/1,000 live births
comparison ranking: total 203

Life expectancy at birth: *total population:* 83.4 years (2024 est.)
male: 80.9 years
female: 85.9 years
comparison ranking: total population 14

Total fertility rate: 1.63 children born/woman (2024 est.)
comparison ranking: 175

Gross reproduction rate: 0.79 (2024 est.)

Drinking water source: *improved: urban:* 100% of population
rural: 98.6% of population
total: 99.9% of population
unimproved: urban: 0% of population
rural: 1.4% of population
total: 0.1% of population (2020 est.)

Current health expenditure: 5.8% of GDP (2020)

Physician density: 3.01 physicians/1,000 population (2017)

Hospital bed density: 4.3 beds/1,000 population (2019)

Sanitation facility access: *improved: urban:* 100% of population
rural: 99.9% of population
total: 100% of population
unimproved: urban: 0% of population
rural: 0.1% of population
total: 0% of population (2020 est.)

Obesity - adult prevalence rate: 22.6% (2016)
comparison ranking: 74

Alcohol consumption per capita: *total:* 11 liters of pure alcohol (2019 est.)
beer: 4.04 liters of pure alcohol (2019 est.)
wine: 4.73 liters of pure alcohol (2019 est.)
spirits: 2.14 liters of pure alcohol (2019 est.)
other alcohols: 0 liters of pure alcohol (2019 est.)
comparison ranking: total 11

Tobacco use: *total:* 21.1% (2020 est.)
male: 22.4% (2020 est.)
female: 19.8% (2020 est.)
comparison ranking: total 78

Currently married women (ages 15-49): 51.4% (2023 est.)

Education expenditures: 5% of GDP (2020 est.)
comparison ranking: 78

School life expectancy (primary to tertiary education): *total:* 15 years
male: 15 years
female: 15 years (2020)

ENVIRONMENT

Environment - current issues: air and water pollution in urban areas, soil pollution of farmland; unsustainable patterns of consumption (transport, energy, recreation, space) threaten biodiversity and landscapes

Environment - international agreements: *party to:* Air Pollution, Air Pollution-Heavy Metals, Air Pollution-Multi-effect Protocol, Air Pollution-Nitrogen Oxides, Air Pollution-Persistent Organic Pollutants, Air Pollution-Sulphur 85, Air Pollution-Sulphur 94, Air Pollution-Volatile Organic Compounds, Biodiversity, Climate Change, Climate Change-Kyoto Protocol, Climate Change-Paris Agreement, Comprehensive Nuclear Test Ban, Desertification, Endangered Species, Hazardous Wastes, Law of the Sea, Marine Dumping-London Convention, Marine Dumping-London Protocol, Nuclear Test Ban, Ozone Layer Protection, Ship Pollution, Tropical Timber 2006, Wetlands, Whaling
signed, but not ratified: Environmental Modification

Climate: modified continental with mild winters, cool summers

Urbanization: *urban population:* 92.1% of total population (2023)
rate of urbanization: 1.43% annual rate of change (2020-25 est.)

Revenue from forest resources: 0.01% of GDP (2018 est.)
comparison ranking: 155

Revenue from coal: 0% of GDP (2018 est.)
comparison ranking: 81

Air pollutants: *particulate matter emissions:* 8.89 micrograms per cubic meter (2019 est.)
carbon dioxide emissions: 8.99 megatons (2016 est.)
methane emissions: 0.61 megatons (2020 est.)

Waste and recycling: *municipal solid waste generated annually:* 356,000 tons (2015 est.)
municipal solid waste recycled annually: 100,997 tons (2015 est.)
percent of municipal solid waste recycled: 28.4% (2015 est.)

Major watersheds (area sq km): Atlantic Ocean drainage: Rhine-Maas (198,735 sq km)

Total water withdrawal: *municipal:* 50 million cubic meters (2020 est.)
industrial: 1.6 million cubic meters (2017 est.)
agricultural: 400,000 cubic meters (2017 est.)

Total renewable water resources: 3.5 billion cubic meters (2020 est.)

Geoparks: *total global geoparks and regional networks:* 1
global geoparks and regional networks: Mëllerdall (2023)

GOVERNMENT

Country name: *conventional long form:* Grand Duchy of Luxembourg
conventional short form: Luxembourg

local long form: Grand Duché de Luxembourg
local short form: Luxembourg
etymology: the name derives from the Celtic "lucilem" (little) and the German "burg" (castle or fortress) to produce the meaning of the "little castle"; the name is actually ironic, since for centuries the Fortress of Luxembourg was one of Europe's most formidable fortifications; the name passed to the surrounding city and then to the country itself

Government type: constitutional monarchy

Capital: *name:* Luxembourg
geographic coordinates: 49 36 N, 6 07 E
time difference: UTC+1 (6 hours ahead of Washington, DC, during Standard Time)
daylight saving time: +1hr, begins last Sunday in March; ends last Sunday in October
etymology: the name derives from the Celtic *lucilem* (little) and the German *burg* (castle or fortress) to produce the meaning of the "little castle"; the name is actually ironic, since for centuries the Fortress of Luxembourg was one of Europe's most formidable fortifications; the name passed to the city that grew around the fortress

Administrative divisions: 12 cantons (cantons, singular - canton); Capellen, Clervaux, Diekirch, Echternach, Esch-sur-Alzette, Grevenmacher, Luxembourg, Mersch, Redange, Remich, Vianden, Wiltz

Independence: 1839 (from the Netherlands)

National holiday: National Day (birthday of Grand Duke HENRI), 23 June; note - this date of birth is not the true date of birth for any of the Royals, but the national festivities were shifted in 1962 to allow observance during a more favorable time of year

Legal system: civil law system

Constitution: *history:* previous 1842 (heavily amended 1848, 1856); latest effective 17 October 1868
amendments: proposed by the Chamber of Deputies or by the monarch to the Chamber; passage requires at least two-thirds majority vote by the Chamber in two successive readings three months apart; a referendum can be substituted for the second reading if approved by more than a quarter of the Chamber members or by 25,000 valid voters; adoption by referendum requires a majority of all valid voters; amended many times, last in 2020

International law organization participation: accepts compulsory ICJ jurisdiction; accepts ICCt jurisdiction

Citizenship: *citizenship by birth:* limited to situations where the parents are either unknown, stateless, or when the nationality law of the parents' state of origin does not permit acquisition of citizenship by descent when the birth occurs outside of national territory
citizenship by descent only: at least one parent must be a citizen of Luxembourg
dual citizenship recognized: yes
residency requirement for naturalization: 7 years

Suffrage: 18 years of age; universal and compulsory

Executive branch: *chief of state:* Grand Duke HENRI (since 7 October 2000)
head of government: Prime Minister Luc FRIEDEN (since 17 November 2023)
cabinet: Council of Ministers recommended by the prime minister, appointed by the monarch
elections/appointments: the monarchy is hereditary; following elections to the Chamber of Deputies, the leader of the majority party or majority coalition usually appointed prime minister by the monarch; deputy prime minister appointed by the monarch; prime minister and deputy prime minister are responsible to the Chamber of Deputies

Legislative branch: *description:* unicameral Chamber of Deputies or Chambre des Deputes (60 seats; members directly elected in multi-seat constituencies by party-list proportional representation vote; members serve 5-year terms); note - a 21-member Council of State appointed by the Grand Duke on the advice of the prime minister serves as an advisory body to the Chamber of Deputies
elections: last held on 8 October 2023 (next to be held by 31 October 2028)
election results: percent of vote by party - CSV 29.2%, LSAP 18.9%, DP 18.7%, ADR 9.3%, Green Party 8.6%, Pirate Party 6.7%, The Left 3.9%; seats by party - CSV 21, DP 14, LSAP 11, ADR 5, Green Party 4, Pirate Party 3, The Left 2; composition - men 40, women 20, percentage women 33.3%

Judicial branch: *highest court(s):* Supreme Court of Justice includes Court of Appeal and Court of Cassation (consists of 27 judges on 9 benches); Constitutional Court (consists of 9 members)
judge selection and term of office: judges of both courts appointed by the monarch for life
subordinate courts: Court of Accounts; district and local tribunals and courts

Political parties: Alternative Democratic Reform Party or ADR
Christian Social People's Party or CSV
Democratic Party or DP
Green Party
Luxembourg Socialist Workers' Party or LSAP
Pirate Party
The Left (dei Lenk/la Gauche)

International organization participation: ADB (nonregional member), Australia Group, Benelux, BIS, CD, CE, EAPC, EBRD, ECB, EIB, EMU, ESA, EU, FAO, FATF, IAEA, IBRD, ICAO, ICC (national committees), ICCt, ICRM, IDA, IEA, IFAD, IFC, IFRCS, ILO, IMF, IMO, Interpol, IOC, IOM, IPU, ISO, ITSO, ITU, ITUC (NGOs), MIGA, NATO, NEA, NSG, OAS (observer), OECD, OIF, OPCW, OSCE, PCA, Schengen Convention, UN, UNCTAD, UNESCO, UNHCR, UNHRC, UNIDO, UNRWA, UPU, Wassenaar Arrangement, WCO, WHO, WIPO, WMO, WTO, ZC

Diplomatic representation in the US: *chief of mission:* Ambassador Nicole BINTNER-BAKSHIAN (since 15 August 2021)
chancery: 2200 Massachusetts Avenue NW, Washington, DC 20008
telephone: [1] (202) 265-4171
FAX: [1] (202) 328-8270
email address and website:
washington.amb@mae.etat.lu
https://washington.mae.lu/en.html
consulate(s) general: New York, San Francisco

Diplomatic representation from the US: *chief of mission:* Ambassador Thomas M. BARRETT (since 10 February 2022)
embassy: 22 Boulevard Emmanuel Servais, L-2535 Luxembourg City
mailing address: 5380 Luxembourg Place, Washington DC 20521-5380
telephone: [352] 46-01-23-00
FAX: [352] 46-14-01
email address and website: Luxembourgconsular@state.gov
https://lu.usembassy.gov/

Flag description: three equal horizontal bands of red (top), white, and light blue; similar to the flag of the Netherlands, which uses a darker blue and is shorter; the coloring is derived from the Grand Duke's coat of arms (a red lion on a white and blue striped field)

National symbol(s): red, rampant lion; national colors: red, white, light blue

National anthem: *name:* "Ons Heemecht" (Our Motherland); "De Wilhelmus" (The William)
lyrics/music: Michel LENTZ/Jean-Antoine ZINNEN; Nikolaus WELTER/unknown
note: "Ons Heemecht," adopted 1864, is the national anthem, while "De Wilhelmus," adopted 1919, serves as a royal anthem for use when members of the grand ducal family enter or exit a ceremony in Luxembourg

National heritage: *total World Heritage Sites:* 1 (cultural)
selected World Heritage Site locales: Luxembourg City Old Quarters and Fortifications

ECONOMY

Economic overview: high-income EU and eurozone economy; global, highly capitalized banking sector; one of highest GDP-per-capita countries; trending toward recovery after economic contraction from energy-driven inflation, reduced exports and investments, and financial sector weakness

Real GDP (purchasing power parity): $88.533 billion (2023 est.)
$89.514 billion (2022 est.)
$88.295 billion (2021 est.)
note: data in 2021 dollars
comparison ranking: 99

Real GDP growth rate: -1.1% (2023 est.)
1.38% (2022 est.)
7.17% (2021 est.)
note: annual GDP % growth based on constant local currency
comparison ranking: 201

Real GDP per capita: $132,400 (2023 est.)
$137,100 (2022 est.)
$137,900 (2021 est.)
note: data in 2021 dollars
comparison ranking: 1

GDP (official exchange rate): $85.755 billion (2023 est.)
note: data in current dollars at official exchange rate

Inflation rate (consumer prices): 3.74% (2023 est.)
6.34% (2022 est.)
2.53% (2021 est.)
note: annual % change based on consumer prices
comparison ranking: 75

Credit ratings: Fitch rating: AAA (1994)

Moody's rating: Aaa (1989)

Standard & Poors rating: AAA (1994)
note: The year refers to the year in which the current credit rating was first obtained.

GDP - composition, by sector of origin: *agriculture:* 0.2% (2023 est.)
industry: 10.5% (2023 est.)
services: 80.6% (2023 est.)
note: figures may not total 100% due to non-allocated consumption not captured in sector-reported data
comparison rankings: services 14; industry 191; agriculture 209

GDP - composition, by end use: *household consumption:* 32.2% (2023 est.)
government consumption: 19% (2023 est.)
investment in fixed capital: 18.1% (2023 est.)
investment in inventories: -0.2% (2023 est.)
exports of goods and services: 212.5% (2023 est.)
imports of goods and services: -181.7% (2023 est.)
note: figures may not total 100% due to rounding or gaps in data collection

Agricultural products: milk, wheat, barley, triticale, potatoes, pork, grapes, beef, oats, rapeseed (2022)
note: top ten agricultural products based on tonnage

Industries: banking and financial services, construction, real estate services, iron, metals, and steel, information technology, telecommunications, cargo transportation and logistics, chemicals, engineering, tires, glass, aluminum, tourism, biotechnology

Industrial production growth rate: 0.49% (2023 est.)
note: annual % change in industrial value added based on constant local currency
comparison ranking: 149

Labor force: 352,000 (2023 est.)
note: number of people ages 15 or older who are employed or seeking work
comparison ranking: 166

Unemployment rate: 5.19% (2023 est.)
4.59% (2022 est.)
5.25% (2021 est.)
note: % of labor force seeking employment
comparison ranking: 98

Youth unemployment rate (ages 15-24): *total:* 19% (2023 est.)
male: 15.7% (2023 est.)
female: 22.9% (2023 est.)
note: % of labor force ages 15-24 seeking employment
comparison ranking: total 70

Population below poverty line: 17.3% (2021 est.)
note: % of population with income below national poverty line

Gini Index coefficient - distribution of family income: 32.7 (2021 est.)
note: index (0-100) of income distribution; higher values represent greater inequality
comparison ranking: 104

Household income or consumption by percentage share: *lowest 10%:* 2.8% (2021 est.)
highest 10%: 24.6% (2021 est.)
note: % share of income accruing to lowest and highest 10% of population

Remittances: 2.72% of GDP (2023 est.)
2.72% of GDP (2022 est.)
2.83% of GDP (2021 est.)
note: personal transfers and compensation between resident and non-resident individuals/households/entities

Budget: *revenues:* $33.533 billion (2022 est.)
expenditures: $33.054 billion (2022 est.)
note: central government revenues (excluding grants) and expenses converted to US dollars at average official exchange rate for year indicated

Public debt: 23% of GDP (2017 est.)
note: data cover general government debt and include debt instruments issued (or owned) by government entities other than the treasury; the data include treasury debt held by foreign entities; the data include debt issued by subnational entities, as well as intragovernmental debt; intragovernmental debt consists of treasury borrowings from surpluses in the social funds, such as for retirement, medical care, and unemployment; debt instruments for the social funds are not sold at public auctions
comparison ranking: 179

Taxes and other revenues: 25.97% (of GDP) (2022 est.)
note: central government tax revenue as a % of GDP
comparison ranking: 40

Current account balance: $5.826 billion (2023 est.)
$6.168 billion (2022 est.)
$6.819 billion (2021 est.)
note: balance of payments - net trade and primary/secondary income in current dollars
comparison ranking: 31

Exports: $176.133 billion (2023 est.)
$172.145 billion (2022 est.)
$184.932 billion (2021 est.)
note: balance of payments - exports of goods and services in current dollars
comparison ranking: 36

Exports - partners: Germany 20%, France 15%, Belgium 10%, Netherlands 8%, Italy 4% (2022)
note: top five export partners based on percentage share of exports

Exports - commodities: iron blocks, plastic products, rubber tires, plastics, gas turbines (2022)
note: top five export commodities based on value in dollars

Imports: $146.807 billion (2023 est.)
$141.761 billion (2022 est.)
$152.01 billion (2021 est.)
note: balance of payments - imports of goods and services in current dollars
comparison ranking: 39

Imports - partners: Belgium 26%, Germany 26%, France 11%, Netherlands 6%, US 3% (2022)
note: top five import partners based on percentage share of imports

Imports - commodities: refined petroleum, cars, electricity, natural gas, scrap iron (2022)
note: top five import commodities based on value in dollars

Reserves of foreign exchange and gold: $2.977 billion (2023 est.)
$2.874 billion (2022 est.)
$2.921 billion (2021 est.)
note: holdings of gold (year-end prices)/foreign exchange/special drawing rights in current dollars
comparison ranking: 137

Exchange rates: euros (EUR) per US dollar -

Exchange rates: 0.925 (2023 est.)
0.95 (2022 est.)
0.845 (2021 est.)
0.876 (2020 est.)
0.893 (2019 est.)

ENERGY

Electricity access: *electrification - total population:* 100% (2022 est.)

Electricity: *installed generating capacity:* 2.002 million kW (2022 est.)
consumption: 6.122 billion kWh (2022 est.)
exports: 1.639 billion kWh (2022 est.)
imports: 7.146 billion kWh (2022 est.)
transmission/distribution losses: 147.934 million kWh (2022 est.)
comparison rankings: transmission/distribution losses 58; imports 36; exports 60; consumption 124; installed generating capacity 122

Electricity generation sources: *fossil fuels:* 13.6% of total installed capacity (2022 est.)
solar: 28% of total installed capacity (2022 est.)
wind: 43.4% of total installed capacity (2022 est.)
hydroelectricity: -40.1% of total installed capacity (2022 est.) note: Luxembourg has negative net hydroelectric power generation based on losses from use of pumped storage hydropower
biomass and waste: 55.1% of total installed capacity (2022 est.)

Coal: *consumption:* 62,000 metric tons (2022 est.)
exports: 30.2 metric tons (2022 est.)
imports: 3,000 metric tons (2022 est.)

Petroleum: *refined petroleum consumption:* 51,000 bbl/day (2023 est.)

Natural gas: *consumption:* 594.24 million cubic meters (2022 est.)
imports: 590.144 million cubic meters (2022 est.)

Carbon dioxide emissions: 8.694 million metric tonnes of CO2 (2022 est.)
from coal and metallurgical coke: 135,000 metric tonnes of CO2 (2022 est.)
from petroleum and other liquids: 7.338 million metric tonnes of CO2 (2022 est.)
from consumed natural gas: 1.221 million metric tonnes of CO2 (2022 est.)
comparison ranking: total emissions 111

Energy consumption per capita: 232.384 million Btu/person (2022 est.)
comparison ranking: 14

COMMUNICATIONS

Telephones - fixed lines: *total subscriptions:* 261,000 (2022 est.)
subscriptions per 100 inhabitants: 40 (2022 est.)
comparison ranking: total subscriptions 114

Telephones - mobile cellular: *total subscriptions:* 876,000 (2021 est.)
subscriptions per 100 inhabitants: 137 (2021 est.)
comparison ranking: total subscriptions 166

Telecommunication systems: *general assessment:* Luxembourg has a small telecom sector; there remains some pressure from regulatory measures, though no further reductions to fixed and mobile interconnection tariffs have been imposed through to 2024; high mobile penetration has slowed subscriber growth in the mobile market since 2005, though a recent law requiring SIM card registration has not had an adverse effect on the number of mobile subscribers despite network operators deactivating unregistered cards (2021)
domestic: fixed-line teledensity about 42 per 100 persons; 140 per 100 mobile-cellular subscriptions (2021)
international: country code - 352

Broadcast media: Luxembourg has a long tradition of operating radio and TV services for pan-European audiences and is home to Europe's largest privately owned broadcast media group, the RTL Group, which operates 46 TV stations and 29 radio stations in Europe; also home to Europe's largest satellite operator, Societe Europeenne des Satellites (SES); domestically, the RTL Group operates TV and radio networks; other domestic private radio and TV operators and French and German stations available; satellite and cable TV services available

Internet country code: .lu

Internet users: *total:* 633,600 (2021 est.)
percent of population: 99% (2021 est.)

comparison ranking: total 163

Broadband - fixed subscriptions: *total:* 235,155 (2020 est.)
subscriptions per 100 inhabitants: 38 (2020 est.)
comparison ranking: total 113

TRANSPORTATION

National air transport system: *number of registered air carriers:* 4 (2020)
inventory of registered aircraft operated by air carriers: 66
annual passenger traffic on registered air carriers: 2,099,102 (2018)
annual freight traffic on registered air carriers: 7,323,040,000 (2018) mt-km

Civil aircraft registration country code prefix: LX

Airports: 3 (2024)
comparison ranking: 194

Heliports: 11 (2024)

Pipelines: 142 km gas, 27 km refined products (2013)

Railways: *total:* 271 km (2020) 262 km electrified
comparison ranking: total 125

Roadways: *total:* 2,746 km (2022)
comparison ranking: total 168

Waterways: 37 km (2010) (on Moselle River)
comparison ranking: 115

Merchant marine: *total:* 147 (2023)
by type: bulk carrier 3, container ship 1, general cargo 24, oil tanker 4, other 115
comparison ranking: total 76

MILITARY AND SECURITY

Military and security forces: Luxembourg Army (l'Armée Luxembourgeoise) (2024)
note: the Grand Ducal Police maintain internal security and report to the Ministry of Internal Security

Military expenditures: 1.3% of GDP (2024 est.)
1% of GDP (2023)
0.6% of GDP (2022)
0.5% of GDP (2021)
0.6% of GDP (2020)
comparison ranking: 112

Military and security service personnel strengths: approximately 900 active-duty personnel (2024)

Military equipment inventories and acquisitions: the inventory of Luxembourg's Army is a small mix of Western origin equipment (2024)

Military service age and obligation: 18-26 years of age for voluntary military service for men and women; no conscription (abolished 1969) (2024)
note 1: since 2003, the Army has allowed EU citizens 18-24 years of age who have been a resident in the country for at least 36 months to volunteer
note 2: 2024, women made up about 12% of the military's full-time personnel

Military - note: founded in 1881, the Luxembourg Army is responsible for the defense of the country and fulfilling the Grand Duchy's commitments to NATO, European security, and international peacekeeping, as well as providing support to civil authorities in the event of emergencies, such as floods or disease outbreaks; the Army is an active participant in EU, NATO, and UN missions and has contributed small numbers of troops to multinational operations in such places as Afghanistan, Bosnia and Herzegovina, Chad, Croatia, the Democratic Republic of the Congo, Iraq, Kosovo, Lebanon, North Macedonia, Mali, Mozambique, and Uganda; it trains and exercises regularly with EU and NATO partners and has contributed to the NATO battlegroup forward deployed in Lithuania since 2017; Luxembourg was one of the original 12 countries to sign the North Atlantic Treaty (also known as the Washington Treaty) establishing NATO in 1949
in 2015, Belgium, the Netherlands, and Luxembourg signed an agreement to conduct joint air policing of their territories; under the agreement, which went into effect in January 2017, the Belgian and Dutch Air Forces trade responsibility for patrolling the skies over the three countries (2024)

SPACE

Space agency/agencies: the Luxembourg Space Agency (LSA; established 2018) (2024)

Space program overview: aims to be the commercial space hub for Europe; LSA established largely to develop space policy, encourage and coordinate commercial space ventures, support space education, and to promote the country's space-related capabilities internationally; has a national space strategy; has set up policy and funding initiatives (such as LuxIMPULSE) aimed at encouraging space research, development, innovation, and entrepreneurship and attracting space-based industries; focused on developing commercial satellites and infrastructure (Luxembourg is home to some of the largest commercial satellite companies in the world), as well as other space sector capabilities and technologies, such as autonomous vehicles, robotics, remote sensing (RS), communications, and software; member of the European Space Agency (ESA), participates in ESA programs, and cooperates with individual ESA and EU member states; also has relations with other foreign space agencies and industries, including those of Canada, China, Japan, New Zealand, South Korea, the UAE, and the US (2024)
note: further details about the key activities, programs, and milestones of the country's space program, as well as government spending estimates on the space sector, appear in the Space Programs reference guide

TRANSNATIONAL ISSUES

Refugees and internally displaced persons: *refugees (country of origin):* 6,065 (Ukraine) (as of 11 August 2023)
stateless persons: 174 (2022)

MACAU

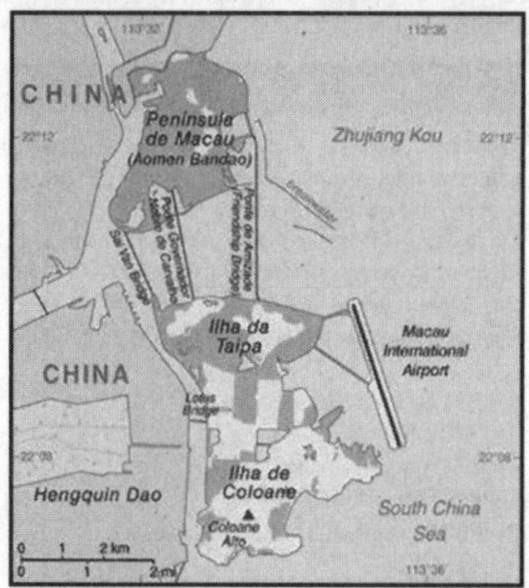

INTRODUCTION

Background: Portuguese ships began arriving in 1513. In the 1550s, Portuguese paying tribute to China settled in Macau, which became the official entrepôt for all international trade with China and Japan and the first European settlement in the Far East. The first governor was appointed in the 17th century, but the Portuguese remained largely under the control of the Chinese. In the 1930s and '40s Macau was declared a neutral territory during the Sino-Japanese War and World War II and became a refuge for both Chinese and Europeans. Portugal officially made Macau an overseas province in 1951.

In April 1987, Portugal and China reached an agreement to return Macau to Chinese rule in 1999, using the Hong Kong Joint Declaration between China and the UK as a model. In this agreement, China promised that, under its "one country, two systems" formula, China's political and economic system would not be imposed on Macau, and that Macau would enjoy a "high degree of autonomy" in all matters except foreign affairs and defense for the next 50 years. However, after China's multi-year crackdown against the pro-democracy movement in nearby Hong Kong, the governments of China and the Macau Special Administrative Region worked to limit Macau's political autonomy by suppressing opposition activity in the 2021 legislative elections.

GEOGRAPHY

Location: Eastern Asia, bordering the South China Sea and China

Geographic coordinates: 22 10 N, 113 33 E

Map references: Southeast Asia

Area: *total:* 28 sq km
land: 28.2 sq km
water: 0 sq km
comparison ranking: total 235

Area - comparative: less than one-sixth the size of Washington, DC

Land boundaries: *total:* 3 km
regional borders (l): China 3 km

Coastline: 41 km

Maritime claims: not specified

Climate: subtropical; marine with cool winters, warm summers

Terrain: generally flat

Elevation: *highest point:* Alto Coloane 172 m
lowest point: South China Sea 0 m

Natural resources: NEGL

Land use: *agricultural land:* 0% (2018 est.)
other: 100% (2018 est.)

Irrigated land: 0 sq km (2012)

Population distribution: population fairly equally distributed

Natural hazards: typhoons

Geography - note: essentially urban; an area of land reclaimed from the sea measuring 5.2 sq km and known as Cotai now connects the islands of Coloane and Taipa; the island area is connected to the mainland peninsula by three bridges

PEOPLE AND SOCIETY

Population: *total:* 644,426
male: 304,988
female: 339,438 (2024 est.)
comparison rankings: female 168; male 170; total 170

Nationality: *noun:* Chinese
adjective: Chinese

Ethnic groups: Chinese 89.4%, Chinese and Portuguese 1%, Portuguese 0.8%, Chinese and non-Portuguese 0.2%, Portuguese and others 0.2%, other 8.5% (2021 est.)

Languages: Cantonese 81%, Mandarin 4.7%, other Chinese dialects 5.4%, English 3.6%, Tagalog 2.9%, Portuguese 0.6%, other 1.8% (2021 est.)
major-language sample(s):
世界概况, 必須擁有的基本資料参考书
(Cantonese)
note: Chinese and Portuguese are official languages; Macanese or Patua, a Portuguese-based Creole, is also spoken

Religions: folk religion 58.9%, Buddhist 17.3%, Christian 7.2%, other 1.2%, none 15.4% (2020 est.)

Age structure: *0-14 years:* 14.4% (male 47,346/female 45,216)
15-64 years: 69.9% (male 210,059/female 240,577)
65 years and over: 15.7% (2024 est.) (male 47,583/female 53,645)

Dependency ratios: *total dependency ratio:* 36.9
youth dependency ratio: 20
elderly dependency ratio: 16.9
potential support ratio: 5.9 (2021 est.)

Median age: *total:* 42.5 years (2024 est.)
male: 41.5 years
female: 43.1 years
comparison ranking: total 43

Population growth rate: 0.67% (2024 est.)
comparison ranking: 132

Birth rate: 8.6 births/1,000 population (2024 est.)
comparison ranking: 204

Death rate: 4.9 deaths/1,000 population (2024 est.)
comparison ranking: 197

Net migration rate: 3.1 migrant(s)/1,000 population (2024 est.)
comparison ranking: 35

Population distribution: population fairly equally distributed

Urbanization: *urban population:* 100% of total population (2023)
rate of urbanization: 1.46% annual rate of change (2020-25 est.)

Major urban areas - population: 682,000 Macau (2023)

Sex ratio: *at birth:* 1.05 male(s)/female
0-14 years: 1.05 male(s)/female
15-64 years: 0.87 male(s)/female
65 years and over: 0.89 male(s)/female
total population: 0.9 male(s)/female (2024 est.)

Infant mortality rate: *total:* 4.4 deaths/1,000 live births (2024 est.)
male: 4.5 deaths/1,000 live births
female: 4.3 deaths/1,000 live births
comparison ranking: total 183

Life expectancy at birth: *total population:* 85.3 years (2024 est.)
male: 82.5 years
female: 88.3 years
comparison ranking: total population 3

Total fertility rate: 1.24 children born/woman (2024 est.)
comparison ranking: 222

Gross reproduction rate: 0.6 (2024 est.)

Contraceptive prevalence rate: NA

Drinking water source: *improved: urban:* 100% of population
rural: NA
total: 100% of population

Currently married women (ages 15-49): 53.5% (2023 est.)

Education expenditures: 6.3% of GDP (2020 est.)
comparison ranking: 36

Literacy: *definition:* age 15 and over can read and write
total population: 97.1%
male: 98.5%
female: 95.9% (2021)

School life expectancy (primary to tertiary education): *total:* 18 years
male: 17 years
female: 19 years (2021)

ENVIRONMENT

Environment - current issues: air pollution; coastal waters pollution; insufficient policies in reducing and recycling solid wastes; increasing population density worsening noise pollution

Climate: subtropical; marine with cool winters, warm summers

Urbanization: *urban population:* 100% of total population (2023)
rate of urbanization: 1.46% annual rate of change (2020-25 est.)

Revenue from forest resources: 0% of GDP (2018 est.)
comparison ranking: 204

Revenue from coal: 0% of GDP (2018 est.)
comparison ranking: 120

Air pollutants: *carbon dioxide emissions:* 2.07 megatons (2016 est.)

Waste and recycling: *municipal solid waste generated annually:* 377,942 tons (2016 est.)
municipal solid waste recycled annually: 75,588 tons (2014 est.)
percent of municipal solid waste recycled: 20% (2014 est.)

GOVERNMENT

Country name: *conventional long form:* Macau Special Administrative Region
conventional short form: Macau
official long form: Aomen Tebie Xingzhengqu (Chinese)/ Regiao Administrativa Especial de Macau (Portuguese)
official short form: Aomen (Chinese)/ Macau (Portuguese)
etymology: name is thought to derive from the A-Ma Temple - built in 1488 and dedicated to Mazu, the goddess of seafarers and fishermen - which is referred to locally as "Maa Gok" - and in Portuguese became "Macau"; the Chinese name Aomen means "inlet gates"

Government type: executive-led limited democracy; a special administrative region of the People's Republic of China

Dependency status: special administrative region of the People's Republic of China

Administrative divisions: none (special administrative region of the People's Republic of China)

Independence: none (special administrative region of China)

National holiday: National Day (anniversary of the Founding of the People's Republic of China), 1 October (1949); note - 20 December (1999) is celebrated as Macau Special Administrative Region Establishment Day

Legal system: civil law system based on the Portuguese model

Constitution: *history:* previous 1976 (Organic Statute of Macau, under Portuguese authority); latest adopted 31 March 1993, effective 20 December 1999 (Basic Law of the Macau Special Administrative Region of the People's Republic of China serves as Macau's constitution)
amendments: proposed by the Standing Committee of the National People's Congress (NPC), the People's Republic of China State Council, and the Macau Special Administrative Region; submittal of proposals to the NPC requires two-thirds majority vote by the Legislative Assembly of Macau, approval by two thirds of Macau's deputies to the NPC, and consent of the Macau chief executive; final passage requires approval by the NPC; amended 2005, 2012

Citizenship: see China

Suffrage: 18 years of age in direct elections for some legislative positions, universal for permanent residents living in Macau for the past 7 years; note - indirect elections are limited to organizations registered as "corporate voters" and an election committee for the chief executive drawn from broad regional groupings, municipal organizations, central government bodies, and elected Macau officials

Executive branch: *chief of state:* President of China XI Jinping (since 14 March 2013)
head of government: Chief Executive HO Iat Seng (since 20 December 2019)
cabinet: Executive Council appointed by the chief executive
elections/appointments: president indirectly elected by National People's Congress for a 5-year term (eligible for a second term); election last held on 10 March 2023 (next to be held in March 2028); chief executive chosen by a 400- member Election Committee for a 5-year term (eligible for a second term); election last held on 24 August 2019 (next to be held in 2024)
election results:
2019: HO Iat Seng (unopposed; received 392 out of 400 votes)
2014: Fernando CHUI Sai (unopposed; received 380 of 396 votes)

Legislative branch: *description:* unicameral Legislative Assembly or Regiao Administrativa Especial de Macau (33 seats; 14 members directly elected by proportional representation vote, 12 indirectly elected by an electoral college of professional and commercial interest groups, and 7 appointed by the chief executive; members serve 4-year terms)
elections: last held on 12 September 2021 (next to be held in September 2025)
election results: percent of vote - ACUM 20.1%, UPD 18%, NE 13.8%, UMG 12.7%, UPP 11.4%, ABL 10.8%, PS 6.6%, other 6.6%; seats by political group - ACUM 3, UPD 2, UGM 2, UPP 2, ABL 2, NE 2, PS 1; composition - men NA, women NA, percentage women NA%

Judicial branch: *highest court(s):* Court of Final Appeal of Macau Special Administrative Region (consists of the court president and 2 associate justices)
judge selection and term of office: justices appointed by the Macau chief executive upon the recommendation of an independent commission of judges, lawyers, and "eminent" persons; judge tenure NA
subordinate courts: Court of Second Instance; Court of First instance; Lower Court; Administrative Court

Political parties: Alliance for a Happy Home or ABL
Association of Synergy of Macau ("Synergy Power" or Poder da Singeria) or PS
Macau-Guangdong Union or UGM
New Hope or NE
Union for Development or UPD
Union for Promoting Progress or UPP or UNIPRO
United Citizens Association of Macau or ACUM
note: there is no political party ordinance, so there are no registered political parties; politically active groups register as societies or companies

International organization participation: ICC (national committees), IHO, IMF, IMO (associate), Interpol (subbureau), ISO (correspondent), UNESCO (associate), UNWTO (associate), UPU, WCO, WMO, WTO

Diplomatic representation in the US: none (Special Administrative Region of China)

Diplomatic representation from the US: *embassy:* the US has no offices in Macau; US Consulate General in Hong Kong is accredited to Macau

Flag description: *green with a lotus flower above a stylized bridge and water in white, beneath an arc of five gold, five-pointed stars:* one large in the center of the arc and two smaller on either side; the lotus is the floral emblem of Macau, the three petals represent the peninsula and two islands that make up Macau; the five stars echo those on the flag of China

National symbol(s): lotus blossom; national colors: green, white, yellow

National anthem: *note:* as a Special Administrative Region of China, "Yiyongjun Jinxingqu" is the official anthem (see China)

ECONOMY

Economic overview: high-income, Chinese special administrative region economy; known for apparel exports and gambling tourism; currency pegged to Hong Kong dollar; significant recession due to 2015 Chinese anticorruption campaign; COVID-19 further halved economic activity

Real GDP (purchasing power parity): $71.837 billion (2023 est.)
$39.791 billion (2022 est.)
$50.626 billion (2021 est.)
note: data in 2021 dollars
comparison ranking: 108

Real GDP growth rate: 80.53% (2023 est.)
-21.4% (2022 est.)
23.54% (2021 est.)
note: annual GDP % growth based on constant local currency
comparison ranking: 1

Real GDP per capita: $102,000 (2023 est.)
$57,200 (2022 est.)
$73,700 (2021 est.)
note: data in 2021 dollars
comparison ranking: 6

GDP (official exchange rate): $47.062 billion (2023 est.)
note: data in current dollars at official exchange rate

Inflation rate (consumer prices): 1.05% (2022 est.)
0.03% (2021 est.)
0.81% (2020 est.)
note: annual % change based on consumer prices
comparison ranking: 21

Credit ratings: Fitch rating: AA (2018)

Moody's rating: Aa3 (2016)
note: The year refers to the year in which the current credit rating was first obtained.

GDP - composition, by sector of origin: *industry:* 9.5% (2022 est.)
services: 90.1% (2022 est.)
note: figures may not total 100% due to non-allocated consumption not captured in sector-reported data
comparison rankings: services 8; industry 197

GDP - composition, by end use: *household consumption:* 29% (2023 est.)
government consumption: 13.7% (2023 est.)
investment in fixed capital: 13.5% (2023 est.)
investment in inventories: 0.4% (2023 est.)
exports of goods and services: 92.7% (2023 est.)
imports of goods and services: -49.3% (2023 est.)
note: figures may not total 100% due to rounding or gaps in data collection

Agricultural products: pork, chicken, beef, eggs, pork offal, pork fat, pepper, beef offal, cattle hides, goose meat (2022)
note: top ten agricultural products based on tonnage

Industries: tourism, gambling, clothing, textiles, electronics, footwear, toys

Industrial production growth rate: -5.63% (2022 est.)
note: annual % change in industrial value added based on constant local currency
comparison ranking: 199

Labor force: 407,000 (2023 est.)
note: number of people ages 15 or older who are employed or seeking work
comparison ranking: 162

Unemployment rate: 2.25% (2023 est.)
2.48% (2022 est.)
2.25% (2021 est.)
note: % of labor force seeking employment
comparison ranking: 25

Youth unemployment rate (ages 15-24): *total:* 7% (2023 est.)
male: 9% (2023 est.)
female: 5.3% (2023 est.)
note: % of labor force ages 15-24 seeking employment
comparison ranking: total 159

Remittances: 0.19% of GDP (2023 est.)
0.34% of GDP (2022 est.)
0.24% of GDP (2021 est.)
note: personal transfers and compensation between resident and non-resident individuals/households/entities

Budget: *revenues:* $5.135 billion (2022 est.)
expenditures: $12.259 billion (2022 est.)
note: central government revenues (excluding grants) and expenses converted to US dollars at average official exchange rate for year indicated

Public debt: 0% of GDP (2017 est.)
comparison ranking: 207

Taxes and other revenues: 17.07% (of GDP) (2022 est.)
note: central government tax revenue as a % of GDP
comparison ranking: 115

Current account balance: $2.782 billion (2022 est.)
$2.683 billion (2021 est.)
$3.635 billion (2020 est.)
note: balance of payments - net trade and primary/secondary income in current dollars
comparison ranking: 44

Exports: $20.985 billion (2022 est.)
$28.163 billion (2021 est.)
$15.578 billion (2020 est.)
note: balance of payments - exports of goods and services in current dollars
comparison ranking: 89

Exports - partners: Hong Kong 65%, China 8%, US 7%, Switzerland 3%, Israel 2% (2022)
note: top five export partners based on percentage share of exports

Exports - commodities: jewelry, garments, broadcasting equipment, precious metal watches, trunks and cases (2022)
note: top five export commodities based on value in dollars

Imports: $21.795 billion (2022 est.)
$23.769 billion (2021 est.)
$15.214 billion (2020 est.)
note: balance of payments - imports of goods and services in current dollars
comparison ranking: 95

Imports - partners: China 39%, Hong Kong 25%, France 5%, Italy 4%, US 3% (2022)
note: top five import partners based on percentage share of imports

Imports - commodities: jewelry, garments, electricity, broadcasting equipment, trunks and cases (2022)
note: top five import commodities based on value in dollars

Reserves of foreign exchange and gold: $27.771 billion (2023 est.)
$25.971 billion (2022 est.)
$26.665 billion (2021 est.)
note: holdings of gold (year-end prices)/foreign exchange/special drawing rights in current dollars
comparison ranking: 61

Exchange rates: patacas (MOP) per US dollar -

Exchange rates: 8.063 (2023 est.)
8.065 (2022 est.)
8.006 (2021 est.)
7.989 (2020 est.)
8.07 (2019 est.)

ENERGY

Electricity access: *electrification - total population:* 100% (2022 est.)

Electricity: *installed generating capacity:* 437,000 kW (2022 est.)
consumption: 5.581 billion kWh (2022 est.)
imports: 5.238 billion kWh (2022 est.)
transmission/distribution losses: 150.268 million kWh (2022 est.)
comparison rankings: transmission/distribution losses 59; imports 46; consumption 128; installed generating capacity 155

Electricity generation sources: *fossil fuels:* 58.5% of total installed capacity (2022 est.)
biomass and waste: 41.5% of total installed capacity (2022 est.)

Coal: *imports:* (2022 est.) less than 1 metric ton

Petroleum: *refined petroleum consumption:* 12,000 bbl/day (2022 est.)

Natural gas: *consumption:* 120.337 million cubic meters (2022 est.)
imports: 117.085 million cubic meters (2022 est.)

Carbon dioxide emissions: 1.746 million metric tonnes of CO2 (2022 est.)
from petroleum and other liquids: 1.511 million metric tonnes of CO2 (2022 est.)
from consumed natural gas: 236,000 metric tonnes of CO2 (2022 est.)
comparison ranking: total emissions 162

Energy consumption per capita: 69.034 million Btu/person (2022 est.)
comparison ranking: 73

COMMUNICATIONS

Telephones - fixed lines: *total subscriptions:* 92,000 (2022 est.)
subscriptions per 100 inhabitants: 13 (2022 est.)
comparison ranking: total subscriptions 139

Telephones - mobile cellular: *total subscriptions:* 1.213 million (2022 est.)
subscriptions per 100 inhabitants: 175 (2022 est.)
comparison ranking: total subscriptions 162

Telecommunication systems: general assessment: Macau's economy and GDP have been on a roller coaster ride since the start of the Covid-19 pandemic in 2020; the Special Administrative Region (SAR) of China is heavily dependent on tourists coming from the mainland and Hong Kong to play in Macau's many casinos, but the ensuing lock downs contributed to a dramatic fall in visitor numbers as well as income; this too, has had a major effect on the telecom sector (particularly in the mobile segment) with short-stay visitors as well as foreign workers on temporary-stay visas being forced to stay away.; total mobile subscription numbers are estimated to have dropped from a high of 2.8 million in 2019 (representing a whopping 442% penetration rate in a region with a population of just 700,000) to less than half that by the end of 2021: 1.3 million subscribers; Macau had almost the highest mobile penetration rate in the world; it is now sitting at a more 'reasonable' level of 200%; a significant bounce back can be expected to follow the easing of travel restrictions, although perhaps not up to the same lofty heights achieved in 2019; asecond factor behind the steep fall in 2020 was the introduction of a Cyber Security Law that required all prepaid SIM cards to become registered or face being deactivated in October 2020; the combined effect of the pandemic and the new restrictions meant that prepaid subscriber numbers fell by more than 80%; postpaid accounts, largely the domain of Macau's permanent residents, were barely affected by the external upheaval; they continued to increase in number, year-on-year, and provided better returns to the operators thanks to substantially increased data usage during the lock downs; the mobile broadband market has experienced the same dramatic fluctuations as the broader mobile segment over the last two years, at least in terms of subscriber numbers; but this is largely because mobile broadband uptake is inextricably tied to the base mobile offering in Macau; with total mobile broadband data traffic going up, not down, between 2019 and 2021, that again points to the strength of the contract segment helping to drive future growth in Macau's telecom sector (2022)
domestic: fixed-line nearly 16 per 100 and mobile-cellular roughly 410 per 100 persons (2021)
international: country code - 853; landing point for the SEA-ME-WE-3 submarine cable network that provides links to Asia, Africa, Australia, the Middle East, and Europe; HF radiotelephone communication facility; satellite earth station - 1 Intelsat (Indian Ocean) (2019)

Broadcast media: local government dominates broadcast media; 2 television stations operated by the government with one broadcasting in Portuguese and the other in Cantonese and Mandarin; 1 cable TV and 4 satellite TV services available; 3 radio stations broadcasting, of which 2 are government-operated (2019)

Internet country code: .mo

Internet users: *total:* 607,200 (2021 est.)
percent of population: 88% (2021 est.)
comparison ranking: total 164

Broadband - fixed subscriptions: *total:* 208,000 (2020 est.)
subscriptions per 100 inhabitants: 32 (2020 est.)
comparison ranking: total 119

TRANSPORTATION

National air transport system: *number of registered air carriers:* 1 (2020) (registered in China)
inventory of registered aircraft operated by air carriers: 21 (registered in China)
annual passenger traffic on registered air carriers: 3,157,724 (2018)
annual freight traffic on registered air carriers: 31.84 million (2018) mt-km

Civil aircraft registration country code prefix: B-M

Airports: 1 (2024)
comparison ranking: 210

Heliports: 4 (2024)

Roadways: *total:* 428 km
paved: 428 km (2017)

comparison ranking: total 199

Merchant marine: *total:* 5 (2023)
by type: other 5
comparison ranking: total 167

Ports: *total ports:* 1 (2024)
large: 0
medium: 1
small: 0
very small: 0
ports with oil terminals: 1
key ports: Macau

MILITARY AND SECURITY

Military and security forces: no regular indigenous military forces; Macau Public Security Police Force (includes the Police Intervention Tactical Unit or UTIP for counterterrorism operations)

Military - note: defense is the responsibility of China; the Chinese People's Liberation Army (PLA) maintains a garrison in Macau

TRANSNATIONAL ISSUES

Trafficking in persons: tier rating: Tier 3 — Macau does not fully meet the minimum standards for the elimination of trafficking and is not making significant efforts to do so, therefore, Macau remained on Tier 3; for more details, go to: https://www.state.gov/reports/2024-trafficking-in-persons-report/macau/

Illicit drugs: Asian organized crime groups involved in drug trafficking and money laundering

MADAGASCAR

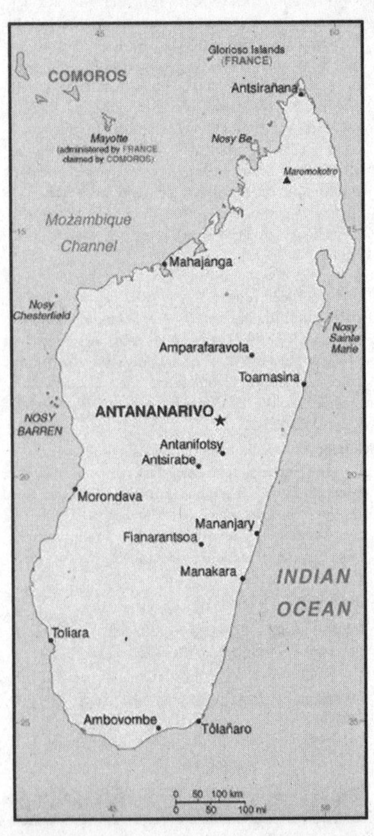

INTRODUCTION

Background: Madagascar was one of the last major habitable landmasses on earth to be settled by humans. While there is some evidence of human presence on the island in the millennia B.C., large-scale settlement began between A.D. 350 and 550 with settlers from present-day Indonesia. The island attracted Arab and Persian traders as early as the 7th century, and migrants from Africa arrived around A.D. 1000. Madagascar was a pirate stronghold during the late 17th and early 18th centuries and served as a slave trading center into the 19th century. From the 16th to the late 19th century, a native Merina Kingdom dominated much of Madagascar. The French conquered the island in 1896 and made it a colony; independence was regained in 1960.

Free presidential and National Assembly elections were held in 1992-93, ending 17 years of single-party rule. In 1997, in the second presidential race, Didier RATSIRAKA, the leader during the 1970s and 1980s, returned to the presidency. The 2001 presidential election was contested between the followers of RATSIRAKA and Marc RAVALOMANANA, nearly causing half the country to secede. In 2002, the High Constitutional Court announced RAVALOMANANA the winner. He won a second term in 2006 but, following protests in 2009, handed over power to the military, which then conferred the presidency on the mayor of Antananarivo, Andry RAJOELINA, in what amounted to a coup d'etat. After a lengthy mediation process, Madagascar held UN-supported presidential and parliamentary elections in 2013. Former de facto finance minister Hery RAJAONARIMAMPIANINA won in a runoff and was inaugurated in 2014. In 2019, RAJOELINA was declared the winner against RAVALOMANANA. In 2023, RAJOELINA won another term in an election that most of the opposition boycotted, including RAJAONARIMAMPIANINA and RAVALOMANANA, who claimed it was rigged in favor of RAJOELINA. International observers, however, saw no evidence of systemic fraud, leading the international community to accept the election results.

GEOGRAPHY

Location: Southern Africa, island in the Indian Ocean, east of Mozambique

Geographic coordinates: 20 00 S, 47 00 E

Map references: Africa

Area: *total:* 587,041 sq km
land: 581,540 sq km
water: 5,501 sq km
comparison ranking: total 49

Area - comparative: almost four times the size of Georgia; slightly less than twice the size of Arizona

Land boundaries: *total:* 0 km

Coastline: 4,828 km

Maritime claims: *territorial sea:* 12 nm
contiguous zone: 24 nm
exclusive economic zone: 200 nm
continental shelf: 200 nm or 100 nm from the 2,500-m isobath

Climate: tropical along coast, temperate inland, arid in south

Terrain: narrow coastal plain, high plateau and mountains in center

Elevation: *highest point:* Maromokotro 2,876 m
lowest point: Indian Ocean 0 m
mean elevation: 615 m

Natural resources: graphite, chromite, coal, bauxite, rare earth elements, salt, quartz, tar sands, semiprecious stones, mica, fish, hydropower

Land use: *agricultural land:* 71.1% (2018 est.)
arable land: 6% (2018 est.)
permanent crops: 1% (2018 est.)
permanent pasture: 64.1% (2018 est.)
forest: 21.5% (2018 est.)
other: 7.4% (2018 est.)

Irrigated land: 10,860 sq km (2012)

Population distribution: most of population lives on the eastern half of the island; significant clustering is found in the central highlands and eastern coastline as shown in this population distribution map

Natural hazards: periodic cyclones; drought; and locust infestation
volcanism: Madagascar's volcanoes have not erupted in historical times

Geography - note: world's fourth-largest island; strategic location along Mozambique Channel; despite Madagascar's close proximity to the African continent, ocean currents isolate the island resulting in high rates of endemic plant and animal species; approximately 90% of the flora and fauna on the island are found nowhere else

PEOPLE AND SOCIETY

Population: *total:* 29,452,714
male: 14,760,501
female: 14,692,213 (2024 est.)
comparison rankings: female 53; male 53; total 53

Nationality: *noun:* Malagasy (singular and plural)
adjective: Malagasy

Ethnic groups: Malayo-Indonesian (Merina and related Betsileo), Cotiers (mixed African, Malayo-Indonesian, and Arab ancestry - Betsimisaraka, Tsimihety, Antaisaka, Sakalava), French, Indian, Creole, Comoran

Languages: Malagasy (official) 99.9%, French (official) 23.6%, English 8.2%, other 0.6% (2018 est.)
note: shares sum to more than 100% because some respondents gave more than one answer on the census

Religions: Church of Jesus Christ in Madagascar/ Malagasy Lutheran Church/Anglican Church 34%, Roman Catholic 32.3%, other Christian 8.1%, traditional/Animist 1.7%, Muslim 1.4%, other 0.6%, none 21.9% (2021 est.)

Demographic profile: Madagascar's youthful population – nearly 60% are under the age of 25 as of 2020 – and moderately high total fertility rate of more than 3.6 children per woman ensures that the Malagasy population will continue its rapid growth trajectory for the foreseeable future. The population is predominantly rural and poor; chronic malnutrition is prevalent, and large families are the norm. Many young Malagasy girls are withdrawn from school, marry early (often pressured to do so by their parents), and soon begin having children. Early childbearing, coupled with Madagascar's widespread poverty and lack of access to skilled health care providers during delivery, increases the risk of death and serious health problems for young mothers and their babies.

Child marriage perpetuates gender inequality and is prevalent among the poor, the uneducated, and rural households – as of 2018, 40% of Malagasy women aged 20 to 24 were married. Although the legal age for marriage is 18, parental consent is often given for earlier marriages or the law is flouted, especially in rural areas that make up approximately 60% of the country. Forms of arranged marriage whereby young girls are married to older men in exchange for oxen or money are traditional. If a union does not work out, a girl can be placed in another marriage, but the dowry paid to her family diminishes with each unsuccessful marriage.

Madagascar's population consists of 18 main ethnic groups, all of whom speak the same Malagasy language. Most Malagasy are multi-ethnic, however, reflecting the island's diversity of settlers and historical contacts (see Background). Madagascar's legacy of hierarchical societies practicing domestic slavery (most notably the Merina Kingdom of the 16th to the 19th century) is evident today in persistent class tension, with some ethnic groups maintaining a caste system. Slave descendants are vulnerable to unequal access to education and jobs, despite Madagascar's constitutional guarantee of free compulsory primary education and its being party to several international conventions on human rights. Historical distinctions also remain between central highlanders and coastal people.

Age structure: *0-14 years:* 37% (male 5,507,847/ female 5,400,551)
15-64 years: 59.1% (male 8,720,012/female 8,673,880)
65 years and over: 3.9% (2024 est.) (male 532,642/ female 617,782)

Dependency ratios: *total dependency ratio:* 74.5
youth dependency ratio: 68.8
elderly dependency ratio: 5.8
potential support ratio: 17.4 (2021 est.)

Median age: *total:* 21.3 years (2024 est.)
male: 21.1 years
female: 21.5 years
comparison ranking: total 193

Population growth rate: 2.18% (2024 est.)
comparison ranking: 33

Birth rate: 27.6 births/1,000 population (2024 est.)
comparison ranking: 34

Death rate: 5.8 deaths/1,000 population (2024 est.)
comparison ranking: 163

Net migration rate: 0 migrant(s)/1,000 population (2024 est.)
comparison ranking: 85

Population distribution: most of population lives on the eastern half of the island; significant clustering is found in the central highlands and eastern coastline as shown in this population distribution map

Urbanization: *urban population:* 40.6% of total population (2023)
rate of urbanization: 4.26% annual rate of change (2020-25 est.)

Major urban areas - population: 3.872 million ANTANANARIVO (capital) (2023)

Sex ratio: *at birth:* 1.03 male(s)/female
0-14 years: 1.02 male(s)/female
15-64 years: 1.01 male(s)/female
65 years and over: 0.86 male(s)/female
total population: 1.01 male(s)/female (2024 est.)

Mother's mean age at first birth: 19.5 years (2021 est.)
note: data represents median age at first birth among women 25-29

Maternal mortality ratio: 392 deaths/100,000 live births (2020 est.)
comparison ranking: 24

Infant mortality rate: *total:* 37.5 deaths/1,000 live births (2024 est.)
male: 40.9 deaths/1,000 live births
female: 34 deaths/1,000 live births
comparison ranking: total 31

Life expectancy at birth: *total population:* 68.8 years (2024 est.)
male: 67.3 years
female: 70.3 years
comparison ranking: total population 186

Total fertility rate: 3.47 children born/woman (2024 est.)
comparison ranking: 35

Gross reproduction rate: 1.71 (2024 est.)

Contraceptive prevalence rate: 49.7% (2020)

Drinking water source: *improved: urban:* 85% of population
rural: 38% of population
total: 56.1% of population
unimproved: urban: 15% of population
rural: 62% of population
total: 43.9% of population (2020 est.)

Current health expenditure: 3.9% of GDP (2020)

Physician density: 0.2 physicians/1,000 population (2018)

Hospital bed density: 0.2 beds/1,000 population

Sanitation facility access: *improved: urban:* 49.2% of population
rural: 22.1% of population
total: 32.6% of population
unimproved: urban: 50.8% of population
rural: 77.9% of population
total: 67.4% of population (2020 est.)

Obesity - adult prevalence rate: 5.3% (2016)
comparison ranking: 181

Alcohol consumption per capita: *total:* 0.89 liters of pure alcohol (2019 est.)
beer: 0.5 liters of pure alcohol (2019 est.)
wine: 0.07 liters of pure alcohol (2019 est.)
spirits: 0.32 liters of pure alcohol (2019 est.)
other alcohols: 0 liters of pure alcohol (2019 est.)
comparison ranking: total 155

Tobacco use: *total:* 27.8% (2020 est.)
male: 42.7% (2020 est.)
female: 12.8% (2020 est.)
comparison ranking: total 38

Children under the age of 5 years underweight: 22.6% (2021)
comparison ranking: 9

Currently married women (ages 15-49): 60.1% (2023 est.)

Child marriage: *women married by age 15:* 12.7%
women married by age 18: 38.8%
men married by age 18: 11.2% (2021 est.)

Education expenditures: 3.1% of GDP (2020 est.)
comparison ranking: 157

Literacy: *definition:* age 15 and over can read and write
total population: 77.3%
male: 78.8%
female: 75.8% (2021)

School life expectancy (primary to tertiary education): *total:* 10 years
male: 10 years
female: 10 years (2018)

ENVIRONMENT

Environment - current issues: erosion and soil degradation results from deforestation and overgrazing; desertification; agricultural fires; surface water contaminated with raw sewage and other organic wastes; wildlife preservation (endangered species of flora and fauna unique to the island)

Environment - international agreements: *party to:* Biodiversity, Climate Change, Climate Change-Kyoto Protocol, Climate Change-Paris Agreement, Comprehensive Nuclear Test Ban, Desertification, Endangered Species, Hazardous Wastes, Law of the Sea, Marine Dumping-London Protocol, Marine Life Conservation, Nuclear Test Ban, Ozone Layer Protection, Ship Pollution, Tropical Timber 2006, Wetlands
signed, but not ratified: none of the selected agreements

Climate: tropical along coast, temperate inland, arid in south

Urbanization: *urban population:* 40.6% of total population (2023)
rate of urbanization: 4.26% annual rate of change (2020-25 est.)

Food insecurity: *severe localized food insecurity: due to the effects of extreme weather events and slow economic recovery* - according to the latest May 2022 analysis, the prevalence of food insecurity in the southern regions is projected to peak at 2.1 million people by December 2022 until at least March 2023; overall, the number of people requiring humanitarian assistance by the end of 2022 is expected to be about 30 percent higher compared to the peak number in 2021; the poor food security situation is mainly the consequence of six consecutive poor agricultural seasons that culminated in very tight food supplies for rural households and curbed incomes from crop sales; high rates of poverty and increased prices of essential food commodities, combined with a high reliance on market supplies due to low harvests for own consumption, are also contributing to the high rates of food insecurity across the southern regions (2022)

Revenue from forest resources: 4.34% of GDP (2018 est.)
comparison ranking: 17

Revenue from coal: 0% of GDP (2018 est.)
comparison ranking: 155

Air pollutants: *particulate matter emissions:* 16.02 micrograms per cubic meter (2019 est.)
carbon dioxide emissions: 3.91 megatons (2016 est.)
methane emissions: 10.14 megatons (2020 est.)

Waste and recycling: *municipal solid waste generated annually:* 3,768,759 tons (2016 est.)

Total water withdrawal: *municipal:* 400 million cubic meters (2020 est.)
industrial: 160 million cubic meters (2020 est.)
agricultural: 13 billion cubic meters (2020 est.)

Total renewable water resources: 337 billion cubic meters (2020 est.)

GOVERNMENT

Country name: *conventional long form:* Republic of Madagascar
conventional short form: Madagascar
local long form: République de Madagascar/Repoblikan'i Madagasikara
local short form: Madagascar/Madagasikara
former: Malagasy Republic
etymology: the name "Madageiscar" was first used by the 13th-century Venetian explorer Marco POLO, as a corrupted transliteration of Mogadishu, the Somali port with which POLO confused the island

Government type: semi-presidential republic

Capital: *name:* Antananarivo
geographic coordinates: 18 55 S, 47 31 E
time difference: UTC+3 (8 hours ahead of Washington, DC, during Standard Time)
etymology: the name, which means "City of the Thousand," was bestowed by 17th century King ADRIANJAKA to honor the soldiers assigned to guard the city

Administrative divisions: 6 provinces (faritany); Antananarivo, Antsiranana, Fianarantsoa, Mahajanga, Toamasina, Toliara

Independence: 26 June 1960 (from France)

National holiday: Independence Day, 26 June (1960)

Legal system: civil law system based on the old French civil code and customary law in matters of marriage, family, and obligation

Constitution: *history:* previous 1992; latest passed by referendum 17 November 2010, promulgated 11 December 2010
amendments: proposed by the president of the republic in consultation with the cabinet or supported by a least two thirds of both the Senate and National Assembly membership; passage requires at least three-fourths approval of both the Senate and National Assembly and approval in a referendum; constitutional articles, including the form and powers of government, the sovereignty of the state, and the autonomy of Madagascar's collectivities, cannot be amended

International law organization participation: accepts compulsory ICJ jurisdiction with reservations; accepts ICCt jurisdiction

Citizenship: *citizenship by birth:* no
citizenship by descent only: the father must be a citizen of Madagascar; in the case of a child born out of wedlock, the mother must be a citizen
dual citizenship recognized: no
residency requirement for naturalization: unknown

Suffrage: 18 years of age; universal

Executive branch: *chief of state:* President Andry RAJOELINA (since 16 December 2023)
head of government: Prime Minister Christian NTSAY (since 6 June 2018)
cabinet: Council of Ministers appointed by the prime minister
elections/appointments: president directly elected by absolute majority popular vote in 2 rounds if needed for a 5-year term (eligible for a second term); election last held on 16 November 2023 (next to be held in November 2028); prime minister nominated by the National Assembly, appointed by the president
election results:
2023: Andry RAJOELINA reelected president in first round; percent of vote - Andry RAJOELINA (TGV) 59.0%, Siteny Thierry RANDRIANASOLONIAIKO 14.4%, Marc RAVALOMANANA (TIM) 12.1%, other 14.5%
2018: Andry RAJOELINA elected president in second round; percent of vote in first round - Andry RAJOELINA (TGV) 39.2%, Marc RAVALOMANANA (TIM) 35.4%, other 25.4%; percent of vote in second round - Andry RAJOELINA 55.7%, Marc RAVALOMANANA 44.3%

Legislative branch: *description:* bicameral Parliament consists of:
Senate or Antenimierandoholona (18 seats; 12 members indirectly elected by an electoral college of municipal, communal, regional, and provincial leaders and 6 appointed by the president; members serve 5-year terms) National Assembly or Antenimierampirenena (151 seats; 87 members directly elected in single-seat constituencies by simple majority vote and 64 directly elected in multi-seat constituencies by closed-list proportional representation vote; members serve 5-year terms)
elections: Senate - last held on 11 December 2020 (next to be held in December 2025)
National Assembly - last held on 27 May 2019 (next to be held on 29 May 2024)
election results: Senate - percent of vote by party - NA; elected seats by party - Irmar 10, Malagasy Miara Miainga 2; composition - men 17, women 1, percentage women 5.6%
National Assembly - percent of vote by party/coalition - IRD 55.6%, TIM 10.6%, independent 30.5%, other 3.3%; seats by party/coalition - IRD 84, TIM 16, independent 46, other 5; composition - men 123, women 28, percentage women 18.5%; total Parliament percentage women 10.7%

Judicial branch: *highest court(s):* Supreme Court or Cour Supreme (consists of 11 members; addresses judicial administration issues only); High Constitutional Court or Haute Cour Constitutionnelle (consists of 9 members); High Court of Justice (consists of 11 members; addresses cases brought against the president of Madagascar and high officials for high treason, grave violations of the Constitution, or breach of duties incompatible with the exercise of the presidential mandate)
judge selection and term of office: Supreme Court heads elected by the president and judiciary officials to serve 3- year, single renewable terms; High Constitutional Court members appointed - 3 each by the president, by both legislative bodies, and by the Council of Magistrates; members serve single, 7-year terms; High Court of Justice members include: first president of the Supreme Court; 2 presidents from the Court of Cassation; 2 presidents from the Court of Appeal; 2 deputies from the National Assembly; 2 senators from the Senate; 2 members from the High Council for the Defense of Democracy and the State of law
subordinate courts: Courts of Appeal; Court of Cassation; Courts of First Instance; military courts; traditional (dina) courts; Trade Court

Political parties: Group of Young Malagasy Patriots (Groupe des Jeunes Malgaches Patriotes) or GJMP
I Love Madagascar (Tiako I Madagasikara) or TIM
Isika Rehetra Miaraka amin'i Andry Rajoelina coalition or IRD
Malagasy Aware (Malagasy Tonga Saina) or MTS
Malagasy Tia Tanindrazana or MATITA or ANGADY
Movement for Democracy in Madagascar (Mouvement pour la Démocratie à Madagascar) or MDM
Rally for Democratic Socialism (Rassemblement pour Socialisme Démocratique - Nouveau) or RPSD Vaovao
Young Malagasies Determined (Tanora Malagasy Vonona) or TGV

International organization participation: ACP, AfDB, AU, CD, COMESA, EITI (candidate country), FAO, G-77, IAEA, IBRD, ICAO, ICC (NGOs), ICCt, ICRM, IDA, IFAD, IFC, IFRCS, ILO, IMF, IMO, InOC, Interpol, IOC, IOM, IPU, ISO (correspondent), ITSO, ITU, ITUC (NGOs), MIGA, NAM, OIF, OPCW, PCA, SADC, UN, UNCTAD, UNESCO, UNHCR, UNIDO, UNWTO, UPU, WCO, WFTU (NGOs), WHO, WIPO, WMO, WTO

Diplomatic representation in the US: *chief of mission:* Ambassador (vacant); Chargé d'Affaires Amielle Pelenne NIRINIAVISOA MARCEDA (since 31 October 2019)
chancery: 2374 Massachusetts Avenue NW, Washington, DC 20008
telephone: [1] (202) 265-5525
FAX: [1] (202) 265-3034
email address and website:
madagascar.embassy.dc@gmail.com
https://us-madagascar-embassy.org/

Diplomatic representation from the US: *chief of mission:* Ambassador Claire PIERANGELO (since 2 May 2022)
embassy: Lot 207A, Andranoro, Antehiroka, 105 Antananarivo - Madagascar
mailing address: 2040 Antananarivo Place, Washington DC 20521-2040
telephone: [261] 33-44-320-00
FAX: [261] 33-44-320-35
email address and website:
antanACS@state.gov
https://mg.usembassy.gov/

Flag description: two equal horizontal bands of red (top) and green with a vertical white band of the same width on hoist side; by tradition, red stands for sovereignty, green for hope, white for purity

National symbol(s): traveller's palm, zebu; national colors: red, green, white

National anthem: *name:* "Ry Tanindraza nay malala o" (Oh, Our Beloved Fatherland)
lyrics/music: Pasteur RAHAJASON/Norbert RAHARISOA
note: adopted 1959

National heritage: *total World Heritage Sites:* 3 (1 cultural, 2 natural)
selected World Heritage Site locales: Tsingy de Bemaraha Strict Nature Reserve (n); Ambohimanga Royal Hill (c); Atsinanana Rainforests (n)

ECONOMY

Economic overview: low-income East African island economy; natural resource rich; extreme poverty; return of political stability has helped growth; sharp tax revenue drop due to COVID-19; leading vanilla producer; environmentally fragile

Real GDP (purchasing power parity): $51.255 billion (2023 est.)
$49.291 billion (2022 est.)
$47.488 billion (2021 est.)
note: data in 2021 dollars
comparison ranking: 123

Real GDP growth rate: 3.99% (2023 est.)
3.8% (2022 est.)
5.74% (2021 est.)
note: annual GDP % growth based on constant local currency
comparison ranking: 77

Real GDP per capita: $1,700 (2023 est.)
$1,700 (2022 est.)
$1,600 (2021 est.)
note: data in 2021 dollars
comparison ranking: 212

GDP (official exchange rate): $16.032 billion (2023 est.)
note: data in current dollars at official exchange rate

Inflation rate (consumer prices): 9.87% (2023 est.)
8.16% (2022 est.)
5.81% (2021 est.)
note: annual % change based on consumer prices
comparison ranking: 176

GDP - composition, by sector of origin: *agriculture:* 21.1% (2023 est.)
industry: 14.9% (2023 est.)
services: 54.9% (2023 est.)
note: figures may not total 100% due to non-allocated consumption not captured in sector-reported data
comparison rankings: services 119; industry 171; agriculture 36

GDP - composition, by end use: *household consumption:* 66.5% (2023 est.)
government consumption: 18.7% (2023 est.)
investment in fixed capital: 20.3% (2023 est.)
investment in inventories: 1% (2023 est.)
exports of goods and services: 32.5% (2023 est.)
imports of goods and services: -39.1% (2023 est.)
note: figures may not total 100% due to rounding or gaps in data collection

Agricultural products: rice, sugarcane, cassava, sweet potatoes, milk, bananas, vegetables, mangoes/guavas, tropical fruits, potatoes (2022)
note: top ten agricultural products based on tonnage

Industries: meat processing, seafood, soap, beer, leather, sugar, textiles, glassware, cement, automobile assembly plant, paper, petroleum, tourism, mining

Industrial production growth rate: -33.28% (2023 est.)
note: annual % change in industrial value added based on constant local currency
comparison ranking: 218

Labor force: 15.83 million (2023 est.)
note: number of people ages 15 or older who are employed or seeking work
comparison ranking: 40

Unemployment rate: 3.06% (2023 est.)
3.19% (2022 est.)
3.42% (2021 est.)
note: % of labor force seeking employment
comparison ranking: 48

Youth unemployment rate (ages 15-24): *total:* 5.5% (2023 est.)
male: 5.4% (2023 est.)
female: 5.6% (2023 est.)
note: % of labor force ages 15-24 seeking employment
comparison ranking: total 174

Remittances: 2.37% of GDP (2023 est.)
2.52% of GDP (2022 est.)
3.02% of GDP (2021 est.)
note: personal transfers and compensation between resident and non-resident individuals/households/entities

Budget: *revenues:* $1.756 billion (2022 est.)
expenditures: $1.523 billion (2022 est.)
note: central government revenues and expenses (excluding grants/extrabudgetary units/social security funds) converted to US dollars at average official exchange rate for year indicated

Public debt: 36% of GDP (2017 est.)
comparison ranking: 148

Taxes and other revenues: 9.25% (of GDP) (2022 est.)
note: central government tax revenue as a % of GDP
comparison ranking: 182

Current account balance: -$829.376 million (2022 est.)
-$721.953 million (2021 est.)
-$623.653 million (2020 est.)
note: balance of payments - net trade and primary/secondary income in current dollars
comparison ranking: 134

Exports: $4.689 billion (2022 est.)
$3.362 billion (2021 est.)
$2.589 billion (2020 est.)
note: balance of payments - exports of goods and services in current dollars
comparison ranking: 142

Exports - partners: US 18%, France 15%, China 13%, Japan 11%, Germany 4% (2022)
note: top five export partners based on percentage share of exports

Exports - commodities: nickel, garments, vanilla, cloves, cobalt (2022)
note: top five export commodities based on value in dollars

Imports: $6.041 billion (2022 est.)
$4.769 billion (2021 est.)
$3.718 billion (2020 est.)
note: balance of payments - imports of goods and services in current dollars
comparison ranking: 142

Imports - partners: China 24%, India 10%, France 9%, Oman 6%, South Africa 6% (2022)
note: top five import partners based on percentage share of imports

Imports - commodities: refined petroleum, rice, fabric, palm oil, cotton fabric (2022)
note: top five import commodities based on value in dollars

Reserves of foreign exchange and gold: $2.632 billion (2023 est.)
$2.16 billion (2022 est.)
$2.335 billion (2021 est.)
note: holdings of gold (year-end prices)/foreign exchange/special drawing rights in current dollars
comparison ranking: 126

Debt - external: $2.972 billion (2022 est.)
note: present value of external debt in current US dollars
comparison ranking: 66

Exchange rates: Malagasy ariary (MGA) per US dollar -

Exchange rates: 4,429.579 (2023 est.)
4,096.116 (2022 est.)
3,829.978 (2021 est.)
3,787.754 (2020 est.)
3,618.322 (2019 est.)

ENERGY

Electricity access: *electrification - total population:* 36.1% (2022 est.)
electrification - urban areas: 71.6%
electrification - rural areas: 10.9%

Electricity: *installed generating capacity:* 663,000 kW (2022 est.)
consumption: 2.248 billion kWh (2022 est.)
transmission/distribution losses: 118.792 million kWh (2022 est.)
comparison rankings: transmission/distribution losses 52; consumption 146; installed generating capacity 144

Electricity generation sources: *fossil fuels:* 63.1% of total installed capacity (2022 est.)
solar: 1.6% of total installed capacity (2022 est.)
hydroelectricity: 33.1% of total installed capacity (2022 est.)
biomass and waste: 2.2% of total installed capacity (2022 est.)

Coal: *consumption:* 511,000 metric tons (2022 est.)
exports: (2022 est.) less than 1 metric ton
imports: 511,000 metric tons (2022 est.)
proven reserves: 150 million metric tons (2022 est.)

Petroleum: *refined petroleum consumption:* 19,000 bbl/day (2022 est.)

Carbon dioxide emissions: 4.054 million metric tonnes of CO2 (2022 est.)
from coal and metallurgical coke: 1.155 million metric tonnes of CO2 (2022 est.)
from petroleum and other liquids: 2.899 million metric tonnes of CO2 (2022 est.)
comparison ranking: total emissions 140

Energy consumption per capita: 1.887 million Btu/person (2022 est.)
comparison ranking: 187

COMMUNICATIONS

Telephones - fixed lines: *total subscriptions:* 26,000 (2022 est.)
subscriptions per 100 inhabitants: (2022 est.) less than 1
comparison ranking: total subscriptions 170

Telephones - mobile cellular: *total subscriptions:* 20.783 million (2022 est.)
subscriptions per 100 inhabitants: 70 (2022 est.)
comparison ranking: total subscriptions 60

Telecommunication systems: *general assessment:* internet service is fast compared to other African countries, and telecom services in Madagascar have benefited from intensifying competition

between the main operators; there have been positive developments with the country's link to international submarine cables, particularly the METiSs cable connecting to South Africa and Mauritius; in addition, the country's connection to the Africa-1 cable, which arrived in 2023, provides links to Kenya, Djibouti, countries in north and south Africa, as well as Pakistan, the UAE, Saudi Arabia, and France; a national fiber backbone has been implemented connecting the major cities, however much of the fiber in country has been installed by Huawei, which also manages data centers for the government; in addition, the government has progressed with its five- year plan to develop a digital platform running to 2024; various schemes within the program have been managed by a unit within the President's office; penetration rates in all market sectors remain below the average for the African region, and so there remains considerable growth potential; much progress was made in 2020, stimulated by the particular conditions related to the pandemic, which encouraged greater use of voice and data services (2022)
domestic: less than 1 per 100 for fixed-line and mobile-cellular teledensity about 56 per 100 persons (2021)
international: country code - 261; landing points for the EASSy, METISS, and LION fiber-optic submarine cable systems connecting to numerous Indian Ocean Islands, South Africa, and Eastern African countries; satellite earth stations - 2 (1 Intelsat - Indian Ocean, 1 Intersputnik - Atlantic Ocean region) (2019)

Broadcast media: state-owned Radio Nationale Malagasy (RNM) and Television Malagasy (TVM) have an extensive national network reach; privately owned radio and TV broadcasters in cities and major towns; state-run radio dominates in rural areas; relays of 2 international broadcasters are available in Antananarivo (2019)

Internet country code: .mg

Internet users: *total:* 5.8 million (2021 est.)
percent of population: 20% (2021 est.)
comparison ranking: total 83

Broadband - fixed subscriptions: *total:* 32,000 (2020 est.)
subscriptions per 100 inhabitants: 0.1 (2020 est.)
comparison ranking: total 151

TRANSPORTATION

National air transport system: *number of registered air carriers:* 4 (2020)
inventory of registered aircraft operated by air carriers: 18
annual passenger traffic on registered air carriers: 541,290 (2018)
annual freight traffic on registered air carriers: 16.25 million (2018) mt-km

Civil aircraft registration country code prefix: 5R

Airports: 91 (2024)
comparison ranking: 57

Railways: *total:* 836 km (2018)
narrow gauge: 836 km (2018) 1.000-m gauge
comparison ranking: total 95

Roadways: *total:* 31,640 km (2017)
comparison ranking: total 99

Waterways: 600 km (2011) (432 km navigable)
comparison ranking: 86

Merchant marine: *total:* 29 (2023)
by type: general cargo 16, oil tanker 2, other 11
comparison ranking: total 135

Ports: *total ports:* 13 (2024)
large: 0
medium: 0
small: 2
very small: 11
ports with oil terminals: 5
key ports: Andoany, Antsiranana, Antsohim Bondrona, Iharana, Mahajanga, Maintirano, Manakara, Mananjary, Maroantsetra, Morondava, Toamasina, Tolanaro, Toliara

MILITARY AND SECURITY

Military and security forces: Madagascar People's Armed Forces (PAF): Army, Navy, Air Force; National Gendarmerie (2024)
note: the National Gendarmerie is separate from the PAF under the Ministry of Defense and is responsible for maintaining law and order in rural areas at the village level, protecting government facilities, and operating a maritime police contingent; the National Police under the Ministry of Security is responsible for maintaining law and order in urban areas

Military expenditures: 0.7% of GDP (2023 est.)
0.7% of GDP (2022 est.)
0.7% of GDP (2021 est.)
0.7% of GDP (2020 est.)
0.5% of GDP (2019 est.)
comparison ranking: 144

Military and security service personnel strengths: estimated 13,000 personnel (12,000 Army; 500 Navy; 500 Air Force); estimated 10,000 Gendarmerie (2023)

Military equipment inventories and acquisitions: the PAF's inventory consists of a mix of older or second-hand weapons from several suppliers, such as France, Japan, South Africa, the UAE, the UK, the US, and the former Soviet Union (2023)

Military service age and obligation: 18-25 years of age for men and women; service obligation 18 months; no conscription; women are permitted to serve in all branches (2023)

Military - note: the PAF's responsibilities include ensuring sovereignty and territorial integrity and protecting Madagascar's maritime domain, particularly against piracy, drug trafficking, and smuggling; it also assists the Gendarmerie with maintaining law and order in rural areas, largely in areas affected by banditry, cattle rustling, and criminal groups; the PAF has a history of having influence in domestic politics and a lack of accountability; members of the Army and the Gendarmerie were arrested for coup plotting as recently as 2021; its closest defense partners have been India and Russia; the PAF's small Navy has traditionally looked to India for assistance with maritime security (2023)

TRANSNATIONAL ISSUES

Trafficking in persons: tier rating: Tier 2 Watch List — the government has devoted sufficient resources to a written plan that, if implemented, would constitute significant efforts to meet the minimum standards; therefore, Madagascar was granted a waiver per the Trafficking Victims Protection Act from an otherwise required downgrade to Tier 3 and remained on Tier 2 Watch List for the third consecutive year; for more details, go to: https://www.state.gov/reports/2024-trafficking-in-persons-report/madagascar/

Illicit drugs: illicit producer of cannabis (cultivated and wild varieties) used mostly for domestic consumption; transshipment point for Southwest Asian heroin

MALAWI

INTRODUCTION

Background: Malawi shares its name with the Chewa word for flames and is linked to the Maravi people from whom the Chewa language originated. The Maravi settled in what is now Malawi around 1400, during one of the later waves of Bantu migration across central and southern Africa. A powerful Maravi kingdom established around 1500 reached its zenith around 1700, when it controlled what is now southern and central Malawi and portions of neighboring Mozambique and Zambia. The kingdom eventually declined because of destabilization from the escalating global trade in enslaved people. In the early 1800s, widespread conflict in southern Africa displaced various ethnic Ngoni groups, some of which moved into Malawi and further undermined the Maravi. Members of the Yao ethnic group – which had long traded with Malawi from Mozambique – introduced Islam and began to settle in Malawi in significant numbers in the mid-1800s, followed by members of the Lomwe ethnic group. British missionary and trading activity increased in the area around Lake Nyasa in the mid-1800s, and in 1891, Britain declared a protectorate called British Central Africa over what is now Malawi. The British renamed the territory Nyasaland in 1907, and it was part of the colonial Federation of Rhodesia and Nyasaland – including present-day Zambia and Zimbabwe – from 1953 to 1963 before gaining independence as Malawi in 1964.

Hastings Kamuzu BANDA served as prime minister at independence and then as president when the country became a republic in 1966. He later instituted one-party rule under his Malawi Congress Party (MCP) and was declared president for life. After three decades of one-party rule, the country held multiparty presidential and parliamentary elections in 1994 under a provisional constitution that came into full effect the following year. Bakili MULUZI of the United Democratic Front party became the first freely elected president of Malawi when he defeated

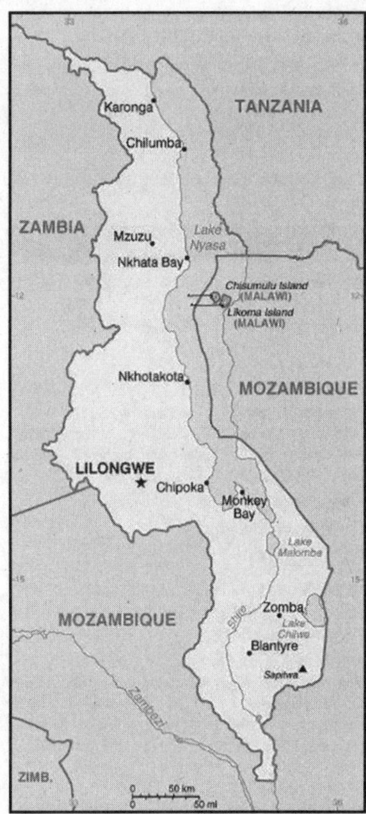

BANDA at the polls in 1994; he won reelection in 1999. President Bingu wa MUTHARIKA was elected in 2004 and reelected to a second term in 2009. He died abruptly in 2012 and was succeeded by Vice President Joyce BANDA. MUTHARIKA's brother, Peter MUTHARIKA, defeated BANDA in the election in 2014. Peter MUTHARIKA was reelected in a disputed election in 2019 that resulted in countrywide protests. The courts ordered a new election, and in 2020, Lazarus CHAKWERA of the MCP was elected president. Population growth, increasing pressure on agricultural lands, corruption, and HIV/AIDS pose major problems for Malawi.

GEOGRAPHY

Location: Southern Africa, east of Zambia, west and north of Mozambique

Geographic coordinates: 13 30 S, 34 00 E

Map references: Africa

Area: *total:* 118,484 sq km
land: 94,080 sq km
water: 24,404 sq km
comparison ranking: total 100

Area - comparative: slightly smaller than Pennsylvania

Land boundaries: *total:* 2,857 km
border countries (3): Mozambique 1,498 km; Tanzania 512 km; Zambia 847 km

Coastline: 0 km (landlocked)

Maritime claims: none (landlocked)

Climate: sub-tropical; rainy season (November to May); dry season (May to November)

Terrain: narrow elongated plateau with rolling plains, rounded hills, some mountains

Elevation: *highest point:* Sapitwa (Mount Mlanje) 3,002 m
lowest point: junction of the Shire River and international boundary with Mozambique 37 m
mean elevation: 779 m

Natural resources: limestone, arable land, hydropower, unexploited deposits of uranium, coal, and bauxite

Land use: *agricultural land:* 59.2% (2018 est.)
arable land: 38.2% (2018 est.)
permanent crops: 1.4% (2018 est.)
permanent pasture: 19.6% (2018 est.)
forest: 34% (2018 est.)
other: 6.8% (2018 est.)

Irrigated land: 740 sq km (2012)

Major lakes (area sq km): *fresh water lake(s):* Lake Malawi (shared with Mozambique and Tanzania) - 22,490
salt water lake(s): Lake Chilwa - 1,040 sq km

Major rivers (by length in km): Zambezi (shared with Zambia [s], Angola, Zimbabwe, Namibia, Tanzania, and Mozambique [m]) - 2,740 km
note – [s] after country name indicates river source; [m] after country name indicates river mouth

Major watersheds (area sq km): Atlantic Ocean drainage: Congo (3,730,881 sq km)

Indian Ocean drainage: Zambezi (1,332,412 sq km)

Population distribution: population density is highest south of Lake Nyasa as shown in this population distribution map

Natural hazards: flooding; droughts; earthquakes

Geography - note: landlocked; Lake Nyasa, some 580 km long, is the country's most prominent physical feature; it contains more fish species than any other lake on earth

PEOPLE AND SOCIETY

Population: *total:* 21,763,309
male: 10,674,594
female: 11,088,715 (2024 est.)
comparison rankings: female 62; male 61; total 62

Nationality: *noun:* Malawian(s)
adjective: Malawian

Ethnic groups: Chewa 34.3%, Lomwe 18.8%, Yao 13.2%, Ngoni 10.4%, Tumbuka 9.2%, Sena 3.8%, Mang'anja 3.2%, Tonga 1.8%, Nyanja 1.8%, Nkhonde 1%, other 2.2%, foreign 0.3% (2018 est.)

Languages: English (official), Chewa (dominant), Lambya, Lomwe, Ngoni, Nkhonde, Nyakyusa, Nyanja, Sena, Tonga, Tumbuka, Yao
note: Chewa and Nyanja are mutually intelligible dialects; Nkhonde and Nyakyusa are mutually intelligible dialects

Religions: Protestant 33.5% (includes Church of Central Africa Presbyterian 14.2%, Seventh Day Adventist/Baptist 9.4%, Pentecostal 7.6%, Anglican 2.3%), Roman Catholic 17.2%, other Christian 26.6%, Muslim 13.8%, traditionalist 1.1%, other 5.6%, none 2.1% (2018 est.)

Demographic profile: Malawi has made great improvements in maternal and child health, but has made less progress in reducing its high fertility rate. In both rural and urban areas, very high proportions of mothers are receiving prenatal care and skilled birth assistance, and most children are being vaccinated. Malawi's fertility rate, however, has only declined slowly, decreasing from more than 7 children per woman in the 1980s to about 5.5 today. Nonetheless, Malawians prefer smaller families than in the past, and women are increasingly using contraceptives to prevent or space pregnancies. Rapid population growth and high population density is putting pressure on Malawi's land, water, and forest resources. Reduced plot sizes and increasing vulnerability to climate change, further threaten the sustainability of Malawi's agriculturally based economy and will worsen food shortages. About 80% of the population is employed in agriculture.

Historically, Malawians migrated abroad in search of work, primarily to South Africa and present-day Zimbabwe, but international migration became uncommon after the 1970s, and most migration in recent years has been internal. During the colonial period, Malawians regularly migrated to southern Africa as contract farm laborers, miners, and domestic servants. In the decade and a half after independence in 1964, the Malawian Government sought to transform its economy from one dependent on small-scale farms to one based on estate agriculture. The resulting demand for wage labor induced more than 300,000 Malawians to return home between the mid-1960s and the mid-1970s. In recent times, internal migration has generally been local, motivated more by marriage than economic reasons.

Age structure: *0-14 years:* 37.7% (male 4,080,567/female 4,132,710)
15-64 years: 58.4% (male 6,217,761/female 6,487,273)
65 years and over: 3.9% (2024 est.) (male 376,266/female 468,732)

Dependency ratios: *total dependency ratio:* 84.7
youth dependency ratio: 79.7
elderly dependency ratio: 5
potential support ratio: 20.1 (2021 est.)

Median age: *total:* 20.3 years (2024 est.)
male: 20 years
female: 20.6 years
comparison ranking: total 204

Population growth rate: 2.22% (2024 est.)
comparison ranking: 31

Birth rate: 26.6 births/1,000 population (2024 est.)
comparison ranking: 40

Death rate: 4.5 deaths/1,000 population (2024 est.)
comparison ranking: 207

Net migration rate: 0 migrant(s)/1,000 population (2024 est.)
comparison ranking: 88

Population distribution: population density is highest south of Lake Nyasa as shown in this population distribution map

Urbanization: *urban population:* 18.3% of total population (2023)
rate of urbanization: 4.41% annual rate of change (2020-25 est.)

Major urban areas - population: 1.276 million LILONGWE (capital), 1.031 million Blantyre-Limbe (2023)

Sex ratio: *at birth:* 1.01 male(s)/female
0-14 years: 0.99 male(s)/female
15-64 years: 0.96 male(s)/female
65 years and over: 0.8 male(s)/female
total population: 0.96 male(s)/female (2024 est.)

Mother's mean age at first birth: 19.1 years (2015/16 est.)
note: data represents median age at first birth among women 20-49

Maternal mortality ratio: 381 deaths/100,000 live births (2020 est.)
comparison ranking: 25

Infant mortality rate: *total:* 31.9 deaths/1,000 live births (2024 est.)
male: 36.4 deaths/1,000 live births
female: 27.4 deaths/1,000 live births
comparison ranking: total 44

Life expectancy at birth: *total population:* 73 years (2024 est.)
male: 69.9 years
female: 76.1 years
comparison ranking: total population 155

Total fertility rate: 3.19 children born/woman (2024 est.)
comparison ranking: 44

Gross reproduction rate: 1.58 (2024 est.)

Contraceptive prevalence rate: 65.6% (2019/20)

Drinking water source: *improved: urban:* 96.7% of population
rural: 91% of population
total: 92% of population
unimproved: urban: 3.3% of population
rural: 9% of population
total: 8% of population (2020 est.)

Current health expenditure: 5.4% of GDP (2020)

Physician density: 0.05 physicians/1,000 population (2020)

Hospital bed density: 1.3 beds/1,000 population (2011)

Sanitation facility access: *improved: urban:* 59.9% of population
rural: 35.9% of population
total: 40% of population
unimproved: urban: 40.1% of population
rural: 64.1% of population
total: 60% of population (2020 est.)

Obesity - adult prevalence rate: 5.8% (2016)
comparison ranking: 174

Alcohol consumption per capita: *total:* 2.04 liters of pure alcohol (2019 est.)
beer: 0.08 liters of pure alcohol (2019 est.)
wine: 0 liters of pure alcohol (2019 est.)
spirits: 0.25 liters of pure alcohol (2019 est.)
other alcohols: 1.7 liters of pure alcohol (2019 est.)
comparison ranking: total 129

Tobacco use: *total:* 10.8% (2020 est.)
male: 17.5% (2020 est.)
female: 4.1% (2020 est.)
comparison ranking: total 132

Children under the age of 5 years underweight: 11.7% (2020)
comparison ranking: 47

Currently married women (ages 15-49): 60.7% (2022 est.)

Child marriage: *women married by age 15:* 7.5%
women married by age 18: 37.7%
men married by age 18: 7% (2020 est.)

Education expenditures: 2.9% of GDP (2020 est.)
comparison ranking: 160

Literacy: *definition:* age 15 and over can read and write
total population: 67.3%
male: 71.2%
female: 63.7% (2021)

School life expectancy (primary to tertiary education): *total:* 11 years
male: 11 years
female: 11 years (2011)

ENVIRONMENT

Environment - current issues: deforestation; land degradation; water pollution from agricultural runoff, sewage, industrial wastes; siltation of spawning grounds endangers fish populations; negative effects of climate change (extreme high temperatures, changing precipitation patterns)

Environment - international agreements: *party to:* Biodiversity, Climate Change, Climate Change-Kyoto Protocol, Climate Change-Paris Agreement, Comprehensive Nuclear Test Ban, Desertification, Endangered Species, Environmental Modification, Hazardous Wastes, Law of the Sea, Marine Life Conservation, Nuclear Test Ban, Ozone Layer Protection, Ship Pollution, Wetlands
signed, but not ratified: none of the selected agreements

Climate: sub-tropical; rainy season (November to May); dry season (May to November)

Urbanization: *urban population:* 18.3% of total population (2023)
rate of urbanization: 4.41% annual rate of change (2020-25 est.)

Food insecurity: *widespread lack of access: due to weather extremes and high food prices* - the latest analysis indicates that about 3.8 million people (20 percent of the population) are estimated to have faced high levels of acute food insecurity between January and March 2023; this figure is more than double the number in the corresponding months of 2022; high food prices are the key reason for the deterioration in food insecurity, which, in the absence of a substantial increase in incomes, are severely constraining households' economic access to food; production shortfalls in southern districts in 2022, areas that have the highest prevalence of food insecurity, are a further contributing factor; the impact of Cyclone Freddy (February-March 2023) on southern districts, including crop losses and destruction of infrastructure as well as high food prices, are expected to aggravate food insecurity conditions in 2023 (2023)

Revenue from forest resources: 6.19% of GDP (2018 est.)
comparison ranking: 10

Revenue from coal: 0.03% of GDP (2018 est.)
comparison ranking: 37

Air pollutants: *particulate matter emissions:* 18.57 micrograms per cubic meter (2019 est.)
carbon dioxide emissions: 1.3 megatons (2016 est.)
methane emissions: 11.12 megatons (2020 est.)

Waste and recycling: *municipal solid waste generated annually:* 1,297,844 tons (2013 est.)

Major lakes (area sq km): *fresh water lake(s):* Lake Malawi (shared with Mozambique and Tanzania) - 22,490
salt water lake(s): Lake Chilwa - 1,040 sq km

Major rivers (by length in km): Zambezi (shared with Zambia [s], Angola, Zimbabwe, Namibia, Tanzania, and Mozambique [m]) - 2,740 km
note – [s] after country name indicates river source; [m] after country name indicates river mouth

Major watersheds (area sq km): Atlantic Ocean drainage: Congo (3,730,881 sq km)

Indian Ocean drainage: Zambezi (1,332,412 sq km)

Total water withdrawal: *municipal:* 140 million cubic meters (2020 est.)
industrial: 50 million cubic meters (2020 est.)
agricultural: 1.17 billion cubic meters (2020 est.)

Total renewable water resources: 17.28 billion cubic meters (2020 est.)

GOVERNMENT

Country name: *conventional long form:* Republic of Malawi
conventional short form: Malawi
local long form: Dziko la Malawi
local short form: Malawi
former: British Central African Protectorate, Nyasaland Protectorate, Nyasaland
etymology: named for the East African Maravi Kingdom of the 16th century; the word "maravi" means "fire flames"

Government type: presidential republic

Capital: *name:* Lilongwe
geographic coordinates: 13 58 S, 33 47 E
time difference: UTC+2 (7 hours ahead of Washington, DC, during Standard Time)
etymology: named after the Lilongwe River that flows through the city

Administrative divisions: 28 districts; Balaka, Blantyre, Chikwawa, Chiradzulu, Chitipa, Dedza, Dowa, Karonga, Kasungu, Likoma, Lilongwe, Machinga, Mangochi, Mchinji, Mulanje, Mwanza, Mzimba, Neno, Ntcheu, Nkhata Bay, Nkhotakota, Nsanje, Ntchisi, Phalombe, Rumphi, Salima, Thyolo, Zomba

Independence: 6 July 1964 (from the UK)

National holiday: Independence Day, 6 July (1964); note - also called Republic Day since 6 July 1966

Legal system: mixed legal system of English common law and customary law; judicial review of legislative acts in the Supreme Court of Appeal

Constitution: *history:* previous 1953 (pre-independence), 1964, 1966; latest drafted January to May 1994, approved 16 May 1994, entered into force 18 May 1995
amendments: proposed by the National Assembly; passage of amendments affecting constitutional articles, including the sovereignty and territory of the state, fundamental constitutional principles, human rights, voting rights, and the judiciary, requires majority approval in a referendum and majority approval by the Assembly; passage of other amendments requires at least two-thirds majority vote of the Assembly; amended several times, last in 2017

International law organization participation: accepts compulsory ICJ jurisdiction with reservations; accepts ICCt jurisdiction

Citizenship: *citizenship by birth:* no
citizenship by descent only: at least one parent must be a citizen of Malawi
dual citizenship recognized: no
residency requirement for naturalization: 7 years

Suffrage: 18 years of age; universal

Executive branch: *chief of state:* President Lazarus CHAKWERA (since 28 June 2020)
head of government: President Lazarus CHAKWERA (since 28 June 2020)
cabinet: Cabinet named by the president

elections/appointments: president directly elected by simple majority popular vote for a 5-year term (eligible for a second term); election last held on 23 June 2020 (next to be held in 2025) note - the president is both chief of state and head of government
election results:
2020: Lazarus CHAKWERA elected president; Lazarus CHAKWERA (MCP) 59.3%, Peter Mutharika (DPP) 39.9%, other 0.8%
2014: Peter MUTHARIKA elected president; percent of vote - Peter MUTHARIKA (DPP) 36.4%, Lazarus CHAKWERA (MCP) 27.8%, Joyce BANDA (PP) 20.2%, Atupele MULUZI (UDF) 13.7%, other 1.9%

Legislative branch: *description:* unicameral National Assembly (193 seats; members directly elected in single-seat constituencies by simple majority vote to serve 5-year terms)
elections: last held on 21 May 2019 (next to be held in May 2025)
election results: percent of vote by party - DPP 26%, MCP 22.3%, UTM 9.9%, UDF 4.6%, PP 2.4%, ADF 0.5%, independent 33.4%; seats by party - DPP 62, MCP 56, UDF 10, UTM 4, PP 5, ADF 1, independent 55; composition - men 153, women 40, percentage women 20.7%

Judicial branch: *highest court(s):* Supreme Court of Appeal (consists of the chief justice and at least 3 judges)
judge selection and term of office: Supreme Court chief justice appointed by the president and confirmed by the National Assembly; other judges appointed by the president upon the recommendation of the Judicial Service Commission, which regulates judicial officers; judges serve until age 65
subordinate courts: High Court; magistrate courts; Industrial Relations Court; district and city traditional or local courts

Political parties: Democratic Progressive Party or DPP
Malawi Congress Party or mCP
People's Party or PP
United Democratic Front or UDF
United Transformation Movement or UTM

International organization participation: ACP, AfDB, AU, C, CD, COMESA, FAO, G-77, IAEA, IBRD, ICAO, ICCt, ICRM, IDA, IFAD, IFC, IFRCS, ILO, IMF, IMO, Interpol, IOC, IOM, IPU, ISO (correspondent), ITSO, ITU, ITUC (NGOs), MIGA, MINURSO, MONUSCO, NAM, OPCW, SADC, UN, UNCTAD, UNESCO, UNHCR, UNHRC, UNIDO, UNISFA, UNOCI, UNWTO, UPU, WCO, WFTU (NGOs), WHO, WIPO, WMO, WTO

Diplomatic representation in the US: *chief of mission:* Ambassador Esme Jynet CHOMBO (since 19 April 2022)
chancery: 2408 Massachusetts Avenue NW, Washington, DC 20008
telephone: [1] (202) 451- 0409
email address and website:
malawidc@aol.com
Home | Malawi Embassy USA

Diplomatic representation from the US: *chief of mission:* Ambassador David YOUNG (since 5 May 2022)
embassy: 16 Jomo Kenyatta Road, Lilongwe 3
mailing address: 2280 Lilongwe Place, Washington DC 20521-2280
telephone: [265] (0) 177-3166
FAX: [265] (0) 177-0471
email address and website:
LilongweConsular@state.gov
https://mw.usembassy.gov/

Flag description: three equal horizontal bands of black (top), red, and green with a radiant, rising, red sun centered on the black band; black represents the native peoples, red the blood shed in their struggle for freedom, and green the color of nature; the rising sun represents the hope of freedom for the continent of Africa

National symbol(s): lion; national colors: black, red, green

National anthem: *name:* "Mulungu dalitsa Malawi" (Oh God Bless Our Land of Malawi)
lyrics/music: Michael-Fredrick Paul SAUKA
note: adopted 1964

National heritage: *total World Heritage Sites:* 2 (1 cultural, 1 natural)
selected World Heritage Site locales: Lake Malawi National Park (n); Chongoni Rock-Art Area (c)

ECONOMY

Economic overview: low-income East African economy; primarily agrarian; investing in human capital; urban poverty increasing due to COVID-19; high public debt; endemic corruption and poor property rights; poor hydroelectric grid; localized pharmaceutical industry

Real GDP (purchasing power parity): $35.238 billion (2023 est.)
$34.703 billion (2022 est.)
$34.386 billion (2021 est.)
note: data in 2021 dollars
comparison ranking: 142

Real GDP growth rate: 1.54% (2023 est.)
0.92% (2022 est.)
2.75% (2021 est.)
note: annual GDP % growth based on constant local currency
comparison ranking: 152

Real GDP per capita: $1,700 (2023 est.)
$1,700 (2022 est.)
$1,700 (2021 est.)
note: data in 2021 dollars
comparison ranking: 210

GDP (official exchange rate): $14.084 billion (2023 est.)
note: data in current dollars at official exchange rate

Inflation rate (consumer prices): 28.79% (2023 est.)
20.95% (2022 est.)
9.33% (2021 est.)
note: annual % change based on consumer prices
comparison ranking: 205

GDP - composition, by sector of origin: *agriculture:* 22.1% (2023 est.)
industry: 18.3% (2023 est.)
services: 52.2% (2023 est.)
note: figures may not total 100% due to non-allocated consumption not captured in sector-reported data
comparison rankings: services 131; industry 151; agriculture 31

GDP - composition, by end use: *household consumption:* 84.3% (2017 est.)
government consumption: 16.3% (2017 est.)
investment in fixed capital: 15.3% (2017 est.)
exports of goods and services: 27.9% (2017 est.)
imports of goods and services: -43.8% (2017 est.)

Agricultural products: sweet potatoes, cassava, maize, sugarcane, mangoes/guavas, potatoes, tomatoes, pigeon peas, bananas, pumpkins/ squash (2022)
note: top ten agricultural products based on tonnage

Industries: tobacco, tea, sugar, sawmill products, cement, consumer goods

Industrial production growth rate: 1.58% (2023 est.)
note: annual % change in industrial value added based on constant local currency
comparison ranking: 125

Labor force: 8.366 million (2023 est.)
note: number of people ages 15 or older who are employed or seeking work
comparison ranking: 64

Unemployment rate: 5.04% (2023 est.)
5.05% (2022 est.)
5.59% (2021 est.)
note: % of labor force seeking employment
comparison ranking: 94

Youth unemployment rate (ages 15-24): *total:* 6.8% (2023 est.)
male: 6.4% (2023 est.)
female: 7.2% (2023 est.)
note: % of labor force ages 15-24 seeking employment
comparison ranking: total 162

Population below poverty line: 50.7% (2019 est.)
note: % of population with income below national poverty line

Gini Index coefficient - distribution of family income: 38.5 (2019 est.)
note: index (0-100) of income distribution; higher values represent greater inequality
comparison ranking: 52

Household income or consumption by percentage share: *lowest 10%:* 2.9% (2019 est.)
highest 10%: 31% (2019 est.)
note: % share of income accruing to lowest and highest 10% of population

Remittances: 1.85% of GDP (2023 est.)
2.01% of GDP (2022 est.)
2.53% of GDP (2021 est.)
note: personal transfers and compensation between resident and non-resident individuals/households/entities

Budget: *revenues:* $1.688 billion (2020 est.)
expenditures: $1.941 billion (2020 est.)
note: central government revenues and expenses (excluding grants/extrabudgetary units/social security funds) converted to US dollars at average official exchange rate for year indicated

Public debt: 52.63% of GDP (2022 est.)
note: central government debt as a % of GDP
comparison ranking: 96

Taxes and other revenues: 12.78% (of GDP) (2022 est.)
note: central government tax revenue as a % of GDP
comparison ranking: 157

Current account balance: -$2.276 billion (2022 est.)
-$1.918 billion (2021 est.)
-$1.639 billion (2020 est.)
note: balance of payments - net trade and primary/secondary income in current dollars
comparison ranking: 163

Exports: $1.487 billion (2022 est.)
$1.587 billion (2021 est.)
$1.308 billion (2020 est.)
note: balance of payments - exports of goods and services in current dollars
comparison ranking: 169

Exports - partners: UAE 21%, Belgium 12%, Tanzania 6%, Kenya 5%, South Africa 5% (2022)
note: top five export partners based on percentage share of exports

Exports - commodities: tobacco, gold, tea, ground nuts, dried legumes (2022)
note: top five export commodities based on value in dollars

Imports: $3.706 billion (2022 est.)
$3.768 billion (2021 est.)
$3.373 billion (2020 est.)
note: balance of payments - imports of goods and services in current dollars
comparison ranking: 159

Imports - partners: South Africa 20%, China 15%, UAE 11%, India 6%, Kuwait 5% (2022)
note: top five import partners based on percentage share of imports

Imports - commodities: refined petroleum, fertilizers, crude petroleum, packaged medicine, plastic products (2022)
note: top five import commodities based on value in dollars

Reserves of foreign exchange and gold: $594.498 million (2020 est.)
$846.84 million (2019 est.)
$766.155 million (2018 est.)
note: holdings of gold (year-end prices)/foreign exchange/special drawing rights in current dollars
comparison ranking: 155

Debt - external: $1.971 billion (2022 est.)
note: present value of external debt in current US dollars
comparison ranking: 72

Exchange rates: Malawian kwachas (MWK) per US dollar -

Exchange rates: 749.527 (2020 est.)
745.541 (2019 est.)
732.333 (2018 est.)
730.273 (2017 est.)
718.005 (2016 est.)

ENERGY

Electricity access: *electrification - total population:* 14% (2022 est.)
electrification - urban areas: 54%
electrification - rural areas: 5.6%

Electricity: *installed generating capacity:* 758,000 kW (2022 est.)
consumption: 1.101 billion kWh (2022 est.)
exports: 20 million kWh (2022 est.)
transmission/distribution losses: 231.84 million kWh (2022 est.)
comparison rankings: transmission/distribution losses 66; exports 95; consumption 158; installed generating capacity 141

Electricity generation sources: *fossil fuels:* 5.7% of total installed capacity (2022 est.)
solar: 12.7% of total installed capacity (2022 est.)
hydroelectricity: 77.7% of total installed capacity (2022 est.)
biomass and waste: 4% of total installed capacity (2022 est.)

Coal: *production:* 50,000 metric tons (2022 est.)
consumption: 50,000 metric tons (2022 est.)
exports: (2022 est.) less than 1 metric ton
imports: 2.5 metric tons (2022 est.)
proven reserves: 801.999 million metric tons (2022 est.)

Petroleum: *refined petroleum consumption:* 11,000 bbl/day (2022 est.)

Carbon dioxide emissions: 1.617 million metric tonnes of CO2 (2022 est.)
from coal and metallurgical coke: 112,000 metric tonnes of CO2 (2022 est.)
from petroleum and other liquids: 1.505 million metric tonnes of CO2 (2022 est.)
comparison ranking: total emissions 163

Energy consumption per capita: 1.331 million Btu/person (2022 est.)
comparison ranking: 191

COMMUNICATIONS

Telephones - fixed lines: *total subscriptions:* 9,000 (2022 est.)
subscriptions per 100 inhabitants: (2022 est.) less than 1
comparison ranking: total subscriptions 191

Telephones - mobile cellular: *total subscriptions:* 12.269 million (2022 est.)
subscriptions per 100 inhabitants: 60 (2022 est.)
comparison ranking: total subscriptions 81

Telecommunication systems: *general assessment:* with few resources, Malawi is one of the world's least developed countries; there has been little investment in fixed-line telecom infrastructure, and as a result, the country's two mobile networks Airtel Malawi and TMN provide the vast majority of connections for voice and data services; both operators have invested in LTE technologies to improve the quality of data services; the lack of market competition, together with limited international internet bandwidth, has also resulted in some of the highest prices for telecom services in the region; the government in late 2020 secured an average 80% reduction in the cost of data bundles offered by the MNOs; following continuing customer complaints, the regulator in mid-2021 ensured that costs were again reduced, this time by about a third; mobile penetration remains low in comparison to the regional average and so there are considerable opportunities for further growth, particularly in the mobile broadband sector, though there is the possibility that a new play come launch services by the end of 2022; the internet sector is reasonably competitive, with about 50 licensed ISPs, though the limited availability and high cost of international bandwidth has held back growth and kept broadband access prices among the highest in the region; these limitations are being addressed, with the second phase of the national fiber backbone having started in mid-2021 (2022)
domestic: limited fixed-line subscribership less than 1 per 100 households; mobile-cellular subscribership roughly 60 per 100 households (2021)
international: country code - 265; satellite earth stations - 2 Intelsat (1 Indian Ocean, 1 Atlantic Ocean) (2019)

Broadcast media: radio is the main broadcast medium; privately owned Zodiak radio has the widest national broadcasting reach, followed by state-run radio; numerous private and community radio stations broadcast in cities and towns around the country; the largest TV network is government-owned, but at least 4 private TV networks broadcast in urban areas; relays of multiple international broadcasters are available (2019)

Internet country code: .mw

Internet users: *total:* 4.8 million (2021 est.)
percent of population: 24% (2021 est.)
comparison ranking: total 100

Broadband - fixed subscriptions: *total:* 12,255 (2020 est.)
subscriptions per 100 inhabitants: 0.1 (2020 est.)
comparison ranking: total 176

TRANSPORTATION

National air transport system: *number of registered air carriers:* 2 (2020)
inventory of registered aircraft operated by air carriers: 9
annual passenger traffic on registered air carriers: 10,545 (2018)
annual freight traffic on registered air carriers: 10,000 (2018) mt-km

Civil aircraft registration country code prefix: 7Q

Airports: 28 (2024)
comparison ranking: 123

Railways: *total:* 767 km (2014)
narrow gauge: 767 km (2014) 1.067-m gauge
comparison ranking: total 97

Roadways: *total:* 15,451 km
paved: 4,038 km
unpaved: 11,413 km (2022)
comparison ranking: total 122

Waterways: 700 km (2010) (on Lake Nyasa [Lake Malawi] and Shire River)
comparison ranking: 82

MILITARY AND SECURITY

Military and security forces: Malawi Defense Force (MDF): Land Forces (Army), Maritime Force, Air Force, National Service (reserve force)

Ministry of Homeland Security: Malawi Police Service (2024)
note: the MDF reports directly to the president as commander in chief

Military expenditures: 0.7% of GDP (2023 est.)
0.7% of GDP (2022 est.)
0.9% of GDP (2021 est.)
0.9% of GDP (2020 est.)
1.1% of GDP (2019 est.)
comparison ranking: 147

Military and security service personnel strengths: estimated 10,000 active military personnel (2023)

Military equipment inventories and acquisitions: the MDF's inventory is comprised of mostly obsolescent or secondhand equipment originating from such countries as France, South Africa, and the UK (2023)

Military service age and obligation: 18-30years of age for men and women for voluntary military service; high school equivalent required for enlisted recruits and college equivalent for officer recruits; initial engagement is 7 years for enlisted personnel and 10 years for officers (2023)

Military deployments: 740 Democratic Republic of the Congo (MONUSCO; note - as of early 2024, MONUSCO forces were drawing down towards a complete withdrawal by the end of 2024) (2024)

Military - note: the MDF's primary responsibility is external security; it is also tasked as necessary with providing support to civilian authorities during emergencies, supporting the Police Service, protecting national forest reserves, and participating in regional peacekeeping missions, as well as assisting with

infrastructure development; it is generally considered to be a professional and effective service, although most of its equipment is aging and obsolescent; Malawi contributes regularly to African Union and UN peace support operations
the MDF was established in 1964 from elements of the Kings African Rifles (KAR), a British colonial regiment raised from Great Britain's various possessions in East Africa from 1902 until independence in the 1960s; the KAR conducted both military and internal security functions within the colonial territories, and served outside the territories during the World Wars (2023)

TRANSNATIONAL ISSUES

Refugees and internally displaced persons: *refugees (country of origin):* 11,502 (Burundi) (refugees and asylum seekers), 6,594 (Rwanda) (refugees and asylum seekers) (2023); 34,605 (Democratic Republic of the Congo) (refugees and asylum seekers)

Illicit drugs: NA

MALAYSIA

INTRODUCTION

Background: Malaysia's location has long made it an important cultural, economic, historical, social, and trade link between the islands of Southeast Asia and the mainland. Through the Strait of Malacca, which separates the Malay Peninsula from the archipelago, flowed maritime trade and with it influences from China, India, the Middle East, and the east coast of Africa. Prior to the 14th century, several powerful maritime empires existed in what is modern-day Malaysia, including the Srivijayan, which controlled much of the southern part of the peninsula between the 7th and 13th centuries, and the Majapahit Empire, which took control over most of the peninsula and the Malay Archipelago between the 13th and 14th centuries. The adoption of Islam between the 13th and 17th centuries also saw the rise of a number of powerful maritime states and sultanates on the Malay Peninsula and the island of Borneo, such as the port city of Malacca (Melaka), which at its height in the 15th century had a navy and hosted thousands of Chinese, Arab, Persian, and Indian merchants.

The Portuguese in the 16th century and the Dutch in the 17th century were the first European colonial powers to establish themselves on the Malay Peninsula and in Southeast Asia. However, it was the British who ultimately secured hegemony across the territory and during the late 18th and 19th centuries established colonies and protectorates in the area that is now Malaysia. Japan occupied these holdings from 1942 to 1945. In 1948, the British-ruled territories on the Malay Peninsula (except Singapore) formed the Federation of Malaya, which became independent in 1957. Malaysia was formed in 1963 when the former British colonies of Singapore, as well as Sabah and Sarawak on the northern coast of Borneo, joined the Federation.

A communist insurgency, confrontations with Indonesia, Philippine claims to Sabah, and Singapore's expulsion in 1965 marred the first several years of the country's independence. During the 22-year term of Prime Minister MAHATHIR Mohamad (1981-2003), Malaysia was successful in diversifying its economy from dependence on exports of raw materials to the development of manufacturing, services, and tourism. Former Prime Minister MAHATHIR and a newly formed coalition of opposition parties defeated Prime Minister Mohamed NAJIB bin Abdul Razak's United Malays National Organization (UMNO) in 2018, ending over 60 years of uninterrupted UMNO rule. From 2018-2022, Malaysia underwent considerable political upheaval, with a succession of coalition governments holding power. Following legislative elections in 2022, ANWAR Ibrahim was appointed prime minister after more than 20 years in opposition. His political coalition, Pakatan Harapan (PH), joined its longtime UNMO rival to form a government, but the two groups have remained deeply divided on many issues.

GEOGRAPHY

Location: Southeastern Asia, peninsula bordering Thailand and northern one-third of the island of Borneo, bordering Indonesia, Brunei, and the South China Sea, south of Vietnam

Geographic coordinates: 2 30 N, 112 30 E

Map references: Southeast Asia

Area: *total:* 329,847 sq km
land: 328,657 sq km
water: 1,190 sq km
comparison ranking: total 68

Area - comparative: slightly larger than New Mexico

Land boundaries: *total:* 2,742 km
border countries (3): Brunei 266 km; Indonesia 1,881 km; Thailand 595 km

Coastline: 4,675 km (Peninsular Malaysia 2,068 km, East Malaysia 2,607 km)

Maritime claims: *territorial sea:* 12 nm
exclusive economic zone: 200 nm
continental shelf: 200-m depth or to the depth of exploitation; specified boundary in the South China Sea

Climate: tropical; annual southwest (April to October) and northeast (October to February) monsoons

Terrain: coastal plains rising to hills and mountains

Elevation: *highest point:* Gunung Kinabalu 4,095 m
lowest point: Indian Ocean 0 m
mean elevation: 419 m

Natural resources: tin, petroleum, timber, copper, iron ore, natural gas, bauxite

Land use: *agricultural land:* 23.2% (2018 est.)
arable land: 2.9% (2018 est.)
permanent crops: 19.4% (2018 est.)
permanent pasture: 0.9% (2018 est.)
forest: 62% (2018 est.)
other: 14.8% (2018 est.)

Irrigated land: 4,420 sq km (2020)

Population distribution: a highly uneven distribution with over 80% of the population residing on the Malay Peninsula

Natural hazards: flooding; landslides; forest fires

Geography - note: strategic location along Strait of Malacca and southern South China Sea

PEOPLE AND SOCIETY

Population: *total:* 34,564,810
male: 17,666,212
female: 16,898,598 (2024 est.)
comparison rankings: female 45; male 43; total 45

Nationality: *noun:* Malaysian(s)
adjective: Malaysian

Ethnic groups: Bumiputera 63.8% (Malay 52.8% and indigenous peoples, including Orang Asli, Dayak, Anak Negeri, 11%), Chinese 20.6%, Indian 6%, other 0.6%, non-citizens 9% (2023 est.)

Languages: Bahasa Malaysia (official), English, Chinese (Cantonese, Mandarin, Hokkien, Hakka, Hainan, Foochow), Tamil, Telugu, Malayalam, Panjabi, Thai
major-language sample(s):
Buku Fakta Dunia, sumber yang diperlukan untuk maklumat asas. (Bahasa Malaysia)
note: Malaysia has 134 languages (112 indigenous and 22 non-indigenous); in East Malaysia, there are several indigenous languages, and the most widely spoken are Iban and Kadazan

Religions: Muslim (official) 63.5%, Buddhist 18.7%, Christian 9.1%, Hindu 6.1%, other (Confucianism, Taoism, other traditional Chinese religions) 0.9%, none/unspecified 1.8% (2020 est.)

Demographic profile: Malaysia's multi-ethnic population consists of the bumiputera – Malays and other indigenous peoples – (62%), ethnic Chinese (21%), ethnic Indians (6%), and foreigners (10%). The majority of Malaysia's ethnic Chinese and Indians trace their roots to the British colonialists' recruitment of hundreds of thousands of Chinese and Indians as mine and plantation workers between the early-19th century and the 1930s. Most Malays have maintained their rural lifestyle, while the entrepreneurial Chinese have achieved greater wealth and economic dominance. In order to eradicate Malay poverty, the Malaysian Government in 1971 adopted policies that gave preference to the bumiputera in public university admissions, government jobs and contracts, and property ownership. Affirmative action continues to benefit well-off urban bumiputera but has done little to alleviate poverty for their more numerous rural counterparts. The policies have pushed ethnic Chinese and Indians to study at private or foreign universities (many do not return) and have created and sustained one of the world's largest civil services, which is 85-90% Malay.

The country's age structure has changed significantly since the 1960s, as fertility and mortality rates have declined. Malaysia's total fertility rate (TFR) has dropped from 5 children per woman in 1970, to 3 in 1998, to 2.1 in 2015 as a result of increased educational attainment and labor participation among women, later marriages, increased use of contraception, and changes in family size preference related to urbanization. The TFR is higher among Malays, rural residents (who are mainly Malay), the poor, and the less-educated. Despite the reduced fertility rate, Malaysia's population will continue to grow, albeit at a decreasing rate, for the next few decades because of its large number of reproductive-age women. The youth population has been shrinking, and the working-age population (15-64 year olds) has been growing steadily. Malaysia's labor market has successfully absorbed the increasing number of job seekers, leading to sustained economic growth. However, the favorable age structure is changing, and around 2020, Malaysia will start to become a rapidly aging society. As the population ages, Malaysia will need to better educate and train its labor force, raise productivity, and continue to increase the number of women workers in order to further develop its economy.

More than 1.8 million Malaysians lived abroad as of 2015, including anywhere from 350,000 to 785,000 workers, more than half of whom have an advanced level of education. The vast majority of emigrants are ethnic Chinese, seeking better educational and job opportunities abroad because of institutionalized ethnic discrimination favoring the Malays. The primary destination country is nearby Singapore, followed by Bangladesh and Australia. Hundreds of thousands of Malaysians also commute across the causeway to Singapore daily for work.

Brain drain is an impediment to Malaysia's goal of becoming a high-income country. The situation is compounded by a migrant inflow that is composed almost entirely of low-skilled laborers who work mainly in manufacturing, agriculture, and construction. Officially, Malaysia had about 1.8 million legal foreign workers as of mid-year 2017 – largely from Indonesia, Nepal, the Philippines, and Bangladesh – but as many as 3 to 4 million are estimated to be in the country illegally. Immigrants outnumber ethnic Indians and could supplant the ethnic Chinese as Malaysia's second largest population group around 2035.

Age structure: *0-14 years:* 22.2% (male 3,947,914/female 3,730,319)
15-64 years: 69.4% (male 12,308,938/female 11,666,947)
65 years and over: 8.4% (2024 est.) (male 1,409,360/female 1,501,332)

Dependency ratios: *total dependency ratio:* 43.3
youth dependency ratio: 32.9
elderly dependency ratio: 10.4
potential support ratio: 9.6 (2021 est.)

Median age: *total:* 31.8 years (2024 est.)
male: 31.7 years
female: 31.9 years
comparison ranking: total 122

Population growth rate: 0.99% (2024 est.)
comparison ranking: 94

Birth rate: 14.2 births/1,000 population (2024 est.)
comparison ranking: 120

Death rate: 5.8 deaths/1,000 population (2024 est.)
comparison ranking: 166

Net migration rate: 1.5 migrant(s)/1,000 population (2024 est.)
comparison ranking: 57

Population distribution: a highly uneven distribution with over 80% of the population residing on the Malay Peninsula

Urbanization: *urban population:* 78.7% of total population (2023)
rate of urbanization: 1.87% annual rate of change (2020-25 est.)

Major urban areas - population: 8.622 million KUALA LUMPUR (capital), 1.086 million Johor Bahru, 857,000 Ipoh (2023)

Sex ratio: *at birth:* 1.07 male(s)/female
0-14 years: 1.06 male(s)/female
15-64 years: 1.06 male(s)/female
65 years and over: 0.94 male(s)/female
total population: 1.05 male(s)/female (2024 est.)

Maternal mortality ratio: 21 deaths/100,000 live births (2020 est.)
comparison ranking: 124

Infant mortality rate: *total:* 6.4 deaths/1,000 live births (2024 est.)
male: 6.8 deaths/1,000 live births
female: 6 deaths/1,000 live births
comparison ranking: total 164

Life expectancy at birth: *total population:* 76.6 years (2024 est.)
male: 75 years
female: 78.4 years
comparison ranking: total population 106

Total fertility rate: 1.73 children born/woman (2024 est.)
comparison ranking: 156

Gross reproduction rate: 0.84 (2024 est.)

Contraceptive prevalence rate: 52.2% (2014)

Drinking water source: *improved: urban:* 99.4% of population
rural: 90.7% of population
total: 97.5% of population
unimproved: urban: 0.6% of population
rural: 9.3% of population
total: 2.5% of population (2020 est.)

Current health expenditure: 4.1% of GDP (2020)

Physician density: 1.54 physicians/1,000 population (2020)

Hospital bed density: 1.9 beds/1,000 population (2017)

Sanitation facility access: *improved: urban:* 99% of population
unimproved: urban: 0.1% of population

Obesity - adult prevalence rate: 15.6% (2016)
comparison ranking: 125

Alcohol consumption per capita: *total:* 0.64 liters of pure alcohol (2019 est.)
beer: 0.48 liters of pure alcohol (2019 est.)
wine: 0.04 liters of pure alcohol (2019 est.)
spirits: 0.11 liters of pure alcohol (2019 est.)
other alcohols: 0.01 liters of pure alcohol (2019 est.)
comparison ranking: total 158

Tobacco use: *total:* 22.5% (2020 est.)
male: 43.8% (2020 est.)
female: 1.1% (2020 est.)
comparison ranking: total 68

Children under the age of 5 years underweight: 14.1% (2019)
comparison ranking: 38

Currently married women (ages 15-49): 59.3% (2023 est.)

Education expenditures: 3.9% of GDP (2020 est.)
comparison ranking: 124

Literacy: *definition:* age 15 and over can read and write
total population: 95%
male: 96.2%
female: 93.6% (2019)

School life expectancy (primary to tertiary education): *total:* 13 years
male: 13 years
female: 14 years (2020)

ENVIRONMENT

Environment - current issues: air pollution from industrial and vehicular emissions; water pollution from raw sewage; deforestation; smoke/haze from Indonesian forest fires; endangered species; coastal reclamation damaging mangroves and turtle nesting sites

Environment - international agreements: *party to:* Antarctic-Environmental Protection, Antarctic Treaty, Biodiversity, Climate Change, Climate Change-Kyoto Protocol, Climate Change-Paris Agreement, Comprehensive Nuclear Test Ban, Desertification, Endangered Species, Hazardous Wastes, Law of the Sea, Marine Life Conservation, Nuclear Test Ban, Ozone Layer Protection, Ship Pollution, Tropical Timber 2006, Wetlands
signed, but not ratified: none of the selected agreements

Climate: tropical; annual southwest (April to October) and northeast (October to February) monsoons

Urbanization: *urban population:* 78.7% of total population (2023)
rate of urbanization: 1.87% annual rate of change (2020-25 est.)

Revenue from forest resources: 1.57% of GDP (2018 est.)
comparison ranking: 40

Revenue from coal: 0.02% of GDP (2018 est.)
comparison ranking: 45

Air pollutants: *particulate matter emissions:* 21.52 micrograms per cubic meter (2019 est.)
carbon dioxide emissions: 248.29 megatons (2016 est.)
methane emissions: 51.51 megatons (2020 est.)

Waste and recycling: *municipal solid waste generated annually:* 12,982,685 tons (2014 est.)
municipal solid waste recycled annually: 2,271,970 tons (2016 est.)
percent of municipal solid waste recycled: 17.5% (2016 est.)

Total water withdrawal: *municipal:* 1.34 billion cubic meters (2020 est.)
industrial: 1.64 billion cubic meters (2020 est.)
agricultural: 2.51 billion cubic meters (2020 est.)

Total renewable water resources: 580 billion cubic meters (2020 est.)

Geoparks: *total global geoparks and regional networks:* 2

global geoparks and regional networks: Kinabalu; Langkawi (2023)

GOVERNMENT

Country name: *conventional long form:* none
conventional short form: Malaysia
local long form: none
local short form: Malaysia
former: British Malaya, Malayan Union, Federation of Malaya
etymology: the name means "Land of the Malays"

Government type: federal parliamentary constitutional monarchy
note: all Peninsular Malaysian states have hereditary rulers (commonly referred to as sultans) except Melaka (Malacca) and Pulau Pinang (Penang); those two states along with Sabah and Sarawak in East Malaysia have governors appointed by government; powers of state governments are limited by the federal constitution; under terms of federation, Sabah and Sarawak retain certain constitutional prerogatives (e.g., right to maintain their own immigration controls)

Capital: *name:* Kuala Lumpur; note - nearby Putrajaya is referred to as a federal government administrative center but not the capital; Parliament meets in Kuala Lumpur
geographic coordinates: 3 10 N, 101 42 E
time difference: UTC+8 (13 hours ahead of Washington, DC, during Standard Time)
etymology: the Malay word for "river junction or estuary" is *kuala* and *lumpur* means "mud"; together the words render the meaning of "muddy confluence"

Administrative divisions: 13 states (negeri-negeri, singular - negeri); Johor, Kedah, Kelantan, Melaka, Negeri Sembilan, Pahang, Perak, Perlis, Pulau Pinang, Sabah, Sarawak, Selangor, Terengganu; and 1 federal territory (Wilayah Persekutuan) with 3 components, Kuala Lumpur, Labuan, and Putrajaya

Independence: 31 August 1957 (from the UK)

National holiday: Independence Day (or Merdeka Day), 31 August (1957) (independence of Malaya); Malaysia Day, 16 September (1963) (formation of Malaysia)

Legal system: mixed legal system of English common law, Islamic law (sharia), and customary law; judicial review of legislative acts in the Federal Court at request of supreme head of the federation

Constitution: *history:* previous 1948; latest drafted 21 February 1957, effective 27 August 1957
amendments: proposed as a bill by Parliament; passage requires at least two-thirds majority vote by the Parliament membership in the bill's second and third readings; a number of constitutional sections are excluded from amendment or repeal; amended many times, last in 2019

International law organization participation: has not submitted an ICJ jurisdiction declaration; non-party state to the ICCt

Citizenship: *citizenship by birth:* no
citizenship by descent only: at least one parent must be a citizen of Malaysia
dual citizenship recognized: no
residency requirement for naturalization: 10 out 12 years preceding application

Suffrage: 18 years of age; universal

Executive branch: *chief of state:* King Sultan IBRAHIM ibni al-Marhum Sultan Iskandar (since 31 January 2024)
head of government: Prime Minister ANWAR Ibrahim (since 25 November 2022)
cabinet: Cabinet appointed by the prime minister from among members of Parliament with the consent of the king
elections/appointments: king elected by and from the hereditary rulers of 9 states for a 5-year term; election is on a rotational basis among rulers of the 9 states; election last held on 24 October 2023 (next to be held in October 2028 with installation in January 2029); prime minister designated from among members of the House of Representatives; following legislative elections, the leader who commands support of the majority of members in the House becomes prime minister
note: the position of the king is primarily ceremonial, but he is the final arbiter on the appointment of the prime minister

Legislative branch: *description:* bicameral Parliament of Malaysia or Parlimen Malaysia consists of:
Senate or Dewan Negara (70 seats; 44 members appointed by the king and 26 indirectly elected by 13 state legislatures; members serve 3-year terms)
House of Representatives or Dewan Rakyat (222 seats; members directly elected in single-seat constituencies by simple majority vote to serve 5-year terms)
elections: Senate - appointed
House of Representatives - last held on 19 Nov 2022 (next to be held in 2027)
election results: Senate - appointed; composition - men 51, women 10, percentage women 16.4%
House of Representatives - percent of vote by party/coalition - PH 37.5%, PN 30.4%, BN 22.4%, GPS 4%, WARISAN 1.8%, GRS 1.3%, other 2.6%; seats by party/coalition - PH 90, PN 50, BN 42, GPS 18, WARISAN 7, PEJUANG 4, PBM 3, PSB 1, MUDA 1, independent 4, vacant 2; composition - 192 men, 30 women; percentage women 13.5%; total Parliament percentage women 9.2%

Judicial branch: *highest court(s):* Federal Court (consists of the chief justice, president of the Court of Appeal, chief justice of the High Court of Malaya, chief judge of the High Court of Sabah and Sarawak, 8 judges, and 1 "additional" judge); note - Malaysia has a dual judicial hierarchy of civil and religious (sharia) courts
judge selection and term of office: Federal Court justices appointed by the monarch on advice of the prime minister; judges serve until mandatory retirement at age 66 with the possibility of a single 6-month extension
subordinate courts: Court of Appeal; High Court; Sessions Court; Magistrates' Court

Political parties: National Front (Barisan Nasional) or BN: Malaysian Chinese Association (Persatuan Cina Malaysia) or MCA
Malaysian Indian Congress (Kongres India Malaysia) or MIC
United Malays National Organization (Pertubuhan Kebansaan Melayu Bersatu) or UMNO
United Sabah People's Party (Parti Bersatu Rakyat Sabah) or PBRS

Alliance of Hope (Pakatan Harapan) or PH: Democratic Action Party (Parti Tindakan Demokratik) or DAP
National Trust Party (Parti Amanah Negara) or AMANAH
People's Justice Party (Parti Keadilan Rakyat) or PKR
United Progressive Kinabalu Organization (Pertubuhan Kinabalu Progresif Bersatu) or UPKO

National Alliance (Perikatan Nasional) or PN: Malaysian People's Movement Party (Parti Gerakan Rakyat Malaysia) or GERAKAN or PGRM
Malaysian United Indigenous Party (Parti Pribumi Bersatu Malaysia) or PPBM or BERSATU
Pan-Malaysian Islamic Party (Parti Islam Se-Malaysia) or PAS

Sabah People's Alliance (Gabungan Rakya Sabah) or GRS: Homeland Solidarity Party (Parti Solidariti Tanah Airku) or STAR
Love Sabah Party (Parti Cinta Sabah) or PCS
Sabah People's Ideas Party (Parti Gagasan Rakyat Sabah) or GAGASAN or PGRS

Sarawak Parties Alliance (Gabungan Parti Sarawak) or GPS: Progressive Democratic Party (Parti Demokratik Progresif) or PDP
Sarawak People's Party (Parti Rakyat Sarawak) or PRS
Sarawak United People's Party (Parti Rakyat Bersatu Sarawak) or SUPP
United Bumiputera Heritage Party (Parti Pesaka Bumiputera Bersata) or PBB

Others: Malaysian Nation Party (Parti Bangsa Malaysia) or PBM
Heritage Party (Parti Warisan) or WARISAN
Homeland Fighter's Party (Parti Pejuang Tanah Air) or PEJUANG
Malaysian United Democratic Alliance (Ikatan Demokratik Malaysia) or MUDA
United Sarawak Party (PSB)

International organization participation: ADB, APEC, ARF, ASEAN, BIS, C, CICA (observer), CP, D-8, EAS, FAO, G-15, G-77, IAEA, IBRD, ICAO, ICC (national committees), ICRM, IDA, IDB, IFAD, IFC, IFRCS, IHO, ILO, IMF, IMO, IMSO, Interpol, IOC, IPU, ISO, ITSO, ITU, ITUC (NGOs), MIGA, MINURSO, MONUSCO, NAM, OIC, OPCW, PCA, PIF (partner), UN, UNAMID, UNCTAD, UNESCO, UNHRC, UNIDO, UNIFIL, UNISFA, UNMIL, UNWTO, UPU, WCO, WFTU (NGOs), WHO, WIPO, WMO, WTO

Diplomatic representation in the US: *chief of mission:* Ambassador Mohamed NAZRI Bin Abdul Aziz (since 19 April 2023)
chancery: 3516 International Court NW, Washington, DC 20008
telephone: [1] (202) 572-9700
FAX: [1] (202) 572-9882
email address and website:
mwwashington@kln.gov.my
https://www.kln.gov.my/web/usa_washington/home
consulate(s) general: Los Angeles, New York

Diplomatic representation from the US: *chief of mission:* Ambassador Edgard D. KAGAN (since 20 March 2024)
embassy: 376 Jalan Tun Razak, 50400 Kuala Lumpur
mailing address: 4210 Kuala Lumpur, Washington DC 20521-4210
telephone: [60] (3) 2168-5000
FAX: [60] (3) 2142-2207
email address and website:
KLACS@state.gov
https://my.usembassy.gov/

Flag description: 14 equal horizontal stripes of red (top) alternating with white (bottom); there is a dark blue rectangle in the upper hoistside corner bearing a yellow crescent and a yellow 14-pointed star; the

flag is often referred to as Jalur Gemilang (Stripes of Glory); the 14 stripes stand for the equal status in the federation of the 13 member states and the federal government; the 14 points on the star represent the unity between these entities; the crescent is a traditional symbol of Islam; blue symbolizes the unity of the Malay people and yellow is the royal color of Malay rulers
note: the design is based on the flag of the US

National symbol(s): tiger, hibiscus; national colors: gold, black

National anthem: *name:* "Negaraku" (My Country)
lyrics/music: collective, led by Tunku ABDUL RAHMAN/Pierre Jean DE BERANGER
note: adopted 1957; full version only performed in the presence of the king; the tune, which was adopted from a popular French melody titled "La Rosalie," was originally the anthem of Perak, one of Malaysia's 13 states

National heritage: *total World Heritage Sites:* 4 (2 cultural, 2 natural)
selected World Heritage Site locales: Gunung Mulu National Park (n); Kinabalu Park (n); Malacca and George Town, Historic Cities of the Straits of Malacca (c); Archaeological Heritage of the Lenggong Valley (c)

ECONOMY

Economic overview: upper middle-income Southeast Asian economy; implementing key anticorruption policies; major electronics, oil, and chemicals exporter; trade sector employs over 40% of jobs; key economic equity initiative; high labor productivity

Real GDP (purchasing power parity): $1.152 trillion (2023 est.)
$1.111 trillion (2022 est.)
$1.023 trillion (2021 est.)
note: data in 2021 dollars
comparison ranking: 29

Real GDP growth rate: 3.68% (2023 est.)
8.65% (2022 est.)
3.3% (2021 est.)
note: annual GDP % growth based on constant local currency
comparison ranking: 87

Real GDP per capita: $33,600 (2023 est.)
$32,700 (2022 est.)
$30,500 (2021 est.)
note: data in 2021 dollars
comparison ranking: 73

GDP (official exchange rate): $399.649 billion (2023 est.)
note: data in current dollars at official exchange rate

Inflation rate (consumer prices): 2.49% (2023 est.)
3.38% (2022 est.)
2.48% (2021 est.)
note: annual % change based on consumer prices
comparison ranking: 52

Credit ratings: Fitch rating: BBB+ (2020)

Moody's rating: A3 (2004)

Standard & Poors rating: A- (2003)
note: The year refers to the year in which the current credit rating was first obtained.

GDP - composition, by sector of origin: *agriculture:* 7.7% (2023 est.)
industry: 37.7% (2023 est.)
services: 53.5% (2023 est.)
note: figures may not total 100% due to non-allocated consumption not captured in sector-reported data
comparison rankings: services 125; industry 36; agriculture 94

GDP - composition, by end use: *household consumption:* 60.4% (2023 est.)
government consumption: 12% (2023 est.)
investment in fixed capital: 19.2% (2023 est.)
investment in inventories: 3.3% (2023 est.)
exports of goods and services: 68.4% (2023 est.)
imports of goods and services: -63.4% (2023 est.)
note: figures may not total 100% due to rounding or gaps in data collection

Agricultural products: oil palm fruit, rice, chicken, eggs, coconuts, tropical fruits, vegetables, rubber, bananas, pineapples (2022)
note: top ten agricultural products based on tonnage

Industries: Peninsular Malaysia - rubber and oil palm processing and manufacturing, petroleum and natural gas, light manufacturing, pharmaceuticals, medical technology, electronics and semiconductors, timber processing; Sabah - logging, petroleum and natural gas production; Sarawak - agriculture processing, petroleum and natural gas production, logging

Industrial production growth rate: 1.43% (2023 est.)
note: annual % change in industrial value added based on constant local currency
comparison ranking: 130

Labor force: 17.308 million (2023 est.)
note: number of people ages 15 or older who are employed or seeking work
comparison ranking: 37

Unemployment rate: 3.86% (2023 est.)
3.93% (2022 est.)
4.64% (2021 est.)
note: % of labor force seeking employment
comparison ranking: 73

Youth unemployment rate (ages 15-24): *total:* 12.5% (2023 est.)
male: 11.4% (2023 est.)
female: 14.2% (2023 est.)
note: % of labor force ages 15-24 seeking employment
comparison ranking: total 110

Population below poverty line: 6.2% (2021 est.)
note: % of population with income below national poverty line

Gini Index coefficient - distribution of family income: 40.7 (2021 est.)
note: index (0-100) of income distribution; higher values represent greater inequality
comparison ranking: 39

Average household expenditures: *on food:* 24.5% of household expenditures (2022 est.)
on alcohol and tobacco: 1.8% of household expenditures (2022 est.)

Household income or consumption by percentage share: *lowest 10%:* 2.3% (2021 est.)
highest 10%: 30.9% (2021 est.)
note: % share of income accruing to lowest and highest 10% of population

Remittances: 0.44% of GDP (2023 est.)
0.4% of GDP (2022 est.)
0.42% of GDP (2021 est.)
note: personal transfers and compensation between resident and non-resident individuals/households/entities

Budget: *revenues:* $66.883 billion (2022 est.)
expenditures: $72.986 billion (2022 est.)
note: central government revenues and expenses (excluding grants/extrabudgetary units/social security funds) converted to US dollars at average official exchange rate for year indicated

Public debt: 60.27% of GDP (2022 est.)
note: central government debt as a % of GDP
comparison ranking: 81

Taxes and other revenues: 11.65% (of GDP) (2022 est.)
note: central government tax revenue as a % of GDP
comparison ranking: 168

Current account balance: $12.271 billion (2022 est.)
$14.493 billion (2021 est.)
$14.138 billion (2020 est.)
note: balance of payments - net trade and primary/secondary income in current dollars
comparison ranking: 26

Exports: $312.857 billion (2022 est.)
$263.836 billion (2021 est.)
$208.217 billion (2020 est.)
note: balance of payments - exports of goods and services in current dollars
comparison ranking: 30

Exports - partners: Singapore 14%, China 13%, US 12%, Japan 6%, Hong Kong 6% (2022)
note: top five export partners based on percentage share of exports

Exports - commodities: integrated circuits, refined petroleum, natural gas, palm oil, crude petroleum (2022)
note: top five export commodities based on value in dollars

Imports: $283.601 billion (2022 est.)
$236.855 billion (2021 est.)
$186.613 billion (2020 est.)
note: balance of payments - imports of goods and services in current dollars
comparison ranking: 30

Imports - partners: China 28%, Singapore 12%, US 6%, Taiwan 6%, Japan 5% (2022)
note: top five import partners based on percentage share of imports

Imports - commodities: integrated circuits, refined petroleum, crude petroleum, coal, vehicle parts/accessories (2022)
note: top five import commodities based on value in dollars

Reserves of foreign exchange and gold: $113.438 billion (2023 est.)
$114.659 billion (2022 est.)
$116.916 billion (2021 est.)
note: holdings of gold (year-end prices)/foreign exchange/special drawing rights in current dollars
comparison ranking: 26

Exchange rates: ringgits (MYR) per US dollar -

Exchange rates: 4.561 (2023 est.)
4.401 (2022 est.)
4.143 (2021 est.)
4.203 (2020 est.)
4.142 (2019 est.)

ENERGY

Electricity access: *electrification - total population:* 100% (2022 est.)

Electricity: *installed generating capacity:* 36.301 million kW (2022 est.)
consumption: 181.004 billion kWh (2022 est.)
exports: 1.062 billion kWh (2022 est.)

imports: 38.028 million kWh (2022 est.)
transmission/distribution losses: 12.262 billion kWh (2022 est.)
comparison rankings: transmission/distribution losses 185; imports 117; exports 68; consumption 24; installed generating capacity 33

Electricity generation sources: *fossil fuels:* 81.4% of total installed capacity (2022 est.)
solar: 1.1% of total installed capacity (2022 est.)
hydroelectricity: 16.9% of total installed capacity (2022 est.)
biomass and waste: 0.6% of total installed capacity (2022 est.)

Coal: *production:* 3.731 million metric tons (2022 est.)
consumption: 35.05 million metric tons (2022 est.)
exports: 168,000 metric tons (2022 est.)
imports: 31.834 million metric tons (2022 est.)
proven reserves: 226 million metric tons (2022 est.)

Petroleum: *total petroleum production:* 582,000 bbl/day (2023 est.)
refined petroleum consumption: 717,000 bbl/day (2022 est.)
crude oil estimated reserves: 3.6 billion barrels (2021 est.)

Natural gas: *production:* 75.456 billion cubic meters (2022 est.)
consumption: 42.499 billion cubic meters (2022 est.)
exports: 38.603 billion cubic meters (2022 est.)
imports: 4.529 billion cubic meters (2022 est.)
proven reserves: 1.189 trillion cubic meters (2021 est.)

Carbon dioxide emissions: 262.458 million metric tonnes of CO2 (2022 est.)
from coal and metallurgical coke: 82.481 million metric tonnes of CO2 (2022 est.)
from petroleum and other liquids: 96.127 million metric tonnes of CO2 (2022 est.)
from consumed natural gas: 83.85 million metric tonnes of CO2 (2022 est.)
comparison ranking: total emissions 27

Energy consumption per capita: 116.494 million Btu/person (2022 est.)
comparison ranking: 39

COMMUNICATIONS

Telephones - fixed lines: *total subscriptions:* 8.453 million (2022 est.)
subscriptions per 100 inhabitants: 25 (2022 est.)
comparison ranking: total subscriptions 19

Telephones - mobile cellular: *total subscriptions:* 47.952 million (2022 est.)
subscriptions per 100 inhabitants: 141 (2022 est.)
comparison ranking: total subscriptions 38

Telecommunication systems: *general assessment:* as part of a diverse range of initiatives designed to move the country from developing to developed status by 2025, Malaysia has enabled and encouraged open competition in its telecommunications market; the result is very high penetration levels in both the mobile (147%) and mobile broadband (127%) segments, and nearuniversal coverage of 4G LTE networks; steady growth is occurring as more fiber optic cable networks are being deployed around the country; consumers are the main beneficiaries of the highly competitive market; they enjoy widespread access to high-speed mobile services as well as attractive offers on bundles to keep data use up but prices low; the downside is that most of Malaysia's MNOs and MVNOs have struggled to increase revenue in line with growth in subscriber numbers as well as demand for broadband data; while the operators have been very successful in moving a significant proportion (now over 30%) of customers from prepaid over to higher-value postpaid accounts, ARPU continues to fall year after year as a result of competitive pricing pressures; the mobile market, in particular, has become overcrowded and the government is keen to see further rationalization and consolidation with the operators; while customers will no doubt continue to enjoy high quality services at competitive rates, the new entity will be hopeful of squeezing better margins through improved economies of scale; in 2022, the government abandoned its single wholesale 5G network model and committed to deploying a dual 5G network; currently, 80 percent of Malaysia's population is covered by 5G (2023)
domestic: fixed-line roughly 25 per 100 and mobile-cellular teledensity roughly 141 per 100 persons (2021)
international: country code - 60; landing points for BBG, FEA, SAFE, SeaMeWe-3 & 4 & 5, AAE-1, JASUKA, BDM, Dumai-Melaka Cable System, BRCS, aCe, AAG, East-West Submarine Cable System, SEAX-1, SKR1M, APCN-2, APG, BtoBe, BaSICS, and Labuan-Brunei Submarine and MCT submarine cables providing connectivity to Asia, the Middle East, Southeast Asia, Australia and Europe; satellite earth stations - 2 Intelsat (1 Indian Ocean, 1 Pacific Ocean); launch of Kacific-1 satellite in 2019 (2019)

Broadcast media: state-owned TV broadcaster operates 2 TV networks with relays throughout the country, and the leading private commercial media group operates 4 TV stations with numerous relays throughout the country; satellite TV subscription service is available; state-owned radio broadcaster operates multiple national networks, as well as regional and local stations; many private commercial radio broadcasters and some subscription satellite radio services are available; about 55 radio stations overall (2019)

Internet country code: .my

Internet users: *total:* 32.98 million (2021 est.)
percent of population: 97% (2021 est.)
comparison ranking: total 30

Broadband - fixed subscriptions: *total:* 3,358,800 (2020 est.)
subscriptions per 100 inhabitants: 10 (2020 est.)
comparison ranking: total 43

TRANSPORTATION

National air transport system: *number of registered air carriers:* 13 (2020)
inventory of registered aircraft operated by air carriers: 270
annual passenger traffic on registered air carriers: 60,481,772 (2018)
annual freight traffic on registered air carriers: 1,404,410,000 (2018) mt-km

Civil aircraft registration country code prefix: 9M

Airports: 102 (2024)
comparison ranking: 52

Heliports: 24 (2024)

Pipelines: 354 km condensate, 6,439 km gas, 155 km liquid petroleum gas, 1,937 km oil, 43 km oil/gas/water, 114 km refined products, 26 km water (2013)

Railways: *total:* 1,851 km (2014)
standard gauge: 59 km (2014) 1.435-m gauge (59 km electrified)
narrow gauge: 1,792 km (2014) 1.000-m gauge (339 km electrified)
comparison ranking: total 76

Roadways: *total:* 144,403 km (excludes local roads)
paved: 116,169 km (includes 1,821 km of expressways)
unpaved: 28,234 km (2010)
comparison ranking: total 37

Waterways: 7,200 km (2011) (Peninsular Malaysia 3,200 km; Sabah 1,500 km; Sarawak 2,500 km)
comparison ranking: 21

Merchant marine: *total:* 1,750 (2023)
by type: bulk carrier 14, container ship 35, general cargo 169, oil tanker 148, other 1,384
comparison ranking: total 16

Ports: *total ports:* 35 (2024)
large: 3
medium: 4
small: 10
very small: 18
ports with oil terminals: 24
key ports: Johor, Kota Kinabalu, Port Dickson, Port Klang, Pulau Pinang, Tanjung Pelepas, Tapis Marine Terminal A

MILITARY AND SECURITY

Military and security forces: Malaysian Armed Forces (Angkatan Tentera Malaysia, ATM): Malaysian Army (Tentera Darat Malaysia), Royal Malaysian Navy (Tentera Laut Diraja Malaysia, TLDM), Royal Malaysian Air Force (Tentera Udara Diraja Malaysia, TUDM) (2024)
note 1: the Royal Malaysia Police (RMP or Polis Diraja Malaysia, PDRM) are under the Ministry of Home Affairs; the PRMD includes the General Operations Force, a paramilitary force with a variety of roles, including patrolling borders, counter-terrorism, maritime security, and counterinsurgency; the Ministry of Home Affairs also includes the Malaysian Maritime Enforcement Agency (MMEA; aka Malaysian Coast Guard)
note 2: Malaysia created a National Special Operations Force in 2016 for combating terrorism threats; the force is comprised of personnel from the ATM, the PRMD, and the MMEA

Military expenditures: 0.9% of GDP (2023 est.)
1.1% of GDP (2022 est.)
1% of GDP (2021 est.)
1.1% of GDP (2020 est.)
1% of GDP (2019 est.)
comparison ranking: 133

Military and security service personnel strengths: approximately 110,000 active-duty troops (80,000 Army; 15,000 Navy; 15,000 Air Force) (2023)

Military equipment inventories and acquisitions: the military fields a diverse array of mostly older but growing mix of modern weapons and equipment; its inventory originates from a wide variety of suppliers across Europe, Asia, and the US; Malaysia has a domestic defense industry that has some co-production agreements with countries such as France, Germany, and Turkey in such areas armored vehicles and naval vessels (2024)

Military service age and obligation: 17 years 6 months of age for voluntary military service for men and women (younger with parental consent and

proof of age); maximum age of 27 to enlist; mandatory retirement age 60; no conscription (2023)
note: in 2020, the military announced a goal of having 10% of the active force comprised of women

Military deployments: 830 Lebanon (UNIFIL) (2024)

Military - note: the Malaysian military is responsible for defense of the country's national interests, sovereignty, and territorial integrity; it also has some domestic responsibilities, such as responding to natural disasters; while the Army has traditionally been the dominant service, air and maritime security have received increased emphasis in recent years, particularly anti-piracy operations in the Strait of Malacca and countering Chinese incursions into Malaysia's Economic Exclusion Zone, as well as addressing other identified shortfalls in air and maritime capabilities; as such, Malaysia has undertaken efforts to procure more modern fighters and ships, improve air and maritime surveillance, expand the Navy's support infrastructure (particularly bases/ports) and domestic ship-building capacities, restructure naval command and control, and increase air and naval cooperation with regional and international partners such as Indonesia, the Philippines, and the US
Malaysia is a member of the Five Powers Defense Arrangements (FPDA), a series of mutual assistance agreements reached in 1971 embracing Australia, Malaysia, New Zealand, Singapore, and the UK; the FPDA commits the members to consult with one another in the event or threat of an armed attack on any of the members and to mutually decide what measures should be taken, jointly or separately; there is no specific obligation to intervene militarily (2024)

SPACE

Space agency/agencies: Malaysian Space Agency (MYSA); MYSA was established in 2019 through the merging of the National Space Agency (ANGKASA; established 2002) and Malaysian Remote Sensing Agency (MRSA; established 1998); Astronautic Technology Sd Bhd (ATSB; established 1995) (2024)

Space program overview: has a growing space program focused on the areas of remote sensing (RS), communication, and navigational services to support domestic economic sectors; also seeks to promote a domestic space industry; acquires, manufactures, and operates satellites; conducts research in RS capabilities and space sciences such as astronomy, atmospherics, space environment, and weather; has an astronaut training exchange program with Russia and has relations with a variety of foreign space agencies and industries, including those of the European Space Agency and some of its individual member states, India, Japan, Russia, South Korea, the UK, and the US (2024)
note: further details about the key activities, programs, and milestones of the country's space program, as well as government spending estimates on the space sector, appear in the Space Programs reference guide

TERRORISM

Terrorist group(s): Islamic State of Iraq and ash-Sham (ISIS); Jemaah Islamiyah (JI); Abu Sayyaf Group (ASG)
note: details about the history, aims, leadership, organization, areas of operation, tactics, targets, weapons, size, and sources of support of the group(s) appear(s) in the Terrorism reference guide

TRANSNATIONAL ISSUES

Refugees and internally displaced persons: *refugees (country of origin):* 157,731 (Burma) (refugees and asylum seekers) (2023)
stateless persons: 113,930 (2022); note - Malaysia's stateless population consists of Rohingya refugees from Burma, ethnic Indians, and the children of Filipino and Indonesian illegal migrants; Burma stripped the Rohingya of their nationality in 1982; Filipino and Indonesian children who have not been registered for birth certificates by their parents or who received birth certificates stamped "foreigner" are not eligible to attend government schools; these children are vulnerable to statelessness should they not be able to apply to their parents' country of origin for passports

Illicit drugs: not a source country for illicit drugs bound for the United States but is a significant transit country for drugs destined for Australia; drugs trafficked to Malaysia include crystal methamphetamine and lesser quantities of MDMA (ecstasy), cannabis, heroin, and ketamine; significant number of the population abuse drugs especially methamphetamine

MALDIVES

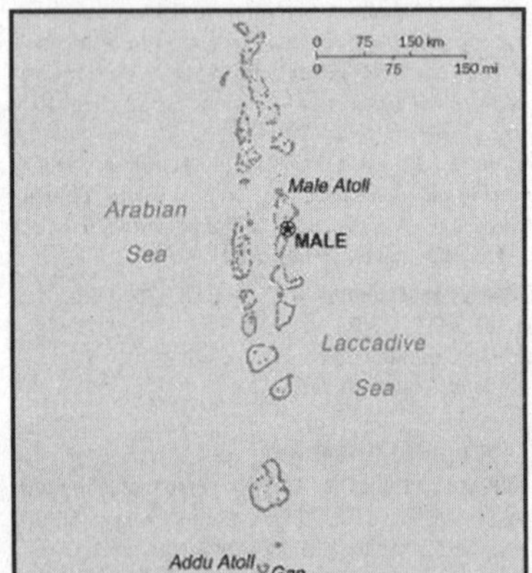

INTRODUCTION

Background: A sultanate since the 12th century, the Maldives became a British protectorate in 1887 and a republic in 1968, three years after independence. President Maumoon Abdul GAYOOM dominated Maldives' political scene for 30 years, elected to six successive terms by single-party referendums. After political demonstrations in the capital Male in 2003, GAYOOM and his government pledged to embark upon a process of liberalization and democratic reforms, including a more representative political system and expanded political freedoms. Political parties were legalized in 2005.

In 2008, a constituent assembly – termed the "Special Majlis" – finalized a new constitution ratified by GAYOOM. The first-ever presidential elections under a multi-candidate, multi-party system were held later that year. GAYOOM was defeated in a runoff by Mohamed NASHEED, a political activist whom the regime had jailed several years earlier. In 2012, after several weeks of street protests in response to a top judge's arrest, NASHEED resigned the presidency and handed over power to Vice President Mohammed WAHEED Hassan Maniku. A government-appointed Commission of National Inquiry concluded that there was no evidence of a coup, but NASHEED contended that police and military personnel forced him to resign. NASHEED, WAHEED, and Abdulla YAMEEN Abdul Gayoom ran in the 2013 elections with YAMEEN ultimately winning the presidency after three rounds of voting. In 2018, YAMEEN lost his reelection bid to parliamentarian Ibrahim Mohamed SOLIH. YAMEEN was arrested and jailed in 2022 on corruption charges. Maldives' fourth democratic election was held in September 2023. The winner, Male City Mayor Dr. Mohamed MUIZZU, campaigned on a platform of Maldivian sovereignty, vowing to remove Indian military personnel from the country. MUIZZU represents a joint Progressive Pary of Maldives and People's National Congress (PPM/PNC) coalition.

GEOGRAPHY

Location: Southern Asia, group of atolls in the Indian Ocean, south-southwest of India

Geographic coordinates: 3 15 N, 73 00 E

Map references: Asia

Area: *total:* 298 sq km
land: 298 sq km
water: 0 sq km
comparison ranking: total 209

Area - comparative: about 1.7 times the size of Washington, DC

Land boundaries: *total:* 0 km

Coastline: 644 km

Maritime claims: *territorial sea:* 12 nm
contiguous zone: 24 nm
exclusive economic zone: 200 nm
measured from claimed archipelagic straight baselines

Climate: tropical; hot, humid; dry, northeast monsoon (November to March); rainy, southwest monsoon (June to August)

Terrain: flat coral atolls, with white sandy beaches; sits atop the submarine volcanic Chagos-Laccadive Ridge

Elevation: *highest point:* 8th tee, golf course, Villingi Island 5 m
lowest point: Indian Ocean 0 m
mean elevation: 2 m

Natural resources: fish

Land use: *agricultural land:* 23.3% (2018 est.)
arable land: 10% (2018 est.)
permanent crops: 10% (2018 est.)
permanent pasture: 3.3% (2018 est.)
forest: 3% (2018 est.)
other: 73.7% (2018 est.)

Irrigated land: 0 sq km (2012)

Population distribution: about a third of the population lives in the centrally located capital city of Male and almost a tenth in southern Addu City; the remainder of the populace is spread over the 200 or so populated islands of the archipelago

Natural hazards: tsunamis; low elevation of islands makes them sensitive to sea level rise

Geography - note: smallest Asian country; archipelago of 1,190 coral islands grouped into 26 atolls (200 inhabited islands, plus 80 islands with tourist resorts); strategic location astride and along major sea lanes in Indian Ocean

PEOPLE AND SOCIETY

Population: *total:* 388,858
male: 197,739
female: 191,119 (2024 est.)
comparison rankings: female 177; male 176; total 177

Nationality: *noun:* Maldivian(s)
adjective: Maldivian

Ethnic groups: homogeneous mixture of Sinhalese, Dravidian, Arab, Australasian, and African resulting from historical changes in regional hegemony over marine trade routes

Languages: Dhivehi (official, closely related to Sinhala, script derived from Arabic), English (spoken by most government officials)

Religions: Sunni Muslim (official)

Age structure: *0-14 years:* 22.4% (male 44,321/female 42,626)
15-64 years: 71.5% (male 143,021/female 135,044)
65 years and over: 6.1% (2024 est.) (male 10,397/female 13,449)

Dependency ratios: *total dependency ratio:* 35.6
youth dependency ratio: 29.5
elderly dependency ratio: 6.2
potential support ratio: 16.2 (2021 est.)

Median age: *total:* 31.9 years (2024 est.)
male: 31.3 years
female: 32.4 years
comparison ranking: total 120

Population growth rate: -0.2% (2024 est.)
comparison ranking: 210

Birth rate: 15.1 births/1,000 population (2024 est.)
comparison ranking: 108

Death rate: 4.3 deaths/1,000 population (2024 est.)
comparison ranking: 210

Net migration rate: -12.8 migrant(s)/1,000 population (2024 est.)
comparison ranking: 225

Population distribution: about a third of the population lives in the centrally located capital city of Male and almost a tenth in southern Addu City; the remainder of the populace is spread over the 200 or so populated islands of the archipelago

Urbanization: *urban population:* 42% of total population (2023)
rate of urbanization: 2.34% annual rate of change (2020-25 est.)

Major urban areas - population: 177,000 MALE (capital) (2018)

Sex ratio: *at birth:* 1.05 male(s)/female
0-14 years: 1.04 male(s)/female
15-64 years: 1.06 male(s)/female
65 years and over: 0.77 male(s)/female
total population: 1.04 male(s)/female (2024 est.)

Mother's mean age at first birth: 23.2 years (2016/17 est.)
note: data represents median age at first birth among women 25-49

Maternal mortality ratio: 57 deaths/100,000 live births (2020 est.)
comparison ranking: 95

Infant mortality rate: *total:* 24.4 deaths/1,000 live births (2024 est.)
male: 27.3 deaths/1,000 live births
female: 21.3 deaths/1,000 live births
comparison ranking: total 62

Life expectancy at birth: *total population:* 77.4 years (2024 est.)
male: 75.1 years
female: 79.9 years
comparison ranking: total population 90

Total fertility rate: 1.7 children born/woman (2024 est.)
comparison ranking: 165

Gross reproduction rate: 0.83 (2024 est.)

Contraceptive prevalence rate: 18.8% (2016/17)

Drinking water source: *improved: urban:* 99% of population
rural: 100% of population
total: 99.6% of population
unimproved: urban: 1% of population
rural: 0% of population
total: 0.4% of population (2020 est.)

Current health expenditure: 11.4% of GDP (2020)

Physician density: 2.05 physicians/1,000 population (2019)

Hospital bed density: 4.3 beds/1,000 population

Sanitation facility access: *improved: urban:* 100% of population
rural: 99.1% of population
total: 99.5% of population
unimproved: urban: 0% of population
rural: 0.9% of population
total: 0.5% of population (2020 est.)

Obesity - adult prevalence rate: 8.6% (2016)
comparison ranking: 149

Alcohol consumption per capita: *total:* 1.38 liters of pure alcohol (2019 est.)
beer: 0.33 liters of pure alcohol (2019 est.)
wine: 0.59 liters of pure alcohol (2019 est.)
spirits: 0.45 liters of pure alcohol (2019 est.)
other alcohols: 0 liters of pure alcohol (2019 est.)
comparison ranking: total 142

Tobacco use: *total:* 25.2% (2020 est.)
male: 44.4% (2020 est.)
female: 6% (2020 est.)
comparison ranking: total 50

Children under the age of 5 years underweight: 14.8% (2016/17)
comparison ranking: 34

Currently married women (ages 15-49): 71.9% (2023 est.)

Child marriage: *women married by age 18:* 2.2%
men married by age 18: 2.2% (2017 est.)

Education expenditures: 5.8% of GDP (2020 est.)
comparison ranking: 50

Literacy: *definition:* age 15 and over can read and write
total population: 97.9%
male: 97.6%
female: 98.4% (2021)

School life expectancy (primary to tertiary education): *total:* 13 years
male: 12 years
female: 14 years (2019)

ENVIRONMENT

Environment - current issues: rising sea levels threaten land; depletion of freshwater aquifers threatens water supplies; inadequate sewage treatment; coral reef bleaching

Environment - international agreements: *party to:* Biodiversity, Climate Change, Climate Change-Kyoto Protocol, Climate Change-Paris Agreement, Comprehensive Nuclear Test Ban, Desertification, Endangered Species, Hazardous Wastes, Law of the Sea, Ozone Layer Protection, Ship Pollution
signed, but not ratified: none of the selected agreements

Climate: tropical; hot, humid; dry, northeast monsoon (November to March); rainy, southwest monsoon (June to August)

Urbanization: *urban population:* 42% of total population (2023)
rate of urbanization: 2.34% annual rate of change (2020-25 est.)

Revenue from forest resources: 0% of GDP (2018 est.)
comparison ranking: 183

Revenue from coal: 0% of GDP (2018 est.)
comparison ranking: 79

Air pollutants: *particulate matter emissions:* 13 micrograms per cubic meter (2019 est.)
carbon dioxide emissions: 1.44 megatons (2016 est.)
methane emissions: 0.14 megatons (2020 est.)

Waste and recycling: *municipal solid waste generated annually:* 211,506 tons (2015 est.)

Total water withdrawal: *municipal:* 10 million cubic meters (2020 est.)
industrial: 300,000 cubic meters (2017 est.)
agricultural: 0 cubic meters (2017 est.)

Total renewable water resources: 30 million cubic meters (2020 est.)

GOVERNMENT

Country name: *conventional long form:* Republic of Maldives
conventional short form: Maldives
local long form: Dhivehi Raajjeyge Jumhooriyyaa
local short form: Dhivehi Raajje
etymology: archipelago apparently named after the main island (and capital) of Male; the word "Maldives" means "the islands (dives) of Male"; alternatively, the name may derive from the Sanskrit word

"maladvipa" meaning "garland of islands"; Dhivehi Raajje in Dhivehi means "Kingdom of the Dhivehi people"

Government type: presidential republic

Capital: *name:* Male
geographic coordinates: 4 10 N, 73 30 E
time difference: UTC+5 (10 hours ahead of Washington, DC, during Standard Time)
etymology: derived from the Sanskrit word "mahaalay" meaning "big house"

Administrative divisions: 21 administrative atolls (atholhuthah, singular - atholhu); Addu (Addu City), Ariatholhu Dhekunuburi (South Ari Atoll), Ariatholhu Uthuruburi (North Ari Atoll), Faadhippolhu, Felidhuatholhu (Felidhu Atoll), Fuvammulah, Hahdhunmathi, Huvadhuatholhu Dhekunuburi (South Huvadhu Atoll), Huvadhuatholhu Uthuruburi (North Huvadhu Atoll), Kolhumadulu, Maale (Male), Maaleatholhu (Male Atoll), Maalhosmadulu Dhekunuburi (South Maalhosmadulu), Maalhosmadulu Uthuruburi (North Maalhosmadulu), Miladhunmadulu Dhekunuburi (South Miladhunmadulu), Miladhunmadulu Uthuruburi (North Miladhunmadulu), Mulakatholhu (Mulaku Atoll), Nilandheatholhu Dhekunuburi (South Nilandhe Atoll), Nilandheatholhu Uthuruburi (North Nilandhe Atoll), Thiladhunmathee Dhekunuburi (South Thiladhunmathi), Thiladhunmathee Uthuruburi (North Thiladhunmathi)

Independence: 26 July 1965 (from the UK)

National holiday: Independence Day, 26 July (1965)

Legal system: Islamic (sharia) legal system with English common law influences, primarily in commercial matters

Constitution: *history:* many previous; latest ratified 7 August 2008
amendments: proposed by Parliament; passage requires at least three-quarters majority vote by its membership and the signature of the president of the republic; passage of amendments to constitutional articles on rights and freedoms and the terms of office of Parliament and of the president also requires a majority vote in a referendum; amended 2015

International law organization participation: has not submitted an ICJ jurisdiction declaration; accepts ICCt jurisdiction

Citizenship: *citizenship by birth:* no
citizenship by descent only: at least one parent must be a citizen of Maldives
dual citizenship recognized: yes
residency requirement for naturalization: unknown

Suffrage: 18 years of age; universal

Executive branch: *chief of state:* President Mohamed MUIZZU (since 17 November 2023)
head of government: President Mohamed MUIZZU (since 17 November 2023)
cabinet: Cabinet of Ministers appointed by the president, approved by Parliament
elections/appointments: president directly elected by absolute majority popular vote in 2 rounds if needed for a 5-year term (eligible for a second term); first round held on 9 September 2023 and runoff held on 30 September 2023 (next to be held in 2028)
election results:
2023: Mohamed MUIZZU elected president in the second round; percent of vote in first round - Mohamed MUIZZU (PNC) 46.1%, Ibrahim Mohamed SOLIH (MDP) 39.1%, Ilyas LABEEB (DEMS) 7.1%, other 7.7%; percent of vote in the second round - Mohamed MUIZZU 54%, Ibrahim Mohamed SOLIH 46%
2018: Ibrahim Mohamed SOLIH elected president in first round; Ibrahim Mohamed SOLIH (MDP) 58.3%, Abdulla YAMEEN Abdul Gayoom (PPM) 41.7%

Legislative branch: *description:* unicameral People's Assembly or People's Majlis (93 seats; members directly elected in single-seat constituencies by simple majority vote to serve 5-year terms)
elections: last held on 21 April 2024 (next to be held in 2029)
election results: percent of vote by party - NA; seats by party - PNC 66, MDP 12, MDA 2, JP 1, MNP 1, independent 11; composition - men 90, women 3, percentage women 3.3%

Judicial branch: *highest court(s):* Supreme Court (consists of the chief justice and 6 justices
judge selection and term of office: Supreme Court judges appointed by the president in consultation with the Judicial Service Commission - a 10-member body of selected high government officials and the public - and upon confirmation by voting members of the People's Majlis; judges serve until mandatory retirement at age 70
subordinate courts: High Court; Criminal, Civil, Family, Juvenile, and Drug Courts; Magistrate Courts (on each of the inhabited islands)

Political parties: Adhaalath (Justice) Party or AP
Dhivehi Rayyithunge Party or DRP
Maldives Development Alliance or MDA
Maldivian Democratic Party or MDP
Maldives Third Way Democrats or MTD
People's National Congress or PNC
People's National Front
Republican (Jumhooree) Party or JP

International organization participation: ADB, AOSIS, C, CP, FAO, G-77, IBRD, ICAO, ICC (NGOs), ICCt, IDA, IDB, IFAD, IFC, IFRCS, ILO, IMF, IMO, Interpol, IOC, IOM, IPU, ITU, MIGA, NAM, OIC, OPCW, SAARC, SACEP, UN, UNCTAD, UNESCO, UNIDO, UNWTO, UPU, WCO, WHO, WIPO, WMO, WTO

Diplomatic representation in the US: *chief of mission:* Ambassador Abdul GHAFOOR Mohamed (since 15 June 2023)
chancery: 1100 H Street NW, Suite 250, Washington, D.C. 20005
telephone: [1] (202) 516-5458
email address and website:
WashingtonInfo@foreign.gov.mv
The Embassy (mdvmission.gov.mv)

Diplomatic representation from the US: *chief of mission:* Ambassador Hugo Yue-Ho YON (since 6 September 2023); note - Ambassador YON is the first resident US ambassador to the Republic of Maldives
embassy: 210 Galle Road, Colombo 03, Sri Lanka; note - as of early November 2023, the US has no consular or diplomatic offices in Maldives; the US Mission to Maldives operates from US Embassy Colombo, Sri Lanka
telephone: [94] (11) 249-8500
FAX: [94] (11) 243-7345

Flag description: red with a large green rectangle in the center bearing a vertical white crescent moon; the closed side of the crescent is on the hoist side of the flag; red recalls those who have sacrificed their lives in defense of their country, the green rectangle represents peace and prosperity, and the white crescent signifies Islam

National symbol(s): coconut palm, yellowfin tuna; national colors: red, green, white

National anthem: *name:* "Gaumee Salaam" (National Salute)
lyrics/music: Mohamed Jameel DIDI/ Wannakuwattawaduge DON AMARADEVA
note: lyrics adopted 1948, music adopted 1972; between 1948 and 1972, the lyrics were sung to the tune of "Auld Lang Syne"

ECONOMY

Economic overview: upper middle-income Indian Ocean island economy; major tourism, fishing, and shipping industries; high public debt; systemic corruption; crippled by COVID-19; ongoing deflation; poverty has tripled since pandemic began

Real GDP (purchasing power parity): $11.651 billion (2023 est.)
$11.206 billion (2022 est.)
$9.838 billion (2021 est.)
note: data in 2021 dollars
comparison ranking: 164

Real GDP growth rate: 3.97% (2023 est.)
13.91% (2022 est.)
37.69% (2021 est.)
note: annual GDP % growth based on constant local currency
comparison ranking: 79

Real GDP per capita: $22,400 (2023 est.)
$21,400 (2022 est.)
$18,900 (2021 est.)
note: data in 2021 dollars
comparison ranking: 95

GDP (official exchange rate): $6.6 billion (2023 est.)
note: data in current dollars at official exchange rate

Inflation rate (consumer prices): 2.33% (2022 est.)
0.54% (2021 est.)
-1.37% (2020 est.)
note: annual % change based on consumer prices
comparison ranking: 48

Credit ratings: Fitch rating: CCC (2020)

Moody's rating: B3 (2020)
note: The year refers to the year in which the current credit rating was first obtained.

GDP - composition, by sector of origin: *agriculture:* 4.9% (2022 est.)
industry: 10.3% (2022 est.)
services: 73.3% (2022 est.)
note: figures may not total 100% due to non-allocated consumption not captured in sector-reported data
comparison rankings: services 28; industry 193; agriculture 118

GDP - composition, by end use: *exports of goods and services:* 93.6% (2016 est.)
imports of goods and services: 89% (2016 est.)

Agricultural products: fruits, vegetables, nuts, other meats, tomatoes, bananas, maize, pulses, coconuts, papayas (2022)
note: top ten agricultural products based on tonnage

Industries: tourism, fish processing, shipping, boat building, coconut processing, woven mats, rope, handicrafts, coral and sand mining

Industrial production growth rate: 7.26% (2023 est.)
note: annual % change in industrial value added based on constant local currency

comparison ranking: 33

Labor force: 260,000 (2023 est.)
note: number of people ages 15 or older who are employed or seeking work
comparison ranking: 170

Unemployment rate: 4.13% (2023 est.)
4.42% (2022 est.)
5.02% (2021 est.)
note: % of labor force seeking employment
comparison ranking: 80

Youth unemployment rate (ages 15-24): *total:* 14.9% (2023 est.)
male: 18.6% (2023 est.)
female: 9.2% (2023 est.)
note: % of labor force ages 15-24 seeking employment
comparison ranking: total 96

Population below poverty line: 5.4% (2019 est.)
note: % of population with income below national poverty line

Gini Index coefficient - distribution of family income: 29.3 (2019 est.)
note: index (0-100) of income distribution; higher values represent greater inequality
comparison ranking: 127

Household income or consumption by percentage share: *lowest 10%:* 3.8% (2019 est.)
highest 10%: 23.3% (2019 est.)
note: % share of income accruing to lowest and highest 10% of population

Remittances: 0.07% of GDP (2023 est.)
0.08% of GDP (2022 est.)
0.09% of GDP (2021 est.)
note: personal transfers and compensation between resident and non-resident individuals/households/entities

Budget: *revenues:* $1.407 billion (2021 est.)
expenditures: $1.548 billion (2021 est.)
note: central government revenues and expenses (excluding grants/extrabudgetary units/social security funds) converted to US dollars at average official exchange rate for year indicated

Public debt: 63.9% of GDP (2017 est.)
comparison ranking: 68

Taxes and other revenues: 19.45% (of GDP) (2021 est.)
comparison ranking: 91

Current account balance: -$1.033 billion (2022 est.)
-$455.003 million (2021 est.)
-$1.327 billion (2020 est.)
note: balance of payments - net trade and primary/secondary income in current dollars
comparison ranking: 143

Exports: $5.096 billion (2022 est.)
$3.985 billion (2021 est.)
$1.787 billion (2020 est.)
note: balance of payments - exports of goods and services in current dollars
comparison ranking: 140

Exports - partners: India 71%, Thailand 12%, Germany 3%, Oman 2%, UK 2% (2022)
note: top five export partners based on percentage share of exports

Exports - commodities: aircraft, fish, natural gas, scrap iron, refined petroleum (2022)
note: top five export commodities based on value in dollars

Imports: $4.904 billion (2022 est.)
$3.484 billion (2021 est.)
$2.449 billion (2020 est.)
note: balance of payments - imports of goods and services in current dollars
comparison ranking: 153

Imports - partners: India 16%, China 16%, UAE 10%, Oman 9%, Malaysia 6% (2022)
note: top five import partners based on percentage share of imports

Imports - commodities: refined petroleum, ships, aircraft, plastic products, broadcasting equipment (2022)
note: top five import commodities based on value in dollars

Reserves of foreign exchange and gold: $590.523 million (2023 est.)
$832.094 million (2022 est.)
$805.808 million (2021 est.)
note: holdings of gold (year-end prices)/foreign exchange/special drawing rights in current dollars
comparison ranking: 147

Exchange rates: rufiyaa (MVR) per US dollar -

Exchange rates: 15.387 (2023 est.)
15.387 (2022 est.)
15.373 (2021 est.)
15.381 (2020 est.)
15.382 (2019 est.)

ENERGY

Electricity access: *electrification - total population:* 100% (2022 est.)

Electricity: *installed generating capacity:* 566,000 kW (2022 est.)
consumption: 821.397 million kWh (2022 est.)
transmission/distribution losses: 25.867 million kWh (2022 est.)
comparison rankings: transmission/distribution losses 29; consumption 164; installed generating capacity 149

Electricity generation sources: *fossil fuels:* 93.2% of total installed capacity (2022 est.)
solar: 6.6% of total installed capacity (2022 est.)
wind: 0.2% of total installed capacity (2022 est.)

Coal: *imports:* 1 metric tons (2022 est.)

Petroleum: *refined petroleum consumption:* 14,000 bbl/day (2022 est.)

Carbon dioxide emissions: 2.247 million metric tonnes of CO2 (2022 est.)
from petroleum and other liquids: 2.247 million metric tonnes of CO2 (2022 est.)
comparison ranking: total emissions 157

Energy consumption per capita: 56.264 million Btu/person (2022 est.)
comparison ranking: 89

COMMUNICATIONS

Telephones - fixed lines: *total subscriptions:* 13,000 (2022 est.)
subscriptions per 100 inhabitants: 3 (2022 est.)
comparison ranking: total subscriptions 184

Telephones - mobile cellular: *total subscriptions:* 715,000 (2022 est.)
subscriptions per 100 inhabitants: 137 (2022 est.)
comparison ranking: total subscriptions 170

Telecommunication systems: *general assessment:* with its economy so heavily dependent on tourism, the Maldives has suffered heavy economic as well as health casualties during the pandemic; the country had a relatively short period of lock down and was willing to welcome visitors back as early as July 2020; but the effective shutdown of international air travel for most of the year resulted in the bottom falling out of the Maldives' tourism industry, taking GDP down 32% in the process; the economy fared better in 2021, with a return to growth, yet it may still be a few years before the country's key industries can return to the same level of prosperity that they previously enjoyed; the country's high number of tourists and expatriate workers has inflated the penetration rate for mobile services, making it one of the highest in the world; that rate crashed in 2020 as demand for SIM cards (primarily prepaid) dried up; however, the number of contract subscribers increased as locals took advantage of competitive pricing offers from operators; with commercial 5G services already launched and fiber networks rapidly expanding around the country, the Maldives is primed to deliver world-class telecommunications services to its domestic and international customers (2021)
domestic: fixed-line is at nearly 3 per 100 persons and mobile-cellular subscriptions stands at nearly 135 per 100 persons (2021)
international: country code - 960; landing points for Dhiraagu Cable Network, NaSCOM, Dhiraagu-SLT Submarine Cable Networks and WARF submarine cables providing connections to 8 points in Maldives, India, and Sri Lanka; satellite earth station - 3 Intelsat (Indian Ocean) (2019)

Broadcast media: state-owned radio and TV monopoly until recently; 4 state-operated and 7 privately owned TV stations and 4 state-operated and 7 privately owned radio stations (2019)

Internet country code: .mv

Internet users: *total:* 447,200 (2021 est.)
percent of population: 86% (2021 est.)
comparison ranking: total 169

Broadband - fixed subscriptions: *total:* 63,685 (2020 est.)
subscriptions per 100 inhabitants: 12 (2020 est.)
comparison ranking: total 139

TRANSPORTATION

National air transport system: *number of registered air carriers:* 3 (2020)
inventory of registered aircraft operated by air carriers: 36
annual passenger traffic on registered air carriers: 1,147,247 (2018)
annual freight traffic on registered air carriers: 7.75 million (2018)

Civil aircraft registration country code prefix: 8Q

Airports: 19 (2024)
comparison ranking: 140

Roadways: *total:* 93 km
paved: 93 km (2018) - 60 km in Malée; 16 km on Addu Atolis; 17 km on Laamu
note: island roads are mainly compacted coral
comparison ranking: total 216

Merchant marine: *total:* 82 (2023)
by type: general cargo 30, oil tanker 20, other 32
comparison ranking: total 98

Ports: *total ports:* 1 (2024)
large: 0
medium: 0
small: 0
very small: 1
ports with oil terminals: 1

key ports: Male

MILITARY AND SECURITY

Military and security forces: Maldives National Defense Force (MNDF): the MNDF has combined force structure with seven services divided into Combat and Maneuver Forces (Coast Guard, Marine Corps, and Fire and Rescue Service) and Support Services (Service Corps, Defense Intelligence Service, Medical Corps, Adjutant General's Corps); there is also a separate Special Forces command and a Special Protection Service (2024)
note: the Maldives Police Service is responsible for internal security and reports to the Ministry of Homeland Security and Technology

Military expenditures: not available

Military and security service personnel strengths: approximately 3-4,000 personnel (2023)

Military equipment inventories and acquisitions: the Defense Force has a limited inventory consisting of a mix of mostly secondhand or donated equipment from suppliers such as Germany, India, Japan, and the UK; in 2024, the Maldives received surveillance drones from Turkey (2024)

Military service age and obligation: 18-28 years of age for voluntary service; no conscription; 10th grade or equivalent education required; must not be a member of a political party (2023)

Military - note: the Maldives National Defense Force (MNDF) is responsible for defending and safeguarding the Maldives' territorial integrity, economic exclusion zone, and people; it is also responsible for disaster relief, and if requested, assisting the Maldives Police Service in maintaining internal security and law and order; the MNDF is organized into four area commands and a functional Special Forces command; the head of the MNDF reports to the Minister of Defense (2024)

TERRORISM

Terrorist group(s): Islamic State of Iraq and ash-Sham (ISIS)
note: details about the history, aims, leadership, organization, areas of operation, tactics, targets, weapons, size, and sources of support of the group(s) appear(s) in the Terrorism reference guide

TRANSNATIONAL ISSUES

Trafficking in persons: tier rating: Tier 2 Watch List — the Maldives did not demonstrate overall increasing efforts to eliminate trafficking compared with the previous reporting period and was downgraded to Tier 2 Watch List; for more details, go to: https:// www.state.gov/reports/2024-trafficking-in-persons-report/maldives/

Illicit drugs: NA

MALI

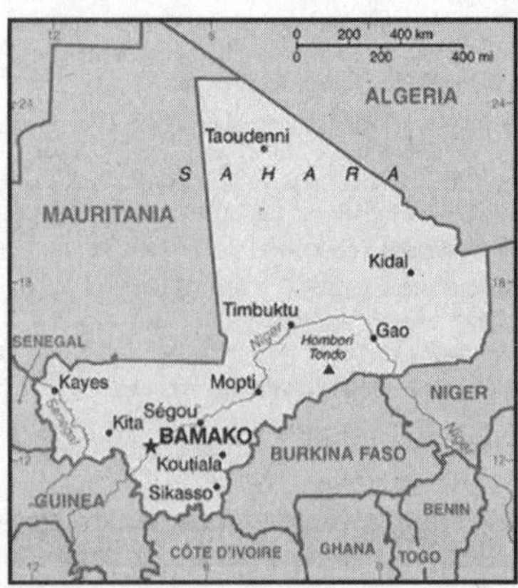

INTRODUCTION

Background: Present-day Mali is named after the Mali Empire that ruled the region between the 13th and 16th centuries. At its peak in the 14th century, it was the largest and wealthiest empire in West Africa and controlled an area about twice the size of modern-day France. Primarily a trading empire, Mali derived its wealth from gold and maintained several goldfields and trade routes in the Sahel. The empire also influenced West African culture through the spread of its language, laws, and customs, but by the 16th century, it had fragmented into mostly small chiefdoms. The Songhai Empire, previously a Mali dependency centered in Timbuktu, gained prominence in the 15th and 16th centuries. Under Songhai rule, Timbuktu became a large commercial center, well-known for its scholarship and religious teaching. Timbuktu remains a center of culture in West Africa today. In the late 16th century, the Songhai Empire fell to Moroccan invaders and disintegrated into independent sultanates and kingdoms.

France, expanding from Senegal, seized control of the area in the 1890s and incorporated it into French West Africa as French Sudan. In 1960, French Sudan gained independence from France and became the Mali Federation. When Senegal withdrew after only a few months, the remaining area was renamed the Republic of Mali. Mali saw 31 years of dictatorship until 1991, when a military coup led by Amadou Toumani TOURE ousted the government, established a new constitution, and instituted a multiparty democracy. Alpha Oumar KONARE won Mali's first two democratic presidential elections in 1992 and 1997. In keeping with Mali's two-term constitutional limit, he stepped down in 2002 and was succeeded by Amadou Toumani TOURE, who won a second term in 2007.

In 2012, rising ethnic tensions and an influx of fighters – some linked to Al-Qa'ida – from Libya led to a rebellion and military coup. Following the coup, rebels expelled the military from the country's three northern regions, allowing terrorist organizations to develop strongholds in the area. With a 2013 French-led military intervention, the Malian government managed to retake most of the north. However, the government's grasp in the region remains weak with local militias, terrorists, and insurgent groups competing for control. In 2015, the Malian Government and northern rebels signed an internationally mediated peace accord. Despite a 2017 target for implementation of the agreement, the signatories have made little progress. Terrorist groups were left out of the peace process, and terrorist attacks remain common.

Ibrahim Boubacar KEITA won the Malian presidential elections in 2013 and 2018. Aside from security and logistic shortfalls, international observers deemed these elections credible. Terrorism, banditry, ethnic-based violence, and extra-judicial military killings plagued the country during KEITA's second term. In 2020, the military arrested KEITA, his prime minister, and other senior members of the government and established a military junta called the National Committee for the Salvation of the People (CNSP). The junta then established a transition government and appointed Bah N'DAW, a retired army officer and former defense minister, as interim president and Colonel Assimi GOITA, the coup leader and chairman of the CNSP, as interim vice president. The transition government's charter allowed it to rule for up to 18 months before calling a general election.

In 2021, GOITA led a military takeover, arresting the interim president after a Cabinet shake-up removed GOITA's key allies. GOITA was sworn in as transition president, and Choguel Kokalla MAIGA was sworn in as prime minister. In 2022, the Economic Community of West African States (ECOWAS) imposed sanctions on the transition government, and member states closed their borders with Mali after the transition government presented a five-year extension to the electoral calendar. The transition government and ECOWAS agreed to a new two-year timeline, which would have included presidential elections in February 2024, but the transition government postponed the elections indefinitely in September 2023 and withdrew from ECOWAS in January 2024.

GEOGRAPHY

Location: interior Western Africa, southwest of Algeria, north of Guinea, Cote d'Ivoire, and Burkina Faso, west of Niger

Geographic coordinates: 17 00 N, 4 00 W

Map references: Africa

Area: *total:* 1,240,192 sq km
land: 1,220,190 sq km
water: 20,002 sq km
comparison ranking: total 25

Area - comparative: slightly less than twice the size of Texas

Land boundaries: *total:* 7,908 km
border countries (6): Algeria 1,359 km; Burkina Faso 1,325 km; Cote d'Ivoire 599 km; Guinea 1,062 km; Mauritania 2,236 km; Niger 838 km, Senegal 489 km

Coastline: 0 km (landlocked)

Maritime claims: none (landlocked)

Climate: subtropical to arid; hot and dry (February to June); rainy, humid, and mild (June to November); cool and dry (November to February)

Terrain: mostly flat to rolling northern plains covered by sand; savanna in south, rugged hills in northeast

Elevation: *highest point:* Hombori Tondo 1,155 m
lowest point: Senegal River 23 m
mean elevation: 343 m

Natural resources: gold, phosphates, kaolin, salt, limestone, uranium, gypsum, granite, hydropower
note: bauxite, iron ore, manganese, tin, and copper deposits are known but not exploited

Land use: *agricultural land:* 34.1% (2018 est.)
arable land: 5.6% (2018 est.)
permanent crops: 0.1% (2018 est.)
permanent pasture: 28.4% (2018 est.)
forest: 10.2% (2018 est.)
other: 55.7% (2018 est.)

Irrigated land: 3,780 sq km (2012)

Major lakes (area sq km): *fresh water lake(s):* Lac Faguibine - 590 sq km
note - the Niger River is the only source of water for the lake; in recent years the lake is dry

Major rivers (by length in km): Niger (shared with Guinea [s], Niger, and Nigeria [m]) - 4,200 km; Senegal (shared with Guinea [s], Senegal, and Mauritania [m]) - 1,641 km
note – [s] after country name indicates river source; [m] after country name indicates river mouth

Major watersheds (area sq km): Atlantic Ocean drainage: Niger (2,261,741 sq km), Senegal (456,397 sq km), Volta (410,991 sq km)

Major aquifers: Lullemeden-Irhazer Basin, Taodeni-Tanezrouft Basin

Population distribution: the overwhelming majority of the population lives in the southern half of the country, with greater density along the border with Burkina Faso as shown in this population distribution map

Natural hazards: hot, dust-laden harmattan haze common during dry seasons; recurring droughts; occasional Niger River flooding

Geography - note: *landlocked; divided into three natural zones:* the southern, cultivated Sudanese; the central, semiarid Sahelian; and the northern, arid Saharan

PEOPLE AND SOCIETY

Population: *total:* 21,990,607
male: 10,688,755
female: 11,301,852 (2024 est.)
comparison rankings: female 61; male 60; total 60

Nationality: *noun:* Malian(s)
adjective: Malian

Ethnic groups: Bambara 33.3%, Fulani (Peuhl) 13.3%, Sarakole/Soninke/Marka 9.8%, Senufo/Manianka 9.6%, Malinke 8.8%, Dogon 8.7%, Sonrai 5.9%, Bobo 2.1%, Tuareg/Bella 1.7%, other Malian 6%, from members of Economic Community of West Africa 0.4%, other 0.3% (2018 est.)

Languages: Bambara (official), French 17.2%, Peuhl/Foulfoulbe/Fulani 9.4%, Dogon 7.2%, Maraka/Soninke 6.4%, Malinke 5.6%, Sonrhai/Djerma 5.6%, Minianka 4.3%, Tamacheq 3.5%, Senoufo 2.6%, Bobo 2.1%, other 6.3%, unspecified 0.7% (2009 est.)
note: Mali has 13 national languages in addition to its official language

Religions: Muslim 93.9%, Christian 2.8%, animist 0.7%, none 2.5% (2018 est.)

Demographic profile: Mali's total population is expected to double by 2035; its capital Bamako is one of the fastest-growing cities in Africa. A young age structure, a declining mortality rate, and a sustained high total fertility rate of 5.5 children per woman – the fourth highest in the world, as of 2022 – ensure continued rapid population growth for the foreseeable future. Significant outmigration only marginally tempers this growth. Despite decreases, Mali's infant, child, and maternal mortality rates remain among the highest in Sub-Saharan Africa because of limited access to and adoption of family planning, early childbearing, short birth intervals, the prevalence of female genital cutting, infrequent use of skilled birth attendants, and a lack of emergency obstetrical and neonatal care.
Mali's high total fertility rate has been virtually unchanged for decades, as a result of the ongoing preference for large families, early childbearing, the lack of female education and empowerment, poverty, and extremely low contraceptive use. Slowing Mali's population growth by lowering its birth rate will be essential for poverty reduction, improving food security, and developing human capital and the economy.
Mali has a long history of seasonal migration and emigration driven by poverty, conflict, demographic pressure, unemployment, food insecurity, and droughts. Many Malians from rural areas migrate during the dry period to nearby villages and towns to do odd jobs or to adjoining countries to work in agriculture or mining. Pastoralists and nomads move seasonally to southern Mali or nearby coastal states. Others migrate long term to Mali's urban areas, Cote d'Ivoire, other neighboring countries, and in smaller numbers to France, Mali's former colonial ruler. Since the early 1990s, Mali's role has grown as a transit country for regional migration flows and illegal migration to Europe. Human smugglers and traffickers exploit the same regional routes used for moving contraband drugs, arms, and cigarettes.
Between early 2012 and 2013, renewed fighting in northern Mali between government forces and Tuareg secessionists and their Islamist allies, a French-led international military intervention, as well as chronic food shortages, caused the displacement of hundreds of thousands of Malians. Most of those displaced domestically sought shelter in urban areas of southern Mali, except for pastoralist and nomadic groups, who abandoned their traditional routes, gave away or sold their livestock, and dispersed into the deserts of northern Mali or crossed into neighboring countries. Almost all Malians who took refuge abroad (mostly Tuareg and Maure pastoralists) stayed in the region, largely in Mauritania, Niger, and Burkina Faso.

Age structure: *0-14 years:* 46.8% (male 5,175,714/female 5,114,128)
15-64 years: 50.1% (male 5,178,742/female 5,842,456)
65 years and over: 3.1% (2024 est.) (male 334,299/female 345,268)

Dependency ratios: *total dependency ratio:* 99.3
youth dependency ratio: 94.5
elderly dependency ratio: 4.9
potential support ratio: 20.6 (2021 est.)

Median age: *total:* 16.4 years (2024 est.)
male: 15.7 years
female: 17.1 years
comparison ranking: total 226

Population growth rate: 2.9% (2024 est.)
comparison ranking: 9

Birth rate: 40 births/1,000 population (2024 est.)
comparison ranking: 4

Death rate: 8.1 deaths/1,000 population (2024 est.)
comparison ranking: 86

Net migration rate: -2.9 migrant(s)/1,000 population (2024 est.)
comparison ranking: 177

Population distribution: the overwhelming majority of the population lives in the southern half of the country, with greater density along the border with Burkina Faso as shown in this population distribution map

Urbanization: *urban population:* 46.2% of total population (2023)
rate of urbanization: 4.57% annual rate of change (2020-25 est.)

Major urban areas - population: 2.929 million BAMAKO (capital) (2023)

Sex ratio: *at birth:* 1.03 male(s)/female
0-14 years: 1.01 male(s)/female
15-64 years: 0.89 male(s)/female
65 years and over: 0.97 male(s)/female
total population: 0.95 male(s)/female (2024 est.)

Mother's mean age at first birth: 19.2 years (2018 est.)
note: data represents median age at first birth among women 20-49

Maternal mortality ratio: 440 deaths/100,000 live births (2020 est.)
comparison ranking: 20

Infant mortality rate: *total:* 57.4 deaths/1,000 live births (2024 est.)
male: 62.6 deaths/1,000 live births
female: 52 deaths/1,000 live births
comparison ranking: total 10

Life expectancy at birth: *total population:* 63.2 years (2024 est.)
male: 60.9 years
female: 65.6 years
comparison ranking: total population 211

Total fertility rate: 5.35 children born/woman (2024 est.)
comparison ranking: 4

Gross reproduction rate: 2.64 (2024 est.)

Contraceptive prevalence rate: 17.2% (2018)

Drinking water source: *improved: urban:* 99.9% of population
rural: 75.9% of population
total: 86.4% of population
unimproved: urban: 0.1% of population
rural: 24.1% of population
total: 13.6% of population (2020 est.)

Current health expenditure: 4.3% of GDP (2020)

Physician density: 0.13 physicians/1,000 population (2018)

Hospital bed density: 0.1 beds/1,000 population

Sanitation facility access: *improved: urban:* 85.7% of population
rural: 44.7% of population
total: 62.7% of population
unimproved: urban: 14.3% of population
rural: 55.3% of population
total: 37.3% of population (2020 est.)

Obesity - adult prevalence rate: 8.6% (2016)
comparison ranking: 150

Alcohol consumption per capita: *total:* 0.6 liters of pure alcohol (2019 est.)

beer: 0.09 liters of pure alcohol (2019 est.)
wine: 0 liters of pure alcohol (2019 est.)
spirits: 0.02 liters of pure alcohol (2019 est.)
other alcohols: 0.49 liters of pure alcohol (2019 est.)
comparison ranking: total 159

Tobacco use: *total:* 8.3% (2020 est.)
male: 15.6% (2020 est.)
female: 1% (2020 est.)
comparison ranking: total 146

Children under the age of 5 years underweight: 18.5% (2022)
comparison ranking: 24

Currently married women (ages 15-49): 77.9% (2023 est.)

Child marriage: *women married by age 15:* 15.9%
women married by age 18: 53.7%
men married by age 18: 2.1% (2018 est.)

Education expenditures: 4.4% of GDP (2021 est.)
comparison ranking: 105

Literacy: *definition:* age 15 and over can read and write
total population: 35.5%
male: 46.2%
female: 25.7% (2018)

School life expectancy (primary to tertiary education): *total:* 7 years
male: 8 years
female: 7 years (2017)

ENVIRONMENT

Environment - current issues: deforestation; soil erosion; desertification; loss of pasture land; inadequate supplies of potable water

Environment - international agreements: *party to:* Biodiversity, Climate Change, Climate Change-Kyoto Protocol, Climate Change-Paris Agreement, Comprehensive Nuclear Test Ban, Desertification, Endangered Species, Hazardous Wastes, Law of the Sea, Ozone Layer Protection, Tropical Timber 2006, Wetlands, Whaling
signed, but not ratified: Nuclear Test Ban

Climate: subtropical to arid; hot and dry (February to June); rainy, humid, and mild (June to November); cool and dry (November to February)

Urbanization: *urban population:* 46.2% of total population (2023)
rate of urbanization: 4.57% annual rate of change (2020-25 est.)

Food insecurity: *severe localized food insecurity: due to civil insecurity and high food prices* - according to the latest analysis, about 1.26 million people are projected to face acute food insecurity during the June to August 2023 lean season period; in total however, the number of food insecure is lower in 2023 compared to 2022; food insecurity conditions are primarily underpinned by the impact of the conflict in central and northern areas, which has caused the displacement of over 375,000 people, as of April 2023; persistent high food prices affect vulnerable households across the country, but limit in particular the food access of people in conflict-affected areas due to market disruptions and limited access to sources of income and humanitarian assistance
(2023)

Revenue from forest resources: 2.02% of GDP (2018 est.)
comparison ranking: 35

Revenue from coal: 0% of GDP (2018 est.)
comparison ranking: 115

Air pollutants: *particulate matter emissions:* 38.55 micrograms per cubic meter (2019 est.)
carbon dioxide emissions: 3.18 megatons (2016 est.)
methane emissions: 19.16 megatons (2020 est.)

Waste and recycling: *municipal solid waste generated annually:* 1,937,354 tons (2012 est.)

Major lakes (area sq km): *fresh water lake(s):* Lac Faguibine - 590 sq km
note - the Niger River is the only source of water for the lake; in recent years the lake is dry

Major rivers (by length in km): Niger (shared with Guinea [s], Niger, and Nigeria [m]) - 4,200 km; Senegal (shared with Guinea [s], Senegal, and Mauritania [m]) - 1,641 km
note – [s] after country name indicates river source; [m] after country name indicates river mouth

Major watersheds (area sq km): Atlantic Ocean drainage: Niger (2,261,741 sq km), Senegal (456,397 sq km), Volta (410,991 sq km)

Major aquifers: Lullemeden-Irhazer Basin, Taodeni-Tanezrouft Basin

Total water withdrawal: *municipal:* 110 million cubic meters (2020 est.)
industrial: 4 million cubic meters (2020 est.)
agricultural: 5.08 billion cubic meters (2020 est.)

Total renewable water resources: 120 billion cubic meters (2020 est.)

GOVERNMENT

Country name: *conventional long form:* Republic of Mali
conventional short form: Mali
local long form: République de Mali
local short form: Mali
former: French Sudan, Sudanese Republic, Mali Federation
etymology: name derives from the West African Mali Empire of the 13th to 16th centuries A.D.

Government type: semi-presidential republic

Capital: *name:* Bamako
geographic coordinates: 12 39 N, 8 00 W
time difference: UTC 0 (5 hours ahead of Washington, DC, during Standard Time)
etymology: the name in the Bambara language can mean either "crocodile tail" or "crocodile river" and three crocodiles appear on the city seal

Administrative divisions: 10 regions (regions, singular - region), 1 district*; District de Bamako*, Gao, Kayes, Kidal, Koulikoro, Menaka, Mopti, Segou, Sikasso, Taoudenni, Tombouctou (Timbuktu); note - Menaka and Taoudenni were legislated in 2016, but implementation has not been confirmed by the US Board on Geographic Names

Independence: 22 September 1960 (from France)

National holiday: Independence Day, 22 September (1960)

Legal system: civil law system based on the French civil law model and influenced by customary law; judicial review of legislative acts in the Constitutional Court

Constitution: *history:* several previous; latest drafted 13 October 2022 and submitted to Transition President Assimi GOITA; final draft completed 1 March 2023; referendum held on 18 June 2023 and approved; referendum results validated by Constitutional Court on 22 July 2023; note - the new constitution includes provisions for the extension of presidential and military powers and the creation of a "senate"
amendments: procedure for amending the 2023 constitution NA

International law organization participation: has not submitted an ICJ jurisdiction declaration; accepts ICCt jurisdiction

Citizenship: *citizenship by birth:* no
citizenship by descent only: at least one parent must be a citizen of Mali
dual citizenship recognized: yes
residency requirement for naturalization: 5 years

Suffrage: 18 years of age; universal

Executive branch: *chief of state:* Transition President Assimi GOITA (since 7 June 2021)
head of government: Transition Prime Minister Choguel MAIGA (since 7 June 2021)
cabinet: Council of Ministers appointed by the prime minister
elections/appointments: president directly elected by absolute majority popular vote in 2 rounds if needed for a 5-year term (eligible for a second term); election last held on 29 July 2018 with runoff on 12 August 2018; prime minister appointed by the president; note - on 21 February 2022, the transition government adopted a charter allowing transition authorities to rule for up to 5 years, but a referendum pushed through by the junta in June 2023 consolidated power in the presidency and would allow junta leaders to serve in a new government, creating the potential for transition President GOITA to maintain his hold on power indefinitely
election results:
2018: Ibrahim Boubacar KEITA reelected president in second round; percent of vote in first round - Ibrahim Boubacar KEITA (RPM) 41.7%, Soumaila CISSE (URD) 17.8%, other 40.5%; percent of vote in second round - Ibrahim Boubacar KEITA 67.2%, Soumaila CISSE 32.8%
2013: Ibrahim Boubacar KEITA elected president in second round; percent of vote in first round - Ibrahim Boubacar KEITA (RPM) 39.8%, Soumaila CISSE (URD) 19.7%, other 40.5%; percent of vote in second round - Ibrahim Boubacar KEITA (RPM) 77.6%, Soumaila CISSE (URD) 22.4%
note: an August 2020 coup d'état deposed President Ibrahim Boubacar KEITA; on 21 September 2020, a group of 17 electors chosen by the Malian military junta, known as the National Committee for the Salvation of the People (CNSP) and led by Colonel Assimi GOITA, selected Bah NDAW as transition president; GOITA served as vice president of the transition government which was inaugurated on 25 September 2020; Vice President GOITA seized power on 25 May 2021; NDAW resigned on 26 May 2021; on 6 June 2022, GOITA's government announced a transition period of 24 months with a planned return to civilian rule by March 2024

Legislative branch: *description:* unicameral National Assembly or Assemblee Nationale (147 seats; members directly elected in single and multi-seat constituencies by absolute majority vote in 2 rounds if needed; 13 seats reserved for citizens living abroad; members serve 5-year terms)
note 1 - the National Assembly was dissolved on 18 August 2020 following a military coup and the resignation of President KEITA; the transition government created a National Transition Council (CNT) whose 121 members were selected by then transition Vice President Assimi GOITA; the CNT acts as

the transitional government's legislative body, with Malick DIAW serving as the president; in February 2022, the CNT increased the number of seats to 147, but some of the additional seats have not yet been filled
note 2 - passage of a constitutional referendum held on 18 June 2023 calls for the creation of a "Senate"
elections: last held on 30 March and 19 April 2020; note - following the dissolution of the National Assembly in August 2020 and the ratification of a new constitution in July 2023 expanding the powers of the military junta, no plans for legislative elections have been announced
election results: percent of vote by party - NA; seats by party - NA; composition - NA

Judicial branch: *highest court(s):* Supreme Court or Cour Supreme (consists of 19 judges organized into judicial, administrative, and accounting sections); Constitutional Court (consists of 9 judges)
judge selection and term of office: Supreme Court judges appointed by the Ministry of Justice to serve 5-year terms; Constitutional Court judges selected - 3 each by the president, the National Assembly, and the Supreme Council of the Magistracy; members serve single renewable 7-year terms
subordinate courts: Court of Appeal; High Court of Justice (jurisdiction limited to cases of high treason or criminal offenses by the president or ministers while in office); administrative courts (first instance and appeal); commercial courts; magistrate courts; labor courts; juvenile courts; special court of state security

Political parties: African Solidarity for Democracy and Independence or SADI
Alliance for Democracy and Progress or ADP-Maliba
Alliance for Democracy in Mali-Pan-African Party for Liberty, Solidarity, and Justice or ADEMA-PASJ
Alliance for the Solidarity of Mali-Convergence of Patriotic Forces or ASMA-CFP
Convergence for the Development of Mali or CODEM
Democratic Alliance for Peace or ADP-Maliba
Movement for Mali or MPM
Party for National Renewal (also Rebirth or Renaissance or PARENA)
Rally for Mali or RPM
Social Democratic Convention or CDS
Union for Democracy and Development or UDD
Union for Republic and Democracy or URD
Yéléma
note 1: only parties with 2 or more seats in the last National Assembly parliamentary elections (30 March and 19 April 2020) included
note 2: the National Assembly was dissolved on 18 August 2020 following a military coup and replaced with a National Transition Council; currently 121 members, party affiliations unknown

International organization participation: ACP, AfDB, AU (suspended), CD, EITI (compliant country), FAO, FZ, G-77, IAEA, IBRD, ICAO, ICCt, ICRM, IDA, IDB, IFAD, IFC, IFRCS, ILO, IMF, Interpol, IOC, IOM, IPU, ISO, ITSO, ITU, ITUC (NGOs), MIGA, MINUSCA, MONUSCO, NAM, OIC, OPCW, UN, UNCTAD, UNDP, UNESCO, UNFPA, UNHCR, UNIDO, UNOPS, UN Women, UNWTO, UPU, WADB (regional), WAEMU, World Bank Group, WCO, WFTU (NGOs), WHO, WIPO, WMO, WTO

Diplomatic representation in the US: *chief of mission:* Ambassador Sékou BERTHE (since 16 September 2022)
chancery: 2130 R Street NW, Washington, DC 20008
telephone: [1] (202) 332-2249
FAX: [1] (202) 332-6603
email address and website:
administration@maliembassy.us
https://www.maliembassy.us/

Diplomatic representation from the US: *chief of mission:* Ambassador Rachna KORHONEN (since 16 March 2023)
embassy: ACI 2000, Rue 243, (located off the Roi Bin Fahad Aziz Bridge west of the Bamako central district), Porte 297, Bamako
mailing address: 2050 Bamako Place, Washington DC 20521-2050
telephone: [223] 20-70-23-00
FAX: [223] 20-70-24-79
email address and website:
ACSBamako@state.gov
https://ml.usembassy.gov/

Flag description: three equal vertical bands of green (hoist side), yellow, and red
note: uses the popular Pan-African colors of Ethiopia; the colors from left to right are the same as those of neighboring Senegal (which has an additional green central star) and the reverse of those on the flag of neighboring Guinea

National symbol(s): Great Mosque of Djenne; national colors: green, yellow, red

National anthem: *name:* "Le Mali" (Mali)
lyrics/music: Seydou Badian KOUYATE/ Banzoumana SISSOKO
note: adopted 1962; also known as "Pour L'Afrique et pour toi, Mali" (For Africa and for You, Mali) and "A ton appel Mali" (At Your Call, Mali)

National heritage: *total World Heritage Sites:* 4 (3 cultural, 1 mixed)
selected World Heritage Site locales: Old Towns of Djenné (c); Timbuktu (c); Cliff of Bandiagara (Land of the Dogons) (m); Tomb of Askia (c)

ECONOMY

Economic overview: low-income Saharan economy; recession due to COVID-19 and political instability; extreme poverty; environmentally fragile; high public debt; agricultural and gold exporter; terrorism and warfare are common

Real GDP (purchasing power parity): $57.235 billion (2023 est.)
$54.387 billion (2022 est.)
$52.56 billion (2021 est.)
note: data in 2021 dollars
comparison ranking: 118

Real GDP growth rate: 5.24% (2023 est.)
3.47% (2022 est.)
3.05% (2021 est.)
note: annual GDP % growth based on constant local currency
comparison ranking: 43

Real GDP per capita: $2,500 (2023 est.)
$2,400 (2022 est.)
$2,400 (2021 est.)
note: data in 2021 dollars
comparison ranking: 206

GDP (official exchange rate): $20.905 billion (2023 est.)
note: data in current dollars at official exchange rate

Inflation rate (consumer prices): 2.06% (2023 est.)
9.62% (2022 est.)
3.93% (2021 est.)
note: annual % change based on consumer prices
comparison ranking: 38

Credit ratings: Moody's rating: Caa1 (2020)
note: The year refers to the year in which the current credit rating was first obtained.

GDP - composition, by sector of origin: *agriculture:* 36.8% (2023 est.)
industry: 19.4% (2023 est.)
services: 36.1% (2023 est.)
note: figures may not total 100% due to non-allocated consumption not captured in sector-reported data
comparison rankings: services 204; industry 141; agriculture 5

GDP - composition, by end use: *household consumption:* 74.3% (2023 est.)
government consumption: 17.1% (2023 est.)
investment in fixed capital: 20.1% (2023 est.)
investment in inventories: -1.9% (2023 est.)
exports of goods and services: 28.2% (2023 est.)
imports of goods and services: -37.8% (2023 est.)
note: figures may not total 100% due to rounding or gaps in data collection

Agricultural products: maize, rice, millet, sorghum, okra, sugarcane, mangoes/guavas, onions, cotton, bananas (2022)
note: top ten agricultural products based on tonnage

Industries: food processing; construction; phosphate and gold mining

Industrial production growth rate: -0.82% (2023 est.)
note: annual % change in industrial value added based on constant local currency
comparison ranking: 164

Labor force: 8.277 million (2023 est.)
note: number of people ages 15 or older who are employed or seeking work
comparison ranking: 66

Unemployment rate: 3.01% (2023 est.)
3.09% (2022 est.)
2.29% (2021 est.)
note: % of labor force seeking employment
comparison ranking: 46

Youth unemployment rate (ages 15-24): *total:* 4.1% (2023 est.)
male: 4.1% (2023 est.)
female: 4.2% (2023 est.)
note: % of labor force ages 15-24 seeking employment
comparison ranking: total 183

Population below poverty line: 44.6% (2021 est.)
note: % of population with income below national poverty line

Gini Index coefficient - distribution of family income: 35.7 (2021 est.)
note: index (0-100) of income distribution; higher values represent greater inequality
comparison ranking: 72

Household income or consumption by percentage share: *lowest 10%:* 3.2% (2021 est.)
highest 10%: 28.3% (2021 est.)
note: % share of income accruing to lowest and highest 10% of population

Remittances: 5.52% of GDP (2023 est.)
5.89% of GDP (2022 est.)
5.86% of GDP (2021 est.)
note: personal transfers and compensation between resident and non-resident individuals/households/ entities

Budget: *revenues:* $2.841 billion (2020 est.)

expenditures: $2.533 billion (2020 est.)
note: central government revenues and expenses (excluding grants/extrabudgetary units/social security funds) converted to US dollars at average official exchange rate for year indicated

Public debt: 35.4% of GDP (2017 est.)
comparison ranking: 151

Taxes and other revenues: 14.16% (of GDP) (2020 est.)
note: central government tax revenue as a % of GDP
comparison ranking: 148

Current account balance: -$1.475 billion (2022 est.)
-$1.469 billion (2021 est.)
-$379.683 million (2020 est.)
note: balance of payments - net trade and primary/secondary income in current dollars
comparison ranking: 149

Exports: $5.855 billion (2022 est.)
$5.381 billion (2021 est.)
$5.196 billion (2020 est.)
note: balance of payments - exports of goods and services in current dollars
comparison ranking: 134

Exports - partners: UAE 74%, Switzerland 17%, Australia 5%, China 1%, Turkey 1% (2022)
note: top five export partners based on percentage share of exports

Exports - commodities: gold, cotton, oil seeds, wood, fertilizers (2022)
note: top five export commodities based on value in dollars

Imports: $7.942 billion (2022 est.)
$7.596 billion (2021 est.)
$6.339 billion (2020 est.)
note: balance of payments - imports of goods and services in current dollars
comparison ranking: 132

Imports - partners: Cote d'Ivoire 24%, Senegal 19%, China 10%, France 6%, Burkina Faso 5% (2022)
note: top five import partners based on percentage share of imports

Imports - commodities: refined petroleum, cotton fabric, broadcasting equipment, packaged medicine, gold (2022)
note: top five import commodities based on value in dollars

Reserves of foreign exchange and gold: $647.8 million (31 December 2017 est.)
$395.7 million (31 December 2016 est.)
comparison ranking: 154

Debt - external: $3.923 billion (2022 est.)
note: present value of external debt in current US dollars
comparison ranking: 57

Exchange rates: Communaute Financiere Africaine francs (XOF) per US dollar -

Exchange rates: 606.57 (2023 est.)
623.76 (2022 est.)
554.531 (2021 est.)
575.586 (2020 est.)
585.911 (2019 est.)

ENERGY

Electricity access: *electrification - total population:* 53% (2022 est.)
electrification - urban areas: 99.7%
electrification - rural areas: 18.3%

Electricity: *installed generating capacity:* 1.145 million kW (2022 est.)
consumption: 3.5 billion kWh (2022 est.)
exports: 600 million kWh (2022 est.)
imports: 775.87 million kWh (2022 est.)
transmission/distribution losses: 433.773 million kWh (2022 est.)
comparison rankings: transmission/distribution losses 78; imports 86; exports 74; consumption 136; installed generating capacity 134

Electricity generation sources: *fossil fuels:* 60.2% of total installed capacity (2022 est.)
solar: 0.9% of total installed capacity (2022 est.)
hydroelectricity: 37.3% of total installed capacity (2022 est.)
biomass and waste: 1.6% of total installed capacity (2022 est.)

Coal: *exports:* (2022 est.) less than 1 metric ton
imports: 100 metric tons (2022 est.)

Petroleum: *refined petroleum consumption:* 46,000 bbl/day (2022 est.)

Carbon dioxide emissions: 6.868 million metric tonnes of CO2 (2022 est.)
from petroleum and other liquids: 6.868 million metric tonnes of CO2 (2022 est.)
comparison ranking: total emissions 127

Energy consumption per capita: 4.476 million Btu/person (2022 est.)
comparison ranking: 172

COMMUNICATIONS

Telephones - fixed lines: *total subscriptions:* 307,000 (2022 est.)
subscriptions per 100 inhabitants: 1 (2022 est.)
comparison ranking: total subscriptions 105

Telephones - mobile cellular: *total subscriptions:* 25.869 million (2022 est.)
subscriptions per 100 inhabitants: 114 (2022 est.)
comparison ranking: total subscriptions 51

Telecommunication systems: *general assessment:* Mali's telecom systems are challenged by recent conflict, geography, areas of low population, poverty, security issues, and high illiteracy; telecom infrastructure is barely adequate in urban areas and not available in most of the country with underinvestment in fixed-line networks; high mobile penetration and potential for mobile broadband service; local plans for IXP; dependent on neighboring countries for international bandwidth and access to submarine cables (2022)
domestic: fixed-line subscribership is 1 per 100 persons; mobile-cellular subscribership has increased sharply to 100 per 100 persons (2021)
international: country code - 223; satellite communications center and fiber-optic links to neighboring countries; satellite earth stations - 2 Intelsat (1 Atlantic Ocean, 1 Indian Ocean) (2020)

Broadcast media: national public TV broadcaster; 2 privately owned companies provide subscription services to foreign multi-channel TV packages; national public radio broadcaster supplemented by a large number of privately owned and community broadcast stations; transmissions of multiple international broadcasters are available (2019)

Internet country code: .ml

Internet users: *total:* 7.48 million (2021 est.)
percent of population: 34% (2021 est.)
comparison ranking: total 79

Broadband - fixed subscriptions: *total:* 243,806 (2020 est.)
subscriptions per 100 inhabitants: 1 (2020 est.)
comparison ranking: total 112

TRANSPORTATION

National air transport system: *number of registered air carriers:* 0 (2020)

Civil aircraft registration country code prefix: TZ, TT

Airports: 30 (2024)
comparison ranking: 120

Heliports: 3 (2024)

Railways: *total:* 593 km (2014)
narrow gauge: 593 km (2014) 1.000-m gauge
comparison ranking: total 109

Roadways: *total:* 139,107 km (2014)
comparison ranking: total 38

Waterways: 1,800 km (2011) (downstream of Koulikoro; low water levels on the River Niger cause problems in dry years; in the months before the rainy season the river is not navigable by commercial vessels)
comparison ranking: 45

MILITARY AND SECURITY

Military and security forces: Malian Armed Forces (Forces Armées Maliennes or FAMa): Land Forces (l'Armée de Terre), Air Force (l'Armée de l'Air); National Guard (la Garde Nationale du Mali or GNM); General Directorate of the National Gendarmerie (la Direction Générale de la Gendarmerie Nationale or DGGN) (2024)
note 1: the Gendarmerie and the National Guard are under the authority of the Ministry of Defense and Veterans Affairs (Ministere De La Defense Et Des Anciens Combattants, MDAC), but operational control is shared with the Ministry of Internal Security and Civil Protection which also controls the National Police; the National Police has responsibility for law enforcement and maintenance of order in urban areas and supports the FAMa in internal military operations
note 2: the Gendarmerie's primary mission is internal security and public order; its duties also include territorial defense, humanitarian operations, intelligence gathering, and protecting private property, mainly in rural areas; it also has a specialized border security unit
note 3: the National Guard is a military force responsible for providing security to government facilities and institutions, prison service, public order, humanitarian operations, some border security, and intelligence gathering; its forces include a camel corps for patrolling the deserts and borders of northern Mali
note 4: there are also pro-government militias operating in Mali, such as the Imghad Tuareg Self-Defense Group and Allies (GATIA); the leader of GATIA is also a general in the national army

Military expenditures: 4% of GDP (2023 est.)
3.5% of GDP (2022 est.)
3.5% of GDP (2021 est.)
3.4% of GDP (2020 est.)
3.1% of GDP (2019 est.)
comparison ranking: 18

Military and security service personnel strengths: information varies; estimated 35-40,000 total active military and paramilitary personnel, including approximately 20-25,000 FAMa (up to 2,000 Air Force), 5-7,000 Gendarmerie, and 10,000 National Guard (2023)

Military equipment inventories and acquisitions: the FAMa's inventory includes a large amount of Soviet-era weapons and equipment; in recent years it has received limited quantities of newer armaments from more than a dozen countries, including China, Czechia, Russia, and Turkey (2024)

Military service age and obligation: 18 years of age for men and women for selective compulsory and voluntary military service; 24-month compulsory service obligation (2023)

Military deployments: *note:* until announcing its withdrawal in May of 2022, Mali was part of a five-nation anti-jihadist task force known as the G5 Sahel Group, set up in 2014 with Burkina Faso, Chad, Mauritania, and Niger; Mali had committed 1,100 troops and 200 gendarmes to the force

Military - note: the FAMa is responsible for defense of the country's sovereignty and territory, but also has some domestic security duties, including the maintenance of public order and support to law enforcement if required, as well as counterterrorism and counterinsurgency operations; it also participates in socio-economic development projects; the military has traditionally played a large role in Mali's politics; prior to the coup in August 2020 and military takeover in May 2021, it had intervened in the political arena at least five times since the country gained independence in 1960 (1968, 1976, 1978, 1991, 2012)
the FAMa and other security forces are actively engaged in operations against several insurgent/terrorist groups affiliated with al-Qa'ida and the Islamic State of Iraq and ash-Sham (ISIS), as well as other rebel organizations, communal militias, and criminal bands spread across the central, northern, and southern regions of the country; the government is reportedly in control of only an estimated 10-20% of the country's central and northern territories, and attacks have increased in the more heavily populated south, including around the capital Bamako; the Macina Liberation Front (FLM), part of the Jama'at Nusrat al Islam wal Muslimin (JNIM) coalition of al-Qa'ida-linked terror groups, has played a large role in a surge in violence in Mali's central and southern regions; in the north, ISIS in the Greater Sahara (ISIS-GS) has regained strength in recent years
the FAMa and the remainder of the security forces collapsed in 2012 during the fighting against Tuareg rebels and Islamic militants and have since been rebuilt with considerable external assistance, including the EU, France, and the UN; for example, the EU Training Mission in Mali (EUTM) from 2013-2022 trained as many as 15,000 Malian soldiers and eight combined arms battalions/battlegroups (Groupement Tactique InterArmes, GTIA), each of which was structured to be self-sufficient with its own motorized/mechanized infantry, light armor, commandos, artillery, engineers, and other support forces; the EUTM and the French military ended their missions in 2022 citing issues with the ruling military government, including human rights abuses and the presence of Russian private military contractors; the UN Multidimensional Integrated Stabilization Mission in Mali (MINUSMA) operated in the country from 2013-2023 with the mission of providing security, rebuilding Malian security forces, protecting civilians, supporting national political dialogue, and assisting in the reestablishment of Malian government authority; MINUSMA had more than 15,000 personnel at its peak strength and lost over 300 peacekeepers during the course of the mission, which was concluded at the end of 2023 after the ruling junta demanded the withdrawal of foreign forces
the military government has increased security ties with Russia; Russia has provided military equipment, and in December 2021, Mali contracted with a Russian private military company to provide training and other support for local armed forces, as well as security for senior Malian officials (2024)

TERRORISM

Terrorist group(s): Ansar al-Dine; Islamic State of Iraq and ash-Sham in the Greater Sahara (ISIS-GS); Jama'at Nusrat al-Islam wal-Muslimin (JNIM); al-Mulathamun Battalion (al-Mourabitoun)
note: details about the history, aims, leadership, organization, areas of operation, tactics, targets, weapons, size, and sources of support of the group(s) appear(s) in the Terrorism reference guide

TRANSNATIONAL ISSUES

Refugees and internally displaced persons: *refugees (country of origin):* 29,138 (Burkina Faso) (refugees and asylum seekers), 20,617 (Niger) (refugees and asylum seekers), 14,956 (Mauritania) (refugees and asylum seekers) (2023)
IDPs: 375,539 (Tuareg rebellion since 2012) (2023)

Trafficking in persons: tier rating: Tier 2 Watch list — Mali did not demonstrate overall increasing efforts to eliminate trafficking compared with the previous reporting period and was downgraded to Tier 2 Watch List; for more details, go to: https://www.state.gov/ reports/2024-trafficking-in-persons-report/mali/

Illicit drugs: a transit point for illicit drugs trafficked to Europe; trafficking controlled by armed groups, criminal organizations, terrorist groups and government officials that facilitate, protect and profit from the activity

MALTA

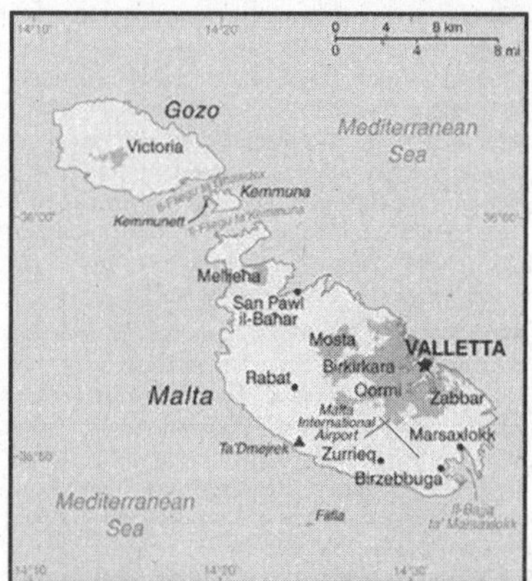

INTRODUCTION

Background: With a civilization that dates back thousands of years, Malta boasts some of the oldest megalithic sites in the world. Situated in the center of the Mediterranean, Malta's islands have long served as a strategic military asset, with the islands at various times falling under the control of the Phoenicians, Carthaginians, Greeks, Romans, Byzantines, Moors, Normans, Sicilians, Spanish, Knights of St. John, and French. Most recently a British colony (since 1814), Malta gained its independence in 1964 and declared itself a republic 10 years later. While under British rule, the island staunchly supported the UK through both world wars. Since the mid-1980s, the island has transformed itself into a freight transshipment point, a financial center, and a tourist destination, as its key industries moved toward more service-oriented activities. Malta became an EU member in 2004 and joined the eurozone in 2008.

GEOGRAPHY

Location: Southern Europe, islands in the Mediterranean Sea, south of Sicily (Italy)

Geographic coordinates: 35 50 N, 14 35 E

Map references: Europe

Area: *total:* 316 sq km
land: 316 sq km
water: 0 sq km
comparison ranking: total 208

Area - comparative: slightly less than twice the size of Washington, DC

Land boundaries: *total:* 0 km

Coastline: 196.8 km (excludes 56 km for the island of Gozo)

Maritime claims: *territorial sea:* 12 nm
contiguous zone: 24 nm
continental shelf: 200-m depth or to the depth of exploitation
exclusive fishing zone: 25 nm

Climate: Mediterranean; mild, rainy winters; hot, dry summers

Terrain: mostly low, rocky, flat to dissected plains; many coastal cliffs

Elevation: *highest point:* Ta'Dmejrek on Dingli Cliffs 253 m
lowest point: Mediterranean Sea 0 m

Natural resources: limestone, salt, arable land

Land use: *agricultural land:* 32.3% (2018 est.)
arable land: 28.4% (2018 est.)
permanent crops: 3.9% (2018 est.)
permanent pasture: 0% (2018 est.)
forest: 0.9% (2018 est.)
other: 66.8% (2018 est.)

Irrigated land: 35 sq km (2020)

Population distribution: most of the population lives on the eastern half of Malta, the largest of the three inhabited islands

Natural hazards: occasional droughts

Geography - note: the country is an archipelago, with only the three largest islands (Malta, Ghawdex or Gozo, and Kemmuna or Comino) inhabited; numerous bays provide good harbors

PEOPLE AND SOCIETY

Population: *total:* 469,730
male: 237,023
female: 232,707 (2024 est.)
comparison rankings: female 174; male 174; total 174

Nationality: *noun:* Maltese (singular and plural)
adjective: Maltese

Ethnic groups: Maltese (descendants of ancient Carthaginians and Phoenicians with strong elements of Italian and other Mediterranean stock)

Languages: Maltese (official) 90.1%, English (official) 6%, multilingual 3%, other 0.9% (2005 est.)

Religions: Roman Catholic (official) more than 90% (2006 est.)

Age structure: *0-14 years:* 14.5% (male 35,034/female 33,181)
15-64 years: 62.4% (male 151,836/female 141,248)
65 years and over: 23.1% (2024 est.) (male 50,153/female 58,278)

Dependency ratios: *total dependency ratio:* 47.1
youth dependency ratio: 19.3
elderly dependency ratio: 27.7
potential support ratio: 3.6 (2021 est.)

Median age: *total:* 43.5 years (2024 est.)
male: 42.4 years
female: 44.7 years
comparison ranking: total 35

Population growth rate: 0.51% (2024 est.)
comparison ranking: 150

Birth rate: 9.4 births/1,000 population (2024 est.)
comparison ranking: 193

Death rate: 8.8 deaths/1,000 population (2024 est.)
comparison ranking: 67

Net migration rate: 4.4 migrant(s)/1,000 population (2024 est.)
comparison ranking: 21

Population distribution: most of the population lives on the eastern half of Malta, the largest of the three inhabited islands

Urbanization: *urban population:* 94.9% of total population (2023)
rate of urbanization: 0.28% annual rate of change (2020-25 est.)

Major urban areas - population: 213,000 VALLETTA (capital) (2018)

Sex ratio: *at birth:* 1.04 male(s)/female
0-14 years: 1.06 male(s)/female
15-64 years: 1.07 male(s)/female
65 years and over: 0.86 male(s)/female
total population: 1.02 male(s)/female (2024 est.)

Mother's mean age at first birth: 29.3 years (2020 est.)
note: data refers to the average of the different child-bearing ages of first-order births

Maternal mortality ratio: 3 deaths/100,000 live births (2020 est.)
comparison ranking: 181

Infant mortality rate: *total:* 4.4 deaths/1,000 live births (2024 est.)
male: 4.3 deaths/1,000 live births
female: 4.5 deaths/1,000 live births
comparison ranking: total 182

Life expectancy at birth: *total population:* 83.6 years (2024 est.)
male: 81.5 years
female: 85.8 years
comparison ranking: total population 12

Total fertility rate: 1.51 children born/woman (2024 est.)
comparison ranking: 201

Gross reproduction rate: 0.74 (2024 est.)

Drinking water source: *improved: urban:* 100% of population
rural: 100% of population
total: 100% of population

Current health expenditure: 10.8% of GDP (2020)

Physician density: 2.86 physicians/1,000 population (2015)

Hospital bed density: 4.5 beds/1,000 population (2017)

Sanitation facility access: *improved: urban:* 100% of population
rural: 100% of population
total: 100% of population

Obesity - adult prevalence rate: 28.9% (2016)
comparison ranking: 29

Alcohol consumption per capita: *total:* 8.07 liters of pure alcohol (2019 est.)
beer: 2.8 liters of pure alcohol (2019 est.)
wine: 2.34 liters of pure alcohol (2019 est.)
spirits: 2.51 liters of pure alcohol (2019 est.)
other alcohols: 0.42 liters of pure alcohol (2019 est.)
comparison ranking: total 43

Tobacco use: *total:* 24% (2020 est.)
male: 26.4% (2020 est.)
female: 21.6% (2020 est.)
comparison ranking: total 56

Currently married women (ages 15-49): 63.2% (2023 est.)

Education expenditures: 5.9% of GDP (2020 est.)
comparison ranking: 45

Literacy: *definition:* age 15 and over can read and write
total population: 94.9%
male: 93.4%
female: 96.4% (2021)

School life expectancy (primary to tertiary education): *total:* 17 years
male: 17 years
female: 18 years (2020)

ENVIRONMENT

Environment - current issues: limited natural freshwater resources; increasing reliance on desalination; deforestation; wildlife preservation

Environment - international agreements: *party to:* Air Pollution, Biodiversity, Climate Change, Climate Change-Kyoto Protocol, Climate Change-Paris Agreement, Comprehensive Nuclear Test Ban, Desertification, Endangered Species, Hazardous Wastes, Law of the Sea, Marine Dumping-London Convention, Nuclear Test Ban, Ozone Layer Protection, Ship Pollution, Tropical Timber 2006, Wetlands
signed, but not ratified: none of the selected agreements

Climate: Mediterranean; mild, rainy winters; hot, dry summers

Urbanization: *urban population:* 94.9% of total population (2023)
rate of urbanization: 0.28% annual rate of change (2020-25 est.)

Revenue from forest resources: 0% of GDP (2018 est.)
comparison ranking: 192

Revenue from coal: 0% of GDP (2018 est.)
comparison ranking: 112

Air pollutants: *particulate matter emissions:* 12.93 micrograms per cubic meter (2019 est.)
carbon dioxide emissions: 1.34 megatons (2016 est.)
methane emissions: 0.2 megatons (2020 est.)

Waste and recycling: *municipal solid waste generated annually:* 269,000 tons (2015 est.)
municipal solid waste recycled annually: 17,996 tons (2015 est.)
percent of municipal solid waste recycled: 6.7% (2015 est.)

Total water withdrawal: *municipal:* 40 million cubic meters (2020 est.)
industrial: 1 million cubic meters (2020 est.)
agricultural: 20 million cubic meters (2020 est.)

Total renewable water resources: 50 million cubic meters (2020 est.)

GOVERNMENT

Country name: *conventional long form:* Republic of Malta
conventional short form: Malta
local long form: Repubblika ta' Malta
local short form: Malta
etymology: the ancient Greeks called the island "Melite" meaning "honey-sweet" from the Greek word "meli" meaning "honey" and referring to the island's honey production

Government type: parliamentary republic

Capital: *name:* Valletta
geographic coordinates: 35 53 N, 14 30 E
time difference: UTC+1 (6 hours ahead of Washington, DC, during Standard Time)
daylight saving time: +1hr, begins last Sunday in March; ends last Sunday in October
etymology: named in honor of Jean de VALETTE, the Grand Master of the Order of Saint John (crusader knights), who successfully led a defense of the island from an Ottoman invasion in 1565

Administrative divisions: 68 localities (Il-lokalita); Attard, Balzan, Birgu, Birkirkara, Birzebbuga, Bormla, Dingli, Fgura, Floriana, Fontana, Ghajnsielem, Gharb, Gharghur, Ghasri, Ghaxaq, Gudja, Gzira, Hamrun, Iklin, Imdina, Imgarr, Imqabba, Imsida, Imtarfa, Isla, Kalkara, Kercem, Kirkop, Lija, Luqa, Marsa, Marsaskala, Marsaxlokk, Mellieha, Mosta, Munxar, Nadur, Naxxar, Paola, Pembroke, Pieta, Qala, Qormi, Qrendi, Rabat, Rabat (Ghawdex), Safi, San Giljan/Saint Julian, San Gwann/Saint John, San Lawrenz/Saint Lawrence, Sannat, San Pawl il-Bahar/Saint Paul's Bay, Santa Lucija/Saint Lucia, Santa Venera/Saint Venera, Siggiewi, Sliema, Swieqi, Tarxien, Ta' Xbiex, Valletta, Xaghra, Xewkija, Xghajra, Zabbar, Zebbug, Zebbug (Ghawdex), Zejtun, Zurrieq

Independence: 21 September 1964 (from the UK)

National holiday: Independence Day, 21 September (1964); Republic Day, 13 December (1974)

Legal system: mixed legal system of English common law and civil law based on the Roman and Napoleonic civil codes; subject to European Union law

Constitution: *history:* many previous; latest adopted 21 September 1964
amendments: proposals (Acts of Parliament) require at least two-thirds majority vote by the House of Representatives; passage of Acts requires majority vote by referendum, followed by final majority vote by the House and assent of the president of the republic; amended many times, last in 2020

International law organization participation: accepts compulsory ICJ jurisdiction with reservations; accepts ICCt jurisdiction

Citizenship: *citizenship by birth:* no
citizenship by descent only: at least one parent must be a citizen of Malta
dual citizenship recognized: no
residency requirement for naturalization: 5 years

Suffrage: 18 years of age (16 in local council elections); universal

Executive branch: *chief of state:* President Myriam Spiteri DEBONO (since 4 April 2024)
head of government: Prime Minister Robert ABELA (13 January 2020)
cabinet: Cabinet appointed by the president on the advice of the prime minister
elections/appointments: president indirectly elected by the House of Representatives for a single 5-year term; election last held on 27 March 2024 (next to be held by March 2029); following legislative elections, the leader of the majority party or majority coalition usually appointed prime minister by the president for a 5-year term; deputy prime minister appointed by the president on the advice of the prime minister
election results:
2024: Myriam SPITERI DEBONO (PL) elected president; House of Representatives vote - unanimous
2019: George VELLA (PL) elected president; House of Representatives vote - unanimous

Legislative branch: *description:* unicameral House of Representatives or Il-Kamra Tad-Deputati, a component of the Parliament of Malta (65 seats statutory, 79 for 2022-2027 term; members directly elected in 5 multi-seat constituencies by proportional representation vote; members serve 5-year terms)
elections: last held on 26 March 2022 (next to be held in 2027)
election results: percent of vote by party - PL 55.1%, PN 41.7%, other 3.2%; seats by party - PL 38, PN 29; composition as of February 2024 - men 57, women 22, percentage women 27.9%; note - due to underepresentation by women in the combined general on 26 March and two casual elections on 7 and 12 April (10 seats or 14.9%), an additional 12 seats were awarded because their percentage did not meet the 40% threshold required by the Malta Constitution or the General Elections Amendment Act 2021

Judicial branch: *highest court(s):* Court of Appeal (consists of either 1 or 3 judges); Constitutional Court (consists of 3 judges); Court of Criminal Appeal (consists of either 1 or 3 judges)
judge selection and term of office: Court of Appeal and Constitutional Court judges appointed by the president, usually upon the advice of the prime minister; judges of both courts serve until age 65
subordinate courts: Civil Court (divided into the General Jurisdiction Section, Family Section, and Voluntary Section); Criminal Court; Court of Magistrates; Gozo Courts (for the islands of Gozo and Comino)

Political parties: AD+PD or ADPD (formed from the merger of Democratic Alternative or AD and Democratic Party (Partit Demokratiku) or PD)
Labor Party (Partit Laburista) or PL
Nationalist Party (Partit Nazzjonalista) or PN

International organization participation: Australia Group, C, CD, CE, EAPC, EBRD, ECB, EIB, EMU, EU, FAO, IAEA, IBRD, ICAO, ICC (NGOs), ICCt, ICRM, IDA, IFAD, IFC, IFRCS, ILO, IMF, IMO, IMSO, Interpol, IOC, IOM, IPU, ISO, ITSO, ITU, ITUC (NGOs), MIGA, NATO (partner), NSG, OAS (observer), OPCW, OSCE, PCA, PFP, Schengen Convention, UN, UNCTAD, UNESCO, UNIDO, Union Latina (observer), UNWTO, UPU, Wassenaar Arrangement, WCO, WHO, WIPO, WMO, WTO

Diplomatic representation in the US: *chief of mission:* Ambassador Godfrey C. XUEREB (since 19 April 2023)
chancery: 2017 Connecticut Avenue NW, Washington, DC 20008
telephone: [1] (771) 213-4050
FAX: [1] (202) 530-9753
email address and website:
maltaembassy.washington@gov.mt
The Embassy (gov.mt)

Diplomatic representation from the US: *chief of mission:* Ambassador Constance J. MILSTEIN (since October 27, 2022)
embassy: Ta' Qali National Park, Attard, ATD 4000
mailing address: 5800 Valletta Place, Washington DC 20521-5800
telephone: [356] 2561-4000
email address and website:
ACSMalta@state.gov
https://mt.usembassy.gov/

Flag description: two equal vertical bands of white (hoist side) and red; in the upper hoist-side corner is a representation of the George Cross, edged in red; according to legend, the colors are taken from the red and white checkered banner of Count Roger of Sicily who removed a bi-colored corner and granted it to Malta in 1091; an uncontested explanation is that the colors are those of the Knights of Saint John who ruled Malta from 1530 to 1798; in 1942, King George VI of the UK awarded the George Cross to the islanders for their exceptional bravery and gallantry in World War II; since independence in 1964, the George Cross bordered in red has appeared directly on the white field

National symbol(s): Maltese eight-pointed cross; national colors: red, white

National anthem: *name:* "L-Innu Malti" (The Maltese Anthem)
lyrics/music: Dun Karm PSAILA/Robert SAMMUT
note: adopted 1945; written in the form of a prayer

National heritage: *total World Heritage Sites:* 3 (all cultural)
selected World Heritage Site locales: City of Valletta; Hal Saflieni Hypogeum; Megalithic Temples of Malta

ECONOMY

Economic overview: high-income, EU-member European economy; diversified portfolio; euro user; dependent on food and energy imports; strong tourism, trade, and manufacturing sectors; high North African immigration; large welfare system; educated workforce

Real GDP (purchasing power parity): $31.661 billion (2023 est.)
$29.978 billion (2022 est.)
$27.738 billion (2021 est.)
note: data in 2021 dollars
comparison ranking: 146

Real GDP growth rate: 5.61% (2023 est.)
8.08% (2022 est.)
12.51% (2021 est.)
note: annual GDP % growth based on constant local currency
comparison ranking: 36

Real GDP per capita: $57,200 (2023 est.)
$56,400 (2022 est.)
$53,500 (2021 est.)
note: data in 2021 dollars
comparison ranking: 32

GDP (official exchange rate): $20.957 billion (2023 est.)
note: data in current dollars at official exchange rate

Inflation rate (consumer prices): 5.09% (2023 est.)
6.15% (2022 est.)
1.5% (2021 est.)
note: annual % change based on consumer prices
comparison ranking: 111

Credit ratings: Fitch rating: A+ (2017)

Moody's rating: A2 (2019)

Standard & Poors rating: A- (2016)
note: The year refers to the year in which the current credit rating was first obtained.

GDP - composition, by sector of origin: *agriculture:* 0.7% (2023 est.)
industry: 12.1% (2023 est.)
services: 79.7% (2023 est.)
note: figures may not total 100% due to non-allocated consumption not captured in sector-reported data
comparison rankings: services 16; industry 180; agriculture 192

GDP - composition, by end use: *household consumption:* 43.4% (2023 est.)
government consumption: 17.7% (2023 est.)
investment in fixed capital: 18.5% (2023 est.)
investment in inventories: 1% (2023 est.)
exports of goods and services: 166.7% (2023 est.)
imports of goods and services: -147.3% (2023 est.)
note: figures may not total 100% due to rounding or gaps in data collection

Agricultural products: milk, tomatoes, onions, potatoes, cauliflower/broccoli, pork, chicken, cabbages, pumpkins/squash, grapes (2022)
note: top ten agricultural products based on tonnage

Industries: tourism, electronics, ship building and repair, construction, food and beverages, pharmaceuticals, footwear, clothing, tobacco, aviation services, financial services, information technology services

Industrial production growth rate: 4.3% (2014 est.)
note: annual % change in industrial value added based on constant local currency
comparison ranking: 63

Labor force: 313,000 (2023 est.)
note: number of people ages 15 or older who are employed or seeking work
comparison ranking: 167

Unemployment rate: 3.13% (2023 est.)
2.93% (2022 est.)
3.4% (2021 est.)
note: % of labor force seeking employment
comparison ranking: 52

Youth unemployment rate (ages 15-24): *total:* 9.3% (2023 est.)
male: 13.8% (2023 est.)
female: 4.3% (2023 est.)
note: % of labor force ages 15-24 seeking employment
comparison ranking: total 141

Population below poverty line: 16.7% (2021 est.)
note: % of population with income below national poverty line

Gini Index coefficient - distribution of family income: 31.4 (2020 est.)
note: index (0-100) of income distribution; higher values represent greater inequality
comparison ranking: 115

Household income or consumption by percentage share: *lowest 10%:* 3.1% (2020 est.)
highest 10%: 25.1% (2020 est.)
note: % share of income accruing to lowest and highest 10% of population

Remittances: 1.11% of GDP (2023 est.)
1.23% of GDP (2022 est.)
1.49% of GDP (2021 est.)
note: personal transfers and compensation between resident and non-resident individuals/households/entities

Budget: *revenues:* $6.106 billion (2022 est.)
expenditures: $6.922 billion (2022 est.)
note: central government revenues (excluding grants) and expenses converted to US dollars at average official exchange rate for year indicated

Public debt: 50.7% of GDP (2017 est.)
note: Malta reports public debt at nominal value outstanding at the end of the year, according to guidelines set out in the Maastricht Treaty for general government gross debt; the data include the following categories of government liabilities (as defined in ESA95): currency and deposits (AF.2), securities other than shares excluding financial derivatives (AF.3, excluding AF.34), and loans (AF.4); general government comprises the central, state, and local governments, and social security funds
comparison ranking: 103

Taxes and other revenues: 23.37% (of GDP) (2022 est.)
note: central government tax revenue as a % of GDP
comparison ranking: 58

Current account balance: -$1.02 billion (2022 est.)
$214.463 million (2021 est.)
$348.601 million (2020 est.)
note: balance of payments - net trade and primary/secondary income in current dollars
comparison ranking: 141

Exports: $25.417 billion (2022 est.)
$25.533 billion (2021 est.)
$22.735 billion (2020 est.)
note: balance of payments - exports of goods and services in current dollars
comparison ranking: 85

Exports - partners: Germany 12%, Italy 6%, France 6%, Japan 5%, Singapore 5% (2022)
note: top five export partners based on percentage share of exports

Exports - commodities: integrated circuits, packaged medicine, refined petroleum, fish, postage stamps/documents (2022)
note: top five export commodities based on value in dollars

Imports: $23.883 billion (2022 est.)
$22.958 billion (2021 est.)
$20.164 billion (2020 est.)
note: balance of payments - imports of goods and services in current dollars
comparison ranking: 88

Imports - partners: Italy 14%, China 11%, South Korea 11%, Germany 10%, Canada 5% (2022)
note: top five import partners based on percentage share of imports

Imports - commodities: ships, refined petroleum, aircraft, integrated circuits, packaged medicine (2022)
note: top five import commodities based on value in dollars

Reserves of foreign exchange and gold: $1.223 billion (2023 est.)
$1.199 billion (2022 est.)
$1.149 billion (2021 est.)
note: holdings of gold (year-end prices)/foreign exchange/special drawing rights in current dollars
comparison ranking: 144

Exchange rates: euros (EUR) per US dollar -

Exchange rates: 0.925 (2023 est.)
0.95 (2022 est.)
0.845 (2021 est.)
0.876 (2020 est.)
0.893 (2019 est.)

ENERGY

Electricity access: *electrification - total population:* 100% (2022 est.)

Electricity: *installed generating capacity:* 805,000 kW (2022 est.)
consumption: 2.786 billion kWh (2022 est.)
exports: 7 million kWh (2022 est.)
imports: 646 million kWh (2022 est.)
transmission/distribution losses: 95.168 million kWh (2022 est.)
comparison rankings: transmission/distribution losses 46; imports 88; exports 98; consumption 141; installed generating capacity 139

Electricity generation sources: *fossil fuels:* 86.8% of total installed capacity (2022 est.)
solar: 12.9% of total installed capacity (2022 est.)
biomass and waste: 0.3% of total installed capacity (2022 est.)

Coal: *consumption:* 8.4 metric tons (2021 est.)
exports: (2022 est.) less than 1 metric ton
imports: 3.9 metric tons (2022 est.)

Petroleum: *refined petroleum consumption:* 46,000 bbl/day (2022 est.)

Natural gas: *consumption:* 399.719 million cubic meters (2022 est.)
imports: 399.719 million cubic meters (2022 est.)

Carbon dioxide emissions: 8.352 million metric tonnes of CO2 (2022 est.)
from petroleum and other liquids: 7.586 million metric tonnes of CO2 (2022 est.)
from consumed natural gas: 766,000 metric tonnes of CO2 (2022 est.)
comparison ranking: total emissions 114

Energy consumption per capita: 226.072 million Btu/person (2022 est.)
comparison ranking: 15

COMMUNICATIONS

Telephones - fixed lines: *total subscriptions:* 259,000 (2022 est.)
subscriptions per 100 inhabitants: 49 (2022 est.)
comparison ranking: total subscriptions 115

Telephones - mobile cellular: *total subscriptions:* 702,000 (2022 est.)
subscriptions per 100 inhabitants: 132 (2022 est.)
comparison ranking: total subscriptions 171

Telecommunication systems: *general assessment:* Malta's small telecom sector is among the most advanced in Europe; this has been helped by the topography, which has made it relatively easy for operators to expand the reach of their fiber infrastructure; with high mobile and broadband penetration rates, the government and regulator have effective strategies in place to capitalize on these infrastructure developments to ensure that the population has among the fastest data rates in Europe, and is well positioned to take advantage of emerging e-commerce opportunities; the sector has also been stimulated by regulatory measures designed to reduce consumer prices; the incumbent telco is investing in a sub sea cable to connect the islands to France and Egypt; expected to be ready for service in 2022, the cable will further enhance Malta's internet bandwidth and lead to reduced prices for end-users; there has also been some encouragement to increase market competition (2021)
domestic: fixed-line approximately 49 per 100 persons and mobile-cellular subscribership 122 per 100 persons (2021)
international: country code - 356; landing points for the Malta-Gozo Cable, VMSCS, GO-1 Mediterranean Cable System, Malta Italy Interconnector, Melita-1, and the Italy-Malta submarine cable connections to Italy; satellite earth station - 1 Intelsat (Atlantic Ocean) (2019)

Broadcast media: 2 publicly owned TV stations, Television Malta broadcasting nationally plus an educational channel; several privately owned national television stations, 2 of which are owned by political parties; Italian and British broadcast programs are available; multi-channel cable and satellite TV services are available; publicly owned radio broadcaster operates 3 stations; roughly 20 commercial radio stations (2019)

Internet country code: .mt

Internet users: *total:* 461,100 (2021 est.)
percent of population: 87% (2021 est.)
comparison ranking: total 168

Broadband - fixed subscriptions: *total:* 213,419 (2020 est.)
subscriptions per 100 inhabitants: 48 (2020 est.)
comparison ranking: total 117

TRANSPORTATION

National air transport system: *number of registered air carriers:* 13 (2020)
inventory of registered aircraft operated by air carriers: 180
annual passenger traffic on registered air carriers: 2,576,898 (2018)
annual freight traffic on registered air carriers: 5.14 million (2018) mt-km

Civil aircraft registration country code prefix: 9H

Airports: 1 (2024)
comparison ranking: 219

Heliports: 2 (2024)

Roadways: *total:* 2,855 km (2021)
comparison ranking: total 167

Merchant marine: *total:* 1,957 (2023)
by type: bulk carrier 490, container ship 348, general cargo 152, oil tanker 354, other 613
comparison ranking: total 14

Ports: *total ports:* 2 (2024)
large: 0
medium: 1
small: 1
very small: 0
ports with oil terminals: 0
key ports: Marsaxlokk, Valletta Harbors

MILITARY AND SECURITY

Military and security forces: the Armed Forces of Malta (AFM) is a joint force with land, maritime, and air elements, plus a Volunteer Reserve Force (2024)
note: the Malta Police Force maintains internal security; both the Police and the AFM report to the Ministry of Home Affairs, National Security, and Law Enforcement

Military expenditures: 0.8% of GDP (2023 est.)
0.7% of GDP (2022)
0.5% of GDP (2021)
0.6% of GDP (2020)
0.5% of GDP (2019)
comparison ranking: 138

Military and security service personnel strengths: approximately 2,000 active-duty personnel (2023)

Military equipment inventories and acquisitions: the military has a small inventory that consists of equipment from a mix of European countries, particularly Italy, and the US (2024)

Military service age and obligation: 18-30 years of age for men and women for voluntary military service; no conscription (2024)

Military - note: the Armed Forces of Malta (AFM) are responsible for external security but also have some domestic security responsibilities; the AFM's primary roles include maintaining the country's sovereignty and territorial integrity, monitoring and policing its territorial waters, participating in overseas peacekeeping and stability operations, and providing search and rescue and explosive ordnance disposal capabilities; secondary missions include assisting civil authorities during emergencies, supporting the police and other security services, and providing ceremonial and other public support duties
Malta maintains a security policy of neutrality but contributes to EU and UN military missions and joined NATO's Partnership for Peace program in 1995 (suspended in 1996, but reactivated in 2008); it also participates in various bilateral and multinational military exercises; Malta cooperates closely with Italy on defense matters; in 1973, Italy established a military mission in Malta to provide advice, training, and search and rescue assistance (2024)

TRANSNATIONAL ISSUES

Refugees and internally displaced persons: *refugees (country of origin):* 5,890 (Ukraine) (as of 16 July 2023)
stateless persons: 11 (2022)
note: 8,556 estimated refugee and migrant arrivals by sea (January 2015-November 2022)

Trafficking in persons: tier rating: Tier 2 Watch list — Malta did not demonstrate overall increasing efforts to eliminate trafficking compared with the previous reporting period and was downgraded to Tier 2 Watch List; for more details, go to: https://www.state.gov/reports/2024-trafficking-in-persons-report/malta/

Illicit drugs: minor transshipment point for hashish from North Africa to Western Europe

MARSHALL ISLANDS

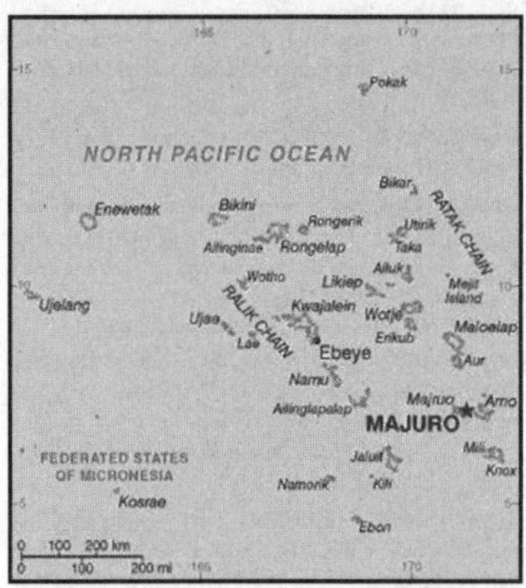

INTRODUCTION

Background: Humans arrived in the Marshall Islands in the first millennium B.C. and gradually created permanent settlements on the various atolls. The early inhabitants were skilled navigators who frequently traveled between atolls using stick charts to map the islands. Society became organized under two paramount chiefs, one each for the Ratak (Sunrise) Chain and the Ralik (Sunset) Chain. Spain formally claimed the islands in 1592. Germany established a supply station on Jaluit Atoll and bought the islands from Spain in 1884, although paramount chiefs continued to rule.

Japan seized the Marshall Islands in 1914 and was granted a League of Nations Mandate to administer the islands in 1920. The US captured the islands in heavy fighting during World War II, and the islands came under US administration as part of the Trust Territory of the Pacific Islands (TTPI) in 1947. Between 1946 and 1958, the US resettled populations from Bikini and Enewetak Atolls and conducted 67 nuclear tests; people from Ailinginae, Rongelap, and Utrik Atolls were also evacuated because of nuclear fallout, and Bikini and Rongelap remain largely uninhabited. In 1979, the Marshall Islands drafted a constitution separate from the rest of the TTPI and declared independence under President Amata KABUA, a paramount chief. In 2000, Kessai NOTE became the first commoner elected president. In 2016, Hilda HEINE was the first woman elected president.

GEOGRAPHY

Location: Oceania, consists of 29 atolls and five isolated islands in the North Pacific Ocean, about halfway between Hawaii and Australia; the atolls and islands are situated in two, almost-parallel island chains - the Ratak (Sunrise) group and the Ralik (Sunset) group; the total number of islands and islets is about 1,225; 22 of the atolls and four of the islands are uninhabited

Geographic coordinates: 9 00 N, 168 00 E

Map references: Oceania

Area: *total:* 181 sq km
land: 181 sq km
water: 0 sq km
note: the archipelago includes 11,673 sq km of lagoon waters and encompasses the atolls of Bikini, Enewetak, Kwajalein, Majuro, Rongelap, and Utrik
comparison ranking: total 217

Area - comparative: about the size of Washington, DC

Land boundaries: *total:* 0 km

Coastline: 370.4 km

Maritime claims: *territorial sea:* 12 nm
contiguous zone: 24 nm
exclusive economic zone: 200 nm

Climate: tropical; hot and humid; wet season May to November; islands border typhoon belt

Terrain: low coral limestone and sand islands

Elevation: *highest point:* East-central Airik Island, Maloelap Atoll 14 m
lowest point: Pacific Ocean 0 m
mean elevation: 2 m

Natural resources: coconut products, marine products, deep seabed minerals

Land use: *agricultural land:* 50.7% (2018 est.)
arable land: 7.8% (2018 est.)
permanent crops: 31.2% (2018 est.)
permanent pasture: 11.7% (2018 est.)
forest: 49.3% (2018 est.)
other: 0% (2018 est.)

Irrigated land: 0 sq km (2022)

Population distribution: most people live in urban clusters found on many of the country's islands; more than two-thirds of the population lives on the atolls of Majuro and Ebeye

Natural hazards: infrequent typhoons

Geography - note: the islands of Bikini and Enewetak are former US nuclear test sites; Kwajalein atoll surrounds the world's largest lagoon and is used as a US missile test range; the island city of Ebeye is the second largest settlement in the Marshall Islands, after the capital of Majuro, and one of the most densely populated locations in the Pacific

PEOPLE AND SOCIETY

Population: *total:* 82,011
male: 41,581
female: 40,430 (2024 est.)
comparison rankings: female 200; male 200; total 200

Nationality: *noun:* Marshallese (singular and plural)
adjective: Marshallese

Ethnic groups: Marshallese 95.6%, Filipino 1.1%, other 3.3% (2021 est.)

Languages: Marshallese (official) 98.2%, other languages 1.8% (1999)
major-language sample(s):
Bok eo an Lalin kin Melele ko Rejimwe ej jikin ebōk melele ko raurōk. (Marshallese)
note: English (official), widely spoken as a second language

Religions: Protestant 79.3% (United Church of Christ 47.9%, Assembly of God 14.1%, Full Gospel 5%, Bukot Nan Jesus 3%, Salvation Army 2.3%, Reformed Congressional Church 2.2%, Seventh Day Adventist 1.7%, New Beginning Church 1.4%, other Protestant 1.6%), Roman Catholic 9.3%, Church of Jesus Christ 5.7%, Jehovah's Witness 1.3%, other 3.3%, none 1.1% (2021 est.)

Age structure: *0-14 years:* 30% (male 12,538/female 12,072)
15-64 years: 64.3% (male 26,750/female 25,944)
65 years and over: 5.7% (2024 est.) (male 2,293/female 2,414)

Dependency ratios: *total dependency ratio:* 59.9
youth dependency ratio: 53
elderly dependency ratio: 6.8
potential support ratio: 14.7 (2021)

Median age: *total:* 25.5 years (2024 est.)
male: 25.4 years
female: 25.6 years
comparison ranking: total 169

Population growth rate: 1.26% (2024 est.)
comparison ranking: 76

Birth rate: 21.2 births/1,000 population (2024 est.)
comparison ranking: 61

Death rate: 4.3 deaths/1,000 population (2024 est.)
comparison ranking: 211

Net migration rate: -4.3 migrant(s)/1,000 population (2024 est.)
comparison ranking: 197

Population distribution: most people live in urban clusters found on many of the country's islands; more than two-thirds of the population lives on the atolls of Majuro and Ebeye

Urbanization: *urban population:* 78.9% of total population (2023)
rate of urbanization: 0.61% annual rate of change (2020-25 est.)

Major urban areas - population: 31,000 MAJURO (capital) (2018)

Sex ratio: *at birth:* 1.05 male(s)/female
0-14 years: 1.04 male(s)/female
15-64 years: 1.03 male(s)/female
65 years and over: 0.95 male(s)/female
total population: 1.03 male(s)/female (2024 est.)

Infant mortality rate: *total:* 20.6 deaths/1,000 live births (2024 est.)
male: 24 deaths/1,000 live births
female: 17.1 deaths/1,000 live births
comparison ranking: total 77

Life expectancy at birth: *total population:* 75.2 years (2024 est.)
male: 73 years
female: 77.5 years
comparison ranking: total population 130

Total fertility rate: 2.67 children born/woman (2024 est.)
comparison ranking: 61

Gross reproduction rate: 1.3 (2024 est.)

Contraceptive prevalence rate: NA

Drinking water source: *improved: urban:* 100% of population
rural: 99.8% of population
total: 100% of population
unimproved: urban: 0% of population
rural: 0.2% of population
total: 0% of population (2020 est.)

Current health expenditure: 13% of GDP (2020)

Physician density: 0.42 physicians/1,000 population (2012)

Hospital bed density: 2.7 beds/1,000 population

Sanitation facility access: *improved: urban:* 96.6% of population
rural: 65.4% of population
total: 89.7% of population
unimproved: urban: 3.4% of population
rural: 34.6% of population
total: 10.3% of population (2020 est.)

Obesity - adult prevalence rate: 52.9% (2016)
comparison ranking: 4

Tobacco use: *total:* 28.5% (2020 est.)
male: 48.7% (2020 est.)
female: 8.3% (2020 est.)
comparison ranking: total 36

Children under the age of 5 years underweight: 11.9% (2017)
comparison ranking: 45

Currently married women (ages 15-49): 68.3% (2022 est.)

Education expenditures: 13.6% of GDP (2020 est.)
comparison ranking: 1

Literacy: *definition:* age 15 and over can read and write
total population: 98.3%
male: 98.3%
female: 98.2% (2011)

School life expectancy (primary to tertiary education): *total:* 10 years
male: 10 years
female: 10 years (2019)

ENVIRONMENT

Environment - current issues: inadequate supplies of potable water; pollution of Majuro lagoon from household waste and discharges from fishing vessels; sea level rise

Environment - international agreements: *party to:* Biodiversity, Climate Change, Climate Change-Kyoto Protocol, Climate Change-Paris Agreement, Comprehensive Nuclear Test Ban, Desertification, Hazardous Wastes, Law of the Sea, Marine Dumping-London Protocol, Ozone Layer Protection, Ship Pollution, Wetlands, Whaling
signed, but not ratified: none of the selected agreements

Climate: tropical; hot and humid; wet season May to November; islands border typhoon belt

Urbanization: *urban population:* 78.9% of total population (2023)
rate of urbanization: 0.61% annual rate of change (2020-25 est.)

Revenue from forest resources: 0% of GDP (2018 est.)
comparison ranking: 187

Air pollutants: *particulate matter emissions:* 7.21 micrograms per cubic meter (2019 est.)
carbon dioxide emissions: 0.14 megatons (2016 est.)
methane emissions: 0.03 megatons (2020 est.)

Waste and recycling: *municipal solid waste generated annually:* 8,614 tons (2013 est.)
municipal solid waste recycled annually: 2,653 tons (2007 est.)
percent of municipal solid waste recycled: 30.8% (2007 est.)

Total renewable water resources: 0 cubic meters (2017 est.)

GOVERNMENT

Country name: *conventional long form:* Republic of the Marshall Islands
conventional short form: Marshall Islands
local long form: Republic of the Marshall Islands
local short form: Marshall Islands
former: Trust Territory of the Pacific Islands, Marshall Islands District
abbreviation: RMI
etymology: named after British Captain John MARSHALL, who charted many of the islands in 1788

Government type: mixed presidential-parliamentary system in free association with the US

Capital: name: Majuro; note - the capital is an atoll of 64 islands; governmental buildings are housed on three fused islands on the eastern side of the atoll: Djarrit, Uliga, and Delap
geographic coordinates: 7 06 N, 171 23 E
time difference: UTC+12 (17 hours ahead of Washington, DC, during Standard Time)
etymology: Majuro means "two openings" or "two eyes" and refers to the two major northern passages through the atoll into the Majuro lagoon

Administrative divisions: 24 municipalities; Ailinglaplap, Ailuk, Arno, Aur, Bikini & Kili, Ebon, Enewetak & Ujelang, Jabat, Jaluit, Kwajalein, Lae, Lib, Likiep, Majuro, Maloelap, Mejit, Mili, Namorik, Namu, Rongelap, Ujae, Utrik, Wotho, Wotje

Independence: 21 October 1986 (from the US-administered UN trusteeship)

National holiday: Constitution Day, 1 May (1979)

Legal system: mixed legal system of US and English common law, customary law, and local statutes

Constitution: *history:* effective 1 May 1979
amendments: proposed by the National Parliament or by a constitutional convention; passage by Parliament requires at least two-thirds majority vote of the total membership in each of two readings and approval by a majority of votes in a referendum; amendments submitted by a constitutional convention require approval of at least two thirds of votes in a referendum; amended several times, last in 2018

International law organization participation: accepts compulsory ICJ jurisdiction with reservations; accepts ICCt jurisdiction

Citizenship: *citizenship by birth:* no
citizenship by descent only: at least one parent must be a citizen of the Marshall Islands
dual citizenship recognized: no
residency requirement for naturalization: 5 years

Suffrage: 18 years of age; universal

Executive branch: *chief of state:* President Hilda C. HEINE (since 3 January 2023)
head of government: President Hilda C. HEINE (since 3 January 2023)
cabinet: Cabinet nominated by the president from among members of the Nitijela, appointed by Nitijela speaker
elections/appointments: president indirectly elected by the Nitijela from among its members for a 4-year term (no term limits); election last held on 2 January 2023 (next to be held in 2027)
election results:
2023: Hilda C. HEINE elected president; National Parliament vote - Hilda C. HEINE (independent) 17, David KABUA (independent) 16
2020: David KABUA elected president; National Parliament vote - David KABUA (independent) 20, Hilda C. HEINE (independent) 12
note: the president is both chief of state and head of government

Legislative branch: *description:* unicameral National Parliament or Nitijela (33 seats; members in 19 single- and 5 multi-seat constituencies directly elected by simple majority vote to serve 4-year terms)
elections: last held on 20 November 2023 (next to be held in November 2027)
election results: percent of vote by party - NA; seats by part - independent 33; composition - men 29, women 4, percent of women 12.1%
note: the Council of Iroij is a 12-member consultative group of tribal leaders that advises the Presidential Cabinet and reviews legislation affecting customary law or any traditional practice

Judicial branch: *highest court(s):* Supreme Court (consists of the chief justice and 2 associate justices)
judge selection and term of office: judges appointed by the Cabinet upon the recommendation of the Judicial Service Commission (consists of the chief justice of the High Court, the attorney general and a private citizen selected by the Cabinet) and upon approval of the Nitijela; the current chief justice, appointed in 2013, serves for 10 years; Marshallese citizens appointed as justices serve until retirement at age 72
subordinate courts: High Court; District Courts; Traditional Rights Court; Community Courts

Political parties: traditionally there have been no formally organized political parties; what has existed more closely resembles factions or interest groups because they do not have party headquarters, formal platforms, or party structures

International organization participation: ACP, ADB, AOSIS, FAO, G-77, IAEA, IBRD, ICAO, ICCt, IDA, IFAD, IFC, ILO, IMF, IMO, IMSO, Interpol, IOC, IOM, ITU, OPCW, PIF, Sparteca, SPC, UN, UNCTAD, UNESCO, UNHRC, WHO

Diplomatic representation in the US: *chief of mission:* Ambassador Charles Rudolph PAUL (since 27 February 2024)
chancery: 2433 Massachusetts Avenue NW, Washington, DC 20008
telephone: [1] (202) 234-5414
FAX: [1] (202) 232-3236
email address and website:
info@rmiembassyus.org
consulate(s) general: Honolulu, Springdale (AR)

Diplomatic representation from the US: *chief of mission:* Ambassador (vacant); Chargé d'Affaires Lance POSEY (since 18 August 2023)
embassy: Mejen Weto, Ocean Side, Majuro
mailing address: 4380 Majuro Place, Washington DC 20521-4380
telephone: [692] 247-4011
FAX: [692] 247-4012
email address and website:
MAJConsular@state.gov
https://mh.usembassy.gov/

Flag description: blue with two stripes radiating from the lower hoist-side corner - orange (top) and white; a white star with four large rays and 20 small rays appears on the hoist side above the two stripes; blue represents the Pacific Ocean, the orange stripe signifies the Ralik Chain or sunset and courage, while the white stripe signifies the Ratak Chain or sunrise and peace; the star symbolizes the cross of Christianity, each of the 24 rays designates one of the electoral districts in the country and the four larger rays highlight the principal cultural centers of Majuro, Jaluit, Wotje, and Ebeye; the rising diagonal band can also be interpreted as representing the equator, with the star showing the archipelago's position just to the north

National symbol(s): a 24-rayed star; national colors: blue, white, orange

National anthem: *name:* "Forever Marshall Islands"
lyrics/music: Amata KABUA
note: adopted 1981

National heritage: *total World Heritage Sites:* 1 (cultural)
selected World Heritage Site locales: Bikini Atoll Nuclear Test Site

ECONOMY

Economic overview: upper middle-income Pacific island economy; US aid reliance; large public sector; coconut oil production as diesel fuel substitute; growing offshore banking locale; fishing rights seller; import-dependent

Real GDP (purchasing power parity): $283.577 million (2023 est.)
$274.715 million (2022 est.)
$276.583 million (2021 est.)
note: data in 2021 dollars
comparison ranking: 217

Real GDP growth rate: 3.23% (2023 est.)
-0.68% (2022 est.)
1.11% (2021 est.)
note: annual GDP % growth based on constant local currency
comparison ranking: 101

Real GDP per capita: $6,800 (2023 est.)
$6,600 (2022 est.)
$6,600 (2021 est.)
note: data in 2021 dollars
comparison ranking: 160

GDP (official exchange rate): $284 million (2023 est.)
note: data in current dollars at official exchange rate

Inflation rate (consumer prices): 0% (2017 est.)
-1.5% (2016 est.)
comparison ranking: 6

GDP - composition, by sector of origin: *agriculture:* 20.6% (2022 est.)
industry: 10.3% (2022 est.)
services: 68.7% (2022 est.)
note: figures may not total 100% due to non-allocated consumption not captured in sector-reported data
comparison rankings: services 42; industry 192; agriculture 38

GDP - composition, by end use: *household consumption:* 71.7% (2022 est.)
government consumption: 57.4% (2022 est.)
investment in fixed capital: 19.8% (2022 est.)
investment in inventories: 0.3% (2022 est.)
exports of goods and services: 46.3% (2022 est.)
imports of goods and services: -73.7% (2022 est.)
note: figures may not total 100% due to rounding or gaps in data collection

Agricultural products: coconuts (2022)
note: top ten agricultural products based on tonnage

Industries: copra, tuna processing, tourism, craft items (from seashells, wood, and pearls)

Industrial production growth rate: 10.24% (2022 est.)
note: annual % change in industrial value added based on constant local currency
comparison ranking: 16

Youth unemployment rate (ages 15-24): *total:* 26% (2019 est.)
male: 31%
female: 14.2%
comparison ranking: total 39

Population below poverty line: 7.2% (2019 est.)
note: % of population with income below national poverty line

Gini Index coefficient - distribution of family income: 35.5 (2019 est.)
note: index (0-100) of income distribution; higher values represent greater inequality
comparison ranking: 73

Household income or consumption by percentage share: *lowest 10%:* 2.8% (2019 est.)
highest 10%: 27.5% (2019 est.)
note: % share of income accruing to lowest and highest 10% of population

Remittances: 10.56% of GDP (2023 est.)
3.23% of GDP (2022 est.)
13.36% of GDP (2021 est.)
note: personal transfers and compensation between resident and non-resident individuals/households/entities

Budget: *revenues:* $186.971 million (2018 est.)
expenditures: $177.91 million (2018 est.)
note: central government revenues (excluding grants) and expenses converted to US dollars at average official exchange rate for year indicated

Public debt: 41.73% of GDP (2019 est.)
note: central government debt as a % of GDP
comparison ranking: 128

Taxes and other revenues: 17.23% (of GDP) (2020 est.)
note: central government tax revenue as a % of GDP
comparison ranking: 113

Current account balance: $76.263 million (2021 est.)
$90.281 million (2020 est.)
$86.133 million (2019 est.)
note: balance of payments - net trade and primary/secondary income in current dollars
comparison ranking: 74

Exports: $130.016 million (2021 est.)
$88.042 million (2020 est.)
$91.394 million (2019 est.)
note: balance of payments - exports of goods and services in current dollars
comparison ranking: 210

Exports - partners: Germany 30%, Denmark 15%, UK 14%, Malta 6%, Indonesia 5% (2022)
note: top five export partners based on percentage share of exports

Exports - commodities: ships, refined petroleum, fish, coated flat-rolled iron, wood carpentry (2022)
note: top five export commodities based on value in dollars

Imports: $206.025 million (2021 est.)
$132.845 million (2020 est.)
$129.682 million (2019 est.)
note: balance of payments - imports of goods and services in current dollars
comparison ranking: 213

Imports - partners: China 33%, South Korea 31%, Japan 12%, Taiwan 4%, Brazil 4% (2022)
note: top five import partners based on percentage share of imports

Imports - commodities: ships, refined petroleum, additive manufacturing machines, centrifuges, iron structures (2022)
note: top five import commodities based on value in dollars

Exchange rates: the US dollar is used

ENERGY

Electricity access: *electrification - total population:* 100% (2022 est.)
electrification - urban areas: 96.1%
electrification - rural areas: 100%

Carbon dioxide emissions: 293,700 metric tonnes of CO2 (2017 est.)
comparison ranking: total emissions 199

COMMUNICATIONS

Telephones - fixed lines: *total subscriptions:* 2,000 (2014 est.)
subscriptions per 100 inhabitants: 5 (2014 est.)
comparison ranking: total subscriptions 214

Telephones - mobile cellular: *total subscriptions:* 16,000 (2021 est.)
subscriptions per 100 inhabitants: 38 (2021 est.)
comparison ranking: total subscriptions 218

Telecommunication systems: *general assessment:* the National Telecommunications Act, through Bill No. 66, ushered in a new era in telecommunications in the Marshall Islands; this will enable an open, competitive market for telecommunications that is regulated by a Telecommunications Commissioner; telecom officials announced that they would be able to offer satellite internet services beginning in mid-2023; the World Bank has been promoting telecommunications reform here for a decade and has a multi-million-dollar telecommunications reform grant program in progress (2022)
domestic: fixed-line roughly 5 per 100 persons and mobile-cellular is nearly 38 per 100 persons (2021)
international: country code - 692; satellite earth stations - 2 Intelsat (Pacific Ocean); US Government satellite communications system on Kwajalein

Broadcast media: no TV broadcast station; a cable network is available on Majuro with programming via videotape replay and satellite relays; 4 radio broadcast stations; American Armed Forces Radio and Television Service (AFRTS) provides satellite radio and television service to Kwajalein Atoll (2019)

Internet country code: .mh

Internet users: *total:* 16,254 (2021 est.)
percent of population: 38.7% (2021 est.)
comparison ranking: total 214

Broadband - fixed subscriptions: *total:* 1,000 (2020 est.)
subscriptions per 100 inhabitants: 2 (2020 est.)
comparison ranking: total 207

Communications - note: Kwajalein hosts one of four dedicated ground antennas that assist in the operation of the Global Positioning System (GPS) navigation system (the others are at Cape Canaveral, Florida (US), on Ascension (Saint Helena, Ascension, and Tristan da Cunha), and at Diego Garcia (British Indian Ocean Territory))

TRANSPORTATION

National air transport system: *number of registered air carriers:* 1 (2020)
inventory of registered aircraft operated by air carriers: 3
annual passenger traffic on registered air carriers: 24,313 (2018)
annual freight traffic on registered air carriers: 130,000 (2018) mt-km

Civil aircraft registration country code prefix: V7

Airports: 33 (2024)
comparison ranking: 114

Roadways: *total:* 2,028 km
paved: 75 km
unpaved: 1,953 km (2007)
comparison ranking: total 174

Merchant marine: *total:* 4,180 (2023)
by type: bulk carrier 1,939, container ship 277, general cargo 66, oil tanker 1039, other 859
comparison ranking: total 6

Ports: *total ports:* 3 (2024)
large: 0
medium: 0
small: 0
very small: 3
ports with oil terminals: 2
key ports: Enitwetak Island, Kwajalein, Majuro Atoll

MILITARY AND SECURITY

Military and security forces: no regular military forces; the national police (Marshall Islands Police Department, MIPD), local police forces, and the Sea Patrol (maritime police) are responsible for security; the MIPD and Sea Patrol report to the Ministry of Justice; local police report to their respective local government councils (2024)

Military - note: defense is the responsibility of the US; in 1982, the Marshall Islands signed a Compact of Free Association (COFA) with the US, which granted the Marshall Islands financial assistance and access to many US domestic programs in exchange for exclusive US military access and defense responsibilities; the COFA entered into force in 1986, and its funding was renewed in 2003; the Marshall Islands hosts a US Army missile test site
the Marshall Islands have a "shiprider" agreement with the US, which allows local maritime law enforcement officers to embark on US Coast Guard (USCG) and US Navy (USN) vessels, including to board and search vessels suspected of violating laws or regulations within its designated exclusive economic zone (EEZ) or on the high seas; "shiprider" agreements also enable USCG personnel and USN vessels with embarked USCG law enforcement personnel to work with host nations to protect critical regional resources (2024)

TRANSNATIONAL ISSUES

Trafficking in persons: tier rating: Tier 2 Watch List — Tier 2 Watch List — the government did not demonstrate overall increasing efforts to eliminate trafficking compared with the previous reporting period, therefore Marshall Islands remained on Tier 2 Watch List for the second consecutive year; for more details, go to: https://www.state.gov/reports/2024-trafficking-in-persons-report/marshall-islands/

MAURITANIA

INTRODUCTION

Background: The Amazigh and Bafour people were among the earliest settlers in what is now Mauritania and among the first in recorded history to convert from a nomadic to agricultural lifestyle. These groups account for roughly one third of Mauritania's ethnic makeup. The remainder of Mauritania's ethnic groups derive from Sub-Saharan ethnic groups originating mainly from the Senegal River Valley, including descendants of former enslaved peoples. These three groups are organized according to a strict caste system with deep ethnic divides that impact access to resources and power dynamics.

A former French colony, Mauritania achieved independence from France in 1960. Mauritania initially began as a single-party, authoritarian regime and experienced 49 years of dictatorships, flawed elections, failed attempts at democracy, and military coups. Ould Abdel AZIZ led the last coup in 2008, was elected president in 2009, and was reelected in 2014. Mohamed Ould Cheikh GHAZOUANI was elected president in 2019, and his inauguration marked the first peaceful transition of power from one democratically elected president to another, solidifying the country's status as an emerging democracy. International observers recognized the elections

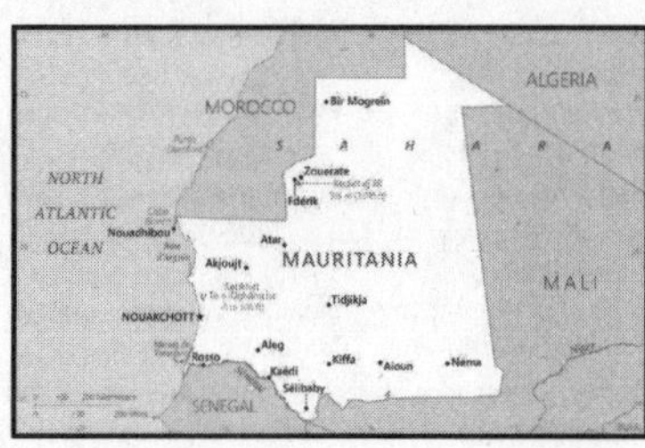

as relatively free and fair. GHAZOUANI is seeking re-election in June 2024 for a second, and final, five-year term.

The country is working to address vestigial practices of slavery and its hereditary impacts. Mauritania officially abolished slavery in 1981, but the practice was not criminalized until 2007. Between 2005 and 2011, Al-Qaeda in the Islamic Maghreb (AQIM) launched a series of attacks killing western tourists and aid workers, attacking diplomatic and government facilities, and ambushing Mauritanian soldiers and gendarmes. Although Mauritania has not seen an attack since 2011, AQIM and similar groups remain active in the Sahel region.

GEOGRAPHY

Location: Western Africa, bordering the North Atlantic Ocean, between Senegal and Western Sahara

Geographic coordinates: 20 00 N, 12 00 W

Map references: Africa

Area: *total:* 1,030,700 sq km
land: 1,030,700 sq km
water: 0 sq km
comparison ranking: total 30

Area - comparative: slightly larger than three times the size of New Mexico; about six times the size of Florida

Land boundaries: *total:* 5,002 km
border countries (4): Algeria 460 km; Mali 2,236 km; Morocco 1,564 km; Senegal 742 km

Coastline: 754 km

Maritime claims: *territorial sea:* 12 nm
contiguous zone: 24 nm
exclusive economic zone: 200 nm
continental shelf: 200 nm or to the edge of the continental margin

Climate: desert; constantly hot, dry, dusty

Terrain: mostly barren, flat plains of the Sahara; some central hills

Elevation: *highest point:* Kediet Ijill 915 m
lowest point: Sebkhet Te-n-Dghamcha -5 m
mean elevation: 276 m

Natural resources: iron ore, gypsum, copper, phosphate, diamonds, gold, oil, fish

Land use: *agricultural land:* 38.5% (2018 est.)
arable land: 0.4% (2018 est.)
permanent crops: 0% (2018 est.)
permanent pasture: 38.1% (2018 est.)
forest: 0.2% (2018 est.)
other: 61.3% (2018 est.)

Irrigated land: 450 sq km (2012)

Major rivers (by length in km): Senegal river mouth (shared with Guinea [s], Senegal and Mali) - 1,641 km
note – [s] after country name indicates river source; [m] after country name indicates river mouth

Major watersheds (area sq km): Atlantic Ocean drainage: Niger (2,261,741 sq km), Senegal (456,397 sq km)

Major aquifers: Senegalo-Mauritanian Basin, Taodeni-Tanzerouft Basin

Population distribution: with most of the country being a desert, vast areas of the country, particularly in the central, northern, and eastern areas, are without sizeable population clusters; half the population lives in or around the coastal capital of Nouakchott; smaller clusters are found near the southern border with Mali and Senegal as shown in this population distribution map

Natural hazards: hot, dry, dust/sand-laden sirocco wind primarily in March and April; periodic droughts

Geography - note: Mauritania is considered both a part of North Africa's Maghreb region and West Africa's Sahel region; most of the population is concentrated in the cities of Nouakchott and Nouadhibou and along the Senegal River in the southern part of the country

PEOPLE AND SOCIETY

Population: *total:* 4,328,040
male: 2,083,690
female: 2,244,350 (2024 est.)
comparison rankings: female 127; male 129; total 128

Nationality: *noun:* Mauritanian(s)
adjective: Mauritanian

Ethnic groups: Black Moors (Haratines - Arabic-speaking descendants of African origin who are or were enslaved by White Moors) 40%, White Moors (of Arab-Amazigh descent, known as Beydane) 30%, Sub-Saharan Mauritanians (non-Arabic speaking, largely resident in or originating from the Senegal River Valley, including Halpulaar, Fulani, Soninke, Wolof, and Bambara ethnic groups) 30%

Languages: Arabic (official and national), Pular, Soninke, Wolof (all national languages), French
major-language sample(s):
يمكن الاستغناء عنه للمعلومات الأساسية
كتاب حقائق العالم، المصدر الذي لا
(Arabic)
note: the spoken Arabic in Mauritania differs considerably from Modern Standard Arabic; the Mauritanian dialect, which incorporates many Tamazight words, is referred to as Hassaniya

Religions: Muslim (official) 100%

Demographic profile: With a sustained total fertility rate of about 3.5 children per woman and almost 60% of the population under the age of 25 as of 2020, Mauritania's population is likely to continue growing for the foreseeable future. Mauritania's large youth cohort is vital to its development prospects, but available schooling does not adequately prepare students for the workplace. Girls continue to be underrepresented in the classroom, educational quality remains poor, and the dropout rate is high. The literacy rate is only about 50%, even though access to primary education has improved since the mid-2000s. Women's restricted access to education and discriminatory laws maintain gender inequality - worsened by early and forced marriages and female genital cutting.

The denial of education to black Moors also helps to perpetuate slavery. Although Mauritania abolished slavery in 1981 (the last country in the world to do so) and made it a criminal offense in 2007, the millenniums-old practice persists largely because anti-slavery laws are rarely enforced and the custom is so ingrained. According to a 2018 nongovernmental organization's report, a little more than 2% of Mauritania's population is enslaved, which includes individuals subjected to forced labor and forced marriage, while many thousands of individuals who are legally free contend with discrimination, poor education, and a lack of identity papers and, therefore, live in de facto slavery. The UN and international press outlets have claimed that up to 20% of Mauritania's population is enslaved, which would be the highest rate worldwide.

Drought, poverty, and unemployment have driven outmigration from Mauritania since the 1970s. Early flows were directed toward other West African countries, including Senegal, Mali, Cote d'Ivoire, and Gambia. The 1989 Mauritania-Senegal conflict forced thousands of black Mauritanians to take refuge in Senegal and pushed labor migrants toward the Gulf, Libya, and Europe in the late 1980s and early 1990s. Mauritania has accepted migrants from neighboring countries to fill labor shortages since its independence in 1960 and more recently has received refugees escaping civil wars, including tens of thousands of Tuaregs who fled Mali in 2012.

Mauritania was an important transit point for Sub-Saharan migrants moving illegally to North Africa and Europe. In the mid-2000s, as border patrols increased in the Strait of Gibraltar, security increased around Spain's North African enclaves (Ceuta and Melilla), and Moroccan border controls intensified, illegal migration flows shifted from the Western Mediterranean to Spain's Canary Islands. In 2006, departure points moved southward along the West African coast from Morocco and then Western Sahara to Mauritania's two key ports (Nouadhibou and the capital Nouakchott), and illegal migration to the Canaries peaked at almost 32,000. The numbers fell dramatically in the following years because of joint patrolling off the West African coast by Frontex (the EU's border protection agency), Spain, Mauritania, and Senegal; the expansion of Spain's border surveillance system; and the 2008 European economic downturn.

Age structure: *0-14 years:* 35.7% (male 776,035/female 770,132)
15-64 years: 59.9% (male 1,227,347/female 1,363,938)
65 years and over: 4.4% (2024 est.) (male 80,308/female 110,280)

Dependency ratios: *total dependency ratio:* 82.7
youth dependency ratio: 76.8
elderly dependency ratio: 6
potential support ratio: 16.8 (2021 est.)

Median age: *total:* 22.1 years (2024 est.)
male: 21.1 years
female: 23.1 years
comparison ranking: total 185

Population growth rate: 1.92% (2024 est.)
comparison ranking: 43

Birth rate: births/1,000 population (2024 est.)
comparison ranking: 37

Death rate: 7.2 deaths/1,000 population (2024 est.)
comparison ranking: 115

Net migration rate: -0.7 migrant(s)/1,000 population (2024 est.)
comparison ranking: 133

Population distribution: with most of the country being a desert, vast areas of the country, particularly in the central, northern, and eastern areas, are without sizeable population clusters; half the population lives in or around the coastal capital of Nouakchott; smaller clusters are found near the southern border with Mali and Senegal as shown in this population distribution map

Urbanization: *urban population:* 57.7% of total population (2023)
rate of urbanization: 3.84% annual rate of change (2020-25 est.)

Major urban areas - population: 1.492 million NOUAKCHOTT (capital) (2023)

Sex ratio: *at birth:* 1.03 male(s)/female
0-14 years: 1.01 male(s)/female
15-64 years: 0.9 male(s)/female
65 years and over: 0.73 male(s)/female
total population: 0.93 male(s)/female (2024 est.)

Mother's mean age at first birth: 21.8 years (2019/21)
note: data represents median age at first birth among women 25-49

Maternal mortality ratio: 465 deaths/100,000 live births (2020 est.)
comparison ranking: 16

Infant mortality rate: *total:* 48.9 deaths/1,000 live births (2024 est.)
male: 54.8 deaths/1,000 live births
female: 42.9 deaths/1,000 live births
comparison ranking: total 19

Life expectancy at birth: *total population:* 65.9 years (2024 est.)
male: 63.4 years
female: 68.5 years
comparison ranking: total population 204

Total fertility rate: 3.4 children born/woman (2024 est.)
comparison ranking: 38

Gross reproduction rate: 1.68 (2024 est.)

Contraceptive prevalence rate: 11.5% (2019/20)

Drinking water source: *improved: urban:* 98.7% of population
rural: 68.4% of population
total: 85.2% of population
unimproved: urban: 1.3% of population
rural: 31.6% of population
total: 14.8% of population (2020 est.)

Current health expenditure: 3.4% of GDP (2020)

Physician density: 0.19 physicians/1,000 population (2018)

Sanitation facility access: *improved: urban:* 83.5% of population
rural: 25.2% of population
total: 57.5% of population
unimproved: urban: 16.5% of population
rural: 74.8% of population
total: 42.5% of population (2020 est.)

Obesity - adult prevalence rate: 12.7% (2016)
comparison ranking: 132

Alcohol consumption per capita: *total:* 0 liters of pure alcohol (2019 est.)
beer: 0 liters of pure alcohol (2019 est.)
wine: 0 liters of pure alcohol (2019 est.)
spirits: 0 liters of pure alcohol (2019 est.)
other alcohols: 0 liters of pure alcohol (2019 est.)
comparison ranking: total 186

Tobacco use: *total:* 10.7% (2020 est.)
male: 19.3% (2020 est.)
female: 2.1% (2020 est.)
comparison ranking: total 133

Children under the age of 5 years underweight: 22.4% (2022)
comparison ranking: 11

Currently married women (ages 15-49): 66% (2023 est.)

Child marriage: *women married by age 15:* 15.5%
women married by age 18: 36.6%
men married by age 18: 1.2% (2021 est.)

Education expenditures: 1.9% of GDP (2020 est.)
comparison ranking: 189

Literacy: *definition:* age 15 and over can read and write
total population: 67%
male: 71.8%
female: 62.2% (2021)

School life expectancy (primary to tertiary education): *total:* 9 years
male: 8 years
female: 9 years (2020)

ENVIRONMENT

Environment - current issues: overgrazing, deforestation, and soil erosion aggravated by drought are contributing to desertification; limited natural freshwater resources away from the Senegal, which is the only perennial river; locust infestation

Environment - international agreements: *party to:* Biodiversity, Climate Change, Climate Change-Kyoto Protocol, Climate Change-Paris Agreement, Comprehensive Nuclear Test Ban, Desertification, Endangered Species, Hazardous Wastes, Law of the Sea, Nuclear Test Ban, Ozone Layer Protection, Ship Pollution, Wetlands, Whaling
signed, but not ratified: none of the selected agreements

Climate: desert; constantly hot, dry, dusty

Urbanization: *urban population:* 57.7% of total population (2023)
rate of urbanization: 3.84% annual rate of change (2020-25 est.)

Food insecurity: *widespread lack of access: due to high food prices* - according to the latest analysis, nearly 695,000 people are projected to be in need of humanitarian assistance during the June to August 2023 lean season; this would be an improvement compared to the previous year, mostly due to the substantial cereal production increase in 2022; high food prices continue to worsen food security, while flooding in 2022, which affected about 54,000 people, has further aggravated the conditions of vulnerable households (2023)

Revenue from forest resources: 1.3% of GDP (2018 est.)
comparison ranking: 48

Revenue from coal: 0% of GDP (2018 est.)
comparison ranking: 174

Air pollutants: *particulate matter emissions:* 41.98 micrograms per cubic meter (2019 est.)
carbon dioxide emissions: 2.74 megatons (2016 est.)
methane emissions: 6.16 megatons (2020 est.)

Waste and recycling: *municipal solid waste generated annually:* 454,000 tons (2009 est.)
municipal solid waste recycled annually: 36,320 tons (2009 est.)
percent of municipal solid waste recycled: 8% (2009 est.)

Major rivers (by length in km): Senegal river mouth (shared with Guinea [s], Senegal and Mali) - 1,641 km
note – [s] after country name indicates river source; [m] after country name indicates river mouth

Major watersheds (area sq km): Atlantic Ocean drainage: Niger (2,261,741 sq km), Senegal (456,397 sq km)

Major aquifers: Senegalo-Mauritanian Basin, Taodeni-Tanzerouft Basin

Total water withdrawal: *municipal:* 100 million cubic meters (2020 est.)
industrial: 30 million cubic meters (2020 est.)
agricultural: 1.2 billion cubic meters (2020 est.)

Total renewable water resources: 11.4 billion cubic meters (2020 est.)

GOVERNMENT

Country name: *conventional long form:* Islamic Republic of Mauritania
conventional short form: Mauritania
local long form: Al Jumhuriyah al Islamiyah al Muritaniyah
local short form: Muritaniyah
etymology: named for the ancient kingdom of Mauretania (3rd century B.C. to 1st century A.D.) and the subsequent Roman province (1st-7th centuries A.D.), which existed further north in present-day Morocco; the name derives from the Mauri (Moors), the Berber-speaking peoples of northwest Africa

Government type: presidential republic

Capital: *name:* Nouakchott
geographic coordinates: 18 04 N, 15 58 W
time difference: UTC 0 (5 hours ahead of Washington, DC, during Standard Time)
etymology: may derive from the Berber "nawakshut" meaning "place of the winds"

Administrative divisions: 15 regions (wilayas, singular - wilaya); Adrar, Assaba, Brakna, Dakhlet Nouadhibou, Gorgol, Guidimaka, Hodh ech Chargui, Hodh El Gharbi, Inchiri, Nouakchott Nord, Nouakchott Ouest, Nouakchott Sud, Tagant, Tiris Zemmour, Trarza

Independence: 28 November 1960 (from France)

National holiday: Independence Day, 28 November (1960)

Legal system: mixed legal system of Islamic and French civil law

Constitution: *history:* previous 1964; latest adopted 12 July 1991
amendments: proposed by the president of the republic or by Parliament; consideration of amendments by Parliament requires approval of at least one third of the membership; a referendum is held only if the amendment is approved by two-thirds majority vote; passage by referendum requires simple majority vote by eligible voters; passage of amendments proposed by the president can bypass a referendum if approved by at least three-fifths majority vote by Parliament; amended 2006, 2012, 2017

International law organization participation: has not submitted an ICJ jurisdiction declaration; non-party state to the ICCt

Citizenship: *citizenship by birth:* no

citizenship by descent only: at least one parent must be a citizen of Mauritania
dual citizenship recognized: no
residency requirement for naturalization: 5 years

Suffrage: 18 years of age; universal

Executive branch: *chief of state:* President Mohamed Ould Cheikh el GHAZOUANI (since 1 August 2019)
head of government: Prime Minister Moctar Ould DIAY (since 2 August 2024)
cabinet: Council of Ministers - nominees suggested by the prime minister, appointed by the president
elections/appointments: president directly elected by absolute majority popular vote in 2 rounds if needed for a 5-year term (eligible for a second term); election last held on 29 June 2024 (next to be held in June 2029); prime minister appointed by the president
election results:
2024: Mohamed Ould Cheikh el GHAZOUANI re-elected president in first round; percent of vote - Mohamed Ould Cheikh el GHAZOUANI (UPR) 56.1%, Biram Dah Ould ABEID (independent) 22.1%, Hamadi Sidi el MOKHTAR independent) 12.8%, other 9.0%
2019: Mohamed Ould Cheikh el GHAZOUANI elected president in first round; percent of vote - Mohamed Ould Cheikh el GHAZOUANI (UPR) 52%, Biram Dah Ould ABEID (independent) 18.6%, Sidi Mohamed Ould BOUBACAR (independent) 17.9%, other 11.5%

Legislative branch: *description:* bicameral Parliament or Barlamane consists of:
Senate or Majlis al-Shuyukh (56 seats, 53 members elected for a six-year term by municipal councilors, with one third renewed every two years)
National Assembly or Al Jamiya Al Wataniya (176 seats statutory; 88 members filled from one or two seat constituencies elected by a two-round majority system and the other 88 members filled from a single, nationwide constituency directly elected by proportional representation vote); 20 seats are reserved for women candidates in the nationwide constituency, 11 seats are reserved for young candidates (aged between 25 and 35), and 4 members directly elected by the diaspora; all members serve 5-year terms
elections: last held on 13 May 2023 with a second round on 27 May 2023 (next to be held in May 2028)
election results: National Assembly - percent of vote by party - NA; seats by party - El Insaf 107, Tawassoul 11, UDP 10, FRUD 7, El Islah 6, AND 6, El Karama 5, Nida Al-Watan 5, Sawab 5, AJD/MR 4, HIWAR 3, HATEM 3, El Vadila 2, UPC 1, Hakam 1; composition- men 135, women 41, percentage women 23.3%
note: the early parliamentary elections in 2023 were the first to be held under President Mohamed Ould Cheikh El GHAZOUANI, elected in 2019 in the first peaceful transition of power; the elections followed the agreement between the government and parties in September 2022 to renew the Independent National Electoral Commission (CENI) and hold the elections in the first semester of 2023 for climatic and logistical reasons

Judicial branch: highest court(s): Supreme Court or Cour Supreme (subdivided into 7 chambers: 2 civil, 2 labor, 1 commercial, 1 administrative, and 1 criminal, each with a chamber president and 2 councilors); Constitutional Council (consists of 9 members); High Court of Justice (consists of 9 members)
judge selection and term of office: Supreme Court president appointed by the president of the republic to serve a 5-year renewable term; Constitutional Council members appointed - 3 by the president of the republic, 2 by the president of the National Assembly, 1 by the prime minister, 1 by the leader of the democratic opposition, 1 by the largest opposition party in the National Assembly, and 1 by the second largest party in the National Assembly; members serve single, 9-year terms with one-third of membership renewed every 3 years; High Court of Justice members appointed by Parliament - 6 by the ruling Coalition of Majority Parties and 3 by opposition parties
subordinate courts: Courts of Appeal; courts of first instance or wilya courts are established in the regions' headquarters and include commercial and labor courts, criminal courts, Moughataa (district) Courts, and informal/customary courts

Political parties: Alliance for Justice and Democracy/Movement for Renewal or AJD/MR
El Insaf or Equity Party
El Islah or Reform Party
El Karama or Dignity Party
El Vadila or Virtue Party
Mauritanian Party of Union and Change or HATEM
National Democratic Alliance or AND
National Rally for Reform and Development or RNRD or TAWASSOUL
Nida El-Watan
Party for Conciliation and Prosperity or HIWAR
Party of the Mauritanian Masses or Hakam
Republican Front for Unity and Democracy or FRUD
Sawab Party
Union for Democracy and Progress or UDP
Union of Planning and Construction or UPC

International organization participation: ABEDA, ACP, AfDB, AFESD, AIIB, AMF, AMU, AU, CAEU, EITI (compliant country), FAO, G-77, IAEA, IBRD, ICAO, ICC (NGOs), ICRM, IDA, IDB, IFAD, IFC, IFRCS, IHO (pending member), ILO, IMF, IMO, Interpol, IOC, IOM, IPU, ISO (correspondent), ITSO, ITU, ITUC (NGOs), LAS, MIGA, NAM, OIC, OIF, OPCW, UN, UNCTAD, UNESCO, UNHRC, UNIDO, UNWTO, UPU, WCO, WHO, WIPO, WMO, WTO

Diplomatic representation in the US: *chief of mission:* Ambassador Cissé Mint Cheikh Ould BOIDE (since 15 September 2021)
chancery: 2129 Leroy Place NW, Washington, DC 20008
telephone: [1] (202) 232-5700
FAX: [1] (202) 319-2623
email address and website:
ambarimwashington@diplomatie.gov.mr
mauritaniaembassyus.org – Mauritania Embassy washington

Diplomatic representation from the US: *chief of mission:* Ambassador Cynthia KIERSCHT (since 27 January 2021)
embassy: Nouadhibou Road, Avenue Al Quds, NOT PRTZ, Nouakchott
mailing address: 2430 Nouakchott Place, Washington DC 20521-2430
telephone: [222] 4525-2660
FAX: [222] 4525-1592
email address and website:
consularnkc@state.gov
https://mr.usembassy.gov/

Flag description: green with a yellow, five-pointed star between the horns of a yellow, upward-pointing crescent moon; red stripes along the top and bottom edges; the crescent, star, and color green are traditional symbols of Islam; green also represents hope for a bright future; the yellow color stands for the sands of the Sahara; red symbolizes the blood shed in the struggle for independence

National symbol(s): five-pointed star between the horns of a horizontal crescent moon; national colors: green, yellow

National anthem: *name:* "Bilāda l-'ubāti l-hudāti l-kirām" (Land of the Proud, Guided by Noblemen)
lyrics/music: unknown/traditional, Rageh DAOUD
note: adopted 28 November 2017, preceded by "National Anthem of the Islamic Republic of Mauritania"

National heritage: *total World Heritage Sites:* 2 (1 cultural, 1 natural)
selected World Heritage Site locales: Ancient Ksour (Fortified Villages) of Ouadane, Chinguetti, Tichitt, and Oualata (c); Banc d'Arguin National Park (n)

ECONOMY

Economic overview: lower middle-income West African economy; primarily agrarian; rising urbanization; poor property rights; systemic corruption; endemic social and workforce tensions; wide-scale terrorism; foreign over-fishing; environmentally fragile

Real GDP (purchasing power parity): $30.395 billion (2023 est.)
$29.4 billion (2022 est.)
$27.635 billion (2021 est.)
note: data in 2021 dollars
comparison ranking: 147

Real GDP growth rate: 3.38% (2023 est.)
6.39% (2022 est.)
0.74% (2021 est.)
note: annual GDP % growth based on constant local currency
comparison ranking: 98

Real GDP per capita: $6,300 (2023 est.)
$6,200 (2022 est.)
$6,000 (2021 est.)
note: data in 2021 dollars
comparison ranking: 166

GDP (official exchange rate): $10.453 billion (2023 est.)
note: data in current dollars at official exchange rate

Inflation rate (consumer prices): 4.95% (2023 est.)
9.53% (2022 est.)
3.57% (2021 est.)
note: annual % change based on consumer prices
comparison ranking: 106

GDP - composition, by sector of origin: *agriculture:* 19.9% (2023 est.)
industry: 30.9% (2023 est.)
services: 42.5% (2023 est.)
note: figures may not total 100% due to non-allocated consumption not captured in sector-reported data
comparison rankings: services 183; industry 62; agriculture 40

GDP - composition, by end use: *household consumption:* 53.3% (2023 est.)
government consumption: 18.1% (2023 est.)
investment in fixed capital: 27.4% (2023 est.)
investment in inventories: 9.1% (2023 est.)

exports of goods and services: 44.2% (2023 est.)
imports of goods and services: -52.2% (2023 est.)
note: figures may not total 100% due to rounding or gaps in data collection

Agricultural products: rice, milk, sorghum, goat milk, sheep milk, lamb/mutton, beef, camel meat, camel milk, dates (2022)
note: top ten agricultural products based on tonnage

Industries: fish processing, oil production, mining (iron ore, gold, copper)
note: gypsum deposits have never been exploited

Industrial production growth rate: -0.48% (2023 est.)
note: annual % change in industrial value added based on constant local currency
comparison ranking: 161

Labor force: 1.179 million (2023 est.)
note: number of people ages 15 or older who are employed or seeking work
comparison ranking: 142

Unemployment rate: 10.51% (2023 est.)
10.6% (2022 est.)
11.07% (2021 est.)
note: % of labor force seeking employment
comparison ranking: 166

Youth unemployment rate (ages 15-24): *total:* 23.7% (2023 est.)
male: 20.3% (2023 est.)
female: 30.9% (2023 est.)
note: % of labor force ages 15-24 seeking employment
comparison ranking: total 48

Population below poverty line: 31.8% (2019 est.)
note: % of population with income below national poverty line

Gini Index coefficient - distribution of family income: 32 (2019 est.)
note: index (0-100) of income distribution; higher values represent greater inequality
comparison ranking: 108

Household income or consumption by percentage share: *lowest 10%:* 3.1% (2019 est.)
highest 10%: 24.6% (2019 est.)
note: % share of income accruing to lowest and highest 10% of population

Remittances: 0.57% of GDP (2023 est.)
1.12% of GDP (2022 est.)
0.14% of GDP (2021 est.)
note: personal transfers and compensation between resident and non-resident individuals/households/entities

Budget: *revenues:* $1.617 billion (2019 est.)
expenditures: $1.407 billion (2019 est.)

Public debt: 96.6% of GDP (2017 est.)
comparison ranking: 23

Taxes and other revenues: 27.4% (of GDP) (2017 est.)
comparison ranking: 30

Current account balance: -$1.424 billion (2022 est.)
-$807.862 million (2021 est.)
-$576.175 million (2020 est.)
note: balance of payments - net trade and primary/secondary income in current dollars
comparison ranking: 148

Exports: $4.132 billion (2022 est.)
$3.18 billion (2021 est.)
$2.784 billion (2020 est.)
note: balance of payments - exports of goods and services in current dollars
comparison ranking: 145

Exports - partners: China 24%, Canada 12%, UAE 12%, Spain 9%, Turkey 6% (2022)
note: top five export partners based on percentage share of exports

Exports - commodities: gold, iron ore, fish, processed crustaceans, animal meal (2022)
note: top five export commodities based on value in dollars

Imports: $5.77 billion (2022 est.)
$4.312 billion (2021 est.)
$3.675 billion (2020 est.)
note: balance of payments - imports of goods and services in current dollars
comparison ranking: 145

Imports - partners: China 18%, Spain 7%, Morocco 6%, UAE 6%, Indonesia 6% (2022)
note: top five import partners based on percentage share of imports

Imports - commodities: refined petroleum, iron pipes, wheat, raw sugar, palm oil (2022)
note: top five import commodities based on value in dollars

Reserves of foreign exchange and gold: $2.039 billion (2021 est.)
$1.493 billion (2020 est.)
$1.029 billion (2019 est.)
note: holdings of gold (year-end prices)/foreign exchange/special drawing rights in current dollars
comparison ranking: 123

Debt - external: $3.172 billion (2022 est.)
note: present value of external debt in current US dollars
comparison ranking: 65

Exchange rates: ouguiyas (MRO) per US dollar -

Exchange rates: 36.063 (2021 est.)
37.189 (2020 est.)
36.691 (2019 est.)
35.678 (2018 est.)
35.794 (2017 est.)

ENERGY

Electricity access: *electrification - total population:* 49% (2022 est.)
electrification - urban areas: 91.6%

Electricity: *installed generating capacity:* 675,000 kW (2022 est.)
consumption: 1.658 billion kWh (2022 est.)
imports: 193.742 million kWh (2022 est.)
transmission/distribution losses: 231.44 million kWh (2022 est.)
comparison rankings: transmission/distribution losses 65; imports 106; consumption 152; installed generating capacity 143

Electricity generation sources: *fossil fuels:* 70.1% of total installed capacity (2022 est.)
solar: 8.3% of total installed capacity (2022 est.)
wind: 9.2% of total installed capacity (2022 est.)
hydroelectricity: 12.4% of total installed capacity (2022 est.)

Coal: *imports:* 58 metric tons (2022 est.)

Petroleum: *refined petroleum consumption:* 29,000 bbl/day (2022 est.)
crude oil estimated reserves: 20 million barrels (2021 est.)

Natural gas: *proven reserves:* 28.317 billion cubic meters (2021 est.)

Carbon dioxide emissions: 4.322 million metric tonnes of CO2 (2022 est.)
from petroleum and other liquids: 4.322 million metric tonnes of CO2 (2022 est.)
comparison ranking: total emissions 139

Energy consumption per capita: 13.306 million Btu/person (2022 est.)
comparison ranking: 143

COMMUNICATIONS

Telephones - fixed lines: *total subscriptions:* 48,000 (2022 est.)
subscriptions per 100 inhabitants: 1 (2022 est.)
comparison ranking: total subscriptions 157

Telephones - mobile cellular: *total subscriptions:* 5.358 million (2022 est.)
subscriptions per 100 inhabitants: 113 (2022 est.)
comparison ranking: total subscriptions 123

Telecommunication systems: *general assessment:* Mauritania's small population and low economic output has limited the country's ability to develop sustained growth in the telecom sector; low disposable income has restricted growth in the use of services; this has impacted their ability to invest in network upgrades and improvements to service offerings; this has been reflected in the repeated fines imposed against them by the regulator for failing to ensure a good quality of service; there are also practical challenges related to transparency and tax burdens which have hindered foreign investment; financial support has been forthcoming from the government as well as the World Bank and European Investment Bank; their efforts have focused on implementing appropriate regulatory measures and promoting the further penetration of fixed-line broadband services by improving the national backbone network, ensuring connectivity to international telecom cables, and facilitating operator access to infrastructure; progress has been made to improve internet bandwidth capacity, including the completion of a cable link at the border with Algeria, and the connection to the EllaLink submarine cable; the final stage of the national backbone network was completed in December 2021, which now runs to some 4,000km; penetration of fixed telephony and broadband service is very low and is expected to remain so in coming years, though growth is anticipated following improvements to backbone infrastructure and the reduction in access pricing; most voice and data services are carried over the mobile networks (2022)
domestic: fixed-line teledensity 1 per 100 persons; mobile-cellular teledensity of roughly 141 per 100 persons (2021)
international: country code - 222; landing point for the ACE submarine cable for connectivity to 19 West African countries and 2 European countries; satellite earth stations - 3 (1 Intelsat - Atlantic Ocean, 2 Arabsat) (2019)

Broadcast media: *12 TV stations:* 6 government-owned and 6 private (the 6th was started in early 2022, owed by the President of Mauritanian Businessmen); in October 2017, the government suspended most private TV stations due to non-payment of broadcasting fees, but they later negotiated payment options with the government and are back since 2019. There are 19 radio broadcasters: 15 government-owned, 4 (Radio Nouakchott Libre, Radio Tenwir, Radio Kobeni and Mauritanid) private; all 4 private radio stations broadcast from Nouakchott; of the 15 government stations, 4 broadcast from Nouakchott (Radio Mauritanie, Radio Jeunesse, Radio Koran and

Mauritanid) and the other 12 broadcast from each of the 12 regions outside Nouakchott; Radio Jeunesse and Radio Koran are now also being re-broadcast in all the regions. (2022)

Internet country code: .mr

Internet users: *total:* 2.714 million (2021 est.)
percent of population: 59% (2021 est.)
comparison ranking: total 125

Broadband - fixed subscriptions: *total:* 18,457 (2020 est.)
subscriptions per 100 inhabitants: 0.4 (2020 est.)
comparison ranking: total 168

TRANSPORTATION

National air transport system: *number of registered air carriers:* 1 (2020)
inventory of registered aircraft operated by air carriers: 6
annual passenger traffic on registered air carriers: 454,435 (2018)

Civil aircraft registration country code prefix: 5T

Airports: 25 (2024)
comparison ranking: 130

Heliports: 3 (2024)

Railways: *total:* 728 km (2014)
standard gauge: 728 km (2014) 1.435-m gauge
comparison ranking: total 98

Roadways: *total:* 12,253 km
paved: 3,988 km
unpaved: 8,265 km
comparison ranking: total 130

Waterways: 1,086 km (2022) (some navigation possible on the Senegal River)
comparison ranking: 67

Merchant marine: *total:* 11 (2023)
by type: general cargo 2, other 9
comparison ranking: total 158

Ports: *total ports:* 2 (2024)
large: 0
medium: 1
small: 1
very small: 0
ports with oil terminals: 2
key ports: Nouadhibou, Nouakchott

MILITARY AND SECURITY

Military and security forces: Mauritanian Armed Forces (aka Armée Nationale Mauritanienne): National Army, National Navy (Marine Nationale), Mauritania Islamic Air Force; Gendarmerie (Ministry of Defense)

Ministry of Interior and Decentralization: National Police, National Guard (2024)
note 1: the National Police are responsible for enforcing the law and maintaining order in urban areas, while the paramilitary Gendarmerie is responsible for maintaining civil order around metropolitan areas and providing law enforcement services in rural areas; like the Mauritanian Armed Forces, the Gendarmerie is under the Ministry of Defense, but also supports the ministries of Interior and Justice
note 2: the National Guard performs a limited police function in keeping with its peacetime role of providing security at government facilities, to include prisons; regional authorities may call upon the National Guard to restore civil order during riots and other large-scale disturbances

Military expenditures: 2.5% of GDP (2023 est.)
2.5% of GDP (2022 est.)
2.4% of GDP (2021 est.)
2.5% of GDP (2020 est.)
2.1% of GDP (2019 est.)
comparison ranking: 46

Military and security service personnel strengths: approximately 16,000 Mauritanian Armed Forces personnel (15,000 Army; 700 Navy; 300 Air Force); estimated 3,000 Gendarmerie; estimated 2,000 National Guard (2023)

Military equipment inventories and acquisitions: the military's inventory is limited and made up largely of older French and Soviet-era equipment; in recent years, Mauritania has received some secondhand and new military equipment, including unmanned aircraft (drones), from several suppliers, including China and the UAE (2024)

Military service age and obligation: 18 is the legal minimum age for voluntary military service; has a compulsory two-year military service law, but the law has reportedly never been applied (2023)

Military deployments: 450 (plus about 325 police) Central African Republic (MINUSCA) (2024)

Military - note: founded in 1960, the Mauritanian military is responsible for territorial defense and internal security; it also assists in economic development projects, humanitarian missions, and disaster response; securing the border and countering terrorist groups operating in the Sahel, particularly from Mali, are key operational priorities; since a spate of deadly terrorist attacks on civilian and military targets in the 2005-2011 timeframe, the Mauritanian Government has increased the defense budget (up 40% between 2008 and 2018) and military equipment acquisitions, enhanced military training, heightened security cooperation with its neighbors and the international community, and built up the military's counterinsurgency and counterterrorism forces and capabilities; equipment acquisitions have prioritized mobility and intelligence collection, including light ground attack and reconnaissance aircraft, assault helicopters, patrol vessels, light trucks, and surveillance radars; Mauritania has received foreign security assistance from France, NATO, and the US in areas such as commando/special forces operations, counterterrorism, and professional military education (2023)

TERRORISM

Terrorist group(s): Al-Qa'ida in the Islamic Maghreb (AQIM)

TRANSNATIONAL ISSUES

Refugees and internally displaced persons: *refugees (country of origin):* 26,000 (Sahrawis) (2021); 104,080 (Mali) (2023)

Illicit drugs: NA

MAURITIUS

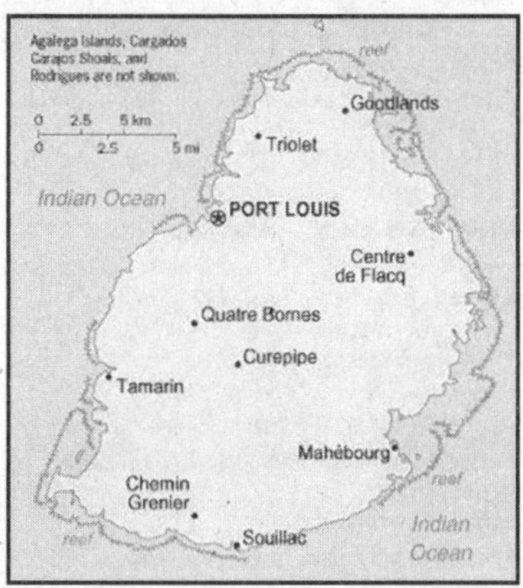

INTRODUCTION

Background: Although known to Arab and European sailors since at least the early 1500s, the island of Mauritius was uninhabited until 1638 when the Dutch established a settlement named in honor of Prince Maurits van NASSAU. Their presence led to the rapid disappearance of the flightless dodo bird that has since become one of the most well-known examples of extinction in modern times. The Dutch abandoned their financially distressed settlement in 1710, although a number of formerly enslaved people remained. In 1722, the French established what would become a highly profitable settlement focused on sugar cane plantations that were reliant on the labor of enslaved people brought to Mauritius from other parts of Africa. In the 1790s, the island had a brief period of autonomous rule when plantation owners rejected French control because of laws ending slavery that were temporarily in effect during the French Revolution. Britain captured the island in 1810 as part of the Napoleonic Wars but kept most of the French administrative structure, which remains to this day in the form of the country's legal codes and widespread use of the French Creole language. The abolition of slavery in 1835 – later than most other British colonies – led to increased reliance on contracted laborers from the Indian subcontinent to work on plantations. Today their descendants form the majority of the population. Mauritius remained a strategically important British naval base and later an air station, and it played a role during World War II in anti-submarine and convoy operations, as well as in the collection of signals intelligence.

Mauritius gained independence from the UK in 1968 as a Parliamentary Republic and has remained a stable democracy with regular free elections and a positive human rights record. The country also attracted considerable foreign investment and now has one of Africa's highest per capita incomes. Mauritius' often-fractious coalition politics has been dominated by two prominent families, each of which has had father-son pairs who have been prime minister over multiple, often nonconsecutive, terms. Seewoosagur RAMGOOLAM (1968-76) was Mauritius' first prime minister, and he was succeeded by Anerood JUGNAUTH (1982-95, 2000-03, 2014-17); his son Navin RAMGOOLAM (1995-2000, 2005-14); and Paul Raymond BERENGER (2003-05), the only non-Hindu prime minister of post-independence Mauritius. In 2017, Pravind JUGNAUTH became prime minister after his father stepped down short of completing his term, and he was elected in his own right in 2019.

Mauritius claims the French island of Tromelin and the British Chagos Archipelago (British Indian Ocean Territory). Since 2017, Mauritius has secured favorable UN General Assembly resolutions and an International Court of Justice advisory opinion relating to its sovereignty dispute with the UK.

GEOGRAPHY

Location: Southern Africa, island in the Indian Ocean, about 800 km (500 mi) east of Madagascar

Geographic coordinates: 20 17 S, 57 33 E

Map references: Africa

Area: *total:* 2,040 sq km
land: 2,030 sq km
water: 10 sq km
note: includes Agalega Islands, Cargados Carajos Shoals (Saint Brandon), and Rodrigues
comparison ranking: total 180

Area - comparative: almost 11 times the size of Washington, DC

Land boundaries: *total:* 0 km

Coastline: 177 km

Maritime claims: *territorial sea:* 12 nm
exclusive economic zone: 200 nm
continental shelf: 200 nm or to the edge of the continental margin
measured from claimed archipelagic straight baselines

Climate: tropical, modified by southeast trade winds; warm, dry winter (May to November); hot, wet, humid summer (November to May)

Terrain: small coastal plain rising to discontinuous mountains encircling central plateau

Elevation: *highest point:* Mont Piton 828 m
lowest point: Indian Ocean 0 m

Natural resources: arable land, fish

Land use: *agricultural land:* 43.8% (2018 est.)
arable land: 38.4% (2018 est.)
permanent crops: 2% (2018 est.)
permanent pasture: 3.4% (2018 est.)
forest: 17.3% (2018 est.)
other: 38.9% (2018 est.)

Irrigated land: 158 sq km (2020)

Population distribution: population density is one of the highest in the world; urban clusters are found throughout the main island, with a greater density in and around Port Luis; population on Rodrigues Island is spread across the island with a slightly denser cluster on the north coast as shown in this population distribution map

Natural hazards: cyclones (November to April); almost completely surrounded by reefs that may pose maritime hazards

Geography - note: the main island, from which the country derives its name, is of volcanic origin and is almost entirely surrounded by coral reefs; former home of the dodo, a large flightless bird related to pigeons, driven to extinction by the end of the 17th century through a combination of hunting and the introduction of predatory species

PEOPLE AND SOCIETY

Population: *total:* 1,310,504
male: 639,270
female: 671,234 (2024 est.)
comparison rankings: female 156; male 159; total 159

Nationality: *noun:* Mauritian(s)
adjective: Mauritian

Ethnic groups: Indo-Mauritian (compose approximately two thirds of the total population), Creole, Sino-Mauritian, Franco-Mauritian
note: Mauritius has not had a question on ethnicity on its national census since 1972

Languages: Creole 86.5%, Bhojpuri 5.3%, French 4.1%, two languages 1.4%, other 2.6% (includes English, one of the two official languages of the National Assembly, which is spoken by less than 1% of the population), unspecified 0.1% (2011 est.)

Religions: Hindu 48.5%, Roman Catholic 26.3%, Muslim 17.3%, other Christian 6.4%, other 0.6%, none 0.7%, unspecified 0.1% (2011 est.)

Demographic profile: Mauritius has transitioned from a country of high fertility and high mortality rates in the 1950s and mid-1960s to one with among the lowest population growth rates in the developing world today. After World War II, Mauritius' population began to expand quickly due to increased fertility and a dramatic drop in mortality rates as a result of improved health care and the eradication of malaria. This period of heightened population growth – reaching about 3% a year – was followed by one of the world's most rapid birth rate declines.

The total fertility rate fell from 6.2 children per women in 1963 to 3.2 in 1972 – largely the result of improved educational attainment, especially among young women, accompanied by later marriage and the adoption of family planning methods. The family planning programs' success was due to support from the government and eventually the traditionally pronatalist religious communities, which both recognized that controlling population growth was necessary because of Mauritius' small size and limited resources. Mauritius' fertility rate has consistently been below replacement level since the late 1990s, a rate that is substantially lower than nearby countries in southern Africa.

With no indigenous population, Mauritius' ethnic mix is a product of more than two centuries of European colonialism and continued international labor migration. Sugar production relied on slave labor mainly from Madagascar, Mozambique, and East Africa from the early 18th century until its abolition in 1835, when slaves were replaced with indentured Indians. Most of the influx of indentured labor – peaking between the late 1830s and early 1860s – settled permanently creating massive population growth of more than 7% a year and reshaping the island's social and cultural composition. While Indians represented about 12% of Mauritius' population in 1837, they and their descendants accounted for roughly two-thirds by the end of the 19th century. Most were Hindus, but the majority of the free Indian traders were Muslims.

Mauritius again turned to overseas labor when its success in clothing and textile exports led to a labor shortage in the mid-1980s. Clothing manufacturers brought in contract workers (increasingly women) from China, India, and, to a lesser extent Bangladesh and Madagascar, who worked longer hours for lower wages under poor conditions and were viewed as more productive than locals. Downturns in the sugar and textile industries in the mid-2000s and a lack of highly qualified domestic workers for Mauritius' growing services sector led to the emigration of low-skilled workers and a reliance on skilled foreign labor. Since 2007, Mauritius has pursued a circular migration program to enable citizens to acquire new skills and savings abroad and then return home to start businesses and to invest in the country's development.

Age structure: *0-14 years:* 15.1% (male 100,973/female 96,711)
15-64 years: 71% (male 462,833/female 467,509)
65 years and over: 13.9% (2024 est.) (male 75,464/female 107,014)

Dependency ratios: *total dependency ratio:* 40.7
youth dependency ratio: 23.4
elderly dependency ratio: 17.3
potential support ratio: 5.8 (2021 est.)

Median age: *total:* 39.6 years (2024 est.)
male: 38.1 years
female: 41 years
comparison ranking: total 66

Population growth rate: 0.07% (2024 est.)
comparison ranking: 189

Birth rate: 9.8 births/1,000 population (2024 est.)
comparison ranking: 191

Death rate: 9 deaths/1,000 population (2024 est.)
comparison ranking: 59

Net migration rate: 0 migrant(s)/1,000 population (2024 est.)
comparison ranking: 78

Population distribution: population density is one of the highest in the world; urban clusters are found throughout the main island, with a greater density in and around Port Luis; population on Rodrigues Island is spread across the island with a slightly denser cluster on the north coast as shown in this population distribution map

Urbanization: *urban population:* 40.9% of total population (2023)
rate of urbanization: 0.28% annual rate of change (2020-25 est.)

Major urban areas - population: 149,000 PORT LOUIS (capital) (2018)

Sex ratio: *at birth:* 1.07 male(s)/female
0-14 years: 1.04 male(s)/female
15-64 years: 0.99 male(s)/female
65 years and over: 0.71 male(s)/female
total population: 0.95 male(s)/female (2024 est.)

Maternal mortality ratio: 84 deaths/100,000 live births (2020 est.)
comparison ranking: 73

Infant mortality rate: *total:* 11.6 deaths/1,000 live births (2024 est.)
male: 13.1 deaths/1,000 live births

female: 10 deaths/1,000 live births
comparison ranking: total 116

Life expectancy at birth: *total population:* 75.4 years (2024 est.)
male: 72.6 years
female: 78.4 years
comparison ranking: total population 127

Total fertility rate: 1.36 children born/woman (2024 est.)
comparison ranking: 215

Gross reproduction rate: 0.66 (2024 est.)

Contraceptive prevalence rate: 63.8% (2014)

Drinking water source: *improved: urban:* 99.9% of population
rural: 99.8% of population
total: 99.9% of population
unimproved: urban: 0.1% of population
rural: 0.2% of population
total: 0.1% of population (2020 est.)

Current health expenditure: 6.7% of GDP (2020)

Physician density: 2.71 physicians/1,000 population (2020)

Hospital bed density: 3.7 beds/1,000 population (2020)

Sanitation facility access: *improved: urban:* 99.9% of population
rural: NA
total: NA
unimproved: urban: 0.1% of population
rural: NA
total: (2020 est.) NA

Obesity - adult prevalence rate: 10.8% (2016)
comparison ranking: 137

Alcohol consumption per capita: *total:* 3.39 liters of pure alcohol (2019 est.)
beer: 1.94 liters of pure alcohol (2019 est.)
wine: 0.23 liters of pure alcohol (2019 est.)
spirits: 0.88 liters of pure alcohol (2019 est.)
other alcohols: 0.03 liters of pure alcohol (2019 est.)
comparison ranking: total 106

Tobacco use: *total:* 20.2% (2020 est.)
male: 37.3% (2020 est.)
female: 3% (2020 est.)
comparison ranking: total 88

Children under the age of 5 years underweight: NA

Currently married women (ages 15-49): 62% (2023 est.)

Education expenditures: 4.9% of GDP (2021 est.)
comparison ranking: 80

Literacy: *definition:* age 15 and over can read and write
total population: 92.2%
male: 93.5%
female: 90.5% (2021)

School life expectancy (primary to tertiary education): *total:* 15 years
male: 14 years
female: 16 years (2017)

ENVIRONMENT

Environment - current issues: water pollution, degradation of coral reefs; soil erosion; wildlife preservation; solid waste disposal

Environment - international agreements: *party to:* Antarctic-Marine Living Resources, Biodiversity, Climate Change, Climate Change-Kyoto Protocol, Climate Change-Paris Agreement, Desertification, Endangered Species, Environmental Modification, Hazardous Wastes, Law of the Sea, Marine Life Conservation, Nuclear Test Ban, Ozone Layer Protection, Ship Pollution, Wetlands
signed, but not ratified: none of the selected agreements

Climate: tropical, modified by southeast trade winds; warm, dry winter (May to November); hot, wet, humid summer (November to May)

Urbanization: *urban population:* 40.9% of total population (2023)
rate of urbanization: 0.28% annual rate of change (2020-25 est.)

Revenue from forest resources: 0% of GDP (2018 est.)
comparison ranking: 171

Revenue from coal: 0% of GDP (2018 est.)
comparison ranking: 77

Air pollutants: *particulate matter emissions:* 10.48 micrograms per cubic meter (2019 est.)
carbon dioxide emissions: 4.35 megatons (2016 est.)
methane emissions: 2.06 megatons (2020 est.)

Waste and recycling: *municipal solid waste generated annually:* 438,000 tons (2016 est.)

Total water withdrawal: *municipal:* 290 million cubic meters (2020 est.)
industrial: 10 million cubic meters (2020 est.)
agricultural: 310 million cubic meters (2020 est.)

Total renewable water resources: 2.75 billion cubic meters (2020 est.)

GOVERNMENT

Country name: *conventional long form:* Republic of Mauritius
conventional short form: Mauritius
local long form: Republic of Mauritius
local short form: Mauritius
etymology: island named after Prince Maurice VAN NASSAU, stadtholder of the Dutch Republic, in 1598
note: pronounced mah-rish-us

Government type: parliamentary republic

Capital: *name:* Port Louis
geographic coordinates: 20 09 S, 57 29 E
time difference: UTC+4 (9 hours ahead of Washington, DC, during Standard Time)
etymology: named after LOUIS XV, who was king of France in 1736 when the port became the administrative center of Mauritius and a major reprovisioning stop for French ships traveling between Europe and Asia

Administrative divisions: 9 districts and 3 dependencies*; Agalega Islands*, Black River, Cargados Carajos Shoals*, Flacq, Grand Port, Moka, Pamplemousses, Plaines Wilhems, Port Louis, Riviere du Rempart, Rodrigues*, Savanne

Independence: 12 March 1968 (from the UK)

National holiday: Independence and Republic Day, 12 March (1968 & 1992); note - became independent and a republic on the same date in 1968 and 1992 respectively

Legal system: civil legal system based on French civil law with some elements of English common law

Constitution: *history:* several previous; latest adopted 12 March 1968
amendments: proposed by the National Assembly; passage of amendments affecting constitutional articles, including the sovereignty of the state, fundamental rights and freedoms, citizenship, or the branches of government, requires approval in a referendum by at least three-fourths majority of voters followed by a unanimous vote by the Assembly; passage of other amendments requires only two-thirds majority vote by the Assembly; amended many times, last in 2016

International law organization participation: accepts compulsory ICJ jurisdiction with reservations; accepts ICCt jurisdiction

Citizenship: *citizenship by birth:* yes
citizenship by descent only: yes
dual citizenship recognized: yes
residency requirement for naturalization: 5 out of the previous 7 years including the last 12 months

Suffrage: 18 years of age; universal

Executive branch: *chief of state:* President Prithvirajsing ROOPUN (since 2 December 2019)
head of government: Prime Minister Pravind JUGNAUTH (since 23 January 2017)
cabinet: Cabinet of Ministers (Council of Ministers) appointed by the president on the recommendation of the prime minister
elections/appointments: president and vice president indirectly elected by the National Assembly for 5-year renewable terms; election last held on 7 November 2019 (next to be held in 2024); the president appoints the prime minister and deputy prime minister who have the majority support in the National Assembly
election results:
2019: Prithvirajsing ROOPUN (MSM) elected president by the National Assembly - unanimous vote
2015: Ameenah GURIB-FAKIM (independent) elected president by the National Assembly - unanimous vote; note - GURIB-FAKIM, who was Mauritius' first female president, resigned on 23 March 2018; acting presidents served from March 2018 until ROOPUN's appointment in 2019

Legislative branch: *description:* unicameral National Assembly or Assemblee Nationale (70 seats maximum; 62 members directly elected multi-seat constituencies by simple majority vote and up to 8 seats allocated to non-elected party candidates by the Office of Electoral Commissioner; members serve a 5-year term)
elections: last held on 7 November 2019 (next to be held by late 2024)
election results: percent of vote by party - Mauritian Alliance 2019 (MSM, ML, MAG, and PM) 37.7%, National Alliance (PTR, PMSD, and MJCB) 32.8%, MMM 20.6%, OPR 1%, other 7.9%; seats by party - MSM 38, PTR 14, MMM 8, OPR 2; composition - men 56, women 14, percentage women 20% (2019)

Judicial branch: *highest court(s):* Supreme Court of Mauritius (consists of the chief justice, a senior puisne judge, and 24 puisne judges); note - the Judicial Committee of the Privy Council (in London) serves as the final court of appeal
judge selection and term of office: chief justice appointed by the president after consultation with the prime minister; senior puisne judge appointed by the president with the advice of the chief justice; other puisne judges appointed by the president with the advice of the Judicial and Legal Commission, a 4-member body of judicial officials including the

chief justice; all judges serve until retirement at age 67
subordinate courts: lower regional courts known as District Courts, Court of Civil Appeal; Court of Criminal Appeal; Public Bodies Appeal Tribunal

Political parties: Alliance Morisien (Mauritian Alliance)
Jean-Claude Barbier Movement (Mouvement Jean-Claude Barbier) or MJCB
Mauritian Militant Movement (Mouvement Militant Mauricien) or MMM
Mauritian Social Democratic Party (Parti Mauricien Social Democrate) or PMSD
Mauritius Labor Party (Parti Travailliste) or PTR or MLP
Militant Platform (Plateforme Militante) or PM
Militant Socialist Movement (Mouvement Socialist Mauricien) or MSM
Muvman Liberater or ML
National Alliance
Patriotic Movement (Mouvement Patriotique) or MAG
Rodrigues Peoples Organization (Organisation du Peuple Rodriguais) or OPR

International organization participation: ACP, AfDB, AOSIS, AU, CD, COMESA, CPLP (associate), FAO, G-77, IAEA, IBRD, ICAO, ICC (NGOs), ICCt, ICRM, IDA, IFAD, IFC, IFRCS, IHO, ILO, IMF, IMO, IMSO, InOC, Interpol, IOC, IOM, IPU, ISO, ITSO, ITU, ITUC (NGOs), MIGA, NAM, OIF, OPCW, PCA, SAARC (observer), SADC, UN, UNCTAD, UNESCO, UNIDO, UNWTO, UPU, WCO, WFTU (NGOs), WHO, WIPO, WMO, WTO

Diplomatic representation in the US: *chief of mission:* Ambassador Purmanund JHUGROO (since 7 July 2021)
chancery: 1709 N Street NW, Washington, DC 20036
telephone: [1] (202) 244-1491
FAX: [1] (202) 966-0983
email address and website:
mauritius.embassy@verizon.net
https://mauritius-washington.govmu.org/Pages/index.aspx

Diplomatic representation from the US: *chief of mission:* Ambassador Henry V. JARDINE (since 22 February 2023); note - also accredited to Seychelles
embassy: 4th Floor, Rogers House, John Kennedy Avenue, Port Louis
mailing address: 2450 Port Louis Place, Washington, DC 20521-2450
telephone: [230] 202-4400
FAX: [230] 208-9534
email address and website:
PTLConsular@state.gov
https://mu.usembassy.gov/

Flag description: four equal horizontal bands of red (top), blue, yellow, and green; red represents self-determination and independence, blue the Indian Ocean surrounding the island, yellow has been interpreted as the new light of independence, golden sunshine, or the bright future, and green can symbolize either agriculture or the lush vegetation of the island
note: while many national flags consist of three - and in some cases five - horizontal bands of color, the flag of Mauritius is the world's only national flag to consist of four horizontal color bands

National symbol(s): dodo bird, Trochetia Boutoniana flower; national colors: red, blue, yellow, green

National anthem: *name:* "Motherland"
lyrics/music: Jean Georges PROSPER/Philippe GENTIL
note: adopted 1968

National heritage: *total World Heritage Sites:* 2 (both cultural)
selected World Heritage Site locales: Aapravasi Ghat; Le Morne Cultural Landscape

ECONOMY

Economic overview: upper middle-income Indian Ocean island economy; diversified portfolio; investing in maritime security; strong tourism sector decimated by COVID-19; expanding in information and financial services; environmentally fragile

Real GDP (purchasing power parity): $33.53 billion (2023 est.)
$31.35 billion (2022 est.)
$28.793 billion (2021 est.)
note: data in 2021 dollars
comparison ranking: 144

Real GDP growth rate: 6.95% (2023 est.)
8.88% (2022 est.)
3.4% (2021 est.)
note: annual GDP % growth based on constant local currency
comparison ranking: 22

Real GDP per capita: $26,600 (2023 est.)
$24,800 (2022 est.)
$22,700 (2021 est.)
note: data in 2021 dollars
comparison ranking: 85

GDP (official exchange rate): $14.397 billion (2023 est.)
note: data in current dollars at official exchange rate

Inflation rate (consumer prices): 7.05% (2023 est.)
10.77% (2022 est.)
4.03% (2021 est.)
note: annual % change based on consumer prices
comparison ranking: 143

Credit ratings: Moody's rating: Baa1 (2012)
note: The year refers to the year in which the current credit rating was first obtained.

GDP - composition, by sector of origin: *agriculture:* 3.8% (2023 est.)
industry: 18.6% (2023 est.)
services: 64.6% (2023 est.)
note: figures may not total 100% due to non-allocated consumption not captured in sector-reported data
comparison rankings: services 59; industry 148; agriculture 130

GDP - composition, by end use: *household consumption:* 67.6% (2023 est.)
government consumption: 14.2% (2023 est.)
investment in fixed capital: 23.5% (2023 est.)
investment in inventories: -0.2% (2023 est.)
exports of goods and services: 53.3% (2023 est.)
imports of goods and services: -55.2% (2023 est.)
note: figures may not total 100% due to rounding or gaps in data collection

Agricultural products: sugarcane, chicken, pumpkins/squash, eggs, potatoes, tomatoes, bananas, onions, tea, cucumbers/gherkins (2022)
note: top ten agricultural products based on tonnage

Industries: food processing (largely sugar milling), textiles, clothing, mining, chemicals, metal products, transport equipment, nonelectrical machinery, tourism

Industrial production growth rate: 10.47% (2023 est.)
note: annual % change in industrial value added based on constant local currency
comparison ranking: 12

Labor force: 588,000 (2023 est.)
note: number of people ages 15 or older who are employed or seeking work
comparison ranking: 159

Unemployment rate: 6.06% (2023 est.)
6.32% (2022 est.)
7.72% (2021 est.)
note: % of labor force seeking employment
comparison ranking: 125

Youth unemployment rate (ages 15-24): *total:* 20.9% (2023 est.)
male: 19% (2023 est.)
female: 23.6% (2023 est.)
note: % of labor force ages 15-24 seeking employment
comparison ranking: total 60

Population below poverty line: 10.3% (2017 est.)
note: % of population with income below national poverty line

Gini Index coefficient - distribution of family income: 36.8 (2017 est.)
note: index (0-100) of income distribution; higher values represent greater inequality
comparison ranking: 64

Household income or consumption by percentage share: *lowest 10%:* 2.9% (2017 est.)
highest 10%: 29.9% (2017 est.)
note: % share of income accruing to lowest and highest 10% of population

Remittances: 1.94% of GDP (2023 est.)
2.12% of GDP (2022 est.)
2.37% of GDP (2021 est.)
note: personal transfers and compensation between resident and non-resident individuals/households/entities

Budget: *revenues:* $3.134 billion (2022 est.)
expenditures: $3.647 billion (2022 est.)
note: central government revenues (excluding grants) and expenses converted to US dollars at average official exchange rate for year indicated

Public debt: 57.96% of GDP (2019 est.)
note: central government debt as a % of GDP
comparison ranking: 85

Taxes and other revenues: 19.05% (of GDP) (2022 est.)
note: central government tax revenue as a % of GDP
comparison ranking: 93

Current account balance: -$654.051 million (2023 est.)
-$1.437 billion (2022 est.)
-$1.497 billion (2021 est.)
note: balance of payments - net trade and primary/secondary income in current dollars
comparison ranking: 126

Exports: $5.499 billion (2023 est.)
$5.004 billion (2022 est.)
$3.194 billion (2021 est.)
note: balance of payments - exports of goods and services in current dollars

comparison ranking: 139

Exports - partners: Zimbabwe 11%, South Africa 11%, France 10%, Madagascar 8%, US 7% (2022)
note: top five export partners based on percentage share of exports

Exports - commodities: garments, fish, raw sugar, fertilizers, diamonds (2022)
note: top five export commodities based on value in dollars

Imports: $8.038 billion (2023 est.)
$8.052 billion (2022 est.)
$6.057 billion (2021 est.)
note: balance of payments - imports of goods and services in current dollars
comparison ranking: 131

Imports - partners: China 16%, South Africa 10%, UAE 9%, India 9%, Oman 8% (2022)
note: top five import partners based on percentage share of imports

Imports - commodities: refined petroleum, coal, fish, cars, packaged medicine (2022)
note: top five import commodities based on value in dollars

Reserves of foreign exchange and gold: $7.248 billion (2023 est.)
$7.793 billion (2022 est.)
$8.563 billion (2021 est.)
note: holdings of gold (year-end prices)/foreign exchange/special drawing rights in current dollars
comparison ranking: 86

Debt - external: $2.827 billion (2022 est.)
note: present value of external debt in current US dollars
comparison ranking: 67

Exchange rates: Mauritian rupees (MUR) per US dollar -

Exchange rates: 45.267 (2023 est.)
44.183 (2022 est.)
41.692 (2021 est.)
39.347 (2020 est.)
35.474 (2019 est.)

ENERGY

Electricity access: *electrification - total population:* 100% (2022 est.)
electrification - urban areas: 99%
electrification - rural areas: 100%

Electricity: *installed generating capacity:* 956,000 kW (2022 est.)
consumption: 3.288 billion kWh (2022 est.)
transmission/distribution losses: 208.205 million kWh (2022 est.)
comparison rankings: transmission/distribution losses 63; consumption 139; installed generating capacity 137

Electricity generation sources: *fossil fuels:* 80.9% of total installed capacity (2022 est.)
solar: 4.4% of total installed capacity (2022 est.)
wind: 0.5% of total installed capacity (2022 est.)
hydroelectricity: 3.7% of total installed capacity (2022 est.)
biomass and waste: 10.6% of total installed capacity (2022 est.)

Coal: *consumption:* 580,000 metric tons (2022 est.)
imports: 580,000 metric tons (2022 est.)

Petroleum: *refined petroleum consumption:* 25,000 bbl/day (2022 est.)

Carbon dioxide emissions: 5.091 million metric tonnes of CO_2 (2022 est.)
from coal and metallurgical coke: 1.31 million metric tonnes of CO_2 (2022 est.)
from petroleum and other liquids: 3.781 million metric tonnes of CO_2 (2022 est.)
comparison ranking: total emissions 133

Energy consumption per capita: 54.401 million Btu/person (2022 est.)
comparison ranking: 91

COMMUNICATIONS

Telephones - fixed lines: *total subscriptions:* 462,000 (2022 est.)
subscriptions per 100 inhabitants: 36 (2022 est.)
comparison ranking: total subscriptions 95

Telephones - mobile cellular: *total subscriptions:* 2.097 million (2022 est.)
subscriptions per 100 inhabitants: 161 (2022 est.)
comparison ranking: total subscriptions 149

Telecommunication systems: *general assessment:* the telecom sector in Mauritius has long been supported by the varied needs of tourists; this has stimulated the mobile market, leading to a particularly high penetration rate; the response of the country's telcos to tourist requirements also contributed to the country being among the first in the region to provide services based on 3G and WiMAX technologies; the incumbent telco provides comprehensive LTE and fiber broadband coverage, and in late 2021 it launched a gigabit fiber-based broadband service; the country has seen improved international internet capacity in recent years, with direct cables linking to India, Madagascar, and South Africa, as well as other connections to Rodrigues and Reunion; mobile subscribers in Mauritius secured 5G services in mid-2021; this followed the regulator's award of spectrum in two bands to the MNOs (2022)
domestic: fixed-line teledensity over 36 per 100 persons and mobile-cellular services teledensity 152 per 100 persons (2021)
international: country code - 230; landing points for the SAFE, MARS, IOX Cable System, METISS and LION submarine cable system that provides links to Asia, Africa, Southeast Asia, Indian Ocean Islands of Reunion, Madagascar, and Mauritius; satellite earth station - 1 Intelsat (Indian Ocean); new microwave link to Reunion; HF radiotelephone links to several countries (2019)

Broadcast media: the Mauritius Broadcasting Corporation is the national public television and radio broadcaster; it broadcasts programming in French, English, Hindi, Creole and Chinese, it provides 17 television channels in Mauritius; there are nine Mauritian FM radio stations and two operating on the AM band
(2022)

Internet country code: .mu

Internet users: *total:* 884,000 (2021 est.)
percent of population: 68% (2021 est.)
comparison ranking: total 150

Broadband - fixed subscriptions: *total:* 323,200 (2020 est.)
subscriptions per 100 inhabitants: 25 (2020 est.)
comparison ranking: total 105

TRANSPORTATION

National air transport system: *number of registered air carriers:* 1 (2020)
inventory of registered aircraft operated by air carriers: 13
annual passenger traffic on registered air carriers: 1,745,291 (2018)
annual freight traffic on registered air carriers: 233.72 million (2018) mt-km

Civil aircraft registration country code prefix: 3B

Airports: 4 (2024)
comparison ranking: 183

Heliports: 1 (2024)

Roadways: *total:* 2,428 km
paved: 2,379 km (includes 99 km of expressways)
unpaved: 49 km (2015)
comparison ranking: total 171

Merchant marine: *total:* 32 (2023)
by type: general cargo 1, oil tanker 4, other 27
comparison ranking: total 132

Ports: *total ports:* 2 (2024)
large: 0
medium: 0
small: 1
very small: 1
ports with oil terminals: 1
key ports: Port Louis, Port Mathurin

MILITARY AND SECURITY

Military and security forces: no regular military forces; the Mauritius Police Force (MPF) under the Ministry of Defense includes a paramilitary unit known as the Special Mobile Force, which includes some motorized infantry and light armored units; the MPF also has a Police Helicopter Squadron, a Special Support Unit (riot police), and the National Coast Guard (also includes an air squadron) (2024)
note: the MPF is responsible for law enforcement and maintenance of order within the country; a police commissioner heads the force and has authority over all police and other security forces, including the Coast Guard and Special Mobile Forces; the Special Mobile Forces share responsibility with police for internal security

Military equipment inventories and acquisitions: the MPF's inventory is comprised of mostly secondhand equipment from Western European countries and India (2023)

Military - note: the MPF's primary security partner is India, which provides training and other support to the National Coast Guard; Indian naval vessels often patrol the country's waters; the MPF has also received assistance and training from France, the UK, and the US; the MPF's chief security concerns are piracy and narcotics trafficking
the Special Mobile Force was created in 1960 following the withdrawal of the British garrison (2024)

TRANSNATIONAL ISSUES

Illicit drugs: consumer and transshipment point for heroin from South Asia; small amounts of cannabis produced and consumed locally; significant offshore financial industry creates potential for money laundering

MEXICO

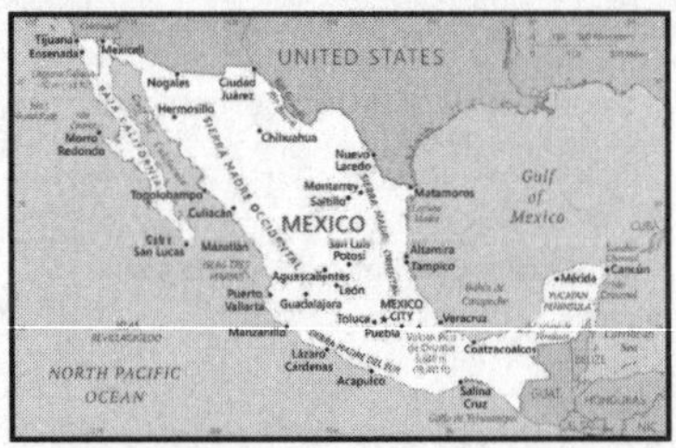

INTRODUCTION

Background: Mexico was the site of several advanced Amerindian civilizations – including the Olmec, Toltec, Teotihuacan, Zapotec, Maya, and Aztec – until Spain conquered and colonized the area in the early 16th century. Administered as the Viceroyalty of New Spain for three centuries, it achieved independence early in the 19th century. Elections held in 2000 marked the first time since Mexican Revolution in 1910 that an opposition candidate – Vicente FOX of the National Action Party (PAN) – defeated the party in government, the Institutional Revolutionary Party (PRI). He was succeeded in 2006 by another PAN candidate Felipe CALDERON, but Enrique PEÑA NIETO regained the presidency for the PRI in 2012. Left-leaning anti-establishment politician and former mayor of Mexico City (2000-05) Andrés Manuel LÓPEZ OBRADOR, from the National Regeneration Movement (MORENA), became president in 2018.

The US-Mexico-Canada Agreement (USMCA, or T-MEC by its Spanish acronym) entered into force in 2020 and replaced its predecessor, the North American Free Trade Agreement (NAFTA). Mexico amended its constitution in 2019 to facilitate the implementation of the labor components of USMCA.

Mexico is currently the US's second-largest goods trading partner, after Canada. Ongoing economic and social concerns include low real wages, high underemployment, inequitable income distribution, and few advancement opportunities, particularly for the largely indigenous population in the impoverished southern states. Since 2007, Mexico's powerful transnational criminal organizations have engaged in a struggle to control criminal markets, resulting in tens of thousands of drug-related homicides and forced disappearances.

GEOGRAPHY

Location: North America, bordering the Caribbean Sea and the Gulf of Mexico, between Belize and the United States and bordering the North Pacific Ocean, between Guatemala and the United States

Geographic coordinates: 23 00 N, 102 00 W

Map references: North America

Area: *total:* 1,964,375 sq km
land: 1,943,945 sq km
water: 20,430 sq km
comparison ranking: total 15

Area - comparative: slightly less than three times the size of Texas

Land boundaries: *total:* 4,389 km
border countries (3): Belize 276 km; Guatemala 958 km; US 3,155 km

Coastline: 9,330 km

Maritime claims: *territorial sea:* 12 nm
contiguous zone: 24 nm
exclusive economic zone: 200 nm
continental shelf: 200 nm or to the edge of the continental margin

Climate: varies from tropical to desert

Terrain: high, rugged mountains; low coastal plains; high plateaus; desert

Elevation: *highest point:* Volcan Pico de Orizaba 5,636 m
lowest point: Laguna Salada -10 m
mean elevation: 1,111 m

Natural resources: petroleum, silver, antimony, copper, gold, lead, zinc, natural gas, timber

Land use: *agricultural land:* 54.9% (2018 est.)
arable land: 11.8% (2018 est.)
permanent crops: 1.4% (2018 est.)
permanent pasture: 41.7% (2018 est.)
forest: 33.3% (2018 est.)
other: 11.8% (2018 est.)

Irrigated land: 60,620 sq km (2020)

Major lakes (area sq km): *fresh water lake(s):* Laguna de Chapala - 1,140 sq km
salt water lake(s): Laguna de Terminos - 1,550 sq km

Major rivers (by length in km): Rio Grande river mouth (shared with US [s]) - 3,057 km; Colorado river mouth (shared with US [s]) - 2,333 km
note – [s] after country name indicates river source; [m] after country name indicates river mouth

Major watersheds (area sq km): Atlantic Ocean drainage: *(Gulf of Mexico)* Rio Grande/Bravo (607,965 sq km)
Pacific Ocean drainage: *(Gulf of California)* Colorado (703,148 sq km)

Major aquifers: Atlantic and Gulf Coastal Plains Aquifer

Population distribution: most of the population is found in the middle of the country between the states of Jalisco and Veracruz; approximately a quarter of the population lives in and around Mexico City

Natural hazards: tsunamis along the Pacific coast, volcanoes and destructive earthquakes in the center and south, and hurricanes on the Pacific, Gulf of Mexico, and Caribbean coasts
volcanism: volcanic activity in the central-southern part of the country; the volcanoes in Baja California are mostly dormant; Colima (3,850 m), which erupted in 2010, is Mexico's most active volcano and is responsible for causing periodic evacuations of nearby villagers; it has been deemed a Decade Volcano by the International Association of Volcanology and Chemistry of the Earth's Interior, worthy of study due to its explosive history and close proximity to human populations; Popocatepetl (5,426 m) poses a threat to Mexico City; other historically active volcanoes include Barcena, Ceboruco, El Chichon, Michoacan-Guanajuato, Pico de Orizaba, San Martin, Socorro, and Tacana; see note 2 under "Geography - note"

Geography - note: *note 1:* strategic location on southern border of the US; Mexico is one of the countries along the Ring of Fire, a belt of active volcanoes and earthquake epicenters bordering the Pacific Ocean; up to 90% of the world's earthquakes and some 75% of the world's volcanoes occur within the Ring of Fire
note 2: some of the world's most important food crops were first domesticated in Mexico; the "Three Sisters" companion plants – winter squash, maize (corn), and climbing beans – served as the main agricultural crops for various North American Indian groups; all three apparently originated in Mexico but then were widely disseminated through much of North America; avocado, amaranth, and chili peppers also emanate from Mexico, as does vanilla, the world's most popular aroma and flavor spice; although cherry tomatoes originated in Ecuador, their domestication in Mexico transformed them into the larger modern tomato
note 3: the Sac Actun cave system at 348 km (216 mi) is the longest underwater cave in the world and the second longest cave worldwide, after Mammoth Cave in the United States (see "Geography - note" under United States)
note 4: the prominent Yucatán Peninsula that divides the Gulf of Mexico from the Caribbean Sea is shared by Mexico, Guatemala, and Belize; just on the northern coast of Yucatan, near the town of Chicxulub (pronounce cheek-sha-loob), lie the remnants of a massive crater (some 150 km in diameter and extending well out into the Gulf of Mexico); formed by an asteroid or comet when it struck the earth 66 million years ago, the impact is now widely accepted as initiating a worldwide climate disruption that caused a mass extinction of 75% of all the earth's plant and animal species – including the non-avian dinosaurs

PEOPLE AND SOCIETY

Population: *total:* 130,739,927
male: 63,899,138
female: 66,840,789 (2024 est.)
comparison rankings: female 10; male 10; total 10

Nationality: *noun:* Mexican(s)
adjective: Mexican

Ethnic groups: Mestizo (Indigenous-Spanish) 62%, predominantly Indigenous 21%, Indigenous 7%, other 10% (mostly European) (2012 est.)
note: Mexico does not collect census data on ethnicity

Languages: Spanish only 93.8%, Spanish and indigenous languages (including Mayan, Nahuatl, and others) 5.4%, indigenous only 0.6%, unspecified 0.2% (2020 est.)
major-language sample(s):
La Libreta Informativa del Mundo, la fuente indispensable de información básica. (Spanish)

Religions: Roman Catholic 78%, Protestant/evangelical Christian 11.2%, other 0.002%, unaffiliated (includes atheism) 10.6% (2020 est.)

Age structure: *0-14 years:* 23.3% (male 15,647,805/female 14,754,004)
15-64 years: 68.6% (male 43,651,105/female 45,983,174)
65 years and over: 8.2% (2024 est.) (male 4,600,228/female 6,103,611)

Dependency ratios: *total dependency ratio:* 49.4

youth dependency ratio: 37.3
elderly dependency ratio: 12.2
potential support ratio: 8.2 (2021 est.)

Median age: *total:* 30.8 years (2024 est.)
male: 28.8 years
female: 32.7 years
comparison ranking: total 132

Population growth rate: 0.72% (2024 est.)
comparison ranking: 122

Birth rate: 14.3 births/1,000 population (2024 est.)
comparison ranking: 118

Death rate: 6.5 deaths/1,000 population (2024 est.)
comparison ranking: 134

Net migration rate: -0.7 migrant(s)/1,000 population (2024 est.)
comparison ranking: 131

Population distribution: most of the population is found in the middle of the country between the states of Jalisco and Veracruz; approximately a quarter of the population lives in and around Mexico City

Urbanization: *urban population:* 81.6% of total population (2023)
rate of urbanization: 1.4% annual rate of change (2020-25 est.)

Major urban areas - population: 22.281 million MEXICO CITY (capital), 5.420 million Guadalajara, 5.117 million Monterrey, 3.345 million Puebla, 2.626 million Toluca de Lerdo, 2.260 million Tijuana (2023)

Sex ratio: *at birth:* 1.05 male(s)/female
0-14 years: 1.06 male(s)/female
15-64 years: 0.95 male(s)/female
65 years and over: 0.75 male(s)/female
total population: 0.96 male(s)/female (2024 est.)

Mother's mean age at first birth: 21.3 years (2008 est.)

Maternal mortality ratio: 59 deaths/100,000 live births (2020 est.)
comparison ranking: 94

Infant mortality rate: *total:* 12.1 deaths/1,000 live births (2024 est.)
male: 13.4 deaths/1,000 live births
female: 10.9 deaths/1,000 live births
comparison ranking: total 109

Life expectancy at birth: *total population:* 74.6 years (2024 est.)
male: 71.6 years
female: 77.7 years
comparison ranking: total population 140

Total fertility rate: 1.79 children born/woman (2024 est.)
comparison ranking: 142

Gross reproduction rate: 0.88 (2024 est.)

Contraceptive prevalence rate: 73.1% (2018)

Drinking water source: *improved: urban:* 100% of population
rural: 98.3% of population
total: 99.7% of population
unimproved: urban: 0% of population
rural: 1.7% of population
total: 0.3% of population (2020 est.)

Current health expenditure: 6.2% of GDP (2020)

Physician density: 2.43 physicians/1,000 population (2019)

Hospital bed density: 1 beds/1,000 population (2018)

Sanitation facility access: *improved: urban:* 99.9% of population
rural: 96.4% of population
total: 99.2% of population
unimproved: urban: 0.1% of population
rural: 3.6% of population
total: 0.8% of population (2020 est.)

Obesity - adult prevalence rate: 28.9% (2016)
comparison ranking: 28

Alcohol consumption per capita: *total:* 4.25 liters of pure alcohol (2019 est.)
beer: 3.72 liters of pure alcohol (2019 est.)
wine: 0.19 liters of pure alcohol (2019 est.)
spirits: 0.19 liters of pure alcohol (2019 est.)
other alcohols: 0.15 liters of pure alcohol (2019 est.)
comparison ranking: total 91

Tobacco use: *total:* 13.1% (2020 est.)
male: 19.9% (2020 est.)
female: 6.2% (2020 est.)
comparison ranking: total 116

Children under the age of 5 years underweight: 4.2% (2021)
comparison ranking: 79

Currently married women (ages 15-49): 56.6% (2023 est.)

Child marriage: *women married by age 15:* 3.6%
women married by age 18: 20.7% (2018 est.)

Education expenditures: 4.3% of GDP (2018 est.)
comparison ranking: 107

Literacy: *definition:* age 15 and over can read and write
total population: 95.2%
male: 96.1%
female: 94.5% (2020)

School life expectancy (primary to tertiary education): *total:* 15 years
male: 15 years
female: 15 years (2020)

ENVIRONMENT

Environment - current issues: scarcity of hazardous waste disposal facilities; rural to urban migration; natural freshwater resources scarce and polluted in north, inaccessible and poor quality in center and extreme southeast; raw sewage and industrial effluents polluting rivers in urban areas; deforestation; widespread erosion; desertification; deteriorating agricultural lands; serious air and water pollution in the national capital and urban centers along US-Mexico border; land subsidence in Valley of Mexico caused by groundwater depletion
note: the government considers the lack of clean water and deforestation national security issues

Environment - international agreements: *party to:* Biodiversity, Climate Change, Climate Change-Kyoto Protocol, Climate Change-Paris Agreement, Comprehensive Nuclear Test Ban, Desertification, Endangered Species, Hazardous Wastes, Law of the Sea, Marine Dumping-London Convention, Marine Dumping-London Protocol, Marine Life Conservation, Nuclear Test Ban, Ozone Layer Protection, Ship Pollution, Tropical Timber 2006, Wetlands, Whaling
signed, but not ratified: none of the selected agreements

Climate: varies from tropical to desert

Urbanization: *urban population:* 81.6% of total population (2023)
rate of urbanization: 1.4% annual rate of change (2020-25 est.)

Revenue from forest resources: 0.1% of GDP (2018 est.)
comparison ranking: 111

Revenue from coal: 0.03% of GDP (2018 est.)
comparison ranking: 36

Air pollutants: *particulate matter emissions:* 17.83 micrograms per cubic meter (2019 est.)
carbon dioxide emissions: 486.41 megatons (2016 est.)
methane emissions: 135.77 megatons (2020 est.)

Waste and recycling: *municipal solid waste generated annually:* 53.1 million tons (2015 est.)
municipal solid waste recycled annually: 2.655 million tons (2013 est.)
percent of municipal solid waste recycled: 5% (2013 est.)

Major lakes (area sq km): *fresh water lake(s):* Laguna de Chapala - 1,140 sq km
salt water lake(s): Laguna de Terminos - 1,550 sq km

Major rivers (by length in km): Rio Grande river mouth (shared with US [s]) - 3,057 km; Colorado river mouth (shared with US [s]) - 2,333 km
note – [s] after country name indicates river source; [m] after country name indicates river mouth

Major watersheds (area sq km): Atlantic Ocean drainage: *(Gulf of Mexico)* Rio Grande/Bravo (607,965 sq km)

Pacific Ocean drainage: *(Gulf of California)* Colorado (703,148 sq km)

Major aquifers: Atlantic and Gulf Coastal Plains Aquifer

Total water withdrawal: *municipal:* 13.17 billion cubic meters (2020 est.)
industrial: 8.56 billion cubic meters (2020 est.)
agricultural: 67.83 billion cubic meters (2020 est.)

Total renewable water resources: 461.89 billion cubic meters (2020 est.)

Geoparks: *total global geoparks and regional networks:* 2
global geoparks and regional networks: Comarca Minera, Hidalgo; Mixteca Alta, Oaxaca (2023)

GOVERNMENT

Country name: *conventional long form:* United Mexican States
conventional short form: Mexico
local long form: Estados Unidos Mexicanos
local short form: Mexico
former: Mexican Republic, Mexican Empire
etymology: named after the capital city, whose name stems from the Mexica, the largest and most powerful branch of the Aztecs; the meaning of the name is uncertain

Government type: federal presidential republic

Capital: *name:* Mexico City (Ciudad de Mexico)
geographic coordinates: 19 26 N, 99 08 W
time difference: UTC-6 (1 hour behind Washington, DC, during Standard Time)
daylight saving time: DST was permanently removed in October 2022
time zone note: Mexico has four time zones
etymology: named after the Mexica, the largest and most powerful branch of the Aztecs; the meaning of the name is uncertain

Administrative divisions: 32 states (estados, singular - estado); Aguascalientes, Baja California, Baja California Sur, Campeche, Chiapas, Chihuahua, Coahuila, Colima, Cuidad de Mexico, Durango,

Guanajuato, Guerrero, Hidalgo, Jalisco, Mexico, Michoacan, Morelos, Nayarit, Nuevo Leon, Oaxaca, Puebla, Queretaro, Quintana Roo, San Luis Potosi, Sinaloa, Sonora, Tabasco, Tamaulipas, Tlaxcala, Veracruz, Yucatan, Zacatecas

Independence: 16 September 1810 (declared independence from Spain); 27 September 1821 (recognized by Spain)

National holiday: Independence Day, 16 September (1810)

Legal system: civil law system with US constitutional law influence; judicial review of legislative acts

Constitution: *history:* several previous; latest approved 5 February 1917
amendments: proposed by the Congress of the Union; passage requires approval by at least two thirds of the members present and approval by a majority of the state legislatures; amended many times, last in 2024

International law organization participation: accepts compulsory ICJ jurisdiction with reservations; accepts ICCt jurisdiction

Citizenship: *citizenship by birth:* yes
citizenship by descent only: yes
dual citizenship recognized: not specified
residency requirement for naturalization: 5 years

Suffrage: 18 years of age; universal and compulsory

Executive branch: *chief of state:* President Claudia SHEINBAUM Pardo (since 1 October 2024)
head of government: President Claudia SHEINBAUM Pardo (since 1 October 2024)
cabinet: Cabinet appointed by the president
elections/appointments: president directly elected by simple majority popular vote for a single 6-year term; election last held on 2 June 2024 (next to be held in 2030)
election results:
2024: Claudia SHEINBAUM Pardo elected president; percent of vote - Claudia SHEINBAUM Pardo (MORENA) 59.4%, Xóchitl GÁLVEZ Ruiz (PAN) 27.9%, Jorge Álvarez MÁYNEZ (MC) 10.4%, other 2.3%
2018: Andrés Manuel LÓPEZ OBRADOR elected president; percent of vote - Andrés Manuel LÓPEZ OBRADOR (MORENA) 53.2%, Ricardo ANAYA Cortés (PAN) 22.3%, José Antonio MEADE Kuribreña (PRI) 16.4%, Jaime RODRÍGUEZ Calderón 5.2% (independent), other 2.9%
2012: Enrique PEÑA NIETO elected president; percent of vote - Enrique PEÑA NIETO (PRI) 38.2%, Andrés Manuel LÓPEZ OBRADOR (PRD) 31.6%, Josefina Eugenia VÁZQUEZ Mota (PAN) 25.4%, other 4.8%
note: the president is both chief of state and head of government

Legislative branch: *description:*
bicameral National Congress or Congreso de la Unión consists of:
Senate or Cámara de Senadores (128 seats; 96 members directly elected in multi-seat constituencies by simple majority vote and 32 directly elected in a single, nationwide constituency by proportional representation vote; members serve 6-year terms)
Chamber of Deputies or Cámara de Diputados (500 seats; 300 members directly elected in single-seat constituencies by simple majority vote and 200 directly elected in a single, nationwide constituency by proportional representation vote; members serve 3-year terms)
elections: Senate - last held on 2 June 2024 (next to be held in 2030)
Chamber of Deputies - last held on 2 June 2024 (next to be held in 2027)
election results: Senate - percent of vote by party - NA; seats by party - NA; note - awaiting official results from the 2 June 2024 election
Chamber of Deputies - percent of vote by party - NA; seats by party - NA; note - awaiting official results from the 2 June 2024 election
note: as of the 2018 election, senators will be eligible for a second term and deputies up to 4 consecutive terms

Judicial branch: *highest court(s):* Supreme Court of Justice or Suprema Corte de Justicia de la Nación (consists of the chief justice and 11 justices and organized into civil, criminal, administrative, and labor panels) and the Electoral Tribunal of the Federal Judiciary (organized into the superior court, with 7 judges including the court president, and 5 regional courts, each with 3 judges)
judge selection and term of office: Supreme Court justices nominated by the president of the republic and approved by two-thirds vote of the members present in the Senate; justices serve 15-year terms; Electoral Tribunal superior and regional court judges nominated by the Supreme Court and elected by two-thirds vote of members present in the Senate; superior court president elected from among its members to hold office for a 4-year term; other judges of the superior and regional courts serve staggered, 9-year terms
subordinate courts: federal level includes circuit, collegiate, and unitary courts; state and district level courts
note: in April 2021, the Mexican congress passed a judicial reform which changed 7 articles of the constitution and preceded a new Organic Law on the Judicial Branch of the Federation

Political parties: Citizen's Movement (Movimiento Ciudadano) or MC
Institutional Revolutionary Party (Partido Revolucionario Institucional) or PRI
Labor Party (Partido del Trabajo) or PT
Mexican Green Ecological Party (Partido Verde Ecologista de México) or PVEM
Movement for National Regeneration (Movimiento Regeneración Nacional) or MORENA
National Action Party (Partido Acción Nacional) or PAN
Party of the Democratic Revolution (Partido de la Revolución Democrática) or PRD
This Is For Mexico (Va Por México) (alliance that includes PAN, PRI, and PRD)
Together We Make History (Juntos Hacemos Historia) (alliance that included MORENA, PT, PVEM) (dissolved 23 December 2020)

International organization participation: ACS, APEC, Australia Group, BCIE, BIS, CABEI, CAN (observer), Caricom (observer), CD, CDB, CE (observer), CELAC, CSN (observer), EBRD, FAO, FATF, G-3, G-15, G-20, G-24, G-5, IADB, IAEA, IBRD, ICAO, ICC (national committees), ICCt, ICRM, IDA, IFAD, IFC, IFRCS, IHO, ILO, IMF, IMO, IMSO, Interpol, IOC, IOM, IPU, ISO, ITSO, ITU, ITUC (NGOs), LAES, LAIA, MIGA, NAFTA, NAM (observer), NEA, NSG, OAS, OECD, OPANAL, OPCW, Pacific Alliance, Paris Club (associate), PCA, SICA (observer), UN, UNASUR (observer), UNCTAD, UNESCO, UNHCR, UNIDO, Union Latina (observer), UNOOSA, UNWTO, UPU, USMCA, Wassenaar Arrangement, WCO, WFTU (NGOs), WHO, WIPO, WMO, WTO

Diplomatic representation in the US: *chief of mission:* Ambassador Esteban MOCTEZUMA Barragán (since 20 April 2021)
chancery: 1911 Pennsylvania Avenue NW, Washington, DC 20006
telephone: [1] (202) 728-1600
FAX: [1] (202) 728-1698
email address and website:
mexembusa@sre.gob.mx
https://embamex.sre.gob.mx/eua/index.php/en/
consulate(s) general: Atlanta (GA), Austin (TX), Boston (MA), Chicago (IL), Dallas (TX), Denver (GA), El Paso (TX), Houston (TX), Laredo (TX), Miami (FL), New York (NY), Nogales (AZ), Phoenix (AZ), Raleigh (NC), Sacramento (CA), San Antonio (TX), San Diego (CA), San Francisco (CA), San Jose (CA), San Juan (Puerto Rico)
consulate(s): Albuquerque (NM), Boise (ID), Brownsville (TX), Calexico (CA), Del Rio (TX), Detroit (MI), Douglas (AZ), Eagle Pass (TX), Fresno (CA), Indianapolis (IN), Kansas City (MO), Las Vegas (NV), Little Rock (AR), Los Angeles (CA), McAllen (TX), Milwaukee (WI), New Orleans (LA), Oklahoma City (OK), Omaha (NE), Orlando (FL), Oxnard (CA), Philadelphia (PA), Portland (OR), Presidio (TX), Salt Lake City (UT), San Bernardino (CA), Santa Ana (CA), Seattle (WA), St. Paul (MN), Tucson (AZ), Yuma (AZ)

Diplomatic representation from the US: *chief of mission:* Ambassador Ken SALAZAR (since 14 September 2021)
embassy: Paseo de la Reforma 305, Colonia Cuauhtémoc, 06500 Mexico, CDMX
mailing address: 8700 Mexico City Place, Washington DC 20521-8700
telephone: (011) [52]-55-5080-2000
FAX: (011) 52-55-5080-2005
email address and website:
ACSMexicoCity@state.gov
https://mx.usembassy.gov/
consulate(s) general: Ciudad Juárez, Guadalajara, Hermosillo, Matamoros, Mérida, Monterrey, Nogales, Nuevo Laredo, Tijuana

Flag description: three equal vertical bands of green (hoist side), white, and red; Mexico's coat of arms (an eagle with a snake in its beak perched on a cactus) is centered in the white band; green signifies hope, joy, and love; white represents peace and honesty; red stands for hardiness, bravery, strength, and valor; the coat of arms is derived from a legend that the wandering Aztec people were to settle at a location where they would see an eagle on a cactus eating a snake; the city they founded, Tenochtitlan, is now Mexico City
note: similar to the flag of Italy, which is shorter, uses lighter shades of green and red, and does not display anything in its white band

National symbol(s): golden eagle, dahlia; national colors: green, white, red

National anthem: *name:* "Himno Nacional Mexicano" (National Anthem of Mexico)
lyrics/music: Francisco Gonzalez BOCANEGRA/ Jaime Nuno ROCA
note: adopted 1943, in use since 1854; also known as "Mexicanos, al grito de Guerra" (Mexicans, to the War Cry); according to tradition, Francisco Gonzalez BOCANEGRA, an accomplished poet, was uninterested in submitting lyrics to a national anthem

contest; his fiancee locked him in a room and refused to release him until the lyrics were completed

National heritage: *total World Heritage Sites:* 35 (27 cultural, 6 natural, 2 mixed)
selected World Heritage Site locales: Historic Mexico City (c); Earliest 16th-Century Monasteries on the Slopes of Popocatepetl (c); Teotihuacan (c); Whale Sanctuary of El Vizcaino (n); Monarch Butterfly Biosphere Reserve (n); Tehuacán-Cuicatlán Valley (m); Historic Puebla (c); El Tajin (c); Historic Tlacotalpan (c); Historic Oaxaca and Monte Albán (c); Palenque (c); Chichen-Itza (c); Uxmal (c)

ECONOMY

Economic overview: upper-middle income economy; highly integrated with US via trade and nearshore manufacturing; low unemployment; inflation gradually decreasing amid tight monetary policy; state intervention in energy sector and public infrastructure projects; challenges from income inequality, corruption, and cartel-based violence

Real GDP (purchasing power parity): $2.873 trillion (2023 est.)
$2.783 trillion (2022 est.)
$2.678 trillion (2021 est.)
note: data in 2021 dollars
comparison ranking: 13

Real GDP growth rate: 3.23% (2023 est.)
3.95% (2022 est.)
5.74% (2021 est.)
note: annual GDP % growth based on constant local currency
comparison ranking: 100

Real GDP per capita: $22,400 (2023 est.)
$21,800 (2022 est.)
$21,100 (2021 est.)
note: data in 2021 dollars
comparison ranking: 94

GDP (official exchange rate): $1.789 trillion (2023 est.)
note: data in current dollars at official exchange rate

Inflation rate (consumer prices): 5.53% (2023 est.)
7.9% (2022 est.)
5.69% (2021 est.)
note: annual % change based on consumer prices
comparison ranking: 117

Credit ratings: Fitch rating: BBB- (2020)

Moody's rating: Baa1 (2020)

Standard & Poors rating: BBB (2020)
note: The year refers to the year in which the current credit rating was first obtained.

GDP - composition, by sector of origin: *agriculture:* 4% (2023 est.)
industry: 31.8% (2023 est.)
services: 58.3% (2023 est.)
note: figures may not total 100% due to non-allocated consumption not captured in sector-reported data
comparison rankings: services 99; industry 56; agriculture 127

GDP - composition, by end use: *household consumption:* 70.4% (2023 est.)
government consumption: 11% (2023 est.)
investment in fixed capital: 24.4% (2023 est.)
investment in inventories: 0.4% (2023 est.)
exports of goods and services: 36.2% (2023 est.)
imports of goods and services: -37.9% (2023 est.)
note: figures may not total 100% due to rounding or gaps in data collection

Agricultural products: sugarcane, maize, milk, oranges, sorghum, tomatoes, chicken, wheat, chilies/peppers, lemons/limes (2022)
note: top ten agricultural products based on tonnage

Industries: food and beverages, tobacco, chemicals, iron and steel, petroleum, mining, textiles, clothing, motor vehicles, consumer durables, tourism

Industrial production growth rate: 3.52% (2023 est.)
note: annual % change in industrial value added based on constant local currency
comparison ranking: 93

Labor force: 60.042 million (2023 est.)
note: number of people ages 15 or older who are employed or seeking work
comparison ranking: 12

Unemployment rate: 2.81% (2023 est.)
3.26% (2022 est.)
4.02% (2021 est.)
note: % of labor force seeking employment
comparison ranking: 37

Youth unemployment rate (ages 15-24): *total:* 6.1% (2023 est.)
male: 5.8% (2023 est.)
female: 6.7% (2023 est.)
note: % of labor force ages 15-24 seeking employment
comparison ranking: total 166

Population below poverty line: 36.3% (2022 est.)
note: % of population with income below national poverty line

Gini Index coefficient - distribution of family income: 43.5 (2022 est.)
note: index (0-100) of income distribution; higher values represent greater inequality
comparison ranking: 28

Average household expenditures: *on food:* 25.7% of household expenditures (2022 est.)
on alcohol and tobacco: 3.6% of household expenditures (2022 est.)

Household income or consumption by percentage share: *lowest 10%:* 2.1% (2022 est.)
highest 10%: 34.4% (2022 est.)
note: % share of income accruing to lowest and highest 10% of population

Remittances: 3.7% of GDP (2023 est.)
4.2% of GDP (2022 est.)
4.19% of GDP (2021 est.)
note: personal transfers and compensation between resident and non-resident individuals/households/entities

Budget: *revenues:* $282.751 billion (2022 est.)
expenditures: $327.211 billion (2022 est.)
note: central government revenues (excluding grants) and expenses converted to US dollars at average official exchange rate for year indicated

Public debt: 44.05% of GDP (2022 est.)
note: central government debt as a % of GDP
comparison ranking: 123

Taxes and other revenues: 13.44% (of GDP) (2022 est.)
note: central government tax revenue as a % of GDP
comparison ranking: 151

Current account balance: -$5.716 billion (2023 est.)
-$17.667 billion (2022 est.)
-$4.493 billion (2021 est.)
note: balance of payments - net trade and primary/secondary income in current dollars
comparison ranking: 186

Exports: $649.312 billion (2023 est.)
$630.384 billion (2022 est.)
$537.714 billion (2021 est.)
note: balance of payments - exports of goods and services in current dollars
comparison ranking: 16

Exports - partners: US 77%, Canada 4%, China 2%, Taiwan 1%, South Korea 1% (2022)
note: top five export partners based on percentage share of exports

Exports - commodities: cars, computers, vehicle parts/accessories, crude petroleum, trucks (2022)
note: top five export commodities based on value in dollars

Imports: $673.828 billion (2023 est.)
$672.914 billion (2022 est.)
$560.842 billion (2021 est.)
note: balance of payments - imports of goods and services in current dollars
comparison ranking: 13

Imports - partners: US 56%, China 17%, Germany 3%, South Korea 3%, Japan 2% (2022)
note: top five import partners based on percentage share of imports

Imports - commodities: refined petroleum, vehicle parts/accessories, machine parts, integrated circuits, natural gas (2022)
note: top five import commodities based on value in dollars

Reserves of foreign exchange and gold: $214.317 billion (2023 est.)
$201.119 billion (2022 est.)
$207.799 billion (2021 est.)
note: holdings of gold (year-end prices)/foreign exchange/special drawing rights in current dollars
comparison ranking: 16

Debt - external: $286.005 billion (2022 est.)
note: present value of external debt in current US dollars
comparison ranking: 2

Exchange rates: Mexican pesos (MXN) per US dollar -

Exchange rates: 17.759 (2023 est.)
20.127 (2022 est.)
20.272 (2021 est.)
21.486 (2020 est.)
19.264 (2019 est.)

ENERGY

Electricity access: *electrification - total population:* 100% (2022 est.)
electrification - urban areas: 99.8%
electrification - rural areas: 100%

Electricity: *installed generating capacity:* 104.318 million kW (2022 est.)
consumption: 296.969 billion kWh (2022 est.)
exports: 1.447 billion kWh (2022 est.)
imports: 4.551 billion kWh (2022 est.)
transmission/distribution losses: 39.275 billion kWh (2022 est.)
comparison rankings: transmission/distribution losses 204; imports 48; exports 63; consumption 15; installed generating capacity 14

Electricity generation sources: *fossil fuels:* 75% of total installed capacity (2022 est.)
nuclear: 3.2% of total installed capacity (2022 est.)
solar: 3.5% of total installed capacity (2022 est.)
wind: 6.1% of total installed capacity (2022 est.)
hydroelectricity: 10.2% of total installed capacity (2022 est.)

geothermal: 1.5% of total installed capacity (2022 est.)
biomass and waste: 0.6% of total installed capacity (2022 est.)

Nuclear energy: Number of operational nuclear reactors: 2 (2023)

Net capacity of operational nuclear reactors: 1.55GW (2023 est.)

Percent of total electricity production: 4.9% (2023 est.)

Coal: *production:* 7.453 million metric tons (2022 est.)
consumption: 18.423 million metric tons (2022 est.)
exports: 2,000 metric tons (2022 est.)
imports: 9.917 million metric tons (2022 est.)
proven reserves: 1.211 billion metric tons (2022 est.)

Petroleum: *total petroleum production:* 2.101 million bbl/day (2023 est.)
refined petroleum consumption: 1.737 million bbl/day (2023 est.)
crude oil estimated reserves: 5.786 billion barrels (2021 est.)

Natural gas: *production:* 31.422 billion cubic meters (2022 est.)
consumption: 90.566 billion cubic meters (2022 est.)
exports: 30.129 million cubic meters (2022 est.)
imports: 59.436 billion cubic meters (2022 est.)
proven reserves: 180.322 billion cubic meters (2021 est.)

Carbon dioxide emissions: 453.6 million metric tonnes of CO2 (2022 est.)
from coal and metallurgical coke: 38.781 million metric tonnes of CO2 (2022 est.)
from petroleum and other liquids: 246.324 million metric tonnes of CO2 (2022 est.)
from consumed natural gas: 168.494 million metric tonnes of CO2 (2022 est.)
comparison ranking: total emissions 14

Energy consumption per capita: 59.319 million Btu/person (2022 est.)
comparison ranking: 81

COMMUNICATIONS

Telephones - fixed lines: *total subscriptions:* 27.185 million (2022 est.)
subscriptions per 100 inhabitants: 21 (2022 est.)
comparison ranking: total subscriptions 10

Telephones - mobile cellular: *total subscriptions:* 127.872 million (2022 est.)
subscriptions per 100 inhabitants: 100 (2022 est.)
comparison ranking: total subscriptions 14

Telecommunication systems: *general assessment:* with a large population and relatively low broadband and mobile penetration, (86 lines for mobile broadband for every 100 habitants in June 2021) Mexico's telecom sector has potential for growth; adequate telephone service for business and government; improving quality and increasing mobile cellular availability, with mobile subscribers far outnumbering fixed-line subscribers (24.6 million fixed line subscribers and 125 million mobile line subscribers in June 2021); relatively low broadband and mobile penetration, potential for growth and international investment; extensive microwave radio relay network; considerable use of fiber-optic cable and coaxial cable; 5G development slow in part due to high costs (2021)
domestic: fixed-line teledensity 19 lines per every 100; mobile-cellular teledensity is 98 per 100 persons (2021)
international: country code - 52; Columbus-2 fiber-optic submarine cable with access to the US, Virgin Islands, Canary Islands, Spain, and Italy; the ARCOS-1 and the MAYA-1 submarine cable system together provide access to Central America, parts of South America and the Caribbean, and the U.S.; Pan-American Crossing (PAC) submarine cable system provides access to Panama, California, U.S., and Costa Rica; Lazaro Cardenas-Manzanillo Santiago submarines cable system (LCMSSCS) provides access to Michoacan, Guerrero, and Colima, Mexico; AMX-1 submarine cable system with access to Colombia, Brazil, Puerto Rico, Gulf of California Cable submarine cable systems that connects La Paz, Baja California Sur and Topolobambo, Sinaloa; and Aurora submarine cable system provides access to Guatemala, Panama, Ecuador, Colombia, Mexico, and the U.S. satellite earth stations - 124 (36 Intelsat, 1 Solidaridad (giving Mexico improved access to South America, Central America, and much of the US as well as enhancing domestic communications), 9 Panamsat, numerous Inmarsat mobile earth stations); linked to Central American Microwave System of trunk connections (2022)

Broadcast media: telecom reform in 2013 enabled the creation of new broadcast television channels after decades of a quasi-monopoly; Mexico has 885 TV stations and 1,841 radio stations and most are privately owned; the Televisa group once had a virtual monopoly in TV broadcasting, but new broadcasting groups and foreign satellite and cable operators are now available; in 2016, Mexico became the first country in Latin America to complete the transition from analog to digital transmissions, allowing for better image and audio quality and a wider selection of programming from networks (2022)

Internet country code: .mx

Internet users: *total:* 98.8 million (2021 est.)
percent of population: 76% (2021 est.)
comparison ranking: total 9

Broadband - fixed subscriptions: *total:* 21,936,131 (2020 est.)
subscriptions per 100 inhabitants: 17 (2020 est.)
comparison ranking: total 11

TRANSPORTATION

National air transport system: *number of registered air carriers:* 16 (2020)
inventory of registered aircraft operated by air carriers: 370
annual passenger traffic on registered air carriers: 64,569,640 (2018)
annual freight traffic on registered air carriers: 1,090,380,000 (2018) mt-km

Civil aircraft registration country code prefix: XA

Airports: 1,485 (2024)
comparison ranking: 4

Heliports: 460 (2024)

Pipelines: 17,210 km natural gas (2022), 9,757 km oil (2017), 10,237 km refined products (2020)

Railways: *total:* 23,389 km (2017)
standard gauge: 23,389 km (2017) 1.435-m gauge (27 km electrified)
comparison ranking: total 12

Roadways: *total:* 704,884 km
paved: 175,526 km (includes 10,845 km of expressways)
unpaved: 529,358 km (2017)
comparison ranking: total 12

Waterways: 2,900 km (2012) (navigable rivers and coastal canals mostly connected with ports on the country's east coast)
comparison ranking: 35

Merchant marine: *total:* 674 (2023)
by type: bulk carrier 4, general cargo 11, oil tanker 32, other 627
comparison ranking: total 34

Ports: *total ports:* 35 (2024)
large: 0
medium: 7
small: 10
very small: 14
size unknown: 4
ports with oil terminals: 21
key ports: Acapulco, Ensenada, Manzanillo, Mazatlan, Tampico, Tuxpan, Veracruz

MILITARY AND SECURITY

Military and security forces: the Mexican Armed Forces (Fuerzas Armadas de México) are divided between the Secretariat of National Defense and the Secretariat of the Navy:
Secretariat of National Defense (Secretaria de Defensa Nacional, SEDENA): Army (Ejercito), Mexican Air Force (Fuerza Aerea Mexicana, FAM); Secretariat of the Navy (Secretaria de Marina, SEMAR): Mexican Navy (Armada de Mexico (ARM), includes Naval Air Force (FAN), Mexican Naval Infantry Corps (Cuerpo de Infanteria de Marina, Mexmar or CIM))
Secretariat of Security and Civilian Protection/SEDENA: National Guard (2024)
note: the National Guard was formed in 2019 of personnel from the former Federal Police (disbanded in December 2019) and military police units of the Army and Navy; the Guard was placed under the civilian-led Secretariat of Security and Civilian Protection, while the SEDENA had day-to-day operational control and provided the commanders and the training; in September 2022, Mexico's Congress passed legislation shifting complete control of the National Guard to the military; however, in 2023 the move was ruled unconstitutional by the Supreme Court; the Guard, along with state and municipal police, is responsible for enforcing the law and maintaining order; the regular military also actively supports police operations

Military expenditures: 0.6% of GDP (2023 est.)
0.7% of GDP (2022 est.)
0.7% of GDP (2021 est.)
0.6% of GDP (2020 est.)
0.5% of GDP (2019 est.)
comparison ranking: 158

Military and security service personnel strengths: information varies; approximately 240,000 armed forces personnel (180,000 Army; 10,000 Air Force; 50,000 Navy, including about 20,000 marines); approximately 110,000 National Guard personnel (2023)

Military equipment inventories and acquisitions: the Mexican military inventory includes a mix of domestically produced and imported weapons and equipment from a variety of mostly Western suppliers, particularly the US; a considerable portion of its inventory, such as ships and fighter aircraft, are older, secondhand items from the US; over the past decade, the Mexican military has made efforts to acquire more modern equipment; Mexico's defense industry produces some naval vessels and light armored vehicles, as well as small arms and other miscellaneous equipment (2023)

Military service age and obligation: *18 years of age (16 with parental consent) for voluntary enlistment for men and women; 18 years of age for compulsory military service for men (selection for service determined by lottery); conscript service obligation is 12 months; those selected serve on Saturdays in a Batallón del Servicio Militar Nacional (National Military Service Battalion) composed entirely of 12-month Servicio Militar Nacional (SMN) conscripts; conscripts remain in reserve status until the age of 40; cadets enrolled in military schools from the age of 15 are considered members of the armed forces; National Guard:* single men and women 18-30 years of age may volunteer (2023)
note: as of 2023, women comprised about 10% of the active-duty Army, Air Force, and Navy, and about 14% of the National Guard

Military - note: the Mexican military is responsible for defending the independence, integrity, and sovereignty of Mexico, as well as providing for internal security, disaster response, humanitarian assistance, and socio-economic development; in recent years, internal security duties have been a key focus, particularly in countering narcotics trafficking and organized crime groups, as well as border control and immigration enforcement; the constitution was amended in 2019 to grant the president the authority to use the armed forces to protect internal and national security, and courts have upheld the legality of the armed forces' role in law enforcement activities in support of civilian authorities through 2028; the military also provides security for strategic facilities, such as oil production infrastructure, and administers most of the country's land and sea ports and customs services, plus a state-owned development bank; in addition, President LÓPEZ OBRADOR placed the military in charge of a growing number of infrastructure projects, such as building and operating a new airport for Mexico City and sections of a train line in the country's southeast (2024)

SPACE

Space agency/agencies: Mexican Space Agency (Agencia Espacial Mexicana or AEM; established 2010 and began operating in 2013) (2024)

Space program overview: the AEM's focus is on coordinating Mexico's space policy and the country's commercial space sector, including developing specialists, technologies, and infrastructure, and acquiring satellites; manufactures and operates communications and scientific satellites; conducts research in a range of space-related capabilities and technologies, including satellites and satellite payloads, telecommunications, remote sensing, robotics, Earth and weather sciences, astronomy, and astrophysics; has relations with a variety of foreign space agencies and commercial space industries, including those of Argentina, Brazil, Chile, the European Space Agency (ESA) and its member states (particularly France, Germany, and the UK), India, Peru, Russia, Ukraine, and the US; leading member of the Latin American and Caribbean Space Agency (ALCE) (2024)
note: further details about the key activities, programs, and milestones of the country's space program, as well as government spending estimates on the space sector, appear in the Space Programs reference guide

TRANSNATIONAL ISSUES

Refugees and internally displaced persons: *refugees (country of origin):* 35,755 (Honduras), 13,531 (El Salvador) (mid-year 2022); 113,108 (Venezuela) (economic and political crisis; includes Venezuelans who have claimed asylum, are recognized as refugees, or have received alternative legal stay) (2023)

IDPs: 386,000 (government's quashing of Zapatista uprising in 1994 in eastern Chiapas Region; drug cartel violence and government's military response since 2007; violence between and within indigenous groups) (2022)
stateless persons: 13 (2022)

Illicit drugs: significant source and transit country for fentanyl, fentanyl-laced counterfeit pills, other synthetic opioids, cocaine from South America, heroin, marijuana, and methamphetamine destined for the United States; a destination for synthetic drug precursor chemicals from China, India, and other countries

MICRONESIA, FEDERATED STATES OF

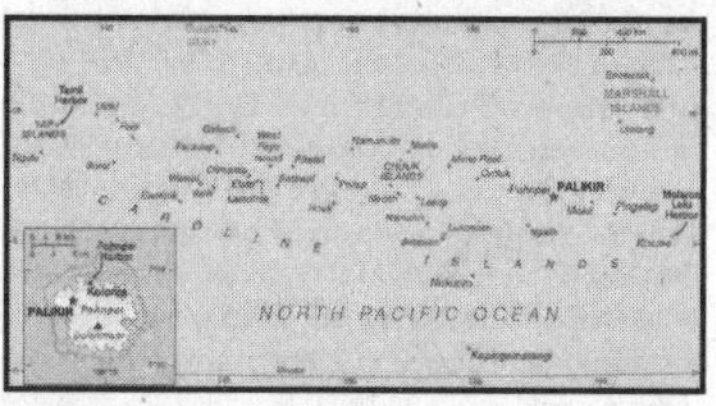

INTRODUCTION

Background: Each of the four states that compose the Federated States of Micronesia (FSM) – Chuuk, Kosrae, Pohnpei, and Yap – has its own unique history and cultural traditions. The first humans arrived in what is now the FSM in the second millennium B.C. In the 800s A.D., construction of the artificial islets at the Nan Madol complex in Pohnpei began, with the main architecture being built around 1200. At its height, Nan Madol united the approximately 25,000 people of Pohnpei under the Saudeleur Dynasty. By 1250, Kosrae was united in a kingdom centered in Leluh. Yap's society became strictly hierarchical, with chiefs receiving tributes from islands up to 1,100 km (700 mi) away. Widespread human settlement in Chuuk began in the 1300s, and the different islands in the Chuuk Lagoon were frequently at war with one another.

Portuguese and Spanish explorers visited a few of the islands in the 1500s, and Spain began exerting nominal, but not day-to-day, control over some of the islands – which they named the Caroline Islands – in the 1600s. In 1899, Spain sold all of the FSM to Germany. Japan seized the islands in 1914 and was granted a League of Nations mandate to administer them in 1920. The Japanese navy built bases across most of the islands and headquartered their Pacific naval operations in Chuuk. The US bombed Chuuk in 1944 but largely bypassed the other islands in its leapfrog campaign across the Pacific.

In 1947, the FSM came under US administration as part of the Trust Territory of the Pacific Islands, which comprised six districts: Chuuk, the Marshall Islands, the Northern Mariana Islands, Palau, Pohnpei, and Yap; Kosrae was separated from Pohnpei into a separate district in 1977. In 1979, Chuuk, Kosrae, Pohnpei, and Yap ratified the FSM Constitution and declared independence while the other three districts opted to pursue separate political status. There are significant inter-island rivalries stemming from their different histories and cultures. Chuuk, the most populous but poorest state, has pushed for secession, but an independence referendum has been repeatedly postponed.

GEOGRAPHY

Location: Oceania, island group in the North Pacific Ocean, about three-quarters of the way from Hawaii to Indonesia

Geographic coordinates: 6 55 N, 158 15 E

Map references: Oceania

Area: *total:* 702 sq km
land: 702 sq km
water: 0 sq km (fresh water only)
note: includes Pohnpei (Ponape), Chuuk (Truk) Islands, Yap Islands, and Kosrae (Kosaie)
comparison ranking: total 191

Area - comparative: four times the size of Washington, DC (land area only)

Land boundaries: *total:* 0 km

Coastline: 6,112 km

Maritime claims: *territorial sea:* 12 nm
exclusive economic zone: 200 nm

Climate: tropical; heavy year-round rainfall, especially in the eastern islands; located on southern edge of the typhoon belt with occasionally severe damage

Terrain: islands vary geologically from high mountainous islands to low, coral atolls; volcanic outcroppings on Pohnpei, Kosrae, and Chuuk

Elevation: *highest point:* Nanlaud on Pohnpei 782 m
lowest point: Pacific Ocean 0 m

Natural resources: timber, marine products, deep-seabed minerals, phosphate

Land use: *agricultural land:* 25.5% (2018 est.)
arable land: 2.3% (2018 est.)
permanent crops: 19.7% (2018 est.)
permanent pasture: 3.5% (2018 est.)
forest: 74.5% (2018 est.)
other: 0% (2018 est.)

Irrigated land: 0 sq km (2022)

Population distribution: the majority of the population lives in the coastal areas of the high islands; the mountainous interior is largely uninhabited; less than half of the population lives in urban areas

Natural hazards: typhoons (June to December)

Geography - note: composed of four major island groups totaling 607 islands

PEOPLE AND SOCIETY

Population: *total:* 99,603
male: 48,708
female: 50,895 (2024 est.)
comparison rankings: female 195; male 196; total 196

Nationality: *noun:* Micronesian(s)
adjective: Micronesian; Chuukese, Kosraen(s), Pohnpeian(s), Yapese

Ethnic groups: Chuukese/Mortlockese 49.3%, Pohnpeian 29.8%, Kosraean 6.3%, Yapese 5.7%, Yap outer islanders 5.1%, Polynesian 1.6%, Asian 1.4%, other 0.8% (2010 est.)

Languages: English (official and common language), Chuukese, Kosrean, Pohnpeian, Yapese, Ulithian, Woleaian, Nukuoro, Kapingamarangi

Religions: Roman Catholic 54.7%, Protestant 41.1% (includes Congregational 38.5%, Baptist 1.1%, Seventh Day Adventist 0.8%, Assembly of God 0.7%), Church of Jesus Christ 1.5%, other 1.9%, none 0.7%, unspecified 0.1% (2010 est.)

Age structure: *0-14 years:* 27% (male 13,673/female 13,239)
15-64 years: 67.3% (male 32,527/female 34,487)
65 years and over: 5.7% (2024 est.) (male 2,508/female 3,169)

Dependency ratios: *total dependency ratio:* 57.7
youth dependency ratio: 48.4
elderly dependency ratio: 9.3
potential support ratio: 10.8 (2021 est.)

Median age: *total:* 28.2 years (2024 est.)
male: 27.3 years
female: 29.1 years
comparison ranking: total 152

Population growth rate: -0.73% (2024 est.)
comparison ranking: 227

Birth rate: births/1,000 population (2024 est.)
comparison ranking: 80

Death rate: 4.2 deaths/1,000 population (2024 est.)
comparison ranking: 213

Net migration rate: -21 migrant(s)/1,000 population (2024 est.)
comparison ranking: 228

Population distribution: the majority of the population lives in the coastal areas of the high islands; the mountainous interior is largely uninhabited; less than half of the population lives in urban areas

Urbanization: *urban population:* 23.4% of total population (2023)
rate of urbanization: 1.52% annual rate of change (2020-25 est.)

Major urban areas - population: 7,000 PALIKIR (capital) (2018)

Sex ratio: *at birth:* 1.05 male(s)/female
0-14 years: 1.03 male(s)/female
15-64 years: 0.94 male(s)/female
65 years and over: 0.79 male(s)/female
total population: 0.96 male(s)/female (2024 est.)

Maternal mortality ratio: 74 deaths/100,000 live births (2020 est.)
comparison ranking: 81

Infant mortality rate: *total:* 20.9 deaths/1,000 live births (2024 est.)
male: 23.8 deaths/1,000 live births
female: 17.8 deaths/1,000 live births
comparison ranking: total 76

Life expectancy at birth: *total population:* 75 years (2024 est.)
male: 72.9 years
female: 77.2 years
comparison ranking: total population 133

Total fertility rate: 2.19 children born/woman (2024 est.)
comparison ranking: 86

Gross reproduction rate: 1.07 (2024 est.)

Drinking water source: *improved: total:* 78.6% of population
unimproved: total: 21.4% of population (2017 est.)

Current health expenditure: 11.6% of GDP (2020)

Hospital bed density: 3.2 beds/1,000 population

Sanitation facility access: *improved:*
total: 88.3% of population
unimproved:
total: 11.7% of population (2017 est.)

Obesity - adult prevalence rate: 45.8% (2016)
comparison ranking: 10

Alcohol consumption per capita: *total:* 1.59 liters of pure alcohol (2019 est.)
beer: 0.92 liters of pure alcohol (2019 est.)
wine: 0.13 liters of pure alcohol (2019 est.)
spirits: 0.52 liters of pure alcohol (2019 est.)
other alcohols: 0.01 liters of pure alcohol (2019 est.)
comparison ranking: total 138

Currently married women (ages 15-49): 51.7% (2023 est.)

Education expenditures: 9.7% of GDP (2018 est.)
comparison ranking: 6

ENVIRONMENT

Environment - current issues: overfishing; sea level rise due to climate change threatens land; water pollution, toxic pollution from mining; solid waste disposal

Environment - international agreements: *party to:* Biodiversity, Climate Change, Climate Change-Kyoto Protocol, Climate Change-Paris Agreement, Comprehensive Nuclear Test Ban, Desertification, Hazardous Wastes, Law of the Sea, Ozone Layer Protection
signed, but not ratified: none of the selected agreements

Climate: tropical; heavy year-round rainfall, especially in the eastern islands; located on southern edge of the typhoon belt with occasionally severe damage

Urbanization: *urban population:* 23.4% of total population (2023)
rate of urbanization: 1.52% annual rate of change (2020-25 est.)

Revenue from forest resources: 0.02% of GDP (2018 est.)
comparison ranking: 141

Air pollutants: *particulate matter emissions:* 7.79 micrograms per cubic meter (2019 est.)
carbon dioxide emissions: 0.14 megatons (2016 est.)
methane emissions: 0.02 megatons (2020 est.)

Waste and recycling: *municipal solid waste generated annually:* 26,040 tons (2016 est.)

Total renewable water resources: 0 cubic meters (2017 est.)

GOVERNMENT

Country name: *conventional long form:* Federated States of Micronesia
conventional short form: none
local long form: Federated States of Micronesia
local short form: none
former: New Philippines; Caroline Islands; Trust Territory of the Pacific Islands, Ponape, Truk, and Yap Districts
abbreviation: FSM
etymology: the term "Micronesia" is a 19th-century construct of two Greek words, "micro" (small) and "nesoi" (islands), and refers to thousands of small islands in the western Pacific Ocean

Government type: federal republic in free association with the US

Capital: *name:* Palikir
geographic coordinates: 6 55 N, 158 09 E
time difference: UTC+11 (16 hours ahead of Washington, DC, during Standard Time)
time zone note: Micronesia has two time zones
note: Palikir became the new capital of the country in 1989, three years after independence; Kolonia, the former capital, remains the site for many foreign embassies; it also serves as the Pohnpei state capital

Administrative divisions: 4 states; Chuuk (Truk), Kosrae (Kosaie), Pohnpei (Ponape), Yap

Independence: 3 November 1986 (from the US-administered UN trusteeship)

National holiday: Constitution Day, 10 May (1979)

Legal system: mixed legal system of common and customary law

Constitution: *history:* drafted June 1975, ratified 1 October 1978, entered into force 10 May 1979
amendments: proposed by Congress, by a constitutional convention, or by public petition; passage requires approval by at least three-fourths majority vote in at least three fourths of the states; amended 1990; note – at least every 10 years as part of a general or special election, voters are asked whether to hold a constitution convention; a majority of affirmative votes is required to proceed; amended many times, last in 2019 (approval by referendum to hold a constitutional convention)

International law organization participation: has not submitted an ICJ jurisdiction declaration; non-party state to the ICCt

Citizenship: *citizenship by birth:* no
citizenship by descent only: at least one parent must be a citizen of FSM
dual citizenship recognized: no
residency requirement for naturalization: 5 years

Suffrage: 18 years of age; universal

Executive branch: *chief of state:* President Wesley W. SIMINA (since 12 May 2023)
head of government: President Wesley W. SIMINA (since 12 May 2023)
cabinet: Cabinet includes the vice president and the heads of the 8 executive departments
elections/appointments: president and vice president indirectly elected by Congress from among the 4 'at large' senators for a 4-year term (eligible for a

second term); election last held on 12 May 2023 (next to be held in 2027)
election results:
2023: David W. PANUELO elected president by Congress; Yosiwo P. GEORGE reelected vice president
2019: David W. PANUELO elected president by Congress; Yosiwo P. GEORGE reelected vice president
note: the president is both chief of state and head of government

Legislative branch: *description:* unicameral Congress (14 seats; 10 members directly elected in single-seat constituencies by simple majority vote to serve 2-year terms and 4 at- large members directly elected from each of the 4 states by proportional representation vote to serve 4-year terms)
elections: last held on 7 March 2023 (next to be held in March 2025)
election results: percent of vote - NA; seats by party - independent 14; composition - men 11, women 2; percentage women 15.4%

Judicial branch: *highest court(s):* Federated States of Micronesia (FSM) Supreme Court (consists of the chief justice and not more than 5 associate justices and organized into appellate and criminal divisions)
judge selection and term of office: justices appointed by the FSM president with the approval of two-thirds of Congress; justices appointed for life
subordinate courts: the highest state-level courts are: Chuuk Supreme Court; Korsae State Court; Pohnpei State Court; Yap State Court

Political parties: no formal parties

International organization participation: ACP, ADB, AOSIS, FAO, G-77, IBRD, ICAO, ICRM, IDA, IFC, IFRCS, IMF, IOC, IOM, IPU, ITSO, ITU, MIGA, OPCW, PIF, Sparteca, SPC, UN, UNCTAD, UNESCO, WHO, WMO

Diplomatic representation in the US: *chief of mission:* Ambassador Jackson T. SORAM (since 27 February 2024)
chancery: 1725 N Street NW, Washington, DC 20036
telephone: [1] (202) 223-4383
FAX: [1] (202) 223-4391
email address and website:
dcmission@fsmembassy.fm
https://fsmembassy.fm/
consulate(s) general: Honolulu, Portland (OR), Tamuning (Guam)

Diplomatic representation from the US: *chief of mission:* Ambassador Jennifer JOHNSON (since 13 September 2023)
embassy: 1286 US Embassy Place, Kolonia, Pohnpei, FM 96941
mailing address: 4120 Kolonia Place, Washington, D.C. 20521-4120
telephone: [691] 320-2187
FAX: [691] 320-2186
email address and website:
koloniaacs@state.gov
https://fm.usembassy.gov/

Flag description: light blue with four white five-pointed stars centered; the stars are arranged in a diamond pattern; blue symbolizes the Pacific Ocean, the stars represent the four island groups of Chuuk, Kosrae, Pohnpei, and Yap

National symbol(s): four, five-pointed, white stars on a light blue field, hibiscus flower; national colors: light blue, white

National anthem: *name:* "Patriots of Micronesia"
lyrics/music: unknown/August Daniel BINZER
note: adopted 1991; also known as "Across All Micronesia"; the music is based on the 1820 German patriotic song "Ich hab mich ergeben", which was the West German national anthem from 1949-1950; variants of this tune are used in Johannes BRAHMS' "Festival Overture" and Gustav MAHLER's "Third Symphony"

National heritage: total World Heritage Sites: 1 (cultural)
selected World Heritage Site locales: Nan Madol: Ceremonial Center of Eastern Micronesia

ECONOMY

Economic overview: lower middle-income Pacific island economy; US aid reliance, sunsetting in 2024; low entrepreneurship; mostly fishing and farming; US dollar user; no patent laws; tourism remains underdeveloped; significant corruption

Real GDP (purchasing power parity): $437.922 million (2023 est.)
$434.514 million (2022 est.)
$437.922 million (2021 est.)
note: data in 2021 dollars
comparison ranking: 214

Real GDP growth rate: 0.78% (2023 est.)
-0.78% (2022 est.)
2.8% (2021 est.)
note: annual GDP % growth based on constant local currency
comparison ranking: 170

Real GDP per capita: $3,800 (2023 est.)
$3,800 (2022 est.)
$3,900 (2021 est.)
note: data in 2021 dollars
comparison ranking: 187

GDP (official exchange rate): $460 million (2023 est.)
note: data in current dollars at official exchange rate

Inflation rate (consumer prices): 5.41% (2022 est.)
3.19% (2021 est.)
0.55% (2020 est.)
note: annual % change based on consumer prices
comparison ranking: 114

GDP - composition, by sector of origin: *agriculture:* 22.5% (2023 est.)
industry: 4.9% (2023 est.)
services: 66.8% (2023 est.)
note: figures may not total 100% due to non-allocated consumption not captured in sector-reported data
comparison rankings: services 52; industry 214; agriculture 30

GDP - composition, by end use: *exports of goods and services:* 27.3% (2023 est.)
imports of goods and services: -67.5% (2023 est.)
note: figures may not total 100% due to rounding or gaps in data collection

Agricultural products: coconuts, cassava, vegetables, sweet potatoes, bananas, pork, plantains, fruits, beef, eggs (2022)
note: top ten agricultural products based on tonnage

Industries: tourism, construction; specialized aquaculture, craft items (shell and wood)

Industrial production growth rate: 0.78% (2023 est.)
note: annual % change in industrial value added based on constant local currency
comparison ranking: 142

Youth unemployment rate (ages 15-24): *total:* 18.9% (2014)
male: 10.4%
female: 29.9%
comparison ranking: total 72

Remittances: 5.07% of GDP (2023 est.)
5.43% of GDP (2022 est.)
5.98% of GDP (2021 est.)
note: personal transfers and compensation between resident and non-resident individuals/households/entities

Budget: *revenues:* $137.795 million (2020 est.)
expenditures: $87.355 million (2020 est.)
note: central government revenues and expenses (excluding grants/extrabudgetary units/social security funds) converted to US dollars at average official exchange rate for year indicated

Public debt: 27.86% of GDP (2020 est.)
note: central government debt as a % of GDP
comparison ranking: 171

Taxes and other revenues: 7.05% (of GDP) (2020 est.)
note: central government tax revenue as a % of GDP
comparison ranking: 197

Current account balance: $12 million (2017 est.)
$11 million (2016 est.)
$22.408 million (2014 est.)
note: balance of payments - net trade and primary/secondary income in current dollars
comparison ranking: 78

Exports: $179 million (2021 est.)
$122 million (2020 est.)
$130 million (2019 est.)
note: balance of payments - exports of goods and services in current dollars
comparison ranking: 206

Exports - partners: Thailand 78%, Philippines 12%, Japan 5%, Ecuador 2%, US 1% (2022)
note: top five export partners based on percentage share of exports

Exports - commodities: fish, integrated circuits, garments, aircraft parts, broadcasting equipment (2022)
note: top five export commodities based on value in dollars

Imports: $126 million (2021 est.)
$133 million (2020 est.)
$121 million (2019 est.)
note: balance of payments - imports of goods and services in current dollars
comparison ranking: 215

Imports - partners: US 37%, China 21%, Japan 10%, South Korea 8%, Taiwan 5% (2022)
note: top five import partners based on percentage share of imports

Imports - commodities: plastic products, ships, poultry, refined petroleum, fish (2022)
note: top five import commodities based on value in dollars

Reserves of foreign exchange and gold: $497.434 million (2021 est.)
$451.913 million (2020 est.)
$397.158 million (2019 est.)
note: holdings of gold (year-end prices)/foreign exchange/special drawing rights in current dollars
comparison ranking: 163

Exchange rates: the US dollar is used

ENERGY

Electricity access: *electrification - total population:* 85.3% (2022 est.)
electrification - urban areas: 98.6%
electrification - rural areas: 79.4%

Petroleum: *refined petroleum consumption:* 1,000 bbl/day (2022 est.)

Carbon dioxide emissions: 166,000 metric tonnes of CO2 (2022 est.)
from petroleum and other liquids: 166,000 metric tonnes of CO2 (2022 est.)
comparison ranking: total emissions 206

Energy consumption per capita: (2019 est.)

COMMUNICATIONS

Telephones - fixed lines: *total subscriptions:* 7,000 (2021 est.)
subscriptions per 100 inhabitants: 6 (2021 est.)
comparison ranking: total subscriptions 197

Telephones - mobile cellular: *total subscriptions:* 22,000 (2021 est.)
subscriptions per 100 inhabitants: 19 (2021 est.)
comparison ranking: total subscriptions 215

Telecommunication systems: *general assessment:* Australia, Japan, and the United States are committed to working in partnership with the Federated States of Micronesia (FSM), Kiribati, and Nauru to improve internet connectivity to these three Pacific nations by providing funding to build a new undersea cable; the proposed undersea cable will provide faster, higher quality, and more reliable and secure communications to approximately 100,000 people across three countries; this will support increased economic growth, drive development opportunities, and help to improve living standards as the region recovers from the severe impacts of COVID-19; the new cable will connect Kosrae (FSM), Nauru, and Tarawa (Kiribati) with the existing HANTRU-1 cable at Pohnpei (FSM), providing internet connectivity through a submarine cable for the first time (2021)
domestic: fixed line teledensity roughly 6 per 100 and mobile-cellular nearly 19 per 100 (2021)
international: country code - 691; landing points for the Chuukk-Pohnpei Cable and HANTRU-1 submarine cable system linking the Federated States of Micronesia and the US; satellite earth stations - 5 Intelsat (Pacific Ocean) (2019)

Broadcast media: no TV broadcast stations; each state has a multi-channel cable service with TV transmissions carrying roughly 95% imported programming and 5% local programming; about a half-dozen radio stations (2009)

Internet country code: .fm

Internet users: *total:* 44,000 (2021 est.)
percent of population: 40% (2021 est.)
comparison ranking: total 202

Broadband - fixed subscriptions: *total:* 6,000 (2020 est.)
subscriptions per 100 inhabitants: 5 (2020 est.)
comparison ranking: total 183

TRANSPORTATION

Civil aircraft registration country code prefix: V6

Airports: 7 (2024)
comparison ranking: 169

Roadways: *total:* 388 km (2022)
note - paved and unpaved circumferential roads, most interior roads are unpaved
comparison ranking: total 201

Merchant marine: *total:* 38 (2023)
by type: general cargo 17, oil tanker 4, other 17
comparison ranking: total 128

Ports: *total ports:* 4 (2024)
large: 0
medium: 0
small: 1
very small: 3
ports with oil terminals: 3
key ports: Colonia, Lele Harbor, Moen, Pohnpei Harbor

MILITARY AND SECURITY

Military and security forces: no military forces; Federated States of Micronesia National Police (includes a maritime wing); the Department of Justice oversees the National Police; State police forces are responsible for law enforcement in their respective states and are under the jurisdiction of each state's director of public safety (2024)

Military - note: defense is the responsibility of the US; in 1982, the FSM signed a Compact of Free Association (COFA) with the US, which granted the FSM financial assistance and access to many US domestic programs in exchange for exclusive US military access and defense responsibilities; the COFA entered into force in 1986 and its funding was renewed in 2003; Micronesians can serve in the US armed forces
the FSM has a "shiprider" agreement with the US, which allows local maritime law enforcement officers to embark on US Coast Guard (USCG) and US Navy (USN) vessels, including to board and search vessels suspected of violating laws or regulations within the FSM's designated exclusive economic zone (EEZ) or on the high seas; "shiprider" agreements also enable USCG personnel and USN vessels with embarked USCG law enforcement personnel to work with host nations to protect critical regional resources (2024)

TRANSNATIONAL ISSUES

Illicit drugs: major consumer of cannabis

MOLDOVA

INTRODUCTION

Background: A large portion of present-day Moldovan territory became a province of the Russian Empire in 1812 and then unified with Romania in 1918 in the aftermath of World War I. This territory was then incorporated into the Soviet Union at the close of World War II. Although Moldova has been independent from the Soviet Union since 1991, Russian forces have remained on Moldovan territory east of the Nistru River in the breakaway region of Transnistria.

Years of Communist Party rule in Moldova from 2001 to 2009 ultimately ended with election-related violent protests and a rerun of parliamentary elections in 2009. A series of pro-Europe ruling coalitions governed Moldova from 2010 to 2019, but pro-Russia candidate Igor DODON won the presidency in 2016, and his Socialist Party of the Republic of Moldova won a plurality in the legislative election in 2019. Pro-EU reformist candidate Maia SANDU defeated DODON in his reelection bid in 2020, and SANDU's Party of Action and Solidarity won a parliamentary majority in an early legislative election in 2021. Prime Minister Natalia GAVRILITA and her cabinet took office in 2021. In early 2023, Moldova's parliament confirmed a new cabinet led by Prime Minister Dorin RECEAN, which retained the majority of the former ministers.

GEOGRAPHY

Location: Eastern Europe, northeast of Romania

Geographic coordinates: 47 00 N, 29 00 E

Map references: Europe

Area: *total:* 33,851 sq km
land: 32,891 sq km
water: 960 sq km
comparison ranking: total 139

Area - comparative: slightly larger than Maryland

Land boundaries: *total:* 1,885 km
border countries (2): Romania 683 km; Ukraine 1202 km

Coastline: 0 km (landlocked)

Maritime claims: none (landlocked)

Climate: moderate winters, warm summers

Terrain: rolling steppe, gradual slope south to Black Sea

Elevation: *highest point:* Dealul Balanesti 430 m
lowest point: Dniester (Nistru) 2 m
mean elevation: 139 m

Natural resources: lignite, phosphorites, gypsum, limestone, arable land

Land use: *agricultural land:* 74.9% (2018 est.)
arable land: 55.1% (2018 est.)
permanent crops: 9.1% (2018 est.)
permanent pasture: 10.7% (2018 est.)
forest: 11.9% (2018 est.)
other: 13.2% (2018 est.)

Irrigated land: 2,155 sq km (2020)

Major rivers (by length in km): Dunărea (Danube) (shared with Germany [s], Austria, Slovakia, Hungary, Croatia, Serbia, Bulgaria, Ukraine, and Romania [m]) - 2,888 km; Nistru (Dniester) (shared with Ukraine [s/m]) - 1,411 km
note – [s] after country name indicates river source; [m] after country name indicates river mouth

Major watersheds (area sq km): Atlantic Ocean drainage: *(Black Sea)* Danube (795,656 sq km)

Population distribution: pockets of agglomeration exist throughout the country, the largest being in the center of the country around the capital of Chisinau, followed by Tiraspol and Balti

Natural hazards: landslides

Geography - note: landlocked; well-endowed with various sedimentary rocks and minerals including sand, gravel, gypsum, and limestone

PEOPLE AND SOCIETY

Population: *total:* 3,599,528
male: 1,698,249
female: 1,901,279 (2024 est.)
comparison rankings: female 131; male 134; total 132

Nationality: *noun:* Moldovan(s)
adjective: Moldovan

Ethnic groups: Moldovan 75.1%, Romanian 7%, Ukrainian 6.6%, Gagauz 4.6%, Russian 4.1%, Bulgarian 1.9%, other 0.8% (2014 est.)

Languages: Moldovan/Romanian 80.2% (official) (56.7% Moldovan; 23.5% Romanian), Russian 9.7%, Gagauz 4.2% (a Turkish language), Ukrainian 3.9%, Bulgarian 1.5%, Romani 0.3%, other 0.2% (2014)
major-language sample(s):
Cartea informativa a lumii, sursa indispensabila pentru informatii de baza. (Moldovan/Romanian)
note: data represent mother tongue; as of March 2023, "Romanian" replaced "Moldovan" as the name of Moldova's official language

Religions: Orthodox 90.1%, other Christian 2.6%, other 0.1%, agnostic <0.1%, atheist 0.2%, unspecified 6.9% (2014 est.)

Age structure: *0-14 years:* 14.8% (male 266,493/ female 266,166)
15-64 years: 70.2% (male 1,225,535/female 1,300,640)
65 years and over: 15% (2024 est.) (male 206,221/ female 334,473)

Dependency ratios: *total dependency ratio:* 39.6
youth dependency ratio: 29.7
elderly dependency ratio: 20.4
potential support ratio: 4.9 (2021 est.)

Median age: *total:* 39.9 years (2024 est.)
male: 38.6 years
female: 41.3 years
comparison ranking: total 63

Population growth rate: -0.58% (2024 est.)
comparison ranking: 224

Birth rate: 8.4 births/1,000 population (2024 est.)
comparison ranking: 208

Death rate: 14.2 deaths/1,000 population (2024 est.)
comparison ranking: 8

Net migration rate: 0 migrant(s)/1,000 population (2024 est.)
comparison ranking: 81

Population distribution: pockets of agglomeration exist throughout the country, the largest being in the center of the country around the capital of Chisinau, followed by Tiraspol and Balti

Urbanization: *urban population:* 43.4% of total population (2023)
rate of urbanization: 0.09% annual rate of change (2020-25 est.)

Major urban areas - population: 488,000 CHISINAU (capital) (2023)

Sex ratio: *at birth:* 1.07 male(s)/female
0-14 years: 1 male(s)/female
15-64 years: 0.94 male(s)/female
65 years and over: 0.62 male(s)/female
total population: 0.89 male(s)/female (2024 est.)

Mother's mean age at first birth: 25.2 years (2019 est.)

Maternal mortality ratio: 12 deaths/100,000 live births (2020 est.)
comparison ranking: 140

Infant mortality rate: *total:* 13.8 deaths/1,000 live births (2024 est.)
male: 16 deaths/1,000 live births
female: 11.5 deaths/1,000 live births
comparison ranking: total 102

Life expectancy at birth: *total population:* 70.1 years (2024 est.)
male: 66.1 years
female: 74.4 years
comparison ranking: total population 179

Total fertility rate: 1.26 children born/woman (2024 est.)
comparison ranking: 221

Gross reproduction rate: 0.61 (2024 est.)

Contraceptive prevalence rate: 56% (2020)

Drinking water source: *improved: urban:* 98.9% of population
rural: 87% of population
total: 92.1% of population
unimproved: urban: 1.1% of population
rural: 13% of population
total: 7.9% of population (2020 est.)

Current health expenditure: 6.8% of GDP (2020)

Physician density: 3.1 physicians/1,000 population (2020)

Hospital bed density: 5.7 beds/1,000 population (2014)

Sanitation facility access: *improved: urban:* 99% of population
rural: 83.1% of population
total: 89.9% of population
unimproved: urban: 1% of population
rural: 16.9% of population
total: 10.1% of population (2020 est.)

Obesity - adult prevalence rate: 18.9% (2016)
comparison ranking: 113

Alcohol consumption per capita: *total:* 7.45 liters of pure alcohol (2019 est.)
beer: 1.53 liters of pure alcohol (2019 est.)
wine: 3.57 liters of pure alcohol (2019 est.)
spirits: 2.25 liters of pure alcohol (2019 est.)
other alcohols: 0.1 liters of pure alcohol (2019 est.)
comparison ranking: total 54

Tobacco use: *total:* 29% (2020 est.)
male: 51.7% (2020 est.)
female: 6.2% (2020 est.)
comparison ranking: total 35

Currently married women (ages 15-49): 67% (2023 est.)

Education expenditures: 6.4% of GDP (2020 est.)
comparison ranking: 33

Literacy: *definition:* age 15 and over can read and write
total population: 99.6%
male: 99.7%
female: 99.5% (2021)

School life expectancy (primary to tertiary education): *total:* 14 years
male: 14 years
female: 15 years (2021)

ENVIRONMENT

Environment - current issues: heavy use of agricultural chemicals has contaminated soil and groundwater; extensive soil erosion and declining soil fertility from poor farming methods

Environment - international agreements: *party to:* Air Pollution, Air Pollution-Heavy Metals, Air Pollution-Persistent Organic Pollutants, Biodiversity, Climate Change, Climate Change-Kyoto Protocol, Climate Change-Paris Agreement, Comprehensive Nuclear Test Ban, Desertification, Endangered Species, Hazardous Wastes, Law of the Sea, Ozone Layer Protection, Ship Pollution, Wetlands
signed, but not ratified: Air Pollution-Multi-effect Protocol

Climate: moderate winters, warm summers

Urbanization: *urban population:* 43.4% of total population (2023)
rate of urbanization: 0.09% annual rate of change (2020-25 est.)

Revenue from forest resources: 0.26% of GDP (2018 est.)
comparison ranking: 86

Revenue from coal: 0% of GDP (2018 est.)
comparison ranking: 146

Air pollutants: *particulate matter emissions:* 12.37 micrograms per cubic meter (2019 est.)
carbon dioxide emissions: 5.12 megatons (2016 est.)
methane emissions: 3.29 megatons (2020 est.)

Waste and recycling: *municipal solid waste generated annually:* 3,981,200 tons (2015 est.)
municipal solid waste recycled annually: 609,920 tons (2015 est.)
percent of municipal solid waste recycled: 15.3% (2015 est.)

Major rivers (by length in km): Dunărea (Danube) (shared with Germany [s], Austria, Slovakia, Hungary, Croatia, Serbia, Bulgaria, Ukraine, and Romania [m]) - 2,888 km; Nistru (Dniester) (shared with Ukraine [s/m]) - 1,411 km
note – [s] after country name indicates river source; [m] after country name indicates river mouth

Major watersheds (area sq km): Atlantic Ocean drainage: *(Black Sea)* Danube (795,656 sq km)

Total water withdrawal: *municipal:* 160 million cubic meters (2020 est.)
industrial: 580 million cubic meters (2020 est.)
agricultural: 60 million cubic meters (2020 est.)

Total renewable water resources: 12.27 billion cubic meters (2020 est.)

GOVERNMENT

Country name: *conventional long form:* Republic of Moldova
conventional short form: Moldova
local long form: Republica Moldova
local short form: Moldova
former: Moldavian Soviet Socialist Republic, Moldovan Soviet Socialist Republic
etymology: named for the Moldova River in neighboring eastern Romania

Government type: parliamentary republic

Capital: *name:* Chisinau in Romanian (Kishinev in Russian)
geographic coordinates: 47 00 N, 28 51 E
time difference: UTC+2 (7 hours ahead of Washington, DC, during Standard Time)
daylight saving time: +1hr, begins last Sunday in March; ends last Sunday in October
etymology: origin unclear but may derive from the archaic Romanian word *chisla* ("spring" or "water source") and *noua* ("new") because the original settlement was built at the site of a small spring
note: pronounced KEE-shee-now (KIH-shi-nyov)

Administrative divisions: 32 raions (raioane, singular - raion), 3 municipalities (municipii, singular - municipiul), 1 autonomous territorial unit (unitatea teritoriala autonoma), and 1 territorial unit (unitatea teritoriala)
raions: Anenii Noi, Basarabeasca, Briceni, Cahul, Cantemir, Calarasi, Causeni, Cimislia, Criuleni, Donduseni, Drochia, Dubasari, Edinet, Falesti, Floresti, Glodeni, Hincesti, Ialoveni, Leova, Nisporeni, Ocnita, Orhei, Rezina, Riscani, Singerei, Soldanesti, Soroca, Stefan Voda, Straseni, Taraclia, Telenesti, Ungheni
municipalities: Balti, Bender, Chisinau
autonomous territorial unit: Gagauzia
territorial unit: Stinga Nistrului (Transnistria)

Independence: 27 August 1991 (from the Soviet Union)

National holiday: Independence Day, 27 August (1991)

Legal system: civil law system with Germanic law influences; Constitutional Court review of legislative acts

Constitution: *history:* previous 1978; latest adopted 29 July 1994, effective 27 August 1994
amendments: proposed by voter petition (at least 200,000 eligible voters), by at least one third of Parliament members, or by the government; passage requires two-thirds majority vote of Parliament within one year of initial proposal; revisions to constitutional articles on sovereignty, independence, and neutrality require majority vote by referendum; articles on fundamental rights and freedoms cannot be amended; amended many times, last in 2018

International law organization participation: has not submitted an ICJ jurisdiction declaration; accepts ICCt jurisdiction

Citizenship: *citizenship by birth:* no
citizenship by descent only: at least one parent must be a citizen of Moldova
dual citizenship recognized: no
residency requirement for naturalization: 10 years

Suffrage: 18 years of age; universal

Executive branch: *chief of state:* President Maia SANDU (since 24 December 2020)
head of government: Prime Minister Dorin RECEAN (since 16 February 2023)
cabinet: Cabinet proposed by the prime minister-designate, nominated by the president, approved through a vote of confidence in Parliament
elections/appointments: president directly elected for a 4-year term (eligible for a second term); election last held on 15 November 2020 (first round held on 20 October 2024, the runoff will be held on 3 November 2024); prime minister designated by the president upon consultation with Parliament; within 15 days from designation, the prime minister-designate must request a vote of confidence for his/her proposed work program from the Parliament
election results:
2024: In the first round of presidential elections, incumbent Maia SANDU (Action and Solidarity Party) wins 42.5% of the vote, Alexandr STOIANOGLO (Party of Socialists of the Republic of Moldova) 26.0%, Renato USATII (Our Party) 13.8%, and Irina VLAH (independent) 5.4%; turnout is 51.7%; the runoff will take place on November 3.
2020: Maia SANDU elected president in second round; percent of vote in second round - Maia SANDU (PAS) 57.7%, Igor DODON (PSRM) 42.3%
2016: Igor DODON elected president in second round; percent of vote - Igor DODON (PSRM) 52.1%, Maia SANDU (PAS) 47.9%

Legislative branch: *description:* unicameral Parliament (101 seats; 51 members directly elected in single-seat constituencies by simple majority vote and 50 members directly elected in a single, nationwide constituency by closed party-list proportional representation vote; all members serve 4-year terms
elections: last held on 11 July 2021 (next to be held in July 2025)
election results: percent of vote by party - PAS 52.8%, BECS 27.1%, SOR 5.7%, other 14.4%; seats by party - PAS 63, BECS 32, SOR 6; composition - men 58, women 40, percent of women 40.8%

Judicial branch: *highest court(s):* Supreme Court of Justice (consists of the chief judge, 3 deputy-chief judges, 45 judges, and 7 assistant judges); Constitutional Court (consists of the court president and 6 judges); note - the Constitutional Court is autonomous to the other branches of government; the Court interprets the Constitution and reviews the constitutionality of parliamentary laws and decisions, decrees of the president, and acts of the government
judge selection and term of office: Supreme Court of Justice judges appointed by the president upon the recommendation of the Superior Council of Magistracy, an 11-member body of judicial officials; all judges serve 4-year renewable terms; Constitutional Court judges appointed 2 each by Parliament, the president, and the Higher Council of Magistracy for 6-year terms; court president elected by other court judges for a 3-year term
subordinate courts: Courts of Appeal; Court of Business Audit; municipal courts

Political parties: Bloc of Communists and Socialists or BCS
Party of Action and Solidarity or PAS

International organization participation: BSEC, CD, CE, CEI, CIS, EAEU (observer), EAPC, EBRD, FAO, GCTU, GUAM, IAEA, IBRD, ICAO, ICC (NGOs), ICCt, ICRM, IDA, IFAD, IFC, IFRCS, ILO, IMF, IMO, Interpol, IOC, IOM, IPU, ISO (correspondent), ITU, ITUC (NGOs), MIGA, OIF, OPCW, OSCE, PFP, SELEC, UN, UNCTAD, UNESCO, UNHCR, UNIDO, Union Latina, UNMIL, UNMISS, UNOCI, UNWTO, UPU, WCO, WHO, WIPO, WMO, WTO
note: Moldova is an EU candidate country whose satisfactory completion of accession criteria is required before being granted full EU membership

Diplomatic representation in the US: *chief of mission:* Ambassador Viorel URSU (since 12 December 2022)
chancery: 2101 S Street NW, Washington, DC 20008
telephone: [1] (202) 667-1130
FAX: [1] (202) 667-2624
email address and website:
washington@mfa.gov.md
https://sua.mfa.gov.md/en

Diplomatic representation from the US: *chief of mission:* Ambassador Kent D. LOGSDON (since 16 February 2022)
embassy: 103 Mateevici Street, Chisinau MD-2009
mailing address: 7080 Chisinau Place, Washington DC 20521-7080
telephone: [373] (22) 408-300
FAX: [373] (22) 233-044
email address and website:
ChisinauACS@state.gov
https://md.usembassy.gov/

Flag description: three equal vertical bands of Prussian blue (hoist side), chrome yellow, and vermilion red; emblem in center of flag is of a Roman eagle of dark gold (brown) outlined in black with a red beak and talons carrying a yellow cross in its beak and a green olive branch in its right talons and a yellow scepter in its left talons; on its breast is a shield divided horizontally red over blue with a stylized aurochs head, star, rose, and crescent all in black-outlined yellow; based on the color scheme of the flag of Romania - with which Moldova shares a history and culture - but Moldova's blue band is lighter; the reverse of the flag displays a mirrored image of the coat of arms
note: one of only three national flags that differ on their obverse and reverse sides - the others are Paraguay and Saudi Arabia

National symbol(s): aurochs (a type of wild cattle); national colors: blue, yellow, red

National anthem: *name:* "Limba noastra" (Our Language)
lyrics/music: Alexei MATEEVICI/Alexandru CRISTEA
note: adopted 1994

National heritage: *total World Heritage Sites:* 1 (cultural)
selected World Heritage Site locales: Struve Geodetic Arc

ECONOMY

Economic overview: upper middle-income Eastern European economy; sustained growth reversed by COVID-19; significant remittances; Russian energy and regional dependence; agricultural exporter; declining workforce due to emigration and low fertility

Real GDP (purchasing power parity): $38.969 billion (2023 est.)
$38.666 billion (2022 est.)
$40.708 billion (2021 est.)
note: data in 2021 dollars
comparison ranking: 139

Real GDP growth rate: 0.78% (2023 est.)
-5.02% (2022 est.)
13.93% (2021 est.)
note: annual GDP % growth based on constant local currency
comparison ranking: 171

Real GDP per capita: $15,700 (2023 est.)
$15,200 (2022 est.)
$15,700 (2021 est.)
note: data in 2021 dollars
comparison ranking: 121

GDP (official exchange rate): $16.539 billion (2023 est.)
note: data in current dollars at official exchange rate

Inflation rate (consumer prices): 13.42% (2023 est.)
28.74% (2022 est.)
5.11% (2021 est.)
note: annual % change based on consumer prices
comparison ranking: 191

Credit ratings: Moody's rating: B3 (2010)
note: The year refers to the year in which the current credit rating was first obtained.

GDP - composition, by sector of origin: *agriculture:* 7.6% (2023 est.)
industry: 17.4% (2023 est.)
services: 61.1% (2023 est.)
note: figures may not total 100% due to non-allocated consumption not captured in sector-reported data
comparison rankings: services 80; industry 157; agriculture 96

GDP - composition, by end use: *household consumption:* 85.3% (2023 est.)
government consumption: 18.1% (2023 est.)
investment in fixed capital: 19.7% (2023 est.)
investment in inventories: 1.1% (2023 est.)
exports of goods and services: 35.5% (2023 est.)
imports of goods and services: -59.6% (2023 est.)
note: figures may not total 100% due to rounding or gaps in data collection

Agricultural products: wheat, maize, sunflower seeds, grapes, sugar beets, apples, milk, potatoes, barley, plums (2022)
note: top ten agricultural products based on tonnage

Industries: sugar processing, vegetable oil, food processing, agricultural machinery; foundry equipment, refrigerators and freezers, washing machines; hosiery, shoes, textiles

Industrial production growth rate: -11.74% (2023 est.)
note: annual % change in industrial value added based on constant local currency
comparison ranking: 213

Labor force: 1.464 million (2023 est.)
note: number of people ages 15 or older who are employed or seeking work
comparison ranking: 135

Unemployment rate: 1.62% (2023 est.)
0.91% (2022 est.)
0.79% (2021 est.)
note: % of labor force seeking employment
comparison ranking: 18

Youth unemployment rate (ages 15-24): *total:* 4.2% (2023 est.)
male: 5% (2023 est.)
female: 3.4% (2023 est.)
note: % of labor force ages 15-24 seeking employment
comparison ranking: total 180

Population below poverty line: 31.1% (2022 est.)
note: % of population with income below national poverty line

Gini Index coefficient - distribution of family income: 25.7 (2021 est.)
note: index (0-100) of income distribution; higher values represent greater inequality
comparison ranking: 147

Household income or consumption by percentage share: *lowest 10%:* 4.3% (2021 est.)
highest 10%: 22.1% (2021 est.)
note: % share of income accruing to lowest and highest 10% of population

Remittances: 12.27% of GDP (2023 est.)
14.04% of GDP (2022 est.)
15.48% of GDP (2021 est.)
note: personal transfers and compensation between resident and non-resident individuals/households/entities

Budget: *revenues:* $4.487 billion (2022 est.)
expenditures: $4.684 billion (2022 est.)
note: central government revenues (excluding grants) and expenses converted to US dollars at average official exchange rate for year indicated

Public debt: 34.52% of GDP (2022 est.)
note: central government debt as a % of GDP
comparison ranking: 157

Taxes and other revenues: 18.94% (of GDP) (2022 est.)
note: central government tax revenue as a % of GDP
comparison ranking: 94

Current account balance: -$1.974 billion (2023 est.)
-$2.482 billion (2022 est.)
-$1.699 billion (2021 est.)
note: balance of payments - net trade and primary/secondary income in current dollars
comparison ranking: 158

Exports: $5.865 billion (2023 est.)
$5.981 billion (2022 est.)
$4.197 billion (2021 est.)
note: balance of payments - exports of goods and services in current dollars
comparison ranking: 133

Exports - partners: Romania 27%, Ukraine 15%, Italy 7%, Turkey 6%, Germany 5% (2022)
note: top five export partners based on percentage share of exports

Exports - commodities: refined petroleum, insulated wire, garments, seed oils, corn (2022)
note: top five export commodities based on value in dollars

Imports: $9.867 billion (2023 est.)
$10.265 billion (2022 est.)
$7.915 billion (2021 est.)
note: balance of payments - imports of goods and services in current dollars
comparison ranking: 125

Imports - partners: Romania 23%, Russia 11%, Ukraine 10%, China 8%, Turkey 7% (2022)
note: top five import partners based on percentage share of imports

Imports - commodities: refined petroleum, natural gas, cars, plastic products, insulated wire (2022)
note: top five import commodities based on value in dollars

Reserves of foreign exchange and gold: $5.453 billion (2023 est.)
$4.474 billion (2022 est.)
$3.902 billion (2021 est.)
note: holdings of gold (year-end prices)/foreign exchange/special drawing rights in current dollars
comparison ranking: 114

Debt - external: $1.899 billion (2022 est.)
note: present value of external debt in current US dollars
comparison ranking: 73

Exchange rates: Moldovan lei (MDL) per US dollar -

Exchange rates: 18.164 (2023 est.)
18.897 (2022 est.)
17.68 (2021 est.)
17.322 (2020 est.)
17.573 (2019 est.)

ENERGY

Electricity access: *electrification - total population:* 100% (2022 est.)

Electricity: *installed generating capacity:* 625,000 kW (2022 est.)
consumption: 5.579 billion kWh (2022 est.)
exports: 94 million kWh (2022 est.)
imports: 936 million kWh (2022 est.)
transmission/distribution losses: 576.529 million kWh (2022 est.)
comparison rankings: transmission/distribution losses 83; imports 78; exports 88; consumption 129; installed generating capacity 147

Electricity generation sources: *fossil fuels:* 90.8% of total installed capacity (2022 est.)
solar: 0.6% of total installed capacity (2022 est.)
wind: 1.2% of total installed capacity (2020 est.)
hydroelectricity: 5.5% of total installed capacity (2022 est.)
biomass and waste: 0.5% of total installed capacity (2022 est.)

Coal: *consumption:* 120,000 metric tons (2022 est.)
imports: 121,000 metric tons (2022 est.)

Petroleum: *refined petroleum consumption:* 22,000 bbl/day (2022 est.)

Natural gas: *production:* 10,000 cubic meters (2021 est.)
consumption: 2.344 billion cubic meters (2022 est.)
imports: 2.344 billion cubic meters (2022 est.)

Carbon dioxide emissions: 7.319 million metric tonnes of CO_2 (2022 est.)
from coal and metallurgical coke: 293,000 metric tonnes of CO_2 (2022 est.)
from petroleum and other liquids: 3.035 million metric tonnes of CO_2 (2022 est.)
from consumed natural gas: 3.991 million metric tonnes of CO_2 (2022 est.)
comparison ranking: total emissions 121

Energy consumption per capita: 34.021 million Btu/person (2022 est.)
comparison ranking: 108

COMMUNICATIONS

Telephones - fixed lines: *total subscriptions:* 951,000 (2022 est.)
subscriptions per 100 inhabitants: 29 (2022 est.)

comparison ranking: total subscriptions 71

Telephones - mobile cellular: *total subscriptions:* 4.17 million (2022 est.)
subscriptions per 100 inhabitants: 127 (2022 est.)
comparison ranking: total subscriptions 134

Telecommunication systems: *general assessment:* the telecom market has been affected by a combination of high unemployment and economic difficulties which have led to constraints on consumer spending; Moldova's aspirations to join the EU have encouraged the government and regulator to adopt a range of measures to bring the country's telecoms sector into line with EU principles and standards; in July 2017 the Electronic Communications Act was amended to accommodate the 2009 European regulatory framework, while further amendments were adopted in December 2017 and additional changes were proposed in 2019; Moldova is also part of the Eastern Partnership group of countries, and as such has set in train a glidepath to reducing roaming charges, effective between 2022 and 2026; the country's broadband strategy through to 2025 has been supported by the ITU and industry counterparts from Korea; the internet market is developing rapidly, and though the penetration rate is well below the average for most European countries there are many opportunities for further development; the number of cable broadband subscribers is increasing steadily, though fiber is now by far the strongest sector; by the end of 2020 fiber accounted for about 72.3% of all fixed broadband connections; the mobile market has also grown rapidly, and the sector accounts for the majority of total telecoms revenue; the launch of LTE services has opened up a new revenue growth opportunity centered on mobile broadband; the near comprehensive geographical reach of their mobile networks, market brand recognition and existing customer relationships will make for steady subscriber growth in coming years
(2024)
domestic: fixed-line service is 29 per 100; mobile cellular tele density is 127 per 100 persons (2022)
international: country code - 373; service through Romania and Russia via landline; satellite earth stations - at least 3 - Intelsat, Eutelsat, and Intersputnik

Broadcast media: state-owned national radio-TV broadcaster operates 1 TV and 1 radio station; a total of nearly 70 terrestrial TV channels and some 50 radio stations are in operation; Russian and Romanian channels also are available (2019)

Internet country code: .md

Internet users: *total:* 1.891 million (2021 est.)
percent of population: 61% (2021 est.)
comparison ranking: total 135

Broadband - fixed subscriptions: *total:* 719,001 (2020 est.)
subscriptions per 100 inhabitants: 18 (2020 est.)
comparison ranking: total 80

TRANSPORTATION

National air transport system: *number of registered air carriers:* 6 (2020)
inventory of registered aircraft operated by air carriers: 21
annual passenger traffic on registered air carriers: 1,135,999 (2018)
annual freight traffic on registered air carriers: 640,000 (2018) mt-km

Civil aircraft registration country code prefix: ER

Airports: 11 (2024)
comparison ranking: 155

Pipelines: 2,026 km gas (2021) (2021)

Railways: *total:* 1,171 km (2014)
standard gauge: 14 km (2014) 1.435-m gauge
broad gauge: 1,157 km (2014) 1.520-m gauge
comparison ranking: total 87

Roadways: *total:* 9,488 km (2022)
comparison ranking: total 138

Waterways: 558 km (2011) (in public use on Danube, Dniester and Prut Rivers)
comparison ranking: 91

Merchant marine: *total:* 75 (2023)
by type: bulk carrier 1, container ship 1, general cargo 44, oil tanker 7, other 22
comparison ranking: total 102

MILITARY AND SECURITY

Military and security forces: Armed Forces of the Republic of Moldova (Forțele Armate ale Republicii Moldova): National Army (comprised of a General Staff, a Land Forces Command, and an Air Force Command)

Ministry of Internal Affairs: General Carabinieri Inspectorate (aka Carabinieri Troops or Trupele de Carabinieri), General Police Inspectorate (GPI), General Inspectorate of the Border Police (2024)
note: the Carabinieri is a quasi-militarized gendarmerie responsible for protecting public buildings, maintaining public order, and other national security functions; the GPI is the primary law enforcement body, responsible for internal security, public order, traffic, and criminal investigations; prior to 2012, the Border Police were under the armed forces and known as the Border Troops

Military expenditures: 0.5% of GDP (2023 est.)
0.4% of GDP (2022 est.)
0.4% of GDP (2021 est.)
0.4% of GDP (2020 est.)
0.4% of GDP (2019 est.)
comparison ranking: 160

Military and security service personnel strengths: approximately 6,500 active-duty troops; approximately 2,000 Carabinieri (2023)

Military equipment inventories and acquisitions: the military's inventory is limited and almost entirely comprised of Soviet-era equipment; in recent years, it has received donated equipment from Western European nations and the US (2024)

Military service age and obligation: 18-27 years of age for compulsory or voluntary military service; male registration required at age 16; 12-month service obligation (2024)
note: as of 2024, women made up about 23% of the military's full-time personnel

Military - note: the National Army is responsible for defense against external aggression, suppressing illegal military violence along the state border or inside the country, and supporting other internal security forces in maintaining public order if necessary; its primary focuses are Transnistrian separatist forces and their Russian backers; the 1992 war between Moldovan forces and the Transnistrian separatists backed by Russian troops ended with a cease-fire; the separatists maintain several armed paramilitary combat units, plus other security forces and reserves; Russia maintains approximately 1,500 troops in the breakaway region, including some Transnistrian locals who serve as Russian troops; some of those troops are under the authority of a peacekeeping force known as a Joint Control Commission that also includes Moldovan and separatist personnel, while the remainder of the Russian contingent guard a depot of Soviet-era ammunition and train Transnistrian separatist forces
Moldova is constitutionally neutral but has maintained a relationship with NATO since 1992; bilateral cooperation started when Moldova joined NATO's Partnership for Peace program in 1994; Moldova has contributed small numbers of troops to NATO's Kosovo Force (KFOR) since 2014, and a civilian NATO liaison office was established in Moldova in 2017 at the request of the Moldovan Government to promote practical cooperation and facilitate support (2024)

TRANSNATIONAL ISSUES

Refugees and internally displaced persons: *refugees (country of origin):* 116,855 (Ukraine) (as of 7 April 2024)
stateless persons: 1,701 (2022)

Illicit drugs: limited cultivation of opium poppy and cannabis, mostly for CIS consumption; transshipment point for illicit drugs from Southwest Asia via Central Asia to Russia, Western Europe, and possibly the US; widespread crime and underground economic activity

MONACO

INTRODUCTION

Background: The Genoese built a fortress on the site of present-day Monaco in 1215. The current ruling GRIMALDI family first seized control in 1297 but was not able to permanently secure its holding until 1419. Economic development was spurred in the late 19th century with a railroad linkup to France and the opening of a casino. Since then, the principality's mild climate, coastal Mediterranean scenery, and gambling facilities have made Monaco world-famous as a tourist and recreation center.

GEOGRAPHY

Location: Western Europe, bordering the Mediterranean Sea on the southern coast of France, near the border with Italy

Geographic coordinates: 43 44 N, 7 24 E

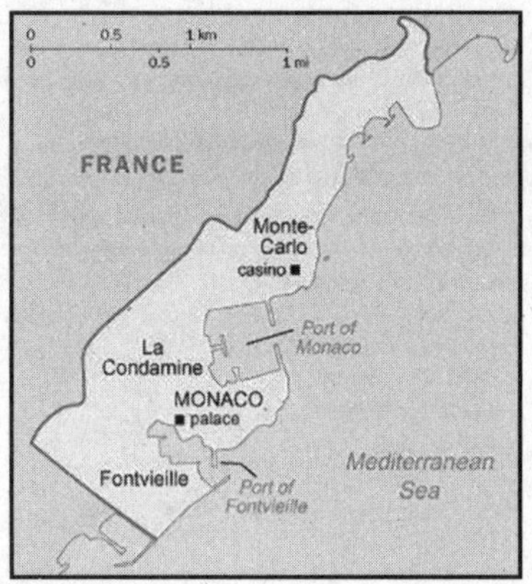

Map references: Europe

Area: *total:* 2 sq km
land: 2 sq km
water: 0 sq km
comparison ranking: total 253

Area - comparative: about three times the size of the National Mall in Washington, DC

Land boundaries: *total:* 6 km
border countries (1): France 6 km

Coastline: 4.1 km

Maritime claims: *territorial sea:* 12 nm
exclusive economic zone: 12 nm

Climate: Mediterranean with mild, wet winters and hot, dry summers

Terrain: hilly, rugged, rocky

Elevation: *highest point:* Chemin des Revoires on Mont Agel 162 m
lowest point: Mediterranean Sea 0 m

Natural resources: none

Land use: *agricultural land:* 1% (2018 est.)
arable land: 0% (2018 est.)
permanent crops: 1% (2018 est.)
permanent pasture: 0% (2018 est.)
forest: 0% (2018 est.)
other: 99% (2018 est.)

Irrigated land: 0 sq km (2022)

Population distribution: the second most densely populated country in the world (after Macau); its entire population living on 2 square km

Natural hazards: none

Geography - note: second-smallest independent state in the world (after the Holy See); smallest country with a coastline; almost entirely urban

PEOPLE AND SOCIETY

Population: *total:* 31,813
male: 15,366
female: 16,447 (2024 est.)
comparison rankings: female 216; male 216; total 216

Nationality: *noun:* Monegasque(s) or Monacan(s)
adjective: Monegasque or Monacan

Ethnic groups: Monegasque 32.1%, French 19.9%, Italian 15.3%, British 5%, Belgian 2.3%, Swiss 2%, German 1.9%, Russian 1.8%, American 1.1%, Dutch 1.1%, Moroccan 1%, other 16.6% (2016 est.)
note: data represent population by country of birth

Languages: French (official), English, Italian, Monegasque
major-language sample(s):
The World Factbook, une source indispensable d'informations de base. (French)

Religions: Roman Catholic 90% (official), other 10%

Age structure: *0-14 years:* 9.1% (male 1,485/female 1,408)
15-64 years: 53.8% (male 8,620/female 8,490)
65 years and over: 37.1% (2024 est.) (male 5,261/female 6,549)
2023 population pyramid:

Dependency ratios: *total dependency ratio:* 95.2
youth dependency ratio: 25
elderly dependency ratio: 70.2
potential support ratio: 1.4 (2021)

Median age: *total:* 56.9 years (2024 est.)
male: 55 years
female: 58.4 years
comparison ranking: total 1

Population growth rate: 0.71% (2024 est.)
comparison ranking: 124

Birth rate: 6.5 births/1,000 population (2024 est.)
comparison ranking: 226

Death rate: 11.1 deaths/1,000 population (2024 est.)
comparison ranking: 25

Net migration rate: 11.7 migrant(s)/1,000 population (2024 est.)
comparison ranking: 7

Population distribution: the second most densely populated country in the world (after Macau); its entire population living on 2 square km

Urbanization: *urban population:* 100% of total population (2023)
rate of urbanization: 0.5% annual rate of change (2020-25 est.)

Major urban areas - population: 39,000 MONACO (capital) (2018)

Sex ratio: *at birth:* 1.04 male(s)/female
0-14 years: 1.05 male(s)/female
15-64 years: 1.02 male(s)/female
65 years and over: 0.8 male(s)/female
total population: 0.93 male(s)/female (2024 est.)

Infant mortality rate: *total:* 1.7 deaths/1,000 live births (2024 est.)
male: 2 deaths/1,000 live births
female: 1.4 deaths/1,000 live births
comparison ranking: total 224

Life expectancy at birth: *total population:* 89.8 years (2024 est.)
male: 86 years
female: 93.7 years
comparison ranking: total population 1

Total fertility rate: 1.54 children born/woman (2024 est.)
comparison ranking: 196

Gross reproduction rate: 0.76 (2024 est.)

Contraceptive prevalence rate: NA

Drinking water source: *improved: urban:* 100% of population
total: 100% of population

Current health expenditure: 1.7% of GDP (2020)

Physician density: physicians/1,000 population (2014)

Hospital bed density: 13.8 beds/1,000 population (2012)

Sanitation facility access: *improved: urban:* 100% of population
rural: NA
total: 100% of population

Children under the age of 5 years underweight: NA

Education expenditures: 1.2% of GDP (2019 est.)
comparison ranking: 195

ENVIRONMENT

Environment - current issues: no serious issues; actively monitors pollution levels in air and water

Environment - international agreements: *party to:* Air Pollution, Air Pollution-Heavy Metals, Air Pollution-Sulphur 94, Air Pollution-Volatile Organic Compounds, Antarctic-Environmental Protection, Antarctic Treaty, Biodiversity, Climate Change, Climate Change-Kyoto Protocol, Climate Change-Paris Agreement, Comprehensive Nuclear Test Ban, Desertification, Endangered Species, Hazardous Wastes, Law of the Sea, Marine Dumping-London Convention, Ozone Layer Protection, Ship Pollution, Wetlands, Whaling
signed, but not ratified: none of the selected agreements

Climate: Mediterranean with mild, wet winters and hot, dry summers

Urbanization: *urban population:* 100% of total population (2023)
rate of urbanization: 0.5% annual rate of change (2020-25 est.)

Revenue from forest resources: 0% of GDP (2018 est.)
comparison ranking: 196

Air pollutants: *particulate matter emissions:* 9.21 micrograms per cubic meter (2019 est.)
methane emissions: 0.05 megatons (2020 est.)

Waste and recycling: *municipal solid waste generated annually:* 46,000 tons (2012 est.)
municipal solid waste recycled annually: 2,484 tons (2012 est.)
percent of municipal solid waste recycled: 5.4% (2012 est.)

Total water withdrawal: *municipal:* 10 million cubic meters (2020 est.)
industrial: 0 cubic meters (2017 est.)
agricultural: 0 cubic meters (2017 est.)

GOVERNMENT

Country name: *conventional long form:* Principality of Monaco
conventional short form: Monaco
local long form: Principauté de Monaco
local short form: Monaco
etymology: founded as a Greek colony in the 6th century B.C., the name derives from two Greek words "monos" (single, alone) and "oikos" (house) to convey the sense of a people "living apart" or in a "single habitation"

Government type: constitutional monarchy

Capital: *name:* Monaco
geographic coordinates: 43 44 N, 7 25 E
time difference: UTC+1 (6 hours ahead of Washington, DC, during Standard Time)
daylight saving time: +1hr, begins last Sunday in March; ends last Sunday in October
etymology: founded as a Greek colony in the 6th century B.C., the name derives from two Greek words *monos* (single, alone) and *oikos* (house) to convey

the sense of a people "living apart" or in a "single habitation"

Administrative divisions: none; there are no first-order administrative divisions as defined by the US Government, but there are 4 quarters (quartiers, singular - quartier); Fontvieille, La Condamine, Monaco-Ville, Monte-Carlo; note - Moneghetti, a part of La Condamine, is sometimes called the 5th quarter of Monaco

Independence: 1419 (beginning of permanent rule by the House of GRIMALDI)

National holiday: National Day (Saint Rainier's Day), 19 November (1857)

Legal system: civil law system influenced by French legal tradition

Constitution: *history:* previous 1911 (suspended 1959); latest adopted 17 December 1962
amendments: proposed by joint agreement of the chief of state (the prince) and the National Council; passage requires two-thirds majority vote of National Council members; amended 2002

International law organization participation: has not submitted an ICJ jurisdiction declaration; non-party state to the ICCt

Citizenship: *citizenship by birth:* no
citizenship by descent only: the father must be a citizen of Monaco; in the case of a child born out of wedlock, the mother must be a citizen and father unknown
dual citizenship recognized: no
residency requirement for naturalization: 10 years

Suffrage: 18 years of age; universal

Executive branch: *chief of state:* Prince ALBERT II (since 6 April 2005)
head of government: Minister of State Didier GUILLAUME (since 2 September 2024)
cabinet: Council of Government under the authority of the monarch
elections/appointments: the monarchy is hereditary; minister of state appointed by the monarch from a list of three French national candidates presented by the French Government

Legislative branch: *description:* unicameral National Council or Conseil National (24 seats; 16 members directly elected in multi-seat constituencies by simple majority vote and 8 directly elected by proportional representation vote; members serve 5-year terms)
elections: last held on 5 February 2023 (next to be held in February 2028)
election results: percent of vote by coalition - Monegasque National Union 100%; seats by coalition - Monegasque National Union 24; composition - men 13, women 11, percent of women 45.8%

Judicial branch: *highest court(s):* Supreme Court (consists of 5 permanent members and 2 substitutes)
judge selection and term of office: Supreme Court members appointed by the monarch upon the proposals of the National Council, State Council, Crown Council, Court of Appeal, and Trial Court
subordinate courts: Court of Appeal; Civil Court of First Instance

Political parties: Monegasque National Union (includes Horizon Monaco, Primo!, Union Monegasque)
Horizon Monaco
Priorite Monaco or Primo!
Union Monegasque

International organization participation: CD, CE, FAO, IAEA, ICAO, ICC (national committees), ICRM, IFRCS, IHO, IMO, IMSO, Interpol, IOC, IPU, ITSO, ITU, OAS (observer), OIF, OPCW, OSCE, Schengen Convention (de facto member), UN, UNCTAD, UNESCO, UNIDO, Union Latina, UNWTO, UPU, WHO, WIPO, WMO

Diplomatic representation in the US: *chief of mission:* Ambassador Maguy MACCARIO DOYLE (since 3 December 2013)
chancery: 888 17th Street NW, Suite 500, Washington, DC 20006
telephone: [1] (202) 234-1530
FAX: [1] (202) 244-7656
email address and website:
info@monacodc.org
https://monacodc.org/index.html
consulate(s) general: New York

Diplomatic representation from the US: *embassy:* US does not have an embassy in Monaco; the US Ambassador to France is accredited to Monaco; the US Consul General in Marseille (France), under the authority of the US Ambassador to France, handles diplomatic and consular matters concerning Monaco; +(33)(1) 43-12-22-22, enter zero "0" after the automated greeting; US Embassy Paris, 2 Avenue Gabriel, 75008 Paris, France

Flag description: two equal horizontal bands of red (top) and white; the colors are those of the ruling House of Grimaldi and have been in use since 1339, making the flag one of the world's oldest national banners
note: similar to the flag of Indonesia which is longer and the flag of Poland which is white (top) and red

National symbol(s): red and white lozenges (diamond shapes); national colors: red, white

National anthem: *name:* "A Marcia de Muneghu" (The March of Monaco)
lyrics/music: Louis NOTARI/Charles ALBRECHT
note: music adopted 1867, lyrics adopted 1931; although French is commonly spoken, only the Monegasque lyrics are official; the French version is known as "Hymne Monegasque" (Monegasque Anthem); the words are generally only sung on official occasions

ECONOMY

Economic overview: high-income European economy; non-EU euro user; considered a tax haven; tourism and banking are largest sectors; negatively impacted by COVID-19; major oceanographic museum; among most expensive real estate; major state-owned enterprises

Real GDP (purchasing power parity): $7.672 billion (2015 est.)
note: data are in 2015 dollars
comparison ranking: 171

Real GDP growth rate: 11.1% (2022 est.)
21.87% (2021 est.)
-13.01% (2020 est.)
note: annual GDP % growth based on constant local currency
comparison ranking: 4

Real GDP per capita: $115,700 (2015 est.)
$109,200 (2014 est.)
comparison ranking: 3

GDP (official exchange rate): $8.784 billion (2022 est.)
note: data in current dollars at official exchange rate

GDP - composition, by sector of origin: *industry:* 12.3% (2022 est.)
services: 87.7% (2022 est.)
note: figures may not total 100% due to non-allocated consumption not captured in sector-reported data
comparison rankings: services 10; industry 176

Agricultural products: none

Industries: banking, insurance, tourism, construction, small-scale industrial and consumer products

Industrial production growth rate: -3.16% (2014 est.)
note: annual % change in industrial value added based on constant local currency
comparison ranking: 192

Labor force: 52,000 (2014 est.)
note: includes all foreign workers
comparison ranking: 191

Youth unemployment rate (ages 15-24): *total:* 26.6% (2016 est.)
male: 25.7%
female: 27.9%
comparison ranking: total 36

Exports: $964.6 million (2017 est.)
note: full customs integration with France, which collects and rebates Monegasque trade duties; also participates in EU market system through customs union with France
comparison ranking: 181

Exports - partners: Italy, Switzerland, Germany, Belgium, Spain
(2021)

Exports - commodities: jewelry, perfumes, watches, packaged medicines, cars (2021)

Imports: $1.371 billion (2017 est.)
note: full customs integration with France, which collects and rebates Monegasque trade duties; also participates in EU market system through customs union with France
comparison ranking: 186

Imports - partners: Italy, Switzerland, United Kingdom, Germany, China (2021)

Imports - commodities: jewelry, cars and vehicle parts, recreational boats, plastic products, artwork (2021)

Exchange rates: euros (EUR) per US dollar -

Exchange rates: 0.925 (2023 est.)
0.95 (2022 est.)
0.845 (2021 est.)
0.876 (2020 est.)
0.893 (2019 est.)
note: while not an EU member state, Monaco, due to its preexisting monetary and banking agreements with France, has a 1998 monetary agreement with the EU to produce limited euro coinage—but not banknotes—that began enforcement in January 2002 and superseded by a new EU agreement in 2012

ENERGY

Electricity access: *electrification - total population:* 100% (2022 est.)

COMMUNICATIONS

Telephones - fixed lines: *total subscriptions:* 45,000 (2022 est.)
subscriptions per 100 inhabitants: 122 (2022 est.)
comparison ranking: total subscriptions 159

Telephones - mobile cellular: *total subscriptions:* 39,000 (2022 est.)
subscriptions per 100 inhabitants: 107 (2022 est.)

comparison ranking: total subscriptions 209

Telecommunication systems: *general assessment:* modern automatic telephone system: the country's sole fixed-line operator offers a full range of services to residential and business customers; competitive mobile telephony market; 4G LTE widely available (2020)
domestic: fixed-line a little over 117 per 100 and mobile-cellular teledensity is 99 per 100 persons (2021)
international: country code - 377; landing points for the EIG and Italy-Monaco submarine cables connecting Monaco to Europe, Africa, the Middle East and Asia; no satellite earth stations; connected by cable into the French communications system (2019)

Broadcast media: TV Monte-Carlo operates a TV network; cable TV available; Radio Monte-Carlo has extensive radio networks in France and Italy with French-language broadcasts to France beginning in the 1960s and Italian-language broadcasts to Italy beginning in the 1970s; other radio stations include Riviera Radio and Radio Monaco

Internet country code: .mc

Internet users: *total:* 31,820 (2021 est.)
percent of population: 86% (2021 est.)
comparison ranking: total 208

Broadband - fixed subscriptions: *total:* 20,877 (2020 est.)
subscriptions per 100 inhabitants: 53 (2020 est.)
comparison ranking: total 166

TRANSPORTATION

Civil aircraft registration country code prefix: 3A

Heliports: 3 (2024)

Railways: *note:* Monaco has a single railway station but does not operate its own train service; the French operator SNCF operates rail services in Monaco

Merchant marine: *total:* 1
comparison ranking: total 185

Ports: *total ports:* 1 (2024)
large: 0
medium: 0
small: 0
very small: 1
ports with oil terminals: 0
key ports: Monaco

MILITARY AND SECURITY

Military and security forces: *no regular military forces; Ministry of Interior:* Compagnie des Carabiniers du Prince (Prince's Company of Carabiniers), Corps des Sapeurs-pompiers de Monaco (Fire and Emergency), Police Department (2024)
note: the primary responsibility for the Compagnie des Carabiniers du Prince is guarding the palace; the Police maintain public order

Military service age and obligation: the Compagnie des Carabiniers du Prince is staffed by French nationals (2024)

Military - note: by treaty, France is responsible for defending the independence and sovereignty of Monaco

MONGOLIA

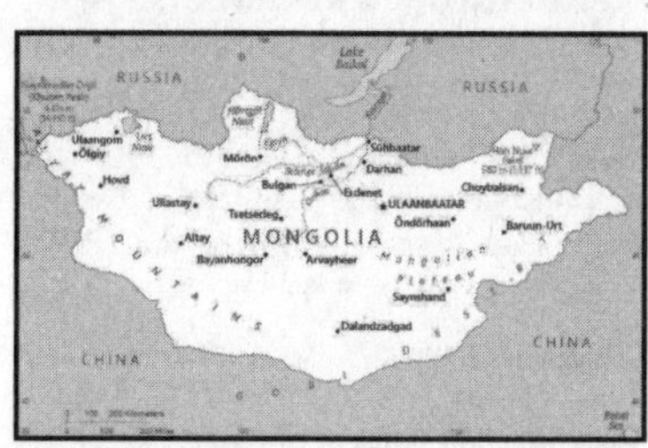

INTRODUCTION

Background: The peoples of Mongolia have a long history under a number of nomadic empires dating back to the Xiongnu in the 4th century B.C., and the name Mongol goes back to at least the 11th century A.D. The most famous Mongol, TEMÜÜJIN (aka Genghis Khan), emerged as the ruler of all Mongols in the early 1200s. By the time of his death in 1227, he had created through conquest a Mongol Empire that extended across much of Eurasia. His descendants, including ÖGÖDEI and KHUBILAI (aka Kublai Khan), continued to conquer Eastern Europe, the Middle East, and the rest of China, where KHUBILAI established the Yuan Dynasty in the 1270s. The Mongols attempted to invade Japan and Java before their empire broke apart in the 14th century. In the 17th century, Mongolia fell under the rule of the Manchus of the Chinese Qing Dynasty. After Manchu rule collapsed in 1911, Mongolia declared independence, finally winning it in 1921 with help from the Soviet Union. Mongolia became a socialist state (the Mongolian People's Republic) in 1924. Until the collapse of the Soviet Union in 1989, Mongolia was a Soviet satellite state and relied heavily on economic, military, and political assistance from Moscow. The period was also marked by purges, political repression, economic stagnation, and tensions with China.

Mongolia peacefully transitioned to an independent democracy in 1990. In 1992, it adopted a new constitution and established a free-market economy. Since the country's transition, it has conducted a series of successful presidential and legislative elections. Throughout the period, the ex-communist Mongolian People's Revolutionary Party – which took the name Mongolian People's Party (MPP) in 2010 – has competed for political power with the Democratic Party and several other smaller parties. For most of its democratic history, Mongolia has had a divided government, with the presidency and the parliamentary majority held by different parties but that changed in 2021, when the MPP won the presidency after having secured a supermajority in parliament in 2020. Mongolia's June 2021 presidential election delivered a decisive victory for MPP candidate Ukhnaagiin KHURELSUKH.

Mongolia maintains close cultural, political, and military ties with Russia, while China is its largest economic partner. Mongolia's foreign relations are focused on preserving its autonomy by balancing relations with China and Russia, as well as its other major partners, Japan, South Korea, and the US.

GEOGRAPHY

Location: Northern Asia, between China and Russia

Geographic coordinates: 46 00 N, 105 00 E

Map references: Asia

Area: *total:* 1,564,116 sq km
land: 1,553,556 sq km
water: 10,560 sq km
comparison ranking: total 20

Area - comparative: slightly smaller than Alaska; more than twice the size of Texas

Land boundaries: *total:* 8,082 km
border countries (2): China 4,630 km; Russia 3,452 km

Coastline: 0 km (landlocked)

Maritime claims: none (landlocked)

Climate: desert; continental (large daily and seasonal temperature ranges)

Terrain: vast semidesert and desert plains, grassy steppe, mountains in west and southwest; Gobi Desert in south-central

Elevation: *highest point:* Nayramadlin Orgil (Khuiten Peak) 4,374 m
lowest point: Hoh Nuur 560 m
mean elevation: 1,528 m

Natural resources: oil, coal, copper, molybdenum, tungsten, phosphates, tin, nickel, zinc, fluorspar, gold, silver, iron

Land use: *agricultural land:* 73% (2018 est.)
arable land: 0.4% (2018 est.)
permanent crops: 0% (2018 est.)
permanent pasture: 72.6% (2018 est.)
forest: 7% (2018 est.)
other: 20% (2018 est.)

Irrigated land: 602 sq km (2020)

Major lakes (area sq km): *fresh water lake(s):* Hovsgol Nuur - 2,620 sq km; Har Us Nuur - 1,760 sq km;
salt water lake(s): Uvs Nuur - 3,350 sq km; Hyargas Nuur - 1,360 sq km

Major rivers (by length in km): Amur (shared with China [s] and Russia [m]) - 4,444 km

note – [s] after country name indicates river source; [m] after country name indicates river mouth

Population distribution: sparsely distributed population throughout the country; the capital of Ulaanbaatar and the northern city of Darhan support the highest population densities

Natural hazards: dust storms; grassland and forest fires; drought; "zud," which is harsh winter conditions

Geography - note: landlocked; strategic location between China and Russia

PEOPLE AND SOCIETY

Population: *total:* 3,281,676

male: 1,595,596
female: 1,686,080 (2024 est.)
comparison rankings: female 134; male 137; total 134

Nationality: *noun:* Mongolian(s)
adjective: Mongolian

Ethnic groups: Khalkh 83.8%, Kazak 3.8%, Durvud 2.6%, Bayad 2%, Buriad 1.4%, Zakhchin 1.2%, Dariganga 1.1%, other 4.1% (2020 est.)

Languages: Mongolian 90% (official, Khalkha dialect is predominant), Turkic, Russian (1999)
major-language sample(s):
major-language sample(s): Дэлхийн баримтат ном, үндсэн мэдээллийн зайлшгүй эх сурвалж. (Mongolian)

Religions: Buddhist 51.7%, Muslim 3.2%, Shamanist 2.5%, Christian 1.3%, other 0.7%, none 40.6% (2020 est.)

Age structure: *0-14 years:* 25.7% (male 429,867/female 412,943)
15-64 years: 68.4% (male 1,087,487/female 1,156,547)
65 years and over: 5.9% (2024 est.) (male 78,242/female 116,590)

Dependency ratios: *total dependency ratio:* 58.4
youth dependency ratio: 51.4
elderly dependency ratio: 7
potential support ratio: 14.3 (2021 est.)

Median age: *total:* 31.5 years (2024 est.)
male: 30.1 years
female: 32.8 years
comparison ranking: total 126

Population growth rate: 0.78% (2024 est.)
comparison ranking: 113

Birth rate: 14.9 births/1,000 population (2024 est.)
comparison ranking: 109

Death rate: 6.4 deaths/1,000 population (2024 est.)
comparison ranking: 144

Net migration rate: -0.8 migrant(s)/1,000 population (2024 est.)
comparison ranking: 138

Population distribution: sparsely distributed population throughout the country; the capital of Ulaanbaatar and the northern city of Darhan support the highest population densities

Urbanization: *urban population:* 69.1% of total population (2023)
rate of urbanization: 1.4% annual rate of change (2020-25 est.)

Major urban areas - population: 1.673 million ULAANBAATAR (capital) (2023)

Sex ratio: *at birth:* 1.05 male(s)/female
0-14 years: 1.04 male(s)/female
15-64 years: 0.94 male(s)/female
65 years and over: 0.67 male(s)/female
total population: 0.95 male(s)/female (2024 est.)

Mother's mean age at first birth: 20.5 years (2008 est.)
note: data represents median age at first birth among women 20-24

Maternal mortality ratio: 39 deaths/100,000 live births (2020 est.)
comparison ranking: 104

Infant mortality rate: *total:* 19.4 deaths/1,000 live births (2024 est.)
male: 22.4 deaths/1,000 live births
female: 16.2 deaths/1,000 live births
comparison ranking: total 78

Life expectancy at birth: *total population:* 71.9 years (2024 est.)
male: 67.8 years
female: 76.3 years
comparison ranking: total population 168

Total fertility rate: 1.87 children born/woman (2024 est.)
comparison ranking: 128

Gross reproduction rate: 0.91 (2024 est.)

Contraceptive prevalence rate: 48.1% (2018)

Drinking water source: *improved: urban:* 98.4% of population
rural: 64.2% of population
total: 87.6% of population
unimproved: urban: 1.6% of population
rural: 35.8% of population
total: 12.4% of population (2020 est.)

Current health expenditure: 4.9% of GDP (2020)

Physician density: 3.85 physicians/1,000 population (2018)

Hospital bed density: 8 beds/1,000 population (2017)

Sanitation facility access: *improved: urban:* 97.4% of population
rural: 69.9% of population
total: 88.8% of population
unimproved: urban: 2.6% of population
rural: 30.1% of population
total: 11.2% of population (2020 est.)

Obesity - adult prevalence rate: 20.6% (2016)
comparison ranking: 97

Alcohol consumption per capita: *total:* 5.46 liters of pure alcohol (2019 est.)
beer: 2.18 liters of pure alcohol (2019 est.)
wine: 1.46 liters of pure alcohol (2019 est.)
spirits: 1.82 liters of pure alcohol (2019 est.)
other alcohols: 0 liters of pure alcohol (2019 est.)
comparison ranking: total 80

Tobacco use: *total:* 29.4% (2020 est.)
male: 51.7% (2020 est.)
female: 7.1% (2020 est.)
comparison ranking: total 33

Children under the age of 5 years underweight: 1.8% (2018)
comparison ranking: 108

Currently married women (ages 15-49): 58.9% (2023 est.)

Child marriage: *women married by age 15:* 0.9%
women married by age 18: 12%
men married by age 18: 2.1% (2018 est.)

Education expenditures: 4.7% of GDP (2020 est.)
comparison ranking: 88

Literacy: *definition:* age 15 and over can read and write
total population: 99.2%
male: 99.1%
female: 99.2% (2020)

School life expectancy (primary to tertiary education): *total:* 15 years
male: 14 years
female: 16 years (2019)

ENVIRONMENT

Environment - current issues: limited natural freshwater resources in some areas; the burning of soft coal in power plants and the lack of enforcement of environmental laws leads to air pollution in Ulaanbaatar; deforestation and overgrazing increase soil erosion from wind and rain; water pollution; desertification and mining activities have a deleterious effect on the environment

Environment - international agreements: *party to:* Antarctic Treaty, Biodiversity, Climate Change, Climate Change-Kyoto Protocol, Climate Change-Paris Agreement, Comprehensive Nuclear Test Ban, Desertification, Endangered Species, Environmental Modification, Hazardous Wastes, Law of the Sea, Nuclear Test Ban, Ozone Layer Protection, Ship Pollution, Wetlands, Whaling
signed, but not ratified: none of the selected agreements

Climate: desert; continental (large daily and seasonal temperature ranges)

Urbanization: *urban population:* 69.1% of total population (2023)
rate of urbanization: 1.4% annual rate of change (2020-25 est.)

Revenue from forest resources: 0.14% of GDP (2018 est.)
comparison ranking: 104

Revenue from coal: 8.62% of GDP (2018 est.)
comparison ranking: 1

Air pollutants: *particulate matter emissions:* 41.3 micrograms per cubic meter (2019 est.)
carbon dioxide emissions: 25.37 megatons (2016 est.)
methane emissions: 13.72 megatons (2020 est.)

Waste and recycling: *municipal solid waste generated annually:* 2.9 million tons (2016 est.)

Major lakes (area sq km): *fresh water lake(s):* Hovsgol Nuur - 2,620 sq km; Har Us Nuur - 1,760 sq km;
salt water lake(s): Uvs Nuur - 3,350 sq km; Hyargas Nuur - 1,360 sq km

Major rivers (by length in km): Amur (shared with China [s] and Russia [m]) - 4,444 km
note – [s] after country name indicates river source; [m] after country name indicates river mouth

Total water withdrawal: *municipal:* 50 million cubic meters (2020 est.)
industrial: 170 million cubic meters (2020 est.)
agricultural: 250 million cubic meters (2020 est.)

Total renewable water resources: 34.8 billion cubic meters (2020 est.)

GOVERNMENT

Country name: *conventional long form:* none
conventional short form: Mongolia
local long form: none
local short form: Mongol Uls
former: Outer Mongolia, Mongolian People's Republic
etymology: the name means "Land of the Mongols" in Latin; the Mongolian name Mongol Uls translates as "Mongol State"

Government type: semi-presidential republic

Capital: *name:* Ulaanbaatar
geographic coordinates: 47 55 N, 106 55 E
time difference: UTC+8 (13 hours ahead of Washington, DC, during Standard Time)
daylight saving time: +1hr, begins last Saturday in March; ends last Saturday in September

time zone note: Mongolia has two time zones - Ulaanbaatar Time (8 hours in advance of UTC) and Hovd Time (7 hours in advance of UTC)
etymology: the name means "red hero" in Mongolian and honors national hero Damdin SUKHBAATAR, leader of the partisan army that with Soviet Red Army help, liberated Mongolia from Chinese occupation in the early 1920s

Administrative divisions: 21 provinces (aymguud, singular - aymag) and 1 municipality* (singular - hot); Arhangay, Bayanhongor, Bayan-Olgiy, Bulgan, Darhan-Uul, Dornod, Dornogovi, Dundgovi, Dzavhan (Zavkhan), Govi-Altay, Govisumber, Hentiy, Hovd, Hovsgol, Omnogovi, Orhon, Ovorhangay, Selenge, Suhbaatar, Tov, Ulaanbaatar*, Uvs

Independence: 29 December 1911 (independence declared from China; in actuality, autonomy attained); 11 July 1921 (from China)

National holiday: Naadam (games) holiday (commemorates independence from China in the 1921 Revolution), 11-15 July; Constitution Day (marks the date that the Mongolian People's Republic was created under a new constitution), 26 November (1924)

Legal system: civil law system influenced by Soviet and Romano-Germanic legal systems; constitution ambiguous on judicial review of legislative acts

Constitution: *history:* several previous; latest adopted 13 January 1992, effective 12 February 1992
amendments: proposed by the State Great Hural, by the president of the republic, by the government, or by petition submitted to the State Great Hural by the Constitutional Court; conducting referenda on proposed amendments requires at least two-thirds majority vote of the State Great Hural; passage of amendments by the State Great Hural requires at least three-quarters majority vote; passage by referendum requires majority participation of qualified voters and a majority of votes; amended 1999, 2000, 2019, 2023; note - an amendment passed in a referendum held in May 2023 increased the seats in the State Great Hural from 76 to 126

International law organization participation: has not submitted an ICJ jurisdiction declaration; accepts ICCt jurisdiction

Citizenship: *citizenship by birth:* no
citizenship by descent only: both parents must be citizens of Mongolia; one parent if born within Mongolia
dual citizenship recognized: no
residency requirement for naturalization: 5 years

Suffrage: 18 years of age; universal

Executive branch: *chief of state:* President Ukhnaagiin KHURELSUKH (since 25 June 2021)
head of government: Prime Minister Luvsannamsrai OYUN-ERDENE (since 27 January 2021)
cabinet: directly appointed by the prime minister following a constitutional amendment ratified in November 2019; prior to the amendment, the cabinet was nominated by the prime minister in consultation with the president and confirmed by the State Great Hural (parliament)
elections/appointments: presidential candidates nominated by political parties represented in the State Great Hural and directly elected by simple majority popular vote for one 6-year term; election last held on 9 June 2021 (next to be held in 2027); following legislative elections, the leader of the majority party or majority coalition is usually elected prime minister by the State Great Hural
election results:
2021: Ukhnaagiin KHURELSUKH elected president in first round; percent of vote - Ukhnaagiin KHURELSUKH (MPP) 68%, Dangaasuren ENKHBAT (RPEC) 20.1%, Sodnomzundui ERDENE (DP) 6%
2017: Khaltmaa BATTULGA elected president in second round; percent of vote in first round - Khaltmaa BATTULGA (DP) 38.1%, Miyegombo ENKHBOLD (MPP) 30.3%, Sainkhuu GANBAATAR (MPRP) 30.2%, invalid 1.4%; percent of vote in second round - Khaltmaa BATTULGA 55.2%, Miyegombo ENKHBOLD 44.8%

Legislative branch: *description:* unicameral State Great Hural or Ulsyn Ikh Khural (126 seats; 78 members directly elected in a selected constituency by simple majority vote and 48 members directly elected by proportional representation vote; members serve 4-year terms)
elections: last held on 28 June 2024 (next to be held June 2028)
election results: percent of vote by party - MPP 35.0%, DP 30.1%, HUN Party 10.4%, National Coalition 5.2%, CWGP 5%, other 14.3%; seats by party - MPP 68, DP 42, HUN Party 8, National Coalition 4, CWGP 4; composition - N/A

Judicial branch: *highest court(s):* Supreme Court (consists of the Chief Justice and 24 judges organized into civil, criminal, and administrative chambers); Constitutional Court or Tsets (consists of the chairman and 8 members)
judge selection and term of office: Supreme Court chief justice and judges appointed by the president upon recommendation by the General Council of Courts - a 14-member body of judges and judicial officials - to the State Great Hural; appointment is for life; chairman of the Constitutional Court elected from among its members; members appointed from nominations by the State Great Hural - 3 each by the president, the State Great Hural, and the Supreme Court; appointment is 6 years; chairmanship limited to a single renewable 3-year term
subordinate courts: aimag (provincial) and capital city appellate courts; soum, inter-soum, and district courts; Administrative Cases Courts

Political parties: Democratic Party or DP
Mongolian People's Party or MPP
National Coalition (consists of Mongolian Green Party or MGP and the Mongolian National Democratic Party or MNDP)
National Labor Party or HUN
Civil Will-Green Party or CWGP

International organization participation: ADB, ARF, CD, CICA, CP, EBRD, EITI (compliant country), FAO, G-77, IAEA, IBRD, ICAO, ICC (NGOs), ICCt, ICRM, IDA, IFAD, IFC, IFRCS, ILO, IMF, IMO, IMSO, Interpol, IOC, IOM, IPU, ISO, ITSO, ITU, ITUC, MIGA, MINURSO, MONUSCO, NAM, OPCW, OSCE, SCO (observer), UN, UNAMID, UNCTAD, UNESCO, UNIDO, UNISFA, UNMISS, UNWTO, UPU, WCO, WHO, WIPO, WMO, WTO

Diplomatic representation in the US: *chief of mission:* Ambassador BATBAYAR Ulziidelger (since 1 December 2021)
chancery: 2833 M Street NW, Washington, DC 20007
telephone: [1] (202) 333-7117
FAX: [1] (202) 298-9227
email address and website:
washington@mfa.gov.mn
http://mongolianembassy.us/
consulate(s) general: New York, San Francisco

Diplomatic representation from the US: *chief of mission:* Ambassador Richard L. BUANGAN (since November 2022)
embassy: Denver Street #3, 11th Micro-District, Ulaanbaatar 14190
mailing address: 4410 Ulaanbaatar Place, Washington DC 20521-4410
telephone: [976] 7007-6001
FAX: [976] 7007-6174
email address and website:
UlaanbaatarACS@state.gov
https://mn.usembassy.gov/

Flag description: three, equal vertical bands of red (hoist side), blue, and red; centered on the hoist-side red band in yellow is the national emblem ("soyombo" - a columnar arrangement of abstract and geometric representation for fire, sun, moon, earth, water, and the yin-yang symbol); blue represents the sky, red symbolizes progress and prosperity

National symbol(s): soyombo emblem; national colors: red, blue, yellow

National anthem: *name:* "Mongol ulsyn toriin duulal" (National Anthem of Mongolia)
lyrics/music: Tsendiin DAMDINSUREN/Bilegiin DAMDINSUREN and Luvsanjamts MURJORJ
note: music adopted 1950, lyrics adopted 2006; lyrics altered on numerous occasions

National heritage: *total World Heritage Sites:* 6 (4 cultural, 2 natural)
selected World Heritage Site locales: Uvs Nuur Basin (n); Orkhon Valley Cultural Landscape (c); Petroglyphic Complexes of the Mongolian Altai (c); Great Burkhan Khaldun Mountain and surrounding sacred landscape (c); Landscapes of Dauria (n); Deer Stone Monuments and Related Bronze Age Sites (c)

ECONOMY

Economic overview: lower middle-income East Asian economy; large human capital improvements over last 3 decades; agricultural and natural resource rich; export and consumption-led growth; high inflation due to supply bottlenecks and increased food and energy prices; currency depreciation

Real GDP (purchasing power parity): $56.264 billion (2023 est.)
$52.572 billion (2022 est.)
$50.053 billion (2021 est.)
note: data in 2021 dollars
comparison ranking: 121

Real GDP growth rate: 7.02% (2023 est.)
5.03% (2022 est.)
1.64% (2021 est.)
note: annual GDP % growth based on constant local currency
comparison ranking: 21

Real GDP per capita: $16,300 (2023 est.)
$15,500 (2022 est.)
$15,000 (2021 est.)
note: data in 2021 dollars
comparison ranking: 114

GDP (official exchange rate): $19.872 billion (2023 est.)
note: data in current dollars at official exchange rate

Inflation rate (consumer prices): 10.35% (2023 est.)
15.15% (2022 est.)
7.35% (2021 est.)
note: annual % change based on consumer prices
comparison ranking: 178

Credit ratings: Fitch rating: B (2018)

Moody's rating: B3 (2018)

Standard & Poors rating: B (2018)
note: The year refers to the year in which the current credit rating was first obtained.

GDP - composition, by sector of origin: *agriculture:* 10.2% (2023 est.)
industry: 40% (2023 est.)
services: 40.1% (2023 est.)
note: figures may not total 100% due to non-allocated consumption not captured in sector-reported data
comparison rankings: services 193; industry 30; agriculture 75

GDP - composition, by end use: *household consumption:* 47.8% (2023 est.)
government consumption: 13.3% (2023 est.)
investment in fixed capital: 27.4% (2023 est.)
investment in inventories: 5% (2023 est.)
exports of goods and services: 78% (2023 est.)
imports of goods and services: -69.2% (2023 est.)
note: figures may not total 100% due to rounding or gaps in data collection

Agricultural products: milk, wheat, potatoes, lamb/mutton, goat milk, beef, goat meat, bison milk, sheep milk, horse meat (2022)
note: top ten agricultural products based on tonnage

Industries: construction and construction materials; mining (coal, copper, molybdenum, fluorspar, tin, tungsten, gold); oil; food and beverages; processing of animal products, cashmere and natural fiber manufacturing

Industrial production growth rate: 12.57% (2023 est.)
note: annual % change in industrial value added based on constant local currency
comparison ranking: 8

Labor force: 1.403 million (2023 est.)
note: number of people ages 15 or older who are employed or seeking work
comparison ranking: 136

Unemployment rate: 6.13% (2023 est.)
6.21% (2022 est.)
7.75% (2021 est.)
note: % of labor force seeking employment
comparison ranking: 126

Youth unemployment rate (ages 15-24): *total:* 11.4% (2023 est.)
male: 10.3% (2023 est.)
female: 12.9% (2023 est.)
note: % of labor force ages 15-24 seeking employment
comparison ranking: total 118

Population below poverty line: 27.8% (2020 est.)
note: % of population with income below national poverty line

Gini Index coefficient - distribution of family income: 31.4 (2022 est.)
note: index (0-100) of income distribution; higher values represent greater inequality
comparison ranking: 114

Household income or consumption by percentage share: *lowest 10%:* 3.4% (2022 est.)
highest 10%: 24.6% (2022 est.)
note: % share of income accruing to lowest and highest 10% of population

Remittances: 2.21% of GDP (2023 est.)
2.33% of GDP (2022 est.)
3.08% of GDP (2021 est.)
note: personal transfers and compensation between resident and non-resident individuals/households/entities

Budget: *revenues:* $4.721 billion (2021 est.)
expenditures: $4.845 billion (2021 est.)
note: central government revenues (excluding grants) and expenses converted to US dollars at average official exchange rate for year indicated

Public debt: 67.57% of GDP (2021 est.)
note: central government debt as a % of GDP
comparison ranking: 59

Taxes and other revenues: 16.91% (of GDP) (2021 est.)
note: central government tax revenue as a % of GDP
comparison ranking: 116

Current account balance: $121.266 million (2023 est.)
-$2.303 billion (2022 est.)
-$2.108 billion (2021 est.)
note: balance of payments - net trade and primary/secondary income in current dollars
comparison ranking: 71

Exports: $15.501 billion (2023 est.)
$10.989 billion (2022 est.)
$8.95 billion (2021 est.)
note: balance of payments - exports of goods and services in current dollars
comparison ranking: 98

Exports - partners: China 78%, Switzerland 15%, Singapore 3%, South Korea 2%, Russia 1% (2022)
note: top five export partners based on percentage share of exports

Exports - commodities: coal, copper ore, gold, animal hair, iron ore (2022)
note: top five export commodities based on value in dollars

Imports: $13.545 billion (2023 est.)
$12.112 billion (2022 est.)
$9.256 billion (2021 est.)
note: balance of payments - imports of goods and services in current dollars
comparison ranking: 108

Imports - partners: China 36%, Russia 29%, Japan 7%, South Korea 5%, US 3% (2022)
note: top five import partners based on percentage share of imports

Imports - commodities: refined petroleum, cars, trucks, trailers, raw iron bars (2022)
note: top five import commodities based on value in dollars

Reserves of foreign exchange and gold: $4.782 billion (2023 est.)
$3.398 billion (2022 est.)
$4.38 billion (2021 est.)
note: holdings of gold (year-end prices)/foreign exchange/special drawing rights in current dollars
comparison ranking: 101

Debt - external: $9.085 billion (2022 est.)
note: present value of external debt in current US dollars
comparison ranking: 42

Exchange rates: togrog/tugriks (MNT) per US dollar -

Exchange rates: 3,465.737 (2023 est.)
3,140.678 (2022 est.)
2,849.289 (2021 est.)
2,813.29 (2020 est.)
2,663.541 (2019 est.)

ENERGY

Electricity access: *electrification - total population:* 100% (2022 est.)

Electricity: *installed generating capacity:* 1.61 million kW (2022 est.)
consumption: 8.602 billion kWh (2022 est.)
exports: 24 million kWh (2022 est.)
imports: 1.861 billion kWh (2022 est.)
transmission/distribution losses: 1.036 billion kWh (2022 est.)
comparison rankings: transmission/distribution losses 97; imports 62; exports 94; consumption 113; installed generating capacity 128

Electricity generation sources: *fossil fuels:* 88.9% of total installed capacity (2022 est.)
solar: 2.2% of total installed capacity (2022 est.)
wind: 7.8% of total installed capacity (2022 est.)
hydroelectricity: 1% of total installed capacity (2022 est.)

Coal: *production:* 28.276 million metric tons (2022 est.)
consumption: 6.393 million metric tons (2022 est.)
exports: 19.47 million metric tons (2022 est.)
imports: 2,000 metric tons (2022 est.)
proven reserves: 2.52 billion metric tons (2022 est.)

Petroleum: *total petroleum production:* 15,000 bbl/day (2023 est.)
refined petroleum consumption: 36,000 bbl/day (2022 est.)

Carbon dioxide emissions: 15.918 million metric tonnes of CO2 (2022 est.)
from coal and metallurgical coke: 10.63 million metric tonnes of CO2 (2022 est.)
from petroleum and other liquids: 5.289 million metric tonnes of CO2 (2022 est.)
comparison ranking: total emissions 95

Energy consumption per capita: 57.093 million Btu/person (2022 est.)
comparison ranking: 87

COMMUNICATIONS

Telephones - fixed lines: *total subscriptions:* 475,000 (2022 est.)
subscriptions per 100 inhabitants: 14 (2022 est.)
comparison ranking: total subscriptions 93

Telephones - mobile cellular: *total subscriptions:* 4.836 million (2022 est.)
subscriptions per 100 inhabitants: 142 (2022 est.)
comparison ranking: total subscriptions 124

Telecommunication systems: *general assessment:* liberalized and competitive telecoms market comprises of a number of operators; fixed-line penetration increased steadily in the years to 2018 as more people took on fixed-line access for voice calls and to access copper-based broadband services; the number of lines fell in 2019, and again and more sharply in 2020, partly through the economic consequences of the pandemic (GDP fell 5.3% in

2020, year-on-year) and partly due to the migration to the mobile platform and to VoIP; fixed broadband penetration remains low, mainly due to a limited number of fixed lines and the dominance of the mobile platform; the attraction of fixed broadband as a preferred access where it is available is waning as the mobile networks are upgraded with greater capacity and capabilities; the growing popularity of mobile broadband continues to underpin overall broadband and telecom sector growth, with Mongolia's market very much being dominated by mobile services, supported by widely available LTE; this will largely determine and shape the future direction of Mongolia's developing digital economy (2021)
domestic: fixed-line teledensity of 12 per 100; mobile-cellular subscribership is 140 per 100 persons (2021)
international: country code - 976; satellite earth stations - 7 (2016)

Broadcast media: following a law passed in 2005, Mongolia's state-run radio and TV provider converted to a public service provider; also available are 68 radio and 160 TV stations, including multi-channel satellite and cable TV providers; transmissions of multiple international broadcasters are available (2019)

Internet country code: .mn

Internet users: *total:* 2.772 million (2021 est.)
percent of population: 84% (2021 est.)
comparison ranking: total 124

Broadband - fixed subscriptions: *total:* 307,166 (2020 est.)
subscriptions per 100 inhabitants: 9 (2020 est.)
comparison ranking: total 106

TRANSPORTATION

National air transport system: *number of registered air carriers:* 4 (2020)
inventory of registered aircraft operated by air carriers: 12
annual passenger traffic on registered air carriers: 670,360 (2018)
annual freight traffic on registered air carriers: 7.82 million (2018) mt-km

Civil aircraft registration country code prefix: JU

Airports: 35 (2024)
comparison ranking: 112

Railways: *total:* 1,815 km (2017)
broad gauge: 1,815 km (2017) 1.520-m gauge
note: national operator Ulaanbaatar Railway is jointly owned by the Mongolian Government and by the Russian State Railway
comparison ranking: total 77

Roadways: *total:* 113,200 km
paved: 10,600 km
unpaved: 102,600 km (2017)
comparison ranking: total 45

Waterways: 580 km (2010) (the only waterway in operation is Lake Hovsgol) (135 km); Selenge River (270 km) and Orhon River (175 km) are navigable but carry little traffic; lakes and rivers ice-free from May to September)
comparison ranking: 88

Merchant marine: *total:* 318 (2023)
by type: bulk carrier 8, container ship 8, general cargo 151, oil tanker 58, other 93
comparison ranking: total 55

MILITARY AND SECURITY

Military and security forces: Mongolian Armed Forces (MAF): Ground Force, Air Force, Cyber Security Forces, Special Forces, Construction-Engineering Forces (2024)
note: the National Police Agency and the General Authority for Border Protection, which operate under the Ministry of Justice and Home Affairs, are primarily responsible for internal security; they are assisted by the General Intelligence Agency under the prime minister; the MAF assists the internal security forces in providing domestic emergency assistance and disaster relief

Military expenditures: 0.6% of GDP (2023 est.)
0.6% of GDP (2022 est.)
0.8% of GDP (2021 est.)
0.8% of GDP (2020 est.)
0.7% of GDP (2019 est.)
comparison ranking: 154

Military and security service personnel strengths: information varies; estimated 10,000 active troops (2023)

Military equipment inventories and acquisitions: the MAF's inventory is comprised largely of Soviet-era and Russian equipment (2024)

Military service age and obligation: 18-25 years of age for compulsory and voluntary military service (can enter military schools at age 17); 12-month conscript service obligation for men can be extended 3 months under special circumstances; conscription service can be exchanged for a 24-month stint in the civil service or a cash payment determined by the Mongolian Government; after conscription, soldiers can contract into military service for 2 or 4 years; volunteer military service for men and women is 24 months, which can be extended for another two years up to the age of 31 (2024)

Military deployments: 875 South Sudan (UNMISS) (2024)
note: since 2002, Mongolia has deployed more than 20,000 peacekeepers and observers to UN operations in more than a dozen countries

Military - note: the Mongolian Armed Forces (MAF) are responsible for ensuring the country's independence, security, and territorial integrity, and supporting Mongolia's developmental goals and diplomacy; it has a range of missions, including counterterrorism, disaster response, and international peacekeeping duties; the Ground Force is the military's primary service and is centered on a motorized infantry brigade; it also has a battalion devoted to peacekeeping duties and hosts an annual international peacekeeping exercise known as "Khaan Quest"; Mongolia's primary military partner is Russia, and in addition to receiving Russian military equipment, the MAF participates in Russia's large "Vostok" exercise, which is conducted every four years; the MAF has a growing relationship with the US military
Mongolia has been engaged in dialogue and cooperation with NATO since 2005 and is considered by NATO to be a global partner; Mongolia supported the NATO-led Kosovo Force from 2005-2007 and contributed troops to the NATO-led International Security Assistance Force in Afghanistan from 2009-2014, as well as to the follow-on Resolute Support Mission that provided training, advice, and other assistance to the Afghan security forces (2015-2021) (2023)

TRANSNATIONAL ISSUES

Refugees and internally displaced persons: *stateless persons:* 17 (2022)

Illicit drugs: NA

MONTENEGRO

INTRODUCTION

Background: The use of the name Crna Gora or Black Mountain (Montenegro) began in the 13th century in reference to a highland region in the Serbian province of Zeta. Under Ottoman control beginning in 1496, Montenegro was a semi-autonomous theocracy ruled by a series of bishop princes until 1852, when it became a secular principality. Montenegro fought a series of wars with the Ottomans and eventually won recognition as an independent sovereign principality at the Congress of Berlin in 1878. In 1918, the country was absorbed by the Kingdom of Serbs, Croats, and Slovenes, which became the Kingdom of Yugoslavia in 1929. At the end of World War II, Montenegro joined the Socialist Federal Republic of Yugoslavia (SFRY). When the SFRY dissolved in 1992, Montenegro and Serbia created the Federal Republic of Yugoslavia (FRY), which shifted in 2003 to a looser State Union of Serbia and Montenegro. Montenegro voted to restore its independence on 3 June 2006. Montenegro became an official EU candidate in 2010 and joined NATO in 2017.

GEOGRAPHY

Location: Southeastern Europe, between the Adriatic Sea and Serbia

Geographic coordinates: 42 30 N, 19 18 E

Map references: Europe

Area: *total:* 13,812 sq km
land: 13,452 sq km
water: 360 sq km
comparison ranking: total 161

Area - comparative: slightly smaller than Connecticut; slightly larger than twice the size of Delaware

Land boundaries: *total:* 680 km
border countries (5): Albania 186 km; Bosnia and Herzegovina 242 km; Croatia 19 km; Kosovo 76 km; Serbia 157 km

Coastline: 293.5 km

Maritime claims: *territorial sea:* 12 nm
continental shelf: defined by treaty

Climate: Mediterranean climate, hot dry summers and autumns and relatively cold winters with heavy snowfalls inland

Terrain: highly indented coastline with narrow coastal plain backed by rugged high limestone mountains and plateaus

Elevation: *highest point:* Zia Kolata 2,534 m
lowest point: Adriatic Sea 0 m
mean elevation: 1,086 m

Natural resources: bauxite, hydroelectricity

Land use: *agricultural land:* 38.2% (2018 est.)
arable land: 12.9% (2018 est.)
permanent crops: 1.2% (2018 est.)
permanent pasture: 24.1% (2018 est.)
forest: 40.4% (2018 est.)
other: 21.4% (2018 est.)

Irrigated land: 24 sq km (2012)

Major lakes (area sq km): *fresh water lake(s):* Lake Scutari (shared with Albania) - 400 sq km
note - largest lake in the Balkans

Major watersheds (area sq km): Atlantic Ocean drainage: *(Black Sea)* Danube (795,656 sq km)

Population distribution: highest population density is concentrated in the south, southwest; the extreme eastern border is the least populated area

Natural hazards: destructive earthquakes

Geography - note: strategic location along the Adriatic coast

PEOPLE AND SOCIETY

Population: *total:* 599,849
male: 294,482
female: 305,367 (2024 est.)
comparison rankings: female 172; male 172; total 172

Nationality: *noun:* Montenegrin(s)
adjective: Montenegrin

Ethnic groups: Montenegrin 45%, Serbian 28.7%, Bosniak 8.7%, Albanian 4.9%, Muslim 3.3%, Romani 1%, Croat 1%, other 2.6%, unspecified 4.9% (2011 est.)

Languages: Serbian 42.9%, Montenegrin (official) 37%, Bosnian 5.3%, Albanian 5.3%, Serbo-Croat 2%, other 3.5%, unspecified 4% (2011 est.)
major-language sample(s):
Knjiga svetskih činjenica, neophodan izvor osnovnih informacija. (Serbian)
Knjiga svjetskih činjenica, neophodan izvor osnovnih informacija. (Montenegrin/Bosnian)

Religions: Orthodox 72.1%, Muslim 19.1%, Catholic 3.4%, atheist 1.2%, other 1.5%, unspecified 2.6% (2011 est.)

Age structure: *0-14 years:* 17.7% (male 54,608/ female 51,594)
15-64 years: 64.4% (male 192,631/female 193,515)
65 years and over: 17.9% (2024 est.) (male 47,243/ female 60,258)

Dependency ratios: *total dependency ratio:* 52.5
youth dependency ratio: 27.7
elderly dependency ratio: 24.8
potential support ratio: 4 (2021 est.)

Median age: *total:* 41.1 years (2024 est.)
male: 39.5 years
female: 42.5 years
comparison ranking: total 54

Population growth rate: -0.44% (2024 est.)
comparison ranking: 219

Birth rate: 10.9 births/1,000 population (2024 est.)
comparison ranking: 165

Death rate: 10.3 deaths/1,000 population (2024 est.)
comparison ranking: 31

Net migration rate: -5 migrant(s)/1,000 population (2024 est.)
comparison ranking: 203

Population distribution: highest population density is concentrated in the south, southwest; the extreme eastern border is the least populated area

Urbanization: *urban population:* 68.5% of total population (2023)
rate of urbanization: 0.45% annual rate of change (2020-25 est.)

Major urban areas - population: 177,000 PODGORICA (capital) (2018)

Sex ratio: *at birth:* 1.04 male(s)/female
0-14 years: 1.06 male(s)/female
15-64 years: 1 male(s)/female
65 years and over: 0.78 male(s)/female
total population: 0.96 male(s)/female (2024 est.)

Mother's mean age at first birth: 26.3 years (2010 est.)

Maternal mortality ratio: 6 deaths/100,000 live births (2020 est.)
comparison ranking: 161

Infant mortality rate: *total:* 3.2 deaths/1,000 live births (2024 est.)
male: 2.7 deaths/1,000 live births
female: 3.7 deaths/1,000 live births
comparison ranking: total 202

Life expectancy at birth: *total population:* 78.2 years (2024 est.)
male: 75.8 years
female: 80.7 years
comparison ranking: total population 82

Total fertility rate: 1.8 children born/woman (2024 est.)
comparison ranking: 141

Gross reproduction rate: 0.89 (2024 est.)

Contraceptive prevalence rate: 20.7% (2018)

Drinking water source: *improved: urban:* 100% of population
rural: 98.2% of population
total: 99.4% of population
unimproved: urban: 0% of population
rural: 1.8% of population
total: 0.6% of population (2020 est.)

Current health expenditure: 11.4% of GDP (2020)

Physician density: 2.74 physicians/1,000 population (2020)

Hospital bed density: 3.9 beds/1,000 population (2017)

Sanitation facility access: *improved: urban:* 100% of population
rural: 93.9% of population
total: 98% of population
unimproved: urban: 0% of population
rural: 6.1% of population
total: 2% of population (2020 est.)

Obesity - adult prevalence rate: 23.3% (2016)
comparison ranking: 66

Alcohol consumption per capita: *total:* 9.91 liters of pure alcohol (2019 est.)
beer: 3.83 liters of pure alcohol (2019 est.)
wine: 2.68 liters of pure alcohol (2019 est.)
spirits: 3.22 liters of pure alcohol (2019 est.)
other alcohols: 0.16 liters of pure alcohol (2019 est.)
comparison ranking: total 23

Tobacco use: *total:* 31.4% (2020 est.)
male: 31.6% (2020 est.)
female: 31.1% (2020 est.)
comparison ranking: total 26

Children under the age of 5 years underweight: 3.7% (2018/19)
comparison ranking: 82

Currently married women (ages 15-49): 57.1% (2023 est.)

Child marriage: *women married by age 15:* 1.9%
women married by age 18: 5.8%
men married by age 18: 3.2% (2018 est.)

Education expenditures: NA

Literacy: *definition:* age 15 and over can read and write
total population: 99%
male: 99.4%
female: 98.5% (2021)

School life expectancy (primary to tertiary education): *total:* 15 years
male: 15 years
female: 16 years (2021)

ENVIRONMENT

Environment - current issues: pollution of coastal waters from sewage outlets, especially in tourist-related areas such as Kotor; serious air pollution in Podgorica, Pljevlja and Niksie; air pollution in Pljevlja is caused by the nearby lignite power plant and the domestic use of coal and wood for household heating

Environment - international agreements: *party to:* Air Pollution, Air Pollution-Heavy Metals, Air Pollution-Persistent Organic Pollutants, Biodiversity, Climate Change, Climate Change-Kyoto Protocol, Climate Change-Paris Agreement, Comprehensive Nuclear Test Ban, Desertification, Endangered Species, Hazardous Wastes, Law of the Sea, Marine Dumping-London Convention, Marine Life Conservation, Nuclear Test Ban, Ozone Layer Protection, Ship Pollution, Wetlands
signed, but not ratified: none of the selected agreements

Climate: Mediterranean climate, hot dry summers and autumns and relatively cold winters with heavy snowfalls inland

Urbanization: *urban population:* 68.5% of total population (2023)
rate of urbanization: 0.45% annual rate of change (2020-25 est.)

Revenue from forest resources: 0.43% of GDP (2018 est.)
comparison ranking: 70

Revenue from coal: 0.12% of GDP (2018 est.)
comparison ranking: 25

Air pollutants: *particulate matter emissions:* 19.3 micrograms per cubic meter (2019 est.)
carbon dioxide emissions: 2.02 megatons (2016 est.)
methane emissions: 0.75 megatons (2020 est.)

Waste and recycling: *municipal solid waste generated annually:* 332,000 tons (2015 est.)
municipal solid waste recycled annually: 17,994 tons (2015 est.)
percent of municipal solid waste recycled: 5.4% (2015 est.)

Major lakes (area sq km): *fresh water lake(s):* Lake Scutari (shared with Albania) - 400 sq km
note - largest lake in the Balkans

Major watersheds (area sq km): Atlantic Ocean drainage: *(Black Sea)* Danube (795,656 sq km)

Total water withdrawal: *municipal:* 100 million cubic meters (2020 est.)
industrial: 60 million cubic meters (2020 est.)
agricultural: 1.7 million cubic meters (2017 est.)

GOVERNMENT

Country name: *conventional long form:* none
conventional short form: Montenegro
local long form: none
local short form: Crna Gora
former: People's Republic of Montenegro, Socialist Republic of Montenegro, Republic of Montenegro
etymology: the country's name locally as well as in most Western European languages means "black mountain" and refers to the dark coniferous forests on Mount Lovcen and the surrounding area

Government type: parliamentary republic

Capital: *name:* Podgorica; note - Cetinje retains the status of "Old Royal Capital"
geographic coordinates: 42 26 N, 19 16 E
time difference: UTC+1 (6 hours ahead of Washington, DC, during Standard Time)
daylight saving time: +1 hr, begins last Sunday in March; ends last Sunday in October
etymology: the name translates as "beneath Gorica"; the meaning of Gorica is "hillock"; the reference is to the small hill named Gorica that the city is built around

Administrative divisions: 25 municipalities (opstine, singular - opstina); Andrijevica, Bar, Berane, Bijelo Polje, Budva, Cetinje, Danilovgrad, Gusinje, Herceg Novi, Kolasin, Kotor, Mojkovac, Niksic, Petnjica, Plav, Pljevlja, Pluzine, Podgorica, Rozaje, Savnik, Tivat, Tuzi, Ulcinj, Zabljak, Zeta

Independence: *3 June 2006 (from the State Union of Serbia and Montenegro); notable earlier dates:* 13 March 1852 (Principality of Montenegro established); 13 July 1878 (Congress of Berlin recognizes Montenegrin independence); 28 August 1910 (Kingdom of Montenegro established)

National holiday: Statehood Day, 13 July (1878, the day the Berlin Congress recognized Montenegro as the 27th independent state in the world, and 1941, the day the Montenegrins staged an uprising against fascist occupiers and sided with the partisan communist movement)

Legal system: civil law

Constitution: *history:* several previous; latest adopted 22 October 2007
amendments: proposed by the president of Montenegro, by the government, or by at least 25 members of the Assembly; passage of draft proposals requires two-thirds majority vote of the Assembly, followed by a public hearing; passage of draft amendments requires two-thirds majority vote of the Assembly; changes to certain constitutional articles, such as sovereignty, state symbols, citizenship, and constitutional change procedures, require three-fifths majority vote in a referendum; amended 2013

International law organization participation: has not submitted an ICJ jurisdiction declaration; accepts ICCt jurisdiction

Citizenship: *citizenship by birth:* no
citizenship by descent only: at least one parent must be a citizen of Montenegro
dual citizenship recognized: no
residency requirement for naturalization: 10 years

Suffrage: 18 years of age; universal

Executive branch: *chief of state:* President Jakov MILATOVIC (since 20 May 2023)
head of government: Prime Minister Milojko SPAJIC (since 31 October 2023)
cabinet: ministers act as cabinet
elections/appointments: president directly elected by absolute majority popular vote in 2 rounds if needed for a 5-year term (eligible for a second term); election last held on 19 March 2023 with a runoff on 2 April 2023 (next to be held in 2028); prime minister nominated by the president, approved by the Assembly
election results:
2023: Jakov MILATOVIC elected president in second round; percent of vote in first round - Milo DUKANOVIC (DPS) 35.4%, Jakov MILATOVIC (Europe Now!) 28.9%, Andrija MANDIC (DF) 19.3%, Aleksa BECIC (DCG) 11.1%, other 5.3%; percent of vote in second round - Jakov MILATOVIC 58.9%, Milo DUKANOVIC 41.1%
2018: Milo DJUKANOVIC elected president in first round; percent of vote - Milo DJUKANOVIC (DPS) 53.9%, Mladen BOJANIC (independent) 33.4%, Draginja VUKSANOVIC (SDP) 8.2%, Marko MILACIC (PRAVA) 2.8%, other 1.7%

Legislative branch: *description:* unicameral Assembly or Skupstina (81 seats; members directly elected in a single nationwide constituency by proportional representation vote; members serve 4-year terms)
elections: last held on 11 June 2023 (next to be held in June 2027)
election results: percent of vote by party/coalition - Europe Now! 25.5%, Together! 23.2%, For the Future of Montenegro 14.7%, Aleksa and Dritan - Count Bravely 12.5%, BP 7.1%, SNP-DEMOS 3.1%, Albanian Forum 1.9%, HGI 0.7%; seats by party/coalition Europe Now! 24, Together! 21, For the Future of Montenegro 13, Aleksa and Dritan - Count Bravely 11, BP 6, SNP-DEMOS 2, Albanian Forum 2, Albanian Alliance 1, HGI 1; composition - men 59, women 22, percentage women 27.2%

Judicial branch: *highest court(s):* Supreme Court or Vrhovni Sud (consists of the court president, deputy president, and 15 judges); Constitutional Court or Ustavni Sud (consists of the court president and 7 judges)
judge selection and term of office: Supreme Court president proposed by general session of the Supreme Court and elected by the Judicial Council, a 9-member body consisting of judges, lawyers designated by the Assembly, and the minister of judicial affairs; Supreme Court president elected for a single renewable, 5-year term; other judges elected by the Judicial Council for life; Constitutional Court judges - 2 proposed by the president of Montenegro and 5 by the Assembly, and elected by the Assembly; court president elected from among the court members; court president elected for a 3-year term, other judges serve 9-year terms
subordinate courts: Administrative Courts; Appellate Court; Commercial Courts; High Courts; basic courts

Political parties: Albanian Alliance (electoral coalition includes FORCA, PD, DSCG)
Albanian Alternative or AA
Albanian Democratic League or LDSH
Albanian Forum (electoral coalition includes AA, LDSH, UDSH)
Aleksa and Dritan - Count Bravely! (electoral coalition includes Democrats, URA)
Bosniak Party or BS
Civic Movement United Reform Action or United Reform Action or URA
Croatian Civic Initiative or HGI
Democratic Alliance or DEMOS
Democratic League in Montenegro or DSCG
Democratic Montenegro or Democrats
Democratic Party of Socialists or DPS
Democratic People's Party or DNP
Democratic Union of Albanians or UDSH
Europe Now!
For the Future of Montenegro or ZBCG (coalition includes NSD, DNP, RP)
Liberal Party or LP
New Democratic Power or FORCA
New Serb Democracy or NSD or NOVA
Social Democrats or SD
Socialist People's Party or SNP
Together! (electoral coalition includes DPS, SD, LP, UDSH)
United Montenegro or UCG (split from DEMOS)
Workers' Party or RP

International organization participation: CE, CEI, EAPC, EBRD, FAO, IAEA, IBRD, ICAO, ICC (NGOs), ICCt, ICRM, IDA, IFC, IFRCS, IHO, ILO, IMF, IMO, IMSO, Interpol, IOC, IOM, IPU, ISO (correspondent), ITSO, ITU, ITUC (NGOs), MIGA, NATO, OAS (observer), OIF (observer), OPCW, OSCE, PCA, PFP, SELEC, UN, UNCTAD, UNESCO, UNHCR, UNHRC, UNIDO, UNWTO, UPU, WCO, WHO, WIPO, WMO, WTO
note: Montenegro is an EU candidate country whose satisfactory completion of accession criteria is required before being granted full EU membership

Diplomatic representation in the US: *chief of mission:* Ambassador Jovan MIRKOVIC (since 18 September 2024)
chancery: 1610 New Hampshire Avenue NW, Washington, DC, 20009
telephone: [1] (202) 234-6108
FAX: [1] (202) 234-6109
email address and website:
usa@mfa.gov.me

United States of America - Embassies and consulates of Montenegro and visa regimes for foreign citizens (www.gov.me)
consulate(s) general: New York

Diplomatic representation from the US: *chief of mission:* Ambassador Judy Rising REINKE (since 20 December 2018)
embassy: Dzona Dzeksona 2, 81000 Podgorica
mailing address: 5570 Podgorica Place, Washington DC 20521-5570
telephone: [382] (0) 20-410-500
FAX: [382] (0) 20-241-358
email address and website:
PodgoricaACS@state.gov
https://me.usembassy.gov/

Flag description: a red field bordered by a narrow golden-yellow stripe with the Montenegrin coat of arms centered; the arms consist of a double-headed golden eagle - symbolizing the unity of church and state - surmounted by a crown; the eagle holds a golden scepter in its right claw and a blue orb in its left; the breast shield over the eagle shows a golden lion passant on a green field in front of a blue sky; the lion is a symbol of episcopal authority and harkens back to the three and a half centuries when Montenegro was ruled as a theocracy

National symbol(s): double-headed eagle; national colors: red, gold

National anthem: *name:* "Oj, svijetla majska zoro" (Oh, Bright Dawn of May)
lyrics/music: Sekula DRLJEVIC/unknown, arranged by Zarko MIKOVIC
note: adopted 2004; music based on a Montenegrin folk song

National heritage: *total World Heritage Sites:* 4 (3 cultural, 1 natural)
selected World Heritage Site locales: Natural and Culturo-Historical Region of Kotor (c); Durmitor National Park (n); Stecci Medieval Tombstones Graveyards (c); Fortified City of Kotor Venetian Defense Works (c)

ECONOMY

Economic overview: upper middle-income, small Balkan economy; uses euro as de facto currency; strong growth driven by tourism and consumption; new impetus for EU accession under Europe Now government; influx of affluent migrants from Russia and Ukraine; progress in fiscal position subject to risks from pension costs, debt service, and informal sector

Real GDP (purchasing power parity): $17.115 billion (2023 est.)
$16.149 billion (2022 est.)
$15.177 billion (2021 est.)
note: data in 2021 dollars
comparison ranking: 158

Real GDP growth rate: 5.98% (2023 est.)
6.41% (2022 est.)
13.04% (2021 est.)
note: annual GDP % growth based on constant local currency
comparison ranking: 33

Real GDP per capita: $27,800 (2023 est.)
$26,200 (2022 est.)
$24,500 (2021 est.)
note: data in 2021 dollars
comparison ranking: 82

GDP (official exchange rate): $7.405 billion (2023 est.)
note: data in current dollars at official exchange rate

Inflation rate (consumer prices): 8.58% (2023 est.)
13.04% (2022 est.)
2.41% (2021 est.)
note: annual % change based on consumer prices
comparison ranking: 161

Credit ratings: Moody's rating: B1 (2016)

Standard & Poors rating: B+ (2014)
note: The year refers to the year in which the current credit rating was first obtained.

GDP - composition, by sector of origin: *agriculture:* 5.6% (2023 est.)
industry: 11.9% (2023 est.)
services: 62.4% (2023 est.)
note: figures may not total 100% due to non-allocated consumption not captured in sector-reported data
comparison rankings: services 72; industry 183; agriculture 112

GDP - composition, by end use: *household consumption:* 73.6% (2023 est.)
government consumption: 18.1% (2023 est.)
investment in fixed capital: 19.3% (2023 est.)
investment in inventories: 7.7% (2023 est.)
exports of goods and services: 50.7% (2023 est.)
imports of goods and services: -69.3% (2023 est.)
note: figures may not total 100% due to rounding or gaps in data collection

Agricultural products: milk, potatoes, grapes, watermelons, sheep milk, cabbages, oranges, eggs, goat milk, figs (2022)
note: top ten agricultural products based on tonnage

Industries: steelmaking, aluminum, agricultural processing, consumer goods, tourism

Industrial production growth rate: 3.34% (2023 est.)
note: annual % change in industrial value added based on constant local currency
comparison ranking: 99

Labor force: 286,000 (2023 est.)
note: number of people ages 15 or older who are employed or seeking work
comparison ranking: 169

Unemployment rate: 15.25% (2023 est.)
15.29% (2022 est.)
16.54% (2021 est.)
note: % of labor force seeking employment
comparison ranking: 191

Youth unemployment rate (ages 15-24): *total:* 27.9% (2023 est.)
male: 29% (2023 est.)
female: 26.3% (2023 est.)
note: % of labor force ages 15-24 seeking employment
comparison ranking: total 33

Population below poverty line: 21.2% (2020 est.)
note: % of population with income below national poverty line

Gini Index coefficient - distribution of family income: 34.3 (2021 est.)
note: index (0-100) of income distribution; higher values represent greater inequality
comparison ranking: 83

Average household expenditures: *on food:* 24.8% of household expenditures (2022 est.)
on alcohol and tobacco: 5.6% of household expenditures (2022 est.)

Household income or consumption by percentage share: *lowest 10%:* 2.1% (2021 est.)
highest 10%: 24.7% (2021 est.)
note: % share of income accruing to lowest and highest 10% of population

Remittances: 10.87% of GDP (2023 est.)
13.33% of GDP (2022 est.)
13.52% of GDP (2021 est.)
note: personal transfers and compensation between resident and non-resident individuals/households/entities

Budget: *revenues:* $1.463 billion (2015 est.)
expenditures: $1.491 billion (2015 est.)
note: central government revenues and expenses (excluding grants/extrabudgetary units/social security funds) converted to US dollars at average official exchange rate for year indicated

Public debt: 67.2% of GDP (2017 est.)
note: data cover general government debt, and includes debt instruments issued (or owned) by government entities other than the treasury; the data include treasury debt held by foreign entities; the data include debt issued by subnational entities, as well as intragovernmental debt; intragovernmental debt consists of treasury borrowings from surpluses in the social funds, such as for retirement, medical care, and unemployment; debt instruments for the social funds are not sold at public auctions
comparison ranking: 60

Taxes and other revenues: 37.2% (of GDP) (2017 est.)
comparison ranking: 14

Current account balance: -$841.765 million (2023 est.)
-$817.858 million (2022 est.)
-$541.201 million (2021 est.)
note: balance of payments - net trade and primary/secondary income in current dollars
comparison ranking: 135

Exports: $3.775 billion (2023 est.)
$3.178 billion (2022 est.)
$2.502 billion (2021 est.)
note: balance of payments - exports of goods and services in current dollars
comparison ranking: 148

Exports - partners: South Korea 24%, Serbia 12%, Italy 9%, Switzerland 9%, Bosnia and Herzegovina 7% (2022)
note: top five export partners based on percentage share of exports

Exports - commodities: copper ore, electricity, aluminum, aluminum ore, packaged medicine (2022)
note: top five export commodities based on value in dollars

Imports: $5.163 billion (2023 est.)
$4.614 billion (2022 est.)
$3.637 billion (2021 est.)
note: balance of payments - imports of goods and services in current dollars
comparison ranking: 149

Imports - partners: Serbia 24%, China 8%, Italy 8%, Croatia 7%, Greece 7% (2022)
note: top five import partners based on percentage share of imports

Imports - commodities: electricity, refined petroleum, aluminum, cars, garments (2022)
note: top five import commodities based on value in dollars

Reserves of foreign exchange and gold: $1.574 billion (2023 est.)
$2.041 billion (2022 est.)
$1.982 billion (2021 est.)
note: holdings of gold (year-end prices)/foreign exchange/special drawing rights in current dollars
comparison ranking: 127

Debt - external: $3.401 billion (2022 est.)
note: present value of external debt in current US dollars
comparison ranking: 62

Exchange rates: euros (EUR) per US dollar -

Exchange rates: 0.925 (2023 est.)
0.951 (2022 est.)
0.845 (2021 est.)
0.877 (2020 est.)
0.893 (2019 est.)
note: Montenegro, which is neither an EU member state nor a party to a formal EU monetary agreement, uses the euro as its de facto currency

ENERGY

Electricity access: *electrification - total population:* 100% (2022 est.)

Electricity: *installed generating capacity:* 1.066 million kW (2022 est.)
consumption: 2.963 billion kWh (2022 est.)
exports: 8.326 billion kWh (2022 est.)
imports: 8.467 billion kWh (2022 est.)
transmission/distribution losses: 507.151 million kWh (2022 est.)
comparison rankings: transmission/distribution losses 79; imports 30; exports 28; consumption 140; installed generating capacity 136

Electricity generation sources: *fossil fuels:* 47% of total installed capacity (2022 est.)
solar: 0.1% of total installed capacity (2022 est.)
wind: 9.8% of total installed capacity (2022 est.)
hydroelectricity: 43.1% of total installed capacity (2022 est.)

Coal: *production:* 1.734 million metric tons (2022 est.)
consumption: 1.517 million metric tons (2022 est.)
exports: 234,000 metric tons (2022 est.)
imports: 2.8 metric tons (2022 est.)
proven reserves: 337 million metric tons (2022 est.)

Petroleum: *refined petroleum consumption:* 8,000 bbl/day (2022 est.)

Carbon dioxide emissions: 2.566 million metric tonnes of CO_2 (2022 est.)
from coal and metallurgical coke: 1.401 million metric tonnes of CO_2 (2022 est.)
from petroleum and other liquids: 1.165 million metric tonnes of CO_2 (2022 est.)
comparison ranking: total emissions 151

Energy consumption per capita: 59.174 million Btu/person (2022 est.)
comparison ranking: 82

COMMUNICATIONS

Telephones - fixed lines: *total subscriptions:* 191,000 (2022 est.)
subscriptions per 100 inhabitants: 30 (2022 est.)
comparison ranking: total subscriptions 119

Telephones - mobile cellular: *total subscriptions:* 1.274 million (2022 est.)
subscriptions per 100 inhabitants: 203 (2022 est.)
comparison ranking: total subscriptions 161

Telecommunication systems: *general assessment:* a small telecom market supported by a population of only 623,000; fixed broadband services are available via a variety of technology platforms, though fiber is the dominant platform, accounting for almost 40% of connections; the growth of fiber has largely been at the expense of DSL as customers are migrated to fiber networks as these are built out progressively; mobile penetration is particularly high, though this is partly due to the significant number of tourists visiting the country seasonally, as also to the popularity of subscribers having multiple prepaid cards; in the wake of the pandemic and associated restrictions on travel, the number of mobile subscribers fell in 2020, as also in the first quarter of 2021, year-on-year; networks support a vibrant mobile broadband services sector, largely based on LTE; two of the MNOs began trialing 5G in May 2021, though commercial services will not gain traction until after the multi-spectrum auction is completed at the end of 2021; spectrum is available in the 694-790MHz and 3400-3800MHz ranges, as well as in the 26.5-27.5GHz range (2021)
domestic: fixed-line over 30 per 100 and mobile-cellular 178 per 100 persons (2021)
international: country code - 382; 2 international switches connect the national system

Broadcast media: state-funded national radio-TV broadcaster operates 2 terrestrial TV networks, 1 satellite TV channel, and 2 radio networks; 4 local public TV stations and 14 private TV stations; 14 local public radio stations, 35 private radio stations, and several on-line media (2019)

Internet country code: .me

Internet users: *total:* 516,600 (2021 est.)
percent of population: 82% (2021 est.)
comparison ranking: total 166

Broadband - fixed subscriptions: *total:* 184,176 (2020 est.)
subscriptions per 100 inhabitants: 29 (2020 est.)
comparison ranking: total 121

TRANSPORTATION

National air transport system: *number of registered air carriers:* 1 (2020)
inventory of registered aircraft operated by air carriers: 4
annual passenger traffic on registered air carriers: 565,522 (2018)
annual freight traffic on registered air carriers: 130,000 (2018) mt-km

Civil aircraft registration country code prefix: 4O

Airports: 5 (2024)
comparison ranking: 177

Heliports: 1 (2024)

Railways: *total:* 250 km (2017)
standard gauge: 250 km (2017) 1.435-m gauge (224 km electrified)
comparison ranking: total 126

Roadways: *total:* 9,825 km (2022)
comparison ranking: total 137

Merchant marine: *total:* 18 (2023)
by type: bulk carrier 4, other 14
comparison ranking: total 148

Ports: *total ports:* 4 (2024)
large: 0
medium: 0
small: 1
very small: 3
ports with oil terminals: 1
key ports: Bar, Kotor, Risan, Tivat

MILITARY AND SECURITY

Military and security forces: Army of Montenegro (Vojska Crne Gore or VCG): Ground Forces (Kopnene snage), Air Force (Vazduhoplovstvo), Navy (Mornarica) (2024)
note: the National Police Force, which includes Border Police, is responsible for maintaining internal security; it is organized under the Police Administration within the Ministry of Interior and reports to the police director and, through the director, to the minister of interior and prime minister

Military expenditures: 2% of GDP (2024 est.)
1.6% of GDP (2023)
1.4% of GDP (2022)
1.6% of GDP (2021)
1.7% of GDP (2020)
comparison ranking: 70

Military and security service personnel strengths: approximately 1,600 active-duty troops (2024)

Military equipment inventories and acquisitions: the military's inventory is small and consists largely of Soviet-era equipment inherited from the former Yugoslavia military, along with a limited but growing mix of imported Western systems (2024)

Military service age and obligation: 18 is the legal minimum age for voluntary military service; conscription abolished in 2006 (2024)
note: as of 2024, women made up over 11% of the military's full-time personnel

Military - note: the Army of Montenegro is a small, lightly armed military focused on the defense of Montenegro's sovereignty and territorial integrity, cooperating in international and multinational security, and assisting civil authorities during emergencies such as natural disasters; since Montenegro joined NATO in 2017, another focus has been integrating into the Alliance, including adapting NATO standards for planning and professionalization, structural reforms, and modernization by replacing its Soviet-era equipment; the Army trains and exercises with NATO partners and actively supports NATO missions and operations, committing small numbers of troops in Afghanistan, Kosovo, and NATO's Enhanced Forward Presence mission in Eastern Europe; a few personnel have also been deployed on EU- and UN-led operations (2024)

TRANSNATIONAL ISSUES

Refugees and internally displaced persons: *refugees (country of origin):* 65,105 (Ukraine) (as of 29 January 2024)
stateless persons: 468 (2022)
note: 34,511 estimated refugee and migrant arrivals (January 2015-March 2024)

Illicit drugs: drug trafficking groups are major players in the procurement and transportation of of large quantities of cocaine destined for European markets

MONTSERRAT

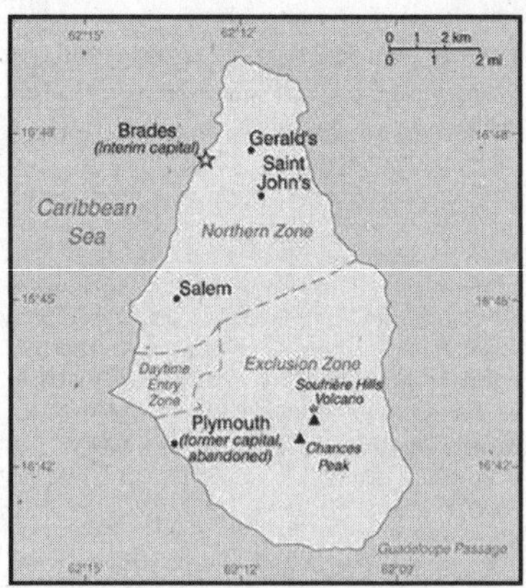

INTRODUCTION

Background: English and Irish colonists from St. Kitts first settled on Montserrat in 1632; the first African slaves arrived three decades later. The British and French fought for possession of the island for most of the 18th century, but it finally was confirmed as a British possession in 1783. The island's sugar plantation economy was converted to small farm landholdings in the mid-19th century. The Soufriere Hills Volcano erupted in 1995, devastating much of the island; two thirds of the population fled abroad. Montserrat has endured volcanic activity since, with the last eruption occurring in 2013.

GEOGRAPHY

Location: Caribbean, island in the Caribbean Sea, southeast of Puerto Rico

Geographic coordinates: 16 45 N, 62 12 W

Map references: Central America and the Caribbean

Area: *total:* 102 sq km
land: 102 sq km
water: 0 sq km
comparison ranking: total 224

Area - comparative: about 0.6 times the size of Washington, DC

Land boundaries: *total:* 0 km

Coastline: 40 km

Maritime claims: *territorial sea:* 12 nm
exclusive fishing zone: 200 nm

Climate: tropical; little daily or seasonal temperature variation

Terrain: volcanic island, mostly mountainous, with small coastal lowland

Elevation: *highest point:* Soufriere Hills volcano pre-eruption height was 915 m; current lava dome is subject to periodic build up and collapse; estimated dome height was 1,050 m in 2015
lowest point: Caribbean Sea 0 m

Natural resources: NEGL

Land use: *agricultural land:* 30% (2018 est.)
arable land: 20% (2018 est.)
permanent crops: 0% (2018 est.)
permanent pasture: 10% (2018 est.)
forest: 25% (2018 est.)
other: 45% (2018 est.)

Irrigated land: 0 sq km (2022)

Population distribution: only the northern half of the island is populated, the southern portion is uninhabitable due to volcanic activity

Natural hazards: volcanic eruptions; severe hurricanes (June to November)
volcanism: Soufriere Hills volcano (915 m), has erupted continuously since 1995; a massive eruption in 1997 destroyed most of the capital, Plymouth, and resulted in approximately half of the island becoming uninhabitable; the island of Montserrat is part of the volcanic island arc of the Lesser Antilles that extends from Saba in the north to Grenada in the south

Geography - note: the island is entirely volcanic in origin and composed of three major volcanic centers of differing ages

PEOPLE AND SOCIETY

Population: *total:* 5,468
male: 2,728
female: 2,740 (2024 est.)
note: an estimated 8,000 refugees left the island following the resumption of volcanic activity in July 1995; some have returned
comparison rankings: female 226; male 226; total 226

Nationality: *noun:* Montserratian(s)
adjective: Montserratian

Ethnic groups: African/Black 86.2%, mixed 4.8%, Hispanic/Spanish 3%, Caucasian/White 2.7%, East Indian/Indian 1.6%, other 1.8% (2018 est.)

Languages: English

Religions: Protestant 71.4% (includes Anglican 17.7%, Pentecostal/Full Gospel 16.1%, Seventh Day Adventist 15%, Methodist 13.9%, Church of God 6.7%, other Protestant 2%), Roman Catholic 11.4%, Rastafarian 1.4%, Hindu 1.2%, Jehovah's Witness 1%, Muslim 0.4%, other/not stated 5.1%, none 7.9% (2018 est.)

Age structure: *0-14 years:* 15.8% (male 446/female 420)
15-64 years: 76.1% (male 2,062/female 2,101)
65 years and over: 8% (2024 est.) (male 220/female 219)

Dependency ratios: *total dependency ratio:* 43.9
youth dependency ratio: 19.2
elderly dependency ratio: 24.7
potential support ratio: 4 (2021)

Median age: *total:* 36.8 years (2024 est.)
male: 35.4 years
female: 37.8 years
comparison ranking: total 87

Population growth rate: 0.59% (2024 est.)
comparison ranking: 141

Birth rate: 11.9 births/1,000 population (2024 est.)
comparison ranking: 149

Death rate: 6 deaths/1,000 population (2024 est.)
comparison ranking: 156

Net migration rate: 0 migrant(s)/1,000 population (2024 est.)
comparison ranking: 83

Population distribution: only the northern half of the island is populated, the southern portion is uninhabitable due to volcanic activity

Urbanization: *urban population:* 9.3% of total population (2023)
rate of urbanization: 0.94% annual rate of change (2020-25 est.)

Sex ratio: *at birth:* 1.03 male(s)/female
0-14 years: 1.06 male(s)/female
15-64 years: 0.98 male(s)/female
65 years and over: 1 male(s)/female
total population: 1 male(s)/female (2024 est.)

Infant mortality rate: *total:* 9.7 deaths/1,000 live births (2024 est.)
male: 8 deaths/1,000 live births
female: 11.6 deaths/1,000 live births
comparison ranking: total 134

Life expectancy at birth: *total population:* 76.1 years (2024 est.)
male: 76.9 years
female: 75.3 years
comparison ranking: total population 116

Total fertility rate: 1.33 children born/woman (2024 est.)
comparison ranking: 216

Gross reproduction rate: 0.63 (2024 est.)

Drinking water source: *improved:*
total: 98.1% of population
unimproved:
total: 1.9% of population (2020 est.)

Currently married women (ages 15-49): 35.8% (2023 est.)

Education expenditures: 5.4% of GDP (2020 est.)
comparison ranking: 62

School life expectancy (primary to tertiary education): *total:* 14 years
male: 13 years
female: 15 years (2019)

ENVIRONMENT

Environment - current issues: land erosion occurs on slopes that have been cleared for cultivation

Climate: tropical; little daily or seasonal temperature variation

Urbanization: *urban population:* 9.3% of total population (2023)
rate of urbanization: 0.94% annual rate of change (2020-25 est.)

GOVERNMENT

Country name: *conventional long form:* none
conventional short form: Montserrat
etymology: island named by explorer Christopher COLUMBUS in 1493 after the Benedictine abbey Santa Maria de Montserrat, near Barcelona, Spain

Government type: parliamentary democracy; self-governing overseas territory of the UK

Dependency status: overseas territory of the UK

Capital: *name:* Plymouth; note - Plymouth was abandoned in 1997 because of volcanic activity; interim government buildings have been built at

Brades Estate, the de facto capital, in the Carr's Bay/Little Bay vicinity at the northwest end of Montserrat
geographic coordinates: 16 42 N, 62 13 W
time difference: UTC-4 (1 hour ahead of Washington, DC, during Standard Time)
etymology: now entirely deserted because of volcanic activity, the city was originally named after Plymouth, England; *de jure,* Plymouth remains the capital city of Montserrat; it is therefore the only ghost town that serves as the capital of a political entity

Administrative divisions: 3 parishes; Saint Anthony, Saint Georges, Saint Peter

Independence: none (overseas territory of the UK)

National holiday: Birthday of Queen ELIZABETH II, usually celebrated the Monday after the second Saturday in June (1926)

Legal system: English common law

Constitution: *history:* previous 1960; latest put into force 20 October 2010 (The Montserrat Constitution Order 2010)
amendments: amended 2011, 2020

Citizenship: see United Kingdom

Suffrage: 18 years of age; universal

Executive branch: *chief of state:* King CHARLES III (since 8 September 2022); represented by Governor Sarah TUCKER (since 6 April 2023)
head of government: Premier Easton TAYLOR-FARRELL (since 19 November 2019)
cabinet: Executive Council consists of the governor, the premier, 3 other ministers, the attorney general, and the finance secretary
elections/appointments: the monarchy is hereditary; governor appointed by the monarch; following legislative elections, the leader of the majority party usually becomes premier
note: effective with Constitution Order 2010, October 2010, the office of premier replaced the office of chief minister

Legislative branch: *description:* unicameral Legislative Assembly (12 seats; 9 members directly elected in a single constituency by absolute majority vote in 2 rounds to serve 5-year terms; the speaker, normally elected from the outside by the Assembly for a 5- year term, and 2 ex-officio members - the attorney general and financial secretary)
elections: last held on 18 November 2019 (next to be held in 2024)
election results: percent of vote by party - MCAP 42.7%, PDM 29.9%, other 17.1%; seats by party - MCAP 5, PDM 3, independent 1; composition - men 8, women 4, percentage women 33.3%

Judicial branch: *highest court(s):* the Eastern Caribbean Supreme Court (ECSC) is the superior court of the Organization of Eastern Caribbean States; the ECSC - headquartered on St. Lucia - consists of the Court of Appeal - headed by the chief justice and 4 judges - and the High Court with 18 judges; the Court of Appeal is itinerant, traveling to member states on a schedule to hear appeals from the High Court and subordinate courts; High Court judges reside in the member states, with 1 assigned to Montserrat; Montserrat is also a member of the Caribbean Court of Justice
judge selection and term of office: chief justice of Eastern Caribbean Supreme Court appointed by the Her Majesty, Queen ELIZABETH II; other justices and judges appointed by the Judicial and Legal Services Commission, and independent body of judicial officials; Court of Appeal justices appointed for life with mandatory retirement at age 65; High Court judges appointed for life with mandatory retirement at age 62
subordinate courts: magistrate's court

Political parties: Movement for Change and Prosperity or MCAP
People's Democratic Movement or PDM

International organization participation: Caricom, CDB, Interpol (subbureau), OECS, UPU

Diplomatic representation in the US: none (overseas territory of the UK)

Diplomatic representation from the US: *embassy:* none (overseas territory of the UK); alternate contact is the US Embassy in Barbados [1] (246) 227-4000; US Embassy Bridgetown, Wildey Business Park, St. Michael BB 14006, Barbados, WI

Flag description: blue with the flag of the UK in the upper hoist-side quadrant and the Montserratian coat of arms centered in the outer half of the flag; the arms feature a woman in green dress, Erin, the female personification of Ireland, standing beside a yellow harp and embracing a large dark cross with her right arm; Erin and the harp are symbols of Ireland reflecting the territory's Irish ancestry; blue represents awareness, trustworthiness, determination, and righteousness

National anthem: *note:* as a territory of the UK, "God Save the King" is official (see United Kingdom)

ECONOMY

Economic overview: formerly high-income economy; volcanic activity destroyed much of original infrastructure and economy; new capital and port is being developed; key geothermal and solar power generation; key music recording operations

Real GDP per capita: (2011)
(2010)
(2009)

Inflation rate (consumer prices): 1.2% (2017 est.)
-0.2% (2016 est.)
comparison ranking: 23

Credit ratings: Standard & Poors rating: BBB- (2020)
note: The year refers to the year in which the current credit rating was first obtained.

GDP - composition, by sector of origin: *agriculture:* 1.9% (2017 est.)
industry: 7.8% (2017 est.)
services: 90.3% (2017 est.)
comparison rankings: services 7; industry 206; agriculture 161

GDP - composition, by end use: *household consumption:* 90.8% (2017 est.)
government consumption: 50.4% (2017 est.)
investment in fixed capital: 17.9% (2017 est.)
investment in inventories: -0.1% (2017 est.)
exports of goods and services: 29.5% (2017 est.)
imports of goods and services: -88.6% (2017 est.)

Agricultural products: cabbages, carrots, cucumbers, tomatoes, onions, peppers; livestock products

Industries: tourism, rum, textiles, electronic appliances

Industrial production growth rate: -21% (2017 est.)
comparison ranking: 217

Unemployment rate: 5.6% (2017 est.)
comparison ranking: 109

Budget: *revenues:* $55.651 million (2014 est.)
expenditures: $43.652 million (2014 est.)
note: central government revenues and expenses (excluding grants/extrabudgetary units/social security funds) converted to US dollars at average official exchange rate for year indicated

Current account balance: -$15.4 million (2017 est.)
-$12.2 million (2016 est.)
comparison ranking: 86

Exports: $11.9 million (2021 est.)
$4.4 million (2017 est.)
$5.2 million (2016 est.)
comparison ranking: 218

Exports - partners: US 23%, France 21%, Antigua and Barbuda 19%, Ireland 15%, UK 7% (2022)
note: top five export partners based on percentage share of exports

Exports - commodities: sand, gravel and crushed stone, packaged medicine, lead products, liquid pumps (2022)
note: top five export commodities based on value in dollars

Imports: $15.3 million (2021 est.)
$39.44 million (2017 est.)
$36.1 million (2016 est.)
comparison ranking: 220

Imports - partners: US 54%, UK 8%, Singapore 4%, Antigua and Barbuda 4%, Trinidad and Tobago 4% (2022)
note: top five import partners based on percentage share of imports

Imports - commodities: refined petroleum, machine parts, plastic products, machinery, natural gas (2022)
note: top five import commodities based on value in dollars

Reserves of foreign exchange and gold: $47.58 million (31 December 2017 est.)
$51.47 million (31 December 2015 est.)
comparison ranking: 193

Exchange rates: East Caribbean dollars (XCD) per US dollar -

Exchange rates: 2.7 (2023 est.)
2.7 (2022 est.)
2.7 (2021 est.)
2.7 (2020 est.)
2.7 (2019 est.)

ENERGY

Electricity access: *electrification - total population:* 100% (2020)

Electricity: *installed generating capacity:* 6,000 kW (2022 est.)
consumption: 13.968 million kWh (2022 est.)
transmission/distribution losses: 370,000 kWh (2022 est.)
comparison rankings: transmission/distribution losses 1; consumption 209; installed generating capacity 210

Electricity generation sources: *fossil fuels:* 100% of total installed capacity (2022 est.)

Coal: *imports:* (2022 est.) less than 1 metric ton

Petroleum: *refined petroleum consumption:* 200 bbl/day (2022 est.)

Carbon dioxide emissions: 26,000 metric tonnes of CO2 (2022 est.)
from petroleum and other liquids: 26,000 metric tonnes of CO2 (2022 est.)
comparison ranking: total emissions 214

Energy consumption per capita: (2019)

COMMUNICATIONS

Telephones - fixed lines: *total subscriptions:* 3,000 (2020 est.)
subscriptions per 100 inhabitants: 67 (2020 est.)
comparison ranking: total subscriptions 211

Telephones - mobile cellular: *total subscriptions:* 5,000 (2020 est.)
subscriptions per 100 inhabitants: 110 (2020 est.)
comparison ranking: total subscriptions 222

Telecommunication systems: *general assessment:* telecom market one of growth in Caribbean and fully digitalized; high dependency on tourism and offshore financial services; operators expand FttP (Fiber to Home) services; LTE launches and operators invest in mobile networks; effective competition in all sectors (2020)
domestic: fixed-line is 67 per 100 and mobile-cellular teledensity is 110 per 100 persons (2020)
international: country code - 1-664; landing point for the ECFS optic submarine cable with links to 14 other islands in the eastern Caribbean extending from the British Virgin Islands to Trinidad (2019)

Broadcast media: Radio Montserrat, a public radio broadcaster, transmits on 1 station and has a repeater transmission to a second station; repeater transmissions from the GEM Radio Network of Trinidad and Tobago provide another 2 radio stations; cable and satellite TV available (2007)

Internet country code: .ms

Internet users: *total:* 2,473 (2021 est.)
percent of population: 56.2% (2021 est.)
comparison ranking: total 226

Broadband - fixed subscriptions: *total:* 2,700 (2018 est.)
subscriptions per 100 inhabitants: 55 (2018 est.)
comparison ranking: total 196

TRANSPORTATION

National air transport system: *number of registered air carriers:* 1 (2020)
inventory of registered aircraft operated by air carriers: 3

Civil aircraft registration country code prefix: VP-M

Airports: 1 (2024)
comparison ranking: 217

Roadways: *note:* volcanic eruptions that began in 1995 destroyed most of the 227 km road system; a new road infrastructure has been built on the north end of the island

MILITARY AND SECURITY

Military and security forces: no regular military forces; Royal Montserrat Defense Force (ceremonial, civil defense duties), Montserrat Police Force (2024)

Military - note: defense is the responsibility of the UK

TRANSNATIONAL ISSUES

Illicit drugs: transshipment point for South American narcotics destined for the US and Europe

MOROCCO

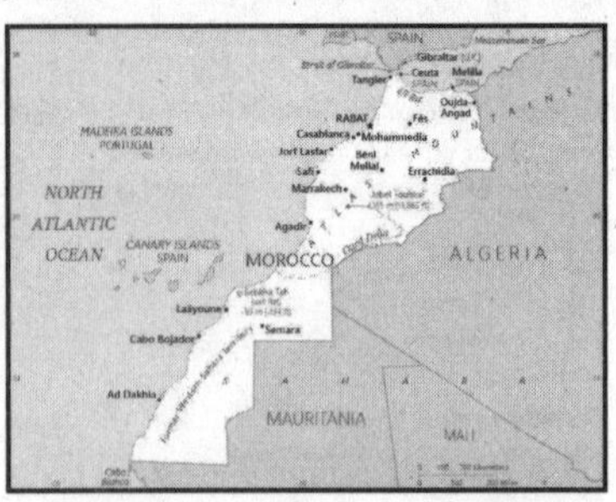

INTRODUCTION

Background: In 788, about a century after the Arab conquest of North Africa, a series of Muslim dynasties began to rule in Morocco. In the 16th century, the Sa'adi monarchy, particularly under Ahmad al-MANSUR (1578-1603), repelled foreign invaders and inaugurated a golden age. The Alaouite Dynasty, to which the current Moroccan royal family belongs, dates from the 17th century. In 1860, Spain occupied northern Morocco and ushered in a half-century of trade rivalry among European powers that saw Morocco's sovereignty steadily erode; in 1912, the French imposed a protectorate over the country. A protracted independence struggle with France ended successfully in 1956. The internationalized city of Tangier and most Spanish possessions were turned over to the new country that same year. Sultan MOHAMMED V, the current monarch's grandfather, organized the new state as a constitutional monarchy and in 1957 assumed the title of king.

Since Spain's 1976 withdrawal from Western Sahara, Morocco has extended its de facto administrative control to roughly 75% of this territory; however, the UN does not recognize Morocco as the administering power for Western Sahara. The UN since 1991 has monitored a cease-fire, which broke down in late 2020, between Morocco and the Polisario Front – an organization advocating the territory's independence – and restarted negotiations over the status of the territory in 2018. In 2020, the US recognized Morocco's sovereignty over all of Western Sahara.

In 2011, King MOHAMMED VI responded to the spread of pro-democracy protests in the North Africa region by implementing a reform program that included a new constitution, passed by popular referendum, under which some new powers were extended to parliament and the prime minister, but ultimate authority remains in the hands of the monarch. Later that year, the Justice and Development Party (PJD) – a moderate Islamist democratic party – won the largest number of seats in parliamentary elections, becoming the first Islamist party to lead the Moroccan Government. In 2015, Morocco held its first direct elections for regional councils, which was one of the reforms included in the 2011 constitution. The PJD again won the largest number of seats in nationwide parliamentary elections in 2016, but it lost its plurality to the probusiness National Rally of Independents (RNI) in 2021. In 2020, Morocco signed a normalization agreement with Israel, similar to those that Bahrain, the United Arab Emirates, and Sudan had concluded with Israel earlier that year.

GEOGRAPHY

Location: Northern Africa, bordering the North Atlantic Ocean and the Mediterranean Sea, between Algeria and Mauritania

Geographic coordinates: 28 30 N, 10 00 W

Map references: Africa

Area: *total:* 716,550 sq km
land: 716,300 sq km
water: 250 sq km
comparison ranking: total 41

Area - comparative: slightly larger than twice the size of California

Land boundaries: *total:* 3,523.5 km
border countries (3): Algeria 1,941 km; Mauritania 1,564 km; Spain (Ceuta) 8 km and Spain (Melilla) 10.5 km
note: an additional 75-meter border segment exists between Morocco and the Spanish exclave of Penon de Velez de la Gomera

Coastline: 2,945 km

Maritime claims: *territorial sea:* 12 nm
contiguous zone: 24 nm
exclusive economic zone: 200 nm
continental shelf: 200-m depth or to the depth of exploitation

Climate: Mediterranean in the north, becoming more extreme in the interior; in the south, hot, dry desert; rain is rare; cold offshore air currents produce fog and heavy dew
note: data does not include former Western Sahara

Terrain: mountainous northern coast (Rif Mountains) and interior (Atlas Mountains) bordered by large plateaus with intermontane valleys, and fertile coastal plains; the south is mostly low, flat desert with large areas of rocky or sandy surfaces

Elevation: *highest point:* Jebel Toubkal 4,165 m
lowest point: Sebkha Tah -59 m
mean elevation: 909 m

Natural resources: phosphates, iron ore, manganese, lead, zinc, fish, salt

Land use: *agricultural land:* 67.5% (2018 est.)
arable land: 17.5% (2018 est.)
permanent crops: 2.9% (2018 est.)
permanent pasture: 47.1% (2018 est.)
forest: 11.5% (2018 est.)
other: 21% (2018 est.)
note: does not include the area of the former Western Sahara, which is almost exclusively desert

Irrigated land: 17,645 sq km (2019)

Major rivers (by length in km): Draa - 1,100 km

Population distribution: the highest population density is found along the Atlantic and Mediterranean coasts; a number of densely populated agglomerations are found scattered through the Atlas Mountains as shown in this population distribution map

Natural hazards: in the north, the mountains are geologically unstable and subject to earthquakes; periodic droughts; windstorms; flash floods; landslides; in the south, a hot, dry, dust/sand-laden sirocco wind can occur during winter and spring; widespread harmattan haze exists 60% of time, often severely restricting visibility

Geography - note: strategic location along Strait of Gibraltar; the only African nation to have both Atlantic and Mediterranean coastlines; the waters off the Atlantic coast are particularly rich fishing areas

PEOPLE AND SOCIETY

Population: *total:* 37,387,585
male: 18,664,263
female: 18,723,322 (2024 est.)
comparison rankings: female 40; male 39; total 39

Nationality: *noun:* Moroccan(s)
adjective: Moroccan

Ethnic groups: Arab-Amazigh 99%, other 1%
note: does not include data from the former Western Sahara

Languages: Arabic (official), Tamazight languages (Tamazight (official), Tachelhit, Tarifit), French (often the language of business, government, and diplomacy)
major-language sample(s):
احسن مصدر متاع المعلومات الأساسية
كتاب ديال لحقائق متاع العالم،
(Arabic)
note: the proportion of Tamazight speakers is disputed

Religions: Muslim 99% (official; virtually all Sunni, <0.1% Shia), other 1% (includes Christian, Jewish, and Baha'i); note - Jewish about 3,000-3,500 (2020 est.)
note: does not include data from the former Western Sahara

Demographic profile: Morocco is undergoing a demographic transition. Its population is growing but at a declining rate, as people live longer and women have fewer children. Infant, child, and maternal mortality rates have been reduced through better health care, nutrition, hygiene, and vaccination coverage, although disparities between urban and rural and rich and poor households persist. Morocco's shrinking child cohort reflects the decline of its total fertility rate from 5 in mid-1980s to 2.2 in 2010, which is a result of increased female educational attainment, higher contraceptive use, delayed marriage, and the desire for smaller families. Young adults (persons aged 15-29) make up almost 26% of the total population and represent a potential economic asset if they can be gainfully employed. Currently, however, many youths are unemployed because Morocco's job creation rate has not kept pace with the growth of its working-age population. Most youths who have jobs work in the informal sector with little security or benefits.
During the second half of the 20th century, Morocco became one of the world's top emigration countries, creating large, widely dispersed migrant communities in Western Europe. The Moroccan Government has encouraged emigration since its independence in 1956, both to secure remittances for funding national development and as an outlet to prevent unrest in rebellious (often Berber) areas. Although Moroccan labor migrants earlier targeted Algeria and France, the flood of Moroccan "guest workers" from the mid-1960s to the early 1970s spread widely across northwestern Europe to fill unskilled jobs in the booming manufacturing, mining, construction, and agriculture industries. Host societies and most Moroccan migrants expected this migration to be temporary, but deteriorating economic conditions in Morocco related to the 1973 oil crisis and tighter European immigration policies resulted in these stays becoming permanent.
A wave of family migration followed in the 1970s and 1980s, with a growing number of second generation Moroccans opting to become naturalized citizens of their host countries. Spain and Italy emerged as new destination countries in the mid-1980s, but their introduction of visa restrictions in the early 1990s pushed Moroccans increasingly to migrate either legally by marrying Moroccans already in Europe or illegally to work in the underground economy. Women began to make up a growing share of these labor migrants. At the same time, some higher-skilled Moroccans went to the US and Quebec, Canada.
In the mid-1990s, Morocco developed into a transit country for asylum seekers from Sub-Saharan Africa and illegal labor migrants from Sub-Saharan Africa and South Asia trying to reach Europe via southern Spain, Spain's Canary Islands, or Spain's North African enclaves, Ceuta and Melilla. Forcible expulsions by Moroccan and Spanish security forces have not deterred these illegal migrants or calmed Europe's security concerns. Rabat remains unlikely to adopt an EU agreement to take back third-country nationals who have entered the EU illegally via Morocco. Thousands of other illegal migrants have chosen to stay in Morocco until they earn enough money for further travel or permanently as a "second-best" option. The launching of a regularization program in 2014 legalized the status of some migrants and granted them equal access to education, health care, and work, but xenophobia and racism remain obstacles.

Age structure: *0-14 years:* 25.7% (male 4,898,154/female 4,701,786)
15-64 years: 65.9% (male 12,236,752/female 12,410,567)
65 years and over: 8.4% (2024 est.) (male 1,529,357/female 1,610,969)

Dependency ratios: *total dependency ratio:* 52.2
youth dependency ratio: 40.9
elderly dependency ratio: 11.3
potential support ratio: 8.9 (2021 est.)
note: does not include data from the former Western Sahara

Median age: *total:* 30.6 years (2024 est.)
male: 30.1 years
female: 31 years
comparison ranking: total 135

Population growth rate: 0.84% (2024 est.)
comparison ranking: 108

Birth rate: 16.8 births/1,000 population (2024 est.)
comparison ranking: 92

Death rate: 6.6 deaths/1,000 population (2024 est.)
comparison ranking: 131

Net migration rate: -1.7 migrant(s)/1,000 population (2024 est.)
comparison ranking: 163

Population distribution: the highest population density is found along the Atlantic and Mediterranean coasts; a number of densely populated agglomerations are found scattered through the Atlas Mountains as shown in this population distribution map

Urbanization: *urban population:* 65.1% of total population (2023)
rate of urbanization: 1.88% annual rate of change (2020-25 est.)
note: data does not include former Western Sahara

Major urban areas - population: 3.893 million Casablanca, 1.959 million RABAT (capital), 1.290 million Fes, 1.314 million Tangier, 1.050 million Marrakech, 979,000 Agadir (2023)

Sex ratio: *at birth:* 1.05 male(s)/female
0-14 years: 1.04 male(s)/female
15-64 years: 0.99 male(s)/female
65 years and over: 0.95 male(s)/female
total population: 1 male(s)/female (2024 est.)

Maternal mortality ratio: 72 deaths/100,000 live births (2020 est.)
note: does not include data from the former Western Sahara
comparison ranking: 83

Infant mortality rate: *total:* 18.3 deaths/1,000 live births (2024 est.)
male: 20.4 deaths/1,000 live births
female: 16 deaths/1,000 live births
comparison ranking: total 84

Life expectancy at birth: *total population:* 74.2 years (2024 est.)
male: 72.5 years
female: 76 years
comparison ranking: total population 145

Total fertility rate: 2.25 children born/woman (2024 est.)
comparison ranking: 80

Gross reproduction rate: 1.1 (2024 est.)

Contraceptive prevalence rate: 70.8% (2018)
note: does not include data from the former Western Sahara

Drinking water source: *improved: urban:* 98.3% of population
rural: 79.1% of population
total: 91% of population
unimproved: urban: 1.7% of population
rural: 20.9% of population
total: 9% of population (2017 est.)
note: does not include data from the former Western Sahara

Current health expenditure: 6% of GDP (2020)
note: does not include data from the former Western Sahara

Physician density: 0.73 physicians/1,000 population (2017)
note: does not include data from the former Western Sahara

Hospital bed density: 1 beds/1,000 population (2017)
note: does not include data from the former Western Sahara

Sanitation facility access: *improved: urban:* 98.2% of population
rural: 72.4% of population
total: 88.8% of population
unimproved: urban: 1.8% of population
rural: 27.6% of population
total: 11.2% of population (2020 est.)
note: does not include data from the former Western Sahara

Obesity - adult prevalence rate: 26.1% (2016)

note: does not include data from the former Western Sahara
comparison ranking: 44

Alcohol consumption per capita: *total:* 0.51 liters of pure alcohol (2019 est.)
beer: 0.18 liters of pure alcohol (2019 est.)
wine: 0.24 liters of pure alcohol (2019 est.)
spirits: 0.09 liters of pure alcohol (2019 est.)
other alcohols: 0 liters of pure alcohol (2019 est.)
comparison ranking: total 163

Tobacco use: *total:* 14.5% (2020 est.)
male: 28.2% (2020 est.)
female: 0.8% (2020 est.)
comparison ranking: total 106

Children under the age of 5 years underweight: 2.8% (2019/20)
note: does not include data from the former Western Sahara
comparison ranking: 92

Currently married women (ages 15-49): 58.8% (2023 est.)

Child marriage: *women married by age 15:* 0.5%
women married by age 18: 13.7% (2018 est.)

Education expenditures: 6.8% of GDP (2020)
note: does not include data from the former Western Sahara
comparison ranking: 23

Literacy: *definition:* age 15 and over can read and write
total population: 75.9%
male: 84.8%
female: 67.4% (2021)
note: does not include data from the former Western Sahara

School life expectancy (primary to tertiary education): *total:* 14 years
male: 14 years
female: 14 years (2021)
note: does not include data from the former Western Sahara

ENVIRONMENT

Environment - current issues: in the north, land degradation/desertification (soil erosion resulting from farming of marginal areas, overgrazing, destruction of vegetation); water and soil pollution due to dumping of industrial wastes into the ocean and inland water sources, and onto the land; in the south, desertification; overgrazing; sparse water and lack of arable land
note: data does not include former Western Sahara

Environment - international agreements: *party to:* Biodiversity, Climate Change, Climate Change-Kyoto Protocol, Climate Change-Paris Agreement, Comprehensive Nuclear Test Ban, Desertification, Endangered Species, Hazardous Wastes, Law of the Sea, Marine Dumping-London Convention, Marine Dumping-London Protocol, Nuclear Test Ban, Ozone Layer Protection, Ship Pollution, Wetlands, Whaling
signed, but not ratified: Environmental Modification

Climate: Mediterranean in the north, becoming more extreme in the interior; in the south, hot, dry desert; rain is rare; cold offshore air currents produce fog and heavy dew
note: data does not include former Western Sahara

Urbanization: *urban population:* 65.1% of total population (2023)
rate of urbanization: 1.88% annual rate of change (2020-25 est.)
note: data does not include former Western Sahara

Revenue from forest resources: 0.13% of GDP (2018 est.)
comparison ranking: 107

Revenue from coal: 0% of GDP (2018 est.)
comparison ranking: 80

Air pollutants: *particulate matter emissions:* 13.44 micrograms per cubic meter (2019 est.)
carbon dioxide emissions: 61.28 megatons (2016 est.)
methane emissions: 17.16 megatons (2020 est.)
note: data does not include former Western Sahara

Waste and recycling: *municipal solid waste generated annually:* 6.852 million tons (2014 est.)
municipal solid waste recycled annually: 548,160 tons (2014 est.)
percent of municipal solid waste recycled: 8% (2014 est.)
note: data does not include former Western Sahara

Major rivers (by length in km): Draa - 1,100 km

Total water withdrawal: *municipal:* 1.06 billion cubic meters (2020 est.)
industrial: 210 million cubic meters (2020 est.)
agricultural: 9.16 billion cubic meters (2020 est.)
note: data does not include former Western Sahara

Total renewable water resources: 29 billion cubic meters (2020 est.)
note: data does not include former Western Sahara

Geoparks: *total global geoparks and regional networks:* 1
global geoparks and regional networks: M'Goun (2023)

GOVERNMENT

Country name: *conventional long form:* Kingdom of Morocco
conventional short form: Morocco
local long form: Al Mamlakah al Maghribiyah
local short form: Al Maghrib
former: French Protectorate in Morocco, Spanish Protectorate in Morocco, Ifni, Spanish Sahara, Western Sahara
etymology: the English name "Morocco" derives from, respectively, the Spanish and Portuguese names "Marruecos" and "Marrocos," which stem from "Marrakesh" the Latin name for the former capital of ancient Morocco; the Arabic name "Al Maghrib" translates as "The West"

Government type: parliamentary constitutional monarchy

Capital: *name:* Rabat
geographic coordinates: 34 01 N, 6 49 W
time difference: UTC+1 (6 hours ahead of Washington, DC, during Standard Time)
etymology: name derives from the Arabic title "Ribat el-Fath," meaning "stronghold of victory," applied to the newly constructed citadel in 1170

Administrative divisions: 12 regions; Beni Mellal-Khenifra, Casablanca-Settat, Dakhla-Oued Ed-Dahab, Draa-Tafilalet, Fes-Meknes, Guelmim-Oued Noun, Laayoune-Sakia El Hamra, Marrakech-Safi, Oriental, Rabat-Sale-Kenitra, Souss-Massa, Tanger-Tetouan-Al Hoceima
note: effective 10 December 2020, the US Government recognizes the sovereignty of Morocco over all of the territory of former Western Sahara

Independence: 2 March 1956 (from France)

National holiday: Throne Day (accession of King MOHAMMED VI to the throne), 30 July (1999)

Legal system: mixed legal system of civil law based on French civil law and Islamic (sharia) law; judicial review of legislative acts by Constitutional Court

Constitution: *history:* several previous; latest drafted 17 June 2011, approved by referendum 1 July 2011; note - sources disagree on whether the 2011 referendum was for a new constitution or for reforms to the existing constitution
amendments: proposed by the king, by the prime minister, or by members in either chamber of Parliament; passage requires at least two-thirds majority vote by both chambers and approval in a referendum; the king can opt to submit selfinitiated proposals directly to a referendum

International law organization participation: has not submitted an ICJ jurisdiction declaration; non-party state to the ICCt

Citizenship: *citizenship by birth:* no
citizenship by descent only: the father must be a citizen of Morocco; if the father is unknown or stateless, the mother must be a citizen
dual citizenship recognized: yes
residency requirement for naturalization: 5 years

Suffrage: 18 years of age; universal

Executive branch: *chief of state:* King MOHAMMED VI (since 30 July 1999)
head of government: Prime Minister Aziz AKHANNOUCH (since 7 October 2021)
cabinet: Council of Ministers chosen by the prime minister in consultation with Parliament and appointed by the monarch; the monarch chooses the ministers of Interior, Foreign Affairs, Islamic Affairs, and National Defense Administration
elections/appointments: the monarchy is hereditary; prime minister appointed by the monarch from the majority party following legislative elections

Legislative branch: *description:* bicameral Parliament consists of:
House of Councilors or Majlis al-Mustacharine (120 seats; members indirectly elected by an electoral college of local councils, professional organizations, and labor unions; members serve 6-year terms)
House of Representatives or Majlis al-Nuwab (395 seats; 305 members directly elected in multi-seat constituencies by proportional representation vote and 90 directly elected in a single nationwide constituency by proportional representation vote; members serve 5-year terms); note - 60 seats reserved for women and 30 seats for those under age 40 in regional multi-seat constituencies, with the seats divided proportionally among the 12 regions by population size of the region
elections: House of Councillors - last held on 5 October 2021 (next to be held by 31 October 2027)
House of Representatives - last held on 8 September 2021 (next to be held by 30 September 2026)
election results: House of Councillors - percent of vote by party - NA; seats by party - RNI 27, PAM 19, PI 17, MP 12, USFP 8, UGIM 6, CDT 3, PJD 3, UC 2, UMT 2, Amal 1, FDT 1, MDS 1, PRD 1, independent 1; composition - men 106, women 14, percentage women 11.7%
House of Representatives - percent of vote by party NA; seats by party - RNI 102, PAM 87, PI 81, USFP 34, MP 28, PPS 22, UC 18, PJD 13, MDS 5, other 5; composition - men 299, women 96, percentage women 24.3%; total Parliament percentage women 21.4%

Judicial branch: *highest court(s):* Supreme Court or Court of Cassation (consists of 5-judge panels organized into civil, family matters, commercial, administrative, social, and criminal sections); Constitutional Court (consists of 12 members)
judge selection and term of office: Supreme Court judges appointed by the Superior Council of Judicial Power, a 20- member body presided over by the monarch, which includes the Supreme Court president, the prosecutor general, representatives of the appeals and first instance courts (among them 1 woman magistrate), the president of the National Council for Human Rights (CNDH), and 5 "notable persons" appointed by the monarch; judges appointed for life; Constitutional Court members - 6 designated by the monarch and 6 elected by Parliament; court president appointed by the monarch from among the court members; members serve 9-year nonrenewable terms
subordinate courts: courts of appeal; High Court of Justice; administrative and commercial courts; regional and Sadad courts (for religious, civil and administrative, and penal adjudication); first instance courts

Political parties: Action Party or PA
Amal (hope) Party
An-Nahj Ad-Dimocrati or An-Nahj or Democratic Way
Authenticity and Modernity Party or PAM
Constitutional Union Party or UC
Democratic and Social Movement or MDS
Democratic Forces Front or FFD
Environment and Sustainable Development Party or PEDD
Federation of the Democratic Left or FGD
Green Left Party or PGV
Istiqlal (Independence) Party or PI
Moroccan Liberal Party or PML
Moroccan Union for Democracy or UMD
National Democratic Party
National Rally of Independents or RNI
Neo-Democrats Party
Party of Development Reform or PRD
Party of Justice and Development or PJD
Party of Liberty and Social Justice or PLJS
Party of Progress and Socialism or PPS
Popular Movement or MP
Renaissance and Virtue Party or PRV
Renaissance Party
Renewal and Equity Party or PRE
Shoura (consultation) and Istiqlal Party
Socialist Union of Popular Forces or USFP
Unified Socialist Party or GSU
Unity and Democracy Party

International organization participation: ABEDA, AfDB, AFESD, AIIB, AMF, AMU, AU, CAEU, CD, EBRD, FAO, G-11, G-77, IAEA, IBRD, ICAO, ICC (national committees), ICRM, IDA, IDB, IFAD, IFC, IFRCS, IHO, ILO, IMF, IMO, IMSO, Interpol, IOC, IOM, IPU, ISO, ITSO, ITU, ITUC (NGOs), LAS, MIGA, MONUSCO, NAM, OAS (observer), OIC, OIF, OPCW, OSCE (partner), Pacific Alliance (observer), Paris Club (associate), PCA, SICA (observer), UN, UNCTAD, UNESCO, UNHCR, UNIDO, UNOCI, UNOOSA, UNSC (temporary), UNWTO, UPU, WCO, WHO, WIPO, WMO, WTO

Diplomatic representation in the US: *chief of mission:* Ambassador Youssef AMRANI (since 27 February 2024)
chancery: 3508 International Drive NW, Washington, DC 20008
telephone: [1] (202) 462-7979
FAX: [1] (202) 265-0161
email address and website:
washingtonembmorocco@maec.gov.ma
Embassy of the Kingdom of Morocco in the United States (diplomatie.ma)
consulate(s) general: New York

Diplomatic representation from the US: *chief of mission:* Ambassador Puneet TALWAR (since 4 October 2023)
embassy: Km 5.7 Avenue Mohammed VI, Souissi, Rabat 10170
mailing address: 9400 Rabat Place, Washington DC 20521-9400
telephone: [212] 0537-637-200
FAX: [212] 0537-637-201
email address and website:
https://ma.usembassy.gov/
consulate(s) general: Casablanca

Flag description: red with a green pentacle (five-pointed, linear star) known as Sulayman's (Solomon's) seal in the center of the flag; red and green are traditional colors in Arab flags, although the use of red is more commonly associated with the Arab states of the Persian Gulf; the pentacle represents the five pillars of Islam and signifies the association between God and the nation; design dates to 1912

National symbol(s): pentacle symbol, lion; national colors: red, green

National anthem: *name:* "Hymne Cherifien" (Hymn of the Sharif)
lyrics/music: Ali Squalli HOUSSAINI/Leo MORGAN
note: music adopted 1956, lyrics adopted 1970

National heritage: *total World Heritage Sites:* 9 (all cultural)
selected World Heritage Site locales: Medina of Fez; Medina of Marrakesh; Ksar of Ait-Ben-Haddou; Historic City of Meknes; Archaeological Site of Volubilis; Medina of Tétouan (formerly known as Titawin); Medina of Essaouira (formerly Mogador); Portuguese City of Mazagan (El Jadida); Historic and Modern Rabat

ECONOMY

Economic overview: lower middle-income North African economy; ongoing recovery from recent drought and earthquake; rebounding via tourism, manufacturing, and raw materials processing; significant trade and investment with EU; reform programs include fiscal rebalancing, state enterprise governance and private sector investments

Real GDP (purchasing power parity): $337.48 billion (2023 est.)
$327.085 billion (2022 est.)
$323.02 billion (2021 est.)
note: data in 2021 dollars
comparison ranking: 57

Real GDP growth rate: 3.18% (2023 est.)
1.26% (2022 est.)
8.02% (2021 est.)
note: annual GDP % growth based on constant local currency
comparison ranking: 104

Real GDP per capita: $8,800 (2023 est.)
$8,600 (2022 est.)
$8,600 (2021 est.)
note: data in 2021 dollars
comparison ranking: 151

GDP (official exchange rate): $141.109 billion (2023 est.)
note: data in current dollars at official exchange rate

Inflation rate (consumer prices): 6.09% (2023 est.)
6.66% (2022 est.)
1.4% (2021 est.)
note: annual % change based on consumer prices
comparison ranking: 130

Credit ratings: Fitch rating: BB+ (2020)

Moody's rating: Ba1 (1999)

Standard & Poors rating: BBB- (2010)
note: The year refers to the year in which the current credit rating was first obtained.

GDP - composition, by sector of origin: *agriculture:* 12% (2023 est.)
industry: 23.8% (2023 est.)
services: 53.9% (2023 est.)
note: figures may not total 100% due to non-allocated consumption not captured in sector-reported data
comparison rankings: services 124; industry 109; agriculture 65

GDP - composition, by end use: *household consumption:* 61.6% (2023 est.)
government consumption: 18.7% (2023 est.)
investment in fixed capital: 27% (2023 est.)
investment in inventories: 1% (2023 est.)
exports of goods and services: 44% (2023 est.)
imports of goods and services: -52.3% (2023 est.)
note: figures may not total 100% due to rounding or gaps in data collection

Agricultural products: wheat, milk, olives, sugar beets, potatoes, tomatoes, tangerines/mandarins, oranges, apples, onions (2022)
note: top ten agricultural products based on tonnage

Industries: automotive parts, phosphate mining and processing, aerospace, food processing, leather goods, textiles, construction, energy, tourism

Industrial production growth rate: 0.96% (2023 est.)
note: annual % change in industrial value added based on constant local currency
comparison ranking: 140

Labor force: 12.284 million (2023 est.)
note: number of people ages 15 or older who are employed or seeking work
comparison ranking: 48

Unemployment rate: 9.11% (2023 est.)
9.53% (2022 est.)
10.54% (2021 est.)
note: % of labor force seeking employment
comparison ranking: 159

Youth unemployment rate (ages 15-24): *total:* 22.6% (2023 est.)
male: 22.5% (2023 est.)
female: 23% (2023 est.)
note: % of labor force ages 15-24 seeking employment
comparison ranking: total 53

Average household expenditures: *on food:* 33.9% of household expenditures (2022 est.)
on alcohol and tobacco: 1.4% of household expenditures (2022 est.)

Remittances: 8.6% of GDP (2023 est.)
8.53% of GDP (2022 est.)
7.69% of GDP (2021 est.)

note: personal transfers and compensation between resident and non-resident individuals/households/ entities

Budget: *revenues:* $35.356 billion (2022 est.)
expenditures: $36.939 billion (2022 est.)
note: central government revenues and expenses (excluding grants/extrabudgetary units/social security funds) converted to US dollars at average official exchange rate for year indicated

Public debt: 65.1% of GDP (2017 est.)
comparison ranking: 63

Taxes and other revenues: 22.12 % (of GDP) (2022 est.)
note: central government tax revenue as a % of GDP
comparison ranking: 66

Current account balance: -$4.775 billion (2022 est.)
-$3.349 billion (2021 est.)
-$1.368 billion (2020 est.)
note: balance of payments - net trade and primary/ secondary income in current dollars
comparison ranking: 180

Exports: $58.556 billion (2022 est.)
$47.09 billion (2021 est.)
$37.545 billion (2020 est.)
note: balance of payments - exports of goods and services in current dollars
comparison ranking: 65

Exports - partners: Spain 18%, France 17%, India 6%, Italy 5%, Brazil 4% (2022)
note: top five export partners based on percentage share of exports

Exports - commodities: fertilizers, cars, garments, insulated wire, phosphoric acid (2022)
note: top five export commodities based on value in dollars

Imports: $73.783 billion (2022 est.)
$60.215 billion (2021 est.)
$46.358 billion (2020 est.)
note: balance of payments - imports of goods and services in current dollars
comparison ranking: 53

Imports - partners: Spain 18%, France 10%, China 10%, US 6%, Saudi Arabia 6% (2022)
note: top five import partners based on percentage share of imports

Imports - commodities: refined petroleum, wheat, natural gas, coal, vehicle parts/accessories (2022)
note: top five import commodities based on value in dollars

Reserves of foreign exchange and gold: $36.328 billion (2023 est.)
$32.314 billion (2022 est.)
$35.648 billion (2021 est.)
note: holdings of gold (year-end prices)/foreign exchange/special drawing rights in current dollars
comparison ranking: 56

Debt - external: $36.29 billion (2022 est.)
note: present value of external debt in current US dollars
comparison ranking: 19

Exchange rates: Moroccan dirhams (MAD) per US dollar -

Exchange rates: 10.131 (2023 est.)
10.161 (2022 est.)
8.988 (2021 est.)
9.497 (2020 est.)
9.617 (2019 est.)

ENERGY

Electricity access: *electrification - total population:* 100% (2022 est.)

Electricity: *installed generating capacity:* 14.237 million kW (2022 est.)
consumption: 35.278 billion kWh (2022 est.)
exports: 471 million kWh (2022 est.)
imports: 1.868 billion kWh (2022 est.)
transmission/distribution losses: 7.366 billion kWh (2022 est.)
comparison rankings: transmission/distribution losses 171; imports 61; exports 77; consumption 62; installed generating capacity 55

Electricity generation sources: *fossil fuels:* 82.1% of total installed capacity (2022 est.)
solar: 3.5% of total installed capacity (2022 est.)
wind: 13% of total installed capacity (2022 est.)
hydroelectricity: 1.3% of total installed capacity (2022 est.)
biomass and waste: 0.1% of total installed capacity (2022 est.)

Coal: *consumption:* 11.94 million metric tons (2022 est.)
exports: 12.8 metric tons (2022 est.)
imports: 11.772 million metric tons (2022 est.)
proven reserves: 96 million metric tons (2022 est.)

Petroleum: *total petroleum production:* 25 bbl/day (2023 est.)
refined petroleum consumption: 318,000 bbl/day (2022 est.)
crude oil estimated reserves: 684,000 barrels (2021 est.)

Natural gas: *production:* 82.595 million cubic meters (2022 est.)
consumption: 243.201 million cubic meters (2022 est.)
imports: 162.157 million cubic meters (2022 est.)
proven reserves: 1.444 billion cubic meters (2021 est.)

Carbon dioxide emissions: 67.688 million metric tonnes of CO_2 (2022 est.)
from coal and metallurgical coke: 27.475 million metric tonnes of CO_2 (2022 est.)
from petroleum and other liquids: 39.727 million metric tonnes of CO_2 (2022 est.)
from consumed natural gas: 485,000 metric tonnes of CO_2 (2022 est.)
comparison ranking: total emissions 50

Energy consumption per capita: 24.936 million Btu/ person (2022 est.)
comparison ranking: 122

COMMUNICATIONS

Telephones - fixed lines: *total subscriptions:* 2.645 million (2022 est.)
subscriptions per 100 inhabitants: 7 (2021 est.)
comparison ranking: total subscriptions 44

Telephones - mobile cellular: *total subscriptions:* 52.959 million (2022 est.)
subscriptions per 100 inhabitants: 137 (2021 est.)
comparison ranking: total subscriptions 31

Telecommunication systems: *general assessment:* national network nearly 100% digital using fiber-optic links; improved rural service employs microwave radio relay; one of the most state-of-the-art markets in Africa; high mobile penetration rates in the region with low cost for broadband Internet access; improvement in LTE reach and capabilities; service providers have all successfully completed 5G proofs of concept and are currently lining up 5G equipment providers for both radio and core technology; regulatory agency expects to conduct the 5G spectrum auction in 2023; mobile Internet accounts for 93% of all Internet connections; World Bank provided funds for Morocco's digital transformation; government supported digital education during pandemic; submarine cables and satellite provide connectivity to Asia, Africa, the Middle East, Europe, and Australia (2022)
domestic: fixed-line teledensity is 7 per 100 persons and mobile-cellular subscribership is 139 per 100 persons (2021)
international: country code - 212; landing point for the Atlas Offshore, Estepona-Tetouan, Canalink and SEA-ME-WE-3 fiber-optic telecommunications undersea cables that provide connectivity to Asia, Africa, the Middle East, Europe and Australia; satellite earth stations - 2 Intelsat (Atlantic Ocean) and 1 Arabsat; microwave radio relay to Gibraltar, Spain, and Western Sahara (2019)

Broadcast media: 2 TV broadcast networks with state-run Radio-Television Marocaine (RTM) operating one network and the state partially owning the other; foreign TV broadcasts are available via satellite dish; 3 radio broadcast networks with RTM operating one; the government-owned network includes 10 regional radio channels in addition to its national service (2019)

Internet country code: .ma

Internet users: *total:* 32.56 million (2021 est.)
percent of population: 88% (2021 est.)
comparison ranking: total 31

Broadband - fixed subscriptions: *total:* 2,102,434 (2020 est.)
subscriptions per 100 inhabitants: 6 (2020 est.)
comparison ranking: total 57

Communications - note: the University of al-Quarawiyyin Library in Fez is recognized as the oldest existing, continually operating library in the world, dating back to A.D. 859; among its holdings are approximately 4,000 ancient Islamic manuscripts

TRANSPORTATION

National air transport system: *number of registered air carriers:* 3 (2020)
inventory of registered aircraft operated by air carriers: 76
annual passenger traffic on registered air carriers: 8,132,917 (2018)
annual freight traffic on registered air carriers: 97.71 million (2018) mt-km

Civil aircraft registration country code prefix: CN

Airports: 49 (2024)
comparison ranking: 89

Heliports: 17 (2024)

Pipelines: 944 km gas, 270 km oil, 175 km refined products (2013)

Railways: *total:* 2,067 km (2014)
standard gauge: 2,067 km (2014) 1.435-m gauge (1,022 km electrified)
comparison ranking: total 72

Roadways: *total:* 57,300 km (2018)
comparison ranking: total 84

Merchant marine: *total:* 94 (2023)
by type: container ship 6, general cargo 5, oil tanker 2, other 81

comparison ranking: total 94

Ports: *total ports:* 12 (2024)
large: 3
medium: 1
small: 3
very small: 5
ports with oil terminals: 2
key ports: Agadir, Casablanca, Tanger, Tangier-Mediterranean

MILITARY AND SECURITY

Military and security forces: Royal Armed Forces (FAR): Royal Moroccan Army (includes the Moroccan Royal Guard), Royal Moroccan Navy (includes Coast Guard, marines), Royal Moroccan Air Force, Royal Moroccan Gendarmerie

Ministry of Interior: National Police (DGSN), Auxiliary Forces (2024)
note 1: the Moroccan Royal Guard is officially part of the Royal Moroccan Army, but is under the direct operational control of the Royal Military Household of His Majesty the King; it provides for the security and safety of the King and royal family; it was established in the 11th century and is considered one of the world's oldest active units still in military service
note 2: the National Police manage internal law enforcement in cities; the Royal Gendarmerie (Administration of National Defense) is responsible for law enforcement in rural regions and on national highways; the Gendarmerie operates mobile and fixed checkpoints along the roads in border areas and at the entrances to major municipalities; it also has a counterterrorism role; the Auxiliary Forces provide support to the Gendarmerie and National Police and includes a Mobile Intervention Corps, a motorized paramilitary security force that supplements the military and the police as needed

Military expenditures: 4% of GDP (2023 est.)
4.5% of GDP (2022 est.)
4.5% of GDP (2021 est.)
4.5% of GDP (2020 est.)
3.4% of GDP (2019 est.)
comparison ranking: 16

Military and security service personnel strengths: approximately 200,000 active personnel (175,000 Army; 10,000 Navy; 15,000 Air Force); estimated 20,000 Gendarmerie; estimated 5,000 Mobile Intervention Corps; estimated 25-30,000 Auxiliary Forces (2023)

Military equipment inventories and acquisitions: the Moroccan military's inventory is comprised of mostly older French and US equipment, although in recent years it has embarked on a modernization program and received quantities of more modern equipment from a variety of countries, particularly France, Spain, and the US (2024)

Military service age and obligation: 19-25 years of age for 12-month compulsory and voluntary military service for men and women (conscription abolished 2006 and reintroduced in 2019) (2023)

Military deployments: 770 Central African Republic (MINUSCA); 930 Democratic Republic of the Congo (MONUSCO) (2024)

Military - note: the Royal Armed Forces (FAR) are responsible for protecting Morocco's national interests, sovereignty, and territorial integrity; key areas of concern for the FAR include regional challenges such as the Polisario Front in Western Sahara and Algeria; Morocco claims the territory of Western Sahara and administers the territory that it controls; the Polisario Front (Popular Front for the Liberation of Saguia el Hamra and Rio de Oro), an organization that seeks the territory's independence, disputes Morocco's claim of sovereignty over the territory; Moroccan and Polisario forces fought intermittently from 1975, when Spain relinquished colonial authority over the territory, until a 1991 cease-fire and the establishment of a UN peacekeeping mission; the Polisario withdrew from the cease-fire in November 2020, and since then there have been reports of intermittent indirect fire between the FAR and Polisario fighters across the 2,500- kilometer-long berm built in 1987 that separates the two sides; Algeria is seen as a regional rival and has openly backed the Polisario Front
the FAR has experience in counterinsurgency, desert warfare, and international peacekeeping and security operations; it participates in both bilateral and multinational exercises and has relations with a variety of partners including the militaries of France, Spain, and the US, as well as NATO, the Arab League, and the African Union; the FAR provided fighter aircraft to the Saudi-led coalition in Yemen from 2015-2019; Morocco has Major Non-NATO Ally (MNNA) status with the US, a designation under US law that provides foreign partners with certain benefits in the areas of defense trade and security cooperation
the FAR was created in May 1956; large numbers of Moroccans were recruited for service in the Spahi and Tirailleur regiments of the French Army of Africa during the period of the French protectorate (1912-1956); many Moroccans fought under the French Army during both World Wars; after World War II, Moroccans formed part of the French Far East Expeditionary Corps during the First Indochina War (1946-1954); the Spanish Army recruited Moroccans from the Spanish Protectorate during both the Rif War (1921-26) and the Spanish Civil War (1936-39)
the UN Mission for the Referendum in Western Sahara (MINURSO) was established by Security Council resolution 690 in April 1991 in accordance with settlement proposals accepted in August 1988 by Morocco and the Polisario Front; MINURSO was unable to carry out all the original settlement proposals, but continues to monitor the cease-fire and reduce the threat of mines and unexploded ordnance, and has provided logistic support to the Office of the UN High Commissioner for Refugees (UNHCR) with personnel and air and ground assets (2024)

TERRORISM

Terrorist group(s): Islamic State of Iraq and ash-Sham (ISIS)
note: details about the history, aims, leadership, organization, areas of operation, tactics, targets, weapons, size, and sources of support of the group(s) appear(s) in the Terrorism reference guide

TRANSNATIONAL ISSUES

Refugees and internally displaced persons: *refugees (country of origin):* 5,250 (Syria) (mid-year 2022)

Illicit drugs: one of the world's largest cannabis-producing country with Europe as the main market; hashish is smuggled to South America and the Caribbean where it is exchanged for cocaine which is distributed in Europe; MDMA (ecstasy), originating in Belgium and the Netherlands is smuggled into northern Morocco for sale on the domestic market

MOZAMBIQUE

INTRODUCTION

Background: In the first half of the second millennium A.D., northern Mozambican port towns were frequented by traders from Somalia, Ethiopia, Egypt, Arabia, Persia, and India. The Portuguese were able to wrest much of the coastal trade from Arab Muslims in the centuries after 1500, and they set up their own colonies. Portugal did not relinquish Mozambique until 1975. Large-scale emigration, economic dependence on South Africa, a severe drought, and a prolonged civil war hindered the country's development until the mid-1990s.

The ruling Front for the Liberation of Mozambique (FRELIMO) party formally abandoned Marxism in 1989, and a new constitution the following year provided for multiparty elections and a free-market economy. A UN-negotiated peace agreement between FRELIMO and rebel Mozambique National Resistance (RENAMO) forces ended the fighting in 1992. In 2004, Mozambique underwent a delicate transition as Joaquim CHISSANO stepped down after 18 years in office. His elected successor, Armando GUEBUZA, served two terms and then passed executive power to Filipe NYUSI in 2015. RENAMO's residual armed forces intermittently engaged in a low-level insurgency after 2012, but a 2016 cease-fire eventually led to the two sides signing a comprehensive peace deal in 2019.

Since 2017, violent extremists – who an official ISIS media outlet recognized as ISIS's network in Mozambique for the first time in 2019 – have been conducting attacks against civilians and security services in the northern province of Cabo Delgado. In 2021, Rwanda and the Southern African Development Community deployed forces to support Mozambique's efforts to counter the extremist group.

GEOGRAPHY

Location: Southeastern Africa, bordering the Mozambique Channel, between South Africa and Tanzania

Geographic coordinates: 18 15 S, 35 00 E

Map references: Africa

Area: *total:* 799,380 sq km
land: 786,380 sq km

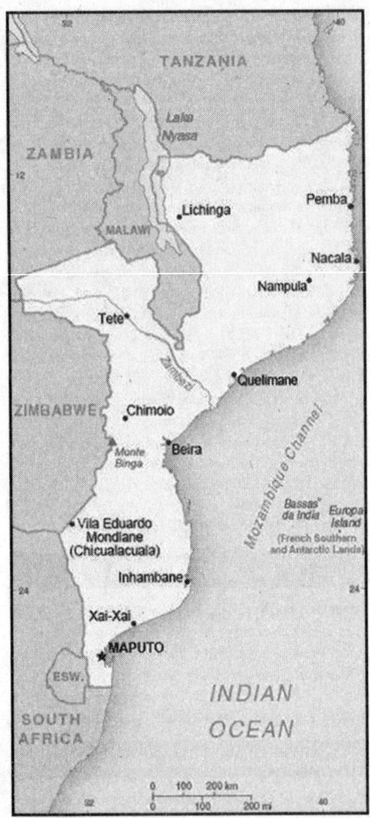

water: 13,000 sq km
comparison ranking: total 36

Area - comparative: slightly more than five times the size of Georgia; slightly less than twice the size of California

Land boundaries: *total:* 4,783 km
border countries (6): Malawi 1498 km; South Africa 496 km; Eswatini 108 km; Tanzania 840 km; Zambia 439 km; Zimbabwe 1,402 km

Coastline: 2,470 km

Maritime claims: *territorial sea:* 12 nm
exclusive economic zone: 200 nm

Climate: tropical to subtropical

Terrain: mostly coastal lowlands, uplands in center, high plateaus in northwest, mountains in west

Elevation: *highest point:* Monte Binga 2,436 m
lowest point: Indian Ocean 0 m
mean elevation: 345 m

Natural resources: coal, titanium, natural gas, hydropower, tantalum, graphite

Land use: *agricultural land:* 56.3% (2018 est.)
arable land: 6.4% (2018 est.)
permanent crops: 0.3% (2018 est.)
permanent pasture: 49.6% (2018 est.)
forest: 43.7% (2018 est.)
other: 0% (2018 est.)

Irrigated land: 1,180 sq km (2012)

Major lakes (area sq km): *fresh water lake(s):* Lake Malawi (shared with Malawi and Tanzania) - 22,490

Major rivers (by length in km): Rio Zambeze (Zambezi) river mouth (shared with Zambia [s]), Angola, Namibia, Botswana, and Zimbabwe) - 2,740 km; Rio Limpopo river mouth (shared with South Africa [s], Botswana, and Zimbabwe) - 1,800 km
note – [s] after country name indicates river source; [m] after country name indicates river mouth

Major watersheds (area sq km): Indian Ocean drainage: Zambezi (1,332,412 sq km)

Population distribution: three large populations clusters are found along the southern coast between Maputo and Inhambane, in the central area between Beira and Chimoio along the Zambezi River, and in and around the northern cities of Nampula, Cidade de Nacala, and Pemba; the northwest and southwest are the least populated areas as shown in this population distribution map

Natural hazards: severe droughts; devastating cyclones and floods in central and southern provinces

Geography - note: the Zambezi River flows through the north-central and most fertile part of the country

PEOPLE AND SOCIETY

Population: *total:* 33,350,954
male: 16,449,734
female: 16,901,220 (2024 est.)
comparison rankings: female 44; male 46; total 46

Nationality: *noun:* Mozambican(s)
adjective: Mozambican

Ethnic groups: African 99% (Makhuwa, Tsonga, Lomwe, Sena, and others), Mestizo 0.8%, other (includes European, Indian, Pakistani, Chinese) 0.2% (2017 est.)

Languages: Makhuwa 26.1%, Portuguese (official) 16.6%, Tsonga 8.6%, Nyanja 8.1, Sena 7.1%, Lomwe 7.1%, Chuwabo 4.7%, Ndau 3.8%, Tswa 3.8%, other Mozambican languages 11.8%, other 0.5%, unspecified 1.8% (2017 est.)

Religions: Roman Catholic 27.2%, Muslim 18.9%, Zionist Christian 15.6%, Evangelical/Pentecostal 15.3%, Anglican 1.7%, other 4.8%, none 13.9%, unspecified 2.5% (2017 est.)

Demographic profile: Mozambique is a poor, sparsely populated country with high fertility and mortality rates and a rapidly growing youthful population – 45% of the population is younger than 15, as of 2020. Mozambique's high poverty rate is sustained by natural disasters, disease, high population growth, low agricultural productivity, and the unequal distribution of wealth. The country's birth rate is among the world's highest, averaging around 5 children per woman (and higher in rural areas) for at least the last three decades. The sustained high level of fertility reflects gender inequality, low contraceptive use, early marriages and childbearing, and a lack of education, particularly among women. The high population growth rate is somewhat restrained by the country's high HIV/AIDS and overall mortality rates. Mozambique ranks among the worst in the world for HIV/AIDS prevalence, HIV/AIDS deaths, and life expectancy at birth, as of 2022.

Mozambique is predominantly a country of emigration, but internal, rural-urban migration has begun to grow. Mozambicans, primarily from the country's southern region, have been migrating to South Africa for work for more than a century. Additionally, approximately 1.7 million Mozambicans fled to Malawi, South Africa, and other neighboring countries between 1979 and 1992 to escape from civil war. Labor migrants have usually been men from rural areas whose crops have failed or who are unemployed and have headed to South Africa to work as miners; multiple generations of the same family often become miners. Since the abolition of apartheid in South Africa in 1991, other job opportunities have opened to Mozambicans, including in the informal and manufacturing sectors, but mining remains their main source of employment.

Age structure: *0-14 years:* 44.7% (male 7,548,247/female 7,350,012)
15-64 years: 52.4% (male 8,428,457/female 9,061,065)
65 years and over: 2.9% (2024 est.) (male 473,030/female 490,143)

Dependency ratios: *total dependency ratio:* 86.1
youth dependency ratio: 81.3
elderly dependency ratio: 4.8
potential support ratio: 20.8 (2021 est.)

Median age: *total:* 17.3 years (2024 est.)
male: 16.7 years
female: 17.9 years
comparison ranking: total 222

Population growth rate: 2.54% (2024 est.)
comparison ranking: 17

Birth rate: 36.5 births/1,000 population (2024 est.)
comparison ranking: 9

Death rate: 9.6 deaths/1,000 population (2024 est.)
comparison ranking: 40

Net migration rate: -1.5 migrant(s)/1,000 population (2024 est.)
comparison ranking: 158

Population distribution: three large populations clusters are found along the southern coast between Maputo and Inhambane, in the central area between Beira and Chimoio along the Zambezi River, and in and around the northern cities of Nampula, Cidade de Nacala, and Pemba; the northwest and southwest are the least populated areas as shown in this population distribution map

Urbanization: *urban population:* 38.8% of total population (2023)
rate of urbanization: 4.24% annual rate of change (2020-25 est.)

Major urban areas - population: 1.852 million Matola, 1.163 million MAPUTO (capital), 969,000 Nampula (2023)

Sex ratio: *at birth:* 1.03 male(s)/female
0-14 years: 1.03 male(s)/female
15-64 years: 0.93 male(s)/female
65 years and over: 0.97 male(s)/female
total population: 0.97 male(s)/female (2024 est.)

Mother's mean age at first birth: 19.2 years (2011 est.)
note: data represents median age at first birth among women 20-49

Maternal mortality ratio: 127 deaths/100,000 live births (2020 est.)
comparison ranking: 58

Infant mortality rate: *total:* 58.2 deaths/1,000 live births (2024 est.)
male: 60.1 deaths/1,000 live births
female: 56.2 deaths/1,000 live births
comparison ranking: total 9

Life expectancy at birth: *total population:* 58.3 years (2024 est.)
male: 57.1 years

female: 59.6 years
comparison ranking: total population 224

Total fertility rate: 4.66 children born/woman (2024 est.)
comparison ranking: 12

Gross reproduction rate: 2.29 (2024 est.)

Contraceptive prevalence rate: 27.1% (2015)

Drinking water source: *improved: urban:* 93.4% of population
rural: 61.5% of population
total: 73.3% of population
unimproved: urban: 6.6% of population
rural: 38.5% of population
total: 26.7% of population (2020 est.)

Current health expenditure: 7.6% of GDP (2020)

Physician density: 0.09 physicians/1,000 population (2020)

Hospital bed density: 0.7 beds/1,000 population (2011)

Sanitation facility access: *improved: urban:* 71.9% of population (2015 est.)
rural: 24.7% of population
total: 42.2% of population
unimproved: urban: 28.1% of population
rural: 75.3% of population
total: 57.8% of population (2020 est.)

Obesity - adult prevalence rate: 7.2% (2016)
comparison ranking: 160

Alcohol consumption per capita: *total:* 1.46 liters of pure alcohol (2019 est.)
beer: 1.03 liters of pure alcohol (2019 est.)
wine: 0.22 liters of pure alcohol (2019 est.)
spirits: 0.21 liters of pure alcohol (2019 est.)
other alcohols: 0 liters of pure alcohol (2019 est.)
comparison ranking: total 140

Tobacco use: *total:* 14.3% (2020 est.)
male: 23% (2020 est.)
female: 5.6% (2020 est.)
comparison ranking: total 109

Children under the age of 5 years underweight: 14.6% (2019/20)
comparison ranking: 35

Currently married women (ages 15-49): 63.7% (2023 est.)

Education expenditures: 6.3% of GDP (2020 est.)
comparison ranking: 35

Literacy: *definition:* age 15 and over can read and write
total population: 63.4%
male: 74.1%
female: 53.8% (2021)

School life expectancy (primary to tertiary education): *total:* 10 years
male: 10 years
female: 9 years (2017)

ENVIRONMENT

Environment - current issues: increased migration of the population to urban and coastal areas with adverse environmental consequences; desertification; soil erosion; deforestation; water pollution caused by artisanal mining; pollution of surface and coastal waters; wildlife preservation (elephant poaching for ivory)

Environment - international agreements: *party to:* Biodiversity, Climate Change, Climate Change-Kyoto Protocol, Climate Change-Paris Agreement, Comprehensive Nuclear Test Ban, Desertification, Endangered Species, Hazardous Wastes, Law of the Sea, Ozone Layer Protection, Ship Pollution, Tropical Timber 2006, Wetlands
signed, but not ratified: none of the selected agreements

Climate: tropical to subtropical

Urbanization: *urban population:* 38.8% of total population (2023)
rate of urbanization: 4.24% annual rate of change (2020-25 est.)

Food insecurity: *severe localized food insecurity: due to shortfall in agricultural production and economic downturn* - the number of people in need of food assistance is expected to rise above the 1.86 million estimated in 2021-2022 because of three key factors; firstly, higher year-on-year prices of food and fuel are reducing households' purchasing power, worsening their economic access to food, particularly for low-income households; secondly, the impact of extreme weather events on agricultural production in central and southern provinces in 2022 is likely to mean that farming households in the affected areas have both low food supplies from their own production and curtailed income-earning opportunities from crop sales, impinging on their food availability and economic access to food; thirdly, there has been an increase in attacks by non-state armed groups in the northern province of Cabo Delgado in 2022 (2022)

Revenue from forest resources: 6.46% of GDP (2018 est.)
comparison ranking: 9

Revenue from coal: 4.17% of GDP (2018 est.)
comparison ranking: 2

Air pollutants: *particulate matter emissions:* 16.45 micrograms per cubic meter (2019 est.)
carbon dioxide emissions: 7.94 megatons (2016 est.)
methane emissions: 16.26 megatons (2020 est.)

Waste and recycling: *municipal solid waste generated annually:* 2.5 million tons (2014 est.)
municipal solid waste recycled annually: 25,000 tons (2014 est.)
percent of municipal solid waste recycled: 1% (2014 est.)

Major lakes (area sq km): *fresh water lake(s):* Lake Malawi (shared with Malawi and Tanzania) - 22,490

Major rivers (by length in km): Rio Zambeze (Zambezi) river mouth (shared with Zambia [s]), Angola, Namibia, Botswana, and Zimbabwe) - 2,740 km; Rio Limpopo river mouth (shared with South Africa [s], Botswana, and Zimbabwe) - 1,800 km

note – [s] after country name indicates river source; [m] after country name indicates river mouth

Major watersheds (area sq km): Indian Ocean drainage: Zambezi (1,332,412 sq km)

Total water withdrawal: *municipal:* 370 million cubic meters (2020 est.)
industrial: 30 million cubic meters (2020 est.)
agricultural: 1.08 billion cubic meters (2020 est.)

Total renewable water resources: 217.1 billion cubic meters (2020 est.)

GOVERNMENT

Country name: *conventional long form:* Republic of Mozambique
conventional short form: Mozambique
local long form: Republica de Mocambique
local short form: Mocambique
former: Portuguese East Africa, People's Republic of Mozambique
etymology: named for the offshore island of Mozambique; the island was apparently named after Mussa al-BIK, an influential Arab slave trader who set himself up as sultan on the island in the 15th century

Government type: presidential republic

Capital: *name:* Maputo
geographic coordinates: 25 57 S, 32 35 E
time difference: UTC+2 (7 hours ahead of Washington, DC, during Standard Time)
etymology: reputedly named after the Maputo River, which drains into Maputo Bay south of the city

Administrative divisions: 10 provinces (provincias, singular - provincia), 1 city (cidade)*; Cabo Delgado, Gaza, Inhambane, Manica, Maputo, Cidade de Maputo*, Nampula, Niassa, Sofala, Tete, Zambezia

Independence: 25 June 1975 (from Portugal)

National holiday: Independence Day, 25 June (1975)

Legal system: mixed legal system of Portuguese civil law and customary law

Constitution: *history:* previous 1975, 1990; latest adopted 16 November 2004, effective 21 December 2004
amendments: proposed by the president of the republic or supported by at least one third of the Assembly of the Republic membership; passage of amendments affecting constitutional provisions, including the independence and sovereignty of the state, the republican form of government, basic rights and freedoms, and universal suffrage, requires at least a two-thirds majority vote by the Assembly and approval in a referendum; referenda not required for passage of other amendments; amended 2007, 2018

International law organization participation: has not submitted an ICJ jurisdiction declaration; non-party state to the ICCt

Citizenship: *citizenship by birth:* no
citizenship by descent only: at least one parent must be a citizen of Mozambique
dual citizenship recognized: no
residency requirement for naturalization: 5 years

Suffrage: 18 years of age; universal

Executive branch: *chief of state:* President Filipe Jacinto NYUSI (since 15 January 2015)
head of government: Prime Minister Adriano MALEIANE (since 3 March 2022)
cabinet: Cabinet appointed by the president
elections/appointments: president elected directly by absolute majority popular vote in 2 rounds if needed for a 5-year term (eligible for 2 consecutive terms); election last held on 15 October 2019 (next to be held on 9 October 2024); prime minister appointed by the president
election results:
2019: Filipe NYUSI reelected president in first round; percent of vote - Filipe NYUSI (FRELIMO) 73.0%, Ossufo MOMADE (RENAMO) 21.9%, Daviz SIMANGO (MDM) 5.1%
2014: Filipe NYUSI elected president in first round; percent of vote - Filipe NYUSI (FRELIMO) 57.0%, Afonso DHLAKAMA (RENAMO) 36.6%, Daviz SIMANGO (MDM) 6.4%

Legislative branch: *description:* unicameral Assembly of the Republic or Assembleia da Republica (250 seats; 248 members elected in

multi-seat constituencies by party-list proportional representation vote and 2 members representing Mozambicans abroad directly elected by simple majority vote; members serve 5-year terms)
elections: last held on 15 October 2019 (next to be held on 9 October 2024)
election results: percent of vote by party - FRELIMO 71%, RENAMO 23%, MDM 4%; seats by party - FRELIMO 184, RENAMO 60, MDM 6; composition - men 142, women 108, percentage women 43.2%

Judicial branch: *highest court(s):* Supreme Court (consists of the court president, vice president, and 5 judges); Constitutional Council (consists of 7 judges); note - the Higher Council of the Judiciary Magistracy is responsible for judiciary management and discipline
judge selection and term of office: Supreme Court president appointed by the president of the republic; vice president appointed by the president in consultation with the Higher Council of the Judiciary (CSMJ) and ratified by the Assembly of the Republic; other judges elected by the Assembly; judges serve 5-year renewable terms; Constitutional Council judges appointed - 1 by the president, 5 by the Assembly, and 1 by the CSMJ; judges serve 5-year nonrenewable terms
subordinate courts: Administrative Court (capital city only); provincial courts or Tribunais Judicias de Provincia; District Courts or Tribunais Judicias de Districto; customs courts; maritime courts; courts marshal; labor courts; community courts

Political parties: Democratic Movement of Mozambique (Movimento Democratico de Mocambique) or MDM
Liberation Front of Mozambique (Frente de Liberatacao de Mocambique) or FRELIMO
Mozambican National Resistance (Resistencia Nacional Mocambicana) or RENAMO

International organization participation: ACP, AfDB, AU, C, CD, CPLP, EITI (compliant country), FAO, G-77, IAEA, IBRD, ICAO, ICC (NGOs), ICRM, IDA, IDB, IFAD, IFC, IFRCS, IHO, ILO, IMF, IMO, IMSO, Interpol, IOC, IOM, IPU, ISO (correspondent), ITSO, ITU, ITUC (NGOs), MIGA, NAM, OIC, OIF (observer), OPCW, SADC, UN, UNCDF, UNCTAD, UNDP, UNDSS, UNECA, UNEP, UNESCO, UNFPA, UNHCR, UNIDO, UNODC, UNOPS, UNV, UNWTO, Union Latina, UPU, WCO, WFP, WFTU (NGOs), WHO, WIPO, WMO, WTO

Diplomatic representation in the US: *chief of mission:* Ambassador Alfredo Fabião NUVUNGA (since 19 April 2023)
chancery: 1525 New Hampshire Avenue NW, Washington, DC 20036
telephone: [1] (202) 293-7147
FAX: [1] (202) 835-0245
email address and website:
washington.dc@embamoc.gov.mz
https://usa.embamoc.gov.mz/

Diplomatic representation from the US: *chief of mission:* Ambassador Peter Hendrick VROOMAN (since 3 March 2022)
embassy: Avenida Marginal 5467, Maputo
mailing address: 2330 Maputo Place, Washington DC 20521-2330
telephone: [258] (84) 095-8000
email address and website:
MaputaConsular@state.gov
https://mz.usembassy.gov/

Flag description: three equal horizontal bands of green (top), black, and yellow with a red isosceles triangle based on the hoist side; the black band is edged in white; centered in the triangle is a yellow five-pointed star bearing a crossed rifle and hoe in black superimposed on an open white book; green represents the riches of the land, white peace, black the African continent, yellow the country's minerals, and red the struggle for independence; the rifle symbolizes defense and vigilance, the hoe refers to the country's agriculture, the open book stresses the importance of education, and the star represents Marxism and internationalism
note: one of only two national flags featuring a firearm, the other is Guatemala

National symbol(s): national colors: green, black, yellow, white, red

National anthem: *name:* "Patria Amada" (Lovely Fatherland)
lyrics/music: Salomao J. MANHICA/unknown
note: adopted 2002

National heritage: *total World Heritage Sites:* 1 (cultural)
selected World Heritage Site locales: Island of Mozambique

ECONOMY

Economic overview: low-income East African economy; subsistence farming dominates labor force; return to growth led by agriculture and extractive industries; Islamist insurgency threatens natural gas projects in north; ongoing foreign debt restructuring and resolution under IMF Highly Indebted Poor Countries (HIPC) initiative

Real GDP (purchasing power parity): $50.631 billion (2023 est.)
$48.22 billion (2022 est.)
$46.206 billion (2021 est.)
note: data in 2021 dollars
comparison ranking: 125

Real GDP growth rate: 5% (2023 est.)
4.36% (2022 est.)
2.38% (2021 est.)
note: annual GDP % growth based on constant local currency
comparison ranking: 55

Real GDP per capita: $1,500 (2023 est.)
$1,500 (2022 est.)
$1,400 (2021 est.)
note: data in 2021 dollars
comparison ranking: 218

GDP (official exchange rate): $20.625 billion (2023 est.)
note: data in current dollars at official exchange rate

Inflation rate (consumer prices): 7.13% (2023 est.)
10.28% (2022 est.)
6.41% (2021 est.)
note: annual % change based on consumer prices
comparison ranking: 145

Credit ratings: Fitch rating: CCC (2019)

Moody's rating: Caa2 (2019)

Standard & Poors rating: CCC+ (2019)
note: The year refers to the year in which the current credit rating was first obtained.

GDP - composition, by sector of origin: *agriculture:* 26.7% (2022 est.)
industry: 22.8% (2022 est.)
services: 40.6% (2022 est.)
note: figures may not total 100% due to non-allocated consumption not captured in sector-reported data
comparison rankings: services 189; industry 116; agriculture 17

GDP - composition, by end use: *household consumption:* 75.2% (2022 est.)
government consumption: 16.7% (2022 est.)
investment in fixed capital: 38.6% (2022 est.)
exports of goods and services: 52.5% (2022 est.)
imports of goods and services: -83% (2022 est.)
note: figures may not total 100% due to rounding or gaps in data collection

Agricultural products: cassava, sugarcane, maize, tomatoes, sweet potatoes, beans, bananas, onions, rice, coconuts (2022)
note: top ten agricultural products based on tonnage

Industries: aluminum, petroleum products, chemicals (fertilizer, soap, paints), textiles, cement, glass, asbestos, tobacco, food, beverages

Industrial production growth rate: 10.43% (2023 est.)
note: annual % change in industrial value added based on constant local currency
comparison ranking: 13

Labor force: 15.191 million (2023 est.)
note: number of people ages 15 or older who are employed or seeking work
comparison ranking: 42

Unemployment rate: 3.54% (2023 est.)
3.62% (2022 est.)
3.98% (2021 est.)
note: % of labor force seeking employment
comparison ranking: 61

Youth unemployment rate (ages 15-24): *total:* 7.6% (2023 est.)
male: 7.9% (2023 est.)
female: 7.3% (2023 est.)
note: % of labor force ages 15-24 seeking employment
comparison ranking: total 154

Population below poverty line: 46.1% (2014 est.)
note: % of population with income below national poverty line

Gini Index coefficient - distribution of family income: 50.5 (2019 est.)
note: index (0-100) of income distribution; higher values represent greater inequality
comparison ranking: 11

Household income or consumption by percentage share: *lowest 10%:* 1.6% (2019 est.)
highest 10%: 41.2% (2019 est.)
note: % share of income accruing to lowest and highest 10% of population

Remittances: 3.22% of GDP (2023 est.)
1.34% of GDP (2022 est.)
4.57% of GDP (2021 est.)
note: personal transfers and compensation between resident and non-resident individuals/households/entities

Budget: *revenues:* $5.388 billion (2022 est.)
expenditures: $4.91 billion (2022 est.)
note: central government revenues and expenses (excluding grants/extrabudgetary units/social security funds) converted to US dollars at average official exchange rate for year indicated

Public debt: 78.62% of GDP (2022 est.)
note: central government debt as a % of GDP
comparison ranking: 41

Taxes and other revenues: 23.25% (of GDP) (2022 est.)

note: central government tax revenue as a % of GDP
comparison ranking: 59

Current account balance: -$2.426 billion (2023 est.)
-$6.88 billion (2022 est.)
-$3.436 billion (2021 est.)
note: balance of payments - net trade and primary/ secondary income in current dollars
comparison ranking: 165

Exports: $9.289 billion (2023 est.)
$9.409 billion (2022 est.)
$6.526 billion (2021 est.)
note: balance of payments - exports of goods and services in current dollars
comparison ranking: 117

Exports - partners: India 22%, South Africa 9%, South Korea 8%, Italy 7%, China 6% (2022)
note: top five export partners based on percentage share of exports

Exports - commodities: coal, aluminum, coke, natural gas, gold (2022)
note: top five export commodities based on value in dollars

Imports: $11.18 billion (2023 est.)
$15.932 billion (2022 est.)
$10.534 billion (2021 est.)
note: balance of payments - imports of goods and services in current dollars
comparison ranking: 116

Imports - partners: South Africa 23%, South Korea 20%, China 12%, India 10%, Democratic Republic of the Congo 5% (2022)
note: top five import partners based on percentage share of imports

Imports - commodities: ships, refined petroleum, iron alloys, chromium ore, refined copper (2022)
note: top five import commodities based on value in dollars

Reserves of foreign exchange and gold: $3.515 billion (2023 est.)
$2.939 billion (2022 est.)
$3.781 billion (2021 est.)
note: holdings of gold (year-end prices)/foreign exchange/special drawing rights in current dollars
comparison ranking: 63

Exchange rates: meticais (MZM) per US dollar -

Exchange rates: 63.886 (2023 est.)
63.851 (2022 est.)
65.465 (2021 est.)
69.465 (2020 est.)
62.548 (2019 est.)

ENERGY

Electricity access: *electrification - total population:* 33.2% (2022 est.)
electrification - urban areas: 79.4%
electrification - rural areas: 5%

Electricity: *installed generating capacity:* 2.77 million kW (2022 est.)
consumption: 13.09 billion kWh (2022 est.)
exports: 11.096 billion kWh (2022 est.)
imports: 8.219 billion kWh (2022 est.)
transmission/distribution losses: 3.052 billion kWh (2022 est.)
comparison rankings: transmission/distribution losses 141; imports 32; exports 23; consumption 90; installed generating capacity 112

Electricity generation sources: *fossil fuels:* 17.6% of total installed capacity (2022 est.)
solar: 0.4% of total installed capacity (2022 est.)
hydroelectricity: 81.4% of total installed capacity (2022 est.)
biomass and waste: 0.6% of total installed capacity (2022 est.)

Coal: *production:* 9.015 million metric tons (2022 est.)
consumption: 11,000 metric tons (2022 est.)
exports: 9.413 million metric tons (2022 est.)
imports: 9,000 metric tons (2022 est.)
proven reserves: 1.792 billion metric tons (2022 est.)

Petroleum: *refined petroleum consumption:* 40,000 bbl/day (2022 est.)

Natural gas: *production:* 5.338 billion cubic meters (2022 est.)
consumption: 1.347 billion cubic meters (2022 est.)
exports: 3.963 billion cubic meters (2022 est.)
proven reserves: 2.832 trillion cubic meters (2021 est.)

Carbon dioxide emissions: 8.423 million metric tonnes of CO2 (2022 est.)
from coal and metallurgical coke: 59,000 metric tonnes of CO2 (2022 est.)
from petroleum and other liquids: 5.568 million metric tonnes of CO2 (2022 est.)
from consumed natural gas: 2.796 million metric tonnes of CO2 (2022 est.)
comparison ranking: total emissions 113

Energy consumption per capita: 5.426 million Btu/ person (2022 est.)
comparison ranking: 169

COMMUNICATIONS

Telephones - fixed lines: *total subscriptions:* 29,000 (2022 est.)
subscriptions per 100 inhabitants: (2022 est.) less than 1
comparison ranking: total subscriptions 166

Telephones - mobile cellular: *total subscriptions:* 13.871 million (2022 est.)
subscriptions per 100 inhabitants: 42 (2022 est.)
comparison ranking: total subscriptions 75

Telecommunication systems: *general assessment:* one of the first countries in the region to embark upon telecom reform and to open the sector to competition; the mobile segment in particular has shown strong growth; additional competition followed in late 2020; a new licensing regime ensured that by mid-2019 all operators had been provided with universal licenses, enabling them to offer all types of telephony and data services; mobile, fixed-line and broadband penetration rates remain far below the average for the region; in recent years the government has enforced the registration of SIM cards, but with varying success; at the end of 2016 almost five million unregistered SIM cards were deactivated but poor monitoring meant that the process was revisited in mid-2019 and again in late 2020; the high cost of international bandwidth had long hampered internet use, though the landing of two international submarine cables (SEACOM and EASSy) has reduced the cost of bandwidth and so led to drastic reductions in broadband retail prices as well as a significant jump in available bandwidth; there is some cross-platform competition, with DSL, cable, fibre, WiMAX, and mobile broadband options available, though fixed broadband options can be limited to urban areas; improvements can be expected from the ongoing rollout of a national fiber backbone networks and of upgrades to mobile infrastructure (2022)
domestic: fixed-line less than 1 per 100 and nearly 43 per 100 mobile-cellular teledensity (2021)
international: country code - 258; landing points for the EASSy and SEACOM/ Tata TGN-Eurasia fiber-optic submarine cable systems linking numerous east African countries, the Middle East and Asia ; satellite earth stations - 5 Intelsat (2 Atlantic Ocean and 3 Indian Ocean); TdM contracts for Itelsat for satellite broadband and bulk haul services (2020)

Broadcast media: state-run TV station supplemented by private TV station; Portuguese state TV's African service, RTP Africa, and Brazilian-owned TV Miramar are available; state-run radio provides nearly 100% territorial coverage and broadcasts in multiple languages; a number of privately owned and community-operated stations; transmissions of multiple international broadcasters are available (2019)

Internet country code: .mz

Internet users: *total:* 5.44 million (2021 est.)
percent of population: 17% (2021 est.)
comparison ranking: total 87

Broadband - fixed subscriptions: *total:* 70,000 (2020 est.)
subscriptions per 100 inhabitants: 0.2 (2020 est.)
comparison ranking: total 136

TRANSPORTATION

National air transport system: *number of registered air carriers:* 2 (2020)
inventory of registered aircraft operated by air carriers: 11
annual passenger traffic on registered air carriers: 540,124 (2018)
annual freight traffic on registered air carriers: 4.78 million (2018) mt-km

Civil aircraft registration country code prefix: C9

Airports: 92 (2024)
comparison ranking: 56

Pipelines: 972 km gas, 278 km refined products (2013)

Railways: *total:* 4,787 km (2014)
narrow gauge: 4,787 km (2014) 1.067-m gauge
comparison ranking: total 40

Roadways: *total:* 30,562 km
paved: 5,958 km
unpaved: 24,604 km (2018)
comparison ranking: total 100

Waterways: 460 km (2010) (Zambezi River navigable to Tete and along Cahora Bassa Lake)
comparison ranking: 94

Merchant marine: *total:* 36 (2023)
by type: general cargo 9, other 27
comparison ranking: total 130

Ports: *total ports:* 11 (2024)
large: 0
medium: 2
small: 5
very small: 4
ports with oil terminals: 3
key ports: Beira, Chinde, Inhambane, Maputo, Mocambique, Pebane, Porto Belo

MILITARY AND SECURITY

Military and security forces: Armed Forces for the Defense of Mozambique (Forcas Armadas de Defesa

de Mocambique, FADM): Mozambique Army (Ramo do Exercito), Mozambique Navy (Marinha de Guerra de Mocambique, MGM), Mozambique Air Force (Forca Aerea de Mocambique, FAM)

Ministry of Interior: Mozambique National Police (PRM), the National Criminal Investigation Service (SERNIC), Rapid Intervention Unit (UIR; police special forces), Border Security Force; other security forces include the Presidential Guard and the Force for the Protection of High-Level Individuals (2024)
note 1: the FADM and other security forces are referred to collectively as the Defense and Security Forces (DFS)
note 2: the PRM, SERNIC, and the UIR are responsible for law enforcement and internal security; the Border Security Force is responsible for protecting the country's international borders and for carrying out police duties within 24 miles of borders
note 3: the Presidential Guard provides security for the president, and the Force for the Protection of High-level Individuals provides security for senior-level officials at the national and provincial levels
note 4: in 2023, the Mozambique Government legalized local militias that have been assisting security forces operating in Cabo Delgado against Islamic militants since 2020; this Local Force is comprised of ex-combatants and other civilians and receives training, uniforms, weapons, and logistical support from the FADM

Military expenditures: 1.5% of GDP (2023 est.)
1.3% of GDP (2022 est.)
1.2% of GDP (2021 est.)
1.1% of GDP (2020 est.)
1.2% of GDP (2019 est.)
comparison ranking: 94

Military and security service personnel strengths: information limited and varied; estimated 12,000 active personnel (11,000 Army and about 1,000 Air Force and Navy) (2023)

Military equipment inventories and acquisitions: the FADM's inventory consists primarily of Russian and Soviet-era equipment, although in recent years it has received limited quantities of more modern equipment from a variety of countries, mostly as aid/donations (2024)

Military service age and obligation: registration for military service is mandatory for all men and women at 18 years of age; 18-35 years of age for selective compulsory military service; 18 years of age for voluntary service for men and women; 24-month service obligation (note - in 2023, the Mozambique Government said it intended to raise the length of service from two to five years) (2023)

Military - note: the FADM is responsible for external security, cooperating with police on internal security, and responding to natural disasters and other emergencies; the current primary focus of the FADM is countering an insurgency driven by militants with ties to the Islamic State of Iraq and ash-Sham (ISIS) terrorist group in the northern province of Cabo Delgado, an area known for rich liquid natural gas deposits; insurgent attacks in the province began in 2017, and the fighting has left an estimated 6,000 dead and 1 million displaced; several countries from the Southern Africa Development Community (SADC) and the EU, as well as Rwanda and the US have provided various forms of military assistance to the FADM; the SADC countries and Rwanda have sent more than 3,000 military and security personnel, while some EU member states and the US have provided training assistance; in the first half of 2024, the SADC began withdrawing personnel, although the insurgency remained active (2024)

TERRORISM

Terrorist group(s): Islamic State of Iraq and ash-Sham - Mozambique (ISIS-M)
note: details about the history, aims, leadership, organization, areas of operation, tactics, targets, weapons, size, and sources of support of the group(s) appear(s) in the Terrorism reference guide

TRANSNATIONAL ISSUES

Refugees and internally displaced persons: *refugees (country of origin):* 10,655 (Burundi) (refugees and asylum seekers) (2023); 9,340 (Democratic Republic of Congo) (refugees and asylum seekers) (2024)
IDPs: 850,599 (north Mozambique, violence between the government and an opposition group, violence associated with extremists groups in 2018, political violence 2019) (2023)

Illicit drugs: a transit country for large shipments of heroin and methamphetamine originating from Afghanistan to primarily South Africa

NAMIBIA

INTRODUCTION

Background: Various ethnic groups occupied southwestern Africa prior to Germany establishing a colony over most of the territory in 1884. South Africa occupied the colony, then known as German South West Africa, in 1915 during World War I and administered it as a mandate until after World War II, when it annexed the territory. In 1966, the Marxist South-West Africa People's Organization (SWAPO) guerrilla group launched a war of independence for the area that became Namibia, but it was not until 1988 that South Africa agreed to end its administration in accordance with a UN peace plan for the entire region. Namibia gained independence in 1990, and SWAPO has governed it since, although the party has dropped much of its Marxist ideology. President Hage GEINGOB was elected in 2014 in a landslide victory, replacing Hifikepunye POHAMBA, who stepped down after serving two terms. SWAPO retained its parliamentary super majority in the 2014 elections. In 2019 elections, GEINGOB was reelected but by a substantially reduced majority, and SWAPO narrowly lost its super majority in parliament.

GEOGRAPHY

Location: Southern Africa, bordering the South Atlantic Ocean, between Angola and South Africa

Geographic coordinates: 22 00 S, 17 00 E

Map references: Africa

Area: *total:* 824,292 sq km
land: 823,290 sq km
water: 1,002 sq km
comparison ranking: total 35

Area - comparative: almost seven times the size of Pennsylvania; slightly more than half the size of Alaska

Land boundaries: *total:* 4,220 km
border countries (4): Angola 1,427 km; Botswana 1,544 km; South Africa 1,005 km; Zambia 244 km

Coastline: 1,572 km

Maritime claims: *territorial sea:* 12 nm
contiguous zone: 24 nm
exclusive economic zone: 200 nm

Climate: desert; hot, dry; rainfall sparse and erratic

Terrain: mostly high plateau; Namib Desert along coast; Kalahari Desert in east

Elevation: *highest point:* Konigstein on Brandberg 2,573 m
lowest point: Atlantic Ocean 0 m
mean elevation: 1,141 m

Natural resources: diamonds, copper, uranium, gold, silver, lead, tin, lithium, cadmium, tungsten, zinc, salt, hydropower, fish
note: suspected deposits of oil, coal, and iron ore

Land use: *agricultural land:* 47.2% (2018 est.)
arable land: 1% (2018 est.)
permanent crops: 0% (2018 est.)
permanent pasture: 46.2% (2018 est.)
forest: 8.8% (2018 est.)
other: 44% (2018 est.)

Irrigated land: 80 sq km (2012)

Major rivers (by length in km): Zambezi (shared with Zambia [s]), Angola, Botswana, Zimbabwe, and Mozambique [m]) - 2,740 km; Orange river mouth (shared with Lesotho [s], and South Africa) - 2,092 km; Okavango (shared with Angola [s], and Botswana [m]) - 1,600 km
note – [s] after country name indicates river source; [m] after country name indicates river mouth

Major watersheds (area sq km): Atlantic Ocean drainage: Orange (941,351 sq km)

Indian Ocean drainage: Zambezi (1,332,412 sq km)

Internal (endorheic basin) drainage: Okavango Basin (863,866 sq km)

Major aquifers: Lower Kalahari-Stampriet Basin, Upper Kalahari-Cuvelai-Upper Zambezi Basin

Population distribution: population density is very low, with the largest clustering found in the extreme north-central area along the border with Angola as shown in this population distribution map

Natural hazards: prolonged periods of drought

Geography - note: the Namib Desert, after which the country is named, is considered to be the oldest desert in the world; Namibia is the first country in the world to incorporate the protection of the environment into its constitution; some 14% of the land is protected, including virtually the entire Namib Desert coastal strip; Namib-Naukluft National Park (49,768 sq km), is the largest game park in Africa and one of the largest in the world

PEOPLE AND SOCIETY

Population: *total:* 2,803,660
male: 1,377,286
female: 1,426,374 (2024 est.)
comparison rankings: female 139; male 142; total 141

Nationality: *noun:* Namibian(s)
adjective: Namibian

Ethnic groups: Ovambo 50%, Kavangos 9%, Herero 7%, Damara 7%, mixed European and African ancestry 6.5%, European 6%, Nama 5%, Caprivian 4%, San 3%, Baster 2%, Tswana 0.5%

Languages: Oshiwambo languages 49.7%, Nama/Damara 11%, Kavango languages 10.4%, Afrikaans 9.4%, Herero languages 9.2%, Zambezi languages 4.9%, English (official) 2.3%, other African languages 1.5%, other European languages 0.7%, other 1% (2016 est.)
note: Namibia has 13 recognized national languages, including 10 indigenous African languages and 3 European languages

Religions: Christian 97.5%, other 0.6% (includes Muslim, Baha'i, Jewish, Buddhist), unaffiliated 1.9% (2020 est.)

Demographic profile: Planning officials view Namibia's reduced population growth rate as sustainable based on the country's economic growth over the past decade. Prior to independence in 1990, Namibia's relatively small population grew at about 3% annually, but declining fertility and the impact of HIV/AIDS slowed this growth to 1.4% by 2011, rebounding to close to 2% by 2016. Namibia's fertility rate has fallen over the last two decades – from about 4.5 children per woman in 1996 to 3.4 in 2016 and to 3 in 2022 – due to increased contraceptive use, higher educational attainment among women, and greater female participation in the labor force. The average age at first birth has stayed fairly constant, but the age at first marriage continues to increase, indicating a rising incidence of premarital childbearing.

The majority of Namibians are rural dwellers (about 55%) and live in the better-watered north and northeast parts of the country. Migration, historically male-dominated, generally flows from northern communal areas – non-agricultural lands where blacks were sequestered under the apartheid system – to agricultural, mining, and manufacturing centers in the center and south. After independence from South Africa, restrictions on internal movement eased, and rural-urban migration increased, bolstering urban growth.

Some Namibians – usually persons who are better-educated, more affluent, and from urban areas – continue to legally migrate to South Africa temporarily to visit family and friends and, much less frequently, to pursue tertiary education or better economic opportunities. Namibians concentrated along the country's other borders make unauthorized visits to Angola, Zambia, Zimbabwe, or Botswana, to visit family and to trade agricultural goods. Few Namibians express interest in permanently settling in other countries; they prefer the safety of their homeland, have a strong national identity, and enjoy a well-supplied retail sector. Although Namibia is receptive to foreign investment and cross-border trade, intolerance toward non-citizens is widespread.

Age structure: *0-14 years:* 34.1% (male 482,790/female 473,306)
15-64 years: 62% (male 846,810/female 890,099)
65 years and over: 3.9% (2024 est.) (male 47,686/female 62,969)

Dependency ratios: *total dependency ratio:* 67.3
youth dependency ratio: 60.6
elderly dependency ratio: 6.7
potential support ratio: 14.8 (2021 est.)

Median age: *total:* 22.8 years (2024 est.)
male: 22.1 years
female: 23.5 years
comparison ranking: total 182

Population growth rate: 1.72% (2024 est.)
comparison ranking: 54

Birth rate: 24.3 births/1,000 population (2024 est.)
comparison ranking: 47

Death rate: 7.1 deaths/1,000 population (2024 est.)
comparison ranking: 117

Net migration rate: 0 migrant(s)/1,000 population (2024 est.)
comparison ranking: 87

Population distribution: population density is very low, with the largest clustering found in the extreme north-central area along the border with Angola as shown in this population distribution map

Urbanization: *urban population:* 54.9% of total population (2023)
rate of urbanization: 3.64% annual rate of change (2020-25 est.)

Major urban areas - population: 477,000 WINDHOEK (capital) (2023)

Sex ratio: *at birth:* 1.03 male(s)/female
0-14 years: 1.02 male(s)/female
15-64 years: 0.95 male(s)/female
65 years and over: 0.76 male(s)/female
total population: 0.97 male(s)/female (2024 est.)

Mother's mean age at first birth: 21.6 years (2013 est.)
note: data represents median age at first birth among women 25-49

Maternal mortality ratio: 215 deaths/100,000 live births (2020 est.)
comparison ranking: 44

Infant mortality rate: *total:* 27.9 deaths/1,000 live births (2024 est.)
male: 31 deaths/1,000 live births
female: 24.7 deaths/1,000 live births
comparison ranking: total 55

Life expectancy at birth: *total population:* 65.9 years (2024 est.)
male: 64.2 years
female: 67.6 years
comparison ranking: total population 203

Total fertility rate: 2.89 children born/woman (2024 est.)
comparison ranking: 51

Gross reproduction rate: 1.43 (2024 est.)

Contraceptive prevalence rate: 56.1% (2013)

Drinking water source: *improved: urban:* 98.9% of population
rural: 83.2% of population
total: 91.4% of population
unimproved: urban: 1.1% of population
rural: 16.8% of population
total: 8.6% of population (2020 est.)

Current health expenditure: 8.9% of GDP (2020)

Physician density: 0.59 physicians/1,000 population (2018)

Hospital bed density: 2.7 beds/1,000 population

Sanitation facility access: *improved: urban:* 70.6% of population
rural: 23.6% of population
total: 48.1% of population
unimproved: urban: 29.4% of population
rural: 76.4% of population
total: 51.9% of population (2020 est.)

Obesity - adult prevalence rate: 17.2% (2016)
comparison ranking: 119

Alcohol consumption per capita: *total:* 2.38 liters of pure alcohol (2019 est.)
beer: 1.37 liters of pure alcohol (2019 est.)
wine: 0.16 liters of pure alcohol (2019 est.)
spirits: 0.53 liters of pure alcohol (2019 est.)
other alcohols: 0.32 liters of pure alcohol (2019 est.)
comparison ranking: total 126

Tobacco use: *total:* 15.1% (2020 est.)
male: 24.2% (2020 est.)
female: 6% (2020 est.)
comparison ranking: total 103

Children under the age of 5 years underweight: 13.2% (2013)
comparison ranking: 39

Currently married women (ages 15-49): 33.3% (2023 est.)

Education expenditures: 9.6% of GDP (2021 est.)
comparison ranking: 7

Literacy: *definition:* age 15 and over can read and write
total population: 92.3%
male: 90.6%
female: 92.3% (2021)

ENVIRONMENT

Environment - current issues: depletion and degradation of water and aquatic resources; desertification; land degradation; loss of biodiversity and biotic resources; wildlife poaching

Environment - international agreements: *party to:* Antarctic-Marine Living Resources, Biodiversity, Climate Change, Climate Change-Kyoto Protocol, Climate Change-Paris Agreement, Comprehensive Nuclear Test Ban, Desertification, Endangered Species, Hazardous Wastes, Law of the Sea, Ozone Layer Protection, Ship Pollution, Wetlands
signed, but not ratified: none of the selected agreements

Climate: desert; hot, dry; rainfall sparse and erratic

Urbanization: *urban population:* 54.9% of total population (2023)
rate of urbanization: 3.64% annual rate of change (2020-25 est.)

Food insecurity: *severe localized food insecurity: due to localized shortfalls in cereal production and rising food prices* - cereal production increased in 2022 and this is expected to have a positive impact on food security, however, rising prices of basic foods is likely to limit a more substantial improvement (2022)

Revenue from forest resources: 0.47% of GDP (2018 est.)
comparison ranking: 68

Revenue from coal: 0% of GDP (2018 est.)
comparison ranking: 124

Air pollutants: *particulate matter emissions:* 11.81 micrograms per cubic meter (2019 est.)
carbon dioxide emissions: 4.23 megatons (2016 est.)
methane emissions: 10.4 megatons (2020 est.)

Waste and recycling: *municipal solid waste generated annually:* 256,729 tons (1993 est.)
municipal solid waste recycled annually: 11,553 tons (2005 est.)
percent of municipal solid waste recycled: 4.5% (2005 est.)

Major rivers (by length in km): Zambezi (shared with Zambia [s]), Angola, Botswana, Zimbabwe, and Mozambique [m]) - 2,740 km; Orange river mouth (shared with Lesotho [s], and South Africa) - 2,092 km; Okavango (shared with Angola [s], and Botswana [m]) - 1,600 km
note – [s] after country name indicates river source; [m] after country name indicates river mouth

Major watersheds (area sq km): Atlantic Ocean drainage: Orange (941,351 sq km)

Indian Ocean drainage: Zambezi (1,332,412 sq km)

Internal (endorheic basin) drainage: Okavango Basin (863,866 sq km)

Major aquifers: Lower Kalahari-Stampriet Basin, Upper Kalahari-Cuvelai-Upper Zambezi Basin

Total water withdrawal: *municipal:* 70 million cubic meters (2020 est.)
industrial: 10 million cubic meters (2020 est.)
agricultural: 201 million cubic meters (2020 est.)

Total renewable water resources: 39.91 billion cubic meters (2020 est.)

GOVERNMENT

Country name: *conventional long form:* Republic of Namibia
conventional short form: Namibia
local long form: Republic of Namibia
local short form: Namibia
former: German South-West Africa (Deutsch-Suedwestafrika), South-West Africa
etymology: named for the coastal Namib Desert; the name "namib" means "vast place" in the Nama/Damara language

Government type: presidential republic

Capital: *name:* Windhoek
geographic coordinates: 22 34 S, 17 05 E
time difference: UTC+1 (6 hours ahead of Washington, DC, during Standard Time)
daylight saving time: +1hr, begins first Sunday in September; ends first Sunday in April
etymology: may derive from the Afrikaans word "wind-hoek" meaning "windy corner"

Administrative divisions: 14 regions; Erongo, Hardap, //Karas, Kavango East, Kavango West, Khomas, Kunene, Ohangwena, Omaheke, Omusati, Oshana, Oshikoto, Otjozondjupa, Zambezi; note - the Karas Region was renamed //Karas in September 2013 to include the alveolar lateral click of the Khoekhoegowab language

Independence: 21 March 1990 (from South African mandate)

National holiday: Independence Day, 21 March (1990)

Legal system: mixed legal system of uncodified civil law based on Roman-Dutch law and customary law

Constitution: *history:* adopted 9 February 1990, entered into force 21 March 1990
amendments: passage requires majority vote of the National Assembly membership and of the National Council of Parliament and assent of the president of the republic; if the National Council fails to pass an amendment, the president can call for a referendum; passage by referendum requires two-thirds majority of votes cast; amendments that detract from or repeal constitutional articles on fundamental rights and freedoms cannot be amended, and the requisite majorities needed by Parliament to amend the constitution cannot be changed; amended 1998, 2010, 2014

International law organization participation: has not submitted an ICJ jurisdiction declaration; accepts ICCt jurisdiction

Citizenship: *citizenship by birth:* no

citizenship by descent only: at least one parent must be a citizen of Namibia
dual citizenship recognized: no
residency requirement for naturalization: 5 years

Suffrage: 18 years of age; universal

Executive branch: *chief of state:* Acting President Nangolo MBUMBA (since 4 February 2024)
head of government: Acting President Nangolo MBUMBA (since 4 February 2024)
cabinet: Cabinet appointed by the president from among members of the National Assembly
elections/appointments: president directly elected by absolute majority popular vote in 2 rounds if needed for a 5-year term (eligible for a second term); election last held on 28 November 2019 (next to be held in November 2024) note - the president is both chief of state and head of government; note-President Hage GEINGOB died on 4 February 2024, and Vice President MBUMBA was sworn in to run the government until the next presidential election in November 2024
election results:
2019: Hage GEINGOB reelected president in the first round; percent of vote - Hage GEINGOB (SWAPO) 56.3%, Panduleni ITULA (independent) 29.4%, McHenry VENAANI (PDM) 5.3%, other .9%
2014: Hage GEINGOB elected president in the first round; percent of vote - Hage GEINGOB (SWAPO) 86.7%, McHenry VENAANI (DTA) 5%, Hidipo HAMUTENYA (RDP) 3.4%, Asser MBAI (NUDO)1.9%, Henk MUDGE (RP) 1%, other 2%

Legislative branch: *description:* bicameral Parliament consists of:
National Council (42 seats); members indirectly elected 3 each by the 14 regional councils to serve 5-year terms); note - the Council primarily reviews legislation passed and referred by the National Assembly
National Assembly (104 seats; 96 members directly elected in multi-seat constituencies by closed list, proportional representation vote to serve 5-year terms and 8 nonvoting members appointed by the president)
elections: National Council - elections for regional councils to determine members of the National Council held on 25 November 2020 (next to be held on 25 November 2025)
National Assembly - last held on 27 November 2019 (next to be held in November 2024)
election results: Nstional Council - percent of vote by party - NA; seats by party - SWAPO 28, LPM 6, IPC 2, PDM 2, UDF 2, NUDO 1, independent 1; composition - men 36, women 6, percentage women 14.3%
National Assembly - percent of vote by party - SWAPO 65.5%, PDM 16.6%, LPM 4.7%, NUDO 1.9%, APP 1.8%, UDF 1.8%, RP 1.8%, NEFF 1.7%, RDP 1.1%, CDV .7%, SWANU .6%, other 1.8%; seats by party - SWAPO 63, PDM 16, LPM 4, NUDO 2, APP 2, UDF 2, RP 2, NEFF 2, RDP 1, CDV 1, SWANU 1; composition - men 58, women 46, percentage women 44.2%; total Parliament percentage women 35.6%

Judicial branch: *highest court(s):* Supreme Court (consists of the chief justice and at least 3 judges in quorum sessions)
judge selection and term of office: judges appointed by the president of Namibia upon the recommendation of the Judicial Service Commission; judges serve until age 65, but terms can be extended by the president until age 70
subordinate courts: High Court; Electoral Court, Labor Court; regional and district magistrates' courts; community courts

Political parties: All People's Party or APP
Christian Democratic Voice or CDV
Landless People's Movement or LPM
National Unity Democratic Organization or NUDO
Namibian Economic Freedom Fighters or NEFF
Popular Democratic Movement or PDM (formerly Democratic Turnhalle Alliance or DTA)
Rally for Democracy and Progress or RDP
Republican Party or RP
South West Africa National Union or SWANU
South West Africa People's Organization or SWAPO
United Democratic Front or UDF
United People's Movement or UPM

International organization participation: ACP, AfDB, AU, C, CD, CPLP (associate observer), FAO, G-77, IAEA, IBRD, ICAO, ICCt, ICRM, IDA, IFAD, IFC, IFRCS, ILO, IMF, IMO, Interpol, IOC, IOM, IPU, ISO, ITSO, ITU, ITUC (NGOs), MIGA, NAM, OPCW, SACU, SADC, UN, UNAMID, UNCTAD, UNESCO, UNHCR, UNHRC, UNIDO, UNISFA, UNMIL, UNMISS, UNOCI, UNWTO, UPU, WCO, WHO, WIPO, WMO, WTO

Diplomatic representation in the US: *chief of mission:* Ambassador Margareth Natalie MENSAH-WILLIAMS (since 18 January 2021)
chancery: 1605 New Hampshire Avenue NW, Washington, DC 20009
telephone: [1] (202) 986-0540
FAX: [1] (202) 986-0443
email address and website:
info@namibiaembassyusa.org
https://namibiaembassyusa.org/

Diplomatic representation from the US: *chief of mission:* Ambassador Randy William BERRY (since 9 February 2023)
embassy: 38 Metje Street, Klein Windhoek, Windhoek
mailing address: 2540 Windhoek Place, Washington DC 20521-2540
telephone: [264] (61) 202-5000
FAX: [264] (61) 202-5219
email address and website:
ConsularWindhoek@state.gov
https://na.usembassy.gov/

Flag description: a wide red stripe edged by narrow white stripes divides the flag diagonally from lower hoist corner to upper fly corner; the upper hoist-side triangle is blue and charged with a golden-yellow, 12-rayed sunburst; the lower fly-side triangle is green; red signifies the heroism of the people and their determination to build a future of equal opportunity for all; white stands for peace, unity, tranquility, and harmony; blue represents the Namibian sky and the Atlantic Ocean, the country's precious water resources and rain; the golden-yellow sun denotes power and existence; green symbolizes vegetation and agricultural resources

National symbol(s): oryx (antelope); national colors: blue, red, green, white, yellow

National anthem: *name:* "Namibia, Land of the Brave"
lyrics/music: Axali DOESEB
note: adopted 1991

National heritage: *total World Heritage Sites:* 2 (1 cultural, 1 natural)
selected World Heritage Site locales: Twyfelfontein or /Ui-//aes (c); Namib Sand Sea (n)

ECONOMY

Economic overview: upper middle-income, export-driven Sub-Saharan economy; natural resource rich; Walvis Bay port expansion for trade; high potential for renewable power generation and energy independence; major nature-based tourist locale; natural resource rich; shortage of skilled labor

Real GDP (purchasing power parity): $29.944 billion (2023 est.)
$28.748 billion (2022 est.)
$27.288 billion (2021 est.)
note: data in 2021 dollars
comparison ranking: 148

Real GDP growth rate: 4.16% (2023 est.)
5.35% (2022 est.)
3.6% (2021 est.)
note: annual GDP % growth based on constant local currency
comparison ranking: 73

Real GDP per capita: $11,500 (2023 est.)
$11,200 (2022 est.)
$10,800 (2021 est.)
note: data in 2021 dollars
comparison ranking: 140

GDP (official exchange rate): $12.351 billion (2023 est.)
note: data in current dollars at official exchange rate

Inflation rate (consumer prices): 5.88% (2023 est.)
6.08% (2022 est.)
3.62% (2021 est.)
note: annual % change based on consumer prices
comparison ranking: 125

Credit ratings: Fitch rating: BB (2019)

Moody's rating: Ba3 (2020)
note: The year refers to the year in which the current credit rating was first obtained.

GDP - composition, by sector of origin: *agriculture:* 7.7% (2023 est.)
industry: 30% (2023 est.)
services: 53.4% (2023 est.)
note: figures may not total 100% due to non-allocated consumption not captured in sector-reported data
comparison rankings: services 127; industry 67; agriculture 93

GDP - composition, by end use: *household consumption:* 73.3% (2023 est.)
government consumption: 21.8% (2023 est.)
investment in fixed capital: 26.2% (2023 est.)
investment in inventories: 1.5% (2023 est.)
exports of goods and services: 43.4% (2023 est.)
imports of goods and services: -66.2% (2023 est.)
note: figures may not total 100% due to rounding or gaps in data collection

Agricultural products: root vegetables, milk, maize, millet, grapes, beef, onions, wheat, fruits, pulses (2022)
note: top ten agricultural products based on tonnage

Industries: mining, tourism, fishing, agriculture

Industrial production growth rate: 9.19% (2023 est.)
note: annual % change in industrial value added based on constant local currency
comparison ranking: 20

Labor force: 989,000 (2023 est.)
note: number of people ages 15 or older who are employed or seeking work
comparison ranking: 147

Unemployment rate: 19.42% (2023 est.)
19.75% (2022 est.)
20.88% (2021 est.)
note: % of labor force seeking employment
comparison ranking: 199

Youth unemployment rate (ages 15-24): *total:* 38% (2023 est.)
male: 37.4% (2023 est.)
female: 38.8% (2023 est.)
note: % of labor force ages 15-24 seeking employment
comparison ranking: total 11

Population below poverty line: 17.4% (2015 est.)
note: % of population with income below national poverty line

Gini Index coefficient - distribution of family income: 59.1 (2015 est.)
note: index (0-100) of income distribution; higher values represent greater inequality
comparison ranking: 2

Household income or consumption by percentage share: *lowest 10%:* 1% (2015 est.)
highest 10%: 47.3% (2015 est.)
note: % share of income accruing to lowest and highest 10% of population

Remittances: 0.5% of GDP (2023 est.)
0.43% of GDP (2022 est.)
0.37% of GDP (2021 est.)
note: personal transfers and compensation between resident and non-resident individuals/households/entities

Budget: *revenues:* $3.998 billion (2022 est.)
expenditures: $4.535 billion (2022 est.)
note: central government revenues (excluding grants) and expenses converted to US dollars at average official exchange rate for year indicated

Public debt: 4.64% of GDP (2019 est.)
note: central government debt as a % of GDP
comparison ranking: 201

Taxes and other revenues: 27.17% (of GDP) (2022 est.)
note: central government tax revenue as a % of GDP
comparison ranking: 33

Current account balance: -$1.848 billion (2023 est.)
-$1.628 billion (2022 est.)
-$1.391 billion (2021 est.)
note: balance of payments - net trade and primary/secondary income in current dollars
comparison ranking: 155

Exports: $5.641 billion (2023 est.)
$5.314 billion (2022 est.)
$4.341 billion (2021 est.)
note: balance of payments - exports of goods and services in current dollars
comparison ranking: 138

Exports - partners: South Africa 28%, Botswana 11%, China 10%, Zambia 5%, France 4% (2022)
note: top five export partners based on percentage share of exports

Exports - commodities: diamonds, gold, fish, radioactive chemicals, ships (2022)
note: top five export commodities based on value in dollars

Imports: $8.281 billion (2023 est.)
$7.423 billion (2022 est.)
$6.467 billion (2021 est.)
note: balance of payments - imports of goods and services in current dollars
comparison ranking: 129

Imports - partners: South Africa 41%, China 7%, Nigeria 5%, India 4%, UAE 4% (2022)
note: top five import partners based on percentage share of imports

Imports - commodities: refined petroleum, ships, copper ore, trucks, electricity (2022)
note: top five import commodities based on value in dollars

Reserves of foreign exchange and gold: $2.956 billion (2023 est.)
$2.803 billion (2022 est.)
$2.764 billion (2021 est.)
note: holdings of gold (year-end prices)/foreign exchange/special drawing rights in current dollars
comparison ranking: 122

Exchange rates: Namibian dollars (NAD) per US dollar -

Exchange rates: 18.446 (2023 est.)
16.356 (2022 est.)
14.779 (2021 est.)
16.463 (2020 est.)
14.449 (2019 est.)

ENERGY

Electricity access: *electrification - total population:* 56.2% (2022 est.)
electrification - urban areas: 74.8%
electrification - rural areas: 33.2%

Electricity: *installed generating capacity:* 646,000 kW (2022 est.)
consumption: 3.433 billion kWh (2022 est.)
exports: 382 million kWh (2022 est.)
imports: 2.835 billion kWh (2022 est.)
transmission/distribution losses: 370.694 million kWh (2022 est.)
comparison rankings: transmission/distribution losses 73; imports 55; exports 82; consumption 137; installed generating capacity 145

Electricity generation sources: *fossil fuels:* 3.8% of total installed capacity (2022 est.)
solar: 36.8% of total installed capacity (2022 est.)
wind: 1.6% of total installed capacity (2022 est.)
hydroelectricity: 57.8% of total installed capacity (2022 est.)

Coal: *consumption:* 32,000 metric tons (2022 est.)
exports: (2022 est.) less than 1 metric ton
imports: 33,000 metric tons (2022 est.)
proven reserves: 350 million metric tons (2022 est.)

Petroleum: *refined petroleum consumption:* 25,000 bbl/day (2022 est.)

Natural gas: *proven reserves:* 62.297 billion cubic meters (2021 est.)

Carbon dioxide emissions: 3.61 million metric tonnes of CO_2 (2022 est.)
from coal and metallurgical coke: 72,000 metric tonnes of CO_2 (2022 est.)
from petroleum and other liquids: 3.538 million metric tonnes of CO_2 (2022 est.)
comparison ranking: total emissions 146

Energy consumption per capita: 24.695 million Btu/person (2022 est.)
comparison ranking: 125

COMMUNICATIONS

Telephones - fixed lines: *total subscriptions:* 86,000 (2022 est.)
subscriptions per 100 inhabitants: 3 (2022 est.)
comparison ranking: total subscriptions 141

Telephones - mobile cellular: *total subscriptions:* 2.906 million (2022 est.)
subscriptions per 100 inhabitants: 113 (2022 est.)
comparison ranking: total subscriptions 142

Telecommunication systems: *general assessment:* the government's Broadband Policy aims to provide 95% population coverage by 2024; mobile network coverage has increased sharply in recent years; by 2023, 3G infrastructure provided 89% population coverage while LTE infrastructure provided 79% coverage; despite the relatively advanced nature of the market, progress towards 5G has been slow, partly due to unsubstantiated public concerns over health implications of the technology which caused the government to order an environmental assessment of 5G in mid-2020; the government has requested the regulator to speed up its 5G development strategy; Namibia's internet and broadband sector is reasonably competitive, its development was for many years held back by high prices for international bandwidth caused by the lack of a direct connection to international submarine cables; this market situation improved after operators invested in diversifying terrestrial access routes to adjacent countries; in June 2022 Namibia was connected to a 1,050km branch line of cable running between Portugal and South Africa (2022)
domestic: fixed-line subscribership is 4 per 100 and mobile-cellular roughly 113 per 100 persons (2022) (2021)
international: country code - 264; landing points for the ACE and WACS fiber-optic submarine cable linking southern and western African countries to Europe; satellite earth stations - 4 Intelsat (2019)

Broadcast media: 1 private and 1 state-run TV station; satellite and cable TV service available; state-run radio service broadcasts in multiple languages; about a dozen private radio stations; transmissions of multiple international broadcasters available

Internet country code: .na

Internet users: *total:* 1.325 million (2021 est.)
percent of population: 53% (2021 est.)
comparison ranking: total 145

Broadband - fixed subscriptions: *total:* 71,063 (2020 est.)
subscriptions per 100 inhabitants: 3 (2020 est.)
comparison ranking: total 135

TRANSPORTATION

National air transport system: *number of registered air carriers:* 2 (2020)
inventory of registered aircraft operated by air carriers: 21
annual passenger traffic on registered air carriers: 602,893 (2018)
annual freight traffic on registered air carriers: 26.29 million (2018) mt-km

Civil aircraft registration country code prefix: V5

Airports: 255 (2024)
comparison ranking: 26

Railways: *total:* 2,628 km (2014)
narrow gauge: 2,628 km (2014) 1.067-m gauge
comparison ranking: total 62

Roadways: *total:* 48,875 km
paved: 7,893 km
unpaved: 40,982 km (2018)
comparison ranking: total 85

Merchant marine: *total:* 15 (2023)
by type: general cargo 1, other 14
comparison ranking: total 152

Ports: *total ports:* 2 (2024)
large: 0
medium: 0
small: 2
very small: 0
ports with oil terminals: 2
key ports: Luderitz Bay, Walvis Bay

MILITARY AND SECURITY

Military and security forces: Namibian Defense Force (NDF): Army, Navy, Air Force (2024)
note: the Namibian Police Force is under the Ministry of Home Affairs, Immigration, Safety, and Security; it has a paramilitary Special Field Force responsible for protecting borders and government installations

Military expenditures: 2.8% of GDP (2023 est.)
3% of GDP (2022 est.)
3% of GDP (2021 est.)
3.4% of GDP (2020 est.)
3.3% of GDP (2019 est.)
comparison ranking: 40

Military and security service personnel strengths: information varies; approximately 12,000 personnel (10,000 Army; 1,000 Navy; 1,000 Air Force) (2024)

Military equipment inventories and acquisitions: the NDF's inventory consists of a mix of Soviet-era and some more modern systems from a variety of countries, including Brazil, China, Germany, India, and South Africa; most of the Navy's vessels and the Air Force's fighter aircraft were acquired from China; Namibia has a small defense industry that produces items such as armored personnel carriers (2024)

Military service age and obligation: 18-25 years of age for men and women for voluntary military service; no conscription (2024)
note: as of 2022, women comprised about 23% of the active-duty military

Military - note: the NDF's primary responsibility is defending Namibia's territorial integrity and national interests; it has participated in UN and regional peacekeeping and security missions and provides assistance to civil authorities as needed; it also participates in multinational training exercises
the NDF was created in 1990, largely from demobilized former members of the People's Liberation Army of Namibia (PLAN) and the South West Africa Territorial Force (SWATF); the PLAN was the armed wing of the South West Africa People's Organization (SWAPO), while SWATF was an auxiliary of the South African Defense Force and comprised the armed forces of the former South West Africa, 1977-1989; from 1990-1995, the British military assisted with the forming and training the NDF (2024)

TRANSNATIONAL ISSUES

Refugees and internally displaced persons: *refugees (country of origin):* 6,288 (Democratic Republic of the Congo) (refugees and asylum seekers) (2024)

NAURU

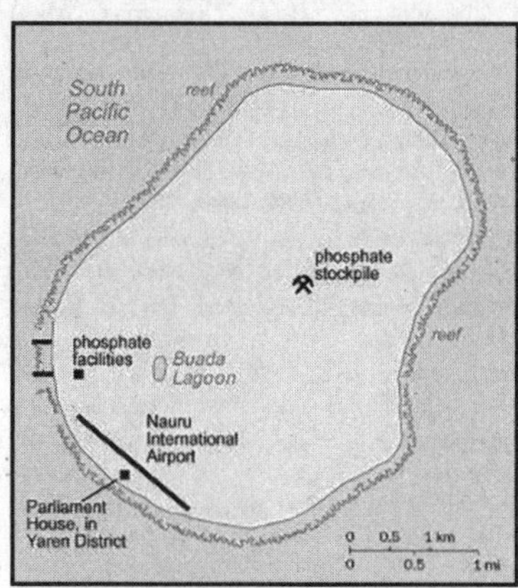

INTRODUCTION

Background: By 1000 B.C., Micronesian and Polynesian settlers inhabited Nauru, and the island was divided among 12 clans. Nauru developed in relative isolation because ocean currents made landfall on the island difficult. As a result, the Nauruan language does not clearly resemble any other in the Pacific region. In 1798, a British mariner was the first European to spot the island and by 1830, European whalers used Nauru as a supply stop, trading firearms for food. A civil war in 1878 reduced the population by more than a third. Germany forcibly annexed Nauru in 1888 by holding the 12 chiefs under house arrest until they consented to the annexation. Phosphate was discovered in 1900 and was heavily mined, although Nauru and Nauruans earned about one tenth of one percent of the profits from the phosphate deposits.

Australian forces captured Nauru from Germany during World War I, and in 1919, it was placed under a joint Australian- British-New Zealand mandate with Australian administration. Japan occupied Nauru during World War II and used its residents as forced labor elsewhere in the Pacific while destroying much of the infrastructure on the island. After the war, Nauru became a UN trust territory under Australian administration. In 1962, recognizing the phosphate stocks would eventually be depleted, Australian Prime Minister Robert MENZIES offered to resettle all Nauruans on Curtis Island in Queensland, but Nauruans rejected that plan and opted for independence, which was achieved in 1968. In 1970, Nauru purchased the phosphate mining assets, and income from the mines made Nauruans among the richest people in the world. However, a series of unwise investments led to near bankruptcy by 2000. Widespread phosphate mining officially ceased in 2006. Widespread phosphate mining officially ceased in 2006.

As its economy faltered, Nauru briefly tried to rebrand itself as an offshore banking haven, an initiative that ended in 2005, and the country made a successful bid for Russian humanitarian aid in 2008. In 2001, Australia set up the Nauru Regional Processing Center (NRPC), an offshore refugee detention facility, paying Nauru per person at the center. The NRPC closed in 2008 but reopened in 2012. The number of refugees steadily declined after 2014, and in 2020, the remaining people were moved to Brisbane, Australia, effectively shuttering the NRPC. However, in 2023, Australia agreed to continue funding NRPC for two years and restarted settling asylees in the center in mid-2023. The center remains the Government of Nauru's largest source of income.

GEOGRAPHY

Location: Oceania, island in the South Pacific Ocean, south of the Marshall Islands

Geographic coordinates: 0 32 S, 166 55 E

Map references: Oceania

Area: *total:* 21 sq km
land: 21 sq km
water: 0 sq km
comparison ranking: total 238

Area - comparative: about 0.1 times the size of Washington, DC

Land boundaries: *total:* 0 km

Coastline: 30 km

Maritime claims: *territorial sea:* 12 nm
contiguous zone: 24 nm
exclusive economic zone: 200 nm

Climate: tropical with a monsoonal pattern; rainy season (November to February)

Terrain: sandy beach rises to fertile ring around raised coral reefs with phosphate plateau in center

Elevation: *highest point:* Command Ridge 70 m
lowest point: Pacific Ocean 0 m

Natural resources: phosphates, fish

Land use: *agricultural land:* 20% (2018 est.)
arable land: 0% (2018 est.)
permanent crops: 20% (2018 est.)
permanent pasture: 0% (2018 est.)
forest: 0% (2018 est.)
other: 80% (2018 est.)

Irrigated land: 0 sq km (2022)

Population distribution: extensive phosphate mining made approximately 90% of the island unsuitable for farming; most people live in the fertile coastal areas, especially along the southwest coast

Natural hazards: periodic droughts

Geography - note: Nauru is the third-smallest country in the world behind the Holy See (Vatican City) and Monaco; it is the smallest country in the Pacific Ocean, the smallest country outside Europe, the world's smallest island country, and the world's smallest independent republic; situated just 53 km south of the Equator, Nauru is one of the three great phosphate rock islands in the Pacific Ocean – the others are Banaba (Ocean Island) in Kiribati and Makatea in French Polynesia

PEOPLE AND SOCIETY

Population: *total:* 9,892
male: 4,856
female: 5,036 (2024 est.)
comparison rankings: female 222; male 222; total 222

Nationality: *noun:* Nauruan(s)
adjective: Nauruan

Ethnic groups: Nauruan 94.6%, I-Kiribati 2.2%, Fijian 1.3%, other 1.9% (2021 est.)

Languages: Nauruan 93% (official, a distinct Pacific Island language), English 2% (widely understood, spoken, and used for most government and commercial purposes), other 5% (includes Gilbertese 2% and Chinese 2%) (2011 est.)
note: data represent main language spoken at home; Nauruan is spoken by 95% of the population, English by 66%, and other languages by 12%

Religions: Protestant 60.4% (Nauruan Congregational 34.7%, Assemblies of God 11.6%, Pacific Light House 6.3%, Nauru Independent 3.6%, Baptist 1.5, Seventh Day Adventist 1.3%, other Protestant 1.4%), Roman Catholic 33.9%, other 4.2%, none 1.3%, no answer 0.3% (2021 est.)

Age structure: *0-14 years:* 29.6% (male 1,493/female 1,433)
15-64 years: 66% (male 3,220/female 3,309)
65 years and over: 4.4% (2024 est.) (male 143/ female 294)

Dependency ratios: *total dependency ratio:* 69.9
youth dependency ratio: 66
elderly dependency ratio: 3.9
potential support ratio: 25.8 (2021)

Median age: *total:* 27.8 years (2024 est.)
male: 27.3 years
female: 28.4 years
comparison ranking: total 156

Population growth rate: 0.39% (2024 est.)
comparison ranking: 161

Birth rate: births/1,000 population (2024 est.)
comparison ranking: 66

Death rate: 6.5 deaths/1,000 population (2024 est.)
comparison ranking: 138

Net migration rate: -9.8 migrant(s)/1,000 population (2024 est.)
comparison ranking: 222

Population distribution: extensive phosphate mining made approximately 90% of the island unsuitable for farming; most people live in the fertile coastal areas, especially along the southwest coast

Urbanization: *urban population:* 100% of total population (2023)
rate of urbanization: 0.18% annual rate of change (2020-25 est.)

Sex ratio: *at birth:* 1.04 male(s)/female
0-14 years: 1.04 male(s)/female
15-64 years: 0.97 male(s)/female
65 years and over: 0.49 male(s)/female
total population: 0.96 male(s)/female (2024 est.)

Infant mortality rate: *total:* 7.6 deaths/1,000 live births (2024 est.)
male: 9.8 deaths/1,000 live births
female: 5.3 deaths/1,000 live births
comparison ranking: total 151

Life expectancy at birth: *total population:* 68.6 years (2024 est.)
male: 65 years
female: 72.3 years
comparison ranking: total population 187

Total fertility rate: 2.55 children born/woman (2024 est.)
comparison ranking: 68

Gross reproduction rate: 1.25 (2024 est.)

Drinking water source: *improved: urban:* 100% of population
rural: NA
total: 100% of population

Current health expenditure: 12% of GDP (2020)

Physician density: 1.35 physicians/1,000 population (2015)

Sanitation facility access: *improved: urban:* 96.3% of population
rural: NA
total: 96.3% of population

Obesity - adult prevalence rate: 61% (2016)
comparison ranking: 1

Alcohol consumption per capita: *total:* 2.44 liters of pure alcohol (2019 est.)
beer: 0.54 liters of pure alcohol (2019 est.)
wine: 0.09 liters of pure alcohol (2019 est.)
spirits: 1.81 liters of pure alcohol (2019 est.)
other alcohols: 0 liters of pure alcohol (2019 est.)
comparison ranking: total 125

Tobacco use: *total:* 48.5% (2020 est.)
male: 47.8% (2020 est.)
female: 49.1% (2020 est.)
comparison ranking: total 1

Currently married women (ages 15-49): 59.6% (2023 est.)

Education expenditures: 7.1% of GDP (2021) NA
comparison ranking: 20

ENVIRONMENT

Environment - current issues: limited natural freshwater resources, roof storage tanks that collect rainwater and desalination plants provide water; a century of intensive phosphate mining beginning in 1906 left the central 90% of Nauru a wasteland; cadmium residue, phosphate dust, and other contaminants have caused air and water pollution with negative impacts on health; climate change has brought on rising sea levels and inland water shortages

Environment - international agreements: *party to:* Biodiversity, Climate Change, Climate Change-Kyoto Protocol, Climate Change-Paris Agreement, Comprehensive Nuclear Test Ban, Desertification, Hazardous Wastes, Law of the Sea, Marine Dumping-London Convention, Ozone Layer Protection, Whaling
signed, but not ratified: none of the selected agreements

Climate: tropical with a monsoonal pattern; rainy season (November to February)

Land use: *agricultural land:* 20% (2018 est.)
arable land: 0% (2018 est.)
permanent crops: 20% (2018 est.)
permanent pasture: 0% (2018 est.)
forest: 0% (2018 est.)
other: 80% (2018 est.)

Urbanization: *urban population:* 100% of total population (2023)
rate of urbanization: 0.18% annual rate of change (2020-25 est.)

Revenue from forest resources: 0% of GDP (2018 est.)
comparison ranking: 172

Air pollutants: *particulate matter emissions:* 7.4 micrograms per cubic meter (2019 est.)
carbon dioxide emissions: 0.05 megatons (2016 est.)
methane emissions: 0.01 megatons (2020 est.)

Waste and recycling: *municipal solid waste generated annually:* 6,192 tons (2016 est.)

Total renewable water resources: 10 million cubic meters (2020 est.)

GOVERNMENT

Country name: *conventional long form:* Republic of Nauru
conventional short form: Nauru
local long form: Republic of Nauru
local short form: Nauru
former: Pleasant Island
etymology: the island name may derive from the Nauruan word "anaoero" meaning "I go to the beach"

Government type: parliamentary republic

Capital: *name:* no official capital; government offices in the Yaren District
time difference: UTC+12 (17 hours ahead of Washington, DC, during Standard Time)

Administrative divisions: 14 districts; Aiwo, Anabar, Anetan, Anibare, Baitsi, Boe, Buada, Denigomodu, Ewa, Ijuw, Meneng, Nibok, Uaboe, Yaren

Independence: 31 January 1968 (from the Australia-, NZ-, and UK-administered UN trusteeship)

National holiday: Independence Day, 31 January (1968)

Legal system: mixed legal system of common law based on the English model and customary law

Constitution: *history:* effective 29 January 1968
amendments: proposed by Parliament; passage requires two-thirds majority vote of Parliament; amendments to constitutional articles, such as the republican form of government, protection of fundamental rights and freedoms, the structure and authorities of the executive and legislative branches, also require two-thirds majority of votes in a referendum; amended several times, last in 2018

International law organization participation: has not submitted an ICJ jurisdiction declaration; accepts ICCt jurisdiction

Suffrage: 20 years of age; universal and compulsory

Executive branch: *chief of state:* President David ADEANG (since 30 October 2023)
head of government: President David ADEANG (since 30 October 2023)
cabinet: Cabinet appointed by the president from among members of Parliament
elections/appointments: president indirectly elected by Parliament for 3-year term (eligible for a second term); election last held on 30 October 2023 (next to be held in 2026)
election results:
2023: David ADEAGN elected president over Delvin THOMA, 10-8
2022: Russ KUN elected president unopposed

note: the president is both chief of state and head of government

Legislative branch: *description:* unicameral Parliament (19 seats; members directly elected in multi-seat constituencies by majority vote using the "Dowdall" counting system by which voters rank candidates on their ballots; members serve 3-year terms)
elections: last held on 24 September 2022 (next to be held in September 2025)
election results: percent of vote - NA; seats - independent 19; composition - men 17, women 2, percentage women 10.5%

Judicial branch: *highest court(s):* Supreme Court (consists of the chief justice and several justices); note - in late 2017, the Nauruan Government revoked the 1976 High Court Appeals Act, which had allowed appeals beyond the Nauruan Supreme Court, and in early 2018, the government formed its own appeals court
judge selection and term of office: judges appointed by the president to serve until age 65
subordinate courts: District Court, Family Court

Political parties: Nauru does not have formal political parties; alliances within the government are often formed based on extended family ties

International organization participation: ACP, ADB, AOSIS, C, FAO, G-77, ICAO, ICCt, IFAD, Interpol, IOC, IOM, ITU, OPCW, PIF, Sparteca, SPC, UN, UNCTAD, UNESCO, UPU, WHO

Diplomatic representation in the US: *chief of mission:* Ambassador Margo DEIYE (since 1 December 2021); note - also Permanent Representative to the UN
chancery: 801 2nd Avenue, Third Floor, New York, NY 10017
telephone: [1] (212) 937-0074
FAX: [1] (212) 937-0079
email address and website:
nauru@onecommonwealth.org
https://www.un.int/nauru/

Diplomatic representation from the US: *embassy:* the US does not have an embassy in Nauru; the US Ambassador to Fiji is accredited to Nauru

Flag description: blue with a narrow, horizontal, gold stripe across the center and a large white 12-pointed star below the stripe on the hoist side; blue stands for the Pacific Ocean, the star indicates the country's location in relation to the Equator (the gold stripe) and the 12 points symbolize the 12 original tribes of Nauru; the star's white color represents phosphate, the basis of the island's wealth

National symbol(s): frigatebird, calophyllum flower; national colors: blue, yellow, white

National anthem: *name:* "Nauru Bwiema" (Song of Nauru)
lyrics/music: Margaret HENDRIE/Laurence Henry HICKS
note: adopted 1968

ECONOMY

Economic overview: upper-middle-income Pacific island country; phosphate resource exhaustion made island interior uninhabitable; licenses fishing rights; houses Australia's Regional Processing Centre; former tax haven; largely dependent on foreign subsidies

Real GDP (purchasing power parity): $145.958 million (2023 est.)
$144.937 million (2022 est.)
$141.875 million (2021 est.)
note: data in 2021 dollars
comparison ranking: 221

Real GDP growth rate: 0.7% (2023 est.)
2.16% (2022 est.)
7.75% (2021 est.)
note: annual GDP % growth based on constant local currency
comparison ranking: 175

Real GDP per capita: $11,400 (2023 est.)
$11,400 (2022 est.)
$11,300 (2021 est.)
note: data in 2021 dollars
comparison ranking: 141

GDP (official exchange rate): $154.128 million (2023 est.)
note: data in current dollars at official exchange rate

Inflation rate (consumer prices): 5.1% (2017 est.)
8.2% (2016 est.)
comparison ranking: 112

GDP - composition, by end use: *exports of goods and services:* 54.7% (2022 est.)
imports of goods and services: -113.2% (2022 est.)
note: figures may not total 100% due to rounding or gaps in data collection

Agricultural products: coconuts, tropical fruits, pork, eggs, pork offal, pork fat, chicken, papayas, vegetables, cabbages (2022)
note: top ten agricultural products based on tonnage

Industries: phosphate mining, offshore banking, coconut products

Industrial production growth rate: 4.3% (2014 est.)
note: annual % change in industrial value added based on constant local currency
comparison ranking: 74

Remittances: 4.99% of GDP (2018 est.)
9.46% of GDP (2017 est.)
12.04% of GDP (2016 est.)
note: personal transfers and compensation between resident and non-resident individuals/households/entities

Budget: *revenues:* $199.728 million (2020 est.)
expenditures: $132.607 million (2020 est.)
note: central government revenues (excluding grants) and expenses converted to US dollars at average official exchange rate for year indicated

Public debt: 62% of GDP (2017 est.)
comparison ranking: 76

Taxes and other revenues: 44.35% (of GDP) (2020 est.)
note: central government tax revenue as a % of GDP
comparison ranking: 6

Current account balance: $8.406 million (2018 est.)
$14.11 million (2017 est.)
$2.079 million (2016 est.)
note: balance of payments - net trade and primary/secondary income in current dollars
comparison ranking: 79

Exports: $187 million (2021 est.)
$105 million (2020 est.)
$32.7 million (2019 est.)
note: balance of payments - exports of goods and services in current dollars
comparison ranking: 203

Exports - partners: Thailand 59%, Philippines 19%, South Korea 11%, India 3%, Japan 2% (2022)
note: top five export partners based on percentage share of exports

Exports - commodities: fish, phosphates, gas turbines, power equipment, plastic products (2022)
note: top five export commodities based on value in dollars

Imports: $94.2 million (2021 est.)
$103 million (2020 est.)
$88.2 million (2019 est.)
note: balance of payments - imports of goods and services in current dollars
comparison ranking: 216

Imports - partners: Australia 47%, China 17%, Japan 12%, Fiji 11%, NZ 2% (2022)
note: top five import partners based on percentage share of imports

Imports - commodities: ships, plastic products, other foods, cars, refined petroleum (2022)
note: top five import commodities based on value in dollars

Exchange rates: Australian dollars (AUD) per US dollar -

Exchange rates: 1.505 (2023 est.)
1.442 (2022 est.)
1.331 (2021 est.)
1.453 (2020 est.)
1.439 (2019 est.)

ENERGY

Electricity access: *electrification - total population:* 100% (2022 est.)

Electricity: *installed generating capacity:* 19,000 kW (2022 est.)
consumption: 37.48 million kWh (2022 est.)
transmission/distribution losses: 3.922 million kWh (2022 est.)
comparison rankings: transmission/distribution losses 8; consumption 206; installed generating capacity 205

Electricity generation sources: *fossil fuels:* 88.9% of total installed capacity (2022 est.)
solar: 11.1% of total installed capacity (2022 est.)

Petroleum: *refined petroleum consumption:* 500 bbl/day (2022 est.)

Carbon dioxide emissions: 70,000 metric tonnes of CO2 (2022 est.)
from petroleum and other liquids: 70,000 metric tonnes of CO2 (2022 est.)
comparison ranking: total emissions 211

Energy consumption per capita: (2019)

COMMUNICATIONS

Telephones - fixed lines: *total subscriptions:* (2018 est.) 0
subscriptions per 100 inhabitants: (2014 est.) less than 1

Telephones - mobile cellular: *total subscriptions:* 10,000 (2021 est.)
subscriptions per 100 inhabitants: 80 (2021 est.)
comparison ranking: total subscriptions 219

Telecommunication systems: *general assessment:* relies on satellite as the primary Internet service provider and mobile operator; internet connectivity on the island is very limited and unstable due to the vulnerability of the network infrastructure to bad

weather and limited network coverage, with several blind spots (2022)
domestic: fixed-line 0 per 100 and mobile-cellular subscribership approximately 80 per 100 (2021)
international: country code - 674; satellite earth station - 1 Intelsat (Pacific Ocean)

Broadcast media: 1 government-owned TV station broadcasting programs from New Zealand sent via satellite or on videotape; 1 government-owned radio station, broadcasting on AM and FM, utilizes Australian and British programs (2019)

Internet country code: .nr

Internet users: *total:* 10,920 (2021 est.)
percent of population: 84% (2021 est.)
comparison ranking: total 218

Broadband - fixed subscriptions: *total:* 950 (2010 est.)
subscriptions per 100 inhabitants: 10 (2010 est.)
comparison ranking: total 209

TRANSPORTATION

National air transport system: *number of registered air carriers:* 1 (2020)
inventory of registered aircraft operated by air carriers: 5
annual passenger traffic on registered air carriers: 45,457 (2018)
annual freight traffic on registered air carriers: 7.94 million (2018) mt-km

Civil aircraft registration country code prefix: C2

Airports: 1 (2024)
comparison ranking: 226

Roadways: *total:* 30 km
paved: 24 km
unpaved: 6 km (2002)
comparison ranking: total 221

Merchant marine: *total:* 6 (2023)
by type: other 6
comparison ranking: total 164

Ports: *total ports:* 1 (2024)
large: 0
medium: 0
small: 0
very small: 1
ports with oil terminals: 1
key ports: Nauru

MILITARY AND SECURITY

Military and security forces: no regular military forces; the police force, under the Minister for Police and Emergency Services, maintains internal security and, as necessary, external security (2024)

Military - note: under an informal agreement, defense is the responsibility of Australia
Nauru has a "shiprider" agreement with the US, which allows local maritime law enforcement officers to embark on US Coast Guard (USCG) and US Navy (USN) vessels, including to board and search vessels suspected of violating laws or regulations within Nauru's designated exclusive economic zone (EEZ) or on the high seas; "shiprider" agreements also enable USCG personnel and USN vessels with embarked USCG law enforcement personnel to work with host nations to protect critical regional resources (2024)

TRANSNATIONAL ISSUES

Refugees and internally displaced persons: *stateless persons:* 140 (2022)

NAVASSA ISLAND

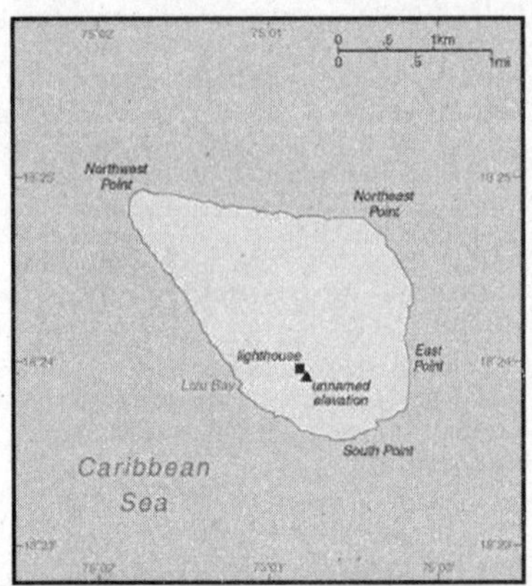

INTRODUCTION

Background: The US claimed uninhabited Navassa Island in 1857 for its guano. Mining took place between 1865 and 1898. The lighthouse, built in 1917, was shut down in 1996, and administration of Navassa Island was transferred from the US Coast Guard to the Department of the Interior, Office of Insular Affairs. A 1998 scientific expedition to the island described it as a "unique preserve of Caribbean biodiversity." The following year it became a National Wildlife Refuge, and annual scientific expeditions have continued.

GEOGRAPHY

Location: Caribbean, island in the Caribbean Sea, 30 nm west of Tiburon Peninsula of Haiti

Geographic coordinates: 18 25 N, 75 02 W

Map references: Central America and the Caribbean

Area: *total:* 5 sq km
land: 5.4 sq km
water: 0 sq km
comparison ranking: total 248

Area - comparative: about nine times the size of the National Mall in Washington, DC

Land boundaries: *total:* 0 km

Coastline: 8 km

Maritime claims: *territorial sea:* 12 nm
exclusive economic zone: 200 nm

Climate: marine, tropical

Terrain: raised flat to undulating coral and limestone plateau; ringed by vertical white cliffs (9 to 15 m high)

Elevation: *highest point:* 200 m NNW of lighthouse 85 m
lowest point: Caribbean Sea 0 m

Natural resources: guano (mining discontinued in 1898)

Land use: *other:* 100% (2018 est.)

Natural hazards: hurricanes

Geography - note: strategic location 160 km south of the US Naval Base at Guantanamo Bay, Cuba; mostly exposed rock with numerous solution holes (limestone sinkholes) but with enough grassland to support goat herds; dense stands of fig trees, scattered cactus

PEOPLE AND SOCIETY

Population: *total:* uninhabited; transient Haitian fishermen and others camp on the island

ENVIRONMENT

Environment - current issues: some coral bleaching

Climate: marine, tropical

GOVERNMENT

Country name: *conventional long form:* none
conventional short form: Navassa Island
etymology: the flat island was named "Navaza" by some of Christopher COLUMBUS' sailors in 1504; the name derives from the Spanish term "nava" meaning "flat land, plain, or field"

Dependency status: unorganized, unincorporated territory of the US; administered by the Fish and Wildlife Service, US Department of the Interior from the Caribbean Islands National Wildlife Refuge in Boqueron, Puerto Rico; in September 1996, the Coast Guard ceased operations and maintenance of the Navassa Island Light, a 46-meter-tall lighthouse on the southern side of the island; Haiti has claimed the island since the 19th century

Legal system: the laws of the US apply where applicable

Diplomatic representation from the US: *embassy:* none (territory of the US)

Flag description: the flag of the US is used

MILITARY AND SECURITY

Military - note: defense is the responsibility of the US

NEPAL

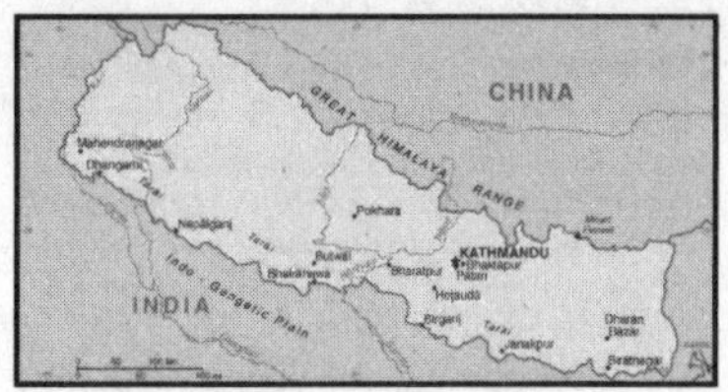

INTRODUCTION

Background: During the late 18th and early 19th centuries, the principality of Gorkha united many of the other principalities and states of the sub-Himalayan region into a Nepali Kingdom. Nepal retained its independence after the Anglo-Nepalese War of 1814-16, and the subsequent peace treaty laid the foundations for two centuries of amicable relations between Britain and Nepal. (The Brigade of Gurkhas continues to serve in the British Army to the present day.) In 1951, the Nepali monarch ended the century-old system of hereditary rule and instituted a cabinet system that brought political parties into the government. That arrangement lasted until 1960, when political parties were again banned, but it was reinstated in 1990 with the establishment of a multiparty democracy within the framework of a constitutional monarchy.

A Maoist-led insurgency broke out in 1996. During the ensuing 10-year civil war between Maoist and government forces, the monarchy dissolved the cabinet and parliament. In 2001, Crown Prince DIPENDRA first massacred the royal family and then shot himself. His brother GYANENDRA became king, and the monarchy reassumed absolute power the next year. A peace accord in 2006 led to the promulgation of an interim constitution in 2007. After a nationwide Constituent Assembly (CA) election in 2008, the newly formed CA declared Nepal a federal democratic republic, abolished the monarchy, and elected the country's first president.

When the CA failed to draft a Supreme Court-mandated constitution, then-Prime Minister Baburam BHATTARAI dissolved the CA. An interim government held elections in 2013, in which the Nepali Congress (NC) won the largest share of seats. In 2014, NC formed a coalition government with the second-place Communist Party of Nepal-Unified Marxist-Leninist (UML). Nepal's new constitution came into effect in 2015, at which point the CA became the Parliament and Khagda Prasad Sharma OLI the first post-constitution prime minister (2015-16). He resigned ahead of a no-confidence motion, and Parliament elected Communist Party of Nepal-Maoist (CPN-M) leader Pushpa Kamal DAHAL as prime minister.

The parties headed by OLI and DAHAL ran in coalition and swept the parliamentary elections in 2017, and OLI was sworn in as prime minister in 2018. OLI's efforts to dissolve parliament and hold elections were declared unconstitutional in 2021, and the opposition-supported NC leader Sher Bahadur DEUBA was named prime minister. The NC won a majority of seats in the parliamentary elections in 2022, but DAHAL then broke with the ruling coalition and partnered with OLI and the CPN-UML to become prime minister. DAHAL's first cabinet lasted about two months, until OLI withdrew his support over disagreements about ministerial assignments. In early 2023, DAHAL survived a vote of confidence and formed a coalition with the NC to remain prime minister.

GEOGRAPHY

Location: Southern Asia, between China and India

Geographic coordinates: 28 00 N, 84 00 E

Map references: Asia

Area: *total:* 147,181 sq km
land: 143,351 sq km
water: 3,830 sq km
comparison ranking: total 95

Area - comparative: slightly larger than New York state

Land boundaries: *total:* 3,159 km
border countries (2): China 1,389 km; India 1,770 km

Coastline: 0 km (landlocked)

Maritime claims: none (landlocked)

Climate: varies from cool summers and severe winters in north to subtropical summers and mild winters in south

Terrain: Tarai or flat river plain of the Ganges in south; central hill region with rugged Himalayas in north

Elevation: *highest point:* Mount Everest (highest peak in Asia and highest point on earth above sea level) 8,849 m
lowest point: Kanchan Kalan 70 m
mean elevation: 2,565 m

Natural resources: quartz, water, timber, hydropower, scenic beauty, small deposits of lignite, copper, cobalt, iron ore

Land use: *agricultural land:* 28.8% (2018 est.)
arable land: 15.1% (2018 est.)
permanent crops: 1.2% (2018 est.)
permanent pasture: 12.5% (2018 est.)
forest: 25.4% (2018 est.)
other: 45.8% (2018 est.)

Irrigated land: 13,320 sq km (2012)

Major watersheds (area sq km): Indian Ocean drainage: Brahmaputra (651,335 sq km), Ganges (1,016,124 sq km), Indus (1,081,718 sq km)

Major aquifers: Indus-Ganges-Brahmaputra Basin

Population distribution: most of the population is divided nearly equally between a concentration in the southern-most plains of the Tarai region and the central hilly region; overall density is quite low

Natural hazards: severe thunderstorms; flooding; landslides; drought and famine depending on the timing, intensity, and duration of the summer monsoons

Geography - note: landlocked; strategic location between China and India; contains eight of world's 10 highest peaks, including Mount Everest and Kanchenjunga – the world's tallest and third tallest mountains – on the borders with China and India respectively

PEOPLE AND SOCIETY

Population: *total:* 31,122,387
male: 15,240,643
female: 15,881,744 (2024 est.)
comparison rankings: female 48; male 51; total 50

Nationality: *noun:* Nepali (singular and plural)
adjective: Nepali

Ethnic groups: Chhetri 16.5%, Brahman-Hill 11.3%, Magar 6.9%, Tharu 6.2%, Tamang 5.6%, Bishwokarma 5%, Musalman 4.9%, Newar 4.6%, Yadav 4.2%, Rai 2.2%, Pariyar 1.9%, Gurung 1.9%, Thakuri 1.7%, Mijar 1.6%, Teli 1.5%, Yakthung/Limbu 1.4%, Chamar/Harijan/Ram 1.4%, Koiri/Kushwaha 1.2%, other 20% (2021 est.)
note: 141 caste/ethnic groups were reported in the 2021 national census

Languages: Nepali (official) 44.9%, Maithali 11.1%, Bhojpuri 6.2%, Tharu 5.9%, Tamang 4.9%, Bajjika 3.9%, Avadhi 3%, Nepalbhasha (Newari) 3%, Magar Dhut 2.8%, Doteli 1.7%, Urdu 1.4%, Yakthung/Limbu 1.2%, Gurung 1.1%, other 8.9% (2021 est.)
major-language sample(s):
विश्व तथ्य पुस्तक,आधारभूत जानकारीको लागि अपरिहार्य स्रोत
(Nepali)
note: 123 languages reported as mother tongue in 2021 national census; many in government and business also speak English

Religions: Hindu 81.2%, Buddhist 8.2%, Muslim 5.1%, Kirat 3.2%, Christian 1.8%, other 0.5% (2021 est.)

Age structure: *0-14 years:* 25.8% (male 4,125,244/female 3,909,135)
15-64 years: 67.8% (male 10,153,682/female 10,957,011)
65 years and over: 6.4% (2024 est.) (male 961,717/female 1,015,598)

Dependency ratios: *total dependency ratio:* 54.9
youth dependency ratio: 45.5
elderly dependency ratio: 9.4
potential support ratio: 10.7 (2021 est.)

Median age: *total:* 27.6 years (2024 est.)
male: 26.5 years
female: 28.6 years
comparison ranking: total 157

Population growth rate: 0.7% (2024 est.)
comparison ranking: 128

Birth rate: 17 births/1,000 population (2024 est.)
comparison ranking: 91

Death rate: 5.6 deaths/1,000 population (2024 est.)
comparison ranking: 178

Net migration rate: -4.4 migrant(s)/1,000 population (2024 est.)
comparison ranking: 198

Population distribution: most of the population is divided nearly equally between a concentration in the southern-most plains of the Tarai region and the central hilly region; overall density is quite low

Urbanization: *urban population:* 21.9% of total population (2023)

rate of urbanization: 3.09% annual rate of change (2020-25 est.)

Major urban areas - population: 1.571 million KATHMANDU (capital) (2023)

Sex ratio: *at birth:* 1.06 male(s)/female
0-14 years: 1.06 male(s)/female
15-64 years: 0.93 male(s)/female
65 years and over: 0.95 male(s)/female
total population: 0.96 male(s)/female (2024 est.)

Mother's mean age at first birth: 20.4 years (2016 est.)
note: data represents median age at first birth among women 25-49

Maternal mortality ratio: 174 deaths/100,000 live births (2020 est.)
comparison ranking: 51

Infant mortality rate: *total:* 24 deaths/1,000 live births (2024 est.)
male: 25.2 deaths/1,000 live births
female: 22.7 deaths/1,000 live births
comparison ranking: total 64

Life expectancy at birth: *total population:* 73 years (2024 est.)
male: 72.2 years
female: 73.7 years
comparison ranking: total population 154

Total fertility rate: 1.85 children born/woman (2024 est.)
comparison ranking: 132

Gross reproduction rate: 0.9 (2024 est.)

Contraceptive prevalence rate: 46.7% (2019)

Drinking water source: *improved: urban:* 92.7% of population
rural: 94.4% of population
total: 94.1% of population
unimproved: urban: 7.3% of population
rural: 5.6% of population
total: 5.9% of population (2020 est.)

Current health expenditure: 5.2% of GDP (2020)

Physician density: 0.85 physicians/1,000 population (2020)

Hospital bed density: 0.3 beds/1,000 population (2012)

Sanitation facility access: *improved: urban:* 95.1% of population
rural: 85.7% of population
total: 87.7% of population
unimproved: urban: 4.9% of population
rural: 14.3% of population
total: 12.3% of population (2020 est.)

Obesity - adult prevalence rate: 4.1% (2016)
comparison ranking: 187

Alcohol consumption per capita: *total:* 0.36 liters of pure alcohol (2019 est.)
beer: 0.22 liters of pure alcohol (2019 est.)
wine: 0 liters of pure alcohol (2019 est.)
spirits: 0.13 liters of pure alcohol (2019 est.)
other alcohols: 0 liters of pure alcohol (2019 est.)
comparison ranking: total 167

Tobacco use: *total:* 30.4% (2020 est.)
male: 47.9% (2020 est.)
female: 12.8% (2020 est.)
comparison ranking: total 31

Children under the age of 5 years underweight: 18.7% (2022)
comparison ranking: 23

Currently married women (ages 15-49): 74.6% (2023 est.)

Child marriage: *women married by age 15:* 7.9%
women married by age 18: 32.8%
men married by age 18: 9% (2019 est.)

Education expenditures: 4.2% of GDP (2020 est.)
comparison ranking: 110

Literacy: *definition:* age 15 and over can read and write
total population: 71.2%
male: 81%
female: 63.3% (2021)

School life expectancy (primary to tertiary education): *total:* 13 years
male: 13 years
female: 13 years (2020)

ENVIRONMENT

Environment - current issues: deforestation (overuse of wood for fuel and lack of alternatives); forest degradation; soil erosion; contaminated water (with human and animal wastes, agricultural runoff, and industrial effluents); unmanaged solid-waste; wildlife conservation; vehicular emissions

Environment - international agreements: *party to:* Biodiversity, Climate Change, Climate Change-Kyoto Protocol, Climate Change-Paris Agreement, Desertification, Endangered Species, Hazardous Wastes, Law of the Sea, Nuclear Test Ban, Ozone Layer Protection, Wetlands
signed, but not ratified: Comprehensive Nuclear Test Ban, Marine Life Conservation

Climate: varies from cool summers and severe winters in north to subtropical summers and mild winters in south

Urbanization: *urban population:* 21.9% of total population (2023)
rate of urbanization: 3.09% annual rate of change (2020-25 est.)

Revenue from forest resources: 0.45% of GDP (2018 est.)
comparison ranking: 69

Revenue from coal: 0% of GDP (2018 est.)
comparison ranking: 157

Air pollutants: *particulate matter emissions:* 36.43 micrograms per cubic meter (2019 est.)
carbon dioxide emissions: 9.11 megatons (2016 est.)
methane emissions: 41.15 megatons (2020 est.)

Waste and recycling: *municipal solid waste generated annually:* 1,768,977 tons (2016 est.)

Major watersheds (area sq km): Indian Ocean drainage: Brahmaputra (651,335 sq km), Ganges (1,016,124 sq km), Indus (1,081,718 sq km)

Major aquifers: Indus-Ganges-Brahmaputra Basin

Total water withdrawal: *municipal:* 150 million cubic meters (2020 est.)
industrial: 30 million cubic meters (2020 est.)
agricultural: 9.32 billion cubic meters (2020 est.)

Total renewable water resources: 210.2 billion cubic meters (2020 est.)

GOVERNMENT

Country name: *conventional long form:* none
conventional short form: Nepal
local long form: none
local short form: Nepal
etymology: the Newar people of the Kathmandu Valley and surrounding areas apparently gave their name to the country; the terms "Nepal," "Newar," "Nepar," and "Newal" are phonetically different forms of the same word

Government type: federal parliamentary republic

Capital: *name:* Kathmandu
geographic coordinates: 27 43 N, 85 19 E
time difference: UTC+5.75 (10.75 hours ahead of Washington, DC, during Standard Time)
etymology: name derives from the Kasthamandap temple that stood in Durbar Square; in Sanskrit, *kastha* means "wood" and *mandapa* means "pavilion"; the three-story structure was made entirely of wood, without iron nails or supports, and dated to the late 16th century; it collapsed during a 2015 earthquake

Administrative divisions: 7 provinces (pradesh, singular - pradesh); Bagmati, Gandaki, Karnali, Koshi, Lumbini, Madhesh, Sudurpashchim

Independence: 1768 (unified by Prithvi Narayan SHAH)

National holiday: Constitution Day, 20 September (2015); note - marks the promulgation of Nepal's constitution in 2015 and replaces the previous 28 May Republic Day as the official national day in Nepal; the Gregorian day fluctuates based on Nepal's Hindu calendar

Legal system: English common law and Hindu legal concepts; note - new criminal and civil codes came into effect on 17 August 2018

Constitution: *history:* several previous; latest approved by the Second Constituent Assembly 16 September 2015, signed by the president and effective 20 September 2015
amendments: proposed as a bill by either house of the Federal Parliament; bills affecting a state border or powers delegated to a state must be submitted to the affected state assembly; passage of such bills requires a majority vote of that state assembly membership; bills not requiring state assembly consent require at least two-thirds majority vote by the membership of both houses of the Federal Parliament; parts of the constitution on the sovereignty, territorial integrity, independence, and sovereignty vested in the people cannot be amended; amended 2016, 2020

International law organization participation: has not submitted an ICJ jurisdiction declaration; non-party state to the ICCt

Citizenship: *citizenship by birth:* yes
citizenship by descent only: yes
dual citizenship recognized: no
residency requirement for naturalization: 15 years

Suffrage: 18 years of age; universal

Executive branch: *chief of state:* President Ram Chandra POUDEL (since 13 March 2023)
head of government: Prime Minister Khadga Prasad Sharma OLI (since 15 July 2024)
cabinet: Council of Ministers appointed by the prime minister; cabinet split between Nepali Congress, Communist Party of Nepal-Maoist Centre, and various coalition partners
elections/appointments: president indirectly elected by an electoral college of the Federal Parliament and of the state assemblies for a 5-year term (eligible for a second term); election last held on 9 March 2023 (next to be held in 2028)
election results:

2023: Ram Chandra POUDEL elected president; electoral college vote - Ram Chandra POUDEL (NC) 33,802, Subash Chandra NEMBANG (CPN-UML) 15,518
2018: Bidhya Devi BHANDARI reelected president; electoral vote - Bidhya Devi BHANDARI (CPN-UML) 39,275, Kumari Laxmi RAI (NC) 11,730

Legislative branch: *description:* bicameral Federal Parliament consists of:
National Assembly (59 seats; 56 members, including at least 3 women, 1 Dalit, 1 member with disabilities, or 1 minority indirectly elected by an electoral college of state and municipal government leaders, and 3 members, including 1 woman, nominated by the president of Nepal on the recommendation of the government; members serve 6-year terms with renewal of one-third of the membership every 2 years)
House of Representatives (275 seats statutory, current 272; 165 members directly elected in single-seat constituencies by simple majority vote and 110 members directly elected in a single nationwide constituency by closed-list proportional representation vote, with a threshold of 3% overall valid vote to be allocated a seat; members serve 5-year terms); note - the House of Representatives was dissolved on 22 May 2021, but on 13 July, the Supreme Court directed its reinstatement
elections: National Assembly - last held on 25 January 2024 (next to be held in January 2026)
House of Representatives - last held on 20 November 2022 (next to be held in November 2027)
election results: National Assembly - percent of vote by party - NA; seats by party - CPN-MC 17, NC 16, CON-UML 10, CPN-US 8, other 5, nominated members 3; composition - men 37, women 22, percentage women 37.3%
House of Representatives - percent of vote by party - NA; seats by party - NC 89, CPN-UML 78, CPN-MC 32, RSP 20, RPP 14, PSP-N 12, CPN (Unified Socialist) 10, Janamat Party 6, Loktantrik Samajwadi Party 4, other 10 other 10; composition - men 182, women 90, percentage women 33.1%; total Federal Parliament percentage women 33.5%

Judicial branch: *highest court(s):* Supreme Court (consists of the chief justice and up to 20 judges)
judge selection and term of office: Supreme Court chief justice appointed by the president upon the recommendation of the Constitutional Council, a 5-member, high-level advisory body headed by the prime minister; other judges appointed by the president upon the recommendation of the Judicial Council, a 5-member advisory body headed by the chief justice; the chief justice serves a 6-year term; judges serve until age 65
subordinate courts: High Court; district courts

Political parties: Communist Party of Nepal (Maoist Centre) or CPN-MC
Communist Party of Nepal (Unified Marxist-Leninist) or CPN-UML
Communist Party of Nepal (Unified Socialist) or CPN-US
Janamat Party
Janata Samajbaadi Party or JSP
Loktantrik Samajwadi Party or LSP
Naya Shakti Party, Nepal
Nepali Congress or NC
Nepal Mazdoor Kisan Party (Nepal Workers' and Peasants' Party) or NWPP
Rastriya Janamorcha (National People's Front)
Rastriya Prajatantra Party (National Democratic Party) or RPP
Rastriya Swatantra Party or RSP

International organization participation: ADB, BIMSTEC, CD, CP, FAO, G-77, IAEA, IBRD, ICAO, ICC (NGOs), ICRM, IDA, IFAD, IFC, IFRCS, ILO, IMF, IMO, Interpol, IOC, IOM, IPU, ISO, ITSO, ITU, ITUC (NGOs), MIGA, MINURSO, MINUSTAH, MONUSCO, NAM, OPCW, SAARC, SACEP, UN, UNAMID, UNCTAD, UNDOF, UNESCO, UNIDO, UNIFIL, UNISFA, UNMIL, UNMISS, UNOCI, UNSOM, UNTSO, UNWTO, UPU, WCO, WFTU (NGOs), WHO, WIPO, WMO, WTO

Diplomatic representation in the US: *chief of mission:* Ambassador (vacant); Chargé d'Affaires Kumar Raj KHAREL (since 26 June 2024)
chancery: 2730 34th Place NW, Washington, DC 20007
telephone: [1] (202) 667-4550
FAX: [1] (202) 667-5534
email address and website:
info@nepalembassyusa.org
https://us.nepalembassy.gov.np/
consulate(s) general: New York

Diplomatic representation from the US: *chief of mission:* Ambassador Dean R. THOMPSON (since October 2022)
embassy: Maharajgunj, Kathmandu
mailing address: 6190 Kathmandu Place, Washington DC 20521-6190
telephone: [977] (1) 423-4000
FAX: [977] (1) 400-7272
email address and website:
usembktm@state.gov
https://np.usembassy.gov/

Flag description: crimson red with a blue border around the unique shape of two overlapping right triangles; the smaller, upper triangle bears a white stylized moon and the larger, lower triangle displays a white 12-pointed sun; the color red represents the rhododendron (Nepal's national flower) and is a sign of victory and bravery, the blue border signifies peace and harmony; the two right triangles are a combination of two single pennons (pennants) that originally symbolized the Himalaya Mountains while their charges represented the families of the king (upper) and the prime minister, but today they are understood to denote Hinduism and Buddhism, the country's two main religions; the moon represents the serenity of the Nepalese people and the shade and cool weather in the Himalayas, while the sun depicts the heat and higher temperatures of the lower parts of Nepal; the moon and the sun are also said to express the hope that the nation will endure as long as these heavenly bodies
note: Nepal is the only country in the world whose flag is not rectangular or square

National symbol(s): rhododendron blossom; national color: red

National anthem: *name:* "Sayaun Thunga Phool Ka" (Hundreds of Flowers)
lyrics/music: Pradeep Kumar RAI/Ambar GURUNG
note: adopted 2007; after the abolition of the monarchy in 2006, a new anthem was required because of the previous anthem's praise for the king

National heritage: *total World Heritage Sites:* 4 (2 cultural, 2 natural)
selected World Heritage Site locales: Kathmandu Valley (c); Sagarmatha National Park (n); Chitwan National Park (n); Lumbini, Buddha Birthplace (c)

ECONOMY

Economic overview: low-income South Asian economy; post-conflict fiscal federalism increasing stability; COVID-19 hurt trade and tourism; widening current account deficits; environmentally fragile economy from earthquakes; growing Chinese relations and investments

Real GDP (purchasing power parity): $144.31 billion (2023 est.)
$141.546 billion (2022 est.)
$134 billion (2021 est.)
note: data in 2021 dollars
comparison ranking: 84

Real GDP growth rate: 1.95% (2023 est.)
5.63% (2022 est.)
4.84% (2021 est.)
note: annual GDP % growth based on constant local currency
comparison ranking: 141

Real GDP per capita: $4,700 (2023 est.)
$4,600 (2022 est.)
$4,500 (2021 est.)
note: data in 2021 dollars
comparison ranking: 180

GDP (official exchange rate): $40.908 billion (2023 est.)
note: data in current dollars at official exchange rate

Inflation rate (consumer prices): 7.11% (2023 est.)
7.65% (2022 est.)
4.15% (2021 est.)
note: annual % change based on consumer prices
comparison ranking: 144

GDP - composition, by sector of origin: *agriculture:* 21.2% (2023 est.)
industry: 12.1% (2023 est.)
services: 55.4% (2023 est.)
note: figures may not total 100% due to non-allocated consumption not captured in sector-reported data
comparison rankings: services 118; industry 181; agriculture 35

GDP - composition, by end use: *household consumption:* 85.9% (2023 est.)
government consumption: 6.6% (2023 est.)
investment in fixed capital: 25.1% (2023 est.)
investment in inventories: 6.6% (2023 est.)
exports of goods and services: 7% (2023 est.)
imports of goods and services: -34.7% (2023 est.)
note: figures may not total 100% due to rounding or gaps in data collection

Agricultural products: rice, vegetables, potatoes, sugarcane, maize, wheat, bison milk, milk, mangoes/guavas, fruits (2022)
note: top ten agricultural products based on tonnage

Industries: tourism, carpets, textiles, small rice, jute, sugar, oilseed mills, cigarettes, cement and brick production

Industrial production growth rate: 1.38% (2023 est.)
note: annual % change in industrial value added based on constant local currency
comparison ranking: 131

Labor force: 8.937 million (2023 est.)
note: number of people ages 15 or older who are employed or seeking work

comparison ranking: 59

Unemployment rate: 10.69% (2023 est.)
10.92% (2022 est.)
12.32% (2021 est.)
note: % of labor force seeking employment
comparison ranking: 167

Youth unemployment rate (ages 15-24): *total:* 20.4% (2023 est.)
male: 18.7% (2023 est.)
female: 23.3% (2023 est.)
note: % of labor force ages 15-24 seeking employment
comparison ranking: total 62

Remittances: 26.89% of GDP (2023 est.)
22.56% of GDP (2022 est.)
22.28% of GDP (2021 est.)
note: personal transfers and compensation between resident and non-resident individuals/households/entities

Budget: *revenues:* $7.625 billion (2021 est.)
expenditures: $7.163 billion (2021 est.)
note: central government revenues (excluding grants) and expenses converted to US dollars at average official exchange rate for year indicated

Public debt: 39.92% of GDP (2021 est.)
note: central government debt as a % of GDP
comparison ranking: 131

Taxes and other revenues: 17.49% (of GDP) (2021 est.)
note: central government tax revenue as a % of GDP
comparison ranking: 107

Current account balance: $939.38 million (2023 est.)
-$2.518 billion (2022 est.)
-$5.363 billion (2021 est.)
note: balance of payments - net trade and primary/secondary income in current dollars
comparison ranking: 58

Exports: $2.999 billion (2023 est.)
$2.733 billion (2022 est.)
$2.52 billion (2021 est.)
note: balance of payments - exports of goods and services in current dollars
comparison ranking: 155

Exports - partners: India 67%, US 11%, Germany 3%, Turkey 2%, UK 2% (2022)
note: top five export partners based on percentage share of exports

Exports - commodities: palm oil, soybean oil, garments, synthetic fibers, knotted carpets (2022)
note: top five export commodities based on value in dollars

Imports: $14.098 billion (2023 est.)
$15.462 billion (2022 est.)
$16.993 billion (2021 est.)
note: balance of payments - imports of goods and services in current dollars
comparison ranking: 107

Imports - partners: India 64%, China 13%, UAE 3%, Indonesia 2%, US 2% (2022)
note: top five import partners based on percentage share of imports

Imports - commodities: refined petroleum, natural gas, gold, rice, soybean oil (2022)
note: top five import commodities based on value in dollars

Reserves of foreign exchange and gold: $12.456 billion (2023 est.)
$9.319 billion (2022 est.)
$9.639 billion (2021 est.)
note: holdings of gold (year-end prices)/foreign exchange/special drawing rights in current dollars
comparison ranking: 81

Debt - external: $5.677 billion (2022 est.)
note: present value of external debt in current US dollars
comparison ranking: 51

Exchange rates: Nepalese rupees (NPR) per US dollar -

Exchange rates: 132.115 (2023 est.)
125.199 (2022 est.)
118.134 (2021 est.)
118.345 (2020 est.)
112.609 (2019 est.)

ENERGY

Electricity access: *electrification - total population:* 91.3% (2022 est.)
electrification - urban areas: 97.7%
electrification - rural areas: 93.7%

Electricity: *installed generating capacity:* 2.389 million kW (2022 est.)
consumption: 9.327 billion kWh (2022 est.)
exports: 347.784 million kWh (2022 est.)
imports: 1.601 billion kWh (2022 est.)
transmission/distribution losses: 1.738 billion kWh (2022 est.)
comparison rankings: transmission/distribution losses 119; imports 64; exports 83; consumption 106; installed generating capacity 117

Electricity generation sources: *solar:* 1.4% of total installed capacity (2022 est.)
wind: 0.1% of total installed capacity (2022 est.)
hydroelectricity: 98.5% of total installed capacity (2022 est.)

Coal: *production:* 15,000 metric tons (2022 est.)
consumption: 1.095 million metric tons (2022 est.)
imports: 1.015 million metric tons (2022 est.)
proven reserves: 8 million metric tons (2022 est.)

Petroleum: *refined petroleum consumption:* 62,000 bbl/day (2022 est.)

Carbon dioxide emissions: 10.515 million metric tonnes of CO2 (2022 est.)
from coal and metallurgical coke: 2.179 million metric tonnes of CO2 (2022 est.)
from petroleum and other liquids: 8.336 million metric tonnes of CO2 (2022 est.)
comparison ranking: total emissions 105

Energy consumption per capita: 5.881 million Btu/person (2022 est.)
comparison ranking: 167

COMMUNICATIONS

Telephones - fixed lines: *total subscriptions:* 726,000 (2021 est.)
subscriptions per 100 inhabitants: 2 (2021 est.)
comparison ranking: total subscriptions 80

Telephones - mobile cellular: *total subscriptions:* 38.213 million (2021 est.)
subscriptions per 100 inhabitants: 127 (2021 est.)
comparison ranking: total subscriptions 42

Telecommunication systems: *general assessment:* in relation to its telecom sector, Nepal has several topographical and economic constraints which have impeded efforts to expand network infrastructure and improve the quality of service for end-users; the fixed line market remains underdeveloped, and as a result most traffic is channeled via mobile networks; fixed broadband penetration remains very low, though to address this the government has initiated several programs as part of the Digital Nepal Framework and the wider Optical Fiber Backbone Network Expansion Project, started in 2012; supported by the Rural Telecommunications Development Fund, the programs include building out fiber backbone infrastructure and using this to provide broadband to schools and community centers nationally; telcos have also invested in fiber networks, and competition in the market is intensifying; cheap fiber-based services launched in mid-2021 prompted responses from other ISPs to provide faster and more competitively priced offers; Nepal's mobile market is relatively developed, with a focus on LTE; in 2021, the regulator considered a range of spectrum bands which could be used for 5G (2021)
domestic: fixed-line is 2 per 100 persons and mobile-cellular nearly 130 per 100 persons (2021)
international: country code - 977; Nepal, China and Tibet connected across borders with underground and all-dielectric self-supporting (ADSS) fiber-optic cables; radiotelephone communications; microwave and fiber landlines to India; satellite earth station - 1 Intelsat (Indian Ocean) (2019)

Broadcast media: state operates 3 TV stations, as well as national and regional radio stations; 117 television channels are licensed, among those 71 are cable television channels, three are distributed through Direct-To-Home (DTH) system, and four are digital terrestrial; 736 FM radio stations are licensed and at least 314 of those radio stations are community radio stations (2019)

Internet country code: .np

Internet users: *total:* 15.6 million (2021 est.)
percent of population: 52% (2021 est.)
comparison ranking: total 49

Broadband - fixed subscriptions: *total:* 1.27 million (2020 est.)
subscriptions per 100 inhabitants: 4 (2020 est.)
comparison ranking: total 69

TRANSPORTATION

National air transport system: *number of registered air carriers:* 6 (2020)
inventory of registered aircraft operated by air carriers: 39
annual passenger traffic on registered air carriers: 3,296,953 (2018)
annual freight traffic on registered air carriers: 4.66 million (2018) mt-km

Civil aircraft registration country code prefix: 9N

Airports: 51 (2024)
comparison ranking: 87

Heliports: 14 (2024)

Railways: *total:* 59 km (2018)
narrow gauge: 59 km (2018) 0.762-m gauge
comparison ranking: total 132

Roadways: *total:* 64,500 km (2020)
comparison ranking: total 76

MILITARY AND SECURITY

Military and security forces: Nepalese Armed Forces (Ministry of Defense): Nepali Army (includes Air Wing)

Ministry of Home Affairs: Nepal Police, Nepal Armed Police Force (2024) *note:* the Nepal Police are responsible for enforcing law and order across the country; the Armed Police Force is responsible for combating terrorism, providing security during riots and public disturbances, assisting in natural disasters, and protecting vital infrastructure, public officials, and the borders; it also conducts counterinsurgency and counterterrorism operations and would assist the Army in the event of an external invasion

Military expenditures: 1% of GDP (2023 est.)
1.1% of GDP (2022 est.)
1.3% of GDP (2021 est.)
1.3% of GDP (2020 est.)
1.6% of GDP (2019 est.)
comparison ranking: 129

Military and security service personnel strengths: approximately 95,000 active troops (including a small air wing of about 500 personnel) (2023)

Military equipment inventories and acquisitions: the Army's inventory includes a mix of mostly older equipment largely of British, Chinese, Indian, Russian, and South African origin; in recent years, Nepal has received limited amounts of newer hardware from several countries, including China, Indonesia, Italy, and Russia (2023)

Military service age and obligation: 18 years of age for voluntary military service for men and women; no conscription (2023)
note: as of 2022, women comprised about 7% of the active duty military

Military deployments: 1240 Central African Republic (MINUSCA); 1,150 Democratic Republic of the Congo (MONUSCO); 400 Golan Heights (UNDOF); 875 Lebanon (UNIFIL); 225 Liberia (UNSMIL); 100 South Sudan/Sudan (UNISFA); 1,725 (plus about 220 police) South Sudan (UNMISS); note - Nepal has over 6,000 total personnel deployed on 15 UN missions (2024)

Military - note: the Nepali Army is a lightly equipped force responsible for territorial defense, although it has some domestic duties such as disaster relief/humanitarian assistance and nature conservation efforts; during the 10-year civil war that ended in 2006, it conducted extensive counterinsurgency operations against Maoist guerrillas; the Army also has a long and distinguished history of supporting UN missions, having sent its first UN observers to Lebanon in 1958 and its first troop contingent to Egypt in 1974; as of 2024, about 150,000 Nepali military personnel had deployed on over 40 UN missions; the Army conducts training with foreign partners, including China, India, and the US
the British began to recruit Nepalese citizens (Gurkhas) into the East India Company Army during the Anglo-Nepalese War (1814-1816); the Gurkhas subsequently were brought into the British Indian Army and by 1914, there were 10 Gurkha regiments, collectively known as the Gurkha Brigade; following the partition of India in 1947, an agreement between Nepal, India, and Great Britain allowed for the transfer of the 10 regiments from the British Indian Army to the separate British and Indian armies; four regiments were transferred to the British Army, where they have since served continuously as the Brigade of Gurkhas; six Gurkha (aka Gorkha in India) regiments went to the new Indian Army; a seventh regiment was later added; Gurkhas are also recruited into the Singaporean Police and a special guard in the Sultanate of Brunei known as the Gurkha Reserve Unit (2024)

TERRORISM

Terrorist group(s): Indian Mujahedeen
note: details about the history, aims, leadership, organization, areas of operation, tactics, targets, weapons, size, and sources of support of the group(s) appear(s) in the Terrorism reference guide

TRANSNATIONAL ISSUES

Refugees and internally displaced persons: *refugees (country of origin):* 12,540 (Tibet/China), 6,365 (Bhutan) (mid-year 2022)
stateless persons: undetermined (mid-year 2021)

Trafficking in persons: tier rating: Tier 2 Watch List — the government did not demonstrate overall increasing efforts to eliminate trafficking compared with the previous reporting period, therefore Nepal was downgraded to Tier 2 Watch List; for more details, go to: https://www.state.gov/reports/2024-trafficking-in-persons-report/nepal/

Illicit drugs: illicit producer of cannabis and hashish for the domestic and international drug markets; transit point for opiates from Southeast Asia to the West; destination country for Indian-produced heroin smuggled in for domestic consumption

NETHERLANDS

INTRODUCTION

Background: The Dutch United Provinces declared their independence from Spain in 1581; during the 17th century, they became a leading seafaring and commercial power, with settlements and colonies around the world. After 18 years of French domination, the Netherlands regained its independence in 1813. In 1830, Belgium seceded and formed a separate kingdom. The Netherlands remained neutral in World War I but suffered German invasion and occupation in World War II. A modern, industrialized nation, the Netherlands is also a large exporter of agricultural products. The country was a founding member of NATO and the EEC (now the EU) and participated in the introduction of the euro in 1999. In 2010, the former Netherlands Antilles was dissolved and the three smallest islands – Bonaire, Sint Eustatius, and Saba – became special municipalities in the Netherlands administrative structure. The larger islands of Sint Maarten and Curacao joined the Netherlands and Aruba as constituent countries forming the Kingdom of the Netherlands.

In 2018, the Sint Eustatius island council (governing body) was dissolved and replaced by a government commissioner to restore the integrity of public administration. According to the Dutch Government, the intervention will be as "short as possible and as long as needed."

GEOGRAPHY

Location: Western Europe, bordering the North Sea, between Belgium and Germany

Geographic coordinates: 52 31 N, 5 46 E

Map references: Europe

Area: *total:* 41,543 sq km
land: 33,893 sq km
water: 7,650 sq km
comparison ranking: total 134

Area - comparative: slightly less than twice the size of New Jersey

Land boundaries: *total:* 1,053 km
border countries (2): Belgium 478 km; Germany 575 km

Coastline: 451 km

Maritime claims: *territorial sea:* 12 nm
contiguous zone: 24 nm
exclusive fishing zone: 200 nm

Climate: temperate; marine; cool summers and mild winters

Terrain: mostly coastal lowland and reclaimed land (polders); some hills in southeast

Elevation: *highest point:* Mount Scenery (on the island of Saba in the Caribbean, now considered an integral part of the Netherlands following the dissolution of the Netherlands Antilles) 862 m
lowest point: Zuidplaspolder -7 m
mean elevation: 30 m
note: the highest point on continental Netherlands is Vaalserberg at 322 m

Natural resources: natural gas, petroleum, peat, limestone, salt, sand and gravel, arable land

Land use: *agricultural land:* 55.1% (2018 est.)
arable land: 29.8% (2018 est.)
permanent crops: 1.1% (2018 est.)
permanent pasture: 24.2% (2018 est.)
forest: 10.8% (2018 est.)
other: 34.1% (2018 est.)

Irrigated land: 2,969 sq km (2019)

Major rivers (by length in km): Rijn (Rhine) river mouth (shared with Switzerland [s], Germany, and France) - 1,233 km
note – [s] after country name indicates river source; [m] after country name indicates river mouth

Major watersheds (area sq km): Atlantic Ocean drainage: Rhine-Maas (198,735 sq km)

Population distribution: an area known as the Randstad, anchored by the cities of Amsterdam, Rotterdam, the Hague, and Utrecht, is the most densely populated region; the north tends to be less dense, though sizeable communities can be found throughout the entire country

Natural hazards: flooding
volcanism: Mount Scenery (887 m), located on the island of Saba in the Caribbean, last erupted in 1640; Round Hill (601 m), a dormant volcano also known as The Quill, is located on the island of St. Eustatius in the Caribbean; these islands are at the northern end of the volcanic island arc of the Lesser Antilles that extends south to Grenada

Geography - note: located at mouths of three major European rivers (Rhine (Rijn), Meuse (Maas), and Scheldt (Schelde)); about a quarter of the country lies below sea level and only about half of the land exceeds one meter above sea level

PEOPLE AND SOCIETY

Population: *total:* 17,772,378
male: 8,844,100
female: 8,928,278 (2024 est.)
comparison rankings: female 71; male 70; total 71

Nationality: *noun:* Dutchman(men), Dutchwoman (women)
adjective: Dutch

Ethnic groups: Dutch 75.4%, EU (excluding Dutch) 6.4%, Turkish 2.4%, Moroccan 2.4%, Surinamese 2.1%, Indonesian 2%, other 9.3% (2021 est.)

Languages: Dutch (official), Frisian (official in Fryslan province)
major-language sample(s): Het Wereld Feitenboek, een onmisbare bron van informatie. (Dutch)
note: Frisian, Low Saxon, Limburgish, Romani, and Yiddish have protected status; Dutch is the official language of the three special municipalities of the Caribbean Netherlands; English is a recognized regional language on Sint Eustatius and Saba; Papiamento is a recognized regional language on Bonaire

Religions: Roman Catholic 20.1%, Protestant 14.8% (includes Dutch Reformed, Protestant Church of The Netherlands, Calvinist), Muslim 5%, other 5.9% (includes Hindu, Buddhist, Jewish), none 54.1% (2019 est.)

Age structure: *0-14 years:* 15.2% (male 1,384,142/female 1,312,455)
15-64 years: 64.1% (male 5,750,034/female 5,640,691)
65 years and over: 20.7% (2024 est.) (male 1,709,924/female 1,975,132)

Dependency ratios: *total dependency ratio:* 54.9
youth dependency ratio: 24
elderly dependency ratio: 30.9
potential support ratio: 3.2 (2021 est.)

Median age: *total:* 42.2 years (2024 est.)
male: 40.9 years
female: 43.5 years
comparison ranking: total 44

Population growth rate: 0.39% (2024 est.)
comparison ranking: 160

Birth rate: 10.6 births/1,000 population (2024 est.)
comparison ranking: 175

Death rate: 9.7 deaths/1,000 population (2024 est.)
comparison ranking: 38

Net migration rate: 3 migrant(s)/1,000 population (2024 est.)
comparison ranking: 37

Population distribution: an area known as the Randstad, anchored by the cities of Amsterdam, Rotterdam, the Hague, and Utrecht, is the most densely populated region; the north tends to be less dense, though sizeable communities can be found throughout the entire country

Urbanization: *urban population:* 93.2% of total population (2023)
rate of urbanization: 0.59% annual rate of change (2020-25 est.)

Major urban areas - population: 1.174 million AMSTERDAM (capital), 1.018 million Rotterdam (2023)

Sex ratio: *at birth:* 1.05 male(s)/female
0-14 years: 1.05 male(s)/female
15-64 years: 1.02 male(s)/female
65 years and over: 0.87 male(s)/female
total population: 0.99 male(s)/female (2024 est.)

Mother's mean age at first birth: 30.2 years (2020 est.)

Maternal mortality ratio: 4 deaths/100,000 live births (2020 est.)
comparison ranking: 174

Infant mortality rate: *total:* 3.6 deaths/1,000 live births (2024 est.)
male: 3.9 deaths/1,000 live births
female: 3.3 deaths/1,000 live births
comparison ranking: total 194

Life expectancy at birth: *total population:* 81.9 years (2024 est.)
male: 80.3 years
female: 83.5 years
comparison ranking: total population 39

Total fertility rate: 1.61 children born/woman (2024 est.)
comparison ranking: 180

Gross reproduction rate: 0.78 (2024 est.)

Contraceptive prevalence rate: 73% (2013)
note: percent of women aged 18-45

Drinking water source: *improved: urban:* 100% of population
rural: 100% of population
total: 100% of population

Current health expenditure: 11.1% of GDP (2020)

Physician density: 4.08 physicians/1,000 population (2020)

Hospital bed density: 3.2 beds/1,000 population (2018)

Sanitation facility access: *improved: urban:* 100% of population
rural: 100% of population
total: 100% of population

Obesity - adult prevalence rate: 20.4% (2016)
comparison ranking: 99

Alcohol consumption per capita: *total:* 8.23 liters of pure alcohol (2019 est.)
beer: 3.95 liters of pure alcohol (2019 est.)
wine: 2.92 liters of pure alcohol (2019 est.)
spirits: 1.36 liters of pure alcohol (2019 est.)
other alcohols: 0 liters of pure alcohol (2019 est.)
comparison ranking: total 40

Tobacco use: *total:* 22.2% (2020 est.)
male: 24.4% (2020 est.)
female: 19.9% (2020 est.)
comparison ranking: total 70

Currently married women (ages 15-49): 53.7% (2023 est.)

Education expenditures: 5.3% of GDP (2020 est.)
comparison ranking: 64

School life expectancy (primary to tertiary education): *total:* 19 years
male: 18 years
female: 19 years (2020)

ENVIRONMENT

Environment - current issues: water and air pollution are significant environmental problems; pollution of the country's rivers from industrial and agricultural chemicals, including heavy metals, organic compounds, nitrates, and phosphates; air pollution from vehicles and refining activities

Environment - international agreements: *party to:* Air Pollution, Air Pollution-Heavy Metals, Air Pollution-Multi-effect Protocol, Air Pollution-Nitrogen Oxides, Air Pollution-Persistent Organic Pollutants, Air Pollution-Sulphur 85, Air Pollution-Sulphur 94, Air Pollution-Volatile Organic Compounds, Antarctic-Environmental Protection, Antarctic-Marine Living Resources, Antarctic Treaty, Biodiversity, Climate Change, Climate Change-Kyoto Protocol, Climate Change-Paris Agreement, Comprehensive Nuclear Test Ban, Desertification, Endangered Species, Environmental Modification, Hazardous Wastes, Law of the Sea, Marine Dumping-London Convention, Marine Dumping-London Protocol, Marine Life Conservation, Nuclear Test Ban, Ozone Layer Protection, Ship Pollution, Tropical Timber 2006, Wetlands, Whaling
signed, but not ratified: none of the selected agreements

Climate: temperate; marine; cool summers and mild winters

Urbanization: *urban population:* 93.2% of total population (2023)
rate of urbanization: 0.59% annual rate of change (2020-25 est.)

Revenue from forest resources: 0.01% of GDP (2018 est.)
comparison ranking: 156

Revenue from coal: 0% of GDP (2018 est.)
comparison ranking: 160

Air pollutants: *particulate matter emissions:* 10.74 micrograms per cubic meter (2019 est.)
carbon dioxide emissions: 170.78 megatons (2016 est.)
methane emissions: 17.79 megatons (2020 est.)

Waste and recycling: *municipal solid waste generated annually:* 8.855 million tons (2015 est.)
municipal solid waste recycled annually: 2,179,216 tons (2015 est.)
percent of municipal solid waste recycled: 24.6% (2015 est.)

Major rivers (by length in km): Rijn (Rhine) river mouth (shared with Switzerland [s], Germany, and France) - 1,233 km

note – [s] after country name indicates river source; [m] after country name indicates river mouth

Major watersheds (area sq km): Atlantic Ocean drainage: Rhine-Maas (198,735 sq km)

Total water withdrawal: *municipal:* 2.05 billion cubic meters (2020 est.)
industrial: 5.94 billion cubic meters (2020 est.)
agricultural: 31 million cubic meters (2020 est.)

Total renewable water resources: 91 billion cubic meters (2020 est.)

Geoparks: *total global geoparks and regional networks:* 2 (2024)
global geoparks and regional networks: De Hondsrug; Schelde Delta (includes Belgium) (2024)

GOVERNMENT

Country name: *conventional long form:* Kingdom of the Netherlands
conventional short form: Netherlands
local long form: Koninkrijk der Nederlanden
local short form: Nederland
abbreviation: NL
etymology: the country name literally means "the lowlands" and refers to the geographic features of the land being both flat and down river from higher areas (i.e., at the estuaries of the Scheldt, Meuse, and Rhine Rivers; only about half of the Netherlands is more than 1 meter above sea level)

Government type: parliamentary constitutional monarchy; part of the Kingdom of the Netherlands

Capital: *name:* Amsterdam; note - The Hague is the seat of government
geographic coordinates: 52 21 N, 4 55 E
time difference: UTC+1 (6 hours ahead of Washington, DC, during Standard Time)
daylight saving time: +1hr, begins last Sunday in March; ends last Sunday in October
time zone note: time descriptions apply to the continental Netherlands only, for the constituent countries in the Caribbean, the time difference is UTC-4
etymology: the original Dutch name, Amstellerdam, meaning "a dam on the Amstel River," dates to the 13th century; over time the name simplified to Amsterdam

Administrative divisions: 12 provinces (provincies, singular - provincie), 3 public entities* (openbare lichamen, singular - openbaar lichaam (Dutch); entidatnan publiko, singular - entidat publiko (Papiamento)); Bonaire*, Drenthe, Flevoland, Fryslan (Friesland), Gelderland, Groningen, Limburg, Noord-Brabant (North Brabant), Noord-Holland (North Holland), Overijssel, Saba*, Sint Eustatius*, Utrecht, Zeeland (Zealand), Zuid-Holland (South Holland)
note 1: the Netherlands is one of four constituent countries of the Kingdom of the Netherlands; the other three, Aruba, Curacao, and Sint Maarten, are all islands in the Caribbean; while all four parts are considered equal partners, in practice, most of the Kingdom's affairs are administered by the Netherlands, which makes up about 98% of the Kingdom's total land area and population
note 2: although Bonaire, Saba, and Sint Eustatius are officially incorporated into the country of the Netherlands under the broad designation of "public entities," Dutch Government sources regularly apply to them the more descriptive term of "special municipalities"; Bonaire, Saba, and Sint Eustatius are collectively referred to as the Caribbean Netherlands

Independence: 26 July 1581 (the northern provinces of the Low Countries formally declared their independence with an Act of Abjuration; however, it was not until 30 January 1648 and the Peace of Westphalia that Spain recognized this independence)

National holiday: King's Day (birthday of King WILLEM-ALEXANDER), 27 April (1967); note - King's or Queen's Day is observed on the ruling monarch's birthday; currently celebrated on 26 April if 27 April is a Sunday

Legal system: civil law system based on the French system; constitution does not permit judicial review of acts of the States General

Constitution: *history:* many previous to adoption of the "Basic Law of the Kingdom of the Netherlands" on 24 August 1815; revised 8 times, the latest in 1983
amendments: proposed as an Act of Parliament by or on behalf of the king or by the Second Chamber of the States General; the Second Chamber is dissolved after its first reading of the Act; passage requires a second reading by both the First Chamber and the newly elected Second Chamber, followed by at least two-thirds majority vote of both chambers, and ratification by the king; amended many times, last in 2023

International law organization participation: accepts compulsory ICJ jurisdiction with reservations; accepts ICCt jurisdiction

Citizenship: *citizenship by birth:* no
citizenship by descent only: at least one parent must be a citizen of the Netherlands
dual citizenship recognized: no
residency requirement for naturalization: 5 years

Suffrage: 18 years of age; universal

Executive branch: *chief of state:* King WILLEM-ALEXANDER (since 30 April 2013)
head of government: Prime Minister Dick SCHOOF (since 2 July 2024)
cabinet: Council of Ministers appointed by the monarch
elections/appointments: the monarchy is hereditary; following Second Chamber elections, the leader of the majority party or majority coalition is usually appointed prime minister by the monarch; deputy prime ministers are appointed by the monarch
note: Mark RUTTE's ruling coalition collapsed on 8 July 2023; he is serving as prime minister in a caretaker status until a new prime minister is sworn into office

Legislative branch: *description:* bicameral States General or Staten Generaal consists of:
Senate or Eerste Kamer (75 seats; members indirectly elected by the country's 12 provincial council members by proportional representation vote; members serve 4-year terms)
House of Representatives or Tweede Kamer (150 seats; members directly elected in multi-seat constituencies by openlist proportional representation vote to serve up to 4-year terms)
elections: Senate - last held on 30 May 2023 (next to be held in May 2027)
House of Representatives - last held on 22 November 2023 (next to be held on 30 November 2027)
election results: Senate - percent of vote by party - BBB 21.3%, VVD 13.3%, GL 9.3%, PvdA 9.3%, CDA 8.0%, D66 6.7%, PVV 5.3%, SP 4%, CU 4%, PvdD 4%, JA21 4%, Volt 2.7%, SGP 2.7%, FvD 2.7%, other 2.6%; seats by party - BBB 16, VVD 10, GL 7, PvdA 7, CDA 6, D66 5, PVV 4, SP 3, CU 3, PvdD 3, JA21 3, Volt 2, SGP 2, FvD 2 other 2; composition - men 45, women 30, percentage women 40%
House of Representatives - percent of vote by party - PVV 23.6%, GL/PvdA 15.5%, VVD 15.2%, NSC 12.8%, D66 6.2%, BBB 4.7%, CDA 3.3%, SP 3.1%, Denk 2.4%, FvD 2.2%, PvdD 2.3%, CU 2.1%, SGP 2.2%, other 6.4%; seats by party - PVV 37, GL/PvdA 25, VVD 24, NSC 20, D66 9, BBB 7, CDA 5, SP 5, Denk 3, PvdD 3, CU 3, FvD 3, SGP 3, other 6; composition - men 91, women 58, percentage women 38.7%; total States General percentage women 39.3%

Judicial branch: highest court(s): Supreme Court or Hoge Raad (consists of 41 judges: the president, 6 vice presidents, 31 justices or raadsheren, and 3 justices in exceptional service, referred to as buitengewone dienst); the court is divided into criminal, civil, tax, and ombuds chambers
judge selection and term of office: justices appointed by the monarch from a list provided by the House of Representatives of the States General; justices appointed for life or until mandatory retirement at age 70
subordinate courts: courts of appeal; district courts, each with up to 5 subdistrict courts; Netherlands Commercial Court

Political parties: Christian Democratic Appeal or CDA
Christian Union or CU
Correct Answer 2021 or JA21
Democrats 66 or D66
Denk
Farmer-Citizen Movement or BBB
50Plus
Forum for Democracy or FvD
Green Left (GroenLinks) or GL
Labor Party or PvdA
New Social Contract or NSC
Party for Freedom or PVV
Party for the Animals or PvdD
People's Party for Freedom and Democracy or VVD
Reformed Political Party or SGP
Socialist Party or SP
Together or BIJ1
Volt Netherlands or Volt

International organization participation: ADB (nonregional member), AfDB (nonregional member), Arctic Council (observer), Australia Group, Benelux, BIS, CBSS (observer), CD, CE, CERN, EAPC, EBRD, ECB, EIB, EITI (implementing country), EMU, ESA, EU, FAO, FATF, G-10, IADB, IAEA, IBRD, ICAO, ICC (national committees), ICCt, ICRM, IDA, IEA, IFAD, IFC, IFRCS, IGAD (partners), IHO, ILO, IMF, IMO, IMSO, Interpol, IOC, IOM, IPU, ISO, ITSO, ITU, ITUC (NGOs), MIGA, NATO, NEA, NSG, OAS (observer), OECD, OPCW, OSCE, Pacific Alliance (observer), Paris Club, PCA, Schengen Convention, SELEC (observer), UN, UNCTAD, UNESCO, UNHCR, UNHRC, UNIDO, UNMISS, UNOOSA, UNRWA, UN Security Council (temporary), UNTSO, UNWTO, UPU, Wassenaar Arrangement, WCO, WHO, WIPO, WMO, WTO, ZC

Diplomatic representation in the US: *chief of mission:* Ambassador Birgitta TAZELAAR (since 15 September 2023)
chancery: 4200 Linnean Avenue NW, Washington, DC 20008
telephone: [1] (202) 244-5300
FAX: [1] (202) 362-3430
email address and website:

was@minbuza.nl
https://www.netherlandsworldwide.nl/countries/united-states/about-us/embassy-in-washington-dc
consulate(s) general: Atlanta, Chicago, Miami, New York, San Francisco

Diplomatic representation from the US: *chief of mission:* Ambassador Shefali RAZDAN DUGGAL (since 19 October 2022)
embassy: John Adams Park 1, 2244 BZ Wassenaar
mailing address: 5780 Amsterdam Place, Washington DC 20521-5780
telephone: [31] (70) 310-2209
FAX: [31] (70) 310-2207
email address and website: AmsterdamUSC@state.gov
https://nl.usembassy.gov/
consulate(s) general: Amsterdam

Flag description: three equal horizontal bands of red (bright vermilion; top), white, and blue (cobalt); similar to the flag of Luxembourg, which uses a lighter blue and is longer; the colors were derived from those of WILLIAM I, Prince of Orange, who led the Dutch Revolt against Spanish sovereignty in the latter half of the 16th century; originally the upper band was orange, but because its dye tended to turn red over time, the red shade was eventually made the permanent color; the banner is perhaps the oldest tricolor in continuous use

National symbol(s): lion, tulip; national color: orange

National anthem: *name:* "Het Wilhelmus" (The William)
lyrics/music: Philips VAN MARNIX van Sint Aldegonde (presumed)/unknown
note: adopted 1932, in use since the 17th century, making it the oldest national anthem in the world; also known as "Wilhelmus van Nassouwe" (William of Nassau), it is in the form of an acrostic, where the first letter of each stanza spells the name of the leader of the Dutch Revolt

National heritage: *total World Heritage Sites:* 13 (12 cultural, 1 natural); note - includes one site in Curacao
selected World Heritage Site locales: Schokland and Surroundings (c); Dutch Water Defense Lines (c); Van Nellefabriek (c); Mill Network at Kinderdijk-Elshout (c); Droogmakerij de Beemster (Beemster Polder) (c); Rietveld Schröderhuis (Rietveld Schröder House) (c); Wadden Sea (n); Seventeenth Century Canal Ring Area of Amsterdam inside the Singelgracht (c); Colonies of Benevolence (c); Frontiers of the Roman Empire - The Lower German Limes (c)

ECONOMY

Economic overview: high-income, core EU- and eurozone-member economy; trade-oriented with strong services, logistics, and high tech sectors; exiting mild recession triggered by inflation and weak export demand; tight labor market; low deficits and manageable public debt; strong ratings for innovation, competitiveness, and business climate

Real GDP (purchasing power parity): $1.24 trillion (2023 est.)
$1.238 trillion (2022 est.)
$1.187 trillion (2021 est.)
note: data in 2021 dollars
comparison ranking: 27

Real GDP growth rate: 0.12% (2023 est.)
4.33% (2022 est.)
6.19% (2021 est.)
note: annual GDP % growth based on constant local currency
comparison ranking: 186

Real GDP per capita: $69,300 (2023 est.)
$70,000 (2022 est.)
$67,700 (2021 est.)
note: data in 2021 dollars
comparison ranking: 18

GDP (official exchange rate): $1.118 trillion (2023 est.)
note: data in current dollars at official exchange rate

Inflation rate (consumer prices): 3.84% (2023 est.)
10% (2022 est.)
2.68% (2021 est.)
note: annual % change based on consumer prices
comparison ranking: 77

Credit ratings: Fitch rating: AAA (1994)

Moody's rating: Aaa (1986)

Standard & Poors rating: AAA (2015)
note: The year refers to the year in which the current credit rating was first obtained.

GDP - composition, by sector of origin: *agriculture:* 1.5% (2023 est.)
industry: 19.4% (2023 est.)
services: 69.3% (2023 est.)
note: figures may not total 100% due to non-allocated consumption not captured in sector-reported data
comparison rankings: services 40; industry 139; agriculture 174

GDP - composition, by end use: *household consumption:* 43.5% (2023 est.)
government consumption: 25.3% (2023 est.)
investment in fixed capital: 20.5% (2023 est.)
investment in inventories: -0.4% (2023 est.)
exports of goods and services: 85% (2023 est.)
imports of goods and services: -73.9% (2023 est.)
note: figures may not total 100% due to rounding or gaps in data collection

Agricultural products: milk, sugar beets, potatoes, pork, onions, wheat, chicken, tomatoes, carrots/turnips, goat milk (2022)
note: top ten agricultural products based on tonnage

Industries: agroindustries, metal and engineering products, electrical machinery and equipment, chemicals, petroleum, construction, microelectronics, fishing

Industrial production growth rate: -2.02% (2023 est.)
note: annual % change in industrial value added based on constant local currency
comparison ranking: 182

Labor force: 9.999 million (2023 est.)
note: number of people ages 15 or older who are employed or seeking work
comparison ranking: 55

Unemployment rate: 3.56% (2023 est.)
3.52% (2022 est.)
4.21% (2021 est.)
note: % of labor force seeking employment
comparison ranking: 63

Youth unemployment rate (ages 15-24): *total:* 8.9% (2023 est.)
male: 9.4% (2023 est.)
female: 8.5% (2023 est.)
note: % of labor force ages 15-24 seeking employment
comparison ranking: total 144

Population below poverty line: 14.5% (2021 est.)
note: % of population with income below national poverty line

Gini Index coefficient - distribution of family income: 25.7 (2021 est.)
note: index (0-100) of income distribution; higher values represent greater inequality
comparison ranking: 148

Average household expenditures: *on food:* 11.8% of household expenditures (2022 est.)
on alcohol and tobacco: 3% of household expenditures (2022 est.)

Household income or consumption by percentage share: *lowest 10%:* 3.6% (2021 est.)
highest 10%: 21.4% (2021 est.)
note: % share of income accruing to lowest and highest 10% of population

Remittances: 0.24% of GDP (2023 est.)
0.23% of GDP (2022 est.)
0.22% of GDP (2021 est.)
note: personal transfers and compensation between resident and non-resident individuals/households/entities

Budget: *revenues:* $399.616 billion (2022 est.)
expenditures: $398.696 billion (2022 est.)
note: central government revenues (excluding grants) and expenses converted to US dollars at average official exchange rate for year indicated

Public debt: 56.5% of GDP (2017 est.)
note: data cover general government debt and include debt instruments issued (or owned) by government entities other than the treasury; the data include treasury debt held by foreign entities; the data include debt issued by subnational entities, as well as intragovernmental debt; intragovernmental debt consists of treasury borrowings from surpluses in the social funds, such as for retirement, medical care, and unemployment, debt instruments for the social funds are not sold at public auctions
comparison ranking: 87

Taxes and other revenues: 24.11% (of GDP) (2022 est.)
note: central government tax revenue as a % of GDP
comparison ranking: 54

Current account balance: $112.952 billion (2023 est.)
$93.836 billion (2022 est.)
$124.924 billion (2021 est.)
note: balance of payments - net trade and primary/secondary income in current dollars
comparison ranking: 4

Exports: $949.983 billion (2023 est.)
$944.421 billion (2022 est.)
$865.094 billion (2021 est.)
note: balance of payments - exports of goods and services in current dollars
comparison ranking: 6

Exports - partners: Germany 19%, Belgium 14%, France 9%, UK 6%, Italy 5% (2022)
note: top five export partners based on percentage share of exports

Exports - commodities: refined petroleum, broadcasting equipment, machinery, packaged medicine, crude petroleum (2022)
note: top five export commodities based on value in dollars

Imports: $825.799 billion (2023 est.)
$835.47 billion (2022 est.)
$749.324 billion (2021 est.)

note: balance of payments - imports of goods and services in current dollars
comparison ranking: 8

Imports - partners: Germany 14%, China 12%, US 9%, Belgium 9%, UK 5% (2022)
note: top five import partners based on percentage share of imports

Imports - commodities: crude petroleum, refined petroleum, natural gas, broadcasting equipment, computers (2022)
note: top five import commodities based on value in dollars

Reserves of foreign exchange and gold: $69.83 billion (2023 est.)
$63.353 billion (2022 est.)
$64.469 billion (2021 est.)
note: holdings of gold (year-end prices)/foreign exchange/special drawing rights in current dollars
comparison ranking: 45

Exchange rates: euros (EUR) per US dollar -

Exchange rates: 0.925 (2023 est.)
0.95 (2022 est.)
0.845 (2021 est.)
0.876 (2020 est.)
0.893 (2019 est.)

ENERGY

Electricity access: *electrification - total population:* 100% (2022 est.)

Electricity: *installed generating capacity:* 57.194 million kW (2022 est.)
consumption: 111.757 billion kWh (2022 est.)
exports: 22.811 billion kWh (2022 est.)
imports: 18.544 billion kWh (2022 est.)
transmission/distribution losses: 4.817 billion kWh (2022 est.)
comparison rankings: transmission/distribution losses 165; imports 11; exports 11; consumption 32; installed generating capacity 27

Electricity generation sources: *fossil fuels:* 55.3% of total installed capacity (2022 est.)
nuclear: 3.3% of total installed capacity (2022 est.)
solar: 14.6% of total installed capacity (2022 est.)
wind: 17.6% of total installed capacity (2022 est.)
biomass and waste: 9.2% of total installed capacity (2022 est.)

Nuclear energy: Number of operational nuclear reactors: 1 (2023)

Net capacity of operational nuclear reactors: 0.48GW (2023 est.)

Percent of total electricity production: 3.4% (2023 est.)

Number of nuclear reactors permanently shut down: 1 (2023)

Coal: *production:* 1.825 million metric tons (2022 est.)
consumption: 10.61 million metric tons (2022 est.)
exports: 16.123 million metric tons (2022 est.)
imports: 24.908 million metric tons (2022 est.)
proven reserves: 3.247 billion metric tons (2022 est.)

Petroleum: *total petroleum production:* 70,000 bbl/day (2023 est.)
refined petroleum consumption: 872,000 bbl/day (2023 est.)
crude oil estimated reserves: 137.747 million barrels (2021 est.)

Natural gas: *production:* 17.774 billion cubic meters (2022 est.)
consumption: 33.243 billion cubic meters (2022 est.)
exports: 43.026 billion cubic meters (2022 est.)
imports: 65.807 billion cubic meters (2022 est.)
proven reserves: 132.608 billion cubic meters (2021 est.)

Carbon dioxide emissions: 186.092 million metric tonnes of CO2 (2022 est.)
from coal and metallurgical coke: 20.014 million metric tonnes of CO2 (2022 est.)
from petroleum and other liquids: 110.348 million metric tonnes of CO2 (2022 est.)
from consumed natural gas: 55.73 million metric tonnes of CO2 (2022 est.)
comparison ranking: total emissions 31

Energy consumption per capita: 186.89 million Btu/person (2022 est.)
comparison ranking: 20

COMMUNICATIONS

Telephones - fixed lines: *total subscriptions:* 4.57 million (2022 est.)
subscriptions per 100 inhabitants: 26 (2022 est.)
comparison ranking: total subscriptions 31

Telephones - mobile cellular: *total subscriptions:* 20.737 million (2022 est.)
subscriptions per 100 inhabitants: 118 (2022 est.)
comparison ranking: total subscriptions 61

Telecommunication systems: *general assessment:* telecom infrastructure in the Netherlands continues to be upgraded as modernization schemes undertaken by telcos make steady progress; other fiber providers have been supported by regulatory measures which have encouraged municipal governments to intervene with telcos' fiber builds, facilitating open access networks in a bid to make rollouts cheaper, and completed sooner; while the Mobile Network Operators (MNOs) are also closing down their Global System for Mobile Communication (MSM) and 3G networks and repurposing their spectrum and physical assets for LTE and 5G, the regulator has also encouraged GSM/3G roaming in the interim, thus safeguarding services such as machine to machine and other low data-use applications while individual MNOs disable their own GSM/3G networks; the country has one of the highest fixed broadband penetration rates in the world, with effective cross-platform competition between Digital Subscriber Line (DSL), Hybrid Fiber Coazial (HFC), and fiber networks; in the third quarter of 2020 the number of cable broadband connections fell for the first time, while the DSL segment has long been eclipsed by fiber; by the end of 2021, over a quarter of fixed broadband connections were on fiber infrastructure, while DSL accounted for only about 29%; almost 49% of fixed connections provided data above 100Mb/s, while an additional 43.7% provided data of at least 30Mb/s (2022)
domestic: fixed-line is 29 per 100 and mobile-cellular at 125 per 100 persons (2021)
international: country code - 31; landing points for Farland North, TAT-14, Circe North, Concerto, Ulysses 2, AC-1, UK- Netherlands 14, and COBRAcable submarine cables which provide links to the US and Europe; satellite earth stations - 5 (3 Intelsat - 1 Indian Ocean and 2 Atlantic Ocean, 1 Eutelsat, and 1 Inmarsat) (2019)

Broadcast media: more than 90% of households are connected to cable or satellite TV systems that provide a wide range of domestic and foreign channels; public service broadcast system includes multiple broadcasters, 3 with a national reach and the remainder operating in regional and local markets; 2 major nationwide commercial television companies, each with 3 or more stations, and many commercial TV stations in regional and local markets; nearly 600 radio stations with a mix of public and private stations providing national or regional coverage

Internet country code: .nl

Internet users: *total:* 16.56 million (2021 est.)
percent of population: 92% (2021 est.)
comparison ranking: total 47

Broadband - fixed subscriptions: *total:* 7,525,016 (2020 est.)
subscriptions per 100 inhabitants: 44 (2020 est.)
comparison ranking: total 29

TRANSPORTATION

National air transport system: *number of registered air carriers:* 8 (2020)
inventory of registered aircraft operated by air carriers: 238
annual passenger traffic on registered air carriers: 43,996,044 (2018)
annual freight traffic on registered air carriers: 5,886,510,000 (2018) mt-km

Civil aircraft registration country code prefix: PH

Airports: 45 (2024)
note: Includes 3 airports in Bonaire, Sint Eustatius and Saba
comparison ranking: 93

Heliports: 184 (2024)

Pipelines: 14,000 km gas, 2,500 km oil and refined products, 3,000 km chemicals (2017)

Railways: *total:* 3,055 km (2020) 2,310 km electrified
comparison ranking: total 58

Roadways: *total:* 139,027 km (2022)
comparison ranking: total 39

Waterways: 6,237 km (2012) (navigable by ships up to 50 tons)
comparison ranking: 23

Merchant marine: *total:* 1,187 (2023)
by type: bulk carrier 11, container ship 36, general cargo 521, oil tanker 27, other 592
comparison ranking: total 21

Ports: *total ports:* 18 (2024)
large: 2
medium: 4
small: 5
very small: 7
ports with oil terminals: 12
key ports: Amsterdam, Dordrecht, Europoort, Rotterdam, Terneuzen, Vlissingen

MILITARY AND SECURITY

Military and security forces: Netherlands (Dutch) Armed Forces (Nederlandse Krijgsmacht): Royal Netherlands Army, Royal Netherlands Navy (includes Marine Corps), Royal Netherlands Air Force, Royal Netherlands Marechaussee (Military Constabulary) (2024)
note 1: the Netherlands Coast Guard and the Dutch Caribbean Coast Guard are civilian in nature but managed by the Royal Netherlands Navy
note 2: the core missions of the Royal Netherlands Marechaussee are border security, security and surveillance, and international and military police tasks;

it has 21 brigades based in eight Dutch provinces, plus Curaçao in the Caribbean, a special missions security brigade, and separate security platoons to guard and protect domestic sites that are most likely to be the targets of attacks, such as government buildings
note 3: the national police maintain internal security in the Netherlands and report to the Ministry of Justice and Security, which oversees law enforcement organizations, as do the justice ministries in Aruba, Curacao, and Sint Maarten

Military expenditures: 2.1% of GDP (2024 est.)
1.6% of GDP (2023)
1.5% of GDP (2022)
1.4% of GDP (2021)
1.4% of GDP (2020)
comparison ranking: 64

Military and security service personnel strengths: approximately 45,000 active-duty personnel (19,000 Army; 8,000 Navy; 8,000 Air Force; 6,000 Constabulary; 4,000 other) (2024)
note: the total figures include about 6,000 reservists on active duty; the Navy figures include about 2,300 marines

Military equipment inventories and acquisitions: the military's inventory consists of a mix of domestically produced and modern European- and US-sourced equipment; in recent years, the US has been the leading supplier of weapons systems; the Netherlands has an advanced domestic defense industry that focuses on armored vehicles, naval ships, and air defense systems; it also participates with the US and other European countries on joint development and production of advanced weapons systems (2024)

Military service age and obligation: 17 years of age for voluntary service for men and women; the military is an all-volunteer force; conscription remains in place, but the requirement to show up for compulsory military service was suspended in 1997; must be a citizen of the Netherlands (2024)
note: in 2023, women made up about 14% of the military's full-time personnel

Military deployments: 350 Lithuania (NATO); 200 Romania (NATO) (2024)
note: as of 2024, the Dutch military had close to 1,000 total military personnel deployed abroad

Military - note: the Dutch military is charged with the three core tasks of defending the country's national territory and that of its allies, enforcing the national and international rule of law, and providing assistance during disasters and other crises; it also has some domestic security duties, including in the Dutch Caribbean territories; the military operates globally but rarely carries out military operations independently and focuses on cooperating with the armed forces of other countries, particularly with Belgium, Denmark, Germany, and the UK
the Netherlands has been a member of NATO since its founding in 1949, and the Dutch military is heavily involved in NATO missions and operations with air, ground, and naval forces, including air policing missions over the Benelux countries and Eastern Europe, NATO's Enhanced Forward Presence initiative in the Baltic States and Eastern Europe, and several NATO naval flotillas, as well as standby units for NATO's rapid response force; the military has previously deployed forces to NATO-led operations in Afghanistan, Iraq, and Kosovo and also regularly contributes to EU- and UNled missions; Royal Netherlands Marechaussee detachments have been included in international police units deployed by NATO
the Dutch Army has especially close ties with the German Army, including having its air mobile and mechanized brigades assigned to German divisional headquarters; in addition, the Army shares with the Germans command of a NATO high-readiness corps-level headquarters, which can be ready for deployment inside or outside NATO territory within 20 days; in 2020, Belgium, Denmark, and the Netherlands formed a joint composite special operations component command
founded in the late 1400s, the Royal Netherlands Navy is one of the oldest naval forces in the World and conducts a variety of missions worldwide; in addition to its close ties with NATO, the Navy cooperates closely with the Belgian Navy, including a joint staff known as the Admiralty Benelux; it has a command responsible for the activities of Dutch naval units in the Caribbean, which includes combating drug trafficking, environmental crime, and illegal fishing, as well as providing search and rescue and disaster relief capabilities; the Netherlands has naval bases on Curaçao and Aruba; since 1973, the Dutch Marine Corps has worked closely with the British Royal Marines, including jointly in the UK-Netherlands amphibious landing force
the Dutch military is also part of the UK-led Joint Expeditionary Force, a defense framework of 10 Northern European nations designed to provide security to the High North, North Atlantic, and the Baltic Sea Region in response to a crisis (2024)

SPACE

Space agency/agencies: Netherlands Space Office (NSO; established 2009); Netherlands Institute for Space Research (SRON; advises NSO on scientific space research; established 1983) (2024)

Space program overview: has an active space program focused on the added value of space on science, the economy, and society, as well as the development of cutting edge space technologies and services based on satellite data; builds and operates satellites; researches and develops technologies related to astrophysics, telecommunications, remote sensing (RS), propulsion systems, atmospheric measuring instruments (such as spectrometers), planetary/exoplanetary research, and robotics; active member of the European Space Agency (ESA) and participates in the construction of ESA satellite launch vehicles (Arienne and VEGA) and in the ESA astronaut training program; participates in international space programs and with other foreign space agencies and industries, including those of Japan, the US, and members of the EU; has a robust commercial space sector tied in to the larger European space economy (2024)
note: further details about the key activities, programs, and milestones of the country's space program, as well as government spending estimates on the space sector, appear in the Space Programs reference guide

TERRORISM

Terrorist group(s): Islamic State of Iraq and ash-Sham (ISIS)
note: details about the history, aims, leadership, organization, areas of operation, tactics, targets, weapons, size, and sources of support of the group(s) appear(s) in the Terrorism reference guide

TRANSNATIONAL ISSUES

Refugees and internally displaced persons: *refugees (country of origin):* 53,496 (Syria), 19,204 (Eritrea), 7,106 (Turkey), 5,593 (Iran), 5,152 (Iraq) (mid-year 2022); 117,950 (Ukraine) (as of 21 February 2024)
stateless persons: 4,570 (2022)

Illicit drugs: a major transit hub for illicit substances, especially cocaine from South and Central America and methamphetamine from Mexico; homegrown synthetic drug makers and illegal chemical precursor manufacturers selling dangerous drugs, including synthetic opioids, via the internet to customers in the United States and worldwide

NEW CALEDONIA

INTRODUCTION

Background: The first humans settled in New Caledonia around 1600 B.C. The Lapita were skilled navigators, and evidence of their pottery around the Pacific has served as a guide for understanding human expansion in the region. Successive waves of migrants from other islands in Melanesia intermarried with the Lapita, giving rise to the Kanak ethnic group considered indigenous to New Caledonia. British explorer James COOK was the first European to visit New Caledonia in 1774, giving it the Latin name for Scotland. Missionaries first landed in New Caledonia in 1840. In 1853, France annexed New Caledonia to preclude any British attempt to claim the island. France declared it a penal colony in 1864 and sent more than 20,000 prisoners to New Caledonia in the ensuing three decades.

Nickel was discovered in 1864, and French prisoners were directed to mine it. France brought in indentured servants and enslaved labor from elsewhere in Southeast Asia to work the mines, blocking Kanaks from accessing the most profitable part of the local economy. In 1878, High Chief ATAI led a rebellion against French rule. The Kanaks were relegated to reservations, leading to periodic smaller uprisings and culminating in a large revolt in 1917

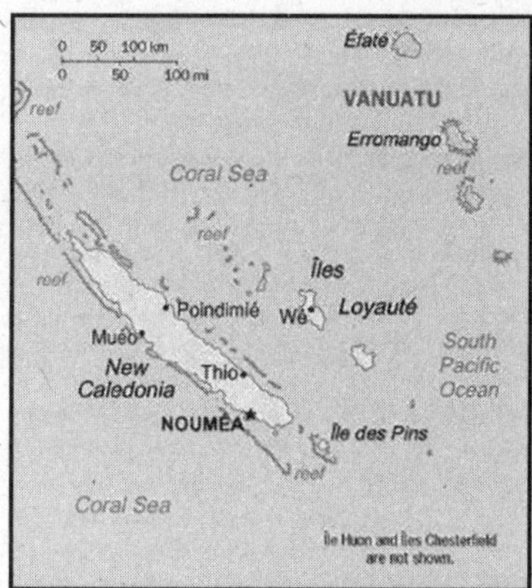

that colonial authorities brutally suppressed. During World War II, New Caledonia became an important base for Allied troops, and the US moved its South Pacific headquarters to the island in 1942. Following the war, France made New Caledonia an overseas territory and granted French citizenship to all inhabitants in 1953, thereby permitting the Kanaks to move off the reservations.

The Kanak nationalist movement began in the 1950s, but most voters chose to remain a territory in an independence referendum in 1958. The European population of New Caledonia boomed in the 1970s with a renewed focus on nickel mining, reigniting Kanak nationalism. Key Kanak leaders were assassinated in the early 1980s, leading to escalating violence and dozens of fatalities. The Matignon Accords of 1988 provided for a 10-year transition period. The Noumea Accord of 1998 transferred increasing governing responsibility from France to New Caledonia over a 20-year period and provided for three independence referenda. In the first held in 2018, voters rejected independence by 57% to 43%; in the second held in 2020, voters rejected independence 53% to 47%. In the third referendum held in 2021, voters rejected independence 96% to 4%; however, a boycott by key Kanak groups spurred challenges about the legitimacy of the vote. Pro-independence parties subsequently won a majority in the New Caledonian Government for the first time. France and New Caledonia officials remain in talks about the status of the territory.

GEOGRAPHY

Location: Oceania, islands in the South Pacific Ocean, east of Australia

Geographic coordinates: 21 30 S, 165 30 E

Map references: Oceania

Area: *total:* 18,575 sq km
land: 18,275 sq km
water: 300 sq km
comparison ranking: total 155

Area - comparative: slightly smaller than New Jersey

Land boundaries: *total:* 0 km

Coastline: 2,254 km

Maritime claims: *territorial sea:* 12 nm
exclusive economic zone: 200 nm

Climate: tropical; modified by southeast trade winds; hot, humid

Terrain: coastal plains with interior mountains

Elevation: *highest point:* Mont Panie 1,628 m
lowest point: Pacific Ocean 0 m

Natural resources: nickel, chrome, iron, cobalt, manganese, silver, gold, lead, copper

Land use: *agricultural land:* 10.4% (2018 est.)
arable land: 0.4% (2018 est.)
permanent crops: 0.2% (2018 est.)
permanent pasture: 9.8% (2018 est.)
forest: 45.9% (2018 est.)
other: 43.7% (2018 est.)

Irrigated land: 100 sq km (2012)

Population distribution: most of the populace lives in the southern part of the main island, in and around the capital of Noumea

Natural hazards: cyclones, most frequent from November to March
volcanism: Matthew and Hunter Islands are historically active

Geography - note: consists of the main island of New Caledonia (one of the largest in the Pacific Ocean), the archipelago of Iles Loyaute, and numerous small, sparsely populated islands and atolls

PEOPLE AND SOCIETY

Population: *total:* 304,167
male: 151,389
female: 152,778 (2024 est.)
comparison rankings: female 181; male 181; total 180

Nationality: *noun:* New Caledonian(s)
adjective: New Caledonian

Ethnic groups: Kanak 39.1%, European 27.1%, Wallisian, Futunian 8.2%, Tahitian 2.1%, Indonesian 1.4%, Ni-Vanuatu 1%, Vietnamese 0.9%, other 17.7%, unspecified 2.5% (2014 est.)

Languages: French (official), 33 Melanesian-Polynesian dialects
major-language sample(s):
The World Factbook, une source indispensable d'informations de base. (French)

Religions: Christian 85.2%, Muslim 2.8%, other 1.6%, unaffiliated 10.4% (2020 est.)

Age structure: *0-14 years:* 20.7% (male 32,238/female 30,858)
15-64 years: 68.4% (male 104,825/female 103,349)
65 years and over: 10.8% (2024 est.) (male 14,326/female 18,571)

Dependency ratios: *total dependency ratio:* 49.6
youth dependency ratio: 33.6
elderly dependency ratio: 16
potential support ratio: 6.3 (2021 est.)

Median age: *total:* 34.3 years (2024 est.)
male: 33.5 years
female: 35.1 years
comparison ranking: total 103

Population growth rate: 1.14% (2024 est.)
comparison ranking: 80

Birth rate: 13.8 births/1,000 population (2024 est.)
comparison ranking: 123

Death rate: 6 deaths/1,000 population (2024 est.)
comparison ranking: 157

Net migration rate: 3.6 migrant(s)/1,000 population (2024 est.)
comparison ranking: 30

Population distribution: most of the populace lives in the southern part of the main island, in and around the capital of Noumea

Urbanization: *urban population:* 72.7% of total population (2023)
rate of urbanization: 1.72% annual rate of change (2020-25 est.)

Major urban areas - population: 198,000 NOUMEA (capital) (2018)

Sex ratio: *at birth:* 1.05 male(s)/female
0-14 years: 1.04 male(s)/female
15-64 years: 1.01 male(s)/female
65 years and over: 0.77 male(s)/female
total population: 0.99 male(s)/female (2024 est.)

Infant mortality rate: *total:* 4.8 deaths/1,000 live births (2024 est.)
male: 5.8 deaths/1,000 live births
female: 3.9 deaths/1,000 live births
comparison ranking: total 178

Life expectancy at birth: *total population:* 79.3 years (2024 est.)
male: 75.4 years
female: 83.3 years
comparison ranking: total population 65

Total fertility rate: 1.83 children born/woman (2024 est.)
comparison ranking: 135

Gross reproduction rate: 0.89 (2024 est.)

Drinking water source: *improved:*
total: 99.3% of population
unimproved:
total: 0.7% of population (2020 est.)

Sanitation facility access: *improved:*
total: 100% of population
unimproved:
total: 0% of population (2020 est.)

Currently married women (ages 15-49): 22.5% (2023 est.)

Literacy: *definition:* age 15 and over can read and write
total population: 96.9%
male: 97.3%
female: 96.5% (2015)

ENVIRONMENT

Environment - current issues: preservation of coral reefs; prevention of invasive species; limiting erosion caused by nickel mining and forest fires

Climate: tropical; modified by southeast trade winds; hot, humid

Urbanization: *urban population:* 72.7% of total population (2023)
rate of urbanization: 1.72% annual rate of change (2020-25 est.)

Air pollutants: *carbon dioxide emissions:* 5.33 megatons (2016 est.)

Waste and recycling: *municipal solid waste generated annually:* 108,157 tons (2016 est.)

GOVERNMENT

Country name: *conventional long form:* Territory of New Caledonia and Dependencies
conventional short form: New Caledonia
local long form: Territoire des Nouvelle-Calédonie et dépendances

local short form: Nouvelle-Calédonie
etymology: British explorer Captain James COOK discovered and named New Caledonia in 1774; he used the appellation because the northeast of the island reminded him of Scotland (Caledonia is the Latin designation for Scotland)

Government type: parliamentary democracy (Territorial Congress); an overseas collectivity of France

Dependency status: special collectivity (or a sui generis collectivity) of France since 1998; note - independence referenda took place on 4 November 2018, 4 October 2020, and 12 December 2021 with a majority voting in each case to reject independence in favor of maintaining the status quo; an 18-month transition period is now in place (ending 30 June 2023), during which a referendum on the new status of New Caledonia within France will take place

Capital: *name:* Noumea
geographic coordinates: 22 16 S, 166 27 E
time difference: UTC+11 (16 hours ahead of Washington, DC, during Standard Time)
etymology: established in 1854 as Port-de-France, the settlement was renamed Noumea in 1866, in order to avoid any confusion with Fort-de-France in Martinique; the New Caledonian language of Ndrumbea (also spelled Ndumbea, Dubea, and Drubea) spoken in the area gave its name to the capital city, Noumea, as well as to the neighboring town (suburb) of Dumbea

Administrative divisions: 3 provinces; Province Iles (Islands Province), Province Nord (North Province), and Province Sud (South Province)

Independence: none (overseas collectivity of France); note - in three independence referenda, on 4 November 2018, 4 October 2020, and 12 December 2021, the majority voted to reject independence in favor of maintaining the status quo; an 18-month transition period is now in place (ending 30 June 2023), during which a referendum on the new status of New Caledonia within France will take place

National holiday: Fête de la Fédération, 14 July (1790); note - the local holiday is New Caledonia Day, 24 September (1853)

Legal system: civil law system based on French civil law

Constitution: *history:* 4 October 1958 (French Constitution with changes as reflected in the Noumea Accord of 5 May 1998)
amendments: French constitution amendment procedures apply

Citizenship: see France

Suffrage: 18 years of age; universal

Executive branch: *chief of state:* President Emmanuel MACRON (since 14 May 2017); represented by High Commissioner Louise LEFRANC (since 6 February 2023)
head of government: President of the Government Louis MAPOU (since 22 July 2021)
cabinet: Cabinet elected from and by the Territorial Congress
elections/appointments: French president directly elected by absolute majority popular vote in 2 rounds if needed for a 5-year term (eligible for a second term); high commissioner appointed by the French president on the advice of the French Ministry of Interior; president of New Caledonia elected by Territorial Congress for a 5-year term (no term limits); election last held on 8 July 2021 (next to be held in 2026)
election results:
2021: Louis MAPOU (PALIKA) elected president by Territorial Congress with 6 of 11 votes
2019: Thierry SANTA (The Republicans) elected president by Territorial Congress with 6 of 11 votes

Legislative branch: *description:* unicameral Territorial Congress or Congrès du Territoire (54 seats; members indirectly selected proportionally by the partisan makeup of the 3 Provincial Assemblies or Assemblés Provinciales; members of the 3 Provincial Assemblies directly elected by party-list proportional representation vote; members serve 5-year terms); note - the Customary Senate is the assembly of the various traditional councils of the Kanaks, the indigenous population, which rules on laws affecting the indigenous population
New Caledonia indirectly elects 2 members to the French Senate by an electoral colleges for a 6-year term with one seat renewed every 3 years and directly elects 2 members to the French National Assembly by absolute majority vote in 2 rounds if needed for a 5-year term
elections: Territorial Congress - last held on 12 May 2019 (next to be held by 15 December 2024)
French Senate - election last held on 24 September 2023 (next to be held on 30 September 2026)
French National Assembly - election last held on 12 and 19 June 2022 (next to be held by June 2027)
election results: Territorial Congress - percent of vote by party - NA; seats by party - Future With Confidence 18, UNI 9, UC 9, CE 7, FLNKS 6, Oceanic Awakening 3, PT 1, LKS 1 (Anti-Independence 28, Pro-Independence 26)
French Senate - percent of vote by party - NA; seats by party - UMP 2
French National Assembly - percent of vote by party - NA; seats by party - CE 2

Judicial branch: *highest court(s):* Court of Appeal in Noumea or Cour d'Appel; organized into civil, commercial, social, and pre-trial investigation chambers; court bench normally includes the court president and 2 counselors); Administrative Court (number of judges NA); note - final appeals beyond the Court of Appeal are referred to the Court of Cassation or Cour de Cassation (in Paris); final appeals beyond the Administrative Court are referred to the Administrative Court of Appeal (in Paris)
judge selection and term of office: judge appointment and tenure based on France's judicial system
subordinate courts: Courts of First Instance include: civil, juvenile, commercial, labor, police, criminal, assizes, and also a pre-trial investigation chamber; Joint Commerce Tribunal; administrative courts

Political parties: Caledonia Together or CE
Caledonian Union or UC
Future With Confidence or AEC
Kanak Socialist Front for National Liberation or FLNKS (alliance includes PALIKA, UNI, UC, and UPM)
Labor Party or PT
National Union for Independence or UNI
Oceanian Awakening
Party of Kanak Liberation or PALIKA
Socialist Kanak Liberation or LKS
The Republicans (formerly The Rally or UMP)

International organization participation: ITUC (NGOs), PIF, SPC, UPU, WFTU (NGOs), WMO

Diplomatic representation in the US: none (overseas territory of France)

Diplomatic representation from the US: *embassy:* none (overseas territory of France)

Flag description: New Caledonia has two official flags; alongside the flag of France, the Kanak (indigenous Melanesian) flag has equal status; the latter consists of three equal horizontal bands of blue (top), red, and green; a large yellow disk - diameter two-thirds the height of the flag - shifted slightly to the hoist side is edged in black and displays a black fleche faitiere symbol, a native rooftop adornment

National symbol(s): fleche faitiere (native rooftop adornment), kagu bird; national colors: gray, red

National anthem: *name:* "Soyons unis, devenons freres" (Let Us Be United, Let Us Become Brothers)
lyrics/music: Chorale Melodia (a local choir)
note: adopted 2008; contains a mixture of lyrics in both French and Nengone (an indigenous language); as a selfgoverning territory of France, in addition to the local anthem, "La Marseillaise" is official (see France)

National heritage: *total World Heritage Sites:* 1 (natural); note - excerpted from the France entry
selected World Heritage Site locales: Lagoons of New Caledonia

ECONOMY

Economic overview: upper-middle-income French Pacific territorial economy; enormous nickel reserves; ongoing French independence negotiations; large Chinese nickel exporter; luxury eco-tourism destination; large French aid recipient; high cost-of-living; lingering wealth disparities

Real GDP (purchasing power parity): $10.266 billion (2021 est.)
$11.11 billion (2017 est.)
$10.89 billion (2016 est.)
note: data are in 2015 dollars
comparison ranking: 167

Real GDP growth rate: 3.5% (2022 est.)
-2.1% (2021 est.)
-2.4% (2020 est.)
note: annual GDP % growth based on constant local currency
comparison ranking: 91

Real GDP per capita: $35,700 (2021 est.)
$31,100 (2015 est.)
$32,100 (2014 est.)
comparison ranking: 68

GDP (official exchange rate): $9.623 billion (2022 est.)
note: data in current dollars at official exchange rate

Inflation rate (consumer prices): 1.4% (2017 est.)
0.58% (2016 est.)
0.57% (2015 est.)
note: annual % change based on consumer prices
comparison ranking: 27

GDP - composition, by sector of origin: *agriculture:* 1.8% (2019 est.)
industry: 22.3% (2019 est.)
services: 65.2% (2019 est.)
note: figures may not total 100% due to non-allocated consumption not captured in sector-reported data
comparison rankings: services 56; industry 122; agriculture 162

GDP - composition, by end use: *household consumption:* 65.6% (2017 est.)
government consumption: 23.5% (2017 est.)
investment in fixed capital: 27.9% (2017 est.)
investment in inventories: -0.1% (2017 est.)
exports of goods and services: 21% (2017 est.)
imports of goods and services: -37.9% (2017 est.)
note: figures may not total 100% due to rounding or gaps in data collection

Agricultural products: coconuts, vegetables, fruits, maize, beef, pork, eggs, yams, bananas, mangoes/guavas (2022)
note: top ten agricultural products based on tonnage

Industries: nickel mining and smelting

Industrial production growth rate: 4.3% (2014 est.)
note: annual % change in industrial value added based on constant local currency
comparison ranking: 64

Labor force: 119,000 (2023 est.)
note: number of people ages 15 or older who are employed or seeking work
comparison ranking: 182

Unemployment rate: 11.22% (2023 est.)
11.29% (2022 est.)
12.54% (2021 est.)
note: % of labor force seeking employment
comparison ranking: 171

Youth unemployment rate (ages 15-24): *total:* 32.6% (2023 est.)
male: 29.8% (2023 est.)
female: 35.7% (2023 est.)
note: % of labor force ages 15-24 seeking employment
comparison ranking: total 21

Remittances: 6.45% of GDP (2022 est.)
6.17% of GDP (2021 est.)
6.57% of GDP (2020 est.)
note: personal transfers and compensation between resident and non-resident individuals/households/entities

Budget: *revenues:* $1.995 billion (2015 est.)
expenditures: $1.993 billion (2015 est.)

Public debt: 6.5% of GDP (2015 est.)
comparison ranking: 199

Taxes and other revenues: 20.4% (of GDP) (2015 est.)
comparison ranking: 82

Current account balance: -$654.237 million (2016 est.)
-$1.119 billion (2015 est.)
-$1.3 billion (2014 est.)
note: balance of payments - net trade and primary/secondary income in current dollars
comparison ranking: 127

Exports: $1.92 billion (2021 est.)
$1.8 billion (2020 est.)
$1.79 billion (2019 est.)
note: balance of payments - exports of goods and services in current dollars
comparison ranking: 167

Exports - partners: China 62%, South Korea 14%, Japan 12%, Taiwan 2%, Spain 2% (2022)
note: top five export partners based on percentage share of exports

Exports - commodities: iron alloys, nickel ore, nickel, aircraft, essential oils (2022)
note: top five export commodities based on value in dollars

Imports: $2.26 billion (2021 est.)
$2.1 billion (2020 est.)
$2.48 billion (2019 est.)
note: balance of payments - imports of goods and services in current dollars
comparison ranking: 172

Imports - partners: France 30%, Australia 22%, Singapore 13%, China 6%, Malaysia 6% (2022)
note: top five import partners based on percentage share of imports

Imports - commodities: refined petroleum, coal, cars, packaged medicine, trucks (2022)
note: top five import commodities based on value in dollars

Exchange rates: Comptoirs Francais du Pacifique francs (XPF) per US dollar -

Exchange rates: 110.347 (2023 est.)
113.474 (2022 est.)
100.88 (2021 est.)
104.711 (2020 est.)
106.589 (2019 est.)

ENERGY

Electricity access: *electrification - total population:* 100% (2022 est.)

Electricity: *installed generating capacity:* 1.069 million kW (2022 est.)
consumption: 2.666 billion kWh (2022 est.)
transmission/distribution losses: 66.3 million kWh (2022 est.)
comparison rankings: transmission/distribution losses 42; consumption 142; installed generating capacity 135

Electricity generation sources: *fossil fuels:* 83.4% of total installed capacity (2022 est.)
solar: 6.5% of total installed capacity (2022 est.)
wind: 2% of total installed capacity (2022 est.)
hydroelectricity: 8.1% of total installed capacity (2022 est.)

Coal: *consumption:* 1.039 million metric tons (2022 est.)
imports: 1.039 million metric tons (2022 est.)
proven reserves: 2 million metric tons (2022 est.)

Petroleum: *refined petroleum consumption:* 16,000 bbl/day (2022 est.)

Carbon dioxide emissions: 4.806 million metric tonnes of CO_2 (2022 est.)
from coal and metallurgical coke: 2.366 million metric tonnes of CO_2 (2022 est.)
from petroleum and other liquids: 2.44 million metric tonnes of CO_2 (2022 est.)
comparison ranking: total emissions 136

Energy consumption per capita: (2019)

COMMUNICATIONS

Telephones - fixed lines: *total subscriptions:* 46,000 (2021 est.)
subscriptions per 100 inhabitants: 16 (2021 est.)
comparison ranking: total subscriptions 158

Telephones - mobile cellular: *total subscriptions:* 260,000 (2021 est.)
subscriptions per 100 inhabitants: 90 (2021 est.)
comparison ranking: total subscriptions 181

Telecommunication systems: *general assessment:* New Caledonia's telecom sector provides fixed and mobile voice services, mobile internet, fixed broadband access, and wholesale services for other ISPs; the territory is well serviced by extensive 3G and LTE networks, and is considered to have one of the highest smartphone adoption rates in the Pacific region; by 2025, smart phone penetration is expected to reach 71%; while DSL is still the dominant fixed broadband technology, and a nationwide FttP network; the South Pacific region has become a hub for submarine cable system developments in recent years, with further networks scheduled to come online later in 2021 and into 2022; these new cables are expected to increase competition in the region with regards to international capacity; in 2020, the government owned telco commissioned Alcatel Submarine Networks (ASN) to build the Gondwana-2 cable system to provide additional network capacity and complement the Gondwana-1 cable (2022)
domestic: fixed-line is 16 per 100 and mobile-cellular telephone subscribership 90 per 100 persons (2021)
international: country code - 687; landing points for the Gondwana-1 and Picot-1 providing connectivity via submarine cables around New Caledonia and to Australia; satellite earth station - 1 Intelsat (Pacific Ocean) (2019)

Broadcast media: the publicly owned French Overseas Network (RFO), which operates in France's overseas departments and territories, broadcasts over the RFO Nouvelle-Calédonie TV and radio stations; a small number of privately owned radio stations also broadcast

Internet country code: .nc

Internet users: *total:* 237,800 (2021 est.)
percent of population: 82% (2021 est.)
comparison ranking: total 178

Broadband - fixed subscriptions: *total:* 55,000 (2020 est.)
subscriptions per 100 inhabitants: 19 (2020 est.)
comparison ranking: total 142

TRANSPORTATION

National air transport system: *number of registered air carriers:* 3 (2020) (registered in France)
inventory of registered aircraft operated by air carriers: 15 (registered in France)

Airports: 21 (2024)
comparison ranking: 133

Heliports: 2 (2024)

Roadways: *total:* 5,622 km (2006)
comparison ranking: total 149

Merchant marine: *total:* 23 (2023)
by type: general cargo 5, oil tanker 1, other 17
comparison ranking: total 146

Ports: *total ports:* 3 (2024)
large: 0
medium: 0
small: 1
very small: 2
ports with oil terminals: 1
key ports: Baie de Kouaoua, Baie Ugue, Noumea

MILITARY AND SECURITY

Military and security forces: no regular military forces; France bases land, air, and naval forces on New Caledonia (Forces Armées de la Nouvelle-Calédonie, FANC) (2024)

Military - note: defense is the responsibility of France

NEW ZEALAND

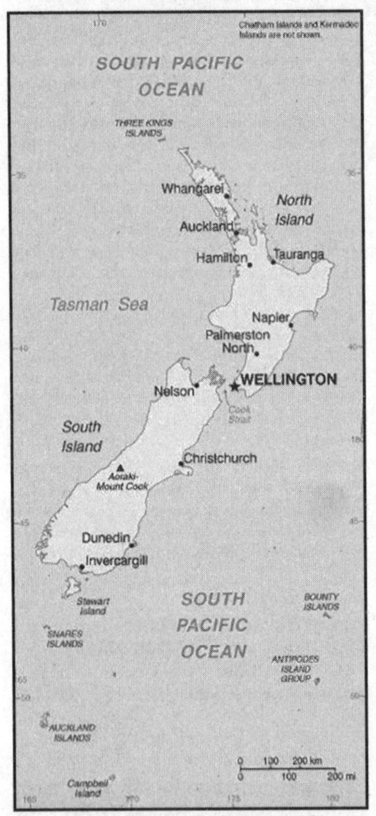

INTRODUCTION

Background: Polynesians settled New Zealand between the late 1200s and the mid-1300s. They called the land Aotearoa, which legend holds is the name of the canoe that Kupe, the first Polynesian in New Zealand, used to sail to the country; the name Aotearoa is now in widespread use as the local Maori name for the country. By the 1500s, competition for land and resources led to intermittent fighting between different Maori tribes as large game became extinct. Dutch explorer Abel TASMAN was the first European to see the islands in 1642 but left after an encounter with local Maori. British sea captain James COOK arrived in 1769, followed by whalers, sealers, and traders. The UK only nominally claimed New Zealand and included it as part of New South Wales in Australia. Concerns about increasing lawlessness led the UK to appoint its first British Resident in New Zealand in 1832, although the position had few legal powers. In 1835, some Maori tribes from the North Island declared independence. Fearing an impending French settlement and takeover, the majority of Maori chiefs signed the Treaty of Waitangi with the British in 1840. Land tenure issues stemming from the treaty are still being actively negotiated in New Zealand.

The UK declared New Zealand a separate colony in 1841 and granted limited self-government in 1852. Different traditions of authority and land use led to a series of wars between Europeans and various Maori tribes from the 1840s to the 1870s. Along with disease, these conflicts halved the Maori population. In the 1890s, New Zealand initially expressed interest in joining independence talks with Australia but ultimately opted against it and changed its status to an independent dominion in 1907. New Zealand provided more than 100,000 troops during each World War, many of whom fought as part of the Australia and New Zealand Army Corps (ANZAC). New Zealand reaffirmed its independence in 1947 and signed the Australia, New Zealand, and US (ANZUS) Treaty in 1951.

Beginning in 1984, New Zealand began to adopt nuclear-free policies, contributing to a dispute with the US over naval ship visits that led the US to suspend its defense obligations to New Zealand in 1986, but bilateral relations and military ties have been revitalized since the 2010s with new security agreements. A key challenge for Auckland that has emerged over the past decade is balancing concerns over China's growing influence in the Pacific region with its role as New Zealand's largest export destination. New Zealand has close ties with Australia based to a large extent on the two nations' common origins as British colonies and their shared military history.

GEOGRAPHY

Location: Oceania, islands in the South Pacific Ocean, southeast of Australia

Geographic coordinates: 41 00 S, 174 00 E

Map references: Oceania

Area: *total:* 268,838 sq km
land: 264,537 sq km
water: 4,301 sq km
note: includes Antipodes Islands, Auckland Islands, Bounty Islands, Campbell Island, Chatham Islands, and Kermadec Islands
comparison ranking: total 77

Area - comparative: almost twice the size of North Carolina; about the size of Colorado

Land boundaries: *total:* 0 km

Coastline: 15,134 km

Maritime claims: *territorial sea:* 12 nm
contiguous zone: 24 nm
exclusive economic zone: 200 nm
continental shelf: 200 nm or to the edge of the continental margin

Climate: temperate with sharp regional contrasts

Terrain: predominately mountainous with large coastal plains

Elevation: *highest point:* Aoraki/Mount Cook 3,724 m; note - the mountain's height was 3,764 m until 14 December 1991 when it lost about 10 m in an avalanche of rock and ice; erosion of the ice cap since then has brought the height down another 30 m
lowest point: Pacific Ocean 0 m
mean elevation: 388 m

Natural resources: natural gas, iron ore, sand, coal, timber, hydropower, gold, limestone

Land use: *agricultural land:* 43.2% (2018 est.)
arable land: 1.8% (2018 est.)
permanent crops: 0.3% (2018 est.)
permanent pasture: 41.1% (2018 est.)
forest: 31.4% (2018 est.)
other: 25.4% (2018 est.)

Irrigated land: 7,000 sq km (2014)

Major lakes (area sq km): *fresh water lake(s):* Lake Taupo - 610 sq km

Population distribution: over three-quarters of New Zealanders, including the indigenous Maori, live on the North Island, primarily in urban areas

Natural hazards: earthquakes are common, though usually not severe; volcanic activity
volcanism: significant volcanism on North Island; Ruapehu (2,797 m), which last erupted in 2007, has a history of large eruptions in the past century; Taranaki has the potential to produce dangerous avalanches and lahars; other historically active volcanoes include Okataina, Raoul Island, Tongariro, and White Island; see note 2 under "Geography - note"

Geography - note: *note 1:* consists of two main islands and a number of smaller islands; South Island, the larger main island, is the 12th largest island in the world and is divided along its length by the Southern Alps; North Island is the 14th largest island in the world and is not as mountainous, but it is marked by volcanism
note 2: New Zealand lies along the Ring of Fire, a belt of active volcanoes and earthquake epicenters bordering the Pacific Ocean; up to 90% of the world's earthquakes and some 75% of the world's volcanoes occur within the Ring of Fire
note 3: almost 90% of the population lives in cities and over three-quarters on North Island; Wellington is the southernmost national capital in the world

PEOPLE AND SOCIETY

Population: *total:* 5,161,211
male: 2,584,607
female: 2,576,604 (2024 est.)
comparison rankings: female 125; male 125; total 125

Nationality: *noun:* New Zealander(s)
adjective: New Zealand

Ethnic groups: European 64.1%, Maori 16.5%, Chinese 4.9%, Indian 4.7%, Samoan 3.9%, Tongan 1.8%, Cook Islands Maori 1.7%, English 1.5%, Filipino 1.5%, New Zealander 1%, other 13.7% (2018 est.)
note: based on the 2018 census of the usually resident population; percentages add up to more than 100% because respondents were able to identify more than one ethnic group

Languages: English (de facto official) 95.4%, Maori (de jure official) 4%, Samoan 2.2%, Northern Chinese 2%, Hindi 1.5%, French 1.2%, Yue 1.1%, New Zealand Sign Language (de jure official) 0.5%, other or not stated 17.2% (2018 est.)
note: shares sum to 124.1% due to multiple responses on the 2018 census

Religions: Christian 37.3% (Catholic 10.1%, Anglican 6.8%, Presbyterian and Congregational 5.2%, Pentecostal 1.8%, Methodist 1.6%, Church of Jesus Christ 1.2%, other 10.7%), Hindu 2.7%, Maori 1.3%, Muslim, 1.3%, Buddhist 1.1%, other

religion 1.6% (includes Judaism, Spiritualism and New Age religions, Baha'i, Asian religions other than Buddhism), no religion 48.6%, objected to answering 6.7% (2018 est.)
note: based on the 2018 census of the usually resident population; percentages add up to more than 100% because respondents were able to identify more than one religion

Age structure: *0-14 years:* 19% (male 503,120/female 475,490)
15-64 years: 64.2% (male 1,674,407/female 1,638,276)
65 years and over: 16.9% (2024 est.) (male 407,080/female 462,838)

Dependency ratios: *total dependency ratio:* 53.4
youth dependency ratio: 29
elderly dependency ratio: 24.4
potential support ratio: 4.1 (2021 est.)

Median age: *total:* 37.9 years (2024 est.)
male: 37.2 years
female: 38.6 years
comparison ranking: total 80

Population growth rate: 0.95% (2024 est.)
comparison ranking: 96

Birth rate: births/1,000 population (2024 est.)
comparison ranking: 137

Death rate: 6.9 deaths/1,000 population (2024 est.)
comparison ranking: 126

Net migration rate: 3.8 migrant(s)/1,000 population (2024 est.)
comparison ranking: 29

Population distribution: over three-quarters of New Zealanders, including the indigenous Maori, live on the North Island, primarily in urban areas

Urbanization: *urban population:* 87% of total population (2023)
rate of urbanization: 0.92% annual rate of change (2020-25 est.)

Major urban areas - population: 1.673 million Auckland, 422,000 WELLINGTON (capital) (2023)

Sex ratio: *at birth:* 1.05 male(s)/female
0-14 years: 1.06 male(s)/female
15-64 years: 1.02 male(s)/female
65 years and over: 0.88 male(s)/female
total population: 1 male(s)/female (2024 est.)

Mother's mean age at first birth: years

Maternal mortality ratio: 7 deaths/100,000 live births (2020 est.)
comparison ranking: 156

Infant mortality rate: *total:* 3.3 deaths/1,000 live births (2024 est.)
male: 3.5 deaths/1,000 live births
female: 3.1 deaths/1,000 live births
comparison ranking: total 199

Life expectancy at birth: *total population:* 82.9 years (2024 est.)
male: 81.2 years
female: 84.8 years
comparison ranking: total population 23

Total fertility rate: 1.85 children born/woman (2024 est.)
comparison ranking: 131

Gross reproduction rate: 0.9 (2024 est.)

Contraceptive prevalence rate: 79.9% (2014/15)
note: percent of women aged 16-49

Drinking water source: *improved: urban:* 100% of population
rural: 100% of population
total: 100% of population

Current health expenditure: 10% of GDP (2020)

Physician density: 3.62 physicians/1,000 population (2020)

Hospital bed density: 2.6 beds/1,000 population (2019)

Sanitation facility access: *improved: urban:* 100% of population
rural: 100% of population
total: 100% of population

Obesity - adult prevalence rate: 30.8% (2016)
comparison ranking: 22

Alcohol consumption per capita: *total:* 9.17 liters of pure alcohol (2019 est.)
beer: 3.41 liters of pure alcohol (2019 est.)
wine: 2.88 liters of pure alcohol (2019 est.)
spirits: 1.62 liters of pure alcohol (2019 est.)
other alcohols: 1.26 liters of pure alcohol (2019 est.)
comparison ranking: total 32

Tobacco use: *total:* 13.7% (2020 est.)
male: 15% (2020 est.)
female: 12.3% (2020 est.)
comparison ranking: total 111

Currently married women (ages 15-49): % (2023 est.)

Education expenditures: 6% of GDP (2020 est.)
comparison ranking: 42

School life expectancy (primary to tertiary education): *total:* 20 years
male: 20 years
female: 21 years (2020)

ENVIRONMENT

Environment - current issues: water quality and availability; rapid urbanization; deforestation; soil erosion and degradation; native flora and fauna hard-hit by invasive species

Environment - international agreements: *party to:* Antarctic-Environmental Protection, Antarctic-Marine Living Resources, Antarctic Treaty, Biodiversity, Climate Change, Climate Change-Kyoto Protocol, Climate Change-Paris Agreement, Comprehensive Nuclear Test Ban, Desertification, Endangered Species, Environmental Modification, Hazardous Wastes, Law of the Sea, Marine Dumping-London Convention, Marine Dumping-London Protocol, Nuclear Test Ban, Ozone Layer Protection, Ship Pollution, Tropical Timber 2006, Wetlands, Whaling
signed, but not ratified: Antarctic Seals, Marine Life Conservation

Climate: temperate with sharp regional contrasts

Urbanization: *urban population:* 87% of total population (2023)
rate of urbanization: 0.92% annual rate of change (2020-25 est.)

Revenue from forest resources: 0.5% of GDP (2018 est.)
comparison ranking: 65

Revenue from coal: 0.03% of GDP (2018 est.)
comparison ranking: 38

Air pollutants: *particulate matter emissions:* 8.61 micrograms per cubic meter (2019 est.)
carbon dioxide emissions: 34.38 megatons (2016 est.)
methane emissions: 34.3 megatons (2020 est.)

Waste and recycling: *municipal solid waste generated annually:* 3.405 million tons (2016 est.)

Major lakes (area sq km): *fresh water lake(s):* Lake Taupo - 610 sq km

Total water withdrawal: *municipal:* 500 million cubic meters (2020 est.)
industrial: 1.18 billion cubic meters (2020 est.)
agricultural: 3.2 billion cubic meters (2020 est.)

Total renewable water resources: 327 billion cubic meters (2020 est.)

GOVERNMENT

Country name: *conventional long form:* none
conventional short form: New Zealand
abbreviation: NZ
etymology: Dutch explorer Abel TASMAN was the first European to reach New Zealand in 1642; he named it Staten Landt, but Dutch cartographers renamed it Nova Zeelandia in 1645 after the Dutch province of Zeeland; British explorer Captain James COOK subsequently anglicized the name to New Zealand when he mapped the islands in 1769

Government type: parliamentary democracy under a constitutional monarchy; a Commonwealth realm

Capital: *name:* Wellington
geographic coordinates: 41 18 S, 174 47 E
time difference: UTC+12 (17 hours ahead of Washington, DC, during Standard Time)
daylight saving time: +1hr, begins last Sunday in September; ends first Sunday in April
time zone note: New Zealand has two time zones: New Zealand standard time (UTC+12) and Chatham Islands time (45 minutes in advance of New Zealand standard time; UTC+12:45)
etymology: named in 1840 after Arthur WELLESLEY, the first Duke of Wellington and victorious general at the Battle of Waterloo

Administrative divisions: 16 regions and 1 territory*; Auckland, Bay of Plenty, Canterbury, Chatham Islands*, Gisborne, Hawke's Bay, Manawatu-Wanganui, Marlborough, Nelson, Northland, Otago, Southland, Taranaki, Tasman, Waikato, Wellington, West Coast

Dependent areas: Tokelau (1)

Independence: 26 September 1907 (from the UK)

National holiday: Waitangi Day (Treaty of Waitangi established British sovereignty over New Zealand), 6 February (1840); Anzac Day (commemorated as the anniversary of the landing of troops of the Australian and New Zealand Army Corps during World War I at Gallipoli, Turkey), 25 April (1915)

Legal system: common law system, based on English model, with special legislation and land courts for the Maori

Constitution: *history:* New Zealand has no single constitution document; the Constitution Act 1986, effective 1 January 1987, includes only part of the uncodified constitution; others include a collection of statutes or "acts of Parliament," the Treaty of Waitangi, Orders in Council, letters patent, court decisions, and unwritten conventions
amendments: proposed as bill by Parliament or by referendum called either by the government or by citizens; passage of a bill as an act normally requires two separate readings with committee reviews in between to make changes and corrections, a third reading approved by the House of Representatives membership or by the majority of votes in a referendum, and assent of the governor-general; passage

of amendments to reserved constitutional provisions affecting the term of Parliament, electoral districts, and voting restrictions requires approval by 75% of the House membership or the majority of votes in a referendum; amended many times, last in 2020

International law organization participation: accepts compulsory ICJ jurisdiction with reservations; accepts ICCt jurisdiction

Citizenship: *citizenship by birth:* no
citizenship by descent only: at least one parent must be a citizen of New Zealand
dual citizenship recognized: yes
residency requirement for naturalization: 3 years

Suffrage: 18 years of age; universal

Executive branch: *chief of state:* King CHARLES III (since 8 September 2022); represented by Governor-General Dame Cindy KIRO (since 21 October 2021)
head of government: Prime Minister Christopher LUXON (since 27 November 2023)
cabinet: Executive Council appointed by the governor-general on the recommendation of the prime minister
elections/appointments: the monarchy is hereditary; governor-general appointed by the monarch on the advice of the prime minister; following legislative elections, the leader of the majority party or majority coalition usually appointed prime minister by the governor-general; deputy prime minister appointed by the governor-general
note: according to Prime Minister LUXON, the Winston PETERS of the New Zealand First Party would be the deputy prime minister in the first half of the term while Act party leader, David SEYMOUR, would take the role for the second half of the term

Legislative branch: *description:* unicameral House of Representatives - commonly called Parliament (121 seats for 2023-26 term); 72 members directly elected in 65 single-seat constituencies and 7 Maori constituencies by simple majority vote and 49 directly elected by closed party-list proportional representation vote; members serve 3-year terms)
elections: last held on 14 October 2023 (next scheduled for October 2026)
election results: percent of vote by party - National Party 38.1%, Labor Party 26.9%, Green Party 11.6%, ACT Party 8.6%, New Zealand First 6.1%; Maori Party 3.1%; seats by party - National Party 48, Labor Party 34, Green Party 15, ACT Party 11, New Zealand First 8, Maori Party 6; composition - 67 men, 56 women; percentage of women 45.5%

Judicial branch: *highest court(s):* Supreme Court (consists of 5 justices, including the chief justice); note - the Supreme Court in 2004 replaced the Judicial Committee of the Privy Council (in London) as the final appeals court
judge selection and term of office: justices appointed by the governor-general upon the recommendation of the attorney- general; justices appointed until compulsory retirement at age 70
subordinate courts: Court of Appeal; High Court; tribunals and authorities; district courts; specialized courts for issues related to employment, environment, family, Maori lands, youth, military; tribunals

Political parties: ACT New Zealand
Green Party
New Zealand First Party or NZ First
New Zealand Labor Party
New Zealand National Party
Te Pati Maori

International organization participation: ADB, ANZUS, APEC, ARF, ASEAN (dialogue partner), Australia Group, BIS, C, CD, CP, EAS, EBRD, FAO, FATF, IAEA, IBRD, ICAO, ICC (national committees), ICCt, ICRM, IDA, IEA, IFAD, IFC, IFRCS, IHO, ILO, IMF, IMO, IMSO, Interpol, IOC, IOM, IPU, ISO, ITSO, ITU, ITUC (NGOs), MIGA, NSG, OECD, OPCW, Pacific Alliance (observer), Paris Club (associate), PCA, PIF, SICA (observer), Sparteca, SPC, UN, UNCTAD, UNESCO, UNHCR, UNIDO, UNMISS, UNTSO, UPU, Wassenaar Arrangement, WCO, WFTU (NGOs), WHO, WIPO, WMO, WTO

Diplomatic representation in the US: *chief of mission:* Ambassador Rosemary BANKS (since 17 June 2024)
chancery: 37 Observatory Circle NW, Washington, DC 20008
telephone: [1] (202) 328-4800
FAX: [1] (202) 667-5277
email address and website:
wshinfo@mfat.govt.nz
https://www.mfat.govt.nz/en/countries-and-regions/americas/united-states-of-america/
consulate(s) general: Honolulu, Los Angeles, New York

Diplomatic representation from the US: *chief of mission:* Ambassador Thomas Stewart UDALL (since 1 December 2021); note - also accredited to Samoa
embassy: 29 Fitzherbert Terrace, Thorndon, Wellington 6011
mailing address: 4370 Auckland Place, Washington DC 20521-4370
telephone: [64] (4) 462-6000
FAX: [64] (4) 499-0490
email address and website:
AucklandACS@state.gov
https://nz.usembassy.gov/
consulate(s) general: Auckland

Flag description: blue with the flag of the UK in the upper hoist-side quadrant with four red five-pointed stars edged in white centered in the outer half of the flag; the stars represent the Southern Cross constellation

National symbol(s): Southern Cross constellation (four, five-pointed stars), kiwi (bird), silver fern; national colors: black, white, red (ochre)

National anthem: *name:* "God Defend New Zealand"
lyrics/music: Thomas BRACKEN [English], Thomas Henry SMITH [Maori]/John Joseph WOODS
note: adopted 1940 as national song, adopted 1977 as co-national anthem; New Zealand has two national anthems with equal status; as a commonwealth realm, in addition to "God Defend New Zealand," "God Save the King" serves as a royal anthem (see United Kingdom); "God Save the King" normally played only when a member of the royal family or the governor-general is present; in all other cases, "God Defend New Zealand" is played

National heritage: *total World Heritage Sites:* 3 (2 natural, 1 mixed)
selected World Heritage Site locales: Te Wahipounamu – South West New Zealand (n); Tongariro National Park (m); New Zealand Sub-Antarctic Islands (n)

ECONOMY

Economic overview: high-income, globally integrated Pacific island economy; strong agriculture, manufacturing, and tourism sectors; reliant on Chinese market for exports; slow recovery from post-COVID recession and inflation; challenges of fiscal deficits, below-average productivity, and curbing greenhouse gas emissions

Real GDP (purchasing power parity): $254.77 billion (2023 est.)
$253.17 billion (2022 est.)
$246.334 billion (2021 est.)
note: data in 2021 dollars
comparison ranking: 68

Real GDP growth rate: 0.63% (2023 est.)
2.77% (2022 est.)
4.55% (2021 est.)
note: annual GDP % growth based on constant local currency
comparison ranking: 176

Real GDP per capita: $48,800 (2023 est.)
$49,500 (2022 est.)
$48,200 (2021 est.)
note: data in 2021 dollars
comparison ranking: 44

GDP (official exchange rate): $253.466 billion (2023 est.)
note: data in current dollars at official exchange rate

Inflation rate (consumer prices): 5.73% (2023 est.)
7.17% (2022 est.)
3.94% (2021 est.)
note: annual % change based on consumer prices
comparison ranking: 121

Credit ratings: Fitch rating: AA (2011)

Moody's rating: Aaa (2002)

Standard & Poors rating: AA (2011)
note: The year refers to the year in which the current credit rating was first obtained.

GDP - composition, by sector of origin: *agriculture:* 5.8% (2021 est.)
industry: 19% (2021 est.)
services: 67.1% (2021 est.)
note: figures may not total 100% due to non-allocated consumption not captured in sector-reported data
comparison rankings: services 50; industry 142; agriculture 109

GDP - composition, by end use: *household consumption:* 58.2% (2022 est.)
government consumption: 21.1% (2022 est.)
investment in fixed capital: 25.4% (2022 est.)
investment in inventories: 0.4% (2022 est.)
exports of goods and services: 24.4% (2022 est.)
imports of goods and services: -29.7% (2022 est.)
note: figures may not total 100% due to rounding or gaps in data collection

Agricultural products: milk, beef, kiwifruit, apples, grapes, lamb/mutton, potatoes, wheat, barley, onions (2022)
note: top ten agricultural products based on tonnage

Industries: agriculture, forestry, fishing, logs and wood articles, manufacturing, mining, construction, financial services, real estate services, tourism

Industrial production growth rate: -2.56% (2022 est.)
note: annual % change in industrial value added based on constant local currency
comparison ranking: 187

Labor force: 3.068 million (2023 est.)
note: number of people ages 15 or older who are employed or seeking work
comparison ranking: 109

Unemployment rate: 3.74% (2023 est.)

3.3% (2022 est.)
3.78% (2021 est.)
note: % of labor force seeking employment
comparison ranking: 72

Youth unemployment rate (ages 15-24): *total:* 10.7% (2023 est.)
male: 10.9% (2023 est.)
female: 10.5% (2023 est.)
note: % of labor force ages 15-24 seeking employment
comparison ranking: total 126

Average household expenditures: *on food:* 12.5% of household expenditures (2022 est.)
on alcohol and tobacco: 4.9% of household expenditures (2022 est.)

Remittances: 0.24% of GDP (2023 est.)
0.23% of GDP (2022 est.)
0.26% of GDP (2021 est.)
note: personal transfers and compensation between resident and non-resident individuals/households/entities

Budget: *revenues:* $83.157 billion (2022 est.)
expenditures: $88.64 billion (2022 est.)
note: central government revenues (excluding grants) and expenses converted to US dollars at average official exchange rate for year indicated

Public debt: 54.57% of GDP (2022 est.)
note: central government debt as a % of GDP
comparison ranking: 89

Taxes and other revenues: 29.93% (of GDP) (2022 est.)
note: central government tax revenue as a % of GDP
comparison ranking: 25

Current account balance: -$16.982 billion (2023 est.)
-$21.627 billion (2022 est.)
-$14.804 billion (2021 est.)
note: balance of payments - net trade and primary/secondary income in current dollars
comparison ranking: 199

Exports: $59.043 billion (2023 est.)
$57.485 billion (2022 est.)
$54.923 billion (2021 est.)
note: balance of payments - exports of goods and services in current dollars
comparison ranking: 62

Exports - partners: China 28%, Australia 11%, US 11%, Japan 6%, South Korea 4% (2022)
note: top five export partners based on percentage share of exports

Exports - commodities: milk, beef, wood, sheep and goat meat, butter (2022)
note: top five export commodities based on value in dollars

Imports: $68.429 billion (2023 est.)
$71.35 billion (2022 est.)
$62.984 billion (2021 est.)
note: balance of payments - imports of goods and services in current dollars
comparison ranking: 59

Imports - partners: China 21%, Australia 14%, US 8%, South Korea 7%, Singapore 6% (2022)
note: top five import partners based on percentage share of imports

Imports - commodities: refined petroleum, cars, plastic products, garments, trucks (2022)
note: top five import commodities based on value in dollars

Reserves of foreign exchange and gold: $15.487 billion (2023 est.)
$14.4 billion (2022 est.)
$16.114 billion (2021 est.)
note: holdings of gold (year-end prices)/foreign exchange/special drawing rights in current dollars
comparison ranking: 65

Exchange rates: New Zealand dollars (NZD) per US dollar -

Exchange rates: 1.628 (2023 est.)
1.577 (2022 est.)
1.414 (2021 est.)
1.542 (2020 est.)
1.518 (2019 est.)

ENERGY

Electricity access: *electrification - total population:* 100% (2022 est.)

Electricity: *installed generating capacity:* 10.412 million kW (2022 est.)
consumption: 41.466 billion kWh (2022 est.)
transmission/distribution losses: 2.712 billion kWh (2022 est.)
comparison rankings: transmission/distribution losses 133; consumption 58; installed generating capacity 66

Electricity generation sources: *fossil fuels:* 13.2% of total installed capacity (2022 est.)
solar: 0.5% of total installed capacity (2022 est.)
wind: 6.5% of total installed capacity (2022 est.)
hydroelectricity: 58.5% of total installed capacity (2022 est.)
geothermal: 17.7% of total installed capacity (2022 est.)
biomass and waste: 3.5% of total installed capacity (2022 est.)

Coal: *production:* 3.036 million metric tons (2022 est.)
consumption: 2.441 million metric tons (2022 est.)
exports: 1.278 million metric tons (2022 est.)
imports: 727,000 metric tons (2022 est.)
proven reserves: 7.575 billion metric tons (2022 est.)

Petroleum: *total petroleum production:* 12,000 bbl/day (2023 est.)
refined petroleum consumption: 154,000 bbl/day (2023 est.)
crude oil estimated reserves: 40.993 million barrels (2021 est.)

Natural gas: *production:* 3.77 billion cubic meters (2022 est.)
consumption: 3.819 billion cubic meters (2022 est.)
proven reserves: 31.149 billion cubic meters (2021 est.)

Carbon dioxide emissions: 31.998 million metric tonnes of CO2 (2022 est.)
from coal and metallurgical coke: 3.687 million metric tonnes of CO2 (2022 est.)
from petroleum and other liquids: 21.018 million metric tonnes of CO2 (2022 est.)
from consumed natural gas: 7.293 million metric tonnes of CO2 (2022 est.)
comparison ranking: total emissions 71

Energy consumption per capita: 120.219 million Btu/person (2022 est.)
comparison ranking: 36

COMMUNICATIONS

Telephones - fixed lines: *total subscriptions:* 757,000 (2022 est.)
subscriptions per 100 inhabitants: 15 (2022 est.)
comparison ranking: total subscriptions 78

Telephones - mobile cellular: *total subscriptions:* 5.947 million (2022 est.)
subscriptions per 100 inhabitants: 115 (2022 est.)
comparison ranking: total subscriptions 119

Telecommunication systems: *general assessment:* the growth areas in in New Zealand's telecom market have been in mobile broadband and fiber; New Zealand's mobile market continues to undergo significant developments; the coverage of LTE networks has been supported by the Rural Broadband Initiative rollout, which added a significant number of mobile sites to new or underserved areas; the market is undergoing additional consolidation; offering fixed and mobile services
(2023)
domestic: fixed-line roughly 13 per 100 and mobile-cellular telephone subscribership 114 per 100 persons (2021)
international: country code - 64; landing points for the Southern Cross NEXT, Aqualink, Nelson-Levin, SCCN and Hawaiki submarine cable system providing links to Australia, Fiji, American Samoa, Kiribati, Samo, Tokelau, US and around New Zealand; satellite earth stations - 8 (1 Inmarsat - Pacific Ocean, 7 other) (2019)

Broadcast media: state-owned Television New Zealand operates multiple TV networks and state-owned Radio New Zealand operates 3 radio networks and an external shortwave radio service to the South Pacific region; a small number of national commercial TV and radio stations and many regional commercial television and radio stations are available; cable and satellite TV systems are available, as are a range of streaming services (2019)

Internet country code: .nz

Internet users: *total:* 4.896 million (2021 est.)
percent of population: 96% (2021 est.)
comparison ranking: total 95

Broadband - fixed subscriptions: *total:* 1,764,984 (2020 est.)
subscriptions per 100 inhabitants: 37 (2020 est.)
comparison ranking: total 61

TRANSPORTATION

National air transport system: *number of registered air carriers:* 15 (2020)
inventory of registered aircraft operated by air carriers: 199
annual passenger traffic on registered air carriers: 17,249,049 (2018)
annual freight traffic on registered air carriers: 1,349,300,000 (2018) mt-km

Civil aircraft registration country code prefix: ZK

Airports: 202 (2024)
comparison ranking: 31

Heliports: 62 (2024)

Pipelines: 331 km condensate, 2,500 km gas, 172 km liquid petroleum gas, 288 km oil, 198 km refined products (2018)

Railways: *total:* 4,128 km (2018)
narrow gauge: 4,128 km (2018) 1.067-m gauge (506 km electrified)
comparison ranking: total 42

Roadways: *total:* 94,000 km
paved: 61,600 km (includes 199 km of expressways)
unpaved: 32,400 km (2017)
comparison ranking: total 54

Merchant marine: *total:* 117 (2023)

by type: container ship 2, general cargo 12, oil tanker 3, other 100
comparison ranking: total 84

Ports: *total ports:* 22 (2024)
large: 2
medium: 1
small: 10
very small: 9
ports with oil terminals: 14
key ports: Auckland, Bluff Harbor, Gisborne, Manukau Harbor, Napier, Nelson, New Plymouth, Otago Harbor, Picton, Tauranga, Timaru, Wellington, Whangarei

MILITARY AND SECURITY

Military and security forces: New Zealand Defense Force (NZDF): New Zealand Army, Royal New Zealand Navy, Royal New Zealand Air Force (2024)
note: the New Zealand Police, under the Minister of Police, are responsible for internal security

Military expenditures: 1.3% of GDP (2023)
1.3% of GDP (2022)
1.3% of GDP (2021)
1.5% of GDP (2020)
1.4% of GDP (2019)
comparison ranking: 106

Military and security service personnel strengths: approximately 8,800 active-duty (Regular Force) troops (4,300 Army; 2,100 Navy; 2,400 Air Force) (2024)
note: the total NZDF complement is about 15,300 including the Regular Force, Reserves, and civilians

Military equipment inventories and acquisitions: the NZDF's inventory is comprised of domestically produced and Western-supplied weapons and equipment, including from Australia, Canada, the US, and the UK (2024)

Military service age and obligation: 17 years of age for voluntary military service for men and women; soldiers cannot be deployed until the age of 18; no conscription (2024)
note: New Zealand opened up all military occupations to women in 2000; as of 2024, women accounted for about 20% of Regular Force personnel

Military deployments: small numbers of NZ military personnel are deployed on a variety of international missions in Africa, Antarctica, the Asia- Pacific region, and the Middle East (2024)

Military - note: the NZDF is a small military with considerable overseas experience; it supports the country's national security objectives by protecting New Zealand's sovereignty, promoting its interests, safeguarding peace and security, and conducting peacekeeping, humanitarian, and other international missions
New Zealand is a member of the Five Powers Defense Arrangements (FPDA), a series of mutual assistance agreements reached in 1971 embracing Australia, Malaysia, New Zealand, Singapore, and the UK; the FPDA commits the members to consult with one another in the event or threat of an armed attack on any of the members and to mutually decide what measures should be taken, jointly or separately; there is no specific obligation to intervene militarily
New Zealand has been part of the Australia, New Zealand, and US Security (ANZUS) Treaty since 1951; however, the US suspended its ANZUS security obligations to New Zealand in 1986 after New Zealand implemented a policy barring nuclear-armed and nuclear-powered warships from its ports; the US and New Zealand signed the Wellington Declaration in 2010, which reaffirmed close ties between the two countries, and in 2012 signed the Washington Declaration, which provided a framework for future security cooperation and defense dialogues; in 2016, a US naval ship conducted the first bilateral warship visit to New Zealand since the 1980s; New Zealand has Major Non-NATO Ally (MNNA) status with the US, a designation under US law that provides foreign partners with certain benefits in the areas of defense trade and security cooperation (2024)

SPACE

Space agency/agencies: New Zealand Space Agency (NZSA; established 2016 under the Ministry of Business, Innovation, and Employment); Center for Space Science and Technology (CSST; established 2017) (2024)

Space launch site(s): Mahia Peninsula Launch Complex (Hawke's Bay) (2024)

Space program overview: the New Zealand space sector model is mostly based on commercial space; NZSA and CSST primarily focus on developing space policy and strategy, bringing commercial space talent to New Zealand, and encouraging the commercial development of space technologies, particularly satellites and satellite/space launch vehicles (SLV); manufactures and launches satellites; builds and launches commercial SLVs; researches and develops a range of other space-related technologies, including propulsion systems; has a national space strategy; participates in international space programs and partners with a range of foreign space agencies and industries, including those of Australia, Canada, the EU and its member states, the European Space Agency (ESA) and its member states, South Africa, and the US; has a small, but growing commercial space sector (2024)
note: further details about the key activities, programs, and milestones of the country's space program, as well as government spending estimates on the space sector, appear in the Space Programs reference guide

TERRORISM

Terrorist group(s): Islamic State of Iraq and ash-Sham (ISIS)
note: details about the history, aims, leadership, organization, areas of operation, tactics, targets, weapons, size, and sources of support of the group(s) appear(s) in the Terrorism reference guide

TRANSNATIONAL ISSUES

Refugees and internally displaced persons: *stateless persons:* 5 (2022)

Illicit drugs: significant consumer of amphetamines

NICARAGUA

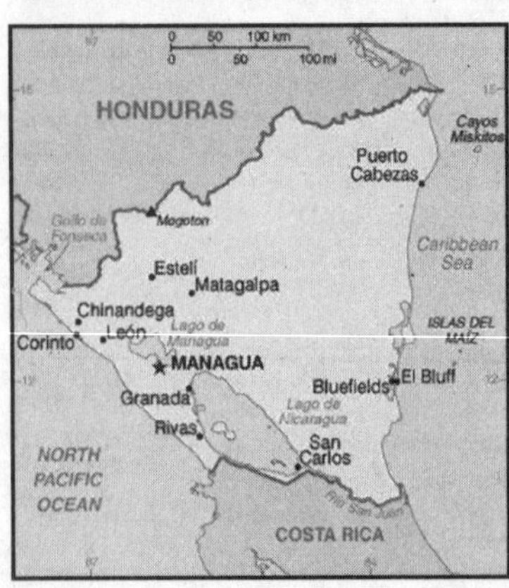

INTRODUCTION

Background: The Pacific coast of Nicaragua was settled as a Spanish colony in the early 16th century. Independence from Spain was declared in 1821, and the country became an independent republic in 1838. Britain occupied the Caribbean Coast in the first half of the 19th century, but gradually ceded control of the region in subsequent decades. By 1978, violent opposition to governmental manipulation and corruption resulted in a short-lived civil war that brought a civil-military coalition to power in 1979, spearheaded by Marxist Sandinista guerrillas led by Daniel ORTEGA Saavedra. Nicaraguan aid to leftist rebels in El Salvador prompted the US to sponsor anti-Sandinista Contra guerrillas through much of the 1980s.

After losing free and fair elections in 1990, 1996, and 2001, ORTEGA was elected president in 2006, 2011, 2016, and most recently in 2021. Municipal, regional, and national-level elections since 2008 have been marred by widespread irregularities. Democratic institutions have lost their independence under the ORTEGA regime as the president has assumed full control over all branches of government, as well as cracking down on a nationwide pro-democracy protest movement in 2018 and shuttering over 3,300 civil society organizations between 2018 and 2024. In the lead-up to the 2021 presidential election, authorities arrested over 40 individuals linked to the opposition, including presidential candidates, private sector leaders, NGO workers, human rights defenders, and journalists. Only five lesser-known presidential candidates from mostly small parties allied to ORTEGA's Sandinistas were allowed to run against ORTEGA. He then awarded the Sandinistas control of all 153 of Nicaraguan municipalities in the 2022 municipal elections, consolidating one-party rule.

GEOGRAPHY

Location: Central America, bordering both the Caribbean Sea and the North Pacific Ocean, between Costa Rica and Honduras

Geographic coordinates: 13 00 N, 85 00 W

Map references: Central America and the Caribbean

Area: *total:* 130,370 sq km
land: 119,990 sq km
water: 10,380 sq km
comparison ranking: total 98

Area - comparative: slightly larger than Pennsylvania; slightly smaller than New York state

Land boundaries: *total:* 1,253 km
border countries (2): Costa Rica 313 km; Honduras 940 km

Coastline: 910 km

Maritime claims: *territorial sea:* 12 nm
contiguous zone: 24 nm
continental shelf: natural prolongation

Climate: tropical in lowlands, cooler in highlands

Terrain: extensive Atlantic coastal plains rising to central interior mountains; narrow Pacific coastal plain interrupted by volcanoes

Elevation: *highest point:* Mogoton 2,085 m
lowest point: Pacific Ocean 0 m
mean elevation: 298 m

Natural resources: gold, silver, copper, tungsten, lead, zinc, timber, fish

Land use: *agricultural land:* 42.2% (2018 est.)
arable land: 12.5% (2018 est.)
permanent crops: 2.5% (2018 est.)
permanent pasture: 27.2% (2018 est.)
forest: 25.3% (2018 est.)
other: 32.5% (2018 est.)

Irrigated land: 1,990 sq km (2012)

Major lakes (area sq km): *fresh water lake(s):* Lago de Nicaragua - 8,150 sq km; Lago de Managua - 1,040 sq km

Population distribution: the overwhelming majority of the population resides in the western half of the country, with much of the urban growth centered in the capital city of Managua; coastal areas also show large population clusters

Natural hazards: destructive earthquakes; volcanoes; landslides; extremely susceptible to hurricanes
volcanism: significant volcanic activity; Cerro Negro (728 m), which last erupted in 1999, is one of Nicaragua's most active volcanoes; its lava flows and ash have been known to cause significant damage to farmland and buildings; other historically active volcanoes include Concepcion, Cosiguina, Las Pilas, Masaya, Momotombo, San Cristobal, and Telica

Geography - note: largest country in Central America; contains the largest freshwater body in Central America, Lago de Nicaragua

PEOPLE AND SOCIETY

Population: *total:* 6,676,948
male: 3,273,900
female: 3,403,048 (2024 est.)
comparison rankings: female 109; male 108; total 108

Nationality: *noun:* Nicaraguan(s)
adjective: Nicaraguan

Ethnic groups: Mestizo (mixed Indigenous and White) 69%, White 17%, Black 9%, Indigenous 5%

Languages: Spanish (official) 99.5%, Indigenous 0.3%, Portuguese 0.1%, other 0.1% (2020 est.)
major-language sample(s):
La Libreta Informativa del Mundo, la fuente indispensable de información básica. (Spanish)
note: English and indigenous languages found on the Caribbean coast

Religions: Roman Catholic 44.9%, Protestant 38.7% (Evangelical 38.2, Adventist 0.5%), other 1.2%, (includes Jehovah's Witness and Church of Jesus Christ), believer but not belonging to a church 1%, agnostic or atheist 0.4%, none 13.7%, unspecified 0.2% (2020 est.)

Demographic profile: Despite being one of the poorest countries in Latin America, Nicaragua has improved its access to potable water and sanitation and has ameliorated its life expectancy, infant and child mortality, and immunization rates. However, income distribution is very uneven, and the poor, agriculturalists, and indigenous people continue to have less access to healthcare services. Nicaragua's total fertility rate has fallen from around 6 children per woman in 1980 to below replacement level today, but the high birth rate among adolescents perpetuates a cycle of poverty and low educational attainment.
Nicaraguans emigrate primarily to Costa Rica and to a lesser extent the United States. Nicaraguan men have been migrating seasonally to Costa Rica to harvest bananas and coffee since the early 20th century. Political turmoil, civil war, and natural disasters from the 1970s through the 1990s dramatically increased the flow of refugees and permanent migrants seeking jobs, higher wages, and better social and healthcare benefits. Since 2000, Nicaraguan emigration to Costa Rica has slowed and stabilized. Today roughly 300,000 Nicaraguans are permanent residents of Costa Rica - about 75% of the foreign population - and thousands more migrate seasonally for work, many illegally.

Age structure: *0-14 years:* 25.1% (male 855,256/female 818,714)
15-64 years: 68.9% (male 2,240,297/female 2,360,244)
65 years and over: 6% (2024 est.) (male 178,347/female 224,090)

Dependency ratios: *total dependency ratio:* 54.4
youth dependency ratio: 46.4
elderly dependency ratio: 8
potential support ratio: 12.6 (2021 est.)

Median age: *total:* 29 years (2024 est.)
male: 28.1 years
female: 29.9 years
comparison ranking: total 147

Population growth rate: 0.95% (2024 est.)
comparison ranking: 97

Birth rate: 16.4 births/1,000 population (2024 est.)
comparison ranking: 97

Death rate: 5.1 deaths/1,000 population (2024 est.)
comparison ranking: 191

Net migration rate: -1.8 migrant(s)/1,000 population (2024 est.)
comparison ranking: 166

Population distribution: the overwhelming majority of the population resides in the western half of the country, with much of the urban growth centered in the capital city of Managua; coastal areas also show large population clusters

Urbanization: *urban population:* 59.8% of total population (2023)
rate of urbanization: 1.45% annual rate of change (2020-25 est.)

Major urban areas - population: 1.095 million MANAGUA (capital) (2023)

Sex ratio: *at birth:* 1.05 male(s)/female
0-14 years: 1.04 male(s)/female
15-64 years: 0.95 male(s)/female
65 years and over: 0.8 male(s)/female
total population: 0.96 male(s)/female (2024 est.)

Mother's mean age at first birth: 19.2 years (2011/12 est.)
note: data represents median age at first birth among women 25-29

Maternal mortality ratio: 78 deaths/100,000 live births (2020 est.)
comparison ranking: 74

Infant mortality rate: *total:* 14.4 deaths/1,000 live births (2024 est.)
male: 15.9 deaths/1,000 live births
female: 12.8 deaths/1,000 live births
comparison ranking: total 96

Life expectancy at birth: *total population:* 74.7 years (2024 est.)
male: 73.2 years
female: 76.4 years
comparison ranking: total population 139

Total fertility rate: 1.83 children born/woman (2024 est.)
comparison ranking: 134

Gross reproduction rate: 0.89 (2024 est.)

Contraceptive prevalence rate: 80.4% (2011/12)

Drinking water source: *improved: urban:* 97.5% of population
rural: 62.6% of population
total: 83.2% of population
unimproved: urban: 2.5% of population
rural: 37.4% of population
total: 16.8% of population (2020 est.)

Current health expenditure: 8.6% of GDP (2020)

Physician density: 1.67 physicians/1,000 population (2018)

Hospital bed density: 0.9 beds/1,000 population (2017)

Sanitation facility access: *improved: urban:* 89.9% of population
rural: 66.5% of population
total: 80.3% of population
unimproved: urban: 10.1% of population
rural: 33.5% of population
total: 19.7% of population (2020 est.)

Obesity - adult prevalence rate: 23.7% (2016)
comparison ranking: 63

Alcohol consumption per capita: *total:* 3.69 liters of pure alcohol (2019 est.)
beer: 1.57 liters of pure alcohol (2019 est.)
wine: 0.02 liters of pure alcohol (2019 est.)
spirits: 2.1 liters of pure alcohol (2019 est.)
other alcohols: 0 liters of pure alcohol (2019 est.)
comparison ranking: total 101

Currently married women (ages 15-49): 56% (2023 est.)

Education expenditures: 4.6% of GDP (2020 est.)
comparison ranking: 96

Literacy: *definition:* age 15 and over can read and write

total population: 82.6%
male: 82.4%
female: 82.8% (2015)

ENVIRONMENT

Environment - current issues: deforestation; soil erosion; water pollution; drought

Environment - international agreements: *party to:* Biodiversity, Climate Change, Climate Change-Kyoto Protocol, Climate Change-Paris Agreement, Comprehensive Nuclear Test Ban, Desertification, Endangered Species, Environmental Modification, Hazardous Wastes, Law of the Sea, Nuclear Test Ban, Ozone Layer Protection, Ship Pollution, Wetlands, Whaling
signed, but not ratified: none of the selected agreements

Climate: tropical in lowlands, cooler in highlands

Urbanization: *urban population:* 59.8% of total population (2023)
rate of urbanization: 1.45% annual rate of change (2020-25 est.)

Revenue from forest resources: 1.26% of GDP (2018 est.)
comparison ranking: 49

Revenue from coal: 0% of GDP (2018 est.)
comparison ranking: 98

Air pollutants: *particulate matter emissions:* 16 micrograms per cubic meter (2019 est.)
carbon dioxide emissions: 5.59 megatons (2016 est.)
methane emissions: 6.46 megatons (2020 est.)

Waste and recycling: *municipal solid waste generated annually:* 1,528,816 tons (2010 est.)

Major lakes (area sq km): *fresh water lake(s):* Lago de Nicaragua - 8,150 sq km; Lago de Managua - 1,040 sq km

Total water withdrawal: *municipal:* 286 million cubic meters (2020 est.)
industrial: 50 million cubic meters (2020 est.)
agricultural: 1.08 billion cubic meters (2020 est.)

Total renewable water resources: 164.52 billion cubic meters (2020 est.)

Geoparks: *total global geoparks and regional networks:* 1
global geoparks and regional networks: Rio Coco (2023)

GOVERNMENT

Country name: *conventional long form:* Republic of Nicaragua
conventional short form: Nicaragua
local long form: República de Nicaragua
local short form: Nicaragua
etymology: Nicarao was the name of the largest indigenous settlement at the time of Spanish arrival; conquistador Gil GONZALEZ Davila, who explored the area (1622-23), combined the name of the community with the Spanish word "agua" (water), referring to the two large lakes in the west of the country (Lake Managua and Lake Nicaragua)

Government type: presidential republic

Capital: *name:* Managua
geographic coordinates: 12 08 N, 86 15 W
time difference: UTC-6 (1 hour behind Washington, DC, during Standard Time)
etymology: may derive from the indigenous Nahuatl term "mana-ahuac," which translates as "adjacent to the water" or a site "surrounded by water"; the city is situated on the southwestern shore of Lake Managua

Administrative divisions: 15 departments (departamentos, singular - departamento) and 2 autonomous regions* (regiones autonomistas, singular - region autonoma); Boaco, Carazo, Chinandega, Chontales, Costa Caribe Norte*, Costa Caribe Sur*, Esteli, Granada, Jinotega, Leon, Madriz, Managua, Masaya, Matagalpa, Nueva Segovia, Rio San Juan, Rivas

Independence: 15 September 1821 (from Spain)

National holiday: Independence Day, 15 September (1821)

Legal system: civil law system; Supreme Court may review administrative acts

Constitution: *history:* several previous; latest adopted 19 November 1986, effective 9 January 1987
amendments: proposed by the president of the republic or assent of at least half of the National Assembly membership; passage requires approval by 60% of the membership of the next elected Assembly and promulgation by the president of the republic; amended several times, last in 2021

International law organization participation: accepts compulsory ICJ jurisdiction with reservations; non-party state to the ICCt

Citizenship: *citizenship by birth:* yes
citizenship by descent only: yes
dual citizenship recognized: no, except in cases where bilateral agreements exist
residency requirement for naturalization: 4 years

Suffrage: 16 years of age; universal

Executive branch: *chief of state:* President Jose Daniel ORTEGA Saavedra (since 10 January 2007)
head of government: President Jose Daniel ORTEGA Saavedra (since 10 January 2007)
cabinet: Council of Ministers appointed by the president
elections/appointments: president and vice president directly elected on the same ballot by qualified plurality vote for a 5-year term (no term limits); election last held on 7 November 2021 (next to be held on 1 November 2026)
election results:
2021: Jose Daniel ORTEGA Saavedra reelected president for a fourth consecutive term; percent of vote - Jose Daniel ORTEGA Saavedra (FSLN) 75.9%, Walter ESPINOZA (PLC) 14.3%, Guillermo OSORNO (CCN) 3.3%, Marcelo MONTIEL (ALN) 3.1%, other 3.4%
2016: Jose Daniel ORTEGA Saavedra reelected president for a third consecutive term; percent of vote - Jose Daniel ORTEGA Saavedra (FSLN) 72.4%, Maximino RODRIGUEZ (PLC) 15%, Jose del Carmen ALVARADO (PLI) 4.5%, Saturnino CERRATO Hodgson (ALN) 4.3%, other 3.7%
note: the president is both chief of state and head of government

Legislative branch: *description:* unicameral National Assembly or Asamblea Nacional (92 statutory seats, current 91; 70 members in multiseat constituencies, representing the country's 15 departments and 2 autonomous regions, and 20 members in a single nationwide constituency directly elected by party-list proportional representation vote; up to 2 seats reserved for the previous president and the runner-up candidate in the previous presidential election; members serve 5-year terms)
elections: last held on 7 November 2021 (next to be held on 1 November 2026)
election results: percent of vote by party - NA; seats by party - FSLN 75, PLC 9, ALN 2, APRE 1, CCN 1, PLI 1, YATAMA 1; composition - men 42, women 49, percentage women 53.9%

Judicial branch: *highest court(s):* Supreme Court or Corte Suprema de Justicia (consists of 16 judges organized into administrative, civil, criminal, and constitutional chambers)
judge selection and term of office: Supreme Court judges elected by the National Assembly to serve 5-year staggered terms
subordinate courts: Appeals Court; first instance civil, criminal, and labor courts; military courts are independent of the Supreme Court

Political parties: Alliance for the Republic or APRE
Alternative for Change or AC (operates in a political alliance with the FSLN)
Autonomous Liberal Party or PAL
Caribbean Unity Movement or PAMUC
Christian Unity Party or PUC (operates in a political alliance with the FSLN)
Independent Liberal Party or PLI
Liberal Constitutionalist Party or PLC
Moskitia Indigenous Progressive Movement or MOSKITIA PAWANKA (operates in a political alliance with the FSLN)
Multiethnic Indigenous Party or PIM (operates in a political alliance with the FSLN)
Nationalist Liberal Party or PLN (operates in a political alliance with the FSLN)
Nicaraguan Liberal Alliance or ALN
Nicaraguan Party of the Christian Path or CCN
Nicaraguan Resistance Party or PRN (operates in a political alliance with the FSLN)
Sandinista National Liberation Front or FSLN
Sons of Mother Earth or YATAMA
The New Sons of Mother Earth Movement or MYATAMARAN (operates in a political alliance with the FSLN)

International organization participation: ACS, BCIE, CACM, CD, CELAC, FAO, G-77, IADB, IAEA, IBRD, ICAO, ICRM, IDA, IFAD, IFC, IFRCS, ILO, IMF, IMO, Interpol, IOC, IOM, IPU, ISO (correspondent), ITSO, ITU, ITUC (NGOs), LAES, LAIA (observer), MIGA, NAM, OAS, OPANAL, OPCW, PCA, Petrocaribe, SICA, UN, UNCTAD, UNESCO, UNHCR, UNIDO, Union Latina, UNOOSA, UNWTO, UPU, WCO, WHO, WIPO, WMO, WTO

Diplomatic representation in the US: *chief of mission:* Ambassador (vacant); Chargé d'Affaires M. Lautaro SANDINO Montes (since 23 February 2024)
chancery: 1627 New Hampshire Avenue NW, Washington, DC 20009
telephone: [1] (202) 939-6570
FAX: [1] (202) 939-6545
email address and website:
mperalta@cancilleria.gob.ni
United States of America | ConsuladoDeNicaragua.com
consulate(s) general: Houston, Los Angeles, Miami, New York, San Francisco

Diplomatic representation from the US: *chief of mission:* Ambassador (vacant); Chargé d'Affaires Kevin Michael O'REILLY (since 28 June 2023)
embassy: Kilometer 5.5 Carretera Sur, Managua
mailing address: 3240 Managua Place, Washington DC 20521-3240
telephone: [505] 2252-7100,
FAX: [505] 2252-7250

email address and website:
ACS.Managua@state.gov
https://ni.usembassy.gov/

Flag description: three equal horizontal bands of blue (top), white, and blue with the national coat of arms centered in the white band; the coat of arms features a triangle encircled by the words REPUBLICA DE NICARAGUA on the top and AMERICA CENTRAL on the bottom; the banner is based on the former blue-white-blue flag of the Federal Republic of Central America; the blue bands symbolize the Pacific Ocean and the Caribbean Sea, while the white band represents the land between the two bodies of water
note: similar to the flag of El Salvador, which features a round emblem encircled by the words REPUBLICA DE EL SALVADOR EN LA AMERICA CENTRAL centered in the white band; also similar to the flag of Honduras, which has five blue stars arranged in an X pattern centered in the white band

National symbol(s): turquoise-browed motmot (bird); national colors: blue, white

National anthem: *name:* "Salve a ti, Nicaragua" (Hail to Thee, Nicaragua)
lyrics/music: Salomon Ibarra MAYORGA/traditional, arranged by Luis Abraham DELGADILLO
note: although only officially adopted in 1971, the music was approved in 1918 and the lyrics in 1939; the tune, originally from Spain, was used as an anthem for Nicaragua from the 1830s until 1876

National heritage: *total World Heritage Sites:* 2 (both cultural)
selected World Heritage Site locales: Ruins of León Viejo; León Cathedral

ECONOMY

Economic overview: low-income Central American economy; until 2018, nearly 20 years of sustained GDP growth; recent struggles due to COVID-19, political instability, and hurricanes; significant remittances; increasing poverty and food scarcity since 2005; sanctions limit investment

Real GDP (purchasing power parity): $51.088 billion (2023 est.)
$48.856 billion (2022 est.)
$47.089 billion (2021 est.)
note: data in 2021 dollars
comparison ranking: 124

Real GDP growth rate: 4.57% (2023 est.)
3.75% (2022 est.)
10.32% (2021 est.)
note: annual GDP % growth based on constant local currency
comparison ranking: 65

Real GDP per capita: $7,300 (2023 est.)
$7,000 (2022 est.)
$6,900 (2021 est.)
note: data in 2021 dollars
comparison ranking: 157

GDP (official exchange rate): $17.829 billion (2023 est.)
note: data in current dollars at official exchange rate

Inflation rate (consumer prices): 8.39% (2023 est.)
10.47% (2022 est.)
4.93% (2021 est.)
note: annual % change based on consumer prices
comparison ranking: 159

Credit ratings: Fitch rating: B- (2018)

Moody's rating: B3 (2020)

Standard & Poors rating: B- (2018)
note: The year refers to the year in which the current credit rating was first obtained.

GDP - composition, by sector of origin: *agriculture:* 15.3% (2023 est.)
industry: 27.3% (2023 est.)
services: 46.3% (2023 est.)
note: figures may not total 100% due to non-allocated consumption not captured in sector-reported data
comparison rankings: services 164; industry 82; agriculture 55

GDP - composition, by end use: *household consumption:* 78.1% (2023 est.)
government consumption: 12.2% (2023 est.)
investment in fixed capital: 21.2% (2023 est.)
investment in inventories: 1.8% (2023 est.)
exports of goods and services: 45.8% (2023 est.)
imports of goods and services: -59.1% (2023 est.)
note: figures may not total 100% due to rounding or gaps in data collection

Agricultural products: sugarcane, milk, rice, oil palm fruit, maize, plantains, cassava, groundnuts, beans, coffee (2022)
note: top ten agricultural products based on tonnage

Industries: food processing, chemicals, machinery and metal products, knit and woven apparel, petroleum refining and distribution, beverages, footwear, wood, electric wire harness manufacturing, mining

Industrial production growth rate: 6.07% (2023 est.)
note: annual % change in industrial value added based on constant local currency
comparison ranking: 41

Labor force: 3.264 million (2023 est.)
note: number of people ages 15 or older who are employed or seeking work
comparison ranking: 102

Unemployment rate: 4.8% (2023 est.)
4.98% (2022 est.)
6.06% (2021 est.)
note: % of labor force seeking employment
comparison ranking: 90

Youth unemployment rate (ages 15-24): *total:* 9.5% (2023 est.)
male: 8.3% (2023 est.)
female: 12.6% (2023 est.)
note: % of labor force ages 15-24 seeking employment
comparison ranking: total 140

Population below poverty line: 24.9% (2016 est.)
note: % of population with income below national poverty line

Gini Index coefficient - distribution of family income: 46.2 (2014 est.)
note: index (0-100) of income distribution; higher values represent greater inequality
comparison ranking: 17

Household income or consumption by percentage share: *lowest 10%:* 2% (2014 est.)
highest 10%: 37.2% (2014 est.)
note: % share of income accruing to lowest and highest 10% of population

Remittances: 26.18% of GDP (2023 est.)
20.62% of GDP (2022 est.)
15.2% of GDP (2021 est.)
note: personal transfers and compensation between resident and non-resident individuals/households/entities

Budget: *revenues:* $3.396 billion (2022 est.)
expenditures: $2.609 billion (2022 est.)
note: central government revenues and expenses (excluding grants/extrabudgetary units/social security funds) converted to US dollars at average official exchange rate for year indicated

Public debt: 33.3% of GDP (2017 est.)
note: official data; data cover general government debt and include debt instruments issued (or owned) by Government entities other than the treasury; the data include treasury debt held by foreign entities, as well as intragovernmental debt; intragovernmental debt consists of treasury borrowings from surpluses in the social funds, such as retirement, medical care, and unemployment, debt instruments for the social funds are not sold at public auctions; Nicaragua rebased its GDP figures in 2012, which reduced the figures for debt as a percentage of GDP
comparison ranking: 160

Taxes and other revenues: 19.84% (of GDP) (2022 est.)
note: central government tax revenue as a % of GDP
comparison ranking: 85

Current account balance: $1.381 billion (2023 est.)
-$386.9 million (2022 est.)
-$540.879 million (2021 est.)
note: balance of payments - net trade and primary/secondary income in current dollars
comparison ranking: 51

Exports: $8.25 billion (2023 est.)
$7.87 billion (2022 est.)
$6.618 billion (2021 est.)
note: balance of payments - exports of goods and services in current dollars
comparison ranking: 124

Exports - partners: US 52%, Mexico 12%, Honduras 7%, El Salvador 6%, Costa Rica 3% (2022)
note: top five export partners based on percentage share of exports

Exports - commodities: garments, gold, coffee, insulated wire, beef (2022)
note: top five export commodities based on value in dollars

Imports: $10.517 billion (2023 est.)
$10.212 billion (2022 est.)
$8.342 billion (2021 est.)
note: balance of payments - imports of goods and services in current dollars
comparison ranking: 120

Imports - partners: US 26%, China 11%, Honduras 10%, Guatemala 9%, Mexico 9% (2022)
note: top five import partners based on percentage share of imports

Imports - commodities: garments, refined petroleum, fabric, plastic products, crude petroleum (2022)
note: top five import commodities based on value in dollars

Reserves of foreign exchange and gold: $5.447 billion (2023 est.)
$4.404 billion (2022 est.)
$4.047 billion (2021 est.)
note: holdings of gold (year-end prices)/foreign exchange/special drawing rights in current dollars
comparison ranking: 119

Debt - external: $6.106 billion (2022 est.)
note: present value of external debt in current US dollars
comparison ranking: 47

Exchange rates: cordobas (NIO) per US dollar -

Exchange rates: 36.441 (2023 est.)
35.874 (2022 est.)

35.171 (2021 est.)
34.342 (2020 est.)
33.122 (2019 est.)

ENERGY

Electricity access: *electrification - total population:* 86.5% (2022 est.)
electrification - urban areas: 100%
electrification - rural areas: 66.3%

Electricity: *installed generating capacity:* 1.841 million kW (2022 est.)
consumption: 4.169 billion kWh (2022 est.)
imports: 995.1 million kWh (2022 est.)
transmission/distribution losses: 1.11 billion kWh (2022 est.)
comparison rankings: transmission/distribution losses 103; imports 76; consumption 133; installed generating capacity 123

Electricity generation sources: *fossil fuels:* 31.4% of total installed capacity (2022 est.)
solar: 0.7% of total installed capacity (2022 est.)
wind: 15.3% of total installed capacity (2022 est.)
hydroelectricity: 14% of total installed capacity (2022 est.)
geothermal: 16.9% of total installed capacity (2022 est.)
biomass and waste: 21.6% of total installed capacity (2022 est.)

Petroleum: *total petroleum production:* 200 bbl/day (2023 est.)
refined petroleum consumption: 36,000 bbl/day (2022 est.)

Carbon dioxide emissions: 4.987 million metric tonnes of CO_2 (2022 est.)
from petroleum and other liquids: 4.987 million metric tonnes of CO_2 (2022 est.)
comparison ranking: total emissions 135

Energy consumption per capita: 12.903 million Btu/person (2022 est.)
comparison ranking: 144

COMMUNICATIONS

Telephones - fixed lines: *total subscriptions:* 216,000 (2022 est.)
subscriptions per 100 inhabitants: 3 (2022 est.)
comparison ranking: total subscriptions 118

Telephones - mobile cellular: *total subscriptions:* 6.652 million (2021 est.)
subscriptions per 100 inhabitants: 97 (2021 est.)
comparison ranking: total subscriptions 114

Telecommunication systems: *general assessment:* Nicaragua's telecoms market has mirrored the country's poor economic achievements, with fixed-line teledensity and mobile penetration also being the lowest in Central America; the fixed line broadband market remains nascent, with population penetration below 4%; most internet users are concentrated in the largest cities, given that rural and marginal areas lack access to the most basic telecom infrastructure; internet cafés provide public access to internet and email services, but these also tend to be restricted to the larger population centers; to address poor infrastructure, the World Bank has funded a project aimed at improving connectivity via a national fiber broadband network; there are separate schemes to improve broadband in eastern regions and provide links to Caribbean submarine cables; the number of mobile subscribers overtook the number of fixed lines in early 2002, and the mobile sector now accounts for most lines in service (2021)
domestic: fixed-line teledensity is 3 per 100 persons; mobile-cellular telephone subscribership is 91 per 100 persons (2021)
international: country code - 505; landing point for the ARCOS fiber-optic submarine cable which provides connectivity to South and Central America, parts of the Caribbean, and the US; satellite earth stations - 1 Intersputnik (Atlantic Ocean region) and 1 Intelsat (Atlantic Ocean) (2019)

Broadcast media: multiple terrestrial TV stations, supplemented by cable TV in most urban areas; nearly all are government-owned or affiliated; more than 300 radio stations, both government-affiliated and privately owned (2019)

Internet country code: .ni

Internet users: *total:* 3.933 million (2021 est.)
percent of population: 57% (2021 est.)
comparison ranking: total 112

Broadband - fixed subscriptions: *total:* 290,351 (2020 est.)
subscriptions per 100 inhabitants: 4 (2020 est.)
comparison ranking: total 108

TRANSPORTATION

National air transport system: *number of registered air carriers:* 1 (2020)
inventory of registered aircraft operated by air carriers: 7

Civil aircraft registration country code prefix: YN

Airports: 39 (2024)
comparison ranking: 104

Pipelines: 54 km oil (2013)

Roadways: *total:* 24,033 km
paved: 3,447 km
unpaved: 20,586 km (2013)
comparison ranking: total 109

Waterways: 2,220 km (2011) (navigable waterways as well as the use of the large Lake Managua and Lake Nicaragua; rivers serve only the sparsely populated eastern part of the country)
comparison ranking: 41

Merchant marine: *total:* 5 (2023)
by type: general cargo 1, oil tanker 1, other 3
comparison ranking: total 168

Ports: *total ports:* 5 (2024)
large: 0
medium: 0
small: 2
very small: 3
ports with oil terminals: 4
key ports: Bluefields, Corinto, El Bluff, Puerto Cabezas, Puerto Sandino

MILITARY AND SECURITY

Military and security forces: Armed Forces of Nicaragua (formal name is Army of Nicaragua or Ejercito de Nicaragua, EN): Land Forces (Fuerza Terrestre); Naval Forces (Fuerza Naval); Air Forces (Fuerza Aérea) (2024)
note: both the military and the Nicaraguan National Police (Policía Nacional de Nicaragua or PNN) report directly to the president; Parapolice, which are non-uniformed, armed, and masked units with marginal tactical training and loose hierarchical organization, act in coordination with government security forces and report directly to the National Police; they have been used to suppress anti-government protesters

Military expenditures: 0.6% of GDP (2023 est.)
0.6% of GDP (2022 est.)
0.6% of GDP (2021 est.)
0.6% of GDP (2020 est.)
0.6% of GDP (2019 est.)
comparison ranking: 151

Military and security service personnel strengths: approximately 12,000 active personnel (10,000 Army; 800 Navy; 1,200 Air Force) (2023)

Military equipment inventories and acquisitions: the military's air and ground force inventories include mostly secondhand Russian or Soviet-era equipment; its naval force has a miscellaneous mix of patrol boats from several foreign suppliers, as well as some commercial vessels converted into gunboats domestically (2024)
note: in 2024, the US imposed restrictions on the import and export of US origin defense articles and defense services destined for or originating in Nicaragua

Military service age and obligation: 18-30 years of age for voluntary military service; no conscription; tour of duty 18-36 months (2024)

Military - note: the military is responsible for defending Nicaragua's independence, sovereignty, and territory, but also has some domestic security responsibilities; key tasks include border security, assisting the police, protecting natural resources, and providing disaster relief and humanitarian assistance; it has ties with the militaries of Cuba, Venezuela, and Russia; Russia has provided training support and equipment
the modern Army of Nicaragua was created in 1979 as the Sandinista Popular Army (1979-1984); prior to 1979, the military was known as the National Guard, which was organized and trained by the US in the 1920s and 1930s; the first commander of the National Guard, Anastasio SOMOZA GARCIA, seized power in 1937 and ran the country as a military dictator until his assassination in 1956; his sons ran the country either directly or through figureheads until the Sandinistas came to power in 1979; the defeated National Guard was disbanded by the Sandinistas (2024)

SPACE

Space agency/agencies: National Secretariat for Extraterrestrial Space Affairs, The Moon and Other Celestial Bodies (Secretaría Nacional para Asuntos del Espacio Ultraterrestre, la Luna y otros Cuerpos Celestes, established 2021; operates under the military's control) (2024)

Space program overview: stated mission of the space agency is to promote the development of space activities with the aim of broadening the country's capacities in the fields of education, industry, science, and technology; has cooperated with China and Russia; is a signatory of the convention establishing the Latin American and Caribbean Space Agency (ALCE) (2024)
note: further details about the key activities, programs, and milestones of the country's space program, as well as government spending estimates on the space sector, appear in the Space Programs reference guide

TRANSNATIONAL ISSUES

Trafficking in persons: tier rating: Tier 3 — Nicaragua does not fully meet the minimum standards for the elimination of trafficking and is not making significant efforts to do so, therefore, Nicaragua remained on Tier 3; for more details, go to: https:// www.state.gov/reports/2024-trafficking-in-persons-report/nicaragua/

Illicit drugs: transit route for illicit drugs originating from South America destined for the United States

NIGER

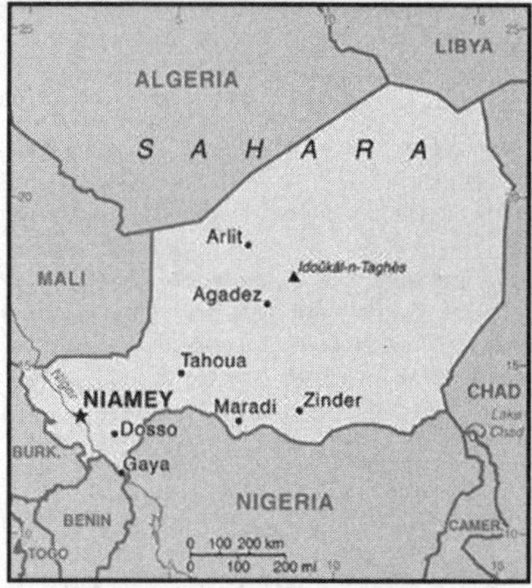

INTRODUCTION

Background: Nomadic peoples from the Saharan north and agriculturalists from the south settled present-day Niger. The Taureg kingdom of Takedda was one of the largest kingdoms in the north and played a prominent role in regional trade in the 14th century. In the south, the primary ethnic groups were the Songhai-Zarma in the west, the Hausa in the center, and the Kanuri in the east. When European colonizers arrived in the 19th century, the region was an assemblage of disparate local kingdoms.

In the late 19th century, the British and French agreed to partition the middle regions of the Niger River, and France began its conquest of what would become the colony of Niger. France experienced determined local resistance – particularly during the Tuareg uprising (1916-1917) – but established a colonial administration in 1922.

After achieving independence from France in 1960, Niger experienced single-party or military rule until 1991, when political pressure forced General Ali SAIBOU to allow multiparty elections. Political infighting and democratic backsliding led to coups in 1996 and 1999. In 1999, military officers restored democratic rule and held elections that brought Mamadou TANDJA to power. TANDJA was reelected in 2004 and spearheaded a 2009 constitutional amendment allowing him to extend his presidential term. In 2010, military officers led another coup that deposed TANDJA. ISSOUFOU Mahamadou was elected in 2011 and reelected in 2016. In 2021, BAZOUM Mohamed won the presidential election, marking Niger's first transition from one democratically elected president to another. Nonetheless, a military junta led by General Abdourahamane TIANI once again seized power in July 2023, detaining President BAZOUM and announcing the creation of a National Council for the Safeguarding of the Homeland (CNSP).

Niger is one of the poorest countries in the world with minimal government services and insufficient funds to develop its resource base. It is ranked fourth to last in the world on the UN Development Program's Human Development Index of 2023/2024. The largely agrarian and subsistence-based economy is frequently disrupted by extended droughts common to the Sahel region of Africa. The Nigerien Government continues its attempts to diversify the economy through increased oil production and mining projects. In addition, Niger is facing increased security concerns on its borders from various external threats including insecurity in Libya, spillover from the conflict and terrorism in Mali, and violent extremism in northeastern Nigeria.

GEOGRAPHY

Location: Western Africa, southeast of Algeria

Geographic coordinates: 16 00 N, 8 00 E

Map references: Africa

Area: *total:* 1.267 million sq km
land: 1,266,700 sq km
water: 300 sq km
comparison ranking: total 23

Area - comparative: slightly less than twice the size of Texas

Land boundaries: *total:* 5,834 km
border countries (7): Algeria 951 km; Benin 277 km; Burkina Faso 622 km; Chad 1,196 km; Libya 342 km; Mali 838 km; Nigeria 1,608 km

Coastline: 0 km (landlocked)

Maritime claims: none (landlocked)

Climate: desert; mostly hot, dry, dusty; tropical in extreme south

Terrain: predominately desert plains and sand dunes; flat to rolling plains in south; hills in north

Elevation: *highest point:* Idoukal-n-Taghes 2,022 m
lowest point: Niger River 200 m
mean elevation: 474 m

Natural resources: uranium, coal, iron ore, tin, phosphates, gold, molybdenum, gypsum, salt, petroleum

Land use: *agricultural land:* 35.1% (2018 est.)
arable land: 12.3% (2018 est.)
permanent crops: 0.1% (2018 est.)
permanent pasture: 22.7% (2018 est.)
forest: 1% (2018 est.)
other: 63.9% (2018 est.)

Irrigated land: 2,666 sq km (2020)

Major lakes (area sq km): *fresh water lake(s):* Lake Chad (endorheic lake shared with Chad, Nigeria, and Cameroon) - 10,360-25,900 sq km
note - area varies by season and year to year

Major rivers (by length in km): Niger (shared with Guinea [s], Mali, Benin, and Nigeria [m]) - 4,200 km
note – [s] after country name indicates river source; [m] after country name indicates river mouth

Major watersheds (area sq km): Atlantic Ocean drainage: Niger (2,261,741 sq km)
Internal (endorheic basin) drainage: Lake Chad (2,497,738 sq km)

Major aquifers: Lake Chad Basin, Lullemeden-Irhazer Basin, Murzuk-Djado Basin

Population distribution: majority of the populace is located in the southernmost extreme of the country along the border with Nigeria and Benin as shown in this population distribution map

Natural hazards: recurring droughts

Geography - note: landlocked; one of the hottest countries in the world; northern four-fifths is desert, southern one-fifth is savanna, suitable for livestock and limited agriculture

PEOPLE AND SOCIETY

Population: *total:* 26,342,784
male: 13,056,203
female: 13,286,581 (2024 est.)
comparison rankings: female 56; male 55; total 55

Nationality: *noun:* Nigerien(s)
adjective: Nigerien

Ethnic groups: Hausa 53.1%, Zarma/Songhai 21.2%, Tuareg 11%, Fulani (Peuhl) 6.5%, Kanuri 5.9%, Gurma 0.8%, Arab 0.4%, Tubu 0.4%, other/unavailable 0.9% (2006 est.)

Languages: Hausa, Zarma, French (official), Fufulde, Tamashek, Kanuri, Gurmancema, Tagdal
note: represents the most-spoken languages; Niger has 10 national languages: Arabic, Buduma, Fulfuldé, Guimancema, Hausa, Kanuri, Sonay-Zarma, Tamajaq, Tassawaq, and Tubu

Religions: Muslim 95.5%, ethnic religionist 4.1%, Christian 0.3%, agnostics and other 0.1% (2020 est.)

Demographic profile: Niger has the highest total fertility rate (TFR) of any country in the world, averaging close to 7 children per woman in 2022. A slight decline in fertility over the last few decades has stalled. This leveling off of the high fertility rate is in large part a product of the continued desire for large families. In Niger, the TFR is lower than the desired fertility rate, which makes it unlikely that contraceptive use will increase. The high TFR sustains rapid population growth and a large youth population – almost 70% of the populace is under the age of 25, as of 2020. Gender inequality, including a lack of educational opportunities for women and early marriage and childbirth, also contributes to high population growth.
Because of large family sizes, children are inheriting smaller and smaller parcels of land. The dependence of most Nigeriens on subsistence farming on increasingly small landholdings, coupled with declining rainfall and the resultant shrinkage of arable land, are all preventing food production from keeping up with population growth.

For more than half a century, Niger's lack of economic development has led to steady net outmigration. In the 1960s, Nigeriens mainly migrated to coastal West African countries to work on a seasonal basis. Some headed to Libya and Algeria in the 1970s to work in the booming oil industry until its decline in the 1980s. Since the 1990s, the principal destinations for Nigerien labor migrants have been West African countries, especially Burkina Faso and Cote d'Ivoire, while emigration to Europe and North America has remained modest. During the same period, Niger's desert trade route town Agadez became a hub for West African and other Sub-Saharan migrants crossing the Sahara to North Africa and sometimes onward to Europe.

More than 60,000 Malian refugees have fled to Niger since violence between Malian government troops and armed rebels began in early 2012. Ongoing attacks by the Boko Haram Islamist insurgency, dating to 2013 in northern Nigeria and February 2015 in southeastern Niger, pushed tens of thousands of Nigerian refugees and Nigerien returnees across the border to Niger and displaced thousands of locals in Niger's already impoverished Diffa region.

Age structure: *0-14 years:* 49.5% (male 6,567,460/female 6,463,877)
15-64 years: 47.8% (male 6,146,355/female 6,451,574)
65 years and over: 2.7% (2024 est.) (male 342,388/female 371,130)

Dependency ratios: *total dependency ratio:* 105.4
youth dependency ratio: 100.4
elderly dependency ratio: 5
potential support ratio: 20.1 (2021 est.)

Median age: *total:* 15.2 years (2024 est.)
male: 14.9 years
female: 15.6 years
comparison ranking: total 229

Population growth rate: 3.66% (2024 est.)
comparison ranking: 2

Birth rate: 46.6 births/1,000 population (2024 est.)
comparison ranking: 1

Death rate: 9.5 deaths/1,000 population (2024 est.)
comparison ranking: 44

Net migration rate: -0.6 migrant(s)/1,000 population (2024 est.)
comparison ranking: 125

Population distribution: majority of the populace is located in the southernmost extreme of the country along the border with Nigeria and Benin as shown in this population distribution map

Urbanization: *urban population:* 17.1% of total population (2023)
rate of urbanization: 4.72% annual rate of change (2020-25 est.)

Major urban areas - population: 1.437 million NIAMEY (capital) (2023)

Sex ratio: *at birth:* 1.03 male(s)/female
0-14 years: 1.02 male(s)/female
15-64 years: 0.95 male(s)/female
65 years and over: 0.92 male(s)/female
total population: 0.98 male(s)/female (2024 est.)

Mother's mean age at first birth: 18.5 years (2012 est.)
note: data represents median age at first birth among women 20-49

Maternal mortality ratio: 441 deaths/100,000 live births (2020 est.)
comparison ranking: 19

Infant mortality rate: *total:* 64.3 deaths/1,000 live births (2024 est.)
male: 69.2 deaths/1,000 live births
female: 59.2 deaths/1,000 live births
comparison ranking: total 6

Life expectancy at birth: *total population:* 60.9 years (2024 est.)
male: 59.3 years
female: 62.5 years
comparison ranking: total population 218

Total fertility rate: 6.64 children born/woman (2024 est.)
comparison ranking: 1

Gross reproduction rate: 3.27 (2024 est.)

Contraceptive prevalence rate: 11% (2021)

Drinking water source: *improved: urban:* 95.8% of population
rural: 63.1% of population
total: 68.6% of population
unimproved: urban: 4.2% of population
rural: 36.9% of population
total: 31.4% of population (2020 est.)

Current health expenditure: 6.2% of GDP (2020)

Physician density: 0.04 physicians/1,000 population (2020)

Hospital bed density: 0.4 beds/1,000 population (2017)

Sanitation facility access: *improved: urban:* 81.9% of population
rural: 13.5% of population
total: 24.8% of population
unimproved: urban: 18.1% of population
rural: 86.5% of population
total: 75.2% of population (2020 est.)

Obesity - adult prevalence rate: 5.5% (2016)
comparison ranking: 176

Alcohol consumption per capita: *total:* 0.11 liters of pure alcohol (2019 est.)
beer: 0.04 liters of pure alcohol (2019 est.)
wine: 0.01 liters of pure alcohol (2019 est.)
spirits: 0.06 liters of pure alcohol (2019 est.)
other alcohols: 0 liters of pure alcohol (2019 est.)
comparison ranking: total 177

Tobacco use: *total:* 7.4% (2020 est.)
male: 13.7% (2020 est.)
female: 1.1% (2020 est.)
comparison ranking: total 154

Children under the age of 5 years underweight: 34.6% (2022)
comparison ranking: 2

Currently married women (ages 15-49): 80.3% (2023 est.)

Education expenditures: 3.8% of GDP (2020 est.)
comparison ranking: 125

Literacy: *definition:* age 15 and over can read and write
total population: 37.3%
male: 45.8%
female: 29% (2018)

School life expectancy (primary to tertiary education): *total:* 6 years
male: 7 years
female: 6 years (2017)

ENVIRONMENT

Environment - current issues: overgrazing; soil erosion; deforestation; desertification; contaminated water; inadequate potable water; wildlife populations (such as elephant, hippopotamus, giraffe, and lion) threatened because of poaching and habitat destruction

Environment - international agreements: *party to:* Biodiversity, Climate Change, Climate Change-Kyoto Protocol, Climate Change-Paris Agreement, Comprehensive Nuclear Test Ban, Desertification, Endangered Species, Environmental Modification, Hazardous Wastes, Law of the Sea, Nuclear Test Ban, Ozone Layer Protection, Wetlands
signed, but not ratified: none of the selected agreements

Climate: desert; mostly hot, dry, dusty; tropical in extreme south

Urbanization: *urban population:* 17.1% of total population (2023)
rate of urbanization: 4.72% annual rate of change (2020-25 est.)

Food insecurity: *widespread lack of access: due to internal conflict, high food prices, and floods* - about 2.87 million people are projected to be acutely food insecure during the June to August 2023 lean season period; this would be an improvement on the situation in 2022, mostly reflecting the sharp upturn in crop yields following the below-average cereal output in 2021; persistent insecurity continues to disrupt livelihoods and has displaced over 360,000 people as of January 2023, mostly in the Diffa, Tahoua and Tillabery regions; high food prices, as well as the floods in 2022 that affected about 327,000 people, are additional factors that have aggravated food insecurity (2023)

Revenue from forest resources: 4.41% of GDP (2018 est.)
comparison ranking: 16

Revenue from coal: 0.03% of GDP (2018 est.)
comparison ranking: 34

Air pollutants: *particulate matter emissions:* 50.15 micrograms per cubic meter (2019 est.)
carbon dioxide emissions: 2.02 megatons (2016 est.)
methane emissions: 22.99 megatons (2020 est.)

Waste and recycling: *municipal solid waste generated annually:* 1,865,646 tons (1993 est.)
municipal solid waste recycled annually: 74,626 tons (2005 est.)
percent of municipal solid waste recycled: 4% (2005 est.)

Major lakes (area sq km): *fresh water lake(s):* Lake Chad (endorheic lake shared with Chad, Nigeria, and Cameroon) - 10,360-25,900 sq km note - area varies by season and year to year

Major rivers (by length in km): Niger (shared with Guinea [s], Mali, Benin, and Nigeria [m]) - 4,200 km
note – [s] after country name indicates river source; [m] after country name indicates river mouth

Major watersheds (area sq km): Atlantic Ocean drainage: Niger (2,261,741 sq km)

Internal (endorheic basin) drainage: Lake Chad (2,497,738 sq km)

Major aquifers: Lake Chad Basin, Lullemeden-Irhazer Basin, Murzuk-Djado Basin

Total water withdrawal: *municipal:* 190 million cubic meters (2020 est.)
industrial: 40 million cubic meters (2020 est.)
agricultural: 2.35 billion cubic meters (2020 est.)

Total renewable water resources: 34.05 billion cubic meters (2020 est.)

GOVERNMENT

Country name: *conventional long form:* Republic of Niger
conventional short form: Niger
local long form: République du Niger
local short form: Niger
etymology: named for the Niger River that passes through the southwest of the country; from a native term "Ni Gir" meaning "River Gir"
note: pronounced nee-zhair

Government type: formerly, semi-presidential republic

Note: on 26 July 2023, the National Council for the Safeguard of the Homeland, a military junta which took control of Niger's government, dissolved all government institutions, and rules by decree

Capital: *name:* Niamey
geographic coordinates: 13 31 N, 2 07 E
time difference: UTC+1 (6 hours ahead of Washington, DC, during Standard Time)
etymology: according to tradition, the site was originally a fishing village named after a prominent local tree referred to as "nia niam"

Administrative divisions: 7 regions (regions, singular - region) and 1 capital district* (communaute urbaine); Agadez, Diffa, Dosso, Maradi, Niamey*, Tahoua, Tillaberi, Zinder

Independence: 3 August 1960 (from France)

National holiday: Republic Day, 18 December (1958); note - commemorates the founding of the Republic of Niger which predated independence from France in 1960

Legal system: note - following the 26 July 2023 military coup, the National Council for the Safeguard of the Homeland assumed control of all government institutions and rules by decree; formerly, mixed legal system of civil law, based on French civil law, Islamic law, and customary law

Constitution: *history:* several previous; passed by referendum 31 October 2010, entered into force 25 November 2010
amendments: formerly proposed by the president of the republic or by the National Assembly; consideration of amendments requires at least three-fourths majority vote by the Assembly; passage requires at least four-fifths majority vote; if disapproved, the proposed amendment is dropped or submitted to a referendum; constitutional articles on the form of government, the multiparty system, the separation of state and religion, disqualification of Assembly members, amendment procedures, and amnesty of participants in the 2010 coup cannot be amended; amended 2011, 2017

Note: on 26 July 2023, the National Council for the Safeguard of the Homeland, a military junta which took control of Niger's government, dissolved the country's constitution

International law organization participation: has not submitted an ICJ jurisdiction declaration; accepts ICCt jurisdiction

Citizenship: *citizenship by birth:* no
citizenship by descent only: at least one parent must be a citizen of Niger
dual citizenship recognized: yes
residency requirement for naturalization: unknown

Suffrage: 18 years of age; universal

Executive branch: *chief of state:* President of the National Council for the Safeguard of the Homeland (CNSP) General Abdourahame TIANI (since 28 July 2023)
head of government: CNSP Prime Minister Ali Mahaman Lamine ZEINE (since 9 August 2023)
cabinet: Cabinet appointed by the CNSP; Cabinet previously appointed by the elected president
elections/appointments: the CNSP rules by decree; previously, the president directly elected by absolute majority popular vote in 2 rounds if needed for a 5-year term (eligible for a second term); election last held on 27 December 2020 with a runoff held on 21 February 2021 (next election was to be held in 2025); prime minister appointed by the president, authorized by the National Assembly
election results:
2020/2021: Mohamed BAZOUM elected president in second round; percent of vote in first round - Mohamed BAZOUM (PNDS-Tarrayya) 39.3%, Mahamane OUSMANE (MODEN/FA Lumana Africa) 17%, Seini OUMAROU (MNSD-Nassara) 9%, Albade ABOUDA (MPR-Jamhuriya) 7.1%, other 27.6%; percent of vote in second round - Mohamed BAZOUM 55.7%, Mahamane OUSMANE 44.3%
2016: ISSOUFOU Mahamadou reelected president in second round; percent of vote in first round - ISSOUFOU Mahamadou (PNDS-Tarrayya) 48.6%, Hama AMADOU (MODEN/FA Lumana Africa) 17.8%, Seini OUMAROU (MNSD-Nassara) 11.3%, other 22.3%; percent of vote in second round - ISSOUFOU Mahamadou 92%, Hama AMADOU 8%
note: deposed president BAZOUM has been under house arrest since a military coup on 26 July 2023

Legislative branch: *description:* formerly the unicameral National Assembly (171 statutory seats - 166 currently; 158 members directly elected from 8 multi-member constituencies in 7 regions and Niamey by party-list proportional representation, 8 reserved for minorities elected in special single-seat constituencies by simple majority vote, 5 seats reserved for Nigeriens living abroad - 1 seat per continent - elected in single-seat constituencies by simple majority vote; members serve 5-year terms)
elections: last held on 27 December 2020 (prior to the military coup, next elections were to be held in December 2025)
election results: percent of vote by party - PNDS-Tarrayya 37%, MODEN/FA Lumana 8.7%, MPR-Jamhuriya 7.6%, MNSD-Nassara 6.8%, RDR-Tchanji 4.4%, CPR-Inganci 4.2%, MPN-Kishin Kassa 4%, PJP Generation Dubara 2.9%, ANDP Zaman Lahya 2.5%, RPP Farrilla 2.1%, ARD Adaltchi-Mutuntchi 1.7%, AMEN AMIN 1.4%, MDEN Falala 1.4%, other 15.3%; seats by party - PNDS-Tarrayya 79, MODEN/FA Lumana 19, MPR-Jamhuriya 14, MNSD-Nassara 13, CPR-Inganci 8, MPN-Kishin Kassa 6, ANDP-Zaman Lahiya 3, RPP Farrilla 2, PJP Generation Dubara 2, ARD Adaltchi- Mutuntchi 2, AMEN AMIN 2, other 16; composition - men 115, women 51, percentage women 30.7%

Note: on 26 July 2023, the National Council for the Safeguard of the Homeland, a military junta which took control of Niger's government, dissolved the National Assembly

Judicial branch: *highest court(s):* formerly the Constitutional Court (consists of 7 judges); High Court of Justice (consists of 7 members)
judge selection and term of office: formerly, Constitutional Court judges nominated/elected - 1 by the president of the Republic, 1 by the president of the National Assembly, 2 by peer judges, 2 by peer lawyers, 1 law professor by peers, and 1 from within Nigerien society; all appointed by the president; judges serve 6-year nonrenewable terms with one-third of membership renewed every 2 years; High Judicial Court members selected from among the legislature and judiciary; members serve 5-year terms
subordinate courts: formerly, Court of Cassation; Council of State; Court of Finances; various specialized tribunals and customary courts

Note: on 26 July 2023, the National Council for the Safeguard of the Homeland, a military junta which took control of Niger's government, dissolved the country's judicial system

Political parties: Alliance for Democracy and the Republic
Alliance for Democratic Renewal or ARD-Adaltchi-Mutuntchi
Alliance of Movements for the Emergence of Niger or AMEN AMIN
Congress for the Republic or CPR-Inganci
Democratic Alternation for Equity in Niger
Democratic and Republican Renewal-RDR-Tchanji
Democratic Movement for the Emergence of Niger Falala
Democratic Patriots' Rally or RPD Bazara
National Movement for the Development of Society-Nassara or MNSD-Nassara
Nigerien Alliance for Democracy and Progress-Zaman Lahiya or ANDP-Zaman Lahiya
Nigerien Democratic Movement for an African Federation or MODEN/FA Lumana
Nigerien Party for Democracy and Socialism or PNDS-Tarrayya
Nigerien Patriotic Movement or MPN-Kishin Kassa
Nigerien Rally for Democracy and Peace
Patriotic Movement for the Republic or MPR-Jamhuriya
Peace, Justice, Progress–Generation Doubara
Rally for Democracy and Progress-Jama'a or RDP-Jama'a
Rally for Peace and Progress or RPP Farilla
Social Democratic Rally or RSD-Gaskiyya
Social Democratic Party or PSD-Bassira

Note: after the 26 July 2023 military coup, the National Council for the Safeguard of the Homeland dissolved the National Assembly and prohibited all political party activity

International organization participation: ACP, AfDB, AU (suspended), CD, EITI (compliant country), Entente, FAO, FZ, G-77, IAEA, IBRD, ICAO, ICCt, ICRM, IDA, IDB, IFAD, IFC, IFRCS, ILO, IMF, Interpol, IOC, IOM, IPU, ISO (correspondent), ITSO, ITU, ITUC (NGOs), LCBC, MIGA, MINUSCA, MNJTF, MONUSCO, NAM, OIC, OIF, OPCW, UN, UNCTAD, UNESCO, UNIDO, UNOOSA, UNWTO, UPU, WADB (regional), WAEMU, WCO, WFTU (NGOs), WHO, WIPO, WMO, WTO

Diplomatic representation in the US: *chief of mission:* Ambassador (vacant); Chargé d'Affaires Hassane IDI (since 3 August 2023)
chancery: 2204 R Street NW, Washington, DC 20008
telephone: [1] (202) 483-4224
FAX: [1] (202) 483-3169
email address and website:
communication@embassyofniger.org

http://www.embassyofniger.org/

Diplomatic representation from the US: *chief of mission:* Ambassador Kathleen FITZGIBBON (since 2 December 2023)
embassy: BP 11201, Niamey
mailing address: 2420 Niamey Place, Washington DC 20521-2420
telephone: [227] 20-72-26-61
FAX: [227] 20-73-55-60
email address and website:
consulateniamey@state.gov
https://ne.usembassy.gov/

Flag description: three equal horizontal bands of orange (top), white, and green with a small orange disk centered in the white band; the orange band denotes the drier northern regions of the Sahara; white stands for purity and innocence; green symbolizes hope and the fertile and productive southern and western areas, as well as the Niger River; the orange disc represents the sun and the sacrifices made by the people
note: similar to the flag of India, which has a blue spoked wheel centered in the white band

National symbol(s): zebu; national colors: orange, white, green

National anthem: *name:* "La Nigerienne" (The Nigerien)
lyrics/music: Maurice Albert THIRIET/Robert JACQUET and Nicolas Abel Francois FRIONNET
note: adopted 1961

National heritage: *total World Heritage Sites:* 3 (1 cultural, 2 natural)
selected World Heritage Site locales: Air and Ténéré Natural Reserves (n); W-Arly-Pendjari Complex (n); Historic Agadez (c)

ECONOMY

Economic overview: low-income Sahel economy; major instability and humanitarian crises limit economic activity; COVID-19 eliminated recent anti-poverty gains; economy rebounding since December 2020 Nigerian border reopening and new investments; uranium resource rich

Real GDP (purchasing power parity): $44.561 billion (2023 est.)
$43.474 billion (2022 est.)
$38.851 billion (2021 est.)
note: data in 2021 dollars
comparison ranking: 132

Real GDP growth rate: 2.5% (2023 est.)
11.9% (2022 est.)
1.38% (2021 est.)
note: annual GDP % growth based on constant local currency
comparison ranking: 125

Real GDP per capita: $1,600 (2023 est.)
$1,700 (2022 est.)
$1,500 (2021 est.)
note: data in 2021 dollars
comparison ranking: 217

GDP (official exchange rate): $16.819 billion (2023 est.)
note: data in current dollars at official exchange rate

Inflation rate (consumer prices): 3.7% (2023 est.)
4.23% (2022 est.)
3.84% (2021 est.)
note: annual % change based on consumer prices
comparison ranking: 74

Credit ratings: Moody's rating: B3 (2019)
note: The year refers to the year in which the current credit rating was first obtained.

GDP - composition, by sector of origin: *agriculture:* 47.8% (2023 est.)
industry: 20.2% (2023 est.)
services: 26.9% (2023 est.)
note: figures may not total 100% due to non-allocated consumption not captured in sector-reported data
comparison rankings: services 212; industry 137; agriculture 2

GDP - composition, by end use: *household consumption:* 72% (2021 est.)
government consumption: 17.3% (2021 est.)
investment in fixed capital: 26.4% (2023 est.)
exports of goods and services: 8.8% (2023 est.)
imports of goods and services: -21.6% (2023 est.)
note: figures may not total 100% due to rounding or gaps in data collection

Agricultural products: millet, cowpeas, sorghum, onions, milk, groundnuts, sugarcane, cabbages, cassava, potatoes (2022)
note: top ten agricultural products based on tonnage

Industries: uranium mining, petroleum, cement, brick, soap, textiles, food processing, chemicals, slaughterhouses

Industrial production growth rate: 2.9% (2023 est.)
note: annual % change in industrial value added based on constant local currency
comparison ranking: 108

Labor force: 10.237 million (2023 est.)
note: number of people ages 15 or older who are employed or seeking work
comparison ranking: 54

Unemployment rate: 0.55% (2023 est.)
0.55% (2022 est.)
0.82% (2021 est.)
note: % of labor force seeking employment
comparison ranking: 3

Youth unemployment rate (ages 15-24): *total:* 0.8% (2023 est.)
male: 0.9% (2023 est.)
female: 0.8% (2023 est.)
note: % of labor force ages 15-24 seeking employment
comparison ranking: total 199

Population below poverty line: 40.8% (2018 est.)
note: % of population with income below national poverty line

Gini Index coefficient - distribution of family income: 32.9 (2021 est.)
note: index (0-100) of income distribution; higher values represent greater inequality
comparison ranking: 102

Household income or consumption by percentage share: *lowest 10%:* 3.8% (2021 est.)
highest 10%: 27.8% (2021 est.)
note: % share of income accruing to lowest and highest 10% of population

Remittances: 3.15% of GDP (2023 est.)
4.7% of GDP (2022 est.)
2.37% of GDP (2021 est.)
note: personal transfers and compensation between resident and non-resident individuals/households/entities

Budget: *revenues:* $2.325 billion (2019 est.)
expenditures: $2.785 billion (2019 est.)

Public debt: 45.3% of GDP (2017 est.)
comparison ranking: 122

Taxes and other revenues: 21.4% (of GDP) (2017 est.)
comparison ranking: 73

Current account balance: -$2.5 billion (2022 est.)
-$2.099 billion (2021 est.)
-$1.816 billion (2020 est.)
note: balance of payments - net trade and primary/secondary income in current dollars
comparison ranking: 166

Exports: $1.376 billion (2022 est.)
$1.487 billion (2021 est.)
$1.338 billion (2020 est.)
note: balance of payments - exports of goods and services in current dollars
comparison ranking: 173

Exports - partners: UAE 69%, France 9%, China 9%, Nigeria 3%, Mali 2% (2022)
note: top five export partners based on percentage share of exports

Exports - commodities: gold, oil seeds, radioactive chemicals, refined petroleum, uranium and thorium ore (2022)
note: top five export commodities based on value in dollars

Imports: $4.194 billion (2022 est.)
$4.027 billion (2021 est.)
$3.542 billion (2020 est.)
note: balance of payments - imports of goods and services in current dollars
comparison ranking: 156

Imports - partners: China 22%, France 14%, Nigeria 8%, Germany 5%, UAE 5% (2022)
note: top five import partners based on percentage share of imports

Imports - commodities: weapons parts and accessories, rice, aircraft, tobacco, iron pipes (2022)
note: top five import commodities based on value in dollars

Reserves of foreign exchange and gold: $1.314 billion (31 December 2017 est.)
$1.186 billion (31 December 2016 est.)
comparison ranking: 135

Debt - external: $3.688 billion (2022 est.)
note: present value of external debt in current US dollars
comparison ranking: 59

Exchange rates: Communaute Financiere Africaine francs (XOF) per US dollar -

Exchange rates: 606.57 (2023 est.)
623.76 (2022 est.)
554.531 (2021 est.)
575.586 (2020 est.)
585.911 (2019 est.)

ENERGY

Electricity access: *electrification - total population:* 19.5% (2022 est.)
electrification - urban areas: 66.1%
electrification - rural areas: 7.7%

Electricity: *installed generating capacity:* 359,000 kW (2022 est.)
consumption: 1.594 billion kWh (2022 est.)
imports: 1.173 billion kWh (2022 est.)
transmission/distribution losses: 364.8 million kWh (2022 est.)
comparison rankings: transmission/distribution losses 72; imports 73; consumption 153; installed generating capacity 158

Electricity generation sources: *fossil fuels:* 94.1% of total installed capacity (2022 est.)
solar: 5.9% of total installed capacity (2022 est.)

Coal: *production:* 457,000 metric tons (2022 est.)
consumption: 457,000 metric tons (2022 est.)
imports: 3,000 metric tons (2022 est.)
proven reserves: 90 million metric tons (2022 est.)

Petroleum: *total petroleum production:* 6,000 bbl/day (2023 est.)
refined petroleum consumption: 13,000 bbl/day (2022 est.)
crude oil estimated reserves: 150 million barrels (2021 est.)

Natural gas: *production:* 29.509 million cubic meters (2022 est.)
consumption: 29.858 million cubic meters (2022 est.)

Carbon dioxide emissions: 2.454 million metric tonnes of CO_2 (2022 est.)
from coal and metallurgical coke: 674,000 metric tonnes of CO_2 (2022 est.)
from petroleum and other liquids: 1.722 million metric tonnes of CO_2 (2022 est.)
from consumed natural gas: 58,000 metric tonnes of CO_2 (2022 est.)
comparison ranking: total emissions 154

Energy consumption per capita: 1.405 million Btu/person (2022 est.)
comparison ranking: 190

COMMUNICATIONS

Telephones - fixed lines: *total subscriptions:* 58,000 (2021 est.)
subscriptions per 100 inhabitants: (2021 est.) less than 1
comparison ranking: total subscriptions 151

Telephones - mobile cellular: *total subscriptions:* 14.239 million (2021 est.)
subscriptions per 100 inhabitants: 56 (2021 est.)
comparison ranking: total subscriptions 73

Telecommunication systems: *general assessment:* Niger is one of the largest countries in West Africa but also one of the poorest in the world; as with many African markets, a lack of fixed telecoms infrastructure has led to growth in mobile services; Niger's mobile penetration is modest compared to other countries in the region, while fixed broadband penetration is negligible; recent international investment to complete the Trans-Saharan Dorsal optical fiber (SDR) network has extended the reach of fiber infrastructure in the country, and also increased international capacity; new cables linking the country with Chad and Burkina Faso have extended Niger's connectivity with international cable infrastructure (2022)
domestic: fixed-line less than 1 per 100 persons and mobile-cellular at nearly 56 per 100 persons (2021)
international: country code - 227; satellite earth stations - 2 Intelsat (1 Atlantic Ocean and 1 Indian Ocean)

Broadcast media: state-run TV station; 3 private TV stations provide a mix of local and foreign programming; state-run radio has only radio station with national coverage; about 30 private radio stations operate locally; as many as 100 community radio stations broadcast; transmissions of multiple international broadcasters are available

Internet country code: .ne

Internet users: *total:* 5.5 million (2021 est.)
percent of population: 22% (2021 est.)
comparison ranking: total 86

Broadband - fixed subscriptions: *total:* 12,000 (2020 est.)
subscriptions per 100 inhabitants: 0.1 (2020 est.)
comparison ranking: total 177

TRANSPORTATION

National air transport system: *number of registered air carriers:* 2 (2020)
inventory of registered aircraft operated by air carriers: 3

Civil aircraft registration country code prefix: 5U

Airports: 26 (2024)
comparison ranking: 126

Pipelines: 2,444 km oil (2024)

Roadways: *total:* 18,949 km
paved: 3,979 km
unpaved: 14,969 km (2018)
comparison ranking: total 117

Waterways: 563 km (2024) (the Niger, the only major river, is navigable to Gaya between September and March)
comparison ranking: 90

MILITARY AND SECURITY

Military and security forces: Nigerien Armed Forces (Forces Armees Nigeriennes, FAN): Army, Nigerien Air Force, Niger Gendarmerie (GN)

Ministry of Interior: Niger National Guard (GNN), National Police (2024)
note 1: the Gendarmerie (GN) and the National Guard (GNN) are paramilitary forces; the GN has primary responsibility for rural security while the GNN is responsible for domestic security and the protection of high-level officials and government buildings; the GNN in past years was known as the National Forces of Intervention and Security and the Republican Guard
note 2: the National Police includes the Directorate of Territorial Surveillance, which is charged with border management

Military expenditures: 2% of GDP (2023 est.)
1.7% of GDP (2022 est.)
1.8% of GDP (2021 est.)
2% of GDP (2020 est.)
1.7% of GDP (2019 est.)
comparison ranking: 67

Military and security service personnel strengths: information varies; estimated 30-35,000 active FAN troops; estimated 5-10,000 paramilitary Gendarmerie and National Guard personnel (2024)
note: in 2020, the Nigerien Government announced it intended to increase the size of the FAN to 50,000 by 2025 and 100,000 by 2030

Military equipment inventories and acquisitions: the FAN's inventory consists of a wide variety of older weapons, including French, Russian, and Soviet era; in recent years, it has received small amounts of mostly secondhand equipment from several countries, including China, Egypt, and the US (2023)

Military service age and obligation: 18 is the legal minimum age for selective compulsory or voluntary military service for unmarried men and women; 24-month service term (2023)

Military deployments: Niger has committed about 1,000 troops to the Multinational Joint Task Force (MNJTF) against Boko Haram and other terrorist groups operating in the general area of the Lake Chad Basin and along Nigeria's northeast border; national MNJTF troop contingents are deployed within their own country territories, although cross-border operations are conducted periodically (2024)

Military - note: the military seized control of the government in 2023; since its establishment in 1960-61, it has played a significant role in the country's politics, attempting coups in 1974, 1996, 1999, 2010, and 2021, and ruling Niger for much of the period before 1999
while the FAN is responsible for ensuring external security, most of its focus is on internal counterinsurgency/ counterterrorism operations against terrorist groups operating in the areas bordering Burkina Faso, Libya, Mali, and Nigeria, as well as much of northern Niger and the Diffa and Lake Chad regions; these groups include the Islamic State of Iraq and ash-Sham in the Greater Sahara (ISIS-GS), Boko Haram, ISIS-West Africa, and Jama'at Nusrat al-Islam wal- Muslimin (JNIM)
since the 2010s, Niger has placed considerable emphasis on improving the effectiveness and mobility of its security forces for countering terrorism and protecting the country's borders; with training support and material assistance from the US and the EU, each security service has created new units or reconfigured existing units with an emphasis on mobility, hybridization, and specialized training; the Army has established a special operations command, several special intervention battalions, and an anti-terrorism unit known as the 1st Expeditionary Force of Niger (EFoN); the National Gendarmerie has created mobile units modeled on European gendarmerie forces known as the Rapid Action Group— Surveillance and Response in the Sahel (Groupe d'action Rapides—Surveillance et Intervention au Sahel or GAR-SI Sahel); the National Guard (GNN) has established mobile Multipurpose Squadrons (Escadrons Polyvalentes de la Garde Nationale de Niger or EP-GNN), while the National Police have created Mobile Border Control Companies (Compagnie Mobile de Contrôle des Frontières or CMCF); Niger has also established training centers for special forces in Tillia and peacekeeping in Ouallam; meanwhile, the Air Force has received armed UAVs from Turkey (2024)

TERRORISM

Terrorist group(s): Boko Haram; Islamic State of Iraq and ash-Sham in the Greater Sahara (ISIS-GS); Islamic State of Iraq and ash-Sham – West Africa (ISIS-WA); Jama'at Nusrat al-Islam wal-Muslimin (JNIM); al-Mulathamun Battalion (al- Mourabitoun)
note: details about the history, aims, leadership, organization, areas of operation, tactics, targets, weapons, size, and sources of support of the group(s) appear(s) in the Terrorism reference guide

TRANSNATIONAL ISSUES

Refugees and internally displaced persons: *refugees (country of origin):* 67,191 (Mali) (refugees and asylum seekers) (2023); 200,423 (Nigeria) (2024)
IDPs: 335,277 (includes the regions of Diffa, Tillaberi, and Tahoua; unknown how many of the 11,000 people displaced by clashes between government forces and the Tuareg militant group, Niger Movement for Justice, in 2007 are still displaced; inter-communal

violence; Boko Haram attacks in southern Niger, 2015) (2023)

Trafficking in persons: tier rating: Tier 2 Watch List — the government did not demonstrate overall increasing efforts to eliminate trafficking compared with the previous reporting period, therefore Niger was downgraded to Tier 2 Watch List; for more details, go to: https://www.state.gov/reports/2024-trafficking-in-persons-report/niger/

Illicit drugs: a transit country for illegal drugs shipped through Niger to Africa, Europe, and the Middle East; drugs from South America, cocaine, heroin, cannabis, and various synthetics transit through Niger to European and Middle Eastern markets; hashish from Morocco is trafficked through Niger to Libya and Egypt and Europe and the Middle East; Nigerien citizens and migrants crossing Niger consume significant quantities of the opioid tramadol from neighboring Nigeria

NIGERIA

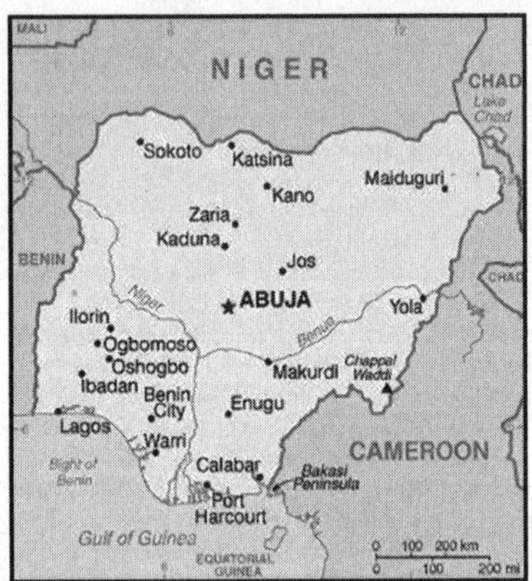

INTRODUCTION

Background: In ancient and pre-colonial times, the area of present-day Nigeria was occupied by a variety of ethnic groups with different languages and traditions. These included large Islamic kingdoms such as Borno, Kano, and the Sokoto Caliphate dominating the north, the Benin and Oyo Empires that controlled much of modern western Nigeria, and more decentralized political entities and city states in the south and southeast. In 1914, the British amalgamated their separately administered northern and southern territories into a Colony and Protectorate of Nigeria.

Nigeria achieved independence from Britain in 1960 and transitioned to a federal republic with three constituent states in 1963 under President Nnamdi AZIKIWE. This structure served to enflame regional and ethnic tension, contributing to a bloody coup led by predominately southeastern military officers in 1966 and a countercoup later that year masterminded by northern officers. In the aftermath of this tension, the governor of Nigeria's Eastern Region, centered on the southeast, declared the region independent as the Republic of Biafra. The ensuring civil war (1967-1970), resulted in more than a million deaths, many from starvation. While the war forged a stronger Nigerian state and national identity, it contributed to long-lasting mistrust of the southeast's predominantly Igbo population. Wartime military leader Yakubu GOWON ruled until a bloodless coup by frustrated junior officers in 1975. This generation of officers, including Olusegun OBASANJO, Ibrahim BABANGIDA, and Muhammadu BUHARI, who would all later serve as president, continue to exert significant influence in Nigeria to the present day.

Military rule predominated until the first durable transition to civilian government and adoption of a new constitution in 1999. The elections of 2007 marked the first civilian-to-civilian transfer of power in the country's history. National and state elections in 2011 and 2015 were generally regarded as credible. The 2015 election was also heralded for the fact that the then-umbrella opposition party, the All Progressives Congress, defeated the long-ruling (since 1999) People's Democratic Party and assumed the presidency, marking the first peaceful transfer of power from one party to another. Presidential and legislative elections in 2019 and 2023 were deemed broadly free and fair despite voting irregularities, intimidation, and violence. The government of Africa's most populous nation continues to face the daunting task of institutionalizing democracy and reforming a petroleum-based economy whose revenues have been squandered through decades of corruption and mismanagement. In addition, Nigeria faces increasing violence from Islamic terrorism, largely in the northeast, large scale criminal banditry, secessionist violence in the southeast, and competition over land and resources nationwide.

GEOGRAPHY

Location: Western Africa, bordering the Gulf of Guinea, between Benin and Cameroon

Geographic coordinates: 10 00 N, 8 00 E

Map references: Africa

Area: *total:* 923,768 sq km
land: 910,768 sq km
water: 13,000 sq km
comparison ranking: total 33

Area - comparative: about six times the size of Georgia; slightly more than twice the size of California

Land boundaries: *total:* 4,477 km
border countries (4): Benin 809 km; Cameroon 1,975 km; Chad 85 km; Niger 1,608 km

Coastline: 853 km

Maritime claims: *territorial sea:* 12 nm
exclusive economic zone: 200 nm
continental shelf: 200-m depth or to the depth of exploitation

Climate: varies; equatorial in south, tropical in center, arid in north

Terrain: southern lowlands merge into central hills and plateaus; mountains in southeast, plains in north

Elevation: *highest point:* Chappal Waddi 2,419 m
lowest point: Atlantic Ocean 0 m
mean elevation: 380 m

Natural resources: natural gas, petroleum, tin, iron ore, coal, limestone, niobium, lead, zinc, arable land

Land use: *agricultural land:* 78% (2018 est.)
arable land: 37.3% (2018 est.)
permanent crops: 7.4% (2018 est.)
permanent pasture: 33.3% (2018 est.)
forest: 9.5% (2018 est.)
other: 12.5% (2018 est.)

Irrigated land: 2,930 sq km (2012)

Major lakes (area sq km): *fresh water lake(s):* Lake Chad (endorheic lake shared with Niger, Chad, and Cameroon) - 10,360-25,900 sq km note - area varies by season and year to year

Major rivers (by length in km): Niger river mouth (shared with Guinea [s], Mali, Benin, and Niger) - 4,200 km
note – [s] after country name indicates river source; [m] after country name indicates river mouth

Major watersheds (area sq km): Atlantic Ocean drainage: Niger (2,261,741 sq km)

Internal (endorheic basin) drainage: Lake Chad (2,497,738 sq km)

Major aquifers: Lake Chad Basin, Lullemeden-Irhazer Aquifer System

Population distribution: largest population of any African nation; significant population clusters are scattered throughout the country, with the highest density areas being in the south and southwest as shown in this population distribution map

Natural hazards: periodic droughts; flooding

Geography - note: the Niger River enters the country in the northwest and flows southward through tropical rain forests and swamps to its delta in the Gulf of Guinea

PEOPLE AND SOCIETY

Population: *total:* 236,747,130
male: 119,514,449
female: 117,232,681 (2024 est.)
comparison rankings: female 6; male 6; total 6

Nationality: *noun:* Nigerian(s)
adjective: Nigerian

Ethnic groups: Hausa 30%, Yoruba 15.5%, Igbo (Ibo) 15.2%, Fulani 6%, Tiv 2.4%, Kanuri/Beriberi 2.4%, Ibibio 1.8%, Ijaw/Izon 1.8%, other 24.9% (2018 est.)
note: Nigeria, Africa's most populous country, is composed of more than 250 ethnic groups

Languages: English (official), Hausa, Yoruba, Igbo (Ibo), Fulani, over 500 additional indigenous languages

Religions: Muslim 53.5%, Roman Catholic 10.6%, other Christian 35.3%, other 0.6% (2018 est.)

Demographic profile: Nigeria's population is projected to grow from more than 186 million people in 2016 to 392 million in 2050, becoming the world's fourth most populous country. Nigeria's sustained high population growth rate will continue for the foreseeable future because of population momentum and its high birth rate. Abuja has not successfully implemented family planning programs to reduce and space births because of a lack of political will, government financing, and the availability and affordability of services and products, as well as a cultural preference for large families. Increased educational attainment, especially among women, and improvements in health care are needed to encourage and to better enable parents to opt for smaller families.

Nigeria needs to harness the potential of its burgeoning youth population in order to boost economic development, reduce widespread poverty, and channel large numbers of unemployed youth into productive activities and away from ongoing religious and ethnic violence. While most movement of Nigerians is internal, significant emigration regionally and to the West provides an outlet for Nigerians looking for economic opportunities, seeking asylum, and increasingly pursuing higher education. Immigration largely of West Africans continues to be insufficient to offset emigration and the loss of highly skilled workers. Nigeria also is a major source, transit, and destination country for forced labor and sex trafficking.

Age structure: *0-14 years:* 40.4% (male 48,856,606/ female 46,770,810)
15-64 years: 56.2% (male 66,897,900/female 66,187,584)
65 years and over: 3.4% (2024 est.) (male 3,759,943/ female 4,274,287)

Dependency ratios: *total dependency ratio:* 86
youth dependency ratio: 80.6
elderly dependency ratio: 5.5
potential support ratio: 18 (2021 est.)

Median age: *total:* 19.3 years (2024 est.)
male: 19.1 years
female: 19.6 years
comparison ranking: total 211

Population growth rate: 2.52% (2024 est.)
comparison ranking: 19

Birth rate: 33.8 births/1,000 population (2024 est.)
comparison ranking: 17

Death rate: 8.4 deaths/1,000 population (2024 est.)
comparison ranking: 75

Net migration rate: -0.2 migrant(s)/1,000 population (2024 est.)
comparison ranking: 110

Population distribution: largest population of any African nation; significant population clusters are scattered throughout the country, with the highest density areas being in the south and southwest as shown in this population distribution map

Urbanization: *urban population:* 54.3% of total population (2023)
rate of urbanization: 3.92% annual rate of change (2020-25 est.)

Major urban areas - population: 15.946 million Lagos, 4.348 million Kano, 3.875 million Ibadan, 3.840 million ABUJA (capital), 3.480 million Port Harcourt, 1.905 million Benin City (2023)

Sex ratio: *at birth:* 1.06 male(s)/female
0-14 years: 1.04 male(s)/female
15-64 years: 1.01 male(s)/female
65 years and over: 0.88 male(s)/female
total population: 1.02 male(s)/female (2024 est.)

Mother's mean age at first birth: 20.4 years (2018 est.)
note: data represents median age at first birth among women 25-49

Maternal mortality ratio: 1,047 deaths/100,000 live births (2020 est.)
comparison ranking: 3

Infant mortality rate: *total:* 53.7 deaths/1,000 live births (2024 est.)
male: 58.9 deaths/1,000 live births
female: 48.2 deaths/1,000 live births
comparison ranking: total 15

Life expectancy at birth: *total population:* 62.2 years (2024 est.)
male: 60.4 years
female: 64.2 years
comparison ranking: total population 216

Total fertility rate: 4.52 children born/woman (2024 est.)
comparison ranking: 14

Gross reproduction rate: 2.19 (2024 est.)

Contraceptive prevalence rate: 16.6% (2018)

Drinking water source: *improved: urban:* 95.3% of population
rural: 68.8% of population
total: 82.6% of population
unimproved: urban: 4.7% of population
rural: 31.2% of population
total: 17.4% of population (2020 est.)

Current health expenditure: 3.4% of GDP (2020)

Physician density: 0.38 physicians/1,000 population (2018)

Sanitation facility access: *improved: urban:* 81.6% of population
rural: 41.4% of population
total: 62.3% of population
unimproved: urban: 18.4% of population
rural: 58.6% of population
total: 37.7% of population (2020 est.)

Obesity - adult prevalence rate: 8.9% (2016)
comparison ranking: 145

Alcohol consumption per capita: *total:* 4.49 liters of pure alcohol (2019 est.)
beer: 0.73 liters of pure alcohol (2019 est.)
wine: 0.09 liters of pure alcohol (2019 est.)
spirits: 0.4 liters of pure alcohol (2019 est.)
other alcohols: 3.27 liters of pure alcohol (2019 est.)
comparison ranking: total 88

Tobacco use: *total:* 3.7% (2020 est.)
male: 6.9% (2020 est.)
female: 0.5% (2020 est.)
comparison ranking: total 163

Children under the age of 5 years underweight: 18.4% (2019/20)
comparison ranking: 25

Currently married women (ages 15-49): 66.2% (2023 est.)

Child marriage: *women married by age 15:* 12.3%
women married by age 18: 30.3%
men married by age 18: 1.6% (2021 est.)
note: due to prolonged insecurity concerns, some parts of states, including Borno state, were not sampled

Education expenditures: 0.5% of GDP (2013)
comparison ranking: 196

Literacy: *definition:* age 15 and over can read and write
total population: 62%
male: 71.3%
female: 52.7% (2018)

ENVIRONMENT

Environment - current issues: serious overpopulation and rapid urbanization have led to numerous environmental problems; urban air and water pollution; rapid deforestation; soil degradation; loss of arable land; oil pollution - water, air, and soil have suffered serious damage from oil spills

Environment - international agreements: *party to:* Biodiversity, Climate Change, Climate Change-Kyoto Protocol, Climate Change-Paris Agreement, Comprehensive Nuclear Test Ban, Desertification, Endangered Species, Hazardous Wastes, Law of the Sea, Marine Dumping-London Convention, Marine Dumping-London Protocol, Marine Life Conservation, Nuclear Test Ban, Ozone Layer Protection, Ship Pollution, Wetlands
signed, but not ratified: Tropical Timber 2006

Climate: varies; equatorial in south, tropical in center, arid in north

Urbanization: *urban population:* 54.3% of total population (2023)
rate of urbanization: 3.92% annual rate of change (2020-25 est.)

Food insecurity: *widespread lack of access: due to persistent civil conflict in the northern areas, floods, high food prices, and an economic slowdown* - about 25.3 million people are projected to face acute food insecurity during the June to August 2023 lean season; this would be a significant deterioration compared to last year, when 19.45 million people were estimated to be acutely food insecure; acute food insecurity is mostly driven by the deterioration of security conditions and conflicts in northern states, which have led to the displacement of about 3.17 million people as of March 2022 (the latest data available) and are constraining farmers' access to their lands; widespread flooding in 2022, affecting about 4.5 million people across the country, has further compounded conditions, particularly in areas already facing high levels of insecurity; high food prices and the expected slowdown in economic growth in 2023 are additional drivers of acute food insecurity (2023)

Revenue from forest resources: 1.02% of GDP (2018 est.)
comparison ranking: 53

Revenue from coal: 0% of GDP (2018 est.)
comparison ranking: 86

Air pollutants: *particulate matter emissions:* 55.64 micrograms per cubic meter (2019 est.)
carbon dioxide emissions: 120.37 megatons (2016 est.)
methane emissions: 143.99 megatons (2020 est.)

Waste and recycling: *municipal solid waste generated annually:* 27,614,830 tons (2009 est.)

Major lakes (area sq km): *fresh water lake(s):* Lake Chad (endorheic lake shared with Niger, Chad, and Cameroon) - 10,360-25,900 sq km note - area varies by season and year to year

Major rivers (by length in km): Niger river mouth (shared with Guinea [s], Mali, Benin, and Niger) - 4,200 km
note – [s] after country name indicates river source; [m] after country name indicates river mouth

Major watersheds (area sq km): Atlantic Ocean drainage: Niger (2,261,741 sq km)

Internal (endorheic basin) drainage: Lake Chad (2,497,738 sq km)

Major aquifers: Lake Chad Basin, Lullemeden-Irhazer Aquifer System

Total water withdrawal: *municipal:* 5 billion cubic meters (2020 est.)
industrial: 1.97 billion cubic meters (2020 est.)
agricultural: 5.51 billion cubic meters (2020 est.)

Total renewable water resources: 286.2 billion cubic meters (2020 est.)

GOVERNMENT

Country name: *conventional long form:* Federal Republic of Nigeria
conventional short form: Nigeria
etymology: named for the Niger River that flows through the west of the country to the Atlantic Ocean; from a native term "Ni Gir" meaning "River Gir"

Government type: federal presidential republic

Capital: *name:* Abuja
geographic coordinates: 9 05 N, 7 32 E
time difference: UTC+1 (6 hours ahead of Washington, DC, during Standard Time)
etymology: Abuja is a planned capital city, it replaced Lagos in 1991; situated in the center of the country, Abuja takes its name from a nearby town, now renamed Suleja

Administrative divisions: 36 states and 1 territory*; Abia, Adamawa, Akwa Ibom, Anambra, Bauchi, Bayelsa, Benue, Borno, Cross River, Delta, Ebonyi, Edo, Ekiti, Enugu, Federal Capital Territory*, Gombe, Imo, Jigawa, Kaduna, Kano, Katsina, Kebbi, Kogi, Kwara, Lagos, Nasarawa, Niger, Ogun, Ondo, Osun, Oyo, Plateau, Rivers, Sokoto, Taraba, Yobe, Zamfara

Independence: 1 October 1960 (from the UK)

National holiday: Independence Day (National Day), 1 October (1960)

Legal system: mixed legal system of English common law, Islamic law (in 12 northern states), and traditional law

Constitution: *history:* several previous; latest adopted 5 May 1999, effective 29 May 1999
amendments: proposed by the National Assembly; passage requires at least two-thirds majority vote of both houses and approval by the Houses of Assembly of at least two thirds of the states; amendments to constitutional articles on the creation of a new state, fundamental constitutional rights, or constitution-amending procedures requires at least four-fifths majority vote by both houses of the National Assembly and approval by the Houses of Assembly in at least two thirds of the states; passage of amendments limited to the creation of a new state require at least two-thirds majority vote by the proposing National Assembly house and approval by the Houses of Assembly in two thirds of the states; amended several times, last in 2018

International law organization participation: accepts compulsory ICJ jurisdiction with reservations; accepts ICCt jurisdiction

Citizenship: *citizenship by birth:* no
citizenship by descent only: at least one parent must be a citizen of Nigeria
dual citizenship recognized: yes
residency requirement for naturalization: 15 years

Suffrage: 18 years of age; universal

Executive branch: *chief of state:* President Bola Ahmed Adekunle TINUBU (since 29 May 2023)
head of government: President Bola Ahmed Adekunle TINUBU (since 29 May 2023)
cabinet: Federal Executive Council appointed by the president but constrained constitutionally to include at least one member from each of the 36 states
elections/appointments: president directly elected by qualified majority popular vote and at least 25% of the votes cast in 24 of Nigeria's 36 states; president elected for a 4-year term (eligible for a second term); election last held on 25 February 2023 (next to be held on 27 February 2027) note - the president is chief of state, head of government, and commander-in-chief of the armed forces
election results:
2023: Bola Ahmed Adekunle TINUBU elected president; percent of vote - Bola Ahmed Adekunle TINUBU (APC) 36.6%, Atiku ABUBAKAR (PDP) 29.1%, Peter OBI (LP) 25.4%, Rabiu KWANKWASO (NNPP) 6.4%, other 2.5%
2019: Muhammadu BUHARI elected president; percent of vote - Muhammadu BUHARI (APC) 53%, Atiku ABUBAKAR (PDP) 39%, other 8%

Legislative branch: *description:* bicameral National Assembly consists of:
Senate (109 seats - 3 each for the 36 states and 1 for Abuja-Federal Capital Territory; members directly elected in single-seat constituencies by simple majority vote to serve 4-year terms)
House of Representatives (360 seats statutory, 258 current; members directly elected in single-seat constituencies by simple majority vote to serve 4-year terms)
elections: Senate - last held on 25 February 2023 (next to be held in February 2027)
House of Representatives - last held on 25 February 2023 (next to be held in February 2027)
election results: Senate - percent of vote by party - NA; seats by party - APC 59, PDP 36, LP 8, NNPP 2, SDP 2, YPP 1, APGA 1; composition - men 105, women 4, percentage women 3.7%
House of Representatives - percent of vote by party - NA; seats by party - APC 178, PDP 114, LP 35, NNPP 19, APGA 5, other 7, vacant 2; composition - men 344, women 14, percentage women 3.8%; note - total National Assembly percentage women 3.9%

Judicial branch: *highest court(s):* Supreme Court (consists of the chief justice and 15 justices)
judge selection and term of office: judges appointed by the president upon the recommendation of the National Judicial Council, a 23-member independent body of federal and state judicial officials; judge appointments confirmed by the Senate; judges serve until age 70
subordinate courts: Court of Appeal; Federal High Court; High Court of the Federal Capital Territory; Sharia Court of Appeal of the Federal Capital Territory; Customary Court of Appeal of the Federal Capital Territory; state court system similar in structure to federal system

Political parties: Accord Party or ACC
Africa Democratic Congress or ADC
All Progressives Congress or APC
All Progressives Grand Alliance or APGA
Labor Party or LP
New Nigeria People's Party or NNPP
Peoples Democratic Party or PDP
Young Progressive Party or YPP

International organization participation: ACP, AfDB, ATMIS, AU, C, CD, D-8, ECOWAS, EITI (compliant country), FAO, G-15, G-24, G-77, IAEA, IBRD, ICAO, ICC (national committees), ICCt, ICRM, IDA, IDB, IFAD, IFC, IFRCS, IHO, ILO, IMF, IMO, IMSO, Interpol, IOC, IOM, IPU, ISO, ITSO, ITU, ITUC (NGOs), LCBC, MIGA, MINURSO, MNJTF, MONUSCO, NAM, OAS (observer), OIC, OPCW, OPEC, PCA, UN, UNAMID, UNCTAD, UNESCO, UNHCR, UNIDO, UNIFIL, UNISFA, UNITAR, UNMIL, UNMISS, UNOCI, UNOOSA, UNWTO, UPU, WCO, WFTU (NGOs), WHO, WIPO, WMO, WTO

Diplomatic representation in the US: *chief of mission:* Ambassador-designate Samson ITEGBOJE, (since October 2024)
chancery: 3519 International Court NW, Washington, DC 20008
telephone: [1] (202) 800-7201 (ext. 100)
FAX: [1] (202) 362-6541
email address and website:
info@nigeriaembassyusa.org
https://www.nigeriaembassyusa.org/
consulate(s) general: Atlanta, New York

Diplomatic representation from the US: *chief of mission:* Ambassador Richard MILLS, Jr. (since 25 July 2024)
embassy: Plot 1075 Diplomatic Drive, Central District Area, Abuja
mailing address: 8320 Abuja Place, Washington DC 20521-8320
telephone: [234] (9) 461-4000
FAX: [234] (9) 461-4036
email address and website:
AbujaACS@state.gov
https://ng.usembassy.gov/
consulate(s) general: Lagos

Flag description: three equal vertical bands of green (hoist side), white, and green; the color green represents the forests and abundant natural wealth of the country, white stands for peace and unity

National symbol(s): eagle; national colors: green, white

National anthem: *name:* "Arise Oh Compatriots, Nigeria's Call Obey"
lyrics/music: John A. ILECHUKWU, Eme Etim AKPAN, B.A. OGUNNAIKE, Sotu OMOIGUI and P.O. ADERIBIGBE/ Benedict Elide ODIASE
note: adopted 1978; lyrics are a mixture of the five top entries in a national contest

National heritage: *total World Heritage Sites:* 2 (both cultural)
selected World Heritage Site locales: Sukur Cultural Landscape; Osun-Osogbo Sacred Grove

ECONOMY

Economic overview: largest African market economy; enormous but mostly lower middle income labor force; major oil exporter; key telecommunications and finance industries; susceptible to energy prices; regional leader in critical infrastructure; primarily agrarian employment

Real GDP (purchasing power parity): $1.275 trillion (2023 est.)
$1.239 trillion (2022 est.)
$1.2 trillion (2021 est.)
note: data in 2021 dollars
comparison ranking: 26

Real GDP growth rate: 2.86% (2023 est.)
3.25% (2022 est.)
3.65% (2021 est.)
note: annual GDP % growth based on constant local currency

comparison ranking: 113

Real GDP per capita: $5,700 (2023 est.)
$5,700 (2022 est.)
$5,600 (2021 est.)
note: data in 2021 dollars
comparison ranking: 171

GDP (official exchange rate): $362.815 billion (2023 est.)
note: data in current dollars at official exchange rate

Inflation rate (consumer prices): 24.66% (2023 est.)
18.85% (2022 est.)
16.95% (2021 est.)
note: annual % change based on consumer prices
comparison ranking: 200

Credit ratings: Fitch rating: B (2020)

Moody's rating: B2 (2017)

Standard & Poors rating: B- (2020)
note: The year refers to the year in which the current credit rating was first obtained.

GDP - composition, by sector of origin: *agriculture:* 22.7% (2023 est.)
industry: 32.6% (2023 est.)
services: 42.8% (2023 est.)
note: figures may not total 100% due to non-allocated consumption not captured in sector-reported data
comparison rankings: services 179; industry 52; agriculture 28

GDP - composition, by end use: *household consumption:* 80% (2017 est.)
government consumption: 5.8% (2017 est.)
investment in fixed capital: 14.8% (2017 est.)
investment in inventories: 0.7% (2017 est.)
exports of goods and services: 11.9% (2017 est.)
imports of goods and services: -13.2% (2017 est.)

Agricultural products: yams, cassava, maize, oil palm fruit, rice, taro, bananas, vegetables, sorghum, groundnuts (2022)
note: top ten agricultural products based on tonnage

Industries: crude oil, coal, tin, columbite; rubber products, wood; hides and skins, textiles, cement and other construction materials, food products, footwear, chemicals, fertilizer, printing, ceramics, steel

Industrial production growth rate: 0.72% (2023 est.)
note: annual % change in industrial value added based on constant local currency
comparison ranking: 146

Labor force: 75.721 million (2023 est.)
note: number of people ages 15 or older who are employed or seeking work
comparison ranking: 7

Unemployment rate: 3.07% (2023 est.)
3.83% (2022 est.)
5.39% (2021 est.)
note: % of labor force seeking employment
comparison ranking: 49

Youth unemployment rate (ages 15-24): *total:* 5.8% (2023 est.)
male: 4.8% (2023 est.)
female: 7.1% (2023 est.)
note: % of labor force ages 15-24 seeking employment
comparison ranking: total 171

Population below poverty line: 40.1% (2018 est.)
note: % of population with income below national poverty line

Gini Index coefficient - distribution of family income: 35.1 (2018 est.)
note: index (0-100) of income distribution; higher values represent greater inequality
comparison ranking: 76

Average household expenditures: *on food:* 59% of household expenditures (2022 est.)
on alcohol and tobacco: 1% of household expenditures (2022 est.)

Household income or consumption by percentage share: *lowest 10%:* 2.9% (2018 est.)
highest 10%: 26.7% (2018 est.)
note: % share of income accruing to lowest and highest 10% of population

Remittances: 5.65% of GDP (2023 est.)
4.26% of GDP (2022 est.)
4.42% of GDP (2021 est.)
note: personal transfers and compensation between resident and non-resident individuals/households/entities

Budget: *revenues:* $37.298 billion (2019 est.)
expenditures: $59.868 billion (2019 est.)

Public debt: 21.8% of GDP (2017 est.)
comparison ranking: 182

Taxes and other revenues: 3.4% (of GDP) (2017 est.)
comparison ranking: 204

Current account balance: -$805.777 million (2023 est.)
$1.019 billion (2022 est.)
-$3.254 billion (2021 est.)
note: balance of payments - net trade and primary/secondary income in current dollars
comparison ranking: 132

Exports: $60.261 billion (2023 est.)
$69.091 billion (2022 est.)
$50.856 billion (2021 est.)
note: balance of payments - exports of goods and services in current dollars
comparison ranking: 60

Exports - partners: Spain 13%, India 12%, France 7%, US 7%, Netherlands 6% (2022)
note: top five export partners based on percentage share of exports

Exports - commodities: crude petroleum, natural gas, fertilizers, refined petroleum, gold (2022)
note: top five export commodities based on value in dollars

Imports: $72.251 billion (2023 est.)
$77.049 billion (2022 est.)
$67.478 billion (2021 est.)
note: balance of payments - imports of goods and services in current dollars
comparison ranking: 55

Imports - partners: China 32%, Belgium 11%, Netherlands 10%, India 8%, US 5% (2022)
note: top five import partners based on percentage share of imports

Imports - commodities: refined petroleum, wheat, garments, plastics, cars (2022)
note: top five import commodities based on value in dollars

Reserves of foreign exchange and gold: $35.564 billion (2022 est.)
$40.476 billion (2021 est.)
$36.73 billion (2020 est.)
note: holdings of gold (year-end prices)/foreign exchange/special drawing rights in current dollars
comparison ranking: 49

Debt - external: $37.911 billion (2022 est.)
note: present value of external debt in current US dollars
comparison ranking: 16

Exchange rates: nairas (NGN) per US dollar -

Exchange rates: 425.979 (2022 est.)
401.152 (2021 est.)
358.811 (2020 est.)
306.921 (2019 est.)
306.084 (2018 est.)

ENERGY

Electricity access: *electrification - total population:* 60.5% (2022 est.)
electrification - urban areas: 89%
electrification - rural areas: 27%

Electricity: *installed generating capacity:* 11.697 million kW (2022 est.)
consumption: 31.57 billion kWh (2022 est.)
transmission/distribution losses: 5.41 billion kWh (2022 est.)
comparison rankings: transmission/distribution losses 167; consumption 65; installed generating capacity 61

Electricity generation sources: *fossil fuels:* 78.3% of total installed capacity (2022 est.)
solar: 0.1% of total installed capacity (2022 est.)
hydroelectricity: 21.5% of total installed capacity (2022 est.)
biomass and waste: 0.1% of total installed capacity (2022 est.)

Coal: *production:* 3.043 million metric tons (2022 est.)
consumption: 3.044 million metric tons (2022 est.)
exports: (2022 est.) less than 1 metric ton
imports: 1,000 metric tons (2022 est.)
proven reserves: 2.144 billion metric tons (2022 est.)

Petroleum: *total petroleum production:* 1.514 million bbl/day (2023 est.)
refined petroleum consumption: 515,000 bbl/day (2022 est.)
crude oil estimated reserves: 36.89 billion barrels (2021 est.)

Natural gas: *production:* 39.951 billion cubic meters (2022 est.)
consumption: 20.719 billion cubic meters (2022 est.)
exports: 19.722 billion cubic meters (2022 est.)
proven reserves: 5.761 trillion cubic meters (2021 est.)

Carbon dioxide emissions: 118.699 million metric tonnes of CO_2 (2022 est.)
from coal and metallurgical coke: 6.8 million metric tonnes of CO_2 (2022 est.)
from petroleum and other liquids: 71.255 million metric tonnes of CO_2 (2022 est.)
from consumed natural gas: 40.645 million metric tonnes of CO_2 (2022 est.)
comparison ranking: total emissions 37

Energy consumption per capita: 8.564 million Btu/person (2022 est.)
comparison ranking: 154

COMMUNICATIONS

Telephones - fixed lines: *total subscriptions:* 97,000 (2022 est.)
subscriptions per 100 inhabitants: (2022 est.) less than 1
comparison ranking: total subscriptions 134

Telephones - mobile cellular: *total subscriptions:* 222.225 million (2022 est.)
subscriptions per 100 inhabitants: 102 (2022 est.)
comparison ranking: total subscriptions 6

Telecommunication systems: *general assessment:* one of the larger telecom markets in Africa subject to sporadic access to electricity and vandalism of infrastructure; most Internet connections are via mobile networks; market competition with affordable access; LTE technologies available but GSM is dominant; mobile penetration high due to use of multiple SIM cards and phones; government committed to expanding broadband penetration; operators to deploy fiber optic cable in six geopolitical zones and Lagos; operators invested in base stations to deplete network congestion; submarine cable break in 2020 slowed speeds and interrupted connectivity; Nigeria concluded its first 5G spectrum auction in 2021 and granted licenses to two firms; construction of 5G infrastructure has not yet been completed (2022)
domestic: fixed-line subscribership remains less than 1 per 100 persons; mobile-cellular subscribership is 91 per 100 persons (2021)
international: country code - 234; landing point for the SAT-3/WASC, NCSCS, MainOne, Glo-1 & 2, ACE, and Equiano fiber-optic submarine cable that provides connectivity to Europe and South and West Africa; satellite earth stations - 3 Intelsat (2 Atlantic Ocean and 1 Indian Ocean) (2019)

Broadcast media: nearly 70 federal government-controlled national and regional TV stations; all 36 states operate TV stations; several private TV stations operational; cable and satellite TV subscription services are available; network of federal government-controlled national, regional, and state radio stations; roughly 40 state government-owned radio stations typically carry their own programs except for news broadcasts; about 20 private radio stations; transmissions of international broadcasters are available; digital broadcasting migration process completed in three states in 2018 (2019)

Internet country code: .ng

Internet users: *total:* 115.5 million (2021 est.)
percent of population: 55% (2021 est.)
comparison ranking: total 7

Broadband - fixed subscriptions: *total:* 65,313 (2020 est.)
subscriptions per 100 inhabitants: 0.03 (2020 est.)
comparison ranking: total 137

TRANSPORTATION

National air transport system: *number of registered air carriers:* 13 (2020)
inventory of registered aircraft operated by air carriers: 104
annual passenger traffic on registered air carriers: 8,169,192 (2018)
annual freight traffic on registered air carriers: 19.42 million (2018) mt-km

Civil aircraft registration country code prefix: 5N

Airports: 47 (2024)
comparison ranking: 91

Heliports: 15 (2024)

Pipelines: 124 km condensate, 4,045 km gas, 164 km liquid petroleum gas, 4,441 km oil, 3,940 km refined products (2013)

Railways: *total:* 3,798 km (2014)
standard gauge: 293 km (2014) 1.435-m gauge
narrow gauge: 3,505 km (2014) 1.067-m gauge
note: as of the end of 2018, there were only six operational locomotives in Nigeria primarily used for passenger service; the majority of the rail lines are in a severe state of disrepair and need to be replaced
comparison ranking: total 52

Roadways: *total:* 195,000 km
paved: 60,000 km
unpaved: 135,000 km (2019)
comparison ranking: total 28

Waterways: 8,600 km (2011) (Niger and Benue Rivers and smaller rivers and creeks)
comparison ranking: 17

Merchant marine: *total:* 928 (2023)
by type: general cargo 23, oil tanker 128, other 777
comparison ranking: total 25

Ports: *total ports:* 28 (2024)
large: 2
medium: 1
small: 1
very small: 24
ports with oil terminals: 23
key ports: Antan Oil Terminal, Bonny, Lagos, Pennington Oil Terminal

MILITARY AND SECURITY

Military and security forces: Armed Forces of Nigeria (AFN): Army, Navy (includes Coast Guard), Air Force

Ministry of Interior: Nigeria Security and Civil Defense Corps (NSCDC); Ministry of Police Affairs: Nigeria Police Force (NPF) (2024)
note 1: the NSCDC is a paramilitary agency commissioned to assist the military in the management of threats to internal security, including attacks and natural disasters
note 2: the Office of the National Security Advisor is responsible for coordinating all security and enforcement agencies, including the Department of State Security (DSS), the NSCDC, the Ministry of Justice, and the Police; border security responsibilities are shared among the NPF, the DSS, the NSCDC, Nigeria Customs Service, Immigration Service, and the AFN
note 3: some states have created local security forces akin to neighborhood watches in response to increased violence, insecurity, and criminality that have exceeded the response capacity of federal government security forces, but official security forces remained the constitutional prerogative of the federal government; in 2023, the federal government began deploying thousands of "agro rangers" across 19 states and the Federal Capital Territory to help safeguard farmland and mediate conflicts, especially in areas hit by farmer-herder clashes

Military expenditures: 0.7% of GDP (2023 est.)
0.6% of GDP (2022 est.)
0.7% of GDP (2021 est.)
0.6% of GDP (2020 est.)
0.5% of GDP (2019 est.)
comparison ranking: 149

Military and security service personnel strengths: information varies; approximately 135,000 active-duty armed forces personnel (100,000 Army; 20,000 Navy/Coast Guard; 15,000 Air Force); approximately 80,000 Security and Civil Defense Corps; approximately 370,000 police (2023)

Military equipment inventories and acquisitions: the military's inventory consists of a wide variety of imported weapons systems of Chinese, European, Middle Eastern, Russian (including Soviet-era), and US origin; the military is undergoing a modernization program, and in recent years has received equipment from a range of suppliers, including Brazil, China, France, Italy, Russia, Turkey, and the US; Nigeria is also developing a defense-industry capacity, including small arms, armored personnel vehicles, and smallscale naval production (2024)

Military service age and obligation: 18-26 years of age for voluntary military service for men and women; no conscription (2023)

Military deployments: 190 Sudan/South Sudan (UNISFA) (2024)
note: Nigeria has committed an Army combat brigade (approximately 3,000 troops) to the Multinational Joint Task Force (MNJTF), a regional counter-terrorism force comprised of troops from Benin, Cameroon, Chad, and Niger; MNJTF conducts operations against Boko Haram and other terrorist groups operating in the general area of the Lake Chad Basin and along Nigeria's northeast border; national MNJTF troop contingents are deployed within their own country territories, although cross-border operations are conducted periodically

Military - note: the Nigerian military is sub-Saharan Africa's largest and regarded as one of its most capable forces; the military's primary concerns are internal and maritime security, and it faces a number of challenges; the Army is deployed in all 36 of the country's states; in the northeast, it is conducting counterinsurgency/counterterrorist operations against the Boko Haram (BH) and Islamic State of Iraq and ash-Sham in West Africa (ISIS-WA) terrorist groups, where it has deployed as many as 70,000 troops at times and jihadist-related violence has killed an estimated 35-40,000 people, mostly civilians, since 2009; in the northwest, it faces threats from criminal gangs–locally referred to as bandits–and violence associated with long-standing farmer-herder conflicts, as well as BH and ISIS-WA terrorists; bandits in northwestern Nigeria are estimated to number as many as 30,000 and violence there has killed approximately 14,000 people since the mid-2010s; the military also continues to protect the oil industry in the Niger Delta region against militants and criminal activity; since 2021, additional troops and security forces have been deployed to eastern Nigeria to quell renewed agitation for a state of Biafra (Biafra seceded from Nigeria in the late 1960s, sparking a civil war that caused more than 1 million deaths)
the Navy is focused on maritime security in the Gulf of Guinea; since 2016, it has developed a maritime strategy, boosted naval training and its naval presence in the Gulf, increased participation in regional maritime security efforts, and acquired a number of new naval platforms, including offshore and coastal patrol craft, fast attack boats, and air assets
the Nigerian military traces its origins to the Nigeria Regiment of the West African Frontier Force (WAFF), a multiregiment force formed by the British colonial office in 1900 to garrison Great Britain's West African colonies; the WAFF (the honorary title "Royal" was added later) served in both World Wars; in 1956, the Nigeria Regiment of the Royal WAFF was renamed the Nigerian Military Forces (NMF) and in 1958, the colonial government of Nigeria took over control of the NMF from the British War Office; the Nigerian Armed Forces were established following independence in 1960 (2024)

SPACE

Space agency/agencies: National Space Research and Development Agency (NARSDA; established 1999); NARSDA originated from the National Centre for Remote Sensing and National Committee on Space Applications (both established in 1987), and the Directorate of Science (established 1993); Defense Space Administration (DSA; established 2014) (2024)

Space program overview: has a formal national space program, which is one of the largest in Africa; focused on acquiring satellites for agricultural, environmental, meteorology, mining and disaster monitoring, socio-economic development, and security purposes; designs, builds (mostly with foreign assistance), and operates satellites; processes overhead imagery data for analysis and sharing; developing additional capabilities in satellite and satellite payload production, including remote sensing (RS) technologies; has a sounding rocket program for researching rockets and rocket propulsion systems with goal of launching domestically produced satellites into space from a Nigerian spaceport by 2030; has relations and/or cooperation agreements with a variety of foreign space agencies and industries, including those of Algeria, Bangladesh, Belarus, China, Ghana, India, Japan, Kenya, Mongolia, South Africa, Thailand, Turkey, the UK, the US, and Vietnam; has a government-owned satellite company and a small commercial aerospace sector (2024)
note: further details about the key activities, programs, and milestones of the country's space program, as well as government spending estimates on the space sector, appear in the Space Programs reference guide

TERRORISM

Terrorist group(s): Boko Haram; Islamic State of Iraq and ash-Sham – West Africa; Jama'atu Ansarul Muslimina Fi Biladis-Sudan (Ansaru)
note: details about the history, aims, leadership, organization, areas of operation, tactics, targets, weapons, size, and sources of support of the group(s) appear(s) in the Terrorism reference guide

TRANSNATIONAL ISSUES

Refugees and internally displaced persons: *refugees (country of origin):* 89,045 (Cameroon) (2023)
IDPs: 3.09 million (northeast Nigeria; Boko Haram attacks and counterinsurgency efforts in northern Nigeria; communal violence between Christians and Muslims in the middle belt region, political violence; flooding; forced evictions; cattle rustling; competition for resources) (2024)

Illicit drugs: Nigeria is a major hub for transnational drug trafficking networks entrenched throughout the world and supplying cocaine to Asia and Europe, heroin to Europe and North America, and methamphetamine to South Africa, Southeast Asia, Australia, and New Zealand; also exporting massive quantities of opioids such as tramadol and captagon along with crack cocaine; a major source of precursor or essential chemicals used in the production of illicit narcotics

NIUE

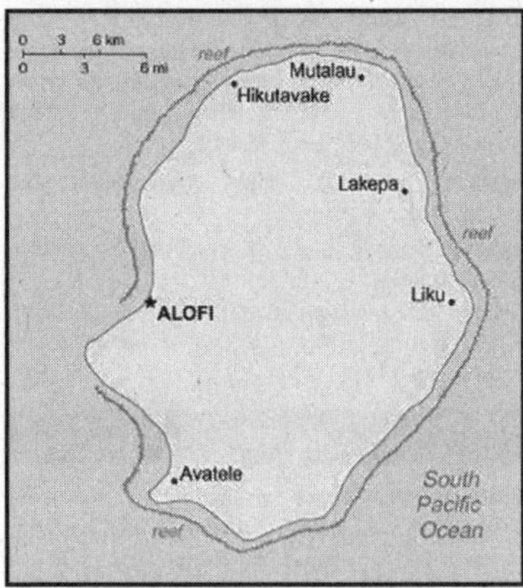

INTRODUCTION

Background: Voyagers from Samoa first settled on Niue around A.D. 900, and a second main group of settlers came from Tonga around 1500. With only one reliable source of fresh water, conflict was high on the island. Samoan and Tongan customs heavily influenced Niuean culture, including the formation of an island-wide elected kingship system in the early 1700s. In 1774, British explorer James COOK landed on the island and named it Savage Island because of the Niueans' hostility. Missionaries arrived in 1830 but were also largely unsuccessful at staying on the island until 1846, when a Niuean trained as a Samoan missionary returned to the island and provided a space from which the missionaries could work. In addition to converting the population, the missionaries worked to stop the violent conflicts and helped establish the first parliament in 1849.

Great Britain established a protectorate over Niue in 1900. The following year, Niue was annexed to New Zealand and included as part of the Cook Islands. Niue's remoteness and cultural and linguistic differences with the Cook Islands led New Zealand to separate Niue into its own administration in 1904. The island became internally self-governing in 1974; it is an independent member of international organizations but is in free association with New Zealand, which is responsible for defense and foreign affairs. In September 2023, the US recognized Niue as a sovereign and independent state.

GEOGRAPHY

Location: Oceania, island in the South Pacific Ocean, east of Tonga

Geographic coordinates: 19 02 S, 169 52 W

Map references: Oceania

Area: *total:* 260 sq km
land: 260 sq km
water: 0 sq km
comparison ranking: total 212

Area - comparative: 1.5 times the size of Washington, DC

Land boundaries: *total:* 0 km

Coastline: 64 km

Maritime claims: *territorial sea:* 12 nm
exclusive economic zone: 200 nm

Climate: tropical; modified by southeast trade winds

Terrain: steep limestone cliffs along coast, central plateau

Elevation: *highest point:* unnamed elevation 1.4 km east of Hikutavake 80 m
lowest point: Pacific Ocean 0 m

Natural resources: arable land, fish

Land use: *agricultural land:* 19.1% (2018 est.)
arable land: 3.8% (2018 est.)
permanent crops: 11.5% (2018 est.)
permanent pasture: 3.8% (2018 est.)
forest: 71.2% (2018 est.)
other: 9.7% (2018 est.)

Irrigated land: 0 sq km (2022)

Population distribution: population distributed around the peripheral coastal areas of the island

Natural hazards: tropical cyclones

Geography - note: one of world's largest coral islands; the only major break in the surrounding coral reef occurs in the central western part of the coast

PEOPLE AND SOCIETY

Population: *total:* 2,000 (2022 est.)
note: because of the island's limited economic and educational opportunities, Niueans have emigrated for decades - primarily to New Zealand but also to Australia and other Pacific island states; Niue's population peaked in 1966 at 5,194, but by 2005 had fallen to 1,508; since then, it has rebounded slightly; as of 2013, 23,883 people of Niuean ancestry lived in New Zealand - with more than 20% Niue-born - or about 15 times as many persons of Niuean ancestry living in New Zealand as in Niue
comparison ranking: total 230

Nationality: *noun:* Niuean(s)
adjective: Niuean

Ethnic groups: Niuean 65.4%, part-Niuean 14%, non-Niuean 20.6% (2017 est.)
note: data represent the resident population

Languages: Niuean 46% (official, a Polynesian language closely related to Tongan and Samoan), Niuean and English 32%, English (official) 11%, Niuean and others 5%, other 6% (2011 est.)

Religions: Ekalesia Niue (Congregational Christian Church of Niue - a Protestant church founded by missionaries from the London Missionary Society) 61.7%, Church of Jesus Christ 8.7%, Roman Catholic 8.4%, Jehovah's Witness 2.7%, Seventh Day Adventist 1.4%, other 8.2%, none 8.9% (2017 est.)

Dependency ratios: *total dependency ratio:* 70.4
youth dependency ratio: 44.9
elderly dependency ratio: 25.4

potential support ratio: 3.9 (2021)

Population growth rate: -0.03% (2021 est.)
comparison ranking: 198

Population distribution: population distributed around the peripheral coastal areas of the island

Urbanization: *urban population:* 48.2% of total population (2023)
rate of urbanization: 1.43% annual rate of change (2020-25 est.)

Major urban areas - population: 1,000 ALOFI (capital) (2018)

Drinking water source: *improved:* improved: *total:* 97% of population
unimproved: unimproved: total: 3% of population (2020 est.)

Current health expenditure: 7.8% of GDP (2020)

Sanitation facility access: *improved:* improved: *total:* 95.5% of population
unimproved: unimproved: total: 4.5% of population (2020 est.)

Obesity - adult prevalence rate: 50% (2016)
comparison ranking: 6

Alcohol consumption per capita: *total:* 8.5 liters of pure alcohol (2019 est.)
beer: 4.28 liters of pure alcohol (2019 est.)
wine: 1.89 liters of pure alcohol (2019 est.)
spirits: 2.33 liters of pure alcohol (2019 est.)
other alcohols: 0 liters of pure alcohol (2019 est.)
comparison ranking: total 38

ENVIRONMENT

Environment - current issues: increasing attention to conservationist practices to counter loss of soil fertility from traditional slash and burn agriculture

Environment - international agreements: *party to:* Biodiversity, Climate Change, Climate Change-Kyoto Protocol, Climate Change-Paris Agreement, Comprehensive Nuclear Test Ban, Desertification, Law of the Sea, Ozone Layer Protection, Ship Pollution
signed, but not ratified: none of the selected agreements

Climate: tropical; modified by southeast trade winds

Urbanization: *urban population:* 48.2% of total population (2023)
rate of urbanization: 1.43% annual rate of change (2020-25 est.)

Air pollutants: *particulate matter emissions:* 6.74 micrograms per cubic meter (2019 est.)

Total renewable water resources: 0 cubic meters (2017 est.)

GOVERNMENT

Country name: *conventional long form:* none
conventional short form: Niue
former: Savage Island
etymology: the origin of the name is obscure; in Niuean, the word supposedly translates as "behold the coconut"
note: pronunciation falls between nyu-way and new-way, but not like new-wee

Government type: parliamentary democracy

Dependency status: self-governing in free association with New Zealand since 1974; Niue is fully responsible for internal affairs; New Zealand retains responsibility for external affairs and defense; however, these responsibilities confer no rights of control and are only exercised at the request of the Government of Niue

Capital: *name:* Alofi
geographic coordinates: 19 01 S, 169 55 W
time difference: UTC-11 (6 hours behind Washington, DC, during Standard Time)

Administrative divisions: none; there are no first-order administrative divisions as defined by the US Government, but there are 14 villages at the second order

Independence: 19 October 1974 (Niue became a self-governing state in free association with New Zealand)

National holiday: Waitangi Day (Treaty of Waitangi established British sovereignty over New Zealand), 6 February (1840)

Legal system: English common law

Constitution: *history:* several previous (New Zealand colonial statutes); latest 19 October 1974 (Niue Constitution Act 1974)
amendments: proposed by the Assembly; passage requires at least two-thirds majority vote of the Assembly membership in each of three readings and approval by at least two-thirds majority votes in a referendum; passage of amendments to a number of sections, including Niue's self-governing status, British nationality and New Zealand citizenship, external affairs and defense, economic and administrative assistance by New Zealand, and amendment procedures, requires at least two-thirds majority vote by the Assembly and at least two thirds of votes in a referendum; amended 1992, 2007; note - in early 2021, the constitution review committee of the Assembly requested suggestions from the public about changes to the constitution

Suffrage: 18 years of age; universal

Executive branch: *chief of state:* King CHARLES III (since 8 September 2022); represented by Governor-General of New Zealand Cindy KIRO (since 21 October 2021); the UK and New Zealand are represented by New Zealand High Commissioner Mark GIBBS (since 5 March 2024)
head of government: Prime Minister Dalton TAGELAGI (since 10 June 2020)
cabinet: Cabinet chosen by the premier
elections/appointments: the monarchy is hereditary; premier indirectly elected by the Legislative Assembly for a 3-year term; election last held on 8 May 2023 (next to be held in 2026)
election results: Dalton TAGELAGI reelected premier; Legislative Assembly vote - Dalton TAGELAGI (independent) 16, O'Love JACOBSEN (independent) 4

Legislative branch: *description:* unicameral Assembly or Fono Ekepule (20 seats; 14 members directly elected in single-seat constituencies by simple majority vote and 6 directly elected from the National Register or "common roll" by majority vote; members serve 3-year terms)
elections: last held on 29 April 2023 (next to be held in 2026)
election results: percent of vote - NA; seats - independent 20; composition - men 17, women 3, percentage women 15%

Judicial branch: *highest court(s):* Court of Appeal (consists of the chief justice and up to 3 judges); note - the Judicial Committee of the Privy Council (in London) is the final appeal court beyond the Niue Court of Appeal
judge selection and term of office: Niue chief justice appointed by the governor general on the advice of the Cabinet and tendered by the premier; other judges appointed by the governor general on the advice of the Cabinet and tendered by the chief justice and the minister of justice; judges serve until age 68
subordinate courts: High Court
note: Niue is a participant in the Pacific Judicial Development Program, which is designed to build governance and the rule of law in 15 Pacific island countries

Political parties: none

International organization participation: ACP, AOSIS, FAO, IFAD, OPCW, PIF, Sparteca, SPC, UNESCO, UPU, WHO, WIPO, WMO

Diplomatic representation in the US: none (self-governing territory in free association with New Zealand)

Diplomatic representation from the US: *embassy:* none (self-governing territory in free association with New Zealand)
note: on 25 September 2023, the US officially established diplomatic relations with Niue

Flag description: yellow with the flag of the UK in the upper hoist-side quadrant; the flag of the UK bears five yellow five-pointed stars - a large star on a blue disk in the center and a smaller star on each arm of the bold red cross; the larger star stands for Niue, the smaller stars recall the Southern Cross constellation on the New Zealand flag and symbolize links with that country; yellow represents the bright sunshine of Niue and the warmth and friendship between Niue and New Zealand

National symbol(s): yellow, five-pointed star; national color: yellow

National anthem: *name:* "Ko e Iki he Lagi" (The Lord in Heaven)
lyrics/music: unknown/unknown, prepared by Sioeli FUSIKATA
note: adopted 1974

ECONOMY

Economic overview: upper-middle-income self-governing New Zealand territorial economy; environmentally fragile; massive emigration; postpandemic tourism rebound; postage stamps, small-scale agricultural processing, and subsistence farming; most recent Asian Development Bank member

Real GDP (purchasing power parity): $18.7 million (2021 est.)
$19.9 million (2020 est.)
$20.9 million (2019 est.)
comparison ranking: 223

Real GDP per capita: $11,100 (2021 est.)
$11,800 (2020 est.)
$12,400 (2019 est.)
note: data are in 2009 dollars
comparison ranking: 144

Agricultural products: taro, coconuts, fruits, sweet potatoes, tropical fruits, yams, vegetables, lemons/limes, bananas, pork (2022)
note: top ten agricultural products based on tonnage

Industries: handicrafts, food processing

Exports: $5.68 million (2021 est.)
comparison ranking: 220

Exports - partners: US 56%, Brazil 9%, UK 6%, Kuwait 4%, Australia 4% (2022)

note: top five export partners based on percentage share of exports

Exports - commodities: broadcasting equipment, abrasive powder, collector's items, coin, milling stones (2022)
note: top five export commodities based on value in dollars

Imports: $43.8 million (2021 est.)
comparison ranking: 218

Imports - partners: UK 46%, NZ 31%, Japan 19%, Brazil 1%, US 1% (2022)
note: top five import partners based on percentage share of imports

Imports - commodities: iron structures, ships, refined petroleum, plastic products, cars (2022)
note: top five import commodities based on value in dollars

Exchange rates: New Zealand dollars (NZD) per US dollar -

Exchange rates: 1.628 (2023 est.)
1.577 (2022 est.)
1.414 (2021 est.)
1.542 (2020 est.)
1.518 (2019 est.)

ENERGY

Electricity: *installed generating capacity:* 3,000 kW (2022 est.)
consumption: 3 million kWh (2022 est.)
transmission/distribution losses: 400,000 kWh (2022 est.)
comparison rankings: transmission/distribution losses 2; consumption 211; installed generating capacity 211

Electricity generation sources: *fossil fuels:* 100% of total installed capacity (2022 est.)

Petroleum: *refined petroleum consumption:* 58.2 bbl/day (2022 est.)

Carbon dioxide emissions: 8,000 metric tonnes of CO2 (2022 est.)
from petroleum and other liquids: 8,000 metric tonnes of CO2 (2022 est.)
comparison ranking: total emissions 217

Energy consumption per capita: (2019)

COMMUNICATIONS

Telephones - fixed lines: *total subscriptions:* 1,000 (2021 est.)
subscriptions per 100 inhabitants: 52 (2021 est.)
comparison ranking: total subscriptions 219

Telecommunication systems: *general assessment:* in 2020, the Manatua One Polynesia Fiber Cable provided Niue with high speed Internet access for the first time replacing a 4 megabit satellite link with gigabit fiber connectivity; the government set out a strategy to upgrade to a new infrastructure that would be robust enough to operate reliably in a challenging climate: 40 40°C heat, 40% humidity, salty air, frequent power outages during storms, and no air conditioning (2022)
domestic: single-line (fixed line) telephone system connects all villages on island; fixed teledensity at nearly 52 per 100 (2021)
international: country code - 683; landing point for the Manatua submarine cable linking Niue to several South Pacific Ocean Islands; expansion of satellite services (2019)

Broadcast media: 1 government-owned TV station with many of the programs supplied by Television New Zealand; 1 government-owned radio station broadcasting in AM and FM (2019)

Internet country code: .nu

Internet users: *total:* 1,512 (2021 est.)
percent of population: 79.6% (2021 est.)
comparison ranking: total 228

TRANSPORTATION

Airports: 1 (2024)
comparison ranking: 223

Roadways: *total:* 234 km
paved: 210 km
unpaved: 24 km (2017)
comparison ranking: total 208

Merchant marine: *total:* 70 (2023)
by type: bulk carrier 5, container ship 2, general cargo 29, oil tanker 4, other 30
comparison ranking: total 109

Ports: *total ports:* 1 (2024)
large: 0
medium: 0
small: 0
very small: 1
ports with oil terminals: 0
key ports: Alofi

MILITARY AND SECURITY

Military and security forces: no regular indigenous military forces; Police Force

Military - note: defense is the responsibility of New Zealand

NORFOLK ISLAND

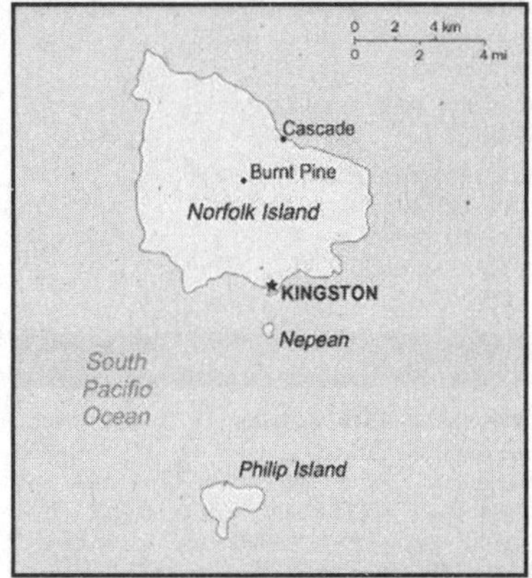

INTRODUCTION

Background: Polynesians lived on Norfolk Island between 1200 and 1500, but the remote island was uninhabited by the time British explorer James COOK landed on the island in 1774. Two British attempts at establishing the island as a penal colony (1788-1814 and 1825-55) were ultimately abandoned.

In 1856, almost 200 Pitcairn Islanders – descendants of the *Bounty* mutineers and their Tahitian companions – were relocated to Norfolk Island because of overcrowding on the Pitcairn Islands. Some returned to the Pitcairn Islands over the next few years, but most settled permanently on Norfolk Island and recreated their previous land tenure and governance structures. Norfolk Island retained a great degree of local control until 1897, when it became a dependency of New South Wales. During World War II, Norfolk Island was an airbase and an important refueling stop in the South Pacific. In 1976, an Australian judge recommended Norfolk Island be incorporated fully into Australia, which Norfolk Islanders rejected. After an appeal to the UN, Australia granted limited self-government to Norfolk Island in 1979.

With growing financial troubles during the 2000s, Australia abolished the Norfolk Island Legislative Assembly in 2015, reduced Norfolk Island's autonomy in 2016, and suspended the local council in 2020. Most services are provided by a mix of the Australian Capital Territory and the states of New South Wales and Queensland. These moves were unpopular on Norfolk Island, which has sought to have its self-government restored and as of 2024, the Australian Government was working with Norfolk Island to establish a new local governing body.

GEOGRAPHY

Location: Oceania, island in the South Pacific Ocean, east of Australia

Geographic coordinates: 29 02 S, 167 57 E

Map references: Oceania

Area: *total:* 36 sq km
land: 36 sq km
water: 0 sq km
comparison ranking: total 233

Area - comparative: about 0.2 times the size of Washington, DC

Land boundaries: *total:* 0 km

Coastline: 32 km

Maritime claims: *territorial sea:* 12 nm
contiguous zone: 24 nm
exclusive fishing zone: 200 nm

Climate: subtropical; mild, little seasonal temperature variation

Terrain: volcanic island with mostly rolling plains

Elevation: *highest point:* Mount Bates 319 m
lowest point: Pacific Ocean 0 m

Natural resources: fish

Land use: *agricultural land:* 25% (2018 est.)
arable land: 0% (2018 est.)
permanent crops: 0% (2018 est.)
permanent pasture: 25% (2018 est.)
forest: 11.5% (2018 est.)
other: 63.5% (2018 est.)

Irrigated land: 0 sq km (2022)

Population distribution: population concentrated around the capital of Kingston

Natural hazards: tropical cyclones (especially May to July)

Geography - note: most of the 32 km coastline consists of almost inaccessible cliffs, but the land slopes down to the sea in one small southern area on Sydney Bay, where the capital of Kingston is situated

PEOPLE AND SOCIETY

Population: *total:* 1,748 (2016 est.)
comparison ranking: total 231

Nationality: *noun:* Norfolk Islander(s)
adjective: Norfolk Islander(s)

Ethnic groups: Australian 22.8%, English 22.4%, Pitcairn Islander 20%, Scottish 6%, Irish 5.2% (2011 est.)
note: respondents were able to identify up to two ancestries; percentages represent a proportion of all responses from people in Norfolk Island, including those who did not identify an ancestry; only top responses are shown

Languages: English (official) 44.9%, Norfolk (official, a mixture of 18th century English and ancient Tahitian) 40.3%, Fijian 1.8%, other 6.8%, unspecified 6.2% (2016 est.)
note: data represent language spoken at home

Religions: Protestant 46.8% (Anglican 29.2%, Uniting Church in Australia 9.8%, Presbyterian 2.9%, Seventh Day Adventist 2.7%, other 2.2%), Roman Catholic 12.6%, other Christian 2.9%, other 1.4%, none 26.7%, unspecified 9.5% (2016 est.)

Population growth rate: 0.01% (2014 est.)
comparison ranking: 192

Population distribution: population concentrated around the capital of Kingston

ENVIRONMENT

Environment - current issues: inadequate solid waste management; most freshwater obtained through rainwater catchment; preservation of unique ecosystem

Climate: subtropical; mild, little seasonal temperature variation

GOVERNMENT

Country name: *conventional long form:* Territory of Norfolk Island
conventional short form: Norfolk Island
etymology: named by British explorer Captain James COOK after Mary HOWARD, Duchess of Norfolk, in 1774

Government type: non-self-governing overseas territory of Australia; note - the Norfolk Island Regional Council, which began operations 1 July 2016, is responsible for planning and managing a variety of public services, including those funded by the Government of Australia

Dependency status: self-governing territory of Australia; administered from Canberra by the Department of Infrastructure, Transport, Cities & Regional Development

Capital: *name:* Kingston
geographic coordinates: 29 03 S, 167 58 E
time difference: UTC+11 (16 hours ahead of Washington, DC, during Standard Time)
daylight saving time: +1hr, begins first Sunday in October; ends first Sunday in April
etymology: the name is a blending of the words "king's" and "town"; the British king at the time of the town's settlement in the late 18th century was GEORGE III

Administrative divisions: none (territory of Australia)

Independence: none (territory of Australia)

National holiday: Bounty Day (commemorates the arrival of Pitcairn Islanders), 8 June (1856)

Legal system: English common law and the laws of Australia

Constitution: *history:* previous 1913, 1957; latest effective 7 August 1979
amendments: amended many times, last in 2020

Citizenship: see Australia

Suffrage: 18 years of age; universal

Executive branch: *chief of state:* King CHARLES III (since 8 September 2022); represented by Governor General of the Commonwealth of Australia General David HURLEY (since 1 July 2019)
head of government: Administrator Eric HUTCHINSON (since 1 April 2017)
cabinet: Executive Council consists of 4 Legislative Assembly members
elections/appointments: the monarchy is hereditary; governor general appointed by the monarch; administrator appointed by the governor general of Australia for a 2-year term and represents the monarch and Australia

Legislative branch: *description:* unicameral Norfolk Island Regional Council (5 seats; councillors directly elected by simple majority vote to serve 4-year terms); mayor elected annually by the councillors
elections: last held on 28 May 2016 (next originally scheduled for 13 March 2021 but was postponed)
election results: seats by party - independent 5; composition - men 4, women 1, percentage women 20%

Judicial branch: *highest court(s):* Supreme Court of Norfolk Island (consists of the chief justice and several justices); note – appeals beyond the Supreme Court of Norfolk Island are heard by the Federal Court and the High Court of Australia
judge selection and term of office: justices appointed by the governor general of Australia from among justices of the Federal Court of Australia; justices serve until mandatory retirement at age 70
subordinate courts: Petty Court of Sessions; specialized courts, including a Coroner's Court and the Employment Tribunal

Political parties: Norfolk Island Labor Party
Norfolk Liberals

International organization participation: UPU

Diplomatic representation in the US: none (territory of Australia)

Diplomatic representation from the US: *embassy:* none (territory of Australia)

Flag description: three vertical bands of green (hoist side), white, and green with a large green Norfolk Island pine tree centered in the slightly wider white band; green stands for the rich vegetation on the island, and the pine tree - endemic to the island - is a symbol of Norfolk Island
note: somewhat reminiscent of the flag of Canada with its use of only two colors and depiction of a prominent local floral symbol in the central white band; also resembles the green and white triband of Nigeria

National symbol(s): Norfolk Island pine

National anthem: *name:* "Come Ye Blessed"
lyrics/music: New Testament/John Prindle SCOTT
*note: the local anthem, whose lyrics consist of the words from Matthew 25:*34-36, 40, is also known as "The Pitcairn Anthem;" the island does not recognize "Advance Australia Fair" (which other Australian territories use); instead "God Save the King" is official (see United Kingdom)

ECONOMY

Economic overview: high-income Australian territorial economy; key tourism and re-exportation industries; small labor force and declining participation creating more part-time jobs; former tax haven; increasing medical cannabis exporter; little transportation infrastructure

Agricultural products: Norfolk Island pine seed, Kentia palm seed, cereals, vegetables, fruit; cattle, poultry

Industries: tourism, light industry, ready mixed concrete

Exports - partners: India 16%, Belgium 14%, US 14%, Malaysia 13%, Singapore 10% (2022)
note: top five export partners based on percentage share of exports

Exports - commodities: pine seeds, lumber, cars and vehicle parts, soybeans, lactose syrup, cleaning products, scrap aluminum (2021)

Imports - partners: Australia 34%, Philippines 19%, NZ 17%, Fiji 9%, Brazil 7% (2022)
note: top five import partners based on percentage share of imports

Imports - commodities: clothing and apparel, chemical analysis instruments, refined petroleum, cars, kitchen machinery (2019)

Exchange rates: Australian dollars (AUD) per US dollar -

Exchange rates: 1.505 (2023 est.)
1.442 (2022 est.)
1.331 (2021 est.)
1.453 (2020 est.)
1.439 (2019 est.)

COMMUNICATIONS

Telecommunication systems: *general assessment:* the current infrastructure consists of fixed line telephone utilizing copper twisted pair cable and optic fiber, two Satellite Earth Station, GSM Mobile switch with five remote base stations and 2 micro cells, central public exchange which switches international as well as national calls, ADSL Broadband internet connection (Asynchronous Digital Subscriber Line), and an ISP (Internet Service Provider); 3G/4G telecommunications network went live on Tuesday 12 January, 2021 (2021)
domestic: free local calls
international: country code - 672; submarine cable links with Australia and New Zealand; satellite earth station - 1

Broadcast media: 1 local radio station; broadcasts of several Australian radio and TV stations available via satellite (2009)

Internet country code: .nf

Internet users: *total:* 806 (2021 est.)
percent of population: 46.1% (2021 est.)
comparison ranking: total 230

TRANSPORTATION

Airports: 1 (2024)
comparison ranking: 215

Roadways: *total:* 80 km
paved: 53 km
unpaved: 27 km (2008)
comparison ranking: total 217

Ports: *total ports:* 1 (2024)
large: 0
medium: 0
small: 0
very small: 1
ports with oil terminals: 1
key ports: Kingston

MILITARY AND SECURITY

Military - note: defense is the responsibility of Australia

NORTH MACEDONIA

INTRODUCTION

Background: North Macedonia gained its independence peacefully from Yugoslavia in 1991 under the name of "Macedonia." Greece objected to the new country's name, insisting it implied territorial pretensions to the northern Greek province of Macedonia, and democratic backsliding for several years stalled North Macedonia's movement toward Euro-Atlantic integration. Immediately after Macedonia declared independence, Greece sought to block its efforts to gain UN membership if the name "Macedonia" was used. The country was eventually admitted to the UN in 1993 as "The former Yugoslav Republic of Macedonia," and at the same time it agreed to UN-sponsored negotiations on the name dispute. In 1995, Greece lifted a 20-month trade embargo and the two countries agreed to normalize relations, but the issue of the name remained unresolved amid ongoing negotiations. As an interim measure, the US and over 130 other nations recognized Macedonia by its constitutional name, Republic of Macedonia.

Ethnic Albanian grievances over perceived political and economic inequities escalated into an armed conflict in 2001 that eventually led to the internationally brokered Ohrid Framework Agreement, which ended the fighting and established guidelines for constitutional amendments and new laws that enhanced the rights of minorities. In 2018, the government adopted a new law on languages, which elevated the Albanian language to an official language at the national level and kept the Macedonian language as the sole official language in international relations, but ties between ethnic Macedonians and ethnic Albanians remain complicated.

In 2018, Macedonia and Greece signed the Prespa Agreement whereby Macedonia agreed to change its name to North Macedonia, and the agreement went in to force on 12 February 2019. North Macedonia joined NATO in 2020 after amending its constitution as agreed and opened EU accession talks in 2022 after a two-year veto by Bulgaria over identity, language, and historical disputes. The 2014 legislative and presidential election triggered a political crisis that lasted almost three years and escalated in 2015 when the opposition party began releasing wiretapped material revealing alleged widespread government corruption and abuse. The country still faces challenges, including fully implementing reforms to overcome years of democratic backsliding, stimulating economic growth and development, and fighting organized crime and corruption.

GEOGRAPHY

Location: Southeastern Europe, north of Greece

Geographic coordinates: 41 50 N, 22 00 E

Map references: Europe

Area: *total:* 25,713 sq km
land: 25,433 sq km
water: 280 sq km
comparison ranking: total 149

Area - comparative: slightly larger than Vermont; almost four times the size of Delaware

Land boundaries: *total:* 838 km
border countries (5): Albania 181 km; Bulgaria 162 km; Greece 234 km; Kosovo 160 km; Serbia 101 km

Coastline: 0 km (landlocked)

Maritime claims: none (landlocked)

Climate: warm, dry summers and autumns; relatively cold winters with heavy snowfall

Terrain: mountainous with deep basins and valleys; three large lakes, each divided by a frontier line; country bisected by the Vardar River

Elevation: *highest point:* Golem Korab (Maja e Korabit) 2,764 m
lowest point: Vardar River 50 m
mean elevation: 741 m

Natural resources: low-grade iron ore, copper, lead, zinc, chromite, manganese, nickel, tungsten, gold, silver, asbestos, gypsum, timber, arable land

Land use: *agricultural land:* 44.3% (2018 est.)
arable land: 16.4% (2018 est.)
permanent crops: 1.4% (2018 est.)
permanent pasture: 26.5% (2018 est.)
forest: 39.8% (2018 est.)
other: 15.9% (2018 est.)

Irrigated land: 844 sq km (2016)

Major watersheds (area sq km): Atlantic Ocean drainage: *(Black Sea)* Danube (795,656 sq km)

Population distribution: a fairly even distribution throughout most of the country, with urban areas attracting larger and denser populations

Natural hazards: high seismic risks

Geography - note: landlocked; major transportation corridor from Western and Central Europe to Aegean Sea and Southern Europe to Western Europe

PEOPLE AND SOCIETY

Population: *total:* 2,135,622
male: 1,064,727
female: 1,070,895 (2024 est.)
comparison rankings: female 148; male 149; total 149

Nationality: *noun:* Macedonian(s)
adjective: Macedonian

Ethnic groups: Macedonian 58.4%, Albanian 24.3%, Turkish 3.9%, Romani 2.5%, Serb 1.3%, other 2.3%, no ethnic affiliation data available 7.2% (2021 est.)
note: data represent total resident population; Romani populations are usually underestimated in official statistics and may represent 6.5–13% of North Macedonia's population

Languages: Macedonian (official) 61.4%, Albanian (official) 24.3%, Turkish 3.4%, Romani 1.7%, other (includes Aromanian (Vlach) and Bosnian) 2%, unspecified 7.2% (2021 est.)
major-language sample(s):
основни информации. (Macedonian)
note: data represent mother tongue; minority languages are co-official with Macedonian in municipalities where at least 20% of the population are speakers, with Albanian co-official in Tetovo, Brvenica, Vrapciste, and other municipalities, Turkish in Centar Zupa and Plasnica, Romani in Suto Orizari, Aromanian in Krusevo, Serbian in Cucer Sandevo

Religions: Macedonian Orthodox 46.1%, Muslim 32.2%, other Christian 13.8%, other and non-believers 0.5%, unspecified 7.4% (2021 est.)

Age structure: *0-14 years:* 16% (male 176,423/female 164,945)
15-64 years: 68.4% (male 740,649/female 719,627)
65 years and over: 15.6% (2024 est.) (male 147,655/female 186,323)

Dependency ratios: *total dependency ratio:* 44.6
youth dependency ratio: 23.2
elderly dependency ratio: 21.4
potential support ratio: 4.7 (2021 est.)

Median age: *total:* 40.5 years (2024 est.)
male: 39.4 years
female: 41.6 years
comparison ranking: total 59

Population growth rate: 0.1% (2024 est.)
comparison ranking: 187

Birth rate: births/1,000 population (2024 est.)
comparison ranking: 181

Death rate: 9.6 deaths/1,000 population (2024 est.)
comparison ranking: 43

Net migration rate: 0.4 migrant(s)/1,000 population (2024 est.)
comparison ranking: 72

Population distribution: a fairly even distribution throughout most of the country, with urban areas attracting larger and denser populations

Urbanization: *urban population:* 59.5% of total population (2023)
rate of urbanization: 0.61% annual rate of change (2020-25 est.)

Major urban areas - population: 611,000 SKOPJE (capital) (2023)

Sex ratio: *at birth:* 1.07 male(s)/female
0-14 years: 1.07 male(s)/female
15-64 years: 1.03 male(s)/female
65 years and over: 0.79 male(s)/female
total population: 0.99 male(s)/female (2024 est.)

Mother's mean age at first birth: years (2020 est.)

Maternal mortality ratio: 3 deaths/100,000 live births (2020 est.)
comparison ranking: 179

Infant mortality rate: *total:* 7 deaths/1,000 live births (2024 est.)
male: 7.9 deaths/1,000 live births
female: 6 deaths/1,000 live births
comparison ranking: total 156

Life expectancy at birth: *total population:* 77.3 years (2024 est.)
male: 75.3 years
female: 79.6 years
comparison ranking: total population 92

Total fertility rate: 1.53 children born/woman (2024 est.)
comparison ranking: 198

Gross reproduction rate: 0.74 (2024 est.)

Contraceptive prevalence rate: 59.9% (2018/19)

Drinking water source: *improved: urban:* 99.7% of population
rural: 99% of population
total: 99.4% of population
unimproved: urban: 0.3% of population
rural: 1% of population
total: 0.6% of population (2020 est.)

Current health expenditure: 7.9% of GDP (2020)

Physician density: 2.87 physicians/1,000 population (2015)

Hospital bed density: 4.3 beds/1,000 population (2017)

Sanitation facility access: *improved: urban:* 100% of population
rural: 98% of population
total: 99.2% of population
unimproved: urban: 0% of population
rural: 2% of population
total: 0.8% of population (2020 est.)

Obesity - adult prevalence rate: 22.4% (2016)
comparison ranking: 77

Alcohol consumption per capita: *total:* 3.9 liters of pure alcohol (2019 est.)
beer: 1.93 liters of pure alcohol (2019 est.)
wine: 1.03 liters of pure alcohol (2019 est.)
spirits: 0.9 liters of pure alcohol (2019 est.)
other alcohols: 0.03 liters of pure alcohol (2019 est.)
comparison ranking: total 97

Children under the age of 5 years underweight: 0.9% (2018/19)
comparison ranking: 119

Currently married women (ages 15-49): 66.5% (2023 est.)

Child marriage: *women married by age 15:* 0.3%
women married by age 18: 7.5% (2019 est.)

Literacy: *definition:* age 15 and over can read and write
total population: 98.4%
male: 99.1%
female: 97.6% (2020)

School life expectancy (primary to tertiary education): *total:* 13 years
male: 13 years
female: 14 years (2020)

ENVIRONMENT

Environment - current issues: air pollution from metallurgical plants; Skopje has severe air pollution problems every winter as a result of industrial emissions, smoke from wood-buring stoves, and exhaust fumes from old cars

Environment - international agreements: *party to:* Air Pollution, Air Pollution-Heavy Metals, Air Pollution-Multi-effect Protocol, Air Pollution-Nitrogen Oxides, Air Pollution-Persistent Organic Pollutants, Air Pollution-Sulphur 85, Air Pollution-Sulphur 94, Air Pollution-Volatile Organic Compounds, Biodiversity, Climate Change, Climate Change-Kyoto Protocol, Climate Change-Paris Agreement, Comprehensive Nuclear Test Ban, Desertification, Endangered Species, Hazardous Wastes, Law of the Sea, Ozone Layer Protection, Wetlands
signed, but not ratified: none of the selected agreements

Climate: warm, dry summers and autumns; relatively cold winters with heavy snowfall

Urbanization: *urban population:* 59.5% of total population (2023)
rate of urbanization: 0.61% annual rate of change (2020-25 est.)

Revenue from forest resources: 0.15% of GDP (2018 est.)
comparison ranking: 100

Revenue from coal: 0% of GDP (2018 est.)
comparison ranking: 119

Air pollutants: *particulate matter emissions:* 25.17 micrograms per cubic meter (2019 est.)
carbon dioxide emissions: 7.05 megatons (2016 est.)
methane emissions: 2.28 megatons (2020 est.)

Waste and recycling: *municipal solid waste generated annually:* 796,585 tons (2016 est.)
municipal solid waste recycled annually: 1,434 tons (2013 est.)
percent of municipal solid waste recycled: 0.2% (2013 est.)

Major watersheds (area sq km): Atlantic Ocean drainage: *(Black Sea)* Danube (795,656 sq km)

Total water withdrawal: *municipal:* 310 million cubic meters (2020 est.)
industrial: 20 million cubic meters (2020 est.)
agricultural: 140 million cubic meters (2020 est.)

Total renewable water resources: 6.4 billion cubic meters (2020 est.)

GOVERNMENT

Country name: *conventional long form:* Republic of North Macedonia
conventional short form: North Macedonia
local long form: Republika Severna Makedonija
local short form: Severna Makedonija
former: Democratic Federal Macedonia, People's Republic of Macedonia, Socialist Republic of Macedonia, Republic of Macedonia
etymology: the country name derives from the ancient kingdom of Macedon (7th to 2nd centuries B.C.)

Government type: parliamentary republic

Capital: *name:* Skopje
geographic coordinates: 42 00 N, 21 26 E
time difference: UTC+1 (6 hours ahead of Washington, DC, during Standard Time)
daylight saving time: +1hr, begins last Sunday in March; ends last Sunday in October
etymology: Skopje derives from its ancient name Scupi, the Latin designation of a Dardanian and classical era Greco-Roman frontier fortress town; the name goes back to a pre-Hellenic, Illyrian times

Administrative divisions: 80 *municipalities (opstini, singular - opstina) and 1 city* (grad); Aracinovo, Berovo, Bitola, Bogdanci, Bogovinje, Bosilovo, Brvenica, Caska, Centar Zupa, Cesinovo-Oblesevo, Cucer Sandevo, Debar, Debarca, Delcevo, Demir Hisar, Demir Kapija, Dojran, Dolneni, Gevgelija, Gostivar, Gradsko, Ilinden, Jegunovce, Karbinci, Kavadarci, Kicevo, Kocani, Konce, Kratovo, Kriva Palanka, Krivogastani, Krusevo, Kumanovo, Lipkovo, Lozovo, Makedonska Kamenica, Makedonski Brod, Mavrovo i Rostuse, Mogila, Negotino, Novaci, Novo Selo, Ohrid, Pehcevo, Petrovec, Plasnica, Prilep, Probistip, Radovis, Rankovce, Resen, Rosoman, Skopje*, Sopiste, Staro Nagoricane, Stip, Struga, Strumica, Studenicani, Sveti Nikole, Tearce, Tetovo, Valandovo, Vasilevo, Veles, Vevcani, Vinica, Vrapciste, Zelenikovo, Zelino, Zrnovci. The Greater Skopje area is comprised of 10 municipalities:* Aerodrom, Butel, Centar, Chair, Gazi Baba, Gjorce Petrov, Karposh, Kisela Voda, Saraj, and Shuto Orizari.

Independence: 8 September 1991 (referendum by registered voters endorsed independence from Yugoslavia)

National holiday: Independence Day, 8 September (1991), also known as National Day

Legal system: civil law system; judicial review of legislative acts

Constitution: *history:* several previous (since 1944); latest adopted 17 November 1991, effective 20 November 1991
amendments: proposed by the president of the republic, by the government, by at least 30 members of the Assembly, or by petition of at least 150,000

citizens; final approval requires a two-thirds majority vote by the Assembly; amended several times, last in 2019; this amendment was the result of the 2018 Prespa Agreement with Greece, in which the constitutional name of the country would be modified to Republic of North Macedonia in exchange for assurances that Greece would no longer object to its integration in international organizations; note - a referendum on amendments to the constitution is expected in 2024

International law organization participation: has not submitted an ICJ jurisdiction declaration; accepts ICCt jurisdiction

Citizenship: *citizenship by birth:* no
citizenship by descent only: at least one parent must be a citizen of North Macedonia
dual citizenship recognized: no
residency requirement for naturalization: 8 years

Suffrage: 18 years of age; universal

Executive branch: *chief of state:* President Gordana SILJANOVSKA-DAVKOVA (since 12 May 2024)
head of government: President Gordana SILJANOVSKA-DAVKOVA (since 12 May 2024)
cabinet: Council of Ministers elected by the Assembly by simple majority vote
elections/appointments: president directly elected using a modified 2-round system; a candidate can only be elected in the first round with an absolute majority from all registered voters; in the second round, voter turnout must be at least 40% for the result to be deemed valid; president elected for a 5-year term (eligible for a second term); election last held on 24 April and 8 May 2024 (next to be held in 2029); following legislative elections, the leader of the majority party or majority coalition is usually elected prime minister by the Assembly
election results:
2024: Gordana SILJANOVSKA-DAVKOVA elected president in the second round; percent of vote - Gordana SILJANOVSKA-DAVKOVA (VMRO-DPMNE) 69%, Stevo PENDAROVSKI (SDSM) 31%
2024: Talat XHAFERI elected caretaker Prime Minister; Assembly vote - 65 for (opposition boycott)
2022: Dimitar KOVACEVSKI elected Prime Minister; Assembly vote - NA

Legislative branch: *description:* unicameral Assembly - Sobranie in Macedonian, Kuvend in Albanian (between 120 and 140 seats, current 123; members directly elected in multi-seat constituencies by closed-list proportional representation vote; possibility of 3 directly elected in diaspora constituencies by simple majority vote provided there is sufficient voter turnout; members serve 4-year terms)
elections: last held on 8 May 2024 (next to be held on 31 May 2028)
election results: percent of vote by party/coalition - Your Macedonia 44.6%, For a European Future 15.8%, European Front 14%, VLEN 10.9%, The Left 7%, For Our Macedonia 5.7%, other 1.9%; seats by party/coalition - Your Macedonia 58, For a European Future 18, European Front 18, VLEN 14, The Left 6, For Our Macedonia 6; composition - TBD

Judicial branch: *highest court(s):* Supreme Court (consists of 22 judges); Constitutional Court (consists of 9 judges)
judge selection and term of office: Supreme Court judges nominated by the Judicial Council, a 7-member body of legal professionals, and appointed by the Assembly; judge tenure NA; Constitutional Court judges appointed by the Assembly for nonrenewable, 9-year terms
subordinate courts: Courts of Appeal; Basic Courts

Political parties: Alliance for Albanians or AfA or ASH
Alternative (Alternativa) or AAA
Besa Movement or BESA
Citizen Option for Macedonia or GROM
Democratic Alliance or DS
Democratic Movement or LD
Democratic Party of Albanians or PDSH
Democratic Party of Serbs or DPSM
Democratic Renewal of Macedonia or DOM
Democratic Union for Integration or BDI
European Democratic Party or PDE
Internal Macedonian Revolutionary Organization - Democratic Party for Macedonian National Unity or VMRO-DPMNE
Internal Macedonian Revolutionary Organization - People's Party or VMRO-NP
Liberal Democratic Party or LDP
New Social-Democratic Party or NSDP
Social Democratic Union of Macedonia or SDSM
Socialist Party of Macedonia or SPM
Srpska Stranka in Macedonia or SSM
The Left (Levica)
The People Movement or LP
Turkish Democratic Party or TDP
Turkish Movement Party or THP
We Can! (coalition includes SDSM/BESA/VMRO-NP, DPT, LDP)

International organization participation: BIS, CD, CE, CEI, EAPC, EBRD, EU (candidate country), FAO, IAEA, IBRD, ICAO, ICC (NGOs), ICCt, ICRM, IDA, IFAD, IFC, IFRCS, ILO, IMF, IMO, Interpol, IOC, IOM, IPU, ISO, ITU, ITUC (NGOs), MIGA, NATO, OAS (observer), OIF, OPCW, OSCE, PCA, PFP, SELEC, UN, UNCTAD, UNESCO, UNHCR, UNIDO, UNIFIL, UNWTO, UPU, WCO, WHO, WIPO, WMO, WTO
note: North Macedonia is an EU candidate country whose satisfactory completion of accession criteria is required before being granted full EU membership

Diplomatic representation in the US: *chief of mission:* Ambassador Zoran POPOV (since 16 September 2022)
chancery: 2129 Wyoming Avenue NW, Washington, DC 20008
telephone: [1] (202) 667-0501
FAX: [1] (202) 667-2104
email address and website:
washington@mfa.gov.mk
United States (mfa.gov.mk)
consulate(s) general: Chicago, Detroit, New York

Diplomatic representation from the US: *chief of mission:* Ambassador Angela AGGELER (since 8 November 2022)
embassy: Str. Samoilova, Nr. 21, 1000 Skopje
mailing address: 7120 Skopje Place, Washington, DC 20521-7120
telephone: [389] (2) 310-2000
FAX: [389] (2) 310-2499
email address and website:
SkopjeACS@state.gov
https://mk.usembassy.gov/

Flag description: a yellow sun (the Sun of Liberty) with eight broadening rays extending to the edges of the red field; the red and yellow colors have long been associated with Macedonia

National symbol(s): eight-rayed sun; national colors: red, yellow

National anthem: *name:* "Denes nad Makedonija" (Today Over Macedonia)
lyrics/music: Vlado MALESKI/Todor SKALOVSKI
note: written in 1943 and adopted in 1991, the song previously served as the anthem of the Socialist Republic of Macedonia while part of Yugoslavia

National heritage: *total World Heritage Sites:* 2 (both natural)
selected World Heritage Site locales: Natural and Cultural Heritage of the Ohrid Region; Ancient and Primeval Beech Forests of the Carpathians

ECONOMY

Economic overview: upper-middle-income European economy; recovering from energy-driven inflation; macroeconomic support from IMF and EU lending facilities; stalled progress on EU accession; fiscal consolidation hampered by deficit spending on public works; structural challenges of emigration, low productivity growth, and governance

Real GDP (purchasing power parity): $42.444 billion (2023 est.)
$42.012 billion (2022 est.)
$41.099 billion (2021 est.)
note: data in 2021 dollars
comparison ranking: 136

Real GDP growth rate: 1.03% (2023 est.)
2.22% (2022 est.)
4.51% (2021 est.)
note: annual GDP % growth based on constant local currency
comparison ranking: 164

Real GDP per capita: $23,400 (2023 est.)
$22,900 (2022 est.)
$22,400 (2021 est.)
note: data in 2021 dollars
comparison ranking: 90

GDP (official exchange rate): $14.761 billion (2023 est.)
note: data in current dollars at official exchange rate

Inflation rate (consumer prices): 9.36% (2023 est.)
14.2% (2022 est.)
3.23% (2021 est.)
note: annual % change based on consumer prices
comparison ranking: 171

Credit ratings: Fitch rating: BB+ (2019)

Standard & Poors rating: BB- (2013)
note: The year refers to the year in which the current credit rating was first obtained.

GDP - composition, by sector of origin: *agriculture:* 7% (2023 est.)
industry: 21.4% (2023 est.)
services: 58.2% (2023 est.)
note: figures may not total 100% due to non-allocated consumption not captured in sector-reported data
comparison rankings: services 102; industry 127; agriculture 101

GDP - composition, by end use: *household consumption:* 72.9% (2023 est.)
government consumption: 16.8% (2023 est.)
investment in fixed capital: 23.5% (2021 est.)
investment in inventories: 0.4% (2023 est.)
exports of goods and services: 72.8% (2023 est.)
imports of goods and services: -86.3% (2023 est.)
note: figures may not total 100% due to rounding or gaps in data collection

Agricultural products: milk, grapes, chilies/peppers, wheat, potatoes, apples, tomatoes, cabbages, maize, barley (2022)
note: top ten agricultural products based on tonnage

Industries: food processing, beverages, textiles, chemicals, iron, steel, cement, energy, pharmaceuticals, automotive parts

Industrial production growth rate: -1.07% (2023 est.)
note: annual % change in industrial value added based on constant local currency
comparison ranking: 166

Labor force: 801,000 (2023 est.)
note: number of people ages 15 or older who are employed or seeking work
comparison ranking: 151

Unemployment rate: 13.08% (2023 est.)
14.48% (2022 est.)
15.8% (2021 est.)
note: % of labor force seeking employment
comparison ranking: 183

Youth unemployment rate (ages 15-24): *total:* 28.6% (2023 est.)
male: 27% (2023 est.)
female: 31.5% (2023 est.)
note: % of labor force ages 15-24 seeking employment
comparison ranking: total 29

Population below poverty line: 21.8% (2019 est.)
note: % of population with income below national poverty line

Gini Index coefficient - distribution of family income: 33.5 (2019 est.)
note: index (0-100) of income distribution; higher values represent greater inequality
comparison ranking: 97

Average household expenditures: *on food:* 33% of household expenditures (2022 est.)
on alcohol and tobacco: 6% of household expenditures (2022 est.)

Household income or consumption by percentage share: *lowest 10%:* 1.9% (2019 est.)
highest 10%: 22.9% (2019 est.)
note: % share of income accruing to lowest and highest 10% of population

Remittances: 3.13% of GDP (2023 est.)
3.33% of GDP (2022 est.)
3.5% of GDP (2021 est.)
note: personal transfers and compensation between resident and non-resident individuals/households/entities

Budget: *revenues:* $4.141 billion (2021 est.)
expenditures: $4.666 billion (2021 est.)
note: central government revenues (excluding grants) and expenses converted to US dollars at average official exchange rate for year indicated

Public debt: 39.3% of GDP (2017 est.)
note: official data from Ministry of Finance; data cover central government debt; this data excludes debt instruments issued (or owned) by government entities other than the treasury; includes treasury debt held by foreign entitites; excludes debt issued by sub-national entities; there are no debt instruments sold for social funds
comparison ranking: 135

Taxes and other revenues: 17.39% (of GDP) (2021 est.)
note: central government tax revenue as a % of GDP
comparison ranking: 108

Current account balance: $99.23 million (2023 est.)
-$864.777 million (2022 est.)
-$374.85 million (2021 est.)
note: balance of payments - net trade and primary/secondary income in current dollars
comparison ranking: 73

Exports: $10.748 billion (2023 est.)
$10.126 billion (2022 est.)
$9.208 billion (2021 est.)
note: balance of payments - exports of goods and services in current dollars
comparison ranking: 113

Exports - partners: Germany 42%, Serbia 8%, Greece 7%, Bulgaria 5%, Italy 3% (2022)
note: top five export partners based on percentage share of exports

Exports - commodities: reaction and catalytic products, insulated wire, electricity, garments, vehicle parts/accessories (2022)
note: top five export commodities based on value in dollars

Imports: $12.745 billion (2023 est.)
$13.008 billion (2022 est.)
$11.362 billion (2021 est.)
note: balance of payments - imports of goods and services in current dollars
comparison ranking: 111

Imports - partners: UK 16%, Greece 13%, Germany 9%, Serbia 8%, China 6% (2022)
note: top five import partners based on percentage share of imports

Imports - commodities: platinum, refined petroleum, electricity, precious metal compounds, natural gas (2022)
note: top five import commodities based on value in dollars

Reserves of foreign exchange and gold: $5.015 billion (2023 est.)
$4.12 billion (2022 est.)
$4.129 billion (2021 est.)
note: holdings of gold (year-end prices)/foreign exchange/special drawing rights in current dollars
comparison ranking: 105

Exchange rates: Macedonian denars (MKD) per US dollar -

Exchange rates: 56.947 (2023 est.)
58.574 (2022 est.)
52.102 (2021 est.)
54.144 (2020 est.)
54.947 (2019 est.)

ENERGY

Electricity access: *electrification - total population:* 100% (2022 est.)

Electricity: *installed generating capacity:* 2.153 million kW (2022 est.)
consumption: 5.791 billion kWh (2022 est.)
exports: 5.662 billion kWh (2022 est.)
imports: 7.074 billion kWh (2022 est.)
transmission/distribution losses: 1.064 billion kWh (2022 est.)
comparison rankings: transmission/distribution losses 101; imports 37; exports 36; consumption 127; installed generating capacity 120

Electricity generation sources: *fossil fuels:* 71.9% of total installed capacity (2022 est.)
solar: 0.6% of total installed capacity (2022 est.)
wind: 2% of total installed capacity (2022 est.)
hydroelectricity: 24.6% of total installed capacity (2022 est.)
biomass and waste: 0.9% of total installed capacity (2022 est.)

Coal: *production:* 5.075 million metric tons (2022 est.)
consumption: 5.776 million metric tons (2022 est.)
exports: 53,000 metric tons (2022 est.)
imports: 750,000 metric tons (2022 est.)
proven reserves: 332 million metric tons (2022 est.)

Petroleum: *refined petroleum consumption:* 22,000 bbl/day (2022 est.)

Natural gas: *consumption:* 274.928 million cubic meters (2022 est.)
imports: 274.918 million cubic meters (2022 est.)

Carbon dioxide emissions: 6.775 million metric tonnes of CO_2 (2022 est.)
from coal and metallurgical coke: 3.132 million metric tonnes of CO_2 (2022 est.)
from petroleum and other liquids: 3.111 million metric tonnes of CO_2 (2022 est.)
from consumed natural gas: 532,000 metric tonnes of CO_2 (2022 est.)
comparison ranking: total emissions 128

Energy consumption per capita: 46.564 million Btu/person (2022 est.)
comparison ranking: 98

COMMUNICATIONS

Telephones - fixed lines: *total subscriptions:* 436,000 (2022 est.)
subscriptions per 100 inhabitants: 21 (2022 est.)
comparison ranking: total subscriptions 99

Telephones - mobile cellular: *total subscriptions:* 2.048 million (2022 est.)
subscriptions per 100 inhabitants: 98 (2022 est.)
comparison ranking: total subscriptions 151

Telecommunication systems: *general assessment:* as part of the EU pre-accession process, North Macedonia has built closer economic ties with the Union which accounts for 79% of Macedonia's exports and 49% of its imports; closer regulatory and administrative ties with European Commission (EC) institutions have done much to develop the telecom sector and prepare the market for the competitive environment encouraged in the EU; as part of EU integration legislation North Macedonia has implemented the principles of the EU's regulatory framework for communications, established an independent regulator and set out several provisions to provide for a competitive telecom market, including wholesale access to the incumbent's fixed-line network; broadband services are widely available, with effective competition between DSL and cable platforms complemented by wireless broadband and a developing fiber sector; the number of DSL subscribers has continued to fall in recent years as customers are migrated to fiber networks; the MNOs are increasingly focused on expanding their 5G networks, seeking stronger coverage across North Macedonia's high value urban areas; mobile data services are also becoming increasingly important following investments in LTE network rollouts and in upgrades to LTE-A technology (2022)
domestic: fixed-line roughly 20 per 100 and mobile-cellular 92 per 100 subscriptions (2021)
international: country code - 389

Broadcast media: public service TV broadcaster Macedonian Radio and Television operates 5 national terrestrial TV channels and 2 satellite TV channels; additionally, there are 11 regional TV stations broadcasting nationally, 29 regional and local broadcasters, a large number of cable operators offer domestic and international programming; the public radio broadcaster operates 3 stations; there are 4 privately owned national radio stations that broadcast and 60 regional and local operators (2023)

Internet country code: .mk

Internet users: *total:* 1.743 million (2021 est.)
percent of population: 83% (2021 est.)
comparison ranking: total 140

Broadband - fixed subscriptions: *total:* 475,569 (2020 est.)
subscriptions per 100 inhabitants: 23 (2020 est.)
comparison ranking: total 93

TRANSPORTATION

Civil aircraft registration country code prefix: Z3

Airports: 13 (2024)
comparison ranking: 151

Heliports: 8 (2024)

Pipelines: 262 km gas, 120 km oil (2017)

Railways: *total:* 699 km (2020) 313 km electrified
comparison ranking: total 99

Roadways: *total:* 15,170 km (2022)
comparison ranking: total 124

MILITARY AND SECURITY

Military and security forces: Army of the Republic of North Macedonia (ARSM or ARNM): joint force with air, ground, reserve, special operations, and support forces (2024)
note: the Police of Macedonia maintain internal security, including migration and border enforcement, and report to the Ministry of the Interior

Military expenditures: 2.2% of GDP (2024 est.)
1.7% of GDP (2023)
1.6% of GDP (2022)
1.5% of GDP (2021)
1.2% of GDP (2020)
comparison ranking: 56

Military and security service personnel strengths: approximately 6,000 active-duty personnel (2024)

Military equipment inventories and acquisitions: the military's inventory is a mix of Soviet-era and increasing amounts of modern equipment from countries such as Turkey, the UK, and the US, with more on order (2024)

Military service age and obligation: 18 years of age for voluntary military service; conscription abolished in 2007 (2024)
note: as of 2024, women made up about 10% of the military's full-time personnel

Military - note: the Army of the Republic of North Macedonia (ARSM) is responsible for the defense of the country's territory and independence, fulfilling North Macedonia's commitments to NATO and European security, and contributing to EU, NATO, and UN peace and security missions; the ARSM has participated in multinational missions and operations in Afghanistan (NATO), Bosnia and Herzegovina (EU), Eastern Europe (NATO), Iraq (NATO), Kosovo (NATO), and Lebanon (UN); a key area of focus over the past decade has been improving capabilities and bringing the largely Soviet-era-equipped ARSM up to NATO standards; it has increased its participation in NATO training exercises since becoming the 30th member of the Alliance in 2020 and currently has small numbers of combat troops deployed to Bulgaria and Romania as part of NATO's Enhance Forward Presence mission implemented because of Russian military aggression against Ukraine (2024)

TERRORISM

Terrorist group(s): Islamic State of Iraq and ash-Sham (ISIS)
note: details about the history, aims, leadership, organization, areas of operation, tactics, targets, weapons, size, and sources of support of the group(s) appear(s) in the Terrorism reference guide

TRANSNATIONAL ISSUES

Refugees and internally displaced persons: *refugees (country of origin):* 18,915 (Ukraine) (as of 22 February 2024)
stateless persons: 521 (2022)
note: 579,828 estimated refugee and migrant arrivals (January 2015-February 2024)

Illicit drugs: major transshipment point for Southwest Asian heroin and hashish; minor transit point for South American cocaine destined for Europe; although not a financial center and most criminal activity is thought to be domestic, money laundering is a problem due to a mostly cash-based economy and weak enforcement

NORTHERN MARIANA ISLANDS

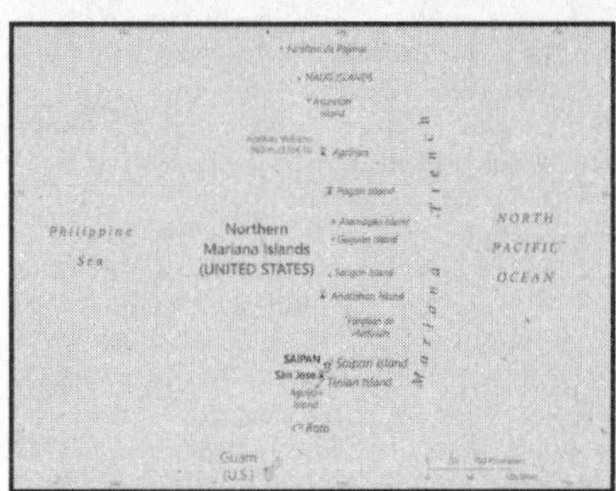

INTRODUCTION

Background: Austronesian people settled the Northern Mariana Islands around 1500 B.C. These people became the indigenous Chamorro and were influenced by later migrations, including Micronesians in the first century A.D. and island Southeast Asians around 900. Spanish explorer Ferdinand MAGELLAN sailed through the Mariana Islands in 1521, and Spain claimed them in 1565. Spain formally colonized the Mariana Islands in 1668 and administered the archipelago from Guam. Spain's brutal repression of the Chamorro, along with new diseases and intermittent warfare, reduced the indigenous population by about 90% in the 1700s. With a similar dynamic occurring on Guam, Spain forced the Chamorro from the Northern Mariana Islands to resettle there. By the time they returned, many other Micronesians, including Chuukese and Yapese, had already settled on their islands.

In 1898, Spain ceded Guam to the US after the Spanish-American War but sold the Northern Mariana Islands to Germany under the German-Spanish Treaty of 1899. Germany administered the territory from German New Guinea but took a hands-off approach to dayto-day life. Following World War I, Japan administered the islands under a League of Nations mandate. Japan focused on sugar production and brought in thousands of Japanese laborers, who quickly outnumbered the Chamorro on the islands. During World War II, Japan invaded Guam from the Northern Mariana Islands and used Marianan Chamorro as translators with Guamanian Chamorro, creating friction between the two Chamorro communities that continues to this day. The US captured the Northern Mariana Islands in 1944 after the Battle of Saipan and later administered them as part of the Trust Territory of the Pacific Islands (TTPI).

On four occasions in the 1950s and 1960s, voters opted for integration with Guam, which Guam rejected in 1969. In 1978, the Northern Mariana Islands was granted self-governance separate from the rest of the TTPI, and in 1986, islanders were granted US citizenship, with the territory coming under US sovereignty as the Commonwealth of the Northern Mariana Islands (CNMI). In 2009, the CNMI became the final US territory to elect a nonvoting delegate to the US Congress.

GEOGRAPHY

Location: Oceania, islands in the North Pacific Ocean, about three-quarters of the way from Hawaii to the Philippines

Geographic coordinates: 15 12 N, 145 45 E

Map references: Oceania

Area: *total:* 464 sq km
land: 464 sq km
water: 0 sq km
note: consists of 14 islands including Saipan, Rota, and Tinian
comparison ranking: total 196

Area - comparative: 2.5 times the size of Washington, DC

Land boundaries: *total:* 0 km

Coastline: 1,482 km

Maritime claims: *territorial sea:* 12 nm
exclusive economic zone: 200 nm

Climate: tropical marine; moderated by northeast trade winds, little seasonal temperature variation; dry season December to June, rainy season July to October

Terrain: the southern islands in this north-south trending archipelago are limestone, with fringing coral reefs; the northern islands are volcanic, with active volcanoes on several islands

Elevation: *highest point:* Agrihan Volcano 965 m
lowest point: Pacific Ocean 0 m

Natural resources: arable land, fish

Land use: *agricultural land:* 6.6% (2018 est.)
arable land: 2.2% (2018 est.)
permanent crops: 2.2% (2018 est.)
permanent pasture: 2.2% (2018 est.)
forest: 65.5% (2018 est.)
other: 27.9% (2018 est.)

Irrigated land: 1 sq km (2012)

Population distribution: approximately 90% of the population lives on the island of Saipan

Natural hazards: active volcanoes on Pagan and Agrihan; typhoons (especially August to November)

Geography - note: strategic location in the North Pacific Ocean

PEOPLE AND SOCIETY

Population: *total:* 51,118
male: 27,044
female: 24,074 (2024 est.)
comparison rankings: female 209; male 209; total 209

Nationality: *noun:* NA (US citizens)
adjective: NA

Ethnic groups: Asian 50% (includes Filipino 35.3%, Chinese 6.8%, Korean 4.2%, and other Asian 3.7%), Native Hawaiian or other Pacific Islander 34.9% (includes Chamorro 23.9%, Carolinian 4.6%, and other Native Hawaiian or Pacific Islander 6.4%), other 2.5%, two or more ethnicities or races 12.7% (2010 est.)

Languages: Philippine languages 32.8%, Chamorro (official) 24.1%, English (official) 17%, other Pacific island languages 10.1% (includes Carolinian (official), Chinese 6.8%, other Asian languages 7.3%, other 1.9% (2010 est.)

Religions: Christian (Roman Catholic majority, although traditional beliefs and taboos may still be found)

Age structure: *0-14 years:* 22.1% (male 6,066/female 5,231)
15-64 years: 67.7% (male 18,206/female 16,377)
65 years and over: 10.2% (2024 est.) (male 2,772/female 2,466)

Dependency ratios: *total dependency ratio:* 46
youth dependency ratio: 31.7
elderly dependency ratio: 14.3
potential support ratio: 7 (2021)

Median age: *total:* 32.4 years (2024 est.)
male: 31.8 years
female: 33.2 years
comparison ranking: total 116

Population growth rate: -0.34% (2024 est.)
comparison ranking: 214

Birth rate: 15.7 births/1,000 population (2024 est.)
comparison ranking: 104

Death rate: 5.7 deaths/1,000 population (2024 est.)
comparison ranking: 172

Net migration rate: -13.4 migrant(s)/1,000 population (2024 est.)
comparison ranking: 226

Population distribution: approximately 90% of the population lives on the island of Saipan

Urbanization: *urban population:* 92.1% of total population (2023)
rate of urbanization: 0.36% annual rate of change (2020-25 est.)

Major urban areas - population: 51,000 SAIPAN (capital) (2018)

Sex ratio: *at birth:* 1.17 male(s)/female
0-14 years: 1.16 male(s)/female
15-64 years: 1.11 male(s)/female
65 years and over: 1.12 male(s)/female
total population: 1.12 male(s)/female (2024 est.)

Infant mortality rate: *total:* 11.9 deaths/1,000 live births (2024 est.)
male: 14.4 deaths/1,000 live births
female: 9 deaths/1,000 live births
comparison ranking: total 110

Life expectancy at birth: *total population:* 77.1 years (2024 est.)
male: 75 years
female: 79.5 years
comparison ranking: total population 98

Total fertility rate: 2.56 children born/woman (2024 est.)
comparison ranking: 67

Gross reproduction rate: (2024 est.)

Drinking water source: *improved:*
total: 100% of population

Sanitation facility access: *improved:*
total: 97.9% of population
unimproved:
total: 2.1% of population (2020 est.)

ENVIRONMENT

Environment - current issues: contamination of groundwater on Saipan may contribute to disease; clean-up of landfill; protection of endangered species conflicts with development

Climate: tropical marine; moderated by northeast trade winds, little seasonal temperature variation; dry season December to June, rainy season July to October

Land use: *agricultural land:* 6.6% (2018 est.)
arable land: 2.2% (2018 est.)
permanent crops: 2.2% (2018 est.)
permanent pasture: 2.2% (2018 est.)
forest: 65.5% (2018 est.)
other: 27.9% (2018 est.)

Urbanization: *urban population:* 92.1% of total population (2023)
rate of urbanization: 0.36% annual rate of change (2020-25 est.)

Revenue from forest resources: 0% of GDP (2018 est.)
comparison ranking: 177

Waste and recycling: *municipal solid waste generated annually:* 32,761 tons (2013 est.)
municipal solid waste recycled annually: 11,794 tons (2016 est.)
percent of municipal solid waste recycled: 36% (2016 est.)

GOVERNMENT

Country name: *conventional long form:* Commonwealth of the Northern Mariana Islands
conventional short form: Northern Mariana Islands
former: Trust Territory of the Pacific Islands, Mariana Islands District
abbreviation: CNMI
etymology: formally claimed and named by Spain in 1667 in honor of the Spanish Queen, MARIANA of Austria

Government type: a commonwealth in political union with and under the sovereignty of the US; republican form of government with separate executive, legislative, and judicial branches

Dependency status: commonwealth in political union with and under the sovereignty of the US; federal funds to the Commonwealth administered by the US Department of the Interior, Office of Insular Affairs, Washington, DC

Capital: *name:* Saipan
geographic coordinates: 15 12 N, 145 45 E
time difference: UTC+10 (15 hours ahead of Washington, DC, during Standard Time)
etymology: the entire island of Saipan is organized as a single municipality and serves as the capital; according to legend, when the first native voyagers arrived in their outrigger canoes they found an uninhabited island; to them it was like an empty voyage, so they named the island *saay* meaning "a voyage," and *peel* meaning "empty"; over time *Saaypeel* - "island of the empty voyage" - became Saipan

Administrative divisions: *none (commonwealth in political union with the US); there are no first-order administrative divisions as defined by the US Government, but there are 4 municipalities at the second order:* Northern Islands, Rota, Saipan, Tinian

Independence: none (commonwealth in political union with the US)

National holiday: Commonwealth Day, 8 January (1978)

Legal system: the laws of the US apply, except for customs and some aspects of taxation

Constitution: *history:* partially effective 9 January 1978 (Constitution of the Commonwealth of the Northern Mariana Islands); fully effective 4 November 1986 (Covenant Agreement)
amendments: proposed by constitutional convention, by public petition, or by the Legislature; ratification of proposed amendments requires approval by voters at the next general election or special election; amendments proposed by constitutional convention or by petition become effective if approved by a majority of voters and at least two-thirds majority of voters in each of two senatorial districts; amendments proposed by the Legislature are effective if approved by majority vote; amended several times, last in 2012

Citizenship: see United States

Suffrage: 18 years of age; universal; note - indigenous inhabitants are US citizens but do not vote in US presidential elections

Executive branch: *chief of state:* President Joseph R. BIDEN Jr. (since 20 January 2021)
head of government: Governor Arnold PALACIOS (since 9 January 2023)
cabinet: Cabinet appointed by the governor with the advice and consent of the Senate
elections/appointments: president and vice president indirectly elected on the same ballot by an Electoral College of 'electors' chosen from each state; president and vice president serve a 4-year term (eligible for a second term); under the US Constitution, residents of the Northern Mariana Islands do not vote in elections for US president and vice president; however, they may vote in Democratic and

Republican party presidential primary elections; governor directly elected by absolute majority vote in 2 rounds if needed; election last held on 8 November 2022 with a runoff held on 25 November 2022 (next to be held in 2026)
election results:
2022: Arnold PALACIOS elected governor in second round; percent of vote in first round - Ralph TORRES (Republican) 38.8%; Arnold PALACIOS (independent) 32.2%, Tina SABLAN (Democrat) 28%; percent of vote - Arnold PALACIOS 54%, Ralph TORRES 46%; David APATANG (independent) elected lieutenant governor
2018: Ralph TORRES elected governor; percent of vote - Ralph TORRES (Republican) 62.2%, Juan BABAUTA (Independent) 37.8%; Arnold PALACIOS elected Lieutenant Governor

Legislative branch: *description:* bicameral Northern Marianas Commonwealth Legislature consists of:
Senate (9 seats; members directly elected in single-seat constituencies by simple majority vote to serve 4-year terms) House of Representatives (20 seats; members directly elected in single-seat constituencies by simple majority vote to serve 2-year terms) the Northern Mariana Islands directly elects 1 delegate to the US House of Representatives by simple majority vote to serve a 2-year term
elections: CNMI Senate - last held on 8 November 2020 (next to be held on 5 November 2024)
CNMI House of Representatives - last held on 8 November 2022 (next to be held on 5 November 2024)
Commonwealth of Northern Mariana Islands delegate to the US House of Representatives - last held on 8 November 2022 (next to be held on 5 November 2024)
election results: CNMI Senate - percent of vote by party - NA; seats by party - Republican Party 6, independent 3; composition - men 6, women 3, percentage women 33.3%
CNMI House of Representatives - percent of vote by party - NA; seats by party - Republican Party 9, Democrat Party 8, independent 3; composition - men 17, women 3, percentage women 15%; total Commonwealth Legislature percentage women 20.7%
Northern Mariana Islands delegate to US House of Representatives - seat won by independent; composition - 1 man

Judicial branch: *highest court(s):* Supreme Court of the Commonwealth of the Northern Mariana Islands (CNMI) (consists of the chief justice and 2 associate justices); US Federal District Court (consists of 1 judge); note - US Federal District Court jurisdiction limited to US federal laws; appeals beyond the CNMI Supreme Court are referred to the US Supreme Court
judge selection and term of office: CNMI Supreme Court judges appointed by the governor and confirmed by the CNMI Senate; judges appointed for 8-year terms and another term if directly elected in a popular election; US Federal District Court judges appointed by the US president and confirmed by the US Senate; judges appointed for renewable 10-year terms
subordinate courts: Superior Court

Political parties: Democratic Party
Republican Party

International organization participation: PIF (observer), SPC, UPU

Diplomatic representation from the US: *embassy:* none (commonwealth in political union with the US)

Flag description: *blue with a white, five-pointed star superimposed on a gray latte stone (the traditional foundation stone used in building) in the center, surrounded by a mwáár or head lei (wreath); blue symbolizes the Pacific Ocean, the star represents the Commonwealth; the Chamorro latte stone and the Carolinian mwáár (head lei) represent elements of Marianas culture; the mwáár is composed of the flowers from four flowering plants:* flores mayo (*Plumeria*), ylang-ylang or langilang (*Cananga odorata*), angagha or peacock flower (*Caesalpinia pulcherrima*), and teibwo or Pacific basil (*Ocimum tenuiflorum*)

National symbol(s): latte stone; national colors: blue, white

National anthem: *name:* "Gi Talo Gi Halom Tasi" (In the Middle of the Sea)
lyrics/music: Jose S. PANGELINAN [Chamoru], David PETER [Carolinian]/Wilhelm GANZHORN
note: adopted 1996; the Carolinian version of the song is known as "Satil Matawal Pacifico;" as a commonwealth of the US, in addition to the local anthem, "The Star-Spangled Banner" is official (see United States)

ECONOMY

Economic overview: US Pacific island commonwealth economy; growing Chinese and Korean tourist destination; hit hard by 2018 typhoon; dependent on energy imports; exempt from some US labor and immigration laws; longstanding garment production

Real GDP (purchasing power parity): $1.242 billion (2016 est.)
$933 million (2015 est.)
$845 million (2014 est.)
note: GDP estimate includes US subsidy; data are in 2013 dollars
comparison ranking: 207

Real GDP growth rate: -29.68% (2020 est.)
-11.32% (2019 est.)
-19.27% (2018 est.)
note: annual GDP % growth based on constant local currency
comparison ranking: 220

Real GDP per capita: $24,500 (2016 est.)
$18,400 (2015 est.)
$16,600 (2014 est.)
comparison ranking: 89

GDP (official exchange rate): $858 million (2020 est.)
note: data in current dollars at official exchange rate

Inflation rate (consumer prices): 0.3% (2016 est.)
0.1% (2015 est.)
comparison ranking: 10

GDP - composition, by sector of origin: *agriculture:* 1.7% (2016)
industry: 58.1% (2016 est.)
services: 40.2% (2016)
comparison rankings: services 192; industry 6; agriculture 167

GDP - composition, by end use: *household consumption:* 75.1% (2020 est.)
government consumption: 28.9% (2016 est.)
investment in fixed capital: 26.3% (2016 est.)
exports of goods and services: 14.9% (2020 est.)
imports of goods and services: -62.5% (2020 est.)
note: figures may not total 100% due to rounding or gaps in data collection

Agricultural products: vegetables and melons, fruits and nuts; ornamental plants; livestock, poultry, eggs; fish and aquaculture products

Industries: tourism, banking, construction, fishing, handicrafts, other services

Industrial production growth rate: 4.3% (2014 est.)
note: annual % change in industrial value added based on constant local currency
comparison ranking: 61

Budget: *revenues:* $389.6 million (2016 est.)
expenditures: $344 million (2015 est.)

Public debt: 7.1% of GDP (2017 est.)
comparison ranking: 197

Taxes and other revenues: 31.4% (of GDP) (2016 est.)
comparison ranking: 19

Exports: $128 million (2020 est.)
$500 million (2019 est.)
$660 million (2018 est.)
note: GDP expenditure basis - exports of goods and services in current dollars
comparison ranking: 211

Exports - partners: South Korea 48%, Thailand 9%, Germany 6%, Cyprus 6%, India 6% (2022)
note: top five export partners based on percentage share of exports

Exports - commodities: scrap iron, refined petroleum, scrap copper, hydraulic engines, integrated circuits, peas, scrap aluminum (2021)

Imports: $536 million (2020 est.)
$735 million (2019 est.)
$754 million (2018 est.)
note: GDP expenditure basis - imports of goods and services in current dollars
comparison ranking: 204

Imports - partners: Singapore 42%, Japan 20%, South Korea 16%, Hong Kong 7%, Taiwan 3% (2022)
note: top five import partners based on percentage share of imports

Imports - commodities: refined petroleum, trunks/cases, cars, watches, jewelry (2019)

Exchange rates: the US dollar is used

ENERGY

Electricity access: *electrification - total population:* 100% (2022 est.)

Coal: *production:* 0 metric tons (2020 est.)
consumption: 0 metric tons (2020 est.)
exports: 0 metric tons (2020 est.)
imports: 0 metric tons (2020 est.)

Petroleum: *total petroleum production:* 0 bbl/day (2021 est.)
refined petroleum consumption: 2,100 bbl/day (2019 est.)
crude oil estimated reserves: 0 barrels (2021 est.)

Natural gas: *production:* 0 cubic meters (2021 est.)
consumption: 0 cubic meters (2021 est.)
exports: 0 cubic meters (2021 est.)
imports: 0 cubic meters (2021 est.)
proven reserves: 0 cubic meters (2021 est.)

Carbon dioxide emissions: 0 metric tonnes of CO_2 (2019 est.)
from coal and metallurgical coke: 0 metric tonnes of CO_2 (2019 est.)

from consumed natural gas: 0 metric tonnes of CO_2 (2019 est.)
comparison ranking: total emissions 218

Energy consumption per capita: (2019)

COMMUNICATIONS

Telephones - fixed lines: *total subscriptions:* 20,000 (2021 est.)
subscriptions per 100 inhabitants: 40 (2021 est.)
comparison ranking: total subscriptions 174

Telephones - mobile cellular: *total subscriptions:* 20,474 (2004 est.)
subscriptions per 100 inhabitants: 28 (2004)
comparison ranking: total subscriptions 216

Telecommunication systems: *general assessment:* digital fiber-optic cables and satellites connect the islands to worldwide networks; demand for broadband growing given that mobile services are the source for Internet across region; future launch of 5G; as of April 2024 the Northern Mariana Islands Broadband Policy and Development Office (BPD) received an award of $81 million from the National Telecommunications and Information Administration (NTIA) Broadband Equity, Access, and Deployment (BEAD) Program; CNMI submitted its BEAD Five-Year Action Plan to NTIA; this plan aims to improve Internet services in the Commonwealth by outlining strategies for enhancing Internet accessibility and affordability for all members of the CNMI community (2024)
domestic: fixed-line teledensity is 40 per 100 persons; mobile cellular subscriptions are 28 per 100 (2021)
international: country code - 1-670; landing points for the Atisa and Mariana-Guam submarine cables linking Mariana islands to Guam; satellite earth stations - 2 Intelsat (Pacific Ocean) (2019)

Broadcast media: 1 TV broadcast station on Saipan; multi-channel cable TV services are available on Saipan; 9 licensed radio broadcast stations (2009)

Internet country code: .mp

Internet users: *total:* 12,299 (2021 est.)
percent of population: 25.1% (2021 est.)
comparison ranking: total 216

TRANSPORTATION

Airports: 4 (2024)
comparison ranking: 181

Heliports: 7 (2024)

Roadways: *total:* 536 km (2008)
comparison ranking: total 195

Ports: *total ports:* 3 (2024)
large: 0
medium: 0
small: 1
very small: 2
ports with oil terminals: 1
key ports: Rota, Saipan, Tinian

MILITARY AND SECURITY

Military - note: defense is the responsibility of the US

NORWAY

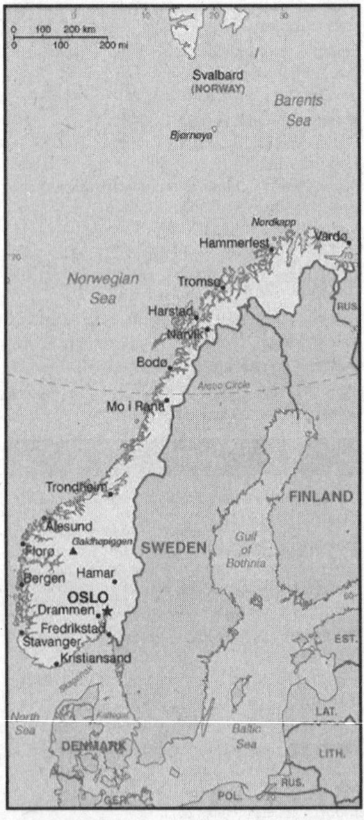

INTRODUCTION

Background: Two centuries of Viking raids into Europe tapered off after King Olav TRYGGVASON adopted Christianity in 994; conversion of the Norwegian kingdom occurred over the next several decades. In 1397, Norway was absorbed into a union with Denmark that lasted more than four centuries. In 1814, Norwegians resisted the cession of their country to Sweden and adopted a new constitution. Sweden then invaded Norway but agreed to let Norway keep its constitution in return for accepting the union under a Swedish king. Rising nationalism throughout the 19th century led to a 1905 referendum granting Norway independence. Norway remained neutral in World War I and proclaimed its neutrality at the outset of World War II, but Nazi Germany nonetheless occupied the country for five years (1940-45). In 1949, Norway abandoned neutrality and became a member of NATO. Discovery of oil and gas in adjacent waters in the late 1960s boosted Norway's economic fortunes. In referenda held in 1972 and 1994, Norway rejected joining the EU. Key domestic issues include immigration and integration of ethnic minorities, maintaining the country's extensive social safety net with an aging population, and preserving economic competitiveness.

GEOGRAPHY

Location: Northern Europe, bordering the North Sea and the North Atlantic Ocean, west of Sweden

Geographic coordinates: 62 00 N, 10 00 E

Map references: Europe

Area: *total:* 323,802 sq km
land: 304,282 sq km
water: 19,520 sq km
comparison ranking: total 69

Area - comparative: slightly larger than twice the size of Georgia; slightly larger than New Mexico

Land boundaries: *total:* 2,566 km
border countries (3): Finland 709 km; Sweden 1,666 km; Russia 191 km

Coastline: 25,148 km (includes mainland 2,650 km, as well as long fjords, numerous small islands, and minor indentations 22,498 km; length of island coastlines 58,133 km)

Maritime claims: *territorial sea:* 12 nm
contiguous zone: 10 nm
exclusive economic zone: 200 nm
continental shelf: 200 nm

Climate: temperate along coast, modified by North Atlantic Current; colder interior with increased precipitation and colder summers; rainy year-round on west coast

Terrain: glaciated; mostly high plateaus and rugged mountains broken by fertile valleys; small, scattered plains; coastline deeply indented by fjords; arctic tundra in north

Elevation: *highest point:* Galdhopiggen 2,469 m
lowest point: Norwegian Sea 0 m
mean elevation: 460 m

Natural resources: petroleum, natural gas, iron ore, copper, lead, zinc, titanium, pyrites, nickel, fish, timber, hydropower

Land use: *agricultural land:* 2.7% (2018 est.)
arable land: 2.2% (2018 est.)
permanent crops: 0% (2018 est.)
permanent pasture: 0.5% (2018 est.)
forest: 27.8% (2018 est.)
other: 69.5% (2018 est.)

Irrigated land: 337 sq km (2016)

Population distribution: most Norwegians live in the south where the climate is milder and there is better connectivity to mainland Europe; population clusters are found all along the North Sea coast in the southwest, and Skaggerak in the southeast; the interior areas of the north remain sparsely populated

Natural hazards: rockslides, avalanches
volcanism: Beerenberg (2,227 m) on Jan Mayen Island in the Norwegian Sea is the country's only active volcano

Geography - note: about two-thirds mountains; some 50,000 islands off its much-indented coastline; strategic location adjacent to sea lanes and air routes in

North Atlantic; one of the most rugged and longest coastlines in the world

PEOPLE AND SOCIETY

Population: *total:* 5,509,733
male: 2,780,972
female: 2,728,761 (2024 est.)
comparison rankings: female 120; male 118; total 120

Nationality: *noun:* Norwegian(s)
adjective: Norwegian

Ethnic groups: Norwegian 81.5% (includes about 60,000 Sami), other European 8.9%, other 9.6% (2021 est.)

Languages: Bokmal Norwegian (official), Nynorsk Norwegian (official), small Sami- and Finnish-speaking minorities
major-language sample(s):
Verdens Faktabok, den essensielle kilden for grunnleggende informasjon. (Norwegian)
note: Sami has three dialects (Lule, North Sami, and South Sami) and is an official language in nine municipalities in the northernmost counties of Finnmark, Nordland, and Troms

Religions: Church of Norway (Evangelical Lutheran - official) 67.5%, Muslim 3.1%, Roman Catholic 3.1%, other Christian 3.8%, other 2.6%, unspecified 19.9% (2021 est.)

Demographic profile: Norway is a trendsetter country in gender equality, especially in workforce participation. Of particular value to families are the child and parental leave benefits. This supplement is a monthly allowance paid to families from a month after birth until the child reaches 18 to defray some of the costs of raising children. This is helpful to families with young children where the mother works limited hours. The parental leave benefit is available to qualified mothers in a child's first year, enabling parents to share at-home childcare for up to 49 weeks at full salary (or 59 weeks with 80% of their salary). Afterward, parents can put their child in high-quality subsidized daycare or receive funding toward private child care or as compensation for one parent staying home to care for their child.
Norway was originally a country of emigration with almost 850,000 Norwegians going abroad between 1825 and 1945. At the turn of the 20th century, most Norwegians emigrated temporarily to work in the US. Immigrants to Norway in the 1960s were mostly from neighboring Nordic countries, with whom they shared a common labor market. By the end of the 1960s, with a strong economy and population shortage, Norway admitted guest workers from Pakistan, Morocco, then Yugoslavia, and Turkey. The labor migrants were expected to be temporary, but many settled in Norway. Eventually, Norway imposed immigration restrictions and the majority of migrants came in as refugees or for family reunification. Beginning in the 1990s, Norway's migration policy aimed at achieving integration – including language instruction and integration into the job market – as well as combatting racism and xenophobia.

Age structure: *0-14 years:* 16.3% (male 461,979/female 438,243)
15-64 years: 64.5% (male 1,820,692/female 1,734,818)
65 years and over: 19.1% (2024 est.) (male 498,301/female 555,700)

Dependency ratios: *total dependency ratio:* 54
youth dependency ratio: 26.1
elderly dependency ratio: 27.9
potential support ratio: 3.6 (2021 est.)
note: data include Svalbard and Jan Mayen Islands

Median age: *total:* 40.8 years (2024 est.)
male: 40.1 years
female: 41.5 years
comparison ranking: total 57

Population growth rate: 0.59% (2024 est.)
comparison ranking: 142

Birth rate: 10.4 births/1,000 population (2024 est.)
comparison ranking: 179

Death rate: 8.4 deaths/1,000 population (2024 est.)
comparison ranking: 74

Net migration rate: 3.9 migrant(s)/1,000 population (2024 est.)
comparison ranking: 28

Population distribution: most Norwegians live in the south where the climate is milder and there is better connectivity to mainland Europe; population clusters are found all along the North Sea coast in the southwest, and Skaggerak in the southeast; the interior areas of the north remain sparsely populated

Urbanization: *urban population:* 84% of total population (2023)
rate of urbanization: 1.32% annual rate of change (2020-25 est.)
note: data include Svalbard and Jan Mayen Islands

Major urban areas - population: 1.086 million OSLO (capital) (2023)

Sex ratio: *at birth:* 1.05 male(s)/female
0-14 years: 1.05 male(s)/female
15-64 years: 1.05 male(s)/female
65 years and over: 0.9 male(s)/female
total population: 1.02 male(s)/female (2024 est.)

Mother's mean age at first birth: 29.8 years (2020 est.)
note: data is calculated based on actual age at first births

Maternal mortality ratio: 2 deaths/100,000 live births (2020 est.)
comparison ranking: 185

Infant mortality rate: *total:* 1.8 deaths/1,000 live births (2024 est.)
male: 2.1 deaths/1,000 live births
female: 1.5 deaths/1,000 live births
comparison ranking: total 223

Life expectancy at birth: *total population:* 82.9 years (2024 est.)
male: 81.3 years
female: 84.6 years
comparison ranking: total population 22

Total fertility rate: 1.57 children born/woman (2024 est.)
comparison ranking: 191

Gross reproduction rate: 0.77 (2024 est.)

Drinking water source: *improved: urban:* 100% of population
rural: 100% of population
total: 100% of population

Current health expenditure: 11.4% of GDP (2020)

Physician density: 5.04 physicians/1,000 population (2020)

Hospital bed density: 3.5 beds/1,000 population (2018)

Sanitation facility access: *improved: urban:* 100% of population
rural: 100% of population
total: 100% of population

Obesity - adult prevalence rate: 23.1% (2016)
comparison ranking: 67

Alcohol consumption per capita: *total:* 6.05 liters of pure alcohol (2019 est.)
beer: 2.63 liters of pure alcohol (2019 est.)
wine: 2.23 liters of pure alcohol (2019 est.)
spirits: 1 liters of pure alcohol (2019 est.)
other alcohols: 0.19 liters of pure alcohol (2019 est.)
comparison ranking: total 70

Tobacco use: *total:* 16.2% (2020 est.)
male: 17% (2020 est.)
female: 15.4% (2020 est.)
comparison ranking: total 101

Currently married women (ages 15-49): 50.2% (2023 est.)

Education expenditures: 5.9% of GDP (2020 est.)
comparison ranking: 48

School life expectancy (primary to tertiary education): *total:* 18 years
male: 18 years
female: 19 years (2020)

ENVIRONMENT

Environment - current issues: water pollution; acid rain damaging forests and adversely affecting lakes, threatening fish stocks; air pollution from vehicle emissions

Environment - international agreements: *party to:* Air Pollution, Air Pollution-Heavy Metals, Air Pollution-Multi-effect Protocol, Air Pollution-Nitrogen Oxides, Air Pollution-Persistent Organic Pollutants, Air Pollution-Sulphur 85, Air Pollution-Sulphur 94, Air Pollution-Volatile Organic Compounds, Antarctic-Environmental Protection, Antarctic-Marine Living Resources, Antarctic Seals, Antarctic Treaty, Biodiversity, Climate Change, Climate Change-Kyoto Protocol, Climate Change-Paris Agreement, Comprehensive Nuclear Test Ban, Desertification, Endangered Species, Environmental Modification, Hazardous Wastes, Law of the Sea, Marine Dumping-London Convention, Marine Dumping-London Protocol, Nuclear Test Ban, Ozone Layer Protection, Ship Pollution, Tropical Timber 2006, Wetlands, Whaling
signed, but not ratified: none of the selected agreements

Climate: temperate along coast, modified by North Atlantic Current; colder interior with increased precipitation and colder summers; rainy year-round on west coast

Land use: *agricultural land:* 2.7% (2018 est.)
arable land: 2.2% (2018 est.)
permanent crops: 0% (2018 est.)
permanent pasture: 0.5% (2018 est.)
forest: 27.8% (2018 est.)
other: 69.5% (2018 est.)

Urbanization: *urban population:* 84% of total population (2023)
rate of urbanization: 1.32% annual rate of change (2020-25 est.)
note: data include Svalbard and Jan Mayen Islands

Revenue from forest resources: 0.05% of GDP (2018 est.)
comparison ranking: 128

Revenue from coal: 0% of GDP (2018 est.)
comparison ranking: 56

Air pollutants: *particulate matter emissions:* 6.3 micrograms per cubic meter (2019 est.)
carbon dioxide emissions: 41.02 megatons (2016 est.)
methane emissions: 4.81 megatons (2020 est.)

Waste and recycling: *municipal solid waste generated annually:* 2.187 million tons (2015 est.)
municipal solid waste recycled annually: 572,119 tons (2015 est.)
percent of municipal solid waste recycled: 26.2% (2015 est.)

Total water withdrawal: *municipal:* 780 million cubic meters (2020 est.)
industrial: 1.07 billion cubic meters (2020 est.)
agricultural: 840 million cubic meters (2020 est.)

Total renewable water resources: 393 billion cubic meters (2020 est.)

Geoparks: *total global geoparks and regional networks:* 4
global geoparks and regional networks: Gea Norvegica; Magma; Sunnhordland; Trollfjell (2023)

GOVERNMENT

Country name: *conventional long form:* Kingdom of Norway
conventional short form: Norway
local long form: Kongeriket Norge
local short form: Norge
etymology: derives from the Old Norse words "nordr" and "vegr" meaning "northern way" and refers to the long coastline of western Norway

Government type: parliamentary constitutional monarchy

Capital: *name:* Oslo
geographic coordinates: 59 55 N, 10 45 E
time difference: UTC+1 (6 hours ahead of Washington, DC, during Standard Time)
daylight saving time: +1hr, begins last Sunday in March; ends last Sunday in October
etymology: the medieval name was spelt "Aslo"; the *as* component refered either to the Ekeberg ridge southeast of the town ("as" in modern Norwegian), or to the Aesir (Norse gods); *lo* refered to "meadow," so the most likely interpretations would have been either "the meadow beneath the ridge" or "the meadow of the gods"; both explanations are considered equally plausible

Administrative divisions: 12 counties (fylker, singular - fylke); Agder, Innlandet, More og Romsdal, Nordland, Oslo, Rogaland, Romsdal, Troms og Finnmark, Trondelag, Vestfold og Telemark, Vestland, Viken (2024)

Dependent areas: Bouvet Island, Jan Mayen, Svalbard (3)

Independence: *7 June 1905 (union with Sweden declared dissolved); 26 October 1905 (Sweden agreed to the repeal of the union); notable earlier dates:* ca. 872 (traditional unification of petty Norwegian kingdoms by HARALD Fairhair); 1397 (Kalmar Union of Denmark, Norway, and Sweden); 1524 (Denmark-Norway); 17 May 1814 (Norwegian constitution adopted); 4 November 1814 (Sweden-Norway union confirmed)

National holiday: Constitution Day, 17 May (1814)

Legal system: mixed legal system of civil, common, and customary law; Supreme Court can advise on legislative acts

Constitution: *history:* drafted spring 1814, adopted 16 May 1814, signed by Constituent Assembly 17 May 1814
amendments: proposals submitted by members of Parliament or by the government within the first three years of Parliament's four-year term; passage requires two-thirds majority vote of a two-thirds quorum in the next elected Parliament; amended over 400 times, last in 2023

International law organization participation: accepts compulsory ICJ jurisdiction with reservations; accepts ICCt jurisdiction

Citizenship: *citizenship by birth:* no
citizenship by descent only: at least one parent must be a citizen of Norway
dual citizenship recognized: no
residency requirement for naturalization: 7 years

Suffrage: 18 years of age; universal

Executive branch: *chief of state:* King HARALD V (since 17 January 1991)
head of government: Prime Minister Jonas Gahr STORE (since 14 October 2021)
cabinet: Council of State appointed by the monarch, approved by Parliament
elections/appointments: the monarchy is hereditary; following parliamentary elections, the leader of the majority party or majority coalition usually appointed prime minister by the monarch with the approval of the parliament

Legislative branch: *description:* unicameral Parliament or Storting (169 seats; members directly elected in multi-seat constituencies by list proportional representation vote; members serve 4-year terms)
elections: last held on 13 September 2021 (next to be held by September 2025)
election results: percent of vote by party - Ap 26.3%, H 20.5%, SP 13.6%, FrP 11.7%, SV 7.6%, R 4.7%, V 4.6%, MDG 3.9%, KrF 3.8%, PF 0.2%, other 3.1%; seats by party - Ap 48, H 36, SP 28, FrP 21, SV 13, R 8, V 8, , KrF 3, MDG 3, PF 1; composition - men 94, women 75, percentage women 44.4%

Judicial branch: *highest court(s):* Supreme Court or Hoyesterett (consists of the chief justice and 18 associate justices)
judge selection and term of office: justices appointed by the monarch (King in Council) upon the recommendation of the Judicial Appointments Board; justices can serve until mandatory retirement at age 70
subordinate courts: Courts of Appeal or Lagmennsrett; regional and district courts; Conciliation Boards; ordinary and special courts; note - in addition to professionally trained judges, elected lay judges sit on the bench with professional judges in the Courts of Appeal and district courts

Political parties: Center Party or Sp
Christian Democratic Party or KrF
Conservative Party or H
Green Party or MDG
Labor Party or Ap
Liberal Party or V
Patient Focus or PF
Progress Party or FrP
Red Party or R
Socialist Left Party or SV

International organization participation: ADB (nonregional member), AfDB (nonregional member), Arctic Council, Australia Group, BIS, CBSS, CD, CE, CERN, EAPC, EBRD, EFTA, EITI (implementing country), ESA, FAO, FATF, IADB, IAEA, IBRD, ICAO, ICC (national committees), ICCt, ICRM, IDA, IEA, IFAD, IFC, IFRCS, IGAD (partners), IHO, ILO, IMF, IMO, IMSO, Interpol, IOC, IOM, IPU, ISO, ITSO, ITU, ITUC (NGOs), MIGA, NATO, NC, NEA, NIB, NSG, OAS (observer), OECD, OPCW, OSCE, Paris Club, PCA, Schengen Convention, UN, UNCTAD, UNESCO, UNHCR, UNIDO, UNITAR, UNMISS, UNOOSA, UNRWA, UNTSO, UNWTO, UPU, Wassenaar Arrangement, WCO, WHO, WIPO, WMO, WTO, ZC

Diplomatic representation in the US: *chief of mission:* Ambassador Anniken Scharning HUITFELDT (since 18 September 2024)
chancery: 2720 34th Street NW, Washington, DC 20008
telephone: [1] (202) 333-6000
FAX: [1] (202) 469-3990
email address and website:
emb.washington@mfa.no
https://www.norway.no/en/usa/
consulate(s) general: New York, San Francisco

Diplomatic representation from the US: *chief of mission:* Ambassador (vacant); Chargé d'Affaires Sharon HUDSON-DEAN (since February 2024)
embassy: Morgedalsvegen 36, 0378 Oslo
mailing address: 5460 Oslo Place, Washington DC 20521-5460
telephone: [47] 21-30-85-40
FAX: [47] 22-56-27-51
email address and website:
OsloACS@state.gov
https://no.usembassy.gov/

Flag description: red with a blue cross outlined in white that extends to the edges of the flag; the vertical part of the cross is shifted to the hoist side in the style of the Dannebrog (Danish flag); the colors recall Norway's past political unions with Denmark (red and white) and Sweden (blue)

National symbol(s): lion; national colors: red, white, blue

National anthem: *name:* "Ja, vi elsker dette landet" (Yes, We Love This Country)
lyrics/music: *lyrics/music:* Bjornstjerne BJORNSON/Rikard NORDRAAK
note: adopted 1864; in addition to the national anthem, "Kongesangen" (Song of the King), which uses the tune of "God Save the King," serves as the royal anthem

National heritage: *total World Heritage Sites:* 8 (7 cultural, 1 natural)
selected World Heritage Site locales: Bryggen (c); Urnes Stave Church (c); Røros Mining Town and the Circumference (c); Rock Art of Alta (c); Vegaøyan – The Vega Archipelago (c); Struve Geodetic Arc (c); West Norwegian Fjords – Geirangerfjord and Nærøyfjord (n); Rjukan-Notodden Industrial Heritage Site (c)

ECONOMY

Economic overview: high-income, non-EU economy with trade links via European Economic Area (EEA); key European energy security role as leader in oil, gas, and electricity exports; major fishing, forestry, and extraction industries; oil sovereign fund supports generous welfare system; low unemployment; inflation and response hampering growth in non-energy sectors

Real GDP (purchasing power parity): $499.528 billion (2023 est.)
$496.973 billion (2022 est.)

$482.472 billion (2021 est.)
note: data in 2021 dollars
comparison ranking: 49

Real GDP growth rate: 0.51% (2023 est.)
3.01% (2022 est.)
3.91% (2021 est.)
note: annual GDP % growth based on constant local currency
comparison ranking: 180

Real GDP per capita: $90,500 (2023 est.)
$91,100 (2022 est.)
$89,200 (2021 est.)
note: data in 2021 dollars
comparison ranking: 8

GDP (official exchange rate): $485.513 billion (2023 est.)
note: data in current dollars at official exchange rate

Inflation rate (consumer prices): 5.52% (2023 est.)
5.76% (2022 est.)
3.48% (2021 est.)
note: annual % change based on consumer prices
comparison ranking: 116

Credit ratings: Fitch rating: AAA (1995)

Moody's rating: Aaa (1997)

Standard & Poors rating: AAA (1975)
note: The year refers to the year in which the current credit rating was first obtained.

GDP - composition, by sector of origin: *agriculture:* 2.1% (2023 est.)
industry: 39% (2023 est.)
services: 50% (2023 est.)
note: figures may not total 100% due to non-allocated consumption not captured in sector-reported data
comparison rankings: services 147; industry 31; agriculture 154

GDP - composition, by end use: *household consumption:* 37.5% (2023 est.)
government consumption: 21.9% (2023 est.)
investment in fixed capital: 23.4% (2023 est.)
investment in inventories: 2.4% (2023 est.)
exports of goods and services: 47.2% (2023 est.)
imports of goods and services: -32.5% (2023 est.)
note: figures may not total 100% due to rounding or gaps in data collection

Agricultural products: milk, barley, wheat, potatoes, oats, pork, chicken, beef, eggs, rye (2022)
note: top ten agricultural products based on tonnage

Industries: petroleum and gas, shipping, fishing, aquaculture, food processing, shipbuilding, pulp and paper products, metals, chemicals, timber, mining, textiles

Industrial production growth rate: 0.22% (2023 est.)
note: annual % change in industrial value added based on constant local currency
comparison ranking: 151

Labor force: 3.009 million (2023 est.)
note: number of people ages 15 or older who are employed or seeking work
comparison ranking: 111

Unemployment rate: 3.58% (2023 est.)
3.23% (2022 est.)
4.37% (2021 est.)
note: % of labor force seeking employment
comparison ranking: 65

Youth unemployment rate (ages 15-24): *total:* 11% (2023 est.)
male: 11.3% (2023 est.)
female: 10.6% (2023 est.)
note: % of labor force ages 15-24 seeking employment
comparison ranking: total 120

Population below poverty line: 12.2% (2021 est.)
note: % of population with income below national poverty line

Gini Index coefficient - distribution of family income: 27.7 (2019 est.)
note: index (0-100) of income distribution; higher values represent greater inequality
comparison ranking: 140

Average household expenditures: *on food:* 12.4% of household expenditures (2022 est.)
on alcohol and tobacco: 4% of household expenditures (2022 est.)

Household income or consumption by percentage share: *lowest 10%:* 3.4% (2019 est.)
highest 10%: 22.4% (2019 est.)
note: % share of income accruing to lowest and highest 10% of population

Remittances: 0.12% of GDP (2023 est.)
0.11% of GDP (2022 est.)
0.13% of GDP (2021 est.)
note: personal transfers and compensation between resident and non-resident individuals/households/entities

Budget: *revenues:* $334.543 billion (2022 est.)
expenditures: $174.546 billion (2022 est.)
note: central government revenues (excluding grants) and expenses converted to US dollars at average official exchange rate for year indicated

Public debt: 36.5% of GDP (2017 est.)
note: data cover general government debt and include debt instruments issued (or owned) by government entities other than the treasury; the data exclude treasury debt held by foreign entities; the data exclude debt issued by subnational entities, as well as intragovernmental debt; intragovernmental debt consists of treasury borrowings from surpluses in the social funds, such as for retirement, medical care, and unemployment; debt instruments for the social funds are not sold at public auctions
comparison ranking: 144

Taxes and other revenues: 31.27% (of GDP) (2022 est.)
note: central government tax revenue as a % of GDP
comparison ranking: 22

Current account balance: $86.368 billion (2023 est.)
$177.149 billion (2022 est.)
$66.254 billion (2021 est.)
note: balance of payments - net trade and primary/secondary income in current dollars
comparison ranking: 6

Exports: $228.625 billion (2023 est.)
$327.706 billion (2022 est.)
$203.228 billion (2021 est.)
note: balance of payments - exports of goods and services in current dollars
comparison ranking: 35

Exports - partners: Germany 27%, UK 21%, France 9%, Belgium 7%, Sweden 6% (2022)
note: top five export partners based on percentage share of exports

Exports - commodities: natural gas, crude petroleum, fish, refined petroleum, aluminum (2022)
note: top five export commodities based on value in dollars

Imports: $157.032 billion (2023 est.)
$161.645 billion (2022 est.)
$140.331 billion (2021 est.)
note: balance of payments - imports of goods and services in current dollars
comparison ranking: 36

Imports - partners: Sweden 18%, Germany 11%, China 10%, Denmark 6%, Netherlands 6% (2022)
note: top five import partners based on percentage share of imports

Imports - commodities: cars, refined petroleum, ships, garments, nickel (2022)
note: top five import commodities based on value in dollars

Reserves of foreign exchange and gold: $80.459 billion (2023 est.)
$72.077 billion (2022 est.)
$84.271 billion (2021 est.)
note: holdings of gold (year-end prices)/foreign exchange/special drawing rights in current dollars
comparison ranking: 35

Exchange rates: Norwegian kroner (NOK) per US dollar -

Exchange rates: 10.563 (2023 est.)
9.614 (2022 est.)
8.59 (2021 est.)
9.416 (2020 est.)
8.8 (2019 est.)

ENERGY

Electricity access: *electrification - total population:* 100% (2022 est.)

Electricity: *installed generating capacity:* 40.54 million kW (2022 est.)
consumption: 121.899 billion kWh (2022 est.)
exports: 25.792 billion kWh (2022 est.)
imports: 13.259 billion kWh (2022 est.)
transmission/distribution losses: 8.951 billion kWh (2022 est.)
comparison rankings: transmission/distribution losses 175; imports 19; exports 9; consumption 31; installed generating capacity 31

Electricity generation sources: *fossil fuels:* 0.5% of total installed capacity (2022 est.)
solar: 0.1% of total installed capacity (2022 est.)
wind: 10.3% of total installed capacity (2022 est.)
hydroelectricity: 88.7% of total installed capacity (2022 est.)
biomass and waste: 0.3% of total installed capacity (2022 est.)

Coal: *production:* 117,000 metric tons (2022 est.)
consumption: 1.201 million metric tons (2022 est.)
exports: 84,000 metric tons (2022 est.)
imports: 1.204 million metric tons (2022 est.)
proven reserves: 2 million metric tons (2022 est.)

Petroleum: *total petroleum production:* 2.02 million bbl/day (2023 est.)
refined petroleum consumption: 229,000 bbl/day (2023 est.)
crude oil estimated reserves: 8.122 billion barrels (2021 est.)

Natural gas: *production:* 123.727 billion cubic meters (2022 est.)
consumption: 4.548 billion cubic meters (2022 est.)
exports: 121.285 billion cubic meters (2022 est.)
imports: 67.96 million cubic meters (2022 est.)
proven reserves: 1.544 trillion cubic meters (2021 est.)

Carbon dioxide emissions: 38.928 million metric tonnes of CO2 (2022 est.)

from coal and metallurgical coke: 3.231 million metric tonnes of CO2 (2022 est.)
from petroleum and other liquids: 26.72 million metric tonnes of CO2 (2022 est.)
from consumed natural gas: 8.977 million metric tonnes of CO2 (2022 est.)
comparison ranking: total emissions 65

Energy consumption per capita: 201.034 million Btu/person (2022 est.)
comparison ranking: 19

COMMUNICATIONS

Telephones - fixed lines: *total subscriptions:* 140,000 (2022 est.)
subscriptions per 100 inhabitants: 3 (2022 est.)
comparison ranking: total subscriptions 127

Telephones - mobile cellular: *total subscriptions:* 6.015 million (2022 est.)
subscriptions per 100 inhabitants: 111 (2022 est.)
comparison ranking: total subscriptions 117

Telecommunication systems: *general assessment:* Norway has a sophisticated telecom market with high broadband and mobile penetration rates and a highly developed digital media sector. Although not a member of the European Union, the country's telecoms sector is synchronized with relevant EC legislation; Norway enjoys near comprehensive LTE coverage with upgrades to 5G technologies in the future (2023)
domestic: fixed-line is 7 per 100 and mobile-cellular nearly 110 per 100 (2021)
international: country code - 47; landing points for the Svalbard Undersea Cable System, Polar Circle Cable, Bodo-Rost Cable, NOR5KE Viking, Celtic Norse, Tempnet Offshore FOC Network, England Cable, Denmark-Norway6, Havfrue/ AEC-2, Skagerrak 4, and the Skagenfiber West & East submarine cables providing links to other Nordic countries, Europe and the US; satellite earth stations - Eutelsat, Intelsat (Atlantic Ocean), and 1 Inmarsat (Atlantic and Indian Ocean regions); note - Norway shares the Inmarsat earth station with the other Nordic countries (Denmark, Finland, Iceland, and Sweden) (2019)

Broadcast media: state-owned public radio-TV broadcaster operates 3 nationwide TV stations, 3 nationwide radio stations, and 16 regional radio stations; roughly a dozen privately owned TV stations broadcast nationally and roughly another 25 local TV stations broadcasting; nearly 75% of households have access to multi-channel cable or satellite TV; 2 privately owned radio stations broadcast nationwide and another 240 stations operate locally; Norway is the first country in the world to phase out FM radio in favor of Digital Audio Broadcasting (DAB), a process scheduled for completion in late 2017 (2019)

Internet country code: .no

Internet users: *total:* 5.346 million (2021 est.)
percent of population: 99% (2021 est.)
comparison ranking: total 89

Broadband - fixed subscriptions: *total:* 2,387,661 (2020 est.)
subscriptions per 100 inhabitants: 44 (2020 est.)
comparison ranking: total 54

TRANSPORTATION

National air transport system: *number of registered air carriers:* 8 (2020)
inventory of registered aircraft operated by air carriers: 125

Civil aircraft registration country code prefix: LN

Airports: 145 (2024)
comparison ranking: 36

Heliports: 77 (2024)

Pipelines: 8,520 km gas, 1,304 km oil/condensate (2017)

Railways: *total:* 3,848 km (2020) 2,482 km electrified
comparison ranking: total 50

Roadways: *total:* 95,120 km (2022)
comparison ranking: total 53

Waterways: 1,577 km (2010)
comparison ranking: 54

Merchant marine: *total:* 1,720 (2022)
by type: bulk carrier 109, container ship 1, general cargo 274, oil tanker 95, other 1,241
comparison ranking: total 17

Ports: *total ports:* 141 (2024)
large: 1
medium: 10
small: 34
very small: 90
size unknown: 6
ports with oil terminals: 54
key ports: Bergen, Drammen, Hammerfest, Harstad, Horten, Karsto, Mongstad, Oslo, Stavanger, Tromso, Trondheim

MILITARY AND SECURITY

Military and security forces: Norwegian Armed Forces (Forsvaret or "the Defense"): Norwegian Army (Haeren), Royal Norwegian Navy (Kongelige Norske Sjoeforsvaret; includes Coastal Rangers and Coast Guard (Kystvakt)), Royal Norwegian Air Force (Kongelige Norske Luftforsvaret), Norwegian Special Forces, Norwegian Cyber Defense Force, Home Guard (Heimevernet, HV) (2024)
note: the national police have primary responsibility for internal security; the National Police Directorate, an entity under the Ministry of Justice and Public Security, oversees the police force

Military expenditures: 2.2% of GDP (2024 est.)
1.8% of GDP (2023)
1.5% of GDP (2022)
1.7% of GDP (2021)
2% of GDP (2020)
comparison ranking: 54

Military and security service personnel strengths: approximately 27,000 active personnel (9,000 Army; 4,300 Navy; 4,700 Air Force; 9,000 other, including special operations, cyber, joint staff, intelligence, logistics support, active Home Guard, etc.); approximately 40,000 Home Guard (2024)
note: active personnel include about 10,000 conscripts

Military equipment inventories and acquisitions: the military's inventory includes a mix of modern, imported Western European and US, as well as domestically produced weapons systems and equipment; in 2024, the Norwegian Government announced a new defense plan which would double defense spending over the following 12 years with priorities placed in such areas as the acquisition of air defenses and naval capabilities; Norway has a defense industry with a focus in niche capabilities and participates in joint development and production of weapons systems with other European countries (2024)

Military service age and obligation: 19-35 years of age for selective compulsory military service for men and women; 17 years of age for male volunteers; 18 years of age for women volunteers; 12-19 month service obligation; conscripts first serve 12 months between the ages of 19 and 28, and then up to 4-5 refresher training periods until age 35, 44, 55, or 60 depending on rank and function (2024)
note 1: Norway has had compulsory military service since 1907; individuals conscripted each year are selected from a larger cohort who are evaluated through online assessments and physical tests
note 2: Norway was the first NATO country to allow women to serve in all combat arms branches of the military (1985); it also has an all-female special operations unit known as Jegertroppen (The Hunter Troop), which was established in 2014; as of 2023, women comprised about 20% of the military's full-time personnel
note 3: beginning in 1995, the military began offering Icelandic citizens the opportunity to apply for admission to officer schools in Norway with an associated education and service contract under special reasons and based on recommendations from Icelandic authorities; as early as 1996, Norway and Iceland entered into a cooperation agreement on the voluntary participation of Icelandic personnel in Norwegian force contributions in foreign operations

Military deployments: up to 200 Lithuania (NATO); Norway also has deployed air and naval assets in support of other NATO operations such as the Iceland Air Policing and the Mine Counter Measures Group missions (2024)

Military - note: the Norwegian Armed Forces (Forsvaret) are responsible for protecting Norway and its allies, including monitoring Norway's airspace, digital, land, and maritime areas, maintaining the country's borders and sovereignty, contributing to NATO and UN missions, and providing support to civil society, such as assisting the police, search and rescue, and maritime counterterrorism efforts; the military's territorial and sovereignty defense missions are complicated by Norway's vast sea areas, numerous islands, long and winding fjords, and difficult and mountainous terrain; a key area of emphasis is its far northern border with Russia
Norway is one of the original members of NATO, and the Alliance is a key component of Norway's defense policy; the Forsvaret participates regularly in NATO exercises, missions, and operations, including air policing of NATO territory, NATO's Enhanced Forward Presence mission in the Baltic States and Eastern Europe, and standing naval missions, as well as operations in non-NATO areas, such as the Middle East
the Forsvaret also cooperates closely with the militaries of other Nordic countries through the Nordic Defense Cooperation (NORDEFCO; established 2009), which consists of Denmark, Finland, Iceland, Norway, and Sweden; areas of cooperation include armaments, education, human resources, training and exercises, and operations; Norway contributes to the UK-led Joint Expeditionary Force, a pool of high-readiness military forces from 10 Baltic and Scandinavian countries designed to respond to a wide range of contingencies both in peacetime and in times of crisis or conflict with a focus on the High North, North Atlantic, and Baltic Sea regions; Norway has close military ties with the US, including rotational US military deployments and an agreement allowing for mutual defense activities and US military forces to access some Norwegian facilities

the Forsvaret's origins go back to the leidangen, defense forces which were established along the coastline in the 10th century to protect the Norwegian coast (2024)

SPACE

Space agency/agencies: the Norwegian Space Agency (NOSA, aka Norsk Romsenter; established 1987) (2024)

Space launch site(s): Andøya Space Center (Andøya Island; note - first operational spaceport in continental Europe) (2024)

Space program overview: has a broad and active space program coordinated with the European Space Agency (ESA) and the EU; jointly designs and builds satellites with foreign partners, including communications, remote sensing (RS), scientific, and navigational/ positional; operates satellites; develops and launches sounding rockets; researches and produces a range of other space-related technologies, including satellite/space launch vehicle (SLV) and space station components, telescopes, and robotics; conducts solar and telecommunications research; participates in international space programs, such as the International Space Station; hosts training for Mars landing missions on the island of Svalbard; active member of the ESA and cooperates with a variety of foreign space agencies and industries, including those of Canada, ESA/EU member states, Japan, Russia, and the US; has an active and advanced space industry that cooperates with both the NOSA and foreign space programs and produces a variety of space-related products, from terminals for satellite communications and technologies for RS satellites to sensors for gamma radiation in deep space (2024)
note: further details about the key activities, programs, and milestones of the country's space program, as well as government spending estimates on the space sector, appear in the Space Programs reference guide

TRANSNATIONAL ISSUES

Refugees and internally displaced persons: *refugees (country of origin):* 15,901 (Syria), 10,883 (Eritrea) (mid-year 2022); 70,085 (Ukraine) (as of 8 March 2024)
stateless persons: 3,901 (2022)

OMAN

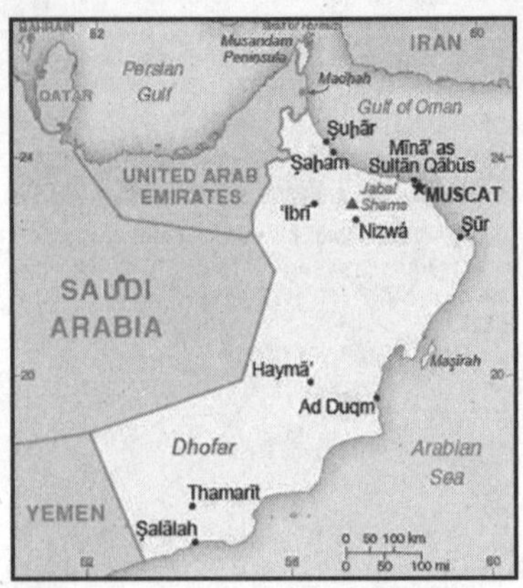

INTRODUCTION

Background: The inhabitants of the area of present-day Oman have long prospered from Indian Ocean trade. In the late 18th century, the nascent sultanate in Muscat signed the first in a series of friendship treaties with Britain. Over time, Oman's dependence on British political and military advisors increased, although the sultanate never became a British colony. In 1970, QABOOS bin Said Al Said overthrew his father and ruled as sultan for the next five decades. His extensive modernization program opened the country to the outside world. He prioritized strategic ties to the UK and US, and his moderate, independent foreign policy allowed Oman to maintain good relations with its neighbors and avoid external entanglements.

In 2011, the popular uprisings that swept the Middle East and North Africa inspired demonstrations in Oman that called for more jobs and economic benefits and an end to corruption. In response, QABOOS implemented economic and political reforms such as granting Oman's legislative body more power and authorizing direct elections for its lower house. Additionally, the sultan increased unemployment benefits and issued a royal directive mandating a national public- and private-sector job creation plan. As part of the government's efforts to decentralize authority and allow greater citizen participation in local governance, Oman successfully conducted its first municipal council elections in 2012. QABOOS, Oman's longest reigning monarch, died on in 2020. His cousin, HAYTHAM bin Tariq Al Said, former Minister of Heritage and Culture, was sworn in as Oman's new sultan the same day.

GEOGRAPHY

Location: Middle East, bordering the Arabian Sea, Gulf of Oman, and Persian Gulf, between Yemen and the UAE

Geographic coordinates: 21 00 N, 57 00 E

Map references: Middle East

Area: *total:* 309,500 sq km
land: 309,500 sq km
water: 0 sq km
comparison ranking: total 72

Area - comparative: twice the size of Georgia

Land boundaries: *total:* 1,561 km
border countries (3): Saudi Arabia 658 km; UAE 609 km; Yemen 294 km

Coastline: 2,092 km

Maritime claims: *territorial sea:* 12 nm
contiguous zone: 24 nm
exclusive economic zone: 200 nm

Climate: dry desert; hot, humid along coast; hot, dry interior; strong southwest summer monsoon (May to September) in far south

Terrain: central desert plain, rugged mountains in north and south

Elevation: *highest point:* Jabal Shams 3,004 m
lowest point: Arabian Sea 0 m
mean elevation: 310 m

Natural resources: petroleum, copper, asbestos, some marble, limestone, chromium, gypsum, natural gas

Land use: *agricultural land:* 4.7% (2018 est.)
arable land: 0.1% (2018 est.)
permanent crops: 0.1% (2018 est.)
permanent pasture: 4.5% (2018 est.)
forest: 0% (2018 est.)
other: 95.3% (2018 est.)

Irrigated land: 1,079 sq km (2020)

Major aquifers: Arabian Aquifer System

Population distribution: the vast majority of the population is located in and around the Al Hagar Mountains in the north of the country; another smaller cluster is found around the city of Salalah in the far south; most of the country remains sparsely poplulated

Natural hazards: summer winds often raise large sandstorms and dust storms in interior; periodic droughts

Geography - note: consists of Oman proper and two northern exclaves, Musandam and Al Madhah; the former is a peninsula that occupies a strategic location adjacent to the Strait of Hormuz, a vital transit point for world crude oil

PEOPLE AND SOCIETY

Population: *total:* 3,901,992
male: 2,096,126
female: 1,805,866 (2024 est.)
comparison rankings: female 132; male 128; total 130

Nationality: *noun:* Omani(s)
adjective: Omani

Ethnic groups: Arab, Baluchi, South Asian (Indian, Pakistani, Sri Lankan, Bangladeshi), African

Languages: Arabic (official), English, Baluchi, Swahili, Urdu, Indian dialects
major-language sample(s):
يمكن الاستغناء عنه للمعلومات الأساسية
كتاب حقائق العالم، المصدر الذي لا
(Arabic)

Religions: Muslim 85.9%, Christian 6.4%, Hindu 5.7%, other and unaffiliated 2% (2020 est.)
note: Omani citizens represent approximately 56.4% of the population and are overwhelming Muslim (Ibadhi and Sunni sects each constitute about 45% and Shia about 5%); Christians, Hindus, and Buddhists account for roughly 5% of Omani citizens

Age structure: *0-14 years:* 29.8% (male 594,909/female 566,682)
15-64 years: 66.2% (male 1,428,141/female 1,155,438)
65 years and over: 4% (2024 est.) (male 73,076/female 83,746)

Dependency ratios: *total dependency ratio:* 42
youth dependency ratio: 38
elderly dependency ratio: 4
potential support ratio: 25.2 (2021 est.)

Median age: *total:* 27.3 years (2024 est.)
male: 28.1 years
female: 26.3 years
comparison ranking: total 159

Population growth rate: 1.75% (2024 est.)
comparison ranking: 52

Birth rate: 21.1 births/1,000 population (2024 est.)
comparison ranking: 62

Death rate: 3.2 deaths/1,000 population (2024 est.)
comparison ranking: 224

Net migration rate: -0.5 migrant(s)/1,000 population (2024 est.)
comparison ranking: 121

Population distribution: the vast majority of the population is located in and around the Al Hagar Mountains in the north of the country; another smaller cluster is found around the city of Salalah in the far south; most of the country remains sparsely poplulated

Urbanization: *urban population:* 88.4% of total population (2023)
rate of urbanization: 2.32% annual rate of change (2020-25 est.)

Major urban areas - population: 1.650 million MUSCAT (capital) (2023)

Sex ratio: *at birth:* 1.05 male(s)/female
0-14 years: 1.05 male(s)/female
15-64 years: 1.24 male(s)/female
65 years and over: 0.87 male(s)/female
total population: 1.16 male(s)/female (2024 est.)

Maternal mortality ratio: 17 deaths/100,000 live births (2020 est.)
comparison ranking: 132

Infant mortality rate: *total:* 13.9 deaths/1,000 live births (2024 est.)
male: 15.1 deaths/1,000 live births
female: 12.6 deaths/1,000 live births
comparison ranking: total 100

Life expectancy at birth: *total population:* 77.4 years (2024 est.)
male: 75.5 years
female: 79.4 years
comparison ranking: total population 91

Total fertility rate: 2.64 children born/woman (2024 est.)
comparison ranking: 64

Gross reproduction rate: 1.29 (2024 est.)

Contraceptive prevalence rate: 29.7% (2014)

Drinking water source: *improved: urban:* 100% of population
rural: 97.9% of population
total: 99.7% of population
unimproved: urban: 0% of population
rural: 2.1% of population
total: 0.3% of population (2020 est.)

Current health expenditure: 5.3% of GDP (2020)

Physician density: 1.77 physicians/1,000 population (2020)

Hospital bed density: 1.5 beds/1,000 population (2017)

Sanitation facility access: *improved: urban:* 100% of population
rural: 100% of population
total: 100% of population

Obesity - adult prevalence rate: 27% (2016)
comparison ranking: 39

Alcohol consumption per capita: *total:* 0.47 liters of pure alcohol (2019 est.)
beer: 0.17 liters of pure alcohol (2019 est.)
wine: 0.02 liters of pure alcohol (2019 est.)
spirits: 0.29 liters of pure alcohol (2019 est.)
other alcohols: 0 liters of pure alcohol (2019 est.)
comparison ranking: total 164

Tobacco use: *total:* 8% (2020 est.)
male: 15.5% (2020 est.)
female: 0.4% (2020 est.)
comparison ranking: total 150

Children under the age of 5 years underweight: 11.2% (2016/17)
comparison ranking: 52

Currently married women (ages 15-49): 56.4% (2023 est.)

Education expenditures: 5,4% of GDP (2019 est.)
comparison ranking: 61

Literacy: *definition:* age 15 and over can read and write
total population: 95.7%
male: 97%
female: 92.7% (2018)

School life expectancy (primary to tertiary education): *total:* 15 years
male: 15 years
female: 15 years (2021)

ENVIRONMENT

Environment - current issues: limited natural freshwater resources; high levels of soil and water salinity in the coastal plains; beach pollution from oil spills; industrial effluents seeping into the water tables and aquifers; desertificaiton due to high winds driving desert sand into arable lands

Environment - international agreements: *party to:* Biodiversity, Climate Change, Climate Change-Kyoto Protocol, Climate Change-Paris Agreement, Comprehensive Nuclear Test Ban, Desertification, Endangered Species, Hazardous Wastes, Law of the Sea, Marine Dumping-London Convention, Ozone Layer Protection, Ship Pollution, Wetlands, Whaling
signed, but not ratified: none of the selected agreements

Climate: dry desert; hot, humid along coast; hot, dry interior; strong southwest summer monsoon (May to September) in far south

Urbanization: *urban population:* 88.4% of total population (2023)
rate of urbanization: 2.32% annual rate of change (2020-25 est.)

Revenue from forest resources: 0% of GDP (2018 est.)
comparison ranking: 174

Revenue from coal: 0% of GDP (2018 est.)
comparison ranking: 167

Air pollutants: *particulate matter emissions:* 34.88 micrograms per cubic meter (2019 est.)
carbon dioxide emissions: 63.46 megatons (2016 est.)
methane emissions: 5.6 megatons (2020 est.)

Waste and recycling: *municipal solid waste generated annually:* 1,734,885 tons (2014 est.)

Major aquifers: Arabian Aquifer System

Total water withdrawal: *municipal:* 130 million cubic meters (2020 est.)
industrial: 240 million cubic meters (2020 est.)
agricultural: 1.55 billion cubic meters (2020 est.)

Total renewable water resources: 1.4 billion cubic meters (2020 est.)

GOVERNMENT

Country name: *conventional long form:* Sultanate of Oman
conventional short form: Oman
local long form: Saltanat Uman
local short form: Uman
former: Sultanate of Muscat and Oman
etymology: the origin of the name is uncertain, but it apparently dates back at least 2,000 years since an "Omana" is mentioned by Pliny the Elder (1st century A.D.) and an "Omanon" by Ptolemy (2nd century A.D.)

Government type: absolute monarchy

Capital: *name:* Muscat
geographic coordinates: 23 37 N, 58 35 E
time difference: UTC+4 (9 hours ahead of Washington, DC, during Standard Time)
etymology: the name, whose meaning is uncertain, traces back almost two millennia; two 2nd century A.D. scholars, the geographer PTOLEMY and the historian ARRIAN, both mention an Arabian Sea coastal town of Moscha, which most likely referred to Muscat

Administrative divisions: 11 governorates (muhafazat, singular - muhafaza); Ad Dakhiliyah, Al Buraymi, Al Wusta, Az Zahirah, Janub al Batinah (Al Batinah South), Janub ash Sharqiyah (Ash Sharqiyah South), Masqat (Muscat), Musandam, Shamal al Batinah (Al Batinah North), Shamal ash Sharqiyah (Ash Sharqiyah North), Zufar (Dhofar)

Independence: 1650 (expulsion of the Portuguese)

National holiday: National Day, 18 November; note - celebrates Oman's independence from Portugal in 1650 and the birthday of Sultan QABOOS bin Said al Said, who reigned from 1970 to 2020

Legal system: mixed legal system of Anglo-Saxon law and Islamic law

Constitution: *history:* promulgated by royal decree 6 November 1996 (the Basic Law of the Sultanate of Oman serves as the constitution); amended by royal decree in 2011
amendments: promulgated by the sultan or proposed by the Council of Oman and drafted by a technical committee as stipulated by royal decree and then promulgated through royal decree; amended by royal decree 2011, 2021

International law organization participation: has not submitted an ICJ jurisdiction declaration; non-party state to the ICCt

Citizenship: *citizenship by birth:* no
citizenship by descent only: the father must be a citizen of Oman
dual citizenship recognized: no
residency requirement for naturalization: unknown

Suffrage: 21 years of age; universal; note - members of the military and security forces by law cannot vote

Executive branch: *chief of state:* Sultan and Prime Minister HAITHAM bin Tarik Al Said (since 11 January 2020)
head of government: Sultan and Prime HAITHAM bin Tarik Al Said (since 11 January 2020)
cabinet: Cabinet appointed by the monarch

Legislative branch: *description:* bicameral Council of Oman or Majlis Oman consists of:
Council of State or Majlis al-Dawla (87 seats including the chairman; members appointed by the sultan from among former government officials and prominent educators, businessmen, and citizens; members serve 4-year term) Consultative Assembly or Majlis al-Shura (90 seats; members directly elected in single- and 2-seat constituencies by simple majority popular vote to serve renewable 4-year terms)
elections: Council of State - last appointments on 8 November 2023 (next appointments in November 2027) Consultative Assembly - last held on 29 October 2023 (next to be held in October 2027)
election results: Council of State - 87 nonpartisan members were appointed by the sultan; composition - men 68, women 18, percentage women 20.9%
Consultative Assembly percent of vote by party - NA; seats by party - NA; 90 nonpartisan members were elected (organized political parties in Oman are legally banned); composition - 90 men, 0 women, percentage women 0%; total Council of Oman percentage women 10.2%

Judicial branch: *highest court(s):* Supreme Court (consists of 5 judges)
judge selection and term of office: judges nominated by the 9-member Supreme Judicial Council (chaired by the monarch) and appointed by the monarch; judges appointed for life
subordinate courts: Courts of Appeal; Administrative Court; Courts of First Instance; sharia courts; magistrates' courts; military courts

Political parties: none; note - organized political parties are legally banned in Oman, and loyalties tend to form around tribal affiliations

International organization participation: ABEDA, AFESD, AMF, CAEU, FAO, G-77, GCC, IAEA, IBRD, ICAO, ICC (NGOs), IDA, IDB, IFAD, IFC, IHO, ILO, IMF, IMO, IMSO, Interpol, IOC, IPU, ISO, ITSO, ITU, LAS, MIGA, NAM, OIC, OPCW, UN, UNCTAD, UNESCO, UNIDO, UNWTO, UPU, WCO, WFTU (NGOs), WHO, WIPO, WMO, WTO

Diplomatic representation in the US: *chief of mission:* Ambassador Moosa Hamdan Moosa AL TAI (since 17 February 2021)
chancery: 2535 Belmont Road, NW, Washington, DC 20008
telephone: [1] (202) 387-1980
FAX: [1] (202) 745-4933

email address and website:
washington@fm.gov.om
Embassy of the Sultanate of Oman, Washington, USA - FM.gov.om

Diplomatic representation from the US: *chief of mission:* Ambassador Ana ESCROGIMA (since 4 December 2023)
embassy: P.C. 115, Madinat Al Sultan Qaboos, Muscat
mailing address: 6220 Muscat Place, Washington DC 20521
telephone: [968] 2464-3400
FAX: [968] 2464-3740
email address and website:
ConsularMuscat@state.gov
https://om.usembassy.gov/

Flag description: three horizontal bands of white (top), red, and green of equal width with a broad, vertical, red band on the hoist side; the national emblem (a khanjar dagger in its sheath superimposed on two crossed swords in scabbards) in white is centered near the top of the vertical band; white represents peace and prosperity, red recalls battles against foreign invaders, and green symbolizes the Jebel al Akhdar (Green Mountains) and fertility

National symbol(s): khanjar dagger superimposed on two crossed swords; national colors: red, white, green

National anthem: *name:* "Nashid as-Salaam as-Sultani" (The Sultan's Anthem)
lyrics/music: Rashid bin Uzayyiz al KHUSAIDI/ James Frederick MILLS, arranged by Bernard EBBINGHAUS
note: adopted 1932; new lyrics written after QABOOS bin Said al Said gained power in 1970; first performed by the band of a British ship as a salute to the Sultan during a 1932 visit to Muscat; the bandmaster of the HMS Hawkins was asked to write a salutation to the Sultan on the occasion of his ship visit

National heritage: *total World Heritage Sites:* 5 (all cultural)
selected World Heritage Site locales: Bahla Fort; Archaeological Sites of Bat; Land of Frankincense; Aflaj Irrigation Systems of Oman; Ancient Qalhat

ECONOMY

Economic overview: high-income, oil-based economy; large welfare system; growing government debt; citizenship-based labor force growth policy; US free trade agreement; diversifying portfolio; high female labor force participation

Real GDP (purchasing power parity): $185.96 billion (2023 est.)
$183.574 billion (2022 est.)
$175.986 billion (2021 est.)
note: data in 2021 dollars
comparison ranking: 78

Real GDP growth rate: 1.3% (2023 est.)
4.31% (2022 est.)
3.09% (2021 est.)
note: annual GDP % growth based on constant local currency
comparison ranking: 158

Real GDP per capita: $40,000 (2023 est.)
$40,100 (2022 est.)
$38,900 (2021 est.)
note: data in 2021 dollars
comparison ranking: 62

GDP (official exchange rate): $108.192 billion (2023 est.)
note: data in current dollars at official exchange rate

Inflation rate (consumer prices): 0.94% (2023 est.)
2.51% (2022 est.)
1.68% (2021 est.)
note: annual % change based on consumer prices
comparison ranking: 16

Credit ratings: Fitch rating: BB- (2020)
Moody's rating: Ba3 (2020)
Standard & Poors rating: B+ (2020)
note: The year refers to the year in which the current credit rating was first obtained.

GDP - composition, by sector of origin: *agriculture:* 1.8% (2022 est.)
industry: 57% (2022 est.)
services: 44.5% (2022 est.)
note: figures may not total 100% due to non-allocated consumption not captured in sector-reported data
comparison rankings: services 172; industry 7; agriculture 164

GDP - composition, by end use: *household consumption:* 44.3% (2021 est.)
government consumption: 22.1% (2021 est.)
investment in fixed capital: 25.6% (2021 est.)
investment in inventories: -3.2% (2021 est.)
exports of goods and services: 52.5% (2021 est.)
imports of goods and services: -41.4% (2021 est.)
note: figures may not total 100% due to rounding or gaps in data collection

Agricultural products: dates, tomatoes, milk, sorghum, vegetables, goat milk, cucumbers/gherkins, chilies/peppers, watermelons, cantaloupes/ melons (2022)
note: top ten agricultural products based on tonnage

Industries: crude oil production and refining, natural and liquefied natural gas production; construction, cement, copper, steel, chemicals, optic fiber

Industrial production growth rate: 5.05% (2022 est.)
note: annual % change in industrial value added based on constant local currency
comparison ranking: 49

Labor force: 2.316 million (2023 est.)
note: number of people ages 15 or older who are employed or seeking work
comparison ranking: 123

Unemployment rate: 1.46% (2023 est.)
1.51% (2022 est.)
1.9% (2021 est.)
note: % of labor force seeking employment
comparison ranking: 14

Youth unemployment rate (ages 15-24): *total:* 6.8% (2023 est.)
male: 5.5% (2023 est.)
female: 13.3% (2023 est.)
note: % of labor force ages 15-24 seeking employment
comparison ranking: total 161

Average household expenditures: *on food:* 21.8% of household expenditures (2022 est.)
on alcohol and tobacco: 0.2% of household expenditures (2022 est.)

Remittances: 0.04% of GDP (2023 est.)
0.03% of GDP (2022 est.)
0.04% of GDP (2021 est.)
note: personal transfers and compensation between resident and non-resident individuals/households/ entities

Budget: *revenues:* $29.334 billion (2018 est.)
expenditures: $35.984 billion (2018 est.)

Public debt: 46.9% of GDP (2017 est.)
note: excludes indebtedness of state-owned enterprises
comparison ranking: 116

Taxes and other revenues: 31.3% (of GDP) (2017 est.)
comparison ranking: 21

Current account balance: $5.652 billion (2022 est.)
-$4.834 billion (2021 est.)
-$12.514 billion (2020 est.)
note: balance of payments - net trade and primary/ secondary income in current dollars
comparison ranking: 33

Exports: $69.701 billion (2022 est.)
$46.572 billion (2021 est.)
$35.691 billion (2020 est.)
note: balance of payments - exports of goods and services in current dollars
comparison ranking: 56

Exports - partners: China 40%, India 11%, South Korea 6%, UAE 4%, US 4% (2022)
note: top five export partners based on percentage share of exports

Exports - commodities: crude petroleum, natural gas, refined petroleum, fertilizers, semi-finished iron (2022)
note: top five export commodities based on value in dollars

Imports: $46.326 billion (2022 est.)
$37.216 billion (2021 est.)
$33.827 billion (2020 est.)
note: balance of payments - imports of goods and services in current dollars
comparison ranking: 71

Imports - partners: UAE 27%, Saudi Arabia 11%, India 10%, China 9%, Qatar 5% (2022)
note: top five import partners based on percentage share of imports

Imports - commodities: refined petroleum, cars, iron ore, milk, iron pipes (2022)
note: top five import commodities based on value in dollars

Reserves of foreign exchange and gold: $17.455 billion (2023 est.)
$17.606 billion (2022 est.)
$19.731 billion (2021 est.)
note: holdings of gold (year-end prices)/foreign exchange/special drawing rights in current dollars
comparison ranking: 66

Exchange rates: Omani rials (OMR) per US dollar -

Exchange rates: 0.385 (2023 est.)
0.385 (2022 est.)
0.385 (2021 est.)
0.385 (2020 est.)
0.385 (2019 est.)

ENERGY

Electricity access: *electrification - total population:* 100% (2022 est.)

Electricity: *installed generating capacity:* 9.129 million kW (2022 est.)
consumption: 39.012 billion kWh (2022 est.)
transmission/distribution losses: 4.043 billion kWh (2022 est.)

comparison rankings: transmission/distribution losses 155; consumption 59; installed generating capacity 68

Electricity generation sources: *fossil fuels:* 99.4% of total installed capacity (2022 est.)
solar: 0.6% of total installed capacity (2022 est.)

Coal: *consumption:* 31,000 metric tons (2022 est.)
exports: 73,000 metric tons (2022 est.)
imports: 105,000 metric tons (2022 est.)

Petroleum: *total petroleum production:* 1.056 million bbl/day (2023 est.)
refined petroleum consumption: 211,000 bbl/day (2022 est.)
crude oil estimated reserves: 5.373 billion barrels (2021 est.)

Natural gas: *production:* 40.754 billion cubic meters (2022 est.)
consumption: 27.364 billion cubic meters (2022 est.)
exports: 15.446 billion cubic meters (2022 est.)
imports: 1.506 billion cubic meters (2022 est.)
proven reserves: 651.287 billion cubic meters (2021 est.)

Carbon dioxide emissions: 79.559 million metric tonnes of CO_2 (2022 est.)
from coal and metallurgical coke: 24,000 metric tonnes of CO_2 (2022 est.)
from petroleum and other liquids: 27.188 million metric tonnes of CO_2 (2022 est.)
from consumed natural gas: 52.348 million metric tonnes of CO_2 (2022 est.)
comparison ranking: total emissions 48

Energy consumption per capita: 285.886 million Btu/person (2022 est.)
comparison ranking: 9

COMMUNICATIONS

Telephones - fixed lines: *total subscriptions:* 563,000 (2022 est.)
subscriptions per 100 inhabitants: 13 (2021 est.)
comparison ranking: total subscriptions 86

Telephones - mobile cellular: *total subscriptions:* 6.75 million (2022 est.)
subscriptions per 100 inhabitants: 135 (2021 est.)
comparison ranking: total subscriptions 113

Telecommunication systems: *general assessment:* Oman has a modern mobile sector which comprises substantial coverage of both 3G and LTE networks; in February 2021 commercial 5G services were launched; the Covid-19 pandemic has caused a spike in mobile data traffic; while Oman's fixed broadband infrastructure penetration is considered low, it is being improved with the building of fiber-based networks as part of Oman's Vision 2040 program; Oman has also established itself as an important communications hub in the Middle East, with access to numerous submarine cables including the 2Africa submarine cable, which should become available during 2023-2024; the 9,800km Oman Australia Cable running from Muscat to Perth, with the potential for a branch line to Djibouti, is making progress and is expected to be completed in December 2021; this additional infrastructure will provide considerable additional bandwidth (2021)
domestic: fixed-line is 13 per 100 and mobile-cellular is 135 per 100 (2021)
international: country code - 968; landing points for GSA, AAE-1, SeaMeWe-5, Tata TGN-Gulf, FALCON, GBICS/ MENA, MENA/Guld Bridge International, TW1, BBG, EIG, OMRAN/EPEG, and POI submarine cables providing connectivity to Asia, Africa, the Middle East, Southeast Asia and Europe; satellite earth stations - 2 Intelsat (Indian Ocean) (2019)

Broadcast media: 1 state-run TV broadcaster; TV stations transmitting from Saudi Arabia, the UAE, Iran, and Yemen available via satellite TV; state-run radio operates multiple stations; first private radio station began operating in 2007 and several additional stations now operating (2019)

Internet country code: .om

Internet users: *total:* 4.32 million (2021 est.)
percent of population: 96% (2021 est.)
comparison ranking: total 105

Broadband - fixed subscriptions: *total:* 508,949 (2020 est.)
subscriptions per 100 inhabitants: 11 (2020 est.)
comparison ranking: total 90

TRANSPORTATION

National air transport system: *number of registered air carriers:* 2 (2020)
inventory of registered aircraft operated by air carriers: 57
annual passenger traffic on registered air carriers: 10,438,241 (2018)
annual freight traffic on registered air carriers: 510.43 million (2018) mt-km

Civil aircraft registration country code prefix: A4O

Airports: 36 (2024)
comparison ranking: 110

Heliports: 20 (2024)

Pipelines: 106 km condensate, 4,224 km gas, 3,558 km oil, 33 km oil/gas/water, 264 km refined products (2013)

Roadways: *total:* 60,230 km
paved: 29,685 km (includes 1,943 km of expressways)
unpaved: 30,545 km (2012)
comparison ranking: total 78

Merchant marine: *total:* 57 (2023)
by type: general cargo 11, other 46
comparison ranking: total 117

Ports: *total ports:* 7 (2024)
large: 0
medium: 1
small: 4
very small: 2
ports with oil terminals: 6
key ports: Duqm, Khawr Khasab, Mina Al Fahl, Mina Raysut, Sohar

MILITARY AND SECURITY

Military and security forces: Sultan's Armed Forces (SAF): Royal Army of Oman (RAO), Royal Navy of Oman (RNO), Royal Air Force of Oman (RAFO), Royal Guard of Oman (RGO), Sultan's Special Forces

Royal Oman Police (ROP): Civil Defense, Immigration, Customs, Royal Oman Police Coast Guard, Special Task Force (2024)
note 1: the Sultan's Special Forces and the ROP Special Task Force are Oman's primary tactical counterterrorism response forces
note 2: in addition to its policing duties, the ROP conducts many administrative functions similar to the responsibilities of a Ministry of Interior in other countries

Military expenditures: 5.5% of GDP (2023 est.)
5.5% of GDP (2022 est.)
8% of GDP (2021 est.)
11% of GDP (2020 est.)
11.8% of GDP (2019 est.)
comparison ranking: 6

Military and security service personnel strengths: approximately 40,000 active-duty troops (25,000 Army, 5,000 Navy; 5,000 Air Force; 5,000 Royal Guard) (2023)

Military equipment inventories and acquisitions: the SAF's inventory includes a mix of older and some more modern weapons systems from a variety of suppliers, particularly the UK and the US; other suppliers have included China, EU countries, South Africa, and Turkey (2024)

Military service age and obligation: 18 for voluntary military service for men and women (women have been allowed to serve since 2011); no conscription (2023)

Military - note: the Sultan's Armed Forces (SAF) are responsible for defending the country, ensuring internal security, and protecting the monarchy; it is a small but well-equipped military that often trains with foreign partners such as the Gulf Cooperation Council countries, the UK, and the US; the SAF has a longstanding security relationship with the British military going back to the 18th century; today, the SAF and the British maintain a joint training base in Oman; in 2017, Oman and the UK signed an agreement allowing the British military the use of facilities at Al Duqm Port; in 2019, the US obtained access to the port, expanding on previous military cooperation agreements in 2014, 2010, and 1980; Oman also allows other nations to use some of its maritime facilities, including China
Oman has a small but relatively modern navy that conducts maritime security operations along the country's long coastline, including patrolling, ensuring freedom of navigation in the key naval chokepoint of the Strait of Hormuz, and countering piracy and smuggling; while Oman is not a member of the US-led, multinational Combined Maritime Forces (CMF), which operates task forces to counter piracy and smuggling, the Omani Navy has at times participated in CMF-led joint exercises (2024)

TERRORISM

Terrorist group(s): Islamic State of Iraq and ash-Sham (ISIS)
note: details about the history, aims, leadership, organization, areas of operation, tactics, targets, weapons, size, and sources of support of the group(s) appear(s) in the Terrorism reference guide

TRANSNATIONAL ISSUES

Refugees and internally displaced persons: *refugees (country of origin):* 5,000 (Yemen) (2017)

PACIFIC OCEAN

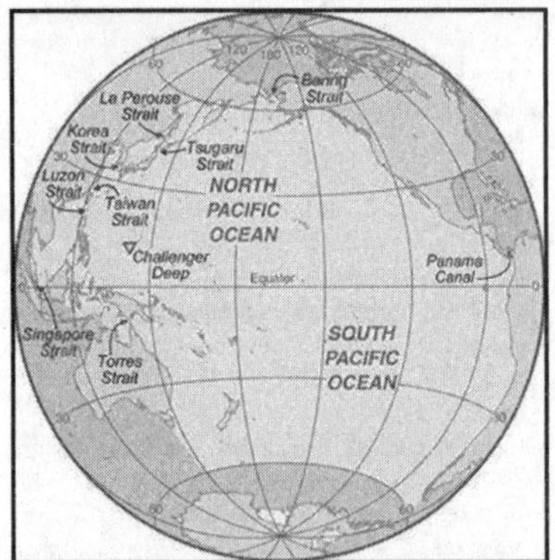

INTRODUCTION

Background: The Pacific Ocean is the largest of the world's five ocean basins (followed by the Atlantic Ocean, Indian Ocean, Southern Ocean, and Arctic Ocean). Strategically important access waterways include the La Perouse, Tsugaru, Tsushima, Taiwan, Singapore, and Torres Straits. The International Hydrographic Organization decision in 2000 to delimit a fifth world ocean basin, the Southern Ocean, removed the portion of the Pacific Ocean south of 60 degrees south. For convenience and because of its immense size, the Pacific Ocean is often divided at the Equator and designated as the North Pacific Ocean and the South Pacific Ocean.

GEOGRAPHY

Location: body of water between the Southern Ocean, Asia, Australia, and the Western Hemisphere

Geographic coordinates: 0 00 N, 160 00 W

Map references: Map of the world oceans

Area: *total:* 168.723 million sq km
note: includes Arafura Sea, Bali Sea, Banda Sea, Bering Sea, Bering Strait, Celebes Sea, Coral Sea, East China Sea, Flores Sea, Gulf of Alaska, Gulf of Thailand, Gulf of Tonkin, Java Sea, Philippine Sea, Sea of Japan, Sea of Okhotsk, Solomon Sea, South China Sea, Sulu Sea, Tasman Sea, and other tributary water bodies

Area - comparative: about 15 times the size of the US; covers about 28% of the global surface; almost equal to the total land area of the world

Coastline: 135,663 km

Climate: planetary air pressure systems and resultant wind patterns exhibit remarkable uniformity in the south and east; trade winds and westerly winds are well-developed patterns, modified by seasonal fluctuations; tropical cyclones (hurricanes) may form south of Mexico from June to October and affect Mexico and Central America; continental influences cause climatic uniformity to be much less pronounced in the eastern and western regions at the same latitude in the North Pacific Ocean; the western Pacific is monsoonal - a rainy season occurs during the summer months, when moistureladen winds blow from the ocean over the land, and a dry season during the winter months, when dry winds blow from the Asian landmass back to the ocean; tropical cyclones (typhoons) may strike southeast and east Asia from May to December

Ocean volume: *ocean volume:* 669.88 million cu km
percent of World Ocean total volume: 50.1%

Major ocean currents: the clockwise North Pacific Gyre formed by the warm northward flowing Kuroshio Current in the west, the eastward flowing North Pacific Current in the north, the southward flowing cold California Current in the east, and the westward flowing North Equatorial Current in the south; the counterclockwise South Pacific Gyre composed of the southward flowing warm East Australian Current in the west, the eastward flowing South Pacific Current in the south, the northward flowing cold Peru (Humbolt) Current in the east, and the westward flowing South Equatorial Current in the north

Elevation: *highest point:* sea level
lowest point: Challenger Deep in the Mariana Trench -10,924 m; note - the Pacific Ocean is the deepest ocean basin
mean depth: -4,080 m
ocean zones: Composed of water and in a fluid state, the ocean is delimited differently than the solid continents. It is divided into three zones based on depth and light level. Sunlight entering the water may travel about 1,000 m into the oceans under the right conditions, but there is rarely any significant light beyond 200 m.
The upper 200 m (656 ft) of the ocean is called the euphotic, or "sunlight," zone. This zone contains the vast majority of commercial fisheries and is home to many protected marine mammals and sea turtles. Only a small amount of light penetrates beyond this depth.
The zone between 200 m (656 ft) and 1,000 m (3,280 ft) is usually referred to as the "twilight" zone, but is officially the dysphotic zone. In this zone, the intensity of light rapidly dissipates as depth increases. Such a minuscule amount of light penetrates beyond a depth of 200 m that photosynthesis is no longer possible.
The aphotic, or "midnight," zone exists in depths below 1,000 m (3,280 ft). Sunlight does not penetrate to these depths, and the zone is bathed in darkness.

Natural resources: oil and gas fields, polymetallic nodules, sand and gravel aggregates, placer deposits, fish

Natural hazards: surrounded by a zone of violent volcanic and earthquake activity sometimes referred to as the "Pacific Ring of Fire"; up to 90% of the world's earthquakes and some 75% of the world's volcanoes occur within the Ring of Fire; 80% of tsunamis, caused by volcanic or seismic events, occur within the "Pacific Ring of Fire"; subject to tropical cyclones (typhoons) in southeast and east Asia from May to December (most frequent from July to October); tropical cyclones (hurricanes) may form south of Mexico and strike Central America and Mexico from June to October (most common in August and September); cyclical El Niño/La Niña phenomenon occurs in the equatorial Pacific, influencing weather in the Western Hemisphere and the western Pacific; ships subject to superstructure icing in extreme north from October to May; persistent fog in the northern Pacific can be a maritime hazard from June to December

Geography - note: the major chokepoints are the Bering Strait, Panama Canal, Luzon Strait, and the Singapore Strait; the Equator divides the Pacific Ocean into the North Pacific Ocean and the South Pacific Ocean; dotted with low coral islands and rugged volcanic islands in the southwestern Pacific Ocean; much of the Pacific Ocean's rim lies along the Ring of Fire, a belt of active volcanoes and earthquake epicenters that accounts for up to 90% of the world's earthquakes and some 75% of the world's volcanoes; the Pacific Ocean is the deepest ocean basin averaging 4,000 m in depth

ENVIRONMENT

Environment - current issues: pollution from land- and sea-based sources (such as sewage, nutrient runoff from agriculture, plastic pollution, and toxic waste); habitat destruction; over-fishing; climate change leading to sea level rise, ocean acidification, and warming; endangered marine species include the dugong, sea lion, sea otter, seals, turtles, and whales; oil pollution in Philippine Sea and South China Sea

Climate: planetary air pressure systems and resultant wind patterns exhibit remarkable uniformity in the south and east; trade winds and westerly winds are well-developed patterns, modified by seasonal fluctuations; tropical cyclones (hurricanes) may form south of Mexico from June to October and affect Mexico and Central America; continental influences cause climatic uniformity to be much less pronounced in the eastern and western regions at the same latitude in the North Pacific Ocean; the western Pacific is monsoonal - a rainy season occurs during the summer months, when moistureladen winds blow from the ocean over the land, and a dry season during the winter months, when dry winds blow from the Asian landmass back to the ocean; tropical cyclones (typhoons) may strike southeast and east Asia from May to December

Marine fisheries: *the Pacific Ocean fisheries are the most important in the world, accounting for 58.1%, or 45,800,000 mt, of the global marine capture in 2020; of the six regions delineated by the Food and Agriculture Organization in the Pacific Ocean, the following are the most important:*
Northwest Pacific region (Region 61) is the world's most important fishery, producing 24.3% of the global catch or 19,150,000 mt in 2020; it encompasses the waters north of 20º north latitude and west of 175º west longitude, with the major producers including China (29,080726 mt), Japan (3,417,871 mt), South Korea (1,403,892 mt), and Taiwan (487,739 mt); the principal catches include Alaska pollock, Japanese anchovy, chub mackerel, and scads
Western Central Pacific region (Region 71) is the world's second most important fishing region producing 16.8%, or 13,260,000 mt, of the global catch in 2020; tuna is the most important species in this region; the region includes the waters between 20º North and 25º South latitude and west of 175º West longitude with the major producers including Indonesia (6,907,932 mt), Vietnam (4,571,497 mt), Philippines (2,416,879 mt), Thailand (1,509,574 mt), and Malaysia (692,553 mt); the principal

catches include skipjack and yellowfin tuna, sardinellas, and cephalopods
Southeast Pacific region (Region 87) is the third largest fishery in the world, producing 10.7%, or 8,400,000 mt, of the global catch in 2020; this region includes the nutrient-rich waters off the west coast of South America between 5º North and 60º South latitude and east of 120º West longitude, with the major producers including Peru (4,888,730 mt), Chile (3,298,795 mt), and Ecuador (1,186,249 mt); the principal catches include Peruvian anchovy (68.5% of the catch), jumbo flying squid, and Chilean jack mackerel
Pacific Northeast region (Region 67) is the eighth largest fishery in the world, producing 3.6% of the global catch or 2,860,000 mt in 2020; this region encompasses the waters north of 40º North latitude and east of 175º West longitude, including the Gulf of Alaska and Bering Sea, with the major producers including the US (3,009,568 mt), Canada (276,677 mt), and Russia (6,908 mt); the principal catches include Alaska pollock, Pacific cod, and North Pacific hake

Regional fisheries bodies: Commission for the Conservation of Southern Bluefin Tuna, Inter-American Tropical Tuna Commission, International Council for the Exploration of the Seas, North Pacific Anadromous Fish Commission, North Pacific Fisheries Commission, South Pacific Regional Fisheries Management Organization, Southeast Asian Fisheries Development Center, Western and Central Pacific Fisheries Commission

GOVERNMENT

Country name: *etymology:* named by Portuguese explorer Ferdinand MAGELLAN during the Spanish circumnavigation of the world in 1521; encountering favorable winds upon reaching the ocean, he called it "Mar Pacifico," which means "peaceful sea" in both Portuguese and Spanish

PAKISTAN

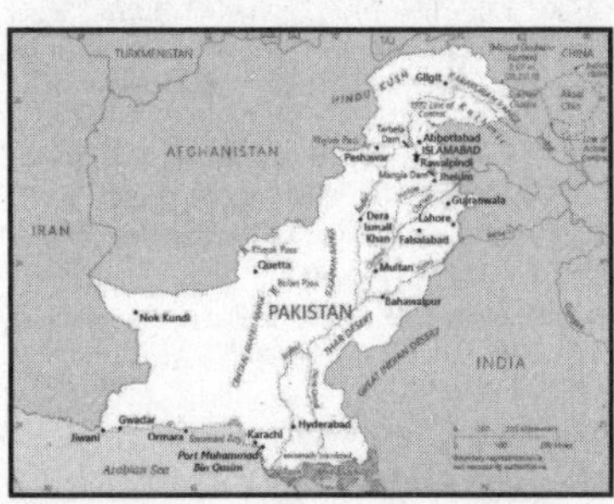

INTRODUCTION

Background: The Indus Valley civilization, one of the oldest in the world and dating back at least 5,000 years, spread over much of modern-day Pakistan. During the second millennium B.C., remnants of this culture fused with the migrating Indo-Aryan peoples. The area underwent successive invasions in subsequent centuries from the Persians, Greeks, Scythians, Arabs (who brought Islam), Afghans, and Turks. The Mughal Empire flourished in the 16th and 17th centuries; the British came to dominate the region in the 18th century. The partition in 1947 of British India into the Muslim state of Pakistan (with West and East sections) and largely Hindu India created lasting tension between the two countries. They have fought two wars and a limited conflict – in 1947-48, 1965, and 1999 respectively – over the Kashmir territory, a dispute that continues to this day. A third war in 1971 – in which India assisted an indigenous movement reacting to Bengali marginalization in Pakistani politics – resulted in East Pakistan becoming the separate nation of Bangladesh.

In response to Indian nuclear weapons testing, Pakistan conducted its own tests in 1998. Pakistan has been engaged in a decades-long armed conflict with militant groups, including the Tehreek-e-Taliban Pakistan (TTP) and other militant networks that target government institutions and civilians.

GEOGRAPHY

Location: Southern Asia, bordering the Arabian Sea, between India on the east and Iran and Afghanistan on the west and China in the north

Geographic coordinates: 30 00 N, 70 00 E

Map references: Asia

Area: *total:* 796,095 sq km
land: 770,875 sq km
water: 25,220 sq km
comparison ranking: total 37

Area - comparative: slightly more than five times the size of Georgia; slightly less than twice the size of California

Land boundaries: *total:* 7,257 km
border countries (4): Afghanistan 2,670 km; China 438 km; India 3,190 km; Iran 959 km

Coastline: 1,046 km

Maritime claims: *territorial sea:* 12 nm
contiguous zone: 24 nm
exclusive economic zone: 200 nm
continental shelf: 200 nm or to the edge of the continental margin

Climate: mostly hot, dry desert; temperate in northwest; arctic in north

Terrain: *divided into three major geographic areas:* the northern highlands, the Indus River plain in the center and east, and the Balochistan Plateau in the south and west

Elevation: *highest point:* K2 (Mt. Godwin-Austen) 8,611 m
lowest point: Arabian Sea 0 m
mean elevation: 900 m

Natural resources: arable land, extensive natural gas reserves, limited petroleum, poor quality coal, iron ore, copper, salt, limestone

Land use: *agricultural land:* 35.2% (2018 est.)
arable land: 27.6% (2018 est.)
permanent crops: 1.1% (2018 est.)
permanent pasture: 6.5% (2018 est.)
forest: 2.1% (2018 est.)
other: 62.7% (2018 est.)

Irrigated land: 193,400 sq km (2020)

Major rivers (by length in km): Indus river mouth (shared with China [s] and India) - 3,610 km; Sutlej river mouth (shared with China [s] and India) - 1,372 km; Chenab river mouth (shared with India [s]) - 1,086 km
note – [s] after country name indicates river source; [m] after country name indicates river mouth

Major watersheds (area sq km): Indian Ocean drainage: Indus (1,081,718 sq km)

Internal (endorheic basin) drainage: Tarim Basin (1,152,448 sq km), *(Aral Sea basin)* Amu Darya (534,739 sq km)

Major aquifers: Indus Basin

Population distribution: the Indus River and its tributaries attract most of the settlement, with Punjab province the most densely populated

Natural hazards: frequent earthquakes, occasionally severe especially in north and west; flooding along the Indus after heavy rains (July and August)

Geography - note: controls Khyber Pass and Bolan Pass, traditional invasion routes between Central Asia and the Indian Subcontinent

PEOPLE AND SOCIETY

Population: *total:* 252,363,571
male: 128,387,797
female: 123,975,774 (2024 est.)
note: results of Pakistan's 2017 national census estimate the country's total population to be 207,684,626
comparison rankings: female 5; male 5; total 5

Nationality: *noun:* Pakistani(s)
adjective: Pakistani

Ethnic groups: Punjabi 44.7%, Pashtun (Pathan) 15.4%, Sindhi 14.1%, Saraiki 8.4%, Muhajirs 7.6%, Baloch 3.6%, other 6.3%

Languages: Punjabi 38.8%, Pashto (alternate name, Pashtu) 18.2%, Sindhi 14.6%, Saraiki (a Punjabi variant) 12.2%, Urdu 7.1%, Balochi 3%, Hindko 2.4%, Brahui 1.2%, other 2.4%
major-language sample(s):
دنیا کا قاموس، ایک لازمی زریہ بنیادی معلومات کا
note: data represent population by mother tongue; English (official; lingua franca of Pakistani elite and most government ministries)

Religions: Muslim (official) 96.5% (Sunni 85-90%, Shia 10-15%), other (includes Christian and Hindu) 3.5% (2020 est.)

Age structure: *0-14 years:* 34.4% (male 44,330,669/female 42,529,007)
15-64 years: 60.7% (male 78,321,834/female 74,833,003)
65 years and over: 4.9% (2024 est.) (male 5,735,294/female 6,613,764)

Dependency ratios: *total dependency ratio:* 70
youth dependency ratio: 62.8
elderly dependency ratio: 7.2
potential support ratio: 13.9 (2021 est.)

Median age: *total:* 22.9 years (2024 est.)
male: 22.8 years

female: 23 years
comparison ranking: total 180

Population growth rate: % (2024 est.)
comparison ranking: 46

Birth rate: 25.5 births/1,000 population (2024 est.)
comparison ranking: 45

Death rate: 5.9 deaths/1,000 population (2024 est.)
comparison ranking: 159

Net migration rate: -1.1 migrant(s)/1,000 population (2024 est.)
comparison ranking: 148

Population distribution: the Indus River and its tributaries attract most of the settlement, with Punjab province the most densely populated

Urbanization: *urban population:* 38% of total population (2023)
rate of urbanization: 2.1% annual rate of change (2020-25 est.)

Major urban areas - population: 17.236 million Karachi, 13.979 million Lahore, 3.711 million Faisalabad, 2.415 million Gujranwala, 2.412 million Peshawar, 1.232 million ISLAMABAD (capital) (2023)

Sex ratio: *at birth:* 1.05 male(s)/female
0-14 years: 1.04 male(s)/female
15-64 years: 1.05 male(s)/female
65 years and over: 0.87 male(s)/female
total population: 1.04 male(s)/female (2024 est.)

Mother's mean age at first birth: 22.8 years (2017/18 est.)
note: data represents median age at first birth among women 25-49

Maternal mortality ratio: 154 deaths/100,000 live births (2020 est.)
comparison ranking: 54

Infant mortality rate: *total:* 51.5 deaths/1,000 live births (2024 est.)
male: 56 deaths/1,000 live births
female: 46.8 deaths/1,000 live births
comparison ranking: total 18

Life expectancy at birth: *total population:* 70.3 years (2024 est.)
male: 68.2 years
female: 72.5 years
comparison ranking: total population 178

Total fertility rate: 3.32 children born/woman (2024 est.)
comparison ranking: 40

Gross reproduction rate: 1.62 (2024 est.)

Contraceptive prevalence rate: 34% (2018/19)

Drinking water source: *improved: urban:* 96.5% of population
rural: 92.5% of population
total: 94% of population
unimproved: urban: 3.5% of population
rural: 7.5% of population
total: 6% of population (2020 est.)

Current health expenditure: 2.8% of GDP (2020)

Physician density: 1.12 physicians/1,000 population (2019)

Hospital bed density: 0.6 beds/1,000 population (2017)

Sanitation facility access: *improved: urban:* 88.6% of population
rural: 73.2% of population
total: 78.9% of population
unimproved: urban: 11.4% of population
rural: 26.8% of population
total: 21.1% of population (2020 est.)

Obesity - adult prevalence rate: 8.6% (2016)
comparison ranking: 148

Alcohol consumption per capita: *total:* 0.04 liters of pure alcohol (2019 est.)
beer: 0 liters of pure alcohol (2019 est.)
wine: 0 liters of pure alcohol (2019 est.)
spirits: 0.04 liters of pure alcohol (2019 est.)
other alcohols: 0 liters of pure alcohol (2019 est.)
comparison ranking: total 180

Tobacco use: *total:* 20.2% (2020 est.)
male: 33% (2020 est.)
female: 7.3% (2020 est.)
comparison ranking: total 86

Children under the age of 5 years underweight: 23.1% (2017/18)
comparison ranking: 8

Currently married women (ages 15-49): 63.5% (2023 est.)

Child marriage: *women married by age 15:* 3.6%
women married by age 18: 18.3%
men married by age 18: 4.7% (2018 est.)

Education expenditures: 2.4% of GDP (2021 est.)
comparison ranking: 177

Literacy: *definition:* age 15 and over can read and write
total population: 58%
male: 69.3%
female: 46.5% (2019)

School life expectancy (primary to tertiary education): *total:* 9 years
male: 9 years
female: 8 years (2019)

ENVIRONMENT

Environment - current issues: water pollution from raw sewage, industrial wastes, and agricultural runoff; limited natural freshwater resources; most of the population does not have access to potable water; deforestation; soil erosion; desertification; air pollution and noise pollution in urban areas

Environment - international agreements: *party to:* Antarctic-Environmental Protection, Antarctic-Marine Living Resources, Antarctic Treaty, Biodiversity, Climate Change, Climate Change-Kyoto Protocol, Climate Change-Paris Agreement, Desertification, Endangered Species, Environmental Modification, Hazardous Wastes, Law of the Sea, Marine Dumping-London Convention, Nuclear Test Ban, Ozone Layer Protection, Ship Pollution, Wetlands
signed, but not ratified: Marine Life Conservation

Climate: mostly hot, dry desert; temperate in northwest; arctic in north

Urbanization: *urban population:* 38% of total population (2023)
rate of urbanization: 2.1% annual rate of change (2020-25 est.)

Food insecurity: *severe localized food insecurity: due to population displacements, economic constraints, and high prices of the main food staple* - according to the latest analysis, about 4.7 million people, 25% of the population, are estimated to be facing high levels of acute food insecurity, between April and June 2022 in 25 districts analyzed in Balochistan, Sindh and Khyber Pakhtunkhwa provinces; prices of wheat flour, the country's main staple, were at high levels in most markets in May 2022, constraining access to the staple food (2022)

Revenue from forest resources: 0.1% of GDP (2018 est.)
comparison ranking: 114

Revenue from coal: 0.06% of GDP (2018 est.)
comparison ranking: 29

Air pollutants: *particulate matter emissions:* 50.13 micrograms per cubic meter (2019 est.)
carbon dioxide emissions: 201.15 megatons (2016 est.)
methane emissions: 142.12 megatons (2020 est.)

Waste and recycling: *municipal solid waste generated annually:* 30.76 million tons (2017 est.)
municipal solid waste recycled annually: 2,460,800 tons (2017 est.)
percent of municipal solid waste recycled: 8% (2017 est.)

Major rivers (by length in km): Indus river mouth (shared with China [s] and India) - 3,610 km; Sutlej river mouth (shared with China [s] and India) - 1,372 km; Chenab river mouth (shared with India [s]) - 1,086 km
note – [s] after country name indicates river source; [m] after country name indicates river mouth

Major watersheds (area sq km): Indian Ocean drainage: Indus (1,081,718 sq km)

Internal (endorheic basin) drainage: Tarim Basin (1,152,448 sq km), *(Aral Sea basin)* Amu Darya (534,739 sq km)

Major aquifers: Indus Basin

Total water withdrawal: *municipal:* 9.65 billion cubic meters (2020 est.)
industrial: 1.4 billion cubic meters (2020 est.)
agricultural: 172.4 billion cubic meters (2020 est.)

Total renewable water resources: 246.8 billion cubic meters (2020 est.)

GOVERNMENT

Country name: *conventional long form:* Islamic Republic of Pakistan
conventional short form: Pakistan
local long form: Jamhuryat Islami Pakistan
local short form: Pakistan
former: West Pakistan
etymology: the word "pak" means "pure" in Persian or Pashto, while the Persian suffix "-stan" means "place of" or "country," so the word Pakistan literally means "Land of the Pure"

Government type: federal parliamentary republic

Capital: *name:* Islamabad
geographic coordinates: 33 41 N, 73 03 E
time difference: UTC+5 (10 hours ahead of Washington, DC, during Standard Time)
etymology: derived from two words: Islam, an Urdu word referring to the religion of Islam, and *-abad*, a Persian suffix indicating an "inhabited place" or "city," to render the meaning "City of Islam"

Administrative divisions: 4 provinces, 2 Pakistan-administered areas*, and 1 capital territory**; Azad Kashmir*, Balochistan, Gilgit-Baltistan*, Islamabad Capital Territory**, Khyber Pakhtunkhwa, Punjab, Sindh

Independence: 14 August 1947 (from British India)

National holiday: Pakistan Day (also referred to as Pakistan Resolution Day or Republic Day), 23 March (1940); note - commemorates both the adoption of the Lahore Resolution by the All-India Muslim

League during its 22-24 March 1940 session, which called for the creation of independent Muslim states, and the adoption of the first constitution of Pakistan on 23 March 1956 during the transition to the Islamic Republic of Pakistan

Legal system: common law system with Islamic law influence

Constitution: *history:* several previous; latest endorsed 12 April 1973, passed 19 April 1973, entered into force 14 August 1973 (suspended and restored several times)
amendments: proposed by the Senate or by the National Assembly; passage requires at least two-thirds majority vote of both houses; amended many times, last in 2018

International law organization participation: accepts compulsory ICJ jurisdiction with reservations; non-party state to the ICCt

Citizenship: *citizenship by birth:* yes
citizenship by descent only: at least one parent must be a citizen of Pakistan
dual citizenship recognized: yes, but limited to select countries
residency requirement for naturalization: 4 out of the previous 7 years and including the 12 months preceding application

Suffrage: 18 years of age; universal; note - there are joint electorates and reserved parliamentary seats for women and non-Muslims

Executive branch: *chief of state:* President Asif Ali ZARDARI (since 10 March 2024)
head of government: Prime Minister Shahbaz SHARIF (since 3 March 2024)
cabinet: Cabinet appointed by the president upon the advice of the prime minister
elections/appointments: president indirectly elected by the Electoral College consisting of members of the Senate, National Assembly, and provincial assemblies for a 5-year term (limited to 2 consecutive terms); election last held on 9 March 2024 (next to be held in 2029)
election results:
2024: Asif Ali ZARDARI elected president; National Assembly vote - Asif Ali ZARDARI (PPP) 411 votes, Mehmood Khan ACHAKZALI (PMAP) -181 votes; Shahbaz SHARIF elected prime minister on 3 March 2024; National Assembly vote - Shahbaz SHARIF (PML-N) 201, Omar AYUB (PTI) 92
2018: Arif ALVI elected president; Electoral College vote - Arif ALVI (PTI) 352, Fazl-ur-REHMAN (MMA) 184, Aitzaz AHSAN (PPP) 124; Imran KHAN elected prime minister; National Assembly vote - Imran KHAN (PTI) 176, Shehbaz SHARIF (PML-N) 96

Legislative branch: *description:* bicameral Parliament or Majlis-e-Shoora consists of:
Senate (96 seats current; members indirectly elected by the 4 provincial assemblies and the federal capital territory indirectly elected by the National Assembly using proportional representation vote; members serve 6-year terms with one-half of the membership renewed every 3 years)
National Assembly (336 seats; 266 members directly elected in single-seat constituencies by simple majority vote and 70 members - 60 women and 10 non-Muslims - directly elected by proportional representation vote; all members serve 5- year terms)
elections: Senate - last held on 2 and 9 April 2024 (next to be held in 2027)
National Assembly - last held on 8 February 2024 (next to be held in 2029)
election results: Senate - percent of vote by party - NA; seats by party - NA; composition - men 79, women 17, percent of women 17.7%
National Assembly - percent of vote by party - NA; seats by party - PML-N 75, PPP 54, MQM-P 17, JUI-F 4, Pakistan Muslim League 3, Istehkam-e-Pakistan Party 2, BNP-A 2, BAP 1, PMAP 1, PML-Z 1, NP 1, independent (PTI-backed) 101, other 8, vacant 2 (excludes 60 seats reserved for women and 10 non-Muslims); composition - men 276, women 60, percent of women 17.9%; note - total Parliament percent of women 17.8%
note: in May 2018, the Parliament of Pakistan and the Khyber Pakhtunkhwa Assembly passed a constitutional amendment to merge the Federally Administrated Tribal Areas and Provincially Administered Tribal Areas with the province of Khyber Pakhtunkhwa; the amendment reduces the Senate from 104 to 96 members - 4 in the 2024 election and 4 in the 2027 election

Judicial branch: *highest court(s):* Supreme Court of Pakistan (consists of the chief justice and 16 judges)
judge selection and term of office: justices nominated by an 8-member parliamentary committee upon the recommendation of the Judicial Commission, a 9-member body of judges and other judicial professionals, and appointed by the president; justices can serve until age 65
subordinate courts: High Courts; Federal Shariat Court; provincial and district civil and criminal courts; specialized courts for issues, such as taxation, banking, and customs

Political parties: Awami National Party or ANP
Awami Muslim League or AML
Balochistan Awami Party or BAP
Balochistan National Party-Awami or BNP-A
Balochistan National Party-Mengal or BNP-M
Grand Democratic Alliance or GDA (alliance of several parties)
Hazara Democratic Party or HDP
Istehkam-e-Pakistan Party
Jamaat-e-Islami or JI
Jamhoori Wattan Party or JWP
Jamiat Ulema-e-Islam-Fazl or JUI-F
Majlis Wahdat-e-Muslimeen Pakistan or MWM
Muttahida Majlis-e-Amal or MMA (alliance of several parties)
Muttahida Qaumi Movement-Pakistan or MQM-P
National Party or NP
Pakistan Muslim League or PML-Z
Pakistan Muslim League-Functional or PML-F
Pakistan Muslim League-Nawaz or PML-N
Pakistan Muslim League-Quaid-e-Azam or PML-Q
Pakistan Peoples Party or PPP
Pakistan Rah-e-Haq Party or PRHP
Pakistan Tehrik-e Insaaf or PTI (Pakistan Movement for Justice)
Pashtoonkhwa Milli Awami Party or PMAP or PKMAP
Tehreek-e-Labbaik Pakistan or TLP

International organization participation: ADB, AIIB, ARF, ASEAN (sectoral dialogue partner), C, CERN (associate member), CICA, CP, D-8, ECO, FAO, G-11, G-24, G-77, IAEA, IBRD, ICAO, ICC (national committees), ICRM, IDA, IDB, IFAD, IFC, IFRCS, IHO, ILO, IMF, IMO, IMSO, Interpol, IOC, IOM, IPU, ISO, ITSO, ITU, ITUC (NGOs), MIGA, MINURCAT, MINURSO, MINUSCA, MONUSCO, NAM, OAS (observer), OIC, OPCW, PCA, SAARC, SACEP, SCO, UN, UNAMID, UNCTAD, UNESCO, UNFICYP, UNHCR, UNIDO, UNISFA, UNISFA, UNMISS, UNOOSA, UNSOS, UNWTO, UPU, WCO, WFTU (NGOs), WHO, WIPO, WMO, WTO

Diplomatic representation in the US: *chief of mission:* Ambassador Rizwan Saeed SHEIKH (since 18 September 2024)
chancery: 3517 International Court NW, Washington, DC 20008
telephone: [1] (202) 243-6500
FAX: [1] (202) 686-1534
email address and website:
consularsection@embassyofpakistanusa.org
https://embassyofpakistanusa.org/
consulate(s) general: Chicago, Houston, Los Angeles, New York

Diplomatic representation from the US: *chief of mission:* Ambassador Donald BLOME (since 2 July 2022)
embassy: Diplomatic Enclave, Ramna 5, Islamabad
mailing address: 8100 Islamabad Place, Washington, DC 20521-8100
telephone: [92] 051-201-4000
FAX: [92] 51-2338071
email address and website:
ACSIslamabad@state.gov
https://pk.usembassy.gov/
consulate(s) general: Karachi, Lahore, Peshawar

Flag description: green with a vertical white band (symbolizing the role of religious minorities) on the hoist side; a large white crescent and star are centered in the green field; the crescent, star, and color green are traditional symbols of Islam

National symbol(s): five-pointed star between the horns of a waxing crescent moon, jasmine; national colors: green, white

National anthem: *name:* "Qaumi Tarana" (National Anthem)
lyrics/music: Abu-Al-Asar Hafeez JULLANDHURI/ Ahmed Ghulamali CHAGLA
note: adopted 1954; also known as "Pak sarzamin shad bad" (Blessed Be the Sacred Land)

National heritage: *total World Heritage Sites:* 6 (all cultural)
selected World Heritage Site locales: Archaeological Ruins at Moenjodaro; Buddhist Ruins of Takht-i-Bahi; Taxila; Fort and Shalamar Gardens in Lahore; Historical Monuments at Makli, Thatta; Rohtas Fort

ECONOMY

Economic overview: lower middle-income South Asian economy; extremely high debt; endemic corruption; major currency devaluation; major food insecurity and inflation; environmentally fragile agricultural sector; regional disputes with India and Afghanistan hinder investment

Real GDP (purchasing power parity): $1.347 trillion (2023 est.)
$1.347 trillion (2022 est.)
$1.285 trillion (2021 est.)
note: data in 2021 dollars
comparison ranking: 25

Real GDP growth rate: 0% (2023 est.)
4.77% (2022 est.)
6.51% (2021 est.)
note: annual GDP % growth based on constant local currency
comparison ranking: 188

Real GDP per capita: $5,600 (2023 est.)
$5,700 (2022 est.)
$5,600 (2021 est.)

note: data in 2021 dollars
comparison ranking: 172

GDP (official exchange rate): $338.368 billion (2023 est.)
note: data in current dollars at official exchange rate

Inflation rate (consumer prices): 30.77% (2023 est.)
19.87% (2022 est.)
9.5% (2021 est.)
note: annual % change based on consumer prices
comparison ranking: 207

Credit ratings: Fitch rating: B- (2018)

Moody's rating: B3 (2015)

Standard & Poors rating: B- (2019)
note: The year refers to the year in which the current credit rating was first obtained.

GDP - composition, by sector of origin: *agriculture:* 23.4% (2023 est.)
industry: 20.8% (2023 est.)
services: 50.6% (2023 est.)
note: figures may not total 100% due to non-allocated consumption not captured in sector-reported data
comparison rankings: services 145; industry 131; agriculture 24

GDP - composition, by end use: *household consumption:* 83.4% (2023 est.)
government consumption: 10.2% (2023 est.)
investment in fixed capital: 12% (2023 est.)
investment in inventories: 1.7% (2023 est.)
exports of goods and services: 10.4% (2023 est.)
imports of goods and services: -17.7% (2023 est.)
note: figures may not total 100% due to rounding or gaps in data collection

Agricultural products: sugarcane, bison milk, wheat, milk, rice, maize, potatoes, mangoes/guavas, cotton, onions (2022)
note: top ten agricultural products based on tonnage

Industries: textiles and apparel, food processing, pharmaceuticals, surgical instruments, construction materials, paper products, fertilizer, shrimp

Industrial production growth rate: -3.76% (2023 est.)
note: annual % change in industrial value added based on constant local currency
comparison ranking: 193

Labor force: 80.99 million (2023 est.)
note: number of people ages 15 or older who are employed or seeking work
comparison ranking: 6

Unemployment rate: 5.5% (2023 est.)
5.55% (2022 est.)
6.34% (2021 est.)
note: % of labor force seeking employment
comparison ranking: 105

Youth unemployment rate (ages 15-24): *total:* 9.7% (2023 est.)
male: 9.3% (2023 est.)
female: 10.7% (2023 est.)
note: % of labor force ages 15-24 seeking employment
comparison ranking: total 139

Population below poverty line: 21.9% (2018 est.)
note: % of population with income below national poverty line

Gini Index coefficient - distribution of family income: 29.6 (2018 est.)
note: index (0-100) of income distribution; higher values represent greater inequality
comparison ranking: 124

Average household expenditures: *on food:* 39.1% of household expenditures (2022 est.)
on alcohol and tobacco: 1.2% of household expenditures (2022 est.)

Household income or consumption by percentage share: *lowest 10%:* 4.2% (2018 est.)
highest 10%: 25.5% (2018 est.)
note: % share of income accruing to lowest and highest 10% of population

Remittances: 7.85% of GDP (2023 est.)
8.05% of GDP (2022 est.)
8.98% of GDP (2021 est.)
note: personal transfers and compensation between resident and non-resident individuals/households/entities

Budget: *revenues:* $40.774 billion (2015 est.)
expenditures: $49.558 billion (2015 est.)
note: central government revenues and expenses (excluding grants/extrabudgetary units/social security funds) converted to US dollars at average official exchange rate for year indicated

Public debt: 67% of GDP (2017 est.)
comparison ranking: 61

Taxes and other revenues: 15.4% (of GDP) (2017 est.)
comparison ranking: 135

Current account balance: -$350.044 million (2023 est.)
-$12.216 billion (2022 est.)
-$12.283 billion (2021 est.)
note: balance of payments - net trade and primary/secondary income in current dollars
comparison ranking: 117

Exports: $36.442 billion (2023 est.)
$38.967 billion (2022 est.)
$35.612 billion (2021 est.)
note: balance of payments - exports of goods and services in current dollars
comparison ranking: 74

Exports - partners: US 17%, Germany 7%, China 7%, UAE 7%, UK 6% (2022)
note: top five export partners based on percentage share of exports

Exports - commodities: garments, fabric, cotton fabric, rice, refined petroleum (2022)
note: top five export commodities based on value in dollars

Imports: $57.806 billion (2023 est.)
$76.594 billion (2022 est.)
$76.514 billion (2021 est.)
note: balance of payments - imports of goods and services in current dollars
comparison ranking: 64

Imports - partners: China 28%, UAE 8%, Indonesia 6%, Saudi Arabia 6%, Kuwait 5% (2022)
note: top five import partners based on percentage share of imports

Imports - commodities: refined petroleum, crude petroleum, natural gas, palm oil, cotton (2022)
note: top five import commodities based on value in dollars

Reserves of foreign exchange and gold: $13.73 billion (2023 est.)
$9.927 billion (2022 est.)
$22.812 billion (2021 est.)
note: holdings of gold (year-end prices)/foreign exchange/special drawing rights in current dollars
comparison ranking: 67

Debt - external: $74.852 billion (2022 est.)
note: present value of external debt in current US dollars
comparison ranking: 10

Exchange rates: Pakistani rupees (PKR) per US dollar -

Exchange rates: 280.356 (2023 est.)
204.867 (2022 est.)
162.906 (2021 est.)
161.838 (2020 est.)
150.036 (2019 est.)

ENERGY

Electricity access: *electrification - total population:* 95% (2022 est.)
electrification - urban areas: 100%
electrification - rural areas: 93%

Electricity: *installed generating capacity:* 43.478 million kW (2022 est.)
consumption: 145.999 billion kWh (2022 est.)
imports: 498.228 million kWh (2022 est.)
transmission/distribution losses: 23.021 billion kWh (2022 est.)
comparison rankings: transmission/distribution losses 190; imports 91; consumption 28; installed generating capacity 30

Electricity generation sources: *fossil fuels:* 62.5% of total installed capacity (2022 est.)
nuclear: 13.2% of total installed capacity (2022 est.)
solar: 0.8% of total installed capacity (2022 est.)
wind: 1.9% of total installed capacity (2022 est.)
hydroelectricity: 20.5% of total installed capacity (2022 est.)
biomass and waste: 1.1% of total installed capacity (2022 est.)

Nuclear energy: Number of operational nuclear reactors: 6 (2023)

Net capacity of operational nuclear reactors: 3.26GW (2023 est.)

Percent of total electricity production: 17.4% (2023 est.)

Number of nuclear reactors permanently shut down: 1 (2023)

Coal: *production:* 12.712 million metric tons (2022 est.)
consumption: 34.027 million metric tons (2022 est.)
exports: 1,000 metric tons (2022 est.)
imports: 21.944 million metric tons (2022 est.)
proven reserves: 3.064 billion metric tons (2022 est.)

Petroleum: *total petroleum production:* 101,000 bbl/day (2023 est.)
refined petroleum consumption: 473,000 bbl/day (2022 est.)
crude oil estimated reserves: 540 million barrels (2021 est.)

Natural gas: *production:* 36.937 billion cubic meters (2022 est.)
consumption: 46.448 billion cubic meters (2022 est.)
imports: 10.851 billion cubic meters (2022 est.)
proven reserves: 592.219 billion cubic meters (2021 est.)

Carbon dioxide emissions: 213.498 million metric tonnes of CO2 (2022 est.)
from coal and metallurgical coke: 71.24 million metric tonnes of CO2 (2022 est.)
from petroleum and other liquids: 66.804 million metric tonnes of CO2 (2022 est.)
from consumed natural gas: 75.454 million metric tonnes of CO2 (2022 est.)
comparison ranking: total emissions 30

Energy consumption per capita: 14.902 million Btu/person (2022 est.)
comparison ranking: 141

COMMUNICATIONS

Telephones - fixed lines: *total subscriptions:* 2.799 million (2022 est.)
subscriptions per 100 inhabitants: 1 (2022 est.)
comparison ranking: total subscriptions 43

Telephones - mobile cellular: *total subscriptions:* 192.78 million (2022 est.)
subscriptions per 100 inhabitants: 82 (2022 est.)
comparison ranking: total subscriptions 9

Telecommunication systems: *general assessment:* Pakistan's telecom market transitioned from a regulated state-owned monopoly to a deregulated competitive structure in 2003, now aided by foreign investment; moderate growth over the last six years, supported by a young population and a rising use of mobile services; telecom infrastructure is improving, with investments in mobile-cellular networks, fixed-line subscriptions declining; system consists of microwave radio relay, coaxial cable, fiber-optic cable, cellular, and satellite networks; 4G mobile services broadly available; 5G tests ongoing; data centers in major cities; mobile and broadband doing well and dominate over fixed-broadband sector; future growth (in market size as well as revenue) is likely to come from the wider availability of value-added services on top of the expansion of 4G LTE and (from 2023) 5G mobile networks; the Universal Service Fund (USF) continues to direct investment towards the development of mobile broadband (and, to a lesser extent, fiber-based networks) in under-served and even under served areas of the country, with multiple projects being approved to start in 2021 and 2022 (2021)
domestic: mobile-cellular subscribership has increased; more than 90% of Pakistanis live within areas that have cell phone coverage; fiber-optic networks are being constructed throughout the country to increase broadband access and broadband penetration in Pakistan is increasing–by the end of 2021, 50% of the population had access to broadband services; fixed-line teledensity is a little over 1 per 100 and mobile-cellular roughly 82 per 100 persons (2021)
international: country code - 92; landing points for the SEA-ME-WE-3, -4, -5, AAE-1, IMEWE, Orient Express, PEACE Cable, and TW1 submarine cable systems that provide links to Europe, Africa, the Middle East, Asia, Southeast Asia, and Australia; satellite earth stations - 3 Intelsat (1 Atlantic Ocean and 2 Indian Ocean); 3 operational international gateway exchanges (1 at Karachi and 2 at Islamabad); microwave radio relay to neighboring countries (2019)

Broadcast media: television is the most popular and dominant source of news in Pakistan with over 120 satellite tv stations licensed by the country's electronic media regulatory body, PEMRA ,and 42 media companies/channels with landing rights permission; state-run Pakistan Television Corporation (PTV) is the largest television network in the country and serves over 85 percent of the population with the largest terrestrial infrastructure of the country; PTV consists of nine TV Channels and PTV networks give special coverage to Kashmir; Pakistanis have access to over 100 private cable and satellite channels; six channels are considered the leaders for news reporting and current affairs programing in the country; state-owned Pakistan Broadcasting Corporation (PBC or Radio Pakistan) has the largest radio audience in the country, particularly in the rural areas; Radio Pakistan's AM/SW/FM stations cover 98 percent of the population and 80 percent of the total area in the country; all major newspapers have online editions and all major print publications operate websites; freedom of the press and freedom of speech in the country are fragile (2022)

Internet country code: .pk

Internet users: *total:* 48.3 million (2021 est.)
percent of population: 21% (2021 est.)
comparison ranking: total 21

Broadband - fixed subscriptions: *total:* 2,523,027 (2020 est.)
subscriptions per 100 inhabitants: 1 (2020 est.)
comparison ranking: total 53

TRANSPORTATION

National air transport system: *number of registered air carriers:* 5 (2020)
inventory of registered aircraft operated by air carriers: 52
annual passenger traffic on registered air carriers: 6,880,637 (2018)
annual freight traffic on registered air carriers: 217.53 million (2018) mt-km

Civil aircraft registration country code prefix: AP

Airports: 116 (2024)
comparison ranking: 45

Heliports: 48 (2024)

Pipelines: 13,452 km gas transmission and 177,029 km gas distribution, 3,663 km oil, 1,150 km refined products (2022)

Railways: *total:* 11,881 km (2021)
narrow gauge: 389 km (2021) 1.000-m gauge
broad gauge: 11,492 km (2021) 1.676-m gauge (286 km electrified)
comparison ranking: total 20

Roadways: *total:* 264,175 km
paved: 185,463 km (includes 708 km of expressways)
unpaved: 78,712 km (2021)
comparison ranking: total 17

Merchant marine: *total:* 60 (2023)
by type: bulk carrier 5, oil tanker 9, other 46
comparison ranking: total 113

Ports: *total ports:* 3 (2024)
large: 0
medium: 2
small: 1
very small: 0
ports with oil terminals: 2
key ports: Gwadar, Karachi, Muhamamad Bin Qasim

MILITARY AND SECURITY

Military and security forces: Pakistan Armed Forces: Pakistan Army (includes National Guard), Pakistan Navy (includes marines, Maritime Security Agency), Pakistan Air Force (Pakistan Fizaia)

Ministry of Interior: Frontier Corps, Pakistan Rangers (2024)
note 1: the National Guard is a paramilitary force and one of the Army's reserve forces, along with the Pakistan Army Reserve, the Frontier Corps, and the Pakistan Rangers
note 2: the Frontier Corps is a paramilitary force manned mostly by individuals from the tribal areas and commanded by Pakistan Army officers; its primary mission is security of the border with Afghanistan; the Frontier Corps is under the Ministry of Interior, but would report to the Army in times of conflict
note 3: the paramilitary Pakistan Rangers operate in Sindh and Punjab

Military expenditures: 3% of GDP (2023 est.)
4% of GDP (2022 est.)
4% of GDP (2021 est.)
4% of GDP (2020 est.)
4.1% of GDP (2019 est.)
comparison ranking: 34

Military and security service personnel strengths: information varies; approximately 630,000 active-duty personnel (550,000 Army; 30,000 Navy; 50,000 Air Force); approximately 150,000 Frontier Corps and Pakistan Rangers (2023)

Military equipment inventories and acquisitions: the military's inventory is a broad mix of mostly imported and some domestically produced weapons and equipment; most of its imported weapons are from China; other suppliers include France, Russia, Turkey, Ukraine, the UK, and the US; Pakistan also has a large domestic defense industry, which produces or co-produces such items as armored vehicles, aircraft, missiles, naval vessels (2024)

Military service age and obligation: 16 (or 17 depending on service) to 23 years of age for voluntary military service; soldiers cannot be deployed for combat until age 18; women serve in all three armed forces; reserve obligation to age 45 for enlisted men, age 50 for officers (2023)

Military deployments: 1,300 Central African Republic (MINUSCA); 290 South Sudan (UNMISS); 590 Sudan (UNISFA) (2024)

Military - note: the Pakistan military operates largely independently and without effective civilian oversight; it has ruled the country for more than 30 years since independence in 1947 and continues to play a significant role in Pakistan's political arena; it also has a large stake in the country's economic sector and is involved in a diverse array of commercial activities, including banking, construction of public projects, employment services, energy and power generation, fertilizer, food, housing, real estate, and security services
the military is responsible for external defense but also has a large role in domestic security; its chief external focus is on the perceived threat posed by India; the military is the lead security agency in many areas of the former Federally Administered Tribal Areas (FATA); it has considerable operational experience, having engaged in several conflicts with India and conducted counterinsurgency and counterterrorism operations for decades against various internal militant groups; it is also one of the longest serving and largest contributors to UN peacekeeping missions; China is its closest security partner
Pakistan and India have fought several conflicts since 1947, including the Indo-Pakistan War of 1965 and the Indo-Pakistan and Bangladesh War of Independence of 1971, as well as two clashes over the disputed region of Kashmir (First Kashmir War of 1947 and the Kargil Conflict of 1999); a fragile cease-fire in Kashmir was reached in 2003, revised in 2018, and reaffirmed in 2021, although the Line of Control remains contested, and India has accused Pakistan of backing armed separatists and terrorist organizations in Jammu and Kashmir; in addition, India and Pakistan have battled over the Siachen Glacier of Kashmir, which was seized by India in 1984 with

Pakistan attempting to retake the area several times between 1985-1995; despite a cease-fire, both sides continue to maintain a permanent military presence there with outposts at altitudes above 20,000 feet (over 6,000 meters) where most casualties are due to extreme weather or the hazards of operating in the high mountain terrain of the world's highest conflict, including avalanches, exposure, and altitude sickness Pakistan has Major Non-NATO Ally (MNNA) status with the US, a designation under US law that provides foreign partners with certain benefits in the areas of defense trade and security cooperation (2024)

SPACE

Space agency/agencies: Pakistan Space & Upper Atmosphere Research Commission (SUPARCO; established 1961); National Remote Sensing Center (aka Resacent; established 1980) (2024)

Space launch site(s): Somiani Flight Test Range (Balochistan); Tilla Satellite Launch Center (aka Tilla Range; Punjab) (2024)

Space program overview: space program dates back to the early 1960s but funding shortfalls and shifts in priority toward ballistic missile development in the 1980s and 1990s hampered the program's development; more recently, the program has regained attention and become more ambitious, particularly in acquiring satellites and reaching agreements with other space powers for additional capabilities; manufactures and operates satellites; researching and developing other space-related capabilities and technologies, such as satellite payloads and probably satellite/space launch vehicles (SLVs); also conducts research in such areas as astronomy, astrophysics, environmental monitoring, and space sciences; has relations or cooperation agreements on space with China, Russia, and Turkey (cooperated with the UK and US prior to the 1990s) (2024)
note: further details about the key activities, programs, and milestones of the country's space program, as well as government spending estimates on the space sector, appear in the Space Programs reference guide

TERRORISM

Terrorist group(s): Haqqani Network; Harakat ul-Jihad-i-Islami; Harakat ul-Mujahidin; Hizbul Mujahideen; Indian Mujahedeen; Islamic State of Iraq and ash-Sham-Khorasan (ISIS-K); Islamic State of ash-Sham – India; Islamic State of ash-Sham – Pakistan; Islamic Movement of Uzbekistan; Jaish-e-Mohammed; Jaysh al Adl (Jundallah); Lashkar i Jhangvi; Lashkar-e Tayyiba; Tehrik-e-Taliban Pakistan (TTP); al-Qa'ida; al-Qa'ida in the Indian Subcontinent (AQIS)
note: details about the history, aims, leadership, organization, areas of operation, tactics, targets, weapons, size, and sources of support of the group(s) appear(s) in the Terrorism reference guide

TRANSNATIONAL ISSUES

Refugees and internally displaced persons: *refugees (country of origin):* 2.64-2.9 million (1.3 million registered, 1.34-1.6 million undocumented or otherwise categorized) (Afghanistan) (2023)
IDPs: 21,000 (primarily those who remain displaced by counter-terrorism and counter-insurgency operations and violent conflict between armed non-state groups in the Federally Administered Tribal Areas and Khyber-Paktunkwa Province; more than 1 million displaced in northern Waziristan in 2014; individuals also have been displaced by repeated monsoon floods) (2022)
stateless persons: 48 (2022)

Illicit drugs: one of the world's top transit corridors for opiates and cannabis products trafficked with Afghanistan and Iran; increased synthetic drug smuggling primarily methamphetamine; a major source of precursor or essential chemicals used in the production of heroin and amphetamine-type stimulants

PALAU

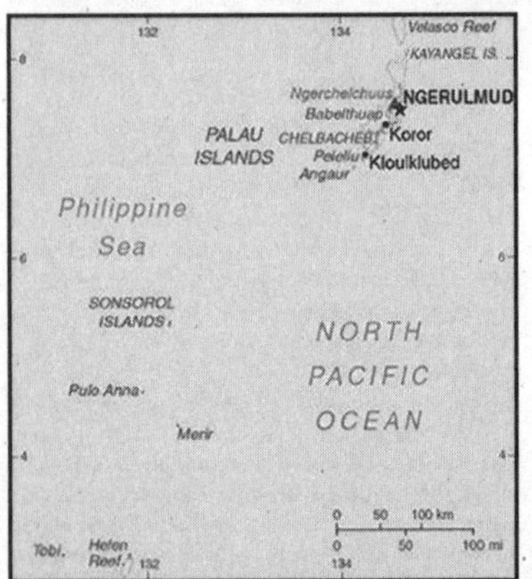

INTRODUCTION

Background: Humans arrived in the Palauan archipelago from Southeast Asia around 1000 B.C. and developed a complex, highly organized matrilineal society where high-ranking women picked the chiefs. The islands were the westernmost part of the widely scattered Pacific islands north of New Guinea that Spanish explorers named the Caroline Islands in the 17th century. The 18th and 19th centuries saw occasional visits of whalers and traders as Spain gained some influence in the islands and administered it from the Philippines. Spain sold Palau to Germany in 1899 after losing the Philippines in the Spanish-American War.

Japan seized Palau in 1914, was granted a League of Nations mandate to administer the islands in 1920, and made Koror the capital of its South Seas Mandate in 1922. By the outbreak of World War II, there were four times as many Japanese living in Koror as Palauans. In 1944, the US invasion of the island of Peleliu was one of the bloodiest island fights of the Pacific War. After the war, Palau became part of the US-administered Trust Territory of the Pacific Islands.

Palau voted against joining the Federated States of Micronesia in 1978 and adopted its own constitution in 1981, which stated that Palau was a nuclear-free country. In 1982, Palau signed a Compact of Free Association (COFA) with the US, which granted Palau financial assistance and access to many US domestic programs in exchange for exclusive US military access and defense responsibilities. However, many Palauans saw the COFA as incompatible with the Palauan Constitution because of the US military's nuclear arsenal, and seven referenda failed to achieve ratification. Following a constitutional amendment and eighth referendum in 1993, the COFA was ratified and entered into force in 1994 when the islands gained their independence. Its funding was renewed in 2010.

Palau has been on the frontlines of combatting climate change and protecting marine resources. In 2011, Palau banned commercial shark fishing and created the world's first shark sanctuary. In 2017, Palau began stamping the Palau Pledge into passports, reminding visitors to act in ecologically and culturally responsible ways. In 2020, Palau banned coral reef-toxic sunscreens and expanded its fishing prohibition to include 80% of its exclusive economic zone.

GEOGRAPHY

Location: Oceania, group of islands in the North Pacific Ocean, southeast of the Philippines

Geographic coordinates: 7 30 N, 134 30 E

Map references: Oceania

Area: *total:* 459 sq km
land: 459 sq km
water: 0 sq km
comparison ranking: total 197

Area - comparative: slightly more than 2.5 times the size of Washington, DC

Land boundaries: *total:* 0 km

Coastline: 1,519 km

Maritime claims: *territorial sea:* 12 nm
contiguous zone: 24 nm
exclusive economic zone: 200 nm
continental shelf: 200 nm

Climate: tropical; hot and humid; wet season May to November

Terrain: varying topography from the high, mountainous main island of Babelthuap to low, coral islands usually fringed by large barrier reefs

Elevation: *highest point:* Mount Ngerchelchuus 242 m
lowest point: Pacific Ocean 0 m

Natural resources: forests, minerals (especially gold), marine products, deep-seabed minerals

Land use: *agricultural land:* 10.8% (2018 est.)
arable land: 2.2% (2018 est.)
permanent crops: 4.3% (2018 est.)
permanent pasture: 4.3% (2018 est.)
forest: 87.6% (2018 est.)
other: 1.6% (2018 est.)

Irrigated land: 0 sq km (2022)

Population distribution: most of the population is located on the southern end of the main island of Babelthuap

Natural hazards: typhoons (June to December)

Geography - note: westernmost archipelago in the Caroline chain, consists of six island groups totaling more than 300 islands; includes world-famous Rock Islands

PEOPLE AND SOCIETY

Population: *total:* 21,864
male: 11,235
female: 10,629 (2024 est.)
comparison rankings: female 218; male 218; total 218

Nationality: *noun:* Palauan(s)
adjective: Palauan

Ethnic groups: Palauan (Micronesian with Malayan and Melanesian admixtures) 70.6%, Carolinian 1.2%, Asian 26.5%, other 1.7% (2020 est.)

Languages: Palauan (official on most islands) 65.2%, other Micronesian 1.9%, English (official) 19.1%, Filipino 9.9%, Chinese 1.2%, other 2.8% (2015 est.)
note: Sonsoralese is official in Sonsoral; Tobian is official in Tobi; Angaur and Japanese are official in Angaur

Religions: Roman Catholic 46.9%, Protestant 30.9% (Evangelical 24.6%, Seventh Day Adventist 5%, other Protestant 1.4%), Modekngei 5.1% (indigenous to Palau), Muslim 4.9%, other 12.3% (2020 est.)

Age structure: *0-14 years:* 17.5% (male 1,976/female 1,849)
15-64 years: 71.3% (male 8,647/female 6,935)
65 years and over: 11.2% (2024 est.) (male 612/female 1,845)

Dependency ratios: *total dependency ratio:* 43.8
youth dependency ratio: 30.2
elderly dependency ratio: 13.7
potential support ratio: 7.3 (2021)

Median age: *total:* 35.3 years (2024 est.)
male: 34.1 years
female: 37.4 years
comparison ranking: total 99

Population growth rate: 0.38% (2024 est.)
comparison ranking: 162

Birth rate: 11.6 births/1,000 population (2024 est.)
comparison ranking: 157

Death rate: 8.4 deaths/1,000 population (2024 est.)
comparison ranking: 77

Net migration rate: 0.7 migrant(s)/1,000 population (2024 est.)
comparison ranking: 71

Population distribution: most of the population is located on the southern end of the main island of Babelthuap Urbanization
urban population: 82.4% of total population (2023)
rate of urbanization: 1.59% annual rate of change (2020-25 est.)

Major urban areas - population: 277 NGERULMUD (capital) (2018)

Sex ratio: *at birth:* 1.06 male(s)/female
0-14 years: 1.07 male(s)/female
15-64 years: 1.25 male(s)/female
65 years and over: 0.33 male(s)/female
total population: 1.06 male(s)/female (2024 est.)

Infant mortality rate: *total:* 10.8 deaths/1,000 live births (2024 est.)
male: 12.7 deaths/1,000 live births
female: 8.8 deaths/1,000 live births
comparison ranking: total 126

Life expectancy at birth: *total population:* 75.2 years (2024 est.)
male: 72 years
female: 78.5 years
comparison ranking: total population 131

Total fertility rate: 1.7 children born/woman (2024 est.)
comparison ranking: 166

Gross reproduction rate: 0.83 (2024 est.)

Contraceptive prevalence rate: NA

Drinking water source: *improved: urban:* 99.6% of population
rural: 99.8% of population
total: 99.7% of population
unimproved: urban: 0.4% of population
rural: 0.2% of population
total: 0.3% of population (2020 est.)

Current health expenditure: 18.4% of GDP (2020)

Physician density: 1.77 physicians/1,000 population (2020)

Sanitation facility access: *improved: urban:* 99.8% of population
rural: 99% of population
total: 99.6% of population
unimproved: urban: 0.2% of population
rural: 1% of population
total: 0.4% of population (2020 est.)

Obesity - adult prevalence rate: 55.3% (2016)
comparison ranking: 3

Tobacco use: *total:* 17.6% (2020 est.)
male: 27.3% (2020 est.)
female: 7.9% (2020 est.)
comparison ranking: total 95

Currently married women (ages 15-49): 45.6% (2023 est.)

Education expenditures: 6.8% of GDP (2019)
comparison ranking: 24

Literacy: *definition:* age 15 and over can read and write
total population: 96.6%
male: 96.8%
female: 96.3% (2015)

School life expectancy (primary to tertiary education): *total:* 17 years
male: 16 years
female: 17 years (2013)

ENVIRONMENT

Environment - current issues: inadequate facilities for disposal of solid waste; threats to the marine ecosystem from sand and coral dredging, illegal and destructive fishing practices, and overfishing; climate change contributes to rising sea level and coral bleaching; drought

Environment - international agreements: *party to:* Biodiversity, Climate Change, Climate Change-Kyoto Protocol, Climate Change-Paris Agreement, Comprehensive Nuclear Test Ban, Desertification, Endangered Species, Hazardous Wastes, Law of the Sea, Ozone Layer Protection, Ship Pollution, Wetlands, Whaling
signed, but not ratified: none of the selected agreements

Climate: tropical; hot and humid; wet season May to November

Urbanization: *urban population:* 82.4% of total population (2023)
rate of urbanization: 1.59% annual rate of change (2020-25 est.)

Revenue from forest resources: 0% of GDP (2018 est.)
comparison ranking: 169

Air pollutants: *particulate matter emissions:* 7.82 micrograms per cubic meter (2019 est.)
carbon dioxide emissions: 0.22 megatons (2016 est.)
methane emissions: 0.06 megatons (2020 est.)

Waste and recycling: *municipal solid waste generated annually:* 9,427 tons (2016 est.)

Total renewable water resources: 0 cubic meters (2017 est.)

GOVERNMENT

Country name: *conventional long form:* Republic of Palau
conventional short form: Palau
local long form: Beluu er a Belau
local short form: Belau
former: Trust Territory of the Pacific Islands, Palau District
etymology: from the Palauan name for the islands, Belau, which likely derives from the Palauan word "beluu" meaning "village"

Government type: presidential republic in free association with the US

Capital: *name:* Ngerulmud
geographic coordinates: 7 30 N, 134 37 E
time difference: UTC+9 (14 hours ahead of Washington, DC, during Standard Time)
etymology: the Palauan meaning is "place of fermented 'mud'" ('mud' being the native name for the keyhole angelfish); the site of the new capitol (established in 2006) had been a large hill overlooking the ocean, Ngerulmud, on which women would communally gather to offer fermented angelfish to the gods
note: Ngerulmud, on Babeldaob Island, is the smallest national capital on earth by population, with only a few hundred people; the name is pronounced en-jer-al-mud; Koror, on Koror Island, with over 11,000 residents is by far the largest settlement in Palau; it served as the country's capital from independence in 1994 to 2006

Administrative divisions: 16 states; Aimeliik, Airai, Angaur, Hatohobei, Kayangel, Koror, Melekeok, Ngaraard, Ngarchelong, Ngardmau, Ngatpang, Ngchesar, Ngeremlengui, Ngiwal, Peleliu, Sonsorol

Independence: 1 October 1994 (from the US-administered UN trusteeship)

National holiday: Constitution Day, 9 July (1981), day of a national referendum to pass the new constitution; Independence Day, 1 October (1994)

Legal system: mixed legal system of civil, common, and customary law

Constitution: *history:* ratified 9 July 1980, effective 1 January 1981
amendments: proposed by a constitutional convention (held at least once every 15 years with voter approval), by public petition of at least 25% of eligible voters, or by a resolution adopted by at least three fourths of National Congress members; passage requires approval by a majority of votes in at least three fourths of the states in the next regular general election; amended several times, last in 2020

International law organization participation: has not submitted an ICJ jurisdiction declaration; non-party state to the ICCt

Citizenship: *citizenship by birth:* no
citizenship by descent only: at least one parent must be a citizen of Palau
dual citizenship recognized: no
residency requirement for naturalization: note - no procedure for naturalization

Suffrage: 18 years of age; universal

Executive branch: *chief of state:* President Surangel WHIPPS Jr. (since 21 January 2021)
head of government: President Surangel WHIPPS Jr. (since 21 January 2021)
cabinet: Cabinet appointed by the president with the advice and consent of the Senate; also includes the vice president; the Council of Chiefs consists of chiefs from each of the states who advise the president on issues concerning traditional laws, customs, and their relationship to the constitution and laws of Palau
elections/appointments: president and vice president directly elected on separate ballots by absolute majority popular vote in 2 rounds if needed for a 4-year term (eligible for a second term); election last held on 5 November 2024 (next to be held November 2028)
election results: 2024: Surangel WHIPPS, Jr. elected president in second round; percent of vote - Surangel WHIPPS, Jr. (independent) 56.7%, Tommy REMENGESAU (independent) 41.7%
2020: Surangel WHIPPS, Jr. elected president in second round; percent of vote - Surangel WHIPPS, Jr. (independent) 56.7%, Raynold OILUCH (independent) 43.3%
note: the president is both chief of state and head of government

Legislative branch: *description:* bicameral National Congress or Olbiil Era Kelulau consists of:
Senate (13 seats; members directly elected in single-seat constituencies by majority vote to serve 4-year terms)
House of Delegates (16 seats; members directly elected in single-seat constituencies by simple majority vote to serve 4-year terms)
elections: Senate - last held on 3 November 2020 (next to be held in November 2024)
House of Delegates - last held on 3 November 2020 (next to be held in November 2024)
election results: Senate - percent of vote - NA; seats - independent 13; composition - men 12, women 1; percentage women 7.7%
House of Delegates - percent of vote - NA; seats - independent 16; composition - men 15, women 1; percentage women 6.3%; note - total National Congress percentage women 6.9%

Judicial branch: *highest court(s):* Supreme Court (consists of the chief justice and 3 associate justices organized into appellate trial divisions; the Supreme Court organization also includes the Common Pleas and Land Courts)
judge selection and term of office: justices nominated by a 7-member independent body consisting of judges, presidential appointees, and lawyers and appointed by the president; judges can serve until mandatory retirement at age 65
subordinate courts: National Court and other 'inferior' courts

Political parties: none

International organization participation: ACP, ADB, AOSIS, FAO, IAEA, IBRD, ICAO, ICRM, IDA, IFC, IFRCS, ILO, IMF, IMO, IMSO, IOC, IPU, MIGA, OPCW, PIF, Sparteca, SPC, UN, UNAMID, UNCTAD, UNESCO, WHO

Diplomatic representation in the US: *chief of mission:* Ambassador Hersey KYOTA (since 12 November 1997)
chancery: 1701 Pennsylvania Avenue NW, Suite 200, Washington, DC 20006
telephone: [1] (202) 349-8598
FAX: [1] (202) 452-6281
email address and website:
info@palauembassy.org
https://www.palauembassy.org/
consulate(s): Tamuning (Guam)

Diplomatic representation from the US: *chief of mission:* Ambassador (vacant); Chargé d'Affaires James BOUGHNER (since 9 September 2022)
embassy: Omsangel/Beklelachieb, Airai 96940
mailing address: 4260 Koror Place, Washington, DC 20521-4260
telephone: [680] 587-2920
FAX: [680] 587-2911
email address and website:
ConsularKoror@state.gov
https://pw.usembassy.gov/

Flag description: light blue with a large yellow disk shifted slightly to the hoist side; the blue color represents the ocean, the disk represents the moon; Palauans consider the full moon to be the optimum time for human activity; it is also considered a symbol of peace, love, and tranquility

National symbol(s): bai (native meeting house); national colors: blue, yellow

National anthem: *name:* "Belau rekid" (Our Palau)
lyrics/music: multiple/Ymesei O. EZEKIEL
note: adopted 1980

National heritage: *total World Heritage Sites:* 1 (mixed)
selected World Heritage Site locales: Rock Islands Southern Lagoon

ECONOMY

Economic overview: high-income Pacific island economy; environmentally fragile; subsistence agriculture and fishing industries; US aid reliance; rebounding post-pandemic tourism industry and services sector; very high living standard and low unemployment

Real GDP (purchasing power parity): $284.695 million (2023 est.)
$283.424 million (2022 est.)
$284.454 million (2021 est.)
note: data in 2021 dollars
comparison ranking: 216

Real GDP growth rate: 0.45% (2023 est.)
-0.36% (2022 est.)
-14.16% (2021 est.)
note: annual GDP % growth based on constant local currency
comparison ranking: 181

Real GDP per capita: $15,800 (2023 est.)
$15,700 (2022 est.)
$15,800 (2021 est.)
note: data in 2021 dollars
comparison ranking: 119

GDP (official exchange rate): $263.021 million (2023 est.)
note: data in current dollars at official exchange rate

Inflation rate (consumer prices): 12.8% (2023 est.)
12.35% (2022 est.)
2.61% (2021 est.)
note: annual % change based on consumer prices
comparison ranking: 189

GDP - composition, by sector of origin: *agriculture:* 3.4% (2022 est.)
industry: 12.3% (2022 est.)
services: 80.1% (2022 est.)
note: figures may not total 100% due to non-allocated consumption not captured in sector-reported data
comparison rankings: services 15; industry 177; agriculture 134

GDP - composition, by end use: *household consumption:* 82% (2022 est.)
government consumption: 38.3% (2022 est.)
investment in fixed capital: 38.7% (2022 est.)
investment in inventories: 1.2% (2022 est.)
exports of goods and services: 14.2% (2022 est.)
imports of goods and services: -78.3% (2022 est.)
note: figures may not total 100% due to rounding or gaps in data collection

Agricultural products: coconuts, cassava (manioc, tapioca), sweet potatoes; fish, pigs, chickens, eggs, bananas, papaya, breadfruit, calamansi, soursop, Polynesian chestnuts, Polynesian almonds, mangoes, taro, guava, beans, cucumbers, squash/pumpkins (various), eggplant, green onions, kangkong (watercress), cabbages (various), radishes, betel nuts, melons, peppers, noni, okra

Industries: tourism, fishing, subsistence agriculture

Industrial production growth rate: -19.56% (2022 est.)
note: annual % change in industrial value added based on constant local currency
comparison ranking: 216

Labor force: 11,610 (2016)
comparison ranking: 202

Unemployment rate: 1.7% (2015 est.)
comparison ranking: 19

Youth unemployment rate (ages 15-24): *total:* 5.6% (2014)
comparison ranking: total 173

Remittances: 0.38% of GDP (2023 est.)
0.81% of GDP (2022 est.)
0.82% of GDP (2021 est.)
note: personal transfers and compensation between resident and non-resident individuals/households/entities

Budget: *revenues:* $173.256 million (2019 est.)
expenditures: $175.508 million (2019 est.)
note: central government revenues (excluding grants) and expenses converted to US dollars at average official exchange rate for year indicated

Public debt: 85.24% of GDP (2019 est.)
note: central government debt as a % of GDP
comparison ranking: 33

Taxes and other revenues: 17.93% (of GDP) (2020 est.)
note: central government tax revenue as a % of GDP
comparison ranking: 104

Current account balance: -$135.428 million (2022 est.)
-$115.739 million (2021 est.)
-$115.61 million (2020 est.)
note: balance of payments - net trade and primary/secondary income in current dollars
comparison ranking: 99

Exports: $24.48 million (2022 est.)
$10.566 million (2021 est.)
$52.897 million (2020 est.)
note: balance of payments - exports of goods and services in current dollars
comparison ranking: 215

Exports - partners: Greece 27%, Japan 26%, France 18%, Taiwan 8%, US 7% (2022)
note: top five export partners based on percentage share of exports

Exports - commodities: ships, computers, machine parts, scrap iron, fish (2022)

note: top five export commodities based on value in dollars

Imports: $216.681 million (2022 est.)
$169.938 million (2021 est.)
$207.224 million (2020 est.)
note: balance of payments - imports of goods and services in current dollars
comparison ranking: 211

Imports - partners: China 35%, US 14%, South Korea 13%, Japan 8%, Italy 6% (2022)
note: top five import partners based on percentage share of imports

Imports - commodities: ships, refined petroleum, iron structures, plastic products, electric batteries (2022)
note: top five import commodities based on value in dollars

Reserves of foreign exchange and gold: $580.9 million (31 December 2015 est.)
comparison ranking: 156

Exchange rates: the US dollar is used

ENERGY

Electricity access: *electrification - total population:* 100% (2022 est.)
electrification - urban areas: 99.9%
electrification - rural areas: 100%

COMMUNICATIONS

Telephones - fixed lines: *total subscriptions:* 8,000 (2022 est.)
subscriptions per 100 inhabitants: 44 (2022 est.)
comparison ranking: total subscriptions 192

Telephones - mobile cellular: *total subscriptions:* 24,000 (2022 est.)
subscriptions per 100 inhabitants: 133 (2022 est.)
comparison ranking: total subscriptions 214

Telecommunication systems: *general assessment:* Palau telecommunications is a small, formerly unregulated sector undertaking significant growth with the improvement and cost reduction in technology; mobile services have taken over the share of the market from landlines, with both 2-3G cell services throughout the islands; sim cards are easily available and offer 3G and data options; there are pre-paid and post-paid options for both voice and data; there are three data options for using a wireless hotspot network throughout Palau; connection from hotel and restaurant premises is available, enabling users to connect via WiFi throughout the main Islands of Palau (2022)
domestic: fixed-line nearly 44 per 100 and mobile-cellular services roughly 130 per 100 persons (2021)
international: country code - 680; landing point for the SEA-US submarine cable linking Palau, Philippines, Micronesia, Indonesia, Hawaii (US), Guam (US) and California (US); satellite earth station - 1 Intelsat (Pacific Ocean) (2019)

Broadcast media: no broadcast TV stations; a cable TV network covers the major islands and provides access to 4 local cable stations, rebroadcasts (on a delayed basis) of a number of US stations, as well as access to a number of real-time satellite TV channels; about a half dozen radio stations (1 government-owned) (2019)

Internet country code: .pw

Internet users: *total:* 6,696 (2021 est.)
percent of population: 37.2% (2021 est.)
comparison ranking: total 221

Broadband - fixed subscriptions: *total:* 1,224 (2015 est.)
subscriptions per 100 inhabitants: 7 (2015 est.)
comparison ranking: total 200

TRANSPORTATION

National air transport system: *number of registered air carriers:* 1 (2020)
inventory of registered aircraft operated by air carriers: 1

Civil aircraft registration country code prefix: T8

Airports: 3 (2024)
comparison ranking: 189

Roadways: *total:* 121 km
paved: 85 km
unpaved: 36 km (2018)
comparison ranking: total 214

Merchant marine: *total:* 427 (2023)
by type: bulk carrier 49, container ship 8, general cargo 200, oil tanker 52, other 118
comparison ranking: total 47

Ports: *total ports:* 1 (2024)
large: 0
medium: 0
small: 0
very small: 1
ports with oil terminals: 1
key ports: Malakal Harbor

MILITARY AND SECURITY

Military and security forces: no regular military forces; the Ministry of Justice includes divisions/bureaus for public security, police functions, and maritime law enforcement (2024)

Military - note: under the Compact of Free Association between Palau and the US, the US is responsible for the defense of Palau and the US military is granted access to the islands; the COFA also allows citizens of Palau to serve in the US armed forces
Palau has a "shiprider" agreement with the US, which allows local maritime law enforcement officers to embark on US Coast Guard (USCG) and US Navy (USN) vessels, including to board and search vessels suspected of violating laws or regulations within Palau's designated exclusive economic zone (EEZ) or on the high seas; "shiprider" agreements also enable USCG personnel and USN vessels with embarked USCG law enforcement personnel to work with host nations to protect critical regional resources (2024)

PANAMA

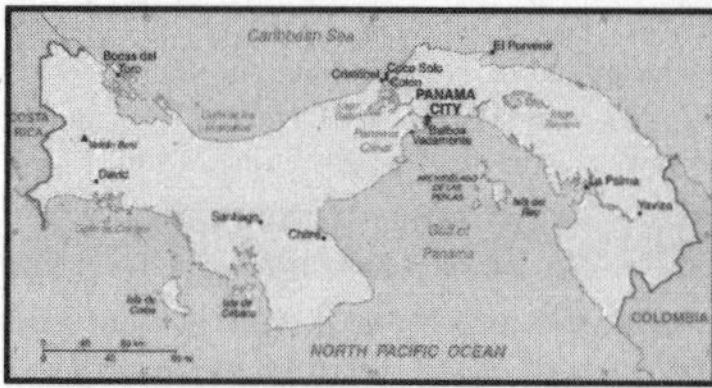

INTRODUCTION

Background: Explored and settled by the Spanish in the 16th century, Panama broke with Spain in 1821 and joined a union of Colombia, Ecuador, and Venezuela that was named the Republic of Gran Colombia. When the union dissolved in 1830, Panama remained part of Colombia. With US backing, Panama seceded from Colombia in 1903 and promptly signed a treaty with the US allowing for the construction of a canal and US sovereignty over a strip of land known as the Panama Canal Zone on either side of the structure. The US Army Corps of Engineers built the Panama Canal between 1904 and 1914. In 1977, an agreement was signed for the complete transfer of the Canal from the US to Panama by the end of the century. Certain portions of the Zone and increasing responsibility over the Canal were turned over in the subsequent decades. With US help, Panamanian dictator Manuel NORIEGA was deposed in 1989. The entire Panama Canal, the area supporting the Canal, and remaining US military bases were transferred to Panama by the end of 1999. An ambitious expansion project to more than double the Canal's capacity by allowing for more Canal transits and larger ships was carried out between 2007 and 2016.

GEOGRAPHY

Location: Central America, bordering both the Caribbean Sea and the North Pacific Ocean, between Colombia and Costa Rica

Geographic coordinates: 9 00 N, 80 00 W

Map references: Central America and the Caribbean

Area: *total:* 75,420 sq km
land: 74,340 sq km
water: 1,080 sq km
comparison ranking: total 118

Area - comparative: slightly smaller than South Carolina

Land boundaries: *total:* 687 km
border countries (2): Colombia 339 km; Costa Rica 348 km

Coastline: 2,490 km

Maritime claims: *territorial sea:* 12 nm
contiguous zone: 24 nm
exclusive economic zone: 200 nm or edge of continental margin

Climate: tropical maritime; hot, humid, cloudy; prolonged rainy season (May to January), short dry season (January to May)

Terrain: interior mostly steep, rugged mountains with dissected, upland plains; coastal plains with rolling hills

Elevation: *highest point:* Volcan Baru 3,475 m
lowest point: Pacific Ocean 0 m
mean elevation: 360 m

Natural resources: copper, mahogany forests, shrimp, hydropower

Land use: *agricultural land:* 30.5% (2018 est.)
arable land: 7.3% (2018 est.)
permanent crops: 2.5% (2018 est.)
permanent pasture: 20.7% (2018 est.)
forest: 43.6% (2018 est.)
other: 25.9% (2018 est.)

Irrigated land: 407 sq km (2020)

Major lakes (area sq km): *salt water lake(s):* Laguna de Chiriqui - 900 sq km

Population distribution: population is concentrated towards the center of the country, particularly around the Canal, but a sizeable segment of the populace also lives in the far west around David; the eastern third of the country is sparsely inhabited

Natural hazards: occasional severe storms and forest fires in the Darien area

Geography - note: strategic location on eastern end of isthmus forming land bridge connecting North and South America; controls Panama Canal that links North Atlantic Ocean via Caribbean Sea with North Pacific Ocean

PEOPLE AND SOCIETY

Population: *total:* 4,470,241
male: 2,251,257
female: 2,218,984 (2024 est.)
comparison rankings: female 128; male 127; total 127

Nationality: *noun:* Panamanian(s)
adjective: Panamanian

Ethnic groups: Mestizo (mixed Indigenous and White) 65%, Indigenous 12.3% (Ngabe 7.6%, Kuna 2.4%, Embera 0.9%, Bugle 0.8%, other 0.4%, unspecified 0.2%), Black or African descent 9.2%, Mulatto 6.8%, White 6.7% (2010 est.)

Languages: Spanish (official), Indigenous languages (including Ngabere (Guaymi), Buglere, Kuna, Embera, Wounaan, Naso (Teribe), and Bri Bri), Panamanian English Creole (a mixture of English and Spanish with elements of Ngabere, also known as Guari Guari and Colon Creole), English, Chinese (Yue and Hakka), Arabic, French Creole, other (Yiddish, Hebrew, Korean, Japanese)
major-language sample(s):
La Libreta Informativa del Mundo, la fuente indispensable de información básica. (Spanish)

Religions: Evangelical 55%, Roman Catholic 33.4%, none 10.1%, unspecified 1.5% (2023 est.)

Demographic profile: Panama is a country of demographic and economic contrasts. It is in the midst of a demographic transition, characterized by steadily declining rates of fertility, mortality, and population growth, but disparities persist based on wealth, geography, and ethnicity. Panama has one of the fastest growing economies in Latin America and dedicates substantial funding to social programs, yet poverty and inequality remain prevalent. The indigenous population accounts for a growing share of Panama's poor and extreme poor, while the non-indigenous rural poor have been more successful at rising out of poverty through rural-to-urban labor migration. The government's large expenditures on untargeted, indirect subsidies for water, electricity, and fuel have been ineffective, but its conditional cash transfer program has shown some promise in helping to decrease extreme poverty among the indigenous population. Panama has expanded access to education and clean water, but the availability of sanitation and, to a lesser extent, electricity remains poor. The increase in secondary schooling - led by female enrollment - is spreading to rural and indigenous areas, which probably will help to alleviate poverty if educational quality and the availability of skilled jobs improve. Inadequate access to sanitation contributes to a high incidence of diarrhea in Panama's children, which is one of the main causes of Panama's elevated chronic malnutrition rate, especially among indigenous communities.

Age structure: *0-14 years:* 25% (male 574,336/female 544,180)
15-64 years: 64.8% (male 1,465,907/female 1,433,023)
65 years and over: 10.1% (2024 est.) (male 211,014/female 241,781)

Dependency ratios: *total dependency ratio:* 53.8
youth dependency ratio: 40.6
elderly dependency ratio: 13.2
potential support ratio: 7.6 (2021 est.)

Median age: *total:* 31.5 years (2024 est.)
male: 31 years
female: 31.9 years
comparison ranking: total 127

Population growth rate: 1.48% (2024 est.)
comparison ranking: 66

Birth rate: 17.4 births/1,000 population (2024 est.)
comparison ranking: 86

Death rate: 5.7 deaths/1,000 population (2024 est.)
comparison ranking: 170

Net migration rate: 3 migrant(s)/1,000 population (2024 est.)
comparison ranking: 36

Population distribution: population is concentrated towards the center of the country, particularly around the Canal, but a sizeable segment of the populace also lives in the far west around David; the eastern third of the country is sparsely inhabited

Urbanization: *urban population:* 69.5% of total population (2023)
rate of urbanization: 1.92% annual rate of change (2020-25 est.)

Major urban areas - population: 1.977 million PANAMA CITY (capital) (2023)

Sex ratio: *at birth:* 1.06 male(s)/female
0-14 years: 1.06 male(s)/female
15-64 years: 1.02 male(s)/female
65 years and over: 0.87 male(s)/female
total population: 1.02 male(s)/female (2024 est.)

Maternal mortality ratio: 50 deaths/100,000 live births (2020 est.)
comparison ranking: 96

Infant mortality rate: *total:* 14.2 deaths/1,000 live births (2024 est.)
male: 15.4 deaths/1,000 live births
female: 12.9 deaths/1,000 live births
comparison ranking: total 98

Life expectancy at birth: *total population:* 79.2 years (2024 est.)
male: 76.4 years
female: 82.2 years
comparison ranking: total population 66

Total fertility rate: 2.35 children born/woman (2024 est.)
comparison ranking: 74

Gross reproduction rate: 1.14 (2024 est.)

Contraceptive prevalence rate: 50.8% (2014/15)

Drinking water source: *improved: urban:* 100% of population
rural: 88.1% of population
total: 96.2% of population
unimproved: urban: 0% of population
rural: 11.9% of population
total: 3.8% of population (2020 est.)

Current health expenditure: 9.7% of GDP (2020)

Physician density: 1.63 physicians/1,000 population (2019)

Hospital bed density: 2.3 beds/1,000 population (2016)

Sanitation facility access: *improved: urban:* 95.5% of population
rural: 69.1% of population
total: 87.2% of population
unimproved: urban: 4.5% of population
rural: 30.9% of population
total: 12.8% of population (2020 est.)

Obesity - adult prevalence rate: 22.7% (2016)
comparison ranking: 73

Alcohol consumption per capita: *total:* 6.54 liters of pure alcohol (2019 est.)
beer: 5.29 liters of pure alcohol (2019 est.)
wine: 0.02 liters of pure alcohol (2019 est.)
spirits: 1.2 liters of pure alcohol (2019 est.)
other alcohols: 0.02 liters of pure alcohol (2019 est.)
comparison ranking: total 63

Tobacco use: *total:* 5% (2020 est.)
male: 7.7% (2020 est.)
female: 2.2% (2020 est.)
comparison ranking: total 162

Children under the age of 5 years underweight: 3% (2019)
comparison ranking: 90

Currently married women (ages 15-49): 58.6% (2023 est.)

Education expenditures: 3.9% of GDP (2020 est.)
comparison ranking: 120

Literacy: *definition:* age 15 and over can read and write
total population: 95.7%
male: 98.8%
female: 95.4% (2019)

School life expectancy (primary to tertiary education): *total:* 13 years
male: 12 years
female: 13 years (2016)

ENVIRONMENT

Environment - current issues: water pollution from agricultural runoff threatens fishery resources; deforestation of tropical rain forest; land degradation and soil erosion threatens siltation of Panama Canal; air pollution in urban areas; mining threatens natural resources

Environment - international agreements: *party to:* Antarctic-Marine Living Resources, Biodiversity, Climate Change, Climate Change-Kyoto Protocol, Climate Change-Paris Agreement, Comprehensive Nuclear Test Ban, Desertification, Endangered Species, Environmental Modification, Hazardous Wastes, Law of the Sea, Marine Dumping-London Convention, Nuclear Test Ban, Ozone Layer Protection, Ship Pollution, Tropical Timber 2006, Wetlands, Whaling
signed, but not ratified: Marine Life Conservation

Climate: tropical maritime; hot, humid, cloudy; prolonged rainy season (May to January), short dry season (January to May)

Urbanization: *urban population:* 69.5% of total population (2023)
rate of urbanization: 1.92% annual rate of change (2020-25 est.)

Revenue from forest resources: 0.08% of GDP (2018 est.)
comparison ranking: 121

Revenue from coal: 0% of GDP (2018 est.)
comparison ranking: 122

Air pollutants: *particulate matter emissions:* 11.78 micrograms per cubic meter (2019 est.)
carbon dioxide emissions: 10.71 megatons (2016 est.)
methane emissions: 5.97 megatons (2020 est.)

Waste and recycling: *municipal solid waste generated annually:* 1,472,262 tons (2015 est.)

Major lakes (area sq km): *salt water lake(s):* Laguna de Chiriqui - 900 sq km

Total water withdrawal: *municipal:* 760 million cubic meters (2020 est.)
industrial: 10 million cubic meters (2020 est.)
agricultural: 450 million cubic meters (2020 est.)

Total renewable water resources: 139.3 billion cubic meters (2020 est.)

GOVERNMENT

Country name: *conventional long form:* Republic of Panama
conventional short form: Panama
local long form: República de Panama
local short form: Panama
etymology: named after the capital city which was itself named after a former indigenous fishing village

Government type: presidential republic

Capital: *name:* Panama City
geographic coordinates: 8 58 N, 79 32 W
time difference: UTC-5 (same time as Washington, DC, during Standard Time)
etymology: according to tradition, the name derives from a former fishing area near the present capital - an indigenous village and its adjacent beach - that were called "panama" meaning "an abundance of fish"

Administrative divisions: 10 provinces (provincias, singular - provincia) and 4 indigenous regions* (comarcas); Bocas del Toro, Chiriqui, Cocle, Colon, Darien, Embera-Wounaan*, Guna Yala*, Herrera, Los Santos, Naso Tjer Di*, Ngabe-Bugle*, Panama, Panama Oeste, Veraguas

Independence: 3 November 1903 (from Colombia; became independent from Spain on 28 November 1821)

National holiday: Independence Day (Separation Day), 3 November (1903)

Legal system: civil law system; judicial review of legislative acts in the Supreme Court of Justice

Constitution: *history:* several previous; latest effective 11 October 1972
amendments: proposed by the National Assembly, by the Cabinet, or by the Supreme Court of Justice; passage requires approval by one of two procedures: 1) absolute majority vote of the Assembly membership in each of three readings and by absolute majority vote of the next elected Assembly in a single reading without textual modifications; 2) absolute majority vote of the Assembly membership in each of three readings, followed by absolute majority vote of the next elected Assembly in each of three readings with textual modifications, and approval in a referendum; amended several times, last in 2004

International law organization participation: accepts compulsory ICJ jurisdiction with reservations; accepts ICCt jurisdiction

Citizenship: *citizenship by birth:* yes
citizenship by descent only: yes
dual citizenship recognized: no
residency requirement for naturalization: 5 years

Suffrage: 18 years of age; universal

Executive branch: *chief of state:* President José Raúl MULINO Quintero (since 1 July 2024)
head of government: President José Raúl MULINO Quintero (since 1 July 2024)
cabinet: Cabinet appointed by the president
elections/appointments: president and vice president directly elected on the same ballot by simple majority popular vote for a 5-year term; president eligible for a single non-consecutive term); election last held on 5 May 2024 (next to be held in May 2029)
election results:
2024: José Raúl MULINO Quintero elected president; percent of vote - José Raúl MULINO Quintero (RM) 34.2%, Ricardo Alberto LOMBANA González (MOCA) 24.6%, Martín Erasto TORRIJOS Espino (PP) 16%, Rómulo Alberto ROUX Moses (CD) 11.4%, Zulay RODRÍGUEZ Lu (independent) 6.6%, José Gabriel CARRIZO Jaén (PRD) 5.9%, other 1.3%
2019: Laurentino "Nito" CORTIZO Cohen elected president; percent of vote - Laurentino CORTIZO Cohen (PRD) 33.3%, Romulo ROUX (CD) 31%, Ricardo LOMBANA (independent) 18.8%, Jose BLANDON (Panameñista Party) 10.8%, Ana Matilde GOMEZ Ruiloba (independent) 4.8%, other 1.3%
note: the president is both chief of state and head of government

Legislative branch: *description:* unicameral National Assembly or Asamblea Nacional (71 seats; 45 members directly elected in multi-seat constituencies - populous towns and cities - by open list proportional representation vote and 26 directly elected in single-seat constituencies - outlying rural districts - by simple majority vote; members serve 5-year terms)
elections: last held on 5 May 2024 (next to be held in May 2029)
election results: percent of vote by party - NA; seats by party - independents 21, PRD 13, RM 13, CD 8, Panameñista 8, MOCA 3, PA 2, PP 2, MOLIRENA 1

Judicial branch: *highest court(s):* Supreme Court of Justice or Corte Suprema de Justicia (consists of 9 magistrates and 9 alternates and divided into civil, criminal, administrative, and general business chambers)
judge selection and term of office: magistrates appointed by the president for staggered 10-year terms
subordinate courts: appellate courts or Tribunal Superior; Labor Supreme Courts; Court of Audit; circuit courts or Tribunal Circuital (2 each in 9 of the 10 provinces); municipal courts; electoral, family, maritime, and adolescent courts

Political parties: Alliance Party or PA
Alternative Independent Socialist Party or PAIS
Another Way Movement or MOCA
Democratic Change or CD
Democratic Revolutionary Party or PRD
Nationalist Republican Liberal Movement or MOLIRENA
Panameñista Party (formerly the Arnulfista Party)
Popular Party or PP (formerly Christian Democratic Party or PDC)
Realizing Goals Party or RM

International organization participation: ACS, BCIE, CAN (observer), CD, CELAC, FAO, G-77, IADB, IAEA, IBRD, ICAO, ICC (national committees), ICCt, ICRM, IDA, IFAD, IFC, IFRCS, ILO, IMF, IMO, IMSO, Interpol, IOC, IOM, IPU, ISO, ITSO, ITU, ITUC (NGOs), LAES, LAIA, MIGA, NAM, OAS, OPANAL, OPCW, Pacific Alliance (observer), PCA, SICA, UN, UNASUR (observer), UNCTAD, UNESCO, UNIDO, Union Latina, UNOOSA, UNWTO, UPU, WCO, WFTU (NGOs), WHO, WIPO, WMO, WTO

Diplomatic representation in the US: *chief of mission:* Ambassador José Miguel ALEMÁN HEALY (since 18 September 2024)
chancery: 2862 McGill Terrace NW, Washington, DC 20008
telephone: [1] (202) 483-1407
FAX: [1] (202) 483-8413
email address and website:
info@embassyofpanama.org
https://www.embassyofpanama.org/
consulate(s) general: Houston, Los Angeles, Miami, New Orleans, New York, Philadelphia, Tampa

Diplomatic representation from the US: *chief of mission:* Ambassador Mari Carmen APONTE (since 21 November 2022)
embassy: Building 783, Demetrio Basilio Lakas Avenue, Clayton
mailing address: 9100 Panama City PL, Washington, DC 20521-9100
telephone: [507] 317-5000
FAX: [507] 317-5568
email address and website:
Panama-ACS@state.gov
https://pa.usembassy.gov/

Flag description: divided into four, equal rectangles; the top quadrants are white (hoist side) with a blue five-pointed star in the center and plain red; the bottom quadrants are plain blue (hoist side) and white with a red five-pointed star in the center; the blue and red colors are those of the main political parties (Conservatives and Liberals respectively) and the white denotes peace between them; the blue star stands for the civic virtues of purity and honesty, the red star signifies authority and law

National symbol(s): harpy eagle; national colors: blue, white, red

National anthem: *name:* "Himno Istmeno" (Isthmus Hymn)
lyrics/music: Jeronimo DE LA OSSA/Santos A. JORGE
note: adopted 1925

National heritage: *total World Heritage Sites:* 5 (2 cultural, 3 natural)
selected World Heritage Site locales: Caribbean Fortifications (c); Darien National Park (n); Talamanca Range-La Amistad National Park (n); Panamá Viejo and Historic District of Panamá (c); Coiba National Park (n)

ECONOMY

Economic overview: upper middle-income Central American economy; increasing Chinese trade; US dollar user; canal expansion fueling broader infrastructure investment; services sector dominates economy; historic money-laundering and illegal drug hub

Real GDP (purchasing power parity): $159.867 billion (2023 est.)
$148.968 billion (2022 est.)
$134.436 billion (2021 est.)
note: data in 2021 dollars
comparison ranking: 80

Real GDP growth rate: 7.32% (2023 est.)
10.81% (2022 est.)
15.84% (2021 est.)
note: annual GDP % growth based on constant local currency
comparison ranking: 19

Real GDP per capita: $35,800 (2023 est.)
$33,800 (2022 est.)
$30,900 (2021 est.)
note: data in 2021 dollars
comparison ranking: 67

GDP (official exchange rate): $83.382 billion (2023 est.)
note: data in current dollars at official exchange rate

Inflation rate (consumer prices): 1.49% (2023 est.)
2.86% (2022 est.)
1.63% (2021 est.)
note: annual % change based on consumer prices
comparison ranking: 28

Credit ratings: Fitch rating: BBB (2011)

Moody's rating: Baa1 (2019)

Standard & Poors rating: BBB (2020)
note: The year refers to the year in which the current credit rating was first obtained.

GDP - composition, by sector of origin: *agriculture:* 2.4% (2023 est.)
industry: 27.1% (2023 est.)
services: 67.9% (2023 est.)
note: figures may not total 100% due to non-allocated consumption not captured in sector-reported data
comparison rankings: services 46; industry 83; agriculture 149

GDP - composition, by end use: *household consumption:* 46.1% (2022 est.)
government consumption: 12.8% (2022 est.)
investment in fixed capital: 29.5% (2022 est.)
investment in inventories: 11.7% (2022 est.)
exports of goods and services: 47.9% (2022 est.)
imports of goods and services: -48% (2022 est.)
note: figures may not total 100% due to rounding or gaps in data collection

Agricultural products: sugarcane, bananas, rice, oranges, oil palm fruit, plantains, chicken, milk, pineapples, maize (2022)
note: top ten agricultural products based on tonnage

Industries: construction, brewing, cement and other construction materials, sugar milling

Industrial production growth rate: 13.06% (2023 est.)
note: annual % change in industrial value added based on constant local currency
comparison ranking: 7

Labor force: 2.096 million (2023 est.)
note: number of people ages 15 or older who are employed or seeking work
comparison ranking: 126

Unemployment rate: 6.7% (2023 est.)
8.2% (2022 est.)
10.45% (2021 est.)
note: % of labor force seeking employment
comparison ranking: 134

Youth unemployment rate (ages 15-24): *total:* 16.6% (2023 est.)
male: 13.5% (2023 est.)
female: 22% (2023 est.)
note: % of labor force ages 15-24 seeking employment
comparison ranking: total 85

Population below poverty line: 21.5% (2019 est.)
note: % of population with income below national poverty line

Gini Index coefficient - distribution of family income: 48.9 (2023 est.)
note: index (0-100) of income distribution; higher values represent greater inequality
comparison ranking: 13

Average household expenditures: *on food:* 15.6% of household expenditures (2022 est.)
on alcohol and tobacco: 1.7% of household expenditures (2022 est.)

Household income or consumption by percentage share: *lowest 10%:* 1.2% (2023 est.)
highest 10%: 36.9% (2023 est.)
note: % share of income accruing to lowest and highest 10% of population

Remittances: 0.64% of GDP (2023 est.)
0.69% of GDP (2022 est.)
0.84% of GDP (2021 est.)
note: personal transfers and compensation between resident and non-resident individuals/households/entities

Budget: *revenues:* $7.57 billion (2021 est.)
expenditures: $11.553 billion (2021 est.)
note: central government revenues and expenses (excluding grants/extrabudgetary units/social security funds) converted to US dollars at average official exchange rate for year indicated

Public debt: 37.8% of GDP (2017 est.)
comparison ranking: 138

Taxes and other revenues: 7.46% (of GDP) (2021 est.)
note: central government tax revenue as a % of GDP
comparison ranking: 193

Current account balance: -$3.739 billion (2023 est.)
-$475.146 million (2022 est.)
-$778.779 million (2021 est.)
note: balance of payments - net trade and primary/secondary income in current dollars
comparison ranking: 170

Exports: $36.569 billion (2023 est.)
$35.731 billion (2022 est.)
$27.488 billion (2021 est.)
note: balance of payments - exports of goods and services in current dollars
comparison ranking: 73

Exports - partners: China 17%, Japan 12%, South Korea 8%, US 5%, Spain 5% (2022)
note: top five export partners based on percentage share of exports

Exports - commodities; copper ore, ships, fish, bananas, refined petroleum (2022)
note: top five export commodities based on value in dollars

Imports: $36.135 billion (2023 est.)
$32.693 billion (2022 est.)
$24.459 billion (2021 est.)
note: balance of payments - imports of goods and services in current dollars
comparison ranking: 73

Imports - partners: China 20%, US 20%, Guyana 11%, Colombia 11%, Ecuador 9% (2022)
note: top five import partners based on percentage share of imports

Imports - commodities: crude petroleum, refined petroleum, ships, garments, packaged medicine (2022)
note: top five import commodities based on value in dollars

Reserves of foreign exchange and gold: $6.757 billion (2023 est.)
$6.876 billion (2022 est.)
$8.832 billion (2021 est.)
note: holdings of gold (year-end prices)/foreign exchange/special drawing rights in current dollars
comparison ranking: 111

Exchange rates: balboas (PAB) per US dollar -

Exchange rates: 1 (2023 est.)
1 (2022 est.)
1 (2021 est.)
1 (2020 est.)
1 (2019 est.)

ENERGY

Electricity access: *electrification - total population:* 95% (2022 est.)
electrification - urban areas: 99%
electrification - rural areas: 100%

Electricity: *installed generating capacity:* 4.434 million kW (2022 est.)
consumption: 11.608 billion kWh (2022 est.)
exports: 502 million kWh (2022 est.)
imports: 69.81 million kWh (2022 est.)
transmission/distribution losses: 1.315 billion kWh (2022 est.)
comparison rankings: transmission/distribution losses 111; imports 111; exports 76; consumption 95; installed generating capacity 92

Electricity generation sources: *fossil fuels:* 21.8% of total installed capacity (2022 est.)
solar: 4.9% of total installed capacity (2022 est.)
wind: 4% of total installed capacity (2022 est.)
hydroelectricity: 69.2% of total installed capacity (2022 est.)
biomass and waste: 0.2% of total installed capacity (2022 est.)

Coal: *consumption:* 837,000 metric tons (2022 est.)
exports: (2022 est.) less than 1 metric ton
imports: 845,000 metric tons (2022 est.)

Petroleum: *refined petroleum consumption:* 146,000 bbl/day (2022 est.)

Natural gas: *consumption:* 389.611 million cubic meters (2022 est.)
imports: 389.611 million cubic meters (2022 est.)

Carbon dioxide emissions: 25.763 million metric tonnes of CO2 (2022 est.)
from coal and metallurgical coke: 1.89 million metric tonnes of CO2 (2022 est.)
from petroleum and other liquids: 23.114 million metric tonnes of CO2 (2022 est.)
from consumed natural gas: 759,000 metric tonnes of CO2 (2022 est.)
comparison ranking: total emissions 77

Energy consumption per capita: 87.16 million Btu/person (2022 est.)
comparison ranking: 62

COMMUNICATIONS

Telephones - fixed lines: *total subscriptions:* 811,000 (2022 est.)
subscriptions per 100 inhabitants: 18 (2022 est.)
comparison ranking: total subscriptions 76

Telephones - mobile cellular: *total subscriptions:* 6.891 million (2022 est.)
subscriptions per 100 inhabitants: 156 (2022 est.)

comparison ranking: total subscriptions 112

Telecommunication systems: *general assessment:* Panama has seen a steady increase in revenue from the telecom sector in recent years; mobile services and broadband remain the key growth sectors, with mobile connections accounting for 90% of all connections, and over half of telecom sector revenue; the mobile market has effective competition; internet services have grown in recent years as consumers responded to government fixed-line projects, improved mobile broadband connectivity and mobile applications (2021)
domestic: fixed-line is 18 per 100 and subscribership of mobile-cellular telephone is 138 per 100 (2021)
international: country code - 507; landing points for the PAN-AM, ARCOS, SAC, AURORA, PCCS, PAC, and the MAYA-1 submarine cable systems that together provide links to the US and parts of the Caribbean, Central America, and South America; satellite earth stations - 2 Intelsat (Atlantic Ocean); connected to the Central American Microwave System (2019)

Broadcast media: multiple privately owned TV networks and a government-owned educational TV station; multi-channel cable and satellite TV subscription services are available; more than 100 commercial radio stations (2019)

Internet country code: .pa

Internet users: *total:* 2.992 million (2021 est.)
percent of population: 68% (2021 est.)
comparison ranking: total 122

Broadband - fixed subscriptions: *total:* 562,413 (2020 est.)
subscriptions per 100 inhabitants: 13 (2020 est.)
comparison ranking: total 88

TRANSPORTATION

National air transport system: *number of registered air carriers:* 4 (2020)
inventory of registered aircraft operated by air carriers: 122
annual passenger traffic on registered air carriers: 12,939,350 (2018)
annual freight traffic on registered air carriers: 47.63 million (2018) mt-km

Civil aircraft registration country code prefix: HP

Airports: 76 (2024)
comparison ranking: 67

Heliports: 1 (2024)

Pipelines: 128 km oil (2013)

Railways: *total:* 77 km (2014)
standard gauge: 77 km (2014) 1.435-m gauge
comparison ranking: total 129

Waterways: 800 km (2011) (includes the 82-km Panama Canal that is being widened)
comparison ranking: 78

Merchant marine: *total:* 8,174 (2023)
by type: bulk carrier 2732, container ship 671, general cargo 1,428, oil tanker 866, other 2,477
comparison ranking: total 3

Ports: *total ports:* 12 (2024)
large: 0
medium: 3
small: 3
very small: 5
size unknown: 1
ports with oil terminals: 5
key ports: Bahia de las Minas, Balboa, Pedregal, Puerto Armuelles, Puerto Colon, Puerto Cristobal

MILITARY AND SECURITY

Military and security forces: no regular military forces; the paramilitary Panamanian Public Forces are under the Ministry of Public Security and include the Panama National Police (La Policía Nacional de Panamá, PNP), National Aeronaval Service (Servicio Nacional Aeronaval, SENAN), and National Border Service (Servicio Nacional de Fronteras, SENAFRONT) (2024)
note: the PNP includes a special forces directorate with counterterrorism and counternarcotics units; SENAFRONT has three regionally based border security brigades, plus a specialized brigade comprised of special forces, counternarcotics, maritime, and rapid reaction units

Military expenditures: 1.1% of GDP (2023 est.)
1.2% of GDP (2022 est.)
1.3% of GDP (2021 est.)
1.4% of GDP (2020 est.)
1.2% of GDP (2019 est.)
comparison ranking: 121

Military and security service personnel strengths: approximately 27,000 Ministry of Public Security personnel (2023)

Military - note: the Panama National Police is principally responsible for internal law enforcement and public order, while the National Border Service handles border security; the Aeronaval Service is responsible for carrying out air and naval operations that include some internal security responsibilities; key areas of focus are countering narcotics trafficking and securing the border, particularly along the southern border with Colombia (the area is known as the Darién Gap) where the National Border Service (SENAFRONT) maintains a significant presence
Panama created a paramilitary National Guard (Guardia Nacional de Panamá) in the 1950s from the former National Police (established 1904); the National Guard subsequently evolved into more of a military force with some police responsibilities; it seized power in a coup in 1968 and military officers ran the country until 1989; in 1983, the National Guard was renamed the Panama Defense Force (PDF); the PDF was disbanded after the 1989 US invasion and the current national police forces were formed in 1990; the armed forces were officially abolished under the 1994 Constitution (2024)

TRANSNATIONAL ISSUES

Refugees and internally displaced persons: *refugees (country of origin):* 58,158 (Venezuela) (economic and political crisis; includes Venezuelans who have claimed asylum or have received alternative legal stay) (2023)

Illicit drugs: not a major consumer or producer of illicit drugs; a prime sea and land passage for drugs, primarily cocaine, from South America to North America and Europe; drug traffickers also use millions of shipping containers to smuggle drugs to North America and Europe through the Panama

PAPUA NEW GUINEA

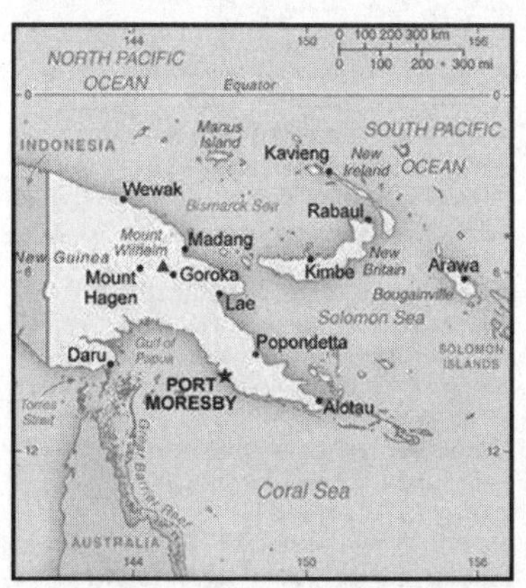

INTRODUCTION

Background: Papua New Guinea (PNG) occupies the eastern half of the island of New Guinea; the western half is part of Indonesia. PNG was first settled between 50,000 and 60,000 years ago. Its harsh geography of mountains, jungles, and numerous river valleys kept many of the arriving groups isolated, giving rise to PNG's ethnic and linguistic diversity. Around 500 B.C., Austronesian voyagers settled along the coast. Spanish and Portuguese explorers periodically visited the island starting in the 1500s, but none made it into the country's interior. American and British whaling ships frequented the islands off the coast of New Guinea in the mid-1800s. In 1884, Germany declared a protectorate – and eventually a colony – over the northern part of what would become PNG and named it German New Guinea; days later the UK followed suit on the southern part and nearby islands and called it Papua. Most of their focus was on the coastal regions, leaving the highlands largely unexplored.

The UK put its colony under Australian administration in 1902 and formalized the act in 1906. At the outbreak of World War I, Australia occupied German New Guinea and continued to rule it after the war as a League of Nations Mandate. The discovery of gold along the Bulolo River in the 1920s led prospectors to venture into the highlands, where they found about 1 million people living in isolated communities. The New Guinea campaign of World War II lasted from January 1942 to the Japanese surrender in August 1945. After the war, Australia combined the two territories and administered PNG as a UN trusteeship. In 1975, PNG gained independence and became a member of the Commonwealth.

Between 1988-1997, a secessionist movement on the island province of Bougainville, located off the eastern PNG coast, fought the PNG Government, resulting in 15,000-20,000 deaths. In 1997, the PNG Government and Bougainville leaders reached a cease-fire and subsequently signed a peace agreement in 2001. The Autonomous Bougainville Government was formally established in 2005. Bougainvilleans voted in favor of independence in a 2019 non-binding referendum. The Bougainville and PNG governments are in the process of negotiating a roadmap for independence, which requires approval by the PNG parliament.

GEOGRAPHY

Location: Oceania, group of islands including the eastern half of the island of New Guinea between the Coral Sea and the South Pacific Ocean, east of Indonesia

Geographic coordinates: 6 00 S, 147 00 E

Map references: Oceania

Area: *total:* 462,840 sq km
land: 452,860 sq km
water: 9,980 sq km
comparison ranking: total 57

Area - comparative: slightly larger than California

Land boundaries: *total:* 824 km
border countries (1): Indonesia 824 km

Coastline: 5,152 km

Maritime claims: *territorial sea:* 12 nm
continental shelf: 200-m depth or to the depth of exploitation
exclusive fishing zone: 200 nm
measured from claimed archipelagic baselines

Climate: tropical; northwest monsoon (December to March), southeast monsoon (May to October); slight seasonal temperature variation

Terrain: mostly mountains with coastal lowlands and rolling foothills

Elevation: *highest point:* Mount Wilhelm 4,509 m
lowest point: Pacific Ocean 0 m
mean elevation: 667 m

Natural resources: gold, copper, silver, natural gas, timber, oil, fisheries

Land use: *agricultural land:* 2.6% (2018 est.)
arable land: 0.7% (2018 est.)
permanent crops: 1.5% (2018 est.)
permanent pasture: 0.4% (2018 est.)
forest: 63.1% (2018 est.)
other: 34.3% (2018 est.)

Irrigated land: 0 sq km (2022)

Major rivers (by length in km): Sepik river source and mouth (shared with Indonesia) - 1,126 km; Fly river source and mouth (shared with Indonesia) - 1,050 km

Population distribution: population concentrated in the highlands and eastern coastal areas on the island of New Guinea; predominantly a rural distribution with only about one-fifth of the population residing in urban areas

Natural hazards: active volcanism; the country is subject to frequent and sometimes severe earthquakes; mud slides; tsunamis
volcanism: severe volcanic activity; Ulawun (2,334 m), one of Papua New Guinea's potentially most dangerous volcanoes, has been deemed a Decade Volcano by the International Association of Volcanology and Chemistry of the Earth's Interior, worthy of study due to its explosive history and close proximity to human populations; Rabaul (688 m) destroyed the city of Rabaul in 1937 and 1994; Lamington erupted in 1951 killing 3,000 people; Manam's 2004 eruption forced the island's abandonment; other historically active volcanoes include Bam, Bagana, Garbuna, Karkar, Langila, Lolobau, Long Island, Pago, St. Andrew Strait, Victory, and Waiowa; see note 2 under "Geography - note"

Geography - note: *note 1:* shares island of New Guinea with Indonesia; generally east-west trending highlands break up New Guinea into diverse ecoregions; one of world's largest swamps along southwest coast
note 2: two major food crops apparently developed on the island of New Guinea: bananas and sugarcane
note 3: Papua New Guinea is one of the countries along the Ring of Fire, a belt of active volcanoes and earthquake epicenters bordering the Pacific Ocean; up to 90% of the world's earthquakes and some 75% of the world's volcanoes occur within the Ring of Fire

PEOPLE AND SOCIETY

Population: *total:* 10,046,233
male: 5,092,262
female: 4,953,971 (2024 est.)
comparison rankings: female 95; male 93; total 93

Nationality: *noun:* Papua New Guinean(s)
adjective: Papua New Guinean

Ethnic groups: Melanesian, Papuan, Negrito, Micronesian, Polynesian

Languages: Tok Pisin (official), English (official), Hiri Motu (official), some 839 living indigenous languages are spoken (about 12% of the world's total)
note: Tok Pisin, a creole language, is widely used and understood; English is spoken by 1%-2%; Hiri Motu is spoken by less than 2%

Religions: Protestant 64.3% (Evangelical Lutheran 18.4%, Seventh Day Adventist 12.9%, Pentecostal 10.4%, United Church 10.3%, Evangelical Alliance 5.9%, Anglican 3.2%, Baptist 2.8%, Salvation Army 0.4%), Roman Catholic 26%, other Christian 5.3%, non-Christian 1.4%, unspecified 3.1% (2011 est.)
note: data represent only the citizen population; roughly 0.3% of the population are non-citizens, consisting of Christian 52% (predominantly Roman Catholic), other 10.7% , none 37.3%

Age structure: *0-14 years:* 37.1% (male 1,902,272/female 1,825,471)
15-64 years: 58.9% (male 2,991,479/female 2,923,410)
65 years and over: 4% (2024 est.) (male 198,511/female 205,090)

Dependency ratios: *total dependency ratio:* 60.5
youth dependency ratio: 55.5
elderly dependency ratio: 5
potential support ratio: 20.1 (2021 est.)

Median age: *total:* 21.7 years (2024 est.)
male: 21.6 years
female: 21.9 years
comparison ranking: total 190

Population growth rate: 2.26% (2024 est.)
comparison ranking: 30

Birth rate: 28.1 births/1,000 population (2024 est.)
comparison ranking: 31

Death rate: 5.4 deaths/1,000 population (2024 est.)
comparison ranking: 186

Net migration rate: 0 migrant(s)/1,000 population (2024 est.)
comparison ranking: 94

Population distribution: population concentrated in the highlands and eastern coastal areas on the island of New Guinea; predominantly a rural distribution with only about one-fifth of the population residing in urban areas

Urbanization: *urban population:* 13.7% of total population (2023)
rate of urbanization: 2.91% annual rate of change (2020-25 est.)

Major urban areas - population: 410,000 PORT MORESBY (capital) (2023)

Sex ratio: *at birth:* 1.05 male(s)/female
0-14 years: 1.04 male(s)/female
15-64 years: 1.02 male(s)/female
65 years and over: 0.97 male(s)/female
total population: 1.03 male(s)/female (2024 est.)

Mother's mean age at first birth: 21.9 years (2016/18)
note: data represents median age a first birth among women 25-49

Maternal mortality ratio: 192 deaths/100,000 live births (2020 est.)
comparison ranking: 47

Infant mortality rate: *total:* 32 deaths/1,000 live births (2024 est.)
male: 35.3 deaths/1,000 live births
female: 28.6 deaths/1,000 live births
comparison ranking: total 43

Life expectancy at birth: *total population:* 70.1 years (2024 est.)
male: 68.3 years
female: 71.9 years
comparison ranking: total population 181

Total fertility rate: 3.79 children born/woman (2024 est.)
comparison ranking: 28

Gross reproduction rate: 1.85 (2024 est.)

Contraceptive prevalence rate: 36.7% (2016/18)

Drinking water source: *improved: urban:* 86.2% of population
rural: 41.5% of population
total: 47.5% of population
unimproved: urban: 13.8% of population
rural: 58.5% of population
total: 52.5% of population (2020 est.)

Current health expenditure: 2.5% of GDP (2020)

Physician density: 0.07 physicians/1,000 population (2019)

Sanitation facility access: *improved: urban:* 57.8% of population
rural: 18.2% of population
total: 23.5% of population
unimproved: urban: 42.2% of population
rural: 81.8% of population
total: 76.5% of population (2020 est.)

Obesity - adult prevalence rate: 21.3% (2016)
comparison ranking: 90

Alcohol consumption per capita: *total:* 1.26 liters of pure alcohol (2019 est.)
beer: 0.6 liters of pure alcohol (2019 est.)
wine: 0.06 liters of pure alcohol (2019 est.)
spirits: 0.6 liters of pure alcohol (2019 est.)
other alcohols: 0 liters of pure alcohol (2019 est.)
comparison ranking: total 144

Tobacco use: *total:* 39.3% (2020 est.)
male: 53.5% (2020 est.)
female: 25.1% (2020 est.)
comparison ranking: total 5

Currently married women (ages 15-49): 65.5% (2023 est.)

Child marriage: *women married by age 15:* 8%
women married by age 18: 27.3%
men married by age 18: 3.7% (2018 est.)

Education expenditures: 1.4% of GDP (2020 est.)
comparison ranking: 193

Literacy: *definition:* age 15 and over can read and write
total population: 64.2%
male: 65.6%
female: 62.8% (2015)

People - note: the indigenous population of Papua New Guinea (PNG) is one of the most heterogeneous in the world; PNG has several thousand separate communities, most with only a few hundred people; divided by language, customs, and tradition, some of these communities have engaged in low-scale tribal conflict with their neighbors for millennia; the advent of modern weapons and modern migrants into urban areas has greatly magnified the impact of this lawlessness

ENVIRONMENT

Environment - current issues: rain forest loss as a result of growing commercial demand for tropical timber; unsustainable logging practices result in soil erosion, water quality degredation, and loss of habitat and biodiversity; large-scale mining projects cause adverse impacts on forests and water quality (discharge of heavy metals, cyanide, and acids into rivers); severe drought; inappropriate farming practices accelerate land degradion (soil erosion, siltation, loss of soil fertility); destructive fishing practices and coastal pollution due to run-off from land-based activities and oil spills

Environment - international agreements: *party to:* Antarctic Treaty, Biodiversity, Climate Change, Climate Change-Kyoto Protocol, Climate Change-Paris Agreement, Desertification, Endangered Species, Environmental Modification, Hazardous Wastes, Law of the Sea, Marine Dumping-London Convention, Nuclear Test Ban, Ozone Layer Protection, Ship Pollution, Tropical Timber 2006, Wetlands
signed, but not ratified: Comprehensive Nuclear Test Ban

Climate: tropical; northwest monsoon (December to March), southeast monsoon (May to October); slight seasonal temperature variation

Urbanization: *urban population:* 13.7% of total population (2023)
rate of urbanization: 2.91% annual rate of change (2020-25 est.)

Revenue from forest resources: 2.08% of GDP (2018 est.)
comparison ranking: 33

Revenue from coal: 0% of GDP (2018 est.)
comparison ranking: 95

Air pollutants: *particulate matter emissions:* 8.89 micrograms per cubic meter (2019 est.)
carbon dioxide emissions: 7.54 megatons (2016 est.)
methane emissions: 11.05 megatons (2020 est.)

Waste and recycling: *municipal solid waste generated annually:* 1 million tons (2014 est.)
municipal solid waste recycled annually: 20,000 tons (2016 est.)
percent of municipal solid waste recycled: 2% (2016 est.)

Major rivers (by length in km): Sepik river source and mouth (shared with Indonesia) - 1,126 km; Fly river source and mouth (shared with Indonesia) - 1,050 km

Total water withdrawal: *municipal:* 220 million cubic meters (2020 est.)
industrial: 170 million cubic meters (2020 est.)
agricultural: 1 million cubic meters (2020 est.)

Total renewable water resources: 801 billion cubic meters (2020 est.)

GOVERNMENT

Country name: *conventional long form:* Independent State of Papua New Guinea
conventional short form: Papua New Guinea
local short form: Papuaniugini
former: German New Guinea, British New Guinea, Territory of Papua and New Guinea
abbreviation: PNG
etymology: the word "papua" derives from the Malay "papuah" describing the frizzy hair of the Melanesians; Spanish explorer Ynigo ORTIZ de RETEZ applied the term "Nueva Guinea" to the island of New Guinea in 1545 after noting the resemblance of the locals to the peoples of the Guinea coast of Africa

Government type: parliamentary democracy under a constitutional monarchy; a Commonwealth realm

Capital: *name:* Port Moresby
geographic coordinates: 9 27 S, 147 11 E
time difference: UTC+10 (15 hours ahead of Washington, DC, during Standard Time)
time zone note: Papua New Guinea has two time zones, including Bougainville (UTC+11)
etymology: named in 1873 by Captain John MORESBY (1830-1922) in honor of his father, British Admiral Sir Fairfax MORESBY (1786-1877)

Administrative divisions: 20 provinces, 1 autonomous region*, and 1 district**; Bougainville*, Central, Chimbu, Eastern Highlands, East New Britain, East Sepik, Enga, Gulf, Hela, Jiwaka, Madang, Manus, Milne Bay, Morobe, National Capital**, New Ireland, Northern, Southern Highlands, Western, Western Highlands, West New Britain, West Sepik

Independence: 16 September 1975 (from the Australia-administered UN trusteeship)

National holiday: Independence Day, 16 September (1975)

Legal system: mixed legal system of English common law and customary law

Constitution: *history:* adopted 15 August 1975, effective at independence 16 September 1975
amendments: proposed by the National Parliament; passage has prescribed majority vote requirements depending on the constitutional sections being amended – absolute majority, two-thirds majority, or three-fourths majority; amended many times, last in 2016

International law organization participation: has not submitted an ICJ jurisdiction declaration; non-party state to the ICCt

Citizenship: *citizenship by birth:* no
citizenship by descent only: at least one parent must be a citizen of Papua New Guinea
dual citizenship recognized: no
residency requirement for naturalization: 8 years

Suffrage: 18 years of age; universal

Executive branch: *chief of state:* King CHARLES III (since 8 September 2022); represented by Governor General Grand Chief Sir Bob DADAE (since 28 February 2017)
head of government: Prime Minister James MARAPE (since 30 May 2019)
cabinet: National Executive Council appointed by the governor general on the recommendation of the prime minister
elections/appointments: the monarchy is hereditary; governor general nominated by the National Parliament and appointed by the chief of state; following legislative elections, the leader of the majority party or majority coalition usually appointed prime minister by the governor general pending the outcome of a National Parliament vote
election results: James MARAPE reelected prime minister; National Parliament vote - 105 out of 118

Legislative branch: *description:* unicameral National Parliament (111 seats; 89 members directly elected from single-seat open constituencies and 22 governors directly elected from 20 provincial constituencies, 1 autonomous region, and 1 district - all by instant runoff preferential vote; members serve 5-year terms)
elections: last held from 4-22 July 2022 (next to be held in June 2027)
election results: percent of vote by party - NA; seats by party - PANGU PATI - 39, PNC - 17, URP - 11, NAP - 6, SDP - 4, PFP - 4, PP – 4, PNGP – 3, ULP - 3, Advance PNG - 2, National Party - 2, Liberal Party - 2, AP - 1, Destiny Party - 1, Greens - 1, MAP - 1, NGP - 1, ODP - 1, PLP - 1, PMC - 1, PPP - 1, PRP - 1, THE - 1, independent - 10; composition - men 108, women 3, percentage women 2.7%

Judicial branch: *highest court(s):* Supreme Court (consists of the chief justice, deputy chief justice, 35 justices, and 5 acting justices); National Courts (consists of 13 courts located in the provincial capitals, with a total of 19 resident judges)
judge selection and term of office: Supreme Court chief justice appointed by the governor general upon advice of the National Executive Council (cabinet) after consultation with the National Justice Administration minister; deputy chief justice and other justices appointed by the Judicial and Legal Services Commission, a 5-member body that includes the Supreme Court chief and deputy chief justices, the chief ombudsman, and a member of the National Parliament; full-time citizen judges appointed for 10-year renewable terms; non-citizen judges initially appointed for 3-year renewable terms and after first renewal can serve until age 70; appointment and tenure of National Court resident judges NA
subordinate courts: district, village, and juvenile courts, military courts, taxation courts, coronial courts, mining warden courts, land courts, traffic courts, committal courts, grade five courts

Political parties: Destiny Party
Liberal Party
Melanesian Alliance Party or MAP
Melanesian Liberal Party or MLP
National Alliance Party or NAP
Our Development Party or ODP
Papua and Niugini Union Party or PANGU PATI
Papua New Guinea Greens Party
Papua New Guinea National Party
Papua New Guinea Party or PNGP
People's First Party or PFP
People's Movement for Change or PMC
People's National Congress Party or PNC
People's National Party
People's Party or PP
People's Progress Party or PPP
People's Reform Party or PRP
PNG Party

Social Democratic Party or SDP
Triumph Heritage Empowerment Party or THE
United Labor Party or ULP
United Resources Party or URP

International organization participation: ACP, ADB, AOSIS, APEC, ARF, ASEAN (observer), C, CD, CP, EITI (candidate country), FAO, G-77, IAEA, IBRD, ICAO, ICRM, IDA, IFAD, IFC, IFRCS, IHO, ILO, IMF, IMO, Interpol, IOC, IOM, IPU, ISO (correspondent), ITSO, ITU, MIGA, NAM, OPCW, PIF, Sparteca, SPC, UN, UNCTAD, UNESCO, UNIDO, UNMISS, UNWTO, UPU, WCO, WFTU (NGOs), WHO, WIPO, WMO, WTO

Diplomatic representation in the US: *chief of mission:* Ambassador (vacant); Chargé d'Affaires Cephas KAYO (since 31 January 2018)
chancery: 1825 K Street NW, Suite 1010, Washington, DC 20006
telephone: [1] (202) 745-3680
FAX: [1] (202) 745-3679
email address and website:
info@pngembassy.org
http://www.pngembassy.org/

Diplomatic representation from the US: *chief of mission:* Ambassador Ann Marie YASTISHOCK (since 22 February 2024); note - also accredited to the Solomon Islands and Vanuatu
embassy: Harbour City Road, Konedobu, Port Moresby, NCD, Papua New Guinea
mailing address: 4240 Port Moresby Pl, Washington DC 20521-4240
telephone: [675] 308-9100
email address and website:
ConsularPortMoresby@state.gov
https://pg.usembassy.gov/

Flag description: divided diagonally from upper hoist-side corner; the upper triangle is red with a soaring yellow bird of paradise centered; the lower triangle is black with five, white, five-pointed stars of the Southern Cross constellation centered; red, black, and yellow are traditional colors of Papua New Guinea; the bird of paradise - endemic to the island of New Guinea - is an emblem of regional tribal culture and represents the emergence of Papua New Guinea as a nation; the Southern Cross, visible in the night sky, symbolizes Papua New Guinea's connection with Australia and several other countries in the South Pacific

National symbol(s): bird of paradise; national colors: red, black

National anthem: *name:* "O Arise All You Sons"
lyrics/music: Thomas SHACKLADY
note: adopted 1975

National heritage: *total World Heritage Sites:* 1 (cultural)
selected World Heritage Site locales: Kuk Early Agricultural Site

ECONOMY

Economic overview: lower middle-income Pacific island economy; primarily informal agrarian sector; natural resource-rich; key liquified natural gas exporter; growing young workforce; slow post-pandemic recovery; increasingly impoverished citizenry; sustainable inflation

Real GDP (purchasing power parity): $42.9 billion (2023 est.)
$41.779 billion (2022 est.)
$39.728 billion (2021 est.)
note: data in 2021 dollars
comparison ranking: 134

Real GDP growth rate: 2.68% (2023 est.)
5.17% (2022 est.)
-0.78% (2021 est.)
note: annual GDP % growth based on constant local currency
comparison ranking: 119

Real GDP per capita: $4,200 (2023 est.)
$4,100 (2022 est.)
$4,000 (2021 est.)
note: data in 2021 dollars
comparison ranking: 184

GDP (official exchange rate): $30.932 billion (2023 est.)
note: data in current dollars at official exchange rate

Inflation rate (consumer prices): 2.3% (2023 est.)
5.25% (2022 est.)
4.48% (2021 est.)
note: annual % change based on consumer prices
comparison ranking: 46

Credit ratings: Moody's rating: B2 (2016)

Standard & Poors rating: B- (2020)
note: The year refers to the year in which the current credit rating was first obtained.

GDP - composition, by sector of origin: *agriculture:* 16.9% (2022 est.)
industry: 40.3% (2022 est.)
services: 39% (2022 est.)
note: figures may not total 100% due to non-allocated consumption not captured in sector-reported data
comparison rankings: services 196; industry 27; agriculture 47

GDP - composition, by end use: *household consumption:* 43.7% (2017 est.)
government consumption: 19.7% (2017 est.)
investment in fixed capital: 10% (2017 est.)
investment in inventories: 0.4% (2017 est.)
exports of goods and services: 49.3% (2017 est.)
imports of goods and services: -22.3% (2017 est.)

Agricultural products: oil palm fruit, coconuts, bananas, fruits, sweet potatoes, game meat, yams, root vegetables, sugarcane, vegetables (2022)
note: top ten agricultural products based on tonnage

Industries: oil and gas; mining (gold, copper, and nickel); palm oil processing; plywood and wood chip production; copra crushing; construction; tourism; fishing; livestock (pork, poultry, cattle) and dairy farming; spice products (turmeric, vanilla, ginger, cardamom, chili, pepper, citronella, and nutmeg)

Industrial production growth rate: 6.61% (2022 est.)
note: annual % change in industrial value added based on constant local currency
comparison ranking: 36

Labor force: 3.229 million (2023 est.)
note: number of people ages 15 or older who are employed or seeking work
comparison ranking: 103

Unemployment rate: 2.65% (2023 est.)
2.69% (2022 est.)
2.91% (2021 est.)
note: % of labor force seeking employment
comparison ranking: 33

Youth unemployment rate (ages 15-24): *total:* 3.7% (2023 est.)
male: 4.5% (2023 est.)
female: 2.9% (2023 est.)
note: % of labor force ages 15-24 seeking employment
comparison ranking: total 188

Remittances: 0.01% of GDP (2023 est.)
0.01% of GDP (2022 est.)
0.05% of GDP (2021 est.)
note: personal transfers and compensation between resident and non-resident individuals/households/entities

Budget: *revenues:* $5.268 billion (2022 est.)
expenditures: $6.156 billion (2022 est.)
note: central government revenues and expenses (excluding grants/extrabudgetary units/social security funds) converted to US dollars at average official exchange rate for year indicated

Public debt: 48.26% of GDP (2022 est.)
note: central government debt as a % of GDP
comparison ranking: 111

Taxes and other revenues: 14.79% (of GDP) (2022 est.)
note: central government tax revenue as a % of GDP
comparison ranking: 142

Current account balance: $4.499 billion (2021 est.)
$3.419 billion (2020 est.)
$3.559 billion (2019 est.)
note: balance of payments - net trade and primary/secondary income in current dollars
comparison ranking: 36

Exports: $11.625 billion (2021 est.)
$9.175 billion (2020 est.)
$11.236 billion (2019 est.)
note: balance of payments - exports of goods and services in current dollars
comparison ranking: 110

Exports - partners: Japan 26%, China 22%, Australia 11%, South Korea 10%, Taiwan 9% (2022)
note: top five export partners based on percentage share of exports

Exports - commodities: natural gas, gold, palm oil, crude petroleum, copper ore (2022)
note: top five export commodities based on value in dollars

Imports: $6.303 billion (2021 est.)
$5.282 billion (2020 est.)
$6.329 billion (2019 est.)
note: balance of payments - imports of goods and services in current dollars
comparison ranking: 140

Imports - partners: China 26%, Australia 23%, Singapore 16%, Malaysia 9%, Indonesia 4% (2022)
note: top five import partners based on percentage share of imports

Imports - commodities: refined petroleum, rice, plastic products, excavation machinery, trucks (2022)
note: top five import commodities based on value in dollars

Reserves of foreign exchange and gold: $3.983 billion (2022 est.)
$3.24 billion (2021 est.)
$2.686 billion (2020 est.)
note: holdings of gold (year-end prices)/foreign exchange/special drawing rights in current dollars
comparison ranking: 121

Debt - external: $6.35 billion (2022 est.)
note: present value of external debt in current US dollars
comparison ranking: 46

Exchange rates: kina (PGK) per US dollar -

Exchange rates: 3.519 (2022 est.)
3.509 (2021 est.)

3.46 (2020 est.)
3.388 (2019 est.)
3.293 (2018 est.)

ENERGY

Electricity access: *electrification - total population:* 19% (2022 est.)
electrification - urban areas: 65.1%
electrification - rural areas: 14.2%

Electricity: *installed generating capacity:* 1.263 million kW (2022 est.)
consumption: 4.524 billion kWh (2022 est.)
transmission/distribution losses: 318.563 million kWh (2022 est.)
comparison rankings: transmission/distribution losses 71; consumption 132; installed generating capacity 131

Electricity generation sources: *fossil fuels:* 74.8% of total installed capacity (2022 est.)
solar: 0.1% of total installed capacity (2022 est.)
hydroelectricity: 16.5% of total installed capacity (2022 est.)
geothermal: 8.3% of total installed capacity (2022 est.)
biomass and waste: 0.3% of total installed capacity (2022 est.)

Coal: *imports:* 9,000 metric tons (2022 est.)

Petroleum: *total petroleum production:* 32,000 bbl/day (2023 est.)
refined petroleum consumption: 27,000 bbl/day (2022 est.)
crude oil estimated reserves: 159.656 million barrels (2021 est.)

Natural gas: *production:* 10.837 billion cubic meters (2022 est.)
consumption: 166.98 million cubic meters (2022 est.)
exports: 10.67 billion cubic meters (2022 est.)
proven reserves: 183.125 billion cubic meters (2021 est.)

Carbon dioxide emissions: 4.375 million metric tonnes of CO2 (2022 est.)
from petroleum and other liquids: 4.048 million metric tonnes of CO2 (2022 est.)
from consumed natural gas: 328,000 metric tonnes of CO2 (2022 est.)
comparison ranking: total emissions 138

Energy consumption per capita: 6.565 million Btu/person (2022 est.)
comparison ranking: 161

COMMUNICATIONS

Telephones - fixed lines: *total subscriptions:* 166,000 (2021 est.)
subscriptions per 100 inhabitants: 2 (2021 est.)
comparison ranking: total subscriptions 124

Telephones - mobile cellular: *total subscriptions:* 4.818 million (2021 est.)
subscriptions per 100 inhabitants: 48 (2021 est.)
comparison ranking: total subscriptions 126

Telecommunication systems: *general assessment:* fixed-line teledensity in Papua New Guinea has seen little change over the past two decades; progress in the country's telecom sector has come primarily from mobile networks, where accessibility has expanded considerably in recent years, with population coverage increasing from less than 3% in 2006 to more than 90% by early 2021; the MNOs operate networks offering services based on GSM, 3G, and 4G, depending on location; GSM is prevalent in many rural and remote areas, while 3G and 4G are centered more on urban areas; MNOs' investments in 4G are growing, though GSM still represents the bulk of all mobile connections owing to the low penetration of smartphones and the concentration of high-speed data networks predominantly in high value urban areas; a lack of sufficient competition and investment in the wire line segment has driven up prices and hampered network coverage and quality; infrastructure deployment costs are high, partly due to the relatively low subscriber base, the difficult terrain, and the high proportion of the population living in rural areas; fixed telecom infrastructure is almost non-existent outside urban centers, leaving most of the population under served; PNG is the Pacific region's largest poorly developed telecom market, with only around 22% of its people connected to the internet; this falls far behind the recommended targets set in the country's draft National Broadband Policy, which aimed to provide universal mobile broadband access; low international capacity has meant that internet services are slow and unreliable; two subsea cables connect PNG to Australia (landing at Sydney) and the United States (Guam); despite the improvement in recent years, the country is still impacted by a connectivity infrastructure deficit, making it reliant on more expensive alternatives such as satellites, also weighing on the affordability of services for end-users; the government granted a license to Starlink at the beginning of 2024, which should improve digital access in rural areas (2023)
domestic: fixed-line nearly 2 per 100 and mobile-cellular is 48 per 100 persons (2021)
international: country code - 675; landing points for the Kumul Domestic Submarine Cable System, PNG-LNG, APNG-2, CSCS the PPC-1 submarine cables to Australia, Guam, PNG and Solomon Islands; and CS2 to PNG, Solomon Islands, and Australia; satellite earth station - 1 Intelsat (Pacific Ocean) (2023)

Broadcast media: *5 TV stations:* 1 commercial station (TV Wan), 2 state-run stations, (National Broadcasting Corporation and EMTV - formerly a commercial TV station previously owned by Fiji Television Limited but PNG's Telikom purchased it in Jan 2016, hence being state-run); 1 digital free-to-view network launched in 2014, and 1 satellite network Click TV (PNGTV) launched in 2015; the state-run NBC operates 3 radio networks with multiple repeaters and about 20 provincial stations; several commercial radio stations with multiple transmission points as well as several community stations; transmissions of several international broadcasters are accessible (2023)

Internet country code: .pg

Internet users: *total:* 3.168 million (2021 est.)
percent of population: 32% (2021 est.)
comparison ranking: total 116

Broadband - fixed subscriptions: *total:* 21,000 (2020 est.)
subscriptions per 100 inhabitants: 0.2 (2020 est.)
comparison ranking: total 165

TRANSPORTATION

National air transport system: *number of registered air carriers:* 6 (2020)
inventory of registered aircraft operated by air carriers: 48
annual passenger traffic on registered air carriers: 964,713 (2018)
annual freight traffic on registered air carriers: 30.93 million (2018) mt-km

Civil aircraft registration country code prefix: P2

Airports: 535 (2024)
comparison ranking: 14

Heliports: 3 (2024)

Pipelines: 264 km oil (2013)

Roadways: *total:* 24,862 km
paved: 2,647 km
unpaved: 22,215 km (2015)
comparison ranking: total 108

Waterways: 11,000 km (2011)
comparison ranking: 14

Merchant marine: *total:* 205 (2023)
by type: container ship 6, general cargo 89, oil tanker 4, other 106
comparison ranking: total 65

Ports: *total ports:* 22 (2024)
large: 0
medium: 0
small: 6
very small: 16
ports with oil terminals: 8
key ports: Kavieng Harbor, Kieta, Port Moresby, Rabaul, Vanimo, Wewak Harbor

MILITARY AND SECURITY

Military and security forces: Papua New Guinea Defense Force (PNGDF): Land Element, Maritime Element, Air Element

Ministry of Internal Security: Royal Papua New Guinea Constabulary (RPNGC) (2024)

Military expenditures: 0.3% of GDP (2023 est.)
0.3% of GDP (2022 est.)
0.4% of GDP (2021 est.)
0.4% of GDP (2020 est.)
0.3% of GDP (2019 est.)
comparison ranking: 164

Military and security service personnel strengths: approximately 2,500 active-duty PNGDF troops (2023)

Military equipment inventories and acquisitions: the PNGDF is lightly armed; the Land Force has no heavy weapons while the Air and the Maritime forces have a handful of light aircraft and small patrol boats provided by Australia (2024)

Military service age and obligation: 18-27 for voluntary military service for men and women; no conscription (2024)

Military - note: the Papua New Guinea Defense Force (PNGDF) is a small and lightly armed force tasked with defense of the country and its territories against external attack, as well as internal security and socio-economic development duties; following some inter-tribal violence in Wapenamanda in early 2024, the PNGDF was given arrest powers
the PNGDF was established in 1973, and its primary combat unit, the Royal Pacific Islands Regiment (RPIR), is descended from Australian Army infantry battalions comprised of native soldiers and led by Australian officers and non-commissioned officers formed during World War II to help fight the Japanese; the RPIR was disbanded after the war, but reestablished in 1951 as part of the Australian Army where it continued to serve until Papua New Guinea

(PNG) gained its independence in 1975, when it became part of the PNGDF
PNG's security partners include Australia, France, Indonesia, New Zealand, the UK, and the US; the US and PNG signed a defense cooperation agreement in 2023, which included a shiprider agreement that provides the opportunity for PNG personnel to work on US Coast Guard and US Navy vessels, and vice versa, to tackle maritime crime such as illegal fishing; the agreement also allowed the US military to develop and operate out of bases in PNG with the PNG Government's approval (2024)

TRANSNATIONAL ISSUES

Refugees and internally displaced persons: *refugees (country of origin):* 11,432 (Indonesia) (mid-year 2022)
IDPs: 91,000 (tribal conflict, inter-communal violence) (2022)
stateless persons: 15 (2022)

Trafficking in persons: tier rating: Tier 3 — Papua New Guinea does not fully meet the minimum standards for the elimination of trafficking and is not making significant efforts to do so; therefore, Papua New Guinea remained on Tier 3; for more details, go to: https://www.state.gov/reports/2024-trafficking-in-persons-report/papua-new-guinea/

Illicit drugs: transit point for smuggling drugs such as methamphetamine and cocaine; major consumer of cannabis

PARACEL ISLANDS

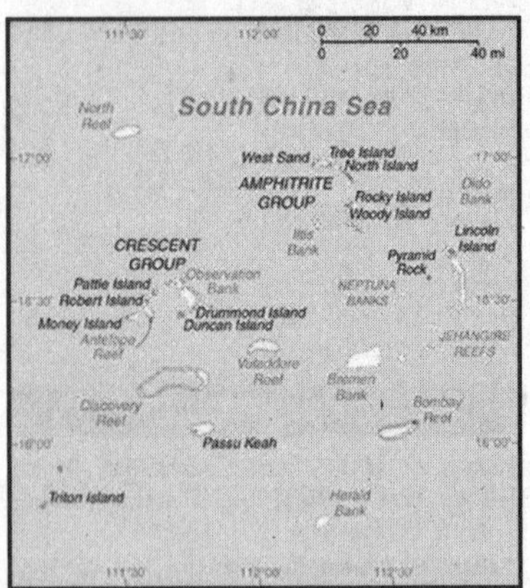

INTRODUCTION

Background: The Paracel Islands are surrounded by productive fishing grounds and potential oil and gas reserves. In 1932, French Indochina annexed the islands and set up a weather station on Pattle Island. China has occupied all the Paracel Islands since 1974, when its troops seized a South Vietnamese garrison occupying the western islands. China has built a military installation on Woody Island with an airfield and artificial harbor, and it has scattered garrisons on some of the other islands. Taiwan and Vietnam also claim the Paracel Islands.

GEOGRAPHY

Location: Southeastern Asia, group of small islands and reefs in the South China Sea, about one-third of the way from central Vietnam to the northern Philippines

Geographic coordinates: 16 30 N, 112 00 E

Map references: Southeast Asia

Area: *total:* 8 sq km ca.
land: 7.75 sq km ca.
water: 0 sq km
comparison ranking: total 242

Area - comparative: land area is about 13 times the size of the National Mall in Washington, DC

Land boundaries: *total:* 0 km

Coastline: 518 km

Climate: tropical

Terrain: mostly low and flat

Elevation: *highest point:* unnamed location on Rocky Island 14 m
lowest point: South China Sea 0 m

Natural resources: none

Land use: *other:* 100% (2018 est.)

Irrigated land: 0 sq km (2022)

Population distribution: a population of over 1,000 Chinese resides on Woody Island, the largest of the Paracels; there are scattered Chinese garrisons on some other islands

Natural hazards: typhoons

Geography - note: composed of 130 small coral islands and reefs divided into the northeast Amphitrite Group and the western Crescent Group

PEOPLE AND SOCIETY

Population: *total:* 1,440 (July 2014 est.)
note: Chinese activity has increased in recent years, particularly on Woody Island, where the population exceeds 1,000; some other islands have scattered Chinese garrisons comparison ranking: total 234

Population growth rate: 0.75% (2021 est.)
comparison ranking: 118

Net migration rate: -0.66 migrant(s)/1,000 population (2021 est.)
comparison ranking: 130

Population distribution: a population of over 1,000 Chinese resides on Woody Island, the largest of the Paracels; there are scattered Chinese garrisons on some other islands

ENVIRONMENT

Environment - current issues: China's use of dredged sand and coral to build artificial islands harms reef systems; ongoing human activities, including military operations, infrastructure construction, and tourism endangers local ecosystem including birds, fish, marine mammals, and marine reptiles

Climate: tropical

GOVERNMENT

Country name: *conventional long form:* none
conventional short form: Paracel Islands
etymology: Portuguese navigators began to refer to the "Ilhas do Pracel" in the 16th century as a designation of low lying islets, sandbanks, and reefs scattered over a wide area; over time the name changed to "parcel" and then "paracel"

MILITARY AND SECURITY

Military - note: occupied by China, which is assessed to maintain 20 outposts in the Paracels (Antelope, Bombay, and North reefs; Drummond, Duncan, Lincoln, Middle, Money, North, Pattle, Quanfu, Robert, South, Tree, Triton, Woody, and Yagong islands; South Sand and West Sand; Observation Bank); the outposts range in size from one or two buildings to bases with significant military infrastructure; Woody Island is the main base in the Paracels and includes an airstrip with fighter aircraft hangers, naval facilities, surveillance radars, and defenses such as surface-to-air missiles and anti-ship cruise missiles; combat aircraft have deployed to the island (2024)

PARAGUAY

INTRODUCTION

Background: Several Indigenous groups, principally belonging to the Guarani language family, inhabited the area of modern Paraguay before the arrival of the Spanish in the early 16th century, when the territory was incorporated into the Viceroyalty of Peru. Paraguay achieved its independence from Spain in 1811 with the help of neighboring states. In the aftermath of independence, a series of military dictators ruled the country until 1870. During the disastrous War of the Triple Alliance (1864-70) – fought against Argentina, Brazil, and Uruguay – Paraguay lost two thirds of its adult males and much of its territory. The country stagnated economically for the next half-century and experienced a tumultuous series of political regimes. Following the Chaco War of 1932-35 with Bolivia, Paraguay gained a large part of the Chaco lowland region. The 35-year military dictatorship of Alfredo STROESSNER ended in 1989, and Paraguay has held relatively free and regular presidential elections since the country's return to democracy.

GEOGRAPHY

Location: Central South America, northeast of Argentina, southwest of Brazil

Geographic coordinates: 23 00 S, 58 00 W

Map references: South America

Area: *total:* 406,752 sq km
land: 397,302 sq km
water: 9,450 sq km
comparison ranking: total 61

Area - comparative: about three times the size of New York state; slightly smaller than California

Land boundaries: *total:* 4,655 km
border countries (3): Argentina 2,531 km; Bolivia 753 km; Brazil 1,371 km

Coastline: 0 km (landlocked)

Maritime claims: none (landlocked)

Climate: subtropical to temperate; substantial rainfall in the eastern portions, becoming semiarid in the far west

Terrain: grassy plains and wooded hills east of Rio Paraguay; Gran Chaco region west of Rio Paraguay mostly low, marshy plain near the river, and dry forest and thorny scrub elsewhere

Elevation: *highest point:* Cerro Pero 842 m
lowest point: junction of Río Paraguay and Río Paraná 46 m
mean elevation: 178 m

Natural resources: hydropower, timber, iron ore, manganese, limestone

Land use: *agricultural land:* 53.8% (2018 est.)
arable land: 10.8% (2018 est.)
permanent crops: 0.2% (2018 est.)
permanent pasture: 42:8% (2018 est.)
forest: 43.8% (2018 est.)
other: 2.4% (2018 est.)

Irrigated land: 1,362 sq km (2012)

Major rivers (by length in km): Río de la Plata/Paraná (shared with Brazil [s], Argentina, and Uruguay [m]) - 4,880 km; Paraguay river mouth (shared with Brazil [s] and Argentina) - 2,549 km
note – [s] after country name indicates river source; [m] after country name indicates river mouth

Major watersheds (area sq km): Atlantic Ocean drainage: Paraná (2,582,704 sq km)

Major aquifers: Guarani Aquifer System

Population distribution: most of the population resides in the eastern half of the country; to the west lies the Gran Chaco (a semi-arid lowland plain), which accounts for 60% of the land territory, but only 2% of the overall population

Natural hazards: local flooding in southeast (early September to June); poorly drained plains may become boggy (early October to June)

Geography - note: *note 1:* landlocked; lies between Argentina, Bolivia, and Brazil; population concentrated in eastern and southern part of country
note 2: pineapples are probably indigenous to the southern Brazil-Paraguay region

PEOPLE AND SOCIETY

Population: *total:* 7,522,549
male: 3,769,376
female: 3,753,173 (2024 est.)
comparison rankings: female 104; male 104; total 104

Nationality: *noun:* Paraguayan(s)
adjective: Paraguayan

Ethnic groups: Mestizo (mixed Spanish and Indigenous ancestry) 95%, other 5%

Languages: Spanish (official) and Guarani (official) 46.3%, only Guarani 34%, only Spanish 15.2%, other (includes Portuguese, German, other Indigenous languages) 4.1%, no response 0.4% (2012 est.)
major-language sample(s):
La Libreta Informativa del Mundo, la fuente indispensable de información básica. (Spanish)
note: data represent predominant household language

Religions: Roman Catholic 80.4%, Protestant 7% (Evangelical (non-specific) 6.7%, Evangelical Pentecostal <0.1%, Adventist <0.1%, Protestant (non-specific) <0.1%), Believer (not belonging to the church) 5.7%, other 0.6%, agnostic <0.1%, none 0.2%, unspecified 6.2% (2023 est.)

Demographic profile: Paraguay falls below the Latin American average in several socioeconomic categories, including immunization rates, potable water, sanitation, and secondary school enrollment, and has greater rates of income inequality and child and maternal mortality. Paraguay's poverty rate has declined in recent years but remains high, especially in rural areas, with more than a third of the population below the poverty line. However, the well-being of the poor in many regions has improved in terms of housing quality and access to clean water, telephone service, and electricity. The fertility rate continues to drop, declining sharply from an average 4.3 births per woman in the late 1990s to about 2 in 2013, as a result of the greater educational attainment of women, increased use of contraception, and a desire for smaller families among young women.

Paraguay is a country of emigration; it has not attracted large numbers of immigrants because of political instability, civil wars, years of dictatorship, and the greater appeal of neighboring countries. Paraguay first tried to encourage immigration in 1870 in order to rebound from the heavy death toll it suffered during the War of the Triple Alliance, but it received few European and Middle Eastern immigrants. In the 20th century, limited numbers of immigrants arrived from Lebanon, Japan, South Korea, and China, as well as Mennonites from Canada, Russia, and Mexico. Large flows of Brazilian immigrants have been arriving since the 1960s, mainly to work in agriculture. Paraguayans continue to emigrate to Argentina, Brazil, Uruguay, the United States, Italy, Spain, and France.

Age structure: *0-14 years:* 22.2% (male 850,191/ female 821,237)
15-64 years: 68.4% (male 2,582,021/female 2,561,962)
65 years and over: 9.4% (2024 est.) (male 337,164/ female 369,974)

Dependency ratios: *total dependency ratio:* 54.4
youth dependency ratio: 44.8
elderly dependency ratio: 9.6
potential support ratio: 10.4 (2021 est.)

Median age: *total:* 31.8 years (2024 est.)
male: 31.6 years
female: 32 years
comparison ranking: total 123

Population growth rate: 1.09% (2024 est.)
comparison ranking: 86

Birth rate: births/1,000 population (2024 est.)
comparison ranking: 100

Death rate: 4.9 deaths/1,000 population (2024 est.)
comparison ranking: 196

Net migration rate: -0.1 migrant(s)/1,000 population (2024 est.)
comparison ranking: 95

Population distribution: most of the population resides in the eastern half of the country; to the west lies the Gran Chaco (a semi-arid lowland plain), which accounts for 60% of the land territory, but only 2% of the overall population

Urbanization: *urban population:* 63.1% of total population (2023)
rate of urbanization: 1.64% annual rate of change (2020-25 est.)

Major urban areas - population: 3.511 million ASUNCION (capital) (2023)

Sex ratio: *at birth:* 1.05 male(s)/female

0-14 years: 1.04 male(s)/female
15-64 years: 1.01 male(s)/female
65 years and over: 0.91 male(s)/female
total population: 1 male(s)/female (2024 est.)

Mother's mean age at first birth: 22.9 years (2008 est.)
note: data represents median age at first birth among women 25-29

Maternal mortality ratio: 71 deaths/100,000 live births (2020 est.)
comparison ranking: 87

Infant mortality rate: *total:* 22 deaths/1,000 live births (2024 est.)
male: 26.1 deaths/1,000 live births
female: 17.7 deaths/1,000 live births
comparison ranking: total 70

Life expectancy at birth: *total population:* 78.8 years (2024 est.)
male: 76.2 years
female: 81.6 years
comparison ranking: total population 73

Total fertility rate: 1.88 children born/woman (2024 est.)
comparison ranking: 126

Gross reproduction rate: 0.92 (2024 est.)

Contraceptive prevalence rate: 68.4% (2016)

Drinking water source: *improved: urban:* 100% of population
rural: 100% of population
total: 100% of population

Current health expenditure: 7.6% of GDP (2020)

Physician density: 1.05 physicians/1,000 population (2020)

Hospital bed density: 0.8 beds/1,000 population (2016)

Sanitation facility access: *improved: urban:* 99.6% of population
rural: 90.6% of population
total: 96.2% of population
unimproved: urban: 0.4% of population
rural: 9.4% of population
total: 3.8% of population (2020 est.)

Obesity - adult prevalence rate: 20.3% (2016)
comparison ranking: 100

Alcohol consumption per capita: *total:* 5.47 liters of pure alcohol (2019 est.)
beer: 3.27 liters of pure alcohol (2019 est.)
wine: 0.59 liters of pure alcohol (2019 est.)
spirits: 1.59 liters of pure alcohol (2019 est.)
other alcohols: 0.03 liters of pure alcohol (2019 est.)
comparison ranking: total 79

Tobacco use: *total:* 11.5% (2020 est.)
male: 18.6% (2020 est.)
female: 4.4% (2020 est.)
comparison ranking: total 126

Children under the age of 5 years underweight: 1.3% (2016)
comparison ranking: 115

Currently married women (ages 15-49): 59.4% (2023 est.)

Child marriage: *women married by age 15:* 3.6%
women married by age 18: 21.6% (2016 est.)

Education expenditures: 3.3% of GDP (2020 est.)
comparison ranking: 147

Literacy: *definition:* age 15 and over can read and write
total population: 94.5%
male: 94.9%
female: 94.2% (2020)

ENVIRONMENT

Environment - current issues: deforestation; water pollution; rivers suffer from toxic dumping; tanneries release mercury and chromium into rivers and streams; loss of wetlands; inadequate means for waste disposal pose health risks for many urban residents

Environment - international agreements: *party to:* Biodiversity, Climate Change, Climate Change-Kyoto Protocol, Climate Change-Paris Agreement, Comprehensive Nuclear Test Ban, Desertification, Endangered Species, Hazardous Wastes, Law of the Sea, Ozone Layer Protection, Wetlands
signed, but not ratified: Nuclear Test Ban, Tropical Timber 2006

Climate: subtropical to temperate; substantial rainfall in the eastern portions, becoming semiarid in the far west

Urbanization: *urban population:* 63.1% of total population (2023)
rate of urbanization: 1.64% annual rate of change (2020-25 est.)

Revenue from forest resources: 1.21% of GDP (2018 est.)
comparison ranking: 50

Revenue from coal: 0% of GDP (2018 est.)
comparison ranking: 109

Air pollutants: *particulate matter emissions:* 12.31 micrograms per cubic meter (2019 est.)
carbon dioxide emissions: 7.41 megatons (2016 est.)
methane emissions: 27.65 megatons (2020 est.)

Waste and recycling: *municipal solid waste generated annually:* 1,818,501 tons (2015 est.)

Major rivers (by length in km): Río de la Plata/Paraná (shared with Brazil [s], Argentina, and Uruguay [m]) - 4,880 km; Paraguay river mouth (shared with Brazil [s] and Argentina) - 2,549 km
note – [s] after country name indicates river source; [m] after country name indicates river mouth

Major watersheds (area sq km): Atlantic Ocean drainage: Paraná (2,582,704 sq km)

Major aquifers: Guarani Aquifer System

Total water withdrawal: *municipal:* 360 million cubic meters (2020 est.)
industrial: 150 million cubic meters (2020 est.)
agricultural: 1.9 billion cubic meters (2020 est.)

Total renewable water resources: 387.77 billion cubic meters (2020 est.)

GOVERNMENT

Country name: *conventional long form:* Republic of Paraguay
conventional short form: Paraguay
local long form: República del Paraguay
local short form: Paraguay
etymology: the precise meaning of the name Paraguay is unclear, but it seems to derive from the river of the same name; one explanation has the name meaning "water of the Payagua" (an indigenous tribe that lived along the river)

Government type: presidential republic

Capital: *name:* Asunción
geographic coordinates: 25 16 S, 57 40 W
time difference: UTC-4 (1 hour ahead of Washington, DC, during Standard Time)
daylight saving time: +1hr, begins first Sunday in October; ends last Sunday in March
etymology: the name means "assumption" and derives from the original name given to the city at its founding in 1537, Nuestra Senora Santa Maria de la Asuncion (Our Lady Saint Mary of the Assumption)

Administrative divisions: 17 departments (departamentos, singular - departamento) and 1 capital city*; Alto Paraguay, Alto Parana, Amambay, Asuncion*, Boqueron, Caaguazu, Caazapa, Canindeyu, Central, Concepcion, Cordillera, Guaira, Itapua, Misiones, Neembucu, Paraguari, Presidente Hayes, San Pedro

Independence: 14-15 May 1811 (from Spain); note - the uprising against Spanish authorities took place during the night of 14-15 May 1811 and both days are celebrated in Paraguay

National holiday: Independence Day, 14-15 May (1811) (observed 15 May); 14 May is celebrated as Flag Day

Legal system: civil law system with influences from Argentine, Spanish, Roman, and French civil law models; judicial review of legislative acts in Supreme Court of Justice

Constitution: *history:* several previous; latest approved and promulgated 20 June 1992
amendments: proposed at the initiative of at least one quarter of either chamber of the National Congress, by the president of the republic, or by petition of at least 30,000 voters; passage requires a two-thirds majority vote by both chambers and approval in a referendum; amended 2011

International law organization participation: accepts compulsory ICJ jurisdiction; accepts ICCt jurisdiction

Citizenship: *citizenship by birth:* yes
citizenship by descent only: at least one parent must be a native-born citizen of Paraguay
dual citizenship recognized: yes
residency requirement for naturalization: 3 years

Suffrage: 18 years of age; universal and compulsory until the age of 75

Executive branch: *chief of state:* President Santiago PEÑA Palacios (since 15 August 2023)
head of government: President Santiago PEÑA Palacios (since 15 August 2023)
cabinet: Council of Ministers appointed by the president
elections/appointments: president and vice president directly elected on the same ballot by simple majority popular vote for a single 5-year term; election last held on 30 April 2023 (next to be held in April 2028)
election results:
2023: Santiago PEÑA Palacios elected president; percent of vote - Santiago PEÑA Palacios (ANR) 43.9%, Efraín ALEGRE (PLRA) 28.3%, Paraguayo "Payo" CUBAS Colomés (PCN) 23.6%, other 4.2%
2018: Mario ABDO BENÍTEZ elected president; percent of vote - Mario ABDO BENÍTEZ (ANR) 49%, Efraín ALEGRE (PLRA) 45.1%, other 5.9%
note: the president is both chief of state and head of government

Legislative branch: *description:* bicameral National Congress or Congreso Nacional consists of:
Chamber of Senators or Camara de Senadores (45 seats; members directly elected in a single nationwide constituency by closed-list proportional representation vote to serve 5-year terms)
Chamber of Deputies or Camara de Diputados (80 seats; members directly elected in 18 multi-seat

constituencies - corresponding to the country's 17 departments and capital city - by closed-list proportional representation vote to serve 5-year terms)
elections: Chamber of Senators - last held on 30 April 2023 (next to be held in April 2028)
Chamber of Deputies - last held on 30 April 2023 (next to be held in April 2028)
election results: Chamber of Senators - percent of vote by party/coalition - ANR 45.7%, PLRA 24.4%, PCN 11.5%, PEN 5.2%, PPQ 2.5%, other 10.7%; seats by party/coalition - ANR 23, PLRA 12, PCN 5, PEN 2, PPQ 1, other 2; composition - men 34, women 11, percentage women 24.4%
Chamber of Deputies - percent of vote by party/coalition - ANR 44%, PLRA 30.9%, PCN 8.3%, PPQ 3.6%, PEN 2.9%; other 10.3%; seats by party/coalition - ANR 49, PLRA 21, PCN 4, PEN 2, PPQ 1, other 3; compositio - men 61, women 19, percentage women 23.8%; note - total National Congress percentage women NA%

Judicial branch: *highest court(s):* Supreme Court of Justice or Corte Suprema de Justicia (consists of 9 justices divided 3 each into the Constitutional Court, Civil and Commercial Chamber, and Criminal Division)
judge selection and term of office: justices proposed by the Council of Magistrates or Consejo de la Magistratura, a 6- member independent body, and appointed by the Chamber of Senators with presidential concurrence; judges can serve until mandatory retirement at age 75
subordinate courts: appellate courts; first instance courts; minor courts, including justices of the peace

Political parties: Asociacion Nacional Republicana (National Republican Association) - Colorado Party or ANR
Avanza Pais coalition or AP
Frente Guasu (Broad Front coalition) or FG
GANAR Alliance (Great Renewed National Alliance) (alliance between PLRA and Guasú Front)
Movimiento Hagamos or MH
Movimiento Union Nacional de Ciudadanos Eticos (National Union of Ethical Citizens) or UNACE
Partido Cruzada Nacional (National Crusade Party) or PCN; note - formerly Movimiento Cruzada Nacional
Partido del Movimiento al Socialismo or P-MAS
Partido Democratica Progresista (Progressive Democratic Party) or PDP
Partido Encuentro Nacional or PEN
Partido Liberal Radical Autentico (Authentic Radical Liberal Party) or PLRA
Partido Pais Solidario or PPS
Partido Popular Tekojoja or PPT
Patria Querida (Beloved Fatherland Party) or PPQ

International organization participation: CAN (associate), CD, CELAC, FAO, G-11, G-77, IADB, IAEA, IBRD, ICAO, ICC (national committees), ICCt, ICRM, IDA, IFAD, IFC, IFRCS, ILO, IMF, IMO, Interpol, IOC, IOM, IPU, ISO (correspondent), ITSO, ITU, ITUC (NGOs), LAES, LAIA, Mercosur, MIGA, MINURSO, MINUSTAH, MONUSCO, NAM (observer), OAS, OPANAL, OPCW, Pacific Alliance (observer), PCA, PROSUR, UN, UNASUR, UNCTAD, UNESCO, UNFICYP, UNHRC, UNIDO, Union Latina, UNISFA, UNMIL, UNMISS, UNOCI, UNWTO, UPU, WCO, WHO, WIPO, WMO, WTO

Diplomatic representation in the US: *chief of mission:* Ambassador José Antonio DOS SANTOS BEDOYA (since 15 September 2021)
chancery: 2209 Massachusetts Avenue, NW, Washington DC 20008
telephone: [1] (202) 483-6960
FAX: [1] (202) 234-4508
email address and website:
gabineteembaparusa@mre.gov.py
Embajada de la República del Paraguay ante los Estados Unidos de América: The Embassy (mre.gov.py)
consulate(s) general: Los Angeles, Miami, New York

Diplomatic representation from the US: *chief of mission:* Ambassador Marc OSTFIELD (since 9 March 2022)
embassy: 1776 Mariscal Lopez Avenue, Asuncion
mailing address: 3020 Asuncion Place, Washington DC 20521-3020
telephone: [595] (21) 248-3000
FAX: [595] (21) 213-728
email address and website:
ParaguayACS@state.gov
https://py.usembassy.gov/

Flag description: three equal, horizontal bands of red (top), white, and blue with an emblem centered in the white band; unusual flag in that the emblem is different on each side; the obverse (hoist side at the left) bears the national coat of arms (a yellow five-pointed star within a green wreath capped by the words REPUBLICA DEL PARAGUAY, all within two circles); the reverse (hoist side at the right) bears a circular seal of the treasury (a yellow lion below a red Cap of Liberty and the words PAZ Y JUSTICIA (Peace and Justice)); red symbolizes bravery and patriotism, white represents integrity and peace, and blue denotes liberty and generosity
note: the three color bands resemble those on the flag of the Netherlands; one of only three national flags that differ on their obverse and reverse sides - the others are Moldova and Saudi Arabia

National symbol(s): lion; national colors: red, white, blue

National anthem: *name:* "Paraguayos, Republica o muerte!" (Paraguayans, The Republic or Death!)
lyrics/music: Francisco Esteban ACUNA de Figueroa/disputed
note: adopted 1934, in use since 1846; officially adopted following its re-arrangement in 1934

National heritage: *total World Heritage Sites:* 1 (cultural)
selected World Heritage Site locales: Jesuit Missions of La Santísima Trinidad de Paraná and Jesús de Tavarangue

ECONOMY

Economic overview: upper middle-income South American economy; COVID-19 hit while still recovering from 2019 Argentina-driven recession; global hydroelectricity leader; major corruption and money-laundering locale; highly agrarian economy; significant income inequality

Real GDP (purchasing power parity): $108.022 billion (2023 est.)
$103.159 billion (2022 est.)
$102.978 billion (2021 est.)
note: data in 2021 dollars
comparison ranking: 94

Real GDP growth rate: 4.71% (2023 est.)
0.18% (2022 est.)
4.02% (2021 est.)
note: annual GDP % growth based on constant local currency
comparison ranking: 63

Real GDP per capita: $15,700 (2023 est.)
$15,200 (2022 est.)
$15,400 (2021 est.)
note: data in 2021 dollars
comparison ranking: 120

GDP (official exchange rate): $42.956 billion (2023 est.)
note: data in current dollars at official exchange rate

Inflation rate (consumer prices): 4.63% (2023 est.)
9.77% (2022 est.)
4.79% (2021 est.)
note: annual % change based on consumer prices
comparison ranking: 98

Credit ratings: Fitch rating: BB+ (2018)

Moody's rating: Ba1 (2015)

Standard & Poors rating: BB (2014)
note: The year refers to the year in which the current credit rating was first obtained.

GDP - composition, by sector of origin: *agriculture:* 11.3% (2023 est.)
industry: 32.4% (2023 est.)
services: 49% (2023 est.)
note: figures may not total 100% due to non-allocated consumption not captured in sector-reported data
comparison rankings: services 152; industry 54; agriculture 70

GDP - composition, by end use: *household consumption:* 66.3% (2023 est.)
government consumption: 12% (2023 est.)
investment in fixed capital: 20.6% (2023 est.)
investment in inventories: -0.9% (2023 est.)
exports of goods and services: 42.5% (2023 est.)
imports of goods and services: -40.4% (2023 est.)
note: figures may not total 100% due to rounding or gaps in data collection

Agricultural products: sugarcane, maize, soybeans, cassava, rice, wheat, milk, beef, oranges, oil palm fruit (2022)
note: top ten agricultural products based on tonnage

Industries: sugar processing, cement, textiles, beverages, wood products, steel, base metals, electric power

Industrial production growth rate: 3.43% (2023 est.)
note: annual % change in industrial value added based on constant local currency
comparison ranking: 98

Labor force: 3.469 million (2023 est.)
note: number of people ages 15 or older who are employed or seeking work
comparison ranking: 99

Unemployment rate: 5.78% (2023 est.)
6.76% (2022 est.)
7.31% (2021 est.)
note: % of labor force seeking employment
comparison ranking: 114

Youth unemployment rate (ages 15-24): *total:* 13% (2023 est.)
male: 10.4% (2023 est.)
female: 16.9% (2023 est.)
note: % of labor force ages 15-24 seeking employment
comparison ranking: total 106

Population below poverty line: 24.7% (2022 est.)
note: % of population with income below national poverty line

Gini Index coefficient - distribution of family income: 45.1 (2022 est.)
note: index (0-100) of income distribution; higher values represent greater inequality

comparison ranking: 21

Average household expenditures: *on food:* 29.8% of household expenditures (2022 est.)
on alcohol and tobacco: 4.2% of household expenditures (2022 est.)

Household income or consumption by percentage share: *lowest 10%:* 1.8% (2022 est.)
highest 10%: 35.4% (2022 est.)
note: % share of income accruing to lowest and highest 10% of population

Remittances: 1.4% of GDP (2023 est.)
1.41% of GDP (2022 est.)
1.47% of GDP (2021 est.)
note: personal transfers and compensation between resident and non-resident individuals/households/entities

Budget: *revenues:* $7.148 billion (2022 est.)
expenditures: $6.937 billion (2022 est.)
note: central government revenues (excluding grants) and expenses converted to US dollars at average official exchange rate for year indicated

Public debt: 19.5% of GDP (2017 est.)
comparison ranking: 189

Taxes and other revenues: 10.27% (of GDP) (2022 est.)
note: central government tax revenue as a % of GDP
comparison ranking: 178

Current account balance: $109.625 million (2023 est.)
-$2.993 billion (2022 est.)
-$347.383 million (2021 est.)
note: balance of payments - net trade and primary/secondary income in current dollars
comparison ranking: 72

Exports: $18.711 billion (2023 est.)
$14.971 billion (2022 est.)
$14.821 billion (2021 est.)
note: balance of payments - exports of goods and services in current dollars
comparison ranking: 92

Exports - partners: Brazil 36%, Argentina 19%, Chile 12%, Russia 4%, US 3% (2022)
note: top five export partners based on percentage share of exports

Exports - commodities: beef, electricity, soybeans, corn, soybean meal (2022)
note: top five export commodities based on value in dollars

Imports: $17.906 billion (2023 est.)
$17.142 billion (2022 est.)
$14.316 billion (2021 est.)
note: balance of payments - imports of goods and services in current dollars
comparison ranking: 100

Imports - partners: China 28%, Brazil 23%, US 11%, Argentina 8%, Chile 3% (2022)
note: top five import partners based on percentage share of imports

Imports - commodities: refined petroleum, broadcasting equipment, cars, fertilizers, pesticides (2022)
note: top five import commodities based on value in dollars

Reserves of foreign exchange and gold: $9.886 billion (2023 est.)
$9.519 billion (2022 est.)
$9.661 billion (2021 est.)
note: holdings of gold (year-end prices)/foreign exchange/special drawing rights in current dollars

comparison ranking: 84

Debt - external: $12.118 billion (2022 est.)
note: present value of external debt in current US dollars
comparison ranking: 35

Exchange rates: guarani (PYG) per US dollar -

Exchange rates: 7,288.872 (2023 est.)
6,982.752 (2022 est.)
6,774.163 (2021 est.)
6,771.097 (2020 est.)
6,240.722 (2019 est.)

ENERGY

Electricity access: *electrification - total population:* 100% (2022 est.)

Electricity: *installed generating capacity:* 8.833 million kW (2022 est.)
consumption: 17.486 billion kWh (2022 est.)
exports: 21.719 billion kWh (2022 est.)
transmission/distribution losses: 4.8 billion kWh (2022 est.)
comparison rankings: transmission/distribution losses 164; exports 12; consumption 79; installed generating capacity 69

Electricity generation sources: *hydroelectricity:* 99.7% of total installed capacity (2022 est.)
biomass and waste: 0.3% of total installed capacity (2022 est.)

Coal: *consumption:* 1,000 metric tons (2022 est.)
exports: (2022 est.) less than 1 metric ton
imports: 200 metric tons (2022 est.)

Petroleum: *total petroleum production:* 2,000 bbl/day (2023 est.)
refined petroleum consumption: 57,000 bbl/day (2022 est.)

Carbon dioxide emissions: 8.234 million metric tonnes of CO2 (2022 est.)
from coal and metallurgical coke: 3,000 metric tonnes of CO2 (2022 est.)
from petroleum and other liquids: 8.231 million metric tonnes of CO2 (2022 est.)
comparison ranking: total emissions 117

Energy consumption per capita: 28.472 million Btu/person (2022 est.)
comparison ranking: 118

COMMUNICATIONS

Telephones - fixed lines: *total subscriptions:* 169,000 (2022 est.)
subscriptions per 100 inhabitants: 2 (2022 est.)
comparison ranking: total subscriptions 123

Telephones - mobile cellular: *total subscriptions:* 8.659 million (2022 est.)
subscriptions per 100 inhabitants: 128 (2022 est.)
comparison ranking: total subscriptions 97

Telecommunication systems: *general assessment:* limited progress on structural reform and deficient infrastructure of the landlocked country are obstacles to the telecom platform; effective competition in mobile market, serving 96% of population through LTE; deployment of fiber; operator enabled 109 free Internet points across the country and is looking to expand to 430 points in 2022; dependent on neighboring countries for access to submarine cables (2022)
domestic: fixed-line just over 3 per 100 and mobile-cellular is 119 per 100 of the population (2021)
international: country code - 595; Paraguay's landlocked position means they must depend on neighbors for interconnection with submarine cable networks, making it cost more for broadband services; satellite earth station - 1 Intelsat (Atlantic Ocean) (2019)

Broadcast media: 6 privately owned TV stations; about 75 commercial and community radio stations; 1 state-owned radio network (2019)

Internet country code: .py

Internet users: *total:* 5.159 million (2021 est.)
percent of population: 77% (2021 est.)
comparison ranking: total 91

Broadband - fixed subscriptions: *total:* 562,369 (2020 est.)
subscriptions per 100 inhabitants: 8 (2020 est.)
comparison ranking: total 89

TRANSPORTATION

National air transport system: *number of registered air carriers:* 2 (2020)
inventory of registered aircraft operated by air carriers: 8
annual passenger traffic on registered air carriers: 560,631 (2018)
annual freight traffic on registered air carriers: 1.97 million (2018) mt-km

Civil aircraft registration country code prefix: ZP

Airports: 83 (2024)
comparison ranking: 62

Heliports: 27 (2024)

Railways: *total:* 30 km (2014)
standard gauge: 30 km (2014) 1.435-m gauge
comparison ranking: total 134

Roadways: *total:* 78,811 km
paved: 8,573 km
unpaved: 70,238 km (2020)
comparison ranking: total 63

Waterways: 3,100 km (2012) (primarily on the Paraguay and Paraná River systems)
comparison ranking: 34

Merchant marine: *total:* 108 (2023)
by type: container ship 2, general cargo 22, oil tanker 5, other 79
comparison ranking: total 87

Ports: *total ports:* 1 (2024)
large: 0
medium: 0
small: 0
very small: 1
ports with oil terminals: 0
key ports: Puerto de Asuncion

MILITARY AND SECURITY

Military and security forces: Armed Forces of Paraguay (Fuerzas Armadas de Paraguay; aka Armed Forces of the Nation or Fuerzas Armadas de la Nación): Paraguayan Army (Ejército Paraguayo), Paraguayan Navy (Armada Paraguaya; includes marines), Paraguayan Air Force (Fuerza Aérea Paraguaya)

Ministry of Internal Affairs: National Police of Paraguay (Policía Nacional del Paraguay, PNP) (2024)
note: Paraguay also has a National Counterdrug Bureau (Secretaria Nacional Antidrogas or SENAD) that operates under the presidency

Military expenditures: 0.8% of GDP (2023 est.)
0.8% of GDP (2022 est.)
1% of GDP (2021 est.)
1% of GDP (2020 est.)
1% of GDP (2019 est.)
comparison ranking: 143

Military and security service personnel strengths: approximately 20,000 active-duty personnel (13,500 Army; 4,000 Navy; 2,500 Air Force) (2023)

Military equipment inventories and acquisitions: the military's inventory is comprised of mostly older or obsolescent equipment from a variety of foreign suppliers, particularly Brazil and the US; in recent years, the Paraguayan Government has purchased small quantities of more modern equipment (2024)

Military service age and obligation: 18 years of age for compulsory (men) and voluntary (men and women) military service; conscript service obligation is 12 months for Army, 24 months for Navy; conscripts also serve in the National Police (2024)
note: as of 2021, women made up about 6% of the active military

Military - note: the Paraguayan military is responsible for external defense but also has some domestic security duties; while the National Police are responsible for maintaining internal security, the military works with the police through a Joint Task Force (Fuerza de Tarea Conjunta or FTC) in combatting the Paraguayan People's Army (Ejército del Pueblo Paraguayo or EPP) and transnational criminal organizations; the military has an Internal Defense Operations Command (Comando de Defensa Interna or CODI), which includes the Army, Navy, and Air Force, to coordinate internal security support to the police and other security organizations, such as the National Anti-Drug Secretariat or SENAD
the EPP is a domestic criminal/guerrilla group initially dedicated to a Marxist-Leninist revolution in Paraguay that operates in the rural northern part of the country along the border with Brazil; the activities of the EPP and its offshoots—Marsical López's Army (EML) and the Armed Peasant Association (ACA)—have consisted largely of isolated attacks on remote police and army posts, or against ranchers and peasants accused of aiding Paraguayan security forces
the Paraguayan military is a small force by regional standards, and its limited equipment inventory is largely obsolete, with some of it pre-dating World War II; it has deployed small numbers of troops on UN missions and cooperates with neighboring countries, such as Argentina and Brazil, on security issues, particularly organized crime and narco-trafficking in what is known as the Tri-Border Area; Paraguay has not fought a war against a neighboring country since the Chaco War with Bolivia in the 1930s (2024)

SPACE

Space agency/agencies: Space Agency of Paraguay (Agencia Especial del Paraguay, AEP; established 2014) (2024)

Space program overview: has a small, recently established space program focused on the acquisition of satellites, satellite data, and the technologies and capabilities to manufacture satellites, as well as promoting in-country expertise building and space industry; a priority is acquiring remote sensing (RS) capabilities to support socio-economic develop, including resource mapping, weather, and crop monitoring; has built a cube satellite with foreign assistance; operates satellites; cooperates with foreign space agencies and industries, including those of India, Japan, Taiwan, the US, and member states of the Latin American and Caribbean Space Agency (ALCE) (2024)
note: further details about the key activities, programs, and milestones of the country's space program, as well as government spending estimates on the space sector, appear in the Space Programs reference guide

TERRORISM

Terrorist group(s): Hizballah (2022)
note: details about the history, aims, leadership, organization, areas of operation, tactics, targets, weapons, size, and sources of support of the group(s) appear(s) in the Terrorism reference guide

TRANSNATIONAL ISSUES

Refugees and internally displaced persons: *refugees (country of origin):* 5,231 (Venezuela) (2022)

Illicit drugs: marijuana cultivation and the trafficking of Andean cocaine in the tri-border area shared with Argentina, and Brazil facilitates money laundering

PERU

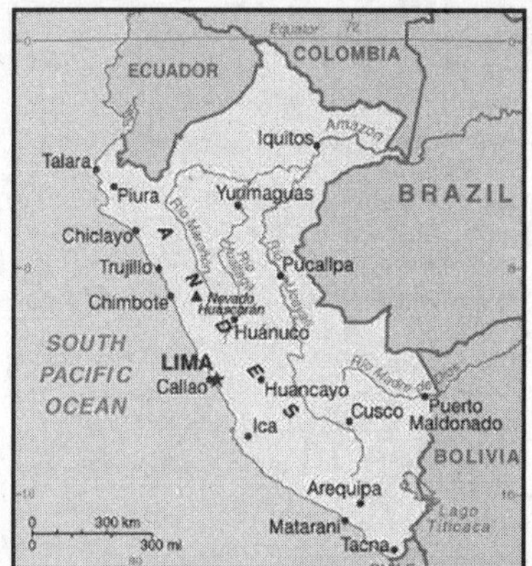

INTRODUCTION

Background: Ancient Peru was the seat of several prominent Andean civilizations, most notably that of the Incas whose empire was captured by Spanish conquistadors in 1533. Peru declared its independence in 1821, and remaining Spanish forces were defeated in 1824. After a dozen years of military rule, Peru returned to democratic leadership in 1980 but experienced economic problems and the growth of a violent insurgency. President Alberto FUJIMORI's election in 1990 ushered in a decade that saw a dramatic turnaround in the economy and significant progress in curtailing guerrilla activity. Nevertheless, an economic slump and the president's increasing reliance on authoritarian measures in the late 1990s generated mounting dissatisfaction with his regime, which led to his resignation in 2000.

A caretaker government oversaw a new election in 2001 that installed Alejandro TOLEDO Manrique as the new head of government - Peru's first democratically elected president of indigenous ethnicity. The presidential election of 2006 saw the return of Alan GARCIA Perez who, after a disappointing presidential term from 1985 to 1990, presided over a robust economic rebound. Former army officer Ollanta HUMALA Tasso was elected president in 2011 and carried on the market-oriented economic policies of the three preceding administrations. Pedro Pablo KUCZYNSKI Godard won a very narrow runoff in the 2016 presidential election. Facing impeachment after evidence surfaced of his involvement in a vote-buying scandal, KUCZYNSKI offered his resignation in 2018, and First Vice President Martin Alberto VIZCARRA Cornejo was sworn in as president. In 2019, VIZCARRA invoked his constitutional authority to dissolve Peru's Congress after months of battling with the body over anti-corruption reforms. New congressional elections in 2020 resulted in an opposition-led legislature. The Congress impeached VIZCARRA for a second time and removed him from office after accusations of corruption and mishandling of the COVID-19 pandemic. Because of vacancies in the vice-presidential positions, the President of the Peruvian Congress, Manuel MERINO, became the next president. His ascension to office was not well received, and large protests forced his resignation later in 2020. Francisco SAGASTI assumed the position of President of Peru after being appointed President of the Congress the previous day. Jose Pedro CASTILLO Terrones won presidential election in 2021 but was impeached and ousted the following year; his vice president, Dina BOLUARTE, assumed the presidency by constitutional succession in 2022.

GEOGRAPHY

Location: Western South America, bordering the South Pacific Ocean, between Chile and Ecuador

Geographic coordinates: 10 00 S, 76 00 W

Map references: South America

Area: *total:* 1,285,216 sq km
land: 1,279,996 sq km
water: 5,220 sq km
comparison ranking: total 21

Area - comparative: almost twice the size of Texas; slightly smaller than Alaska

Land boundaries: *total:* 7,062 km
border countries (5): Bolivia 1,212 km; Brazil 2,659 km; Chile 168 km; Colombia 1,494 km; Ecuador 1,529 km

Coastline: 2,414 km

Maritime claims: *territorial sea:* 200 nm; note: the US does not recognize this claim
exclusive economic zone: 200 nm
continental shelf: 200 nm

Climate: varies from tropical in east to dry desert in west; temperate to frigid in Andes

Terrain: western coastal plain (costa), high and rugged Andes in center (sierra), eastern lowland jungle of Amazon Basin (selva)

Elevation: *highest point:* Nevado Huascaran 6,746 m
lowest point: Pacific Ocean 0 m
mean elevation: 1,555 m

Natural resources: copper, silver, gold, petroleum, timber, fish, iron ore, coal, phosphate, potash, hydropower, natural gas

Land use: *agricultural land:* 18.8% (2018 est.)
arable land: 3.1% (2018 est.)
permanent crops: 1.1% (2018 est.)
permanent pasture: 14.6% (2018 est.)
forest: 53% (2018 est.)
other: 28.2% (2018 est.)

Irrigated land: 25,800 sq km (2012)

Major lakes (area sq km): *fresh water lake(s):* Lago Titicaca (shared with Bolivia) - 8,030 sq km

Major rivers (by length in km): Amazon river source (shared with Brazil [m]) - 6,400 km
note – [s] after country name indicates river source; [m] after country name indicates river mouth

Major watersheds (area sq km): Atlantic Ocean drainage: Amazon (6,145,186 sq km)

Major aquifers: Amazon Basin

Population distribution: approximately one-third of the population resides along the desert coastal belt in the west, with a strong focus on the capital city of Lima; the Andean highlands, or sierra, which is strongly identified with the country's Amerindian population, contains roughly half of the overall population; the eastern slopes of the Andes, and adjoining rainforest, are sparsely populated

Natural hazards: earthquakes, tsunamis, flooding, landslides, mild volcanic activity
volcanism: volcanic activity in the Andes Mountains; Ubinas (5,672 m), which last erupted in 2009, is the country's most active volcano; other historically active volcanoes include El Misti, Huaynaputina, Sabancaya, and Yucamane; see note 2 under "Geography - note"

Geography - note: *note 1:* shares control of Lago Titicaca, world's highest navigable lake, with Bolivia; a remote slope of Nevado Mismi, a 5,316 m peak, is the ultimate source of the Amazon River
note 2: Peru is one of the countries along the Ring of Fire, a belt of active volcanoes and earthquake epicenters bordering the Pacific Ocean; up to 90% of the world's earthquakes and some 75% of the world's volcanoes occur within the Ring of Fire
note 3: on 19 February 1600, Mount Huaynaputina in the southern Peruvian Andes erupted in the largest volcanic explosion in South America in historical times; intermittent eruptions lasted until 5 March 1600 and pumped an estimated 16 to 32 million metric tons of particulates into the atmosphere, reducing the amount of sunlight reaching the earth's surface and affecting weather worldwide; over the next two and a half years, millions died around the globe in famines from bitterly cold winters, cool summers, and the loss of crops and animals
note 4: the southern regions of Peru and the extreme northwestern part of Bolivia are considered to be the place of origin for the common potato

PEOPLE AND SOCIETY

Population: *total:* 32,600,249
male: 15,952,556
female: 16,647,693 (2024 est.)
comparison rankings: female 46; male 48; total 47

Nationality: *noun:* Peruvian(s)
adjective: Peruvian

Ethnic groups: Mestizo (mixed Indigenous and White) 60.2%, Indigenous 25.8%, White 5.9%, African descent 3.6%, other (includes Chinese and Japanese descent) 1.2%, unspecified 3.3% (2017 est.)

Languages: Spanish (official) 82.9%, Quechua (official) 13.6%, Aymara (official) 1.6%, Ashaninka 0.3%, other native languages (includes many minor Amazonian languages) 0.8%, other 0.2%, none 0.1%, unspecified 0.7% (2017 est.)
major-language sample(s):
La Libreta Informativa del Mundo, la fuente indispensable de información básica. (Spanish)

Religions: Roman Catholic 66.4%, Protestant 22.4% (Evangelical 19.6%, other Protestant 1.3%), other 1.9%, agnostic/atheist none 6.8%, unspecified 1.2% (2023 est.)

Demographic profile: Peru's urban and coastal communities have benefited much more from recent economic growth than rural, Afro-Peruvian, indigenous, and poor populations of the Amazon and mountain regions. The poverty rate has dropped substantially during the last decade but remains stubbornly high at about 30% (more than 55% in rural areas). After remaining almost static for about a decade, Peru's malnutrition rate began falling in 2005, when the government introduced a coordinated strategy focusing on hygiene, sanitation, and clean water. School enrollment has improved, but achievement scores reflect ongoing problems with educational quality. Many poor children temporarily or permanently drop out of school to help support their families. About a quarter to a third of Peruvian children aged 6 to 14 work, often putting in long hours at hazardous mining or construction sites.

Peru was a country of immigration in the 19th and early 20th centuries, but has become a country of emigration in the last few decades. Beginning in the 19th century, Peru brought in Asian contract laborers mainly to work on coastal plantations. Populations of Chinese and Japanese descent - among the largest in Latin America - are economically and culturally influential in Peru today. Peruvian emigration began rising in the 1980s due to an economic crisis and a violent internal conflict, but outflows have stabilized in the last few years as economic conditions have improved. Nonetheless, more than 2 million Peruvians have emigrated in the last decade, principally to the US, Spain, and Argentina.

Age structure: *0-14 years:* 25.8% (male 4,293,229/female 4,119,269)
15-64 years: 66.2% (male 10,546,502/female 11,041,106)
65 years and over: 8% (2024 est.) (male 1,112,825/female 1,487,318)

Dependency ratios: *total dependency ratio:* 53
youth dependency ratio: 37.1
elderly dependency ratio: 13.1
potential support ratio: 7.9 (2021 est.)

Median age: *total:* 30.2 years (2024 est.)
male: 29.1 years
female: 31.3 years
comparison ranking: total 139

Population growth rate: 0.48% (2024 est.)
comparison ranking: 151

Birth rate: 16.7 births/1,000 population (2024 est.)
comparison ranking: 96

Death rate: 10.9 deaths/1,000 population (2024 est.)
comparison ranking: 26

Net migration rate: -1 migrant(s)/1,000 population (2024 est.)
comparison ranking: 146

Population distribution: approximately one-third of the population resides along the desert coastal belt in the west, with a strong focus on the capital city of Lima; the Andean highlands, or sierra, which is strongly identified with the country's Amerindian population, contains roughly half of the overall population; the eastern slopes of the Andes, and adjoining rainforest, are sparsely populated

Urbanization: *urban population:* 78.9% of total population (2023)
rate of urbanization: 1.33% annual rate of change (2020-25 est.)

Major urban areas - population: 11.204 million LIMA (capital), 959,000 Arequipa, 904,000 Trujillo (2023)

Sex ratio: *at birth:* 1.05 male(s)/female
0-14 years: 1.04 male(s)/female
15-64 years: 0.96 male(s)/female
65 years and over: 0.75 male(s)/female
total population: 0.96 male(s)/female (2024 est.)

Mother's mean age at first birth: 21.9 years (2013 est.)
note: data represents median age at first birth among women 25-49

Maternal mortality ratio: 69 deaths/100,000 live births (2020 est.)
comparison ranking: 88

Infant mortality rate: *total:* 10.8 deaths/1,000 live births (2024 est.)
male: 11.9 deaths/1,000 live births
female: 9.7 deaths/1,000 live births
comparison ranking: total 125

Life expectancy at birth: *total population:* 68.9 years (2024 est.)
male: 65.4 years
female: 72.7 years
comparison ranking: total population 185

Total fertility rate: 2.15 children born/woman (2024 est.)
comparison ranking: 90

Gross reproduction rate: 1.05 (2024 est.)

Contraceptive prevalence rate: 77.4% (2020)

Drinking water source: *improved: urban:* 97.2% of population
rural: 82.4% of population
total: 94% of population
unimproved: urban: 2.8% of population
rural: 17.6% of population
total: 6% of population (2020 est.)

Current health expenditure: 6.3% of GDP (2020)

Physician density: 1.37 physicians/1,000 population (2018)

Hospital bed density: 1.6 beds/1,000 population (2017)

Sanitation facility access: *improved: urban:* 93.6% of population
rural: 65.3% of population
total: 87.4% of population
unimproved: urban: 6.4% of population
rural: 34.7% of population
total: 12.6% of population (2020 est.)

Obesity - adult prevalence rate: 19.7% (2016)
comparison ranking: 110

Alcohol consumption per capita: *total:* 5.74 liters of pure alcohol (2019 est.)
beer: 3.01 liters of pure alcohol (2019 est.)
wine: 0.46 liters of pure alcohol (2019 est.)
spirits: 2.26 liters of pure alcohol (2019 est.)
other alcohols: 0.01 liters of pure alcohol (2019 est.)
comparison ranking: total 76

Tobacco use: *total:* 8.1% (2020 est.)
male: 13.2% (2020 est.)
female: 3% (2020 est.)
comparison ranking: total 149

Children under the age of 5 years underweight: 2.1% (2021)
comparison ranking: 103

Currently married women (ages 15-49): 51.2% (2023 est.)

Child marriage: *women married by age 15:* 2%
women married by age 18: 14.1% (2020 est.)

Education expenditures: 4% of GDP (2021 est.)
comparison ranking: 114

Literacy: *definition:* age 15 and over can read and write
total population: 94.5%
male: 97%
female: 92% (2020)

School life expectancy (primary to tertiary education): *total:* 15 years
male: 15 years
female: 15 years (2017)

ENVIRONMENT

Environment - current issues: deforestation (some the result of illegal logging); overgrazing leading to soil erosion; desertification; air pollution in Lima; pollution of rivers and coastal waters from municipal and mining wastes; overfishing

Environment - international agreements: *party to:* Antarctic-Environmental Protection, Antarctic-Marine Living Resources, Antarctic Treaty, Biodiversity, Climate Change, Climate Change-Kyoto Protocol, Climate Change-Paris Agreement, Desertification, Endangered Species, Hazardous Wastes, Marine Dumping-London Convention, Marine Dumping-London Protocol, Nuclear Test Ban, Ozone Layer Protection, Ship - Pollution, Tropical Timber 2006, Wetlands, Whaling
signed, but not ratified: none of the selected agreements

Climate: varies from tropical in east to dry desert in west; temperate to frigid in Andes

Urbanization: *urban population:* 78.9% of total population (2023)
rate of urbanization: 1.33% annual rate of change (2020-25 est.)

Revenue from forest resources: 0.12% of GDP (2018 est.)
comparison ranking: 109

Revenue from coal: 0% of GDP (2018 est.)
comparison ranking: 145

Air pollutants: *particulate matter emissions:* 29.07 micrograms per cubic meter (2019 est.)
carbon dioxide emissions: 57.41 megatons (2016 est.)
methane emissions: 30.17 megatons (2020 est.)

Waste and recycling: *municipal solid waste generated annually:* 8,356,711 tons (2014 est.)
municipal solid waste recycled annually: 334,268 tons (2012 est.)
percent of municipal solid waste recycled: 4% (2012 est.)

Major lakes (area sq km): *fresh water lake(s):* Lago Titicaca (shared with Bolivia) - 8,030 sq km

Major rivers (by length in km): Amazon river source (shared with Brazil [m]) - 6,400 km
note – [s] after country name indicates river source; [m] after country name indicates river mouth

Major watersheds (area sq km): Atlantic Ocean drainage: Amazon (6,145,186 sq km)

Major aquifers: Amazon Basin

Total water withdrawal: *municipal:* 2.24 billion cubic meters (2020 est.)
industrial: 3.51 billion cubic meters (2020 est.)
agricultural: 32.8 billion cubic meters (2020 est.)

Total renewable water resources: 1.88 trillion cubic meters (2020 est.)

Geoparks: *total global geoparks and regional networks:* 1
global geoparks and regional networks: Colca y Volcanes de Andagua (2023)

GOVERNMENT

Country name: *conventional long form:* Republic of Peru
conventional short form: Peru
local long form: República del Perú
local short form: Perú
etymology: exact meaning is obscure, but the name may derive from a native word "biru" meaning "river"

Government type: presidential republic

Capital: *name:* Lima
geographic coordinates: 12 03 S, 77 03 W
time difference: UTC-5 (same time as Washington, DC, during Standard Time)
etymology: the word "Lima" derives from the Spanish pronunciation of "Limaq," the native name for the valley in which the city was founded in 1535; "limaq" means "talker" in coastal Quechua and referred to an oracle that was situated in the valley but which was eventually destroyed by the Spanish and replaced with a church

Administrative divisions: 25 regions (regiones, singular - region) and 1 province* (provincia); Amazonas, Ancash, Apurimac, Arequipa, Ayacucho, Cajamarca, Callao, Cusco, Huancavelica, Huanuco, Ica, Junin, La Libertad, Lambayeque, Lima, Lima*, Loreto, Madre de Dios, Moquegua, Pasco, Piura, Puno, San Martin, Tacna, Tumbes, Ucayali
note: Callao, the largest port in Peru, is also referred to as a constitutional province, the only province of the Callao region

Independence: 28 July 1821 (from Spain)

National holiday: Independence Day, 28-29 July (1821)

Legal system: civil law system

Constitution: *history:* several previous; latest promulgated 29 December 1993, enacted 31 December 1993
amendments: proposed by Congress, by the president of the republic with the approval of the Council of Ministers or by petition of at least 0.3% of voters; passage requires absolute majority approval by the Congress membership, followed by approval in a referendum; a referendum is not required if Congress approves the amendment by greater than two-thirds majority vote in each of two successive sessions; amended many times, last in 2021

International law organization participation: accepts compulsory ICJ jurisdiction with reservations; accepts ICCt jurisdiction

Citizenship: *citizenship by birth:* yes
citizenship by descent only: yes
dual citizenship recognized: yes
residency requirement for naturalization: 2 years

Suffrage: 18 years of age; universal and compulsory until the age of 70

Executive branch: *chief of state:* President Dina Ercilia BOLUARTE Zegarra (since 7 December 2022)
head of government: President Dina Ercilia BOLUARTE Zegarra (since 7 December 2022)
cabinet: Council of Ministers appointed by the president
elections/appointments: president directly elected by absolute majority popular vote in 2 rounds if needed for a 5-year term (eligible for nonconsecutive terms); election last held on 11 April 2021 with a runoff on 6 June 2021 (next to be held in April 2026)
election results:
2021: Jose Pedro CASTILLO Terrones elected president in second round; percent of vote in first round - Jose Pedro CASTILLO Terrones (PL) 18.9%, Keiko Sofia FUJIMORI Higuchi (FP) 13.4%, Rafael LOPEZ ALIAGA Cazorla (RP) 11.8%, Hernando DE SOTO Polar (Social Integration Party) 11.6%, Yonhy LESCANO Ancieta (AP) 9.1%, Veronika MENDOZA Frisch (JP) 7.9%, Cesar ACUNA Peralta (APP) 6%, George FORSYTH Sommer (VN) 5.7%, Daniel Belizario URRESTI Elera (PP) 5.6%, other 10%; percent of vote second round - Jose Pedro CASTILLO Terrones 50.1%, Keiko Sofia FUJIMORI Higuchi 49.9%
2016: Pedro Pablo KUCZYNSKI Godard elected president in second round; percent of vote in first round - Keiko FUJIMORI Higuchi (FP) 39.9%, Pedro Pablo KUCZYNSKI Godard (PPK) 21.1%, Veronika MENDOZA (FA) 18.7%, Alfredo BARNECHEA (AP) 7%, Alan GARCIA (APRA) 5.8%, other 7.5%; percent of vote in second round - Pedro Pablo KUCZYNSKI Godard 50.1%, Keiko FUJIMORI Higuchi 49.9%
note 1: First Vice President Dina Ercilia BOLUARTE Zegarra assumed the office of the president on 7 December 2022 after President Jose Pedro CASTILLO Terrones was impeached and arrested; BOLUARTE is the first woman to become president of Peru
note 2: Prime Minister Gustavo ADRIANZÉN (since 6 March 2024) does not exercise executive power; this power rests with the president; on 5 March 2024, Prime Minister Alberto OTÁROLA resigned amid allegations of corruption
note 3: the president is both chief of state and head of government

Legislative branch: *description:* unicameral Congress of the Republic of Peru or Congreso de la República del Perú (130 seats; members directly elected in multi-seat constituencies by closed party-list proportional representation vote to serve single 5-year terms)
elections: last held on 11 April 2021 (next to be held in April 2026)
election results:
percent of vote by party/coalition - NA; seats by party/coalition - Free Peru 32, Popular Force 24, AP 15, APP 15, AvP 10, RP 9, Democratic Peru 7, We Are Peru 5, PP 5, JP 5, Purple Party 3; composition - men 80, women 50, percentage women 40%
note: seats by party/coalition as of January 2024 - Popular Force 23, Free Peru 16, AP 14, APP 11, AvP 9, Democratic Peru 9, RP 9, SP 6, PP 6, PB 5; BMCN 9, independent 25

Judicial branch: *highest court(s):* Supreme Court (consists of 16 judges and divided into civil, criminal, and constitutional-social sectors)
judge selection and term of office: justices proposed by the National Board of Justice (a 7-member independent body), nominated by the president, and confirmed by the Congress; justices can serve until mandatory retirement at age 70
subordinate courts: Court of Constitutional Guarantees; Superior Courts or Cortes Superiores; specialized civil, criminal, and mixed courts; 2 types of peace courts in which professional judges and selected members of the local communities preside

Political parties: Advance the Nation (Avanza País) or AvP
Alliance for Progress (Alianza para el Progreso) or APP
Broad Front (Frente Amplio) or FA
Free Peru (Perú Libre) or PL
Front for Hope (Frente Esperanza)
Magisterial Block of National Concentration (Bloque Magisterial de Concertación Nacional) or BMCN
National Victory (Victoria Nacional) or VN
Peru Bicentennial (Perú Bicentenario) or PB
Popular Action (Acción Popular) or AP
Popular Force (Fuerza Popular) or FP
Popular Renewal (Renovación Popular) or RP
Purple Party (Partido Morado)
Social Integration Party (Avanza País - Partido de Integración Social)
Together For Perú (Juntos por el Peru) or JP
We Are Peru (Somos Perú) of SP
We Can Peru (Podemos Perú) or PP

International organization participation: AIIB, APEC, BIS, CAN, CD, CELAC, EITI (compliant country), FAO, G-24, G-77, IADB, IAEA, IBRD, ICAO, ICC (NGOs), ICCt, ICRM, IDA, IFAD, IFC, IFRCS, IHO, ILO, IMF, IMO, IMSO, Interpol, IOC, IOM, IPU, ISO, ITSO, ITU, ITUC (NGOs), LAES, LAIA, Mercosur (associate), MIGA, MINUSTAH, MONUSCO, NAM, OAS, OPANAL, OPCW, Pacific Alliance, PCA, PROSUR, SICA (observer), UN, UNAMID, UNASUR, UNCTAD, UNESCO, UNHCR, UNIDO, Union Latina, UNISFA, UNMISS, UNOCI, UNOOSA, UN Security Council (temporary), UNWTO, UPU, WCO, WFTU (NGOs), WHO, WIPO, WMO, WTO

Diplomatic representation in the US: *chief of mission:* Ambassador Alfredo Santiago Carlos FERRERO DIEZ CANSECO (since 27 February 2024)
chancery: 1700 Massachusetts Avenue NW, Washington, DC 20036
telephone: [1] (202) 833-9860
FAX: [1] (202) 659-8124
email address and website:
Webadmin@embassyofperu.us
Embassy of Peru in the United States - E-United States - Platform of the Peruvian State (www.gob.pe)
consulate(s) general: Atlanta, Boston, Chicago, Dallas, Denver, Hartford (CT), Houston, Los Angeles, Miami, New York, Paterson (NJ), San Francisco

Diplomatic representation from the US: *chief of mission:* Ambassador Stephanie SYPTAK-RAMNATH (since 20 June 2024)
embassy: Avenida La Encalada, Cuadra 17 s/n, Surco, Lima 33
mailing address: 3230 Lima Place, Washington DC 20521-3230
telephone: [51] (1) 618-2000
FAX: [51] (1) 618-2724
email address and website:
lima_webmaster@state.gov
https://pe.usembassy.gov/

Flag description: three equal, vertical bands of red (hoist side), white, and red with the coat of arms centered in the white band; the coat of arms features a shield bearing a vicuna (representing fauna), a cinchona tree (the source of quinine, signifying flora), and a yellow cornucopia spilling out coins (denoting mineral wealth); red recalls blood shed for independence, white symbolizes peace

National symbol(s): vicuna (a camelid related to the llama); national colors: red, white

National anthem: *name:* "Himno Nacional del Peru" (National Anthem of Peru)
lyrics/music: Jose DE LA TORRE Ugarte/Jose Bernardo ALZEDO
note: adopted 1822; the song won a national anthem contest

National heritage: *total World Heritage Sites:* 13 (9 cultural, 2 natural, 2 mixed)
selected World Heritage Site locales: Cuzco (c); Machu Picchu (m); Chavin (c); Historic Lima (c); Huascarán National Park (n); Chan Chan (c); Manú National Park (n); Lines and Geoglyphs of Nazca (c); Rio Abiseo National Park (m); Historic Arequipa (c); Sacred City of Caral-Supe (c); Qhapaq Ñan/ Andean Road System (c)

ECONOMY

Economic overview: upper-middle-income South American economy; strong post-COVID rebound tempered by political uncertainty and climate risks; exports driven by mineral extraction and agriculture; large informal sector and uneven access to public services; stable fiscal position and financial sector

Real GDP (purchasing power parity): $517.644 billion (2023 est.)
$520.507 billion (2022 est.)
$506.697 billion (2021 est.)
note: data in 2021 dollars
comparison ranking: 48

Real GDP growth rate: -0.55% (2023 est.)
2.73% (2022 est.)
13.36% (2021 est.)
note: annual GDP % growth based on constant local currency
comparison ranking: 196

Real GDP per capita: $15,100 (2023 est.)
$15,300 (2022 est.)
$15,000 (2021 est.)
note: data in 2021 dollars
comparison ranking: 124

GDP (official exchange rate): $267.603 billion (2023 est.)
note: data in current dollars at official exchange rate

Inflation rate (consumer prices): 6.46% (2023 est.)
8.33% (2022 est.)
4.27% (2021 est.)
note: annual % change based on consumer prices
comparison ranking: 136

Credit ratings: Fitch rating: BBB+ (2013)

Moody's rating: A3 (2014)

Standard & Poors rating: BBB+ (2013)
note: The year refers to the year in which the current credit rating was first obtained.

GDP - composition, by sector of origin: *agriculture:* 7.1% (2022 est.)
industry: 35% (2022 est.)
services: 49.6% (2022 est.)
note: figures may not total 100% due to non-allocated consumption not captured in sector-reported data
comparison rankings: services 151; industry 43; agriculture 100

GDP - composition, by end use: *household consumption:* 64.3% (2023 est.)
government consumption: 13.7% (2023 est.)
investment in fixed capital: 21.3% (2023 est.)
investment in inventories: -2.4% (2023 est.)
exports of goods and services: 27.1% (2023 est.)
imports of goods and services: -23.8% (2023 est.)
note: figures may not total 100% due to rounding or gaps in data collection

Agricultural products: sugarcane, potatoes, rice, bananas, milk, chicken, maize, oil palm fruit, cassava, grapes (2022)
note: top ten agricultural products based on tonnage

Industries: mining and refining of minerals; steel, metal fabrication; petroleum extraction and refining, natural gas and natural gas liquefaction; fishing and fish processing, cement, glass, textiles, clothing, food processing, beer, soft drinks, rubber, machinery, electrical machinery, chemicals, furniture

Industrial production growth rate: -1.28% (2023 est.)
note: annual % change in industrial value added based on constant local currency
comparison ranking: 172

Labor force: 18.529 million (2023 est.)
note: number of people ages 15 or older who are employed or seeking work
comparison ranking: 35

Unemployment rate: 4.82% (2023 est.)
3.85% (2022 est.)
5.1% (2021 est.)
note: % of labor force seeking employment
comparison ranking: 91

Youth unemployment rate (ages 15-24): *total:* 8.8% (2023 est.)
male: 7.8% (2023 est.)
female: 10% (2023 est.)
note: % of labor force ages 15-24 seeking employment
comparison ranking: total 145

Population below poverty line: 27.5% (2022 est.)
note: % of population with income below national poverty line

Gini Index coefficient - distribution of family income: 40.3 (2022 est.)
note: index (0-100) of income distribution; higher values represent greater inequality
comparison ranking: 43

Average household expenditures: *on food:* 26.6% of household expenditures (2022 est.)
on alcohol and tobacco: 2.4% of household expenditures (2022 est.)

Household income or consumption by percentage share: *lowest 10%:* 2.1% (2022 est.)
highest 10%: 30.7% (2022 est.)
note: % share of income accruing to lowest and highest 10% of population

Remittances: 1.58% of GDP (2023 est.)
1.5% of GDP (2022 est.)
1.59% of GDP (2021 est.)
note: personal transfers and compensation between resident and non-resident individuals/households/entities

Budget: *revenues:* $48.008 billion (2021 est.)
expenditures: $51.709 billion (2021 est.)
note: central government revenues (excluding grants) and expenses converted to US dollars at average official exchange rate for year indicated

Public debt: 35.25% of GDP (2021 est.)
note: central government debt as a % of GDP
comparison ranking: 153

Taxes and other revenues: 15.92% (of GDP) (2021 est.)
note: central government tax revenue as a % of GDP
comparison ranking: 129

Current account balance: $2.219 billion (2023 est.)
-$9.743 billion (2022 est.)
-$4.674 billion (2021 est.)
note: balance of payments - net trade and primary/secondary income in current dollars
comparison ranking: 47

Exports: $73.326 billion (2023 est.)
$71.129 billion (2022 est.)
$66.061 billion (2021 est.)
note: balance of payments - exports of goods and services in current dollars
comparison ranking: 55

Exports - partners: China 30%, US 15%, Japan 5%, Canada 5%, South Korea 4% (2022)
note: top five export partners based on percentage share of exports

Exports - commodities: copper ore, gold, natural gas, refined copper, refined petroleum (2022)
note: top five export commodities based on value in dollars

Imports: $62.99 billion (2023 est.)
$69.44 billion (2022 est.)
$58.509 billion (2021 est.)
note: balance of payments - imports of goods and services in current dollars
comparison ranking: 61

Imports - partners: China 27%, US 24%, Brazil 6%, Argentina 4%, Chile 3% (2022)
note: top five import partners based on percentage share of imports

Imports - commodities: refined petroleum, crude petroleum, cars, broadcasting equipment, trucks (2022)
note: top five import commodities based on value in dollars

Reserves of foreign exchange and gold: $71.394 billion (2023 est.)
$72.328 billion (2022 est.)
$78.59 billion (2021 est.)
note: holdings of gold (year-end prices)/foreign exchange/special drawing rights in current dollars
comparison ranking: 33

Debt - external: $37.467 billion (2022 est.)
note: present value of external debt in current US dollars
comparison ranking: 18

Exchange rates: nuevo sol (PEN) per US dollar -

Exchange rates: 3.744 (2023 est.)
3.835 (2022 est.)
3.881 (2021 est.)
3.495 (2020 est.)
3.337 (2019 est.)

ENERGY

Electricity access: *electrification - total population:* 96.2% (2022 est.)
electrification - urban areas: 99%
electrification - rural areas: 85.1%

Electricity: *installed generating capacity:* 15.504 million kW (2022 est.)
consumption: 50.868 billion kWh (2022 est.)
imports: 43 million kWh (2022 est.)
transmission/distribution losses: 6.814 billion kWh (2022 est.)
comparison rankings: transmission/distribution losses 170; imports 116; consumption 52; installed generating capacity 54

Electricity generation sources: *fossil fuels:* 38.6% of total installed capacity (2022 est.)
solar: 1.4% of total installed capacity (2022 est.)
wind: 3.1% of total installed capacity (2022 est.)
hydroelectricity: 55.8% of total installed capacity (2022 est.)
biomass and waste: 1% of total installed capacity (2022 est.)

Coal: *production:* 153,000 metric tons (2022 est.)
consumption: 712,000 metric tons (2022 est.)
exports: 1.159 million metric tons (2022 est.)
imports: 356,000 metric tons (2022 est.)
proven reserves: 1.567 billion metric tons (2022 est.)

Petroleum: *total petroleum production:* 118,000 bbl/day (2023 est.)
refined petroleum consumption: 210,000 bbl/day (2022 est.)
crude oil estimated reserves: 858.89 million barrels (2021 est.)

Natural gas: *production:* 12.27 billion cubic meters (2022 est.)
consumption: 7.185 billion cubic meters (2022 est.)
exports: 5.041 billion cubic meters (2022 est.)
proven reserves: 300.159 billion cubic meters (2021 est.)

Carbon dioxide emissions: 45.504 million metric tonnes of CO2 (2022 est.)
from coal and metallurgical coke: 1.481 million metric tonnes of CO2 (2022 est.)
from petroleum and other liquids: 27.786 million metric tonnes of CO2 (2022 est.)
from consumed natural gas: 16.236 million metric tonnes of CO2 (2022 est.)
comparison ranking: total emissions 59

Energy consumption per capita: 24.932 million Btu/person (2022 est.)
comparison ranking: 123

COMMUNICATIONS

Telephones - fixed lines: *total subscriptions:* 1.798 million (2022 est.)
subscriptions per 100 inhabitants: 5 (2022 est.)
comparison ranking: total subscriptions 54

Telephones - mobile cellular: *total subscriptions:* 41.549 million (2022 est.)
subscriptions per 100 inhabitants: 122 (2022 est.)
comparison ranking: total subscriptions 40

Telecommunication systems: *general assessment:* after suffering a sharp retraction in the number of subscriptions and revenue during 2020 due to the pandemic, Peru's telecom sector managed to stage a small recovery in the first half of 2021; it will likely be two to three years before penetration rates return to the peak levels last seen in 2018; this is especially true given the overwhelming influence of mobile on Peru's telecommunications market, which now commands almost 95% of all connections; Peru's fixed-line teledensity continued its slow dropping below 7% at the end of 2021; investment in network infrastructure is mainly focused on rolling out fiber cable for fixed broadband services in (mainly) urban areas; fixed broadband services inched higher to reach 8.4% at the end of 2020, a positive result that reflected the shift to working from home during enforced lock downs at the start of the year; yet Peru has a relatively low level of computer use, and prices for fixed broadband services are among the highest in Latin America; the overwhelmingly preferred internet access platform will remain the smartphone, with a further 8.6% growth in the number of mobile broadband subscriptions expected in 2021 (2021)
domestic: fixed-line teledensity is 7 per 100 persons; mobile-cellular teledensity is 128 telephones per 100 persons (2021)
international: country code - 51; landing points for the SAM-1, IGW, American Movil-Telxius, SAC and PAN-AM submarine cable systems that provide links to parts of Central and South America, the Caribbean, and US; satellite earth stations - 2 Intelsat (Atlantic Ocean) (2019)

Broadcast media: 10 major TV networks of which only one, Television Nacional de Peru, is state owned; multi-channel cable TV services are available; in excess of 5,000 radio stations including a substantial number of indigenous language stations (2021)

Internet country code: .pe

Internet users: *total:* 24.14 million (2021 est.)
percent of population: 71% (2021 est.)
comparison ranking: total 36

Broadband - fixed subscriptions: *total:* 3.044 million (2020 est.)
subscriptions per 100 inhabitants: 9 (2020 est.)
comparison ranking: total 46

TRANSPORTATION

National air transport system: *number of registered air carriers:* 6 (2020)
inventory of registered aircraft operated by air carriers: 62
annual passenger traffic on registered air carriers: 17,758,527 (2018)
annual freight traffic on registered air carriers: 313.26 million (2018) mt-km

Civil aircraft registration country code prefix: OB

Airports: 166 (2024)
comparison ranking: 34

Heliports: 6 (2024)

Pipelines: 786 km extra heavy crude, 1,526 km gas, 679 km liquid petroleum gas, 1,106 km oil, 15 km refined products (2022)

Railways: *total:* 1,854.4 km (2017)
standard gauge: 1,730.4 km (2014) 1.435-m gauge (34 km electrified)
narrow gauge: 124 km (2014) 0.914-m gauge
comparison ranking: total 75

Roadways: *total:* 70,000 km (2021)
paved: 18,699 km (2022)
note: includes 27,109 km of national roads (21,434 km paved), 247,505 km of departmental roads (3,623 km paved), and 113,857 km of local roads (1,858 km paved)
comparison ranking: total 70

Waterways: 8,808 km (2011) (8,600 km of navigable tributaries on the Amazon River system and 208 km on Lago Titicaca)
comparison ranking: 16

Merchant marine: *total:* 111 (2023)
by type: general cargo 1, oil tanker 9, other 101
comparison ranking: total 85

Ports: *total ports:* 20 (2024)
large: 0
medium: 1
small: 3
very small: 16
ports with oil terminals: 16
key ports: Bahia de Matarani, Iquitos, Puerto del Callao, Talara

MILITARY AND SECURITY

Military and security forces: Armed Forces of Peru (Fuerzas Armadas del Perú or FAP): Peruvian Army (Ejercito del Peru), Peruvian Navy (Marina de Guerra del Peru, MGP, includes naval infantry and Coast Guard), Air Force of Peru (Fuerza Aerea del Peru, FAP)

Ministry of the Interior (Ministerio del Interior): Peruvian National Police (Policía Nacional del Perú, PNP) (2024)

Military expenditures: 1% of GDP (2023 est.)
1.1% of GDP (2022 est.)
1.1% of GDP (2021 est.)
1.2% of GDP (2020 est.)
1.2% of GDP (2019 est.)
comparison ranking: 125

Military and security service personnel strengths: information varies; approximately 95,000 active-duty personnel (60,000 Army; 25,000 Navy, including about 4,000 naval infantry and 1,000 Coast Guard; 10,000 Air Force) (2023)

Military equipment inventories and acquisitions: the military has a broad mix of mostly older but some more modern equipment from a range of suppliers, including Brazil, China, France, Germany, Italy, Russia and the former Soviet Union, South Korea, and the US; some deliveries have been secondhand weapons systems; Peru has a small defense industry, including a shipyard that builds and upgrades naval vessels; it also has defense industrial cooperation agreements with several countries, including Russia, South Korea, Spain, and the US (2024)

Military service age and obligation: 18-30 years of age for voluntary military service (12 months); no conscription (abolished in 1999) (2023)
note: as of 2019, women made up about 10% of the active duty military

Military deployments: 225 Central African Republic (MINUSCA) (2024)

Military - note: the Peruvian Armed Forces (FAP) are responsible for external defense in addition to some domestic security responsibilities in designated emergency areas and in exceptional circumstances; key areas of focus include counterinsurgency, counternarcotics, disaster relief, and maritime security operations; the FAP has contributed to UN missions since 1958 and has ties to regional militaries, particularly Colombia, as well as those of numerous other countries such as China, Russia, Spain, and the US; the FAP's last external conflict was a brief border war with Ecuador in 1995; the FAP supported the police during anti-government protests in early 2023 and was accused of human rights violations
the Joint Command of the Armed Forces of Peru (Comando Conjunto de las Fuerzas Armadas del Perú or CCFFAA) has responsibility for the planning, preparation, coordination, and direction of the military's operations; the CCFFAA has oversight over commands for air, air defense, cyber, maritime, and special operations, as well as five regional commands (Amazonas, central, north, south, and Ucayali) and a Special Command of the Valley of the Apurimac, Ene, and Mantaro rivers (CE-VRAEM); CE-VRAEM is responsible for combating the remnants of the Shining Path terrorist group (aka Sendero Luminoso) and includes several thousand air, ground, naval, police, and special forces personnel; the FAP also provides aircraft, vehicles, and logistical support to the command (2024)

SPACE

Space agency/agencies: National Aerospace Research and Development Commission (Comisión Nacional de Investigación y Desarrollo Aeroespacia, CONIDA; established 1974); National Satellite Imagery Operations Center (Centro Nacional de Operaciones de Imágenes Satelitales, CONIS; established 2006) (2024)

Space launch site(s): Punta Lobos Rocket Range (Chilca, Huancayo; used by foreign partners for scientific sounding rocket launches (1970s-1990s; the US used the site for scientific launches in 1975 and 1983) (2023)

Space program overview: has a small space program focused on acquiring satellites, applying space applications such as data satellite imagery, and building small rockets; has built a small science/technology satellite; operates satellites and processes satellite imagery data; builds and launches sounding rockets with goal of developing a satellite/space launch vehicle (SLV); researching, developing, and acquiring technologies for manufacturing satellites and satellite payloads with a focus on remote sensing (RS) capabilities; member of Latin American and Caribbean Space Agency (ALCE); cooperates with a variety of foreign space agencies and industries, including those of Brazil, China, the European Space Agency and individual member states (particularly France and Germany), India, Russia, South Korea, Thailand, and the US, as well as signatories of the Latin American and Caribbean Space Agency (ALCE) (2024)
note: further details about the key activities, programs, and milestones of the country's space program, as well as government spending estimates on the space sector, appear in the Space Programs reference guide

TERRORISM

Terrorist group(s): Shining Path (Sendero Luminoso)
note: details about the history, aims, leadership, organization, areas of operation, tactics, targets, weapons, size, and sources of support of the group(s) appear(s) in the Terrorism reference guide

TRANSNATIONAL ISSUES

Refugees and internally displaced persons: *refugees (country of origin):* 1,542,004 (Venezuela) (economic and political crisis; includes Venezuelans who have claimed asylum, are recognized as refugees, or have received alternative legal stay) (2023)
IDPs: 73,000 (civil war from 1980-2000; most IDPs are indigenous peasants in Andean and Amazonian regions; as of 2011, no new information on the situation of these IDPs) (2022)

Illicit drugs: world's second-largest producer of cocaine and coca (after Colombia), with approximately 84,400 hectares (ha) under cultivation in 2021; Peruvian cocaine is trafficked throughout South America for shipment to Europe, East Asia, Mexico, and the United States; major importer of precursor chemicals for cocaine production; growing domestic drug consumption problem; a major source of precursor or essential chemicals used in the production of illicit narcotics

PHILIPPINES

INTRODUCTION

Background: The Philippine Islands became a Spanish colony during the 16th century; they were ceded to the US in 1898 following the Spanish-American War. Led by Emilio AGUINALDO, the Filipinos conducted an insurgency against US rule from 1899-1902, although some fighting continued in outlying islands as late as 1913. In 1935, the Philippines became a self-governing commonwealth. Manuel QUEZON was elected president and was tasked with preparing the country for independence after a 10-year transition. The islands fell under Japanese occupation during World War II, and US forces and Filipinos fought together during 1944-45 to regain control. On 4 July 1946 the Republic of the Philippines attained its independence.

Twenty-one years of authoritarian rule under Ferdinand MARCOS ended in 1986, when a "people power" movement in Manila ("EDSA 1") forced him into exile and installed Corazon AQUINO as president. Several coup attempts hampered her presidency, and progress on political stability and economic development faltered until Fidel RAMOS was elected president in 1992. The US closed its last military bases on the islands the same year. Joseph ESTRADA was elected president in 1998. His vice-president, Gloria MACAPAGAL-ARROYO, succeded him in 2001 after ESTRADA's stormy impeachment trial on corruption charges broke down and another "people power" movement ("EDSA 2") demanded his resignation. MACAPAGAL-ARROYO was elected president in 2004. Corruption allegations marred her presidency, but the Philippine economy was one of the few to avoid contraction after the 2008 global financial crisis. Benigno AQUINO III was elected as president in 2010, followed by Rodrigo DUTERTE in 2016. During his term, DUTERTE pursued a controversial drug war that garnered international criticism for alleged human rights abuses. Ferdinand MARCOS, Jr. was elected president in 2022 with the largest popular vote in a presidential election since his father's ouster.

For decades, the country has been challenged by armed ethnic separatists, communist rebels, and Islamic terrorist groups, particularly in the southern islands and remote areas of Luzon.

GEOGRAPHY

Location: Southeastern Asia, archipelago between the Philippine Sea and the South China Sea, east of Vietnam

Geographic coordinates: 13 00 N, 122 00 E

Map references: Southeast Asia

Area: *total:* 300,000 sq km
land: 298,170 sq km
water: 1,830 sq km
comparison ranking: total 74

Area - comparative: slightly less than twice the size of Georgia; slightly larger than Arizona

Land boundaries: *total:* 0 km

Coastline: 36,289 km

Maritime claims: *territorial sea:* irregular polygon extending up to 100 nm from coastline as defined by 1898 treaty; since late 1970s has also claimed polygonal-shaped area in South China Sea as wide as 285 nm
exclusive economic zone: 200 nm
continental shelf: to the depth of exploitation

Climate: tropical marine; northeast monsoon (November to April); southwest monsoon (May to October)

Terrain: mostly mountains with narrow to extensive coastal lowlands

Elevation: *highest point:* Mount Apo 2,954 m
lowest point: Philippine Sea 0 m
mean elevation: 442 m

Natural resources: timber, petroleum, nickel, cobalt, silver, gold, salt, copper

Land use: *agricultural land:* 41% (2018 est.)
arable land: 18.2% (2018 est.)
permanent crops: 17.8% (2018 est.)
permanent pasture: 5% (2018 est.)
forest: 25.9% (2018 est.)
other: 33.1% (2018 est.)

Irrigated land: 16,270 sq km (2012)

Major lakes (area sq km): *salt water lake(s):* Laguna de Bay - 890 sq km

Population distribution: population concentrated where good farmlands lie; highest concentrations are northwest and south-central Luzon, the southeastern extension of Luzon, and the islands of the Visayan Sea, particularly Cebu and Negros; Manila is home to one-eighth of the entire national population

Natural hazards: astride typhoon belt, usually affected by 15 and struck by five to six cyclonic storms each year; landslides; active volcanoes; destructive earthquakes; tsunamis
volcanism: significant volcanic activity; Taal (311 m), which has shown recent unrest and may erupt in the near future, has been deemed a Decade Volcano by the International Association of Volcanology and Chemistry of the Earth's Interior, worthy of study due to its explosive history and close proximity to human populations; Mayon (2,462 m), the country's most active volcano, erupted in 2009 forcing over 33,000 to be evacuated; other historically active volcanoes include Biliran, Babuyan Claro, Bulusan, Camiguin, Camiguin de Babuyanes, Didicas, Iraya, Jolo, Kanlaon, Makaturing, Musuan, Parker, Pinatubo, and Ragang; see note 2 under "Geography - note"

Geography - note: *note 1:* for decades, the Philippine archipelago was reported as having 7,107 islands; in 2016, the national mapping authority reported that hundreds of new islands had been discovered and increased the number of islands to 7,641, though not all of the new islands have been verified; the country is favorably located in relation to many of Southeast Asia's main water bodies: the South China Sea, Philippine Sea, Sulu Sea, Celebes Sea, and Luzon Strait
note 2: Philippines is one of the countries along the Ring of Fire, a belt of active volcanoes and earthquake epicenters bordering the Pacific Ocean; up to 90% of the world's earthquakes and some 75% of the world's volcanoes occur within the Ring of Fire
note 3: the Philippines sits astride the Pacific typhoon belt and an average of 9 typhoons make landfall on the islands each year – with about 5 of these being destructive; the country is the most exposed in the world to tropical storms

PEOPLE AND SOCIETY

Population: *total:* 118,277,063
male: 59,227,092
female: 59,049,971 (2024 est.)
comparison rankings: female 13; male 12; total 13

Nationality: *noun:* Filipino(s)
adjective: Philippine

Ethnic groups: Tagalog 26%, Bisaya/Binisaya 14.3%, Ilocano 8%, Cebuano 8%, Illonggo 7.9%, Bikol/Bicol 6.5%, Waray 3.8%, Kapampangan 3%, Maguindanao 1.9%, Pangasinan 1.9%, other local ethnicities 18.5%, foreign ethnicities 0.2% (2020 est.)

Languages: Tagalog 39.9%, Bisaya/Binisaya 16%, Hiligaynon/Ilonggo 7.3%, Ilocano 7.1%, Cebuano 6.5%, Bikol/Bicol 3.9%, Waray 2.6%, Kapampangan 2.4%, Maguindanao 1.4%, Pangasinan/Panggalato 1.3%, other languages/dialects 11.2%, unspecified 0.4% (2020 est.)
major-language sample(s):
Ang World Factbook, ang mapagkukunan ng kailangang impormasyon. (Tagalog)
note: data represent percentage of households; unspecified Filipino (based on Tagalog) and English are official languagesTaga; eight major dialects

- Tagalog, Cebuano, Ilocano, Hiligaynon or Ilonggo, Bicol, Waray, Pampango, and Pangasinan

Religions: Roman Catholic 78.8%, Muslim 6.4%, Iglesia ni Cristo 2.6%, other Christian 3.9%, other 8.2%, none/unspecified <0.1 (2020 est.)

Demographic profile: The Philippines is an ethnically diverse country that is in the early stages of demographic transition. Its fertility rate has dropped steadily since the 1950s. The decline was more rapid after the introduction of a national population program in the 1970s in large part due to the increased use of modern contraceptive methods, but fertility has decreased more slowly in recent years. The country's total fertility rate (TFR) – the average number of births per woman – dropped below 5 in the 1980s, below 4 in the 1990s, and below 3 in the 2010s. TFR continues to be above replacement level at 2.9 and even higher among the poor, rural residents, and the less-educated. Significant reasons for elevated TFR are the desire for more than two children, in part because children are a means of financial assistance and security for parents as they age, particularly among the poor.

The Philippines are the source of one of the world's largest emigrant populations, much of which consists of legal temporary workers known as Overseas Foreign Workers or OFWs. As of 2019, there were 2.2 million OFWs. They work in a wide array of fields, most frequently in services (such as caregivers and domestic work), skilled trades, and construction but also in professional fields, including nursing and engineering. OFWs most often migrate to Middle Eastern countries, but other popular destinations include Hong Kong, China, and Singapore, as well as employment on ships. Filipino seafarers make up 35-40% of the world's seafarers, as of 2014. Women OFWs, who work primarily in domestic services and entertainment, have outnumbered men since 1992.

Migration and remittances have been a feature of Philippine culture for decades. The government has encouraged and facilitated emigration, regulating recruitment agencies and adopting legislation to protect the rights of migrant workers. Filipinos began emigrating to the US and Hawaii early in the 20th century. In 1934, US legislation limited Filipinos to 50 visas per year except during labor shortages, causing emigration to plummet. It was not until the 1960s, when the US and other destination countries – Canada, Australia, and New Zealand – loosened their immigration policies, that Filipino emigration expanded and diversified. The government implemented an overseas employment program in the 1970s, promoting Filipino labor to Gulf countries needing more workers for their oil industries. Filipino emigration increased rapidly. The government had intended for international migration to be temporary, but a lack of jobs and poor wages domestically, the ongoing demand for workers in the Gulf countries, and new labor markets in Asia continue to spur Philippine emigration.

Age structure: *0-14 years:* 30.2% (male 18,234,279/female 17,462,803)
15-64 years: 64.3% (male 38,381,583/female 37,613,294)
65 years and over: 5.6% (2024 est.) (male 2,611,230/female 3,973,874)

Dependency ratios: *total dependency ratio:* 56.2
youth dependency ratio: 47.8
elderly dependency ratio: 8.3
potential support ratio: 12 (2021 est.)

Median age: *total:* 25.7 years (2024 est.)
male: 25.1 years
female: 26.3 years
comparison ranking: total 167

Population growth rate: 1.56% (2024 est.)
comparison ranking: 60

Birth rate: 22.1 births/1,000 population (2024 est.)
comparison ranking: 53

Death rate: 6.2 deaths/1,000 population (2024 est.)
comparison ranking: 146

Net migration rate: -0.2 migrant(s)/1,000 population (2024 est.)
comparison ranking: 109

Population distribution: population concentrated where good farmlands lie; highest concentrations are northwest and south-central Luzon, the southeastern extension of Luzon, and the islands of the Visayan Sea, particularly Cebu and Negros; Manila is home to one-eighth of the entire national population

Urbanization: *urban population:* 48.3% of total population (2023)
rate of urbanization: 2.04% annual rate of change (2020-25 est.)

Major urban areas - population: 14.667 million MANILA (capital), 1.949 million Davao, 1.025 million Cebu City, 931,000 Zamboanga, 960,000 Antipolo, 803,000 Cagayan de Oro City, 803,000 Dasmarinas (2023)

Sex ratio: *at birth:* 1.05 male(s)/female
0-14 years: 1.04 male(s)/female
15-64 years: 1.02 male(s)/female
65 years and over: 0.66 male(s)/female
total population: 1 male(s)/female (2024 est.)

Mother's mean age at first birth: 23.6 years (2022 est.)
note: data represents median age at first birth among women 25-49

Maternal mortality ratio: 78 deaths/100,000 live births (2020 est.)
comparison ranking: 75

Infant mortality rate: *total:* 22 deaths/1,000 live births (2024 est.)
male: 24.4 deaths/1,000 live births
female: 19.6 deaths/1,000 live births
comparison ranking: total 69

Life expectancy at birth: *total population:* 70.8 years (2024 est.)
male: 67.3 years
female: 74.5 years
comparison ranking: total population 170

Total fertility rate: 2.75 children born/woman (2024 est.)
comparison ranking: 58

Gross reproduction rate: 1.34 (2024 est.)

Contraceptive prevalence rate: 54.1% (2017)

Drinking water source: *improved: urban:* 99.1% of population
rural: 95% of population
total: 97% of population
unimproved: urban: 0.9% of population
rural: 5% of population
total: 3% of population (2020 est.)

Current health expenditure: 5.1% of GDP (2020)

Physician density: 0.77 physicians/1,000 population (2020)

Hospital bed density: 1 beds/1,000 population (2014)

Sanitation facility access: *improved: urban:* 96% of population
rural: 91% of population
total: 93.4% of population
unimproved: urban: 4% of population
rural: 9% of population
total: 6.6% of population (2020 est.)

Obesity - adult prevalence rate: 6.4% (2016)
comparison ranking: 167

Alcohol consumption per capita: *total:* 4.85 liters of pure alcohol (2019 est.)
beer: 1.47 liters of pure alcohol (2019 est.)
wine: 0.03 liters of pure alcohol (2019 est.)
spirits: 3.34 liters of pure alcohol (2019 est.)
other alcohols: 0.01 liters of pure alcohol (2019 est.)
comparison ranking: total 84

Tobacco use: *total:* 22.9% (2020 est.)
male: 39.3% (2020 est.)
female: 6.5% (2020 est.)
comparison ranking: total 67

Children under the age of 5 years underweight: 19.1% (2018)
comparison ranking: 17

Currently married women (ages 15-49): 59.3% (2023 est.)

Child marriage: *women married by age 15:* 2.2%
women married by age 18: 16.5% (2017 est.)

Education expenditures: 3.7% of GDP (2020 est.)
comparison ranking: 129

Literacy: *definition:* age 15 and over can read and write
total population: 96.3%
male: 95.7%
female: 96.9% (2019)

School life expectancy (primary to tertiary education): *total:* 13 years
male: 13 years
female: 13 years (2020)

People - note: one of only two predominantly Christian nations in Southeast Asia, the other being Timor-Leste

ENVIRONMENT

Environment - current issues: uncontrolled deforestation especially in watershed areas; illegal mining and logging; soil erosion; air and water pollution in major urban centers; coral reef degradation; increasing pollution of coastal mangrove swamps that are important fish breeding grounds; coastal erosion; dynamite fishing; wildlife extinction

Environment - international agreements: *party to:* Biodiversity, Climate Change, Climate Change-Kyoto Protocol, Climate Change-Paris Agreement, Comprehensive Nuclear Test Ban, Desertification, Endangered Species, Hazardous Wastes, Law of the Sea, Marine Dumping-London Convention, Marine Dumping-London Protocol, Nuclear Test Ban, Ozone Layer Protection, Ship Pollution, Tropical Timber 2006, Wetlands
signed, but not ratified: none of the selected agreements

Climate: tropical marine; northeast monsoon (November to April); southwest monsoon (May to October)

Urbanization: *urban population:* 48.3% of total population (2023)
rate of urbanization: 2.04% annual rate of change (2020-25 est.)

Revenue from forest resources: 0.18% of GDP (2018 est.)

comparison ranking: 96

Revenue from coal: 0.07% of GDP (2018 est.)
comparison ranking: 28

Air pollutants: *particulate matter emissions:* 22.45 micrograms per cubic meter (2019 est.)
carbon dioxide emissions: 122.29 megatons (2016 est.)
methane emissions: 51.32 megatons (2020 est.)

Waste and recycling: *municipal solid waste generated annually:* 14,631,923 tons (2016 est.)
municipal solid waste recycled annually: 4,096,938 tons (2014 est.)
percent of municipal solid waste recycled: 28% (2014 est.)

Major lakes (area sq km): *salt water lake(s):* Laguna de Bay - 890 sq km

Total water withdrawal: *municipal:* 8.16 billion cubic meters (2020 est.)
industrial: 9.88 billion cubic meters (2020 est.)
agricultural: 67.83 billion cubic meters (2020 est.)

Total renewable water resources: 479 billion cubic meters (2020 est.)

Geoparks: *total global geoparks and regional networks:* 1
global geoparks and regional networks: Bohol Island (2023)

GOVERNMENT

Country name: *conventional long form:* Republic of the Philippines
conventional short form: Philippines
local long form: Republika ng Pilipinas
local short form: Pilipinas
etymology: named in honor of King PHILLIP II of Spain by Spanish explorer Ruy LOPEZ de VILLALOBOS, who visited some of the islands in 1543

Government type: presidential republic

Capital: *name:* Manila
geographic coordinates: 14 36 N, 120 58 E
time difference: UTC+8 (13 hours ahead of Washington, DC, during Standard Time)
etymology: derives from the Tagalog "may-nila" meaning "where there is indigo" and refers to the presence of indigo-yielding plants growing in the area surrounding the original settlement

Administrative divisions: 81 provinces and 38 chartered cities
provinces: Abra, Agusan del Norte, Agusan del Sur, Aklan, Albay, Antique, Apayao, Aurora, Basilan, Bataan, Batanes, Batangas, Biliran, Benguet, Bohol, Bukidnon, Bulacan, Cagayan, Camarines Norte, Camarines Sur, Camiguin, Capiz, Catanduanes, Cavite, Cebu, Cotabato, Davao del Norte, Davao del Sur, Davao de Oro, Davao Occidental, Davao Oriental, Dinagat Islands, Eastern Samar, Guimaras, Ifugao, Ilocos Norte, Ilocos Sur, Iloilo, Isabela, Kalinga, Laguna, Lanao del Norte, Lanao del Sur, La Union, Leyte, Maguindanao, Marinduque, Masbate, Mindoro Occidental, Mindoro Oriental, Misamis Occidental, Misamis Oriental, Mountain, Negros Occidental, Negros Oriental, Northern Samar, Nueva Ecija, Nueva Vizcaya, Palawan, Pampanga, Pangasinan, Quezon, Quirino, Rizal, Romblon, Samar, Sarangani, Siquijor, Sorsogon, South Cotabato, Southern Leyte, Sultan Kudarat, Sulu, Surigao del Norte, Surigao del Sur, Tarlac, Tawi-Tawi, Zambales, Zamboanga del Norte, Zamboanga del Sur, Zamboanga Sibugay;
chartered cities: Angeles, Bacolod, Baguio, Butuan, Cagayan de Oro, Caloocan, Cebu, Cotabato, Dagupan, Davao, General Santos, Iligan, Iloilo, Lapu-Lapu, Las Pinas, Lucena, Makati, Malabon, Mandaluyong, Mandaue, Manila, Marikina, Muntinlupa, Naga, Navotas, Olongapo, Ormoc, Paranaque, Pasay, Pasig, Puerto Princesa, Quezon, San Juan, Santiago, Tacloban, Taguig, Valenzuela, Zamboanga

Independence: 4 July 1946 (from the US)

National holiday: Independence Day, 12 June (1898); note - 12 June 1898 was date of declaration of independence from Spain; 4 July 1946 was date of independence from the US

Legal system: mixed legal system of civil, common, Islamic (sharia), and customary law

Constitution: *history:* several previous; latest ratified 2 February 1987, effective 11 February 1987
amendments: proposed by Congress if supported by three fourths of the membership, by a constitutional convention called by Congress, or by public petition; passage by either of the three proposal methods requires a majority vote in a national referendum; note - the constitution has not been amended since its enactment in 1987

International law organization participation: accepts compulsory ICJ jurisdiction with reservations; withdrew from the ICCt in March 2019

Citizenship: *citizenship by birth:* no
citizenship by descent only: at least one parent must be a citizen of the Philippines
dual citizenship recognized: no
residency requirement for naturalization: 10 years

Suffrage: 18 years of age; universal

Executive branch: *chief of state:* President Ferdinand "BongBong" MARCOS, Jr. (since 30 June 2022)
head of government: President Ferdinand "BongBong" MARCOS, Jr. (since 30 June 2022)
cabinet: Cabinet appointed by the president with the consent of the Commission of Appointments, an independent body of 25 Congressional members including the Senate president (ex officio chairman), appointed by the president
elections/appointments: president and vice president directly elected on separate ballots by simple majority popular vote for a single 6-year term; election last held on 9 May 2022 (next to be held on 9 May 2028)
election results:
2022: Ferdinand MARCOS, Jr. elected president; percent of vote - Ferdinand MARCOS, Jr. (PFP) 58.7%, Leni ROBREDO (independent) 27.9%, Manny PACQUIAO (PROMDI) 6.8%, other 6.6%; Sara DUTERTE-Carpio elected vice president; percent of vote Sara DUTERTE-Carpio (Lakas-CMD) 61.5%, Francis PANGILINAN (LP) 17.8%, Tito SOTTO 15.8%, other 4.9%
2016: Rodrigo DUTERTE elected president; percent of vote - Rodrigo DUTERTE (PDP-Laban) 39%, Manuel "Mar" ROXAS (LP) 23.5%, Grace POE (independent) 21.4%, Jejomar BINAY (UNA) 12.7%, Miriam Defensor SANTIAGO (PRP) 3.4%; Leni ROBREDO elected vice president; percent of vote Leni ROBREDO (LP) 35.1%, Bongbong MARCOS (independent) 34.5%, Alan CAYETANO 14.4%, Francis ESCUDERO (independent) 12%, other 4%
note: the president is both chief of state and head of government

Legislative branch: *description:* bicameral Congress or Kongreso consists of:
Senate or Senado (24 seats; members directly elected in multi-seat constituencies by majority vote; members serve 6- year terms with one-half of the membership renewed every 3 years)
House of Representatives or Kapulungan Ng Mga Kinatawan (316 seats; 253 members directly elected in single-seat constituencies by simple majority vote and 63 representing minorities directly elected by party-list proportional representation vote; members serve 3-year terms)
elections: Senate - elections last held on 9 May 2022 (next to be held in May 2025)
House of Representatives - elections last held on 9 May 2022 (next to be held in May 2025)
election results: Senate - percent of vote by party - NA; seats by party - NPC 5, PDP-Laban 5, NP 4, other 5, independent 5; composition - men 17, women 7, percentage women 29.2%
House of Representatives - percent of vote by party - PDP-Laban 22.7%, NP 13.7%, NUP 12.6%, NPC 11.7%, Lakas- CMD 9.4%, LP 3.8%, HNP 2.5%, other 19.6%, independent 4%; seats by party - PDP-Laban 66, NP 36, NPC 35, NUP 33, Lakas-CMD 26, LP 10, HNP 6, other 35, independent 6, party-list 63; composition - men 226, women 85, percentage women 27.3%; total Congress percentage women 27.5%

Judicial branch: *highest court(s):* Supreme Court (consists of a chief justice and 14 associate justices)
judge selection and term of office: justices are appointed by the president on the recommendation of the Judicial and Bar Council, a constitutionally created, 6-member body that recommends Supreme Court nominees; justices serve until age 70
subordinate courts: Court of Appeals; Sandiganbayan (special court for corruption cases of government officials); Court of Tax Appeals; regional, metropolitan, and municipal trial courts; sharia courts

Political parties: Democratic Action (Aksyon Demokratiko)
Alliance for Change (Hugpong ng Pagbabago or HNP)
Lakas ng EDSA-Christian Muslim Democrats or Lakas-CMD
Liberal Party or LP
Nacionalista Party or NP
Nationalist People's Coalition or NPC
National Unity Party or NUP
Partido Demokratiko Pilipino-Lakas ng Bayan or PDP-Laban
Partido Federal ng Pilipinas or PFP
Progressive Movement for the Devolution of Initiatives or PROMDI

International organization participation: ADB, APEC, ARF, ASEAN, BIS, CD, CICA (observer), CP, EAS, FAO, G-24, G-77, IAEA, IBRD, ICAO, ICRM, IDA, IFAD, IFC, IFRCS, IHO, ILO, IMF, IMO, IMSO, Interpol, IOC, IOM, IPU, ISO, ITSO, ITU, ITUC (NGOs), MIGA, MINUSTAH, NAM, OAS (observer), OPCW, PCA, PIF (partner), UN, UNCTAD, UNESCO, UNHCR, UNIDO, Union Latina, UNMIL, UNMOGIP, UNOCI, UNOOSA, UNWTO, UPU, WCO, WFTU (NGOs), WHO, WIPO, WMO, WTO

Diplomatic representation in the US: *chief of mission:* Ambassador Jose Manuel del Gallego ROMUALDEZ (since 29 November 2017)
chancery: 1600 Massachusetts Avenue NW, Washington, DC 20036
telephone: [1] (202) 467-9300

FAX: [1] (202) 328-7614
email address and website:
info@phembassy-us.org
The Embassy of the Republic of the Philippines in Washington D.C. (philippineembassy-dc.org)
consulate(s) general: Chicago, Honolulu, Houston, Los Angeles, New York, San Francisco, Tamuning (Guam)

Diplomatic representation from the US: *chief of mission:* Ambassador MaryKay Loss CARLSON (since 22 July 2022)
embassy: 1201 Roxas Boulevard, Manila 1000
mailing address: 8600 Manila Place, Washington DC 20521-8600
telephone: [63] (2) 5301-2000
FAX: [63] (2) 5301-2017
email address and website:
acsinfomanila@state.gov
https://ph.usembassy.gov/

Flag description: *two equal horizontal bands of blue (top) and red; a white equilateral triangle is based on the hoist side; the center of the triangle displays a yellow sun with eight primary rays; each corner of the triangle contains a small, yellow, five-pointed star; blue stands for peace and justice, red symbolizes courage, the white equal-sided triangle represents equality; the rays recall the first eight provinces that sought independence from Spain, while the stars represent the three major geographical divisions of the country:* Luzon, Visayas, and Mindanao; the design of the flag dates to 1897
note: in wartime the flag is flown upside down with the red band at the top

National symbol(s): three stars and sun, Philippine eagle; national colors: red, white, blue, yellow

National anthem: *name:* "Lupang Hinirang" (Chosen Land)
lyrics/music: Jose PALMA (revised by Felipe PADILLA de Leon)/Julian FELIPE
note: music adopted 1898, original Spanish lyrics adopted 1899, Filipino (Tagalog) lyrics adopted 1956; although the original lyrics were written in Spanish, later English and Filipino versions were created; today, only the Filipino version is used

National heritage: *total World Heritage Sites:* 6 (3 cultural, 3 natural)
selected World Heritage Site locales: Baroque Churches of the Philippines (c); Tubbataha Reefs Natural Park (n); Rice Terraces of the Philippine Cordilleras (c); Historic Vigan (c); Puerto-Princesa Subterranean River National Park (n);
Mount Hamiguitan Range Wildlife Sanctuary (n)

ECONOMY

Economic overview: growing Southeast Asian economy; commercial rebound led by transportation, construction and financial services; electronics exports recovering from sector slowdown; significant remittances; interest rate rises following heightened inflation; uncertainties due to increased regional tensions with China

Real GDP (purchasing power parity): $1.138 trillion (2023 est.)
$1.078 trillion (2022 est.)
$1.002 trillion (2021 est.)
note: data in 2021 dollars
comparison ranking: 31

Real GDP growth rate: 5.55% (2023 est.)
7.58% (2022 est.)
5.71% (2021 est.)
note: annual GDP % growth based on constant local currency
comparison ranking: 37

Real GDP per capita: $9,700 (2023 est.)
$9,300 (2022 est.)
$8,800 (2021 est.)
note: data in 2021 dollars
comparison ranking: 148

GDP (official exchange rate): $437.146 billion (2023 est.)
note: data in current dollars at official exchange rate

Inflation rate (consumer prices): 5.98% (2023 est.)
5.82% (2022 est.)
3.93% (2021 est.)
note: annual % change based on consumer prices
comparison ranking: 128

Credit ratings: Fitch rating: BBB (2017)

Moody's rating: Baa2 (2014)

Standard & Poors rating: BBB+ (2019)
note: The year refers to the year in which the current credit rating was first obtained.

GDP - composition, by sector of origin: *agriculture:* 9.4% (2023 est.)
industry: 28.2% (2023 est.)
services: 62.4% (2023 est.)
note: figures may not total 100% due to non-allocated consumption not captured in sector-reported data
comparison rankings: services 73; industry 77; agriculture 80

GDP - composition, by end use: *household consumption:* 76.5% (2023 est.)
government consumption: 14.2% (2023 est.)
investment in fixed capital: 23.6% (2023 est.)
investment in inventories: -0.3% (2023 est.)
exports of goods and services: 26.7% (2023 est.)
imports of goods and services: -40.7% (2023 est.)
note: figures may not total 100% due to rounding or gaps in data collection

Agricultural products: sugarcane, rice, coconuts, maize, bananas, vegetables, tropical fruits, plantains, pineapples, cassava (2022)
note: top ten agricultural products based on tonnage

Industries: semiconductors and electronics assembly, business process outsourcing, food and beverage manufacturing, construction, electric/gas/water supply, chemical products, radio/television/communications equipment and apparatus, petroleum and fuel, textile and garments, non-metallic minerals, basic metal industries, transport equipment

Industrial production growth rate: 3.59% (2023 est.)
note: annual % change in industrial value added based on constant local currency
comparison ranking: 90

Labor force: 49.477 million (2023 est.)
note: number of people ages 15 or older who are employed or seeking work
comparison ranking: 14

Unemployment rate: 2.23% (2023 est.)
2.6% (2022 est.)
3.4% (2021 est.)
note: % of labor force seeking employment
comparison ranking: 24

Youth unemployment rate (ages 15-24): *total:* 6.9% (2023 est.)
male: 5.9% (2023 est.)
female: 8.4% (2023 est.)
note: % of labor force ages 15-24 seeking employment
comparison ranking: total 160

Population below poverty line: 18.1% (2021 est.)
note: % of population with income below national poverty line

Gini Index coefficient - distribution of family income: 40.7 (2021 est.)
note: index (0-100) of income distribution; higher values represent greater inequality
comparison ranking: 37

Average household expenditures: *on food:* 37.9% of household expenditures (2022 est.)
on alcohol and tobacco: 2% of household expenditures (2022 est.)

Household income or consumption by percentage share: *lowest 10%:* 2.7% (2021 est.)
highest 10%: 32.5% (2021 est.)
note: % share of income accruing to lowest and highest 10% of population

Remittances: 8.94% of GDP (2023 est.)
9.41% of GDP (2022 est.)
9.31% of GDP (2021 est.)
note: personal transfers and compensation between resident and non-resident individuals/households/entities

Budget: *revenues:* $65.051 billion (2022 est.)
expenditures: $75.238 billion (2022 est.)
note: central government revenues and expenses (excluding grants/extrabudgetary units/social security funds) converted to US dollars at average official exchange rate for year indicated

Public debt: 39.9% of GDP (2017 est.)
note: central government debt as a % of GDP
comparison ranking: 132

Taxes and other revenues: 14.62% (of GDP) (2022 est.)
note: central government tax revenue as a % of GDP
comparison ranking: 144

Current account balance: -$11.206 billion (2023 est.)
-$18.261 billion (2022 est.)
-$5.943 billion (2021 est.)
note: balance of payments - net trade and primary/secondary income in current dollars
comparison ranking: 195

Exports: $103.601 billion (2023 est.)
$98.832 billion (2022 est.)
$87.798 billion (2021 est.)
note: balance of payments - exports of goods and services in current dollars
comparison ranking: 49

Exports - partners: US 14%, China 14%, Hong Kong 11%, Japan 10%, Singapore 6% (2022)
note: top five export partners based on percentage share of exports

Exports - commodities: integrated circuits, machine parts, gold, semiconductors, insulated wire (2022)
note: top five export commodities based on value in dollars

Imports: $150.269 billion (2023 est.)
$152.638 billion (2022 est.)
$126.565 billion (2021 est.)
note: balance of payments - imports of goods and services in current dollars
comparison ranking: 38

Imports - partners: China 32%, Indonesia 8%, South Korea 7%, Japan 7%, Singapore 6% (2022)
note: top five import partners based on percentage share of imports

Imports - commodities: integrated circuits, refined petroleum, coal, cars, plastic products (2022)
note: top five import commodities based on value in dollars

Reserves of foreign exchange and gold: $103.742 billion (2023 est.)
$96.04 billion (2022 est.)
$108.755 billion (2021 est.)
note: holdings of gold (year-end prices)/foreign exchange/special drawing rights in current dollars
comparison ranking: 27

Exchange rates: Philippine pesos (PHP) per US dollar -

Exchange rates: 55.63 (2023 est.)
54.478 (2022 est.)
49.255 (2021 est.)
49.624 (2020 est.)
51.796 (2019 est.)

ENERGY

Electricity access: *electrification - total population:* 94.8% (2022 est.)
electrification - urban areas: 98%
electrification - rural areas: 91.1%

Electricity: *installed generating capacity:* 27.542 million kW (2022 est.)
consumption: 102.834 billion kWh (2022 est.)
transmission/distribution losses: 10.174 billion kWh (2022 est.)
comparison rankings: transmission/distribution losses 179; consumption 34; installed generating capacity 38

Electricity generation sources: *fossil fuels:* 78.2% of total installed capacity (2022 est.)
solar: 1.4% of total installed capacity (2022 est.)
wind: 1.1% of total installed capacity (2022 est.)
hydroelectricity: 8% of total installed capacity (2022 est.)
geothermal: 10.2% of total installed capacity (2022 est.)
biomass and waste: 1.1% of total installed capacity (2022 est.)

Coal: *production:* 14.483 million metric tons (2022 est.)
consumption: 37.13 million metric tons (2022 est.)
exports: 8.698 million metric tons (2022 est.)
imports: 31.634 million metric tons (2022 est.)
proven reserves: 361 million metric tons (2022 est.)

Petroleum: *total petroleum production:* 10,000 bbl/day (2023 est.)
refined petroleum consumption: 453,000 bbl/day (2022 est.)
crude oil estimated reserves: 138.5 million barrels (2021 est.)

Natural gas: *production:* 2.251 billion cubic meters (2022 est.)
consumption: 2.251 billion cubic meters (2022 est.)
proven reserves: 98.543 billion cubic meters (2021 est.)

Carbon dioxide emissions: 136.273 million metric tonnes of CO2 (2022 est.)
from coal and metallurgical coke: 70.975 million metric tonnes of CO2 (2022 est.)
from petroleum and other liquids: 60.932 million metric tonnes of CO2 (2022 est.)
from consumed natural gas: 4.365 million metric tonnes of CO2 (2022 est.)
comparison ranking: total emissions 35

Energy consumption per capita: 15.558 million Btu/person (2022 est.)
comparison ranking: 138

COMMUNICATIONS

Telephones - fixed lines: *total subscriptions:* 4.885 million (2022 est.)
subscriptions per 100 inhabitants: 4 (2022 est.)
comparison ranking: total subscriptions 30

Telephones - mobile cellular: *total subscriptions:* 166.454 million (2022 est.)
subscriptions per 100 inhabitants: 144 (2022 est.)
comparison ranking: total subscriptions 11

Telecommunication systems: *general assessment:* the Covid-19 pandemic had a relatively minor impact on the Philippine's telecom sector in 2020; subscriber numbers fell in some areas, but this was offset by strong growth in mobile data and broadband usage since a significant proportion of the population transitioned to working or studying from home; major investment programs covering LTE, 5G, and fiber broadband networks suffered slight delays due to holdups in supply chains, but activity has since ramped up in an attempt to complete the roll outs as per the original schedule; the major telecom operators had mixed financial results for the past year; overall, the number of mobile subscribers is expected to grow to 153 million by the end of 2021, with the penetration rate approaching 144%; the government remains keen, and committed, to seeing strong competition, growth, and service excellence in the telecom sector, so there is likely to be continued support (financially as well as through legislation such as enabling mobile tower sharing and number portability) to ensure that the sector remains viable for emerging players; the mobile sector will remain the Philippines' primary market for telecommunications well into the future; the unique terrain and resulting challenges associated with accessing remote parts of the archipelago means that in many areas fixed networks are neither cost-effective nor logistically viable; the bulk of telecoms investment over the coming years will continue to be in 5G and 5G-enabled LTE networks; coverage of LTE and 5G networks extends to over 95% of the population, and for the vast majority of people mobile will likely remain their only platform for telecom services (2021)
domestic: fixed-line nearly 4 per 100 and mobile-cellular nearly 143 per 100 (2021)
international: country code - 63; landing points for the NDTN, TGN-IA, AAG, PLCN, EAC-02C, DFON, SJC, APCN-2, SeaMeWe, Boracay-Palawan Submarine Cable System, Palawa-Illoilo Cable System, NDTN, SEA-US, SSSFOIP, ASE and JUPITAR submarine cables that together provide connectivity to the US, Southeast Asia, Asia, Europe, Africa, the Middle East, and Australia (2019)

Broadcast media: multiple national private TV and radio networks; multi-channel satellite and cable TV systems available; more than 400 TV stations; about 1,500 cable TV providers with more than 2 million subscribers, and some 1,400 radio stations; the Philippines adopted Japan's Integrated Service Digital Broadcast – Terrestrial standard for digital terrestrial television in November 2013 and is scheduled to complete the switch from analog to digital broadcasting by the end of 2023 (2019)

Internet country code: .ph

Internet users: *total:* 58.3 million (2021 est.)
percent of population: 53% (2021 est.)
comparison ranking: total 18

Broadband - fixed subscriptions: *total:* 7,936,574 (2020 est.)
subscriptions per 100 inhabitants: 7 (2020 est.)
comparison ranking: total 25

TRANSPORTATION

National air transport system: *number of registered air carriers:* 13 (2020)
inventory of registered aircraft operated by air carriers: 200
annual passenger traffic on registered air carriers: 43,080,118 (2018)
annual freight traffic on registered air carriers: 835.9 million (2018) mt-km

Civil aircraft registration country code prefix: RP

Airports: 246 (2024)
comparison ranking: 27

Heliports: 341 (2024)

Pipelines: 530 km gas, 138 km oil (non-operational), 185 km refined products (2017)

Railways: *total:* 77 km (2017)
standard gauge: 49 km (2017) 1.435-m gauge
narrow gauge: 28 km (2017) 1.067-m gauge
comparison ranking: total 130

Roadways: *total:* 216,387 km
paved: 61,093 km
unpaved: 155,294 km (2014)
comparison ranking: total 24

Waterways: 3,219 km (2011) (limited to vessels with draft less than 1.5 m)
comparison ranking: 32

Merchant marine: *total:* 2,203 (2023)
by type: bulk carrier 52, container ship 43, general cargo 955, oil tanker 207, other 946
comparison ranking: total 11

Ports: *total ports:* 70 (2024)
large: 2
medium: 4
small: 8
very small: 56
ports with oil terminals: 22
key ports: Batangas City, Cagayan de Oro, Cebu, Manila, San Fernando Harbor, Subic Bay

MILITARY AND SECURITY

Military and security forces: Armed Forces of the Philippines (AFP): Army, Navy (includes Marine Corps), Air Force

Department of Transportation: Philippine Coast Guard (PCG)

Department of the Interior: Philippine National Police Force (PNP) (2024)
note 1: the PCG is an armed and uniformed service that would be attached to the AFP during a conflict
note 2: the Philippine Government also arms and supports civilian militias; the AFP controls the Civilian Armed Force Geographical Units, while the Civilian Volunteer Organizations fall under PNP command

Military expenditures: 1.5% of GDP (2023 est.)
1.2% of GDP (2022 est.)
1.2% of GDP (2021 est.)
1.1% of GDP (2020 est.)
1.1% of GDP (2019 est.)
comparison ranking: 87

Military and security service personnel strengths: approximately 140,000 active-duty personnel (100,000 Army; 25,000 Navy, including about 8,000 Marine Corps; 15,000 Air Force) (2023)

Military equipment inventories and acquisitions: the AFP is equipped with a wide mix of imported weapons systems; in recent years, it has received equipment from more than a dozen countries, including Israel, South Korea, and the US (2024)

Military service age and obligation: 18-27 years of age for voluntary military service for men and women; no conscription (2023)
note: as of 2023, women made up about 8% of the active military; women have attended the Philippine Military Academy and trained as combat soldiers since 1993

Military - note: the Armed Forces of the Philippines (AFP) were formally organized during the American colonial period as the Philippine Army; they were established by the National Defense Act of 1935 and were comprised of both Filipinos and Americans
the US and Philippines agreed to a mutual defense treaty in 1951; in 2014, the two governments signed an Enhanced Defense Cooperation Agreement (EDCA) that established new parameters for military cooperation; under the EDCA, the Philippine Government may grant US troops access to Philippine military bases on a rotational basis "for security cooperation exercises, joint and combined military training activities, and humanitarian assistance and disaster relief activities"; the Philippines has Major Non-NATO Ally (MNNA) status with the US, a designation under US law that provides foreign partners with certain benefits in the areas of defense trade and security cooperation
the Philippine Government faces internal threats from several armed separatists, terrorists, and criminal groups; as such, much of the AFP's operational focus is internal security, particularly in the south, where several separatist Islamic insurgent and terrorist groups operate and a considerable portion of the AFP is typically deployed; additional combat operations are conducted against the Communist People's Party/New People's Army, which is active mostly on Luzon, as well as the Visayas and areas of Mindanao; prior to a peace deal in 2014, the AFP fought a decades-long conflict against the Moro Islamic Liberation Front (MILF), a separatist organization based mostly on the island of Mindanao; the MILF's armed wing, the Bangsamoro Islamic Armed Forces (BIAF), had up to 40,000 fighters under arms the AFP's naval forces are also involved in interdiction operations against terrorist, insurgent, and criminal groups around the southern islands, including joint maritime patrols with Indonesia and Malaysia, particularly in the Sulu Sea; rising tensions with China over disputed waters and land features in the South China Sea since 2012 have spurred the AFP to place more emphasis on blue-water naval capabilities, including acquiring larger warships such guided missile frigates, corvettes, offshore patrol vessels, and landing platform dock (LPD) amphibious assault ships the Philippines National Police (PNP) has an active role in counterinsurgency and counter-terrorism operations alongside the AFP, particularly the Special Action Force, a PNP commando unit that specializes in urban counter-terrorism operations (2024)

SPACE

Space agency/agencies: Philippine Space Agency (PhilSA; established 2019); Philippine Space Council (PSC; established in 2019 as an advisory body responsible for coordinating and integrating policies, programs and resources affecting space science and technology applications) (2024)

Space program overview: has a small and ambitious space program focused on acquiring satellites and related technologies, largely for the areas of climate studies, national security, and risk management; also prioritizing development of the country's space expertise and industry; manufactures and operates satellites (mostly micro- and nano-sized), including remote sensing (RS) and scientific/experimental; has relations with a variety of foreign space agencies and industries, including those of China, the European Space Agency and some of its member states, Japan, Russia, and the US (2024)
note: further details about the key activities, programs, and milestones of the country's space program, as well as government spending estimates on the space sector, appear in the Space Programs reference guide

TERRORISM

Terrorist group(s): Abu Sayyaf Group; Communist Party of the Philippines/New People's Army (CPP/NPA); Islamic State of Iraq and ash-Sham – East Asia (ISIS-EA) in the Philippines
note 1: ISIS-EA factions include Daulah Islamiya-Lanao (aka Maute Group), Daulah Islamiya-Maguindanao, Daulah Islamiya-Socsargen, ISIS-aligned elements of the Abu Sayyaf Group (ASG), ISIS-aligned elements of the Bangsamoro Islamic Freedom Fighters (BIFF), and rogue elements of the Moro Islamic Liberation Front (MILF)
note 2: details about the history, aims, leadership, organization, areas of operation, tactics, targets, weapons, size, and sources of support of the group(s) appear(s) in the Terrorism reference guide

TRANSNATIONAL ISSUES

Refugees and internally displaced persons: IDPs: 102,000 (government troops fighting the Moro Islamic Liberation Front, the Abu Sayyaf Group, and the New People's Army; clan feuds; armed attacks, political violence, and communal tensions in Mindanao) (2022)
stateless persons: 261 (2022); note - stateless persons are descendants of Indonesian migrants

Illicit drugs: Illegal drugs, including methamphetamine hydrochloride, cannabis, and methylenedioxymethamphetamine (MMDA, or "ecstasy") enter the Philippines from the Golden Triangle (Thailand, Laos, and Burma); drugs entering the Philippines are used locally and transported to other countries in Southeast Asia and Oceania; Chinese transnational organizations are the principal supplier of methamphetamine; not a significant source or transit country for drugs entering the United States

PITCAIRN ISLANDS

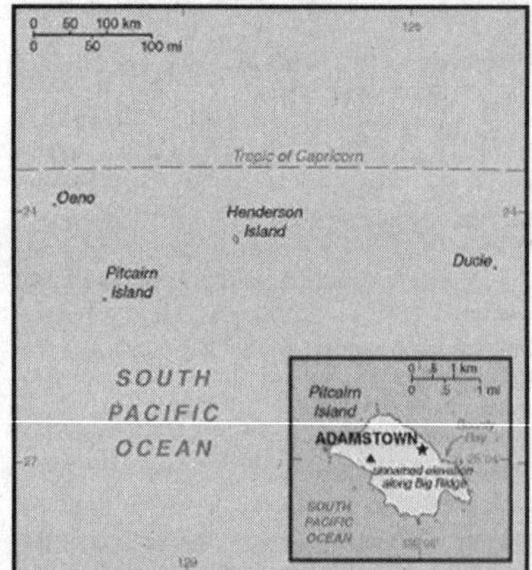

INTRODUCTION

Background: Polynesians were the first settlers on the four tiny islands that are now called the Pitcairn Islands, but all four were uninhabited by the time Europeans discovered them in 1606. Pitcairn Island – the only one now inhabited – was rediscovered by a British explorer in 1767. In 1789, Fletcher CHRISTIAN led a mutiny on the HMS Bounty, and after several months of searching for Pitcairn Island, he landed on it with eight other mutineers and their Tahitian companions. They lived in isolation and evaded detection by English authorities until 1808, when only one man, 10 women, and 23 children remained. In 1831, with the population of 87 proving too big for the island, the British attempted to move all the islanders to Tahiti, but they were soon returned to Pitcairn Island. The island became an official British colony in 1838, and in 1856, the British again determined that the population of 193 was too high and relocated all the residents to Norfolk Island. Several families returned in 1858 and 1864, bringing the island's population to 43, and almost all of the island's current population are descendants of these returnees.

The UK annexed the nearby uninhabited islands of Henderson, Oeno, and Ducie in 1902 and incorporated them into the Pitcairn Islands colony in 1938. The population peaked at 233 in 1937 as outmigration, primarily to New Zealand, has since thinned the population. Only two children were born between 1986 and 2012, and in 2005, a couple became the first outsiders to obtain citizenship in more than a century. Since 2013, the Pitcairn Islands has tried to attract new migrants but has had no applicants because it requires prospective migrants to front significant sums of money and prohibits employment during a two-year trial period, at which point the local council can deny long-term resident status.

GEOGRAPHY

Location: Oceania, islands in the South Pacific Ocean, about midway between Peru and New Zealand

Geographic coordinates: 25 04 S, 130 06 W

Map references: Oceania

Area: *total:* 47 sq km
land: 47 sq km
water: 0 sq km
comparison ranking: total 232

Area - comparative: about three-tenths the size of Washington, DC

Land boundaries: *total:* 0 km

Coastline: 51 km

Maritime claims: *territorial sea:* 12 nm
exclusive economic zone: 200 nm

Climate: tropical; hot and humid; modified by southeast trade winds; rainy season (November to March)

Terrain: rugged volcanic formation; rocky coastline with cliffs

Elevation: *highest point:* Palwala Valley Point on Big Ridge 347 m
lowest point: Pacific Ocean 0 m

Natural resources: miro trees (used for handicrafts), fish
note: manganese, iron, copper, gold, silver, and zinc have been discovered offshore

Land use: *agricultural land:* 0% (2011 est.)
forest: 74.5% (2018 est.)
other: 25.5% (2018 est.)

Irrigated land: 0 sq km (2022)

Population distribution: less than 50 inhabitants on Pitcairn Island, most reside near the village of Adamstown

Natural hazards: occasional tropical cyclones (especially November to March), but generally only heavy tropical storms; landslides

Geography - note: Britain's most isolated dependency; only the larger island of Pitcairn is inhabited but it has no port or natural harbor; supplies must be transported by longboat from larger ships stationed offshore

PEOPLE AND SOCIETY

Population: *total:* 50 (2021 est.)
comparison ranking: total 237

Nationality: *noun:* Pitcairn Islander(s)
adjective: Pitcairn Islander

Ethnic groups: descendants of the Bounty mutineers and their Tahitian wives

Languages: English (official), Pitkern (mixture of an 18th century English dialect and a Tahitian dialect)

Religions: Seventh Day Adventist 100%

Population growth rate: 0% (2014 est.)
comparison ranking: 195

Population distribution: less than 50 inhabitants on Pitcairn Island, most reside near the village of Adamstown

ENVIRONMENT

Environment - current issues: deforestation (only a small portion of the original forest remains because of burning and clearing for settlement)

Climate: tropical; hot and humid; modified by southeast trade winds; rainy season (November to March)

GOVERNMENT

Country name: *conventional long form:* Pitcairn, Henderson, Ducie, and Oeno Islands
conventional short form: Pitcairn Islands
etymology: named after Midshipman Robert PITCAIRN who first sighted the island in 1767

Government type: parliamentary democracy

Dependency status: overseas territory of the UK

Capital: *name:* Adamstown
geographic coordinates: 25 04 S, 130 05 W
time difference: UTC-9 (4 hours behind Washington, DC, during Standard Time)
etymology: named after John ADAMS (1767–1829), the last survivor of the Bounty mutineers who settled on Pitcairn Island in January 1790

Administrative divisions: none (overseas territory of the UK)

Independence: none (overseas territory of the UK)

National holiday: Birthday of King CHARLES III, second Saturday in June (1948); Discovery Day (Pitcairn Day), 2 July (1767)

Legal system: local island by-laws

Constitution: *history:* several previous; latest drafted 10 February 2010, presented 17 February 2010, effective 4 March 2010

Citizenship: see United Kingdom

Suffrage: 18 years of age; universal with three years residency

Executive branch: *chief of state:* King CHARLES III (since 8 September 2022); represented by UK High Commissioner to New Zealand and Governor (nonresident) of the Pitcairn Islands Iona THOMAS (since 9 August 2022)
head of government: Mayor and Chairman of the Island Council Simon YOUNG (since 1 January 2023)
cabinet: none
elections/appointments: the monarchy is hereditary; governor and commissioner appointed by the monarch; island mayor directly elected by majority popular vote for a 3-year term; election last held on 9 November 2022 (next to be held no later than December 2025)
election results: Simon YOUNG elected mayor and chairman of the Island Council; Island Council vote - NA

Legislative branch: *description:* direcunicameral Island Council: 10 seats; (7 members - 5 councilors, the mayor, and the deputy mayor - elected by popular vote, and 3 ex officio non-voting members - the administrator, who serves as both the head of government and the representative of the governor of Pitcairn Islands, the governor, and the deputy governor; the councilors and the deputy mayor serve 2-year terms, the mayor serves a 3-year term, and the administrator is appointed by the governor for an indefinite term)
elections: last held on 6 November 2019 (next to be held in - NA)
election results: percent of vote - NA; seats - independent 5; composition - men 4, women 6, percent of women 60%

Judicial branch: *highest court(s):* Pitcairn Court of Appeal (consists of the court president, 2 judges, and the Supreme Court chief justice, an ex-officio member); Pitcairn Supreme Court (consists of the chief justice and 2 judges); note - appeals beyond the Pitcairn Court of Appeal are referred to the Judicial Committee of the Privy Council (in London)
judge selection and term of office: all judges of both courts appointed by the governor of the Pitcairn Islands on the instructions of the British monarch through the Secretary of State; all judges can serve until retirement, normally at age 75
subordinate courts: Magistrate's Court

Political parties: none

International organization participation: SPC, UPU

Diplomatic representation in the US: none (overseas territory of the UK)

Diplomatic representation from the US: *embassy:* none (overseas territory of the UK)

Flag description: blue with the flag of the UK in the upper hoist-side quadrant and the Pitcairn Islander coat of arms centered on the outer half of the flag; the green, yellow, and blue of the shield represents the island rising from the ocean; the green field features a yellow anchor surmounted by a bible (both the anchor and the bible were items found on the HMS Bounty); sitting on the crest is a Pitcairn Island wheelbarrow from which springs a flowering twig of miro (a local plant)

National anthem: *name:* "We From Pitcairn Island"
lyrics/music: unknown/Frederick M. LEHMAN
note: serves as a local anthem; as an overseas territory of the UK, "God Save the King" is official (see United Kingdom)

ECONOMY

Economic overview: small South Pacific British island territorial economy; exports primarily postage stamps, handicraft goods, honey, and tinctures; extremely limited infrastructure; dependent upon UK and EU aid; recent border reopening post-COVID-19

Agricultural products: honey; wide variety of fruits and vegetables; goats, chickens; fish

Industries: postage stamps, handicrafts, beekeeping, honey

Exports - partners: Zambia 99%, Czechia 0%, UK 0%, US 0%, Australia 0% (2022)
note: top five export partners based on percentage share of exports

Exports - commodities: fertilizers, sulfur, refined petroleum, excavation machinery, ethylene polymers (2022)
note: top five export commodities based on value in dollars

Imports - partners: Zambia 100%, NZ 0%, Brazil 0%, UAE 0%, UK 0% (2022)
note: top five import partners based on percentage share of imports

Imports - commodities: raw copper, refined copper, cobalt oxides and hydroxides, corn, soybean meal (2022)
note: top five import commodities based on value in dollars

Exchange rates: New Zealand dollars (NZD) per US dollar -

Exchange rates: 1.628 (2023 est.)
1.577 (2022 est.)
1.414 (2021 est.)
1.542 (2020 est.)
1.518 (2019 est.)

COMMUNICATIONS

Telecommunication systems: *general assessment:* satellite-based phone services; rural connectivity a challenge; 2G services widespread; demand for mobile broadband due to mobile services providing Internet source; the launch of the Kacific-1 satellite in 2019 will improve telecommunications in the region (2020)
domestic: local phone service with international connections via Internet (2018)
international: country code - 872; satellite earth station - 1 Inmarsat

Broadcast media: satellite TV from Fiji-based Sky Pacific offering a wide range of international channels

Internet country code: .pn

Internet users: *total:* 37 (2021 est.)
percent of population: 96.2% (2021 est.)
comparison ranking: total 234

Communications - note: satellite-based local phone service and broadband Internet connections available in all homes

MILITARY AND SECURITY

Military - note: defense is the responsibility of the UK

POLAND

INTRODUCTION

Background: Poland's history as a state began near the middle of the 10th century. By the mid-16th century, the Polish-Lithuanian Commonwealth ruled a vast tract of land in Central and Eastern Europe. During the 18th century, internal disorder weakened the nation, and in a series of agreements between 1772 and 1795, Russia, Prussia, and Austria partitioned Poland among themselves. Poland regained its independence in 1918 only to be overrun by Germany and the Soviet Union in World War II. It became a Soviet satellite state following the war. Labor turmoil in 1980 led to the formation of the independent trade union Solidarity that over time became a political force with over 10 million members. Free elections in 1989 and 1990 won Solidarity control of the parliament and the presidency, bringing the communist era to a close. A "shock therapy" program during the early 1990s enabled the country to transform its economy into one of the most robust in Central Europe. Poland joined NATO in 1999 and the EU in 2004.

GEOGRAPHY

Location: Central Europe, east of Germany

Geographic coordinates: 52 00 N, 20 00 E

Map references: Europe

Area: *total:* 312,685 sq km
land: 304,255 sq km
water: 8,430 sq km
comparison ranking: total 71

Area - comparative: about twice the size of Georgia; slightly smaller than New Mexico

Land boundaries: *total:* 2,865 km
border countries (6): Belarus 375 km; Czechia 699 km; Germany 467 km; Lithuania 100 km, Russia (Kaliningrad Oblast) 209 km; Slovakia 517 km; Ukraine 498 km

Coastline: 440 km

Maritime claims: *territorial sea:* 12 nm
exclusive economic zone: defined by international treaties

Climate: temperate with cold, cloudy, moderately severe winters with frequent precipitation; mild summers with frequent showers and thundershowers

Terrain: mostly flat plain; mountains along southern border

Elevation: *highest point:* Rysy 2,499 m
lowest point: near Raczki Elblaskie -2 m
mean elevation: 173 m

Natural resources: coal, sulfur, copper, natural gas, silver, lead, salt, amber, arable land

Land use: *agricultural land:* 48.2% (2018 est.)
arable land: 36.2% (2018 est.)
permanent crops: 1.3% (2018 est.)
permanent pasture: 10.7% (2018 est.)
forest: 30.6% (2018 est.)
other: 21.2% (2018 est.)

Irrigated land: 760 sq km (2013)

Major lakes (area sq km): *salt water lake(s):* Zalew Szczecinski/Stettiner Haff (shared with Germany) - 900 sq km

Major rivers (by length in km): Wisla (Vistula) river source and mouth (shared with Belarus and Ukraine) - 1,213 km
note - longest river in Poland

Major watersheds (area sq km): Atlantic Ocean drainage: *(Black Sea)* Danube (795,656 sq km)

Population distribution: population concentrated in the southern area around Krakow and the central area around Warsaw and Lodz, with an extension to the northern coastal city of Gdansk

Natural hazards: flooding

Geography - note: historically, an area of conflict because of flat terrain and the lack of natural barriers on the North European Plain

PEOPLE AND SOCIETY

Population: *total:* 38,746,310
male: 18,441,415
female: 20,304,895 (2024 est.)
comparison rankings: female 36; male 40; total 38

Nationality: *noun:* Pole(s)
adjective: Polish

Ethnic groups: Polish 96.9%, Silesian 1.1%, German 0.2%, Ukrainian 0.1%, other and unspecified 1.7% (2011 est.)
note: represents ethnicity declared first

Languages: Polish (official) 98.2%, Silesian 1.4%, other 1.1%, unspecified 1.2% (2011 est.)
major-language sample(s):
Księga Faktów Świata, niezbędne źródło podstawowych informacji. (Polish)
note 1: shares of languages sum to more than 100% because some respondents gave more than one answer on the census; data represent language spoken at home
note 2: Poland also recognizes Kashub as a regional language; Czech, Hebrew, Yiddish, Belarusian, Lithuanian, German, Armenian, Russian, Slovak, and Ukrainian as national minority languages; and Karaim, Lemko, Romani (Polska Roma and Bergitka Roma), and Tatar as ethnic minority languages

Religions: Catholic 84.6% (Roman Catholic 84.6% and other Catholic 0.3%), Orthodox 1.3% (almost all are Polish Autocephalous Orthodox), Protestant 0.4% (mainly Augsburg Evangelical and Pentecostal), other 0.3%, unspecified 13% (2022 est.)

Age structure: *0-14 years:* 14.2% (male 2,830,048/female 2,676,300)
15-64 years: 65.9% (male 12,513,402/female 13,036,977)
65 years and over: 19.8% (2024 est.) (male 3,097,965/female 4,591,618)

Dependency ratios: *total dependency ratio:* 51.4
youth dependency ratio: 23.4
elderly dependency ratio: 28.6
potential support ratio: 3.5 (2021 est.)

Median age: *total:* 42.9 years (2024 est.)
male: 41.5 years
female: 44.3 years
comparison ranking: total 38

Population growth rate: -1% (2024 est.)
comparison ranking: 230

Birth rate: 8.4 births/1,000 population (2024 est.)
comparison ranking: 207

Death rate: deaths/1,000 population (2024 est.)
comparison ranking: 14

Net migration rate: -6.2 migrant(s)/1,000 population (2024 est.)
comparison ranking: 210

Population distribution: population concentrated in the southern area around Krakow and the central area around Warsaw and Lodz, with an extension to the northern coastal city of Gdansk

Urbanization: *urban population:* 60.2% of total population (2023)
rate of urbanization: -0.16% annual rate of change (2020-25 est.)

Major urban areas - population: 1.798 million WARSAW (capital), 769,000 Krakow (2023)

Sex ratio: *at birth:* 1.06 male(s)/female
0-14 years: 1.06 male(s)/female
15-64 years: 0.96 male(s)/female
65 years and over: 0.67 male(s)/female
total population: 0.91 male(s)/female (2024 est.)

Mother's mean age at first birth: 27.9 years (2020 est.)

Maternal mortality ratio: 2 deaths/100,000 live births (2020 est.)
comparison ranking: 184

Infant mortality rate: *total:* 4.9 deaths/1,000 live births (2024 est.)
male: 5.3 deaths/1,000 live births
female: 4.4 deaths/1,000 live births
comparison ranking: total 177

Life expectancy at birth: *total population:* 76.7 years (2024 est.)
male: 72.8 years
female: 80.9 years
comparison ranking: total population 101

Total fertility rate: 1.32 children born/woman (2024 est.)
comparison ranking: 217

Gross reproduction rate: 0.64 (2024 est.)

Contraceptive prevalence rate: 62.3% (2014)

Drinking water source: *improved: urban:* 99.9% of population
rural: 100% of population
total: 100% of population
unimproved: urban: 0.1% of population
rural: 0% of population
total: 0% of population (2020 est.)

Current health expenditure: 6.5% of GDP (2020)

Physician density: 3.77 physicians/1,000 population (2020)

Hospital bed density: 6.5 beds/1,000 population (2018)

Sanitation facility access: *improved: urban:* 100% of population
rural: 100% of population
total: 100% of population

Obesity - adult prevalence rate: 23.1% (2016)
comparison ranking: 68

Alcohol consumption per capita: *total:* 10.96 liters of pure alcohol (2019 est.)
beer: 5.72 liters of pure alcohol (2019 est.)
wine: 0.88 liters of pure alcohol (2019 est.)
spirits: 4.36 liters of pure alcohol (2019 est.)
other alcohols: 0 liters of pure alcohol (2019 est.)
comparison ranking: total 13

Tobacco use: *total:* 24% (2020 est.)
male: 27.9% (2020 est.)
female: 20.1% (2020 est.)
comparison ranking: total 59

Currently married women (ages 15-49): 56.6% (2023 est.)

Education expenditures: 5.2% of GDP (2020 est.)
comparison ranking: 69

Literacy: *definition:* age 15 and over can read and write
total population: 99.8%
male: 99.8%
female: 99.8% (2021)

School life expectancy (primary to tertiary education): *total:* 16 years
male: 15 years
female: 17 years (2020)

ENVIRONMENT

Environment - current issues: decreased emphasis on heavy industry and increased environmental concern by post-communist governments has improved environment; air pollution remains serious because of emissions from burning low-quality coals in homes and from coal-fired power plants; the resulting acid rain causes forest damage; water pollution from industrial and municipal sources is a problem, as is disposal of hazardous wastes

Environment - international agreements: *party to:* Air Pollution, Air Pollution-Nitrogen Oxides, Air Pollution-Sulphur 94, Antarctic-Environmental Protection, Antarctic- Marine Living Resources, Antarctic Seals, Antarctic Treaty, Biodiversity, Climate Change, Climate Change- Kyoto Protocol, Climate Change-Paris Agreement, Comprehensive Nuclear Test Ban, Desertification, Endangered Species, Environmental Modification, Hazardous Wastes, Law of the Sea, Marine Dumping-London Convention, Nuclear Test Ban, Ozone Layer Protection, Ship Pollution, Tropical Timber 2006, Wetlands, Whaling
signed, but not ratified: Air Pollution-Heavy Metals, Air Pollution-Multi-effect Protocol, Air Pollution-Persistent Organic Pollutants

Climate: temperate with cold, cloudy, moderately severe winters with frequent precipitation; mild summers with frequent showers and thundershowers

Urbanization: *urban population:* 60.2% of total population (2023)
rate of urbanization: -0.16% annual rate of change (2020-25 est.)

Revenue from forest resources: 0.17% of GDP (2018 est.)
comparison ranking: 98

Revenue from coal: 0.27% of GDP (2018 est.)
comparison ranking: 19

Air pollutants: *particulate matter emissions:* 18.83 micrograms per cubic meter (2019 est.)
carbon dioxide emissions: 299.04 megatons (2016 est.)
methane emissions: 46.62 megatons (2020 est.)

Waste and recycling: *municipal solid waste generated annually:* 10.863 million tons (2015 est.)
municipal solid waste recycled annually: 2,866,746 tons (2015 est.)
percent of municipal solid waste recycled: 26.4% (2015 est.)

Major lakes (area sq km): *salt water lake(s):* Zalew Szczecinski/Stettiner Haff (shared with Germany) - 900 sq km

Major rivers (by length in km): Wisla (Vistula) river source and mouth (shared with Belarus and Ukraine) - 1,213 km
note - longest river in Poland

Major watersheds (area sq km): Atlantic Ocean drainage: *(Black Sea)* Danube (795,656 sq km)

Total water withdrawal: *municipal:* 1.96 billion cubic meters (2020 est.)
industrial: 5.87 billion cubic meters (2020 est.)
agricultural: 1.39 billion cubic meters (2020 est.)

Total renewable water resources: 60.5 billion cubic meters (2020 est.)

Geoparks: *total global geoparks and regional networks:* 3 (2024)
global geoparks and regional networks: Land of Extinct Volcanoes; Muskauer Faltenbogen / Łuk Muzakowa (includes Germany); Holy Cross Mountains (2024)

GOVERNMENT

Country name: *conventional long form:* Republic of Poland
conventional short form: Poland
local long form: Rzeczpospolita Polska
local short form: Polska
former: Polish People's Republic
etymology: name derives from the Polanians, a west Slavic tribe that united several surrounding Slavic groups (9th-10th centuries A.D.) and who passed on their name to the country; the name of the tribe likely comes from the Slavic "pole" (field or plain), indicating the flat nature of their country

Government type: parliamentary republic

Capital: *name:* Warsaw
geographic coordinates: 52 15 N, 21 00 E
time difference: UTC+1 (6 hours ahead of Washington, DC, during Standard Time)
daylight saving time: +1hr, begins last Sunday in March; ends last Sunday in October
etymology: the origin of the name is unknown; the Polish designation "Warszawa" was the name of a fishing village and several legends/traditions link the city's founding to a man named Wars or Warsz

Administrative divisions: 16 voivodships [provinces] (wojewodztwa, singular - wojewodztwo); Dolnoslaskie (Lower Silesia), Kujawsko-Pomorskie (Kuyavia-Pomerania), Lodzkie (Lodz), Lubelskie (Lublin), Lubuskie (Lubusz), Malopolskie (Lesser Poland), Mazowieckie (Masovia), Opolskie (Opole), Podkarpackie (Subcarpathia), Podlaskie, Pomorskie (Pomerania), Slaskie (Silesia), Swietokrzyskie (Holy Cross), Warminsko-Mazurskie (Warmia-Masuria), Wielkopolskie (Greater Poland), Zachodniopomorskie (West Pomerania)

Independence: *11 November 1918 (republic proclaimed); notable earlier dates:* 14 April 966 (adoption of Christianity, traditional founding date), 1 July 1569 (Polish-Lithuanian Commonwealth created)

National holiday: Constitution Day, 3 May (1791)

Legal system: civil law system; judicial review of legislative, administrative, and other governmental acts; constitutional law rulings of the Constitutional Tribunal are final

Constitution: *history:* several previous; latest adopted 2 April 1997, approved by referendum 25 May 1997, effective 17 October 1997
amendments: proposed by at least one fifth of Sejm deputies, by the Senate, or by the president of the republic; passage requires at least two-thirds majority vote in the Sejm and absolute majority vote in the Senate; amendments to articles relating to sovereignty, personal freedoms, and constitutional amendment procedures also require passage by majority vote in a referendum; amended 2006, 2009

International law organization participation: accepts compulsory ICJ jurisdiction with reservations; accepts ICCt jurisdiction

Citizenship: *citizenship by birth:* no
citizenship by descent only: both parents must be citizens of Poland
dual citizenship recognized: no
residency requirement for naturalization: 5 years

Suffrage: 18 years of age; universal

Executive branch: *chief of state:* President Andrzej DUDA (since 6 August 2015)
head of government: Prime Minister Donald TUSK (since 11 December 2023)
cabinet: Council of Ministers proposed by the prime minister, appointed by the president, and approved by the Sejm
elections/appointments: president directly elected by absolute majority popular vote in 2 rounds if needed for a 5-year term (eligible for a second term); election last held on 28 June 2020 with a second round on 12 July 2020 (next to be held in 2025); prime minister, deputy prime ministers, and Council of Ministers appointed by the president and confirmed by the Sejm; all presidential candidates resign their party affiliation
election results:

2020: Andrzej DUDA reelected president in second round; percent of vote - Andrzej DUDA (independent) 51%, Rafal TRZASKOWSKI (KO) 49%
2015: Andrzej DUDA elected president in second round; percent of vote - Andrzej DUDA (independent) 51.5%, Bronislaw KOMOROWSKI (independent) 48.5%

Legislative branch: *description:* bicameral Parliament consists of:
Senate or Senat (100 seats; members directly elected in single-seat constituencies by simple majority vote to serve 4- year terms)
Sejm (460 seats; members elected in multi-seat constituencies by party-list proportional representation vote with 5% threshold of total votes needed for parties and 8% for coalitions to gain seats; minority parties exempt from threshold; members serve 4-year terms)
elections: Senate - last held on 15 October 2023 (next to be held in 2027)
Sejm - last held on 15 October 2023 (next to be held in 2027)
election results: Senate - percent of vote by coalition/party - United Right 34.8%, Civic Coalition 28.9%, Third Way 11.5%, The Left 5.3%, Senate Pact Independents 2.7%, independent 3%; seats by coalition/party - Civic Coalition 41, United Right 34, Third Way 11, The Left 9, Senate Pact Independents 4, independent 1
Sejm - percent of vote by coalition/party - PiS 35.4%, KO 30.7%, TD 14.4%, Lewica 8.6%, Konf 7.2%; seats by coalition/ party - United Way 194, Civic Coalition 157, Third Way 65, The Left 26, Confederation 18

Judicial branch: *highest court(s):* Supreme Court or Sad Najwyzszy (consists of the first president of the Supreme Court and 120 justices organized in criminal, civil, labor and social insurance, and extraordinary appeals and public affairs and disciplinary chambers); Constitutional Tribunal (consists of 15 judges, including the court president and vice president)
judge selection and term of office: president of the Supreme Court nominated by the General Assembly of the Supreme Court and selected by the president of Poland; other judges nominated by the 25-member National Judicial Council and appointed by the president of Poland; judges serve until retirement, usually at age 65, but tenure can be extended; Constitutional Tribunal judges chosen by the Sejm for single 9-year terms
subordinate courts: administrative courts; military courts; local, regional and appellate courts subdivided into military, civil, criminal, labor, and family courts

Political parties: AGROunion or AU
Center for Poland or CdP
Civic Platform or PO
Confederation of the Polish Crown or KKP
Kukiz' 15 or K'15
Labor Union or UP
Law and Justice or PiS
Left Together or LR
Modern or .N
National Movement or NN
New Hope or RN
New Left or NL
Poland 2050 or PL2050
Polish Initiative or iPL
Polish People's Party or PSL
Polish Socialist Party or PPS
Renewal of the Republic of Poland or ON RP
Sovereign Poland or SP
The Greens or Zieloni
Union of European Democrats or UED
Yes! For Poland or T!DPL

International organization participation: Arctic Council (observer), Australia Group, BIS, BSEC (observer), CBSS, CD, CE, CEI, CERN, EAPC, EBRD, ECB, EIB, ESA, EU, FAO, IAEA, IBRD, ICAO, ICC (national committees), ICCt, ICRM, IDA, IEA, IFC, IFRCS, IHO, ILO, IMF, IMO, IMSO, Interpol, IOC, IOM, IPU, ISO, ITSO, ITU, ITUC (NGOs), MIGA, MONUSCO, NATO, NEA, NSG, OAS (observer), OECD, OIF (observer), OPCW, OSCE, PCA, Schengen Convention, UN, UNCTAD, UNESCO, UNHCR, UNHRC, UNIDO, UNMIL, UNMISS, UNOCI, UN Security Council (temporary), UNWTO, UPU, Wassenaar Arrangement, WCO, WFTU (NGOs), WHO, WIPO, WMO, WTO, ZC

Diplomatic representation in the US: *chief of mission:* Ambassador (vacant); Chargé d'Affaires Adam KRZYWOSĄDZKI (since 31 July 2024)
chancery: 2640 16th Street NW, Washington, DC 20009
telephone: [1] (202) 499-1700
FAX: [1] (202) 328-2152
email address and website:
washington.amb.sekretariat@msz.gov.pl
https://www.gov.pl/web/usa-en/embassy-washington
consulate(s) general: Chicago, Houston, Los Angeles, New York

Diplomatic representation from the US: *chief of mission:* Ambassador Mark BRZEZINSKI (since 19 January 2022)
embassy: Aleje Ujazdowskie 29/31, 00-540 Warsaw
mailing address: 5010 Warsaw Place, Washington, DC 20521-5010
telephone: [48] (22) 504-2000
FAX: [48] (22) 504-2088
email address and website:
acswarsaw@state.gov
https://pl.usembassy.gov/
consulate(s) general: Krakow

Flag description: two equal horizontal bands of white (top) and red; colors derive from the Polish emblem - a white eagle on a red field
note: similar to the flags of Indonesia and Monaco which are red (top) and white

National symbol(s): white crowned eagle; national colors: white, red

National anthem: *name:* "Mazurek Dabrowskiego" (Dabrowski's Mazurka)
lyrics/music: Jozef WYBICKI/traditional
note: adopted 1927; the anthem, commonly known as "Jeszcze Polska nie zginela" (Poland Has Not Yet Perished), was written in 1797; the lyrics resonate strongly with Poles because they reflect the numerous occasions in which the nation's lands have been occupied

National heritage: *total World Heritage Sites:* 17 (15 cultural, 2 natural)
selected World Heritage Site locales: Historic Krakow (c); Historic Warsaw (c); Medieval Torun (c); Wooden Tserkvas of the Carpathian Region (c); Castle of the Teutonic Order in Malbork (c); Wieliczka and Bochnia Royal Salt Mines (c); Auschwitz Birkenau Concentration Camp (c); Ancient and Primeval Beech Forests of the Carpathians (n); Bialowieza Forest (n); Old City of Zamość (c)

ECONOMY

Economic overview: high-income, diversified, EU-member economy; significant growth in GDP, trade, and investment since joining EU in 2004; rebounding from slowdown triggered by inflation and fall in consumer demand; strong foreign investment supported by EU structural funds; income tax reform and defense spending have added to public debt

Real GDP (purchasing power parity): $1.616 trillion (2023 est.)
$1.613 trillion (2022 est.)
$1.527 trillion (2021 est.)
note: data in 2021 dollars
comparison ranking: 19

Real GDP growth rate: 0.16% (2023 est.)
5.64% (2022 est.)
6.93% (2021 est.)
note: annual GDP % growth based on constant local currency
comparison ranking: 185

Real GDP per capita: $44,100 (2023 est.)
$43,800 (2022 est.)
$40,500 (2021 est.)
note: data in 2021 dollars
comparison ranking: 54

GDP (official exchange rate): $811.229 billion (2023 est.)
note: data in current dollars at official exchange rate

Inflation rate (consumer prices): 11.53% (2023 est.)
14.43% (2022 est.)
5.06% (2021 est.)
note: annual % change based on consumer prices
comparison ranking: 186

Credit ratings: Fitch rating: A- (2007)
Moody's rating: A2 (2002)
Standard & Poors rating: A- (2018)
note: The year refers to the year in which the current credit rating was first obtained.

GDP - composition, by sector of origin: *agriculture:* 2.9% (2023 est.)
industry: 28.7% (2023 est.)
services: 58.8% (2023 est.)
note: figures may not total 100% due to non-allocated consumption not captured in sector-reported data
comparison rankings: services 94; industry 75; agriculture 141

GDP - composition, by end use: *household consumption:* 57.2% (2023 est.)
government consumption: 18.6% (2023 est.)
investment in fixed capital: 17.8% (2023 est.)
investment in inventories: 0.3% (2023 est.)
exports of goods and services: 57.8% (2023 est.)
imports of goods and services: -51.7% (2023 est.)
note: figures may not total 100% due to rounding or gaps in data collection

Agricultural products: milk, sugar beets, wheat, maize, potatoes, triticale, apples, rapeseed, barley, rye (2022)
note: top ten agricultural products based on tonnage

Industries: machine building, iron and steel, coal mining, chemicals, shipbuilding, food processing, glass, beverages, textiles

Industrial production growth rate: 0.55% (2023 est.)
note: annual % change in industrial value added based on constant local currency
comparison ranking: 148

Labor force: 18.387 million (2023 est.)
note: number of people ages 15 or older who are employed or seeking work
comparison ranking: 36

Unemployment rate: 2.91% (2023 est.)
2.89% (2022 est.)
3.36% (2021 est.)
note: % of labor force seeking employment
comparison ranking: 41

Youth unemployment rate (ages 15-24): *total:* 11.6% (2023 est.)
male: 12% (2023 est.)
female: 11.1% (2023 est.)
note: % of labor force ages 15-24 seeking employment
comparison ranking: total 117

Population below poverty line: 11.8% (2022 est.)
note: % of population with income below national poverty line

Gini Index coefficient - distribution of family income: 28.5 (2021 est.)
note: index (0-100) of income distribution; higher values represent greater inequality
comparison ranking: 134

Average household expenditures: *on food:* 19.4% of household expenditures (2022 est.)
on alcohol and tobacco: 6.4% of household expenditures (2022 est.)

Household income or consumption by percentage share: *lowest 10%:* 3.4% (2021 est.)
highest 10%: 22.8% (2021 est.)
note: % share of income accruing to lowest and highest 10% of population

Remittances: 0.84% of GDP (2023 est.)
0.93% of GDP (2022 est.)
1.05% of GDP (2021 est.)
note: personal transfers and compensation between resident and non-resident individuals/households/entities

Budget: *revenues:* $234.98 billion (2022 est.)
expenditures: $250.097 billion (2022 est.)
note: central government revenues (excluding grants) and expenses converted to US dollars at average official exchange rate for year indicated

Public debt: 50.6% of GDP (2017 est.)
note: data cover general government debt and include debt instruments issued (or owned) by government entities other than the treasury; the data include treasury debt held by foreign entities, the data include subnational entities, as well as intragovernmental debt; intragovernmental debt consists of treasury borrowings from surpluses in the social funds, such as for retirement, medical care, and unemployment; debt instruments for the social funds are not sold at public auctions
comparison ranking: 104

Taxes and other revenues: 17.27% (of GDP) (2022 est.)
note: central government tax revenue as a % of GDP
comparison ranking: 111

Current account balance: $12.689 billion (2023 est.)
-$16.697 billion (2022 est.)
-$8.515 billion (2021 est.)
note: balance of payments - net trade and primary/secondary income in current dollars
comparison ranking: 25

Exports: $469.264 billion (2023 est.)
$434.008 billion (2022 est.)
$392.694 billion (2021 est.)
note: balance of payments - exports of goods and services in current dollars
comparison ranking: 19

Exports - partners: Germany 27%, Czechia 6%, France 6%, UK 5%, Netherlands 5% (2022)
note: top five export partners based on percentage share of exports

Exports - commodities: vehicle parts/accessories, plastic products, garments, electric batteries, computers (2022)
note: top five export commodities based on value in dollars

Imports: $419.701 billion (2023 est.)
$421.226 billion (2022 est.)
$369.82 billion (2021 est.)
note: balance of payments - imports of goods and services in current dollars
comparison ranking: 19

Imports - partners: Germany 23%, China 11%, Italy 5%, Netherlands 5%, Czechia 4% (2022)
note: top five import partners based on percentage share of imports

Imports - commodities: garments, crude petroleum, cars, vehicle parts/accessories, plastic products (2022)
note: top five import commodities based on value in dollars

Reserves of foreign exchange and gold: $193.783 billion (2023 est.)
$166.664 billion (2022 est.)
$166.03 billion (2021 est.)
note: holdings of gold (year-end prices)/foreign exchange/special drawing rights in current dollars
comparison ranking: 21

Exchange rates: zlotych (PLN) per US dollar -

Exchange rates: 4.204 (2023 est.)
4.458 (2022 est.)
3.862 (2021 est.)
3.9 (2020 est.)
3.839 (2019 est.)

ENERGY

Electricity access: *electrification - total population:* 100% (2022 est.)

Electricity: *installed generating capacity:* 58.719 million kW (2022 est.)
consumption: 156.869 billion kWh (2022 est.)
exports: 16.915 billion kWh (2022 est.)
imports: 15.238 billion kWh (2022 est.)
transmission/distribution losses: 8.659 billion kWh (2022 est.)
comparison rankings: transmission/distribution losses 174; imports 17; exports 18; consumption 27; installed generating capacity 24

Electricity generation sources: *fossil fuels:* 78.4% of total installed capacity (2022 est.)
solar: 4.9% of total installed capacity (2022 est.)
wind: 11% of total installed capacity (2022 est.)
hydroelectricity: 0.8% of total installed capacity (2022 est.)
biomass and waste: 4.9% of total installed capacity (2022 est.)

Coal: *production:* 116.682 million metric tons (2022 est.)
consumption: 123.782 million metric tons (2022 est.)
exports: 12.047 million metric tons (2022 est.)
imports: 13.347 million metric tons (2022 est.)
proven reserves: 28.531 billion metric tons (2022 est.)

Petroleum: *total petroleum production:* 24,000 bbl/day (2023 est.)
refined petroleum consumption: 722,000 bbl/day (2023 est.)
crude oil estimated reserves: 113 million barrels (2021 est.)

Natural gas: *production:* 5.551 billion cubic meters (2022 est.)
consumption: 20.056 billion cubic meters (2022 est.)
exports: 587.771 million cubic meters (2022 est.)
imports: 14.42 billion cubic meters (2022 est.)
proven reserves: 91.492 billion cubic meters (2021 est.)

Carbon dioxide emissions: 293.356 million metric tonnes of CO_2 (2022 est.)
from coal and metallurgical coke: 163.359 million metric tonnes of CO_2 (2022 est.)
from petroleum and other liquids: 94.138 million metric tonnes of CO_2 (2022 est.)
from consumed natural gas: 35.86 million metric tonnes of CO_2 (2022 est.)
comparison ranking: total emissions 23

Energy consumption per capita: 106.196 million Btu/person (2022 est.)
comparison ranking: 47

COMMUNICATIONS

Telephones - fixed lines: *total subscriptions:* 5.277 million (2022 est.)
subscriptions per 100 inhabitants: 13 (2022 est.)
comparison ranking: total subscriptions 28

Telephones - mobile cellular: *total subscriptions:* 52.589 million (2022 est.)
subscriptions per 100 inhabitants: 132 (2022 est.)
comparison ranking: total subscriptions 32

Telecommunication systems: *general assessment:* the liberalized telecom market has seen considerable development in the broadband and mobile sectors; the regulatory environment has encouraged market competition, partly by encouraging operators to secure spectrum and also by ensuring access to cable and fiber infrastructure; the mobile market in recent years has been characterized by the rapid extension of LTE and 5G networks, and the development of mobile data services based on newly released and re-farmed spectrum; the regulator's attempts to auction spectrum in a range of bands has been delayed, with spectrum in the 5G-suitable 3.4-3.8GHz range having been put back to later in 2023 as a result of the Covid-19 outbreak and changes to legislation (2024)
domestic: fixed-line is 13 per 100 (service lags in rural areas), mobile-cellular is 132 per 100 persons (2022)
international: country code - 48; landing points for the Baltica and the Denmark-Poland2 submarine cables connecting Poland, Denmark and Sweden; international direct dialing with automated exchanges; satellite earth station - 1 with access to Intelsat, Eutelsat, Inmarsat, and Intersputnik (2019)

Broadcast media: state-run public TV operates 2 national channels supplemented by 16 regional channels and several niche channels; privately owned entities operate several national TV networks and a number of special interest channels; many privately owned channels broadcasting locally; roughly half of all households are linked to either satellite or cable TV systems providing access to foreign television networks; state-run public radio operates 5 national networks and 17 regional radio stations; 2 privately owned national radio networks, several commercial stations broadcasting to multiple cities, and many privately owned local radio stations (2019)

Internet country code: .pl

Internet users: *total:* 32.3 million (2021 est.)
percent of population: 85% (2021 est.)
comparison ranking: total 32

Broadband - fixed subscriptions: *total:* 8,369,218 (2020 est.)
subscriptions per 100 inhabitants: 22 (2020 est.)
comparison ranking: total 24

TRANSPORTATION

National air transport system: *number of registered air carriers:* 6 (2020)
inventory of registered aircraft operated by air carriers: 169
annual passenger traffic on registered air carriers: 9,277,538 (2018)
annual freight traffic on registered air carriers: 271.49 million (2018) mt-km

Civil aircraft registration country code prefix: SP

Airports: 288 (2024)
comparison ranking: 23

Heliports: 11 (2024)

Pipelines: 14,198 km gas, 1,374 km oil, 2,483 km refined products (2018)

Railways: *total:* 19,461 km (2020) 11,946 km electrified
comparison ranking: total 14

Roadways: *total:* 427,580 km (2022)
comparison ranking: total 14

Waterways: 3,997 km (2009) (navigable rivers and canals)
comparison ranking: 29

Merchant marine: *total:* 152 (2023)
by type: general cargo 6, oil tanker 6, other 140
comparison ranking: total 75

Ports: *total ports:* 10 (2024)
large: 2
medium: 2
small: 4
very small: 2
ports with oil terminals: 5
key ports: Gdansk, Gdynia, Port Polnochny, Szczecin

MILITARY AND SECURITY

Military and security forces: Polish Armed Forces (Polskie Siły Zbrojne): Land Forces (Wojska Ladowe), Navy (Marynarka Wojenna), Air Force (Sily Powietrzne), Special Forces (Wojska Specjalne), Territorial Defense Forces (Wojska Obrony Terytorialnej), Cyberspace Defense Forces (Wojska Obrony Cyberprzestrzeni)

Ministry of Interior and Administration: Polish National Police (Policja); Border Guard (Straz Graniczna or SG) (2024)

Military expenditures: 4.1% of GDP (2024 est.)
3.9% of GDP (2023 est.)
2.2% of GDP (2022)
2.2% of GDP (2021)
2.2% of GDP (2020)
comparison ranking: 15

Military and security service personnel strengths: approximately 210,000 including air, ground, naval, special forces, and Territorial Defense Forces (2024)
note: a new national defense law in 2022 set a goal to double the size of Poland's armed forces to 300,000 personnel, including 250,000 professional soldiers and 50,000 territorials

Military equipment inventories and acquisitions: the military's inventory consists of a mix of some Soviet-era and a growing amount of more modern, NATO-compatible weapons systems; in recent years, the leading suppliers of armaments have included several European countries, South Korea, and the US; Poland has a large domestic defense sector that produces or provides upgrades to a wide variety of weapons systems, particularly ground systems such as tanks and other armored vehicles; it also cooperates with the European and US defense sectors (2024)
note: in late 2018, Poland announced a 7-year (through 2026) approximately $50 billion defense modernization plan that would include such items as 5th generation combat aircraft, unmanned aerial vehicles, rocket artillery, helicopters, submarines, frigates, and improved cyber security; in 2022-2023, it signed large military weapons contracts with South Korea, the UK, and the US

Military service age and obligation: 18-28 years of age for male and female voluntary military service; conscription phased out in 2009-12; professional soldiers serve on a permanent basis (for an unspecified period of time) or on a contract basis (for a specified period of time); initial contract period is 24 months; women serve in the military on the same terms as men (2024)
note 1: as of 2024, women made up about 16.5% of the military's full-time personnel
note 2: in May 2022, Poland announced a new 12-month voluntary military service program with recruits going through a one-month basic training period with a military unit, followed by 11 months of specialized training; upon completion of service, the volunteers would be allowed to join the Territorial Defense Forces or the active reserve, and have priority to join the professional army and be given preference for employment in the public sector; the program is part of an effort to increase the size of the Polish military

Military deployments: 210 Kosovo (NATO/KFOR); up to 180 Latvia (NATO); 190 Lebanon (UNIFIL); approximately 230 Romania (NATO) (2024)
note 1: Poland has obligated about 2,500 troops to the Lithuania, Poland, and Ukraine joint military brigade (LITPOLUKRBRIG), which was established in 2014; the brigade is headquartered in Poland and is comprised of an international staff, three battalions, and specialized units; units affiliated with the multinational brigade remain within the structures of the armed forces of their respective countries until the brigade is activated for participation in an international operation

Military - note: Poland's geographic location on NATO's eastern flank and its history of foreign invasion underpin the Polish military's heavy focus on territorial and border defense and supporting its NATO and EU security commitments; its chief concern is Russian aggression against neighboring Ukraine since 2014, which has led to efforts to boost border defenses and military capabilities and to increase the NATO and US military presence in Poland
since 2014, Poland has been hosting several NATO military formations designed to enhance the defense of Poland and NATO's eastern flank, including a US-led multinational NATO ground force battlegroup as part of the Alliance's Enhanced Forward Presence initiative, NATO fighter detachments at Malbork Air Base, a NATO-led divisional headquarters (Multinational Division Northeast), which coordinates training and preparation activities of its respective subordinate battlegroups in Poland and Lithuania, and a corps-level NATO field headquarters (Multinational Corps Northeast); since 2022, the US has established a permanent corps headquarters in Poland to command US rotational forces in Europe; Poland also participates in a variety of EU and NATO military deployments in Africa, the Baltic States, Southern Europe, and the Middle East; Poland provided considerable support to the NATO mission in Afghanistan, where more than 30,000 military personnel served over a 20-year period before the mission ended in 2021 (2024)

SPACE

Space agency/agencies: Polish Space Agency (POLSA; established 2014; operational in 2015); Space Research Center (SRC, interdisciplinary research institute of the Polish Academy of Sciences that acted as Poland's space agency until POLSA was established in 1977) (2024)

Space program overview: space program is integrated within the framework of the European Space Agency (ESA); builds satellites, including nano/cube remote sensing (RS) and educational/scientific/technology satellites; researches and develops communications, RS, navigational, and other scientific applications for satellite payloads; creating infrastructure for receiving, storing, processing and distributing data from meteorological and environmental satellites; researches and develops other space-related technologies, including sensors and robotic probes for interplanetary landers, and launcher systems; participates in international space programs and cooperates with a variety of foreign space agencies and industries, including those of Brazil, Canada, China, ESA/EU member states (particularly France, Germany, Italy), India, Japan, Mexico, Russia, Ukraine, UK, and the US; has a growing commercial space sector with more than 300 active enterprises (2024)
note: further details about the key activities, programs, and milestones of the country's space program, as well as government spending estimates on the space sector, appear in the Space Programs reference guide

TERRORISM

Terrorist group(s): Islamic State of Iraq and ash-Sham (ISIS)
note: details about the history, aims, leadership, organization, areas of operation, tactics, targets, weapons, size, and sources of support of the group(s) appear(s) in the Terrorism reference guide

TRANSNATIONAL ISSUES

Refugees and internally displaced persons: *refugees (country of origin):* 956,635 (Ukraine) (as of 15 December 2023)
stateless persons: 1,435 (2022)

Illicit drugs: a major source of precursor or essential chemicals used in the production of illicit narcotics

PORTUGAL

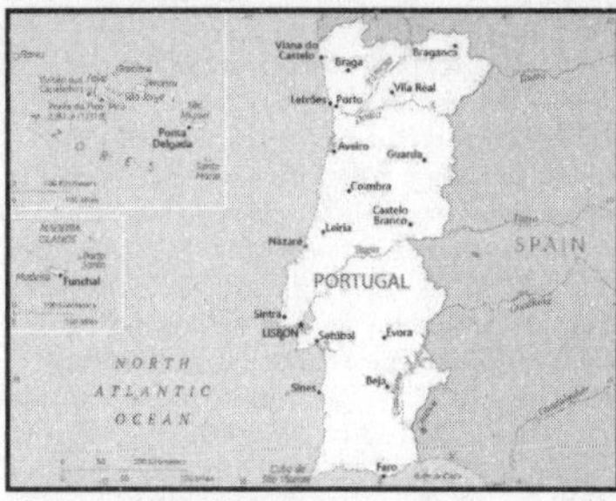

INTRODUCTION

Background: A global maritime power during the 15th and 16th centuries, Portugal lost much of its wealth and status with the destruction of Lisbon in a 1755 earthquake, occupation during the Napoleonic Wars, and the independence of Brazil, its wealthiest colony, in 1822. A revolution deposed the monarchy in 1910, and for most of the next six decades, repressive governments ran the country. In 1974, a left-wing military coup ushered in broad democratic reforms. The following year, Portugal granted independence to all its African colonies. Portugal is a founding member of NATO and entered the EC (now the EU) in 1986.

GEOGRAPHY

Location: Southwestern Europe, bordering the North Atlantic Ocean, west of Spain

Geographic coordinates: 39 30 N, 8 00 W

Map references: Europe

Area: *total:* 92,090 sq km
land: 91,470 sq km
water: 620 sq km
note: includes Azores and Madeira Islands
comparison ranking: total 111

Area - comparative: slightly smaller than Virginia

Land boundaries: *total:* 1,224 km
border countries (1): Spain 1,224 km

Coastline: 1,793 km

Maritime claims: *territorial sea:* 12 nm
contiguous zone: 24 nm
exclusive economic zone: 200 nm
continental shelf: 200-m depth or to the depth of exploitation

Climate: maritime temperate; cool and rainy in north, warmer and drier in south

Terrain: *the west-flowing Tagus River divides the country:* the north is mountainous toward the interior, while the south is characterized by rolling plains

Elevation: *highest point:* Ponta do Pico (Pico or Pico Alto) on Ilha do Pico in the Azores 2,351 m
lowest point: Atlantic Ocean 0 m
mean elevation: 372 m

Natural resources: fish, forests (cork), iron ore, copper, zinc, tin, tungsten, silver, gold, uranium, marble, clay, gypsum, salt, arable land, hydropower

Land use: *agricultural land:* 39.7% (2018 est.)
arable land: 11.9% (2018 est.)
permanent crops: 7.8% (2018 est.)
permanent pasture: 20% (2018 est.)
forest: 37.8% (2018 est.)
other: 22.5% (2018 est.)

Irrigated land: 5,662 sq km (2019)

Population distribution: concentrations are primarily along or near the Atlantic coast; both Lisbon and the second largest city, Porto, are coastal cities

Natural hazards: Azores subject to severe earthquakes
volcanism: limited volcanic activity in the Azores Islands; Fayal or Faial (1,043 m) last erupted in 1958; most volcanoes have not erupted in centuries; historically active volcanoes include Agua de Pau, Furnas, Pico, Picos Volcanic System, San Jorge, Sete Cidades, and Terceira

Geography - note: Azores and Madeira Islands occupy strategic locations along western sea approaches to Strait of Gibraltar; they are two of the four North Atlantic archipelagos that make up Macaronesia; the others are the Canary Islands (Spain) and Cabo Verde

PEOPLE AND SOCIETY

Population: *total:* 10,207,177
male: 4,835,763
female: 5,371,414 (2024 est.)
comparison rankings: female 86; male 94; total 92

Nationality: *noun:* Portuguese (singular and plural)
adjective: Portuguese

Ethnic groups: Portuguese 95%; citizens from Portugal's former colonies in Africa, Asia (Han Chinese), and South America (Brazilian) and other foreign born 5%

Languages: Portuguese (official), Mirandese (official, but locally used)

Religions: Roman Catholic 79.7%, Protestant 2.2%, other Christian 2.5%, other non-Christian, 1.1%, none 14.5% (2021 est.)
note: data represent population 15 years of age and older

Age structure: *0-14 years:* 12.7% (male 662,419/female 631,284)
15-64 years: 65% (male 3,264,766/female 3,371,087)
65 years and over: 22.3% (2024 est.) (male 908,578/female 1,369,043)

Dependency ratios: *total dependency ratio:* 56
youth dependency ratio: 20.8
elderly dependency ratio: 35.2
potential support ratio: 2.8 (2021 est.)

Median age: *total:* 46.4 years (2024 est.)
male: 44.3 years
female: 48.3 years
comparison ranking: total 11

Population growth rate: -0.14% (2024 est.)
comparison ranking: 207

Birth rate: 8 births/1,000 population (2024 est.)
comparison ranking: 214

Death rate: 10.9 deaths/1,000 population (2024 est.)
comparison ranking: 27

Net migration rate: 1.5 migrant(s)/1,000 population (2024 est.)
comparison ranking: 56

Population distribution: concentrations are primarily along or near the Atlantic coast; both Lisbon and the second largest city, Porto, are coastal cities

Urbanization: *urban population:* 67.9% of total population (2023)
rate of urbanization: 0.44% annual rate of change (2020-25 est.)

Major urban areas - population: 3.001 million LISBON (capital), 1.325 million Porto (2023)

Sex ratio: *at birth:* 1.05 male(s)/female
0-14 years: 1.05 male(s)/female
15-64 years: 0.97 male(s)/female
65 years and over: 0.66 male(s)/female
total population: 0.9 male(s)/female (2024 est.)

Mother's mean age at first birth: 29.9 years (2020 est.)

Maternal mortality ratio: 12 deaths/100,000 live births (2020 est.)
comparison ranking: 141

Infant mortality rate: *total:* 2.4 deaths/1,000 live births (2024 est.)
male: 2.8 deaths/1,000 live births
female: 2.1 deaths/1,000 live births
comparison ranking: total 216

Life expectancy at birth: *total population:* 81.9 years (2024 est.)
male: 78.8 years
female: 85.2 years
comparison ranking: total population 37

Total fertility rate: 1.45 children born/woman (2024 est.)
comparison ranking: 207

Gross reproduction rate: 0.71 (2024 est.)

Contraceptive prevalence rate: 73.9% (2014)

Drinking water source: *improved: urban:* 100% of population
rural: 99.7% of population
total: 99.9% of population
unimproved: urban: 0% of population
rural: 0.3% of population
total: 0.1% of population (2020 est.)

Current health expenditure: 10.6% of GDP (2020)

Physician density: 5.48 physicians/1,000 population (2019)

Hospital bed density: 3.5 beds/1,000 population (2018)

Sanitation facility access: *improved: urban:* 99.9% of population
rural: 100% of population
total: 99.9% of population
unimproved: urban: 0.1% of population
rural: 0% of population
total: 0.1% of population (2020 est.)

Obesity - adult prevalence rate: 20.8% (2016)
comparison ranking: 95

Alcohol consumption per capita: *total:* 10.37 liters of pure alcohol (2019 est.)
beer: 2.62 liters of pure alcohol (2019 est.)
wine: 6.04 liters of pure alcohol (2019 est.)
spirits: 1.34 liters of pure alcohol (2019 est.)
other alcohols: 0.37 liters of pure alcohol (2019 est.)
comparison ranking: total 20

Tobacco use: *total:* 25.4% (2020 est.)

male: 30.5% (2020 est.)
female: 20.2% (2020 est.)
comparison ranking: total 47

Children under the age of 5 years underweight: 0.4% (2015/16)
comparison ranking: 124

Currently married women (ages 15-49): 52.6% (2023 est.)

Education expenditures: 5% of GDP (2020 est.)
comparison ranking: 76

Literacy: *definition:* age 15 and over can read and write
total population: 95.9%
male: 97.8%
female: 95.9% (2021)

School life expectancy (primary to tertiary education): *total:* 17 years
male: 17 years
female: 17 years (2020)

ENVIRONMENT

Environment - current issues: soil erosion; air pollution caused by industrial and vehicle emissions; water pollution, especially in urban centers and coastal areas

Environment - international agreements: *party to:* Air Pollution, Air Pollution-Heavy Metals, Air Pollution-Multi-effect Protocol, Antarctic-Environmental Protection, Antarctic Treaty, Biodiversity, Climate Change, Climate Change-Kyoto Protocol, Climate Change-Paris Agreement, Comprehensive Nuclear Test Ban, Desertification, Endangered Species, Hazardous Wastes, Law of the Sea, Marine Dumping-London Convention, Marine Life Conservation, Ozone Layer Protection, Ship Pollution, Tropical Timber 2006, Wetlands, Whaling
signed, but not ratified: Air Pollution-Persistent Organic Pollutants, Air Pollution-Volatile Organic Compounds, Environmental Modification, Nuclear Test Ban

Climate: maritime temperate; cool and rainy in north, warmer and drier in south

Urbanization: *urban population:* 67.9% of total population (2023)
rate of urbanization: 0.44% annual rate of change (2020-25 est.)

Revenue from forest resources: 0.13% of GDP (2018 est.)
comparison ranking: 108

Revenue from coal: 0% of GDP (2018 est.)
comparison ranking: 82

Air pollutants: *particulate matter emissions:* 7.34 micrograms per cubic meter (2019 est.)
carbon dioxide emissions: 48.74 megatons (2016 est.)
methane emissions: 10.93 megatons (2020 est.)

Waste and recycling: *municipal solid waste generated annually:* 4.71 million tons (2014 est.)
municipal solid waste recycled annually: 764,433 tons (2014 est.)
percent of municipal solid waste recycled: 16.2% (2014 est.)

Total water withdrawal: *municipal:* 880 million cubic meters (2020 est.)
industrial: 1.83 billion cubic meters (2020 est.)
agricultural: 3.42 billion cubic meters (2020 est.)

Total renewable water resources: 77.4 billion cubic meters (2020 est.)

Geoparks: *total global geoparks and regional networks:* 6 (2024)
global geoparks and regional networks: Açores; Arouca; Estrela; Naturtejo da Meseta Meridional; Oeste; Terras de Cavaleiros (2024)

GOVERNMENT

Country name: *conventional long form:* Portuguese Republic
conventional short form: Portugal
local long form: Republica Portuguesa
local short form: Portugal
etymology: name derives from the Roman designation "Portus Cale" meaning "Port of Cale"; Cale was an ancient Celtic town and port in present-day northern Portugal

Government type: semi-presidential republic

Capital: *name:* Lisbon
geographic coordinates: 38 43 N, 9 08 W
time difference: UTC 0 (5 hours ahead of Washington, DC, during Standard Time)
daylight saving time: +1hr, begins last Sunday in March; ends last Sunday in October
time zone note: Portugal has two time zones, including the Azores (UTC-1)
etymology: Lisbon is one of Europe's oldest cities (the second oldest capital city after Athens) and the origin of the name is lost in time; it may have been founded as an ancient Celtic settlement that subsequently maintained close commercial relations with the Phoenicians (beginning about 1200 B.C.); the name of the settlement may have been derived from the pre-Roman appellation for the Tagus River that runs through the city, Lisso or Lucio; the Romans named the city "Olisippo" when they took it from the Carthaginians in 205 B.C.; under the Visigoths the city name became "Ulixbona," under the Arabs it was "al-Ushbuna"; the medieval version of "Lissabona" became today's Lisboa

Administrative divisions: 18 districts (distritos, singular - distrito) and 2 autonomous regions* (regioes autonomas, singular - regiao autonoma); Aveiro, Acores (Azores)*, Beja, Braga, Braganca, Castelo Branco, Coimbra, Evora, Faro, Guarda, Leiria, Lisboa (Lisbon), Madeira*, Portalegre, Porto, Santarem, Setubal, Viana do Castelo, Vila Real, Viseu

Independence: 1143 (Kingdom of Portugal recognized); 1 December 1640 (independence reestablished following 60 years of Spanish rule); 5 October 1910 (republic proclaimed)

National holiday: Portugal Day (Dia de Portugal), 10 June (1580); note - also called Camoes Day, the day that revered national poet Luis DE CAMOES (1524-80) died

Legal system: civil law system; Constitutional Court review of legislative acts

Constitution: *history:* several previous; latest adopted 2 April 1976, effective 25 April 1976
amendments: proposed by the Assembly of the Republic; adoption requires two-thirds majority vote of Assembly members; amended several times, last in 2005

International law organization participation: accepts compulsory ICJ jurisdiction with reservations; accepts ICCt jurisdiction

Citizenship: *citizenship by birth:* no
citizenship by descent only: at least one parent must be a citizen of Portugal
dual citizenship recognized: yes
residency requirement for naturalization: 10 years; 6 years if from a Portuguese-speaking country

Suffrage: 18 years of age; universal

Executive branch: *chief of state:* President Marcelo REBELO DE SOUSA (since 9 March 2016)
head of government: Prime Minister Antonio Luis MONTENEGRO (since 2 April 2024)
cabinet: Council of Ministers appointed by the president on the recommendation of the prime minister
elections/appointments: president directly elected by absolute majority popular vote in 2 rounds if needed for a 5-year term (eligible for a second term); election last held on 24 January 2021 (next to be held in January 2026); following legislative elections the leader of the majority party or majority coalition is usually appointed prime minister by the president
election results:
2021: Marcelo REBELO DE SOUSA reelected president in the first round; percent of vote - Marcelo REBELO DE SOUSA (PSD) 60.7%, Ana GOMES (ran as an independent but is a member of PS) 13%, Andre VENTURA (CH) 11.9%, João FERREIRA (PCP-PEV) 4.3%, other 10.1%
2016: Marcelo REBELO DE SOUSA elected president in the first round; percent of vote - Marcelo REBELO DE SOUSA (PSD) 52%, António SAMPAIO DA NOVOA (independent) 22.9%, Marisa MATIAS (BE) 10.1%, Maria DE BELEM ROSEIRA (PS) 4.2%, other 10.8%
note: there is also a Council of State that acts as a consultative body to the president

Legislative branch: *description:* unicameral Assembly of the Republic or Assembleia da Republica (230 seats; 226 members directly elected in multi-seat constituencies by closed-list proportional representation vote and 4 members - 2 each in 2 constituencies representing Portuguese living abroad - directly elected by proportional representation vote; members serve 4-year terms)
elections: last held on 10 March 2024 (next to be held on 30 September 2028); note - early elections were called after Prime Minister Antonio Luis Santos da COSTA resigned on 7 November 2023
election results: percent of vote by party - AD (PSD, CDS-PP, PPM) 28.8%, PS, 28%, Enough 18.1%, IL 4.9%, BE 4.4%, L 3.2%, CDU 3.2%, other 9.4%; seats by party - AD (PSD, CDS-PP, PPM) 80, PS 78, Enough 50, IL 8, BE 5, L 4, CDU 4, other 1; composition - men 155, women 75, percentage women 32.6%

Judicial branch: *highest court(s):* Supreme Court or Supremo Tribunal de Justica (consists of 12 justices); Constitutional Court or Tribunal Constitucional (consists of 13 judges)
judge selection and term of office: Supreme Court justices nominated by the president and appointed by the Assembly of the Republic; judges can serve for life; Constitutional Court judges - 10 elected by the Assembly and 3 elected by the other Constitutional Court judges; judges elected for 6-year nonrenewable terms
subordinate courts: Supreme Administrative Court (Supremo Tribunal Administrativo); Audit Court (Tribunal de Contas); appellate, district, and municipal courts

Political parties: Democratic Alliance or AD (2024 electoral alliance in the Azores, includes PSD, CDS-PP, PPM)
Democratic and Social Center/People's Party (Partido do Centro Democratico Social-Partido Popular) or CDS-PP
Ecologist Party "The Greens" or "Os Verdes" (Partido Ecologista-Os Verdes) or PEV
Enough (Chega)
Liberal Initiative (Iniciativa Liberal) or IL

LIVRE or L
People-Animals-Nature Party (Pessoas-Animais-Natureza) or PAN
People's Monarchist Party or PPM
Portuguese Communist Party (Partido Comunista Portugues) or PCP
Social Democratic Party (Partido Social Democrata) or PSD (formerly the Partido Popular Democratico or PPD)
Socialist Party (Partido Socialista) or PS
The Left Bloc (Bloco de Esquerda) or BE or O Bloco
Unitary Democratic Coalition (Coligacao Democratica Unitaria) or CDU (includes PCP and PEV) (2024)

International organization participation: ADB (nonregional member), AfDB (nonregional member), Australia Group, BIS, CD, CE, CERN, CPLP, EAPC, EBRD, ECB, EIB, EMU, ESA, EU, FAO, FATF, IADB, IAEA, IBRD, ICAO, ICC (national committees), ICCt, ICRM, IDA, IEA, IFAD, IFC, IFRCS, IHO, ILO, IMF, IMO, IMSO, Interpol, IOC, IOM, IPU, ISO, ITSO, ITU, ITUC (NGOs), LAIA (observer), MIGA, NATO, NEA, NSG, OAS (observer), OECD, OPCW, OSCE, Pacific Alliance (observer), Paris Club (associate), PCA, Schengen Convention, SELEC (observer), UN, UNCTAD, UNESCO, UNHCR, UNIDO, Union Latina, UNOOSA, UNWTO, UPU, Wassenaar Arrangement, WCO, WFTU (NGOs), WHO, WIPO, WMO, WTO, ZC

Diplomatic representation in the US: *chief of mission:* Ambassador Francisco Antonio DUARTE LOPES (since 7 June 2022)
chancery: 2012 Massachusetts Avenue NW, Washington, DC 20036
telephone: [1] (202) 350-5400
FAX: [1] (202) 462-3726
email address and website:
info.washington@mne.pt
https://washingtondc.embaixadaportugal.mne.gov.pt/en/
consulate(s) general: Boston, Newark (NJ), New York, San Francisco
consulate(s): New Bedford (MA), Providence (RI)

Diplomatic representation from the US: *chief of mission:* Ambassador Randi Charno LEVINE (since 22 April 2022)
embassy: Avenida das Forcas Armadas, 1600-081 Lisboa
mailing address: 5320 Lisbon Place, Washington DC 20521-5320
telephone: [351] (21) 727-3300
FAX: [351] (21) 726-9109
email address and website:
conslisbon@state.gov
https://pt.usembassy.gov/
consulate(s): Ponta Delgada (Azores)

Flag description: two vertical bands of green (hoist side, two-fifths) and red (three-fifths) with the national coat of arms (armillary sphere and Portuguese shield) centered on the dividing line; explanations for the color meanings are ambiguous, but a popular interpretation has green symbolizing hope and red the blood of those defending the nation

National symbol(s): armillary sphere (a spherical astrolabe modeling objects in the sky and representing the Republic); national colors: red, green

National anthem: *name:* "A Portugesa" (The Song of the Portuguese)
lyrics/music: Henrique LOPES DE MENDOCA/ Alfredo KEIL
note: adopted 1910; "A Portuguesa" was originally written to protest the Portuguese monarchy's acquiescence to the 1890 British ultimatum forcing Portugal to give up areas of Africa; the lyrics refer to the "insult" that resulted from the event

National heritage: *total World Heritage Sites:* 17 (16 cultural, 1 natural)
selected World Heritage Site locales: Historic Évora (c); Central Zone of the Town of Angra do Heroismo in the Azores (c); Cultural Landscape of Sintra (c); Laurisilva of Madeira (n); Historic Guimarães (c); Monastery of the Hieronymites and Tower of Belém in Lisbon (c); Convent of Christ in Tomar (c); Prehistoric Rock Art Sites in the Côa Valley and Siega Verde (c); University of Coimbra – Alta and Sofia (c); Sanctuary of Bom Jesus do Monte in Braga (c)

ECONOMY

Economic overview: high-income EU and eurozone economy; strong services sector led by tourism and banking; tight labor market; private consumption and export recovery driving post-inflation rebound; EU Recovery and Resilience Plan (RRP) funds a key driver of public investment; high public debt but improving fiscal position

Real GDP (purchasing power parity): $439.008 billion (2023 est.)
$429.3 billion (2022 est.)
$401.863 billion (2021 est.)
note: data in 2021 dollars
comparison ranking: 52

Real GDP growth rate: 2.26% (2023 est.)
6.83% (2022 est.)
5.74% (2021 est.)
note: annual GDP % growth based on constant local currency
comparison ranking: 132

Real GDP per capita: $41,700 (2023 est.)
$41,200 (2022 est.)
$38,800 (2021 est.)
note: data in 2021 dollars
comparison ranking: 58

GDP (official exchange rate): $287.08 billion (2023 est.)
note: data in current dollars at official exchange rate

Inflation rate (consumer prices): 4.31% (2023 est.)
7.83% (2022 est.)
1.27% (2021 est.)
note: annual % change based on consumer prices
comparison ranking: 92

Credit ratings: Fitch rating: BBB (2007)
Moody's rating: Baa3 (2018)
Standard & Poors rating: BBB (2019)
note: The year refers to the year in which the current credit rating was first obtained.

GDP - composition, by sector of origin: *agriculture:* 2% (2023 est.)
industry: 18% (2023 est.)
services: 67% (2023 est.)
note: figures may not total 100% due to non-allocated consumption not captured in sector-reported data
comparison rankings: services 51; industry 153; agriculture 155

GDP - composition, by end use: *household consumption:* 62.6% (2023 est.)
government consumption: 17% (2023 est.)
investment in fixed capital: 19.4% (2023 est.)
investment in inventories: 0.2% (2023 est.)
exports of goods and services: 47.4% (2023 est.)
imports of goods and services: -46.6% (2023 est.)
note: figures may not total 100% due to rounding or gaps in data collection

Agricultural products: milk, tomatoes, grapes, olives, maize, oranges, pork, potatoes, chicken, apples (2022)
note: top ten agricultural products based on tonnage

Industries: textiles, clothing, footwear, wood and cork, paper and pulp, chemicals, fuels and lubricants, automobiles and auto parts, base metals, minerals, porcelain and ceramics, glassware, technology, telecommunications; dairy products, wine, other foodstuffs; ship construction and refurbishment; tourism, plastics, financial services, optics

Industrial production growth rate: -1.13% (2023 est.)
note: annual % change in industrial value added based on constant local currency
comparison ranking: 169

Labor force: 5.419 million (2023 est.)
note: number of people ages 15 or older who are employed or seeking work
comparison ranking: 80

Unemployment rate: 6.49% (2023 est.)
6.01% (2022 est.)
6.58% (2021 est.)
note: % of labor force seeking employment
comparison ranking: 132

Youth unemployment rate (ages 15-24): *total:* 20.2% (2023 est.)
male: 20.6% (2023 est.)
female: 19.9% (2023 est.)
note: % of labor force ages 15-24 seeking employment
comparison ranking: total 63

Population below poverty line: 16.4% (2021 est.)
note: % of population with income below national poverty line

Gini Index coefficient - distribution of family income: 34.6 (2021 est.)
note: index (0-100) of income distribution; higher values represent greater inequality
comparison ranking: 81

Average household expenditures: *on food:* 17.6% of household expenditures (2022 est.)
on alcohol and tobacco: 3.4% of household expenditures (2022 est.)

Household income or consumption by percentage share: *lowest 10%:* 2.8% (2021 est.)
highest 10%: 27.6% (2021 est.)
note: % share of income accruing to lowest and highest 10% of population

Remittances: 0.47% of GDP (2023 est.)
0.38% of GDP (2022 est.)
0.3% of GDP (2021 est.)
note: personal transfers and compensation between resident and non-resident individuals/households/entities

Budget: *revenues:* $99.473 billion (2022 est.)
expenditures: $100.796 billion (2022 est.)
note: central government revenues (excluding grants) and expenses converted to US dollars at average official exchange rate for year indicated

Public debt: 125.7% of GDP (2017 est.)
note: data cover general government debt and include debt instruments issued (or owned) by government entities other than the treasury; the data include treasury debt held by foreign entities; the data include debt issued by subnational entities, as well as intragovernmental debt; intragovernmental

debt consists of treasury borrowings from surpluses in the social funds, such as for retirement, medical care, and unemployment; debt instruments for the social funds are not sold at public auctions
comparison ranking: 11

Taxes and other revenues: 23.05% (of GDP) (2022 est.)
note: central government tax revenue as a % of GDP
comparison ranking: 62

Current account balance: $3.974 billion (2023 est.)
-$3.108 billion (2022 est.)
-$2.987 billion (2021 est.)
note: balance of payments - net trade and primary/secondary income in current dollars
comparison ranking: 39

Exports: $136.589 billion (2023 est.)
$126.541 billion (2022 est.)
$105.648 billion (2021 est.)
note: balance of payments - exports of goods and services in current dollars
comparison ranking: 40

Exports - partners: Spain 25%, France 12%, Germany 11%, US 7%, UK 5% (2022)
note: top five export partners based on percentage share of exports

Exports - commodities: cars, garments, refined petroleum, vehicle parts/accessories, plastic products (2022)
note: top five export commodities based on value in dollars

Imports: $133.006 billion (2023 est.)
$131.627 billion (2022 est.)
$112.413 billion (2021 est.)
note: balance of payments - imports of goods and services in current dollars
comparison ranking: 41

Imports - partners: Spain 31%, Germany 11%, France 6%, China 5%, Italy 5% (2022)
note: top five import partners based on percentage share of imports

Imports - commodities: crude petroleum, cars, refined petroleum, natural gas, vehicle parts/accessories (2022)
note: top five import commodities based on value in dollars

Reserves of foreign exchange and gold: $35.243 billion (2023 est.)
$32.232 billion (2022 est.)
$32.535 billion (2021 est.)
note: holdings of gold (year-end prices)/foreign exchange/special drawing rights in current dollars
comparison ranking: 58

Exchange rates: euros (EUR) per US dollar -

Exchange rates: 0.925 (2023 est.)
0.95 (2022 est.)
0.845 (2021 est.)
0.876 (2020 est.)
0.893 (2019 est.)

ENERGY

Electricity access: *electrification - total population:* 100% (2022 est.)

Electricity: *installed generating capacity:* 23.316 million kW (2022 est.)
consumption: 50.255 billion kWh (2022 est.)
exports: 3.062 billion kWh (2022 est.)
imports: 12.314 billion kWh (2022 est.)
transmission/distribution losses: 4.54 billion kWh (2022 est.)
comparison rankings: transmission/distribution losses 159; imports 22; exports 46; consumption 53; installed generating capacity 43

Electricity generation sources: *fossil fuels:* 42.1% of total installed capacity (2022 est.)
solar: 7.4% of total installed capacity (2022 est.)
wind: 28.8% of total installed capacity (2022 est.)
hydroelectricity: 12.8% of total installed capacity (2022 est.)
geothermal: 0.4% of total installed capacity (2022 est.)
biomass and waste: 8.6% of total installed capacity (2022 est.)

Coal: *consumption:* 9,000 metric tons (2022 est.)
exports: 200 metric tons (2022 est.)
imports: 23,000 metric tons (2022 est.)
proven reserves: 3 million metric tons (2022 est.)

Petroleum: *total petroleum production:* 8,000 bbl/day (2023 est.)
refined petroleum consumption: 212,000 bbl/day (2023 est.)

Natural gas: *consumption:* 5.515 billion cubic meters (2022 est.)
imports: 5.97 billion cubic meters (2022 est.)

Carbon dioxide emissions: 42.562 million metric tonnes of CO2 (2022 est.)
from coal and metallurgical coke: 40,000 metric tonnes of CO2 (2022 est.)
from petroleum and other liquids: 31.394 million metric tonnes of CO2 (2022 est.)
from consumed natural gas: 11.128 million metric tonnes of CO2 (2022 est.)
comparison ranking: total emissions 64

Energy consumption per capita: 80.316 million Btu/person (2022 est.)
comparison ranking: 64

COMMUNICATIONS

Telephones - fixed lines: *total subscriptions:* 5.437 million (2022 est.)
subscriptions per 100 inhabitants: 53 (2022 est.)
comparison ranking: total subscriptions 27

Telephones - mobile cellular: *total subscriptions:* 12.792 million (2022 est.)
subscriptions per 100 inhabitants: 125 (2022 est.)
comparison ranking: total subscriptions 80

Telecommunication systems: *general assessment:* Portugal has a medium-sized telecom market with a strong mobile sector and a growing broadband customer base; before the pandemic, the country had seen improving economic growth, following several years of austerity measures; revenue among some operators remains under pressure, though investments in network upgrades are continuing in an effort to attract customers to high-end services; Portugal's broadband services have grown steadily in recent years, largely the result of joint efforts between the regulator and the key market operators which have invested in significant infrastructure upgrades; these operators are focused on fiber-based services, resulting in a migration of subscribers from digital subscriber line DSL infrastructure; the government has also supported open-access wholesale networks; the mobile virtual network operator (MVNO) market remains largely undeveloped, partly because network operators have their own low-cost brands; collectively, MVNOs have about 2.9% share of the market; population coverage by 3G infrastructure is universal, and most investment in the sector is being directed to LTE and 5G technologies; the MNOs have trialed 5G and are looking to launch commercial services (2021)
domestic: fixed-lineis 52 per 100 persons and mobile-cellular is 121 per 100 persons (2021)
international: country code - 351; landing points for the Ella Link, BUGIO, EIG, SAT-3/WASC, SeaMeWe-3, Equino, MainOne, Tat TGN-Western Europe, WACS, ACE, Atlantis2 and Columbus-III submarine cables provide connectivity to Europe, Africa, the Middle East, Asia, Southeast Asia, Australia, South America and the US; satellite earth stations - 3 Intelsat (2 Atlantic Ocean and 1 Indian Ocean), NA Eutelsat; tropospheric scatter to Azores (2019)

Broadcast media: Radio e Televisao de Portugal, the publicly owned TV broadcaster, operates 4 domestic channels and external service channels to Africa; overall, roughly 40 domestic TV stations; viewers have widespread access to international broadcasters with more than half of all households connected to multi-channel cable or satellite TV systems; publicly owned radio operates 3 national networks and provides regional and external services; several privately owned national radio stations and some 300 regional and local commercial radio stations

Internet country code: .pt

Internet users: *total:* 8.2 million (2021 est.)
percent of population: 82% (2021 est.)
comparison ranking: total 74

Broadband - fixed subscriptions: *total:* 4,160,795 (2020 est.)
subscriptions per 100 inhabitants: 41 (2020 est.)
comparison ranking: total 37

TRANSPORTATION

National air transport system: *number of registered air carriers:* 10 (2020)
inventory of registered aircraft operated by air carriers: 168
annual passenger traffic on registered air carriers: 17,367,956 (2018)
annual freight traffic on registered air carriers: 454.21 million (2018) mt-km

Civil aircraft registration country code prefix: CR, CS

Airports: 130 (2024)
comparison ranking: 39

Heliports: 63 (2024)

Pipelines: 1,344 km gas, 11 km oil, 188 km refined products (2013)

Railways: *total:* 2,526 km (2020) 1,696 km electrified
comparison ranking: total 65

Roadways: *total:* 11,217 km (2022)
comparison ranking: total 134

Waterways: 210 km (2011) (on Douro River from Porto)
comparison ranking: 105

Merchant marine: *total:* 888 (2023)
by type: bulk carrier 110, container ship 299, general cargo 191, oil tanker 29, other 259
comparison ranking: total 27

Ports: *total ports:* 18 (2024)
large: 3
medium: 2
small: 4
very small: 9
ports with oil terminals: 5
key ports: Aveiro, Funchal, Lagos, Lisboa, Sines

MILITARY AND SECURITY

Military and security forces: Portuguese Armed Forces (Forças Armadas Portuguesa): Portuguese Army (Exercito Portuguesa), Portuguese Navy (Marinha Portuguesa; includes Marine Corps, aka Corpo de Fuzileiros or Corps of Fusiliers), Portuguese Air Force (Forca Aerea Portuguesa, FAP)

Ministry of Internal Administration: Foreigners and Borders Service, Public Security Service, National Republican Guard (Guarda Nacional Republicana, GNR) (2024)
note: the Foreigners and Borders Service has jurisdiction over immigration and border matters, the Public Security Police has jurisdiction in cities, and the GNR has jurisdiction in rural areas; the GNR is a national gendarmerie force comprised of military personnel with law enforcement, internal security, civil defense, disaster response, and coast guard duties; it is responsible to both the Ministry of Internal Administration and to the Ministry of National Defense; it is not part of the Armed Forces, but may be placed under the operational command of the Chief of the General Staff of the Armed Forces in the event of a national emergency; the GNR describes itself as a hinge between the Armed Forces and the police forces and other security services

Military expenditures: 1.6% of GDP (2024 est.)
1.5% of GDP (2023)
1.4% of GDP (2022 est.)
1.5% of GDP (2021)
1.4% of GDP (2020)
comparison ranking: 85

Military and security service personnel strengths: approximately 28,000 active-duty personnel (15,000 Army; 7,000 Navy, including about 1,000 marines; 6,000 Air Force); 24,500 National Republican Guard (military personnel) (2024)

Military equipment inventories and acquisitions: the military's inventory includes mostly European- and US-origin weapons systems along with a smaller mix of domestically produced equipment; in recent years, leading foreign suppliers have included Germany and the US; Portugal's defense industry is noted for its shipbuilding (2024)
note: in 2023, Portugal announced a modernization program that included the acquisition of land, naval, air, cyber security, and space capabilities, as well as emerging disruptive technologies

Military service age and obligation: 18-30 years of age for voluntary or contract military service; no compulsory military service (abolished 2004) but conscription possible if insufficient volunteers available; women serve in the armed forces but are prohibited from serving in some combatant specialties; contract service lasts for an initial period of 2-6 years, and can be extended to a maximum of 20 years of service; initial voluntary military service lasts 12 months; reserve obligation to age 35 (2023)
note: as of 2023, women made up about 14% of the military's full-time personnel

Military deployments: the Portuguese Armed Forces have more than 1,100 military personnel deployed around the world engaged in missions supporting the EU, NATO, the UN, and partner nations; key deployments include 225 troops in the Central African Republic (MINUSCA), approximately 220 in Lithuania (NATO), and approximately 150 in Romania (NATO); it also participates in NATO air policing and maritime patrolling operations (2024)

Military - note: the Portuguese military is an all-volunteer force with the primary responsibilities of external defense, humanitarian operations, and fulfilling Portugal's commitments to European and international security; maritime security has long been a key component of the military's portfolio, and Portugal has one of the world's oldest navies
Portugal was one of the original signers of the North Atlantic Treaty (also known as the Washington Treaty) in 1949 establishing NATO, and the Alliance forms a key pillar of Portugal's defense policy; Portugal is also a signatory of the EU's Common Security and Defense Policy, and it regularly participates in a variety of EU, NATO, and UN deployments around the world; the military's largest commitments include air, ground, and naval forces under NATO-led missions and standing task forces in the Baltics, Eastern Europe, and the Mediterranean Sea; the military also participates regularly in exercises with NATO partners (2024)

SPACE

Space agency/agencies: Portuguese Space Agency (Agência Espacial Portuguesa; aka Portugal Space; established 2019); Foundation for Science and Technology (FCT; government agency that funds space research established in 2009) (2024)

Space launch site(s): developing a commercial space port on Santa Maria Island in the Azores (first anticipated launch, 2025) (2024)

Space program overview: has a national space program which is is integrated within the framework of the European Space Agency (ESA); builds and operates satellites; researches and develops a range of space-related technologies with an emphasis on small/ micro/nano satellites for remote sensing (RS), navigational, science/technology, and telecommunications, as well as satellite launch services; in addition to the ESA/EU and their member states, cooperates with the space agencies and industries of a variety of countries, including those of Algeria, Angola, Brazil, China, India, Japan, Morocco, South Korea, and the US, as well as such international organizations and projects as the Europe South Observatory (ESO) and the Square Kilometer Array (SKA) Observatory project; one of the objectives of the country's national space strategy (Portugal Space 2030) is to increase the annual outcome of space related activities in the country to about $500 million by 2030 (2024)
note: further details about the key activities, programs, and milestones of the country's space program, as well as government spending estimates on the space sector, appear in the Space Programs reference guide

TERRORISM

Terrorist group(s): Islamic State of Iraq and ash-Sham (ISIS)
note: details about the history, aims, leadership, organization, areas of operation, tactics, targets, weapons, size, and sources of support of the group(s) appear(s) in the Terrorism reference guide

TRANSNATIONAL ISSUES

Refugees and internally displaced persons: *refugees (country of origin):* 59,920 (Ukraine) (as of 31 January 2024)
stateless persons: 55 (2022)

Illicit drugs: a European gateway for Southwest Asian heroin; transshipment point for hashish from North Africa to Europe; consumer of Southwest Asian heroin

PUERTO RICO

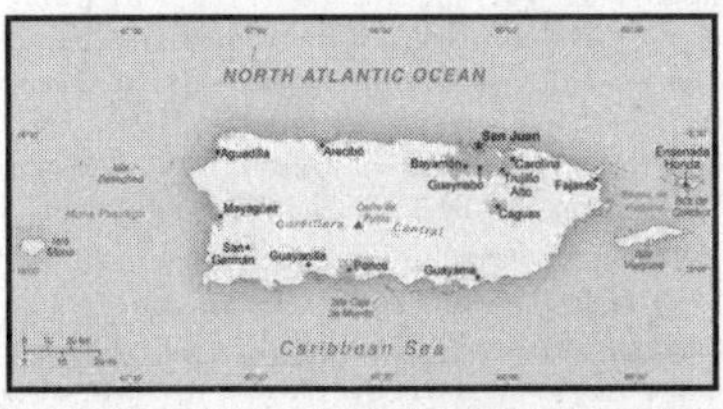

INTRODUCTION

Background: Populated for centuries by aboriginal peoples, Puerto Rico was claimed by the Spanish Crown in 1493 after Christopher COLUMBUS' second voyage to the Americas. In 1898, after 400 years of colonial rule that saw the indigenous population nearly exterminated and African slave labor introduced, Puerto Rico was ceded to the US as a result of the Spanish-American War. Puerto Ricans were granted US citizenship in 1917. Popularly elected governors have served since 1948. In 1952, a constitution was enacted that provided for internal self-government. In plebiscites held in 1967, 1993, and 1998, voters chose not to alter the existing political status with the US, but the results of a 2012 vote left open the possibility of American statehood. A referendum held in late 2020 showed a narrow preference for statehood.

Economic recession on the island has led to a net population loss since about 2005, as large numbers of residents moved to the US mainland. In 2017, Hurricane Maria was the worst storm to hit the island in eight decades, and damage was estimated in the tens of billions of dollars.

GEOGRAPHY

Location: Caribbean, island between the Caribbean Sea and the North Atlantic Ocean, east of the Dominican Republic

Geographic coordinates: 18 15 N, 66 30 W

Map references: Central America and the Caribbean

Area: *total:* 9,104 sq km
land: 8,959 sq km
water: 145 sq km
comparison ranking: total 170

Area - comparative: slightly less than three times the size of Rhode Island

Land boundaries: *total:* 0 km

Coastline: 501 km

Maritime claims: *territorial sea:* 12 nm
exclusive economic zone: 200 nm

Climate: tropical marine, mild; little seasonal temperature variation

Terrain: mostly mountains with coastal plain in north; precipitous mountains to the sea on west coast; sandy beaches along most coastal areas

Elevation: *highest point:* Cerro de Punta 1,338 m
lowest point: Caribbean Sea 0 m
mean elevation: 261 m

Natural resources: some copper and nickel; potential for onshore and offshore oil

Land use: *agricultural land:* 22% (2018 est.)
arable land: 6.6% (2018 est.)
permanent crops: 5.6% (2018 est.)
permanent pasture: 9.8% (2018 est.)
forest: 63.2% (2018 est.)
other: 14.8% (2018 est.)

Irrigated land: 220 sq km (2012)

Population distribution: population clusters tend to be found along the coast, the largest of these is found in and around San Juan; an exception to this is a sizeable population located in the interior of the island immediately south of the capital around Caguas; most of the interior, particularly in the western half of the island, is dominated by the Cordillera Central mountains, where population density is low

Natural hazards: periodic droughts; hurricanes

Geography - note: important location along the Mona Passage – a key shipping lane to the Panama Canal; San Juan is one of the biggest and best natural harbors in the Caribbean; many small rivers and high central mountains ensure land is well watered; south coast relatively dry; fertile coastal plain belt in north

PEOPLE AND SOCIETY

Population: *total:* 3,019,450
male: 1,418,753
female: 1,600,697 (2024 est.)
comparison rankings: female 135; male 140; total 138

Nationality: *noun:* Puerto Rican(s) (US citizens)
adjective: Puerto Rican

Ethnic groups: White 75.8%, Black/African American 12.4%, other 8.5% (includes American Indian, Alaskan Native, Native Hawaiian, other Pacific Islander, and others), mixed 3.3% (2010 est.)
note: 99% of the population is Latino

Languages: Spanish, English
major-language sample(s):
La Libreta Informativa del Mundo, la fuente indispensable de información básica. (Spanish)

Religions: Roman Catholic 56%, Protestant 33% (largely Pentecostal), other 2%, atheist 1%, none 7% (2014 est.)

Age structure: *0-14 years:* 12.5% (male 191,649/female 184,597)
15-64 years: 62.6% (male 904,406/female 986,778)
65 years and over: 24.9% (2024 est.) (male 322,698/female 429,322)

Dependency ratios: *total dependency ratio:* 56.3
youth dependency ratio: 21.3
elderly dependency ratio: 34.9
potential support ratio: 2.9 (2021 est.)

Median age: *total:* 46.1 years (2024 est.)
male: 44.2 years
female: 47.8 years
comparison ranking: total 13

Population growth rate: -1.2% (2024 est.)
comparison ranking: 233

Birth rate: 7.8 births/1,000 population (2024 est.)
comparison ranking: 217

Death rate: 10.2 deaths/1,000 population (2024 est.)
comparison ranking: 33

Net migration rate: -9.6 migrant(s)/1,000 population (2024 est.)
comparison ranking: 221

Population distribution: population clusters tend to be found along the coast, the largest of these is found in and around San Juan; an exception to this is a sizeable population located in the interior of the island immediately south of the capital around Caguas; most of the interior, particularly in the western half of the island, is dominated by the Cordillera Central mountains, where population density is low

Urbanization: *urban population:* 93.6% of total population (2023)
rate of urbanization: -0.12% annual rate of change (2020-25 est.)

Major urban areas - population: 2.440 million SAN JUAN (capital) (2023)

Sex ratio: *at birth:* 1.06 male(s)/female
0-14 years: 1.04 male(s)/female
15-64 years: 0.92 male(s)/female
65 years and over: 0.75 male(s)/female
total population: 0.89 male(s)/female (2024 est.)

Maternal mortality ratio: 34 deaths/100,000 live births (2020 est.)
comparison ranking: 109

Infant mortality rate: *total:* 5.8 deaths/1,000 live births (2024 est.)
male: 6.4 deaths/1,000 live births
female: 5.2 deaths/1,000 live births
comparison ranking: total 170

Life expectancy at birth: *total population:* 82.1 years (2024 est.)
male: 78.9 years
female: 85.5 years
comparison ranking: total population 34

Total fertility rate: 1.26 children born/woman (2024 est.)
comparison ranking: 220

Gross reproduction rate: 0.61 (2024 est.)

Drinking water source: *improved:*
total: 100% of population

Physician density: 3.06 physicians/1,000 population (2018)

Sanitation facility access: *improved:*
total: 100% of population

Currently married women (ages 15-49): 37.4% (2023 est.)

Education expenditures: 3.6% of GDP (2021 est.)
comparison ranking: 139

Literacy: *definition:* age 15 and over can read and write
total population: 92.4%
male: 92.4%
female: 92.4% (2021)

School life expectancy (primary to tertiary education): *total:* 16 years
male: 15 years
female: 18 years (2018)

ENVIRONMENT

Environment - current issues: soil erosion; occasional droughts cause water shortages; industrial pollution

Climate: tropical marine, mild; little seasonal temperature variation

Land use: *agricultural land:* 22% (2018 est.)
arable land: 6.6% (2018 est.)
permanent crops: 5.6% (2018 est.)
permanent pasture: 9.8% (2018 est.)
forest: 63.2% (2018 est.)
other: 14.8% (2018 est.)

Urbanization: *urban population:* 93.6% of total population (2023)
rate of urbanization: -0.12% annual rate of change (2020-25 est.)

Revenue from forest resources: 0% of GDP (2018 est.)
comparison ranking: 186

Revenue from coal: 0% of GDP (2018 est.)
comparison ranking: 63

Waste and recycling: *municipal solid waste generated annually:* 4,170,953 tons (2015 est.)
municipal solid waste recycled annually: 583,933 tons (2013 est.)
percent of municipal solid waste recycled: 14% (2013 est.)

Total water withdrawal: *municipal:* 800 million cubic meters (2020 est.)
industrial: 2.37 billion cubic meters (2020 est.)
agricultural: 110 million cubic meters (2020 est.)

Total renewable water resources: 7.1 billion cubic meters (2020 est.)

GOVERNMENT

Country name: *conventional long form:* Commonwealth of Puerto Rico
conventional short form: Puerto Rico
abbreviation: PR
etymology: Christopher COLUMBUS named the island San Juan Bautista (Saint John the Baptist) and the capital city and main port Cuidad de Puerto Rico (Rich Port City); over time, however, the names were shortened and transposed and the island came to be called Puerto Rico and its capital San Juan

Government type: unincorporated organized territory of the US with local self-government; republican form of territorial government with separate executive, legislative, and judicial branches; note - reference Puerto Rican Federal Relations Act, 2 March 1917, as amended by Public Law 600, 3 July 1950

Dependency status: unincorporated organized territory of the US with commonwealth status; policy relations between Puerto Rico and the US conducted under the jurisdiction of the Office of the President

Capital: *name:* San Juan
geographic coordinates: 18 28 N, 66 07 W
time difference: UTC-4 (1 hour ahead of Washington, DC, during Standard Time)

etymology: the name dates to 1521 and the founding of the city under the name "Ciudad de San Juan Bautista de Puerto Rico" (City of Saint John the Baptist of Puerto Rico)

Administrative divisions: none (territory of the US); there are no first-order administrative divisions as defined by the US Government, but there are 78 municipalities (municipios, singular - municipio) at the second order; Adjuntas, Aguada, Aguadilla, Aguas Buenas, Aibonito, Anasco, Arecibo, Arroyo, Barceloneta, Barranquitas, Bayamon, Cabo Rojo, Caguas, Camuy, Canovanas, Carolina, Catano, Cayey, Ceiba, Ciales, Cidra, Coamo, Comerio, Corozal, Culebra, Dorado, Fajardo, Florida, Guanica, Guayama, Guayanilla, Guaynabo, Gurabo, Hatillo, Hormigueros, Humacao, Isabela, Jayuya, Juana Diaz, Juncos, Lajas, Lares, Las Marias, Las Piedras, Loiza, Luquillo, Manati, Maricao, Maunabo, Mayaguez, Moca, Morovis, Naguabo, Naranjito, Orocovis, Patillas, Penuelas, Ponce, Quebradillas, Rincon, Rio Grande, Sabana Grande, Salinas, San German, San Juan, San Lorenzo, San Sebastian, Santa Isabel, Toa Alta, Toa Baja, Trujillo Alto, Utuado, Vega Alta, Vega Baja, Vieques, Villalba, Yabucoa, Yauco

Independence: none (territory of the US with commonwealth status)

National holiday: US Independence Day, 4 July (1776); Puerto Rico Constitution Day, 25 July (1952)

Legal system: civil law system based on the Spanish civil code and within the framework of the US federal system

Constitution: *history:* previous 1900 (Organic Act, or Foraker Act); latest ratified by referendum 3 March 1952, approved 3 July 1952, effective 25 July 1952
amendments: proposed by a concurrent resolution of at least two-thirds majority by the total Legislative Assembly membership; approval requires at least two-thirds majority vote by the membership of both houses and approval by a majority of voters in a special referendum; if passed by at least three-fourths Assembly vote, the referendum can be held concurrently with the next general election; constitutional articles such as the republican form of government or the bill of rights cannot be amended; amended 1952

Citizenship: see United States

Suffrage: 18 years of age; universal; note - island residents are US citizens but do not vote in US presidential elections

Executive branch: *chief of state:* President Joseph R. BIDEN Jr. (since 20 January 2021)
head of government: Governor Pedro PIERLUISI (since 2 January 2021)
cabinet: Cabinet appointed by governor with the consent of the Legislative Assembly
elections/appointments: president and vice president indirectly elected on the same ballot by an Electoral College of 'electors' chosen from each state; president and vice president serve a 4-year term (eligible for a second term); under the US Constitution, residents of Puerto Rico do not vote in elections for US president and vice president; however, they may vote in Democratic and Republican party presidential primary elections; governor directly elected by simple majority popular vote for a 4-year term (no term limits); election last held on 3 November 2020 (next to be held on 5 November 2024)
election results:
2020: Pedro PIERLUISI elected governor; percent of vote - Pedro PIERLUISI (PNP) 32.9%, Carlos DELGADO (PPD) 31.6%, Alexandra LUGARO (independent) 14.2%, Juan DALMAU (PIP) 13.7%, other 7.6%
2016: Ricardo ROSSELLO elected governor; percent of vote - Ricardo ROSSELLO (PNP) 41.8%, David BERNIER (PPD) 38.9%, Alexandra LUGARO (independent) 11.1%, Manuel CIDRE (independent) 5.7%

Legislative branch: *description:*
bicameral Legislative Assembly or Asamblea Legislativa consists of:
Senate or Senado (30 seats statutory, 27 current; 16 members directly elected in 8 2-seat constituencies by simple majority vote and 11 at-large members directly elected by simple majority vote to serve 4-year terms)
House of Representatives or Camara de Representantes (51 seats; members directly elected in single-seat constituencies by simple majority vote to serve 4-year terms)
elections: Senate - last held on 3 November 2020 (next to be held on 5 November 2024)
House of Representatives - last held on 3 November 2020 (next to be held on 5 November 2024)
election results: Senate - percent of vote by party - NA; seats by party - PPD 12, NP 10, MVC 2, PD 1, PIP 1, independent 1; composition - men 14, women 13, percentage women 48.1%
House of Representatives - percent of vote by party - NA; seats by party - PPD 26, PNP 21, MVC 2, PIP 1, PD 1; composition - men 41, women 10, percentage women 19.6%; total Legislative Assembly percentage women 29.5%
note: Puerto Rico directly elects 1 member by simple majority vote to serve a 4-year term as a commissioner to the US House of Representatives; the commissioner can vote when serving on a committee and when the House meets as the Committee of the Whole House but not when legislation is submitted for a 'full floor' House vote; election of commissioner last held on 6 November 2018 (next to be held in November 2022)

Judicial branch: *highest court(s):* Supreme Court (consists of the chief justice and 8 associate justices)
judge selection and term of office: justices appointed by the governor and confirmed by majority Senate vote; judges serve until compulsory retirement at age 70
subordinate courts: Court of Appeals; First Instance Court comprised of superior and municipal courts

Political parties: Citizens' Victory Movement (Movimiento Victoria Ciudadana) or MVC
Democratic Party of Puerto Rico
New Progressive Party or PNP (pro-US statehood)
Popular Democratic Party or PPD (pro-commonwealth)
Project Dignity (Projecto Dignidad) or PD
Puerto Rican Independence Party or PIP (pro-independence)
Republican Party of Puerto Rico

International organization participation: AOSIS (observer), Caricom (observer), Interpol (subbureau), IOC, UNWTO (associate), UPU, WFTU (NGOs)

Diplomatic representation in the US: none (territory of the US)

Diplomatic representation from the US: *embassy:* none (territory of the US with commonwealth status)

Flag description: five equal horizontal bands of red (top, center, and bottom) alternating with white; a blue isosceles triangle based on the hoist side bears a large, white, five-pointed star in the center; the white star symbolizes Puerto Rico; the three sides of the triangle signify the executive, legislative and judicial parts of the government; blue stands for the sky and the coastal waters; red symbolizes the blood shed by warriors, while white represents liberty, victory, and peace
note: design initially influenced by the US flag, but similar to the Cuban flag, with the colors of the bands and triangle reversed

National symbol(s): Puerto Rican spindalis (bird), coqui (frog); national colors: red, white, blue

National anthem: *name:* "La Borinquena" (The Puerto Rican)
lyrics/music: Manuel Fernandez JUNCOS/Felix Astol ARTES
note: music adopted 1952, lyrics adopted 1977; the local anthem's name is a reference to the indigenous name of the island, Borinquen; the music was originally composed as a dance in 1867 and gained popularity in the early 20th century; there is some evidence that the music was written by Francisco RAMIREZ; as a commonwealth of the US, "The Star-Spangled Banner" is official (see United States)

National heritage: *total World Heritage Sites:* 1 (cultural); note - excerpted from the US entry
selected World Heritage Site locales: La Fortaleza and San Juan National Historic Site

ECONOMY

Economic overview: US Caribbean island territorial economy; hit hard by COVID-19 and hurricanes; declining labor force and job growth after a decade of continuous recession; capital-based industry and tourism; high poverty; energy import-dependent

Real GDP (purchasing power parity): $137.828 billion (2023 est.)
$137.056 billion (2022 est.)
$132.334 billion (2021 est.)
note: data in 2021 dollars
comparison ranking: 86

Real GDP growth rate: 0.56% (2023 est.)
3.57% (2022 est.)
0.39% (2021 est.)
note: annual GDP % growth based on constant local currency
comparison ranking: 179

Real GDP per capita: $43,000 (2023 est.)
$42,600 (2022 est.)
$40,600 (2021 est.)
note: data in 2021 dollars
comparison ranking: 55

GDP (official exchange rate): $117.902 billion (2023 est.)
note: data in current dollars at official exchange rate

Inflation rate (consumer prices): 1.8% (2017 est.)
-0.3% (2016 est.)
comparison ranking: 32

Credit ratings: Standard & Poors rating: D (2015)
note: The year refers to the year in which the current credit rating was first obtained.

GDP - composition, by sector of origin: *agriculture:* 0.7% (2023 est.)
industry: 49.1% (2023 est.)
services: 50.6% (2023 est.)
note: figures may not total 100% due to non-allocated consumption not captured in sector-reported data

comparison rankings: services 146; industry 13; agriculture 194

GDP - composition, by end use: *household consumption:* 80% (2023 est.)
government consumption: 7.1% (2023 est.)
investment in fixed capital: 13.7% (2023 est.)
investment in inventories: 0.5% (2023 est.)
exports of goods and services: 53.9% (2023 est.)
imports of goods and services: -47.8% (2023 est.)
note: figures may not total 100% due to rounding or gaps in data collection

Agricultural products: milk, plantains, bananas, chicken, tomatoes, mangoes/guavas, eggs, oranges, pumpkins/squash, papayas (2022)
note: top ten agricultural products based on tonnage

Industries: pharmaceuticals, electronics, apparel, food products, tourism

Industrial production growth rate: 4.3% (2014 est.)
note: annual % change in industrial value added based on constant local currency
comparison ranking: 72

Labor force: 1.154 million (2023 est.)
note: number of people ages 15 or older who are employed or seeking work
comparison ranking: 144

Unemployment rate: 5.96% (2023 est.)
6% (2022 est.)
7.9% (2021 est.)
note: % of labor force seeking employment
comparison ranking: 119

Youth unemployment rate (ages 15-24): *total:* 13.7% (2023 est.)
male: 14.9% (2023 est.)
female: 10.5% (2023 est.)
note: % of labor force ages 15-24 seeking employment
comparison ranking: total 102

Budget: *revenues:* $9.268 billion (2017 est.)
expenditures: $9.974 billion (2017 est.)

Public debt: 51.6% of GDP (2017 est.)
comparison ranking: 101

Taxes and other revenues: 8.9% (of GDP) (2017 est.)
comparison ranking: 187

Current account balance: $0 (2017 est.)
$0 (2016 est.)
comparison ranking: 82

Exports: $59.787 billion (2022 est.)
$57.916 billion (2021 est.)
$62.237 billion (2020 est.)
note: GDP expenditure basis - exports of goods and services in current dollars
comparison ranking: 61

Exports - partners: Italy 15%, Netherlands 15%, Belgium 9%, Japan 8%, Germany 8%, Austria 8%, Spain 7%, China 5% (2019)

Exports - commodities: packaged medicines, medical cultures/vaccines, hormones, orthopedic and medical appliances, sulfur compounds (2019)

Imports: $51.509 billion (2022 est.)
$45.052 billion (2021 est.)
$44.513 billion (2020 est.)
note: GDP expenditure basis - imports of goods and services in current dollars
comparison ranking: 67

Imports - partners: Ireland 38%, Singapore 9%, Switzerland 8%, South Korea 5% (2019)

Imports - commodities: nitrogen compounds, sulfur compounds, refined petroleum, medical cultures/vaccines, cars (2019)

Exchange rates: the US dollar is used

ENERGY

Electricity access: *electrification - total population:* 100% (2022 est.)

Electricity: *installed generating capacity:* 6.601 million kW (2022 est.)
consumption: 18.1 billion kWh (2022 est.)
transmission/distribution losses: 1.224 billion kWh (2022 est.)
comparison rankings: transmission/distribution losses 107; consumption 78; installed generating capacity 80

Electricity generation sources: *fossil fuels:* 97.4% of total installed capacity (2022 est.)
solar: 1.4% of total installed capacity (2022 est.)
wind: 0.8% of total installed capacity (2022 est.)
hydroelectricity: 0.3% of total installed capacity (2022 est.)
biomass and waste: 0.1% of total installed capacity (2022 est.)

Coal: *consumption:* 1.299 million metric tons (2022 est.)
exports: 3 metric tons (2022 est.)
imports: 1.299 million metric tons (2022 est.)

Petroleum: *refined petroleum consumption:* 80,000 bbl/day (2022 est.)

Natural gas: *consumption:* 1.409 billion cubic meters (2022 est.)
imports: 1.409 billion cubic meters (2022 est.)

Carbon dioxide emissions: 17.26 million metric tonnes of CO2 (2022 est.)
from coal and metallurgical coke: 2.935 million metric tonnes of CO2 (2022 est.)
from petroleum and other liquids: 11.561 million metric tonnes of CO2 (2022 est.)
from consumed natural gas: 2.763 million metric tonnes of CO2 (2022 est.)
comparison ranking: total emissions 91

Energy consumption per capita: 76.228 million Btu/person (2022 est.)
comparison ranking: 67

COMMUNICATIONS

Telephones - fixed lines: *total subscriptions:* 739,000 (2022 est.)
subscriptions per 100 inhabitants: 23 (2022 est.)
comparison ranking: total subscriptions 79

Telephones - mobile cellular: *total subscriptions:* 3.896 million (2022 est.)
subscriptions per 100 inhabitants: 120 (2022 est.)
comparison ranking: total subscriptions 135

Telecommunication systems: *general assessment:* Puerto Rico has a small telecom market which in recent years has been deeply affected by a combination of economic mismanagement and natural disasters, including two hurricanes which landed in late 2017 and an earthquake which struck in January 2020; these disasters caused considerable destruction of telecom infrastructure, which in turn led to a marked decline in the number of subscribers for all services; compounding these difficulties have been a long-term economic downturn which encouraged many people not to resume telecom services after these were restored; after some delay, the FCC in late 2019 issued an order relating to the release of funds to help rebuild telecom infrastructure; although Puerto Rico is a US territory it lags well behind the mainland US states in terms of fixed-line and broadband services; this is partly due to high unemployment rates (and consequently low disposable income) and poor telecoms investment in a market; the mobile market has been impacted by several mergers and acquisitions over the last few years; the activities of large multinational telcos continue to impact the Puerto Rican market; operators have secured spectrum in the 600MHz and 3.5GHz bands, thus enabling them to expand the reach of LTE services and launch services based on 5G; the growing number of submarine cables landing in Puerto Rico is helping to drive down the cost of telecom services, creating a demand for streaming content from abroad; the uptake of cloud-based applications for both business and individuals is also creating a heightened demand for affordable services (2021)
domestic: fixed-line is 22 per 100 and mobile-cellular is 112 per 100 persons (2021)
international: country code - 1-787, 939; landing points for the GTMO-PR, AMX-1, BRUSA, GCN, PCCS, SAm-1, Southern Caribbean Fiber, Americas-II, Antillas, ARCOS, SMPR-1, and Taino-Carib submarine cables providing connectivity to the mainland US, Caribbean, Central and South America; satellite earth station - 1 Intelsat (2019)

Broadcast media: more than 30 TV stations operating; cable TV subscription services are available; roughly 125 radio stations

Internet country code: .pr

Internet users: *total:* 2,564,100 (2021 est.)
percent of population: 77.7% (2021 est.)
comparison ranking: total 127

Broadband - fixed subscriptions: *total:* 671,284 (2020 est.)
subscriptions per 100 inhabitants: 24 (2020 est.)
comparison ranking: total 83

TRANSPORTATION

Airports: 20 (2024)
comparison ranking: 134

Heliports: 38 (2024)

Roadways: *total:* 26,862 km (2012) (includes 454 km of expressways)
comparison ranking: total 104

Ports: *total ports:* 14 (2024)
large: 0
medium: 3
small: 4
very small: 7
ports with oil terminals: 7
key ports: Arroyo, Ensenada Honda, Mayaguez, Playa de Guanica, Playa de Guayanilla, Playa de Ponce, San Juan

MILITARY AND SECURITY

Military and security forces: Puerto Rico Police Bureau (Negociado de la Policía de Puerto Rico); Puerto Rico (US) National Guard (Guardia Nacional de Puerto Rico or GNPR)
note: the GNPR was created by order of the US Congress in June 1919; the organization traces its lineage and history to Spanish militias created in 1511 and is one of the oldest organizations in the US National Guard system

Military - note: defense is the responsibility of the US

QATAR

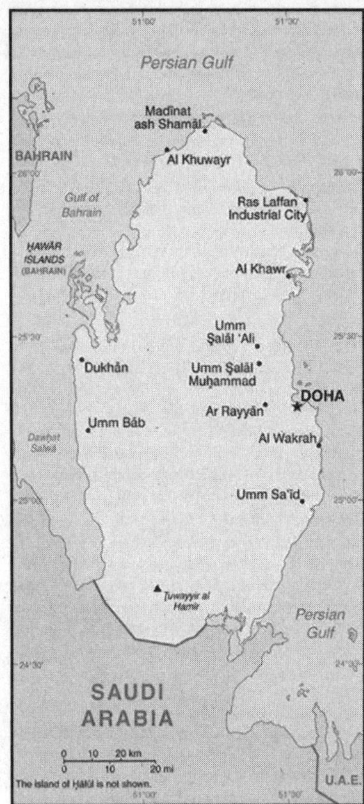

INTRODUCTION

Background: Ruled by the Al Thani family since the mid-1800s, Qatar within the last 60 years transformed itself from a poor British protectorate noted mainly for pearling into an independent state with significant hydrocarbon revenues. Former Amir HAMAD bin Khalifa Al Thani, who overthrew his father in a bloodless coup in 1995, ushered in wide-sweeping political and media reforms, unprecedented economic investment, and a growing Qatari regional leadership role, in part through the creation of the pan-Arab satellite news network Al-Jazeera and Qatar's mediation of some regional conflicts. In the 2000s, Qatar resolved its longstanding border disputes with both Bahrain and Saudi Arabia, and by 2007, Doha had attained the highest per capita income in the world. Qatar did not experience domestic unrest or violence like that seen in other Near Eastern and North African countries in 2011, due in part to its immense wealth and patronage network. In mid-2013, HAMAD peacefully abdicated, transferring power to his son, the current Amir TAMIM bin Hamad. TAMIM is popular with the Qatari public for his role in shepherding the country through an economic embargo from some other regional countries, for his efforts to improve the country's healthcare and education systems, and for his expansion of the country's infrastructure in anticipation of hosting international sporting events. Qatar became the first country in the Arab world to host the FIFA Men's World Cup in 2022.

Following the outbreak of regional unrest in 2011, Doha prided itself on its support for many popular revolutions, particularly in Libya and Syria. This stance was to the detriment of Qatar's relations with Bahrain, Egypt, Saudi Arabia, and the United Arab Emirates (UAE), which temporarily recalled their respective ambassadors from Doha in 2014. TAMIM later oversaw a warming of Qatar's relations with Bahrain, Egypt, Saudi Arabia, and the UAE in November 2014 following Kuwaiti mediation and signing of the Riyadh Agreement. This reconciliation, however, was short-lived. In 2017, Bahrain, Egypt, Saudi Arabia, and the UAE (the "Quartet") cut diplomatic and economic ties with Qatar in response to alleged violations of the agreement, among other complaints. They restored ties in 2021 after signing a declaration at the Gulf Cooperation Council Summit in Al Ula, Saudi Arabia. In 2022, the United States designated Qatar as a major non-NATO ally.

GEOGRAPHY

Location: Middle East, peninsula bordering the Persian Gulf and Saudi Arabia

Geographic coordinates: 25 30 N, 51 15 E

Map references: Middle East

Area: *total:* 11,586 sq km
land: 11,586 sq km
water: 0 sq km
comparison ranking: total 164

Area - comparative: almost twice the size of Delaware; slightly smaller than Connecticut

Land boundaries: *total:* 87 km
border countries (1): Saudi Arabia 87 km

Coastline: 563 km

Maritime claims: *territorial sea:* 12 nm
contiguous zone: 24 nm
exclusive economic zone: as determined by bilateral agreements or the median line

Climate: arid; mild, pleasant winters; very hot, humid summers

Terrain: mostly flat and barren desert

Elevation: *highest point:* Tuwayyir al Hamir 103 m
lowest point: Persian Gulf 0 m
mean elevation: 28 m

Natural resources: petroleum, fish, natural gas

Land use: *agricultural land:* 5.6% (2018 est.)
arable land: 1.1% (2018 est.)
permanent crops: 0.2% (2018 est.)
permanent pasture: 4.3% (2018 est.)
forest: 0% (2018 est.)
other: 94.4% (2018 est.)

Irrigated land: 130 sq km (2020)

Major aquifers: Arabian Aquifer System

Population distribution: most of the population is clustered in or around the capital of Doha on the eastern side of the peninsula

Natural hazards: haze, dust storms, sandstorms common

Geography - note: the peninsula occupies a strategic location in the central Persian Gulf near major petroleum deposits

PEOPLE AND SOCIETY

Population: *total:* 2,552,088
male: 1,961,135
female: 590,953 (2024 est.)
comparison rankings: female 161; male 131; total 143

Nationality: *noun:* Qatari(s)
adjective: Qatari

Ethnic groups: non-Qatari 88.4%, Qatari 11.6% (2015 est.)

Languages: Arabic (official), English commonly used as a second language
major-language sample(s):
كتاب حقائق العالم، المصدر الذي لا يمكن الاستغناء عنه للمعلومات الأساسية
(Arabic)

Religions: Muslim 65.2%, Christian 13.7%, Hindu 15.9%, Buddhist 3.8%, folk religion <0.1%, Jewish <0.1%, other <1%, unaffiliated <1% (2020 est.)

Age structure: *0-14 years:* 13.1% (male 168,844/female 165,905)
15-64 years: 85.4% (male 1,767,294/female 411,977)
65 years and over: 1.5% (2024 est.) (male 24,997/female 13,071)

Dependency ratios: *total dependency ratio:* 20.7
youth dependency ratio: 16.1
elderly dependency ratio: 2
potential support ratio: 50.1 (2021 est.)

Median age: *total:* 34.3 years (2024 est.)
male: 35.7 years
female: 28.1 years
comparison ranking: total 105

Population growth rate: 0.71% (2024 est.)
comparison ranking: 126

Birth rate: 9.2 births/1,000 population (2024 est.)
comparison ranking: 197

Death rate: 1.4 deaths/1,000 population (2024 est.)
comparison ranking: 229

Net migration rate: -0.7 migrant(s)/1,000 population (2024 est.)
comparison ranking: 135

Population distribution: most of the population is clustered in or around the capital of Doha on the eastern side of the peninsula

Urbanization: *urban population:* 99.4% of total population (2023)
rate of urbanization: 1.66% annual rate of change (2020-25 est.)

Major urban areas - population: 798,000 Ar-Rayyan, 658,000 DOHA (capital) (2023)

Sex ratio: *at birth:* 1.02 male(s)/female
0-14 years: 1.02 male(s)/female
15-64 years: 4.29 male(s)/female
65 years and over: 1.91 male(s)/female
total population: 3.32 male(s)/female (2024 est.)

Maternal mortality ratio: 8 deaths/100,000 live births (2020 est.)
comparison ranking: 148

Infant mortality rate: *total:* 6.4 deaths/1,000 live births (2024 est.)

male: 7 deaths/1,000 live births
female: 5.8 deaths/1,000 live births
comparison ranking: total 163

Life expectancy at birth: *total population:* 80.3 years (2024 est.)
male: 78.2 years
female: 82.4 years
comparison ranking: total population 53

Total fertility rate: 1.9 children born/woman (2024 est.)
comparison ranking: 120

Gross reproduction rate: 0.94 (2024 est.)

Contraceptive prevalence rate: 37.5% (2012)

Drinking water source: *improved:*
total: 99.6% of population
unimproved:
total: 0.4% of population (2020 est.)

Current health expenditure: 4.2% of GDP (2020)

Physician density: 2.49 physicians/1,000 population (2018)

Hospital bed density: 1.3 beds/1,000 population (2017)

Sanitation facility access: *improved:*
total: 100% of population
unimproved:
total: 0% of population (2020 est.)

Obesity - adult prevalence rate: 35.1% (2016)
comparison ranking: 15

Alcohol consumption per capita: *total:* 0.96 liters of pure alcohol (2019 est.)
beer: 0.29 liters of pure alcohol (2019 est.)
wine: 0.07 liters of pure alcohol (2019 est.)
spirits: 0.59 liters of pure alcohol (2019 est.)
other alcohols: 0.01 liters of pure alcohol (2019 est.)
comparison ranking: total 151

Tobacco use: *total:* 11.8% (2020 est.)
male: 21.7% (2020 est.)
female: 1.9% (2020 est.)
comparison ranking: total 124

Children under the age of 5 years underweight: NA

Currently married women (ages 15-49): 65.8% (2023 est.)

Education expenditures: 3.2% of GDP (2020 est.)
comparison ranking: 149

Literacy: *definition:* age 15 and over can read and write
total population: 93.5%
male: 92.4%
female: 94.7% (2017)

School life expectancy (primary to tertiary education): *total:* 13 years
male: 12 years
female: 15 years (2021)

ENVIRONMENT

Environment - current issues: air, land, and water pollution are significant environmental issues; limited natural freshwater resources are increasing dependence on large-scale desalination facilities; other issues include conservation of oil supplies and preservation of the natural wildlife heritage

Environment - international agreements: *party to:* Biodiversity, Climate Change, Climate Change-Kyoto Protocol, Comprehensive Nuclear Test Ban, Desertification, Endangered Species, Hazardous Wastes, Law of the Sea, Ozone Layer Protection, Ship Pollution
signed, but not ratified: none of the selected agreements

Climate: arid; mild, pleasant winters; very hot, humid summers

Urbanization: *urban population:* 99.4% of total population (2023)
rate of urbanization: 1.66% annual rate of change (2020-25 est.)

Revenue from forest resources: 0% of GDP (2018 est.)
comparison ranking: 173

Revenue from coal: 0% of GDP (2018 est.)
comparison ranking: 113

Air pollutants: *particulate matter emissions:* 59.04 micrograms per cubic meter (2019 est.)
carbon dioxide emissions: 103.26 megatons (2016 est.)
methane emissions: 8.34 megatons (2020 est.)

Waste and recycling: *municipal solid waste generated annually:* 1,000,990 tons (2012 est.)
municipal solid waste recycled annually: 30,030 tons (2014 est.)
percent of municipal solid waste recycled: 3% (2014 est.)

Major aquifers: Arabian Aquifer System

Total water withdrawal: *municipal:* 530 million cubic meters (2020 est.)
industrial: 400 million cubic meters (2020 est.)
agricultural: 320 million cubic meters (2020 est.)

Total renewable water resources: 60 million cubic meters (2020 est.)

GOVERNMENT

Country name: *conventional long form:* State of Qatar
conventional short form: Qatar
local long form: Dawlat Qatar
local short form: Qatar
etymology: the origin of the name is uncertain, but it dates back at least 2,000 years since a term "Catharrei" was used to describe the inhabitants of the peninsula by Pliny the Elder (1st century A.D.), and a "Catara" peninsula is depicted on a map by Ptolemy (2nd century A.D.)
note: closest approximation of the native pronunciation is gat-tar or cot-tar

Government type: absolute monarchy

Capital: *name:* Doha
geographic coordinates: 25 17 N, 51 32 E
time difference: UTC+3 (8 hours ahead of Washington, DC, during Standard Time)
etymology: derives from the Arabic term "dohat," meaning "roundness," and refers to the small rounded bays along the area's coastline

Administrative divisions: 8 municipalities (baladiyat, singular - baladiyah); Ad Dawhah, Al Khawr wa adh Dhakhirah, Al Wakrah, Ar Rayyan, Ash Shamal, Ash Shihaniyah, Az Za'ayin, Umm Salal

Independence: 3 September 1971 (from the UK)

National holiday: National Day, 18 December (1878), anniversary of Al Thani family accession to the throne; Independence Day, 3 September (1971)

Legal system: mixed legal system of civil law and Islamic (sharia) law (in family and personal matters)

Constitution: *history:* previous 1972 (provisional); latest drafted 2 July 2002, approved by referendum 29 April 2003, endorsed 8 June 2004, effective 9 June 2005
amendments: proposed by the Amir or by one third of Advisory Council members; passage requires two-thirds majority vote of Advisory Council members and approval and promulgation by the emir; articles pertaining to the rule of state and its inheritance, functions of the emir, and citizen rights and liberties cannot be amended

International law organization participation: has not submitted an ICJ jurisdiction declaration; non-party state to the ICCt

Citizenship: *citizenship by birth:* no
citizenship by descent only: the father must be a citizen of Qatar
dual citizenship recognized: no
residency requirement for naturalization: 20 years; 15 years if an Arab national

Suffrage: 18 years of age; universal

Executive branch: *chief of state:* Amir TAMIM bin Hamad Al Thani (since 25 June 2013)
head of government: Prime Minister and Foreign Minister MUHAMMAD bin Abd al-Rahman Al Thani (since 7 March 2023)
cabinet: Council of Ministers appointed by the amir
elections/appointments: the monarchy is hereditary; prime minister appointed by the amir

Legislative branch: *description:* unicameral Advisory Council or Majlis al-Shura (45 seats; 30 members directly elected by popular vote for 4-year re-electable terms; 15 members appointed by the monarch to serve until resignation or until relieved; note - legislative drafting authority rests with the Council of Ministers and is reviewed by the Advisory Council
elections: last held for 30 elected members on 2 October 2021 (next to be held in 2025); last members appointed - 14 October 2021 (next appointments - NA)
election results:
30 nonpartisan members elected; composition - men 30, women 0, percentage women 0%
15 appointed members; composition men 13, women 2, percentage women 13.3%

Judicial branch: *highest court(s):* Supreme Court or Court of Cassation (consists of the court president and several judges); Supreme Constitutional Court (consists of the chief justice and 6 members)
judge selection and term of office: Supreme Court judges nominated by the Supreme Judiciary Council, a 9-member independent body consisting of judiciary heads appointed by the amir; judges appointed for 3-year renewable terms; Supreme Constitutional Court members nominated by the Supreme Judiciary Council and appointed by the monarch; term of appointment NA
subordinate courts: Courts of Appeal; Administrative Court; Courts of First Instance; sharia courts; Courts of Justice; Qatar International Court and Dispute Resolution Center, established in 2009, provides dispute resolution services for institutions and bodies in Qatar, as well as internationally

Political parties: political parties are banned

International organization participation: ABEDA, AFESD, AMF, CAEU, CD, CICA (observer), EITI (implementing country), FAO, G-77, GCC, IAEA, IBRD, ICAO, ICC (national committees), ICRM, IDA, IDB, IFAD, IFC, IFRCS, IHO, ILO, IMF, IMO, IMSO, Interpol, IOC, IOM (observer), IPU, ISO, ITSO, ITU, LAS, MIGA, NAM, OAPEC, OAS (observer), OIC, OIF, OPCW, OPEC, PCA, UN, UNCTAD, UNESCO, UNHRC, UNIDO, UNIFIL, UNWTO, UPU, WCO, WHO, WIPO, WMO, WTO

Diplomatic representation in the US: *chief of mission:* Ambassador Meshal bin Hamad AL THANI (since 24 April 2017)
chancery: 2555 M Street NW, Washington, DC 20037
telephone: [1] (202) 274-1600
FAX: [1] (202) 237-0682
email address and website:
info.dc@mofa.gov.qa
https://washington.embassy.qa/en/home
consulate(s) general: Houston, Los Angeles, New York

Diplomatic representation from the US: *chief of mission:* Ambassador Timmy DAVIS (since 5 September 2022)
embassy: 22 February Street, Al Luqta District, P.O. Box 2399, Doha
mailing address: 6130 Doha Place, Washington DC 20521-6130
telephone: [974] 4496-6000
FAX: [974] 4488-4298
email address and website:
PasDoha@state.gov
https://qa.usembassy.gov/

Flag description: maroon with a broad white serrated band (nine white points) on the hoist side; maroon represents the blood shed in Qatari wars, white stands for peace; the nine-pointed serrated edge signifies Qatar as the ninth member of the "reconciled emirates" in the wake of the Qatari-British treaty of 1916
note: the other eight emirates are the seven that compose the UAE and Bahrain; according to some sources, the dominant color was formerly red, but this darkened to maroon upon exposure to the sun and the new shade was eventually adopted

National symbol(s): a maroon field surmounted by a white serrated band with nine white points; national colors: maroon, white

National anthem: *name:* "Al-Salam Al-Amiri" (The Amiri Salute)
lyrics/music: Sheikh MUBARAK bin Saif al-Thani/ Abdul Aziz Nasser OBAIDAN
note: adopted 1996; anthem first performed that year at a meeting of the Gulf Cooperative Council hosted by Qatar

National heritage: *total World Heritage Sites:* 1 (cultural)
selected World Heritage Site locales: Al Zubarah Archaeological Site

ECONOMY

Economic overview: high-income, oil-and-gas-based Middle Eastern economy; National Vision 2030 government strategy for economic development, diversification, favorable business conditions to grow investment and employment; infrastructure investments; Islamic finance leader; citizenship-based labor force growth

Real GDP (purchasing power parity): $304.973 billion (2022 est.)
$292.655 billion (2021 est.)
$287.97 billion (2020 est.)
note: data in 2021 dollars
comparison ranking: 61

Real GDP growth rate: 4.21% (2022 est.)
1.63% (2021 est.)
-3.56% (2020 est.)
note: annual GDP % growth based on constant local currency
comparison ranking: 72

Real GDP per capita: $113,200 (2022 est.)
$108,900 (2021 est.)
$104,300 (2020 est.)
note: data in 2021 dollars
comparison ranking: 5

GDP (official exchange rate): $235.77 billion (2022 est.)
note: data in current dollars at official exchange rate

Inflation rate (consumer prices): 3.03% (2023 est.)
5% (2022 est.)
2.3% (2021 est.)
note: annual % change based on consumer prices
comparison ranking: 60

Credit ratings: Fitch rating: AA- (2017)

Moody's rating: Aa3 (2017)

Standard & Poors rating: AA- (2017)
note: The year refers to the year in which the current credit rating was first obtained.

GDP - composition, by sector of origin: *agriculture:* 0.3% (2022 est.)
industry: 65.4% (2022 est.)
services: 38.5% (2022 est.)
note: figures may not total 100% due to non-allocated consumption not captured in sector-reported data
comparison rankings: services 199; industry 4; agriculture 205

GDP - composition, by end use: *household consumption:* 19.5% (2022 est.)
government consumption: 12.9% (2022 est.)
investment in fixed capital: 30.7% (2022 est.)
exports of goods and services: 68.6% (2022 est.)
imports of goods and services: -31.6% (2022 est.)
note: figures may not total 100% due to rounding or gaps in data collection

Agricultural products: tomatoes, dates, chicken, cucumbers/gherkins, camel milk, eggs, sheep milk, goat milk, pumpkins/squash, milk (2022)
note: top ten agricultural products based on tonnage

Industries: liquefied natural gas, crude oil production and refining, ammonia, fertilizer, petrochemicals, steel reinforcing bars, cement, commercial ship repair

Industrial production growth rate: 1.69% (2022 est.)
note: annual % change in industrial value added based on constant local currency
comparison ranking: 120

Labor force: 2.035 million (2023 est.)
note: number of people ages 15 or older who are employed or seeking work
comparison ranking: 127

Unemployment rate: 0.13% (2023 est.)
0.13% (2022 est.)
0.14% (2021 est.)
note: % of labor force seeking employment
comparison ranking: 1

Youth unemployment rate (ages 15-24): *total:* 0.6% (2023 est.)
male: 0.3% (2023 est.)
female: 1.5% (2023 est.)
note: % of labor force ages 15-24 seeking employment
comparison ranking: total 201

Average household expenditures: *on food:* 12.3% of household expenditures (2022 est.)
on alcohol and tobacco: 0.3% of household expenditures (2022 est.)

Remittances: 0.44% of GDP (2022 est.)
0.48% of GDP (2021 est.)
0.45% of GDP (2020 est.)
note: personal transfers and compensation between resident and non-resident individuals/households/ entities

Budget: *revenues:* $65.922 billion (2019 est.)
expenditures: $57.258 billion (2019 est.)

Public debt: 53.8% of GDP (2017 est.)
comparison ranking: 93

Taxes and other revenues: 26.4% (of GDP) (2017 est.)
comparison ranking: 35

Current account balance: $36.47 billion (2023 est.)
$63.118 billion (2022 est.)
$26.319 billion (2021 est.)
note: balance of payments - net trade and primary/ secondary income in current dollars
comparison ranking: 16

Exports: $128.726 billion (2023 est.)
$161.693 billion (2022 est.)
$105.549 billion (2021 est.)
note: balance of payments - exports of goods and services in current dollars
comparison ranking: 41

Exports - partners: China 18%, India 15%, Japan 10%, South Korea 9%, UK 6% (2022)
note: top five export partners based on percentage share of exports

Exports - commodities: natural gas, crude petroleum, refined petroleum, fertilizers, ethylene polymers (2022)
note: top five export commodities based on value in dollars

Imports: $72.174 billion (2023 est.)
$74.52 billion (2022 est.)
$61.204 billion (2021 est.)
note: balance of payments - imports of goods and services in current dollars
comparison ranking: 56

Imports - partners: UAE 13%, China 11%, US 10%, UK 8%, India 5% (2022)
note: top five import partners based on percentage share of imports

Imports - commodities: gas turbines, jewelry, cars, garments, aircraft (2022)
note: top five import commodities based on value in dollars

Reserves of foreign exchange and gold: $51.539 billion (2023 est.)
$47.389 billion (2022 est.)
$42.213 billion (2021 est.)
note: holdings of gold (year-end prices)/foreign exchange/special drawing rights in current dollars
comparison ranking: 48

Exchange rates: Qatari rials (QAR) per US dollar -

Exchange rates: 3.64 (2023 est.)
3.64 (2022 est.)
3.64 (2021 est.)
3.64 (2020 est.)
3.64 (2019 est.)

ENERGY

Electricity access: *electrification - total population:* 100% (2022 est.)

Electricity: *installed generating capacity:* 11.414 million kW (2022 est.)
consumption: 51.079 billion kWh (2022 est.)
transmission/distribution losses: 2.968 billion kWh (2022 est.)
comparison rankings: transmission/distribution losses 139; consumption 51; installed generating capacity 64

Electricity generation sources: *fossil fuels:* 99.7% of total installed capacity (2022 est.)
biomass and waste: 0.3% of total installed capacity (2022 est.)

Coal: *exports:* 3,000 metric tons (2022 est.)
imports: 4,000 metric tons (2022 est.)

Petroleum: *total petroleum production:* 1.851 million bbl/day (2023 est.)
refined petroleum consumption: 297,000 bbl/day (2022 est.)
crude oil estimated reserves: 25.244 billion barrels (2021 est.)

Natural gas: *production:* 169.595 billion cubic meters (2022 est.)
consumption: 41.515 billion cubic meters (2022 est.)
exports: 126.221 billion cubic meters (2022 est.)
proven reserves: 23.861 trillion cubic meters (2021 est.)

Carbon dioxide emissions: 122.122 million metric tonnes of CO2 (2022 est.)
from coal and metallurgical coke: 3,000 metric tonnes of CO2 (2022 est.)
from petroleum and other liquids: 35.699 million metric tonnes of CO2 (2022 est.)
from consumed natural gas: 86.42 million metric tonnes of CO2 (2022 est.)
comparison ranking: total emissions 36

Energy consumption per capita: 767.202 million Btu/person (2022 est.)
comparison ranking: 1

COMMUNICATIONS

Telephones - fixed lines: *total subscriptions:* 524,000 (2022 est.)
subscriptions per 100 inhabitants: 19 (2022 est.)
comparison ranking: total subscriptions 90

Telephones - mobile cellular: *total subscriptions:* 4.693 million (2022 est.)
subscriptions per 100 inhabitants: 174 (2022 est.)
comparison ranking: total subscriptions 128

Telecommunication systems: *general assessment:* Qatar had developed a mature telecom sector which has been able to absorb the additional data demands made on it during the pandemic; mobile services based on LTE are universally available to migrate to 5G; in combination with a strong fiber rollout, the country is aiming to provide gigabit services nationally; 5G services are largely based on 3.5GHz spectrum made available following an auction in early 2019 (2022)
domestic: fixed-line is 17 per 100 and mobile-cellular telephone subscribership is 144 telephones per 100 persons (2021)
international: country code - 974; landing points for the Qatar-UAE Submarine Cable System, AAE-1, FOG, GBICS/East North Africa MENA and the FALCON submarine cable network that provides links to Asia, Africa, the Middle East, Europe and Southeast Asia; tropospheric scatter to Bahrain; microwave radio relay to Saudi Arabia and the UAE; satellite earth stations - 2 Intelsat (1 Atlantic Ocean and 1 Indian Ocean) and 1 Arabsat; retains full ownership of two commercial satellites, Es'hailSat 1 and 2 (2019)

Broadcast media: TV and radio broadcast licensing and access to local media markets are state controlled; home of the satellite TV channel Al-Jazeera, which was originally owned and financed by the Qatari government but has evolved to independent corporate status; Al-Jazeera claims editorial independence in broadcasting; local radio transmissions include state, private, and international broadcasters on FM frequencies in Doha; in August 2013, Qatar's satellite company Es'hailSat launched its first communications satellite Es'hail 1 (manufactured in the US), which entered commercial service in December 2013 to provide improved television broadcasting capability and expand availability of voice and Internet; Es'hailSat launched its second commercial satellite in 2018 with aid of SpaceX (2019)

Internet country code: .qa

Internet users: *total:* 2.7 million (2021 est.)
percent of population: 100% (2021 est.)
comparison ranking: total 126

Broadband - fixed subscriptions: *total:* 296,126 (2020 est.)
subscriptions per 100 inhabitants: 10 (2020 est.)
comparison ranking: total 107

TRANSPORTATION

National air transport system: *number of registered air carriers:* 3 (2020)
inventory of registered aircraft operated by air carriers: 251
annual passenger traffic on registered air carriers: 29,178,923 (2018)
annual freight traffic on registered air carriers: 12,666,710,000 (2018) mt-km

Civil aircraft registration country code prefix: A7

Airports: 8 (2024)
comparison ranking: 166

Heliports: 12 (2024)

Pipelines: 288 km condensate, 221 km condensate/gas, 2,383 km gas, 90 km liquid petroleum gas, 745 km oil, 103 km refined products (2013)

Roadways: *total:* 7,039 km (2016)
comparison ranking: total 145

Merchant marine: *total:* 123 (2023)
by type: bulk carrier 5, container ship 4, general cargo 4, oil tanker 2, other 108
comparison ranking: total 80

Ports: *total ports:* 6 (2024)
large: 0
medium: 1
small: 2
very small: 3
ports with oil terminals: 5
key ports: Al Rayyan Terminal, Al Shaheen Terminal, Doha, Jazirat Halul, Ras Laffan, Umm Said

MILITARY AND SECURITY

Military and security forces: Qatar Armed Forces (QAF): Qatari Amiri Land Force (QALF, includes Emiri Guard), Qatari Amiri Navy (QAN, includes Coast Guard), Qatari Amiri Air Force (QAAF)

Ministry of Interior: General Directorate of Public Security, General Directorate of Coasts and Border Security, Internal Security Forces (includes Mobile Gendarmerie) (2024)
note: the national police and Ministry of Interior forces maintain internal security, including preventing terrorism, cyberattacks, and espionage

Military expenditures: 4% of GDP (2023 est.)
4% of GDP (2022 est.)
4% of GDP (2021 est.)
4% of GDP (2020 est.)
3.4% of GDP (2019 est.)
comparison ranking: 20

Military and security service personnel strengths: information varies; approximately 15,000 active-duty personnel (10,000 Land Force, including Emiri Guard; 3,000 Navy; 2,000 Air Force) (2023)

Military equipment inventories and acquisitions: the Qatari military's inventory includes a broad mix of older and modern weapons systems, mostly from the US and Europe; in the 2010s, Qatar embarked on a military expansion and modernization program with large air, ground, and naval equipment purchases; in recent years, major suppliers have included France, Germany, Italy, the UK, and the US; Qatar is one of the world's largest arms importers (2024)

Military service age and obligation: conscription for men aged 18-35 introduced in 2013; compulsory service times range from 4-12 months, depending on educational and professional circumstances; since 2018, women have been permitted to serve as volunteers in the armed forces, including as uniformed officers and pilots (2023)
note: the military incorporates about 2,000 conscripts annually and recruits foreign contract soldiers to overcome manpower limitations

Military - note: Qatar's military is a small and well-equipped force that is responsible for defense against external threats; following the downturn in ties with Bahrain, Egypt, Saudi Arabia, and the UAE in the mid-2010s, the Qatari Government embarked on an arms acquisition and modernization program to increase the military's capabilities and regional standing; the Air Force's inventory of combat aircraft, for example, grew from 12 older models in 2017 to more than 60 modern multirole fighter aircraft from Europe and the US by the 2020s; it is slated to further increase to about 100 such aircraft; other aircraft acquisitions have included US attack helicopters; the Land Force has re-equipped its armored, mechanized, and artillery units with modern tanks, armored vehicles, and self-propelled artillery, mostly with purchases from Germany and Turkey; meanwhile, the Navy over the same period has received several corvettes and offshore patrol vessels from Italy and Turkey
Qatar hosts the regional headquarters for the US Central Command (CENTCOM; established 1983) and several thousand US military forces at various military facilities, including the Al Udeid Air Base; it has Major Non-NATO Ally status with the US, a designation under US law that provides foreign partners with certain benefits in the areas of defense trade and security cooperation; Qatar also has close security ties with Turkey and hosts Turkish military forces at two bases established in 2014 and 2019 (2024)

TRANSNATIONAL ISSUES

Refugees and internally displaced persons: *stateless persons:* 1,200 (2022)

ROMANIA

INTRODUCTION

Background: The principalities of Wallachia and Moldavia – for centuries under the control of the Turkish Ottoman Empire – secured their autonomy through the Treaty of Paris in 1856. They were de facto linked in 1859 and formally united in 1862 under the new name of Romania. The country joined the Allied Powers in World War I and subsequently acquired new territories – most notably Transylvania – that more than doubled its size. In 1940, Romania allied with the Axis powers and participated in the 1941 German invasion of the USSR. Three years later, overrun by the Soviets, Romania signed an armistice. The post-war Soviet occupation led to the formation of a communist "people's republic" in 1947 and the abdication of the king. The decades-long rule of dictator Nicolae CEAUSESCU, who took power in 1965, and his Securitate police state became increasingly oppressive and draconian through the 1980s. CEAUSESCU was overthrown and executed in late 1989. Former communists dominated the government until 1996 when they were swept from power. Romania joined NATO in 2004, the EU in 2007, and the Schengen Area for air and sea travel in 2024.

GEOGRAPHY

Location: Southeastern Europe, bordering the Black Sea, between Bulgaria and Ukraine

Geographic coordinates: 46 00 N, 25 00 E

Map references: Europe

Area: *total:* 238,391 sq km
land: 229,891 sq km
water: 8,500 sq km
comparison ranking: total 83

Area - comparative: twice the size of Pennsylvania; slightly smaller than Oregon

Land boundaries: *total:* 2,844 km
border countries (5): Bulgaria 605 km; Hungary 424 km; Moldova 683 km; Serbia 531 km; Ukraine 601 km

Coastline: 225 km

Maritime claims: *territorial sea:* 12 nm
contiguous zone: 24 nm
exclusive economic zone: 200 nm
continental shelf: 200-m depth or to the depth of exploitation

Climate: temperate; cold, cloudy winters with frequent snow and fog; sunny summers with frequent showers and thunderstorms

Terrain: central Transylvanian Basin is separated from the Moldavian Plateau on the east by the Eastern Carpathian Mountains and separated from the Walachian Plain on the south by the Transylvanian Alps

Elevation: *highest point:* Moldoveanu 2,544 m
lowest point: Black Sea 0 m
mean elevation: 414 m

Natural resources: petroleum (reserves declining), timber, natural gas, coal, iron ore, salt, arable land, hydropower

Land use: *agricultural land:* 60.7% (2018 est.)
arable land: 39.1% (2018 est.)
permanent crops: 1.9% (2018 est.)
permanent pasture: 19.7% (2018 est.)
forest: 28.7% (2018 est.)
other: 10.6% (2018 est.)

Irrigated land: 4,730 sq km (2020)

Major rivers (by length in km): Dunărea (Danube) river mouth (shared with Germany [s], Austria, Slovakia, Hungary, Croatia, Serbia, Bulgaria, Moldova, and Ukraine) - 2,888 km
note – [s] after country name indicates river source; [m] after country name indicates river mouth

Major watersheds (area sq km): Atlantic Ocean drainage: *(Black Sea)* Danube (795,656 sq km)

Population distribution: urbanization is not particularly high, and a fairly even population distribution can be found throughout most of the country, with urban areas attracting larger and denser populations; Hungarians, the country's largest minority, have a particularly strong presence in eastern Transylvania

Natural hazards: earthquakes, most severe in south and southwest; geologic structure and climate promote landslides

Geography - note: controls the most easily traversable land route between the Balkans, Moldova, and Ukraine; the Carpathian Mountains dominate the center of the country, while the Danube River forms much of the southern boundary with Serbia and Bulgaria

PEOPLE AND SOCIETY

Population: *total:* 18,148,155
male: 8,747,795
female: 9,400,360 (2024 est.)
comparison rankings: female 68; male 71; total 70

Nationality: *noun:* Romanian(s)
adjective: Romanian

Ethnic groups: Romanian 89.3%, Hungarian 6%, Romani 3.4%, Ukrainian 0.3%, German 0.1%, other 0.9% (2021 est.)
note: data represent individuals who declared an ethnic group in the 2021 national census; 13% did not respond; Romani populations are usually underestimated in official statistics and may represent 5–11% of Romania's population

Languages: Romanian (official) 91.6%, Hungarian 6.3%, Romani 1.2%, other 0.7% (2021 est.)
major-language sample(s):
Cartea informativa a lumii, sursa indispensabila pentru informatii de baza. (Romanian)
note: data represent individuals who declared a maternal language in the 2021 national census; 13.1% did not respond

Religions: Romanian Orthodox 85.3%, Roman Catholic 4.5%, Reformed 3%, Pentecostal 2.5%, other 4.7% (2021 est.)
note: data represent individuals who declared a religion in the 2021 national census; 13.9% did not respond

Age structure: *0-14 years:* 15.4% (male 1,441,359/female 1,362,304)
15-64 years: 62% (male 5,618,366/female 5,632,718)
65 years and over: 22.6% (2024 est.) (male 1,688,070/female 2,405,338)

Dependency ratios: *total dependency ratio:* 53.7
youth dependency ratio: 24.6
elderly dependency ratio: 29.1
potential support ratio: 3.4 (2021 est.)

Median age: *total:* 45.5 years (2024 est.)
male: 44 years
female: 46.9 years
comparison ranking: total 16

Population growth rate: -0.94% (2024 est.)
comparison ranking: 229

Birth rate: 8.5 births/1,000 population (2024 est.)
comparison ranking: 206

Death rate: deaths/1,000 population (2024 est.)
comparison ranking: 5

Net migration rate: -3.3 migrant(s)/1,000 population (2024 est.)
comparison ranking: 187

Population distribution: urbanization is not particularly high, and a fairly even population distribution can be found throughout most of the country, with urban areas attracting larger and denser populations; Hungarians, the country's largest minority, have a particularly strong presence in eastern Transylvania

Urbanization: *urban population:* 54.7% of total population (2023)
rate of urbanization: -0.15% annual rate of change (2020-25 est.)

Major urban areas - population: 1.776 million BUCHAREST (capital) (2023)

Sex ratio: *at birth:* 1.06 male(s)/female
0-14 years: 1.06 male(s)/female
15-64 years: 1 male(s)/female
65 years and over: 0.7 male(s)/female
total population: 0.93 male(s)/female (2024 est.)

Mother's mean age at first birth: years (2020 est.)

Maternal mortality ratio: 10 deaths/100,000 live births (2020 est.)
comparison ranking: 144

Infant mortality rate: *total:* 5.5 deaths/1,000 live births (2024 est.)
male: 5.8 deaths/1,000 live births
female: 5.2 deaths/1,000 live births
comparison ranking: total 172

Life expectancy at birth: *total population:* 76.9 years (2024 est.)

male: 73.4 years
female: 80.5 years
comparison ranking: total population 99

Total fertility rate: 1.63 children born/woman (2024 est.)
comparison ranking: 176

Gross reproduction rate: 0.79 (2024 est.)

Drinking water source: *improved: urban:* 100% of population
rural: 100% of population
total: 100% of population

Current health expenditure: 6.3% of GDP (2020)

Physician density: 2.98 physicians/1,000 population (2017)

Hospital bed density: 6.9 beds/1,000 population (2017)

Sanitation facility access: *improved: urban:* 96.9% of population
rural: 76% of population
total: 87.3% of population
unimproved: urban: 3.1% of population
rural: 24% of population
total: 12.7% of population (2020 est.)

Obesity - adult prevalence rate: 22.5% (2016)
comparison ranking: 76

Alcohol consumption per capita: *total:* 10.96 liters of pure alcohol (2019 est.)
beer: 5.33 liters of pure alcohol (2019 est.)
wine: 3.38 liters of pure alcohol (2019 est.)
spirits: 2.25 liters of pure alcohol (2019 est.)
other alcohols: 0 liters of pure alcohol (2019 est.)
comparison ranking: total 14

Tobacco use: *total:* 28% (2020 est.)
male: 35.9% (2020 est.)
female: 20% (2020 est.)
comparison ranking: total 37

Currently married women (ages 15-49): 54.8% (2023)

Education expenditures: 3.7% of GDP (2020 est.)
comparison ranking: 130

Literacy: *definition:* age 15 and over can read and write
total population: 98.9%
male: 99.1%
female: 98.7% (2021)

School life expectancy (primary to tertiary education): *total:* 14 years
male: 14 years
female: 15 years (2020)

ENVIRONMENT

Environment - current issues: soil erosion, degradation, and desertification; water pollution; air pollution in south from industrial effluents; contamination of Danube delta wetlands

Environment - international agreements: *party to:* Air Pollution, Air Pollution-Heavy Metals, Air Pollution-Multi-effect Protocol, Air Pollution-Persistent Organic Pollutants, Antarctic-Environmental Protection, Antarctic Treaty, Biodiversity, Climate Change, Climate Change-Kyoto Protocol, Climate Change-Paris Agreement, Comprehensive Nuclear Test Ban, Desertification, Endangered Species, Environmental Modification, Hazardous Wastes, Law of the Sea, Nuclear Test Ban, Ozone Layer Protection, Ship Pollution, Tropical Timber 2006, Wetlands, Whaling
signed, but not ratified: none of the selected agreements

Climate: temperate; cold, cloudy winters with frequent snow and fog; sunny summers with frequent showers and thunderstorms

Urbanization: *urban population:* 54.7% of total population (2023)
rate of urbanization: -0.15% annual rate of change (2020-25 est.)

Revenue from forest resources: 0.16% of GDP (2018 est.)
comparison ranking: 99

Revenue from coal: 0.03% of GDP (2018 est.)
comparison ranking: 39

Air pollutants: *particulate matter emissions:* 13.3 micrograms per cubic meter (2019 est.)
carbon dioxide emissions: 69.26 megatons (2016 est.)
methane emissions: 27.62 megatons (2020 est.)

Waste and recycling: *municipal solid waste generated annually:* 4.895 million tons (2015 est.)
municipal solid waste recycled annually: 277,547 tons (2015 est.)
percent of municipal solid waste recycled: 5.7% (2015 est.)

Major rivers (by length in km): Dunărea (Danube) river mouth (shared with Germany [s], Austria, Slovakia, Hungary, Croatia, Serbia, Bulgaria, Moldova, and Ukraine) - 2,888 km
note – [s] after country name indicates river source; [m] after country name indicates river mouth

Major watersheds (area sq km): Atlantic Ocean drainage: *(Black Sea)* Danube (795,656 sq km)

Total water withdrawal: *municipal:* 1.09 billion cubic meters (2020 est.)
industrial: 3.9 billion cubic meters (2020 est.)
agricultural: 1.43 billion cubic meters (2020 est.)

Total renewable water resources: 212 billion cubic meters (2020 est.)

Geoparks: *total global geoparks and regional networks:* 2
global geoparks and regional networks: Buzău; Hateg (2023)

GOVERNMENT

Country name: *conventional long form:* none
conventional short form: Romania
local long form: none
local short form: Romania
former: Kingdom of Romania, Romanian People's Republic, Socialist Republic of Romania
etymology: the name derives from the Latin "Romanus" meaning "citizen of Rome" and was used to stress the common ancient heritage of Romania's three main regions - Moldavia, Transylvania, and Wallachia - during their gradual unification between the mid-19th century and early 20th century

Government type: semi-presidential republic

Capital: *name:* Bucharest
geographic coordinates: 44 26 N, 26 06 E
time difference: UTC+2 (7 hours ahead of Washington, DC, during Standard Time)
daylight saving time: +1hr, begins last Sunday in March; ends last Sunday in October
etymology: related to the Romanian word "bucura" that is believed to be of Dacian origin and whose meaning is "to be glad (happy)"; Bucharest's meaning is thus akin to "city of joy"

Administrative divisions: 41 counties (judete, singular - judet) and 1 municipality* (municipiu); Alba, Arad, Arges, Bacau, Bihor, Bistrita-Nasaud, Botosani, Braila, Brasov, Bucuresti (Bucharest)*, Buzau, Calarasi, Caras-Severin, Cluj, Constanta, Covasna, Dambovita, Dolj, Galati, Gorj, Giurgiu, Harghita, Hunedoara, Ialomita, Iasi, Ilfov, Maramures, Mehedinti, Mures, Neamt, Olt, Prahova, Salaj, Satu Mare, Sibiu, Suceava, Teleorman, Timis, Tulcea, Vaslui, Valcea, Vrancea

Independence: 9 May 1877 (independence proclaimed from the Ottoman Empire; 13 July 1878 (independence recognized by the Treaty of Berlin); 26 March 1881 (kingdom proclaimed); 30 December 1947 (republic proclaimed)

National holiday: Unification Day (unification of Romania and Transylvania), 1 December (1918)

Legal system: civil law system

Constitution: *history:* several previous; latest adopted 21 November 1991, approved by referendum and effective 8 December 1991
amendments: initiated by the president of Romania through a proposal by the government, by at least one fourth of deputies or senators in Parliament, or by petition of eligible voters representing at least half of Romania's counties; passage requires at least two-thirds majority vote by both chambers or – if mediation is required - by three-fourths majority vote in a joint session, followed by approval in a referendum; articles, including those on national sovereignty, form of government, political pluralism, and fundamental rights and freedoms cannot be amended; amended 2003

International law organization participation: accepts compulsory ICJ jurisdiction with reservations; accepts ICCt jurisdiction

Citizenship: *citizenship by birth:* no
citizenship by descent only: at least one parent must be a citizen of Romania
dual citizenship recognized: yes
residency requirement for naturalization: 5 years

Suffrage: 18 years of age; universal

Executive branch: *chief of state:* President Klaus Werner IOHANNIS (since 21 December 2014)
head of government: Prime Minister Marcel CIOLACU (since 15 June 2023)
cabinet: Council of Ministers appointed by the prime minister
elections/appointments: president directly elected by absolute majority popular vote in 2 rounds if needed for a 5-year term (eligible for a second term); election last held on 10 November 2019 with a runoff on 24 November 2019 (next to be held in November 2024); prime minister appointed by the president with consent of Parliament
election results:
2019: Klaus IOHANNIS reelected president in second round; percent of vote - Klaus IOHANNIS (PNL) 66.1%, Viorica DANCILA (PSD) 33.9%
2014: Klaus IOHANNIS elected president in second round; percent of vote - Klaus IOHANNIS (PNL) 54.4%, Victor PONTA (PSD) 45.6%

Legislative branch: *description:* bicameral Parliament or Parlament consists of:
Senate or Senat (136 seats; members directly elected in single- and multi-seat constituencies - including 2 seats for diaspora - by party-list, proportional representation vote; members serve 4-year terms)
Chamber of Deputies or Camera Deputatilor (330 seats; members directly elected in single- and

multi-seat constituencies - including 4 seats for diaspora - by party-list, proportional representation vote; members serve 4-year terms)
elections: Senate - last held on 6 December 2020 (next to be held in 2024)
Chamber of Deputies - last held on 6 December 2020 (next to be held in 2024)
election results: Senate - percent of vote by party - PSD 29.3%, PNL 25.6%, 2020 USR-PLUS Alliance 15.9%, AUR 9.2%, UDMR 5.9%, other 14.1%; seats by party - PSD 47, PNL 41, 2020 USR-PLUS Alliance 25, AUR 14, UDMR 9; composition - men 111, women 24, percentage women 17.8%
Chamber of Deputies - percent of vote by party - PSD 28.9%, PNL 25.2%, 2020 USR-PLUS Alliance 15.4%, AUR 9.1%, UDMR 5.7%, other 15.7%; seats by party - PSD 110, PNL 93, 2020 USR-PLUS Alliance 55, AUR 33, UDMR 21, other 18; composition - men 265, women 63, percentage women 19.2%; total Parliament percentage women 18.8%

Judicial branch: *highest court(s):* High Court of Cassation and Justice (consists of 111 judges organized into civil, penal, commercial, contentious administrative and fiscal business, and joint sections); Supreme Constitutional Court (consists of 9 members)
judge selection and term of office: High Court of Cassation and Justice judges appointed by the president upon nomination by the Superior Council of Magistracy, a 19-member body of judges, prosecutors, and law specialists; judges appointed for 6-year renewable terms; Constitutional Court members - 6 elected by Parliament and 3 appointed by the president; members serve 9-year, nonrenewable terms
subordinate courts: Courts of Appeal; regional tribunals; first instance courts; military and arbitration courts

Political parties: Alliance for the Fatherland or APP
Alliance for the Unity of Romanians or AUR
Christian-Democratic National Peasants' Party or PNT-CD
Civic Hungarian Party
Democratic Union of Hungarians in Romania or UDMR
Ecologist Party of Romania or PER
Force of the Right or FD
Greater Romania Party or PRM
Green Party
National Liberal Party or PNL
Popular Movement Party or PMP
PRO Romania or PRO
Romanian Nationhood Party or PNR
Save Romania Union Party or USR
Social Democratic Party or PSD
Social Liberal Humanist Party or PUSL (formerly Humanist Power Party (Social-Liberal) or PPU-SL)
S.O.S. Romania
The Right Alternative or AD
United Romania Party or PRU
We are Renewing the European Project in Romania or REPER

International organization participation: Australia Group, BIS, BSEC, CBSS (observer), CD, CE, CEI, EAPC, EBRD, ECB, EIB, ESA, EU, FAO, G-9, IAEA, IBRD, ICAO, ICC (national committees), ICCt, ICRM, IDA, IFAD, IFC, IFRCS, IHO, ILO, IMF, IMO, IMSO, Interpol, IOC, IOM, IPU, ISO, ITSO, ITU, ITUC (NGOs), LAIA (observer), MIGA, MONUSCO, NATO, NSG, OAS (observer), OIF, OPCW, OSCE, PCA, SELEC, UN, UNCTAD, UNESCO, UNHCR, UNIDO, Union Latina, UNMIL, UNMISS, UNOCI, UNWTO, UPU, Wassenaar Arrangement, WCO, WFTU (NGOs), WHO, WIPO, WMO, WTO, ZC

Diplomatic representation in the US: *chief of mission:* Ambassador Dan-Andrei MURARU (since 15 September 2021)
chancery: 1607 23rd Street NW, Washington, DC 20008
telephone: [1] (202) 332-4829
FAX: [1] (202) 232-4748
email address and website:
washington@mae.ro
https://washington.mae.ro/en
consulate(s) general: Chicago, Los Angeles, Miami, New York

Diplomatic representation from the US: *chief of mission:* Ambassador Kathleen KAVALEC (since 14 February 2023)
embassy: 4-6, Dr. Liviu Librescu Blvd., District 1, Bucharest, 015118
mailing address: 5260 Bucharest Place, Washington, DC 20521-5260
telephone: [40] (21) 200-3300
FAX: [40] (21) 200-3442
email address and website:
ACSBucharest@state.gov
https://ro.usembassy.gov/

Flag description: three equal vertical bands of cobalt blue (hoist side), chrome yellow, and vermilion red; modeled after the flag of France, the colors are those of the principalities of Walachia (red and yellow) and Moldavia (red and blue), which united in 1862 to form Romania; the national coat of arms that used to be centered in the yellow band has been removed
note: now similar to the flag of Chad, whose blue band is darker; also resembles the flags of Andorra and Moldova

National symbol(s): golden eagle; national colors: blue, yellow, red

National anthem: *name:* "Desteapta-te romane!" (Wake up, Romanian!)
lyrics/music: Andrei MURESIANU/Anton PANN
note: adopted 1990; the anthem was written during the 1848 Revolution

National heritage: *total World Heritage Sites:* 9 (7 cultural, 2 natural)
selected World Heritage Site locales: Danube Delta (n); Churches of Moldavia (c); Monastery of Horezu (c); Villages with Fortified Churches in Transylvania (c); Dacian Fortresses of the Orastie Mountains (c); Historic Center of Sighişoara (c); Wooden Churches of Maramureş (c); Ancient and Primeval Beech Forests of the Carpathians (n); Roşia Montană Mining Landscape (c)

ECONOMY

Economic overview: high-income EU member economy; joined Schengen area as of March 2024; euro membership delayed over convergence criteria; persistent inflation but recovery driven by consumption and EU-funded investments; skilled labor shortage; regional economic disparities; fiscal reforms to address rising deficits

Real GDP (purchasing power parity): $772.107 billion (2023 est.)
$755.867 billion (2022 est.)
$726.048 billion (2021 est.)
note: data in 2021 dollars
comparison ranking: 34

Real GDP growth rate: 2.15% (2023 est.)
4.11% (2022 est.)
5.71% (2021 est.)
note: annual GDP % growth based on constant local currency
comparison ranking: 135

Real GDP per capita: $40,500 (2023 est.)
$39,700 (2022 est.)
$38,000 (2021 est.)
note: data in 2021 dollars
comparison ranking: 61

GDP (official exchange rate): $351.003 billion (2023 est.)
note: data in current dollars at official exchange rate

Inflation rate (consumer prices): 10.4% (2023 est.)
13.8% (2022 est.)
5.05% (2021 est.)
note: annual % change based on consumer prices
comparison ranking: 179

Credit ratings: Fitch rating: BBB- (2011)

Moody's rating: Baa3 (2006)

Standard & Poors rating: BBB- (2014)
note: The year refers to the year in which the current credit rating was first obtained.

GDP - composition, by sector of origin: *agriculture:* 3.9% (2023 est.)
industry: 27.6% (2023 est.)
services: 59.8% (2023 est.)
note: figures may not total 100% due to non-allocated consumption not captured in sector-reported data
comparison rankings: services 88; industry 80; agriculture 129

GDP - composition, by end use: *household consumption:* 62.2% (2023 est.)
government consumption: 16.9% (2023 est.)
investment in fixed capital: 26.9% (2023 est.)
investment in inventories: -1.2% (2023 est.)
exports of goods and services: 39.1% (2023 est.)
imports of goods and services: -43.9% (2023 est.)
note: figures may not total 100% due to rounding or gaps in data collection

Agricultural products: wheat, maize, milk, sunflower seeds, barley, potatoes, rapeseed, grapes, plums, apples (2022)
note: top ten agricultural products based on tonnage

Industries: electric machinery and equipment, auto assembly, textiles and footwear, light machinery, metallurgy, chemicals, food processing, petroleum refining, mining, timber, construction materials

Industrial production growth rate: 1.15% (2023 est.)
note: annual % change in industrial value added based on constant local currency
comparison ranking: 136

Labor force: 8.282 million (2023 est.)
note: number of people ages 15 or older who are employed or seeking work
comparison ranking: 65

Unemployment rate: 5.6% (2023 est.)
5.61% (2022 est.)
5.59% (2021 est.)
note: % of labor force seeking employment
comparison ranking: 110

Youth unemployment rate (ages 15-24): *total:* 21.3% (2023 est.)
male: 21.2% (2023 est.)
female: 21.4% (2023 est.)
note: % of labor force ages 15-24 seeking employment
comparison ranking: total 58

Population below poverty line: 21.2% (2021 est.)
note: % of population with income below national poverty line

Gini Index coefficient - distribution of family income: 33.9 (2021 est.)
note: index (0-100) of income distribution; higher values represent greater inequality
comparison ranking: 89

Average household expenditures: *on food:* 25.1% of household expenditures (2022 est.)
on alcohol and tobacco: 5.5% of household expenditures (2022 est.)

Household income or consumption by percentage share: *lowest 10%:* 1.9% (2021 est.)
highest 10%: 24% (2021 est.)
note: % share of income accruing to lowest and highest 10% of population

Remittances: 2.76% of GDP (2023 est.)
2.94% of GDP (2022 est.)
3.19% of GDP (2021 est.)
note: personal transfers and compensation between resident and non-resident individuals/households/entities

Budget: *revenues:* $93.681 billion (2022 est.)
expenditures: $110.163 billion (2022 est.)
note: central government revenues (excluding grants) and expenses converted to US dollars at average official exchange rate for year indicated

Public debt: 50.45% of GDP (2022 est.)
note: central government debt as a % of GDP
comparison ranking: 105

Taxes and other revenues: 16.02% (of GDP) (2022 est.)
note: central government tax revenue as a % of GDP
comparison ranking: 127

Current account balance: -$24.487 billion (2023 est.)
-$27.326 billion (2022 est.)
-$20.627 billion (2021 est.)
note: balance of payments - net trade and primary/secondary income in current dollars
comparison ranking: 202

Exports: $137.337 billion (2023 est.)
$129.286 billion (2022 est.)
$115.879 billion (2021 est.)
note: balance of payments - exports of goods and services in current dollars
comparison ranking: 39

Exports - partners: Germany 19%, Italy 10%, Hungary 7%, France 6%, Bulgaria 4% (2022)
note: top five export partners based on percentage share of exports

Exports - commodities: vehicle parts/accessories, cars, insulated wire, refined petroleum, wheat (2022)
note: top five export commodities based on value in dollars

Imports: $154.106 billion (2023 est.)
$149.209 billion (2022 est.)
$132.056 billion (2021 est.)
note: balance of payments - imports of goods and services in current dollars
comparison ranking: 37

Imports - partners: Germany 17%, Italy 8%, Hungary 6%, Turkey 6%, Poland 6% (2022)
note: top five import partners based on percentage share of imports

Imports - commodities: crude petroleum, vehicle parts/accessories, refined petroleum, packaged medicine, cars (2022)
note: top five import commodities based on value in dollars

Reserves of foreign exchange and gold: $73 billion (2023 est.)
$55.81 billion (2022 est.)
$51.886 billion (2021 est.)
note: holdings of gold (year-end prices)/foreign exchange/special drawing rights in current dollars
comparison ranking: 46

Exchange rates: lei (RON) per US dollar -

Exchange rates: 4.574 (2023 est.)
4.688 (2022 est.)
4.16 (2021 est.)
4.244 (2020 est.)
4.238 (2019 est.)

ENERGY

Electricity access: *electrification - total population:* 100% (2022 est.)

Electricity: *installed generating capacity:* 19.126 million kW (2022 est.)
consumption: 49.805 billion kWh (2022 est.)
exports: 7.429 billion kWh (2022 est.)
imports: 8.653 billion kWh (2022 est.)
transmission/distribution losses: 6.204 billion kWh (2022 est.)
comparison rankings: transmission/distribution losses 168; imports 28; exports 29; consumption 54; installed generating capacity 51

Electricity generation sources: *fossil fuels:* 39.1% of total installed capacity (2022 est.)
nuclear: 18.6% of total installed capacity (2022 est.)
solar: 3.2% of total installed capacity (2022 est.)
wind: 12.7% of total installed capacity (2022 est.)
hydroelectricity: 25.3% of total installed capacity (2022 est.)
biomass and waste: 0.9% of total installed capacity (2022 est.)

Nuclear energy: Number of operational nuclear reactors: 2 (2023)

Net capacity of operational nuclear reactors: 1.3GW (2023 est.)

Percent of total electricity production: 18.9% (2023 est.)

Coal: *production:* 18.16 million metric tons (2022 est.)
consumption: 19.404 million metric tons (2022 est.)
exports: 242,000 metric tons (2022 est.)
imports: 1.338 million metric tons (2022 est.)
proven reserves: 291 million metric tons (2022 est.)

Petroleum: *total petroleum production:* 67,000 bbl/day (2023 est.)
refined petroleum consumption: 221,000 bbl/day (2022 est.)
crude oil estimated reserves: 600 million barrels (2021 est.)

Natural gas: *production:* 9.501 billion cubic meters (2022 est.)
consumption: 10.055 billion cubic meters (2022 est.)
exports: 832.421 million cubic meters (2022 est.)
imports: 2.977 billion cubic meters (2022 est.)
proven reserves: 105.48 billion cubic meters (2021 est.)

Carbon dioxide emissions: 62.594 million metric tonnes of CO2 (2022 est.)
from coal and metallurgical coke: 15.319 million metric tonnes of CO2 (2022 est.)
from petroleum and other liquids: 28.604 million metric tonnes of CO2 (2022 est.)
from consumed natural gas: 18.67 million metric tonnes of CO2 (2022 est.)
comparison ranking: total emissions 52

Energy consumption per capita: 60.67 million Btu/person (2022 est.)
comparison ranking: 80

COMMUNICATIONS

Telephones - fixed lines: *total subscriptions:* 2.222 million (2022 est.)
subscriptions per 100 inhabitants: 11 (2022 est.)
comparison ranking: total subscriptions 50

Telephones - mobile cellular: *total subscriptions:* 23.219 million (2022 est.)
subscriptions per 100 inhabitants: 118 (2022 est.)
comparison ranking: total subscriptions 55

Telecommunication systems: *general assessment:* Romania's telecom market has undergone several significant changes in recent years; the mobile market is served by network operators that have extensive LTE networks in place, while services based on 5G have been offered under their existing spectrum concessions since 2019; the delayed multi-spectrum auction, expected to be completed later in 2021, will enable the operators to expand 5G network capacity and enable consumers to make far greater use of the technology's potential; in line with legislation passed in July 2021 the MNOs will have to replace equipment provided by vendors deemed to be a security risk (2021)
domestic: fixed-line teledensity is 13 telephones per 100 persons; mobile-cellular teledensity is119 telephones per 100 persons (2021)
international: country code - 40; landing point for the Diamond Link Global submarine cable linking Romania with Georgia; satellite earth stations - 10; digital, international, direct-dial exchanges operate in Bucharest (2019)

Broadcast media: a mixture of public and private TV stations; there are 7 public TV stations (2 national, 5 regional) using terrestrial broadcasting and 187 private TV stations (out of which 171 offer local coverage) using terrestrial broadcasting, plus 11 public TV stations using satellite broadcasting and 86 private TV stations using satellite broadcasting; state-owned public radio broadcaster operates 4 national networks and regional and local stations, having in total 20 public radio stations by terrestrial broadcasting plus 4 public radio stations by satellite broadcasting; there are 502 operational private radio stations using terrestrial broadcasting and 26 private radio stations using satellite broadcasting

Internet country code: .ro

Internet users: *total:* 15.96 million (2021 est.)
percent of population: 84% (2021 est.)
comparison ranking: total 48

Broadband - fixed subscriptions: *total:* 5,684,782 (2020 est.)
subscriptions per 100 inhabitants: 30 (2020 est.)
comparison ranking: total 32

TRANSPORTATION

National air transport system: *number of registered air carriers:* 8 (2020)
inventory of registered aircraft operated by air carriers: 60

annual passenger traffic on registered air carriers: 4,908,235 (2018)
annual freight traffic on registered air carriers: 2.71 million (2018) mt-km

Civil aircraft registration country code prefix: YR

Airports: 82 (2024)
comparison ranking: 65

Heliports: 18 (2024)

Pipelines: 3,726 km gas, 2,451 km oil (2013)

Railways: *total:* 10,628 km (2020) 4,030 km electrified
comparison ranking: total 23

Roadways: *total:* 85,387 km (2022)
comparison ranking: total 59

Waterways: 1,731 km (2010) (includes 1,075 km on the Danube River, 524 km on secondary branches, and 132 km on canals)
comparison ranking: 47

Merchant marine: *total:* 127 (2023)
by type: general cargo 9, oil tanker 7, other 111
comparison ranking: total 79

Ports: *total ports:* 11 (2024)
large: 0
medium: 2
small: 1
very small: 8
ports with oil terminals: 4
key ports: Basarabi, Braila, Cernavoda, Constanta, Danube-Black Sea Canal, Galati, Mangalia, Medgidia, Midia, Sulina, Tulcea

MILITARY AND SECURITY

Military and security forces: Romanian Armed Forces (Forțele Armate Române or Armata Română): Land Forces, Naval Forces, Air Force

Ministry of Internal Affairs: General Inspectorate of the Romanian Police, the Romanian Gendarmerie (Jandarmeria Română), the Romanian Border Police, the General Directorate for Internal Protection, and the Directorate General for Anticorruption (2024)

Military expenditures: 2.3% of GDP (2024 est.)
1.6% of GDP (2023)
1.7% of GDP (2022)
1.9% of GDP (2021)
2% of GDP (2020)
comparison ranking: 51

Military and security service personnel strengths: approximately 68,000 active-duty military personnel (53,000 Land Forces; 7,000 Naval Forces; 8,000 Air Force) (2024)

Military equipment inventories and acquisitions: the military's inventory includes a considerable amount of Soviet-era and older domestically produced weapons systems, although in recent years Romania has launched an effort to acquire more modern and NATO-standard equipment from European countries and the US, including aircraft and armored vehicles (2024)

Military service age and obligation: 18 years of age for voluntary service for men and women; all military inductees contract for an initial 5-year term of service, with subsequent successive 3-year terms until age 36; conscription ended in 2006 (2023)

Military deployments: up to 120 Poland (NATO); Romania also has small numbers of military personnel deployed on other international missions under the EU, NATO, and UN (2024)

Military - note: the Romanian Armed Forces are responsible for territorial defense, fulfilling the country's commitments to European security, and contributing to multinational peacekeeping operations; the military has a variety of concerns, including cyber attacks and terrorism, but its primary focus is Russian aggression against neighboring Ukraine and Russia's activities in the Black Sea and Romania's other eastern neighbor, Moldova
Romania joined NATO in 2004, and the Alliance forms a key pillar of the country's defense policy; it hosts a NATO multinational divisional headquarters (Multinational Division Southeast) and a French-led ground force battlegroup as part of NATO's Enhanced Forward Presence initiative in the southeastern part of the Alliance, which came about in response to Russia's 2022 invasion of Ukraine; NATO allies have also sent detachments of fighters to augment the Romanian Air Force since 2014 because of aggressive Russian activity in the Black Sea region; the Romanian military trains regularly with NATO and its member states and has participated in NATO- and EU-led multinational missions in Bosnia and Herzegovina, Kosovo, and Poland (2024)

SPACE

Space agency/agencies: Romanian Space Agency (Agentia Spatiala Romania, ROSA; established 1991) (2024)

Space program overview: space program is integrated into the European Space Agency (ESA) and dates back to the 1960s; program is involved in the development and production of a wide range of capabilities and technologies, including satellites, satellite/space launch vehicles (SLVs), remote sensing, human space flight, navigation, telecommunications, and other space-related applications; in addition to the ESA/EU and their member states (particularly Bulgaria, France, Germany, Hungary, Italy), it cooperates with a variety of other space agencies and commercial space entities, including those of Azerbaijan, China, Japan, Russia, and the US; also participates in international programs; has an active space industry sector with over 50 entities involved in space-related activities (2024)
note: further details about the key activities, programs, and milestones of the country's space program, as well as government spending estimates on the space sector, appear in the Space Programs reference guide

TERRORISM

Terrorist group(s): Islamic State of Iraq and ash-Sham (ISIS)
note: details about the history, aims, leadership, organization, areas of operation, tactics, targets, weapons, size, and sources of support of the group(s) appear(s) in the Terrorism reference guide

TRANSNATIONAL ISSUES

Refugees and internally displaced persons: *refugees (country of origin):* 77,250 (Ukraine) (as of 14 April 2024)
stateless persons: 297 (2022)
note: 16,085 estimated refugee and migrant arrivals (January 2015-March 2024)

Illicit drugs: a source country for cannabis

RUSSIA

INTRODUCTION

Background: Founded in the 12th century, the Principality of Muscovy emerged from over 200 years of Mongol domination (13th-15th centuries) and gradually conquered and absorbed surrounding principalities. In the early 17th century, a new ROMANOV dynasty continued this policy of expansion across Siberia to the Pacific. Under PETER I (1682-1725), hegemony was extended to the Baltic Sea and the country was renamed the Russian Empire. During the 19th century, more territorial acquisitions were made in Europe and Asia. Defeat in the Russo-Japanese War of 1904-05 contributed to the Revolution of 1905, which resulted in the formation of a parliament and other reforms. Devastating defeats and food shortages in World War I led to widespread rioting in the major cities of the Russian Empire and to the overthrow of the ROMANOV Dynasty in 1917. The communists under Vladimir LENIN seized power soon after and formed the Union of Soviet Socialist Republics (USSR).

The brutal rule of Iosif STALIN (1928-53) strengthened communist control and Russian dominance of the Soviet Union at a cost of tens of millions of lives. After defeating Germany in World War II as part of an alliance with the US (1939-1945), the USSR expanded its territory and influence in Eastern Europe and emerged as a global power. The USSR was the principal US adversary during the Cold War (1947-1991). The Soviet economy and society stagnated in the decades following Stalin's rule, until General Secretary Mikhail GORBACHEV (1985-91) introduced glasnost (openness) and perestroika (restructuring) in an attempt to modernize communism. His initiatives inadvertently released political and economic forces that by December 1991 led to the dissolution of the USSR into Russia and 14 other independent states. In response to the ensuing turmoil during President Boris YELTSIN's term (1991-99), Russia shifted toward a centralized authoritarian state under President Vladimir PUTIN (2000-2008, 2012-present) in which the regime seeks to legitimize its rule through managed elections, populist appeals, a foreign policy focused on enhancing the country's geopolitical influence, and commodity-based economic growth.

In 2014, Russia purported to annex Ukraine's Crimean Peninsula and occupied large portions of two eastern Ukrainian oblasts. In sporadic fighting over the next eight years, more than 14,000 civilians were killed or wounded as a result of the Russian invasion in eastern Ukraine. On 24 February 2022, Russia escalated its conflict with Ukraine by invading the country on several fronts in what has become the largest conventional military attack on a sovereign state in Europe since World War II. The invasion received near-universal international condemnation, and many countries imposed sanctions on Russia and supplied humanitarian and military aid to Ukraine. In September 2022, Russia unilaterally declared its annexation of four Ukrainian oblasts – Donetsk, Kherson, Luhansk, and Zaporizhzhia – even though none were fully under Russian control. The annexations remain unrecognized by the international community.

GEOGRAPHY

Location: North Asia bordering the Arctic Ocean, extending from Eastern Europe (the portion west of the Urals) to the North Pacific Ocean

Geographic coordinates: 60 00 N, 100 00 E

Map references: Asia

Area: *total:* 17,098,242 sq km
land: 16,377,742 sq km
water: 720,500 sq km
comparison ranking: total 1

Area - comparative: approximately 1.8 times the size of the US

Land boundaries: *total:* 22,407 km
border countries (14): Azerbaijan 338 km; Belarus 1,312 km; China (southeast) 4,133 km and China (south) 46 km; Estonia 324 km; Finland 1,309 km; Georgia 894 km; Kazakhstan 7,644 km; North Korea 18 km; Latvia 332 km; Lithuania (Kaliningrad Oblast) 261 km; Mongolia 3,452 km; Norway 191 km; Poland (Kaliningrad Oblast) 209 km; Ukraine 1,944 km

Coastline: 37,653 km

Maritime claims: *territorial sea:* 12 nm
contiguous zone: 24 nm
exclusive economic zone: 200 nm
continental shelf: 200-m depth or to the depth of exploitation

Climate: ranges from steppes in the south through humid continental in much of European Russia; subarctic in Siberia to tundra climate in the polar north; winters vary from cool along Black Sea coast to frigid in Siberia; summers vary from warm in the steppes to cool along Arctic coast

Terrain: broad plain with low hills west of Urals; vast coniferous forest and tundra in Siberia; uplands and mountains along southern border regions

Elevation: *highest point:* Gora El'brus (highest point in Europe) 5,642 m
lowest point: Caspian Sea -28 m
mean elevation: 600 m

Natural resources: wide natural-resource base including major deposits of oil, natural gas, coal, and many strategic minerals, bauxite, reserves of rare earth elements, timber
note: formidable obstacles of climate, terrain, and distance hinder exploitation of natural resources

Land use: *agricultural land:* 13.1% (2018 est.)
arable land: 7.3% (2018 est.)
permanent crops: 0.1% (2018 est.)
permanent pasture: 5.7% (2018 est.)
forest: 49.4% (2018 est.)
other: 37.5% (2018 est.)

Irrigated land: 43,000 sq km (2012)

Major lakes (area sq km): *fresh water lake(s):* Lake Baikal - 31,500 sq km; Lake Ladoga - 18,130 sq km; Lake Onega - 9,720 sq km; Lake Khanka (shared with China) - 5,010 sq km; Lake Peipus - 4,300 sq km (shared with Estonia); Ozero Vygozero - 1,250 sq km; Ozero Beloye - 1,120 sq km
salt water lake(s): Caspian Sea (shared with Iran, Azerbaijan, Turkmenistan, and Kazakhstan) - 374,000 sq km; Ozero Malyye Chany - 2,500 sq km; Curonian Lagoon (shared with Lithuania) - 1,620 sq km
note - the Caspian Sea is the World's largest lake

Major rivers (by length in km): Yenisey-Angara - 5,539 km; Ob-Irtysh - 5,410 km; Amur river mouth (shared with China [s] and Mongolia) - 4,444 km; Lena - 4,400 km; Volga - 3,645 km; Kolyma - 2,513 km; Ural river source (shared with Kazakhstan [m]) - 2,428 km; Dnepr (Dnieper) river source (shared with Belarus and Ukraine [m]) - 2,287 km; Don - 1,870 km; Pechora - 1,809 km
note – [s] after country name indicates river source; [m] after country name indicates river mouth

Major watersheds (area sq km): Arctic Ocean drainage: Kolyma (679,934 sq km), Lena (2,306,743 sq km), Ob (2,972,493 sq km), Pechora (289,532 sq km), Yenisei (2,554,388 sq km)

Atlantic Ocean drainage: *(Black Sea)* Don (458,694 sq km), Dnieper (533,966 sq km)

Pacific Ocean drainage: Amur (1,929,955 sq km)

Internal (endorheic basin) drainage: *(Caspian Sea basin)* Volga (1,410,951 sq km)

Major aquifers: Angara-Lena Basin, Pechora Basin, North Caucasus Basin, East European Aquifer System, West Siberian Basin, Tunguss Basin, Yakut Basin

Population distribution: population is heavily concentrated in the westernmost fifth of the country extending from the Baltic Sea, south to the Caspian Sea, and eastward parallel to the Kazakh border; elsewhere, sizeable pockets are isolated and generally found in the south

Natural hazards: permafrost over much of Siberia is a major impediment to development; volcanic activity in the Kuril Islands; volcanoes and earthquakes on the Kamchatka Peninsula; spring floods and summer/autumn forest fires throughout Siberia and parts of European Russia
volcanism: significant volcanic activity on the Kamchatka Peninsula and Kuril Islands; the peninsula alone is home to some 29 historically active volcanoes, with dozens more in the Kuril Islands; Kliuchevskoi (4,835 m), which erupted in 2007 and 2010, is Kamchatka's most active volcano; Avachinsky and Koryaksky volcanoes, which pose a threat to the city of Petropavlovsk-Kamchatsky, have been deemed Decade Volcanoes by the International Association of Volcanology and Chemistry of the Earth's Interior, worthy of study due to their explosive history and close proximity to human populations; other notable historically active volcanoes include Bezymianny, Chikurachki, Ebeko, Gorely, Grozny, Karymsky, Ketoi, Kronotsky, Ksudach, Medvezhia, Mutnovsky, Sarychev Peak, Shiveluch, Tiatia, Tolbachik, and Zheltovsky; see note 2 under "Geography - note"

Geography - note: *note 1:* largest country in the world in terms of area but unfavorably located in relation to major sea lanes of the world; despite its size, much of the country lacks proper soils and climates (either too cold or too dry) for agriculture
note 2: Russia's far east, particularly the Kamchatka Peninsula, lies along the Ring of Fire, a belt of active volcanoes and earthquake epicenters bordering the Pacific Ocean; up to 90% of the world's earthquakes and some 75% of the world's volcanoes occur within the Ring of Fire
note 3: Mount El'brus is Europe's tallest peak; Lake Baikal, the deepest lake in the world, is estimated to hold one fifth of the world's fresh surface water
note 4: Kaliningrad oblast is an exclave annexed from Germany following World War II (it was formerly part of East Prussia); its capital city of Kaliningrad – formerly Koenigsberg – is the only Baltic port in Russia that remains ice free in the winter

PEOPLE AND SOCIETY

Population: *total:* 140,820,810
male: 65,496,805
female: 75,324,005 (2024 est.)
comparison rankings: female 9; male 9; total 9

Nationality: *noun:* Russian(s)
adjective: Russian

Ethnic groups: Russian 77.7%, Tatar 3.7%, Ukrainian 1.4%, Bashkir 1.1%, Chuvash 1%, Chechen 1%, other 10.2%, unspecified 3.9% (2010 est.)
note: nearly 200 national and/or ethnic groups are represented in Russia's 2010 census

Languages: Russian (official) 85.7%, Tatar 3.2%, Chechen 1%, other 10.1% (2010 est.)
major-language sample(s):
Книга фактов о мире – незаменимый источник базовой информации (Russian)
note: data represent native language spoken

Religions: Russian Orthodox 15-20%, Muslim 10-15%, other Christian 2% (2006 est.)
note: estimates are of practicing worshipers; Russia has large populations of non-practicing believers and non-believers, a legacy of over seven decades of official atheism under Soviet rule; Russia officially recognizes Orthodox Christianity, Islam, Judaism, and Buddhism as the country's traditional religions

Age structure: *0-14 years:* 16.5% (male 11,956,284/female 11,313,829)
15-64 years: 65.7% (male 45,007,073/female 47,518,221)
65 years and over: 17.8% (2024 est.) (male 8,533,448/female 16,491,955)

Dependency ratios: *total dependency ratio:* 50
youth dependency ratio: 26.6
elderly dependency ratio: 23.4
potential support ratio: 4.3 (2021 est.)

Median age: *total:* 41.9 years (2024 est.)
male: 39.4 years
female: 44.5 years
comparison ranking: total 48

Population growth rate: -0.49% (2024 est.)
comparison ranking: 221

Birth rate: 8.4 births/1,000 population (2024 est.)
comparison ranking: 209

Death rate: 14 deaths/1,000 population (2024 est.)
comparison ranking: 9

Net migration rate: 0.8 migrant(s)/1,000 population (2024 est.)
comparison ranking: 68

Population distribution: population is heavily concentrated in the westernmost fifth of the country extending from the Baltic Sea, south to the Caspian Sea, and eastward parallel to the Kazakh border; elsewhere, sizeable pockets are isolated and generally found in the south

Urbanization: *urban population:* 75.3% of total population (2023)
rate of urbanization: 0.11% annual rate of change (2020-25 est.)

Major urban areas - population: 12.680 million MOSCOW (capital), 5.561 million Saint Petersburg, 1.695 million Novosibirsk, 1.528 million Yekaterinburg, 1.292 million Kazan, 1.251 million Nizhniy Novgorod (2023)

Sex ratio: *at birth:* 1.06 male(s)/female
0-14 years: 1.06 male(s)/female
15-64 years: 0.95 male(s)/female
65 years and over: 0.52 male(s)/female
total population: 0.87 male(s)/female (2024 est.)

Mother's mean age at first birth: years (2013 est.)

Maternal mortality ratio: 14 deaths/100,000 live births (2020 est.)
comparison ranking: 138

Infant mortality rate: *total:* 6.5 deaths/1,000 live births (2024 est.)
male: 7.2 deaths/1,000 live births
female: 5.8 deaths/1,000 live births
comparison ranking: total 162

Life expectancy at birth: *total population:* 72.3 years (2024 est.)
male: 67.4 years
female: 77.4 years
comparison ranking: total population 164

Total fertility rate: 1.52 children born/woman (2024 est.)
comparison ranking: 199

Gross reproduction rate: 0.74 (2024 est.)

Contraceptive prevalence rate: 68% (2011)
note: percent of women aged 15-44

Drinking water source: *improved: urban:* 99.1% of population
rural: 93.1% of population
total: 97.6% of population
unimproved: urban: 0.9% of population
rural: 6.9% of population
total: 2.4% of population (2020 est.)

Current health expenditure: 7.6% of GDP (2020)

Physician density: 3.82 physicians/1,000 population (2020)

Hospital bed density: 7.1 beds/1,000 population (2018)

Sanitation facility access: *improved: urban:* 95.2% of population
rural: 72.3% of population
total: 89.4% of population
unimproved: urban: 4.8% of population
rural: 27.7% of population
total: 10.6% of population (2020 est.)

Obesity - adult prevalence rate: % (2016)
comparison ranking: 70

Alcohol consumption per capita: *total:* 7.29 liters of pure alcohol (2019 est.)
beer: 3.04 liters of pure alcohol (2019 est.)
wine: 0.97 liters of pure alcohol (2019 est.)
spirits: 3.16 liters of pure alcohol (2019 est.)
other alcohols: 0.12 liters of pure alcohol (2019 est.)
comparison ranking: total 56

Tobacco use: *total:* 26.8% (2020 est.)
male: 40.8% (2020 est.)
female: 12.8% (2020 est.)
comparison ranking: total 41

Currently married women (ages 15-49): % (2023 est.)

Child marriage: *women married by age 15:* 0.3%
women married by age 18: 6.2% (2017 est.)

Education expenditures: 3.7% of GDP (2020 est.)
comparison ranking: 132

Literacy: *definition:* age 15 and over can read and write
total population: 99.7%
male: 99.7%
female: 99.7% (2018)

School life expectancy (primary to tertiary education): *total:* 16 years
male: 16 years
female: 16 years (2019)

ENVIRONMENT

Environment - current issues: air pollution from heavy industry, emissions of coal-fired electric plants, and transportation in major cities; industrial, municipal, and agricultural pollution of inland waterways and seacoasts; deforestation; soil erosion; soil contamination from improper application of agricultural chemicals; nuclear waste disposal; scattered areas of sometimes intense radioactive contamination; groundwater contamination from toxic waste; urban solid waste management; abandoned stocks of obsolete pesticides

Environment - international agreements: *party to:* Air Pollution, Air Pollution-Nitrogen Oxides, Air Pollution-Sulphur 85, Antarctic-Environmental Protection, Antarctic-Marine Living Resources, Antarctic Seals, Antarctic Treaty, Biodiversity, Climate Change, Climate Change-Kyoto Protocol, Climate Change-Paris Agreement, Comprehensive Nuclear Test Ban, Desertification, Endangered Species, Environmental Modification, Hazardous Wastes, Law of the Sea, Marine Dumping-London Convention, Nuclear Test Ban, Ozone Layer Protection, Ship Pollution, Wetlands, Whaling
signed, but not ratified: Air Pollution-Sulfur 94

Climate: ranges from steppes in the south through humid continental in much of European Russia; subarctic in Siberia to tundra climate in the polar north; winters vary from cool along Black Sea coast to frigid in Siberia; summers vary from warm in the steppes to cool along Arctic coast

Urbanization: *urban population:* 75.3% of total population (2023)
rate of urbanization: 0.11% annual rate of change (2020-25 est.)

Revenue from forest resources: 0.29% of GDP (2018 est.)
comparison ranking: 81

Revenue from coal: 0.53% of GDP (2018 est.)
comparison ranking: 11

Air pollutants: *particulate matter emissions:* 8.88 micrograms per cubic meter (2019 est.)
carbon dioxide emissions: 1,732.03 megatons (2016 est.)
methane emissions: 851.52 megatons (2020 est.)

Waste and recycling: *municipal solid waste generated annually:* 60 million tons (2012 est.)
municipal solid waste recycled annually: 2.7 million tons (2012 est.)
percent of municipal solid waste recycled: 4.5% (2012 est.)

Major lakes (area sq km): *fresh water lake(s):* Lake Baikal - 31,500 sq km; Lake Ladoga - 18,130 sq km; Lake Onega - 9,720 sq km; Lake Khanka (shared with China) - 5,010 sq km; Lake Peipus - 4,300 sq km (shared with Estonia); Ozero Vygozero - 1,250 sq km; Ozero Beloye - 1,120 sq km
salt water lake(s): Caspian Sea (shared with Iran, Azerbaijan, Turkmenistan, and Kazakhstan) - 374,000 sq km; Ozero Malyye Chany - 2,500 sq km; Curonian Lagoon (shared with Lithuania) - 1,620 sq km
note - the Caspian Sea is the World's largest lake

Major rivers (by length in km): Yenisey-Angara - 5,539 km; Ob-Irtysh - 5,410 km; Amur river mouth (shared with China [s] and Mongolia) - 4,444 km; Lena - 4,400 km; Volga - 3,645 km; Kolyma - 2,513 km; Ural river source (shared with Kazakhstan [m]) - 2,428 km; Dnepr (Dnieper) river source (shared with Belarus and Ukraine [m]) - 2,287 km; Don - 1,870 km; Pechora - 1,809 km
note – [s] after country name indicates river source; [m] after country name indicates river mouth

Major watersheds (area sq km): Arctic Ocean drainage: Kolyma (679,934 sq km), Lena (2,306,743 sq km), Ob (2,972,493 sq km), Pechora (289,532 sq km), Yenisei (2,554,388 sq km)

Atlantic Ocean drainage: *(Black Sea)* Don (458,694 sq km), Dnieper (533,966 sq km)

Pacific Ocean drainage: Amur (1,929,955 sq km)

Internal (endorheic basin) drainage: *(Caspian Sea basin)* Volga (1,410,951 sq km)

Major aquifers: Angara-Lena Basin, Pechora Basin, North Caucasus Basin, East European Aquifer System, West Siberian Basin, Tunguss Basin, Yakut Basin

Total water withdrawal: *municipal:* 17.15 billion cubic meters (2020 est.)
industrial: 29.03 billion cubic meters (2020 est.)
agricultural: 18.64 billion cubic meters (2020 est.)

Total renewable water resources: 4.53 trillion cubic meters (2020 est.)

Geoparks: *total global geoparks and regional networks:* 1
global geoparks and regional networks: Yangan-Tau (2023)

GOVERNMENT

Country name: *conventional long form:* Russian Federation
conventional short form: Russia
local long form: Rossiyskaya Federatsiya
local short form: Rossiya
former: Russian Empire, Russian Soviet Federative Socialist Republic

etymology: Russian lands were generally referred to as Muscovy until PETER I officially declared the Russian Empire in 1721; the new name sought to invoke the patrimony of the medieval eastern European Rus state centered on Kyiv in present-day Ukraine; the Rus were a Varangian (eastern Viking) elite that imposed their rule and eventually their name on their Slavic subjects

Government type: semi-presidential federation

Capital: *name:* Moscow
geographic coordinates: 55 45 N, 37 36 E
time difference: UTC+3 (8 hours ahead of Washington, DC, during Standard Time)
daylight saving time: does not observe daylight savings time (DST)
time zone note: Russia has 11 time zones, the largest number of contiguous time zones of any country in the world; in 2014, two time zones were added and DST dropped
etymology: named after the Moskva River; the origin of the river's name is obscure but may derive from the appellation "Mustajoki" given to the river by the Finno-Ugric people who originally inhabited the area and whose meaning may have been "dark" or "turbid"

Administrative divisions: 46 provinces (oblasti, singular - oblast), 21 republics (respubliki, singular - respublika), 4 autonomous okrugs (avtonomnyye okrugi, singular - avtonomnyy okrug), 9 krays (kraya, singular - kray), 2 federal cities (goroda, singular - gorod), and 1 autonomous oblast (avtonomnaya oblast')
oblasts: Amur (Blagoveshchensk), Arkhangelsk, Astrakhan, Belgorod, Bryansk, Chelyabinsk, Irkutsk, Ivanovo, Kaliningrad, Kaluga, Kemerovo, Kirov, Kostroma, Kurgan, Kursk, Leningrad (Gatchina), Lipetsk, Magadan, Moscow, Murmansk, Nizhniy Novgorod, Novgorod, Novosibirsk, Omsk, Orenburg, Orel, Penza, Pskov, Rostov, Ryazan, Sakhalin (Yuzhno-Sakhalinsk), Samara, Saratov, Smolensk, Sverdlovsk (Yekaterinburg), Tambov, Tomsk, Tula, Tver, Tyumen, Ulyanovsk, Vladimir, Volgograd, Vologda, Voronezh, Yaroslavl
republics: Adygeya (Maykop), Altay (Gorno-Altaysk), Bashkortostan (Ufa), Buryatiya (Ulan-Ude), Chechnya (Groznyy), Chuvashiya (Cheboksary), Dagestan (Makhachkala), Ingushetiya (Magas), Kabardino-Balkariya (Nal'chik), Kalmykiya (Elista), Karachayevo- Cherkesiya (Cherkessk), Kareliya (Petrozavodsk), Khakasiya (Abakan), Komi (Syktyvkar), Mariy-El (Yoshkar-Ola), Mordoviya (Saransk), North Ossetia (Vladikavkaz), Sakha [Yakutiya] (Yakutsk), Tatarstan (Kazan), Tyva (Kyzyl), Udmurtiya (Izhevsk)
autonomous okrugs: Chukotka (Anadyr'), Khanty-Mansi-Yugra (Khanty-Mansiysk), Nenets (Nar'yan-Mar), Yamalo-Nenets (Salekhard)
krays: Altay (Barnaul), Kamchatka (Petropavlovsk-Kamchatskiy), Khabarovsk, Krasnodar, Krasnoyarsk, Perm, Primorskiy [Maritime] (Vladivostok), Stavropol, Zabaykalsk [Transbaikal] (Chita)
federal cities: Moscow [Moskva], Saint Petersburg [Sankt-Peterburg]
autonomous oblast: Yevreyskaya [Jewish] (Birobidzhan)
note 1: administrative divisions have the same names as their administrative centers (exceptions have the administrative center name following in parentheses)
note 2: the United States does not recognize Russia's annexation of Ukraine's Autonomous Republic of Crimea and the municipality of Sevastopol, nor their redesignation as the "Republic of Crimea" and the "Federal City of Sevastopol"; it similarly does not recognize the annexation of the Ukrainian oblasts Donetsk, Luhansk, Zaporizhzhia, and Kherson

Independence: *25 December 1991 (from the Soviet Union; Russian SFSR renamed Russian Federation); notable earlier dates:* 1157 (Principality of Vladimir-Suzdal created); 16 January 1547 (Tsardom of Muscovy established); 22 October 1721 (Russian Empire proclaimed); 30 December 1922 (Soviet Union established)

National holiday: Russia Day, 12 June (1990); note - commemorates the adoption of the Declaration of State Sovereignty of the Russian Soviet Federative Socialist Republic (RSFSR)

Legal system: civil law system; judicial review of legislative acts

Constitution: *history:* several previous (during Russian Empire and Soviet era); latest drafted 12 July 1993, adopted by referendum 12 December 1993, effective 25 December 1993
amendments: proposed by the president of the Russian Federation, by either house of the Federal Assembly, by the government of the Russian Federation, or by legislative (representative) bodies of the Federation's constituent entities; proposals to amend the government's constitutional system, human and civil rights and freedoms, and procedures for amending or drafting a new constitution require formation of a Constitutional Assembly; passage of such amendments requires two-thirds majority vote of its total membership; passage in a referendum requires participation of an absolute majority of eligible voters and an absolute majority of valid votes; approval of proposed amendments to the government structure, authorities, and procedures requires approval by the legislative bodies of at least two thirds of the Russian Federation's constituent entities; amended several times, last in 2020 (major revisions)

International law organization participation: has not submitted an ICJ jurisdiction declaration; non-party state to the ICCt

Citizenship: *citizenship by birth:* no
citizenship by descent only: at least one parent must be a citizen of Russia
dual citizenship recognized: yes
residency requirement for naturalization: 3-5 years

Suffrage: 18 years of age; universal

Executive branch: *chief of state:* President Vladimir Vladimirovich PUTIN (since 7 May 2012)
head of government: Premier Mikhail Vladimirovich MISHUSTIN (since 16 January 2020)
cabinet: the government is composed of the premier, his deputies, and ministers, all appointed by the president; the premier is also confirmed by the Duma
elections/appointments: president directly elected by absolute majority popular vote in 2 rounds if needed for a 6-year term (2020 constitutional amendments allow a second consecutive term); election last held on 15 to 17 March 2024 (next to be held 2030)
election results:
2024: Vladimir PUTIN reelected president; percent of vote - Vladimir PUTIN (independent) 88.5%, Nikolay KHARITONOV (Communist Party) 4.4%, Vladislav DAVANKOV (New People party) 3.9%, Leonid SLUTSKY (Liberal Democrats) 3.2%
2018: Vladimir PUTIN reelected president; percent of vote - Vladimir PUTIN (independent) 77.5%, Pavel GRUDININ (CPRF) 11.9%, Vladimir ZHIRINOVSKIY (LDPR) 5.7%, other 4.9%; Mikhail MISHUSTIN (independent) approved as premier by Duma; vote - 383 to 0
2012: Vladimir PUTIN elected president; percent of vote - Vladimir PUTIN (United Russia) 63.6%, Gennadiy ZYUGANOV (CPRF) 17.2%, Mikhail PROKHOROV (CP) 8%, Vladimir ZHIRINOVSKIY (LDPR) 6.2%, Sergey MIRONOV (A Just Russia) 3.9%, other 1.1%; Dmitriy MEDVEDEV (United Russia) approved as premier by Duma; vote - 299 to 144
note: there is also a Presidential Administration that provides staff and policy support to the president, drafts presidential decrees, and coordinates policy among government agencies; a Security Council also reports directly to the president

Legislative branch: *description:* bicameral Federal Assembly or Federalnoye Sobraniye consists of:
Federation Council or Sovet Federatsii (170 seats statutory, 169 as of April 2023; 2 members in each of the 83 federal administrative units (see note below) - oblasts, krays, republics, autonomous okrugs and oblasts, and federal cities of Moscow and Saint Petersburg - appointed by the top executive and legislative officials; members serve 4-year terms)
State Duma or Gosudarstvennaya Duma (450 seats (see note below); as of February 2014, the electoral system reverted to a mixed electoral system for the 2016 election, in which one-half of the members are directly elected by simple majority vote and one-half directly elected by proportional representation vote; members serve 5-year terms)
elections: State Duma - last held 17 - 19 September 2021 (next to be held in September 2026)
election results: Federation Council - composition - men 137, women 32, percentage women 18.9%
State Duma - percent vote by party - United Russia 50.9%, CPRF 19.3%, LDPR 7.7%, A Just Russia 7.6%, New People 5.3% other minor parties and independents 9.2%; seats by party - United Russia 324, CPRF 57, LDPR 21, A Just Russia 27, New People 13; Rodina 1, CP 1, Party of Growth 1, independent 5; composition - men 376, women 74, percentage women 16.4%; total Federal Assembly percentage women 17.1%
note 1: the State Duma now includes 3 representatives from the "Republic of Crimea," while the Federation Council includes 2 each from the "Republic of Crimea" and the "Federal City of Sevastopol," both regions that Russia occupied and attempted to annex from Ukraine and that the US does not recognize as part of Russia

Judicial branch: *highest court(s):* Supreme Court of the Russian Federation (consists of 170 members organized into the Judicial Panel for Civil Affairs, the Judicial Panel for Criminal Affairs, and the Military Panel); Constitutional Court (consists of 11 members, including the chairperson and deputy); note - in February 2014, Russia's Higher Court of Arbitration was abolished and its former authorities transferred to the Supreme Court, which in addition is the country's highest judicial authority for appeals, civil, criminal, administrative, and military cases, and the disciplinary judicial board, which has jurisdiction over economic disputes
judge selection and term of office: all members of Russia's 3 highest courts nominated by the president and appointed by the Federation Council (the upper house of the legislature); members of all 3 courts appointed for life
subordinate courts: regional (kray) and provincial (oblast) courts; Moscow and St. Petersburg city

courts; autonomous province and district courts; note - the 21 Russian Republics have court systems specified by their own constitutions

Political parties: A Just Russia or SRZP
Civic Platform or GP
Communist Party of the Russian Federation or KPRF
Liberal Democratic Party of Russia or LDPR
New People NL
Party of Growth PR
Rodina
United Russia ER

International organization participation: APEC, Arctic Council, ARF, ASEAN (dialogue partner), BIS, BRICS, BSEC, CBSS, CD, CE, CERN (observer), CICA, CIS, CSTO, EAEC, EAEU, EAPC, EAS, EBRD, FAO, FATF, G-20, GCTU, IAEA, IBRD, ICAO, ICC (national committees), ICRM, IDA, IFAD, IFC, IFRCS, IHO, ILO, IMF, IMO, IMSO, Interpol, IOC, IOM (observer), IPU, ISO, ITSO, ITU, ITUC (NGOs), LAIA (observer), MIGA, MINURSO, MONUSCO, NEA, NSG, OAS (observer), OIC (observer), OPCW, OSCE, Paris Club, PCA, PFP, SCO, UN, UNCTAD, UNESCO, UNHCR, UNIDO, UNISFA, UNMIL, UNMISS, UNOCI, UN Security Council (permanent), UNTSO, UNWTO, UPU, Wassenaar Arrangement, WCO, WFTU (NGOs), WHO, WIPO, WMO, WTO, ZC

Diplomatic representation in the US: *chief of mission:* Ambassador Anatoly Ivanovich ANTONOV (since 8 September 2017)
chancery: 2650 Wisconsin Avenue NW, Washington, DC 20007
telephone: [1] (202) 298-5700
FAX: [1] (202) 298-5735
email address and website:
rusembusa@mid.ru
https://washington.mid.ru/en/
consulate(s) general: Houston, New York

Diplomatic representation from the US: *chief of mission:* Ambassador Lynne M. TRACY (30 January 2023)
embassy: 55,75566° N, 37,58028° E
mailing address: 5430 Moscow Place, Washington DC 20521-5430
telephone: [7] (495) 728-5000
FAX: [7] (495) 728-5090
email address and website:
MoscowACS@state.gov
https://ru.usembassy.gov/
consulate(s) general: Vladivostok (suspended status), Yekaterinburg (suspended status)

Flag description: three equal horizontal bands of white (top), blue, and red
note: the Russian flag was created when Russia built its first naval vessels, and was used mostly as a naval ensign until the nineteenth century; the colors may have been based on those of the Dutch flag; despite many popular interpretations, there is no official meaning assigned to the colors of the Russian flag; the flag inspired several other Slavic countries to adopt horizontal tricolors of the same colors but in different arrangements, and so red, blue, and white became the Pan-Slav colors

National symbol(s): bear, double-headed eagle; national colors: white, blue, red

National anthem: *name:* "Gimn Rossiyskoy Federatsii" (National Anthem of the Russian Federation)
lyrics/music: Sergey Vladimirovich MIKHALKOV/ Aleksandr Vasilyevich ALEKSANDROV
note: in 2000, Russia adopted the tune of the anthem of the former Soviet Union (composed in 1939); the lyrics, also adopted in 2000, were written by the same person who authored the Soviet lyrics in 1943

National heritage: *total World Heritage Sites:* 31 (20 cultural, 11 natural)
selected World Heritage Site locales: Kremlin and Red Square, Moscow (c); Historic Saint Petersburg (c); Novodevichy Convent (c); Historic Monuments of Novgorod (c); Trinity Sergius Lavra in Sergiev Posad (c); Volcanoes of Kamchatka (n); Lake Baikal (n); Central Sikhote-Alin (n); Historic Derbent (c); Kazan Kremlin (c)

ECONOMY

Economic overview: natural resource-rich Eurasian economy; leading energy exporter to Europe and Asia; decreased oil export reliance; endemic corruption, Ukrainian invasion, and lack of green infrastructure limit investment and have led to sanctions

Real GDP (purchasing power parity): $5.816 trillion (2023 est.)
$5.614 trillion (2022 est.)
$5.732 trillion (2021 est.)
note: data in 2021 dollars
comparison ranking: 4

Real GDP growth rate: 3.6% (2023 est.)
-2.07% (2022 est.)
5.61% (2021 est.)
note: annual GDP % growth based on constant local currency
comparison ranking: 88

Real GDP per capita: $39,800 (2023 est.)
$38,300 (2022 est.)
$38,900 (2021 est.)
note: data in 2021 dollars
comparison ranking: 63

GDP (official exchange rate): $2.021 trillion (2023 est.)
note: data in current dollars at official exchange rate

Inflation rate (consumer prices): 6.69% (2021 est.)
3.38% (2020 est.)
4.47% (2019 est.)
note: annual % change based on consumer prices
comparison ranking: 140

Credit ratings: Fitch rating: BBB (2019)

Moody's rating: Baa3 (2019)

Standard & Poors rating: BBB- (2018)
note: The year refers to the year in which the current credit rating was first obtained.

GDP - composition, by sector of origin: *agriculture:* 3.3% (2023 est.)
industry: 30.6% (2023 est.)
services: 56.9% (2023 est.)
note: figures may not total 100% due to non-allocated consumption not captured in sector-reported data
comparison rankings: services 106; industry 63; agriculture 135

GDP - composition, by end use: *household consumption:* 49.8% (2023 est.)
government consumption: 18.5% (2023 est.)
investment in fixed capital: 21.9% (2023 est.)
investment in inventories: 3.8% (2023 est.)
exports of goods and services: 23.1% (2023 est.)
imports of goods and services: -18.7% (2023 est.)
note: figures may not total 100% due to rounding or gaps in data collection

Agricultural products: wheat, sugar beets, milk, barley, potatoes, sunflower seeds, maize, soybeans, chicken, pork (2022)
note: top ten agricultural products based on tonnage

Industries: complete range of mining and extractive industries producing coal, oil, gas, chemicals, and metals; all forms of machine building from rolling mills to high-performance aircraft and space vehicles; defense industries (including radar, missile production, advanced electronic components), shipbuilding; road and rail transportation equipment; communications equipment; agricultural machinery, tractors, and construction equipment; electric power generating and transmitting equipment; medical and scientific instruments; consumer durables, textiles, foodstuffs, handicrafts

Industrial production growth rate: 3.56% (2023 est.)
note: annual % change in industrial value added based on constant local currency
comparison ranking: 92

Labor force: 72.408 million (2023 est.)
note: number of people ages 15 or older who are employed or seeking work
comparison ranking: 9

Unemployment rate: 3.33% (2023 est.)
3.87% (2022 est.)
4.72% (2021 est.)
note: % of labor force seeking employment
comparison ranking: 55

Youth unemployment rate (ages 15-24): *total:* 12.7% (2023 est.)
male: 12.3% (2023 est.)
female: 13.2% (2023 est.)
note: % of labor force ages 15-24 seeking employment
comparison ranking: total 109

Population below poverty line: 11% (2021 est.)
note: % of population with income below national poverty line

Gini Index coefficient - distribution of family income: 36 (2020 est.)
note: index (0-100) of income distribution; higher values represent greater inequality
comparison ranking: 69

Average household expenditures: *on food:* 28.9% of household expenditures (2022 est.)
on alcohol and tobacco: 7.3% of household expenditures (2022 est.)

Household income or consumption by percentage share: *lowest 10%:* 3.1% (2020 est.)
highest 10%: 29% (2020 est.)
note: % share of income accruing to lowest and highest 10% of population

Remittances: 0.34% of GDP (2023 est.)
0.15% of GDP (2022 est.)
0.52% of GDP (2021 est.)
note: personal transfers and compensation between resident and non-resident individuals/households/entities

Budget: *revenues:* $776.897 billion (2022 est.)
expenditures: $719.521 billion (2022 est.)
note: central government revenues (excluding grants) and expenses converted to US dollars at average official exchange rate for year indicated

Public debt: 19.51% of GDP (2022 est.)
note: central government debt as a % of GDP
comparison ranking: 188

Taxes and other revenues: 10.97% (of GDP) (2022 est.)
note: central government tax revenue as a % of GDP
comparison ranking: 176

Current account balance: $50.224 billion (2023 est.)
$237.678 billion (2022 est.)
$124.953 billion (2021 est.)
note: balance of payments - net trade and primary/secondary income in current dollars
comparison ranking: 12

Exports: $465.432 billion (2023 est.)
$640.709 billion (2022 est.)
$549.717 billion (2021 est.)
note: balance of payments - exports of goods and services in current dollars
comparison ranking: 20

Exports - partners: China 21%, India 8%, Germany 6%, Turkey 5%, Italy 5% (2022)
note: top five export partners based on percentage share of exports

Exports - commodities: crude petroleum, natural gas, refined petroleum, coal, fertilizers (2022)
note: top five export commodities based on value in dollars

Imports: $378.615 billion (2023 est.)
$347.384 billion (2022 est.)
$376.923 billion (2021 est.)
note: balance of payments - imports of goods and services in current dollars
comparison ranking: 21

Imports - partners: China 39%, Germany 8%, Turkey 5%, Kazakhstan 5%, South Korea 3% (2022)
note: top five import partners based on percentage share of imports

Imports - commodities: packaged medicine, broadcasting equipment, cars, garments, plastic products (2022)
note: top five import commodities based on value in dollars

Reserves of foreign exchange and gold: $597.217 billion (2023 est.)
$581.71 billion (2022 est.)
$632.242 billion (2021 est.)
note: holdings of gold (year-end prices)/foreign exchange/special drawing rights in current dollars
comparison ranking: 4

Debt - external: $135.301 billion (2022 est.)
note: present value of external debt in current US dollars
comparison ranking: 5

Exchange rates: Russian rubles (RUB) per US dollar -

Exchange rates: 85.162 (2023 est.)
68.485 (2022 est.)
73.654 (2021 est.)
72.105 (2020 est.)
64.738 (2019 est.)

ENERGY

Electricity access: *electrification - total population:* 100% (2022 est.)
electrification - urban areas: 99.1%
electrification - rural areas: 100%

Electricity: *installed generating capacity:* 301.123 million kW (2022 est.)
consumption: 1.026 trillion kWh (2022 est.)
exports: 18.582 billion kWh (2022 est.)
imports: 1.532 billion kWh (2022 est.)
transmission/distribution losses: 95.804 billion kWh (2022 est.)
comparison rankings: transmission/distribution losses 207; imports 67; exports 16; consumption 4; installed generating capacity 5

Electricity generation sources: *fossil fuels:* 60.3% of total installed capacity (2022 est.)
nuclear: 19.6% of total installed capacity (2022 est.)
solar: 0.2% of total installed capacity (2022 est.)
wind: 0.3% of total installed capacity (2022 est.)
hydroelectricity: 19.2% of total installed capacity (2022 est.)
biomass and waste: 0.3% of total installed capacity (2022 est.)

Nuclear energy: Number of operational nuclear reactors: 36 (2023)

Number of nuclear reactors under construction: 4 (2023)

Net capacity of operational nuclear reactors: 26.8GW (2023 est.)

Percent of total electricity production: 18.4% (2023 est.)

Number of nuclear reactors permanently shut down: 11 (2023)

Coal: *production:* 508.19 million metric tons (2022 est.)
consumption: 310.958 million metric tons (2022 est.)
exports: 220.306 million metric tons (2022 est.)
imports: 23.074 million metric tons (2022 est.)
proven reserves: 162.166 billion metric tons (2022 est.)

Petroleum: *total petroleum production:* 10.727 million bbl/day (2023 est.)
refined petroleum consumption: 3.684 million bbl/day (2022 est.)
crude oil estimated reserves: 80 billion barrels (2021 est.)

Natural gas: *production:* 617.83 billion cubic meters (2022 est.)
consumption: 472.239 billion cubic meters (2022 est.)
exports: 176.056 billion cubic meters (2022 est.)
imports: 8.129 billion cubic meters (2022 est.)
proven reserves: 47.805 trillion cubic meters (2021 est.)

Carbon dioxide emissions: 1.84 billion metric tonnes of CO_2 (2022 est.)
from coal and metallurgical coke: 517.718 million metric tonnes of CO_2 (2022 est.)
from petroleum and other liquids: 414.253 million metric tonnes of CO_2 (2022 est.)
from consumed natural gas: 907.83 million metric tonnes of CO_2 (2022 est.)
comparison ranking: total emissions 4

Energy consumption per capita: 225.235 million Btu/person (2022 est.)
comparison ranking: 16

COMMUNICATIONS

Telephones - fixed lines: *total subscriptions:* 23.864 million (2021 est.)
subscriptions per 100 inhabitants: 16 (2021 est.)
comparison ranking: total subscriptions 11

Telephones - mobile cellular: *total subscriptions:* 245.267 million (2022 est.)
subscriptions per 100 inhabitants: 169 (2021 est.)
comparison ranking: total subscriptions 5

Telecommunication systems: *general assessment:* the telecom market is the largest in Europe, supported by a population of about 143 million; the overall market is dominated by the western regions, particularly Moscow and St Petersburg which are the main cities and economic centers; many other regions in the east and north of the country were settled during the Soviet period; the telecommunication companies continue to deploy and modernize fixed-line network infrastructure to offer improved broadband services as well as a range of IP-delivered content; the number of Digital Subscriber Line (DSL) connections continues to decrease as subscribers are migrated to fiber; the development of 5G services has been hindered by the lack of frequencies; the 3.4GHz range commonly used for 5G in Europe has been restricted for use in Russia by the military and intelligence agencies; the Mobile Network Operators (MNOs) have an equal share in a joint venture, New Digital Solutions, aimed at developing a strategy to deploy 5G using a shared network
(2024)
domestic: 16 per 100 for fixed-line and mobile-cellular is 169 per 100 persons (2022)
international: country code - 7; landing points for the Far East Submarine Cable System, HSCS, Sakhalin-Kuril Island Cable, RSCN, BCS North-Phase 2, Kerch Strait Cable and the Georgia-Russian submarine cable system connecting Russia, Japan, Finland, Georgia and Ukraine; satellite earth stations provide access to Intelsat, Intersputnik, Eutelsat, Inmarsat, and Orbita systems (2019)

Broadcast media: 13 national TV stations with the federal government owning 1 and holding a controlling interest in a second; state-owned Gazprom maintains a controlling interest in 2 of the national channels; government-affiliated Bank Rossiya owns controlling interest in a fourth and fifth, while a sixth national channel is owned by the Moscow city administration; the Russian Orthodox Church and the Russian military, respectively, own 2 additional national channels; roughly 3,300 national, regional, and local TV stations with over two-thirds completely or partially controlled by the federal or local governments; satellite TV services are available; 2 state-run national radio networks with a third majority-owned by Gazprom; roughly 2,400 public and commercial radio stations

Internet country code: .ru; note - Russia also has responsibility for a legacy domain ".su" that was allocated to the Soviet Union and is being phased out

Internet users: *total:* 132 million (2021 est.)
percent of population: 88% (2021 est.)
comparison ranking: total 6

Broadband - fixed subscriptions: *total:* 33,893,305 (2020 est.)
subscriptions per 100 inhabitants: 23 (2020 est.)
comparison ranking: total 6

TRANSPORTATION

National air transport system: *number of registered air carriers:* 32 (2020)
inventory of registered aircraft operated by air carriers: 958
annual passenger traffic on registered air carriers: 99,327,311 (2018)
annual freight traffic on registered air carriers: 6,810,610,000 (2018) mt-km

Civil aircraft registration country code prefix: RA

Airports: 904 (2024)

comparison ranking: 7

Heliports: 383 (2024)

Pipelines: 177,700 km gas, 54,800 km oil, 19,300 km refined products (2017)

Railways: *total:* 85,494 km (2019)
narrow gauge: 957 km
comparison ranking: total 3

Roadways: *total:* 1,283,387 km
paved: 927,721 km (includes 39,143 km of expressways)
unpaved: 355,666 km (2012)
comparison ranking: total 5

Waterways: 102,000 km (2009) (including 48,000 km with guaranteed depth; the 72,000-km system in European Russia links Baltic Sea, White Sea, Caspian Sea, Sea of Azov, and Black Sea)
comparison ranking: 1

Merchant marine: *total:* 2,910 (2023)
by type: bulk carrier 15, container ship 20, general cargo 976, oil tanker 387, other 1,512
comparison ranking: total 9

Ports: *total ports:* 67 (2024)
large: 4
medium: 5
small: 19
very small: 38
size unknown: 1
ports with oil terminals: 32
key ports: Arkhangels'k, De Kastri, Dudinka, Kaliningrad, Murmansk, Novorossiysk, Sankt-Peterburg, Vladivostok, Vyborg

Transportation - note: Russia operates the largest polar-class icebreaker fleet in the world with 52 vessels, seven of which are the world's only nuclear-powered heavy icebreakers; the primary mission includes keeping open ports, terminals, and shipping lanes along the Northern Sea Route (see Arctic Ocean map), in the Baltic Sea, and in the Russian Far East, including the Sea of Okhotsk

Russian icebreaker Yamal:

MILITARY AND SECURITY

Military and security forces: Armed Forces of the Russian Federation: Ground Troops (Sukhoputnyye Voyskia, SV), Navy (Voyenno-Morskoy Flot, VMF), Aerospace Forces (Vozdushno-Kosmicheskiye Sily, VKS); Airborne Troops (Vozdushno-Desantnyye Voyska, VDV), and Missile Troops of Strategic Purpose (Raketnyye Voyska Strategicheskogo Naznacheniya, RVSN) referred to commonly as Strategic Rocket Forces, are independent "combat arms," not subordinate to any of the three branches
Federal National Guard Troops Service of the Russian Federation (FSVNG, National Guard, Russian Guard, or Rosgvardiya)

Federal Security Services (FSB): Federal Border Guard Service (includes land and maritime forces) (2023)
note 1: the Air Force and Aerospace Defense Forces were merged into the VKS in 2015; VKS responsibilities also include launching military and dual-use satellites, maintaining military satellites, and monitoring and defending against space threats
note 2: the Ministry of Internal Affairs, Federal Security Service, Investigative Committee, Office of the Prosecutor General, and National Guard are responsible for law enforcement; the Federal Security Service is responsible for state security, counterintelligence, and counterterrorism, as well as for fighting organized crime and corruption; the national police force, under the Ministry of Internal Affairs, is responsible for combating all crime
note 3: the National Guard was created in 2016 as an independent agency for internal/regime security, combating terrorism and narcotics trafficking, protecting important state facilities and government personnel, and supporting border security; it also participates in armed defense of the country's territory in coordination with the Armed Forces; forces under the National Guard include the Special Purpose Mobile Units (OMON), Special Rapid Response Detachment (SOBR), and Interior Troops (VV); these troops were originally under the command of the Interior Ministry (MVD)

Military expenditures: 5% of GDP (2023 est.)
4% of GDP (2022 est.)
4% of GDP (2021 est.)
4% of GDP (2020 est.)
3.8% of GDP (2019 est.)
comparison ranking: 9

Military and security service personnel strengths: approximately 1.1-1.3 million Armed Forces personnel; estimated 350,000-plus Federal National Guard Troops (2024)

Military equipment inventories and acquisitions: the Russian Federation's military and paramilitary services are equipped with domestically produced weapons systems, although in recent years Russia has imported considerable amounts of military hardware from external suppliers such as Iran and North Korea; the Russian defense industry is capable of designing, developing, and producing a full range of advanced air, land, missile, and naval systems; Russia is the world's second largest exporter of military hardware (2024)

Military service age and obligation: 18-27 years of age for compulsory service for men; 18-40 for voluntary/contractual service; women and non-Russian citizens (18-30) may volunteer; men are registered for the draft at 17 years of age; 12-month service obligation (Russia offers the option of serving on a 24-month contract instead of completing a 12-month conscription period); reserve obligation for non-officers to age 50 (Russian men who have completed their compulsory service to re-enter the army up to the age of 55); enrollment in military schools from the age of 16 (2023)
note 1: in May 2022, Russia's parliament approved a law removing the upper age limit for contractual service in the military; in November 2022, President Vladimir PUTIN signed a decree allowing dual-national Russians and those with permanent residency status in foreign countries to be drafted into the army for military service
note 2: historically, the Russian military has taken in about 260,000 conscripts each year in two semi-annual drafts (Spring and Fall)
note 3: prior to the invasion of Ukraine in 2022, approximately 40-45,000 women served in the Russian Armed Forces
note 4: since 2015, foreigners 18-30 with a good command of Russian have been allowed to join the military on five-year contracts and become eligible for Russian citizenship after serving three years; in October 2022, the Interior Ministry opened up recruitment centers for foreigners to sign a one-year service contract with the armed forces, other troops, or military formations participating in the invasion of Ukraine with the promise of simplifying the process of obtaining Russian citizenship

Military deployments: information varies and may not reflect troops transferred to support Russian military operations in Ukraine; approximately 3,000 Armenia; up to 5,000 Belarus; up to 10,000 Georgia; approximately 500 Kyrgyzstan; approximately 1,500 Moldova (Transnistria); estimated 2,000-5,000 Syria; approximately 3-5,000 Tajikistan (2024)
note 1: in February 2022, Russia invaded Ukraine with an estimated 150,000 troops, some of which were staged out of Belarus; prior to the invasion, it maintained an estimated 30,000 troops in areas of Ukraine occupied since 2014; in 2024, the Russian Government claimed to have more than 600,000 troops in the occupied portions of Ukraine
note 2: as of 2024, Russia was assessed to have thousands private military contractors and other security personnel conducting operations in Africa and the Middle East, including in Burkina Faso, the Central African Republic, Libya, Mali, Niger, Sudan, and Syria

Military - note: the Russian military is a mixed force of conscripts and professionals (contract servicemen) that is capable of conducting the full range of air, land, maritime, and strategic missile operations; it is also active in the areas of cyber warfare, electronic warfare, and space; in addition to protecting Russia's sovereignty and territorial integrity, the military supports Moscow's national security objectives, which include maintaining and projecting influence and power outside Russia, particularly in the former Soviet republics, and deterring perceived external threats from the US and NATO
in recent years, the Russian military has conducted combat operations in both Ukraine and Syria; in February 2022, Russia launched a full-scale invasion of Ukraine, and the military continues to be heavily engaged there in what is the largest war in Europe since World War II ended in 1945; Russia has occupied Ukraine's province of Crimea and backed separatist forces in the Donbas region of Ukraine since 2014 with arms, equipment, and training, as well as Russian military troops, although Moscow denied their presence prior to 2022; Russia intervened in the Syrian civil war at the request of the ASAD government in September 2015 in what was Moscow's first overseas expeditionary operation since the Soviet era; Russian assistance has included air support, arms and equipment, intelligence, military advisors, private military contractors, special operations forces, and training
prior to its military operations in Syria and Ukraine, Russia seized the Georgian regions of Abkhazia and South Ossetia by force in 2008 (2024)

SPACE

Space agency/agencies: State Space Corporation of the Russian Federation (Roscosmos); Roscosmos was established in 2015 from a merger of the Federal Space Agency and the state-owned United Rocket and Space Corporation; began as the Russian Space Agency (RSA or RKA) in 1992 and restructured in 1999 and 2004 as the Russian Aviation and Space Agency and then the Federal Space Agency); the Russian Space Forces (Kosmicheskie voyska Rossii, KV) are part of the Russian Aerospace Forces (Vozdushno-Kosmicheskiye Sily, VKS) (2024)
note: Russia's space strategy is defined jointly by Roscosmos and the Ministry of Defense; prior to the breakup of the Soviet Union in 1991, the USSR's space program was dispersed amongst several civil and military organizations

Space launch site(s): Baikonur Cosmodrome (Kazakhstan); Vostochny Cosmodrome (Amur Oblast); Plesetsk Cosmodrome (Arkhangel'sk Oblast); Kapustin Yar (Astrakhan Oblast); Yasny Launch Base (Orenburg Oblast) (2024)
note 1: the Baikonur cosmodrome and the surrounding area are leased and administered by Russia until 2050 for approximately $115 million/year; the cosmodrome was originally built by the Soviet Union in the mid-1950s and is the site of the World's first successful satellite launch (Sputnik) in 1957; it is also the largest space launch facility in the World, comprising 15 launch pads for space launch vehicles, four launch pads for testing intercontinental ballistic missiles, more than 10 assembly and test facilities, and other infrastructure
note 2: in 2018, Kazakhstan and Russia agreed that Kazakhstan would build, maintain, and operate a new space launch facility (Baiterek) at the Baikonur space center (estimated to be ready for operations in 2025)

Space program overview: has one of the world's largest space programs and is active across all areas of the space sector; builds, launches, and operates rockets/space launch vehicles (SLVs), satellites, space stations, interplanetary probes, and manned, robotic, and re-usable spacecraft; has astronaut (cosmonaut) training program and conducts human space flight; researching and developing a broad range of other space-related technologies; participates in international space programs such as the International Space Station (ISS); prior to Russia's 2022 full-scale invasion of Ukraine, Russia had relations with dozens of foreign space agencies and commercial entities, including those of China, the European Space Agency (ESA), India, Japan, and the US; Roscosmos and its public subsidiaries comprise the majority of the Russian space industry; Roscosmos has eight operating areas, including manned space flights, launch systems, unmanned spacecraft, rocket propulsion, military missiles, space avionics, special military space systems, and flight control systems; private companies are also involved in a range of space systems, including satellites, telecommunications, remote-sensing, and geo-spatial services (2024)
note: further details about the key activities, programs, and milestones of the country's space program, as well as government spending estimates on the space sector, appear in the Space Programs reference guide

TERRORISM

Terrorist group(s): Islamic State of Iraq and ash-Sham (ISIS)
note: details about the history, aims, leadership, organization, areas of operation, tactics, targets, weapons, size, and sources of support of the group(s) appear(s) in the Terrorism reference guide

TRANSNATIONAL ISSUES

Refugees and internally displaced persons: *refugees (country of origin):* 1,212,585 (Ukraine) (as of 30 June 2023)
IDPs: 7,500 (2022)
stateless persons: 56,960 (mid-year 2021); note - Russia's stateless population consists of Roma, Meskhetian Turks, and ex-Soviet citizens from the former republics; between 2003 and 2010 more than 600,000 stateless people were naturalized; most Meskhetian Turks, followers of Islam with origins in Georgia, fled or were evacuated from Uzbekistan after a 1989 pogrom and have lived in Russia for more than the required five-year residency period; they continue to be denied registration for citizenship and basic rights by local Krasnodar Krai authorities on the grounds that they are temporary illegal migrants

Trafficking in persons: tier rating: Tier 3 — Russia does not fully meet the minimum standards for the elimination of trafficking and is not making significant efforts to do so, therefore, Russia remained on Tier 3; for more details, go to: https://www.state.gov/reports/2024-trafficking-in-persons-report/russia/

Illicit drugs: a destination country for heroin and other Afghan opiates; a transit country for cocaine from South America, especially Ecuador to Europe, Belgium and Netherlands; synthetic drugs are produced in clandestine drug laboratories throughout the country; marijuana cultivated in Russian Far East and the North Caucasus; the majority of hashish is smuggled in from Northern Africa

RWANDA

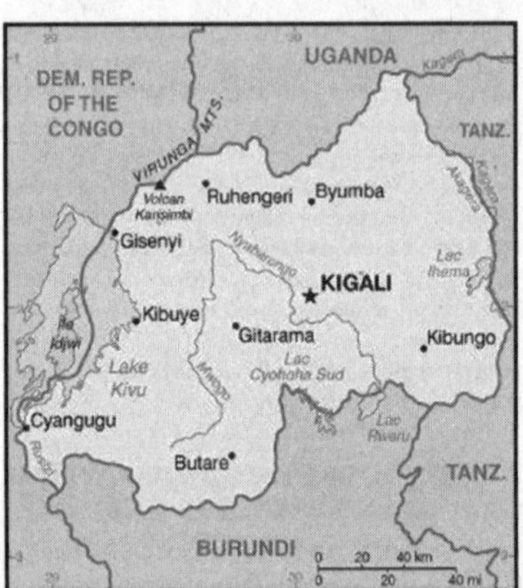

INTRODUCTION

Background: Rwanda – a small and centralized country dominated by rugged hills and fertile volcanic soil – has exerted disproportionate influence over the African Great Lakes region for centuries. A Rwandan kingdom increasingly dominated the region from the mid-18th century onward, with the Tutsi monarchs gradually extending the power of the royal court into peripheral areas and expanding their borders through military conquest. While the current ethnic labels Hutu and Tutsi predate colonial rule, their flexibility and importance have varied significantly over time and often manifested more as a hierarchical class distinction than an ethnic or cultural distinction. The majority Hutu and minority Tutsi have long shared a common language and culture, and intermarriage was frequent. The Rwandan royal court centered on the Tutsi king (*mwami*), who relied on an extensive network of political, cultural, and economic relationships. Social categories became more rigid during the reign of RWABUGIRI (1860-1895), who focused on aggressive expansion and solidifying Rwanda's bureaucratic structures. German colonial conquest began in the late 1890s, but the territory was ceded to Belgian forces in 1916 during World War I. Both European nations quickly realized the benefits of ruling through the already centralized Rwandan Tutsi kingdom. Colonial rule reinforced existing trends toward autocratic and exclusionary rule, leading to the elimination of traditional positions of authority for Hutus and a calcification of ethnic identities. Belgian administrators significantly increased requirements for communal labor and instituted harsh taxes, increasing frustration and inequality. Changing political attitudes in Belgium contributed to colonial and Catholic officials shifting their support from Tutsi to Hutu leaders in the years leading up to independence.

Newly mobilized political parties and simmering resentment of minority rule exploded in 1959, three years before independence from Belgium, when Hutus overthrew the Tutsi king. Thousands of Tutsis were killed over the next several years, and some 150,000 were driven into exile in neighboring countries. Army Chief of Staff Juvenal HABYARIMANA seized power in a coup in 1973 and ruled Rwanda as a single-party state for two decades. HABYARIMANA increasingly discriminated against Tutsis, and extremist Hutu factions gained prominence after multiple parties were introduced in the early 1990s. The children of Tutsi exiles later formed a rebel group, the Rwandan Patriotic Front (RPF) and began a civil war in 1990. The civil war exacerbated ethnic tensions and culminated in the shooting down of HABYARIMANA's private jet in 1994. The event sparked a state-orchestrated genocide in which Rwandans killed more than 800,000 of their fellow citizens, including approximately three-quarters of the Tutsi population. The genocide ended later that same year when the predominantly Tutsi RPF, operating out of Uganda and northern Rwanda, defeated the national army and Hutu militias and established an RPF-led government of national unity. Rwanda held its first local elections in 1999 and its first post-genocide presidential and legislative elections in 2003, formalizing President Paul KAGAME's de facto role as head of government. KAGAME was formally elected in 2010, and again in 2017 after changing the constitution to allow him to run for a third term.

GEOGRAPHY

Location: Central Africa, east of the Democratic Republic of the Congo, north of Burundi
Geographic coordinates: 2 00 S, 30 00 E
Map references: Africa

Area: *total:* 26,338 sq km
land: 24,668 sq km
water: 1,670 sq km
comparison ranking: total 148

Area - comparative: slightly smaller than Maryland

Land boundaries: *total:* 930 km
border countries (4): Burundi 315 km; Democratic Republic of the Congo 221 km; Tanzania 222 km; Uganda 172 km

Coastline: 0 km (landlocked)

Maritime claims: none (landlocked)

Climate: temperate; two rainy seasons (February to April, November to January); mild in mountains with frost and snow possible

Terrain: mostly grassy uplands and hills; relief is mountainous with altitude declining from west to east

Elevation: *highest point:* Volcan Karisimbi 4,519 m
lowest point: Rusizi River 950 m
mean elevation: 1,598 m

Natural resources: gold, cassiterite (tin ore), wolframite (tungsten ore), methane, hydropower, arable land

Land use: *agricultural land:* 74.5% (2018 est.)
arable land: 47% (2018 est.)
permanent crops: 10.1% (2018 est.)
permanent pasture: 17.4% (2018 est.)
forest: 18% (2018 est.)
other: 7.5% (2018 est.)

Irrigated land: 96 sq km (2012)

Major lakes (area sq km): *fresh water lake(s):* Lake Kivu (shared with Democratic Republic of Congo) - 2,220 sq km

Major rivers (by length in km): Nile river source (shared with Tanzania, Uganda, South Sudan, Sudan, and Egypt [m]) - 6,650 km
note – [s] after country name indicates river source; [m] after country name indicates river mouth

Major watersheds (area sq km):Atlantic Ocean drainage: Congo (3,730,881 sq km), *(Mediterranean Sea)* Nile (3,254,853 sq km)

Population distribution: one of Africa's most densely populated countries; large concentrations tend to be in the central regions and along the shore of Lake Kivu in the west as shown in this population distribution map

Natural hazards: periodic droughts; the volcanic Virunga Mountains are in the northwest along the border with Democratic Republic of the Congo
volcanism: Visoke (3,711 m), located on the border with the Democratic Republic of the Congo, is the country's only historically active volcano

Geography - note: landlocked; most of the country is intensively cultivated and rugged, with the population predominantly rural

PEOPLE AND SOCIETY

Population: *total:* 13,623,302
male: 6,684,655
female: 6,938,647 (2024 est.)
comparison rankings: female 76; male 78; total 76

Nationality: *noun:* Rwandan(s)
adjective: Rwandan

Ethnic groups: Hutu, Tutsi, Twa

Languages: Kinyarwanda (official, universal Bantu vernacular) 93.2%, French (official) <0.1%, English (official) <0.1%, Swahili/Kiswahili (official, used in commercial centers) <0.1%, more than one language, other 6.3%, unspecified 0.3% (2002 est.)
major-language sample(s):
Inkoranya nzimbuzi y'isi, isoko fatizo y'amakuru y'ibanze. (Kinyarwanda)

Religions: Christian 95.9% (Protestant 57.7% [includes Adventist 12.6%], Roman Catholic 38.2%), Muslim 2.1%, other 1% (includes traditional, Jehovah's Witness), none 1.1% (2019-20 est.)

Demographic profile: Rwanda's fertility rate declined sharply during the last decade, as a result of the government's commitment to family planning, the increased use of contraceptives, and a downward trend in ideal family size. Increases in educational attainment, particularly among girls, and exposure to social media also contributed to the reduction in the birth rate. The average number of births per woman decreased from a 5.6 in 2005 to 4.5 in 2016 and 3.3 in 2022. Despite these significant strides in reducing fertility, Rwanda's birth rate remains very high and will continue to for an extended period of time because of its large population entering reproductive age. Because Rwanda is one of the most densely populated countries in Africa, its persistent high population growth and increasingly small agricultural landholdings will put additional strain on families' ability to raise foodstuffs and access potable water. These conditions will also hinder the government's efforts to reduce poverty and prevent environmental degradation.
The UNHCR recommended that effective 30 June 2013 countries invoke a cessation of refugee status for those Rwandans who fled their homeland between 1959 and 1998, including the 1994 genocide, on the grounds that the conditions that drove them to seek protection abroad no longer exist. The UNHCR's decision is controversial because many Rwandan refugees still fear persecution if they return home, concerns that are supported by the number of Rwandans granted asylum since 1998 and by the number exempted from the cessation. Rwandan refugees can still seek an exemption or local integration, but host countries are anxious to send the refugees back to Rwanda and are likely to avoid options that enable them to stay. Conversely, Rwanda itself hosts approximately 125,000 refugees as of 2022; virtually all of them fleeing conflict in neighboring Burundi and the Democratic Republic of the Congo.

Age structure: *0-14 years:* 37.2% (male 2,561,884/female 2,508,218)
15-64 years: 59.7% (male 3,954,608/female 4,179,844)
65 years and over: 3.1% (2024 est.) (male 168,163/female 250,585)

Dependency ratios: *total dependency ratio:* 72.5
youth dependency ratio: 67.1
elderly dependency ratio: 5.4
potential support ratio: 18.4 (2021 est.)

Median age: *total:* 20.8 years (2024 est.)
male: 20.1 years
female: 21.5 years
comparison ranking: total 198

Population growth rate: 1.62% (2024 est.)
comparison ranking: 58

Birth rate: 25 births/1,000 population (2024 est.)
comparison ranking: 46

Death rate: 5.7 deaths/1,000 population (2024 est.)
comparison ranking: 169

Net migration rate: -3.1 migrant(s)/1,000 population (2024 est.)
comparison ranking: 182

Population distribution: one of Africa's most densely populated countries; large concentrations tend to be in the central regions and along the shore of Lake Kivu in the west as shown in this population distribution map

Urbanization: *urban population:* 17.9% of total population (2023)
rate of urbanization: 3.07% annual rate of change (2020-25 est.)

Major urban areas - population: 1.248 million KIGALI (capital) (2023)

Sex ratio: *at birth:* 1.03 male(s)/female
0-14 years: 1.02 male(s)/female
15-64 years: 0.95 male(s)/female
65 years and over: 0.67 male(s)/female
total population: 0.96 male(s)/female (2024 est.)

Mother's mean age at first birth: 23 years (2019/20 est.)
note: data represents median age at first birth among women 25-49

Maternal mortality ratio: 259 deaths/100,000 live births (2020 est.)
comparison ranking: 37

Infant mortality rate: *total:* 24.9 deaths/1,000 live births (2024 est.)
male: 27.3 deaths/1,000 live births
female: 22.5 deaths/1,000 live births
comparison ranking: total 60

Life expectancy at birth: *total population:* 66.6 years (2024 est.)
male: 64.6 years
female: 68.6 years
comparison ranking: total population 200

Total fertility rate: children born/woman (2024 est.)
comparison ranking: 46

Gross reproduction rate: (2024 est.)

Contraceptive prevalence rate: 64.1% (2019/20)

Drinking water source: *improved: urban:* 92.3% of population
rural: 80.7% of population
total: 82.7% of population
unimproved: urban: 7.7% of population
rural: 19.3% of population
total: 17.3% of population (2020 est.)

Current health expenditure: 7.3% of GDP (2020)

Physician density: 0.12 physicians/1,000 population (2019)

Sanitation facility access: *improved: urban:* 89.1% of population
rural: 83.2% of population
total: 84.2% of population
unimproved: urban: 10.9% of population
rural: 16.8% of population
total: 15.8% of population (2020 est.)

Obesity - adult prevalence rate: 5.8% (2016)
comparison ranking: 172

Alcohol consumption per capita: *total:* 6.35 liters of pure alcohol (2019 est.)
beer: 0.23 liters of pure alcohol (2019 est.)
wine: 0.03 liters of pure alcohol (2019 est.)
spirits: 0.09 liters of pure alcohol (2019 est.)
other alcohols: 6 liters of pure alcohol (2019 est.)
comparison ranking: total 65

Tobacco use: *total:* 13.7% (2020 est.)
male: 20.1% (2020 est.)

female: 7.2% (2020 est.)
comparison ranking: total 112

Children under the age of 5 years underweight: 7.7% (2019/20)
comparison ranking: 61

Currently married women (ages 15-49): 50.4% (2023 est.)

Child marriage: *women married by age 18:* 0.4% (2020 est.)

Education expenditures: 3.8% of GDP (2021 est.)
comparison ranking: 127

Literacy: *definition:* age 15 and over can read and write
total population: 75.9%
male: 78.7%
female: 73.3% (2021)

School life expectancy (primary to tertiary education): *total:* 11 years
male: 11 years
female: 11 years (2019)

ENVIRONMENT

Environment - current issues: deforestation results from uncontrolled cutting of trees for fuel; overgrazing; land degradation; soil erosion; a decline in soil fertility (soil exhaustion); wetland degradation and loss of biodiversity; widespread poaching

Environment - international agreements: *party to:* Biodiversity, Climate Change, Climate Change-Kyoto Protocol, Comprehensive Nuclear Test Ban, Desertification, Endangered Species, Hazardous Wastes, Nuclear Test Ban, Ozone Layer Protection, Wetlands
signed, but not ratified: Law of the Sea

Climate: temperate; two rainy seasons (February to April, November to January); mild in mountains with frost and snow possible

Urbanization: *urban population:* 17.9% of total population (2023)
rate of urbanization: 3.07% annual rate of change (2020-25 est.)

Revenue from forest resources: 3.75% of GDP (2018 est.)
comparison ranking: 20

Revenue from coal: 0% of GDP (2018 est.)
comparison ranking: 168

Air pollutants: *particulate matter emissions:* 35.66 micrograms per cubic meter (2019 est.)
carbon dioxide emissions: 1.11 megatons (2016 est.)
methane emissions: 2.92 megatons (2020 est.)

Waste and recycling: *municipal solid waste generated annually:* 4,384,969 tons (2016 est.)

Major lakes (area sq km): *fresh water lake(s):* Lake Kivu (shared with Democratic Republic of Congo) - 2,220 sq km

Major rivers (by length in km): Nile river source (shared with Tanzania, Uganda, South Sudan, Sudan, and Egypt [m]) - 6,650 km
note – [s] after country name indicates river source; [m] after country name indicates river mouth

Major watersheds (area sq km):Atlantic Ocean drainage: Congo (3,730,881 sq km), *(Mediterranean Sea)* Nile (3,254,853 sq km)

Total water withdrawal: *municipal:* 230 million cubic meters (2020 est.)
industrial: 10 million cubic meters (2020 est.)
agricultural: 360 million cubic meters (2020 est.)

Total renewable water resources: 13.3 billion cubic meters (2020 est.)

GOVERNMENT

Country name: *conventional long form:* Republic of Rwanda
conventional short form: Rwanda
local long form: Republika y'u Rwanda
local short form: Rwanda
former: Kingdom of Rwanda, Ruanda, German East Africa
etymology: the name translates as "'domain"' in the native Kinyarwanda language

Government type: presidential republic

Capital: *name:* Kigali
geographic coordinates: 1 57 S, 30 03 E
time difference: UTC+2 (7 hours ahead of Washington, DC, during Standard Time)
etymology: the city takes its name from nearby Mount Kigali; the name "'Kigali"' is composed of the Bantu prefix *ki* and the Rwandan *gali* meaning "'broad"' and likely refers to the broad, sprawling hill that has been dignified with the title of "'mount"'

Administrative divisions: 4 provinces (in French - provinces, singular - province; in Kinyarwanda - intara for singular and plural) and 1 city* (in French - ville; in Kinyarwanda - umujyi); Est (Eastern), Kigali*, Nord (Northern), Ouest (Western), Sud (Southern)

Independence: 1 July 1962 (from Belgium-administered UN trusteeship)

National holiday: Independence Day, 1 July (1962)

Legal system: mixed legal system of civil law, based on German and Belgian models, and customary law; judicial review of legislative acts in the Supreme Court

Constitution: *history:* several previous; latest adopted by referendum 26 May 2003, effective 4 June 2003
amendments: proposed by the president of the republic (with Council of Ministers approval) or by two-thirds majority vote of both houses of Parliament; passage requires at least three-quarters majority vote in both houses; changes to constitutional articles on national sovereignty, the presidential term, the form and system of government, and political pluralism also require approval in a referendum; amended several times, last in 2015

International law organization participation: has not submitted an ICJ jurisdiction declaration; non-party state to the ICCt

Citizenship: *citizenship by birth:* no
citizenship by descent only: the father must be a citizen of Rwanda; if the father is stateless or unknown, the mother must be a citizen
dual citizenship recognized: no
residency requirement for naturalization: 10 years

Suffrage: 18 years of age; universal

Executive branch: *chief of state:* President Paul KAGAME (since 22 April 2000)
head of government: Prime Minister Edouard NGIRENTE (since 30 August 2017)
cabinet: Council of Ministers appointed by the president
elections/appointments: president directly elected by simple majority popular vote for a 5-year term (eligible for a second term); note - a constitutional amendment approved in December 2016 reduced the presidential term from 7 to 5 years but included an exception that allowed President KAGAME to serve another 7-year term in 2017, potentially followed by two additional 5-year terms; election last held on 4 August 2017 (next to be held on 15 July 2029); prime minister appointed by the president
election results:
2024: Paul KAGAME reelected president; Paul KAGAME (RPF) 99.2%, Frank HABINEZA (DGPR) 0.50%, Philippe MPAYIMANA (independent) 0.32%
2017: Paul KAGAME reelected president; Paul KAGAME (RPF) 98.8%, Philippe MPAYIMANA (independent), other 1.2%

Legislative branch: *description:* bicameral Parliament consists of:
Senate or Senat (26 seats; 12 members indirectly elected by local councils, 8 appointed by the president, 4 appointed by the Political Organizations Forum - a body of registered political parties, and 2 selected by institutions of higher learning; members serve 8-year terms)
Chamber of Deputies or Chambre des Deputes (80 seats; 53 members directly elected by proportional representation vote, 24 women selected by special interest groups, and 3 selected by youth and disability organizations; members serve 5-year terms)
elections: Senate - last held on 16-18 September 2019 (next to be held 30 September 2024)
Chamber of Deputies - last held on 15 July 2024 (next to be held 31 July 2029)
election results: Senate - percent of vote by party - NA; seats by party - NA; composition - men 17, women 9, percentage women 34.6%
Chamber of Deputies - percent of vote by party - NA; seats by party - FPR 37, PSD 5, PL 5, DGPR 2, PDI 2, PS 2 composition - men 36, women 44, percentage women 55%; total Parliament percentage women 50%

Judicial branch: *highest court(s):* Supreme Court (consists of the chief and deputy chief justices and 5 judges; normally organized into 3-judge panels); High Court (consists of the court president, vice president, and a minimum of 24 judges and organized into 5 chambers)
judge selection and term of office: Supreme Court judges nominated by the president after consultation with the Cabinet and the Superior Council of the Judiciary (SCJ), a 27-member body of judges, other judicial officials, and legal professionals) and approved by the Senate; chief and deputy chief justices appointed for 8-year nonrenewable terms; tenure of judges NA; High Court president and vice president appointed by the president of the republic upon approval by the Senate; judges appointed by the Supreme Court chief justice upon approval of the SCJ; judge tenure NA
subordinate courts: High Court of the Republic; commercial courts including the High Commercial Court; intermediate courts; primary courts; and military specialized courts

Political parties: Democratic Green Party of Rwanda or DGPR
Liberal Party or PL
Party for Progress and Concord or PPC
Rwandan Patriotic Front or RPF
Rwandan Patriotic Front Coalition (includes RPF, PPC, PSP, UDPR, PDI, PSR, PDC)
Social Democratic Party or PSD
Social Party Imberakuri or PS-Imberakuri

International organization participation: ACP, AfDB, AU, CEPGL, COMESA, EAC, EADB, FAO,

G-77, IAEA, IBRD, ICAO, ICRM, IDA, IFAD, IFC, IFRCS, ILO, IMF, Interpol, IOC, IOM, IPU, ISO, ITSO, ITU, ITUC (NGOs), MIGA, MINUSMA, NAM, OIF, OPCW, PCA, UN, UNCTAD, UNESCO, UNHCR, UNIDO, UNISFA, UNMISS, UNOOSA, UNWTO, UPU, WCO, WHO, WIPO, WMO, WTO

Diplomatic representation in the US: *chief of mission:* Ambassador Mathilde MUKANTABANA (since 18 July 2013)
chancery: 1714 New Hampshire Avenue NW, Washington, DC 20009
telephone: [1] (202) 232-2882
FAX: [1] (202) 232-4544
email address and website:
info@rwandaembassy.org
https://rwandaembassy.org/

Diplomatic representation from the US: *chief of mission:* Ambassador Eric KNEEDLER (since 3 October 2023)
embassy: 2657 Avenue de la Gendarmerie (Kaciyiru), P. O. Box 28 Kigali
mailing address: 2210 Kigali Place, Washington DC 20521-2210
telephone: [250] 252 596-400
FAX: [250] 252 580-325
email address and website:
consularkigali@state.gov
https://rw.usembassy.gov/

Flag description: three horizontal bands of sky blue (top, double width), yellow, and green, with a golden sun with 24 rays near the fly end of the blue band; blue represents happiness and peace, yellow economic development and mineral wealth, green hope of prosperity and natural resources; the sun symbolizes unity, as well as enlightenment and transparency from ignorance

National symbol(s): traditional woven basket with peaked lid; national colors: blue, yellow, green

National anthem: *name:* ""Rwanda nziza"" (Rwanda, Our Beautiful Country)
lyrics/music: Faustin MURIGO/Jean-Bosco HASHAKAIMANA
note: adopted 2001

National heritage: *total World Heritage Sites:* 2 (1 cultural, 1 natural)
selected World Heritage Site locales: Memorial sites of the Genocide: Nyamata, Murambi, Gisozi and Bisesero (c); Nyungwe National Park (n)

ECONOMY

Economic overview: fast-growing Sub-Saharan economy; major public investments; trade and tourism hit hard by COVID-19; increasing poverty after 2 decades of declines; Ugandan competition for regional influence; major coffee exporter; contested GDP figures

Real GDP (purchasing power parity): $42.701 billion (2023 est.)
$39.45 billion (2022 est.)
$36.474 billion (2021 est.)
note: data in 2021 dollars
comparison ranking: 135

Real GDP growth rate: 8.24% (2023 est.)
8.16% (2022 est.)
10.86% (2021 est.)
note: annual GDP % growth based on constant local currency
comparison ranking: 11

Real GDP per capita: $3,000 (2023 est.)
$2,900 (2022 est.)
$2,700 (2021 est.)
note: data in 2021 dollars
comparison ranking: 194

GDP (official exchange rate): $14.098 billion (2023 est.)
note: data in current dollars at official exchange rate

Inflation rate (consumer prices): 19.79% (2023 est.)
17.69% (2022 est.)
-0.39% (2021 est.)
note: annual % change based on consumer prices
comparison ranking: 197

Credit ratings: Fitch rating: B+ (2014)

Moody's rating: B2 (2016)

Standard & Poors rating: B+ (2019)
note: The year refers to the year in which the current credit rating was first obtained.

GDP - composition, by sector of origin: *agriculture:* 27.1% (2023 est.)
industry: 21.5% (2023 est.)
services: 44.3% (2023 est.)
note: figures may not total 100% due to non-allocated consumption not captured in sector-reported data
comparison rankings: services 173; industry 126; agriculture 15

GDP - composition, by end use: *household consumption:* 75.3% (2023 est.)
government consumption: 16.6% (2023 est.)
investment in fixed capital: 27.1% (2023 est.)
investment in inventories: -3.8% (2023 est.)
exports of goods and services: 25.4% (2023 est.)
imports of goods and services: -40.6% (2023 est.)
note: figures may not total 100% due to rounding or gaps in data collection

Agricultural products: bananas, cassava, sweet potatoes, potatoes, plantains, maize, beans, pumpkins/squash, taro, sorghum (2022)
note: top ten agricultural products based on tonnage

Industries: cement, agricultural products, small-scale beverages, soap, furniture, shoes, plastic goods, textiles, cigarettes

Industrial production growth rate: % (2023 est.)
note: annual % change in industrial value added based on constant local currency
comparison ranking: 15

Labor force: 5.283 million (2023 est.)
note: number of people ages 15 or older who are employed or seeking work
comparison ranking: 83

Unemployment rate: % (2023 est.)
15.09% (2022 est.)
15.79% (2021 est.)
note: % of labor force seeking employment
comparison ranking: 189

Youth unemployment rate (ages 15-24): *total:* 22% (2023 est.)
male: 20.8% (2023 est.)
female: 23.3% (2023 est.)
note: % of labor force ages 15-24 seeking employment
comparison ranking: total 55

Population below poverty line: 38.2% (2016 est.)
note: % of population with income below national poverty line

Gini Index coefficient - distribution of family income: 43.7 (2016 est.)
note: index (0-100) of income distribution; higher values represent greater inequality
comparison ranking: 27

Household income or consumption by percentage share: *lowest 10%:* 2.4% (2016 est.)
highest 10%: 35.6% (2016 est.)
note: % share of income accruing to lowest and highest 10% of population

Remittances: 3.93% of GDP (2023 est.)
3.56% of GDP (2022 est.)
3.53% of GDP (2021 est.)
note: personal transfers and compensation between resident and non-resident individuals/households/entities

Budget: *revenues:* $2.676 billion (2020 est.)
expenditures: $2.191 billion (2020 est.)
note: central government revenues (excluding grants) and expenses converted to US dollars at average official exchange rate for year indicated

Public debt: 40.5% of GDP (2017 est.)
comparison ranking: 130

Taxes and other revenues: 15.07% (of GDP) (2020 est.)
note: central government tax revenue as a % of GDP
comparison ranking: 137

Current account balance: -$1.654 billion (2023 est.)
-$1.246 billion (2022 est.)
-$1.209 billion (2021 est.)
note: balance of payments - net trade and primary/secondary income in current dollars
comparison ranking: 152

Exports: $3.509 billion (2023 est.)
$2.993 billion (2022 est.)
$2.11 billion (2021 est.)
note: balance of payments - exports of goods and services in current dollars
comparison ranking: 152

Exports - partners: UAE 32%, Democratic Republic of the Congo 25%, Thailand 5%, US 3%, Ethiopia 3% (2022)
note: top five export partners based on percentage share of exports

Exports - commodities: gold, tin ores, coffee, malt extract, rare earth ores (2022)
note: top five export commodities based on value in dollars

Imports: $5.783 billion (2023 est.)
$4.978 billion (2022 est.)
$3.856 billion (2021 est.)
note: balance of payments - imports of goods and services in current dollars
comparison ranking: 144

Imports - partners: China 19%, Tanzania 11%, Kenya 10%, UAE 10%, India 7% (2022)
note: top five import partners based on percentage share of imports

Imports - commodities: refined petroleum, gold, palm oil, rice, raw sugar (2022)
note: top five import commodities based on value in dollars

Reserves of foreign exchange and gold: $1.834 billion (2023 est.)
$1.726 billion (2022 est.)
$1.867 billion (2021 est.)
note: holdings of gold (year-end prices)/foreign exchange/special drawing rights in current dollars
comparison ranking: 130

Debt - external: $4.254 billion (2022 est.)

note: present value of external debt in current US dollars
comparison ranking: 56

Exchange rates: Rwandan francs (RWF) per US dollar -

Exchange rates: 1,160.099 (2023 est.)
1,030.308 (2022 est.)
988.625 (2021 est.)
943.278 (2020 est.)
899.351 (2019 est.)

ENERGY

Electricity access: *electrification - total population:* 50.6% (2022 est.)
electrification - urban areas: 98%
electrification - rural areas: 38.2%

Electricity: *installed generating capacity:* 273,000 kW (2022 est.)
consumption: 861.285 million kWh (2022 est.)
exports: 9 million kWh (2022 est.)
imports: 31 million kWh (2022 est.)
transmission/distribution losses: 140.605 million kWh (2022 est.)
comparison rankings: transmission/distribution losses 55; imports 119; exports 97; consumption 162; installed generating capacity 169

Electricity generation sources: *fossil fuels:* 45.5% of total installed capacity (2022 est.)
solar: 1.8% of total installed capacity (2022 est.)
hydroelectricity: 52.5% of total installed capacity (2022 est.)
biomass and waste: 0.2% of total installed capacity (2022 est.)

Coal: *consumption:* 41,000 metric tons (2022 est.)
imports: 64,000 metric tons (2022 est.)

Petroleum: *refined petroleum consumption:* 9,000 bbl/day (2022 est.)

Natural gas: *production:* 60.145 million cubic meters (2022 est.)
consumption: 59.715 million cubic meters (2022 est.)
proven reserves: 56.634 billion cubic meters (2021 est.)

Carbon dioxide emissions: 1.442 million metric tonnes of CO_2 (2022 est.)
from coal and metallurgical coke: 77,000 metric tonnes of CO_2 (2022 est.)
from petroleum and other liquids: 1.249 million metric tonnes of CO_2 (2022 est.)
from consumed natural gas: 116,000 metric tonnes of CO_2 (2022 est.)
comparison ranking: total emissions 164

Energy consumption per capita: 1.659 million Btu/person (2022 est.)
comparison ranking: 188

COMMUNICATIONS

Telephones - fixed lines: *total subscriptions:* 10,000 (2022 est.)
subscriptions per 100 inhabitants: (2022 est.) less than 1
comparison ranking: total subscriptions 189

Telephones - mobile cellular: *total subscriptions:* 11.002 million (2022 est.)
subscriptions per 100 inhabitants: 80 (2022 est.)
comparison ranking: total subscriptions 91

Telecommunication systems: *general assessment:* Rwanda was slow to liberalize the mobile sector; there was effective competition among three operators; the fixed broadband sector has suffered from limited fixed-line infrastructure and high prices; operators are rolling out national backbone networks which also allow them to connect to the international submarine cables on Africa's east coast; these cables gave the entire region greater internet bandwidth and ended the dependency on satellites; while the country also has a new cable link with Tanzania, and via Tanzania's national broadband backbone it has gained connectivity to the networks of several other countries in the region; the number of subscribers on LTE infrastructure has increased sharply, helped by national LTE coverage achieved in mid-2018; mobile remains the dominant platform for voice and data services; the regulator noted that the number of mobile subscribers increased 2.7% in 2021, year-on-year; there was a slight fall in the beginning of 2022 (2022)
domestic: fixed-line less than 1 per 100 and mobile-cellular telephone density is 81 telephones per 100 persons (2021)
international: country code - 250; international connections employ microwave radio relay to neighboring countries and satellite communications to more distant countries; satellite earth stations - 1 Intelsat (Indian Ocean) in Kigali (includes telex and telefax service); international submarine fiber-optic cables on the African east coast has brought international bandwidth and lessened the dependency on satellites

Broadcast media: 13 TV stations; 35 radio stations registered, including international broadcasters, government owns most popular TV and radio stations; regional satellite-based TV services available

Internet country code: .rw

Internet users: *total:* 3.9 million (2021 est.)
percent of population: 30% (2021 est.)
comparison ranking: total 113

Broadband - fixed subscriptions: *total:* 17,685 (2020 est.)
subscriptions per 100 inhabitants: 0.1 (2020 est.)
comparison ranking: total 171

TRANSPORTATION

National air transport system: *number of registered air carriers:* 1 (2020)
inventory of registered aircraft operated by air carriers: 12
annual passenger traffic on registered air carriers: 1,073,528 (2018)

Civil aircraft registration country code prefix: 9XR

Airports: 8 (2024)
comparison ranking: 165

Roadways: *total:* 7,797 km
paved: 2,652 km
unpaved: 5,145 km (2024)
comparison ranking: total 141

Waterways: 90 km (2022) (Lake Kivu navigable by shallow-draft barges and native craft)
comparison ranking: 112

MILITARY AND SECURITY

Military and security forces: Rwanda Defense Force (RDF; Ingabo z'u Rwanda): Rwanda Army (Rwanda Land Force), Rwanda Air Force (Force Aerienne Rwandaise, FAR), Rwanda Reserve Force, Special Units

Ministry of Internal Security: Rwanda National Police (2024)

Military expenditures: 1.4% of GDP (2023 est.)
1.4% of GDP (2022 est.)
1.4% of GDP (2021 est.)
1.3% of GDP (2020 est.)
1.2% of GDP (2019 est.)
comparison ranking: 97

Military and security service personnel strengths: approximately 33,000 active RDF personnel (32,000 Army; 1,000 Air Force) (2023)

Military equipment inventories and acquisitions: the RDF's inventory includes a mix of older and some modern equipment from suppliers such as China, France, Israel, Russia and the former Soviet Union, South Africa, and Turkey (2024)

Military service age and obligation: 18 years of age for men and women for voluntary military service; no conscription; Rwandan citizenship is required; enlistment is either as contract (5-years, renewable twice) or career (2023)
note: as of 2022, women comprised approximately 6% of the Rwanda Defense Force

Military deployments: approximately 3,200 Central African Republic (about 2,200 under MINUSCA, plus some 700 police; approximately 1,000 under a bi-lateral agreement); approximately 3,000 Mozambique (bilateral agreement to assist with combating an insurgency; includes both military and police forces); 2,600 (plus about 450 police) South Sudan (UNMISS) (2024)

Military - note: the RDF is widely regarded as one of East Africa's best trained and most experienced militaries; its principle responsibilities are ensuring territorial integrity and national sovereignty and preventing infiltrations of illegal armed groups from neighboring countries, particularly the Democratic Republic of the Congo (DRC); since 2021, Rwanda has deployed troops to the border region with the DRC to combat the rebel Democratic Forces for the Liberation of Rwanda (FDLR), which it has accused the DRC of backing; the RDF has been accused by the DRC, the UN, and the US of making incursions into the DRC and providing material support to the March 23 Movement (M23, aka Congolese Revolutionary Army) rebel group, which has been fighting with DRC troops and UN peacekeeping forces; the RDF also participates in UN and regional military operations, as well as multinational exercises the Rwandan Armed Forces (FAR) were established following independence in 1962; after the 1990-1994 civil war and genocide, the victorious Tutsi-dominated Rwandan Patriotic Front's military wing, the Rwandan Patriotic Army (RPA), became the country's military force; the RPA participated in the First (1996-1997) and Second (1998-2003) Congolese Wars; the RPA was renamed the Rwanda Defense Force (RDF) in 2003, by which time it had assumed a more national character with the inclusion of many former Hutu officers as well as newly recruited soldiers (2024)

SPACE

Space agency/agencies: Rwanda Space Agency (L'Agence Spatiale Rwandaise; RSA; established 2020 and approved by legislature in 2021) (2024)

Space program overview: has a small program focused on developing and utilizing space technologies, such as satellite imagery for socioeconomic development and security purposes; operates communications and

remote sensing (RS) satellites; the RSA is responsible for regulating and coordinating the country's space activities and encouraging commercial and industrial development; has established ties with the space agencies or industries of several countries, including France, Israel, Japan, the UAE, and the US (2024)
note: further details about the key activities, programs, and milestones of the country's space program, as well as government spending estimates on the space sector, appear in the Space Programs reference guide

TRANSNATIONAL ISSUES

Refugees and internally displaced persons: *refugees (country of origin):* 79,720 (Democratic Republic of the Congo), 48,533 (Burundi) (2024)
stateless persons: 9,500 (2022)

Trafficking in persons: tier rating: Tier 2 Watch List — the government did not demonstrate overall increasing efforts to eliminate trafficking compared with the previous reporting period, therefore Rwanda was downgraded to Tier 2 Watch List; for more details, go to: https://www.state.gov/reports/2024-trafficking-in-persons-report/rwanda/

S

SAINT BARTHELEMY

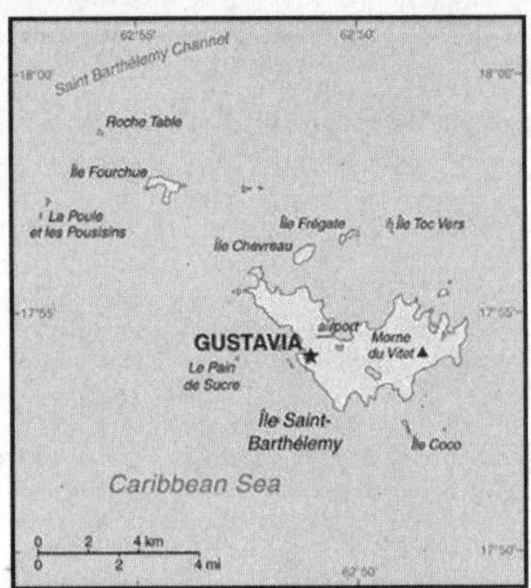

INTRODUCTION

Background: In 1493, Christopher COLUMBUS named Saint Barthelemy for his brother Bartolomeo, but the island was first settled by the French in 1648. In 1784, France sold the island to Sweden, which renamed the largest town Gustavia after the Swedish King GUSTAV III and made it a free port; the island prospered as a trade and supply center during the colonial wars of the 18th century. France repurchased the island in 1877 and took control the following year, placing it under the administration of Guadeloupe. Saint Barthelemy retained its free port status along with various Swedish appellations such as Swedish street and town names, and the three-crown symbol on the coat of arms. In 2003, the islanders voted to secede from Guadeloupe, and in 2007, the island became a French overseas collectivity. In 2012, it became an overseas territory of the EU, allowing it to exert local control over the permanent and temporary immigration of foreign workers, including non-French European citizens. Hurricane Irma hit the island in 2017 and caused extensive damage.

GEOGRAPHY

Location: Caribbean, island between the Caribbean Sea and the North Atlantic Ocean; located in the Leeward Islands (northern) group; Saint Barthelemy lies east of the US Virgin Islands

Geographic coordinates: 17 90 N, 62 85 W

Map references: Central America and the Caribbean

Area: *total:* 25 sq km
land: 25 sq km
water: negligible
comparison ranking: total 237

Area - comparative: less than one-eighth the size of Washington, DC

Land boundaries: *total:* 0 km

Climate: tropical, with practically no variation in temperature; has two seasons (dry and humid)

Terrain: hilly, almost completely surrounded by shallow-water reefs, with plentiful beaches

Elevation: *highest point:* Morne du Vitet 286 m
lowest point: Caribbean Ocean 0 m

Natural resources: few natural resources; beaches foster tourism

Population distribution: most of the populace concentrated in and around the capital of Gustavia, but scattered settlements exist around the island periphery

Geography - note: a 1,200-hectare marine nature reserve, the Reserve Naturelle, is made up of five zones around the island that form a network to protect the island's coral reefs, seagrass, and endangered marine species

PEOPLE AND SOCIETY

Population: *total:* 7,086
male: 3,737
female: 3,349 (2024 est.)
comparison rankings: female 225; male 225; total 225

Ethnic groups: French, Portuguese, Caribbean, Afro-Caribbean

Languages: French (primary), English
major-language sample(s):
The World Factbook, une source indispensable d'informations de base. (French)

Religions: Roman Catholic, Protestant, Jehovah's Witnesses

Age structure: *0-14 years:* 13.9% (male 506/female 479)
15-64 years: 63.1% (male 2,413/female 2,057)
65 years and over: 23% (2024 est.) (male 818/female 813)

Dependency ratios: *total dependency ratio:* 30.8
youth dependency ratio: 17.5
elderly dependency ratio: 13.3
potential support ratio: 7.5 (2021)

Median age: *total:* 47.4 years (2024 est.)
male: 47 years
female: 47.8 years
comparison ranking: total 6

Population growth rate: -0.11% (2024 est.)
comparison ranking: 204

Birth rate: 9.3 births/1,000 population (2024 est.)
comparison ranking: 195

Death rate: 9.5 deaths/1,000 population (2024 est.)
comparison ranking: 47

Net migration rate: -1 migrant(s)/1,000 population (2024 est.)
comparison ranking: 144

Population distribution: most of the populace concentrated in and around the capital of Gustavia, but scattered settlements exist around the island periphery

Sex ratio: *at birth:* 1.06 male(s)/female
0-14 years: 1.06 male(s)/female
15-64 years: 1.17 male(s)/female
65 years and over: 1.01 male(s)/female
total population: 1.12 male(s)/female (2024 est.)

Infant mortality rate: *total:* 6.5 deaths/1,000 live births (2024 est.)
male: 7.6 deaths/1,000 live births
female: 5.3 deaths/1,000 live births
comparison ranking: total 161

Life expectancy at birth: *total population:* 81 years (2024 est.)
male: 78 years
female: 84.2 years
comparison ranking: total population 47

Total fertility rate: 1.64 children born/woman (2024 est.)
comparison ranking: 173

Gross reproduction rate: 0.79 (2024 est.)

Drinking water source: *improved: urban:* 100% of population
total: 100% of population

Sanitation facility access: *improved: urban:* 100% of population
total: 100% of population

ENVIRONMENT

Environment - current issues: land-based pollution; urbanization; with no natural rivers or streams, fresh water is in short supply, especially in summer, and is provided by the desalination of sea water, the collection of rain water, or imported via water tanker; overfishing

Climate: tropical, with practically no variation in temperature; has two seasons (dry and humid)

GOVERNMENT

Country name: *conventional long form:* Overseas Collectivity of Saint Barthelemy
conventional short form: Saint Barthelemy
local long form: Collectivité d'outre mer de Saint-Barthélemy
local short form: Saint-Barthélemy
abbreviation: Saint-Barth (French)/ St. Barts or St. Barths (English)
etymology: explorer Christopher COLUMBUS named the island in honor of his brother Bartolomeo's namesake saint in 1493

Government type: parliamentary democracy (Territorial Council); overseas collectivity of France

Dependency status: overseas collectivity of France

Capital: *name:* Gustavia
geographic coordinates: 17 53 N, 62 51 W
time difference: UTC-4 (1 hour ahead of Washington, DC, during Standard Time)
etymology: named in honor of King Gustav III (1746-1792) of Sweden during whose reign the island was obtained from France in 1784; the name was retained when in 1878 the island was sold back to France

Independence: none (overseas collectivity of France)

National holiday: Fête de la Fédération, 14 July (1790); note - local holiday is St. Barthelemy Day, 24 August (1572)

Legal system: French civil law

Constitution: *history:* 4 October 1958 (French Constitution)
amendments: amendment procedures of France's constitution apply

Citizenship: see France

Suffrage: 18 years of age, universal

Executive branch: *chief of state:* President Emmanuel MACRON (since 14 May 2017), represented by Prefect Vincent BERTON (since 28 March 2022)
head of government: President of Territorial Council Xavier LEDEE (since 3 April 2022)
cabinet: Executive Council elected by the Territorial Council; note - there is also an advisory, economic, social, and cultural council
elections/appointments: French president directly elected by absolute majority popular vote in 2 rounds if needed for a 5-year term (eligible for a second term); prefect appointed by the French president on the advice of French Ministry of Interior; president of Territorial Council indirectly elected by its members for a 5-year term; election last held on 27 March 2022 (next to be held in 2027)
election results:
2022: Xavier LEDEE (Saint Barth United) elected president; Territorial Council vote - 13 votes for, 6 blank votes
2017: Bruno MAGRAS (Saint Barth First!) elected president; Territorial Council vote - 14 out of 19 votes

Legislative branch: *description:* unicameral Territorial Council (19 seats; members elected by absolute majority vote in the first-round vote and proportional representation vote in the second round; members serve 5-year terms); Saint Barthelemy indirectly elects 1 senator to the French Senate by an electoral college for a 6-year term and directly elects 1 deputy (shared with Saint Martin) to the French National Assembly
elections: Territorial Council - first round held on 20 March 2022 and second round held on 27 March 2022 (next to be held in 2027)
French Senate - election last held on 24 September 2023 (next to be held on 30 September 2026)
French National Assembly - election last held on 12 and 19 June 2022 (next to be held by June 2027)
election results: Territorial Council - percent of vote by party in first round - SBA 46.2%, Saint Barth Action Equilibre 27.1%, Unis pour Saint Barthelemy 26.8%; percent of vote by party in second round - Saint Barth Action Equilibre and Unis pour Saint Barthelemy 50.9%, SBA 49.2%, seats by party - Saint Barth Action Equilibre and Unis pour Saint Barthelemy 13, SBA 6; composition - men NA, women NA, percentage women NA%
French Senate - percent of vote by party - NA; seats by party - UMP 1
French National Assembly - percent of vote by party NA; seats by party - UMP 1

Political parties: All for Saint Barth (Tous pour Saint-Barth)
Saint Barth Action Equilibre
Saint Barth First! (Saint-Barth d'Abord!) or SBA (affiliated with France's Republican party, Les Republicans)
Saint Barth United (Unis pour Saint-Barthelemy)

International organization participation: ACS (associate), UPU

Diplomatic representation in the US: none (overseas collectivity of France)

Diplomatic representation from the US: *embassy:* none (overseas collectivity of France)

Flag description: the flag of France is used

National symbol(s): pelican

National anthem: *name:* "L'Hymne a St. Barthelemy" (Hymn to St. Barthelemy)
lyrics/music: Isabelle Massart DERAVIN/Michael VALENTI
note: local anthem in use since 1999; as a collectivity of France, "La Marseillaise" is official (see France)

ECONOMY

Economic overview: high-income French Caribbean territorial economy; duty-free luxury commerce and tourism industries; import-dependent for food, water, energy, and manufacturing; large Brazilian and Portuguese labor supply; environmentally fragile

Exports - partners: Nigeria 98%, Suriname 1%, France 0%, Switzerland 0%, Poland 0% (2022)
note: top five export partners based on percentage share of exports

Exports - commodities: refined petroleum, fruit juice, precious metal watches, beauty products, special pharmaceuticals (2022)
note: top five export commodities based on value in dollars

Imports - partners: Switzerland 37%, Italy 14%, Portugal 11%, Suriname 9%, Brazil 5% (2022)
note: top five import partners based on percentage share of imports

Imports - commodities: precious metal watches, base metal watches, jewelry, refined petroleum, cars (2022)
note: top five import commodities based on value in dollars

Exchange rates: euros (EUR) per US dollar -

Exchange rates: 0.925 (2023 est.)
0.95 (2022 est.)
0.845 (2021 est.)
0.876 (2020 est.)
0.893 (2019 est.)

ENERGY

Electricity access: *electrification - total population:* 100% (2021)

COMMUNICATIONS

Telecommunication systems: *general assessment:* fully integrated access; 4G and LTE services (2019)
domestic: direct dial capability with both fixed and wireless systems, 3 FM channels, no broadcasting (2018)
international: country code - 590; landing points for the SSCS and the Southern Caribbean Fiber submarine cables providing voice and data connectivity to numerous Caribbean Islands (2019)

Broadcast media: 2 local TV broadcasters; 5 FM radio channels (2021)

Internet country code: .bl; note - .gp, the Internet country code for Guadeloupe, and .fr, the Internet country code for France, might also be encountered

Internet users: *total:* 7,077 (2022 est.)
percent of population: 71.3% (2022 est.)
comparison ranking: total 220

TRANSPORTATION

Airports: 1 (2024)
comparison ranking: 212

Roadways: *total:* 40 km
comparison ranking: total 220

Transportation - note: nearest airport for international flights is Princess Juliana International Airport (SXM) located on Sint Maarten

MILITARY AND SECURITY

Military - note: defense is the responsibility of France

SAINT HELENA, ASCENSION, AND TRISTAN DA CUNHA

INTRODUCTION

Background: Saint Helena is a British Overseas Territory off the coast of Africa in the South Atlantic Ocean, and it consists of Saint Helena, Ascension Island, and the island group of Tristan da Cunha.

Saint Helena: The island was uninhabited when the Portuguese first discovered it in 1502, and the British garrisoned troops on Saint Helena during the 17th century. It acquired fame as the place of Napoleon BONAPARTE's exile from 1815 until his death in 1821, but its importance as a port of call declined after the opening of the Suez Canal in 1869. During the Anglo-Boer War in South Africa, several thousand Boer prisoners were confined on the island between 1900 and 1903.
Saint Helena is one of the most remote populated places in the world. The British Government committed to building an airport on Saint Helena in 2005. After more than a decade of delays and construction, a commercial air service to South Africa via Namibia was inaugurated in 2017. The weekly service to Saint Helena from Johannesburg via Windhoek in Namibia takes just over six hours (including the refueling stop in Windhoek) and replaces the mail ship that had made a five-day journey to the island every three weeks.

Ascension Island: This barren and uninhabited island was discovered and named by the Portuguese in 1503. The British garrisoned the island in 1815 to prevent a rescue of NAPOLEON from Saint Helena. It served as a provisioning station for the Royal Navy's West Africa Squadron on anti-slavery patrol. The island remained under Admiralty control until 1922, when it became a dependency of Saint Helena. During World War II, the UK permitted the US to construct an airfield on Ascension in support of transatlantic flights to Africa and anti-submarine operations in the South Atlantic. In the 1960s, the island became an important space tracking station for the US. In 1982, Ascension was an essential staging area for British forces during the Falklands War. It

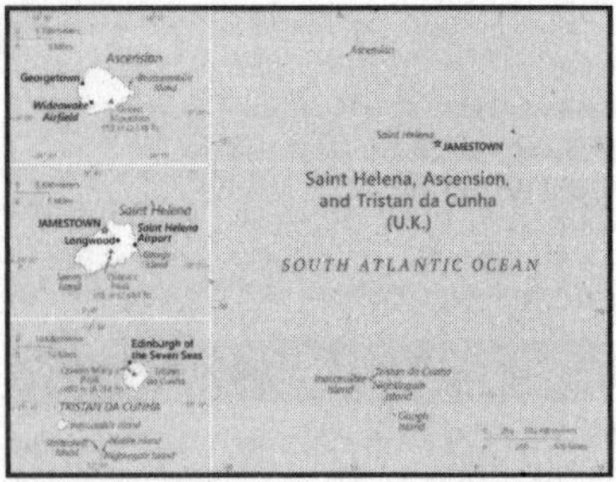

remains a critical refueling point in the air-bridge from the UK to the South Atlantic.

The island hosts one of four dedicated ground antennas that assist in the operation of the Global Positioning System (GPS) navigation system – the others are on Diego Garcia (British Indian Ocean Territory), Kwajalein (Marshall Islands), and at Cape Canaveral, Florida (US). NASA and the US Air Force also operate a Meter-Class Autonomous Telescope (MCAT) on Ascension as part of the deep space surveillance system for tracking orbital debris, which can be a hazard to spacecraft and astronauts.

Tristan da Cunha: The island group consists of Tristan da Cunha, Nightingale, Inaccessible, and Gough Islands. Tristan da Cunha, named after its Portuguese discoverer (1506), was garrisoned by the British in 1816 to prevent any attempt to rescue NAPOLEON from Saint Helena. Gough and Inaccessible Islands have been designated World Heritage Sites. South Africa leases a site for a meteorological station on Gough Island.

GEOGRAPHY

Location: islands in the South Atlantic Ocean, about midway between South America and Africa; Ascension Island lies 1,300 km (800 mi) northwest of Saint Helena; Tristan da Cunha lies 4,300 km (2,700 mi) southwest of Saint Helena

Geographic coordinates: Saint Helena: 15 57 S, 5 42 W;

Ascension Island: 7 57 S, 14 22 W;

Tristan da Cunha island group: 37 15 S, 12 30 W

Map references: Africa

Area: *total:* 394 sq km
land: 122 sq km Saint Helena Island
water: 0 sq km
88 sq km Ascension Island, 184 sq km Tristan da Cunha island group (includes Tristan (98 sq km), Inaccessible, Nightingale, and Gough islands)
comparison ranking: total 203

Area - comparative: slightly more than twice the size of Washington, DC

Land boundaries: *total:* 0 km

Coastline: Saint Helena: 60 km

Ascension Island: NA

Tristan da Cunha (island only): 34 km

Maritime claims: *territorial sea:* 12 nm
exclusive fishing zone: 200 nm

Climate: Saint Helena: tropical marine; mild, tempered by trade winds;

Ascension Island: tropical marine; mild, semi-arid;

Tristan da Cunha: temperate marine; mild, tempered by trade winds (tends to be cooler than Saint Helena)

Terrain: the islands of this group are of volcanic origin associated with the Atlantic Mid-Ocean Ridge

Saint Helena: rugged, volcanic; small scattered plateaus and plains;

Ascension: surface covered by lava flows and cinder cones of 44 dormant volcanoes; terrain rises to the east;

Tristan da Cunha: sheer cliffs line the coastline of the nearly circular island; the flanks of the central volcanic peak are deeply dissected; narrow coastal plain lies between The Peak and the coastal cliffs

Elevation: *highest point:* Queen Mary's Peak on Tristan da Cunha 2,060 m; Green Mountain on Ascension Island 859 m; Diana's Peak on Saint Helena Island 818 m
lowest point: Atlantic Ocean 0 m

Natural resources: fish, lobster

Land use: *agricultural land:* 30.8% (2018 est.)
arable land: 10.3% (2018 est.)
permanent crops: 0% (2018 est.)
permanent pasture: 20.5% (2018 est.)
forest: 5.1% (2018 est.)
other: 64.1% (2018 est.)

Irrigated land: 0 sq km (2022)

Population distribution: Saint Helena - population is concentrated in and around the capital Jamestown in the northwest, with another significant cluster in the interior Longwood area; Ascension - largest settlement, and location of most of the population, is Georgetown; Tristan da Cunha - most of the nearly 300 inhabitants live in the northern coastal town of Edinburgh of the Seven Seas

Natural hazards: active volcanism on Tristan da Cunha
volcanism: the island volcanoes of Tristan da Cunha (2,060 m) and Nightingale Island (365 m) experience volcanic activity; Tristan da Cunha erupted in 1962 and Nightingale in 2004

Geography - note: Saint Helena harbors at least 40 species of plants unknown elsewhere in the world; Ascension is a breeding ground for sea turtles and sooty terns; Queen Mary's Peak on Tristan da Cunha is the highest island mountain in the South Atlantic and a prominent landmark on the sea lanes around southern Africa

PEOPLE AND SOCIETY

Population: *total:* 7,943
male: 3,978
female: 3,965 (2024 est.)
comparison rankings: female 223; male 224; total 223

Nationality: *noun:* Saint Helenian(s)
adjective: Saint Helenian
note: referred to locally as "Saints"

Ethnic groups: St. Helena 82.1%, UK 7.6%, South Africa 3.6%, Ascension 2.8%, other 3.9% (2021 est.)
note: data represent population of Saint Helena by country of birth

Languages: English

Religions: Protestant 69.4% (includes Anglican 63.2%, Baptist 2.3%, Salvation Army 2%, Seventh Day Adventist 1.9%), Jehovah's Witness 3.8%, Roman Catholic 2.2%, New Apostolic 1.6%, other Christian 1.4%, other 1.1%, none 9%, unspecified 11.4% (2021 est.)
note: data represent Saint Helena only

Demographic profile: The vast majority of the population of Saint Helena, Ascension, and Tristan da Cunha live on Saint Helena. Ascension has no indigenous or permanent residents and is inhabited only by persons contracted to work on the island (mainly with the UK and US military or in the space and communications industries) or their dependents, while Tristan da Cunha – the main island in a small archipelago – has fewer than 300 residents. The population of Saint Helena consists of the descendants of 17th century British sailors and settlers from the East India Company, African slaves, and indentured servants and laborers from India, Indonesia, and China. Most of the population of Ascension are Saint Helenians, Britons, and Americans, while that of Tristan da Cunha descends from shipwrecked sailors and Saint Helenians.

Change in Saint Helena's population size is driven by net outward migration. Since the 1980s, Saint Helena's population steadily has shrunk and aged as the birth rate has decreased and many working-age residents left for better opportunities elsewhere. The restoration of British citizenship in 2002 accelerated family emigration; from 1998 to 2008 alone, population declined by about 20%.

In the 2010s, the population experienced some temporary growth, as foreigners and returning Saint Helenians, came to build an international airport, but numbers faded as the project reached completion and workers departed. With the airport fully operational, increased access to the remote island has the potential to boost tourism and fishing, provide more jobs for Saint Helenians domestically, and could encourage some ex-patriots to return home. In the meantime, however, Saint Helena, Ascension, and Tristan da Cunha have to contend with the needs of an aging population. The elderly population of the islands has risen from an estimated 9.4% in 1998 to 18% in 2022.

Age structure: *0-14 years:* 14.3% (male 579/female 556)
15-64 years: 66.5% (male 2,626/female 2,655)
65 years and over: 19.2% (2024 est.) (male 773/female 754)
2023 population pyramid:

Dependency ratios: *total dependency ratio:* 68.6
youth dependency ratio: 23.6
elderly dependency ratio: 45.1
potential support ratio: 2.2 (2021)

Median age: *total:* 45.1 years (2024 est.)
male: 44.8 years
female: 45.4 years
comparison ranking: total 21

Population growth rate: 0.1% (2024 est.)
comparison ranking: 186

Birth rate: 9.3 births/1,000 population (2024 est.)
comparison ranking: 196

Death rate: 8.3 deaths/1,000 population (2024 est.)
comparison ranking: 80

Net migration rate: 0 migrant(s)/1,000 population (2024 est.)
comparison ranking: 90

Population distribution: Saint Helena - population is concentrated in and around the capital Jamestown in the northwest, with another significant cluster in the interior Longwood area; Ascension - largest settlement, and location of most of the population, is Georgetown; Tristan da Cunha - most of the nearly 300 inhabitants live in the northern coastal town of Edinburgh of the Seven Seas

Urbanization: *urban population:* 40.7% of total population (2023)
rate of urbanization: 0.98% annual rate of change (2020-25 est.)

Major urban areas - population: 1,000 JAMESTOWN (capital) (2018)

Sex ratio: *at birth:* 1.06 male(s)/female
0-14 years: 1.04 male(s)/female
15-64 years: 0.99 male(s)/female
65 years and over: 1.03 male(s)/female
total population: 1 male(s)/female (2024 est.)

Infant mortality rate: *total:* 18.1 deaths/1,000 live births (2024 est.)
male: 21.7 deaths/1,000 live births
female: 14.2 deaths/1,000 live births
comparison ranking: total 86

Life expectancy at birth: *total population:* 80.9 years (2024 est.)
male: 78.1 years
female: 83.9 years
comparison ranking: total population 50

Total fertility rate: 1.61 children born/woman (2024 est.)
comparison ranking: 181

Gross reproduction rate: 0.78 (2024 est.)

Drinking water source: *improved:*
total: 99.1% of population
unimproved:
total: 0.9% of population (2020)

Sanitation facility access: *improved:*
total: 100% of population
unimproved:
total: 0% of population (2020)

ENVIRONMENT

Environment - current issues: development threatens unique biota on Saint Helena

Climate: Saint Helena: tropical marine; mild, tempered by trade winds;

Ascension Island: tropical marine; mild, semi-arid;

Tristan da Cunha: temperate marine; mild, tempered by trade winds (tends to be cooler than Saint Helena)

Urbanization: *urban population:* 40.7% of total population (2023)
rate of urbanization: 0.98% annual rate of change (2020-25 est.)

GOVERNMENT

Country name: *conventional long form:* Saint Helena, Ascension, and Tristan da Cunha
conventional short form: none
etymology: Saint Helena was discovered in 1502 by Galician navigator Joao da NOVA, sailing in the service of the Kingdom of Portugal, who named it "Santa Helena"; Ascension was named in 1503 by Portuguese navigator Afonso de ALBUQUERQUE who sighted the island on the Feast Day of the Ascension; Tristan da Cunha was discovered in 1506 by Portuguese explorer Tristao da CUNHA who christened the main island after himself (the name was subsequently anglicized)

Government type: parliamentary democracy

Dependency status: overseas territory of the UK

Capital: *name:* Jamestown
geographic coordinates: 15 56 S, 5 43 W
time difference: UTC 0 (5 hours ahead of Washington, DC, during Standard Time)
etymology: founded in 1659 and named after James, Duke of York, who would become King JAMES II of England (r. 1785-1788)

Administrative divisions: 3 administrative areas; Ascension, Saint Helena, Tristan da Cunha

Independence: none (overseas territory of the UK)

National holiday: Official birthday of King Charles III, April or June as designated by the governor

Legal system: English common law and local statutes

Constitution: *history:* several previous; latest effective 1 September 2009 (St Helena, Ascension and Tristan da Cunha Constitution Order 2009)

Citizenship: see United Kingdom

Suffrage: 18 years of age

Executive branch: *chief of state:* King CHARLES III (since 8 September 2022)
head of government: Governor Nigel PHILLIPS (since 13 August 2022)
cabinet: Executive Council consists of the governor, 3 ex-officio officers, and 5 elected members of the Legislative Council
elections/appointments: none; the monarchy is hereditary; governor appointed by the monarch
note: the constitution order provides for an administrator for Ascension and Tristan da Cunha, appointed by the governor

Legislative branch: *description:* unicameral Legislative Council (17 seats including the speaker and deputy speaker; 12 members directly elected in a single countrywide constituency by simple majority vote and 3 ex-officio members - the chief secretary, financial secretary, and attorney general; members serve 4-year terms)
elections: last held on 13 October 2021 (next to be held in 2025)
election results: vote - NA; seats - independent 12; composition - men 8, women 6, percent women 42.9%
note: the Constitution Order provides for separate Island Councils for both Ascension and Tristan da Cunha

Judicial branch: *highest court(s):* Court of Appeal (consists of the court president and 2 justices); Supreme Court (consists of the chief justice - a nonresident - and NA judges); note - appeals beyond the Court of Appeal are heard by the Judicial Committee of the Privy Council (in London)
judge selection and term of office: Court of Appeal and Supreme Court justices appointed by the governor acting upon the instructions from a secretary of state acting on behalf of King CHARLES III; justices of both courts serve until retirement at age 70, but terms can be extended
subordinate courts: Magistrates' Court; Small Claims Court; Juvenile Court

Political parties: none

International organization participation: UPU

Diplomatic representation in the US: none (overseas territory of the UK)

Diplomatic representation from the US: *embassy:* none (overseas territory of the UK)

Flag description: blue with the flag of the UK in the upper hoist-side quadrant and the Saint Helenian shield centered on the outer half of the flag; the upper third of the shield depicts a white plover (wire bird) on a yellow field; the remainder of the shield depicts a rocky coastline on the left, offshore is a three-masted sailing ship with sails furled but flying an English flag

National symbol(s): Saint Helena plover (bird)

Coat of Arms of Saint Helena: National anthem: note: as an overseas territory of the UK, "God Save the King" is official (see United Kingdom)

ECONOMY

Economic overview: upper middle-income, British Atlantic Ocean territorial economy; native (but pegged to British pound) currency user on 2 of 3 islands; significant UK financial support; unique land/farming commune structure; military-related economic activity; sport fishing locale

Agricultural products: coffee, corn, potatoes, vegetables; fish, lobster; livestock; timber

Industries: construction, crafts (furniture, lacework, fancy woodwork), fishing, collectible postage stamps

Exports - partners: US 55%, Netherlands 17%, Singapore 10%, Japan 8%, Senegal 2% (2022)
note: top five export partners based on percentage share of exports

Exports - commodities: fish, shellfish, iron alloys, glass working machines, corn (2022)
note: top five export commodities based on value in dollars

Imports - partners: UK 44%, South Africa 25%, US 21%, Czechia 4%, Namibia 2% (2022)
note: top five import partners based on percentage share of imports

Imports - commodities: asphalt, baked goods, air pumps, plastic products, iron sheet piling (2022)
note: top five import commodities based on value in dollars

Exchange rates: Saint Helena pounds (SHP) per US dollar -

Exchange rates: 0.805 (2023 est.)
0.811 (2022 est.)
0.727 (2021 est.)
0.78 (2020 est.)
0.783 (2019 est.)

ENERGY

Electricity access: *electrification - total population:* 100% (2021)

Electricity: *installed generating capacity:* 8,000 kW (2022 est.)
consumption: 6.963 million kWh (2022 est.)
transmission/distribution losses: 1.5 million kWh (2022 est.)
comparison rankings: transmission/distribution losses 4; consumption 210; installed generating capacity 209

Electricity generation sources: *fossil fuels:* 100% of total installed capacity (2022 est.)

Coal: *imports:* 69.9 metric tons (2022 est.)

Petroleum: *refined petroleum consumption:* 81 bbl/day (2022 est.)

Carbon dioxide emissions: 13,000 metric tonnes of CO2 (2022 est.)
from petroleum and other liquids: 13,000 metric tonnes of CO2 (2022 est.)
comparison ranking: total emissions 215

Energy consumption per capita: (2019)

COMMUNICATIONS

Telephones - fixed lines: *total subscriptions:* 4,000 (2021 est.)
subscriptions per 100 inhabitants: 74 (2021 est.)
comparison ranking: total subscriptions 207

Telephones - mobile cellular: *total subscriptions:* 4,000 (2021 est.)
subscriptions per 100 inhabitants: 74 (2021 est.)
comparison ranking: total subscriptions 223

Telecommunication systems: *general assessment:* capability to communicate worldwide; ADSL-broadband service; LTE coverage of 95% of population, includes voice calls, text messages, mobile data as well as inbound and outbound roaming; Wi-Fi hotspots in Jamestown, 1 ISP, many services are not offered locally but made available for visitors; some sun outages due to the reliance of international telephone and Internet communication relying on single satellite link (2020)
domestic: automatic digital network; fixed-line is 74 per 100 and mobile-cellular is 74 per 100 persons (2021)
international: country code (Saint Helena) - 290, (Ascension Island) - 247; landing point for the SaEx1 submarine cable providing connectivity to South Africa, Brazil, Virginia Beach (US) and islands in Saint Helena, Ascension and Tristan de Cunha; international direct dialing; satellite voice and data communications; satellite earth stations - 5 (Ascension Island - 4, Saint Helena - 1) (2019)

Broadcast media: Saint Helena has no local TV station; 2 local radio stations, one of which is relayed to Ascension Island; satellite TV stations rebroadcast terrestrially; Ascension Island has no local TV station but has 1 local radio station and receives relays of broadcasts from 1 radio station on Saint Helena; broadcasts from the British Forces Broadcasting Service (BFBS) are available, as well as TV services for the US military; Tristan da Cunha has 1 local radio station and receives BFBS TV and radio broadcasts

Internet country code: .sh; note - Ascension Island assigned .ac

Internet users: *total:* 2,287 (2021 est.)
percent of population: 37.6% (2021 est.)
comparison ranking: total 227

Broadband - fixed subscriptions: *total:* 1,000 (2018 est.)
subscriptions per 100 inhabitants: 17 (2020 est.)
comparison ranking: total 205

Communications - note: Ascension Island hosts one of four dedicated ground antennas that assist in the operation of the Global Positioning System (GPS) navigation system (the others are on Diego Garcia (British Indian Ocean Territory), Kwajalein (Marshall Islands), and at Cape Canaveral, Florida (US)); South Africa maintains a meteorological station on Gough Island in the Tristan da Cunha archipelago

TRANSPORTATION

Civil aircraft registration country code prefix: VQ-H

Airports: 2 (2024)
comparison ranking: 197

Heliports: 2 (2024)

Roadways: *total:* 198 km (Saint Helena 138 km, Ascension 40 km, Tristan da Cunha 20 km)
paved: 168 km (Saint Helena 118 km, Ascension 40 km, Tristan da Cunha 10 km)
unpaved: 30 km (2002) (Saint Helena 20 km, Tristan da Cunha 10 km)
comparison ranking: total 210

Ports: *total ports:* 4 (2024)
large: 1
medium: 1
small: 1
very small: 1
ports with oil terminals: 2
key ports: Edinburgh of the Seven Seas, Georgetown, Jamestown, North Point

Transportation - note: the new airport on Saint Helena opened for limited operations in July 2016, and the first commercial flight took place on 14 October 2017, marking the start of weekly air service between Saint Helena and South Africa via Namibia; the military airport on Ascension Island is closed to civilian traffic; there is no air connection to Tristan da Cunha and very limited sea connections making it one of the most isolated communities on the planet

MILITARY AND SECURITY

Military - note: defense is the responsibility of the UK

SAINT KITTS AND NEVIS

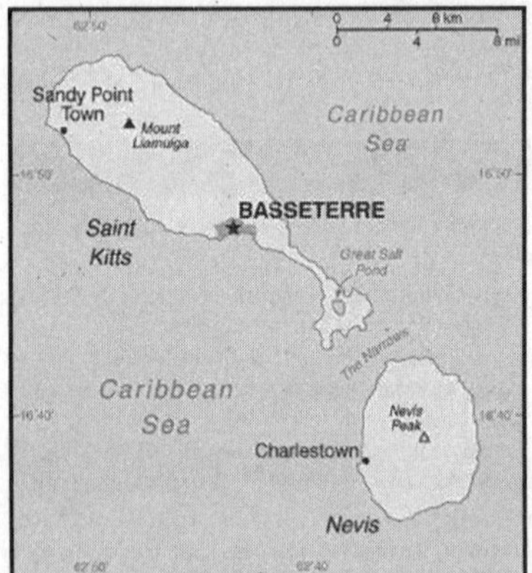

INTRODUCTION

Background: Carib Indians occupied the islands of the West Indies for hundreds of years before the British and French began settlement in 1623. During the 17th century, Saint Kitts became the premier base for British and French expansion into the Caribbean. The French ceded the territory to the UK in 1713. At the turn of the 18th century, Saint Kitts was the richest British Crown Colony per capita in the Caribbean, a result of the sugar trade. Although small in size and separated by only 3 km (2 mi) of water, Saint Kitts and Nevis were viewed and governed as different states until the late-19th century, when the British forcibly unified them along with the island of Anguilla. In 1967, the island territory of Saint Christopher-Nevis-Anguilla became an associated state of the UK with full internal autonomy. The island of Anguilla rebelled and was allowed to secede in 1971. The remaining islands achieved independence in 1983 as Saint Kitts and Nevis. In 1998, a referendum on Nevis to separate from Saint Kitts fell short of the necessary two-thirds majority.

GEOGRAPHY

Location: Caribbean, islands in the Caribbean Sea, about one-third of the way from Puerto Rico to Trinidad and Tobago

Geographic coordinates: 17 20 N, 62 45 W

Map references: Central America and the Caribbean

Area: *total:* 261 sq km (Saint Kitts 168 sq km; Nevis 93 sq km)
land: 261 sq km
water: 0 sq km
comparison ranking: total 211

Area - comparative: 1.5 times the size of Washington, DC

Land boundaries: *total:* 0 km

Coastline: 135 km

Maritime claims: *territorial sea:* 12 nm
contiguous zone: 24 nm
exclusive economic zone: 200 nm
continental shelf: 200 nm or to the edge of the continental margin

Climate: tropical, tempered by constant sea breezes; little seasonal temperature variation; rainy season (May to November)

Terrain: volcanic with mountainous interiors

Elevation: *highest point:* Mount Liamuiga 1,156 m
lowest point: Caribbean Sea 0 m

Natural resources: arable land

Land use: *agricultural land:* 23.1% (2018 est.)
arable land: 19.2% (2018 est.)
permanent crops: 0.4% (2018 est.)
permanent pasture: 3.5% (2018 est.)
forest: 42.3% (2018 est.)
other: 34.6% (2018 est.)

Irrigated land: 8 sq km (2012)

Population distribution: population clusters are found in the small towns located on the periphery of both islands

Natural hazards: hurricanes (July to October)
volcanism: Mount Liamuiga (1,156 m) on Saint Kitts, and Nevis Peak (985 m) on Nevis, are both volcanoes that are part of the volcanic island arc of the Lesser Antilles, which extends from Saba in the north to Grenada in the south

Geography - note: smallest country in the Western Hemisphere both in terms of area and population;

with coastlines in the shape of a baseball bat and ball, the two volcanic islands are separated by a 3-km-wide channel called The Narrows; on the southern tip of baseball-bat-shaped Saint Kitts lies the Great Salt Pond; Nevis Peak sits in the center of its almost circular namesake island and its ball shape complements that of its sister island

PEOPLE AND SOCIETY

Population: *total:* 55,133
male: 27,599
female: 27,534 (2024 est.)
comparison rankings: female 207; male 207; total 207

Nationality: *noun:* Kittitian(s), Nevisian(s)
adjective: Kittitian, Nevisian

Ethnic groups: African descent 92.5%, mixed 3%, White 2.1%, East Indian 1.5%, other 0.6%, unspecified 0.3% (2001 est.)

Languages: English (official)

Religions: Protestant 75.6% (includes Anglican 16.6%, Methodist 15.8%, Pentecostal 10.8%, Church of God 7.4%, Baptist 5.4%, Seventh Day Adventist 5.4%, Wesleyan Holiness 5.3%, Moravian 4.8%, Evangelical 2.1%, Brethren 1.7%, Presbyterian 0.3%), Roman Catholic 5.9%, Hindu 1.8%, Jehovah's Witness 1.4%, Rastafarian 1.3%, other 5%, none 8.8%, unspecified 0.1% (2011 est.)

Age structure: *0-14 years:* 19.2% (male 5,314/female 5,277)
15-64 years: 68.1% (male 18,944/female 18,575)
65 years and over: 12.7% (2024 est.) (male 3,341/female 3,682)

Dependency ratios: *total dependency ratio:* 41.7
youth dependency ratio: 28
elderly dependency ratio: 13.7
potential support ratio: 7.3 (2021)

Median age: *total:* 38.6 years (2024 est.)
male: 38.8 years
female: 38.3 years
comparison ranking: total 72

Population growth rate: 0.56% (2024 est.)
comparison ranking: 147

Birth rate: 11.8 births/1,000 population (2024 est.)
comparison ranking: 153

Death rate: 7.4 deaths/1,000 population (2024 est.)
comparison ranking: 106

Net migration rate: 1.1 migrant(s)/1,000 population (2024 est.)
comparison ranking: 64

Population distribution: population clusters are found in the small towns located on the periphery of both islands

Urbanization: *urban population:* 31.1% of total population (2023)
rate of urbanization: 1.06% annual rate of change (2020-25 est.)

Major urban areas - population: 14,000 BASSETERRE (capital) (2018)

Sex ratio: *at birth:* 1.02 male(s)/female
0-14 years: 1.01 male(s)/female
15-64 years: 1.02 male(s)/female
65 years and over: 0.91 male(s)/female
total population: 1 male(s)/female (2024 est.)

Infant mortality rate: *total:* 8 deaths/1,000 live births (2024 est.)
male: 5.5 deaths/1,000 live births
female: 10.6 deaths/1,000 live births
comparison ranking: total 147

Life expectancy at birth: *total population:* 77.6 years (2024 est.)
male: 75.2 years
female: 80.1 years
comparison ranking: total population 89

Total fertility rate: 1.76 children born/woman (2024 est.)
comparison ranking: 146

Gross reproduction rate: 0.87 (2024 est.)

Drinking water source: *improved: urban:* 98.3% of population
rural: 98.3% of population
total: 98.3% of population
unimproved: urban: 1.7% of population
rural: 1.7% of population
total: 1.7% of population (2015 est.)

Current health expenditure: 5.4% of GDP (2020)

Physician density: 2.77 physicians/1,000 population (2018)

Hospital bed density: 4.8 beds/1,000 population (2012)

Sanitation facility access: *improved: urban:* 87.3% of population
rural: 87.3% of population
total: 87.3% of population
unimproved: urban: 12.7% of population
rural: 12.7% of population
total: 12.7% of population (2017 est.)

Obesity - adult prevalence rate: 22.9% (2016)
comparison ranking: 71

Alcohol consumption per capita: *total:* 8.84 liters of pure alcohol (2019 est.)
beer: 3.73 liters of pure alcohol (2019 est.)
wine: 1.02 liters of pure alcohol (2019 est.)
spirits: 3.89 liters of pure alcohol (2019 est.)
other alcohols: 0.21 liters of pure alcohol (2019 est.)
comparison ranking: total 36

Currently married women (ages 15-49): 57.2% (2023 est.)

Education expenditures: 2.5% of GDP (2021 est.)
comparison ranking: 176

Literacy: *total population:* NA
male: NA
female: NA

School life expectancy (primary to tertiary education): *total:* 17 years
male: 16 years
female: 19 years (2015)

ENVIRONMENT

Environment - current issues: deforestation; soil erosion and silting affects marine life on coral reefs; water pollution from uncontrolled dumping of sewage

Environment - international agreements: *party to:* Biodiversity, Climate Change, Climate Change-Kyoto Protocol, Climate Change-Paris Agreement, Comprehensive Nuclear Test Ban, Desertification, Endangered Species, Hazardous Wastes, Law of the Sea, Marine Dumping-London Protocol, Ozone Layer Protection, Ship Pollution, Whaling
signed, but not ratified: none of the selected agreements

Climate: tropical, tempered by constant sea breezes; little seasonal temperature variation; rainy season (May to November)

Urbanization: *urban population:* 31.1% of total population (2023)
rate of urbanization: 1.06% annual rate of change (2020-25 est.)

Revenue from forest resources: 0% of GDP (2018 est.)
comparison ranking: 193

Revenue from coal: 0% of GDP (2018 est.)
comparison ranking: 111

Air pollutants: *particulate matter emissions:* 8.05 micrograms per cubic meter (2019 est.)
carbon dioxide emissions: 0.24 megatons (2016 est.)
methane emissions: 0.1 megatons (2020 est.)

Waste and recycling: *municipal solid waste generated annually:* 32,892 tons (2015 est.)

Total water withdrawal: *municipal:* 20 million cubic meters (2020 est.)
industrial: 0 cubic meters (2017 est.)
agricultural: 200,000 cubic meters (2017 est.)

Total renewable water resources: 20 million cubic meters (2020 est.)

GOVERNMENT

Country name: *conventional long form:* Federation of Saint Kitts and Nevis
conventional short form: Saint Kitts and Nevis
former: Federation of Saint Christopher and Nevis
etymology: Saint Kitts was, and still is, referred to as Saint Christopher and this name was well established by the 17th century (although who first applied the name is unclear); in the 17th century a common nickname for Christopher was Kit or Kitt, so the island began to be referred to as "Saint Kitt's Island" or just "Saint Kitts"; Nevis is derived from the original Spanish name "Nuestra Senora de las Nieves" (Our Lady of the Snows) and refers to the white halo of clouds that generally wreathes Nevis Peak
note: Nevis is pronounced nee-vis

Government type: federal parliamentary democracy under a constitutional monarchy; a Commonwealth realm

Capital: *name:* Basseterre
geographic coordinates: 17 18 N, 62 43 W
time difference: UTC-4 (1 hour ahead of Washington, DC, during Standard Time)
etymology: the French name translates as "low land" in English; the reference is to the city's low-lying location within a valley, as well as to the fact that the city is on the leeward (downwind) part of the island, and is thus a safe anchorage

Administrative divisions: 14 parishes; Christ Church Nichola Town, Saint Anne Sandy Point, Saint George Basseterre, Saint George Gingerland, Saint James Windward, Saint John Capesterre, Saint John Figtree, Saint Mary Cayon, Saint Paul Capesterre, Saint Paul Charlestown, Saint Peter Basseterre, Saint Thomas Lowland, Saint Thomas Middle Island, Trinity Palmetto Point

Independence: 19 September 1983 (from the UK)

National holiday: Independence Day, 19 September (1983)

Legal system: English common law

Constitution: *history:* several previous (preindependence); latest presented 22 June 1983, effective 23 June 1983
amendments: proposed by the National Assembly; passage requires approval by at least two-thirds majority vote of the total Assembly membership

and assent of the governor general; amendments to constitutional provisions such as the sovereignty of the federation, fundamental rights and freedoms, the judiciary, and the Nevis Island Assembly also require approval in a referendum by at least two thirds of the votes cast in Saint Kitts and in Nevis

International law organization participation: has not submitted an ICJ jurisdiction declaration; accepts ICCt jurisdiction

Citizenship: *citizenship by birth:* yes
citizenship by descent only: yes
dual citizenship recognized: yes
residency requirement for naturalization: 14 years

Suffrage: 18 years of age; universal

Executive branch: *chief of state:* King CHARLES III (since 8 September 2022); represented by Governor General Marcella LIBURD (since 1 February 2023)
head of government: Prime Minister Dr. Terrance DREW (since 6 August 2022)
cabinet: Cabinet appointed by governor general in consultation with prime minister
elections/appointments: the monarchy is hereditary; governor general appointed by the monarch; following legislative elections, the leader of the majority party or majority coalition usually appointed prime minister by governor general; deputy prime minister appointed by governor general

Legislative branch: *description:* unicameral National Assembly (15 seats, including the attorney general; 11 members directly elected in single-seat constituencies by simple majority vote and 3 appointed by the governor general - 2 on the advice of the prime minister and the third on the advice of the opposition leader; members serve 5-year terms)
elections: last held on 5 August 2022 (next to be held on 2027)
election results: percent of vote by party - SKNLP 44.4%, PLP 16.1%, PAM 16.2%, CCM 12.7%, other 10.6%; seats by party - SKNLP 6, CCM 3, PLP 1, CCM 1; composition - men 11, women 5, percentage women 31.3%

Judicial branch: *highest court(s):* the Eastern Caribbean Supreme Court (ECSC) is the superior court of the Organization of Eastern Caribbean States; the ECSC - headquartered on St. Lucia - consists of the Court of Appeal - headed by the chief justice and 4 judges - and the High Court with 18 judges; the Court of Appeal is itinerant, traveling to member states on a schedule to hear appeals from the High Court and subordinate courts; High Court judges reside in the member states, with 2 assigned to Saint Kitts and Nevis; note - the ECSC in 2003 replaced the Judicial Committee of the Privy Council (in London) as the final court of appeal on Saint Kitts and Nevis; Saint Kitts and Nevis is also a member of the Caribbean Court of Justice
judge selection and term of office: chief justice of Eastern Caribbean Supreme Court appointed by His Majesty, King Charles III; other justices and judges appointed by the Judicial and Legal Services Commission, an independent body of judicial officials; Court of Appeal justices appointed for life with mandatory retirement at age 65; High Court judges appointed for life with mandatory retirement at age 62
subordinate courts: magistrates' courts

Political parties: Concerned Citizens Movement or CCM
Nevis Reformation Party or NRP
People's Action Movement or PAM
People's Labour Party or PLP
Saint Kitts and Nevis Labor Party or SKNLP

International organization participation: ACP, ACS, AOSIS, C, Caricom, CDB, CELAC, FAO, G-77, IBRD, ICAO, ICCt, ICRM, IDA, IFAD, IFC, IFRCS, ILO, IMF, IMO, Interpol, IOC, ITU, MIGA, OAS, OECS, OPANAL, OPCW, Petrocaribe, UN, UNCTAD, UNESCO, UNIDO, UPU, WHO, WIPO, WTO

Diplomatic representation in the US: *chief of mission:* Ambassador Jacinth HENRY-MARTIN (since 15 September 2023)
chancery: 1203 19th St. NW, 5th Floor, Washington, DC 20036
telephone: [1] (202) 686-2636
FAX: [1] (202) 686-5740
email address and website:
stkittsnevis@embskn.com
Embassy of St.Kitts and Nevis to the USA – and Permanent Mission to the OAS (embassydc.gov.kn)
consulate(s) general: Los Angeles, New York

Diplomatic representation from the US: *embassy:* the US does not have an embassy in Saint Kitts and Nevis; the US Ambassador to Barbados is accredited to Saint Kitts and Nevis

Flag description: divided diagonally from the lower hoist side by a broad black band bearing two white, five-pointed stars; the black band is edged in yellow; the upper triangle is green, the lower triangle is red; green signifies the island's fertility, red symbolizes the struggles of the people from slavery, yellow denotes year-round sunshine, and black represents the African heritage of the people; the white stars stand for the islands of Saint Kitts and Nevis, but can also express hope and liberty, or independence and optimism

National symbol(s): brown pelican, royal poinciana (flamboyant) tree; national colors: green, yellow, red, black, white

National anthem: *name:* "Oh Land of Beauty!"
lyrics/music: Kenrick Anderson GEORGES
note: adopted 1983

National heritage: *total World Heritage Sites:* 1 (cultural)
selected World Heritage Site locales: Brimstone Hill Fortress National Park

ECONOMY

Economic overview: high-income, tourism-based Caribbean OECS economy; better debt balancing; CARICOM and ECCU member; growing offshore financial and telecommunications hub; environmentally fragile; unique citizenship-driven growth model

Real GDP (purchasing power parity): $1.438 billion (2023 est.)
$1.39 billion (2022 est.)
$1.258 billion (2021 est.)
note: data in 2021 dollars
comparison ranking: 204

Real GDP growth rate: 3.43% (2023 est.)
10.52% (2022 est.)
0.48% (2021 est.)
note: annual GDP % growth based on constant local currency
comparison ranking: 94

Real GDP per capita: $30,100 (2023 est.)
$29,200 (2022 est.)
$26,400 (2021 est.)
note: data in 2021 dollars
comparison ranking: 77

GDP (official exchange rate): $1.077 billion (2023 est.)
note: data in current dollars at official exchange rate

Inflation rate (consumer prices): 3.56% (2023 est.)
2.67% (2022 est.)
1.2% (2021 est.)
note: annual % change based on consumer prices
comparison ranking: 69

GDP - composition, by sector of origin: *agriculture:* 1.4% (2023 est.)
industry: 19.8% (2023 est.)
services: 64.9% (2023 est.)
note: figures may not total 100% due to non-allocated consumption not captured in sector-reported data
comparison rankings: services 57; industry 138; agriculture 175

GDP - composition, by end use: *household consumption:* 41.4% (2017 est.)
government consumption: 25.9% (2017 est.)
investment in fixed capital: 30.8% (2017 est.)
exports of goods and services: 62.5% (2017 est.)
imports of goods and services: -60.4% (2017 est.)

Agricultural products: coconuts, tropical fruits, root vegetables, vegetables, eggs, pulses, tomatoes, beef, sweet potatoes, watermelons (2022)
note: top ten agricultural products based on tonnage

Industries: tourism, cotton, salt, copra, clothing, footwear, beverages

Industrial production growth rate: -2.4% (2023 est.)
note: annual % change in industrial value added based on constant local currency
comparison ranking: 186

Remittances: 3.48% of GDP (2023 est.)
3.83% of GDP (2022 est.)
4.32% of GDP (2021 est.)
note: personal transfers and compensation between resident and non-resident individuals/households/entities

Budget: *revenues:* $262 million (2020 est.)
expenditures: $236.444 million (2020 est.)
note: central government revenues and expenses (excluding grants/extrabudgetary units/social security funds) converted to US dollars at average official exchange rate for year indicated

Public debt: 62.9% of GDP (2017 est.)
note: central government debt as a % of GDP
comparison ranking: 71

Taxes and other revenues: 15.04% (of GDP) (2020 est.)
note: central government tax revenue as a % of GDP
comparison ranking: 139

Current account balance: -$143.262 million (2023 est.)
-$105.744 million (2022 est.)
-$43.725 million (2021 est.)
note: balance of payments - net trade and primary/secondary income in current dollars
comparison ranking: 103

Exports: $577.568 million (2023 est.)
$546.373 million (2022 est.)
$389.355 million (2021 est.)
note: balance of payments - exports of goods and services in current dollars
comparison ranking: 190

Exports - partners: US 61%, India 7%, Trinidad and Tobago 5%, Germany 4%, Canada 3% (2022)

note: top five export partners based on percentage share of exports

Exports - commodities: measuring instruments, broadcasting equipment, electrical transformers, electrical control boards, ships (2022)
note: top five export commodities based on value in dollars

Imports: $674.134 million (2023 est.)
$606.301 million (2022 est.)
$407.417 million (2021 est.)
note: balance of payments - imports of goods and services in current dollars
comparison ranking: 198

Imports - partners: US 47%, Italy 9%, Turkey 6%, Trinidad and Tobago 6%, China 5% (2022)
note: top five import partners based on percentage share of imports

Imports - commodities: ships, refined petroleum, plastic products, cars, jewelry (2022)
note: top five import commodities based on value in dollars

Reserves of foreign exchange and gold: $286.075 million (2023 est.)
$293.98 million (2022 est.)
$337.533 million (2021 est.)
note: holdings of gold (year-end prices)/foreign exchange/special drawing rights in current dollars
comparison ranking: 168

Exchange rates: East Caribbean dollars (XCD) per US dollar -

Exchange rates: 2.7 (2023 est.)
2.7 (2022 est.)
2.7 (2021 est.)
2.7 (2020 est.)
2.7 (2019 est.)

ENERGY

Electricity access: *electrification - total population:* 100% (2022 est.)

Electricity: *installed generating capacity:* 72,000 kW (2022 est.)
consumption: 177.455 million kWh (2022 est.)
transmission/distribution losses: 39.522 million kWh (2022 est.)
comparison rankings: transmission/distribution losses 32; consumption 190; installed generating capacity 190

Electricity generation sources: *fossil fuels:* 97.2% of total installed capacity (2022 est.)
wind: 2.8% of total installed capacity (2022 est.)

Petroleum: *refined petroleum consumption:* 2,000 bbl/day (2022 est.)

Carbon dioxide emissions: 272,000 metric tonnes of CO_2 (2022 est.)
from petroleum and other liquids: 272,000 metric tonnes of CO_2 (2022 est.)
comparison ranking: total emissions 200

Energy consumption per capita: 77.743 million Btu/person (2022 est.)
comparison ranking: 66

COMMUNICATIONS

Telephones - fixed lines: *total subscriptions:* 16,000 (2021 est.)
subscriptions per 100 inhabitants: 33 (2021 est.)
comparison ranking: total subscriptions 180

Telephones - mobile cellular: *total subscriptions:* 57,000 (2021 est.)
subscriptions per 100 inhabitants: 119 (2021 est.)
comparison ranking: total subscriptions 206

Telecommunication systems: *general assessment:* good interisland and international connections; broadband access; expanded FttP (Fiber to the Home) and LTE markets; regulatory development; telecom sector contributes greatly to the overall GDP; telecom sector is a growth area (2020)
domestic: fixed-line teledensity is 33 per 100 persons; mobile-cellular teledensity is 120 per 100 persons (2021)
international: country code - 1-869; landing points for the ECFS, Southern Caribbean Fiber and the SSCS submarine cables providing connectivity for numerous Caribbean Islands (2019)

Broadcast media: the government operates a national TV network that broadcasts on 2 channels; cable subscription services provide access to local and international channels; the government operates a national radio network; a mix of government-owned and privately owned broadcasters operate roughly 15 radio stations (2019)

Internet country code: .kn

Internet users: *total:* 37,920 (2021 est.)
percent of population: 79% (2021 est.)
comparison ranking: total 205

Broadband - fixed subscriptions: *total:* 30,000 (2020 est.)
subscriptions per 100 inhabitants: 56 (2020 est.)
comparison ranking: total 154

TRANSPORTATION

Civil aircraft registration country code prefix: V4

Airports: 2 (2024)
comparison ranking: 206

Heliports: 1 (2024)

Railways: *total:* 50 km (2008)
narrow gauge: 50 km (2008) 0.762-m gauge on Saint Kitts for tourists
comparison ranking: total 133

Roadways: *total:* 383 km
paved: 163 km
unpaved: 220 km (2002)
comparison ranking: total 202

Merchant marine: *total:* 341 (2023)
by type: bulk carrier 22, container ship 16, general cargo 85, oil tanker 59, other 159
comparison ranking: total 53

Ports: *total ports:* 2 (2024)
large: 0
medium: 0
small: 0
very small: 2
ports with oil terminals: 2
key ports: Basseterre, Charlestown

MILITARY AND SECURITY

Military and security forces: Ministry of National Security: St. Kitts and Nevis Defense Force (SKNDF), St. Kitts and Nevis Coast Guard, the Royal St. Christopher and Nevis Police Force (2024)
note: the Nevis Police Force includes the paramilitary Special Services Unit

Military and security service personnel strengths: less than 500 active personnel (2023)

Military equipment inventories and acquisitions: the SKNDF is lightly armed with equipment from Belgium, the UK, and the US (2024)

Military service age and obligation: 18 years of age for voluntary military service for men and women (under 18 with written parental permission); no conscription (2023)

Military - note: SKNDF's missions include defense of the country's territorial integrity and sovereignty, protecting natural resources, interdicting narcotics trafficking, and providing humanitarian relief as needed
St. Kitts joined the Caribbean Regional Security System (RSS) in 1984; RSS signatories (Antigua and Barbuda, Barbados, Dominica, Grenada, Guyana, Saint Lucia, and Saint Vincent and the Grenadines) agreed to prepare contingency plans and assist one another, on request, in national emergencies, prevention of smuggling, search and rescue, immigration control, fishery protection, customs and excise control, maritime policing duties, protection of off-shore installations, pollution control, national and other disasters, and threats to national security (2024)

TRANSNATIONAL ISSUES

Illicit drugs: a transit point for cocaine and marijuana destined for North America, Europe, and elsewhere in the Caribbean; some local demand for cocaine and some use of synthetic drugs

SAINT LUCIA

INTRODUCTION

Background: England and France contested Saint Lucia – with its fine natural harbor at Castries and burgeoning sugar industry – throughout the 17th and early 18th centuries, with possession changing 14 times; it was finally ceded to the UK in 1814 and became part of the British Windward Islands colony. Even after the abolition of slavery on its plantations in 1834, Saint Lucia remained an agricultural island, dedicated to producing tropical commodity crops. In the mid-20th century, Saint Lucia joined the West Indies Federation (1958–1962) and in 1967 became one of the six members of the West Indies Associated States, with internal self-government. In 1979, Saint Lucia gained full independence.

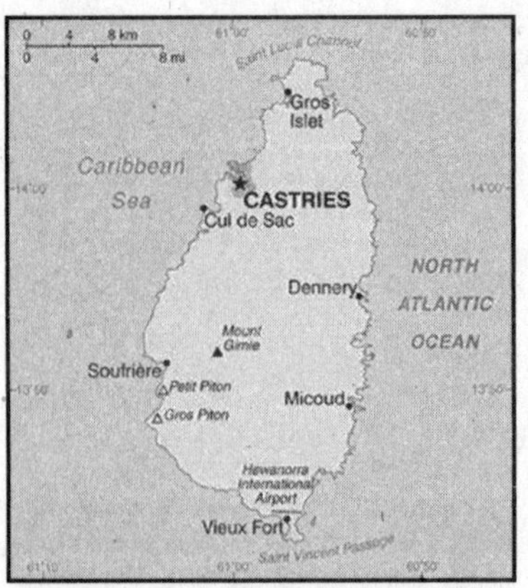

GEOGRAPHY

Location: Caribbean, island between the Caribbean Sea and North Atlantic Ocean, north of Trinidad and Tobago

Geographic coordinates: 13 53 N, 60 58 W

Map references: Central America and the Caribbean

Area: *total:* 616 sq km
land: 606 sq km
water: 10 sq km
comparison ranking: total 192

Area - comparative: three and a half times the size of Washington, DC

Land boundaries: *total:* 0 km

Coastline: 158 km

Maritime claims: *territorial sea:* 12 nm
contiguous zone: 24 nm
exclusive economic zone: 200 nm
continental shelf: 200 nm or to the edge of the continental margin

Climate: tropical, moderated by northeast trade winds; dry season January to April, rainy season May to August

Terrain: volcanic and mountainous with broad, fertile valleys

Elevation: *highest point:* Mount Gimie 948 m
lowest point: Caribbean Sea 0 m

Natural resources: forests, sandy beaches, minerals (pumice), mineral springs, geothermal potential

Land use: *agricultural land:* 17.4% (2018 est.)
arable land: 4.9% (2018 est.)
permanent crops: 11.5% (2018 est.)
permanent pasture: 1% (2018 est.)
forest: 77% (2018 est.)
other: 5.6% (2018 est.)

Irrigated land: 30 sq km (2012)

Population distribution: most of the population is found on the periphery of the island, with a larger concentration in the north around the capital of Castries

Natural hazards: hurricanes
volcanism: Mount Gimie (948 m), also known as Qualibou, is a caldera on the west of the island; the iconic twin pyramidal peaks of Gros Piton (771 m) and Petit Piton (743 m) are lava dome remnants associated with the Soufriere volcano; there have been no historical magmatic eruptions, but a minor steam eruption in 1766 spread a thin layer of ash over a wide area; Saint Lucia is part of the volcanic island arc of the Lesser Antilles that extends from Saba in the north to Grenada in the south

Geography - note: the twin Pitons (Gros Piton and Petit Piton), striking cone-shaped peaks south of Soufriere, are one of the scenic natural highlights of the Caribbean

PEOPLE AND SOCIETY

Population: *total:* 168,038
male: 81,517
female: 86,521 (2024 est.)
comparison rankings: female 185; male 186; total 186

Nationality: *noun:* Saint Lucian(s)
adjective: Saint Lucian

Ethnic groups: Black/African descent 85.3%, mixed 10.9%, East Indian 2.2%, other 1.6%, unspecified 0.1% (2010 est.)

Languages: English (official), Saint Lucian Creole

Religions: Roman Catholic 61.5%, Protestant 25.5% (includes Seventh Day Adventist 10.4%, Pentecostal 8.9%, Baptist 2.2%, Anglican 1.6%, Church of God 1.5%, other Protestant 0.9%), other Christian 3.4% (includes Evangelical 2.3% and Jehovah's Witness 1.1%), Rastafarian 1.9%, other 0.4%, none 5.9%, unspecified 1.4% (2010 est.)

Age structure: *0-14 years:* 17.9% (male 15,505/female 14,607)
15-64 years: 66.7% (male 54,260/female 57,747)
65 years and over: 15.4% (2024 est.) (male 11,752/female 14,167)

Dependency ratios: *total dependency ratio:* 37.7
youth dependency ratio: 25.2
elderly dependency ratio: 12.5
potential support ratio: 8 (2021 est.)

Median age: *total:* 39.7 years (2024 est.)
male: 38.4 years
female: 40.9 years
comparison ranking: total 65

Population growth rate: 0.26% (2024 est.)
comparison ranking: 171

Birth rate: births/1,000 population (2024 est.)
comparison ranking: 159

Death rate: 8.3 deaths/1,000 population (2024 est.)
comparison ranking: 78

Net migration rate: -0.6 migrant(s)/1,000 population (2024 est.)
comparison ranking: 128

Population distribution: most of the population is found on the periphery of the island, with a larger concentration in the north around the capital of Castries

Urbanization: *urban population:* 19.2% of total population (2023)
rate of urbanization: 0.98% annual rate of change (2020-25 est.)

Major urban areas - population: 22,000 CASTRIES (capital) (2018)

Sex ratio: *at birth:* 1.06 male(s)/female
0-14 years: 1.06 male(s)/female
15-64 years: 0.94 male(s)/female
65 years and over: 0.83 male(s)/female
total population: 0.94 male(s)/female (2024 est.)

Maternal mortality ratio: 73 deaths/100,000 live births (2020 est.)
comparison ranking: 82

Infant mortality rate: *total:* 11.5 deaths/1,000 live births (2024 est.)
male: 10.8 deaths/1,000 live births
female: 12.2 deaths/1,000 live births
comparison ranking: total 118

Life expectancy at birth: *total population:* 79.4 years (2024 est.)
male: 76.7 years
female: 82.3 years
comparison ranking: total population 64

Total fertility rate: 1.71 children born/woman (2024 est.)
comparison ranking: 161

Gross reproduction rate: 0.83 (2024 est.)

Contraceptive prevalence rate: 55.5% (2011/12)

Drinking water source: *improved: urban:* 99.4% of population
rural: 98.5% of population
total: 98.7% of population
unimproved: urban: 0.6% of population
rural: 1.5% of population
total: 1.3% of population (2020 est.)

Current health expenditure: 6.7% of GDP (2020)

Physician density: 0.64 physicians/1,000 population (2017)

Hospital bed density: 1.3 beds/1,000 population (2017)

Sanitation facility access: *improved: urban:* 97.6% of population
rural: 92.9% of population
total: 93.8% of population
unimproved: urban: 2.4% of population
rural: 7.1% of population
total: 6.2% of population (2020 est.)

Obesity - adult prevalence rate: 19.7% (2016)
comparison ranking: 111

Alcohol consumption per capita: *total:* 9.3 liters of pure alcohol (2019 est.)
beer: 3.21 liters of pure alcohol (2019 est.)
wine: 0.4 liters of pure alcohol (2019 est.)
spirits: 5.1 liters of pure alcohol (2019 est.)
other alcohols: 0.6 liters of pure alcohol (2019 est.)
comparison ranking: total 31

Currently married women (ages 15-49): 53.6% (2023 est.)

Education expenditures: 3.6% of GDP (2020 est.)
comparison ranking: 138

School life expectancy (primary to tertiary education): *total:* 13 years
male: 12 years
female: 13 years (2020)

ENVIRONMENT

Environment - current issues: deforestation; soil erosion, particularly in the northern region

Environment - international agreements: *party to:* Biodiversity, Climate Change, Climate Change-Kyoto Protocol, Climate Change-Paris Agreement, Comprehensive Nuclear Test Ban, Desertification, Endangered Species, Environmental Modification, Hazardous Wastes, Law of the Sea, Marine Dumping-London Convention, Ozone Layer Protection, Ship Pollution, Wetlands, Whaling
signed, but not ratified: none of the selected agreements

Climate: tropical, moderated by northeast trade winds; dry season January to April, rainy season May to August

Urbanization: *urban population:* 19.2% of total population (2023)
rate of urbanization: 0.98% annual rate of change (2020-25 est.)

Revenue from forest resources: 0.01% of GDP (2018 est.)
comparison ranking: 153

Revenue from coal: 0% of GDP (2018 est.)
comparison ranking: 66

Air pollutants: *particulate matter emissions:* 8.98 micrograms per cubic meter (2019 est.)
carbon dioxide emissions: 0.41 megatons (2016 est.)
methane emissions: 0.27 megatons (2020 est.)

Waste and recycling: *municipal solid waste generated annually:* 77,616 tons (2015 est.)

Total water withdrawal: *municipal:* 10 million cubic meters (2020 est.)
industrial: 0 cubic meters (2017 est.)
agricultural: 30 million cubic meters (2020 est.)

Total renewable water resources: 300 million cubic meters (2020 est.)

GOVERNMENT

Country name: *conventional long form:* none
conventional short form: Saint Lucia
etymology: named after Saint LUCY of Syracuse by French sailors who were shipwrecked on the island on 13 December 1502, the saint's feast day; Saint Lucia is the only country named specifically after a woman
note: pronounced saynt-looshuh

Government type: parliamentary democracy under a constitutional monarchy; a Commonwealth realm

Capital: *name:* Castries
geographic coordinates: 14 00 N, 61 00 W
time difference: UTC-4 (1 hour ahead of Washington, DC, during Standard Time)
etymology: in 1785, the village of Carenage was renamed Castries, after Charles Eugene Gabriel de La Croix de CASTRIES (1727-1801), who was then the French Minister of the Navy and Colonies

Administrative divisions: 10 districts; Anse-la-Raye, Canaries, Castries, Choiseul, Dennery, Gros-Islet, Laborie, Micoud, Soufriere, Vieux-Fort

Independence: 22 February 1979 (from the UK)

National holiday: Independence Day, 22 February (1979)

Legal system: English common law

Constitution: *history:* previous 1958, 1960 (preindependence); latest presented 20 December 1978, effective 22 February 1979
amendments: proposed by Parliament; passage requires at least two-thirds majority vote by the House of Assembly membership in the final reading and assent of the governor general; passage of amendments to various constitutional sections, such as those on fundamental rights and freedoms, government finances, the judiciary, and procedures for amending the constitution, require at least three-quarters majority vote by the House and assent of the governor general; passage of amendments approved by the House but rejected by the Senate require a majority of votes cast in a referendum; amended several times, last in 2008

International law organization participation: has not submitted an ICJ jurisdiction declaration; accepts ICCt jurisdiction

Citizenship: *citizenship by birth:* yes
citizenship by descent only: at least one parent must be a citizen of Saint Lucia
dual citizenship recognized: yes
residency requirement for naturalization: 8 years

Suffrage: 18 years of age; universal

Executive branch: *chief of state:* King CHARLES III (since 8 September 2022); represented by Acting Governor General Errol CHARLES (since 11 November 2021)
head of government: Prime Minister Philip J. PIERRE (since 28 July 2021)
cabinet: Cabinet appointed by the governor general on the advice of the prime minister
elections/appointments: the monarchy is hereditary; governor general appointed by the monarch; following legislative elections, the leader of the majority party or majority coalition usually appointed prime minister by governor general; deputy prime minister appointed by governor general

Legislative branch: *description:* bicameral Houses of Parliament consists of:
Senate (11 seats; all members appointed by the governor general; 6 on the advice of the prime minister, 3 on the advice of the leader of the opposition, and 2 upon consultation with religious, economic, and social groups; members serve 5- year terms)
House of Assembly (18 seats; 17 members directly elected in single-seat constituencies by simple majority vote and the speaker, designated from outside the Parliament; members serve 5-year terms)
elections: Senate - last appointments on 17 August 2021 (next to be held in 2026)
House of Assembly - last held on 26 July 2021 (next to be held in 2026)
election results: Senate - percent of vote by party - NA; seats by party - NA; composition - men 6, women 5, percentage women 45.5%
House of Assembly - percent of vote by party - SLP 50.1%, UWP 42.9%, other 0.3%, independent 6.6%; seats by party - SLP 13, UWP 2, independent 2; composition - men 16, women 2, percentage women 11.1%; note - total Parliament percentage women 24.1%

Judicial branch: *highest court(s):* the Eastern Caribbean Supreme Court (ECSC) is the superior court of the Organization of Eastern Caribbean States; the ECSC - headquartered on St. Lucia - consists of the Court of Appeal - headed by the chief justice and 4 judges - and the High Court with 18 judges; the Court of Appeal is itinerant, traveling to member states on a schedule to hear appeals from the High Court and subordinate courts; High Court judges reside in the member states with 4 on Saint Lucia; Saint Lucia is a member of the Caribbean Court of Justice
judge selection and term of office: chief justice of Eastern Caribbean Supreme Court appointed by Her Majesty, Queen ELIZABETH II; other justices and judges appointed by the Judicial and Legal Services Commission, an independent body of judicial officials; Court of Appeal justices appointed for life with mandatory retirement at age 65; High Court judges appointed for life with mandatory retirement at age 62
subordinate courts: magistrate's court

Political parties: Saint Lucia Labor Party or SLP
United Workers Party or UWP

International organization participation: ACP, ACS, AOSIS, C, Caricom, CD, CDB, CELAC, FAO, G-77, IBRD, ICAO, ICCt, ICRM, IDA, IFAD, IFC, IFRCS, ILO, IMF, IMO, Interpol, IOC, ISO, ITU, ITUC (NGOs), MIGA, NAM, OAS, OECS, OIF, OPANAL, OPCW, Petrocaribe, UN, UNCTAD, UNESCO, UNIDO, UPU, WCO, WFTU (NGOs), WHO, WIPO, WMO, WTO

Diplomatic representation in the US: *chief of mission:* Ambassador Elizabeth DARIUS-CLARKE (since 7 June 2022)
chancery: 1629 K Street NW, Suite 1250, Washington, DC 20006
telephone: [1] (202) 364-6792
FAX: [1] (202) 364-6723
email address and website:
embassydc@gosl.gov.lc
https://www.embassyofstlucia.org/
consulate(s) general: Miami, New York

Diplomatic representation from the US: *embassy:* the US does not have an embassy in Saint Lucia; the US Ambassador to Barbados is accredited to Saint Lucia

Flag description: cerulean blue with a gold isosceles triangle below a black arrowhead; the upper edges of the arrowhead have a white border; the blue color represents the sky and sea, gold stands for sunshine and prosperity, and white and black the racial composition of the island (with the latter being dominant); the two major triangles invoke the twin Pitons (Gros Piton and Petit Piton), cone-shaped volcanic plugs that are a symbol of the island

National symbol(s): twin pitons (volcanic peaks), Saint Lucia parrot; national colors: cerulean blue, gold, black, white

National anthem: *name:* "Sons and Daughters of St. Lucia"
lyrics/music: Charles JESSE/Leton Felix THOMAS
note: adopted 1967

National heritage: *total World Heritage Sites:* 1 (natural)
selected World Heritage Site locales: Pitons Management Area

ECONOMY

Economic overview: upper middle-income, tourism-based Caribbean island economy; environmentally fragile; energy import-dependent; major banana producer; well-educated labor force; key infrastructure, IT, and communications investments

Real GDP (purchasing power parity): $4.083 billion (2023 est.)
$3.957 billion (2022 est.)
$3.351 billion (2021 est.)
note: data in 2021 dollars
comparison ranking: 191

Real GDP growth rate: 3.19% (2023 est.)
18.08% (2022 est.)
12.23% (2021 est.)
note: annual GDP % growth based on constant local currency
comparison ranking: 103

Real GDP per capita: $22,700 (2023 est.)
$22,000 (2022 est.)
$18,700 (2021 est.)
note: data in 2021 dollars
comparison ranking: 92

GDP (official exchange rate): $2.52 billion (2023 est.)
note: data in current dollars at official exchange rate

Inflation rate (consumer prices): 4.07% (2023 est.)
6.38% (2022 est.)
2.41% (2021 est.)
note: annual % change based on consumer prices
comparison ranking: 83

GDP - composition, by sector of origin: *agriculture:* 0.9% (2023 est.)
industry: 8.6% (2023 est.)
services: 74.1% (2023 est.)
note: figures may not total 100% due to non-allocated consumption not captured in sector-reported data
comparison rankings: services 25; industry 201; agriculture 184

GDP - composition, by end use: *household consumption:* 66.1% (2017 est.)
government consumption: 11.2% (2017 est.)
investment in fixed capital: 16.9% (2017 est.)
investment in inventories: 0.1% (2017 est.)
exports of goods and services: 62.7% (2017 est.)
imports of goods and services: -56.9% (2017 est.)

Agricultural products: coconuts, bananas, tropical fruits, fruits, plantains, root vegetables, chicken, vegetables, cassava, pork (2022)
note: top ten agricultural products based on tonnage

Industries: tourism; clothing, assembly of electronic components, beverages, corrugated cardboard boxes, lime processing, coconut processing

Industrial production growth rate: 3.5% (2023 est.)
note: annual % change in industrial value added based on constant local currency
comparison ranking: 94

Labor force: 101,000 (2023 est.)
note: number of people ages 15 or older who are employed or seeking work
comparison ranking: 183

Unemployment rate: 11.09% (2023 est.)
15.93% (2022 est.)
20.51% (2021 est.)
note: % of labor force seeking employment
comparison ranking: 170

Youth unemployment rate (ages 15-24): *total:* 28.2% (2023 est.)
male: 29.5% (2023 est.)
female: 26.5% (2023 est.)
note: % of labor force ages 15-24 seeking employment
comparison ranking: total 31

Population below poverty line: 25% (2016 est.)
note: % of population with income below national poverty line

Gini Index coefficient - distribution of family income: 51.2 (2016 est.)
note: index (0-100) of income distribution; higher values represent greater inequality
comparison ranking: 10

Household income or consumption by percentage share: *lowest 10%:* 2.1% (2015 est.)
highest 10%: 34.1% (2015 est.)
note: % share of income accruing to lowest and highest 10% of population

Remittances: 2.5% of GDP (2023 est.)
2.64% of GDP (2022 est.)
3.45% of GDP (2021 est.)
note: personal transfers and compensation between resident and non-resident individuals/households/entities

Budget: *revenues:* $414.77 million (2017 est.)
expenditures: $351.956 million (2017 est.)
note: central government revenues and expenses (excluding grants/extrabudgetary units/social security funds) converted to US dollars at average official exchange rate for year indicated

Public debt: 70.7% of GDP (2017 est.)
comparison ranking: 54

Taxes and other revenues: 18.23% (of GDP) (2017 est.)
note: central government tax revenue as a % of GDP
comparison ranking: 100

Current account balance: -$45.381 million (2023 est.)
-$67.064 million (2022 est.)
-$221.371 million (2021 est.)
note: balance of payments - net trade and primary/secondary income in current dollars
comparison ranking: 91

Exports: $1.415 billion (2023 est.)
$1.296 billion (2022 est.)
$710.754 million (2021 est.)
note: balance of payments - exports of goods and services in current dollars
comparison ranking: 172

Exports - partners: US 17%, Guyana 16%, Trinidad and Tobago 14%, Barbados 9%, Suriname 7% (2022)
note: top five export partners based on percentage share of exports

Exports - commodities: beer, gravel and crushed stone, paper containers, refined petroleum, liquor (2022)
note: top five export commodities based on value in dollars

Imports: $1.274 billion (2023 est.)
$1.194 billion (2022 est.)
$891.761 million (2021 est.)
note: balance of payments - imports of goods and services in current dollars
comparison ranking: 189

Imports - partners: US 76%, Trinidad and Tobago 4%, China 3%, UK 2%, Barbados 2% (2022)
note: top five import partners based on percentage share of imports

Imports - commodities: refined petroleum, cars, plastic products, poultry, flavored water (2022)
note: top five import commodities based on value in dollars

Reserves of foreign exchange and gold: $424.324 million (2023 est.)
$389.083 million (2022 est.)
$433.117 million (2021 est.)
note: holdings of gold (year-end prices)/foreign exchange/special drawing rights in current dollars
comparison ranking: 174

Debt - external: $687.824 million (2022 est.)
note: present value of external debt in current US dollars
comparison ranking: 87

Exchange rates: East Caribbean dollars (XCD) per US dollar -

Exchange rates: 2.7 (2023 est.)
2.7 (2022 est.)
2.7 (2021 est.)
2.7 (2020 est.)
2.7 (2019 est.)

ENERGY

Electricity access: *electrification - total population:* 100% (2022 est.)

Electricity: *installed generating capacity:* 92,000 kW (2022 est.)
consumption: 360.34 million kWh (2022 est.)
transmission/distribution losses: 31.038 million kWh (2022 est.)
comparison rankings: transmission/distribution losses 30; consumption 182; installed generating capacity 186

Electricity generation sources: *fossil fuels:* 99.2% of total installed capacity (2022 est.)
solar: 0.8% of total installed capacity (2022 est.)

Petroleum: *refined petroleum consumption:* 4,000 bbl/day (2022 est.)

Carbon dioxide emissions: 617,000 metric tonnes of CO_2 (2022 est.)
from petroleum and other liquids: 617,000 metric tonnes of CO_2 (2022 est.)
comparison ranking: total emissions 186

Energy consumption per capita: 48.251 million Btu/person (2022 est.)
comparison ranking: 95

COMMUNICATIONS

Telephones - fixed lines: *total subscriptions:* 14,000 (2021 est.)
subscriptions per 100 inhabitants: 8 (2021 est.)
comparison ranking: total subscriptions 183

Telephones - mobile cellular: *total subscriptions:* 172,000 (2021 est.)
subscriptions per 100 inhabitants: 96 (2021 est.)
comparison ranking: total subscriptions 186

Telecommunication systems: *general assessment:* an adequate system that is automatically switched; good interisland and international connections; broadband access; expanded FttP (Fiber to the Home) and LTE markets; regulatory development; telecom sector contributes to the overall GDP; telecom sector is a growth area (2020)
domestic: fixed-line teledensity is 8 per 100 persons and mobile-cellular teledensity is roughly 96 per 100 persons (2021)
international: country code - 1-758; landing points for the ECFS and Southern Caribbean Fiber submarine cables providing connectivity to numerous Caribbean islands; direct microwave radio relay link with Martinique and Saint Vincent and the Grenadines; tropospheric scatter to Barbados (2019)

Broadcast media: 3 privately owned TV stations; 1 public TV station operating on a cable network; multi-channel cable TV service available; a mix of state-owned and privately owned broadcasters operate nearly 25 radio stations including repeater transmission stations (2019)

Internet country code: .lc

Internet users: *total:* 140,400 (2021 est.)
percent of population: 78% (2021 est.)
comparison ranking: total 183

Broadband - fixed subscriptions: *total:* 33,000 (2020 est.)
subscriptions per 100 inhabitants: 18 (2020 est.)
comparison ranking: total 149

TRANSPORTATION

Civil aircraft registration country code prefix: J6

Airports: 2 (2024)
comparison ranking: 205

Roadways: *total:* 1,210 km
paved: 847 km
unpaved: 363 km (2011)
comparison ranking: total 181

Ports: *total ports:* 3 (2024)
large: 0
medium: 0
small: 2
very small: 1
ports with oil terminals: 2
key ports: Castries, Grand Cul de Sac Bay, Vieux Fort

MILITARY AND SECURITY

Military and security forces: no regular military forces; Royal Saint Lucia Police Force (RSLPF) (2024)
note: the RSLPF has responsibility for law enforcement and maintenance of order within the country; it is under the Ministry of Home Affairs, Justice, and National Security and includes a Special Service Unit and a Marine Unit (coast guard)

Military - note: Saint Lucia has been a member of the Caribbean Regional Security System (RSS) since its creation in 1982; RSS signatories (Antigua and Barbuda, Barbados, Dominica, Grenada, Guyana, Saint Kitts, and Saint Vincent and the Grenadines) agreed to prepare contingency plans and assist one another, on request, in national emergencies, prevention of smuggling, search and rescue, immigration control, fishery protection, customs and excise control, maritime policing duties, protection of off-shore installations, pollution control, national and other disasters, and threats to national security (2024)

TRANSNATIONAL ISSUES

Illicit drugs: a transit point for cocaine and marijuana destined for North America, Europe, and elsewhere in the Caribbean; some local demand for cocaine and some use of synthetic drugs

SAINT MARTIN

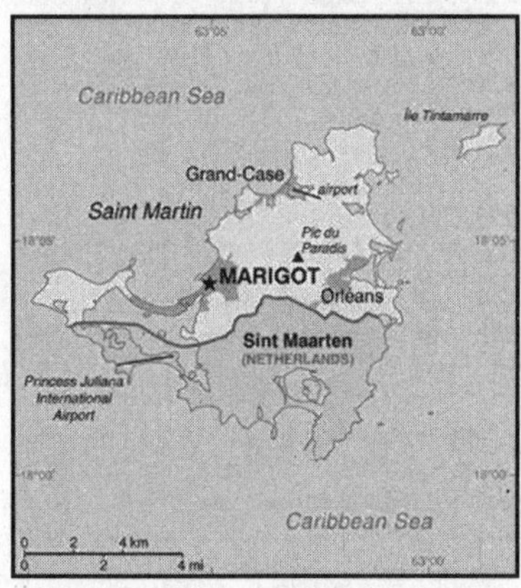

INTRODUCTION

Background: Christopher COLUMBUS claimed Saint Martin for Spain in 1493, naming it after the feast day of St. Martin of Tours, but it was the Dutch who occupied the island in 1631 to exploit its salt deposits. The Spanish retook Saint Martin in 1633, but the Dutch continued to assert their claims. The Spanish finally relinquished the island to the French and Dutch, who divided it between themselves in 1648. The border frequently fluctuated over the next 200 years because of friction between the two countries, with the French eventually holding the greater portion of the island (about 61%).

The cultivation of sugarcane introduced African slavery to the island in the late 18th century; the practice was not abolished until 1848. The island became a free port in 1939, and the tourism industry was dramatically expanded during the 1970s and 1980s. In 2003, the populace of Saint Martin voted to secede from Guadeloupe, and in 2007, the northern portion of the island became a French overseas collectivity. In 2010, the southern Dutch portion of the island became the independent nation of Sint Maarten within the Kingdom of the Netherlands. In 2017, Hurricane Irma passed over the island of Saint Martin, causing extensive damage to roads, communications, electrical power, and housing; the UN estimated that 90% of the buildings were damaged or destroyed.

GEOGRAPHY

Location: Caribbean, located in the Leeward Islands (northern) group; French part of the island of Saint Martin in the Caribbean Sea; Saint Martin lies east of the US Virgin Islands

Geographic coordinates: 18 05 N, 63 57 W

Map references: Central America and the Caribbean

Area: *total:* 50 sq km
land: 50 sq km
water: negligible
comparison ranking: total 230

Area - comparative: more than one-third the size of Washington, DC

Land boundaries: *total:* 16 km
border countries (1): Sint Maarten 16 km

Coastline: 58.9 km (for entire island)

Climate: temperature averages 27-29 degrees Celsius all year long; low humidity, gentle trade winds, brief, intense rain showers; hurricane season stretches from July to November

Elevation: *highest point:* Pic du Paradis 424 m
lowest point: Caribbean Ocean 0 m

Natural resources: salt

Population distribution: most of the population is found along the coast, with a largest concentrations around the capital Marigot, Orleans, and Grand-Case

Natural hazards: subject to hurricanes from July to November

Geography - note: *note 1:* the southern border is shared with Sint Maarten, a country within the Kingdom of the Netherlands; together, these two entities make up the smallest landmass in the world shared by two self-governing states
note 2: Simpson Bay Lagoon (aka as Simson Bay Lagoon or The Great Pond) is one of the largest inland lagoons in the West Indies; the border between the French and Dutch halves of the island of Saint Martin runs across the center of the lagoon, which is shared by both of the island's entities

PEOPLE AND SOCIETY

Population: *total:* 32,996
male: 15,791
female: 17,205 (2024 est.)
comparison rankings: female 215; male 215; total 215

Ethnic groups: Creole (Mulatto), Black, Guadeloupe Mestizo (French-East Asian), White, East Indian, other

Languages: French (official), Dutch, English, Guadeloupian Creole, Haitian Creole, Italian, Martiniquan Creole, Papiamento (dialect of Netherlands Antilles), Spanish
major-language sample(s):
The World Factbook, une source indispensable d'informations de base. (French)

Religions: Roman Catholic, Jehovah's Witness, Protestant, Hindu

Age structure: *0-14 years:* 24.7% (male 4,039/female 4,100)
15-64 years: 64.5% (male 10,216/female 11,068)
65 years and over: 10.8% (2024 est.) (male 1,536/female 2,037)

Dependency ratios: *total dependency ratio:* 49.1 N
youth dependency ratio: 33.5
elderly dependency ratio: 15.6
potential support ratio: 6.4 (2021)

Median age: *total:* 34.2 years (2024 est.)
male: 33.4 years
female: 34.9 years
comparison ranking: total 106

Population growth rate: 0.3% (2024 est.)
comparison ranking: 166

Birth rate: 13.9 births/1,000 population (2024 est.)
comparison ranking: 121

Death rate: 4.8 deaths/1,000 population (2024 est.)
comparison ranking: 202

Net migration rate: -6.2 migrant(s)/1,000 population (2024 est.)
comparison ranking: 211

Population distribution: most of the population is found along the coast, with a largest concentrations around the capital Marigot, Orleans, and Grand-Case

Sex ratio: *at birth:* 1.04 male(s)/female
0-14 years: 0.99 male(s)/female

15-64 years: 0.92 male(s)/female
65 years and over: 0.75 male(s)/female
total population: 0.92 male(s)/female (2024 est.)

Infant mortality rate: *total:* 6.5 deaths/1,000 live births (2024 est.)
male: 7.6 deaths/1,000 live births
female: 5.3 deaths/1,000 live births
comparison ranking: total 160

Life expectancy at birth: *total population:* 81 years (2024 est.)
male: 78 years
female: 84.2 years
comparison ranking: total population 46

Total fertility rate: 1.8 children born/woman (2024 est.)
comparison ranking: 140

Gross reproduction rate: 0.88 (2024 est.)

Contraceptive prevalence rate: NA

Drinking water source: *improved: urban:* 100% of population
rural: NA
total: 100% of population

Sanitation facility access: *improved: urban:* 100% of population
rural: NA
total: 100% of population

ENVIRONMENT

Environment - current issues: excessive population pressure (increasing settlement); waste management; salinity intrusions into the mainland of the island; fresh water supply is dependent on desalination of sea water; over-exploitation of marine resources (reef fisheries, coral and shell); indiscriminate anchoring of boats damages coral reefs, causing underwater pollution and sedimentation

Climate: temperature averages 27-29 degrees Celsius all year long; low humidity, gentle trade winds, brief, intense rain showers; hurricane season stretches from July to November

Waste and recycling: *municipal solid waste generated annually:* 15,480 tons (2012 est.)

GOVERNMENT

Country name: *conventional long form:* Overseas Collectivity of Saint Martin
conventional short form: Saint Martin
local long form: Collectivité d'outre mer de Saint-Martin
local short form: Saint-Martin
etymology: explorer Christopher COLUMBUS named the island after Saint MARTIN of Tours because the 11 November 1493 day of discovery was the saint's feast day

Government type: parliamentary democracy (Territorial Council); overseas collectivity of France

Dependency status: overseas collectivity of France
note: the only French overseas collectivity that is part of the EU

Capital: *name:* Marigot
geographic coordinates: 18 04 N, 63 05 W
time difference: UTC-4 (1 hour ahead of Washington, DC, during Standard Time)
etymology: marigot is a French term referring to a body of water, a watercourse, a side-stream, or a tributary rivulet; the name likely refers to a stream at the site of the city's original founding

Independence: none (overseas collectivity of France)

National holiday: Fête de la Fédération, 14 July (1790); note - local holiday is Schoelcher Day (Slavery Abolition Day) 12 July (1848), as well as St. Martin's Day, 11 November (1985), which commemorates the discovery of the island by COLUMBUS on Saint Martin's Day, 11 November 1493; the latter holiday celebrated on both halves of the island

Legal system: French civil law

Constitution: *history:* 4 October 1958 (French Constitution)
amendments: amendment procedures of France's constitution apply

Citizenship: see France

Suffrage: 18 years of age, universal

Executive branch: *chief of state:* President Emmanuel MACRON (since 14 May 2017); represented by Prefect Vincent BERTON (since 28 March 2022)
head of government: President of Territorial Council Louis MUSSINGTON (since 3 April 2022)
cabinet: Executive Council; note - there is also an advisory economic, social, and cultural council
elections/appointments: French president directly elected by absolute majority popular vote in 2 rounds if needed for a 5-year term (eligible for a second term); prefect appointed by French president on the advice of French Ministry of Interior; president of Territorial Council elected by its members for a 5-year term; election last held on 3 April 2022 (next to be held in 2027)
election results:
2022: Louis MUSSINGTON (RSM) elected president; Territorial Council vote - unanimous
2017: Daniel Gibbs (UD) elected president; Territorial Council vote - 18 of 23 votes

Legislative branch: *description:* unicameral Territorial Council (23 seats; members directly elected by absolute majority vote in 2 rounds if needed to serve 5-year terms); Saint Martin elects 1 member to the French Senate and 1 member (shared with Saint Barthelemy) to the French National Assembly
elections: Territorial Council - first round held on 20 March and second round held on 27 March 2022 (next to be held in March 2027)
French Senate - last held on 27 September 2020 (next to be held not later than September 2023)
French National Assembly - last held on 12 and 19 June 2022 (next to be held by June 2027)
election results: Territorial Council - percent of vote by party in first round - RSM 25.4%, UD 24.7%, HOPE 17.5%, Saint Martin with You 13.8%, Alternative 11.2%, Future Saint Martin 7.5%; percent of vote by party in second round - RSM and Alternative 49.1%; UD 33.3%; HOPE, Saint Martin with You, and Future Saint Martin 17.6%; seats by party - RSM and Alternative 16; UD 5, HOPE, Saint Martin with You, and Future Saint Martin 2; composition - men 13, women 10, percentage women 43.5%
French Senate - 1 seat - UMP 1
French National Assembly - 1 seat - UMP 1

Political parties: Alternative
Future Saint Martin (Avenir Saint Martin)
Generation Hope or HOPE
Rassemblement Saint-Martinois or RSM (formerly Movement for Justice and Prosperity or MJP) Saint Martin with You
Union for Democracy or UD

International organization participation: ACS (associate), UPU

Diplomatic representation in the US: none (overseas collectivity of France)

Diplomatic representation from the US: *embassy:* none (overseas collectivity of France)

Flag description: the flag of France is used

National symbol(s): brown pelican

National anthem: *name:* "O Sweet Saint Martin's Land"
lyrics/music: Gerard KEMPS
note: the song, written in 1958, is used as an unofficial anthem for the entire island (both French and Dutch sides); as a collectivity of France, in addition to the local anthem, "La Marseillaise" remains official on the French side (see France); as a constituent part of the Kingdom of the Netherlands, in addition to the local anthem, "Het Wilhelmus" remains official on the Dutch side (see Netherlands)

ECONOMY

Economic overview: high-income French Caribbean territorial economy; extremely reliant on tourism, with severe COVID-19 impacts; near-total destruction from Hurricane Irma in 2017; some offshore banking; import-dependent; duty-free commerce; yachting destination

Real GDP growth rate: 4.9% (2021 est.)
-12.5% (2020 est.)
6.5% (2019 est.)
note: annual GDP % growth based on constant local currency
comparison ranking: 59

GDP (official exchange rate): $649.206 million (2021 est.)
note: data in current dollars at official exchange rate

Industries: tourism, light industry and manufacturing, heavy industry

Industrial production growth rate: 4.3% (2014 est.)
note: annual % change in industrial value added based on constant local currency
comparison ranking: 69

Exports - partners: United States 35%, Netherlands 26%, Antigua and Barbuda 21%, France 10% (2019)

Exports - commodities: gold, special use vessels, furniture, scrap aluminum, rum (2019)

Imports - partners: United States 76%, Netherlands 7%, France 7% (2019)

Imports - commodities: jewelry, diamonds, pearls, recreational boats, cars (2019)

Exchange rates: euros (EUR) per US dollar -

Exchange rates: 0.925 (2023 est.)
0.95 (2022 est.)
0.845 (2021 est.)
0.876 (2020 est.)
0.893 (2019 est.)

ENERGY

Electricity access: *electrification - total population:* 100% (2022 est.)

COMMUNICATIONS

Telephones - mobile cellular: *total subscriptions:* 68,840 (2012 est.)
subscriptions per 100 inhabitants: 196 (2012 est.)
comparison ranking: total subscriptions 198

Telecommunication systems: *general assessment:* fully integrated access; good interisland and

international connections; broadband access; expanded FttP (Fiber to the Home) and LTE markets; regulatory development; telecom sector contributes greatly to the overall GDP; telecom sector is a growth area (2020)
domestic: direct dial capability with both fixed and wireless systems (2018)
international: country code - 590; landing points for the SMPR-1, Southern Caribbean Fiber and the Saba, Statia Cable System submarine cables providing connectivity to numerous Caribbean islands (2019)

Broadcast media: 1 local TV station; access to about 20 radio stations, including RFO Guadeloupe radio broadcasts via repeater

Internet country code: .mf; note - .gp, the Internet country code for Guadeloupe, and .fr, the Internet country code for France, might also be encountered

Internet users: *total:* 19,284 (2022 est.)
percent of population: 48.5% (2022 est.)
comparison ranking: total 212

TRANSPORTATION

Airports: 1 (2024)
comparison ranking: 230

Transportation - note: nearest airport for international flights is Princess Juliana International Airport (SXM) located on Sint Maarten

MILITARY AND SECURITY

Military and security forces: no armed forces; Saint Martin Police Force (Korps Politie Sint Marteen)

Military - note: defense is the responsibility of France

TRANSNATIONAL ISSUES

Illicit drugs: transshipment point for cocaine, heroin, and marijuana destined for Puerto Rico and the U.S. Virgin Islands as well as Europe.

SAINT PIERRE AND MIQUELON

INTRODUCTION

Background: First settled by the French in the early 17th century, Saint Pierre and Miquelon are the sole remaining vestige of France's once vast North American possessions. They attained the status of an overseas collectivity in 2003.

GEOGRAPHY

Location: Northern North America, islands in the North Atlantic Ocean, south of Newfoundland (Canada)

Geographic coordinates: 46 50 N, 56 20 W

Map references: North America

Area: *total:* 242 sq km
land: 242 sq km
water: 0 sq km
note: includes eight small islands in the Saint Pierre and the Miquelon groups
comparison ranking: total 214

Area - comparative: one and half times the size of Washington, DC

Land boundaries: *total:* 0 km

Coastline: 120 km

Maritime claims: *territorial sea:* 12 nm
exclusive economic zone: 200 nm

Climate: cold and wet, with considerable mist and fog; spring and autumn are often windy

Terrain: mostly barren rock

Elevation: *highest point:* Morne de la Grande Montagne 240 m
lowest point: Atlantic Ocean 0 m

Natural resources: fish, deepwater ports

Land use: *agricultural land:* 8.7% (2018 est.)
arable land: 8.7% (2018 est.)
permanent crops: 0% (2018 est.)
permanent pasture: 0% (2018 est.)
forest: 12.5% (2018 est.)
other: 78.8% (2018 est.)

Irrigated land: 0 sq km (2022)

Population distribution: most of the population is found on Saint Pierre Island; a small settlement is located on the north end of Miquelon Island

Natural hazards: persistent fog throughout the year can be a maritime hazard

Geography - note: vegetation scanty; the islands are part of the northern Appalachians, along with Newfoundland

PEOPLE AND SOCIETY

Population: *total:* 5,132
male: 2,476
female: 2,656 (2024 est.)
comparison rankings: female 227; male 227; total 227

Nationality: *noun:* Frenchman(men), Frenchwoman(women)
adjective: French

Ethnic groups: Basques and Bretons (French fishermen)

Languages: French (official)
major-language sample(s):
The World Factbook, une source indispensable d'informations de base. (French)

Religions: Roman Catholic 99%, other 1%

Age structure: *0-14 years:* 13.1% (male 346/female 328)
15-64 years: 61.6% (male 1,559/female 1,600)
65 years and over: 25.3% (2024 est.) (male 571/female 728)

Dependency ratios: *total dependency ratio:* 52
youth dependency ratio: 26.1
elderly dependency ratio: 25.9
potential support ratio: 3.9 (2021)

Median age: *total:* 51.2 years (2024 est.)
male: 50.5 years
female: 51.9 years
comparison ranking: total 2

Population growth rate: -1.21% (2024 est.)
comparison ranking: 234

Birth rate: 6.4 births/1,000 population (2024 est.)
comparison ranking: 227

Death rate: deaths/1,000 population (2024 est.)
comparison ranking: 20

Net migration rate: -6.8 migrant(s)/1,000 population (2024 est.)
comparison ranking: 215

Population distribution: most of the population is found on Saint Pierre Island; a small settlement is located on the north end of Miquelon Island

Urbanization: *urban population:* 90.1% of total population (2023)
rate of urbanization: 0.75% annual rate of change (2020-25 est.)

Major urban areas - population: 6,000 SAINT-PIERRE (capital) (2018)

Sex ratio: *at birth:* 1.06 male(s)/female
0-14 years: 1.05 male(s)/female
15-64 years: 0.97 male(s)/female
65 years and over: 0.78 male(s)/female
total population: 0.93 male(s)/female (2024 est.)

Infant mortality rate: *total:* 7.8 deaths/1,000 live births (2024 est!)
male: 9.6 deaths/1,000 live births
female: 5.8 deaths/1,000 live births
comparison ranking: total 148

Life expectancy at birth: *total population:* 81.8 years (2024 est.)
male: 79.5 years
female: 84.3 years
comparison ranking: total population 41

Total fertility rate: 1.6 children born/woman (2024 est.)
comparison ranking: 183

Gross reproduction rate: 0.78 (2024 est.)

Drinking water source: *improved:*
total: 91.4% of population
unimproved:
total: 8.6% of population (2017 est.)

Sanitation facility access: *improved:*
total: 100% of population

Currently married women (ages 15-49): 64.1% (2023 est.)

ENVIRONMENT

Environment - current issues: overfishing; recent test drilling for oil in waters around Saint Pierre and Miquelon may bring future development that would impact the environment

Climate: cold and wet, with considerable mist and fog; spring and autumn are often windy

Urbanization: *urban population:* 90.1% of total population (2023)
rate of urbanization: 0.75% annual rate of change (2020-25 est.)

GOVERNMENT

Country name: *conventional long form:* Territorial Collectivity of Saint Pierre and Miquelon
conventional short form: Saint Pierre and Miquelon
local long form: Département de Saint-Pierre et Miquelon
local short form: Saint-Pierre et Miquelon
etymology: Saint-Pierre is named after Saint PETER, the patron saint of fishermen; Miquelon may be a corruption of the Basque name Mikelon

Government type: parliamentary democracy (Territorial Council); overseas collectivity of France

Dependency status: overseas collectivity of France

Capital: *name:* Saint-Pierre
geographic coordinates: 46 46 N, 56 11 W
time difference: UTC-3 (2 hours ahead of Washington, DC, during Standard Time)
daylight saving time: +1hr, begins second Sunday in March; ends first Sunday in November
etymology: named after Saint Peter, the patron saint of fisherman

Administrative divisions: none (territorial overseas collectivity of France); note - there are no first-order administrative divisions as defined by the US Government, but there are 2 communes at the second order - Saint Pierre, Miquelon

Independence: none (overseas collectivity collectivity of France; has been under French control since 1763)

National holiday: Fête de la Fédération, 14 July (1790)

Legal system: French civil law

Constitution: *history:* 4 October 1958 (French Constitution)
amendments: amendment procedures of France's constitution apply

Citizenship: see France

Suffrage: 18 years of age; universal

Executive branch: *chief of state:* President Emmanuel MACRON (since 14 May 2017); represented by Prefect Christian POUGET (since 6 January 2021)
head of government: President of Territorial Council Bernard BRIAND (since 13 October 2020)
cabinet: Le Cabinet du Prefet
elections/appointments: French president directly elected by absolute majority popular vote in 2 rounds if needed for a 5-year term (eligible for a second term); election last held on 10 April and 24 April 2022 (next to be held in 2027); prefect appointed by French president on the advice of French Ministry of Interior; Territorial Council president elected by Territorial Council councilors by absolute majority vote; term NA; election last held on 13 October 2020 (next to be held in NA)
election results:
2020: Bernard BRIAND elected President of Territorial Council; Territorial Council vote - 17 for, 2 abstentions
2017: Stephane LENORMAND elected President of Territorial Council vote - NA

Legislative branch: *description:* unicameral Territorial Council or Conseil Territorial (19 seats - Saint Pierre 15, Miquelon 4; members directly elected in single-seat constituencies by absolute majority vote in 2 rounds if needed to serve 6-year terms); Saint Pierre and Miquelon indirectly elects 1 senator to the French Senate by an electoral college to serve a 6-year term and directly elects 1 deputy to the French National Assembly by absolute majority vote to serve a 5-year term
elections: Territorial Council - first round held on 20 March and second round held on 27 March 2022 (next to be held in March 2028)
French Senate - last held on 27 September 2020 (next to be held no later than September 2025)
French National Assembly - last held on 12 and 19 June 2022 (next to be held by June 2027)
election results: Territorial Council - percent of vote by party in first round - AD 45.9%, Focus on the Future 37%, Together to Build 17.1%; percent of vote by party in second round - AD 51.8%, Focus on the Future 38.1%, Together to Build 10.1%, seats by party - AD 15, Focus on the Future 4; composition - men NA, women NA, percent of women NA%
French Senate - percent of vote by party - NA; seats by party - PS 1 (affiliated with UMP)
French National Assembly - percent of vote by party - NA; seats by party - AD 1

Judicial branch: *highest court(s):* Superior Tribunal of Appeals or Tribunal Superieur d'Appel (composition NA)
judge selection and term of office: judge selection and tenure NA
subordinate courts: NA

Political parties: Archipelago Tomorrow (Archipel Domain) or AD (affiliated with The Republicans)
Focus on the Future (Cap sur l'Avenir) (affiliated with Left Radical Party)
Together to Build (Ensemble pour Construire)

International organization participation: UPU, WFTU (NGOs)

Diplomatic representation in the US: none (overseas territory of France)

Diplomatic representation from the US: *embassy:* none (territorial overseas collectivity of France)

Flag description: *a yellow three-masted sailing ship facing the hoist side rides on a blue background with scattered, white, wavy lines under the ship; a continuous black-over-white wavy line divides the ship from the white wavy lines; on the hoist side, a vertical band is divided into three parts:* the top part (called ikkurina) is red with a green diagonal cross extending to the corners overlaid by a white cross dividing the rectangle into four sections; the middle part has a white background with an ermine pattern; the third part has a red background with two stylized yellow lions outlined in black, one above the other; these three heraldic arms represent settlement by colonists from the Basque Country (top), Brittany, and Normandy; the blue on the main portion of the flag symbolizes the Atlantic Ocean and the stylized ship represents the Grande Hermine in which Jacques Cartier "discovered" the islands in 1536
note: the flag of France used for official occasions

National symbol(s): 16th-century sailing ship

National anthem: *note:* as a collectivity of France, "La Marseillaise" is official (see France)

ECONOMY

Economic overview: high-income, French North American territorial economy; primarily fishing exports; substantial French Government support; highly seasonal labor force; euro user; increasing tourism and aquaculture investments

Real GDP (purchasing power parity): $261.3 million (2015 est.)
(2006)
note: supplemented by annual payments from France of about $60 million
comparison ranking: 219

GDP (official exchange rate): $261.3 million (2015 est.)

Inflation rate (consumer prices): 1.5% (2015) (2010)
comparison ranking: 30

Agricultural products: vegetables; poultry, cattle, sheep, pigs; fish

Industries: fish processing and supply base for fishing fleets; tourism

Labor force: 4,429 (2015)
comparison ranking: 204

Unemployment rate: 8.7% (2015 est.)
comparison ranking: 154

Exports - partners: Canada 84%, France 11%, Ireland 3%, Slovakia 1%, Democratic Republic of the Congo 0% (2022)
note: top five export partners based on percentage share of exports

Exports - commodities: processed crustaceans, shellfish, fish, special purpose motor vehicles, vehicle parts/accessories (2022)
note: top five export commodities based on value in dollars

Imports - partners: France 52%, Canada 42%, Netherlands 2%, Germany 1%, Belgium 1% (2022)
note: top five import partners based on percentage share of imports

Imports - commodities: refined petroleum, packaged medicine, other foods, plastic products, cars (2022)
note: top five import commodities based on value in dollars

Exchange rates: euros (EUR) per US dollar -

Exchange rates: 0.925 (2023 est.)
0.95 (2022 est.)
0.845 (2021 est.)
0.876 (2020 est.)
0.893 (2019 est.)

ENERGY

Electricity: *installed generating capacity:* 26,000 kW (2022 est.)
consumption: 48.714 million kWh (2022 est.)
transmission/distribution losses: 2 million kWh (2022 est.)
comparison rankings: transmission/distribution losses 5; consumption 204; installed generating capacity 204

Electricity generation sources: *fossil fuels:* 100% of total installed capacity (2022 est.)

Petroleum: *refined petroleum consumption:* 400 bbl/day (2022 est.)

Carbon dioxide emissions: 59,000 metric tonnes of CO2 (2022 est.)
from petroleum and other liquids: 59,000 metric tonnes of CO2 (2022 est.)
comparison ranking: total emissions 212

Energy consumption per capita: (2019)

COMMUNICATIONS

Telephones - fixed lines: *total subscriptions:* 4,800 (2015 est.)
subscriptions per 100 inhabitants: 76 (2015 est.)
comparison ranking: total subscriptions 206

Telecommunication systems: *general assessment:* adequate (2019)
domestic: fixed-line teledensity 76 per 100 persons (2019)
international: country code - 508; landing point for the St Pierre and Miquelon Cable connecting Saint Pierre & Miquelon and Canada; radiotelephone communication with most countries in the world; satellite earth station - 1 in French domestic satellite system (2019)

Broadcast media: 8 TV stations, all part of the French Overseas Network, and local cable provided by SPM Telecom; 3 of 4 radio stations on St. Pierre and on Miquelon are part of the French Overseas Network (2021)

Internet country code: .pm

Internet users: *total:* 5,099 (2022 est.)
percent of population: 88.7% (2022 est.)
comparison ranking: total 223

TRANSPORTATION

Airports: 2 (2024)
comparison ranking: 203

Roadways: *total:* 117 km
paved: 80 km
unpaved: 37 km (2009)
comparison ranking: total 215

Ports: *total ports:* 2 (2024)
large: 0
medium: 0
small: 1
very small: 0
size unknown: 1
ports with oil terminals: 1
key ports: Miquelon, St. Pierre

MILITARY AND SECURITY

Military - note: defense is the responsibility of France

SAINT VINCENT AND THE GRENADINES

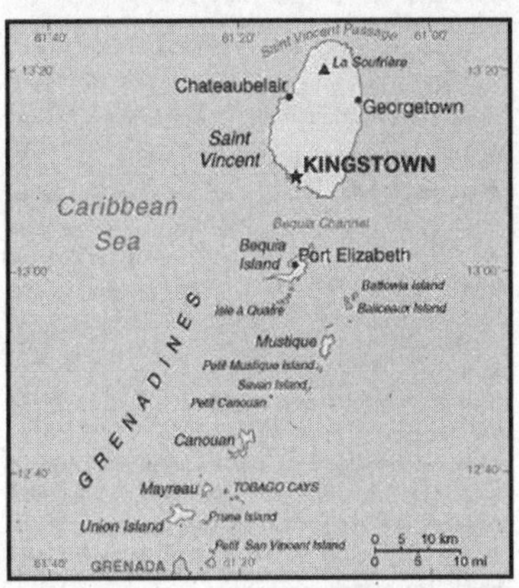

INTRODUCTION

Background: Resistance from native Caribs prevented colonization on Saint Vincent until 1719. France and England disputed the island for most of the 18th century, but it was ceded to England in 1783. The British prized Saint Vincent because of its fertile soil, which allowed for thriving slave-run plantations of sugar, coffee, indigo, tobacco, cotton, and cocoa. In 1834, the British abolished slavery. Immigration of indentured servants eased the ensuing labor shortage, as did subsequent immigrant waves from Portugal and East India. Conditions remained harsh for both former slaves and immigrant agricultural workers, however, as depressed world sugar prices kept the economy stagnant until the early 1900s. The economy then went into a period of decline, with many landowners abandoning their estates and leaving the land to be cultivated by liberated slaves.

Between 1960 and 1962, Saint Vincent and the Grenadines was a separate administrative unit of the Federation of the West Indies. Autonomy was granted in 1969 and independence in 1979. In 2021, the eruption of the La Soufrière volcano in the north of Saint Vincent destroyed much of Saint Vincent's most productive agricultural lands. Unlike most of its tourism-dependent neighbors, the Vincentian economy is primarily agricultural.

GEOGRAPHY

Location: Caribbean, islands between the Caribbean Sea and North Atlantic Ocean, north of Trinidad and Tobago

Geographic coordinates: 13 15 N, 61 12 W

Map references: Central America and the Caribbean

Area: *total:* 389 sq km (Saint Vincent 344 sq km)
land: 389 sq km
water: 0 sq km
comparison ranking: total 204

Area - comparative: twice the size of Washington, DC

Land boundaries: *total:* 0 km

Coastline: 84 km

Maritime claims: *territorial sea:* 12 nm
contiguous zone: 24 nm
exclusive economic zone: 200 nm
continental shelf: 200 nm

Climate: tropical; little seasonal temperature variation; rainy season (May to November)

Terrain: volcanic, mountainous

Elevation: *highest point:* La Soufriere 1,234 m
lowest point: Caribbean Sea 0 m

Natural resources: hydropower, arable land

Land use: *agricultural land:* 25.6% (2018 est.)
arable land: 12.8% (2018 est.)
permanent crops: 7.7% (2018 est.)
permanent pasture: 5.1% (2018 est.)
forest: 68.7% (2018 est.)
other: 5.7% (2018 est.)

Irrigated land: 10 sq km (2012)

Population distribution: most of the population is concentrated in and around the capital of Kingstown

Natural hazards: hurricanes; La Soufriere volcano on the island of Saint Vincent is a constant threat
volcanism: La Soufriere (1,234 m) on the island of Saint Vincent last erupted in 1979; the island of Saint Vincent is part of the volcanic island arc of the Lesser Antilles that extends from Saba in the north to Grenada in the south

Geography - note: the administration of the islands of the Grenadines group is divided between Saint Vincent and the Grenadines and Grenada; Saint Vincent and the Grenadines is comprised of 32 islands and cays

PEOPLE AND SOCIETY

Population: *total:* 100,647
male: 51,249
female: 49,398 (2024 est.)
comparison rankings: female 196; male 192; total 195

Nationality: *noun:* Saint Vincentian(s) or Vincentian(s)
adjective: Saint Vincentian or Vincentian

Ethnic groups: African descent 71.2%, mixed 23%, Indigenous 3%, East Indian/Indian 1.1%, European 1.5%, other 0.2% (2012 est.)

Languages: English, Vincentian Creole English, French patois

Religions: Protestant 75% (Pentecostal 27.6%, Anglican 13.9%, Seventh Day Adventist 11.6%, Baptist 8.9%, Methodist 8.7%, Evangelical 3.8%, Salvation Army 0.3%, Presbyterian/Congregational 0.3%), Roman Catholic 6.3%, Rastafarian 1.1%, Jehovah's Witness 0.8%, other 4.7%, none 7.5%, unspecified 4.7% (2012 est.)

Age structure: *0-14 years:* 18.8% (male 9,527/female 9,353)
15-64 years: 68.2% (male 35,401/female 33,288)
65 years and over: 13% (2024 est.) (male 6,321/female 6,757)

Dependency ratios: *total dependency ratio:* 49
youth dependency ratio: 32.9
elderly dependency ratio: 16.1
potential support ratio: 6.2 (2021 est.)

Median age: *total:* 37.6 years (2024 est.)

male: 37.7 years
female: 37.4 years
comparison ranking: total 82

Population growth rate: -0.15% (2024 est.)
comparison ranking: 208

Birth rate: 11.9 births/1,000 population (2024 est.)
comparison ranking: 150

Death rate: 7.7 deaths/1,000 population (2024 est.)
comparison ranking: 96

Net migration rate: -5.8 migrant(s)/1,000 population (2024 est.)
comparison ranking: 208

Population distribution: most of the population is concentrated in and around the capital of Kingstown

Urbanization: *urban population:* 54.3% of total population (2023)
rate of urbanization: 0.94% annual rate of change (2020-25 est.)

Major urban areas - population: 27,000 KINGSTOWN (capital) (2018)

Sex ratio: *at birth:* 1.03 male(s)/female
0-14 years: 1.02 male(s)/female
15-64 years: 1.06 male(s)/female
65 years and over: 0.94 male(s)/female
total population: 1.04 male(s)/female (2024 est.)

Maternal mortality ratio: 62 deaths/100,000 live births (2020 est.)
comparison ranking: 91

Infant mortality rate: *total:* 12.3 deaths/1,000 live births (2024 est.)
male: 13.9 deaths/1,000 live births
female: 10.7 deaths/1,000 live births
comparison ranking: total 108

Life expectancy at birth: *total population:* 77.2 years (2024 est.)
male: 75.2 years
female: 79.3 years
comparison ranking: total population 96

Total fertility rate: 1.74 children born/woman (2024 est.)
comparison ranking: 152

Gross reproduction rate: 0.85 (2024 est.)

Contraceptive prevalence rate: NA

Drinking water source: *improved: total:* 95.1% of population
unimproved: total: 4.9% of population (2017 est.)

Current health expenditure: 4.8% of GDP (2020)

Physician density: 0.66 physicians/1,000 population (2012)

Hospital bed density: 4.3 beds/1,000 population (2016)

Sanitation facility access: *improved:*
total: 90.2% of population
unimproved:
total: 9.8% of population (2017 est.)

Obesity - adult prevalence rate: 23.7% (2016)
comparison ranking: 64

Alcohol consumption per capita: *total:* 7.48 liters of pure alcohol (2019 est.)
beer: 2.52 liters of pure alcohol (2019 est.)
wine: 0.24 liters of pure alcohol (2019 est.)
spirits: 4.48 liters of pure alcohol (2019 est.)
other alcohols: 0.23 liters of pure alcohol (2019 est.)
comparison ranking: total 52

Currently married women (ages 15-49): 53.3% (2023 est.)

Education expenditures: 5.7% of GDP (2018 est.)
comparison ranking: 52

Literacy: *total population:* NA
male: NA
female: NA

School life expectancy (primary to tertiary education): *total:* 14 years
male: 14 years
female: 15 years (2015)

ENVIRONMENT

Environment - current issues: pollution of coastal waters and shorelines from discharges by pleasure yachts and other effluents; in some areas, pollution is severe enough to make swimming prohibitive; poor land use planning; deforestation; watershed management and squatter settlement control

Environment - international agreements: *party to:* Biodiversity, Climate Change, Climate Change-Kyoto Protocol, Climate Change-Paris Agreement, Comprehensive Nuclear Test Ban, Desertification, Endangered Species, Environmental Modification, Hazardous Wastes, Law of the Sea, Marine Dumping-London Convention, Ozone Layer Protection, Ship Pollution, Whaling
signed, but not ratified: none of the selected agreements

Climate: tropical; little seasonal temperature variation; rainy season (May to November)

Urbanization: *urban population:* 54.3% of total population (2023)
rate of urbanization: 0.94% annual rate of change (2020-25 est.)

Revenue from forest resources: 0.02% of GDP (2018 est.)
comparison ranking: 145

Revenue from coal: 0% of GDP (2018 est.)
comparison ranking: 105

Air pollutants: *particulate matter emissions:* 9.41 micrograms per cubic meter (2019 est.)
carbon dioxide emissions: 0.22 megatons (2016 est.)
methane emissions: 0.09 megatons (2020 est.)

Waste and recycling: *municipal solid waste generated annually:* 31,561 tons (2015 est.)

Total water withdrawal: *municipal:* 10 million cubic meters (2020 est.)
industrial: 2,000 cubic meters (2017 est.)
agricultural: 0 cubic meters (2017 est.)

Total renewable water resources: 100 million cubic meters (2020 est.)

GOVERNMENT

Country name: *conventional long form:* none
conventional short form: Saint Vincent and the Grenadines
etymology: Saint Vincent was named by explorer Christopher COLUMBUS after Saint VINCENT of Saragossa because the 22 January 1498 day of discovery was the saint's feast day

Government type: parliamentary democracy under a constitutional monarchy; a Commonwealth realm

Capital: *name:* Kingstown
geographic coordinates: 13 08 N, 61 13 W
time difference: UTC-4 (1 hour ahead of Washington, DC, during Standard Time)
etymology: an earlier French settlement was renamed Kingstown by the British in 1763 when they assumed control of the island; the king referred to in the name is GEORGE III (r. 1760-1820)

Administrative divisions: 6 parishes; Charlotte, Grenadines, Saint Andrew, Saint David, Saint George, Saint Patrick

Independence: 27 October 1979 (from the UK)

National holiday: Independence Day, 27 October (1979)

Legal system: English common law

Constitution: *history:* previous 1969, 1975; latest drafted 26 July 1979, effective 27 October 1979 (The Saint Vincent Constitution Order 1979)
amendments: proposed by the House of Assembly; passage requires at least two-thirds majority vote of the Assembly membership and assent of the governor general; passage of amendments to constitutional sections on fundamental rights and freedoms, citizen protections, various government functions and authorities, and constitutional amendment procedures requires approval by the Assembly membership, approval in a referendum of at least two thirds of the votes cast, and assent of the governor general

International law organization participation: has not submitted an ICJ jurisdiction declaration; accepts ICCt jurisdiction

Citizenship: *citizenship by birth:* yes
citizenship by descent only: at least one parent must be a citizen of Saint Vincent and the Grenadines
dual citizenship recognized: yes
residency requirement for naturalization: 7 years

Suffrage: 18 years of age; universal

Executive branch: *chief of state:* King CHARLES III (since 8 September 2022); represented by Governor General Susan DOUGAN (since 1 August 2019)
head of government: Prime Minister Ralph Everard GONSALVES (since 29 March 2001)
cabinet: Cabinet appointed by the governor general on the advice of the prime minister
elections/appointments: the monarchy is hereditary; governor general appointed by the monarch; following legislative elections, the leader of the majority party usually appointed prime minister by the governor general; deputy prime minister appointed by the governor general on the advice of the prime minister

Legislative branch: *description:* unicameral House of Assembly (23 seats; 15 representatives directly elected in single-seat constituencies by simple majority vote, 6 senators appointed by the governor general, and 2 ex officio members - the speaker of the house and the attorney general; members serve 5-year terms)
elections: last held on 5 November 2020 (next to be held in 2025)
election results: percent of vote by party - ULP 49.58%, NDP 50.34%, other 0.8%; seats by party - ULP 9, NDP 6;
composition - men 18, women 5, percentage women 21.7%

Judicial branch: *highest court(s):* the Eastern Caribbean Supreme Court (ECSC) is the superior court of the Organization of Eastern Caribbean States; the ECSC - headquartered on St. Lucia - consists of the Court of Appeal - headed by the chief justice and 4 judges - and the High Court with 18 judges; the Court of Appeal is itinerant, traveling to member states on a schedule to hear appeals from the High Court and subordinate courts; High Court judges reside in the member states, with 2 assigned to Saint Vincent and the Grenadines; note - Saint

Vincent and the Grenadines is also a member of the Caribbean Court of Justice
judge selection and term of office: chief justice of Eastern Caribbean Supreme Court appointed by Her Majesty, Queen ELIZABETH II; other justices and judges appointed by the Judicial and Legal Services Commission, an independent body of judicial officials; Court of Appeal justices appointed for life with mandatory retirement at age 65; High Court judges appointed for life with mandatory retirement at age 62
subordinate courts: magistrates' courts

Political parties: New Democratic Party or NDP
SVG Green Party or SVGP
Unity Labor Party or ULP (formed in 1994 by the coalition of Saint Vincent Labor Party or SVLP and the Movement for National Unity or MNU)

International organization participation: ACP, ACS, AOSIS, C, Caricom, CDB, CELAC, FAO, G-77, IBRD, ICAO, ICCt, ICRM, IDA, IFAD, IFRCS, ILO, IMF, IMO, Interpol, IOC, IOM, ISO (subscriber), ITU, MIGA, NAM, OAS, OECS, OPANAL, OPCW, Petrocaribe, UN, UNCTAD, UNESCO, UNIDO, UPU, WFTU (NGOs), WHO, WIPO, WTO

Diplomatic representation in the US: *chief of mission:* Ambassador Lou-Anne Gaylene GILCHRIST (since 18 January 2017)
chancery: 1627 K Street, NW, Suite 704, Washington, DC 20006
telephone: [1] (202) 364-6730
FAX: [1] (202) 364-6736
email address and website:
mail@embsvg.com
http://wa.embassy.gov.vc/washington/
consulate(s) general: New York

Diplomatic representation from the US: *embassy:* the US does not have an embassy in Saint Vincent and the Grenadines; the US Ambassador to Barbados is accredited to Saint Vincent and the Grenadines

Flag description: three vertical bands of blue (hoist side), gold (double width), and green; the gold band bears three green diamonds arranged in a V pattern, which stands for Vincent; the diamonds recall the islands as "the Gems of the Antilles" and are set slightly lowered in the gold band to reflect the nation's position in the Antilles; blue conveys the colors of a tropical sky and crystal waters, yellow signifies the golden Grenadine sands, and green represents lush vegetation

National symbol(s): Saint Vincent parrot; national colors: blue, gold, green

National anthem: *name:* "St. Vincent! Land So Beautiful!"
lyrics/music: Phyllis Joyce MCCLEAN PUNNETT/ Joel Bertram MIGUEL
note: adopted 1967

ECONOMY

Economic overview: upper middle-income Caribbean island economy; key agriculture and tourism sectors; environmentally fragile; diversifying economy across services, science and knowledge, and creative industries; CARICOM member and US Caribbean Basin Initiative beneficiary

Real GDP (purchasing power parity): $1.858 billion (2023 est.)
$1.752 billion (2022 est.)
$1.635 billion (2021 est.)
note: data in 2021 dollars
comparison ranking: 203

Real GDP growth rate: 6.02% (2023 est.)
7.16% (2022 est.)
0.75% (2021 est.)
note: annual GDP % growth based on constant local currency
comparison ranking: 31

Real GDP per capita: $17,900 (2023 est.)
$16,900 (2022 est.)
$15,700 (2021 est.)
note: data in 2021 dollars
comparison ranking: 108

GDP (official exchange rate): $1.066 billion (2023 est.)
note: data in current dollars at official exchange rate

Inflation rate (consumer prices): 4.56% (2023 est.)
5.66% (2022 est.)
1.57% (2021 est.)
note: annual % change based on consumer prices
comparison ranking: 96

Credit ratings: Moody's rating: B3 (2014)
note: The year refers to the year in which the current credit rating was first obtained.

GDP - composition, by sector of origin: *agriculture:* 4.2% (2023 est.)
industry: 14.2% (2023 est.)
services: 64.2% (2023 est.)
note: figures may not total 100% due to non-allocated consumption not captured in sector-reported data
comparison rankings: services 62; industry 173; agriculture 125

GDP - composition, by end use: *household consumption:* 87.3% (2017 est.)
government consumption: 16.6% (2017 est.)
investment in fixed capital: 10.8% (2017 est.)
investment in inventories: -0.2% (2017 est.)
exports of goods and services: 37.1% (2017 est.)
imports of goods and services: -51.7% (2017 est.)

Agricultural products: bananas, root vegetables, plantains, vegetables, fruits, coconuts, mangoes/guavas, yams, spices, sweet potatoes (2022)
note: top ten agricultural products based on tonnage

Industries: tourism; food processing, cement, furniture, clothing, starch

Industrial production growth rate: 3.91% (2023 est.)
note: annual % change in industrial value added based on constant local currency
comparison ranking: 79

Labor force: 53,000 (2023 est.)
note: number of people ages 15 or older who are employed or seeking work
comparison ranking: 190

Unemployment rate: 18.67% (2023 est.)
19.51% (2022 est.)
20.28% (2021 est.)
note: % of labor force seeking employment
comparison ranking: 196

Youth unemployment rate (ages 15-24): *total:* 42.3% (2023 est.)
male: 42.5% (2023 est.)
female: 42% (2023 est.)
note: % of labor force ages 15-24 seeking employment
comparison ranking: total 7

Remittances: 6.7% of GDP (2023 est.)
9.17% of GDP (2022 est.)
8.03% of GDP (2021 est.)
note: personal transfers and compensation between resident and non-resident individuals/households/ entities

Budget: *revenues:* $226.404 million (2017 est.)
expenditures: $208.744 million (2017 est.)
note: central government revenues and expenses (excluding grants/extrabudgetary units/social security funds) converted to US dollars at average official exchange rate for year indicated

Public debt: 73.8% of GDP (2017 est.)
comparison ranking: 48

Taxes and other revenues: 23.8% (of GDP) (2017 est.)
note: central government tax revenue as a % of GDP
comparison ranking: 55

Current account balance: -$142.763 million (2023 est.)
-$186.777 million (2022 est.)
-$197.13 million (2021 est.)
note: balance of payments - net trade and primary/ secondary income in current dollars
comparison ranking: 102

Exports: $347.827 million (2023 est.)
$278.292 million (2022 est.)
$140.607 million (2021 est.)
note: balance of payments - exports of goods and services in current dollars
comparison ranking: 194

Exports - partners: Malaysia 34%, US 10%, Greece 9%, Barbados 8%, Spain 6% (2022)
note: top five export partners based on percentage share of exports

Exports - commodities: refined petroleum, ships, fish, shellfish, wheat (2022)
note: top five export commodities based on value in dollars

Imports: $566.477 million (2023 est.)
$537.929 million (2022 est.)
$425.694 million (2021 est.)
note: balance of payments - imports of goods and services in current dollars
comparison ranking: 201

Imports - partners: US 40%, Trinidad and Tobago 10%, China 6%, UK 6%, Turkey 5% (2022)
note: top five import partners based on percentage share of imports

Imports - commodities: refined petroleum, poultry, ships, raw sugar, plastic products (2022)
note: top five import commodities based on value in dollars

Reserves of foreign exchange and gold: $280.564 million (2023 est.)
$320.193 million (2022 est.)
$311.903 million (2021 est.)
note: holdings of gold (year-end prices)/foreign exchange/special drawing rights in current dollars
comparison ranking: 180

Debt - external: $414.492 million (2022 est.)
note: present value of external debt in current US dollars
comparison ranking: 93

Exchange rates: East Caribbean dollars (XCD) per US dollar -

Exchange rates: 2.7 (2023 est.)
2.7 (2022 est.)
2.7 (2021 est.)
2.7 (2020 est.)
2.7 (2019 est.)

ENERGY

Electricity access: *electrification - total population:* 100% (2022 est.)

Electricity: *installed generating capacity:* 54,000 kW (2022 est.)
consumption: 162.316 million kWh (2022 est.)
transmission/distribution losses: 10.868 million kWh (2022 est.)
comparison rankings: transmission/distribution losses 19; consumption 193; installed generating capacity 192

Electricity generation sources: *fossil fuels:* 75.2% of total installed capacity (2022 est.)
solar: 1.7% of total installed capacity (2022 est.)
hydroelectricity: 23.1% of total installed capacity (2022 est.)

Coal: *exports:* 16.8 metric tons (2022 est.)
imports: 16 metric tons (2022 est.)

Petroleum: *refined petroleum consumption:* 2,000 bbl/day (2022 est.)

Carbon dioxide emissions: 246,000 metric tonnes of CO2 (2022 est.)
from petroleum and other liquids: 246,000 metric tonnes of CO2 (2022 est.)
comparison ranking: total emissions 202

Energy consumption per capita: 35.826 million Btu/person (2022 est.)
comparison ranking: 106

COMMUNICATIONS

Telephones - fixed lines: *total subscriptions:* 11,000 (2022 est.)
subscriptions per 100 inhabitants: 11 (2022 est.)
comparison ranking: total subscriptions 186

Telephones - mobile cellular: *total subscriptions:* 104,000 (2022 est.)
subscriptions per 100 inhabitants: 100 (2022 est.)
comparison ranking: total subscriptions 192

Telecommunication systems: *general assessment:* adequate island-wide, fully automatic telephone system; broadband access; expanded FttP (Fiber to the Home) markets; LTE launches; regulatory development; telecom sector contributes greatly to the overall GDP; telecom sector is a growth area (2020)
domestic: fixed-line teledensity is 11 per 100 persons and mobile-cellular teledensity is 110 per 100 persons (2021)
international: country code - 1-784; landing points for the ECFS, CARCIP and Southern Caribbean Fiber submarine cables providing connectivity to US and Caribbean Islands; connectivity also provided by VHF/UHF radiotelephone from Saint Vincent to Barbados; SHF radiotelephone to Grenada and Saint Lucia; access to Intelsat earth station in Martinique through Saint Lucia (2019)

Broadcast media: St. Vincent and the Grenadines Broadcasting Corporation operates 1 TV station and 5 repeater stations that provide near total coverage to the multi-island state; multi-channel cable TV service available; a partially government-funded national radio service broadcasts on 1 station and has 2 repeater stations; about a dozen privately owned radio stations and repeater stations

Internet country code: .vc

Internet users: *total:* 85,000 (2021 est.)
percent of population: 85% (2021 est.)
comparison ranking: total 192

Broadband - fixed subscriptions: *total:* 24,733 (2020 est.)
subscriptions per 100 inhabitants: 22 (2020 est.)
comparison ranking: total 161

TRANSPORTATION

National air transport system: *number of registered air carriers:* 2 (2020)
inventory of registered aircraft operated by air carriers: 11

Civil aircraft registration country code prefix: J8

Airports: 5 (2024)
comparison ranking: 176

Merchant marine: *total:* 830 (2023)
by type: bulk carrier 30, container ship 18, general cargo 137, oil tanker 16, other 629
comparison ranking: total 30

Ports: *total ports:* 1 (2024)
large: 0
medium: 0
small: 1
very small: 0
ports with oil terminals: 1
key ports: Kingstown

MILITARY AND SECURITY

Military and security forces: no regular military forces; Royal Saint Vincent and the Grenadines Police Force (RSVPF; includes the Coast Guard, Special Services Unit, Rapid Response Unit, Drug Squad, and Anti-Trafficking Unit) (2024)
note: the RSVPF is the only security force in the country and is responsible for maintaining internal security; it reports to the Minister of National Security, a portfolio held by the prime minister

Military - note: the country has been a member of the Caribbean Regional Security System (RSS) since its creation in 1982; RSS signatories (Antigua and Barbuda, Barbados, Dominica, Grenada, Guyana, Saint Kitts and Nevis, and Saint Lucia) agreed to prepare contingency plans and assist one another, on request, in national emergencies, prevention of smuggling, search and rescue, immigration control, fishery protection, customs and excise control, maritime policing duties, protection of off-shore installations, pollution control, national and other disasters, and threats to national security (2024)

TRANSNATIONAL ISSUES

Illicit drugs: a transit point for cocaine and marijuana destined for North America, Europe, and elsewhere in the Caribbean; some local demand for cocaine and some use of synthetic drugs

SAMOA

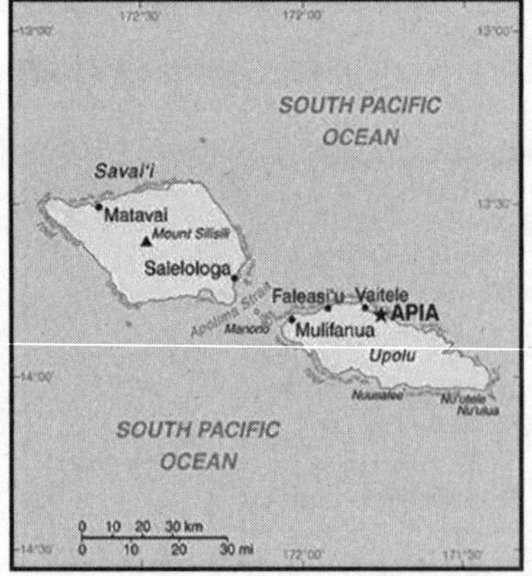

INTRODUCTION

Background: The first Austronesian settlers arrived in Samoa around 1000 B.C., and early Samoans traded and intermarried with Fijian and Tongan nobility. The fa'amatai system of titles and nobility developed, which dominates Samoan politics to this day; all but two seats in the legislature are reserved for matai, or heads of families. A Dutch explorer was the first European to spot the islands in 1722. Christian missionaries arrived in the 1830s and were followed by an influx of American and European settlers and influence. By the 1880s, Germany, the UK, and the US had trading posts and claimed parts of the kingdom. In 1886, an eight-year civil war broke out, with rival matai factions fighting over royal succession and the three foreign powers providing support to the factions. Germany, the UK, and the US all sent warships to Apia in 1889 and came close to conflict, but a cyclone damaged or destroyed the ships of all three navies.

At the end of the civil war in 1894, Malietoa LAUPEPA was installed as king, but upon his death in 1898, a second civil war over succession broke out. When the war ended in 1899, the Western powers abolished the monarchy, giving the western Samoan islands to Germany and the eastern Samoan islands to the US. The UK abandoned claims in Samoa and received former German territory in the Solomon Islands.

New Zealand occupied Samoa during World War I but was accused of negligence and opposed by many Samoans, particularly an organized political movement called the Mau ("Strongly Held View") that advocated for independence. During the 1918-1919 influenza pandemic, about 20% of the population died. In 1929, New Zealand police shot into a crowd of peaceful Mau protestors, killing 11, in an event known as Black Sunday. In 1962, Samoa became the first Polynesian nation to reestablish its independence as Western Samoa but dropped the "Western" from its name in 1997. The Human Rights Protection Party dominated politics from 1982 until Prime Minister FIAME Naomi Mata'afa's Fa'atuatua i le Atua Samoa ua Tasi (FAST) party gained a majority in elections in 2021.

GEOGRAPHY

Location: Oceania, group of islands in the South Pacific Ocean, about halfway between Hawaii and New Zealand

Geographic coordinates: 13 35 S, 172 20 W

Map references: Oceania

Area: *total:* 2,831 sq km
land: 2,821 sq km
water: 10 sq km
comparison ranking: total 177

Area - comparative: slightly smaller than Rhode Island

Land boundaries: *total:* 0 km

Coastline: 403 km

Maritime claims: *territorial sea:* 12 nm
contiguous zone: 24 nm
exclusive economic zone: 200 nm

Climate: tropical; rainy season (November to April), dry season (May to October)

Terrain: two main islands (Savaii, Upolu) and several smaller islands and uninhabited islets; narrow coastal plain with volcanic, rugged mountains in interior

Elevation: *highest point:* Mount Silisili 1,857 m
lowest point: Pacific Ocean 0 m

Natural resources: hardwood forests, fish, hydropower

Land use: *agricultural land:* 12.4% (2018 est.)
arable land: 2.8% (2018 est.)
permanent crops: 7.8% (2018 est.)
permanent pasture: 1.8% (2018 est.)
forest: 60.4% (2018 est.)
other: 27.2% (2018 est.)

Irrigated land: 0 sq km (2022)

Population distribution: about three-quarters of the population lives on the island of Upolu

Natural hazards: occasional cyclones; active volcanism
volcanism: Savai'I Island (1,858 m), which last erupted in 1911, is historically active

Geography - note: occupies an almost central position within Polynesia

PEOPLE AND SOCIETY

Population: *total:* 208,853
male: 105,920
female: 102,933 (2024 est.)
comparison rankings: female 184; male 184; total 184

Nationality: *noun:* Samoan(s)
adjective: Samoan

Ethnic groups: Samoan 96%, Samoan/New Zealander 2%, other 1.9% (2011 est.)
note: data represent the population by country of citizenship

Languages: Samoan (Polynesian) (official) 91.1%, Samoan/English 6.7%, English (official) 0.5%, other 0.2%, unspecified 1.6% (2006 est.)

Religions: Protestant 54.9% (Congregationalist 29%, Methodist 12.4%, Assembly of God 6.8%, Seventh Day Adventist 4.4%, other Protestant 2.3%), Roman Catholic 18.8%, Church of Jesus Christ 16.9%, Worship Centre 2.8%, other Christian 3.6%, other 2.9% (includes Baha'i, Muslim), none 0.2% (2016 est.)

Age structure: *0-14 years:* 26.9% (male 28,952/female 27,173)
15-64 years: 65.9% (male 70,225/female 67,427)
65 years and over: 7.2% (2024 est.) (male 6,743/female 8,333)

Dependency ratios: *total dependency ratio:* 74.9
youth dependency ratio: 66
elderly dependency ratio: 8.9
potential support ratio: 11.2 (2020 est.)

Median age: *total:* 27.4 years (2024 est.)
male: 27 years
female: 27.8 years
comparison ranking: total 158

Population growth rate: 0.65% (2024 est.)
comparison ranking: 134

Birth rate: 18.8 births/1,000 population (2024 est.)
comparison ranking: 75

Death rate: 5.4 deaths/1,000 population (2024 est.)
comparison ranking: 184

Net migration rate: -6.9 migrant(s)/1,000 population (2024 est.)
comparison ranking: 216

Population distribution: about three-quarters of the population lives on the island of Upolu

Urbanization: *urban population:* 17.5% of total population (2023)
rate of urbanization: -0.03% annual rate of change (2020-25 est.)

Major urban areas - population: 36,000 APIA (capital) (2018)

Sex ratio: *at birth:* 1.05 male(s)/female
0-14 years: 1.07 male(s)/female
15-64 years: 1.04 male(s)/female
65 years and over: 0.81 male(s)/female
total population: 1.03 male(s)/female (2024 est.)

Maternal mortality ratio: 59 deaths/100,000 live births (2020 est.)
comparison ranking: 93

Infant mortality rate: *total:* 17.3 deaths/1,000 live births (2024 est.)
male: 20.9 deaths/1,000 live births
female: 13.6 deaths/1,000 live births
comparison ranking: total 87

Life expectancy at birth: *total population:* 75.7 years (2024 est.)
male: 72.8 years
female: 78.7 years
comparison ranking: total population 124

Total fertility rate: 2.33 children born/woman (2024 est.)
comparison ranking: 77

Gross reproduction rate: 1.14 (2024 est.)

Contraceptive prevalence rate: 16.6% (2019/20)

Drinking water source: *improved: urban:* 100% of population
rural: 98% of population
total: 98.4% of population
unimproved: urban: 0% of population
rural: 2% of population
total: 1.6% of population (2020 est.)

Current health expenditure: 5.3 % of GDP (2020)

Physician density: 0.6 physicians/1,000 population (2020)

Sanitation facility access: *improved: urban:* 99.5% of population
rural: 99.5% of population
total: 99.5% of population
unimproved: urban: 0.5% of population
rural: 0.5% of population
total: 0.5% of population (2020 est.)

Obesity - adult prevalence rate: 47.3% (2016)
comparison ranking: 8

Alcohol consumption per capita: *total:* 2.18 liters of pure alcohol (2019 est.)
beer: 2.01 liters of pure alcohol (2019 est.)
wine: 0 liters of pure alcohol (2019 est.)
spirits: 0.17 liters of pure alcohol (2019 est.)
other alcohols: 0 liters of pure alcohol (2019 est.)
comparison ranking: total 127

Tobacco use: *total:* 25.3% (2020 est.)
male: 36.1% (2020 est.)
female: 14.5% (2020 est.)
comparison ranking: total 49

Children under the age of 5 years underweight: 3.4% (2019/20)
comparison ranking: 84

Currently married women (ages 15-49): 61.7% (2023 est.)

Child marriage: *women married by age 15:* 0.9%
women married by age 18: 7.4%
men married by age 18: 2% (2020 est.)

Education expenditures: 4.8% of GDP (2020 est.)
comparison ranking: 85

Literacy: *definition:* age 15 and over can read and write
total population: 99.1%
male: 99%
female: 99.3% (2021)

ENVIRONMENT

Environment - current issues: soil erosion, deforestation, invasive species, overfishing

Environment - international agreements: *party to:* Biodiversity, Climate Change, Climate Change-Kyoto Protocol, Climate Change-Paris Agreement, Comprehensive Nuclear Test Ban, Desertification, Endangered Species, Hazardous Wastes, Law of the Sea, Nuclear Test Ban, Ozone Layer Protection, Ship Pollution, Wetlands
signed, but not ratified: none of the selected agreements

Climate: tropical; rainy season (November to April), dry season (May to October)

Urbanization: *urban population:* 17.5% of total population (2023)
rate of urbanization: -0.03% annual rate of change (2020-25 est.)

Revenue from forest resources: 0.27% of GDP (2018 est.)
comparison ranking: 84

Revenue from coal: 0% of GDP (2018 est.)
comparison ranking: 180

Air pollutants: *particulate matter emissions:* 7.78 micrograms per cubic meter (2019 est.)
carbon dioxide emissions: 0.25 megatons (2016 est.)
methane emissions: 0.27 megatons (2020 est.)

Waste and recycling: *municipal solid waste generated annually:* 27,399 tons (2011 est.)
municipal solid waste recycled annually: 9,864 tons (2013 est.)
percent of municipal solid waste recycled: 36% (2013 est.)

Total renewable water resources: 0 cubic meters (2017 est.)

GOVERNMENT

Country name: *conventional long form:* Independent State of Samoa
conventional short form: Samoa
local long form: Malo Sa'oloto Tuto'atasi o Samoa
local short form: Samoa
former: Western Samoa
etymology: the meaning of Samoa is disputed; some modern explanations are that the "sa" connotes "sacred" and "moa" indicates "center," so the name can mean "Holy Center"; alternatively, some assertions state that it can mean "place of the sacred moa bird" of Polynesian mythology; the name, however, may go back to Proto-Polynesian (PPn) times (before 1000 B.C.); a plausible PPn reconstruction has the first syllable as "sa'a" meaning "tribe or people" and "moa" meaning "deep sea or ocean" to convey the meaning "people of the deep sea"

Government type: parliamentary republic

Capital: *name:* Apia
geographic coordinates: 13 49 S, 171 46 W
time difference: UTC+13 (18 hours ahead of Washington, DC, during Standard Time)
etymology: name derives from the native village around which the capital was constructed in the 1850s; the village still exists within the larger modern capital

Administrative divisions: 11 districts; A'ana, Aiga-i-le-Tai, Atua, Fa'asaleleaga, Gaga'emauga, Gagaifomauga, Palauli, Satupa'itea, Tuamasaga, Va'a-o-Fonoti, Vaisigano

Independence: 1 January 1962 (from New Zealand-administered UN trusteeship)

National holiday: Independence Day Celebration, 1 June (1962); note - 1 January 1962 is the date of independence from the New Zealand-administered UN trusteeship, but it is observed in June

Legal system: mixed legal system of English common law and customary law; judicial review of legislative acts with respect to fundamental rights of the citizen

Constitution: *history:* several previous (preindependence); latest 1 January 1962
amendments: proposed as an act by the Legislative Assembly; passage requires at least two-thirds majority vote by the Assembly membership in the third reading - provided at least 90 days have elapsed since the second reading, and assent of the chief of state; passage of amendments affecting constitutional articles on customary land or constitutional amendment procedures also requires at least two-thirds majority approval in a referendum; amended several times, last in 2020

International law organization participation: has not submitted an ICJ jurisdiction declaration; accepts ICCt jurisdiction

Citizenship: *citizenship by birth:* no
citizenship by descent only: at least one parent must be a citizen of Samoa
dual citizenship recognized: no
residency requirement for naturalization: 5 years

Suffrage: 21 years of age; universal

Executive branch: *chief of state:* TUIMALEALI'IFANO Va'aletoa Sualauvi II (since 21 July 2017)
head of government: Prime Minister FIAME Naomi Mata'afa (since 24 May 2021)
cabinet: Cabinet appointed by the chief of state on the advice of the prime minister
elections/appointments: chief of state indirectly elected by the Legislative Assembly to serve a 5-year term (2-term limit); election last held on 23 August 2022 (next to be held in 2026); following legislative elections, the leader of the majority party is usually appointed prime minister by the chief of state, approved by the Legislative Assembly
election results: TUIMALEALI'IFANO Va'aletoa Sualauvi II (independent) unanimously reelected by the Legislative Assembly

Legislative branch: *description:* unicameral Legislative Assembly or Fono (54 seats); members from single-seat constituencies directly elected by simple majority vote, with a minimum 10% representation of women in the Assembly required; members serve 5-year terms)
elections: election last held on 9 April 2021 (next election to be held in 2026)
election results: percent of vote by party - HRPP 55%, FAST 37%, TSP 3%, independent 5%; seats by party – 35 FAST, HRPP 18, independent 1; composition - men 47, women 7, percentage women 13%

Judicial branch: *highest court(s):* Court of Appeal (consists of the chief justice and 2 Supreme Court judges and meets once or twice a year); Supreme Court (consists of the chief justice and several judges)
judge selection and term of office: chief justice appointed by the chief of state upon the advice of the prime minister; other Supreme Court judges appointed by the Judicial Service Commission, a 3-member body chaired by the chief justice and includes the attorney general and an appointee of the Minister of Justice; judges normally serve until retirement at age 68
subordinate courts: District Court; Magistrates' Courts; Land and Titles Courts; village fono or village chief councils

Political parties: Fa'atuatua i le Atua Samoa ua Tasi or FAST
Human Rights Protection Party or HRPP
Tautua Samoa Party or TSP

International organization participation: ACP, ADB, AOSIS, C, FAO, G-77, IBRD, ICAO, ICCt, ICRM, IDA, IFAD, IFC, IFRCS, ILO, IMF, IMO, Interpol, IOC, IPU, ITU, ITUC (NGOs), MIGA, OPCW, PIF, Sparteca, SPC, UN, UNCTAD, UNESCO, UNIDO, UPU, WCO, WHO, WIPO, WMO, WTO

Diplomatic representation in the US: *chief of mission:* Ambassador Pa'olelei LUTERU (since 7 July 2021); note - also Permanent Representative to the UN
chancery: 685 Third Avenue, 44th Street, 11th Floor, Suite 1102, New York, NY 10017
telephone: [1] (212) 599-6196
FAX: [1] (212) 599-0797
email address and website:
samoa@samoanymission.ws
About | Samoa Permanent Mission to the United Nations
consulate(s) general: Pago Pago (American Samoa)

Diplomatic representation from the US: *chief of mission:* the US Ambassador to New Zealand is accredited to Samoa
embassy: 5th Floor, Accident Corporation Building, Matafele Apia
mailing address: 4400 Apia Place, Washington DC 20521-4400
telephone: [685] 21-436
FAX: [685] 22-030
email address and website:
ApiaConsular@state.gov
https://ws.usembassy.gov/

Flag description: red with a blue rectangle in the upper hoist-side quadrant bearing five white, five-pointed stars representing the Southern Cross constellation; red stands for courage, blue represents freedom, and white signifies purity
note: similar to the flag of Taiwan

National symbol(s): Southern Cross constellation (five, five-pointed stars); national colors: red, white, blue

National anthem: *name:* "O le Fu'a o le Sa'olotoga o Samoa" (The Banner of Freedom)
lyrics/music: Sauni Liga KURESA
note: adopted 1962; also known as "Samoa Tula'i" (Samoa Arise)

ECONOMY

Economic overview: ower middle-income Pacific island economy; enormous fishing and agriculture industries; significant remittances; growing offshore financial hub; recently hosted Pacific Games to drive tourism and infrastructure growth

Real GDP (purchasing power parity): $1.359 billion (2023 est.)
$1.258 billion (2022 est.)
$1.329 billion (2021 est.)
note: data in 2021 dollars
comparison ranking: 205

Real GDP growth rate: 7.99% (2023 est.)
-5.31% (2022 est.)
-7.08% (2021 est.)
note: annual GDP % growth based on constant local currency
comparison ranking: 13

Real GDP per capita: $6,000 (2023 est.)
$5,700 (2022 est.)
$6,100 (2021 est.)
note: data in 2021 dollars
comparison ranking: 169

GDP (official exchange rate): $934.1 million (2023 est.)
note: data in current dollars at official exchange rate

Inflation rate (consumer prices): 8.12% (2023 est.)
10.96% (2022 est.)
3.13% (2021 est.)
note: annual % change based on consumer prices
comparison ranking: 157

GDP - composition, by sector of origin: *agriculture:* 11% (2023 est.)
industry: 11% (2023 est.)
services: 67.6% (2023 est.)
note: figures may not total 100% due to non-allocated consumption not captured in sector-reported data
comparison rankings: services 48; industry 187; agriculture 71

GDP - composition, by end use: *household consumption:* 86.2% (2023 est.)

government consumption: 18.2% (2023 est.)
investment in fixed capital: 34.7% (2023 est.)
investment in inventories: 2.6% (2023 est.)
exports of goods and services: 28.9% (2023 est.)
imports of goods and services: -62.2% (2023 est.)
note: figures may not total 100% due to rounding or gaps in data collection

Agricultural products: coconuts, taro, bananas, tropical fruits, pineapples, mangoes/guavas, papayas, root vegetables, milk, pork (2022)
note: top ten agricultural products based on tonnage

Industries: food processing, building materials, auto parts

Industrial production growth rate: -1.9% (2023 est.)
note: annual % change in industrial value added based on constant local currency
comparison ranking: 178

Labor force: 77,000 (2023 est.)
note: number of people ages 15 or older who are employed or seeking work
comparison ranking: 187

Unemployment rate: 9.75% (2023 est.)
9.92% (2022 est.)
10.37% (2021 est.)
note: % of labor force seeking employment
comparison ranking: 163

Youth unemployment rate (ages 15-24): *total:* 19.8% (2023 est.)
male: 13.4% (2023 est.)
female: 29.9% (2023 est.)
note: % of labor force ages 15-24 seeking employment
comparison ranking: total 64

Population below poverty line: 21.9% (2018 est.)
note: % of population with income below national poverty line

Remittances: 28.36% of GDP (2023 est.)
33.61% of GDP (2022 est.)
29.44% of GDP (2021 est.)
note: personal transfers and compensation between resident and non-resident individuals/households/entities

Budget: *revenues:* $342.18 million (2021 est.)
expenditures: $297.736 million (2021 est.)
note: central government revenues (excluding grants) and expenses converted to US dollars at average official exchange rate for year indicated

Public debt: 49.1% of GDP (2017 est.)
comparison ranking: 107

Taxes and other revenues: 25.02% (of GDP) (2021 est.)
note: central government tax revenue as a % of GDP
comparison ranking: 46

Current account balance: $46.511 million (2023 est.)
-$86.678 million (2022 est.)
-$114.383 million (2021 est.)
note: balance of payments - net trade and primary/secondary income in current dollars
comparison ranking: 77

Exports: $347.19 million (2023 est.)
$162.803 million (2022 est.)
$97.774 million (2021 est.)
note: balance of payments - exports of goods and services in current dollars
comparison ranking: 195

Exports - partners: India 23%, US 19%, NZ 12%, Hungary 8%, Poland 6% (2022)
note: top five export partners based on percentage share of exports

Exports - commodities: coconut oil, integrated circuits, insulated wire, citrus, power equipment (2022)
note: top five export commodities based on value in dollars

Imports: $560.488 million (2023 est.)
$512.002 million (2022 est.)
$430.011 million (2021 est.)
note: balance of payments - imports of goods and services in current dollars
comparison ranking: 202

Imports - partners: China 25%, Singapore 16%, NZ 14%, South Korea 7%, US 7% (2022)
note: top five import partners based on percentage share of imports

Imports - commodities: refined petroleum, coated flat-rolled iron, fish, poultry, ships (2022)
note: top five import commodities based on value in dollars

Reserves of foreign exchange and gold: $447.09 million (2023 est.)
$321.163 million (2022 est.)
$294.682 million (2021 est.)
note: holdings of gold (year-end prices)/foreign exchange/special drawing rights in current dollars
comparison ranking: 184

Debt - external: $279.335 million (2022 est.)
note: present value of external debt in current US dollars
comparison ranking: 96

Exchange rates: tala (SAT) per US dollar -

Exchange rates: 2.738 (2023 est.)
2.689 (2022 est.)
2.556 (2021 est.)
2.665 (2020 est.)
2.649 (2019 est.)

ENERGY

Electricity access: *electrification - total population:* 98.3% (2022 est.)
electrification - urban areas: 100%
electrification - rural areas: 97.9%

Electricity: *installed generating capacity:* 53,000 kW (2022 est.)
consumption: 177.279 million kWh (2022 est.)
transmission/distribution losses: 17.175 million kWh (2022 est.)
comparison rankings: transmission/distribution losses 24; consumption 191; installed generating capacity 193

Electricity generation sources: *fossil fuels:* 66.9% of total installed capacity (2022 est.)
solar: 12.3% of total installed capacity (2022 est.)
wind: 0.1% of total installed capacity (2022 est.)
hydroelectricity: 20.6% of total installed capacity (2022 est.)
biomass and waste: 0.1% of total installed capacity (2022 est.)

Petroleum: *refined petroleum consumption:* 2,000 bbl/day (2022 est.)

Carbon dioxide emissions: 311,000 metric tonnes of CO_2 (2022 est.)
from petroleum and other liquids: 311,000 metric tonnes of CO_2 (2022 est.)
comparison ranking: total emissions 197

Energy consumption per capita: 20.949 million Btu/person (2022 est.)
comparison ranking: 130

COMMUNICATIONS

Telephones - fixed lines: *total subscriptions:* 5,000 (2022 est.)
subscriptions per 100 inhabitants: 2 (2022 est.)
comparison ranking: total subscriptions 203

Telephones - mobile cellular: *total subscriptions:* 134,000 (2022 est.)
subscriptions per 100 inhabitants: 60 (2022 est.)
comparison ranking: total subscriptions 189

Telecommunication systems: *general assessment:* Samoa was one of the first Pacific Island countries to establish a regulatory infrastructure and to liberalize its telecom market; the advent of competition in the mobile market saw prices fall by around 50% and network coverage increase to more than 90% of the population; Samoa also boasts one of the highest rates of mobile phone coverage in the Pacific region; the growth of fixed-line internet has been impeded by factors including the high costs for bandwidth, under investment in fixed-line infrastructure; Samoa's telecoms sector has been inhibited by a lack of international connectivity; Samoa has had access to the Samoa-America-Samoa (SAS) cable laid in 2009, this cable has insufficient capacity to meet the country's future bandwidth needs; this issue was addressed with two new submarine cables that became available in 2018 and 2019; combined with the Samoa National Broadband Highway (SNBH), have improved internet data rates and reliability, and have helped to reduce the high costs previously associated with internet access in Samoa; in April 2022, the Samoan government announced its decision to take over control of the Samoa Submarine Cable Company, looking to the cable to generate additional revenue for the state (2022)
domestic: fixed-line is 3 per 100 and mobile-cellular teledensity 32 telephones per 100 persons (2021)
international: country code - 685; landing points for the Tui-Samo, Manatua, SAS, and Southern Cross NEXT submarine cables providing connectivity to Samoa, Fiji, Wallis & Futuna, Cook Islands, Niue, French Polynesia, American Samoa, Australia, New Zealand, Kiribati, Los Angeles (US), and Tokelau; satellite earth station - 1 Intelsat (Pacific Ocean) (2019)

Broadcast media: state-owned TV station privatized in 2008; 4 privately owned television broadcast stations; about a half-dozen privately owned radio stations and one state-owned radio station; TV and radio broadcasts of several stations from American Samoa are available (2019)

Internet country code: .ws

Internet users: *total:* 171,600 (2021 est.)
percent of population: 78% (2021 est.)
comparison ranking: total 182

Broadband - fixed subscriptions: *total:* 1,692 (2020 est.)
subscriptions per 100 inhabitants: 1 (2020 est.)
comparison ranking: total 199

TRANSPORTATION

National air transport system: *number of registered air carriers:* 1 (2020)
inventory of registered aircraft operated by air carriers: 4
annual passenger traffic on registered air carriers: 137,770 (2018)

Civil aircraft registration country code prefix: 5W

Airports: 3 (2024)
comparison ranking: 186

Roadways: *total:* 1,150 km (2018)
comparison ranking: total 183

Merchant marine: *total:* 13 (2023)
by type: general cargo 3, oil tanker 1, other 9
comparison ranking: total 155

Ports: *total ports:* 1 (2024)
large: 0
medium: 0
small: 0
very small: 1
ports with oil terminals: 1
key ports: Apia

MILITARY AND SECURITY

Military and security forces: *no regular military forces; Ministry of Police, Prisons, and Correction Services:* Samoa Police Force (2024)

Military - note: informal defense ties exist with New Zealand, which is required to consider any Samoan request for assistance under the 1962 Treaty of Friendship

Samoa has a "shiprider" agreement with the US, which allows local maritime law enforcement officers to embark on US Coast Guard (USCG) and US Navy (USN) vessels, including to board and search vessels suspected of violating laws or regulations within Somoa's designated exclusive economic zone (EEZ) or on the high seas; "shiprider" agreements also enable USCG personnel and USN vessels with embarked USCG law enforcement personnel to work with host nations to protect critical regional resources (2024)

SAN MARINO

INTRODUCTION

Background: Geographically the third-smallest state in Europe (after the Holy See and Monaco), San Marino also claims to be the world's oldest republic. According to tradition, it was founded by a Christian stonemason named MARINUS in A.D. 301. San Marino's foreign policy is aligned with that of the EU, although it is not a member. San Marino is negotiating an Association Agreement that is expected to allow participation in the EU's internal market and cooperation in other policy areas by late 2024. Social and political trends in the republic track closely with those of its larger neighbor, Italy.

GEOGRAPHY

Location: Southern Europe, an enclave in central Italy

Geographic coordinates: 43 46 N, 12 25 E

Map references: Europe

Area: *total:* 61 sq km
land: 61 sq km
water: 0 sq km
comparison ranking: total 227

Area - comparative: about one-third the size of Washington, DC

Land boundaries: *total:* 37 km
border countries (1): Italy 37 km

Coastline: 0 km (landlocked)

Maritime claims: none (landlocked)

Climate: Mediterranean; mild to cool winters; warm, sunny summers

Terrain: rugged mountains

Elevation: *highest point:* Monte Titano 739 m
lowest point: Torrente Ausa 55 m

Natural resources: building stone

Land use: *agricultural land:* 16.7% (2018 est.)
arable land: 16.7% (2018 est.)
permanent crops: 0% (2018 est.)
permanent pasture: 0% (2018 est.)
forest: 0% (2018 est.)
other: 83.3% (2018 est.)

Irrigated land: 0 sq km (2022)

Natural hazards: occasional earthquakes

Geography - note: landlocked; an enclave of (completely surrounded by) Italy; smallest independent state in Europe after the Holy See and Monaco; dominated by the Apennine Mountains

PEOPLE AND SOCIETY

Population: *total:* 35,095
male: 16,944
female: 18,151 (2024 est.)
comparison rankings: female 214; male 214; total 214

Nationality: *noun:* Sammarinese (singular and plural)
adjective: Sammarinese

Ethnic groups: Sammarinese, Italian

Languages: Italian
major-language sample(s):
L'Almanacco dei fatti del mondo, l'indispensabile fonte per le informazioni di base. (Italian)

Religions: Roman Catholic

Age structure: *0-14 years:* 14.2% (male 2,614/female 2,387)
15-64 years: 64.3% (male 10,916/female 11,648)
65 years and over: 21.5% (2024 est.) (male 3,414/female 4,116)

Dependency ratios: *total dependency ratio:* 49.6
youth dependency ratio: 19.6
elderly dependency ratio: 30
potential support ratio: 3.3 (2021)

Median age: *total:* 46.1 years (2024 est.)
male: 44.5 years
female: 47.4 years
comparison ranking: total 14

Population growth rate: 0.57% (2024 est.)
comparison ranking: 144

Birth rate: 9 births/1,000 population (2024 est.)
comparison ranking: 199

Death rate: 8.9 deaths/1,000 population (2024 est.)
comparison ranking: 63

Net migration rate: 5.6 migrant(s)/1,000 population (2024 est.)
comparison ranking: 18

Urbanization: *urban population:* 97.8% of total population (2023)
rate of urbanization: 0.41% annual rate of change (2020-25 est.)

Major urban areas - population: 4,000 SAN MARINO (2018)

Sex ratio: *at birth:* 1.09 male(s)/female
0-14 years: 1.1 male(s)/female
15-64 years: 0.94 male(s)/female
65 years and over: 0.83 male(s)/female
total population: 0.93 male(s)/female (2024 est.)

Mother's mean age at first birth: 31.9 years (2019)

Infant mortality rate: *total:* 6.2 deaths/1,000 live births (2024 est.)
male: 7.4 deaths/1,000 live births
female: 5 deaths/1,000 live births
comparison ranking: total 168

Life expectancy at birth: *total population:* 84.2 years (2024 est.)
male: 81.7 years
female: 87 years
comparison ranking: total population 6

Total fertility rate: 1.54 children born/woman (2024 est.)
comparison ranking: 195

Gross reproduction rate: 0.74 (2024 est.)

Drinking water source: *improved:*
total: 100% of population

Current health expenditure: 8.7% of GDP (2020)

Physician density: 6.11 physicians/1,000 population (2014)

Hospital bed density: 3.8 beds/1,000 population (2012)

Sanitation facility access: *improved:*
total: 100% of population

Currently married women (ages 15-49): 47.7% (2023 est.)

Education expenditures: 3.4% of GDP (2020 est.)
comparison ranking: 143

Literacy: *total population:* 99.9%

male: 99.9%
female: 99.9% (2018)

School life expectancy (primary to tertiary education): *total:* 12 years
male: 13 years
female: 12 years (2021)

ENVIRONMENT

Environment - current issues: air pollution; urbanization decreasing rural farmlands; water shortage

Environment - international agreements: *party to:* Biodiversity, Climate Change, Climate Change-Kyoto Protocol, Climate Change-Paris Agreement, Comprehensive Nuclear Test Ban, Desertification, Endangered Species, Nuclear Test Ban, Ozone Layer Protection, Whaling
signed, but not ratified: Air Pollution

Climate: Mediterranean; mild to cool winters; warm, sunny summers

Land use: *agricultural land:* 16.7% (2018 est.)
arable land: 16.7% (2018 est.)
permanent crops: 0% (2018 est.)
permanent pasture: 0% (2018 est.)
forest: 0% (2018 est.)
other: 83.3% (2018 est.)

Urbanization: *urban population:* 97.8% of total population (2023)
rate of urbanization: 0.41% annual rate of change (2020-25 est.)

Revenue from forest resources: 0% of GDP (2018 est.)
comparison ranking: 170

Air pollutants: *particulate matter emissions:* 9.85 micrograms per cubic meter (2019 est.)
methane emissions: 0.02 megatons (2020 est.)

Waste and recycling: *municipal solid waste generated annually:* 17,175 tons (2016 est.)
municipal solid waste recycled annually: 7,737 tons (2016 est.)
percent of municipal solid waste recycled: 45.1% (2016 est.)

GOVERNMENT

Country name: *conventional long form:* Republic of San Marino
conventional short form: San Marino
local long form: Repubblica di San Marino
local short form: San Marino
etymology: named after Saint MARINUS, who in A.D. 301 founded the monastic settlement around which the city and later the state of San Marino coalesced

Government type: parliamentary republic

Capital: *name:* San Marino (city)
geographic coordinates: 43 56 N, 12 25 E
time difference: UTC+1 (6 hours ahead of Washington, DC, during Standard Time)
daylight saving time: +1hr, begins last Sunday in March; ends last Sunday in October
etymology: named after Saint MARINUS, who in A.D. 301 founded a monastic settlement around which the city and later the state of San Marino coalesced

Administrative divisions: 9 municipalities (castelli, singular - castello); Acquaviva, Borgo Maggiore, Chiesanuova, Domagnano, Faetano, Fiorentino, Montegiardino, San Marino Citta, Serravalle

Independence: 3 September 301 (traditional founding date)

National holiday: Founding of the Republic (or Feast of Saint Marinus), 3 September (A.D. 301)

Legal system: civil law system with Italian civil law influences

Constitution: *history:* San Marino's principal legislative instruments consist of old customs (antiche consuetudini), the Statutory Laws of San Marino (Leges Statutae Sancti Marini), old statutes (antichi statute) from the1600s, Brief Notes on the Constitutional Order and Institutional Organs of the Republic of San Marino (Brevi Cenni sull'Ordinamento Costituzionale e gli Organi Istituzionali della Repubblica di San Marino) and successive legislation, chief among them is the Declaration of the Rights of Citizens and Fundamental Principles of the San Marino Legal Order (Dichiarazione dei Diritti dei Cittadini e dei Principi Fondamentali dell'Ordinamento Sammarinese), approved 8 July 1974
amendments: proposed by the Great and General Council; passage requires two-thirds majority Council vote; Council passage by absolute majority vote also requires passage in a referendum; Declaration of Civil Rights amended several times, last in 2019

International law organization participation: has not submitted an ICJ jurisdiction declaration; accepts ICCt jurisdiction

Citizenship: *citizenship by birth:* no
citizenship by descent only: at least one parent must be a citizen of San Marino
dual citizenship recognized: no
residency requirement for naturalization: 30 years

Suffrage: 18 years of age; universal

Executive branch: *chief of state:* co-chiefs of state Captains Regent Francesca CIVERCHIA and Dalibor RICCARDI (for the period 1 October 2024 - 30 March 2025)
head of government: Secretary of State for Foreign and Political Affairs Luca BECCARI (since 8 January 2020)
cabinet: Congress of State elected by the Grand and General Council
elections/appointments: co-chiefs of state (captains regent) indirectly elected by the Grand and General Council for a single 6-month term; election last held in March 2024 (next to be held in September 2024; Secretary of State for Foreign and Political Affairs indirectly elected by the Grand and General Council for a single 5-year term; election last held on 28 December 2019 (next to be held by November 2024)
election results: March 2024: Alessandro ROSSI (Demos) and Milena GASPERONI (We for the Republic) elected captains regent; percent of Grand and General Council vote - NA

September 2023: Filippo TAMAGNINI and Gaetano TROINA elected captains regent; percent of Grand and General Council vote - NA
2019: Luca BECCARI (PDCS) elected Secretary of State for Foreign and Political Affairs; percent of Grand and General Council vote - NA
note: the captains regent preside over meetings of the Grand and General Council and its cabinet (Congress of State), which has seven other members who are selected by the Grand and General Council; assisting the captains regent are seven secretaries of state; the secretary of state for Foreign Affairs has some prime ministerial roles

Legislative branch: *description:* unicameral Grand and General Council or Consiglio Grande e Generale (60 seats; members directly elected in single- and multi-seat constituencies by list proportional representation vote in 2 rounds if needed; members serve 5-year terms)
elections: last held on 9 June 2024 (next to be held by 30 June 2029)
election results: percent of vote by party/coalition - (PDCS 34.1% & AR 6.9% coalition), (PS 15.8% & PSD 12.2% coalition), RF 12%, DML 8.5%, RETE 5.1% seats by party/coalition - (PDCS 22 & AR 4 coalition), (PS 10 & PSD 8 coalition), RF 8, DML 5, RETE 3, composition - men 42, women 18, percentage women 30%

Judicial branch: *highest court(s):* Council of Twelve or Consiglio dei XII (consists of 12 members); note - the College of Guarantors for the Constitutionality and General Norms functions as San Marino's constitutional court
judge selection and term of office: judges elected by the Grand and General Council from among its own to serve 5- year terms
subordinate courts: first instance and first appeal criminal, administrative, and civil courts; Court for the Trust and Trustee Relations; justices of the peace or conciliatory judges

Political parties: Domani - Modus Liberi or DML
Free San Marino (Libera San Marino) or Libera
Future Republic or RF
Party of Socialists and Democrats or PSD
Reformist Alliance or AR
RETE Movement
Sammarinese Christian Democratic Party or PDCS
Socialist Party or PS
Tomorrow in Movement coalition (includes RETE Movement, DML)

International organization participation: CE, FAO, IAEA, IBRD, ICAO, ICC (NGOs), ICCt, ICRM, IDA, IFRCS, ILO, IMF, IMO, Interpol, IOC, IOM (observer), IPU, ITU, ITUC (NGOs), LAIA (observer), OPCW, OSCE, Schengen Convention (de facto member), UN, UNCTAD, UNESCO, Union Latina, UNWTO, UPU, WHO, WIPO

Diplomatic representation in the US: *chief of mission:* Ambassador Damiano BELEFFI (since 21 July 2017); note - also Permanent Representative to the UN
chancery: 327 E 50th Street, New York, NY 10022
telephone: [1] (212) 751-1234
FAX: [1] (212) 751-1436
email address and website:
sanmarinoun@gmail.com
Republic of San Marino Permanent Mission to the United Nations

Diplomatic representation from the US: *chief of mission:* Ambassador Jack Markell (since September 2023); note - also accredited to Italy
embassy: the United States does not have an Embassy in San Marino; the US Ambassador to Italy is accredited to San Marino, and the US Consulate General in Florence maintains day-to-day ties

Flag description: *two equal horizontal bands of white (top) and light blue with the national coat of arms superimposed in the center; the main colors derive from the shield of the coat of arms, which features three white towers on three peaks on a blue field; the towers represent three castles built on San Marino's highest feature, Mount Titano:* Guaita, Cesta, and Montale; the coat of arms is flanked by a wreath, below a crown and above a scroll bearing the word LIBERTAS (Liberty); the white and blue colors are also said to stand for peace and liberty respectively

National symbol(s): three peaks each displaying a tower; national colors: white, blue

National anthem: *name:* "Inno Nazionale della Repubblica" (National Anthem of the Republic)
lyrics/music: no lyrics/Federico CONSOLO
note: adopted 1894; the music for the lyric-less anthem is based on a 10th century chorale piece

National heritage: *total World Heritage Sites:* 1 (cultural)
selected World Heritage Site locales: San Marino Historic Center and Mount Titano

ECONOMY

Economic overview: high-income, non-EU European economy; surrounded by Italy, which is the dominant importer and exporter; open border to EU and a euro user; strong financial sector; high foreign investments; low taxation; increasingly high and risky debt

Real GDP (purchasing power parity): $2.218 billion (2021 est.)
$2.045 billion (2020 est.)
$2.19 billion (2019 est.)
note: data in 2021 dollars
comparison ranking: 198

Real GDP growth rate: 8.46% (2021 est.)
-6.65% (2020 est.)
2.07% (2019 est.)
note: annual GDP % growth based on constant local currency
comparison ranking: 9

Real GDP per capita: $65,700 (2021 est.)
$60,100 (2020 est.)
$64,100 (2019 est.)
note: data in 2021 dollars
comparison ranking: 21

GDP (official exchange rate): $1.855 billion (2021 est.)
note: data in current dollars at official exchange rate

Inflation rate (consumer prices): 1.05% (2017 est.)
0.57% (2016 est.)
0.15% (2015 est.)
note: annual % change based on consumer prices
comparison ranking: 22

Credit ratings: Fitch rating: BB+ (2020)
note: The year refers to the year in which the current credit rating was first obtained.

GDP - composition, by sector of origin: *agriculture:* 0% (2021 est.)
industry: 36.6% (2021 est.)
services: 56.5% (2021 est.)
note: figures may not total 100% due to non-allocated consumption not captured in sector-reported data
comparison rankings: services 111; industry 40; agriculture 211

GDP - composition, by end use: *household consumption:* 33.1% (2021 est.)
government consumption: 18.5% (2021 est.)
investment in fixed capital: 17.5% (2021 est.)
investment in inventories: 4.7% (2021 est.)
exports of goods and services: 184.3% (2021 est.)
imports of goods and services: -158.2% (2021 est.)
note: figures may not total 100% due to rounding or gaps in data collection

Agricultural products: wheat, grapes, corn, olives; cattle, pigs, horses, beef, cheese, hides

Industries: tourism, banking, textiles, electronics, ceramics, cement, wine

Industrial production growth rate: 11.57% (2021 est.)
note: annual % change in industrial value added based on constant local currency
comparison ranking: 10

Unemployment rate: 8.1% (2017 est.)
8.6% (2016 est.)
comparison ranking: 147

Youth unemployment rate (ages 15-24): *total:* 27.4% (2016 est.)
male: 21.4%
female: 36%
comparison ranking: total 34

Remittances: 1.13% of GDP (2021 est.)
1.15% of GDP (2020 est.)
1.08% of GDP (2019 est.)
note: personal transfers and compensation between resident and non-resident individuals/households/entities

Budget: *revenues:* $817.27 million (2022 est.)
expenditures: $816.572 million (2022 est.)
note: central government revenues (excluding grants) and expenses converted to US dollars at average official exchange rate for year indicated

Public debt: 95.12% of GDP (2021 est.)
note: central government debt as a % of GDP
comparison ranking: 24

Taxes and other revenues: 17.3% (of GDP) (2021 est.)
note: central government tax revenue as a % of GDP
comparison ranking: 109

Current account balance: $0 (2017 est.)
$0 (2016 est.)
comparison ranking: 81

Exports: $3.42 billion (2021 est.)
$2.535 billion (2020 est.)
$2.651 billion (2019 est.)
note: GDP expenditure basis - exports of goods and services in current dollars
comparison ranking: 153

Exports - partners: US 10%, Germany 9%, France 9%, Austria 9%, Romania 7% (2022)
note: top five export partners based on percentage share of exports

Exports - commodities: washing and bottling machines, woodworking machines, furniture, other foods, packaged medicine (2022)
note: top five export commodities based on value in dollars

Imports: $2.934 billion (2021 est.)
$2.164 billion (2020 est.)
$2.315 billion (2019 est.)
note: GDP expenditure basis - imports of goods and services in current dollars
comparison ranking: 163

Imports - partners: Italy 22%, Germany 20%, Poland 7%, Spain 7%, Netherlands 7% (2022)
note: top five import partners based on percentage share of imports

Imports - commodities: electricity, garments, cars, aluminum, footwear (2022)
note: top five import commodities based on value in dollars

Reserves of foreign exchange and gold: $836.088 million (2023 est.)
$716.066 million (2022 est.)
$954.383 million (2021 est.)
note: holdings of gold (year-end prices)/foreign exchange/special drawing rights in current dollars
comparison ranking: 164

Exchange rates: euros (EUR) per US dollar -

Exchange rates: 0.925 (2023 est.)
0.951 (2022 est.)
0.845 (2021 est.)
0.877 (2020 est.)
0.893 (2019 est.)
note: while not an EU member state, San Marino, due to its preexisting monetary and banking agreements with Italy, has a 2000 monetary agreement with the EU to produce limited euro coinage—but not banknotes—that began enforcement in January 2002 and was superseded by a new EU agreement in 2012

ENERGY

Electricity access: *electrification - total population:* 100% (2022 est.)

COMMUNICATIONS

Telephones - fixed lines: *total subscriptions:* 16,000 (2022 est.)
subscriptions per 100 inhabitants: 48 (2022 est.)
comparison ranking: total subscriptions 179

Telephones - mobile cellular: *total subscriptions:* 41,000 (2022 est.)
subscriptions per 100 inhabitants: 122 (2022 est.)
comparison ranking: total subscriptions 208

Telecommunication systems: *general assessment:* automatic telephone system completely integrated into Italian system (2018)
domestic: fixed-line is 47 per 100 and mobile-cellular teledensity is 119 telephones per 100 persons (2021)
international: country code - 378; connected to Italian international network

Broadcast media: state-owned public broadcaster operates 1 TV station and 3 radio stations; receives radio and TV broadcasts from Italy (2019)

Internet country code: .sm

Internet users: *total:* 25,500 (2021 est.)
percent of population: 75% (2021 est.)
comparison ranking: total 210

Broadband - fixed subscriptions: *total:* 11,000 (2020 est.)
subscriptions per 100 inhabitants: 32 (2020 est.)
comparison ranking: total 179

TRANSPORTATION

Civil aircraft registration country code prefix: T7

Airports: 1 (2024)
comparison ranking: 214

Heliports: 1 (2024)

Roadways: *total:* 292 km
paved: 292 km (2006)
comparison ranking: total 205

MILITARY AND SECURITY

Military and security forces: Military Corps (National Guard): Guard of the Rock (or Fortress Guard), Uniformed Militia, Guard of the Great and General Council, Corps of the Gendarmerie

Ministry of Internal Affairs: Civil Police Corps (2024)

note: the captains regent oversees the Gendarmerie and National Guard when they are performing duties related to public order and security; the Ministry of Foreign Affairs exercises control over such administrative functions as personnel and equipment, and the courts exercise control over the Gendarmerie when it acts as judicial police

Military service age and obligation: 18 is the legal minimum age for voluntary military service; no conscription; government has the authority to call up all San Marino citizens from 16-60 years of age to serve in the military (2024)

Military - note: defense is the responsibility of Italy

SAO TOME AND PRINCIPE

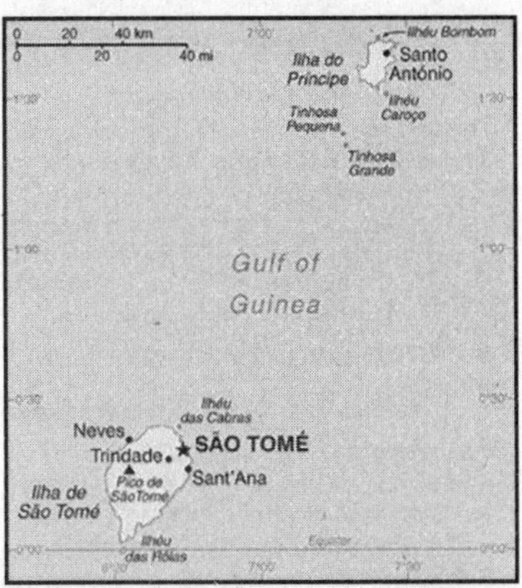

INTRODUCTION

Background: Portugal discovered and colonized the uninhabited Sao Tome and Principe islands in the late 15th century, setting up a sugar-based economy that gave way to coffee and cocoa in the 19th century – all grown with African slave labor, a form of which lingered into the 20th century. While independence was achieved in 1975, democratic reforms were not instituted until the late 1980s.

The country held its first free elections in 1991, but frequent internal wrangling among the various political parties precipitated repeated changes in leadership and failed, non-violent coup attempts in 1995, 1998, 2003, and 2009. In 2012, three opposition parties combined in a no-confidence vote to bring down the majority government of former Prime Minister Patrice TROVOADA, but legislative elections returned him to the office two years later. President Evaristo CARVALHO, of the same political party as TROVOADA, was elected in 2016, marking a rare instance in which the same party held the positions of president and prime minister. TROVOADA resigned in 2018 and was replaced by Jorge BOM JESUS. Carlos Vila NOVA was elected president in 2021. TROVOADA began his fourth stint as prime minister in 2022, after his party's victory in legislative elections.

GEOGRAPHY

Location: Central Africa, islands in the Gulf of Guinea, just north of the Equator, west of Gabon

Geographic coordinates: 1 00 N, 7 00 E

Map references: Africa

Area: *total:* 964 sq km
land: 964 sq km
water: 0 sq km
comparison ranking: total 184

Area - comparative: more than five times the size of Washington, DC

Land boundaries: *total:* 0 km

Coastline: 209 km

Maritime claims: *territorial sea:* 12 nm
exclusive economic zone: 200 nm
measured from claimed archipelagic baselines

Climate: tropical; hot, humid; one rainy season (October to May)

Terrain: volcanic, mountainous

Elevation: *highest point:* Pico de Sao Tome 2,024 m
lowest point: Atlantic Ocean 0 m

Natural resources: fish, hydropower

Land use: *agricultural land:* 50.7% (2018 est.)
arable land: 9.1% (2018 est.)
permanent crops: 40.6% (2018 est.)
permanent pasture: 1% (2018 est.)
forest: 28.1% (2018 est.)
other: 21.2% (2018 est.)

Irrigated land: 100 sq km (2012)

Population distribution: Sao Tome, the capital city, has roughly a quarter of the nation's population; Santo Antonio is the largest town on Principe; the northern areas of both islands have the highest population densities as shown in this population distribution map

Natural hazards: flooding

Geography - note: the second-smallest African country (after the Seychelles); the two main islands form part of a chain of extinct volcanoes, and both are mountainous

PEOPLE AND SOCIETY

Population: *total:* 223,561
male: 111,553
female: 112,008 (2024 est.)
comparison rankings: female 183; male 183; total 183

Nationality: *noun:* Sao Tomean(s)
adjective: Sao Tomean

Ethnic groups: Mestico, Angolares (descendants of Angolan slaves), Forros (descendants of freed slaves), Servicais (contract laborers from Angola, Mozambique, and Cabo Verde), Tongas (children of servicais born on the islands), Europeans (primarily Portuguese), Asians (mostly Chinese)

Languages: Portuguese 98.4% (official), Forro 36.2%, Cabo Verdian 8.5%, French 6.8%, Angolar 6.6%, English 4.9%, Lunguie 1%, other (including sign language) 2.4%; other Portuguese-based Creoles are also spoken (2012 est.)
note: shares of language sum to more than 100% because some respondents gave more than one answer on the census

Religions: Catholic 55.7%, Adventist 4.1%, Assembly of God 3.4%, New Apostolic 2.9%, Mana 2.3%, Universal Kingdom of God 2%, Jehovah's Witness 1.2%, other 6.2%, none 21.2%, unspecified 1% (2012 est.)

Demographic profile: Sao Tome and Principe's youthful age structure – more than 60% of the population is under the age of 25 as of 2020 – and high fertility rate ensure future population growth. Although Sao Tome has a net negative international migration rate, emigration is not a sufficient safety valve to reduce already high levels of unemployment and poverty. While literacy and primary school attendance have improved in recent years, Sao Tome still struggles to improve its educational quality and to increase its secondary school completion rate. Despite some improvements in education and access to healthcare, Sao Tome and Principe has much to do to decrease its high poverty rate, create jobs, and increase its economic growth.

The population of Sao Tome and Principe descends primarily from the islands' colonial Portuguese settlers, who first arrived in the late 15th century, and the much larger number of African slaves brought in for sugar production and the slave trade. For about 100 years after the abolition of slavery in 1876, the population was further shaped by the widespread use of imported unskilled contract laborers from Portugal's other African colonies, who worked on coffee and cocoa plantations. In the first decades after abolition, most workers were brought from Angola under a system similar to slavery. While Angolan laborers were technically free, they were forced or coerced into long contracts that were automatically renewed and extended to their children. Other contract workers from Mozambique and famine-stricken Cape Verde first arrived in the early 20th century under short-term contracts and had the option of repatriation, although some chose to remain in Sao Tome and Principe.

Today's Sao Tomean population consists of mesticos (creole descendants of the European immigrants and African slaves that first inhabited the islands), forros (descendants of freed African slaves), angolares (descendants of runaway African slaves that formed a community in the south of Sao Tome Island and today are fishermen), servicais (contract laborers from Angola, Mozambique, and Cape Verde), tongas (locally born children of contract laborers), and lesser numbers of Europeans and Asians.

Age structure: *0-14 years:* 36.4% (male 41,337/female 40,106)
15-64 years: 60.3% (male 67,101/female 67,775)
65 years and over: 3.2% (2024 est.) (male 3,115/female 4,127)

Dependency ratios: *total dependency ratio:* 77.9
youth dependency ratio: 71.2
elderly dependency ratio: 6.7
potential support ratio: 14.9 (2021 est.)

Median age: *total:* 20.8 years (2024 est.)
male: 20.4 years
female: 21.2 years
comparison ranking: total 197

Population growth rate: 1.42% (2024 est.)
comparison ranking: 70

Birth rate: 26.7 births/1,000 population (2024 est.)
comparison ranking: 39

Death rate: 6 deaths/1,000 population (2024 est.)
comparison ranking: 155

Net migration rate: -6.5 migrant(s)/1,000 population (2024 est.)
comparison ranking: 213

Population distribution: Sao Tome, the capital city, has roughly a quarter of the nation's population; Santo Antonio is the largest town on Principe; the northern areas of both islands have the highest population densities as shown in this population distribution map

Urbanization: *urban population:* 76.4% of total population (2023)
rate of urbanization: 2.96% annual rate of change (2020-25 est.)

Major urban areas - population: 80,000 SAO TOME (capital) (2018)

Sex ratio: *at birth:* 1.03 male(s)/female
0-14 years: 1.03 male(s)/female
15-64 years: 0.99 male(s)/female
65 years and over: 0.75 male(s)/female
total population: 1 male(s)/female (2024 est.)

Mother's mean age at first birth: 19.4 years (2008/09 est.)
note: data represents median age at first birth among women 25-29

Maternal mortality ratio: 146 deaths/100,000 live births (2020 est.)
comparison ranking: 55

Infant mortality rate: *total:* 42.6 deaths/1,000 live births (2024 est.)
male: 46.1 deaths/1,000 live births
female: 39 deaths/1,000 live births
comparison ranking: total 27

Life expectancy at birth: *total population:* 67.7 years (2024 est.)
male: 66 years
female: 69.4 years
comparison ranking: total population 195

Total fertility rate: 3.31 children born/woman (2024 est.)
comparison ranking: 41

Gross reproduction rate: 1.63 (2024 est.)

Contraceptive prevalence rate: 49.7% (2019)

Drinking water source: *improved: urban:* 100% of population
rural: 94% of population
total: 98.5% of population
unimproved: urban: 0% of population
rural: 6% of population
total: 1.5% of population (2020 est.)

Current health expenditure: 4.9% of GDP (2020)

Physician density: 0.49 physicians/1,000 population (2019)

Hospital bed density: 2.9 beds/1,000 population (2011)

Sanitation facility access: *improved: urban:* 57.1% of population
rural: 42.8% of population
total: 53.4% of population
unimproved: urban: 42.9% of population
rural: 57.2% of population
total: 46.6% of population (2020 est.)

Obesity - adult prevalence rate: 12.4% (2016)
comparison ranking: 133

Alcohol consumption per capita: *total:* 4.23 liters of pure alcohol (2019 est.)
beer: 0.42 liters of pure alcohol (2019 est.)
wine: 3.58 liters of pure alcohol (2019 est.)
spirits: 0.23 liters of pure alcohol (2019 est.)
other alcohols: 0 liters of pure alcohol (2019 est.)
comparison ranking: total 92

Tobacco use: *total:* 5.7% (2020 est.)
male: 10.1% (2020 est.)
female: 1.3% (2020 est.)
comparison ranking: total 159

Children under the age of 5 years underweight: 5.4% (2019)
comparison ranking: 72

Currently married women (ages 15-49): 51.9% (2023 est.)

Child marriage: *women married by age 15:* 5.4%
women married by age 18: 28%
men married by age 18: 3.1% (2019 est.)

Education expenditures: 5% of GDP (2020 est.)
comparison ranking: 73

Literacy: *definition:* age 15 and over can read and write
total population: 94.8%
male: 96.5%
female: 91.1% (2021)

School life expectancy (primary to tertiary education): *total:* 12 years
male: 12 years
female: 13 years (2015)

ENVIRONMENT

Environment - current issues: deforestation and illegal logging; soil erosion and exhaustion; inadequate sewage treatment in cities; biodiversity preservation

Environment - international agreements: *party to:* Biodiversity, Climate Change, Climate Change-Kyoto Protocol, Climate Change-Paris Agreement, Desertification, Endangered Species, Environmental Modification, Hazardous Wastes, Law of the Sea, Ozone Layer Protection, Ship Pollution, Wetlands, Whaling
signed, but not ratified: Comprehensive Nuclear Test Ban

Climate: tropical; hot, humid; one rainy season (October to May)

Urbanization: *urban population:* 76.4% of total population (2023)
rate of urbanization: 2.96% annual rate of change (2020-25 est.)

Revenue from forest resources: 1.9% of GDP (2018 est.)
comparison ranking: 36

Revenue from coal: 0% of GDP (2018 est.)
comparison ranking: 110

Air pollutants: *particulate matter emissions:* 33.75 micrograms per cubic meter (2019 est.)
carbon dioxide emissions: 0.12 megatons (2016 est.)
methane emissions: 0.04 megatons (2020 est.)

Waste and recycling: *municipal solid waste generated annually:* 25,587 tons (2014 est.)

Total water withdrawal: *municipal:* 10 million cubic meters (2020 est.)
industrial: 600,000 cubic meters (2017 est.)
agricultural: 30 million cubic meters (2020 est.)

Total renewable water resources: 2.18 billion cubic meters (2020 est.)

GOVERNMENT

Country name: *conventional long form:* Democratic Republic of Sao Tome and Principe
conventional short form: Sao Tome and Principe
local long form: Republica Democratica de Sao Tome e Principe
local short form: Sao Tome e Principe
etymology: Sao Tome was named after Saint THOMAS the Apostle by the Portuguese who discovered the island on 21 December 1470 (or 1471), the saint's feast day; Principe is a shortening of the original Portuguese name of "Ilha do Principe" (Isle of the Prince) referring to the Prince of Portugal to whom duties on the island's sugar crop were paid

Government type: semi-presidential republic

Capital: *name:* Sao Tome
geographic coordinates: 0 20 N, 6 44 E
time difference: UTC 0 (5 hours ahead of Washington, DC, during Standard Time)
etymology: named after Saint Thomas the Apostle

Administrative divisions: 6 districts (distritos, singular - distrito), 1 autonomous region* (regiao autonoma); Agua Grande, Cantagalo, Caue, Lemba, Lobata, Me-Zochi, Principe*

Independence: 12 July 1975 (from Portugal)

National holiday: Independence Day, 12 July (1975)

Legal system: mixed legal system of civil law based on the Portuguese model and customary law

Constitution: *history:* approved 5 November 1975
amendments: proposed by the National Assembly; passage requires two-thirds majority vote by the Assembly; the Assembly can propose to the president of the republic that an amendment be submitted to a referendum; revised several times, last in 2006

International law organization participation: has not submitted an ICJ jurisdiction declaration; non-party state to the ICCt

Citizenship: *citizenship by birth:* no
citizenship by descent only: at least one parent must be a citizen of Sao Tome and Principe
dual citizenship recognized: no
residency requirement for naturalization: 5 years

Suffrage: 18 years of age; universal

Executive branch: *chief of state:* President Carlos Manuel VILA NOVA (since 2 October 2021)
head of government: Prime Minister Patrice TROVOADA (since 11 November 2022)
cabinet: Council of Ministers proposed by the prime minister, appointed by the president
elections/appointments: president directly elected by absolute majority popular vote in 2 rounds if needed for a 5-year term (eligible for a second term); election last held on 18 July 2021 with a runoff on 5 September 2021 (next to be held in 2026); prime minister chosen by the National Assembly and approved by the president
election results:
2021: Carlos Manuel VILA NOVA elected president in the second round; percent of vote in the first round - Carlos Manuel VILA NOVA (IDA) 39.5%; Guilherme POSSER DA COSTA (MLSTP-PSD)

20.8%; Delfim NEVES (PCD-GR) 16.9%; Abel BOM JESUS (independent) 3.6%; Maria DAS NEVES (independent) 3.3%; other 15.9%; percent of the vote in second round - Carlos Manuel VILA NOVA 57.5%, Guilherme POSSER DA COSTA 42.5%
2016: Evaristo CARVALHO elected president; percent of vote - Evaristo CARVALHO (ADI) 49.8%, Manuel Pinto DA COSTA (independent) 24.8%, Maria DAS NEVES (MLSTP-PSD) 24.1%; note - first round results for CARVALHO were revised downward from just over 50%, prompting the 7 August runoff; however, on 1 August 2016 DA COSTA withdrew from the runoff, citing voting irregularities, and Evaristo CARVALHO was declared the winner

Legislative branch: *description:* unicameral National Assembly or Assembleia Nacional (55 seats; members directly elected in multi-seat constituencies by closed party-list proportional representation vote to serve 4-year terms)
elections: last held on 25 September 2022 (next to be held 30 September 2026)
election results: percent of vote by party - ADI 46.8%, MLSTP-PSD 32.7%, MCI-PS-PUN 6.6%, BASTA Movement 8.8%, other 5.1%; seats by party - ADI 30, MLSTP-PSD 18, MCI-PS-PUN 5, BASTA Movement 2; composition - men 47, women 8, percentage women 14.6%

Judicial branch: *highest court(s):* Supreme Court or Supremo Tribunal Justica (consists of 5 judges); Constitutional Court or Tribunal Constitucional (consists of 5 judges, 3 of whom are from the Supreme Court)
judge selection and term of office: Supreme Court judges appointed by the National Assembly; judge tenure NA; Constitutional Court judges nominated by the president and elected by the National Assembly for 5-year terms
subordinate courts: Court of First Instance; Audit Court

Political parties: BASTA Movement
Independent Democratic Action or ADI
Movement for the Liberation of Sao Tome and Principe-Social Democratic Party or MLSTP-PSD
Movement of Independent Citizens of São Tomé and Príncipe - Socialist Party or MCI-PS
National Unity Party or PUN

International organization participation: ACP, AfDB, AOSIS, AU, CD, CEMAC, CPLP, EITI (candidate country), FAO, G-77, IBRD, ICAO, ICRM, IDA, IFAD, IFC, IFRCS, ILO, IMF, IMO, Interpol, IOC, IOM (observer), IPU, ITU, ITUC (NGOs), MIGA, NAM, OIF, OPCW, PCA, UN, UNCTAD, UNESCO, UNIDO, Union Latina, UNWTO, UPU, WCO, WHO, WIPO, WMO, WTO (observer)

Diplomatic representation in the US: *chief of mission:* Ambassador (vacant)
chancery: 122 East 42nd Street, Suite 1604
New York, NY 101168
telephone: [1] (212) 317-0533
FAX: [1] (212) 317-0580
email address and website:
stp1@attglobal.net
Sao Tome and Principe Permanent Mission to the United Nations

Diplomatic representation from the US: *embassy:* the US does not have an embassy in Sao Tome and Principe; the US Ambassador to Angola is accredited to Sao Tome and Principe
mailing address: 2290 Sao Tome Place, Washington DC 20521-2290

Flag description: three horizontal bands of green (top), yellow (double width), and green with two black five-pointed stars placed side by side in the center of the yellow band and a red isosceles triangle based on the hoist side; green stands for the country's rich vegetation, red recalls the struggle for independence, and yellow represents cocoa, one of the country's main agricultural products; the two stars symbolize the two main islands
note: uses the popular Pan-African colors of Ethiopia

National symbol(s): palm tree; national colors: green, yellow, red, black

National anthem: *name:* "Independencia total" (Total Independence)
lyrics/music: Alda Neves DA GRACA do Espirito Santo/Manuel dos Santos Barreto de Sousa e ALMEIDA
note: adopted 1975

ECONOMY

Economic overview: lower middle-income Central African island economy; falling cocoa production due to drought and mismanagement; joint oil venture with Nigeria; government owns 90% of land; high debt, partly from fuel subsidies; tourism gutted by COVID-19

Real GDP (purchasing power parity): $1.267 billion (2023 est.)
$1.273 billion (2022 est.)
$1.272 billion (2021 est.)
note: data in 2021 dollars
comparison ranking: 206

Real GDP growth rate: -0.47% (2023 est.)
0.07% (2022 est.)
1.9% (2021 est.)
note: annual GDP % growth based on constant local currency
comparison ranking: 195

Real GDP per capita: $5,500 (2023 est.)
$5,600 (2022 est.)
$5,700 (2021 est.)
note: data in 2021 dollars
comparison ranking: 173

GDP (official exchange rate): $603.241 million (2023 est.)
note: data in current dollars at official exchange rate

Inflation rate (consumer prices): 21.26% (2023 est.)
18.01% (2022 est.)
8.14% (2021 est.)
note: annual % change based on consumer prices
comparison ranking: 198

GDP - composition, by sector of origin: *agriculture:* 13.9% (2022 est.)
industry: 4.4% (2022 est.)
services: 79% (2022 est.)
note: figures may not total 100% due to non-allocated consumption not captured in sector-reported data
comparison rankings: services 17; industry 215; agriculture 60

GDP - composition, by end use: *household consumption:* 81.4% (2017 est.)
government consumption: 17.6% (2017 est.)
investment in fixed capital: 33.4% (2017 est.)
investment in inventories: 0% (2017 est.)
exports of goods and services: 7.9% (2017 est.)
imports of goods and services: -40.4% (2017 est.)

Agricultural products: plantains, oil palm fruit, taro, bananas, fruits, cocoa beans, coconuts, yams, cassava, carrots/turnips (2022)
note: top ten agricultural products based on tonnage

Industries: light construction, textiles, soap, beer, fish processing, timber

Industrial production growth rate: 6.59% (2022 est.)
note: annual % change in industrial value added based on constant local currency
comparison ranking: 37

Labor force: 76,000 (2023 est.)
note: number of people ages 15 or older who are employed or seeking work
comparison ranking: 188

Unemployment rate: 14.21% (2023 est.)
14.12% (2022 est.)
15.04% (2021 est.)
note: % of labor force seeking employment
comparison ranking: 185

Youth unemployment rate (ages 15-24): *total:* 21.1% (2023 est.)
male: 15.3% (2023 est.)
female: 33.5% (2023 est.)
note: % of labor force ages 15-24 seeking employment
comparison ranking: total 59

Population below poverty line: 55.5% (2017 est.)
note: % of population with income below national poverty line

Gini Index coefficient - distribution of family income: 40.7 (2017 est.)
note: index (0-100) of income distribution; higher values represent greater inequality
comparison ranking: 38

Household income or consumption by percentage share: *lowest 10%:* 2.6% (2017 est.)
highest 10%: 32.8% (2017 est.)
note: % share of income accruing to lowest and highest 10% of population

Remittances: 1.35% of GDP (2023 est.)
1.87% of GDP (2022 est.)
2.02% of GDP (2021 est.)
note: personal transfers and compensation between resident and non-resident individuals/households/entities

Budget: *revenues:* $128.764 million (2022 est.)
expenditures: $122.193 million (2022 est.)
note: central government revenues and expenses (excluding grants/extrabudgetary units/social security funds) converted to US dollars at average official exchange rate for year indicated

Public debt: 88.4% of GDP (2017 est.)
comparison ranking: 27

Taxes and other revenues: 26.2% (of GDP) (2017 est.)
comparison ranking: 37

Current account balance: -$79.437 million (2022 est.)
-$95.248 million (2021 est.)
-$59.595 million (2020 est.)
note: balance of payments - net trade and primary/secondary income in current dollars
comparison ranking: 92

Exports: $96.977 million (2022 est.)
$75.256 million (2021 est.)
$49.337 million (2020 est.)
note: balance of payments - exports of goods and services in current dollars
comparison ranking: 212

Exports - partners: Netherlands 26%, France 11%, Belgium 11%, Portugal 8%, Angola 6% (2022)
note: top five export partners based on percentage share of exports

Exports - commodities: cocoa beans, palm oil, gas turbines, integrated circuits, coconut oil (2022)
note: top five export commodities based on value in dollars

Imports: $219.322 million (2022 est.)
$201.145 million (2021 est.)
$160.097 million (2020 est.)
note: balance of payments - imports of goods and services in current dollars
comparison ranking: 210

Imports - partners: Portugal 35%, Angola 18%, Togo 13%, China 6%, Italy 5% (2022)
note: top five import partners based on percentage share of imports

Imports - commodities: refined petroleum, ships, electric generating sets, rice, cars (2022)
note: top five import commodities based on value in dollars

Reserves of foreign exchange and gold: $64.476 million (2022 est.)
$75.017 million (2021 est.)
$75.288 million (2020 est.)
note: holdings of gold (year-end prices)/foreign exchange/special drawing rights in current dollars
comparison ranking: 194

Debt - external: $249.404 million (2022 est.)
note: present value of external debt in current US dollars
comparison ranking: 98

Exchange rates: dobras (STD) per US dollar -

Exchange rates: 23.29 (2022 est.)
20.71 (2021 est.)
21.507 (2020 est.)
21.885 (2019 est.)
20.751 (2018 est.)

ENERGY

Electricity access: *electrification - total population:* 78% (2022 est.)
electrification - urban areas: 80%
electrification - rural areas: 73.7%

Electricity: *installed generating capacity:* 30,000 kW (2022 est.)
consumption: 95.235 million kWh (2022 est.)
transmission/distribution losses: 40.95 million kWh (2022 est.)
comparison rankings: transmission/distribution losses 34; consumption 199; installed generating capacity 202

Electricity generation sources: *fossil fuels:* 95.6% of total installed capacity (2022 est.)
hydroelectricity: 4.4% of total installed capacity (2022 est.)

Coal: *imports:* (2022 est.) less than 1 metric ton

Petroleum: *refined petroleum consumption:* 1,000 bbl/day (2022 est.)

Carbon dioxide emissions: 162,000 metric tonnes of CO2 (2022 est.)
from petroleum and other liquids: 162,000 metric tonnes of CO2 (2022 est.)
comparison ranking: total emissions 207

Energy consumption per capita: 9.873 million Btu/person (2022 est.)
comparison ranking: 149

COMMUNICATIONS

Telephones - fixed lines: *total subscriptions:* 3,000 (2022 est.)
subscriptions per 100 inhabitants: 1 (2022 est.)
comparison ranking: total subscriptions 212

Telephones - mobile cellular: *total subscriptions:* 197,000 (2022 est.)
subscriptions per 100 inhabitants: 87 (2022 est.)
comparison ranking: total subscriptions 184

Telecommunication systems: *general assessment:* local telephone network of adequate quality with most lines connected to digital switches; mobile cellular superior choice to landline; dial-up quality low; broadband expensive (2018)
domestic: fixed-line is 1 per 100 and mobile-cellular teledensity is 85 telephones per 100 persons (2021)
international: country code - 239; landing points for the Ultramar GE and ACE submarine cables from South Africa to over 20 West African countries and Europe; satellite earth station - 1 Intelsat (Atlantic Ocean) (2019)

Broadcast media: 1 government-owned TV station; 2 government-owned radio stations; 7 independent local radio stations; transmissions of multiple international broadcasters are available

Internet country code: .st

Internet users: *total:* 112,200 (2021 est.)
percent of population: 51% (2021 est.)
comparison ranking: total 185

Broadband - fixed subscriptions: *total:* 2,512 (2020 est.)
subscriptions per 100 inhabitants: 1 (2020 est.)
comparison ranking: total 197

TRANSPORTATION

National air transport system: *number of registered air carriers:* 1 (2020)
inventory of registered aircraft operated by air carriers: 1

Civil aircraft registration country code prefix: S9

Airports: 2 (2024)
comparison ranking: 201

Roadways: *total:* 1,300 km
paved: 230 km
unpaved: 1,070 km (2018)
comparison ranking: total 179

Merchant marine: *total:* 25 (2023)
by type: general cargo 15, oil tanker 4, other 6
comparison ranking: total 141

Ports: *total ports:* 2 (2024)
large: 0
medium: 0
small: 0
very small: 2
ports with oil terminals: 0
key ports: Santo Antonio, Sao Tome

MILITARY AND SECURITY

Military and security forces: Armed Forces of Sao Tome and Principe (Forcas Armadas de Sao Tome e Principe, FASTP): Army, Coast Guard of Sao Tome e Principe (Guarda Costeira de Sao Tome e Principe, GCSTP), Presidential Guard, National Guard (2024)
note: the Army and Coast Guard are responsible for external security while the public security police and judicial police maintain internal security; both the public security police and the military report to the Ministry of Defense and Internal Affairs; the judicial police report to the Ministry of Justice, Public Administration, and Human Rights

Military and security service personnel strengths: the FASTP has approximately 500 personnel (2023)

Military equipment inventories and acquisitions: the FASTP has a limited inventory of mostly older weapons and equipment (2023)

Military service age and obligation: 18 is the legal minimum age for compulsory military service (reportedly not enforced); 17 is the legal minimum age for voluntary service (2023)

Military - note: the FASTP is one of the smallest militaries in Africa and consists of only a few companies of ground troops and some small patrol boats
in November 2022, the FASTP's headquarters was attacked shortly after the prime minister's inauguration in what São Tomé authorities described as an attempted coup; in 2024, the governments of Russia and São Tomé and Principe signed a military cooperation agreement, which included training, materiel and logistics support, and information sharing (2024)

SAUDI ARABIA

INTRODUCTION

Background: Saudi Arabia is the birthplace of Islam and home to Islam's two holiest shrines in Mecca and Medina. The king's official title is the Custodian of the Two Holy Mosques. ABD AL-AZIZ bin Abd al-Rahman AL SAUD (Ibn Saud) founded the modern Saudi state in 1932 after a 30-year campaign to unify most of the Arabian Peninsula. One of his male descendants rules the country today, as required by the country's 1992 Basic Law. After Iraq invaded Kuwait in 1990, Saudi Arabia took in the Kuwaiti royal family and 400,000 refugees, while allowing Western and Arab troops to deploy on its soil and liberate Kuwait the following year. Major terrorist attacks in 2003 spurred a strong ongoing campaign against domestic terrorism and extremism. US troops returned to the Kingdom in 2019 after attacks on Saudi oil infrastructure.

From 2005 to 2015, King ABDALLAH bin Abd al-Aziz Al Saud incrementally modernized the Kingdom through a series of social and economic initiatives that included expanding employment and social opportunities for women, attracting

foreign investment, increasing the private sector's role in the economy, and discouraging the hiring of foreign workers. Saudi Arabia saw some protests during the 2011 Arab Spring but not the level of bloodshed seen in protests elsewhere in the region; Riyadh took a cautious but firm approach, arresting and quickly releasing some protesters and using its state-sponsored clerics to counter political and Islamist activism. The government held its first-ever elections in 2005 and 2011, when Saudis voted for municipal councilors. King ABDALLAH's reforms accelerated under King SALMAN bin Abd al-Aziz, who ascended to the throne in 2015 and lifted the Kingdom's ban on women driving, implemented education reforms, funded green initiatives, and allowed cinemas to operate for the first time in decades. In 2015, women were allowed to vote and stand as candidates for the first time in municipal elections, with 19 women winning seats. King SALMAN initially named his nephew, MUHAMMAD BIN NAYIF bin Abd al-Aziz Al Saud, as the Crown Prince, but a palace coup in 2017 resulted in King SALMAN's son, Deputy Crown Prince MUHAMMAD BIN SALMAN bin Abd al-Aziz Al Saud, taking over as Crown Prince. King SALMAN appointed MUHAMMAD BIN SALMAN as prime minister in 2022.

In 2015, Saudi Arabia led a coalition of 10 countries in a military campaign to restore Yemen's legitimate government, which had been ousted by Houthi forces. The war in Yemen has drawn international criticism for civilian casualties and its effect on the country's dire humanitarian situation. The same year, MUHAMMAD BIN SALMAN announced that Saudi Arabia would lead a multi-nation Islamic Coalition to fight terrorism, and in 2017, Saudi Arabia inaugurated the Global Center for Combatting Extremist Ideology (also known as "Etidal").

The country remains a leading producer of oil and natural gas and holds about 17% of the world's proven oil reserves as of 2020. The government continues to pursue economic reform and diversification – particularly since Saudi Arabia's accession to the WTO in 2005 – and promotes foreign investment in the Kingdom. In 2016, the Saudi Government announced broad socio-economic reforms known as Vision 2030. Low global oil prices in 2015 and 2016 significantly lowered Saudi Arabia's governmental revenue, prompting cuts to subsidies on water, electricity, and gasoline; reduced government-employee compensation; and new land taxes. In coordination with OPEC and some key non-OPEC countries, Saudi Arabia agreed to cut oil output in 2017 to regulate supply and help boost global prices. In 2020, this agreement collapsed, and Saudi Arabia launched a price war by flooding the market with low-priced oil before returning to the negotiating table to agree to a major output cut that helped buoy prices.

GEOGRAPHY

Location: Middle East, bordering the Persian Gulf and the Red Sea, north of Yemen

Geographic coordinates: 25 00 N, 45 00 E

Map references: Middle East

Area: *total:* 2,149,690 sq km
land: 2,149,690 sq km
water: 0 sq km
comparison ranking: total 14

Area - comparative: slightly more than one-fifth the size of the US

Land boundaries: *total:* 4,272 km
border countries (7): Iraq 811 km; Jordan 731 km; Kuwait 221 km; Oman 658 km; Qatar 87 km; UAE 457 km; Yemen 1,307 km

Coastline: 2,640 km

Maritime claims: *territorial sea:* 12 nm
contiguous zone: 18 nm
continental shelf: not specified

Climate: harsh, dry desert with great temperature extremes

Terrain: mostly sandy desert

Elevation: *highest point:* As Sarawat range, 3,000 m
lowest point: Persian Gulf 0 m
mean elevation: 665 m

Natural resources: petroleum, natural gas, iron ore, gold, copper

Land use: *agricultural land:* 80.7% (2018 est.)
arable land: 1.5% (2018 est.)
permanent crops: 0.1% (2018 est.)
permanent pasture: 79.1% (2018 est.)
forest: 0.5% (2018 est.)
other: 18.8% (2018 est.)

Irrigated land: 11,910 sq km (2018)

Major watersheds (area sq km): Indian Ocean drainage: *(Persian Gulf)* Tigris and Euphrates (918,044 sq km)

Major aquifers: Arabian Aquifer System

Population distribution: historically a population that was mostly nomadic or semi-nomadic, the Saudi population has become more settled since petroleum was discovered in the 1930s; most of the economic activities - and with it the country's population - is concentrated in a wide area across the middle of the peninsula, from Ad Dammam in the east, through Riyadh in the interior, to Mecca-Medina in the west near the Red Sea

Natural hazards: frequent sand and dust storms
volcanism: despite many volcanic formations, there has been little activity in the past few centuries; volcanoes include Harrat Rahat, Harrat Khaybar, Harrat Lunayyir, and Jabal Yar

Geography - note: Saudi Arabia is the largest country in the world without a river; extensive coastlines on the Persian Gulf and Red Sea allow for considerable shipping (especially of crude oil) through the Persian Gulf and Suez Canal

PEOPLE AND SOCIETY

Population: *total:* 36,544,431
male: 20,700,838
female: 15,843,593 (2024 est.)
comparison rankings: female 49; male 36; total 41

Nationality: *noun:* Saudi(s)
adjective: Saudi or Saudi Arabian

Ethnic groups: Arab 90%, Afro-Asian 10%

Languages: Arabic (official)
major-language sample(s):
كتاب حقائق العالم، المصدر الذي لا يمكن الاستغناء عنه للمعلومات الأساسية
(Arabic)

Religions: Muslim (official; citizens are 85-90% Sunni and 10-12% Shia), other (includes Eastern Orthodox, Protestant, Roman Catholic, Jewish, Hindu, Buddhist, and Sikh) (2020 est.)
note: despite having a large expatriate community of various faiths (more than 30% of the population), most forms of public religious expression inconsistent with the government-sanctioned interpretation of Sunni Islam are restricted; non-Muslims are not allowed to have Saudi citizenship and non-Muslim places of worship are not permitted (2013)

Age structure: *0-14 years:* 22.9% (male 4,266,720/female 4,097,270)
15-64 years: 72.7% (male 15,577,133/female 10,994,061)
65 years and over: 4.4% (2024 est.) (male 856,985/female 752,262)

Dependency ratios: *total dependency ratio:* 40.4
youth dependency ratio: 36.8
elderly dependency ratio: 3.7
potential support ratio: 27.4 (2021 est.)

Median age: *total:* 32.4 years (2024 est.)
male: 34.6 years
female: 29.3 years
comparison ranking: total 115

Population growth rate: 1.68% (2024 est.)
comparison ranking: 55

Birth rate: 13.6 births/1,000 population (2024 est.)
comparison ranking: 125

Death rate: 3.5 deaths/1,000 population (2024 est.)
comparison ranking: 220

Net migration rate: 6.7 migrant(s)/1,000 population (2024 est.)
comparison ranking: 12

Population distribution: historically a population that was mostly nomadic or semi-nomadic, the Saudi population has become more settled since petroleum was discovered in the 1930s; most of the economic activities - and with it the country's population - is concentrated in a wide area across the middle of the peninsula, from Ad Dammam in the east, through Riyadh in the interior, to Mecca-Medina in the west near the Red Sea

Urbanization: *urban population:* 85% of total population (2023)
rate of urbanization: 1.69% annual rate of change (2020-25 est.)

Major urban areas - population: 7.682 million RIYADH (capital), 4.863 million Jeddah, 2.150 million Mecca, 1.573 million Medina, 1.329 million Ad Dammam, 872,000 million Hufuf-Mubarraz (2023)

Sex ratio: *at birth:* 1.05 male(s)/female
0-14 years: 1.04 male(s)/female
15-64 years: 1.42 male(s)/female
65 years and over: 1.14 male(s)/female

total population: 1.31 male(s)/female (2024 est.)

Maternal mortality ratio: 16 deaths/100,000 live births (2020 est.)
comparison ranking: 134

Infant mortality rate: *total:* 11.7 deaths/1,000 live births (2024 est.)
male: 12.8 deaths/1,000 live births
female: 10.5 deaths/1,000 live births
comparison ranking: total 113

Life expectancy at birth: *total population:* 77.2 years (2024 est.)
male: 75.6 years
female: 78.8 years
comparison ranking: total population 97

Total fertility rate: 1.87 children born/woman (2024 est.)
comparison ranking: 130

Gross reproduction rate: 0.91 (2024 est.)

Contraceptive prevalence rate: 27.9% (2019)

Drinking water source: *improved:*
total: 100% of population

Current health expenditure: 5.5% of GDP (2018)

Physician density: 2.74 physicians/1,000 population (2020)

Hospital bed density: 2.2 beds/1,000 population (2017)

Sanitation facility access: *improved:*
total: 100% of population

Obesity - adult prevalence rate: 35.4% (2016)
comparison ranking: 14

Alcohol consumption per capita: *total:* 0 liters of pure alcohol (2019 est.)
beer: 0 liters of pure alcohol (2019 est.)
wine: 0 liters of pure alcohol (2019 est.)
spirits: 0 liters of pure alcohol (2019 est.)
other alcohols: 0 liters of pure alcohol (2019 est.)
comparison ranking: total 185

Tobacco use: *total:* 14.3% (2020 est.)
male: 26.5% (2020 est.)
female: 2% (2020 est.)
comparison ranking: total 110

Children under the age of 5 years underweight: 3.5% (2020) NA
comparison ranking: 83

Currently married women (ages 15-49): 63.2% (2023 est.)

Education expenditures: 7.8% of GDP (2020) NA
comparison ranking: 12

Literacy: *definition:* age 15 and over can read and write
total population: 97.6%
male: 98.6%
female: 96% (2020)

School life expectancy (primary to tertiary education): *total:* 17 years
male: 17 years
female: 16 years (2021)

ENVIRONMENT

Environment - current issues: desertification; depletion of underground water resources; the lack of perennial rivers or permanent water bodies has prompted the development of extensive seawater desalination facilities; coastal pollution from oil spills; air pollution; waste management

Environment - international agreements: *party to:* Biodiversity, Climate Change, Climate Change-Kyoto Protocol, Climate Change-Paris Agreement, Desertification, Endangered Species, Hazardous Wastes, Law of the Sea, Marine Dumping-London Protocol, Ozone Layer Protection, Ship Pollution
signed, but not ratified: none of the selected agreements

Climate: harsh, dry desert with great temperature extremes

Urbanization: *urban population:* 85% of total population (2023)
rate of urbanization: 1.69% annual rate of change (2020-25 est.)

Revenue from forest resources: 0% of GDP (2018 est.)
comparison ranking: 178

Revenue from coal: 0% of GDP (2018 est.)
comparison ranking: 84

Air pollutants: *particulate matter emissions:* 57.16 micrograms per cubic meter (2019 est.)
carbon dioxide emissions: 563.45 megatons (2016 est.)
methane emissions: 45.47 megatons (2020 est.)

Waste and recycling: *municipal solid waste generated annually:* 16,125,701 tons (2015 est.)
municipal solid waste recycled annually: 2,418,855 tons (2015 est.)
percent of municipal solid waste recycled: 15% (2015 est.)

Major watersheds (area sq km): Indian Ocean drainage: *(Persian Gulf)* Tigris and Euphrates (918,044 sq km)

Major aquifers: Arabian Aquifer System

Total water withdrawal: *municipal:* 3.39 billion cubic meters (2020 est.)
industrial: 1.4 billion cubic meters (2020 est.)
agricultural: 21.2 billion cubic meters (2020 est.)

Total renewable water resources: 2.4 billion cubic meters (2020 est.)

GOVERNMENT

Country name: *conventional long form:* Kingdom of Saudi Arabia
conventional short form: Saudi Arabia
local long form: Al Mamlakah al Arabiyah as Suudiyah
local short form: Al Arabiyah as Suudiyah
etymology: named after the ruling dynasty of the country, the House of Saud; the name "Arabia" can be traced back many centuries B.C., the ancient Egyptians referred to the region as "Ar Rabi"

Government type: absolute monarchy

Capital: *name:* Riyadh
geographic coordinates: 24 39 N, 46 42 E
time difference: UTC+3 (8 hours ahead of Washington, DC, during Standard Time)
etymology: the name derives from the Arabic word "riyadh," meaning "gardens," and refers to various oasis towns in the area that merged to form the city

Administrative divisions: 13 regions (manatiq, singular - mintaqah); Al Bahah, Al Hudud ash Shamaliyah (Northern Border), Al Jawf, Al Madinah al Munawwarah (Medina), Al Qasim, Ar Riyad (Riyadh), Ash Sharqiyah (Eastern), 'Asir, Ha'il, Jazan, Makkah al Mukarramah (Mecca), Najran, Tabuk

Independence: 23 September 1932 (unification of the kingdom)

National holiday: Saudi National Day (Unification of the Kingdom), 23 September (1932)

Legal system: Islamic (sharia) legal system with some elements of Egyptian, French, and customary law; note - several secular codes have been introduced; commercial disputes handled by special committees

Constitution: *history:* 1 March 1992 - Basic Law of Government, issued by royal decree, serves as the constitutional framework and is based on the Qur'an and the life and traditions of the Prophet Muhammad
amendments: proposed by the king directly or proposed to the king by the Consultative Assembly or by the Council of Ministers; passage by the king through royal decree; Basic Law amended many times, last in 2017

International law organization participation: has not submitted an ICJ jurisdiction declaration; non-party state to the ICCt

Citizenship: *citizenship by birth:* no
citizenship by descent only: the father must be a citizen of Saudi Arabia; a child born out of wedlock in Saudi Arabia to a Saudi mother and unknown father
dual citizenship recognized: no
residency requirement for naturalization: 5 years

Suffrage: 18 years of age; universal for municipal elections
https://www.wilsoncenter.org/publication/saudi-women-go-to-the-polls-finally

Executive branch: *chief of state:* King SALMAN bin Abd al-Aziz Al Saud (since 23 January 2015)
head of government: Crown Prince and Prime Minister MUHAMMAD BIN SALMAN bin Abd al-Aziz Al Saud (since 27 September 2022)
cabinet: Council of Ministers appointed by the monarch every 4 years and includes many royal family members
elections/appointments: none; the monarchy is hereditary; an Allegiance Council created by royal decree in October 2006 established a committee of Saudi princes for a voice in selecting future Saudi kings

Legislative branch: *description:* unicameral Shura Council (Majlis Ash-Shura) (150 seats plus a speaker; members appointed by the monarch to serve 4-year terms); note - in early 2013, the monarch granted women 30 seats on the Council
election results: composition - men 121, women 30, percentage women 19.9%

Judicial branch: *highest court(s):* High Court (consists of the court chief and organized into circuits with 3-judge panels, except for the criminal circuit, which has a 5-judge panel for cases involving major punishments)
judge selection and term of office: High Court chief and chiefs of the High Court Circuits appointed by royal decree upon the recommendation of the Supreme Judiciary Council, a 10-member body of high-level judges and other judicial heads; new judges and assistant judges serve 1- and 2-year probations, respectively, before permanent assignment
subordinate courts: Court of Appeals; Specialized Criminal Court, first-degree courts composed of general, criminal, personal status, and commercial courts; Labor Court; a hierarchy of administrative courts

Political parties: none

International organization participation: ABEDA, AfDB (nonregional member), AFESD, AMF, BIS, BRICS, CAEU, CP, FAO, G-20, G-77, GCC, IAEA, IBRD, ICAO, ICC (national committees), ICRM, IDA, IDB, IFAD, IFC, IFRCS, IHO, ILO, IMF, IMO, IMSO, Interpol, IOC, IOM (observer), IPU, ISO, ITSO, ITU, LAS, MIGA, NAM, OAPEC, OAS (observer), OIC, OPCW, OPEC, PCA, UN, UNCTAD, UNESCO, UNIDO, UNOOSA, UNRWA, UNWTO, UPU, WCO, WFTU (NGOs), WHO, WIPO, WMO, WTO

Diplomatic representation in the US: *chief of mission:* Ambassador Reema Bint Bandar Bin Sultan AL SAUD (since 8 July 2019)
chancery: 601 New Hampshire Avenue NW, Washington, DC 20037
telephone: [1] (202) 342-3800
FAX: [1] (202) 295-3625
email address and website:
saudisusemb@mofa.gov.sa
https://www.saudiembassy.net/
consulate(s) general: Houston, Los Angeles, New York

Diplomatic representation from the US: *chief of mission:* Ambassador Michael RATNEY (since 27 April 2023)
embassy: Riyadh 11564
mailing address: 6300 Riyadh Place, Washington DC 20521-6300
telephone: [966] (11) 835-4000
FAX: [966] (11) 488-7360
email address and website:
RiyadhACS@state.gov
https://sa.usembassy.gov/
consulate(s) general: Dhahran, Jeddah

Flag description: green, a traditional color in Islamic flags, with the Shahada or Muslim creed in large white Arabic script (translated as "There is no god but God; Muhammad is the Messenger of God") above a white horizontal saber (the tip points to the hoist side); design dates to the early twentieth century and is closely associated with the Al Saud family, which established the kingdom in 1932; the flag is manufactured with differing obverse and reverse sides so that the Shahada reads - and the sword points - correctly from right to left on both sides
note: the only national flag to display an inscription as its principal design; one of only three national flags that differ on their obverse and reverse sides - the others are Moldova and Paraguay

National symbol(s): palm tree surmounting two crossed swords; national colors: green, white

National anthem: *name:* "Aash Al Maleek" (Long Live Our Beloved King)
lyrics/music: Ibrahim KHAFAJI/Abdul Rahman al-KHATEEB
note: music adopted 1947, lyrics adopted 1984

National heritage: *total World Heritage Sites:* 7 (6 cultural, 1 natural)
selected World Heritage Site locales: Hegra Archaeological Site (al-Hijr / Madā ' in Ṣāliḥ) (c); At-Turaif District in ad-Dir'iyah (c); Historic Jeddah, the Gate to Makkah (c); Rock Art in the Hail Region (c); Al-Ahsa Oasis (c); Ḥimā Cultural Area (c); 'Uruq Bani Ma'arid (n)

ECONOMY

Economic overview: high-income, oil-based Middle Eastern economy; OPEC leader; diversifying portfolio; declining per-capita incomes; young labor force; key human capital gaps; heavy bureaucracy and increasing corruption; substantial poverty; low innovation economy

Real GDP (purchasing power parity): $1.831 trillion (2023 est.)
$1.845 trillion (2022 est.)
$1.717 trillion (2021 est.)
note: data in 2021 dollars
comparison ranking: 18

Real GDP growth rate: -0.75% (2023 est.)
7.49% (2022 est.)
5.08% (2021 est.)
note: annual GDP % growth based on constant local currency
comparison ranking: 197

Real GDP per capita: $49,600 (2023 est.)
$50,700 (2022 est.)
$47,800 (2021 est.)
note: data in 2021 dollars
comparison ranking: 43

GDP (official exchange rate): $1.068 trillion (2023 est.)
note: data in current dollars at official exchange rate

Inflation rate (consumer prices): 2.33% (2023 est.)
2.47% (2022 est.)
3.06% (2021 est.)
note: annual % change based on consumer prices
comparison ranking: 47

Credit ratings: Fitch rating: A (2019)

Moody's rating: A1 (2016)

Standard & Poors rating: A- (2016)
note: The year refers to the year in which the current credit rating was first obtained.

GDP - composition, by sector of origin: *agriculture:* 2.7% (2023 est.)
industry: 47% (2023 est.)
services: 44.9% (2023 est.)
note: figures may not total 100% due to non-allocated consumption not captured in sector-reported data
comparison rankings: services 169; industry 16; agriculture 146

GDP - composition, by end use: *household consumption:* 40% (2023 est.)
government consumption: 23.3% (2023 est.)
investment in fixed capital: 27.9% (2023 est.)
investment in inventories: 1.4% (2023 est.)
exports of goods and services: 34.7% (2023 est.)
imports of goods and services: -27.4% (2023 est.)
note: figures may not total 100% due to rounding or gaps in data collection

Agricultural products: milk, dates, chicken, wheat, tomatoes, potatoes, watermelons, olives, eggs, onions (2022)
note: top ten agricultural products based on tonnage

Industries: crude oil production, petroleum refining, basic petrochemicals, ammonia, industrial gases, sodium hydroxide (caustic soda), cement, fertilizer, plastics, metals, commercial ship repair, commercial aircraft repair, construction

Industrial production growth rate: -1.51% (2023 est.)
note: annual % change in industrial value added based on constant local currency
comparison ranking: 175

Labor force: 16.934 million (2023 est.)
note: number of people ages 15 or older who are employed or seeking work
comparison ranking: 38

Unemployment rate: 4.88% (2023 est.)
5.59% (2022 est.)
6.62% (2021 est.)
note: % of labor force seeking employment
comparison ranking: 93

Youth unemployment rate (ages 15-24): *total:* 16.3% (2023 est.)
male: 12.9% (2023 est.)
female: 24.4% (2023 est.)
note: % of labor force ages 15-24 seeking employment
comparison ranking: total 88

Average household expenditures: *on food:* 20.4% of household expenditures (2022 est.)
on alcohol and tobacco: 0.7% of household expenditures (2022 est.)

Remittances: 0.03% of GDP (2023 est.)
0.03% of GDP (2022 est.)
0.03% of GDP (2021 est.)
note: personal transfers and compensation between resident and non-resident individuals/households/entities

Budget: *revenues:* $398.023 billion (2022 est.)
expenditures: $315.007 billion (2022 est.)
note: central government revenues (excluding grants) and expenses converted to US dollars at average official exchange rate for year indicated

Public debt: 17.2% of GDP (2017 est.)
comparison ranking: 191

Taxes and other revenues: 7.77% (of GDP) (2022 est.)
note: central government tax revenue as a % of GDP
comparison ranking: 190

Current account balance: $34.07 billion (2023 est.)
$151.519 billion (2022 est.)
$41.718 billion (2021 est.)
note: balance of payments - net trade and primary/secondary income in current dollars
comparison ranking: 19

Exports: $370.974 billion (2023 est.)
$445.881 billion (2022 est.)
$286.502 billion (2021 est.)
note: balance of payments - exports of goods and services in current dollars
comparison ranking: 25

Exports - partners: China 19%, India 13%, Japan 10%, South Korea 10%, US 7% (2022)
note: top five export partners based on percentage share of exports

Exports - commodities: crude petroleum, refined petroleum, ethylene polymers, plastics, fertilizers (2022)
note: top five export commodities based on value in dollars

Imports: $291.565 billion (2023 est.)
$258.213 billion (2022 est.)
$213.516 billion (2021 est.)
note: balance of payments - imports of goods and services in current dollars
comparison ranking: 28

Imports - partners: China 22%, UAE 16%, US 6%, India 6%, Germany 4% (2022)
note: top five import partners based on percentage share of imports

Imports - commodities: cars, broadcasting equipment, garments, gold, refined petroleum (2022)
note: top five import commodities based on value in dollars

Reserves of foreign exchange and gold: $457.949 billion (2023 est.)
$478.232 billion (2022 est.)

$473.89 billion (2021 est.)
note: holdings of gold (year-end prices)/foreign exchange/special drawing rights in current dollars
comparison ranking: 6

Exchange rates: Saudi riyals (SAR) per US dollar -

Exchange rates: 3.75 (2023 est.)
3.75 (2022 est.)
3.75 (2021 est.)
3.75 (2020 est.)
3.75 (2019 est.)

ENERGY

Electricity access: *electrification - total population:* 100% (2022 est.)

Electricity: *installed generating capacity:* 80.11 million kW (2022 est.)
consumption: 393.213 billion kWh (2022 est.)
exports: 382.556 million kWh (2022 est.)
imports: 334.737 million kWh (2022 est.)
transmission/distribution losses: 38.658 billion kWh (2022 est.)
comparison rankings: transmission/distribution losses 203; imports 100; exports 81; consumption 11; installed generating capacity 19

Electricity generation sources: *fossil fuels:* 99.7% of total installed capacity (2022 est.)
solar: 0.2% of total installed capacity (2022 est.)
wind: 0.1% of total installed capacity (2022 est.)

Coal: *consumption:* 164,000 metric tons (2022 est.)
exports: 200 metric tons (2022 est.)
imports: 164,000 metric tons (2022 est.)

Petroleum: *total petroleum production:* 11.113 million bbl/day (2023 est.)
refined petroleum consumption: 3.649 million bbl/day (2022 est.)
crude oil estimated reserves: 258.6 billion barrels (2021 est.)

Natural gas: *production:* 121.87 billion cubic meters (2022 est.)
consumption: 121.87 billion cubic meters (2022 est.)
proven reserves: 9.423 trillion cubic meters (2021 est.)

Carbon dioxide emissions: 638.449 million metric tonnes of CO_2 (2022 est.)
from coal and metallurgical coke: 437,000 metric tonnes of CO_2 (2022 est.)
from petroleum and other liquids: 398.933 million metric tonnes of CO_2 (2022 est.)
from consumed natural gas: 239.078 million metric tonnes of CO_2 (2022 est.)
comparison ranking: total emissions 10

Energy consumption per capita: 313.903 million Btu/person (2022 est.)
comparison ranking: 8

COMMUNICATIONS

Telephones - fixed lines: *total subscriptions:* 6.773 million (2022 est.)
subscriptions per 100 inhabitants: 19 (2022 est.)
comparison ranking: total subscriptions 23

Telephones - mobile cellular: *total subscriptions:* 48.198 million (2022 est.)
subscriptions per 100 inhabitants: 132 (2022 est.)
comparison ranking: total subscriptions 37

Telecommunication systems: *general assessment:* Saudi Arabia's telecom and ICT sectors continue to benefit from the range of programs aimed at diversifying the economy away from a dependence on oil, and establishing a wider digital transformation over the next decade; an essential element of this has been the widening reach of 5G networks, which by mid-2021 reached about half of the population and the majority of cities; the MNOs have focused investment on upgrading LTE infrastructure and further developing 5G; this in part is aimed at generating additional revenue from mobile data services, and also to their contribution to the Vision 2030 program; the ongoing pandemic has resulted in more people working and schooling from home during periods of restricted travel; this has stimulated growth in mobile data traffic, while the government has encouraged non-cash transactions and so helped develop the vast e-commerce market; while Saudi Arabia's fixed broadband penetration remains relatively low, there has been a concentration of fiber infrastructure and the Kingdom has developed one of the fastest services in the region (2022)
domestic: fixed-line are 18 per 100 and mobile-cellular subscribership is 126 per 100 persons (2021)
international: country code - 966; landing points for the SeaMeWe-3, -4, -5, AAE-1, EIG, FALCON, FEA, IMEWE, MENA/Gulf Bridge International, SEACOM, SAS-1, -2, GBICS/MENA, and the Tata TGN-Gulf submarine cables providing connectivity to Europe, Africa, the Middle East, Asia, Southeast Asia and Australia; microwave radio relay to Bahrain, Jordan, Kuwait, Qatar, UAE, Yemen, and Sudan; coaxial cable to Kuwait and Jordan; satellite earth stations - 5 Intelsat (3 Atlantic Ocean and 2 Indian Ocean), 1 Arabsat, and 1 Inmarsat (Indian Ocean region) (2019)

Broadcast media: broadcast media are state-controlled; state-run TV operates 4 networks; Saudi Arabia is a major market for pan-Arab satellite TV broadcasters; state-run radio operates several networks; multiple international broadcasters are available

Internet country code: .sa

Internet users: *total:* 36 million (2021 est.)
percent of population: 100% (2021 est.)
comparison ranking: total 27

Broadband - fixed subscriptions: *total:* 7,890,261 (2020 est.)
subscriptions per 100 inhabitants: 23 (2020 est.)
comparison ranking: total 26

Communications - note: the innovative King Abdulaziz Center for World Culture (informally known as Ithra, meaning "enrichment") opened on 1 December 2017 in Dhahran, Eastern Region; its facilities include a grand library, several museums, an archive, an Idea Lab, a theater, a cinema, and an Energy Exhibit, all which are meant to provide visitors an immersive and transformative experience

TRANSPORTATION

National air transport system: *number of registered air carriers:* 12 (2020)
inventory of registered aircraft operated by air carriers: 230
annual passenger traffic on registered air carriers: 39,141,660 (2018)
annual freight traffic on registered air carriers: 1,085,470,000 (2018) mt-km

Civil aircraft registration country code prefix: HZ

Airports: 86 (2024)
comparison ranking: 59

Heliports: 67 (2024)

Pipelines: 209 km condensate, 2,940 km gas, 1,183 km liquid petroleum gas, 5,117 km oil, 1,151 km refined products (2013)

Railways: *total:* 5,410 km (2016)
standard gauge: 5,410 km (2016) 1.435-m gauge (with branch lines and sidings)
comparison ranking: total 35

Roadways: *total:* 221,372 km
paved: 47,529 km (includes 3,891 km of expressways)
unpaved: 173,843 km (2006)
comparison ranking: total 22

Merchant marine: *total:* 433 (2023)
by type: bulk carrier 9, container ship 1, general cargo 20, oil tanker 55, other 348
comparison ranking: total 46

Ports: *total ports:* 16 (2024)
large: 0
medium: 1
small: 7
very small: 8
ports with oil terminals: 10
key ports: Dammam, Duba, Jiddah, Jizan, Ju Aymah Oil Terminal, Ras Tannurah, Ras Al Khafji, Ras Al Mishab

MILITARY AND SECURITY

Military and security forces: *the Saudi Arabian Armed Forces (SAAF) are divided into two ministries:*

Ministry of Defense: Royal Saudi Land Forces, Royal Saudi Naval Forces (includes marines, special forces, naval aviation), Royal Saudi Air Force, Royal Saudi Air Defense Forces, Royal Saudi Strategic Missiles Force; Ministry of the National Guard: Saudi Arabian National Guard (SANG)
Other security forces include:

Ministry of Interior: Special Forces for Security and Protection; Special Forces for Environmental Security; Special Forces for Roads Security; General Directorate of Border Guard

State Security Presidency (SSP): General Directorate of Investigation (Mabahith), Special Security Forces, Special Emergency Forces (2024)
note 1: the SANG (also known as the White Army) is a land force comprised off tribal elements loyal to the House of Saud; it is responsible for internal security, protecting the royal family, and external defense
note 2: the SAAF includes the Saudi Royal Guard Command, a unit which provides security and protection to the ruling family and other dignitaries

Military expenditures: 7% of GDP (2023 est.)
6% of GDP (2022 est.)
6% of GDP (2021 est.)
8% of GDP (2020 est.)
8.8% of GDP (2019 est.)
comparison ranking: 3

Military and security service personnel strengths: the Saudi Armed Forces have about 250,000 total active troops; approximately 125,000 under the Ministry of Defense (75,000 Land Forces; 15,000 Naval Forces, including about 3,000 marines; 35,000 Air Force/Air Defense/Strategic Missile Forces) and up to 125,000 in the Saudi Arabia National Guard (SANG) (2023)
note: SANG also has an irregular force (Fowj), primarily Bedouin tribal volunteers, with a total strength of approximately 25,000

Military equipment inventories and acquisitions: the inventory of the Saudi military forces, including the SANG, includes a mix of mostly modern weapons systems from the US and Europe; in recent years, the US has been the leading supplier of armaments; other major suppliers include France, Spain, and the UK; Saudi Arabia is one of the world's largest importers of arms (2024)
note: the Saudi Navy is in the midst of a multi-year and multi-billion-dollar expansion and modernization program to purchase new frigates, corvettes, and other naval craft from such suppliers as Spain and the US

Military service age and obligation: men (17-40) and women (21-40) may volunteer for military service; no conscription (2023)
note 1: in 2021, women were allowed to serve in the Army, Air Defense, Navy, Strategic Missile Force, medical services, and internal security forces up to the rank of non-commissioned officer
note 2: the National Guard is restricted to citizens, but the regular Saudi military has hired foreigners on contract for operations associated with its intervention in Yemen

Military deployments: continues to maintain a military presence in Yemen; has also established and supports several local militias, including the National Shield Forces in Aden and the Amajid Brigade in Abyan (2023)

Military - note: the Saudi Arabian Armed Forces (SAAF) are divided into the regular forces under the Ministry of Defense and the Saudi Arabian National Guard (SANG); the regular forces are responsible for territorial defense, although they can be called for domestic security duties if needed; they include land, naval, air, air defense, and strategic missile forces
the SANG is responsible for both internal security and external defense; its duties include protecting the royal family, guarding against military coups, defending strategic facilities and resources, and providing security for the cities of Mecca and Medina; the SANG is primarily comprised of tribal elements loyal to the Saud family and is comprised of brigades of light infantry, mechanized or motorized infantry, and security forces; it is supplemented by combat helicopter units and tribal levies/militias known as Fowj
Saudi Arabia has close security ties with the US; the SAAF conducts bilateral exercises with the US military and hosts US forces; the US has participated in a cooperative program to equip and train the SANG since 1973; much of the equipment for both the regular forces and the SANG has been acquired from the US; Saudi Arabia also has defense relationships with China, France, India, the UK, and fellow Gulf Cooperation Council members
in 2015, Saudi Arabia led a military intervention into Yemen by a coalition of Arab states in support of the Republic of Yemen Government against the separatist Houthis; Saudi forces from both the Ministry of Defense and the SANG participated in combat operations in Yemen; Saudi Arabia also raised and equipped paramilitary/militia security forces in Yemen–based largely on tribal or regional affiliation–to deploy along the Saudi-Yemen border (2024)

SPACE

Space agency/agencies: Saudi Space Agency (SSA; elevated to agency level from previous Saudi Space Commission or SSC, which was established in 2018); King Abdulaziz City for Science and Technology (KACST; established 1977); KACST includes the Space and Aeronautics Research Institute (SARI; established 2000) (2024)

Space program overview: has an ambitious and growing space program; manufactures and operates communications, remote sensing (RS), and scientific satellites; develops a range of satellite subsystems and payload technologies; SSA's missions also include accelerating economic diversification, enhancing research and development, and raising private sector participation in the global space industry; is the main founder and financier of the Arab Satellite Communications Organization (Arabsat; launched in 1976; headquartered in Riyadh, Saudi Arabia and the primary satellite communications service provider for over 170 million persons in the Arab world); cooperates with the space agencies and industries of a wide range of countries, including those of Belarus, China, Egypt, the European Space Agency and its member states (particularly France, Germany, Greece, and Hungary), India, Kazakhstan, Morocco, Russia, South Africa, South Korea, Ukraine, the UAE, the UK, and the US; member of the Arab Space Cooperation Group (established by the UAE in 2019 and includes Algeria, Bahrain, Egypt, Jordan, Kuwait, Lebanon, Morocco, and Sudan) (2024)
note: further details about the key activities, programs, and milestones of the country's space program, as well as government spending estimates on the space sector, appear in the Space Programs reference guide

TERRORISM

Terrorist group(s): Islamic State of Iraq and ash-Sham (ISIS); al-Qa'ida; al-Qa'ida in the Arabian Peninsula (AQAP)
note: details about the history, aims, leadership, organization, areas of operation, tactics, targets, weapons, size, and sources of support of the group(s) appear(s) in the Terrorism reference guide

TRANSNATIONAL ISSUES

Refugees and internally displaced persons: *stateless persons:* 70,000 (2022); note - thousands of biduns (stateless Arabs) are descendants of nomadic tribes who were not officially registered when national borders were established, while others migrated to Saudi Arabia in search of jobs; some have temporary identification cards that must be renewed every five years, but their rights remain restricted; most Palestinians have only legal resident status; some naturalized Yemenis were made stateless after being stripped of their passports when Yemen backed Iraq in its invasion of Kuwait in 1990; Saudi women cannot pass their citizenship on to their children, so if they marry a non-national, their children risk statelessness

Illicit drugs: regularly sentences drug traffickers to the death penalty, although a moratorium on executions for drug offences has been in place since at least 2020; improving anti-money-laundering legislation and enforcement

SENEGAL

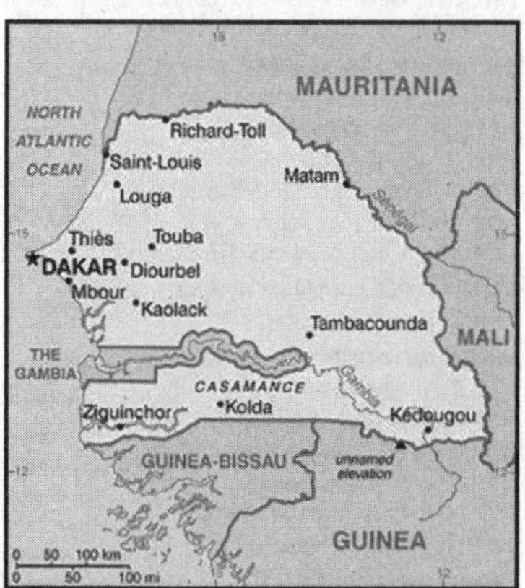

INTRODUCTION

Background: Senegal is one of the few countries in the world with evidence of continuous human life from the Paleolithic period to present. Between the 14th and 16th centuries, the Jolof Empire ruled most of Senegal. Starting in the 15th century, Portugal, the Netherlands, France, and Great Britain traded along the Senegalese coast. Senegal's location on the western tip of Africa made it a favorable base for the European slave trade. European powers used the Senegalese island of Goree as a base to purchase slaves from the warring chiefdoms on the mainland, and at the height of the slave trade in Senegal, over one-third of the Senegalese population was enslaved. In 1815, France abolished slavery and began expanding inland. During the second half of the 19th century, France took possession of Senegal as a French colony. In 1959, the French colonies of Senegal and French Sudan were merged and granted independence in 1960 as the Mali Federation. The union broke up after only a few months. In 1982, Senegal joined with The Gambia to form the nominal confederation of Senegambia. The envisaged integration of the two countries was never implemented, and the union dissolved in 1989.

Since the 1980s, the Movement of Democratic Forces in the Casamance – a separatist movement based in southern Senegal – has led a low-level insurgency. Several attempts at reaching a comprehensive peace agreement have failed. Since 2012, despite sporadic incidents of violence, an unofficial ceasefire has remained largely in effect. Senegal is one of the most stable democracies in Africa and has a long history of participating in international peacekeeping and regional mediation. The Socialist Party of Senegal ruled for 40 years until Abdoulaye WADE was elected president in 2000 and re-elected in 2007.

WADE amended Senegal's constitution over a dozen times to increase executive power and weaken the opposition. In 2012, WADE's decision to run for a third presidential term sparked public backlash that led to his loss to current President Macky SALL. A 2016 constitutional referendum limited future presidents to two consecutive five-year terms. President Bassirou Diomaye FAYE took office in April 2024.

GEOGRAPHY

Location: Western Africa, bordering the North Atlantic Ocean, between Guinea-Bissau and Mauritania

Geographic coordinates: 14 00 N, 14 00 W

Map references: Africa

Area: *total:* 196,722 sq km
land: 192,530 sq km
water: 4,192 sq km
comparison ranking: total 88

Area - comparative: slightly smaller than South Dakota; slightly larger than twice the size of Indiana

Land boundaries: *total:* 2,684 km
border countries (5): The Gambia 749 km; Guinea 363 km; Guinea-Bissau 341 km; Mali 489 km; Mauritania 742 km

Coastline: 531 km

Maritime claims: *territorial sea:* 12 nm
contiguous zone: 24 nm
exclusive economic zone: 200 nm
continental shelf: 200 nm or to the edge of the continental margin

Climate: tropical; hot, humid; rainy season (May to November) has strong southeast winds; dry season (December to April) dominated by hot, dry, harmattan wind

Terrain: generally low, rolling, plains rising to foothills in southeast

Elevation: *highest point:* unnamed elevation 2.8 km southeast of Nepen Diaka 648 m
lowest point: Atlantic Ocean 0 m
mean elevation: 69 m

Natural resources: fish, phosphates, iron ore

Land use: *agricultural land:* 46.8% (2018 est.)
arable land: 17.4% (2018 est.)
permanent crops: 0.3% (2018 est.)
permanent pasture: 29.1% (2018 est.)
forest: 43.8% (2018 est.)
other: 9.4% (2018 est.)

Irrigated land: 1,200 sq km (2012)

Major rivers (by length in km): Senegal (shared with Guinea [s], Mali, and Mauritania [m]) - 1,641 km; Gambie (Gambia) (shared with Guinea [s] and The Gambia [m]) - 1,094 km
note – [s] after country name indicates river source; [m] after country name indicates river mouth

Major watersheds (area sq km): Atlantic Ocean drainage: Senegal (456,397 sq km)

Major aquifers: Senegalo-Mauritanian Basin

Population distribution: the population is concentrated in the west, with Dakar anchoring a well-defined core area; approximately 70% of the population is rural as shown in this population distribution map

Natural hazards: lowlands seasonally flooded; periodic droughts

Geography - note: westernmost country on the African continent; The Gambia is almost an enclave within Senegal

PEOPLE AND SOCIETY

Population: *total:* 18,847,519
male: 9,283,314
female: 9,564,205 (2024 est.)
comparison rankings: female 66; male 66; total 66

Nationality: *noun:* Senegalese (singular and plural)
adjective: Senegalese

Ethnic groups: Wolof 39.7%, Pulaar 27.5%, Sereer 16%, Mandinka 4.9%, Jola 4.2%, Soninke 2.4%, other 5.4% (includes Europeans and persons of Lebanese descent) (2019 est.)

Languages: French (official), Wolof, Pulaar, Jola, Mandinka, Serer, Soninke

Religions: Muslim 97.2% (most adhere to one of the four main Sufi brotherhoods), Christian 2.7% (mostly Roman Catholic) (2019 est.)

Demographic profile: Senegal has a large and growing youth population but has not been successful in developing its potential human capital. Senegal's high total fertility rate of almost 4.5 children per woman continues to bolster the country's large youth cohort – more than 60% of the population is under the age of 25. Fertility remains high because of the continued desire for large families, the low use of family planning, and early childbearing. Because of the country's high illiteracy rate (more than 40%), high unemployment (even among university graduates), and widespread poverty, Senegalese youths face dim prospects; women are especially disadvantaged.
Senegal historically was a destination country for economic migrants, but in recent years West African migrants more often use Senegal as a transit point to North Africa – and sometimes illegally onward to Europe. The country also has been host to several thousand black Mauritanian refugees since they were expelled from their homeland during its 1989 border conflict with Senegal. The country's economic crisis in the 1970s stimulated emigration; departures accelerated in the 1990s. Destinations shifted from neighboring countries, which were experiencing economic decline, civil wars, and increasing xenophobia, to Libya and Mauritania because of their booming oil industries and to developed countries (most notably former colonial ruler France, as well as Italy and Spain). The latter became attractive in the 1990s because of job opportunities and their periodic regularization programs (legalizing the status of illegal migrants).

Age structure: *0-14 years:* 40.7% (male 3,907,986/female 3,760,594)
15-64 years: 55.9% (male 5,098,038/female 5,437,195)
65 years and over: 3.4% (2024 est.) (male 277,290/female 366,416)

Dependency ratios: *total dependency ratio:* 81.5
youth dependency ratio: 75.8
elderly dependency ratio: 5.7
potential support ratio: 17.4 (2021 est.)

Median age: *total:* 19.2 years (2024 est.)
male: 18.4 years
female: 20 years
comparison ranking: total 213

Population growth rate: 2.46% (2024 est.)
comparison ranking: 20

Birth rate: 30.2 births/1,000 population (2024 est.)
comparison ranking: 25

Death rate: 4.9 deaths/1,000 population (2024 est.)
comparison ranking: 198

Net migration rate: -0.7 migrant(s)/1,000 population (2024 est.)
comparison ranking: 134

Population distribution: the population is concentrated in the west, with Dakar anchoring a well-defined core area; approximately 70% of the population is rural as shown in this population distribution map

Urbanization: *urban population:* 49.6% of total population (2023)
rate of urbanization: 3.59% annual rate of change (2020-25 est.)

Major urban areas - population: 3.340 million DAKAR (capital) (2023)

Sex ratio: *at birth:* 1.05 male(s)/female
0-14 years: 1.04 male(s)/female
15-64 years: 0.94 male(s)/female
65 years and over: 0.76 male(s)/female
total population: 0.97 male(s)/female (2024 est.)

Mother's mean age at first birth: 21.9 years (2019 est.)
note: data represents median age at first birth among women 25-49

Maternal mortality ratio: 261 deaths/100,000 live births (2020 est.)
comparison ranking: 35

Infant mortality rate: *total:* 31.1 deaths/1,000 live births (2024 est.)
male: 34.4 deaths/1,000 live births
female: 27.6 deaths/1,000 live births
comparison ranking: total 47

Life expectancy at birth: *total population:* 70.6 years (2024 est.)
male: 68.8 years
female: 72.4 years
comparison ranking: total population 172

Total fertility rate: 4.06 children born/woman (2024 est.)
comparison ranking: 22

Gross reproduction rate: 1.98 (2024 est.)

Contraceptive prevalence rate: 26.9% (2019)

Drinking water source: *improved: urban:* 95.9% of population
rural: 79.3% of population
total: 87.3% of population
unimproved: urban: 4.1% of population
rural: 20.7% of population
total: 12.7% of population (2020 est.)

Current health expenditure: 5.2% of GDP (2020)

Physician density: 0.09 physicians/1,000 population (2019)

Sanitation facility access: *improved: urban:* 94.1% of population
rural: 55.5% of population
total: 74.1% of population
unimproved: urban: 5.9% of population
rural: 44.5% of population
total: 25.9% of population (2020 est.)

Obesity - adult prevalence rate: 8.8% (2016)
comparison ranking: 146

Alcohol consumption per capita: *total:* 0.25 liters of pure alcohol (2019 est.)
beer: 0.21 liters of pure alcohol (2019 est.)
wine: 0.02 liters of pure alcohol (2019 est.)
spirits: 0.02 liters of pure alcohol (2019 est.)
other alcohols: 0 liters of pure alcohol (2019 est.)
comparison ranking: total 170

Tobacco use: *total:* 6.9% (2020 est.)
male: 13.1% (2020 est.)

female: 0.7% (2020 est.)
comparison ranking: total 156

Children under the age of 5 years underweight: 14.4% (2019)
comparison ranking: 37

Currently married women (ages 15-49): 65.3% (2023 est.)

Child marriage: *women married by age 15:* 8.8%
women married by age 18: 30.5%
men married by age 18: 0.7% (2019 est.)

Education expenditures: 5.5% of GDP (2020 est.)
comparison ranking: 59

Literacy: *definition:* age 15 and over can read and write
total population: 56.3%
male: 68.4%
female: 45.4% (2021)

School life expectancy (primary to tertiary education): *total:* 9 years
male: 8 years
female: 10 years (2021)

ENVIRONMENT

Environment - current issues: deforestation; overgrazing; soil erosion; desertification; periodic droughts; seasonal flooding; overfishing; weak environmental protective laws; wildlife populations threatened by poaching

Environment - international agreements: *party to:* Biodiversity, Climate Change, Climate Change-Kyoto Protocol, Climate Change-Paris Agreement, Comprehensive Nuclear Test Ban, Desertification, Endangered Species, Hazardous Wastes, Law of the Sea, Marine Life Conservation, Nuclear Test Ban, Ozone Layer Protection, Ship Pollution, Wetlands, Whaling
signed, but not ratified: none of the selected agreements

Climate: tropical; hot, humid; rainy season (May to November) has strong southeast winds; dry season (December to April) dominated by hot, dry, harmattan wind

Urbanization: *urban population:* 49.6% of total population (2023)
rate of urbanization: 3.59% annual rate of change (2020-25 est.)

Food insecurity: *severe localized food insecurity: due to localized shortfalls in cereal production and reduced incomes* - according to the latest analysis, about 881,000 people are estimated to be in need of humanitarian assistance between June and August 2022, mostly on account of localized shortfalls in cereal production in 2021 and reduced incomes owing to the impact of the COVID-19 pandemic (2022)

Revenue from forest resources: 1.46% of GDP (2018 est.)
comparison ranking: 45

Revenue from coal: 0% of GDP (2018 est.)
comparison ranking: 76

Air pollutants: *particulate matter emissions:* 38.21 micrograms per cubic meter (2019 est.)
carbon dioxide emissions: 10.9 megatons (2016 est.)
methane emissions: 11.74 megatons (2020 est.)

Waste and recycling: *municipal solid waste generated annually:* 2,454,059 tons (2016 est.)

Major rivers (by length in km): Senegal (shared with Guinea [s], Mali, and Mauritania [m]) - 1,641 km; Gambie (Gambia) (shared with Guinea [s] and The Gambia [m]) - 1,094 km
note – [s] after country name indicates river source; [m] after country name indicates river mouth

Major watersheds (area sq km): Atlantic Ocean drainage: Senegal (456,397 sq km)

Major aquifers: Senegalo-Mauritanian Basin

Total water withdrawal: *municipal:* 260 million cubic meters (2020 est.)
industrial: 58 million cubic meters (2017 est.)
agricultural: 2.76 billion cubic meters (2020 est.)

Total renewable water resources: 38.97 billion cubic meters (2020 est.)

GOVERNMENT

Country name: *conventional long form:* Republic of Senegal
conventional short form: Senegal
local long form: République du Sénégal
local short form: Sénégal
former: Senegambia (along with The Gambia), Mali Federation
etymology: named for the Senegal River that forms the northern border of the country; many theories exist for the origin of the river name; perhaps the most widely cited derives the name from "Azenegue," the Portuguese appellation for the Berber Zenaga people who lived north of the river

Government type: presidential republic

Capital: *name:* Dakar
geographic coordinates: 14 44 N, 17 38 W
time difference: UTC 0 (5 hours ahead of Washington, D.C., during Standard Time)
etymology: the Atlantic coast trading settlement of Ndakaaru came to be called "Dakar" by French colonialists

Administrative divisions: 14 regions (regions, singular - region); Dakar, Diourbel, Fatick, Kaffrine, Kaolack, Kéedougou, Kolda, Louga, Matam, Saint-Louis, Sedhiou, Tambacounda, Thies, Ziguinchor

Independence: 4 April 1960 (from France); note - complete independence achieved upon dissolution of federation with Mali on 20 August 1960

National holiday: Independence Day, 4 April (1960)

Legal system: civil law system based on French law; judicial review of legislative acts in Constitutional Council

Constitution: *history:* previous 1959 (pre-independence), 1963; latest adopted by referendum 7 January 2001, promulgated 22
January 2001
amendments: proposed by the president of the republic or by the National Assembly; passage requires Assembly approval and approval in a referendum; the president can bypass a referendum and submit an amendment directly to the Assembly, which requires at least three-fifths majority vote; the republican form of government is not amendable; amended several times, last in 2019

International law organization participation: accepts compulsory ICJ jurisdiction with reservations; accepts ICCt jurisdiction

Citizenship: *citizenship by birth:* no
citizenship by descent only: at least one parent must be a citizen of Senegal
dual citizenship recognized: no, but Senegalese citizens do not automatically lose their citizenship if they acquire citizenship in another state
residency requirement for naturalization: 5 years

Suffrage: 18 years of age; universal

Executive branch: *chief of state:* President Bassirou Diomaye FAYE (since 2 April 2024)
head of government: Prime Minister Ousmane SONKO (since 2 April 2024)
cabinet: Council of Ministers appointed by the president
elections/appointments: president directly elected by absolute majority popular vote in 2 rounds if needed for a single, renewable 5-year term; election last held on 24 March 2024 (next to be held in 2029)
election results:
2024: Bassirou Diomaye FAYE elected president in first round; percent of vote - Bassirou Diomaye FAYE (PASTEF) 54%, Amadou BA (APR) 36%, other 10%
2019: Macky SALL reelected president in first round; percent of vote - Macky SALL (APR) 58.3%, Idrissa SECK (Rewmi) 20.5%, Ousmane SONKO (PASTEF) 15.7%, other 5.5%

Legislative branch: *description:* unicameral National Assembly or Assemblée Nationale (165 seats; 112 members including 15 representing Senegalese diaspora directly elected by plurality vote in single- and multi-seat constituencies and 53 members directly elected by proportional representation vote in a single nationwide constituency; member term is 5-years)
elections: last held on 31 July 2022 (next scheduled to be held in July 2027)
election results: percent of vote by party/coalition - BBY 46.6%, YAW 32.9%, WS 14.5%, other 6%; seats by party/ coalition - BBY 82, YAW 42, WS 24, other 17; composition - men 89, women 76, percentage women 46.1%

Judicial branch: *highest court(s):* Supreme Court or *Cour Suprême* (consists of the court president and 12 judges and organized into civil and commercial, criminal, administrative, and social chambers); Constitutional Council or *Conseil Constitutionnel* (consists of 7 members, including the court president, vice president, and 5 judges)
judge selection and term of office: Supreme Court judges appointed by the president of the republic upon recommendation of the Superior Council of the Magistrates, a body chaired by the president and minister of justice; judge tenure varies, with mandatory retirement either at 65 or 68 years; Constitutional Council members appointed - 5 by the president and 2 by the National Assembly speaker; judges serve 6-year terms, with renewal of 2 members every 2 years
subordinate courts: High Court of Justice (for crimes of high treason by the president); Courts of Appeal; Court of Auditors; assize courts; regional and district courts; Labor Court

Political parties: Alliance for Citizenship and Work or ACT
Alliance for the Republic-Yakaar or APR
Alliance of Forces of Progress or AFP
AND (National Alliance for Democracy)
And-Jef/African Party for Democracy and Socialism or AJ/PADS
ARC (Alternative for the next generation of citizens)
Awalé
Benno Bokk Yakaar or BBY (United in Hope); coalition includes AFP, APR, BGC, LD-MPT, PIT, PS, and UNP

Bokk Gis Gis coalition
Citizen Movement for National Reform or MCRN-Bes Du Nakk
Coalition Mimi 2024
Dare the Future movement
Democratic League-Labor Party Movement or LD-MPT
Democratic Renaissance Congress
Front for Socialism and Democracy/Benno Jubel or FSD/BJ
Gainde Centrist Bloc or BCG
General Alliance for the Interests of the Republic or AGIR
Grand Party or GP
Gueum sa Bopp (Believe in yourself)
Independence and Labor Party or PIT
Jotna Coalition
Liberate the People (Yewwi Askan Wi) or YAW
Madicke 2019 coalition
National Union for the People or UNP
Only Senegal Movement
Party for Truth and Development or PVD
Party of Unity and Rally or PUR
Patriotic Convergence Kaddu Askan Wi or CP-Kaddu Askan Wi
PRP (Republican party for Progress)
Rewmi Party
Save Senegal (Wallu Senegal Grand Coalition) or WS; coalition includes PDS, Jotna Coalition, Democratic Renaissance Congress
Senegalese Democratic Party or PDS
Socialist Party or PS
Tekki Movement
Réewum Ngor (Republic of Values)
Servants (Les Serviteurs)

International organization participation: ACP, AfDB, AU, CD, CPLP (associate), ECOWAS, EITI (candidate country), FAO, FZ, G-15, G-77, IAEA, IBRD, ICAO, ICC (national committees), ICCt, ICRM, IDA, IDB, IFAD, IFC, IFRCS, ILO, IMF, IMO, IMSO, Interpol, IOC, IOM, IPU, ISO, ITSO, ITU, ITUC (NGOs), MIGA, MONUSCO, NAM, OIC, OIF, OPCW, PCA, UN, UNAMID, UNCTAD, UNESCO, UNHCR, UNIDO, UNMIL, UNMISS, UNOCI, UNOOSA, UNWTO, UPU, WADB (regional), WAEMU, WCO, WFTU (NGOs), WHO, WIPO, WMO, WTO

Diplomatic representation in the US: *chief of mission:* Ambassador (vacant); Chargé d'Affaires Isidor Marcel SENE (since 31 August 2024)
chancery: 2215 M ST NW, Washington, D.C. 20037
telephone: [1] (202) 234-0540
FAX: [1] (202) 629-2961
email address and website:
contact@ambasenegal-us.org
http://www.ambasenegal-us.org/index.php
consulate(s) general: New York

Diplomatic representation from the US: *chief of mission:* Ambassador Michael RAYNOR (since 10 March 2022); note - also accredited to Guinea-Bissau
embassy: Route des Almadies, Dakar
mailing address: 2130 Dakar Place, Washington D.C. 20521-2130
telephone: [221] 33-879-4000
email address and website:
DakarACS@state.gov
https://sn.usembassy.gov/

Flag description: three equal vertical bands of green (hoist side), yellow, and red with a small green five-pointed star centered in the yellow band; green represents Islam, progress, and hope; yellow signifies natural wealth and progress; red symbolizes sacrifice and determination; the star denotes unity and hope
note: uses the popular Pan-African colors of Ethiopia; the colors from left to right are the same as those of neighboring Mali and the reverse of those on the flag of neighboring Guinea

National symbol(s): lion; national colors: green, yellow, red

National anthem: *name:* "Pincez Tous vos Koras, Frappez les Balafons" (Pluck Your Koras, Strike the Balafons)
lyrics/music: Leopold Sedar SENGHOR/Herbert PEPPER
note: adopted 1960; lyrics written by Leopold Sedar SENGHOR, Senegal's first president; the anthem sometimes played incorporating the Koras (harp-like stringed instruments) and Balafons (types of xylophones) mentioned in the title

National heritage: *total World Heritage Sites:* 7 (5 cultural, 2 natural)
selected World Heritage Site locales: Island of Gorée (c); Niokolo-Koba National Park (n); Djoudj National Bird Sanctuary (n); Island of Saint-Louis (c); Stone Circles of Senegambia (c); Saloum Delta (c); Bassari Country: Bassari, Fula, and Bedik Cultural Landscapes (c)

ECONOMY

Economic overview: lower middle-income, services-driven West African economy; key mining, construction, agriculture, and fishing industries; tourism and exports hit hard by COVID-19; large informal economy; developing offshore oil and gas fields; systemic corruption

Real GDP (purchasing power parity): $77.382 billion (2023 est.)
$74.621 billion (2022 est.)
$71.874 billion (2021 est.)
note: data in 2021 dollars
comparison ranking: 104

Real GDP growth rate: 3.7% (2023 est.)
3.82% (2022 est.)
6.54% (2021 est.)
note: annual GDP % growth based on constant local currency
comparison ranking: 86

Real GDP per capita: $4,400 (2023 est.)
$4,300 (2022 est.)
$4,300 (2021 est.)
note: data in 2021 dollars
comparison ranking: 183

GDP (official exchange rate): $31.014 billion (2023 est.)
note: data in current dollars at official exchange rate

Inflation rate (consumer prices): 9.7% (2022 est.)
2.18% (2021 est.)
2.54% (2020 est.)
note: annual % change based on consumer prices
comparison ranking: 174

Credit ratings: Moody's rating: Ba3 (2017)

Standard & Poors rating: B+ (2000)
note: The year refers to the year in which the current credit rating was first obtained.

GDP - composition, by sector of origin: *agriculture:* 16.4% (2023 est.)
industry: 23.7% (2023 est.)
services: 50.8% (2023 est.)
note: figures may not total 100% due to non-allocated consumption not captured in sector-reported data
comparison rankings: services 144; industry 111; agriculture 49

GDP - composition, by end use: *household consumption:* 55.9% (2023 est.)
government consumption: 14.7% (2023 est.)
investment in fixed capital: 38.4% (2023 est.)
investment in inventories: 9% (2023 est.)
exports of goods and services: 25.6% (2023 est.)
imports of goods and services: -43.9% (2023 est.)
note: figures may not total 100% due to rounding or gaps in data collection

Agricultural products: groundnuts, watermelons, rice, cassava, sugarcane, millet, maize, onions, sorghum, milk (2022)
note: top ten agricultural products based on tonnage

Industries: agricultural and fish processing, phosphate mining, fertilizer production, petroleum refining, zircon, and gold mining, construction materials, ship construction and repair

Industrial production growth rate: 2.9% (2023 est.)
note: annual % change in industrial value added based on constant local currency
comparison ranking: 109

Labor force: 5.257 million (2023 est.)
note: number of people ages 15 or older who are employed or seeking work
comparison ranking: 84

Unemployment rate: 2.93% (2023 est.)
2.97% (2022 est.)
3.37% (2021 est.)
note: % of labor force seeking employment
comparison ranking: 42

Youth unemployment rate (ages 15-24): *total:* 4.1% (2023 est.)
male: 2.9% (2023 est.)
female: 6.7% (2023 est.)
note: % of labor force ages 15-24 seeking employment
comparison ranking: total 181

Gini Index coefficient - distribution of family income: 36.2 (2021 est.)
note: index (0-100) of income distribution; higher values represent greater inequality
comparison ranking: 67

Household income or consumption by percentage share: *lowest 10%:* 3% (2021 est.)
highest 10%: 28.8% (2021 est.)
note: % share of income accruing to lowest and highest 10% of population

Remittances: 9.47% of GDP (2023 est.)
10.89% of GDP (2022 est.)
11.25% of GDP (2021 est.)
note: personal transfers and compensation between resident and non-resident individuals/households/entities

Budget: *revenues:* $6.423 billion (2022 est.)
expenditures: $6.424 billion (2022 est.)
note: central government revenues (excluding grants) and expenses converted to US dollars at average official exchange rate for year indicated

Public debt: 48.3% of GDP (2017 est.)
comparison ranking: 110

Taxes and other revenues: 18.7% (of GDP) (2022 est.)
note: central government tax revenue as a % of GDP
comparison ranking: 95

Current account balance: -$3.327 billion (2021 est.)

-$2.662 billion (2020 est.)
-$1.898 billion (2019 est.)
note: balance of payments - net trade and primary/secondary income in current dollars
comparison ranking: 169

Exports: $6.78 billion (2021 est.)
$5.063 billion (2020 est.)
$5.836 billion (2019 est.)
note: balance of payments - exports of goods and services in current dollars
comparison ranking: 127

Exports - partners: Mali 18%, India 16%, Switzerland 11%, US 8%, China 4% (2022)
note: top five export partners based on percentage share of exports

Exports - commodities: gold, phosphoric acid, refined petroleum, fish, precious metal products (2022)
note: top five export commodities based on value in dollars

Imports: $12.278 billion (2021 est.)
$9.627 billion (2020 est.)
$9.17 billion (2019 est.)
note: balance of payments - imports of goods and services in current dollars
comparison ranking: 112

Imports - partners: China 22%, India 8%, France 7%, Belgium 5%, Netherlands 4% (2022)
note: top five import partners based on percentage share of imports

Imports - commodities: refined petroleum, ships, rice, crude petroleum, plastic products (2022)
note: top five import commodities based on value in dollars

Reserves of foreign exchange and gold: $1.827 billion (31 December 2017 est.)
$116.9 million (31 December 2016 est.)
comparison ranking: 124

Debt - external: $12.652 billion (2022 est.)
note: present value of external debt in current US dollars
comparison ranking: 33

Exchange rates: Communaute Financiere Africaine francs (XOF) per US dollar -

Exchange rates: 606.57 (2023 est.)
623.76 (2022 est.)
554.531 (2021 est.)
575.586 (2020 est.)
585.911 (2019 est.)

ENERGY

Electricity access: *electrification - total population:* 67.9% (2022 est.)
electrification - urban areas: 96.6%
electrification - rural areas: 43.4%

Electricity: *installed generating capacity:* 1.668 million kW (2022 est.)
consumption: 7.025 billion kWh (2022 est.)
imports: 326.425 million kWh (2022 est.)
transmission/distribution losses: 1.057 billion kWh (2022 est.)
comparison rankings: transmission/distribution losses 99; imports 101; consumption 117; installed generating capacity 127

Electricity generation sources: *fossil fuels:* 74.3% of total installed capacity (2022 est.)
solar: 10.9% of total installed capacity (2022 est.)
wind: 9.5% of total installed capacity (2022 est.)
hydroelectricity: 4% of total installed capacity (2022 est.)
biomass and waste: 1.4% of total installed capacity (2022 est.)

Coal: *consumption:* 502,000 metric tons (2022 est.)
imports: 502,000 metric tons (2022 est.)

Petroleum: *total petroleum production:* 9,000 bbl/day (2023 est.)
refined petroleum consumption: 55,000 bbl/day (2022 est.)

Natural gas: *production:* 54.646 million cubic meters (2022 est.)
consumption: 54.498 million cubic meters (2022 est.)

Carbon dioxide emissions: 9.152 million metric tonnes of CO2 (2022 est.)
from coal and metallurgical coke: 1.134 million metric tonnes of CO2 (2022 est.)
from petroleum and other liquids: 7.926 million metric tonnes of CO2 (2022 est.)
from consumed natural gas: 92,000 metric tonnes of CO2 (2022 est.)
comparison ranking: total emissions 108

Energy consumption per capita: 7.836 million Btu/person (2022 est.)
comparison ranking: 156

COMMUNICATIONS

Telephones - fixed lines: *total subscriptions:* 297,000 (2022 est.)
subscriptions per 100 inhabitants: 2 (2022 est.)
comparison ranking: total subscriptions 108

Telephones - mobile cellular: *total subscriptions:* 20.855 million (2022 est.)
subscriptions per 100 inhabitants: 120 (2022 est.)
comparison ranking: total subscriptions 59

Telecommunication systems: *general assessment:* Senegal's telecom market continues to show steady growth in all sectors; this has been supported by the particular demands made on consumers during the pandemic, which resulted in a particularly strong increase in the number of subscribers; the mobile subscriber base increased 6.7% in 2020, year-on-year, and by 4.1% in 2021, while the number of fixed broadband subscribers increased 17.5% year-on-year in 2021; mobile internet platforms account for the vast majority of all internet accesses; quality of service issues continue to plague the market, with the regulator periodically issuing fines to the market players (2022)
domestic: fixed-line is 2 per 100 and mobile-cellular 118 per 100 persons (2021)
international: country code - 221; landing points for the ACE, Atlantis-2, MainOne and SAT-3/WASC submarine cables providing connectivity from South Africa, numerous western African countries, Europe and South America; satellite earth station - 1 Intelsat (Atlantic Ocean) (2019)

Broadcast media: Senegal's media environment includes over 25 private television stations, hundreds of radio stations, and more than 45 newspapers. State-run Radiodiffusion Television Senegalaise (RTS) broadcasts from five cities in Senegal and a wide range of independent TV programming is available via satellite; transmissions of several international broadcasters are accessible on FM in Dakar

Internet country code: .sn

Internet users: *total:* 9.86 million (2021 est.)
percent of population: 58% (2021 est.)
comparison ranking: total 59

Broadband - fixed subscriptions: *total:* 153,813 (2020 est.)
subscriptions per 100 inhabitants: 1 (2020 est.)
comparison ranking: total 122

TRANSPORTATION

National air transport system: *number of registered air carriers:* 2 (2020)
inventory of registered aircraft operated by air carriers: 11
annual passenger traffic on registered air carriers: 21,038 (2018)
annual freight traffic on registered air carriers: 40,000 (2018) mt-km

Civil aircraft registration country code prefix: 6V

Airports: 19 (2024)
comparison ranking: 136

Pipelines: 43 km gas, 8 km refined products (2017)

Railways: *total:* 906 km (2017) (713 km operational in 2017)
narrow gauge: 906 km (2017) 1.000-m gauge
comparison ranking: total 93

Roadways: *total:* 16,665 km
paved: 6,126 km (includes 241 km of expressways)
unpaved: 10,539 km (2017)
comparison ranking: total 119

Waterways: 1,000 km (2012) (primarily on the Senegal, Saloum, and Casamance Rivers)
comparison ranking: 68

Merchant marine: *total:* 36 (2023)
by type: general cargo 5, oil tanker 1, other 30
comparison ranking: total 129

Ports: *total ports:* 6 (2024)
large: 0
medium: 1
small: 1
very small: 4
ports with oil terminals: 4
key ports: Dakar, Karabane, Lyndiane, M'bao Oil Terminal, Rufisque, St. Louis

MILITARY AND SECURITY

Military and security forces: Senegalese Armed Forces (les Forces Armées Sénégalaises, FAS): Army (l'Armée de Terre, AT), Senegalese National Navy (Marine Séenéegalaise, MNS), Senegalese Air Force (l'Arméee de l'Air du Séenéegal, AAS), National Gendarmerie (includes Territorial and Mobile components)

Ministry of Interior: National Police (2024)
note: the National Police operates in major cities, while the Gendarmerie under the FAS primarily operates outside urban areas; both services have specialized anti-terrorism units

Military expenditures: 1.5% of GDP (2023 est.)
1.6% of GDP (2022 est.)
1.7% of GDP (2021 est.)
1.5% of GDP (2020 est.)
1.5% of GDP (2019 est.)
comparison ranking: 93

Military and security service personnel strengths: approximately 27,000 active personnel (15,000 Army; 1,500 Navy; 1,500 Air Force; 16,000 National Gendarmerie); 15,000 National Police (2023)

Military equipment inventories and acquisitions: the military's inventory includes a mix of older, secondhand, and more modern equipment from a variety of countries, including France, South Africa, and Russia/former Soviet Union; in recent years, the military has undertaken a modernization program and has received newer equipment from more than 10 countries, including France and the US (2024)

Military service age and obligation: 18 years of age for voluntary military service for men and women; 20 years of age for selective compulsory service for men and possibly women; 24-month service obligation (2023)

Military deployments: 200 Central African Republic (MINUSCA; plus about 525 police); 800 (ECOWAS Military Intervention in The Gambia– ECOMIG); 500 (ECOWAS Stabilization Support Mission in Guinea-Bissau–EESMGB); 450 police Democratic Republic of the Congo (MONUSCO) (2024)

Military - note: despite limited resources, the Senegalese military is considered to be a well-equipped, experienced, and effective force; the military has a tradition of non-interference in the country's political process and positive relations with civil authorities; it participates in foreign deployments and multinational exercises and has received assistance from France, which maintains a military presence in the country, as well as Germany, Spain, the UK, and the US; the military's primary focuses are border, internal, and maritime security; it also works with the civilian government in areas such as preventive healthcare, infrastructure development, environmental protection, and disaster response

Senegal's security concerns include the prevalence of multiple active terrorist groups across the region and political instability in neighboring Mali and Guinea; Senegal has recently established new military and gendarmerie camps along its eastern border with Mali

Senegalese security forces have been engaged in a low-level counterinsurgency campaign in the southern Casamance region against various factions of the separatist Movement of Democratic Forces of the Casamance (MDFC) since 1982; the conflict is one of longest running low-level insurgencies in the World, having claimed more than 5,000 lives while leaving another 60,000 displaced; in May 2023, a faction of the MFDC agreed to a peace deal (2024)

SPACE

Space agency/agencies: Senegalese Space Study Agency (Agence Sénégalaise d'Etudes Spatiales or ASES; launched in 2023 under the Ministry of Higher Education, Research, and Innovation) (2024)

Space program overview: small, nascent program focused on acquiring satellites, largely for socio-economic development and research; conducts research in such fields as astronomy and planetary sciences; has cooperated with the European Space Agency, and the space agencies of China, France, Turkey, and the US (2024)

TERRORISM

Terrorist group(s): Jama'at Nusrat al-Islam wal-Muslimin (JNIM)

TRANSNATIONAL ISSUES

Refugees and internally displaced persons: *refugees (country of origin):* 11,518 (Mauritania) (2023)
IDPs: 8,400 (2022)

Illicit drugs: a transit point on the cocaine route from South America to Europe; large production of cannabis in southern Casamance region; the high domestic use of cannabis, ecstasy, and to a lesser extent crack cocaine

SERBIA

INTRODUCTION

Background: In 1918, the Croats, Serbs, and Slovenes formed a kingdom known after 1929 as Yugoslavia. The monarchy remained in power until 1945, when the communist Partisans headed by Josip Broz (aka TITO) took control of the newly created Socialist Federal Republic of Yugoslavia (SFRY). After TITO died in 1980, communism in Yugoslavia gradually gave way to resurgent nationalism. In 1989, Slobodan MILOSEVIC became president of the Republic of Serbia, and his calls for Serbian domination led to the violent breakup of Yugoslavia along ethnic lines. In 1991, Croatia, Slovenia, and Macedonia declared independence, followed by Bosnia in 1992. The remaining republics of Serbia and Montenegro declared a new Federal Republic of Yugoslavia (FRY) in 1992, and MILOSEVIC led military campaigns to unite ethnic Serbs in neighboring republics into a "Greater Serbia." These actions ultimately failed, and international intervention led to the signing of the Dayton Accords in 1995.

In 1998, an ethnic Albanian insurgency in the formerly autonomous Serbian province of Kosovo resulted in a brutal Serbian counterinsurgency campaign. Serbia rejected a proposed international settlement, and NATO responded with a bombing campaign that forced Serbian forces to withdraw from Kosovo in June 1999. In 2003, the FRY became the State Union of Serbia and Montenegro, a loose federation of the two republics. In 2006, Montenegro seceded and declared itself an independent nation.

In 2008, Kosovo also declared independence – an action Serbia still refuses to recognize. In 2013, Serbia and Kosovo signed the first agreement of principles governing the normalization of relations between the two countries. Additional agreements were reached in 2015 and 2023, but implementation remains incomplete. Serbia has been an official candidate for EU membership since 2012, and President Aleksandar VUCIC has promoted the ambitious goal of Serbia joining the EU by 2025.

GEOGRAPHY

Location: Southeastern Europe, between Macedonia and Hungary

Geographic coordinates: 44 00 N, 21 00 E

Map references: Europe

Area: *total:* 77,474 sq km
land: 77,474 sq km
water: 0 sq km
comparison ranking: total 117

Area - comparative: slightly smaller than South Carolina

Land boundaries: *total:* 2,322 km
border countries (8): Bosnia and Herzegovina 345 km; Bulgaria 344 km; Croatia 314 km; Hungary 164 km; Kosovo 366 km; North Macedonia 101 km; Montenegro 157 km; Romania 531 km

Coastline: 0 km (landlocked)

Maritime claims: none (landlocked)

Climate: in the north, continental climate (cold winters and hot, humid summers with well-distributed rainfall); in other parts, continental and Mediterranean climate (relatively cold winters with heavy snowfall and hot, dry summers and autumns)

Terrain: extremely varied; to the north, rich fertile plains; to the east, limestone ranges and basins; to the southeast, ancient mountains and hills

Elevation: *highest point:* Midzor 2,169 m
lowest point: Danube and Timok Rivers 35 m
mean elevation: 442 m

Natural resources: oil, gas, coal, iron ore, copper, zinc, antimony, chromite, gold, silver, magnesium, pyrite, limestone, marble, salt, arable land

Land use: *agricultural land:* 57.9% (2018 est.)
arable land: 37.7% (2018 est.)
permanent crops: 3.4% (2018 est.)
permanent pasture: 16.8% (2018 est.)
forest: 31.6% (2018 est.)
other: 10.5% (2018 est.)

Irrigated land: 520 sq km (2020)

Major rivers (by length in km): Dunav (Danube) (shared with Germany [s], Austria, Slovakia, Hungary, Croatia, Bulgaria, Ukraine, Moldova, and Romania [m]) - 2,888 km
note – [s] after country name indicates river source; [m] after country name indicates river mouth

Major watersheds (area sq km): Atlantic Ocean drainage: *(Black Sea)* Danube (795,656 sq km)

Population distribution: a fairly even distribution throughout most of the country, with urban areas attracting larger and denser populations

Natural hazards: destructive earthquakes

Geography - note: landlocked; controls one of the major land routes from Western Europe to Turkey and the Near East

PEOPLE AND SOCIETY

Population: *total:* 6,652,212
male: 3,242,751
female: 3,409,461 (2024 est.)
comparison rankings: female 108; male 109; total 109

Nationality: *noun:* Serb(s)
adjective: Serbian

Ethnic groups: Serb 83.3%, Hungarian 3.5%, Romani 2.1%, Bosniak 2%, other 5.7%, undeclared or unknown 3.4% (2011 est.)
note: most ethnic Albanians boycotted the 2011 census; Romani populations are usually underestimated in official statistics and may represent 5–11% of Serbia's population

Languages: Serbian (official) 88.1%, Hungarian 3.4%, Bosnian 1.9%, Romani 1.4%, other 3.4%, undeclared or unknown 1.8% (2011 est.)
major-language sample(s):
Knjiga svetskih činjenica, neophodan izvor osnovnih informacija. (Serbian)
note: Serbian, Hungarian, Slovak, Romanian, Croatian, and Ruthenian (Rusyn) are official in the Autonomous Province of Vojvodina; most ethnic Albanians boycotted the 2011 census

Religions: Orthodox 84.6%, Catholic 5%, Muslim 3.1%, Protestant 1%, atheist 1.1%, other 0.8% (includes agnostics, other Christians, Eastern, Jewish), undeclared or unknown 4.5% (2011 est.)
note: most ethnic Albanians boycotted the 2011 census

Age structure: *0-14 years:* 14.4% (male 492,963/female 463,995)
15-64 years: 65.6% (male 2,198,591/female 2,168,113)
65 years and over: 20% (2024 est.) (male 551,197/female 777,353)

Dependency ratios: *total dependency ratio:* 53.8
youth dependency ratio: 21.9
elderly dependency ratio: 31.9
potential support ratio: 3.1 (2021 est.)
note: data include Kosovo

Median age: *total:* 43.9 years (2024 est.)
male: 42.4 years
female: 45.4 years
comparison ranking: total 33

Population growth rate: -0.61% (2024 est.)
comparison ranking: 225

Birth rate: 8.8 births/1,000 population (2024 est.)
comparison ranking: 202

Death rate: 14.9 deaths/1,000 population (2024 est.)
comparison ranking: 3

Net migration rate: 0 migrant(s)/1,000 population (2024 est.)
comparison ranking: 82

Population distribution: a fairly even distribution throughout most of the country, with urban areas attracting larger and denser populations

Urbanization: *urban population:* 57.1% of total population (2023)
rate of urbanization: 0.04% annual rate of change (2020-25 est.)
note: data include Kosovo

Major urban areas - population: 1.408 million BELGRADE (capital) (2023)

Sex ratio: *at birth:* 1.06 male(s)/female
0-14 years: 1.06 male(s)/female
15-64 years: 1.01 male(s)/female
65 years and over: 0.71 male(s)/female
total population: 0.95 male(s)/female (2024 est.)

Mother's mean age at first birth: 28.2 years (2020 est.)
note: data does not cover Kosovo or Metohija

Maternal mortality ratio: 10 deaths/100,000 live births (2020 est.)
comparison ranking: 143

Infant mortality rate: *total:* 4.5 deaths/1,000 live births (2024 est.)
male: 5.1 deaths/1,000 live births
female: 3.9 deaths/1,000 live births
comparison ranking: total 181

Life expectancy at birth: *total population:* 75.3 years (2024 est.)
male: 72.7 years
female: 78.1 years
comparison ranking: total population 128

Total fertility rate: 1.46 children born/woman (2024 est.)
comparison ranking: 205

Gross reproduction rate: 0.71 (2024 est.)

Contraceptive prevalence rate: 62.3% (2019)

Drinking water source: *improved: urban:* 99.7% of population
rural: 99.4% of population
total: 99.5% of population
unimproved: urban: 0.3% of population
rural: 0.6% of population
total: 0.5% of population (2020 est.)

Current health expenditure: 8.7% of GDP (2020)

Physician density: 3.11 physicians/1,000 population (2016)

Hospital bed density: 5.6 beds/1,000 population (2017)

Sanitation facility access: *improved: urban:* 99.6% of population
rural: 95.7% of population
total: 97.9% of population
unimproved: urban: 0.4% of population
rural: 4.3% of population
total: 2.1% of population (2020 est.)

Obesity - adult prevalence rate: 21.5% (2016)
comparison ranking: 88

Alcohol consumption per capita: *total:* 7.45 liters of pure alcohol (2019 est.)
beer: 3.24 liters of pure alcohol (2019 est.)
wine: 1.62 liters of pure alcohol (2019 est.)
spirits: 2.37 liters of pure alcohol (2019 est.)
other alcohols: 0.22 liters of pure alcohol (2019 est.)
comparison ranking: total 55

Tobacco use: *total:* 39.8% (2020 est.)
male: 40.5% (2020 est.)
female: 39.1% (2020 est.)
comparison ranking: total 4

Children under the age of 5 years underweight: 1% (2019)
comparison ranking: 116

Currently married women (ages 15-49): 60.8% (2023 est.)

Child marriage: *women married by age 15:* 1.2%
women married by age 18: 5.5% (2019 est.)

Education expenditures: 3.6% of GDP (2019 est.)
comparison ranking: 134

Literacy: *definition:* age 15 and over can read and write
total population: 99.5%
male: 99.9%
female: 99.1% (2019)

School life expectancy (primary to tertiary education): *total:* 14 years
male: 14 years
female: 15 years (2021)

ENVIRONMENT

Environment - current issues: air pollution around Belgrade and other industrial cities; water pollution from industrial wastes dumped into the Sava which flows into the Danube; inadequate management of domestic, industrial, and hazardous waste

Environment - international agreements: *party to:* Air Pollution, Air Pollution-Heavy Metals, Air Pollution-Persistent Organic Pollutants, Biodiversity, Climate Change, Climate Change-Kyoto Protocol, Climate Change-Paris Agreement, Comprehensive Nuclear Test Ban, Desertification, Endangered Species, Hazardous Wastes, Law of the Sea, Marine Dumping-London Convention, Marine Life Conservation, Nuclear Test Ban, Ozone Layer Protection, Ship Pollution, Wetlands
signed, but not ratified: none of the selected agreements

Climate: in the north, continental climate (cold winters and hot, humid summers with well-distributed rainfall); in other parts, continental and Mediterranean climate (relatively cold winters with heavy snowfall and hot, dry summers and autumns)

Urbanization: *urban population:* 57.1% of total population (2023)
rate of urbanization: 0.04% annual rate of change (2020-25 est.)
note: data include Kosovo

Revenue from forest resources: 0.38% of GDP (2018 est.)
comparison ranking: 73

Revenue from coal: 0.25% of GDP (2018 est.)
comparison ranking: 20

Air pollutants: *particulate matter emissions:* 21.74 micrograms per cubic meter (2019 est.)
carbon dioxide emissions: 45.22 megatons (2016 est.)
methane emissions: 11.96 megatons (2020 est.)

Waste and recycling: *municipal solid waste generated annually:* 1.84 million tons (2015 est.)
municipal solid waste recycled annually: 13,984 tons (2015 est.)
percent of municipal solid waste recycled: 0.8% (2015 est.)

Major rivers (by length in km): Dunav (Danube) (shared with Germany [s], Austria, Slovakia, Hungary, Croatia, Bulgaria, Ukraine, Moldova, and Romania [m]) - 2,888 km
note – [s] after country name indicates river source; [m] after country name indicates river mouth

Major watersheds (area sq km): Atlantic Ocean drainage: *(Black Sea)* Danube (795,656 sq km)

Total water withdrawal: *municipal:* 680 million cubic meters (2020 est.)
industrial: 3.99 billion cubic meters (2020 est.)
agricultural: 660 million cubic meters (2020 est.)

Total renewable water resources: 162.2 billion cubic meters (2020 est.) (note - includes Kosovo)

Geoparks: *total global geoparks and regional networks:* 1
global geoparks and regional networks: Djerdap (2023)

GOVERNMENT

Country name: *conventional long form:* Republic of Serbia
conventional short form: Serbia
local long form: Republika Srbija
local short form: Srbija
former: People's Republic of Serbia, Socialist Republic of Serbia
etymology: the origin of the name is uncertain, but seems to be related to the name of the West Slavic Sorbs who reside in the Lusatian region in present-day eastern Germany; by tradition, the Serbs migrated from that region to the Balkans in about the 6th century A.D.

Government type: parliamentary republic

Capital: *name:* Belgrade (Beograd)
geographic coordinates: 44 50 N, 20 30 E
time difference: UTC+1 (6 hours ahead of Washington, DC, during Standard Time)
daylight saving time: +1hr, begins last Sunday in March; ends last Sunday in October
etymology: the Serbian "Beograd" means "white fortress" or "white city" and dates back to the 9th century; the name derives from the white fortress wall that once enclosed the city

Administrative divisions: 117 municipalities (opstine, singular - opstina) and 28 cities (gradovi, singular - grad)
municipalities: Ada*, Aleksandrovac, Aleksinac, Alibunar*, Apatin*, Arandelovac, Arilje, Babusnica, Bac*, Backa Palanka*, Backa Topola*, Backi Petrovac*, Bajina Basta, Batocina, Becej*, Bela Crkva*, Bela Palanka, Beocin*, Blace, Bogatic, Bojnik, Boljevac, Bosilegrad, Brus, Bujanovac, Cajetina, Cicevac, Coka*, Crna Trava, Cuprija, Despotovac, Dimitrov, Doljevac, Gadzin Han, Golubac, Gornji Milanovac, Indija*, Irig*, Ivanjica, Kanjiza*, Kladovo, Knic, Knjazevac, Koceljeva, Kosjeric, Kovacica*, Kovin*, Krupanj, Kucevo, Kula*, Kursumlija, Lajkovac, Lapovo, Lebane, Ljig, Ljubovija, Lucani, Majdanpek, Mali Idos*, Mali Zvornik, Malo Crnice, Medveda, Merosina, Mionica, Negotin, Nova Crnja*, Nova Varos, Novi Becej*, Novi Knezevac*, Odzaci*, Opovo*, Osecina, Paracin, Pecinci*, Petrovac na Mlavi, Plandiste*, Pozega, Presevo, Priboj, Prijepolje, Raca, Raska, Razanj, Rekovac, Ruma*, Secanj*, Senta*, Sid*, Sjenica, Smederevska Palanka, Sokobanja, Srbobran*, Sremski Karlovci*, Stara Pazova*, Surdulica, Svilajnac, Svrljig, Temerin*, Titel*, Topola, Trgoviste, Trstenik, Tutin, Ub, Varvarin, Velika Plana, Veliko Gradiste, Vladicin Han, Vladimirci, Vlasotince, Vrbas*, Vrnjacka Banja, Zabalj*, Zabari, Zagubica, Zitiste*, Zitorada
cities: Beograd (Belgrade), Bor, Cacak, Jagodina, Kikinda*, Kragujevac, Kraljevo, Krusevac, Leskovac, Loznica, Nis, Novi Pazar, Novi Sad*, Pancevo*, Pirot, Pozarevac, Prokuplje, Sabac, Smederevo, Sombor*, Sremska Mitrovica*, Subotica*, Uzice, Valjevo, Vranje, Vrsac*, Zajecar, Zrenjanin*
note: the northern 37 municipalities and 8 cities - about 28% of Serbia's area - compose the Autonomous Province of Vojvodina and are indicated with *

Independence: *5 June 2006 (from the State Union of Serbia and Montenegro); notable earlier dates:* 1217 (Serbian Kingdom established); 16 April 1346 (Serbian Empire established); 13 July 1878 (Congress of Berlin recognizes Serbian independence); 1 December 1918 (Kingdom of Serbs, Croats, and Slovenes (Yugoslavia) established)

National holiday: Statehood Day, 15 February (1835), the day the first constitution of the country was adopted

Legal system: civil law system

Constitution: *history:* many previous; latest adopted 30 September 2006, approved by referendum 28-29 October 2006, effective 8 November 2006
amendments: proposed by at least one third of deputies in the National Assembly, by the president of the republic, by the government, or by petition of at least 150,000 voters; passage of proposals and draft amendments each requires at least two-thirds majority vote in the Assembly; amendments to constitutional articles including the preamble, constitutional principles, and human and minority rights and freedoms also require passage by simple majority vote in a referendum

International law organization participation: has not submitted an ICJ jurisdiction declaration; accepts ICCt jurisdiction

Citizenship: *citizenship by birth:* no
citizenship by descent only: at least one parent must be a citizen of Serbia
dual citizenship recognized: yes
residency requirement for naturalization: 3 years

Suffrage: 18 years of age, 16 if employed; universal

Executive branch: *chief of state:* President Aleksandar VUCIC (since 31 May 2017)
head of government: Prime Minister Milos Vucevic (since 2 May 2024)
cabinet: Cabinet elected by the National Assembly
elections/appointments: president directly elected by absolute majority popular vote in 2 rounds if needed for a 5-year term (eligible for a second term); election last held on 17 December 2023 (next to be held in 2028); prime minister elected by the National Assembly
election results:
2022: Aleksandar VUCIC reelected in first round; percent of vote - Aleksandar VUCIC (SNS) 60%, Zdravko PONOS (US) 18.9%, Milos JOVANOVIC (NADA) 6.1%, Bosko OBRADOVIC (Dveri-POKS) 4.5%, Milica DJURDJEVIC STAMENKOVSKI (SSZ) 4.3%, other 6.2%
2017: Aleksandar VUCIC elected president in first round; percent of vote - Aleksandar VUCIC (SNS) 55.1%, Sasa JANKOVIC (independent) 16.4%, Luka MAKSIMOVIC (independent) 9.4%, Vuk JEREMIC (independent) 5.7%, Vojislav SESELJ (SRS) 4.5%, other 7.3%, invalid/blank 1.6%; Prime Minister Ana BRNABIC reelected by the National Assembly on 5 October 2020; National Assembly vote - NA

Legislative branch: *description:* unicameral National Assembly or Narodna Skupstina (250 seats; members directly elected by party list proportional representation vote in a single nationwide constituency to serve 4-year terms)
elections: last held on 17 December 2023 (next to be held in 2027)
election results: percent of vote by party/coalition - Serbia Must Stop 48%, SPN 24.4%, SPS-JS-ZS 6.7%, NADA 5.2%, MI-GIN 4.8%, Alliance of Vojvodina Hungarians 1.7%, SPP-DSHV 0.8%, SDAS 0.6%, Political Battle of the Albanians Continues 0.4%, RS-NKPJ 0.3%, other 7.1%; seats by party/coalition - Serbia Must Stop 128, SPN 65, SPS-JS-ZS 18, NADA 13, MI-GIN 13, Alliance of Vojvodina Hungarians 6, SPP-DSHV 3, SDAS 2, Political Battle of the Albanians Continues 1, RS-NKPJ 1; composition - men 155, women 95; percentage of women 38%

Judicial branch: *highest court(s):* Supreme Court of Cassation (consists of 36 judges, including the court president); Constitutional Court (consists of 15 judges, including the court president and vice president)
judge selection and term of office: Supreme Court justices proposed by the High Judicial Council (HJC), an 11- member independent body consisting of 8 judges elected by the National Assembly and 3 ex-officio members; justices appointed by the National Assembly; Constitutional Court judges elected - 5 each by the National Assembly, the president, and the Supreme Court of Cassation; initial appointment of Supreme Court judges by the HJC is 3 years and beyond that period tenure is permanent; Constitutional Court judges elected for 9-year terms
subordinate courts: basic courts, higher courts, appellate courts; courts of special jurisdiction include the Administrative Court, commercial courts, and misdemeanor courts

Political parties: Alliance of Vojvodina Hungarians or SVM or VMSZ
Democratic Alliance of Croats in Vojvodina or DSHV
Democratic Party or DS
Ecological Uprising or EU
Green - Left Front or ZLF
Greens of Serbia or ZS
Justice and Reconciliation Party or SPP (formerly Bosniak Democratic Union of Sandzak or BDZS)
Movement for Reversal or PZP
Movement for the Restoration of the Kingdom of Serbia or POKS
Movement of Free Citizens or PSG
Movement of Socialists or PS
National Democratic Alternative or NADA (electoral coalition includes NDSS and POKS)
New Communist Party of Yugoslavia or NKPJ
New Democratic Party of Serbia or NDSS or New DSS (formerly Democratic Party of Serbia or DSS)
New Face of Serbia or NLS
Party of Democratic Action of the Sandzak or SDAS
Party of Freedom and Justice or SSP
Party of United Pensioners, Farmers, and Proletarians of Serbia – Solidarity and Justice or PUPS - Solidarity and Justice (formerly Party of United Pensioners of Serbia or PUPS)
People's Movement of Serbia or NPS
People's Movement of Serbs from Kosovo and Metohija or Fatherland
People's Peasant Party or NSS
Political Battle of the Albanians Continues
Russian Party or RS
Serbia Against Violence or SPN (electoral coalition includes DS, SSP, ZLF, Zajedno, NPS, PSG, EU, PZP, USS Sloga, NLS, Fatherland)

Serbia Must Not Stop (electoral coalitions includes SNS, SDPS, PUPS, PSS, SNP, SPO, PS, NSS, USS)
Serbian People's Party or SNP
Serbian Progressive Party or SNS
Serbian Renewal Movement or SPO
Social Democratic Party of Serbia or SDPS
Socialist Party of Serbia or SPS
Strength of Serbia or PSS
Together or ZAJEDNO
United Peasant Party or USS
United Serbia or JS
United Trade Unions of Serbia "Sloga" or USS Sloga
We - The Voice from the People or MI-GIN

International organization participation: BIS, BSEC, CD, CE, CEI, EAPC, EBRD, EU (candidate country), FAO, G-9, IAEA, IBRD, ICAO, ICC (national committees), ICCt, ICRM, IDA, IFC, IFRCS, IHO, ILO, IMF, IMO, IMSO, Interpol, IOC, IOM, IPU, ISO, ITSO, ITU, ITUC (NGOs), MIGA, MONUSCO, NAM (observer), NSG, OAS (observer), OIF (observer), OPCW, OSCE, PCA, PFP, SELEC, UN, UNCTAD, UNESCO, UNFICYP, UNHCR, UNIDO, UNIFIL, UNMIL, UNOCI, UNTSO, UNWTO, UPU, WCO, WHO, WIPO, WMO, WTO (observer)
note: Serbia is an EU candidate country whose satisfactory completion of accession criteria is required before being granted full EU membership

Diplomatic representation in the US: *chief of mission:* Ambassador (vacant); Chargé d'Affaires Vladimir MARIC (since 30 April 2024)
chancery: 1333 16th Street, NW Washington, D.C. 20036
telephone: [1] (202) 507-8654
FAX: [1] (202) 332-3933
email address and website:
info@serbiaembusa.org
http://www.washington.mfa.gov.rs/
consulate(s) general: Chicago, New York

Diplomatic representation from the US: *chief of mission:* Ambassador Christopher R. HILL (since 1 April 2022)
embassy: 92 Bulevar kneza Aleksandra Karadjordjevica, 11040 Belgrade
mailing address: 5070 Belgrade Place, Washington, DC 20521-5070
telephone: [381] (11) 706-4000
FAX: [381] (11) 706-4481
email address and website:
belgradeacs@state.gov
https://rs.usembassy.gov/

Flag description: three equal horizontal stripes of red (top), blue, and white - the Pan-Slav colors representing freedom and revolutionary ideals; charged with the coat of arms of Serbia shifted slightly to the hoist side; the principal field of the coat of arms represents the Serbian state and displays a white two-headed eagle on a red shield; a smaller red shield on the eagle represents the Serbian nation, and is divided into four quarters by a white cross; interpretations vary as to the meaning and origin of the white, curved symbols resembling firesteels (fire strikers) or Cyrillic "C's" in each quarter; a royal crown surmounts the coat of arms
note: the Pan-Slav colors were inspired by the 19th-century flag of Russia

National symbol(s): white double-headed eagle; national colors: red, blue, white

National anthem: *name:* "Boze pravde" (God of Justice)
lyrics/music: Jovan DORDEVIC/Davorin JENKO
note: adopted 1904; song originally written as part of a play in 1872 and has been used as an anthem by the Serbian people throughout the 20th and 21st centuries

National heritage: *total World Heritage Sites:* 4 (all cultural)
selected World Heritage Site locales: Stari Ras and Sopocani; Studenica Monastery; Gamzigrad-Romuliana, Palace of Galerius; Stecci Medieval Tombstone Graveyards

ECONOMY

Economic overview: upper middle-income Balkan economy; current EU accession candidate; hit by COVID-19; pursuing green growth development; manageable public debt; new anticorruption efforts; falling unemployment; historic Russian relations; energy import-dependent

Real GDP (purchasing power parity): $162.213 billion (2023 est.)
$158.214 billion (2022 est.)
$154.28 billion (2021 est.)
note: data in 2021 dollars
comparison ranking: 79

Real GDP growth rate: 2.53% (2023 est.)
2.55% (2022 est.)
7.73% (2021 est.)
note: annual GDP % growth based on constant local currency
comparison ranking: 123

Real GDP per capita: $24,500 (2023 est.)
$23,700 (2022 est.)
$22,600 (2021 est.)
note: data in 2021 dollars
comparison ranking: 88

GDP (official exchange rate): $75.187 billion (2023 est.)
note: data in current dollars at official exchange rate

Inflation rate (consumer prices): 12.37% (2023 est.)
11.98% (2022 est.)
4.09% (2021 est.)
note: annual % change based on consumer prices
comparison ranking: 188

Credit ratings: Fitch rating: BB+ (2019)

Moody's rating: Ba3 (2017)

Standard & Poors rating: BB+ (2019)
note: The year refers to the year in which the current credit rating was first obtained.

GDP - composition, by sector of origin: *agriculture:* 5.2% (2023 est.)
industry: 26.4% (2023 est.)
services: 51.2% (2023 est.)
note: figures may not total 100% due to non-allocated consumption not captured in sector-reported data
comparison rankings: services 140; industry 86; agriculture 116

GDP - composition, by end use: *household consumption:* 67.3% (2023 est.)
government consumption: 15.9% (2023 est.)
investment in fixed capital: 22.7% (2023 est.)
investment in inventories: -1.3% (2023 est.)
exports of goods and services: 59.9% (2023 est.)
imports of goods and services: -64.4% (2023 est.)
note: figures may not total 100% due to rounding or gaps in data collection

Agricultural products: maize, wheat, sugar beets, milk, sunflower seeds, potatoes, plums, apples, barley, soybeans (2022)
note: top ten agricultural products based on tonnage

Industries: automobiles, base metals, furniture, food processing, machinery, chemicals, sugar, tires, clothes, pharmaceuticals

Industrial production growth rate: 3.62% (2023 est.)
note: annual % change in industrial value added based on constant local currency
comparison ranking: 89

Labor force: 3.333 million (2023 est.)
note: number of people ages 15 or older who are employed or seeking work
comparison ranking: 100

Unemployment rate: 8.68% (2023 est.)
8.68% (2022 est.)
10.06% (2021 est.)
note: % of labor force seeking employment
comparison ranking: 153

Youth unemployment rate (ages 15-24): *total:* 24.3% (2023 est.)
male: 23.2% (2023 est.)
female: 26.1% (2023 est.)
note: % of labor force ages 15-24 seeking employment
comparison ranking: total 46

Population below poverty line: 21.2% (2020 est.)
note: % of population with income below national poverty line

Gini Index coefficient - distribution of family income: 33.1 (2021 est.)
note: index (0-100) of income distribution; higher values represent greater inequality
comparison ranking: 100

Average household expenditures: *on food:* 22.9% of household expenditures (2022 est.)
on alcohol and tobacco: 8.4% of household expenditures (2022 est.)

Household income or consumption by percentage share: *lowest 10%:* 2.5% (2021 est.)
highest 10%: 25.9% (2021 est.)
note: % share of income accruing to lowest and highest 10% of population

Remittances: 7.68% of GDP (2023 est.)
8.97% of GDP (2022 est.)
7.29% of GDP (2021 est.)
note: personal transfers and compensation between resident and non-resident individuals/households/entities

Budget: *revenues:* $26.077 billion (2022 est.)
expenditures: $23.693 billion (2022 est.)
note: central government revenues (excluding grants) and expenses converted to US dollars at average official exchange rate for year indicated

Public debt: 62.5% of GDP (2017 est.)
comparison ranking: 75

Taxes and other revenues: 25.11% (of GDP) (2022 est.)
note: central government tax revenue as a % of GDP
comparison ranking: 45

Current account balance: -$1.954 billion (2023 est.)
-$4.457 billion (2022 est.)
-$2.654 billion (2021 est.)
note: balance of payments - net trade and primary/secondary income in current dollars
comparison ranking: 157

Exports: $44.343 billion (2023 est.)
$39.905 billion (2022 est.)

$34.035 billion (2021 est.)
note: balance of payments - exports of goods and services in current dollars
comparison ranking: 70

Exports - partners: Germany 13%, Bosnia and Herzegovina 7%, Italy 7%, Hungary 6%, Romania 4% (2022)
note: top five export partners based on percentage share of exports

Exports - commodities: insulated wire, copper ore, plastic products, electricity, rubber tires (2022)
note: top five export commodities based on value in dollars

Imports: $48.216 billion (2023 est.)
$47.395 billion (2022 est.)
$39.476 billion (2021 est.)
note: balance of payments - imports of goods and services in current dollars
comparison ranking: 68

Imports - partners: Germany 11%, China 8%, Hungary 8%, Russia 7%, Italy 6% (2022)
note: top five import partners based on percentage share of imports

Imports - commodities: electricity, crude petroleum, natural gas, plastic products, packaged medicine (2022)
note: top five import commodities based on value in dollars

Reserves of foreign exchange and gold: $27.569 billion (2023 est.)
$20.68 billion (2022 est.)
$18.617 billion (2021 est.)
note: holdings of gold (year-end prices)/foreign exchange/special drawing rights in current dollars
comparison ranking: 70

Debt - external: (2019)

Exchange rates: Serbian dinars (RSD) per US dollar -

Exchange rates: 108.403 (2023 est.)
111.662 (2022 est.)
99.396 (2021 est.)
103.163 (2020 est.)
105.25 (2019 est.)

ENERGY

Electricity access: *electrification - total population:* 100% (2022 est.)

Electricity: *installed generating capacity:* 8.075 million kW (2022 est.)
consumption: 30.678 billion kWh (2022 est.)
exports: 5.613 billion kWh (2022 est.)
imports: 8.236 billion kWh (2022 est.)
transmission/distribution losses: 4.494 billion kWh (2022 est.)
comparison rankings: transmission/distribution losses 158; imports 31; exports 37; consumption 67; installed generating capacity 72

Electricity generation sources: *fossil fuels:* 68.8% of total installed capacity (2022 est.)
wind: 2.9% of total installed capacity (2022 est.)
hydroelectricity: 27.5% of total installed capacity (2022 est.)
biomass and waste: 0.8% of total installed capacity (2022 est.)

Coal: *production:* 35.129 million metric tons (2022 est.)
consumption: 38.297 million metric tons (2022 est.)
exports: 9,000 metric tons (2022 est.)
imports: 1.641 million metric tons (2022 est.)
proven reserves: 7.514 billion metric tons (2022 est.)

Petroleum: *total petroleum production:* 13,000 bbl/day (2023 est.)
refined petroleum consumption: 82,000 bbl/day (2022 est.)
crude oil estimated reserves: 77.5 million barrels (2021 est.)

Natural gas: *production:* 353.376 million cubic meters (2022 est.)
consumption: 2.939 billion cubic meters (2022 est.)
imports: 2.652 billion cubic meters (2022 est.)
proven reserves: 48.139 billion cubic meters (2021 est.)

Carbon dioxide emissions: 42.933 million metric tonnes of CO2 (2022 est.)
from coal and metallurgical coke: 27.399 million metric tonnes of CO2 (2022 est.)
from petroleum and other liquids: 10.06 million metric tonnes of CO2 (2022 est.)
from consumed natural gas: 5.474 million metric tonnes of CO2 (2022 est.)
comparison ranking: total emissions 63

Energy consumption per capita: 89.037 million Btu/person (2022 est.)
comparison ranking: 60

COMMUNICATIONS

Telephones - fixed lines: *total subscriptions:* 2.539 million (2022 est.)
subscriptions per 100 inhabitants: 37 (2021 est.)
comparison ranking: total subscriptions 46

Telephones - mobile cellular: *total subscriptions:* 8.621 million (2022 est.)
subscriptions per 100 inhabitants: 124 (2021 est.)
comparison ranking: total subscriptions 98

Telecommunication systems: *general assessment:* Serbia's telecom industry has been liberalized in line with the principles of the EU's regulatory framework for communications, focused on encouraging competition in telecom products and services, and ensuring universal access; considerable network investment has been undertaken in Serbia by incumbent and alternative operators in recent years, despite economic difficulties; this has helped to stimulate internet usage, which has also been bolstered by improved affordability as prices are reduced through competition; the pandemic has stimulated consumer take up of services, particularly mobile data; the government's various initiatives to improve rural broadband availability have also been supported by European development loans; Serbia's high mobile services, partly the result of multiple SIM card use, has weighed on revenue growth in recent years, placing further pressure on operators to develop business models which encourage consumer use of mobile data services also in response to the continued substitution of fixed-line for mobile voice calls; the regulator has yet to auction 5G-suitable frequencies, though operators are already investing in their networks in preparation for this next growth frontier; during 2021 the regulator resumed the process towards a 5G spectrum auction, which had been delayed owing to the onset of the covid-19 pandemic (2022)
domestic: fixed-line over 37 per 100 and mobile-cellular is 124 per 100 persons (2021)
international: country code - 381

Internet country code: .rs

Internet users: *total:* 5.589 million (2021 est.)
percent of population: 81% (2021 est.)
comparison ranking: total 85

Broadband - fixed subscriptions: *total:* 1,730,496 (2020 est.)
subscriptions per 100 inhabitants: 25 (2020 est.)
comparison ranking: total 62

TRANSPORTATION

National air transport system: *number of registered air carriers:* 4 (2020)
inventory of registered aircraft operated by air carriers: 43
annual passenger traffic on registered air carriers: 2,262,703 (2018)
annual freight traffic on registered air carriers: 17.71 million (2018) mt-km

Civil aircraft registration country code prefix: YU

Airports: 43 (2024)
comparison ranking: 95

Heliports: 8 (2024)

Pipelines: 1,936 km gas, 413 km oil

Railways: *total:* 3,333 km (2020) 1,274 km electrified
comparison ranking: total 56

Roadways: *total:* 45,022 km (2022)
comparison ranking: total 87

Waterways: 587 km (2009) (primarily on the Danube and Sava Rivers)
comparison ranking: 87

MILITARY AND SECURITY

Military and security forces: Serbian Armed Forces (Vojska Srbije, VS): Army (aka Land Forces; includes Riverine Component, consisting of a naval flotilla on the Danube), Air and Air Defense Forces, Serbian Guard

Serbian Ministry of Internal Affairs: General Police Directorate (2024)
note: the Serbian Guard is a brigade-sized unit that is directly subordinate to the Serbian Armed Forces Chief of General Staff; its duties include safeguarding key defense facilities and rendering military honors to top foreign, state, and military officials

Military expenditures: 2.4% of GDP (2023 est.)
2.2% of GDP (2022 est.)
2.2% of GDP (2021 est.)
2% of GDP (2020 est.)
2.2% of GDP (2019 est.)
comparison ranking: 47

Military and security service personnel strengths: approximately 25,000 active-duty troops (15,000 Land Forces; 5,000 Air/Air Defense; 5,000 other); approximately 3,000 Gendarmerie (2023)

Military equipment inventories and acquisitions: the military's inventory consists of a mix of domestically produced, Russian/Soviet-era, and Yugoslav equipment and weapons systems; in recent years, it has purchased some weapons systems from China, such as anti-aircraft missiles and armed aerial drones (2024)

Military service age and obligation: 18 years of age for voluntary military service for men and women; conscription abolished in 2011 (2024)
note: as of 2024, women made up about 11% of the military's full-time personnel

Military deployments: 180 Lebanon (UNIFIL) (2024)

Military - note: the Serbian military is responsible for defense and deterrence against external threats, supporting international peacekeeping operations, and providing support to civil authorities for internal security; specific threat concerns of the military include extremism, separatism, and deepening international recognition of Kosovo; Serbia has cooperated with NATO since 2006, when it joined the Partnership for Peace program, and the military trains with NATO countries, particularly other Balkan states; Serbia has participated in EU peacekeeping missions, as well as missions under the Organization for Security and Cooperation in Europe and the UN; it also maintains close security ties with Russia and has a growing security relationship with China

the modern Serbian military was established in 2006 but traces its origins back through World War II, World War I, the Balkan Wars of 1912-1913, and the Bulgarian-Serb War of 1885 to the First (1804-1813) and Second (1815-1817) Uprisings against the Ottoman Empire (2024)

TRANSNATIONAL ISSUES

Refugees and internally displaced persons: *refugees (country of origin):* 17,334 (Croatia), 7,997 (Bosnia and Herzegovina) (mid-year 2022)
IDPs: 196,066 (most are Kosovar Serbs, some are Roma, Ashkalis, and Egyptian (RAE); some RAE IDPs are unregistered) (2022)
stateless persons: 2,594 (includes stateless persons in Kosovo) (2022)
note: 1,045,323 estimated refugee and migrant arrivals (January 2015-March 2024)

Trafficking in persons: tier rating: Tier 2 Watch List — the government has devoted sufficient resources to a written plan that, if implemented, would constitute significant efforts to meet the minimum standards; therefore, Serbia was granted a waiver per the Trafficking Victims Protection Act from an otherwise required downgrade to Tier 3 and remained on Tier 2 Watch List for the third consecutive year; for more details, go to: https://www.state.gov/reports/2024-trafficking-in-persons-report/ serbia/

Illicit drugs: drug trafficking groups are major players in the procurement and transportation of of large quantities of cocaine destined for European markets

SEYCHELLES

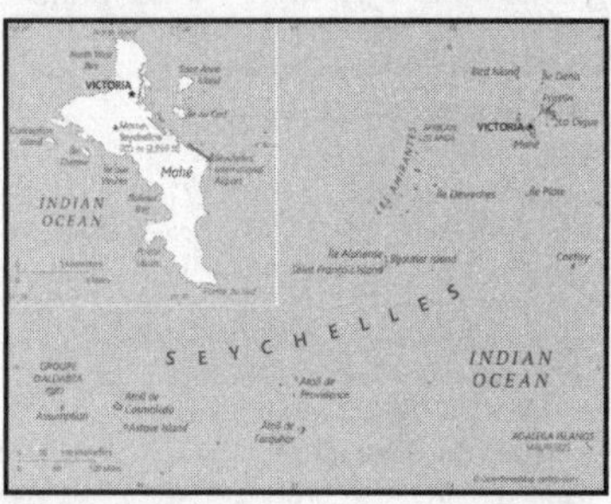

INTRODUCTION

Background: Seychelles was uninhabited before Europeans discovered the islands early in the 16th century. After a lengthy struggle, France eventually ceded control of the islands to Great Britain in 1814. During colonial rule, a plantation-based economy developed that relied on imported labor, primarily from European colonies in Africa. Seychelles gained independence in 1976 through negotiations with Great Britain. In 1977, Prime Minister France-Albert RENE launched a coup against the country's first president, and Seychelles became a socialist one-party state until adopting a new constitution and holding elections in 1993. RENE continued to lead Seychelles through two election cycles until he stepped down in 2004. Vice President James Alix MICHEL took over the presidency and in 2006 was elected to a new five-year term; he was reelected in 2011 and again in 2015. In 2016, James MICHEL resigned and handed over the presidency to his vice-president, Danny FAURE. In 2020, Wavel RAMKALAWAN was elected president, the first time an opposition candidate has won the presidency.

GEOGRAPHY

Location: archipelago in the Indian Ocean, northeast of Madagascar

Geographic coordinates: 4 35 S, 55 40 E

Map references: Africa

Area: *total:* 455 sq km
land: 455 sq km
water: 0 sq km
comparison ranking: total 198

Area - comparative: 2.5 times the size of Washington, DC

Land boundaries: *total:* 0 km

Coastline: 491 km

Maritime claims: *territorial sea:* 12 nm
contiguous zone: 24 nm
exclusive economic zone: 200 nm
continental shelf: 200 nm or to the edge of the continental margin

Climate: tropical marine; humid; cooler season during southeast monsoon (late May to September); warmer season during northwest monsoon (March to May)

Terrain: Mahe Group is volcanic with a narrow coastal strip and rocky, hilly interior; others are relatively flat coral atolls, or elevated reefs; sits atop the submarine Mascarene Plateau

Elevation: *highest point:* Morne Seychellois 905 m
lowest point: Indian Ocean 0 m

Natural resources: fish, coconuts (copra), cinnamon trees

Land use: *agricultural land:* 6.5% (2018 est.)
arable land: 2.2% (2018 est.)
permanent crops: 4.3% (2018 est.)
permanent pasture: 0% (2018 est.)
forest: 88.5% (2018 est.)
other: 5% (2018 est.)

Irrigated land: 3 sq km (2012)

Population distribution: more than three-quarters of the population lives on the main island of Mahe; Praslin contains less than 10%; a smaller percent on La Digue and the outer islands as shown in this population distribution map

Natural hazards: lies outside the cyclone belt, so severe storms are rare; occasional short droughts

Geography - note: the smallest African country in terms of both area and population; the constitution of the Republic of Seychelles lists 155 islands, 42 granitic and 113 coralline; by far the largest island is Mahe, which is home to about 90% of the population and the site of the capital city of Victoria

PEOPLE AND SOCIETY

Population: *total:* 98,187
male: 50,973
female: 47,214 (2024 est.)
comparison rankings: female 197; male 194; total 197

Nationality: *noun:* Seychellois (singular and plural)
adjective: Seychellois

Ethnic groups: predominantly Creole (mainly of East African and Malagasy heritage); also French, Indian, Chinese, and Arab populations

Languages: Seychellois Creole (official) 89.1%, English (official) 5.1%, French (official) 0.7%, other 3.8%, unspecified 1.4% (2010 est.)

Religions: Roman Catholic 76.2%, Protestant 10.5% (Anglican 6.1%, Pentecostal Assembly 1.5%, Seventh Day Adventist 1.2%, other Protestant 1.7%), other Christian 2.4%, Hindu 2.4%, Muslim 1.6%, other non-Christian 1.1%, unspecified 4.8%, none 0.9% (2010 est.)

Demographic profile: Seychelles has no indigenous population and was first permanently settled by a small group of French planters, African slaves, and South Indians in 1770. Seychelles' modern population is composed of the descendants of French and later British settlers, Africans, and Indian, Chinese, and Middle Eastern traders and is concentrated on three of its 155 islands – the vast majority on Mahe and lesser numbers on Praslin and La Digue. Seychelles' population grew rapidly during the second half of the 20th century, largely due to natural increase, but the pace has slowed because of fertility decline. The total fertility rate dropped sharply from 4.0 children per woman in 1980 to 1.9 in 2015, mainly as a result of a family planning program, free education and health care, and increased female labor force participation. Life expectancy has increased steadily, but women on average live 9 years longer than men, a difference that is higher than that typical of developed countries.
The combination of reduced fertility and increased longevity has resulted in an aging population, which will put pressure on the government's provision of pensions and health care. Seychelles' sustained investment in social welfare services, such as free primary health care and education up to the

post-secondary level, have enabled the country to achieve a high human development index score – among the highest in Africa. Despite some of its health and education indicators being nearly on par with Western countries, Seychelles has a high level of income inequality.

An increasing number of migrant workers – mainly young men – have been coming to Seychelles in recent years to work in the construction and tourism industries. As of 2011, foreign workers made up nearly a quarter of the workforce. Indians are the largest non-Seychellois population – representing half of the country's foreigners – followed by Malagasy.

Age structure: *0-14 years:* 17.7% (male 8,912/female 8,439)
15-64 years: 72.4% (male 37,841/female 33,210)
65 years and over: 10% (2024 est.) (male 4,220/female 5,565)

Dependency ratios: *total dependency ratio:* 45
youth dependency ratio: 33.6
elderly dependency ratio: 11.4
potential support ratio: 8.7 (2021 est.)

Median age: *total:* 38.7 years (2024 est.)
male: 38.2 years
female: 39.4 years
comparison ranking: total 71

Population growth rate: 0.56% (2024 est.)
comparison ranking: 145

Birth rate: 11.8 births/1,000 population (2024 est.)
comparison ranking: 152

Death rate: 7 deaths/1,000 population (2024 est.)
comparison ranking: 121

Net migration rate: 0.8 migrant(s)/1,000 population (2024 est.)
comparison ranking: 69

Population distribution: more than three-quarters of the population lives on the main island of Mahe; Praslin contains less than 10%; a smaller percent on La Digue and the outer islands as shown in this population distribution map

Urbanization: *urban population:* 58.8% of total population (2023)
rate of urbanization: 0.99% annual rate of change (2020-25 est.)

Major urban areas - population: 28,000 VICTORIA (capital) (2018)

Sex ratio: *at birth:* 1.03 male(s)/female
0-14 years: 1.06 male(s)/female
15-64 years: 1.14 male(s)/female
65 years and over: 0.76 male(s)/female
total population: 1.08 male(s)/female (2024 est.)

Maternal mortality ratio: 3 deaths/100,000 live births (2020)
comparison ranking: 183

Infant mortality rate: *total:* 10.2 deaths/1,000 live births (2024 est.)
male: 12.8 deaths/1,000 live births
female: 7.4 deaths/1,000 live births
comparison ranking: total 131

Life expectancy at birth: *total population:* 76.6 years (2024 est.)
male: 72.2 years
female: 81.1 years
comparison ranking: total population 105

Total fertility rate: 1.81 children born/woman (2024 est.)
comparison ranking: 139

Gross reproduction rate: 0.89 (2024 est.)

Drinking water source: *improved:*
total: 96.2% of population
unimproved:
total: 3.8% of population (2017 est.)

Current health expenditure: 6.4% of GDP (2020)

Physician density: 2.25 physicians/1,000 population (2019)

Hospital bed density: 3.6 beds/1,000 population (2011)

Sanitation facility access: *improved: urban:* NA
rural: NA
total: 100% of population
unimproved: urban: NA
rural: NA
total: 0% of population (2020 est.)

Obesity - adult prevalence rate: 14% (2016)
comparison ranking: 130

Alcohol consumption per capita: *total:* 9.48 liters of pure alcohol (2019 est.)
beer: 4.11 liters of pure alcohol (2019 est.)
wine: 0.49 liters of pure alcohol (2019 est.)
spirits: 4.62 liters of pure alcohol (2019 est.)
other alcohols: 0.25 liters of pure alcohol (2019 est.)
comparison ranking: total 28

Tobacco use: *total:* 20.2% (2020 est.)
male: 34% (2020 est.)
female: 6.4% (2020 est.)
comparison ranking: total 87

Currently married women (ages 15-49): 45% (2023 est.)

Education expenditures: 5.2% of GDP (2020 est.)
comparison ranking: 67

Literacy: *definition:* age 15 and over can read and write
total population: 95.9%
male: 95.4%
female: 96.4% (2018)

School life expectancy (primary to tertiary education): *total:* 15 years
male: 13 years
female: 16 years (2021)

ENVIRONMENT

Environment - current issues: water supply depends on catchments to collect rainwater; water pollution; biodiversity maintainance

Environment - international agreements: *party to:* Biodiversity, Climate Change, Climate Change-Kyoto Protocol, Climate Change-Paris Agreement, Comprehensive Nuclear Test Ban, Desertification, Endangered Species, Hazardous Wastes, Law of the Sea, Marine Dumping-London Convention, Nuclear Test Ban, Ozone Layer Protection, Ship Pollution, Wetlands
signed, but not ratified: none of the selected agreements

Climate: tropical marine; humid; cooler season during southeast monsoon (late May to September); warmer season during northwest monsoon (March to May)

Urbanization: *urban population:* 58.8% of total population (2023)
rate of urbanization: 0.99% annual rate of change (2020-25 est.)

Revenue from forest resources: 0.09% of GDP (2018 est.)
comparison ranking: 116

Revenue from coal: 0% of GDP (2018 est.)
comparison ranking: 59

Air pollutants: *particulate matter emissions:* 16.96 micrograms per cubic meter (2019 est.)
carbon dioxide emissions: 0.61 megatons (2016 est.)
methane emissions: 0.1 megatons (2020 est.)

Waste and recycling: *municipal solid waste generated annually:* 48,000 tons (2012 est.)

Total water withdrawal: *municipal:* 10 million cubic meters (2020 est.)
industrial: 3.8 million cubic meters (2017 est.)
agricultural: 900,000 cubic meters (2017 est.)

Total renewable water resources: 0 cubic meters (2017 est.)

GOVERNMENT

Country name: *conventional long form:* Republic of Seychelles
conventional short form: Seychelles
local long form: Republic of Seychelles
local short form: Seychelles
etymology: named by French Captain Corneille Nicholas MORPHEY after Jean Moreau de SECHELLES, the finance minister of France, in 1756

Government type: presidential republic

Capital: *name:* Victoria
geographic coordinates: 4 37 S, 55 27 E
time difference: UTC+4 (9 hours ahead of Washington, DC, during Standard Time)
etymology: founded as L'etablissement in 1778 by French colonists, the town was renamed in 1841 by the British after Queen VICTORIA (1819-1901); "victoria" is the Latin word for "victory"

Administrative divisions: 27 administrative districts; Anse aux Pins, Anse Boileau, Anse Etoile, Anse Royale, Au Cap, Baie Lazare, Baie Sainte Anne, Beau Vallon, Bel Air, Bel Ombre, Cascade, Glacis, Grand Anse Mahe, Grand Anse Praslin, Ile Perseverance I, Ile Perseverance II, La Digue, La Riviere Anglaise, Les Mamelles, Mont Buxton, Mont Fleuri, Plaisance, Pointe Larue, Port Glaud, Roche Caiman, Saint Louis, Takamaka

Independence: 29 June 1976 (from the UK)

National holiday: Constitution Day, 18 June (1993); Independence Day (National Day), 29 June (1976)

Legal system: mixed legal system of English common law, French civil law, and customary law

Constitution: *history:* previous 1970, 1979; latest drafted May 1993, approved by referendum 18 June 1993, effective 23 June 1993
amendments: proposed by the National Assembly; passage requires at least two-thirds majority vote by the National Assembly; passage of amendments affecting the country's sovereignty, symbols and languages, the supremacy of the constitution, fundamental rights and freedoms, amendment procedures, and dissolution of the Assembly also requires approval by at least 60% of voters in a referendum; amended several times, last in 2018

International law organization participation: has not submitted an ICJ jurisdiction declaration; accepts ICCt jurisdiction

Citizenship: *citizenship by birth:* no
citizenship by descent only: at least one parent must be a citizen of the Seychelles
dual citizenship recognized: no
residency requirement for naturalization: 5 years

Suffrage: 18 years of age; universal

Executive branch: *chief of state:* President Wavel RAMKALAWAN (since 26 October 2020)
head of government: President Wavel RAMKALAWAN (since 26 October 2020)
cabinet: Council of Ministers appointed by the president
elections/appointments: president directly elected by absolute majority popular vote in 2 rounds if needed for a 5-year term (eligible for a second term); election last held on 22 to 24 October 2020 (next to be held in 2025)
election results:
2020: Wavel RAMKALAWAN elected president; Wavel RAMKALAWAN (LDS) 54.9%, Danny FAURE (US) 43.5%, other 1.6%
2015: President James Alix MICHEL reelected president in second round; percent of vote in first round - James Alix MICHEL (PL) 47.8%, Wavel RAMKALAWAN (SNP) 35.3%, other 16.9%; percent of vote in second round - James Alix MICHEL 50.2%, Wavel RAMKALAWAN 49.8%
note: the president is both chief of state and head of government

Legislative branch: *description:* unicameral National Assembly or Assemblee Nationale (35 seats in the 2020-25 term; 26 members directly elected in single-seat constituencies by simple majority vote and up to 9 members elected by proportional representation vote; members serve 5-year terms)
elections: last held on 22-24 October 2020 (next to be held in October 2025); note - the election was originally scheduled for 2021 but was moved up a year and held alongside the presidential election in order to cut election costs
election results: percent of vote by party - LDS 54.8%, US 42.3%, other 2.9%; seats by party - LDS 25, US 10;
composition - men 27, women 7, percentage women 20.6%

Judicial branch: *highest court(s):* Seychelles Court of Appeal (consists of the court president and 4 justices); Supreme Court of Seychelles (consists of the chief justice and 9 puisne judges); Constitutional Court (consists of 3 Supreme Court judges)
judge selection and term of office: all judges appointed by the president of the republic upon the recommendation of the Constitutional Appointments Authority, a 3-member body, with 1 member appointed by the president of the republic, 1 by the opposition leader in the National Assembly, and 1 by the other 2 appointees; judges serve until retirement at age 70
subordinate courts: Magistrates' Courts of Seychelles; Family Tribunal for issues such as domestic violence, child custody, and maintenance; Employment Tribunal for labor-related disputes

Political parties: Seychelles Party for Social Justice and Democracy or SPSJD
Seychellois Democratic Alliance or LDS (Linyon Demokratik Seselwa/Union Démocratique Seychelloise)
Seychelles National Party or SNP
United Seychelles or US

International organization participation: ACP, AfDB, AOSIS, AU, C, CD, COMESA, EITI (candidate country), FAO, G-77, IAEA, IBRD, ICAO, ICC (NGOs), ICCt, ICRM, IDA, IFAD, IFC, IFRCS, ILO, IMF, IMO, InOC, Interpol, IOC, IOM, IPU, ISO (correspondent), ITU, MIGA, NAM, OIF, OPCW, SADC, UN, UNCTAD, UNESCO, UNIDO, UNWTO, UPU, WCO, WHO, WIPO, WMO, WTO

Diplomatic representation in the US: *chief of mission:* Ambassador Ian Dereck Joseph MADELEINE (since 1 December 2021); note - also Permanent Representative to the UN
chancery: 685 Third Avenue, Suite 1107, 11th Floor, New York, NY 10017
telephone: [1] (212) 972-1785
FAX: [1] (212) 972-1786
email address and website: seychellesmission@sycun.org
Foreign Affairs Department Republic of Seychelles » United States of America (mfa.gov.sc)

Diplomatic representation from the US: *chief of mission:* Ambassador Henry V. JARDINE (since 22 February 2023); Chargé d'Affaires Adham LOUTFI (since 6 October 2023) note - Ambassador JARDINE is posted in Mauritius and is accredited to Seychelles, and Chargé d'Affaires LOUTFI is posted in Victoria, Seychelles to manage the expanding policy interests
embassy: 2nd Floor, Oliaji Trade Center, Victoria Mahe, Seychelles; note - US Embassy in Seychelles reopened on 1
June 2023 after having been closed in 1996
telephone: [248] 422 5256

Flag description: five oblique bands of blue (hoist side), yellow, red, white, and green (bottom) radiating from the bottom of the hoist side; the oblique bands are meant to symbolize a dynamic new country moving into the future; blue represents sky and sea, yellow the sun giving light and life, red the peoples' determination to work for the future in unity and love, white social justice and harmony, and green the land and natural environment

National symbol(s): coco de mer (sea coconut); national colors: blue, yellow, red, white, green

National anthem: *name:* "Koste Seselwa" (Seychellois Unite)
lyrics/music: David Francois Marc ANDRE and George Charles Robert PAYET
note: adopted 1996

National heritage: *total World Heritage Sites:* 2 (both natural)
selected World Heritage Site locales: Aldabra Atoll; Vallée de Mai Nature Reserve

ECONOMY

Economic overview: high-income Indian Ocean island economy; rapidly growing tourism sector; major tuna exporter; offshore financial hub; environmentally fragile and investing in ocean rise mitigation; recently discovered offshore oil potential; successful anticorruption efforts

Real GDP (purchasing power parity): $3.53 billion (2023 est.)
$3.421 billion (2022 est.)
$2.976 billion (2021 est.)
note: data in 2021 dollars
comparison ranking: 194

Real GDP growth rate: 3.16% (2023 est.)
14.98% (2022 est.)
0.55% (2021 est.)
note: annual GDP % growth based on constant local currency
comparison ranking: 105

Real GDP per capita: $29,500 (2023 est.)
$28,500 (2022 est.)
$30,000 (2021 est.)
note: data in 2021 dollars
comparison ranking: 78

GDP (official exchange rate): $2.141 billion (2023 est.)
note: data in current dollars at official exchange rate

Inflation rate (consumer prices): 8.28% (2020 est.)
2.07% (2019 est.)
3.7% (2018 est.)
note: annual % change based on consumer prices
comparison ranking: 158

Credit ratings: Fitch rating: B+ (2020)
note: The year refers to the year in which the current credit rating was first obtained.

GDP - composition, by sector of origin: *agriculture:* 2.8% (2023 est.)
industry: 12% (2023 est.)
services: 68% (2023 est.)
note: figures may not total 100% due to non-allocated consumption not captured in sector-reported data
comparison rankings: services 44; industry 182; agriculture 143

GDP - composition, by end use: *household consumption:* 73.8% (2023 est.)
government consumption: 21.3% (2023 est.)
investment in fixed capital: 16.1% (2023 est.)
exports of goods and services: 85.9% (2023 est.)
imports of goods and services: -97.1% (2023 est.)
note: figures may not total 100% due to rounding or gaps in data collection

Agricultural products: coconuts, vegetables, bananas, eggs, chicken, pork, fruits, tomatoes, tropical fruits, cassava (2022)
note: top ten agricultural products based on tonnage

Industries: fishing, tourism, beverages

Industrial production growth rate: 2.13% (2023 est.)
note: annual % change in industrial value added based on constant local currency
comparison ranking: 115

Labor force: 51,000 (2018 est.)
comparison ranking: 192

Unemployment rate: 3% (2017 est.)
2.7% (2016 est.)
comparison ranking: 44

Youth unemployment rate (ages 15-24): *total:* 16.5% (2020 est.)
male: 17.5%
female: 15.6%
comparison ranking: total 86

Population below poverty line: 25.3% (2018 est.)
note: % of population with income below national poverty line

Gini Index coefficient - distribution of family income: 32.1 (2018 est.)
note: index (0-100) of income distribution; higher values represent greater inequality
comparison ranking: 107

Household income or consumption by percentage share: *lowest 10%:* 2.6% (2018 est.)
highest 10%: 23.9% (2018 est.)
note: % share of income accruing to lowest and highest 10% of population

Remittances: 0.49% of GDP (2023 est.)
0.49% of GDP (2022 est.)
0.64% of GDP (2021 est.)
note: personal transfers and compensation between resident and non-resident individuals/households/entities

Budget: *revenues:* $431.07 million (2020 est.)
expenditures: $611.548 million (2020 est.)
note: central government revenues (excluding grants) and expenses converted to US dollars at average official exchange rate for year indicated

Public debt: 63.6% of GDP (2017 est.)
note: central government debt as a % of GDP
comparison ranking: 70

Taxes and other revenues: 26.18% (of GDP) (2020 est.)
note: central government tax revenue as a % of GDP
comparison ranking: 38

Current account balance: -$155.194 million (2023 est.)
-$141.648 million (2022 est.)
-$160.168 million (2021 est.)
note: balance of payments - net trade and primary/secondary income in current dollars
comparison ranking: 105

Exports: $2.375 billion (2023 est.)
$2.247 billion (2022 est.)
$1.751 billion (2021 est.)
note: balance of payments - exports of goods and services in current dollars
comparison ranking: 160

Exports - partners: UAE 18%, France 17%, UK 9%, Mauritius 9%, Japan 8% (2022)
note: top five export partners based on percentage share of exports

Exports - commodities: fish, refined petroleum, ships, aircraft, animal meal (2022)
note: top five export commodities based on value in dollars

Imports: $2.437 billion (2023 est.)
$2.298 billion (2022 est.)
$1.821 billion (2021 est.)
note: balance of payments - imports of goods and services in current dollars
comparison ranking: 167

Imports - partners: UAE 22%, Netherlands 14%, Cayman Islands 7%, France 6%, China 6% (2022)
note: top five import partners based on percentage share of imports

Imports - commodities: ships, refined petroleum, fish, plastic products, cars (2022)
note: top five import commodities based on value in dollars

Reserves of foreign exchange and gold: $638.961 million (2022 est.)
$702.585 million (2021 est.)
$559.682 million (2020 est.)
note: holdings of gold (year-end prices)/foreign exchange/special drawing rights in current dollars
comparison ranking: 157

Exchange rates: Seychelles rupees (SCR) per US dollar -

Exchange rates: 14.273 (2022 est.)
16.921 (2021 est.)
17.617 (2020 est.)
14.033 (2019 est.)
13.911 (2018 est.)

ENERGY

Electricity access: *electrification - total population:* 100% (2022 est.)

Electricity: *installed generating capacity:* 158,000 kW (2022 est.)
consumption: 571.297 million kWh (2022 est.)
transmission/distribution losses: 44.034 million kWh (2022 est.)
comparison rankings: transmission/distribution losses 37; consumption 172; installed generating capacity 178

Electricity generation sources: *fossil fuels:* 86.1% of total installed capacity (2022 est.)
solar: 12.9% of total installed capacity (2022 est.)
wind: 1% of total installed capacity (2022 est.)

Coal: *imports:* (2022 est.) less than 1 metric ton

Petroleum: *refined petroleum consumption:* 6,000 bbl/day (2022 est.)

Carbon dioxide emissions: 867,000 metric tonnes of CO2 (2022 est.)
from petroleum and other liquids: 867,000 metric tonnes of CO2 (2022 est.)
comparison ranking: total emissions 173

Energy consumption per capita: 111.2 million Btu/person (2022 est.)
comparison ranking: 44

COMMUNICATIONS

Telephones - fixed lines: *total subscriptions:* 19,000 (2022 est.)
subscriptions per 100 inhabitants: 18 (2022 est.)
comparison ranking: total subscriptions 175

Telephones - mobile cellular: *total subscriptions:* 205,000 (2022 est.)
subscriptions per 100 inhabitants: 192 (2022 est.)
comparison ranking: total subscriptions 183

Telecommunication systems: *general assessment:* effective system; direct international calls to over 100 countries; radiotelephone communications between islands in the archipelago; 3 ISPs; use of Internet cafes' for access to Internet; 4G services and 5G pending (2020)
domestic: fixed-line is 18 per 100 and mobile-cellular teledensity is 173 telephones per 100 persons (2021)
international: country code - 248; landing points for the PEACE and the SEAS submarine cables providing connectivity to Europe, the Middle East, Africa and Asia; direct radiotelephone communications with adjacent island countries and African coastal countries; satellite earth station - 1 Intelsat (Indian Ocean) (2019)

Broadcast media: the national broadcaster, Seychelles Broadcasting Corporation (SBC), which is funded by taxpayer money, operates the only terrestrial TV station, which provides local programming and airs broadcasts from international services; a privately owned Internet Protocol Television (IPTV) channel also provides local programming multi-channel cable and satellite TV are available through 2 providers; the national broadcaster operates 1 AM and 1 FM radio station; there are 2 privately operated radio stations; transmissions of 2 international broadcasters are accessible in Victoria
(2019)

Internet country code: .sc

Internet users: *total:* 90,200 (2021 est.)
percent of population: 82% (2021 est.)
comparison ranking: total 190

Broadband - fixed subscriptions: *total:* 34,966 (2020 est.)
subscriptions per 100 inhabitants: 36 (2020 est.)
comparison ranking: total 148

TRANSPORTATION

National air transport system: *number of registered air carriers:* 1 (2020)
inventory of registered aircraft operated by air carriers: 7
annual passenger traffic on registered air carriers: 455,201 (2018)
annual freight traffic on registered air carriers: 7.79 million (2018) mt-km

Civil aircraft registration country code prefix: S7

Airports: 16 (2024)
comparison ranking: 148

Heliports: 6 (2024)

Roadways: *total:* 526 km
paved: 514 km
unpaved: 12 km (2015)
comparison ranking: total 196

Merchant marine: *total:* 30 (2023)
by type: general cargo 6, oil tanker 6, other 18
comparison ranking: total 134

Ports: *total ports:* 1 (2024)
large: 0
medium: 0
small: 0
very small: 1
ports with oil terminals: 1
key ports: Victoria

MILITARY AND SECURITY

Military and security forces: Seychelles Defense Forces (SDF): Army (includes infantry, special forces, and a presidential security unit), Coast Guard, and Air Force Ministry of Internal Affairs: Seychelles Police Force (includes unarmed police and an armed paramilitary Police Special Support Wing, and the Marine Police Unit) (2024)
note: the SDF reports to the president, who acts as minister of defense

Military expenditures: 1.6% of GDP (2023 est.)
1.4% of GDP (2022 est.)
1.5% of GDP (2021 est.)
1.6% of GDP (2020 est.)
1.3% of GDP (2019 est.)
comparison ranking: 83

Military and security service personnel strengths: approximately 500-1,000 personnel (2023)

Military equipment inventories and acquisitions: the SDF's inventory primarily consists of Soviet-era equipment delivered in the 1970s and 1980s; in recent years, the SDF has received limited amounts of more modern equipment, mostly donations of patrol boats and aircraft, from several suppliers, including Bahrain, China, India, and the UAE (2024)

Military service age and obligation: 18-28 (18-25 for officers) years of age for voluntary military service for men and women; 6-year initial commitment; no conscription (2023)

Military - note: formed in 1977, the SDF is one of the World's smallest militaries; its primary responsibility is maritime security, including countering illegal fishing, piracy, and drug smuggling; it was given police powers in 2022; the Seychelles has close security ties with India (2024)

SIERRA LEONE

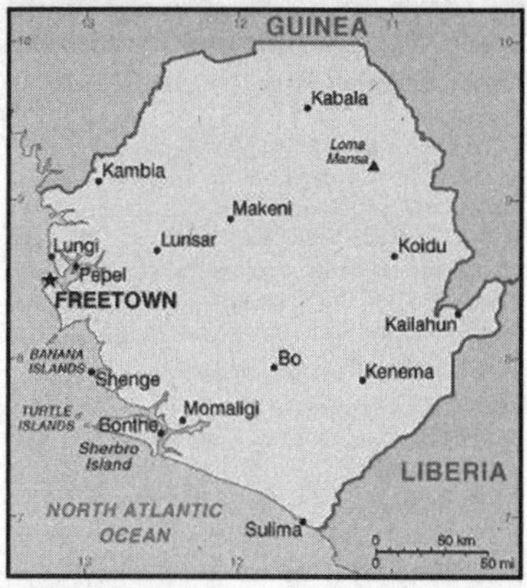

INTRODUCTION

Background: Continuously populated for at least 2,500 years, the area now known as Sierra Leone is covered with dense jungle that allowed the region to remain relatively protected from invading West African empires. Traders introduced Sierra Leone to Islam, which occupies a central role in Sierra Leonean culture and history. In the 17th century, the British set up a trading post near present-day Freetown. The trade originally involved timber and ivory but later expanded to enslaved people. In 1787, after the American Revolution, Sierra Leone became a destination for Black British loyalists from the new United States. When Britain abolished the slave trade in 1807, British ships delivered thousands of liberated Africans to Sierra Leone. During the 19th century, the colony gradually expanded inland.

In 1961, Sierra Leone became independent of the UK. Sierra Leone held free and fair elections in 1962 and 1967, but Siaka STEVENS – Sierra Leone's second prime minister – quickly reverted to authoritarian tendencies, outlawing most political parties and ruling from 1967 to 1985. In 1991, Sierra Leonean soldiers launched a civil war against STEVENS' ruling party. The war caused tens of thousands of deaths and displaced more than 2 million people (about one third of the population). In 1998, a Nigerian-led West African coalition military force intervened, installing Tejan KABBAH – who was originally elected in 1996 – as prime minister. In 2002, KABBAH officially announced the end of the war. Since 1998, Sierra Leone has conducted democratic elections dominated by the two main political parties, the Sierra Leone People's Party (SLPP) and the All People's Congress (APC) party. In 2018, Julius Maada BIO of the Sierra Leone People's Party won the presidential election that saw a high voter turnout despite some allegations of voter intimidation. BIO won again in June 2023, although irregularities were noted that called into question the integrity of the results. In October 2023, the Government of Sierra Leone and the main opposition party, the All People's Congress, signed the Agreement for National Unity to boost cooperation between political parties and begin the process of reforming the country's electoral system.

GEOGRAPHY

Location: Western Africa, bordering the North Atlantic Ocean, between Guinea and Liberia

Geographic coordinates: 8 30 N, 11 30 W

Map references: Africa

Area: *total:* 71,740 sq km
land: 71,620 sq km
water: 120 sq km
comparison ranking: total 119

Area - comparative: slightly smaller than South Carolina

Land boundaries: *total:* 1,093 km
border countries (2): Guinea 794 km; Liberia 299 km

Coastline: 402 km

Maritime claims: *territorial sea:* 12 nm
contiguous zone: 24 nm
exclusive economic zone: 200 nm
continental shelf: 200 nm

Climate: tropical; hot, humid; summer rainy season (May to December); winter dry season (December to April)

Terrain: coastal belt of mangrove swamps, wooded hill country, upland plateau, mountains in east

Elevation: *highest point:* Loma Mansa (Bintimani) 1,948 m
lowest point: Atlantic Ocean 0 m
mean elevation: 279 m

Natural resources: diamonds, titanium ore, bauxite, iron ore, gold, chromite

Land use: *agricultural land:* 56.2% (2018 est.)
arable land: 23.4% (2018 est.)
permanent crops: 2.3% (2018 est.)
permanent pasture: 30.5% (2018 est.)
forest: 37.5% (2018 est.)
other: 6.3% (2018 est.)

Irrigated land: 300 sq km (2012)

Major watersheds (area sq km): Atlantic Ocean drainage: Niger (2,261,741 sq km)

Population distribution: population clusters are found in the lower elevations of the south and west; the northern third of the country is less populated as shown on this population distribution map

Natural hazards: dry, sand-laden harmattan winds blow from the Sahara (December to February); sandstorms, dust storms

Geography - note: rainfall along the coast can reach 495 cm (195 inches) a year, making it one of the wettest places along coastal, western Africa

PEOPLE AND SOCIETY

Population: *total:* 9,121,049
male: 4,515,726
female: 4,605,323 (2024 est.)
comparison rankings: female 98; male 98; total 99

Nationality: *noun:* Sierra Leonean(s)
adjective: Sierra Leonean

Ethnic groups: Temne 35.4%, Mende 30.8%, Limba 8.8%, Kono 4.3%, Korankoh 4%, Fullah 3.8%, Mandingo 2.8%, Loko 2%, Sherbro 1.9%, Creole 1.2% (descendants of freed Jamaican slaves who were settled in the Freetown area in the late-18th century; also known as Krio), other 5% (2019 est.)

Languages: English (official, regular use limited to literate minority), Mende (principal vernacular in the south), Temne (principal vernacular in the north), Krio (English-based Creole, spoken by the descendants of freed Jamaican slaves; a first language for 10% of the population but understood by 95%)

Religions: Muslim 77.1%, Christian 22.9% (2019 est.)

Demographic profile: Sierra Leone's youthful and growing population is driven by its high total fertility rate (TFR) of almost 4 children per woman as of 2022, which has declined little over the last two decades. Its elevated TFR is sustained by the continued desire for large families, the low level of contraceptive use, and the early start of childbearing. Despite its high TFR, Sierra Leone's population growth is somewhat tempered by high infant, child, and maternal mortality rates that are among the world's highest and are a result of poverty, a lack of potable water and sanitation, poor nutrition, limited access to quality health care services, and the prevalence of female genital cutting.

Sierra Leone's large youth cohort – about 60% of the population is under the age of 25 – continues to struggle with high levels of unemployment, which was one of the major causes of the country's 1991-2002 civil war and remains a threat to stability today. Its estimated 60% youth unemployment rate is attributed to high levels of illiteracy and unskilled labor, a lack of private sector jobs, and low pay.

Sierra Leone has been a source of and destination for refugees. Sierra Leone's civil war internally displaced as many as 2 million people, or almost half the population, and forced almost another half million to seek refuge in neighboring countries (370,000 Sierra Leoneans fled to Guinea and 120,000 to Liberia). The UNHCR has helped almost 180,000 Sierra Leoneans to return home, while more than 90,000 others have repatriated on their own. Of the more than 65,000 Liberians who took refuge in Sierra Leone during their country's civil war (1989-2003), about 50,000 have been voluntarily repatriated by the UNHCR and others have returned home independently.

Age structure: *0-14 years:* 40.1% (male 1,843,606/female 1,812,304)
15-64 years: 57.4% (male 2,557,715/female 2,675,418)
65 years and over: 2.5% (2024 est.) (male 114,405/female 117,601)

Dependency ratios: *total dependency ratio:* 74
youth dependency ratio: 68.5
elderly dependency ratio: 5.5
potential support ratio: 18.3 (2020 est.)

Median age: *total:* 19.4 years (2024 est.)
male: 19 years
female: 19.9 years
comparison ranking: total 210

Population growth rate: 2.32% (2024 est.)
comparison ranking: 29

Birth rate: 30.8 births/1,000 population (2024 est.)
comparison ranking: 24

Death rate: 9 deaths/1,000 population (2024 est.)
comparison ranking: 58

Net migration rate: 1.4 migrant(s)/1,000 population (2024 est.)
comparison ranking: 60

Population distribution: population clusters are found in the lower elevations of the south and west; the northern third of the country is less populated as shown on this population distribution map

Urbanization: *urban population:* 44.3% of total population (2023)
rate of urbanization: 3.02% annual rate of change (2020-25 est.)

Major urban areas - population: 1.309 million FREETOWN (capital) (2023)

Sex ratio: *at birth:* 1.03 male(s)/female
0-14 years: 1.02 male(s)/female
15-64 years: 0.96 male(s)/female
65 years and over: 0.97 male(s)/female
total population: 0.98 male(s)/female (2024 est.)

Mother's mean age at first birth: 19.6 years (2019 est.)
note: data represents median age at first birth among women 20-49

Maternal mortality ratio: 443 deaths/100,000 live births (2020 est.)
comparison ranking: 18

Infant mortality rate: *total:* 71.2 deaths/1,000 live births (2024 est.)
male: 76 deaths/1,000 live births
female: 66.2 deaths/1,000 live births
comparison ranking: total 5

Life expectancy at birth: *total population:* 59.4 years (2024 est.)
male: 57.8 years
female: 61 years
comparison ranking: total population 223

Total fertility rate: 3.61 children born/woman (2024 est.)
comparison ranking: 30

Gross reproduction rate: 1.78 (2024 est.)

Contraceptive prevalence rate: 21.2% (2019)

Drinking water source: *improved: urban:* 92.5% of population
rural: 58% of population
total: 72.8% of population
unimproved: urban: 7.5% of population
rural: 42% of population
total: 27.2% of population (2020 est.)

Current health expenditure: 8.8% of GDP (2020)

Physician density: 0.07 physicians/1,000 population (2018)

Sanitation facility access: *improved: urban:* 79.5% of population
rural: 35.5% of population
total: 54.4% of population
unimproved: urban: 20.5% of population
rural: 64.5% of population
total: 45.6% of population (2020 est.)

Obesity - adult prevalence rate: 8.7% (2016)
comparison ranking: 147

Alcohol consumption per capita: *total:* 3.22 liters of pure alcohol (2019 est.)
beer: 0.17 liters of pure alcohol (2019 est.)
wine: 0.01 liters of pure alcohol (2019 est.)
spirits: 0.15 liters of pure alcohol (2019 est.)
other alcohols: 2.9 liters of pure alcohol (2019 est.)
comparison ranking: total 107

Tobacco use: *total:* 13.5% (2020 est.)
male: 20.5% (2020 est.)
female: 6.4% (2020 est.)
comparison ranking: total 115

Children under the age of 5 years underweight: 12% (2021)
comparison ranking: 44

Currently married women (ages 15-49): 58.9% (2023 est.)

Child marriage: *women married by age 15:* 8.6%
women married by age 18: 29.6%
men married by age 18: 4.1% (2019 est.)

Education expenditures: 9.1% of GDP (2021 est.)
comparison ranking: 8

Literacy: *definition:* age 15 and over can read and write English, Mende, Temne, or Arabic
total population: 48.6%
male: 56.3%
female: 41.3% (2022)

ENVIRONMENT

Environment - current issues: rapid population growth pressuring the environment; overharvesting of timber, expansion of cattle grazing, and slash-and-burn agriculture have resulted in deforestation, soil exhaustion, and flooding; loss of biodiversity; air pollution; water pollution; overfishing

Environment - international agreements: *party to:* Biodiversity, Climate Change, Climate Change-Kyoto Protocol, Climate Change-Paris Agreement, Comprehensive Nuclear Test Ban, Desertification, Endangered Species, Hazardous Wastes, Law of the Sea, Marine Dumping-London Convention, Marine Dumping-London Protocol, Marine Life Conservation, Nuclear Test Ban, Ozone Layer Protection, Ship Pollution, Wetlands
signed, but not ratified: Environmental Modification

Climate: tropical; hot, humid; summer rainy season (May to December); winter dry season (December to April)

Urbanization: *urban population:* 44.3% of total population (2023)
rate of urbanization: 3.02% annual rate of change (2020-25 est.)

Food insecurity: *severe localized food insecurity: due to high food prices and reduced incomes* - according to the latest analysis, about 1.18 million people are projected to be in need of humanitarian assistance between the June to August 2023 lean season; acute food insecurity is underpinned by elevated food prices, in part driven by a weak currency, and low purchasing power of vulnerable households (2023)

Revenue from forest resources: 6.92% of GDP (2018 est.)
comparison ranking: 8

Revenue from coal: 0% of GDP (2018 est.)
comparison ranking: 133

Air pollutants: *particulate matter emissions:* 39.42 micrograms per cubic meter (2019 est.)
carbon dioxide emissions: 1.09 megatons (2016 est.)
methane emissions: 3.16 megatons (2020 est.)

Waste and recycling: *municipal solid waste generated annually:* 610,222 tons (2004 est.)

Major watersheds (area sq km): Atlantic Ocean drainage: Niger (2,261,741 sq km)

Total water withdrawal: *municipal:* 110 million cubic meters (2020 est.)
industrial: 60 million cubic meters (2020 est.)
agricultural: 50 million cubic meters (2020 est.)

Total renewable water resources: 160 billion cubic meters (2020 est.)

GOVERNMENT

Country name: *conventional long form:* Republic of Sierra Leone
conventional short form: Sierra Leone
local long form: Republic of Sierra Leone
local short form: Sierra Leone
etymology: the Portuguese explorer Pedro de SINTRA named the country "Serra Leoa" (Lion Mountains) for the impressive mountains he saw while sailing the West African coast in 1462

Government type: presidential republic

Capital: *name:* Freetown
geographic coordinates: 8 29 N, 13 14 W
time difference: UTC 0 (5 hours ahead of Washington, DC, during Standard Time)
etymology: name derived from the fact that the original settlement served as a haven for free-born and freed African Americans, as well as for liberated Africans rescued from slave ships

Administrative divisions: 4 provinces and 1 area*; Eastern, Northern, North Western, Southern, Western*

Independence: 27 April 1961 (from the UK)

National holiday: Independence Day, 27 April (1961)

Legal system: mixed legal system of English common law and customary law

Constitution: *history:* several previous; latest effective 1 October 1991
amendments: proposed by Parliament; passage of amendments requires at least two-thirds majority vote of Parliament in two successive readings and assent of the president of the republic; passage of amendments affecting fundamental rights and freedoms and many other constitutional sections also requires approval in a referendum with participation of at least one half of qualified voters and at least two thirds of votes cast; amended several times, last in 2016

International law organization participation: has not submitted an ICJ jurisdiction declaration; accepts ICCt jurisdiction

Citizenship: *citizenship by birth:* no
citizenship by descent only: at least one parent or grandparent must be a citizen of Sierra Leone
dual citizenship recognized: yes
residency requirement for naturalization: 5 years

Suffrage: 18 years of age; universal

Executive branch: *chief of state:* President Julius Maada BIO (since 27 June 2023)
head of government: President Julius Maada BIO (since 27 June 2023)
cabinet: Ministers of State appointed by the president, approved by Parliament; the cabinet is responsible to the president
elections/appointments: president directly elected by 55% in the first round or absolute majority popular vote in 2 rounds if needed for a 5-year term (eligible for a second term); election last held on 24 June 2023 (next to be held in 2028) note - the president is chief of state, head of government, and Minister of Defense
election results:
2023: Julius Maada BIO reelected president in first round; percent of vote - Julius Maada BIO (SLPP) 56.2%, Samura KAMARA (APC) 41.2%, other 2.6%

2018: Julius Maada BIO elected president in second round; percent of vote - Julius Maada BIO (SLPP) 51.8%, Samura KAMARA (APC) 48.2%

Legislative branch: *description:* unicameral Parliament (149 seats; 135 members directly elected in single-seat constituencies by a district block proportional representation vote and 14 seats for "paramount chiefs" indirectly elected to represent the 14 provincial districts; members serve 5-year terms)
elections: last held on 24 June 2023 (next to be held in 2028)
election results: percent of vote by party - NA; seats by party - SLPP 81, APC 54; composition - men 105, women 44, percentage women 29.5%

Judicial branch: *highest court(s):* Superior Court of Judicature (consists of the Supreme Court - at the apex - with the chief justice and 4 other judges, the Court of Appeal with the chief justice and 7 other judges, and the High Court of Justice with the chief justice and 9 other judges); note – the Judicature has jurisdiction in all civil, criminal, and constitutional matters
judge selection and term of office: Supreme Court chief justice and other judges of the Judicature appointed by the president on the advice of the Judicial and Legal Service Commission, a 7-member independent body of judges, presidential appointees, and the Commission chairman, and are subject to approval by Parliament; all Judicature judges serve until retirement at age 65
subordinate courts: magistrates' courts; District Appeals Court; local courts

Political parties: All People's Congress or APC
Sierra Leone People's Party or SLPP

International organization participation: ACP, AfDB, ATMIS, AU, C, ECOWAS, EITI (compliant country), FAO, G-77, IAEA, IBRD, ICAO, ICCt, ICRM, IDA, IDB, IFAD, IFC, IFRCS, IHO (pending member), ILO, IMF, IMO, Interpol, IOC, IOM, IPU, ISO (correspondent), ITU, ITUC (NGOs), MIGA, NAM, OIC, OPCW, UN, UNAMID, UNCTAD, UNESCO, UNIDO, UNIFIL, UNISFA, UNOOSA, UNSOM, UNWTO, UPU, WCO, WFTU (NGOs), WHO, WIPO, WMO, WTO

Diplomatic representation in the US: *chief of mission:* Ambassador Sidique Abou-Bakarr WAI (since 8 April 2019)
chancery: 1701 19th Street NW, Washington, DC 20009-1605
telephone: [1] (202) 939-9261
FAX: [1] (202) 483-1793
email address and website:
info@embassyofsierraleone.net
https://embassyofsierraleone.net/

Diplomatic representation from the US: *chief of mission:* Ambassador Bryan David HUNT (since 8 September 2023)
embassy: Southridge-Hill Station, Freetown
mailing address: 2160 Freetown Place, Washington DC 20521-2160
telephone: [232] 99 105 000
email address and website:
consularfreetown@state.gov
https://sl.usembassy.gov/

Flag description: three equal horizontal bands of light green (top), white, and light blue; green symbolizes agriculture, mountains, and natural resources, white represents unity and justice, and blue the sea and the natural harbor in Freetown

National symbol(s): lion; national colors: green, white, blue

National anthem: *name:* "High We Exalt Thee, Realm of the Free"
lyrics/music: Clifford Nelson FYLE/John Joseph AKA
note: adopted 1961

ECONOMY

Economic overview: low-income West African economy; primarily subsistent agriculture; key iron and diamond mining activities suspended; slow recovery from 1990s civil war; systemic corruption; high-risk debt; high youth unemployment; natural resource rich

Real GDP (purchasing power parity): $14.633 billion (2023 est.)
$14.148 billion (2022 est.)
$13.675 billion (2021 est.)
note: data in 2021 dollars
comparison ranking: 159

Real GDP growth rate: 3.43% (2023 est.)
3.46% (2022 est.)
4.1% (2021 est.)
note: annual GDP % growth based on constant local currency
comparison ranking: 95

Real GDP per capita: $1,700 (2023 est.)
$1,600 (2022 est.)
$1,600 (2021 est.)
note: data in 2021 dollars
comparison ranking: 213

GDP (official exchange rate): $3.81 billion (2023 est.)
note: data in current dollars at official exchange rate

Inflation rate (consumer prices): 47.64% (2023 est.)
27.21% (2022 est.)
11.87% (2021 est.)
note: annual % change based on consumer prices
comparison ranking: 214

GDP - composition, by sector of origin: *agriculture:* 64.4% (2023 est.)
industry: 7.8% (2023 est.)
services: 24.7% (2023 est.)
note: figures may not total 100% due to non-allocated consumption not captured in sector-reported data
comparison rankings: services 213; industry 205; agriculture 1

GDP - composition, by end use: *household consumption:* 106.2% (2023 est.)
government consumption: 8.8% (2023 est.)
investment in fixed capital: 11.5% (2023 est.)
investment in inventories: 0.3% (2023 est.)
exports of goods and services: 40.5% (2023 est.)
imports of goods and services: -67.3% (2023 est.)
note: figures may not total 100% due to rounding or gaps in data collection

Agricultural products: cassava, rice, oil palm fruit, vegetables, sweet potatoes, milk, citrus fruits, groundnuts, fruits, sugarcane (2022)
note: top ten agricultural products based on tonnage

Industries: diamond mining; iron ore, rutile and bauxite mining; small-scale manufacturing (beverages, textiles, footwear)

Industrial production growth rate: 3.27% (2023 est.)
note: annual % change in industrial value added based on constant local currency
comparison ranking: 101

Labor force: 2.913 million (2023 est.)
note: number of people ages 15 or older who are employed or seeking work
comparison ranking: 112

Unemployment rate: 3.17% (2023 est.)
3.19% (2022 est.)
3.52% (2021 est.)
note: % of labor force seeking employment
comparison ranking: 53

Youth unemployment rate (ages 15-24): *total:* 3.6% (2023 est.)
male: 4.7% (2023 est.)
female: 2.5% (2023 est.)
note: % of labor force ages 15-24 seeking employment
comparison ranking: total 189

Population below poverty line: 56.8% (2018 est.)
note: % of population with income below national poverty line

Gini Index coefficient - distribution of family income: 35.7 (2018 est.)
note: index (0-100) of income distribution; higher values represent greater inequality
comparison ranking: 71

Household income or consumption by percentage share: *lowest 10%:* 3.4% (2018 est.)
highest 10%: 29.4% (2018 est.)
note: % share of income accruing to lowest and highest 10% of population

Remittances: 6.1% of GDP (2023 est.)
7.85% of GDP (2022 est.)
5.47% of GDP (2021 est.)
note: personal transfers and compensation between resident and non-resident individuals/households/entities

Budget: *revenues:* $740 million (2019 est.)
expenditures: $867 million (2019 est.)

Public debt: 63.9% of GDP (2017 est.)
comparison ranking: 67

Taxes and other revenues: 15.6% (of GDP) (2017 est.)
comparison ranking: 134

Current account balance: -$156.702 million (2022 est.)
-$395.465 million (2021 est.)
-$320.411 million (2020 est.)
note: balance of payments - net trade and primary/secondary income in current dollars
comparison ranking: 106

Exports: $1.195 billion (2022 est.)
$1.114 billion (2021 est.)
$661.505 million (2020 est.)
note: balance of payments - exports of goods and services in current dollars
comparison ranking: 178

Exports - partners: China 54%, Belgium 12%, UAE 6%, Germany 4%, Netherlands 4% (2022)
note: top five export partners based on percentage share of exports

Exports - commodities: iron ore, titanium ore, diamonds, wood, aluminum ore (2022)
note: top five export commodities based on value in dollars

Imports: $2.013 billion (2022 est.)
$1.906 billion (2021 est.)
$1.386 billion (2020 est.)
note: balance of payments - imports of goods and services in current dollars
comparison ranking: 178

Imports - partners: China 33%, India 12%, Turkey 9%, US 6%, UAE 5% (2022)
note: top five import partners based on percentage share of imports

Imports - commodities: rice, plastic products, refined petroleum, vaccines, packaged medicine (2022)
note: top five import commodities based on value in dollars

Reserves of foreign exchange and gold: $495.699 million (2023 est.)
$624.496 million (2022 est.)
$945.908 million (2021 est.)
note: holdings of gold (year-end prices)/foreign exchange/special drawing rights in current dollars
comparison ranking: 160

Debt - external: $1.072 billion (2022 est.)
note: present value of external debt in current US dollars
comparison ranking: 81

Exchange rates: leones (SLL) per US dollar -

Exchange rates: 21.305 (2023 est.)
14.048 (2022 est.)
10.439 (2021 est.)
9.83 (2020 est.)
9.01 (2019 est.)

ENERGY

Electricity access: *electrification - total population:* 29.4% (2022 est.)
electrification - urban areas: 55.3%
electrification - rural areas: 5%

Electricity: *installed generating capacity:* 138,000 kW (2022 est.)
consumption: 122.083 million kWh (2022 est.)
transmission/distribution losses: 76.158 million kWh (2022 est.)
comparison rankings: transmission/distribution losses 43; consumption 197; installed generating capacity 181

Electricity generation sources: *fossil fuels:* 3.7% of total installed capacity (2022 est.)
solar: 3% of total installed capacity (2022 est.)
hydroelectricity: 90.8% of total installed capacity (2022 est.)
biomass and waste: 2.5% of total installed capacity (2022 est.)

Coal: *imports:* (2022 est.) less than 1 metric ton

Petroleum: *refined petroleum consumption:* 9,000 bbl/day (2022 est.)

Carbon dioxide emissions: 1.352 million metric tonnes of CO2 (2022 est.)
from petroleum and other liquids: 1.352 million metric tonnes of CO2 (2022 est.)
comparison ranking: total emissions 165

Energy consumption per capita: 2.229 million Btu/person (2022 est.)
comparison ranking: 185

COMMUNICATIONS

Telephones - fixed lines: *total subscriptions:* 269 (2021 est.)
subscriptions per 100 inhabitants: (2021 est.) less than 1
comparison ranking: total subscriptions 221

Telephones - mobile cellular: *total subscriptions:* 8.227 million (2021 est.)
subscriptions per 100 inhabitants: 98 (2021 est.)
comparison ranking: total subscriptions 100

Telecommunication systems: *general assessment:* the telecom sector has only gradually recovered from the destruction caused during the war years, and only since 2019 has there been an effective terrestrial fiber backbone infrastructure, while the cable link to neighboring Guinea was not completed until February 2020; there is considerable available capacity from the ACE submarine cable and the national fiber network, but this is used inefficiently and so the price of internet connectivity remains one of the highest in the region; the theft of equipment and cabling, compounded by neglect, mismanagement, and under investment, means that telecommunications companies continue to operate in difficult conditions; the telecom regulator has made efforts to improve the market, including the liberalization of the international gateway and regular checks on QoS; the regulator reduced the price floor for mobile voice calls in early 2020, though consumers objected to the MNOs withdrawing a number of cheap packages as a response; the mobile sector has been the main driver of overall telecom revenue (2022)
domestic: fixed-line less than 0 per 100 and mobile-cellular just over 98 per 100 (2021)
international: country code - 232; landing point for the ACE submarine cable linking to South Africa, over 20 western African countries and Europe; satellite earth station - 1 Intelsat (Atlantic Ocean) (2019)

Broadcast media: 1 government-owned TV station; 3 private TV stations; a pay-TV service began operations in late 2007; 1 government-owned national radio station; about two-dozen private radio stations primarily clustered in major cities; transmissions of several international broadcasters are available (2019)

Internet country code: .sl

Internet users: *total:* 1,047,499 (2022 est.)
percent of population: 12.7% (2022 est.)
comparison ranking: total 149

TRANSPORTATION

National air transport system: *annual passenger traffic on registered air carriers:* 50,193 (2015)
annual freight traffic on registered air carriers: 0 (2015) mt-km

Civil aircraft registration country code prefix: 9L

Airports: 8 (2024)
comparison ranking: 167

Heliports: 3 (2024)

Roadways: *total:* 11,701 km
paved: 1,051 km
unpaved: 10,650 km (2015)
urban: 3,000 km (2015)
non-urban: 8,700 km (2015)
comparison ranking: total 133

Waterways: 800 km (2011) (600 km navigable year-round)
comparison ranking: 79

Merchant marine: *total:* 584 (2023)
by type: bulk carrier 33, container ship 8, general cargo 320, oil tanker 97, other 126
comparison ranking: total 39

Ports: *total ports:* 3 (2024)
large: 0
medium: 0
small: 1
very small: 2
ports with oil terminals: 2
key ports: Bonthe, Freetown, Pepel

MILITARY AND SECURITY

Military and security forces: Republic of Sierra Leone Armed Forces (RSLAF): Land Forces, Maritime Forces, Air Wing

Ministry of Internal Affairs: Sierra Leone Police (2024)

Military expenditures: 0.6% of GDP (2023 est.)
0.6% of GDP (2022 est.)
0.3% of GDP (2021 est.)
0.3% of GDP (2020 est.)
0.3% of GDP (2019 est.)
comparison ranking: 157

Military and security service personnel strengths: approximately 8,500 personnel, mostly ground forces (2023)

Military equipment inventories and acquisitions: the RSLAF has a small inventory that includes a mix of Soviet-origin and other older-foreign-supplied equipment; in recent years, it has received limited amounts of newer equipment, mostly as donations (2024)

Military service age and obligation: 18-30 for voluntary military service for men and women (25-40 for specialists); no conscription (2023)

Military - note: the RSLAF's principle responsibilities are securing the borders and the country's territorial waters, supporting civil authorities during emergencies and reconstruction efforts, and participating in peacekeeping missions; it is small, lightly armed, and has a limited budget; since being reduced in size and restructured with British assistance after the end of the civil war in 2002, it has received assistance from several foreign militaries, including those of Canada, China, France, the UK, and the US; the RSLAF has participated in peacekeeping operations in Somalia and Sudan
the RSLAF's origins lie in the Sierra Leone Battalion of the Royal West African Frontier Force (RWAFF), a multi-regiment force formed by the British colonial office in 1900 to garrison the West African colonies of Gold Coast (Ghana), Nigeria (Lagos and the protectorates of Northern and Southern Nigeria), Sierra Leone, and The Gambia; the RWAFF fought in both World Wars (2024)

TRANSNATIONAL ISSUES

Refugees and internally displaced persons: IDPs: IDPs: 3000 currently displaced due to post-electoral violence in 2018 and clashes in the Pujehun region in 2019); 900 internal displacements due to flood in 2022 (2022)
5,500 (displacement caused by post-electoral violence in 2018 and clashes in the Pujehun region in 2019) (2021)

SINGAPORE

INTRODUCTION

Background: A Malay trading port known as Temasek existed on the island of Singapore by the 14th century. The settlement changed hands several times in the ensuing centuries and was eventually burned in the 17th century, falling into obscurity. In 1819, the British founded modern Singapore as a trading colony on the same site and granted it full internal self-government for all matters except defense and foreign affairs in 1959. Singapore joined the Malaysian Federation in 1963 but was ousted two years later and became independent. Singapore subsequently became one of the world's most prosperous countries, with strong international trading links and per capita GDP among the highest globally. The People's Action Party has won every general election in Singapore since the end of the British colonial era, aided by its success in delivering consistent economic growth, as well as the city-state's fragmented opposition and electoral procedures that strongly favor the ruling party.

GEOGRAPHY

Location: Southeastern Asia, islands between Malaysia and Indonesia

Geographic coordinates: 1 22 N, 103 48 E

Map references: Southeast Asia

Area: *total:* 719 sq km
land: 709.2 sq km
water: 10 sq km
comparison ranking: total 190

Area - comparative: slightly more than 3.5 times the size of Washington, DC\

Land boundaries: *total:* 0 km

Coastline: 193 km

Maritime claims: *territorial sea:* 3 nm
exclusive fishing zone: within and beyond territorial sea, as defined in treaties and practice

Climate: tropical; hot, humid, rainy; two distinct monsoon seasons - northeastern monsoon (December to March) and southwestern monsoon (June to September); inter-monsoon - frequent afternoon and early evening thunderstorms

Terrain: lowlying, gently undulating central plateau

Elevation: *highest point:* Bukit Timah 166 m
lowest point: Singapore Strait 0 m

Natural resources: fish, deepwater ports

Land use: *agricultural land:* 1% (2018 est.)
arable land: 0.9% (2018 est.)
permanent crops: 0.1% (2018 est.)
permanent pasture: 0% (2018 est.)
forest: 3.3% (2018 est.)
other: 95.7% (2018 est.)

Irrigated land: 0 sq km (2022)

Population distribution: most of the urbanization is along the southern coast, with relatively dense population clusters found in the central areas

Natural hazards: flash floods

Geography - note: focal point for Southeast Asian sea routes; consists of about 60 islands, the largest of which by far is Pulau Ujong; land reclamation has removed many former islands and created a number of new ones

PEOPLE AND SOCIETY

Population: *total:* 6,028,459
male: 3,013,630
female: 3,014,829 (2024 est.)
comparison rankings: female 114; male 114; total 114

Nationality: *noun:* Singaporean(s)
adjective: Singapore

Ethnic groups: Chinese 74.2%, Malay 13.7%, Indian 8.9%, other 3.2% (2021 est.)
note: data represent population by self-identification; the population is divided into four categories: Chinese, Malay (includes indigenous Malays and Indonesians), Indian (includes Indian, Pakistani, Bangladeshi, or Sri Lankan), and other ethnic groups (includes Eurasians, Caucasians, Japanese, Filipino, Vietnamese)

Languages: English (official) 48.3%, Mandarin (official) 29.9%, other Chinese dialects (includes Hokkien, Cantonese, Teochew, Hakka) 8.7%, Malay (official) 9.2%, Tamil (official) 2.5%, other 1.4% (2020 est.)
major-language sample(s):
世界概況 — 不可缺少的基本消息來源 (Mandarin)
note: data represent language most frequently spoken at home

Religions: Buddhist 31.1%, Christian 18.9%, Muslim 15.6%, Taoist 8.8%, Hindu 5%, other 0.6%, none 20% (2020 est.)

Demographic profile: Singapore has one of the lowest total fertility rates (TFR) in the world – an average of 1.15 children born per woman – and a rapidly aging population. Women's expanded educations, widened aspirations, and a desire to establish careers has contributed to delayed marriage and smaller families. Most married couples have only one or two children in order to invest more in each child, including the high costs of education. In addition, more and more Singaporeans, particularly women, are staying single. Factors contributing to this trend are a focus on careers, long working hours, the high cost of living, and long waits for public housing. With fertility at such a low rate and rising life expectancy, the proportion of the population aged 65 or over is growing and the youth population is shrinking. Singapore is projected to experience one of the largest percentage point increases in the elderly share of the population at 21% between 2019 and 2050, according to the UN. The working-age population (aged 15-64) will gradually decrease, leaving fewer workers to economically support the elderly population.
Migration has played a key role in Singapore's development. As Singapore's economy expanded during the 19th century, more and more Chinese, Indian, and Malay labor immigrants arrived. Most of Singapore's pre-World War II population growth was a result of immigration. During World War II, immigration came to a halt when the Japanese occupied the island but revived in the postwar years. Policy was restrictive during the 1950s and 1960s, aiming to protect jobs for residents by reducing the intake of low-skilled foreign workers and focusing instead on attracting professionals from abroad with specialist skills. Consequently, the nonresident share of Singapore's population plummeted to less than 3%.
As the country industrialized, however, it loosened restrictions on the immigration of manual workers. From the 1980s through the 2000s, the foreign population continued to grow as a result of policies aimed at attracting foreign workers of all skill levels. More recently, the government has instituted immigration policies that target highly skilled workers. Skilled workers are encouraged to stay and are given the opportunity to become permanent residents or citizens. The country, however, imposes restrictions on unskilled and low-skilled workers to ensure they do not establish roots, including prohibiting them from bringing their families and requiring employers to pay a monthly foreign worker levy and security bond. The country has also become increasingly attractive to international students. The growth of the foreign-born population has continued to be rapid; as of 2015, the foreign-born composed 46% of the total population. At the same time, growing numbers of Singaporeans are emigrating for education and work experience in highly skilled sectors such finance, information technology, and medicine. Increasingly, the moves abroad are permanent.

Age structure: *0-14 years:* 14.6% (male 455,536/female 424,969)
15-64 years: 71.1% (male 2,157,441/female 2,126,799)
65 years and over: 14.3% (2024 est.) (male 400,653/female 463,061)

Dependency ratios: *total dependency ratio:* 35.4
youth dependency ratio: 16.2
elderly dependency ratio: 19.1
potential support ratio: 5.2 (2021 est.)

Median age: *total:* 39.4 years (2024 est.)
male: 38 years
female: 40.6 years
comparison ranking: total 68

Population growth rate: 0.87% (2024 est.)
comparison ranking: 105

Birth rate: 8.8 births/1,000 population (2024 est.)
comparison ranking: 203

Death rate: 4.3 deaths/1,000 population (2024 est.)
comparison ranking: 209

Net migration rate: 4.2 migrant(s)/1,000 population (2024 est.)
comparison ranking: 24

Population distribution: most of the urbanization is along the southern coast, with relatively dense population clusters found in the central areas

Urbanization: *urban population:* 100% of total population (2023)
rate of urbanization: 0.74% annual rate of change (2020-25 est.)

Major urban areas - population: 6.081 million SINGAPORE (capital) (2023)

Sex ratio: *at birth:* 1.05 male(s)/female
0-14 years: 1.07 male(s)/female
15-64 years: 1.01 male(s)/female
65 years and over: 0.87 male(s)/female
total population: 1 male(s)/female (2024 est.)

Mother's mean age at first birth: 30.5 years (2015 est.)
note: data represents median age

Maternal mortality ratio: 7 deaths/100,000 live births (2020 est.)
comparison ranking: 157

Infant mortality rate: *total:* 1.5 deaths/1,000 live births (2024 est.)
male: 1.7 deaths/1,000 live births
female: 1.4 deaths/1,000 live births
comparison ranking: total 226

Life expectancy at birth: *total population:* 86.7 years (2024 est.)
male: 84 years
female: 89.5 years
comparison ranking: total population 2

Total fertility rate: 1.17 children born/woman (2024 est.)
comparison ranking: 225

Gross reproduction rate: 0.57 (2024 est.)

Drinking water source: *improved:* *urban:* 100% of population
total: 100% of population

Current health expenditure: 6.1% of GDP (2020)

Physician density: 2.46 physicians/1,000 population (2019)

Hospital bed density: 2.5 beds/1,000 population (2017)

Sanitation facility access: *improved:* *urban:* 100% of population
total: 100% of population

Obesity - adult prevalence rate: 6.1% (2016)
comparison ranking: 170

Alcohol consumption per capita: *total:* 1.81 liters of pure alcohol (2019 est.)
beer: 1.26 liters of pure alcohol (2019 est.)
wine: 0.27 liters of pure alcohol (2019 est.)
spirits: 0.24 liters of pure alcohol (2019 est.)
other alcohols: 0.04 liters of pure alcohol (2019 est.)
comparison ranking: total 132

Tobacco use: *total:* 16.5% (2020 est.)
male: 28% (2020 est.)
female: 5% (2020 est.)
comparison ranking: total 99

Currently married women (ages 15-49): 54.3% (2023 est.)

Child marriage: *women married by age 18:* 0.1% (2022 est.)

Education expenditures: 2.8% of GDP (2021 est.)
comparison ranking: 165

Literacy: *definition:* age 15 and over can read and write
total population: 97.5%
male: 98.9%
female: 96.1% (2019)

School life expectancy (primary to tertiary education): *total:* 17 years
male: 16 years
female: 17 years (2020)

ENVIRONMENT

Environment - current issues: water pollution; industrial pollution; limited natural freshwater resources; limited land availability presents waste disposal problems; air pollution; deforestation; seasonal smoke/haze resulting from forest fires in Indonesia

Environment - international agreements: *party to:* Biodiversity, Climate Change, Climate Change-Kyoto Protocol, Climate Change-Paris Agreement, Comprehensive Nuclear Test Ban, Desertification, Endangered Species, Hazardous Wastes, Law of the Sea, Nuclear Test Ban, Ozone Layer Protection, Ship Pollution
signed, but not ratified: none of the selected agreements

Climate: tropical; hot, humid, rainy; two distinct monsoon seasons - northeastern monsoon (December to March) and southwestern monsoon (June to September); inter-monsoon - frequent afternoon and early evening thunderstorms

Urbanization: *urban population:* 100% of total population (2023)
rate of urbanization: 0.74% annual rate of change (2020-25 est.)

Revenue from forest resources: 0% of GDP (2018 est.)
comparison ranking: 190

Revenue from coal: 0% of GDP (2018 est.)
comparison ranking: 131

Air pollutants: *particulate matter emissions:* 13.33 micrograms per cubic meter (2019 est.)
carbon dioxide emissions: 37.54 megatons (2016 est.)
methane emissions: 4.4 megatons (2020 est.)

Waste and recycling: *municipal solid waste generated annually:* 7,704,300 tons (2017 est.)
municipal solid waste recycled annually: 4,699,623 tons (2015 est.)
percent of municipal solid waste recycled: 61% (2015 est.)

Total water withdrawal: *municipal:* 300 million cubic meters (2020 est.)
industrial: 340 million cubic meters (2020 est.)
agricultural: 30 million cubic meters (2020 est.)

Total renewable water resources: 600 million cubic meters (2020 est.)

GOVERNMENT

Country name: *conventional long form:* Republic of Singapore
conventional short form: Singapore
local long form: Republic of Singapore
local short form: Singapore
etymology: name derives from the Sanskrit words "simha" (lion) and "pura" (city) to describe the city-state's leonine symbol

Government type: parliamentary republic

Capital: *name:* Singapore
geographic coordinates: 1 17 N, 103 51 E
time difference: UTC+8 (13 hours ahead of Washington, DC, during Standard Time)
etymology: name derives from the Sanskrit words *simha* (lion) and *pura* (city), thus creating the city's epithet "lion city"

Administrative divisions: *no first order administrative divisions; there are five community development councils:* Central Singapore Development Council, North East Development Council, North West Development Council, South East Development Council, South West Development Council (2019)

Independence: 9 August 1965 (from Malaysian Federation)

National holiday: National Day, 9 August (1965)

Legal system: English common law

Constitution: *history:* several previous; latest adopted 22 December 1965
amendments: proposed by Parliament; passage requires two-thirds majority vote in the second and third readings by the elected Parliament membership and assent of the president of the republic; passage of amendments affecting sovereignty or control of the Police Force or the Armed Forces requires at least two-thirds majority vote in a referendum; amended many times, last in 2020

International law organization participation: has not submitted an ICJ jurisdiction declaration; non-party state to the ICCt

Citizenship: *citizenship by birth:* no
citizenship by descent only: at least one parent must be a citizen of Singapore
dual citizenship recognized: no
residency requirement for naturalization: 10 years

Suffrage: 21 years of age; universal and compulsory

Executive branch: *chief of state:* President THARMAN Shanmugaratnam (since 14 September 2023)
head of government: Prime Minister Lawrence WONG (since 15 May 2024)
cabinet: Cabinet appointed by the president on the advice of the prime minister; Cabinet responsible to Parliament
elections/appointments: president directly elected by simple majority popular vote for a 6-year term (no term limits); election last held on 1 September 2023 (next to be held in 2029); following legislative elections, the leader of the majority party or majority coalition appointed prime minister by the president; deputy prime ministers appointed by the president
election results:
2023: THARMAN Shanmugaratnam elected president; percent of vote - THARMAN Shanmugaratnam (independent) 70.4%, NG Kok Song (independent) 15.7%, TAN Kin Lian (independent) 13.9%
2017: HALIMAH Yacob declared president on 13 September 2017, being the only eligible candidate

Legislative branch: *description:* unicameral Parliament (104 seats statutory; 93 members directly elected by simple majority popular vote, up to 9 nominated by a parliamentary selection committee and appointed by the president, and up to 12 non-constituency members from opposition parties to ensure political diversity; members serve 5-year terms)
elections: last held on 10 July 2020 (next must be held by 24 November 2025)

election results: percent of vote by party - PAP 89.2%, WP 10.6%, other 0.2%; seats by party - PAP 79, WP 10, PSP 2, independent 9; composition - men 70, women 29, percentage women 29.3%

Judicial branch: *highest court(s):* Supreme Court (although the number of judges varies - as of April 2019, the court totaled 20 judges, 7 judicial commissioners, 4 judges of appeal, and 16 international judges); the court is organized into an upper tier Appeal Court and a lower tier High Court
judge selection and term of office: judges appointed by the president from candidates recommended by the prime minister after consultation with the chief justice; judges usually serve until retirement at age 65, but terms can be extended
subordinate courts: district, magistrates', juvenile, family, community, and coroners' courts; small claims tribunals; employment claims tribunals

Political parties: People's Action Party or PAP
Progress Singapore Party or PSP
Workers' Party or WP
note: the PAP has won every general election since the end of the British colonial era in 1959

International organization participation: ADB, AOSIS, APEC, Arctic Council (observer), ARF, ASEAN, BIS, C, CP, EAS, FAO, FATF, G-77, IAEA, IBRD, ICAO, ICC (national committees), ICCt, ICRM, IDA, IFC, IFRCS, IHO, ILO, IMF, IMO, IMSO, Interpol, IOC, IPU, ISO, ITSO, ITU, ITUC (NGOs), MIGA, NAM, OPCW, Pacific Alliance (observer), PCA, UN, UNCTAD, UNESCO, UNHCR, UPU, WCO, WHO, WIPO, WMO, WTO

Diplomatic representation in the US: *chief of mission:* Ambassador LUI Tuck Yew (since 30 June 2023)
chancery: 3501 International Place NW, Washington, DC 20008
telephone: [1] (202) 537-3100
FAX: [1] (202) 537-0876
email address and website:
singemb_was@mfa.sg
https://www.mfa.gov.sg/washington/
consulate(s) general: San Francisco
consulate(s): New York

Diplomatic representation from the US: *chief of mission:* Ambassador Jonathan KAPLAN (since December 2021)
embassy: 27 Napier Road, Singapore 258508
mailing address: 4280 Singapore Place, Washington DC 20521-4280
telephone: [65] 6476-9100
FAX: [65] 6476-9340
email address and website:
singaporeusembassy@state.gov
https://sg.usembassy.gov/

Flag description: two equal horizontal bands of red (top) and white; near the hoist side of the red band, there is a vertical, white crescent (closed portion is toward the hoist side) partially enclosing five white five-pointed stars arranged in a circle; red denotes brotherhood and equality; white signifies purity and virtue; the waxing crescent moon symbolizes a young nation on the ascendancy; the five stars represent the nation's ideals of democracy, peace, progress, justice, and equality

National symbol(s): lion, merlion (mythical half lion-half fish creature), orchid; national colors: red, white

National anthem: *name:* "Majulah Singapura" (Onward Singapore)
lyrics/music: ZUBIR Said
note: adopted 1965; first performed in 1958 at the Victoria Theatre, the anthem is sung only in Malay

National heritage: *total World Heritage Sites:* 1 (cultural)
selected World Heritage Site locales: Singapore Botanic Gardens

ECONOMY

Economic overview: high-income, service-based Southeast Asian economy; renowned for financial markets and Asian Infrastructure Exchange; business-driven regulations; low unemployment; electronics, oil, and chemicals exporter; continuing education investment

Real GDP (purchasing power parity): $754.758 billion (2023 est.)
$746.73 billion (2022 est.)
$719.13 billion (2021 est.)
note: data in 2021 dollars
comparison ranking: 35

Real GDP growth rate: 1.08% (2023 est.)
3.84% (2022 est.)
9.69% (2021 est.)
note: annual GDP % growth based on constant local currency
comparison ranking: 162

Real GDP per capita: $127,500 (2023 est.)
$132,500 (2022 est.)
$131,900 (2021 est.)
note: data in 2021 dollars
comparison ranking: 2

GDP (official exchange rate): $501.428 billion (2023 est.)
note: data in current dollars at official exchange rate

Inflation rate (consumer prices): 4.82% (2023 est.)
6.12% (2022 est.)
2.3% (2021 est.)
note: annual % change based on consumer prices
comparison ranking: 102

Credit ratings: Fitch rating: AAA (2003)

Moody's rating: Aaa (2002)

Standard & Poors rating: AAA (1995)
note: The year refers to the year in which the current credit rating was first obtained.

GDP - composition, by sector of origin: *agriculture:* 0% (2023 est.)
industry: 22.4% (2023 est.)
services: 72.4% (2023 est.)
note: figures may not total 100% due to non-allocated consumption not captured in sector-reported data
comparison rankings: services 31; industry 120; agriculture 213

GDP - composition, by end use: *household consumption:* 31.3% (2023 est.)
government consumption: 10.2% (2023 est.)
investment in fixed capital: 22.2% (2023 est.)
investment in inventories: -1.2% (2023 est.)
exports of goods and services: 174.3% (2023 est.)
imports of goods and services: -136.9% (2023 est.)
note: figures may not total 100% due to rounding or gaps in data collection

Agricultural products: chicken, eggs, pork, vegetables, duck, spinach, pork offal, pork fat, cabbages, lettuce (2022)
note: top ten agricultural products based on tonnage

Industries: electronics, chemicals, financial services, oil drilling equipment, petroleum refining, biomedical products, scientific instruments, telecommunication equipment, processed food and beverages, ship repair, offshore platform construction, entrepot trade

Industrial production growth rate: -2.89% (2023 est.)
note: annual % change in industrial value added based on constant local currency
comparison ranking: 191

Labor force: 3.619 million (2023 est.)
note: number of people ages 15 or older who are employed or seeking work
comparison ranking: 98

Unemployment rate: 3.47% (2023 est.)
3.59% (2022 est.)
4.64% (2021 est.)
note: % of labor force seeking employment
comparison ranking: 59

Youth unemployment rate (ages 15-24): *total:* 8.3% (2023 est.)
male: 6.5% (2023 est.)
female: 10.4% (2023 est.)
note: % of labor force ages 15-24 seeking employment
comparison ranking: total 149

Gini Index coefficient - distribution of family income: 45.9 (2017)
comparison ranking: 18

Average household expenditures: *on food:* 7% of household expenditures (2022 est.)
on alcohol and tobacco: 1.9% of household expenditures (2022 est.)

Household income or consumption by percentage share: *lowest 10%:* 1.6%
highest 10%: 27.5% (2017)

Remittances: 0% of GDP (2023 est.)
0% of GDP (2022 est.)
0% of GDP (2021 est.)
note: personal transfers and compensation between resident and non-resident individuals/households/entities

Budget: *revenues:* $80.855 billion (2022 est.)
expenditures: $75.448 billion (2022 est.)
note: central government revenues (excluding grants) and expenses converted to US dollars at average official exchange rate for year indicated

Public debt: 150.14% of GDP (2021 est.)
note: central government debt as a % of GDP
comparison ranking: 3

Taxes and other revenues: 12.03% (of GDP) (2022 est.)
note: central government tax revenue as a % of GDP
comparison ranking: 164

Current account balance: $99.128 billion (2023 est.)
$89.701 billion (2022 est.)
$86.137 billion (2021 est.)
note: balance of payments - net trade and primary/secondary income in current dollars
comparison ranking: 5

Exports: $873.989 billion (2023 est.)
$925.952 billion (2022 est.)
$794.47 billion (2021 est.)
note: balance of payments - exports of goods and services in current dollars
comparison ranking: 8

Exports - partners: Hong Kong 14%, China 13%, Malaysia 9%, US 8%, Indonesia 6% (2022)
note: top five export partners based on percentage share of exports

Exports - commodities: integrated circuits, refined petroleum, machinery, gold, gas turbines (2022)
note: top five export commodities based on value in dollars

Imports: $686.656 billion (2023 est.)
$733.876 billion (2022 est.)
$637.165 billion (2021 est.)
note: balance of payments - imports of goods and services in current dollars
comparison ranking: 12

Imports - partners: China 17%, Malaysia 13%, US 10%, Taiwan 9%, South Korea 5% (2022)
note: top five import partners based on percentage share of imports

Imports - commodities: integrated circuits, refined petroleum, crude petroleum, gold, machinery (2022)
note: top five import commodities based on value in dollars

Reserves of foreign exchange and gold: $359.835 billion (2023 est.)
$296.629 billion (2022 est.)
$425.098 billion (2021 est.)
note: holdings of gold (year-end prices)/foreign exchange/special drawing rights in current dollars
comparison ranking: 12

Debt - external: (2019)

Exchange rates: Singapore dollars (SGD) per US dollar -

Exchange rates: 1.343 (2023 est.)
1.379 (2022 est.)
1.343 (2021 est.)
1.38 (2020 est.)
1.364 (2019 est.)

ENERGY

Electricity access: *electrification - total population:* 100% (2022 est.)

Electricity: *installed generating capacity:* 12.538 million kW (2022 est.)
consumption: 57.029 billion kWh (2022 est.)
transmission/distribution losses: 656.085 million kWh (2022 est.)
comparison rankings: transmission/distribution losses 88; consumption 49; installed generating capacity 57

Electricity generation sources: *fossil fuels:* 94.7% of total installed capacity (2022 est.)
solar: 2.1% of total installed capacity (2022 est.)
biomass and waste: 3.2% of total installed capacity (2022 est.)

Coal: *consumption:* 784,000 metric tons (2022 est.)
exports: 2,000 metric tons (2022 est.)
imports: 595,000 metric tons (2022 est.)

Petroleum: *refined petroleum consumption:* 1.47 million bbl/day (2022 est.)

Natural gas: *consumption:* 13.724 billion cubic meters (2022 est.)
exports: 352.812 million cubic meters (2022 est.)
imports: 15.124 billion cubic meters (2022 est.)

Carbon dioxide emissions: 241.71 million metric tonnes of CO2 (2022 est.)
from coal and metallurgical coke: 1.558 million metric tonnes of CO2 (2022 est.)
from petroleum and other liquids: 213.229 million metric tonnes of CO2 (2022 est.)
from consumed natural gas: 26.923 million metric tonnes of CO2 (2022 est.)
comparison ranking: total emissions 28

Energy consumption per capita: 653.844 million Btu/person (2022 est.)
comparison ranking: 2

COMMUNICATIONS

Telephones - fixed lines: *total subscriptions:* 1.906 million (2022 est.)
subscriptions per 100 inhabitants: 32 (2022 est.)
comparison ranking: total subscriptions 53

Telephones - mobile cellular: *total subscriptions:* 9.351 million (2022 est.)
subscriptions per 100 inhabitants: 156 (2022 est.)
comparison ranking: total subscriptions 95

Telecommunication systems: *general assessment:* a wealthy city-state, Singapore has a highly developed ICT infrastructure; government supported near universal home broadband penetration and free public access to wireless network; the government's telecommunication regulator, Infocomm Media Development Authority (IMDA), issued awards in mid-2020 to telecom operators with the goal of having at least 50% of the city-state covered with a standalone 5G network by the end of 2022; government actively promoting Smart Nation initiative supporting digital innovation; government oversees service providers and controls Internet content; well served by submarine cable and satellite connections (2021)
domestic: fixed-line is 32 per 100 and mobile-cellular 146 per 100 teledensity (2021)
international: country code - 65; landing points for INDIGO-West, SeaMeWe -3,-4,-5, SIGMAR, SJC, i2icn, PGASCOM, BSCS, IGG, B3JS, SAEx2, APCN-2, APG, ASC, SEAX-1, ASE, EAC-C2C, Matrix Cable System and SJC2 submarine cables providing links throughout Asia, Southeast Asia, Africa, Australia, the Middle East, and Europe; satellite earth stations - 3, Bukit Timah, Seletar, and Sentosa; supplemented by VSAT coverage (2019)

Broadcast media: state controls broadcast media; 6 domestic TV stations operated by MediaCorp which is wholly owned by a state investment company; broadcasts from Malaysian and Indonesian stations available; satellite dishes banned; multi-channel cable TV services available; a total of 19 domestic radio stations broadcasting, with MediaCorp operating 11, Singapore Press Holdings, also government-linked, another 5, 2 controlled by the Singapore Armed Forces Reservists Association and one owned by BBC Radio; Malaysian and Indonesian radio stations are available as is BBC; a number of Internet service radio stations are also available (2019)

Internet country code: .sg

Internet users: *total:* 5.369 million (2021 est.)
percent of population: 91% (2021 est.)
comparison ranking: total 88

Broadband - fixed subscriptions: *total:* 1,509,700 (2020 est.)
subscriptions per 100 inhabitants: 26 (2020 est.)
comparison ranking: total 66

TRANSPORTATION

National air transport system: *number of registered air carriers:* 4 (2020)
inventory of registered aircraft operated by air carriers: 230
annual passenger traffic on registered air carriers: 40,401,515 (2018)
annual freight traffic on registered air carriers: 5,194,900,000 (2018) mt-km

Civil aircraft registration country code prefix: 9V

Airports: 9 (2024)
comparison ranking: 164

Heliports: 1 (2024)

Pipelines: 3,220 km domestic gas (2014), 1,122 km cross-border pipelines (2017), 8 km refined products (2013)

Roadways: *total:* 3,500 km
paved: 3,500 km (2017) (includes 164 km of expressways)
comparison ranking: total 160

Merchant marine: *total:* 3,202 (2023)
by type: bulk carrier 591, container ship 604, general cargo 107, oil tanker 600, other 1,300
comparison ranking: total 8

Ports: *total ports:* 5 (2024)
large: 2
medium: 1
small: 1
very small: 1
ports with oil terminals: 3
key ports: Jurong Island, Keppel - (East Singapore), Pulau Bukom, Pulau Sebarok

MILITARY AND SECURITY

Military and security forces: Singapore Armed Forces (SAF; aka Singapore Defense Force): Singapore Army, Republic of Singapore Navy, Republic of Singapore Air Force (includes air defense), Digital and Intelligence Service

Ministry of Home Affairs: Singapore Police Force (SPF; includes Police Coast Guard and the Gurkha Contingent) (2024)
note 1: the Digital and Intelligence Service (DIS) was stood up as the fourth SAF service in October of 2022
note 2: the Gurkha Contingent of the Singapore Police Force (GCSPF) is a paramilitary unit for riot control and acts as a rapid reaction force
note 3: in 2009, Singapore established a multi-agency national Maritime Security Task Force (MSTF) to work with law enforcement and maritime agencies to guard Singapore's waters, including conducting daily patrols, as well as boarding and escort operations in the Singapore Strait; the MSTF is subordinate to the Singapore Navy

Military expenditures: 3% of GDP (2024 est.)
3% of GDP (2023 est.)
3% of GDP (2022 est.)
3% of GDP (2021 est.)
3% of GDP (2020 est.)
comparison ranking: 35

Military and security service personnel strengths: information varies; approximately 60,000 active-duty troops (45,000 Army; 7,000 Navy; 8,000 Air Force) (2023)

Military equipment inventories and acquisitions: the SAF has a diverse and largely modern mix of domestically produced and imported Western weapons systems; in recent years, France, Germany, and the US have been among the top suppliers of arms; Singapore has the most developed arms industry in Southeast Asia and is also its largest importer of weapons (2024)

Military service age and obligation: 18-21 years of age for compulsory military service for men; 16.5 years of age for voluntary enlistment (with parental consent); 24-month conscript service obligation,

with a reserve obligation to age 40 (enlisted) or age 50 (officers); women are not conscripted, but they are allowed to volunteer for all services and branches, including combat arms (2023)
note 1: under the Enlistment Act, all male Singaporean citizens and permanent residents, unless exempted, are required to enter National Service (NS) upon attaining the age of 18; most NS conscripts serve in the Armed Forces, but some go into the Police Force or Civil Defense Force; conscripts comprise over half of the defense establishment
note 2: women began serving in the SAF in 1986; as of 2022, women made up about 8% of the regular force
note 3: the Singapore Armed Forces (SAF) also has a uniformed volunteer auxiliary branch known as the Volunteer Corps (SAFVC); the SAFVC allows citizens and residents not subject to the National Service obligation, including Singaporean women, first generation permanent residents, and naturalized citizens, to contribute towards Singapore's defense; the volunteers must be 18-45 and physically fit
note 4: members of the Gurkha Contingent (GC) of the Singapore Police Force are mostly recruited from a small number of hill tribes in Nepal; the GC was formed in 1949 originally from selected ex-British Army Gurkhas

Military deployments: maintains permanent training detachments of military personnel in Australia, France, and the US (2023)

Military - note: the SAF's primary responsibility is external defense, but it has trained for certain domestic security operations, including joint deterrence patrols with police in instances of heightened terrorism alerts; the Army includes a "people's defense force," which is a divisional headquarters responsible for homeland security and counterterrorism
the SAF's roots go back to 1854 when the Singapore Volunteer Rifle Corps was formed under colonial rule; the first battalion of regular soldiers, the First Singapore Infantry Regiment, was organized in 1957; the modern SAF was established in 1965 and is today widely viewed as the best equipped military in Southeast Asia
Singapore is a member of the Five Powers Defense Arrangements (FPDA), a series of mutual assistance agreements reached in 1971 embracing Australia, Malaysia, New Zealand, Singapore, and the UK; the FPDA commits the members to consult with one another in the event or threat of an armed attack on any of the members and to mutually decide what measures should be taken, jointly or separately; there is no specific obligation to intervene militarily; Singapore also has close security ties with the US, including granting the US military access, basing, and overflight privileges (2024)

TRANSNATIONAL ISSUES

Refugees and internally displaced persons: *stateless persons:* 1,109 (2022)

Illicit drugs: drug abuse limited because of aggressive law enforcement efforts, including carrying out death sentences; as a transportation and financial services hub, Singapore is vulnerable, despite strict laws and enforcement, as a venue for money laundering

SINT MAARTEN

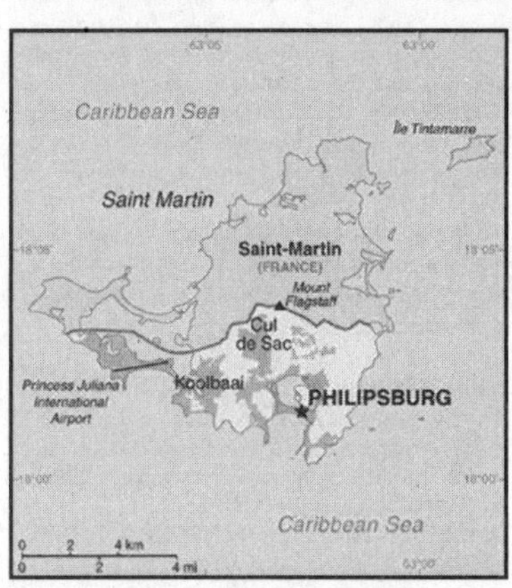

INTRODUCTION

Background: Christopher COLUMBUS claimed Saint Martin for Spain in 1493, naming it after the feast day of St. Martin of Tours, but it was the Dutch who occupied the island in 1631 to exploit its salt deposits. The Spanish retook Saint Martin in 1633, but the Dutch continued to assert their claims. The Spanish finally relinquished the island to the French and Dutch, who divided it between themselves in 1648. The border frequently fluctuated over the next 200 years because of friction between the two countries, with the Dutch eventually holding the smaller portion of the island (about 39%) and adopting the Dutch spelling of the island's name for their territory.

The establishment of cotton, tobacco, and sugar plantations dramatically expanded African slavery on the island in the 18th and 19th centuries; the practice was not abolished in the Dutch half until 1863. The island's economy declined until 1939 when it became a free port; the tourism industry was dramatically expanded beginning in the 1950s. In 1954, Sint Maarten and several other Dutch Caribbean possessions became part of the Kingdom of the Netherlands as the Netherlands Antilles. In a 2000 referendum, the citizens of Sint Maarten voted to become a self-governing country within the Kingdom of the Netherlands, effective in 2010. In 2017, Hurricane Irma hit Saint Martin/Sint Maarten, causing extensive damage to roads, communications, electrical power, and housing; the UN estimated that 90% of the buildings were damaged or destroyed.

GEOGRAPHY

Location: Caribbean, located in the Leeward Islands (northern) group; Dutch part of the island of Saint Martin in the Caribbean Sea; Sint Maarten lies east of the US Virgin Islands

Geographic coordinates: 18 4 N, 63 4 W

Map references: Central America and the Caribbean

Area: *total:* 34 sq km
land: 34 sq km
water: 0 sq km
note: Dutch part of the island of Saint Martin
comparison ranking: total 234

Area - comparative: one-fifth the size of Washington, DC

Land boundaries: *total:* 16 km
border countries (1): Saint Martin (France) 16 km

Coastline: 58.9 km (for entire island)

Maritime claims: *territorial sea:* 12 nm
exclusive economic zone: 200 nm

Climate: tropical marine climate, ameliorated by northeast trade winds, results in moderate temperatures; average rainfall of 150 cm/year; hurricane season stretches from July to November

Terrain: low, hilly terrain, volcanic origin

Elevation: *highest point:* Mount Flagstaff 383 m
lowest point: Caribbean Sea 0 m

Natural resources: fish, salt

Population distribution: most populous areas are Lower Prince's Quarter (north of Philipsburg), followed closely by Cul de Sac

Natural hazards: subject to hurricanes from July to November

Geography - note: *note 1:* the northern border is shared with the French overseas collectivity of Saint Martin; together, these two entities make up the smallest landmass in the world shared by two self-governing states
note 2: Simpson Bay Lagoon (aka Simson Bay Lagoon or The Great Pond) is one of the largest inland lagoons in the West Indies; the border between the French and Dutch halves of the island of Saint Martin runs across the center of the lagoon, which is shared by both entities

PEOPLE AND SOCIETY

Population: *total:* 46,215
male: 22,817
female: 23,398 (2024 est.)
comparison rankings: female 210; male 210; total 210

Ethnic groups: Saint Maarten 29.9%, Dominican Republic 10.2%, Haiti 7.8%, Jamaica 6.6%, Saint Martin 5.9%, Guyana 5%, Dominica 4.4%, Curacao 4.1%, Aruba 3.4%, Saint Kitts and Nevis 2.8%, India 2.6%, Netherlands 2.2%, US 1.6%, Suriname 1.4%, Saint Lucia 1.3%, Anguilla 1.1%, other 8%, unspecified 1.7% (2011 est.)
note: data represent population by country of birth

Languages: English (official) 67.5%, Spanish 12.9%, Creole 8.2%, Dutch (official) 4.2%, Papiamento (a Spanish-Portuguese-Dutch- English dialect) 2.2%, French 1.5%, other 3.5% (2001 est.)

Religions: Protestant 41.9% (Pentecostal 14.7%, Methodist 10.0%, Seventh Day Adventist 6.6%, Baptist 4.7%, Anglican 3.1%, other Protestant 2.8%), Roman Catholic 33.1%, Hindu 5.2%, Christian 4.1%, Jehovah's Witness 1.7%, Evangelical 1.4%, Muslim/Jewish 1.1%, other 1.3% (includes

Buddhist, Sikh, Rastafarian), none 7.9%, no response 2.4% (2011 est.)

Age structure: *0-14 years:* 18.4% (male 4,409/female 4,114)
15-64 years: 66.3% (male 15,158/female 15,496)
65 years and over: 15.2% (2024 est.) (male 3,250/female 3,788)

Dependency ratios: *total dependency ratio:* 27.2
youth dependency ratio: 14.9
elderly dependency ratio: 12.3
potential support ratio: 8.1 (2021)

Median age: *total:* 41 years (2024 est.)
male: 39 years
female: 42.8 years
comparison ranking: total 55

Population growth rate: 1.15% (2024 est.)
comparison ranking: 79

Birth rate: 12.2 births/1,000 population (2024 est.)
comparison ranking: 144

Death rate: 6.4 deaths/1,000 population (2024 est.)
comparison ranking: 141

Net migration rate: 5.7 migrant(s)/1,000 population (2024 est.)
comparison ranking: 16

Population distribution: most populous areas are Lower Prince's Quarter (north of Philipsburg), followed closely by Cul de Sac

Urbanization: *urban population:* 100% of total population (2023)
rate of urbanization: 1.16% annual rate of change (2020-25 est. est.)

Major urban areas - population: 1,327 PHILIPSBURG (capital) (2011)

Sex ratio: *at birth:* 1.05 male(s)/female
0-14 years: 1.07 male(s)/female
15-64 years: 0.98 male(s)/female
65 years and over: 0.86 male(s)/female
total population: 0.98 male(s)/female (2024 est.)

Infant mortality rate: *total:* 7.6 deaths/1,000 live births (2024 est.)
male: 8.4 deaths/1,000 live births
female: 6.8 deaths/1,000 live births
comparison ranking: total 150

Life expectancy at birth: *total population:* 79.7 years (2024 est.)
male: 77.4 years
female: 82.2 years
comparison ranking: total population 62

Total fertility rate: 1.97 children born/woman (2024 est.)
comparison ranking: 107

Gross reproduction rate: 0.96 (2024 est.)

Drinking water source: *improved: total:* 95.1% of population
unimproved: total: 4.9% of population (2017)

Sanitation facility access: *improved:*
total: 98.8% of population
unimproved:
total: 1.2% of population (2017)

School life expectancy (primary to tertiary education): *total:* 12 years
male: 12 years
female: 12 years (2014)

ENVIRONMENT

Environment - current issues: scarcity of potable water (increasing percentage provided by desalination); inadequate solid waste management; pollution from construction, chemical runoff, and sewage harms reefs

Climate: tropical marine climate, ameliorated by northeast trade winds, results in moderate temperatures; average rainfall of 150 cm/year; hurricane season stretches from July to November

Urbanization: *urban population:* 100% of total population (2023)
rate of urbanization: 1.16% annual rate of change (2020-25 est. est.)

GOVERNMENT

Country name: *conventional long form:* Country of Sint Maarten
conventional short form: Sint Maarten
local long form: Land Sint Maarten (Dutch)/ Country of Sint Maarten (English)
local short form: Sint Maarten (Dutch and English)
former: Netherlands Antilles; Curacao and Dependencies
etymology: explorer Christopher COLUMBUS named the island after Saint MARTIN of Tours because the 11 November 1493 day of discovery was the saint's feast day

Government type: parliamentary democracy under a constitutional monarchy

Dependency status: constituent country within the Kingdom of the Netherlands; full autonomy in internal affairs granted in 2010; Dutch Government responsible for defense and foreign affairs

Capital: *name:* Philipsburg
geographic coordinates: 18 1 N, 63 2 W
time difference: UTC-4 (1 hour ahead of Washington, DC, during Standard Time)
etymology: founded and named in 1763 by John PHILIPS, a Scottish captain in the Dutch navy

Administrative divisions: none (part of the Kingdom of the Netherlands)
note: Sint Maarten is one of four constituent countries of the Kingdom of the Netherlands; the other three are the Netherlands, Aruba, and Curacao

Independence: none (part of the Kingdom of the Netherlands)

National holiday: King's Day (birthday of King WILLEM-ALEXANDER), 27 April (1967); note - King's or Queen's Day are observed on the ruling monarch's birthday; celebrated on 26 April if 27 April is a Sunday; local holiday Sint Maarten's Day, 11 November (1985), commemorates the discovery of the island by COLUMBUS on Saint Martin's Day, 11 November 1493; celebrated on both halves of the island

Legal system: based on Dutch civil law system with some English common law influence

Constitution: *history:* previous 1947, 1955; latest adopted 21 July 2010, entered into force 10 October 2010 (regulates governance of Sint Maarten but is subordinate to the Charter for the Kingdom of the Netherlands)
amendments: proposals initiated by the Government or by Parliament; passage requires at least a two-thirds majority of the Parliament membership; passage of amendments relating to fundamental rights, authorities of the governor and of Parliament must include the "views" of the Kingdom of the Netherlands Government prior to ratification by Parliament

Citizenship: see the Netherlands

Suffrage: 18 years of age; universal

Executive branch: *chief of state:* King WILLEM-ALEXANDER of the Netherlands (since 30 April 2013); represented by Governor Ajamu G. BALY (since 10 October 2022)
head of government: Prime Minister Luc MERCELINA (since 3 May 2024)
cabinet: Cabinet nominated by the prime minister and appointed by the governor
elections/appointments: the monarch is hereditary; governor appointed by the monarch for a 6-year term; following parliamentary elections, the leader of the majority party usually elected prime minister by Parliament

Legislative branch: *description:* unicameral Parliament of Sint Maarten (15 seats; members directly elected by proportional representation vote to serve 4-year terms)
elections: last held 11 January 2024 (next to be held in 2028)
election results: percent of vote by party - NA 23.9%, UPP 19.6%, URSM 13.9%, DP 13.6%, PFP 11.9%, NOW 10.3%, other 6.8%; seats by party - NA 4, UPP 3, URSM 2, DP 2, PFP2, NOW 2; composition - men 8, women 7, percentage women 46.7% (additional member is suspended)

Judicial branch: *highest court(s):* Joint Court of Justice of Aruba, Curacao, Sint Maarten, and of Bonaire, Sint Eustatius and Saba or "Joint Court of Justice" (consists of the presiding judge, other members, and their substitutes); final appeals heard by the Supreme Court (in The Hague, Netherlands); note - prior to 2010, the Joint Court of Justice was the Common Court of Justice of the Netherlands Antilles and Aruba
judge selection and term of office: Joint Court judges appointed by the monarch serve for life
subordinate courts: Courts in First Instance

Political parties: Democratic Party or DP
National Alliance or NA
National Opportunity Wealth or NOW
Party for Progress or PFP
Sint Maarten Christian Party or SMCP
Unified Resilient St Maarten Movement or URSM
United People's Party or UPP
United Sint Maarten Party or US Party

International organization participation: Caricom (observer), ILO, Interpol, UNESCO (associate), UPU, WMO

Diplomatic representation in the US: none (represented by the Kingdom of the Netherlands)

Diplomatic representation from the US: *embassy:* the US does not have an embassy in Sint Maarten; the Consul General to Curacao is accredited to Sint Maarten

Flag description: *two equal horizontal bands of red (top) and blue with a white isosceles triangle based on the hoist side; the center of the triangle displays the Sint Maarten coat of arms; the arms consist of an orange-bordered blue shield prominently displaying the white court house in Philipsburg, as well as a bouquet of yellow sage (the national flower) in the upper left, and the silhouette of a Dutch-French friendship monument in the upper right; the shield is surmounted by a yellow rising sun in front of which is a brown pelican in flight; a yellow scroll below the shield bears the motto:* SEMPER PROGREDIENS (Always Progressing); the three main colors are identical to those on the Dutch flag *note:* the flag somewhat resembles that of the Philippines but with the main red and blue bands reversed; the banner more closely evokes the wartime Philippine flag

National symbol(s): brown pelican, yellow sage (flower); national colors: red, white, blue

National anthem: *name:* O Sweet Saint Martin's Land
lyrics/music: Gerard KEMPS
note: the song, written in 1958, is used as an unofficial anthem for the entire island (both French and Dutch sides); as a collectivity of France, in addition to the local anthem, "La Marseillaise" is official on the French side (see France); as a constituent part of the Kingdom of the Netherlands, in addition to the local anthem, "Het Wilhelmus" is official on the Dutch side (see Netherlands)

ECONOMY

Economic overview: high-income, tourism-based Dutch autonomous constituent economy; severe hurricane- and COVID-19-related
economic recessions; multilateral trust fund helping offset economic downturn; no property taxation; re-exporter to Saint Martin

Real GDP (purchasing power parity): $1.912 billion (2023 est.)
$1.849 billion (2022 est.)
$1.684 billion (2021 est.)
note: data in 2021 dollars
comparison ranking: 202

Real GDP growth rate: 3.4% (2023 est.)
9.8% (2022 est.)
4.58% (2021 est.)
note: annual GDP % growth based on constant local currency
comparison ranking: 97

Real GDP per capita: $46,400 (2023 est.)
$45,200 (2022 est.)
$41,400 (2021 est.)
note: data in 2021 dollars
comparison ranking: 50

GDP (official exchange rate): $1.623 billion (2023 est.)
note: data in current dollars at official exchange rate

Inflation rate (consumer prices): 2.19% (2017 est.)
0.11% (2016 est.)
0.33% (2015 est.)
note: annual % change based on consumer prices
comparison ranking: 43

GDP - composition, by sector of origin: *industry:* 6% (2021 est.)
services: 89.3% (2021 est.)
note: figures may not total 100% due to non-allocated consumption not captured in sector-reported data
comparison rankings: services 9; industry 211

Agricultural products: sugar

Industries: tourism, light industry

Industrial production growth rate: 0.46% (2021 est.)
note: annual % change in industrial value added based on constant local currency
comparison ranking: 150

Remittances: 2.9% of GDP (2023 est.)
3.15% of GDP (2022 est.)
3.44% of GDP (2021 est.)
note: personal transfers and compensation between resident and non-resident individuals/households/entities

Current account balance: -$41.64 million (2022 est.)
-$300.6 million (2021 est.)
-$290.458 million (2020 est.)
note: balance of payments - net trade and primary/secondary income in current dollars
comparison ranking: 90

Exports: $1.372 billion (2022 est.)
$790.938 million (2021 est.)
$527.044 million (2020 est.)
note: balance of payments - exports of goods and services in current dollars
comparison ranking: 174

Exports - partners: France 41%, Antigua and Barbuda 18%, US 13%, Morocco 9%, UK 7% (2022)
note: top five export partners based on percentage share of exports

Exports - commodities: gas turbines, scrap iron, jewelry, coconuts/Brazil nuts/cashews, flavored water (2022)
note: top five export commodities based on value in dollars

Imports: $1.318 billion (2022 est.)
$1.003 billion (2021 est.)
$760.824 million (2020 est.)
note: balance of payments - imports of goods and services in current dollars
comparison ranking: 187

Imports - partners: US 77%, Netherlands 7%, France 4%, Trinidad and Tobago 2%, Switzerland 2% (2022)
note: top five import partners based on percentage share of imports

Imports - commodities: refined petroleum, jewelry, pearl products, diamonds, cars (2022)
note: top five import commodities based on value in dollars

Exchange rates: Netherlands Antillean guilders (ANG) per US dollar -

Exchange rates: 1.79 (2023 est.)
1.79 (2022 est.)
1.79 (2021 est.)
1.79 (2020 est.)
1.79 (2019 est.)

ENERGY

Electricity access: *electrification - total population:* 100% (2022 est.)

COMMUNICATIONS

Telephones - mobile cellular: *total subscriptions:* 68,840 (2012 est.)
subscriptions per 100 inhabitants: 196 (2012 est.)
comparison ranking: total subscriptions 199

Telecommunication systems: *general assessment:* generally adequate facilities; growth sectors include mobile telephone and data segments; effective competition; LTE expansion; tourism and telecom sector contribute greatly to the GDP (2018)
domestic: 196 per 100 mobile-cellular teledensity (2012)
international: country code - 1-721; landing points for SMPR-1 and the ECFS submarine cables providing connectivity to the Caribbean; satellite earth stations - 2 Intelsat (Atlantic Ocean) (2019)

Internet country code: .sx; note - IANA has designated .sx for Sint Maarten, but has not yet assigned it to a sponsoring organization

Internet users: *total:* 39,089 (2022)
percent of population: 89.5% (2022)
comparison ranking: total 203

TRANSPORTATION

Airports: 1 (2024)
comparison ranking: 232

Roadways: *total:* 53 km
comparison ranking: total 218

Ports: *total ports:* 2 (2024)
large: 0
medium: 0
small: 2
very small: 0
ports with oil terminals: 1
key ports: Coles Bay Oil Terminal, Philipsburg

MILITARY AND SECURITY

Military and security forces: no regular military forces; Police Department for local law enforcement, supported by the Royal Netherlands Marechaussee (Gendarmerie), the Dutch Caribbean Police Force (Korps Politie Caribisch Nederland, KPCN), and the Dutch Caribbean Coast Guard (DCCG or Kustwacht Caribisch Gebied (KWCARIB)) (2024)

Military - note: defense is the responsibility of the Kingdom of the Netherlands

TRANSNATIONAL ISSUES

Trafficking in persons: tier rating: Tier 3 — Sint Maarten does not fully meet the minimum standards for the elimination of trafficking and is not making significant efforts to do so, therefore, Sint Maarten remained on Tier 3; for more details, go to: https://www.state.gov/reports/2024-trafficking-in-persons-report/sint-maarten/

SLOVAKIA

INTRODUCTION

Background: Slovakia traces its roots to the 9th century state of Great Moravia. The Slovaks then became part of the Hungarian Kingdom, where they remained for the next 1,000 years. After the formation of the dual Austro-Hungarian monarchy in 1867, language and education policies favoring the use of Hungarian (known as "Magyarization") led to a public backlash that boosted Slovak nationalism and strengthened Slovak cultural ties with the closely related Czechs, who fell administratively

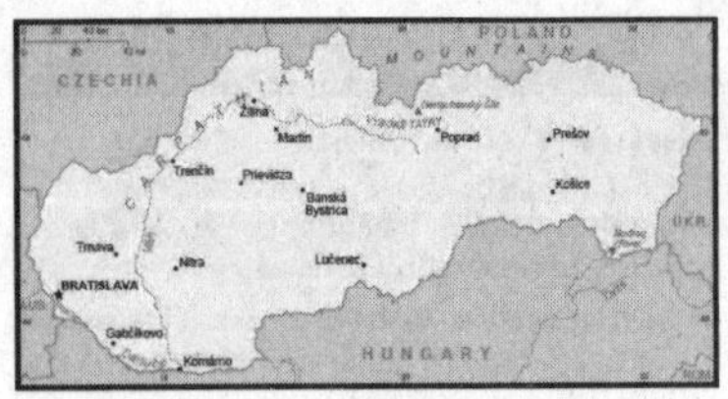

under the Austrian half of the empire. When the Austro-Hungarian Empire dissolved at the end of World War I, the Slovaks joined the Czechs to form Czechoslovakia. During the interwar period, Slovak nationalist leaders pushed for autonomy within Czechoslovakia, and in 1939, in the wake of Germany's annexation of the Sudetenland, the newly established Slovak Republic became a German client state for the remainder of World War II.

After World War II, Czechoslovakia was reconstituted and came under communist rule within Soviet-dominated Eastern Europe. In 1968, Warsaw Pact troops invaded and ended the efforts of Czechoslovakia's leaders to liberalize communist rule and create "socialism with a human face," ushering in a period of repression known as "normalization." The peaceful Velvet Revolution swept the Communist Party from power at the end of 1989 and inaugurated a return to democratic rule and a market economy. On 1 January 1993, Czechoslovakia underwent a nonviolent "velvet divorce" into its two national components, Slovakia and the Czech Republic. Slovakia joined both NATO and the EU in 2004 and the euro zone in 2009.

GEOGRAPHY

Location: Central Europe, south of Poland

Geographic coordinates: 48 40 N, 19 30 E

Map references: Europe

Area: *total:* 49,035 sq km
land: 48,105 sq km
water: 930 sq km
comparison ranking: total 130

Area - comparative: about one and a half times the size of Maryland; about twice the size of New Hampshire

Land boundaries: *total:* 1,587 km
border countries (5): Austria 105 km; Czechia 241 km; Hungary 627 km; Poland 517 km; Ukraine 97 km

Coastline: 0 km (landlocked)

Maritime claims: none (landlocked)

Climate: temperate; cool summers; cold, cloudy, humid winters

Terrain: rugged mountains in the central and northern part and lowlands in the south

Elevation: *highest point:* Gerlachovsky Stit 2,655 m
lowest point: Bodrok River 94 m
mean elevation: 458 m

Natural resources: lignite, small amounts of iron ore, copper and manganese ore; salt; arable land

Land use: *agricultural land:* 40.1% (2018 est.)
arable land: 28.9% (2018 est.)
permanent crops: 0.4% (2018 est.)
permanent pasture: 10.8% (2018 est.)
forest: 40.2% (2018 est.)
other: 19.7% (2018 est.)

Irrigated land: 211 sq km (2015)

Major rivers (by length in km): Dunaj (Danube) (shared with Germany [s], Austria, Hungary, Croatia, Serbia, Bulgaria, Ukraine, Moldova, and Romania [m]) - 2,888 km
note – [s] after country name indicates river source; [m] after country name indicates river mouth

Major watersheds (area sq km): Atlantic Ocean drainage: *(Black Sea)* Danube (795,656 sq km)

Population distribution: a fairly even distribution throughout most of the country; slightly larger concentration in the west in proximity to the Czech border

Natural hazards: flooding

Geography - note: landlocked; most of the country is rugged and mountainous; the Tatra Mountains in the north are interspersed with many scenic lakes and valleys

PEOPLE AND SOCIETY

Population: *total:* 5,563,649
male: 2,684,747
female: 2,878,902 (2024 est.)
comparison rankings: female 117; male 121; total 119

Nationality: *noun:* Slovak(s)
adjective: Slovak

Ethnic groups: Slovak 83.8%, Hungarian 7.8%, Romani 1.2%, other 1.8% (includes Czech, Ruthenian, Ukrainian, Russian, German, Polish), unspecified 5.4% (2021 est.)
note: data represent population by nationality; Romani populations are usually underestimated in official statistics and may represent 7–11% of Slovakia's population

Languages: Slovak (official) 81.8%, Hungarian 8.5%, Roma 1.8%, other 2.2%, unspecified 5.7% (2021 est.)
major-language sample(s):
Svetova Kniha Faktov, nenahraditelny zdroj zakladnej informacie. (Slovak)

Religions: Roman Catholic 55.8%, Evangelical Church of the Augsburg Confession 5.3%, Greek Catholic 4%, Reformed Christian 1.6%, other 3%, none 23.8%, unspecified 6.5% (2021 est.)

Age structure: *0-14 years:* 15.3% (male 444,033/ female 408,902)
15-64 years: 66.5% (male 1,834,359/female 1,867,158)
65 years and over: 18.1% (2024 est.) (male 406,355/ female 602,842)

Dependency ratios: *total dependency ratio:* 49.5
youth dependency ratio: 23.7
elderly dependency ratio: 25.8
potential support ratio: 3.9 (2021 est.)

Median age: *total:* 42.8 years (2024 est.)
male: 41.3 years
female: 44.4 years
comparison ranking: total 39

Population growth rate: -0.08% (2024 est.)
comparison ranking: 202

Birth rate: 10 births/1,000 population (2024 est.)
comparison ranking: 187

Death rate: 11.2 deaths/1,000 population (2024 est.)
comparison ranking: 24

Net migration rate: 0.4 migrant(s)/1,000 population (2024 est.)
comparison ranking: 73

Population distribution: a fairly even distribution throughout most of the country; slightly larger concentration in the west in proximity to the Czech border

Urbanization: *urban population:* 54% of total population (2023)
rate of urbanization: 0.17% annual rate of change (2020-25 est.)

Major urban areas - population: 441,000 BRATISLAVA (capital) (2023)

Sex ratio: *at birth:* 1.07 male(s)/female
0-14 years: 1.09 male(s)/female
15-64 years: 0.98 male(s)/female
65 years and over: 0.67 male(s)/female
total population: 0.93 male(s)/female (2024 est.)

Mother's mean age at first birth: 27.2 years (2020 est.)

Maternal mortality ratio: 5 deaths/100,000 live births (2020 est.)
comparison ranking: 171

Infant mortality rate: *total:* 5.1 deaths/1,000 live births (2024 est.)
male: 5.7 deaths/1,000 live births
female: 4.5 deaths/1,000 live births
comparison ranking: total 174

Life expectancy at birth: *total population:* 77.2 years (2024 est.)
male: 73.7 years
female: 81 years
comparison ranking: total population 94

Total fertility rate: 1.6 children born/woman (2024 est.)
comparison ranking: 184

Gross reproduction rate: 0.77 (2024 est.)

Contraceptive prevalence rate: NA

Drinking water source: *improved: urban:* 100% of population
rural: 100% of population
total: 100% of population

Current health expenditure: 7.2% of GDP (2020)

Physician density: 3.57 physicians/1,000 population (2019)

Hospital bed density: 5.7 beds/1,000 population (2018)

Sanitation facility access: *improved: urban:* 99.9% of population
rural: 100% of population
total: 100% of population

Obesity - adult prevalence rate: 20.5% (2016)
comparison ranking: 98

Alcohol consumption per capita: *total:* 10.3 liters of pure alcohol (2019 est.)
beer: 4.14 liters of pure alcohol (2019 est.)
wine: 2.01 liters of pure alcohol (2019 est.)
spirits: 4.14 liters of pure alcohol (2019 est.)
other alcohols: 0 liters of pure alcohol (2019 est.)
comparison ranking: total 21

Tobacco use: *total:* 31.5% (2020 est.)
male: 37.4% (2020 est.)
female: 25.6% (2020 est.)
comparison ranking: total 25

Currently married women (ages 15-49): 47.9% (2023 est.)

Education expenditures: 4.6% of GDP (2020 est.)
comparison ranking: 94

School life expectancy (primary to tertiary education): *total:* 15 years
male: 14 years
female: 15 years (2020)

ENVIRONMENT

Environment - current issues: air pollution and acid rain present human health risks and damage forests; land erosion caused by agricultural and mining practices; water pollution

Environment - international agreements: *party to:* Air Pollution, Air Pollution-Heavy Metals, Air Pollution-Multi-effect Protocol, Air Pollution-Nitrogen Oxides, Air Pollution-Persistent Organic Pollutants, Air Pollution-Sulphur 85, Air Pollution-Sulphur 94, Air Pollution-Volatile Organic Compounds, Antarctic Treaty, Biodiversity, Climate Change, Climate Change-Kyoto Protocol, Climate Change-Paris Agreement, Comprehensive Nuclear Test Ban, Desertification, Endangered Species, Environmental Modification, Hazardous Wastes, Law of the Sea, Nuclear Test Ban, Ozone Layer Protection, Ship Pollution, Tropical Timber 2006, Wetlands, Whaling
signed, but not ratified: Antarctic-Environmental Protection

Climate: temperate; cool summers; cold, cloudy, humid winters

Urbanization: *urban population:* 54% of total population (2023)
rate of urbanization: 0.17% annual rate of change (2020-25 est.)

Revenue from forest resources: 0.22% of GDP (2018 est.)
comparison ranking: 89

Revenue from coal: 0.01% of GDP (2018 est.)
comparison ranking: 48

Air pollutants: *particulate matter emissions:* 15.89 micrograms per cubic meter (2019 est.)
carbon dioxide emissions: 32.42 megatons (2016 est.)
methane emissions: 4.43 megatons (2020 est.)

Waste and recycling: *municipal solid waste generated annually:* 1.784 million tons (2015 est.)
municipal solid waste recycled annually: 135,941 tons (2015 est.)
percent of municipal solid waste recycled: 7.6% (2015 est.)

Major rivers (by length in km): Dunaj (Danube) (shared with Germany [s], Austria, Hungary, Croatia, Serbia, Bulgaria, Ukraine, Moldova, and Romania [m]) - 2,888 km
note – [s] after country name indicates river source; [m] after country name indicates river mouth

Major watersheds (area sq km): Atlantic Ocean drainage: *(Black Sea)* Danube (795,656 sq km)

Total water withdrawal: *municipal:* 290 million cubic meters (2020 est.)
industrial: 230 million cubic meters (2020 est.)
agricultural: 30 million cubic meters (2020 est.)

Total renewable water resources: 50.1 billion cubic meters (2020 est.)

Geoparks: *total global geoparks and regional networks:* 1
global geoparks and regional networks: Novohrad-Nógrád (includes Hungary) (2023)

GOVERNMENT

Country name: *conventional long form:* Slovak Republic
conventional short form: Slovakia
local long form: Slovenska republika
local short form: Slovensko
etymology: may derive from the medieval Latin word "Slavus" (Slav), which had the local form "Sloven", used since the 13th century to refer to the territory of Slovakia and its inhabitants

Government type: parliamentary republic

Capital: *name:* Bratislava
geographic coordinates: 48 09 N, 17 07 E
time difference: UTC+1 (6 hours ahead of Washington, DC, during Standard Time)
daylight saving time: +1hr, begins last Sunday in March; ends last Sunday in October
etymology: the name was adopted in 1919 after Czechoslovakia gained its independence and may derive from later transliterations of the 9th century military commander, Braslav, or the 11th century Bohemian Duke BRETISLAV I; alternatively, the name may derive from the Slovak words *brat* (brother) and *slava* (glory)

Administrative divisions: 8 regions (kraje, singular - kraj); Banska Bystrica, Bratislava, Kosice, Nitra, Presov, Trencin, Trnava, Zilina

Independence: 1 January 1993 (Czechoslovakia split into the Czech Republic and Slovakia)

National holiday: Constitution Day, 1 September (1992)

Legal system: civil law system based on Austro-Hungarian codes; note - legal code modified to comply with the obligations of Organization on Security and Cooperation in Europe

Constitution: *history:* several previous (preindependence); latest passed by the National Council 1 September 1992, signed 3 September 1992, effective 1 October 1992
amendments: proposed by the National Council; passage requires at least three-fifths majority vote of Council members; amended many times, last in 2020

International law organization participation: accepts compulsory ICJ jurisdiction with reservations; accepts ICCt jurisdiction

Citizenship: *citizenship by birth:* no
citizenship by descent only: at least one parent must be a citizen of Slovakia
dual citizenship recognized: no
residency requirement for naturalization: 5 years

Suffrage: 18 years of age; universal

Executive branch: *chief of state:* President Peter PELLEGRINI (since 15 June 2024)
head of government: Prime Minister Robert FICO (since 25 October 2023)
cabinet: Cabinet appointed by the president on the recommendation of the prime minister
elections/appointments: president directly elected by absolute majority popular vote in 2 rounds if needed for a 5-year term (eligible for a second term); election first round 23 March 2024 with a runoff on 6 April 2024 (next to be held in 2029); following National Council elections (every 4 years), the president designates a prime minister candidate, usually the leader of the party or coalition that wins the most votes, who must win a vote of confidence in the National Council
election results:
2024: Peter PELLEGRINI elected president in the second round; percent of vote in first round - Ivan KORCOK (independent) 42.5%; Peter PELLEGRINI (Hlas-SD) 37%; Stefan HARABIN (independent) 11.7%, other 8.8%; percent of vote in second round Peter PELLEGRINI (Hlas-SD) 53.1%; Ivan KORCOK (independent) 46.9%
2019: Zuzana CAPUTOVA elected president in second round; percent of vote - Zuzana CAPUTOVA (PS) 58.4%, Maros SEFCOVIC (independent) 41.6%

Legislative branch: *description:* unicameral National Council or Narodna Rada (150 seats; members directly elected in a single- and multi-seat constituencies by closed, party-list proportional representation vote; members serve 4-year terms); 76 seats needed for a majority
elections: last held on 30 September 2023 (next to be held by 2027)
election results: percent of vote by party - SMER-SSD 23%, PS 18%, Hlas-SD 14.7%, OL'aNO 8.9%, KDH 6.8%, SaS 6.3%, SNS 5.6%; seats by party - SMER-SSD 42, PS 32, Hlas-SD 27, OL'aNO 16, KDH 12, SaS 11, SNS 10;
composition - men 116, women 34, percentage women 22.7%

Judicial branch: *highest court(s):* Supreme Court of the Slovak Republic (consists of the court president, vice president, and approximately 80 judges organized into criminal, civil, commercial, and administrative divisions with 3- and 5-judge panels); Constitutional Court of the Slovak Republic (consists of 13 judges organized into 3-judge panels)
judge selection and term of office: Supreme Court judge candidates nominated by the Judicial Council of the Slovak Republic, an 18-member self-governing body that includes the Supreme Court chief justice and presidential, governmental, parliamentary, and judiciary appointees; judges appointed by the president serve for life subject to removal by the president at age 65; Constitutional Court judges nominated by the National Council of the Republic and appointed by the president; judges serve 12-year terms
subordinate courts: regional and district civil courts; Special Criminal Court; Higher Military Court; military district courts; Court of Audit;

Political parties: Alliance-Szovetseg or A-S
Christian Union or KÚ
Civic Conservative Party or OKS
Democrats
Direction-Social Democracy or Smer-SSD
For the People or Za Ludi
Freedom and Solidarity or SaS
Life National Party or Zivot–NS (formerly Christian Democracy - Life and Prosperity - Alliance for Slovkia)
New Majority or NOVA
Ordinary People and Independent Personalities - New Majority or OLaNO-NOVA
People's Party Our Slovakia or LSNS
Progressive Slovakia or PS
Republic
Slovak National Party or SNS
Voice - Social Democracy or Hlas-SD
We Are Family or Sme-Rodina (formerly Party of Citizens of Slovakia)

International organization participation: Australia Group, BIS, BSEC (observer), CBSS (observer), CD, CE, CEI, CERN, EAPC, EBRD, ECB, EIB, EMU,

EU, FAO, IAEA, IBRD, ICAO, ICC (national committees), ICRM, IDA, IEA, IFC, IFRCS, ILO, IMF, IMO, IMSO, Interpol, IOC, IOM, IPU, ISO, ITU, ITUC (NGOs), MIGA, NATO, NEA, NSG, OAS (observer), OECD, OIF (observer), OPCW, OSCE, PCA, Schengen Convention, SELEC (observer), UN, UNCTAD, UNESCO, UNFICYP, UNIDO, UNTSO, UNWTO, UPU, Wassenaar Arrangement, WCO, WFTU (NGOs), WHO, WIPO, WMO, WTO, ZC

Diplomatic representation in the US: *chief of mission:* Ambassador Radovan JAVORČÍK (since 18 January 2021)
chancery: 3523 International Court NW, Washington, DC 20008
telephone: [1] (202) 237-1054
FAX: [1] (202) 237-6438
email address and website:
emb.washington@mzv.sk
https://www.mzv.sk/web/washington-en
consulate(s) general: New York

Diplomatic representation from the US: *chief of mission:* Ambassador Gautam A. RANA (since 28 September 2022)
embassy: P.O. Box 309, 814 99 Bratislava
mailing address: 5840 Bratislava Place, Washington DC 20521-5840
telephone: [421] (2) 5443-3338
FAX: [421] (2) 5441-8861
email address and website:
consulbratislava@state.gov
https://sk.usembassy.gov/

Flag description: three equal horizontal bands of white (top), blue, and red derive from the Pan-Slav colors; the Slovakian coat of arms (consisting of a red shield bordered in white and bearing a white double-barred cross of St. Cyril and St. Methodius surmounting three blue hills) is centered over the bands but offset slightly to the hoist side
note: the Pan-Slav colors were inspired by the 19th-century flag of Russia

National symbol(s): double-barred cross (Cross of St. Cyril and St. Methodius) surmounting three peaks; national colors: white, blue, red

National anthem: *name:* "Nad Tatrou sa blyska" (Lightning Over the Tatras)
lyrics/music: Janko MATUSKA/traditional
note: adopted 1993, in use since 1844; music based on the Slovak folk song "Kopala studienku" (She was digging a well)

National heritage: *total World Heritage Sites:* 8 (6 cultural, 2 natural)
selected World Heritage Site locales: Historic Town of Banská Štiavnica (c); Levoča, Spišský Hrad, and the Associated Cultural Monuments (c); Vlkolínec (c); Caves of Aggtelek Karst and Slovak Karst (n); Bardejov Town (c); Ancient and Primeval Beech Forests of the Carpathians (n); Wooden Churches of the Slovak Carpathians (c); Frontiers of the Roman Empire - The Danube Limes (Western Segment) (c)

ECONOMY

Economic overview: high-income EU- and eurozone-member economy; manufacturing and exports led by automotive sector; weakening of anti-corruption laws may impact foreign investment and status of EU funds; influx of foreign labor offsets aging workforce; widening fiscal deficit from social spending and EU-financed public investments

Real GDP (purchasing power parity): $213.053 billion (2023 est.)
$209.705 billion (2022 est.)
$205.856 billion (2021 est.)
note: data in 2021 dollars
comparison ranking: 76

Real GDP growth rate: 1.6% (2023 est.)
1.87% (2022 est.)
4.77% (2021 est.)
note: annual GDP % growth based on constant local currency
comparison ranking: 150

Real GDP per capita: $39,300 (2023 est.)
$38,600 (2022 est.)
$37,800 (2021 est.)
note: data in 2021 dollars
comparison ranking: 64

GDP (official exchange rate): $132.794 billion (2023 est.)
note: data in current dollars at official exchange rate

Inflation rate (consumer prices): 10.53% (2023 est.)
12.77% (2022 est.)
3.15% (2021 est.)
note: annual % change based on consumer prices
comparison ranking: 180

Credit ratings: Fitch rating: A (2020)

Moody's rating: A2 (2012)

Standard & Poors rating: A+ (2015)
note: The year refers to the year in which the current credit rating was first obtained.

GDP - composition, by sector of origin: *agriculture:* 2% (2023 est.)
industry: 32.7% (2023 est.)
services: 56.5% (2023 est.)
note: figures may not total 100% due to non-allocated consumption not captured in sector-reported data
comparison rankings: services 112; industry 51; agriculture 156

GDP - composition, by end use: *household consumption:* 58.9% (2023 est.)
government consumption: 20.1% (2023 est.)
investment in fixed capital: 22% (2023 est.)
investment in inventories: -2.3% (2023 est.)
exports of goods and services: 91.4% (2023 est.)
imports of goods and services: -90.1% (2023 est.)
note: figures may not total 100% due to rounding or gaps in data collection

Agricultural products: wheat, sugar beets, milk, maize, barley, rapeseed, sunflower seeds, potatoes, soybeans, pork (2022)
note: top ten agricultural products based on tonnage

Industries: automobiles; metal and metal products; electricity, gas, coke, oil, nuclear fuel; chemicals, synthetic fibers, wood and paper products; machinery; earthenware and ceramics; textiles; electrical and optical apparatus; rubber products; food and beverages; pharmaceutical

Industrial production growth rate: 15.61% (2023 est.)
note: annual % change in industrial value added based on constant local currency
comparison ranking: 3

Labor force: 2.823 million (2023 est.)
note: number of people ages 15 or older who are employed or seeking work
comparison ranking: 115

Unemployment rate: 5.84% (2023 est.)
6.14% (2022 est.)
6.89% (2021 est.)
note: % of labor force seeking employment
comparison ranking: 116

Youth unemployment rate (ages 15-24): *total:* 19.4% (2023 est.)
male: 21.6% (2023 est.)
female: 15.8% (2023 est.)
note: % of labor force ages 15-24 seeking employment
comparison ranking: total 65

Population below poverty line: 13.7% (2021 est.)
note: % of population with income below national poverty line

Gini Index coefficient - distribution of family income: 24.1 (2021 est.)
note: index (0-100) of income distribution; higher values represent greater inequality
comparison ranking: 152

Average household expenditures: *on food:* 20% of household expenditures (2022 est.)
on alcohol and tobacco: 5% of household expenditures (2022 est.)

Household income or consumption by percentage share: *lowest 10%:* 3.4% (2021 est.)
highest 10%: 19.2% (2021 est.)
note: % share of income accruing to lowest and highest 10% of population

Remittances: 1.69% of GDP (2023 est.)
2% of GDP (2022 est.)
2.05% of GDP (2021 est.)
note: personal transfers and compensation between resident and non-resident individuals/households/entities

Budget: *revenues:* $43.882 billion (2022 est.)
expenditures: $46.056 billion (2022 est.)
note: central government revenues (excluding grants) and expenses converted to US dollars at average official exchange rate for year indicated

Public debt: 64.51% of GDP (2022 est.)
note: central government debt as a % of GDP
comparison ranking: 65

Taxes and other revenues: 19.5% (of GDP) (2022 est.)
note: central government tax revenue as a % of GDP
comparison ranking: 90

Current account balance: -$2.088 billion (2023 est.)
-$8.452 billion (2022 est.)
-$4.655 billion (2021 est.)
note: balance of payments - net trade and primary/secondary income in current dollars
comparison ranking: 161

Exports: $121.238 billion (2023 est.)
$114.678 billion (2022 est.)
$109.565 billion (2021 est.)
note: balance of payments - exports of goods and services in current dollars
comparison ranking: 45

Exports - partners: Germany 20%, Czechia 11%, Hungary 9%, Poland 7%, France 6% (2022)
note: top five export partners based on percentage share of exports

Exports - commodities: cars, vehicle parts/accessories, video displays, broadcasting equipment, electricity (2022)
note: top five export commodities based on value in dollars

Imports: $118.869 billion (2023 est.)
$120.622 billion (2022 est.)
$109.265 billion (2021 est.)
note: balance of payments - imports of goods and services in current dollars

comparison ranking: 44

Imports - partners: Czechia 18%, Germany 15%, Poland 9%, Russia 7%, Austria 7% (2022)
note: top five import partners based on percentage share of imports

Imports - commodities: vehicle parts/accessories, broadcasting equipment, natural gas, cars, electricity (2022)
note: top five import commodities based on value in dollars

Reserves of foreign exchange and gold: $11.288 billion (2023 est.)
$10.28 billion (2022 est.)
$9.61 billion (2021 est.)
note: holdings of gold (year-end prices)/foreign exchange/special drawing rights in current dollars
comparison ranking: 88

Exchange rates: euros (EUR) per US dollar -

Exchange rates: 0.925 (2023 est.)
0.95 (2022 est.)
0.845 (2021 est.)
0.876 (2020 est.)
0.893 (2019 est.)

ENERGY

Electricity access: *electrification - total population:* 100% (2022 est.)

Electricity: *installed generating capacity:* 8.029 million kW (2022 est.)
consumption: 26.372 billion kWh (2022 est.)
exports: 15.336 billion kWh (2022 est.)
imports: 16.709 billion kWh (2022 est.)
transmission/distribution losses: 1.236 billion kWh (2022 est.)
comparison rankings: transmission/distribution losses 108; imports 14; exports 20; consumption 69; installed generating capacity 73

Electricity generation sources: *fossil fuels:* 17.8% of total installed capacity (2022 est.)
nuclear: 60.7% of total installed capacity (2022 est.)
solar: 2.5% of total installed capacity (2022 est.)
hydroelectricity: 11.8% of total installed capacity (2022 est.)
biomass and waste: 7.2% of total installed capacity (2022 est.)

Nuclear energy: Number of operational nuclear reactors: 5 (2023)

Number of nuclear reactors under construction: 1 (2023)

Net capacity of operational nuclear reactors: 2.31GW (2023 est.)

Percent of total electricity production: 61.3% (2023 est.)

Number of nuclear reactors permanently shut down: 3 (2023)

Coal: *production:* 2.343 million metric tons (2022 est.)
consumption: 5.794 million metric tons (2022 est.)
exports: 20,000 metric tons (2022 est.)
imports: 3.414 million metric tons (2022 est.)
proven reserves: 19 million metric tons (2022 est.)

Petroleum: *total petroleum production:* 7,000 bbl/day (2023 est.)
refined petroleum consumption: 94,000 bbl/day (2023 est.)
crude oil estimated reserves: 9 million barrels (2021 est.)

Natural gas: *production:* 52.556 million cubic meters (2022 est.)
consumption: 60.424 million cubic meters (2022 est.)
imports: 6.241 billion cubic meters (2022 est.)
proven reserves: 14.158 billion cubic meters (2021 est.)

Carbon dioxide emissions: 21.405 million metric tonnes of CO_2 (2022 est.)
from coal and metallurgical coke: 9.253 million metric tonnes of CO_2 (2022 est.)
from petroleum and other liquids: 12.033 million metric tonnes of CO_2 (2022 est.)
from consumed natural gas: 118,000 metric tonnes of CO_2 (2022 est.)
comparison ranking: total emissions 84

Energy consumption per capita: 93.681 million Btu/person (2022 est.)
comparison ranking: 57

COMMUNICATIONS

Telephones - fixed lines: *total subscriptions:* 541,000 (2022 est.)
subscriptions per 100 inhabitants: 10 (2022 est.)
comparison ranking: total subscriptions 88

Telephones - mobile cellular: *total subscriptions:* 7.445 million (2022 est.)
subscriptions per 100 inhabitants: 132 (2022 est.)
comparison ranking: total subscriptions 108

Telecommunication systems: *general assessment:* the broadband market has shown steady growth in recent years; fiber has become the principal platform for fixed broadband services, followed by DSL; the cable sector is a distant third in terms of subscribers, though cable is particularly strong in urban areas; mobile broadband access and content services are developing rapidly in line with operators having upgraded their networks; the regulator prepared the groundwork for 5G services in line with European Union requirements, with concessions in the 3.5GHz range followed by those in the 700MHz, 900MHz and 1800MHz bands; 5G was launched in late 2021 and is expected to cover about a fifth of the population by the end of 2022 (2024)
domestic: fixed-line is 10 per 100 and mobile-cellular is 132 per 100 tele density (2022)
international: country code - 421; 3 international exchanges (1 in Bratislava and 2 in Banska Bystrica) are available; Slovakia is participating in several international telecommunications projects that will increase the availability of external services; connects to DREAM cable (2017)

Broadcast media: state-owned public broadcaster, Radio and Television of Slovakia (RTVS), operates 2 national TV stations and multiple national and regional radio networks; roughly 50 privately owned TV stations operating nationally, regionally, and locally; about 40% of households are connected to multi-channel cable or satellite TV; 32 privately owned radio stations

Internet country code: .sk

Internet users: *total:* 4.806 million (2021 est.)
percent of population: 89% (2021 est.)
comparison ranking: total 98

Broadband - fixed subscriptions: *total:* 1,701,561 (2020 est.)
subscriptions per 100 inhabitants: 31 (2020 est.)
comparison ranking: total 63

TRANSPORTATION

National air transport system: *number of registered air carriers:* 4 (2020)
inventory of registered aircraft operated by air carriers: 45

Civil aircraft registration country code prefix: OM

Airports: 114 (2024)
comparison ranking: 47

Heliports: 2 (2024)

Pipelines: 2,270 km gas transmission pipelines, 6,278 km high-pressure gas distribution pipelines, 27,023 km mid- and low-pressure gas distribution pipelines (2016), 510 km oil (2015) (2016)

Railways: *total:* 3,627 km (2020) 1,585 km electrified
comparison ranking: total 53

Roadways: *total:* 45,106 km (2022)
comparison ranking: total 86

Waterways: 172 km (2012) (on Danube River)
comparison ranking: 109

MILITARY AND SECURITY

Military and security forces: Armed Forces of the Slovak Republic (Ozbrojene Sily Slovenskej Republiky): Land Forces (Slovenské Pozemné Sily), Air Forces (Slovenské Vzdušné Sily), Special Operations Forces (Sily Pre Speciálne Operácie)

Ministry of Interior: Slovak Police Force (SPF or Policajný Zbor) (2024)
note: the SPF has sole responsibility for internal and border security

Military expenditures: 2% of GDP (2024 est.)
2.1% of GDP (2023)
1.8% of GDP (2022)
1.7% of GDP (2021)
1.9% of GDP (2020)
comparison ranking: 69

Military and security service personnel strengths: approximately 15,000 active-duty personnel (8,000 Land Forces; 4,000 Air Forces; 3,000 other, including staff, special operations, and support forces) (2024)

Military equipment inventories and acquisitions: the military's inventory consists mostly of Soviet-era platforms; in recent years it has imported limited quantities of more modern, NATO-compatible equipment, particularly from Italy and the US (2024)

Military service age and obligation: 18-30 years of age for voluntary military service for men and women; conscription in peacetime suspended in 2004 (2023)
note: as of 2021, women made up around 12% of the military's full-time personnel

Military deployments: 240 Cyprus (UNFICYP); up to 150 Latvia (NATO) (2024)

Military - note: the Slovak military was created from the Czechoslovak Army after the dissolution of Czechoslovakia in January 1993; it is responsible for external defense and fulfilling Slovakia's commitments to European and international security; Slovakia has been a member of both the EU and NATO since 2004; a key focus of the Slovak military is fulfilling the country's security responsibilities to NATO, including modernizing and acquiring NATO-compatible equipment, participating in training exercises, and providing forces for security missions such as NATO's Enhanced Forward Presence in the Baltic States; since 2022, Slovakia has hosted a

NATO ground force battlegroup comprised of troops from Czechia, Germany, the Netherlands, Poland, Slovakia, Slovenia, and the US as part of the NATO effort to boost the defenses of Eastern Europe since the Russian invasion of Ukraine; Slovakia also contributes to EU and UN peacekeeping missions
the Slovak Air Force has only a handful of fighter aircraft and is assisted by NATO's air policing mission over Slovakia, which includes fighter aircraft from Czechia and Poland; in 2022, Slovakia signed a defense agreement with the US that allows the US to use two Slovak military air bases (2024)

SPACE

Space agency/agencies: no national government agency; the Slovak Space Office is responsible for inter-ministerial political coordination and multilateral international cooperation; it serves as the official national contact point for international cooperation between space agencies, offices, associations, businesses, and research entities, and is part of the Ministry of Education, Science, Research, and Sport (2023)

Space program overview: focused on the development of satellites, satellite subcomponents, and other space-related technologies; as a member state of the EU, it is actively involved in all key components of the EU space program, and Slovak researchers actively participate in a variety of EU and/or European Space Agency (ESA) space missions including the Galileo global navigational system program, Copernicus Earth observation satellite program, Rosetta comet probe, BepiColombo (Mercury planetary orbiter), and Jupiter Icy Moons Explorer (JUICE) mission; has more than 40 established companies actively involved in the space sector (2023)

note: further details about the key activities, programs, and milestones of the country's space program, as well as government spending estimates on the space sector, appear in the Space Programs reference guide

TRANSNATIONAL ISSUES

Refugees and internally displaced persons: *refugees (country of origin):* 117,265 (Ukraine) (as of 14 April 2024)
stateless persons: 2,940 (2022)

Illicit drugs: transshipment point for Southwest Asian heroin bound for Western Europe; producer of synthetic drugs for regional market; consumer of MDMA (ecstasy)

SLOVENIA

INTRODUCTION

Background: The Slovene lands were part of the Austro-Hungarian Empire until the latter's dissolution at the end of World War I. In 1918, Slovenia became part of the Kingdom of Serbs, Croats, and Slovenes, which was renamed Yugoslavia in 1929. After World War II, Slovenia joined Bosnia and Herzegovina, Croatia, Macedonia, Montenegro, and Serbia as one of the constituent republics in the new Socialist Federal Republic of Yugoslavia (SFRY). In 1990, Slovenia held its first multiparty elections, as well as a referendum on independence. Serbia responded with an economic blockade and military action, but after a short 10-day war, Slovenia declared independence in 1991. Slovenia acceded to both NATO and the EU in the spring of 2004; it joined the euro zone and the Schengen Area in 2007.

GEOGRAPHY

Location: south Central Europe, Julian Alps between Austria and Croatia

Geographic coordinates: 46 07 N, 14 49 E

Map references: Europe

Area: *total:* 20,273 sq km
land: 20,151 sq km
water: 122 sq km
comparison ranking: total 154

Area - comparative: slightly smaller than New Jersey

Land boundaries: *total:* 1,211 km
border countries (4): Austria 299 km; Croatia 600 km; Hungary 94 km; Italy 218 km

Coastline: 46.6 km

Maritime claims: *territorial sea:* 12 nm

Climate: Mediterranean climate on the coast, continental climate with mild to hot summers and cold winters in the plateaus and valleys to the east

Terrain: a short southwestern coastal strip of Karst topography on the Adriatic; an alpine mountain region lies adjacent to Italy and Austria in the north; mixed mountains and valleys with numerous rivers to the east

Elevation: *highest point:* Triglav 2,864 m
lowest point: Adriatic Sea 0 m
mean elevation: 492 m

Natural resources: lignite, lead, zinc, building stone, hydropower, forests

Land use: *agricultural land:* 22.8% (2018 est.)
arable land: 8.4% (2018 est.)
permanent crops: 1.3% (2018 est.)
permanent pasture: 13.1% (2018 est.)
forest: 62.3% (2018 est.)
other: 14.9% (2018 est.)

Irrigated land: 39 sq km (2020)

Major watersheds (area sq km): Atlantic Ocean drainage: *(Black Sea)* Danube (795,656 sq km)

Population distribution: a fairly even distribution throughout most of the country, with urban areas attracting larger and denser populations; pockets in the mountainous northwest exhibit less density than elsewhere

Natural hazards: flooding; earthquakes

Geography - note: despite its small size, this eastern Alpine country controls some of Europe's major transit routes

PEOPLE AND SOCIETY

Population: *total:* 2,097,893
male: 1,051,044
female: 1,046,849 (2024 est.)
comparison rankings: female 150; male 150; total 151

Nationality: *noun:* Slovene(s)
adjective: Slovenian

Ethnic groups: Slovene 83.1%, Serb 2%, Croat 1.8%, Bosniak 1.1%, other or unspecified 12% (2002 est.)

Languages: Slovene (official) 87.7%, Croatian 2.8%, Serbo-Croatian 1.8%, Bosnian 1.6%, Serbian 1.6%, Hungarian 0.4% (official, only in municipalities where Hungarian nationals reside), Italian 0.2% (official, only in municipalities where Italian nationals reside), other or unspecified 3.9% (2002 est.)
major-language sample(s):
Svetovni informativni zvezek - neobhoden vir osnovnih informacij. (Slovene)

Religions: Catholic 69%, Orthodox 4%, Muslim 3%, Christian 1%, other 3%, atheist 14%, non-believer/agnostic 4%, refused to answer 2% (2019 est.)

Age structure: *0-14 years:* 14.3% (male 153,852/female 146,628)
15-64 years: 62.5% (male 683,573/female 627,788)
65 years and over: 23.2% (2024 est.) (male 213,619/female 272,433)

Dependency ratios: *total dependency ratio:* 55.5
youth dependency ratio: 23.6
elderly dependency ratio: 31.9
potential support ratio: 3.1 (2021 est.)

Median age: *total:* 46.3 years (2024 est.)
male: 45 years
female: 47.9 years
comparison ranking: total 12

Population growth rate: -0.1% (2024 est.)
comparison ranking: 203

Birth rate: 8 births/1,000 population (2024 est.)
comparison ranking: 215

Death rate: 10.5 deaths/1,000 population (2024 est.)
comparison ranking: 29

Net migration rate: 1.5 migrant(s)/1,000 population (2024 est.)

comparison ranking: 58

Population distribution: a fairly even distribution throughout most of the country, with urban areas attracting larger and denser populations; pockets in the mountainous northwest exhibit less density than elsewhere

Urbanization: *urban population:* 56.1% of total population (2023)
rate of urbanization: 0.54% annual rate of change (2020-25 est.)

Major urban areas - population: 286,000 LJUBLJANA (capital) (2018)

Sex ratio: *at birth:* 1.04 male(s)/female
0-14 years: 1.05 male(s)/female
15-64 years: 1.09 male(s)/female
65 years and over: 0.78 male(s)/female
total population: 1 male(s)/female (2024 est.)

Mother's mean age at first birth: 29 years (2020 est.)

Maternal mortality ratio: 5 deaths/100,000 live births (2020 est.)
comparison ranking: 172

Infant mortality rate: *total:* 1.5 deaths/1,000 live births (2024 est.)
male: 1.6 deaths/1,000 live births
female: 1.4 deaths/1,000 live births
comparison ranking: total 227

Life expectancy at birth: *total population:* 82.2 years (2024 est.)
male: 79.4 years
female: 85.2 years
comparison ranking: total population 32

Total fertility rate: 1.6 children born/woman (2024 est.)
comparison ranking: 185

Gross reproduction rate: 0.79 (2024 est.)

Contraceptive prevalence rate: NA

Drinking water source: *improved: urban:* NA
total: 99.5% of population
unimproved: urban: NA
rural: NA
total: 0.5% of population (2020 est.)

Current health expenditure: 9.5% of GDP (2020)

Physician density: 3.28 physicians/1,000 population (2019)

Hospital bed density: 4.4 beds/1,000 population (2018)

Sanitation facility access: *improved: urban:* NA
rural: NA
total: 99% of population
unimproved: urban: NA
rural: NA
total: 1% of population (2020 est.)

Obesity - adult prevalence rate: 20.2% (2016)
comparison ranking: 104

Alcohol consumption per capita: *total:* 11.05 liters of pure alcohol (2019 est.)
beer: 4.54 liters of pure alcohol (2019 est.)
wine: 5.26 liters of pure alcohol (2019 est.)
spirits: 1.26 liters of pure alcohol (2019 est.)
other alcohols: 0 liters of pure alcohol (2019 est.)
comparison ranking: total 10

Tobacco use: *total:* 22% (2020 est.)
male: 24.4% (2020 est.)
female: 19.6% (2020 est.)
comparison ranking: total 73

Currently married women (ages 15-49): 46.4% (2023 est.)

Education expenditures: 5.8% of GDP (2020 est.)
comparison ranking: 49

Literacy: *definition:* NA
total population: 99.7%
male: 99.7%
female: 99.7% (2015)

School life expectancy (primary to tertiary education): *total:* 18 years
male: 17 years
female: 18 years (2020)

ENVIRONMENT

Environment - current issues: air pollution from road traffic, domestic heating (wood buring), power generation, and industry; water pollution; biodiversity protection

Environment - international agreements: *party to:* Air Pollution, Air Pollution-Heavy Metals, Air Pollution-Multi-effect Protocol, Air Pollution-Nitrogen Oxides, Air Pollution-Persistent Organic Pollutants, Air Pollution-Sulphur 94, Antarctic Treaty, Biodiversity, Climate Change, Climate Change-Kyoto Protocol, Climate Change-Paris Agreement, Comprehensive Nuclear Test Ban, Desertification, Endangered Species, Environmental Modification, Hazardous Wastes, Law of the Sea, Marine Dumping-London Convention, Marine Dumping-London Protocol, Nuclear Test Ban, Ozone Layer Protection, Ship Pollution, Tropical Timber 2006, Wetlands, Whaling
signed, but not ratified: none of the selected agreements

Climate: Mediterranean climate on the coast, continental climate with mild to hot summers and cold winters in the plateaus and valleys to the east

Urbanization: *urban population:* 56.1% of total population (2023)
rate of urbanization: 0.54% annual rate of change (2020-25 est.)

Revenue from forest resources: 0.2% of GDP (2018 est.)
comparison ranking: 93

Revenue from coal: 0.03% of GDP (2018 est.)
comparison ranking: 41

Air pollutants: *particulate matter emissions:* 14.08 micrograms per cubic meter (2019 est.)
carbon dioxide emissions: 12.63 megatons (2016 est.)
methane emissions: 2.1 megatons (2020 est.)

Waste and recycling: *municipal solid waste generated annually:* 926,000 tons (2015 est.)
municipal solid waste recycled annually: 430,034 tons (2015 est.)
percent of municipal solid waste recycled: 46.4% (2015 est.)

Major watersheds (area sq km): Atlantic Ocean drainage: *(Black Sea)* Danube (795,656 sq km)

Total water withdrawal: *municipal:* 170 million cubic meters (2020 est.)
industrial: 830 million cubic meters (2020 est.)
agricultural: 3.9 million cubic meters (2017 est.)

Total renewable water resources: 31.87 billion cubic meters (2020 est.)

Geoparks: *total global geoparks and regional networks:* 2
global geoparks and regional networks: Idrija; Karawanken / Karavanke (includes Austria) (2023)

GOVERNMENT

Country name: *conventional long form:* Republic of Slovenia
conventional short form: Slovenia
local long form: Republika Slovenija
local short form: Slovenija
former: People's Republic of Slovenia, Socialist Republic of Slovenia
etymology: the country's name means "Land of the Slavs" in Slovene

Government type: parliamentary republic

Capital: *name:* Ljubljana
geographic coordinates: 46 03 N, 14 31 E
time difference: UTC+1 (6 hours ahead of Washington, DC, during Standard Time)
daylight saving time: +1hr, begins last Sunday in March; ends last Sunday in October
etymology: likely related to the Slavic root "ljub", meaning "to like" or "to love"; by tradition, the name is related to the Slovene word "ljubljena" meaning "beloved"

Administrative divisions: 200 municipalities (obcine, singular - obcina) and 12 urban municipalities (mestne obcine, singular - mestna obcina)
municipalities: Ajdovscina, Ankaran, Apace, Beltinci, Benedikt, Bistrica ob Sotli, Bled, Bloke, Bohinj, Borovnica, Bovec, Braslovce, Brda, Brezice, Brezovica, Cankova, Cerklje na Gorenjskem, Cerknica, Cerkno, Cerkvenjak, Cirkulane, Crensovci, Crna na Koroskem, Crnomelj, Destrnik, Divaca, Dobje, Dobrepolje, Dobrna, Dobrova-Polhov Gradec, Dobrovnik/Dobronak, Dolenjske Toplice, Dol pri Ljubljani, Domzale, Dornava, Dravograd, Duplek, Gorenja Vas-Poljane, Gorisnica, Gorje, Gornja Radgona, Gornji Grad, Gornji Petrovci, Grad, Grosuplje, Hajdina, Hoce-Slivnica, Hodos, Horjul, Hrastnik, Hrpelje-Kozina, Idrija, Ig, Ilirska Bistrica, Ivancna Gorica, Izola/Isola, Jesenice, Jezersko, Jursinci, Kamnik, Kanal ob Soci, Kidricevo, Kobarid, Kobilje, Kocevje, Komen, Komenda, Kosanjevica na Krki, Kostel, Kozje, Kranjska Gora, Krizevci, Kungota, Kuzma, Lasko, Lenart, Lendava/Lendva, Litija, Ljubno, Ljutomer, Log- Dragomer, Logatec, Loska Dolina, Loski Potok, Lovrenc na Pohorju, Luce, Lukovica, Majsperk, Makole, Markovci, Medvode, Menges, Metlika, Mezica, Miklavz na Dravskem Polju, Miren-Kostanjevica, Mirna, Mirna Pec, Mislinja, Mokronog-Trebelno, Moravce, Moravske Toplice, Mozirje, Muta, Naklo, Nazarje, Odranci, Oplotnica, Ormoz, Osilnica, Pesnica, Piran/Pirano, Pivka, Podcetrtek, Podlehnik, Podvelka, Poljcane, Polzela, Postojna, Prebold, Preddvor, Prevalje, Puconci, Race-Fram, Radece, Radenci, Radlje ob Dravi, Radovljica, Ravne na Koroskem, Razkrizje, Recica ob Savinji, Rence-Vogrsko, Ribnica, Ribnica na Pohorju, Rogaska Slatina, Rogasovci, Rogatec, Ruse, Salovci, Selnica ob Dravi, Semic, Sempeter-Vrtojba, Sencur, Sentilj, Sentjernej, Sentjur, Sentrupert, Sevnica, Sezana, Skocjan, Skofja Loka, Skofljica, Slovenska Bistrica, Slovenske Konjice, Smarje pri Jelsah, Smarjeske Toplice, Smartno ob Paki, Smartno pri Litiji, Sodrazica, Solcava, Sostanj, Sredisce ob Dravi, Starse, Store, Straza, Sveta Ana, Sveta Trojica v Slovenskih Goricah, Sveti Andraz v Slovenskih Goricah, Sveti Jurij ob Scavnici, Sveti Jurij v Slovenskih Goricah, Sveti Tomaz, Tabor, Tisina, Tolmin, Trbovlje, Trebnje, Trnovska Vas, Trzic, Trzin, Turnisce, Velika Polana, Velike Lasce, Verzej, Videm, Vipava, Vitanje, Vodice, Vojnik, Vransko, Vrhnika,

Vuzenica, Zagorje ob Savi, Zalec, Zavrc, Zelezniki, Zetale, Ziri, Zirovnica, Zrece, Zuzemberk
urban municipalities: Celje, Koper, Kranj, Krsko, Ljubljana, Maribor, Murska Sobota, Nova Gorica, Novo Mesto, Ptuj, Slovenj Gradec, Velenje

Independence: 25 June 1991 (from Yugoslavia)

National holiday: Independence Day/Statehood Day, 25 June (1991)

Legal system: civil law system

Constitution: *history:* previous 1974 (preindependence); latest passed by Parliament 23 December 1991
amendments: proposed by at least 20 National Assembly members, by the government, or by petition of at least 30,000 voters; passage requires at least two-thirds majority vote by the Assembly; referendum required if agreed upon by at least 30 Assembly members; passage in a referendum requires participation of a majority of eligible voters and a simple majority of votes cast; amended several times, last in 2016

International law organization participation: has not submitted an ICJ jurisdiction declaration; accepts ICCt jurisdiction

Citizenship: *citizenship by birth:* no
citizenship by descent only: at least one parent must be a citizen of Slovenia; both parents if the child is born outside of Slovenia
dual citizenship recognized: yes, for select cases
residency requirement for naturalization: 10 years, the last 5 of which have been continuous

Suffrage: 18 years of age; universal

Executive branch: *chief of state:* President Natasa PIRC MUSAR (since 23 December 2022)
head of government: Prime Minister Robert GOLOB (since 1 June 2022)
cabinet: Council of Ministers nominated by the prime minister, elected by the National Assembly
elections/appointments: president directly elected by absolute majority popular vote in 2 rounds if needed for a 5-year term (eligible for a second consecutive term); election last held on 23 October 2022 with a runoff on 13 November 2022 (next to be held in 2027); following National Assembly elections, the leader of the majority party or majority coalition usually nominated prime minister by the president and elected by the National Assembly
election results:
2022: Natasa PIRC MUSAR elected president in second round: percent of vote in first round - Anze LOGAR (SDS) 34%, Natasa PIRC MUSAR (independent) 26.9%, Milan BRGLEZ (SD) 15.5%, Vladimir PREBILIC (independent) 10.6%, Sabina SENCAR (Resni.ca) 5.9%, Janez CIGLER KRALJ (NSi) 4.4%, other 2.7%; percent of vote in second round - Natasa PIRC MUSAR 53.9%, Anze LOGAR 46.1%; Robert GOLOB (GS) elected prime minister on 25 May 2022, National Assembly vote - 54-30
2017: Borut PAHOR reelected president in second round; percent of vote in first round - Borut PAHOR (independent) 47.1%, Marjan SAREC (Marjan Sarec List) 25%, Romana TOMC (SDS) 13.7%, Ljudmila NOVAK (NSi) 7.2%, other 7%; percent of vote in second round - Borut PAHOR 52.9%, Marjan SAREC 47.1%

Legislative branch: *description:* bicameral Parliament consists of:
National Council (State Council) or Drzavni Svet (40 seats; members indirectly elected by an electoral college to serve 5- year terms); note - the Council is primarily an advisory body with limited legislative powers
National Assembly or Drzavni Zbor (90 seats; 88 members directly elected in single-seat constituencies by proportional representation vote and 2 directly elected in special constituencies for Italian and Hungarian minorities by simple majority vote; members serve 4-year terms)
elections: National Council - last held on 24 November 2022 (next to be held in 2027) National Assembly - last held on 24 April 2022 (next to be held in 2026)
election results: National Council - percent of vote by party - NA; seats by party - NA; composition - men 33, women 7, percentage women 17.5%
National Assembly - percent of vote by party - GS 34.5%, SDS 23.5%, NSi 6.9%, SD 6.7%, Levica 4.4%, other 24%; seats by party - GS 41, SDS 27, NSi 8, SD 7, Levica 5; composition - men 56, women 34, percentage women 37.8%; total Parliament percentage women 31.5%

Judicial branch: *highest court(s):* Supreme Court (consists of the court president and 37 judges organized into civil, criminal, commercial, labor and social security, administrative, and registry departments); Constitutional Court (consists of the court president, vice president, and 7 judges)
judge selection and term of office: Supreme Court president and vice president appointed by the National Assembly upon the proposal of the Minister of Justice based on the opinions of the Judicial Council, an 11-member independent body elected by the National Assembly from proposals submitted by the president, attorneys, law universities, and sitting judges; other Supreme Court judges elected by the National Assembly from candidates proposed by the Judicial Council; Supreme Court judges serve for life; Constitutional Court judges appointed by the National Assembly from nominations by the president of the republic; Constitutional Court president selected from among its own membership for a 3-year term; other judges elected for single 9-year terms
subordinate courts: county, district, regional, and high courts; specialized labor-related and social courts; Court of Audit; Administrative Court

Political parties: Democratic Party of Pensioners of Slovenia or DeSUS
Freedom Movement or GS (formerly Greens Actions Party or Z.DEJ)
List of Marjan Sarec or LMS
New Slovenia - Christian Democrats or NSi
Party of Alenka Bratusek or SAB (formerly Alliance of Social Liberal Democrats or ZSD and before that Alliance of Alenka Bratusek or ZaAB)
Resni.ca
Slovenian Democratic Party or SDS (formerly the Social Democratic Party of Slovenia or SDSS)
Slovenian National Party or SNS
Social Democrats or SD
The Left or Levica (successor to United Left or ZL)

International organization participation: Australia Group, BIS, CD, CE, CEI, EAPC, EBRD, ECB, EIB, EMU, ESA (cooperating state), EU, FAO, IADB, IAEA, IBRD, ICAO, ICC (national committees), ICCt, ICRM, IDA, IFC, IFRCS, IHO, ILO, IMF, IMO, Interpol, IOC, IOM, IPU, ISO, ITU, MIGA, NATO, NEA, NSG, OAS (observer), OECD, OIF (observer), OPCW, OSCE, PCA, Schengen Convention, SELEC, UN, UNCTAD, UNESCO, UNHCR, UNIDO, UNIFIL, UNTSO, UNWTO, UPU, Wassenaar Arrangement, WCO, WHO, WIPO, WMO, WTO, ZC

Diplomatic representation in the US: *chief of mission:* Ambassador Iztok MIROŠIČ (since 15 September 2023)
chancery: 2410 California Street NW, Washington, DC 20008
telephone: [1] (202) 386-6611
FAX: [1] (202) 386-6633
email address and website:
sloembassy.washington@gov.si
http://www.washington.embassy.si/
consulate(s) general: Cleveland (OH)

Diplomatic representation from the US: *chief of mission:* Ambassador Jamie L. HARPOOTLIAN (since 17 February 2022)
embassy: Presernova 31, 1000 Ljubljana
mailing address: 7140 Ljubljana Place, Washington, DC 20521-7140
telephone: [386] (1) 200-5500
FAX: [386] (1) 200-5555
email address and website:
LjubljanaACS@state.gov
https://si.usembassy.gov/

Flag description: three equal horizontal bands of white (top), blue, and red, derive from the medieval coat of arms of the Duchy of Carniola; the Slovenian seal (a shield with the image of Triglav, Slovenia's highest peak, in white against a blue background at the center; beneath it are two wavy blue lines depicting seas and rivers, and above it are three six-pointed stars arranged in an inverted triangle, which are taken from the coat of arms of the Counts of Celje, the prominent Slovene dynastic house of the late 14th and early 15th centuries) appears in the upper hoist side of the flag centered on the white and blue bands

National symbol(s): Mount Triglav; national colors: white, blue, red

National anthem: *name:* "Zdravljica" (A Toast)
lyrics/music: France PRESEREN/Stanko PREMRL
note: adopted in 1989 while still part of Yugoslavia; originally written in 1848; the full poem, whose seventh verse is used as the anthem, speaks of pan-Slavic nationalism

National heritage: *total World Heritage Sites:* 5 (3 cultural, 2 natural)
selected World Heritage Site locales: Škocjan Caves (n); Ancient and Primeval Beech Forests of the Carpathians and Other Regions of Europe (n); Prehistoric Pile Dwellings around the Alps (c); Heritage of Mercury: Almadén and Idrija (c); The works of Jože Plečnik in Ljubljana (c)

ECONOMY

Economic overview: high-income, EU and eurozone member economy; high per-capita income and low inequality; key exports in automotive and pharmaceuticals; tight labor market with low unemployment; growth supported by EU funds and reconstruction from 2023 floods; pressures over public sector wage demands

Real GDP (purchasing power parity): $102.036 billion (2023 est.)
$100.442 billion (2022 est.)
$98.03 billion (2021 est.)
note: data in 2021 dollars
comparison ranking: 97

Real GDP growth rate: 1.59% (2023 est.)

2.46% (2022 est.)
8.23% (2021 est.)
note: annual GDP % growth based on constant local currency
comparison ranking: 151

Real GDP per capita: $48,100 (2023 est.)
$47,600 (2022 est.)
$46,500 (2021 est.)
note: data in 2021 dollars
comparison ranking: 46

GDP (official exchange rate): $68.217 billion (2023 est.)
note: data in current dollars at official exchange rate

Inflation rate (consumer prices): 7.45% (2023 est.)
8.83% (2022 est.)
1.92% (2021 est.)
note: annual % change based on consumer prices
comparison ranking: 147

Credit ratings: Fitch rating: A (2019)

Moody's rating: A3 (2020)

Standard & Poors rating: AA- (2019)
note: The year refers to the year in which the current credit rating was first obtained.

GDP - composition, by sector of origin: *agriculture:* 1.9% (2023 est.)
industry: 29.1% (2023 est.)
services: 57.8% (2023 est.)
note: figures may not total 100% due to non-allocated consumption not captured in sector-reported data
comparison rankings: services 103; industry 73; agriculture 159

GDP - composition, by end use: *household consumption:* 53% (2023 est.)
government consumption: 19.5% (2023 est.)
investment in fixed capital: 22.5% (2023 est.)
investment in inventories: -1.7% (2023 est.)
exports of goods and services: 84% (2023 est.)
imports of goods and services: -77.3% (2023 est.)
note: figures may not total 100% due to rounding or gaps in data collection

Agricultural products: milk, maize, wheat, barley, grapes, chicken, potatoes, apples, beef, pork (2022)
note: top ten agricultural products based on tonnage

Industries: ferrous metallurgy and aluminum products, lead and zinc smelting; electronics (including military electronics), trucks, automobiles, electric power equipment, wood products, textiles, chemicals, machine tools

Industrial production growth rate: 3.8% (2023 est.)
note: annual % change in industrial value added based on constant local currency
comparison ranking: 85

Labor force: 1.055 million (2023 est.)
note: number of people ages 15 or older who are employed or seeking work
comparison ranking: 145

Unemployment rate: 3.63% (2023 est.)
4.01% (2022 est.)
4.75% (2021 est.)
note: % of labor force seeking employment
comparison ranking: 67

Youth unemployment rate (ages 15-24): *total:* 9.9% (2023 est.)
male: 9.9% (2023 est.)
female: 9.9% (2023 est.)
note: % of labor force ages 15-24 seeking employment
comparison ranking: total 136

Population below poverty line: 12.7% (2022 est.)
note: % of population with income below national poverty line

Gini Index coefficient - distribution of family income: 24.3 (2021 est.)
note: index (0-100) of income distribution; higher values represent greater inequality
comparison ranking: 151

Average household expenditures: *on food:* 14.1% of household expenditures (2022 est.)
on alcohol and tobacco: 4.5% of household expenditures (2022 est.)

Household income or consumption by percentage share: *lowest 10%:* 4.2% (2021 est.)
highest 10%: 20.7% (2021 est.)
note: % share of income accruing to lowest and highest 10% of population

Remittances: 1.3% of GDP (2023 est.)
1.3% of GDP (2022 est.)
1.34% of GDP (2021 est.)
note: personal transfers and compensation between resident and non-resident individuals/households/entities

Budget: *revenues:* $23.529 billion (2022 est.)
expenditures: $24.369 billion (2022 est.)
note: central government revenues (excluding grants) and expenses converted to US dollars at average official exchange rate for year indicated

Public debt: 73.6% of GDP (2017 est.)
note: defined by the EU's Maastricht Treaty as consolidated general government gross debt at nominal value, outstanding at the end of the year in the following categories of government liabilities: currency and deposits, securities other than shares excluding financial derivatives, and loans; general government sector comprises the central, state, local government, and social security funds
comparison ranking: 49

Taxes and other revenues: 18.14% (of GDP) (2022 est.)
note: central government tax revenue as a % of GDP
comparison ranking: 103

Current account balance: $3.057 billion (2023 est.)
-$617.374 million (2022 est.)
$2.073 billion (2021 est.)
note: balance of payments - net trade and primary/secondary income in current dollars
comparison ranking: 43

Exports: $57.489 billion (2023 est.)
$56.51 billion (2022 est.)
$51.662 billion (2021 est.)
note: balance of payments - exports of goods and services in current dollars
comparison ranking: 66

Exports - partners: Switzerland 18%, Germany 14%, Italy 11%, Croatia 8%, Austria 7% (2022)
note: top five export partners based on percentage share of exports

Exports - commodities: packaged medicine, cars, refined petroleum, electricity, vehicle parts/accessories (2022)
note: top five export commodities based on value in dollars

Imports: $52.826 billion (2023 est.)
$55.158 billion (2022 est.)
$47.997 billion (2021 est.)
note: balance of payments - imports of goods and services in current dollars
comparison ranking: 65

Imports - partners: Switzerland 17%, China 11%, Italy 10%, Germany 10%, Austria 7% (2022)
note: top five import partners based on percentage share of imports

Imports - commodities: packaged medicine, nitrogen compounds, refined petroleum, cars, electricity (2022)
note: top five import commodities based on value in dollars

Reserves of foreign exchange and gold: $2.37 billion (2023 est.)
$2.268 billion (2022 est.)
$2.267 billion (2021 est.)
note: holdings of gold (year-end prices)/foreign exchange/special drawing rights in current dollars
comparison ranking: 140

Exchange rates: euros (EUR) per US dollar -

Exchange rates: 0.925 (2023 est.)
0.95 (2022 est.)
0.845 (2021 est.)
0.876 (2020 est.)
0.893 (2019 est.)

ENERGY

Electricity access: *electrification - total population:* 100% (2022 est.)

Electricity: *installed generating capacity:* 4.322 million kW (2022 est.)
consumption: 13.081 billion kWh (2022 est.)
exports: 8.752 billion kWh (2022 est.)
imports: 10.198 billion kWh (2022 est.)
transmission/distribution losses: 834.794 million kWh (2022 est.)
comparison rankings: transmission/distribution losses 90; imports 26; exports 27; consumption 91; installed generating capacity 94

Electricity generation sources: *fossil fuels:* 26.7% of total installed capacity (2022 est.)
nuclear: 42.6% of total installed capacity (2022 est.)
solar: 4.3% of total installed capacity (2022 est.)
hydroelectricity: 24.1% of total installed capacity (2022 est.)
biomass and waste: 2.2% of total installed capacity (2022 est.)

Nuclear energy: Number of operational nuclear reactors: 1 (2023)

Net capacity of operational nuclear reactors: 0.69GW (2023 est.)

Percent of total electricity production: 36.8% (2023 est.)

Coal: *production:* 2.358 million metric tons (2022 est.)
consumption: 2.553 million metric tons (2022 est.)
exports: 5,000 metric tons (2022 est.)
imports: 486,000 metric tons (2022 est.)
proven reserves: 95 million metric tons (2022 est.)

Petroleum: *refined petroleum consumption:* 45,000 bbl/day (2023 est.)

Natural gas: *production:* 3.863 million cubic meters (2022 est.)
consumption: 840.902 million cubic meters (2022 est.)
exports: 11.387 million cubic meters (2018 est.)
imports: 840.606 million cubic meters (2022 est.)

Carbon dioxide emissions: 12.26 million metric tonnes of CO_2 (2022 est.)
from coal and metallurgical coke: 2.97 million metric tonnes of CO_2 (2022 est.)

from petroleum and other liquids: 7.689 million metric tonnes of CO2 (2022 est.)
from consumed natural gas: 1.601 million metric tonnes of CO2 (2022 est.)
comparison ranking: total emissions 102

Energy consumption per capita: 114.991 million Btu/person (2022 est.)
comparison ranking: 41

COMMUNICATIONS

Telephones - fixed lines: *total subscriptions:* 676,000 (2022 est.)
subscriptions per 100 inhabitants: 32 (2022 est.)
comparison ranking: total subscriptions 83

Telephones - mobile cellular: *total subscriptions:* 2.675 million (2022 est.)
subscriptions per 100 inhabitants: 126 (2022 est.)
comparison ranking: total subscriptions 145

Telecommunication systems: *general assessment:* Slovenia's telecom sector is dominated by four operators; the mobile market has four MNOs and a small number of MVNOs, operating in a country with a potential market of just over two million people; the regulator in recent years has addressed the need for mobile operators to have more spectrum, so enabling them to improve the quality and range of services; a multi-spectrum auction was concluded in mid-2021, aimed at supporting 5G services; the broadband market continues to be dominated by a small number of players; DSL lost its dominance some years ago, being taken over by fiber as subscribers are migrated to new fiber-based networks; fiber accounted for almost half of all fixed broadband connections by March 2022 (2022)
domestic: fixed-line is 32 per 100 and mobile-cellular is 126 per 100 teledensity (2022)
international: country code - 386 (2016)

Broadcast media: public TV broadcaster, Radiotelevizija Slovenija (RTV), operates a system of national and regional TV stations; 35 domestic commercial TV stations operating nationally, regionally, and locally; about 60% of households are connected to multi-channel cable TV; public radio broadcaster operates 3 national and 4 regional stations; more than 75 regional and local commercial and non-commercial radio stations

Internet country code: .si

Internet users: *total:* 1.869 million (2021 est.)
percent of population: 89% (2021 est.)
comparison ranking: total 136

Broadband - fixed subscriptions: *total:* 651,604 (2020 est.)
subscriptions per 100 inhabitants: 31 (2020 est.)
comparison ranking: total 84

TRANSPORTATION

National air transport system: *number of registered air carriers:* 2 (2020)
inventory of registered aircraft operated by air carriers: 21
annual passenger traffic on registered air carriers: 1,094,762 (2018)
annual freight traffic on registered air carriers: 540,000 (2018) mt-km

Civil aircraft registration country code prefix: S5

Airports: 42 (2024)
comparison ranking: 99

Heliports: 4 (2024)

Pipelines: 1,155 km gas, 5 km oil (2018)

Railways: *total:* 1,207 km (2020) 609 km electrified
comparison ranking: total 86

Roadways: *total:* 38,125 km (2022)
comparison ranking: total 93

Waterways: 710 km (2022) (some transport on the Drava River)
comparison ranking: 81

Merchant marine: *total:* 8 (2023)
by type: other 8
comparison ranking: total 163

Ports: *total ports:* 2 (2024)
large: 0
medium: 0
small: 1
very small: 1
ports with oil terminals: 0
key ports: Koper, Piran

MILITARY AND SECURITY

Military and security forces: Slovenian Armed Forces (Slovenska Vojska, SV): structured as a combined force with air, land, maritime, special operations, combat support, and combat service support elements

Ministry of Interior: National Police (2024)

Military expenditures: 1.3% of GDP (2024 est.)
1.3% of GDP (2023)
1.3% of GDP (2022)
1.2% of GDP (2021)
1% of GDP (2020)
comparison ranking: 108

Military and security service personnel strengths: approximately 6,000 active-duty troops (2024)

Military equipment inventories and acquisitions: the military's inventory is a mix of Soviet-era and smaller quantities of more modern, mostly Western equipment; in recent years, Slovenia has begun a modernization program and imported growing amounts of NATO-standard European and US equipment (2024)

Military service age and obligation: 18-30 years of age for voluntary military service for men and women; must be a citizen of the Republic of Slovenia; recruits sign up for 3-, 5-, or 10-year service contracts; conscription abolished in 2003 (2023)
note: as of 2023, women comprised about 16% of the military's full-time personnel

Military deployments: 100 Kosovo (NATO); 100 Slovakia (NATO) (2024)
note: in response to Russia's 2022 invasion of Ukraine, some NATO countries, including Slovenia, have sent additional troops and equipment to the battlegroups deployed in NATO territory in eastern Europe

Military - note: the Slovenian Armed Forces (Slovenska Vojska or SV) are responsible for the defense of the country's sovereignty and territory, deterring external threats, and contributing to European security and other international peacekeeping missions; the SV is also active in civil-military cooperation, such as the maintenance of local infrastructure; Slovenia has been a member of the EU and NATO since 2004, and one of the SV's key missions is fulfilling the country's commitments to NATO, including equipment modernization, participating in training exercises, and contributing to NATO operations; the SV provides troops to NATO's efforts to enhance its presence in the Baltics (Latvia) and Eastern Europe (Slovakia); it has also participated in other international security missions with small numbers of personnel in such places as Africa, southern Europe, the Mediterranean Sea, and the Middle East; because the SV air component has no fighter aircraft, NATO allies Hungary and Italy provide air policing for Slovenia
the SV was formally established in 1993 as a reorganization of the Slovenia Defense Force; the Defense Force, along with the Slovenian police, comprised the majority of the forces that engaged with the Yugoslav People's Army during the 10-Day War after Slovenia declared its independence in 1991 (2024)

TRANSNATIONAL ISSUES

Refugees and internally displaced persons: *refugees (country of origin):* 11,035 (Ukraine) (as of 1 March 2024)
stateless persons: 10 (2020)
note: 634,128 estimated refugee and migrant arrivals (January 2015-February 2024)

Illicit drugs: minor transit point for cocaine and Southwest Asian heroin bound for Western Europe, and for precursor chemicals

SOLOMON ISLANDS

INTRODUCTION

Background: Settlers from Papua arrived on the Solomon Islands around 30,000 years ago. About 6,000 years ago, Austronesian settlers came to the islands, and the two groups mixed extensively. Despite significant inter-island trade, no attempts were made to unite the islands into a single political entity. In 1568, a Spanish explorer became the first European to spot the islands. After a failed Spanish attempt at creating a permanent European settlement in the late 1500s, the Solomon Islands remained free of European contact until a British explorer arrived in 1767. European explorers and US and British whaling ships regularly visited the islands into the 1800s.

Germany declared a protectorate over the northern Solomon Islands in 1885, and the UK established a protectorate over the southern islands in 1893. In 1899, Germany transferred its islands to the UK in exchange for the UK relinquishing all claims in Samoa. In 1942, Japan invaded the islands, and the Guadalcanal Campaign (August 1942-February 1943) proved a turning point in the Pacific war. The

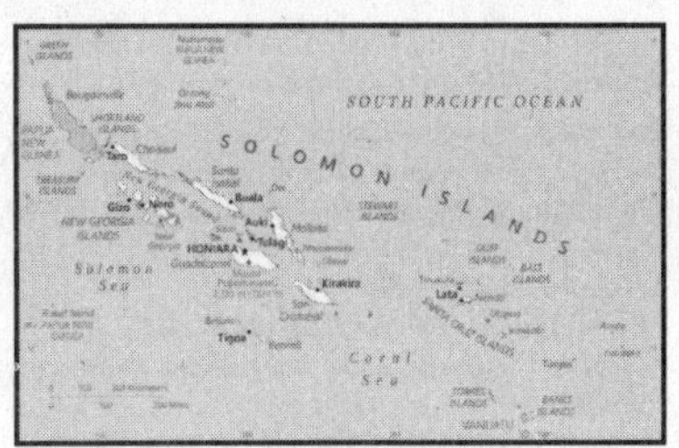

fighting destroyed large parts of the Solomon Islands, and a nationalist movement emerged near the end of the war. By 1960, the British allowed some local autonomy. The islands were granted self-government in 1976 and independence two years later under Prime Minister Sir Peter KENILOREA.

In 1999, longstanding tensions between ethnic Guale in Honiara and ethnic Malaitans in Honiara's suburbs erupted in civil war, leading thousands of Malaitans to take refuge in Honiara and prompting Guale to flee the city. In 2000, newly elected Prime Minister Manasseh SOGAVARE focused on peace agreements and distributing resources equally among groups, but his actions bankrupted the government in 2001 and led to his ouster. In 2003, the Solomon Islands requested international assistance to reestablish law and order; the Australian-led Regional Assistance Mission to the Solomon Islands, which ended in 2017, improved the security situation. In 2006, however, riots broke out in Honiara, and the city's Chinatown was burned amid allegations that the prime minister took money from China. SOGAVARE was reelected prime minister for a fourth time in 2019. When a small group of protestors, mostly from the island of Malaita, approached parliament to lodge a petition calling for SOGAVARE's removal and more development in Malaita in 2021, police fired tear gas into the crowd which sparked rioting and looting in Honiara.

GEOGRAPHY

Location: Oceania, group of islands in the South Pacific Ocean, east of Papua New Guinea

Geographic coordinates: 8 00 S, 159 00 E

Map references: Oceania

Area: *total:* 28,896 sq km
land: 27,986 sq km
water: 910 sq km
comparison ranking: total 143

Area - comparative: slightly smaller than Maryland

Land boundaries: *total:* 0 km

Coastline: 5,313 km

Maritime claims: *territorial sea:* 12 nm
exclusive economic zone: 200 nm
continental shelf: 200 nm
measured from claimed archipelagic baselines

Climate: tropical monsoon; few temperature and weather extremes

Terrain: mostly rugged mountains with some low coral atolls

Elevation: *highest point:* Mount Popomanaseu 2,335 m
lowest point: Pacific Ocean 0 m

Natural resources: fish, forests, gold, bauxite, phosphates, lead, zinc, nickel

Land use: *agricultural land:* 3.9% (2018 est.)
arable land: 0.7% (2018 est.)
permanent crops: 2.9% (2018 est.)
permanent pasture: 0.3% (2018 est.)
forest: 78.9% (2018 est.)
other: 17.2% (2018 est.)

Irrigated land: 0 sq km (2022)

Population distribution: most of the population lives along the coastal regions; about one in five live in urban areas, and of these some two-thirds reside in Honiara, the largest town and chief port

Natural hazards: tropical cyclones, but rarely destructive; geologically active region with frequent earthquakes, tremors, and volcanic activity; tsunamis
volcanism: Tinakula (851 m) has frequent eruption activity, while an eruption of Savo (485 m) could affect the capital Honiara on nearby Guadalcanal

Geography - note: strategic location on sea routes between the South Pacific Ocean, the Solomon Sea, and the Coral Sea; Rennell Island, the southernmost in the Solomon Islands chain, is one of the world's largest raised coral atolls; the island's Lake Tegano, formerly a lagoon on the atoll, is the largest lake in the insular Pacific (15,500 hectares)

PEOPLE AND SOCIETY

Population: *total:* 726,799
male: 370,970
female: 355,829 (2024 est.)
comparison rankings: female 167; male 167; total 167

Nationality: *noun:* Solomon Islander(s)
adjective: Solomon Islander

Ethnic groups: Melanesian 95.3%, Polynesian 3.1%, Micronesian 1.2%, other 0.3% (2009 est.)

Languages: Melanesian pidgin (lingua franca in much of the country), English (official but spoken by only 1%-2% of the population), 120 indigenous languages

Religions: Protestant 73.4% (Church of Melanesia 31.9%, South Sea Evangelical 17.1%, Seventh Day Adventist 11.7%, United Church 10.1%, Christian Fellowship Church 2.5%), Roman Catholic 19.6%, other Christian 2.9%, other 4%, unspecified 0.1% (2009 est.)

Age structure: *0-14 years:* 30.6% (male 114,246/female 108,020)
15-64 years: 64.2% (male 238,708/female 227,636)
65 years and over: 5.3% (2024 est.) (male 18,016/female 20,173)

Dependency ratios: *total dependency ratio:* 74.8
youth dependency ratio: 68.8
elderly dependency ratio: 6
potential support ratio: 16.5 (2021 est.)

Median age: *total:* 25.2 years (2024 est.)
male: 25 years
female: 25.4 years
comparison ranking: total 171

Population growth rate: 1.65% (2024 est.)
comparison ranking: 57

Birth rate: 22 births/1,000 population (2024 est.)
comparison ranking: 54

Death rate: 3.9 deaths/1,000 population (2024 est.)
comparison ranking: 216

Net migration rate: -1.5 migrant(s)/1,000 population (2024 est.)
comparison ranking: 157

Population distribution: most of the population lives along the coastal regions; about one in five live in urban areas, and of these some two-thirds reside in Honiara, the largest town and chief port

Urbanization: *urban population:* 26% of total population (2023)
rate of urbanization: 3.57% annual rate of change (2020-25 est.)

Major urban areas - population: 82,000 HONIARA (capital) (2018)

Sex ratio: *at birth:* 1.05 male(s)/female
0-14 years: 1.06 male(s)/female
15-64 years: 1.05 male(s)/female
65 years and over: 0.89 male(s)/female
total population: 1.04 male(s)/female (2024 est.)

Mother's mean age at first birth: 22.6 years (2015 est.)
note: data represents median age at first birth among women 25-29

Maternal mortality ratio: 122 deaths/100,000 live births (2020 est.)
comparison ranking: 64

Infant mortality rate: *total:* 19.1 deaths/1,000 live births (2024 est.)
male: 22.7 deaths/1,000 live births
female: 15.2 deaths/1,000 live births
comparison ranking: total 79

Life expectancy at birth: *total population:* 77.2 years (2024 est.)
male: 74.6 years
female: 80 years
comparison ranking: total population 95

Total fertility rate: 2.77 children born/woman (2024 est.)
comparison ranking: 56

Gross reproduction rate: 1.35 (2024 est.)

Contraceptive prevalence rate: 29.3% (2015)

Drinking water source: *improved: urban:* 95% of population
rural: 65.9% of population
total: 73.1% of population
unimproved: urban: 5% of population
rural: 34.1% of population
total: 26.9% of population (2020 est.)

Current health expenditure: 4.4% of GDP (2020)

Physician density: 0.19 physicians/1,000 population (2016)

Hospital bed density: 1.4 beds/1,000 population (2012)

Sanitation facility access: *improved: urban:* 95.6% of population
rural: 22.6% of population
total: 40.6% of population
unimproved: urban: 4.4% of population
rural: 77.4% of population
total: 59.4% of population (2020 est.)

Obesity - adult prevalence rate: 22.5% (2016)
comparison ranking: 75

Alcohol consumption per capita: *total:* 1.19 liters of pure alcohol (2019 est.)
beer: 1.1 liters of pure alcohol (2019 est.)
wine: 0.06 liters of pure alcohol (2019 est.)
spirits: 0.02 liters of pure alcohol (2019 est.)
other alcohols: 0 liters of pure alcohol (2019 est.)
comparison ranking: total 146

Tobacco use: *total:* 36.5% (2020 est.)
male: 53.8% (2020 est.)
female: 19.2% (2020 est.)

comparison ranking: total 12

Children under the age of 5 years underweight: 16.2% (2015)
comparison ranking: 32

Currently married women (ages 15-49): 64.1% (2023 est.)

Education expenditures: 12.8% of GDP (2020 est.)
comparison ranking: 2

ENVIRONMENT

Environment - current issues: deforestation; soil erosion; many of the surrounding coral reefs are dead or dying, exhibiting the effects of climate change and rising sea levels

Environment - international agreements: *party to:* Biodiversity, Climate Change, Climate Change-Kyoto Protocol, Climate Change-Paris Agreement, Desertification, Endangered Species, Environmental Modification, Law of the Sea, Marine Dumping-London Convention, Marine Life Conservation, Ozone Layer Protection, Ship Pollution, Whaling
signed, but not ratified: Comprehensive Nuclear Test Ban

Climate: tropical monsoon; few temperature and weather extremes

Urbanization: *urban population:* 26% of total population (2023)
rate of urbanization: 3.57% annual rate of change (2020-25 est.)

Revenue from forest resources: 20.27% of GDP (2018 est.)
comparison ranking: 1

Revenue from coal: 0% of GDP (2018 est.)
comparison ranking: 150

Air pollutants: *particulate matter emissions:* 7.83 micrograms per cubic meter (2019 est.)
carbon dioxide emissions: 0.17 megatons (2016 est.)
methane emissions: 0.43 megatons (2020 est.)

Waste and recycling: *municipal solid waste generated annually:* 179,972 tons (2013 est.)

Total renewable water resources: 44.7 billion cubic meters (2020 est.)

GOVERNMENT

Country name: *conventional long form:* none
conventional short form: Solomon Islands
local long form: none
local short form: Solomon Islands
former: British Solomon Islands
etymology: Spanish explorer Alvaro de MENDANA named the isles in 1568 after the wealthy biblical King SOLOMON in the mistaken belief that the islands contained great riches

Government type: parliamentary democracy under a constitutional monarchy; a Commonwealth realm

Capital: *name:* Honiara
geographic coordinates: 9 26 S, 159 57 E
time difference: UTC+11 (16 hours ahead of Washington, DC, during Standard Time)
etymology: the name derives from "nagho ni ara," which in one of the Guadalcanal languages roughly translates as "facing the eastern wind"

Administrative divisions: 9 provinces and 1 city*; Central, Choiseul, Guadalcanal, Honiara*, Isabel, Makira and Ulawa, Malaita, Rennell and Bellona, Temotu, Western

Independence: 7 July 1978 (from the UK)

National holiday: Independence Day, 7 July (1978)

Legal system: mixed legal system of English common law and customary law

Constitution: *history:* adopted 31 May 1978, effective 7 July 1978; note - in late 2017, provincial leaders agreed to adopt a new federal constitution; progress has been stalled, but as of February 2023, the draft constitution was with the Constitutional Review Unit in the prime minister's office
amendments: proposed by the National Parliament; passage of constitutional sections, including those on fundamental rights and freedoms, the legal system, Parliament, alteration of the constitution and the ombudsman, requires three-fourths majority vote by Parliament and assent of the governor general; passage of other amendments requires two-thirds majority vote and assent of the governor general; amended several times, last in 2018

International law organization participation: has not submitted an ICJ jurisdiction declaration; non-party state to the ICCt

Citizenship: *citizenship by birth:* no
citizenship by descent only: at least one parent must be a citizen of the Solomon Islands
dual citizenship recognized: no
residency requirement for naturalization: 7 years

Suffrage: 21 years of age; universal

Executive branch: *chief of state:* King CHARLES III (since 8 September 2022); represented by Governor General David Tiva KAPU (since 7 July 2024)
head of government: Prime Minister Jeremiah MANELE (since 2 May 2024)
cabinet: Cabinet appointed by the governor general on the advice of the prime minister
elections/appointments: the monarchy is hereditary; governor general appointed by the monarch on the advice of the National Parliament for up to 5 years (eligible for a second term); following legislative elections, the leader of the majority party or majority coalition usually elected prime minister by the National Parliament; deputy prime minister appointed by the governor general on the advice of the prime minister from among members of the National Parliament

Legislative branch: *description:* unicameral National Parliament (50 seats; members directly elected in single-seat constituencies by simple majority vote to serve 4-year terms)
elections: last held on 17 April 2024 (next to be held in 2028)
election results: percent of vote by party - OUR: 24.1%, independent 21.9%, SIDP 19.3%, SIUP 13.5%, KAD 4.5%, SIPRA 4.5%, PFP 3.2%, U4C 3.0%, DAP 1.6%, others 4.0%; seats by party - OUR Party 15, SIDP 8, SIUP 6, DAP 4, KAD 1, SIPRA 1, PFP 3, U4C 1, independents 11; composition - men 46, women 4, percentage women 8%

Judicial branch: *highest court(s):* Court of Appeal (consists of the court president and ex officio members including the High Court chief justice and its puisne judges); High Court (consists of the chief justice and puisne judges, as prescribed by the National Parliament)
judge selection and term of office: Court of Appeal and High Court president, chief justices, and puisne judges appointed by the governor general upon recommendation of the Judicial and Legal Service Commission, chaired by the chief justice and includes 5 members, mostly judicial officials and legal professionals; all judges serve until retirement at age 60
subordinate courts: Magistrates' Courts; Customary Land Appeal Court; local courts

Political parties: Democratic Alliance Party or DAP
Kadere Party of Solomon Islands or KAD
Ownership, Unity, and Responsibility Party (OUR Party)
People First Party or PFP
Solomon Islands Democratic Party or SIDP
Solomon Islands Party for Rural Advancement or SIPRA
Solomon Islands United Party or SIUP
United for Change Party or U4C
Coalition for Accountability Reform and Empowerment (CARE) is comprised of DAP, SIDP, and U4C
note: in general, Solomon Islands politics is characterized by fluid coalitions

International organization participation: ACP, ADB, AOSIS, C, EITI (candidate country), ESCAP, FAO, G-77, IBRD, ICAO, ICRM, IDA, IFAD, IFC, IFRCS, ILO, IMF, IMO, IOC, ITU, MIGA, OPCW, PIF, Sparteca, SPC, UN, UNCTAD, UNESCO, UPU, WFTU, WHO, WMO, WTO

Diplomatic representation in the US: *chief of mission:* Ambassador Jane Mugafalu Kabui WAETARA (since 16 September 2022); note - also Permanent Representative to the UN
chancery: 685 Third Avenue, 11th Floor, Suite 1102, New York, NY 10017
telephone: [1] (212) 599-6192
FAX: [1] (212) 661-8925
email address and website:
simun@solomons.com

Diplomatic representation from the US: *chief of mission:* Ambassador Ann Marie YASTISHOCK (since 14 March 2024); note - also accredited to the Papua New Guinea and Vanuatu, based in Port Moresby, Papua New Guinea
embassy: BJS Building
Commonwealth Avenue
Honiara, Solomon Islands
telephone: [677] 23426
FAX: [677] 27429

Flag description: divided diagonally by a thin yellow stripe from the lower hoist-side corner; the upper triangle (hoist side) is blue with five white five-pointed stars arranged in an X pattern; the lower triangle is green; blue represents the ocean, green the land, and yellow sunshine; the five stars stand for the five main island groups of the Solomon Islands

National symbol(s): national colors: blue, yellow, green, white

National anthem: *name:* "God Save Our Solomon Islands"
lyrics/music: Panapasa BALEKANA and Matila BALEKANA/Panapasa BALEKANA
note: adopted 1978

National heritage: *total World Heritage Sites:* 1 (natural)
selected World Heritage Site locales: East Rennell

ECONOMY

Economic overview: lower middle-income Pacific island economy; natural resource rich but environmentally fragile; key agrarian sector; growing Chinese economic relationship; infrastructure damage due to social unrest; metal mining operations

Real GDP (purchasing power parity): $2.025 billion (2023 est.)

$1.967 billion (2022 est.)
$1.921 billion (2021 est.)
note: data in 2021 dollars
comparison ranking: 200

Real GDP growth rate: 2.95% (2023 est.)
2.4% (2022 est.)
2.56% (2021 est.)
note: annual GDP % growth based on constant local currency
comparison ranking: 110

Real GDP per capita: $2,700 (2023 est.)
$2,700 (2022 est.)
$2,700 (2021 est.)
note: data in 2021 dollars
comparison ranking: 202

GDP (official exchange rate): $1.631 billion (2023 est.)
note: data in current dollars at official exchange rate

Inflation rate (consumer prices): 5.89% (2023 est.)
5.52% (2022 est.)
-0.12% (2021 est.)
note: annual % change based on consumer prices
comparison ranking: 126

Credit ratings: Moody's rating: B3 (2015)
note: The year refers to the year in which the current credit rating was first obtained.

GDP - composition, by sector of origin: *agriculture:* 33.8% (2022 est.)
industry: 18.7% (2022 est.)
services: 47.3% (2022 est.)
note: figures may not total 100% due to non-allocated consumption not captured in sector-reported data
comparison rankings: services 162; industry 147; agriculture 8

GDP - composition, by end use: *household consumption:* 61.7% (2022 est.)
government consumption: 29.2% (2022 est.)
investment in fixed capital: 24.4% (2022 est.)
investment in inventories: -1% (2022 est.) NA
exports of goods and services: 26.3% (2022 est.)
imports of goods and services: -51.7% (2022 est.)
note: figures may not total 100% due to rounding or gaps in data collection

Agricultural products: oil palm fruit, coconuts, sweet potatoes, taro, yams, fruits, pulses, vegetables, cocoa beans, cassava (2022)
note: top ten agricultural products based on tonnage

Industries: fish (tuna), mining, timber

Industrial production growth rate: 4.7% (2022 est.)
note: annual % change in industrial value added based on constant local currency
comparison ranking: 55

Labor force: 382,000 (2023 est.)
note: number of people ages 15 or older who are employed or seeking work
comparison ranking: 165

Unemployment rate: 1.55% (2023 est.)
1.58% (2022 est.)
0.87% (2021 est.)
note: % of labor force seeking employment
comparison ranking: 16

Youth unemployment rate (ages 15-24): *total:* 3% (2023 est.)
male: 2.6% (2023 est.)
female: 3.5% (2023 est.)
note: % of labor force ages 15-24 seeking employment
comparison ranking: total 193

Gini Index coefficient - distribution of family income: (2013)

Remittances: 5.18% of GDP (2023 est.)
5.18% of GDP (2022 est.)
3.35% of GDP (2021 est.)
note: personal transfers and compensation between resident and non-resident individuals/households/entities

Budget: *revenues:* $436.2 million (2022 est.)
expenditures: $423.726 million (2022 est.)
note: central government revenues and expenses (excluding grants/extrabudgetary units/social security funds) converted to US dollars at average official exchange rate for year indicated

Public debt: 15.39% of GDP (2022 est.)
note: central government debt as a % of GDP
comparison ranking: 194

Taxes and other revenues: 20.67% (of GDP) (2022 est.)
note: central government tax revenue as a % of GDP
comparison ranking: 81

Current account balance: -$178.197 million (2023 est.)
-$218.534 million (2022 est.)
-$78.192 million (2021 est.)
note: balance of payments - net trade and primary/secondary income in current dollars
comparison ranking: 108

Exports: $546.025 million (2023 est.)
$411.359 million (2022 est.)
$413.657 million (2021 est.)
note: balance of payments - exports of goods and services in current dollars
comparison ranking: 191

Exports - partners: China 51%, India 9%, Italy 8%, Australia 5%, Netherlands 4% (2022)
note: top five export partners based on percentage share of exports

Exports - commodities: wood, fish, palm oil, gold, coconut oil (2022)
note: top five export commodities based on value in dollars

Imports: $883.611 million (2023 est.)
$764.641 million (2022 est.)
$619.46 million (2021 est.)
note: balance of payments - imports of goods and services in current dollars
comparison ranking: 194

Imports - partners: China 37%, Singapore 16%, Malaysia 12%, Australia 10%, NZ 4% (2022)
note: top five import partners based on percentage share of imports

Imports - commodities: refined petroleum, plastic products, fish, iron structures, construction vehicles (2022)
note: top five import commodities based on value in dollars

Reserves of foreign exchange and gold: $661.604 million (2022 est.)
$694.515 million (2021 est.)
$660.996 million (2020 est.)
note: holdings of gold (year-end prices)/foreign exchange/special drawing rights in current dollars
comparison ranking: 159

Debt - external: $117.742 million (2022 est.)
note: present value of external debt in current US dollars
comparison ranking: 102

Exchange rates: Solomon Islands dollars (SBD) per US dollar -

Exchange rates: 8.376 (2023 est.)
8.156 (2022 est.)
8.03 (2021 est.)
8.213 (2020 est.)
8.173 (2019 est.)

ENERGY

Electricity access: *electrification - total population:* 76% (2022 est.)
electrification - urban areas: 79%
electrification - rural areas: 75.4%

Electricity: *installed generating capacity:* 37,000 kW (2022 est.)
consumption: 89.565 million kWh (2022 est.)
transmission/distribution losses: 19.55 million kWh (2022 est.)
comparison rankings: transmission/distribution losses 25; consumption 200; installed generating capacity 200

Electricity generation sources: *fossil fuels:* 93.8% of total installed capacity (2022 est.)
solar: 2.7% of total installed capacity (2022 est.)
biomass and waste: 3.5% of total installed capacity (2022 est.)

Petroleum: *refined petroleum consumption:* 2,000 bbl/day (2022 est.)

Carbon dioxide emissions: 322,000 metric tonnes of CO_2 (2022 est.)
from petroleum and other liquids: 322,000 metric tonnes of CO_2 (2022 est.)
comparison ranking: total emissions 195

Energy consumption per capita: 6.172 million Btu/person (2022 est.)
comparison ranking: 165

COMMUNICATIONS

Telephones - fixed lines: *total subscriptions:* 7,000 (2021 est.)
subscriptions per 100 inhabitants: (2021 est.) less than 1
comparison ranking: total subscriptions 195

Telephones - mobile cellular: *total subscriptions:* 474,000 (2021 est.)
subscriptions per 100 inhabitants: 67 (2021 est.)
comparison ranking: total subscriptions 175

Telecommunication systems: *general assessment:* mobile services have continually expanded in the Solomon Islands; 3G services became available in 2010, leading to an increase in mobile broadband uptake; Solomon Islands currently host three ISPs; fixed broadband services are largely limited to government, corporations, and educational organizations in the Solomon Islands; telecommunication infrastructure in the Solomon Islands requires significant investment due to the geographical make-up of the islands; this presents a great challenge to rural connectivity in the country; although various international organizations such as the World Bank and the Asian Development Bank have taken a special interest in having communication services improved in both the Solomon Islands and the Pacific region in general, internet and broadband penetration remain low; the provision of broadband infrastructure, particularly to rural areas, is also hindered by land disputes; internet services have, improved with the build-out of the

Coral Sea Cable System linking Papua New Guinea to the Solomon Islands, as also with a connecting cable to a landing station at Sydney; the Australian government provided most of the funding for the Coral Sea Cable System, with contributions and support from the Solomon Islands and Papua New Guinea governments; the launch of the Kacific-1 satellite in late 2019 also improved broadband satellite capacity for the region, though for telcos in Solomon Islands satellite services are now largely used as backup for international traffic; in recent years, the country has stabilized both politically and economically and this, along with improvements to mobile infrastructure, has led to a rise in mobile services and the slow uptake of broadband services; while the first LTE services were launched in late 2017 in the capital Honiara, the main platform for mobile voice and data services remains 3G, while in outlying areas GSM is still an important technology for the provision of services (2022)
domestic: fixed-line is less than 1 per 100 persons and mobile-cellular telephone density 67 per 100 persons (2021)
international: country code - 677; landing points for the CSCS and ICNS2 submarine cables providing connectivity from Solomon Islands, to PNG, Vanuatu and Australia; satellite earth station - 1 Intelsat (Pacific Ocean) (2019)

Broadcast media: Solomon Islands Broadcasting Corporation (SIBC) does not broadcast television; multi-channel pay-TV is available; SIBC operates 2 national radio stations and 2 provincial stations; there are 2 local commercial radio stations; Radio Australia is available via satellite feed (since 2009) (2019)

Internet country code: .sb

Internet users: *total:* 255,600 (2021 est.)
percent of population: 36% (2021 est.)
comparison ranking: total 175

Broadband - fixed subscriptions: *total:* 1,000 (2020 est.)
subscriptions per 100 inhabitants: 0.2 (2020 est.)
comparison ranking: total 206

TRANSPORTATION

National air transport system: *number of registered air carriers:* 1 (2020)
inventory of registered aircraft operated by air carriers: 6
annual passenger traffic on registered air carriers: 427,806 (2018)
annual freight traffic on registered air carriers: 3.84 million (2018) mt-km

Civil aircraft registration country code prefix: H4

Airports: 35 (2024)
comparison ranking: 111

Heliports: 1 (2024)

Roadways: *total:* 1,390 km
paved: 34 km
unpaved: 1,356 km (2011)
note: includes 920 km of private plantation roads
comparison ranking: total 177

Merchant marine: *total:* 25 (2023)
by type: general cargo 8, oil tanker 1, other 16
comparison ranking: total 142

Ports: *total ports:* 6 (2024)
large: 0
medium: 0
small: 2
very small: 4
ports with oil terminals: 1
key ports: Gizo Harbor, Honiara, Port Noro, Ringgi Cove, Tulaghi, Yandina

MILITARY AND SECURITY

Military and security forces: no regular military forces; the Royal Solomon Islands Police Force (RSIPF) is responsible for internal and external security and reports to the Ministry of Police, National Security, and Correctional Services (2024)

Military - note: from 2003 to 2017, at the request of the Solomon Islands Governor-General, the Regional Assistance Mission to Solomon Islands (RAMSI), consisting of police, military, and civilian advisors drawn from 15 countries, assisted in reestablishing and maintaining civil and political order while reinforcing regional stability and security; from November 2021 to August 2024, an Australian-led Solomon Islands Assistance Force (SIAF) provided support to the Royal Solomon Islands Police Force (RSIPF) in maintaining stability; the SIAF also included military and police personnel from New Zealand, Fiji, and Papua New Guinea; following the conclusion of the SIAF mission, Australia continued to provide security assistance to the Solomon Islands; the Solomon Islands Government has also signed police and security agreements with China (2024)

TRANSNATIONAL ISSUES

Trafficking in persons: tier rating: Tier 2 Watch List—the government did not demonstrate overall increasing efforts to eliminate trafficking compared with the previous reporting period, therefore Solomon Islands remained on Tier 2 Watch List for the second consecutive year; for more details, go to: https://www.state.gov/reports/2024-trafficking-in-persons-report/solomon-islands/

SOMALIA

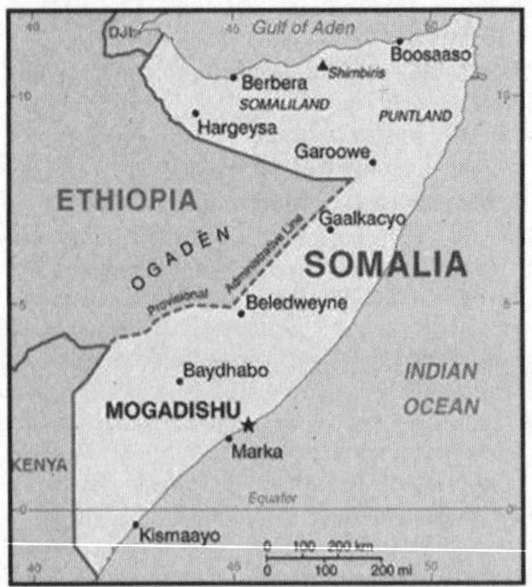

INTRODUCTION

Background: Between A.D. 800 and 1100, immigrant Muslim Arabs and Persians set up coastal trading posts along the Gulf of Aden and the Indian Ocean, solidifying present-day Somalia's close trading relationship with the Arab Peninsula. In the late 19th century, Britain, France, and Italy established colonies in the Somali Peninsula that lasted until 1960, when British Somaliland gained independence and joined with Italian Somaliland to form the Republic of Somalia.

The country functioned as a parliamentary democracy until 1969, when General Mohamed SIAD Barre took control in a coup, beginning a 22-year socialist dictatorship. In an effort to centralize power, SIAD called for the eradication of the clan, the key cultural and social organizing principle in Somali society. Resistance to SIAD's socialist leadership, which was causing a rapid deterioration of the country, prompted allied clan militias to overthrow SIAD in 1991, resulting in state collapse. Subsequent fighting between rival clans for resources and territory overwhelmed the country, causing a manmade famine and prompting international intervention. Beginning in 1993, the UN spearheaded an international humanitarian mission, but the international community largely withdrew by 1995 after an incident that became known as Black Hawk Down, in which two US military helicopters were shot down in Mogadishu. The fighting and subsequent siege and rescue resulted in 21 deaths and 82 wounded among the international forces.

International peace conferences in the 2000s resulted in a number of transitional governments that operated outside Somalia. Left largely to themselves, Somalis in the country established alternative governance structures; some areas formed their own administrations, such as Somaliland and Puntland, while others developed localized institutions. Many local populations turned to sharia courts, an Islamic judicial system that implements religious law. Several of these courts came together in 2006 to form the Islamic Courts Union (ICU). The ICU established order in many areas of central and southern Somalia, including Mogadishu, but was forced out when Ethiopia intervened militarily in 2006 on behalf of the Somali Transitional Federal Government (TFG). As the TFG settled in the capital, the ICU fled to rural areas or left Somalia altogether, but the organization reemerged less than a year later as the Islamic insurgent and terrorist movement al-Shabaab, which is still active today.

In 2007, the African Union (AU) established a peacekeeping force, took over security responsibility for the country, and gave the TFG space to develop Somalia's new government. By 2012, Somali powerbrokers agreed on a provisional constitution with a loose federal structure and established a central government in Mogadishu called the Somali Federal

Government (SFG). Since then, the country has seen several interim regional administrations and three presidential elections, but significant governance and security problems remain because al-Shabaab still controls large portions of the country.

GEOGRAPHY

Location: Eastern Africa, bordering the Gulf of Aden and the Indian Ocean, east of Ethiopia

Geographic coordinates: 10 00 N, 49 00 E

Map references: Africa

Area: *total:* 637,657 sq km
land: 627,337 sq km
water: 10,320 sq km
comparison ranking: total 46

Area - comparative: almost five times the size of Alabama; slightly smaller than Texas

Land boundaries: *total:* 2,385 km
border countries (3): Djibouti 61 km; Ethiopia 1,640 km; Kenya 684 km

Coastline: 3,025 km

Maritime claims: *territorial sea:* 200 nm; note: the US does not recognize this claim
exclusive economic zone: 200 nm

Climate: principally desert; northeast monsoon (December to February), moderate temperatures in north and hot in south; southwest monsoon (May to October), torrid in the north and hot in the south, irregular rainfall, hot and humid periods (tangambili) between monsoons

Terrain: mostly flat to undulating plateau rising to hills in north

Elevation: *highest point:* Mount Shimbiris 2,460 m
lowest point: Indian Ocean 0 m
mean elevation: 410 m

Natural resources: uranium and largely unexploited reserves of iron ore, tin, gypsum, bauxite, copper, salt, natural gas, likely oil reserves

Land use: *agricultural land:* 70.3% (2018 est.)
arable land: 1.8% (2018 est.)
permanent crops: 0% (2018 est.)
permanent pasture: 68.5% (2018 est.)
forest: 10.6% (2018 est.)
other: 19.1% (2018 est.)

Irrigated land: 2,000 sq km (2012)

Major aquifers: Ogaden-Juba Basin

Population distribution: distribution varies greatly throughout the country; least densely populated areas are in the northeast and central regions, as well as areas along the Kenyan border; most populated areas are in and around the cities of Mogadishu, Marka, Boorama, Hargeysa, and Baidoa as shown on this population distribution map

Natural hazards: recurring droughts; frequent dust storms over eastern plains in summer; floods during rainy season

Geography - note: strategic location on Horn of Africa along southern approaches to Bab el Mandeb and route through Red Sea and Suez Canal

PEOPLE AND SOCIETY

Population: *total:* 13,017,273
male: 6,546,312
female: 6,470,961 (2024 est.)
comparison rankings: female 78; male 79; total 78

Nationality: *noun:* Somali(s)
adjective: Somali

Ethnic groups: predominantly Somali with lesser numbers of Arabs, Bantus, and others

Languages: Somali (official), Arabic (official), Italian, English
major-language sample(s):
Buugga Xaqiiqda Aduunka, waa laga maarmaanka macluumaadka assasiga. (Somali)

Religions: Muslim 99.9% (Sunni Muslim 98.1%, Shia Muslim 1.2%, Islamic schismatic 0.6%), ethnic religionist 0.1% (2020 est.)

Demographic profile: Somalia scores very low for most humanitarian indicators, suffering from poor governance, protracted internal conflict, underdevelopment, economic decline, poverty, social and gender inequality, and environmental degradation. Despite civil war and famine raising its mortality rate, Somalia's high fertility rate and large proportion of people of reproductive age maintain rapid population growth, with each generation being larger than the prior one. More than 60% of Somalia's population is younger than 25 as of 2020, and the fertility rate is among the world's highest at almost 5.5 children per woman – a rate that has decreased little since the 1970s.

A lack of educational and job opportunities is a major source of tension for Somalia's large youth cohort, making them vulnerable to recruitment by extremist and pirate groups. Somalia has one of the world's lowest primary school enrollment rates – just over 40% of children are in school – and one of the world's highest youth unemployment rates. Life expectancy is low as a result of high infant and maternal mortality rates, the spread of preventable diseases, poor sanitation, chronic malnutrition, and inadequate health services.

During the two decades of conflict that followed the fall of the SIAD regime in 1991, hundreds of thousands of Somalis fled their homes. Today Somalia is the world's fourth highest source country for refugees, after Ukraine, Syria and Afghanistan. Insecurity, drought, floods, food shortages, and a lack of economic opportunities are the driving factors.

As of 2022, more than 660,000 Somali refugees were hosted in the region, mainly in Kenya, Yemen, Egypt, Ethiopia, Djibouti, and Uganda, while nearly 3 million Somalis were internally displaced. Since the implementation of a tripartite voluntary repatriation agreement among Kenya, Somalia, and the UNHCR in 2013, many Somali refugees have returned home, some 80,000 between 2014 and 2022. The Kenyan Government in March 2021 ordered the closure of its two largest refugee camps, Dadaab and Kakuma, which then hosted more than 410,000 mainly Somali refugees. However, the UN refugee agency presented a road map, including voluntary repatriation, relocation to third countries, and alternative stay options that persuaded the Kenyan Government to delay the closures. The plan was supposed to lead to both camps being closed by 30 June 2022. Yet, as of May 2022, few Somali refugees had decided to return home because of security concerns and the lack of job prospects, instead waiting in the camps unsure of what the future held for them. Other Somali asylum seekers brave the dangers of crossing the Gulf of Aden to reach Yemen – despite its internal conflict – with aspirations to move onward to Saudi Arabia and other locations.

Age structure: *0-14 years:* 41.4% (male 2,689,086/female 2,694,372)
15-64 years: 55.8% (male 3,699,721/female 3,568,163)
65 years and over: 2.8% (2024 est.) (male 157,505/female 208,426)

Dependency ratios: *total dependency ratio:* 99.4
youth dependency ratio: 94.2
elderly dependency ratio: 5.2
potential support ratio: 19.3 (2021 est.)

Median age: *total:* 19.1 years (2024 est.)
male: 19.3 years
female: 18.9 years
comparison ranking: total 215

Population growth rate: 2.55% (2024 est.)
comparison ranking: 15

Birth rate: 37.4 births/1,000 population (2024 est.)
comparison ranking: 8

Death rate: 11.2 deaths/1,000 population (2024 est.)
comparison ranking: 23

Net migration rate: -0.7 migrant(s)/1,000 population (2024 est.)
comparison ranking: 136

Population distribution: distribution varies greatly throughout the country; least densely populated areas are in the northeast and central regions, as well as areas along the Kenyan border; most populated areas are in and around the cities of Mogadishu, Marka, Boorama, Hargeysa, and Baidoa as shown on this population distribution map

Urbanization: *urban population:* 47.9% of total population (2023)
rate of urbanization: 4.2% annual rate of change (2020-25 est.)

Major urban areas - population: 2.610 million MOGADISHU (capital), 1.127 million Hargeysa (2023)

Sex ratio: *at birth:* 1.03 male(s)/female
0-14 years: 1 male(s)/female
15-64 years: 1.04 male(s)/female
65 years and over: 0.76 male(s)/female
total population: 1.01 male(s)/female (2024 est.)

Maternal mortality ratio: 621 deaths/100,000 live births (2020 est.)
comparison ranking: 7

Infant mortality rate: *total:* 83.6 deaths/1,000 live births (2024 est.)
male: 93.2 deaths/1,000 live births
female: 73.7 deaths/1,000 live births
comparison ranking: total 2

Life expectancy at birth: *total population:* 56.5 years (2024 est.)
male: 54.1 years
female: 59 years
comparison ranking: total population 225

Total fertility rate: 5.12 children born/woman (2024 est.)
comparison ranking: 8

Gross reproduction rate: 2.52 (2024 est.)

Contraceptive prevalence rate: 6.9% (2018/19)

Drinking water source: *improved: urban:* 96.4% of population
rural: 73.7% of population
total: 84.2% of population
unimproved: urban: 3.6% of population
rural: 26.3% of population
total: 15.8% of population (2020 est.)

Physician density: 0.02 physicians/1,000 population (2014)

Hospital bed density: 0.9 beds/1,000 population (2017)

Sanitation facility access: *improved: urban:* 82.4% of population
rural: 33.8% of population
total: 56.2% of population
unimproved: urban: 17.6% of population
rural: 66.2% of population
total: 43.8% of population (2020 est.)

Obesity - adult prevalence rate: 8.3% (2016)
comparison ranking: 153

Alcohol consumption per capita: *total:* 0 liters of pure alcohol (2019 est.)
beer: 0 liters of pure alcohol (2019 est.)
wine: 0 liters of pure alcohol (2019 est.)
spirits: 0 liters of pure alcohol (2019 est.)
other alcohols: 0 liters of pure alcohol (2019 est.)
comparison ranking: total 188

Currently married women (ages 15-49): 62.9% (2023 est.)

Child marriage: *women married by age 15:* 16.8%
women married by age 18: 35.5%
men married by age 18: 5.6% (2020 est.)

Education expenditures: 0.3% of GDP (2019) NA
comparison ranking: 197

ENVIRONMENT

Environment - current issues: water scarcity; contaminated water contributes to human health problems; improper waste disposal; deforestation; land degradation; overgrazing; soil erosion; desertification

Environment - international agreements: *party to:* Biodiversity, Climate Change, Climate Change-Kyoto Protocol, Climate Change-Paris Agreement, Desertification, Endangered Species, Hazardous Wastes, Law of the Sea, Ozone Layer Protection
signed, but not ratified: Nuclear Test Ban

Climate: principally desert; northeast monsoon (December to February), moderate temperatures in north and hot in south; southwest monsoon (May to October), torrid in the north and hot in the south, irregular rainfall, hot and humid periods (tangambili) between monsoons

Urbanization: *urban population:* 47.9% of total population (2023)
rate of urbanization: 4.2% annual rate of change (2020-25 est.)

Food insecurity: *exceptional shortfall in aggregate food production/supplies: due to drought conditions and internal conflict* - about 6.5 million people are estimated to face severe acute food insecurity between April and June 2023 as a result of consecutive poor rainy seasons since late 2020 and heightened conflict since early 2021 (2023)

Air pollutants: *particulate matter emissions:* 14.28 micrograms per cubic meter (2019 est.)
carbon dioxide emissions: 0.65 megatons (2016 est.)
methane emissions: 20.13 megatons (2020 est.)

Waste and recycling: *municipal solid waste generated annually:* 2,326,099 tons (2016 est.)

Major aquifers: Ogaden-Juba Basin

Total water withdrawal: *municipal:* 20 million cubic meters (2020 est.)
industrial: 2 million cubic meters (2017 est.)
agricultural: 3.28 billion cubic meters (2020 est.)

Total renewable water resources: 14.7 billion cubic meters (2020 est.)

GOVERNMENT

Country name: *conventional long form:* Federal Republic of Somalia
conventional short form: Somalia
local long form: Jamhuuriyadda Federaalka Soomaaliya (Somali)/ Jumhuriyat as Sumal al Fidiraliyah (Arabic)
local short form: Soomaaliya (Somali)/ As Sumal (Arabic)
former: British Somaliland, Italian Somaliland, Somali Republic, Somali Democratic Republic
etymology: "Land of the Somali" (ethnic group)

Government type: federal parliamentary republic

Capital: *name:* Mogadishu
geographic coordinates: 2 04 N, 45 20 E
time difference: UTC+3 (8 hours ahead of Washington, DC, during Standard Time)
etymology: several theories attempt to explain the city's name; one of the more plausible is that it derives from "maq'ad-i-shah" meaning "the seat of the shah," reflecting the city's links with Persia

Administrative divisions: 18 regions (plural - gobollo, singular - gobol); Awdal, Bakool, Banaadir, Bari, Bay, Galguduud, Gedo, Hiiraan, Jubbada Dhexe (Middle Jubba), Jubbada Hoose (Lower Jubba), Mudug, Nugaal, Sanaag, Shabeellaha Dhexe (Middle Shabeelle), Shabeellaha Hoose (Lower Shabeelle), Sool, Togdheer, Woqooyi Galbeed

Independence: 1 July 1960 (from a merger of British Somaliland, which became independent from the UK on 26 June 1960, and Italian Somaliland, which became independent from the Italian-administered UN trusteeship on 1 July 1960 to form the Somali Republic)

National holiday: Foundation of the Somali Republic, 1 July (1960); note - 26 June (1960) in Somaliland

Legal system: mixed legal system of civil law, Islamic (sharia) law, and customary law (referred to as Xeer)

Constitution: *history:* previous 1961, 1979; latest drafted 12 June 2012, adopted 1 August 2012 (provisional)
amendments: proposed by the federal government, by members of the state governments, the Federal Parliament, or by public petition; proposals require review by a joint committee of Parliament with inclusion of public comments and state legislatures' comments; passage requires at least two-thirds majority vote in both houses of Parliament and approval by a majority of votes cast in a referendum; constitutional clauses on Islamic principles, the federal system, human rights and freedoms, powers and authorities of the government branches, and inclusion of women in national institutions cannot be amended; amended 2024

International law organization participation: accepts compulsory ICJ jurisdiction with reservations; non-party state to the ICCt

Citizenship: *citizenship by birth:* no
citizenship by descent only: the father must be a citizen of Somalia
dual citizenship recognized: no
residency requirement for naturalization: 7 years

Suffrage: 18 years of age; universal suffrage starting with 24 June 2024 local elections

Executive branch: *chief of state:* President HASSAN SHEIKH Mohamud (since 23 May 2022)
head of government: Prime Minister Hamza Abdi BARRE (since 25 June 2022)
cabinet: Cabinet appointed by the prime minister, approved by the House of the People
elections/appointments: president indirectly elected by the Federal Parliament by two-thirds majority vote in 2 rounds if needed for a single 4-year term; election last held on 15 May 2022 (next to be held in 2026); prime minister appointed by the president, approved by the House of the People
election results:
2022: HASSAN SHEIKH Mohamud elected president in third round - Federal Parliament percent of vote in first round - Said ABDULLAHI DENI (Kaah) 20.2%, Mohamed ABDULLAHI Mohamed "Farmaajo" (TPP) 18.3%, HASSAN SHEIKH Mohamud (PDP) 16.2%, Hassan Ali KHAYRE (independent) 14.6%, other 30.7%; Federal Parliament percent of vote in second round - HASSAN SHEIKH Mohamud 34.1%, Mohamed ABDULLAHI Mohamed "Farmaajo" 25.7%, Said ABDULLAHI DENI 21%, Hassan Ali KHAYRE 19.2%; Federal Parliament percent of vote in third round - HASSAN SHEIKH Mohamud 66%, Mohamed ABDULLAHI Mohamed "Farmaajo" 34%
2017: Mohamed ABDULLAHI Mohamed "Farmaajo" elected president in second round; Federal Parliament number of votes in first round - HASSAN SHEIKH Mohamud (PDP) 88, Mohamed ABDULLAHI Mohamed "Farmaajo" (TPP) 72, Sheikh SHARIF Sheikh Ahmed (ARS) 49, other 37; Federal Parliament number of votes in second round - Mohamed ABDULLAHI Mohamed "Farmaajo" 184, HASSAN SHEIKH Mohamud 97, Sheikh SHARIF Sheikh Ahmed 45

Legislative branch: *description:* bicameral Federal Parliament to consist of:
Senate (54 seats; senators indirectly elected by state assemblies to serve 4-year terms)
House of the People (275 seats; members indirectly elected by electoral colleges, each consisting of 51 delegates selected by the 136 Traditional Elders in consultation with sub-clan elders; members serve 4-year terms)
elections: Senate - first held on 10 October 2016; last held 27 July - 13 November 2021 (next to be held in 2024) House of the People - first held 23 October - 10 November 2016 (next scheduled for September - October 2021 but postponed to November 2021 and then extended several times until April 2022; next to be held in June 2024)
election results: Senate - percent of vote by party - NA; seats by party - NA; composition - men 40, women 14, percentage women 25.9%
House of the People - percent of vote by party - NA; seats by party - NA; composition - men 221, women 54, percentage women 19.6%; total Federal Parliament percentage women 20.7%
note: despite the formation of political parties in 2020, the 2021 parliamentary elections maintained a primarily clan-based system of appointments; seats in the legislature were apportioned to Somali member states and not by party representation

Judicial branch: *highest court(s):* the provisional constitution stipulates the establishment of the Constitutional Court (consists of 5 judges, including the chief judge and deputy chief judge); note - under the terms of the 2004 Transitional National Charter, a Supreme Court based in Mogadishu and the Appeal Court were established; yet most regions have reverted to local forms of conflict resolution, either secular, traditional Somali customary law, or Islamic law

judge selection and term of office: judges appointed by the president upon proposal of the Judicial Service Commission, a 9-member judicial and administrative body; judge tenure NA
subordinate courts: federal courts; federal member state-level courts; military courts; sharia courts

Political parties: Cosmopolitan Democratic Party
Green Party
Himilo Qaran Party
Ilays Party
Justice and Reconciliation Party
National Progressive Party
Peace and Unity Party
Qaransoor Party
Qiimo Qaran Party
Security and Justice Party
Social Justice Party
Somali Labour Party
Somali Republic Party
Somali Social Unity Party or SSUP
Union for Peace and Development Party or PDP
Wadajir Party
note: in 2017 an independent electoral commission (the NIEC) was inaugurated with a mandate to oversee the process of registration of political parties in the country; as of 2021, the NIEC had registered a total of 110 parties

International organization participation: ACP, AfDB, AFESD, AMF, AU, CAEU (candidate), EAC, FAO, G-77, IBRD, ICAO, ICRM, IDA, IDB, IFAD, IFC, IFRCS, IGAD, ILO, IMF, IMO, Interpol, IOC, IOM, IPU, ITSO, ITU, LAS, NAM, OIC, OPCW, OPCW (signatory), UN, UNCTAD, UNESCO, UNHCR, UNHRC, UNIDO, UPU, WFTU (NGOs), WHO, WIPO, WMO

Diplomatic representation in the US: *chief of mission:* Ambassador DAHIR Hassan Abdi (since 18 September 2024)
chancery: 1609 22nd Street NW, Washington, DC 20008
telephone: [1] (202) 853-9164
email address and website:
info@somaliembassydc.net
https://somaliembassydc.net/

Diplomatic representation from the US: *chief of mission:* Ambassador (vacant); Chargé d'Affaires Shane L. DIXON (since 25 July 2023)
embassy: Mogadishu, (reopened October 2019 on the grounds of the Mogadishu Airport)
mailing address: P.O. Box 606 Village Market
00621 Nairobi, Kenya
telephone: [254] 20 363-6451
email address and website:
SomaliaPublicAffairs@state.gov
https://so.usembassy.gov/

Flag description: *light blue with a large white five-pointed star in the center; the blue field was originally influenced by the flag of the UN but today is said to denote the sky and the neighboring Indian Ocean; the five points of the star represent the five regions in the horn of Africa that are inhabited by Somali people:* the former British Somaliland and Italian Somaliland (which together make up Somalia), Djibouti, Ogaden (Ethiopia), and the North East Province (Kenya)

National symbol(s): leopard; national colors: blue, white

National anthem: *name:* "Qolobaa Calankeed" (Every Nation Has its own Flag)
lyrics/music: Abdullahi QARSHE
note: adopted 2012; written in 1959

Government - note: regional and local governing bodies continue to exist and control various areas of the country, including the self-declared Republic of Somaliland in northwestern Somalia

ECONOMY

Economic overview: low-income African Horn economy; 30 years of war and instability crippled economic potential; high remittances for basic survival; new fiscal federalism approach; cleared some unsustainable debt; environmentally fragile; digitally driven urbanization efforts

Real GDP (purchasing power parity): $26.351 billion (2023 est.)
$25.558 billion (2022 est.)
$24.949 billion (2021 est.)
note: data in 2021 dollars
comparison ranking: 153

Real GDP growth rate: 3.1% (2023 est.)
2.44% (2022 est.)
3.31% (2021 est.)
note: annual GDP % growth based on constant local currency
comparison ranking: 106

Real GDP per capita: $1,500 (2023 est.)
$1,500 (2022 est.)
$1,500 (2021 est.)
note: data in 2021 dollars
comparison ranking: 220

GDP (official exchange rate): $11.68 billion (2023 est.)
note: data in current dollars at official exchange rate

Inflation rate (consumer prices): 1.5% (2017 est.)
-71.1% (2016 est.)
comparison ranking: 29

GDP - composition, by end use: *household consumption:* 126.4% (2023 est.)
government consumption: 7% (2023 est.)
investment in fixed capital: 25.3% (2023 est.)
exports of goods and services: 17.9% (2023 est.)
imports of goods and services: -76.7% (2023 est.)
note: figures may not total 100% due to rounding or gaps in data collection

Agricultural products: camel milk, milk, goat milk, sheep milk, sugarcane, fruits, sorghum, cassava, vegetables, maize (2022)
note: top ten agricultural products based on tonnage

Industries: light industries, including sugar refining, textiles, wireless communication

Industrial production growth rate: 4.3% (2014 est.)
note: annual % change in industrial value added based on constant local currency
comparison ranking: 67

Labor force: 3.277 million (2023 est.)
note: number of people ages 15 or older who are employed or seeking work
comparison ranking: 101

Unemployment rate: 19.03% (2023 est.)
19.13% (2022 est.)
19.55% (2021 est.)
note: % of labor force seeking employment
comparison ranking: 198

Youth unemployment rate (ages 15-24): *total:* 34.3% (2023 est.)
male: 32.4% (2023 est.)
female: 37.4% (2023 est.)
note: % of labor force ages 15-24 seeking employment
comparison ranking: total 18

Population below poverty line: 54.4% (2022 est.)
note: % of population with income below national poverty line

Gini Index coefficient - distribution of family income: 36.8 (2017 est.)
comparison ranking: 63

Remittances: 14.85% of GDP (2023 est.)
16.65% of GDP (2022 est.)
17.63% of GDP (2021 est.)
note: personal transfers and compensation between resident and non-resident individuals/households/entities

Public debt: 76.7% of GDP (2017 est.)
comparison ranking: 42

Taxes and other revenues: 0% (of GDP) (2020 est.)
note: central government tax revenue as a % of GDP
comparison ranking: 208

Current account balance: -$464 million (2017 est.)
-$427 million (2016 est.)
comparison ranking: 119

Exports: $819 million (2014 est.)
comparison ranking: 186

Exports - partners: UAE 50%, Oman 30%, Bulgaria 3%, India 3%, Kuwait 2% (2022)
note: top five export partners based on percentage share of exports

Exports - commodities: gold, sheep and goats, cattle, gum resins, shellfish (2022)
note: top five export commodities based on value in dollars

Imports: $94.43 billion (2018 est.)
$80.07 billion (2017 est.)
comparison ranking: 49

Imports - partners: UAE 33%, China 19%, India 16%, Turkey 7%, Ethiopia 5% (2022)
note: top five import partners based on percentage share of imports

Imports - commodities: tobacco, raw sugar, palm oil, rice, milk (2022)
note: top five import commodities based on value in dollars

Reserves of foreign exchange and gold: $30.45 million (2014 est.)
comparison ranking: 195

Exchange rates: Somali shillings (SOS) per US dollar -

Exchange rates: 23,097.987 (2017 est.)
23,061.784 (2016 est.)
22,254.236 (2015 est.)
20,230.929 (2014 est.)

ENERGY

Electricity access: *electrification - total population:* 48.9% (2022 est.)
electrification - urban areas: 76.7%
electrification - rural areas: 30.6%

Electricity: *installed generating capacity:* 131,000 kW (2022 est.)
consumption: 362.985 million kWh (2022 est.)
transmission/distribution losses: 15.408 million kWh (2022 est.)
comparison rankings: transmission/distribution losses 22; consumption 181; installed generating capacity 183

Electricity generation sources: *fossil fuels:* 90.4% of total installed capacity (2022 est.)
solar: 8% of total installed capacity (2022 est.)
wind: 1.6% of total installed capacity (2022 est.)

Coal: *imports:* (2022 est.) less than 1 metric ton

Petroleum: *refined petroleum consumption:* 6,000 bbl/day (2022 est.)

Natural gas: *proven reserves:* 5.663 billion cubic meters (2021 est.)

Carbon dioxide emissions: 815,000 metric tonnes of CO2 (2022 est.)
from petroleum and other liquids: 815,000 metric tonnes of CO2 (2022 est.)
comparison ranking: total emissions 175

Energy consumption per capita: 661,000 Btu/person (2022 est.)
comparison ranking: 195

COMMUNICATIONS

Telephones - fixed lines: *total subscriptions:* 91,000 (2022 est.)
subscriptions per 100 inhabitants: (2022 est.) less than 1
comparison ranking: total subscriptions 140

Telephones - mobile cellular: *total subscriptions:* 8.844 million (2022 est.)
subscriptions per 100 inhabitants: 50 (2022 est.)
comparison ranking: total subscriptions 96

Telecommunication systems: *general assessment:* Somalia's economic difficulties in recent years have made it difficult for telcos and the government to sustain investment in infrastructure; the government has also had to contend with militant groups which continue on occasion to force the closure of internet services in many areas of the country; in recent years, though, the government has addressed the lack of guidance which had prevailed since 1991, when a dictatorial regime was overthrown; the National Communications Law was passed in October 2017, aimed at setting a legal and regulatory framework for the telecoms sector, while provision was made in the following year to set up a regulatory authority to oversee the telecom sector; more recently, three types of licenses were mandated to provide clarity to operators, and to bring the market closer into line with international standards; all operators were given until August 2020 to secure one of the three license types; given the poor condition of fixed-line infrastructure, operators have concentrated on mobile connectivity; their investment plans have involved the development of LTE services to provide mobile data and broadband services; the telecom market has flourished; tariffs are among the lowest in Africa, and new cable systems coming on stream in the next few years, as well as planned investments from local operators to bolster the country's national fiber backbone, will lead to downward pressure on retail pricing; on the consumer side, spending on telecoms services and devices are under pressure from the financial effect of large-scale job losses and the consequent restriction on disposable incomes as the remnants of the impact of the Covid-19 pandemic remain and as global events, such as the Russian invasion of Ukraine, continue to play out; the market is continuing a positive growth trajectory, supported by a slow economic rebound in the country (2022)
domestic: fixed-line is 1 per 100 and mobile-cellular is 50 per 100 (2022)
international: country code - 252; landing points for the G2A, DARE1, PEACE, and EASSy fiber-optic submarine cable system linking East Africa, Indian Ocean Islands, the Middle East, North Africa and Europe (2019)

Broadcast media: 2 private TV stations rebroadcast Al-Jazeera and CNN; Somaliland has 1 government-operated TV station and Puntland has 1 private TV station; the transitional government operates Radio Mogadishu; 1 SW and roughly 10 private FM radio stations broadcast in Mogadishu; several radio stations operate in central and southern regions; Somaliland has 1 government-operated radio station; Puntland has roughly a half-dozen private radio stations; transmissions of at least 2 international broadcasters are available (2019)

Internet country code: .so

Internet users: *total:* 2.465 million (2021 est.)
percent of population: 14.5% (2021 est.)
comparison ranking: total 129

Broadband - fixed subscriptions: *total:* 119,000 (2020 est.)
subscriptions per 100 inhabitants: 1 (2020 est.)
comparison ranking: total 127

TRANSPORTATION

National air transport system: *number of registered air carriers:* 6 (2020)
inventory of registered aircraft operated by air carriers: 7
annual passenger traffic on registered air carriers: 4,486 (2018)

Civil aircraft registration country code prefix: 6O

Airports: 38 (2024)
comparison ranking: 106

Roadways: *total:* 15,000 km (2013)
comparison ranking: total 125

Merchant marine: *total:* 4 (2023)
by type: general cargo 1, other 3
comparison ranking: total 172

Ports: *total ports:* 6 (2024)
large: 1
medium: 0
small: 2
very small: 3
ports with oil terminals: 2
key ports: Baraawe, Berbera, Boosaaso, Kismaayo, Marka, Muqdisho

MILITARY AND SECURITY

Military and security forces: Somali National Armed Forces (SNAF; aka Somali National Defense Force): Land Forces (Somali National Army or SNA), Somali Navy, Somali Air Force

Ministry of Internal Security: Somali National Police (SNP, includes Coast Guard and a commando unit known as Harmacad or Cheetah)
National Security and Intelligence Agency (includes a commando/counterterrorism unit) (2024)
note 1: the Somali Navy and Air Force have only a few hundred personnel, little equipment, and are not operational; in early 2024, Somalia signed an agreement with Turkey to build, train and equip the Somali Navy
note 2: Somalia has numerous militia ("macawisley") and regional forces operating throughout the country; these forces include ones that are clan- and warlord-based, semi-official paramilitary and special police forces ("darwish"), and externally sponsored militias
note 3: Somaliland and Puntland have separate military and security forces

Military expenditures: 6% of GDP (2021 est.)
6% of GDP (2020 est.)
5.6% of GDP (2019 est.)
6% of GDP (2018 est.)
5.9% of GDP (2017 est.)
comparison ranking: 5

Military and security service personnel strengths: estimated 20,000 regular military personnel (2024)
note: tens of thousands of militia forces are also active in Somalia

Military equipment inventories and acquisitions: the SNA's inventory includes a variety of mostly older, secondhand equipment largely from Italy, Russia, South Africa, and the UK; in recent years, it has received limited quantities of more modern equipment as aid/donations from a variety of countries, including the US (2024)

Military service age and obligation: 18 is the legal minimum age for voluntary military service for men and women; conscription of men aged 18-40 and women aged 18-30 is authorized, but not currently utilized (2023)

Military - note: the Somali National Army (SNA) and supporting security and militia forces are actively conducting operations against the al-Shabaab terrorist group; al-Shabaab controls large parts of southern and central Somalia
the SNA is a lightly armed force of more than a dozen brigades; its most effective units are assessed to be the US-trained Danab ("Lightning") Advanced Infantry Brigade and those of the Turkish-trained Gorgor ("Eagle") Special Division; as of 2023, the Danab Brigade numbered about 2,000 troops with an eventual projected strength of 3,000, while the Gorgor Division was estimated to have up to 5,000 trained troops; SNA soldiers have also received training from Egypt, Eritrea, Ethiopia, the EU, Uganda, and the UK
the African Union Mission in Somalia (AMISOM) operated in the country with the approval of the UN from 2007-2022; its mission included assisting Somali forces in providing security for a stable political process, enabling the gradual handing over of security responsibilities from AMISOM to the Somali security forces, and reducing the threat posed by al-Shabaab and other armed opposition groups; in April 2022, AMISOM was reconfigured and replaced with the AU Transition Mission in Somalia (ATMIS); the ATMIS mission is to support the Somalia Federal Government (FGS) in implementing the security objectives of the FGS's security transition plan, a comprehensive strategy developed by the FGS and its international partners in 2018 and updated in 2021 to gradually transfer security responsibilities from ATMIS to Somali security forces; originally about 20,000-strong (civilians, military, and police), ATMIS began reducing its staffing levels in mid-2023; it is slated to end its mission at the end of 2024; the follow-on force for ATMIS will be the Support and Stabilization Mission in Somalia (AUSSOM)
UN Assistance Mission in Somalia (UNSOM; established 2013) is mandated by the Security Council to work with the FGS to support national reconciliation,

provide advice on peace-building and state-building, monitor the human rights situation, and help coordinate the efforts of the international community; the UN Support Office in Somalia (UNSOS; established 2015) is responsible for providing logistical field support to ATMIS, UNSOM, and the Somali security forces on joint operations with ATMIS (2024)

TERRORISM

Terrorist group(s): al-Shabaab; Islamic State of Iraq and ash-Sham – Somalia
note: details about the history, aims, leadership, organization, areas of operation, tactics, targets, weapons, size, and sources of support of the group(s) appear(s) in the Terrorism reference guide

TRANSNATIONAL ISSUES

Refugees and internally displaced persons: *refugees (country of origin):* 23,364 (Ethiopia), 9,969 (Yemen) (2023)
IDPs: 3.864 million (civil war since 1988, clan-based competition for resources; famine; insecurity because of fighting between al-Shabaab and the Transitional Federal Government's allied forces) (2022)

SOUTH AFRICA

INTRODUCTION

Background: Some of the earliest human remains in the fossil record were found in South Africa. By about A.D. 500, Bantu-speaking groups began settling into what is now northeastern South Africa, displacing Khoisan-speaking groups to the southwest. Dutch traders landed at the southern tip of present-day South Africa in 1652 and established a stopover point on the spice route between the Netherlands and the Far East, founding the city of Cape Town. After the British seized the Cape of Good Hope area in 1806, many settlers of Dutch descent – known then as "Boers," or farmers, but later called Afrikaners – trekked north to found their own republics, Transvaal and Orange Free State. In the 1820s, several decades of wars began as the Zulus expanded their territory, moving out of what is today southeastern South Africa and clashing with other indigenous peoples and the growing European settlements. The discovery of diamonds (1867) and gold (1886) spurred mass immigration, predominantly from Europe.

The Zulu kingdom's territory was incorporated into the British Empire after the Anglo-Zulu War in 1879, and the Afrikaner republics were incorporated after their defeat in the Second South African War (1899-1902). Beginning in 1910, the British and the Afrikaners ruled together under the Union of South Africa, which left the British Commonwealth to become a fully self-governing republic in 1961 after a Whites-only referendum. In 1948, the National Party was voted into power and instituted a policy of apartheid – billed as "separate development" of the races – which favored the White minority and suppressed the Black majority and other non-White groups. The African National Congress (ANC) led the resistance to apartheid, and many top ANC leaders such as Nelson MANDELA spent decades in South Africa's prisons. Internal protests and insurgency, as well as boycotts from some Western nations and institutions, led to the regime's eventual willingness to unban the ANC and negotiate a peaceful transition to majority rule.

The first multi-racial elections in 1994 ushered in majority rule under an ANC-led government. South Africa has since struggled to address apartheid-era imbalances in wealth, housing, education, and health care under successive administrations. President Cyril RAMAPHOSA, who was reelected as the ANC leader in 2022, has made some progress in reigning in corruption.

GEOGRAPHY

Location: Southern Africa, at the southern tip of the continent of Africa

Geographic coordinates: 29 00 S, 24 00 E

Map references: Africa

Area: *total:* 1,219,090 sq km
land: 1,214,470 sq km
water: 4,620 sq km
note: includes Prince Edward Islands (Marion Island and Prince Edward Island)
comparison ranking: total 26

Area - comparative: slightly less than twice the size of Texas

Land boundaries: *total:* 5,244 km
border countries (6): Botswana 1,969 km; Lesotho 1,106 km; Mozambique 496 km; Namibia 1,005 km; Eswatini 438 km; Zimbabwe 230 km

Coastline: 2,798 km

Maritime claims: *territorial sea:* 12 nm
contiguous zone: 24 nm
exclusive economic zone: 200 nm
continental shelf: 200 nm or to edge of the continental margin

Climate: mostly semiarid; subtropical along east coast; sunny days, cool nights

Terrain: vast interior plateau rimmed by rugged hills and narrow coastal plain

Elevation: *highest point:* Ntheledi (Mafadi) 3,450 m
lowest point: Atlantic Ocean 0 m
mean elevation: 1,034 m

Natural resources: gold, chromium, antimony, coal, iron ore, manganese, nickel, phosphates, tin, rare earth elements, uranium, gem diamonds, platinum, copper, vanadium, salt, natural gas
note: South Africa was the World's leading chromite ore producer in 2022 with an output of 18,000 mt

Land use: *agricultural land:* 79.4% (2018 est.)
arable land: 9.9% (2018 est.)
permanent crops: 0.3% (2018 est.)
permanent pasture: 69.2% (2018 est.)
forest: 7.6% (2018 est.)
other: 13% (2018 est.)

Irrigated land: 16,700 sq km (2012)

Major rivers (by length in km): Orange (shared with Lesotho [s], and Namibia [m]) - 2,092 km; Limpoporivier (Limpopo) river source (shared with Botswana, Zimbabwe, and Mozambique [m]) - 1,800 km; Vaal [s] - 1,210 km
note – [s] after country name indicates river source; [m] after country name indicates river mouth

Major watersheds (area sq km): Atlantic Ocean drainage: Orange (941,351 sq km)

Major aquifers: Karoo Basin, Lower Kalahari-Stampriet Basin

Population distribution: the population concentrated along the southern and southeastern coast, and inland around Pretoria; the eastern half of the country is more densely populated than the west as shown in this population distribution map

Natural hazards: prolonged droughts
volcanism: the volcano forming Marion Island in the Prince Edward Islands, which last erupted in 2004, is South Africa's only active volcano

Geography - note: South Africa completely surrounds Lesotho and almost completely surrounds Eswatini

PEOPLE AND SOCIETY

Population: *total:* 60,442,647
male: 29,664,388
female: 30,778,259 (2024 est.)
comparison rankings: female 25; male 24; total 25

Nationality: *noun:* South African(s)
adjective: South African

Ethnic groups: Black African 80.9%, Colored 8.8%, White 7.8%, Indian/Asian 2.6% (2021 est.)
note: Colored is a term used in South Africa, including on the national census, for persons of mixed race ancestry who developed a distinct cultural identity over several hundred years

Languages: isiZulu or Zulu (official) 25.3%, isiXhosa or Xhosa (official) 14.8%, Afrikaans (official) 12.2%, Sepedi or Pedi (official) 10.1%, Setswana or Tswana (official) 9.1%, English (official) 8.1%, Sesotho or

Sotho (official) 7.9%, Xitsonga or Tsonga (official) 3.6%, siSwati or Swati (official) 2.8%, Tshivenda or Venda (official) 2.5%, isiNdebele or Ndebele (official) 1.6%, other (includes South African sign language (official) and Khoi or Khoisan or Khoe languages) 2% (2018 est.)
major-language sample(s):
Die Wereld Feite Boek, n' onontbeerlike bron vir basiese informasie. (Afrikaans)
note: data represent language spoken most often at home

Religions: Christian 86%, ancestral, tribal, animist, or other traditional African religions 5.4%, Muslim 1.9%, other 1.5%, nothing in particular 5.2% (2015 est.)

Demographic profile: South Africa's youthful population is gradually aging, as the country's total fertility rate (TFR) has declined dramatically from about 6 children per woman in the 1960s to roughly 2.2 in 2014, and has remained at this level as of 2022. This pattern is similar to fertility trends in South Asia, the Middle East, and North Africa, and sets South Africa apart from the rest of Sub-Saharan Africa, where the average TFR remains higher than other regions of the world. Today, South Africa's decreasing number of reproductive age women is having fewer children, as women increase their educational attainment, workforce participation, and use of family planning methods; delay marriage; and opt for smaller families.
As the proportion of working-age South Africans has grown relative to children and the elderly, South Africa has been unable to achieve a demographic dividend because persistent high unemployment and the prevalence of HIV/AIDs have created a larger-than-normal dependent population. HIV/AIDS was also responsible for South Africa's average life expectancy plunging to less than 43 years in 2008; it has rebounded to 65 years as of 2022. HIV/AIDS continues to be a serious public health threat, although awareness-raising campaigns and the wider availability of anti-retroviral drugs is stabilizing the number of new cases, enabling infected individuals to live longer, healthier lives, and reducing mother-child transmissions.
Migration to South Africa began in the second half of the 17th century when traders from the Dutch East India Company settled in the Cape and started using slaves from South and southeast Asia (mainly from India but also from present-day Indonesia, Bangladesh, Sri Lanka, and Malaysia) and southeast Africa (Madagascar and Mozambique) as farm laborers and, to a lesser extent, as domestic servants. The Indian subcontinent remained the Cape Colony's main source of slaves in the early 18th century, while slaves were increasingly obtained from southeast Africa in the latter part of the 18th century and into the 19th century under British rule.
After slavery was completely abolished in the British Empire in 1838, South Africa's colonists turned to temporary African migrants and indentured labor through agreements with India and later China, countries that were anxious to export workers to alleviate domestic poverty and overpopulation. Of the more than 150,000 indentured Indian laborers hired to work in Natal's sugar plantations between 1860 and 1911, most exercised the right as British subjects to remain permanently (a small number of Indian immigrants came freely as merchants). Because of growing resentment toward Indian workers, the 63,000 indentured Chinese workers who mined gold in Transvaal between 1904 and 1911 were under more restrictive contracts and generally were forced to return to their homeland.
In the late 19th century and nearly the entire 20th century, South Africa's then British colonies' and Dutch states' enforced selective immigration policies that welcomed "assimilable" white Europeans as permanent residents but excluded or restricted other immigrants. Following the Union of South Africa's passage of a law in 1913 prohibiting Asian and other non-white immigrants and its elimination of the indenture system in 1917, temporary African contract laborers from neighboring countries became the dominant source of labor in the burgeoning mining industries. Others worked in agriculture and smaller numbers in manufacturing, domestic service, transportation, and construction. Throughout the 20th century, at least 40% of South Africa's miners were foreigners; the numbers peaked at over 80% in the late 1960s. Mozambique, Lesotho, Botswana, and Eswatini were the primary sources of miners, and Malawi and Zimbabwe were periodic suppliers.
Under apartheid, a "two gates" migration policy focused on policing and deporting illegal migrants rather than on managing migration to meet South Africa's development needs. The exclusionary 1991 Aliens Control Act limited labor recruitment to the highly skilled as defined by the ruling white minority, while bilateral labor agreements provided exemptions that enabled the influential mining industry and, to a lesser extent, commercial farms, to hire temporary, low-paid workers from neighboring states. Illegal African migrants were often tacitly allowed to work for low pay in other sectors but were always under threat of deportation.
The abolishment of apartheid in 1994 led to the development of a new inclusive national identity and the strengthening of the country's restrictive immigration policy. Despite South Africa's protectionist approach to immigration, the downsizing and closing of mines, and rising unemployment, migrants from across the continent believed that the country held work opportunities. Fewer African labor migrants were issued temporary work permits and, instead, increasingly entered South Africa with visitors' permits or came illegally, which drove growth in cross-border trade and the informal job market. A new wave of Asian immigrants has also arrived over the last two decades, many operating small retail businesses.
In the post-apartheid period, increasing numbers of highly skilled white workers emigrated, citing dissatisfaction with the political situation, crime, poor services, and a reduced quality of life. The 2002 Immigration Act and later amendments were intended to facilitate the temporary migration of skilled foreign labor to fill labor shortages, but instead the legislation continues to create regulatory obstacles. Although the education system has improved and brain drain has slowed in the wake of the 2008 global financial crisis, South Africa continues to face skills shortages in several key sectors, such as health care and technology.
South Africa's stability and economic growth has acted as a magnet for refugees and asylum seekers from nearby countries, despite the prevalence of discrimination and xenophobic violence. Refugees have included an estimated 350,000 Mozambicans during its 1980s civil war and, more recently, several thousand Somalis, Congolese, and Ethiopians. Nearly all of the tens of thousands of Zimbabweans who have applied for asylum in South Africa have been categorized as economic migrants and denied refuge.

Age structure: *0-14 years:* 27.2% (male 8,227,690/female 8,194,392)
15-64 years: 65.3% (male 19,524,873/female 19,947,839)
65 years and over: 7.5% (2024 est.) (male 1,911,825/female 2,636,028)

Dependency ratios: *total dependency ratio:* 52.2
youth dependency ratio: 43.9
elderly dependency ratio: 8.4
potential support ratio: 10.9 (2021 est.)

Median age: *total:* 30.4 years (2024 est.)
male: 30.1 years
female: 30.6 years
comparison ranking: total 136

Population growth rate: 1.07% (2024 est.)
comparison ranking: 90

Birth rate: 17.7 births/1,000 population (2024 est.)
comparison ranking: 82

Death rate: 6.9 deaths/1,000 population (2024 est.)
comparison ranking: 124

Net migration rate: -0.2 migrant(s)/1,000 population (2024 est.)
comparison ranking: 104

Population distribution: the population concentrated along the southern and southeastern coast, and inland around Pretoria; the eastern half of the country is more densely populated than the west as shown in this population distribution map

Urbanization: *urban population:* 68.8% of total population (2023)
rate of urbanization: 1.72% annual rate of change (2020-25 est.)

Major urban areas - population: 10.316 million Johannesburg (includes Ekurhuleni), 4.890 million Cape Town (legislative capital), 3.228 million Durban, 2.818 million PRETORIA (administrative capital), 1.296 million Port Elizabeth, 934,000 West Rand (2023)

Sex ratio: *at birth:* 1.02 male(s)/female
0-14 years: 1 male(s)/female
15-64 years: 0.98 male(s)/female
65 years and over: 0.73 male(s)/female
total population: 0.96 male(s)/female (2024 est.)

Maternal mortality ratio: 127 deaths/100,000 live births (2020 est.)
comparison ranking: 59

Infant mortality rate: *total:* 21.9 deaths/1,000 live births (2024 est.)
male: 23.9 deaths/1,000 live births
female: 20 deaths/1,000 live births
comparison ranking: total 71

Life expectancy at birth: *total population:* 71.9 years (2024 est.)
male: 70.3 years
female: 73.5 years
comparison ranking: total population 166

Total fertility rate: 2.27 children born/woman (2024 est.)
comparison ranking: 78

Gross reproduction rate: 1.12 (2024 est.)

Contraceptive prevalence rate: 54.6% (2016)

Drinking water source: *improved: urban:* 99.7% of population
rural: 90.3% of population
total: 96.7% of population

unimproved: urban: 0.3% of population
rural: 9.7% of population
total: 3.3% of population (2020 est.)

Current health expenditure: 8.6% of GDP (2020)

Physician density: 0.79 physicians/1,000 population (2019)

Sanitation facility access: *improved: urban:* 96.6% of population
rural: 86.4% of population
total: 93.2% of population
unimproved: urban: 3.4% of population
rural: 13.6% of population
total: 6.8% of population (2020 est.)

Obesity - adult prevalence rate: 28.3% (2016)
comparison ranking: 30

Alcohol consumption per capita: *total:* 7.21 liters of pure alcohol (2019 est.)
beer: 3.99 liters of pure alcohol (2019 est.)
wine: 1.21 liters of pure alcohol (2019 est.)
spirits: 1.31 liters of pure alcohol (2019 est.)
other alcohols: 0.7 liters of pure alcohol (2019 est.)
comparison ranking: total 58

Tobacco use: *total:* 20.3% (2020 est.)
male: 34% (2020 est.)
female: 6.5% (2020 est.)
comparison ranking: total 84

Children under the age of 5 years underweight: 5.5% (2017)
comparison ranking: 71

Currently married women (ages 15-49): 36.9% (2023 est.)

Child marriage: *women married by age 15:* 0.9%
women married by age 18: 3.6%
men married by age 18: 0.6% (2016 est.)

Education expenditures: 6.6% of GDP (2021 est.)
comparison ranking: 27

Literacy: *definition:* age 15 and over can read and write
total population: 95%
male: 95.5%
female: 94.5% (2019)

School life expectancy (primary to tertiary education): *total:* 13 years
male: 13 years
female: 14 years (2020)

ENVIRONMENT

Environment - current issues: lack of important arterial rivers or lakes requires extensive water conservation and control measures; growth in water usage outpacing supply; pollution of rivers from agricultural runoff and urban discharge; air pollution resulting in acid rain; deforestation; soil erosion; land degradation; desertification; solid waste pollution; disruption of fragile ecosystem has resulted in significant floral extinctions

Environment - international agreements: *party to:* Antarctic-Environmental Protection, Antarctic-Marine Living Resources, Antarctic Seals, Antarctic Treaty, Biodiversity, Climate Change, Climate Change-Kyoto Protocol, Climate Change-Paris Agreement, Comprehensive Nuclear Test Ban, Desertification, Endangered Species, Hazardous Wastes, Law of the Sea, Marine Dumping-London Convention, Marine Dumping-London Protocol, Marine Life Conservation, Nuclear Test Ban, Ozone Layer Protection, Ship Pollution, Wetlands, Whaling
signed, but not ratified: none of the selected agreements

Climate: mostly semiarid; subtropical along east coast; sunny days, cool nights

Urbanization: *urban population:* 68.8% of total population (2023)
rate of urbanization: 1.72% annual rate of change (2020-25 est.)

Revenue from coal: 2.4% of GDP (2018 est.)
comparison ranking: 3

Air pollutants: *particulate matter emissions:* 19.75 micrograms per cubic meter (2019 est.)
carbon dioxide emissions: 476.64 megatons (2016 est.)
methane emissions: 55.89 megatons (2020 est.)

Waste and recycling: *municipal solid waste generated annually:* 18,457,232 tons (2011 est.)
municipal solid waste recycled annually: 5,168,025 tons (2011 est.)
percent of municipal solid waste recycled: 28% (2011 est.)

Major rivers (by length in km): Orange (shared with Lesotho [s], and Namibia [m]) - 2,092 km; Limpoporivier (Limpopo) river source (shared with Botswana, Zimbabwe, and Mozambique [m]) - 1,800 km; Vaal [s] - 1,210 km
note – [s] after country name indicates river source; [m] after country name indicates river mouth

Major watersheds (area sq km): Atlantic Ocean drainage: Orange (941,351 sq km)

Major aquifers: Karoo Basin, Lower Kalahari-Stampriet Basin

Total water withdrawal: *municipal:* 3.11 billion cubic meters (2020 est.)
industrial: 4.09 billion cubic meters (2020 est.)
agricultural: 11.99 billion cubic meters (2020 est.)

Total renewable water resources: 51.35 billion cubic meters (2020 est.)

GOVERNMENT

Country name: *conventional long form:* Republic of South Africa
conventional short form: South Africa
former: Union of South Africa
abbreviation: RSA
etymology: self-descriptive name from the country's location on the continent; "Africa" is derived from the Roman designation of the area corresponding to present-day Tunisia "Africa terra," which meant "Land of the Afri" (the tribe resident in that area), but which eventually came to mean the entire continent

Government type: parliamentary republic

Capital: *name:* Pretoria (administrative capital); Cape Town (legislative capital); Bloemfontein (judicial capital)
geographic coordinates: 25 42 S, 28 13 E
time difference: UTC+2 (7 hours ahead of Washington, DC, during Standard Time)
etymology: Pretoria is named in honor of Andries PRETORIUS, the father of voortrekker (pioneer) leader Marthinus PRETORIUS; Cape Town reflects its location on the Cape of Good Hope; Bloemfontein is a combination of the Dutch words *bloem* (flower) and *fontein* (fountain) meaning "fountain of flowers"

Administrative divisions: 9 provinces; Eastern Cape, Free State, Gauteng, KwaZulu-Natal, Limpopo, Mpumalanga, Northern Cape, North West, Western Cape

Independence: *31 May 1910 (Union of South Africa formed from four British colonies:* Cape Colony, Natal, Transvaal, and Orange Free State); 22 August 1934 (Status of the Union Act); 31 May 1961 (republic declared); 27 April 1994 (majority rule)

National holiday: Freedom Day, 27 April (1994)

Legal system: mixed legal system of Roman-Dutch civil law, English common law, and customary law

Constitution: *history:* several previous; latest drafted 8 May 1996, approved by the Constitutional Court 4 December 1996, effective 4 February 1997
amendments: proposed by the National Assembly of Parliament; passage of amendments affecting constitutional sections on human rights and freedoms, non-racism and non-sexism, supremacy of the constitution, suffrage, the multi-party system of democratic government, and amendment procedures requires at least 75% majority vote of the Assembly, approval by at least six of the nine provinces represented in the National Council of Provinces, and assent of the president of the republic; passage of amendments affecting the Bill of Rights, and those related to provincial boundaries, powers, and authorities requires at least two-thirds majority vote of the Assembly, approval by at least six of the nine provinces represented in the National Council, and assent of the president; amended many times, last in 2020

International law organization participation: has not submitted an ICJ jurisdiction declaration; accepts ICCt jurisdiction

Citizenship: *citizenship by birth:* no
citizenship by descent only: at least one parent must be a citizen of South Africa
dual citizenship recognized: yes, but requires prior permission of the government
residency requirement for naturalization: 5 year

Suffrage: 18 years of age; universal

Executive branch: *chief of state:* President Matamela Cyril RAMAPHOSA (since 19 June 2024)
head of government: President Matamela Cyril RAMAPHOSA (since 19 June 2024)
cabinet: Cabinet appointed by the president
elections/appointments: president indirectly elected by the National Assembly for a 5-year term (eligible for a second term); election last held on 29 May 2024 (next to be held in 2029) note - the president is both chief of state and head of government
election results:
2024: Matamela Cyril RAMAPHOSA (ANC) elected president by the National Assembly unopposed
2019: Matamela Cyril RAMAPHOSA (ANC) elected president by the National Assembly unopposed
2014: Jacob ZUMA (ANC) reelected president by the National Assembly unopposed

Legislative branch: *description:* bicameral Parliament consists of:
National Council of Provinces (90 seats; nine 10-member delegations, each with 6 permanent delegates and 4 special delegates, appointed by each of the 9 provincial legislatures to serve 5-year terms; note - the Council has special powers to protect regional interests, including safeguarding cultural and linguistic traditions among ethnic minorities)

National Assembly (400 seats; half the members directly elected in multi-seat constituencies and half in a single nationwide constituency, both by proportional representation popular vote; members serve 5-year terms)
elections: National Council of Provinces and National Assembly - last held on 15 June 2024 (next to be held on 30 June 2029)
election results:
National Council of Provinces - percent of vote by party - NA; seats by party - ANC 29, DA 13, EFF 9, FF+ 2, IFP 1; composition - men 30, women 24, percentage women 44.4%; note - 36 appointed seats not filled
National Assembly - percent of vote by party - ANC 40.1% DA 21.8%, MK 14.5%, EFF 9.5%, IFP 3.8%, PA, 2.06%, FF+ 1.3%, Action SA 1.2%, ACDP 0.60%, UCM 0.49%, RISE 0.42%, BOSA 0.041%, ATM 0.40%, Al Jam-ah 0.24%, NCC 0.23%, PAC 0.23%, UAT 0.22%, GOOD 0.18% other 4.38%; seats by party - ANC 159, DA 87, MK 58, EFF 39, IFP 17, PA 9, FF+ 6, Action SA 6, ACDP 3, UDM 3, RISE 2, BOSA 2, ATM 2, AL Jam-ah 2, NCC 2, PAC 1, UAT 1, GOOD 1; composition - men 210, women 181, percentage women 46.3%; total Parliament percentage women 46.1%

Judicial branch: *highest court(s):* Supreme Court of Appeals (consists of the court president, deputy president, and 21 judges); Constitutional Court (consists of the chief and deputy chief justices and 9 judges)
judge selection and term of office: Supreme Court of Appeals president and vice president appointed by the national president after consultation with the Judicial Services Commission (JSC), a 23-member body chaired by the chief justice and includes other judges and judicial executives, members of parliament, practicing lawyers and advocates, a teacher of law, and several members designated by the president of South Africa; other Supreme Court judges appointed by the national president on the advice of the JSC and hold office until discharged from active service by an Act of Parliament; Constitutional Court chief and deputy chief justices appointed by the president of South Africa after consultation with the JSC and with heads of the National Assembly; other Constitutional Court judges appointed by the national president after consultation with the chief justice and leaders of the National Assembly; Constitutional Court judges serve 12-year nonrenewable terms or until age 70
subordinate courts: High Courts; Magistrates' Courts; labor courts; land claims courts

Political parties: African Christian Democratic Party or ACDP
African Independent Congress or AIC
African National Congress or ANC
African People's Convention or APC
Agang SA
Congress of the People or COPE
Democratic Alliance or DA
Economic Freedom Fighters or EFF
Freedom Front Plus or FF+
GOOD
Inkatha Freedom Party or IFP
National Freedom Party or NFP
Pan-Africanist Congress of Azania or PAC
United Christian Democratic Party or UCDP
United Democratic Movement or UDM

International organization participation: ACP, AfDB, AIIB, AU, BIS, BRICS, C, CD, FAO, FATF, G-20, G-24, G-5, G-77, IAEA, IBRD, ICAO, ICC (national committees), ICCt, ICRM, IDA, IFAD, IFC, IFRCS, IHO, ILO, IMF, IMO, IMSO, Interpol, IOC, IOM, IPU, ISO, ITSO, ITU, ITUC (NGOs), MIGA, MONUSCO, NAM, NSG, OECD (enhanced engagement), OPCW, Paris Club (associate), PCA, SACU, SADC, UN, UNAMID, UNCTAD, UNESCO, UNHCR, UNIDO, UNISFA, UNITAR, UNOOSA, UNWTO, UPU, Wassenaar Arrangement, WCO, WFTU (NGOs), WHO, WIPO, WMO, WTO, ZC

Diplomatic representation in the US: *chief of mission:* Ambassador (vacant); Chargé d'Affaires Ismail ESAU (since 3 May 2024)
chancery: 3051 Massachusetts Avenue NW, Washington, DC 20008
telephone: [1] (240) 937-5760
FAX: [1] (202) 265-1607
email address and website:
Info.saembassyDC@dirco.gov.za
https://www.saembassy.org/
consulate(s) general: Los Angeles, New York

Diplomatic representation from the US: *chief of mission:* Ambassador Reuben E. BRIGETY II (since 11 August 2022)
embassy: 877 Pretorius Street, Arcadia, Pretoria
mailing address: 9300 Pretoria Place, Washington DC 20521-9300
telephone: [27] (12) 431-4000
FAX: [27] (12) 342-2299
email address and website:
ACSJohannesburg@state.gov
https://za.usembassy.gov/
consulate(s) general: Cape Town, Durban, Johannesburg

Flag description: two equal width horizontal bands of red (top) and blue separated by a central green band that splits into a horizontal Y, the arms of which end at the corners of the hoist side; the Y embraces a black isosceles triangle from which the arms are separated by narrow yellow bands; the red and blue bands are separated from the green band and its arms by narrow white stripes; the flag colors do not have any official symbolism, but the Y stands for the "convergence of diverse elements within South African society, taking the road ahead in unity"; black, yellow, and green are found on the flag of the African National Congress, while red, white, and blue are the colors in the flags of the Netherlands and the UK, whose settlers ruled South Africa during the colonial era
note: the South African flag is one of only two national flags to display six colors as part of its primary design, the other is South Sudan's

National symbol(s): springbok (antelope), king protea flower; national colors: red, green, blue, yellow, black, white

National anthem: *name:* "National Anthem of South Africa"
lyrics/music: Enoch SONTONGA and Cornelius Jacob LANGENHOVEN/Enoch SONTONGA and Marthinus LOURENS de Villiers
note: adopted 1994; a combination of "N'kosi Sikelel' iAfrica" (God Bless Africa) and "Die Stem van Suid Afrika" (The Call of South Africa), which were respectively the anthems of the non-white and white communities under apartheid; official lyrics contain a mixture of Xhosa, Zulu, Sesotho, Afrikaans, and English (i.e., the five most widely spoken of South Africa's 11 official languages); music incorporates the melody used in the Tanzanian and Zambian anthems

National heritage: *total World Heritage Sites:* 10 (5 cultural, 4 natural, 1 mixed)
selected World Heritage Site locales: Fossil Hominid Sites of South Africa (c); iSimangaliso Wetland Park (n); Robben Island (c); Maloti-Drakensberg Park (m); Mapungubwe Cultural Landscape (c); Cape Floral Region Protected Areas (n); Vredefort Dome (n); Richtersveld Cultural and Botanical Landscape (c); Khomani Cultural Landscape (c); Barberton Makhonjwa Mountains (n)

ECONOMY

Economic overview: upper middle-income South African economy; hard hit by COVID-19; poor utilities management; key rare earth goods exporter; high income inequality; hosts Africa's largest stock exchange; rising unemployment, especially youth; land rights changes

Real GDP (purchasing power parity): $862.981 billion (2023 est.)
$857.82 billion (2022 est.)
$841.739 billion (2021 est.)
note: data in 2021 dollars
comparison ranking: 33

Real GDP growth rate: 0.6% (2023 est.)
1.91% (2022 est.)
4.7% (2021 est.)
note: annual GDP % growth based on constant local currency
comparison ranking: 178

Real GDP per capita: $14,300 (2023 est.)
$14,300 (2022 est.)
$14,200 (2021 est.)
note: data in 2021 dollars
comparison ranking: 126

GDP (official exchange rate): $377.782 billion (2023 est.)
note: data in current dollars at official exchange rate

Inflation rate (consumer prices): 6.07% (2023 est.)
7.04% (2022 est.)
4.61% (2021 est.)
note: annual % change based on consumer prices
comparison ranking: 129

Credit ratings: Fitch rating: BB- (2020)
Moody's rating: Ba2 (2020)
Standard & Poors rating: BB- (2020)
note: The year refers to the year in which the current credit rating was first obtained.

GDP - composition, by sector of origin: *agriculture:* 2.5% (2023 est.)
industry: 24.6% (2023 est.)
services: 63% (2023 est.)
note: figures may not total 100% due to non-allocated consumption not captured in sector-reported data
comparison rankings: services 67; industry 100; agriculture 148

GDP - composition, by end use: *household consumption:* 64.7% (2023 est.)
government consumption: 19.7% (2023 est.)
investment in fixed capital: 15.2% (2023 est.)
investment in inventories: 0.5% (2023 est.)
exports of goods and services: 33% (2023 est.)
imports of goods and services: -32.7% (2023 est.)
note: figures may not total 100% due to rounding or gaps in data collection

Agricultural products: sugarcane, maize, milk, potatoes, wheat, grapes, chicken, oranges, apples, soybeans (2022)
note: top ten agricultural products based on tonnage

Industries: mining (world's largest producer of platinum, gold, chromium), automobile assembly, metalworking, machinery, textiles, iron and steel, chemicals, fertilizer, foodstuffs, commercial ship repair

Industrial production growth rate: -0.15% (2023 est.)
note: annual % change in industrial value added based on constant local currency
comparison ranking: 156

Labor force: 25.158 million (2023 est.)
note: number of people ages 15 or older who are employed or seeking work
comparison ranking: 28

Unemployment rate: 27.99% (2023 est.)
28.84% (2022 est.)
28.77% (2021 est.)
note: % of labor force seeking employment
comparison ranking: 207

Youth unemployment rate (ages 15-24): *total:* 49.1% (2023 est.)
male: 45.8% (2023 est.)
female: 53.2% (2023 est.)
note: % of labor force ages 15-24 seeking employment
comparison ranking: total 4

Population below poverty line: 55.5% (2014 est.)
note: % of population with income below national poverty line

Gini Index coefficient - distribution of family income: 63 (2014 est.)
note: index (0-100) of income distribution; higher values represent greater inequality
comparison ranking: 1

Average household expenditures: *on food:* 21.6% of household expenditures (2022 est.)
on alcohol and tobacco: 5% of household expenditures (2022 est.)

Household income or consumption by percentage share: *lowest 10%:* 0.9% (2014 est.)
highest 10%: 50.5% (2014 est.)
note: % share of income accruing to lowest and highest 10% of population

Remittances: 0.22% of GDP (2023 est.)
0.22% of GDP (2022 est.)
0.22% of GDP (2021 est.)
note: personal transfers and compensation between resident and non-resident individuals/households/entities

Budget: *revenues:* $123.264 billion (2022 est.)
expenditures: $136.236 billion (2022 est.)
note: central government revenues (excluding grants) and expenses converted to US dollars at average official exchange rate for year indicated

Public debt: 76.55% of GDP (2022 est.)
note: central government debt as a % of GDP
comparison ranking: 43

Taxes and other revenues: 26.11% (of GDP) (2022 est.)
note: central government tax revenue as a % of GDP
comparison ranking: 39

Current account balance: -$6.16 billion (2023 est.)
-$1.698 billion (2022 est.)
$15.5 billion (2021 est.)
note: balance of payments - net trade and primary/secondary income in current dollars
comparison ranking: 188

Exports: $124.731 billion (2023 est.)
$136.112 billion (2022 est.)
$130.882 billion (2021 est.)
note: balance of payments - exports of goods and services in current dollars
comparison ranking: 43

Exports - partners: China 16%, US 7%, Germany 7%, India 6%, Japan 6% (2022)
note: top five export partners based on percentage share of exports

Exports - commodities: gold, platinum, coal, cars, diamonds (2022)
note: top five export commodities based on value in dollars

Imports: $123.541 billion (2023 est.)
$127.596 billion (2022 est.)
$104.867 billion (2021 est.)
note: balance of payments - imports of goods and services in current dollars
comparison ranking: 43

Imports - partners: China 21%, Germany 9%, India 7%, US 5%, Saudi Arabia 4% (2022)
note: top five import partners based on percentage share of imports

Imports - commodities: refined petroleum, cars, crude petroleum, vehicle parts/accessories, broadcasting equipment (2022)
note: top five import commodities based on value in dollars

Reserves of foreign exchange and gold: $62.492 billion (2023 est.)
$60.553 billion (2022 est.)
$57.597 billion (2021 est.)
note: holdings of gold (year-end prices)/foreign exchange/special drawing rights in current dollars
comparison ranking: 39

Debt - external: $53.43 billion (2022 est.)
note: present value of external debt in current US dollars
comparison ranking: 12

Exchange rates: rand (ZAR) per US dollar -

Exchange rates: 18.45 (2023 est.)
16.356 (2022 est.)
14.779 (2021 est.)
16.459 (2020 est.)
14.448 (2019 est.)

ENERGY

Electricity access: *electrification - total population:* 86.5% (2022 est.)
electrification - urban areas: 87.1%
electrification - rural areas: 93.4%

Electricity: *installed generating capacity:* 63.411 million kW (2022 est.)
consumption: 200.565 billion kWh (2022 est.)
exports: 13.967 billion kWh (2022 est.)
imports: 10.331 billion kWh (2022 est.)
transmission/distribution losses: 25.285 billion kWh (2022 est.)
comparison rankings: transmission/distribution losses 191; imports 25; exports 21; consumption 22; installed generating capacity 21

Electricity generation sources: *fossil fuels:* 87.8% of total installed capacity (2022 est.)
nuclear: 4.4% of total installed capacity (2022 est.)
solar: 2.7% of total installed capacity (2022 est.)
wind: 4.2% of total installed capacity (2022 est.)
hydroelectricity: 0.7% of total installed capacity (2022 est.)
biomass and waste: 0.2% of total installed capacity (2022 est.)

Nuclear energy: Number of operational nuclear reactors: 2 (2023)

Net capacity of operational nuclear reactors: 1.85GW (2023 est.)

Percent of total electricity production: 4.4% (2023 est.)

Coal: *production:* 245.467 million metric tons (2022 est.)
consumption: 176.148 million metric tons (2022 est.)
exports: 75.512 million metric tons (2022 est.)
imports: 3.026 million metric tons (2022 est.)
proven reserves: 9.893 billion metric tons (2022 est.)

Petroleum: *total petroleum production:* 95,000 bbl/day (2023 est.)
refined petroleum consumption: 601,000 bbl/day (2022 est.)
crude oil estimated reserves: 15 million barrels (2021 est.)

Natural gas: *production:* 59.128 million cubic meters (2022 est.)
consumption: 4.487 billion cubic meters (2022 est.)
imports: 4.428 billion cubic meters (2022 est.)

Carbon dioxide emissions: 476.987 million metric tonnes of CO2 (2022 est.)
from coal and metallurgical coke: 392.305 million metric tonnes of CO2 (2022 est.)
from petroleum and other liquids: 75.88 million metric tonnes of CO2 (2022 est.)
from consumed natural gas: 8.803 million metric tonnes of CO2 (2022 est.)
comparison ranking: total emissions 13

Energy consumption per capita: 95.511 million Btu/person (2022 est.)
comparison ranking: 55

COMMUNICATIONS

Telephones - fixed lines: *total subscriptions:* 1.31 million (2022 est.)
subscriptions per 100 inhabitants: 2 (2022 est.)
comparison ranking: total subscriptions 61

Telephones - mobile cellular: *total subscriptions:* 100.26 million (2022 est.)
subscriptions per 100 inhabitants: 167 (2022 est.)
comparison ranking: total subscriptions 18

Telecommunication systems: *general assessment:* South Africa's telecom sector boasts one of the most advanced infrastructures on the continent; the focus in recent years has been on back haul capacity and on fiber and LTE networks to extend and improve internet service connectivity; several satellite solutions also appeared in 2023, aimed at providing additional backhaul and improving connectivity in rural areas; the mobile sector has developed strongly in recent years, partly due to the poor availability and level of service of fixed-line networks, which meant that many people had no alternative to mobile networks for voice and data services (2024)
domestic: fixed-line is 2 per 100 persons and mobile-cellular is 167 telephones per 100 persons (2022)
international: country code - 27; landing points for the WACS, ACE, SAFE, SAT-3, Equiano, SABR, SAEx1, SAEx2, IOX Cable System, METISS,

EASSy, and SEACOM/ Tata TGN-Eurasia fiber-optic submarine cable systems connecting South Africa, East Africa, West Africa, Europe, Southeast Asia, Asia, South America, Indian Ocean Islands, and the US; satellite earth stations - 3 Intelsat (1 Indian Ocean and 2 Atlantic Ocean) (2019)

Broadcast media: the South African Broadcasting Corporation (SABC) operates 6 free-to-air TV stations; e.tv, a private station, is accessible to more than half the population; multiple subscription TV services provide a mix of local and international channels; well-developed mix of public and private radio stations at the national, regional, and local levels; the SABC radio network, state-owned and controlled but nominally independent, operates 18 stations, one for each of the 11 official languages, 4 community stations, and 3 commercial stations; more than 100 community-based stations extend coverage to rural areas

Internet country code: .za

Internet users: *total:* 42.48 million (2021 est.)
percent of population: 72% (2021 est.)
comparison ranking: total 24

Broadband - fixed subscriptions: *total:* 1,303,057 (2020 est.)
subscriptions per 100 inhabitants: 2 (2020 est.)
comparison ranking: total 68

TRANSPORTATION

National air transport system: *number of registered air carriers:* 17 (2020)
inventory of registered aircraft operated by air carriers: 243
annual passenger traffic on registered air carriers: 23,921,748 (2018)
annual freight traffic on registered air carriers: 716.25 million (2018) mt-km

Civil aircraft registration country code prefix: ZS

Airports: 575 (2024)
comparison ranking: 13

Heliports: 49 (2024)

Pipelines: 94 km condensate, 1,293 km gas, 992 km oil, 1,460 km refined products (2013)

Railways: *total:* 30,400 km (2021)
standard gauge: 80 km (2021) 1.435-m gauge (80 km electrified)
narrow gauge: 19,756 km (2014) 1.065-m gauge (8,271 km electrified)
comparison ranking: total 8

Roadways: *total:* 750,000 km
paved: 158,124 km
unpaved: 591,876 km (2016)
comparison ranking: total 11

Merchant marine: *total:* 110 (2023)
by type: bulk carrier 3, general cargo 1, oil tanker 7, other 99
comparison ranking: total 86

Ports: *total ports:* 8 (2024)
large: 2
medium: 4
small: 1
very small: 1
ports with oil terminals: 7
key ports: Cape Town, Durban, Mossel Bay, Port Elizabeth, Richards Bay, Saldanha Bay

MILITARY AND SECURITY

Military and security forces: South African National Defense Force (SANDF): South African Army (includes Reserve Force), South African Navy (SAN), South African Air Force (SAAF), South African Military Health Services

Ministry of Police: South African Police Service (2024)
note: the South African Police Service includes a Special Task Force for counterterrorism, counterinsurgency, and hostage rescue operations

Military expenditures: 0.7% of GDP (2023 est.)
0.8% of GDP (2022 est.)
0.9% of GDP (2021 est.)
1.1% of GDP (2020 est.)
1% of GDP (2019 est.)
comparison ranking: 146

Military and security service personnel strengths: approximately 73,000 active-duty personnel (40,000 Army; 7,000 Navy; 10,000 Air Force; 8,000 Military Health Service; 8,000 other, including administrative, logistics, military police); 180,000 South African Police Service (2024)

Military equipment inventories and acquisitions: the SANDF's inventory consists of a mix of domestically produced and foreign-supplied equipment; South Africa's domestic defense industry produced most of the Army's major weapons systems (some were jointly produced with foreign companies), while the Air Force and Navy inventories include a mix of aging European-, Israeli-, and US-origin weapons and equipment; South Africa has one of Africa's leading defense industries (2024)

Military service age and obligation: 18-22 (18-26 for college graduates) years of age for voluntary military service for men and women; 2-year service obligation (2023)
note: in 2023, women comprised nearly 30% of the military

Military deployments: 1,150 Democratic Republic of the Congo (MONUSCO) (2024)

Military - note: the SANDF's primary responsibilities include territorial and maritime defense, supporting the Police Service, protecting key infrastructure, and participating in international peacekeeping missions; the SANDF historically has been one of Africa's most capable militaries, but in recent years its operational readiness and modernization programs have been widely viewed as hampered by funding shortfalls
the SANDF participates regularly in African and UN peacekeeping missions and is a member of the Southern Africa Development Community (SADC) Standby Force; in 2021, it sent about 1,500 troops to Mozambique as part of a multinational SADC force to help combat an insurgency, and South African forces have been a key component of the UN's Force Intervention Brigade in the Democratic Republic of the Congo; in recent years, the SANDF has been deployed internally to assist the Police Service with quelling unrest and assisting with border security
the SANDF was created in 1994 to replace the South African Defense Force (SADF); the SANDF was opened to all South Africans who met military requirements, while the SADF was a mostly white force (only whites were subject to conscription) with non-whites only allowed to join in a voluntary capacity; the SANDF also absorbed members of the guerrilla and militia forces of the various anti-apartheid opposition groups, including the African National Congress, the Pan Africanist Congress, and the Inkatha Freedom Party, as well as the security forces of the formerly independent Bantustan homelands (2024)

SPACE

Space agency/agencies: South African National Space Agency (SANSA; established 2010); South Africa Council for Space Affairs (SACSA; statutory body established 1995); South African Radio Telescope Observatory (SARAO) (2024)

Space launch site(s): Arniston launch facility (Western Cape) used to support space launch vehicle and ballistic missile program (1980s-1990s); it is now a weapons testing facility called the Denel Overberg Test Range (2024)

Space program overview: the largest producer of satellites (particularly nanosatellites) in Africa; areas of focus for development include remote sensing (RS) capabilities, such as optical instruments and synthetic aperture radar systems, space engineering, ground support to space operations (tracking, telemetry, etc.), and space science, particularly astronomy; SANSA is responsible for aggregating RS data for southern African countries; has a sounding rocket program for carrying experimental payloads for research purposes; cooperates with foreign space agencies and industries, including those of China, France, India, Russia, and the US; participates in international programs such as the Square Kilometer Array (SKA) Project, an international effort to build the world's largest radio telescope by 2030; has a substantial number of state- and privately-owned aerospace companies, as well as academic and research institutions involved in space-related activities (2024)
note: further details about the key activities, programs, and milestones of the country's space program, as well as government spending estimates on the space sector, appear in the Space Programs reference guide

TERRORISM

Terrorist group(s): Islamic State of Iraq and ash-Sham (ISIS)
note: details about the history, aims, leadership, organization, areas of operation, tactics, targets, weapons, size, and sources of support of the group(s) appear(s) in the Terrorism reference guide

TRANSNATIONAL ISSUES

Refugees and internally displaced persons: *refugees (country of origin):* 22,388 (Somalia), 15,240 (Ethiopia) (mid-year 2022); 42,132 (Democratic Republic of the Congo) (refugees and asylum seekers) (2024)
IDPs: 5,000 (2020)

Illicit drugs: leading regional importer of chemicals used in the production of illicit drugs especially synthetic drugs;

SOUTH GEORGIA AND SOUTH SANDWICH ISLANDS

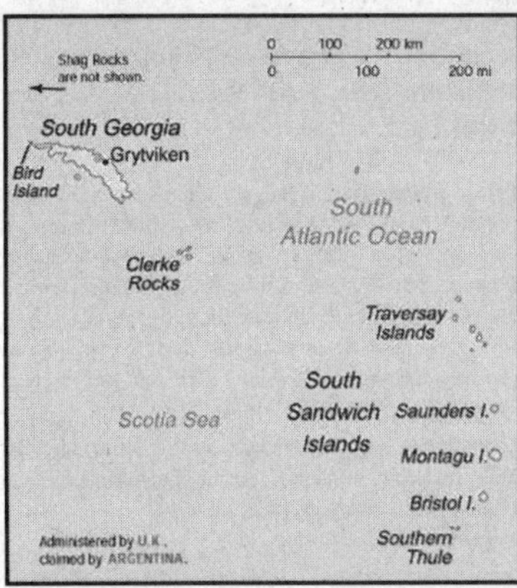

INTRODUCTION

Background: South Georgia and the South Sandwich Islands lie approximately 1,000 km east of the Falkland Islands and have been under British administration since 1908 – except for a brief period in 1982 when Argentina occupied them. Grytviken, on South Georgia, was a 19th- and early 20th-century whaling station. Famed explorer Ernest SHACKLETON stopped there in 1914 en route to his ill-fated attempt to cross Antarctica on foot. He returned some 20 months later with a few companions in a small boat and arranged a successful rescue for the rest of his crew, which was stranded off the Antarctic Peninsula. He died in 1922 on a subsequent expedition and is buried in Grytviken. Today, the station houses scientists from the British Antarctic Survey. Recognizing the importance of preserving the marine stocks in adjacent waters, the UK extended the exclusive fishing zone in 1993, from 12 nm to 200 nm around each island.

GEOGRAPHY

Location: Southern South America, islands in the South Atlantic Ocean, east of the tip of South America

Geographic coordinates: 54 30 S, 37 00 W

Map references: Antarctic Region

Area: *total:* 3,903 sq km
land: 3,903 sq km
water: 0 sq km
note: includes Shag Rocks, Black Rock, Clerke Rocks, South Georgia Island, Bird Island, and the South Sandwich Islands, which consist of 11 islands
comparison ranking: total 176

Area - comparative: slightly larger than Rhode Island

Land boundaries: *total:* 0 km

Coastline: NA

Maritime claims: *territorial sea:* 12 nm
exclusive fishing zone: 200 nm

Climate: variable, with mostly westerly winds throughout the year interspersed with periods of calm; nearly all precipitation falls as snow

Terrain: most of the islands are rugged and mountainous rising steeply from the sea; South Georgia is largely barren with steep, glacier-covered mountains; the South Sandwich Islands are of volcanic origin with some active volcanoes

Elevation: *highest point:* Mount Paget (South Georgia) 2,934 m
lowest point: Atlantic Ocean 0 m

Natural resources: fish

Land use: *other:* 100% (2018 est.)

Irrigated land: 0 sq km (2022)

Natural hazards: the South Sandwich Islands have prevailing weather conditions that generally make them difficult to approach by ship; they are also subject to active volcanism

Geography - note: the north coast of South Georgia has several large bays, which provide good anchorage

PEOPLE AND SOCIETY

Population: *total:* (July 2021 est.) no indigenous inhabitants
note: the small military garrison on South Georgia withdrew in March 2001 and was replaced by a permanent group of scientists from the British Antarctic Survey, which also has a biological station on Bird Island; the South Sandwich Islands are uninhabited

ENVIRONMENT

Environment - current issues: reindeer - introduced to the islands in the 20th century - devastated the native flora and bird species; some reindeer were translocated to the Falkland Islands in 2001, the rest were exterminated (2013-14); a parallel effort (2010-15) eradicated rats and mice that came to the islands as stowaways on ships as early as the late 18th century

Climate: variable, with mostly westerly winds throughout the year interspersed with periods of calm; nearly all precipitation falls as snow

GOVERNMENT

Country name: *conventional long form:* South Georgia and the South Sandwich Islands
conventional short form: South Georgia and South Sandwich Islands
abbreviation: SGSSI
etymology: South Georgia was named "the Isle of Georgia" in 1775 by Captain James COOK in honor of British King GEORGE III; the explorer also discovered the Sandwich Islands Group that year, which he named "Sandwich Land" after John MONTAGU, the Earl of Sandwich and First Lord of the Admiralty; the word "South" was later added to distinguish these islands from the other Sandwich Islands, now known as the Hawaiian Islands

Dependency status: overseas territory of the UK, also claimed by Argentina; administered from the Falkland Islands by a commissioner, who is concurrently governor of the Falkland Islands, representing King CHARLES III

Legal system: the laws of the UK, where applicable, apply

International organization participation: UPU

Diplomatic representation in the US: none (administered by the UK, claimed by Argentina)

Diplomatic representation from the US: none (administered by the UK, claimed by Argentina)

Flag description: blue with the flag of the UK in the upper hoist-side quadrant and the South Georgia and South Sandwich Islands coat of arms centered on the outer half of the flag; the coat of arms features a shield with a golden lion rampant, holding a torch; the shield is supported by a fur seal on the left and a Macaroni penguin on the right; a reindeer appears above the crest, and below the shield on a scroll is the motto LEO TERRAM PROPRIAM PROTEGAT (Let the Lion Protect its Own Land); the lion with the torch represents the UK and discovery; the background of the shield, blue and white estoiles, are found in the coat of arms of James Cook, discoverer of the islands; all the outer supporting animals represented are native to the islands

TRANSPORTATION

Heliports: 1 (2024)

Ports: *total ports:* 3 (2024)
large: 0
medium: 0
small: 0
very small: 3
ports with oil terminals: 1
key ports: Grytviken, Prince Olav Harbor, Stromness Harbor

MILITARY AND SECURITY

Military - note: defense is the responsibility of the UK

SOUTH SUDAN

INTRODUCTION

Background: South Sudan, which gained independence from Sudan in 2011, is the world's newest country. Home to a diverse array of mainly Nilotic ethnolinguistic groups that settled in the territory in the 15th through 19th centuries, South Sudanese society is heavily dependent on seasonal migration and seasonal fluctuations in precipitation. Modern-day South Sudan was conquered first by Egypt and later ruled jointly by Egyptian-British colonial administrators in the late 19th century. Christian

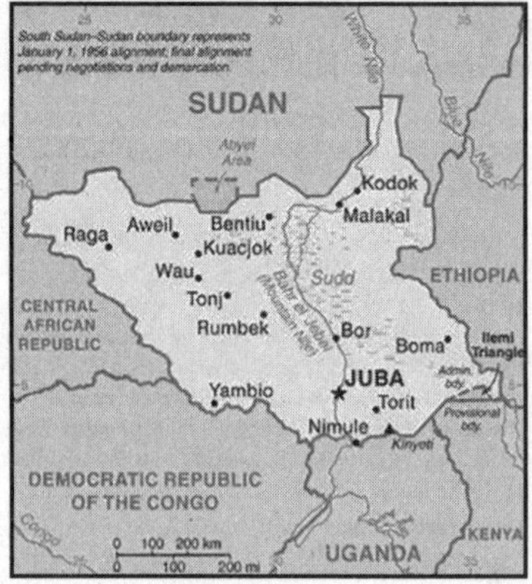

missionaries helped spread the English language and Christianity in the area, leading to significant cultural differences with the northern part of Sudan, where Arabic and Islam are dominant. When Sudan gained its independence in 1956, the southern region received assurances that it would participate fully in the political system. However, the Arab government in Khartoum reneged on its promises, prompting two periods of civil war (1955-1972 and 1983-2005) in which as many as 2.5 million people died – mostly civilians – due largely to starvation and drought. The second Sudanese civil war was one of the deadliest since WWII and left southern Sudanese society devastated. Peace talks resulted in a US-backed Comprehensive Peace Agreement in 2005, which granted the South six years of autonomy followed by a referendum on final status. The result of this referendum, held in 2011, was a vote of 98% in favor of secession.

Since independence, South Sudan has struggled to form a viable governing system and has been plagued by widespread corruption, political conflict, and communal violence. In 2013, conflict erupted between forces loyal to President Salva KIIR, a Dinka, and forces loyal to Vice President Riek MACHAR, a Nuer. The conflict quickly spread through the country along ethnic lines, killing tens of thousands and creating a humanitarian crisis with millions of South Sudanese displaced. KIIR and MACHAR signed a peace agreement in 2015 that created a Transitional Government of National Unity the next year. However, renewed fighting broke out in Juba between KIIR and MACHAR's forces, plunging the country back into conflict and drawing in additional armed opposition groups. A "revitalized" peace agreement was signed in 2018, mostly ending the fighting and laying the groundwork for a unified national army, a transitional government, and elections. The transitional government was formed in 2020, when MACHAR returned to Juba as first vice president. Since 2020, implementation of the peace agreement has been stalled amid wrangling over power-sharing, which has contributed to an uptick in communal violence and the country's worst food crisis since independence, with 7 of 11 million South Sudanese citizens in need of humanitarian assistance. The transitional period was extended an additional two years in 2022, pushing elections to late 2024.

GEOGRAPHY

Location: East-Central Africa; south of Sudan, north of Uganda and Kenya, west of Ethiopia

Geographic coordinates: 8 00 N, 30 00 E

Map references: Africa

Area: *total:* 644,329 sq km
land: NA
water: NA
comparison ranking: total 44

Area - comparative: more than four times the size of Georgia; slightly smaller than Texas

Land boundaries: *total:* 6,018 km
border countries (6): Central African Republic 1,055 km; Democratic Republic of the Congo 714 km; Ethiopia 1,299 km; Kenya 317 km; Sudan 2,158 km; Uganda 475 km
note: South Sudan-Sudan boundary represents 1 January 1956 alignment; final alignment pending negotiations and demarcation; final sovereignty status of Abyei Area pending negotiations between South Sudan and Sudan

Coastline: 0 km (landlocked)

Maritime claims: none (landlocked)

Climate: hot with seasonal rainfall influenced by the annual shift of the Inter-Tropical Convergence Zone; rainfall heaviest in upland areas of the south and diminishes to the north

Terrain: plains in the north and center rise to southern highlands along the border with Uganda and Kenya; the White Nile, flowing north out of the uplands of Central Africa, is the major geographic feature of the country; The Sudd (a name derived from floating vegetation that hinders navigation) is a large swampy area of more than 100,000 sq km fed by the waters of the White Nile that dominates the center of the country

Elevation: *highest point:* Kinyeti 3,187 m
lowest point: White Nile 381 m

Natural resources: hydropower, fertile agricultural land, gold, diamonds, petroleum, hardwoods, limestone, iron ore, copper, chromium ore, zinc, tungsten, mica, silver

Land use: *agricultural land:* 45% (2018)
arable land: 4.4% (2018)
permanent pasture: 40.7% (2018)
forest: 11.3% (2018)
other: 43.5% (2018)

Irrigated land: 1,000 sq km (2012)

Major rivers (by length in km): Nile (shared with Rwanda [s], Tanzania, Uganda, Sudan, and Egypt [m]) - 6,650 km

note – [s] after country name indicates river source; [m] after country name indicates river mouth

Major watersheds (area sq km):Atlantic Ocean drainage: Congo (3,730,881 sq km), *(Mediterranean Sea)* Nile (3,254,853 sq km)

Population distribution: clusters found in urban areas, particularly in the western interior and around the White Nile as shown in this population distribution map

Geography - note: landlocked; The Sudd is a vast swamp in the north central region of South Sudan, formed by the White Nile; its size is variable but can reach some 15% of the country's total area during the rainy season; it is one of the world's largest wetlands

PEOPLE AND SOCIETY

Population: *total:* 12,703,714
male: 6,476,341
female: 6,227,373 (2024 est.)
comparison rankings: female 79; male 80; total 79

Nationality: *noun:* South Sudanese (singular and plural)
adjective: South Sudanese

Ethnic groups: Dinka (Jieng) approximately 35-40%, Nuer (Naath) approximately 15%, Shilluk (Chollo), Azande, Bari, Kakwa, Kuku, Murle, Mandari, Didinga, Ndogo, Bviri, Lndi, Anuak, Bongo, Lango, Dungotona, Acholi, Baka, Fertit (2011 est.)
note: Figures are estimations due to population changes during South Sudan's civil war and the lack of updated demographic studies

Languages: English (official), Arabic (includes Juba and Sudanese variants), ethnic languages include Dinka, Nuer, Bari, Zande, Shilluk
major-language sample(s):
كتاب حقائق العالم، المصدر الذي لا يمكن الاستغناء عنه للمعلومات الأساسية
(Arabic)

Religions: Christian 60.5%, folk religion 32.9%, Muslim 6.2%, other <1%, unaffiliated <1% (2020 est.)

Demographic profile: South Sudan, independent from Sudan since July 2011 after decades of civil war, is one of the world's poorest countries and ranks among the lowest in many socioeconomic categories. Problems are exacerbated by ongoing tensions with Sudan over oil revenues and land borders, fighting between government forces and rebel groups, and inter-communal violence. Most of the population lives off of farming, while smaller numbers rely on animal husbandry; abput 80% of the populace lives in rural areas. The maternal mortality rate is among the world's highest for a variety of reasons, including a shortage of health care workers, facilities, and supplies; poor roads and a lack of transport; and cultural beliefs that prevent women from seeking obstetric care. Most women marry and start having children early, giving birth at home with the assistance of traditional birth attendants, who are unable to handle complications.
Educational attainment is extremely poor due to the lack of schools, qualified teachers, and materials. Only one-third of the population is literate (the rate is even lower among women), and half live below the poverty line. Teachers and students are also struggling with the switch from Arabic to English as the language of instruction. Many adults missed out on schooling because of warfare and displacement.
More than 2 million South Sudanese have sought refuge in neighboring countries since the current conflict began in December 2013. Another 2.2 million South Sudanese are internally displaced as of October 2022. Despite South Sudan's instability and lack of infrastructure and social services, more than 275,000 people had fled to South Sudan to escape fighting in Sudan as of December 2022.

Age structure: *0-14 years:* 42.1% (male 2,725,520/female 2,619,035)
15-64 years: 55.3% (male 3,568,064/female 3,458,804)
65 years and over: 2.6% (2024 est.) (male 182,757/female 149,534)

Dependency ratios: *total dependency ratio:* 80.8
youth dependency ratio: 74.7

elderly dependency ratio: 6.1
potential support ratio: 18.4 (2021 est.)

Median age: *total:* 18.7 years (2024 est.)
male: 18.7 years
female: 18.7 years
comparison ranking: total 217

Population growth rate: 4.65% (2024 est.)
comparison ranking: 1

Birth rate: 36.4 births/1,000 population (2024 est.)
comparison ranking: 10

Death rate: 8.9 deaths/1,000 population (2024 est.)
comparison ranking: 65

Net migration rate: 19.1 migrant(s)/1,000 population (2024 est.)
comparison ranking: 2

Population distribution: clusters found in urban areas, particularly in the western interior and around the White Nile as shown in this population distribution map

Urbanization: *urban population:* 21.2% of total population (2023)
rate of urbanization: 4.12% annual rate of change (2020-25 est.)

Major urban areas - population: 459,000 JUBA (capital) (2023)

Sex ratio: *at birth:* 1.05 male(s)/female
0-14 years: 1.04 male(s)/female
15-64 years: 1.03 male(s)/female
65 years and over: 1.22 male(s)/female
total population: 1.04 male(s)/female (2024 est.)

Maternal mortality ratio: 1,223 deaths/100,000 live births (2020 est.)
comparison ranking: 1

Infant mortality rate: *total:* 60.1 deaths/1,000 live births (2024 est.)
male: 65.8 deaths/1,000 live births
female: 54.1 deaths/1,000 live births
comparison ranking: total 8

Life expectancy at birth: *total population:* 60.3 years (2024 est.)
male: 58.4 years
female: 62.2 years
comparison ranking: total population 220

Total fertility rate: 5.09 children born/woman (2024 est.)
comparison ranking: 9

Gross reproduction rate: 2.48 (2024 est.)

Drinking water source: *improved: urban:* 88.7% of population
rural: 75.8% of population
total: 78.4% of population
unimproved: urban: 11.3% of population
rural: 24.2% of population
total: 21.6% of population (2020 est.)

Current health expenditure: 5.3% of GDP (2020)

Sanitation facility access: *improved: urban:* 60.6% of population
rural: 15.5% of population
total: 24.6% of population
unimproved: urban: 39.4% of population
rural: 84.5% of population
total: 75.4% of population (2020 est.)

Obesity - adult prevalence rate: 6.6% (2014)
comparison ranking: 166

Currently married women (ages 15-49): 72% (2023 est.)

Education expenditures: 1.5% of GDP (2016 est.)
comparison ranking: 191

Literacy: *definition:* age 15 and over can read and write
total population: 34.5%
male: 40.3%
female: 28.9% (2018)

ENVIRONMENT

Environment - current issues: water pollution; inadequate supplies of potable water; wildlife conservation and loss of biodiversity; deforestation; soil erosion; desertification; periodic drought

Environment - international agreements: *party to:* Biodiversity, Climate Change, Climate Change-Paris Agreement, Desertification, Ozone Layer Protection, Wetlands
signed, but not ratified: none of the selected agreements

Climate: hot with seasonal rainfall influenced by the annual shift of the Inter-Tropical Convergence Zone; rainfall heaviest in upland areas of the south and diminishes to the north

Urbanization: *urban population:* 21.2% of total population (2023)
rate of urbanization: 4.12% annual rate of change (2020-25 est.)

Food insecurity: *widespread lack of access: due to economic downturn, the lingering effects of floods, and prolonged internal conflict* - despite sustained humanitarian assistance, food insecurity still affects large segments of the population, owing to rampant inflation and insufficient food supplies due to stagnant agricultural production, the effects of consecutive years with widespread floods, and the escalation of organized violence at the subnational level since 2020; about 7.76 million people, almost two thirds of the total population, are expected to face severe acute food insecurity in the lean season between April and July 2023 (2023)

Revenue from forest resources: 2.65% of GDP (2015 est.)
comparison ranking: 25

Air pollutants: *particulate matter emissions:* 20.18 micrograms per cubic meter (2019 est.)
carbon dioxide emissions: 1.73 megatons (2016 est.)
methane emissions: 7.61 megatons (2020 est.)

Waste and recycling: *municipal solid waste generated annually:* 2,680,681 tons (2013 est.)

Major rivers (by length in km): Nile (shared with Rwanda [s], Tanzania, Uganda, Sudan, and Egypt [m]) - 6,650 km
note – [s] after country name indicates river source; [m] after country name indicates river mouth

Major watersheds (area sq km):Atlantic Ocean drainage: Congo (3,730,881 sq km), *(Mediterranean Sea)* Nile (3,254,853 sq km)

Total water withdrawal: *municipal:* 190 million cubic meters (2020 est.)
industrial: 230 million cubic meters (2020 est.)
agricultural: 240 million cubic meters (2020 est.)

Total renewable water resources: 49.5 billion cubic meters (2020 est.)

GOVERNMENT

Country name: *conventional long form:* Republic of South Sudan
conventional short form: South Sudan
etymology: self-descriptive name from the country's former position within Sudan prior to independence; the name "Sudan" derives from the Arabic "bilad-as-sudan" meaning "Land of the Black [peoples]"

Government type: presidential republic

Capital: *name:* Juba
geographic coordinates: 04 51 N, 31 37 E
time difference: UTC+2 (8 hours ahead of Washington, DC, during Standard Time)
etymology: the name derives from Djouba, another name for the Bari people of South Sudan

Administrative divisions: 10 states; Central Equatoria, Eastern Equatoria, Jonglei, Lakes, Northern Bahr el Ghazal, Unity, Upper Nile, Warrap, Western Bahr el Ghazal, Western Equatoria; note - in 2015, the creation of 28 new states was announced and in 2017 four additional states; following the February 2020 peace agreement, the country was again reorganized into the 10 original states, plus 2 administrative areas, Pibor and Ruweng, and 1 special administrative status area, Abyei (which is disputed between South Sudan and Sudan); this latest administrative revision has not yet been vetted by the US Board on Geographic Names

Independence: 9 July 2011 (from Sudan)

National holiday: Independence Day, 9 July (2011)

Constitution: *history:* previous 2005 (preindependence); latest signed 7 July 2011, effective 9 July 2011 (Transitional Constitution of the Republic of South Sudan, 2011); note - new constitution pending establishment under the 2018 peace agreement
amendments: proposed by the National Legislature or by the president of the republic; passage requires submission of the proposal to the Legislature at least one month prior to consideration, approval by at least two-thirds majority vote in both houses of the Legislature, and assent of the president; amended 2013, 2015, 2018

Citizenship: *citizenship by birth:* no
citizenship by descent only: at least one parent must be a citizen of South Sudan
dual citizenship recognized: yes
residency requirement for naturalization: 10 years

Suffrage: 18 years of age; universal

Executive branch: *chief of state:* President Salva KIIR Mayardit (since 9 July 2011)
head of government: President Salva KIIR Mayardit (since 9 July 2011)
cabinet: National Council of Ministers appointed by the president, approved by the Transitional National Legislative Assembly
elections/appointments: president directly elected by simple majority popular vote for a 4-year term (eligible for a second term); election last held on 11 to 15 April 2010 (originally scheduled for 2015 but postponed several times, currently to be held in December 2024)
election results: 2010: Salva KIIR Mayardit elected leader of then-Southern Sudan; percent of vote - Salva KIIR Mayardit (SPLM) 93%, Lam AKOL (SPLM-DC) 7%
note: the president is both chief of state and head of government

Legislative branch: *description:* bicameral National Legislature consists of:
Council of States, pending establishment as stipulated by the 2018 peace deal
Transitional National Legislative Assembly (TNLA), established on 4 August 2016, in accordance with

the August 2015 Agreement on the Resolution of the Conflict in the Republic of South Sudan; note - originally 400 seats; the TNLA was expanded to 550 members from 400 and reestablished in May 2020 under the 2018 peace agreement
elections: Council of States - pending establishment as stipulated by the 2018 peace deal
Transitional National Legislative Assembly - percent of vote by party - NA; seats by party - 332 SPLM, 128 SPLM-IO, 90 other political parties; composition - NA
election results: Council of States - percent of vote by party - NA; seats by party - SPLM 20, unknown 30; composition - men 57, women 27, percentage women 32.1%
National Legislative Assembly - percent of vote by party - NA; seats by party - SPLM 251, DCP 10, independent 6, unknown 133; composition - men 372, women 178, percentage women 32.4%; total National Legislature percentage women 32.3%

Judicial branch: *highest court(s):* Supreme Court of South Sudan (consists of a chief justice, deputy chief justice, and 5 additional justices); note - consistent with the 2008 Judiciary Act, the Transitional Constitution of South Sudan calls for 9, rather than 5 additional justices
judge selection and term of office: justices appointed by the president (the 2011 Transitional Constitution of South Sudan calls for the establishment of a Judicial Service Council to recommend prospective justices to the president, and for the justices' tenures to be set by the National Legislature; neither of these steps have been effectively implemented as of mid-2023)
subordinate courts: national level - Courts of Appeal; High Courts; County Courts; state level - High Courts; County Courts; customary courts; other specialized courts and tribunals

Note: in mid-2022, the Government of South Sudan inaugurated an Ad-hoc Judiciary Committee, a 12-member body led by two eminent jurists, which is charged with reviewing relevant laws, advising on judicial reform and restructuring of the judiciary

Political parties: Democratic Change or DC
Democratic Forum or DF
Labour Party or LPSS
South Sudan Opposition Alliance or SSOA
Sudan African National Union or SANU
Sudan People's Liberation Movement or SPLM
Sudan People's Liberation Movement-In Opposition or SPLM-IO
United Democratic Salvation Front or UDSF
United South Sudan African Party or USSAP
United South Sudan Party or USSP

International organization participation: AU, EAC, FAO, G-77, IBRD, ICAO, IDA, IFAD, IFC, IFRCS, IGAD, ILO, IMF, Interpol, IOM, IPU, ITU, MIGA, UN, UNCTAD, UNESCO, UPU, WCO, WHO, WMO

Diplomatic representation in the US: *chief of mission:* Ambassador Santino Fardol Watod DICKEN (since 18 September 2024)
chancery: 1015 31st Street NW, Suite 300, Washington, DC 20007
telephone: [1] (202) 600-2238
FAX: [1] (202) 644-9910
email address and website:
info.ssdembassy@gmail.com
https://www.ssembassydc.org/

Diplomatic representation from the US: *chief of mission:* Ambassador Michael J. ADLER (since 24 August 2022)
embassy: Kololo Road adjacent to the EU's compound, Juba
mailing address: 4420 Juba Place, Washington DC 20521-4420
telephone: [211] 912-105-188
email address and website:
ACSJuba@state.gov
https://ss.usembassy.gov/

Flag description: three equal horizontal bands of black (top), red, and green; the red band is edged in white; a blue isosceles triangle based on the hoist side contains a gold, five-pointed star; black represents the people of South Sudan, red the blood shed in the struggle for freedom, green the verdant land, and blue the waters of the Nile; the gold star represents the unity of the states making up South Sudan
note: resembles the flag of Kenya; one of only two national flags to display six colors as part of its primary design, the other is South Africa's

National symbol(s): African fish eagle; national colors: red, green, blue, yellow, black, white

National anthem: *name:* "South Sudan Oyee!" (Hooray!)
lyrics/music: collective of 49 poets/Juba University students and teachers
note: adopted 2011; anthem selected in a national contest

ECONOMY

Economic overview: low-income, oil-based Sahelian economy; extreme poverty and food insecurity; COVID-19 and ongoing violence threaten socioeconomic potential; environmentally fragile; ongoing land and property rights issues; natural resource rich but lacks infrastructure

Real GDP (purchasing power parity): $20.01 billion (2017 est.)
$21.1 billion (2016 est.)
$24.52 billion (2015 est.)
note: data are in 2017 dollars
comparison ranking: 157

Real GDP growth rate: -5.2% (2017 est.)
-13.9% (2016 est.)
-10.79% (2015 est.)
note: annual GDP % growth based on constant local currency
comparison ranking: 212

Real GDP per capita: $1,600 (2017 est.)
$1,700 (2016 est.)
$2,100 (2015 est.)
note: data are in 2017 dollars
comparison ranking: 215

GDP (official exchange rate): $11.998 billion (2015 est.)
note: data in current dollars at official exchange rate

Inflation rate (consumer prices): 2.38% (2023 est.)
-6.69% (2022 est.)
10.52% (2021 est.)
note: annual % change based on consumer prices
comparison ranking: 50

GDP - composition, by sector of origin: *agriculture:* 10.4% (2015 est.)
industry: 33.1% (2015 est.)
services: 56.6% (2015 est.)
note: figures may not total 100% due to non-allocated consumption not captured in sector-reported data
comparison rankings: services 110; industry 48; agriculture 74

GDP - composition, by end use: *investment in fixed capital:* 5.8% (2015 est.)
exports of goods and services: 36.7% (2015 est.)
imports of goods and services: -28.9% (2015 est.)
note: figures may not total 100% due to rounding or gaps in data collection

Agricultural products: milk, cassava, sorghum, goat milk, vegetables, fruits, maize, groundnuts, sesame seeds, beef (2022)
note: top ten agricultural products based on tonnage

Industrial production growth rate: -36.78% (2015 est.)
note: annual % change in industrial value added based on constant local currency
comparison ranking: 219

Labor force: 4.471 million (2023 est.)
note: number of people ages 15 or older who are employed or seeking work
comparison ranking: 94

Unemployment rate: 12.27% (2023 est.)
12.4% (2022 est.)
13.87% (2021 est.)
note: % of labor force seeking employment
comparison ranking: 181

Youth unemployment rate (ages 15-24): *total:* 18.3% (2023 est.)
male: 19.4% (2023 est.)
female: 17.2% (2023 est.)
note: % of labor force ages 15-24 seeking employment
comparison ranking: total 74

Population below poverty line: 82.3% (2016 est.)
note: % of population with income below national poverty line

Gini Index coefficient - distribution of family income: 44.1 (2016 est.)
note: index (0-100) of income distribution; higher values represent greater inequality
comparison ranking: 25

Household income or consumption by percentage share: *lowest 10%:* 1.7% (2016 est.)
highest 10%: 33.1% (2016 est.)

Remittances: 9.49% of GDP (2015 est.)
0.01% of GDP (2014 est.)
note: personal transfers and compensation between resident and non-resident individuals/households/entities

Budget: *revenues:* $1.94 billion (2019 est.)
expenditures: $1.938 billion (2019 est.)

Public debt: 62.7% of GDP (2017 est.)
comparison ranking: 73

Taxes and other revenues: 8.5% (of GDP) (FY2017/18 est.)
comparison ranking: 188

Current account balance: -$596.748 million (2022 est.)
-$6.55 million (2021 est.)
-$1.718 billion (2020 est.)
note: balance of payments - net trade and primary/secondary income in current dollars
comparison ranking: 125

Exports: $5.811 billion (2022 est.)
$4.652 billion (2021 est.)
$2.344 billion (2020 est.)

note: balance of payments - exports of goods and services in current dollars
comparison ranking: 136

Exports - partners: China 44%, Italy 26%, Singapore 12%, Japan 9%, UAE 8% (2022)
note: top five export partners based on percentage share of exports

Exports - commodities: crude petroleum, refined petroleum, gold, forage crops, barley (2022)
note: top five export commodities based on value in dollars

Imports: $6.402 billion (2022 est.)
$4.037 billion (2021 est.)
$4.245 billion (2020 est.)
note: balance of payments - imports of goods and services in current dollars
comparison ranking: 139

Imports - partners: UAE 39%, Kenya 18%, China 17%, US 4%, India 3% (2022)
note: top five import partners based on percentage share of imports

Imports - commodities: garments, cars, trucks, packaged medicine, malt extract (2022)
note: top five import commodities based on value in dollars

Reserves of foreign exchange and gold: $183.615 million (2020 est.)
$378.282 million (2019 est.)
$36.396 million (2018 est.)
note: holdings of gold (year-end prices)/foreign exchange/special drawing rights in current dollars
comparison ranking: 182

Exchange rates: South Sudanese pounds (SSP) per US dollar -

Exchange rates: 534.511 (2022 est.)
306.355 (2021 est.)
165.907 (2020 est.)
157.999 (2019 est.)
141.386 (2018 est.)

ENERGY

Electricity access: *electrification - total population:* 8.4% (2022 est.)
electrification - urban areas: 15%
electrification - rural areas: 1.7%

Electricity: *installed generating capacity:* 134,000 kW (2022 est.)
consumption: 595.604 million kWh (2022 est.)
transmission/distribution losses: 24.506 million kWh (2022 est.)
comparison rankings: transmission/distribution losses 27; consumption 170; installed generating capacity 182

Electricity generation sources: *fossil fuels:* 97.1% of total installed capacity (2022 est.)
solar: 2.9% of total installed capacity (2022 est.)

Coal: *imports:* 100 metric tons (2022 est.)

Petroleum: *total petroleum production:* 146,000 bbl/day (2023 est.)
refined petroleum consumption: 14,000 bbl/day (2022 est.)
crude oil estimated reserves: 3.75 billion barrels (2021 est.)

Carbon dioxide emissions: 1.97 million metric tonnes of CO2 (2022 est.)
from petroleum and other liquids: 1.97 million metric tonnes of CO2 (2022 est.)
comparison ranking: total emissions 160

Energy consumption per capita: 2.627 million Btu/person (2022 est.)
comparison ranking: 180

COMMUNICATIONS

Telephones - fixed lines: *subscriptions per 100 inhabitants:* (2018 est.) less than 1

Telephones - mobile cellular: *total subscriptions:* 3.276 million (2022 est.)
subscriptions per 100 inhabitants: 30 (2022 est.)
comparison ranking: total subscriptions 139

Telecommunication systems: *general assessment:* following a referendum, oil-rich South Sudan seceded from Sudan in 2011 and became an independent nation; having been deprived of investment for decades, it inherited one of the least developed telecom markets in the world; there was once investment activity among mobile network operators who sought to expand their networks in some areas of the country; operators in the telecom sector placed themselves in survival mode and are hoping for a political settlement and a return to some degree of social stability; South Sudan has one of the lowest mobile penetration rates in Africa; growth in the sector in coming years is premised on a resolution to the political crisis and a recovery of the country's economy; the virtually untapped internet and broadband market also depends to a large extent on the country gaining access to international fiber cables and on a national backbone network being in place; sophisticated infrastructure solutions are needed to reach the 80% of the population that live outside of the main urban centers; some improvement has followed from the cable link in February 2020 which connects Juba directly to the company's submarine landing station at Mombasa; the cable was South Sudan's first direct international fiber link, and has helped drive down the price of retail internet services for residential and business customers; a second cable linking to the border with Kenya was completed in December 2021 (2022)
domestic: fixed-line less than 1 per 100 subscriptions, mobile-cellular is 30 per 100 persons (2021)
international: country code - 211 (2017)

Broadcast media: a single TV channel and a radio station are controlled by the government; several community and commercial FM stations are operational, mostly sponsored by outside aid donors; some foreign radio broadcasts are available
(2019)

Internet country code: .ss

Internet users: *total:* 869,000 (2021 est.)
percent of population: 7.9% (2021 est.)
comparison ranking: total 151

Broadband - fixed subscriptions: *total:* 200 (2019 est.)
subscriptions per 100 inhabitants: (2019 est.)
comparison ranking: total 212

TRANSPORTATION

National air transport system: *number of registered air carriers:* 2 (2020)
inventory of registered aircraft operated by air carriers: 2
annual freight traffic on registered air carriers: 0 mt-km

Civil aircraft registration country code prefix: Z8

Airports: 82 (2024)
comparison ranking: 64

Heliports: 1 (2024)

Railways: *total:* 248 km (2018)
note: a narrow gauge, single-track railroad between Babonosa (Sudan) and Wau, the only existing rail system, was repaired in 2010 with $250 million in UN funds, but is not currently operational
comparison ranking: total 127

Roadways: *total:* 90,200 km
paved: 300 km
unpaved: 89,900 km (2015)
note: most of the road network is unpaved and much of it is in disrepair; the Juba-Nimule highway connecting Juba to the border with Uganda is the main paved road in South Sudan
comparison ranking: total 56

Waterways: see entry for Sudan

MILITARY AND SECURITY

Military and security forces: South Sudan People's Defense Force (SSPDF): Land Forces (includes Presidential Guard), Air Forces, Marines (Riverine Forces), Reserve Forces; National (or Necessary) Unified Forces (NUF)

Ministry of Interior: South Sudan National Police Service (SSNPS) (2024)
note 1: the NUF are being formed by retraining rebel and pro-government militia fighters into military, police, and other government security forces; the first operational NUF deployed in November 2023
note 2: numerous irregular forces operate in the country with official knowledge, including militias operated by the National Security Service (an internal security force under the Ministry of National Security) and proxy forces

Military expenditures: 2.5% of GDP (2022 est.)
2% of GDP (2021 est.)
2% of GDP (2020 est.)
3.1% of GDP (2019 est.)
3.2% of GDP (2018 est.)
comparison ranking: 44

Military and security service personnel strengths: estimated 150-200,000 active personnel, mostly ground forces with small contingents of air and riverine forces (2023)
note: some active SSPDF personnel may be militia; the National/Necessary Unified Forces (NUF) are expected to have up to 80,000 personnel when training and integration is completed; the first batch of approximately 20,000 NUF personnel completed training in late 2022

Military equipment inventories and acquisitions: the SSPDF inventory is comprised primarily of Soviet-era equipment; South Sudan has been under a UN arms embargo since 2018 (2024)

Military service age and obligation: 18 is the legal minimum age for compulsory (men) and voluntary (men and women) military service; 12-24 months service (2023)

Military - note: the South Sudan People's Defense Forces (SSPDF) are largely focused on internal security
the SSPDF, formerly the Sudan People's Liberation Army (SPLA), was founded as a guerrilla movement against the Sudanese Government in 1983 and participated in the Second Sudanese Civil War (1983-2005); the Juba Declaration that followed the Comprehensive Peace Agreement of 2005 unified the SPLA and the South Sudan Defense Forces

(SSDF), the second-largest rebel militia remaining from the civil war, under the SPLA name; in 2017, the SPLA was renamed the South Sudan Defense Forces (SSDF) and in September 2018 was renamed again as the SSPDF
the UN Mission in South Sudan (UNMISS) has operated in the country since 2011 with the objectives of consolidating peace and security and helping establish conditions for the successful economic and political development of South Sudan; UNMISS had about 15,000 personnel deployed in the country as of 2024
the UN Interim Security Force for Abyei (UNISFA) has operated in the disputed Abyei region along the border between Sudan and South Sudan since 2011; UNISFA's mission includes ensuring security, protecting civilians, strengthening the capacity of the Abyei Police Service, de-mining, monitoring/verifying the redeployment of armed forces from the area, and facilitating the flow of humanitarian aid; as of 2024, UNISFA had approximately 3,200 personnel assigned (2024)

TRANSNATIONAL ISSUES

Refugees and internally displaced persons: *refugees (country of origin):* 564,738 (Sudan) (refugees since 15 April 2023), 13,833 (Democratic Republic of the Congo) (2024)
IDPs: 2.258 million (alleged coup attempt and ethnic conflict beginning in December 2013; information is lacking on those displaced in earlier years by: fighting in Abyei between the Sudanese Armed Forces and the Sudan People's Liberation Army (SPLA) in May 2011; clashes between the SPLA and dissident militia groups in South Sudan; interethnic conflicts over resources and cattle; attacks from the Lord's Resistance Army; floods and drought) (2023)
stateless persons: 10,000 (2022)

Trafficking in persons: tier rating: Tier 3 — South Sudan does not fully meet the minimum standards for the elimination of trafficking and is not making significant efforts to do so, therefore, South Sudan remains on Tier 3; for more details, go to: https:// www.state.gov/reports/2024-trafficking-in-persons-report/south-sudan/

SOUTHERN OCEAN

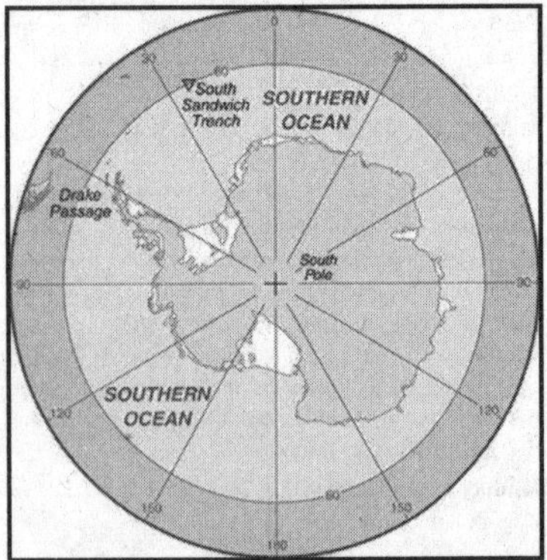

INTRODUCTION

Background: A large body of recent oceanographic research has shown that the Antarctic Circumpolar Current (ACC), an ocean current that flows from west to east around Antarctica, plays a crucial role in global ocean circulation. The region where the cold waters of the ACC meet and mingle with the warmer waters of the north defines a distinct border – the Antarctic Convergence – which fluctuates with the seasons but encompasses a discrete body of water and a unique ecologic region. The Convergence concentrates nutrients, which promotes marine plant life, which in turn allows for a greater abundance of animal life. In 2000, the International Hydrographic Organization delimited the waters within the Convergence as a fifth world ocean basin – the Southern Ocean – by combining the southern portions of the Atlantic Ocean, Indian Ocean, and Pacific Ocean. The Southern Ocean extends from the coast of Antarctica north to 60 degrees south latitude, which coincides with the Antarctic Treaty region and which approximates the extent of the Antarctic Convergence. As such, the Southern Ocean is now the fourth largest of the world's five ocean basins (after the Pacific Ocean, Atlantic Ocean, and Indian Ocean). It should be noted that inclusion of the Southern Ocean does not imply US Government recognition of this feature as one of the world's primary ocean basins.

GEOGRAPHY

Location: body of water between 60 degrees south latitude and Antarctica

Geographic coordinates: 60 00 S, 90 00 E (nominally), but the Southern Ocean has the unique distinction of being a large circumpolar body of water totally encircling the continent of Antarctica; this ring of water lies between 60 degrees south latitude and the coast of Antarctica and encompasses 360 degrees of longitude

Map references: Antarctic Region

Area: *total:* 21.96 million sq km
note: includes Amundsen Sea, Bellingshausen Sea, part of the Drake Passage, Ross Sea, a small part of the Scotia Sea, Weddell Sea, and other tributary water bodies

Area - comparative: slightly more than twice the size of the US

Coastline: 17,968 km

Climate: sea temperatures vary from about 10 degrees Celsius to -2 degrees Celsius; cyclonic storms travel eastward around the continent and frequently are intense because of the temperature contrast between ice and open ocean; the ocean area from about latitude 40 south to the Antarctic Circle has the strongest average winds found anywhere on Earth; in winter the ocean freezes outward to 65 degrees south latitude in the Pacific sector and 55 degrees south latitude in the Atlantic sector, lowering surface temperatures well below 0 degrees Celsius; at some coastal points intense persistent drainage winds from the interior keep the shoreline ice-free throughout the winter

Ocean volume: *ocean volume:* 71.8 million cu km
percent of World Ocean total volume: 5.4%

Major ocean currents: the cold, clockwise-flowing Antarctic Circumpolar Current (West Wind Drift; 21,000 km long) moves perpetually eastward around the continent and is the world's largest and strongest ocean current, transporting 130 million cubic meters of water per second - 100 times the flow of all the world's rivers; it is also the only current that flows all the way around the planet and connects the Atlantic, Pacific, and Indian Ocean basins; the cold Antarctic Coastal Current (East Wind Drift) is the southernmost current in the world, flowing westward and parallel to the Antarctic coastline

Elevation: *highest point:* sea level
lowest point: southern end of the South Sandwich Trench -7,434 m unnamed deep
mean depth: -3,270 m
ocean zones: Composed of water and in a fluid state, the ocean is delimited differently than the solid continents. It is divided into three zones based on depth and light level. Sunlight entering the water may travel about 1,000 m into the oceans under the right conditions, but there is rarely any significant light beyond 200 m.
The upper 200 m (656 ft) of the ocean is called the euphotic, or "sunlight," zone. This zone contains the vast majority of commercial fisheries and is home to many protected marine mammals and sea turtles. Only a small amount of light penetrates beyond this depth.
The zone between 200 m (656 ft) and 1,000 m (3,280 ft) is usually referred to as the "twilight" zone, but is officially the dysphotic zone. In this zone, the intensity of light rapidly dissipates as depth increases. Such a minuscule amount of light penetrates beyond a depth of 200 m that photosynthesis is no longer possible.
The aphotic, or "midnight," zone exists in depths below 1,000 m (3,280 ft). Sunlight does not penetrate to these depths, and the zone is bathed in darkness.

Natural resources: probable large oil and gas fields on the continental margin; manganese nodules, possible placer deposits, sand and gravel, fresh water as icebergs; krill, fish

Natural hazards: huge icebergs with drafts up to several hundred meters; smaller bergs and iceberg fragments; sea ice (generally 0.5 to 1 m thick) with sometimes dynamic short-term variations and with large annual and interannual variations; deep continental shelf floored by glacial deposits varying widely over short distances; high winds and large waves much of the year; ship icing, especially May-October; most of region is remote from sources of search and rescue

Geography - note: the major chokepoint is the Drake Passage between South America and Antarctica; the Polar Front (Antarctic Convergence) is the best natural definition of the northern extent of the Southern Ocean; it is a distinct region at the middle of the Antarctic Circumpolar Current that separates the cold polar surface waters to the south from the warmer waters to the north; the Front and the Current extend entirely around Antarctica, reaching south of 60 degrees south near New Zealand and near 48 degrees south in the far South Atlantic, coinciding with the path of the maximum westerly winds

ENVIRONMENT

Environment - current issues: changes to the ocean's physical, chemical, and biological systems have taken place because of climate change, ocean acidification, and commercial exploitation

Environment - international agreements: *the Southern Ocean is subject to all international agreements regarding the world's oceans; in addition, it is subject to these agreements specific to the Antarctic region:* International Whaling Commission (prohibits commercial whaling south of 40 degrees south [south of 60 degrees south between 50 degrees and 130 degrees west]); Convention on the Conservation of Antarctic Seals (limits sealing); Convention on the Conservation of Antarctic Marine Living Resources (regulates fishing)
note: mineral exploitation except for scientific research is banned by the Environmental Protocol to the Antarctic Treaty; additionally, many nations (including the US) prohibit mineral resource exploration and exploitation south of the fluctuating Polar Front (Antarctic Convergence), which is in the middle of the Antarctic Circumpolar Current and serves as the dividing line between the cold polar surface waters to the south and the warmer waters to the north

Climate: sea temperatures vary from about 10 degrees Celsius to -2 degrees Celsius; cyclonic storms travel eastward around the continent and frequently are intense because of the temperature contrast between ice and open ocean; the ocean area from about latitude 40 south to the Antarctic Circle has the strongest average winds found anywhere on Earth; in winter the ocean freezes outward to 65 degrees south latitude in the Pacific sector and 55 degrees south latitude in the Atlantic sector, lowering surface temperatures well below 0 degrees Celsius; at some coastal points intense persistent drainage winds from the interior keep the shoreline ice-free throughout the winter

Marine fisheries: the Southern Ocean fishery is relatively small with a total catch of 388,901 mt in 2021; the Food and Agriculture Organization has delineated three regions in the Southern Ocean (Regions 48, 58, 88) that generally encompass the waters south of 40° to 60° South latitude; the most important producers in these regions include Norway (241,408 mt), China (47,605 mt), and South Korea (39,487 mt); Antarctic krill made up 95.5% of the total catch in 2021, while other important species include Patagonian and Antarctic toothfish

Regional fisheries bodies: Commission for the Conservation of Antarctic Marine Living Resources

GOVERNMENT

Country name: *etymology:* the International Hydrographic Organization (IHO) included the ocean and its definition as the waters south of 60 degrees south in its year 2000 revision, but this has not formally been adopted; the 2000 IHO definition, however, was circulated in a draft edition of the IHO's *Names and Limits of Oceans and Seas* in 2002 and has acquired de facto usage by many nations and organizations, including the CIA

TRANSPORTATION

Transportation - note: Drake Passage offers alternative to transit through the Panama Canal

SPAIN

INTRODUCTION

Background: Spain's powerful world empire of the 16th and 17th centuries ultimately yielded command of the seas to England. Spain remained neutral during both World Wars but suffered through a devastating civil war (1936-39) resulting in a dictatorship. A peaceful transition to democracy after the death of dictator Francisco FRANCO in 1975 and rapid economic modernization after Spain joined the EU in 1986 gave Spain a dynamic and rapidly growing economy. After a severe recession in the wake of the global financial crisis in 2008, Spain has posted solid years of GDP growth above the EU average. Unemployment has fallen but remains high, especially among youth. Spain is the eurozone's fourth-largest economy. The country has faced increased domestic turmoil in recent years due to the independence movement in its restive Catalonia region.

GEOGRAPHY

Location: Southwestern Europe, bordering the Mediterranean Sea, North Atlantic Ocean, Bay of Biscay, and Pyrenees Mountains; southwest of France

Geographic coordinates: 40 00 N, 4 00 W

Map references: Europe

Area: *total:* 505,370 sq km
land: 498,980 sq km
water: 6,390 sq km
note: there are two autonomous cities - Ceuta and Melilla - and 17 autonomous communities including Balearic Islands and Canary Islands, and three small Spanish possessions off the coast of Morocco - Islas Chafarinas, Penon de Alhucemas, and Penon de Velez de la Gomera
comparison ranking: total 54

Area - comparative: almost five times the size of Kentucky; slightly more than twice the size of Oregon

Land boundaries: *total:* 1,952.7 km
border countries (5): Andorra 63 km; France 646 km; Gibraltar 1.2 km; Portugal 1,224 km; Morocco (Ceuta) 8 km and Morocco (Melilla) 10.5 km
note: an additional 75-meter border segment exists between Morocco and the Spanish exclave of Penon de Velez de la Gomera

Coastline: 4,964 km

Maritime claims: *territorial sea:* 12 nm
contiguous zone: 24 nm
exclusive economic zone: 200 nm (applies only to the Atlantic Ocean)

Climate: temperate; clear, hot summers in interior, more moderate and cloudy along coast; cloudy, cold winters in interior, partly cloudy and cool along coast

Terrain: large, flat to dissected plateau surrounded by rugged hills; Pyrenees Mountains in north

Elevation: *highest point:* Pico de Teide (Tenerife) on Canary Islands 3,718 m
lowest point: Atlantic Ocean 0 m
mean elevation: 660 m

Natural resources: coal, lignite, iron ore, copper, lead, zinc, uranium, tungsten, mercury, pyrites, magnesite, fluorspar, gypsum, sepiolite, kaolin, potash, hydropower, arable land

Land use: *agricultural land:* 54.1% (2018 est.)
arable land: 24.9% (2018 est.)
permanent crops: 9.1% (2018 est.)
permanent pasture: 20.1% (2018 est.)
forest: 36.8% (2018 est.)
other: 9.1% (2018 est.)

Irrigated land: 37,593 sq km (2020)

Major rivers (by length in km): Tagus river source (shared with Portugal [m]) - 1,006
note – [s] after country name indicates river source; [m] after country name indicates river mouth

Population distribution: with the notable exception of Madrid, Sevilla, and Zaragoza, the largest urban agglomerations are found along the Mediterranean and Atlantic coasts; numerous smaller cities are spread throughout the interior reflecting Spain's agrarian heritage; very dense settlement around the capital of Madrid, as well as the port city of Barcelona

Natural hazards: periodic droughts, occasional flooding

volcanism: volcanic activity in the Canary Islands, located off Africa's northwest coast; Teide (3,715 m) has been deemed a Decade Volcano by the International Association of Volcanology and Chemistry of the Earth's Interior, worthy of study due to its explosive history and close proximity to human populations; La Palma (2,426 m), which last erupted in 1971, is the most active of the Canary Islands volcanoes; Lanzarote is the only other historically active volcano

Geography - note: strategic location along approaches to Strait of Gibraltar; Spain controls a number of territories in northern Morocco including the enclaves of Ceuta and Melilla, and the islands of Penon de Velez de la Gomera, Penon de Alhucemas, and Islas Chafarinas; Spain's Canary Islands are one of four North Atlantic archipelagos that make up Macaronesia; the others are Azores (Portugal), Madeira (Portugal), and Cabo Verde

PEOPLE AND SOCIETY

Population: *total:* 47,280,433
male: 23,069,327
female: 24,211,106 (2024 est.)
comparison rankings: female 32; male 34; total 32

Nationality: *noun:* Spaniard(s)
adjective: Spanish

Ethnic groups: Spanish 84.8%, Moroccan 1.7%, Romanian 1.2%, other 12.3% (2021 est.)
note: data represent population by country of birth

Languages: Castilian Spanish (official) 74%, Catalan (official in Catalonia, the Balearic Islands, and the Valencian Community) 17%, Galician (official in Galicia) 7%, Basque (official in the Basque Country and Navarre) 2%, Aranese (official in part of Catalonia) <5,000 speakers
major-language sample(s):
La Libreta Informativa del Mundo, la fuente indispensable de información básica. (Spanish)
note: Aragonese, Aranese Asturian, Calo, and Valencian are also recognized as regional languages

Religions: Roman Catholic 58.2%, atheist 16.2%, agnostic 10.8%, other 2.7%, non-believer 10.5%, unspecified 1.7% (2021 est.)

Age structure: *0-14 years:* 13% (male 3,147,019/female 3,012,821)
15-64 years: 66.1% (male 15,662,492/female 15,585,138)
65 years and over: 20.9% (2024 est.) (male 4,259,816/female 5,613,147)

Dependency ratios: *total dependency ratio:* 52.4
youth dependency ratio: 21.9
elderly dependency ratio: 30.2
potential support ratio: 3.3 (2021 est.)

Median age: *total:* 46.8 years (2024 est.)
male: 45.7 years
female: 47.8 years
comparison ranking: total 8

Population growth rate: 0.12% (2024 est.)
comparison ranking: 182

Birth rate: 7.1 births/1,000 population (2024 est.)
comparison ranking: 221

Death rate: 10 deaths/1,000 population (2024 est.)
comparison ranking: 36

Net migration rate: 4.1 migrant(s)/1,000 population (2024 est.)
comparison ranking: 25

Population distribution: with the notable exception of Madrid, Sevilla, and Zaragoza, the largest urban agglomerations are found along the Mediterranean and Atlantic coasts; numerous smaller cities are spread throughout the interior reflecting Spain's agrarian heritage; very dense settlement around the capital of Madrid, as well as the port city of Barcelona

Urbanization: *urban population:* 81.6% of total population (2023)
rate of urbanization: 0.24% annual rate of change (2020-25 est.)
note: data include Canary Islands, Ceuta, and Melilla

Major urban areas - population: 6.751 million MADRID (capital), 5.687 million Barcelona, 838,000 Valencia (2023)

Sex ratio: *at birth:* 1.05 male(s)/female
0-14 years: 1.04 male(s)/female
15-64 years: 1 male(s)/female
65 years and over: 0.76 male(s)/female
total population: 0.95 male(s)/female (2024 est.)

Mother's mean age at first birth: 31.2 years (2020 est.)

Maternal mortality ratio: 3 deaths/100,000 live births (2020 est.)
comparison ranking: 177

Infant mortality rate: *total:* 2.4 deaths/1,000 live births (2024 est.)
male: 2.7 deaths/1,000 live births
female: 2.1 deaths/1,000 live births
comparison ranking: total 217

Life expectancy at birth: *total population:* 83 years (2024 est.)
male: 80.3 years
female: 85.8 years
comparison ranking: total population 18

Total fertility rate: 1.3 children born/woman (2024 est.)
comparison ranking: 218

Gross reproduction rate: 0.64 (2024 est.)

Contraceptive prevalence rate: 62.1% (2018)
note: percent of women aged 18-49

Drinking water source: *improved: urban:* 99.9% of population
rural: 100% of population
total: 99.9% of population
unimproved: urban: 0.1% of population
rural: 0% of population
total: 0.1% of population (2020 est.)

Current health expenditure: 10.7% of GDP (2020)

Physician density: 4.44 physicians/1,000 population (2019)

Hospital bed density: 3 beds/1,000 population (2018)

Sanitation facility access: *improved: urban:* 100% of population
rural: 100% of population
total: 100% of population

Obesity - adult prevalence rate: 23.8% (2016)
comparison ranking: 62

Alcohol consumption per capita: *total:* 10.72 liters of pure alcohol (2019 est.)
beer: 4.67 liters of pure alcohol (2019 est.)
wine: 3.52 liters of pure alcohol (2019 est.)
spirits: 2.34 liters of pure alcohol (2019 est.)
other alcohols: 0.19 liters of pure alcohol (2019 est.)
comparison ranking: total 17

Tobacco use: *total:* 27.7% (2020 est.)
male: 28.6% (2020 est.)
female: 26.7% (2020 est.)
comparison ranking: total 39

Currently married women (ages 15-49): 50.1% (2023 est.)

Education expenditures: 4.6% of GDP (2020 est.)
comparison ranking: 95

Literacy: *definition:* age 15 and over can read and write
total population: 98.6%
male: 99%
female: 98.2% (2020)

School life expectancy (primary to tertiary education): *total:* 18 years
male: 18 years
female: 19 years (2020)

ENVIRONMENT

Environment - current issues: pollution of the Mediterranean Sea from raw sewage and effluents from the offshore production of oil and gas and drought are negatively impacting water quality and quantity nationwide; air pollution; deforestation; desertification

Environment - international agreements: *party to:* Air Pollution, Air Pollution-Heavy Metals, Air Pollution-Multi-effect Protocol, Air Pollution-Nitrogen Oxides, Air Pollution-Persistent Organic Pollutants, Air Pollution-Sulphur 94, Air Pollution-Volatile Organic Compounds, Antarctic-Environmental Protection, Antarctic-Marine Living Resources, Antarctic Treaty, Biodiversity, Climate Change, Climate Change-Kyoto Protocol, Climate Change-Paris Agreement, Comprehensive Nuclear Test Ban, Desertification, Endangered Species, Environmental Modification, Hazardous Wastes, Law of the Sea, Marine Dumping-London Convention, Marine Dumping-London Protocol, Marine Life Conservation, Nuclear Test Ban, Ozone Layer Protection, Ship Pollution, Tropical Timber 2006, Wetlands, Whaling
signed, but not ratified: none of the selected agreements

Climate: temperate; clear, hot summers in interior, more moderate and cloudy along coast; cloudy, cold winters in interior, partly cloudy and cool along coast

Urbanization: *urban population:* 81.6% of total population (2023)
rate of urbanization: 0.24% annual rate of change (2020-25 est.)
note: data include Canary Islands, Ceuta, and Melilla

Revenue from forest resources: 0.02% of GDP (2018 est.)
comparison ranking: 144

Revenue from coal: 0% of GDP (2018 est.)
comparison ranking: 163

Air pollutants: *particulate matter emissions:* 9.34 micrograms per cubic meter (2019 est.)
carbon dioxide emissions: 244 megatons (2016 est.)
methane emissions: 36.94 megatons (2020 est.)

Waste and recycling: *municipal solid waste generated annually:* 20.151 million tons (2015 est.)
municipal solid waste recycled annually: 3,393,428 tons (2015 est.)
percent of municipal solid waste recycled: 16.8% (2015 est.)

Major rivers (by length in km): Tagus river source (shared with Portugal [m]) - 1,006

note – [s] after country name indicates river source; [m] after country name indicates river mouth

Total water withdrawal: *municipal:* 4.56 billion cubic meters (2020 est.)
industrial: 5.5 billion cubic meters (2020 est.)
agricultural: 18.96 billion cubic meters (2020 est.)

Total renewable water resources: 111.5 billion cubic meters (2020 est.)

Geoparks: *total global geoparks and regional networks:* 17 (2024)
global geoparks and regional networks: Basque Coast UNESCO; Cabo de Gata-Níjar; Cabo Ortegal; Calatrava Volcanoes. Ciudad Real; Central Catalonia; Courel Mountains; El Hierro; Granada; Lanzarote and Chinijo Islands; Las Loras; Maestrazgo; Molina-Alto; Origens; Sierra Norte de Sevilla; Sierras Subbéticas; Sobrarbe-Pirineos: Villuercas Ibores Jara (2024)

GOVERNMENT

Country name: *conventional long form:* Kingdom of Spain
conventional short form: Spain
local long form: Reino de Espana
local short form: Espana
etymology: derivation of the name "Espana" is uncertain, but may come from the Phoenician term "span," related to the word "spy," meaning "to forge metals," so, "i-spn-ya" would mean "place where metals are forged"; the ancient Phoenicians long exploited the Iberian Peninsula for its mineral wealth

Government type: parliamentary constitutional monarchy

Capital: *name:* Madrid
geographic coordinates: 40 24 N, 3 41 W
time difference: UTC+1 (6 hours ahead of Washington, DC, during Standard Time)
daylight saving time: +1hr, begins last Sunday in March; ends last Sunday in October
time zone note: Spain has two time zones, including the Canary Islands (UTC 0)
etymology: the Romans named the original settlement "Matrice" after the river that ran through it; under Arab rule it became "Majerit," meaning "source of water"; in medieval Romance dialects (Mozarabic) it became "Matrit," which over time changed to "Madrid"

Administrative divisions: 17 autonomous communities (comunidades autonomas, singular - comunidad autonoma) and 2 autonomous cities* (ciudades autonomas, singular - ciudad autonoma); Andalucia; Aragon; Asturias; Canarias (Canary Islands); Cantabria; Castilla-La Mancha; Castilla-Leon; Cataluna (Castilian), Catalunya (Catalan), Catalonha (Aranese) [Catalonia]; Ceuta*; Comunidad Valenciana (Castilian), Comunitat Valenciana (Valencian) [Valencian Community]; Extremadura; Galicia; Illes Baleares (Balearic Islands); La Rioja; Madrid; Melilla*; Murcia; Navarra (Castilian), Nafarroa (Basque) [Navarre]; Pais Vasco (Castilian), Euskadi (Basque) [Basque Country]
note: the autonomous cities of Ceuta and Melilla plus three small islands of Islas Chafarinas, Penon de Alhucemas, and Penon de Velez de la Gomera, administered directly by the Spanish central government, are all along the coast of Morocco and are collectively referred to as Places of Sovereignty (Plazas de Soberania)

Independence: 1492; the Iberian peninsula was characterized by a variety of independent kingdoms prior to the Muslim occupation that began in the early 8th century A.D. and lasted nearly seven centuries; the small Christian redoubts of the north began the reconquest almost immediately, culminating in the seizure of Granada in 1492; this event completed the unification of several kingdoms and is traditionally considered the forging of present-day Spain

National holiday: National Day (Hispanic Day), 12 October (1492); note - commemorates the arrival of COLUMBUS in the Americas

Legal system: civil law system with regional variations

Constitution: *history:* several previous; latest approved by the General Courts 31 October 1978, passed by referendum 6 December 1978, signed by the king 27 December 1978, effective 29 December 1978
amendments: proposed by the government, by the General Courts (the Congress or the Senate), or by the self-governing communities submitted through the government; passage requires three-fifths majority vote by both houses and passage by referendum if requested by one tenth of the members of either house; proposals disapproved by both houses are submitted to a joint committee, which submits an agreed upon text for another vote; passage requires two-thirds majority vote in Congress and simple majority vote in the Senate; amended 1992, 2011

International law organization participation: accepts compulsory ICJ jurisdiction with reservations; accepts ICCt jurisdiction

Citizenship: *citizenship by birth:* no
citizenship by descent only: at least one parent must be a citizen of Spain
dual citizenship recognized: only with select Latin American countries
residency requirement for naturalization: 10 years for persons with no ties to Spain

Suffrage: 18 years of age; universal

Executive branch: *chief of state:* King FELIPE VI (since 19 June 2014)
head of government: President of the Government of Spain (prime minister-equivalent) Pedro SANCHEZ PEREZ-CASTEJON (since 2 June 2018)
cabinet: Council of Ministers designated by the president
elections/appointments: the monarchy is hereditary; following legislative elections, the monarch usually proposes as president the leader of the majority party or coalition, who is then indirectly elected by the Congress of Deputies; election last held on 23 July 2023 (next to be held on 31 July 2027); vice president and Council of Ministers appointed by the president
election results: Congress of Deputies vote - 179 to 171 (16 November 2023)
note: there is also a Council of State that is the supreme consultative organ of the government, but its recommendations are non-binding

Legislative branch: *description:* bicameral General Courts or Las Cortes Generales consists of:
Senate or Senado (265 seats; 208 members directly elected in multi-seat constituencies by simple majority vote and 57 members indirectly elected by the legislatures of the autonomous communities; members serve 4-year terms) Congress of Deputies or Congreso de los Diputados (350 seats; 348 members directly elected in 50 multi-seat constituencies by closed-list proportional representation vote, with a 3% threshold needed to gain a seat, and 2 directly elected from the North African Ceuta and Melilla enclaves by simple majority vote; members serve 4-year terms or until the government is dissolved)
elections: Senate - last held on 23 July 2023 (next to be held no later than July 2027)
Congress of Deputies - last held on 23 July 2023 (next to be held no later than July 2027)
election results: Senate - percent of vote by party - NA; seats by party - PP 120, PSOE 72, ERC 7, PNV 4, other 5; composition - men 153, women 112; percentage women 42.3%
Congress of Deputies - percent of vote by party - PP 33.1%, PSOE 31.7%, Vox 12.4%, Sumar 12.3%, ERC 1.7%, Junts 1.6%, EH-Bildu 1.4%, PNV 1.1% other 4.7%; seats by party - PP 137, PSOE 121, Vox 33, Sumar 31, ERC 7, Junts 7, EH-Bildu 6, PNV 5, other 3; composition - men 195, women 155, percentage women 44.3%; total General Courts percentage women 42%

Judicial branch: *highest court(s):* Supreme Court or Tribunal Supremo (consists of the court president and organized into the Civil Room, with a president and 9 judges; the Penal Room, with a president and 14 judges; the Administrative Room, with a president and 32 judges; the Social Room, with a president and 12 judges; and the Military Room, with a president and 7 judges); Constitutional Court or Tribunal Constitucional de Espana (consists of 12 judges)
judge selection and term of office: Supreme Court judges appointed by the monarch from candidates proposed by the General Council of the Judiciary Power, a 20-member governing board chaired by the monarch that includes presidential appointees, lawyers, and jurists confirmed by the National Assembly; judges can serve until age 70; Constitutional Court judges nominated by the National Assembly, executive branch, and the General Council of the Judiciary, and appointed by the monarch for 9-year terms
subordinate courts: National High Court; High Courts of Justice (in each of the autonomous communities); provincial courts; courts of first instance

Political parties: Asturias Forum or FAC
Basque Country Unite (Euskal Herria Bildu) or EH Bildu (coalition of 4 Basque pro-independence parties)
Basque Nationalist Party or PNV or EAJ
Canarian Coalition or CC (coalition of 5 parties)
Ciudadanos Party (Citizens Party) or Cs
Compromis - Compromise Coalition
Navarrese People's Union or UPN
Together for Catalonia or Junts
People's Party or PP
Republican Left of Catalonia or ERC
Spanish Socialist Workers Party or PSOE
Teruel Existe or TE
Unidas (Unite) or Sumar (electoral coalition formed in March 2022) (formerly Unidas Podemos or UP)
Vox or VOX

International organization participation: ADB (nonregional member), AfDB (nonregional member), Arctic Council (observer), Australia Group, BCIE, BIS, CABEI, CAN (observer), CBSS (observer), CD, CE, CERN, EAPC, EBRD, ECB, EIB, EITI (implementing country), EMU, ESA, EU, FAO, FATF, IADB, IAEA, IBRD, ICAO, ICC (national committees), ICCt, ICRM, IDA, IEA, IFAD, IFC, IFRCS, IHO, ILO, IMF, IMO, IMSO, Interpol,

IOC, IOM, IPU, ISO, ITSO, ITU, ITUC (NGOs), LAIA (observer), MIGA, NATO, NEA, NSG, OAS (observer), OECD, OPCW, OSCE, Pacific Alliance (observer), Paris Club, PCA, PIF (partner), Schengen Convention, SELEC (observer), SICA (observer), UN, UNCTAD, UNESCO, UNHCR, UNIDO, UNIFIL, Union Latina, UNOCI, UNOOSA, UNRWA, UNWTO, UPU, Wassenaar Arrangement, WCO, WHO, WIPO, WMO, WTO, ZC

Diplomatic representation in the US: *chief of mission:* Ambassador Ángeles MORENO Bau (since 27 February 2024)
chancery: 2375 Pennsylvania Avenue NW, Washington, DC 20037
telephone: [1] (202) 452-0100
FAX: [1] (202) 833-5670
email address and website:
emb.washington@maec.es
https://www.exteriores.gob.es/Embajadas/washington/en/Paginas/index.aspx
consulate(s) general: Boston, Chicago, Houston, Los Angeles, Miami, New York, San Francisco, San Juan (Puerto Rico)

Diplomatic representation from the US: *chief of mission:* Ambassador Julissa REYNOSO (since 2 February 2022); note - also accredited to Andorra
embassy: Calle de Serrano, 75, 28006 Madrid
mailing address: 8500 Madrid Place, Washington DC 20521-8500
telephone: [34] (91) 587-2200
FAX: [34] (91) 587-2303
email address and website:
askACS@state.gov
https://es.usembassy.gov/
consulate(s) general: Barcelona

Flag description: three horizontal bands of red (top), yellow (double width), and red with the national coat of arms on the hoist side of the yellow band; the coat of arms is quartered to display the emblems of the traditional kingdoms of Spain (clockwise from upper left, Castile, Leon, Navarre, and Aragon) while Granada is represented by the stylized pomegranate at the bottom of the shield; the arms are framed by two columns representing the Pillars of Hercules, which are the two promontories (Gibraltar and Ceuta) on either side of the eastern end of the Strait of Gibraltar; the red scroll across the two columns bears the imperial motto of "Plus Ultra" (further beyond) referring to Spanish lands beyond Europe; the triband arrangement with the center stripe twice the width of the outer dates to the 18th century
note: the red and yellow colors are related to those of the oldest Spanish kingdoms: Aragon, Castile, Leon, and Navarre

National symbol(s): Pillars of Hercules; national colors: red, yellow

National anthem: *name:* "Himno Nacional Espanol" (National Anthem of Spain)
lyrics/music: no lyrics/unknown
note: officially in use between 1770 and 1931, restored in 1939; the Spanish anthem is the first anthem to be officially adopted, but it has no lyrics; in the years prior to 1931 it became known as "Marcha Real" (The Royal March); it first appeared in a 1761 military bugle call book and was replaced by "Himno de Riego" in the years between 1931 and 1939; the long version of the anthem is used for the king, while the short version is used for the prince, prime minister, and occasions such as sporting events

National heritage: *total World Heritage Sites:* 50 (44 cultural, 4 natural, 2 mixed)
selected World Heritage Site locales: Cave of Altamira and Paleolithic Cave Art of Northern Spain (c); Works of Antoni Gaudí (c); Santiago de Compostela (Old Town) (c); Historic City of Toledo (c); Archaeological Ensemble of Mérida (c); Tower of Hercules (c); Doñana National Park (n); Pyrénées - Mont Perdu (m); Alhambra, Generalife, and Albayzín in Granada (c); Old City of Salamanca (c); Teide National Park (n); Historic Walled Town of Cuenca (c); Old Town of Segovia and its Aqueduct (c); Historic Cordoba (c); El Escorial (c)

ECONOMY

Economic overview: high-income core EU and eurozone economy; strong growth driven by public consumption, tourism, and other service exports; tight labor market despite high structural unemployment; government debt remains high amid deficit reductions; innovation and economic freedom ranked lower than EU and OECD peers

Real GDP (purchasing power parity): $2.242 trillion (2023 est.)
$2.188 trillion (2022 est.)
$2.068 trillion (2021 est.)
note: data in 2021 dollars
comparison ranking: 15

Real GDP growth rate: 2.5% (2023 est.)
5.77% (2022 est.)
6.4% (2021 est.)
note: annual GDP % growth based on constant local currency
comparison ranking: 124

Real GDP per capita: $46,400 (2023 est.)
$45,800 (2022 est.)
$43,600 (2021 est.)
note: data in 2021 dollars
comparison ranking: 49

GDP (official exchange rate): $1.581 trillion (2023 est.)
note: data in current dollars at official exchange rate

Inflation rate (consumer prices): 3.53% (2023 est.)
8.39% (2022 est.)
3.09% (2021 est.)
note: annual % change based on consumer prices
comparison ranking: 67

Credit ratings: Fitch rating: A- (2018)

Moody's rating: Baa1 (2018)

Standard & Poors rating: A (2019)
note: The year refers to the year in which the current credit rating was first obtained.

GDP - composition, by sector of origin: *agriculture:* 2.3% (2023 est.)
industry: 20.2% (2023 est.)
services: 68.5% (2023 est.)
note: figures may not total 100% due to non-allocated consumption not captured in sector-reported data
comparison rankings: services 43; industry 135; agriculture 151

GDP - composition, by end use: *household consumption:* 55.6% (2023 est.)
government consumption: 19.9% (2023 est.)
investment in fixed capital: 19.3% (2023 est.)
investment in inventories: 1% (2023 est.)
exports of goods and services: 39% (2023 est.)
imports of goods and services: -34.8% (2023 est.)
note: figures may not total 100% due to rounding or gaps in data collection

Agricultural products: milk, barley, wheat, grapes, pork, olives, tomatoes, maize, oranges, sugar beets (2022)
note: top ten agricultural products based on tonnage

Industries: textiles and apparel (including footwear), food and beverages, metals and metal manufactures, chemicals, shipbuilding, automobiles, machine tools, tourism, clay and refractory products, footwear, pharmaceuticals, medical equipment

Industrial production growth rate: 1.94% (2023 est.)
note: annual % change in industrial value added based on constant local currency
comparison ranking: 117

Labor force: 24.108 million (2023 est.)
note: number of people ages 15 or older who are employed or seeking work
comparison ranking: 29

Unemployment rate: 12.14% (2023 est.)
12.92% (2022 est.)
14.78% (2021 est.)
note: % of labor force seeking employment
comparison ranking: 180

Youth unemployment rate (ages 15-24): *total:* 28.7% (2023 est.)
male: 28.8% (2023 est.)
female: 28.6% (2023 est.)
note: % of labor force ages 15-24 seeking employment
comparison ranking: total 28

Population below poverty line: 20.2% (2022 est.)
note: % of population with income below national poverty line

Gini Index coefficient - distribution of family income: 33.9 (2021 est.)
note: index (0-100) of income distribution; higher values represent greater inequality
comparison ranking: 91

Average household expenditures: *on food:* 15.4% of household expenditures (2022 est.)
on alcohol and tobacco: 4.3% of household expenditures (2022 est.)

Household income or consumption by percentage share: *lowest 10%:* 2.2% (2021 est.)
highest 10%: 24.7% (2021 est.)
note: % share of income accruing to lowest and highest 10% of population

Remittances: 0.31% of GDP (2023 est.)
0.3% of GDP (2022 est.)
0.27% of GDP (2021 est.)
note: personal transfers and compensation between resident and non-resident individuals/households/entities

Budget: *revenues:* $467.609 billion (2022 est.)
expenditures: $514.452 billion (2022 est.)
note: central government revenues (excluding grants) and expenses converted to US dollars at average official exchange rate for year indicated

Public debt: 111.43% of GDP (2022 est.)
note: central government debt as a % of GDP
comparison ranking: 14

Taxes and other revenues: 15.82% (of GDP) (2022 est.)
note: central government tax revenue as a % of GDP
comparison ranking: 132

Current account balance: $41.094 billion (2023 est.)
$8.095 billion (2022 est.)
$10.893 billion (2021 est.)

note: balance of payments - net trade and primary/secondary income in current dollars
comparison ranking: 14

Exports: $615.83 billion (2023 est.)
$578.039 billion (2022 est.)
$493.359 billion (2021 est.)
note: balance of payments - exports of goods and services in current dollars
comparison ranking: 17

Exports - partners: France 17%, Germany 10%, Portugal 9%, Italy 8%, UK 6% (2022)
note: top five export partners based on percentage share of exports

Exports - commodities: cars, refined petroleum, garments, packaged medicine, vehicle parts/accessories (2022)
note: top five export commodities based on value in dollars

Imports: $550.576 billion (2023 est.)
$561.49 billion (2022 est.)
$479.392 billion (2021 est.)
note: balance of payments - imports of goods and services in current dollars
comparison ranking: 16

Imports - partners: Germany 11%, China 10%, France 10%, Italy 7%, US 6% (2022)
note: top five import partners based on percentage share of imports

Imports - commodities: crude petroleum, natural gas, garments, cars, vehicle parts/accessories (2022)
note: top five import commodities based on value in dollars

Reserves of foreign exchange and gold: $103.089 billion (2023 est.)
$92.905 billion (2022 est.)
$92.201 billion (2021 est.)
note: holdings of gold (year-end prices)/foreign exchange/special drawing rights in current dollars
comparison ranking: 31

Exchange rates: euros (EUR) per US dollar -

Exchange rates: 0.925 (2023 est.)
0.95 (2022 est.)
0.845 (2021 est.)
0.876 (2020 est.)
0.893 (2019 est.)

ENERGY

Electricity access: *electrification - total population:* 100% (2022 est.)

Electricity: *installed generating capacity:* 118.141 million kW (2022 est.)
consumption: 232.66 billion kWh (2022 est.)
exports: 27.916 billion kWh (2022 est.)
imports: 8.043 billion kWh (2022 est.)
transmission/distribution losses: 26.117 billion kWh (2022 est.)
comparison rankings: transmission/distribution losses 193; imports 33; exports 8; consumption 21; installed generating capacity 12

Electricity generation sources: *fossil fuels:* 37.8% of total installed capacity (2022 est.)
nuclear: 20.1% of total installed capacity (2022 est.)
solar: 11.8% of total installed capacity (2022 est.)
wind: 22% of total installed capacity (2022 est.)
hydroelectricity: 5.6% of total installed capacity (2022 est.)
biomass and waste: 2.8% of total installed capacity (2022 est.)

Nuclear energy: Number of operational nuclear reactors: 7 (2023)

Net capacity of operational nuclear reactors: 7.12GW (2023 est.)

Percent of total electricity production: 20.3% (2023 est.)

Number of nuclear reactors permanently shut down: 3 (2023)

Coal: *production:* 1.293 million metric tons (2022 est.)
consumption: 8.255 million metric tons (2022 est.)
exports: 1.45 million metric tons (2022 est.)
imports: 10.775 million metric tons (2022 est.)
proven reserves: 1.187 billion metric tons (2022 est.)

Petroleum: *total petroleum production:* 47,000 bbl/day (2023 est.)
refined petroleum consumption: 1.269 million bbl/day (2023 est.)
crude oil estimated reserves: 150 million barrels (2021 est.)

Natural gas: *production:* 41.009 million cubic meters (2022 est.)
consumption: 32.833 billion cubic meters (2022 est.)
exports: 6.066 billion cubic meters (2022 est.)
imports: 39.662 billion cubic meters (2022 est.)
proven reserves: 2.549 billion cubic meters (2021 est.)

Carbon dioxide emissions: 266.476 million metric tonnes of CO_2 (2022 est.)
from coal and metallurgical coke: 15.6 million metric tonnes of CO_2 (2022 est.)
from petroleum and other liquids: 184.054 million metric tonnes of CO_2 (2022 est.)
from consumed natural gas: 66.823 million metric tonnes of CO_2 (2022 est.)
comparison ranking: total emissions 25

Energy consumption per capita: 105.979 million Btu/person (2022 est.)
comparison ranking: 48

COMMUNICATIONS

Telephones - fixed lines: *total subscriptions:* 18.687 million (2022 est.)
subscriptions per 100 inhabitants: 39 (2022 est.)
comparison ranking: total subscriptions 14

Telephones - mobile cellular: *total subscriptions:* 59.02 million (2022 est.)
subscriptions per 100 inhabitants: 124 (2022 est.)
comparison ranking: total subscriptions 29

Telecommunication systems: *general assessment:* Spain's telecom sector has tracked the performance of the overall economy, which has been one of the most heavily impacted by the pandemic in all of Europe; GDP dropped by 10.8% in 2020, while telecom revenue reversed the previous five years' positive results by falling 5.3%; fixed-line services were the hardest hit, with revenue falling 13.7%; mobile voice services did not fare much better, falling 4.7%; this is despite relatively small shifts in the number of subscribers, though the harsh lockdown conditions resulted in a significant drop in usage; it had appeared that a return to growth might be possible in 2021 following lifting the state of emergency in May, but the most recent surge in cases and the continued restrictions on travel may once again put the brakes on growth until at least 2022; Spain's fixed-line broadband market managed to extend its decade-long pattern of steady growth into 2020, with a slight increase in demand caused by the need for fast internet access to support working and learning from home; while most of Spain's larger telcos delivered negative revenue and profit in 2020 (2021)
domestic: fixed-line is 39 per 100 and mobile-cellular 124 telephones per 100 persons (2022)
international: country code - 34; landing points for the MAREA, Tata TGN-Western Europe, Pencan-9, SAT-3/WASC, Canalink, Atlantis-2, Columbus -111, Estepona-Tetouan, FLAG Europe-Asia (FEA), Balalink, ORVAL and PENBAL-5 submarine cables providing connectivity to Europe, the Middle East, Africa, South America, Asia, Southeast Asia and the US; satellite earth stations - 2 Intelsat (1 Atlantic Ocean and 1 Indian Ocean), Eutelsat; tropospheric scatter to adjacent countries (2019)

Broadcast media: a mixture of both publicly operated and privately owned TV and radio stations; overall, hundreds of TV channels are available including national, regional, local, public, and international channels; satellite and cable TV systems available; multiple national radio networks, a large number of regional radio networks, and a larger number of local radio stations; overall, hundreds of radio stations (2019)

Internet country code: .es

Internet users: *total:* 44.18 million (2021 est.)
percent of population: 94% (2021 est.)
comparison ranking: total 23

Broadband - fixed subscriptions: *total:* 16,188,502 (2020 est.)
subscriptions per 100 inhabitants: 35 (2020 est.)
comparison ranking: total 15

TRANSPORTATION

National air transport system: *number of registered air carriers:* 21 (2020)
inventory of registered aircraft operated by air carriers: 552
annual passenger traffic on registered air carriers: 80,672,105 (2018)
annual freight traffic on registered air carriers: 1.117 billion (2018) mt-km

Civil aircraft registration country code prefix: EC

Airports: 363 (2024)
comparison ranking: 20

Heliports: 121 (2024)

Pipelines: 10,481 km gas, 358 km oil, 4,378 km refined products (2017)

Railways: *total:* 15,489 km (2020) 9,953 km electrified
comparison ranking: total 19

Roadways: *total:* 150,110 km (2021)
comparison ranking: total 35

Waterways: 1,000 km (2012)
comparison ranking: 69

Merchant marine: *total:* 503 (2023)
by type: bulk carrier 1, general cargo 33, oil tanker 24, other 445
comparison ranking: total 42

Ports: *total ports:* 52 (2024)
large: 3
medium: 14
small: 9
very small: 24

size unknown: 2
ports with oil terminals: 13
key ports: Alicante, Barcelona, Cadiz, Ceuta, Ferrol, Huelva, Las Palmas, Malaga, Palma de Mallorca, Puerto de Bilbao, Puerto de Pasajes, Santa Cruz de Tenerife, Santander, Sevilla, Tarragona, Valencia, Vigo

MILITARY AND SECURITY

Military and security forces: Spanish Armed Forces (Fuerzas Armadas de España): Army (Ejército de Tierra), Spanish Navy (Armada Espanola; includes Marine Corps), Air and Space Force (Ejército del Aire y del Espacio), Emergency Response Unit (Unidad Militar de Emergencias); Civil Guard (Guardia Civil) (2024)
note 1: the Civil Guard is a military force with police duties (including coast guard) under both the Ministry of Defense and the Ministry of the Interior; it also responds to the needs of the Ministry of Finance
note 2: the Emergency Response Unit was established in 2006 as a separate branch of service for responding to natural disasters and providing disaster relief both domestically and abroad; it has personnel from all the other military services
note 3: the Spanish National Police (Cuerpo Nacional de Policía, CNP) and the Civil Guard maintain internal security as well as migration and border enforcement under the authority of the Ministry of the Interior; the regional police under the authority of the Catalan and the Basque Country regional governments and municipal police throughout the country also support domestic security
note 4: the military has a Common Corps of four specialized corps that provide professional services to all the branches of the Armed Forces and the Civil Guard, including comptroller, legal, medical, and music services
note 5: the Royal Guard is an independent regiment of the military dedicated to the protection of the King and members of the royal family; it is made up of members of the Army, Navy, Air Force, and Common Corps

Military expenditures: 1.3% of GDP (2024 est.)
1.2% of GDP (2023)
1.2% of GDP (2022)
1% of GDP (2021)
1% of GDP (2020)
comparison ranking: 102

Military and security service personnel strengths: approximately 118,000 active-duty troops (70,000 Army; 25,000 Navy, including about 5,500 marines; 23,000 Air and Space Force); 80,000 Guardia Civil (2024)
note: military figures include about 3,500 Emergency Response Unit and 1,500-2,000 Royal Guard personnel

Military equipment inventories and acquisitions: the military's inventory is comprised of weapons and equipment that were produced domestically, co-produced with or imported from other EU countries, or purchased from the US; in recent years, leading suppliers have included France, Germany, and the US; Spain's defense industry manufactures land, air, and sea weapons systems and is integrated within the European defense-industrial sector (2024)

Military service age and obligation: 18 years of age for voluntary military service for men and women; 24-36 month initial obligation; women allowed to serve in all branches, including combat units; no conscription (abolished 2001), but the Spanish Government retains the right to mobilize citizens 19-25 years of age in a national emergency; 18-58 for the voluntary reserves (2024)
note 1: as of 2024, women comprised about 13% of the military's full-time personnel
note 2: the military recruits foreign nationals with residency in Spain from countries of its former empire, including Argentina, Costa Rica, Bolivia, Colombia, Chile, Cuba, Dominican Republic, Ecuador, El Salvador, Equatorial Guinea, Guatemala, Honduras, Mexico, Nicaragua, Panama, Paraguay, Peru, Uruguay, and Venezuela

Military deployments: Spain has up to 3,000 military personnel deployed on 17 missions supporting the EU, NATO, and the UN on four continents, as well as naval missions in the Mediterranean and the seas off the Horn of Africa; its largest deployments are up to 700 troops in Lebanon (UNIFIL) and about 1,700 personnel in Eastern Europe supporting NATO missions in Latvia, Romania, and Slovakia (2024)

Military - note: the Spanish Armed Forces have a wide variety of responsibilities, including protecting the country's national interests, sovereignty, and territory, providing support during natural disasters, and fulfilling Spain's responsibilities to European and international security; the military conducts operations worldwide, and its air, ground, and naval forces participate in a variety of EU-, NATO-, and UN-led missions; Spain joined NATO in 1982 and is fully integrated into the NATO structure; it routinely conducts exercises with EU and NATO partners, and hosts one of NATO's two combined air operations centers
the military is organized into commands for air, cyberspace, joint, land, maritime, and space operations; it maintains garrisons in the Balearic Islands, the Canary Islands, Ceuta, and Melilla
the Spanish military has a rich history that goes back to the 13th century; the Army has an infantry regiment, formed in the 13th century, that is considered the oldest still active military unit in the Western world; the Marine Corps, which traces its roots back to 1537, is the oldest naval infantry force in the World; Spain created a Spanish Legion for foreigners in 1920, but early on the Legion was primarily filled by native Spaniards due to difficulties in recruiting foreigners, and most of its foreign members were from the Republic of Cuba; it was modeled after the French Foreign Legion and its purpose was to provide a corps of professional troops to fight in Spain's colonial campaigns in North Africa; in more recent years, it has been used in NATO peacekeeping deployments; today's Legion includes a mix of native Spaniards and foreigners with Spanish residency (2024)

SPACE

Space agency/agencies: Spanish Space Agency (AEE; became operational in April 2023); previously, the National Institute of Aerospace Technology (Instituto Nacional de Técnica Aeroespacial or INTA, established 1942), a public research organization that depends on the Ministry of Defense, acted as Spain's space agency; Space Command (Mando del Espacio or MESPA; established January 2024); Center for the Development of Industrial Technology (CDTI); Catalan Space Agency (established 2021); Valencian Space Consortium (established 2009) (2024)

Space launch site(s): El Arenosillo Test Center/Range (Andalusia); private launch site (Teruel province) (2024)

Space program overview: space program is integrated into the European Space Agency (ESA) and dates back to the 1940s; manufactures and operates communications, remote sensing (RS), and scientific/technology satellites; has developed sounding rockets; conducts research and development in a broad range of space-related capabilities, including astrobiology, astronomy, imaging/RS, materials, meteorology, optics, propulsion, robotics, satellites (particularly micro- and nano-satellites), satellite systems and subsystems, satellite/space launch vehicles (SLVs), and space sciences; participates in ESA, EU, and other international programs; hosts the European Space Astronomy Center (ESOC) and the ESA's Space Surveillance and Tracking Data Centre (ESAC); cooperates with foreign space agencies and industries, including those of ESA and EU member states and the US; has a considerable commercial space industry, which is involved in a wide range of space-related research, development, and production, including satellites and SLVs; the CDTI coordinates the activities of the commercial space sector (2024)
note: further details about the key activities, programs, and milestones of the country's space program, as well as government spending estimates on the space sector, appear in the Space Programs reference guide

TERRORISM

Terrorist group(s): Islamic State of Iraq and ash-Sham (ISIS); al-Qa'ida
note: details about the history, aims, leadership, organization, areas of operation, tactics, targets, weapons, size, and sources of support of the group(s) appear(s) in the Terrorism reference guide

TRANSNATIONAL ISSUES

Refugees and internally displaced persons: *refugees (country of origin):* 14,994 (Syria) (mid-year 2022); 438,400 (Venezuela) (economic and political crisis; includes Venezuelans who have claimed asylum, are recognized as refugees, or have received alternative legal stay) (2022); 192,390 (Ukraine) (as of 29 February 2024)
stateless persons: 6,489 (2022)
note: 351,562 estimated refugee and migrant arrivals, including Canary Islands (January 2015-March 2024)

Illicit drugs: a European transit point for cocaine from South America and for hashish from Morocco; cocaine is shipped in raw or liquid form with mixed cargo to avoid detection or altered to escape detection after which chemists within Spain extract and reconstitute any altered form of cocaine, preparing it for distribution within Europe; minor domestic drug production; occasionally synthetic drugs, including ketamine, new psychoactive substances (NPS), and MDMA transit through Spain to the United States

SPRATLY ISLANDS

INTRODUCTION

Background: The Spratly Islands consist of more than 100 small islands or reefs surrounded by rich fishing grounds – and potentially by gas and oil deposits. China, Taiwan, and Vietnam all claim the islands in their entirety, while portions are claimed by Malaysia and the Philippines. Around 70 disputed islets and reefs in the Spratly Islands are occupied by China, Malaysia, the Philippines, Taiwan, and Vietnam. Since 1985, Brunei has claimed a continental shelf that overlaps a southern reef but has not made any formal claim to the reef. Brunei claims an exclusive economic zone over this area.

GEOGRAPHY

Location: Southeastern Asia, group of reefs and islands in the South China Sea, about two-thirds of the way from southern Vietnam to the southern Philippines

Geographic coordinates: 8 38 N, 111 55 E

Map references: Southeast Asia

Area: *total:* 5 sq km less than
land: 5 sq km less than
water: 0 sq km
note: includes 100 or so islets, coral reefs, and sea mounts scattered over an area of nearly 410,000 sq km (158,000 sq mi) of the central South China Sea
comparison ranking: total 249

Area - comparative: land area is about seven times the size of the National Mall in Washington, DC

Land boundaries: *total:* 0 km

Coastline: 926 km

Maritime claims: NA

Climate: tropical

Terrain: small, flat islands, islets, cays, and reefs

Elevation: *highest point:* unnamed location on Southwest Cay 6 m
lowest point: South China Sea 0 m

Natural resources: fish, guano, undetermined oil and natural gas potential

Land use: *other:* 100% (2018 est.)

Natural hazards: typhoons; numerous reefs and shoals pose a serious maritime hazard

Geography - note: strategically located near several primary shipping lanes in the central South China Sea; includes numerous small islands, atolls, shoals, and coral reefs

PEOPLE AND SOCIETY

Population: *total:* (July 2021 est.) no indigenous inhabitants
note: scattered garrisons are occupied by military personnel of several claimant states

ENVIRONMENT

Environment - current issues: China's use of dredged sand and coral to build artificial islands harms reef systems; illegal fishing practices indiscriminately harvest endangered species, including sea turtles and giant clams

Climate: tropical

GOVERNMENT

Country name: *conventional long form:* none
conventional short form: Spratly Islands
etymology: named after a British whaling captain Richard SPRATLY, who sighted Spratly Island in 1843; the name of the island eventually passed to the entire archipelago

MILITARY AND SECURITY

Military - note: around 70 disputed islets and reefs in the Spratly Islands are occupied by China, Malaysia, the Philippines, Taiwan, and Vietnam

China: occupies seven outposts (Fiery Cross, Mischief, Subi, Cuarteron, Gavin, Hughes, and Johnson reefs); the outposts on Fiery Cross, Mischief, and Subi include air bases with helipads and aircraft hangers, naval port facilities, surveillance radars, air defense and anti-ship missile sites, and other military infrastructure such as communications, barracks, maintenance facilities, and ammunition and fuel bunkers

Malaysia: occupies five outposts in the southern portion of the archipelago, closest to the Malaysian state of Sabah (Ardasier Reef, Eric Reef, Mariveles Reef, Shallow Reef, and Investigator Shoal); all the outposts have helicopter landing pads, while Shallow Reef also has an airstrip

Philippines: occupies nine features (Commodore Reef, Second Thomas Shoal, Flat Island, Loaita Cay, Loaita Island, Nanshan Island, Northeast Cay, Thitu Island, and West York Island); Thitu Island has an airstrip and a coast guard station

Taiwan: maintains a coast guard outpost with an airstrip on Itu Aba Island

Vietnam: occupies about 50 outposts, plus some 14 platforms known as "economic, scientific, and technological service stations" (Dịch vụ-Khoa) that sit on underwater banks to the southeast that Vietnam does not consider part of the disputed island chain, although China and Taiwan disagree; Spratly Islands outposts are on Alison Reef, Amboyna Cay, Barque Canada Reef, Central Reef, Collins Reef, Cornwallis South Reef, Discovery Great Reef, East Reef, Grierson Reef, Ladd Reef, Landsdowne Reef, Namyit Island, Pearson Reef, Petley Reef, Sand Cay, Sin Cowe Island, South Reef, Southwest Cay, Spratly Island, Tennent Reef, West Reef; the underwater banks with stations include Vanguard, Rifleman, Prince of Wales, Prince Consort, Grainger, and Alexandra; in recent years, Vietnam has continued to make improvements to its outposts, including defensive positions and infrastructure (2024)

SRI LANKA

INTRODUCTION

Background: The first Sinhalese arrived in Sri Lanka late in the 6th century B.C., probably from northern India. Buddhism was introduced circa 250 B.C., and the first kingdoms developed at the cities of Anuradhapura (from about 200 B.C. to about A.D. 1000) and Polonnaruwa (from about A.D. 1070 to 1200). In the 14th century, a South Indian dynasty established a Tamil kingdom in northern Sri Lanka. The Portuguese controlled the coastal areas of the island in the 16th century, followed by the Dutch in the 17th century. The island was ceded to the British in 1796, became a crown colony in 1802, and was formally united under British rule by 1815. As Ceylon, it became independent in 1948; the name was changed to Sri Lanka in 1972. Prevailing tensions between the Sinhalese majority and Tamil separatists erupted into war in 1983. Fighting between the government and Liberation Tigers of Tamil Eelam (LTTE) continued for over a quarter-century. Although Norway brokered peace negotiations that led to a cease-fire in 2002, the fighting slowly resumed and was again in full force by 2006. The government defeated the LTTE in 2009.

During the post-conflict years under then-President Mahinda RAJAPAKSA, the government initiated infrastructure development projects, many of which were financed by loans from China. His regime faced allegations of human rights violations and a shrinking democratic space for civil society. In 2015, a new coalition government headed by President Maithripala SIRISENA of the Sri

Lanka Freedom Party and Prime Minister Ranil WICKREMESINGHE of the United National Party came to power with pledges to advance economic, political, and judicial reforms. However, implementation of these reforms was uneven. In 2019, Gotabaya RAJAPAKSA won the presidential election and appointed his brother Mahinda prime minister. Civil society raised concerns about the RAJAPAKSA administration's commitment to pursuing justice, human rights, and accountability reforms, as well as the risks to foreign creditors that Sri Lanka faced given its ongoing economic crisis. A combination of factors including the COVID-19 pandemic; severe shortages of food, medicine, and fuel; and power outages triggered increasingly violent protests in Columbo beginning in 2022. In response, WICKREMESINGHE – who had already served as prime minister five times – was named to replace the prime minister, but he became president within a few months when Gotabaya RAJAPAKSA fled the country.

GEOGRAPHY

Location: Southern Asia, island in the Indian Ocean, south of India

Geographic coordinates: 7 00 N, 81 00 E

Map references: Asia

Area: *total:* 65,610 sq km
land: 64,630 sq km
water: 980 sq km
comparison ranking: total 122

Area - comparative: slightly larger than West Virginia

Land boundaries: *total:* 0 km

Coastline: 1,340 km

Maritime claims: *territorial sea:* 12 nm
contiguous zone: 24 nm
exclusive economic zone: 200 nm
continental shelf: 200 nm or to the edge of the continental margin

Climate: tropical monsoon; northeast monsoon (December to March); southwest monsoon (June to October)

Terrain: mostly low, flat to rolling plain; mountains in south-central interior

Elevation: *highest point:* Pidurutalagala 2,524 m
lowest point: Indian Ocean 0 m
mean elevation: 228 m

Natural resources: limestone, graphite, mineral sands, gems, phosphates, clay, hydropower, arable land

Land use: *agricultural land:* 43.5% (2018 est.)
arable land: 20.7% (2018 est.)
permanent crops: 15.8% (2018 est.)
permanent pasture: 7% (2018 est.)
forest: 29.4% (2018 est.)
other: 27.1% (2018 est.)

Irrigated land: 5,700 sq km (2012)

Population distribution: the population is primarily concentrated within a broad wet zone in the southwest, urban centers along the eastern coast, and on the Jaffna Peninsula in the north

Natural hazards: occasional cyclones and tornadoes

Geography - note: strategic location near major Indian Ocean sea lanes; Adam's Bridge is a chain of limestone shoals between the southeastern coast of India and the northwestern coast of Sri Lanka; geological evidence suggests that this 50-km long Bridge once connected India and Sri Lanka; ancient records seem to indicate that a foot passage was possible between the two land masses until the 15th century when the land bridge broke up in a cyclone

PEOPLE AND SOCIETY

Population: *total:* 21,982,608
male: 10,642,043
female: 11,340,565 (2024 est.)
comparison rankings: female 60; male 62; total 61

Nationality: *noun:* Sri Lankan(s)
adjective: Sri Lankan

Ethnic groups: Sinhalese 74.9%, Sri Lankan Tamil 11.2%, Sri Lankan Moors 9.2%, Indian Tamil 4.2%, other 0.5% (2012 est.)

Languages: Sinhala (official) 87%, Tamil (official) 28.5%, English 23.8% (2012 est.)
note: data represent main languages spoken by the population aged 10 years and older; shares sum to more than 100% because some respondents gave more than one answer on the census; English is commonly used in government and is referred to as the "link language" in the constitution

Religions: Buddhist (official) 70.2%, Hindu 12.6%, Muslim 9.7%, Roman Catholic 6.1%, other Christian 1.3%, other 0.05% (2012 est.)

Age structure: *0-14 years:* 22.6% (male 2,537,918/female 2,423,615)
15-64 years: 65% (male 6,954,869/female 7,336,897)
65 years and over: 12.4% (2024 est.) (male 1,149,256/female 1,580,053)

Dependency ratios: *total dependency ratio:* 53.7
youth dependency ratio: 35.4
elderly dependency ratio: 17
potential support ratio: 5.9 (2021 est.)

Median age: *total:* 34.1 years (2024 est.)
male: 32.2 years
female: 35.8 years
comparison ranking: total 107

Population growth rate: 0.39% (2024 est.)
comparison ranking: 159

Birth rate: 14.5 births/1,000 population (2024 est.)
comparison ranking: 116

Death rate: 7.5 deaths/1,000 population (2024 est.)
comparison ranking: 101

Net migration rate: -3 migrant(s)/1,000 population (2024 est.)
comparison ranking: 179

Population distribution: the population is primarily concentrated within a broad wet zone in the southwest, urban centers along the eastern coast, and on the Jaffna Peninsula in the north

Urbanization: *urban population:* 19.2% of total population (2023)
rate of urbanization: 1.22% annual rate of change (2020-25 est.)

Major urban areas - population: 103,000 Sri Jayewardenepura Kotte (legislative capital) (2018), 633,000 COLOMBO (capital) (2023)

Sex ratio: *at birth:* 1.05 male(s)/female
0-14 years: 1.05 male(s)/female
15-64 years: 0.95 male(s)/female
65 years and over: 0.73 male(s)/female
total population: 0.94 male(s)/female (2024 est.)

Mother's mean age at first birth: 25.6 years (2016 est.)
note: data represents median age at first birth among women 30-34

Maternal mortality ratio: 29 deaths/100,000 live births (2020 est.)
comparison ranking: 112

Infant mortality rate: *total:* 6.8 deaths/1,000 live births (2024 est.)
male: 7.5 deaths/1,000 live births
female: 6.1 deaths/1,000 live births
comparison ranking: total 157

Life expectancy at birth: *total population:* 76.8 years (2024 est.)
male: 73.7 years
female: 79.9 years
comparison ranking: total population 100

Total fertility rate: 2.13 children born/woman (2024 est.)
comparison ranking: 93

Gross reproduction rate: 1.04 (2024 est.)

Contraceptive prevalence rate: 64.6% (2016)

Drinking water source: *improved: urban:* 99.7% of population
rural: 91.2% of population
total: 92.8% of population
unimproved: urban: 0.3% of population
rural: 8.8% of population
total: 7.2% of population (2020 est.)

Current health expenditure: 4.1% of GDP (2020)

Physician density: 1.23 physicians/1,000 population (2020)

Hospital bed density: 4.2 beds/1,000 population (2017)

Sanitation facility access: *improved: urban:* 96.6% of population
rural: 97.9% of population
total: 97.6% of population
unimproved: urban: 3.4% of population
rural: 2.1% of population
total: 2.4% of population (2020 est.)

Obesity - adult prevalence rate: 5.2% (2016)
comparison ranking: 182

Alcohol consumption per capita: *total:* 2.58 liters of pure alcohol (2019 est.)
beer: 0.22 liters of pure alcohol (2019 est.)
wine: 0.01 liters of pure alcohol (2019 est.)
spirits: 2.32 liters of pure alcohol (2019 est.)
other alcohols: 0.03 liters of pure alcohol (2019 est.)
comparison ranking: total 122

Tobacco use: *total:* 22% (2020 est.)
male: 41.4% (2020 est.)
female: 2.6% (2020 est.)
comparison ranking: total 72

Children under the age of 5 years underweight: 20.5% (2016)
comparison ranking: 16

Currently married women (ages 15-49): 65.1% (2023 est.)

Child marriage: *women married by age 15:* 0.9%
women married by age 18: 9.8% (2016 est.)

Education expenditures: 1.9% of GDP (2019 est.)
comparison ranking: 187

Literacy: *definition:* age 15 and over can read and write
total population: 92.3%
male: 93%
female: 91.6% (2019)

School life expectancy (primary to tertiary education): *total:* 14 years
male: 14 years
female: 14 years (2018)

ENVIRONMENT

Environment - current issues: deforestation; soil erosion; wildlife populations threatened by poaching and urbanization; coastal degradation from mining activities and increased pollution; coral reef destruction; freshwater resources being polluted by industrial wastes and sewage runoff; waste disposal; air pollution in Colombo

Environment - international agreements: *party to:* Biodiversity, Climate Change, Climate Change-Kyoto Protocol, Climate Change-Paris Agreement, Desertification, Endangered Species, Environmental Modification, Hazardous Wastes, Law of the Sea, Nuclear Test Ban, Ozone Layer Protection, Ship Pollution, Wetlands
signed, but not ratified: Comprehensive Nuclear Test Ban, Marine Life Conservation

Climate: tropical monsoon; northeast monsoon (December to March); southwest monsoon (June to October)

Urbanization: *urban population:* 19.2% of total population (2023)
rate of urbanization: 1.22% annual rate of change (2020-25 est.)

Food insecurity: *widespread lack of access: due to serious macroeconomic challenges, significant reduction in 2022 cereal output, and high food prices* - severe macroeconomic challenges, mostly reflecting dwindling foreign currency reserves after revenues from merchandise exports, remittances, and from the tourist sector declined dramatically over the last year, have had a negative impact on the country's capacity to import cereals; the 2022 cereal production sharply declined due to a government ordered reduction in the application of chemical fertilizers; unprecedentedly high food prices are constraining economic access to food for a majority of households

Revenue from forest resources: 0.06% of GDP (2018 est.)
comparison ranking: 126

Revenue from coal: 0% of GDP (2018 est.)
comparison ranking: 178

Air pollutants: *particulate matter emissions:* 23.88 micrograms per cubic meter (2019 est.)
carbon dioxide emissions: 23.36 megatons (2016 est.)
methane emissions: 10.95 megatons (2020 est.)

Waste and recycling: *municipal solid waste generated annually:* 2,631,650 tons (2016 est.)
municipal solid waste recycled annually: 336,588 tons (2016 est.)
percent of municipal solid waste recycled: 12.8% (2016 est.)

Total water withdrawal: *municipal:* 810 million cubic meters (2020 est.)
industrial: 830 million cubic meters (2020 est.)
agricultural: 11.31 billion cubic meters (2020 est.)

Total renewable water resources: 52.8 billion cubic meters (2020 est.)

GOVERNMENT

Country name: *conventional long form:* Democratic Socialist Republic of Sri Lanka
conventional short form: Sri Lanka
local long form: Shri Lanka Prajatantrika Samajavadi Janarajaya (Sinhala)/ Ilankai Jananayaka Choshalichak Kutiyarachu (Tamil)
local short form: Shri Lanka (Sinhala)/ Ilankai (Tamil)
former: Serendib, Ceylon
etymology: the name means "resplendent island" in Sanskrit

Government type: presidential republic

Capital: *name:* Colombo (commercial capital); Sri Jayewardenepura Kotte (legislative capital)
geographic coordinates: 6 55 N, 79 50 E
time difference: UTC+5.5 (10.5 hours ahead of Washington, DC, during Standard Time)
etymology: Colombo may derive from the Sinhala "kolon thota," meaning "port on the river" (referring to the Kelani River that empties into the Indian Ocean at Colombo); alternatively, the name may derive from the Sinhala "kola amba thota" meaning "harbor with mango trees"; it is also possible that the Portuguese named the city after Christopher COLUMBUS, who lived in Portugal for many years (as Cristovao COLOMBO) before discovering the Americas for the Spanish crown in 1492 - not long before the Portuguese made their way to Sri Lanka in 1505; Sri Jayewardenepura Kotte translates as "Resplendent City of Growing Victory" in Sinhala

Administrative divisions: 9 provinces; Central, Eastern, North Central, Northern, North Western, Sabaragamuwa, Southern, Uva, Western

Independence: 4 February 1948 (from the UK)

National holiday: Independence Day (National Day), 4 February (1948)

Legal system: mixed legal system of Roman-Dutch civil law, English common law, Jaffna Tamil customary law, and Muslim personal law

Constitution: *history:* several previous; latest adopted 16 August 1978, certified 31 August 1978
amendments: proposed by Parliament; passage requires at least two-thirds majority vote of its total membership, certification by the president of the republic or the Parliament speaker, and in some cases approval in a referendum by absolute majority of valid votes; amended many times, last in 2020

International law organization participation: has not submitted an ICJ jurisdiction declaration; non-party state to the ICCt

Citizenship: *citizenship by birth:* no
citizenship by descent only: at least one parent must be a citizen of Sri Lanka
dual citizenship recognized: no, except in cases where the government rules it is to the benefit of Sri Lanka
residency requirement for naturalization: 7 years

Suffrage: 18 years of age; universal

Executive branch: *chief of state:* President Anura Kumara DISSANAYAKE (since 23 September 2024)
head of government: Prime Minister Harini AMARASURIYA (since 24 September 2024)
cabinet: Cabinet appointed by the president in consultation with the prime minister
elections/appointments: president directly elected by preferential majority popular vote for a 5-year term (eligible for a second term); election last held on 21 September 2024 (next to be held in 2029)
election results:
2024: Anura Kumara DISSANAYAKE elected president; percent of vote after reallocation - Anura Kumara DISSANAYAKE (JVP) 55.9%, Sajith PREMADASA (SJB) 44.1%
2022: Ranil WICKREMESINGHE elected president by Parliament on 20 July 2022; Parliament vote - WICKREMESINGHE (UNP) 134, Dullas ALAHAPPERUMA (SLPP) 82

Legislative branch: *description:* unicameral Parliament (225 seats; 196 members directly elected in multi-seat district constituencies by proportional representation vote using a preferential method in which voters select 3 candidates in order of preference; remaining 29 seats, referred to as the "national list" are allocated by each party secretary according to the island wide proportional vote the party obtains; members serve 5-year terms)
elections: last held on 5 August 2020 (next to be held on 14 November 2024)
election results: percent of vote by party/coalition - SLFPA 59.1%, SJB 23.9%, JVP 3.8%, TNA 2.8%, UNP 2.2%, TNPF 0.6%, EPDP 0.5%, other 7.1%; seats by party/coalition - SLFPA 145, SJB 54, TNA 10, JVP 3, other 13; compositionmen 213, women 12, percentage women 5.3%

Judicial branch: *highest court(s):* Supreme Court of the Republic (consists of the chief justice and 9 justices); note - the court has exclusive jurisdiction to review legislation
judge selection and term of office: chief justice nominated by the Constitutional Council (CC), a 9-member high-level advisory body, and appointed by the president; other justices nominated by the CC and appointed by the president on the advice of the chief justice; all justices can serve until age 65
subordinate courts: Court of Appeals; High Courts; Magistrates' Courts; municipal and primary courts

Political parties: Crusaders for Democracy or CFD
Eelam People's Democratic Party or EPDP
Eelam People's Revolutionary Liberation Front or EPRLF
Illankai Tamil Arasu Kachchi or ITAK
Janatha Vimukthi Peramuna or JVP
Jathika Hela Urumaya or JHU
National People's Power or NPP (also known as Jathika Jana Balawegaya or JJB)
People's Liberation Organisation of Tamil Eelam or PLOTE
Samagi Jana Balawegaya or SJB
Sri Lanka Freedom Party or SLFP
Sri Lanka Muslim Congress or SLMC
Sri Lanka People's Freedom Alliance or SLPFA (includes SLPFP, SLPP, and several smaller parties)

Sri Lanka Podujana Peramuna (Sri Lanka's People's Front) or SLPP
Tamil Eelam Liberation Organization or TELO
Tamil National Alliance or TNA (includes ITAK, PLOTE, TELO)
Tamil National People's Front or TNPF
Tamil People's National Alliance or TPNA
United National Front for Good Governance or UNFGG (coalition includes JHU, UNP)
United National Party or UNP

International organization participation: ABEDA, ADB, ARF, BIMSTEC, C, CD, CICA (observer), CP, FAO, G-11, G-15, G-24, G-77, IAEA, IBRD, ICAO, ICC (national committees), ICRM, IDA, IFAD, IFC, IFRCS, IHO, ILO, IMF, IMO, IMSO, Interpol, IOC, IOM, IPU, ISO, ITSO, ITU, ITUC (NGOs), MIGA, MINURSO, MINUSTAH, MONUSCO, NAM, OAS (observer), OPCW, PCA, SAARC, SACEP, SCO (dialogue member), UN, UNCTAD, UNESCO, UNIDO, UNIFIL, UNISFA, UNMISS, UNWTO, UPU, WCO, WFTU (NGOs), WHO, WIPO, WMO, WTO

Diplomatic representation in the US: *chief of mission:* Ambassador Mahinda SAMARASINGHE (since 13 January 2022)
chancery: 3025 Whitehaven Street NW, Washington, DC 20008
telephone: [1] (202) 483-4025
FAX: [1] 202-232-2329
email address and website:
slemb.washington@mfa.gov.lk
https://slembassyusa.org/new/
consulate(s) general: Los Angeles
consulate(s): New York

Diplomatic representation from the US: *chief of mission:* Ambassador Julie J. CHUNG (since 17 February 2022)
embassy: 210 Galle Road, Colombo 03
mailing address: 6100 Colombo Place, Washington DC 20521-6100
telephone: [94] (11) 249-8500
FAX: [94] (11) 243-7345
email address and website:
colomboacs@state.gov
https://lk.usembassy.gov/

Flag description: yellow with two panels; the smaller hoist-side panel has two equal vertical bands of green (hoist side) and orange; the other larger panel depicts a yellow lion holding a sword on a maroon rectangular field that also displays a yellow bo leaf in each corner; the yellow field appears as a border around the entire flag and extends between the two panels; the lion represents Sinhalese ethnicity, the strength of the nation, and bravery; the sword demonstrates the sovereignty of the nation; the four bo leaves - symbolizing Buddhism and its influence on the country - stand for the four virtues of kindness, friendliness, happiness, and equanimity; orange signifies Sri Lankan Tamils, green Sri Lankan Moors, and maroon the Sinhalese majority; yellow denotes other ethnic groups; also referred to as the Lion Flag

National symbol(s): lion, water lily; national colors: maroon, yellow

National anthem: *name:* "Sri Lanka Matha" (Mother Sri Lanka)
lyrics/music: Ananda SAMARKONE
note: adopted 1951

National heritage: *total World Heritage Sites:* 8 (6 cultural, 2 natural)
selected World Heritage Site locales: Ancient City of Polonnaruwa (c); Ancient City of Sigiriya (c); Sacred City of Anuradhapura (c); Old Town of Galle and its Fortifications (c); Sacred City of Kandy (c); Sinharaja Forest Reserve (n); Rangiri Dambulla Cave Temple (c); Central Highlands of Sri Lanka (n)

ECONOMY

Economic overview: economic contraction in 2022-23 marked by increased poverty and significant inflation; IMF two-year debt relief program following 2022 sovereign default; structural challenges from non-diversified economy and rigid labor laws; heavy dependence on tourism receipts and remittances

Real GDP (purchasing power parity): $287.132 billion (2023 est.)
$293.885 billion (2022 est.)
$317.188 billion (2021 est.)
note: data in 2021 dollars
comparison ranking: 63

Real GDP growth rate: -2.3% (2023 est.)
-7.35% (2022 est.)
4.21% (2021 est.)
note: annual GDP % growth based on constant local currency
comparison ranking: 208

Real GDP per capita: $13,000 (2023 est.)
$13,200 (2022 est.)
$14,300 (2021 est.)
note: data in 2021 dollars
comparison ranking: 133

GDP (official exchange rate): $84.357 billion (2023 est.)
note: data in current dollars at official exchange rate

Inflation rate (consumer prices): 16.54% (2023 est.)
49.72% (2022 est.)
7.01% (2021 est.)
note: annual % change based on consumer prices
comparison ranking: 194

Credit ratings: Fitch rating: CCC (2020)

Moody's rating: Caa1 (2020)

Standard & Poors rating: CCC+ (2020)
note: The year refers to the year in which the current credit rating was first obtained.

GDP - composition, by sector of origin: *agriculture:* 8.3% (2023 est.)
industry: 25.6% (2023 est.)
services: 59.9% (2023 est.)
note: figures may not total 100% due to non-allocated consumption not captured in sector-reported data
comparison rankings: services 84; industry 91; agriculture 88

GDP - composition, by end use: *household consumption:* 69.3% (2023 est.)
government consumption: 6.9% (2023 est.)
investment in fixed capital: 17.6% (2023 est.)
investment in inventories: 7.7% (2023 est.)
exports of goods and services: 20.4% (2023 est.)
imports of goods and services: -21.9% (2023 est.)
note: figures may not total 100% due to rounding or gaps in data collection

Agricultural products: rice, coconuts, plantains, tea, sugarcane, milk, cassava, fiber crops, maize, chicken (2022)
note: top ten agricultural products based on tonnage

Industries: processing of rubber, tea, coconuts, tobacco and other agricultural commodities; tourism; clothing and textiles; mining

Industrial production growth rate: -9.23% (2023 est.)
note: annual % change in industrial value added based on constant local currency
comparison ranking: 207

Labor force: 8.707 million (2023 est.)
note: number of people ages 15 or older who are employed or seeking work
comparison ranking: 62

Unemployment rate: 6.36% (2023 est.)
6.33% (2022 est.)
5.26% (2021 est.)
note: % of labor force seeking employment
comparison ranking: 130

Youth unemployment rate (ages 15-24): *total:* 25.3% (2023 est.)
male: 20.9% (2023 est.)
female: 33.9% (2023 est.)
note: % of labor force ages 15-24 seeking employment
comparison ranking: total 43

Population below poverty line: 14.3% (2019 est.)
note: % of population with income below national poverty line

Gini Index coefficient - distribution of family income: 37.7 (2019 est.)
note: index (0-100) of income distribution; higher values represent greater inequality
comparison ranking: 57

Average household expenditures: *on food:* 26.8% of household expenditures (2022 est.)
on alcohol and tobacco: 3.4% of household expenditures (2022 est.)

Household income or consumption by percentage share: *lowest 10%:* 3.1% (2019 est.)
highest 10%: 30.8% (2019 est.)
note: % share of income accruing to lowest and highest 10% of population

Remittances: 6.4% of GDP (2023 est.)
5.15% of GDP (2022 est.)
6.23% of GDP (2021 est.)
note: personal transfers and compensation between resident and non-resident individuals/households/entities

Budget: *revenues:* $7.365 billion (2021 est.)
expenditures: $15.477 billion (2021 est.)
note: central government revenues and expenses (excluding grants/extrabudgetary units/social security funds) converted to US dollars at average official exchange rate for year indicated

Public debt: 79.1% of GDP (2017 est.)
note: central government debt as a % of GDP
comparison ranking: 40

Taxes and other revenues: 7.28% (of GDP) (2022 est.)
note: central government tax revenue as a % of GDP
comparison ranking: 195

Current account balance: $1.559 billion (2023 est.)
-$1.448 billion (2022 est.)
-$3.284 billion (2021 est.)
note: balance of payments - net trade and primary/secondary income in current dollars
comparison ranking: 49

Exports: $17.327 billion (2023 est.)
$16.169 billion (2022 est.)
$14.974 billion (2021 est.)
note: balance of payments - exports of goods and services in current dollars
comparison ranking: 94

Exports - partners: US 24%, India 8%, UK 7%, Germany 6%, Italy 4% (2022)
note: top five export partners based on percentage share of exports

Exports - commodities: garments, tea, used rubber tires, rubber products, precious stones (2022)
note: top five export commodities based on value in dollars

Imports: $18.823 billion (2023 est.)
$19.244 billion (2022 est.)
$21.526 billion (2021 est.)
note: balance of payments - imports of goods and services in current dollars
comparison ranking: 98

Imports - partners: India 34%, China 19%, UAE 5%, Malaysia 4%, Singapore 4% (2022)
note: top five import partners based on percentage share of imports

Imports - commodities: refined petroleum, fabric, ships, cotton fabric, synthetic fabric (2022)
note: top five import commodities based on value in dollars

Reserves of foreign exchange and gold: $3.137 billion (2021 est.)
$5.664 billion (2020 est.)
$7.648 billion (2019 est.)
note: holdings of gold (year-end prices)/foreign exchange/special drawing rights in current dollars
comparison ranking: 113

Debt - external: $37.487 billion (2022 est.)
note: present value of external debt in current US dollars
comparison ranking: 17

Exchange rates: Sri Lankan rupees (LKR) per US dollar -

Exchange rates: 198.764 (2021 est.)
185.593 (2020 est.)
178.745 (2019 est.)
162.465 (2018 est.)
152.446 (2017 est.)

ENERGY

Electricity access: *electrification - total population:* 100% (2022 est.)

Electricity: *installed generating capacity:* 5.04 million kW (2022 est.)
consumption: 10.401 billion kWh (2022 est.)
transmission/distribution losses: 1.62 billion kWh (2022 est.)
comparison rankings: transmission/distribution losses 117; consumption 103; installed generating capacity 90

Electricity generation sources: *fossil fuels:* 47.4% of total installed capacity (2022 est.)
solar: 5.3% of total installed capacity (2022 est.)
wind: 5.8% of total installed capacity (2022 est.)
hydroelectricity: 40.6% of total installed capacity (2022 est.)
biomass and waste: 0.8% of total installed capacity (2022 est.)

Coal: *consumption:* 2.084 million metric tons (2022 est.)
exports: (2022 est.) less than 1 metric ton
imports: 2.205 million metric tons (2022 est.)

Petroleum: *refined petroleum consumption:* 121,000 bbl/day (2022 est.)

Carbon dioxide emissions: 21.766 million metric tonnes of CO2 (2022 est.)
from coal and metallurgical coke: 4.663 million metric tonnes of CO2 (2022 est.)
from petroleum and other liquids: 17.103 million metric tonnes of CO2 (2022 est.)
comparison ranking: total emissions 82

Energy consumption per capita: 14.449 million Btu/person (2022 est.)
comparison ranking: 142

COMMUNICATIONS

Telephones - fixed lines: *total subscriptions:* 2.582 million (2022 est.)
subscriptions per 100 inhabitants: 12 (2022 est.)
comparison ranking: total subscriptions 45

Telephones - mobile cellular: *total subscriptions:* 31.237 million (2022 est.)
subscriptions per 100 inhabitants: 143 (2022 est.)
comparison ranking: total subscriptions 47

Telecommunication systems: *general assessment:* Sri Lanka's fixed-line telephony market was one of the very few in the world to experience a significant upsurge in subscriptions in 2020; while the country suffers from a relatively poor fixed-line infrastructure and a correspondingly strong mobile sector, demand for traditional phone services increased 14% in 2020; preliminary results suggest a further jump of up to 13% can also be expected in 2021; this will take Sri Lanka's fixed-line penetration to levels not seen since 2013; the most reason behind the market's reversal of fortunes is the Covid-19 crisis and Sri Lanka's ensuring lock downs; these forced much of the population back inside and reverting to 'traditional' methods of communication for both voice and data services; the fixed broadband market was equally robust, growing 20% in 2020 alone; Sri Lanka possesses a relatively low number of computers per household so the fixed broadband market's success comes off a small base; the one area of the telecommunications market that experienced a fall was the mobile segment; up until the start of the pandemic, Sri Lanka had a very high mobile penetration rate of 155%; this near-saturation level reflected the preponderance for subscribers to carry multiple SIM cards to take advantage of cheaper on-net call rates; the reduction in demand and traffic because of the pandemic led to a sharp drop in the number of active subscriptions, down to just 135% – a 17% decline in just one year; the market is expected to bounce back quickly, as soon as the country eases back on its lock down measures and reduces travel restrictions; it will also be boosted, come 2022, by the anticipated launch of commercial 5G mobile services (2021)
domestic: fixed-line is 12 per 100 and mobile-cellular is 143 per 100 (2022)
international: country code - 94; landing points for the SeaMeWe -3,-5, Dhiraagu-SLT Submarine Cable Network, WARF Submarine Cable, Bharat Lanka Cable System and the Bay of Bengal Gateway submarine cables providing connectivity to Asia, Africa, Southeast Asia, Australia, the Middle East, and Europe; satellite earth stations - 2 Intelsat (Indian Ocean) (2019)

Broadcast media: government operates 5 TV channels and 19 radio channels; multi-channel satellite and cable TV subscription services available; 25 private TV stations and about 43 radio stations; 6 non-profit TV stations and 4 radio stations

Internet country code: .lk

Internet users: *total:* 14.74 million (2021 est.)
percent of population: 67% (2021 est.)
comparison ranking: total 51

Broadband - fixed subscriptions: *total:* 1,781,530 (2020 est.)
subscriptions per 100 inhabitants: 8 (2020 est.)
comparison ranking: total 60

TRANSPORTATION

National air transport system: *number of registered air carriers:* 3 (2020)
inventory of registered aircraft operated by air carriers: 34
annual passenger traffic on registered air carriers: 5,882,376 (2018)
annual freight traffic on registered air carriers: 436.2 million (2018) mt-km

Civil aircraft registration country code prefix: 4R

Airports: 18 (2024)
comparison ranking: 141

Heliports: 1 (2024)

Pipelines: 7 km refined products

Railways: *total:* 1,562 km (2016)
broad gauge: 1,562 km (2016) 1.676-m gauge
comparison ranking: total 81

Roadways: *total:* 114,093 km
paved: 16,977 km
unpaved: 97,116 km (2010)
comparison ranking: total 44

Waterways: 160 km (2012) (primarily on rivers in southwest)
comparison ranking: 110

Merchant marine: *total:* 96 (2023)
by type: bulk carrier 5, general cargo 15, oil tanker 11, other 65
comparison ranking: total 92

Ports: *total ports:* 6 (2024)
large: 0
medium: 2
small: 1
very small: 1
size unknown: 2
ports with oil terminals: 2
key ports: Batticaloa Roads, Colombo, Galle Harbor, Hambantota, Kankesanturai, Trincomalee Harbor

MILITARY AND SECURITY

Military and security forces: Sri Lanka Armed Forces: Sri Lanka Army (includes National Guard and the Volunteer Force), Sri Lanka Navy (includes Marine Corps), Sri Lanka Air Force, Sri Lanka Coast Guard; Civil Security Department (Home Guard)

Ministry of Public Security: Sri Lanka National Police (2024)
note 1: the Civil Security Department, also known as the Civil Defense Force, is an auxiliary force administered by the Ministry of Defense
note 2: the Sri Lanka Police includes the Special Task Force, a paramilitary unit responsible for counterterrorism and counterinsurgency operations; it coordinates internal security operations with the military

Military expenditures: 1.6% of GDP (2023 est.)
1.7% of GDP (2022 est.)
1.9% of GDP (2021 est.)
2% of GDP (2020 est.)
2% of GDP (2019 est.)
comparison ranking: 84

Military and security service personnel strengths: approximately 260,000 total personnel (200,000 Army; 30,000 Navy; 30,000 Air Force); approximately 11,000 Special Task Force personnel (2023)
note: in January 2023, Sri Lanka's Ministry of Defense announced plans to decrease the size of the Army to 135,000 by 2024 and 100,000 by 2030

Military equipment inventories and acquisitions: the military's inventory consists mostly of Chinese- and Russian-origin equipment with a smaller mix of material from countries such as India and the US, including donations; defense acquisitions have been limited over the past decade (2024)

Military service age and obligation: 18-22 years of age for voluntary military service for men and women; no conscription (2023)

Military deployments: 110 Central African Republic (MINUSCA); 125 Lebanon (UNIFIL); 240 Mali (MINUSMA) (2024)

Military - note: the military of Sri Lanka is responsible for external defense and may be called upon to handle specifically delineated domestic security responsibilities that generally do not include arrest authority; it has sent small numbers of personnel on UN peacekeeping missions; from 1983 to 2009, the military fought against the Liberation Tigers of Tamil Eelam (LTTE), a conflict that involved both guerrilla and conventional warfare, as well as acts of terrorism and human rights abuses, and cost the military nearly 30,000 killed; since the end of the war, a large portion of the Army reportedly remains deployed in the majority Tamil-populated northern and eastern provinces; the military over the past decade also has increased its role in a range of commercial sectors including agriculture, hotels, leisure, and restaurants
Sri Lanka traditionally has had close security ties to India; India participated in the LTTE war in 1987-1991, losing over 1,000 soldiers; the Sri Lankan and Indian militaries continue to conduct exercises together, and India trains over 1,000 Sri Lankan soldiers per year; in recent years, Sri Lanka has increased military ties with China, including acquiring military equipment, hosting naval port calls, and sending personnel to China for training (2024)

TERRORISM

Terrorist group(s): Islamic State of Iraq and ash-Sham (ISIS); Liberation Tigers of Tamil Eelam (LTTE)
note: details about the history, aims, leadership, organization, areas of operation, tactics, targets, weapons, size, and sources of support of the group(s) appear(s) in the Terrorism reference guide

TRANSNATIONAL ISSUES

Refugees and internally displaced persons: IDPs: 12,000 (civil war; more than half displaced prior to 2008; many of the more than 480,000 IDPs registered as returnees have not reached durable solutions) (2022)
stateless persons: 35 (2022)

SUDAN

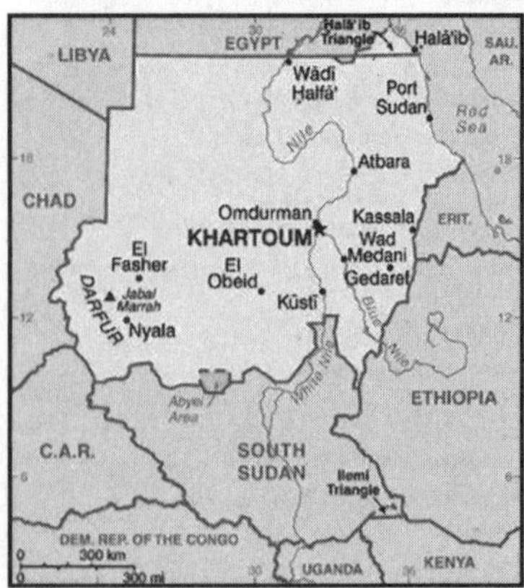

INTRODUCTION

Background: Long referred to as Nubia, modern-day Sudan was the site of the Kingdom of Kerma (ca. 2500-1500 B.C.) until it was absorbed into the New Kingdom of Egypt. By the 11th century B.C., the Kingdom of Kush gained independence from Egypt; it lasted in various forms until the middle of the 4th century A.D. After the fall of Kush, the Nubians formed three Christian kingdoms of Nobatia, Makuria, and Alodia, with the latter two enduring until around 1500. Between the 14th and 15th centuries, Arab nomads settled much of Sudan, leading to extensive Islamization between the 16th and 19th centuries. Following Egyptian occupation early in the 19th century, an agreement in 1899 set up a joint British-Egyptian government in Sudan, but it was effectively a British colony.

Military regimes favoring Islamic-oriented governments have dominated national politics since Sudan gained independence from Anglo-Egyptian co-rule in 1956. During most of the second half of the 20th century, Sudan was embroiled in two prolonged civil wars rooted in northern domination of the largely non-Muslim, non-Arab southern portion of the country. The first civil war ended in 1972, but another broke out in 1983. Peace talks gained momentum in 2002-04, and the final North/South Comprehensive Peace Agreement in 2005 granted the southern rebels autonomy for six years, followed by a referendum on independence for Southern Sudan. South Sudan became independent in 2011, but Sudan and South Sudan have yet to fully implement security and economic agreements to normalize relations between the two countries. Sudan has also faced conflict in Darfur, Southern Kordofan, and Blue Nile starting in 2003.

In 2019, after months of nationwide protests, the 30-year reign of President Omar Hassan Ahmad al-BASHIR ended when the military forced him out. Economist and former international civil servant Abdalla HAMDOUK al-Kinani was selected to serve as the prime minister of a transitional government as the country prepared for elections in 2022. In late 2021, however, the Sudanese military ousted HAMDOUK and his government and replaced civilian members of the Sovereign Council (Sudan's collective Head of State) with individuals selected by the military. HAMDOUK was briefly reinstated but resigned in January 2022. General Abd-al-Fatah alBURHAN Abd-al-Rahman, the Chair of Sudan's Sovereign Council and Commander-in-Chief of the Sudanese Armed Forces, currently serves as de facto head of state and government. He presides over a Sovereign Council consisting of military leaders, former armed opposition group representatives, and military-appointed civilians. A cabinet of acting ministers handles day-to-day administration.

GEOGRAPHY

Location: north-eastern Africa, bordering the Red Sea, between Egypt and Eritrea

Geographic coordinates: 15 00 N, 30 00 E

Map references: Africa

Area: *total:* 1,861,484 sq km
land: 1,731,671 sq km
water: 129,813 sq km
comparison ranking: total 17

Area - comparative: slightly less than one-fifth the size of the US

Land boundaries: *total:* 6,819 km
border countries (7): Central African Republic 174 km; Chad 1,403 km; Egypt 1,276 km; Eritrea 682 km; Ethiopia 744 km; Libya 382 km; South Sudan 2,158 km
note: Sudan-South Sudan boundary represents 1 January 1956 alignment; final alignment pending negotiations and demarcation; final sovereignty status of Abyei region pending negotiations between Sudan and South Sudan

Coastline: 853 km

Maritime claims: *territorial sea:* 12 nm
contiguous zone: 18 nm
continental shelf: 200-m depth or to the depth of exploitation

Climate: hot and dry; arid desert; rainy season varies by region (April to November)

Terrain: generally flat, featureless plain; desert dominates the north

Elevation: *highest point:* Jabal Marrah 3,042 m
lowest point: Red Sea 0 m
mean elevation: 568 m

Natural resources: petroleum; small reserves of iron ore, copper, chromium ore, zinc, tungsten, mica, silver, gold; hydropower

Land use: *agricultural land:* 100% (2018 est.)
arable land: 15.7% (2018 est.)
permanent crops: 0.2% (2018 est.)
permanent pasture: 84.2% (2018 est.)
forest: 0% (2018 est.)
other: 0% (2018 est.)

Irrigated land: 15,666 sq km (2020)

Major rivers (by length in km): An Nīl (Nile) (shared with Rwanda [s], Tanzania, Uganda, South Sudan, and Egypt [m]) - 6,650 km; Blue Nile river mouth (shared with Ethiopia [s]) - 1,600 km
note – [s] after country name indicates river source; [m] after country name indicates river mouth

Major watersheds (area sq km): Atlantic Ocean drainage: *(Mediterranean Sea)* Nile (3,254,853 sq km)

Internal (endorheic basin) drainage: Lake Chad (2,497,738 sq km)

Major aquifers: Nubian Aquifer System, Sudd Basin (Umm Ruwaba Aquifer)

Population distribution: with the exception of a ribbon of settlement that corresponds to the banks of the Nile, northern Sudan, which extends into the dry Sahara, is sparsely populated; more abundant vegetation and broader access to water increases population distribution in the south extending habitable range along nearly the entire border with South Sudan; sizeable areas of population are found around Khartoum, southeast between the Blue and White Nile Rivers, and throughout South Darfur as shown on this population distribution map

Natural hazards: dust storms and periodic persistent droughts

Geography - note: the Nile is Sudan's primary water source; its major tributaries, the White Nile and the Blue Nile, meet at Khartoum to form the River Nile, which flows northward through Egypt to the Mediterranean Sea

PEOPLE AND SOCIETY

Population: *total:* 50,467,278
male: 25,335,092
female: 25,132,186 (2024 est.)
comparison rankings: female 31; male 29; total 29

Nationality: *noun:* Sudanese (singular and plural)
adjective: Sudanese

Ethnic groups: Sudanese Arab (approximately 70%), Fur, Beja, Nuba, Ingessana, Uduk, Fallata, Masalit, Dajo, Gimir, Tunjur, Berti; there are over 500 ethnic groups

Languages: Arabic (official), English (official), Nubian, Ta Bedawie, Fur
major-language sample(s):
كتاب حقائق العالم، المصدر الذي لا يمكن الاستغناء عنه للمعلومات الأساسية
(Arabic)

Religions: Sunni Muslim, small Christian minority

Demographic profile: Sudan's population grew almost fourfold between 1956 and 2008, the date of its last census. Even after the southern part of the country became independent South Sudan in 2011, the population of Sudan has continued to grow. The gender balance overall is fairly even. Females, however, are more prevalent in rural areas because of males migrating to urban areas in search of work. The total fertility rate (TFR) remains high despite falling from 7 children per woman in Sudan's first census in 1955 to about 4.5 in 2022, which can be attributed to early marriage and a low contraceptive prevalence rate. Among the factors that led to the reduction in fertility are family planning, improvement in women's education and participation in the labor force outside the home, and migration and urbanization.
The continued slow decline in fertility accompanied by a drop in mortality and increased life expectancy has produced an age structure where approximately 55% of the population was of working age (15-64) as of 2020. This share will grow as the sizable youth population becomes working age. As Sudan's working age population increasingly outnumbers the youth and elderly populations (the dependent populations), the country will approach the possibility of a demographic dividend. The window of opportunity for potential economic growth depends not only on a favorable age structure but also on having a trained and educated workforce, job creation (particularly in the formal market), and investment in health, as well as generating savings to invest in schooling and care for the elderly. As of 2018, Sudan's literacy rate was just over 60%, and even lower among women. Improvements in school enrollment, student-teacher ratio, infrastructure, funding, and educational quality could help the country to realize a demographic dividend.

Age structure: *0-14 years:* 40.1% (male 10,278,453/female 9,949,343)
15-64 years: 56.7% (male 14,211,514/female 14,390,486)
65 years and over: 3.2% (2024 est.) (male 845,125/female 792,357)

Dependency ratios: *total dependency ratio:* 76.9
youth dependency ratio: 74
elderly dependency ratio: 6.2
potential support ratio: 16.2 (2021 est.)

Median age: *total:* 19.3 years (2024 est.)
male: 19 years
female: 19.6 years
comparison ranking: total 212

Population growth rate: 2.55% (2024 est.)
comparison ranking: 16

Birth rate: 33.1 births/1,000 population (2024 est.)
comparison ranking: 18

Death rate: 6.1 deaths/1,000 population (2024 est.)
comparison ranking: 148

Net migration rate: -1.6 migrant(s)/1,000 population (2024 est.)
comparison ranking: 159

Population distribution: with the exception of a ribbon of settlement that corresponds to the banks of the Nile, northern Sudan, which extends into the dry Sahara, is sparsely populated; more abundant vegetation and broader access to water increases population distribution in the south extending habitable range along nearly the entire border with South Sudan; sizeable areas of population are found around Khartoum, southeast between the Blue and White Nile Rivers, and throughout South Darfur as shown on this population distribution map

Urbanization: *urban population:* 36.3% of total population (2023)
rate of urbanization: 3.43% annual rate of change (2020-25 est.)

Major urban areas - population: 6.344 million KHARTOUM (capital), 1.057 million Nyala (2023)

Sex ratio: *at birth:* 1.05 male(s)/female
0-14 years: 1.03 male(s)/female
15-64 years: 0.99 male(s)/female
65 years and over: 1.07 male(s)/female
total population: 1.01 male(s)/female (2024 est.)

Maternal mortality ratio: 270 deaths/100,000 live births (2020 est.)
comparison ranking: 31

Infant mortality rate: *total:* 40.6 deaths/1,000 live births (2024 est.)
male: 46 deaths/1,000 live births
female: 34.8 deaths/1,000 live births
comparison ranking: total 28

Life expectancy at birth: *total population:* 67.8 years (2024 est.)
male: 65.5 years
female: 70.2 years
comparison ranking: total population 194

Total fertility rate: 4.47 children born/woman (2024 est.)
comparison ranking: 15

Gross reproduction rate: 2.18 (2024 est.)

Contraceptive prevalence rate: 12.2% (2014)

Drinking water source: *improved: urban:* 99% of population
rural: 80.7% of population
total: 87.1% of population
unimproved: urban: 1% of population
rural: 19.3% of population
total: 12.9% of population (2020 est.)

Current health expenditure: 3% of GDP (2020)

Physician density: 0.26 physicians/1,000 population (2017)

Hospital bed density: 0.7 beds/1,000 population (2017)

Sanitation facility access: *improved: urban:* 72.1% of population
rural: 30.6% of population
total: 45.3% of population
unimproved: urban: 27.9% of population
rural: 69.4% of population
total: 54.7% of population (2020 est.)

Obesity - adult prevalence rate: 6.6% (2014)
comparison ranking: 165

Alcohol consumption per capita: *total:* 1.93 liters of pure alcohol (2019 est.)
beer: 0 liters of pure alcohol (2019 est.)
wine: 0 liters of pure alcohol (2019 est.)
spirits: 0.29 liters of pure alcohol (2019 est.)
other alcohols: 1.63 liters of pure alcohol (2019 est.)
comparison ranking: total 131

Children under the age of 5 years underweight: 33% (2014)
comparison ranking: 3

Currently married women (ages 15-49): 61.4% (2023 est.)

Literacy: *definition:* age 15 and over can read and write
total population: 60.7%
male: 65.4%
female: 56.1% (2018)

School life expectancy (primary to tertiary education): *total:* 8 years
male: 8 years
female: 7 years (2015)

ENVIRONMENT

Environment - current issues: water pollution; inadequate supplies of potable water; water scarcity and periodic drought; wildlife populations threatened by excessive hunting; soil erosion; desertification; deforestation; loss of biodiversity

Environment - international agreements: *party to:* Biodiversity, Climate Change, Climate Change-Kyoto Protocol, Climate Change-Paris Agreement, Comprehensive Nuclear Test Ban, Desertification, Endangered Species, Hazardous Wastes, Law of the

Sea, Nuclear Test Ban, Ozone Layer Protection, Wetlands
signed, but not ratified: none of the selected agreements

Climate: hot and dry; arid desert; rainy season varies by region (April to November)

Urbanization: *urban population:* 36.3% of total population (2023)
rate of urbanization: 3.43% annual rate of change (2020-25 est.)

Food insecurity: *severe localized food insecurity: due to conflict, civil insecurity, and soaring food prices* - according to the results of the latest analysis, about 11.7 million people (24% of the analyzed population) are estimated to be severely food insecure during June to September 2022; the main drivers are macroeconomic challenges resulting in rampant food and non-food inflation, tight supplies due to a poor 2021 harvest and the escalation of intercommunal violence (2022)

Revenue from forest resources: 3.01% of GDP (2018 est.)
comparison ranking: 24

Revenue from coal: 0% of GDP (2018 est.)
comparison ranking: 173

Air pollutants: *particulate matter emissions:* 21.43 micrograms per cubic meter (2019 est.)
carbon dioxide emissions: 20 megatons (2016 est.)
methane emissions: 75.1 megatons (2020 est.)

Waste and recycling: *municipal solid waste generated annually:* 2,831,291 tons (2015 est.)

Major rivers (by length in km): An Nīl (Nile) (shared with Rwanda [s], Tanzania, Uganda, South Sudan, and Egypt [m]) - 6,650 km; Blue Nile river mouth (shared with Ethiopia [s]) - 1,600 km
note – [s] after country name indicates river source; [m] after country name indicates river mouth

Major watersheds (area sq km): Atlantic Ocean drainage: *(Mediterranean Sea)* Nile (3,254,853 sq km)

Internal (endorheic basin) drainage: Lake Chad (2,497,738 sq km)

Major aquifers: Nubian Aquifer System, Sudd Basin (Umm Ruwaba Aquifer)

Total water withdrawal: *municipal:* 950 million cubic meters (2020 est.)
industrial: 80 million cubic meters (2020 est.)
agricultural: 25.91 billion cubic meters (2020 est.)

Total renewable water resources: 37.8 billion cubic meters (2020 est.)

GOVERNMENT

Country name: *conventional long form:* Republic of the Sudan
conventional short form: Sudan
local long form: Jumhuriyat as-Sudan
local short form: As-Sudan
former: Anglo-Egyptian Sudan, Democratic Republic of the Sudan
etymology: the name "Sudan" derives from the Arabic "bilad-as-sudan" meaning "Land of the Black [peoples]"

Government type: presidential republic

Capital: *name:* Khartoum
geographic coordinates: 15 36 N, 32 32 E
time difference: UTC+3 (8 hours ahead of Washington, DC, during Standard Time)
etymology: several explanations of the name exist; two of the more plausible are that it is derived from Arabic "al-jartum" meaning "elephant's trunk" or "hose," and likely referring to the narrow strip of land extending between the Blue and White Niles; alternatively, the name could derive from the Dinka words "khar-tuom," indicating a "place where rivers meet"

Administrative divisions: 18 states (wilayat, singular - wilayah); Blue Nile, Central Darfur, East Darfur, Gedaref, Gezira, Kassala, Khartoum, North Darfur, North Kordofan, Northern, Red Sea, River Nile, Sennar, South Darfur, South Kordofan, West Darfur, West Kordofan, White Nile
note: the peace Agreement signed in October 2020 included a provision to establish a system of governance to restructure the country's current 18 provinces/states into regions

Independence: 1 January 1956 (from Egypt and the UK)

National holiday: Independence Day, 1 January (1956)

Legal system: mixed legal system of Islamic law and English common law; note - in mid-July 2020, Sudan amended 15 provisions of its 1991 penal code

Constitution: *history:* previous 1973, 1998, 2005 (interim constitution, which was suspended in April 2019); latest initial draft completed by Transitional Military Council in May 2019; revised draft known as the "Draft Constitutional Charter for the 2019 Transitional Period," or "2019 Constitutional Declaration" was signed by the Council and opposition coalition on 4 August 2019
amendments: amended 2020 to incorporate the Juba Agreement for Peace in Sudan; the military suspended several provisions of the Constitutional Declaration in October 2021

International law organization participation: accepts compulsory ICJ jurisdiction with reservations; withdrew acceptance of ICCt jurisdiction in 2008

Citizenship: *citizenship by birth:* no
citizenship by descent only: the father must be a citizen of Sudan
dual citizenship recognized: no
residency requirement for naturalization: 10 years

Suffrage: 17 years of age; universal

Executive branch: *chief of state:* Sovereign Council Chair and Commander-in-Chief of the Sudanese Armed Forces General Abd-al-Fattah al-BURHAN Abd-al-Rahman
head of government: Sovereign Council Chair and Commander-in-Chief of the Sudanese Armed Forces General Abd-al-Fattah al-BURHAN Abd-al-Rahman
cabinet: most members of the Council of Ministers were forced from office in October 2021 by the military and subsequently resigned in November 2021; the military allowed a handful of ministers appointed by former armed opposition groups to retain their posts; at present, most of the members of the Council are senior civil servants serving in an acting minister capacity appointed either by Prime Minister HAMDOUK prior to his resignation or by the military
elections/appointments: the 2019 Constitutional Declaration originally called for elections to be held in late 2022 at the end of the transitional period; that date was pushed back to late 2023 by the Juba Peace Agreement; the methodology for future elections has not yet been defined; according to the 2019 Constitutional Declaration, civilian members of the Sovereign Council and the prime minister were to have been nominated by an umbrella coalition of civilian actors known as the Forces for Freedom and Change; this methodology was followed in selecting HAMDOUK as prime minister in August 2019; the military purports to have suspended this provision of the 2019 Constitutional Declaration in October 2021; Prime Minister HAMDOUK's restoration to office in November 2021 was the result of an agreement signed between him and Sovereign Council Chair BURHAN; military members of the Sovereign Council are selected by the leadership of the security forces; representatives of former armed groups to the Sovereign Council are selected by the signatories of the Juba Peace Agreement
election results: NA
note 1: the 2019 Constitutional Declaration established a collective chief of state of the "Sovereign Council," which was chaired by al-BURHAN; on 25 October 2021, al-BURHAN dissolved the Sovereign Council but reinstated it on 11 November 2021, replacing its civilian members (previously selected by the umbrella civilian coalition the Forces for Freedom and Change) with civilians of the military's choosing but then relieved the newly appointed civilian members of their duties on 6 July 2022
note 2: Sovereign Council currently consists of only the 5 generals
note 3: former Prime Minister Abdallah HAMDOUK resigned on 2 January 2022; HAMDOUK served as prime minister from August 2019 to October 2019 before he was kidnapped; he was later freed and reinstated as prime minister on 21 November 2021

Legislative branch: *description:* according to the August 2019 Constitutional Declaration, which established Sudan's transitional government, the Transitional Legislative Council (TLC) was to have served as the national legislature during the transitional period until elections could be held; as of June 2023, the TLC had not been established
elections: Council of State - last held 1 June 2015; dissolved in April 2019
National Assembly - last held on 13-15 April 2015; dissolved in April 2019
note: according to the 2019 Constitutional Declaration, elections for a new legislature are to be held in 2023
election results: Council of State - percent of vote by party - NA; seats by party - NA; composition - men 35, women 19, percentage women 35.2%
National Assembly - percent of vote by party - NA; former seats by party - NCP 323, DUP 25, Democratic Unionist Party 15, other 44, independent 19; composition - men 296 women 130, percentage women 30.5%; total National Legislature percentage women 31%

Judicial branch: *highest court(s):* National Supreme Court (consists of 70 judges organized into panels of 3 judges and includes 4 circuits that operate outside the capital); Constitutional Court (consists of 9 justices including the court president); note - the Constitutional Court resides outside the national judiciary and has not been appointed since the signature of the 2019 Constitutional Declaration
judge selection and term of office: National Supreme Court and Constitutional Court judges selected by the Supreme Judicial Council, which replaced the National Judicial Service Commission upon enactment of the 2019 Constitutional Declaration
subordinate courts: Court of Appeal; other national courts; public courts; district, town, and rural courts

Political parties: Democratic Unionist Party
Democratic Unionist Party or DUP
Federal Umma Party
Muslim Brotherhood or MB
National Congress Party or NCP
National Umma Party or NUP
Popular Congress Party or PCP
Reform Movement Now
Sudan National Front
Sudanese Communist Party or SCP
Sudanese Congress Party or SCoP Umma Party for Reform and Development
Unionist Movement Party or UMP
note: in November 2019, the transitional government banned the National Congress Party

International organization participation: ABEDA, ACP, AfDB, AFESD, AMF, AU (suspended), CAEU, COMESA, FAO, G-77, IAEA, IBRD, ICAO, ICC (NGOs), ICRM, IDA, IDB, IFAD, IFC, IFRCS, IGAD, ILO, IMF, IMO, Interpol, IOC, IOM, IPU, ISO, ITSO, ITU, LAS, MIGA, NAM, OIC, OPCW, PCA, UN, UNCTAD, UNESCO, UNHCR, UNHRC, UNIDO, UNOOSA, UNWTO, UPU, WCO, WFTU (NGOs), WHO, WIPO, WMO, WTO (observer)

Diplomatic representation in the US: *chief of mission:* Ambassador Mohamed Abdalla IDRIS (since 16 September 2022)
chancery: 2210 Massachusetts Avenue NW, Washington, DC 20008
telephone: [1] (202) 338-8565
FAX: [1] (202) 667-2406
email address and website:
consular@sudanembassy.org
https://www.sudanembassy.org/

Diplomatic representation from the US: *chief of mission:* Ambassador (vacant); Chargé d'Affaires Colleen Crenwelge (since May 2024)
embassy: P.O. Box 699, Kilo 10, Soba, Khartoum
mailing address: 2200 Khartoum Place, Washington DC 20521-2200
telephone: [249] 187-0-22000
email address and website:
ACSKhartoum@state.gov
https://sd.usembassy.gov/
note: the U.S. Embassy in Khartoum suspended operations on 22 April 2023, and the Department of State ordered the departure of U.S. employees due to the continued threat from armed conflict in Sudan

Flag description: three equal horizontal bands of red (top), white, and black with a green isosceles triangle based on the hoist side; colors and design based on the Arab Revolt flag of World War I, but the meanings of the colors are expressed as follows: red signifies the struggle for freedom, white is the color of peace, light, and love, black represents the people of Sudan (in Arabic 'Sudan' means black), green is the color of Islam, agriculture, and prosperity

National symbol(s): secretary bird; national colors: red, white, black, green

National anthem: *name:* "Nahnu Djundulla Djundulwatan" (We Are the Army of God and of Our Land)
lyrics/music: Sayed Ahmad Muhammad SALIH/ Ahmad MURJAN
note: adopted 1956; originally served as the anthem of the Sudanese military

National heritage: *total World Heritage Sites:* 3 (2 cultural, 1 natural)
selected World Heritage Site locales: Gebel Barkal and the Sites of the Napatan Region (c); Archaeological Sites of the Island of Meroe (c); Sanganeb Marine National Park and Dungonab Bay – Mukkawar Island Marine National Park (n)

ECONOMY

Economic overview: low-income Sahel economy devastated by ongoing civil war; major impacts on rural income, basic commodity prices, industrial production, agricultural supply chain, communications and commerce; hyperinflation and currency depreciation worsening food access and humanitarian conditions

Real GDP (purchasing power parity): $136.039 billion (2023 est.)
$154.672 billion (2022 est.)
$156.168 billion (2021 est.)
note: data in 2021 dollars
comparison ranking: 88

Real GDP growth rate: -12.05% (2023 est.)
-0.96% (2022 est.)
-1.87% (2021 est.)
note: annual GDP % growth based on constant local currency
comparison ranking: 217

Real GDP per capita: $2,800 (2023 est.)
$3,300 (2022 est.)
$3,400 (2021 est.)
note: data in 2021 dollars
comparison ranking: 199

GDP (official exchange rate): $109.327 billion (2023 est.)
note: data in current dollars at official exchange rate

Inflation rate (consumer prices): 138.81% (2022 est.)
359.09% (2021 est.)
163.26% (2020 est.)
note: annual % change based on consumer prices
comparison ranking: 218

GDP - composition, by sector of origin: *agriculture:* 5.6% (2023 est.)
industry: 5.2% (2023 est.)
services: 7.6% (2023 est.)
note: figures may not total 100% due to non-allocated consumption not captured in sector-reported data
comparison rankings: services 216; industry 213; agriculture 114

GDP - composition, by end use: *household consumption:* 81.7% (2023 est.)
government consumption: 16.2% (2023 est.)
investment in fixed capital: 2% (2023 est.)
exports of goods and services: 1.2% (2023 est.)
imports of goods and services: -1% (2023 est.)
note: figures may not total 100% due to rounding or gaps in data collection

Agricultural products: sorghum, sugarcane, milk, groundnuts, millet, onions, sesame seeds, goat milk, bananas, mangoes/guavas (2022)
note: top ten agricultural products based on tonnage

Industries: oil, cotton ginning, textiles, cement, edible oils, sugar, soap distilling, shoes, petroleum refining, pharmaceuticals, armaments, automobile/light truck assembly, milling

Industrial production growth rate: -11.6% (2023 est.)
note: annual % change in industrial value added based on constant local currency
comparison ranking: 212

Labor force: 13.59 million (2023 est.)
note: number of people ages 15 or older who are employed or seeking work
comparison ranking: 46

Unemployment rate: 11.45% (2023 est.)
7.53% (2022 est.)
11.47% (2021 est.)
note: % of labor force seeking employment
comparison ranking: 172

Youth unemployment rate (ages 15-24): *total:* 18.2% (2023 est.)
male: 18.5% (2023 est.)
female: 17.5% (2023 est.)
note: % of labor force ages 15-24 seeking employment
comparison ranking: total 75

Gini Index coefficient - distribution of family income: 34.2 (2014 est.)
note: index (0-100) of income distribution; higher values represent greater inequality
comparison ranking: 87

Household income or consumption by percentage share: *lowest 10%:* 3.2% (2014 est.)
highest 10%: 27.8% (2014 est.)
note: % share of income accruing to lowest and highest 10% of population

Remittances: 0.91% of GDP (2023 est.)
2.9% of GDP (2022 est.)
3.27% of GDP (2021 est.)
note: personal transfers and compensation between resident and non-resident individuals/households/entities

Budget: *revenues:* $9.045 billion (2015 est.)
expenditures: $9.103 billion (2015 est.)
note: central government revenues and expenses (excluding grants/extrabudgetary units/social security funds) converted to US dollars at average official exchange rate for year indicated

Public debt: 121.6% of GDP (2017 est.)
comparison ranking: 12

Taxes and other revenues: 7.39% (of GDP) (2016 est.)
note: central government tax revenue as a % of GDP
comparison ranking: 194

Current account balance: -$4.443 billion (2022 est.)
-$2.62 billion (2021 est.)
-$5.841 billion (2020 est.)
note: balance of payments - net trade and primary/secondary income in current dollars
comparison ranking: 179

Exports: $5.908 billion (2022 est.)
$6.664 billion (2021 est.)
$5.065 billion (2020 est.)
note: balance of payments - exports of goods and services in current dollars
comparison ranking: 132

Exports - partners: UAE 43%, China 16%, Italy 8%, Egypt 8%, Turkey 4% (2022)
note: top five export partners based on percentage share of exports

Exports - commodities: gold, crude petroleum, oil seeds, ground nuts, cotton (2022)
note: top five export commodities based on value in dollars

Imports: $11.575 billion (2022 est.)
$10.271 billion (2021 est.)
$10.52 billion (2020 est.)
note: balance of payments - imports of goods and services in current dollars
comparison ranking: 115

Imports - partners: China 22%, UAE 20%, India 18%, Egypt 9%, Turkey 5% (2022)
note: top five import partners based on percentage share of imports

Imports - commodities: raw sugar, wheat, refined petroleum, garments, jewelry (2022)
note: top five import commodities based on value in dollars

Reserves of foreign exchange and gold: $177.934 million (2017 est.)
$168.284 million (2016 est.)
$173.516 million (2015 est.)
note: holdings of gold (year-end prices)/foreign exchange/special drawing rights in current dollars
comparison ranking: 183

Debt - external: $19.642 billion (2022 est.)
note: present value of external debt in current US dollars
comparison ranking: 26

Exchange rates: Sudanese pounds (SDG) per US dollar -

Exchange rates: 546.759 (2022 est.)
370.791 (2021 est.)
53.996 (2020 est.)
45.767 (2019 est.)
24.329 (2018 est.)

ENERGY

Electricity access: *electrification - total population:* 63.2% (2022 est.)
electrification - urban areas: 84%
electrification - rural areas: 49.4%

Electricity: *installed generating capacity:* 3.815 million kW (2022 est.)
consumption: 14.875 billion kWh (2022 est.)
imports: 933 million kWh (2022 est.)
transmission/distribution losses: 3.913 billion kWh (2022 est.)
comparison rankings: transmission/distribution losses 153; imports 79; consumption 85; installed generating capacity 102

Electricity generation sources: *fossil fuels:* 37.6% of total installed capacity (2022 est.)
solar: 0.2% of total installed capacity (2022 est.)
hydroelectricity: 61.6% of total installed capacity (2022 est.)
biomass and waste: 0.6% of total installed capacity (2022 est.)

Coal: *exports:* 35 metric tons (2022 est.)
imports: 300 metric tons (2022 est.)

Petroleum: *total petroleum production:* 68,000 bbl/day (2023 est.)
refined petroleum consumption: 127,000 bbl/day (2022 est.)
crude oil estimated reserves: 1.25 billion barrels (2021 est.)

Natural gas: *proven reserves:* 84.951 billion cubic meters (2021 est.)

Carbon dioxide emissions: 16.497 million metric tonnes of CO_2 (2022 est.)
from coal and metallurgical coke: 1,000 metric tonnes of CO_2 (2022 est.)
from petroleum and other liquids: 16.496 million metric tonnes of CO_2 (2022 est.)
comparison ranking: total emissions 93

Energy consumption per capita: 6.271 million Btu/person (2022 est.)
comparison ranking: 163

COMMUNICATIONS

Telephones - fixed lines: *total subscriptions:* 156,000 (2022 est.)
subscriptions per 100 inhabitants: (2022 est.) less than 1
comparison ranking: total subscriptions 125

Telephones - mobile cellular: *total subscriptions:* 34.671 million (2022 est.)
subscriptions per 100 inhabitants: 74 (2022 est.)
comparison ranking: total subscriptions 45

Telecommunication systems: *general assessment:* Sudan emerged as a poorer country when South Sudan separated from it in 2011; although Sudan has about four times the population of South Sudan, the latter benefits from its control of the majority of known oil reserves; the Sudanese economy has been affected by hyperinflation in recent years, partly the result of the loss of oil revenue but also due to domestic volatility and social unrest; the difficult economic conditions have meant that for several years telcos have reported revenue under hyper inflationary reporting standards; pressure on revenue has made it difficult for operators to invest in infrastructure upgrades, and so provide improved services to customers; despite this, the number of mobile subscribers increased 7% in 2021, year-on-year; this level of growth is expected to have been maintained in 2022, though could slow from 2023; the country's poor fixed-line infrastructure has helped the development of mobile broadband services; after fighting started in April 2023, much of the telecommunications infrastructure was damaged (2023)
domestic: teledensity fixed-line is 1 per 100 and mobile-cellular is 74 telephones per 100 persons (2022)
international: country code - 249; landing points for the EASSy, FALCON and SAS-1,-2, fiber-optic submarine cable systems linking Africa, the Middle East, Indian Ocean Islands and Asia; satellite earth stations - 1 Intelsat (Atlantic Ocean) (2019)

Broadcast media: Following the establishment of Sudan's transitional government in August 2019, government-owned broadcasters became increasingly independent from government and military control. Following the October 2021 military takeover, additional restrictions were imposed on these government-owned broadcasters, which now practice a heightened degree of self-censorship but still operate more independently than in the pre-2019 environment. (2022)

Internet country code: .sd

Internet users: *total:* 13.248 million (2021 est.)
percent of population: 28.8% (2021 est.)
comparison ranking: total 53

Broadband - fixed subscriptions: *total:* 28,782 (2020 est.)
subscriptions per 100 inhabitants: 0.1 (2020 est.)
comparison ranking: total 156

TRANSPORTATION

National air transport system: *number of registered air carriers:* 9 (2020)
inventory of registered aircraft operated by air carriers: 42
annual passenger traffic on registered air carriers: 269,958 (2018)

Civil aircraft registration country code prefix: ST

Airports: 41 (2024)
comparison ranking: 100

Heliports: 4 (2024)

Pipelines: 156 km gas, 4,070 km oil, 1,613 km refined products (2013)

Railways: *total:* 7,251 km (2014)
narrow gauge: 5,851 km (2014) 1.067-m gauge
1,400 km 0.600-m gauge for cotton plantations
comparison ranking: total 31

Roadways: *total:* 30,000 km
paved: 8,000 km
unpaved: 22,000 km
urban: 1,000 km (2019)
comparison ranking: total 101

Waterways: 4,068 km (2011) (1,723 km open year-round on White and Blue Nile Rivers)
comparison ranking: 27

Merchant marine: *total:* 14 (2023)
by type: other 14
comparison ranking: total 153

Ports: *total ports:* 4 (2024)
large: 0
medium: 2
small: 2
very small: 0
ports with oil terminals: 3
key ports: Al Khair Oil Terminal, Beshayer Oil Terminal, Port Sudan, Sawakin Harbor

MILITARY AND SECURITY

Military and security forces: Sudanese Armed Forces (SAF): Ground Force, Navy, Sudanese Air Force; Rapid Support Forces (RSF); Border Guards

Ministry of Interior: security police, special forces police, traffic police, Central Reserve Police (2024)
note 1: the RSF is a semi-autonomous paramilitary force formed in 2013 to fight armed rebel groups in Sudan, with Mohammed Hamdan DAGALO (aka Hemeti) as its commander; it was initially placed under the National Intelligence and Security Service, then came under the direct command of former president Omar al-BASHIR, who boosted the RSF as his own personal security force; as a result, the RSF was better funded and equipped than the regular armed forces; the RSF has since recruited from all parts of Sudan beyond its original Darfuri Arab groups but remains under the personal patronage and control of DAGALO; the RSF has participated in combat operations in Yemen and in counterinsurgency operations in Darfur, South Kordofan, and the Blue Nile State; it has also been active along the borders with Libya and the Central African Republic and has been used to respond to anti-regime demonstrations; the RSF has been accused of committing human rights abuses against civilians and is reportedly involved in business enterprises, such as gold mining; in 2023, heavy fighting broke out between the SAF and the RSF
note 2: the Central Reserve Police (aka Abu Tira) is a combat-trained paramilitary force that has been used against demonstrators and sanctioned by the US for human rights abuses

Military expenditures: 1% of GDP (2021 est.)
1% of GDP (2020 est.)
2.4% of GDP (2019 est.)
2% of GDP (2018 est.)
3.6% of GDP (2017 est.)
note: many defense expenditures are probably off-budget
comparison ranking: 132

Military and security service personnel strengths: *prior to the outbreak of fighting between the SAF and the RSF in 2023, size estimates for Sudanese armed forces varied widely:* up to 200,000 SAF personnel; up to 100,000 RSF fighters; up to 80,000 Central Reserve Police (2023)

Military equipment inventories and acquisitions: the SAF's inventory includes a mix of mostly Chinese, Russian, Soviet-era, and domestically produced weapons systems; Sudan has one of the largest defense industries in Africa, which includes state-owned companies with military involvement; it has mostly manufactured weapons systems under license from China, Russia, Turkey, and Ukraine (2024)
note 1: Sudan has been under a UN Security Council approved arms embargo since 2005 as a result of violence in Darfur; in September 2024, the embargo was extended for another year
note 2: the RSF traditionally has been a lightly armed paramilitary force but over the years is reported to have acquired some heavier weapons and equipment such as armored vehicles, artillery, and anti-aircraft guns, although their origins are not available; it has captured some SAF arms and equipment during the ongoing conflict; since the start of the conflict, both the RSF and the SAF are reported to have received additional weaponry from various foreign suppliers

Military service age and obligation: 18-33 years of age for compulsory or voluntary military service for men and women; 12-24 month service obligation (2023)
note: implementation of conscription is reportedly uneven

Military - note: the primary responsibilities of the Sudanese Armed Forces (SAF) are internal security, border control, and countering potential external threats from its neighbors; SAF operations have traditionally been supported by militia and paramilitary forces, particularly the Rapid Support Forces (RSF); in the Spring of 2023, heavy fighting broke out between the SAF and the paramilitary RSF, particularly around the capital Khartoum and in the western region of Darfur, amid disputes over an internationally-backed plan for a transition towards civilian rule; fighting has since spread and continued into 2024 with reports of atrocities, ethnic cleansing, food insecurity, heavy civilian casualties, and millions of internally displaced persons
the Sudanese military has been a dominant force in the ruling of the country since its independence in 1956; in addition, the military has a large role in the country's economy, reportedly controlling over 200 commercial companies, including businesses involved in gold mining, rubber production, agriculture, and meat exports
the UN Interim Security Force for Abyei (UNISFA) has operated in the disputed Abyei region along the border between Sudan and South Sudan since 2011; UNISFA's mission includes ensuring security, protecting civilians, strengthening the capacity of the Abyei Police Service, de-mining, monitoring/verifying the redeployment of armed forces from the area, and facilitating the flow of humanitarian aid; as of 2024, UNISFA had approximately 3,200 personnel assigned
the October 2020 peace agreement provided for the establishment of a Joint Security Keeping Forces (JSKF) comprised of 12,000 personnel tasked with securing the Darfur region in the place of the UN African Union Hybrid Operation in Darfur (UNAMID), a joint African Union-UN peacekeeping force that operated in the war-torn region between 2007 and the end of its mandate in December 2020; in June 2021, Sudan's transitional government announced it would increase the size of this force to 20,000 and expand its mission scope to include the capital and other parts of the country suffering from violence; the force would include the SAF, RSF, police, intelligence, and representatives from armed groups involved in peace negotiations; in September 2022, the first 2,000 members of the JSKF completed training; the status of the JSKF since the start of the civil war is not available (2024)

TERRORISM

Terrorist group(s): Islamic State of Iraq and ash-Sham (ISIS); al-Qa'ida; Harakat Sawa'd Misr
note: details about the history, aims, leadership, organization, areas of operation, tactics, targets, weapons, size, and sources of support of the group(s) appear(s) in the Terrorism reference guide

TRANSNATIONAL ISSUES

Refugees and internally displaced persons: *refugees (country of origin):* 696,246 (South Sudan) (refugees and asylum seekers), 137,402 (Eritrea) (refugees and asylum seekers), 93,477 (Syria) (refugees and asylum seekers), 72,334 (Ethiopia) (refugees and asylum seekers), 18,279 (Central African Republic) (2023)
IDPs: 6.5 million (armed conflict between rival factions of the military government of Sudan since 15 April 2023) (2024); note - includes some non-Sudanese nationals

Trafficking in persons: tier rating: Tier 3 — Sudan does not fully meet the minimum standards for the elimination of trafficking and is not making significant efforts to do so; therefore, Sudan was downgraded to Tier 3; for more details, go to: https://www.state.gov/ reports/2024-trafficking-in-persons-report/sudan/

SURINAME

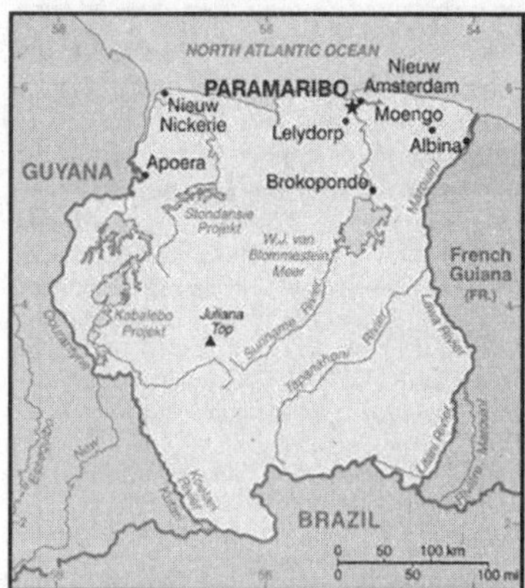

INTRODUCTION

Background: The Spaniards first explored Suriname in the 16th century, and the English then settled it in the mid-17th century. Suriname became a Dutch colony in 1667. With the abolition of African slavery in 1863, workers were brought in from India and Java. The Netherlands granted the colony independence in 1975. Five years later, the civilian government was replaced by a military regime that soon declared Suriname a socialist republic. It continued to exert control through a succession of nominally civilian administrations until 1987, when international pressure finally forced a democratic election. In 1990, the military overthrew the civilian leadership, but a democratically elected government – a four-party coalition – returned to power in 1991. The coalition expanded to eight parties in 2005 and ruled until 2010, when voters returned former military leader Desire BOUTERSE and his opposition coalition to power. President BOUTERSE ran unopposed in 2015 and was reelected. Opposition parties campaigned hard against BOUTERSE in the run-up to the 2020 elections, and a multi-party coalition led by Chandrikapersad SANTOKHI's VHP and Ronnie Brunswijk's ABOP was installed.

GEOGRAPHY

Location: Northern South America, bordering the North Atlantic Ocean, between French Guiana and Guyana

Geographic coordinates: 4 00 N, 56 00 W

Map references: South America

Area: *total:* 163,820 sq km
land: 156,000 sq km
water: 7,820 sq km
comparison ranking: total 92

Area - comparative: slightly larger than Georgia

Land boundaries: *total:* 1,907 km
border countries (3): Brazil 515 km; French Guiana 556 km; Guyana 836 km

Coastline: 386 km

Maritime claims: *territorial sea:* 12 nm
exclusive economic zone: 200 nm

Climate: tropical; moderated by trade winds

Terrain: mostly rolling hills; narrow coastal plain with swamps

Elevation: *highest point:* Juliana Top 1,230 m
lowest point: unnamed location in the coastal plain -2 m
mean elevation: 246 m

Natural resources: timber, hydropower, fish, kaolin, shrimp, bauxite, gold, and small amounts of nickel, copper, platinum, iron ore

Land use: *agricultural land:* 0.5% (2018 est.)

arable land: 0.4% (2018 est.)
permanent crops: 0% (2018 est.)
permanent pasture: 0.1% (2018 est.)
forest: 94.6% (2018 est.)
other: 4.9% (2018 est.)

Irrigated land: 600 sq km (2020)

Major watersheds (area sq km): Atlantic Ocean drainage: Amazon (6,145,186 sq km)

Population distribution: population concentrated along the nothern coastal strip; the remainder of the country is sparsely populated

Natural hazards: flooding

Geography - note: smallest independent country on South American continent; mostly tropical rain forest; great diversity of flora and fauna that, for the most part, is increasingly threatened by new development; relatively small population, mostly along the coast

PEOPLE AND SOCIETY

Population: *total:* 646,758
male: 320,352
female: 326,406 (2024 est.)
comparison rankings: female 170; male 169; total 169

Nationality: *noun:* Surinamer(s)
adjective: Surinamese

Ethnic groups: Hindustani (also known locally as "East Indians"; their ancestors emigrated from northern India in the latter part of the 19th century) 27.4%, Maroon (their African ancestors were brought to the country in the 17th and 18th centuries as slaves and escaped to the interior) 21.7%, Creole (mixed White and Black) 15.7%, Javanese 13.7%, mixed 13.4%, other 7.6%, unspecified 0.6% (2012 est.)

Languages: Dutch (official), English (widely spoken), Sranang Tongo (Surinamese, sometimes called Taki-Taki, is the native language of Creoles and much of the younger population), Caribbean Hindustani (a dialect of Hindi), Javanese
major-language sample(s):
Het Wereld Feitenboek, een omnisbare bron van informatie. (Dutch)

Religions: Protestant 23.6% (includes Evangelical 11.2%, Moravian 11.2%, Reformed 0.7%, Lutheran 0.5%), Hindu 22.3%, Roman Catholic 21.6%, Muslim 13.8%, other Christian 3.2%, Winti 1.8%, Jehovah's Witness 1.2%, other 1.7%, none 7.5%, unspecified 3.2% (2012 est.)

Demographic profile: Suriname is a pluralistic society consisting primarily of Creoles (persons of mixed African and European heritage), the descendants of escaped African slaves known as Maroons, and the descendants of Indian and Javanese (Indonesian) contract workers. The country overall is in full, post-industrial demographic transition, with a low fertility rate, a moderate mortality rate, and a rising life expectancy. However, the Maroon population of the rural interior lags behind because of lower educational attainment and contraceptive use, higher malnutrition, and significantly less access to electricity, potable water, sanitation, infrastructure, and health care.

Some 350,000 people of Surinamese descent live in the Netherlands, Suriname's former colonial ruler. In the 19th century, better-educated, largely Dutch-speaking Surinamese began emigrating to the Netherlands. World War II interrupted the outflow, but it resumed after the war when Dutch labor demands grew - emigrants included all segments of the Creole population. Suriname still is strongly influenced by the Netherlands because most Surinamese have relatives living there and it is the largest supplier of development aid. Other emigration destinations include French Guiana and the United States. Suriname's immigration rules are flexible, and the country is easy to enter illegally because rainforests obscure its borders. Since the mid-1980s, Brazilians have settled in Suriname's capital, Paramaribo, or eastern Suriname, where they mine gold. This immigration is likely to slowly re-orient Suriname toward its Latin American roots.

Age structure: *0-14 years:* 22.5% (male 73,864/female 71,573)
15-64 years: 70% (male 226,417/female 226,235)
65 years and over: 7.5% (2024 est.) (male 20,071/female 28,598)

Dependency ratios: *total dependency ratio:* 50.9
youth dependency ratio: 40
elderly dependency ratio: 11
potential support ratio: 9.1 (2021 est.)

Median age: *total:* 32 years (2024 est.)
male: 31 years
female: 32.9 years
comparison ranking: total 118

Population growth rate: 1.07% (2024 est.)
comparison ranking: 89

Birth rate: 14.9 births/1,000 population (2024 est.)
comparison ranking: 110

Death rate: 6.7 deaths/1,000 population (2024 est.)
comparison ranking: 129

Net migration rate: 2.5 migrant(s)/1,000 population (2024 est.)
comparison ranking: 46

Population distribution: population concentrated along the nothern coastal strip; the remainder of the country is sparsely populated

Urbanization: *urban population:* 66.4% of total population (2023)
rate of urbanization: 0.88% annual rate of change (2020-25 est.)

Major urban areas - population: 239,000 PARAMARIBO (capital) (2018)

Sex ratio: *at birth:* 1.07 male(s)/female
0-14 years: 1.03 male(s)/female
15-64 years: 1 male(s)/female
65 years and over: 0.7 male(s)/female
total population: 0.98 male(s)/female (2024 est.)

Maternal mortality ratio: 96 deaths/100,000 live births (2020 est.)
comparison ranking: 71

Infant mortality rate: *total:* 29.6 deaths/1,000 live births (2024 est.)
male: 37.6 deaths/1,000 live births
female: 21 deaths/1,000 live births
comparison ranking: total 50

Life expectancy at birth: *total population:* 72.7 years (2024 est.)
male: 69 years
female: 76.7 years
comparison ranking: total population 159

Total fertility rate: 1.89 children born/woman (2024 est.)
comparison ranking: 122

Gross reproduction rate: 0.91 (2024 est.)

Contraceptive prevalence rate: 39.1% (2018)

Drinking water source: *improved: urban:* 99.5% of population
rural: 98.2% of population
total: 99.1% of population
unimproved: urban: 0.5% of population
rural: 1.8% of population
total: 0.9% of population (2020 est.)

Current health expenditure: 6.8% of GDP (2020)

Physician density: 0.82 physicians/1,000 population (2018)

Hospital bed density: 3 beds/1,000 population (2017)

Sanitation facility access: *improved: urban:* 98.5% of population
rural: 91.2% of population
total: 96% of population
unimproved: urban: 1.5% of population
rural: 8.8% of population
total: 4% of population (2020 est.)

Obesity - adult prevalence rate: 26.4% (2016)
comparison ranking: 41

Alcohol consumption per capita: *total:* 6.6 liters of pure alcohol (2019 est.)
beer: 3.4 liters of pure alcohol (2019 est.)
wine: 0.14 liters of pure alcohol (2019 est.)
spirits: 2.87 liters of pure alcohol (2019 est.)
other alcohols: 0.18 liters of pure alcohol (2019 est.)
comparison ranking: total 62

Children under the age of 5 years underweight: 6.7% (2018)
comparison ranking: 68

Currently married women (ages 15-49): 52.1% (2023 est.)

Child marriage: *women married by age 15:* 8.8%
women married by age 18: 36%
men married by age 18: 19.6% (2018 est.)

Education expenditures: 5% of GDP (2020 est.)
comparison ranking: 74

Literacy: *definition:* age 15 and over can read and write
total population: 95%
male: 96.5%
female: 93.4% (2021)

ENVIRONMENT

Environment - current issues: deforestation as timber is cut for export; pollution of inland waterways by small-scale mining activities

Environment - international agreements: *party to:* Biodiversity, Climate Change, Climate Change-Kyoto Protocol, Climate Change-Paris Agreement, Comprehensive Nuclear Test Ban, Desertification, Endangered Species, Hazardous Wastes, Law of the Sea, Marine Dumping-London Convention, Marine Dumping-London Protocol, Nuclear Test Ban, Ozone Layer Protection, Ship Pollution, Tropical Timber 2006, Wetlands, Whaling
signed, but not ratified: none of the selected agreements

Climate: tropical; moderated by trade winds

Urbanization: *urban population:* 66.4% of total population (2023)
rate of urbanization: 0.88% annual rate of change (2020-25 est.)

Revenue from forest resources: 2.36% of GDP (2018 est.)
comparison ranking: 29

Revenue from coal: 0% of GDP (2018 est.)

comparison ranking: 140

Air pollutants: *particulate matter emissions:* 12.17 micrograms per cubic meter (2019 est.)
carbon dioxide emissions: 1.74 megatons (2016 est.)
methane emissions: 2.28 megatons (2020 est.)

Waste and recycling: *municipal solid waste generated annually:* 78,620 tons (2010 est.)

Major watersheds (area sq km): Atlantic Ocean drainage: Amazon (6,145,186 sq km)

Total water withdrawal: *municipal:* 50 million cubic meters (2020 est.)
industrial: 140 million cubic meters (2020 est.)
agricultural: 430 million cubic meters (2020 est.)

Total renewable water resources: 99 billion cubic meters (2020 est.)

GOVERNMENT

Country name: *conventional long form:* Republic of Suriname
conventional short form: Suriname
local long form: Republiek Suriname
local short form: Suriname
former: Netherlands Guiana, Dutch Guiana
etymology: name may derive from the indigenous "Surinen" people who inhabited the area at the time of European contact

Government type: presidential republic

Capital: *name:* Paramaribo
geographic coordinates: 5 50 N, 55 10 W
time difference: UTC-3 (2 hours ahead of Washington, DC, during Standard Time)
etymology: the name may be the corruption of a Carib (Kalina) village or tribe named Parmirbo

Administrative divisions: 10 districts (distrikten, singular - distrikt); Brokopondo, Commewijne, Coronie, Marowijne, Nickerie, Para, Paramaribo, Saramacca, Sipaliwini, Wanica

Independence: 25 November 1975 (from the Netherlands)

National holiday: Independence Day, 25 November (1975)

Legal system: civil law system influenced by Dutch civil law; note - a new criminal code was enacted in 2017

Constitution: *history:* previous 1975; latest ratified 30 September 1987, effective 30 October 1987
amendments: proposed by the National Assembly; passage requires at least two-thirds majority vote of the total membership; amended 1992

International law organization participation: accepts compulsory ICJ jurisdiction with reservations; accepts ICCt jurisdiction

Citizenship: *citizenship by birth:* no
citizenship by descent only: at least one parent must be a citizen of Suriname
dual citizenship recognized: no
residency requirement for naturalization: 5 years

Suffrage: 18 years of age; universal

Executive branch: *chief of state:* President Chandrikapersad "Chan" SANTOKHI (since 16 July 2020)
head of government: President Chandrikapersad "Chan" SANTOKHI (since 16 July 2020)
cabinet: Cabinet of Ministers appointed by the president
elections/appointments: president and vice president indirectly elected by the National Assembly; president and vice president serve a 5-year term (no term limits); election last held on 13 July 2020 (next to be held in May 2025)
election results:
2020: Chandrikapersad "Chan" SANTOKHI elected president unopposed; National Assembly vote - NA
2015: Desire Delano BOUTERSE reelected president unopposed; National Assembly vote - NA
note: the president is both chief of state and head of government

Legislative branch: *description:* unicameral National Assembly or Nationale Assemblee (51 seats; members directly elected in 10 multi-seat constituencies by party-list proportional representation vote, using the D'Hondt method, to serve 5-year terms)
elections: last held on 25 May 2020 (next to be held in May 2025)
election results: percent of vote by party - VHP 41.1%, NDP 29.4%, ABOP 17.6%, NPS 7.8%, other 3.9%; seats by party - VHP 20, NDP 16, ABOP 9, NPS 3, BEP 2, PL 2; composition - men 35, women 16, percentage women 31.4%

Judicial branch: *highest court(s):* High Court of Justice of Suriname (consists of the court president, vice president, and 4 judges); note - appeals beyond the High Court are referred to the Caribbean Court of Justice; human rights violations can be appealed to the Inter-American Commission on Human Rights with judgments issued by the Inter-American Court on Human Rights
judge selection and term of office: court judges appointed by the national president in consultation with the National Assembly, the State Advisory Council, and the Order of Private Attorneys; judges serve for life
subordinate courts: cantonal courts

Political parties: Brotherhood and Unity in Politics or BEP
Democratic Alternative '91 or DA91
General Liberation and Development Party or ABOP
National Democratic Party or NDP
National Party of Suriname or NPS
Party for Democracy and Development in Unity or DOE
Party for National Unity and Solidarity or KTPI
People's Alliance (Pertjajah Luhur) or PL
Progressive Workers' and Farmers' Union or PALU
Progressive Reform Party or VHP
Reform and Renewal Movement or HVB
Surinamese Labor Party or SPA

International organization participation: ACP, ACS, AOSIS, Caricom, CD, CDB, CELAC, FAO, G-77, IADB, IBRD, ICAO, ICCt, ICRM, IDA, IDB, IFAD, IFC, IFRCS, IHO, ILO, IMF, IMO, Interpol, IOC, IOM, IPU, ISO (correspondent), ITU, ITUC (NGOs), LAES, MIGA, NAM, OAS, OIC, OPANAL, OPCW, PCA, Petrocaribe, UN, UNASUR, UNCTAD, UNESCO, UNIDO, UPU, WHO, WIPO, WMO, WTO

Diplomatic representation in the US: *chief of mission:* Ambassador Jan Marten Willem SCHALKWIJK (since 19 April 2022)
chancery: 4301 Connecticut Avenue NW, Suite 400, Washington, DC 20008
telephone: [1] (202) 629-4302
FAX: [1] (202) 629-4769
email address and website:
amb.vs@gov.sr
https://surinameembassy.org/index.html
consulate(s) general: Miami

Diplomatic representation from the US: *chief of mission:* Ambassador Robert J. FAUCHER (since 31 January 2023)
embassy: 165 Kristalstraat, Paramaribo
mailing address: 3390 Paramaribo Place, Washington DC 20521-3390
telephone: [597] 556-700
FAX: [597] 551-524
email address and website:
caparamar@state.gov
https://sr.usembassy.gov/

Flag description: five horizontal bands of green (top, double width), white, red (quadruple width), white, and green (double width); a large, yellow, five-pointed star is centered in the red band; red stands for progress and love, green symbolizes hope and fertility, white signifies peace, justice, and freedom; the star represents the unity of all ethnic groups; from its yellow light the nation draws strength to bear sacrifices patiently while working toward a golden future

National symbol(s): royal palm, faya lobi (flower); national colors: green, white, red, yellow

National anthem: *name:* "God zij met ons Suriname!" (God Be With Our Suriname)
lyrics/music: Cornelis Atses HOEKSTRA and Henry DE ZIEL/Johannes Corstianus DE PUY
note: adopted 1959; originally adapted from a Sunday school song written in 1893 and contains lyrics in both Dutch and Sranang Tongo

National heritage: *total World Heritage Sites:* 3 (2 cultural, 1 natural)
selected World Heritage Site locales: Central Suriname Nature Reserve (n); Historic Inner City of Paramaribo (c); Jodensavanne Archaeological Site: Jodensavanne Settlement and Cassipora Creek Cemetery (c)

ECONOMY

Economic overview: upper middle-income South American economy; new floating currency regime; key aluminum goods, gold, and hydrocarbon exporter; new IMF plan for economic recovery and fiscal sustainability; controversial hardwood industry

Real GDP (purchasing power parity): $11.824 billion (2023 est.)
$11.583 billion (2022 est.)
$11.308 billion (2021 est.)
note: data in 2021 dollars
comparison ranking: 163

Real GDP growth rate: 2.08% (2023 est.)
2.43% (2022 est.)
-2.44% (2021 est.)
note: annual GDP % growth based on constant local currency
comparison ranking: 137

Real GDP per capita: $19,000 (2023 est.)
$18,700 (2022 est.)
$18,400 (2021 est.)
note: data in 2021 dollars
comparison ranking: 103

GDP (official exchange rate): $3.782 billion (2023 est.)
note: data in current dollars at official exchange rate

Inflation rate (consumer prices): 52.45% (2022 est.)
59.12% (2021 est.)
34.89% (2020 est.)
note: annual % change based on consumer prices
comparison ranking: 215

Credit ratings: Fitch rating: C (2020)

Moody's rating: Caa3 (2020)
Standard & Poors rating: SD (2020)
note: The year refers to the year in which the current credit rating was first obtained.

GDP - composition, by sector of origin: *agriculture:* 8.1% (2022 est.)
industry: 44.8% (2022 est.)
services: 44.7% (2022 est.)
note: figures may not total 100% due to non-allocated consumption not captured in sector-reported data
comparison rankings: services 171; industry 22; agriculture 91

GDP - composition, by end use: *household consumption:* 27.6% (2017 est.)
government consumption: 11.7% (2017 est.)
investment in fixed capital: 52.5% (2017 est.)
investment in inventories: 26.5% (2017 est.)
exports of goods and services: 68.9% (2017 est.)
imports of goods and services: -60.6% (2017 est.)

Agricultural products: rice, sugarcane, oranges, chicken, plantains, vegetables, bananas, coconuts, cassava, eggs (2022)
note: top ten agricultural products based on tonnage

Industries: gold mining, oil, lumber, food processing, fishing

Industrial production growth rate: 3.05% (2022 est.)
note: annual % change in industrial value added based on constant local currency
comparison ranking: 107

Labor force: 250,000 (2023 est.)
note: number of people ages 15 or older who are employed or seeking work
comparison ranking: 173

Unemployment rate: 7.7% (2023 est.)
8.23% (2022 est.)
8.46% (2021 est.)
note: % of labor force seeking employment
comparison ranking: 144

Youth unemployment rate (ages 15-24): *total:* 25.3% (2023 est.)
male: 17.8% (2023 est.)
female: 37.8% (2023 est.)
note: % of labor force ages 15-24 seeking employment
comparison ranking: total 42

Gini Index coefficient - distribution of family income: 39.2 (2022 est.)
comparison ranking: 46

Household income or consumption by percentage share: *lowest 10%:* 2.2% (2022 est.)
highest 10%: 30.1% (2022 est.)

Remittances: 3.88% of GDP (2023 est.)
4.09% of GDP (2022 est.)
4.79% of GDP (2021 est.)
note: personal transfers and compensation between resident and non-resident individuals/households/entities

Budget: *revenues:* $863 million (2019 est.)
expenditures: $1.648 billion (2019 est.)

Public debt: 69.3% of GDP (2017 est.)
comparison ranking: 58

Taxes and other revenues: 16.4% (of GDP) (2017 est.)
comparison ranking: 123

Current account balance: $146.749 million (2023 est.)
$76.321 million (2022 est.)
$176.058 million (2021 est.)
note: balance of payments - net trade and primary/secondary income in current dollars
comparison ranking: 69

Exports: $2.534 billion (2023 est.)
$2.6 billion (2022 est.)
$2.299 billion (2021 est.)
note: balance of payments - exports of goods and services in current dollars
comparison ranking: 158

Exports - partners: Switzerland 39%, UAE 21%, Belgium 10%, Guyana 5%, Trinidad and Tobago 4% (2022)
note: top five export partners based on percentage share of exports

Exports - commodities: gold, refined petroleum, excavation machinery, wood, fish (2022)
note: top five export commodities based on value in dollars

Imports: $2.218 billion (2023 est.)
$2.342 billion (2022 est.)
$1.876 billion (2021 est.)
note: balance of payments - imports of goods and services in current dollars
comparison ranking: 175

Imports - partners: US 25%, China 15%, Netherlands 13%, Trinidad and Tobago 6%, Japan 3% (2022)
note: top five import partners based on percentage share of imports

Imports - commodities: refined petroleum, excavation machinery, cars, plastic products, tobacco (2022)
note: top five import commodities based on value in dollars

Reserves of foreign exchange and gold: $1.346 billion (2023 est.)
$1.195 billion (2022 est.)
$992.257 million (2021 est.)
note: holdings of gold (year-end prices)/foreign exchange/special drawing rights in current dollars
comparison ranking: 153

Exchange rates: Surinamese dollars (SRD) per US dollar -

Exchange rates: 36.776 (2023 est.)
24.709 (2022 est.)
18.239 (2021 est.)
9.31 (2020 est.)
7.458 (2019 est.)

ENERGY

Electricity access: *electrification - total population:* 99% (2022 est.)
electrification - urban areas: 100%
electrification - rural areas: 98%

Electricity: *installed generating capacity:* 537,000 kW (2022 est.)
consumption: 1.853 billion kWh (2022 est.)
transmission/distribution losses: 245.841 million kWh (2022 est.)
comparison rankings: transmission/distribution losses 69; consumption 150; installed generating capacity 150

Electricity generation sources: *fossil fuels:* 51.8% of total installed capacity (2022 est.)
solar: 0.6% of total installed capacity (2022 est.)
hydroelectricity: 47.3% of total installed capacity (2022 est.)
biomass and waste: 0.3% of total installed capacity (2022 est.)

Petroleum: *total petroleum production:* 14,000 bbl/day (2023 est.)
refined petroleum consumption: 15,000 bbl/day (2022 est.)
crude oil estimated reserves: 89 million barrels (2021 est.)

Natural gas: *production:* 7.109 million cubic meters (2022 est.)
consumption: 6.967 million cubic meters (2022 est.)

Carbon dioxide emissions: 2.19 million metric tonnes of CO_2 (2022 est.)
from petroleum and other liquids: 2.176 million metric tonnes of CO_2 (2022 est.)
from consumed natural gas: 14,000 metric tonnes of CO_2 (2022 est.)
comparison ranking: total emissions 158

Energy consumption per capita: 55.101 million Btu/person (2022 est.)
comparison ranking: 90

COMMUNICATIONS

Telephones - fixed lines: *total subscriptions:* 108,000 (2022 est.)
subscriptions per 100 inhabitants: 18 (2022 est.)
comparison ranking: total subscriptions 133

Telephones - mobile cellular: *total subscriptions:* 929,000 (2022 est.)
subscriptions per 100 inhabitants: 150 (2022 est.)
comparison ranking: total subscriptions 164

Telecommunication systems: *general assessment:* Suriname is the smallest nation on the South American continent, with about 580,000 inhabitants; the only Dutch-speaking nation in South America, it has close affinities with the Caribbean, and is a member of the Caribbean Community and Common Market (CARICOM); the country's fixed-line infrastructure is reasonably reliable in the more populated coastal region, though poor in the interior; fixed teledensity and broadband penetration are slightly lower than average for Latin America and the Caribbean, while mobile penetration is significantly above the regional average and much higher than would be expected given the country's relatively low GDP per capita; many Surinamese have up to three mobile lines with different providers, which has pushed up penetration figures although the number of subscribers has fallen in recent years as consumers have responded to economic pressures
(2021)
domestic: fixed-line is 18 per 100 and mobile-cellular teledensity is 150 telephones per 100 persons (2022)
international: country code - 597; landing point for the SG-SCS submarine cable linking South America with the Caribbean; satellite earth stations - 2 Intelsat (Atlantic Ocean) (2019)

Broadcast media: 2 state-owned TV stations; 1 state-owned radio station; multiple private radio and TV stations (2019)

Internet country code: .sr

Internet users: *total:* 402,600 (2021 est.)
percent of population: 66% (2021 est.)
comparison ranking: total 172

Broadband - fixed subscriptions: *total:* 92,270 (2020 est.)
subscriptions per 100 inhabitants: 16 (2020 est.)
comparison ranking: total 129

TRANSPORTATION

National air transport system: *number of registered air carriers:* 4 (2020)
inventory of registered aircraft operated by air carriers: 20
annual passenger traffic on registered air carriers: 272,347 (2018)
annual freight traffic on registered air carriers: 33.2 million (2018) mt-km

Civil aircraft registration country code prefix: PZ

Airports: 55 (2024)
comparison ranking: 82

Heliports: 1 (2024)

Pipelines: 50 km oil (2013)

Roadways: *total:* 4,304 km
paved: 1,119 km
unpaved: 3,185 km (2003)
comparison ranking: total 154

Waterways: 1,200 km (2011) (most navigable by ships with drafts up to 7 m)
comparison ranking: 63

Merchant marine: *total:* 13 (2023)
by type: general cargo 5, oil tanker 3, other 5
comparison ranking: total 154

Ports: *total ports:* 4 (2024)
large: 0
medium: 0
small: 1
very small: 3
ports with oil terminals: 3
key ports: Moengo, Nieuw Nickerie, Paramaribo, Paranam

MILITARY AND SECURITY

Military and security forces: Suriname National Army (Nationaal Leger or NL); Army (Landmacht), Navy (Marine); Air Force (Luchtmacht), Military Police (Korps Militaire Politie)

Ministry of Justice and Police: Suriname Police Force (Korps Politie Suriname or KPS) (2024)

Military expenditures: 1.2% of GDP (2019 est.)
1.1% of GDP (2018 est.)
1.1% of GDP (2017 est.)
1.2% of GDP (2016 est.)
1.4% of GDP (2015 est.)
comparison ranking: 115

Military and security service personnel strengths: approximately 2,000 total personnel (2023)

Military equipment inventories and acquisitions: the Suriname Army has a limited inventory comprised of a mix of older weapons and equipment, largely originating from such suppliers as Brazil, the Netherlands, and India; France also provides material assistance (2024)

Military service age and obligation: 18 is the legal minimum age for voluntary military service for men and women; no conscription (2024)

Military - note: the National Leger is responsible for defending the sovereignty and territorial integrity of Suriname against foreign aggression; other special tasks include border control and supporting domestic security as required; the military police, for example, have direct responsibility for immigration control at the country's ports of entry, and the military assists the police in combating crime, particularly narco-trafficking, including joint military and police patrols, as well as joint special security teams; in addition, the military provides aid and assistance during times of natural emergencies and participates in socio-economic development projects (2024)

TRANSNATIONAL ISSUES

Illicit drugs: a transit country for South American cocaine en route to Europe; illicit drugs are smuggled in cargo containers, commercial and private air transport and human couriers

SVALBARD

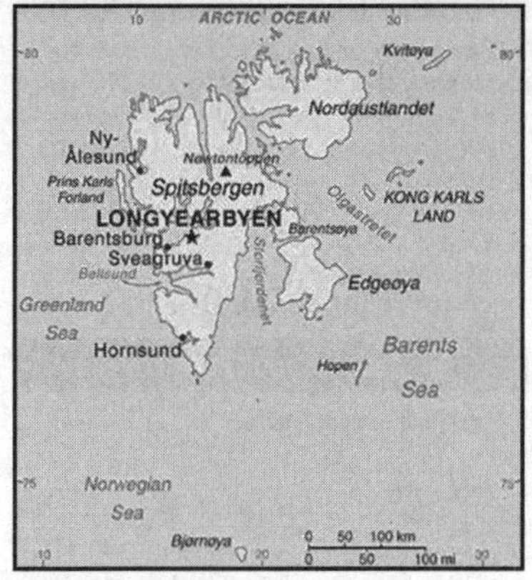

INTRODUCTION

Background: Norse explorers may have first discovered the Svalbard archipelago in the 12th century. The islands served as an international whaling base during the 17th and 18th centuries. Norway's sovereignty was internationally recognized by treaty in 1920, and five years later Norway officially took over the territory. Coal mining started in the 20th century, and a Norwegian company and a Russian company are still in operation today. Travel between the settlements is accomplished with snowmobiles, aircraft, and boats.

GEOGRAPHY

Location: Northern Europe, islands between the Arctic Ocean, Barents Sea, Greenland Sea, and Norwegian Sea, north of Norway

Geographic coordinates: 78 00 N, 20 00 E

Map references: Arctic Region

Area: *total:* 62,045 sq km
land: 62,045 sq km
water: 0 sq km
note: includes Spitsbergen and Bjornoya (Bear Island)
comparison ranking: total 125

Area - comparative: slightly smaller than West Virginia

Land boundaries: *total:* 0 km

Coastline: 3,587 km

Maritime claims: *territorial sea:* 12 nm
contiguous zone: 24 nm
continental shelf: extends to depth of exploitation
exclusive fishing zone: 200 nm

Climate: arctic, tempered by warm North Atlantic Current; cool summers, cold winters; North Atlantic Current flows along west and north coasts of Spitsbergen, keeping water open and navigable most of the year

Terrain: rugged mountains; much of the upland areas are ice covered; west coast clear of ice about half the year; fjords along west and north coasts

Elevation: *highest point:* Newtontoppen 1,717 m
lowest point: Arctic Ocean 0 m

Natural resources: coal, iron ore, copper, zinc, phosphate, wildlife, fish

Land use: *agricultural land:* 0% (2018 est.)
other: 100% (2018 est.)

Population distribution: the small population is primarily concentrated on the island of Spitsbergen in a handful of settlements on the south side of the Isfjorden, with Longyearbyen being the largest

Natural hazards: ice floes often block the entrance to Bellsund (a transit point for coal export) on the west coast and occasionally make parts of the northeastern coast inaccessible to maritime traffic

Geography - note: northernmost part of the Kingdom of Norway; consists of nine main islands; glaciers and snowfields cover 60% of the total area; Spitsbergen Island is the site of the Svalbard Global Seed Vault, a seed repository established by the Global Crop Diversity Trust and the Norwegian Government

PEOPLE AND SOCIETY

Population: *total:* 2,926 (2021 est.)
comparison ranking: total 229

Ethnic groups: Norwegian 61.1%, foreign population 38.9% (consists primarily of Russians, Thais, Swedes, Filipinos, and Ukrainians) (2021 est.)
note: foreigners account for almost one third of the population of the Norwegian settlements, Longyearbyen and Ny-Alesund (where the majority of Svalbard's resident population lives), as of mid-2021

Languages: Norwegian, Russian
major-language sample(s):
Verdens Faktabok, den essensielle kilden for grunnleggende informasjon. (Norwegian)

Population growth rate: -0.03% (2019 est.)

comparison ranking: 199

Net migration rate: -5.57 migrant(s)/1,000 population (2021 est.)
comparison ranking: 207

Population distribution: the small population is primarily concentrated on the island of Spitsbergen in a handful of settlements on the south side of the Isfjorden, with Longyearbyen being the largest

ENVIRONMENT

Environment - current issues: ice floes are a maritime hazard; past exploitation of mammal species (whale, seal, walrus, and polar bear) severely depleted the populations, but a gradual recovery seems to be occurring

Climate: arctic, tempered by warm North Atlantic Current; cool summers, cold winters; North Atlantic Current flows along west and north coasts of Spitsbergen, keeping water open and navigable most of the year

Land use: *agricultural land:* 0% (2018 est.)
other: 100% (2018 est.)

GOVERNMENT

Country name: *conventional long form:* none
conventional short form: Svalbard (sometimes referred to as Spitsbergen, the largest island in the archipelago)
etymology: 12th century Norse accounts speak of the discovery of a "Svalbard" - literally "cold shores" - but they may have referred to Jan Mayen Island or eastern Greenland; the archipelago was traditionally known as Spitsbergen, but Norway renamed it Svalbard in the 1920s when it assumed sovereignty of the islands

Government type: non-self-governing territory of Norway

Dependency status: territory of Norway; administered by the Polar Department of the Ministry of Justice, through a governor (sysselmann) residing in Longyearbyen, Spitsbergen; by treaty (9 February 1920), sovereignty was awarded to Norway

Capital: *name:* Longyearbyen
geographic coordinates: 78 13 N, 15 38 E
time difference: UTC+1 (6 hours ahead of Washington, DC, during Standard Time)
daylight saving time: +1hr, begins last Sunday in March; ends last Sunday in October
etymology: the name in Norwegian means Longyear Town; the site was established by and named after John LONGYEAR, whose Arctic Coal Company began mining operations there in 1906

Independence: none (territory of Norway)

Legal system: only the laws of Norway made explicitly applicable to Svalbard have effect there; the Svalbard Act and the Svalbard Environmental Protection Act, and certain regulations, apply only to Svalbard; the Spitsbergen Treaty and the Svalbard Treaty grant certain rights to citizens and corporations of signatory nations; as of June 2017, 45 nations had ratified the Svalbard Treaty

Citizenship: see Norway

Executive branch: *chief of state:* King HARALD V of Norway (since 17 January 1991)
head of government: Governor Lars FAUSE (since 24 June 2021)
elections/appointments: none; the monarchy is hereditary; governor and assistant governor responsible to the Polar Department of the Ministry of Justice

Legislative branch: *description:* unicameral Longyearbyen Community Council (15 seats; members directly elected by majority vote to serve 4-year-terms); note - the Council acts very much like a Norwegian municipality, responsible for infrastructure and utilities, including power, land-use and community planning, education, and child welfare; however, healthcare services are provided by the state
elections: last held on 9 October 2023 (next to be held in October 2027)
election results: seats by party - Liberal 7, Labor 3, Social Liberal 3, Conservative 2

Judicial branch: *highest court(s):* none; note - Svalbard is subordinate to Norway's Nord-Troms District Court and Halogaland Court of Appeal, both located in Tromso

Political parties: Conservative
Labor
Liberal
Progress
Socialist Left

International organization participation: none

Flag description: the flag of Norway is used

National anthem: *note:* as a territory of Norway, "Ja, vi elsker dette landet" is official (see Norway)

ECONOMY

Economic overview: high-income Norwegian island economy; major coal mining, tourism, and research sectors; recently established northernmost brewery; key whaling and fishing base; home to the Global Seed Vault

Exchange rates: Norwegian kroner (NOK) per US dollar -

Exchange rates: 10.563 (2023 est.)
9.614 (2022 est.)
8.59 (2021 est.)
9.416 (2020 est.)
8.8 (2019 est.)

COMMUNICATIONS

Telecommunication systems: *general assessment:* Svalbard Undersea Cable System is a twin submarine communications cable which connects Svalbard to the mainland of Norway (2022)
domestic: the Svalbard Satellite Station - connected to the mainland via the Svalbard Undersea Cable System - is the only Arctic ground station that can see low-altitude, polar-orbiting satellites; it provides ground services to more satellites than any other facility in the world (2022)
international: country code - 47-790; the Svalbard Undersea Cable System is a twin communications cable that connects Svalbard to mainland Norway; the system is the sole telecommunications link to the archipelago (2019)

Broadcast media: the Norwegian Broadcasting Corporation (NRK) began direct TV transmission to Svalbard via satellite in 1984; Longyearbyen households have access to 3 NRK radio and 2 TV stations

Internet country code: .sj

TRANSPORTATION

Roadways: *total:* 40 km (2020)
comparison ranking: total 219

Ports: *total ports:* 3 (2024)
large: 0
medium: 0
small: 0
very small: 3
ports with oil terminals: 0
key ports: Barentsburg, Longyearbyen, Ny Alesund

MILITARY AND SECURITY

Military and security forces: no regular military forces

Military - note: Svalbard is a territory of Norway, demilitarized by treaty on 9 February 1920; Norwegian military activity is limited to fisheries surveillance by the Norwegian Coast Guard (2024)

SWEDEN

INTRODUCTION

Background: A military power during the 17th century, Sweden maintained a policy of military non-alignment until it applied to join NATO in 2022. Sweden has not participated in any war for two centuries. Stockholm preserved an armed neutrality in both World Wars. Since then, Sweden has pursued a successful economic formula consisting of a capitalist system intermixed with substantial welfare elements. Sweden joined the EU in 1995, but the public rejected the introduction of the euro in a 2003 referendum. The share of Sweden's population born abroad increased from 11.3% in 2000 to 20% in 2022.

GEOGRAPHY

Location: Northern Europe, bordering the Baltic Sea, Gulf of Bothnia, Kattegat, and Skagerrak, between Finland and Norway

Geographic coordinates: 62 00 N, 15 00 E

Map references: Europe

Area: *total:* 450,295 sq km
land: 410,335 sq km
water: 39,960 sq km
comparison ranking: total 58

Area - comparative: almost three times the size of Georgia; slightly larger than California

Land boundaries: *total:* 2,211 km
border countries (2): Finland 545 km; Norway 1,666 km

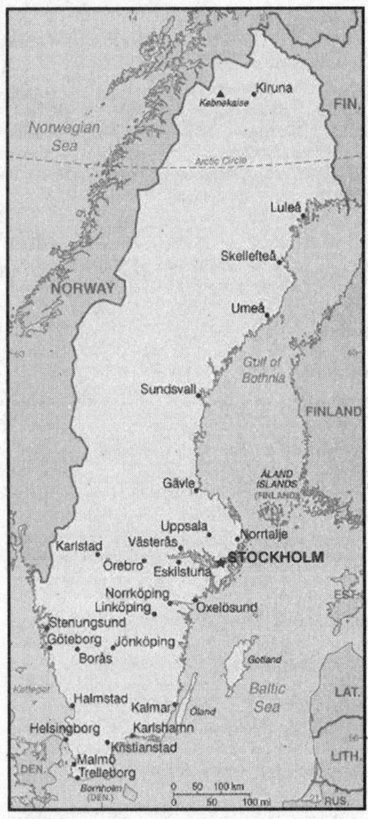

Coastline: 3,218 km

Maritime claims: *territorial sea:* 12 nm (adjustments made to return a portion of straits to high seas)
exclusive economic zone: agreed boundaries or midlines
continental shelf: 200-m depth or to the depth of exploitation

Climate: temperate in south with cold, cloudy winters and cool, partly cloudy summers; subarctic in north

Terrain: mostly flat or gently rolling lowlands; mountains in west

Elevation: *highest point:* Kebnekaise South 2,100 m
lowest point: reclaimed bay of Lake Hammarsjon, near Kristianstad -2.4 m
mean elevation: 320 m

Natural resources: iron ore, copper, lead, zinc, gold, silver, tungsten, uranium, arsenic, feldspar, timber, hydropower

Land use: *agricultural land:* 7.5% (2018 est.)
arable land: 6.4% (2018 est.)
permanent crops: 0% (2018 est.)
permanent pasture: 1.1% (2018 est.)
forest: 68.7% (2018 est.)
other: 23.8% (2018 est.)

Irrigated land: 519 sq km (2013)

Major lakes (area sq km): *fresh water lake(s):* Vanern - 5,580 sq km; Vattern - 1,910 sq km; Malaren - 1,140 sq km

Population distribution: most Swedes live in the south where the climate is milder and there is better connectivity to mainland Europe; population clusters are found all along the Baltic coast in the east; the interior areas of the north remain sparsely populated

Natural hazards: ice floes in the surrounding waters, especially in the Gulf of Bothnia, can interfere with maritime traffic

Geography - note: strategic location along Danish Straits linking Baltic and North Seas; Sweden has almost 100,000 lakes, the largest of which, Vanern, is the third largest in Europe

PEOPLE AND SOCIETY

Population: *total:* 10,589,835
male: 5,332,701
female: 5,257,134 (2024 est.)
comparison rankings: female 91; male 89; total 89

Nationality: *noun:* Swede(s)
adjective: Swedish

Ethnic groups: Swedish 79.6%, Syrian 1.9%, Iraqi 1.4%, Finnish 1.3%, other 15.8%
(2022 est.)
note: data represent the population by country of birth; the indigenous Sami people are estimated to number between 20,000 and 40,000

Languages: Swedish (official)
major-language sample(s):
The World Factbook, den obestridliga källan för grundläggande information. (Swedish)
note: Finnish, Sami, Romani, Yiddish, and Meankieli are official minority languages

Religions: Church of Sweden (Lutheran) 53.9%, other (includes Roman Catholic, Orthodox, Baptist, Muslim, Jewish, and Buddhist) 8.9%, none or unspecified 37.2% (2021 est.)
note: estimates reflect registered members of faith communities eligible for state funding (not all religions are state-funded and not all people who identify with a particular religion are registered members) and the Church of Sweden

Demographic profile: Sweden, the largest Nordic country in terms of size and population, is also Europe's most sparsely populated. Most Swedish men and women agree that both partners should contribute to household income. Swedish society is very gender equal, which is reflected in the country's public policies. A generous leave policy and high-quality subsidized childcare allows mothers and fathers to balance work and family life. Sweden's income-replacement-based parental leave policy encourages women to establish themselves in the workforce before having children. In fact, Swedish women have one of the highest labor participation rates in Europe and one of its highest total fertility rates (TFR), the number of children women have in their lifetime. Postponement of parenthood has increased steadily. Since the late 1960s, marriage and divorce rates have declined, while non-marital cohabitation and births out of wedlock have increased rapidly. Sweden's TFR has hovered for decades around 2, which is close to replacement level and among Europe's highest.

Sweden experienced "the great emigration" between 1850 and the 1930s when, faced with famines, approximately 1.5 million Swedes sought a better life in the Americas and Australia. However, since World War II, Sweden has been a country of immigration. During World War II, thousands of refugees from neighboring countries worked in Swedish factories, agriculture, and forestry, replacing Swedish men who were called up for military service. During the 1950s and 1960s, Sweden joined the Geneva Convention and granted permanent residence to refugees from the USSR and the Warsaw Pact countries. During this period, Sweden also welcomed labor migrants, mainly from Finland and other Nordic countries, who bolstered the tax base needed to fund the country's welfare programs.

Until 1971, labor migrants, particularly from Finland, southern Europe (including then Yugoslavia, Italy, and Greece) the Baltics, and Turkey, came to Sweden as its industries flourished. Companies recruited many of the workers, but others came on their own. Sweden's labor demand eventually decreased, and the job market became saturated. The government restricted the flow of labor migrants, putting an end to labor migration from non-Nordic countries in 1972. From then until the 1990s, inflows consisted largely of asylum seekers from the Middle East, the Balkans, and South America, as well as persons looking to reunite with family members already in Sweden. The country began a new era of labor immigration in 2008, as companies were encouraged to hire non-EU workers. Among the largest source countries have been India, Thailand, and China. As of 2020, over a quarter of Sweden's population had a migrant background.

Age structure: *0-14 years:* 17.1% (male 934,668/female 880,310)
15-64 years: 62.1% (male 3,365,754/female 3,208,248)
65 years and over: 20.8% (2024 est.) (male 1,032,279/female 1,168,576)

Dependency ratios: *total dependency ratio:* 60.8
youth dependency ratio: 28.5
elderly dependency ratio: 32.3
potential support ratio: 3.1 (2021 est.)

Median age: *total:* 41.1 years (2024 est.)
male: 40.1 years
female: 42.1 years
comparison ranking: total 52

Population growth rate: 0.51% (2024 est.)
comparison ranking: 149

Birth rate: 10.7 births/1,000 population (2024 est.)
comparison ranking: 173

Death rate: 9.6 deaths/1,000 population (2024 est.)
comparison ranking: 39

Net migration rate: 4 migrant(s)/1,000 population (2024 est.)
comparison ranking: 26

Population distribution: most Swedes live in the south where the climate is milder and there is better connectivity to mainland Europe; population clusters are found all along the Baltic coast in the east; the interior areas of the north remain sparsely populated

Urbanization: *urban population:* 88.7% of total population (2023)
rate of urbanization: 0.89% annual rate of change (2020-25 est.)

Major urban areas - population: 1.700 million STOCKHOLM (capital) (2023)

Sex ratio: *at birth:* 1.06 male(s)/female
0-14 years: 1.06 male(s)/female
15-64 years: 1.05 male(s)/female
65 years and over: 0.88 male(s)/female
total population: 1.01 male(s)/female (2024 est.)

Mother's mean age at first birth: 29.7 years (2020 est.)

Maternal mortality ratio: 5 deaths/100,000 live births (2020 est.)
comparison ranking: 170

Infant mortality rate: *total:* 2.3 deaths/1,000 live births (2024 est.)
male: 2.5 deaths/1,000 live births
female: 2 deaths/1,000 live births
comparison ranking: total 218

Life expectancy at birth: *total population:* 82.9 years (2024 est.)
male: 81.2 years
female: 84.7 years
comparison ranking: total population 21

Total fertility rate: 1.67 children born/woman (2024 est.)
comparison ranking: 169

Gross reproduction rate: 0.8 (2024 est.)

Contraceptive prevalence rate: 70.3% (2017)
note: percent of women aged 16-49

Drinking water source: *improved: urban:* 99.8% of population
rural: 99.7% of population
total: 99.8% of population
unimproved: urban: 0.2% of population
rural: 0.3% of population
total: 0.2% of population (2020 est.)

Current health expenditure: 11.4% of GDP (2020)

Physician density: 70.9 physicians/1,000 population (2019)

Hospital bed density: 2.1 beds/1,000 population (2018)

Sanitation facility access: *improved: urban:* 100% of population
rural: 100% of population
total: 100% of population

Obesity - adult prevalence rate: 20.6% (2016)
comparison ranking: 96

Alcohol consumption per capita: *total:* 7.1 liters of pure alcohol (2019 est.)
beer: 2.6 liters of pure alcohol (2019 est.)
wine: 3.4 liters of pure alcohol (2019 est.)
spirits: 1 liters of pure alcohol (2019 est.)
other alcohols: 0.1 liters of pure alcohol (2019 est.)
comparison ranking: total 59

Tobacco use: *total:* 24% (2020 est.)
male: 29.8% (2020 est.)
female: 18.2% (2020 est.)
comparison ranking: total 57

Currently married women (ages 15-49): 53.4% (2023 est.)

Education expenditures: 7.2% of GDP (2020 est.)
comparison ranking: 18

School life expectancy (primary to tertiary education): *total:* 20 years
male: 18 years
female: 21 years (2020)

ENVIRONMENT

Environment - current issues: marine pollution (Baltic Sea and North Sea); acid rain damage to soils and lakes; air pollution; inappropriate timber harvesting practices

Environment - international agreements: *party to:* Air Pollution, Air Pollution-Heavy Metals, Air Pollution-Multi-effect Protocol, Air Pollution-Nitrogen Oxides, Air Pollution-Persistent Organic Pollutants, Air Pollution-Sulphur 85, Air Pollution-Sulphur 94, Air Pollution-Volatile Organic Compounds, Antarctic-Environmental Protection, Antarctic-Marine Living Resources, Antarctic Treaty, Biodiversity, Climate Change, Climate Change-Kyoto Protocol, Climate Change-Paris Agreement, Comprehensive Nuclear Test Ban, Desertification, Endangered Species, Environmental Modification, Hazardous Wastes, Law of the Sea, Marine Dumping- London Convention, Marine Dumping-London Protocol, Nuclear Test Ban, Ozone Layer Protection, Ship Pollution, Tropical Timber 2006, Wetlands, Whaling
signed, but not ratified: none of the selected agreements

Climate: temperate in south with cold, cloudy winters and cool, partly cloudy summers; subarctic in north

Urbanization: *urban population:* 88.7% of total population (2023)
rate of urbanization: 0.89% annual rate of change (2020-25 est.)

Revenue from forest resources: 0.21% of GDP (2018 est.)
comparison ranking: 91

Revenue from coal: 0% of GDP (2018 est.)
comparison ranking: 161

Air pollutants: *particulate matter emissions:* 5.96 micrograms per cubic meter (2019 est.)
carbon dioxide emissions: 43.25 megatons (2016 est.)
methane emissions: 4.42 megatons (2020 est.)

Waste and recycling: *municipal solid waste generated annually:* 4.377 million tons (2015 est.)
municipal solid waste recycled annually: 1,416,835 tons (2015 est.)
percent of municipal solid waste recycled: 32.4% (2015 est.)

Major lakes (area sq km): *fresh water lake(s):* Vanern - 5,580 sq km; Vattern - 1,910 sq km; Malaren - 1,140 sq km

Total water withdrawal: *municipal:* 700 million cubic meters (2020 est.)
industrial: 1.27 billion cubic meters (2020 est.)
agricultural: 100 million cubic meters (2020 est.)

Total renewable water resources: 174 billion cubic meters (2020 est.)

Geoparks: *total global geoparks and regional networks:* 1
global geoparks and regional networks: Platåbergens (2023)

GOVERNMENT

Country name: *conventional long form:* Kingdom of Sweden
conventional short form: Sweden
local long form: Konungariket Sverige
local short form: Sverige
etymology: name ultimately derives from the North Germanic Svear tribe, which inhabited central Sweden and is first mentioned in the first centuries A.D.

Government type: parliamentary constitutional monarchy

Capital: *name:* Stockholm
geographic coordinates: 59 20 N, 18 03 E
time difference: UTC+1 (6 hours ahead of Washington, DC, during Standard Time)
daylight saving time: +1hr, begins last Sunday in March; ends last Sunday in October
etymology: *stock* and *holm* literally mean "log" and "islet" in Swedish, but there is no consensus as to what the words refer to

Administrative divisions: 21 counties (lan, singular and plural); Blekinge, Dalarna, Gavleborg, Gotland, Halland, Jamtland, Jonkoping, Kalmar, Kronoberg, Norrbotten, Orebro, Ostergotland, Skane, Sodermanland, Stockholm, Uppsala, Varmland, Vasterbotten, Vasternorrland, Vastmanland, Vastra Gotaland

Independence: 6 June 1523 (Gustav VASA elected king of Sweden, marking the abolishment of the Kalmar Union between Denmark, Norway, and Sweden)

National holiday: National Day, 6 June (1983); note - from 1916 to 1982 this date was celebrated as Swedish Flag Day

Legal system: civil law system influenced by Roman-Germanic law and customary law

Constitution: **history:** Sweden has four fundamental laws which together make up the Constitution: The Instrument of Government (several previous; latest 1974); The Act of Succession (enacted 1810; changed in 1937 and 1980); The Freedom of the Press Act (many previous; latest in 1949); The Fundamental Law on Freedom of Expression (adopted 1991)
amendments: proposed by Parliament; passage requires simple majority vote in two consecutive parliamentary terms with an intervening general election; passage also requires approval by simple majority vote in a referendum if Parliament approves a motion for a referendum by one third of its members; the results of such a referendum are only binding if a majority vote against the proposal; there has not been a referendum on constitutional matters; The Instrument of Government - amended several times, last in 2018; The Act of Succession - changed in 1937, 1980; The Freedom of the Press Act - amended several times, last in 2019; The Fundamental Law on Freedom of Expression - amended several times, last in 2023

International law organization participation: accepts compulsory ICJ jurisdiction with reservations; accepts ICCt jurisdiction

Citizenship: *citizenship by birth:* no
citizenship by descent only: the father must be a citizen of Sweden; in the case of a child born out of wedlock, the mother must be a citizen of Sweden and the father unknown
dual citizenship recognized: no, unless the other citizenship was acquired involuntarily
residency requirement for naturalization: 5 years

Suffrage: 18 years of age; universal

Executive branch: *chief of state:* King CARL XVI GUSTAF (since 15 September 1973)
head of government: Prime Minister Ulf KRISTERSSON (since 18 October 2022)
cabinet: Cabinet appointed by the prime minister
elections/appointments: the monarchy is hereditary; following legislative elections, the leader of the majority party or majority coalition usually becomes the prime minister

Legislative branch: *description:* unicameral Parliament or Riksdag (349 seats; 310 members directly elected in multi-seat constituencies by open party-list proportional representation vote and 39 members in "at-large" seats directly elected by open party-list proportional representation vote; members serve 4-year terms)

elections: last held on 11 September 2022 (next to be held on 13 September 2026)
election results: percent of vote by party - S/SAP 30.3%, M 19.1%, SD 20.5%, C 6.7%, V 6.7%, KD 5.3%, L 4.6%, MP 5.1%, other 1.7%; seats by party - S/SAP 107, M 68, SD 73, C 24, V 24, KD 19, L 16, MP 18; composition - men 186, women 163, percentage women 46.7%

Judicial branch: *highest court(s):* Supreme Court of Sweden (consists of 16 justices, including the court chairman); Supreme Administrative Court (consists of 18 justices, including the court president)
judge selection and term of office: Supreme Court and Supreme Administrative Court justices nominated by the Judges Proposal Board, a 9-member nominating body consisting of high-level judges, prosecutors, and members of Parliament; justices appointed by the Government; following a probationary period, justices' appointments are permanent
subordinate courts: first instance, appellate, general, and administrative courts; specialized courts that handle cases such as land and environment, immigration, labor, markets, and patents

Political parties: Center Party (Centerpartiet) or C
Christian Democrats (Kristdemokraterna) or KD
Green Party (Miljopartiet de Grona) or MP
Left Party (Vansterpartiet) or V
Moderate Party (Moderaterna) or M
Sweden Democrats (Sverigedemokraterna) or SD
Swedish Social Democratic Party (Socialdemokraterna) or S/SAP
The Liberals (Liberalerna) or L

International organization participation: ADB (nonregional member), AfDB (nonregional member), Arctic Council, Australia Group, BIS, CBSS, CD, CE, CERN, EAPC, EBRD, ECB, EIB, EITI (implementing country), EMU, ESA, EU, FAO, FATF, G-9, G-10, IADB, IAEA, IBRD, ICAO, ICC (national committees), ICCt, ICRM, IDA, IEA, IFAD, IFC, IFRCS, IGAD (partners), IHO, ILO, IMF, IMO, IMSO, Interpol, IOC, IOM, IPU, ISO, ITSO, ITU, ITUC (NGOs), MIGA, MONUSCO, NATO, NC, NEA, NIB, NSG, OAS (observer), OECD, OPCW, OSCE, Paris Club, PCA, PFP, Schengen Convention, UN, UNCTAD, UNESCO, UNHCR, UNIDO, UNMISS, UNMOGIP, UNOOSA, UNRWA, UN Security Council (temporary), UNSOM, UNTSO, UPU, Wassenaar Arrangement, WCO, WFTU (NGOs), WHO, WIPO, WMO, WTO, ZC

Diplomatic representation in the US: *chief of mission:* Ambassador Urban AHLIN (since 15 September 2023)
chancery: 2900 K Street NW, Washington, DC 20007
telephone: [1] (202) 467-2600
FAX: [1] (202) 467-2699
email address and website:
ambassaden.washington@gov.se
https://www.swedenabroad.se/en/embassies/usa-washington/
consulate(s) general: New York, San Francisco

Diplomatic representation from the US: *chief of mission:* Ambassador Erik D. RAMANATHAN (since 20 January 2022)
embassy: Dag Hammarskjolds Vag 31, SE-115 89 Stockholm
mailing address: 5750 Stockholm Place, Washington, DC 20521-5750
telephone: [46] (08) 783-53-00
FAX: [46] (08) 661-19-64
email address and website:
STKACSinfo@state.gov
https://se.usembassy.gov/

Flag description: blue with a golden yellow cross extending to the edges of the flag; the vertical part of the cross is shifted to the hoist side in the style of the Dannebrog (Danish flag); the colors reflect those of the Swedish coat of arms - three gold crowns on a blue field

National symbol(s): three crowns, lion; national colors: blue, yellow

National anthem: *name:* "Du Gamla, Du Fria" (Thou Ancient, Thou Free)
lyrics/music: Richard DYBECK/traditional
note: in use since 1844; also known as "Sang till Norden" (Song of the North), is based on a Swedish folk tune; it has never been officially adopted by the government; "Kungssangen" (The King's Song) serves as the royal anthem and is played in the presence of the royal family and during certain state ceremonies

National heritage: *total World Heritage Sites:* 15 (13 cultural, 1 natural, 1 mixed)
selected World Heritage Site locales: Royal Domain of Drottningholm (c); Laponian Area (m); High Coast/Kvarken Archipelago (n); Birka and Hovgården (c); Hanseatic Town of Visby (c); Church Town of Gammelstad, Luleå (c); Naval Port of Karlskrona (c); Rock Carvings in Tanum (c); Engelsberg Ironworks (c); Mining Area of the Great Copper Mountain in Falun (c)

ECONOMY

Economic overview: high-income, largest Nordic economy; EU member but non-euro user; export-oriented led by automotive, electronics, machinery and pharmaceuticals; highly ranked for competitiveness, R&D investments and governance; slowdown triggered by high inflation, weak consumption and financial tightening

Real GDP (purchasing power parity): $676.353 billion (2023 est.)
$677.682 billion (2022 est.)
$660.102 billion (2021 est.)
note: data in 2021 dollars
comparison ranking: 41

Real GDP growth rate: -0.2% (2023 est.)
2.66% (2022 est.)
6.15% (2021 est.)
note: annual GDP % growth based on constant local currency
comparison ranking: 190

Real GDP per capita: $64,200 (2023 est.)
$64,600 (2022 est.)
$63,400 (2021 est.)
note: data in 2021 dollars
comparison ranking: 25

GDP (official exchange rate): $593.268 billion (2023 est.)
note: data in current dollars at official exchange rate

Inflation rate (consumer prices): 8.55% (2023 est.)
8.37% (2022 est.)
2.16% (2021 est.)
note: annual % change based on consumer prices
comparison ranking: 160

Credit ratings: Fitch rating: AAA (2004)
Moody's rating: Aaa (2002)
Standard & Poors rating: AAA (2004)
note: The year refers to the year in which the current credit rating was first obtained.

GDP - composition, by sector of origin: *agriculture:* 1.6% (2023 est.)
industry: 22.8% (2023 est.)
services: 65.3% (2023 est.)
note: figures may not total 100% due to non-allocated consumption not captured in sector-reported data
comparison rankings: services 55; industry 117; agriculture 170

GDP - composition, by end use: *household consumption:* 43.2% (2023 est.)
government consumption: 25.7% (2023 est.)
investment in fixed capital: 26.7% (2023 est.)
investment in inventories: 0.1% (2023 est.)
exports of goods and services: 54% (2023 est.)
imports of goods and services: -49.6% (2023 est.)
note: figures may not total 100% due to rounding or gaps in data collection

Agricultural products: wheat, milk, sugar beets, barley, potatoes, oats, rapeseed, pork, chicken, triticale (2022)
note: top ten agricultural products based on tonnage

Industries: iron and steel, precision equipment (bearings, radio and telephone parts, armaments), wood pulp and paper products, processed foods, motor vehicles

Industrial production growth rate: -2.68% (2023 est.)
note: annual % change in industrial value added based on constant local currency
comparison ranking: 188

Labor force: 5.825 million (2023 est.)
note: number of people ages 15 or older who are employed or seeking work
comparison ranking: 74

Unemployment rate: 7.59% (2023 est.)
7.39% (2022 est.)
8.72% (2021 est.)
note: % of labor force seeking employment
comparison ranking: 141

Youth unemployment rate (ages 15-24): *total:* 21.6% (2023 est.)
male: 21.9% (2023 est.)
female: 21.2% (2023 est.)
note: % of labor force ages 15-24 seeking employment
comparison ranking: total 57

Population below poverty line: 16.1% (2022 est.)
note: % of population with income below national poverty line

Gini Index coefficient - distribution of family income: 29.8 (2021 est.)
note: index (0-100) of income distribution; higher values represent greater inequality
comparison ranking: 123

Average household expenditures: *on food:* 12.5% of household expenditures (2022 est.)
on alcohol and tobacco: 3.1% of household expenditures (2022 est.)

Household income or consumption by percentage share: *lowest 10%:* 2.8% (2021 est.)
highest 10%: 22.7% (2021 est.)
note: % share of income accruing to lowest and highest 10% of population

Remittances: 0.62% of GDP (2023 est.)
0.56% of GDP (2022 est.)
0.49% of GDP (2021 est.)
note: personal transfers and compensation between resident and non-resident individuals/households/entities

Budget: *revenues:* $195.463 billion (2022 est.)

expenditures: $186.928 billion (2022 est.)
note: central government revenues (excluding grants) and expenses converted to US dollars at average official exchange rate for year indicated

Public debt: 36.25% of GDP (2022 est.)
note: central government debt as a % of GDP
comparison ranking: 146

Taxes and other revenues: 27.11% (of GDP) (2022 est.)
note: central government tax revenue as a % of GDP
comparison ranking: 34

Current account balance: $40.073 billion (2023 est.)
$31.881 billion (2022 est.)
$45.248 billion (2021 est.)
note: balance of payments - net trade and primary/secondary income in current dollars
comparison ranking: 15

Exports: $324.073 billion (2023 est.)
$314.412 billion (2022 est.)
$299.365 billion (2021 est.)
note: balance of payments - exports of goods and services in current dollars
comparison ranking: 29

Exports - partners: Germany 10%, Norway 10%, US 9%, Denmark 8%, Finland 7% (2022)
note: top five export partners based on percentage share of exports

Exports - commodities: refined petroleum, cars, packaged medicine, paper, electricity (2022)
note: top five export commodities based on value in dollars

Imports: $296.796 billion (2023 est.)
$298.253 billion (2022 est.)
$268.334 billion (2021 est.)
note: balance of payments - imports of goods and services in current dollars
comparison ranking: 27

Imports - partners: Germany 16%, Netherlands 10%, Norway 9%, China 7%, Denmark 6% (2022)
note: top five import partners based on percentage share of imports

Imports - commodities: crude petroleum, cars, refined petroleum, broadcasting equipment, garments (2022)
note: top five import commodities based on value in dollars

Reserves of foreign exchange and gold: $60.863 billion (2023 est.)
$64.289 billion (2022 est.)
$62.053 billion (2021 est.)
note: holdings of gold (year-end prices)/foreign exchange/special drawing rights in current dollars
comparison ranking: 38

Exchange rates: Swedish kronor (SEK) per US dollar -

Exchange rates: 10.61 (2023 est.)
10.114 (2022 est.)
8.577 (2021 est.)
9.21 (2020 est.)
9.458 (2019 est.)

ENERGY

Electricity access: *electrification - total population:* 100% (2022 est.)

Electricity: *installed generating capacity:* 52.706 million kW (2022 est.)
consumption: 129.934 billion kWh (2022 est.)
exports: 39.064 billion kWh (2022 est.)
imports: 6.177 billion kWh (2022 est.)
transmission/distribution losses: 10.932 billion kWh (2022 est.)
comparison rankings: transmission/distribution losses 181; imports 42; exports 3; consumption 29; installed generating capacity 28

Electricity generation sources: *fossil fuels:* 1% of total installed capacity (2022 est.)
nuclear: 28.8% of total installed capacity (2022 est.)
solar: 0.9% of total installed capacity (2022 est.)
wind: 18.9% of total installed capacity (2022 est.)
hydroelectricity: 41.9% of total installed capacity (2022 est.)
biomass and waste: 8.6% of total installed capacity (2022 est.)

Nuclear energy: Number of operational nuclear reactors: 6 (2023)

Net capacity of operational nuclear reactors: 6.94GW (2023 est.)

Percent of total electricity production: 28.6% (2023 est.)

Number of nuclear reactors permanently shut down: 7 (2023)

Coal: *production:* 1.115 million metric tons (2022 est.)
consumption: 3.396 million metric tons (2022 est.)
exports: 43,000 metric tons (2022 est.)
imports: 2.152 million metric tons (2022 est.)
proven reserves: 5 million metric tons (2022 est.)

Petroleum: *total petroleum production:* 11,000 bbl/day (2023 est.)
refined petroleum consumption: 283,000 bbl/day (2023 est.)

Natural gas: *consumption:* 889.924 million cubic meters (2022 est.)
exports: 12.15 million cubic meters (2022 est.)
imports: 680.998 million cubic meters (2022 est.)

Carbon dioxide emissions: 47.364 million metric tonnes of CO2 (2022 est.)
from coal and metallurgical coke: 6.548 million metric tonnes of CO2 (2022 est.)
from petroleum and other liquids: 38.96 million metric tonnes of CO2 (2022 est.)
from consumed natural gas: 1.855 million metric tonnes of CO2 (2022 est.)
comparison ranking: total emissions 58

Energy consumption per capita: 150.621 million Btu/person (2022 est.)
comparison ranking: 26

COMMUNICATIONS

Telephones - fixed lines: *total subscriptions:* 1.261 million (2021 est.)
subscriptions per 100 inhabitants: 12 (2021 est.)
comparison ranking: total subscriptions 63

Telephones - mobile cellular: *total subscriptions:* 13.194 million (2022 est.)
subscriptions per 100 inhabitants: 125 (2022 est.)
comparison ranking: total subscriptions 79

Telecommunication systems: *general assessment:* Sweden's telecom market includes mature mobile and broadband sectors which have been stimulated by the progressive investment of the main telcos in developing new technologies; the country retains one of the best developed LTE infrastructures in the region, while its MNOs have benefited from the January 2021 auction of spectrum in the 3.5GHz band which will enable them to expand services nationally; the country also has one of the highest fiber broadband penetration rates in Europe; the focus of FttP is aimed at fulfilling the government's target of providing a 1Gb/s service to 98% of the population by 2025; the methodology to achieve this has rested on regulatory measures supported by public funds, as well as on the auction of spectrum in different bands; in the fixed-line broadband segment, the number of DSL subscribers is falling steadily as customers continue to migrate to fiber networks; there is also competition from HFC infrastructure, offering fiber-based broadband and investing in services based on the DOCSIS3.1 standard; this report assesses key aspects of the Swedish telecom market, providing data on fixed network services and profiling the main players; it also reviews the key regulatory issues, including interconnection, local loop unbundling, number portability, carrier preselection and NGN open access; the report also analyses the mobile market, providing data on network operators and their strategies in a highly competitive environment; in addition, the report considers the fixed and fixed-wireless broadband markets, including analyses of market dynamics and the main operators, as well as providing subscriber forecasts (2021)
domestic: fixed-line is 12 per 100 and mobile-cellular is 125 per 100 (2022)
international: country code - 46; landing points for Botina, SFL, SFS-4, Baltic Sea Submarine Cable, Eastern Light, Sweden-Latvia, BCS North-Phase1, EE-S1, LV-SE1, BCS East-West Interlink, NordBalt, Baltica, Denmark- Sweden-15,-17,-18, Scandinavian Ring -North,-South, IP-Only Denmark-Sweden, Donica North, Kattegate-1,-2, Energinet Laeso-Varberg and GC2 submarine cables providing links to other Nordic countries and Europe; satellite earth stations - 1 Intelsat (Atlantic Ocean), 1 Eutelsat, and 1 Inmarsat (Atlantic and Indian Ocean regions); note - Sweden shares the Inmarsat earth station with the other Nordic countries (Denmark, Finland, Iceland, and Norway) (2019)

Broadcast media: publicly owned TV broadcaster operates 2 terrestrial networks plus regional stations; multiple privately owned TV broadcasters operating nationally, regionally, and locally; about 50 local TV stations; widespread access to pan-Nordic and international broadcasters through multi-channel cable and satellite TV; publicly owned radio broadcaster operates 3 national stations and a network of 25 regional channels; roughly 100 privately owned local radio stations with some consolidating into near national networks; an estimated 900 community and neighborhood radio stations broadcast intermittently

Internet country code: .se

Internet users: *total:* 8.8 million (2021 est.)
percent of population: 88% (2021 est.)
comparison ranking: total 66

Broadband - fixed subscriptions: *total:* 4,179,574 (2020 est.)
subscriptions per 100 inhabitants: 41 (2020 est.)
comparison ranking: total 36

TRANSPORTATION

National air transport system: *number of registered air carriers:* 11 (2020)
inventory of registered aircraft operated by air carriers: 316

Civil aircraft registration country code prefix: SE

Airports: 203 (2024)
comparison ranking: 30

Heliports: 11 (2024)

Pipelines: 1626 km gas (2013)

Railways: *total:* 10,910 km (2020) 8,184 km electrified
narrow gauge: 65 km
comparison ranking: total 22

Roadways: *total:* 197,964 km (2022)
comparison ranking: total 26

Waterways: 2,052 km (2010)
comparison ranking: 42

Merchant marine: *total:* 361 (2023)
by type: general cargo 44, oil tanker 18, other 299
comparison ranking: total 52

Ports: *total ports:* 92 (2024)
large: 3
medium: 10
small: 30
very small: 49
ports with oil terminals: 49
key ports: Falkenberg, Goteborg, Helsingborg, Karlsborg, Karlshamn, Lulea, Malmo, Norrkoping, Stockholm, Sundsvall, Uddevalla, Varberg, Vasteras

MILITARY AND SECURITY

Military and security forces: Swedish Armed Forces (Försvarsmakten or "the Defense Force"): Army, Navy, Air Force, Home Guard (2024)

Military expenditures: 2.1% of GDP (2024 est.)
1.7% of GDP (2023)
1.3% of GDP (2022)
1.3% of GDP (2021)
1.2% of GDP (2020)
comparison ranking: 59

Military and security service personnel strengths: *the SAF has about 25,000 active-duty personnel:* approximately 14,000 continuous service/full-time and approximately 11,000 temporary service; approximately 21,000 Home Guard (some on active duty) (2024)
note 1: SAF personnel are divided into continuously serving (full-time) and temporary service troops (part-timers who serve periodically and have another main employer or attend school); additional personnel have signed service agreements with the SAF and mostly serve in the Home Guard; the SAF also has about 9,000 civilian employees
note 2: in 2021, Sweden announced plans that increase the total size of the armed forces to about 100,000 personnel by 2030

Military equipment inventories and acquisitions: the SAF's inventory is comprised of domestically produced and imported Western weapons systems, including from Finland, Germany, and the US; Sweden has a defense industry that produces a range of air, land, and naval systems, including armored vehicles, combat aircraft, and submarines; it also produces weapons systems jointly with other countries (2024)

Military service age and obligation: *18-47 years of age for voluntary military service for men and women; service obligation:* 7-15 months (Army), 7-15 months (Navy), 8-12 months (Air Force); after completing initial service, soldiers have a reserve commitment until age 47; compulsory military service, abolished in 2010, was reinstated in January 2018; conscription is selective, includes both men and women (age 18), and requires 6-15 months of service (2024)
note 1: Sweden conscripts about 5,500 men and women each year; it plans to increase this number to 8,000 by 2025; conscientious objectors in Sweden have the right to apply for alternative service (called vapenfri tjänst); after completing alternative service, the conscript then belongs to the civilian reserve
note 2: as of 2023, women made over 20% of the military's personnel

Military deployments: the Swedish military has small numbers of personnel deployed on multiple EU-, NATO-, and UN-led missions (2024)

Military - note: the Swedish military is responsible for the defense of the country and its territories against armed attack, supporting Sweden's national security interests, providing societal support, such as humanitarian aid, and contributing to international peacekeeping and peacemaking operations
the military has a relatively small active duty force that is designed to be rapidly mobilized in a crisis; it is equipped with modern, mostly Swedish-made weapons, exercises regularly, and is backed up by a trained reserve and a Home Guard; the military's main focus is maintaining itself as a credible and visible deterrent through training and exercises, sustaining high levels of readiness, cooperating and collaborating with both domestic and foreign partners
Sweden maintained a policy of military non-alignment for over 200 years before applying for NATO membership in May 2022 following Russia's full-scale invasion of Ukraine; it became a NATO member in March of 2024; prior to membership, Stockholm joined NATO's Partnership for Peace program in 1994 and contributed to NATO-led missions, including those in Afghanistan, Iraq, and Kosovo; the military cooperates closely with the forces of other Nordic countries through the Nordic Defense Cooperation (NORDEFCO; established 2009), which consists of Denmark, Finland, Iceland, Norway, and Sweden; areas of cooperation include armaments, education, human resources, training and exercises, and operations; Sweden is a signatory of the EU's Common Security and Defense Policy (CSDP) and contributes to CSDP missions and operations, including EU battlegroups; it also participates in UN-led missions; Sweden has close bilateral security relations with some NATO member states, particularly Finland, Germany, the UK, and the US (2024)

SPACE

Space agency/agencies: Swedish National Space Agency (SNSA; established 1972; known until 2018 as the Swedish National Space Board) (2024)

Space launch site(s): Esrange Space Center (Kiruna) (2024)

Space program overview: member of the European Space Agency (ESA) and program is integrated within the framework of the ESA; produces and operates satellites; builds and launches sounding rockets; involved in the research, development, production, and operations of a wide variety of other space-related areas and capabilities, including astronomy, atmospheric monitoring, geographic information systems, infrared imaging, meteorology, propulsion systems, remote sensing, satellite subsystems, spacecraft systems and structures, space physics, scientific research, stratospheric balloons, and telecommunications; conducts extensive bilateral and multilateral international cooperation, in particular through the ESA and EU and their member states, as well as with the US; has a robust commercial space industry involved in a broad range of space-related capabilities (2024)
note: further details about the key activities, programs, and milestones of the country's space program, as well as government spending estimates on the space sector, appear in the Space Programs reference guide

TERRORISM

Terrorist group(s): Islamic State of Iraq and ash-Sham (ISIS)
note: details about the history, aims, leadership, organization, areas of operation, tactics, targets, weapons, size, and sources of support of the group(s) appear(s) in the Terrorism reference guide

TRANSNATIONAL ISSUES

Refugees and internally displaced persons: *refugees (country of origin):* 113,213 (Syria), 26,857 (Afghanistan), 25,849 (Eritrea), 10,464 (Iraq), 9,315 (Somalia), 7,146 (Iran) (mid-year 2022); 43,710 (Ukraine) (as of 28 February 2024)
stateless persons: 46,515 (2022); note - the majority of stateless people are from the Middle East and Somalia

SWITZERLAND

INTRODUCTION

Background: The Swiss Confederation was founded in 1291 as a defensive alliance among three cantons. In succeeding years, other localities joined the original three. The Swiss Confederation secured its independence from the Holy Roman Empire in 1499. A constitution of 1848, which was modified in 1874 to allow voters to introduce referenda on proposed laws, replaced the confederation with a centralized federal government. The major European powers have long honored Switzerland's sovereignty and neutrality, and the country was not involved in either World War. The political and economic integration of Europe over the past half-century, as well as Switzerland's role in many UN and international organizations, has strengthened Switzerland's ties with its neighbors. However, the country did not officially become a UN member until 2002. Switzerland remains active in many UN and international organizations but retains a strong commitment to neutrality.

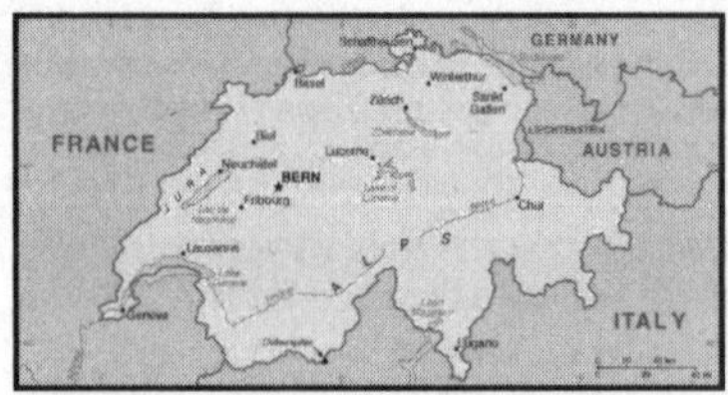

GEOGRAPHY

Location: Central Europe, east of France, north of Italy

Geographic coordinates: 47 00 N, 8 00 E

Map references: Europe

Area: *total:* 41,277 sq km
land: 39,997 sq km
water: 1,280 sq km
comparison ranking: total 135

Area - comparative: slightly less than twice the size of New Jersey

Land boundaries: *total:* 1,770 km
border countries (5): Austria 158 km; France 525 km; Italy 698 km; Liechtenstein 41 km; Germany 348 km

Coastline: 0 km (landlocked)

Maritime claims: none (landlocked)

Climate: temperate, but varies with altitude; cold, cloudy, rainy/snowy winters; cool to warm, cloudy, humid summers with occasional showers

Terrain: mostly mountains (Alps in south, Jura in northwest) with a central plateau of rolling hills, plains, and large lakes

Elevation: *highest point:* Dufourspitze 4,634 m
lowest point: Lake Maggiore 195 m
mean elevation: 1,350 m

Natural resources: hydropower potential, timber, salt

Land use: *agricultural land:* 38.7% (2018 est.)
arable land: 10.2% (2018 est.)
permanent crops: 0.6% (2018 est.)
permanent pasture: 27.9% (2018 est.)
forest: 31.5% (2018 est.)
other: 29.8% (2018 est.)

Irrigated land: 327 sq km (2016)

Major lakes (area sq km): *fresh water lake(s):* Lake Constance (shared with Germany and Austria) - 540 sq km; Lake Geneva (shared with France) - 580 sq km

Major rivers (by length in km): Rhein (Rhine) river source (shared with Germany, France, and Netherlands [m]) - 1,233 km
note – [s] after country name indicates river source; [m] after country name indicates river mouth

Major watersheds (area sq km): Atlantic Ocean drainage: Rhine-Maas (198,735 sq km), *(Black Sea)* Danube (795,656 sq km), *(Adriatic Sea)* Po (76,997 sq km), *(Mediterranean Sea)* Rhone (100,543 sq km)

Population distribution: population distribution corresponds to elevation with the northern and western areas far more heavily populated; the higher Alps of the south limit settlement

Natural hazards: avalanches, landslides; flash floods

Geography - note: landlocked; crossroads of northern and southern Europe; along with southeastern France, northern Italy, and southwestern Austria, has the highest elevations in the Alps

PEOPLE AND SOCIETY

Population: *total:* 8,860,574
male: 4,403,105
female: 4,457,469 (2024 est.)
comparison rankings: female 101; male 100; total 102

Nationality: *noun:* Swiss (singular and plural)
adjective: Swiss

Ethnic groups: Swiss 69.2%, German 4.2%, Italian 3.2%, Portuguese 2.5%, French 2.1%, Kosovan 1.1%, Turkish 1%, other 16.7% (2020 est.)
note: data represent permanent and non-permanent resident population by country of birth

Languages: German (or Swiss German) (official) 62.1%, French (official) 22.8%, Italian (official) 8%, English 5.7%, Portuguese 3.5%, Albanian 3.3%, Serbo-Croatian 2.3%, Spanish 2.3%, Romansh (official) 0.5%, other 7.9% (2019 est.)
major-language sample(s):
Das World Factbook, die unverzichtbare Quelle für grundlegende Informationen. (German)
The World Factbook, une source indispensable d'informations de base. (French)
L'Almanacco dei fatti del mondo, l'indispensabile fonte per le informazioni di base. (Italian)
note: shares sum to more than 100% because respondents could indicate more than one main language

Religions: Roman Catholic 34.4%, Protestant 22.5%, other Christian 5.7%, Muslim 5.4%, other 1.5%, none 29.4%, unspecified 1.1% (2020 est.)

Age structure: *0-14 years:* 15.1% (male 685,221/female 650,802)
15-64 years: 64.6% (male 2,887,767/female 2,834,842)
65 years and over: 20.3% (2024 est.) (male 830,117/female 971,825)

Dependency ratios: *total dependency ratio:* 51.6
youth dependency ratio: 22.8
elderly dependency ratio: 28.7
potential support ratio: 3.5 (2021 est.)

Median age: *total:* 44.2 years (2024 est.)
male: 43.5 years
female: 44.9 years
comparison ranking: total 32

Population growth rate: 0.75% (2024 est.)
comparison ranking: 117

Birth rate: 10.1 births/1,000 population (2024 est.)
comparison ranking: 185

Death rate: 8.5 deaths/1,000 population (2024 est.)
comparison ranking: 73

Net migration rate: 5.9 migrant(s)/1,000 population (2024 est.)
comparison ranking: 14

Population distribution: population distribution corresponds to elevation with the northern and western areas far more heavily populated; the higher Alps of the south limit settlement

Urbanization: *urban population:* 74.2% of total population (2023)
rate of urbanization: 0.79% annual rate of change (2020-25 est.)

Major urban areas - population: 1.432 million Zurich, 441,000 BERN (capital) (2023)

Sex ratio: *at birth:* 1.05 male(s)/female
0-14 years: 1.05 male(s)/female
15-64 years: 1.02 male(s)/female
65 years and over: 0.85 male(s)/female
total population: 0.99 male(s)/female (2024 est.)

Mother's mean age at first birth: 31.1 years (2020 est.)

Maternal mortality ratio: 7 deaths/100,000 live births (2020 est.)
comparison ranking: 154

Infant mortality rate: *total:* 3 deaths/1,000 live births (2024 est.)
male: 3.4 deaths/1,000 live births
female: 2.5 deaths/1,000 live births
comparison ranking: total 209

Life expectancy at birth: *total population:* 83.9 years (2024 est.)
male: 82 years
female: 85.8 years
comparison ranking: total population 9

Total fertility rate: 1.59 children born/woman (2024 est.)
comparison ranking: 187

Gross reproduction rate: 0.77 (2024 est.)

Contraceptive prevalence rate: 71.6% (2017)

Drinking water source: *improved: urban:* 100% of population
rural: 100% of population
total: 100% of population

Current health expenditure: 11.8% of GDP (2020)

Physician density: 4.38 physicians/1,000 population (2020)

Hospital bed density: 4.6 beds/1,000 population (2018)

Sanitation facility access: *improved: urban:* 100% of population
rural: 100% of population
total: 100% of population

Obesity - adult prevalence rate: 19.5% (2016)
comparison ranking: 112

Alcohol consumption per capita: *total:* 9.41 liters of pure alcohol (2019 est.)
beer: 3.17 liters of pure alcohol (2019 est.)
wine: 4.35 liters of pure alcohol (2019 est.)
spirits: 1.76 liters of pure alcohol (2019 est.)
other alcohols: 0.12 liters of pure alcohol (2019 est.)
comparison ranking: total 30

Tobacco use: *total:* 25.5% (2020 est.)
male: 28.1% (2020 est.)
female: 22.9% (2020 est.)
comparison ranking: total 46

Children under the age of 5 years underweight: NA

Currently married women (ages 15-49): 57.5% (2023 est.)

Education expenditures: 5.2% of GDP (2020 est.)
comparison ranking: 68

Literacy: *total population:* NA
male: NA
female: NA

School life expectancy (primary to tertiary education): *total:* 17 years
male: 17 years
female: 17 years (2020)

ENVIRONMENT

Environment - current issues: air pollution from vehicle emissions; water pollution from agricultural fertilizers; chemical contaminants and erosion damage the soil and limit productivity; loss of biodiversity

Environment - international agreements: *party to:* Air Pollution, Air Pollution-Heavy Metals, Air Pollution-Multi-effect Protocol, Air Pollution-Nitrogen Oxides, Air Pollution-Persistent Organic Pollutants, Air Pollution-Sulphur 85, Air Pollution-Sulphur 94, Air Pollution-Volatile Organic Compounds, Antarctic-Environmental Protection, Antarctic Treaty, Biodiversity, Climate Change, Climate Change-Kyoto Protocol, Climate Change-Paris Agreement, Comprehensive Nuclear Test Ban, Desertification, Endangered Species, Environmental Modification, Hazardous Wastes, Law of the Sea, Marine Dumping-London Convention, Marine Dumping-London Protocol, Marine Life Conservation, Nuclear Test Ban, Ozone Layer Protection, Ship Pollution, Tropical Timber 2006, Wetlands, Whaling
signed, but not ratified: none of the selected agreements

Climate: temperate, but varies with altitude; cold, cloudy, rainy/snowy winters; cool to warm, cloudy, humid summers with occasional showers

Urbanization: *urban population:* 74.2% of total population (2023)
rate of urbanization: 0.79% annual rate of change (2020-25 est.)

Revenue from forest resources: 0.01% of GDP (2018 est.)
comparison ranking: 151

Revenue from coal: 0% of GDP (2018 est.)
comparison ranking: 164

Air pollutants: *particulate matter emissions:* 8.97 micrograms per cubic meter (2019 est.)
carbon dioxide emissions: 34.48 megatons (2016 est.)
methane emissions: 4.98 megatons (2020 est.)

Waste and recycling: *municipal solid waste generated annually:* 6.056 million tons (2016 est.)
municipal solid waste recycled annually: 1.938 million tons (2015 est.)
percent of municipal solid waste recycled: 32% (2015 est.)

Major lakes (area sq km): *fresh water lake(s):* Lake Constance (shared with Germany and Austria) - 540 sq km; Lake Geneva (shared with France) - 580 sq km

Major rivers (by length in km): Rhein (Rhine) river source (shared with Germany, France, and Netherlands [m]) - 1,233 km
note – [s] after country name indicates river source; [m] after country name indicates river mouth

Major watersheds (area sq km): Atlantic Ocean drainage: Rhine-Maas (198,735 sq km), *(Black Sea)* Danube (795,656 sq km), *(Adriatic Sea)* Po (76,997 sq km), *(Mediterranean Sea)* Rhone (100,543 sq km)

Total water withdrawal: *municipal:* 970 million cubic meters (2020 est.)
industrial: 640 million cubic meters (2020 est.)
agricultural: 160 million cubic meters (2020 est.)

Total renewable water resources: 53.5 billion cubic meters (2020 est.)

GOVERNMENT

Country name: *conventional long form:* Swiss Confederation
conventional short form: Switzerland
local long form: Schweizerische Eidgenossenschaft (German)/ Confederation Suisse (French)/ Confederazione Svizzera (Italian)/ Confederaziun Svizra (Romansh)
local short form: Schweiz (German)/ Suisse (French)/ Svizzera (Italian)/ Svizra (Romansh)
abbreviation: CH
etymology: name derives from the canton of Schwyz, one of the founding cantons of the Swiss Confederacy that formed in the late 13th century

Government type: federal republic (formally a confederation)

Capital: *name:* Bern
geographic coordinates: 46 55 N, 7 28 E
time difference: UTC+1 (6 hours ahead of Washington, DC, during Standard Time)
daylight saving time: +1hr, begins last Sunday in March; ends last Sunday in October
etymology: origin of the name is uncertain but may derive from a 2nd century B.C. Celtic place name, possibly "berna" meaning "cleft," that was subsequently adopted by a Roman settlement

Administrative divisions: 26 cantons (cantons, singular - canton in French; cantoni, singular - cantone in Italian; Kantone, singular - Kanton in German); Aargau, Appenzell Ausserrhoden, Appenzell Innerrhoden, Basel-Landschaft, Basel-Stadt, Berne/Bern, Fribourg/Freiburg, Geneve (Geneva), Glarus, Graubuenden/Grigioni/Grischun, Jura, Luzern (Lucerne), Neuchatel, Nidwalden, Obwalden, Sankt Gallen, Schaffhausen, Schwyz, Solothurn, Thurgau, Ticino, Uri, Valais/Wallis, Vaud, Zug, Zuerich
note: the canton names are in the official language(s) of the canton with the exception of Geneve and Luzern, where the conventional names (Geneva and Lucerne) have been added in parentheses; 6 of the cantons - Appenzell Ausserrhoden, Appenzell Innerrhoden, Basel-Landschaft, Basel-Stadt, Nidwalden, Obwalden - are referred to as half cantons because they elect only one member (instead of two) to the Council of States and, in popular referendums where a majority of popular votes and a majority of cantonal votes are required, these 6 cantons only have a half vote

Independence: 1 August 1291 (founding of the Swiss Confederation)

National holiday: Founding of the Swiss Confederation in 1291; note - since 1 August 1891 celebrated as Swiss National Day

Legal system: civil law system; judicial review of legislative acts, except for federal decrees of a general obligatory character

Constitution: *history:* previous 1848, 1874; latest adopted by referendum 18 April 1999, effective 1 January 2000
amendments: proposed by the two houses of the Federal Assembly or by petition of at least one hundred thousand voters (called the "federal popular initiative"); passage of proposals requires majority vote in a referendum; following drafting of an amendment by the Assembly, its passage requires approval by majority vote in a referendum and approval by the majority of cantons; amended many times, last in 2018

International law organization participation: accepts compulsory ICJ jurisdiction with reservations; accepts ICCt jurisdiction

Citizenship: *citizenship by birth:* no
citizenship by descent only: at least one parent must be a citizen of Switzerland
dual citizenship recognized: yes
residency requirement for naturalization: 12 years including at least 3 of the last 5 years prior to application

Suffrage: 18 years of age; universal

Executive branch: *chief of state:* President of the Swiss Confederation Viola AMHERD (since 1 January 2024)
head of government: President of the Swiss Confederation Viola AMHERD (since 1 January 2024)
cabinet: Federal Council or Bundesrat (in German), Conseil Federal (in French), Consiglio Federale (in Italian) indirectly elected by the Federal Assembly for a 4-year term
elections/appointments: president and vice president elected by the Federal Assembly from among members of the Federal Council for a 1-year, non-consecutive term; election last held on 13 December 2023 (next to be held in December 2024)
election results:
2023: Viola AMHERD elected president for 2024; Federal Assembly vote - Viola AMHERD (The Center) 158 of 204; Karin Keller-Sutter (FDP.The Liberals) elected vice president for 2024; Federal Assembly vote - 138 of 196
2022: Alain BERSET elected president for 2023; Federal Assembly vote - Alain BERSET (SP) 140 OF 181; Viola AMHERD elected vice president; Federal assembly vote - 207 of 223
note: the Federal Council, comprised of 7 federal councillors, constitutes the federal government of Switzerland; council members rotate the 1-year term of federal president

Legislative branch: *description:* bicameral Federal Assembly or Bundesversammlung (in German), Assemblée Fédérale (in French), Assemblea Federale (in Italian) consists of:
Council of States or Ständerat (in German), Conseil des États (in French), Consiglio degli Stati (in Italian) (46 seats; members in two-seat constituencies representing cantons and single-seat constituencies representing half cantons directly elected by simple majority vote except Jura and Neuchatel cantons, which use list proportional representation vote; member term governed by cantonal law)
National Council or Nationalrat (in German), Conseil National (in French), Consiglio Nazionale (in Italian) (200 seats; 194 members in cantons directly elected by proportional representation vote and 6 in half cantons directly elected by simple majority vote; members serve 4-year terms)
elections: Council of States - last held in most cantons on 22 October 2023 (each canton determines when the next election will be held)
National Council - last held on 22 October 2023 (next to be held on 31 October 2027)
election results: Council of States - percent of vote by party - NA; seats by party - The Center 13, FDP. The Liberals 12, SP 9, SVP 6, Green Party 5, other 1; composition - men 30, women 16, percentage women 34.8%
National Council - percent of vote by party - SVP 28.6%, SP 18%, The Center 14.6%, FDP.The Liberals 14.4%, Green Party 9.4%, GLP 7.2%, EDU 1.2, EDV/PEV 1.9%, MCR/MCG .5%, other 4%; seats by party - SVP 62, SP 41, The Center 29, FDP. The Liberals 28, Green Party 23, GLP 10, EDU 2, EDV/PEV 2, MCR/MCG 2, other 1; composition - men 123, women 77, percentage women 38.5%; note - total Federal Assembly percentage women 37.8%

Judicial branch: *highest court(s):* Federal Supreme Court (consists of 38 justices and 19 deputy justices organized into 7 divisions)
judge selection and term of office: judges elected by the Federal Assembly for 6-year terms; note - judges are affiliated with political parties and are elected according to linguistic and regional criteria in approximate proportion to the level of party representation in the Federal Assembly
subordinate courts: Federal Criminal Court (established in 2004); Federal Administrative Court (established in 2007); note - each of Switzerland's 26 cantons has its own courts

Political parties: The Center (Die Mitte, Alleanza del Centro, Le Centre, Allianza dal Center) (merger of the Christian Democratic People's Party and the Conservative Democratic Party)
Evangelical Peoples' Party or EVP/PEV
Federal Democrats or EDU
Geneva Citizens Movement or MCR/MCG
Green Liberal Party (Gruenliberale Partei or GLP, Parti vert liberale or PVL, Partito Verde-Liberale or PVL, Partida Verde Liberale or PVL)
Green Party (Gruene Partei der Schweiz or Gruene, Parti Ecologiste Suisse or Les Verts, Partito Ecologista Svizzero or I Verdi, Partida Ecologica Svizra or La Verda)
The Liberals or FDP.The Liberals (FDP.Die Liberalen, PLR.Les Liberaux-Radicaux, PLR.I Liberali, Ils Liberals)
Social Democratic Party (Sozialdemokratische Partei der Schweiz or SP, Parti Socialiste Suisse or PSS, Partito
Socialista Svizzero or PSS, Partida Socialdemocratica de la Svizra or PSS)
Swiss People's Party (Schweizerische Volkspartei or SVP, Union Democratique du Centre or UDC, Unione Democratica di Centro or UDC, Uniun Democratica dal Center or UDC)

International organization participation: ADB (nonregional member), AfDB (nonregional member), Australia Group, BIS, CD, CE, CERN, EAPC, EBRD, EFTA, EITI (implementing country), ESA, FAO, FATF, G-10, IADB, IAEA, IBRD, ICAO, ICC (national committees), ICCt, ICRM, IDA, IEA, IFAD, IFC, IFRCS, IGAD (partners), ILO, IMF, IMO, IMSO, Interpol, IOC, IOM, IPU, ISO, ITSO, ITU, ITUC (NGOs), LAIA (observer), MIGA, MONUSCO, NEA, NSG, OAS (observer), OECD, OIF, OPCW, OSCE, Pacific Alliance (observer), Paris Club, PCA, PFP, Schengen Convention, UN, UNCTAD, UNESCO, UNHCR, UNIDO, UNITAR, UNMISS, UNMOGIP, UNOOSA, UNRWA, UNTSO, UNWTO, UPU, Wassenaar Arrangement, WCO, WHO, WIPO, WMO, WTO, ZC

Diplomatic representation in the US: *chief of mission:* Ambassador Ralph HECKNER (since 18 September 2024)
chancery: 2900 Cathedral Ave NW, Washington, DC 20008
telephone: [1] (202) 745-7900
FAX: [1] (202) 387-2564
email address and website:
washington@eda.admin.ch
https://www.eda.admin.ch/washington
consulate(s) general: Atlanta, Chicago, New York, San Francisco
consulate(s): Boston

Diplomatic representation from the US: *chief of mission:* Ambassador Scott C. MILLER (since 11 January 2022) note - also accredited to Liechtenstein
embassy: Sulgeneckstrasse 19, CH-3007 Bern
mailing address: 5110 Bern Place, Washington DC 20521-5110
telephone: [41] (031) 357-70-11
FAX: [41] (031) 357-73-20
email address and website:
https://ch.usembassy.gov/

Flag description: red square with a bold, equilateral white cross in the center that does not extend to the edges of the flag; various medieval legends purport to describe the origin of the flag; a white cross used as identification for troops of the Swiss Confederation is first attested at the Battle of Laupen (1339)
note: in 1863, a newly formed international relief organization convening in Geneva, Switzerland sought to come up with an identifying flag or logo; they chose the inverse of the Swiss flag - a red cross on a white field - as their symbol; today that organization is known throughout the world as the International Red Cross

National symbol(s): Swiss cross (white cross on red field, arms equal length); national colors: red, white

National anthem: *name:* the Swiss anthem has four names: "Schweizerpsalm" [German] "Cantique Suisse" [French] "Salmo svizzero," [Italian] "Psalm svizzer" [Romansch] (Swiss Psalm)
lyrics/music: Leonhard WIDMER [German], Charles CHATELANAT [French], Camillo VALSANGIACOMO [Italian], and Flurin CAMATHIAS [Romansch]/Alberik ZWYSSIG
note: unofficially adopted 1961, officially 1981; the anthem has been popular in a number of Swiss cantons since its composition (in German) in 1841; translated into the other three official languages of the country (French, Italian, and Romansch), it is official in each of those languages

National heritage: *total World Heritage Sites:* 13 (9 cultural, 4 natural)
selected World Heritage Site locales: Old City of Berne (c); Swiss Alps Jungfrau-Aletsch (n); Monte San Giorgio (n); Abbey of St Gall (c); Three Castles, Defensive Wall, and Ramparts of the Market-Town of Bellinzona (c); Rhaetian Railway in the Albula/Bernina Landscapes (c); La Chaux-de-Fonds/Le Locle, Watchmaking Town Planning (c); Prehistoric Pile Dwellings around the Alps (c); Benedictine Convent of St John at Müstair (c); Lavaux, Vineyard Terraces (c)

ECONOMY

Economic overview: high-income, non-EU European economy; top ten in GDP per capita; renowned banking and financial hub; low unemployment and inflation; slowed GDP growth post-pandemic; highly skilled but aging workforce; key pharmaceutical and precision manufacturing exporter; leader in innovation and competitiveness indices

Real GDP (purchasing power parity): $733.779 billion (2023 est.)
$728.562 billion (2022 est.)
$710.319 billion (2021 est.)
note: data in 2021 dollars
comparison ranking: 37

Real GDP growth rate: 0.72% (2023 est.)
2.57% (2022 est.)
5.39% (2021 est.)
note: annual GDP % growth based on constant local currency
comparison ranking: 173

Real GDP per capita: $82,900 (2023 est.)
$83,000 (2022 est.)
$81,600 (2021 est.)
note: data in 2021 dollars
comparison ranking: 10

GDP (official exchange rate): $884.94 billion (2023 est.)
note: data in current dollars at official exchange rate

Inflation rate (consumer prices): 2.14% (2023 est.)
2.84% (2022 est.)
0.58% (2021 est.)
note: annual % change based on consumer prices
comparison ranking: 42

Credit ratings: Fitch rating: AAA (2000)

Moody's rating: Aaa (1982)

Standard & Poors rating: AAA (1988)
note: The year refers to the year in which the current credit rating was first obtained.

GDP - composition, by sector of origin: *agriculture:* 0.6% (2023 est.)
industry: 24.9% (2023 est.)
services: 71.9% (2023 est.)
note: figures may not total 100% due to non-allocated consumption not captured in sector-reported data
comparison rankings: services 33; industry 98; agriculture 196

GDP - composition, by end use: *household consumption:* 51.6% (2023 est.)
government consumption: 11.4% (2023 est.)
investment in fixed capital: 25.9% (2023 est.)
investment in inventories: -1.4% (2023 est.)
exports of goods and services: 75.3% (2023 est.)
imports of goods and services: -62.9% (2023 est.)
note: figures may not total 100% due to rounding or gaps in data collection

Agricultural products: milk, sugar beets, wheat, potatoes, pork, apples, barley, beef, grapes, maize (2022)
note: top ten agricultural products based on tonnage

Industries: machinery, chemicals, watches, textiles, precision instruments, tourism, banking, insurance, pharmaceuticals

Industrial production growth rate: -1.66% (2023 est.)
note: annual % change in industrial value added based on constant local currency
comparison ranking: 177

Labor force: 4.991 million (2023 est.)
note: number of people ages 15 or older who are employed or seeking work
comparison ranking: 87

Unemployment rate: 4.05% (2023 est.)
4.3% (2022 est.)
5.1% (2021 est.)
note: % of labor force seeking employment
comparison ranking: 76

Youth unemployment rate (ages 15-24): *total:* 8% (2023 est.)
male: 8.3% (2023 est.)
female: 7.7% (2023 est.)
note: % of labor force ages 15-24 seeking employment
comparison ranking: total 151

Population below poverty line: 14.7% (2020 est.)
note: % of population with income below national poverty line

Gini Index coefficient - distribution of family income: 33.7 (2020 est.)
note: index (0-100) of income distribution; higher values represent greater inequality
comparison ranking: 94

Average household expenditures: *on food:* 9.3% of household expenditures (2022 est.)
on alcohol and tobacco: 3.5% of household expenditures (2022 est.)

Household income or consumption by percentage share: *lowest 10%:* 2.9% (2020 est.)
highest 10%: 26.4% (2020 est.)
note: % share of income accruing to lowest and highest 10% of population

Remittances: 0.28% of GDP (2023 est.)
0.38% of GDP (2022 est.)
0.39% of GDP (2021 est.)
note: personal transfers and compensation between resident and non-resident individuals/households/entities

Budget: *revenues:* $143.411 billion (2022 est.)
expenditures: $136.348 billion (2022 est.)
note: central government revenues (excluding grants) and expenses converted to US dollars at average official exchange rate for year indicated

Public debt: 17.8% of GDP (2022 est.)
note: central government debt as a % of GDP
comparison ranking: 190

Taxes and other revenues: 9.1% (of GDP) (2022 est.)
note: central government tax revenue as a % of GDP
comparison ranking: 185

Current account balance: $67.821 billion (2023 est.)
$77.245 billion (2022 est.)
$56.091 billion (2021 est.)
note: balance of payments - net trade and primary/secondary income in current dollars
comparison ranking: 7

Exports: $661.628 billion (2023 est.)
$627.788 billion (2022 est.)
$579.011 billion (2021 est.)
note: balance of payments - exports of goods and services in current dollars
comparison ranking: 15

Exports - partners: US 15%, Germany 13%, China 11%, Italy 6%, France 5% (2022)
note: top five export partners based on percentage share of exports

Exports - commodities: gold, vaccines, packaged medicine, nitrogen compounds, base metal watches (2022)
note: top five export commodities based on value in dollars

Imports: $554.358 billion (2023 est.)
$516.517 billion (2022 est.)
$481.27 billion (2021 est.)
note: balance of payments - imports of goods and services in current dollars
comparison ranking: 15

Imports - partners: Germany 21%, US 10%, Italy 8%, France 6%, China 5% (2022)
note: top five import partners based on percentage share of imports

Imports - commodities: gold, packaged medicine, vaccines, cars, garments (2022)
note: top five import commodities based on value in dollars

Reserves of foreign exchange and gold: $863.892 billion (2023 est.)
$923.628 billion (2022 est.)
$1.11 trillion (2021 est.)
note: holdings of gold (year-end prices)/foreign exchange/special drawing rights in current dollars
comparison ranking: 3

Exchange rates: Swiss francs (CHF) per US dollar -

Exchange rates: 0.898 (2023 est.)
0.955 (2022 est.)
0.914 (2021 est.)
0.939 (2020 est.)
0.994 (2019 est.)

ENERGY

Electricity access: *electrification - total population:* 100% (2022 est.)

Electricity: *installed generating capacity:* 24.014 million kW (2022 est.)
consumption: 57.187 billion kWh (2022 est.)
exports: 29.881 billion kWh (2022 est.)
imports: 33.02 billion kWh (2022 est.)
transmission/distribution losses: 4.678 billion kWh (2022 est.)
comparison rankings: transmission/distribution losses 160; imports 6; exports 7; consumption 48; installed generating capacity 42

Electricity generation sources: *fossil fuels:* 0.9% of total installed capacity (2022 est.)
nuclear: 39.4% of total installed capacity (2022 est.)
solar: 6.5% of total installed capacity (2022 est.)
wind: 0.3% of total installed capacity (2022 est.)
hydroelectricity: 48% of total installed capacity (2022 est.)
biomass and waste: 5% of total installed capacity (2022 est.)

Nuclear energy: Number of operational nuclear reactors: 4 (2023)

Net capacity of operational nuclear reactors: 2.97GW (2023 est.)

Percent of total electricity production: 32.4% (2023 est.)

Number of nuclear reactors permanently shut down: 2 (2023)

Coal: *consumption:* 161,000 metric tons (2022 est.)
exports: 3.3 metric tons (2022 est.)
imports: 184,000 metric tons (2022 est.)

Petroleum: *total petroleum production:* 300 bbl/day (2023 est.)
refined petroleum consumption: 193,000 bbl/day (2023 est.)

Natural gas: *consumption:* 3.138 billion cubic meters (2022 est.)
imports: 3.099 billion cubic meters (2022 est.)

Carbon dioxide emissions: 33.609 million metric tonnes of CO2 (2022 est.)
from coal and metallurgical coke: 268,000 metric tonnes of CO2 (2022 est.)
from petroleum and other liquids: 27.331 million metric tonnes of CO2 (2022 est.)
from consumed natural gas: 6.009 million metric tonnes of CO2 (2022 est.)
comparison ranking: total emissions 70

Energy consumption per capita: 101.938 million Btu/person (2022 est.)
comparison ranking: 50

COMMUNICATIONS

Telephones - fixed lines: *total subscriptions:* 2.919 million (2022 est.)
subscriptions per 100 inhabitants: 33 (2022 est.)
comparison ranking: total subscriptions 39

Telephones - mobile cellular: *total subscriptions:* 10.45 million (2022 est.)
subscriptions per 100 inhabitants: 120 (2022 est.)
comparison ranking: total subscriptions 92

Telecommunication systems: *general assessment:* Switzerland has one of the highest broadband penetration rates within Europe, with a focus on services of at least 1Gb/s; this has been supported by sympathetic regulatory measures as well as by cooperative agreements between the main telcos, and with local utilities; fast fiber is complemented by 5G services reaching about 97% of the population by early 2021; together, these networks will soon enable the telcos to provide ultra-fast broadband services nationally, ahead of most other countries in the region; the competitive mobile market is served by three network operators and a small number of MVNOs; 5G services offered by the MNOs offer data rates of up to 2Gb/s, and although various cantons have called a halt to extensions of 5G, citing health concerns, the regulator and environment ministry have put in place measures aimed at ensuring that network roll outs can continue without disruption; with the migration of subscribers to LTE and 5G networks, the MNOs have been able to begin closing down their GSM networks and repurpose physical assets and spectrum; although not a member of the EU, the country's economic integration has meant that its telecom market deregulation has followed the EU's liberalization framework, including the recent regulations on international voice roaming; this report presents an analysis of Switzerland's fixed-line telecom market, including an assessment of network infrastructure (2021)
domestic: fixed-line is 33 per 100 and mobile-cellular subscribership is 120 per 100 persons (2022)
international: country code - 41; satellite earth stations - 2 Intelsat (Atlantic Ocean and Indian Ocean)

Broadcast media: the publicly owned radio and TV broadcaster, Swiss Broadcasting Corporation (SRG/SSR), operates 8 national TV networks, 3 broadcasting in German, 3 in French, and 2 in Italian; private commercial TV stations broadcast regionally and locally; TV broadcasts from stations in Germany, Italy, and France are widely available via multi-channel cable and satellite TV services; SRG/SSR operates 17 radio stations that, along with private broadcasters, provide national to local coverage)
(2019)

Internet country code: .ch

Internet users: *total:* 8.352 million (2021 est.)
percent of population: 96% (2021 est.)
comparison ranking: total 71

Broadband - fixed subscriptions: *total:* 4,028,238 (2020 est.)
subscriptions per 100 inhabitants: 47 (2020 est.)
comparison ranking: total 38

TRANSPORTATION

National air transport system: *number of registered air carriers:* 6 (2020)
inventory of registered aircraft operated by air carriers: 179
annual passenger traffic on registered air carriers: 28,857,994 (2018)
annual freight traffic on registered air carriers: 1,841,310,000 (2018) mt-km

Civil aircraft registration country code prefix: HB

Airports: 62 (2024)
comparison ranking: 76

Heliports: 51 (2024)

Pipelines: 1,800 km gas, 94 km oil (of which 60 are inactive), 17 km refined products (2017)

Railways: *total:* 5,296 km (2020) 5,296 km electrified; Switzerland remains the only country with a fully electrified network
comparison ranking: total 36

Roadways: *total:* 83,131 km (2022)
comparison ranking: total 61

Waterways: 1,292 km (2010) (there are 1,227 km of waterways on lakes and rivers for public transport and 65 km on the Rhine River between Basel-Rheinfelden and Schaffhausen-Bodensee for commercial goods transport)
comparison ranking: 61

Merchant marine: *total:* 17 (2023)
by type: bulk carrier 14, general cargo 1, other 2 (includes Liechtenstein)
comparison ranking: total 149

MILITARY AND SECURITY

Military and security forces: Swiss Armed Forces (aka Swiss Army or Schweizer Armee); Army (Heer; aka Land Forces), Swiss Air Force (Schweizer Luftwaffe) (2024)
note: the federal police maintain internal security and report to the Federal Department of Justice and Police, while the Armed Forces report to the Federal Department of Defense, Civil Protection, and Sport

Military expenditures: 0.7% of GDP (2023)
0.7% of GDP (2022)
0.7% of GDP (2021)
0.7% of GDP (2020)
0.7% of GDP (2019)
comparison ranking: 145

Military and security service personnel strengths: approximately 100,000, including cadre/professionals, conscripts, and militia; the Swiss Armed Forces consist of a small core of cadre/professional personnel along with a mix of militia and up to 20,000 conscripts brought in each year for training (2024)

Military equipment inventories and acquisitions: the military's inventory includes a mix of domestically produced and imported European and US weapons systems; the Swiss defense industry produces a range of military land vehicles (2024)

Military service age and obligation: 18-30 years of age for compulsory military service for men; 18 years of age for voluntary military service for men and women; every Swiss male has to serve at least 245 days in the armed forces; conscripts receive 18 weeks of mandatory training, followed by six 19-day intermittent recalls for training during the next 10 years (2024)
note: conscientious objectors can choose 390 days of community service instead of military service; as of 2023, women comprised about 1% of the active Swiss military

Military deployments: 175 Kosovo (NATO/KFOR) (2024)

Military - note: the Swiss military is responsible for territorial defense, limited support to international disaster response and peacekeeping, and providing support to civil authorities when their resources are not sufficient to ward off threats to internal security or provide sufficient relief during disasters; Switzerland has long maintained a policy of military neutrality but does periodically participate in EU, NATO, Organization for Security and Cooperation in Europe (OSCE), and UN military and peacekeeping operations; however, Swiss units will only participate in operations under the mandate of the UN or OSCE; Switzerland joined NATO's Partnership for Peace program in 1996; it has contributed to the NATO-led force in Kosovo (KFOR) since 1999
the military is comprised of conscripts, militia, and a small professional component; it is led by the Chief of the Armed Forces with an Armed Forces Staff and consists of a Joint Operations Command (JOC), an Armed Forces Logistics Organization, an Armed Forces Command Support Organization, and a Training and Education Command; the JOC controls, among other subordinate commands, the Air Force, the Land Forces, four territorial divisions, the Military Police Command, and the Special Forces Command (2024)

TERRORISM

Terrorist group(s): Islamic State of Iraq and ash-Sham (ISIS)
note: details about the history, aims, leadership, organization, areas of operation, tactics, targets, weapons, size, and sources of support of the group(s) appear(s) in the Terrorism reference guide

TRANSNATIONAL ISSUES

Refugees and internally displaced persons: *refugees (country of origin):* 14,726 (Eritrea), 11,441 (Afghanistan), 8,039 (Syria), (mid-year 2022); 65,615 (Ukraine) (as of 5 March 2024)
stateless persons: 891 (2022)

Illicit drugs: major source of precursor chemicals used in the production of illicit narcotics; a significant importer and exporter of ephedrine and pseudoephedrine;

SYRIA

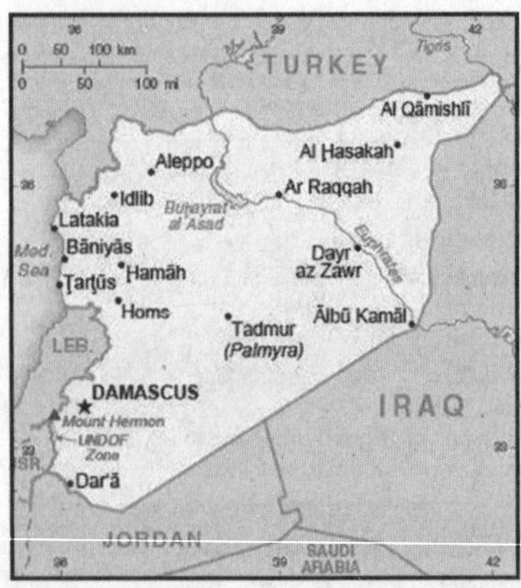

INTRODUCTION

Background: After World War I, France acquired a mandate over the northern portion of the former Ottoman Empire province of Syria. The French administered the area until granting it independence in 1946. The new country lacked political stability and experienced a series of military coups. Syria united with Egypt in 1958 to form the United Arab Republic. In 1961, the two entities separated, and the Syrian Arab Republic was reestablished. In the 1967 Arab-Israeli War, Syria lost control of the Golan Heights region to Israel. During the 1990s, Syria and Israel held occasional, albeit unsuccessful, peace talks over its return. In 1970, Hafiz al-ASAD, a member of the socialist Ba'ath Party and the minority Alawi sect, seized power in a bloodless coup and brought political stability to the country. Following the death of al-ASAD, his son, Bashar al-ASAD, was approved as president by popular referendum in 2000. Syrian troops that were stationed in Lebanon since 1976 in an ostensible peacekeeping role were withdrawn in 2005. During the 2006 conflict between Israel and Hizballah, Syria placed its military forces on alert but did not intervene directly on behalf of its ally Hizballah. In 2007, Bashar al-ASAD's second term as president was again approved in a referendum.

In the wake of major uprisings elsewhere in the region, antigovernment protests broke out in the southern province of Dar'a in 2011. Protesters called for the legalization of political parties, the removal of corrupt local officials, and the repeal of the restrictive Emergency Law allowing arrests without charge. Demonstrations and violent unrest spread across Syria, and the government responded with concessions, but also with military force and detentions that led to extended clashes and eventually civil war. International pressure on the Syrian Government intensified after 2011, as the Arab League, the EU, Turkey, and the US expanded economic sanctions against the ASAD regime and those entities that supported it. In 2012, more than 130 countries recognized the Syrian National Coalition as the sole legitimate representative of the Syrian people. In 2015, Russia launched a military intervention on behalf of the ASAD regime, and domestic and foreign-government-aligned forces recaptured swaths of territory from opposition forces. With foreign support, the regime continued to periodically regain opposition-held territory until 2020, when Turkish firepower halted a regime advance and forced a stalemate between regime and opposition forces. The government lacks territorial control over much of the northeastern part of the country, which the predominantly Kurdish Syrian Democratic Forces (SDF) hold, and a smaller area dominated by Turkey.

Since 2016, Turkey has conducted three large-scale military operations to capture territory along Syria's northern border. Some opposition forces organized under the Turkish-backed Syrian National

Army and Turkish forces have maintained control of northwestern Syria along the Turkish border with the Afrin area of Aleppo Province since 2018. The violent extremist organization Hay'at Tahrir al-Sham (formerly the Nusrah Front) emerged in 2017 as the predominant opposition force in Idlib Province, and still dominates an area also hosting Turkish forces. Negotiations have failed to produce a resolution to the conflict, and the UN estimated in 2022 that at least 306,000 people have died during the civil war. Approximately 6.7 million Syrians were internally displaced as of 2022, and 14.6 million people were in need of humanitarian assistance across the country. An additional 5.6 million Syrians were registered refugees in Turkey, Jordan, Iraq, Egypt, and North Africa. The conflict in Syria remains one of the two largest displacement crises worldwide (the other is the full-scale invasion of Ukraine).

GEOGRAPHY

Location: Middle East, bordering the Mediterranean Sea, between Lebanon and Turkey

Geographic coordinates: 35 00 N, 38 00 E

Map references: Middle East

Area: *total:* 187,437 sq km
land: 185,887 sq km
water: 1,550 sq km
note: includes 1,295 sq km of Israeli-occupied territory
comparison ranking: total 89

Area - comparative: slightly more than 1.5 times the size of Pennsylvania

Land boundaries: *total:* 2,363 km
border countries (5): Iraq 599 km; Israel 83 km; Jordan 379 km; Lebanon 403 km; Turkey 899 km

Coastline: 193 km

Maritime claims: *territorial sea:* 12 nm
contiguous zone: 24 nm

Climate: mostly desert; hot, dry, sunny summers (June to August) and mild, rainy winters (December to February) along coast; cold weather with snow or sleet periodically in Damascus

Terrain: primarily semiarid and desert plateau; narrow coastal plain; mountains in west

Elevation: *highest point:* Mount Hermon (Jabal a-Shayk) 2,814 m
lowest point: Yarmuk River -66 m
mean elevation: 514 m

Natural resources: petroleum, phosphates, chrome and manganese ores, asphalt, iron ore, rock salt, marble, gypsum, hydropower

Land use: *agricultural land:* 75.8% (2018 est.)
arable land: 25.4% (2018 est.)
permanent crops: 5.8% (2018 est.)
permanent pasture: 44.6% (2018 est.)
forest: 2.7% (2018 est.)
other: 21.5% (2018 est.)

Irrigated land: 13,100 sq km (2013)

Major rivers (by length in km): Euphrates (shared with Turkey [s], Iran, and Iraq [m]) - 3,596 km; Tigris (shared with Turkey, Iran, and Iraq [m]) - 1,950 km
note – [s] after country name indicates river source; [m] after country name indicates river mouth

Major watersheds (area sq km): Indian Ocean drainage: *(Persian Gulf)* Tigris and Euphrates (918,044 sq km)

Population distribution: significant population density along the Mediterranean coast; larger concentrations found in the major cities of Damascus, Aleppo (the country's largest city), and Hims (Homs); more than half of the population lives in the coastal plain, the province of Halab, and the Euphrates River valley
note: the ongoing civil war has altered the population distribution

Natural hazards: dust storms, sandstorms
volcanism: Syria's two historically active volcanoes, Es Safa and an unnamed volcano near the Turkish border have not erupted in centuries

Geography - note: the capital of Damascus – located at an oasis fed by the Barada River – is thought to be one of the world's oldest continuously inhabited cities; there are 42 Israeli settlements and civilian land use sites in the Israeli-controlled Golan Heights (2017)

PEOPLE AND SOCIETY

Population: *total:* 23,865,423
male: 11,981,578
female: 11,883,845 (2024 est.)
comparison rankings: female 58; male 57; total 57

Nationality: *noun:* Syrian(s)
adjective: Syrian

Ethnic groups: Arab ~50%, Alawite ~15%, Kurd ~10%, Levantine ~10%, other ~15% (includes Druze, Ismaili, Imami, Nusairi, Assyrian, Turkoman, Armenian)

Languages: Arabic (official), Kurdish, Armenian, Aramaic, Circassian, French, English
major-language sample(s):
كتاب حقائق العالم، المصدر الذي لا يمكن الاستغناء عنه للمعلومات الأساسية
(Arabic)

ڕاستییەکانی جیهان، باشترین سەرچاوەیە بۆ زانیارییە بنەڕەتییەکان
(Kurdish)

Religions: Muslim 87% (official; includes Sunni 74% and Alawi, Ismaili, and Shia 13%), Christian 10% (includes Orthodox, Uniate, and Nestorian), Druze 3%
note: the Christian population may be considerably smaller as a result of Christians fleeing the country during the ongoing civil war

Age structure: *0-14 years:* 33% (male 4,037,493/ female 3,828,777)
15-64 years: 62.8% (male 7,475,355/female 7,522,797)
65 years and over: 4.2% (2024 est.) (male 468,730/ female 532,271)

Dependency ratios: *total dependency ratio:* 55.4
youth dependency ratio: 53
elderly dependency ratio: 7.4
potential support ratio: 13.5 (2021 est.)

Median age: *total:* 24.1 years (2024 est.)
male: 23.6 years
female: 24.7 years
comparison ranking: total 178

Population growth rate: 1.67% (2024 est.)
comparison ranking: 56

Birth rate: 21.7 births/1,000 population (2024 est.)
comparison ranking: 57

Death rate: 4 deaths/1,000 population (2024 est.)
comparison ranking: 214

Net migration rate: -1.1 migrant(s)/1,000 population (2024 est.)
comparison ranking: 147

Population distribution: significant population density along the Mediterranean coast; larger concentrations found in the major cities of Damascus, Aleppo (the country's largest city), and Hims (Homs); more than half of the population lives in the coastal plain, the province of Halab, and the Euphrates River valley
note: the ongoing civil war has altered the population distribution

Urbanization: *urban population:* 57.4% of total population (2023)
rate of urbanization: 5.38% annual rate of change (2020-25 est.)

Major urban areas - population: 2.585 million DAMASCUS (capital), 2.203 million Aleppo, 1.443 million Hims (Homs), 996,000 Hamah (2023)

Sex ratio: *at birth:* 1.06 male(s)/female
0-14 years: 1.05 male(s)/female
15-64 years: 0.99 male(s)/female
65 years and over: 0.88 male(s)/female
total population: 1.01 male(s)/female (2024 est.)

Maternal mortality ratio: 30 deaths/100,000 live births (2020 est.)
comparison ranking: 111

Infant mortality rate: *total:* 15.1 deaths/1,000 live births (2024 est.)
male: 16.6 deaths/1,000 live births
female: 13.5 deaths/1,000 live births
comparison ranking: total 92

Life expectancy at birth: *total population:* 74.8 years (2024 est.)
male: 73.4 years
female: 76.4 years
comparison ranking: total population 137

Total fertility rate: 2.69 children born/woman (2024 est.)
comparison ranking: 60

Gross reproduction rate: 1.31 (2024 est.)

Drinking water source: *improved: urban:* 99.6% of population
rural: 100% of population
total: 99.8% of population
unimproved: urban: 0.4% of population
rural: 0.7% of population
total: 0.2% of population (2020 est.)

Physician density: 1.29 physicians/1,000 population (2016)

Hospital bed density: 1.4 beds/1,000 population (2017)

Sanitation facility access: *improved: urban:* 99.5% of population
rural: 99.5% of population
total: 99.5% of population
unimproved: urban: 0.5% of population
rural: 0.5% of population
total: 0.5% of population (2020 est.)

Obesity - adult prevalence rate: 27.8% (2016)
comparison ranking: 35

Alcohol consumption per capita: *total:* 0.13 liters of pure alcohol (2019 est.)
beer: 0.02 liters of pure alcohol (2019 est.)
wine: 0 liters of pure alcohol (2019 est.)
spirits: 0.11 liters of pure alcohol (2019 est.)
other alcohols: 0 liters of pure alcohol (2019 est.)
comparison ranking: total 176

Currently married women (ages 15-49): 52.6% (2023 est.)

Literacy: *definition:* age 15 and over can read and write

total population: 86.4%
male: 91.7%
female: 81% (2015)

School life expectancy (primary to tertiary education): *total:* 9 years
male: 9 years
female: 9 years (2013)

ENVIRONMENT

Environment - current issues: deforestation; overgrazing; soil erosion; desertification; depletion of water resources; water pollution from raw sewage and petroleum refining wastes; inadequate potable water

Environment - international agreements: *party to:* Biodiversity, Climate Change, Climate Change-Kyoto Protocol, Climate Change-Paris Agreement, Desertification, Endangered Species, Hazardous Wastes, Marine Dumping-London Convention, Nuclear Test Ban, Ozone Layer Protection, Ship Pollution, Wetlands
signed, but not ratified: Environmental Modification

Climate: mostly desert; hot, dry, sunny summers (June to August) and mild, rainy winters (December to February) along coast; cold weather with snow or sleet periodically in Damascus

Urbanization: *urban population:* 57.4% of total population (2023)
rate of urbanization: 5.38% annual rate of change (2020-25 est.)

Food insecurity: *exceptional shortfall in aggregate food production/supplies: due to civil conflict and economic crisis* -the latest available nationwide food security assessment estimated that about 12 million people, 60% of the overall population, were food insecure in 2021, a slight decline from 12.4 million in 2020, but 5 million more than at the end of 2019, mostly due to constrained livelihood opportunities and a rapidly worsening economy (2022)

Air pollutants: *particulate matter emissions:* 25.14 micrograms per cubic meter (2019 est.)
carbon dioxide emissions: 28.83 megatons (2016 est.)
methane emissions: 12.93 megatons (2020 est.)

Waste and recycling: *municipal solid waste generated annually:* 4.5 million tons (2009 est.)
municipal solid waste recycled annually: 112,500 tons (2010 est.)
percent of municipal solid waste recycled: 2.5% (2010 est.)

Major rivers (by length in km): Euphrates (shared with Turkey [s], Iran, and Iraq [m]) - 3,596 km; Tigris (shared with Turkey, Iran, and Iraq [m]) - 1,950 km
note – [s] after country name indicates river source; [m] after country name indicates river mouth

Major watersheds (area sq km): Indian Ocean drainage: *(Persian Gulf)* Tigris and Euphrates (918,044 sq km)

Total water withdrawal: *municipal:* 1.48 billion cubic meters (2020 est.)
industrial: 620 million cubic meters (2020 est.)
agricultural: 14.67 billion cubic meters (2020 est.)

Total renewable water resources: 16.8 billion cubic meters (2020 est.)

GOVERNMENT

Country name: *conventional long form:* Syrian Arab Republic
conventional short form: Syria
local long form: Al Jumhuriyah al Arabiyah as Suriyah
local short form: Suriyah
former: United Arab Republic (with Egypt)
etymology: name ultimately derived from the ancient Assyrians who dominated northern Mesopotamia, but whose reach also extended westward to the Levant; over time, the name came to be associated more with the western area

Government type: presidential republic; highly authoritarian regime

Capital: *name:* Damascus
geographic coordinates: 33 30 N, 36 18 E
time difference: UTC+3 (8 hours ahead of Washington, DC, during Standard Time)
etymology: Damascus is a very old city; its earliest name, Temeseq, first appears in an Egyptian geographical list of the 15th century B.C., but the meaning is uncertain

Administrative divisions: 14 provinces (muhafazat, singular - muhafazah); Al Hasakah, Al Ladhiqiyah (Latakia), Al Qunaytirah, Ar Raqqah, As Suwayda', Dar'a, Dayr az Zawr, Dimashq (Damascus), Halab (Aleppo), Hamah, Hims (Homs), Idlib, Rif Dimashq (Damascus Countryside), Tartus

Independence: 17 April 1946 (from League of Nations mandate under French administration)

National holiday: Independence Day (Evacuation Day), 17 April (1946); note - celebrates the leaving of the last French troops and the proclamation of full independence

Legal system: mixed legal system of civil and Islamic (sharia) law (for family courts)

Constitution: *history:*
several previous; latest issued 15 February 2012, passed by referendum and effective 27 February 2012; note – UN-sponsored talks, which began in late 2019 between delegates from government and opposition forces to draft a new constitution; in June 2022, the 8th round of the Syrian Constitutional Committee ended in Geneva with no results, and the 9th round, scheduled for July 2022, was cancelled due to lack of Russian and regime participation
amendments: proposed by the president of the republic or by one third of the People's Assembly members; following review by a special Assembly committee, passage requires at least three-quarters majority vote by the Assembly and approval by the president

International law organization participation: has not submitted an ICJ jurisdiction declaration; non-party state to the ICC

Citizenship: *citizenship by birth:* no
citizenship by descent only: the father must be a citizen of Syria; if the father is unknown or stateless, the mother must be a citizen of Syria
dual citizenship recognized: yes
residency requirement for naturalization: 10 years

Suffrage: 18 years of age; universal

Executive branch: *chief of state:* President Bashar al-ASAD (since 17 July 2000)
head of government: Prime Minister Hussein ARNOUS (since 30 August 2020)
cabinet: Council of Ministers appointed by the president
elections/appointments: president directly elected by simple majority popular vote for a 7-year term (eligible for a second term); election last held on 26 May 2021 (next to be held in 2028); the president appoints the vice president and prime minister
election results:
2021: Bashar al-ASAD elected president; percent of vote - Bashar al-ASAD (Ba'th Party) 95.2%, Mahmoud Ahmad MAREI (Democratic Arab Socialist Union) 3.3%, other 1.5%
2014: Bashar al-ASAD elected president; percent of vote - Bashar al-ASAD (Ba'th Party) 88.7%, Hassan al-NOURI (independent) 4.3%, Maher HAJJER (independent) 3.2%, other/invalid 3.8%

Legislative branch: *description:* unicameral People's Assembly or Majlis al-Shaab (250 seats; members directly elected in multi-seat constituencies by simple majority preferential vote to serve 4-year terms)
elections: last held on 15 July 2024 (next to be held in July 2028)
election results: percent of vote by party - NA; seats by party - Ba'ath Party 169, SSNP 3, other 13, independent 65; composition - NA

Judicial branch: *highest court(s):* Court of Cassation (organized into civil, criminal, religious, and military divisions, each with 3 judges); Supreme Constitutional Court (consists of 7 members)
judge selection and term of office: Court of Cassation judges appointed by the Supreme Judicial Council (SJC), a judicial management body headed by the minister of justice with 7 members, including the national president; judge tenure NA; Supreme Constitutional Court judges nominated by the president and appointed by the SJC; judges serve 4- year renewable terms
subordinate courts: courts of first instance; magistrates' courts; religious and military courts; Economic Security Court; Counterterrorism Court (established June 2012)

Political parties: *legal parties/alliances:*
Arab Socialist Ba'ath Party
Arab Socialist (Ba'ath) Party – Syrian Regional
Arab Socialist Ba'ath Party – Syrian Regional Branch, Socialist Unionist Democratic Party
Arab Socialist Union of Syria or ASU
Democratic Arab Socialist Union
National Progressive Front or NPF
Socialist Unionist Democratic Party
Socialist Unionist Party
Syrian Communist Party (two branches)
Syrian Social Nationalist Party or SSNP
Unionist Socialist Party
major political organizations:
Kurdish Democratic Union Party or PYD
Kurdish National Council or KNC
Syriac Union Party
Syrian Democratic Council or SDC
Syrian Democratic Party
Syrian Opposition Coalition
de facto governance entities:
Democratic Autonomous Administration of Northeast Syria or DAANES
Syrian Interim Government or SIG
Syrian Salvation Government or SSG

International organization participation: ABEDA, AFESD, AMF, CAEU, FAO, G-24, G-77, IAEA, IBRD, ICAO, ICC (national committees), ICRM, ICSID, IDA, IDB, IFAD, IFC, IFRCS, IHO, ILO, IMF, IMO, Interpol, IOC, IPU, ISO, ITSO, ITU, LAS, MIGA, NAM, OAPEC, OIC, OPCW, UN, UNCTAD, UNESCO, UNIDO, UNRWA, UNWTO, UPU, WBG, WCO, WFTU (NGOs), WHO, WIPO, WMO, WTO (observer)

Diplomatic representation in the US: none

Note: operations at the embassy were suspended on 18 March 2014

Diplomatic representation from the US: *chief of mission:* Ambassador (vacant); note - on 6 February 2012, the US suspended operations at its embassy in Damascus; Czechia serves as a protecting power for US interests in Syria
mailing address: 6110 Damascus Place, Washington DC 20521-6110
email address and website:
USIS_damascus@embassy.mzv.cz
https://sy.usembassy.gov/

Flag description: three equal horizontal bands of red (top), white, and black; two small, green, five-pointed stars in a horizontal line centered in the white band; the band colors derive from the Arab Liberation flag and represent oppression (black), overcome through bloody struggle (red), to be replaced by a bright future (white); identical to the former flag of the United Arab Republic (1958-1961) where the two stars represented the constituent states of Syria and Egypt; the current design dates to 1980
note: similar to the flag of Yemen, which has a plain white band; Iraq, which has an Arabic inscription centered in the white band; and that of Egypt, which has a gold Eagle of Saladin centered in the white band

National symbol(s): hawk; national colors: red, white, black, green

National anthem: *name:* "Humat ad-Diyar" (Guardians of the Homeland)
lyrics/music: Khalil Mardam BEY/Mohammad Salim FLAYFEL and Ahmad Salim FLAYFEL
note: adopted 1936, restored 1961; between 1958 and 1961, while Syria was a member of the United Arab Republic with Egypt, the country had a different anthem

National heritage: *total World Heritage Sites:* 6 (all cultural)
selected World Heritage Site locales: Ancient City of Damascus; Ancient City of Bosra; Site of Palmyra; Ancient City of Aleppo; Crac des Chevaliers and Qal'at Salah El-Din; Ancient Villages of Northern Syria

ECONOMY

Economic overview: low-income Middle Eastern economy; prior infrastructure and economy devastated by 11-year civil war; ongoing US sanctions; sporadic trans-migration during conflict; currently being supported by World Bank trust fund; ongoing hyperinflation

Real GDP (purchasing power parity): $62.151 billion (2021 est.)
$61.353 billion (2020 est.)
$61.465 billion (2019 est.)
note: data in 2021 dollars
comparison ranking: 114

Real GDP growth rate: 1.3% (2021 est.)
-0.18% (2020 est.)
1.22% (2019 est.)
note: annual GDP % growth based on constant local currency
comparison ranking: 157

Real GDP per capita: $2,900 (2021 est.)
$3,000 (2020 est.)
$3,100 (2019 est.)
note: data in 2021 dollars
comparison ranking: 197

GDP (official exchange rate): $8.98 billion (2021 est.)
note: data in current dollars at official exchange rate

Inflation rate (consumer prices): 28.1% (2017 est.)
47.3% (2016 est.)
comparison ranking: 204

GDP - composition, by sector of origin: *agriculture:* 27.8% (2021 est.)
industry: 28.9% (2021 est.)
services: 43.3% (2021 est.)
note: figures may not total 100% due to non-allocated consumption not captured in sector-reported data
comparison rankings: services 177; industry 74; agriculture 14

GDP - composition, by end use: *household consumption:* 128.6% (2021 est.)
government consumption: 10.9% (2021 est.)
investment in fixed capital: 8.7% (2021 est.)
exports of goods and services: 24.8% (2021 est.)
imports of goods and services: -73.1% (2021 est.)
note: figures may not total 100% due to rounding or gaps in data collection

Agricultural products: wheat, milk, olives, sheep milk, tomatoes, potatoes, maize, watermelons, apples, oranges (2022)
note: top ten agricultural products based on tonnage

Industries: petroleum, textiles, food processing, beverages, tobacco, phosphate rock mining, cement, oil seeds crushing, automobile assembly

Industrial production growth rate: -14.03% (2021 est.)
note: annual % change in industrial value added based on constant local currency
comparison ranking: 215

Labor force: 6.315 million (2023 est.)
note: number of people ages 15 or older who are employed or seeking work
comparison ranking: 72

Unemployment rate: 13.54% (2023 est.)
13.81% (2022 est.)
14.8% (2021 est.)
note: % of labor force seeking employment
comparison ranking: 184

Youth unemployment rate (ages 15-24): *total:* 33.5% (2023 est.)
male: 29.8% (2023 est.)
female: 52.6% (2023 est.)
note: % of labor force ages 15-24 seeking employment
comparison ranking: total 19

Population below poverty line: 82.5% (2014 est.)

Gini Index coefficient - distribution of family income: 26.6 (2022 est.)
comparison ranking: 143

Household income or consumption by percentage share: *lowest 10%:* 3.8% (2022 est.)
highest 10%: 21.1% (2022 est.)

Remittances: 0% of GDP (2021 est.)
0% of GDP (2020 est.)
0% of GDP (2019 est.)
note: personal transfers and compensation between resident and non-resident individuals/households/entities

Budget: *revenues:* $1.162 billion (2017 est.)
expenditures: $3.211 billion (2017 est.)
note: government projections for FY2016

Public debt: 94.8% of GDP (2017 est.)
comparison ranking: 25

Taxes and other revenues: 4.2% (of GDP) (2017 est.)
comparison ranking: 203

Current account balance: -$2.123 billion (2017 est.)
-$2.077 billion (2016 est.)
comparison ranking: 162

Exports: $2.224 billion (2021 est.)
$1.649 billion (2020 est.)
$2.94 billion (2019 est.)
note: GDP expenditure basis - exports of goods and services in current dollars
comparison ranking: 162

Exports - partners: Turkey 29%, Kuwait 15%, Lebanon 14%, Jordan 8%, Egypt 7% (2022)
note: top five export partners based on percentage share of exports

Exports - commodities: pure olive oil, nuts, phosphates, cotton, garments (2022)
note: top five export commodities based on value in dollars

Imports: $6.553 billion (2021 est.)
$3.751 billion (2020 est.)
$6.552 billion (2019 est.)
note: GDP expenditure basis - imports of goods and services in current dollars
comparison ranking: 138

Imports - partners: Turkey 45%, UAE 10%, China 9%, Lebanon 8%, Egypt 7% (2022)
note: top five import partners based on percentage share of imports

Imports - commodities: tobacco, plastics, wheat, seed oils, plastic products (2022)
note: top five import commodities based on value in dollars

Reserves of foreign exchange and gold: $407.3 million (31 December 2017 est.)
$504.6 million (31 December 2016 est.)
comparison ranking: 167

Debt - external: $3.619 billion (2022 est.)
note: present value of external debt in current US dollars
comparison ranking: 60

Exchange rates: Syrian pounds (SYP) per US dollar -

Exchange rates: 2,505.747 (2022 est.)
1,256 (2021 est.)
877.945 (2020 est.)
436.5 (2019 est.)
436.5 (2018 est.)

ENERGY

Electricity access: *electrification - total population:* 89% (2022 est.)
electrification - urban areas: 100%
electrification - rural areas: 75%

Electricity: *installed generating capacity:* 10.124 million kW (2022 est.)
consumption: 12.909 billion kWh (2022 est.)
exports: 346 million kWh (2022 est.)
transmission/distribution losses: 3.618 billion kWh (2022 est.)
comparison rankings: transmission/distribution losses 150; exports 84; consumption 92; installed generating capacity 67

Electricity generation sources: *fossil fuels:* 95.3% of total installed capacity (2022 est.)
hydroelectricity: 4.5% of total installed capacity (2022 est.)
biomass and waste: 0.2% of total installed capacity (2022 est.)

Coal: *consumption:* 47,000 metric tons (2022 est.)
exports: (2022 est.) less than 1 metric ton
imports: 30,000 metric tons (2022 est.)

Petroleum: *total petroleum production:* 100,000 bbl/day (2023 est.)
refined petroleum consumption: 138,000 bbl/day (2022 est.)
crude oil estimated reserves: 2.5 billion barrels (2021 est.)

Natural gas: *production:* 3.085 billion cubic meters (2022 est.)
consumption: 3.084 billion cubic meters (2022 est.)
proven reserves: 240.693 billion cubic meters (2021 est.)

Carbon dioxide emissions: 25.628 million metric tonnes of CO2 (2022 est.)
from coal and metallurgical coke: 100,000 metric tonnes of CO2 (2022 est.)
from petroleum and other liquids: 19.478 million metric tonnes of CO2 (2022 est.)
from consumed natural gas: 6.05 million metric tonnes of CO2 (2022 est.)
comparison ranking: total emissions 79

Energy consumption per capita: 18.111 million Btu/person (2022 est.)
comparison ranking: 131

COMMUNICATIONS

Telephones - fixed lines: *total subscriptions:* 2.821 million (2021 est.)
subscriptions per 100 inhabitants: 13 (2021 est.)
comparison ranking: total subscriptions 42

Telephones - mobile cellular: *total subscriptions:* 16.991 million (2021 est.)
subscriptions per 100 inhabitants: 80 (2021 est.)
comparison ranking: total subscriptions 68

Telecommunication systems: *general assessment:* the years of civil war and destruction to infrastructure continue to have a toll on the telecoms sector in Syria; although over the years the major mobile service providers have endeavored to restore and rebuild damaged networks, the operating environment has been difficult; following disputed demands for back taxes, MTN Group in August 2021 exited the country, after its majority stake had been transferred to judicial guardianship; this effectively meant that the mobile market became a monopoly; in February 2022 the regulator awarded a third mobile license following a process which had been ongoing for many years; telecommunication services in Syria are highly regulated; although urban areas can make use of the network built and maintained by the government-owned incumbent, many under served remote areas in the countryside are obliged to rely on satellite communications; the domestic and international fixed-line markets in Syria remain the monopoly of the STE, despite several initiatives over the years aimed at liberalizing the market; mobile broadband penetration in Syria is still quite low, despite quite a high population coverage of 3G networks and some deployment of LTE infrastructure; this may provide potential opportunities for growth once infrastructure and economic reconstruction efforts make headway, and civil issues subside (2022)
domestic: the number of fixed-line connections is 13 per 100; mobile-cellular service is 80 per 100 persons (2021)
international: country code - 963; landing points for the Aletar, BERYTAR and UGART submarine cable connections to Egypt, Lebanon, and Cyprus; satellite earth stations - 1 Intelsat (Indian Ocean) and 1 Intersputnik (Atlantic Ocean region); coaxial cable and microwave radio relay to Iraq, Jordan, Lebanon, and Turkey; participant in Medarabtel (2019)

Broadcast media: state-run TV and radio broadcast networks; state operates 2 TV networks and 5 satellite channels; roughly two-thirds of Syrian homes have a satellite dish providing access to foreign TV broadcasts; 3 state-run radio channels; first private radio station launched in 2005; private radio broadcasters prohibited from transmitting news or political content (2018)

Internet country code: .sy

Internet users: *total:* 8,492,468 (2022 est.)
percent of population: 46.6% (2022 est.)
comparison ranking: total 69

Broadband - fixed subscriptions: *total:* 1,549,356 (2020 est.)
subscriptions per 100 inhabitants: 9 (2020 est.)
comparison ranking: total 64

TRANSPORTATION

National air transport system: *number of registered air carriers:* 3 (2020)
inventory of registered aircraft operated by air carriers: 11
annual passenger traffic on registered air carriers: 17,896 (2018)
annual freight traffic on registered air carriers: 30,000 (2018) mt-km

Civil aircraft registration country code prefix: YK

Airports: 39 (2024)
comparison ranking: 103

Heliports: 12 (2024)

Pipelines: 3,170 km gas, 2029 km oil (2013)

Railways: *total:* 2,052 km (2014)
standard gauge: 1,801 km (2014) 1.435-m gauge
narrow gauge: 251 km (2014) 1.050-m gauge
comparison ranking: total 73

Roadways: *total:* 69,873 km
paved: 63,060 km
unpaved: 6,813 km (2010)
comparison ranking: total 71

Waterways: 900 km (2011) (navigable but not economically significant)
comparison ranking: 75

Merchant marine: *total:* 24 (2023)
by type: bulk carrier 1, container ship 1, general cargo 8, oil tanker 1, other 13
comparison ranking: total 144

Ports: *total ports:* 3 (2024)
large: 1
medium: 1
small: 1
very small: 0
ports with oil terminals: 3
key ports: Al Ladhiqiyah, Baniyas, Tartus

MILITARY AND SECURITY

Military and security forces: Syrian Armed Forces: Syrian Arab Army (includes Republican Guard), Syrian Naval Forces, Syrian Air Forces, Syrian Air Defense Forces, National Defense Forces (NDF), and Local Defense Forces (LDF) (2023)
note: NDF and LDF are pro-government militia and auxiliary forces; some militia and auxiliary forces are backed by Iran; the Syrian military is also supported by the Russian armed forces, the Iran-affiliated Hizballah terrorist group, and Iran's Islamic Revolutionary Guard Corps

Military expenditures: 6.5% of GDP (2019 est.)
6.7% of GDP (2018 est.)
6.8% of GDP (2017 est.)
6.9% of GDP (2016 est.)
7.2% of GDP (2015 est.)
comparison ranking: 4

Military and security service personnel strengths: current estimates not available; the Syrian Armed Forces (SAF) continue to rebuild after suffering significant casualties and desertions since the start of the civil war in 2011; prior to the civil war, the SAF had approximately 300,000 troops, including 200-225,000 Army, plus about 300,000 reserve forces (2023)
note: pro-government militia and auxiliary forces probably number in the tens of thousands

Military equipment inventories and acquisitions: the SAF's inventory is comprised mostly of Russian and Soviet-era equipment (2024)

Military service age and obligation: men 18-42 are obligated to perform military service; compulsory service obligation reportedly up to 30 months; women are not conscripted but may volunteer to serve, including in combat arms (2023)
note 1: the military is comprised largely of conscripts; men in their late 40s and 50s reportedly have been drafted into military service during the civil war
note 2: Syrian women have been serving in combat roles since 2013; in 2015, the Syrian military created an all-female commando brigade

Military - note: the UN Disengagement Observer Force (UNDOF) has operated in the Golan between Israel and Syria since 1974 to monitor the ceasefire following the 1973 Arab-Israeli War and supervise the areas of separation between the two countries; UNDOF has about 1,000 personnel
multiple actors have conducted military operations in Syria in support of the ASAD government or Syrian opposition forces, as well in pursuit of their own security goals, such as counterterrorism and border security; operations have included air strikes, direct ground combat, and sponsoring proxy forces, as well as providing non-lethal military support, including advisors, technicians, arms and equipment, funding, intelligence, and training:
pro-ASAD elements operating in Syria have included the Syrian Arab Army, Lebanese Hizballah, the Iranian military, Iranian-backed Shia militia, and Russian forces; since early in the civil war, the ASAD government has used Lebanese Hizballah and Iranian-backed irregular forces for combat operations and to hold territory; since 2011, Iran has provided military advisors and combat troops from the Iranian Revolutionary Guard Corps (IRGC), as well as intelligence, logistical, material, technical, and financial support; it has funded, trained, equipped, and led Shia militia/paramilitary units comprised of both Syrian and non-Syrian personnel, primarily from Afghanistan, Iraq, and Pakistan; Russia intervened at the request of the ASAD government in 2015 and has since provided air support, special operations forces, military advisors, private military contractors, training, arms, and equipment; Iranian and Russian support has also included assisting Syria in combating the Islamic State of Iraq and ash-Sham (ISIS) terrorist group

Turkey has intervened militarily several times since 2016 to combat Kurdish militants and ISIS, support select Syrian opposition forces, and establish a buffer along portions of its border with Syria; Turkey continues to maintain a considerable military presence in northern Syria; it has armed and trained militia/proxy forces, such as the Syrian National Army, which was formed in late 2017 of Syrian Arab and Turkmen rebel factions in the Halab (Aleppo) province and northwestern Syria

the US and some regional and European states have at times backed Syrian opposition forces militarily and/or conducted military operations, primarily against ISIS; the US has operated in Syria since 2015 with ground forces and air strikes; the majority the US ground forces are deployed in the Eastern Syria Security Area (ESSA, which includes parts of Hasakah and Dayr az Zawr provinces east of the Euphrates River) in support of operations by the Syrian Democratic Forces against ISIS, while the remainder are in southeast Syria around At Tanf supporting counter-ISIS operations by the Syrian Free Army opposition force; the US has also conducted air strikes against Syrian military targets in response to Syrian Government use of chemical weapons against opposition forces and civilians, and since October 2023, against facilities in eastern Syria associated with Iran's IRGC and affiliated militias in response to attacks by Iran-backed militias on US forces in Syria and Iraq; in addition, France, Jordan, Qatar, Saudi Arabia, and the UK have provided forms of military assistance to opposition forces and/or conducted operations against ISIS, including air strikes

Israel has conducted hundreds of military air strikes in Syria against Syrian military, Hizballah, Iranian military, and Iranian-backed militia targets

the Syrian Democratic Forces (SDF), a coalition of forces comprised primarily of Kurdish, Sunni Arab, and Syriac Christian fighters; it is dominated and led by Kurdish forces, particularly the People's Protection Units (YPG) militia; the SDF began to receive US support in 2015 and as of 2024 was the main local US partner in its counter-ISIS campaign; the SDF has internal security, counterterrorism, and commando units; Turkey views the SDF as an extension of the Kurdistan Workers' Party (PKK), a US-designated terrorist organization

the ISIS terrorist group lost its last territorial stronghold to SDF forces in 2019, but continues to maintain a low-level insurgency inside Syria; in addition, the SDF holds about 10,000 captured suspected ISIS fighters in detention facilities across northern Syria, including 2,000 from countries other than Iraq and Syria

the Hay'at Tahrir al-Sham (HTS; formerly known as al-Nusrah Front) terrorist organization is the dominant militant group in northwest Syria and has asserted considerable influence and control over the so-called Syrian Salvation Government in the Iblib de-escalation zone and the Aleppo province (2024)

SPACE

Space agency/agencies: Syrian Space Agency (created in 2014); General Organization of Remote Sensing (GORS; established 1986 to replace the National Remote Sensing Center, established 1981) (2024)

Space program overview: status unclear; has been handicapped by the impact of the civil war, including the loss of students and scientists who fled the country; had previously focused on satellite development and related space technologies, as well as scientific research; has relations with the space agency and space industries of Russia (2024)

note: further details about the key activities, programs, and milestones of the country's space program, as well as government spending estimates on the space sector, appear in the Space Programs reference guide

TERRORISM

Terrorist group(s): Abdallah Azzam Brigades; Ansar al-Islam; Asa'ib Ahl Al-Haq; Hizballah; Hurras al-Din; Islamic Jihad Union; Islamic Revolutionary Guard Corps (IRGC)/Qods Force; Islamic State of Iraq and ash-Sham (ISIS); Kata'ib Hizballah; Kurdistan Workers' Party (PKK); Mujahidin Shura Council in the Environs of Jerusalem; al-Nusrah Front (Hay'at Tahrir al-Sham); al-Qa'ida; Palestine Liberation Front; Popular Front for the Liberation of Palestine (PFLP); PFLP-General Command

note: details about the history, aims, leadership, organization, areas of operation, tactics, targets, weapons, size, and sources of support of the group(s) appear(s) in the Terrorism reference guide

TRANSNATIONAL ISSUES

Refugees and internally displaced persons: *refugees (country of origin):* 580,000 (Palestinian Refugees) (2022); 11,121 (Iraq) (2023)

IDPs: 6.865 million (ongoing civil war since 2011) (2022)

stateless persons: 160,000 (2022); note - Syria's stateless population consists of Kurds and Palestinians; stateless persons are prevented from voting, owning land, holding certain jobs, receiving food subsidies or public healthcare, enrolling in public schools, or being legally married to Syrian citizens; in 1962, some 120,000 Syrian Kurds were stripped of their Syrian citizenship, rendering them and their descendants stateless; in 2011, the Syrian Government granted citizenship to thousands of Syrian Kurds as a means of appeasement; however, resolving the question of statelessness is not a priority given Syria's ongoing civil war

note: the ongoing civil war has resulted in more than 5 million registered Syrian refugees - dispersed mainly in Egypt, Iraq, Jordan, Lebanon, and Turkey - as of March 2024

Trafficking in persons: tier rating: Tier 3 — Syria does not fully meet the minimum standards for the elimination of trafficking and is not making significant efforts to do so, therefore, Syria remained on Tier 3; for more details, go to: https://www.state.gov/reports/2024-trafficking-in-persons-report/syria/

Illicit drugs: increasing drug trafficking particularly the synthetic stimulant captagon, a mixture of various amphetamines, methamphetamine, and/or other stimulants; drug smuggling of captagon and other stimulants linked to the Syrian government and Hizballah

T

TAIWAN

INTRODUCTION

Background: First inhabited by Austronesian people, Taiwan became home to Han immigrants beginning in the late Ming Dynasty (17th century). In 1895, military defeat forced China's Qing Dynasty to cede Taiwan to Japan, which then governed Taiwan for 50 years. Taiwan came under Chinese Nationalist (Kuomintang, KMT) control after World War II. With the communist victory in the Chinese civil war in 1949, the Nationalist-controlled Republic of China government and 2 million Nationalists fled to Taiwan and continued to claim to be the legitimate government for mainland China and Taiwan, based on a 1947 constitution drawn up for all of China. Until 1987, however, the Nationalist Government ruled Taiwan under a civil war martial law declaration dating to 1948. Beginning in the 1970s, Nationalist authorities gradually began to incorporate the native population into the governing structure beyond the local level.

The democratization process expanded rapidly in the 1980s, leading to the then-illegal founding of the Democratic Progressive Party (DPP), Taiwan's first opposition party, in 1986 and the lifting of martial law the following year. Taiwan held legislative elections in 1992, the first in over 40 years, and its first direct presidential election in 1996. In the 2000 presidential elections, Taiwan underwent its first peaceful transfer of power with the KMT loss to the DPP and afterwards experienced two additional democratic transfers of power in 2008 and 2016. Throughout this period, the island prospered and turned into one of East Asia's economic "Tigers," becoming a major investor in mainland China after 2000 as cross-Strait ties matured. The dominant political issues continue to be economic reform and growth, as well as management of sensitive relations between Taiwan and China.

GEOGRAPHY

Location: Eastern Asia, islands bordering the East China Sea, Philippine Sea, South China Sea, and Taiwan Strait, north of the Philippines, off the southeastern coast of China

Geographic coordinates: 23 30 N, 121 00 E

Map references: Southeast Asia

Area: *total:* 35,980 sq km
land: 32,260 sq km
water: 3,720 sq km
note: includes the Pescadores, Matsu, and Kinmen islands
comparison ranking: total 138

Area - comparative: slightly smaller than Maryland and Delaware combined

Land boundaries: *total:* 0 km

Coastline: 1,566.3 km

Maritime claims: *territorial sea:* 12 nm
exclusive economic zone: 200 nm

Climate: tropical; marine; rainy season during southwest monsoon (June to August); persistent and extensive cloudiness all year

Terrain: eastern two-thirds mostly rugged mountains; flat to gently rolling plains in west

Elevation: *highest point:* Yu Shan 3,952 m
lowest point: South China Sea 0 m
mean elevation: 1,150 m

Natural resources: small deposits of coal, natural gas, limestone, marble, asbestos, arable land

Land use: *agricultural land:* 22.7% (2018 est.)
arable land: 16.9% (2018 est.)
permanent crops: 5.8% (2018 est.)
other: 77.3% (2018 est.)

Irrigated land: 3,820 sq km (2012)

Population distribution: distribution exhibits a peripheral coastal settlement pattern, with the largest populations on the north and west coasts

Natural hazards: earthquakes; typhoons
volcanism: Kueishantao Island (401 m), east of Taiwan, is its only historically active volcano, although it has not erupted in centuries

Geography - note: strategic location adjacent to both the Taiwan Strait and the Luzon Strait

PEOPLE AND SOCIETY

Population: *total:* 23,595,274
male: 11,606,491
female: 11,988,783 (2024 est.)
comparison rankings: female 57; male 58; total 58

Nationality: *noun:* Taiwan (singular and plural)
adjective: Taiwan (or Taiwanese)
note: example - he or she is from Taiwan; they are from Taiwan

Ethnic groups: Han Chinese (including Holo, who compose approximately 70% of Taiwan's population, Hakka, and other groups originating in mainland China) more than 95%, indigenous Malayo-Polynesian peoples 2.3%
note 1: there are 16 officially recognized indigenous groups: Amis, Atayal, Bunun, Hla'alua, Kanakaravu, Kavalan, Paiwan, Puyuma, Rukai, Saisiyat, Sakizaya, Seediq, Thao, Truku, Tsou, and Yami; Amis, Paiwan, and Atayal are the largest and account for roughly 70% of the indigenous population
note 2: although not definitive, the majority of current genetic, archeological, and linguistic data support the theory that Taiwan is the ultimate source for the spread of humans across the Pacific to Polynesia; the expansion (ca. 3000 B.C. to A.D. 1200) took place via the Philippines and eastern Indonesia and reached Fiji and Tonga by about 900 B.C.; from there voyagers spread across the rest of the Pacific islands over the next two millennia

Languages: Mandarin (official), Min Nan, Hakka dialects, approximately 16 indigenous languages
major-language sample(s):
世界概況 – 不可缺少的基本消息來源 (Mandarin)

Religions: Buddhist 35.3%, Taoist 33.2%, Christian 3.9%, folk religion (includes Confucian) approximately 10%, none or unspecified 18.2% (2005 est.)

Age structure: *0-14 years:* 12.1% (male 1,472,059/female 1,391,031)
15-64 years: 69% (male 8,132,356/female 8,155,582)
65 years and over: 18.8% (2024 est.) (male 2,002,076/female 2,442,170)

Dependency ratios: *total dependency ratio:* 40.2
youth dependency ratio: 17.8
elderly dependency ratio: 22.4
potential support ratio: 4.5 (2021 est.)

Median age: *total:* 44.6 years (2024 est.)
male: 43.6 years
female: 45.5 years
comparison ranking: total 29

Population growth rate: 0.03% (2024 est.)
comparison ranking: 191

Birth rate: 7.3 births/1,000 population (2024 est.)
comparison ranking: 220

Death rate: 8.1 deaths/1,000 population (2024 est.)
comparison ranking: 88

Net migration rate: 1.1 migrant(s)/1,000 population (2024 est.)
comparison ranking: 66

Population distribution: distribution exhibits a peripheral coastal settlement pattern, with the largest populations on the north and west coasts

Urbanization: *urban population:* 80.1% of total population (2023)
rate of urbanization: 0.65% annual rate of change (2020-25 est.)

Major urban areas - population: 4.504 million New Taipei City, 2.754 million TAIPEI (capital), 2.319 million Taoyuan, 1.553 million Kaohsiung, 1.369 million Taichung, 863,000 Tainan (2023)

Sex ratio: *at birth:* 1.06 male(s)/female
0-14 years: 1.06 male(s)/female
15-64 years: 1 male(s)/female
65 years and over: 0.82 male(s)/female
total population: 0.97 male(s)/female (2024 est.)

Infant mortality rate: *total:* 3.8 deaths/1,000 live births (2024 est.)
male: 4.2 deaths/1,000 live births
female: 3.5 deaths/1,000 live births
comparison ranking: total 191

Life expectancy at birth: *total population:* 81.6 years (2024 est.)
male: 78.6 years
female: 84.7 years
comparison ranking: total population 43

Total fertility rate: 1.11 children born/woman (2024 est.)
comparison ranking: 227

Gross reproduction rate: 0.54 (2024 est.)

Contraceptive prevalence rate: 75.2% (2016)
note: percent of women aged 20-52

Currently married women (ages 15-49): 51% (2023 est.)

Literacy: *definition:* age 15 and over can read and write
total population: 98.5%
male: 99.7%
female: 97.3% (2014)

ENVIRONMENT

Environment - current issues: air pollution; water pollution from industrial emissions, raw sewage; contamination of drinking water supplies; trade in endangered species; low-level radioactive waste disposal

Climate: tropical; marine; rainy season during southwest monsoon (June to August); persistent and extensive cloudiness all year

Urbanization: *urban population:* 80.1% of total population (2023)
rate of urbanization: 0.65% annual rate of change (2020-25 est.)

Waste and recycling: *municipal solid waste generated annually:* 7.336 million tons (2015 est.)

Total renewable water resources: 67 cubic meters (2011)

GOVERNMENT

Country name: *conventional long form:* none
conventional short form: Taiwan
local long form: none
local short form: Taiwan
former: Formosa
etymology: "Tayowan" was the name of the coastal sandbank where the Dutch erected their colonial headquarters on the island in the 17th century; the former name "Formosa" means "beautiful" in Portuguese

Government type: semi-presidential republic

Capital: *name:* Taipei
geographic coordinates: 25 02 N, 121 31 E
time difference: UTC+8 (13 hours ahead of Washington, DC, during Standard Time)
etymology: the Chinese meaning is "Northern Taiwan," reflecting the city's position in the far north of the island

Administrative divisions: includes main island of Taiwan plus smaller islands nearby and off coast of China's Fujian Province; Taiwan is divided into 13 counties (xian, singular and plural), 3 cities (shi, singular and plural), and 6 special municipalities directly under the jurisdiction of the Executive Yuan
counties: Changhua, Chiayi, Hsinchu, Hualien, Kinmen, Lienchiang, Miaoli, Nantou, Penghu, Pingtung, Taitung, Yilan, Yunlin
cities: Chiayi, Hsinchu, Keelung
special municipalities: Kaohsiung (city), New Taipei (city), Taichung (city), Tainan (city), Taipei (city), Taoyuan (city)
note: Taiwan uses a variety of romanization systems; while a modified Wade-Giles system still dominates, the city of Taipei has adopted a Pinyin romanization for street and place names within its boundaries; other local authorities use different romanization systems

National holiday: Republic Day (National Day), 10 October (1911); note - celebrates the anniversary of the Chinese Revolution, also known as Double Ten (10-10) Day

Legal system: civil law system

Constitution: *history:* previous 1912, 1931; latest adopted 25 December 1946, promulgated 1 January 1947, effective 25 December 1947
amendments: proposed by at least one fourth of the Legislative Yuan membership; passage requires approval by at least three-fourths majority vote of at least three fourths of the Legislative Yuan membership and approval in a referendum by more than half of eligible voters; revised several times, last in 2005

International law organization participation: has not submitted an ICJ jurisdiction declaration; non-party state to the ICCt

Citizenship: *citizenship by birth:* no
citizenship by descent only: at least one parent must be a citizen of Taiwan
dual citizenship recognized: yes, except that citizens of Taiwan are not recognized as dual citizens of the People's Republic of China
residency requirement for naturalization: 5 years

Suffrage: 20 years of age; universal; note - in March 2022, the Legislative Yuan approved lowering the voting age to 18, but the change will require a constitutional amendment that must be submitted to a referendum

Executive branch: *chief of state:* President LAI Ching-te (since 19 May 2024)
head of government: Premier CHO Jung-tai (President of the Executive Yuan) (since 20 May 2024)
cabinet: Executive Yuan - ministers appointed by president on recommendation of premier
elections/appointments: president and vice president directly elected on the same ballot by simple majority popular vote for a 4-year term (eligible for a second term); election last held on 13 January 2024 (next to be held in 2028); premier appointed by the president; vice premiers appointed by the president on the recommendation of the premier
election results:
2023: LAI Ching-te elected president; percent of vote - LAI Ching-te (DPP) 40.1%, HOU Yu-ih (KMT) 33.5%, KO Wen-je (TPP) 26.5%; note - LAI takes office on 20 May 2024
2020: TSAI Ing-wen reelected president; percent of vote - TSAI Ing-wen (DPP) 57.1%, HAN Kuo-yu (KMT) 38.6%, James SOONG (PFP) 4.3%; note - TSAI is the first woman elected president of Taiwan

Legislative branch: *description:* unicameral Legislative Yuan (113 seats; 73 members directly elected in single-seat constituencies by simple majority vote, 34 directly elected in a single island-wide constituency by proportional representation vote, and 6 directly elected in multi-seat aboriginal constituencies by proportional representation vote; members serve 4-year terms)
elections: last held on 13 January 2024 (next to be held in 2028)
election results: percent of vote by party - DPP 40.6%, KMT 37.2%, TPP 12.6%, other 5.7%, independent 3.9%; seats by party - KMT 52, DPP 51, TPP 8, independent 2; composition - men 66, women 47, percentage women 41.6%

Judicial branch: *highest court(s):* Supreme Court (consists of the court president, vice president, and approximately 100 judges organized into civil and criminal panels, each with a chief justice and 4 associate justices); Constitutional Court (consists of the court president, vice president, and 13 justices)
judge selection and term of office: Supreme Court justices appointed by the president; Constitutional Court justices appointed by the president, with approval of the Legislative Yuan; Supreme Court justices serve for life; Constitutional Court justices appointed for 8-year terms, with half the membership renewed every 4 years
subordinate courts: high courts; district courts; hierarchy of administrative courts

Political parties: Democratic Progressive Party or DPP
Kuomintang or KMT (Nationalist Party)
Taiwan People's Party or TPP
note: the DPP and the KMT are the two major political parties; more than 30 parties garnered votes in the 2024 election

International organization participation: ADB (Chinese Taipei), APEC (Chinese Taipei), BCIE, CABEI, IOC, ITUC (NGOs), SICA (observer), WTO (Chinese Taipei)
note - separate customs territory of Taiwan, Penghu, Kinmen, and Matsu

Diplomatic representation in the US: *chief of mission:* none

Taipei Economic and Cultural Offices (branch offices): Atlanta, Boston, Chicago, Denver (CO), Hagatna (Guam), Honolulu, Houston, Los Angeles, Miami, New York, San Francisco, Seattle, Washington DC

Note: *commercial and cultural relations with its citizens in the US are maintained through an unofficial instrumentality, the Taipei Economic and Cultural Representative Office in the United States (TECRO), a private nonprofit corporation that performs citizen and consular services similar to those at diplomatic posts, represented by Ambassador Alexander YUI (since 11 December 2023); office:* 4201 Wisconsin Avenue NW, Washington, DC 20016; telephone: [1] (202) 895-1800; fax: [1] (202) 363-0999

Diplomatic representation from the US: *chief of mission:* the US does not have an embassy in Taiwan; commercial and cultural relations with the people of Taiwan are maintained through an unofficial instrumentality, the American Institute in Taiwan (AIT), a private nonprofit corporation that performs citizen and consular services similar to those at diplomatic posts; it is managed by Director Sandra OUDKIRK (since July 2021)
mailing address: 4170 AIT Taipei Place, Washington DC 20521-4170
telephone: [886] 2-2162-2000
FAX: [886] 2-2162-2251
email address and website: TaipeiACS@state.gov
https://www.ait.org.tw/
branch office(s): American Institute in Taiwan
No. 100, Jinhu Road,
Neihu District 11461, Taipei City
other offices: Kaohsiung (Branch Office)

Flag description: red field with a dark blue rectangle in the upper hoist-side corner bearing a white sun with 12 triangular rays; the blue and white design of the canton (symbolizing the sun of progress) dates to 1895; it was later adopted as the flag of the Kuomintang Party; blue signifies liberty, justice, and democracy, red stands for fraternity, sacrifice, and nationalism, and white represents equality, frankness, and the people's livelihood; the 12 rays of the sun are those of the months and the twelve traditional Chinese hours (each ray equals two hours)
note: similar to the flag of Samoa

National symbol(s): white, 12-rayed sun on blue field; national colors: blue, white, red

National anthem: *name:* "Zhonghua Minguo guoge" (National Anthem of the Republic of China)
lyrics/music: HU Han-min, TAI Chi-t'ao, and LIAO Chung-k'ai/CHENG Mao-yun
note: adopted 1930; also the song of the Kuomintang Party; it is informally known as "San Min Chu I" or "San Min Zhu Yi" (Three Principles of the People); because of political pressure from China, "Guo Qi Ge" (National Banner Song) is used at international events rather than the official anthem of Taiwan; the "National Banner Song" has gained popularity in Taiwan and is commonly used during flag raisings

ECONOMY

Economic overview: high-income East Asian economy; most technologically advanced computer microchip manufacturing; increasing Chinese interference threatens market capabilities; minimum wages rising; longstanding regional socioeconomic inequality

Real GDP (purchasing power parity): $1.143 trillion (2019 est.)
$1.113 trillion (2018 est.)
$1.083 trillion (2017 est.)
note: data are in 2010 dollars
comparison ranking: 30

Real GDP growth rate: 2.71% (2019 est.)
2.75% (2018 est.)
3.31% (2017 est.)
comparison ranking: 116

Real GDP per capita: $47,800 (2019 est.)
$46,600 (2018 est.)
$45,400 (2017 est.)
note: data are in 2017 dollars
comparison ranking: 47

GDP (official exchange rate): $611.391 billion (2019 est.)

Inflation rate (consumer prices): 0.5% (2019 est.)
1.3% (2018 est.)
0.6% (2017 est.)
comparison ranking: 12

Credit ratings: Fitch rating: AA- (2016)

Moody's rating: Aa3 (1994)

Standard & Poors rating: AA- (2002)
note: The year refers to the year in which the current credit rating was first obtained.

GDP - composition, by sector of origin: *agriculture:* 1.8% (2017 est.)
industry: 36% (2017 est.)
services: 62.1% (2017 est.)
comparison rankings: services 76; industry 42; agriculture 165

GDP - composition, by end use: *household consumption:* 53% (2017 est.)
government consumption: 14.1% (2017 est.)
investment in fixed capital: 20.5% (2017 est.)
investment in inventories: -0.2% (2017 est.)
exports of goods and services: 65.2% (2017 est.)
imports of goods and services: -52.6% (2017 est.)

Agricultural products: rice, vegetables, pork, chicken, cabbages, sugarcane, milk, eggs, tropical fruits, pineapples (2022)
note: top ten agricultural products based on tonnage

Industries: electronics, communications and information technology products, petroleum refining, chemicals, textiles, iron and steel, machinery, cement, food processing, vehicles, consumer products, pharmaceuticals

Industrial production growth rate: 3.9% (2017 est.)
comparison ranking: 80

Labor force: 11.498 million (2020 est.)
comparison ranking: 52

Unemployment rate: 3.73% (2019 est.)
3.69% (2018 est.)
comparison ranking: 71

Gini Index coefficient - distribution of family income: 33.6 (2014)
comparison ranking: 96

Average household expenditures: *on food:* 14.2% of household expenditures (2022 est.)
on alcohol and tobacco: 2.4% of household expenditures (2022 est.)

Budget: *revenues:* $94.943 billion (2019 est.)
expenditures: $105.833 billion (2019 est.)

Public debt: 35.7% of GDP (2017 est.)
note: data for central government
comparison ranking: 149

Taxes and other revenues: 16% (of GDP) (2017 est.)
comparison ranking: 128

Current account balance: $65.173 billion (2019 est.)
$70.843 billion (2018 est.)
comparison ranking: 8

Exports: $388.49 billion (2019 est.)
$383.484 billion (2018 est.)
$382.736 billion (2017 est.)
comparison ranking: 23

Exports - partners: China 22%, US 15%, Hong Kong 12%, Singapore 7%, Japan 6% (2022)
note: top five export partners based on percentage share of exports

Exports - commodities: integrated circuits, machine parts, computers, refined petroleum, plastics (2022)
note: top five export commodities based on value in dollars

Imports: $308.744 billion (2019 est.)
$305.428 billion (2018 est.)
$303.067 billion (2017 est.)
comparison ranking: 26

Imports - partners: China 19%, Japan 12%, US 10%, South Korea 7%, Australia 6% (2022)
note: top five import partners based on percentage share of imports

Imports - commodities: integrated circuits, crude petroleum, machinery, natural gas, coal (2022)
note: top five import commodities based on value in dollars

Reserves of foreign exchange and gold: $456.7 billion (31 December 2017 est.)
$439 billion (31 December 2016 est.)
comparison ranking: 8

Exchange rates: New Taiwan dollars (TWD) per US dollar -

Exchange rates: 28.211 (2020 est.)
30.472 (2019 est.)
30.8395 (2018 est.)
31.911 (2014 est.)

ENERGY

Electricity: *installed generating capacity:* 61.944 million kW (2022 est.)
consumption: 274.029 billion kWh (2022 est.)
transmission/distribution losses: 9.615 billion kWh (2022 est.)
comparison rankings: transmission/distribution losses 177; consumption 18; installed generating capacity 22

Electricity generation sources: *fossil fuels:* 83.7% of total installed capacity (2022 est.)
nuclear: 8.1% of total installed capacity (2022 est.)
solar: 3.8% of total installed capacity (2022 est.)
wind: 1.2% of total installed capacity (2022 est.)
hydroelectricity: 1.8% of total installed capacity (2022 est.)
biomass and waste: 1.3% of total installed capacity (2022 est.)

Nuclear energy: Number of operational nuclear reactors: 2 (2023)

Number of nuclear reactors under construction: 0

Net capacity of operational nuclear reactors: 1.87GW (2023)

Percent of total electricity production: 11% (2021)

Number of nuclear reactors permanently shut down: 2

Coal: *production:* 5.608 million metric tons (2022 est.)
consumption: 66.855 million metric tons (2022 est.)
exports: 52,000 metric tons (2022 est.)
imports: 63.855 million metric tons (2022 est.)
proven reserves: 1 million metric tons (2022 est.)

Petroleum: *total petroleum production:* 800 bbl/day (2023 est.)
refined petroleum consumption: 1.022 million bbl/day (2022 est.)
crude oil estimated reserves: 2.38 million barrels (2021 est.)

Natural gas: *production:* 63.747 million cubic meters (2022 est.)
consumption: 27.157 billion cubic meters (2022 est.)
imports: 27.085 billion cubic meters (2022 est.)
proven reserves: 6.23 billion cubic meters (2021 est.)

Carbon dioxide emissions: 306.035 million metric tonnes of CO_2 (2022 est.)
from coal and metallurgical coke: 143.069 million metric tonnes of CO_2 (2022 est.)
from petroleum and other liquids: 106.739 million metric tonnes of CO_2 (2022 est.)
from consumed natural gas: 56.227 million metric tonnes of CO_2 (2022 est.)
comparison ranking: total emissions 21

Energy consumption per capita: 208.336 million Btu/person (2022 est.)
comparison ranking: 17

COMMUNICATIONS

Telephones - fixed lines: *total subscriptions:* 10 million (2023 est.)
subscriptions per 100 inhabitants: 43 (2023 est.)
comparison ranking: total subscriptions 18

Telephones - mobile cellular: *total subscriptions:* 30 million (2023 est.)
subscriptions per 100 inhabitants: 128 (2023 est.)
comparison ranking: total subscriptions 48

Telecommunication systems: *general assessment:* Taiwan has a highly developed telecoms sector in both the fixed-line and mobile segments; in part this is due to its early moves to liberalize the market, allowing vigorous competition to flourish; the Taiwan

authorities have also made concerted efforts to take advantage of Taiwan's strengths in the development of high-tech, export-oriented industries to encourage and enable the rapid adoption of advanced telecom platforms, while simultaneously leveraging the same telecoms infrastructure to push even further ahead with Taiwan's industrial development plans; Taiwan has one of the highest teledensities in the region; while fixed-line subscriber numbers are trending downwards, the rate of decline has been slowed by the major fixed-line provider investing strongly in building out a widespread fiber network to allow customers to maintain a terrestrial voice connection as part of a fixed broadband package; fiber is the dominant platform in Taiwan's fixed broadband market; cable services have retained an unusually strong following thanks to the success of cable providers in delivering competitive cable TV and telephony services as a way to get around Chunghwa Telecom's control of the last mile for its copper and fiber networks; Taiwan also has high penetration rates in its mobile and mobile broadband segments, growth in both markets is almost at a standstill because Taiwan reached 100% penetration very early on – way back when GSM was first introduced, in mobile's case; the MNOs moved quickly to roll out 4G and 5G networks and services in rapid succession, but subscriber numbers (and market share) has barely changed; the improved quality and performance available with the new platforms will drive increased usage and ARPU; fierce competition following the launch of 4G saw the opposite happen, with price wars causing telco revenues to fall instead; Taiwan's 5G penetration rate reached 25 percent in October 2023, ranked 5th around the world now; Taiwan's 5G roll-out plan faces challenges as subscribers enjoy 4G unlimited data flow tariff and yet to see a killer app in the 5G world (2023)
domestic: fixed-line over 43 per 100 and mobile-cellular roughly 128 per 100 (2023)
international: country code - 886; landing points for the EAC-C2C, APCN-2, FASTER, SJC2, TSE-1, TPE, APG, SeaMeWe-3, FLAG North Asia Loop/REACH North Asia Loop, HKA, NCP, and PLCN submarine fiber cables provide links throughout Asia, Australia, the Middle East, Europe, Africa and the US; satellite earth stations - 2 (2019)

Broadcast media: 5 nationwide television networks operating roughly 22 TV stations; more than 300 satellite TV channels are available; about 51% of households utilize multi-channel cable TV; 99.9% of households subscribe to digital cable TV; national and regional radio networks with about 171 radio stations (2023)

Internet country code: .tw

Internet users: *total:* 21.6 million (2021 est.)
percent of population: 90% (2021 est.)
comparison ranking: total 40

Broadband - fixed subscriptions: *total:* 5,831,470 (2019 est.)
subscriptions per 100 inhabitants: 25 (2019 est.)
comparison ranking: total 31

TRANSPORTATION

National air transport system: *number of registered air carriers:* 7 (2020)
inventory of registered aircraft operated by air carriers: 216

Civil aircraft registration country code prefix: B

Airports: 53 (2024)
comparison ranking: 85

Heliports: 39 (2024)

Pipelines: 25 km condensate, 2,200 km gas, 13,500 km oil (2018)

Railways: *total:* 1,613.1 km (2018)
standard gauge: 345 km (2018) 1.435-m gauge (345 km electrified)
narrow gauge: 1,118.1 km (2018) 1.067-m gauge (793.9 km electrified)

150 0.762-m gauge note: the 0.762-gauge track belongs to three entities: the Forestry Bureau, Taiwan Cement, and TaiPower
comparison ranking: total 80

Roadways: *total:* 43,206 km
paved: 42,793 km (includes 1,348 km of highways and 737 km of expressways)
unpaved: 413 km (2017)
comparison ranking: total 90

Merchant marine: *total:* 465 (2023)
by type: bulk carrier 29, container ship 53, general cargo 58, oil tanker 35, other 290
comparison ranking: total 44

Ports: *total ports:* 8 (2024)
large: 1
medium: 3
small: 2
very small: 2
ports with oil terminals: 8
key ports: Chi-Lung, Hua-Lien Kang, Kao-Hsiung, Su-Ao

MILITARY AND SECURITY

Military and security forces: Taiwan Armed Forces: Army, Navy (includes Marine Corps), Air Force

Ocean Affairs Council: Coast Guard Administration (CGA)

Ministry of Interior: National Police (2024)
note: the CGA is a law enforcement organization with homeland security functions during peacetime and national defense missions during wartime; it was established in 2000 from the integration of the Coast Guard Command (formerly under the Ministry of Defense), the Marine Police Bureau (formerly under the National Police), and several cutters from the Taiwan Directorate General of Customs (Ministry of Finance)

Military expenditures: 2.5% of GDP (2023 est.)
2.1% of GDP (2022)
2.1% of GDP (2021)
2.1% of GDP (2020)
1.8% of GDP (2019)
comparison ranking: 43

Military and security service personnel strengths: approximately 180,000 active-duty troops (95,000 Army; 45,000 Navy, including approximately 10,000 marines; 40,000 Air Force) (2023)
note: Taiwan trains about 120,000 reservists annually, but in 2022 announced intentions to increase that figure to 260,000

Military equipment inventories and acquisitions: the Taiwan military's inventory is a mix of domestically-produced items and equipment acquired from the US, either as secondhand or direct acquisitions; Taiwan's domestic defense industry produces weapons systems such as aircraft, armored vehicles, missiles, and naval platforms (2024)

Military service age and obligation: men 18-36 years of age may volunteer or must complete 12 months of compulsory military service; civil service can be substituted for military service in some cases; women may enlist but are restricted to noncombat roles in most cases (2024)
note 1: in January 2024, Taiwan extended compulsory service from 4 to 12 months for men born in 2005 and thereafter
note 2: as of 2023, women made up about 15% of the active-duty military

Military - note: the military's primary responsibility is external security, including the defense of the country's sovereignty and territory, and the protection of Taiwan's air space, maritime claims, and sea lines of communication; its main focus is the challenge posed by the People's Republic of China
the US Taiwan Relations Act of April 1979 states that the US shall provide Taiwan with arms of a defensive character and shall maintain the capacity of the US to resist any resort to force or other forms of coercion that would jeopardize the security, or social or economic system, of the people of Taiwan (2024)

SPACE

Space agency/agencies: Taiwan Space Agency (TASA; renamed and reorganized in 2023 from the former National Space Program Organization or NSPO, which was established in 1991) (2024)

Space launch site(s): sounding rockets launched from Jui Peng Air Base (Pingtung); has announced intentions to build a future rocket launch site (2024)

Space program overview: space program focused on the acquisition of satellites and the development of independent space capabilities, such as rocket manufacturing and satellite launch services; manufactures and operates remote sensing (RS) and scientific/research satellites; manufactures and tests sounding rockets; researching and developing other space technologies, including communications satellites, small satellites, satellite payloads and ground station components, spacecraft components, optical RS and telecommunications, navigational control, and rocket propulsion systems; has bi-lateral relations with the space programs of India and the US, but is blocked from participating in most international and regional space organizations due to political pressure from China; has a commercial space industry that provides components and expertise for TASA and is independently developing satellites and a small satellite launch vehicle (2024)
note: further details about the key activities, programs, and milestones of the country's space program, as well as government spending estimates on the space sector, appear in the Space Programs reference guide

TRANSNATIONAL ISSUES

Illicit drugs: major source of precursor chemicals used in the production of illicit narcotics

TAJIKISTAN

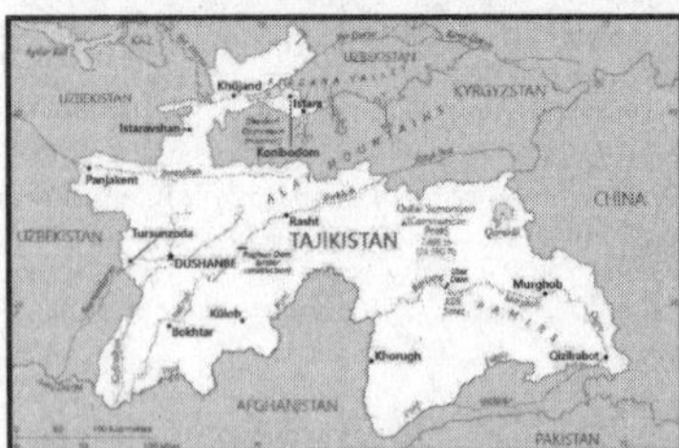

INTRODUCTION

Background: The Tajik people came under Russian imperial rule in the 1860s and 1870s, but Russia's hold on Central Asia weakened following the Revolution of 1917. At that time, bands of indigenous guerrillas (known as "basmachi") fiercely contested Bolshevik control of the area, which was not fully reestablished until 1925. Tajikistan was first established as an autonomous Soviet Socialist Republic within the Uzbek Soviet Socialist Republic in 1924, but in 1929 the Soviet Union made Tajikistan as a separate republic and transferred to it much of present-day Sughd Province. Ethnic Uzbeks form a substantial minority in Tajikistan, and ethnic Tajiks an even larger minority in Uzbekistan. Tajikistan became independent in 1991 after the breakup of the Soviet Union, and the country experienced a civil war among political, regional, and religious factions from 1992 to 1997.

Despite Tajikistan's general elections for both the presidency (once every seven years) and legislature (once every five years), observers note an electoral system rife with irregularities and abuse, and results that are neither free nor fair. President Emomali RAHMON, who came to power in 1992 during the civil war and was first elected president in 1994, used an attack planned by a disaffected deputy defense minister in 2015 to ban the last major opposition party in Tajikistan. RAHMON further strengthened his position by having himself declared "Founder of Peace and National Unity, Leader of the Nation," with limitless terms and lifelong immunity through constitutional amendments ratified in a referendum. The referendum also lowered the minimum age required to run for president from 35 to 30, which made RAHMON's first-born son Rustam EMOMALI, the mayor of the capital city of Dushanbe, eligible to run for president in 2020. RAHMON orchestrated EMOMALI's selection in 2020 as chairman of the Majlisi Milli (the upper chamber of Tajikistan's parliament), positioning EMOMALI as next in line of succession for the presidency. RAHMON opted to run in the presidential election later that year and received 91% of the vote.

The country remains the poorest of the former Soviet republics. Tajikistan became a member of the WTO in 2013, but its economy continues to face major challenges, including dependence on remittances from Tajikistani migrant laborers in Russia and Kazakhstan, pervasive corruption, the opiate trade, and destabilizing violence emanating from neighboring Afghanistan. Tajikistan has endured several domestic security incidents since 2010, including armed conflict between government forces and local strongmen in the Rasht Valley and between government forces and informal leaders in Gorno-Badakhshan Autonomous Oblast. Tajikistan suffered its first ISIS-claimed attack in 2018, when assailants attacked a group of Western bicyclists, killing four. Friction between forces on the border between Tajikistan and the Kyrgyz Republic flared up in 2021, culminating in fatal clashes between border forces in 2021 and 2022.

GEOGRAPHY

Location: Central Asia, west of China, south of Kyrgyzstan

Geographic coordinates: 39 00 N, 71 00 E

Map references: Asia

Area: *total:* 144,100 sq km
land: 141,510 sq km
water: 2,590 sq km
comparison ranking: total 96

Area - comparative: slightly smaller than Wisconsin

Land boundaries: *total:* 4,130 km
border countries (4): Afghanistan 1,357 km; China 477 km; Kyrgyzstan 984 km; Uzbekistan 1,312 km

Coastline: 0 km (landlocked)

Maritime claims: none (landlocked)

Climate: mid-latitude continental, hot summers, mild winters; semiarid to polar in Pamir Mountains

Terrain: mountainous region dominated by the Alay Mountains in the north and the Pamirs in the southeast; western Fergana Valley in north, Kofirnihon and Vakhsh Valleys in southwest

Elevation: *highest point:* Qullai Somoniyon 7,495 m
lowest point: Syr Darya (Sirdaryo) 300 m
mean elevation: 3,186 m

Natural resources: hydropower, some petroleum, uranium, mercury, brown coal, lead, zinc, antimony, tungsten, silver, gold

Land use: *agricultural land:* 34.7% (2018 est.)
arable land: 6.1% (2018 est.)
permanent crops: 0.9% (2018 est.)
permanent pasture: 27.7% (2018 est.)
forest: 2.9% (2018 est.)
other: 62.4% (2018 est.)

Irrigated land: 5,690 sq km (2020)

Major rivers (by length in km): Syr Darya (shared with Kyrgyzstan [s], Uzbekistan, and Kazakhstan [m]) - 3,078 km; Amu Darya river source (shared with Turkmenistan, Afghanistan, and Uzbekistan [m]) - 2,620 km
note – [s] after country name indicates river source; [m] after country name indicates river mouth

Major watersheds (area sq km): Internal (endorheic basin) drainage: Tarim Basin (1,152,448 sq km), *(Aral Sea Basin)* Amu Darya (534,739 sq km), Syr Darya (782,617 sq km)

Population distribution: the country's population is concentrated at lower elevations, with perhaps as much as 90% of the people living in valleys; overall density increases from east to west

Natural hazards: earthquakes; floods

Geography - note: landlocked; highest point, Qullai Ismoili Somoni (formerly Communism Peak), was the tallest mountain in the former USSR

PEOPLE AND SOCIETY

Population: *total:* 10,394,063
male: 5,221,818
female: 5,172,245 (2024 est.)
comparison rankings: female 92; male 91; total 91

Nationality: *noun:* Tajikistani(s)
adjective: Tajikistani

Ethnic groups: Tajik 84.3% (includes Pamiri and Yagnobi), Uzbek 13.8%, other 2% (includes Kyrgyz, Russian, Turkmen, Tatar, Arab) (2014 est.)

Languages: Tajik (official) 84.4%, Uzbek 11.9%, Kyrgyz 0.8%, Russian 0.5%, other 2.4% (2010 est.)
major-language sample(s):
Китоби Фактхои Ҷаҳонӣ, манбаи бебадали маълумоти асосӣ (Tajik)
note: Russian widely used in government and business

Religions: Muslim 98% (Sunni 95%, Shia 3%) other 2% (2014 est.)

Demographic profile: Tajikistan has a youthful age structure with almost 50% of the population under the age of 25. As a Soviet republic, Tajikistan had the highest fertility rate in the Soviet Union. The total fertility rate – the average number of births per woman – was highest in the mid-1970s, when it reached 6.3. In an effort to expand populations to meet economic goals, the Soviets provided resources that made large families affordable. The fertility rate decreased to 5 by the time of independence in 1991 and continued to decline thereafter. In 1996, the Tajik Government discontinued subsidies for large families and having several children became too expensive. The loss of subsidies, the 5-year civil war that followed independence, and other factors caused fertility to continue to fall steadily, but it remains above replacement level at 2.5. The availability of healthcare providers and family planning services is limited, contributing to couples having more children than they would like. As of 2017, 21% of women were using contraceptives.

Tajikistan's ethnic make-up changed with the Soviet's introduction of industrialization. Large numbers of Russian and Ukrainian immigrants arrived in the mid-1920s. Some were forced to immigrate while others came voluntarily to work in the cotton industry and in Tajikistan's Soviet Government. The Russian and Ukrainian immigrants formed urban communities, while Tajiks and Uzbeks continued to live predominantly in rural areas. In addition, thousands of Tatars and Germans were deported to Tajikistan, accused of Nazi complicity during WWII. Tajikistan's ethnic composition was later shaped by the post-independence civil war from 1992-1997 and the economic devastation that followed. Most non-Tajik ethnic groups, including Uzbeks, Russians, Kyrgyz, and Ukrainians, fled to Russia and other former Soviet republics and many never returned, making the country overwhelming Tajik; approximately 80% of the population was Tajik by 2000.

Since the mid-1990s, labor has probably been Tajikistan's main export. Remittances accounted for 30% of GDP in 2018 and are Tajikistan's largest source of external income. Poverty, a lack of jobs, and higher wages abroad push Tajiks to emigrate. Russia – particularly Moscow – is the main destination, while a smaller number of religious Muslims, usually of Uzbek ancestry, migrate to Uzbekistan. The vast majority of labor migrants are unskilled or low-skilled young men who work primarily in construction but also agriculture, transportation, and retail. Many Tajik families are dependent on the money they send home for necessities, such as food and clothing, as well as for education and weddings rather than investment.

Age structure: *0-14 years:* 36.9% (male 1,953,472/ female 1,877,192)
15-64 years: 59.3% (male 3,086,964/female 3,071,642)
65 years and over: 3.9% (2024 est.) (male 181,382/ female 223,411)

Dependency ratios: *total dependency ratio:* 65.9
youth dependency ratio: 60.4
elderly dependency ratio: 5.5
potential support ratio: 18.1 (2021 est.)

Median age: *total:* 22.8 years (2024 est.)
male: 22.3 years
female: 23.2 years
comparison ranking: total 181

Population growth rate: 1.92% (2024 est.)
comparison ranking: 42

Birth rate: 25.8 births/1,000 population (2024 est.)
comparison ranking: 42

Death rate: 4.7 deaths/1,000 population (2024 est.)
comparison ranking: 205

Net migration rate: -2 migrant(s)/1,000 population (2024 est.)
comparison ranking: 167

Population distribution: the country's population is concentrated at lower elevations, with perhaps as much as 90% of the people living in valleys; overall density increases from east to west

Urbanization: *urban population:* 28.2% of total population (2023)
rate of urbanization: 2.73% annual rate of change (2020-25 est.)

Major urban areas - population: 987,000 DUSHANBE (capital) (2023)

Sex ratio: *at birth:* 1.05 male(s)/female
0-14 years: 1.04 male(s)/female
15-64 years: 1 male(s)/female
65 years and over: 0.81 male(s)/female
total population: 1.01 male(s)/female (2024 est.)

Mother's mean age at first birth: 23.2 years (2017 est.)

Maternal mortality ratio: 17 deaths/100,000 live births (2020 est.)
comparison ranking: 131

Infant mortality rate: *total:* 21.7 deaths/1,000 live births (2024 est.)
male: 24.3 deaths/1,000 live births
female: 18.9 deaths/1,000 live births
comparison ranking: total 73

Life expectancy at birth: *total population:* 71.9 years (2024 est.)
male: 70.1 years
female: 73.8 years
comparison ranking: total population 167

Total fertility rate: 3.56 children born/woman (2024 est.)
comparison ranking: 31

Gross reproduction rate: 1.73 (2024 est.)

Contraceptive prevalence rate: 29.3% (2017)

Drinking water source: *improved: urban:* 96.5% of population
rural: 79.9% of population
total: 84.4% of population
unimproved: urban: 3.5% of population
rural: 20.1% of population
total: 15.6% of population (2020 est.)

Current health expenditure: 8.2% of GDP (2020)

Physician density: 1.72 physicians/1,000 population (2014)

Hospital bed density: 4.7 beds/1,000 population (2014)

Sanitation facility access: *improved: urban:* 98.9% of population
rural: 99.6% of population
total: 99.4% of population
unimproved: urban: 1.1% of population
rural: 0.4% of population
total: 0.6% of population (2020 est.)

Obesity - adult prevalence rate: 14.2% (2016)
comparison ranking: 128

Alcohol consumption per capita: *total:* 0.85 liters of pure alcohol (2019 est.)
beer: 0.38 liters of pure alcohol (2019 est.)
wine: 0.01 liters of pure alcohol (2019 est.)
spirits: 0.45 liters of pure alcohol (2019 est.)
other alcohols: 0 liters of pure alcohol (2019 est.)
comparison ranking: total 156

Children under the age of 5 years underweight: 7.6% (2017)
comparison ranking: 63

Currently married women (ages 15-49): 72% (2023 est.)

Child marriage: *women married by age 15:* 0.1%
women married by age 18: 8.7% (2017 est.)

Education expenditures: 5.9% of GDP (2020 est.)
comparison ranking: 47

Literacy: *definition:* age 15 and over can read and write
total population: 99.8%
male: 99.8%
female: 99.7% (2015)

School life expectancy (primary to tertiary education): *total:* 11 years
male: 12 years
female: 11 years (2013)

ENVIRONMENT

Environment - current issues: areas of high air pollution from motor vehicles and industry; water pollution from agricultural runoff and disposal of untreated industrial waste and sewage; poor management of water resources; soil erosion; increasing levels of soil salinity

Environment - international agreements: *party to:* Biodiversity, Climate Change, Climate Change-Kyoto Protocol, Climate Change-Paris Agreement, Comprehensive Nuclear Test Ban, Desertification, Endangered Species, Environmental Modification, Hazardous Wastes, Ozone Layer Protection, Ship Pollution, Wetlands
signed, but not ratified: none of the selected agreements

Climate: mid-latitude continental, hot summers, mild winters; semiarid to polar in Pamir Mountains

Urbanization: *urban population:* 28.2% of total population (2023)
rate of urbanization: 2.73% annual rate of change (2020-25 est.)

Revenue from forest resources: 1.12% of GDP (2018 est.)
comparison ranking: 51

Revenue from coal: 0.54% of GDP (2018 est.)
comparison ranking: 10

Air pollutants: *particulate matter emissions:* 53.65 micrograms per cubic meter (2019 est.)
carbon dioxide emissions: 5.31 megatons (2016 est.)
methane emissions: 4.87 megatons (2020 est.)

Waste and recycling: *municipal solid waste generated annually:* 1,787,400 tons (2013 est.)

Major rivers (by length in km): Syr Darya (shared with Kyrgyzstan [s], Uzbekistan, and Kazakhstan [m]) - 3,078 km; Amu Darya river source (shared with Turkmenistan, Afghanistan, and Uzbekistan [m]) - 2,620 km
note – [s] after country name indicates river source; [m] after country name indicates river mouth

Major watersheds (area sq km): Internal (endorheic basin) drainage: Tarim Basin (1,152,448 sq km), *(Aral Sea Basin)* Amu Darya (534,739 sq km), Syr Darya (782,617 sq km)

Total water withdrawal: *municipal:* 910 million cubic meters (2020 est.)
industrial: 1.61 billion cubic meters (2020 est.)
agricultural: 7.38 billion cubic meters (2020 est.)

Total renewable water resources: 21.91 billion cubic meters (2020 est.)

GOVERNMENT

Country name: *conventional long form:* Republic of Tajikistan
conventional short form: Tajikistan
local long form: Jumhurii Tojikiston
local short form: Tojikiston
former: Tajik Soviet Socialist Republic
etymology: the Persian suffix "-stan" means "place of" or "country," so the word Tajikistan literally means "Land of the Tajik [people]"

Government type: presidential republic

Capital: *name:* Dushanbe
geographic coordinates: 38 33 N, 68 46 E
time difference: UTC+5 (10 hours ahead of Washington, DC, during Standard Time)
etymology: today's city was originally at the crossroads where a large bazaar occurred on Mondays, hence the name Dushanbe, which in Persian means Monday, i.e., the second day (*du*) after Saturday (*shambe*)

Administrative divisions: 2 provinces (viloyatho, singular - viloyat), 1 autonomous province* (viloyati mukhtor), 1 capital region** (viloyati poytakht), and 1 area referred to as Districts Under Republic Administration***; Dushanbe**, Khatlon (Bokhtar), Kuhistoni Badakhshon [Gorno-Badakhshan]* (Khorugh), Nohiyahoi Tobei Jumhuri***, Sughd (Khujand)
note: the administrative center name follows in parentheses

Independence: 9 September 1991 (from the Soviet Union)

National holiday: Independence Day (or National Day), 9 September (1991)

Legal system: civil law system

Constitution: *history:* several previous; latest adopted 6 November 1994
amendments: proposed by the president of the republic or by at least one third of the total membership of both houses of the Supreme Assembly; adoption of any amendment requires a referendum, which includes approval of the president or approval by at least two-thirds majority of the Assembly of Representatives; passage in a referendum requires participation of an absolute majority of eligible voters and an absolute majority of votes; constitutional articles, including Tajikistan's form of government, its territory, and its democratic nature, cannot be amended; amended 1999, 2003, 2016

International law organization participation: has not submitted an ICJ jurisdiction declaration; accepts ICCt jurisdiction

Citizenship: *citizenship by birth:* no
citizenship by descent only: at least one parent must be a citizen of Tajikistan
dual citizenship recognized: no
residency requirement for naturalization: 5 years or 3 years of continuous residence prior to application

Suffrage: 18 years of age; universal

Executive branch: *chief of state:* President Emomali RAHMON (since 6 November 1994; head of state and Supreme Assembly Chairman since 19 November 1992)
head of government: Prime Minister Qohir RASULZODA (since 23 November 2013)
cabinet: Council of Ministers appointed by the president, approved by the Supreme Assembly
elections/appointments: president directly elected by simple majority popular vote for a 7-year term (two-term limit); however, as the "Leader of the Nation" President RAHMON can run an unlimited number of times; election last held on 11 October 2020 (next to be held in 2027); prime minister appointed by the president
election results:
2020: Emomali RAHMON reelected president; percent of vote - Emomali RAHMON (PDPT) 92.1%, Rustam LATIFZODA (APT) 3.1%, and other 4.8%
2013: Emomali RAHMOND reelected president; percent of vote - Emomali RAHMOND (PDPT) 84%, Ismoil TALBAKOV CPT) 5%, other 11%

Legislative branch: *description:* bicameral Supreme Assembly or Majlisi Oli consists of:
National Assembly or Majlisi Milli (34 seats; 25 members indirectly elected by local representative assemblies or majlisi, 8 appointed by the president, and 1 reserved for each living former president; members serve 5-year terms)
Assembly of Representatives or Majlisi Namoyandagon (63 seats; 41 members directly elected in single-seat constituencies by 2-round absolute majority vote and 22 directly elected in a single nationwide constituency by closed-list proportional representation vote; members serve 5-year terms)
elections: National Assembly - last held on 1 March 2020 (next to be held in 2025)
Assembly of Representatives - last held on 1 March 2020 (next to be held in 2025)
election results: National Assembly - percent of vote by party - NA; seats by party - PDPT 47, APT 7, PERT 5, CPT 2, DPT1, SPT 1; composition - men 19, women 6, percentage women 24%
Assembly of Representatives - percent of vote by party - PDPT 50.4%, PERT 16.6%, APT 16.5%, SPT 5.2%, DPT 5.1%, CPT 3.1%, other 3.1%; seats by party - PDPT 47, APT 7, PERT 5, CPT 2, SPT 1, DPT 1; composition - men 48, women 15, percentage women 23.8%; total Supreme Assembly percentage women 27%

Judicial branch: *highest court(s):* Supreme Court (consists of the chairman, deputy chairmen, and 34 judges organized into civil, family, criminal, administrative offense, and military chambers); Constitutional Court (consists of the court chairman, deputy chairman, and 5 judges); High Economic Court (consists of 16 judicial positions)
judge selection and term of office: Supreme Court, Constitutional Court, and High Economic Court judges nominated by the president and approved by the National Assembly; judges of all 3 courts appointed for 10-year renewable terms with no term limits, but the last appointment must occur before the age of 65
subordinate courts: regional and district courts; Dushanbe City Court; viloyat (province level) courts; Court of Gorno- Badakhshan Autonomous Region

Political parties: Agrarian Party of Tajikistan or APT
Communist Party of Tajikistan or CPT
Democratic Party of Tajikistan or DPT
Party of Economic Reform of Tajikistan or PERT
People's Democratic Party of Tajikistan or PDPT
Social Democratic Party of Tajikistan or SDPT
Socialist Party of Tajikistan or SPT

International organization participation: ADB, CICA, CIS, CSTO, EAEC, EAPC, EBRD, ECO, EITI (candidate country), FAO, G-77, GCTU, IAEA, IBRD, ICAO, ICC (NGOs), ICCt, ICRM, IDA, IDB, IFAD, IFC, IFRCS, ILO, IMF, Interpol, IOC, IOM, IPU, ISO (correspondent), ITSO, ITU, MIGA, NAM (observer), OIC, OPCW, OSCE, PFP, SCO, UN, UNCTAD, UNESCO, UNIDO, UNISFA, UNWTO, UPU, WCO, WFTU (NGOs), WHO, WIPO, WMO, WTO

Diplomatic representation in the US: *chief of mission:* Ambassador Farrukh HAMRALIZODA (since 17 February 2021)
chancery: 1005 New Hampshire Avenue NW, Washington, DC 20037
telephone: [1] (202) 223-6090
FAX: [1] (202) 223-6091
email address and website:
tajemus@mfa.tj
https://mfa.tj/en/washington

Diplomatic representation from the US: *chief of mission:* Ambassador Manuel P. MICALLER Jr. (since 9 March 2023)
embassy: 109-A Ismoili Somoni Avenue (Zarafshon district), Dushanbe 734019
mailing address: 7090 Dushanbe Place, Washington DC 20521-7090
telephone: [992] (37) 229-20-00
FAX: [992] (37) 229-20-50
email address and website:
DushanbeConsular@state.gov
https://tj.usembassy.gov/

Flag description: three horizontal stripes of red (top), a wider stripe of white, and green; a gold crown surmounted by seven gold, five-pointed stars is located in the center of the white stripe; red represents the sun, victory, and the unity of the nation, white stands for purity, cotton, and mountain snows, while green is the color of Islam and the bounty of nature; the crown symbolizes the Tajik people; the seven stars signify the Tajik magic number "seven" - a symbol of perfection and the embodiment of happiness

National symbol(s): crown surmounted by an arc of seven, five-pointed stars; snow leopard; national colors: red, white, green

National anthem: *name:* "Surudi milli" (National Anthem)
lyrics/music: Gulnazar KELDI/Sulaimon YUDAKOV
note: adopted 1991; after the fall of the Soviet Union, Tajikistan kept the music of the anthem from its time as a Soviet republic but adopted new lyrics

National heritage: *total World Heritage Sites:* 4 (2 cultural, 2 natural)
selected World Heritage Site locales: Proto-urban Site of Sarazm (c); Tajik National Park (Mountains of the Pamirs) (n); Silk Roads: Zarafshan-Karakum Corridor (c); Tugay forests of the Tigrovaya Balka Nature Reserve (n)

ECONOMY

Economic overview: lower middle-income Central Asian economy; key gold, cotton, and aluminum exporter; declining poverty; sustained high growth; very limited private sector; substantial illicit drug trade; significant remittances; environmentally fragile

Real GDP (purchasing power parity): $46.467 billion (2023 est.)
$42.905 billion (2022 est.)
$39.727 billion (2021 est.)
note: data in 2021 dollars
comparison ranking: 130

Real GDP growth rate: 8.3% (2023 est.)
8% (2022 est.)
9.4% (2021 est.)
note: annual GDP % growth based on constant local currency
comparison ranking: 10

Real GDP per capita: $4,600 (2023 est.)
$4,300 (2022 est.)
$4,100 (2021 est.)
note: data in 2021 dollars
comparison ranking: 181

GDP (official exchange rate): $12.061 billion (2023 est.)
note: data in current dollars at official exchange rate

Inflation rate (consumer prices): 7.7% (2019 est.)
3.9% (2018 est.)
7.3% (2017 est.)
note: annual % change based on consumer prices
comparison ranking: 150

Credit ratings: Moody's rating: B3 (2017)

Standard & Poors rating: B- (2017)
note: The year refers to the year in which the current credit rating was first obtained.

GDP - composition, by sector of origin: *agriculture:* 22.9% (2022 est.)
industry: 34.7% (2022 est.)
services: 34.1% (2022 est.)
note: figures may not total 100% due to non-allocated consumption not captured in sector-reported data
comparison rankings: services 205; industry 44; agriculture 27

GDP - composition, by end use: *household consumption:* 87.6% (2022 est.)
government consumption: 10.1% (2022 est.)
investment in fixed capital: 31.7% (2022 est.)
investment in inventories: 3.8% (2022 est.)
exports of goods and services: 16.4% (2022 est.)

imports of goods and services: -49.1% (2022 est.)
note: figures may not total 100% due to rounding or gaps in data collection

Agricultural products: milk, potatoes, wheat, watermelons, onions, cotton, tomatoes, carrots/turnips, vegetables, beef (2022)
note: top ten agricultural products based on tonnage

Industries: aluminum, cement, coal, gold, silver, antimony, textile, vegetable oil

Industrial production growth rate: 9.26% (2022 est.)
note: annual % change in industrial value added based on constant local currency
comparison ranking: 19

Labor force: 2.677 million (2023 est.)
note: number of people ages 15 or older who are employed or seeking work
comparison ranking: 117

Unemployment rate: 6.98% (2023 est.)
6.98% (2022 est.)
7.25% (2021 est.)
note: % of labor force seeking employment
comparison ranking: 136

Youth unemployment rate (ages 15-24): *total:* 16.9% (2023 est.)
male: 19.5% (2023 est.)
female: 13.2% (2023 est.)
note: % of labor force ages 15-24 seeking employment
comparison ranking: total 84

Population below poverty line: 22.5% (2022 est.)
note: % of population with income below national poverty line

Gini Index coefficient - distribution of family income: 34 (2015 est.)
note: index (0-100) of income distribution; higher values represent greater inequality
comparison ranking: 88

Household income or consumption by percentage share: *lowest 10%:* 3% (2015 est.)
highest 10%: 26.4% (2015 est.)
note: % share of income accruing to lowest and highest 10% of population

Remittances: 38.42% of GDP (2023 est.)
49.9% of GDP (2022 est.)
32.69% of GDP (2021 est.)
note: personal transfers and compensation between resident and non-resident individuals/households/entities

Budget: *revenues:* $2.268 billion (2022 est.)
expenditures: $1.145 billion (2022 est.)
note: central government revenues (excluding grants) and expenses converted to US dollars at average official exchange rate for year indicated

Public debt: 50.4% of GDP (2017 est.)
comparison ranking: 106

Taxes and other revenues: 10.34% (of GDP) (2022 est.)
note: central government tax revenue as a % of GDP
comparison ranking: 177

Current account balance: $584.022 million (2023 est.)
$1.635 billion (2022 est.)
$735.526 million (2021 est.)
note: balance of payments - net trade and primary/secondary income in current dollars
comparison ranking: 62

Exports: $2.105 billion (2023 est.)
$1.753 billion (2022 est.)
$2.161 billion (2021 est.)
note: balance of payments - exports of goods and services in current dollars
comparison ranking: 164

Exports - partners: Kazakhstan 20%, Switzerland 19%, China 17%, Turkey 8%, Uzbekistan 8% (2022)
note: top five export partners based on percentage share of exports

Exports - commodities: gold, precious metal ore, cotton, copper ore, aluminum (2022)
note: top five export commodities based on value in dollars

Imports: $5.931 billion (2023 est.)
$5.261 billion (2022 est.)
$4.258 billion (2021 est.) note: data are in current year dollars
note: balance of payments - imports of goods and services in current dollars
comparison ranking: 143

Imports - partners: China 33%, Russia 22%, Kazakhstan 13%, Uzbekistan 6%, Turkey 6% (2022)
note: top five import partners based on percentage share of imports

Imports - commodities: refined petroleum, garments, wheat, cars, natural gas (2022)
note: top five import commodities based on value in dollars

Reserves of foreign exchange and gold: $3.847 billion (2022 est.)
$2.499 billion (2021 est.)
$2.238 billion (2020 est.)
note: holdings of gold (year-end prices)/foreign exchange/special drawing rights in current dollars
comparison ranking: 129

Exchange rates: Tajikistani somoni (TJS) per US dollar -

Exchange rates: 10.845 (2023 est.)
11.031 (2022 est.)
11.309 (2021 est.)
10.322 (2020 est.)
9.53 (2019 est.)

ENERGY

Electricity access: *electrification - total population:* 100% (2022 est.)
electrification - urban areas: 99%
electrification - rural areas: 100%

Electricity: *installed generating capacity:* 5.993 million kW (2022 est.)
consumption: 14.32 billion kWh (2022 est.)
exports: 3.051 billion kWh (2022 est.)
imports: 883 million kWh (2022 est.)
transmission/distribution losses: 4.399 billion kWh (2022 est.)
comparison rankings: transmission/distribution losses 157; imports 81; exports 47; consumption 87; installed generating capacity 82

Electricity generation sources: *fossil fuels:* 10.7% of total installed capacity (2022 est.)
hydroelectricity: 89.3% of total installed capacity (2022 est.)

Coal: *production:* 2.175 million metric tons (2022 est.)
consumption: 2.245 million metric tons (2022 est.)
exports: 2,000 metric tons (2022 est.)
imports: 105,000 metric tons (2022 est.)
proven reserves: 4.075 billion metric tons (2022 est.)

Petroleum: *total petroleum production:* 300 bbl/day (2023 est.)
refined petroleum consumption: 28,000 bbl/day (2022 est.)
crude oil estimated reserves: 12 million barrels (2021 est.)

Natural gas: *production:* 18.476 million cubic meters (2022 est.)
consumption: 85.567 million cubic meters (2022 est.)
imports: 65.997 million cubic meters (2022 est.)
proven reserves: 5.663 billion cubic meters (2021 est.)

Carbon dioxide emissions: 8.324 million metric tonnes of CO2 (2022 est.)
from coal and metallurgical coke: 4.982 million metric tonnes of CO2 (2022 est.)
from petroleum and other liquids: 3.174 million metric tonnes of CO2 (2022 est.)
from consumed natural gas: 168,000 metric tonnes of CO2 (2022 est.)
comparison ranking: total emissions 115

Energy consumption per capita: 16.255 million Btu/person (2022 est.)
comparison ranking: 137

COMMUNICATIONS

Telephones - fixed lines: *total subscriptions:* 502,000 (2021 est.)
subscriptions per 100 inhabitants: 5 (2021 est.)
comparison ranking: total subscriptions 91

Telephones - mobile cellular: *total subscriptions:* 11.584 million (2021 est.)
subscriptions per 100 inhabitants: 119 (2021 est.)
comparison ranking: total subscriptions 86

Telecommunication systems: *general assessment:* the size of Tajikistan's mobile market dwarfs the fixed line segment, with an estimated penetration rate of nearly 120%; with a number of private sector companies active in the mobile market, there been more commitment to investment in network upgrades and expansion; three MNOs have all launched commercial 5G services, initially in areas of the capital city Dushanbe; the move towards higher speed mobile services should further underpin the growth in the nascent mobile broadband market, which is still estimated to be at a relatively low penetration level of 42% (at least relative to most other Asian nations) but is predicted to be a strong compound annual growth rate of more than 8% for at least the next five years; the ICT ecosystem is a complex mix of foreign operators from the People's Republic of China, the Russian Federation, state-owned enterprises, and telecom systems established by donors and non-governmental organizations (2024)
domestic: fixed-line over 5 per 100 and mobile-cellular over 119 per 100 (2022)
international: country code - 992; linked by cable and microwave radio relay to other CIS republics and by leased connections to the Moscow international gateway switch; Dushanbe linked by Intelsat to international gateway switch in Ankara (Turkey); 3 satellite earth stations - 2 Intelsat and 1 Orbita

Broadcast media: state-run TV broadcasters transmit nationally on 9 TV and 10 radio stations, and regionally on 4 stations; 31 independent TV and 20 radio stations broadcast locally and regionally; many households are able to receive Russian and other foreign stations via cable and satellite (2016)

Internet country code: .tj

Internet users: *total:* 3,009,054 (2022 est.)
percent of population: 30.4% (2022 est.)
comparison ranking: total 121

Broadband - fixed subscriptions: *total:* 6,000 (2020 est.)
subscriptions per 100 inhabitants: 0.1 (2020 est.)
comparison ranking: total 184

TRANSPORTATION

National air transport system: *number of registered air carriers:* 2 (2020)
inventory of registered aircraft operated by air carriers: 6
annual passenger traffic on registered air carriers: 492,320 (2018)
annual freight traffic on registered air carriers: 2.34 million (2018) mt-km

Civil aircraft registration country code prefix: EY

Airports: 19 (2024)
comparison ranking: 139

Pipelines: 549 km gas, 38 km oil (2013)

Railways: *total:* 680 km (2014)
broad gauge: 680 km (2014) 1.520-m gauge
comparison ranking: total 102

Roadways: *total:* 30,000 km (2018)
comparison ranking: total 102

Waterways: 200 km (2011) (along Vakhsh River)
comparison ranking: 108

MILITARY AND SECURITY

Military and security forces: Armed Forces of the Republic of Tajikistan: Land Forces, Mobile Forces, Air and Air Defense Forces; National Guard

Ministry of Internal Affairs: Internal Troops (reserves for Armed Forces in wartime), police

State Committee on National Security: Border Guard Forces (2023)
note: the National Guard, formerly the Presidential Guard, is tasked with ensuring public safety and security, similar to the tasks of the Internal Troops; it also takes part in ceremonial duties

Military expenditures: 1.2% of GDP (2023 est.)
1.1% of GDP (2022 est.)
1.2% of GDP (2021 est.)
1% of GDP (2020 est.)
2.1% of GDP (2019 est.)
comparison ranking: 117

Military and security service personnel strengths: approximately 10,000 active-duty troops (8,000 Land and Mobile Forces; 2,000 Air and Air Defense Forces) (2023)

Military equipment inventories and acquisitions: the military's inventory is comprised mostly of older Russian and Soviet-era weapons and equipment; it also has smaller amounts of items from suppliers such as China, Turkey, and the US; in 2022, Tajikistan opened a plant to produce an Iranian-designed unmanned aerial vehicle under license (2024)

Military service age and obligation: 18-27 years of age for compulsory (men only) or voluntary (men and women) military service; 24-month conscript service obligation (2023)
note: in August 2021, the Tajik Government removed an exemption for university graduates but began allowing men to pay a fee in order to avoid conscription, although there is a cap on the number of individuals who can take advantage of this exemption

Military - note: the military's primary concerns are terrorism, border security, territorial defense, and instability in neighboring countries; Russia is Tajikistan's primary security partner and thousands of Russian troops are stationed in the country, primarily at the 201st military base, which is leased until at least 2042; Russia and Tajikistan have a joint air defense system and they conduct periodic joint exercises; Tajikistan has been a member of the Russian-led Collective Security Treaty Organization (CSTO) since 1994 and contributes troops to CSTO's rapid reaction force

Tajikistan is the only former Soviet republic that did not form its armed forces from old Soviet Army units following the collapse of the USSR in 1991; rather, Russia retained command of the Soviet units there while the Tajik government raised a military from scratch; the first ground forces were officially created in 1993 from groups that fought for the government during the Tajik Civil War (2023)

TERRORISM

Terrorist group(s): Islamic State of Iraq and ash-Sham (ISIS)
note 1: US-designated foreign terrorist groups such as the Islamic Jihad Union, the Islamic Movement of Uzbekistan, and the Islamic State of Iraq and ash-Sham-Khorasan Province have operated in the area where the Uzbek, Kyrgyz, and Tajik borders converge and ill-defined and porous borders allow for the relatively free movement of people and illicit goods
note 2: details about the history, aims, leadership, organization, areas of operation, tactics, targets, weapons, size, and sources of support of the group(s) appear(s) in the Terrorism reference guide

TRANSNATIONAL ISSUES

Refugees and internally displaced persons: *refugees (country of origin):* 6,775 (Afghanistan) (mid-year 2021)
stateless persons: 4,898 (2022)

Trafficking in persons: tier rating: Tier 2 Watch List — the government did not demonstrate overall increasing efforts to eliminate trafficking compared with the previous reporting period, therefore Tajikistan was downgraded to Tier 2 Watch List; for more details, go to: https://www.state.gov/reports/2024-trafficking-in-persons-report/tajikistan/

Illicit drugs: Tajikistan is a primary transit country along the "Northern Route" for Afghanistan-sourced opiates and cannabis for the Russian and Eastern European markets and beyond; minimal domestic recreational drug use though it is increasing

TANZANIA

INTRODUCTION

Background: Tanzania contains some of Africa's most iconic national parks and famous paleoanthropological sites, and its diverse cultural heritage reflects the multiple ethnolinguistic groups that live in the country. Its long history of integration into trade networks spanning the Indian Ocean and the African interior led to the development of Swahili as a common language in much of east Africa and the introduction of Islam into the region. A number of independent coastal and island trading posts in what is now Tanzania came under Portuguese control after 1498 when they began to take control of much of the coast and Indian Ocean trade. By 1700, the Sultanate of Oman had become the dominant power in the region after ousting the Portuguese, who were also facing a series of local uprisings. During the next hundred years, Zanzibar – an archipelago off the coast that is now part of Tanzania – became a hub of Indian Ocean trade, with Arab and Indian traders establishing and consolidating trade routes with communities in mainland Tanzania that contributed to the expansion of the slave trade. Zanzibar briefly became the capital of the Sultanate of Oman before it split into separate Omani and Zanzibar Sultanates in 1856. Beginning in the mid-1800s, European explorers, traders, and Christian missionaries became more active in the region. The Germans eventually established control over mainland Tanzania – which they called Tanganyika – and the British established control over Zanzibar. Tanganyika came under British administration after the German defeat in World War I.

Tanganyika gained independence from Great Britain in 1961, and Zanzibar followed in 1963 as a constitutional monarchy. In Tanganyika, Julius NYERERE, a charismatic and idealistic socialist, established a one-party political system that centralized power and encouraged national self-reliance and rural development. In 1964, a popular uprising overthrew the Sultan in Zanzibar and either killed or expelled many of the Arabs and Indians who had dominated the isles for more than 200 years. Later that year, Tanganyika and Zanzibar combined to form the United Republic of Tanzania, but Zanzibar retained considerable autonomy. Their two ruling parties combined to form the Chama Cha Mapinduzi (CCM) party in 1977, which has since won every presidential election. Tanzania held its first multiparty elections in 1995, but CCM candidates have continued to dominate politics. The ruling party has claimed victory in four contentious elections since 1995, despite international observers' claims of voting irregularities. In 2001, 35 people died in Zanzibar when soldiers fired on protestors. John MAGUFULI won the 2015 and 2020 presidential elections, and the CCM won over two-thirds of the seats in Parliament in both elections. MAGUFULI died in 2021 while in office and was succeeded by his vice president, Samia Suluhu HASSAN.

GEOGRAPHY

Location: Eastern Africa, bordering the Indian Ocean, between Kenya and Mozambique

Geographic coordinates: 6 00 S, 35 00 E

Map references: Africa

Area: *total:* 947,300 sq km
land: 885,800 sq km
water: 61,500 sq km
note: includes the islands of Mafia, Pemba, and Zanzibar
comparison ranking: total 32

Area - comparative: more than six times the size of Georgia; slightly larger than twice the size of California

Land boundaries: *total:* 4,161 km
border countries (8): Burundi 589 km; Democratic Republic of the Congo 479 km; Kenya 775 km; Malawi 512 km; Mozambique 840 km; Rwanda 222 km; Uganda 391 km; Zambia 353 km

Coastline: 1,424 km

Maritime claims: *territorial sea:* 12 nm
exclusive economic zone: 200 nm

Climate: varies from tropical along coast to temperate in highlands

Terrain: plains along coast; central plateau; highlands in north, south

Elevation: *highest point:* Kilimanjaro (highest point in Africa) 5,895 m
lowest point: Indian Ocean 0 m
mean elevation: 1,018 m

Natural resources: hydropower, tin, phosphates, iron ore, coal, diamonds, gemstones (including tanzanite, found only in Tanzania), gold, natural gas, nickel

Land use: *agricultural land:* 43.7% (2018 est.)
arable land: 14.3% (2018 est.)
permanent crops: 2.3% (2018 est.)
permanent pasture: 27.1% (2018 est.)
forest: 37.3% (2018 est.)
other: 19% (2018 est.)

Irrigated land: 1,840 sq km (2012)

Major lakes (area sq km): *fresh water lake(s):* Lake Victoria (shared with Uganda and Kenya) - 62,940 sq km; Lake Tanganyika (shared with Democratic Republic of Congo, Burundi, and Zambia) - 32,000 sq km; Lake Malawi (shared with Mozambique and Malawi) - 22,490
salt water lake(s): Lake Rukwa - 5,760 sq km

Major rivers (by length in km): Nile (shared with Rwanda [s], Uganda, South Sudan, Sudan, and Egypt [m]) - 6,650 km
note – [s] after country name indicates river source; [m] after country name indicates river mouth

Major watersheds (area sq km): Atlantic Ocean drainage: Congo (3,730,881 sq km), *(Mediterranean Sea)* Nile (3,254,853 sq km)

Indian Ocean drainage: Zambezi (1,332,412 sq km)

Population distribution: the largest and most populous East African country; population distribution is extremely uneven, but greater population clusters occur in the northern half of country and along the east coast as shown in this population distribution map

Natural hazards: flooding on the central plateau during the rainy season; drought
volcanism: limited volcanic activity; Ol Doinyo Lengai (2,962 m) has emitted lava in recent years; other historically active volcanoes include Kieyo and Meru

Geography - note: Kilimanjaro is the highest point in Africa and one of only three mountain ranges on the continent that has glaciers (the others are Mount Kenya in Kenya and the Ruwenzori Mountains on the Uganda-Democratic Republic of the Congo border); Tanzania is bordered by three of the largest lakes on the continent: Lake Victoria (the world's second-largest freshwater lake) in the north, Lake Tanganyika (the world's second deepest) in the west, and Lake Nyasa (Lake Malawi) in the southwest

PEOPLE AND SOCIETY

Population: *total:* 67,462,121
male: 33,691,904
female: 33,770,217 (2024 est.)
comparison rankings: female 23; male 22; total 23

Nationality: *noun:* Tanzanian(s)
adjective: Tanzanian

Ethnic groups: mainland - African 99% (of which 95% are Bantu consisting of more than 130 tribes), other 1% (consisting of Asian, European, and Arab); Zanzibar - Arab, African, mixed Arab and African

Languages: Kiswahili or Swahili (official), Kiunguja (name for Swahili in Zanzibar), English (official, primary language of commerce, administration, and higher education), Arabic, many local languages
major-language sample(s):
The World Factbook, Chanzo cha Lazima Kuhusu Habari ya Msingi. (Kiswahili)

Religions: Christian 63.1%, Muslim 34.1%, folk religion 1.1%, Buddhist <1%, Hindu <1%, Jewish <1%, other <1%, unspecified 1.6% (2020 est.)
note: Zanzibar is almost entirely Muslim

Demographic profile: Tanzania has the largest population in East Africa and the lowest population density; more than a third of the population is urban. Tanzania's youthful population – over 60% of the population is under 25 as of 2020 – is growing rapidly because of the high total fertility rate of 4.4 children per woman, as of 2022. Progress in reducing the birth rate has stalled, sustaining the country's nearly 3% annual growth rate. The maternal mortality rate has improved since 2000, yet it remains very high because of early and frequent pregnancies, inadequate maternal health services, and a lack of skilled birth attendants – problems that are worse among poor and rural women. Tanzania has made strides in reducing under-5 and infant mortality rates, but a recent drop in immunization threatens to undermine gains in child health. Malaria is a leading killer of children under 5, while HIV is the main source of adult mortality.
For Tanzania, most migration is internal, rural to urban movement, while some temporary labor migration from towns to plantations takes place seasonally for harvests. Tanzania was Africa's largest refugee-hosting country for decades, hosting hundreds of thousands of refugees from the Great Lakes region, primarily Burundi, over the last fifty years. However, the assisted repatriation and naturalization of tens of thousands of Burundian refugees between 2002 and 2014 dramatically reduced the refugee population. Tanzania is increasingly a transit country for illegal migrants from the Horn of Africa and the Great Lakes region who are heading to southern Africa for security reasons and/or economic opportunities. Some of these migrants choose to settle in Tanzania.

Age structure: *0-14 years:* 41.2% (male 14,039,292/female 13,740,439)
15-64 years: 55.4% (male 18,677,388/female 18,708,390)
65 years and over: 3.4% (2024 est.) (male 975,224/female 1,321,388)

Dependency ratios: *total dependency ratio:* 87.7
youth dependency ratio: 81.9
elderly dependency ratio: 5.9
potential support ratio: 20.4 (2021 est.)

Median age: *total:* 19.1 years (2024 est.)
male: 18.8 years
female: 19.4 years
comparison ranking: total 214

Population growth rate: 2.72% (2024 est.)
comparison ranking: 13

Birth rate: 32.5 births/1,000 population (2024 est.)
comparison ranking: 19

Death rate: 5 deaths/1,000 population (2024 est.)
comparison ranking: 193

Net migration rate: -0.4 migrant(s)/1,000 population (2024 est.)
comparison ranking: 120

Population distribution: the largest and most populous East African country; population distribution is extremely uneven, but greater population clusters occur in the northern half of country and along the east coast as shown in this population distribution map

Urbanization: *urban population:* 37.4% of total population (2023)
rate of urbanization: 4.89% annual rate of change (2020-25 est.)

Major urban areas - population: 262,000 Dodoma (legislative capital) (2018), 7.776 million DAR ES SALAAM (administrative capital), 1.311 million Mwanza, 800,000 Zanzibar (2023)

Sex ratio: *at birth:* 1.03 male(s)/female
0-14 years: 1.02 male(s)/female
15-64 years: 1 male(s)/female
65 years and over: 0.74 male(s)/female
total population: 1 male(s)/female (2024 est.)

Mother's mean age at first birth: 19.9 years (2022 est.)
note: data represents median age at first birth among women 15-49

Maternal mortality ratio: 238 deaths/100,000 live births (2020 est.)

comparison ranking: 38

Infant mortality rate: *total:* 29.6 deaths/1,000 live births (2024 est.)
male: 32.3 deaths/1,000 live births
female: 26.9 deaths/1,000 live births
comparison ranking: total 51

Life expectancy at birth: *total population:* 70.8 years (2024 est.)
male: 69 years
female: 72.6 years
comparison ranking: total population 171

Total fertility rate: 4.27 children born/woman (2024 est.)
comparison ranking: 19

Gross reproduction rate: 2.1 (2024 est.)

Contraceptive prevalence rate: 38.4% (2015/16)

Drinking water source: *improved: urban:* 95.1% of population
rural: 59.4% of population
total: 72% of population
unimproved: urban: 4.9% of population
rural: 40.6% of population
total: 28% of population (2020 est.)

Current health expenditure: 3.8% of GDP (2020)

Physician density: 0.05 physicians/1,000 population (2018)

Hospital bed density: 0.7 beds/1,000 population

Sanitation facility access: *improved: urban:* 89.4% of population
rural: 29.2% of population
total: 50.4% of population
unimproved: urban: 10.6% of population
rural: 70.8% of population
total: 49.6% of population (2020 est.)

Obesity - adult prevalence rate: 8.4% (2016)
comparison ranking: 152

Alcohol consumption per capita: *total:* 7.81 liters of pure alcohol (2019 est.)
beer: 0.74 liters of pure alcohol (2019 est.)
wine: 0.09 liters of pure alcohol (2019 est.)
spirits: 0.38 liters of pure alcohol (2019 est.)
other alcohols: 6.6 liters of pure alcohol (2019 est.)
comparison ranking: total 46

Tobacco use: *total:* 8.7% (2020 est.)
male: 14% (2020 est.)
female: 3.4% (2020 est.)
comparison ranking: total 141

Children under the age of 5 years underweight: 12.1% (2022)
comparison ranking: 43

Currently married women (ages 15-49): 59.5% (2023 est.)

Child marriage: *women married by age 15:* 5.2%
women married by age 18: 30.5%
men married by age 18: 3.9% (2016 est.)

Education expenditures: 3.3% of GDP (2021 est.)
comparison ranking: 146

Literacy: *definition:* age 15 and over can read and write Kiswahili (Swahili), English, or Arabic
total population: 81.8%
male: 85.5%
female: 78.2% (2021)

School life expectancy (primary to tertiary education): *total:* 9 years
male: 9 years
female: 9 years (2021)

ENVIRONMENT

Environment - current issues: water pollution; improper management of liquid waste; indoor air pollution caused by the burning of fuel wood or charcoal for cooking and heating is a large environmental health issue; soil degradation; deforestation; desertification; destruction of coral reefs threatens marine habitats; wildlife threatened by illegal hunting and trade, especially for ivory; loss of biodiversity; solid waste disposal

Environment - international agreements: *party to:* Biodiversity, Climate Change, Climate Change-Kyoto Protocol, Climate Change-Paris Agreement, Comprehensive Nuclear Test Ban, Desertification, Endangered Species, Hazardous Wastes, Law of the Sea, Marine Dumping-London Convention, Nuclear Test Ban, Ozone Layer Protection, Ship Pollution, Wetlands, Whaling
signed, but not ratified: none of the selected agreements

Climate: varies from tropical along coast to temperate in highlands

Urbanization: *urban population:* 37.4% of total population (2023)
rate of urbanization: 4.89% annual rate of change (2020-25 est.)

Food insecurity: *severe localized food insecurity: due to localized shortfalls in staple food production* - about 592,000 people are estimated to be in need of humanitarian assistance between May and September 2022, mainly located in northeastern regions, reflecting crop losses during the October–December "Vuli" 2021 and March–May "Masika" 2022 seasons due to poor rains; high food prices are also constraining households' economic access to food (2022)

Revenue from forest resources: 2.19% of GDP (2018 est.)
comparison ranking: 32

Revenue from coal: 0.02% of GDP (2018 est.)
comparison ranking: 42

Air pollutants: *particulate matter emissions:* 15.36 micrograms per cubic meter (2019 est.)
carbon dioxide emissions: 11.97 megatons (2016 est.)
methane emissions: 59.08 megatons (2020 est.)

Waste and recycling: *municipal solid waste generated annually:* 9,276,995 tons (2012 est.)

Major lakes (area sq km): *fresh water lake(s):* Lake Victoria (shared with Uganda and Kenya) - 62,940 sq km; Lake Tanganyika (shared with Democratic Republic of Congo, Burundi, and Zambia) - 32,000 sq km; Lake Malawi (shared with Mozambique and Malawi) - 22,490
salt water lake(s): Lake Rukwa - 5,760 sq km

Major rivers (by length in km): Nile (shared with Rwanda [s], Uganda, South Sudan, Sudan, and Egypt [m]) - 6,650 km
note – [s] after country name indicates river source; [m] after country name indicates river mouth

Major watersheds (area sq km): Atlantic Ocean drainage: Congo (3,730,881 sq km), (Mediterranean Sea) Nile (3,254,853 sq km) Indian Ocean drainage: Zambezi (1,332,412 sq km)

Total water withdrawal: *municipal:* 530 million cubic meters (2020 est.)
industrial: 30 million cubic meters (2020 est.)
agricultural: 4.63 billion cubic meters (2020 est.)

Total renewable water resources: 96.3 billion cubic meters (2019 est.)

Geoparks: *total global geoparks and regional networks:* 1
global geoparks and regional networks: Ngorongoro Lengai (2023)

GOVERNMENT

Country name: *conventional long form:* United Republic of Tanzania
conventional short form: Tanzania
local long form: Jamhuri ya Muungano wa Tanzania
local short form: Tanzania
former: German East Africa, Trust Territory of Tanganyika, Republic of Tanganyika, People's Republic of Zanzibar, United Republic of Tanganyika and Zanzibar
etymology: the country's name is a combination of the first letters of Tanganyika and Zanzibar, the two states that merged to form Tanzania in 1964

Government type: presidential republic

Capital: *name:* Dodoma; note - Dodoma was designated the national capital in 1996; Dar es Salaam, the original national capital, is the country's largest city and commercial center
geographic coordinates: 6 48 S, 39 17 E
time difference: UTC+3 (8 hours ahead of Washington, DC, during Standard Time)
etymology: Dodoma, in the native Gogo language, means "it has sunk"; supposedly, one day during the rainy season, an elephant drowned in the area; the villagers in that place were so struck by what had occurred, that ever since the locale has been referred to as the place where "it (the elephant) sunk"

Administrative divisions: 31 regions; Arusha, Dar es Salaam, Dodoma, Geita, Iringa, Kagera, Kaskazini Pemba (Pemba North), Kaskazini Unguja (Zanzibar North), Katavi, Kigoma, Kilimanjaro, Kusini Pemba (Pemba South), Kusini Unguja (Zanzibar Central/South), Lindi, Manyara, Mara, Mbeya, Mjini Magharibi (Zanzibar Urban/West), Morogoro, Mtwara, Mwanza, Njombe, Pwani (Coast), Rukwa, Ruvuma, Shinyanga, Simiyu, Singida, Songwe, Tabora, Tanga

Independence: *26 April 1964 (Tanganyika united with Zanzibar to form the United Republic of Tanganyika and Zanzibar); 29 October 1964 (renamed United Republic of Tanzania); notable earlier dates:* 9 December 1961 (Tanganyika became independent from UK-administered UN trusteeship); 10 December 1963 (Zanzibar became independent from UK)

National holiday: Union Day (Tanganyika and Zanzibar), 26 April (1964)

Legal system: English common law; judicial review of legislative acts limited to matters of interpretation

Constitution: *history:* several previous; latest adopted 25 April 1977; note - drafting of a new constitution by the National Assembly in 2014 had stalled, and not until 2021, when President HASSAN expressed the need for broad government reform was there a renewed mandate for a new constitution; a task force drafted and submitted a report in October 2202 with broad government reform recommendations, including a six-pronged approach to a new constitution; the president as recently as mid-2023 reaffirmed her commitment to a new constitution; Tanzania's political opposition in early 2024, called

for protests rallying countrywide support for action on this issue
amendments: proposed by the National Assembly; passage of amendments to constitutional articles including those on sovereignty of the United Republic, the authorities and powers of the government, the president, the Assembly, and the High Court requires two-thirds majority vote of the mainland Assembly membership and of the Zanzibar House of Representatives membership; House of Representatives approval of other amendments is not required; amended several times, last in 2017

International law organization participation: has not submitted an ICJ jurisdiction declaration; accepts ICCt jurisdiction

Citizenship: *citizenship by birth:* no
citizenship by descent only: at least one parent must be a citizen of Tanzania; if a child is born abroad, the father must be a citizen of Tanzania
dual citizenship recognized: no
residency requirement for naturalization: 5 years

Suffrage: 18 years of age; universal

Executive branch: *chief of state:* President Samia Suluhu HASSAN (since 19 March 2021)
head of government: President Samia Suluhu HASSAN (since 19 March 2021)
cabinet: Cabinet appointed by the president from among members of the National Assembly
elections/appointments: president and vice president directly elected on the same ballot by simple majority popular vote for a 5-year term (eligible for a second term); election last held on 28 October 2020 (next to be held in October 2025); prime minister appointed by the president
election results:
2020: John MAGUFULI reelected president; percent of vote - John MAGUFULI (CCM) 84.4%, Tundu LISSU (CHADEMA) 13%, other 2.6%; note - President MAGUFULI died on 17 March 2021 and his Vice President, Samia Suluhu HASSAN, assumed the office of the President on 19 March 2021
2015: John MAGUFULI elected president; percent of vote - John MAGUFULI (CCM) 58.5%, Edward LOWASSA (CHADEMA) 40%, other 1.5%
note 1: Zanzibar elects a president as head of government for internal matters; elections were held on 28 October 2020; Hussein MWINYI (CCM) 76.3%, Maalim Seif SHARIF (ACT-Wazalendo) 19.9%, other 3.8%
note 2: the president is both chief of state and head of government
note 3: following the death of President John MAGUFULI in March 2021, then Vice President Samia Suluhu HASSAN assumed the presidency

Legislative branch: *description:* unicameral National Assembly or Parliament (Bunge) (393 seats; 264 members directly elected in singleseat constituencies by simple majority vote, 113 women indirectly elected by proportional representation vote, 5 indirectly elected by simple majority vote by the Zanzibar House of Representatives, 10 appointed by the president, and 1 seat reserved for the attorney general; members serve 5-year terms)
elections: Tanzania National Assembly - last held on 28 October 2020 (next to be held in October 2025)
election results: National Assembly - percent of vote by party - NA; seats by party - CCM 350, Chadema 20, ACT-Wazalendo 4, CUF 3; composition - men 246, women 147, percentage women 37.4%

Judicial branch: *highest court(s):* Court of Appeal of the United Republic of Tanzania (consists of the chief justice and 14 justices); High Court of the United Republic for Mainland Tanzania (consists of the principal judge and 30 judges organized into commercial, land, and labor courts); High Court of Zanzibar (consists of the chief justice and 10 justices)
judge selection and term of office: Court of Appeal and High Court justices appointed by the national president after consultation with the Judicial Service Commission for Tanzania, a judicial body of high level judges and 2 members appointed by the national president; Court of Appeal and High Court judges serve until mandatory retirement at age 60, but terms can be extended; High Court of Zanzibar judges appointed by the national president after consultation with the Judicial Commission of Zanzibar; judges can serve until mandatory retirement at age 65
subordinate courts: Resident Magistrates Courts; Kadhi courts (for Islamic family matters); district and primary courts

Political parties: Alliance for Change and Transparency (Wazalendo) or ACT-Wazalendo
Civic United Front (Chama Cha Wananchi) or CUF
Party of Democracy and Development (Chama Cha Demokrasia na Maendeleo) or CHADEMA
Revolutionary Party of Tanzania (Chama Cha Mapinduzi) or CCM

International organization participation: ACP, AfDB, AU, C, CD, EAC, EADB, EITI, FAO, G-77, IAEA, IBRD, ICAO, ICC (NGOs), ICCt, ICRM, IDA, IFAD, IFC, IFRCS, ILO, IMF, IMO, IMSO, Interpol, IOC, IOM, IPU, ISO, ITSO, ITU, ITUC (NGOs), MIGA, MONUSCO, NAM, OPCW, SADC, UN, UNAMID, UNCTAD, UNESCO, UNHCR, UNIDO, UNIFIL, UNISFA, UNMISS, UNWTO, UPU, WCO, WFTU (NGOs), WHO, WIPO, WMO, WTO

Diplomatic representation in the US: *chief of mission:* Ambassador Elsie Sia KANZA (since 1 December 2021)
chancery: 1232 22nd Street NW, Washington, DC 20037
telephone: [1] (202) 884-1080
FAX: [1] (202) 797-7408
email address and website:
ubalozi@tanzaniaembassy-us.org
https://us.tzembassy.go.tz/

Diplomatic representation from the US: *chief of mission:* Ambassador Michael A. BATTLE Sr. (since 27 February 2023)
embassy: 686 Old Bagamoyo Road, Msasani, P.O. Box 9123, Dar es Salaam
mailing address: 2140 Dar es Salaam Place, Washington, DC 20521-2140
telephone: [255] (22) 229-4000
FAX: [255] (22) 229-4721
email address and website:
DRSACS@state.gov
https://tz.usembassy.gov/

Flag description: divided diagonally by a yellow-edged black band from the lower hoist-side corner; the upper triangle (hoist side) is green and the lower triangle is blue; the banner combines colors found on the flags of Tanganyika and Zanzibar; green represents the natural vegetation of the country, gold its rich mineral deposits, black the native Swahili people, and blue the country's many lakes and rivers, as well as the Indian Ocean

National symbol(s): Uhuru (Freedom) torch, giraffe; national colors: green, yellow, blue, black

National anthem: *name:* "Mungu ibariki Afrika" (God Bless Africa)
lyrics/music: collective/Enoch Mankayi SONTONGA
note: adopted 1961; the anthem, which is also a popular song in Africa, shares the same melody with that of Zambia but has different lyrics; the melody is also incorporated into South Africa's anthem

National heritage: *total World Heritage Sites:* 7 (3 cultural, 3 natural, 1 mixed)
selected World Heritage Site locales: Ngorongoro Conservation Area (m); Ruins of Kilwa Kisiwani and Songo Mnara (c); Serengeti National Park (n); Selous Game Reserve (n); Kilimanjaro National Park (n); Stone Town of Zanzibar (c); Kondoa Rock-Art Sites (c)

ECONOMY

Economic overview: emerging lower middle-income East African economy; resource-rich and growing tourism; strong post-pandemic recovery from hospitality, electricity, mining, and transit sectors; declining poverty; stable inflation; gender-based violence economic and labor force disruptions

Real GDP (purchasing power parity): $234.05 billion (2023 est.)
$222.506 billion (2022 est.)
$212.79 billion (2021 est.)
note: data in 2021 dollars
comparison ranking: 70

Real GDP growth rate: 5.19% (2023 est.)
4.57% (2022 est.)
4.32% (2021 est.)
note: annual GDP % growth based on constant local currency
comparison ranking: 47

Real GDP per capita: $3,600 (2023 est.)
$3,500 (2022 est.)
$3,500 (2021 est.)
note: data in 2021 dollars
comparison ranking: 189

GDP (official exchange rate): $79.158 billion (2023 est.)
note: data in current dollars at official exchange rate

Inflation rate (consumer prices): 3.8% (2023 est.)
4.35% (2022 est.)
3.69% (2021 est.)
note: annual % change based on consumer prices
comparison ranking: 76

Credit ratings: Moody's rating: B2 (2020)
note: The year refers to the year in which the current credit rating was first obtained.

GDP - composition, by sector of origin: *agriculture:* 23.7% (2023 est.)
industry: 27.7% (2023 est.)
services: 28.9% (2023 est.)
note: figures may not total 100% due to non-allocated consumption not captured in sector-reported data
comparison rankings: services 210; industry 79; agriculture 23

GDP - composition, by end use: *household consumption:* 53.8% (2023 est.)
government consumption: 8.1% (2023 est.)
investment in fixed capital: 42% (2023 est.)
investment in inventories: -1.7% (2023 est.)
exports of goods and services: 17.8% (2023 est.)
imports of goods and services: -20% (2023 est.)

note: figures may not total 100% due to rounding or gaps in data collection

Agricultural products: cassava, maize, sweet potatoes, sugarcane, bananas, milk, rice, vegetables, beans, sunflower seeds (2022)
note: top ten agricultural products based on tonnage

Industries: agricultural processing (sugar, beer, cigarettes, sisal twine); mining (diamonds, gold, and iron), salt, soda ash; cement, oil refining, shoes, apparel, wood products, fertilizer

Industrial production growth rate: 3.9% (2023 est.)
note: annual % change in industrial value added based on constant local currency
comparison ranking: 81

Labor force: 31.219 million (2023 est.)
note: number of people ages 15 or older who are employed or seeking work
comparison ranking: 22

Unemployment rate: 2.61% (2023 est.)
2.61% (2022 est.)
2.81% (2021 est.)
note: % of labor force seeking employment
comparison ranking: 31

Youth unemployment rate (ages 15-24): *total:* 3.5% (2023 est.)
male: 2.6% (2023 est.)
female: 4.4% (2023 est.)
note: % of labor force ages 15-24 seeking employment
comparison ranking: total 190

Population below poverty line: 26.4% (2018 est.)
note: % of population with income below national poverty line

Gini Index coefficient - distribution of family income: 40.5 (2018 est.)
note: index (0-100) of income distribution; higher values represent greater inequality
comparison ranking: 42

Average household expenditures: *on food:* 27.9% of household expenditures (2022 est.)
on alcohol and tobacco: 1.6% of household expenditures (2022 est.)

Household income or consumption by percentage share: *lowest 10%:* 2.9% (2018 est.)
highest 10%: 33.1% (2018 est.)
note: % share of income accruing to lowest and highest 10% of population

Remittances: 0.42% of GDP (2023 est.)
0.92% of GDP (2022 est.)
0.79% of GDP (2021 est.)
note: personal transfers and compensation between resident and non-resident individuals/households/entities

Budget: *revenues:* $9.114 billion (2014 est.)
expenditures: $8.926 billion (2014 est.)
note: central government revenues (excluding grants) and expenses converted to US dollars at average official exchange rate for year indicated

Public debt: 37% of GDP (2017 est.)
comparison ranking: 142

Taxes and other revenues: 11.47% (of GDP) (2023 est.)
note: central government tax revenue as a % of GDP
comparison ranking: 170

Current account balance: -$5.384 billion (2022 est.)
-$2.388 billion (2021 est.)
-$1.459 billion (2020 est.)
note: balance of payments - net trade and primary/secondary income in current dollars
comparison ranking: 183

Exports: $11.986 billion (2022 est.)
$9.874 billion (2021 est.)
$8.555 billion (2020 est.)
note: balance of payments - exports of goods and services in current dollars
comparison ranking: 106

Exports - partners: India 27%, UAE 11%, South Africa 9%, Kenya 5%, Rwanda 5% (2022)
note: top five export partners based on percentage share of exports

Exports - commodities: gold, raw copper, refined copper, copper ore, coconuts/Brazil nuts/cashews (2022)
note: top five export commodities based on value in dollars

Imports: $16.674 billion (2022 est.)
$11.61 billion (2021 est.)
$9.151 billion (2020 est.)
note: balance of payments - imports of goods and services in current dollars
comparison ranking: 104

Imports - partners: China 30%, India 18%, UAE 11%, Democratic Republic of the Congo 5%, Saudi Arabia 2% (2022)
note: top five import partners based on percentage share of imports

Imports - commodities: refined petroleum, refined copper, garments, fertilizers, plastics (2022)
note: top five import commodities based on value in dollars

Reserves of foreign exchange and gold: $5.05 billion (2018 est.)
$5.888 billion (2017 est.)
$4.351 billion (2016 est.)
note: holdings of gold (year-end prices)/foreign exchange/special drawing rights in current dollars
comparison ranking: 99

Debt - external: $15.913 billion (2022 est.)
note: present value of external debt in current US dollars
comparison ranking: 29

Exchange rates: Tanzanian shillings (TZS) per US dollar -

Exchange rates: 2,297.764 (2021 est.)
2,294.146 (2020 est.)
2,288.207 (2019 est.)
2,263.782 (2018 est.)
2,228.857 (2017 est.)

ENERGY

Electricity access: *electrification - total population:* 45.8% (2022 est.)
electrification - urban areas: 74.7%
electrification - rural areas: 36%

Electricity: *installed generating capacity:* 1.677 million kW (2022 est.)
consumption: 7.931 billion kWh (2022 est.)
imports: 148.53 million kWh (2022 est.)
transmission/distribution losses: 1.238 billion kWh (2022 est.)
comparison rankings: transmission/distribution losses 109; imports 108; consumption 114; installed generating capacity 126

Electricity generation sources: *fossil fuels:* 67.4% of total installed capacity (2022 est.)
solar: 0.5% of total installed capacity (2022 est.)
hydroelectricity: 31.3% of total installed capacity (2022 est.)
biomass and waste: 0.8% of total installed capacity (2022 est.)

Coal: *production:* 2.511 million metric tons (2022 est.)
consumption: 802,000 metric tons (2022 est.)
exports: 1.71 million metric tons (2022 est.)
imports: 100 metric tons (2022 est.)
proven reserves: 1.41 billion metric tons (2022 est.)

Petroleum: *refined petroleum consumption:* 58,000 bbl/day (2022 est.)

Natural gas: *production:* 1.808 billion cubic meters (2022 est.)
consumption: 1.808 billion cubic meters (2022 est.)
proven reserves: 6.513 billion cubic meters (2021 est.)

Carbon dioxide emissions: 12.804 million metric tonnes of CO2 (2022 est.)
from coal and metallurgical coke: 1.762 million metric tonnes of CO2 (2022 est.)
from petroleum and other liquids: 7.494 million metric tonnes of CO2 (2022 est.)
from consumed natural gas: 3.547 million metric tonnes of CO2 (2022 est.)
comparison ranking: total emissions 99

Energy consumption per capita: 3.221 million Btu/person (2022 est.)
comparison ranking: 177

COMMUNICATIONS

Telephones - fixed lines: *total subscriptions:* 85,000 (2022 est.)
subscriptions per 100 inhabitants: (2022 est.) less than 1
comparison ranking: total subscriptions 143

Telephones - mobile cellular: *total subscriptions:* 60.192 million (2022 est.)
subscriptions per 100 inhabitants: 92 (2022 est.)
comparison ranking: total subscriptions 28

Telecommunication systems: *general assessment:* Tanzania's telecom sector enjoys effective competition, particularly in the mobile segment; the government has encouraged foreign participation to promote economic growth and social development, and policy reforms have led to the country having one of the most liberal telecom sectors in Africa; the government has sought to increase broadband penetration by a range of measures, including the reduction in VAT charged on the sale of smartphones and other devices, and reductions in the cost of data; the MNOs became the leading ISPs following the launch of mobile broadband services based on 3G and LTE technologies; operators are hoping for revenue growth in the mobile data services market, given that the voice market is almost entirely prepaid; the MNOs have invested in network upgrades, which in turn has supported m-mobile data use, as well as m-money transfer services and banking services. Together, these have become a fast-developing source of revenue; the landing of the first international submarine cables in the country some years ago revolutionized the telecom market, which up to that point had entirely depended on expensive satellite connections; following the signing of infrastructure investment agreements with mobile network operators, the government plans to extend its national ICT broadband backbone to 99 or 185 districts by 2024 and to all districts by 2030
(2022)

domestic: fixed-line telephone network is 2 connections per 100 persons; mobile-cellular service is 92 telephones per 100 persons (2022)
international: country code - 255; landing points for the EASSy, SEACOM/Tata TGN-Eurasia, and SEAS fiber-optic submarine cable system linking East Africa with the Middle East; satellite earth stations - 2 Intelsat (1 Indian Ocean, 1 Atlantic Ocean) (2019)

Broadcast media: according to statistics from the Tanzania Communications Regulatory Authority (TCRA), Tanzania had 45 television stations as of 2020; 13 of those stations provided national content services (commercially broadcasting free-to-air television); there are 196 radio stations, most operating at the district level, but also including 5 independent nationally broadcasting stations and 1 state-owned national radio station; international broadcasting is available through satellite television which is becoming increasingly widespread; there are 3 major satellite TV providers (2020)

Internet country code: .tz

Internet users: *total:* 20.48 million (2021 est.)
percent of population: 32% (2021 est.)
comparison ranking: total 43

Broadband - fixed subscriptions: *total:* 1,135,608 (2020 est.)
subscriptions per 100 inhabitants: 2 (2020 est.)
comparison ranking: total 70

TRANSPORTATION

National air transport system: *number of registered air carriers:* 11 (2020)
inventory of registered aircraft operated by air carriers: 91
annual passenger traffic on registered air carriers: 1,481,557 (2018)
annual freight traffic on registered air carriers: 390,000 (2018) mt-km

Civil aircraft registration country code prefix: 5H

Airports: 206 (2024)
comparison ranking: 29

Pipelines: 311 km gas, 891 km oil, 8 km refined products (2013)

Railways: *total:* 4,097 km (2022)
standard gauge: 421 km (2022)
narrow gauge: 969 km (2022) 1.067 m gauge
broad gauge: 2,707 km (2022) 1.000 m guage
comparison ranking: total 44

Roadways: *total:* 145,203 km
paved: 11,201 km
unpaved: 134,002 km (2022)
comparison ranking: total 36

Waterways: 1,594 km (2022) (Lake Tanganyika 673 km, Lake Victoria 337 km, and Lake Nyasa (Lake Malawi) 584 km are the principal avenues of commerce with neighboring countries; the rivers are not navigable)
comparison ranking: 53

Merchant marine: *total:* 381 (2023)
by type: bulk carrier 4, container ship 17, general cargo 170, oil tanker 58, other 132
comparison ranking: total 51

Ports: *total ports:* 8 (2024)
large: 0
medium: 1
small: 3
very small: 4
ports with oil terminals: 4
key ports: Chake Chake, Dar Es Salaam, Tanga, Zanzibar

MILITARY AND SECURITY

Military and security forces: Tanzania People's Defense Forces (TPDF or Jeshi la Wananchi la Tanzania, JWTZ): Land Forces, Naval Forces, Air Force, National Building Army (Jeshi la Kujenga Taifa, JKT), People's Militia (Reserves)

Ministry of Home Affairs: Tanzania Police Force (2024)
note 1: the National Building Army (aka National Services) is a paramilitary organization under the Defense Forces that provides six months of military and vocational training to individuals as part of their two years of public service; after completion of training, some graduates join the regular Defense Forces while the remainder become part of the People's (or Citizen's) Militia
note 2: the Tanzania Police Force includes the Police Field Force (aka Field Force Unit), a special police division with the responsibility for controlling unlawful demonstrations and riots

Military expenditures: 1.3% of GDP (2023 est.)
1.2% of GDP (2022 est.)
1.1% of GDP (2021 est.)
1.2% of GDP (2020 est.)
1.1% of GDP (2019 est.)
comparison ranking: 103

Military and security service personnel strengths: approximately 25,000 active-duty personnel (21,000 Land Forces; 1,000 Naval Forces; 3,000 Air Force) (2023)

Military equipment inventories and acquisitions: the TPDF's inventory includes mostly Chinese and Russian/Soviet-era weapons and equipment (2024)

Military service age and obligation: 18-25 years of age for voluntary military service for men and women; 6-year commitment (2-year contracts afterwards); selective conscription for 2 years of public service (2024)

Military deployments: 520 Central African Republic (MINUSCA); 850 Democratic Republic of the Congo (MONUSCO; note - the MONUSCO mission is in the process of drawing down forces); 125 Lebanon (UNIFIL); approximately 300 Mozambique (under bilateral agreement to assist with combatting an insurgency) (2024)

Military - note: the TDPF's primary concerns are maritime piracy and smuggling, border security, terrorism, animal poaching, and spillover from instability in neighboring countries, particularly Mozambique and the Democratic Republic of the Congo (DRC); it participates in multinational training exercises, regional peacekeeping deployments, and has ties with a variety of foreign militaries, including those of China, India, and the US; it has contributed troops to the UN's Force Intervention Brigade in the DRC; the TPDF also participated in the former Southern African Development Community intervention force in Mozambique, which assisted the Mozambique military in combating fighters affiliated with the Islamic State of Iraq and ash-Sham (ISIS); the regional force withdrew in 2024, but the TPDF continues to maintain troops in Mozambique as part of a separate bilateral security agreement; since 2020, the TPDF has reinforced the border with Mozambique following several cross-border attacks by ISIS fighters (2024)

TERRORISM

Terrorist group(s): Islamic State of Iraq and ash-Sham - Mozambique (ISIS-M)
note: details about the history, aims, leadership, organization, areas of operation, tactics, targets, weapons, size, and sources of support of the group(s) appear(s) in the Terrorism reference guide

TRANSNATIONAL ISSUES

Refugees and internally displaced persons: *refugees (country of origin):* 89,163 (Democratic Republic of the Congo), 112,779 (Burundi) (2024)

Illicit drugs: significant transit country for illicit drugs in East Africa; international drug trafficking organizations and courier networks transit illicit drugs through mainland Tanzania to markets in within Africa, Europe and North America; cultivates cannabis and khat for domestic consumption and regional and international distribution; domestic drug use continues increasing including methamphetamine heroin use (2023)

THAILAND

INTRODUCTION

Background: Two unified Thai kingdoms emerged in the mid-13th century. The Sukhothai Kingdom, located in the south-central plains, gained its independence from the Khmer Empire to the east. By the late 13th century, Sukhothai's territory extended into present-day Burma and Laos. Sukhothai lasted until the mid-15th century. The Thai Lan Na Kingdom was established in the north with its capital at Chang Mai; the Burmese conquered Lan Na in the 16th century. The Ayutthaya Kingdom (14th-18th centuries) succeeded the Sukhothai and would become known as the Siamese Kingdom. During the Ayutthaya period, the Thai/Siamese peoples consolidated their hold on what is present-day central and north-central Thailand. Following a military defeat at the hands of the Burmese in 1767, the Siamese Kingdom rose to new heights under the military ruler TAKSIN, who defeated the Burmese occupiers and expanded the kingdom's territory into modern-day northern Thailand (formerly the Lan Na Kingdom), Cambodia, Laos, and the Malay Peninsula. In the mid-1800s, Western pressure led to Siam signing trade treaties that reduced the country's sovereignty

and independence. In the 1890s and 1900s, the British and French forced the kingdom to cede Cambodian, Laotian, and Malay territories that had been under Siamese control.

Following a bloodless revolution in 1932 that led to the establishment of a constitutional monarchy, Thailand's political history was marked by a series of mostly bloodless coups with power concentrated among military and bureaucratic elites. Periods of civilian rule were unstable. The Cold War era saw a communist insurgency and the rise of strongman leaders. Thailand became a US treaty ally in 1954 after sending troops to Korea and later fighting alongside the US in Vietnam. In the 21st century, Thailand has experienced additional turmoil, including a military coup in 2006 that ousted then Prime Minister THAKSIN Chinnawat and large-scale street protests led by competing political factions in 2008-2010. In 2011, THAKSIN's youngest sister, YINGLAK Chinnawat, led the Puea Thai Party to an electoral win and assumed control of the government.

In 2014, after months of major anti-government protests in Bangkok, the Constitutional Court removed YINGLAK from office, and the Army, led by Gen. PRAYUT Chan-ocha, then staged a coup against the caretaker government. The military-affiliated National Council for Peace and Order (NCPO) ruled the country under PRAYUT for more than four years, drafting a new constitution that allowed the military to appoint the entire 250-member Senate and required a joint meeting of the House and Senate to select the prime minister – which effectively gave the military a veto on the selection. King PHUMIPHON Adunyadet passed away in 2016 after 70 years on the throne; his only son, WACHIRALONGKON (aka King RAMA X), formally ascended the throne in 2019. The same year, a long-delayed election allowed PRAYUT to continue his premiership, although the results were disputed and widely viewed as skewed in favor of the party aligned with the military. The country again experienced major anti-government protests in 2020. The reformist Move Forward Party won the most seats in the 2023 election but was unable to form a government, and Srettha THRAVISIN from the Pheu Thai Party replaced PRAYUT as prime minister after forming a coalition of moderate and conservative parties.

GEOGRAPHY

Location: Southeastern Asia, bordering the Andaman Sea and the Gulf of Thailand, southeast of Burma

Geographic coordinates: 15 00 N, 100 00 E

Map references: Southeast Asia

Area: *total:* 513,120 sq km
land: 510,890 sq km
water: 2,230 sq km
comparison ranking: total 53

Area - comparative: about three times the size of Florida; slightly more than twice the size of Wyoming

Land boundaries: *total:* 5,673 km
border countries (4): Burma 2,416 km; Cambodia 817 km; Laos 1,845 km; Malaysia 595 km

Coastline: 3,219 km

Maritime claims: *territorial sea:* 12 nm
exclusive economic zone: 200 nm
continental shelf: 200-m depth or to the depth of exploitation

Climate: tropical; rainy, warm, cloudy southwest monsoon (mid-May to September); dry, cool northeast monsoon (November to mid-March); southern isthmus always hot and humid

Terrain: central plain; Khorat Plateau in the east; mountains elsewhere

Elevation: *highest point:* Doi Inthanon 2,565 m
lowest point: Gulf of Thailand 0 m
mean elevation: 287 m

Natural resources: tin, rubber, natural gas, tungsten, tantalum, timber, lead, fish, gypsum, lignite, fluorite, arable land

Land use: *agricultural land:* 41.2% (2018 est.)
arable land: 30.8% (2018 est.)
permanent crops: 8.8% (2018 est.)
permanent pasture: 1.6% (2018 est.)
forest: 37.2% (2018 est.)
other: 21.6% (2018 est.)

Irrigated land: 64,150 sq km (2012)

Major lakes (area sq km): *salt water lake(s):* Thalesap Songkhla - 1,290 sq km

Major rivers (by length in km): Mae Nam Khong (Mekong) (shared with China [s], Burma, Laos, Cambodia, and Vietnam [m]) - 4,350 km; Salween (shared with China [s] and Burma [m]) - 3,060 km; Mun - 1,162 km
note – [s] after country name indicates river source; [m] after country name indicates river mouth

Major watersheds (area sq km): Indian Ocean drainage: Salween (271,914 sq km)

Pacific Ocean drainage: Mekong (805,604 sq km)

Population distribution: highest population density is found in and around Bangkok; significant population clusters found througout large parts of the country, particularly north and northeast of Bangkok and in the extreme southern region of the country

Natural hazards: land subsidence in Bangkok area resulting from the depletion of the water table; droughts

Geography - note: controls only land route from Asia to Malaysia and Singapore; ideas for the construction of a canal across the Kra Isthmus that would create a bypass to the Strait of Malacca and shorten shipping times around Asia continue to be discussed

PEOPLE AND SOCIETY

Population: *total:* 69,920,998
male: 34,065,311
female: 35,855,687 (2024 est.)
comparison rankings: female 20; male 20; total 20

Nationality: *noun:* Thai (singular and plural)
adjective: Thai

Ethnic groups: Thai 97.5%, Burmese 1.3%, other 1.1%, unspecified <0.1% (2015 est.)
note: data represent population by nationality

Languages: Thai (official) only 90.7%, Thai and other languages 6.4%, only other languages 2.9% (includes Malay, Burmese); English is a secondary language among the elite (2010 est.)
major-language sample(s):
สารานุกรมโลก - แหล่งข้อมูลพื้นฐานที่สำคัญ (Thai)
note: data represent population by language(s) spoken at home

Religions: Buddhist 92.5%, Muslim 5.4%, Christian 1.2%, other 0.9% (includes animist, Confucian, Hindu, Jewish, Sikh, and Taoist) (2021 est.)

Demographic profile: Thailand has experienced a substantial fertility decline since the 1960s largely due to the nationwide success of its voluntary family planning program. In just one generation, the total fertility rate (TFR) shrank from 6.5 children per woman in the 1960s to below the replacement level of 2.1 in the late 1980s. Reduced fertility occurred among all segments of the Thai population, despite disparities between urban and rural areas in terms of income, education, and access to public services. The country's "reproductive revolution" gained momentum in the 1970s as a result of the government's launch of an official population policy to reduce population growth, the introduction of new forms of birth control, and the assistance of foreign non-government organizations. Contraceptive use rapidly increased as new ways were developed to deliver family planning services to Thailand's then overwhelmingly rural population. The contraceptive prevalence rate increased from just 14% in 1970 to 58% in 1981 and has remained about 80% since 2000.

Thailand's receptiveness to family planning reflects the predominant faith, Theravada Buddhism, which emphasizes individualism, personal responsibility, and independent decision-making. Thai women have more independence and a higher status than women in many other developing countries and are not usually pressured by their husbands or other family members about family planning decisions. Thailand's relatively egalitarian society also does not have the son preference found in a number of other Asian countries; most Thai ideally want one child of each sex.

Because of its low fertility rate, increasing life expectancy, and growing elderly population, Thailand has become an aging society that will face growing labor shortages. The proportion of the population under 15 years of age has shrunk dramatically, the proportion of working-age individuals has peaked and is starting to decrease, and the proportion of elderly is growing rapidly. In the short-term, Thailand will have to improve educational quality to increase the productivity of its workforce and to compete globally in skills-based industries. An increasing reliance on migrant workers will be necessary to mitigate labor shortfalls.

Thailand is a destination, transit, and source country for migrants. It has 3-4 million migrant workers as of 2017, mainly providing low-skilled labor in the construction, agriculture, manufacturing, services, and fishing and seafood processing sectors. Migrant workers from other Southeast Asian countries with lower wages – primarily Burma and, to a lesser extent, Laos and Cambodia – have been coming to Thailand for decades to work in labor-intensive industries. Many are undocumented and are vulnerable to human trafficking for forced labor, especially in the fisheries industry, or sexual exploitation. A July 2017 migrant worker law stiffening fines on undocumented workers and their employers, prompted tens of thousands of migrants to go home. Fearing a labor shortage, the Thai Government has postponed implementation of the law until January 2018 and is rapidly registering workers. Thailand has also hosted ethnic minority refugees from Burma for more than 30 years; as of 2016, approximately 105,000 mainly Karen refugees from Burma were living in nine camps along the Thailand-Burma border.

Thailand has a significant amount of internal migration, most often from rural areas to urban centers, where there are more job opportunities. Low- and semi-skilled Thais also go abroad to work, mainly in Asia and a smaller number in the Middle East and Africa, primarily to more economically developed countries where they can earn higher wages.

Age structure: *0-14 years:* 15.8% (male 5,669,592/female 5,394,398)
15-64 years: 69% (male 23,681,528/female 24,597,535)
65 years and over: 15.1% (2024 est.) (male 4,714,191/female 5,863,754)

Dependency ratios: *total dependency ratio:* 43.5
youth dependency ratio: 22.7
elderly dependency ratio: 18.4
potential support ratio: 4.8 (2021 est.)

Median age: *total:* 41.5 years (2024 est.)
male: 40.2 years
female: 42.7 years
comparison ranking: total 49

Population growth rate: 0.17% (2024 est.)
comparison ranking: 180

Birth rate: 9.9 births/1,000 population (2024 est.)
comparison ranking: 189

Death rate: 8 deaths/1,000 population (2024 est.)
comparison ranking: 90

Net migration rate: -0.3 migrant(s)/1,000 population (2024 est.)
comparison ranking: 116

Population distribution: highest population density is found in and around Bangkok; significant population clusters found througout large parts of the country, particularly north and northeast of Bangkok and in the extreme southern region of the country

Urbanization: *urban population:* 53.6% of total population (2023)
rate of urbanization: 1.43% annual rate of change (2020-25 est.)

Major urban areas - population: 11.070 million BANGKOK (capital), 1.454 Chon Buri, 1.359 million Samut Prakan, 1.213 million Chiang Mai, 1.005 million Songkla, 1.001 million Nothaburi (2023)

Sex ratio: *at birth:* 1.05 male(s)/female
0-14 years: 1.05 male(s)/female
15-64 years: 0.96 male(s)/female
65 years and over: 0.8 male(s)/female
total population: 0.95 male(s)/female (2024 est.)

Mother's mean age at first birth: 23.3 years (2009 est.)

Maternal mortality ratio: 29 deaths/100,000 live births (2020 est.)
comparison ranking: 113

Infant mortality rate: *total:* 6.3 deaths/1,000 live births (2024 est.)
male: 6.9 deaths/1,000 live births
female: 5.6 deaths/1,000 live births
comparison ranking: total 165

Life expectancy at birth: *total population:* 78.2 years (2024 est.)
male: 75.2 years
female: 81.3 years
comparison ranking: total population 81

Total fertility rate: 1.54 children born/woman (2024 est.)
comparison ranking: 197

Gross reproduction rate: 0.75 (2024 est.)

Contraceptive prevalence rate: 73% (2019)

Drinking water source: *improved: urban:* 100% of population
rural: 100% of population
total: 100% of population

Current health expenditure: 4.4% of GDP (2020)

Physician density: 0.95 physicians/1,000 population (2020)

Sanitation facility access: *improved: urban:* 99.9% of population
rural: 100% of population
total: 100% of population

Obesity - adult prevalence rate: 10% (2016)
comparison ranking: 140

Alcohol consumption per capita: *total:* 6.86 liters of pure alcohol (2019 est.)
beer: 1.85 liters of pure alcohol (2019 est.)
wine: 0.23 liters of pure alcohol (2019 est.)
spirits: 4.78 liters of pure alcohol (2019 est.)
other alcohols: 0 liters of pure alcohol (2019 est.)
comparison ranking: total 60

Tobacco use: *total:* 22.1% (2020 est.)
male: 41.3% (2020 est.)
female: 2.9% (2020 est.)
comparison ranking: total 71

Children under the age of 5 years underweight: 7.7% (2019)
comparison ranking: 62

Currently married women (ages 15-49): 60.8% (2023 est.)

Child marriage: *women married by age 15:* 3%
women married by age 18: 20.2%
men married by age 18: 9.8% (2019 est.)

Education expenditures: 3.2% of GDP (2020 est.)
comparison ranking: 148

Literacy: *definition:* age 15 and over can read and write
total population: 94.1%
male: 95.5%
female: 92.8% (2021)

School life expectancy (primary to tertiary education): *total:* 15 years
male: 15 years
female: 16 years (2016)

ENVIRONMENT

Environment - current issues: air pollution from vehicle emissions; water pollution from organic and factory wastes; water scarcity; deforestation; soil erosion; wildlife populations threatened by illegal hunting; hazardous waste disposal

Environment - international agreements: *party to:* Biodiversity, Climate Change, Climate Change-Kyoto Protocol, Climate Change-Paris Agreement, Comprehensive Nuclear Test Ban, Desertification, Endangered Species, Hazardous Wastes, Law of the Sea, Marine Life Conservation, Nuclear Test Ban, Ozone Layer Protection, Ship Pollution, Tropical Timber 2006, Wetlands
signed, but not ratified: none of the selected agreements

Climate: tropical; rainy, warm, cloudy southwest monsoon (mid-May to September); dry, cool northeast monsoon (November to mid-March); southern isthmus always hot and humid

Land use: *agricultural land:* 41.2% (2018 est.)
arable land: 30.8% (2018 est.)
permanent crops: 8.8% (2018 est.)
permanent pasture: 1.6% (2018 est.)
forest: 37.2% (2018 est.)
other: 21.6% (2018 est.)

Urbanization: *urban population:* 53.6% of total population (2023)
rate of urbanization: 1.43% annual rate of change (2020-25 est.)

Revenue from forest resources: 0.34% of GDP (2018 est.)
comparison ranking: 76

Revenue from coal: 0.03% of GDP (2018 est.)
comparison ranking: 35

Air pollutants: *particulate matter emissions:* 24.64 micrograms per cubic meter (2019 est.)
carbon dioxide emissions: 283.76 megatons (2016 est.)
methane emissions: 86.98 megatons (2020 est.)

Waste and recycling: *municipal solid waste generated annually:* 26,853,366 tons (2015 est.)
municipal solid waste recycled annually: 5,128,993 tons (2012 est.)
percent of municipal solid waste recycled: 19.1% (2012 est.)

Major lakes (area sq km): *salt water lake(s):* Thalesap Songkhla - 1,290 sq km

Major rivers (by length in km): Mae Nam Khong (Mekong) (shared with China [s], Burma, Laos, Cambodia, and Vietnam [m]) - 4,350 km; Salween (shared with China [s] and Burma [m]) - 3,060 km; Mun - 1,162 km
note – [s] after country name indicates river source; [m] after country name indicates river mouth

Major watersheds (area sq km): Indian Ocean drainage: Salween (271,914 sq km)

Pacific Ocean drainage: Mekong (805,604 sq km)

Total water withdrawal: *municipal:* 2.74 billion cubic meters (2020 est.)
industrial: 2.78 billion cubic meters (2020 est.)
agricultural: 51.79 billion cubic meters (2020 est.)

Total renewable water resources: 438.61 billion cubic meters (2020 est.)

Geoparks: *total global geoparks and regional networks:* 2
global geoparks and regional networks: Khorat; Satun (2023)

GOVERNMENT

Country name: *conventional long form:* Kingdom of Thailand
conventional short form: Thailand
local long form: Ratcha Anachak Thai
local short form: Prathet Thai
former: Siam
etymology: Land of the Tai [People]"; the meaning of "tai" is uncertain, but may originally have meant "human beings," "people," or "free people"

Government type: constitutional monarchy

Capital: *name:* Bangkok
geographic coordinates: 13 45 N, 100 31 E
time difference: UTC+7 (12 hours ahead of Washington, DC, during Standard Time)
etymology: Bangkok was likely originally a colloquial name, but one that was widely adopted by foreign visitors; the name may derive from bang ko, where bang is the Thai word for "village on a stream" and ko means "island," both referencing the area's landscape, which was carved by rivers and canals; alternatively, the name may come from bang makok, where makok is the name of the Java plum, a plant bearing olive-like fruit; this possibility is supported by the former name of Wat Arun, a historic temple in the area, that used to be called Wat Makok; Krung Thep Maha Nakhon, the city's Thai name, means "City of Angels, Great City" or simply "Great City of Angels" and is a shortening of the full ceremonial name: Krungthepmahanakhon Amonrattanakosin Mahintharayutthaya Mahadilokphop Noppharatratchathaniburirom Udomratchaniwetmahasathan Amonphimanawatansathit Sakkathattiyawitsanukamprasit; translated the meaning is: "City of angels, great city of immortals, magnificent city of the nine gems, seat of the king, city of royal palaces, home of gods incarnate, erected by Vishvakarman at Indra's behest"; it holds the world's record as the longest place name (169 letters); Krung Thep is used colloquially

Administrative divisions: 76 provinces (changwat, singular and plural) and 1 municipality* (maha nakhon); Amnat Charoen, Ang Thong, Bueng Kan, Buri Ram, Chachoengsao, Chai Nat, Chaiyaphum, Chanthaburi, Chiang Mai, Chiang Rai, Chon Buri, Chumphon, Kalasin, Kamphaeng Phet, Kanchanaburi, Khon Kaen, Krabi, Krung Thep* (Bangkok), Lampang, Lamphun, Loei, Lop Buri, Mae Hong Son, Maha Sarakham, Mukdahan, Nakhon Nayok, Nakhon Pathom, Nakhon Phanom, Nakhon Ratchasima, Nakhon Sawan, Nakhon Si Thammarat, Nan, Narathiwat, Nong Bua Lamphu, Nong Khai, Nonthaburi, Pathum Thani, Pattani, Phangnga, Phatthalung, Phayao, Phetchabun, Phetchaburi, Phichit, Phitsanulok, Phra Nakhon Si Ayutthaya, Phrae, Phuket, Prachin Buri, Prachuap Khiri Khan, Ranong, Ratchaburi, Rayong, Roi Et, Sa Kaeo, Sakon Nakhon, Samut Prakan, Samut Sakhon, Samut Songkhram, Saraburi, Satun, Sing Buri, Si Sa Ket, Songkhla, Sukhothai, Suphan Buri, Surat Thani, Surin, Tak, Trang, Trat, Ubon Ratchathani, Udon Thani, Uthai Thani, Uttaradit, Yala, Yasothon

Independence: 1238 (traditional founding date; never colonized)

National holiday: Birthday of King WACHIRALONGKON, 28 July (1952)

Legal system: civil law system with common law influences

Constitution: *history:* many previous; latest drafted and presented 29 March 2016, approved by referendum 7 August 2016, signed into law by the king on 6 April 2017
amendments: amendments require a majority vote in a joint session of the House and Senate and further require at least one fifth of opposition House members and one third of the Senate vote in favor; a national referendum is additionally required for certain amendments; all amendments require signature by the king; Thailand's 2017 constitution was amended in November 2021 to increase the number of constituency members of parliament (MPs) from 350 to 400, reduce the number of party-list MPs from 150 to 100, and change the election to a two-ballot system

International law organization participation: has not submitted an ICJ jurisdiction declaration; non-party state to the ICCt

Citizenship: *citizenship by birth:* no
citizenship by descent only: at least one parent must be a citizen of Thailand
dual citizenship recognized: no
residency requirement for naturalization: 5 years

Suffrage: 18 years of age; universal and compulsory

Executive branch: *chief of state:* King WACHIRALONGKON; also spelled Vajiralongkorn (since 1 December 2016)
head of government: Prime Minister PHAETHONGTHAN Chinnawat; also spelled PAETONGTARN Shinawatra (since 18 August 2024)
cabinet: Council of Ministers nominated by the prime minister, appointed by the king; a Privy Council advises the king
elections/appointments: the monarchy is hereditary; prime minister candidate approved by the House of Representatives and Senate and appointed by the king; starting in 2024, approval of prime minister needed only by the House of Representatives
note: following its May 2023 election win, the MJP formed an eight-party coalition and put forward its leader PITA Limjaroenrat for prime minister; however, the Senate blocked PITA from becoming prime minister in the first National Assembly vote in July 2023, and the Assembly subsequently voted that he could not submit his name again; the Constitutional Court also suspended PITA after accepting cases accusing him of violating election law; in August 2023, MJP handed over the lead in forming a new government to the second largest party in the coalition, PTP, which then formed a new coalition without MJP; PTP put forward SRETTHA Thavisin for prime minister, and he was approved by the National Assembly 482 votes out of a possible 747

Legislative branch: *description:* bicameral National Assembly or Ratthasapha consists of:
Senate or Wuthisapha (200 seats; members indirectly elected in a three-step process (district, provincial, and national) from 20 eligible groups of professionals (see note) and then certified by Election Commission for a single 5-year term)
House of Representatives or Saphaphuthan Ratsadon (500 seats; 400 members directly elected in single-seat constituencies by simple majority vote and 100 members elected in a single nationwide constituency by party-list proportional representation vote; members serve 4-year terms)
elections: Senate - last election dates 9, 16, and 26 June 2024; certified on 10 July 2024 (next to be held in June 2029) House of Representatives - last held on 14 May 2023 (next to be held in May 2027)
election results: Senate - percent of vote by party - independents; seats by party - NA; composition - NA House of Representatives - percent of vote by party - MFP 36.2%, PTP 27.7%, UTN 11.9%, BJT/PJT 2.9%, DP 2.3%, PPRP 1.4%, PCC 1.5%, other 16%; seats by party - MFP 152, PTP 141, BJT/PJT 71, PPRP 41, UTN 36, DP 24, PCC 9, CTP 10, Thai Sang Thai 6, other 11; composition - 403 men, 97 women, percentage women 19.4%
note: the 20 groups of professionals include agriculture, artists or athletes, business owners, education, employees or workers, independent professionals, industrialists, law and justice, mass communication, public health, science and technology, tourism-related professions, women, and elderly, disabled, or ethnic groups

Judicial branch: *highest court(s):* Supreme Court of Justice (consists of the court president, 6 vice presidents, 60-70 judges, and organized into 10 divisions); Constitutional Court (consists of the court president and 8 judges); Supreme Administrative Court (number of judges determined by Judicial Commission of the Administrative Courts)
judge selection and term of office: Supreme Court judges selected by the Judicial Commission of the Courts of Justice and approved by the monarch; judge term determined by the monarch; Constitutional Court justices - 3 judges drawn from the Supreme Court, 2 judges drawn from the Administrative Court, and 4 judge candidates selected by the Selective Committee for Judges of the Constitutional Court, and confirmed by the Senate; judges appointed by the monarch serve single 9-year terms; Supreme Administrative Court judges selected by the Judicial Commission of the Administrative Courts and appointed by the monarch; judges serve for life
subordinate courts: courts of first instance and appeals courts within both the judicial and administrative systems; military courts

Political parties: Bhumjaithai Party or BJT (aka Phumchai Thai Party or PJT; aka Thai Pride Party)
Chat Thai Phatthana Party (Thai Nation Development Party) or CTP
Move Forward Party or MFP (dissolved by order of the Constitutional Court, August 2024)
Palang Pracharat Party (People's State Power Party) or PPRP
Pheu (Puea) Thai Party (For Thais Party) or PTP
Prachachat Party or PCC
Prachathipat Party (Democrat Party) or DP
Thai Sang Thai Party
United Thai Nation (Ruam Thai Sang Chat) or UTN

International organization participation: ADB, APEC, ARF, ASEAN, BIMSTEC, BIS, CD, CICA, CP, EAS, FAO, G-77, IAEA, IBRD, ICAO, ICC (national committees), ICRM, IDA, IFAD, IFC, IFRCS, IHO, ILO, IMF, IMO, IMSO, Interpol, IOC, IOM, IPU, ISO, ITSO, ITU, ITUC (NGOs), MIGA, NAM, OAS (observer), OIC (observer), OIF (observer), OPCW, OSCE (partner), PCA, PIF (partner), UN, UNAMID, UNCTAD, UNESCO, UNHCR, UNIDO, UNMOGIP, UNOCI, UNWTO, UPU, WCO, WFTU (NGOs), WHO, WIPO, WMO, WTO

Diplomatic representation in the US: *chief of mission:* Ambassador Dr. SURIYA Chindawongse (since 17 June 2024)
chancery: 1024 Wisconsin Avenue NW, Suite 401, Washington, DC 20007
telephone: [1] (202) 944-3600
FAX: [1] (202) 944-3611
email address and website:
thai.wsn@thaiembdc.org
https://washingtondc.thaiembassy.org/en/index
consulate(s) general: Chicago, Los Angeles, New York

Diplomatic representation from the US: *chief of mission:* Ambassador Robert F. GODEC (since 7 October 2022)
embassy: 95 Wireless Road, Bangkok 10330
mailing address: 7200 Bangkok Place, Washington DC 20521-7200
telephone: [66] 2-205-4000
FAX: [66] 2-205-4103
email address and website:
acsbkk@state.gov
https://th.usembassy.gov/
consulate(s) general: Chiang Mai

Flag description: five horizontal bands of red (top), white, blue (double width), white, and red; the red color symbolizes the nation and the blood of life, white represents religion and the purity of Buddhism, and blue stands for the monarchy
note: similar to the flag of Costa Rica but with the blue and red colors reversed

National symbol(s): garuda (mythical half-man, half-bird figure), elephant; national colors: red, white, blue

National anthem: *name:* "Phleng Chat Thai" (National Anthem of Thailand)
lyrics/music: Luang SARANUPRAPAN/Phra JENDURIYANG
note: music adopted 1932, lyrics adopted 1939; by law, people are required to stand for the national anthem at 0800 and 1800 every day; the anthem is played in schools, offices, theaters, and on television and radio during this time; "Phleng Sanlasoen Phra Barami" (A Salute to the Monarch) serves as the royal anthem and is played in the presence of the royal family and during certain state ceremonies

National heritage: *total World Heritage Sites:* 7 (4 cultural, 3 natural)
selected World Heritage Site locales: Historic City of Ayutthaya (c); Historic Sukhothai and Associated Historic Towns (c); Thungyai-Huai Kha Khaeng Wildlife Sanctuaries (n); Ban Chiang Archaeological Site (c); Dong Phayayen-Khao Yai Forest Complex (n); Kaeng Krachan Forest Complex (n); The Ancient Town of Si Thep and its Associated Dvaravati Monuments (n)

ECONOMY

Economic overview: upper middle-income Southeast Asian economy; substantial infrastructure; major electronics, food, and automobile parts exporter; globally used currency; extremely low unemployment, even amid COVID-19; ongoing Thailand 4.0 economic development

Real GDP (purchasing power parity): $1.516 trillion (2023 est.)
$1.488 trillion (2022 est.)
$1.452 trillion (2021 est.)
note: data in 2021 dollars
comparison ranking: 21

Real GDP growth rate: 1.88% (2023 est.)
2.46% (2022 est.)
1.57% (2021 est.)
note: annual GDP % growth based on constant local currency
comparison ranking: 145

Real GDP per capita: $21,100 (2023 est.)
$20,800 (2022 est.)
$20,300 (2021 est.)
note: data in 2021 dollars
comparison ranking: 99

GDP (official exchange rate): $514.945 billion (2023 est.)
note: data in current dollars at official exchange rate

Inflation rate (consumer prices): 1.23% (2023 est.)
6.08% (2022 est.)
1.23% (2021 est.)
note: annual % change based on consumer prices
comparison ranking: 24

Credit ratings: Fitch rating: BBB+ (2013)

Moody's rating: Baa1 (2003)

Standard & Poors rating: BBB+ (2004)
note: The year refers to the year in which the current credit rating was first obtained.

GDP - composition, by sector of origin: *agriculture:* 8.6% (2023 est.)
industry: 32.9% (2023 est.)
services: 58.5% (2023 est.)
note: figures may not total 100% due to non-allocated consumption not captured in sector-reported data
comparison rankings: services 97; industry 49; agriculture 86

GDP - composition, by end use: *household consumption:* 57.7% (2023 est.)
government consumption: 16.6% (2023 est.)
investment in fixed capital: 23% (2023 est.)
investment in inventories: -0.4% (2023 est.)
exports of goods and services: 65.4% (2023 est.)
imports of goods and services: -63.7% (2023 est.)
note: figures may not total 100% due to rounding or gaps in data collection

Agricultural products: sugarcane, rice, cassava, oil palm fruit, maize, rubber, tropical fruits, chicken, pineapples, fruits (2022)
note: top ten agricultural products based on tonnage

Industries: tourism, textiles and garments, agricultural processing, beverages, tobacco, cement, light manufacturing such as jewelry and electric appliances, computers and parts, integrated circuits, furniture, plastics, automobiles and automotive parts, agricultural machinery, air conditioning and refrigeration, ceramics, aluminum, chemical, environmental management, glass, granite and marble, leather, machinery and metal work, petrochemical, petroleum refining, pharmaceuticals, printing, pulp and paper, rubber, sugar, rice, fishing, cassava, world's second-largest tungsten producer and third-largest tin producer

Industrial production growth rate: -2.27% (2023 est.)
note: annual % change in industrial value added based on constant local currency
comparison ranking: 185

Labor force: 40.814 million (2023 est.)
note: number of people ages 15 or older who are employed or seeking work
comparison ranking: 16

Unemployment rate: 0.91% (2023 est.)
0.94% (2022 est.)
1.22% (2021 est.)
note: % of labor force seeking employment
comparison ranking: 4

Youth unemployment rate (ages 15-24): *total:* 5.3% (2023 est.)
male: 3.9% (2023 est.)
female: 7.4% (2023 est.)
note: % of labor force ages 15-24 seeking employment
comparison ranking: total 178

Population below poverty line: 6.3% (2021 est.)
note: % of population with income below national poverty line

Gini Index coefficient - distribution of family income: 34.9 (2021 est.)
note: index (0-100) of income distribution; higher values represent greater inequality
comparison ranking: 78

Average household expenditures: *on food:* 26.8% of household expenditures (2022 est.)
on alcohol and tobacco: 3% of household expenditures (2022 est.)

Household income or consumption by percentage share: *lowest 10%:* 3.2% (2021 est.)
highest 10%: 27.1% (2021 est.)
note: % share of income accruing to lowest and highest 10% of population

Remittances: 1.9% of GDP (2023 est.)
1.8% of GDP (2022 est.)
1.79% of GDP (2021 est.)
note: personal transfers and compensation between resident and non-resident individuals/households/entities

Budget: *revenues:* $90.509 billion (2022 est.)
expenditures: $106.576 billion (2022 est.)
note: central government revenues (excluding grants) and expenses converted to US dollars at average official exchange rate for year indicated

Public debt: 60.35% of GDP (2022 est.)
note: central government debt as a % of GDP
comparison ranking: 79

Taxes and other revenues: 14.38% (of GDP) (2022 est.)
note: central government tax revenue as a % of GDP
comparison ranking: 145

Current account balance: $7.002 billion (2023 est.)
-$15.742 billion (2022 est.)
-$10.268 billion (2021 est.)
note: balance of payments - net trade and primary/secondary income in current dollars
comparison ranking: 30

Exports: $336.871 billion (2023 est.)
$324.063 billion (2022 est.)
$295.972 billion (2021 est.)
note: balance of payments - exports of goods and services in current dollars
comparison ranking: 27

Exports - partners: US 17%, China 11%, Japan 8%, Vietnam 4%, Malaysia 4% (2022)
note: top five export partners based on percentage share of exports

Exports - commodities: machine parts, integrated circuits, cars, trucks, vehicle parts/accessories (2022)
note: top five export commodities based on value in dollars

Imports: $328.009 billion (2023 est.)
$334.478 billion (2022 est.)
$296.115 billion (2021 est.)
note: balance of payments - imports of goods and services in current dollars
comparison ranking: 25

Imports - partners: China 26%, Japan 11%, UAE 6%, US 5%, Malaysia 5% (2022)
note: top five import partners based on percentage share of imports

Imports - commodities: crude petroleum, integrated circuits, gold, natural gas, vehicle parts/accessories (2022)
note: top five import commodities based on value in dollars

Reserves of foreign exchange and gold: $224.47 billion (2023 est.)
$216.501 billion (2022 est.)
$246.025 billion (2021 est.)
note: holdings of gold (year-end prices)/foreign exchange/special drawing rights in current dollars
comparison ranking: 13

Debt - external: $35.388 billion (2022 est.)
note: present value of external debt in current US dollars
comparison ranking: 20

Exchange rates: baht per US dollar -

Exchange rates: 34.802 (2023 est.)
35.061 (2022 est.)
31.977 (2021 est.)
31.294 (2020 est.)
31.048 (2019 est.)

ENERGY

Electricity access: *electrification - total population:* 99.9% (2022 est.)
electrification - urban areas: 100%
electrification - rural areas: 100%

Electricity: *installed generating capacity:* 57.216 million kW (2022 est.)
consumption: 199.672 billion kWh (2022 est.)
exports: 2.02 billion kWh (2022 est.)
imports: 34.223 billion kWh (2022 est.)
transmission/distribution losses: 14.464 billion kWh (2022 est.)
comparison rankings: transmission/distribution losses 186; imports 5; exports 57; consumption 23; installed generating capacity 26

Electricity generation sources: *fossil fuels:* 82.1% of total installed capacity (2022 est.)
solar: 2.8% of total installed capacity (2022 est.)
wind: 1.7% of total installed capacity (2022 est.)
hydroelectricity: 3.7% of total installed capacity (2022 est.)
biomass and waste: 9.7% of total installed capacity (2022 est.)

Coal: *production:* 13.642 million metric tons (2022 est.)
consumption: 36.03 million metric tons (2022 est.)
exports: 96,000 metric tons (2022 est.)
imports: 22.485 million metric tons (2022 est.)
proven reserves: 1.063 billion metric tons (2022 est.)

Petroleum: *total petroleum production:* 386,000 bbl/day (2023 est.)
refined petroleum consumption: 1.248 million bbl/day (2022 est.)
crude oil estimated reserves: 252.75 million barrels (2021 est.)

Natural gas: *production:* 30.797 billion cubic meters (2022 est.)
consumption: 48.898 billion cubic meters (2022 est.)
imports: 17.112 billion cubic meters (2022 est.)
proven reserves: 138.243 billion cubic meters (2021 est.)

Carbon dioxide emissions: 307.934 million metric tonnes of CO2 (2022 est.)
from coal and metallurgical coke: 61.666 million metric tonnes of CO2 (2022 est.)
from petroleum and other liquids: 156.756 million metric tonnes of CO2 (2022 est.)
from consumed natural gas: 89.511 million metric tonnes of CO2 (2022 est.)
comparison ranking: total emissions 20

Energy consumption per capita: 69.958 million Btu/person (2022 est.)
comparison ranking: 71

COMMUNICATIONS

Telephones - fixed lines: *total subscriptions:* 4.368 million (2022 est.)
subscriptions per 100 inhabitants: 6 (2022 est.)
comparison ranking: total subscriptions 32

Telephones - mobile cellular: *total subscriptions:* 126.414 million (2022 est.)
subscriptions per 100 inhabitants: 176 (2022 est.)
comparison ranking: total subscriptions 15

Telecommunication systems: *general assessment:* Thailand's telecom sector is relatively mature and hosts a mix of public and private sector players; the mobile market is highly developed and has experienced strong growth over the last seven years; the market returned to growth in 2021 after it contracted in 2020 driven by the Covid-19 pandemic, and a steep decline in inbound tourism; it remains highly saturated, owing to overall maturity and the popularity of multiple SIM card use, which has resulted in a particularly high penetration rate; in general, the sector retains considerable potential given the impetus of 5G, the recent spectrum auctions, and continued network deployments by the country's network operators; further auctions of spectrum in the 700MHz band (being repurposed from digital TV broadcasting), and in the 3.6GHz range will further improve network capacity; in the wire line segment, the decline in fixed-line penetration is expected to continue as subscribers migrate to mobile networks for voice and data services; the emphasis among operators has been to bolster their fiber footprints in key high-value areas; the transition to fiber from DSL and cable has also been facilitated by changes to the regulatory structure that have removed some barriers to investment; this is supporting the cannibalization of older copper-based DSL lines by fiber; the returns from this investment remain a long-term prospect as consumers still favor entry-level packages; there is also strong interest from the government, as well as private vendors, in establishing Thailand as a data center hub to serve the region; the size, capacity and spread of existing data centers in the Greater Mekong Subregion (GMS) outside of Thailand is small; Thailand retains some advantages to attract investment, including improved fiber connectivity and international bandwidth; increasing submarine capacity, such as the SJC2 cable to come online later in 2023, will considerably improve Thailand's potential as a regional hub (2022)
domestic: fixed-line is 19 per 100 and mobile-cellular is 176 per 100 (2022)
international: country code - 66; landing points for the AAE-1, FEA, SeaMeWe-3,-4, APG, SJC2, TIS, MCT and AAG submarine cable systems providing links throughout Asia, Australia, Africa, Middle East, Europe, and US; satellite earth stations - 2 Intelsat (1 Indian Ocean, 1 Pacific Ocean) (2019)

Broadcast media: 26 digital TV stations in Bangkok broadcast nationally, 6 terrestrial TV stations in Bangkok broadcast nationally via relay stations - 2 of the stations are owned by the military, the other 4 are government-owned or controlled, leased to private enterprise, and all are required to broadcast government-produced news programs twice a day; multi-channel satellite and cable TV subscription services are available; radio frequencies have been allotted for more than 500 government and commercial radio stations; many small community radio stations operate with low-power transmitters (2017)

Internet country code: .th

Internet users: *total:* 61.2 million (2021 est.)
percent of population: 85% (2021 est.)
comparison ranking: total 17

Broadband - fixed subscriptions: *total:* 11,478,265 (2020 est.)
subscriptions per 100 inhabitants: 16 (2020 est.)
comparison ranking: total 18

TRANSPORTATION

National air transport system: *number of registered air carriers:* 15 (2020)
inventory of registered aircraft operated by air carriers: 283
annual passenger traffic on registered air carriers: 76,053,042 (2018)
annual freight traffic on registered air carriers: 2,666,260,000 (2018) mt-km

Civil aircraft registration country code prefix: HS

Airports: 108 (2024)
comparison ranking: 50

Heliports: 5 (2024)

Pipelines: 2 km condensate, 5,900 km gas, 85 km liquid petroleum gas, 1 km oil, 1,097 km refined products (2013)

Railways: *total:* 4,127 km (2017)
standard gauge: 84 km (2017) 1.435-m gauge (84 km electrified)
narrow gauge: 4,043 km (2017) 1.000-m gauge
comparison ranking: total 43

Roadways: *total:* 180,053 km (2006) (includes 450 km of expressways)
comparison ranking: total 29

Waterways: 4,000 km (2011) (3,701 km navigable by boats with drafts up to 0.9 m)
comparison ranking: 28

Merchant marine: *total:* 884 (2023)
by type: bulk carrier 28, container ship 28, general cargo 88, oil tanker 251, other 489
comparison ranking: total 28

Ports: *total ports:* 21 (2024)
large: 1
medium: 2
small: 3
very small: 15

ports with oil terminals: 14
key ports: Bangkok, Laem Chabang, Pattani, Phuket, Sattahip, Si Racha

MILITARY AND SECURITY

Military and security forces: Royal Thai Armed Forces (Kongthap Thai, RTARF): Royal Thai Army (Kongthap Bok Thai, RTA), Royal Thai Navy (Kongthap Ruea Thai, RTN; includes Royal Thai Marine Corps), Royal Thai Air Force (Kongthap Akaat Thai, RTAF)

Office of the Prime Minister: Royal Thai Police (2024)
note 1: the Thai Internal Security Operations Command (ISOC) oversees counter-insurgency operations, as well as countering terrorism, narcotics and weapons trafficking, and other internal security duties; it is primarily run by the Army
note 2: official paramilitary forces in Thailand include the Thai Rangers (Thahan Phran or "Hunter Soldiers") under the Army; the Paramilitary Marines under the Navy; the Border Patrol Police (BPP) under the Royal Thai Police; the Volunteer Defense Corps (VDC or O So) and National Defense Volunteers (NDV), both under the Ministry of Interior; there are also several government-backed volunteer militias created to provide village security against insurgents in the Deep South or to assist the ISOC

Military expenditures: 1.3% of GDP (2023 est.)
1.3% of GDP (2022 est.)
1.3% of GDP (2021 est.)
1.4% of GDP (2020 est.)
1.3% of GDP (2019 est.)
comparison ranking: 105

Military and security service personnel strengths: estimated 350,000 active-duty personnel (250,000 Army; 70,000 Navy; 30,000 Air Force); approximately 230,000 Royal Thai Police (2023)

Military equipment inventories and acquisitions: the RTARF has a diverse array of foreign-supplied weapons and equipment, as well as some domestically produced items; in recent years, Thailand has received arms from a wide variety of countries, including China and the US; Thailand has a domestic defense industry, which produces such items as armored vehicles, artillery systems, naval vessels, unmanned aerial vehicles, and other military technologies (2024)

Military service age and obligation: 18 years of age for voluntary military service for men and women; 21 years of age for compulsory military service for men; men register at 18 years of age; volunteer service obligation may be as short as 6 or 12 months, depending on educational qualifications; conscript service obligation also varies by educational qualifications, but is typically 24 months (2023)
note 1: serving in the armed forces is a national duty of all Thai citizens; conscription was introduced in 1905; it includes women, however, only men over the age of 21 who have not gone through reserve training are conscripted; conscripts are chosen by lottery (on draft day, eligible draftees can request volunteer service, or they may choose to stay for the conscription lottery); approximately 75-100,000 men are drafted for military service each year and conscripts reportedly comprise as much as 50% of the armed forces
note 2: as of 2020, women comprised about 8% of active-duty military personnel

Military deployments: 280 South Sudan (UNMISS) (2024)

Military - note: the RTARF's missions include defending the country's territory and sovereignty, protecting the monarchy, ensuring internal security, and responding to natural disasters; it also plays a large role in domestic politics and has attempted as many as 20 coups since the fall of absolute monarchy in 1932, the most recent being in 2014
since 2004, the military and associated paramilitary forces have fought against separatist insurgents in the southern provinces of Pattani, Yala, and Narathiwat, as well as parts of Songkhla; the insurgency is rooted in ethnic Malay nationalist resistance to Thai rule that followed the extension of Siamese sovereignty over the Patani Sultanate in the 18th century; the insurgency consists of several armed groups, the largest of which is the Barisan Revolusi Nasional- Koordinasi (BRN-C): since 2020, Thai officials have been negotiating with BRN, and has parallel talks with an umbrella organization, MARA Pattani, that claims to represent the insurgency groups; since 2004, violence associated with the insurgency has claimed more than 7,000 lives; the Thai Government has had as many as 100,000 military and paramilitary forces deployed in the south to combat the insurgency
Thailand has Major Non-NATO Ally (MNNA) status with the US, a designation under US law that provides foreign partners with certain benefits in the areas of defense trade and security cooperation; the Thai and US militaries host the annual "Cobra Gold" multinational military exercises in Thailand; the exercise is one of the largest multinational exercises in the Pacific region (2024)

SPACE

Space agency/agencies: Geo-Informatics and Space Technology Development Agency (GISTDA; created in 2000 from the Thailand Remote Sensing Center that was established in 1979; GISTDA is under the Ministry of Higher Education, Science, Research and Innovation); National Space Policy Committee (NSPC; advisory body to the prime minister) (2024)

Space launch site(s): none; in 2023, announced intentions to build a spaceport with South Korean assistance (2024)

Space program overview: has an ambitious and growing space program focused on the acquisition and operation of satellites and the development of related technologies; operates communications and remote sensing (RS) satellites; manufactures scientific/ research/ testing cube satellites and developing the capabilities to produce RS satellites (has historically built satellites with foreign assistance); cooperates with a range of foreign space agencies and industries, including those of other ASEAN countries, China, France, India, the Netherlands, Pakistan, Russia, South Korea, and the US; founding member of the China-led Asia-Pacific Space Cooperation Organization (APSCO); has a growing space industry, including Southeast Asia's first dedicated satellite manufacturing facility, which opened in 2021 (2024)
note: further details about the key activities, programs, and milestones of the country's space program, as well as government spending estimates on the space sector, appear in the Space Programs reference guide

TRANSNATIONAL ISSUES

Refugees and internally displaced persons: *refugees (country of origin):* 91,339 (Burma) (refugees and asylum seekers) (2023)
IDPs: 41,000 (2022)
stateless persons: 566,900 (2022) (estimate represents stateless persons registered with the Thai Government; actual number may be as high as 3.5 million); note - about half of Thailand's northern hill tribe people do not have citizenship and make up the bulk of Thailand's stateless population; most lack documentation showing they or one of their parents were born in Thailand; children born to Burmese refugees are not eligible for Burmese or Thai citizenship and are stateless; most Chao Lay, maritime nomadic peoples, who travel from island to island in the Andaman Sea west of Thailand are also stateless; stateless Rohingya refugees from Burma are considered illegal migrants by Thai authorities and are detained in inhumane conditions or expelled; stateless persons are denied access to voting, property, education, employment, healthcare, and driving
note: Thai nationality was granted to more than 23,000 stateless persons between 2012 and 2016 and more than 18,000 between 2018 and 2021; in 2016, the Government of Thailand approved changes to its citizenship laws that could make 80,000 stateless persons eligible for citizenship, as part of its effort to achieve zero statelessness by 2024 (2021)

Illicit drugs: not a cultivator or producer of significant quantities of opiates, methamphetamine, or other illicit drugs; not a significant source or transit country for drugs entering the United States; drugs smuggled through Thailand heading for Indo-Pacific region markets; large influx of methamphetamine and heroin from neighboring Burma to other markets, but also consumed domestically, most of which transits through Thailand to other markets, but is also consumed domestically; a major source of precursor or essential chemicals used in the production of illicit narcotics

TIMOR-LESTE

INTRODUCTION

Background: The island of Timor was actively involved in Southeast Asian trading networks for centuries, and by the 14th century, it exported sandalwood, slaves, honey, and wax. The sandalwood trade attracted the Portuguese, who arrived in the early 16th century; by midcentury, they had colonized the island, which was previously ruled by local chieftains. In 1859, Portugal ceded the western portion of the island to the Dutch. Imperial Japan occupied Portuguese Timor from 1942 to 1945,

but Portugal resumed colonial authority after the Japanese defeat in World War II. The eastern part of Timor declared itself independent from Portugal on 28 November 1975, but Indonesian forces invaded and occupied the area nine days later. It was incorporated into Indonesia in 1976 as the province of Timor Timur (East Timor or Timor Leste). Indonesia conducted an unsuccessful pacification campaign in the province over the next two decades, during which an estimated 100,000 to 250,000 people died.

In a UN-supervised referendum in 1999, an overwhelming majority of the people of Timor-Leste voted for independence from Indonesia. However, anti-independence Timorese militias – organized and supported by the Indonesian military – began a large-scale, scorched-earth campaign of retribution, killing approximately 1,400 Timorese and displacing nearly 500,000. Most of the country's infrastructure was destroyed, including homes, irrigation systems, water supply systems, schools, and most of the electrical grid.

Australian-led peacekeeping troops eventually deployed to the country and ended the violence. In 2002, Timor-Leste was internationally recognized as an independent state.

In 2006, Australia and the UN had to step in again to stabilize the country, which allowed presidential and parliamentary elections to be conducted in 2007 in a largely peaceful atmosphere. In 2008, rebels staged an unsuccessful attack against the president and prime minister. Since that attack, Timor-Leste has made considerable progress in building stability and democratic institutions, holding a series of successful parliamentary and presidential elections since 2012. Nonetheless, weak and unstable political coalitions have led to periodic episodes of stalemate and crisis. The UN continues to provide assistance on economic development and strengthening governing institutions. Currently, Timor-Leste is one of the world's poorest nations, with an economy that relies heavily on energy resources in the Timor Sea.

GEOGRAPHY

Location: Southeastern Asia, northwest of Australia in the Lesser Sunda Islands at the eastern end of the Indonesian archipelago; note - Timor-Leste includes the eastern half of the island of Timor, the Oecussi (Ambeno) region on the northwest portion of the island of Timor, and the islands of Pulau Atauro and Pulau Jaco

Geographic coordinates: 8 50 S, 125 55 E

Map references: Southeast Asia

Area: *total:* 14,874 sq km
land: 14,874 sq km
water: 0 sq km
comparison ranking: total 159

Area - comparative: slightly larger than Connecticut; almost half the size of Maryland

Land boundaries: *total:* 253 km
border countries (1): Indonesia 253 km

Coastline: 706 km

Maritime claims: *territorial sea:* 12 nm
contiguous zone: 24 nm
exclusive fishing zone: 200 nm

Climate: tropical; hot, humid; distinct rainy and dry seasons

Terrain: mountainous

Elevation: *highest point:* Foho Tatamailau 2,963 m
lowest point: Timor Sea, Savu Sea, and Banda Sea 0 m

Natural resources: gold, petroleum, natural gas, manganese, marble

Land use: *agricultural land:* 25.1% (2018 est.)
arable land: 10.1% (2018 est.)
permanent crops: 4.9% (2018 est.)
permanent pasture: 10.1% (2018 est.)
forest: 49.1% (2018 est.)
other: 25.8% (2018 est.)

Irrigated land: 350 sq km (2012)

Population distribution: most of the population concentrated in the western third of the country, particularly around Dili

Natural hazards: floods and landslides are common; earthquakes; tsunamis; tropical cyclones

Geography - note: the island of Timor is part of the Malay Archipelago and is the largest and easternmost of the Lesser Sunda Islands; the district of Oecussi is an exclave separated from Timor-Leste proper by Indonesia; Timor-Leste has the unique distinction of being the only Asian country located completely in the Southern Hemisphere

PEOPLE AND SOCIETY

Population: *total:* 1,506,909
male: 750,665
female: 756,244 (2024 est.)
comparison rankings: female 154; male 156; total 156

Nationality: *noun:* Timorese
adjective: Timorese

Ethnic groups: Austronesian (Malayo-Polynesian) (includes Tetun, Mambai, Tokodede, Galoli, Kemak, Baikeno), Melanesian-Papuan (includes Bunak, Fataluku, Bakasai), small Chinese minority

Languages: Tetun Prasa 30.6%, Mambai 16.6%, Makasai 10.5%, Tetun Terik 6.1%, Baikenu 5.9%, Kemak 5.8%, Bunak 5.5%, Tokodede 4%, Fataluku 3.5%, Waima'a 1.8%, Galoli 1.4%, Naueti 1.4%, Idate 1.2%, Midiki 1.2%, other 4.5% (2015 est.)
note: data represent population by mother tongue; Tetun and Portuguese are official languages; Indonesian and English are working languages; there are about 32 indigenous languages

Religions: Roman Catholic 97.6%, Protestant/Evangelical 2%, Muslim 0.2%, other 0.2% (2015 est.)

Demographic profile: Timor-Leste's high fertility and population growth rates sustain its very youthful age structure – approximately 40% of the population is below the age of 15 and the country's median age is 20. While Timor-Leste's total fertility rate (TFR) – the average number of births per woman – decreased significantly from over 7 in the early 2000s, it remains high at 4.3 in 2021 and will probably continue to decline slowly. The low use of contraceptives and the traditional preference for large families is keeping fertility elevated. The high TFR and falling mortality rates continue to fuel a high population growth rate of nearly 2.2%, which is the highest in Southeast Asia. The country's high total dependency ratio – a measure of the ratio of dependents to the working-age population – could divert more government spending toward social programs. Timor-Leste's growing, poorly educated working-age population and insufficient job creation are ongoing problems. Some 70% of the population lives in rural areas, where most of people are dependent on the agricultural sector. Malnutrition and poverty are prevalent, with 42% of the population living under the poverty line as of 2014.
During the Indonesian occupation (1975-1999) and Timor-Leste's fight for independence, approximately 250,000 Timorese fled to western Timor and, in lesser numbers, Australia, Portugal, and other countries. Many of these emigrants later returned. Since Timor-Leste's 1999 independence referendum, economic motives and periods of conflict have been the main drivers of emigration. Bilateral labor agreements with Australia, Malaysia, and South Korea and the presence of Timorese populations abroad, are pull factors, but the high cost prevents many young Timorese from emigrating. Timorese communities are found in its former colonizers, Indonesia and Portugal, as well as the Philippines and the UK. The country has also become a destination for migrants in the surrounding region, mainly men seeking work in construction, commerce, and services in Dili.

Age structure: *0-14 years:* 38.7% (male 299,929/female 283,416)
15-64 years: 56.8% (male 418,493/female 437,727)
65 years and over: 4.5% (2024 est.) (male 32,243/female 35,101)

Dependency ratios: *total dependency ratio:* 90.3
youth dependency ratio: 59.4
elderly dependency ratio: 8.9
potential support ratio: 11.2 (2021 est.)

Median age: *total:* 20.6 years (2024 est.)
male: 19.8 years
female: 21.3 years
comparison ranking: total 201

Population growth rate: 2.04% (2024 est.)
comparison ranking: 39

Birth rate: 29.7 births/1,000 population (2024 est.)
comparison ranking: 26

Death rate: 5.5 deaths/1,000 population (2024 est.)
comparison ranking: 180

Net migration rate: -3.8 migrant(s)/1,000 population (2024 est.)
comparison ranking: 192

Population distribution: most of the population concentrated in the western third of the country, particularly around Dili

Urbanization: *urban population:* 32.5% of total population (2023)
rate of urbanization: 3.31% annual rate of change (2020-25 est.)

Major urban areas - population: 281,000 DILI (capital) (2018)

Sex ratio: *at birth:* 1.07 male(s)/female
0-14 years: 1.06 male(s)/female
15-64 years: 0.96 male(s)/female
65 years and over: 0.92 male(s)/female
total population: 0.99 male(s)/female (2024 est.)

Mother's mean age at first birth: 23 years (2016 est.)
note: data represents median age at first birth among women 25-49

Maternal mortality ratio: 204 deaths/100,000 live births (2020 est.)
comparison ranking: 46

Infant mortality rate: *total:* 32.2 deaths/1,000 live births (2024 est.)
male: 35.3 deaths/1,000 live births
female: 28.9 deaths/1,000 live births
comparison ranking: total 41

Life expectancy at birth: *total population:* 70.5 years (2024 est.)
male: 68.9 years
female: 72.3 years
comparison ranking: total population 174

Total fertility rate: 3.98 children born/woman (2024 est.)
comparison ranking: 24

Gross reproduction rate: 1.92 (2024 est.)

Contraceptive prevalence rate: 26.1% (2016)

Drinking water source: *improved: urban:* 98% of population
rural: 82.5% of population
total: 87.4% of population
unimproved: urban: 2% of population
rural: 17.5% of population
total: 12.6% of population (2020 est.)

Current health expenditure: 9.9% of GDP (2020)

Physician density: 0.76 physicians/1,000 population (2020)

Sanitation facility access: *improved: urban:* 88.7% of population
rural: 56.1% of population
total: 66.3% of population
unimproved: urban: 11.3% of population
rural: 43.9% of population
total: 33.7% of population (2020 est.)

Obesity - adult prevalence rate: 3.8% (2016)
comparison ranking: 190

Alcohol consumption per capita: *total:* 0.41 liters of pure alcohol (2019 est.)
beer: 0.27 liters of pure alcohol (2019 est.)
wine: 0.09 liters of pure alcohol (2019 est.)
spirits: 0.05 liters of pure alcohol (2019 est.)
other alcohols: 0 liters of pure alcohol (2019 est.)
comparison ranking: total 166

Tobacco use: *total:* 39.2% (2020 est.)
male: 67.6% (2020 est.)
female: 10.8% (2020 est.)
comparison ranking: total 6

Children under the age of 5 years underweight: 31.9% (2020)
comparison ranking: 4

Currently married women (ages 15-49): 55.9% (2023 est.)

Child marriage: *women married by age 15:* 2.6%
women married by age 18: 14.9%
men married by age 18: 1.2% (2016 est.)

Education expenditures: 4.2% of GDP (2020 est.)
comparison ranking: 109

Literacy: *definition:* age 15 and over can read and write
total population: 68.1%
male: 71.9%
female: 64.2% (2018)

People - note: one of only two predominantly Christian nations in Southeast Asia, the other being the Philippines

ENVIRONMENT

Environment - current issues: air pollution and deterioration of air quality; greenhouse gas emissions; water quality, scarcity, and access; land and soil degradation; forest depletion; widespread use of slash and burn agriculture has led to deforestation and soil erosion; loss of biodiversity

Environment - international agreements: *party to:* Biodiversity, Climate Change, Climate Change-Kyoto Protocol, Climate Change-Paris Agreement, Desertification, Law of the Sea, Ozone Layer Protection
signed, but not ratified: Comprehensive Nuclear Test Ban

Climate: tropical; hot, humid; distinct rainy and dry seasons

Urbanization: *urban population:* 32.5% of total population (2023)
rate of urbanization: 3.31% annual rate of change (2020-25 est.)

Revenue from forest resources: 0.13% of GDP (2018 est.)
comparison ranking: 106

Revenue from coal: 0% of GDP (2018 est.)
comparison ranking: 143

Air pollutants: *particulate matter emissions:* 20.47 micrograms per cubic meter (2019 est.)
carbon dioxide emissions: 0.5 megatons (2016 est.)
methane emissions: 4.74 megatons (2020 est.)

Waste and recycling: *municipal solid waste generated annually:* 63,875 tons (2016 est.)

Total water withdrawal: *municipal:* 100 million cubic meters (2020 est.)
industrial: 2 million cubic meters (2017 est.)
agricultural: 1.07 billion cubic meters (2020 est.)

Total renewable water resources: 8.22 billion cubic meters (2020 est.)

GOVERNMENT

Country name: *conventional long form:* Democratic Republic of Timor-Leste
conventional short form: Timor-Leste
local long form: Republika Demokratika Timor Lorosa'e (Tetum)/ Republica Democratica de Timor-Leste (Portuguese)
local short form: Timor Lorosa'e (Tetum)/ Timor-Leste (Portuguese)
former: East Timor, Portuguese Timor
etymology: timor" derives from the Indonesian and Malay word "timur" meaning "east"; "leste" is the Portuguese word for "east", so "Timor-Leste" literally means "Eastern-East"; the local [Tetum] name "Timor Lorosa'e" translates as "East Rising Sun"
note: pronounced TEE-mor LESS-tay

Government type: semi-presidential republic

Capital: *name:* Dili
geographic coordinates: 8 35 S, 125 36 E
time difference: UTC+9 (14 hours ahead of Washington, DC, during Standard Time)

Administrative divisions: 12 municipalities (municipios, singular municipio) and 1 special adminstrative region* (regiao administrativa especial); Aileu, Ainaro, Baucau, Bobonaro (Maliana), Covalima (Suai), Dili, Ermera (Gleno), Lautem (Lospalos), Liquica, Manatuto, Manufahi (Same), Oe-Cusse Ambeno* (Pante Macassar), Viqueque
note: administrative divisions have the same names as their administrative centers (exceptions have the administrative center name following in parentheses)

Independence: 20 May 2002 (from Indonesia); note - 28 November 1975 was the date independence was proclaimed from Portugal; 20 May 2002 was the date of international recognition of Timor-Leste's independence from Indonesia

National holiday: Restoration of Independence Day, 20 May (2002); Proclamation of Independence Day, 28 November (1975)

Legal system: civil law system based on the Portuguese model; note - penal and civil law codes to replace the Indonesian codes were passed by Parliament and promulgated in 2009 and 2011, respectively

Constitution: *history:* drafted 2001, approved 22 March 2002, entered into force 20 May 2002
amendments: proposed by Parliament and parliamentary groups; consideration of amendments requires at least four-fifths majority approval by Parliament; passage requires two-thirds majority vote by Parliament and promulgation by the president of the republic; passage of amendments to the republican form of government and the flag requires approval in a referendum

International law organization participation: accepts compulsory ICJ jurisdiction with reservations; accepts ICCt jurisdiction

Citizenship: *citizenship by birth:* no
citizenship by descent only: at least one parent must be a citizen of Timor-Leste
dual citizenship recognized: no
residency requirement for naturalization: 10 years

Suffrage: 17 years of age; universal

Executive branch: *chief of state:* President José RAMOS-HORTA (since 20 May 2022)
head of government: Prime Minister Kay Rala Xanana GUSMAO (since 1 July 2023)
cabinet: Council of Ministers; ministers proposed to the prime minister by the coalition in the Parliament and sworn in by the President of the Republic
elections/appointments: president directly elected by absolute majority popular vote in 2 rounds if needed for a 5-year term (eligible for a second term); last election held on 19 March 2022 with a runoff on 19 April 2022 (next to be held in April 2027); following parliamentary elections, the president appoints the leader of the majority party or majority coalition as the prime minister
election results:
2022: José RAMOS-HORTA elected president in second round - RAMOS-HORTA (CNRT) 62.1%, Francisco GUTERRES (FRETILIN) 37.9%
2017: Francisco GUTERRES elected president; Francisco GUTERRES (FRETILIN) 57.1%, António da CONCEICAO (PD) 32.5%, other 10.4%
note: the president is commander in chief of the military and can veto legislation, dissolve parliament, and call national elections

Legislative branch: *description:* unicameral National Parliament (65 seats; members directly elected in a single nationwide constituency by closed, party-list proportional representation vote using the D'Hondt method to serve 5-year terms)
elections: last held on 21 May 2023 (next to be held in May 2028)
election results: percent of vote by party - CNRT 41.5%, FRETILIN 25.8%, PD 9.3%, KHUNTO 7.5%, PLP 6%, other 9.9%; seats by party - CNRT 31, FRETILIN 19, PD 6, KHUNTO 5, PLP 4; composition - men 40, women 25, percentage women 38.5%

Judicial branch: *highest court(s):* Court of Appeals (consists of the court president and NA judges)
judge selection and term of office: court president appointed by the president of the republic from among the other court judges to serve a 4-year term; other court judges appointed - 1 by the Parliament and the others by the Supreme Council for the Judiciary, a body chaired by the court president and that includes mostly presidential and parliamentary appointees; other judges serve for life
subordinate courts: Court of Appeal; High Administrative, Tax, and Audit Court; district courts; magistrates' courts; military courts
note: the UN Justice System Programme, launched in 2003 and being rolled out in 4 phases through 2018, is helping strengthen the country's justice system; the Programme is aligned with the country's long-range Justice Sector Strategic Plan, which includes legal reforms

Political parties: Democratic Party or PD
National Congress for Timorese Reconstruction or CNRT
National Unity of the Sons of Timor (Haburas Unidade Nasional Timor Oan or KHUNTO)
People's Liberation Party or PLP
Revolutionary Front of Independent Timor-Leste or FRETILIN

International organization participation: ACP, ADB, AOSIS, ARF, ASEAN (observer), CPLP, EITI (compliant country), FAO, G-77, IBRD, ICAO, ICCt, ICRM, IDA, IFAD, IFC, IFRCS, ILO, IMF, IMO, Interpol, IOC, IOM, IPU, ITU, MIGA, NAM, OPCW, PIF (observer), UN, UNCTAD, UNESCO, UNIDO, Union Latina, UNWTO, UPU, WCO, WHO, WMO

Diplomatic representation in the US: *chief of mission:* Ambassador José Luis GUTERRES (since 17 June 2024)
chancery: 4201 Connecticut Avenue NW, Suite 504, Washington, DC 20008
telephone: [1] (202) 966-3202
FAX: [1] (202) 966-3205
email address and website:
info@timorlesteembassy.org

Diplomatic representation from the US: *chief of mission:* Ambassador (vacant), Chargé d'Affaires Marc WEINSTOCK (since August 2023)
embassy: Avenida de Portugal, Praia dos Coqueiros, Dili
mailing address: 8250 Dili Place, Washington, DC 20521-8250
telephone: (670) 332-4684, (670) 330-2400
FAX: (670) 331-3206
email address and website:
ConsDili@state.gov
https://tl.usembassy.gov/

Flag description: red with a black isosceles triangle (based on the hoist side) superimposed on a slightly longer yellow arrowhead that extends to the center of the flag; a white star - pointing to the upper hoist-side corner of the flag - is in the center of the black triangle; yellow denotes the colonialism in Timor-Leste's past, black represents the obscurantism that needs to be overcome, red stands for the national liberation struggle; the white star symbolizes peace and serves as a guiding light

National symbol(s): Mount Ramelau; national colors: red, yellow, black, white

National anthem: *name:* "Patria" (Fatherland)
lyrics/music: Fransisco Borja DA COSTA/Afonso DE ARAUJO
note: adopted 2002; the song was first used as an anthem when Timor-Leste declared its independence from Portugal in 1975; the lyricist, Francisco Borja DA COSTA, was killed in the Indonesian invasion just days after independence was declared

ECONOMY

Economic overview: lower middle-income Southeast Asian economy; government expenditures funded via oil fund drawdowns; endemic corruption undermines growth; foreign aid-dependent; wide-scale poverty, unemployment, and illiteracy

Real GDP (purchasing power parity): $6.265 billion (2023 est.)
$7.316 billion (2022 est.)
$9.207 billion (2021 est.)
note: data in 2021 dollars
comparison ranking: 175

Real GDP growth rate: -14.36% (2023 est.)
-20.54% (2022 est.)
5.32% (2021 est.)
note: annual GDP % growth based on constant local currency
comparison ranking: 218

Real GDP per capita: $4,600 (2023 est.)
$5,500 (2022 est.)
$7,000 (2021 est.)
note: data in 2021 dollars
comparison ranking: 182

GDP (official exchange rate): $2.243 billion (2023 est.)
note: data in current dollars at official exchange rate

Inflation rate (consumer prices): 0.96% (2019 est.)
2.29% (2018 est.)
0.52% (2017 est.)
note: annual % change based on consumer prices
comparison ranking: 17

GDP - composition, by sector of origin: *agriculture:* 10.2% (2022 est.)
industry: 53.8% (2022 est.)
services: 37.2% (2022 est.)
note: figures may not total 100% due to non-allocated consumption not captured in sector-reported data
comparison rankings: services 201; industry 9; agriculture 76

GDP - composition, by end use: *household consumption:* 42.5% (2022 est.)
government consumption: 33.1% (2022 est.)
investment in fixed capital: 10% (2022 est.)
investment in inventories: 0.6% (2022 est.)
exports of goods and services: 55.7% (2022 est.)
imports of goods and services: -42% (2022 est.)
note: figures may not total 100% due to rounding or gaps in data collection

Agricultural products: maize, rice, coconuts, root vegetables, vegetables, cassava, other meats, coffee, beans, pork (2022)
note: top ten agricultural products based on tonnage

Industries: printing, soap manufacturing, handicrafts, woven cloth

Industrial production growth rate: -46.25% (2022 est.)
note: annual % change in industrial value added based on constant local currency
comparison ranking: 220

Labor force: 597,000 (2023 est.)
note: number of people ages 15 or older who are employed or seeking work
comparison ranking: 157

Unemployment rate: 1.52% (2023 est.)
1.54% (2022 est.)
2.34% (2021 est.)
note: % of labor force seeking employment
comparison ranking: 15

Youth unemployment rate (ages 15-24): *total:* 3.2% (2023 est.)
male: 3.1% (2023 est.)
female: 3.2% (2023 est.)
note: % of labor force ages 15-24 seeking employment
comparison ranking: total 192

Population below poverty line: 41.8% (2014 est.)
note: % of population with income below national poverty line

Gini Index coefficient - distribution of family income: 28.7 (2014 est.)
note: index (0-100) of income distribution; higher values represent greater inequality
comparison ranking: 133

Household income or consumption by percentage share: *lowest 10%:* 4% (2014 est.)
highest 10%: 24% (2014 est.)
note: % share of income accruing to lowest and highest 10% of population

Remittances: 10.88% of GDP (2023 est.)
5.8% of GDP (2022 est.)
4.85% of GDP (2021 est.)
note: personal transfers and compensation between resident and non-resident individuals/households/entities

Budget: *revenues:* $1.877 billion (2022 est.)
expenditures: $1.684 billion (2022 est.)
note: central government revenues (excluding grants) and expenses converted to US dollars at average official exchange rate for year indicated

Public debt: 3.8% of GDP (2017 est.)
comparison ranking: 202

Taxes and other revenues: 21.67% (of GDP) (2022 est.)
note: central government tax revenue as a % of GDP
comparison ranking: 69

Current account balance: -$227.62 million (2023 est.)
$256.151 million (2022 est.)
$1.328 billion (2021 est.)
note: balance of payments - net trade and primary/secondary income in current dollars
comparison ranking: 112

Exports: $701.808 million (2023 est.)
$1.858 billion (2022 est.)
$2.772 billion (2021 est.)
note: balance of payments - exports of goods and services in current dollars

comparison ranking: 188

Exports - partners: China 25%, Indonesia 20%, Japan 14%, South Korea 13%, Thailand 7% (2022)
note: top five export partners based on percentage share of exports

Exports - commodities: crude petroleum, coffee, natural gas, beer, construction vehicles (2022)
note: top five export commodities based on value in dollars

Imports: $1.179 billion (2023 est.)
$1.405 billion (2022 est.)
$1.298 billion (2021 est.)
note: balance of payments - imports of goods and services in current dollars
comparison ranking: 190

Imports - partners: Indonesia 27%, China 23%, Singapore 9%, Australia 6%, Malaysia 6% (2022)
note: top five import partners based on percentage share of imports

Imports - commodities: refined petroleum, rice, cars, coal, cranes (2022)
note: top five import commodities based on value in dollars

Reserves of foreign exchange and gold: $781.995 million (2023 est.)
$830.81 million (2022 est.)
$934.781 million (2021 est.)
note: holdings of gold (year-end prices)/foreign exchange/special drawing rights in current dollars
comparison ranking: 152

Debt - external: $207.551 million (2022 est.)
note: present value of external debt in current US dollars
comparison ranking: 100

Exchange rates: the US dollar is used

ENERGY

Electricity access: *electrification - total population:* 99.7% (2022 est.)
electrification - urban areas: 100%
electrification - rural areas: 100%

Electricity: *installed generating capacity:* 283,000 kW (2022 est.)
consumption: 414.76 million kWh (2022 est.)
transmission/distribution losses: 100 million kWh (2022 est.)
comparison rankings: transmission/distribution losses 47; consumption 178; installed generating capacity 167

Electricity generation sources: *fossil fuels:* 99.6% of total installed capacity (2022 est.)
solar: 0.4% of total installed capacity (2022 est.)

Coal: *imports:* 122,000 metric tons (2022 est.)

Petroleum: *total petroleum production:* 5,000 bbl/day (2023 est.)
refined petroleum consumption: 4,000 bbl/day (2022 est.)

Natural gas: *production:* 2.925 billion cubic meters (2022 est.)
exports: 2.925 billion cubic meters (2022 est.)

Carbon dioxide emissions: 637,000 metric tonnes of CO2 (2022 est.)
from petroleum and other liquids: 637,000 metric tonnes of CO2 (2022 est.)
comparison ranking: total emissions 184

Energy consumption per capita: 6.497 million Btu/person (2022 est.)
comparison ranking: 162

COMMUNICATIONS

Telephones - fixed lines: *total subscriptions:* 2,000 (2022 est.)
subscriptions per 100 inhabitants: (2022 est.) less than 1
comparison ranking: total subscriptions 213

Telephones - mobile cellular: *total subscriptions:* 1.481 million (2022 est.)
subscriptions per 100 inhabitants: 110 (2022 est.)
comparison ranking: total subscriptions 158

Telecommunication systems: *general assessment:* Timor-Leste has been moving forward with the regeneration of its economy and rebuilding key infrastructure, including telecommunications networks, that were destroyed during the years of civil unrest; fixed-line and fixed broadband penetration in Timor-Leste remains extremely low, mainly due to the limited fixed-line infrastructure and the proliferation of mobile connectivity; in an effort to boost e-government services; the number of subscribers through to 2026 is expected to develop steadily, though from a low base; by August 2020, Timor-Leste had three telecom service providers who jointly achieved a 98% network coverage nationally; the mobile broadband market is still at an early stage of development, strong growth is predicted over the next five years; at the end of 2020, the government issued new policy guidelines to maximize the use of spectrum in Timor-Leste; it invited mobile operators to submit applications for the allocation of spectrum in the 1800MHz, 2300MHz and 2600MHz bands; in November 2020, the government approved the deployment of a submarine fiber link connecting the south of the country to Australia via the North Western Cable System (NWCS) (2021)
domestic: fixed-line services less than 1 per 100 and mobile-cellular services is 110 per 100 (2022)
international: country code - 670; international service is available; partnership with Australia telecom companies for potential deployment of a submarine fiber-optic link (NWCS); geostationary earth orbit satellite

Broadcast media: 7 TV stations (3 nationwide satellite coverage; 2 terrestrial coverage, mostly in Dili; 2 cable) and 21 radio stations (3 nationwide coverage) (2019)

Internet country code: .tl

Internet users: *total:* 507,000 (2021 est.)
percent of population: 39% (2021 est.)
comparison ranking: total 167

Broadband - fixed subscriptions: *total:* 75 (2020 est.)
subscriptions per 100 inhabitants: 0.01 (2020 est.)
comparison ranking: total 214

TRANSPORTATION

National air transport system: *number of registered air carriers:* 2 (2020)
inventory of registered aircraft operated by air carriers: 2

Civil aircraft registration country code prefix: 4W

Airports: 10 (2024)
comparison ranking: 162

Heliports: 2 (2024)

Roadways: *total:* 6,040 km
paved: 2,600 km
unpaved: 3,440 km (2008)
comparison ranking: total 147

Merchant marine: *total:* 1 (2023)
by type: other 1
comparison ranking: total 186

Ports: *total ports:* 1 (2024)
large: 0
medium: 0
small: 1
very small: 0
ports with oil terminals: 0
key ports: Dili

MILITARY AND SECURITY

Military and security forces: Timor-Leste Defense Force (Falintil-Forcas de Defesa de Timor-L'este, Falintil (F-FDTL)): Joint Headquarters with Land, Air, Naval, Service Support, and Education/Training components

Ministry of Interior: National Police (Polícia Nacional de Timor-Leste, PNTL) (2024)

Military expenditures: 1.3% of GDP (2023 est.)
1.8% of GDP (2022 est.)
1.8% of GDP (2021 est.)
1.8% of GDP (2020 est.)
1.7% of GDP (2019 est.)
comparison ranking: 109

Military and security service personnel strengths: approximately 1,500-2,000 personnel (2023)

Military equipment inventories and acquisitions: the military is lightly armed and has a limited inventory consisting mostly of donated equipment from countries such as Australia, China, Portugal, South Korea, and the US (2024)

Military service age and obligation: 18 years of age for voluntary military service for men and women; compulsory service was authorized in 2020 for men and women aged 18-30 for 18 months of service, but the level of implementation is unclear (2023)

Military - note: the F-FDTL is a small and lightly equipped force with both external defense and internal security roles; it has two infantry battalions, a small air component, and a handful of naval patrol boats
since achieving independence, Timor-Leste has received security assistance from or has made defense cooperation arrangements with Australia, China, Indonesia, Malaysia, New Zealand, the Philippines, Portugal, the UN, and the US (2024)

TRANSNATIONAL ISSUES

Illicit drugs: NA

TOGO

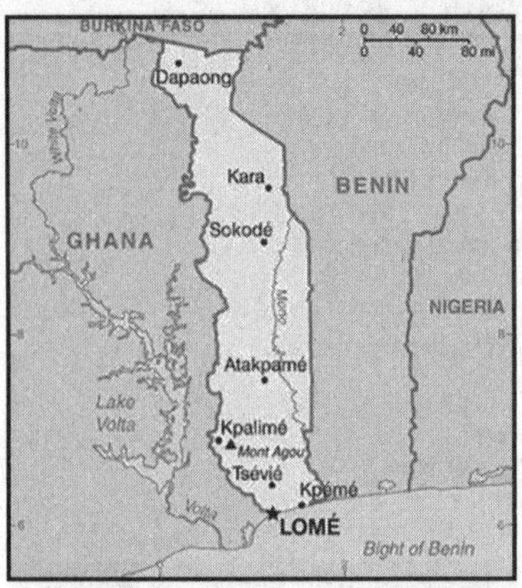

INTRODUCTION

Background: From the 11th to the 16th centuries, various ethnic groups settled the Togo region. From the 16th to the 18th centuries, the coastal region became a major trading center for enslaved people, and the surrounding region took on the name of "The Slave Coast." In 1884, Germany declared the area a protectorate called Togoland, which included present-day Togo. After World War I, colonial rule over Togo was transferred to France. French Togoland became Togo upon independence in 1960.

Gen. Gnassingbe EYADEMA, installed as military ruler in 1967, ruled Togo with a heavy hand for almost four decades. Despite the facade of multi-party elections instituted in the early 1990s, EYADEMA largely dominated the government. His Rally of the Togolese People (RPT) party has been in power almost continually since 1967, with its successor, the Union for the Republic, maintaining a majority of seats in today's legislature. Upon EYADEMA's death in 2005, the military installed his son, Faure GNASSINGBE, as president and then engineered his formal election two months later. Togo held its first relatively free and fair legislative elections in 2007. Since then, GNASSINGBE has started the country along a gradual path to democratic reform. Togo has held multiple presidential and legislative elections, and in 2019, the country held its first local elections in 32 years.

Despite those positive moves, political reconciliation has moved slowly, and the country experiences periodic outbursts of protests from frustrated citizens, leading to violence between security forces and protesters. Constitutional changes in 2019 to institute a runoff system in presidential elections and to establish term limits have done little to reduce the resentment many Togolese feel after more than 50 years of one-family rule. GNASSINGBE became eligible for his current fourth term and one additional fifth term under the new rules. The next presidential election is set for 2025.

GEOGRAPHY

Location: Western Africa, bordering the Bight of Benin, between Benin and Ghana

Geographic coordinates: 8 00 N, 1 10 E

Map references: Africa

Area: *total:* 56,785 sq km
land: 54,385 sq km
water: 2,400 sq km
comparison ranking: total 126

Area - comparative: slightly smaller than West Virginia

Land boundaries: *total:* 1,880 km
border countries (3): Benin 651 km; Burkina Faso 131 km; Ghana 1,098 km

Coastline: 56 km

Maritime claims: *territorial sea:* 30 nm; note: the US does not recognize this claim
exclusive economic zone: 200 nm

Climate: tropical; hot, humid in south; semiarid in north

Terrain: gently rolling savanna in north; central hills; southern plateau; low coastal plain with extensive lagoons and marshes

Elevation: *highest point:* Mont Agou 986 m
lowest point: Atlantic Ocean 0 m
mean elevation: 236 m

Natural resources: phosphates, limestone, marble, arable land

Land use: *agricultural land:* 67.4% (2018 est.)
arable land: 45.2% (2018 est.)
permanent crops: 3.8% (2018 est.)
permanent pasture: 18.4% (2018 est.)
forest: 4.9% (2018 est.)
other: 27.7% (2018 est.)

Irrigated land: 70 sq km (2012)

Major watersheds (area sq km): Atlantic Ocean drainage: Volta (410,991 sq km)

Population distribution: one of the more densely populated African nations with most of the population residing in rural communities, density is highest in the south on or near the Atlantic coast as shown in this population distribution map

Natural hazards: hot, dry harmattan wind can reduce visibility in north during winter; periodic droughts

Geography - note: the country's length allows it to stretch through six distinct geographic regions; climate varies from tropical to savanna

PEOPLE AND SOCIETY

Population: *total:* 8,917,994
male: 4,395,271
female: 4,522,723 (2024 est.)
comparison rankings: female 100; male 101; total 101

Nationality: *noun:* Togolese (singular and plural)
adjective: Togolese

Ethnic groups: Adja-Ewe/Mina 42.4%, Kabye/Tem 25.9%, Para-Gourma/Akan 17.1%, Akposso/Akebu 4.1%, Ana-Ife 3.2%, other Togolese 1.7%, foreigners 5.2%, no response 0.4% (2013-14 est.)
note: Togo has an estimated 37 ethnic groups

Languages: French (official, language of commerce), Ewe and Mina (in the south), Kabye (sometimes spelled Kabiye) and Dagomba (in the north)

Religions: Christian 42.3%, folk religion 36.9%, Muslim 14%, Hindu <1%, Buddhist <1%, Jewish <1%, other <1%, none 6.2% (2020 est.)

Demographic profile: Togo's population is estimated to have grown to four times its size between 1960 and 2010. With nearly 60% of its populace under the age of 25 and a high annual growth rate attributed largely to high fertility, Togo's population is likely to continue to expand for the foreseeable future. Reducing fertility, boosting job creation, and improving education will be essential to reducing the country's high poverty rate. In 2008, Togo eliminated primary school enrollment fees, leading to higher enrollment but increased pressure on limited classroom space, teachers, and materials. Togo has a good chance of achieving universal primary education, but educational quality, the underrepresentation of girls, and the low rate of enrollment in secondary and tertiary schools remain concerns.

Togo is both a country of emigration and asylum. In the early 1990s, southern Togo suffered from the economic decline of the phosphate sector and ethnic and political repression at the hands of dictator Gnassingbe EYADEMA and his northern, Kabye-dominated administration. The turmoil led 300,000 to 350,000 predominantly southern Togolese to flee to Benin and Ghana, with most not returning home until relative stability was restored in 1997. In 2005, another outflow of 40,000 Togolese to Benin and Ghana occurred when violence broke out between the opposition and security forces over the disputed election of EYADEMA's son Faure GNASSINGBE to the presidency. About half of the refugees reluctantly returned home in 2006, many still fearing for their safety. Despite ethnic tensions and periods of political unrest, Togo in December 2022 was home to almost 8,400 refugees from Ghana.

Age structure: *0-14 years:* 38.7% (male 1,749,533/female 1,699,084)
15-64 years: 57% (male 2,486,142/female 2,597,914)
65 years and over: 4.3% (2024 est.) (male 159,596/female 225,725)

Dependency ratios: *total dependency ratio:* 76.5
youth dependency ratio: 71
elderly dependency ratio: 5.5
potential support ratio: 18.3 (2021 est.)

Median age: *total:* 20.7 years (2024 est.)
male: 19.9 years
female: 21.4 years
comparison ranking: total 199

Population growth rate: 2.41% (2024 est.)
comparison ranking: 21

Birth rate: 30.9 births/1,000 population (2024 est.)
comparison ranking: 23

Death rate: 5.1 deaths/1,000 population (2024 est.)
comparison ranking: 192

Net migration rate: -1.7 migrant(s)/1,000 population (2024 est.)
comparison ranking: 164

Population distribution: one of the more densely populated African nations with most of the population residing in rural communities, density is highest in the south on or near the Atlantic coast as shown in this population distribution map

Urbanization: *urban population:* 44.5% of total population (2023)
rate of urbanization: 3.6% annual rate of change (2020-25 est.)

Major urban areas - population: 1.982 million LOME (capital) (2023)

Sex ratio: *at birth:* 1.03 male(s)/female
0-14 years: 1.03 male(s)/female
15-64 years: 0.96 male(s)/female
65 years and over: 0.71 male(s)/female
total population: 0.97 male(s)/female (2024 est.)

Mother's mean age at first birth: 25 years (2017 est.)
note: data represents median age at first birth among women 25-29

Maternal mortality ratio: 399 deaths/100,000 live births (2020 est.)
comparison ranking: 23

Infant mortality rate: *total:* 38.4 deaths/1,000 live births (2024 est.)
male: 43 deaths/1,000 live births
female: 33.7 deaths/1,000 live births
comparison ranking: total 30

Life expectancy at birth: *total population:* 72.1 years (2024 est.)
male: 69.5 years
female: 74.7 years
comparison ranking: total population 165

Total fertility rate: 4.13 children born/woman (2024 est.)
comparison ranking: 20

Gross reproduction rate: 2.03 (2024 est.)

Contraceptive prevalence rate: 23.9% (2017)

Drinking water source: *improved: urban:* 93.8% of population
rural: 60.3% of population
total: 74.6% of population
unimproved: urban: 6.2% of population
rural: 39.7% of population
total: 25.4% of population (2020 est.)

Current health expenditure: 6% of GDP (2020)

Physician density: 0.08 physicians/1,000 population (2020)

Hospital bed density: 0.7 beds/1,000 population (2011)

Sanitation facility access: *improved: urban:* 81.9% of population
rural: 18.3% of population
total: 45.5% of population
unimproved: urban: 18.1% of population
rural: 81.7% of population
total: 54.5% of population (2020 est.)

Obesity - adult prevalence rate: 8.4% (2016)
comparison ranking: 151

Alcohol consumption per capita: *total:* 1.4 liters of pure alcohol (2019 est.)
beer: 0.78 liters of pure alcohol (2019 est.)
wine: 0.09 liters of pure alcohol (2019 est.)
spirits: 0.2 liters of pure alcohol (2019 est.)
other alcohols: 0.33 liters of pure alcohol (2019 est.)
comparison ranking: total 141

Tobacco use: *total:* 6.8% (2020 est.)
male: 12.3% (2020 est.)
female: 1.2% (2020 est.)
comparison ranking: total 158

Children under the age of 5 years underweight: 15.2% (2017)
comparison ranking: 33

Currently married women (ages 15-49): 62% (2023 est.)

Child marriage: *women married by age 15:* 6.4%
women married by age 18: 24.8%
men married by age 18: 2.6% (2017 est.)

Education expenditures: 4% of GDP (2020 est.)
comparison ranking: 118

Literacy: *definition:* age 15 and over can read and write
total population: 66.5%
male: 80%
female: 55.1% (2019)

School life expectancy (primary to tertiary education): *total:* 13 years
male: 14 years
female: 12 years (2017)

ENVIRONMENT

Environment - current issues: deforestation attributable to slash-and-burn agriculture and the use of wood for fuel; very little rain forest still present and what remains is highly degraded; desertification; water pollution presents health hazards and hinders the fishing industry; air pollution increasing in urban areas

Environment - international agreements: *party to:* Biodiversity, Climate Change, Climate Change-Kyoto Protocol, Climate Change-Paris Agreement, Comprehensive Nuclear Test Ban, Desertification, Endangered Species, Hazardous Wastes, Law of the Sea, Nuclear Test Ban, Ozone Layer Protection, Ship Pollution, Tropical Timber 2006, Wetlands, Whaling
signed, but not ratified: none of the selected agreements

Climate: tropical; hot, humid in south; semiarid in north

Land use: *agricultural land:* 67.4% (2018 est.)
arable land: 45.2% (2018 est.)
permanent crops: 3.8% (2018 est.)
permanent pasture: 18.4% (2018 est.)
forest: 4.9% (2018 est.)
other: 27.7% (2018 est.)

Urbanization: *urban population:* 44.5% of total population (2023)
rate of urbanization: 3.6% annual rate of change (2020-25 est.)

Revenue from forest resources: 3.96% of GDP (2018 est.)
comparison ranking: 18

Revenue from coal: 0% of GDP (2018 est.)
comparison ranking: 55

Air pollutants: *particulate matter emissions:* 35.66 micrograms per cubic meter (2019 est.)
carbon dioxide emissions: 3 megatons (2016 est.)
methane emissions: 3.06 megatons (2020 est.)

Waste and recycling: *municipal solid waste generated annually:* 1,109,030 tons (2014 est.)
municipal solid waste recycled annually: 22,181 tons (2012 est.)
percent of municipal solid waste recycled: 2% (2012 est.)

Major watersheds (area sq km): Atlantic Ocean drainage: Volta (410,991 sq km)

Total water withdrawal: *municipal:* 140 million cubic meters (2020 est.)
industrial: 10 million cubic meters (2020 est.)
agricultural: 80 million cubic meters (2020 est.)

Total renewable water resources: 14.7 billion cubic meters (2020 est.)

GOVERNMENT

Country name: *conventional long form:* Togolese Republic
conventional short form: Togo
local long form: République Togolaise
local short form: none
former: French Togoland
etymology: derived from the Ewe words "to" (river) and "godo" (on the other side) to give the sense of "on the other side of the river"; originally, this designation applied to the town of Togodo (now Togoville) on the northern shore of Lake Togo, but the name was eventually extended to the entire nation

Government type: presidential republic

Capital: *name:* Lome
geographic coordinates: 6 07 N, 1 13 E
time difference: UTC 0 (5 hours ahead of Washington, DC, during Standard Time)
etymology: Lome comes from "alotime" which in the native Ewe language means "among the alo plants"; alo trees dominated the city's original founding site

Administrative divisions: 5 regions (regions, singular - region); Centrale, Kara, Maritime, Plateaux, Savanes

Independence: 27 April 1960 (from French-administered UN trusteeship)

National holiday: Independence Day, 27 April (1960)

Legal system: customary law system

Constitution: *history:* several previous; latest adopted 27 September 1992, effective 14 October 1992; revised 6 May 2024
amendments: proposed by the president of the republic or supported by at least one fifth of the National Assembly membership; passage requires four-fifths majority vote by the Assembly; a referendum is required if approved by only two-thirds majority of the Assembly or if requested by the president; constitutional articles on the republican and secular form of government cannot be amended; amended 2002, 2007, last in 2024 (reported as a revision)

International law organization participation: accepts compulsory ICJ jurisdiction with reservations; non-party state to the ICCt

Citizenship: *citizenship by birth:* no
citizenship by descent only: at least one parent must be a citizen of Togo
dual citizenship recognized: yes
residency requirement for naturalization: 5 years

Suffrage: 18 years of age; universal

Executive branch: *chief of state:* President Faure GNASSINGBE (since 4 May 2005)
head of government: Prime Minister Victoire TOMEGAH Dogbé (since 25 September 2020)
cabinet: Council of Ministers appointed by the president on the advice of the prime minister
elections/appointments: president directly elected by simple majority popular vote for a 5-year term (no term limits); election last held on 22 February 2020 (next to be held in 2025); prime minister appointed by the president note- on 21 May 2024 the Prime Minister and her cabinet resigned. The President requested they continue serving during the government transition.
election results:
2020: Faure GNASSINGBE reelected president; percent of vote - Faure GNASSINGBE (UNIR) 70.8%,

Agbeyome KODJO (MPDD) 19.5%, Jean-Pierre FABRE (ANC) 4.7%, other 5%
2015: Faure GNASSINGBE reelected president; percent of vote - Faure GNASSINGBE (UNIR) 58.8%, Jean-Pierre FABRE (ANC) 35.2%, Tchaboure GOGUE (ADDI) 4%, other 2%

Legislative branch: *description:* unicameral National Assembly or Assemblee Nationale (113 seats; members directly elected in multiseat constituencies by closed, party-list proportional representation vote to serve 5-year terms); party lists are required to contain equal numbers of men and women
elections: last held on 29 April 2024 (next election April 2029)
election results: percent of vote by party - NA; seats by party - UNIR 108, ADDI 2, ANC 1, DMP 1, FDR 1 composition - men 92, women 21, percentage of women elected 18.6%

Judicial branch: *highest court(s):* Supreme Court or Cour Supreme (organized into criminal and administrative chambers, each with a chamber president and advisors); Constitutional Court (consists of 9 judges, including the court president)
judge selection and term of office: Supreme Court president appointed by decree of the president of the republic upon the proposal of the Supreme Council of the Magistracy, a 9-member judicial, advisory, and disciplinary body; other judicial appointments and judge tenure NA; Constitutional Court judges appointed by the National Assembly; judge tenure NA
subordinate courts: Court of Assizes (sessions court); Appeal Court; tribunals of first instance (divided into civil, commercial, and correctional chambers; Court of State Security; military tribunal

Political parties: Action Committee for Renewal or CAR
Alliance of Democrats for Integral Development or ADDI
Democratic Convention of African Peoples or CDPA
Democratic Forces for the Republic or FDR
National Alliance for Change or ANC
New Togolese Commitment
Pan-African National Party or PNP
Pan-African Patriotic Convergence or CPP
Patriotic Movement for Democracy and Development or MPDD
Socialist Pact for Renewal or PSR
The Togolese Party
Union of Forces for Change or UFC
Union for the Republic or UNIR

International organization participation: ACP, AfDB, AIIB, AU, ECOWAS, EITI (compliant country), Entente, FAO, FZ, G-77, IAEA, IBRD, ICAO, ICRM, IDA, IDB, IFAD, IFC, IFRCS, ILO, IMF, IMO, Interpol, IOC, IOM, IPU, ISO (correspondent), ITSO, ITU, ITUC (NGOs), MIGA, MINURSO, NAM, OIC, OIF, OPCW, PCA, UN, UNAMID, UNCTAD, UNESCO, UNHCR, UNIDO, UNMIL, UNOCI, UNWTO, UPU, WADB (regional), WAEMU, WCO, WFTU (NGOs), WHO, WIPO, WMO, WTO

Diplomatic representation in the US: *chief of mission:* Ambassador Frédéric Edem HEGBE (since 24 April 2017)
chancery: 2208 Massachusetts Avenue NW, Washington, DC 20008
telephone: [1] (202) 234-4212
FAX: [1] (202) 232-3190
email address and website:
embassyoftogo@hotmail.com
https://embassyoftogousa.com/

Diplomatic representation from the US: *chief of mission:* Ambassador Elizabeth FITZSIMMONS (since 26 April 2022)
embassy: Boulevard Eyadema, B.P. 852, Lome
mailing address: 2300 Lome Place, Washington, DC 20521-2300
telephone: [228] 2261-5470
FAX: [228] 2261-5501
email address and website:
consularLome@state.gov
https://tg.usembassy.gov/

Flag description: five equal horizontal bands of green (top and bottom) alternating with yellow; a white five-pointed star on a red square is in the upper hoist-side corner; the five horizontal stripes stand for the five different regions of the country; the red square is meant to express the loyalty and patriotism of the people, green symbolizes hope, fertility, and agriculture, while yellow represents mineral wealth and faith that hard work and strength will bring prosperity; the star symbolizes life, purity, peace, dignity, and Togo's independence
note: uses the popular Pan-African colors of Ethiopia

National symbol(s): lion; national colors: green, yellow, red, white

National anthem: *name:* "Salut a toi, pays de nos aieux" (Hail to Thee, Land of Our Forefathers)
lyrics/music: Alex CASIMIR-DOSSEH
note: adopted 1960, restored 1992; this anthem was replaced by another during one-party rule between 1979 and 1992

National heritage: *total World Heritage Sites:* 1 (cultural)
selected World Heritage Site locales: Koutammakou; the Land of the Batammariba

ECONOMY

Economic overview: low-income West African economy; primarily agrarian economy; has a deep-water port; growing international shipping locale; improving privatization and public budgeting transparency; key phosphate mining industry; extremely high rural poverty

Real GDP (purchasing power parity): $25.75 billion (2023 est.)
$24.199 billion (2022 est.)
$22.881 billion (2021 est.)
note: data in 2021 dollars
comparison ranking: 155

Real GDP growth rate: 6.41% (2023 est.)
5.76% (2022 est.)
5.99% (2021 est.)
note: annual GDP % growth based on constant local currency
comparison ranking: 27

Real GDP per capita: $2,800 (2023 est.)
$2,700 (2022 est.)
$2,600 (2021 est.)
note: data in 2021 dollars
comparison ranking: 201

GDP (official exchange rate): $9.171 billion (2023 est.)
note: data in current dollars at official exchange rate

Inflation rate (consumer prices): 7.97% (2022 est.)
4.19% (2021 est.)
1.7% (2020 est.)
note: annual % change based on consumer prices
comparison ranking: 155

Credit ratings: Moody's rating: B3 (2019)
Standard & Poors rating: B (2019)
note: The year refers to the year in which the current credit rating was first obtained.

GDP - composition, by sector of origin: *agriculture:* 18.1% (2023 est.)
industry: 20.2% (2023 est.)
services: 51.7% (2023 est.)
note: figures may not total 100% due to non-allocated consumption not captured in sector-reported data
comparison rankings: services 132; industry 136; agriculture 44

GDP - composition, by end use: *household consumption:* 78.1% (2023 est.)
government consumption: 12.6% (2023 est.)
investment in fixed capital: 23% (2023 est.)
exports of goods and services: 23.9% (2023 est.)
imports of goods and services: -37.5% (2023 est.)
note: figures may not total 100% due to rounding or gaps in data collection

Agricultural products: cassava, yams, maize, oil palm fruit, sorghum, soybeans, beans, rice, vegetables, cotton (2022)
note: top ten agricultural products based on tonnage

Industries: phosphate mining, agricultural processing, cement, handicrafts, textiles, beverages

Industrial production growth rate: 6.74% (2023 est.)
note: annual % change in industrial value added based on constant local currency
comparison ranking: 35

Labor force: 3.166 million (2023 est.)
note: number of people ages 15 or older who are employed or seeking work
comparison ranking: 106

Unemployment rate: 2.05% (2023 est.)
2.07% (2022 est.)
2.29% (2021 est.)
note: % of labor force seeking employment
comparison ranking: 21

Youth unemployment rate (ages 15-24): *total:* 3.3% (2023 est.)
male: 4.1% (2023 est.)
female: 2.6% (2023 est.)
note: % of labor force ages 15-24 seeking employment
comparison ranking: total 191

Population below poverty line: 45.5% (2018 est.)
note: % of population with income below national poverty line

Gini Index coefficient - distribution of family income: 37.9 (2021 est.)
note: index (0-100) of income distribution; higher values represent greater inequality
comparison ranking: 55

Household income or consumption by percentage share: *lowest 10%:* 2.8% (2021 est.)
highest 10%: 29.6% (2021 est.)
note: % share of income accruing to lowest and highest 10% of population

Remittances: 6.1% of GDP (2023 est.)
6.81% of GDP (2022 est.)
6.67% of GDP (2021 est.)
note: personal transfers and compensation between resident and non-resident individuals/households/entities

Budget: *revenues:* $1.434 billion (2022 est.)
expenditures: $1.32 billion (2022 est.)
note: central government revenues and expenses (excluding grants/extrabudgetary units/social security

funds) converted to US dollars at average official exchange rate for year indicated

Public debt: 75.7% of GDP (2017 est.)
comparison ranking: 44

Taxes and other revenues: 14.19% (of GDP) (2022 est.)
note: central government tax revenue as a % of GDP
comparison ranking: 147

Current account balance: -$20.738 million (2020 est.)
-$55.444 million (2019 est.)
-$184.852 million (2018 est.)
note: balance of payments - net trade and primary/ secondary income in current dollars
comparison ranking: 87

Exports: $1.722 billion (2020 est.)
$1.665 billion (2019 est.)
$1.703 billion (2018 est.)
note: balance of payments - exports of goods and services in current dollars
comparison ranking: 168

Exports - partners: UAE 26%, India 11%, Cote d'Ivoire 11%, South Africa 6%, Burkina Faso 6% (2022)
note: top five export partners based on percentage share of exports

Exports - commodities: gold, refined petroleum, phosphates, soybeans, plastic products (2022)
note: top five export commodities based on value in dollars

Imports: $2.389 billion (2020 est.)
$2.261 billion (2019 est.)
$2.329 billion (2018 est.)
note: balance of payments - imports of goods and services in current dollars
comparison ranking: 169

Imports - partners: India 30%, China 16%, South Korea 13%, Nigeria 4%, Taiwan 4% (2022)
note: top five import partners based on percentage share of imports

Imports - commodities: refined petroleum, crude petroleum, motorcycles and cycles, garments, rice (2022)
note: top five import commodities based on value in dollars

Reserves of foreign exchange and gold: $77.8 million (31 December 2017 est.)
$42.6 million (31 December 2016 est.)
comparison ranking: 189

Debt - external: $1.462 billion (2022 est.)
note: present value of external debt in current US dollars
comparison ranking: 77

Exchange rates: Communaute Financiere Africaine francs (XOF) per US dollar -

Exchange rates: 606.57 (2023 est.)
623.76 (2022 est.)
554.531 (2021 est.)
575.586 (2020 est.)
585.911 (2019 est.)

ENERGY

Electricity access: *electrification - total population:* 57.2% (2022 est.)
electrification - urban areas: 96.5%
electrification - rural areas: 25%

Electricity: *installed generating capacity:* 309,000 kW (2022 est.)
consumption: 1.562 billion kWh (2022 est.)
imports: 796.563 million kWh (2022 est.)
transmission/distribution losses: 121.682 million kWh (2022 est.)
comparison rankings: transmission/distribution losses 53; imports 85; consumption 154; installed generating capacity 164

Electricity generation sources: *fossil fuels:* 74.4% of total installed capacity (2022 est.)
solar: 6.8% of total installed capacity (2022 est.)
hydroelectricity: 18.4% of total installed capacity (2022 est.)
biomass and waste: 0.4% of total installed capacity (2022 est.)

Coal: *consumption:* 108,000 metric tons (2022 est.)
imports: 108,000 metric tons (2022 est.)

Petroleum: *refined petroleum consumption:* 12,000 bbl/day (2022 est.)

Natural gas: *consumption:* 131.373 million cubic meters (2022 est.)
imports: 131.373 million cubic meters (2022 est.)

Carbon dioxide emissions: 2.306 million metric tonnes of CO2 (2022 est.)
from coal and metallurgical coke: 257,000 metric tonnes of CO2 (2022 est.)
from petroleum and other liquids: 1.793 million metric tonnes of CO2 (2022 est.)
from consumed natural gas: 256,000 metric tonnes of CO2 (2022 est.)
comparison ranking: total emissions 155

Energy consumption per capita: 4.077 million Btu/ person (2022 est.)
comparison ranking: 173

COMMUNICATIONS

Telephones - fixed lines: *total subscriptions:* 66,000 (2022 est.)
subscriptions per 100 inhabitants: (2022 est.) less than 1
comparison ranking: total subscriptions 147

Telephones - mobile cellular: *total subscriptions:* 6.564 million (2022 est.)
subscriptions per 100 inhabitants: 74 (2022 est.)
comparison ranking: total subscriptions 115

Telecommunication systems: *general assessment:* include radio, television, fixed and mobile telephones, and the Internet (2022)
domestic: fixed-line less than 1 per 100 and mobile-cellular is 74 telephones per 100 persons (2022)
international: country code - 228; landing point for the WACS submarine cable, linking countries along the west coast of Africa with each other and with Portugal; satellite earth stations - 1 Intelsat (Atlantic Ocean), 1 Symphonie (2020)

Broadcast media: 1 state-owned TV station with multiple transmission sites; five private TV stations broadcast locally; cable TV service is available; state-owned radio network with two stations (in Lome and Kara); several dozen private radio stations and a few community radio stations; transmissions of multiple international broadcasters available (2019)

Internet country code: .tg

Internet users: *total:* 3.01 million (2021 est.)
percent of population: 35% (2021 est.)
comparison ranking: total 120

Broadband - fixed subscriptions: *total:* 52,706 (2020 est.)
subscriptions per 100 inhabitants: 0.6 (2020 est.)
comparison ranking: total 143

TRANSPORTATION

National air transport system: *number of registered air carriers:* 1 (2020)
inventory of registered aircraft operated by air carriers: 8
annual passenger traffic on registered air carriers: 566,295 (2018)
annual freight traffic on registered air carriers: 10.89 million (2018) mt-km

Civil aircraft registration country code prefix: 5V

Airports: 7 (2024)
comparison ranking: 172

Pipelines: 62 km gas

Railways: *total:* 568 km (2014)
narrow gauge: 568 km (2014) 1.000-m gauge
comparison ranking: total 110

Roadways: *total:* 9,951 km
paved: 1,794 km
unpaved: 8,157 km
urban: 1,783 km (2018)
comparison ranking: total 136

Waterways: 50 km (2011) (seasonally navigable by small craft on the Mono River depending on rainfall)
comparison ranking: 113

Merchant marine: *total:* 397 (2023)
by type: bulk carrier 1, container ship 10, general cargo 250, oil tanker 56, other 80
comparison ranking: total 49

Ports: *total ports:* 2 (2024)
large: 0
medium: 1
small: 0
very small: 1
ports with oil terminals: 2
key ports: Kpeme, Lome

MILITARY AND SECURITY

Military and security forces: Togolese Armed Forces (Forces Armees Togolaise, FAT): Togolese Army (l'Armee de Terre), Togolese Navy (Forces Naval Togolaises), Togolese Air Force (Armee de l'Air), National Gendarmerie (Gendarmerie Nationale Togolaise or GNT)

Ministry of Security and Civil Protection: National Police Directorate (Direction de la Police Nationale) (2024)
note: the Police Directorate and GNT are responsible for law enforcement and maintenance of order within the country; the GNT is also responsible for migration and border enforcement; the GNT falls under the Ministry of the Armed Forces but also reports to the Ministry of Security and Civil Protection on many matters involving law enforcement and internal security; in 2022, the Ministry of the Armed Forces was made part of the Office of the Presidency

Military expenditures: 2.2% of GDP (2023 est.)
2.1% of GDP (2022 est.)
1.9% of GDP (2021 est.)
2% of GDP (2020 est.)
2.6% of GDP (2019 est.)
comparison ranking: 55

Military and security service personnel strengths: estimated 15,000 active-duty personnel, including approximately 3,000 Gendarmerie (2023)

note: in January 2022, the Togolese Government announced its intent to boost the size of the FAT to more than 20,000 by 2025

Military equipment inventories and acquisitions: the FAT has a small inventory of mostly older equipment originating from a variety of countries, including Brazil, Russia/former Soviet Union, Turkey, the US, and some European nations, particularly France (2024)

Military service age and obligation: 18 years of age for military service for men and women; 24-month service obligation; no conscription (2023)
note: as of 2022, about 7% of the military's personnel were women

Military - note: since its creation in 1963, the Togolese military has had a history of involvement in the country's politics with assassinations, coups, influence, and a crackdown in 2005 that killed hundreds of civilians; over the past decade, however, it has made some efforts to reform and professionalize, including increasing its role in UN peacekeeping activities, participating in multinational exercises, and receiving training from foreign partners, including France and the US; in addition, Togo has established a regional peacekeeping training center for military and police in Lome
the FAT's primary concerns are terrorism and maritime security; in recent years, it has increased operations in the northern border region of the country to boost border security and prevent terrorist infiltrations from Jama'at Nasr al-Islam wal Muslimin (JNIM), a coalition of al-Qa'ida-affiliated militant groups based in Mali that also operates in neighboring Burkina Faso; in 2022, the Togolese Government declared a state of emergency in the north due to the threat from JNIM following an attack on a Togolese military post that killed several soldiers; northern Togo has also had problems with banditry, as well as arms, drugs, fuel, and gold smuggling, which has aggravated local disputes and provided terrorist groups with financial resources; the Navy and Air Force have increased focus on combating piracy and smuggling in the Gulf of Guinea (2024)

TERRORISM

Terrorist group(s): Jama'at Nusrat al Islam wal Muslimeen (JNIM)
note: details about the history, aims, leadership, organization, areas of operation, tactics, targets, weapons, size, and sources of support of the group(s) appear(s) in the Terrorism reference guide

TRANSNATIONAL ISSUES

Refugees and internally displaced persons: *refugees (country of origin)*: 9,846 (Burkina Faso), 8,436 (Ghana) (2023)

Illicit drugs: transit hub for Nigerian heroin and cocaine traffickers; money laundering not a significant problem

TOKELAU

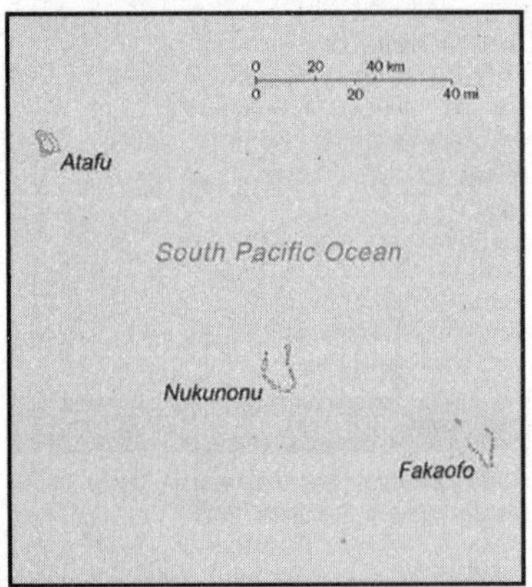

INTRODUCTION

Background: Tokelau is composed of three atolls (Fakaofo, Atafu, and Nukunonu), and it was first settled by Polynesians around A.D. 1000. The atolls operated relatively independently, but Fakaofo Atoll eventually subjugated the others. British explorers first saw the atolls in 1765 and 1791. Catholic and Protestant missionaries arrived in the 1840s and converted the population on the islands on which they landed.

In 1863 Peruvian slave raiders abducted many islanders, and roughly contemporary outbreaks of disease reduced the population to about 200. Settlers of diverse nationalities subsequently intermarried with Tokelauans. In the same period, local governance moved to a system based on a Council of Elders, which still exists today. British interest began in the late 1870s, and Tokelau became a British protectorate in 1889, and in 1916 under the name Union Group, Tokelau became part of the Gilbert and Ellice Islands Colony. In 1925, the UK placed Tokelau under New Zealand administration. The Tokelau Islands Act of 1948 formally transferred sovereignty from the UK to New Zealand, and Tokelauans were granted New Zealand citizenship. In 1979, the US relinquished its claim to Tokelau in the Treaty of Tokehega, and Tokelau relinquished its claim to Swains Island, which is part of American Samoa.

Economic opportunities in Tokelau are sparse, and about 80% of Tokelauans live in New Zealand. Tokelau held self-governance referendums in 2006 and 2007 in which more than 60% of voters chose free association with New Zealand; however, the referendums failed to achieve the two-thirds majority necessary to enact a status change.

GEOGRAPHY

Location: Oceania, group of three atolls in the South Pacific Ocean, about one-half of the way from Hawaii to New Zealand

Geographic coordinates: 9 00 S, 172 00 W

Map references: Oceania

Area: *total:* 12 sq km
land: 12 sq km
water: 0 sq km
comparison ranking: total 240

Area - comparative: about 17 times the size of the National Mall in Washington, DC

Land boundaries: *total:* 0 km

Coastline: 101 km

Maritime claims: *territorial sea:* 12 nm
exclusive economic zone: 200 nm

Climate: tropical; moderated by trade winds (April to November)

Terrain: low-lying coral atolls enclosing large lagoons

Elevation: *highest point:* unnamed location 5 m
lowest point: Pacific Ocean 0 m

Natural resources: fish

Land use: *agricultural land:* 60% (2018 est.)
arable land: 0% (2018 est.)
permanent crops: 60% (2018 est.)
permanent pasture: 0% (2018 est.)
forest: 0% (2018 est.)
other: 40% (2018 est.)

Irrigated land: 0 sq km (2022)

Population distribution: the country's small population is fairly evenly distributed amongst the three atolls

Natural hazards: lies in Pacific cyclone belt

Geography - note: consists of three atolls (Atafu, Fakaofo, Nukunonu), each with a lagoon surrounded by a number of reef-bound islets of varying length and rising to over 3 m above sea level

PEOPLE AND SOCIETY

Population: *total:* 1,647 (2019 est.)
comparison ranking: total 233

Nationality: *noun:* Tokelauan(s)
adjective: Tokelauan

Ethnic groups: Tokelauan 64.5%, part Tokelauan/Samoan 9.7%, part Tokelauan/Tuvaluan 2.8%, Tuvaluan 7.5%, Samoan 5.8%, other Pacific Islander 3.4%, other 5.6%, unspecified 0.8% (2016 est.)

Languages: Tokelauan 88.1% (a Polynesian language), English 48.6%, Samoan 26.7%, Tuvaluan 11.2%, Kiribati 1.5%, other 2.8%, none 2.8%, unspecified 0.8% (2016 ests.)
note: shares sum to more than 100% because some respondents gave more than one answer on the census

Religions: Congregational Christian Church 50.4%, Roman Catholic 38.7%, Presbyterian 5.9%, other Christian 4.2%, unspecified 0.8% (2016 est.)

Dependency ratios: *total dependency ratio:* 60.4
youth dependency ratio: 47
elderly dependency ratio: 13.4
potential support ratio: 7.5 (2021)

Population growth rate: -0.01% (2019 est.)
comparison ranking: 197

Net migration rate: -3.84 migrant(s)/1,000 population (2021 est.)
comparison ranking: 194

Population distribution: the country's small population is fairly evenly distributed amongst the three atolls

Urbanization: *urban population:* 0% of total population (2023)
rate of urbanization: 0% annual rate of change (2020-25 est.)

Drinking water source: *improved: urban:* 0% of population
improved: rural: 99.7% of population
improved: total: 99.7% of population
unimproved: urban: 0% of population
unimproved: rural: 0.3% of population
unimproved: total: 0.3% of population (2020 est.)

Sanitation facility access: *improved:* improved: rural: 100% of population

Currently married women (ages 15-49): 52% (2023 est.)

Child marriage: *women married by age 15:* 0.4%
women married by age 18: 10.1%
men married by age 18: 2.8% (2019 est.)

ENVIRONMENT

Environment - current issues: overexploitation of certain fish and other marine species, coastal sand, and forest resources; pollution of freshwater lenses and coastal waters from improper disposal of chemicals

Climate: tropical; moderated by trade winds (April to November)

Urbanization: *urban population:* 0% of total population (2023)
rate of urbanization: 0% annual rate of change (2020-25 est.)

Total renewable water resources: 0 cubic meters (2017 est.)

GOVERNMENT

Country name: *conventional long form:* none
conventional short form: Tokelau
former: Union Islands, Tokelau Islands
etymology: "tokelau" is a Polynesian word meaning "north wind"

Government type: parliamentary democracy under a constitutional monarchy

Dependency status: self-administering territory of New Zealand; note - Tokelau and New Zealand have agreed to a draft constitution as Tokelau moves toward free association with New Zealand; a UN-sponsored referendum on self governance in October 2007 did not meet the two-thirds majority vote necessary for changing the political status

Capital: *time difference:* UTC+13 (18 hours ahead of Washington, DC during Standard Time)
note: there is no designated, official capital for Tokelau; the location of the capital rotates among the three atolls along with the head of government or Ulu o Tokelau

Administrative divisions: none (territory of New Zealand)

Independence: none (territory of New Zealand)

National holiday: Waitangi Day (Treaty of Waitangi established British sovereignty over New Zealand), 6 February (1840)

Legal system: common law system of New Zealand

Constitution: *history:* many previous; latest effective 1 January 1949 (Tokelau Islands Act 1948)
amendments: proposed as a resolution by the General Fono; passage requires support by each village and approval by the General Fono; amended several times, last in 2007

Citizenship: see New Zealand

Suffrage: 21 years of age; universal

Executive branch: *chief of state:* King CHARLES III (since 8 September 2022); represented by Governor-General of New Zealand Dame Cindy KIRO (since 21 September 2021); New Zealand is represented by Administrator Don HIGGINS (since June 2022)
head of government: (Ulu o Tokelau) Alapati TAVITE (since 12 March 2024)
cabinet: Council for the Ongoing Government of Tokelau (or Tokelau Council) functions as a cabinet; consists of 3 village leaders (Faipule) and 3 village mayors (Pulenuku)
elections/appointments: the monarchy is hereditary; governor general appointed by the monarch; administrator appointed by the Minister of Foreign Affairs and Trade in New Zealand; head of government chosen from the Council of Faipule to serve a 1-year term
note: the meeting place of the Tokelau Council and the head of government position rotates annually among the three atolls; this tradition has given rise to the somewhat misleading description that the capital rotates yearly between the three atolls; in actuality, it is the seat of the government councilors that rotates since Tokelau has no capital

Legislative branch: *description:* unicameral General Fono (20 seats apportioned by island - Atafu 7, Fakaofo 7, Nukunonu 6; members directly elected by simple majority vote to serve 3-year terms)
elections: last held on 26 January 2023 depending on island (next to be held in January 2026)
election results: percent of vote by party - NA; seats by party - independent 20; composition - men 17, women 3, percentage women 15%

Judicial branch: *highest court(s):* Court of Appeal (in New Zealand) (consists of the court president and 8 judges sitting in 3- or 5-judge panels, depending on the case)
judge selection and term of office: judges nominated by the Judicial Selection Committee and approved by three-quarters majority of the Parliament; judges serve for life
subordinate courts: High Court (in New Zealand); Council of Elders or Taupulega

Political parties: none

International organization participation: PIF (associate member), SPC, UNESCO (associate), UPU

Diplomatic representation in the US: none (territory of New Zealand)

Diplomatic representation from the US: none (territory of New Zealand)

Flag description: a yellow stylized Tokelauan canoe on a dark blue field sails toward the manu - the Southern Cross constellation of four, white, five-pointed stars at the hoist side; the Southern Cross represents the role of Christianity in Tokelauan culture and, in conjunction with the canoe, symbolizes the country navigating into the future; the color yellow indicates happiness and peace, and the blue field represents the ocean on which the community relies

National symbol(s): tuluma (fishing tackle box); national colors: blue, yellow, white

National anthem: *name:* "Te Atua" (For the Almighty)
lyrics/music: unknown/Falani KALOLO
note: adopted 2008; in preparation for eventual self governance, Tokelau held a national contest to choose an anthem; as a territory of New Zealand, in addition to "God Defend New Zealand," "God Save the King" serves as a royal anthem (see United Kingdom); "God Save the King" normally played only when a member of the royal family or the governorgeneral is present; in all other cases, "God Defend New Zealand" is played (see New Zealand)

ECONOMY

Economic overview: small New Zealand territorial island economy; labor force can work in New Zealand or Australia; significant remittances; largely solar-powered infrastructure; reliant on New Zealand funding; stamp, coin, and crafts producer

Real GDP (purchasing power parity): $7,711,583 (2017 est.)
note: data are in 2017 dollars.
comparison ranking: 224

Real GDP per capita: $6,004 (2017 est.)
$4,855 (2016 est.)
$4,292 (2015 est.)
note: data are in 2017 dollars
comparison ranking: 168

GDP (official exchange rate): $12.658 million (2017 est.)
note: data uses New Zealand Dollar (NZD) as the currency of exchange.

Inflation rate (consumer prices): 4% (2020 est.)
2.5% (2019 est.)
11% (2017 est.)
note: Tokelau notes that its wide inflation swings are due almost entirely to cigarette prices, a chief import.
comparison ranking: 79

Agricultural products: coconuts, root vegetables, tropical fruits, pork, bananas, eggs, chicken, pork offal, pork fat, fruits (2022)
note: top ten agricultural products based on tonnage

Industries: small-scale enterprises for copra production, woodworking, plaited craft goods; stamps, coins; fishing

Labor force: 1,100 (2019 est.)
comparison ranking: 207

Unemployment rate: 2% (2015 est.)
note: Underemployment may be as high as 6.6%
comparison ranking: 20

Budget: *revenues:* $24,324,473 (2017 est.)
expenditures: $11,666,542 (2017 est.)

Exports: $103,000 (2015 est.)
comparison ranking: 222

Exports - partners: Poland 97%, Singapore 0%, Brazil 0%, South Africa 0%, Rwanda 0% (2022)
note: top five export partners based on percentage share of exports

Exports - commodities: cars, iron fasteners, garments, silver, perfumes (2022)
note: top five export commodities based on value in dollars

Imports: $15,792,720 (2015 est.)
comparison ranking: 219

Imports - partners: Germany 40%, Sweden 10%, Singapore 8%, France 5%, Netherlands 5% (2022)
note: top five import partners based on percentage share of imports

Imports - commodities: cars, orthopedic appliances, surveying equipment, butter, nuts (2022)
note: top five import commodities based on value in dollars

Exchange rates: New Zealand dollars (NZD) per US dollar -

Exchange rates: 1.628 (2023 est.)
1.577 (2022 est.)
1.414 (2021 est.)
1.542 (2020 est.)
1.518 (2019 est.)

COMMUNICATIONS

Telephones - fixed lines: *total subscriptions:* 300 (2010 est.)
subscriptions per 100 inhabitants: 22 (2010 est.)
comparison ranking: total subscriptions 220

Telecommunication systems: *general assessment:* a new submarine cable between New Zealand and Tokelau will provide high speed, reliable internet to Tokelau for the first time; due for completion in 2022, this will provide Tokelau with affordable, high quality internet and telecommunications, and better, more effective access to digital services and platforms (2021)
domestic: fixed-line teledensity is 0 per 100 persons (2019)
international: country code - 690; landing point for the Southern Cross NEXT submarine cable linking Australia, Tokelau, Samoa, Kiribati, Fiji, New Zealand and Los Angeles, CA (USA); radiotelephone service to Samoa; government-regulated telephone service (TeleTok); satellite earth stations - 3 (2020)

Broadcast media: Sky TV access for around 30% of the population; each atoll operates a radio service that provides shipping news and weather reports (2019)

Internet country code: .tk

Internet users: *total:* 800 (2021 est.)
percent of population: 58.3% (2021 est.)
comparison ranking: total 231

TRANSPORTATION

Roadways: *total:* 10 km (2019)
comparison ranking: total 225

MILITARY AND SECURITY

Military - note: defense is the responsibility of New Zealand

TONGA

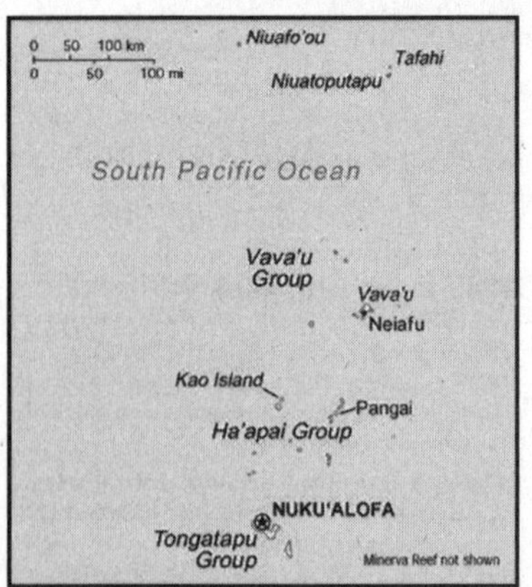

INTRODUCTION

Background: The first humans arrived in Tonga around 1000 B.C. The islands' politics were highly centralized under the Tu'i Tonga, or Tongan king, by A.D. 950, and by 1200, the Tu'i Tonga had expanded his influence throughout Polynesia and into Melanesia and Micronesia. The Tongan Empire began to decline in the 1300s, with civil wars, a military defeat to Samoa, and internal political strife. By the mid-1500s, some Tu'i Tongans were ethnic Samoan, and day-to-day administration of Tonga was transferred to a new position occupied by ethnic Tongans.

Dutch navigators explored the islands in the 1600s, followed by the British in the 1770s, who named them the Friendly Islands. Between 1799 and 1852 Tonga went through a period of war and disorder. In the 1830s, a low-ranking chief from Ha'apai began to consolidate control over the islands and was crowned King George TUPOU I in 1845, establishing the only still-extant Polynesian monarchy. During TUPOU's reign (1845–93), Tonga became a unified and independent country with a modern constitution (1875), legal code, and administrative structure. In separate treaties, Germany (1876), Great Britain (1879), and the US (1888) recognized Tonga's independence. His son and successor, King George TUPOU II, agreed to enter a protectorate agreement with the UK in 1900 after rival Tongan chiefs tried to overthrow him. As a protectorate, Tonga never completely lost its indigenous governance, but it did become more isolated and the social hierarchy became more stratified between a group of nobles and a large class of commoners. Today, about one third of parliamentary seats are reserved for nobles.

Tonga regained full control of domestic and foreign affairs and became a fully independent nation within the Commonwealth in 1970. A pro-democracy movement gained steam in the early 2000s, led by 'Akilisi POHIVA, and in 2006, riots broke out in Nuku'alofa to protest the lack of progress on reform. To appease the activists, in 2008, King George TUPOU V announced he was relinquishing most of his powers leading up to parliamentary elections in 2010 and henceforth most of the monarch's governmental decisions, except those relating to the judiciary, were to be made in consultation with the prime minister. The 2010 Legislative Assembly was called Tonga's first democratically elected Parliament. King George TUPOU V died in 2012 and was succeeded by his brother Crown Prince Tupouto'a Lavaka who ruled as George TUPOU VI. In 2015, 'Akilisi POHIVA became Tonga's first non-noble prime minister.

GEOGRAPHY

Location: Oceania, archipelago in the South Pacific Ocean, about two-thirds of the way from Hawaii to New Zealand

Geographic coordinates: 20 00 S, 175 00 W

Map references: Oceania

Area: *total:* 747 sq km
land: 717 sq km
water: 30 sq km
comparison ranking: total 189

Area - comparative: four times the size of Washington, DC

Land boundaries: *total:* 0 km

Coastline: 419 km

Maritime claims: *territorial sea:* 12 nm
exclusive economic zone: 200 nm
continental shelf: 200-m depth or to the depth of exploitation

Climate: tropical; modified by trade winds; warm season (December to May), cool season (May to December)

Terrain: mostly flat islands with limestone bedrock formed from uplifted coral formation; others have limestone overlying volcanic rock

Elevation: *highest point:* Kao Volcano on Kao Island 1,046 m
lowest point: Pacific Ocean 0 m

Natural resources: arable land, fish

Land use: *agricultural land:* 43.1% (2018 est.)
arable land: 22.2% (2018 est.)
permanent crops: 15.3% (2018 est.)
permanent pasture: 5.6% (2018 est.)
forest: 12.5% (2018 est.)
other: 44.4% (2018 est.)

Irrigated land: 0 sq km (2022)

Population distribution: over two-thirds of the population lives on the island of Tongatapu; only 45 of the nation's 171 islands are occupied

Natural hazards: cyclones (October to April); earthquakes and volcanic activity on Fonuafo'ou
volcanism: moderate volcanic activity; Fonualei (180 m) has shown frequent activity in recent years, while Niuafo'ou (260 m), which last erupted in 1985, has forced evacuations; other historically active volcanoes include Late and Tofua

Geography - note: the western islands (making up the Tongan Volcanic Arch) are all of volcanic origin; the eastern islands are nonvolcanic and are composed of coral limestone and sand

PEOPLE AND SOCIETY

Population: *total:* 104,889
male: 52,606
female: 52,283 (2024 est.)
comparison rankings: female 194; male 191; total 191

Nationality: *noun:* Tongan(s)
adjective: Tongan

Ethnic groups: Tongan 96.5%, other (European, Fijian, Samoan, Indian, Chinese, other Pacific Islander, other Asian, other) 3.5% (2021 est.)

Languages: Tongan only 85%, Tongan and other language 13.9%, Tongan not used at home 1.1% (2021 est.)
note: data represent language use at home of persons aged 5 and older

Religions: Protestant 63.9% (Free Wesleyan Church 34.2%, Free Church of Tonga 11.3%, Church of Tonga 6.8%, Seventh Day Adventist 2.5%, Assembly of God 2.5%, Tokaikolo/Maamafo'ou 1.5%, Constitutional Church of Tonga 1.2%, other Protestant 4%), Church of Jesus Christ 19.7%, Roman Catholic 13.7%, other 2.1%, none 0.6%, no answer 0.1% (2021 est.)

Age structure: *0-14 years:* 29.3% (male 15,627/ female 15,142)
15-64 years: 63.2% (male 33,445/female 32,867)
65 years and over: 7.4% (2024 est.) (male 3,534/ female 4,274)

Dependency ratios: *total dependency ratio:* 68.6
youth dependency ratio: 58.5
elderly dependency ratio: 10.5
potential support ratio: 9.5 (2021 est.)

Median age: *total:* 25.9 years (2024 est.)
male: 25.4 years
female: 26.4 years
comparison ranking: total 166

Population growth rate: -0.34% (2024 est.)
comparison ranking: 213

Birth rate: 19.7 births/1,000 population (2024 est.)
comparison ranking: 71

Death rate: 5 deaths/1,000 population (2024 est.)
comparison ranking: 195

Net migration rate: -18.1 migrant(s)/1,000 population (2024 est.)
comparison ranking: 227

Population distribution: over two-thirds of the population lives on the island of Tongatapu; only 45 of the nation's 171 islands are occupied

Urbanization: *urban population:* 23.2% of total population (2023)
rate of urbanization: 0.99% annual rate of change (2020-25 est.)

Major urban areas - population: 23,000 NUKU'ALOFA (2018)

Sex ratio: *at birth:* 1.03 male(s)/female
0-14 years: 1.03 male(s)/female
15-64 years: 1.02 male(s)/female
65 years and over: 0.83 male(s)/female
total population: 1.01 male(s)/female (2024 est.)

Mother's mean age at first birth: 24.9 years (2012 est.)
note: data represents median age at first birth among women 25-49

Maternal mortality ratio: 126 deaths/100,000 live births (2020 est.)
comparison ranking: 61

Infant mortality rate: *total:* 11.8 deaths/1,000 live births (2024 est.)
male: 12.8 deaths/1,000 live births
female: 10.8 deaths/1,000 live births
comparison ranking: total 111

Life expectancy at birth: *total population:* 78 years (2024 est.)
male: 76.4 years
female: 79.7 years
comparison ranking: total population 84

Total fertility rate: 2.65 children born/woman (2024 est.)
comparison ranking: 62

Gross reproduction rate: 1.3 (2024 est.)

Contraceptive prevalence rate: 29.3% (2019)

Drinking water source: *improved: urban:* 99.8% of population
rural: 99.6% of population
total: 99.6% of population
unimproved: urban: 0.2% of population
rural: 0.4% of population
total: 0.4% of population (2020 est.)

Current health expenditure: 5.3% of GDP (2020)

Physician density: 0.95 physicians/1,000 population (2020)

Sanitation facility access: *improved: urban:* 99.4% of population
rural: 98.8% of population
total: 98.9% of population
unimproved: urban: 0.6% of population
rural: 1.2% of population
total: 1.1% of population (2020 est.)

Obesity - adult prevalence rate: 48.2% (2016)
comparison ranking: 7

Alcohol consumption per capita: *total:* 0.31 liters of pure alcohol (2019 est.)
beer: 0.03 liters of pure alcohol (2019 est.)
wine: 0.17 liters of pure alcohol (2019 est.)
spirits: 0.11 liters of pure alcohol (2019 est.)
other alcohols: 0 liters of pure alcohol (2019 est.)
comparison ranking: total 169

Tobacco use: *total:* 31% (2020 est.)
male: 46.7% (2020 est.)
female: 15.3% (2020 est.)
comparison ranking: total 27

Children under the age of 5 years underweight: 0.8% (2019)
comparison ranking: 120

Currently married women (ages 15-49): 54.9% (2023 est.)

Child marriage: *women married by age 15:* 0.4%
women married by age 18: 10.1%
men married by age 18: 2.8% (2019 est.)

Education expenditures: 6.6% of GDP (2021 est.)
comparison ranking: 28

Literacy: *definition:* can read and write Tongan and/ or English
total population: 99.4%
male: 99.4%
female: 99.5% (2021)

School life expectancy (primary to tertiary education): *total:* 16 years
male: 15 years
female: 17 years (2020)

ENVIRONMENT

Environment - current issues: deforestation from land being cleared for agriculture and settlement; soil exhaustion; water pollution due to salinization, sewage, and toxic chemicals from farming activities; coral reefs and marine populations threatened

Environment - international agreements: *party to:* Biodiversity, Climate Change, Climate Change-Kyoto Protocol, Climate Change-Paris Agreement, Desertification, Endangered Species, Hazardous Wastes, Law of the Sea, Marine Dumping-London Convention, Marine Dumping-London Protocol, Marine Life Conservation, Nuclear Test Ban, Ozone Layer Protection, Ship Pollution
signed, but not ratified: none of the selected agreements

Climate: tropical; modified by trade winds; warm season (December to May), cool season (May to December)

Urbanization: *urban population:* 23.2% of total population (2023)
rate of urbanization: 0.99% annual rate of change (2020-25 est.)

Revenue from forest resources: 0.03% of GDP (2018 est.)
comparison ranking: 134

Revenue from coal: 0% of GDP (2018 est.)
comparison ranking: 88

Air pollutants: *particulate matter emissions:* 7.52 micrograms per cubic meter (2019 est.)
carbon dioxide emissions: 0.13 megatons (2016 est.)
methane emissions: 0.12 megatons (2020 est.)

Waste and recycling: *municipal solid waste generated annually:* 17,238 tons (2012 est.)

Total renewable water resources: 0 cubic meters (2017 est.)

GOVERNMENT

Country name: *conventional long form:* Kingdom of Tonga
conventional short form: Tonga
local long form: Pule'anga Fakatu'i 'o Tonga
local short form: Tonga
former: Friendly Islands
etymology: "tonga" means "south" in the Tongan language and refers to the country's geographic position in relation to central Polynesia

Government type: constitutional monarchy

Capital: *name:* Nuku'alofa
geographic coordinates: 21 08 S, 175 12 W
time difference: UTC+13 (18 hours ahead of Washington, DC, during Standard Time)
daylight saving time: +1hr, begins first Sunday in November; ends second Sunday in January
etymology: composed of the words *nuku*, meaning "residence or abode," and *alofa*, meaning "love," to signify "abode of love"

Administrative divisions: 5 island divisions; 'Eua, Ha'apai, Ongo Niua, Tongatapu, Vava'u

Independence: 4 June 1970 (from UK protectorate status)

National holiday: Official Birthday of King TUPOU VI, 4 July (1959); note - actual birthday of the monarch is 12 July 1959, 4 July (2015) is the day the king was crowned; Constitution Day (National Day), 4 November (1875)

Legal system: English common law

Constitution: *history:* adopted 4 November 1875, revised 1988, 2016
amendments: proposed by the Legislative Assembly; passage requires approval by the Assembly in each of three readings, the unanimous approval of the Privy Council (a high-level advisory body to the monarch), the Cabinet, and assent to by the monarch; revised 1988; amended many times, last in 2013

International law organization participation: has not submitted an ICJ jurisdiction declaration; non-party state to the ICCt

Citizenship: *citizenship by birth:* no
citizenship by descent only: the father must be a citizen of Tonga; if a child is born out of wedlock, the mother must be a citizen of Tonga
dual citizenship recognized: yes
residency requirement for naturalization: 5 years

Suffrage: 21 years of age; universal

Executive branch: *chief of state:* King TUPOU VI (since 18 March 2012)
head of government: Prime Minister Siaosi SOVALENI (since 27 December 2021)
cabinet: Cabinet nominated by the prime minister and appointed by the monarch
elections/appointments: the monarchy is hereditary; prime minister and deputy prime minister indirectly elected by the Legislative Assembly and appointed by the monarch; election last held on 18 November 2021 (next to be held in November 2025)
election results:
2021: Siaosi SOVALENI elected prime minister by the Legislative Assembly; Siaosi SOVALENI 16 votes, Aisake EKE 10
2019: Pohiva TU'I'ONETOA (Peoples Party) elected prime minister by parliament receiving 15 of 23 votes cast
note: a Privy Council advises the monarch

Legislative branch: *description:* unicameral Legislative Assembly or Fale Alea (30 seats statutory, 28 current); 17 people's representatives directly elected in single-seat constituencies by simple majority vote, and 9 indirectly elected by hereditary leaders; members serve 4-year terms)
elections: last held on 18 November 2021 (next to be held in November 2025)
election results: percent of vote - NA; seats by party - independent 12, nobles' representatives 9, DPFI 3, TPPI 3; composition - men 26, women 2, percentage women 7.1%

Judicial branch: *highest court(s):* Court of Appeal (consists of the court president and a number of judges determined by the monarch); note - appeals beyond the Court of Appeal are brought before the King in Privy Council, the monarch's advisory organ that has both judicial and legislative powers
judge selection and term of office: judge appointments and tenures made by the King in Privy Council and subject to consent of the Legislative Assembly
subordinate courts: Supreme Court; Magistrates' Courts; Land Courts

Political parties: Democratic Party of the Friendly Islands or DPFI or PTOA
Tonga People's Party (Paati 'a e Kakai 'o Tonga) or PAK or TPPI

International organization participation: ACP, ADB, AOSIS, C, FAO, G-77, IBRD, ICAO, ICRM, IDA, IFAD, IFC, IFRCS, IHO, IMF, IMO, IMSO, Interpol, IOC, IPU, ITU, ITUC (NGOs), OPCW, PIF, Sparteca, SPC, UN, UNCTAD, UNESCO, UNIDO, UPU, WCO, WHO, WIPO, WMO, WTO

Diplomatic representation in the US: *chief of mission:* Ambassador Viliana Va'inga TONE (since 20 April 2021)
chancery: 250 East 51st Street, New York, NY 10022
telephone: [1] (917) 369-1025
FAX: [1] (917) 369-1024
email address and website:
tongaconsnot@gmail.com
consulate(s) general: San Francisco

Diplomatic representation from the US: *chief of mission:* Ambassador Marie DAMOUR (since 6 December 2022); note - Ambassador DAMOUR is based in the US Embassy in the Republic of Fiji and is accredited to Tonga as well as Kiribati, Nauru, and Tuvalu
embassy: although the US opened an embassy in Tonga on 9 May 2023, the US Ambassador to Fiji is accredited to Tonga while the Embassy is being staffed

Flag description: red with a bold red cross on a white rectangle in the upper hoist-side corner; the cross reflects the deep-rooted Christianity in Tonga, red represents the blood of Christ and his sacrifice, and white signifies purity

National symbol(s): red cross on white field, arms equal length; national colors: red, white

Coat of arms of the Kingdom of Tonga: National anthem: name: "Ko e fasi `o e tu"i `o e `Otu Tonga" (Song of the King of the Tonga Islands)
lyrics/music: Uelingatoni Ngu TUPOUMALOHI/ Karl Gustavus SCHMITT
note: in use since 1875; more commonly known as "Fasi Fakafonua" (National Song)

ECONOMY

Economic overview: upper middle-income Pacific island economy; enormous diaspora and remittance reliance; key tourism and agricultural sectors; major fish exporter; rapidly growing Chinese infrastructure investments; rising methamphetamine hub

Real GDP (purchasing power parity): $700.437 million (2022 est.)
$714.816 million (2021 est.)
$734.406 million (2020 est.)
note: data in 2021 dollars
comparison ranking: 211

Real GDP growth rate: -2.01% (2022 est.)
-2.67% (2021 est.)
0.49% (2020 est.)
note: annual GDP % growth based on constant local currency
comparison ranking: 206

Real GDP per capita: $6,600 (2022 est.)
$6,700 (2021 est.)
$7,000 (2020 est.)
note: data in 2021 dollars
comparison ranking: 162

GDP (official exchange rate): $500.275 million (2022 est.)
note: data in current dollars at official exchange rate

Inflation rate (consumer prices): 6.35% (2023 est.)
10.97% (2022 est.)
5.64% (2021 est.)
note: annual % change based on consumer prices
comparison ranking: 135

GDP - composition, by sector of origin: *agriculture:* 16.3% (2021 est.)
industry: 15.9% (2021 est.)
services: 49.7% (2021 est.)
note: figures may not total 100% due to non-allocated consumption not captured in sector-reported data
comparison rankings: services 149; industry 167; agriculture 50

GDP - composition, by end use: *household consumption:* 109% (2021 est.)
government consumption: 30.7% (2021 est.)
investment in fixed capital: 23.2% (2021 est.)
investment in inventories: -1.3% (2021 est.)
exports of goods and services: 12.5% (2021 est.)
imports of goods and services: -60.8% (2021 est.)
note: figures may not total 100% due to rounding or gaps in data collection

Agricultural products: coconuts, pumpkins/squash, cassava, sweet potatoes, vegetables, yams, taro, root vegetables, plantains, lemons/limes (2022)
note: top ten agricultural products based on tonnage

Industries: tourism, construction, fishing

Industrial production growth rate: 1.23% (2021 est.)
note: annual % change in industrial value added based on constant local currency
comparison ranking: 134

Labor force: 38,000 (2023 est.)
note: number of people ages 15 or older who are employed or seeking work
comparison ranking: 196

Unemployment rate: 2.3% (2023 est.)
2.35% (2022 est.)
2.11% (2021 est.)
note: % of labor force seeking employment
comparison ranking: 26

Youth unemployment rate (ages 15-24): *total:* 6.7% (2023 est.)
male: 4.4% (2023 est.)
female: 10.5% (2023 est.)
note: % of labor force ages 15-24 seeking employment
comparison ranking: total 163

Population below poverty line: 20.6% (2021 est.)

Gini Index coefficient - distribution of family income: 27.1 (2021 est.)
note: index (0-100) of income distribution; higher values represent greater inequality
comparison ranking: 141

Household income or consumption by percentage share: *lowest 10%:* 4% (2021 est.)
highest 10%: 22% (2021 est.)
note: % share of income accruing to lowest and highest 10% of population

Remittances: 45.03% of GDP (2022 est.)
46.95% of GDP (2021 est.)
38.26% of GDP (2020 est.)
note: personal transfers and compensation between resident and non-resident individuals/households/ entities

Budget: *revenues:* $215.007 million (2020 est.)
expenditures: $160.257 million (2020 est.)
note: central government revenues and expenses (excluding grants/extrabudgetary units/social security funds) converted to US dollars at average official exchange rate for year indicated

Public debt: 45.02% of GDP (2020 est.)
note: central government debt as a % of GDP
comparison ranking: 99

Taxes and other revenues: 21.3% (of GDP) (2020 est.)
comparison ranking: 76

Current account balance: -$28.84 million (2022 est.)
-$33.414 million (2021 est.)
-$36.294 million (2020 est.)
note: balance of payments - net trade and primary/secondary income in current dollars
comparison ranking: 89

Exports: $59.926 million (2022 est.)
$57.534 million (2021 est.)
$99.78 million (2020 est.)
note: balance of payments - exports of goods and services in current dollars
comparison ranking: 213

Exports - partners: US 31%, Australia 19%, NZ 12%, Hong Kong 8%, Belgium 8% (2022)
note: top five export partners based on percentage share of exports

Exports - commodities: fish, scrap copper, processed crustaceans, vegetables, perfume plants (2022)
note: top five export commodities based on value in dollars

Imports: $332.743 million (2022 est.)
$299.094 million (2021 est.)
$314.803 million (2020 est.)
note: balance of payments - imports of goods and services in current dollars
comparison ranking: 207

Imports - partners: Fiji 28%, China 23%, NZ 21%, Australia 6%, US 5% (2022)
note: top five import partners based on percentage share of imports

Imports - commodities: refined petroleum, plastic products, poultry, sheep and goat meat, cars (2022)
note: top five import commodities based on value in dollars

Reserves of foreign exchange and gold: $396.53 million (2023 est.)
$375.564 million (2022 est.)
$361.812 million (2021 est.)
note: holdings of gold (year-end prices)/foreign exchange/special drawing rights in current dollars
comparison ranking: 177

Debt - external: $152.877 million (2022 est.)
note: present value of external debt in current US dollars
comparison ranking: 101

Exchange rates: pa'anga (TOP) per US dollar -

Exchange rates: 2.364 (2023 est.)
2.328 (2022 est.)
2.265 (2021 est.)
2.3 (2020 est.)
2.289 (2019 est.)

ENERGY

Electricity access: *electrification - total population:* 100% (2022 est.)

Electricity: *installed generating capacity:* 33,000 kW (2022 est.)
consumption: 69.136 million kWh (2022 est.)
transmission/distribution losses: 6 million kWh (2022 est.)
comparison rankings: transmission/distribution losses 11; consumption 202; installed generating capacity 201

Electricity generation sources: *fossil fuels:* 86.7% of total installed capacity (2022 est.)
solar: 9.3% of total installed capacity (2022 est.)
wind: 4% of total installed capacity (2022 est.)

Petroleum: *refined petroleum consumption:* 900 bbl/day (2022 est.)

Carbon dioxide emissions: 131,000 metric tonnes of CO_2 (2022 est.)
from petroleum and other liquids: 131,000 metric tonnes of CO_2 (2022 est.)
comparison ranking: total emissions 208

Energy consumption per capita: 17.949 million Btu/person (2022 est.)
comparison ranking: 132

COMMUNICATIONS

Telephones - fixed lines: *total subscriptions:* 11,000 (2021 est.)
subscriptions per 100 inhabitants: 10 (2021 est.)
comparison ranking: total subscriptions 187

Telephones - mobile cellular: *total subscriptions:* 64,000 (2021 est.)
subscriptions per 100 inhabitants: 61 (2021 est.)
comparison ranking: total subscriptions 203

Telecommunication systems: *general assessment:* Tonga was only connected to the global submarine telecommunication network in the last decade; though this system is more stable than other technologies such as satellite and fixed infrastructure; the January 2022 eruption of Hunga Tonga-Hunga Ha'apai severed Tonga's connection to the submarine telecommunication network (2023)
domestic: fixed-line 10 per 100 persons and mobile-cellular teledensity 61 telephones per 100 (2021)
international: country code - 676; landing point for the Tonga Cable and the TDCE connecting to Fiji and 3 separate Tonga islands; satellite earth station - 1 Intelsat (Pacific Ocean) (2020)

Broadcast media: 1 state-owned TV station and 3 privately owned TV stations; satellite and cable TV services are available; 1 state-owned and 5 privately owned radio stations; Radio Australia broadcasts available via satellite (2019)

Internet country code: .to

Internet users: *total:* 73,700 (2021 est.)
percent of population: 67% (2021 est.)
comparison ranking: total 194

Broadband - fixed subscriptions: *total:* 5,000 (2020 est.)
subscriptions per 100 inhabitants: 5 (2020 est.)
comparison ranking: total 188

TRANSPORTATION

National air transport system: *number of registered air carriers:* 1 (2020)
inventory of registered aircraft operated by air carriers: 1

Civil aircraft registration country code prefix: A3

Airports: 6 (2024)
comparison ranking: 175

Roadways: *total:* 680 km
paved: 184 km
unpaved: 496 km (2011)
comparison ranking: total 191

Merchant marine: *total:* 29 (2023)
by type: container ship 1, general cargo 13, oil tanker 1, other 14
comparison ranking: total 136

Ports: *total ports:* 3 (2024)
large: 0
medium: 0
small: 0
very small: 3
ports with oil terminals: 0
key ports: Neiafu, Nuku Alofa, Pangai

MILITARY AND SECURITY

Military and security forces: His Majesty's Armed Forces Tonga (aka Tonga Defense Services): Tonga Royal Guard, Land Force (Royal Tongan Marines), Tonga Navy, Air Wing

Ministry of Police and Fire Services: Tonga Police Force (2024)

Military expenditures: 1.6% of GDP (2023 est.)
1.6% of GDP (2022 est.)
1.5% of GDP (2021 est.)
2.1% of GDP (2020 est.)
2.4% of GDP (2019 est.)
comparison ranking: 82

Military and security service personnel strengths: approximately 600 personnel (2024)

Military equipment inventories and acquisitions: the military's inventory consists of light weapons, as well as some naval patrol vessels from Australia and a few US-origin aircraft (2024)

Military service age and obligation: voluntary military service for men and women 18-25; no conscription (2023)

Military - note: the HMAF's primary missions are protecting the King and Tonga's sovereignty; it is also responsible for humanitarian assistance and disaster relief, search and rescue operations, monitoring against illegal fishing, and delivering supplies to the outer islands; the HMAF has contributed limited numbers of personnel to multinational military operations in Afghanistan, Iraq, and the Solomon Islands; it is a small force comprised of royal guards, marines, a few naval patrol boats, and a couple of aircraft for maritime patrolling, search and rescue, and training purposes
Tonga participated in World War I as part of the New Zealand Expeditionary Force, but the Tonga Defense Force (TDF) was not established until 1939 at the beginning of World War II; in 1943, New Zealand helped train about 2,000 Tongan troops who saw action in the Solomon Islands; the TDF was disbanded at the end of the war, but was reactivated in 1946 as the Tonga Defense Services (TDS); in 2013, the name of the TDS was changed to His Majesty's Armed Forces of Tonga (HMAF); Tongan troops deployed to Iraq from 2004-2008 and Afghanistan to support UK forces from 2010-2014
Tonga has a "shiprider" agreement with the US, which allows local maritime law enforcement officers to embark on US Coast Guard (USCG) and US Navy (USN) vessels, including to board and search vessels suspected of violating laws or regulations within Tonga's designated exclusive economic zone (EEZ) or on the high seas; "shiprider" agreements also enable USCG personnel and USN vessels with embarked USCG law enforcement personnel to work with host nations to protect critical regional resources (2024)

TRINIDAD AND TOBAGO

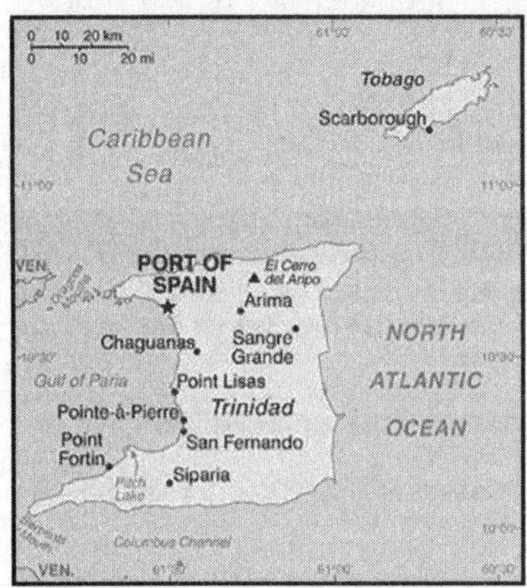

INTRODUCTION

Background: First colonized by the Spanish, Trinidad and Tobago came under British control in the early 19th century. The emancipation of enslaved people in 1834 disrupted the twin islands' sugar industry. Contract workers arriving from India between 1845 and 1917 augmented the labor force, which boosted sugar production as well as the cocoa industry. The discovery of oil on Trinidad in 1910 added another important export that remains the country's dominant industry. Trinidad and Tobago attained independence in 1962. The country is one of the most prosperous in the Caribbean, thanks largely to petroleum and natural gas production and processing. The government is struggling to reverse a surge in violent crime.

GEOGRAPHY

Location: Caribbean, islands between the Caribbean Sea and the North Atlantic Ocean, northeast of Venezuela

Geographic coordinates: 11 00 N, 61 00 W

Map references: Central America and the Caribbean

Area: *total:* 5,128 sq km
land: 5,128 sq km
water: 0 sq km
comparison ranking: total 173

Area - comparative: slightly smaller than Delaware

Land boundaries: *total:* 0 km

Coastline: 362 km

Maritime claims: *territorial sea:* 12 nm
contiguous zone: 24 nm
exclusive economic zone: 200 nm
continental shelf: 200 nm or to the outer edge of the continental margin
measured from claimed archipelagic baselines

Climate: tropical; rainy season (June to December)

Terrain: mostly plains with some hills and low mountains

Elevation: *highest point:* El Cerro del Aripo 940 m
lowest point: Caribbean Sea 0 m
mean elevation: 83 m

Natural resources: petroleum, natural gas, asphalt

Land use: *agricultural land:* 10.6% (2018 est.)
arable land: 4.9% (2018 est.)
permanent crops: 4.3% (2018 est.)
permanent pasture: 1.4% (2018 est.)
forest: 44% (2018 est.)
other: 45.4% (2018 est.)

Irrigated land: 70 sq km (2012)

Population distribution: population on Trinidad is concentrated in the western half of the island, on Tobago in the southern half

Natural hazards: outside usual path of hurricanes and other tropical storms

Geography - note: Pitch Lake, on Trinidad's southwestern coast, is the world's largest natural reservoir of asphalt

PEOPLE AND SOCIETY

Population: *total:* 1,408,966
male: 708,260
female: 700,706 (2024 est.)
comparison rankings: female 155; male 157; total 157

Nationality: *noun:* Trinidadian(s), Tobagonian(s)
adjective: Trinidadian, Tobagonian
note: Trinbagonian is used on occasion to describe a citizen of the country without specifying the island of origin

Ethnic groups: East Indian 35.4%, African descent 34.2%, mixed - other 15.3%, mixed - African/East Indian 7.7%, other 1.3%, unspecified 6.2% (2011 est.)

Languages: English (official), Trinidadian Creole English, Tobagonian Creole English, Caribbean Hindustani (a dialect of Hindi), Trinidadian Creole French, Spanish, Chinese

Religions: Protestant 32.1% (Pentecostal/Evangelical/Full Gospel 12%, Baptist 6.9%, Anglican 5.7%, Seventh Day Adventist 4.1%, Presbyterian/Congregational 2.5%, other Protestant 0.9%), Roman Catholic 21.6%, Hindu 18.2%, Muslim 5%, Jehovah's Witness 1.5%, other 8.4%, none 2.2%, unspecified 11.1% (2011 est.)

Age structure: *0-14 years:* 18.7% (male 134,508/female 129,180)
15-64 years: 67.2% (male 481,606/female 465,150)
65 years and over: 14.1% (2024 est.) (male 92,146/female 106,376)

Dependency ratios: *total dependency ratio:* 43.7
youth dependency ratio: 29.3
elderly dependency ratio: 16.8
potential support ratio: 7.4 (2021 est.)

Median age: *total:* 38.5 years (2024 est.)
male: 38 years
female: 39 years
comparison ranking: total 73

Population growth rate: 0.1% (2024 est.)
comparison ranking: 188

Birth rate: 10.5 births/1,000 population (2024 est.)
comparison ranking: 176

Death rate: 8.6 deaths/1,000 population (2024 est.)
comparison ranking: 71

Net migration rate: -0.9 migrant(s)/1,000 population (2024 est.)
comparison ranking: 142

Population distribution: population on Trinidad is concentrated in the western half of the island, on Tobago in the southern half

Urbanization: *urban population:* 53.4% of total population (2023)
rate of urbanization: 0.23% annual rate of change (2020-25 est.)

Major urban areas - population: 545,000 PORT-OF-SPAIN (capital) (2023)

Sex ratio: *at birth:* 1.04 male(s)/female
0-14 years: 1.04 male(s)/female
15-64 years: 1.04 male(s)/female
65 years and over: 0.87 male(s)/female
total population: 1.01 male(s)/female (2024 est.)

Maternal mortality ratio: 27 deaths/100,000 live births (2020 est.)
comparison ranking: 115

Infant mortality rate: *total:* 15.1 deaths/1,000 live births (2024 est.)
male: 17.1 deaths/1,000 live births
female: 13 deaths/1,000 live births
comparison ranking: total 94

Life expectancy at birth: *total population:* 76.5 years (2024 est.)
male: 74.6 years
female: 78.4 years
comparison ranking: total population 107

Total fertility rate: 1.63 children born/woman (2024 est.)
comparison ranking: 174

Gross reproduction rate: 0.8 (2024 est.)

Drinking water source: *improved:*
total: 100% of population
unimproved:
total: 0% of population (2020 est.)

Current health expenditure: 7.3% of GDP (2020)

Physician density: 4.48 physicians/1,000 population (2019)

Hospital bed density: 3 beds/1,000 population (2017)

Sanitation facility access: *improved:*
total: 99.9% of population
unimproved:
total: 0.1% of population (2020 est.)

Obesity - adult prevalence rate: 18.6% (2016)
comparison ranking: 117

Alcohol consumption per capita: *total:* 5.81 liters of pure alcohol (2019 est.)
beer: 2.92 liters of pure alcohol (2019 est.)
wine: 0.16 liters of pure alcohol (2019 est.)
spirits: 2.65 liters of pure alcohol (2019 est.)
other alcohols: 0.09 liters of pure alcohol (2019 est.)
comparison ranking: total 74

Currently married women (ages 15-49): 48.6% (2023 est.)

Education expenditures: 4.1% of GDP (2020 est.)
comparison ranking: 112

Literacy: *definition:* age 15 and over can read and write
total population: 99%
male: 99.2%

female: 98.7% (2015)

ENVIRONMENT

Environment - current issues: water pollution from agricultural chemicals, industrial wastes, and raw sewage; widespread pollution of waterways and coastal areas; illegal dumping; deforestation; soil erosion; fisheries and wildlife depletion

Environment - international agreements: *party to:* Biodiversity, Climate Change, Climate Change-Kyoto Protocol, Climate Change-Paris Agreement, Comprehensive Nuclear Test Ban, Desertification, Endangered Species, Hazardous Wastes, Law of the Sea, Marine Dumping-London Protocol, Marine Life Conservation, Nuclear Test Ban, Ozone Layer Protection, Ship Pollution, Tropical Timber 2006, Wetlands
signed, but not ratified: none of the selected agreements

Climate: tropical; rainy season (June to December)

Urbanization: *urban population:* 53.4% of total population (2023)
rate of urbanization: 0.23% annual rate of change (2020-25 est.)

Revenue from forest resources: 0.05% of GDP (2018 est.)
comparison ranking: 127

Revenue from coal: 0% of GDP (2018 est.)
comparison ranking: 103

Air pollutants: *particulate matter emissions:* 10.26 micrograms per cubic meter (2019 est.)
carbon dioxide emissions: 43.87 megatons (2016 est.)
methane emissions: 1.35 megatons (2020 est.)

Waste and recycling: *municipal solid waste generated annually:* 727,874 tons (2010 est.)

Total water withdrawal: *municipal:* 240 million cubic meters (2020 est.)
industrial: 130 million cubic meters (202 est.)
agricultural: 20 million cubic meters (2020 est.)

Total renewable water resources: 3.84 billion cubic meters (2020 est.)

GOVERNMENT

Country name: *conventional long form:* Republic of Trinidad and Tobago
conventional short form: Trinidad and Tobago
etymology: explorer Christopher COLUMBUS named the larger island "La Isla de la Trinidad" (The Island of the Trinity) on 31 July 1498 on his third voyage; the tobacco grown and smoked by the natives of the smaller island or its elongated cigar shape may account for the "tobago" name, which is spelled "tobaco" in Spanish

Government type: parliamentary republic

Capital: *name:* Port of Spain
geographic coordinates: 10 39 N, 61 31 W
time difference: UTC-4 (1 hour ahead of Washington, DC, during Standard Time)
etymology: the name dates to the period of Spanish colonial rule (16th to late 18th centuries) when the city was referred to as "Puerto de Espana"; the name was anglicized following the British capture of Trinidad in 1797

Administrative divisions: 9 regions, 3 boroughs, 2 cities, 1 ward
regions: Couva/Tabaquite/Talparo, Diego Martin, Mayaro/Rio Claro, Penal/Debe, Princes Town, Sangre Grande, San Juan/Laventille, Siparia, Tunapuna/Piarco
borough: Arima, Chaguanas, Point Fortin
cities: Port of Spain, San Fernando
ward: Tobago

Independence: 31 August 1962 (from the UK)

National holiday: Independence Day, 31 August (1962)

Legal system: English common law; judicial review of legislative acts in the Supreme Court

Constitution: *history:* previous 1962; latest 1976
amendments: proposed by Parliament; passage of amendments affecting constitutional provisions, such as human rights and freedoms or citizenship, requires at least two-thirds majority vote by the membership of both houses and assent of the president; passage of amendments, such as the powers and authorities of the executive, legislative, and judicial branches of government, and the procedure for amending the constitution, requires at least three-quarters majority vote by the House membership, two-thirds majority vote by the Senate membership, and assent of the president; amended many times, last in 2007

International law organization participation: has not submitted an ICJ jurisdiction declaration; accepts ICCt jurisdiction

Citizenship: *citizenship by birth:* yes
citizenship by descent only: yes
dual citizenship recognized: yes
residency requirement for naturalization: 8 years

Suffrage: 18 years of age; universal

Executive branch: *chief of state:* President Christine KANGALOO (since 20 March 2023)
head of government: Prime Minister Keith ROWLEY (since 9 September 2015)
cabinet: Cabinet appointed from among members of Parliament
elections/appointments: president indirectly elected by an electoral college of selected Senate and House of Representatives members for a 5-year term (eligible for a second term); election last held on 20 January 2023 (next to be held by February 2028); the president usually appoints the leader of the majority party in the House of Representatives as prime minister
election results:
2023: Christine KANGALOO elected president by the electoral college on 20 January 2023; electoral college vote Christine KANGALOO (PNM) 48, Israel KHAN (UNC) 22
2018: Paula-Mae WEEKES (independent) elected president; ran unopposed and was elected without a vote; she was Trinidad and Tabago's first female head of state

Legislative branch: *description:* bicameral Parliament consists of:
Senate (31 seats; 16 members appointed by the ruling party, 9 by the president, and 6 by the opposition party; members serve 5-year terms;)
House of Representatives (42 seats; 41 members directly elected in single-seat constituencies by simple majority vote and the house speaker - usually designated from outside Parliament; members serve 5-year terms)
elections: Senate - last appointments on 28 August 2020 (next appointments in August 2025)
House of Representatives - last held on 10 August 2020 (next to be held in 2025)
election results: Senate - percent by party - NA; seats by party - PNM 16, UNC 6, independent 9; composition - men 19, women 13, percentage women 40.6%
House of Representatives - percent by party - NA; seats by party - PNM 23, UNC 19; composition - men 30, women 12, percentage women 28.6%; total Parliament percentage women 33.8%
note: Tobago has a unicameral House of Assembly (19 seats; 15 assemblymen directly elected by simple majority vote and 4 appointed councilors - 3 on the advice of the chief secretary and 1 on the advice of the minority leader; members serve 4-year terms)

Judicial branch: *highest court(s):* Supreme Court of the Judicature (consists of a chief justice for both the Court of Appeal with 12 judges and the High Court with 24 judges); note - Trinidad and Tobago can file appeals beyond its Supreme Court to the Caribbean Court of Justice, with final appeal to the Judicial Committee of the Privy Council (in London)
judge selection and term of office: Supreme Court chief justice appointed by the president after consultation with the prime minister and the parliamentary leader of the opposition; other judges appointed by the Judicial Legal Services Commission, headed by the chief justice and 5 members with judicial experience; all judges serve for life with mandatory retirement normally at age 65
subordinate courts: Courts of Summary Criminal Jurisdiction; Petty Civil Courts; Family Court

Political parties: People's National Movement or PNM
United National Congress or UNC
Tobago People's Party or Tobago

International organization participation: ACP, ACS, AOSIS, C, Caricom, CDB, CELAC, EITI (compliant country), FAO, G-24, G-77, IADB, IAEA, IBRD, ICAO, ICC (NGOs), ICCt, ICRM, IDA, IFAD, IFC, IFRCS, IHO, ILO, IMF, IMO, Interpol, IOC, IOM, IPU, ISO, ITSO, ITU, ITUC (NGOs), LAES, MIGA, NAM, OAS, OPANAL, OPCW, Pacific Alliance (observer), Paris Club (associate), UN, UNCTAD, UNESCO, UNIDO, UPU, WCO, WFTU (NGOs), WHO, WIPO, WMO, WTO

Diplomatic representation in the US: *chief of mission:* Ambassador (vacant); Chargé d'Affaires Venessa RAMHIT-RAMROOP (since 3 March 2024)
chancery: 1708 Massachusetts Avenue NW, Washington, DC 20036-1975
telephone: [1] (202) 467-6490
FAX: [1] (202) 785-3130
email address and website:
embdcinfo@foreign.gov.tt
https://foreign.gov.tt/missions-consuls/tt-missions-abroad/diplomatic-missions/embassy-washington-dc-us/
consulate(s) general: Miami, New York

Diplomatic representation from the US: *chief of mission:* Ambassador Candace A. BOND (since 8 December 2022)
embassy: 15 Queen's Park West, Port of Spain
mailing address: 3410 Port of Spain Place, Washington DC 20521-3410
telephone: (868) 622-6371
FAX: (868) 822-5905
email address and website:
ptspas@state.gov
https://tt.usembassy.gov/

Flag description: red with a white-edged black diagonal band from the upper hoist side to the lower fly side; the colors represent the elements of earth, water, and fire; black stands for the wealth of the land and the dedication of the people; white symbolizes the sea surrounding the islands, the purity of the country's aspirations, and equality; red symbolizes the warmth and energy of the sun, the vitality of the land, and the courage and friendliness of its people

National symbol(s): scarlet ibis (bird of Trinidad), cocrico (bird of Tobago), Chaconia flower; national colors: red, white, black

National anthem: *name:* "Forged From the Love of Liberty"
lyrics/music: Patrick Stanislaus CASTAGNE
note: adopted 1962; song originally created to serve as an anthem for the West Indies Federation; adopted by Trinidad and Tobago following the Federation's dissolution in 1962

ECONOMY

Economic overview: high-income Caribbean economy; major hydrocarbon exporter; key tourism and finance sectors; high inflation and growing public debt; long foreign currency access delays; large foreign reserves and sovereign wealth fund

Real GDP (purchasing power parity): $43.681 billion (2023 est.)
$42.781 billion (2022 est.)
$42.157 billion (2021 est.)
note: data in 2021 dollars
comparison ranking: 133

Real GDP growth rate: 2.1% (2023 est.)
1.48% (2022 est.)
-1.04% (2021 est.)
note: annual GDP % growth based on constant local currency
comparison ranking: 136

Real GDP per capita: $28,500 (2023 est.)
$27,900 (2022 est.)
$27,600 (2021 est.)
note: data in 2021 dollars
comparison ranking: 81

GDP (official exchange rate): $28.14 billion (2023 est.)
note: data in current dollars at official exchange rate

Inflation rate (consumer prices): 4.63% (2023 est.)
5.83% (2022 est.)
2.06% (2021 est.)
note: annual % change based on consumer prices
comparison ranking: 99

Credit ratings: Moody's rating: Ba1 (2017)

Standard & Poors rating: BBB- (2020)
note: The year refers to the year in which the current credit rating was first obtained.

GDP - composition, by sector of origin: *agriculture:* 1.1% (2022 est.)
industry: 48.9% (2022 est.)
services: 47.8% (2022 est.)
note: figures may not total 100% due to non-allocated consumption not captured in sector-reported data
comparison rankings: services 155; industry 14; agriculture 181

GDP - composition, by end use: *household consumption:* 78.9% (2017 est.)
government consumption: 16.4% (2017 est.)
investment in fixed capital: 19.8% (2021 est.)
exports of goods and services: 45.4% (2017 est.)
imports of goods and services: -48.7% (2017 est.)

Agricultural products: chicken, fruits, coconuts, citrus fruits, plantains, maize, eggs, oranges, tomatoes, bananas (2022)
note: top ten agricultural products based on tonnage

Industries: petroleum and petroleum products, liquefied natural gas, methanol, ammonia, urea, steel products, beverages, food processing, cement, cotton textiles

Industrial production growth rate: 3.18% (2022 est.)
note: annual % change in industrial value added based on constant local currency
comparison ranking: 105

Labor force: 681,000 (2023 est.)
note: number of people ages 15 or older who are employed or seeking work
comparison ranking: 156

Unemployment rate: 4.21% (2023 est.)
4.38% (2022 est.)
4.45% (2021 est.)
note: % of labor force seeking employment
comparison ranking: 82

Youth unemployment rate (ages 15-24): *total:* 10.1% (2023 est.)
male: 9.4% (2023 est.)
female: 11.1% (2023 est.)
note: % of labor force ages 15-24 seeking employment
comparison ranking: total 134

Population below poverty line: 20% (2014 est.)

Remittances: 0.63% of GDP (2023 est.)
0.68% of GDP (2022 est.)
0.96% of GDP (2021 est.)
note: personal transfers and compensation between resident and non-resident individuals/households/entities

Budget: *revenues:* $5.698 billion (2019 est.)
expenditures: $7.822 billion (2019 est.)
note: central government revenues (excluding grants) and expenses converted to US dollars at average official exchange rate for year indicated

Public debt: 41.8% of GDP (2017 est.)
comparison ranking: 126

Taxes and other revenues: 16.55% (of GDP) (2019 est.)
note: central government tax revenue as a % of GDP
comparison ranking: 121

Current account balance: $5.382 billion (2022 est.)
$2.695 billion (2021 est.)
-$1.356 billion (2020 est.)
note: balance of payments - net trade and primary/secondary income in current dollars
comparison ranking: 35

Exports: $17.584 billion (2022 est.)
$11.542 billion (2021 est.)
$6.44 billion (2020 est.)
note: balance of payments - exports of goods and services in current dollars
comparison ranking: 93

Exports - partners: US 35%, Belgium 6%, Morocco 5%, Spain 4%, Brazil 4% (2022)
note: top five export partners based on percentage share of exports

Exports - commodities: ammonia, natural gas, crude petroleum, acyclic alcohols, fertilizers (2022)
note: top five export commodities based on value in dollars

Imports: $10.694 billion (2022 est.)
$8.636 billion (2021 est.)
$6.785 billion (2020 est.)
note: balance of payments - imports of goods and services in current dollars
comparison ranking: 118

Imports - partners: US 40%, China 9%, Italy 7%, Brazil 4%, Canada 3% (2022)
note: top five import partners based on percentage share of imports

Imports - commodities: refined petroleum, iron ore, cars, plastic products, excavation machinery (2022)
note: top five import commodities based on value in dollars

Reserves of foreign exchange and gold: $6.256 billion (2023 est.)
$6.832 billion (2022 est.)
$6.88 billion (2021 est.)
note: holdings of gold (year-end prices)/foreign exchange/special drawing rights in current dollars
comparison ranking: 90

Exchange rates: Trinidad and Tobago dollars (TTD) per US dollar -

Exchange rates: 6.75 (2023 est.)
6.754 (2022 est.)
6.759 (2021 est.)
6.751 (2020 est.)
6.754 (2019 est.)

ENERGY

Electricity access: *electrification - total population:* 100% (2022 est.)

Electricity: *installed generating capacity:* 2.522 million kW (2022 est.)
consumption: 8.981 billion kWh (2022 est.)
transmission/distribution losses: 427.688 million kWh (2022 est.)
comparison rankings: transmission/distribution losses 76; consumption 108; installed generating capacity 114

Electricity generation sources: *fossil fuels:* 99.9% of total installed capacity (2022 est.)
solar: 0.1% of total installed capacity (2022 est.)

Coal: *consumption:* 100 metric tons (2021 est.)
imports: 200 metric tons (2022 est.)

Petroleum: *total petroleum production:* 73,000 bbl/day (2023 est.)
refined petroleum consumption: 32,000 bbl/day (2022 est.)
crude oil estimated reserves: 242.982 million barrels (2021 est.)

Natural gas: *production:* 26.772 billion cubic meters (2022 est.)
consumption: 15.913 billion cubic meters (2022 est.)
exports: 10.878 billion cubic meters (2022 est.)
proven reserves: 298.063 billion cubic meters (2021 est.)

Carbon dioxide emissions: 35.415 million metric tonnes of CO2 (2022 est.)
from petroleum and other liquids: 4.257 million metric tonnes of CO2 (2022 est.)
from consumed natural gas: 31.158 million metric tonnes of CO2 (2022 est.)
comparison ranking: total emissions 69

COMMUNICATIONS

Telephones - fixed lines: *total subscriptions:* 326,000 (2022 est.)
subscriptions per 100 inhabitants: 21 (2022 est.)
comparison ranking: total subscriptions 104

Telephones - mobile cellular: *total subscriptions:* 1.999 million (2022 est.)
subscriptions per 100 inhabitants: 131 (2022 est.)
comparison ranking: total subscriptions 152

Telecommunication systems: *general assessment:* excellent international service; good local service; broadband access; expanded FttP (Fiber to the Home) markets; LTE launch; regulatory development; major growth in mobile telephony and data segments which attacks operation investment in fiber infrastructure; moves to end roaming charges (2020)
domestic: fixed-line is 21 per 100 persons and mobile-cellular teledensity 131 per 100 persons (2022)
international: country code - 1-868; landing points for the EC Link, ECFS, Southern Caribbean Fiber, SG-SCS and Americas II submarine cable systems provide connectivity to US, parts of the Caribbean and South America; satellite earth station - 1 Intelsat (Atlantic Ocean); tropospheric scatter to Barbados and Guyana (2020)

Broadcast media: 6 free-to-air TV networks, 2 of which are state-owned; 24 subscription providers (cable and satellite); over 36 radio frequencies (2019)

Internet country code: .tt

Internet users: *total:* 1.185 million (2021 est.)
percent of population: 79% (2021 est.)
comparison ranking: total 146

Broadband - fixed subscriptions: *total:* 376,771 (2020 est.)
subscriptions per 100 inhabitants: 27 (2020 est.)
comparison ranking: total 101

TRANSPORTATION

National air transport system: *number of registered air carriers:* 1 (2020)
inventory of registered aircraft operated by air carriers: 19
annual passenger traffic on registered air carriers: 2,525,130 (2018)
annual freight traffic on registered air carriers: 41.14 million (2018) mt-km

Civil aircraft registration country code prefix: 9Y

Airports: 3 (2024)
comparison ranking: 193

Pipelines: 257 km condensate, 11 km condensate/gas, 1,567 km gas, 587 km oil (2013)

Merchant marine: *total:* 102 (2023)
by type: general cargo 1, other 101
comparison ranking: total 88

Ports: *total ports:* 10 (2024)
large: 0
medium: 1
small: 4
very small: 5
ports with oil terminals: 8
key ports: Galeota Point Terminal, Point Lisas Industrial Port, Point Lisas Port, Pointe-a-Pierre, Port of Spain

MILITARY AND SECURITY

Military and security forces: Trinidad and Tobago Defense Force (TTDF): Trinidad and Tobago Regiment (Army/Land Forces), Trinidad and Tobago Coast Guard, Trinidad and Tobago Air Guard, Trinidad and Tobago Defense Force Reserves
Trinidad and Tobago Police Service (TTPS) (2024)
note: the Ministry of National Security oversees both the TTDF and the TTPS

Military expenditures: 1% of GDP (2023 est.)
1.1% of GDP (2022 est.)
1% of GDP (2021 est.)
1% of GDP (2020 est.)
1% of GDP (2019 est.)
comparison ranking: 127

Military and security service personnel strengths: approximately 5,000 TTDF personnel (2024)

Military equipment inventories and acquisitions: the TTDF's ground force inventory consists of light weapons, while the Coast Guard and Air Guard field mostly secondhand equipment from a mix of countries, including Australia, China, Italy, the Netherlands, the UK, and the US (2024)

Military service age and obligation: 18-25 years of age for voluntary military service for men and women (some age variations between services, reserves); no conscription (2024)

Military - note: the TTDF's primary responsibilities are conducting border and maritime security, including air and maritime surveillance, assisting civil authorities in times of crisis or disaster, providing search and rescue services, port security, and supporting civil law enforcement, particularly in countering gang-related crime and trafficking of narcotics and other illicit goods; the Police Service maintains internal security (2024)

TRANSNATIONAL ISSUES

Refugees and internally displaced persons: *refugees (country of origin):* 36,218 (Venezuela) (economic and political crisis; includes Venezuelans who have claimed asylum, are recognized as refugees, or have received alternative legal stay) (2023)

Illicit drugs: a transit point for drugs destined for Europe, North America, and the rest of the Caribbean; drug trafficking organizations use the country's proximity to Venezuela, its porous borders, vulnerabilities at ports of entry, a limited law enforcement capacity and resources, and corruption

TUNISIA

INTRODUCTION

Background: Many empires have controlled Tunisia, including the Phoenicians (as early as the 12 century B.C.), Carthaginians, Romans, Vandals, Byzantines, various Arab and Berber kingdoms, and Ottomans (16th to late-19th centuries). Rivalry between French and Italian interests in Tunisia culminated in a French invasion in 1881 and the creation of a protectorate. Agitation for independence in the decades after World War I finally convinced the French to recognize Tunisia as an independent state in 1956. The country's first president, Habib BOURGUIBA, established a strict one-party state. He dominated the country for 31 years, repressing Islamic fundamentalism and establishing rights for women. In 1987, Zine el Abidine BEN ALI replaced BOURGUIBA in a bloodless coup.

Street protests that began in Tunis in 2010 over high unemployment, corruption, widespread poverty, and high food prices escalated in 2011, culminating in rioting that led to hundreds of deaths and later became known as the start of the regional Arab Spring uprising. BEN ALI dismissed the government and fled the country, and a "national unity government" was formed. Elections for the new Constituent Assembly were held later that year, and human rights activist Moncef MARZOUKI was elected as interim president. The Assembly began drafting a new constitution in 2012 and, after several iterations and a months-long political crisis that stalled the transition, ratified the document in 2014. Parliamentary and presidential elections for a permanent government were held at the end of 2014. Beji CAID ESSEBSI was elected as the first president under the country's new constitution. After ESSEBSI's death in office in 2019, Kais SAIED was elected. SAIED's term, as well as that of Tunisia's 217-member parliament, was set to expire in 2024. However, in 2021, SAIED used the exceptional powers allowed under Tunisia's constitution to dismiss the prime minister and suspend the legislature. Tunisians approved a new constitution through public referendum in 2022, expanding presidential powers and creating a new bicameral legislature.

GEOGRAPHY

Location: Northern Africa, bordering the Mediterranean Sea, between Algeria and Libya

Geographic coordinates: 34 00 N, 9 00 E

Map references: Africa

Area: *total:* 163,610 sq km
land: 155,360 sq km
water: 8,250 sq km
comparison ranking: total 93

Area - comparative: slightly larger than Georgia

Land boundaries: *total:* 1,495 km
border countries (2): Algeria 1,034 km; Libya 461 km

Coastline: 1,148 km

Maritime claims: *territorial sea:* 12 nm
contiguous zone: 24 nm
exclusive economic zone: 12 nm

Climate: temperate in north with mild, rainy winters and hot, dry summers; desert in south

Terrain: mountains in north; hot, dry central plain; semiarid south merges into the Sahara

Elevation: *highest point:* Jebel ech Chambi 1,544 m
lowest point: Shatt al Gharsah -17 m
mean elevation: 246 m

Natural resources: petroleum, phosphates, iron ore, lead, zinc, salt

Land use: *agricultural land:* 64.8% (2018 est.)

arable land: 18.3% (2018 est.)
permanent crops: 15.4% (2018 est.)
permanent pasture: 31.1% (2018 est.)
forest: 6.6% (2018 est.)
other: 28.6% (2018 est.)

Irrigated land: 3,920 sq km (2013)

Major aquifers: North Western Sahara Aquifer System

Population distribution: the overwhelming majority of the population is located in the northern half of the country; the south remains largely underpopulated as shown in this population distribution map

Natural hazards: flooding; earthquakes; droughts

Geography - note: strategic location in central Mediterranean; Malta and Tunisia are discussing the commercial exploitation of the continental shelf between their countries, particularly for oil exploration

PEOPLE AND SOCIETY

Population: *total:* 12,048,847
male: 5,972,242
female: 6,076,605 (2024 est.)
comparison rankings: female 81; male 82; total 81

Nationality: *noun:* Tunisian(s)
adjective: Tunisian

Ethnic groups: Arab 98%, European 1%, Jewish and other 1%

Languages: Arabic (official, one of the languages of commerce), French (commerce), Tamazight
major-language sample(s):
كتاب حقائق العالم، أحسن كتاب تتعلم به المعلومات الأساسية
(Arabic)
The World Factbook, une source indispensable d'informations de base. (French)
note: despite having no official status, French plays a major role in the country and is spoken by about two thirds of the population

Religions: Muslim (official; Sunni) 99%, other (includes Christian, Jewish, Shia Muslim, and Baha'i) <1%

Demographic profile: The Tunisian Government took steps in the 1960s to decrease population growth and gender inequality in order to improve socioeconomic development. Through its introduction of a national family planning program (the first in Africa) and by raising the legal age of marriage, Tunisia rapidly reduced its total fertility rate from about 7 children per woman in 1960 to 2 in 2022. Unlike many of its North African and Middle Eastern neighbors, Tunisia will soon be shifting from being a youth-bulge country to having a transitional age structure, characterized by lower fertility and mortality rates, a slower population growth rate, a rising median age, and a longer average life expectancy.

Currently, the sizable young working-age population is straining Tunisia's labor market and education and health care systems. Persistent high unemployment among Tunisia's growing workforce, particularly its increasing number of university graduates and women, was a key factor in the uprisings that led to the overthrow of the BEN ALI regime in 2011. In the near term, Tunisia's large number of jobless young, working-age adults; deficiencies in primary and secondary education; and the ongoing lack of job creation and skills mismatches could contribute to future unrest. In the longer term, a sustained low fertility rate will shrink future youth cohorts and alleviate demographic pressure on Tunisia's labor market, but employment and education hurdles will still need to be addressed.

Tunisia has a history of labor emigration. In the 1960s, workers migrated to European countries to escape poor economic conditions and to fill Europe's need for low-skilled labor in construction and manufacturing. The Tunisian Government signed bilateral labor agreements with France, Germany, Belgium, Hungary, and the Netherlands, with the expectation that Tunisian workers would eventually return home. At the same time, growing numbers of Tunisians headed to Libya, often illegally, to work in the expanding oil industry. In the mid-1970s, with European countries beginning to restrict immigration and Tunisian-Libyan tensions brewing, Tunisian economic migrants turned toward the Gulf countries. After mass expulsions from Libya in 1983, Tunisian migrants increasingly sought family reunification in Europe or moved illegally to southern Europe, while Tunisia itself developed into a transit point for Sub-Saharan migrants heading to Europe.

Following the ousting of BEN ALI in 2011, the illegal migration of unemployed Tunisian youths to Italy and onward to France soared into the tens of thousands. Thousands more Tunisian and foreign workers escaping civil war in Libya flooded into Tunisia and joined the exodus. A readmission agreement signed by Italy and Tunisia in April 2011 helped stem the outflow, leaving Tunisia and international organizations to repatriate, resettle, or accommodate some 1 million Libyans and third-country nationals.

Age structure: *0-14 years:* 24.4% (male 1,516,871/female 1,426,522)
15-64 years: 65.2% (male 3,861,731/female 3,990,802)
65 years and over: 10.4% (2024 est.) (male 593,640/female 659,281)

Dependency ratios: *total dependency ratio:* 50.9
youth dependency ratio: 36.3
elderly dependency ratio: 13.3
potential support ratio: 7.5 (2021 est.)

Median age: *total:* 34.4 years (2024 est.)
male: 33.6 years
female: 35.1 years
comparison ranking: total 102

Population growth rate: 0.58% (2024 est.)
comparison ranking: 143

Birth rate: 13.5 births/1,000 population (2024 est.)
comparison ranking: 127

Death rate: 6.4 deaths/1,000 population (2024 est.)
comparison ranking: 143

Net migration rate: -1.3 migrant(s)/1,000 population (2024 est.)
comparison ranking: 154

Population distribution: the overwhelming majority of the population is located in the northern half of the country; the south remains largely underpopulated as shown in this population distribution map

Urbanization: *urban population:* 70.5% of total population (2023)
rate of urbanization: 1.34% annual rate of change (2020-25 est.)

Major urban areas - population: 2.475 million TUNIS (capital) (2023)

Sex ratio: *at birth:* 1.06 male(s)/female
0-14 years: 1.06 male(s)/female
15-64 years: 0.97 male(s)/female
65 years and over: 0.9 male(s)/female
total population: 0.98 male(s)/female (2024 est.)

Maternal mortality ratio: 37 deaths/100,000 live births (2020 est.)
comparison ranking: 108

Infant mortality rate: *total:* 11.3 deaths/1,000 live births (2024 est.)
male: 12.7 deaths/1,000 live births
female: 9.8 deaths/1,000 live births
comparison ranking: total 119

Life expectancy at birth: *total population:* 77.3 years (2024 est.)
male: 75.7 years
female: 79.1 years
comparison ranking: total population 93

Total fertility rate: 1.93 children born/woman (2024 est.)
comparison ranking: 115

Gross reproduction rate: 0.94 (2024 est.)

Contraceptive prevalence rate: 50.7% (2018)

Drinking water source: *improved: urban:* 100% of population
rural: 97.3% of population
total: 99.2% of population
unimproved: urban: 0% of population
rural: 2.7% of population
total: 0.8% of population (2020 est.)

Current health expenditure: 6.3% of GDP (2020)

Physician density: 1.3 physicians/1,000 population (2017)

Hospital bed density: 2.2 beds/1,000 population (2017)

Sanitation facility access: *improved: urban:* 98.8% of population
rural: 99.4% of population
total: 99% of population
unimproved: urban: 1.2% of population
rural: 0.6% of population
total: 1% of population (2020 est.)

Obesity - adult prevalence rate: 26.9% (2016)
comparison ranking: 40

Alcohol consumption per capita: *total:* 1.51 liters of pure alcohol (2019 est.)
beer: 0.99 liters of pure alcohol (2019 est.)
wine: 0.32 liters of pure alcohol (2019 est.)
spirits: 0.17 liters of pure alcohol (2019 est.)
other alcohols: 0.03 liters of pure alcohol (2019 est.)
comparison ranking: total 139

Tobacco use: *total:* 24.6% (2020 est.)
male: 47.2% (2020 est.)
female: 2% (2020 est.)
comparison ranking: total 52

Children under the age of 5 years underweight: 1.6% (2018)
comparison ranking: 112

Currently married women (ages 15-49): 53.9% (2023 est.)

Child marriage: *women married by age 15:* 1.5% (2018 est.)

Education expenditures: 7.3% of GDP (2016 est.)
comparison ranking: 17

Literacy: *definition:* age 15 and over can read and write
total population: 82.7%
male: 89.1%
female: 82.7% (2021)

School life expectancy (primary to tertiary education): *total:* 15 years
male: 14 years
female: 16 years (2016)

ENVIRONMENT

Environment - current issues: toxic and hazardous waste disposal is ineffective and poses health risks; water pollution from raw sewage; limited natural freshwater resources; deforestation; overgrazing; soil erosion; desertification

Environment - international agreements: *party to:* Biodiversity, Climate Change, Climate Change-Kyoto Protocol, Climate Change-Paris Agreement, Comprehensive Nuclear Test Ban, Desertification, Endangered Species, Environmental Modification, Hazardous Wastes, Law of the Sea, Marine Dumping-London Convention, Nuclear Test Ban, Ozone Layer Protection, Ship Pollution, Wetlands
signed, but not ratified: Marine Life Conservation

Climate: temperate in north with mild, rainy winters and hot, dry summers; desert in south

Urbanization: *urban population:* 70.5% of total population (2023)
rate of urbanization: 1.34% annual rate of change (2020-25 est.)

Revenue from forest resources: 0.21% of GDP (2018 est.)
comparison ranking: 92

Revenue from coal: 0% of GDP (2018 est.)
comparison ranking: 99

Air pollutants: *particulate matter emissions:* 26.52 micrograms per cubic meter (2019 est.)
carbon dioxide emissions: 29.94 megatons (2016 est.)
methane emissions: 7.89 megatons (2020 est.)

Waste and recycling: *municipal solid waste generated annually:* 2.7 million tons (2014 est.)
municipal solid waste recycled annually: 108,000 tons (2014 est.)
percent of municipal solid waste recycled: 4% (2014 est.)

Major aquifers: North Western Sahara Aquifer System

Total water withdrawal: *municipal:* 820 million cubic meters (2020 est.)
industrial: 60 million cubic meters (2020 est.)
agricultural: 2.71 billion cubic meters (2020 est.)

Total renewable water resources: 4.62 billion cubic meters (2020 est.)

GOVERNMENT

Country name: *conventional long form:* Republic of Tunisia
conventional short form: Tunisia
local long form: Al Jumhuriyah at Tunisiyah
local short form: Tunis
etymology: the country name derives from the capital city of Tunis

Government type: parliamentary republic

Capital: *name:* Tunis
geographic coordinates: 36 48 N, 10 11 E
time difference: UTC+1 (6 hours ahead of Washington, DC, during Standard Time)
etymology: three possibilities exist for the derivation of the name; originally a Berber settlement (earliest reference 4th century B.C.), the strategic site fell to the Carthaginians (Phoenicians) and the city could be named after the Punic goddess Tanit, since many ancient cities were named after patron deities; alternatively, the Berber root word "ens," which means "to lie down" or "to pass the night," may indicate that the site was originally a camp or rest stop; finally, the name may be the same as the city of Tynes, mentioned in the writings of some ancient authors

Administrative divisions: 24 governorates (wilayat, singular - wilayah); Beja (Bajah), Ben Arous (Bin 'Arus), Bizerte (Banzart), Gabes (Qabis), Gafsa (Qafsah), Jendouba (Jundubah), Kairouan (Al Qayrawan), Kasserine (Al Qasrayn), Kebili (Qibili), Kef (Al Kaf), L'Ariana (Aryanah), Mahdia (Al Mahdiyah), Manouba (Manubah), Medenine (Madanin), Monastir (Al Munastir), Nabeul (Nabul), Sfax (Safaqis), Sidi Bouzid (Sidi Bu Zayd), Siliana (Silyanah), Sousse (Susah), Tataouine (Tatawin), Tozeur (Tawzar), Tunis, Zaghouan (Zaghwan)

Independence: 20 March 1956 (from France)

National holiday: Independence Day, 20 March (1956); Revolution and Youth Day, 14 January (2011)

Legal system: mixed legal system of civil law, based on the French civil code and Islamic (sharia) law; some judicial review of legislative acts in the Supreme Court in joint session

Constitution: *history:*
several previous; latest - draft published by the president 30 June 2022, approved by referendum 25 July 2022, and adopted 27 July 2022
amendments: proposed by the president of the republic or by one third of the Assembly of the Representatives of the People membership; following review by the Constitutional Court, approval to proceed requires an absolute majority vote by the Assembly and final passage requires a two-thirds Assembly majority vote; the president can opt to submit an amendment to a referendum, which requires an absolute majority of votes cast for passage

International law organization participation: has not submitted an ICJ jurisdiction declaration; accepts ICCt jurisdiction

Citizenship: *citizenship by birth:* no
citizenship by descent only: at least one parent must be a citizen of Tunisia
dual citizenship recognized: yes
residency requirement for naturalization: 5 years

Suffrage: 18 years of age; universal except for active government security forces (including the police and the military), people with mental disabilities, people who have served more than three months in prison (criminal cases only), and people given a suspended sentence of more than six months

Executive branch: *chief of state:* President Kais SAIED (since 23 October 2019)
head of government: Prime Minister Kamel MADDOURI (since 7 August 2024); President Kais SAIED dismissed Prime Minister Ahmed HACHANI the same day he appointed Kamel MADDOURI
cabinet: prime minister appointed by the president; cabinet members appointed by the president in consultation with the prime minister
elections/appointments: president directly elected by absolute majority popular vote in 2 rounds if needed for a 5-year term (eligible for a second term); last held on 6 October 2024 (next to be held in 2029)
election results:
2024: Kais SAIED reelected president in first round - Kais SAIED (independent) 90.7%, Ayachi ZAMMEL (Long Live Tunisia) 7.3%, Zouhair MAGHZAOUI (People's Movement) 2%
2019: Kais SAIED elected president in second round; percent of vote in first round - Kais SAIED (independent) 18.4%, Nabil KAROUI (Heart of Tunisia) 15.6%, Abdelfattah MOUROU (Nahda Movement) 12.9%, Abdelkrim ZBIDI (independent) 10.7%, Youssef CHAHED (Long Live Tunisia) 7.4%, Safi SAID (independent) 7.1%, Lotfi MRAIHI (Republican People's Union) 6.6%, other 21.3%; percent of vote in second round - Kais SAIED 72.7%, Nabil KAROUI 27.3%
note: the president can dismiss any member of government on his own initiative or in consultation with the prime minister

Legislative branch: *description:* bicameral legislature (enacted by the 2022 constitution) consists of:
newly added National Council of Regions and Districts (Le Conseil national des régions et des districts) (77 seats; members indirectly elected by regional and district councils; members of each Regional Council elect 3 members among themselves to the National Council; each District Council elects 1 member among themselves to the National Council; members serve 5-year term)
Assembly of the People's Representatives (161 seats; 151 members in single seat constituencies and 10 members from Tunisian diaspora directly elected by majoritarian two-round voting system; all members serve 5-year terms)

elections: National Council of Regions and Districts - last held on 18 April 2024 for 279 local councils, which indirectly elect the National Council (next to be held in 2029)
Assembly of Representatives of the People - last held on 17 December 2022 with a runoff on 29 January 2023 (next to be held in late 2027)
election results: National Council of Regions and Districts - percent of vote by party NA; seats by party NA
Assembly of Representatives of the People - percent of vote by party NA; seats by party NA

Note: in 2022, President SAIED issued a new electoral law, which requires all legislative candidates to run as independents

Judicial branch: *highest court(s):* Court of Cassation (consists of the first president, chamber presidents, and magistrates and organized into 27 civil and 11 criminal chambers)
judge selection and term of office: Supreme Court judges nominated by the Supreme Judicial Council, an independent 4-part body consisting mainly of elected judges and the remainder legal specialists; judge tenure based on terms of appointment; Constitutional Court (established in the 2014 and 2022 constitutions, but inception has been delayed; note - in mid-February 2022, President SAIED dissolved the Supreme Judicial Council and replaced it with an interim council in early March 2022
subordinate courts: Courts of Appeal; administrative courts; Court of Audit; Housing Court; courts of first instance; lower district courts; military courts
note: the Tunisian constitution of January 2014 called for the establishment of a constitutional court by the end of 2015, but the court was never formed; the new constitution of July 2022 calls for the establishment of a constitutional court consisting of 9 members appointed by presidential decree; members to include former senior judges of other courts

Political parties: Afek Tounes
Al Badil Al-Tounisi (The Tunisian Alternative)
Al-Amal Party
Call for Tunisia Party (Nidaa Tounes)
Current of Love (formerly the Popular Petition party)
Democratic Current
Democratic Patriots' Unified Party
Dignity Coalition or Al Karama Coalition
Ennahda Movement (The Renaissance)
Ettakatol Party
Free Destourian Party or PDL
Green Tunisia Party
Harakat Hak
Heart of Tunisia (Qalb Tounes)
July 25 Movement
Labor and Achievement Party
Long Live Tunisia (Tahya Tounes)
Movement of Socialist Democrats or MDS
National Coalition Party
National Salvation Front
New Carthage Party
Party of the Democratic Arab Vanguard
People's Movement
Republican Party (Al Joumhouri)
The Movement Party (Hizb Harak)
Third Republic Party
Tunisian Ba'ath Movement
Voice of the Republic
Workers' Party
note: President SAIED in 2022 issued a decree that forbids political parties' participation in legislative elections; although parties remain a facet of Tunisian political life, they have lost significant influence

International organization participation: ABEDA, AfDB, AFESD, AIIB, AMF, AMU, AU, BSEC (observer), CAEU, CD, EBRD, FAO, G-11, G-77, IAEA, IBRD, ICAO, ICC (national committees), ICCt, ICRM, IDA, IDB, IFAD, IFC, IFRCS, IHO, ILO, IMF, IMO, IMSO, Interpol, IOC, IOM, IPU, ISO, ITSO, ITU, ITUC (NGOs), LAS, MIGA, MONUSCO, NAM, OAS (observer), OIC, OIF, OPCW, OSCE (partner), UN, UNCTAD, UNESCO, UNHCR, UNIDO, UNOCI, UNOOSA, UNWTO, UPU, WCO, WFTU (NGOs), WHO, WIPO, WMO, WTO

Diplomatic representation in the US: *chief of mission:* Ambassador Hanene TAJOURI BESSASSI (since 1 December 2021)
chancery: 1515 Massachusetts Avenue NW, Washington, DC 20005
telephone: [1] (202) 862-1850
FAX: [1] (202) 862-1858
email address and website:
AT.Washington@Tunisiaembassy.org
https://www.tunisianembassy.org/

Diplomatic representation from the US: *chief of mission:* Ambassador Joey HOOD (since 2 February 2023)
embassy: Les Berges du Lac, 1053 Tunis
mailing address: 6360 Tunis Place, Washington DC 20521-6360
telephone: [216] 71-107-000
FAX: [216] 71-107-090
email address and website:
tuniswebsitecontact@state.gov
https://tn.usembassy.gov/

Flag description: red with a white disk in the center bearing a red crescent nearly encircling a red five-pointed star; resembles the Ottoman flag (red banner with white crescent and star) and recalls Tunisia's history as part of the Ottoman Empire; red represents the blood shed by martyrs in the struggle against oppression, white stands for peace; the crescent and star are traditional symbols of Islam
note: the flag is based on that of Turkey, itself a successor state to the Ottoman Empire

National symbol(s): encircled red crescent moon and five-pointed star; national colors: red, white

National anthem: *name:* "Humat Al Hima" (Defenders of the Homeland)
lyrics/music: Mustafa Sadik AL-RAFII and Aboul-Qacem ECHEBBI/Mohamad Abdel WAHAB
note: adopted 1957, replaced 1958, restored 1987; Mohamad Abdel WAHAB also composed the music for the anthem of the United Arab Emirates

National heritage: *total World Heritage Sites:* 9 (8 cultural, 1 natural)
selected World Heritage Site locales: Amphitheatre of El Jem (c); Archaeological Site of Carthage (c); Medina of Tunis (c); Ichkeul National Park (n); Punic Town of Kerkuane (c); Kairouan (c); Medina of Sousse (c); Dougga / Thugga (c); Djerba: Testimony to a settlement pattern in an island territory (c)

ECONOMY

Economic overview: lower middle-income North African economy; drafting reforms for foreign lenders; high unemployment, especially for youth and women; hit hard by COVID-19; high public sector wages; high public debt; protectionist austerity measures; key EU trade partner

Real GDP (purchasing power parity): $153.637 billion (2023 est.)
$152.988 billion (2022 est.)
$149.106 billion (2021 est.)
note: data in 2021 dollars
comparison ranking: 83

Real GDP growth rate: 0.42% (2023 est.)
2.6% (2022 est.)
4.61% (2021 est.)
note: annual GDP % growth based on constant local currency
comparison ranking: 182

Real GDP per capita: $12,300 (2023 est.)
$12,400 (2022 est.)
$12,200 (2021 est.)
note: data in 2021 dollars
comparison ranking: 137

GDP (official exchange rate): $48.53 billion (2023 est.)
note: data in current dollars at official exchange rate

Inflation rate (consumer prices): 9.33% (2023 est.)
8.31% (2022 est.)
5.71% (2021 est.)
note: annual % change based on consumer prices
comparison ranking: 170

Credit ratings: Fitch rating: B (2020)

Moody's rating: B2 (2018)

Standard & Poors rating: N/A (2013)
note: The year refers to the year in which the current credit rating was first obtained.

GDP - composition, by sector of origin: *agriculture:* 9.5% (2023 est.)
industry: 23.5% (2023 est.)
services: 62.1% (2023 est.)
note: figures may not total 100% due to non-allocated consumption not captured in sector-reported data
comparison rankings: services 75; industry 112; agriculture 79

GDP - composition, by end use: *household consumption:* 78% (2023 est.)
government consumption: 20.6% (2023 est.)
investment in fixed capital: 16.9% (2023 est.)
investment in inventories: -3.4% (2023 est.)
exports of goods and services: 51.1% (2023 est.)
imports of goods and services: -58.1% (2023 est.)
note: figures may not total 100% due to rounding or gaps in data collection

Agricultural products: milk, olives, tomatoes, wheat, barley, watermelons, chilies/peppers, potatoes, dates, oranges (2022)
note: top ten agricultural products based on tonnage

Industries: petroleum, mining (particularly phosphate, iron ore), tourism, textiles, footwear, agribusiness, beverages

Industrial production growth rate: -1.5% (2023 est.)
note: annual % change in industrial value added based on constant local currency
comparison ranking: 174

Labor force: 4.445 million (2023 est.)
note: number of people ages 15 or older who are employed or seeking work
comparison ranking: 95

Unemployment rate: 15.11% (2023 est.)
15.3% (2022 est.)
16.51% (2021 est.)
note: % of labor force seeking employment
comparison ranking: 190

Youth unemployment rate (ages 15-24): *total:* 37.5% (2023 est.)
male: 38.3% (2023 est.)
female: 35.6% (2023 est.)
note: % of labor force ages 15-24 seeking employment
comparison ranking: total 12

Population below poverty line: 16.6% (2021 est.)
note: % of population with income below national poverty line

Gini Index coefficient - distribution of family income: 33.7 (2021 est.)
note: index (0-100) of income distribution; higher values represent greater inequality
comparison ranking: 92

Average household expenditures: *on food:* 23.1% of household expenditures (2022 est.)
on alcohol and tobacco: 3.3% of household expenditures (2022 est.)

Household income or consumption by percentage share: *lowest 10%:* 3.1% (2021 est.)
highest 10%: 27% (2021 est.)
note: % share of income accruing to lowest and highest 10% of population

Remittances: 5.56% of GDP (2023 est.)
6.3% of GDP (2022 est.)
6.34% of GDP (2021 est.)
note: personal transfers and compensation between resident and non-resident individuals/households/entities

Budget: *revenues:* $10.866 billion (2019 est.)
expenditures: $12.375 billion (2019 est.)

Public debt: 70.3% of GDP (2017 est.)
comparison ranking: 56

Taxes and other revenues: 24.7% (of GDP) (2017 est.)
comparison ranking: 51

Current account balance: -$4.018 billion (2022 est.)
-$2.79 billion (2021 est.)
-$2.524 billion (2020 est.)
note: balance of payments - net trade and primary/secondary income in current dollars
comparison ranking: 173

Exports: $17.258 billion (2022 est.)
$14.054 billion (2021 est.)
$11.237 billion (2020 est.)
note: balance of payments - exports of goods and services in current dollars
comparison ranking: 96

Exports - partners: France 22%, Italy 16%, Germany 14%, Spain 4%, Libya 4% (2022)
note: top five export partners based on percentage share of exports

Exports - commodities: garments, insulated wire, refined petroleum, crude petroleum, pure olive oil (2022)
note: top five export commodities based on value in dollars

Imports: $22.5 billion (2022 est.)
$18.198 billion (2021 est.)
$14.574 billion (2020 est.)
note: balance of payments - imports of goods and services in current dollars
comparison ranking: 93

Imports - partners: Italy 14%, France 14%, China 9%, Germany 7%, Turkey 6% (2022)
note: top five import partners based on percentage share of imports

Imports - commodities: refined petroleum, natural gas, plastic products, wheat, cars (2022)
note: top five import commodities based on value in dollars

Reserves of foreign exchange and gold: $9.24 billion (2023 est.)
$8.094 billion (2022 est.)
$8.846 billion (2021 est.)
note: holdings of gold (year-end prices)/foreign exchange/special drawing rights in current dollars
comparison ranking: 83

Debt - external: $18.169 billion (2022 est.)
note: present value of external debt in current US dollars
comparison ranking: 27

Exchange rates: Tunisian dinars (TND) per US dollar -

Exchange rates: 3.106 (2023 est.)
3.104 (2022 est.)
2.794 (2021 est.)
2.812 (2020 est.)
2.934 (2019 est.)

ENERGY

Electricity access: *electrification - total population:* 100% (2022 est.)
electrification - urban areas: 100%
electrification - rural areas: 99.7%

Electricity: *installed generating capacity:* 6.328 million kW (2022 est.)
consumption: 19.061 billion kWh (2022 est.)
exports: 154 million kWh (2022 est.)
imports: 2.726 billion kWh (2022 est.)
transmission/distribution losses: 4.722 billion kWh (2022 est.)
comparison rankings: transmission/distribution losses 162; imports 57; exports 87; consumption 76; installed generating capacity 81

Electricity generation sources: *fossil fuels:* 96.9% of total installed capacity (2022 est.)
solar: 1.5% of total installed capacity (2022 est.)
wind: 1.5% of total installed capacity (2022 est.)
hydroelectricity: 0.1% of total installed capacity (2022 est.)

Coal: *consumption:* 2,000 metric tons (2022 est.)
imports: 2,000 metric tons (2022 est.)

Petroleum: *total petroleum production:* 35,000 bbl/day (2023 est.)
refined petroleum consumption: 108,000 bbl/day (2022 est.)
crude oil estimated reserves: 425 million barrels (2021 est.)

Natural gas: *production:* 1.323 billion cubic meters (2022 est.)
consumption: 5.153 billion cubic meters (2022 est.)
imports: 3.898 billion cubic meters (2022 est.)
proven reserves: 65.129 billion cubic meters (2021 est.)

Carbon dioxide emissions: 23.645 million metric tonnes of CO2 (2022 est.)
from coal and metallurgical coke: 5,000 metric tonnes of CO2 (2022 est.)
from petroleum and other liquids: 13.203 million metric tonnes of CO2 (2022 est.)
from consumed natural gas: 10.437 million metric tonnes of CO2 (2022 est.)
comparison ranking: total emissions 80

Energy consumption per capita: 33.641 million Btu/person (2022 est.)
comparison ranking: 109

COMMUNICATIONS

Telephones - fixed lines: *total subscriptions:* 1.79 million (2022 est.)
subscriptions per 100 inhabitants: 14 (2022 est.)
comparison ranking: total subscriptions 55

Telephones - mobile cellular: *total subscriptions:* 15.971 million (2022 est.)
subscriptions per 100 inhabitants: 129 (2022 est.)
comparison ranking: total subscriptions 69

Telecommunication systems: *general assessment:* Tunisia has one of the most sophisticated telecom infrastructures in North Africa; penetration rates for mobile and Internet services are among the highest in the region; government program of regulation and infrastructure projects aims to improve Internet connectivity to underserved areas; operators built extensive LTE infrastructure in 2019, and continue to discuss plans for future 5G networks and services; one operator has signed an agreement to pursue nano-satellite launches in 2023; internet censorship abolished, though concerns of government surveillance remain; legislation passed in 2017 supporting e-commerce and active e-government; importer of some integrated circuits and broadcasting equipment (including radio, television, and communications transmitters) from the PRC (2022)
domestic: fixed-line is nearly 14 per 100 and mobile-cellular teledensity is 129 telephones per 100 persons (2022)
international: country code - 216; landing points for the SEA-ME-WE-4, Didon, HANNIBAL System and Trapani- Kelibia submarine cable systems that provides links to Europe, Africa, the Middle East, Asia and Southeast Asia; satellite earth stations - 1 Intelsat (Atlantic Ocean) and 1 Arabsat; coaxial cable and microwave radio relay to Algeria and Libya; participant in Medarabtel; 2 international gateway digital switches (2020)

Broadcast media: 2 state-owned TV stations; 10 private TV stations broadcast locally; satellite TV service is available; state-owned radio network with 2 stations; several dozen private radio stations and community radio stations; transmissions of multiple international broadcasters available (2019)

Internet country code: .tn

Internet users: *total:* 9.48 million (2021 est.)
percent of population: 79% (2021 est.)
comparison ranking: total 60

Broadband - fixed subscriptions: *total:* 1,334,059 (2020 est.)
subscriptions per 100 inhabitants: 11 (2020 est.)
comparison ranking: total 67

TRANSPORTATION

National air transport system: *number of registered air carriers:* 7 (2020)
inventory of registered aircraft operated by air carriers: 53
annual passenger traffic on registered air carriers: 4,274,199 (2018)
annual freight traffic on registered air carriers: 13.23 million (2018) mt-km

Civil aircraft registration country code prefix: TS

Airports: 14 (2024)
comparison ranking: 149

Heliports: 11 (2024)

Pipelines: 68 km condensate, 3,111 km gas, 1,381 km oil, 453 km refined products (2013)

Railways: *total:* 2,173 km (2014) (1,991 in use)
standard gauge: 471 km (2014) 1.435-m gauge
narrow gauge: 1,694 km (2014) 1.000-m gauge (65 km electrified)
dual gauge: 8 km (2014) 1.435-1.000-m gauge
comparison ranking: total 70

Roadways: *total:* 32,332 km
paved: 12,264 km
unpaved: 20,068 km (2020)
comparison ranking: total 97

Merchant marine: *total:* 72 (2023)
by type: container ship 1, general cargo 8, oil tanker 1, other 62
comparison ranking: total 107

Ports: *total ports:* 16 (2024)
large: 0
medium: 3
small: 7
very small: 6
ports with oil terminals: 10
key ports: Ashtart Oil Terminal, Banzart, Didon Terminal, Gabes, La Goulette, Menzel Bourguiba, Mersa Sfax, Sousse, Tazerka Oil Terminal, Tunis

MILITARY AND SECURITY

Military and security forces: Tunisian Armed Forces (Forces Armées Tunisiennes, FAT): Tunisian Army (includes Air Defense Force), Tunisian Navy, Tunisia Air Force

Ministry of Interior (MoI): National Police, National Guard (2024)
note: the National Police has primary responsibility for law enforcement in the major cities, while the National Guard (gendarmerie) oversees border security and patrols smaller towns and rural areas; the National Police Anti-Terrorism Brigade and the National Guard Special Unit have the lead for MOI counterterrorism operations

Military expenditures: 2.5% of GDP (2023 est.)
2.7% of GDP (2022 est.)
3% of GDP (2021 est.)
3% of GDP (2020 est.)
3.8% of GDP (2019 est.)
comparison ranking: 45

Military and security service personnel strengths: approximately 35,000 active-duty personnel (25,000 Army; 5,000 Navy; 5,000 Air Force); estimated 10,000 National Guard (2023)

Military equipment inventories and acquisitions: the Tunisian military's inventory consists mostly of older or second-hand equipment from a wide variety of suppliers, including Brazil, China, Turkey, and the US, as well as several European countries, such as France, Germany, and Italy (2024)

Military service age and obligation: 20-23 years of age for compulsory service for men with a 12-month service obligation; individuals engaged in higher education or vocational training programs prior to their military drafting are allowed to delay service until they have completed their programs (up to age 35); exemptions allowed for males considered to a family's sole provider; 18-23 years of age for voluntary service for men and women (2023)
note: women have been allowed in the service since 1975 as volunteers; as of 2023, women constituted about 8% of the military and served in all three services

Military deployments: 775 Central African Republic (MINUSCA) (2024)

Military - note: the FAT is responsible for territorial defense and internal security; its operational areas of focus are countering Islamist terrorist groups and assisting with securing the border; areas of focus include security operations in the mountainous regions along the Algerian border where smuggling and criminal activity has occurred and militants linked to the al-Qa'ida and Islamic State of Iraq and ash-Sham terrorist groups have been active; the military has the lead for security operations in the area and has conducted joint operations with Algerian security forces; the FAT in recent years also has increased its role in securing the southern border with Libya against terrorist activity and infiltrators, criminal gangs, smuggling, and trafficking; in the remote areas of the border with Libya, buffer/exclusion zones have also been established where the military has the lead for security and counter-terrorism operations; outside of these border areas, the Ministry of Interior has responsibility
the FAT conducts bilateral and multinational training exercises with a variety of countries, including Algeria and other North African and Middle Eastern countries, France, and the US, as well as NATO; it also participates in UN peacekeeping operations; Tunisia has Major Non-NATO Ally (MNNA) status with the US, a designation under US law that provides foreign partners with certain benefits in the areas of defense trade and security cooperation (2024)

TERRORISM

Terrorist group(s): Ansar al-Sharia in Tunisia; Islamic State of Iraq and ash-Sham (ISIS) network in Tunisia (known locally as Ajnad al-Khilafah or the Army of the Caliphate); al-Qa'ida in the Islamic Maghreb
note: details about the history, aims, leadership, organization, areas of operation, tactics, targets, weapons, size, and sources of support of the group(s) appear(s) in the Terrorism reference guide

TRANSNATIONAL ISSUES

Illicit drugs: NA

TURKEY (TURKIYE)

INTRODUCTION

Background: Modern Turkey was founded in 1923 from the remnants of the Ottoman Empire by reformer and national hero Mustafa KEMAL, known as Ataturk or "Father of the Turks." One-party rule ended in 1950, and periods of instability and military coups have since fractured the multiparty democracy, in 1960, 1971, 1980, 1997, and 2016.

Turkey joined the UN in 1945 and NATO in 1952. In 1963, Turkey became an associate member of the European Community; it began accession talks with the EU in 2005. Turkey intervened militarily on Cyprus in 1974 to prevent a Greek takeover of the island and has since acted as patron state to the "Turkish Republic of Northern Cyprus," which only Turkey recognizes. The Kurdistan Workers' Party (PKK), a US-designated terrorist organization, began a separatist insurgency in Turkey in 1984, and the struggle has long dominated the attention of Turkish security forces. In 2013, the Turkish Government and the PKK conducted negotiations aimed at ending the violence, but intense fighting resumed in 2015.

The Turkish Government conducted a referendum in 2017 in which voters approved constitutional amendments changing Turkey from a parliamentary to a presidential system.

GEOGRAPHY

Location: Southeastern Europe and Southwestern Asia (that portion of Turkey west of the Bosporus is geographically part of Europe), bordering the Black Sea, between Bulgaria and Georgia, and bordering the Aegean Sea and the Mediterranean Sea, between Greece and Syria

Geographic coordinates: 39 00 N, 35 00 E

Map references: Middle East

Area: *total:* 783,562 sq km
land: 769,632 sq km
water: 13,930 sq km
comparison ranking: total 38

Area - comparative: slightly larger than Texas

Land boundaries: *total:* 2,816 km
border countries (8): Armenia 311 km; Azerbaijan 17 km; Bulgaria 223 km; Georgia 273 km; Greece 192 km; Iran 534 km; Iraq 367 km; Syria 899 km

Coastline: 7,200 km

Maritime claims: *territorial sea:* 6 nm in the Aegean Sea
exclusive economic zone: in Black Sea only: to the maritime boundary agreed upon with the former USSR 12 nm in Black Sea and in Mediterranean Sea

Climate: temperate; hot, dry summers with mild, wet winters; harsher in interior

Terrain: high central plateau (Anatolia); narrow coastal plain; several mountain ranges

Elevation: *highest point:* Mount Ararat 5,137 m
lowest point: Mediterranean Sea 0 m

mean elevation: 1,132 m

Natural resources: coal, iron ore, copper, chromium, antimony, mercury, gold, barite, borate, celestite (strontium), emery, feldspar, limestone, magnesite, marble, perlite, pumice, pyrites (sulfur), clay, arable land, hydropower

Land use: *agricultural land:* 49.7% (2018 est.)
arable land: 26.7% (2018 est.)
permanent crops: 4% (2018 est.)
permanent pasture: 19% (2018 est.)
forest: 14.9% (2018 est.)
other: 35.4% (2018 est.)

Irrigated land: 52,150 sq km (2020)

Major lakes (area sq km): *fresh water lake(s):* Lake Beysehir - 650 sq km; Lake Egridir - 520 sq km
salt water lake(s): Lake Van - 3,740 sq km; Lake Tuz - 1,640 sq km;

Major rivers (by length in km): Euphrates river source (shared with Syria, Iran, and Iraq [m]) - 3,596 km; Tigris river source (shared with Syria, Iran, and Iraq [m]) - 1,950 km
note – [s] after country name indicates river source; [m] after country name indicates river mouth

Major watersheds (area sq km): Indian Ocean drainage: *(Persian Gulf)* Tigris and Euphrates (918,044 sq km)

Population distribution: the most densely populated area is found around the Bosporus in the northwest where 20% of the population lives in Istanbul; with the exception of Ankara, urban centers remain small and scattered throughout the interior of Anatolia; an overall pattern of peripheral development exists, particularly along the Aegean Sea coast in the west, and the Tigris and Euphrates River systems in the southeast

Natural hazards: severe earthquakes, especially in northern Turkey, along an arc extending from the Sea of Marmara to Lake Van; landslides; flooding
volcanism: limited volcanic activity; its three historically active volcanoes; Ararat, Nemrut Dagi, and Tendurek Dagi have not erupted since the 19th century or earlier

Geography - note: strategic location controlling the Turkish Straits (Bosporus, Sea of Marmara, Dardanelles) that link the Black and Aegean Seas; the 3% of Turkish territory north of the Straits lies in Europe and goes by the names of European Turkey, Eastern Thrace, or Turkish Thrace; the 97% of the country in Asia is referred to as Anatolia; Istanbul, which straddles the Bosporus, is the only metropolis in the world located on two continents; Mount Ararat, the legendary landing place of Noah's ark, is in the far eastern portion of the country

PEOPLE AND SOCIETY

Population: *total:* 84,119,531
male: 42,247,430
female: 41,872,101 (2024 est.)
comparison rankings: female 19; male 18; total 18

Nationality: *noun:* Turk(s)
adjective: Turkish

Ethnic groups: Turkish 70-75%, Kurdish 19%, other minorities 6-11% (2016 est.)

Languages: Turkish (official), Kurdish, other minority languages
major-language sample(s):
The World Factbook, temel bilgi edinmek için vazgeçilmez bir kaynak. (Turkish)
ڕاستییەکانی جیهان، باشترین سەرچاوەیە بۆ زانیارییە بنەڕەتییەکان (Kurdish)

Religions: Muslim 99.8% (mostly Sunni), other 0.2% (mostly Christians and Jews)

Age structure: *0-14 years:* 21.7% (male 9,358,711/female 8,933,673)
15-64 years: 68.6% (male 29,219,389/female 28,494,315)
65 years and over: 9.6% (2024 est.) (male 3,669,330/female 4,444,113)
2023 population pyramid:

Dependency ratios: *total dependency ratio:* 49.1
youth dependency ratio: 34.5
elderly dependency ratio: 12.3
potential support ratio: 8.1 (2021 est.)

Median age: *total:* 34 years (2024 est.)
male: 33.4 years
female: 34.6 years
comparison ranking: total 108

Population growth rate: 0.61% (2024 est.)
comparison ranking: 139

Birth rate: births/1,000 population (2024 est.)
comparison ranking: 122

Death rate: 6.1 deaths/1,000 population (2024 est.)
comparison ranking: 151

Net migration rate: -1.5 migrant(s)/1,000 population (2024 est.)
comparison ranking: 156

Population distribution: the most densely populated area is found around the Bosporus in the northwest where 20% of the population lives in Istanbul; with the exception of Ankara, urban centers remain small and scattered throughout the interior of Anatolia; an overall pattern of peripheral development exists, particularly along the Aegean Sea coast in the west, and the Tigris and Euphrates River systems in the southeast

Urbanization: *urban population:* 77.5% of total population (2023)
rate of urbanization: 1.11% annual rate of change (2020-25 est.)

Major urban areas - population: 15.848 million Istanbul, 5.397 million ANKARA (capital), 3.088 million Izmir, 2.086 million Bursa, 1.836 million Adana, 1.805 million Gaziantep (2023)

Sex ratio: *at birth:* 1.05 male(s)/female
0-14 years: 1.05 male(s)/female
15-64 years: 1.03 male(s)/female
65 years and over: 0.83 male(s)/female
total population: 1.01 male(s)/female (2024 est.)

Mother's mean age at first birth: years (2020 est.)

Maternal mortality ratio: 17 deaths/100,000 live births (2020 est.)
comparison ranking: 130

Infant mortality rate: *total:* 18.4 deaths/1,000 live births (2024 est.)
male: 19.9 deaths/1,000 live births
female: 16.7 deaths/1,000 live births
comparison ranking: total 83

Life expectancy at birth: *total population:* 76.7 years (2024 est.)
male: 74.4 years
female: 79.2 years
comparison ranking: total population 103

Total fertility rate: 1.9 children born/woman (2024 est.)
comparison ranking: 119

Gross reproduction rate: 2024 est.)

Contraceptive prevalence rate: 69.8% (2018)

Drinking water source: *improved: urban:* 99.1% of population
rural: 98.7% of population
total: 99% of population
unimproved: urban: 0.9% of population
rural: 1.3% of population
total: 1% of population (2020 est.)

Current health expenditure: 4.6% of GDP (2020)

Physician density: 1.93 physicians/1,000 population (2019)

Hospital bed density: 2.9 beds/1,000 population (2018)

Sanitation facility access: *improved: urban:* 99.8% of population
rural: 98.7% of population
total: 99.6% of population
unimproved: urban: 0.2% of population
rural: 1.3% of population
total: 0.4% of population (2020 est.)

Obesity - adult prevalence rate: 32.1% (2016)
comparison ranking: 17

Alcohol consumption per capita: *total:* 1.18 liters of pure alcohol (2019 est.)
beer: 0.67 liters of pure alcohol (2019 est.)
wine: 0.16 liters of pure alcohol (2019 est.)
spirits: 0.35 liters of pure alcohol (2019 est.)
other alcohols: 0 liters of pure alcohol (2019 est.)
comparison ranking: total 147

Tobacco use: *total:* 30.7% (2020 est.)
male: 42.1% (2020 est.)
female: 19.2% (2020 est.)
comparison ranking: total 28

Children under the age of 5 years underweight: 1.5% (2018/19)
comparison ranking: 113

Currently married women (ages 15-49): 65.4% (2023 est.)

Child marriage: *women married by age 15:* 2%
women married by age 18: 14.7% (2018 est.)

Education expenditures: 3.4% of GDP (2020 est.)
comparison ranking: 145

Literacy: *definition:* age 15 and over can read and write
total population: 96.7%
male: 99.1%
female: 94.4% (2019)

School life expectancy (primary to tertiary education): *total:* 18 years
male: 19 years
female: 18 years (2020)

ENVIRONMENT

Environment - current issues: water pollution from dumping of chemicals and detergents; air pollution, particularly in urban areas; deforestation; land degradation; concern for oil spills from increasing Bosporus ship traffic; conservation of biodiversity

Environment - international agreements: *party to:* Air Pollution, Antarctic-Environmental Protection, Antarctic Treaty, Biodiversity, Climate Change,

Climate Change-Kyoto Protocol, Comprehensive Nuclear Test Ban, Desertification, Endangered Species, Hazardous Wastes, Nuclear Test Ban, Ozone Layer Protection, Ship Pollution, Wetlands
signed, but not ratified: Climate Change-Paris Agreement, Environmental Modification

Climate: temperate; hot, dry summers with mild, wet winters; harsher in interior

Urbanization: *urban population:* 77.5% of total population (2023)
rate of urbanization: 1.11% annual rate of change (2020-25 est.)

Revenue from forest resources: 0.08% of GDP (2018 est.)
comparison ranking: 118

Revenue from coal: 0.05% of GDP (2018 est.)
comparison ranking: 31

Air pollutants: *particulate matter emissions:* 23.25 micrograms per cubic meter (2019 est.)
carbon dioxide emissions: 372.72 megatons (2016 est.)
methane emissions: 57.53 megatons (2020 est.)

Waste and recycling: *municipal solid waste generated annually:* 31.283 million tons (2015 est.)

Major lakes (area sq km): *fresh water lake(s):* Lake Beysehir - 650 sq km; Lake Egridir - 520 sq km
salt water lake(s): Lake Van - 3,740 sq km; Lake Tuz - 1,640 sq km;

Major rivers (by length in km): Euphrates river source (shared with Syria, Iran, and Iraq [m]) - 3,596 km; Tigris river source (shared with Syria, Iran, and Iraq [m]) - 1,950 km
note – [s] after country name indicates river source; [m] after country name indicates river mouth

Major watersheds (area sq km): Indian Ocean drainage: *(Persian Gulf)* Tigris and Euphrates (918,044 sq km)

Total water withdrawal: *municipal:* 6.91 billion cubic meters (2020 est.)
industrial: 1.03 billion cubic meters (2020 est.)
agricultural: 54.27 billion cubic meters (2020 est.)

Total renewable water resources: 211.6 billion cubic meters (2020 est.)

Geoparks: *total global geoparks and regional networks:* 1
global geoparks and regional networks: Kula-Salihli (2023)

GOVERNMENT

Country name: *conventional long form:* Republic of Turkey
conventional short form: Turkey
local long form: Turkey Cumhuriyeti
local short form: Turkey
etymology: the name means "Land of the Turks"
note: Turkiye is an approved English short-form name for Turkey

Government type: presidential republic

Capital: *name:* Ankara
geographic coordinates: 39 56 N, 32 52 E
time difference: UTC+3 (8 hours ahead of Washington, DC, during Standard Time)
etymology: Ankara has been linked with a second millennium B.C. Hittite cult center of Ankuwash, although this connection is uncertain; in classical and medieval times, the city was known as Ankyra (meaning "anchor" in Greek and reflecting the city's position as a junction for multiple trade and military routes); by about the 13th century the city began to be referred to as Angora; following the establishment of the Republic of Turkey in 1923, the city's name became Ankara

Administrative divisions: 81 provinces (iller, singular - ili); Adana, Adiyaman, Afyonkarahisar, Agri, Aksaray, Amasya, Ankara, Antalya, Ardahan, Artvin, Aydin, Balikesir, Bartin, Batman, Bayburt, Bilecik, Bingol, Bitlis, Bolu, Burdur, Bursa, Canakkale, Cankiri, Corum, Denizli, Diyarbakir, Duzce, Edirne, Elazig, Erzincan, Erzurum, Eskisehir, Gaziantep, Giresun, Gumushane, Hakkari, Hatay, Igdir, Isparta, Istanbul, Izmir (Smyrna), Kahramanmaras, Karabuk, Karaman, Kars, Kastamonu, Kayseri, Kilis, Kirikkale, Kirklareli, Kirsehir, Kocaeli, Konya, Kutahya, Malatya, Manisa, Mardin, Mersin, Mugla, Mus, Nevsehir, Nigde, Ordu, Osmaniye, Rize, Sakarya, Samsun, Sanliurfa, Siirt, Sinop, Sirnak, Sivas, Tekirdag, Tokat, Trabzon (Trebizond), Tunceli, Usak, Van, Yalova, Yozgat, Zonguldak

Independence: 29 October 1923 (republic proclaimed, succeeding the Ottoman Empire)

National holiday: Republic Day, 29 October (1923)

Legal system: civil law system based on various European legal systems, notably the Swiss civil code

Constitution: *history:* several previous; latest ratified 9 November 1982
amendments: proposed by written consent of at least one third of Grand National Assembly (GNA) of Turkey (TBMM) members; adoption of draft amendments requires two debates in plenary TBMM session and three-fifths majority vote of all GNA members; the president of the republic can request TBMM reconsideration of the amendment and, if readopted by two-thirds majority TBMM vote, the president may submit the amendment to a referendum; passage by referendum requires absolute majority vote; amended several times, last in 2017

International law organization participation: has not submitted an ICJ jurisdiction declaration; non-party state to the ICCt

Citizenship: *citizenship by birth:* no
citizenship by descent only: at least one parent must be a citizen of Turkey
dual citizenship recognized: yes, but requires prior permission from the government
residency requirement for naturalization: 5 years

Suffrage: 18 years of age; universal

Executive branch: *chief of state:* President Recep Tayyip ERDOGAN (chief of state since 28 August 2014; head of government since 9 July 2018)
head of government: President Recep Tayyip ERDOGAN (head of government since 9 July 2018; chief of state since 28 August 2014)
cabinet: Council of Ministers appointed by the president
elections/appointments: president directly elected by absolute majority popular vote in 2 rounds if needed for a 5-year term (eligible for a second term); election last held on 14 May 2023 with a runoff on 28 May 2023 (next to be held in 2028)
election results:
2023: Recep Tayyip ERDOGAN reelected president in second round - Recep Tayyip ERDOGAN (AKP) 52.2%, Kemal KILICDAROGLU (CHP) 47.8%
2018: Recep Tayyip ERDOGAN reelected president in first round - Recep Tayyip ERDOGAN (AKP) 52.6%, Muharrem INCE (CHP) 30.6%, Selahattin DEMIRTAS (HDP) 8.4%, Meral AKSENER (IYI) 7.3%, other 1.1%

Legislative branch: *description:* unicameral Grand National Assembly of Turkey or Turkey Buyuk Millet Meclisi (600 seats); members directly elected in multi-seat constituencies by closed party-list proportional representation vote, with a 7% threshold required to win a seat; members serve 5-year terms)
elections: last held on 14 May 2023 (next to be held in 2028)
election results: percent of vote by party/coalition - People's Alliance 49.9% (AKP 35.6%, MHP 10.1%, YRP 2.8%, BBP 1%), Nation Alliance 35.4% (CHP 25.3%, IYI 9.7%), Labor and Freedom Alliance 10.7% (YSGP 8.9%, TIP 1.8%); seats by party/coalition - People's Alliance 323 (AKP 268, MHP 50, YRP 5), Nation Alliance 212 (CHP 169, IYI 43), Labor and Freedom Alliance 65 (YSGP 61, TIP 4); composition - men 480, women 119, percentage women 19.9%

Judicial branch: *highest court(s):* Constitutional Court or Anayasa Mahkemesi (consists of the president, 2 vice presidents, and 12 judges); Court of Cassation (consists of about 390 judges and is organized into civil and penal chambers); Council of State (organized into 15 divisions - 14 judicial and 1 consultative - each with a division head and at least 5 members)
judge selection and term of office: Constitutional Court members - 3 appointed by the Grand National Assembly and 12 by the president of the republic; court president and 2 deputy court presidents appointed from among its members for 4-year terms; judges serve 12-year, nonrenewable terms with mandatory retirement at age 65; Court of Cassation judges appointed by the Board of Judges and Prosecutors, a 13-member body of judicial officials; Court of Cassation judges serve until retirement at age 65; Council of State members appointed by the Board and by the president of the republic; members serve renewable, 4-year terms
subordinate courts: regional appeals courts; basic (first instance) courts; peace courts; aggravated crime courts; specialized courts, including administrative and audit; note - a constitutional amendment in 2017 abolished military courts unless established to investigate military personnel actions during war conditions

Political parties: Democracy and Progress Party or DEVA
Democrat Party or DP
Democratic Regions Party or DBP
Felicity Party (Saadet Party) or SP
Free Cause Party or HUDA PAR
Future Party (Gelecek Partisi) or GP
Good Party or IYI
Grand Unity Party or BBP
Justice and Development Party or AKP
Labor and Freedom Alliance (electoral alliance includes YSGP, HDP, TIP)
Nationalist Movement Party or MHP
New Welfare Party or YRP
Party of Greens and the Left Future or YSGP
People's Alliance (electoral alliance includes AKP, BBP, MHP, YRP)
Peoples' Democratic Party or HDP
Republican People's Party or CHP
Workers' Party of Turkey or TIP

International organization participation: ADB (nonregional member), Australia Group, BIS, BSEC, CBSS (observer), CD, CE, CERN (observer), CICA,

CPLP (associate observer), D-8, EAPC, EBRD, ECO, EU (candidate country), FAO, FATF, G-20, IAEA, IBRD, ICAO, ICC (national committees), ICRM, IDA, IDB, IEA, IFAD, IFC, IFRCS, IHO, ILO, IMF, IMO, IMSO, Interpol, IOC, IOM, IPU, ISO, ITSO, ITU, ITUC (NGOs), MIGA, NATO, NEA, NSG, OAS (observer), OECD, OIC, OPCW, OSCE, Pacific Alliance (observer), Paris Club (associate), PCA, PIF (partner), SCO (dialogue member), SELEC, UN, UNCTAD, UNESCO, UNHCR, UNIDO, UNIFIL, UNRWA, UNWTO, UPU, Wassenaar Arrangement, WCO, WFTU (NGOs), WHO, WIPO, WMO, WTO, ZC
note: Turkey is an EU candidate country whose satisfactory completion of accession criteria is required before being granted full EU membership

Diplomatic representation in the US: *chief of mission:* Ambassador Sedat ÖNAL (since 17 June 2024)
chancery: 2525 Massachusetts Avenue NW, Washington, DC 20008
telephone: [1] (202) 612-6700
FAX: [1] (202) 612-6744
email address and website:
embassy.washingtondc@mfa.gov.tr
T.C. Dışişleri Bakanlığı - Turkish Embassy In Washington, D.C. (mfa.gov.tr)
consulate(s) general: Boston, Chicago, Houston, Los Angeles, Miami, New York, San Francisco

Diplomatic representation from the US: *chief of mission:* Ambassador (vacant); Chargé d'Affaires Michael GOLDMAN (since September 2024)
embassy: 1480 Sokak No. 1, Cukurambar Mahallesi, 06530 Cankaya, Ankara
mailing address: 7000 Ankara Place, Washington DC 20512-7000
telephone: [90] (312) 294-0000
FAX: [90] (312) 467-0019
email address and website:
Ankara-ACS@state.gov
https://tr.usembassy.gov/
consulate(s) general: Istanbul
consulate(s): Adana

Flag description: red with a vertical white crescent moon (the closed portion is toward the hoist side) and white five-pointed star centered just outside the crescent opening; the flag colors and designs closely resemble those on the banner of the Ottoman Empire, which preceded modern-day Turkey; the crescent moon and star serve as insignia for Turkic peoples; according to one interpretation, the flag represents the reflection of the moon and a star in a pool of blood of Turkish warriors

National symbol(s): vertical crescent moon with adjacent five-pointed star; national colors: red, white

National anthem: *name:* "Istiklal Marsi" (Independence March)
lyrics/music: Mehmet Akif ERSOY/Zeki UNGOR
note: lyrics adopted 1921, music adopted 1932; the anthem's original music was adopted in 1924; a new composition was agreed upon in 1932

National heritage: *total World Heritage Sites:* 19 (17 cultural, 2 mixed)
selected World Heritage Site locales: Archaeological Site of Troy (c); Ephesus (c); Diyarbakır Fortress and Hevsel Gardens Cultural Landscape (c); Hierapolis-Pamukkale (m); Göreme National Park and the Rock Sites of Cappadocia (m); Göbekli Tepe (c); Historic Areas of Istanbul (c); Selimiye Mosque and its Social Complex (c); Neolithic Site of Çatalhöyük (c); Bursa and Cumalıkızık: the Birth of the Ottoman Empire (c); Gordion (c)

ECONOMY

Economic overview: upper middle-income, diversified Middle Eastern economy; heightened inflation and currency depreciation triggered by expansionary monetary and fiscal policy ahead of 2023 elections, now being reversed; industrializing economy that maintains large agricultural base

Real GDP (purchasing power parity): $2.936 trillion (2023 est.)
$2.81 trillion (2022 est.)
$2.662 trillion (2021 est.)
note: data in 2021 dollars
comparison ranking: 12

Real GDP growth rate: 4.52% (2023 est.)
5.53% (2022 est.)
11.44% (2021 est.)
note: annual GDP % growth based on constant local currency
comparison ranking: 67

Real GDP per capita: $34,400 (2023 est.)
$33,100 (2022 est.)
$31,600 (2021 est.)
note: data in 2021 dollars
comparison ranking: 71

GDP (official exchange rate): $1.108 trillion (2023 est.)
note: data in current dollars at official exchange rate

Inflation rate (consumer prices): 53.86% (2023 est.)
72.31% (2022 est.)
19.6% (2021 est.)
note: annual % change based on consumer prices
comparison ranking: 216

Credit ratings: Fitch rating: BB- (2019)

Moody's rating: B2 (2020)

Standard & Poors rating: B+ (2018)
note: The year refers to the year in which the current credit rating was first obtained.

GDP - composition, by sector of origin: *agriculture:* 6.2% (2023 est.)
industry: 28.3% (2023 est.)
services: 54% (2023 est.)
note: figures may not total 100% due to non-allocated consumption not captured in sector-reported data
comparison rankings: services 123; industry 76; agriculture 105

GDP - composition, by end use: *household consumption:* 59.4% (2023 est.)
government consumption: 13.6% (2023 est.)
investment in fixed capital: 32.4% (2023 est.)
investment in inventories: -3% (2023 est.)
exports of goods and services: 32.3% (2023 est.)
imports of goods and services: -34.7% (2023 est.)
note: figures may not total 100% due to rounding or gaps in data collection

Agricultural products: milk, wheat, sugar beets, tomatoes, barley, maize, potatoes, apples, grapes, watermelons (2022)
note: top ten agricultural products based on tonnage

Industries: textiles, food processing, automobiles, electronics, mining (coal, chromate, copper, boron), steel, petroleum, construction, lumber, paper

Industrial production growth rate: 2.34% (2023 est.)
note: annual % change in industrial value added based on constant local currency
comparison ranking: 112

Labor force: 35.071 million (2023 est.)
note: number of people ages 15 or older who are employed or seeking work
comparison ranking: 19

Unemployment rate: 9.41% (2023 est.)
10.43% (2022 est.)
11.97% (2021 est.)
note: % of labor force seeking employment
comparison ranking: 161

Youth unemployment rate (ages 15-24): *total:* 17.6% (2023 est.)
male: 14.8% (2023 est.)
female: 22.9% (2023 est.)
note: % of labor force ages 15-24 seeking employment
comparison ranking: total 79

Population below poverty line: 14.4% (2020 est.)
note: % of population with income below national poverty line

Gini Index coefficient - distribution of family income: 44.4 (2021 est.)
note: index (0-100) of income distribution; higher values represent greater inequality
comparison ranking: 24

Average household expenditures: *on food:* 25.4% of household expenditures (2022 est.)
on alcohol and tobacco: 3.3% of household expenditures (2022 est.)

Household income or consumption by percentage share: *lowest 10%:* 2% (2021 est.)
highest 10%: 34.7% (2021 est.)
note: % share of income accruing to lowest and highest 10% of population

Remittances: 0.08% of GDP (2023 est.)
0.08% of GDP (2022 est.)
0.09% of GDP (2021 est.)
note: personal transfers and compensation between resident and non-resident individuals/households/entities

Budget: *revenues:* $234.92 billion (2022 est.)
expenditures: $269.146 billion (2022 est.)
note: central government revenues (excluding grants) and expenses converted to US dollars at average official exchange rate for year indicated

Public debt: 35.25% of GDP (2022 est.)
note: central government debt as a % of GDP
comparison ranking: 154

Taxes and other revenues: 16.09% (of GDP) (2022 est.)
note: central government tax revenue as a % of GDP
comparison ranking: 126

Current account balance: -$44.961 billion (2023 est.)
-$45.799 billion (2022 est.)
-$6.433 billion (2021 est.)
note: balance of payments - net trade and primary/secondary income in current dollars
comparison ranking: 205

Exports: $352.514 billion (2023 est.)
$346.369 billion (2022 est.)
$287.318 billion (2021 est.)
note: balance of payments - exports of goods and services in current dollars
comparison ranking: 26

Exports - partners: Germany 8%, US 7%, Iraq 5%, UK 5%, Italy 5% (2022)

note: top five export partners based on percentage share of exports

Exports - commodities: garments, refined petroleum, cars, jewelry, plastic products (2022)
note: top five export commodities based on value in dollars

Imports: $386.828 billion (2023 est.)
$383.02 billion (2022 est.)
$284.019 billion (2021 est.)
note: balance of payments - imports of goods and services in current dollars
comparison ranking: 20

Imports - partners: China 13%, Germany 9%, Russia 8%, US 5%, Italy 5% (2022)
note: top five import partners based on percentage share of imports

Imports - commodities: gold, refined petroleum, plastics, scrap iron, cars (2022)
note: top five import commodities based on value in dollars

Reserves of foreign exchange and gold: $140.858 billion (2023 est.)
$123.735 billion (2022 est.)
$109.535 billion (2021 est.)
note: holdings of gold (year-end prices)/foreign exchange/special drawing rights in current dollars
comparison ranking: 25

Debt - external: $133.882 billion (2022 est.)
note: present value of external debt in current US dollars
comparison ranking: 6

Exchange rates: Turkish liras (TRY) per US dollar -

Exchange rates: 23.739 (2023 est.)
16.549 (2022 est.)
8.85 (2021 est.)
7.009 (2020 est.)
5.674 (2019 est.)

ENERGY

Electricity access: *electrification - total population:* 100% (2022 est.)

Electricity: *installed generating capacity:* 103.817 million kW (2022 est.)
consumption: 280.458 billion kWh (2022 est.)
exports: 3.71 billion kWh (2022 est.)
imports: 6.423 billion kWh (2022 est.)
transmission/distribution losses: 30.452 billion kWh (2022 est.)
comparison rankings: transmission/distribution losses 198; imports 40; exports 43; consumption 17; installed generating capacity 15

Electricity generation sources: *fossil fuels:* 58.2% of total installed capacity (2022 est.)
solar: 4.9% of total installed capacity (2022 est.)
wind: 11.3% of total installed capacity (2022 est.)
hydroelectricity: 21.7% of total installed capacity (2022 est.)
geothermal: 2.9% of total installed capacity (2022 est.)
biomass and waste: 1% of total installed capacity (2022 est.)

Nuclear energy: Number of nuclear reactors under construction: 4 (2023)

Coal: *production:* 88.746 million metric tons (2022 est.)
consumption: 123.976 million metric tons (2022 est.)
exports: 879,000 metric tons (2022 est.)
imports: 38.046 million metric tons (2022 est.)
proven reserves: 11.525 billion metric tons (2022 est.)

Petroleum: *total petroleum production:* 83,000 bbl/day (2023 est.)
refined petroleum consumption: 1.077 million bbl/day (2023 est.)
crude oil estimated reserves: 366 million barrels (2021 est.)

Natural gas: *production:* 379.701 million cubic meters (2022 est.)
consumption: 52.887 billion cubic meters (2022 est.)
exports: 581.666 million cubic meters (2022 est.)
imports: 54.536 billion cubic meters (2022 est.)
proven reserves: 3.794 billion cubic meters (2021 est.)

Carbon dioxide emissions: 391.592 million metric tonnes of CO2 (2022 est.)
from coal and metallurgical coke: 149.781 million metric tonnes of CO2 (2022 est.)
from petroleum and other liquids: 139.954 million metric tonnes of CO2 (2022 est.)
from consumed natural gas: 101.858 million metric tonnes of CO2 (2022 est.)
comparison ranking: total emissions 16

Energy consumption per capita: 70.594 million Btu/person (2022 est.)
comparison ranking: 70

COMMUNICATIONS

Telephones - fixed lines: *total subscriptions:* 11.198 million (2022 est.)
subscriptions per 100 inhabitants: 13 (2022 est.)
comparison ranking: total subscriptions 17

Telephones - mobile cellular: *total subscriptions:* 90.298 million (2022 est.)
subscriptions per 100 inhabitants: 106 (2022 est.)
comparison ranking: total subscriptions 19

Telecommunication systems: *general assessment:* Turkey continues to develop its capabilities within its telecom sector, becoming one of the relatively few countries able to build and develop its own communications satellites; with the successful launch of the Turksat 5A and 5B satellites in 2021, the country has vastly increased its bandwidth capacity; these satellites will be joined by the Turksat 6A in 2023; the country's telcos have invested in fiber infrastructure; deployment of fiber-based broadband networks are well established, with fiber accounting for 26.7% of all fixed broadband connections as of early 2022; the DSL sector still dominates, accounting for about 63% of connections, but its share is steadily declining, year-on-year, while the number of fiber connections has grown strongly; improved fixed and mobile infrastructure is underpinning the country's initiatives relating to Smart City concepts, which have become a key area of focus for the emerging digital economy and the transformation to a knowledge-based economy; Turkey's National Smart Cities Strategy and Action Plan runs through to 2023 (2022)
domestic: fixed-line nearly 14 per 100 and mobile-cellular teledensity is 106 telephones per 100 persons (2022)
international: country code - 90; landing points for the SeaMeWe-3 & -5, MedNautilus Submarine System, Turcyos-1 & -2 submarine cables providing connectivity to Europe, Africa, the Middle East, Asia, Southeast Asia and Australia ; satellite earth stations - 12 Intelsat; mobile satellite terminals - 328 in the Inmarsat and Eutelsat systems (2020)

Broadcast media: Turkish Radio and Television Corporation (TRT) operates multiple TV and radio networks and stations; multiple privately owned national television stations and 567 private regional and local television stations; multi-channel cable TV subscriptions available; 1,007 private radio broadcast stations
(2019)

Internet country code: .tr

Internet users: *total:* 68.85 million (2021 est.)
percent of population: 81% (2021 est.)
comparison ranking: total 14

Broadband - fixed subscriptions: *total:* 16,734,853 (2020 est.)
subscriptions per 100 inhabitants: 20 (2020 est.)
comparison ranking: total 13

TRANSPORTATION

National air transport system: *number of registered air carriers:* 11 (2020)
inventory of registered aircraft operated by air carriers: 618
annual passenger traffic on registered air carriers: 115,595,495 (2018)
annual freight traffic on registered air carriers: 5,949,210,000 (2018) mt-km

Civil aircraft registration country code prefix: TC

Airports: 115 (2024)
comparison ranking: 46

Heliports: 213 (2024)

Pipelines: 14,666 km gas, 3,293 km oil (2017)

Railways: *total:* 11,497 km (2018)
standard gauge: 11,497 km (2018) 1.435-m gauge (1.435 km high speed train)
comparison ranking: total 21

Roadways: *total:* 68,526 km (2023)
paved: 24,082 km (2018) (includes 2,159 km of expressways)
unpaved: 43,251 km (2018)
comparison ranking: total 72

Waterways: 1,200 km (2010)
comparison ranking: 62

Merchant marine: *total:* 1,170 (2023)
by type: bulk carrier 43, container ship 43, general cargo 223, oil tanker 134, other 727
comparison ranking: total 22

Ports: *total ports:* 54 (2024)
large: 3
medium: 3
small: 6
very small: 42
ports with oil terminals: 28
key ports: Haydarpasa, Istanbul, Izmir, Mersin, Nemrut Limani Bay, Samsun

MILITARY AND SECURITY

Military and security forces: Turkish Armed Forces (TAF; Türk Silahlı Kuvvetleri, TSK): Turkish Land

Forces (Türk Kara Kuvvetleri), Turkish Naval Forces (Türk Deniz Kuvvetleri; includes naval air and naval infantry), Turkish Air Forces (Türk Hava Kuvvetleri)

Ministry of Interior: Gendarmerie of the Turkish Republic (aka Gendarmerie General Command), Turkish Coast Guard Command, National Police (2024)

note: the Gendarmerie (Jandarma) is responsible for the maintenance of the public order in areas that fall outside the jurisdiction of police forces (generally in rural areas); in wartime, the Gendarmerie and Coast Guard would be placed under the operational control of the Land Forces and Naval Forces, respectively

Military expenditures: 2.1% of GDP (2024 est.)
1.6% of GDP (2023 est.)
1.4% of GDP (2022)
1.6% of GDP (2021)
1.9% of GDP (2020)
comparison ranking: 60

Military and security service personnel strengths: approximately 480,000 active-duty personnel (380,000 Army; 50,000 Navy; 50,000 Air Force); approximately 150,000 Gendarmerie (2024)

Military equipment inventories and acquisitions: the military's inventory is comprised of domestically produced, European (particularly from Germany), and US weapons and equipment, as well as some Chinese, Russian, and South Korean acquisitions; it is a mix of older and modern weapons systems; Türkiye has a defense industry capable of producing a range of weapons systems for both export and internal use, including armored vehicles, naval vessels, and unmanned aerial vehicles/drones; Türkiye's defense industry also partners with other countries for defense production (2024)

Military service age and obligation: mandatory military service for men at age 20; service can be delayed if in university or in certain professions (researchers, professionals, and athletic, or those with artistic talents have the right to postpone military service until the age of 35); 6-12 months service; women may volunteer (2023)

note 1: after completing six months of service, if a conscripted soldier wants to and is suitable for extending his military service, he may do so for an additional six months in return for a monthly salary; all male Turkish citizens over the age of 20 are required to undergo a one month military training period, but they can obtain an exemption from the remaining 5 months of their mandatory service by paying a fee

note 2: as of 2020, women made up about 0.3% of the military's full-time personnel

Military deployments: approximately 150 (Azerbaijan; monitoring cease-fire, clearing mines); 250 Bosnia-Herzegovina (EUFOR); approximately 30-35,000 Cyprus; 800 Kosovo (NATO/KFOR); 130 Lebanon (UNIFIL); estimated 500 Libya; up to 5,000 Qatar; approximately 200 Somalia (training mission) (2023)

note: Turkey maintains significant military forces in both Iraq and Syria; size estimates vary as some forces are longterm deployments while others are deployed for specific operations; between 2016 and 2020, Turkey conducted four significant military ground campaigns in northern Syria with the stated purpose of securing its southern border; Turkey also has deployed troops into northern Iraq on numerous occasions to combat the Kurdistan Worker's Party (PKK), including large operations involving thousands of troops in 2007, 2011, and 2018, and smaller-scale operations in 2021 and 2022; Turkey has also conducted numerous air strikes in both Iraq and Syria

Military - note: the Turkish Armed Forces (TAF) have a range of responsibilities, including protecting the country's territory and sovereignty, participating in international peacekeeping operations, fulfilling Türkiye's military commitments to NATO, providing disaster/humanitarian relief and assistance to domestic law enforcement if requested by civil authorities, and supporting the country's overall national security interests; the TAF also has overall responsibility for the security of Türkiye's borders; Türkiye is active in international peacekeeping and other security operations under the EU, NATO, and the UN, as well as under bilateral agreements with some countries; the TAF has established expeditionary military bases in northern Cyprus, Qatar, Somalia, and Sudan

Türkiye has been a member of NATO since 1952 and hosts a considerable NATO and US military presence, including the headquarters for a NATO Land Command and a Rapid Deployment Corps, multiple airbases for NATO and US aircraft, NATO air/missile defense systems, and training centers; the TAF is the second-largest military in NATO behind the US and exercises regularly with NATO partners; Türkiye's geographic location at the southeastern flank of the Alliance give it and the TAF a critical role in regional security

the TAF is a large, well-equipped force comprised of a mix of professionals and conscripts; it has considerable operational experience; in addition to peacekeeping and military assistance operations in recent years in such places as Afghanistan (NATO), Bosnia and Herzegovina (EU), Kosovo (NATO), Lebanon (UN), and Somalia (bilateral), it has conducted combat missions of varying duration and scale in Iraq, Libya, and Syria; ; in Syria, it occupies a large swatch of territory and maintain thousands of troops; since the 1980s, the TAF has been involved in a protracted counterinsurgency campaign against the US-designated terrorist group the Kurdistan Worker's Party or PKK, a Kurdish militant political organization and armed guerrilla movement, which historically operated throughout Kurdistan but is now primarily based in the mountainous Kurdish-majority regions of southeastern Türkiye and northern Iraq; other key areas of concern for the TAF include tensions with fellow NATO member Greece over territorial disputes and Cyprus, tensions between neighboring Armenia and Azerbaijan, conflict in the Middle East, threats from the terrorist groups al-Qa'ida and the Islamic State of Iraq and ash-Sham, and the Russia-Ukraine war; under a long-range (2033) strategic plan, the TAF continues an effort to modernize its equipment and force structure

Türkiye's military has a rich history that it traces back to 200 B.C., although the modern TAF was formed following the collapse of the Ottoman Empire at the conclusion of the Turkish War of Independence (1919-1923); the TAF has traditionally had a significant influence in the country as the "guardian" of Turkish politics, but its political role was diminished after the failed 2016 coup attempt; the military has a substantial stake in Türkiye's economy through a holding company that is involved in the automotive, energy, finance, and logistics sectors, as well as iron and steel production (2024)

SPACE

Space agency/agencies: Turkish Space Agency (TUA; established 2018); TÜBİTAK Space Technologies Research Institute (UZAY; established in 1985 as Ankara Electronics Research and Development Institute) (2024)

Space launch site(s): rocket test launch site on the Black Sea in Sinop Province; the 2021 national space program called for the establishment of a space port; has reportedly discussed building a rocket launch site in Somalia or using a sea-launch facility for future space launch vehicles (2024)

Space program overview: has an ambitious space program with a large focus on satellites, software development, ground station technologies, and building up the country's space industries; in recent years has also initiated a space launch program with the goal of placing domestically produced satellites into orbit independently and a probe on the Moon; manufactures and operates remote sensing and telecommunications satellites, as well as satellite components; has a space/satellite launch vehicle program; space sector is heavily import-reliant, particularly at the component level; has established relations with more than 25 foreign space agencies and corporations, including those of Azerbaijan, China, France, India, Japan, Kazakhstan, Pakistan, Russia, South Korea, Ukraine, and the US, as well as the European Space Agency; has state-owned rocket development and satellite communications companies, including some under the Ministry of Defense (2024)

note: further details about the key activities, programs, and milestones of the country's space program, as well as government spending estimates on the space sector, appear in the Space Programs reference guide

TERRORISM

Terrorist group(s): Islamic State of Iraq and ash-Sham (ISIS); Islamic Movement of Uzbekistan (IMU); Islamic Revolutionary Guard Corps (IRGC)/Qods Force; Kurdistan Workers' Party (PKK); al-Qa'ida; Revolutionary People's Liberation Party/Front (DHKP/C)

note: details about the history, aims, leadership, organization, areas of operation, tactics, targets, weapons, size, and sources of support of the group(s) appear(s) in the Terrorism reference guide

TRANSNATIONAL ISSUES

Refugees and internally displaced persons: *refugees (country of origin):* 10,244 (Iraq) (mid-year 2022); 41,665 (Ukraine) (as of 15 February 2024) (2023); 3,122,899 (Syria) (2024)

IDPs: 1.099 million (displaced from 1984-2005 because of fighting between the Kurdish PKK and Turkish military; most IDPs are Kurds from eastern and southeastern provinces; no information available on persons displaced by development projects) (2022)

stateless persons: 117 (2018)

Illicit drugs: a significant transit country for illicit drug trafficking; an increase of heroin and methamphetamine seizures along the Turkiye-Iran border; Syrian drug traffickers play a significant role in Turkiye's drug trade; domestic Illegal drug use relatively low compared to countries in the region

TURKMENISTAN

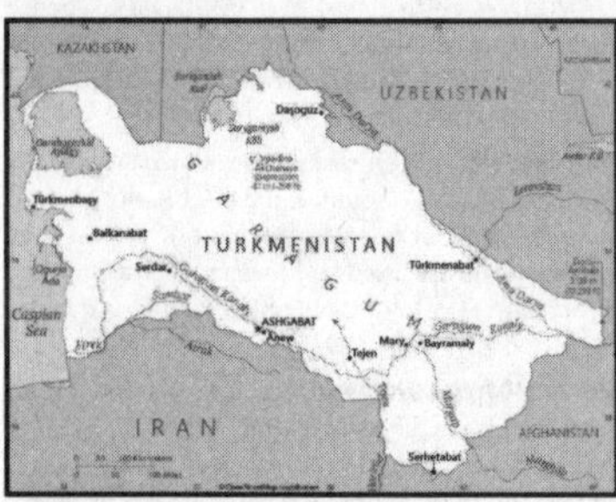

INTRODUCTION

Background: Present-day Turkmenistan has been at the crossroads of civilizations for centuries. Various Persian empires ruled the area in antiquity, and Alexander the Great, Muslim armies, the Mongols, Turkic warriors, and eventually the Russians conquered it. In medieval times, Merv (located in present-day Mary province) was one of the great cities of the Islamic world and an important stop on the Silk Road. Annexed by Russia in the late 1800s, Turkmen territories later figured prominently in the anti-Bolshevik resistance in Central Asia. In 1924, Turkmenistan became a Soviet republic; it achieved independence when the USSR dissolved in 1991.

President for Life Saparmurat NIYAZOV died in 2006, and Gurbanguly BERDIMUHAMEDOV, a deputy chairman under NIYAZOW, emerged as the country's new president. BERDIMUHAMEDOV won Turkmenistan's first multi-candidate presidential election in 2007, and again in 2012 and 2017 with over 97% of the vote in elections widely regarded as undemocratic. In 2022, BERDIMUHAMEDOV announced that he would step down from the presidency and called for an election to replace him. His son, Serdar BERDIMUHAMEDOV, won the ensuing election with 73% of the vote. Gurbanguly BERDIMUHAMEDOV, although no longer head of state, maintains an influential political position as head of the Halk Maslahaty (People's Council) and as National Leader of the Turkmen People, a title that provides additional privileges and immunity for him and his family. Since Gurbanguly BERDIMUHAMEDOV stepped down from the presidency, state-controlled media upgraded his honorific from Arkadag (protector) to Hero-Arkadag, and began referring to Serdar BERDIMUHAMEDOV as Arkadagly Serdar, which can be translated as "Serdar who has a protector to support him."

Turkmenistan has sought new export markets for its extensive hydrocarbon/natural gas reserves, which have yet to be fully exploited. Turkmenistan's reliance on gas exports has made the economy vulnerable to fluctuations in the global energy market, and economic hardships since the drop in energy prices in 2014 have led many citizens of Turkmenistan to emigrate, mostly to Turkey.

GEOGRAPHY

Location: Central Asia, bordering the Caspian Sea, between Iran and Kazakhstan

Geographic coordinates: 40 00 N, 60 00 E

Map references: Asia

Area: *total:* 488,100 sq km
land: 469,930 sq km
water: 18,170 sq km
comparison ranking: total 55

Area - comparative: slightly more than three times the size of Georgia; slightly larger than California

Land boundaries: *total:* 4,158 km
border countries (4): Afghanistan 804 km; Iran 1,148 km; Kazakhstan 413 km; Uzbekistan 1,793 km

Coastline: 0 km (landlocked); note - Turkmenistan borders the Caspian Sea (1,768 km)

Maritime claims: none (landlocked)

Climate: subtropical desert

Terrain: flat-to-rolling sandy desert with dunes rising to mountains in the south; low mountains along border with Iran; borders Caspian Sea in west

Elevation: *highest point:* Gora Ayribaba 3,139 m
lowest point: Vpadina Akchanaya (Sarygamysh Koli is a lake in northern Turkmenistan with a water level that fluctuates above and below the elevation of Vpadina Akchanaya, the lake has dropped as low as -110 m) -81 m
mean elevation: 230 m

Natural resources: petroleum, natural gas, sulfur, salt

Land use: *agricultural land:* 72% (2018 est.)
arable land: 4.1% (2018 est.)
permanent crops: 0.1% (2018 est.)
permanent pasture: 67.8% (2018 est.)
forest: 8.8% (2018 est.)
other: 19.2% (2018 est.)

Irrigated land: 19,950 sq km (2012)

Major lakes (area sq km): *salt water lake(s):* Caspian Sea (shared with Iran, Azerbaijan, Russia, and Kazakhstan) - 374,000 sq km

Major rivers (by length in km): Amu Darya (shared with Tajikistan [s], Afghanistan, and Uzbekistan [m]) - 2,620 km
note – [s] after country name indicates river source; [m] after country name indicates river mouth

Major watersheds (area sq km): Internal (endorheic basin) drainage: *(Aral Sea basin)* Amu Darya (534,739 sq km)

Population distribution: the most densely populated areas are the southern, eastern, and northeastern oases; approximately 50% of the population lives in and around the capital of Ashgabat

Natural hazards: earthquakes; mudslides; droughts; dust storms; floods

Geography - note: landlocked; the western and central low-lying desolate portions of the country make up the great Garagum (Kara-Kum) desert, which occupies over 80% of the country; eastern part is plateau

PEOPLE AND SOCIETY

Population: *total:* 5,744,151
male: 2,842,870
female: 2,901,281 (2024 est.)
comparison rankings: female 116; male 116; total 116

Nationality: *noun:* Turkmenistani(s)
adjective: Turkmenistani

Ethnic groups: Turkmen 85%, Uzbek 5%, Russian 4%, other 6% (2003 est.)

Languages: Turkmen (official) 72%, Russian 12%, Uzbek 9%, other 7%
major-language sample(s):
Dünýä Faktlar Kitaby – esasy maglumatlaryň wajyp çeşmesidir (Turkmen)

Religions: Muslim 93%, Christian 6.4%, Buddhist <1%, folk religion <1%, Jewish <1%, other <1%, unspecified <1% (2020 est.)

Demographic profile: While Turkmenistan reputedly has a population of more than 5.6 million, the figure is most likely considerably less. Getting an accurate population estimate for the country is impossible because then President Gurbanguly BERDIMUHAMEDOW withheld the results of the last two censuses. The 2012 census results reportedly show that nearly 2 million citizens have emigrated in the last decade, which prompted BERDIMUHAMEDOW to order another census. Results of this census, covering 2008-2018, also were not released to the public but purportedly are similar. Another census was held in December 2022.

Authorities have reacted to the dramatic population decline by preventing Turkmen from leaving the country, including removing citizens from international flights and refusing to provide necessary documents. Turkmenistan's rise in outmigration – mainly to Turkey, Russia, and Uzbekistan – coincided with the country's 2013-2014 economic crisis. The outflow has been sustained by poor living standards, inflation, low income, and a lack of health care. At the same time, Ashbagat is encouraging people to have more children to make up for its shrinking population.

Age structure: *0-14 years:* 24.5% (male 711,784/female 692,967)
15-64 years: 68.6% (male 1,956,740/female 1,984,333)
65 years and over: 6.9% (2024 est.) (male 174,346/female 223,981)

Dependency ratios: *total dependency ratio:* 56.6
youth dependency ratio: 48.9
elderly dependency ratio: 7.7
potential support ratio: 13 (2021 est.)

Median age: *total:* 31.2 years (2024 est.)
male: 30.7 years
female: 31.7 years
comparison ranking: total 128

Population growth rate: 0.92% (2024 est.)
comparison ranking: 101

Birth rate: 16.8 births/1,000 population (2024 est.)
comparison ranking: 93

Death rate: 6 deaths/1,000 population (2024 est.)
comparison ranking: 154

Net migration rate: -1.7 migrant(s)/1,000 population (2024 est.)
comparison ranking: 162

Population distribution: the most densely populated areas are the southern, eastern, and northeastern oases; approximately 50% of the population lives in and around the capital of Ashgabat

Urbanization: *urban population:* 54% of total population (2023)
rate of urbanization: 2.23% annual rate of change (2020-25 est.)

Major urban areas - population: 902,000 ASHGABAT (capital) (2023)

Sex ratio: *at birth:* 1.05 male(s)/female
0-14 years: 1.03 male(s)/female
15-64 years: 0.99 male(s)/female
65 years and over: 0.78 male(s)/female
total population: 0.98 male(s)/female (2024 est.)

Mother's mean age at first birth: 24.2 years (2019)

Maternal mortality ratio: 5 deaths/100,000 live births (2020 est.)
comparison ranking: 162

Infant mortality rate: *total:* 35.9 deaths/1,000 live births (2024 est.)
male: 43.6 deaths/1,000 live births
female: 27.7 deaths/1,000 live births
comparison ranking: total 34

Life expectancy at birth: *total population:* 72.4 years (2024 est.)
male: 69.4 years
female: 75.5 years
comparison ranking: total population 162

Total fertility rate: 2.02 children born/woman (2024 est.)
comparison ranking: 103

Gross reproduction rate: 0.99 (2024 est.)

Contraceptive prevalence rate: 49.7% (2019)

Drinking water source: *improved: urban:* 100% of population
rural: 100% of population
total: 100% of population

Current health expenditure: 5.7% of GDP (2020)

Physician density: 2.23 physicians/1,000 population (2014)

Hospital bed density: 4 beds/1,000 population (2014)

Sanitation facility access: *improved: urban:* 99.8% of population
rural: 99.9% of population
total: 99.8% of population
unimproved: urban: 0.2% of population
rural: 0.1% of population
total: 0.2% of population (2020 est.)

Obesity - adult prevalence rate: 18.6% (2016)
comparison ranking: 116

Alcohol consumption per capita: *total:* 2.88 liters of pure alcohol (2019 est.)
beer: 0.65 liters of pure alcohol (2019 est.)
wine: 1.25 liters of pure alcohol (2019 est.)
spirits: 0.98 liters of pure alcohol (2019 est.)
other alcohols: 0 liters of pure alcohol (2019 est.)
comparison ranking: total 117

Tobacco use: *total:* 5.5% (2020 est.)
male: 10.6% (2020 est.)
female: 0.4% (2020 est.)
comparison ranking: total 160

Children under the age of 5 years underweight: 3.1% (2019)
comparison ranking: 88

Currently married women (ages 15-49): 64.3% (2023 est.)

Child marriage: *women married by age 15:* 0.2%
women married by age 18: 6.1% (2019 est.)

Education expenditures: 3.1% of GDP (2019 est.)
comparison ranking: 153

Literacy: *definition:* age 15 and over can read and write
total population: 99.7%
male: 99.8%
female: 99.6% (2015)

School life expectancy (primary to tertiary education): *total:* 13 years
male: 13 years
female: 13 years (2020)

ENVIRONMENT

Environment - current issues: contamination of soil and groundwater with agricultural chemicals, pesticides; salination, water logging of soil due to poor irrigation methods; Caspian Sea pollution; diversion of a large share of the flow of the Amu Darya into irrigation contributes to that river's inability to replenish the Aral Sea; soil erosion; desertification

Environment - international agreements: *party to:* Biodiversity, Climate Change, Climate Change-Kyoto Protocol, Climate Change-Paris Agreement, Comprehensive Nuclear Test Ban, Desertification, Hazardous Wastes, Ozone Layer Protection, Ship Pollution, Wetlands
signed, but not ratified: none of the selected agreements

Climate: subtropical desert

Urbanization: *urban population:* 54% of total population (2023)
rate of urbanization: 2.23% annual rate of change (2020-25 est.)

Revenue from forest resources: 0% of GDP (2018 est.)
comparison ranking: 180

Revenue from coal: 0% of GDP (2018 est.)
comparison ranking: 67

Air pollutants: *particulate matter emissions:* 26.41 micrograms per cubic meter (2019 est.)
carbon dioxide emissions: 70.63 megatons (2016 est.)
methane emissions: 52.09 megatons (2020 est.)

Waste and recycling: *municipal solid waste generated annually:* 500,000 tons (2013 est.)

Major lakes (area sq km): *salt water lake(s):* Caspian Sea (shared with Iran, Azerbaijan, Russia, and Kazakhstan) - 374,000 sq km

Major rivers (by length in km): Amu Darya (shared with Tajikistan [s], Afghanistan, and Uzbekistan [m]) - 2,620 km
note – [s] after country name indicates river source; [m] after country name indicates river mouth

Major watersheds (area sq km): Internal (endorheic basin) drainage: *(Aral Sea basin)* Amu Darya (534,739 sq km)

Total water withdrawal: *municipal:* 450 million cubic meters (2020 est.)
industrial: 810 million cubic meters (2020 est.)
agricultural: 16.12 billion cubic meters (2020 est.)

Total renewable water resources: 24.77 billion cubic meters (2020 est.)

GOVERNMENT

Country name: *conventional long form:* none
conventional short form: Turkmenistan
local long form: none
local short form: Turkmenistan
former: Turkmen Soviet Socialist Republic
etymology: the suffix "-stan" means "place of" or "country," so Turkmenistan literally means the "Land of the Turkmen [people]"

Government type: presidential republic; authoritarian

Capital: *name:* Ashgabat (Ashkhabad)
geographic coordinates: 37 57 N, 58 23 E
time difference: UTC+5 (10 hours ahead of Washington, DC, during Standard Time)
etymology: derived from the Persian words *eshq* meaning "love" and *abad* meaning "inhabited place" or "city," and so loosely translates as "the city of love"

Administrative divisions: *5 provinces (velayatlar, singular - velayat) and 1 independent city*:* Ahal Velayat (Arkadag), Ashgabat*, Balkan Velayat (Balkanabat), Dashoguz Velayat, Lebap Velayat (Turkmenabat), Mary Velayat
note: administrative divisions have the same names as their administrative centers (exceptions have the administrative center name following in parentheses)

Independence: 27 October 1991 (from the Soviet Union)

National holiday: Independence Day, 27 October (1991)

Legal system: civil law system with Islamic (sharia) law influences

Constitution: *history:* several previous; latest adopted 14 September 2016
amendments: proposed by the Assembly or Mejlis; passage requires two-thirds majority vote or absolute majority approval in a referendum; amended several times, last in 2023 (changed legislature from bicameral to unicameral Assembly or Mejlis; reestablished People's Council or Halk Maslahaty and named former president Gurbanguly BERDIMUHAMEDOV as National Leader of the Turkmen people

International law organization participation: has not submitted an ICJ jurisdiction declaration; non-party state to the ICCt

Citizenship: *citizenship by birth:* no
citizenship by descent only: at least one parent must be a citizen of Turkmenistan
dual citizenship recognized: yes
residency requirement for naturalization: 7 years

Suffrage: 18 years of age; universal

Executive branch: *chief of state:* President Serdar BERDIMUHAMEDOV (since 19 March 2022)
head of government: President Serdar BERDIMUHAMEDOV (since 19 March 2022)
cabinet: Cabinet of Ministers appointed by the president
elections/appointments: president directly elected by absolute majority popular vote in 2 rounds if needed for a 7-year term (no term limits); election last held on 12 March 2022 (next to be held in 2029); note - on 11 February 2022, President Gurbanguly BERDIMUHAMEDOV announced his intent to retire, setting up the early presidential election
election results:
2022: Serdar BERDIMUHAMEDOV elected president; percent of vote - Serdar BERDIMUHAMEDOW (DPT) 73%, Khydyr NUNNAYEV (independent) 11.1%, Agadzhan BEKMYRADOV (IAP) 7.2%, other 8.7%; note - Serdar BERDIMUHAMEDOV is the son of previous president Gurbanguly BERDIMUHAMEDOV
2017: Gurbanguly BERDIMUHAMEDOV reelected president in the first round; percent of vote - Gurbanguly BERDIMUHAMEDOW (DPT) 97.7%, other 2.3%

note: the president is both chief of state and head of government

Legislative branch: *description:* unicameral Assembly or Mejlis (125 seats; members directly elected in single-seat constituencies by absolute majority vote in 2 rounds if needed to serve 5-year terms); formerly the Assembly was the lower house of the bicameral National Council or Milli Genes, which consisted of an upper house, the People's Council or Halk Maslahaty, and the Assembly or Mejlis
elections: last held on 26 March 2023 (next to be held in 2028)
election results: percent of vote by party - NA; seats by party - DPT 55, APT 11, PIE 11, independent 48 (individuals nominated by citizen groups); composition men 93, women 32, percentage women 25.6%

Judicial branch: *highest court(s):* Supreme Court of Turkmenistan (consists of the court president and 21 associate judges and organized into civil, criminal, and military chambers)
judge selection and term of office: judges appointed by the president for 5-year terms
subordinate courts: High Commercial Court; appellate courts; provincial, district, and city courts; military courts

Political parties: Agrarian Party of Turkmenistan or APT
Democratic Party of Turkmenistan or DPT
Party of Industrialists and Entrepreneurs or PIE
note: all of these parties support President BERDIMUHAMEDOV; a law authorizing the registration of political parties went into effect in January 2012; unofficial, small opposition movements exist abroad

International organization participation: ADB, CIS (associate member, has not ratified the 1993 CIS charter although it participates in meetings and held the chairmanship of the CIS in 2012), EAPC, EBRD, ECO, FAO, G-77, IBRD, ICAO, ICRM, IDA, IDB, IFC, IFRCS, ILO, IMF, IMO, Interpol, IOC, IOM (observer), ISO (correspondent), ITU, MIGA, NAM, OIC, OPCW, OSCE, PFP, UN, UNCTAD, UNESCO, UNHCR, UNIDO, UNWTO, UPU, WCO, WFTU (NGOs), WHO, WIPO, WMO

Diplomatic representation in the US: *chief of mission:* Ambassador Meret ORAZOV (since 14 February 2001)
chancery: 2207 Massachusetts Avenue NW, Washington, DC 20008
telephone: [1] (202) 588-1500
FAX: [1] (202) 588-1500
email address and website:
turkmenembassyus@verizon.net
https://usa.tmembassy.gov.tm/en

Diplomatic representation from the US: *chief of mission:* Ambassador Matthew S. KLIMOW (since 26 June 2019)
embassy: 9 1984 Street (formerly Pushkin Street), Ashgabat 744000
mailing address: 7070 Ashgabat Place, Washington, DC 20521-7070
telephone: [993] (12) 94-00-45
FAX: [993] (12) 94-26-14
email address and website:
ConsularAshgab@state.gov
https://tm.usembassy.gov/

Flag description: green field with a vertical red stripe near the hoist side, containing five tribal guls (designs used in producing carpets) stacked above two crossed olive branches; five white, five-pointed stars and a white crescent moon appear in the upper corner of the field just to the fly side of the red stripe; the green color and crescent moon represent Islam; the five stars symbolize the regions or welayats of Turkmenistan; the guls reflect the national identity of Turkmenistan where carpetmaking has long been a part of traditional nomadic life
note: the flag of Turkmenistan is the most intricate of all national flags

National symbol(s): Akhal-Teke horse; national colors: green, white

National anthem: *name:* "Garassyz, Bitarap Turkmenistanyn" (Independent, Neutral, Turkmenistan State Anthem)
lyrics/music: collective/Veli MUKHATOV
note: adopted 1997, lyrics revised in 2008, to eliminate references to deceased President Saparmurat NYYAZOW

National heritage: *total World Heritage Sites:* 5 (4 cultural, 1 natural)
selected World Heritage Site locales: Ancient Merv (c); Kunya-Urgench (c); Parthian Fortresses of Nisa (c); Cold Winter Deserts of Turan (n); Silk Roads: Zarafshan-Karakum Corridor (c)

ECONOMY

Economic overview: upper middle-income Central Asian economy; has 10% of global natural gas reserves, exporting to Russia and China; natural resource rich; authoritarian and dominated by state-owned enterprises; major central-south Asian pipeline development

Real GDP (purchasing power parity): $94.79 billion (2022 est.)
$93.205 billion (2021 est.)
$89.192 billion (2020 est.)
note: data in 2017 dollars
comparison ranking: 98

Real GDP growth rate: 6.3% (2023 est.)
6.2% (2022 est.)
6.2% (2021 est.)
note: annual GDP % growth based on constant local currency
comparison ranking: 29

Real GDP per capita: $14,700 (2022 est.)
$14,700 (2021 est.)
$14,300 (2020 est.)
note: data in 2017 dollars
comparison ranking: 125

GDP (official exchange rate): $59.887 billion (2023 est.)
note: data in current dollars at official exchange rate

Inflation rate (consumer prices): 8% (2017 est.)
3.6% (2016 est.)
comparison ranking: 156

GDP - composition, by sector of origin: *agriculture:* 11.6% (2022 est.)
industry: 40.6% (2022 est.)
services: 47.8% (2022 est.)
note: figures may not total 100% due to non-allocated consumption not captured in sector-reported data
comparison rankings: services 157; industry 26; agriculture 69

GDP - composition, by end use: *household consumption:* 50% (2017 est.)
government consumption: 9.8% (2022 est.)
investment in fixed capital: 18.3% (2022 est.)
exports of goods and services: 22.2% (2023 est.)
imports of goods and services: -12.9% (2023 est.)
note: figures may not total 100% due to rounding or gaps in data collection

Agricultural products: milk, cotton, wheat, potatoes, watermelons, tomatoes, grapes, beef, sugar beets, lamb/mutton (2022)
note: top ten agricultural products based on tonnage

Industries: natural gas, oil, petroleum products, textiles, food processing

Industrial production growth rate: 4.3% (2014 est.)
note: annual % change in industrial value added based on constant local currency
comparison ranking: 58

Labor force: 2.163 million (2023 est.)
note: number of people ages 15 or older who are employed or seeking work
comparison ranking: 124

Unemployment rate: 4.12% (2023 est.)
4.12% (2022 est.)
4.45% (2021 est.)
note: % of labor force seeking employment
comparison ranking: 78

Youth unemployment rate (ages 15-24): *total:* 9.1% (2023 est.)
male: 13.9% (2023 est.)
female: 5.7% (2023 est.)
note: % of labor force ages 15-24 seeking employment
comparison ranking: total 143

Average household expenditures: *on food:* 36.7% of household expenditures (2022 est.)
on alcohol and tobacco: 2.2% of household expenditures (2022 est.)

Remittances: 0% of GDP (2022 est.)
0% of GDP (2021 est.)
0% of GDP (2020 est.)
note: personal transfers and compensation between resident and non-resident individuals/households/entities

Budget: *revenues:* $5.954 billion (2019 est.)
expenditures: $6.134 billion (2019 est.)

Public debt: 28.8% of GDP (2017 est.)
comparison ranking: 170

Taxes and other revenues: 14.9% (of GDP) (2017 est.)
comparison ranking: 140

Current account balance: -$4.359 billion (2017 est.)
-$7.207 billion (2016 est.)
comparison ranking: 176

Exports: $10.282 billion (2021 est.)
$8.164 billion (2020 est.)
$11.188 billion (2019 est.)
note: GDP expenditure basis - exports of goods and services in current dollars
comparison ranking: 115

Exports - partners: China 71%, Turkey 7%, Uzbekistan 5%, Azerbaijan 4%, Morocco 2% (2022)
note: top five export partners based on percentage share of exports

Exports - commodities: natural gas, refined petroleum, fertilizers, crude petroleum, electricity (2022)
note: top five export commodities based on value in dollars

Imports: $6.25 billion (2021 est.)
$8.301 billion (2020 est.)
$8.844 billion (2019 est.)
note: GDP expenditure basis - imports of goods and services in current dollars

comparison ranking: 141

Imports - partners: UAE 27%, Turkey 24%, China 19%, Kazakhstan 7%, Germany 4% (2022)
note: top five import partners based on percentage share of imports

Imports - commodities: broadcasting equipment, cars, wheat, computers, iron structures (2022)
note: top five import commodities based on value in dollars

Reserves of foreign exchange and gold: $24.91 billion (31 December 2017 est.)
$25.05 billion (31 December 2016 est.)
comparison ranking: 59

Debt - external: $3.729 billion (2022 est.)
note: present value of external debt in current US dollars
comparison ranking: 58

Exchange rates: Turkmenistani manat (TMM) per US dollar -

Exchange rates: 4.125 (2017 est.)
3.5 (2016 est.)
3.5 (2015 est.)
3.5 (2014 est.)

ENERGY

Electricity access: *electrification - total population:* 100% (2022 est.)

Electricity: *installed generating capacity:* 5.202 million kW (2022 est.)
consumption: 16.977 billion kWh (2022 est.)
exports: 3.201 billion kWh (2022 est.)
transmission/distribution losses: 2.892 billion kWh (2022 est.)
comparison rankings: transmission/distribution losses 137; exports 44; consumption 81; installed generating capacity 89

Electricity generation sources: *fossil fuels:* 100% of total installed capacity (2022 est.)

Coal: *imports:* 100 metric tons (2022 est.)
proven reserves: 799.999 million metric tons (2022 est.)

Petroleum: *total petroleum production:* 272,000 bbl/day (2023 est.)
refined petroleum consumption: 152,000 bbl/day (2022 est.)
crude oil estimated reserves: 600 million barrels (2021 est.)

Natural gas: *production:* 86.472 billion cubic meters (2022 est.)
consumption: 41.561 billion cubic meters (2022 est.)
exports: 44.567 billion cubic meters (2022 est.)
proven reserves: 11.327 trillion cubic meters (2021 est.)

Carbon dioxide emissions: 101.442 million metric tonnes of CO_2 (2022 est.)
from petroleum and other liquids: 19.91 million metric tonnes of CO_2 (2022 est.)
from consumed natural gas: 81.532 million metric tonnes of CO_2 (2022 est.)
comparison ranking: total emissions 40

Energy consumption per capita: 282.657 million Btu/person (2022 est.)
comparison ranking: 11

COMMUNICATIONS

Telephones - fixed lines: *total subscriptions:* 802,000 (2021 est.)
subscriptions per 100 inhabitants: 13 (2021 est.)
comparison ranking: total subscriptions 77

Telephones - mobile cellular: *total subscriptions:* 6.255 million (2021 est.)
subscriptions per 100 inhabitants: 99 (2021 est.)
comparison ranking: total subscriptions 116

Telecommunication systems: *general assessment:* the nation of Turkmenistan, which rivals only North Korea for its isolationism, continues to keep its telecom sector along with the broader populace under tight control; the country inched up just one point off the bottom of the world rankings for press and internet freedom in the most recent report from Reporters Without Borders; most social networks in the country are blocked, although locals do have access to the government-developed platform released in 2019; all internet users, however, need to identify themselves before logging on, and strict censorship over what can be viewed is in force; the end result is that Turkmenistan has one of the lowest usage rates for internet access in the world (2024)
domestic: fixed-line is 13 per 100 and mobile-cellular teledensity is 99 per 100 persons (2022)
international: country code - 993; linked by fiber-optic cable and microwave radio relay to other CIS republics and to other countries by leased connections to the Moscow international gateway switch; an exchange in Ashgabat switches international traffic through Turkey via Intelsat; satellite earth stations - 1 Orbita and 1 Intelsat (2018)

Broadcast media: broadcast media is government controlled and censored; 7 state-owned TV and 4 state-owned radio networks; satellite dishes and programming provide an alternative to the state-run media; officials sometimes limit access to satellite TV by removing satellite dishes

Internet country code: .tm

Internet users: *total:* 1,563,023 (2022 est.)
percent of population: 25.3% (2022 est.)
comparison ranking: total 143

Broadband - fixed subscriptions: *total:* 10,000 (2020 est.)
subscriptions per 100 inhabitants: 0.2 (2020 est.)
comparison ranking: total 180

TRANSPORTATION

National air transport system: *number of registered air carriers:* 1 (2020)
inventory of registered aircraft operated by air carriers: 27
annual passenger traffic on registered air carriers: 2,457,474 (2018)
annual freight traffic on registered air carriers: 16.92 million (2018) mt-km

Civil aircraft registration country code prefix: EZ

Airports: 23 (2024)
comparison ranking: 131

Heliports: 25 (2024)

Pipelines: 7,500 km gas, 1501 km oil (2013)

Railways: *total:* 5,113 km (2017)
broad gauge: 5,113 km (2017) 1.520-m gauge
comparison ranking: total 37

Roadways: *total:* 58,592 km
paved: 47,577 km
unpaved: 11,015 km (2002)
comparison ranking: total 82

Waterways: 1,300 km (2011) (Amu Darya River and Kara Kum Canal are important inland waterways)
comparison ranking: 59

Merchant marine: *total:* 73 (2023)
by type: general cargo 6, oil tanker 8, other 59
comparison ranking: total 106

MILITARY AND SECURITY

Military and security forces: Armed Forces of Turkmenistan (aka Turkmen National Army): Land Forces, Navy, Air and Air Defense Forces

Ministry of Internal Affairs: Internal Troops, national police, Federal/State Border Guard Service (2024)

Military expenditures: 1.9% of GDP (2019 est.)
1.8% of GDP (2018 est.)
1.8% of GDP (2017 est.)
1.8% of GDP (2016 est.)
1.5% of GDP (2015 est.)
comparison ranking: 75

Military and security service personnel strengths: information varies; estimated 35,000 active-duty troops (30,000 Army; 1,000 Navy; 4,000 Air and Air Defense Forces) (2023)

Military equipment inventories and acquisitions: the military's inventory is comprised largely of Russian and Soviet-era weapons systems; in recent years, Turkmenistan has attempted to diversify the military's equipment holdings with acquisitions from more than a dozen countries, including China, Italy, and Turkey (2023)

Military service age and obligation: 18-27 years of age for compulsory military service for men; 24-month conscript service obligation (30 months for the Navy); 20 years of age for voluntary service for men and women; men may enroll in military schools from age 15 (2023)

Military - note: the military is responsible for external defense and works closely with the Border Service on protecting the country's borders; while Turkmenistan has a policy of permanent and "positive" neutrality and has declined to participate in post-Soviet military groupings such as the Collective Security Treaty Organization and the Shanghai Cooperation Organization, it has participated in multinational exercises and bilateral training with neighboring countries, including Russia and Uzbekistan; Turkmenistan joined NATO's Partnership for Peace program in 1994, but it does not offer any military forces to NATO-led operations
in recent years, Turkmenistan has made efforts to strengthen its naval capabilities on the Caspian Sea, including expanding ship building capabilities, building a new naval base, and adding larger vessels to the Navy's inventory; in 2018, Turkmenistan opened its first naval shipyard, and in 2021 the Navy commissioned its largest warship, a corvette that was jointly constructed with Turkey, to complement a small existing force of coastal patrol craft (2023)

SPACE

Space agency/agencies: Turkmenistan National Space Agency (established 2011; in 2019, was transferred to the Space Directorate of Turkmenaragatnashik Agency) (2024)

Space program overview: has a small space program focused on acquiring satellites and developing the

infrastructure to build and operate satellites; particularly interested in remote sensing satellites for such purposes as monitoring its agricultural and transportation sectors, the oil and natural gas industry, and the ecology of the Caspian Sea; has cooperated with the space agencies and/or space industries of France, Italy, Russia, South Korea, and the US (2024)
note: further details about the key activities, programs, and milestones of the country's space program, as well as government spending estimates on the space sector, appear in the Space Programs reference guide

TRANSNATIONAL ISSUES

Refugees and internally displaced persons: *stateless persons:* 4,463 (2022)

Trafficking in persons: tier rating: Tier 3 — Turkmenistan does not fully meet the minimum standards for the elimination of trafficking and is not making significant efforts to do so, therefore, Turkmenistan remained on Tier 3; for more details, go to: https:// www.state.gov/reports/2024-trafficking-in-persons-report/turkmenistan/

Illicit drugs: transit country for Afghan opiates to Turkish, Russian, and European markets, either directly from Afghanistan or through Iran; not a major producer or source country for illegal drugs or precursor chemicals

TURKS AND CAICOS ISLANDS

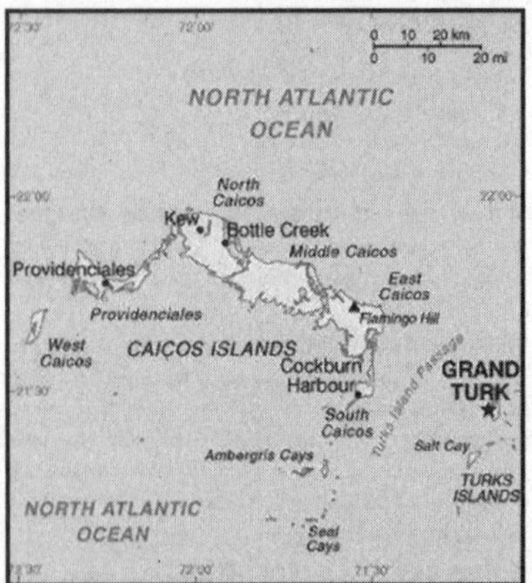

INTRODUCTION

Background: The islands were part of the UK's Jamaican colony until 1962, when they assumed the status of a separate Crown colony upon Jamaica's independence. The governor of The Bahamas oversaw affairs from 1965 to 1973. With Bahamian independence, the islands received a separate governor in 1973. Although independence was agreed upon for 1982, the policy was reversed, and the islands remain a British overseas territory. Grand Turk Island suffered extensive damage from Hurricane Maria in 2017.

GEOGRAPHY

Location: two island groups in the North Atlantic Ocean, southeast of The Bahamas, north of Haiti; note - although the Turks and Caicos Islands do not border the Caribbean Sea, geopolitically they are often designated as being Caribbean

Geographic coordinates: 21 45 N, 71 35 W

Map references: Central America and the Caribbean

Area: *total:* 948 sq km
land: 948 sq km
water: 0 sq km
comparison ranking: total 185

Area - comparative: 2.5 times the size of Washington, DC

Land boundaries: *total:* 0 km

Coastline: 389 km

Maritime claims: *territorial sea:* 12 nm
exclusive fishing zone: 200 nm

Climate: tropical; marine; moderated by trade winds; sunny and relatively dry

Terrain: low, flat limestone; extensive marshes and mangrove swamps

Elevation: *highest point:* Blue Hill on Providenciales and Flamingo Hill on East Caicos 48 m
lowest point: Caribbean Sea 0 m

Natural resources: spiny lobster, conch

Land use: *agricultural land:* 1.1% (2018 est.)
arable land: 1.1% (2018 est.)
permanent crops: 0% (2018 est.)
permanent pasture: 0% (2018 est.)
forest: 36.2% (2018 est.)
other: 62.7% (2018 est.)

Irrigated land: 0 sq km (2022)

Population distribution: eight of the thirty islands are inhabited; the island of Providenciales is the most populated, but the most densely populated is Grand Turk

Natural hazards: frequent hurricanes

Geography - note: include eight large islands and numerous smaller cays, islets, and reefs; only two of the Caicos Islands and six of the Turks group are inhabited

PEOPLE AND SOCIETY

Population: *total:* 60,439
male: 30,389
female: 30,050 (2024 est.)
comparison rankings: female 205; male 205; total 205

Nationality: *noun:* none
adjective: none

Ethnic groups: Black 87.6%, White 7.9%, mixed 2.5%, East Indian 1.3%, other 0.7% (2006 est.)

Languages: English (official)

Religions: Protestant 72.8% (Baptist 35.8%, Church of God 11.7%, Anglican 10%, Methodist 9.3%, Seventh Day Adventist 6%), Roman Catholic 11.4%, Jehovah's Witness 1.8%, other 14% (2006 est.)

Age structure: *0-14 years:* 20.4% (male 6,288/female 6,056)
15-64 years: 73.2% (male 22,232/female 22,011)
65 years and over: 6.4% (2024 est.) (male 1,869/female 1,983)

Dependency ratios: *total dependency ratio:* 36.8
youth dependency ratio: 22.9
elderly dependency ratio: 13.9
potential support ratio: 7.2 (2021)

Median age: *total:* 36.3 years (2024 est.)
male: 36.5 years
female: 36.1 years
comparison ranking: total 93

Population growth rate: 1.77% (2024 est.)
comparison ranking: 49

Birth rate: 13 births/1,000 population (2024 est.)
comparison ranking: 133

Death rate: 3.6 deaths/1,000 population (2024 est.)
comparison ranking: 219

Net migration rate: 8.3 migrant(s)/1,000 population (2024 est.)
comparison ranking: 10

Population distribution: eight of the thirty islands are inhabited; the island of Providenciales is the most populated, but the most densely populated is Grand Turk

Urbanization: *urban population:* 94.2% of total population (2023)
rate of urbanization: 1.46% annual rate of change (2020-25 est.)

Major urban areas - population: 5,000 GRAND TURK (capital) (2018)

Sex ratio: *at birth:* 1.05 male(s)/female
0-14 years: 1.04 male(s)/female
15-64 years: 1.01 male(s)/female
65 years and over: 0.94 male(s)/female
total population: 1.01 male(s)/female (2024 est.)

Infant mortality rate: *total:* 11.1 deaths/1,000 live births (2024 est.)
male: 13.9 deaths/1,000 live births
female: 8.1 deaths/1,000 live births
comparison ranking: total 122

Life expectancy at birth: *total population:* 81.3 years (2024 est.)
male: 78.5 years
female: 84.1 years
comparison ranking: total population 44

Total fertility rate: 1.7 children born/woman (2024 est.)
comparison ranking: 164

Gross reproduction rate: 0.83 (2024 est.)

Contraceptive prevalence rate: 34.4% (2019/20)

Drinking water source: *improved: total:* 94.3% of population
unimproved: total: 5.7% of population (2017)

Sanitation facility access: *improved:*

total: 88% of population
unimproved:
total: 12% of population (2017)

Children under the age of 5 years underweight: 0.4% (2019/20)
comparison ranking: 123

Currently married women (ages 15-49): 59.1% (2023 est.)

Child marriage: *women married by age 18:* 23.3%
men married by age 18: 5.1% (2020 est.)

Education expenditures: 4.5% of GDP (2021 est.)
comparison ranking: 99

School life expectancy (primary to tertiary education): *total:* 9 years

People - note: destination and transit point for illegal Haitian immigrants bound for the Bahamas and the US

ENVIRONMENT

Environment - current issues: limited natural freshwater resources, private cisterns collect rainwater

Climate: tropical; marine; moderated by trade winds; sunny and relatively dry

Urbanization: *urban population:* 94.2% of total population (2023)
rate of urbanization: 1.46% annual rate of change (2020-25 est.)

Revenue from forest resources: 0% of GDP (2018 est.)
comparison ranking: 166

Revenue from coal: 0% of GDP (2018 est.)
comparison ranking: 186

Air pollutants: *carbon dioxide emissions:* 0.22 megatons (2016 est.)

GOVERNMENT

Country name: *conventional long form:* none
conventional short form: Turks and Caicos Islands
abbreviation: TCI
etymology: the Turks Islands are named after the Turk's cap cactus (native to the islands and appearing on the flag and coat of arms), while the Caicos Islands derive from the native term "caya hico" meaning "string of islands"

Government type: parliamentary democracy

Dependency status: overseas territory of the UK

Capital: *name:* Grand Turk (Cockburn Town)
geographic coordinates: 21 28 N, 71 08 W
time difference: UTC-5 (same time as Washington, DC, during Standard Time)
etymology: named after Sir Francis COCKBURN, who served as governor of the Bahamas from 1837 to 1844

Administrative divisions: none (overseas territory of the UK)

Independence: none (overseas territory of the UK)

National holiday: Birthday of Queen ELIZABETH II, usually celebrated the Monday after the second Saturday in June

Legal system: mixed legal system of English common law and civil law

Constitution: *history:* several previous; latest signed 7 August 2012, effective 15 October 2012 (The Turks and Caicos Constitution Order 2011)
amendments: NA

Citizenship: see United Kingdom

Suffrage: 18 years of age; universal

Executive branch: *chief of state:* King CHARLES III (since 8 September 2022); represented by Governor Dileeni Daniel-SELVARATNAM (since 29 June 2023)
head of government: Premier Washington MISICK (since 19 February 2021)
cabinet: Cabinet appointed by the governor from among members of the House of Assembly
elections/appointments: the monarch is hereditary; governor appointed by the monarch; following legislative elections, the leader of the majority party is appointed premier by the governor

Legislative branch: *description:* unicameral House of Assembly (21 seats; 15 members in multi-seat constituencies and a single all-islands constituency directly elected by simple majority vote, 1 member nominated by the premier and appointed by the governor, 1 nominated by the opposition party leader and appointed by the governor, and 2 from the Turks and Caicos Islands Civic Society directly appointed by the governor, and 2 ex-officio members; members serve 4-year terms)
elections: last held on 19 February 2021 (next to be held in 2025)
election results: percent of vote - NA; seats by party - PNP 14, PDM 1; composition - men 11, women 3, percentage women 27.3%

Judicial branch: *highest court(s):* Supreme Court (consists of the chief justice and other judges, as determined by the governor); Court of Appeal (consists of the court president and 2 justices); note - appeals beyond the Supreme Court are referred to the Judicial Committee of the Privy Council (in London)
judge selection and term of office: Supreme Court and Appeals Court judges appointed by the governor in accordance with the Judicial Service Commission, a 3-member body of high-level judicial officials; Supreme Court judges serve until mandatory retirement at age 65, but terms can be extended to age 70; Appeals Court judge tenure determined by individual terms of appointment
subordinate courts: magistrates' courts

Political parties: People's Democratic Movement or PDM
Progressive National Party or PNP

International organization participation: Caricom (associate), CDB, Interpol (subbureau), UPU

Diplomatic representation in the US: none (overseas territory of the UK)

Diplomatic representation from the US: *embassy:* none (overseas territory of the UK)

Flag description: blue with the flag of the UK in the upper hoist-side quadrant and the colonial shield centered on the outer half of the flag; the shield is yellow and displays a conch shell, a spiny lobster, and Turk's cap cactus - three common elements of the islands' biota

National symbol(s): conch shell, Turk's cap cactus

National anthem: *name:* "This Land of Ours"
lyrics/music: Conrad HOWELL
note: serves as a local anthem; as an overseas territory of the UK, "God Save the King" is the official anthem (see United Kingdom)

ECONOMY

Economic overview: British Caribbean island territorial economy; GDP and its tourism industry hit hard by COVID-19 disruptions; major biodiversity locale; US dollar user; fossil fuel dependent; negative trade balance; increasing unemployment

Real GDP (purchasing power parity): $1.03 billion (2023 est.)
$1.018 billion (2022 est.)
$958.811 million (2021 est.)
note: data in 2021 dollars
comparison ranking: 209

Real GDP growth rate: 1.2% (2023 est.)
6.2% (2022 est.)
9.03% (2021 est.)
note: annual GDP % growth based on constant local currency
comparison ranking: 160

Real GDP per capita: $22,400 (2023 est.)
$22,300 (2022 est.)
$21,300 (2021 est.)
note: data in 2021 dollars
comparison ranking: 93

GDP (official exchange rate): $1.402 billion (2023 est.)
note: data in current dollars at official exchange rate

Inflation rate (consumer prices): 4% (2017 est.)
0.7% (2016 est.)
comparison ranking: 80

GDP - composition, by sector of origin: *agriculture:* 0.4% (2016 est.)
industry: 9.5% (2016 est.)
services: 77.9% (2016 est.)
note: figures may not total 100% due to non-allocated consumption not captured in sector-reported data
comparison rankings: services 20; industry 196; agriculture 200

GDP - composition, by end use: *household consumption:* 49% (2017 est.)
government consumption: 21.5% (2017 est.)
investment in fixed capital: 16.5% (2017 est.)
investment in inventories: -0.1% (2017 est.)
exports of goods and services: 69.5% (2017 est.)
imports of goods and services: -56.4% (2017 est.)

Agricultural products: corn, beans, cassava (manioc, tapioca), citrus fruits; fish

Industries: tourism, offshore financial services

Industrial production growth rate: 5.84% (2016 est.)
note: annual % change in industrial value added based on constant local currency
comparison ranking: 43

Remittances: 0% of GDP (2023 est.)
0% of GDP (2022 est.)
0% of GDP (2021 est.)
note: personal transfers and compensation between resident and non-resident individuals/households/entities

Budget: *revenues:* $247.3 million (2017 est.)
expenditures: $224.3 million (2017 est.)

Current account balance: $172.709 million (2018 est.)
$35.016 million (2017 est.)
$247.081 million (2016 est.)
note: balance of payments - net trade and primary/secondary income in current dollars

comparison ranking: 68

Exports: $826.824 million (2018 est.)
$602.581 million (2017 est.)
$741.173 million (2016 est.)
note: balance of payments - exports of goods and services in current dollars
comparison ranking: 185

Exports - partners: Togo 61%, US 13%, Zimbabwe 6%, Democratic Republic of the Congo 3%, Central African Republic 2% (2022)
note: top five export partners based on percentage share of exports

Exports - commodities: fertilizers, shellfish, plastics, sulfur, soybean oil (2022)
note: top five export commodities based on value in dollars

Imports: $544.219 million (2018 est.)
$484.842 million (2017 est.)
$438.041 million (2016 est.)
note: balance of payments - imports of goods and services in current dollars
comparison ranking: 203

Imports - partners: US 75%, Dominican Republic 6%, Italy 3%, Switzerland 2%, China 2% (2022)
note: top five import partners based on percentage share of imports

Imports - commodities: refined petroleum, cars, plastic products, furniture, aluminum structures (2022)
note: top five import commodities based on value in dollars

Exchange rates: the US dollar is used

ENERGY

Electricity access: *electrification - total population:* 99.9% (2022 est.)
electrification - urban areas: 100%
electrification - rural areas: 100%

Electricity: *installed generating capacity:* 91,000 kW (2022 est.)
consumption: 249.998 million kWh (2022 est.)
transmission/distribution losses: 13 million kWh (2022 est.)
comparison rankings: transmission/distribution losses 20; consumption 187; installed generating capacity 187

Electricity generation sources: *fossil fuels:* 99.5% of total installed capacity (2022 est.)
solar: 0.5% of total installed capacity (2022 est.)

Petroleum: *refined petroleum consumption:* 2,000 bbl/day (2022 est.)

Carbon dioxide emissions: 244,000 metric tonnes of CO2 (2022 est.)
from petroleum and other liquids: 244,000 metric tonnes of CO2 (2022 est.)
comparison ranking: total emissions 203

Energy consumption per capita: (2019)

COMMUNICATIONS

Telephones - fixed lines: *total subscriptions:* 4,000 (2021 est.)
subscriptions per 100 inhabitants: 9 (2021 est.)
comparison ranking: total subscriptions 208

Telephones - mobile cellular: *total subscriptions:* 25,085 (2004 est.)
subscriptions per 100 inhabitants: 110 (2004 est.)
comparison ranking: total subscriptions 213

Telecommunication systems: *general assessment:* is connected to the internet via a single submarine fiber-optic cable (Arcos-1), which links the US and several Caribbean countries (2023)
domestic: fixed-line teledensity is 9 per 100 persons (2021)
international: country code - 1-649; landing point for the ARCOS fiber-optic telecommunications submarine cable providing connectivity to South and Central America, parts of the Caribbean, and the US; satellite earth station - 1 Intelsat (Atlantic Ocean) (2020)

Broadcast media: no local terrestrial TV stations, broadcasts from the Bahamas can be received and multi-channel cable and satellite TV services are available; government-run radio network operates alongside private broadcasters with a total of about 15 stations

Internet country code: .tc

Internet users: *total:* 37,008 (2022)
percent of population: 93.5% (2022)
comparison ranking: total 207

TRANSPORTATION

National air transport system: *number of registered air carriers:* 3 (2020)
inventory of registered aircraft operated by air carriers: 22

Civil aircraft registration country code prefix: VQ-T

Airports: 9 (2024)
comparison ranking: 163

Roadways: *total:* 121 km
paved: 24 km
unpaved: 97 km (2003)
comparison ranking: total 213

Merchant marine: *total:* 3 (2023)
by type: general cargo 1, other 2
comparison ranking: total 174

Ports: *total ports:* 3 (2024)
large: 0
medium: 0
small: 0
very small: 2
size unknown: 1
ports with oil terminals: 1
key ports: Cockburn Harbor, Grand Turk, Providenciales

MILITARY AND SECURITY

Military - note: defense is the responsibility of the UK

TRANSNATIONAL ISSUES

Illicit drugs: transshipment point for South American narcotics destined for the US and Europe

TUVALU

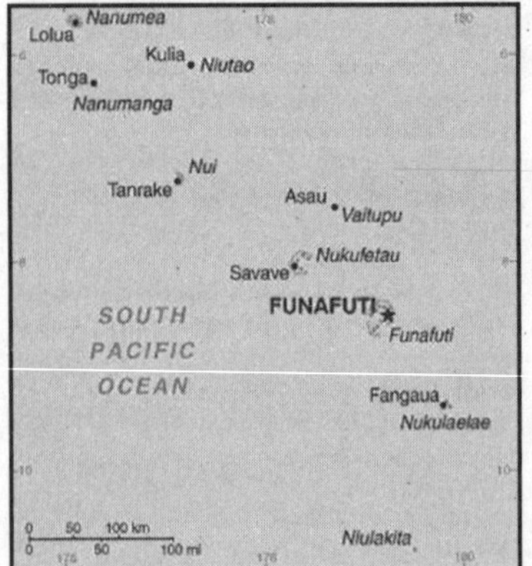

INTRODUCTION

Background: Voyagers from either Samoa or Tonga first populated Tuvalu in the first millennium A.D., and the islands provided a stepping-stone for various Polynesian communities that subsequently settled in Melanesia and Micronesia. Tuvalu eventually came under Samoan and Tongan spheres of influence, although proximity to Micronesia allowed some Micronesian communities to flourish in Tuvalu, in particular on Nui Atoll. In the late 1700s and early 1800s, a series of American, British, Dutch, and Russian ships visited the islands, which were named the Ellice Islands in 1819.

The UK declared a protectorate over islands in 1892 and merged them with the Micronesian Gilbert Islands. The Gilbert and Ellice Islands Protectorate became a colony in 1916. During World War II, the US set up military bases on a few islands, and in 1943, after Japan captured many of the northern Gilbert Islands, the UK transferred administration of the colony southward to Funafuti. After the war, Tarawa in the Gilbert Islands was once again made the colony's capital, and the center of power was firmly in the Gilbert Islands, including the colony's only secondary school. Amid growing tensions with the Gilbertese, Tuvaluans voted to secede from the colony in 1974, were granted self-rule in 1975, and gained independence in 1978 as Tuvalu. In 1979, the US relinquished its claims to the Tuvaluan islands in a treaty of friendship.

GEOGRAPHY

Location: Oceania, island group consisting of nine coral atolls in the South Pacific Ocean, about half way from Hawaii to Australia

Geographic coordinates: 8 00 S, 178 00 E

Map references: Oceania

Area: *total:* 26 sq km
land: 26 sq km
water: 0 sq km
comparison ranking: total 236

Area - comparative: 0.1 times the size of Washington, DC

Land boundaries: *total:* 0 km

Coastline: 24 km

Maritime claims: *territorial sea:* 12 nm
contiguous zone: 24 nm
exclusive economic zone: 200 nm

Climate: tropical; moderated by easterly trade winds (March to November); westerly gales and heavy rain (November to March)

Terrain: low-lying and narrow coral atolls

Elevation: *highest point:* unnamed location 5 m
lowest point: Pacific Ocean 0 m
mean elevation: 2 m

Natural resources: fish, coconut (copra)

Land use: *agricultural land:* 60% (2018 est.)
arable land: 0% (2018 est.)
permanent crops: 60% (2018 est.)
permanent pasture: 0% (2018 est.)
forest: 33.3% (2018 est.)
other: 6.7% (2018 est.)

Irrigated land: 0 sq km (2022)

Population distribution: over half of the population resides on the atoll of Funafuti

Natural hazards: severe tropical storms are usually rare, but in 1997 there were three cyclones; low levels of islands make them sensitive to changes in sea level

Geography - note: one of the smallest and most remote countries on Earth; six of the nine coral atolls – Nanumea, Nui, Vaitupu, Nukufetau, Funafuti, and Nukulaelae – have lagoons open to the ocean; Nanumaya and Niutao have landlocked lagoons; Niulakita does not have a lagoon

PEOPLE AND SOCIETY

Population: *total:* 11,733
male: 5,816
female: 5,917 (2024 est.)
comparison rankings: female 221; male 221; total 221

Nationality: *noun:* Tuvaluan(s)
adjective: Tuvaluan

Ethnic groups: Tuvaluan 97%, Tuvaluan/I-Kiribati 1.6%, Tuvaluan/other 0.8%, other 0.6% (2017 est.)

Languages: Tuvaluan (official), English (official), Samoan, Kiribati (on the island of Nui)

Religions: Protestant 92.7% (Congregational Christian Church of Tuvalu 85.9%, Brethren 2.8%, Seventh Day Adventist 2.5%, Assemblies of God 1.5%), Baha'i 1.5%, Jehovah's Witness 1.5%, other 3.9%, none or refused 0.4% (2017 est.)

Age structure: *0-14 years:* 29.2% (male 1,754/female 1,672)
15-64 years: 63.2% (male 3,736/female 3,675)
65 years and over: 7.6% (2024 est.) (male 326/female 570)

Dependency ratios: *total dependency ratio:* 60.9
youth dependency ratio: 50.9
elderly dependency ratio: 10
potential support ratio: 10 (2021)

Median age: *total:* 27.8 years (2024 est.)
male: 26.8 years
female: 28.8 years
comparison ranking: total 155

Population growth rate: 0.78% (2024 est.)
comparison ranking: 112

Birth rate: 22 births/1,000 population (2024 est.)
comparison ranking: 55

Death rate: 7.8 deaths/1,000 population (2024 est.)
comparison ranking: 94

Net migration rate: -6.3 migrant(s)/1,000 population (2024 est.)
comparison ranking: 212

Population distribution: over half of the population resides on the atoll of Funafuti

Urbanization: *urban population:* 66.2% of total population (2023)
rate of urbanization: 2.08% annual rate of change (2020-25 est.)

Major urban areas - population: 7,000 FUNAFUTI (capital) (2018)

Sex ratio: *at birth:* 1.05 male(s)/female
0-14 years: 1.05 male(s)/female
15-64 years: 1.02 male(s)/female
65 years and over: 0.57 male(s)/female
total population: 0.98 male(s)/female (2024 est.)

Infant mortality rate: *total:* 27.8 deaths/1,000 live births (2024 est.)
male: 31.3 deaths/1,000 live births
female: 24 deaths/1,000 live births
comparison ranking: total 56

Life expectancy at birth: *total population:* 69 years (2024 est.)
male: 66.5 years
female: 71.6 years
comparison ranking: total population 184

Total fertility rate: 2.78 children born/woman (2024 est.)
comparison ranking: 55

Gross reproduction rate: 1.36 (2024 est.)

Contraceptive prevalence rate: 23.7% (2019/20)

Drinking water source: *improved: urban:* 100% of population
rural: 100% of population
total: 100% of population

Current health expenditure: 21.5% of GDP (2020)

Physician density: 1.19 physicians/1,000 population (2020)

Sanitation facility access: *improved: urban:* 91.8% of population
rural: 91% of population
total: 91.5% of population
unimproved: urban: 9.2% of population
rural: 9% of population
total: 8.5% of population (2017 est.)

Obesity - adult prevalence rate: 51.6% (2016)
comparison ranking: 5

Alcohol consumption per capita: *total:* 0.93 liters of pure alcohol (2019 est.)
beer: 0.01 liters of pure alcohol (2019 est.)
wine: 0.69 liters of pure alcohol (2019 est.)
spirits: 0.22 liters of pure alcohol (2019 est.)
other alcohols: 0 liters of pure alcohol (2019 est.)
comparison ranking: total 154

Tobacco use: *total:* 35.6% (2020 est.)
male: 49.8% (2020 est.)
female: 21.3% (2020 est.)
comparison ranking: total 13

Children under the age of 5 years underweight: 3.1% (2019/20) NA
comparison ranking: 87

Currently married women (ages 15-49): 66.1% (2023 est.)

Child marriage: *women married by age 18:* 1.8%
men married by age 18: 1.7% (2020 est.)

ENVIRONMENT

Environment - current issues: water needs met by catchment systems; the use of sand as a building material has led to beachhead erosion; deforestation; damage to coral reefs from increasing ocean temperatures and acidification; rising sea levels threaten water table; in 2000, the government appealed to Australia and New Zealand to take in Tuvaluans if rising sea levels should make evacuation necessary

Environment - international agreements: *party to:* Biodiversity, Climate Change, Climate Change-Kyoto Protocol, Climate Change-Paris Agreement, Desertification, Hazardous Wastes, Law of the Sea, Ozone Layer Protection, Ship Pollution, Whaling
signed, but not ratified: Comprehensive Nuclear Test Ban

Climate: tropical; moderated by easterly trade winds (March to November); westerly gales and heavy rain (November to March)

Urbanization: *urban population:* 66.2% of total population (2023)
rate of urbanization: 2.08% annual rate of change (2020-25 est.)

Revenue from forest resources: 0% of GDP (2018 est.)
comparison ranking: 168

Air pollutants: *particulate matter emissions:* 6.81 micrograms per cubic meter (2019 est.)
carbon dioxide emissions: 0.01 megatons (2016 est.)
methane emissions: 0.01 megatons (2020 est.)

Waste and recycling: *municipal solid waste generated annually:* 3,989 tons (2011 est.)
municipal solid waste recycled annually: 598 tons (2013 est.)
percent of municipal solid waste recycled: 15% (2013 est.)

Total renewable water resources: 0 cubic meters (2017 est.)

GOVERNMENT

Country name: *conventional long form:* none
conventional short form: Tuvalu
local long form: none
local short form: Tuvalu
former: Ellice Islands
etymology: "tuvalu" means "group of eight" or "eight standing together" referring to the country's eight traditionally inhabited islands

Government type: parliamentary democracy under a constitutional monarchy; a Commonwealth realm

Capital: *name:* Funafuti; note - the capital is an atoll of some 29 islets; administrative offices are in Vaiaku Village on Fongafale Islet
geographic coordinates: 8 31 S, 179 13 E
time difference: UTC+12 (17 hours ahead of Washington, DC, during Standard Time)
etymology: the atoll is named after a founding ancestor chief, Funa, from the island of Samoa

Administrative divisions: 7 island councils and 1 town council*; Funafuti*, Nanumaga, Nanumea, Niutao, Nui, Nukufetau, Nukulaelae, Vaitupu

Independence: 1 October 1978 (from the UK)

National holiday: Independence Day, 1 October (1978)

Legal system: mixed legal system of English common law and local customary law

Constitution: *history:* previous 1978 (at independence); latest effective 1 October 1986
amendments: proposed by the House of Assembly; passage requires at least two-thirds majority vote by the Assembly membership in the final reading; amended 2007, 2010, 2013, 2023

International law organization participation: has not submitted an ICJ jurisdiction declaration; non-party state to the ICCt

Citizenship: *citizenship by birth:* yes
citizenship by descent only: yes; for a child born abroad, at least one parent must be a citizen of Tuvalu
dual citizenship recognized: yes
residency requirement for naturalization: na

Suffrage: 18 years of age; universal

Executive branch: *chief of state:* King CHARLES III (since 8 September 2022); represented by Governor General Tofiga Vaevalu FALANI (since 29 August 2021)
head of government: Prime Minister Feleti Penitala TEO (since 27 February 2024)
cabinet: Cabinet appointed by the governor general on recommendation of the prime minister
elections/appointments: the monarchy is hereditary; governor general appointed by the monarch on recommendation of the prime minister; prime minister and deputy prime minister elected by and from members of House of Assembly following parliamentary elections
election results: 2024: TEO was the only candidate nominated by the House of Assembly
2019: Kausea NATANO elected prime minister by House of Assembly; House of Assembly vote - 10 to 6

Legislative branch: *description:* unicameral House of Assembly or Fale I Fono (16 seats; members directly elected in single- and multiseat constituencies by simple majority vote to serve 4-year terms)
elections: last held on 26 January 2024 (next to be held in January 2028)
election results: percent of vote - NA; seats - independent 16; composition - 16 men, 0 women, percentage women 0%

Judicial branch: *highest court(s):* Court of Appeal (consists of the chief justice and not less than 3 appeals judges); High Court (consists of the chief justice); appeals beyond the Court of Appeal are heard by the Judicial Committee of the Privy Council (in London)
judge selection and term of office: Court of Appeal judges appointed by the governor general on the advice of the Cabinet; judge tenure based on terms of appointment; High Court chief justice appointed by the governor general on the advice of the Cabinet; chief justice serves for life; other judges appointed by the governor general on the advice of the Cabinet after consultation with chief justice; judge tenure set by terms of appointment
subordinate courts: magistrates' courts; island courts; land courts

Political parties: there are no political parties, but members of parliament usually align themselves in informal groupings

International organization participation: ACP, ADB, AOSIS, C, FAO, IBRD, IDA, IFAD, IFRCS (observer), ILO, IMF, IMO, IOC, ITU, OPCW, PIF, Sparteca, SPC, UN, UNCTAD, UNESCO, UNIDO, UPU, WHO, WIPO, WMO

Diplomatic representation in the US: *chief of mission:* Ambassador Tapugao FALEFOU (since 19 April 2023); note - also Permanent Representative to UN
chancery: 685 Third Avenue, Suite 1104, New York, NY 10017
telephone: [1] (212) 490-0534
FAX: [1] (212) 808-4975
email address and website:
tuvalumission.un@gmail.com
tuvalu.unmission@gov.tv
https://www.un.int/tuvalu/about
note - the Tuvalu Permanent Mission to the UN serves as the Embassy

Diplomatic representation from the US: *embassy:* the US does not have an embassy in Tuvalu; the US Ambassador to Fiji is accredited to Tuvalu

Flag description: light blue with the flag of the UK in the upper hoist-side quadrant; the outer half of the flag represents a map of the country with nine yellow, five-pointed stars on a blue field symbolizing the nine atolls in the ocean

National symbol(s): maneapa (native meeting house); national colors: light blue, yellow

National anthem: *name:* "Tuvalu mo te Atua" (Tuvalu for the Almighty)
lyrics/music: Afaese MANOA
note: adopted 1978; the anthem's name is also the nation's motto

ECONOMY

Economic overview: upper middle-income Pacific island economy; extremely environmentally fragile; currency pegged to Australian dollar; large international aid recipient; subsistence agrarian sector; Te Kakeega sustainable development; domain name licensing incomes

Real GDP (purchasing power parity): $59.202 million (2023 est.)
$57.006 million (2022 est.)
$56.622 million (2021 est.)
note: data in 2021 dollars
comparison ranking: 222

Real GDP growth rate: 3.85% (2023 est.)
0.68% (2022 est.)
1.8% (2021 est.)
note: annual GDP % growth based on constant local currency
comparison ranking: 82

Real GDP per capita: $5,200 (2023 est.)
$5,000 (2022 est.)
$5,100 (2021 est.)
note: data in 2021 dollars
comparison ranking: 177

GDP (official exchange rate): $62.28 million (2023 est.)
note: data in current dollars at official exchange rate

Inflation rate (consumer prices): 4.1% (2017 est.)
3.5% (2016 est.)
comparison ranking: 84

GDP - composition, by sector of origin: *agriculture:* 15.9% (2015 est.)
industry: 7% (2015 est.)
services: 70% (2012 est.)
note: figures may not total 100% due to non-allocated consumption not captured in sector-reported data
comparison rankings: industry 208; agriculture 54; services 38

Agricultural products: coconuts, vegetables, tropical fruits, bananas, root vegetables, pork, chicken, eggs, pork fat, pork offal (2022)
note: top ten agricultural products based on tonnage

Industries: fishing

Industrial production growth rate: 4.3% (2014 est.)
note: annual % change in industrial value added based on constant local currency
comparison ranking: 62

Labor force: 3,615
comparison ranking: 205

Youth unemployment rate (ages 15-24): *total:* 20.6% (2016)
male: 9.8%
female: 45.9%
comparison ranking: total 61

Remittances: 4.82% of GDP (2023 est.)
4.18% of GDP (2022 est.)
4.9% of GDP (2021 est.)
note: personal transfers and compensation between resident and non-resident individuals/households/entities

Budget: *revenues:* $87 million (2019 est.)
expenditures: $88 million (2019 est.)
note: revenue data include Official Development Assistance from Australia

Public debt: 37% of GDP (2017 est.)
comparison ranking: 141

Current account balance: $2.713 million (2022 est.)
$14.533 million (2021 est.)
$8.46 million (2020 est.)
note: balance of payments - net trade and primary/secondary income in current dollars
comparison ranking: 80

Exports: $2.232 million (2022 est.)
$2.745 million (2021 est.)
$3.089 million (2020 est.)
note: balance of payments - exports of goods and services in current dollars
comparison ranking: 221

Exports - partners: Thailand 69%, Croatia 21%, Philippines 4%, South Korea 2%, Japan 1% (2022)
note: top five export partners based on percentage share of exports

Exports - commodities: fish, ships, computers, integrated circuits, nitrile compounds (2022)
note: top five export commodities based on value in dollars

Imports: $57.388 million (2022 est.)
$63.962 million (2021 est.)
$56.947 million (2020 est.)
note: balance of payments - imports of goods and services in current dollars
comparison ranking: 217

Imports - partners: China 34%, Japan 27%, Fiji 20%, NZ 5%, Australia 5% (2022)
note: top five import partners based on percentage share of imports

Imports - commodities: ships, refined petroleum, iron structures, engine parts, plastic products (2022)
note: top five import commodities based on value in dollars

Exchange rates: Tuvaluan dollars or Australian dollars (AUD) per US dollar -

Exchange rates: 1.505 (2023 est.)
1.442 (2022 est.)
1.331 (2021 est.)
1.453 (2020 est.)
1.439 (2019 est.)

ENERGY

Electricity access: *electrification - total population:* 100% (2022 est.)
electrification - urban areas: 100%
electrification - rural areas: 99.1%

Energy consumption per capita: (2019)

COMMUNICATIONS

Telephones - fixed lines: *total subscriptions:* 2,000 (2021 est.)
subscriptions per 100 inhabitants: 18 (2021 est.)
comparison ranking: total subscriptions 216

Telephones - mobile cellular: *total subscriptions:* 9,000 (2021 est.)
subscriptions per 100 inhabitants: 80 (2021 est.)
comparison ranking: total subscriptions 220

Telecommunication systems: *general assessment:* provides fixed-line telephone communications to subscribers on each of the islands of Tuvalu; each island relies on the use of a satellite dish for inter-island telephone communication, internet access, and mobile phone services (2023)
domestic: fixed-line teledensity is 18 per 100 and mobile-cellular is 80 per 100 (2021)
international: country code - 688; international calls can be made by satellite

Broadcast media: no TV stations; many households use satellite dishes to watch foreign TV stations; 1 government-owned radio station, Radio Tuvalu, includes relays of programming from international broadcasters (2019)

Internet country code: .tv

Internet users: *total:* 7,920 (2021 est.)
percent of population: 49% (2021 est.)
comparison ranking: total 219

Broadband - fixed subscriptions: *total:* 450 (2017 est.)
subscriptions per 100 inhabitants: 4 (2017 est.)
comparison ranking: total 211

TRANSPORTATION

Civil aircraft registration country code prefix: T2

Airports: 1 (2024)
comparison ranking: 213

Roadways: *total:* 16 km (2022)
comparison ranking: total 224

Merchant marine: *total:* 270 (2023)
by type: bulk carrier 21, container ship 3, general cargo 29, oil tanker 19, other 198
comparison ranking: total 61

Ports: *total ports:* 1 (2024)
large: 0
medium: 0
small: 0
very small: 1
ports with oil terminals: 1
key ports: Funafuti Atoll

MILITARY AND SECURITY

Military and security forces: no regular military forces; Tuvalu Police Force (Ministry of Justice, Communications, and Foreign Affairs) (2024)

Military - note: Tuvalu has a security pact with Australia; Australia also provides support to the Tuvalu Police Force, including donations of patrol boats
Tuvalu has a "shiprider" agreement with the US, which allows local maritime law enforcement officers to embark on US Coast Guard (USCG) and US Navy (USN) vessels, including to board and search vessels suspected of violating laws or regulations within Tuvalu's designated exclusive economic zone (EEZ) or on the high seas; "shiprider" agreements also enable USCG personnel and USN vessels with embarked USCG law enforcement personnel to work with host nations to protect critical regional resources (2024)

U

UGANDA

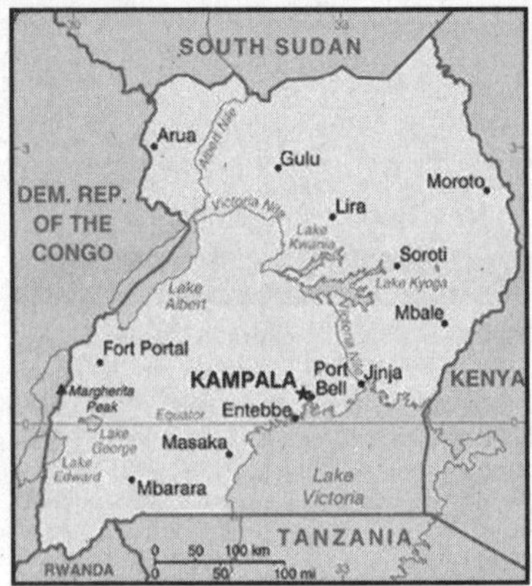

INTRODUCTION

Background: An ancient crossroads for various migrations, Uganda has as many as 65 ethnic groups that speak languages from three of Africa's four major linguistic families. As early as 1200, fertile soils and regular rainfall in the south fostered the formation of several large, centralized kingdoms, including Buganda, from which the country derives its name. Muslim traders from Egypt reached northern Uganda in the 1820s, and Swahili merchants from the Indian Ocean coast arrived in the south by the 1840s. The area attracted the attention of British explorers seeking the source of the Nile River in the 1860s, and this influence expanded in subsequent decades with the arrival of Christian missionaries and trade agreements; Uganda was declared a British protectorate in 1894. Buganda and other southern kingdoms negotiated agreements with Britain to secure privileges and a level of autonomy that were rare during the colonial period in Africa. Uganda's colonial boundaries grouped together a wide range of ethnic groups with different political systems and cultures, and the disparities between how Britain governed southern and northern areas compounded these differences, complicating efforts to establish a cohesive independent country.

Uganda gained independence in 1962 with one of the more developed economies and one of the strongest education systems in Sub-Saharan Africa, but it descended within a few years into political turmoil and internal conflict that lasted more than two decades. In 1966, Prime Minister Milton OBOTE suspended the constitution and violently deposed President Edward MUTESA, who was also the king of Buganda. Idi AMIN seized power in 1971 through a military coup and led the country into economic ruin and rampant mass atrocities that killed as many as 500,000 civilians. AMIN's annexation of Tanzanian territory in 1979 provoked Tanzania to invade Uganda, depose AMIN, and install a coalition government. In the aftermath, Uganda continued to experience atrocities, looting, and political instability and had four different heads of state between 1979 and 1980. OBOTE regained the presidency in 1980 through a controversial election that sparked renewed guerrilla warfare, killing as an estimated 300,000 civilians. Gen. Tito OKELLO seized power in a coup in 1985, but his rule was short-lived, with Yoweri MUSEVENI becoming president in 1986 after his insurgency captured the capital. MUSEVENI is widely credited with restoring relative stability and economic growth to Uganda but has resisted calls to leave office. In 2017, parliament removed presidential age limits, making it possible for MUSEVENI to remain in office for life.

GEOGRAPHY

Location: East-Central Africa, west of Kenya, east of the Democratic Republic of the Congo

Geographic coordinates: 1 00 N, 32 00 E

Map references: Africa

Area: *total:* 241,038 sq km
land: 197,100 sq km
water: 43,938 sq km
comparison ranking: total 81

Area - comparative: slightly more than two times the size of Pennsylvania; slightly smaller than Oregon

Land boundaries: *total:* 2,729 km
border countries (5): Democratic Republic of the Congo 877 km; Kenya 814 km; Rwanda 172 km; South Sudan 475 km; Tanzania 391 km

Coastline: 0 km (landlocked)

Maritime claims: none (landlocked)

Climate: tropical; generally rainy with two dry seasons (December to February, June to August); semiarid in northeast

Terrain: mostly plateau with rim of mountains

Elevation: *highest point:* Margherita Peak on Mount Stanley 5,110 m
lowest point: Albert Nile 614 m

Natural resources: copper, cobalt, hydropower, limestone, salt, arable land, gold

Land use: *agricultural land:* 71.2% (2018 est.)
arable land: 34.3% (2018 est.)
permanent crops: 11.3% (2018 est.)
permanent pasture: 25.6% (2018 est.)
forest: 14.5% (2018 est.)
other: 14.3% (2018 est.)

Irrigated land: 105 sq km (2013)

Major lakes (area sq km): *fresh water lake(s):* Lake Victoria (shared with Tanzania and Kenya) - 62,940 sq km; Lake Albert (shared with Democratic Republic of Congo) - 5,590 sq km; Lake Kyoga - 4,430 sq km; Lake Edward (shared with Democratic Republic of Congo) - 2,150 sq km

Major rivers (by length in km): Nile (shared with Rwanda [s], Tanzania, South Sudan, Sudan, and Egypt [m]) - 6,650 km
note – [s] after country name indicates river source; [m] after country name indicates river mouth

Major watersheds (area sq km):Atlantic Ocean drainage: Congo (3,730,881 sq km), *(Mediterranean Sea)* Nile (3,254,853 sq km)

Population distribution: population density is relatively high in comparison to other African nations; most of the population is concentrated in the central and southern parts of the country, particularly along the shores of Lake Victoria and Lake Albert; the northeast is least populated as shown in this population distribution map

Natural hazards: droughts; floods; earthquakes; landslides; hailstorms

Geography - note: *landlocked; fertile, well-watered country with many lakes and rivers; Lake Victoria, the world's largest tropical lake and the second largest freshwater lake, is shared among three countries:* Kenya, Tanzania, and Uganda

PEOPLE AND SOCIETY

Population: *total:* 49,283,041
male: 24,040,560
female: 25,242,481 (2024 est.)
comparison rankings: female 30; male 31; total 31

Nationality: *noun:* Ugandan(s)
adjective: Ugandan

Ethnic groups: Baganda 16.5%, Banyankole 9.6%, Basoga 8.8%, Bakiga 7.1%, Iteso 7%, Langi 6.3%, Bagisu 4.9%, Acholi 4.4%, Lugbara 3.3%, other 32.1% (2014 est.)

Languages: English (official), Ganda or Luganda (most widely used of the Niger-Congo languages and the language used most often in the capital), other Niger-Congo languages, Nilo-Saharan languages, Swahili (official), Arabic

Religions: Protestant 45.1% (Anglican 32.0%, Pentecostal/Born Again/Evangelical 11.1%, Seventh Day Adventist 1.7%, Baptist .3%), Roman Catholic 39.3%, Muslim 13.7%, other 1.6%, none 0.2% (2014 est.)

Demographic profile: Uganda has one of the youngest and most rapidly growing populations in the world; its total fertility rate is among the world's highest at close to 5.5 children per woman in 2022. Except in urban areas, actual fertility exceeds women's desired fertility by one or two children, which is indicative of the widespread unmet need for contraception, lack of government support for family planning, and a cultural preference for large families. High numbers of births, short birth intervals, and the early age of childbearing contribute to Uganda's high maternal mortality rate. Gender inequities also make fertility reduction difficult; women on average are less-educated, participate less in paid employment, and often have little say in decisions over childbearing and their own reproductive health. However, even if the birth rate were significantly reduced, Uganda's large pool of women entering reproductive age ensures rapid population growth for decades to come.
Unchecked, population increase will further strain the availability of arable land and natural resources and overwhelm the country's limited means for providing food, employment, education, health care, housing, and basic services. The country's north and northeast lag even further behind developmentally than the rest of the country as a result of long-term conflict (the Ugandan Bush War 1981-1986 and more than 20 years of fighting between the Lord's Resistance Army (LRA) and Ugandan Government forces), ongoing inter-communal violence, and periodic natural disasters.
Uganda has been both a source of refugees and migrants and a host country for refugees. In 1972, then President Idi AMIN, in his drive to return Uganda to Ugandans, expelled the South Asian

population that composed a large share of the country's business people and bankers. Since the 1970s, thousands of Ugandans have emigrated, mainly to southern Africa or the West, for security reasons, to escape poverty, to search for jobs, and for access to natural resources. The emigration of Ugandan doctors and nurses due to low wages is a particular concern given the country's shortage of skilled health care workers. Africans escaping conflicts in neighboring states have found refuge in Uganda since the 1950s; the country currently struggles to host tens of thousands from the Democratic Republic of the Congo, South Sudan, and other nearby countries.

Age structure: *0-14 years:* 47% (male 11,747,745/female 11,427,932)
15-64 years: 50.6% (male 11,788,483/female 13,131,051)
65 years and over: 2.4% (2024 est.) (male 504,332/female 683,498)

Dependency ratios: *total dependency ratio:* 88.2
youth dependency ratio: 85.1
elderly dependency ratio: 3.2
potential support ratio: 31.7 (2021 est.)

Median age: *total:* 16.2 years (2024 est.)
male: 15.5 years
female: 17.1 years
comparison ranking: total 228

Population growth rate: 3.18% (2024 est.)
comparison ranking: 6

Birth rate: 39.6 births/1,000 population (2024 est.)
comparison ranking: 5

Death rate: 4.7 deaths/1,000 population (2024 est.)
comparison ranking: 206

Net migration rate: -3.1 migrant(s)/1,000 population (2024 est.)
comparison ranking: 183

Population distribution: population density is relatively high in comparison to other African nations; most of the population is concentrated in the central and southern parts of the country, particularly along the shores of Lake Victoria and Lake Albert; the northeast is least populated as shown in this population distribution map

Urbanization: *urban population:* 26.8% of total population (2023)
rate of urbanization: 5.41% annual rate of change (2020-25 est.)

Major urban areas - population: 3.846 million KAMPALA (capital) (2023)

Sex ratio: *at birth:* 1.03 male(s)/female
0-14 years: 1.03 male(s)/female
15-64 years: 0.9 male(s)/female
65 years and over: 0.74 male(s)/female
total population: 0.95 male(s)/female (2024 est.)

Mother's mean age at first birth: 19.4 years (2016 est.)
note: data represents median age at first birth among women 20-49

Maternal mortality ratio: 284 deaths/100,000 live births (2020 est.)
comparison ranking: 29

Infant mortality rate: *total:* 28.5 deaths/1,000 live births (2024 est.)
male: 31.8 deaths/1,000 live births
female: 25.1 deaths/1,000 live births
comparison ranking: total 53

Life expectancy at birth: *total population:* 69.7 years (2024 est.)
male: 67.5 years
female: 72 years
comparison ranking: total population 182

Total fertility rate: 5.17 children born/woman (2024 est.)
comparison ranking: 7

Gross reproduction rate: 2.55 (2024 est.)

Contraceptive prevalence rate: 50.2% (2021)

Drinking water source: *improved: urban:* 92.5% of population
rural: 80% of population
total: 83.1% of population
unimproved: urban: 7.5% of population
rural: 20% of population
total: 16.9% of population (2020 est.)

Current health expenditure: 4% of GDP (2020)

Physician density: 0.15 physicians/1,000 population (2020)

Hospital bed density: 0.5 beds/1,000 population

Sanitation facility access: *improved: urban:* 67.3% of population
rural: 27.5% of population
total: 37.4% of population
unimproved: urban: 32.7% of population
rural: 72.5% of population
total: 62.6% of population (2020 est.)

Obesity - adult prevalence rate: 5.3% (2016)
comparison ranking: 180

Alcohol consumption per capita: *total:* 6.82 liters of pure alcohol (2019 est.)
beer: 0.85 liters of pure alcohol (2019 est.)
wine: 0.01 liters of pure alcohol (2019 est.)
spirits: 0.5 liters of pure alcohol (2019 est.)
other alcohols: 5.46 liters of pure alcohol (2019 est.)
comparison ranking: total 61

Tobacco use: *total:* 8.4% (2020 est.)
male: 13% (2020 est.)
female: 3.7% (2020 est.)
comparison ranking: total 145

Children under the age of 5 years underweight: 7.6% (2019/20)
comparison ranking: 64

Currently married women (ages 15-49): 58.3% (2023 est.)

Child marriage: *women married by age 15:* 7.3%
women married by age 18: 34%
men married by age 18: 5.5% (2016 est.)

Education expenditures: 2.7% of GDP (2021 est.)
comparison ranking: 169

Literacy: *definition:* age 15 and over can read and write
total population: 79%
male: 84%
female: 74.3% (2021)

ENVIRONMENT

Environment - current issues: draining of wetlands for agricultural use; deforestation; overgrazing; soil erosion; water pollution from industrial discharge and water hyacinth infestation in Lake Victoria; widespread poaching

Environment - international agreements: *party to:* Biodiversity, Climate Change, Climate Change-Kyoto Protocol, Climate Change-Paris Agreement, Comprehensive Nuclear Test Ban, Desertification, Endangered Species, Hazardous Wastes, Law of the Sea, Marine Life Conservation, Nuclear Test Ban, Ozone Layer Protection, Ship Pollution, Wetlands
signed, but not ratified: Environmental Modification

Climate: tropical; generally rainy with two dry seasons (December to February, June to August); semiarid in northeast

Urbanization: *urban population:* 26.8% of total population (2023)
rate of urbanization: 5.41% annual rate of change (2020-25 est.)

Food insecurity: *severe localized food insecurity: due to weather extremes, civil insecurity, and high food prices-* in Karamoja Region, about 518,000 people, 41% of the population, are estimated to be severely food insecure between March and July 2022, as a result of consecutive poor rainy seasons that adversely affected crop and livestock production, frequent episodes of cattle rustling leading to the loss of productive assets, and high food prices (2022)

Revenue from forest resources: 7.32% of GDP (2018 est.)
comparison ranking: 7

Revenue from coal: 0% of GDP (2018 est.)
comparison ranking: 92

Air pollutants: *particulate matter emissions:* 31.31 micrograms per cubic meter (2019 est.)
carbon dioxide emissions: 5.68 megatons (2016 est.)
methane emissions: 30.24 megatons (2020 est.)

Waste and recycling: *municipal solid waste generated annually:* 7,045,050 tons (2016 est.)
municipal solid waste recycled annually: 422,703 tons (2017 est.)
percent of municipal solid waste recycled: 6% (2017 est.)

Major lakes (area sq km): *fresh water lake(s):* Lake Victoria (shared with Tanzania and Kenya) - 62,940 sq km; Lake Albert (shared with Democratic Republic of Congo) - 5,590 sq km; Lake Kyoga - 4,430 sq km; Lake Edward (shared with Democratic Republic of Congo) - 2,150 sq km

Major rivers (by length in km): Nile (shared with Rwanda [s], Tanzania, South Sudan, Sudan, and Egypt [m]) - 6,650 km
note – [s] after country name indicates river source; [m] after country name indicates river mouth

Major watersheds (area sq km):Atlantic Ocean drainage: Congo (3,730,881 sq km), *(Mediterranean Sea)* Nile (3,254,853 sq km)

Total water withdrawal: *municipal:* 330 million cubic meters (2020 est.)
industrial: 50 million cubic meters (2020 est.)
agricultural: 260 million cubic meters (2020 est.)

Total renewable water resources: 60.1 billion cubic meters (2020 est.)

GOVERNMENT

Country name: *conventional long form:* Republic of Uganda
conventional short form: Uganda
etymology: from the name "Buganda," adopted by the British as the designation for their East African colony in 1894; Buganda had been a powerful East African state during the 18th and 19th centuries

Government type: presidential republic

Capital: *name:* Kampala
geographic coordinates: 0 19 N, 32 33 E
time difference: UTC+3 (8 hours ahead of Washington, DC, during Standard Time)

etymology: the site of the original British settlement was referred to by its native name as Akasozi ke'Empala ("hill of the impala" [plural]); over time this designation was shortened to K'empala and finally Kampala

Administrative divisions: 134 districts and 1 capital city*; Abim, Adjumani, Agago, Alebtong, Amolatar, Amudat, Amuria, Amuru, Apac, Arua, Budaka, Bududa, Bugiri, Bugweri, Buhweju, Buikwe, Bukedea, Bukomansimbi, Bukwo, Bulambuli, Buliisa, Bundibugyo, Bunyangabu, Bushenyi, Busia, Butaleja, Butambala, Butebo, Buvuma, Buyende, Dokolo, Gomba, Gulu, Hoima, Ibanda, Iganga, Isingiro, Jinja, Kaabong, Kabale, Kabarole, Kaberamaido, Kagadi, Kakumiro, Kalaki, Kalangala, Kaliro, Kalungu, Kampala*, Kamuli, Kamwenge, Kanungu, Kapchorwa, Kapelebyong, Karenga, Kasese, Kasanda, Katakwi, Kayunga, Kazo, Kibaale, Kiboga, Kibuku, Kikuube, Kiruhura, Kiryandongo, Kisoro, Kitagwenda, Kitgum, Koboko, Kole, Kotido, Kumi, Kwania, Kween, Kyankwanzi, Kyegegwa, Kyenjojo, Kyotera, Lamwo, Lira, Luuka, Luwero, Lwengo, Lyantonde, Madi-Okollo, Manafwa, Maracha, Masaka, Masindi, Mayuge, Mbale, Mbarara, Mitooma, Mityana, Moroto, Moyo, Mpigi, Mubende, Mukono, Nabilatuk, Nakapiripirit, Nakaseke, Nakasongola, Namayingo, Namisindwa, Namutumba, Napak, Nebbi, Ngora, Ntoroko, Ntungamo, Nwoya, Obongi, Omoro, Otuke, Oyam, Pader, Pakwach, Pallisa, Rakai, Rubanda, Rubirizi, Rukiga, Rukungiri, Rwampara, Sembabule, Serere, Sheema, Sironko, Soroti, Tororo, Wakiso, Yumbe, Zombo

Independence: 9 October 1962 (from the UK)

National holiday: Independence Day, 9 October (1962)

Legal system: mixed legal system of English common law and customary law

Constitution: *history:* several previous; latest adopted 27 September 1995, promulgated 8 October 1995
amendments: proposed by the National Assembly; passage requires at least two-thirds majority vote of the Assembly membership in the second and third readings; proposals affecting "entrenched clauses," including the sovereignty of the people, supremacy of the constitution, human rights and freedoms, the democratic and multiparty form of government, presidential term of office, independence of the judiciary, and the institutions of traditional or cultural leaders, also requires passage by referendum, ratification by at least two-thirds majority vote of district council members in at least two thirds of Uganda's districts, and assent of the president of the republic; amended several times, last in 2018

International law organization participation: accepts compulsory ICJ jurisdiction; accepts ICCt jurisdiction

Citizenship: *citizenship by birth:* no
citizenship by descent only: at least one parent or grandparent must be a native-born citizen of Uganda
dual citizenship recognized: yes
residency requirement for naturalization: an aggregate of 20 years and continuously for the last 2 years prior to applying for citizenship

Suffrage: 18 years of age; universal

Executive branch: *chief of state:* President Yoweri Kaguta MUSEVENI (since 26 January 1986)
head of government: Prime Minister Robinah NABBANJA (since 14 June 2021)
cabinet: Cabinet appointed by the president from among elected members of the National Assembly or persons who qualify to be elected as members of the National Assembly
elections/appointments: president directly elected by absolute majority popular vote in 2 rounds if needed for a 5-year term (no term limits); election last held on 14 January 2021 (next to be held in 2026)
election results:
2021: Yoweri Kaguta MUSEVENI reelected president in the first round; percent of vote - Yoweri Kaguta MUSEVENI (NRM) 58.6%, Robert Kyagulanyi SSENTAMU (aka Bobi WINE) (NUP) 34.8%, Patrick Oboi AMURIAT (FDC) 3.2%, other 3.4%
2016: Yoweri Kaguta MUSEVENI reelected president in the first round; percent of vote - Yoweri Kaguta MUSEVENI (NRM) 60.6%, Kizza BESIGYE (FDC) 35.6%, other 3.8%

Legislative branch: *description:* unicameral National Assembly or Parliament (556 seats; 353 members directly elected in single-seat constituencies by simple majority vote, 146 for women directly elected in single-seat districts by simple majority vote, and 30 "representatives" reserved for special interest groups - army 10, disabled 5, youth 5, labor 5, older persons 5; 27 ex officio members appointed by the president; members serve 5-year terms)
elections: last held on 14 January 2021 (next to be held in February 2026)
election results: percent of vote by party - NA; seats by party - NRM 336, NUP 57, FDC 32, DP 9, UPDF 10, UPC 9, independent 76 (excludes 27 ex-officio members); composition- men 368, women 189, percentage women 33.9%

Judicial branch: *highest court(s):* Supreme Court of Uganda (consists of the chief justice and at least 6 justices)
judge selection and term of office: justices appointed by the president of the republic in consultation with the Judicial Service Commission, an 8-member independent advisory body, and approved by the National Assembly; justices serve until mandatory retirement at age 70
subordinate courts: Court of Appeal (also acts as the Constitutional Court); High Court (includes 12 High Court Circuits and 8 High Court Divisions); Industrial Court; Chief Magistrate Grade One and Grade Two Courts throughout the country; qadhis courts; local council courts; family and children courts

Political parties: Democratic Party or DP
Forum for Democratic Change or FDC
Justice Forum or JEEMA
National Resistance Movement or NRM
National Unity Platform
People's Progressive Party or PPP
Uganda People's Congress or UPC

International organization participation: ACP, AfDB, ATMIS, AU, C, COMESA, EAC, EADB, FAO, G-77, IAEA, IBRD, ICAO, ICC (national committees), ICCt, IDA, IDB, IFAD, IFC, IFRCS, IGAD, ILO, IMF, IMO, Interpol, IOC, IOM, IPU, ISO (correspondent), ITC, ITSO, ITU, ITUC (NGOs), MIGA, NAM, OIC, OPCW, PCA, UN, UNCDF, UNCTAD, UNECA, UNDP, UNFPA, UNESCO, UNHCR, UNICEF, UNIDO, UNISFA, UNOCI, UNOPS, UNSOM, UNWTO, UPU, WCO, WFP, WFTU (NGOs), WHO, WIPO, WMO, WTO

Diplomatic representation in the US: *chief of mission:* Ambassador Robie KAKONGE (since 12 December 2022)
chancery: 5911 16th Street NW, Washington, DC 20011
telephone: [1] (202) 726-7100
FAX: [1] (202) 726-1727
email address and website:
washington@mofa.go.ug
https://washington.mofa.go.ug/

Diplomatic representation from the US: *chief of mission:* Ambassador William W. POPP (since 20 September 2023)
embassy: 1577 Ggaba Road, Kampala
mailing address: 2190 Kampala Place, Washington DC 20521-2190
telephone: [256] (0) 312-306-001
FAX: [256] (0) 414-259-794
email address and website:
KampalaWebContact@state.gov
https://ug.usembassy.gov/

Flag description: six equal horizontal bands of black (top), yellow, red, black, yellow, and red; a white disk is superimposed at the center and depicts a grey crowned crane (the national symbol) facing the hoist side; black symbolizes the African people, yellow sunshine and vitality, red African brotherhood; the crane was the military badge of Ugandan soldiers under the UK

National symbol(s): grey crowned crane; national colors: black, yellow, red

National anthem: *name:* "Oh Uganda, Land of Beauty!"
lyrics/music: George Wilberforce KAKOMOA
note: adopted 1962

National heritage: *total World Heritage Sites:* 3 (1 cultural, 2 natural)
selected World Heritage Site locales: Bwindi Impenetrable National Park (n); Rwenzori Mountains National Park (n); Tombs of Buganda Kings at Kasubi (c)

ECONOMY

Economic overview: low-income, primarily agrarian East African economy; COVID-19 hurt economic growth and poverty reduction; lower oil prices threaten prior sector investments; endemic corruption; natural resource rich; high female labor force participation but undervalued

Real GDP (purchasing power parity): $135.668 billion (2023 est.)
$128.923 billion (2022 est.)
$123.267 billion (2021 est.)
note: data in 2021 dollars
comparison ranking: 89

Real GDP growth rate: 5.23% (2023 est.)
4.59% (2022 est.)
3.54% (2021 est.)
note: annual GDP % growth based on constant local currency
comparison ranking: 44

Real GDP per capita: $2,800 (2023 est.)
$2,700 (2022 est.)
$2,700 (2021 est.)
note: data in 2021 dollars
comparison ranking: 200

GDP (official exchange rate): $49.273 billion (2023 est.)
note: data in current dollars at official exchange rate

Inflation rate (consumer prices): 5.35% (2023 est.)
7.2% (2022 est.)
2.2% (2021 est.)
note: annual % change based on consumer prices
comparison ranking: 113

Credit ratings: Fitch rating: B+ (2015)

Moody's rating: B2 (2016)

Standard & Poors rating: B (2014)
note: The year refers to the year in which the current credit rating was first obtained.

GDP - composition, by sector of origin: *agriculture:* 23.8% (2023 est.)
industry: 26% (2023 est.)
services: 42.4% (2023 est.)
note: figures may not total 100% due to non-allocated consumption not captured in sector-reported data
comparison rankings: services 184; industry 90; agriculture 22

GDP - composition, by end use: *household consumption:* 71.3% (2023 est.)
government consumption: 9.5% (2023 est.)
investment in fixed capital: 22.5% (2023 est.)
investment in inventories: 0.7% (2023 est.)
exports of goods and services: 13.4% (2023 est.)
imports of goods and services: -23.8% (2023 est.)
note: figures may not total 100% due to rounding or gaps in data collection

Agricultural products: plantains, sugarcane, maize, cassava, milk, sweet potatoes, beans, vegetables, rice, coffee (2022)
note: top ten agricultural products based on tonnage

Industries: sugar processing, brewing, tobacco, cotton textiles; cement, steel production

Industrial production growth rate: 3.5% (2023 est.)
note: annual % change in industrial value added based on constant local currency
comparison ranking: 95

Labor force: 18.881 million (2023 est.)
note: number of people ages 15 or older who are employed or seeking work
comparison ranking: 34

Unemployment rate: 2.83% (2023 est.)
2.93% (2022 est.)
3.42% (2021 est.)
note: % of labor force seeking employment
comparison ranking: 38

Youth unemployment rate (ages 15-24): *total:* 4.5% (2023 est.)
male: 3.4% (2023 est.)
female: 5.6% (2023 est.)
note: % of labor force ages 15-24 seeking employment
comparison ranking: total 179

Population below poverty line: 20.3% (2019 est.)
note: % of population with income below national poverty line

Gini Index coefficient - distribution of family income: 42.7 (2019 est.)
note: index (0-100) of income distribution; higher values represent greater inequality
comparison ranking: 32

Average household expenditures: *on food:* 44.2% of household expenditures (2022 est.)
on alcohol and tobacco: 0.9% of household expenditures (2022 est.)

Household income or consumption by percentage share: *lowest 10%:* 2.4% (2019 est.)
highest 10%: 34.5% (2019 est.)
note: % share of income accruing to lowest and highest 10% of population

Remittances: 2.63% of GDP (2023 est.)
2.74% of GDP (2022 est.)
2.85% of GDP (2021 est.)
note: personal transfers and compensation between resident and non-resident individuals/households/entities

Budget: *revenues:* $6.895 billion (2022 est.)
expenditures: $7.473 billion (2022 est.)
note: central government revenues (excluding grants) and expenses converted to US dollars at average official exchange rate for year indicated

Public debt: 53.89% of GDP (2022 est.)
note: central government debt as a % of GDP
comparison ranking: 92

Taxes and other revenues: 12.55% (of GDP) (2022 est.)
note: central government tax revenue as a % of GDP
comparison ranking: 158

Current account balance: -$4.172 billion (2022 est.)
-$3.972 billion (2021 est.)
-$3.598 billion (2020 est.)
note: balance of payments - net trade and primary/secondary income in current dollars
comparison ranking: 175

Exports: $6.115 billion (2022 est.)
$6.231 billion (2021 est.)
$5.622 billion (2020 est.)
note: balance of payments - exports of goods and services in current dollars
comparison ranking: 131

Exports - partners: UAE 31%, India 12%, Hong Kong 9%, Kenya 8%, Italy 7% (2022)
note: top five export partners based on percentage share of exports

Exports - commodities: gold, coffee, fish, milk, raw sugar (2022)
note: top five export commodities based on value in dollars

Imports: $11.145 billion (2022 est.)
$10.686 billion (2021 est.)
$10.209 billion (2020 est.)
note: balance of payments - imports of goods and services in current dollars
comparison ranking: 117

Imports - partners: China 23%, Kenya 15%, India 13%, UAE 7%, Tanzania 6% (2022)
note: top five import partners based on percentage share of imports

Imports - commodities: vaccines, packaged medicine, plastic products, cars, motorcycles and cycles (2022)
note: top five import commodities based on value in dollars

Reserves of foreign exchange and gold: $3.359 billion (2018 est.)
$3.721 billion (2017 est.)
$3.098 billion (2016 est.)
note: holdings of gold (year-end prices)/foreign exchange/special drawing rights in current dollars
comparison ranking: 112

Debt - external: $9.636 billion (2022 est.)
note: present value of external debt in current US dollars
comparison ranking: 39

Exchange rates: Ugandan shillings (UGX) per US dollar -

Exchange rates: 3,726.14 (2023 est.)
3,689.817 (2022 est.)
3,587.052 (2021 est.)
3,718.249 (2020 est.)
3,704.049 (2019 est.)

ENERGY

Electricity access: *electrification - total population:* 47.1% (2022 est.)
electrification - urban areas: 72%
electrification - rural areas: 35.9%

Electricity: *installed generating capacity:* 2.436 million kW (2022 est.)
consumption: 3.971 billion kWh (2022 est.)
exports: 336.98 million kWh (2022 est.)
imports: 23 million kWh (2022 est.)
transmission/distribution losses: 1.101 billion kWh (2022 est.)
comparison rankings: transmission/distribution losses 102; imports 120; exports 85; consumption 134; installed generating capacity 116

Electricity generation sources: *fossil fuels:* 1% of total installed capacity (2022 est.)
solar: 2.5% of total installed capacity (2022 est.)
hydroelectricity: 89.3% of total installed capacity (2022 est.)
biomass and waste: 7.2% of total installed capacity (2022 est.)

Coal: *exports:* 85.4 metric tons (2022 est.)
imports: (2022 est.) less than 1 metric ton
proven reserves: 799.999 million metric tons (2022 est.)

Petroleum: *refined petroleum consumption:* 43,000 bbl/day (2022 est.)
crude oil estimated reserves: 2.5 billion barrels (2021 est.)

Natural gas: *proven reserves:* 14.158 billion cubic meters (2021 est.)

Carbon dioxide emissions: 6.19 million metric tonnes of CO2 (2022 est.)
from petroleum and other liquids: 6.19 million metric tonnes of CO2 (2022 est.)
comparison ranking: total emissions 131

Energy consumption per capita: 2.248 million Btu/person (2022 est.)
comparison ranking: 184

COMMUNICATIONS

Telephones - fixed lines: *total subscriptions:* 117,000 (2022 est.)
subscriptions per 100 inhabitants: (2022 est.) less than 1
comparison ranking: total subscriptions 132

Telephones - mobile cellular: *total subscriptions:* 33.068 million (2022 est.)
subscriptions per 100 inhabitants: 70 (2022 est.)
comparison ranking: total subscriptions 46

Telecommunication systems: *general assessment:* a series of reforms within Uganda's telecom sector have provided the country with one of the most competitive markets in the region; in line with the regulator's licensing requirements by which Uganda-based companies should be broadly owned by Ugandans by mid-2022; fixed-line infrastructure remains poor, with low penetration, and as a result fixed-line broadband penetration is also particularly low; consumers have largely depended on mobile infrastructure to provide voice and broadband

services; there is sufficient capacity with LTE infrastructure to match data demand during the next few years; Uganda has anticipated the migration to 5G, having held trials in early 2020 though the roll out of 5G is not expected until later in 2022 (2022)
domestic: fixed-line less than 1 per 100 and mobile cellular systems teledensity is 66 per 100 persons (2021)
international: country code - 256; satellite earth stations - 1 Intelsat (Atlantic Ocean) and 1 Inmarsat; analog and digital links to Kenya and Tanzania

Broadcast media: public broadcaster, Uganda Broadcasting Corporation (UBC), operates radio and TV networks; 31 Free-To-Air (FTA) TV stations, 2 digital terrestrial TV stations, 3 cable TV stations, and 5 digital satellite TV stations; 258 operational FM stations

Internet country code: .ug

Internet users: *total:* 4.6 million (2021 est.)
percent of population: 10% (2021 est.)
comparison ranking: total 102

Broadband - fixed subscriptions: *total:* 58,594 (2020 est.)
subscriptions per 100 inhabitants: 0.1 (2020 est.)
comparison ranking: total 140

TRANSPORTATION

National air transport system: *number of registered air carriers:* 6 (2020)
inventory of registered aircraft operated by air carriers: 26
annual passenger traffic on registered air carriers: 21,537 (2018)

Civil aircraft registration country code prefix: 5X

Airports: 39 (2024)
comparison ranking: 105

Railways: *total:* 1,244 km (2014)
narrow gauge: 1,244 km (2014) 1.000-m gauge
comparison ranking: total 85

Roadways: *total:* 20,544 km (excludes local roads)
paved: 4,257 km
unpaved: 16,287 km (2017)
comparison ranking: total 113

Waterways: 907 km (2022) (there are no long navigable stretches of river in Uganda; parts of the Albert Nile (210 km) that flow out of Lake Albert (160 km) in the northwestern part of the country are navigable; several lakes including Lake Victoria (337 km) and Lake Kyoga (199.5) have substantial traffic; Lake Albert is navigable along a 200-km stretch from its northern tip to its southern shores)
comparison ranking: 74

MILITARY AND SECURITY

Military and security forces: Uganda People's Defense Force (UPDF): Land Force (includes marines), Air Force, Special Forces Command, Reserve Force

Ministry of Internal Affairs: Uganda Police Force (2024)
note 1: the Special Forces Command is a separate branch within the UPDF; it evolved from the former Presidential Guard Brigade and has continued to retain presidential protection duties in addition to its traditional missions, such as counterinsurgency
note 2: the Uganda Police Force includes air, field, territorial, and marine units, as well as a presidential guard force
note 3: in 2018, President MUSEVENI created a volunteer force of Local Defense Units under the military to beef up local security in designated parts of the country

Military expenditures: 2% of GDP (2023 est.)
2.2% of GDP (2022 est.)
2.5% of GDP (2021 est.)
2.5% of GDP (2020 est.)
1.7% of GDP (2019 est.)
comparison ranking: 73

Military and security service personnel strengths: approximately 45-50,000 active-duty troops (2023)

Military equipment inventories and acquisitions: the UPDF's inventory is mostly Russian/Soviet-era equipment with a limited mix of Western-origin arms; in recent years, Belarus and Russia have been the leading supplier of arms to the UPDF; Uganda has a small defense industry that can manufacture light armored vehicles and perform maintenance on some military equipment, including its Russian-made helicopters (2023)

Military service age and obligation: 18-25 years of age for voluntary military duty for men and women; 18-30 for those with degrees/diplomas in specialized fields such as medicine, engineering, chemistry, and education, or possess qualifications in some vocational skills; 9- year service obligation (2024)

Military deployments: as many as 6,000 Somalia (625 for UNSOM; the remainder under ATMIS; note - foreign troop contingents in Somalia under ATMIS are drawing down towards a final withdrawal in December 2024) (2024)

Military - note: the UPDF's missions include defending the sovereignty and territorial integrity of Uganda, assisting the civilian authorities in emergencies and natural disasters, and participating in socio-economic development projects; it supports the police in maintaining internal security and participates in African and UN peacekeeping missions; it is a key contributor to the East Africa Standby Force; the UPDF also has considerable political influence; it is constitutionally granted seats in parliament and is widely viewed as a key constituency for MUSEVENI; it has been used by MUSEVENI and his political party to break up rallies, raid opposition offices, and surveil rival candidates
since the 2010s, the UPDF has participated in several internal and regional military operations in addition to its large commitment to an international peacekeeping force in Somalia; from 2012-2017, it led regional efforts to pursue the Lord's Resistance Army (LRA), a small, violent group of Ugandan origin that conducted widespread attacks against civilians in much of Central Africa; Uganda intervened in the South Sudan civil war in 2013-2016, and UPDF forces have clashed with South Sudanese forces along the border as recently as 2023; since 2021, it is also conducting operations along the border with the Democratic Republic of the Congo (DRC) against the Allied Democratic Front (ADF), which has been designated by the US as the Islamic State of Iraq and ash-Sham in the DRC (see Appendix T); in December 2022, Uganda sent about 1,000 UPDF troops to the DRC as part of a regional force to assist the DRC Government in combating the M23 rebel group; in addition, elements of the UPDF have deployed internally to assist the police against cattle rustlers, poachers, and criminal gangs
the military traces its history back to the formation of the Uganda Rifles in 1895 under the British colonial government; the Uganda Rifles were merged with the Central Africa Regiment and the East Africa Rifles to form the King's African Rifles (KAR) in 1902, which participated in both world wars, as well as the Mau Mau rebellion in Kenya (1952-1960); in 1962, the Ugandan battalion of the KAR was transformed into the country's first military force, the Uganda Rifles, which was subsequently renamed the Uganda Army; the UPDF was established in 1995 from the former rebel National Resistance Army following the enactment of the 1995 Constitution of Uganda (2024)

TERRORISM

Terrorist group(s): al-Shabaab; Islamic State of Iraq and ash-Sham - Democratic Republic of Congo (ISIS-DRC)
note: details about the history, aims, leadership, organization, areas of operation, tactics, targets, weapons, size, and sources of support of the group(s) appear(s) in the Terrorism reference guide

TRANSNATIONAL ISSUES

Refugees and internally displaced persons: *refugees (country of origin):* 34,368 (Eritrea), 23,388 (Rwanda), 8,936 (Ethiopia), 5,776 (Sudan) (2023); 931,666 (South Sudan) (refugees and asylum seekers), 512,445 (Democratic Republic of the Congo), 40,326 (Somalia), 40,326 (Burundi) (2024)
stateless persons: 67,000 (2022)

UKRAINE

INTRODUCTION

Background: Ukraine was the center of the first eastern Slavic state, Kyivan Rus, which was the largest and most powerful state in Europe during the 10th and 11th centuries. Weakened by internecine quarrels and Mongol invasions, Kyivan Rus was incorporated into the Grand Duchy of Lithuania and eventually into the Polish-Lithuanian Commonwealth. The cultural and religious legacy of Kyivan Rus laid the foundation for Ukrainian nationalism. A new Ukrainian state, the Cossack Hetmanate, was established during the mid-17th century after an uprising against the Poles. Despite continuous Muscovite pressure, the Hetmanate managed to remain autonomous

for well over 100 years. During the latter part of the 18th century, the Russian Empire absorbed most Ukrainian territory. After czarist Russia collapsed in 1917, Ukraine – which has long been known as the region's "bread basket" for its agricultural production – achieved a short-lived period of independence (1917-20), but the country was reconquered and endured a Soviet rule that engineered two famines (1921-22 and 1932-33) in which over eight million died. In World War II, German and Soviet armies were responsible for seven to eight million more deaths. In 1986, a sudden power surge during a reactor-systems test at Ukraine's Chernobyl power station triggered the worst nuclear disaster in history, releasing massive amounts of radioactive material. Although Ukraine overwhelmingly voted for independence in 1991 as the Union of Soviet Socialist Republics (USSR) dissolved, democracy and prosperity remained elusive, with the legacy of state control, patronage politics, and endemic corruption stalling efforts at economic reform, privatization, and civil liberties.

In 2004 and 2005, a mass protest dubbed the "Orange Revolution" forced the authorities to overturn a presidential election and allow a new internationally monitored vote that swept into power a reformist slate under Viktor YUSHCHENKO. Rival Viktor YANUKOVYCH became prime minister in 2006 and was elected president in 2010. In 2012, Ukraine held legislative elections that Western observers widely criticized as corrupt. In 2013, YANUKOVYCH backtracked on a trade and cooperation agreement with the EU – in favor of closer economic ties with Russia – and then used force against protestors who supported the agreement, leading to a three-month protestor occupation of Kyiv's central square. The government's use of violence to break up the protest camp in 2014 led to multiple deaths, international condemnation, a failed political deal, and the president's abrupt departure for Russia. Pro-West President Petro POROSHENKO took office later that year; Volodymyr ZELENSKYY succeeded him in 2019.

Shortly after YANUKOVYCH's departure in 2014, Russian President Vladimir PUTIN ordered the invasion of Ukraine's Crimean Peninsula. In response, the UN passed a resolution confirming Ukraine's sovereignty and independence. In mid-2014, Russia began an armed conflict in two of Ukraine's eastern provinces. International efforts to end the conflict failed, and by 2022, more than 14,000 civilians were killed or wounded. On 24 February 2022, Russia escalated the conflict by invading the country on several fronts, in what has become the largest conventional military attack on a sovereign state in Europe since World War II. Russia made substantial gains in the early weeks of the invasion but underestimated Ukrainian resolve and combat capabilities. Despite Ukrainian resistance, Russia has laid claim to four Ukrainian oblasts – Donetsk, Kherson, Luhansk, and Zaporizhzhia – although none is fully under Russian control. The international community has not recognized the annexations. The invasion has also created Europe's largest refugee crisis since World War II, with over six million Ukrainian refugees recorded globally. It remains one of the two largest displacement crises worldwide (the other is the conflict in Syria). President ZELENSKYY has focused on boosting Ukrainian identity to unite the country behind the goals of ending the war through reclaiming territory and advancing Ukraine's candidacy for EU membership.

GEOGRAPHY

Location: Eastern Europe, bordering the Black Sea, between Poland, Belarus, Romania, and Moldova in the west and Russia in the east

Geographic coordinates: 49 00 N, 32 00 E

Map references: AsiaEurope

Area: *total:* 603,550 sq km
land: 579,330 sq km
water: 24,220 sq km
note: Russia annexed Crimea in 2014, an area of approximately 27,000 sq km (10,400 sq miles)
comparison ranking: total 48

Area - comparative: almost four times the size of Georgia; slightly smaller than Texas

Land boundaries: *total:* 5,581 km
border countries (6): Belarus 1,111 km; Hungary 128 km; Moldova 1,202 km; Poland 498 km; Romania 601 km; Russia 1,944 km, Slovakia 97 km

Coastline: 2,782 km

Maritime claims: *territorial sea:* 12 nm
exclusive economic zone: 200 nm
continental shelf: 200 m or to the depth of exploitation

Climate: temperate continental; Mediterranean only on the southern Crimean coast; precipitation disproportionately distributed, highest in west and north, lesser in east and southeast; winters vary from cool along the Black Sea to cold farther inland; warm summers across the greater part of the country, hot in the south

Terrain: mostly fertile plains (steppes) and plateaus, with mountains found only in the west (the Carpathians) or in the extreme south of the Crimean Peninsula

Elevation: *highest point:* Hora Hoverla 2,061 m
lowest point: Black Sea 0 m
mean elevation: 175 m

Natural resources: iron ore, coal, manganese, natural gas, oil, salt, sulfur, graphite, titanium, magnesium, kaolin, nickel, mercury, timber, arable land

Land use: *agricultural land:* 71.2% (2018 est.)
arable land: 56.1% (2018 est.)
permanent crops: 1.5% (2018 est.)
permanent pasture: 13.6% (2018 est.)
forest: 16.8% (2018 est.)
other: 12% (2018 est.)

Irrigated land: 4,350 sq km (2020)

Major rivers (by length in km): Dunay (Danube) (shared with Germany [s], Austria, Slovakia, Hungary, Croatia, Serbia, Bulgaria, Moldova, and Romania [m]) - 2,888 km; Dnipro (Dnieper) river mouth (shared with Russia [s] and Belarus) - 2,287 km; Dnister (Dniester) river source and mouth (shared with Moldova) - 1,411 km; Vistula (shared with Poland [s/m] and Belarus) - 1,213 km

note – [s] after country name indicates river source; [m] after country name indicates river mouth

Major watersheds (area sq km): Atlantic Ocean drainage: *(Black Sea)* Danube (795,656 sq km), Don (458,694 sq km), Dnieper (533,966 sq km)

Population distribution: densest settlement in the eastern (Donbas) and western regions; noteable concentrations in and around major urban areas of Kyiv, Kharkiv, Donets'k, Dnipropetrovs'k, and Odesa

Natural hazards: occasional floods; occasional droughts

Geography - note: strategic position at the crossroads between Europe and Asia; second-largest country in Europe after Russia

PEOPLE AND SOCIETY

Population: *total:* 35,661,826
male: 17,510,149
female: 18,151,677 (2024 est.)
comparison rankings: female 42; male 44; total 43

Nationality: *noun:* Ukrainian(s)
adjective: Ukrainian

Ethnic groups: Ukrainian 77.8%, Russian 17.3%, Belarusian 0.6%, Moldovan 0.5%, Crimean Tatar 0.5%, Bulgarian 0.4%, Hungarian 0.3%, Romanian 0.3%, Polish 0.3%, Jewish 0.2%, other 1.8% (2001 est.)

Languages: Ukrainian (official) 67.5%, Russian (regional language) 29.6%, other (includes Crimean Tatar, Moldovan/Romanian, and Hungarian) 2.9% (2001 est.)
major-language sample(s):
Світова Книга Фактів – найкраще джерело базової інформації. (Ukrainian)

Religions: Orthodox (includes the Orthodox Church of Ukraine (OCU), Ukrainian Autocephalous Orthodox Church (UAOC), and the Ukrainian Orthodox - Moscow Patriarchate (UOC-MP)), Ukrainian Greek Catholic, Roman Catholic, Protestant, Muslim, Jewish (2013 est.)
note: Ukraine's population is overwhelmingly Christian; the vast majority - up to two thirds - identify themselves as Orthodox, but many do not specify a particular branch; the OCU and the UOC-MP each represent less than a quarter of the country's population, the Ukrainian Greek Catholic Church accounts for 8-10%, and the UAOC accounts for 1-2%; Muslim and Jewish adherents each compose less than 1% of the total population

Age structure: *0-14 years:* 12.3% (male 2,278,116/female 2,122,500)
15-64 years: 67.8% (male 12,784,928/female 11,376,460)
65 years and over: 19.9% (2024 est.) (male 2,447,105/female 4,652,717)

Dependency ratios: *total dependency ratio:* 48.4
youth dependency ratio: 22.6
elderly dependency ratio: 25.8
potential support ratio: 3.9 (2021 est.)
note: data include Crimea

Median age: *total:* 44.9 years (2024 est.)
male: 41.4 years
female: 49.2 years
comparison ranking: total 25

Population growth rate: 2.38% (2024 est.)
comparison ranking: 24

Birth rate: 6 births/1,000 population (2024 est.)
comparison ranking: 228

Death rate: 18.6 deaths/1,000 population (2024 est.)
comparison ranking: 1

Net migration rate: 36.5 migrant(s)/1,000 population (2024 est.)
comparison ranking: 1

Population distribution: densest settlement in the eastern (Donbas) and western regions; noteable concentrations in and around major urban areas of Kyiv, Kharkiv, Donets'k, Dnipropetrovs'k, and Odesa

Urbanization: *urban population:* 70.1% of total population (2023)
rate of urbanization: -0.27% annual rate of change (2020-25 est.)

Major urban areas - population: 3.017 million KYIV (capital), 1.421 million Kharkiv, 1.008 million Odesa, 942,000 Dnipropetrovsk, 888,000 Donetsk (2023)

Sex ratio: *at birth:* 1.06 male(s)/female
0-14 years: 1.07 male(s)/female
15-64 years: 1.12 male(s)/female
65 years and over: 0.53 male(s)/female
total population: 0.97 male(s)/female (2024 est.)

Mother's mean age at first birth: 26.2 years (2019 est.)

Maternal mortality ratio: 17 deaths/100,000 live births (2020 est.)
comparison ranking: 133

Infant mortality rate: *total:* 8.7 deaths/1,000 live births (2024 est.)
male: 9.7 deaths/1,000 live births
female: 7.6 deaths/1,000 live births
comparison ranking: total 141

Life expectancy at birth: *total population:* 70.5 years (2024 est.)
male: 65.4 years
female: 75.8 years
comparison ranking: total population 173

Total fertility rate: children born/woman (2024 est.)
comparison ranking: 224

Gross reproduction rate: 2024 est.)

Contraceptive prevalence rate: 65.4% (2012)

Drinking water source: *improved: urban:* 99.4% of population
rural: 100% of population
total: 99.6% of population
unimproved: urban: 0.6% of population
rural: 0% of population
total: 0.4% of population (2020 est.)

Current health expenditure: 7.6% of GDP (2020)

Physician density: 2.99 physicians/1,000 population (2014)

Hospital bed density: 7.5 beds/1,000 population (2014)

Sanitation facility access: *improved: urban:* 100% of population
rural: 100% of population
total: 100% of population
unimproved: urban: 0% of population
rural: 0% of population
total: 0% of population (2020 est.)

Obesity - adult prevalence rate: 24.1% (2016)
comparison ranking: 61

Alcohol consumption per capita: *total:* 5.69 liters of pure alcohol (2019 est.)
beer: 2.44 liters of pure alcohol (2019 est.)
wine: 0.32 liters of pure alcohol (2019 est.)
spirits: 2.88 liters of pure alcohol (2019 est.)
other alcohols: 0.05 liters of pure alcohol (2019 est.)
comparison ranking: total 77

Tobacco use: *total:* 25.8% (2020 est.)
male: 40% (2020 est.)
female: 11.5% (2020 est.)
comparison ranking: total 43

Currently married women (ages 15-49): 61.6% (2023 est.)

Education expenditures: 5.4% of GDP (2020 est.)
comparison ranking: 63

Literacy: *definition:* age 15 and over can read and write
total population: 100%
male: 100%
female: 100% (2021)

School life expectancy (primary to tertiary education): *total:* 15 years
male: 15 years
female: 15 years (2014)

ENVIRONMENT

Environment - current issues: air and water pollution; land degradation; solid waste management; biodiversity loss; deforestation; radiation contamination in the northeast from 1986 accident at Chornobyl' Nuclear Power Plant

Environment - international agreements: *party to:* Air Pollution, Air Pollution-Nitrogen Oxides, Air Pollution-Sulphur 85, Antarctic-Environmental Protection, Antarctic-Marine Living Resources, Antarctic Treaty, Biodiversity, Climate Change, Climate Change-Kyoto Protocol, Climate Change-Paris Agreement, Comprehensive Nuclear Test Ban, Desertification, Endangered Species, Environmental Modification, Hazardous Wastes, Law of the Sea, Marine Dumping-London Convention, Nuclear Test Ban, Ozone Layer Protection, Ship Pollution, Wetlands
signed, but not ratified: Air Pollution-Heavy Metals, Air Pollution-Persistent Organic Pollutants, Air Pollution-Sulfur 94, Air Pollution-Volatile Organic Compounds

Climate: temperate continental; Mediterranean only on the southern Crimean coast; precipitation disproportionately distributed, highest in west and north, lesser in east and southeast; winters vary from cool along the Black Sea to cold farther inland; warm summers across the greater part of the country, hot in the south

Urbanization: *urban population:* 70.1% of total population (2023)
rate of urbanization: -0.27% annual rate of change (2020-25 est.)

Food insecurity: *severe localized food insecurity: due to conflict* - Ukraine continues to be a significant supplier of food commodities for the world; however, according to a 2023 analysis, at least 17.6 million people are estimated to be in need of multi-sectoral humanitarian assistance in 2023 due to the war, including over 11 million in need of food security and livelihood interventions; the harvest of the 2023 winter cereal crops, mostly wheat, is ongoing and will be concluded by August; as a result of a smaller planted area, the 2023 wheat harvest in areas under government control is estimated at 18.5 million mt, about 8% below the already war-affected 2022 output; despite decreased cereal production, food availability at the national level is reported to be adequate, but access remains a major challenge; the country has already experienced elevated levels of food price inflation in the past, due to the economic impact of the conflict in eastern areas; in addition, rising energy costs, amidst high unemployment rates and limited livelihood opportunities, are reducing households' purchasing power and driving more people into poverty
(2023)

Revenue from forest resources: 0.34% of GDP (2018 est.)
comparison ranking: 77

Revenue from coal: 0.42% of GDP (2018 est.)
comparison ranking: 14

Air pollutants: *particulate matter emissions:* 13.51 micrograms per cubic meter (2019 est.)
carbon dioxide emissions: 202.25 megatons (2016 est.)
methane emissions: 63.37 megatons (2020 est.)

Waste and recycling: *municipal solid waste generated annually:* 15,242,025 tons (2016 est.)
municipal solid waste recycled annually: 487,745 tons (2015 est.)
percent of municipal solid waste recycled: 3.2% (2015 est.)

Major rivers (by length in km): Dunay (Danube) (shared with Germany [s], Austria, Slovakia, Hungary, Croatia, Serbia, Bulgaria, Moldova, and Romania [m]) - 2,888 km; Dnipro (Dnieper) river mouth (shared with Russia [s] and Belarus) - 2,287 km; Dnister (Dniester) river source and mouth (shared with Moldova) - 1,411 km; Vistula (shared with Poland [s/m] and Belarus) - 1,213 km
note – [s] after country name indicates river source; [m] after country name indicates river mouth

Major watersheds (area sq km): Atlantic Ocean drainage: *(Black Sea)* Danube (795,656 sq km), Don (458,694 sq km), Dnieper (533,966 sq km)

Total water withdrawal: *municipal:* 2.77 billion cubic meters (2020 est.)
industrial: 4.04 billion cubic meters (2020 est.)
agricultural: 3.06 billion cubic meters (2020 est.)

Total renewable water resources: 175.28 billion cubic meters (2020 est.)

GOVERNMENT

Country name: *conventional long form:* none
conventional short form: Ukraine
local long form: none
local short form: Ukraina
former: Ukrainian National Republic, Ukrainian State, Ukrainian Soviet Socialist Republic
etymology: name derives from the Old East Slavic word "ukraina" meaning "borderland or march (militarized border region)" and began to be used extensively in the 19th century; originally Ukrainians referred to themselves as Rusyny (Rusyns, Ruthenians, or Ruthenes), an endonym derived from the medieval Rus state (Kyivan Rus)

Government type: semi-presidential republic

Capital: *name:* Kyiv (Kiev is the transliteration from Russian)
geographic coordinates: 50 26 N, 30 31 E
time difference: UTC+2 (7 hours ahead of Washington, DC, during Standard Time)
daylight saving time: +1hr, begins last Sunday in March; ends last Sunday in October
etymology: the name is associated with that of Kyi, who along with his brothers Shchek and Khoryv, and their sister Lybid, are the legendary founders of the

medieval city of Kyiv; Kyi being the eldest brother, the city was named after him
note: pronounced KAY-yiv

Administrative divisions: 24 provinces (oblasti, singular - oblast'), 1 autonomous republic* (avtonomna respublika), and 2 municipalities** (mista, singular - misto) with oblast status; Cherkasy, Chernihiv, Chernivtsi, Crimea or Avtonomna Respublika Krym* (Simferopol), Dnipropetrovsk (Dnipro), Donetsk, Ivano-Frankivsk, Kharkiv, Kherson, Khmelnytskyi, Kirovohrad (Kropyvnytskyi), Kyiv**, Kyiv, Luhansk, Lviv, Mykolaiv, Odesa, Poltava, Rivne, Sevastopol**, Sumy, Ternopil, Vinnytsia, Volyn (Lutsk), Zakarpattia (Uzhhorod), Zaporizhzhia, Zhytomyr
note 1: administrative divisions have the same names as their administrative centers (exceptions have the administrative center name following in parentheses); plans include the eventual renaming of Dnipropetrovsk and Kirovohrad oblasts, but because these names are mentioned in the Constitution of Ukraine, the change will require a constitutional amendment
note 2: the US Government does not recognize Russia's illegal annexation of Ukraine's Autonomous Republic of Crimea and the municipality of Sevastopol, nor their redesignation as the "Republic of Crimea" and the "Federal City of Sevastopol"; neither does the US Government recognize Russia's claimed annexation of Donetsk, Kherson, Luhansk, and Zaporizhzhia oblasts

Independence: *24 August 1991 (from the Soviet Union); notable earlier dates:* ca. 982 (VOLODYMYR I consolidates Kyivan Rus); 1199 (Principality (later Kingdom) of Ruthenia formed); 1648 (establishment of the Cossack Hetmanate); 22 January 1918 (from Soviet Russia)

National holiday: Independence Day, 24 August (1991); note - 22 January 1918, the day Ukraine first declared its independence from Soviet Russia, and the date the short-lived Western and Greater (Eastern) Ukrainian republics united (1919), is now celebrated as Unity Day

Legal system: civil law system; judicial review of legislative acts

Constitution: *history:* several previous; latest adopted and ratified 28 June 1996
amendments: proposed by the president of Ukraine or by at least one third of the Supreme Council members; adoption requires simple majority vote by the Council and at least two-thirds majority vote in its next regular session; adoption of proposals relating to general constitutional principles, elections, and amendment procedures requires two-thirds majority vote by the Council and approval in a referendum; constitutional articles on personal rights and freedoms, national independence, and territorial integrity cannot be amended; amended several times, last in 2019

International law organization participation: has not submitted an ICJ jurisdiction declaration; non-party state to the ICCt

Citizenship: *citizenship by birth:* no
citizenship by descent only: at least one parent must be a citizen of Ukraine
dual citizenship recognized: no
residency requirement for naturalization: 5 years

Suffrage: 18 years of age; universal

Executive branch: *chief of state:* President Volodymyr ZELENSKYY (since 20 May 2019)
head of government: Prime Minister Denys SHMYHAL (since 4 March 2020)
cabinet: Cabinet of Ministers nominated by the prime minister, approved by the Verkhovna Rada
elections/appointments: president directly elected by absolute majority popular vote in 2 rounds if needed for a 5-year term (eligible for a second term); election last held on 31 March and 21 April 2019 (next to be held in March 2024); prime minister selected by the Verkhovna Rada
election results:
2019: Volodymyr ZELENSKYY elected president in second round; percent of vote in first round - Volodymyr ZELENSKYY (Servant of the People) 30.2%, Petro POROSHENKO (BPP-Solidarity) 15.6%, Yuliya TYMOSHENKO (Fatherland) 13.4%, Yuriy BOYKO (Opposition Platform-For Life) 11.7%, 35 other candidates 29.1%; percent of vote in the second round - Volodymyr ZELENSKYY 73.2%, Petro POROSHENKO 24.5%, other 2.3%; Denys SHMYHAL (independent) elected prime minister; Verkhovna Rada vote - 291-59
2014: Petro POROSHENKO elected president in first round; percent of vote - Petro POROSHENKO (independent) 54.5%, Yuliya TYMOSHENKO (Fatherland) 12.9%, Oleh LYASHKO (Radical Party) 8.4%, other 24.2%; Volodymyr HROYSMAN (BPP) elected prime minister; Verkhovna Rada vote - 257-50
note: there is also a National Security and Defense Council or NSDC originally created in 1992 as the National Security Council; the NSDC staff is tasked with developing national security policy on domestic and international matters and advising the president; a presidential administration helps draft presidential edicts and provides policy support to the president

Legislative branch: *description:* unicameral Supreme Council or Verkhovna Rada (450 seats; 225 members directly elected in single-seat constituencies by simple majority vote and 225 directly elected in a single nationwide constituency by closed, party-list proportional representation vote; members serve 5-year terms)
elections: last held on 21 July 2019 (the next parliamentary election will take place after the end of the Russo-Ukrainian War)
election results: percent of vote by party - Servant of the People 43.2%, Opposition Platform-For Life 13.1%, Batkivshchyna 8.2%, European Solidarity 8.1%, Voice 5.8%, other 21.6%; Servant of the People 254, Opposition Platform for Life 43, Batkivshchyna 26, European Solidarity 25, Voice 20, Opposition Bloc 6, Svoboda 1, Self Reliance 1, United Centre 1, Bila Tserkva Together 1, independent 46; note - voting not held in Crimea and parts of two Russian-occupied eastern oblasts leaving 26 seats vacant; although this brings the total to 424 elected members (of 450 potential), article 83 of the constitution mandates that a parliamentary majority consists of 226 seats

Judicial branch: *highest court(s):* Supreme Court of Ukraine or SCU (consists of 100 judges, organized into civil, criminal, commercial and administrative chambers, and a grand chamber); Constitutional Court (consists of 18 justices); High Anti-Corruption Court (consists of 39 judges, including 12 in the Appeals Chamber)
judge selection and term of office: Supreme Court judges recommended by the High Qualification Commission of Judges (a 16-member state body responsible for judicial candidate testing and assessment and judicial administration), submitted to the High Council of Justice, a 21-member independent body of judicial officials responsible for judicial self-governance and administration, and appointed by the president; judges serve until mandatory retirement at age 65; High Anti-Corruption Court judges are selected by the same process as Supreme Court justices, with one addition – a majority of a combined High Qualification Commission of Judges and a 6-member Public Council of International Experts must vote in favor of potential judges in order to recommend their nomination to the High Council of Justice; this majority must include at least 3 members of the Public Council of International Experts; Constitutional Court justices appointed - 6 each by the president, by the Congress of Judges, and by the Verkhovna Rada; judges serve 9-year nonrenewable terms
subordinate courts:
Courts of Appeal; district courts
note: specialized courts were abolished as part of Ukraine's judicial reform program; in November 2019, President ZELENSKYY signed a bill on legal reforms

Political parties: Batkivshchyna (Fatherland)
European Solidarity or YeS
Holos (Voice or Vote)
Opposition Bloc (formerly known as Opposition Bloc — Party for Peace and Development, successor of the Industrial
Party of Ukraine, and resulted from a schism in the original Opposition Bloc in 2019; banned in court June 2022; ceased to exist in July 2022)
Opposition Bloc or OB (divided into Opposition Bloc - Party for Peace and Development and Opposition Platform - For Life in 2019; ceased to exist in July 2022)
Opposition Platform - For Life (resulted from a schism in the original Opposition Bloc in 2019; activities suspended by the National Security and Defense Council in March 2022; dissolved in April 2022)
Platform for Life and Peace
Radical Party or RPOL
Samopomich (Self Reliance)
Servant of the People
Svoboda (Freedom)

International organization participation: Australia Group, BSEC, CBSS (observer), CD, CE, CEI, CICA (observer), CIS (participating member, has not signed the 1993 CIS charter), EAEC (observer), EAPC, EBRD, FAO, GCTU, GUAM, IAEA, IBRD, ICAO, ICC (national committees), ICRM, IDA, IFC, IFRCS, IHO, ILO, IMF, IMO, IMSO, Interpol, IOC, IOM, IPU, ISO, ITU, ITUC (NGOs), LAIA (observer), MIGA, MONUSCO, NAM (observer), NSG, OAS (observer), OIF (observer), OPCW, OSCE, PCA, PFP, SELEC (observer), UN, UNCTAD, UNESCO, UNFICYP, UNIDO, UNISFA, UNMIL, UNMISS, UNOCI, UNOOSA, UNWTO, UPU, Wassenaar Arrangement, WCO, WFTU (NGOs), WHO, WIPO, WMO, WTO, ZC
note: Ukraine is an EU candidate country whose satisfactory completion of accession criteria is required before being granted full EU membership

Diplomatic representation in the US: *chief of mission:* Ambassador Oksana MARKAROVA (since 7 July 2021)
chancery: 3350 M Street NW, Washington, DC 20007
telephone: [1] (202) 349-2963
FAX: [1] (202) 333-0817

email address and website:
emb_us@mfa.gov.ua
https://usa.mfa.gov.ua/en
consulate(s) general: Chicago, New York, San Francisco

Diplomatic representation from the US: *chief of mission:* Ambassador Bridget A. BRINK (since 2 June 2022)
embassy: 4 A. I. Igor Sikorsky Street, 04112 Kyiv
mailing address: 5850 Kyiv Place, Washington, DC 20521-5850
telephone: [380] (44) 521-5000
FAX: [380] (44) 521-5544
email address and website:
kyivacs@state.gov
https://ua.usembassy.gov/

Flag description: two equal horizontal bands of azure (top) and golden yellow; although the colors date back to medieval heraldry, in modern times they are sometimes claimed to represent grain fields under a blue sky

National symbol(s): tryzub (trident), sunflower; national colors: blue, yellow

National anthem: *name:* "Shche ne vmerla Ukraina" (Ukraine Has Not Yet Perished)
lyrics/music: Paul CHUBYNSKYI/Mikhail VERBYTSKYI
note: music adopted 1991, lyrics adopted 2003; song first performed in 1864 at the Ukraine Theatre in Lviv; the lyrics, originally written in 1862, were revised in 2003

National heritage: *total World Heritage Sites:* 8 (7 cultural, 1 natural)
selected World Heritage Site locales: Kyiv: Saint Sophia Cathedral and Related Monastic Buildings, Kyiv Pechersk Lavra (c); Lviv Historic Center (c); Residence of Bukovinian and Dalmatian Metropolitans, Chernivtsi (c); Ancient City of Tauric Chersonese, Sevastopol (c); Wooden Tserkvas of the Carpathian Region (c); Ancient and Primeval Beech Forests of the Carpathians (n); Struve Geodetic Arc (c); The Historic Centre of Odesa (c)

ECONOMY

Economic overview: lower-middle-income, non-EU, Eastern European economy; key wheat and corn exporter; gradual recovery after 30% GDP contraction at start of war; damage to infrastructure and agriculture balanced by consumer and business resilience; international aid has stabilized foreign exchange reserves, allowing managed currency float; continued progress on anticorruption reforms

Real GDP (purchasing power parity): $559.981 billion (2023 est.)
$531.796 billion (2022 est.)
$746.471 billion (2021 est.)
note: data in 2021 dollars
comparison ranking: 46

Real GDP growth rate: 5.3% (2023 est.)
-28.76% (2022 est.)
3.45% (2021 est.)
note: annual GDP % growth based on constant local currency
comparison ranking: 41

Real GDP per capita: $16,200 (2023 est.)
$15,000 (2022 est.)
$18,000 (2021 est.)
note: data in 2021 dollars
comparison ranking: 116

GDP (official exchange rate): $178.757 billion (2023 est.)
note: data in current dollars at official exchange rate

Inflation rate (consumer prices): 12.85% (2023 est.)
20.18% (2022 est.)
9.36% (2021 est.)
note: annual % change based on consumer prices
comparison ranking: 190

Credit ratings: Fitch rating: CC (2022)

Moody's rating: Ca (2023)

Standard & Poors rating: CCC (2023)
note: The year refers to the year in which the current credit rating was first obtained.

GDP - composition, by sector of origin: *agriculture:* 7.4% (2023 est.)
industry: 18.8% (2023 est.)
services: 61.3% (2023 est.)
note: figures may not total 100% due to non-allocated consumption not captured in sector-reported data
comparison rankings: services 78; industry 144; agriculture 97

GDP - composition, by end use: *household consumption:* 64.1% (2023 est.)
government consumption: 41.7% (2023 est.)
investment in fixed capital: 16.9% (2023 est.)
investment in inventories: -1.8% (2023 est.)
exports of goods and services: 28.6% (2023 est.)
imports of goods and services: -49.5% (2023 est.)
note: figures may not total 100% due to rounding or gaps in data collection

Agricultural products: maize, potatoes, wheat, sunflower seeds, sugar beets, milk, barley, soybeans, rapeseed, cabbages (2022)
note: top ten agricultural products based on tonnage

Industries: industrial machinery, ferrous and nonferrous metals, automotive and aircraft components, electronics, chemicals, textiles, mining, construction

Industrial production growth rate: 8.61% (2023 est.)
note: annual % change in industrial value added based on constant local currency
comparison ranking: 24

Labor force: 20.312 million (2021 est.)
note: number of people ages 15 or older who are employed or seeking work
comparison ranking: 33

Unemployment rate: 9.83% (2021 est.)
9.48% (2020 est.)
8.19% (2019 est.)
note: % of labor force seeking employment
comparison ranking: 164

Youth unemployment rate (ages 15-24): *total:* 19.1% (2021 est.)
male: 18.1% (2021 est.)
female: 20.4% (2021 est.)
note: % of labor force ages 15-24 seeking employment
comparison ranking: total 68

Population below poverty line: 1.6% (2020 est.)
note: % of population with income below national poverty line

Gini Index coefficient - distribution of family income: 25.6 (2020 est.)
note: index (0-100) of income distribution; higher values represent greater inequality
comparison ranking: 149

Average household expenditures: *on food:* 42.7% of household expenditures (2022 est.)
on alcohol and tobacco: 6.9% of household expenditures (2022 est.)

Household income or consumption by percentage share: *lowest 10%:* 4.3% (2020 est.)
highest 10%: 21.8% (2020 est.)
note: % share of income accruing to lowest and highest 10% of population

Remittances: 8.46% of GDP (2023 est.)
10.36% of GDP (2022 est.)
9.04% of GDP (2021 est.)
note: personal transfers and compensation between resident and non-resident individuals/households/entities

Budget: *revenues:* $68.559 billion (2022 est.)
expenditures: $93.783 billion (2022 est.)
note: central government revenues (excluding grants) and expenses converted to US dollars at average official exchange rate for year indicated

Public debt: 58.72% of GDP (2020 est.)
note: central government debt as a % of GDP
comparison ranking: 82

Taxes and other revenues: 16.69% (of GDP) (2022 est.)
note: central government tax revenue as a % of GDP
comparison ranking: 119

Current account balance: -$9.209 billion (2023 est.)
$7.972 billion (2022 est.)
-$3.882 billion (2021 est.)
note: balance of payments - net trade and primary/secondary income in current dollars
comparison ranking: 192

Exports: $51.093 billion (2023 est.)
$57.517 billion (2022 est.)
$81.504 billion (2021 est.)
note: balance of payments - exports of goods and services in current dollars
comparison ranking: 67

Exports - partners: Poland 14%, Romania 8%, Turkey 6%, China 6%, Germany 5% (2022)
note: top five export partners based on percentage share of exports

Exports - commodities: corn, seed oils, wheat, iron ore, rapeseed (2022)
note: top five export commodities based on value in dollars

Imports: $88.488 billion (2023 est.)
$83.254 billion (2022 est.)
$84.175 billion (2021 est.)
note: balance of payments - imports of goods and services in current dollars
comparison ranking: 51

Imports - partners: Poland 17%, China 12%, Germany 9%, Turkey 6%, Hungary 4% (2022)
note: top five import partners based on percentage share of imports

Imports - commodities: refined petroleum, cars, natural gas, garments, packaged medicine (2022)
note: top five import commodities based on value in dollars

Reserves of foreign exchange and gold: $40.51 billion (2023 est.)
$28.506 billion (2022 est.)
$30.967 billion (2021 est.)
note: holdings of gold (year-end prices)/foreign exchange/special drawing rights in current dollars
comparison ranking: 57

Exchange rates: hryvnia (UAH) per US dollar -

Exchange rates: 36.574 (2023 est.)

32.342 (2022 est.)
27.286 (2021 est.)
26.958 (2020 est.)
25.846 (2019 est.)

ENERGY

Electricity access: *electrification - total population:* 100% (2022 est.)

Electricity: *installed generating capacity:* 58.531 million kW (2022 est.)
consumption: 99.69 billion kWh (2022 est.)
exports: 2.48 billion kWh (2022 est.)
imports: 1.034 billion kWh (2022 est.)
transmission/distribution losses: 11.108 billion kWh (2022 est.)
comparison rankings: transmission/distribution losses 183; imports 75; exports 53; consumption 35; installed generating capacity 25

Electricity generation sources: *fossil fuels:* 32.6% of total installed capacity (2022 est.)
nuclear: 54.5% of total installed capacity (2022 est.)
solar: 4.1% of total installed capacity (2022 est.)
wind: 1.8% of total installed capacity (2022 est.)
hydroelectricity: 6.5% of total installed capacity (2022 est.)
biomass and waste: 0.5% of total installed capacity (2022 est.)

Nuclear energy: Number of operational nuclear reactors: 15 (2023)

Number of nuclear reactors under construction: 2 (2023)

Net capacity of operational nuclear reactors: 13.11GW (2023 est.)

Percent of total electricity production: 55% (2023 est.)

Number of nuclear reactors permanently shut down: 4 (2023)

Coal: *production:* 4.248 million metric tons (2022 est.)
consumption: 10.953 million metric tons (2022 est.)
exports: 9,000 metric tons (2022 est.)
imports: 6.553 million metric tons (2022 est.)
proven reserves: 34.375 billion metric tons (2022 est.)

Petroleum: *total petroleum production:* 3,000 bbl/day (2023 est.)
refined petroleum consumption: 248,000 bbl/day (2022 est.)
crude oil estimated reserves: 395 million barrels (2021 est.)

Natural gas: *production:* 18.725 billion cubic meters (2022 est.)
consumption: 22.856 billion cubic meters (2022 est.)
exports: 95.994 million cubic meters (2022 est.)
imports: 5.404 billion cubic meters (2022 est.)
proven reserves: 1.104 trillion cubic meters (2021 est.)

Carbon dioxide emissions: 93.36 million metric tonnes of CO2 (2022 est.)
from coal and metallurgical coke: 19.401 million metric tonnes of CO2 (2022 est.)
from petroleum and other liquids: 31.22 million metric tonnes of CO2 (2022 est.)
from consumed natural gas: 42.739 million metric tonnes of CO2 (2022 est.)
comparison ranking: total emissions 43

Energy consumption per capita: 53.302 million Btu/person (2022 est.)
comparison ranking: 93

COMMUNICATIONS

Telephones - fixed lines: *total subscriptions:* 1.739 million (2022 est.)
subscriptions per 100 inhabitants: 6 (2021 est.)
comparison ranking: total subscriptions 56

Telephones - mobile cellular: *total subscriptions:* 49.304 million (2022 est.)
subscriptions per 100 inhabitants: 135 (2021 est.)
comparison ranking: total subscriptions 34

Telecommunication systems: *general assessment:* there has been considerable damage and destruction to the communications infrastructure in more than 10 out of 24 regions of Ukraine since the war started; Ukraine estimates it will need $4.67 billion (€4.38 billion) over 10 years to repair an overlooked but expensive casualty in the ongoing Russian invasion: its telecommunications network; forty-five per cent of the total network damage is felt by fixed broadband operators, followed closely by mobile operators at 43 percent; "it will be difficult to restore telecommunications to their pre-war level until there are "conditions for the safe living of consumers and service providers"; the World Bank estimates that roughly 12 per cent of all Ukrainian households have lost mobile service connection: an issue, the report notes, that "affects not only personal communication but also critical services and economic activities"; Ukraine is also one of the biggest users of SpaceX's Starlink, a series of satellites in space that transmit radio signals to users on Earth, with 47,000 units being used by the country; (2024)
domestic: fixed-line teledensity is 6 per 100; the mobile-cellular telephone is 135 mobile phones per 100 persons (2022)
international: country code - 380; landing point for the Kerch Strait Cable connecting Ukraine to Russia; 2 new domestic trunk lines are a part of the fiber-optic TAE system and 3 Ukrainian links have been installed in the fiber-optic TEL project that connects 18 countries; additional international service is provided by the Italy-Turkey-Ukraine-Russia (ITUR) fiberoptic submarine cable and by an unknown number of earth stations in the Intelsat, Inmarsat, and Intersputnik satellite systems

Broadcast media: Ukraine's media landscape is dominated by oligarch-owned news outlets, which are often politically motivated and at odds with one another and/or the government; while polls suggest most Ukrainians still receive news from traditional media sources, social media is a crucial component of information dissemination in Ukraine; almost all Ukrainian politicians and opinion leaders communicate with the public via social media and maintain at least one social media page, if not more; this allows them direct communication with audiences, and news often breaks on Facebook or Twitter before being picked up by traditional news outlets; Kyiv created a unified news platform to broadcast news about the war following Russia's full-scale invasion; the government's "United News" television marathon is a round-the clock framework which untied the Ukrainian public broadcaster and top commercial TV channels' programming; Ukraine television serves as the principal source of news; the largest national networks are controlled by oligarchs: Studio 1+1 is owned by Ihor Kolomoyskyy; Inter is owned by Dmytro Firtash and Serhiy Lyovochkin; and StarlightMedia channels (ICTV, STB, and Novyi Kanal) are owned by Victor Pinchuk; a set of 24-hour news channels also have clear political affiliations: pro-Ukrainian government Channel 5 and Pryamyi are linked to President Petro Poroshenko; 24 is owned by opposition, but not pro-Russian, politicians; UA: Suspilne is a public television station under the umbrella of the National Public Broadcasting Company of Ukraine; while it is often praised by media experts for balanced coverage, it lags in popularity; Ukrainian Radio, institutionally linked to UA: Suspilne, is one of only two national talk radio networks, with the other being the privately owned Radio NV (2021)

Internet country code: .ua

Internet users: *total:* 34,596,356 (2021 est.)
percent of population: 79% (2021 est.)
comparison ranking: total 29

Broadband - fixed subscriptions: *total:* 7,769,401 (2020 est.)
subscriptions per 100 inhabitants: 19 (2020 est.)
comparison ranking: total 27

Communications - note: a sorting code to expeditiously handle large volumes of mail was first set up in Ukraine in the 1930s (then the Ukrainian Soviet Socialist Republic, part of the Soviet Union); the sophisticated, three-part (number-letter-number) postal code system, referred to as an "index," was the world's first postal zip code; the system functioned well and was in use from 1932 to 1939 when it was abruptly discontinued

TRANSPORTATION

National air transport system: *number of registered air carriers:* 14 (2020)
inventory of registered aircraft operated by air carriers: 126
annual passenger traffic on registered air carriers: 7,854,842 (2018)
annual freight traffic on registered air carriers: 75.26 million (2018) mt-km

Civil aircraft registration country code prefix: UR

Airports: 148 (2024)
comparison ranking: 35

Heliports: 42 (2024)

Pipelines: 36,720 km gas, 4,514 km oil, 4,363 km refined products (2013)

Railways: *total:* 21,733 km (2014)
standard gauge: 49 km (2014) 1.435-m gauge (49 km electrified)
broad gauge: 21,684 km (2014) 1.524-m gauge (9,250 km electrified)
comparison ranking: total 13

Roadways: *total:* 169,694 km
paved: 166,095 km (includes 17 km of expressways)
unpaved: 3,599 km (2012)
comparison ranking: total 31

Waterways: 1,672 km (2012) (most on Dnieper River)
comparison ranking: 48

Merchant marine: *total:* 410 (2023)
by type: container ship 1, general cargo 83, oil tanker 14, other 312
comparison ranking: total 48

Ports: *total ports:* 26 (2024)
large: 3
medium: 0
small: 8

very small: 15
ports with oil terminals: 8
key ports: Berdyansk, Dnipro-Buzkyy, Feodosiya, Illichivsk, Kerch, Kherson, Mariupol, Mykolayiv, Odesa, Sevastopol, Yuzhnyy

MILITARY AND SECURITY

Military and security forces: Armed Forces of Ukraine (AFU; Zbroyni Syly Ukrayiny or ZSU): Ground Forces (Sukhoputni Viys'ka), Naval Forces (Viys'kovo-Mors'ki Syly, VMS), Air Forces (Povitryani Syly, PS), Air Assault Forces (Desantno-shturmovi Viyska, DShV), Ukrainian Special Operations Forces (UASOF), Unmanned Systems Forces, Territorial Defense Forces (Reserves)

Ministry of Internal Affairs: National Guard of Ukraine, State Border Guard Service of Ukraine (includes Maritime Border Guard or Sea Guard) (2024)

note 1: in the event that martial law is declared, all National Guard units, with certain exceptions such as those tasked with providing for diplomatic security of embassies and consulates, would come under the command of the Ministry of Defense as auxiliary forces to the Armed Forces

note 2: the Territorial Defense Forces (TDF) were formally established in July 2021; the TDF evolved from former Territorial Defense Battalions and other volunteer militia and paramilitary units that were organized in 2014-2015 to fight Russian-backed separatists in the Donbas; in January 2022, the TDF was activated as a separate military branch; it is organized into at least 25 brigades representing each of the 24 oblasts, plus the city of Kyiv

Military expenditures: 4% of GDP (2021 est.)
4% of GDP (2020 est.)
3.4% of GDP (2019 est.)
3.1% of GDP (2018 est.)
3.1% of GDP (2017 est.)
note: since Russia's invasion of the country in early 2022, defense spending has increased to more than 25% of GDP according to some estimates
comparison ranking: 19

Military and security service personnel strengths: estimated 800,000 active Armed Forces personnel (2024)

note 1: following the Russian invasion of Ukraine in February 2022, President ZELENSKY announced a general mobilization of the country; prior to the invasion, approximately 200,000 active Armed Forces troops (125,000 Army; 25,000 Airborne/Air Assault Forces; 2,000 Special Operations Forces; 10,000 Navy; 40,000 Air Force); approximately 50,000 National Guard; approximately 40,000 State Border Guard

Military equipment inventories and acquisitions: prior to the full-scale Russian invasion in February 2022, the Ukrainian military was equipped largely with Russian-origin and Soviet-era weapons systems; since the invasion, it has received considerable quantities of weapons, including Soviet-era and more modern Western systems, from European countries and the US; Ukraine has a broad defense industry capable of building, maintaining, and upgrading a variety of weapons systems (2024)

Military service age and obligation: 18 years of age for voluntary service; conscription abolished in 2012, but reintroduced for men in 2014; 25 years of age for conscription; prior to the Russian invasion of February 2022, conscript service obligation was 12-18 months, depending on the service (2024)

note 1: following the Russian invasion in 2022, all nonexempt men ages 18 to 60 were required to register with their local recruitment offices and undergo medical screening for possible service; the Territorial Defense Forces (TDF) accepts volunteers, 18-60 years of age; since the invasion, hundreds of thousands of Ukrainians have volunteered for the regular armed forces, the TDF, or to work in civilian defense activities

note 2: women have been able to volunteer for military service since 1993; as of 2024, nearly 70,000 women were serving in the armed forces in both uniformed and civilian positions

note 3: since 2015, the Ukrainian military has allowed foreigners and stateless persons, 18-45 (in special cases up to 60), to join on 3-5-year contracts, based on qualifications; following the Russian invasion in 2022, the military began accepting medically fit foreign volunteers on a larger scale, with an emphasis on persons with combat experience; wartime volunteers typically serve for 6 months

Military deployments: *note:* prior to the Russian invasion in 2022, Ukraine had committed about 500 troops to the Lithuania, Poland, and Ukraine joint military brigade (LITPOLUKRBRIG), which was established in 2014; the brigade is headquartered in Poland and is comprised of an international staff, three battalions, and specialized units; units affiliated with the multinational brigade remain within the structures of the armed forces of their respective countries until the brigade is activated for participation in an international operation

Military - note: the primary focus of the Ukrainian Armed Forces (UAF) is defense against Russian aggression; in February 2022, Russia launched an unprovoked full-scale invasion of Ukraine in what is the largest conflict in Europe since the end of World War II in 1945; as of 2024, the front line of the fighting stretched about 1,000 kilometers (some 600 miles) north and south in eastern and southern Ukraine; Russia's forces have also launched missile and armed drone strikes throughout Ukraine, hitting critical infrastructure, including power, water, and heating facilities, as well as other civilian targets; Russia first invaded Ukraine in 2014, occupying Ukraine's province of Crimea and backing separatist forces in the Donbas region with arms, equipment, and training, as well as special operations forces and regular troops, although Moscow denied their presence prior to 2022; the UAF has received considerable outside military assistance since the Russian invasion, including equipment and training, chiefly from Europe and the US

Ukraine has a relationship with NATO dating back to the early 1990s, when Ukraine joined the North Atlantic Cooperation Council (1991) and the Partnership for Peace program (1994); the relationship intensified in the wake of the 2014 Russia-Ukraine conflict and Russian seizure of Crimea to include NATO support for Ukrainian military capabilities development and capacity-building; NATO further increased its support to the Ukrainian military following Russia's fullscale invasion in 2022 (2024)

SPACE

Space agency/agencies: State Space Agency of Ukraine (SSAU; established 1992 as the National Space Agency of Ukraine or NSAU; renamed in 2010) (2024)

Space program overview: SSAU/NSAU inherited a large and well-developed space program when it took over all of the former Soviet defense/ space industrial industry that was located on the territory of Ukraine upon the country's declaration of independence in 1991; prior to the 2014 Russia takeover of Crimea and support for separatists in Ukraine's Donbas region, Ukraine's space efforts largely provided support to the Russian space program, including the production of satellite/space launch vehicles (SLVs)/rocket carriers and their components; today, it develops and produces SLVs/rocket carriers, spacecraft, satellites, and satellite sub-components both independently and jointly with numerous foreign space agencies and private space industry companies, including those of Brazil, Canada, China, the European Space Agency (ESA) and its member states (particularly Italy and Poland), Japan, Kazakhstan, Russia (curtailed after 2014), Turkey, and the US;

prior to the full scale Russian invasion in February 2022, Ukraine was producing more than 100 SLVs, SLV stages, or SLV engines annually, and since 1991, over 160 rockets and more than 370 spacecraft had been manufactured by Ukraine or produced with its participation; as of 2022, SSAU had 16,000 employees and controlled 20 state-run corporations in Ukraine's "space cluster," a region between the cities of Dnipro, Kharkiv, and Kyiv (note – Dnipro, known as Ukraine's "Rocket City," was one of the Soviet Union's main centers for space, nuclear, and military industries and played a crucial role in the development and manufacture of both civilian and military rockets); in 2019, the Ukrainian Parliament began allowing private companies to engage in space endeavors, including launching rockets into space and allowing companies to negotiate with foreign companies without the state's approval; previously, only state-owned companies could do so (2024)

note: further details about the key activities, programs, and milestones of the country's space program, as well as government spending estimates on the space sector, appear in the Space Programs reference guide

TRANSNATIONAL ISSUES

Refugees and internally displaced persons: IDPs: 1,461,700 (Russian-sponsored separatist violence in Crimea and eastern Ukraine) (2021); 3.67 million (2023) (since Russian invasion that started in February 2022); note – the more recent invasion total may reflect some double counting, since it is impossible to determine how many of the recent IDPs may also include IDPs from the earlier Russian-sponsored violence in Crimea and eastern Ukraine

stateless persons: 36,459 (2022); note - citizens of the former USSR who were permanently resident in Ukraine were granted citizenship upon Ukraine's independence in 1991, but some missed this window of opportunity; people arriving after 1991, Crimean Tatars, ethnic Koreans, people with expired Soviet passports, and people with no documents have difficulty acquiring Ukrainian citizenship; following the fall of the Soviet Union in 1989, thousands of Crimean Tatars and their descendants deported from Ukraine under the STALIN regime returned to their homeland, some being stateless and others holding the citizenship of Uzbekistan or other former Soviet republics; a 1998 bilateral agreement between Ukraine and Uzbekistan simplified the process of renouncing Uzbek citizenship and obtaining Ukrainian citizenship

Illicit drugs: a transit country for non-domestically produced drugs, such as cocaine and heroin, bound for consumer markets in the European Union and Russia; overland corridors for the movement of these drugs exists, but Ukraine's southern ports on the Black Sea, notably Odesa and Pivdennyi, are disrupted due to the war; domestically produced amphetamine, methamphetamine, methadone, alpha-PVP, and new psychoactive substances (NPS) remain threats to Ukrainian society; production and consumption of cannabis remains significant

UNITED ARAB EMIRATES

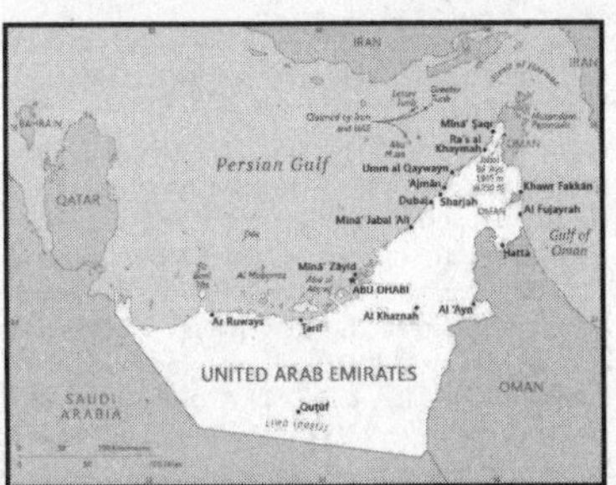

INTRODUCTION

Background: The Trucial States of the Persian Gulf coast granted the UK control of their defense and foreign affairs in 19th-century treaties. In 1971, six of these states – Abu Dhabi, 'Ajman, Al Fujayrah, Ash Shariqah, Dubayy, and Umm al Qaywayn – merged to form the United Arab Emirates (UAE). Ra's al Khaymah joined in 1972.

The UAE's per-capita GDP is on par with those of leading West European nations. For more than three decades, oil and global finance drove the UAE's economy. In 2008-09, the confluence of falling oil prices, collapsing real estate prices, and the international banking crisis hit the UAE especially hard. The UAE did not experience the "Arab Spring" unrest seen elsewhere in the Middle East in 2010-11, partly because of the government's multi-year, $1.6-billion infrastructure investment plan for the poorer northern emirates, and its aggressive pursuit of advocates for political reform.

The UAE in recent years has played a growing role in regional affairs. In addition to donating billions of dollars in economic aid to help stabilize Egypt, the UAE was one of the first countries to join the Defeat ISIS coalition, and to participate as a key partner in a Saudi-led military campaign in Yemen. In 2020, the UAE and Bahrain signed a peace agreement (the Abraham Accords) with Israel – brokered by the US – in Washington, D.C. The UAE and Bahrain thus became the third and fourth Middle Eastern countries, along with Egypt and Jordan, to recognize Israel.

GEOGRAPHY

Location: Middle East, bordering the Gulf of Oman and the Persian Gulf, between Oman and Saudi Arabia

Geographic coordinates: 24 00 N, 54 00 E

Map references: Middle East

Area: *total:* 83,600 sq km
land: 83,600 sq km
water: 0 sq km
comparison ranking: total 115

Area - comparative: slightly larger than South Carolina; slightly smaller than Maine

Land boundaries: *total:* 1,066 km
border countries (2): Oman 609 km; Saudi Arabia 457 km

Coastline: 1,318 km

Maritime claims: *territorial sea:* 12 nm
contiguous zone: 24 nm
exclusive economic zone: 200 nm
continental shelf: 200 nm or to the edge of the continental margin

Climate: desert; cooler in eastern mountains

Terrain: flat, barren coastal plain merging into rolling sand dunes of vast desert; mountains in east Elevation
highest point: Jabal Bil 'Ays 1,905 m
lowest point: Persian Gulf 0 m
mean elevation: 149 m

Natural resources: petroleum, natural gas

Land use: *agricultural land:* 4.6% (2018 est.)
arable land: 0.5% (2018 est.)
permanent crops: 0.5% (2018 est.)
permanent pasture: 3.6% (2018 est.)
forest: 3.8% (2018 est.)
other: 91.6% (2018 est.)

Irrigated land: 898 sq km (2020)

Population distribution: population is heavily concentrated to the northeast on the Musandam Peninsula; the three largest emirates - Abu Dhabi, Dubai, and Sharjah - are home to nearly 85% of the population

Natural hazards: frequent sand and dust storms

Geography - note: strategic location along southern approaches to Strait of Hormuz, a vital transit point for world crude oil; Abu Zaby (Abu Dhabi) and Dubayy (Dubai) together account for over 90% of the area of the country and two-thirds of the population

PEOPLE AND SOCIETY

Population: *total:* 10,032,213
male: 6,824,131
female: 3,208,082 (2024 est.)
comparison rankings: female 111; male 76; total 94

Nationality: *noun:* Emirati(s)
adjective: Emirati

Ethnic groups: Emirati 11.6%, South Asian 59.4% (includes Indian 38.2%, Bangladeshi 9.5%, Pakistani 9.4%, other 2.3%), Egyptian 10.2%, Filipino 6.1%, other 12.8% (2015 est.)
note: data represent the total population; as of 2019, immigrants make up about 87.9% of the total population, according to UN data

Languages: Arabic (official), English, Hindi, Malayalam, Urdu, Pashto, Tagalog, Persian
major-language sample(s):
كتاب حقائق العالم، المصدر الذي لا يمكن الاستغناء عنه للمعلومات الأساسية (Arabic)

Religions: Muslim 74.5% (official) (Sunni 63.3%, Shia 6.7%, other 4.4%), Christian 12.9%, Hindu 6.2%, Buddhist 3.2%, agnostic 1.3%, other 1.9% (2020 est.)
note: data represent the total population; as of 2020, immigrants make up about 88.1% of the total population, according to UN data

Age structure: *0-14 years:* 16.4% (male 842,577/female 802,302)
15-64 years: 81.4% (male 5,812,470/female 2,353,750)
65 years and over: 2.2% (2024 est.) (male 169,084/female 52,030)

Dependency ratios: *total dependency ratio:* 20.3
youth dependency ratio: 18.2
elderly dependency ratio: 2.1
potential support ratio: 47.3 (2021 est.)

Median age: *total:* 35.8 years (2024 est.)
male: 38.1 years
female: 29.8 years
comparison ranking: total 95

Population growth rate: 0.6% (2024 est.)
comparison ranking: 140

Birth rate: 10.7 births/1,000 population (2024 est.)
comparison ranking: 174

Death rate: 1.7 deaths/1,000 population (2024 est.)
comparison ranking: 228

Net migration rate: -3.1 migrant(s)/1,000 population (2024 est.)
comparison ranking: 181

Population distribution: population is heavily concentrated to the northeast on the Musandam Peninsula; the three largest emirates - Abu Dhabi, Dubai, and Sharjah - are home to nearly 85% of the population

Urbanization: *urban population:* 87.8% of total population (2023)
rate of urbanization: 1.5% annual rate of change (2020-25 est.)

Major urban areas - population: 3.008 million Dubai, 1.831 million Sharjah, 1.567 million ABU DHABI (capital) (2023)

Sex ratio: *at birth:* 1.06 male(s)/female
0-14 years: 1.05 male(s)/female
15-64 years: 2.47 male(s)/female
65 years and over: 3.25 male(s)/female
total population: 2.13 male(s)/female (2024 est.)

Maternal mortality ratio: 9 deaths/100,000 live births (2020 est.)
comparison ranking: 147

Infant mortality rate: *total:* 5 deaths/1,000 live births (2024 est.)
male: 5.5 deaths/1,000 live births
female: 4.4 deaths/1,000 live births
comparison ranking: total 175

Life expectancy at birth: *total population:* 79.9 years (2024 est.)
male: 78.6 years
female: 81.4 years
comparison ranking: total population 60

Total fertility rate: 1.61 children born/woman (2024 est.)
comparison ranking: 182

Gross reproduction rate: 0.78 (2024 est.)

Drinking water source: *improved:*
total: 100% of population

Current health expenditure: 5.5% of GDP (2020)

Physician density: 2.6 physicians/1,000 population (2019)

Hospital bed density: 1.4 beds/1,000 population (2017)

Sanitation facility access: *improved:*
total: 100% of population

Obesity - adult prevalence rate: 31.7% (2016)
comparison ranking: 20

Alcohol consumption per capita: *total:* 2.03 liters of pure alcohol (2019 est.)
beer: 0.21 liters of pure alcohol (2019 est.)
wine: 0.14 liters of pure alcohol (2019 est.)
spirits: 1.65 liters of pure alcohol (2019 est.)
other alcohols: 0.02 liters of pure alcohol (2019 est.)
comparison ranking: total 130

Currently married women (ages 15-49): 72.4% (2023 est.)

Education expenditures: 3.9% of GDP (2020 est.)
comparison ranking: 122

Literacy: *definition:* age 15 and over can read and write
total population: 98.1%
male: 98.8%
female: 97.2% (2021)

School life expectancy (primary to tertiary education): *total:* 16 years
male: 15 years
female: 17 years (2020)

ENVIRONMENT

Environment - current issues: air pollution; rapid population growth and high energy demand contribute to water scarcity; lack of natural freshwater resources compensated by desalination plants; land degradation and desertification; waste generation, beach pollution from oil spills

Environment - international agreements: *party to:* Biodiversity, Climate Change, Climate Change-Kyoto Protocol, Climate Change-Paris Agreement, Comprehensive Nuclear Test Ban, Desertification, Endangered Species, Hazardous Wastes, Marine Dumping-London Convention, Ozone Layer Protection, Ship Pollution, Wetlands
signed, but not ratified: Law of the Sea

Climate: desert; cooler in eastern mountains

Land use: *agricultural land:* 4.6% (2018 est.)
arable land: 0.5% (2018 est.)
permanent crops: 0.5% (2018 est.)
permanent pasture: 3.6% (2018 est.)
forest: 3.8% (2018 est.)
other: 91.6% (2018 est.)

Urbanization: *urban population:* 87.8% of total population (2023)
rate of urbanization: 1.5% annual rate of change (2020-25 est.)

Revenue from forest resources: 0% of GDP (2018 est.)
comparison ranking: 159

Revenue from coal: 0% of GDP (2018 est.)
comparison ranking: 57

Air pollutants: *particulate matter emissions:* 41.75 micrograms per cubic meter (2019 est.)
carbon dioxide emissions: 206.32 megatons (2016 est.)
methane emissions: 56.55 megatons (2020 est.)

Waste and recycling: *municipal solid waste generated annually:* 5,413,453 tons (2015 est.)
municipal solid waste recycled annually: 1,082,691 tons (2015 est.)
percent of municipal solid waste recycled: 20% (2015 est.)

Total water withdrawal: *municipal:* 2.63 billion cubic meters (2020 est.)
industrial: 69 million cubic meters (2020 est.)
agricultural: 2.32 billion cubic meters (2020 est.)

Total renewable water resources: 150 million cubic meters (2020 est.)

GOVERNMENT

Country name: *conventional long form:* United Arab Emirates
conventional short form: none
local long form: Al Imarat al Arabiyah al Muttahidah
local short form: none
former: Trucial Oman, Trucial States
abbreviation: UAE
etymology: self-descriptive country name; the name "Arabia" can be traced back many centuries B.C., the ancient Egyptians referred to the region as "Ar Rabi"; "emirates" derives from "amir" the Arabic word for "commander," "lord," or "prince"

Government type: federation of monarchies

Capital: *name:* Abu Dhabi
geographic coordinates: 24 28 N, 54 22 E
time difference: UTC+4 (9 hours ahead of Washington, DC, during Standard Time)
etymology: in Arabic, *abu* means "father" and *dhabi* refers to "gazelle"; the name may derive from an abundance of gazelles that used to live in the area, as well as a folk tale involving the "Father of the Gazelle," Shakhbut BIN DHIYAB AL NAHYAN, whose hunting party tracked a gazelle to a spring on the island where Abu Dhabi was founded

Administrative divisions: 7 emirates (imarat, singular - imarah); Abu Zaby (Abu Dhabi), 'Ajman, Al Fujayrah, Ash Shariqah (Sharjah), Dubayy (Dubai), Ra's al Khaymah, Umm al Qaywayn

Independence: 2 December 1971 (from the UK)

National holiday: Independence Day (National Day), 2 December (1971)

Legal system: mixed legal system of Islamic (sharia) law and civil law

Constitution: *history:* previous 1971 (provisional); latest drafted in 1979, became permanent May 1996
amendments: proposed by the Supreme Council and submitted to the Federal National Council; passage requires at least a two-thirds majority vote of Federal National Council members present and approval of the Supreme Council president; amended 2009

International law organization participation: has not submitted an ICJ jurisdiction declaration; non-party state to the ICCt

Citizenship: *citizenship by birth:* no
citizenship by descent only: the father must be a citizen of the United Arab Emirates; if the father is unknown, the mother must be a citizen
dual citizenship recognized: no
residency requirement for naturalization: 30 years

Suffrage: limited; note - rulers of the seven emirates each select a proportion of voters for the Federal National Council (FNC) that together account for about 12 percent of Emirati citizens

Executive branch: *chief of state:* President MUHAMMAD BIN ZAYID Al Nuhayyan (since 14 May 2022)
head of government: Prime Minister and Co-Vice President MUHAMMAD BIN RASHID Al Maktum (since 5 January 2006)
cabinet: Council of Ministers announced by the prime minister and approved by the president
elections/appointments: president and vice president indirectly elected by the Federal Supreme Council - composed of the rulers of the 7 emirates - for a 5-year term (no term limits); unscheduled election held on 14 May 2022, following the death of President KHALIFA bin Zayid Al-Nuhayyan (next election expected in 2027); prime minister appointed by the president
election results: 2022: MUHAMMAD BIN ZAYID Al-Nuhayyan elected president; Federal Supreme Council vote - NA
note: the Federal Supreme Council (FSC) is composed of the 7 emirate rulers and is the highest constitutional authority in the UAE; the FSC establishes general policies and sanctions federal legislation; meets 4 times a year; Abu Zaby (Abu Dhabi) and Dubayy (Dubai) rulers have effective veto power

Legislative branch: *description:* unicameral Federal National Council (FNC) or Majlis al-Ittihad al-Watani (40 seats; 20 members indirectly elected using single non-transferable vote by an electoral college whose members are selected by each emirate ruler proportional to its FNC membership, and 20 members appointed by the rulers of the 7 constituent states; members serve 4-year terms)
elections: last held for indirectly elected members on 7 October 2023 (next to be held in October 2027); last held for appointed members in October 2023 (next appointments expected in late 2027)
election results: seats by emirate - Abu Dhabi 4, Dubai 4, Sharjah 3, Ras al-Khaimah 3, Ajman 2, Fujairah 2, Umm al- Quwain 2; composition - 13 men, 7 women, percentage elected women 35%; note - to attain overall FNC gender parity, 13 women and 7 men were appointed; total FNC percentage of women 50%

Judicial branch: *highest court(s):* Federal Supreme Court (consists of the court president and 4 judges; jurisdiction limited to federal cases)
judge selection and term of office: judges appointed by the federal president following approval by the Federal Supreme Council, the highest executive and legislative authority consisting of the 7 emirate rulers; judges serve until retirement age or the expiry of their appointment terms
subordinate courts: Federal Court of Cassation (determines the constitutionality of laws promulgated at the federal and emirate level; federal level courts of first instance and appeals courts); the emirates of Abu Dhabi, Dubai, and Ra's al Khaymah have parallel court systems; the other 4 emirates have incorporated their courts into the federal system; note - the Abu Dhabi Global Market Courts and the Dubai International Financial Center Courts, the

country's two largest financial free zones, both adjudicate civil and commercial disputes.

Political parties: none; political parties are banned; all candidates run as independents

International organization participation: ABEDA, AfDB (nonregional member), AFESD, AMF, BIS, BRICS, CAEU, CICA, FAO, G-77, GCC, IAEA, IBRD, ICAO, ICC (national committees), ICRM, IDA, IDB, IFAD, IFC, IFRCS, IHO, ILO, IMF, IMO, IMSO, Interpol, IOC, IPU, ISO, ITSO, ITU, LAS, MIGA, NAM, OAPEC, OIC, OIF (observer), OPCW, OPEC, PCA, UN, UNCTAD, UNESCO, UNHRC, UNIDO, UNOOSA, UNRWA, UNWTO, UPU, WCO, WHO, WIPO, WMO, WTO

Diplomatic representation in the US: *chief of mission:* Ambassador Yousif AL OTAIBA (since 28 July 2008)
chancery: 3522 International Court NW, Suite 400, Washington, DC 20008
telephone: [1] (202) 243-2400
FAX: [1] (202) 243-2408
email address and website:
info@uaeembassy-usa.org
https://www.uae-embassy.org/
consulate(s) general: Houston, Los Angeles, New York

Diplomatic representation from the US: *chief of mission:* Ambassador Martina A. STRONG (since 4 October 2023)
embassy: Embassies District, Plot 38, Sector W59-02, Street No. 4, Abu Dhabi
mailing address: 6010 Abu Dhabi Place, Washington DC 20521-6010
telephone: [971] (2) 414-2200
FAX: [971] (2) 414-2241
email address and website:
abudhabiacs@state.gov
https://ae.usembassy.gov/
consulate(s) general: Dubai

Flag description: three equal horizontal bands of green (top), white, and black with a wider vertical red band on the hoist side; the flag incorporates all four Pan-Arab colors, which in this case represent fertility (green), neutrality (white), petroleum resources (black), and unity (red); red was the traditional color incorporated into all flags of the emirates before their unification

National symbol(s): golden falcon; national colors: green, white, black, red

National anthem: *name:* "Nashid al-watani al-imarati" (National Anthem of the UAE)
lyrics/music: AREF Al Sheikh Abdullah Al Hassan/ Mohamad Abdel WAHAB
note: music adopted 1971, lyrics adopted 1996; Mohamad Abdel WAHAB also composed the music for the anthem of Tunisia

National heritage: *total World Heritage Sites:* 1 (cultural)
selected World Heritage Site locales: Cultural Sites of Al Ain (Hafit, Hili, Bidaa Bint Saud, and Oases Areas)

ECONOMY

Economic overview: historically oil-driven Middle Eastern economy; diversifying into a trade-oriented logistics and supply chain leader; strong foreign direct investment orientation; building trade and investment ties through partnership agreements; growing banking sector; recent economic linkages with Israel slowing due to Gaza conflict

Real GDP (purchasing power parity): $719.733 billion (2023 est.)
$696.041 billion (2022 est.)
$645.376 billion (2021 est.)
note: data in 2021 dollars
comparison ranking: 38

Real GDP growth rate: 3.4% (2023 est.)
7.85% (2022 est.)
4.35% (2021 est.)
note: annual GDP % growth based on constant local currency
comparison ranking: 96

Real GDP per capita: $75,600 (2023 est.)
$73,700 (2022 est.)
$68,900 (2021 est.)
note: data in 2021 dollars
comparison ranking: 13

GDP (official exchange rate): $504.173 billion (2023 est.)
note: data in current dollars at official exchange rate

Inflation rate (consumer prices): 4.83% (2022 est.)
-0.01% (2021 est.)
-2.08% (2020 est.)
note: annual % change based on consumer prices
comparison ranking: 103

Credit ratings: Fitch rating: AA- (2020)

Moody's rating: Aa2 (2007)

Standard & Poors rating: AA (2007)
note: The year refers to the year in which the current credit rating was first obtained.

GDP - composition, by sector of origin: *agriculture:* 0.8% (2022 est.)
industry: 51.5% (2022 est.)
services: 47.7% (2022 est.)
note: figures may not total 100% due to non-allocated consumption not captured in sector-reported data
comparison rankings: services 159; industry 11; agriculture 188

GDP - composition, by end use: *household consumption:* 40.2% (2020 est.)
government consumption: 14.5% (2020 est.)
investment in fixed capital: 20.2% (2020 est.)
investment in inventories: 2.6% (2020 est.)
exports of goods and services: 95.9% (2020 est.)
imports of goods and services: -70.6% (2020 est.)
note: figures may not total 100% due to rounding or gaps in data collection

Agricultural products: dates, cucumbers/gherkins, camel milk, goat milk, tomatoes, eggs, goat meat, milk, chicken, camel meat (2022)
note: top ten agricultural products based on tonnage

Industries: petroleum and petrochemicals; fishing, aluminum, cement, fertilizer, commercial ship repair, construction materials, handicrafts, textiles

Industrial production growth rate: 8.49% (2022 est.)
note: annual % change in industrial value added based on constant local currency
comparison ranking: 25

Labor force: 6.668 million (2023 est.)
note: number of people ages 15 or older who are employed or seeking work
comparison ranking: 70

Unemployment rate: 2.71% (2023 est.)
2.87% (2022 est.)
3.11% (2021 est.)
note: % of labor force seeking employment
comparison ranking: 35

Youth unemployment rate (ages 15-24): *total:* 10.7% (2023 est.)
male: 6.7% (2023 est.)
female: 22.9% (2023 est.)
note: % of labor force ages 15-24 seeking employment
comparison ranking: total 125

Gini Index coefficient - distribution of family income: 26 (2018 est.)
note: index (0-100) of income distribution; higher values represent greater inequality
comparison ranking: 146

Average household expenditures: *on food:* 13.5% of household expenditures (2022 est.)
on alcohol and tobacco: 0.4% of household expenditures (2022 est.)

Household income or consumption by percentage share: *lowest 10%:* 4% (2018 est.)
highest 10%: 20% (2018 est.)
note: % share of income accruing to lowest and highest 10% of population

Budget: *revenues:* $20.165 billion (2022 est.)
expenditures: $19.483 billion (2022 est.)
note: central government revenues (excluding grants) and expenses converted to US dollars at average official exchange rate for year indicated

Public debt: 19.7% of GDP (2017 est.)
note: central government debt as a % of GDP
comparison ranking: 186

Taxes and other revenues: 0.57% (of GDP) (2022 est.)
note: central government tax revenue as a % of GDP
comparison ranking: 207

Current account balance: $26.47 billion (2017 est.)
$13.23 billion (2016 est.)
comparison ranking: 20

Exports: $335.238 billion (2020 est.)
$404.046 billion (2019 est.)
$392.863 billion (2018 est.)
note: GDP expenditure basis - exports of goods and services in current dollars
comparison ranking: 28

Exports - partners: India 13%, Japan 10%, China 8%, Saudi Arabia 7%, Iraq 5% (2022)
note: top five export partners based on percentage share of exports

Exports - commodities: crude petroleum, refined petroleum, gold, broadcasting equipment, natural gas (2022)
note: top five export commodities based on value in dollars

Imports: $246.886 billion (2020 est.)
$295.6 billion (2019 est.)
$281.536 billion (2018 est.)
note: GDP expenditure basis - imports of goods and services in current dollars
comparison ranking: 32

Imports - partners: China 18%, India 10%, US 6%, UK 4%, Saudi Arabia 3% (2022)
note: top five import partners based on percentage share of imports

Imports - commodities: gold, broadcasting equipment, refined petroleum, diamonds, cars (2022)
note: top five import commodities based on value in dollars

Reserves of foreign exchange and gold: $189.491 billion (2023 est.)
$138.433 billion (2022 est.)

$131.117 billion (2021 est.)
note: holdings of gold (year-end prices)/foreign exchange/special drawing rights in current dollars
comparison ranking: 24

Exchange rates: Emirati dirhams (AED) per US dollar -

Exchange rates: 3.673 (2023 est.)
3.673 (2022 est.)
3.673 (2021 est.)
3.673 (2020 est.)
3.673 (2019 est.)

ENERGY

Electricity access: *electrification - total population:* 100% (2022 est.)

Electricity: *installed generating capacity:* 39.915 million kW (2022 est.)
consumption: 161.89 billion kWh (2022 est.)
exports: 657 million kWh (2022 est.)
imports: 868 million kWh (2022 est.)
transmission/distribution losses: 7.524 billion kWh (2022 est.)
comparison rankings: transmission/distribution losses 172; imports 82; exports 71; consumption 26; installed generating capacity 32

Electricity generation sources: *fossil fuels:* 84.6% of total installed capacity (2022 est.)
nuclear: 11.4% of total installed capacity (2022 est.)
solar: 4% of total installed capacity (2022 est.)

Nuclear energy: Number of operational nuclear reactors: 4 (2023)

Net capacity of operational nuclear reactors: 5.32GW (2023 est.)

Percent of total electricity production: 19.7% (2023 est.)

Coal: *consumption:* 3.273 million metric tons (2022 est.)
exports: 99,000 metric tons (2022 est.)
imports: 3.538 million metric tons (2022 est.)

Petroleum: *total petroleum production:* 4.146 million bbl/day (2023 est.)
refined petroleum consumption: 939,000 bbl/day (2022 est.)
crude oil estimated reserves: 97.8 billion barrels (2021 est.)

Natural gas: *production:* 56.683 billion cubic meters (2022 est.)
consumption: 66.091 billion cubic meters (2022 est.)
exports: 6.991 billion cubic meters (2022 est.)
imports: 19.29 billion cubic meters (2022 est.)
proven reserves: 6.091 trillion cubic meters (2021 est.)

Carbon dioxide emissions: 268.041 million metric tonnes of CO2 (2022 est.)
from coal and metallurgical coke: 8.274 million metric tonnes of CO2 (2022 est.)
from petroleum and other liquids: 130.114 million metric tonnes of CO2 (2022 est.)
from consumed natural gas: 129.653 million metric tonnes of CO2 (2022 est.)
comparison ranking: total emissions 24

Energy consumption per capita: 496.365 million Btu/person (2022 est.)
comparison ranking: 4

COMMUNICATIONS

Telephones - fixed lines: *total subscriptions:* 2.286 million (2022 est.)
subscriptions per 100 inhabitants: 24 (2022 est.)
comparison ranking: total subscriptions 49

Telephones - mobile cellular: *total subscriptions:* 20.036 million (2022 est.)
subscriptions per 100 inhabitants: 212 (2022 est.)
comparison ranking: total subscriptions 63

Telecommunication systems: *general assessment:* the UAE has a strong mobile market; while the 5G penetration rate is the second highest globally after China; this has underpinned growth in the mobile broadband sector, and has enabled the strong development in the take-up of rich content and applications, as well as m-commerce; to help increase the capacity of 5G networks in coming years, and so keep up with data demand, the government has allowed for the GSM networks to be closed down and for spectrum and other assets to be re-purposed for 5G by the end of 2022; the fixed-broadband network in the UAE is dominated by fiber, with DSL having a minor and declining presence; this focus on a fully fiber infrastructure has also facilitated growth in e-commerce, and has supported the government's long-term aim of transitioning the economy from its dependence on oil to being knowledge-based and supported by digital services; the country stands to benefit from having signed the Abraham Accord Declaration with Israel, which aims to normalize relations between the two countries; such benefits can be seen in the agreement to enable local ISPs to access Bezeq International's submarine cable infrastructure, and so improve direct connectivity to Europe, South East Asia, and Africa; the UAE's ISPs can also access Bezeq International's data center in Tel Aviv, improving internet services (2022)
domestic: fixed-line is 24 per 100 and mobile-cellular is 190 per 100 (2021)
international: country code - 971; landing points for the FLAG, SEA-ME-WE-3 ,-4 & -5, Qater UAE Submarine Cable System, FALCON, FOG, Tat TGN-Gulf, OMRAN/EPEG Cable System, AAE-1, BBG, EIG, FEA, GBICS/MENA, IMEWE, Orient Express, TEAMS, TW1 and the UAE-Iran submarine cables, linking to Europe, Africa, the Middle East, Asia, Southeast Asia and Australia; satellite earth stations - 3 Intelsat (1 Atlantic Ocean and 2 Indian) (2020)

Broadcast media: except for the many organizations now operating in media free zones in Abu Dhabi and Dubai, most TV and radio stations remain government-owned; widespread use of satellite dishes provides access to pan-Arab and other international broadcasts; restrictions since June 2017 on some satellite channels and websites originating from or otherwise linked to Qatar, but in early 2023 Abu Dhabi unblocked several sites, including Al Jazeera (2022)

Internet country code: .ae

Internet users: *total:* 9.4 million (2021 est.)
percent of population: 100% (2021 est.)
comparison ranking: total 61

Broadband - fixed subscriptions: *total:* 3,245,123 (2020 est.)
subscriptions per 100 inhabitants: 33 (2020 est.)
comparison ranking: total 45

TRANSPORTATION

National air transport system: *number of registered air carriers:* 10 (2020)
inventory of registered aircraft operated by air carriers: 497
annual passenger traffic on registered air carriers: 95,533,069 (2018)
annual freight traffic on registered air carriers: 15,962,900,000 (2018) mt-km

Civil aircraft registration country code prefix: A6

Airports: 42 (2024)
comparison ranking: 97

Heliports: 203 (2024)

Pipelines: 533 km condensate, 3,277 km gas, 300 km liquid petroleum gas, 3287 km oil, 24 km oil/gas/water, 218 km refined products, 99 km water (2013)

Roadways: *total:* 4,080 km
paved: 4,080 km (2008) (includes 253 km of expressways)
comparison ranking: total 156

Merchant marine: *total:* 655 (2023)
by type: bulk carrier 2, container ship 3, general cargo 122, oil tanker 16, other 512
comparison ranking: total 35

Ports: *total ports:* 20 (2024)
large: 1
medium: 4
small: 9
very small: 6
ports with oil terminals: 17
key ports: Abu Zaby, Jabal Az Zannah/Ruways, Khawr Fakkan, Mina Jabal Ali, Zirkuh

MILITARY AND SECURITY

Military and security forces: United Arab Emirates Armed Forces: Land Forces, Navy Forces, Air Force, Presidential Guard (includes special operations forces)

Ministry of Interior: Coast Guard Forces, Critical Infrastructure and Coastal Patrol Agency (CICPA) (2024)
note: each emirate maintains a local police force called a general directorate, which is officially a branch of the federal Ministry of Interior; all emirate-level general directorates of police enforce their respective emirate's laws autonomously; they also enforce federal laws within their emirate in coordination with one another under the federal ministry; the State Security Directorate (SSD) in Abu Dhabi and Dubai State Security (DSS) have primary responsible for counterterrorism law enforcement efforts; local, emirate-level police forces, especially the Abu Dhabi Police and Dubai Police, are the first responders in such cases and provide technical assistance to SSD and DSS

Military expenditures: 4% of GDP (2023 est.)
4% of GDP (2022 est.)
5% of GDP (2021 est.)
5.6% of GDP (2020 est.)
5.4% of GDP (2019 est.)
comparison ranking: 21

Military and security service personnel strengths: approximately 65,000 active personnel (45,000 Land Forces; 3,000 Navy; 5,000 Air Force; 12,000 Presidential Guard) (2024)

Military equipment inventories and acquisitions: the military's inventory is comprised of a wide variety of mostly modern imported equipment; over the past decade, the UAE has acquired military equipment from more than 20 countries with the US as the leading supplier; in recent years, the UAE has tried to boost its domestic defense industry (2023)

Military service age and obligation: 18-30 years of age for compulsory military service for men (compulsory service initiated in 2014); 18-40 for voluntary service; 36-month service obligation for men without a secondary education and 11 months for secondary school graduates; women may volunteer (11-month service obligation regardless of education) (2023)
note 1: compulsory service may be completed in the uniformed military, the Ministry of Interior, or other security institutions designated by the military leadership
note 2: the UAE military employs a considerable number of foreign personnel on contracted service

Military deployments: continues to maintain a small force in Yemen; also maintains some troops at military bases in Eritrea and Somalia (Somaliland) (2023)
note: in 2015, UAE intervened militarily in Yemen as part of the Saudi-led coalition in support of the Republic of Yemen Government with an estimated 3,500 troops, as well as supporting air and naval forces; UAE withdrew its main military force from Yemen in 2019, but has retained a small military presence while working with proxies in southern Yemen, most notably the Southern Transitional Council (STC)

Military - note: the UAE Armed Forces (UAEAF) are responsible for external defense and supporting the UAE's foreign policy objectives; the military's primary concerns include terrorism, regional instability, particularly in neighboring Yemen, and Iran, including a territorial dispute over three islands in the Strait of Hormuz and Iranian support to proxy forces in the region; in recent years, the UAE has undertaken a large military modernization program to go along with an assertive security policy which has included military involvments in Libya, Syria, and Yemen, as well as peacekeeping missions in Afghanistan and Somalia; the UAEAF has organized, trained, and equipped tens of thousands of militia forces in Yemen and offered training and equipment to several countries in Africa; the UAE also hosts the region's first military school for women, which has trained female peacekeepers for deployment in Africa and Asia
the UAE has close security ties to France and the US; it hosts a multi-service French military base, which includes the French naval command for the Indian Ocean (ALINDIEN); the UAE has a defense cooperation agreement with the US and hosts thousands of US military troops, mostly air and naval personnel; it also has defense ties with a variety of other countries, including Australia, China, Egypt, Israel, Jordan, Malaysia, South Korea, and the UK, as well as NATO and fellow members of the Gulf Cooperation Council, particularly Saudi Arabia
the UAEAF traces its origins to the establishment of the Trucial Oman Scouts in 1951, a joint UK-Abu Dhabi organization modeled after Jordan's Arab Legion, which became the Abu Dhabi Defense Force in 1965; the modern UAEAF were formed in 1976 and are considered to be one of the best-trained and most capable forces in the Persian Gulf region (2024)

SPACE

Space agency/agencies: UAE Space Agency (created in 2014); Mohammed bin Rashid Space Centre (MBRSC; established 2006); in 2015, MBRSC combined with the Emirates Institution for Advanced Science and Technology (EIAST; established 2006) (2024)

Space program overview: has an ambitious and growing space program and is recognized as one of the leading programs in the region; focused on satellite development, including communications, remote sensing, and navigational; also placing emphasis on building expertise, infrastructure, ground stations, technology, and research and development capabilities to support its space program domestically; rather than building its own launch capabilities, has elected to utilize foreign partners to launch payloads from spaceports abroad; has looked to invest heavily in foreign commercial space companies and encourage global partnerships; has a foreign-assisted astronaut training program; seeking to establish UAE as an international hub for space education; has signed more than 25 cooperation agreements or memorandums of understanding with major global and regional players in the space sector, including the Arab Space Cooperation Group, China, the European Space Agency (ESA), France, Germany, India, Japan, Russia, South Korea, the UK, and the US; sees the development of its commercial space industry as a key pillar for diversifying and developing the country's non-oil economy; dozens of space companies and entities operate in the UAE, including international and start-ups, plus several space science research centers (2024)
note: further details about the key activities, programs, and milestones of the country's space program, as well as government spending estimates on the space sector, appear in the Space Programs reference guide

TRANSNATIONAL ISSUES

Refugees and internally displaced persons: *stateless persons:* 5 (mid-year 2021)

Illicit drugs: major source of precursor chemicals used in the production of illicit narcotics

UNITED KINGDOM

INTRODUCTION

Background: The United Kingdom of Great Britain and Northern Ireland was created when the Kingdoms of England and Scotland – which previously had been distinct states under a single monarchy – were joined under the 1701 Acts of Union. The island of Ireland was incorporated under the 1800 Acts of Union, while Wales had been part of the Kingdom of England since the 16th century. The United Kingdom has historically played a leading role in developing parliamentary democracy and in advancing literature and science. The 18th and 19th centuries saw the rapid expansion of the British Empire despite the loss of the Thirteen Colonies, and at its zenith in the early 20th century, the British Empire stretched over one fourth of the earth's surface. The first half of the 20th century saw two World Wars seriously deplete the UK's strength and the Irish Republic withdraw from the union. The second half witnessed the dismantling of the Empire and the UK rebuilding itself into a modern and prosperous European nation. As one of five permanent members of the UN Security Council and a founding member of NATO and the Commonwealth of Nations, the UK pursues a global approach to foreign policy. The devolved Scottish Parliament, the National Assembly for Wales, and the Northern Ireland Assembly were established in 1998.

The UK was an active member of the EU after its accession in 1973, although it chose to remain outside the Economic and Monetary Union. However, motivated in part by frustration at a remote bureaucracy in Brussels and massive migration into the country, UK citizens in 2016 voted by 52 to 48 percent to leave the EU. On 31 January 2020, the UK became the only country to depart the EU – a move known as "Brexit" – after prolonged negotiations on EU-UK economic and security relationships.

GEOGRAPHY

Location: Western Europe, islands - including the northern one-sixth of the island of Ireland - between the North Atlantic Ocean and the North Sea; northwest of France

Geographic coordinates: 54 00 N, 2 00 W

Map references: Europe

Area: *total:* 243,610 sq km
land: 241,930 sq km
water: 1,680 sq km
note 1: the percentage area breakdown of the four UK countries is: England 53%, Scotland 32%, Wales 9%, and Northern Ireland 6%
note 2: includes Rockall and the Shetland Islands, which are part of Scotland
comparison ranking: total 80

Area - comparative: twice the size of Pennsylvania; slightly smaller than Oregon

Land boundaries: *total:* 499 km
border countries (1): Ireland 499 km

Coastline: 12,429 km

Maritime claims: *territorial sea:* 12 nm
continental shelf: as defined in continental shelf orders or in accordance with agreed upon boundaries
exclusive fishing zone: 200 nm

Climate: temperate; moderated by prevailing southwest winds over the North Atlantic Current; more than one-half of the days are overcast

Terrain: mostly rugged hills and low mountains; level to rolling plains in east and southeast

Elevation: *highest point:* Ben Nevis 1,345 m
lowest point: The Fens -4 m

mean elevation: 162 m

Natural resources: coal, petroleum, natural gas, iron ore, lead, zinc, gold, tin, limestone, salt, clay, chalk, gypsum, potash, silica sand, slate, arable land

Land use: *agricultural land:* 71% (2018 est.)
arable land: 25.1% (2018 est.)
permanent crops: 0.2% (2018 est.)
permanent pasture: 45.7% (2018 est.)
forest: 11.9% (2018 est.)
other: 17.1% (2018 est.)

Irrigated land: 718 sq km (2018)

Population distribution: the core of the population lies in and around London, with significant clusters found in central Britain around Manchester and Liverpool, in the Scottish lowlands between Edinburgh and Glasgow, southern Wales in and around Cardiff, and far eastern Northern Ireland centered on Belfast

Natural hazards: winter windstorms; floods

Geography - note: lies near vital North Atlantic sea lanes; only 35 km from France and linked by tunnel under the English Channel (the Channel Tunnel or Chunnel); because of heavily indented coastline, no location is more than 125 km from tidal waters

PEOPLE AND SOCIETY

Population: *total:* 68,459,055 United Kingdom
male: 34,005,445
female: 34,453,610 (2024 est.)
comparison rankings: female 22; male 21; total 21

Nationality: *noun:* Briton(s), British (collective plural)
adjective: British

Ethnic groups: White 87.2%, Black/African/Caribbean/black British 3%, Asian/Asian British: Indian 2.3%, Asian/Asian British: Pakistani 1.9%, mixed 2%, other 3.7% (2011 est.)

Languages: English
note: the following are recognized regional languages: Scots (about 30% of the population of Scotland), Scottish Gaelic (about 60,000 speakers in Scotland), Welsh (about 20% of the population of Wales), Irish (about 10% of the population of Northern Ireland), Cornish (some 2,000 to 3,000 people in Cornwall) (2012 est.)

Religions: Christian (includes Anglican, Roman Catholic, Presbyterian, Methodist) 59.5%, Muslim 4.4%, Hindu 1.3%, other 2%, unspecified 7.2%, none 25.7% (2011 est.)

Age structure: *0-14 years:* 16.7% (male 5,872,937/female 5,592,665)
15-64 years: 63.9% (male 22,062,643/female 21,702,401)
65 years and over: 19.3% (2024 est.) (male 6,069,865/female 7,158,544)

Dependency ratios: *total dependency ratio:* 57.7
youth dependency ratio: 27.8
elderly dependency ratio: 29.8
potential support ratio: 3.4 (2021 est.)

Median age: *total:* 40.8 years (2024 est.)
male: 40.1 years
female: 41.5 years
comparison ranking: total 58

Population growth rate: 0.45% (2024 est.)
comparison ranking: 154

Birth rate: 10.8 births/1,000 population (2024 est.)
comparison ranking: 170

Death rate: 9.2 deaths/1,000 population (2024 est.)
comparison ranking: 53

Net migration rate: 2.9 migrant(s)/1,000 population (2024 est.)
comparison ranking: 39

Population distribution: the core of the population lies in and around London, with significant clusters found in central Britain around Manchester and Liverpool, in the Scottish lowlands between Edinburgh and Glasgow, southern Wales in and around Cardiff, and far eastern Northern Ireland centered on Belfast

Urbanization: *urban population:* 84.6% of total population (2023)
rate of urbanization: 0.8% annual rate of change (2020-25 est.)

Major urban areas - population: 9.648 million LONDON (capital), 2.791 million Manchester, 2.665 million Birmingham, 1.929 million West Yorkshire, 1.698 million Glasgow, 952,000 Southampton/Portsmouth (2023)

Sex ratio: *at birth:* 1.05 male(s)/female
0-14 years: 1.05 male(s)/female
15-64 years: 1.02 male(s)/female
65 years and over: 0.85 male(s)/female
total population: 0.99 male(s)/female (2024 est.)

Mother's mean age at first birth: 29 years (2018 est.)
note: data represents England and Wales only

Maternal mortality ratio: 10 deaths/100,000 live births (2020 est.)
comparison ranking: 145

Infant mortality rate: *total:* 3.8 deaths/1,000 live births (2024 est.)
male: 4.2 deaths/1,000 live births
female: 3.3 deaths/1,000 live births
comparison ranking: total 190

Life expectancy at birth: *total population:* 82.2 years (2024 est.)
male: 80.1 years
female: 84.4 years
comparison ranking: total population 33

Total fertility rate: 1.63 children born/woman (2024 est.)
comparison ranking: 177

Gross reproduction rate: 0.8 (2024 est.)

Contraceptive prevalence rate: 76.1% (2010/12)
note: percent of women aged 16-49

Drinking water source: *improved: urban:* 100% of population
rural: 100% of population
total: 100% of population

Current health expenditure: 12% of GDP (2020)

Physician density: 3 physicians/1,000 population (2020)

Hospital bed density: 2.5 beds/1,000 population (2019)

Sanitation facility access: *improved: urban:* 99.8% of population
rural: 99.8% of population
total: 99.8% of population
unimproved: urban: 0.2% of population
rural: 0.2% of population
total: 0.2% of population (2020 est.)

Obesity - adult prevalence rate: 27.8% (2016)
comparison ranking: 36

Alcohol consumption per capita: *total:* 9.8 liters of pure alcohol (2019 est.)
beer: 3.53 liters of pure alcohol (2019 est.)
wine: 3.3 liters of pure alcohol (2019 est.)
spirits: 2.35 liters of pure alcohol (2019 est.)
other alcohols: 0.61 liters of pure alcohol (2019 est.)
comparison ranking: total 24

Tobacco use: *total:* 15.4% (2020 est.)
male: 17.3% (2020 est.)
female: 13.5% (2020 est.)
comparison ranking: total 102

Currently married women (ages 15-49): 50.7% (2023 est.)

Child marriage: *women married by age 18:* 0.1% (2020 est.)

Education expenditures: 5.5% of GDP (2020 est.)
comparison ranking: 55

School life expectancy (primary to tertiary education): *total:* 17 years
male: 17 years
female: 18 years (2020)

ENVIRONMENT

Environment - current issues: air pollution improved but remains a concern, particularly in the London region; soil pollution from pesticides and heavy metals; decline in marine and coastal habitats brought on by pressures from housing, tourism, and industry

Environment - international agreements: *party to:* Air Pollution, Air Pollution-Heavy Metals, Air Pollution-Multi-effect Protocol, Air Pollution-Nitrogen Oxides, Air Pollution-Persistent Organic Pollutants, Air Pollution-Sulphur 94, Air

Pollution-Volatile Organic Compounds, Antarctic-Environmental Protection, Antarctic-Marine Living Resources, Antarctic Seals, Antarctic Treaty, Biodiversity, Climate Change, Climate Change-Kyoto Protocol, Climate Change-Paris Agreement, Comprehensive Nuclear Test Ban, Desertification, Endangered Species, Environmental Modification, Hazardous Wastes, Law of the Sea, Marine Dumping-London Convention, Marine Dumping-London Protocol, Marine Life Conservation, Nuclear Test Ban, Ozone Layer Protection, Ship Pollution, Tropical Timber 2006, Wetlands, Whaling
signed, but not ratified: none of the selected agreements

Climate: temperate; moderated by prevailing southwest winds over the North Atlantic Current; more than one-half of the days are overcast

Urbanization: *urban population:* 84.6% of total population (2023)
rate of urbanization: 0.8% annual rate of change (2020-25 est.)

Revenue from forest resources: 0.01% of GDP (2018 est.)
comparison ranking: 154

Revenue from coal: 0% of GDP (2018 est.)
comparison ranking: 181

Air pollutants: *particulate matter emissions:* 9.52 micrograms per cubic meter (2019 est.)
carbon dioxide emissions: 379.02 megatons (2016 est.)
methane emissions: 49.16 megatons (2020 est.)

Waste and recycling: *municipal solid waste generated annually:* 31.567 million tons (2014 est.)
municipal solid waste recycled annually: 8,602,008 tons (2015 est.)
percent of municipal solid waste recycled: 27.3% (2015 est.)

Total water withdrawal: *municipal:* 6.23 billion cubic meters (2020 est.)
industrial: 1.01 billion cubic meters (2020 est.)
agricultural: 1.18 billion cubic meters (2020 est.)

Total renewable water resources: 147 billion cubic meters (2020 est.)

Geoparks: *total global geoparks and regional networks:* 9
global geoparks and regional networks: Black Country; Cuilcagh Lakelands (includes Ireland); English Riviera; Fforest Fawr; GeoMôn; Mourne Gullion Strangford; North Pennines AONB; North-West Highlands; Shetland (2023)

GOVERNMENT

Country name: *conventional long form:* United Kingdom of Great Britain and Northern Ireland; note - the island of Great Britain includes England, Scotland, and Wales
conventional short form: United Kingdom
abbreviation: UK
etymology: self-descriptive country name; the designation "Great Britain," in the sense of "Larger Britain," dates back to medieval times and was used to distinguish the island from "Little Britain," or Brittany in modern France; the name Ireland derives from the Gaelic "Eriu," the matron goddess of Ireland (goddess of the land)

Government type: parliamentary constitutional monarchy; a Commonwealth realm

Capital: *name:* London
geographic coordinates: 51 30 N, 0 05 W
time difference: UTC 0 (5 hours ahead of Washington, DC, during Standard Time)
daylight saving time: +1hr, begins last Sunday in March; ends last Sunday in October
time zone note: the time statements apply to the United Kingdom proper, not to its crown dependencies or overseas territories
etymology: the name derives from the Roman settlement of Londinium, established on the current site of London around A.D. 43; the original meaning of the name is uncertain

Administrative divisions: England: 24 two-tier counties, 32 London boroughs and 1 City of London or Greater London, 36 metropolitan districts, 59 unitary authorities (including 4 single-tier counties*);
two-tier counties: Cambridgeshire, Cumbria, Derbyshire, Devon, East Sussex, Essex, Gloucestershire, Hampshire, Hertfordshire, Kent, Lancashire, Leicestershire, Lincolnshire, Norfolk, North Yorkshire, Nottinghamshire, Oxfordshire, Somerset, Staffordshire, Suffolk, Surrey, Warwickshire, West Sussex, Worcestershire

London boroughs and City of London or Greater London: Barking and Dagenham, Barnet, Bexley, Brent, Bromley, Camden, Croydon, Ealing, Enfield, Greenwich, Hackney, Hammersmith and Fulham, Haringey, Harrow, Havering, Hillingdon, Hounslow, Islington, Kensington and Chelsea, Kingston upon Thames, Lambeth, Lewisham, City of London, Merton, Newham, Redbridge, Richmond upon Thames, Southwark, Sutton, Tower Hamlets, Waltham Forest, Wandsworth, Westminster
metropolitan districts: Barnsley, Birmingham, Bolton, Bradford, Bury, Calderdale, Coventry, Doncaster, Dudley, Gateshead, Kirklees, Knowsley, Leeds, Liverpool, Manchester, Newcastle upon Tyne, North Tyneside, Oldham, Rochdale, Rotherham, Salford, Sandwell, Sefton, Sheffield, Solihull, South Tyneside, St. Helens, Stockport, Sunderland, Tameside, Trafford, Wakefield, Walsall, Wigan, Wirral, Wolverhampton
unitary authorities: Bath and North East Somerset; Bedford; Blackburn with Darwen; Blackpool; Bournemouth, Christchurch and Poole; Bracknell Forest; Brighton and Hove; City of Bristol; Buckinghamshire; Central Bedfordshire; Cheshire East; Cheshire West and Chester; Cornwall; Darlington; Derby; Dorset; Durham County*; East Riding of Yorkshire; Halton; Hartlepool; Herefordshire*; Isle of Wight*; Isles of Scilly; City of Kingston upon Hull; Leicester; Luton; Medway; Middlesbrough; Milton Keynes; North East Lincolnshire; North Lincolnshire; North Northamptonshire; North Somerset; Northumberland*; Nottingham; Peterborough; Plymouth; Portsmouth; Reading; Redcar and Cleveland; Rutland; Shropshire; Slough; South Gloucestershire; Southampton; Southend-on-Sea; Stockton-on- Tees; Stoke-on-Trent; Swindon; Telford and Wrekin; Thurrock; Torbay; Warrington; West Berkshire; West Northamptonshire; Wiltshire; Windsor and Maidenhead; Wokingham; York

Northern Ireland: 5 borough councils, 4 district councils, 2 city councils;
borough councils: Antrim and Newtownabbey; Ards and North Down; Armagh City, Banbridge, and Craigavon; Causeway Coast and Glens; Mid and East Antrim
district councils: Derry City and Strabane; Fermanagh and Omagh; Mid Ulster; Newry, Murne, and Down
city councils: Belfast; Lisburn and Castlereagh

Scotland: 32 council areas;
council areas: Aberdeen City, Aberdeenshire, Angus, Argyll and Bute, Clackmannanshire, Dumfries and Galloway, Dundee City, East Ayrshire, East Dunbartonshire, East Lothian, East Renfrewshire, City of Edinburgh, Eilean Siar (Western Isles), Falkirk, Fife, Glasgow City, Highland, Inverclyde, Midlothian, Moray, North Ayrshire, North Lanarkshire, Orkney Islands, Perth and Kinross, Renfrewshire, Shetland Islands, South Ayrshire, South Lanarkshire, Stirling, The Scottish Borders, West Dunbartonshire, West Lothian

Wales: 22 unitary authorities;
unitary authorities: Blaenau Gwent, Bridgend, Caerphilly, Cardiff, Carmarthenshire, Ceredigion, Conwy, Denbighshire, Flintshire, Gwynedd, Isle of Anglesey, Merthyr Tydfil, Monmouthshire, Neath Port Talbot, Newport, Pembrokeshire, Powys, Rhondda Cynon Taff, Swansea, The Vale of Glamorgan, Torfaen, Wrexham

Dependent areas: Anguilla; Bermuda; British Indian Ocean Territory; British Virgin Islands; Cayman Islands; Falkland Islands; Gibraltar; Montserrat; Pitcairn Islands; Saint Helena, Ascension, and Tristan da Cunha; South Georgia and the South Sandwich Islands; Turks and Caicos Islands (12)

Independence: *no official date of independence:* 927 (minor English kingdoms unite); 3 March 1284 (enactment of the Statute of Rhuddlan uniting England and Wales); 1536 (Act of Union formally incorporates England and Wales); 1 May 1707 (Acts of Union formally unite England, Scotland, and Wales as Great Britain); 1 January 1801 (Acts of Union formally unite Great Britain and Ireland as the United Kingdom of Great Britain and Ireland); 6 December 1921 (Anglo-Irish Treaty formalizes partition of Ireland; six counties remain part of the United Kingdom and Northern Ireland); 12 April 1927 (Royal and Parliamentary Titles Act establishes current name of the United Kingdom of Great Britain and Northern Ireland)

National holiday: the UK does not celebrate one particular national holiday

Legal system: common law system; has nonbinding judicial review of Acts of Parliament under the Human Rights Act of 1998

Constitution: *history:* uncoded; partly statutes, partly common law and practice
amendments: proposed as a bill for an Act of Parliament by the government, by the House of Commons, or by the House of Lords; passage requires agreement by both houses and by the monarch (Royal Assent); many previous, last in 2020 - The European Union (Withdrawal Agreement) Act 2020, European Union (Future Relationship) Act 2020

International law organization participation: accepts compulsory ICJ jurisdiction with reservations; accepts ICCt jurisdiction

Citizenship: *citizenship by birth:* no
citizenship by descent only: at least one parent must be a citizen of the United Kingdom
dual citizenship recognized: yes
residency requirement for naturalization: 5 years

Suffrage: 18 years of age; universal

Executive branch: *chief of state:* King CHARLES III (since 8 September 2022)

head of government: Prime Minister Keir STARMER (Labor) (since 5 July 2024)
cabinet: Cabinet appointed by the prime minister
elections/appointments: the monarchy is hereditary; following legislative elections, the leader of the majority party or majority coalition usually becomes the prime minister; election last held on 12 December 2019 (next to be held no later than 28 January 2025)
note 1: in addition to serving as the UK head of state, the British sovereign is the constitutional monarch for 14 additional Commonwealth countries (these 15 states are each referred to as a Commonwealth realm)
note 2: King CHARLES succeeded his mother, Queen ELIZABETH II, after serving as Prince of Wales (heir apparent) for over 64 years - the longest such tenure in British history

Legislative branch: *description:* bicameral Parliament consists of:
House of Lords (membership not fixed; as of December 2023, 784 lords were eligible to participate in the work of the House of Lords - 667 life peers, 91 hereditary peers, and 26 clergy; members are appointed by the monarch on the advice of the prime minister and non-party political members recommended by the House of Lords Appointments Commission); note - House of Lords total does not include ineligible members or members on leave of absence House of Commons (650 seats; members directly elected in single-seat constituencies by simple majority popular vote to serve 5-year terms unless the House is dissolved earlier)
elections: House of Lords - no elections; note - in 1999, as provided by the House of Lords Act, elections were held in the House of Lords to determine the 92 hereditary peers who would remain; elections held only as vacancies in the hereditary peerage arise)
House of Commons - last held on 4 July 2024 (next to be held 4 July 2029)
election results: House of Lords - composition - men 556, women 228, percentage women 29%
House of Commons - percent of vote by party - Labor 33.7%, Conservative 23.7%, Lib Dems 12.2%, Green 6.7%, SNP 2.5%, independents 2.0%, Sinn Fein .7%, Plaid Cymru .7%, Workers Party .7%, DUP .6%, other 2.9%; seats by party - Labor 411, Conservative 121, Lib Dems 72, SNP 9, Sinn Fein 7, independents 6, DUP 5, Reform UK 5, Green 4, Plaid Cymru 4, SDLP 2, other 4; composition - men 387, women 263, percentage women 40.3%

Judicial branch: *highest court(s):* Supreme Court (consists of 12 justices, including the court president and deputy president); note - the Supreme Court was established by the Constitutional Reform Act 2005 and implemented in 2009, replacing the Appellate Committee of the House of Lords as the highest court in the United Kingdom
judge selection and term of office: judge candidates selected by an independent committee of several judicial commissions, followed by their recommendations to the prime minister, and appointed by the monarch; justices serve for life
subordinate courts: England and Wales: Court of Appeal (civil and criminal divisions); High Court; Crown Court; County Courts; Magistrates' Courts; Scotland: Court of Sessions; Sheriff Courts; High Court of Justiciary; tribunals; Northern Ireland: Court of Appeal in Northern Ireland; High Court; county courts; magistrates' courts; specialized tribunals

Political parties: Alliance Party or APNI (Northern Ireland)
Conservative and Unionist Party
Democratic Unionist Party or DUP (Northern Ireland)
Green Party of England and Wales or Greens
Labor (Labour) Party
Liberal Democrats (Lib Dems)
Party of Wales (Plaid Cymru)
Reform UK
Scottish National Party or SNP
Sinn Fein (Northern Ireland)
Social Democratic and Labor Party or SDLP (Northern Ireland)
Traditional Unionist Voice or TUV
UK Independence Party or UKIP
Ulster Unionist Party or UUP (Northern Ireland)
Workers Party of Great Britian

International organization participation: ADB (nonregional member), AfDB (nonregional member), Arctic Council (observer), Australia Group, BIS, C, CBSS (observer), CD, CDB, CE, CERN, EAPC, EBRD, ECB, EIB, EITI (implementing country), ESA, EU, FAO, FATF, G-5, G-7, G-8, G-10, G-20, IADB, IAEA, IBRD, ICAO, ICC (national committees), ICCt, ICRM, IDA, IEA, IFAD, IFC, IFRCS, IGAD (partners), IHO, ILO, IMF, IMO, IMSO, Interpol, IOC, IOM, IPU, ISO, ITSO, ITU, ITUC (NGOs), MIGA, MONUSCO, NATO, NEA, NSG, OAS (observer), OECD, OPCW, OSCE, Pacific Alliance (observer), Paris Club, PCA, PIF (partner), SELEC (observer), SICA (observer), UN, UNCTAD, UNESCO, UNFICYP, UNHCR, UNMISS, UNOOSA, UNRWA, UN Security Council (permanent), UNSOM, UPU, Wassenaar Arrangement, WCO, WHO, WIPO, WMO, WTO, ZC

Diplomatic representation in the US: *chief of mission:* Ambassador Karen Elizabeth PIERCE (since 8 April 2020)
chancery: 3100 Massachusetts Avenue NW, Washington, DC 20008
telephone: [1] (202) 588-6500
FAX: [1] (202) 588-7870
email address and website:
ukin.washington@fcdo.gov.uk
https://www.gov.uk/world/organisations/british-embassy-washington
consulate(s) general: Atlanta, Boston, Chicago, Houston, Los Angeles, Miami, New York, San Francisco

Diplomatic representation from the US: *chief of mission:* Ambassador Jane HARTLEY (since 19 July 2022)
embassy: 33 Nine Elms Lane, London, SW11 7US
mailing address: 8400 London Place, Washington DC 20521-8400
telephone: [44] (0) 20-7499-9000
FAX: [44] (0) 20-7891-3845
email address and website:
SCSLondon@state.gov
https://uk.usembassy.gov/
consulate(s) general: Belfast, Edinburgh

Flag description: blue field with the red cross of Saint George (patron saint of England) edged in white superimposed on the diagonal red cross of Saint Patrick (patron saint of Ireland), which is superimposed on the diagonal white cross of Saint Andrew (patron saint of Scotland); properly known as the Union Flag, but commonly called the Union Jack; the design and colors (especially the Blue Ensign) have been the basis for a number of other flags including other Commonwealth countries and their constituent states or provinces, and British overseas territories

National symbol(s): lion (Britain in general); lion, Tudor rose, oak (England); lion, unicorn, thistle (Scotland); dragon, daffodil, leek (Wales); shamrock, flax (Northern Ireland); national colors: red, white, blue (Britain in general); red, white (England); blue, white (Scotland); red, white, green (Wales)

National anthem: *name:* "God Save the King"
lyrics/music: unknown
note: in use since 1745; by tradition, the song serves as both the national and royal anthem of the UK; it is known as either "God Save the Queen" or "God Save the King," depending on the gender of the reigning monarch; it also serves as the royal anthem of many Commonwealth nations

National heritage: *total World Heritage Sites:* 33 (28 cultural, 4 natural, 1 mixed); note - includes one site in Bermuda
selected World Heritage Site locales: Giant's Causeway and Causeway Coast (n); Ironbridge Gorge (c); Stonehenge, Avebury, and Associated Sites (c); Castles and Town Walls of King Edward in Gwynedd (c); Blenheim Palace (c); City of Bath (c); Tower of London (c); St Kilda (m); Maritime Greenwich (c); Old and New Towns of Edinburgh (c); Royal Botanic Gardens, Kew (c); The English Lake District (c)

ECONOMY

Economic overview: high-income, diversified, non-EU European economy; global financial center and dominant service sector; sluggish growth from stringent monetary policy, reduced business investment, low productivity and participation rates, and post-Brexit trade frictions; fiscal austerity in face of high public debt

Real GDP (purchasing power parity): $3.7 trillion (2023 est.)
$3.696 trillion (2022 est.)
$3.542 trillion (2021 est.)
note: data in 2021 dollars
comparison ranking: 10

Real GDP growth rate: 0.1% (2023 est.)
4.35% (2022 est.)
8.67% (2021 est.)
note: annual GDP % growth based on constant local currency
comparison ranking: 187

Real GDP per capita: $54,100 (2023 est.)
$54,500 (2022 est.)
$52,800 (2021 est.)
note: data in 2021 dollars
comparison ranking: 36

GDP (official exchange rate): $3.34 trillion (2023 est.)
note: data in current dollars at official exchange rate

Inflation rate (consumer prices): 6.79% (2023 est.)
7.92% (2022 est.)
2.52% (2021 est.)
note: annual % change based on consumer prices
comparison ranking: 142

Credit ratings: Fitch rating: AA- (2020)

Moody's rating: Aaa (2020)

Standard & Poors rating: AA (2016)
note: The year refers to the year in which the current credit rating was first obtained.

GDP - composition, by sector of origin: *agriculture:* 0.7% (2023 est.)

industry: 16.9% (2023 est.)
services: 72.8% (2023 est.)
note: figures may not total 100% due to non-allocated consumption not captured in sector-reported data
comparison rankings: services 29; industry 161; agriculture 193

GDP - composition, by end use: *household consumption:* 61.8% (2023 est.)
government consumption: 20.7% (2023 est.)
investment in fixed capital: 18.3% (2023 est.)
investment in inventories: -0.5% (2023 est.)
exports of goods and services: 32.2% (2023 est.)
imports of goods and services: -33.4% (2023 est.)
note: figures may not total 100% due to rounding or gaps in data collection

Agricultural products: milk, wheat, barley, sugar beets, potatoes, chicken, rapeseed, oats, pork, beef (2022)
note: top ten agricultural products based on tonnage

Industries: machine tools, electric power equipment, automation equipment, railroad equipment, shipbuilding, aircraft, motor vehicles and parts, electronics and communications equipment, metals, chemicals, coal, petroleum, paper and paper products, food processing, textiles, clothing, other consumer goods

Industrial production growth rate: 0.14% (2023 est.)
note: annual % change in industrial value added based on constant local currency
comparison ranking: 152

Labor force: 35.275 million (2023 est.)
note: number of people ages 15 or older who are employed or seeking work
comparison ranking: 18

Unemployment rate: 4.06% (2023 est.)
3.73% (2022 est.)
4.83% (2021 est.)
note: % of labor force seeking employment
comparison ranking: 77

Youth unemployment rate (ages 15-24): *total:* 12.5% (2023 est.)
male: 14.5% (2023 est.)
female: 10.5% (2023 est.)
note: % of labor force ages 15-24 seeking employment
comparison ranking: total 111

Population below poverty line: 18.6% (2017 est.)
note: % of population with income below national poverty line

Gini Index coefficient - distribution of family income: 32.4 (2021 est.)
note: index (0-100) of income distribution; higher values represent greater inequality
comparison ranking: 105

Average household expenditures: *on food:* 8.5% of household expenditures (2022 est.)
on alcohol and tobacco: 3.4% of household expenditures (2022 est.)

Household income or consumption by percentage share: *lowest 10%:* 3% (2021 est.)
highest 10%: 25% (2021 est.)
note: % share of income accruing to lowest and highest 10% of population

Remittances: 0.12% of GDP (2023 est.)
0.13% of GDP (2022 est.)
0.11% of GDP (2021 est.)
note: personal transfers and compensation between resident and non-resident individuals/households/entities

Budget: *revenues:* $1.136 trillion (2022 est.)
expenditures: $1.291 trillion (2022 est.)
note: central government revenues (excluding grants) and expenses converted to US dollars at average official exchange rate for year indicated

Public debt: 142.28% of GDP (2022 est.)
note: central government debt as a % of GDP
comparison ranking: 6

Taxes and other revenues: 27.3% (of GDP) (2022 est.)
note: central government tax revenue as a % of GDP
comparison ranking: 32

Current account balance: -$110.393 billion (2023 est.)
-$100.436 billion (2022 est.)
-$14.886 billion (2021 est.)
note: balance of payments - net trade and primary/secondary income in current dollars
comparison ranking: 206

Exports: $1.075 trillion (2023 est.)
$1.029 trillion (2022 est.)
$929.185 billion (2021 est.)
note: balance of payments - exports of goods and services in current dollars
comparison ranking: 4

Exports - partners: US 13%, Netherlands 9%, Germany 9%, China 8%, Ireland 7% (2022)
note: top five export partners based on percentage share of exports

Exports - commodities: gold, cars, gas turbines, crude petroleum, packaged medicine (2022)
note: top five export commodities based on value in dollars

Imports: $1.116 trillion (2023 est.)
$1.115 trillion (2022 est.)
$933.904 billion (2021 est.)
note: balance of payments - imports of goods and services in current dollars
comparison ranking: 4

Imports - partners: China 12%, Germany 10%, US 10%, Norway 8%, Netherlands 5% (2022)
note: top five import partners based on percentage share of imports

Imports - commodities: natural gas, cars, crude petroleum, gold, garments (2022)
note: top five import commodities based on value in dollars

Reserves of foreign exchange and gold: $177.915 billion (2023 est.)
$176.41 billion (2022 est.)
$194.181 billion (2021 est.)
note: holdings of gold (year-end prices)/foreign exchange/special drawing rights in current dollars
comparison ranking: 18

Debt - external: (2019)

Exchange rates: British pounds (GBP) per US dollar -

Exchange rates: 0.805 (2023 est.)
0.811 (2022 est.)
0.727 (2021 est.)
0.78 (2020 est.)
0.783 (2019 est.)

ENERGY

Electricity access: *electrification - total population:* 100% (2022 est.)
electrification - urban areas: 99.9%
electrification - rural areas: 100%

Electricity: *installed generating capacity:* 111.02 million kW (2022 est.)
consumption: 287.128 billion kWh (2022 est.)
exports: 20.793 billion kWh (2022 est.)
imports: 15.451 billion kWh (2022 est.)
transmission/distribution losses: 26.125 billion kWh (2022 est.)
comparison rankings: transmission/distribution losses 194; imports 16; exports 13; consumption 16; installed generating capacity 13

Electricity generation sources: *fossil fuels:* 41.5% of total installed capacity (2022 est.)
nuclear: 13.6% of total installed capacity (2022 est.)
solar: 4.3% of total installed capacity (2022 est.)
wind: 25.3% of total installed capacity (2022 est.)
hydroelectricity: 1.7% of total installed capacity (2022 est.)
biomass and waste: 13.5% of total installed capacity (2022 est.)

Nuclear energy: Number of operational nuclear reactors: 9 (2023)

Number of nuclear reactors under construction: 2 (2023)

Net capacity of operational nuclear reactors: 5.88GW (2023 est.)

Percent of total electricity production: 12.5% (2023 est.)

Number of nuclear reactors permanently shut down: 36 (2023)

Coal: *production:* 1.891 million metric tons (2022 est.)
consumption: 8.568 million metric tons (2022 est.)
exports: 691,000 metric tons (2022 est.)
imports: 7.792 million metric tons (2022 est.)
proven reserves: 26 million metric tons (2022 est.)

Petroleum: *total petroleum production:* 753,000 bbl/day (2023 est.)
refined petroleum consumption: 1.397 million bbl/day (2023 est.)
crude oil estimated reserves: 2.5 billion barrels (2021 est.)

Natural gas: *production:* 37.758 billion cubic meters (2022 est.)
consumption: 70.141 billion cubic meters (2022 est.)
exports: 23.475 billion cubic meters (2022 est.)
imports: 56.501 billion cubic meters (2022 est.)
proven reserves: 180.661 billion cubic meters (2021 est.)

Carbon dioxide emissions: 353.407 million metric tonnes of CO_2 (2022 est.)
from coal and metallurgical coke: 19.558 million metric tonnes of CO_2 (2022 est.)
from petroleum and other liquids: 194.001 million metric tonnes of CO_2 (2022 est.)
from consumed natural gas: 139.848 million metric tonnes of CO_2 (2022 est.)
comparison ranking: total emissions 17

Energy consumption per capita: 99.499 million Btu/person (2022 est.)
comparison ranking: 52

COMMUNICATIONS

Telephones - fixed lines: *total subscriptions:* 29.798 million (2022 est.)
subscriptions per 100 inhabitants: 44 (2022 est.)
comparison ranking: total subscriptions 6

Telephones - mobile cellular: *total subscriptions:* 81.564 million (2022 est.)
subscriptions per 100 inhabitants: 121 (2022 est.)
comparison ranking: total subscriptions 20

Telecommunication systems: *general assessment:* UK's telecom market remains one of the largest in Europe, characterized by competition, affordable pricing, and its technologically advanced systems; mobile penetration above the EU average; government to invest in infrastructure and 5G technologies with ambition for a fully-fibered nation by 2033; operators expanded the reach of 5G services in 2020; super-fast broadband available to about 95% of customers; London is developing smart city technology, in collaboration with private, tech, and academic sectors (2021)
domestic: fixed-line is 48 per 100 and mobile-cellular is 120 per 100 (2021)
international: country code - 44; Landing points for the GTT Atlantic, Scotland-Northern Ireland -1, & -2, Lanis 1,-2, &-3, Sirius North, BT-MT-1, SHEFA-2, BT Highlands and Islands Submarine Cable System, Northern Lights, FARICE-1, Celtic Norse, Tampnet Offshore FOC Network, England Cable, CC-2, E-LLan, Sirius South, ESAT -1 & -2, Rockabill, Geo-Eirgrid, UK-Netherlands-14, Circle North & South, Ulysses2, Conceto, Farland North, Pan European Crossing, Solas, Swansea-Bream, GTT Express, Tata TGN-Atlantic & -Western Europe, Apollo, EIG, Glo-1, TAT-14, Yellow, Celtic, FLAG Atlantic-1, FEA, Isle of Scilly Cable, UK-Channel Islands-8 and SeaMeWe-3 submarine cables providing links throughout Europe, Asia, Africa, the Middle East, Southeast Asia, Australia, and US; satellite earth stations - 10 Intelsat (7 Atlantic Ocean and 3 Indian Ocean), 1 Inmarsat (Atlantic Ocean region), and 1 Eutelsat; at least 8 large international switching centers (2019)

Broadcast media: public service broadcaster, British Broadcasting Corporation (BBC), is the largest broadcasting corporation in the world; BBC operates multiple TV networks with regional and local TV service; a mixed system of public and commercial TV broadcasters along with satellite and cable systems provide access to hundreds of TV stations throughout the world; BBC operates multiple national, regional, and local radio networks with multiple transmission sites; a large number of commercial radio stations, as well as satellite radio services are available (2018)

Internet country code: .uk

Internet users: *total:* 64.99 million (2021 est.)
percent of population: 97% (2021 est.)
comparison ranking: total 16

Broadband - fixed subscriptions: *total:* 27,330,297 (2020 est.)
subscriptions per 100 inhabitants: 40 (2020 est.)
comparison ranking: total 8

Communications - note: *note 1:* the British Library claims to be the largest library in the world with well over 150 million items and in most known languages; it receives copies of all books produced in the UK or Ireland, as well as a significant proportion of overseas titles distributed in the UK; in addition to books (print and digital), holdings include: journals, manuscripts, newspapers, magazines, sound and music recordings, videos, maps, prints, patents, and drawings
note 2: on 1 May 1840, the United Kingdom led the world with the introduction of postage stamps; the Austrian Empire had examined the idea of an "adhesive tax postmark" for the prepayment of postage in 1835; while the suggestion was reviewed in detail, it was rejected for the time being; other countries (including Austria) soon followed the UK's example with their own postage stamps; by the 1860s, most countries were issuing stamps; originally, stamps had to be cut from sheets; the UK issued the first postage stamps with perforations in 1854

TRANSPORTATION

National air transport system: *number of registered air carriers:* 20 (2020)
inventory of registered aircraft operated by air carriers: 794
annual passenger traffic on registered air carriers: 165,388,610 (2018)
annual freight traffic on registered air carriers: 6,198,370,000 (2018) mt-km

Civil aircraft registration country code prefix: G

Airports: 1,043 (2024)
comparison ranking: 6

Heliports: 92 (2024)

Pipelines: 502 km condensate, 9 km condensate/gas, 28,603 km gas, 59 km liquid petroleum gas, 5,256 km oil, 175 km oil/gas/ water, 4,919 km refined products, 255 km water (2013)

Railways: *total:* 16,390 km (2020) 6,167 km electrified
comparison ranking: total 18

Roadways: *total:* 416,461 km (2022)
comparison ranking: total 15

Waterways: 3,200 km (2009) (620 km used for commerce)
comparison ranking: 33

Merchant marine: *total:* 868 (2023)
by type: bulk carrier 34, container ship 46, general cargo 62, oil tanker 13, other 713
note: includes Channel Islands (total fleet 2; general cargo 1, other 1); excludes Isle of Man
comparison ranking: total 29

Ports: *total ports:* 185 (2024)
large: 7
medium: 24
small: 67
very small: 86
size unknown: 1
ports with oil terminals: 67
key ports: Aberdeen, Barrow-in-Furness, Barry, Belfast, Blyth, Bristol, Cardiff, Dundee, Falmouth Harbour, Glasgow, Greenock, Grimsby, Immingham, Kingston-upon-Hull, Leith, Lerwick, Liverpool, London, Londonderry, Lyness, Manchester, Milford Haven, Newport, Peterhead, Plymouth, Portland Harbour, Portsmouth Harbour, Southampton, Sunderland, Teesport, Tynemouth

Transportation - note: begun in 1988 and completed in 1994, the Channel Tunnel (nicknamed the Chunnel) is a 50.5-km (31.4-mi) rail tunnel beneath the English Channel at the Strait of Dover that runs from Folkestone, Kent, England to Coquelles, Pas-de-Calais in northern France; it is the only fixed link between the island of Great Britain and mainland Europe

MILITARY AND SECURITY

Military and security forces: United Kingdom Armed Forces (aka British Armed Forces, aka His Majesty's Armed Forces): British Army, Royal Navy (includes Royal Marines), Royal Air Force (2024)

Military expenditures: 2.3% of GDP (2024 est.)
2.3% of GDP (2023)
2.3% of GDP (2022)
2.3% of GDP (2021)
2.4% of GDP (2020)
comparison ranking: 52

Military and security service personnel strengths: approximately 145,000 regular forces (80,000 Army including the Gurkhas; 33,000 Navy including the Royal Marines; 32,000 Air Force) (2024)
note: the military also has approximately 40-45,000 reserves and other personnel on active duty

Military equipment inventories and acquisitions: the inventory of the British military is comprised of a mix of domestically produced and some imported Western weapons systems; in recent years, the US has been the leading supplier of armaments to the UK; the UK defense industry is capable of producing a wide variety of air, land, and sea weapons systems and is one of the world's top weapons suppliers; it also cooperates with other European countries and the US (2024)

Military service age and obligation: some variations by service, but generally 16-36 years of age for enlisted (with parental consent under 18) and 18-29 for officers; minimum length of service 4 years; women serve in all military services including combat roles; conscription abolished in 1963 (2024)
note 1: women made up 11.7% of the military's full-time personnel in 2024
note 2: the British military allows Commonwealth nationals who are current UK residents and have been in the country for at least 5 years to apply; it also accepts Irish citizens
note 3: the British Army has continued the historic practice of recruiting Gurkhas from Nepal to serve in the Brigade of Gurkhas; the British began to recruit Nepalese citizens (Gurkhas) into the East India Company Army during the Anglo- Nepalese War (1814-1816); the Gurkhas subsequently were brought into the British Indian Army and by 1914, there were 10 Gurkha regiments, collectively known as the Gurkha Brigade; following the partition of India in 1947, an agreement between Nepal, India, and Great Britain allowed for the transfer of the 10 regiments from the British Indian Army to the separate British and Indian armies; four of the regiments were transferred to the British Army, where they have since served continuously as the Brigade of Gurkhas

Military deployments: the British military has more than 8,000 personnel on permanent or long-term rotational deployments around the globe in support of NATO, UN, or other commitments and agreements; key deployments include approximately 1,000 in Brunei, approximately 2,500 in Cyprus (includes 250 for UNFICYP), approximately 1,000 in Estonia (NATO), over 1,000 in the Falkland Islands, almost 600 in Gibraltar, and more than 1,000 in the Middle East; its air and naval forces conduct missions on a global basis; the British military also participates in large scale NATO exercises, including providing some 16,000 personnel for the 6-month 2024 Steadfast Defender exercise (2024)

Military - note: the British military has a long history, a global presence, and a wide range of missions and responsibilities; these responsibilities include protecting the UK, its territories, national interests, and values, preventing conflict, providing humanitarian assistance, participating in international peacekeeping, building relationships, and fulfilling

the UK's alliance and treaty commitments; in addition to its role in the UN, the UK is a leading member of NATO and has made considerable military contributions to NATO missions in such places as Afghanistan, the Baltics, and Iraq, as well the Baltic and Mediterranean seas and the waters of the North Atlantic
the UK is a member of the Five Power Defense Arrangements (FPDA), a series of mutual assistance agreements reached in 1971 embracing Australia, Malaysia, New Zealand, Singapore, and the UK; in 2014, the UK led the formation of the Joint Expeditionary Force (JEF), a pool of high-readiness military forces from the Baltic and Scandinavian countries intended to respond to a wide range of contingencies both in peacetime and in times of crisis or conflict; the UK military also has strong bilateral ties with a variety of foreign militaries, particularly the US, with which it has a mutual defense treaty; British and US military forces have routinely operated side-by-side across a wide range of operations; other close military relationships include Australia, France, Germany, and the Netherlands; in 2010, for example, France and the UK signed a declaration on defense and security cooperation that included greater military interoperability and a Combined Joint Expeditionary Force (CJEF), a deployable, combined Anglo-French military force for use in a wide range of crisis scenarios, up to and including high intensity combat operations
the British Armed Forces were formed in 1707 as the armed forces of the Kingdom of Great Britain when England and Scotland merged under the terms of the Treaty of Union; while the origins of the armed forces of England and Scotland stretch back to the Middle Ages, the first standing armies for England and Scotland were organized in the 1600s while the navies were formed in the 1500s; the Royal Marines were established in 1755; the Royal Air Force was created in April 1918 by the merger of the British Army's Royal Flying Corps and the Admiralty's Royal Naval Air Service (2024)

SPACE

Space agency/agencies: UK Space Agency (UKSA; established in 2010); the UKSA replaced the British National Space Center (BNSC; organized in 1985); UK Space Command (formed 2021) (2024)

Space launch site(s): Spaceport 1 (Outer Hebrides, Scotland; operational 2023); Spaceport Machrihanish (Argyll, Scotland; operational 2024); Glasgow Prestwick (South Ayrshire, Scotland; operational 2024 for horizontal launches); Spaceport Snowdonia (Gwynedd, Wales; operational 2024); SaxaVord UK Spaceport (Unst, Shetland Islands; operational 2023); Sutherland Spaceport (Sutherland, Scotland; operational 2024); Sutherland, Scotland (Cornwall Airport Newquay, Cornwall; operational 2023 for horizontal launches) (2024)

Space program overview: has a comprehensive space program and is active across all areas of the space sector outside of launching humans into space, including satellite/space launch vehicles (SLVs)/rockets and their components, space probes, satellites and satellite subcomponents, space sensors, spaceports, and various other space-related technologies; as a founding member of the European Space Agency (ESA), it is heavily involved in ESA programs and has bi-lateral relations with many members; is a close partner of the US NASA and since 2016 has forged over 350 relationships with international organizations across nearly 50 developing countries; has a large commercial space sector that produces SLVs, SLV components, satellites, satellite subcomponents and sensors, and other space-related technologies; the UK has a space industrial plan, and the UKSA has provided funding to encourage and support commercial space projects (2024)
note: further details about the key activities, programs, and milestones of the country's space program, as well as government spending estimates on the space sector, appear in the Space Programs reference guide

TERRORISM

Terrorist group(s): Continuity Irish Republican Army; Islamic State of Iraq and ash-Sham (ISIS); New Irish Republican Army; al-Qa'ida
note: details about the history, aims, leadership, organization, areas of operation, tactics, targets, weapons, size, and sources of support of the group(s) appear(s) in the Terrorism reference guide

TRANSNATIONAL ISSUES

Refugees and internally displaced persons: *refugees (country of origin):* 21,904 (Iran), 15,615 (Eritrea), 11,371 (Sudan), 12,155 (Syria), 10,259 (Afghanistan), 8,009 (Pakistan), 7,699 (Iraq) (mid-year 2022); 255,060 (Ukraine) (as of 12 March 2024)
stateless persons: 5,483 (2022)

Illicit drugs: a major consumer and transshipment point, though not a source, for illicit drugs; among the highest consumer of heroin and cocaine in Europe; one of the largest markets for cannabis; a major source of precursor or essential chemicals used in the production of illicit narcotics

UNITED STATES

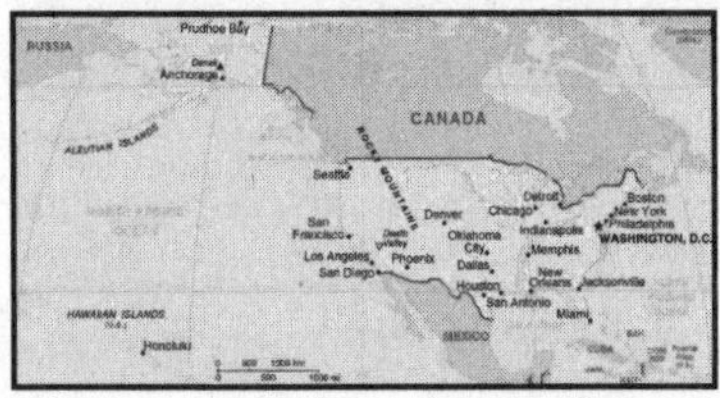

INTRODUCTION

Background: Thirteen of Britain's American colonies broke with the mother country in 1776 and were recognized as the new nation of the United States of America following the Treaty of Paris in 1783. During the 19th and 20th centuries, 37 new states were added as the nation expanded across the North American continent and acquired a number of overseas possessions. Two of the most traumatic experiences in the nation's history were the Civil War (1861-65), in which a northern Union of states defeated a secessionist Confederacy of 11 southern slave states, and the Great Depression of the 1930s, an economic downturn during which about a quarter of the labor force lost its jobs. Buoyed by victories in World Wars I and II and the end of the Cold War in 1991, the US remains the world's most powerful nation state. Since the end of World War II, the economy has achieved relatively steady growth, low unemployment, and rapid advances in technology.

GEOGRAPHY

Location: North America, bordering both the North Atlantic Ocean and the North Pacific Ocean, between Canada and Mexico

Geographic coordinates: 38 00 N, 97 00 W

Map references: North America

Area: *total:* 9,833,517 sq km
land: 9,147,593 sq km
water: 685,924 sq km
note: includes only the 50 states and District of Columbia, no overseas territories
comparison ranking: total 4

Area - comparative: about half the size of Russia; about three-tenths the size of Africa; about half the size of South America (or slightly larger than Brazil); slightly larger than China; more than twice the size of the European Union

Land boundaries: *total:* 12,002 km
border countries (2): Canada 8,891 km (including 2,475 km with Alaska); Mexico 3,111 km
note: US Naval Base at Guantanamo Bay, Cuba is leased by the US and is part of Cuba; the base boundary is 28.5 km

Coastline: 19,924 km

Maritime claims: *territorial sea:* 12 nm
contiguous zone: 24 nm
exclusive economic zone: 200 nm
continental shelf: not specified

Climate: mostly temperate, but tropical in Hawaii and Florida, arctic in Alaska, semiarid in the great plains west of the Mississippi River, and arid in the Great Basin of the southwest; low winter temperatures in the northwest are ameliorated occasionally in January and February by warm chinook winds from the eastern slopes of the Rocky Mountains
note: many consider Denali, the highest peak in the US, to be the world's coldest mountain because of its combination of high elevation and its subarctic location at 63 degrees north latitude; permanent snow and ice cover over 75 percent of the mountain, and enormous glaciers, up to 45 miles long and 3,700 feet thick, spider out from its base in every direction; it is home to some of the world's coldest and most violent weather, where winds of over 150 miles per hour and temperatures of -93°F have been recorded.

Terrain: vast central plain, mountains in west, hills and low mountains in east; rugged mountains and broad river valleys in Alaska; rugged, volcanic topography in Hawaii

Elevation: *highest point:* Denali 6,190 m (Mount McKinley) (highest point in North America)
lowest point: Death Valley (lowest point in North America) -86 m
mean elevation: 760 m
note: Denali is one of the most striking features on the entire planet; at 20,310 feet, it is the crowning peak of the Alaska Range and the highest mountain on North America; it towers three and one-half vertical miles above its base, making it a mile taller from base to summit than Mt. Everest; Denali's base sits at about 2,000 feet above sea level and rises over three and one-half miles to its 20,310 foot summit; Everest begins on a 14,000-foot high plain, then summits at 29,028 feet.
note: the peak of Mauna Kea (4,207 m above sea level) on the island of Hawaii rises about 10,200 m above the Pacific Ocean floor; by this measurement, it is the world's tallest mountain - higher than Mount Everest (8,850 m), which is recognized as the tallest mountain above sea level

Natural resources: coal, copper, lead, molybdenum, phosphates, rare earth elements, uranium, bauxite, gold, iron, mercury, nickel, potash, silver, tungsten, zinc, petroleum, natural gas, timber, arable land
note: the US has the world's largest coal reserves with 491 billion short tons accounting for 27% of the world's total

Land use: *agricultural land:* 44.5% (2018 est.)
arable land: 16.8% (2018 est.)
permanent crops: 0.3% (2018 est.)
permanent pasture: 27.4% (2018 est.)
forest: 33.3% (2018 est.)
other: 22.2% (2018 est.)

Irrigated land: 234,782 sq km (2017)

Major lakes (area sq km): *fresh water lake(s):* Michigan – 57,750 sq km; Superior* – 53,348 sq km; Huron* – 23,597 sq km; Erie* – 12,890 sq km; Ontario* – 9,220 sq km; Lake of the Woods – 4,350 sq km; Iliamna – 2,590 sq km; Okeechobee – 1,810 sq km; Belcharof – 1,190 sq km; Red – 1,170 sq km; Saint Clair – 1,113 sq km; Champlain – 1,100 sq km
note - Great Lakes* area shown as US waters
salt water lake(s): Great Salt – 4,360 sq km; Pontchartrain – 1,620 sq km; Selawik – 1,400 sq km; Salton Sea – 950 sq km

Major rivers (by length in km): Missouri - 3,768 km; Mississippi - 3,544 km; Yukon river mouth (shared with Canada [s]) - 3,190 km; Saint Lawrence (shared with Canada) - 3,058 km; Rio Grande river source (mouth shared with Mexico) - 3,057 km; Colorado river source (shared with Mexico [m]) - 2,333 km; Arkansas - 2,348 km; Columbia river mouth (shared with Canada [s]) - 2,250 km; Red - 2,188 km; Ohio - 2,102 km; Snake - 1,670 km
note – [s] after country name indicates river source; [m] after country name indicates river mouth

Major watersheds (area sq km): Atlantic Ocean drainage: *(Gulf of Mexico)* Mississippi* (3,202,185 sq km); Rio Grande (607,965 sq km); *(Gulf of Saint Lawrence)* Saint Lawrence* (1,049,636 sq km total, US only 505,000 sq km)

Pacific Ocean drainage: Yukon* (847,620 sq km, US only 23,820 sq km); Colorado (703,148 sq km); Columbia* (657,501 sq km, US only 554,501 sq km)
note - watersheds shared with Canada shown with *

Major aquifers: Northern Great Plains Aquifer, Cambrian-Ordovician Aquifer System, Californian Central Valley Aquifer System, Ogallala Aquifer (High Plains), Atlantic and Gulf Coastal Plains Aquifer

Population distribution: large urban clusters are spread throughout the eastern half of the US (particularly the Great Lakes area, northeast, east, and southeast) and the western tier states; mountainous areas, principally the Rocky Mountains and Appalachian chain, deserts in the southwest, the dense boreal forests in the extreme north, and the central prarie states are less densely populated; Alaska's population is concentrated along its southern coast - with particular emphasis on the city of Anchorage - and Hawaii's is centered on the island of Oahu

Natural hazards: tsunamis; volcanoes; earthquake activity around Pacific Basin; hurricanes along the Atlantic and Gulf of Mexico coasts; tornadoes in the Midwest and Southeast; mud slides in California; forest fires in the west; flooding; permafrost in northern Alaska, a major impediment to development
volcanism: volcanic activity in the Hawaiian Islands, Western Alaska, the Pacific Northwest, and in the Northern Mariana Islands; both Mauna Loa (4,170 m) in Hawaii and Mount Rainier (4,392 m) in Washington have been deemed Decade Volcanoes by the International Association of Volcanology and Chemistry of the Earth's Interior, worthy of study due to their explosive history and close proximity to human populations; Pavlof (2,519 m) is the most active volcano in Alaska's Aleutian Arc and poses a significant threat to air travel since the area constitutes a major flight path between North America and East Asia; St. Helens (2,549 m), famous for the devastating 1980 eruption, remains active today; numerous other historically active volcanoes exist, mostly concentrated in the Aleutian arc and Hawaii; they include: in Alaska: Aniakchak, Augustine, Chiginagak, Fourpeaked, Iliamna, Katmai, Kupreanof, Martin, Novarupta, Redoubt, Spurr, Wrangell, Trident, Ugashik-Peulik, Ukinrek Maars, Veniaminof; in Hawaii: Haleakala, Kilauea, Loihi; in the Northern Mariana Islands: Anatahan; and in the Pacific Northwest: Mount Baker, Mount Hood; see note 2 under "Geography - note"

Geography - note: *note 1:* world's third-largest country by size (after Russia and Canada) and by population (after China and India); Denali (Mt. McKinley) is the highest point (6,190 m) in North America and Death Valley the lowest point (-86 m) on the continent
note 2: the western coast of the United States and southern coast of Alaska lie along the Ring of Fire, a belt of active volcanoes and earthquake epicenters bordering the Pacific Ocean; up to 90% of the world's earthquakes and some 75% of the world's volcanoes occur within the Ring of Fire
note 3: the Aleutian Islands are a chain of volcanic islands that divide the Bering Sea (north) from the main Pacific Ocean (south); they extend about 1,800 km westward from the Alaskan Peninsula; the archipelago consists of 14 larger islands, 55 smaller islands, and hundreds of islets; there are 41 active volcanoes on the islands, which together form a large northern section of the Ring of Fire
note 4: Mammoth Cave, in west-central Kentucky, is the world's longest known cave system with more than 650 km (405 miles) of surveyed passageways, which is nearly twice as long as the second-longest cave system, the Sac Actun underwater cave in Mexico – the world's longest underwater cave system (see "Geography - note" under Mexico)
note 5: Kazumura Cave on the island of Hawaii is the world's longest and deepest lava tube cave; it has been surveyed at 66 km (41 mi) long and 1,102 m (3,614 ft) deep
note 6: Bracken Cave outside of San Antonio, Texas is the world's largest bat cave; it is the summer home to the largest colony of bats in the world; an estimated 20 million Mexican free-tailed bats roost in the cave from March to October making it the world's largest known concentration of mammals
note 7: three food crops are generally acknowledged to be native to areas of what is now the United States: cranberries, pecans, and sunflowers

PEOPLE AND SOCIETY

Population: *total:* 341,963,408
male: 168,598,780
female: 173,364,628 (2024 est.)
comparison rankings: female 3; male 3; total 3

Nationality: *noun:* American(s)
adjective: American

Ethnic groups: White 61.6%, Black or African American 12.4%, Asian 6%, Indigenous and Alaska native 1.1%, Native Hawaiian and Other Pacific Islander 0.2%, other 8.4%, two or more races 10.2% (2020 est.)
note: a separate listing for Hispanic is not included because the US Census Bureau considers Hispanic to mean persons of Spanish/Hispanic/Latino origin including those of Mexican, Cuban, Puerto Rican, Dominican Republic, Spanish, and Central or South American origin living in the US who may be of any race or ethnic group (White, Black, Asian, etc.); an estimated 18.7% of the total US population is Hispanic as of 2020

Languages: English only 78.2%, Spanish 13.4%, Chinese 1.1%, other 7.3% (2017 est.)
note: data represent the language spoken at home; the US has no official national language, but English has acquired official status in 32 of the 50 states; Hawaiian is an official language in the state of Hawaii, and 20 indigenous languages are official in Alaska

Religions: Protestant 46.5%, Roman Catholic 20.8%, Jewish 1.9%, Church of Jesus Christ 1.6%, other Christian 0.9%, Muslim 0.9%, Jehovah's Witness 0.8%, Buddhist 0.7%, Hindu 0.7%, other 1.8%, unaffiliated 22.8%, don't know/refused 0.6% (2014 est.)

Age structure: *0-14 years:* 18.1% (male 31,618,532/female 30,254,223)
15-64 years: 63.4% (male 108,553,822/female 108,182,491)
65 years and over: 18.5% (2024 est.) (male 28,426,426/female 34,927,914)

Dependency ratios: *total dependency ratio:* 53.7
youth dependency ratio: 28
elderly dependency ratio: 25.6
potential support ratio: 3.9 (2021 est.)

Median age: *total:* 38.9 years (2022 est.)
male: 37.8 years
female: 40 years
comparison ranking: total 69

Population growth rate: 0.67% (2024 est.)
comparison ranking: 131

Birth rate: 12.2 births/1,000 population (2024 est.)
comparison ranking: 145

Death rate: 8.5 deaths/1,000 population (2024 est.)
comparison ranking: 72

Net migration rate: 3 migrant(s)/1,000 population (2024 est.)
comparison ranking: 38

Population distribution: large urban clusters are spread throughout the eastern half of the US (particularly the Great Lakes area, northeast, east, and southeast) and the western tier states; mountainous areas, principally the Rocky Mountains and Appalachian chain, deserts in the southwest, the dense boreal forests in the extreme north, and the central prarie states are less densely populated; Alaska's population is concentrated along its southern coast - with particular emphasis on the city of Anchorage - and Hawaii's is centered on the island of Oahu

Urbanization: *urban population:* 83.3% of total population (2023)
rate of urbanization: 0.96% annual rate of change (2020-25 est.)

Major urban areas - population: 18.937 million New York-Newark, 12.534 million Los Angeles-Long Beach-Santa Ana, 8.937 million Chicago, 6.707 million Houston, 6.574 million Dallas-Fort Worth, 5.490 million WASHINGTON, D.C. (capital) (2023)

Sex ratio: *at birth:* 1.05 male(s)/female
0-14 years: 1.05 male(s)/female
15-64 years: 1 male(s)/female
65 years and over: 0.81 male(s)/female
total population: 0.97 male(s)/female (2024 est.)

Mother's mean age at first birth: 27 years (2019 est.)

Maternal mortality ratio: 21 deaths/100,000 live births (2020 est.)
comparison ranking: 122

Infant mortality rate: *total:* 5.1 deaths/1,000 live births (2024 est.)
male: 5.4 deaths/1,000 live births
female: 4.7 deaths/1,000 live births
comparison ranking: total 173

Life expectancy at birth: *total population:* 80.9 years (2024 est.)
male: 78.7 years
female: 83.1 years
comparison ranking: total population 49

Total fertility rate: 1.84 children born/woman (2024 est.)
comparison ranking: 133

Gross reproduction rate: 0.9 (2024 est.)

Contraceptive prevalence rate: 73.9% (2017/19)

Drinking water source: *improved: urban:* 99.9% of population
rural: 99.7% of population
total: 99.9% of population
unimproved: urban: 0.1% of population
rural: 0.3% of population
total: 0.1% of population (2020 est.)

Current health expenditure: 18.8% of GDP (2020)

Physician density: 2.61 physicians/1,000 population (2018)

Hospital bed density: 2.9 beds/1,000 population (2017)

Sanitation facility access: *improved: urban:* 99.8% of population
rural: 98.9% of population
total: 99.7% of population
unimproved: urban: 0.2% of population
rural: 11.1% of population
total: 0.3% of population (2020 est.)

Obesity - adult prevalence rate: 36.2% (2016)
comparison ranking: 12

Alcohol consumption per capita: *total:* 8.93 liters of pure alcohol (2019 est.)
beer: 3.97 liters of pure alcohol (2019 est.)
wine: 1.67 liters of pure alcohol (2019 est.)
spirits: 3.29 liters of pure alcohol (2019 est.)
other alcohols: 0 liters of pure alcohol (2019 est.)
comparison ranking: total 35

Tobacco use: *total:* 23% (2020 est.)
male: 28.4% (2020 est.)
female: 17.5% (2020 est.)
comparison ranking: total 66

Children under the age of 5 years underweight: 0.4% (2017/18)
comparison ranking: 125

Currently married women (ages 15-49): 51.9% (2023 est.)

Education expenditures: 6.1% of GDP (2020 est.)
comparison ranking: 40

School life expectancy (primary to tertiary education): *total:* 16 years
male: 16 years
female: 17 years (2020)

ENVIRONMENT

Environment - current issues: air pollution; large emitter of carbon dioxide from the burning of fossil fuels; water pollution from runoff of pesticides and fertilizers; declining natural freshwater resources in much of the western part of the country require careful management; deforestation; mining; desertification; species conservation; invasive species (the Hawaiian Islands are particularly vulnerable)

Environment - international agreements: *party to:* Air Pollution, Air Pollution-Heavy Metals, Air Pollution-Multi-effect Protocol, Air Pollution-Nitrogen Oxides, Antarctic-Environmental Protection, Antarctic-Marine Living Resources, Antarctic Seals, Antarctic Treaty, Climate Change, Climate Change-Paris Agreement, Desertification, Endangered Species, Environmental Modification, Marine Dumping-London Convention, Marine Life Conservation, Nuclear Test Ban, Ozone Layer Protection, Ship Pollution, Tropical Timber 2006, Wetlands, Whaling
signed, but not ratified: Air Pollution-Persistent Organic Pollutants, Air Pollution-Volatile Organic Compounds, Biodiversity, Climate Change-Kyoto Protocol, Comprehensive Nuclear Test Ban, Hazardous Wastes, Marine Dumping- London Protocol

Climate: mostly temperate, but tropical in Hawaii and Florida, arctic in Alaska, semiarid in the great plains west of the Mississippi River, and arid in the Great Basin of the southwest; low winter temperatures in the northwest are ameliorated occasionally in January and February by warm chinook winds from the eastern slopes of the Rocky Mountains
note: many consider Denali, the highest peak in the US, to be the world's coldest mountain because of its combination of high elevation and its subarctic location at 63 degrees north latitude; permanent snow and ice cover over 75 percent of the mountain, and enormous glaciers, up to 45 miles long and 3,700 feet thick, spider out from its base in every direction; it is home to some of the world's coldest and most violent weather, where winds of over 150 miles per hour and temperatures of -93°F have been recorded.

Urbanization: *urban population:* 83.3% of total population (2023)
rate of urbanization: 0.96% annual rate of change (2020-25 est.)

Revenue from forest resources: 0.04% of GDP (2018 est.)
comparison ranking: 132

Revenue from coal: 0.2% of GDP (2018 est.)
comparison ranking: 22

Air pollutants: *particulate matter emissions:* 7.18 micrograms per cubic meter (2019 est.)
carbon dioxide emissions: 5,006.3 megatons (2016 est.)
methane emissions: 685.74 megatons (2020 est.)

Waste and recycling: *municipal solid waste generated annually:* 258 million tons (2015 est.)
municipal solid waste recycled annually: 89.268 million tons (2014 est.)
percent of municipal solid waste recycled: 34.6% (2014 est.)

Major lakes (area sq km): *fresh water lake(s):* Michigan – 57,750 sq km; Superior* – 53,348 sq km; Huron* – 23,597 sq km; Erie* – 12,890 sq km; Ontario* – 9,220 sq km; Lake of the Woods – 4,350 sq km; Iliamna – 2,590 sq km; Okeechobee – 1,810 sq km; Belcharof – 1,190 sq km; Red – 1,170 sq km; Saint Clair – 1,113 sq km; Champlain – 1,100 sq km
note - Great Lakes* area shown as US waters
salt water lake(s): Great Salt – 4,360 sq km; Pontchartrain – 1,620 sq km; Selawik – 1,400 sq km; Salton Sea – 950 sq km

Major rivers (by length in km): Missouri - 3,768 km; Mississippi - 3,544 km; Yukon river mouth (shared with Canada [s]) - 3,190 km; Saint Lawrence (shared with Canada) - 3,058 km; Rio Grande river source (mouth shared with Mexico) - 3,057 km; Colorado river source (shared with Mexico [m]) - 2,333 km; Arkansas - 2,348 km; Columbia river mouth (shared with Canada [s]) - 2,250 km; Red - 2,188 km; Ohio - 2,102 km; Snake - 1,670 km
note – [s] after country name indicates river source; [m] after country name indicates river mouth

Major watersheds (area sq km): Atlantic Ocean drainage: *(Gulf of Mexico)* Mississippi* (3,202,185 sq km); Rio Grande (607,965 sq km); *(Gulf of Saint Lawrence)* Saint Lawrence* (1,049,636 sq km total, US only 505,000 sq km)

Pacific Ocean drainage: Yukon* (847,620 sq km, US only 23,820 sq km); Colorado (703,148 sq km); Columbia* (657,501 sq km, US only 554,501 sq km)
note - watersheds shared with Canada shown with *

Major aquifers: Northern Great Plains Aquifer, Cambrian-Ordovician Aquifer System, Californian Central Valley Aquifer System, Ogallala Aquifer (High Plains), Atlantic and Gulf Coastal Plains Aquifer

Total water withdrawal: *municipal:* 58.39 billion cubic meters (2020 est.)
industrial: 209.7 billion cubic meters (2020 est.)
agricultural: 176.2 billion cubic meters (2020 est.)

Total renewable water resources: 3.07 trillion cubic meters (2020 est.)

GOVERNMENT

Country name: *conventional long form:* United States of America

conventional short form: United States
abbreviation: US or USA
etymology: the name America is derived from that of Amerigo VESPUCCI (1454-1512) - Italian explorer, navigator, and cartographer - using the Latin form of his name, Americus, feminized to America

Government type: constitutional federal republic

Capital: *name:* Washington, DC
geographic coordinates: 38 53 N, 77 02 W
time difference: UTC-5 (during Standard Time)
daylight saving time: +1hr, begins second Sunday in March; ends first Sunday in November
time zone note: the 50 United States cover six time zones
etymology: named after George WASHINGTON (1732-1799), the first president of the United States

Administrative divisions: 50 states and 1 district*; Alabama, Alaska, Arizona, Arkansas, California, Colorado, Connecticut, Delaware, District of Columbia*, Florida, Georgia, Hawaii, Idaho, Illinois, Indiana, Iowa, Kansas, Kentucky, Louisiana, Maine, Maryland, Massachusetts, Michigan, Minnesota, Mississippi, Missouri, Montana, Nebraska, Nevada, New Hampshire, New Jersey, New Mexico, New York, North Carolina, North Dakota, Ohio, Oklahoma, Oregon, Pennsylvania, Rhode Island, South Carolina, South Dakota, Tennessee, Texas, Utah, Vermont, Virginia, Washington, West Virginia, Wisconsin, Wyoming

Dependent areas: American Samoa, Baker Island, Guam, Howland Island, Jarvis Island, Johnston Atoll, Kingman Reef, Midway Islands, Navassa Island, Northern Mariana Islands, Palmyra Atoll, Puerto Rico, Virgin Islands, Wake Island (14)
note: from 18 July 1947 until 1 October 1994, the US administered the Trust Territory of the Pacific Islands; it entered into a political relationship with all four political entities: the Northern Mariana Islands is a commonwealth in political union with the US (effective 3 November 1986); the Republic of the Marshall Islands signed a Compact of Free Association with the US (effective 21 October 1986); the Federated States of Micronesia signed a Compact of Free Association with the US (effective 3 November 1986); Palau concluded a Compact of Free Association with the US (effective 1 October 1994)

Independence: 4 July 1776 (declared independence from Great Britain); 3 September 1783 (recognized by Great Britain)

National holiday: Independence Day, 4 July (1776)

Legal system: common law system based on English common law at the federal level; state legal systems based on common law, except Louisiana, where state law is based on Napoleonic civil code; judicial review of legislative acts

Constitution: *history:* previous 1781 (Articles of Confederation and Perpetual Union); latest drafted July - September 1787, submitted to the Congress of the Confederation 20 September 1787, submitted for states' ratification 28 September 1787, ratification completed by nine of the 13 states 21 June 1788, effective 4 March 1789
amendments: proposed as a "joint resolution" by Congress, which requires a two-thirds majority vote in both the House of Representatives and the Senate or by a constitutional convention called for by at least two thirds of the state legislatures; passage requires ratification by three fourths of the state legislatures or passage in state-held constitutional conventions as specified by Congress; the US president has no role in the constitutional amendment process; amended many times, last in 1992

International law organization participation: withdrew acceptance of compulsory ICJ jurisdiction in 2005; withdrew acceptance of ICCt jurisdiction in 2002

Citizenship: *citizenship by birth:* yes
citizenship by descent only: yes
dual citizenship recognized: no, but the US government acknowledges such situtations exist; US citizens are not encouraged to seek dual citizenship since it limits protection by the US
residency requirement for naturalization: 5 years

Suffrage: 18 years of age; universal

Executive branch: *chief of state:* President Joseph R. BIDEN, Jr. (since 20 January 2021)
head of government: President Joseph R. BIDEN, Jr. (since 20 January 2021)
cabinet: Cabinet appointed by the president, approved by the Senate
elections/appointments: president and vice president indirectly elected on the same ballot by the Electoral College of 'electors' chosen from each state; president and vice president serve a 4-year term (eligible for a second term); election last held on 3 November 2020 (next to be held on 5 November 2024)
election results:
2020: Joseph R. BIDEN, Jr. elected president; electoral vote - Joseph R. BIDEN, Jr. (Democratic Party) 306, Donald J. TRUMP (Republican Party) 232; percent of direct popular vote - Joseph R. BIDEN Jr. 51.3%, Donald J. TRUMP 46.9%, other 1.8%
2016: Donald J. TRUMP elected president; electoral vote - Donald J. TRUMP (Republican Party) 304, Hillary D. CLINTON (Democratic Party) 227, other 7; percent of direct popular vote - Hillary D. CLINTON 48.2%, Donald J. TRUMP 46.1%, other 5.7%
note: the president is both chief of state and head of government

Legislative branch: *description:* bicameral Congress consists of:
Senate (100 seats; 2 members directly elected in each of the 50 state constituencies by simple majority vote except in Georgia and Louisiana which require an absolute majority vote with a second round if needed; members serve 6-year terms with one-third of membership renewed every 2 years)
House of Representatives (435 seats; members directly elected in single-seat constituencies by simple majority vote except in Georgia which requires an absolute majority vote with a second round if needed; members serve 2-year terms)
elections: Senate - last held on 8 November 2022 (next to be held on 5 November 2024)
House of Representatives - last held on 8 November 2022 (next to be held on 5 November 2024)
election results: Senate - percent of vote by party - NA; seats by party - Democratic Party 51, Republican Party 49; composition - men 75, women 25, percentage women 25%
House of Representatives - percent of vote by party - NA; seats by party - Republican Party 222, Democratic Party 213; composition - men 305, women 126, percentage women 29.2%; total US Congress percentage women 28.4%
note: in addition to the regular members of the House of Representatives there are 6 non-voting delegates elected from the District of Columbia and the US territories of American Samoa, Guam, Puerto Rico, the Northern Mariana Islands, and the Virgin Islands; these are single seat constituencies directly elected by simple majority vote to serve a 2-year term (except for the resident commissioner of Puerto Rico who serves a 4-year term); the delegate can vote when serving on a committee and when the House meets as the Committee of the Whole House, but not when legislation is submitted for a "full floor" House vote; election of delegates last held on 8 November 2022 (next to be held on 3 November 2024)

Judicial branch: *highest court(s):* US Supreme Court (consists of 9 justices - the chief justice and 8 associate justices)
judge selection and term of office: president nominates and, with the advice and consent of the Senate, appoints Supreme Court justices; justices serve for life
subordinate courts: Courts of Appeal (includes the US Court of Appeal for the Federal District and 12 regional appeals courts); 94 federal district courts in 50 states and territories
note: the US court system consists of the federal court system and the state court systems; although each court system is responsible for hearing certain types of cases, neither is completely independent of the other, and the systems often interact

Political parties: Democratic Party
Green Party
Libertarian Party
Republican Party

International organization participation: ADB (nonregional member), AfDB (nonregional member), ANZUS, APEC, Arctic Council, ARF, ASEAN (dialogue partner), Australia Group, BIS, BSEC (observer), CBSS (observer), CD, CE (observer), CERN (observer), CICA (observer), CP, EAPC, EAS, EBRD, EITI (implementing country), FAO, FATF, G-5, G-7, G-8, G-10, G-20, IADB, IAEA, IBRD, ICAO, ICC (national committees), ICRM, IDA, IEA, IFAD, IFC, IFRCS, IGAD (partners), IHO, ILO, IMF, IMO, IMSO, Interpol, IOC, IOM, ISO, ITSO, ITU, ITUC (NGOs), MIGA, MINUSTAH, MONUSCO, NAFTA, NATO, NEA, NSG, OAS, OECD, OPCW, OSCE, Pacific Alliance (observer), Paris Club, PCA, PIF (partner), Quad, SAARC (observer), SELEC (observer), SICA (observer), SPC, UN, UNCTAD, UNESCO, UNHCR, UNHRC, UNITAR, UNMIL, UNMISS, UNOOSA, UNRWA, UN Security Council (permanent), UNTSO, UPU, USMCA, Wassenaar Arrangement, WCO, WHO, WIPO, WMO, WTO, ZC

Flag description: 13 equal horizontal stripes of red (top and bottom) alternating with white; there is a blue rectangle in the upper hoist-side corner bearing 50 small, white, five-pointed stars arranged in nine offset horizontal rows of six stars (top and bottom) alternating with rows of five stars; the 50 stars represent the 50 states, the 13 stripes represent the 13 original colonies; blue stands for loyalty, devotion, truth, justice, and friendship, red symbolizes courage, zeal, and fervency, while white denotes purity and rectitude of conduct; commonly referred to by its nickname of Old Glory
note: the design and colors have been the basis for a number of other flags, including Chile, Liberia, Malaysia, and Puerto Rico

National symbol(s): bald eagle; national colors: red, white, blue

National anthem: *name:* "The Star-Spangled Banner"

lyrics/music: Francis Scott KEY/John Stafford SMITH
note: adopted 1931; during the War of 1812, after witnessing the successful American defense of Fort McHenry in Baltimore following British naval bombardment, Francis Scott KEY wrote the lyrics to what would become the national anthem; the lyrics were set to the tune of "The Anacreontic Song"; only the first verse is sung

National heritage: *total World Heritage Sites:* 25 (12 cultural, 12 natural, 1 mixed); note - includes one site in Puerto Rico
selected World Heritage Site locales: Yellowstone National Park (n); Grand Canyon National Park (n); Cahokia Mounds State Historic Site (c); Independence Hall (c); Statue of Liberty (c); Yosemite National Park (n); Papahānaumokuākea (m); Monumental Earthworks of Poverty Point (c); The 20th-Century Architecture of Frank Lloyd Wright (c); Mesa Verde National Park (c); Mammoth Cave National Park (n); Monticello (c); Olympic National Park (n)

ECONOMY

Economic overview: high-income, diversified North American economy; NATO leader; largest importer and second-largest exporter; home to leading financial exchanges; high and growing public debt; rising socioeconomic inequalities; historically low interest rates; hit by COVID-19

Real GDP (purchasing power parity): $24.662 trillion (2023 est.)
$24.051 trillion (2022 est.)
$23.594 trillion (2021 est.)
note: data in 2021 dollars
comparison ranking: 2

Real GDP growth rate: 2.54% (2023 est.)
1.94% (2022 est.)
5.8% (2021 est.)
note: annual GDP % growth based on constant local currency
comparison ranking: 122

Real GDP per capita: $73,600 (2023 est.)
$72,200 (2022 est.)
$71,100 (2021 est.)
note: data in 2021 dollars
comparison ranking: 14

GDP (official exchange rate): $27.361 trillion (2023 est.)
note: data in current dollars at official exchange rate

Inflation rate (consumer prices): 4.12% (2023 est.)
8% (2022 est.)
4.7% (2021 est.)
note: annual % change based on consumer prices
comparison ranking: 86

Credit ratings: Fitch rating: AAA (1994)

Moody's rating: Aaa (1949)

Standard & Poors rating: AA+ (2011)
note: The year refers to the year in which the current credit rating was first obtained.

GDP - composition, by sector of origin: *agriculture:* 0.9% (2021 est.)
industry: 17.7% (2021 est.)
services: 76.7% (2021 est.)
note: figures may not total 100% due to non-allocated consumption not captured in sector-reported data
comparison rankings: services 22; industry 154; agriculture 185

GDP - composition, by end use: *household consumption:* 68% (2022 est.)
government consumption: 13.9% (2022 est.)
investment in fixed capital: 21.3% (2022 est.)
investment in inventories: 0.6% (2022 est.)
exports of goods and services: 11.6% (2022 est.)
imports of goods and services: -15.4% (2022 est.)
note: figures may not total 100% due to rounding or gaps in data collection

Agricultural products: maize, soybeans, milk, wheat, sugarcane, sugar beets, chicken, potatoes, beef, pork (2022)
note: top ten agricultural products based on tonnage

Industries: highly diversified, world leading, high-technology innovator, second-largest industrial output in the world; petroleum, steel, motor vehicles, aerospace, telecommunications, chemicals, electronics, food processing, consumer goods, lumber, mining

Industrial production growth rate: 3.25% (2021 est.)
note: annual % change in industrial value added based on constant local currency
comparison ranking: 103

Labor force: 170.549 million (2023 est.)
note: number of people ages 15 or older who are employed or seeking work
comparison ranking: 3

Unemployment rate: 3.63% (2023 est.)
3.65% (2022 est.)
5.35% (2021 est.)
note: % of labor force seeking employment
comparison ranking: 66

Youth unemployment rate (ages 15-24): *total:* 7.9% (2023 est.)
male: 8.7% (2023 est.)
female: 7.1% (2023 est.)
note: % of labor force ages 15-24 seeking employment
comparison ranking: total 153

Gini Index coefficient - distribution of family income: 39.8 (2021 est.)
note: index (0-100) of income distribution; higher values represent greater inequality
comparison ranking: 45

Average household expenditures: *on food:* 6.7% of household expenditures (2022 est.)
on alcohol and tobacco: 1.8% of household expenditures (2022 est.)

Household income or consumption by percentage share: *lowest 10%:* 2.2% (2021 est.)
highest 10%: 30.1% (2021 est.)
note: % share of income accruing to lowest and highest 10% of population

Remittances: 0.03% of GDP (2023 est.)
0.03% of GDP (2022 est.)
0.03% of GDP (2021 est.)
note: personal transfers and compensation between resident and non-resident individuals/households/entities

Budget: *revenues:* $5.038 trillion (2022 est.)
expenditures: $6.306 trillion (2022 est.)
note: central government revenues (excluding grants) and expenses converted to US dollars at average official exchange rate for year indicated

Public debt: 110.39% of GDP (2022 est.)
note: central government debt as a % of GDP
comparison ranking: 16

Taxes and other revenues: 12.18% (of GDP) (2022 est.)
note: central government tax revenue as a % of GDP
comparison ranking: 162

Current account balance: -$818.822 billion (2023 est.)
-$971.594 billion (2022 est.)
-$831.453 billion (2021 est.)
note: balance of payments - net trade and primary/secondary income in current dollars
comparison ranking: 207

Exports: $3.052 trillion (2023 est.)
$3.018 trillion (2022 est.)
$2.567 trillion (2021 est.)
note: balance of payments - exports of goods and services in current dollars
comparison ranking: 2

Exports - partners: Canada 16%, Mexico 15%, China 8%, Japan 4%, UK 4% (2022)
note: top five export partners based on percentage share of exports

Exports - commodities: refined petroleum, crude petroleum, natural gas, cars, integrated circuits (2022)
note: top five export commodities based on value in dollars

Imports: $3.832 trillion (2023 est.)
$3.97 trillion (2022 est.)
$3.409 trillion (2021 est.)
note: balance of payments - imports of goods and services in current dollars
comparison ranking: 1

Imports - partners: China 18%, Canada 14%, Mexico 14%, Germany 5%, Japan 4% (2022)
note: top five import partners based on percentage share of imports

Imports - commodities: crude petroleum, cars, broadcasting equipment, garments, computers (2022)
note: top five import commodities based on value in dollars

Reserves of foreign exchange and gold: $773.426 billion (2023 est.)
$706.644 billion (2022 est.)
$716.152 billion (2021 est.)
note: holdings of gold (year-end prices)/foreign exchange/special drawing rights in current dollars
comparison ranking: 5

Exchange rates: British pounds per US dollar: 0.805 (2023 est.), 0.811 (2022 est.), 0.727 (2021 est.), 0.780 (2020 est.), 0.783 (2019 est.)

Canadian dollars per US dollar: 1.35 (2023 est.), 1.302 (2022 est.), 1.254 (2021 est.), 1.341 (2020 est.), 1.327 (2019 est.)

Chinese yuan per US dollar: 7.084 (2023 est.), 6.737 (2022 est.), 6.449 (2021 est.), 6.901 (2020 est.), 6.908 (2019 est.)
euros per US dollar: 0.925 (2023 est.), 0.950 (2022 est.), 0.845 (2021 est.), 0.876 (2020 est.), 0.893 (2019 est.)

Japanese yen per US dollar: 140.49 (2023 est.), 131.50 (2022 est.), 109.75 (2021 est.), 106.78 (2020 est.), 109.01 (2019 est.)
note 1: the following countries and territories use the US dollar officially as their legal tender: British Virgin Islands, Ecuador, El Salvador, Marshall Islands, Micronesia, Palau, Timor Leste, Turks and Caicos, and islands of the Caribbean Netherlands (Bonaire, Sint Eustatius, and Saba)
note 2: the following countries and territories use the US dollar as official legal tender alongside local currency: Bahamas, Barbados, Belize, Costa Rica, and Panama

note 3: the following countries and territories widely accept the US dollar as a dominant currency but have yet to declare it as legal tender: Bermuda, Burma, Cambodia, Cayman Islands, Honduras, Nicaragua, and Somalia

ENERGY

Electricity access: *electrification - total population:* 100% (2022 est.)

Electricity: *installed generating capacity:* 1.201 billion kW (2022 est.)
consumption: 4.128 trillion kWh (2022 est.)
exports: 15.758 billion kWh (2022 est.)
imports: 56.97 billion kWh (2022 est.)
transmission/distribution losses: 204.989 billion kWh (2022 est.)
comparison rankings: transmission/distribution losses 209; imports 1; exports 19; consumption 2; installed generating capacity 2

Electricity generation sources: *fossil fuels:* 59.5% of total installed capacity (2022 est.)
nuclear: 18% of total installed capacity (2022 est.)
solar: 4.8% of total installed capacity (2022 est.)
wind: 10.1% of total installed capacity (2022 est.)
hydroelectricity: 5.8% of total installed capacity (2022 est.)
geothermal: 0.4% of total installed capacity (2022 est.)
biomass and waste: 1.5% of total installed capacity (2022 est.)

Nuclear energy: Number of operational nuclear reactors: 94 (2023)

Net capacity of operational nuclear reactors: 96.95GW (2023 est.)

Percent of total electricity production: 18.5% (2023 est.)

Number of nuclear reactors permanently shut down: 41 (2023)

Coal: *production:* 548.849 million metric tons (2022 est.)
consumption: 476.044 million metric tons (2022 est.)
exports: 80.081 million metric tons (2022 est.)
imports: 5.788 million metric tons (2022 est.)
proven reserves: 248.941 billion metric tons (2022 est.)

Petroleum: *total petroleum production:* 20.879 million bbl/day (2023 est.)
refined petroleum consumption: 20.246 million bbl/day (2023 est.)
crude oil estimated reserves: 38.212 billion barrels (2021 est.)

Natural gas: *production:* 1.029 trillion cubic meters (2022 est.)
consumption: 914.301 billion cubic meters (2022 est.)
exports: 195.497 billion cubic meters (2022 est.)
imports: 85.635 billion cubic meters (2022 est.)
proven reserves: 13.402 trillion cubic meters (2021 est.)

Carbon dioxide emissions: 4.941 billion metric tonnes of CO_2 (2022 est.)
from coal and metallurgical coke: 938.649 million metric tonnes of CO_2 (2022 est.)
from petroleum and other liquids: 2.26 billion metric tonnes of CO_2 (2022 est.)
from consumed natural gas: 1.742 billion metric tonnes of CO_2 (2022 est.)
comparison ranking: total emissions 2

Energy consumption per capita: 284.575 million Btu/person (2022 est.)
comparison ranking: 10

COMMUNICATIONS

Telephones - fixed lines: *total subscriptions:* 91.623 million (2022 est.)
subscriptions per 100 inhabitants: 27 (2022 est.)
comparison ranking: total subscriptions 2

Telephones - mobile cellular: *total subscriptions:* 372.682 million (2022 est.)
subscriptions per 100 inhabitants: 110 (2022 est.)
comparison ranking: total subscriptions 3

Telecommunication systems: *general assessment:* the US telecom sector adapted well to the particular demands of the pandemic, which has led to strong growth in the number of mobile, mobile broadband, and fixed broadband subscribers since 2020; the level of growth is expected to taper off from late 2022 as the demand for working and schooling from home subsides; the pandemic also encouraged the Federal government to increase its investment in broadband infrastructure; of particular note was the Infrastructure Investment and Jobs Act of November 2021, which provided $65 billion to a range of programs aimed at delivering broadband to unserved areas, providing fiber-based broadband to upgrade existing service areas, and subsidizing the cost of services to low income households; alongside these fiscal efforts have been the several spectrum auctions undertaken during the last two years, which have greatly assisted the main licensees to improve the reach and quality of their offers based on LTE and 5G; some of this spectrum, auctioned during 2021, was only made available to licensees from February 2022; the widening availability of 5G from the main providers has resulted in a dramatic increase in mobile data traffic; in tandem with the focus on 5G, operators have closed down their GSM and CDMA networks, and have either closed down 3G networks (as AT&T did in January 2022), or plan to in coming months; given the size of the US broadband market, and the growing demand for data on both fixed and mobile networks, there is continuous pressure for operators to invest in fiber networks, and to push connectivity closer to consumers; in recent years the US has seen increased activity from regional players as well as the major telcos and cablecos; although there has been considerable investment in DOCSIS4.0, some of the cablecos are looking to ditch HFC in preference for fiber broadband; the process of migrating from copper (HFC and DSL) to fiber is ongoing, but given the scale of the work involved it will take some years; some operators have investment strategies in place through to 2025, which will see the vast majority of their fixed networks being entirely on fiber; service offerings of up to 2Gb/s are becoming more widely available as the process continues (2024)
domestic: fixed-line just over 27 per 100 and mobile-cellular is 110 per 100 (2022)
international: country code - 1; landing points for the Quintillion Subsea Cable Network, TERRA SW, AU-Aleutian, KKFL, AKORN, Alaska United -West, & -East & -Southeast, North Star, Lynn Canal Fiber, KetchCar 1, PC-1, SCCN, Tat TGN-Pacific & -Atlantic, Jupiter, Hawaiki, NCP, FASTER, HKA, JUS, AAG, BtoBE, Currie, Southern Cross NEXT, SxS, PLCN, Utility EAC-Pacific, SEA-US, Paniolo Cable Network, HICS, HIFN, ASH, Telstra Endeavor, Honotua, AURORA, ARCOS, AMX-1, Americas -I & -II, Columbus IIb & -III, Maya-1, MAC, GTMO-1, BICS, CFX-1, GlobeNet, Monet, SAm-1, Bahamas 2, PCCS, BRUSA, Dunant, MAREA, SAE x1, TAT 14, Apollo, Gemini Bermuda, Havfrue/AEC-2, Seabras-1, WALL-LI, NYNJ-1, FLAG Atalantic-1, Yellow, Atlantic Crossing-1, AE Connect -1, sea2shore, Challenger Bermuda-1, and GTT Atlantic submarine cable systems providing international connectivity to Europe, Africa, the Middle East, Asia, Southeast Asia, Australia, New Zealand, Pacific, & Atlantic, and Indian Ocean Islands, Central and South America, Caribbean, Canada and US; satellite earth stations - 61 Intelsat (45 Atlantic Ocean and 16 Pacific Ocean), 5 Intersputnik (Atlantic Ocean region), and 4 Inmarsat (Pacific and Atlantic Ocean regions) (2020)

Broadcast media: 4 major terrestrial TV networks with affiliate stations throughout the country, plus cable and satellite networks, independent stations, and a limited public broadcasting sector that is largely supported by private grants; overall, thousands of TV stations broadcasting; multiple national radio networks with many affiliate stations; while most stations are commercial, National Public Radio (NPR) has a network of some 900 member stations; satellite radio available; in total, over 15,000 radio stations operating (2018)

Internet country code: .us

Internet users: *total:* 312.8 million (2021 est.)
percent of population: 92% (2021 est.)
comparison ranking: total 3

Broadband - fixed subscriptions: *total:* 121.176 million (2020 est.)
subscriptions per 100 inhabitants: 37 (2020 est.)
comparison ranking: total 2

Communications - note: note 1: The Library of Congress, Washington DC, USA, claims to be the largest library in the world with more than 167 million items (as of 2018); its collections are universal, not limited by subject, format, or national boundary, and include materials from all parts of the world and in over 450 languages; collections include: books, newspapers, magazines, sheet music, sound and video recordings, photographic images, artwork, architectural drawings, and copyright data
note 2: Cape Canaveral, Florida, USA, hosts one of four dedicated ground antennas that assist in the operation of the Global Positioning System (GPS) navigation system (the others are on Ascension (Saint Helena, Ascension, and Tistan da Cunha), Diego Garcia (British Indian Ocean Territory), and at Kwajalein (Marshall Islands)

TRANSPORTATION

National air transport system: *number of registered air carriers:* 99 (2020)
inventory of registered aircraft operated by air carriers: 7,249
annual passenger traffic on registered air carriers: 889.022 million (2018)
annual freight traffic on registered air carriers: 42,985,300,000 (2018) mt-km

Civil aircraft registration country code prefix: N

Airports: 15,873 (2024)
comparison ranking: 1

Heliports: 7,914 (2024)

Pipelines: 1,984,321 km natural gas, 240,711 km petroleum products (2013)

Railways: *total:* 293,564.2 km (2014)

standard gauge: 293,564.2 km (2014) 1.435-m gauge
comparison ranking: total 1

Roadways: *total:* 6,586,610 km
paved: 4,304,715 km (includes 76,334 km of expressways)
unpaved: 2,281,895 km (2012)
comparison ranking: total 1

Waterways: 41,009 km (2012) (19,312 km used for commerce; Saint Lawrence Seaway of 3,769 km, including the Saint Lawrence River of 3,058 km, is shared with Canada)
comparison ranking: 5

Merchant marine: *total:* 3,533 (2023)
by type: bulk carrier 4, container ship 60, general cargo 96, oil tanker 68, other 3,305
note - oceangoing self-propelled, cargo-carrying vessels of 1,000 gross tons and above
comparison ranking: total 7

Ports: *total ports:* 666 (2024)
large: 21
medium: 38
small: 132
very small: 475
ports with oil terminals: 204
key ports: Baltimore, Boston, Brooklyn, Buffalo, Chester, Cleveland, Detroit, Galveston, Houston, Los Angeles, Louisiana Offshore Oil Port (LOOP), Mobile, New Orleans, New York City, Norfolk, Oakland, Philadelphia, Portland, San Francisco, Seattle, Tri-City Port

MILITARY AND SECURITY

Military and security forces: United States Armed Forces (aka US Military): US Army (USA), US Navy (USN; includes US Marine Corps or USMC), US Air Force (USAF), US Space Force (USSF); US Coast Guard (USCG); National Guard (Army National Guard and Air National Guard) (2024)
note 1: the US Coast Guard is administered in peacetime by the Department of Homeland Security, but in wartime reports to the Department of the Navy
note 2: the Army National Guard and the Air National Guard are reserve components of their services and operate in part under state authority; the US military also maintains reserve forces for each branch
note 3: US law enforcement personnel include those of federal agencies, such as the Department of Homeland Security and Department of Justice, the 50 states, special jurisdictions, local sheriff's offices, and municipal, county, regional, and tribal police departments
note 4: some US states have "state defense forces" (SDFs), which are military units that operate under the sole authority of state governments; SDFs are authorized by state and federal law and are under the command of the governor of each state; as of 2023, more than 20 states and the Commonwealth of Puerto Rico had SDFs, which typically have emergency management and homeland security missions; most are organized as ground units, but air and naval units also exist

Military expenditures: 3.4% of GDP (2024 est.)
3.2% of GDP (2023)
3.3% of GDP (2022)
3.5% of GDP (2021)
3.6% of GDP (2020)
comparison ranking: 25

Military and security service personnel strengths: approximately 1.31 million active-duty personnel (446,000 Army; 328,000 Navy; 317,000 Air Force; 9,000 Space Force; 167,000 Marine Corps; 40,000 Coast Guard); 330,000 Army National Guard; 105,000 Air National Guard (2024)

Military equipment inventories and acquisitions: the US military's inventory is comprised almost entirely of domestically produced weapons systems (some assembled with foreign components) along with a smaller mix of imported equipment from a variety of Western countries such as Germany and the UK; the US defense industry is capable of designing, developing, maintaining, and producing the full spectrum of weapons systems; the US is the world's leading arms exporter (2024)

Military service age and obligation: 18 years of age (17 years of age with parental consent) for voluntary service for men and women; no conscription (currently inactive, but males aged 18-25 must register with Selective Service in case conscription is reinstated in the future); maximum enlistment age 34 (Army), 42 (Air Force/Space Force), 39 (Navy), 28 (Marines), 31 (Coast Guard); 8- year service obligation, including 2-5 years active duty (Army), 2 years active duty (Navy), 4 years active duty (Air Force, Coast Guard, Marines, Space Force) (2024)
note 1: the US military has been all-volunteer since 1973, but an act of Congress can reinstate the draft in case of a national emergency
note 2: all military occupations and positions open to women; in 2022, women comprised 17.5% of the total US regular military personnel
note 3: non-citizens living permanently and legally in the US may join as enlisted personnel; they must have permission to work in the US, a high school diploma, and speak, read, and write English fluently; minimum age of 17 with parental consent or 18 without; maximum age 29-39, depending on the service; under the US Nationality Act, honorable service in the military may qualify individuals to obtain expedited citizenship; under the Compact of Free Association, citizens of the Federated States of Micronesia, the Republic of Palau, and the Republic of the Marshall Islands may volunteer; under the Jay Treaty, signed in 1794 between Great Britain and the US, and corresponding legislation, Native Americans/First Nations born in Canada are entitled to freely enter the US and join the US military

Military deployments: the US has more than 200,000 air, ground, and naval personnel deployed overseas on a permanent or a long-term rotational (typically 3-9 months) basis; key areas of deployment include approximately 5,000 in Africa, approximately 100,000 in Europe, approximately 10-15,000 in Southwest Asia, and more than 80,000 in East Asia (2024)

Military - note: *the US military's primary missions are to deter potential enemies, provide for the defense of the US, its Territories, Commonwealths and possessions, and any areas occupied by the US, and to protect US national interests; its responsibilities are worldwide and include providing humanitarian assistance, participating in international military exercises and operations, conducting military diplomacy, and fulfilling the US's alliance and treaty commitments; the US has been a leading member of NATO since the Alliance's formation in 1949; the military has a global presence; the separate services operate jointly under 11 regional- or functionally-based joint service "combatant" commands:* Africa Command; Central Command, Cyber Command, European Command, Indo-Pacific Command, Northern Command, Southern Command, Space Command, Special Operations Command, Strategic Command, and Transportation Command
Congress officially created the US military in September 1789; the US Army was established in June 1775 as the Continental Army; after the declaration of independence in July 1776, the Continental Army and the militia in the service of Congress became known collectively as the Army of the United States; when Congress ordered the Continental Army to disband in 1784, it retained a small number of personnel that would form the nucleus of the 1st American Regiment for national service formed later that year; both the US Navy and the US Marines were also established in 1775, but the Navy fell into disuse after the Revolutionary War, and was reestablished by Congress in 1794; the first US military unit devoted exclusively to aviation began operations in 1913 as part of the US Army; the Army Air Corps (AAC) was the US military service dedicated to aerial warfare between 1926 and 1941; the AAC became the US Army Air Forces in 1941 and remained as a combat arm of the Army until the establishment of the US Air Force in 1947 (2024)

SPACE

Space agency/agencies: National Aeronautics and Space Administration (NASA; established 1958); National Reconnaissance Office (NRO; established in 1961 and responsible for designing, building, launching, and maintaining intelligence satellites); US Space Command (USSPACECOM; established in 2019 and responsible for military operations in outer space, specifically all operations over 100 kilometers or 62 miles above mean sea level) (2024)
note: USSPACECOM was originally created in 1985 but was deactivated in 2002 and its duties were transferred to US Strategic Command

Space launch site(s): has 20 commercial, government, and private space ports hosting Federal Aviation Administration-licensed activity spread across 10 states (Alabama, Alaska, California, Colorado, Florida, Georgia, New Mexico, Oklahoma, Texas, and Virginia) (2024)

Space program overview: has a large and comprehensive space program and is one of the world's top space powers; builds, launches, and operates space launch vehicles (SLVs)/rockets and the full spectrum of spacecraft, including interplanetary probes, manned craft, reusable rockets, satellites, space stations, and space planes; has an astronaut program and a large corps of astronauts; researching and developing a broad range of other space-related capabilities and technologies, such as advanced telecommunications and optics, navigational aids, propulsion, robotics, solar sails, space-based manufacturing, and robotic satellite repair/refueling; has launched orbital or lander probes to the Sun and all planets in the solar system, as well as to asteroids and beyond the solar system; has international missions and projects with dozens of countries and organizations, including such major partners as Canada, Japan, Russia, and South Korea, as well as the European Space Agency (ESA), the EU, and their individual member states; as of October 2024, nearly 50 countries had signed onto the US-led Artemis Accords, whose purpose is to establish principles, guidelines, and best practices to enhance the governance of the civil exploration

and use of outer space with the intention of advancing the Artemis Program, an international effort to establish a sustainable and robust presence on the Moon and an onward human mission to Mars; the US commercial space industry is one of the world's largest and most capable and is active across the entire spectrum of US government space programs; the majority of both NASA and US military space launches are conducted by US commercial companies; the US space economy was valued at over $200 billion in 2021 (2024)
note: further details about the key activities, programs, and milestones of the country's space program, as well as government spending estimates on the space sector, appear in the Space Programs reference guide

TERRORISM

Terrorist group(s): Hizballah; Islamic Revolutionary Guard Corps (IRGC)/Qods Force; Islamic State of Iraq and ash-Sham (ISIS); al-Qa'ida; Lashkar-e Tayyiba (LeT)
note: details about the history, aims, leadership, organization, areas of operation, tactics, targets, weapons, size, and sources of support of the group(s) appear(s) in the Terrorism reference guide

TRANSNATIONAL ISSUES

Refugees and internally displaced persons: *refugees (country of origin):* the US admitted 25,465 refugees during FY2022, including: 7,810 (Democratic Republic of the Congo), 4,556 (Syria), 2,156 (Burma), 1,669 (Sudan), 1,618 (Afghanistan), 1,610 (Ukraine)
stateless persons: 47 (2022)

Illicit drugs: world's largest consumer of cocaine (shipped from Colombia through Mexico and the Caribbean), Colombian heroin, and Mexican heroin and marijuana; major consumer of ecstasy and Mexican methamphetamine; minor consumer of high-quality Southeast Asian heroin; illicit producer of cannabis, marijuana, depressants, stimulants, hallucinogens, and methamphetamine; money-laundering center

UNITED STATES PACIFIC ISLAND WILDLIFE REFUGES

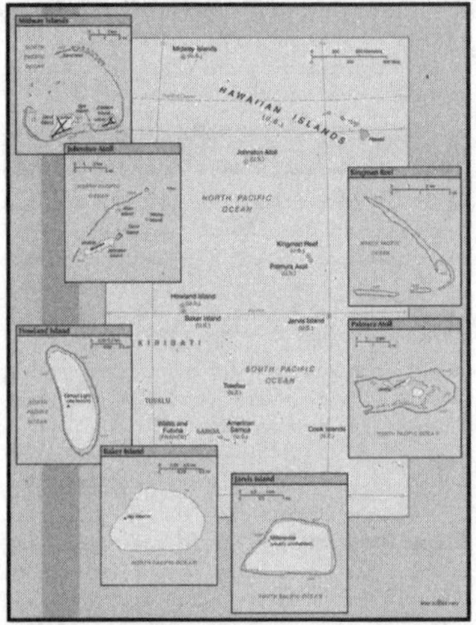

INTRODUCTION

Background: All of the following US Pacific Island territories except Midway Atoll constitute the Pacific Remote Islands National Wildlife Refuge (NWR) Complex and as such are managed by the Fish and Wildlife Service of the US Department of the Interior. Midway Atoll NWR has been included in a Refuge Complex with the Hawaiian Islands NWR and also designated as part of Papahanaumokuakea Marine National Monument. These remote refuges are the most widespread collection of marine- and terrestrial-life protected areas on the planet under a single country's jurisdiction. They sustain many endemic species including corals, fish, shellfish, marine mammals, seabirds, water birds, land birds, insects, and vegetation not found elsewhere.

Baker Island: The US took possession of the island in 1857. US and British companies mined its guano deposits during the second half of the 19th century. In 1935, a short-lived attempt at colonization began but was disrupted by World War II, and the island was thereafter abandoned. Baker Island was declared a National Wildlife Refuge in 1974.

Howland Island: The US discovered the island early in the 19th century and officially claimed it in 1857. Both US and British companies mined guano on the island until about 1890. Earhart Light, a day beacon near the middle of the west coast, was partially destroyed during World War II but subsequently rebuilt; it is named in memory of famed aviatrix Amelia EARHART. The US Department of the Interior administers the island as a National Wildlife Refuge.

Jarvis Island: First discovered by the British in 1821, the uninhabited island was annexed by the US in 1858 but abandoned in 1879 after tons of guano deposits were removed for use in producing fertilizer. The UK annexed the island in 1889 but never carried out plans for further exploitation. The US occupied and reclaimed the island in 1935. Abandoned after World War II, the island is currently a National Wildlife Refuge administered by the US Department of the Interior.

Johnston Atoll: Both the US and the Kingdom of Hawaii annexed Johnston Atoll in 1858, but it was the US that mined the guano deposits until the late 1880s. Johnston Atoll was designated a wildlife refuge in 1926. The US Navy took over the atoll in 1934, and the US Air Force assumed control in 1948. The site was used for high-altitude nuclear tests in the 1950s and 1960s, and until 2000, the atoll was maintained as a storage and disposal site for chemical weapons. Cleanup and closure of the weapons facility ended in 2005.

Kingman Reef: The US annexed Kingman Reef in 1922. Its sheltered lagoon served as a way station for flying boats on Hawaii-to- American Samoa flights during the late 1930s. There are no terrestrial plants on the reef, which is frequently awash, but it does support abundant and diverse marine fauna and flora. In 2001, the waters surrounding the reef out to 12 nm were designated a US National Wildlife Refuge.

Midway Islands: The US took formal possession of the Midway Islands in 1867. The laying of the trans-Pacific cable, which passed through the islands, brought the first residents in 1903. Between 1935 and 1947, Midway was used as a refueling stop for trans-Pacific flights. The US naval victory over a Japanese fleet off Midway in 1942 was one of the turning points of World War II. The islands continued to serve as a naval station until 1993. Today the islands are a US National Wildlife Refuge. The refuge was open to the public from 1996 to 2002 and again from 2008 to 2012, but it is now closed.

Palmyra Atoll: The Kingdom of Hawaii claimed the atoll in 1862, and the US included it among the Hawaiian Islands when it annexed the archipelago in 1898. The Hawaii Statehood Act of 1959 did not include Palmyra Atoll, which is now partly privately owned by the Nature Conservancy and partly US Government-owned and administered as a nature preserve. The lagoons and surrounding waters within the 12-nautical-mile US territorial seas were transferred to the US Fish and Wildlife Service and were designated a National Wildlife Refuge in 2001.

GEOGRAPHY

Location: Oceania

Baker Island: atoll in the North Pacific Ocean 3,390 km southwest of Honolulu, about halfway between Hawaii and Australia;

Howland Island: island in the North Pacific Ocean 3,360 km southwest of Honolulu, about halfway between Hawaii and Australia;

Jarvis Island: island in the South Pacific Ocean 2,415 km south of Honolulu, about halfway between Hawaii and Cook Islands;

Johnston Atoll: atoll in the North Pacific Ocean 1,330 km southwest of Honolulu, about one-third of the way from Hawaii to the Marshall Islands;

Kingman Reef: reef in the North Pacific Ocean 1,720 km south of Honolulu, about halfway between Hawaii and American Samoa;

Midway Islands: atoll in the North Pacific Ocean 2,335 km northwest of Honolulu near the end of the Hawaiian Archipelago, about one-third of the way from Honolulu to Tokyo;

Palmyra Atoll: atoll in the North Pacific Ocean 1,780 km south of Honolulu, about halfway between Hawaii and American Samoa

Geographic coordinates: Baker Island: 0 13 N, 176 28 W;

Howland Island: 0 48 N, 176 38 W;

Jarvis Island: 0 23 S, 160 01 W;

Johnston Atoll: 16 45 N, 169 31 W;

Kingman Reef: 6 23 N, 162 25 W;

Midway Islands: 28 12 N, 177 22 W;
Palmyra Atoll: 5 53 N, 162 05 W

Map references: Oceania

Area: *land:* 6,959.41 sq km (emergent land - 22.41 sq km; submerged - 6,937 sq km)
Baker Island: total - 129.1 sq km; emergent land - 2.1 sq km; submerged - 127 sq km
Howland Island: total - 138.6 sq km; emergent land - 2.6 sq km; submerged - 136 sq km
Jarvis Island: total - 152 sq km; emergent land - 5 sq km; submerged - 147 sq km
Johnston Atoll: total - 276.6 sq km; emergent land - 2.6 sq km; submerged - 274 sq km
Kingman Reef: total - 1,958.01 sq km; emergent land - 0.01 sq km; submerged - 1,958 sq km
Midway Islands: total - 2,355.2 sq km; emergent land - 6.2 sq km; submerged - 2,349 sq km
Palmyra Atoll: total - 1,949.9 sq km; emergent land - 3.9 sq km; submerged - 1,946 sq km

Area - comparative: Baker Island: about 2.5 times the size of the National Mall in Washington, DC;
Howland Island: about three times the size of the National Mall in Washington, DC;
Jarvis Island: about eight times the size of the National Mall in Washington, DC;
Johnston Atoll: about 4.5 times the size of the National Mall in Washington, DC;
Kingman Reef: a little more than 1.5 times the size of the National Mall in Washington, DC;
Midway Islands: about nine times the size of the National Mall in Washington, DC;
Palmyra Atoll: about 20 times the size of the National Mall in Washington, DC

Land boundaries: *total:* 0 km

Coastline: Baker Island: 4.8 km
Howland Island: 6.4 km
Jarvis Island: 8 km
Johnston Atoll: 34 km
Kingman Reef: 3 km
Midway Islands: 15 km
Palmyra Atoll: 14.5 km

Maritime claims: *territorial sea:* 12 nm
exclusive economic zone: 200 nm

Climate: Baker, Howland, and Jarvis Islands: equatorial; scant rainfall, constant wind, burning sun;
Johnston Atoll and Kingman Reef: tropical, but generally dry; consistent northeast trade winds with little seasonal temperature variation;
Midway Islands: subtropical with cool, moist winters (December to February) and warm, dry summers (May to October); moderated by prevailing easterly winds; most of the 107 cm of annual rainfall occurs during the winter;
Palmyra Atoll: equatorial, hot; located within the low pressure area of the Intertropical Convergence Zone (ITCZ) where the northeast and southeast trade winds meet, it is extremely wet with between 400-500 cm of rainfall each year

Terrain: low and nearly flat sandy coral islands with narrow fringing reefs that have developed at the top of submerged volcanic mountains, which in most cases rise steeply from the ocean floor

Elevation: *highest point:* Baker Island, unnamed location 8 m; Howland Island, unnamed location 3 m; Jarvis Island, unnamed location 7 m; Johnston Atoll, Sand Island 10 m; Kingman Reef, unnamed location 2 m; Midway Islands, unnamed location less than 13 m; Palmyra Atoll, unnamed location 3 m
lowest point: Pacific Ocean 0 m

Natural resources: terrestrial and aquatic wildlife

Land use: *other:* 100% (2018 est.)

Natural hazards: Baker, Howland, and Jarvis Islands: the narrow fringing reef surrounding the island poses a maritime hazard;
Kingman Reef: wet or awash most of the time, maximum elevation of less than 2 m makes Kingman Reef a maritime hazard;
Midway Islands, Johnston, and Palmyra Atolls: NA

Geography - note: Baker, Howland, and Jarvis Islands: scattered vegetation consisting of grasses, prostrate vines, and low growing shrubs; primarily a nesting, roosting, and foraging habitat for seabirds, shorebirds, and marine wildlife; closed to the public;
Johnston Atoll: Johnston Island and Sand Island are natural islands, which have been expanded by coral dredging; North Island (Akau) and East Island (Hikina) are manmade islands formed from coral dredging; the egg-shaped reef is 34 km in circumference; closed to the public;
Kingman Reef: barren coral atoll with deep interior lagoon; closed to the public;
Midway Islands: a coral atoll managed as a National Wildlife Refuge and open to the public for wildlife-related recreation in the form of wildlife observation and photography;
Palmyra Atoll: the high rainfall and resulting lush vegetation make the environment of this atoll unique among the US Pacific Island territories; supports a large undisturbed stand of Pisonia beach forest

PEOPLE AND SOCIETY

Population: *total:* no indigenous inhabitants
note: public entry is only by special-use permit from US Fish and Wildlife Service and generally restricted to scientists and educators; visited annually by US Fish and Wildlife Service
Jarvis Island: Millersville settlement on western side of island occasionally used as a weather station from 1935 until World War II, when it was abandoned; reoccupied in 1957 during the International Geophysical Year by scientists who left in 1958; currently unoccupied
Johnston Atoll: in previous years, an average of 1,100 US military and civilian contractor personnel were present; as of May 2005, all US Government personnel had left the island
Midway Islands: approximately 40 people make up the staff of US Fish and Wildlife Service and their services contractor living at the atoll
Palmyra Atoll: 4 to 20 Nature Conservancy, US Fish and Wildlife staff, and researchers

ENVIRONMENT

Environment - current issues: Baker Island: no natural freshwater resources; feral cats, introduced in 1937 during a short-lived colonization effort, ravaged the avian population and were eradicated in 1965
Howland Island: no natural freshwater resources; the island habitat has suffered from invasive exotic species; black rats, introduced in 1854, were eradicated by feral cats within a year of their introduction in 1937; the cats preyed on the bird population and were eliminated by 1985
Jarvis Island: no natural freshwater resources; feral cats, introduced in the 1930s during a short-lived colonization venture, were not completely removed until 1990
Johnston Atoll: no natural freshwater resources; the seven decades under US military administration (1934-2004) left the atoll environmentally degraded and required large-scale remediation efforts; a swarm of Anoplolepis (crazy) ants invaded the island in 2010 damaging native wildlife; eradication has been largely, but not completely, successful
Midway Islands: many exotic species introduced, 75% of the roughly 200 plant species on the island are non-native; plastic pollution harms wildlife, via entanglement, ingestion, and toxic contamination
Kingman Reef: none
Palmyra Atoll: black rats, believed to have been introduced to the atoll during the US military occupation of the 1940s, severely degraded the ecosystem outcompeting native species (seabirds, crabs); following a successful rat removal project in 2011, native flora and fauna have begun to recover

Climate: Baker, Howland, and Jarvis Islands: equatorial; scant rainfall, constant wind, burning sun;
Johnston Atoll and Kingman Reef: tropical, but generally dry; consistent northeast trade winds with little seasonal temperature variation;
Midway Islands: subtropical with cool, moist winters (December to February) and warm, dry summers (May to October); moderated by prevailing easterly winds; most of the 107 cm of annual rainfall occurs during the winter;
Palmyra Atoll: equatorial, hot; located within the low pressure area of the Intertropical Convergence Zone (ITCZ) where the northeast and southeast trade winds meet, it is extremely wet with between 400-500 cm of rainfall each year

GOVERNMENT

Country name: *conventional long form:* none
conventional short form: Baker Island, Howland Island, Jarvis Island, Johnston Atoll, Kingman Reef, Midway Islands, Palmyra Atoll
etymology: self-descriptive name specifying the territories' affiliation and location

Dependency status: with the exception of Palmyra Atoll, the constituent islands are unincorporated, unorganized territories of the US; administered from Washington, DC, by the Fish and Wildlife Service of the US Department of the Interior as part of the National Wildlife Refuge System
note: Palmyra Atoll is partly privately owned and partly federally owned; the federally owned portion is administered from Washington, DC, by the Fish and Wildlife Service of the US Department of the Interior as an incorporated, unorganized territory of the US; the Office of Insular Affairs of the US Department of the Interior continues to administer nine excluded areas comprising certain tidal and submerged lands within the 12 nm territorial sea or within the lagoon

Legal system: the laws of the US apply where applicable

Diplomatic representation from the US: none (territories of the US)

Flag description: the flag of the US is used

ENERGY

Coal: *imports:* 108,000 metric tons (2022 est.)

Petroleum: *refined petroleum consumption:* 2,000 bbl/day (2022 est.)

Carbon dioxide emissions: 297,000 metric tonnes of CO2 (2022 est.)
from petroleum and other liquids: 297,000 metric tonnes of CO2 (2022 est.)
comparison ranking: total emissions 198

TRANSPORTATION

Airports: 2 (2024)
comparison ranking: 208

MILITARY AND SECURITY

Military - note: defense is the responsibility of the US

URUGUAY

INTRODUCTION

Background: The Spanish founded the city of Montevideo in modern-day Uruguay in 1726 as a military stronghold, and it soon became an important commercial center due to its natural harbor. Argentina initially claimed Uruguay, but Brazil annexed the country in 1821. Uruguay declared its independence in 1825 and secured its freedom in 1828 after a three-year struggle. The administrations of President Jose BATLLE in the early 20th century launched widespread political, social, and economic reforms that established a statist tradition. A violent Marxist urban guerrilla movement named the Tupamaros (or Movimiento de Liberación Nacional-Tupamaros) launched in the late 1960s and pushed Uruguay's president to cede control of the government to the military in 1973. By year-end, the rebels had been crushed, but the military continued to expand its hold over the government. Civilian rule was restored in 1985. In 2004, the left-of-center Frente Amplio (FA) Coalition won national elections that effectively ended 170 years of political control by the Colorado and National (Blanco) parties. The left-of-center coalition retained the presidency and control of both chambers of congress until 2019. Uruguay's political and labor conditions are among the freest on the South American continent.

GEOGRAPHY

Location: Southern South America, bordering the South Atlantic Ocean, between Argentina and Brazil

Geographic coordinates: 33 00 S, 56 00 W

Map references: South America

Area: *total:* 176,215 sq km
land: 175,015 sq km
water: 1,200 sq km
comparison ranking: total 91

Area - comparative: about the size of Virginia and West Virginia combined; slightly smaller than the state of Washington

Land boundaries: *total:* 1,591 km
border countries (2): Argentina 541 km; Brazil 1,050 km

Coastline: 660 km

Maritime claims: *territorial sea:* 12 nm
contiguous zone: 24 nm
exclusive economic zone: 200 nm
continental shelf: 200 nm or the edge of continental margin

Climate: warm temperate; freezing temperatures almost unknown

Terrain: mostly rolling plains and low hills; fertile coastal lowland

Elevation: *highest point:* Cerro Catedral 514 m
lowest point: Atlantic Ocean 0 m
mean elevation: 109 m

Natural resources: arable land, hydropower, minor minerals, fish

Land use: *agricultural land:* 87.2% (2018 est.)
arable land: 10.1% (2018 est.)
permanent crops: 0.2% (2018 est.)
permanent pasture: 76.9% (2018 est.)
forest: 10.2% (2018 est.)
other: 2.6% (2018 est.)

Irrigated land: 2,380 sq km (2012)

Major lakes (area sq km): *salt water lake(s):* Lagoa Mirim (shared with Brazil) - 2,970 sq km

Major rivers (by length in km): Rio de la Plata/Parana river mouth (shared with Brazil [s], Argentina, Paraguay) - 4,880 km; Uruguay river mouth (shared with Brazil [s] and Argentina) - 1,610 km
note – [s] after country name indicates river source; [m] after country name indicates river mouth

Major aquifers: Guarani Aquifer System

Population distribution: most of the country's population resides in the southern half of the country; approximately 80% of the populace is urban, living in towns or cities; nearly half of the population lives in and around the capital of Montevideo

Natural hazards: seasonally high winds (the pampero is a chilly and occasional violent wind that blows north from the Argentine pampas), droughts, floods; because of the absence of mountains, which act as weather barriers, all locations are particularly vulnerable to rapid changes from weather fronts

Geography - note: second-smallest South American country (after Suriname); most of the low-lying landscape (three-quarters of the country) is grassland, ideal for cattle and sheep raising

PEOPLE AND SOCIETY

Population: *total:* 3,425,330
male: 1,660,132
female: 1,765,198 (2024 est.)
comparison rankings: female 133; male 135; total 133

Nationality: *noun:* Uruguayan(s)
adjective: Uruguayan

Ethnic groups: White 87.7%, Black 4.6%, Indigenous 2.4%, other 0.3%, none or unspecified 5% (2011 est.)
note: data represent primary ethnic identity

Languages: Spanish (official, Rioplatense is the most widely spoken dialect)
major-language sample(s):
La Libreta Informativa del Mundo, la fuente indispensable de información básica. (Spanish)

Religions: Roman Catholic 36.5%, Protestant 5% (Evangelical (non-specific) 4.6%, Adventist 0.2%, Protestant (non-specific) 0.3%), African American Cults/Umbanda 2.8%, Jehovah's Witness 0.6%, Church of Jesus Christ 0.2%, other 1%, Believer (not belonging to the church) 1.8%, agnostic 0.3%, atheist 1.3%, none 47.3%, unspecified 3.4%
Roman Catholic 42%, Protestant 15%, other 6%, agnostic 3%, atheist 10%, unspecified 24% (2023 est.)

Demographic profile: Uruguay rates high for most development indicators and is known for its secularism, liberal social laws, and well-developed social security, health, and educational systems. It is one of the few countries in Latin America and the Caribbean where the entire population has access to clean water. Uruguay's provision of free primary through university education has contributed to the country's high levels of literacy and educational attainment. However, the emigration of human capital has diminished the state's return on its investment in education. Remittances from the roughly 18% of Uruguayans abroad amount to less than 1 percent of national GDP. The emigration of young adults and a low birth rate are causing Uruguay's population to age rapidly.
In the 1960s, Uruguayans for the first time emigrated en masse - primarily to Argentina and Brazil - because of economic decline and the onset of more than a decade of military dictatorship. Economic crises in the early 1980s and 2002 also triggered waves of emigration, but since 2002 more than 70% of Uruguayan emigrants have selected the US and Spain as destinations because of better job prospects. Uruguay had a tiny population upon its independence in 1828 and welcomed thousands of predominantly Italian

and Spanish immigrants, but the country has not experienced large influxes of new arrivals since the aftermath of World War II. More recent immigrants include Peruvians and Arabs.

Age structure: *0-14 years:* 18.9% (male 329,268/female 317,925)
15-64 years: 65.4% (male 1,112,622/female 1,128,418)
65 years and over: 15.7% (2024 est.) (male 218,242/female 318,855)

Dependency ratios: *total dependency ratio:* 53.6
youth dependency ratio: 29.9
elderly dependency ratio: 23.7
potential support ratio: 4.2 (2021 est.)

Median age: *total:* 36.5 years (2024 est.)
male: 34.9 years
female: 38.2 years
comparison ranking: total 89

Population growth rate: 0.26% (2024 est.)
comparison ranking: 170

Birth rate: births/1,000 population (2024 est.)
comparison ranking: 136

Death rate: 9.1 deaths/1,000 population (2024 est.)
comparison ranking: 57

Net migration rate: -0.9 migrant(s)/1,000 population (2024 est.)
comparison ranking: 140

Population distribution: most of the country's population resides in the southern half of the country; approximately 80% of the populace is urban, living in towns or cities; nearly half of the population lives in and around the capital of Montevideo

Urbanization: *urban population:* 95.8% of total population (2023)
rate of urbanization: 0.4% annual rate of change (2020-25 est.)

Major urban areas - population: 1.774 million MONTEVIDEO (capital) (2023)

Sex ratio: *at birth:* 1.04 male(s)/female
0-14 years: 1.04 male(s)/female
15-64 years: 0.99 male(s)/female
65 years and over: 0.68 male(s)/female
total population: 0.94 male(s)/female (2024 est.)

Maternal mortality ratio: 19 deaths/100,000 live births (2020 est.)
comparison ranking: 127

Infant mortality rate: *total:* 8 deaths/1,000 live births (2024 est.)
male: 9.1 deaths/1,000 live births
female: 6.8 deaths/1,000 live births
comparison ranking: total 145

Life expectancy at birth: *total population:* 78.9 years (2024 est.)
male: 75.8 years
female: 82.1 years
comparison ranking: total population 70

Total fertility rate: 1.75 children born/woman (2024 est.)
comparison ranking: 149

Gross reproduction rate: 0.86 (2024 est.)

Contraceptive prevalence rate: 79.6% (2015)
note: percent of women aged 15-44

Drinking water source: *improved: urban:* 100% of population
rural: 100% of population
total: 100% of population

Current health expenditure: 9.2% of GDP (2020)

Physician density: 4.94 physicians/1,000 population (2017)

Hospital bed density: 2.4 beds/1,000 population (2017)

Sanitation facility access: *improved: urban:* 99.2% of population
rural: 99.6% of population
total: 99.2% of population
unimproved: urban: 0.8% of population
rural: 0.4% of population
total: 0.8% of population (2020 est.)

Obesity - adult prevalence rate: 27.9% (2016)
comparison ranking: 33

Alcohol consumption per capita: *total:* 5.42 liters of pure alcohol (2019 est.)
beer: 1.86 liters of pure alcohol (2019 est.)
wine: 2.86 liters of pure alcohol (2019 est.)
spirits: 0.71 liters of pure alcohol (2019 est.)
other alcohols: 0 liters of pure alcohol (2019 est.)
comparison ranking: total 82

Tobacco use: *total:* 21.5% (2020 est.)
male: 24.4% (2020 est.)
female: 18.5% (2020 est.)
comparison ranking: total 76

Children under the age of 5 years underweight: 1.8% (2018)
comparison ranking: 109

Currently married women (ages 15-49): 55.4% (2023 est.)

Education expenditures: 4.6% of GDP (2020 est.)
comparison ranking: 91

Literacy: *definition:* age 15 and over can read and write
total population: 98.8%
male: 98.5%
female: 99% (2019)

School life expectancy (primary to tertiary education): *total:* 19 years
male: 17 years
female: 20 years (2019)

ENVIRONMENT

Environment - current issues: water pollution from meat packing, tannery industries; heavy metal pollution; inadequate solid and hazardous waste disposal; deforestation

Environment - international agreements: *party to:* Antarctic-Environmental Protection, Antarctic-Marine Living Resources, Antarctic Treaty, Biodiversity, Climate Change, Climate Change-Kyoto Protocol, Climate Change-Paris Agreement, Comprehensive Nuclear Test Ban, Desertification, Endangered Species, Environmental Modification, Hazardous Wastes, Law of the Sea, Marine Dumping-London Protocol, Nuclear Test Ban, Ozone Layer Protection, Ship Pollution, Wetlands, Whaling
signed, but not ratified: Marine Dumping-London Convention, Marine Life Conservation

Climate: warm temperate; freezing temperatures almost unknown

Urbanization: *urban population:* 95.8% of total population (2023)
rate of urbanization: 0.4% annual rate of change (2020-25 est.)

Revenue from forest resources: 1.56% of GDP (2018 est.)
comparison ranking: 41

Revenue from coal: 0% of GDP (2018 est.)
comparison ranking: 104

Air pollutants: *particulate matter emissions:* 8.48 micrograms per cubic meter (2019 est.)
carbon dioxide emissions: 6.77 megatons (2016 est.)
methane emissions: 25.59 megatons (2020 est.)

Waste and recycling: *municipal solid waste generated annually:* 1,260,140 tons (2012 est.)
municipal solid waste recycled annually: 100,811 tons (2011 est.)
percent of municipal solid waste recycled: 8% (2011 est.)

Major lakes (area sq km): *salt water lake(s):* Lagoa Mirim (shared with Brazil) - 2,970 sq km

Major rivers (by length in km): Rio de la Plata/Parana river mouth (shared with Brazil [s], Argentina, Paraguay) - 4,880 km; Uruguay river mouth (shared with Brazil [s] and Argentina) - 1,610 km
note – [s] after country name indicates river source; [m] after country name indicates river mouth

Major aquifers: Guarani Aquifer System

Total water withdrawal: *municipal:* 410 million cubic meters (2020 est.)
industrial: 80 million cubic meters (2020 est.)
agricultural: 3.17 billion cubic meters (2020 est.)

Total renewable water resources: 172.2 billion cubic meters (2020 est.)

Geoparks: *total global geoparks and regional networks:* 1
global geoparks and regional networks: Grutas del Palacio (2023)

GOVERNMENT

Country name: *conventional long form:* Oriental Republic of Uruguay
conventional short form: Uruguay
local long form: República Oriental del Uruguay
local short form: Uruguay
former: Banda Oriental, Cisplatine Province
etymology: name derives from the Spanish pronunciation of the Guarani Indian designation of the Uruguay River, which makes up the western border of the country and whose name later came to be applied to the entire country

Government type: presidential republic

Capital: *name:* Montevideo
geographic coordinates: 34 51 S, 56 10 W
time difference: UTC-3 (2 hours ahead of Washington, DC, during Standard Time)
etymology: the name "Montevidi" was originally applied to the hill that overlooked the bay upon which the city of Montevideo was founded; the earliest meaning may have been "[the place where we] saw the hill"

Administrative divisions: 19 departments (departamentos, singular - departamento); Artigas, Canelones, Cerro Largo, Colonia, Durazno, Flores, Florida, Lavalleja, Maldonado, Montevideo, Paysandú, Rio Negro, Rivera, Rocha, Salto, San José, Soriano, Tacuarembó, Treinta y Tres

Independence: 25 August 1825 (from Brazil)

National holiday: Independence Day, 25 August (1825)

Legal system: civil law system based on the Spanish civil code

Constitution: *history:* several previous; latest approved by plebiscite 27 November 1966, effective

15 February 1967, reinstated in 1985 at the conclusion of military rule
amendments: initiated by public petition of at least 10% of qualified voters, proposed by agreement of at least two fifths of the General Assembly membership, or by existing "constitutional laws" sanctioned by at least two thirds of the membership in both houses of the Assembly; proposals can also be submitted by senators, representatives, or by the executive power and require the formation of and approval in a national constituent convention; final passage by either method requires approval by absolute majority of votes cast in a referendum; amended many times, last in 2004

International law organization participation: accepts compulsory ICJ jurisdiction; accepts ICCt jurisdiction

Citizenship: *citizenship by birth:* yes
citizenship by descent only: yes
dual citizenship recognized: yes
residency requirement for naturalization: 3-5 years

Suffrage: 18 years of age; universal and compulsory

Executive branch: *chief of state:* President Luis Alberto LACALLE POU (since 1 March 2020)
head of government: President Luis Alberto LACALLE POU (since 1 March 2020)
cabinet: Council of Ministers appointed by the president with approval of the General Assembly
elections/appointments: president and vice president directly elected on the same ballot by absolute majority vote in 2 rounds if needed for a 5-year term (eligible for nonconsecutive terms); election last held on 27 October 2024 with a runoff scheduled for 24 November 2024 (next to be held on 28 October 2029 and a runoff, if needed, on 25 November 2029)
election results:
2024: percent of vote in first round - Yamandú Ramón Antonio ORSI Martínez (FA) 46.2%, Álvaro Luis DELGADO Ceretta (PN) 28.2%, Andrés OJEDA Ojeda Spitz (PC) 16.9%, other 8.7%; note - ORSI and DELGADO advance to the second round scheduled for 24 November 2024
2019: Luis Alberto LACALLE POU elected president in second round; percent of vote in first round - Daniel MARTINEZ (FA) 40.7%, Luis Alberto LACALLE POU (PN) 29.7%, Ernesto TALVI (Colorado Party) 12.8%, Guido MANINI RIOS (Open Cabildo) 11.3%, other 5.5%; percent of vote in second round - Luis Alberto LACALLE POU 50.6%, Daniel MARTINEZ 49.4%
2014: Tabare VAZQUEZ elected president in second round; percent of vote - Tabare VAZQUEZ (Socialist Party) 56.5%, Luis Alberto LACALLE Pou (PN) 43.4%
note: the president is both chief of state and head of government

Legislative branch: *description:* bicameral General Assembly or Asamblea General consists of:
Chamber of Senators or Camara de Senadores (30 seats; members directly elected in a single nationwide constituency by proportional representation vote; the vice-president serves as the presiding ex-officio member; elected members serve 5-year terms)
Chamber of Representatives or Camara de Representantes (99 seats; members directly elected in multi-seat constituencies by party-list proportional representation vote using the D'Hondt method; members serve 5-year terms)
elections: Chamber of Senators - last held on 27 October 2019 (next to be held on 27 October 2024)
Chamber of Representatives - last held on 27 October 2019 (next to be held on 27 October 2024)
election results: Chamber of Senators - percent of vote by party/coalition - NA; seats by party/coalition - Frente Amplio 13, National Party 10, Colorado Party 4, Open Cabildo 3; composition - men 21, women 10, percentage women 32.3%
Chamber of Representatives - percent of vote by party/coalition - NA; seats by coalition/party - Frente Amplio 42, National Party 30, Colorado Party 13, Open Cabildo 11, Independent Party 1, other 2; composition - men 74, women 25, percentage women 25.3%; note - total General Assembly percentage women 26.9%

Judicial branch: *highest court(s):* Supreme Court of Justice (consists of 5 judges)
judge selection and term of office: judges nominated by the president and appointed by two-thirds vote in joint conference of the General Assembly; judges serve 10-year terms, with reelection possible after a lapse of 5 years following the previous term
subordinate courts: Courts of Appeal; District Courts (Juzgados Letrados); Peace Courts (Juzgados de Paz); Rural Courts (Juzgados Rurales)

Political parties: Broad Front or FA (Frente Amplio) - (a broad governing coalition that comprises 34 factions including Popular
Participation Movement or MPP, Uruguay Assembly, Progressive Alliance, Broad Social Democratic Space, Socialist Party, Vertiente Artiguista, Christian Democratic Party, Big House, Communist Party, The Federal League, Fuerza Renovadora)
Colorado Party or PC (including Batllistas and Ciudadanos)
Intransigent Radical Ecologist Party (Partido Ecologista Radical Intransigente) or PERI
Independent Party
National Party or PN (including Todos (Everyone) and National Alliance)
Open Cabildo
Popular Unity

International organization participation: CAN (associate), CD, CELAC, FAO, G-77, IADB, IAEA, IBRD, ICAO, ICC (national committees), ICCt, ICRM, IDA, IFAD, IFC, IFRCS, IHO, ILO, IMF, IMO, Interpol, IOC, IOM, IPU, ISO, ITSO, ITU, LAES, LAIA, Mercosur, MIGA, MINUSTAH, MONUSCO, NAM (observer), OAS, OIF (observer), OPANAL, OPCW, Pacific Alliance (observer), PCA, SICA (observer),UN, UNASUR, UNCTAD, UNESCO, UNIDO, Union Latina, UNISFA, UNMOGIP, UNOCI, UNWTO, UPU, WCO, WFTU (NGOs), WHO, WIPO, WMO, WTO

Diplomatic representation in the US: *chief of mission:* Ambassador Andrés Augusto DURÁN Hareau (since 23 December 2020)
chancery: 1913 I Street NW, Washington, DC 20006
telephone: [1] (202) 331-1313
FAX: [1] (202) 331-8142
email address and website:
urueeuu@mrree.gub.uy
https://embassyofuruguay.us/
consulate(s) general: Miami, New York, San Francisco

Diplomatic representation from the US: *chief of mission:* Ambassador Heide B. FULTON (since 22 March 2023)
embassy: Lauro Muller 1776, Montevideo 11200
mailing address: 3360 Montevideo Place, Washington DC 20521-3360
telephone: (+598) 1770-2000
FAX: [+598] 1770-2128
email address and website:
MontevideoACS@state.gov
https://uy.usembassy.gov/

Flag description: nine equal horizontal stripes of white (top and bottom) alternating with blue; a white square in the upper hoist-side corner with a yellow sun bearing a human face (delineated in black) known as the Sun of May with 16 rays that alternate between triangular and wavy; the stripes represent the nine original departments of Uruguay; the sun symbol evokes the legend of the sun breaking through the clouds on 25 May 1810 as independence was first declared from Spain (Uruguay subsequently won its independence from Brazil); the sun features are said to represent those of Inti, the Inca god of the sun
note: the banner was inspired by the national colors of Argentina and by the design of the US flag

National symbol(s): Sun of May (a sun-with-face symbol); national colors: blue, white, yellow

National anthem: *name:* "Himno Nacional" (National Anthem of Uruguay)
lyrics/music: Francisco Esteban ACUNA de Figueroa/Francisco Jose DEBALI
note: adopted 1848; the anthem is also known as "Orientales, la Patria o la tumba!" ("Uruguayans, the Fatherland or Death!"); it is the world's longest national anthem in terms of music (105 bars; almost five minutes); generally only the first verse and chorus are sung

National heritage: *total World Heritage Sites:* 3 (all cultural)
selected World Heritage Site locales: Historic City of Colonia del Sacramento; Fray Bentos Industrial Landscape; The work of engineer Eladio Dieste: Church of Atlántida

ECONOMY

Economic overview: high-income, export-oriented South American economy; South America's largest middle class; low socioeconomic inequality; growing homicide rates; growing Chinese and EU relations; 2019 Argentine recession hurt; key milk, beef, rice, and wool exporter

Real GDP (purchasing power parity): $105.096 billion (2023 est.)
$104.711 billion (2022 est.)
$100.004 billion (2021 est.)
note: data in 2021 dollars
comparison ranking: 96

Real GDP growth rate: 0.37% (2023 est.)
4.71% (2022 est.)
5.56% (2021 est.)
note: annual GDP % growth based on constant local currency
comparison ranking: 183

Real GDP per capita: $30,700 (2023 est.)
$30,600 (2022 est.)
$29,200 (2021 est.)
note: data in 2021 dollars
comparison ranking: 76

GDP (official exchange rate): $77.241 billion (2023 est.)
note: data in current dollars at official exchange rate

Inflation rate (consumer prices): 5.87% (2023 est.)
9.1% (2022 est.)
7.75% (2021 est.)

note: annual % change based on consumer prices
comparison ranking: 124

Credit ratings: Fitch rating: BBB- (2013)

Moody's rating: Baa2 (2014)

Standard & Poors rating: BBB (2015)
note: The year refers to the year in which the current credit rating was first obtained.

GDP - composition, by sector of origin: *agriculture:* 5.6% (2023 est.)
industry: 16.4% (2023 est.)
services: 66.3% (2023 est.)
note: figures may not total 100% due to non-allocated consumption not captured in sector-reported data
comparison rankings: services 53; industry 162; agriculture 113

GDP - composition, by end use: *household consumption:* 66.8% (2015 est.)
government consumption: 13.8% (2015 est.)
investment in fixed capital: 17.4% (2023 est.)
investment in inventories: -0.1% (2023 est.)
exports of goods and services: 27.5% (2023 est.)
imports of goods and services: -24.2% (2023 est.)
note: figures may not total 100% due to rounding or gaps in data collection

Agricultural products: milk, rice, wheat, barley, soybeans, beef, rapeseed, sugarcane, maize, oranges (2022)
note: top ten agricultural products based on tonnage

Industries: food processing, electrical machinery, transportation equipment, petroleum products, textiles, chemicals, beverages

Industrial production growth rate: -3.83% (2023 est.)
note: annual % change in industrial value added based on constant local currency
comparison ranking: 195

Labor force: 1.775 million (2023 est.)
note: number of people ages 15 or older who are employed or seeking work
comparison ranking: 130

Unemployment rate: 8.35% (2023 est.)
7.88% (2022 est.)
9.3% (2021 est.)
note: % of labor force seeking employment
comparison ranking: 150

Youth unemployment rate (ages 15-24): *total:* 26.2% (2023 est.)
male: 24.4% (2023 est.)
female: 28.3% (2023 est.)
note: % of labor force ages 15-24 seeking employment
comparison ranking: total 38

Population below poverty line: 9.9% (2022 est.)
note: % of population with income below national poverty line

Gini Index coefficient - distribution of family income: 40.6 (2022 est.)
note: index (0-100) of income distribution; higher values represent greater inequality
comparison ranking: 41

Average household expenditures: *on food:* 18.6% of household expenditures (2022 est.)
on alcohol and tobacco: 1.3% of household expenditures (2022 est.)

Household income or consumption by percentage share: *lowest 10%:* 2.2% (2022 est.)
highest 10%: 30.5% (2022 est.)
note: % share of income accruing to lowest and highest 10% of population

Remittances: 0.16% of GDP (2023 est.)
0.18% of GDP (2022 est.)
0.21% of GDP (2021 est.)
note: personal transfers and compensation between resident and non-resident individuals/households/entities

Budget: *revenues:* $16.522 billion (2020 est.)
expenditures: $18.58 billion (2020 est.)
note: central government revenues (excluding grants) and expenses converted to US dollars at average official exchange rate for year indicated

Public debt: 60.28% of GDP (2020 est.)
note: central government debt as a % of GDP
comparison ranking: 80

Taxes and other revenues: 18.51% (of GDP) (2020 est.)
note: central government tax revenue as a % of GDP
comparison ranking: 96

Current account balance: -$2.797 billion (2023 est.)
-$2.725 billion (2022 est.)
-$1.472 billion (2021 est.)
note: balance of payments - net trade and primary/secondary income in current dollars
comparison ranking: 167

Exports: $21.286 billion (2023 est.)
$22.611 billion (2022 est.)
$19.639 billion (2021 est.)
note: balance of payments - exports of goods and services in current dollars
comparison ranking: 88

Exports - partners: China 24%, Brazil 14%, Argentina 8%, US 7%, Netherlands 5% (2022)
note: top five export partners based on percentage share of exports

Exports - commodities: beef, wood pulp, soybeans, milk, rice (2022)
note: top five export commodities based on value in dollars

Imports: $18.865 billion (2023 est.)
$18.993 billion (2022 est.)
$15.134 billion (2021 est.)
note: balance of payments - imports of goods and services in current dollars
comparison ranking: 97

Imports - partners: Brazil 20%, China 18%, US 15%, Argentina 11%, Germany 3% (2022)
note: top five import partners based on percentage share of imports

Imports - commodities: crude petroleum, fertilizers, cars, packaged medicine, broadcasting equipment (2022)
note: top five import commodities based on value in dollars

Reserves of foreign exchange and gold: $16.257 billion (2023 est.)
$15.127 billion (2022 est.)
$16.963 billion (2021 est.)
note: holdings of gold (year-end prices)/foreign exchange/special drawing rights in current dollars
comparison ranking: 72

Exchange rates: Uruguayan pesos (UYU) per US dollar -

Exchange rates: 38.824 (2023 est.)
41.171 (2022 est.)
43.555 (2021 est.)
42.013 (2020 est.)
35.255 (2019 est.)

ENERGY

Electricity access: *electrification - total population:* 100% (2022 est.)

Electricity: *installed generating capacity:* 5.36 million kW (2022 est.)
consumption: 11.811 billion kWh (2022 est.)
exports: 2.152 billion kWh (2022 est.)
imports: 55 million kWh (2022 est.)
transmission/distribution losses: 1.281 billion kWh (2022 est.)
comparison rankings: transmission/distribution losses 110; imports 113; exports 55; consumption 94; installed generating capacity 87

Electricity generation sources: *fossil fuels:* 9.1% of total installed capacity (2022 est.)
solar: 3.3% of total installed capacity (2022 est.)
wind: 31.5% of total installed capacity (2022 est.)
hydroelectricity: 37.5% of total installed capacity (2022 est.)
biomass and waste: 18.7% of total installed capacity (2022 est.)

Coal: *consumption:* 18,000 metric tons (2022 est.)
imports: 18,000 metric tons (2022 est.)

Petroleum: *total petroleum production:* 400 bbl/day (2023 est.)
refined petroleum consumption: 52,000 bbl/day (2022 est.)

Natural gas: *consumption:* 86.037 million cubic meters (2022 est.)
imports: 86.89 million cubic meters (2022 est.)

Carbon dioxide emissions: 7.084 million metric tonnes of CO2 (2022 est.)
from coal and metallurgical coke: 45,000 metric tonnes of CO2 (2022 est.)
from petroleum and other liquids: 6.87 million metric tonnes of CO2 (2022 est.)
from consumed natural gas: 169,000 metric tonnes of CO2 (2022 est.)
comparison ranking: total emissions 123

Energy consumption per capita: 47.237 million Btu/person (2022 est.)
comparison ranking: 96

COMMUNICATIONS

Telephones - fixed lines: *total subscriptions:* 1.259 million (2022 est.)
subscriptions per 100 inhabitants: 37 (2022 est.)
comparison ranking: total subscriptions 64

Telephones - mobile cellular: *total subscriptions:* 4.741 million (2022 est.)
subscriptions per 100 inhabitants: 139 (2022 est.)
comparison ranking: total subscriptions 127

Telecommunication systems: *general assessment:* Uruguay has an advanced telecom market, with excellent infrastructure and one of the highest broadband penetration rates in Latin America; fixed-line teledensity is also particularly high for the region, while mobile penetration is the second highest after Panama; in terms of computer penetration, Uruguay tops all other countries in the region by a considerable margin, and this has facilitated growth in fixed-line broadband adoption; the government and telecom regulator have introduced a range of measures to help develop the deployment of fiber infrastructure, partly in a bid to encourage economic growth and stimulate e-commerce; fiber accounted for over 95% of all fixed and fixed-wireless broadband connections as of December 2023; with investment projected to reach

$800 million, the state-owned incumbent Antel is expected to provide national Fiber to the premises (FttP) coverage by 2023; together with the FttP network, the opening of the submarine cable system in early 2012 and August 2017 have helped boost Uruguay's internet bandwidth, and increase the data rate available to end-users; changes in legislation in 2020 allowed cable companies to provide home internet service for the first time, ending the state monopoly; Uruguay's regulator authorized five cable companies to provide broadband service; while the country's broadband network is state owned, other segments of the telecom market have been opened to competition, including international long-distance telephony, mobile telephony, and fixed-wireless broadband; cable networks are well equipped technologically, and digital cable TV is widely available, telecom legislation prohibits data transmission over pay TV networks; all three operators offer mobile broadband through 3G and LTE networks; operators have achieved nationwide 3G coverage and the number of mobile broadband subscribers continues to grow; at the end of 2019, spectrum in the 5G-suitable range was auctioned, enabling operators to launch 5G services; Uruguay's regulators held a 5G spectrum auction in June 2023; the three incumbent operators each acquired 100 Ghz in the 3.5 GHz midband; in 2023, Uruguay's state telecom has deployed hundreds of 5G radio bases, covering all regional capitals (2021)
domestic: fixed-line is 36 per 100 and mobile-cellular teledensity 140 per 100 persons (2021)
international: country code - 598; landing points for the Unisor, Tannat, and Bicentenario submarine cable system providing direct connectivity to Brazil and Argentina; the Firmina cable, which landed in 2023, allowed for direct connectivity to the United States; Bicentenario 2012 and Tannat 2017 cables helped end-users with Internet bandwidth; satellite earth stations - 2 Intelsat (Atlantic Ocean) (2020)

Broadcast media: mixture of privately owned and state-run broadcast media; more than 100 commercial radio stations and about 20 TV channels; cable TV is available; many community radio and TV stations; adopted the hybrid Japanese/Brazilian HDTV standard (ISDB-T) in December 2010 (2019)

Internet country code: .uy

Internet users: *total:* 3.06 million (2021 est.)
percent of population: 90% (2021 est.)
comparison ranking: total 118

Broadband - fixed subscriptions: *total:* 1,063,701 (2020 est.)
subscriptions per 100 inhabitants: 31 (2020 est.)
comparison ranking: total 71

TRANSPORTATION

National air transport system: *number of registered air carriers:* 2 (2020)
inventory of registered aircraft operated by air carriers: 5

Civil aircraft registration country code prefix: CX

Airports: 64 (2024)
comparison ranking: 75

Heliports: 3 (2024)

Pipelines: 257 km gas, 160 km oil (2013)

Railways: *total:* 1,673 km (2016) (operational; government claims overall length is 2,961 km)
standard gauge: 1,673 km (2016) 1.435-m gauge
comparison ranking: total 79

Roadways: *total:* 77,732 km
paved: 7,743 km
unpaved: 69,989 km (2010)
comparison ranking: total 65

Waterways: 1,600 km (2011)
comparison ranking: 50

Merchant marine: *total:* 58 (2023)
by type: container ship 1, general cargo 4, oil tanker 3, other 50
comparison ranking: total 115

Ports: *total ports:* 8 (2024)
large: 0
medium: 1
small: 1
very small: 6
ports with oil terminals: 2
key ports: Colonia, Fray Bentos, Jose Ignacio, La Paloma, Montevideo, Nueva Palmira, Paysandu, Puerto Sauce

MILITARY AND SECURITY

Military and security forces: Armed Forces of Uruguay (Fuerzas Armadas del Uruguay or FF.AA. del Uruguay): National Army (Ejercito Nacional), National Navy (Armada Nacional, includes Coast Guard (Prefectura Nacional Naval or PRENA)), Uruguayan Air Force (Fuerza Aerea)

Ministry of Interior: National Police (2024)
note: the National Police includes the paramilitary National Republican Guard (Guardia Nacional Republicana); the National Police maintains internal security, while the National Directorate for Migration is responsible for migration and border enforcement

Military expenditures: 1% of GDP (2023 est.)
1% of GDP (2022 est.)
2.3% of GDP (2021 est.)
2% of GDP (2020 est.)
2.1% of GDP (2019 est.)
comparison ranking: 130

Military and security service personnel strengths: approximately 23,000 active-duty personnel (15,000 Army; 5,000 Navy; 3,000 Air Force) (2023)

Military equipment inventories and acquisitions: the military's inventory includes a wide variety of older or second-hand equipment; in recent years, it has imported limited amounts of military hardware from a variety of countries with Spain as the leading supplier (2023)

Military service age and obligation: 18-30 years of age (18-22 years of age for Navy) for voluntary military service for men and women; up to 40 years of age for specialists; enlistment is voluntary in peacetime, but the government has the authority to conscript in emergencies (2024)
note: as of 2023, women comprised nearly 20% of the active military

Military deployments: 600 Democratic Republic of the Congo (MONUSCO); 200 Golan Heights (UNDOF) (2024)

Military - note: the armed forces are responsible for defense of the country's independence, national sovereignty, and territorial integrity, as well as protecting strategic resources; it has some domestic responsibilities, including perimeter security for a number of prisons and border security and providing humanitarian/disaster assistance; since 2020, the military has deployed additional troops to the frontiers with Argentina and Brazil to assist the National Police in securing the border; it also assists the Ministry of Interior in combating narcotics trafficking; the military participates in UN peacekeeping missions and multinational exercises with foreign partners; Uruguay has traditionally held security ties with Argentina, Brazil, Peru, and the US; since 2018, it has also signed defense cooperation agreements with China and Russia (2024)

TRANSNATIONAL ISSUES

Refugees and internally displaced persons: *refugees (country of origin):* 32,939 (Venezuela) (economic and political crisis; includes Venezuelans who have claimed asylum or have received alternative legal stay) (2023)
stateless persons: 5 (2022)

Trafficking in persons: tier rating: Tier 2 Watch List — the government did not demonstrate overall increasing efforts to eliminate trafficking compared with the previous reporting period, therefore Uruguay was downgraded to Tier 2 Watch List; for more details, go to: https://www.state.gov/reports/2024-trafficking-in-persons-report/uruguay/

Illicit drugs: transit country for drugs mainly bound for Europe, often through sea-borne containers; limited law enforcement corruption; money laundering; weak border control along Brazilian frontier; increasing consumption of cocaine base and synthetic drugs

UZBEKISTAN

INTRODUCTION

Background: Uzbekistan is the geographic and population center of Central Asia, with a diverse economy and a relatively young population. Russia conquered and united the disparate territories of present-day Uzbekistan in the late 19th century. Stiff resistance to the Red Army after the Bolshevik Revolution was eventually suppressed and a socialist republic established in 1924. During the Soviet era, intensive production of "white gold" (cotton) and grain led to the overuse of agrochemicals and the depletion of water supplies, leaving the land degraded and the Aral Sea and certain rivers half-dry. Independent since the Union of Soviet Socialist Republics (USSR) dissolved in 1991, the country has diversified agricultural production while developing its mineral and petroleum export capacity and increasing its

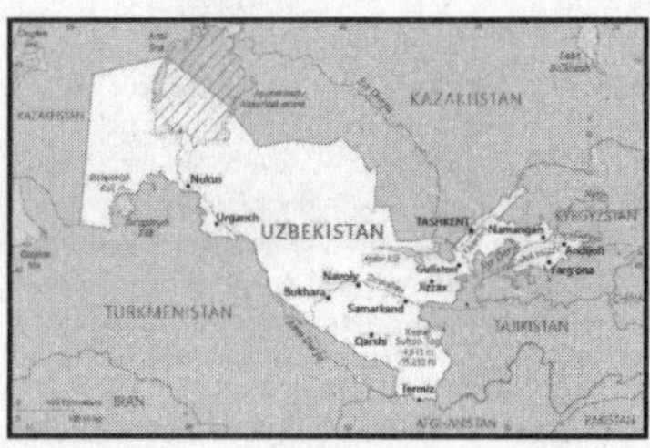

manufacturing base, although cotton remains a major part of its economy. Uzbekistan's first president, Islom KARIMOV, led Uzbekistan for 25 years until his death in 2016. His successor, former Prime Minister Shavkat MIRZIYOYEV, has improved relations with Uzbekistan's neighbors and introduced wide-ranging economic, judicial, and social reforms. MIRZIYOYEV was reelected in 2021 with 80% of the vote and again following a 2023 constitutional referendum with 87% of the vote.

GEOGRAPHY

Location: Central Asia, north of Turkmenistan, south of Kazakhstan

Geographic coordinates: 41 00 N, 64 00 E

Map references: Asia

Area: *total:* 447,400 sq km
land: 425,400 sq km
water: 22,000 sq km
comparison ranking: total 59

Area - comparative: about four times the size of Virginia; slightly larger than California

Land boundaries: *total:* 6,893 km
border countries (5): Afghanistan 144 km; Kazakhstan 2,330 km; Kyrgyzstan 1,314 km; Tajikistan 1,312 km; Turkmenistan 1,793 km

Coastline: 0 km (doubly landlocked); note - Uzbekistan includes the southern portion of the Aral Sea with a 420 km shoreline

Maritime claims: none (doubly landlocked)

Climate: mostly mid-latitude desert, long, hot summers, mild winters; semiarid grassland in east

Terrain: mostly flat-to-rolling sandy desert with dunes; broad, flat intensely irrigated river valleys along course of Amu Darya, Syr Darya (Sirdaryo), and Zaravshan; Fergana Valley in east surrounded by mountainous Tajikistan and Kyrgyzstan; shrinking Aral Sea in west

Elevation: *highest point:* Xazrat Sulton Tog' 4,643 m
lowest point: Sariqamish Kuli -12 m

Natural resources: natural gas, petroleum, coal, gold, uranium, silver, copper, lead and zinc, tungsten, molybdenum

Land use: *agricultural land:* 62.6% (2018 est.)
arable land: 10.1% (2018 est.)
permanent crops: 0.8% (2018 est.)
permanent pasture: 51.7% (2018 est.)
forest: 7.7% (2018 est.)
other: 29.7% (2018 est.)

Irrigated land: 37,320 sq km (2020)

Major lakes (area sq km): *fresh water lake(s):* Aral Sea (shared with Kazakhstan) - largely dried up

Major rivers (by length in km): Syr Darya (shared with Kyrgyzstan [s], Tajikistan, and Kazakhstan [m]) - 3,078 km; Amu Darya river mouth (shared with Tajikistan [s], Afghanistan, and Turkmenistan) - 2,620 km
note – [s] after country name indicates river source; [m] after country name indicates river mouth

Major watersheds (area sq km): Internal (endorheic basin) drainage: *(Aral Sea basin)* Amu Darya (534,739 sq km), Syr Darya (782,617 sq km)

Population distribution: most of the population is concentrated in the fertile Fergana Valley in the easternmost arm of the country; the south has significant clusters of people, while the central and western deserts are sparsely populated

Natural hazards: earthquakes; floods; landslides or mudslides; avalanches; droughts

Geography - note: along with Liechtenstein, one of the only two doubly landlocked countries in the world

PEOPLE AND SOCIETY

Population: *total:* 36,520,593
male: 18,324,813
female: 18,195,780 (2024 est.)
comparison rankings: female 41; male 41; total 42

Nationality: *noun:* Uzbekistani
adjective: Uzbekistani

Ethnic groups: Uzbek 83.8%, Tajik 4.8%, Kazakh 2.5%, Russian 2.3%, Karakalpak 2.2%, Tatar 1.5%, other 2.9% (2017 est.)

Languages: Uzbek (official) 74.3%, Russian 14.2%, Tajik 4.4%, other 7.1%
major-language sample(s):
Jahon faktlari kitobi, asosiy ma'lumotlar uchun zaruriy manba. (Uzbek)
note: in the semi-autonomous Republic of Karakalpakstan, both the Karakalpak language and Uzbek have official status

Religions: Muslim 88% (mostly Sunni), Eastern Orthodox 9%, other 3%

Age structure: *0-14 years:* 29.6% (male 5,597,947/female 5,213,403)
15-64 years: 63.7% (male 11,649,017/female 11,617,411)
65 years and over: 6.7% (2024 est.) (male 1,077,849/female 1,364,966)

Dependency ratios: *total dependency ratio:* 54
youth dependency ratio: 46.3
elderly dependency ratio: 7.2
potential support ratio: 13 (2021 est.)

Median age: *total:* 28.9 years (2024 est.)
male: 28.1 years
female: 29.8 years
comparison ranking: total 148

Population growth rate: 1.43% (2024 est.)
comparison ranking: 69

Birth rate: 20.5 births/1,000 population (2024 est.)
comparison ranking: 64

Death rate: 5.1 deaths/1,000 population (2024 est.)
comparison ranking: 190

Net migration rate: -1.1 migrant(s)/1,000 population (2024 est.)
comparison ranking: 149

Population distribution: most of the population is concentrated in the fertile Fergana Valley in the easternmost arm of the country; the south has significant clusters of people, while the central and western deserts are sparsely populated

Urbanization: *urban population:* 50.5% of total population (2023)
rate of urbanization: 1.25% annual rate of change (2020-25 est.)

Major urban areas - population: 2.603 million TASHKENT (capital) (2023)

Sex ratio: *at birth:* 1.08 male(s)/female
0-14 years: 1.07 male(s)/female
15-64 years: 1 male(s)/female
65 years and over: 0.79 male(s)/female
total population: 1.01 male(s)/female (2024 est.)

Mother's mean age at first birth: 23.7 years (2019 est.)

Maternal mortality ratio: 30 deaths/100,000 live births (2020 est.)
comparison ranking: 110

Infant mortality rate: *total:* 18.2 deaths/1,000 live births (2024 est.)
male: 21.1 deaths/1,000 live births
female: 15.1 deaths/1,000 live births
comparison ranking: total 85

Life expectancy at birth: *total population:* 76.2 years (2024 est.)
male: 73.6 years
female: 79 years
comparison ranking: total population 114

Total fertility rate: 2.76 children born/woman (2024 est.)
comparison ranking: 57

Gross reproduction rate: 1.33 (2024 est.)

Drinking water source: *improved: urban:* 99.6% of population
rural: 96.1% of population
total: 97.8% of population
unimproved: urban: 0.4% of population
rural: 3.9% of population
total: 2.2% of population (2020 est.)

Current health expenditure: 6.8% of GDP (2020)

Physician density: 2.37 physicians/1,000 population (2014)

Hospital bed density: 4 beds/1,000 population (2014)

Sanitation facility access: *improved: urban:* 100% of population
rural: 100% of population
total: 100% of population
unimproved: urban: 0% of population
rural: 0% of population
total: 0% of population (2020 est.)

Obesity - adult prevalence rate: 16.6% (2016)
comparison ranking: 123

Alcohol consumption per capita: *total:* 2.45 liters of pure alcohol (2019 est.)
beer: 0.18 liters of pure alcohol (2019 est.)
wine: 0.09 liters of pure alcohol (2019 est.)
spirits: 2.19 liters of pure alcohol (2019 est.)
other alcohols: 0 liters of pure alcohol (2019 est.)
comparison ranking: total 124

Tobacco use: *total:* 17.6% (2020 est.)
male: 34% (2020 est.)
female: 1.1% (2020 est.)
comparison ranking: total 96

Children under the age of 5 years underweight: 1.8% (2021)
comparison ranking: 107

Currently married women (ages 15-49): 68.6% (2023 est.)

Child marriage: *women married by age 15:* 0.2%

women married by age 18: 3.4% (2022 est.)

Education expenditures: 4.9% of GDP (2020 est.)
comparison ranking: 82

Literacy: *definition:* age 15 and over can read and write
total population: 100%
male: 100%
female: 100% (2019)

School life expectancy (primary to tertiary education): *total:* 12 years
male: 12 years
female: 12 years (2021)

ENVIRONMENT

Environment - current issues: shrinkage of the Aral Sea has resulted in growing concentrations of chemical pesticides and natural salts; these substances are then blown from the increasingly exposed lake bed and contribute to desertification and respiratory health problems; water pollution from industrial wastes and the heavy use of fertilizers and pesticides is the cause of many human health disorders; increasing soil salination; soil contamination from buried nuclear processing and agricultural chemicals, including DDT

Environment - international agreements: *party to:* Biodiversity, Climate Change, Climate Change-Kyoto Protocol, Climate Change-Paris Agreement, Comprehensive Nuclear Test Ban, Desertification, Endangered Species, Environmental Modification, Hazardous Wastes, Ozone Layer Protection, Wetlands
signed, but not ratified: none of the selected agreements

Climate: mostly mid-latitude desert, long, hot summers, mild winters; semiarid grassland in east

Urbanization: *urban population:* 50.5% of total population (2023)
rate of urbanization: 1.25% annual rate of change (2020-25 est.)

Revenue from forest resources: 0% of GDP (2018 est.)
comparison ranking: 176

Revenue from coal: 0.06% of GDP (2018 est.)
comparison ranking: 30

Air pollutants: *particulate matter emissions:* 40.98 micrograms per cubic meter (2019 est.)
carbon dioxide emissions: 91.81 megatons (2016 est.)
methane emissions: 96.16 megatons (2020 est.)

Waste and recycling: *municipal solid waste generated annually:* 4 million tons (2016 est.)

Major lakes (area sq km): *fresh water lake(s):* Aral Sea (shared with Kazakhstan) - largely dried up

Major rivers (by length in km): Syr Darya (shared with Kyrgyzstan [s], Tajikistan, and Kazakhstan [m]) - 3,078 km; Amu Darya river mouth (shared with Tajikistan [s], Afghanistan, and Turkmenistan) - 2,620 km
note – [s] after country name indicates river source; [m] after country name indicates river mouth

Major watersheds (area sq km): Internal (endorheic basin) drainage: *(Aral Sea basin)* Amu Darya (534,739 sq km), Syr Darya (782,617 sq km)

Total water withdrawal: *municipal:* 2.41 billion cubic meters (2020 est.)
industrial: 2.13 billion cubic meters (2020 est.)
agricultural: 54.36 billion cubic meters (2020 est.)

Total renewable water resources: 48.87 billion cubic meters (2020 est.)

GOVERNMENT

Country name: *conventional long form:* Republic of Uzbekistan
conventional short form: Uzbekistan
local long form: O'zbekiston Respublikasi
local short form: O'zbekiston
former: Uzbek Soviet Socialist Republic
etymology: a combination of the Turkic words "uz" (self) and "bek" (master) with the Persian suffix "-stan" (country) to give the meaning "Land of the Free"

Government type: presidential republic; highly authoritarian

Capital: *name:* Tashkent (Toshkent)
geographic coordinates: 41 19 N, 69 15 E
time difference: UTC+5 (10 hours ahead of Washington, DC, during Standard Time)
etymology: *tash* means "stone" and *kent* means "city" in Turkic languages, so the name simply denotes "stone city"

Administrative divisions: 12 provinces (viloyatlar, singular - viloyat), 1 autonomous republic* (avtonom respublikasi), and 3 cities** (shahar); Andijon Viloyati, Buxoro Viloyati [Bukhara Province], Farg'ona Viloyati [Fergana Province], Jizzax Viloyati, Namangan Shahri, Namangan Viloyati, Navoiy Viloyati, Qashqadaryo Viloyati (Qarshi), Qoraqalpog'iston Respublikasi [Karakalpakstan Republic]* (Nukus), Samarqand Shahri [Samarkand City], Samarqand Viloyati [Samarkand Province], Sirdaryo Viloyati (Guliston), Surxondaryo Viloyati (Termiz), Toshkent Shahri [Tashkent City]**, Toshkent Viloyati [Nurafshon], Xorazm Viloyati (Urganch)
note: administrative divisions have the same names as their administrative centers (exceptions have the administrative center name following in parentheses)

Independence: 1 September 1991 (from the Soviet Union)

National holiday: Independence Day, 1 September (1991)

Legal system: *civil law system; note:* in early 2020, the president signed an amendment to the criminal code, criminal procedure code, and code of administrative responsibility; a constitutional referendum passed in April 2023 included criminal code reforms

Constitution: *history:* several previous; latest adopted 8 December 1992
amendments: proposed by the Supreme Assembly or by referendum; passage requires two-thirds majority vote of both houses of the Assembly or passage in a referendum; amended several times, last in 2023
note: in a public referendum passed in April 2023, among the changes were the extension of the presidential term to 7 years from 5 years, and modifications to the structure and powers of the Supreme Assembly and to the criminal code

International law organization participation: has not submitted an ICJ jurisdiction declaration; non-party state to the ICCt

Citizenship: *citizenship by birth:* no
citizenship by descent only: at least one parent must be a citizen of Uzbekistan
dual citizenship recognized: no
residency requirement for naturalization: 5 years

Suffrage: 18 years of age; universal

Executive branch: *chief of state:* President Shavkat MIRZIYOYEV (since 14 December 2016)
head of government: Prime Minister Abdulla ARIPOV (since 14 December 2016)
cabinet: Cabinet of Ministers appointed by the president with most requiring approval of the Senate chamber of the Supreme Assembly (Oliy Majlis)
elections/appointments: president directly elected by absolute majority popular vote in 2 rounds if needed for a 7-year term (eligible for a second term; previously a 5-year term, extended to 7 years by a 2023 constitutional amendment); election last held on 9 July 2023 (next to be held in 2030); prime minister nominated by majority party in legislature since 2011 but appointed along with the ministers and deputy ministers by the president
election results:
2023: Shavkat MIRZIYOYEV reelected president in snap election; percent of vote - Shavkat MIRZIYOYEV (LDPU) 87.71%, Robaxon Maxmudova (Adolat) 4.47%, Ulugbek Inoyatov (PDP) 4.05%, Abdushukur Xamzayev (Ecological Party) 3.77%
2021: Shavkat MIRZIYOYEV reelected president in first round; percent of vote - Shavkat MIRZIYOYEV (LDPU) 80.3%, Maqsuda VORISOVA (PDP) 6.7%, Alisher QODIROV (National Revival Democratic Party) 5.5%, Narzullo OBLOMURODOV (Ecological Party) 4.1%, Bahrom ABDUHALIMOV (Adolat) 3.4%
2016: Shavkat MIRZIYOYEV elected president in first round; percent of vote - Shavkat MIRZIYOYEV (LDPU) 88.6%, Hotamjon KETMONOV (PDP) 3.7%, Narimon UMAROV (Adolat) 3.5%, Sarvar OTAMURODOV (National Revival Democratic Party) 2.4%, other 1.8%

Legislative branch: *description:* bicameral Supreme Assembly or Oliy Majlis consists of:
Senate or Senat (100 seats); 84 members indirectly elected by regional governing councils and 16 appointed by the president; members serve 5-year terms); note - amendments to the constitution approved in April 2023 call for the reduction of Senate seats to 65 from 100
Legislative Chamber or Qonunchilik Palatasi (150 seats statutory, 140 seats current; members directly elected in singleseat constituencies by absolute majority vote with a second round if needed; members serve 5-year terms)
elections: Senate - last held 16-17 January 2020 (next to be held in 2025)
Legislative Chamber - last held on 27 October 2024
election results: Senate - percent of vote by party - NA; seats by party - NA; composition - men 68, women 22, percentage women 24.4%
Legislative Chamber - percent of vote by party - Liberal Democratic Party 34.8%, the National Revival Democratic Party 18.8%, the People's Democratic Party 17.1%, the Adolat (Justice) Social Democratic Party 16.2%, the Ecological Party 13.1%; seats by party - LDP 64, National Revival Democratic Party 29, PDP 20, Adolat 21, the Ecological Party 16

Judicial branch: *highest court(s):* Supreme Court (consists of 67 judges organized into administrative, civil, criminal, and economic sections); Constitutional Court (consists of 7 judges)
judge selection and term of office: judges of the highest courts nominated by the president and confirmed by the Senate of the Oliy Majlis; judges appointed for a single 10-year term; the court

chairman and deputies appointed for 10- year terms without the right to reelection. (Article 132 of the constitution)
subordinate courts: regional, district, city, and town courts

Political parties: Ecological Party of Uzbekistan (O'zbekiston Ekologik Partivasi)
Justice (Adolat) Social Democratic Party of Uzbekistan
Liberal Democratic Party of Uzbekistan (O'zbekiston Liberal-Demokratik Partiyasi) or LDPU
National Revival Democratic Party of Uzbekistan (O'zbekiston Milliy Tiklanish Demokratik Partiyasi)
People's Democratic Party of Uzbekistan (Xalq Demokratik Partiyas) or PDP (formerly Communist Party)

International organization participation: ADB, CICA, CIS, EAEU (observer), EAPC, EBRD, ECO, EEU (observer), FAO, IAEA, IBRD, ICAO, ICC (national committees), ICCt, ICRM, IDA, IDB, IFAD, IFC, IFRCS, ILO, IMF, Interpol, IOC, ISO, ITSO, ITU, MIGA, NAM, OIC, OPCW, OSCE, PFP, SCO, UN, UNCTAD, UNESCO, UNIDO, UNOOSA, UNWTO, UPU, WCO, WFTU (NGOs), WHO, WIPO, WMO, WTO (observer)

Diplomatic representation in the US: *chief of mission:* Ambassador Furqat SIDIKOV (since 19 April 2023)
chancery: 1746 Massachusetts Avenue NW, Washington, DC 20036
telephone: [1] (202) 887-5300
FAX: [1] (202) 293-6804
email address and website:
info.washington@mfa.uz
https://www.uzbekistan.org/
consulate(s) general: New York

Diplomatic representation from the US: *chief of mission:* Ambassador Jonathan HENICK (since 14 October 2022)
embassy: 3 Moyqorghon, 5th Block, Yunusobod District, 100093 Tashkent
mailing address: 7110 Tashkent Place, Washington DC 20521-7110
telephone: [998] 78-120-5450
FAX: [998] 78-120-6335
email address and website:
ACSTashkent@state.gov
https://uz.usembassy.gov/

Flag description: three equal horizontal bands of blue (top), white, and green separated by red fimbriations with a vertical, white crescent moon (closed side to the hoist) and 12 white, five-pointed stars shifted to the hoist on the top band; blue is the color of the Turkic peoples and of the sky, white signifies peace and the striving for purity in thoughts and deeds, while green represents nature and is the color of Islam; the red stripes are the vital force of all living organisms that links good and pure ideas with the eternal sky and with deeds on earth; the crescent represents Islam and the 12 stars the months and constellations of the Uzbek calendar

National symbol(s): khumo (mythical bird); national colors: blue, white, red, green

National anthem: *name:* "O'zbekiston Respublikasining Davlat Madhiyasi" (National Anthem of the Republic of Uzbekistan)
lyrics/music: Abdulla ARIPOV/Mutal BURHANOV
note: adopted 1992; after the fall of the Soviet Union, Uzbekistan kept the music of the anthem from its time as a Soviet Republic but adopted new lyrics

National heritage: *total World Heritage Sites:* 7 (5 cultural, 2 natural)
selected World Heritage Site locales: Itchan Kala (c); Historic Bukhara (c); Historic Shakhrisyabz (c); Samarkand - Crossroad of Cultures (c); Western Tien Shan (n); Cold Winter Deserts of Turan (n); Silk Roads: Zarafshan-Karakum Corridor (c)

ECONOMY

Economic overview: lower middle-income Central Asian economy; CIS Free Trade Area member but no intention of EAEU membership; key natural gas, cotton, and gold exporter; landlocked and environmentally fragile; positive growth through COVID-19, but poverty increasing

Real GDP (purchasing power parity): $319.174 billion (2023 est.)
$301.139 billion (2022 est.)
$284.984 billion (2021 est.)
note: data in 2021 dollars
comparison ranking: 59

Real GDP growth rate: 5.99% (2023 est.)
5.67% (2022 est.)
7.4% (2021 est.)
note: annual GDP % growth based on constant local currency
comparison ranking: 32

Real GDP per capita: $8,800 (2023 est.)
$8,400 (2022 est.)
$8,200 (2021 est.)
note: data in 2021 dollars
comparison ranking: 152

GDP (official exchange rate): $90.889 billion (2023 est.)
note: data in current dollars at official exchange rate

Inflation rate (consumer prices): 11.45% (2022 est.)
10.85% (2021 est.)
12.87% (2020 est.)
note: annual % change based on consumer prices
comparison ranking: 185

Credit ratings: Fitch rating: BB- (2018)

Moody's rating: B1 (2019)

Standard & Poors rating: BB- (2018)
note: The year refers to the year in which the current credit rating was first obtained.

GDP - composition, by sector of origin: *agriculture:* 23% (2023 est.)
industry: 30.5% (2023 est.)
services: 41% (2023 est.)
note: figures may not total 100% due to non-allocated consumption not captured in sector-reported data
comparison rankings: services 188; industry 64; agriculture 26

GDP - composition, by end use: *household consumption:* 59.7% (2023 est.)
government consumption: 16.1% (2023 est.)
investment in fixed capital: 34.8% (2023 est.)
investment in inventories: 8.3% (2023 est.)
exports of goods and services: 26.5% (2023 est.)
imports of goods and services: -45.5% (2023 est.)
note: figures may not total 100% due to rounding or gaps in data collection

Agricultural products: milk, wheat, carrots/turnips, cotton, potatoes, tomatoes, grapes, vegetables, watermelons, apples (2022)
note: top ten agricultural products based on tonnage

Industries: textiles, food processing, machine building, metallurgy, mining, hydrocarbon extraction, chemicals

Industrial production growth rate: 6.15% (2023 est.)
note: annual % change in industrial value added based on constant local currency
comparison ranking: 40

Labor force: 14.27 million (2023 est.)
note: number of people ages 15 or older who are employed or seeking work
comparison ranking: 45

Unemployment rate: 4.53% (2023 est.)
4.54% (2022 est.)
5.35% (2021 est.)
note: % of labor force seeking employment
comparison ranking: 87

Youth unemployment rate (ages 15-24): *total:* 11% (2023 est.)
male: 7.1% (2023 est.)
female: 18.3% (2023 est.)
note: % of labor force ages 15-24 seeking employment
comparison ranking: total 121

Gini Index coefficient - distribution of family income: 31.2 (2022 est.)
comparison ranking: 118

Average household expenditures: *on food:* 46.4% of household expenditures (2022 est.)
on alcohol and tobacco: 3.2% of household expenditures (2022 est.)

Household income or consumption by percentage share: *lowest 10%:* 2.5% (2022 est.)
highest 10%: 23.2% (2022 est.)

Remittances: 17.71% of GDP (2023 est.)
20.63% of GDP (2022 est.)
13.33% of GDP (2021 est.)
note: personal transfers and compensation between resident and non-resident individuals/households/entities

Budget: *revenues:* $20.578 billion (2022 est.)
expenditures: $20.79 billion (2022 est.)
note: central government revenues (excluding grants) and expenses converted to US dollars at average official exchange rate for year indicated

Public debt: 24.3% of GDP (2017 est.)
comparison ranking: 177

Taxes and other revenues: 14.79% (of GDP) (2020 est.)
note: central government tax revenue as a % of GDP
comparison ranking: 141

Current account balance: -$7.788 billion (2023 est.)
-$617.833 million (2022 est.)
-$4.898 billion (2021 est.)
note: balance of payments - net trade and primary/secondary income in current dollars
comparison ranking: 190

Exports: $24.536 billion (2023 est.)
$21.926 billion (2022 est.)
$16.442 billion (2021 est.)
note: balance of payments - exports of goods and services in current dollars
comparison ranking: 86

Exports - partners: Switzerland 25%, Russia 15%, China 12%, Turkey 9%, Kazakhstan 7% (2022)
note: top five export partners based on percentage share of exports

Exports - commodities: gold, cotton yarn, garments, natural gas, refined copper (2022)

note: top five export commodities based on value in dollars

Imports: $42.098 billion (2023 est.)
$35.61 billion (2022 est.)
$27.936 billion (2021 est.)
note: balance of payments - imports of goods and services in current dollars
comparison ranking: 72

Imports - partners: China 24%, Russia 19%, Kazakhstan 12%, South Korea 8%, Turkey 6% (2022)
note: top five import partners based on percentage share of imports

Imports - commodities: vehicle parts/accessories, packaged medicine, cars, wheat, refined petroleum (2022)
note: top five import commodities based on value in dollars

Reserves of foreign exchange and gold: $34.558 billion (2023 est.)
$35.774 billion (2022 est.)
$35.375 billion (2021 est.)
note: holdings of gold (year-end prices)/foreign exchange/special drawing rights in current dollars
comparison ranking: 52

Debt - external: $22.305 billion (2022 est.)
note: present value of external debt in current US dollars
comparison ranking: 24

Exchange rates: Uzbekistani soum (UZS) per US dollar -

Exchange rates: 11,734.833 (2023 est.)
11,050.145 (2022 est.)
10,609.464 (2021 est.)
10,054.261 (2020 est.)
8,836.788 (2019 est.)

ENERGY

Electricity access: *electrification - total population:* 100% (2022 est.)

Electricity: *installed generating capacity:* 16.926 million kW (2022 est.)
consumption: 67.642 billion kWh (2022 est.)
exports: 2.644 billion kWh (2022 est.)
imports: 6.232 billion kWh (2022 est.)
transmission/distribution losses: 10.704 billion kWh (2022 est.)
comparison rankings: transmission/distribution losses 180; imports 41; exports 52; consumption 43; installed generating capacity 53

Electricity generation sources: *fossil fuels:* 93.3% of total installed capacity (2022 est.)
hydroelectricity: 6.7% of total installed capacity (2022 est.)

Coal: *production:* 5.356 million metric tons (2022 est.)
consumption: 7.396 million metric tons (2022 est.)
exports: 9,000 metric tons (2022 est.)
imports: 2.194 million metric tons (2022 est.)
proven reserves: 1.375 billion metric tons (2022 est.)

Petroleum: *total petroleum production:* 64,000 bbl/day (2023 est.)
refined petroleum consumption: 91,000 bbl/day (2022 est.)
crude oil estimated reserves: 594 million barrels (2021 est.)

Natural gas: *production:* 47.5 billion cubic meters (2022 est.)
consumption: 43.227 billion cubic meters (2022 est.)
exports: 5.595 billion cubic meters (2022 est.)
imports: 12,000 cubic meters (2022 est.)
proven reserves: 1.841 trillion cubic meters (2021 est.)

Carbon dioxide emissions: 103.219 million metric tonnes of CO_2 (2022 est.)
from coal and metallurgical coke: 9.807 million metric tonnes of CO_2 (2022 est.)
from petroleum and other liquids: 11.041 million metric tonnes of CO_2 (2022 est.)
from consumed natural gas: 82.37 million metric tonnes of CO_2 (2022 est.)
comparison ranking: total emissions 39

Energy consumption per capita: 53.528 million Btu/person (2022 est.)
comparison ranking: 92

COMMUNICATIONS

Telephones - fixed lines: *total subscriptions:* 5.686 million (2022 est.)
subscriptions per 100 inhabitants: 16 (2022 est.)
comparison ranking: total subscriptions 25

Telephones - mobile cellular: *total subscriptions:* 35.69 million (2022 est.)
subscriptions per 100 inhabitants: 103 (2022 est.)
comparison ranking: total subscriptions 43

Telecommunication systems: *general assessment:* Uzbekistan's telecom markets both wireline and wireless have been playing "catch up" in terms of their development following the country's independence from the former Soviet Union; the government has formally adopted the principles of operating as a market economy, many elements of the old centrally planned economic model remain; this has had the effect of reducing the level of interest from foreign companies and investors in building out the necessary underlying infrastructure, which in turn has constrained the rate of growth in the country's telecoms sector; the last five years has seen an upswing in prospects for the sector as fiber network roll outs continue beyond the main urban centers, while the mobile market experiences some consolidation for stronger, more efficient competitors; growth is present in the fixed broadband segment with penetration projected to reach 24% by 2027 (a 5-year CAGR of 6.2%); despite the promising signs in the fixed markets, it is the mobile segment that continues to dominate Uzbekistan's telecoms sector in terms of penetration, revenue, and growth; there are four major operators providing a modicum of competition; three of the four are government owned entities (2024)
domestic: fixed-line nearly 16 per 100 persons and mobile-cellular teledensity of 103 per 100 persons (2022)
international: country code - 998; linked by fiber-optic cable or microwave radio relay with CIS member states and to other countries by leased connection via the Moscow international gateway switch; the country also has a link to the Trans-Asia-Europe (TAE) fiber-optic cable; Uzbekistan has supported the national fiber-optic backbone project of Afghanistan since 2008

Broadcast media: the government controls media; 17 state-owned broadcasters - 13 TV and 4 radio - provide service to virtually the entire country; about 20 privately owned TV stations, overseen by local officials, broadcast to local markets; privately owned TV stations are required to lease transmitters from the government-owned Republic TV and Radio Industry Corporation; in 2019, the Uzbek Agency for Press and Information was reorganized into the Agency of Information and Mass Communications and became part of the Uzbek Presidential Administration (2019)

Internet country code: .uz

Internet users: *total:* 26.18 million (2021 est.)
percent of population: 77% (2021 est.)
comparison ranking: total 34

Broadband - fixed subscriptions: *total:* 4,820,009 (2020 est.)
subscriptions per 100 inhabitants: 14 (2020 est.)
comparison ranking: total 33

TRANSPORTATION

National air transport system: *number of registered air carriers:* 2 (2020)
inventory of registered aircraft operated by air carriers: 34
annual passenger traffic on registered air carriers: 3,056,558 (2018)
annual freight traffic on registered air carriers: 89.43 million (2018) mt-km

Civil aircraft registration country code prefix: UK

Airports: 74 (2024)
comparison ranking: 68

Heliports: 3 (2024)

Pipelines: 13,700 km gas, 944 km oil (2016)

Railways: *total:* 4,642 km (2018)
broad gauge: 4,642 km (2018) 1.520-m gauge (1,684 km electrified)
comparison ranking: total 41

Roadways: *total:* 225,500 km (2013)
comparison ranking: total 20

Waterways: 1,100 km (2012)
comparison ranking: 66

MILITARY AND SECURITY

Military and security forces: Armed Forces of Uzbekistan: Army, Air and Air Defense Forces; National Guard

Ministry of Internal Affairs: Internal Security Troops, Border Guards, police (2023)
note: the National Guard is under the Defense Ministry, but is independent of the other military services; it is responsible for ensuring public order and the security of diplomatic missions, radio and television broadcasting, and other state entities

Military expenditures: 2.8% of GDP (2019 est.)
2.9% of GDP (2018 est.)
2.7% of GDP (2017 est.)
2.5% of GDP (2016 est.)
2.5% of GDP (2015 est.)
comparison ranking: 39

Military and security service personnel strengths: information varies; approximately 50-60,000 active-duty troops, including 10-15,000 Air Force (2023)

Military equipment inventories and acquisitions: the Uzbek Armed Forces use mainly Soviet-era equipment; in recent years, Russia has been the leading supplier of arms, followed by China (2023)

Military service age and obligation: 18-27 years of age for compulsory military service; 12-month conscript service obligation for men (those conscripted have the option of paying for a shorter service of 1

month while remaining in the reserves until the age of 27) (2023)
note: Uzbek citizens who have completed their service terms in the armed forces have privileges in employment and admission to higher educational institutions

Military - note: the military's primary concerns and responsibilities are border security, ensuring the country's sovereignty and territorial integrity, instability in neighboring countries, and terrorism; the military is equipped largely with Soviet-era arms and its units are based on Soviet Army formations that were in the territory of Uzbekistan when the USSR collapsed in 1991; the armed forces were established in January 1992 when Uzbekistan assumed jurisdiction over all former Soviet ground, air, and air defense units, formations, and installations then deployed on its soil; the building hosting the headquarters for the ex-Soviet Turkestan Military District became the headquarters for the Uzbek armed forces; all former Soviet troops departed Uzbekistan by 1995
Uzbekistan joined the Russian-sponsored Collective Security Treaty Organization (CSTO) in the 1990s but withdrew in 1999; it returned in 2006 but left again in 2012; although it is not part of CSTO, Uzbekistan continues to maintain defense ties with Russia, including joint military exercises and defense industrial cooperation; it also has defense ties with other regional countries, including India, Pakistan, and Turkey; it is part of the Shanghai Cooperation Organization (SCO) and participates in SCO training exercises (2023)

SPACE

Space agency/agencies: Agency for Space Research and Technology (Uzbekcosmos; established 2019) (2024)

Space program overview: has a small space program focused on acquiring satellites and developing the country's space industry; Uzbekcosmos largely sets state policy and shapes the strategic direction, development, and use of the country's space-related industries and technologies in key sectors, including cartography, environmental and disaster monitoring, land use, resource management, and telecommunications; also has an astronomy program; cooperates with foreign space agencies or commercial companies from a variety of countries, including those of Canada, China, France, India, Israel, Kazakhstan, Russia, South Korea, and Spain (2024)
note: further details about the key activities, programs, and milestones of the country's space program, as well as government spending estimates on the space sector, appear in the Space Programs reference guide

TERRORISM

Terrorist group(s): Islamic Jihad Union; Islamic Movement of Uzbekistan; Islamic State of Iraq and ash-Sham - Khorasan (ISIS-K)
note 1: these groups have typically been active in the area where the Uzbek, Kyrgyz, and Tajik borders converge and ill-defined and porous borders allow for the relatively free movement of people and illicit goods
note 2: details about the history, aims, leadership, organization, areas of operation, tactics, targets, weapons, size, and sources of support of the group(s) appear(s) in the Terrorism reference guide

TRANSNATIONAL ISSUES

Refugees and internally displaced persons: *refugees (country of origin):* 13,031 (Afghanistan) (mid-year 2022)
stateless persons: 31,829 (2022)

Illicit drugs: a transit country for Afghan heroin, opium, and hashish destined to Kazakhstan, Russia, and Europe; cannabis and opium poppy are grown domestically for personal use and sale

V

VANUATU

INTRODUCTION

Background: Austronesian speakers from the Solomon Islands first settled Vanuatu around 2000 B.C. By around 1000, localized chieftain systems began to develop on the islands. Around 1600, Melanesian Chief ROI MATA united some of the islands of modern-day Vanuatu under his rule. In 1606, a Portuguese explorer was the first European to see Vanuatu's Banks Islands and Espiritu Santo, setting up a shortlived settlement on the latter. The next European explorers arrived in the 1760s, and the islands – then known as the New Hebrides –were frequented by whalers in the 1800s. European interest in harvesting the islands' sandalwood trees caused conflict with the inhabitants. In the 1860s, European planters in Australia, Fiji, New Caledonia, and Samoa needed labor and kidnapped almost half the adult males on the islands to work as indentured servants.

With growing and overlapping interests in the islands, France and the UK agreed that the New Hebrides would be neutral in 1878 and established a joint naval commission in 1887. In 1906, the two countries created the UK-France condominium to jointly administer the islands, with separate laws, police forces, currencies, and education and health systems. The condominium arrangement was dysfunctional, and the UK used France's initial defeat in World War II to assert greater control over the islands. During the war, the US stationed up to 50,000 soldiers in Vanuatu. In 1945, they withdrew and sold their equipment, leading to the rise of political and religious movements known as "cargo cults," such as the John Frum movement.

The UK-France condominium was reestablished after World War II. The UK was interested in moving the condominium toward independence in the 1960s, but France was hesitant. Political parties agitating for independence began to form, largely divided along linguistic lines. France eventually relented, and elections were held in 1974, with independence granted to the newly named Vanuatu in 1980 under English-speaking Prime Minister Walter LINI. The Nagriamel Movement, with support from French-speaking landowners, then declared the island of Espiritu Santo independent from Vanuatu, but the short-lived state was dissolved 12 weeks later. Linguistic divisions have lessened over time, but highly fractious political parties have led to weak coalition governments that require support from both Anglophone and Francophone parties. Since 2008, prime ministers have been ousted more than a dozen times through no-confidence motions or temporary procedural issues.

GEOGRAPHY

Location: Oceania, group of islands in the South Pacific Ocean, about three-quarters of the way from Hawaii to Australia

Geographic coordinates: 16 00 S, 167 00 E

Map references: Oceania

Area: *total:* 12,189 sq km
land: 12,189 sq km
water: 0 sq km
note: includes more than 80 islands, about 65 of which are inhabited
comparison ranking: total 162

Area - comparative: slightly larger than Connecticut

Land boundaries: *total:* 0 km

Coastline: 2,528 km

Maritime claims: *territorial sea:* 12 nm
contiguous zone: 24 nm
exclusive economic zone: 200 nm
continental shelf: 200 nm or to the edge of the continental margin
measured from claimed archipelagic baselines

Climate: tropical; moderated by southeast trade winds from May to October; moderate rainfall from November to April; may be affected by cyclones from December to April

Terrain: mostly mountainous islands of volcanic origin; narrow coastal plains

Elevation: *highest point:* Tabwemasana 1,877 m
lowest point: Pacific Ocean 0 m

Natural resources: manganese, hardwood forests, fish

Land use: *agricultural land:* 15.3% (2018 est.)
arable land: 1.6% (2018 est.)
permanent crops: 10.3% (2018 est.)
permanent pasture: 3.4% (2018 est.)
forest: 36.1% (2018 est.)
other: 48.6% (2018 est.)

Irrigated land: 0 sq km (2022)

Population distribution: three-quarters of the population lives in rural areas; the urban populace lives primarily in two cities, Port-Vila and Lugenville; three largest islands - Espiritu Santo, Malakula, and Efate - accomodate over half of the populace

Natural hazards: tropical cyclones (January to April); volcanic eruption on Aoba (Ambae) island began on 27 November 2005, volcanism also causes minor earthquakes; tsunamis
volcanism: significant volcanic activity with multiple eruptions in recent years; Yasur (361 m), one of the world's most active volcanoes, has experienced continuous activity in recent centuries; other historically active volcanoes include Aoba, Ambrym, Epi, Gaua, Kuwae, Lopevi, Suretamatai, and Traitor's Head

Geography - note: a Y-shaped chain of four main islands and 80 smaller islands; several of the islands have active volcanoes and there are several underwater volcanoes as well

PEOPLE AND SOCIETY

Population: *total:* 318,007
male: 157,932
female: 160,075 (2024 est.)
comparison rankings: female 179; male 179; total 179

Nationality: *noun:* Ni-Vanuatu (singular and plural)
adjective: Ni-Vanuatu

Ethnic groups: Ni-Vanuatu 99%, other 1% (European, Asian, other Melanesian, Polynesian, Micronesian, other) (2020 est.)

Languages: indigenous languages (more than 100) 82.6%, Bislama (official; creole) 14.5%, English (official) 2.1%, French (official) 0.8% (2020 est.)
note: data represent first language spoken for population aged 3 years and above

Religions: Protestant 39.9% (Presbyterian 27.2%, Seventh Day Adventist 14.8%, Anglican 12%, Churches of Christ 5%, Assemblies of God 4.9%, Neil Thomas Ministry/Inner Life Ministry 3.2%), Roman Catholic 12.1%, Apostolic 2.3%, Church of Jesus Christ 1.8%, customary beliefs (including Jon Frum cargo cult) 3.1%, other 12%, none 1.4%, unspecified 0.1% (2020 est.)

Age structure: *0-14 years:* 31.1% (male 50,584/female 48,475)
15-64 years: 63.8% (male 99,496/female 103,425)
65 years and over: 5% (2024 est.) (male 7,852/female 8,175)

Dependency ratios: *total dependency ratio:* 76.5
youth dependency ratio: 69.9
elderly dependency ratio: 12.3
potential support ratio: 15.2 (2021 est.)

Median age: *total:* 24.6 years (2024 est.)
male: 24.1 years
female: 25 years
comparison ranking: total 176

Population growth rate: 1.55% (2024 est.)
comparison ranking: 61

Birth rate: 20.8 births/1,000 population (2024 est.)
comparison ranking: 63

Death rate: 4 deaths/1,000 population (2024 est.)

comparison ranking: 215

Net migration rate: -1.3 migrant(s)/1,000 population (2024 est.)
comparison ranking: 153

Population distribution: three-quarters of the population lives in rural areas; the urban populace lives primarily in two cities, Port-Vila and Lugenville; three largest islands - Espiritu Santo, Malakula, and Efate - accomodate over half of the populace

Urbanization: *urban population:* 26% of total population (2023)
rate of urbanization: 2.55% annual rate of change (2020-25 est.)

Major urban areas - population: 53,000 PORT-VILA (capital) (2018)

Sex ratio: *at birth:* 1.05 male(s)/female
0-14 years: 1.04 male(s)/female
15-64 years: 0.96 male(s)/female
65 years and over: 0.96 male(s)/female
total population: 0.99 male(s)/female (2024 est.)

Maternal mortality ratio: 94 deaths/100,000 live births (2020 est.)
comparison ranking: 72

Infant mortality rate: *total:* 13.7 deaths/1,000 live births (2024 est.)
male: 15 deaths/1,000 live births
female: 12.3 deaths/1,000 live births
comparison ranking: total 103

Life expectancy at birth: *total population:* 75.7 years (2024 est.)
male: 74 years
female: 77.4 years
comparison ranking: total population 123

Total fertility rate: 2.53 children born/woman (2024 est.)
comparison ranking: 69

Gross reproduction rate: 1.23 (2024 est.)

Contraceptive prevalence rate: 49% (2013)

Drinking water source: *improved: urban:* 100% of population
rural: 89.7% of population
total: 92.3% of population
unimproved: urban: 0% of population
rural: 10.3% of population
total: 7.7% of population (2020 est.)

Current health expenditure: 4% of GDP (2020)

Physician density: 0.17 physicians/1,000 population (2016)

Sanitation facility access: *improved: urban:* 91.1% of population
rural: 60.4% of population
total: 68.2% of population
unimproved: urban: 8.9% of population
rural: 39.6% of population
total: 31.8% of population (2020 est.)

Obesity - adult prevalence rate: 25.2% (2016)
comparison ranking: 52

Alcohol consumption per capita: *total:* 1.6 liters of pure alcohol (2019 est.)
beer: 0.34 liters of pure alcohol (2019 est.)
wine: 0.39 liters of pure alcohol (2019 est.)
spirits: 0.87 liters of pure alcohol (2019 est.)
other alcohols: 0 liters of pure alcohol (2019 est.)
comparison ranking: total 136

Tobacco use: *total:* 17.8% (2020 est.)
male: 33% (2020 est.)
female: 2.6% (2020 est.)
comparison ranking: total 94

Children under the age of 5 years underweight: 11.7% (2013)
comparison ranking: 49

Currently married women (ages 15-49): 69.2% (2023 est.)

Education expenditures: 2.2% of GDP (2020 est.)
comparison ranking: 180

Literacy: *definition:* age 15 and over can read and write
total population: 89.1%
male: 89.8%
female: 88.4% (2021)

ENVIRONMENT

Environment - current issues: population growth; water pollution, most of the population does not have access to a reliable supply of potable water; inadequate sanitation; deforestation

Environment - international agreements: *party to:* Antarctic-Marine Living Resources, Biodiversity, Climate Change, Climate Change-Kyoto Protocol, Climate Change-Paris Agreement, Comprehensive Nuclear Test Ban, Desertification, Endangered Species, Hazardous Wastes, Law of the Sea, Marine Dumping-London Convention, Marine Dumping-London Protocol, Ozone Layer Protection, Ship Pollution, Wetlands
signed, but not ratified: none of the selected agreements

Climate: tropical; moderated by southeast trade winds from May to October; moderate rainfall from November to April; may be affected by cyclones from December to April

Urbanization: *urban population:* 26% of total population (2023)
rate of urbanization: 2.55% annual rate of change (2020-25 est.)

Revenue from forest resources: 0.54% of GDP (2018 est.)
comparison ranking: 64

Revenue from coal: 0% of GDP (2018 est.)
comparison ranking: 144

Air pollutants: *particulate matter emissions:* 8.42 micrograms per cubic meter (2019 est.)
carbon dioxide emissions: 0.15 megatons (2016 est.)
methane emissions: 0.5 megatons (2020 est.)

Waste and recycling: *municipal solid waste generated annually:* 70,225 tons (2012 est.)
municipal solid waste recycled annually: 25,983 tons (2013 est.)
percent of municipal solid waste recycled: 37% (2013 est.)

Total renewable water resources: 10 billion cubic meters (2020 est.)

GOVERNMENT

Country name: *conventional long form:* Republic of Vanuatu
conventional short form: Vanuatu
local long form: Ripablik blong Vanuatu
local short form: Vanuatu
former: New Hebrides
etymology: derived from the words "vanua" (home or land) and "tu" (stand) that occur in several of the Austonesian languages spoken on the islands and which provide a meaning of "the land remains" but which also convey a sense of "independence" or "our land"

Government type: parliamentary republic

Capital: *name:* Port-Vila (on Efate)
geographic coordinates: 17 44 S, 168 19 E
time difference: UTC+11 (16 hours ahead of Washington, DC, during Standard Time)
etymology: there are two possibilities for the origin of the name: early European settlers were Portuguese and "vila" means "village or town" in Portuguese, hence "Port-Vila" would mean "Port Town"; alternatively, the site of the capital is referred to as "Efil" or "Ifira" in native languages, "Vila" is a likely corruption of these names

Administrative divisions: 6 provinces; Malampa, Penama, Sanma, Shefa, Tafea, Torba

Independence: 30 July 1980 (from France and the UK)

National holiday: Independence Day, 30 July (1980)

Legal system: mixed legal system of English common law, French law, and customary law

Constitution: *history:* draft completed August 1979, finalized by constitution conference 19 September 1979, ratified by French and British Governments 23 October 1979, effective 30 July 1980 at independence
amendments: proposed by the prime minister or by the Parliament membership; passage requires at least two-thirds majority vote by Parliament in special session with at least three fourths of the membership; passage of amendments affecting the national and official languages, or the electoral and parliamentary system also requires approval in a referendum; amended several times, last in 2013

International law organization participation: has not submitted an ICJ jurisdiction declaration; accepts ICCt jurisdiction

Citizenship: *citizenship by birth:* no
citizenship by descent only: both parents must be citizens of Vanuatu; in the case of only one parent, it must be the father who is a citizen
dual citizenship recognized: no
residency requirement for naturalization: 10 years

Suffrage: 18 years of age; universal

Executive branch: *chief of state:* President Nikenike VUROBARAVU (since 23 July 2022)
head of government: Prime Minister Charlot SALWAI (since 6 October 2023)
cabinet: Council of Ministers appointed by the prime minister, responsible to Parliament
elections/appointments: president indirectly elected by an electoral college consisting of Parliament and presidents of the 6 provinces; Vanuatu president serves a 5-year term; election last held on 23 July 2022 (next to be held in 2027); following legislative elections, the leader of the majority party or majority coalition usually elected prime minister by Parliament from among its members; election for prime minister last held on 20 April 2020 (next to be held following general elections in 2024)
election results: 2022: Nikenike VUROBARAVU elected president in eighth round; electoral college vote - Nikenike VUROBARAVU (VP) 48 votes, Solas MOLISA (VP) 4 votes; note - Charlot SALWAI (RMC) elected prime minister on 6 October 2023, 29 votes for, 0 against; Prime Minister Sato KILMAN lost no-confidence vote on 6 October 2023, requiring a new election
2017: Bob LOUGHMAN elected prime minister on 20 April 2020; Bob LOUGHMAN 31 votes, Ralph REGENVANU 21 votes
note: the National Council of Chiefs (Malvatu Mauri) is a formal advisory body of chiefs recognized

by the country's constitution; it advises the government on matters of culture and language

Legislative branch: *description:* unicameral Parliament (52 seats; members directly elected in 8 single-seat and 9 multi-seat constituencies by single non-transferable vote to serve 4-year terms (candidates in multi-seat constituencies can be elected with only 4% of the vote)
elections: last held on 13 October 2022 (next to be held in 2026)
election results: percent of vote by party - NA; seats by party - UMP 7, VP 7, LPV 5, RMC 5, GJP 4, NUP 4, RDP 4, IG 3, PPP 2, NCM 2, VNDP 2, LM 1, NAG 1, PUDP 1, UCM 1, VLM 1, VPDP 1, independent 1; composition - men 50, women 1, percentage women 2%; note - political party associations are fluid

Judicial branch: *highest court(s):* Court of Appeal (consists of 2 or more judges of the Supreme Court designated by the chief justice); Supreme Court (consists of the chief justice and 6 puisne judges - 3 local and 3 expatriate)
judge selection and term of office: Supreme Court chief justice appointed by the president after consultation with the prime minister and the leader of the opposition; other judges appointed by the president on the advice of the Judicial Service Commission, a 4-member advisory body; judges serve until the age of retirement
subordinate courts: Magistrates Courts; Island Courts

Political parties: Iauko Group (Eagle Party) or IG
Laverwo Movement or LM
Land and Justice Party (Graon mo Jastis Pati or GJP)
Leaders Party of Vanuatu or LVP
Nagriamel Movement or NAG
National United Party or NUP
Nagwasoanda Custom Movement or NCM
People's Progressive Party or PPP
People Unity Development Party or PUDP
Rural Development Party or RDP
Reunification of Movement for Change or RMC
Union of Moderate Parties or UMP
Unity for Change Movement or UCM
Vanua'aku Pati (Our Land Party) or VP
Vanuatu Liberal Movement or VLM
Vanuatu National Development Party or VNDP
Vanuatu Progressive Development Party or VPDP

International organization participation: ACP, ADB, AOSIS, C, FAO, G-77, IBRD, ICAO, ICRM, IDA, IFC, IFRCS, ILO, IMF, IMO, IMSO, IOC, IOM, ITU, ITUC (NGOs), MIGA, NAM, OAS (observer), OIF, OPCW, PIF, Sparteca, SPC, UN, UNCTAD, UNESCO, UNIDO, UNWTO, UPU, WCO, WFTU (NGOs), WHO, WIPO, WMO, WTO

Diplomatic representation in the US: *chief of mission:* Ambassador Odo TEVI (since 8 September 2017)
note - also Permanent Representative to the UN
chancery: 800 Second Avenue, Suite 400B, New York, NY 10017
telephone: [1] (212) 661-4303
FAX: [1] (212) 422-3427
email address and website:
vanunmis@aol.com
https://www.un.int/vanuatu/
note - the Vanuatu Permanent Mission to the UN serves as the embassy

Diplomatic representation from the US: *chief of mission:* Ambassador Ann Marie YASTISHOCK (since 16 April 2024); note - also accredited to the Papua New Guinea and the Solomon Islands, based in Port Moresby, Papua New Guinea
embassy: Port Vila

Flag description: two equal horizontal bands of red (top) and green with a black isosceles triangle (based on the hoist side) all separated by a black-edged yellow stripe in the shape of a horizontal Y (the two points of the Y face the hoist side and enclose the triangle); centered in the triangle is a boar's tusk encircling two crossed namele fern fronds, all in yellow; red represents the blood of boars and men, as well as unity, green the richness of the islands, and black the ni-Vanuatu people; the yellow Y-shape - which reflects the pattern of the islands in the Pacific Ocean - symbolizes the light of the Gospel spreading through the islands; the boar's tusk is a symbol of prosperity frequently worn as a pendant on the islands; the fern fronds represent peace
note: one of several flags where a prominent component of the design reflects the shape of the country; other such flags are those of Bosnia and Herzegovina, Brazil, and Eritrea

National symbol(s): boar's tusk with crossed fern fronds; national colors: red, black, green, yellow

National anthem: *name:* "Yumi, Yumi, Yumi" (We, We, We)
lyrics/music: Francois Vincent AYSSAV
note: adopted 1980; the anthem is written in Bislama, a Creole language that mixes Pidgin English and French

National heritage: *total World Heritage Sites:* 1 (cultural)
selected World Heritage Site locales: Chief Roi Mata's Domain

ECONOMY

Economic overview: lower-middle income Pacific island economy; extremely reliant on subsistence agriculture and tourism; environmentally fragile; struggling post-pandemic and Tropical Cyclone Harold rebound; sizeable inflation; road infrastructure aid from Australia

Real GDP (purchasing power parity): $999.536 million (2023 est.)
$977.896 million (2022 est.)
$959.511 million (2021 est.)
note: data in 2021 dollars
comparison ranking: 210

Real GDP growth rate: 2.21% (2023 est.)
1.92% (2022 est.)
-1.55% (2021 est.)
note: annual GDP % growth based on constant local currency
comparison ranking: 133

Real GDP per capita: $3,000 (2023 est.)
$3,000 (2022 est.)
$3,000 (2021 est.)
note: data in 2021 dollars
comparison ranking: 193

GDP (official exchange rate): $1.126 billion (2023 est.)
note: data in current dollars at official exchange rate

Inflation rate (consumer prices): 6.68% (2022 est.)
2.34% (2021 est.)
5.33% (2020 est.)
note: annual % change based on consumer prices
comparison ranking: 139

GDP - composition, by sector of origin: *agriculture:* 21.2% (2018 est.)
industry: 10% (2018 est.)
services: 59.8% (2018 est.)
note: figures may not total 100% due to non-allocated consumption not captured in sector-reported data
comparison rankings: services 85; industry 194; agriculture 34

GDP - composition, by end use: *household consumption:* 55.5% (2019 est.)
government consumption: 20.6% (2019 est.)
investment in fixed capital: 55.5% (2022 est.)
investment in inventories: 0.6% (2022 est.)
exports of goods and services: 15.3% (2022 est.)
imports of goods and services: -55.5% (2022 est.)
note: figures may not total 100% due to rounding or gaps in data collection

Agricultural products: coconuts, root vegetables, bananas, vegetables, fruits, pork, groundnuts, milk, beef, tropical fruits (2022)
note: top ten agricultural products based on tonnage

Industries: food and fish freezing, wood processing, meat canning

Industrial production growth rate: 4.92% (2018 est.)
note: annual % change in industrial value added based on constant local currency
comparison ranking: 54

Labor force: 142,000 (2023 est.)
note: number of people ages 15 or older who are employed or seeking work
comparison ranking: 180

Unemployment rate: 5.1% (2023 est.)
5.17% (2022 est.)
4.73% (2021 est.)
note: % of labor force seeking employment
comparison ranking: 96

Youth unemployment rate (ages 15-24): *total:* 10.7% (2023 est.)
male: 8.9% (2023 est.)
female: 13% (2023 est.)
note: % of labor force ages 15-24 seeking employment
comparison ranking: total 128

Population below poverty line: 15.9% (2020 est.)
note: % of population with income below national poverty line

Gini Index coefficient - distribution of family income: 32.3 (2019 est.)
note: index (0-100) of income distribution; higher values represent greater inequality
comparison ranking: 106

Household income or consumption by percentage share: *lowest 10%:* 3% (2019 est.)
highest 10%: 24.7% (2019 est.)
note: % share of income accruing to lowest and highest 10% of population

Remittances: 15.68% of GDP (2023 est.)
19.35% of GDP (2022 est.)
21.03% of GDP (2021 est.)
note: personal transfers and compensation between resident and non-resident individuals/households/entities

Budget: *revenues:* $415.063 million (2021 est.)
expenditures: $325.587 million (2021 est.)
note: central government revenues and expenses (excluding grants/extrabudgetary units/social security funds) converted to US dollars at average official exchange rate for year indicated

Public debt: 87.07% of GDP (2021 est.)

comparison ranking: 29

Taxes and other revenues: 15.88% (of GDP) (2021 est.)
note: central government tax revenue as a % of GDP
comparison ranking: 130

Current account balance: -$127.432 million (2022 est.)
-$75.451 million (2021 est.)
-$57.858 million (2020 est.)
note: balance of payments - net trade and primary/secondary income in current dollars
comparison ranking: 97

Exports: $152.087 million (2022 est.)
$82.08 million (2021 est.)
$132.943 million (2020 est.)
note: balance of payments - exports of goods and services in current dollars
comparison ranking: 209

Exports - partners: Thailand 42%, Japan 27%, South Korea 7%, Philippines 6%, China 5% (2022)
note: top five export partners based on percentage share of exports

Exports - commodities: fish, perfume plants, copra, shellfish, cocoa beans (2022)
note: top five export commodities based on value in dollars

Imports: $579.347 million (2022 est.)
$520.391 million (2021 est.)
$438.373 million (2020 est.)
note: balance of payments - imports of goods and services in current dollars
comparison ranking: 199

Imports - partners: China 24%, Australia 15%, Malaysia 12%, NZ 9%, Fiji 8% (2022)
note: top five import partners based on percentage share of imports

Imports - commodities: refined petroleum, ships, plastic products, poultry, broadcasting equipment (2022)
note: top five import commodities based on value in dollars

Reserves of foreign exchange and gold: $643.768 million (2023 est.)
$638.537 million (2022 est.)
$664.751 million (2021 est.)
note: holdings of gold (year-end prices)/foreign exchange/special drawing rights in current dollars
comparison ranking: 161

Debt - external: $295.759 million (2022 est.)
note: present value of external debt in current US dollars
comparison ranking: 94

Exchange rates: vatu (VUV) per US dollar -

Exchange rates: 119.113 (2023 est.)
115.354 (2022 est.)
109.453 (2021 est.)
115.38 (2020 est.)
114.733 (2019 est.)

ENERGY

Electricity access: *electrification - total population:* 70% (2022 est.)
electrification - urban areas: 97%
electrification - rural areas: 60.7%

Electricity: *installed generating capacity:* 38,000 kW (2022 est.)
consumption: 68.092 million kWh (2022 est.)
transmission/distribution losses: 5.198 million kWh (2022 est.)
comparison rankings: transmission/distribution losses 10; consumption 203; installed generating capacity 198

Electricity generation sources: *fossil fuels:* 81.8% of total installed capacity (2022 est.)
solar: 11.5% of total installed capacity (2022 est.)
wind: 6.5% of total installed capacity (2022 est.)
biomass and waste: 0.1% of total installed capacity (2022 est.)

Petroleum: *refined petroleum consumption:* 2,000 bbl/day (2022 est.)

Carbon dioxide emissions: 248,000 metric tonnes of CO2 (2022 est.)
from petroleum and other liquids: 248,000 metric tonnes of CO2 (2022 est.)
comparison ranking: total emissions 201

Energy consumption per capita: 10.775 million Btu/person (2022 est.)
comparison ranking: 148

COMMUNICATIONS

Telephones - fixed lines: *total subscriptions:* 3,000 (2022 est.)
subscriptions per 100 inhabitants: 1 (2022 est.)
comparison ranking: total subscriptions 210

Telephones - mobile cellular: *total subscriptions:* 256,000 (2022 est.)
subscriptions per 100 inhabitants: 78 (2022 est.)
comparison ranking: total subscriptions 182

Telecommunication systems: *general assessment:* for many years, 2G Global System for Mobile Communications was the primary mobile technology for Vanuatu's 300,000 people; recent infrastructure projects have improved access technologies, with a transition to 3G and 4G; Vanuatu has also benefited from the ICN1 submarine cable and the launch of the Kacific-1 satellite, both of which have considerably improved access to telecom services in recent years; Vanuatu's telecom sector is liberalized, with the two prominent mobile operators; while fixed broadband penetration remains low, the incumbent operator is slowly exchanging copper fixed-lines for fiber; a number of ongoing submarine cable developments will also assist in increasing data rates and reduce internet pricing in coming years (2023)
domestic: fixed-line teledensity is 1 per 100 and mobile-cellular 78 per 100 (2021)
international: country code - 678; landing points for the ICN1 & ICN2 submarine cables providing connectivity to the Solomon Islands and Fiji; cables helped end-users with Internet bandwidth; satellite earth station - 1 Intelsat (Pacific Ocean) (2020)

Broadcast media: 1 state-owned TV station; multi-channel pay TV is available; state-owned Radio Vanuatu operates 2 radio stations; 2 privately owned radio broadcasters (Capital FM 107 and Laef FM); programming from multiple international broadcasters is available (2023)

Internet country code: .vu

Internet users: *total:* 211,200 (2021 est.)
percent of population: 66% (2021 est.)
comparison ranking: total 181

Broadband - fixed subscriptions: *total:* 2,785 (2020 est.)
subscriptions per 100 inhabitants: 1 (2020 est.)
comparison ranking: total 194

TRANSPORTATION

National air transport system: *number of registered air carriers:* 1 (2020)
inventory of registered aircraft operated by air carriers: 8
annual passenger traffic on registered air carriers: 374,603 (2018)
annual freight traffic on registered air carriers: 1.66 million (2018) mt-km

Civil aircraft registration country code prefix: YJ

Airports: 31 (2024)
comparison ranking: 118

Roadways: *total:* 2,958 km (2023)
comparison ranking: total 164

Merchant marine: *total:* 338 (2023)
by type: bulk carrier 11, container ship 3, general cargo 101, other 223
comparison ranking: total 54

Ports: *total ports:* 3 (2024)
large: 0
medium: 0 small: 1
very small: 2
ports with oil terminals: 2
key ports: Forari Bay, Luganville, Port Vila

MILITARY AND SECURITY

Military and security forces: *no regular military forces; Ministry of Internal Affairs:* Vanuatu Police Force (VPF) (2024)
note: the VPF includes the Vanuatu Mobile Force (VMF) and Police Maritime Wing (VPMW); the paramilitary VMF also has external security responsibilities

Military - note: the separate British and French police forces were unified in 1980 as the New Hebrides Constabulary, which was commanded by Ni-Vanuatu officers while retaining some British and French officers as advisors; the Constabulary was subsequently renamed the Vanuatu Police Force later in 1980
the Vanuatu Mobile Force has received training and other support from Australia, China, France, New Zealand, and the US
Vanuatu has a "shiprider" agreement with the US, which allows local maritime law enforcement officers to embark on US Coast Guard (USCG) and US Navy (USN) vessels, including to board and search vessels suspected of violating laws or regulations within Vanuatu's designated exclusive economic zone (EEZ) or on the high seas; "shiprider" agreements also enable USCG personnel and USN vessels with embarked USCG law enforcement personnel to work with host nations to protect critical regional resources (2024)

TRANSNATIONAL ISSUES

Trafficking in persons: tier rating: Tier 2 Watch List — the government did not demonstrate overall increasing efforts to eliminate trafficking compared with the previous reporting period, therefore Vanuatu remained on Tier 2 Watch List for the second consecutive year; for more details, go to: https://www.state.gov/reports/2024-trafficking-in-persons-report/vanuatu/

VENEZUELA

INTRODUCTION

Background: Venezuela was one of three countries that emerged from the collapse of Gran Colombia in 1830, the others being Ecuador and New Granada (Colombia). For most of the first half of the 20th century, military strongmen ruled Venezuela and promoted the oil industry while allowing some social reforms. Democratically elected governments largely held sway until 1999, but Hugo CHAVEZ, who was president from 1999 to 2013, exercised authoritarian control over other branches of government. This trend continued in 2018 when Nicolas MADURO claimed the presidency for his second term in an election boycotted by most opposition parties and widely viewed as fraudulent. The legislative elections in 2020 were also seen as fraudulent, and most opposition parties and many international actors consider the resulting National Assembly illegitimate. In 2021, many opposition parties broke a three-year election boycott and participated in mayoral and gubernatorial elections, despite flawed conditions. As a result, the opposition more than doubled its representation at the mayoral level and retained four of 23 governorships. The 2021 regional elections marked the first time since 2006 that the EU was allowed to send an electoral observation mission to Venezuela.

MADURO has placed strong restrictions on free speech and the press. Since CHAVEZ, the ruling party has expanded the state's role in the economy through expropriations of major enterprises, strict currency exchange and price controls, and over-dependence on the petroleum industry for revenues. Years of economic mismanagement left Venezuela ill-prepared to weather the global drop in oil prices in 2014, sparking an economic decline that has resulted in reduced government social spending, shortages of basic goods, and high inflation. Worsened living conditions have prompted nearly 8 million Venezuelans to emigrate, mainly settling in nearby countries. The US imposed financial sanctions on MADURO and his representatives in 2017 and on sectors of the Venezuelan economy in 2018. Limited sanctions relief followed when the MADURO administration began making democratic and electoral concessions.

The government's mismanagement and lack of investment in infrastructure has also weakened the country's energy sector. Caracas has relaxed some controls to mitigate the impact of its sustained economic crisis, such as allowing increased import flexibility for the private sector and the informal use of US dollars and other international currencies. Ongoing concerns include human rights abuses, rampant violent crime, political manipulation of the judicial and electoral systems, and corruption.

GEOGRAPHY

Location: Northern South America, bordering the Caribbean Sea and the North Atlantic Ocean, between Colombia and Guyana

Geographic coordinates: 8 00 N, 66 00 W

Map references: South America

Area: *total:* 912,050 sq km
land: 882,050 sq km
water: 30,000 sq km
comparison ranking: total 34

Area - comparative: almost six times the size of Georgia; slightly more than twice the size of California

Land boundaries: *total:* 5,267 km
border countries (3): Brazil 2,137 km; Colombia 2,341 km; Guyana 789 km

Coastline: 2,800 km

Maritime claims: *territorial sea:* 12 nm
contiguous zone: 15 nm
exclusive economic zone: 200 nm
continental shelf: 200-m depth or to the depth of exploitation

Climate: tropical; hot, humid; more moderate in highlands

Terrain: Andes Mountains and Maracaibo Lowlands in northwest; central plains (llanos); Guiana Highlands in southeast

Elevation: *highest point:* Pico Bolivar 4,978 m
lowest point: Caribbean Sea 0 m
mean elevation: 450 m

Natural resources: petroleum, natural gas, iron ore, gold, bauxite, other minerals, hydropower, diamonds

Land use: *agricultural land:* 24.5% (2018 est.)
arable land: 3.1% (2018 est.)
permanent crops: 0.8% (2018 est.)
permanent pasture: 20.6% (2018 est.)
forest: 52.1% (2018 est.)
other: 23.4% (2018 est.)

Irrigated land: 10,550 sq km (2012)

Major lakes (area sq km): *salt water lake(s):* Lago de Maracaibo - 13,010 sq km

Major rivers (by length in km): Rio Negro (shared with Colombia [s] and Brazil [m]) - 2,250 km; Orinoco river source and mouth (shared with Colombia) - 2,101 km
note – [s] after country name indicates river source; [m] after country name indicates river mouth

Major watersheds (area sq km): Atlantic Ocean drainage: Amazon (6,145,186 sq km), Orinoco (953,675 sq km)

Population distribution: most of the population is concentrated in the northern and western highlands along an eastern spur at the northern end of the Andes, an area that includes the capital of Caracas

Natural hazards: subject to floods, rockslides, mudslides; periodic droughts

Geography - note: *note 1:* the country lies on major sea and air routes linking North and South America
note 2: Venezuela has some of the most unique geology in the world; tepuis are massive table-top mountains of the western Guiana Highlands that tend to be isolated and thus support unique endemic plant and animal species; their sheer cliffsides account for some of the most spectacular waterfalls in the world including Angel Falls, the world's highest (979 m) that drops off Auyan Tepui

PEOPLE AND SOCIETY

Population: *total:* 31,250,306
male: 15,555,451
female: 15,694,855 (2024 est.)
comparison rankings: female 50; male 49; total 49

Nationality: *noun:* Venezuelan(s)
adjective: Venezuelan

Ethnic groups: unspecified Spanish, Italian, Portuguese, Arab, German, African, Indigenous

Languages: Spanish (official) 98.2%, indigenous 1.3%, Portuguese 0.1%, other 0.4% (2023 est.)
major-language sample(s):
La Libreta Informativa del Mundo, la fuente indispensable de información básica. (Spanish)

Religions: Roman Catholic 48.1%, Protestant 31.6% (Evangelical 31.4%, Adventist 0.2%), Jehovah's Witness 1.4%, African American/umbanda 0.7%, other 0.1%, believer 3.5%, agnostic 0.1%, atheist, 0.4%, none 13.6%, unspecified 0.6% (2023 est.)

Demographic profile: Venezuela's ongoing socio-economic, political, and human rights crises have resulted in widespread poverty and food insecurity and have devastated the country's healthcare system. According to a 2018 national hospital survey, many hospitals were unable to provide basic services, and 20% of operating rooms and intensive care units were non-functional. Hospitals reported shortages in water (79%), medicines (88%), and surgical supplies (79%). The poor conditions in healthcare facilities have motivated many doctors and other health professionals to emigrate, resulting in shortages of specialists, particularly in emergency care. The scarcity of medicines, vaccines, medical supplies, and mosquito controls is leading to a rise in infectious diseases. Tuberculosis cases jumped by 68% between 2014 and 2017, and malaria rates had the largest rise in the world from 2016 to 2017 at 69%. Diptheria, which had been eradicated in the country in 1999, re-emerged in 2016, and new cases have surfaced in 2023. Infectious disease outbreaks, such as measles and malaria, have crossed into neighboring countries. Infant mortality, which had been decreasing since the 1950s, has been on the rise since 2009. Between 2015 and 2016, infant deaths increased 30%, while maternal mortality increased 65%.

As of November 2023, more than 7.7 million Venezuelan migrants, refugees, and asylum seekers had been reported by host governments, with approximately 85% relocating in Latin America and the Caribbean. Colombia has been the largest recipient, accommodating almost 2.5 million as of February 2022, followed by Peru and Ecuador. As of June 2022, almost 212,000 of the refugees and close to 1.04 million of the asylum seekers were recognized by national authorities. An additional 4.3 million Venezuelans have been granted residence permits or other types of regular stay arrangements, as of March 2023. The initial wave of migrants were highly educated professionals. These were followed by university-educated young people. As the economy collapsed in 2017-2018, Venezuelan migrants have been less-educated and from low-income households.

Age structure: *0-14 years:* 25% (male 3,987,361/female 3,811,307)
15-64 years: 65.9% (male 10,264,353/female 10,330,376)
65 years and over: 9.1% (2024 est.) (male 1,303,737/female 1,553,172)

Dependency ratios: *total dependency ratio:* 57.5
youth dependency ratio: 44.4
elderly dependency ratio: 13.1
potential support ratio: 7.6 (2021 est.)

Median age: *total:* 31 years (2024 est.)
male: 30.3 years
female: 31.7 years
comparison ranking: total 129

Population growth rate: 2.34% (2024 est.)
comparison ranking: 27

Birth rate: 16.7 births/1,000 population (2024 est.)
comparison ranking: 94

Death rate: 6.5 deaths/1,000 population (2024 est.)
comparison ranking: 137

Net migration rate: 13.2 migrant(s)/1,000 population (2024 est.)
comparison ranking: 3

Population distribution: most of the population is concentrated in the northern and western highlands along an eastern spur at the northern end of the Andes, an area that includes the capital of Caracas

Urbanization: *urban population:* 88.4% of total population (2023)
rate of urbanization: 1.16% annual rate of change (2020-25 est.)

Major urban areas - population: 2.972 million CARACAS (capital), 2.368 million Maracaibo, 1.983 million Valencia, 1.254 million Barquisimeto, 1.243 million Maracay, 964,000 Ciudad Guayana (2023)

Sex ratio: *at birth:* 1.05 male(s)/female
0-14 years: 1.05 male(s)/female
15-64 years: 0.99 male(s)/female
65 years and over: 0.84 male(s)/female
total population: 0.99 male(s)/female (2024 est.)

Maternal mortality ratio: 259 deaths/100,000 live births (2020 est.)
comparison ranking: 36

Infant mortality rate: *total:* 13.9 deaths/1,000 live births (2024 est.)
male: 15.4 deaths/1,000 live births
female: 12.2 deaths/1,000 live births
comparison ranking: total 101

Life expectancy at birth: *total population:* 74.5 years (2024 est.)
male: 71.5 years
female: 77.7 years
comparison ranking: total population 142

Total fertility rate: 2.18 children born/woman (2024 est.)
comparison ranking: 87

Gross reproduction rate: 1.06 (2024 est.)

Contraceptive prevalence rate: 75% (2010)

Drinking water source: *improved:*
total: 94.2% of population
unimproved:
total: 5.8% of population (2020 est.)

Current health expenditure: 3.8% of GDP (2020)

Physician density: 1.73 physicians/1,000 population (2017)

Hospital bed density: 0.9 beds/1,000 population (2017)

Sanitation facility access: *improved:*
total: 95.8% of population
unimproved:
total: 4.2% of population (2020 est.)

Obesity - adult prevalence rate: 25.6% (2016)
comparison ranking: 49

Alcohol consumption per capita: *total:* 2.51 liters of pure alcohol (2019 est.)
beer: 1.54 liters of pure alcohol (2019 est.)
wine: 0.01 liters of pure alcohol (2019 est.)
spirits: 0.92 liters of pure alcohol (2019 est.)
other alcohols: 0.03 liters of pure alcohol (2019 est.)
comparison ranking: total 123

Currently married women (ages 15-49): 51.5% (2023 est.)

Education expenditures: 1.3% of GDP (2017 est.)
comparison ranking: 194

Literacy: *definition:* age 15 and over can read and write
total population: 97.5%
male: 97.4%
female: 97.7% (2021)

ENVIRONMENT

Environment - current issues: sewage pollution of Lago de Valencia; oil and urban pollution of Lago de Maracaibo; deforestation; soil degradation; urban and industrial pollution, especially along the Caribbean coast; threat to the rainforest ecosystem from irresponsible mining operations

Environment - international agreements: *party to:* Antarctic-Environmental Protection, Antarctic Treaty, Biodiversity, Climate Change, Climate Change-Kyoto Protocol, Climate Change-Paris Agreement, Comprehensive Nuclear Test Ban, Desertification, Endangered Species, Hazardous Wastes, Marine Life Conservation, Nuclear Test Ban, Ozone Layer Protection, Ship Pollution, Tropical Timber 2006, Wetlands
signed, but not ratified: none of the selected agreements

Climate: tropical; hot, humid; more moderate in highlands

Urbanization: *urban population:* 88.4% of total population (2023)
rate of urbanization: 1.16% annual rate of change (2020-25 est.)

Food insecurity: *widespread lack of access: due to severe economic crisis* - the national economy, highly dependent on oil production and exports, was forecast to contract in 2021 for the eighth consecutive year; with the persistent negative effects of the COVID-19 pandemic that have compounded the already severe macro-economic crisis, the access to food of the most vulnerable households is expected to deteriorate throughout 2021 and into 2022 due to widespread losses of income-generating activities and soaring food prices (2022)

Air pollutants: *particulate matter emissions:* 16.21 micrograms per cubic meter (2019 est.)
carbon dioxide emissions: 164.18 megatons (2016 est.)
methane emissions: 68.66 megatons (2020 est.)

Waste and recycling: *municipal solid waste generated annually:* 9,779,093 tons (2010 est.)

Major lakes (area sq km): *salt water lake(s):* Lago de Maracaibo - 13,010 sq km

Major rivers (by length in km): Rio Negro (shared with Colombia [s] and Brazil [m]) - 2,250 km; Orinoco river source and mouth (shared with Colombia) - 2,101 km
note – [s] after country name indicates river source; [m] after country name indicates river mouth

Major watersheds (area sq km): Atlantic Ocean drainage: Amazon (6,145,186 sq km), Orinoco (953,675 sq km)

Total water withdrawal: *municipal:* 5.12 billion cubic meters (2020 est.)
industrial: 790 million cubic meters (2020 est.)
agricultural: 16.71 billion cubic meters (2020 est.)

Total renewable water resources: 1.33 trillion cubic meters (2020 est.)

GOVERNMENT

Country name: *conventional long form:* Bolivarian Republic of Venezuela
conventional short form: Venezuela
local long form: República Bolivariana de Venezuela
local short form: Venezuela
former: State of Venezuela, Republic of Venezuela, United States of Venezuela
etymology: native stilt-houses built on Lake Maracaibo reminded early explorers Alonso de OJEDA and Amerigo VESPUCCI in 1499 of buildings in Venice and so they named the region "Venezuola," which in Italian means "Little Venice"

Government type: federal presidential republic

Capital: *name:* Caracas
geographic coordinates: 10 29 N, 66 52 W
time difference: UTC-4 (1 hour ahead of Washington, DC, during Standard Time)
etymology: named for the native Caracas tribe that originally settled in the city's valley site near the Caribbean coast

Administrative divisions: 23 states (estados, singular - estado), 1 capital district* (distrito capital), and 1 federal dependency** (dependencia federal); Amazonas, Anzoategui, Apure, Aragua, Barinas, Bolivar, Carabobo, Cojedes, Delta Amacuro, Dependencias Federales (Federal Dependencies)**, Distrito Capital (Capital District)*, Falcon, Guarico, La Guaira, Lara, Merida, Miranda, Monagas, Nueva Esparta, Portuguesa, Sucre, Tachira, Trujillo, Yaracuy, Zulia
note: the federal dependency consists of 11 federally controlled island groups with a total of 72 individual islands

Independence: 5 July 1811 (from Spain)

National holiday: Independence Day, 5 July (1811)

Legal system: civil law system based on the Spanish civil code

Constitution: *history:* many previous; latest adopted 15 December 1999, effective 30 December 1999
amendments: proposed through agreement by at least 39% of the National Assembly membership, by the president of the republic in session with the

cabinet of ministers, or by petition of at least 15% of registered voters; passage requires simple majority vote by the Assembly and simple majority approval in a referendum; amended 2009; note - in 2016, President MADURO issued a decree to hold an election to form a constituent assembly to change the constitution; the election in July 2017 approved the formation of a 545-member constituent assembly and elected its delegates, empowering them to change the constitution and dismiss government institutions and officials

International law organization participation: has not submitted an ICJ jurisdiction declaration; accepts ICCt jurisdiction

Citizenship: *citizenship by birth:* yes
citizenship by descent only: yes
dual citizenship recognized: yes
residency requirement for naturalization: 10 years; reduced to five years in the case of applicants from Spain, Portugal, Italy, or a Latin American or Caribbean country

Suffrage: 18 years of age; universal

Executive branch: chief of state: Notification Statement: the United States does not recognize Nicolas MADURO Moros as president of Venezuela President Nicolas MADURO Moros (since 19 April 2013)
head of government: President Nicolas MADURO Moros (since 19 April 2013)
cabinet: Council of Ministers appointed by the president
elections/appointments: president directly elected by simple majority popular vote for a 6-year term (no term limits); election last held on 28 July 2024 (next to be held in 2030)
election results:
2024: official results disputed; Nicolas MADURO Moros was declared the winner by the MADURO-controlled National Electoral Council; percent of vote - Nicolas MADURO Moros (PSUV) 52%, Edmundo GONZÁLEZ Urrutia (Independent) 43.2%, Luis Eduardo MARTÍNEZ (AD) 1.2%, other 3.6%; note – given overwhelming evidence, including more than 80% of the tally sheets received directly from polling stations throughout Venezuela indicating that GONZÁLEZ received the most votes by an insurmountable margin, the United States recognizes that GONZÁLEZ won the most votes in the 28 July 2024 presidential election
2018: Nicolas MADURO Moros reelected president; percent of vote - Nicolas MADURO Moros (PSUV) 67.9%, Henri FALCON (AP) 20.9%, Javier BERTUCCI 10.8%; note - the election was reportedly marred by serious shortcomings and electoral fraud
2013: Nicolas MADURO Moros elected president; percent of vote - Nicolas MADURO Moros (PSUV) 50.6%, Henrique CAPRILES Radonski (PJ) 49.1%, other 0.3%
note: the president is both chief of state and head of government

Legislative branch: *description:* unicameral National Assembly or Asamblea Nacional (277 seats; 3 seats reserved for indigenous peoples of Venezuela; members serve 5-year terms); note - in 2020, the National Electoral Council increased the number of seats in the National Assembly from 167 to 277 for the 6 December 2020 election
elections: last held on 6 December 2020 (next expected to be held in December 2025)
election results: percent of vote by party - GPP (pro-government) 69.3%, Democratic Alliance (opposition coalition) 17.7%, other 13%; seats by party - GPP 253, Democratic Alliance 18, indigenous peoples 3, other 3; composition - NA

Judicial branch: *highest court(s):* Supreme Tribunal of Justice (consists of 32 judges organized into constitutional, politicaladministrative, electoral, civil appeals, criminal appeals, and social divisions)
judge selection and term of office: judges proposed by the Committee of Judicial Postulation (an independent body of organizations dealing with legal issues and of the organs of citizen power) and appointed by the National Assembly; judges serve nonrenewable 12-year terms; note - in July 2017, the National Assembly named 33 judges to the court to replace a series of judges, it argued, had been illegally appointed in late 2015 by the outgoing, socialist-party-led Assembly; MADURO and the Socialist Party-appointed judges refused to recognize these appointments, however, and many of the new judges have since been imprisoned or forced into exile
subordinate courts: Superior or Appeals Courts (Tribunales Superiores); District Tribunals (Tribunales de Distrito); Courts of First Instance (Tribunales de Primera Instancia); Parish Courts (Tribunales de Parroquia); Justices of the Peace (Justicia de Paz) Network

Political parties: A New Era (Un Nuevo Tiempo) or UNT
Cambiemos Movimiento Ciudadano or CMC
Christian Democrats or COPEI (also known as the Social Christian Party)
Citizens Encounter or EC
Clear Accounts or CC
Coalition of parties loyal to Nicolas MADURO - Great Patriotic Pole or GPP
Coalition of opposition parties - Democratic Alliance (Alianza Democratica) (includes AD, EL CAMBIO, COPEI, CMC, and AP)
Come Venezuela (Vente Venezuela) or VV
Communist Party of Venezuela or PCV
Consenso en la Zona or Conenzo
Convergencia
Democratic Action or AD
Fatherland for All (Patria para Todos) or PPT
Fearless People's Alliance or ABP
Fuerza Vecinal or FV
Hope for Change (Esperanza por el Cambio) or EL CAMBIO
Justice First (Primero Justicia) or PJ

LAPIZ

Movement to Socialism (Movimiento al Socialismo) or MAS
Popular Will (Voluntad Popular) or VP
Progressive Advance (Avanzada Progresista) or AP
The Radical Cause or La Causa R
United Socialist Party of Venezuela or PSUV
Venezuela First (Primero Venezuela) or PV
Venezuelan Progressive Movement or MPV
Venezuela Project or PV

International organization participation: ACS, Caricom (observer), CD, CDB, CELAC, FAO, G-15, G-24, G-77, IADB, IAEA, IBRD, ICAO, ICC (national committees), ICCt (signatory), ICRM, IDA, IFAD, IFC, IFRCS, IHO, ILO, IMF, IMO, IMSO, Interpol, IOC, IOM, IPU, ITSO, ITU, ITUC (NGOs), LAES, LAIA, LAS (observer), MIGA, NAM, OAS, OPANAL, OPCW, OPEC, PCA, Petrocaribe, UN, UNASUR, UNCTAD, UNESCO, UNHCR, UNHRC, UNIDO, Union Latina, UNOOSA, UNWTO, UPU, WCO, WFTU (NGOs), WHO, WIPO, WMO, WTO

Diplomatic representation in the US: none

Note: the embassy, which had been run by the Venezuelan political opposition, announced on 5 January 2023, that it had ended all embassy functions

Diplomatic representation from the US: *chief of mission:* Ambassador (vacant); as of 19 May 2023, Francisco L. PALMIERI serves as the chief of mission of the Venezuela Affairs Unit, located in the US Embassy, Bogota
embassy: Venezuela Affairs Unit, US Embassy, Carrera 45 N. 24B-27, Bogota, Colombia
previously - F St. and Suapure St.; Urb. Colinas de Valle Arriba; Caracas 1080
mailing address: 3140 Caracas Place, Washington DC 20521-3140
telephone: 1-888-407-4747
email address and website:
ACSBogota@state.gov
https://ve.usembassy.gov/

Flag description: three equal horizontal bands of yellow (top), blue, and red with the coat of arms on the hoist side of the yellow band and an arc of eight white five-pointed stars centered in the blue band; the flag retains the three equal horizontal bands and three main colors of the banner of Gran Colombia, the South American republic that broke up in 1830; yellow is interpreted as standing for the riches of the land, blue for the courage of its people, and red for the blood shed in attaining independence; the seven stars on the original flag represented the seven provinces in Venezuela that united in the war of independence; in 2006, then President Hugo CHAVEZ ordered an eighth star added to the star arc - a decision that sparked much controversy - to conform with the flag proclaimed by Simon Bolivar in 1827 and to represent the historic province of Guayana

National symbol(s): troupial (bird); national colors: yellow, blue, red

National anthem: *name:* "Gloria al bravo pueblo" (Glory to the Brave People)
lyrics/music: Vicente SALIAS/Juan Jose LANDAETA
note: adopted 1881; lyrics written in 1810, the music some years later; both SALIAS and LANDAETA were executed in 1814 during Venezuela's struggle for independence

National heritage: *total World Heritage Sites:* 3 (2 cultural, 1 natural)
selected World Heritage Site locales: Coro and its Port (c); Canaima National Park (n); Ciudad Universitaria de Caracas (c)

ECONOMY

Economic overview: South American economy; ongoing hyperinflation since mid-2010s; chaotic economy due to political corruption, infrastructure cuts, and human rights abuses; in debt default; oil exporter; hydropower consumer; rising Chinese relations

Real GDP (purchasing power parity): $269.068 billion (2018 est.)
$381.6 billion (2017 est.)
$334.751 billion (2017 est.)
note: data are in 2017 dollars
comparison ranking: 64

Real GDP growth rate: -19.67% (2018 est.)

-14% (2017 est.)
-15.76% (2017 est.)
note: annual GDP % growth based on constant local currency
comparison ranking: 219

Real GDP per capita: $7,704 (2018 est.)
$12,500 (2017 est.)
$9,417 (2017 est.)
note: data are in 2017 dollars
comparison ranking: 156

GDP (official exchange rate): $482.359 billion (2014 est.)
note: data in current dollars at official exchange rate

Inflation rate (consumer prices): 146,101.7% (2019 est.)
45,518.1% (2018 est.)
416.8% (2017 est.)
note: annual % change based on consumer prices
comparison ranking: 220

Credit ratings: Fitch rating: RD (2017)

Moody's rating: WR (2019)

Standard & Poors rating: SD (2017)
note: The year refers to the year in which the current credit rating was first obtained.

GDP - composition, by sector of origin: *agriculture:* 5% (2014 est.)
industry: 37.2% (2014 est.)
services: 51.7% (2014 est.)
note: figures may not total 100% due to non-allocated consumption not captured in sector-reported data
comparison rankings: services 133; industry 38; agriculture 117

GDP - composition, by end use: *household consumption:* 75.3% (2014 est.)
government consumption: 14.6% (2014 est.)
investment in fixed capital: 21.6% (2014 est.)
investment in inventories: 3.2% (2014 est.)
exports of goods and services: 16.7% (2014 est.)
imports of goods and services: -31.4% (2014 est.)
note: figures may not total 100% due to rounding or gaps in data collection

Agricultural products: milk, sugarcane, maize, plantains, oil palm fruit, bananas, rice, potatoes, pineapples, chicken (2022)
note: top ten agricultural products based on tonnage

Industries: agricultural products, livestock, raw materials, machinery and equipment, transport equipment, construction materials, medical equipment, pharmaceuticals, chemicals, iron and steel products, crude oil and petroleum products

Industrial production growth rate: -5.84% (2014 est.)
note: annual % change in industrial value added based on constant local currency
comparison ranking: 201

Labor force: 11.548 million (2023 est.)
note: number of people ages 15 or older who are employed or seeking work
comparison ranking: 51

Unemployment rate: 5.53% (2023 est.)
5.75% (2022 est.)
7.03% (2021 est.)
note: % of labor force seeking employment
comparison ranking: 107

Youth unemployment rate (ages 15-24): *total:* 10.8% (2023 est.)
male: 9.5% (2023 est.)
female: 14.1% (2023 est.)
note: % of labor force ages 15-24 seeking employment
comparison ranking: total 124

Population below poverty line: 33.1% (2015 est.)
note: % of population with income below national poverty line

Average household expenditures: *on food:* 18.4% of household expenditures (2022 est.)
on alcohol and tobacco: 3.8% of household expenditures (2022 est.)

Remittances: 0.03% of GDP (2014 est.)
note: personal transfers and compensation between resident and non-resident individuals/households/entities

Budget: *revenues:* $30 million (2017 est.)
expenditures: $76 million (2017 est.)

Public debt: 38.9% of GDP (2017 est.)
note: data cover central government debt, as well as the debt of state-owned oil company PDVSA; the data include treasury debt held by foreign entities; the data include some debt issued by subnational entities, as well as intragovernmental debt; intragovernmental debt consists of treasury borrowings from surpluses in the social funds, such as for retirement, medical care, and unemployment; some debt instruments for the social funds are sold at public auctions
comparison ranking: 136

Taxes and other revenues: 44.2% (of GDP) (2017 est.)
comparison ranking: 7

Current account balance: -$3.87 billion (2016 est.)
-$3.87 billion (2016 est.)
-$16.051 billion (2015 est.)
note: balance of payments - net trade and primary/secondary income in current dollars
comparison ranking: 171

Exports: $83.401 billion (2018 est.)
$93.485 billion (2017 est.)
$28.684 billion (2016 est.)
note: balance of payments - exports of goods and services in current dollars
comparison ranking: 52

Exports - partners: China 16%, Turkey 14%, Spain 12%, US 10%, Brazil 8% (2022)
note: top five export partners based on percentage share of exports

Exports - commodities: scrap iron, petroleum coke, crude petroleum, acyclic alcohols, aluminum (2022)
note: top five export commodities based on value in dollars

Imports: $18.432 billion (2018 est.)
$18.376 billion (2017 est.)
$25.81 billion (2016 est.)
note: balance of payments - imports of goods and services in current dollars
comparison ranking: 99

Imports - partners: China 31%, US 23%, Brazil 14%, Colombia 7%, Turkey 4% (2022)
note: top five import partners based on percentage share of imports

Imports - commodities: soybean oil, wheat, soybean meal, corn, plastic products (2022)
note: top five import commodities based on value in dollars

Reserves of foreign exchange and gold: $9.794 billion (2017 est.)
$10.15 billion (2016 est.)
$15.625 billion (2015 est.)
note: holdings of gold (year-end prices)/foreign exchange/special drawing rights in current dollars
comparison ranking: 75

Exchange rates: bolivars (VEB) per US dollar -

Exchange rates: 9.975 (2017 est.)
9.257 (2016 est.)
6.284 (2015 est.)
6.284 (2014 est.)

ENERGY

Electricity access: *electrification - total population:* 100% (2022 est.)

Electricity: *installed generating capacity:* 34.742 million kW (2022 est.)
consumption: 56.768 billion kWh (2022 est.)
exports: 652 million kWh (2020 est.)
transmission/distribution losses: 27.882 billion kWh (2022 est.)
comparison rankings: transmission/distribution losses 196; consumption 50; installed generating capacity 35; exports 72

Electricity generation sources: *fossil fuels:* 22.3% of total installed capacity (2022 est.)
wind: 0.1% of total installed capacity (2022 est.)
hydroelectricity: 77.6% of total installed capacity (2022 est.)

Coal: *production:* 197,000 metric tons (2022 est.)
consumption: 82,000 metric tons (2022 est.)
exports: 124,000 metric tons (2022 est.)
imports: 300 metric tons (2022 est.)
proven reserves: 730.999 million metric tons (2022 est.)

Petroleum: *total petroleum production:* 761,000 bbl/day (2023 est.)
refined petroleum consumption: 367,000 bbl/day (2022 est.)
crude oil estimated reserves: 303.806 billion barrels (2021 est.)

Natural gas: *production:* 17.696 billion cubic meters (2022 est.)
consumption: 17.696 billion cubic meters (2022 est.)
proven reserves: 5.674 trillion cubic meters (2021 est.)

Carbon dioxide emissions: 80.769 million metric tonnes of CO_2 (2022 est.)
from coal and metallurgical coke: 188,000 metric tonnes of CO_2 (2022 est.)
from petroleum and other liquids: 44.539 million metric tonnes of CO_2 (2022 est.)
from consumed natural gas: 36.042 million metric tonnes of CO_2 (2022 est.)
comparison ranking: total emissions 46

Energy consumption per capita: 57.282 million Btu/person (2022 est.)
comparison ranking: 86

COMMUNICATIONS

Telephones - fixed lines: *total subscriptions:* 3.147 million (2022 est.)
subscriptions per 100 inhabitants: 11 (2022 est.)
comparison ranking: total subscriptions 37

Telephones - mobile cellular: *total subscriptions:* 17.949 million (2022 est.)
subscriptions per 100 inhabitants: 63 (2022 est.)
comparison ranking: total subscriptions 66

Telecommunication systems: *general assessment:* Venezuela's fixed-line penetration was relatively high for the region at 7.8 million lines in 2014 but the steady growth in the number of lines came to an end in 2015; since then, the number of fixed

lines has plummeted to 2.7 million (2022) or a teledensity of about 9.5%; the cause is largely linked to the country's ongoing economic troubles, which have compelled many people to terminate fixed-line telecom services and others still to flee the country; these pressures have also distorted sector revenue and have placed into disarray operators' investment plans aimed at improving networks and expanding the reach and capabilities of new technologies and services; the fixed broadband penetration rate is lower than the regional average, while data speeds are also relatively low; there is no effective competition in the provision of DSL, and as a result the state-owned incumbent CANTV has had little incentive to improve services from its meager revenue streams; mobile penetration in Venezuela is 67% (2022), below the regional average and ahead of only Honduras, Guatemala, Nicaragua, and Haiti; the number of mobile subscribers decline gradually from 2012 to 2020 as subscribers terminated services in a bid to reduce discretionary spending or left the country; after years of decline, mobile phone lines grew 15% from 2021 to the end of 2022 to reach 18.7 million, as subscribers replaced fixed lines with mobile service and mobile connectivity improved; an estimated 78% of mobile subscribers have smartphones with mobile access to the internet (2021)
domestic: fixed-line is 10 per 100 and mobile-cellular telephone subscribership is 67 per 100 persons (2021)
international: country code - 58; landing points for the Venezuela Festoon, ARCOS, PAN-AM, SAC, GlobeNet, ALBA-1 and Americas II submarine cable system providing connectivity to the Caribbean, Central and South America, and US; satellite earth stations - 1 Intelsat (Atlantic Ocean) and 1 PanAmSat (2020)

Broadcast media: Venezuela has a mixture of state-run and private broadcast media that are subject to high levels of control, including the shuttering of opposition-leaning media outlets; 13 public service networks, 61 privately owned TV networks, a privately owned news channel with limited national coverage, and a Maduro-backed Pan-American channel; 3 Maduro-aligned radio networks officially control roughly 65 news stations and another 30 stations targeted at specific audiences; Maduro-sponsored community broadcasters include 235 radio stations and 44 TV stations; the number of private broadcast radio stations has been declining, but many still remain in operation (2021)

Internet country code: .ve

Internet users: *total:* 22,734,162 (2022 est.)
percent of population: 78.7% (2022 est.)
comparison ranking: total 38

Broadband - fixed subscriptions: *total:* 2,561,556 (2020 est.)
subscriptions per 100 inhabitants: 9 (2020 est.)
comparison ranking: total 52

TRANSPORTATION

National air transport system: *number of registered air carriers:* 12 (2020)
inventory of registered aircraft operated by air carriers: 75
annual passenger traffic on registered air carriers: 2,137,771 (2018)
annual freight traffic on registered air carriers: 1.55 million (2018) mt-km

Civil aircraft registration country code prefix: YV

Airports: 502 (2024)
comparison ranking: 17

Heliports: 88 (2024)

Pipelines: 981 km extra heavy crude, 5941 km gas, 7,588 km oil, 1,778 km refined products (2013)

Railways: *total:* 447 km (2014)
standard gauge: 447 km (2014) 1.435-m gauge (41.4 km electrified)
comparison ranking: total 114

Roadways: *total:* 96,189 km (2014)
comparison ranking: total 51

Waterways: 7,100 km (2011) (Orinoco River (400 km) and Lake de Maracaibo navigable by oceangoing vessels)
comparison ranking: 22

Merchant marine: *total:* 272 (2023)
by type: bulk carrier 3, container ship 1, general cargo 26, oil tanker 17, other 225
comparison ranking: total 60

Ports: *total ports:* 31 (2024)
large: 1
medium: 2
small: 11
very small: 17
ports with oil terminals: 21
key ports: Amuay (Bahia de Amuay), Bahia de Pertigalete, Ciudad Bolivar, Guanta, La Guaira, La Salina, Las Piedras, Maracaibo, Puerto Cabello, Puerto de Hierro, Puerto la Cruz, Puerto Miranda, Puerto Ordaz, Punta Cardon

MILITARY AND SECURITY

Military and security forces: Bolivarian National Armed Forces (Fuerza Armada Nacional Bolivariana, FANB): Bolivarian Army (Ejercito Bolivariano, EB), Bolivarian Navy (Armada Bolivariana, AB; includes marines, Coast Guard), Bolivarian Military Aviation (Aviacion Militar Bolivariana, AMB; includes a joint-service Aerospace Defense Command (Comando de Defensa Aeroespacial Integral, CODAI), Bolivarian Militia (Milicia Bolivariana), Bolivarian National Guard (Guardia Nacional Bolivaria, GNB)

Ministry of Interior, Justice, and Peace: Bolivarian National Police (Policía Nacional Bolivariana, PNB) (2024)
note 1: the Bolivarian Militia was added as a "special component" to the FANB in 2020; it is comprised of armed civilians who receive periodic training in exchange for a small stipend
note 2: the National Guard, established in 1937 and made a component of the FANB in 2007, is responsible for maintaining public order, guarding the exterior of key government installations and prisons, conducting counter-narcotics operations, monitoring borders, and providing law enforcement in remote areas; it reports to both the Ministry of Defense and the Ministry of Interior, Justice, and Peace
note 3: the PNB is a federal force created by Hugo CHAVEZ in 2008 as a "preventative police force," separate from state and local ones; the PNB largely focuses on policing Caracas' Libertador municipality, patrolling Caracas-area highways, railways, and metro system, and protecting diplomatic missions; the PNB includes the Special Action Forces (Fuerzas de Acciones Especiales, FAES), a paramilitary unit created by President MADURO to bolster internal security after the 2017 anti-government protests; it has been accused of multiple human rights abuses

Military expenditures: 5.2% of GDP (2019 est.)
4.4% of GDP (2018 est.)
2.9% of GDP (2017 est.)
2.2% of GDP (2016 est.)
1.8% of GDP (2015 est.)
comparison ranking: 8

Military and security service personnel strengths: information varies; approximately 125-150,000 active military personnel, including about 25-30,000 National Guard; approximately 200-225,000 Bolivarian Militia; approximately 45,000 National Police (2023)
note: in December 2022, President Nicolas MADURO announced that the National Police would be increased to 100,000 in 2024

Military equipment inventories and acquisitions: the FANB inventory is mainly of Chinese and Russian origin with a smaller mix of mostly older equipment from Western countries, including the US; in recent years, leading suppliers has been China (2023)
note: the US prohibited the sale or transfer of military arms or technology to Venezuela in 2006

Military service age and obligation: 18-30 (25 for women) for voluntary service; the minimum service obligation is 24-30 months; all citizens of military service age (18-50) are obligated to register for military service and subject to military training, although "forcible recruitment" is forbidden (2023)

Military - note: the armed forces (FANB) are responsible for ensuring Venezuela's independence, sovereignty, and territorial integrity but also have a domestic role, including assisting with maintaining internal security, conducting counter-narcotics missions, contributing to national socio-economic development, and providing disaster relief/humanitarian assistance; the military conducts internal security operations in large parts of the country and has been deployed against illegal armed groups operating in the Colombian border region and other areas to combat organized crime gangs involved in narcotics trafficking and illegal mining; it has close ties to China and Russia, including weapons acquisitions and technical support
the military has a large role in the country's economy and political sectors; between 2013 and 2017, Venezuela established at least a dozen military-led firms in economic areas such as agriculture, banking, construction, insurance, the media, mining, oil, and tourism; military officers reportedly lead as many as 60 state-owned companies; as of 2023, 14 of 32 government ministries were controlled by the military, including the ministries of agriculture, food, petroleum, and water
the FANB is deployed throughout the country in one maritime and seven geographical regional commands known as Integral Strategic Defense Regions (Regiones Estrategicas de Defensa Integral or REDI) that are mandated to provide for the defense, security, social, and economic needs of their respective areas of responsibility; the REDIs are further broken down into zones and state commands; the National Guard is also organized into regional commands, while the Bolivarian Militia is reportedly divided into a reserve service, a territorial guard component comprised of local battalions and detachments, and a coastal guard force
members of the terrorist organizations National Liberation Army (ELN) and Revolutionary Armed Forces of Colombia dissidents (FARC-People's Army and Segundo Marquetalia) operate in Venezuela, mostly in the states of Amazonas, Apure, Bolivar,

Guarico, Tachira, and Zulia, although the ELN is assessed to be present in 12 of Venezuela's 23 states; the Venezuelan military has been deployed to the border region to patrol border crossings and has clashed with both the ELN and the FARC dissident groups (2023)

SPACE

Space agency/agencies: Bolivarian Agency for Space Activities (Agencia Bolivariana para Actividades Espaciales, ABAE; formed 2007); ABAE was originally known as the Venezuelan Space Center (CEV; created 2005); the ABAE is under the Ministry of Science, Technology, and Innovation (2024)

Space program overview: has a small program primarily focused on the acquisition of satellites and developing the country's space engineering and sciences capabilities; operates satellites and maintains two satellite ground control stations; has relations with the space programs of China and Russia (2024)

note: further details about the key activities, programs, and milestones of the country's space program, as well as government spending estimates on the space sector, appear in the Space Programs reference guide

TERRORISM

Terrorist group(s): National Liberation Army (ELN); Revolutionary Armed Forces of Colombia-People's Army (FARC-EP); Segundo Marquetalia
note: details about the history, aims, leadership, organization, areas of operation, tactics, targets, weapons, size, and sources of support of the group(s) appear(s) in the Terrorism reference guide

TRANSNATIONAL ISSUES

Refugees and internally displaced persons: *refugees (country of origin):* 39,185 (Colombia) (mid-year 2022)
note: As of November 2023, approximately 7.7 million Venezuelan refugees and migrants were residing worldwide with 84.7% in Latin America and the Caribbean

Trafficking in persons: tier rating: Tier 3 — Venezuela does not fully meet the minimum standards for the elimination of trafficking and is not making any efforts to do so, therefore, Venezuela remained on Tier 3; for more details, go to: https://www.state.gov/reports/2024-trafficking-in-persons-report/venezuela/

Illicit drugs: a major drug-transit country and trafficking route in the Western Hemisphere for illegal drugs mainly cocaine; government depends on rents from narco-trafficking, along with other illicit activities, to maintain power; evidence of coca cultivation and cocaine production in domestic drug laboratories suggests the country is now also an illicit drug-producing country; a major source of precursor or essential chemicals used in the production of illicit narcotics

VIETNAM

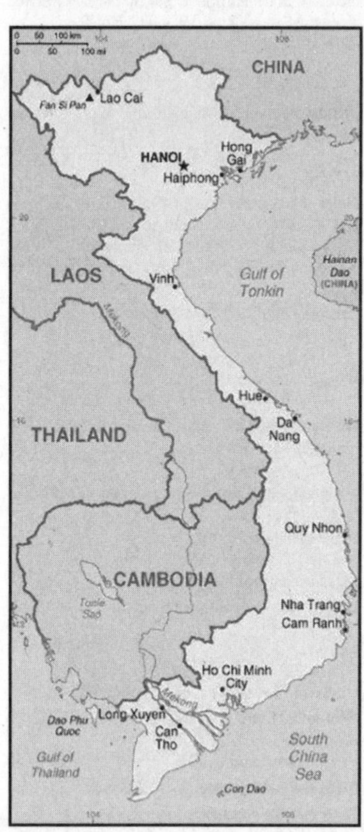

INTRODUCTION

Background: Vietnam's early history included periods of occupation by outside forces and eventual power consolidation under Vietnamese dynastic families. A succession of Han Chinese emperors ruled the area, which was centered on the Red River Valley, until approximately the 10th century. The Ly Dynasty (11th-13th century) created the first independent Vietnamese state, which was known as Dai Viet, and established their capital at Thang Long (Hanoi). Under the Tran Dynasty (13th-15th century), TRAN Hung Dao, one of Vietnam's national heroes, led Dai Viet forces to fight off Mongol invaders in 1279. After a brief Chinese occupation in the early 1400s, Vietnamese resistance leader LE Thai To made himself emperor and established the Le Dynasty, which lasted until the late 18th century despite decades of political turmoil, civil war, and division. During this period, Dai Viet expanded southward to the Central Highlands and Mekong Delta, reaching the approximate boundaries of modern-day Vietnam by the 1750s. Dai Viet suffered additional civil war and division in the latter half of the 18th century, but it was reunited and renamed Vietnam under Emperor NGUYEN Phuc Anh (aka Gia Long) in 1802.

France began its conquest of Vietnam in 1858 and made Vietnam part of French Indochina in 1887. Vietnam declared independence after World War II, but the French continued to rule until communist forces under Ho Chi MINH defeated them in 1954. Under the Geneva Accords of 1954, Vietnam was divided into the communist North and anti-communist South. Fighting erupted between the two governments shortly afterwards with the North supporting communist rebels in the South and eventually committing thousands of combat troops. The US provided to the South significant economic and military assistance, including large numbers of US military forces, which reached a peak strength of over 500,000 troops in 1968. US combat forces were withdrawn following a cease-fire agreement in 1973. Two years later, North Vietnamese forces overran the South, reuniting the country under communist rule. The conflict, known as the Second Indochina War (1955-1975), caused more than 58,000 US combat and non-combat deaths and created deep domestic divisions in the US. It also devastated Vietnam, spilled over into the neighboring countries of Cambodia and Laos, and is estimated to have resulted in the deaths of up to 3 million Vietnamese civilians and soldiers.

Despite the return of peace, the country experienced little economic growth for over a decade because of its diplomatic isolation, leadership policies, and the persecution and mass exodus of citizens, many of them successful South Vietnamese merchants. However, since the enactment of Vietnam's "doi moi" (renovation) policy in 1986, the economy has seen strong growth, particularly in agricultural and industrial production, construction, exports, foreign investment, and tourism. Nevertheless, the Communist Party maintains tight political and social control of the country, and Vietnam faces many related challenges, such as rising income inequality and corruption.

GEOGRAPHY

Location: Southeastern Asia, bordering the Gulf of Thailand, Gulf of Tonkin, and South China Sea, as well as China, Laos, and Cambodia

Geographic coordinates: 16 10 N, 107 50 E

Map references: Southeast Asia

Area: *total:* 331,210 sq km
land: 310,070 sq km
water: 21,140 sq km
comparison ranking: total 67

Area - comparative: about three times the size of Tennessee; slightly larger than New Mexico

Land boundaries: *total:* 4,616 km
border countries (3): Cambodia 1,158 km; China 1,297 km; Laos 2,161 km

Coastline: 3,444 km (excludes islands)

Maritime claims: *territorial sea:* 12 nm
contiguous zone: 24 nm
exclusive economic zone: 200 nm
continental shelf: 200 nm or to the edge of the continental margin

Climate: tropical in south; monsoonal in north with hot, rainy season (May to September) and warm, dry season (October to March)

Terrain: low, flat delta in south and north; central highlands; hilly, mountainous in far north and northwest

Elevation: *highest point:* Fan Si Pan 3,144 m
lowest point: South China Sea 0 m
mean elevation: 398 m

Natural resources: antimony, phosphates, coal, manganese, rare earth elements, bauxite, chromate, offshore oil and gas deposits, timber, hydropower, arable land

Land use: *agricultural land:* 34.8% (2018 est.)
arable land: 20.6% (2018 est.)
permanent crops: 12.1% (2018 est.)
permanent pasture: 2.1% (2018 est.)
forest: 45% (2018 est.)
other: 20.2% (2018 est.)

Irrigated land: 46,000 sq km (2012)

Major rivers (by length in km): Sông Tiên Giang (Mekong) river mouth (shared with China [s], Burma, Laos, Thailand, Cambodia) - 4,350 km; Pearl river source (shared with China [m]) - 2,200 km; Red river mouth (shared with China [s]) - 1,149 km
note – [s] after country name indicates river source; [m] after country name indicates river mouth

Major watersheds (area sq km): Pacific Ocean drainage: Mekong (805,604 sq km)

Population distribution: though it has one of the highest population densities in the world, the population is not evenly dispersed; clustering is heaviest along the South China Sea and Gulf of Tonkin, with the Mekong Delta (in the south) and the Red River Valley (in the north) having the largest concentrations of people

Natural hazards: occasional typhoons (May to January) with extensive flooding, especially in the Mekong River delta

Geography - note: *note 1:* extending 1,650 km north to south, the country is only 50 km across at its narrowest point
note 2: Son Doong in Phong Nha-Ke Bang National Park is the world's largest cave (greatest cross sectional area) and is the largest known cave passage in the world by volume; it currently measures a total of 38.5 million cu m (about 1.35 billion cu ft); it connects to Thung cave (but not yet officially); when recognized, it will add an additional 1.6 million cu m in volume; Son Doong is so massive that it contains its own jungle, underground river, and localized weather system; clouds form inside the cave and spew out from its exits and two dolines (openings, or sinkhole skylights, created by collapsed ceilings that allow sunlight to stream in)

PEOPLE AND SOCIETY

Population: *total:* 105,758,975
male: 53,109,175
female: 52,649,800 (2024 est.)
comparison rankings: female 16; male 16; total 16

Nationality: *noun:* Vietnamese (singular and plural)
adjective: Vietnamese

Ethnic groups: Kinh (Viet) 85.3%, Tay 1.9%, Thai 1.9%, Muong 1.5%, Khmer 1.4%, Mong 1.4%, Nung 1.1%, other 5.5% (2019 est.)
note: 54 ethnic groups are recognized by the Vietnamese Government

Languages: Vietnamese (official); English (often as a second language); some French, Chinese, and Khmer; mountain-area languages (including Mon-Khmer and Malayo-Polynesian)
major-language sample(s):
Dữ kiện thế giới, là nguồn thông tin cơ bản không thể thiếu. (Vietnamese)

Religions: Catholic 6.1%, Buddhist 5.8%, Protestant 1%, other 0.8%, none 86.3% (2019 est.)
note: most Vietnamese are culturally Buddhist

Demographic profile: When Vietnam was reunified in 1975, the country had a youthful age structure and a high fertility rate. The population growth rate slowed dramatically during the next 25 years, as fertility declined and infant mortality and life expectancy improved. The country's adoption of a one-or-two-child policy in 1988 led to increased rates of contraception and abortion. The total fertility rate dropped rapidly from nearly 5 in 1979 to 2.1 or replacement level in 1990, and at 1.8 is below replacement level today. Fertility is higher in the more rural central highlands and northern uplands, which are inhabited primarily by poorer ethnic minorities, and is lower among the majority Kinh, ethnic Chinese, and a few other ethnic groups, particularly in urban centers. With more than two-thirds of the population of working age (15-64), Vietnam has the potential to reap a demographic dividend for approximately three decades (between 2010 and 2040). However, its ability to do so will depend on improving the quality of education and training for its workforce and creating jobs. The Vietnamese Government is also considering changes to the country's population policy because if the country's fertility rate remains below replacement level, it could lead to a worker shortage in the future.

Vietnam has experienced both internal migration and net emigration, both for humanitarian and economic reasons, for the last several decades. Internal migration – rural-rural and rural-urban, temporary and permanent – continues to be a means of coping with Vietnam's extreme weather and flooding. Although Vietnam's population is still mainly rural, increasing numbers of young men and women have been drawn to the country's urban centers where they are more likely to find steady jobs and higher pay in the growing industrial and service sectors.

The aftermath of the Vietnam War in 1975 resulted in an outpouring of approximately 1.6 million Vietnamese refugees over the next two decades. Between 1975 and 1997, programs such as the Orderly Departure Program and the Comprehensive Plan of Action resettled hundreds of thousands of Vietnamese refugees abroad, including the United States (880,000), China (260,000, mainly ethnic Chinese Hoa), Canada (160,000), Australia (155,000), and European countries (150,000).

In the 1980s, some Vietnamese students and workers began to migrate to allied communist countries, including the Soviet Union, Czechoslovakia, Bulgaria, and East Germany. The vast majority returned home following the fall of communism in Eastern Europe in the early 1990s. Since that time, Vietnamese labor migrants instead started to pursue opportunities in Asia and the Middle East. They often perform low-skilled jobs under harsh conditions for low pay and are vulnerable to forced labor, including debt bondage to the private brokers who arrange the work contracts. Despite Vietnam's current labor surplus, the country has in recent years attracted some foreign workers, mainly from China and other Asian countries.

Age structure: *0-14 years:* 23.2% (male 12,953,719/female 11,579,690)
15-64 years: 68.5% (male 36,591,845/female 35,887,201)
65 years and over: 8.3% (2024 est.) (male 3,563,611/female 5,182,909)

Dependency ratios: *total dependency ratio:* 45.6
youth dependency ratio: 32.8
elderly dependency ratio: 12.7
potential support ratio: 7.8 (2021 est.)

Median age: *total:* 33.1 years (2024 est.)
male: 32 years
female: 34.2 years
comparison ranking: total 113

Population growth rate: 0.89% (2024 est.)
comparison ranking: 102

Birth rate: 14.9 births/1,000 population (2024 est.)
comparison ranking: 111

Death rate: 5.8 deaths/1,000 population (2024 est.)
comparison ranking: 165

Net migration rate: -0.2 migrant(s)/1,000 population (2024 est.)
comparison ranking: 106

Population distribution: though it has one of the highest population densities in the world, the population is not evenly dispersed; clustering is heaviest along the South China Sea and Gulf of Tonkin, with the Mekong Delta (in the south) and the Red River Valley (in the north) having the largest concentrations of people

Urbanization: *urban population:* 39.5% of total population (2023)
rate of urbanization: 2.7% annual rate of change (2020-25 est.)

Major urban areas - population: 9.321 million Ho Chi Minh City, 5.253 million HANOI (capital), 1.865 million Can Tho, 1.423 million Hai Phong, 1.221 million Da Nang, 1.111 million Bien Hoa (2023)

Sex ratio: *at birth:* 1.1 male(s)/female
0-14 years: 1.12 male(s)/female
15-64 years: 1.02 male(s)/female
65 years and over: 0.69 male(s)/female
total population: 1.01 male(s)/female (2024 est.)

Maternal mortality ratio: 124 deaths/100,000 live births (2020 est.)
comparison ranking: 62

Infant mortality rate: *total:* 14.1 deaths/1,000 live births (2024 est.)
male: 14.4 deaths/1,000 live births
female: 13.7 deaths/1,000 live births
comparison ranking: total 99

Life expectancy at birth: *total population:* 76.1 years (2024 est.)
male: 73.5 years
female: 78.9 years
comparison ranking: total population 115

Total fertility rate: 2.03 children born/woman (2024 est.)
comparison ranking: 102

Gross reproduction rate: 0.96 (2024 est.)

Contraceptive prevalence rate: 72.8% (2020)

Drinking water source: *improved: urban:* 99.2% of population
rural: 95.5% of population
total: 96.9% of population
unimproved: urban: 0.8% of population
rural: 4.5% of population

total: 3.1% of population (2020 est.)

Current health expenditure: 4.7% of GDP (2020)

Physician density: 0.83 physicians/1,000 population (2016)

Hospital bed density: 3.2 beds/1,000 population (2013)

Sanitation facility access: *improved: urban:* 98.7% of population
rural: 90% of population
total: 93.3% of population
unimproved: urban: 1.3% of population
rural: 10% of population
total: 6.7% of population (2020 est.)

Obesity - adult prevalence rate: 2.1% (2016)
comparison ranking: 192

Alcohol consumption per capita: *total:* 3.41 liters of pure alcohol (2019 est.)
beer: 3.18 liters of pure alcohol (2019 est.)
wine: 0.02 liters of pure alcohol (2019 est.)
spirits: 0.21 liters of pure alcohol (2019 est.)
other alcohols: 0 liters of pure alcohol (2019 est.)
comparison ranking: total 105

Tobacco use: *total:* 24.8% (2020 est.)
male: 47.4% (2020 est.)
female: 2.2% (2020 est.)
comparison ranking: total 51

Children under the age of 5 years underweight: 11.6% (2020)
comparison ranking: 51

Currently married women (ages 15-49): 72.6% (2023 est.)

Child marriage: *women married by age 15:* 1.1%
women married by age 18: 14.6%
men married by age 18: 1.9% (2021 est.)

Education expenditures: 4.1% of GDP (2020 est.)
comparison ranking: 113

Literacy: *definition:* age 15 and over can read and write
total population: 95.8%
male: 97%
female: 94.6% (2019)

ENVIRONMENT

Environment - current issues: logging and slash-and-burn agricultural practices contribute to deforestation and soil degradation; water pollution and overfishing threaten marine life populations; groundwater contamination limits potable water supply; air pollution; growing urban industrialization and population migration are rapidly degrading environment in Hanoi and Ho Chi Minh City

Environment - international agreements: *party to:* Biodiversity, Climate Change, Climate Change-Kyoto Protocol, Climate Change-Paris Agreement, Comprehensive Nuclear Test Ban, Desertification, Endangered Species, Environmental Modification, Hazardous Wastes, Law of the Sea, Ozone Layer Protection, Ship Pollution, Tropical Timber 2006, Wetlands
signed, but not ratified: none of the selected agreements

Climate: tropical in south; monsoonal in north with hot, rainy season (May to September) and warm, dry season (October to March)

Urbanization: *urban population:* 39.5% of total population (2023)
rate of urbanization: 2.7% annual rate of change (2020-25 est.)

Revenue from forest resources: 1.49% of GDP (2018 est.)
comparison ranking: 43

Revenue from coal: 0.35% of GDP (2018 est.)
comparison ranking: 16

Air pollutants: *particulate matter emissions:* 20.89 micrograms per cubic meter (2019 est.)
carbon dioxide emissions: 192.67 megatons (2016 est.)
methane emissions: 110.4 megatons (2020 est.)

Waste and recycling: *municipal solid waste generated annually:* 9,570,300 tons (2011 est.)
municipal solid waste recycled annually: 2,201,169 tons (2014 est.)
percent of municipal solid waste recycled: 23% (2014 est.)

Major rivers (by length in km): Sông Tiên Giang (Mekong) river mouth (shared with China [s], Burma, Laos, Thailand, Cambodia) - 4,350 km; Pearl river source (shared with China [m]) - 2,200 km; Red river mouth (shared with China [s]) - 1,149 km
note – [s] after country name indicates river source; [m] after country name indicates river mouth

Major watersheds (area sq km): Pacific Ocean drainage: Mekong (805,604 sq km)

Total water withdrawal: *municipal:* 1.21 billion cubic meters (2020 est.)
industrial: 3.07 billion cubic meters (2020 est.)
agricultural: 77.75 billion cubic meters (2020 est.)

Total renewable water resources: 884.12 billion cubic meters (2020 est.)

Geoparks: *total global geoparks and regional networks:* 3
global geoparks and regional networks: Dak Nong; Dong Van Karst Plateau; Non nuoc Cao Bang (2023)

GOVERNMENT

Country name: *conventional long form:* Socialist Republic of Vietnam
conventional short form: Vietnam
local long form: Cong Hoa Xa Hoi Chu Nghia Viet Nam
local short form: Viet Nam
former: Democratic Republic of Vietnam (North Vietnam), Republic of Vietnam (South Vietnam)
abbreviation: SRV
etymology: "Viet nam" translates as "Viet south," where "Viet" is an ethnic self identification dating to a second century B.C. kingdom and "nam" refers to its location in relation to other Viet kingdoms

Government type: communist party-led state

Capital: *name:* Hanoi (Ha Noi)
geographic coordinates: 21 02 N, 105 51 E
time difference: UTC+7 (12 hours ahead of Washington, DC, during Standard Time)
etymology: the city has had many names in its history going back to A.D. 1010 when it first became the capital of imperial Vietnam; in 1831, it received its current name of Ha Noi, meaning "between the rivers," which refers to its geographic location

Administrative divisions: 58 provinces (tinh, singular and plural) and 5 municipalities (thanh pho, singular and plural)
provinces: An Giang, Bac Giang, Bac Kan, Bac Lieu, Bac Ninh, Ba Ria-Vung Tau, Ben Tre, Binh Dinh, Binh Duong, Binh Phuoc, Binh Thuan, Ca Mau, Cao Bang, Dak Lak, Dak Nong, Dien Bien, Dong Nai, Dong Thap, Gia Lai, Ha Giang, Ha Nam, Ha Tinh, Hai Duong, Hau Giang, Hoa Binh, Hung Yen, Khanh Hoa, Kien Giang, Kon Tum, Lai Chau, Lam Dong, Lang Son, Lao Cai, Long An, Nam Dinh, Nghe An, Ninh Binh, Ninh Thuan, Phu Tho, Phu Yen, Quang Binh, Quang Nam, Quang Ngai, Quang Ninh, Quang Tri, Soc Trang, Son La, Tay Ninh, Thai Binh, Thai Nguyen, Thanh Hoa, Thua Thien-Hue, Tien Giang, Tra Vinh, Tuyen Quang, Vinh Long, Vinh Phuc, Yen Bai
municipalities: Can Tho, Da Nang, Ha Noi (Hanoi), Hai Phong, Ho Chi Minh City (Saigon)

Independence: 2 September 1945 (from France)

National holiday: Independence Day (National Day), 2 September (1945)

Legal system: civil law system; note - the civil code of 2005 reflects a European-style civil law

Constitution: *history:* several previous; latest adopted 28 November 2013, effective 1 January 2014
amendments: proposed by the president, by the National Assembly's Standing Committee, or by at least two thirds of the National Assembly membership; a decision to draft an amendment requires approval by at least a two-thirds majority vote of the Assembly membership, followed by the formation of a constitutional drafting committee to write a draft and collect citizens' opinions; passage requires at least two-thirds majority of the Assembly membership; the Assembly can opt to conduct a referendum

International law organization participation: has not submitted an ICJ jurisdiction declaration; non-party state to the ICCt

Citizenship: *citizenship by birth:* no
citizenship by descent only: at least one parent must be a citizen of Vietnam
dual citizenship recognized: no
residency requirement for naturalization: 5 years

Suffrage: 18 years of age; universal

Executive branch: *chief of state:* President Luong CUONG (since 21 Oct 2024)
head of government: Prime Minister Pham Minh CHINH (since 26 July 2021)
cabinet: Cabinet proposed by the prime minister, confirmed by the National Assembly, and appointed by the president
elections/appointments: president indirectly elected by the National Assembly from among its members for a single 5- year term; prime minister recommended by the president and confirmed by the National Assembly; deputy prime ministers confirmed by the National Assembly and appointed by the president
note: in August 2024, To LAM was elected general secretary of the Central Committee of the Communist Party of Vietnam, the country's most powerful position

Legislative branch: *description:* unicameral National Assembly or Quoc Hoi (500 seats; members directly elected in multi-seat constituencies by absolute majority vote; members serve 5-year terms)
elections: last held on 23 May 2021 (next to be held in spring 2026)
election results: percent of vote by party - CPV 97.2%, 2.8% non-party; seats by party - CPV 486, non-party 14;
composition- 342 men, 151 women, percentage women 30.6%

Judicial branch: *highest court(s):* Supreme People's Court (consists of the chief justice and 13 judges)

judge selection and term of office: chief justice elected by the National Assembly upon the recommendation of the president for a 5-year, renewable term; deputy chief justice appointed by the president from among the judges for a 5- year term; judges appointed by the president and confirmed by the National Assembly for 5-year terms
subordinate courts: High Courts (administrative, civil, criminal, economic, labor, family, juvenile); provincial courts; district courts; Military Court; note - the National Assembly Standing Committee can establish special tribunals upon the recommendation of the chief justice

Political parties: Communist Party of Vietnam or CPV
note: other parties proscribed

International organization participation: ADB, APEC, ARF, ASEAN, CICA, CP, EAS, FAO, G-77, IAEA, IBRD, ICAO, ICC (NGOs), ICRM, IDA, IFAD, IFC, IFRCS, ILO, IMF, IMO, IMSO, Interpol, IOC, IOM, IPU, ISO, ITSO, ITU, MIGA, NAM, OIF, OPCW, PCA, UN, UNCTAD, UNESCO, UNHRC, UNIDO, UNOOSA, UNWTO, UPU, WCO, WFTU (NGOs), WHO, WIPO, WMO, WTO (2024)

Diplomatic representation in the US: *chief of mission:* Ambassador Nguyen Quoc DZUNG (since 19 April 2022)
chancery: 1233 20th Street NW, Suite 400, Washington, DC 20036
telephone: [1] (202) 861-0737
FAX: [1] (202) 861-0917
email address and website:
vanphong@vietnamembassy.us
http://vietnamembassy-usa.org/
consulate(s) general: Houston, San Francisco
consulate(s): New York

Diplomatic representation from the US: *chief of mission:* Ambassador Marc KNAPPER (since 11 February 2022)
embassy: 7 Lang Ha Street, Hanoi
mailing address: 4550 Hanoi Place, Washington, DC 20521-4550
telephone: [84] (24) 3850-5000
FAX: [84] (24) 3850-5010
email address and website:
ACShanoi@state.gov
https://vn.usembassy.gov/
consulate(s) general: Ho Chi Minh City

Flag description: red field with a large yellow five-pointed star in the center; red symbolizes revolution and blood, the five-pointed star represents the five elements of the populace - peasants, workers, intellectuals, traders, and soldiers - that unite to build socialism

National symbol(s): yellow, five-pointed star on red field; lotus blossom; national colors: red, yellow

National anthem: *name:* "Tien quan ca" (The Song of the Marching Troops)
lyrics/music: Nguyen Van CAO
note: adopted as the national anthem of the Democratic Republic of Vietnam in 1945; it became the national anthem of the unified Socialist Republic of Vietnam in 1976; although it consists of two verses, only the first is used as the official anthem

National heritage: *total World Heritage Sites:* 8 (5 cultural, 2 natural, 1 mixed)
selected World Heritage Site locales: Complex of Hué Monuments (c); Ha Long Bay (n); Hoi An Ancient Town (c); My Son Sanctuary (c); Phong Nha-Ke Bang National Park (n); Imperial Citadel of Thang Long - Hanoi (c); Citadel of the Ho Dynasty (c); Trang An Landscape Complex (m)

ECONOMY

Economic overview: lower middle-income socialist East Asian economy; rapid economic growth since Đổi Mới reforms; strong investment and productivity growth; tourism and manufacturing hub; TPP signatory; declining poverty aside from ethnic minorities; systemic corruption

Real GDP (purchasing power parity): $1.354 trillion (2023 est.)
$1.289 trillion (2022 est.)
$1.192 trillion (2021 est.)
note: data in 2021 dollars
comparison ranking: 24

Real GDP growth rate: 5.05% (2023 est.)
8.12% (2022 est.)
2.55% (2021 est.)
note: annual GDP % growth based on constant local currency
comparison ranking: 54

Real GDP per capita: $13,700 (2023 est.)
$13,100 (2022 est.)
$12,200 (2021 est.)
note: data in 2021 dollars
comparison ranking: 130

GDP (official exchange rate): $429.717 billion (2023 est.)
note: data in current dollars at official exchange rate

Inflation rate (consumer prices): 3.25% (2023 est.)
3.16% (2022 est.)
1.83% (2021 est.)
note: annual % change based on consumer prices
comparison ranking: 62

Credit ratings: Fitch rating: BB (2018)

Moody's rating: Ba3 (2018)

Standard & Poors rating: BB (2019)
note: The year refers to the year in which the current credit rating was first obtained.

GDP - composition, by sector of origin: *agriculture:* 12% (2023 est.)
industry: 37.1% (2023 est.)
services: 42.5% (2023 est.)
note: figures may not total 100% due to non-allocated consumption not captured in sector-reported data
comparison rankings: services 181; industry 39; agriculture 67

GDP - composition, by end use: *household consumption:* 54.8% (2022 est.)
government consumption: 8.9% (2022 est.)
investment in fixed capital: 30.8% (2022 est.)
investment in inventories: 1.8% (2022 est.)
exports of goods and services: 93.8% (2022 est.)
imports of goods and services: -90% (2022 est.)
note: figures may not total 100% due to rounding or gaps in data collection

Agricultural products: rice, vegetables, sugarcane, cassava, maize, pork, fruits, bananas, coffee, coconuts (2022)
note: top ten agricultural products based on tonnage

Industries: food processing, garments, shoes, machine-building; mining, coal, steel; cement, chemical fertilizer, glass, tires, oil, mobile phones

Industrial production growth rate: 3.74% (2023 est.)
note: annual % change in industrial value added based on constant local currency
comparison ranking: 86

Labor force: 56.149 million (2023 est.)
note: number of people ages 15 or older who are employed or seeking work
comparison ranking: 13

Unemployment rate: 1.6% (2023 est.)
1.54% (2022 est.)
2.39% (2021 est.)
note: % of labor force seeking employment
comparison ranking: 17

Youth unemployment rate (ages 15-24): *total:* 6.2% (2023 est.)
male: 6.5% (2023 est.)
female: 5.9% (2023 est.)
note: % of labor force ages 15-24 seeking employment
comparison ranking: total 165

Population below poverty line: 4.8% (2020 est.)
note: % of population with income below national poverty line

Gini Index coefficient - distribution of family income: 36.1 (2022 est.)
note: index (0-100) of income distribution; higher values represent greater inequality
comparison ranking: 68

Average household expenditures: *on food:* 31.1% of household expenditures (2022 est.)
on alcohol and tobacco: 2.1% of household expenditures (2022 est.)

Household income or consumption by percentage share: *lowest 10%:* 2.6% (2022 est.)
highest 10%: 28.1% (2022 est.)
note: % share of income accruing to lowest and highest 10% of population

Remittances: 3.26% of GDP (2023 est.)
3.22% of GDP (2022 est.)
3.47% of GDP (2021 est.)
note: personal transfers and compensation between resident and non-resident individuals/households/entities

Budget: *revenues:* $42.247 billion (2014 est.)
expenditures: $38.025 billion (2014 est.)
note: central government revenues and expenses (excluding grants/extrabudgetary units/social security funds) converted to US dollars at average official exchange rate for year indicated

Public debt: 58.5% of GDP (2017 est.)
note: official data; data cover general government debt and include debt instruments issued (or owned) by government entities other than the treasury; the data include treasury debt held by foreign entities; the data include debt issued by subnational entities, as well as intragovernmental debt; intragovernmental debt consists of treasury borrowings from surpluses in the social funds, such as for retirement, medical care, and unemployment; debt instruments for the social funds are not sold at public auctions
comparison ranking: 83

Taxes and other revenues: 24.8% (of GDP) (2017 est.)
comparison ranking: 49

Current account balance: $25.09 billion (2023 est.)
$1.402 billion (2022 est.)
-$4.628 billion (2021 est.)
note: balance of payments - net trade and primary/secondary income in current dollars
comparison ranking: 21

Exports: $374.265 billion (2023 est.)

$385.241 billion (2022 est.)
$340.126 billion (2021 est.)
note: balance of payments - exports of goods and services in current dollars
comparison ranking: 24

Exports - partners: US 29%, China 15%, South Korea 6%, Japan 6%, Hong Kong 3% (2022)
note: top five export partners based on percentage share of exports

Exports - commodities: broadcasting equipment, garments, telephones, integrated circuits, machine parts (2022)
note: top five export commodities based on value in dollars

Imports: $339.767 billion (2023 est.)
$369.746 billion (2022 est.)
$338.327 billion (2021 est.)
note: balance of payments - imports of goods and services in current dollars
comparison ranking: 24

Imports - partners: China 38%, South Korea 17%, Japan 5%, Taiwan 4%, Thailand 4% (2022)
note: top five import partners based on percentage share of imports

Imports - commodities: integrated circuits, broadcasting equipment, refined petroleum, telephones, fabric (2022)
note: top five import commodities based on value in dollars

Reserves of foreign exchange and gold: $86.54 billion (2022 est.)
$109.371 billion (2021 est.)
$94.834 billion (2020 est.)
note: holdings of gold (year-end prices)/foreign exchange/special drawing rights in current dollars
comparison ranking: 30

Exchange rates: dong (VND) per US dollar -

Exchange rates: 23,787.319 (2023 est.)
23,271.213 (2022 est.)
23,159.783 (2021 est.)
23,208.368 (2020 est.)
23,050.242 (2019 est.)

ENERGY

Electricity access: *electrification - total population:* 100% (2022 est.)

Electricity: *installed generating capacity:* 85.04 million kW (2022 est.)
consumption: 251.549 billion kWh (2022 est.)
exports: 628.664 million kWh (2022 est.)
imports: 1.515 billion kWh (2022 est.)
transmission/distribution losses: 17.084 billion kWh (2022 est.)
comparison rankings: transmission/distribution losses 187; imports 68; exports 73; consumption 19; installed generating capacity 17

Electricity generation sources: *fossil fuels:* 56.8% of total installed capacity (2022 est.)
solar: 11.2% of total installed capacity (2022 est.)
wind: 1.3% of total installed capacity (2022 est.)
hydroelectricity: 29.6% of total installed capacity (2022 est.)
biomass and waste: 1.1% of total installed capacity (2022 est.)

Coal: *production:* 43.614 million metric tons (2022 est.)
consumption: 83.116 million metric tons (2022 est.)
exports: 1.032 million metric tons (2022 est.)
imports: 40.534 million metric tons (2022 est.)
proven reserves: 3.36 billion metric tons (2022 est.)

Petroleum: *total petroleum production:* 187,000 bbl/day (2023 est.)
refined petroleum consumption: 494,000 bbl/day (2022 est.)
crude oil estimated reserves: 4.4 billion barrels (2021 est.)

Natural gas: *production:* 7.676 billion cubic meters (2022 est.)
consumption: 7.676 billion cubic meters (2022 est.)
proven reserves: 699.426 billion cubic meters (2021 est.)

Carbon dioxide emissions: 297.826 million metric tonnes of CO2 (2022 est.)
from coal and metallurgical coke: 219.167 million metric tonnes of CO2 (2022 est.)
from petroleum and other liquids: 63.759 million metric tonnes of CO2 (2022 est.)
from consumed natural gas: 14.9 million metric tonnes of CO2 (2022 est.)
comparison ranking: total emissions 22

Energy consumption per capita: 39.117 million Btu/person (2022 est.)
comparison ranking: 103

COMMUNICATIONS

Telephones - fixed lines: *total subscriptions:* 2.391 million (2022 est.)
subscriptions per 100 inhabitants: 2 (2022 est.)
comparison ranking: total subscriptions 48

Telephones - mobile cellular: *total subscriptions:* 137.412 million (2022 est.)
subscriptions per 100 inhabitants: 140 (2022 est.)
comparison ranking: total subscriptions 13

Telecommunication systems: *general assessment:* even with Covid-19 pandemic-related mobility restrictions in place, Vietnam's economy has continued to outperform the rest of the region in 2020 and 2021; the telecom sector essentially spent most of this period in a holding pattern, focusing on maintaining service throughout the crisis while preparing for some major changes to come in the mobile market in 2022; both fixed-line telephony and mobile have experienced small drops in subscriber numbers since the start of the pandemic, but the similarities between the two markets end there; fixed-line teledensity continued its downwards trajectory towards virtual oblivion, with just 3% penetration (around 3 million subscribers) at the start of 2021; the mobile market has lost about the same number of subscribers since the end of 2019, but has been sitting on much higher penetration levels around 130% for many years; growth is expected to kick in again in 2022 following the anticipated launch of commercial 5G mobile services along with a range of government-led schemes to move consumers completely off 2G and 3G; one example is the planned redistribution of GSM/3G bandwidth to LTE; in addition to propelling Vietnam into having one of the most advanced mobile markets in the world, this should also spur on the mobile broadband segment; with a penetration level of just over 70%, mobile broadband has considerable room to grow; increasing economic prosperity coupled with the latest smartphone technology and networks should see mobile broadband underwriting the country's telecommunications sector for at least the next few years; this report includes the regulator's market data to July 2021, telcos' financial and operating data updates to June 2021, Telecom Maturity Index charts and analyses, assessment of the global impact of Covid-19 on the telecoms sector, and other recent market developments (2021)
domestic: fixed-line is 3 per 100 and mobile-cellular is 140 per 100 (2021)
international: country code - 84; landing points for the SeaMeWe-3, APG, SJC2, AAE-1, AAG and the TGN-IA submarine cable system providing connectivity to Europe, Africa, the Middle East, Asia, Southeast Asia, Australia, and the US; telecom satellite earth stations - 2, (Vinasat 1 and Vinasat 2) (Indian Ocean region) (2023)

Broadcast media: government controls all broadcast media exercising oversight through the Ministry of Information and Communication (MIC); government-controlled national TV provider, Vietnam Television (VTV), operates a network of several channels with regional broadcasting centers; programming is relayed nationwide via a network of provincial and municipal TV stations; law limits access to satellite TV but many households are able to access foreign programming via home satellite equipment; government-controlled Voice of Vietnam, the national radio broadcaster, broadcasts on several channels and is repeated on AM, FM, and shortwave stations throughout Vietnam (2018)

Internet country code: .vn

Internet users: *total:* 71.78 million (2021 est.)
percent of population: 74% (2021 est.)
comparison ranking: total 12

Broadband - fixed subscriptions: *total:* 16,699,249 (2020 est.)
subscriptions per 100 inhabitants: 17 (2020 est.)
comparison ranking: total 14

TRANSPORTATION

National air transport system: *number of registered air carriers:* 5 (2020)
inventory of registered aircraft operated by air carriers: 224
annual passenger traffic on registered air carriers: 47,049,671 (2018)
annual freight traffic on registered air carriers: 481.37 million (2018) mt-km

Civil aircraft registration country code prefix: VN

Airports: 42 (2024)
comparison ranking: 98

Heliports: 25 (2024)

Pipelines: 72 km condensate, 398 km condensate/gas, 955 km gas, 128 km oil, 33 km oil/gas/water, 206 km refined products, 13 km water (2013)

Railways: *total:* 2,600 km (2014)
standard gauge: 178 km (2014) 1.435-m gauge; 253 km mixed gauge
narrow gauge: 2,169 km (2014) 1.000-m gauge
comparison ranking: total 64

Roadways: *total:* 195,468 km
paved: 148,338 km
unpaved: 47,130 km (2013)
comparison ranking: total 27

Waterways: 47,130 km (2011) (30,831 km weight under 50 tons)
comparison ranking: 3

Merchant marine: *total:* 1,973 (2022)
by type: bulk carrier 117, container ship 45, general cargo 1,176, oil tanker 134, other 501
comparison ranking: total 13

Ports: *total ports:* 16 (2024)

large: 0
medium: 1
small: 6
very small: 9
ports with oil terminals: 12
key ports: Da Nang, Hai Phong, Nghe Tinh, Nha Trang, Thanh Ho Chi Minh, Vinh Cam Ranh, Vung Tau

MILITARY AND SECURITY

Military and security forces: People's Army of Vietnam (PAVN; aka Vietnam People's Army, VPA): Ground Forces, Navy (includes naval infantry), Air Defense Force, Border Defense Force, Vietnam Coast Guard
Vietnam People's Ministry of Public Security; Vietnam Civil Defense Force (2024)
note 1: the People's Public Security Ministry is responsible for internal security and controls the national police, a special national security investigative agency, and other internal security units, including specialized riot police regiments
note 2: the Vietnam Coast Guard was established in 1998 as the Vietnam Marine Police and renamed in 2013; Vietnam officially established a maritime self-defense force (civilian militia) in 2010 after the National Assembly passed the Law on Militia and Self-Defense Forces in 2009; the Vietnam Department of Fisheries Resources Surveillance (DFIRES; under the Ministry of Agriculture and Rural Development), established in 2013, is responsible for fisheries enforcement, aquatic conservation roles, and is designated as Vietnam's standing agency for combating illegal, unregulated, and unreported fishing; it is armed, allowed to use force if necessary, and works in tandem with the Vietnam Coast Guard

Military expenditures: 1.8% of GDP (2023 est.)
2.3% of GDP (2022 est.)
2.3% of GDP (2021 est.)
2.4% of GDP (2020 est.)
2.3% of GDP (2019 est.)
comparison ranking: 76

Military and security service personnel strengths: information is limited and varied; estimated 450,000 active-duty troops; estimated 40,000 Border Defense Force and Coast Guard (2023)

Military equipment inventories and acquisitions: the PAVN is armed largely with weapons and equipment from Russia and the former Soviet Union; in recent years, Russia has remained the leading supplier of newer PAVN military equipment, but Vietnam has diversified arms purchases to include more than a dozen other countries including Belarus, Israel, the Netherlands, South Korea, and the US; Vietnam has a limited domestic defense industry (2023)

Military service age and obligation: 18-27 years of age for compulsory and voluntary military service for men and women (in practice only men are drafted); service obligation is between 24 (Army, Air Defense) and 36 (Navy and Air Force) months (2023)

Military deployments: 190 Abyei/South Sudan/Sudan (UNISFA) (2024)

Military - note: since withdrawing its military occupation forces from Cambodia in the late 1980s and the end of Soviet aid in 1991, Vietnam has practiced a non-aligned foreign policy that emphasizes friendly ties with all members of the international community; Hanoi adheres to a security doctrine called the "Four Nos" (no alliances, no siding with one country against another, no foreign bases, and no using force in international relations); despite longstanding tensions with Beijing over maritime boundaries in the South China Sea, Vietnam puts a priority on stable relations with China, given its proximity, size, and status as Vietnam's largest trading partner
the PAVN is one of the region's largest militaries and has participated in numerous conflicts since its founding in the mid-1940s, including the First (1946-54) and Second (1955-1975) Indochina Wars, the Cambodian-Vietnamese War (1978-1989), and the Sino-Vietnamese War (1979); the PAVN's current missions include protecting the country's independence, sovereignty, territorial integrity, and national interests; in recent years, it has placed additional emphasis on protecting the country's maritime economy and sovereignty in the South China Sea, including strengthening air and naval capabilities; the PAVN also assists with natural disasters and is involved in economic projects, such as electrical infrastructure, oil and gas services, hydroelectric projects, aviation and seaport services, telecommunications, and the shipbuilding industry, while military-owned factories and enterprises produce weapons and equipment
the PAVN is the military arm of the ruling Communist Party of Vietnam (CPV) and responsible to the Central Military Commission (CMC), the highest party organ on military policy; the CMC is led by the CPV General Secretary (2024)

SPACE

Space agency/agencies: Vietnam National Space Center (VNSC; established 2011; formerly known as the Vietnam National Satellite Center); Space Technology Institute (STI; established 2006); both the VNSC and the STI operate under the Vietnamese Academy of Science and Technology (VAST); Ministry of Science and Technology (2024)

Space program overview: has a growing space program focused on acquiring, operating, and exploiting satellites, as well as expanding domestic capabilities in satellites and associated sub-system production, space sciences, and technology applications; builds and operates communications and remote sensing satellites; conducting research and development on space science and applied space technologies, such as advanced optics and space data exploitation; has worked closely with Japan on its space program since inception; cooperation has included funding, loans, training, technical expertise, and data sharing; has also established relationships with the space agencies or commercial space sectors of some European countries (such as France), India, and the US (2024)
note: further details about the key activities, programs, and milestones of the country's space program, as well as government spending estimates on the space sector, appear in the Space Programs reference guide

TRANSNATIONAL ISSUES

Refugees and internally displaced persons: *stateless persons:* 35,475 (2022); note - Vietnam's stateless ethnic Chinese Cambodian population dates to the 1970s when thousands of Cambodians fled to Vietnam to escape the Khmer Rouge and were no longer recognized as Cambodian citizens; Vietnamese women who gave up their citizenship to marry foreign men have found themselves stateless after divorcing and returning home to Vietnam; the government addressed this problem in 2009, and Vietnamese women are beginning to reclaim their citizenship

Illicit drugs: a transshipment and destination country for all types of illegal drugs; most transshipments destined for other Asian countries and not the United States; heroin transits from Thailand, Laos, and Burma for domestic use and shipping to r countries in Southeast Asia, Oceania, China and Taiwan; methamphetamine and amphetamine type stimulants from Burma locally consumed and shipped; South American cocaine locally consumed and distributed to Southeast Asia and Oceania

VIRGIN ISLANDS

INTRODUCTION

Background: The Danes secured control over the southern Virgin Islands of Saint Thomas, Saint John, and Saint Croix during the 17th and early 18th centuries. Sugarcane, produced by African slave labor, drove the islands' economy during the 18th and early 19th centuries. In 1917, the US purchased the Danish holdings, which had been in economic decline since the abolition of slavery in 1848. In 2017, Hurricane Irma passed over the northern Virgin Islands of Saint Thomas and Saint John and inflicted severe damage to structures, roads, the airport on Saint Thomas, communications, and electricity. Less than two weeks later, Hurricane Maria passed over the island of Saint Croix in the southern Virgin Islands, inflicting considerable damage with heavy winds and flooding rains.

GEOGRAPHY

Location: Caribbean, islands between the Caribbean Sea and the North Atlantic Ocean, east of Puerto Rico

Geographic coordinates: 18 20 N, 64 50 W

Map references: Central America and the Caribbean

Area: *total:* 1,910 sq km

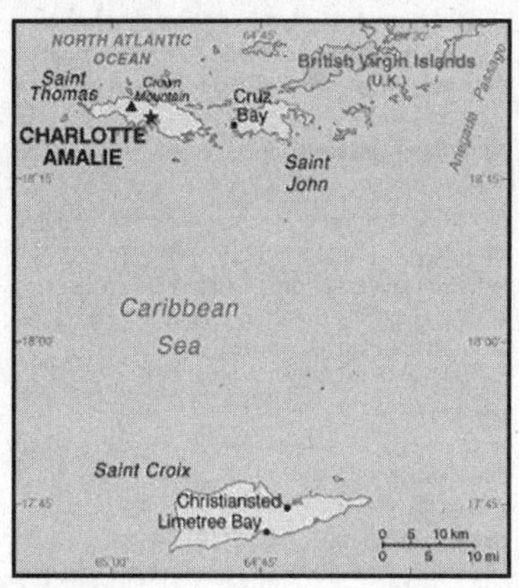

land: 346 sq km
water: 1,564 sq km
comparison ranking: total 181

Area - comparative: twice the size of Washington, DC

Land boundaries: *total:* 0 km

Coastline: 188 km

Maritime claims: *territorial sea:* 12 nm
exclusive economic zone: 200 nm

Climate: subtropical, tempered by easterly trade winds, relatively low humidity, little seasonal temperature variation; rainy season September to November

Terrain: mostly hilly to rugged and mountainous with little flat land

Elevation: *highest point:* Crown Mountain 474 m
lowest point: Caribbean Sea 0 m

Natural resources: pleasant climate, beaches foster tourism

Land use: *agricultural land:* 11.5% (2018 est.)
arable land: 2.9% (2018 est.)
permanent crops: 2.9% (2018 est.)
permanent pasture: 5.7% (2018 est.)
forest: 57.4% (2018 est.)
other: 31.1% (2018 est.)

Irrigated land: 1 sq km (2012)

Population distribution: while overall population density throughout the islands is relatively low, concentrations appear around Charlotte Amalie on St. Thomas and Christiansted on St. Croix

Natural hazards: several hurricanes in recent years; frequent and severe droughts and floods; occasional earthquakes

Geography - note: important location along the Anegada Passage – a key shipping lane for the Panama Canal; Saint Thomas has one of the best natural deepwater harbors in the Caribbean

PEOPLE AND SOCIETY

Population: *total:* 104,377
male: 49,520
female: 54,857 (2024 est.)
comparison rankings: female 191; male 195; total 192

Nationality: *noun:* Virgin Islander(s) (US citizens)
adjective: Virgin Islander

Ethnic groups: African-American or African descent 71.4%, White 13.3%, Indigenous 0.4%, Native Hawaiian and other Pacific Islander 0.1%, other 6.3%, mixed 7.5% (2020 est.)
note: 18.4% self-identify as Latino

Languages: English 71.6%, Spanish or Spanish Creole 17.2%, French or French Creole 8.6%, other 2.5% (2010 est.)

Religions: Protestant 65.5%, Roman Catholic 27.1%, other Christians 2.2%, other 1.5%, none 3.7% (2010 est.)

Age structure: *0-14 years:* 18.7% (male 9,983/female 9,547)
15-64 years: 59.8% (male 29,519/female 32,899)
65 years and over: 21.5% (2024 est.) (male 10,018/female 12,411)

Dependency ratios: *total dependency ratio:* 64.6
youth dependency ratio: 32
elderly dependency ratio: 34
potential support ratio: 3 (2021 est.)

Median age: *total:* 43 years (2024 est.)
male: 42.1 years
female: 43.9 years
comparison ranking: total 37

Population growth rate: -0.54% (2024 est.)
comparison ranking: 223

Birth rate: 11.1 births/1,000 population (2024 est.)
comparison ranking: 162

Death rate: 9.2 deaths/1,000 population (2024 est.)
comparison ranking: 52

Net migration rate: -7.3 migrant(s)/1,000 population (2024 est.)
comparison ranking: 218

Population distribution: while overall population density throughout the islands is relatively low, concentrations appear around Charlotte Amalie on St. Thomas and Christiansted on St. Croix

Urbanization: *urban population:* 96.2% of total population (2023)
rate of urbanization: -0.11% annual rate of change (2020-25 est.)

Major urban areas - population: 52,000 CHARLOTTE AMALIE (capital) (2018)

Sex ratio: *at birth:* 1.06 male(s)/female
0-14 years: 1.05 male(s)/female
15-64 years: 0.9 male(s)/female
65 years and over: 0.81 male(s)/female
total population: 0.9 male(s)/female (2024 est.)

Infant mortality rate: *total:* 7.3 deaths/1,000 live births (2024 est.)
male: 8.3 deaths/1,000 live births
female: 6.3 deaths/1,000 live births
comparison ranking: total 153

Life expectancy at birth: *total population:* 80.7 years (2024 est.)
male: 77.6 years
female: 84.1 years
comparison ranking: total population 51

Total fertility rate: 1.97 children born/woman (2024 est.)
comparison ranking: 108

Gross reproduction rate: 0.95 (2024 est.)

Drinking water source: *improved:*
total: 98.7% of population
unimproved:
total: 1.3% of population (2020 est.)

Sanitation facility access: *improved:*
total: 99.4% of population
unimproved:
total: 0.6% of population (2020 est.)

Currently married women (ages 15-49): 27.4% (2023)

ENVIRONMENT

Environment - current issues: lack of natural freshwater resources; protection of coral reefs; solid waste management; coastal development; increased boating and overfishing

Climate: subtropical, tempered by easterly trade winds, relatively low humidity, little seasonal temperature variation; rainy season September to November

Urbanization: *urban population:* 96.2% of total population (2023)
rate of urbanization: -0.11% annual rate of change (2020-25 est.)

Revenue from forest resources: 0% of GDP (2017 est.)
comparison ranking: 203

Waste and recycling: *municipal solid waste generated annually:* 146,500 tons (2012 est.)

GOVERNMENT

Country name: *conventional long form:* none
conventional short form: Virgin Islands
former: Danish West Indies
abbreviation: VI
etymology: the myriad islets, cays, and rocks surrounding the major islands reminded Christopher COLUMBUS in 1493 of Saint Ursula and her 11,000 virgin followers (Santa Ursula y las Once Mil Virgenes), which over time shortened to the Virgins (las Virgenes)

Government type: unincorporated organized territory of the US with local self-government; republican form of territorial government with separate executive, legislative, and judicial branches

Dependency status: unincorporated organized territory of the US with policy relations between the Virgin Islands and the US Federal Government under the jurisdiction of the Office of Insular Affairs, US Department of the Interior, Washington, DC

Capital: *name:* Charlotte Amalie
geographic coordinates: 18 21 N, 64 56 W
time difference: UTC-4 (1 hour ahead of Washington, DC, during Standard Time)
etymology: originally called Taphus in Danish - meaning "tap house" or "beer house" because of its many beer halls - the town received a more dignified name in 1691 when it was named Charlotte Amalie in honor of Danish King CHRISTIAN V's wife, Charlotte AMALIE of Hesse-Kassel (1650–1714)

Administrative divisions: none (territory of the US); there are no first-order administrative divisions as defined by the US Government, but there are 3 islands at the second order; Saint Croix, Saint John, Saint Thomas

Independence: none (territory of the US)

National holiday: Transfer Day (from Denmark to the US), 31 March (1917)

Legal system: US common law

Constitution: *history:* 22 July 1954 - the Revised Organic Act of the Virgin Islands functions as a constitution for this US territory
amendments: amended several times, last in 2012

Citizenship: see United States

Suffrage: 18 years of age; universal; note - island residents are US citizens but do not vote in US presidential elections

Executive branch: *chief of state:* President Joseph R. BIDEN, Jr. (since 20 January 2021)
head of government: Governor Albert BRYAN, Jr. (since 7 January 2019)
cabinet: Territorial Cabinet appointed by the governor and confirmed by the Senate
elections/appointments: president and vice president indirectly elected on the same ballot by an Electoral College of 'electors' chosen from each state; president and vice president serve a 4-year term (eligible for a second term); under the US Constitution, residents of the Virgin Islands do not vote in elections for US president and vice president; however, they may vote in the Democratic and Republican presidential primary elections; governor and lieutenant governor directly elected on the same ballot by absolute majority vote in 2 rounds if needed for a 4-year term (eligible for a second term); election last held on 8 November 2022 (next to be held in November 2026)
election results:
2022: Albert BRYAN, Jr. reelected governor; percent of vote - Albert BRYAN, Jr. (Democratic Party) 56%, Kurt VIALET (independent) 38%
2018: Albert BRYAN, Jr. elected governor in the second round; percent of vote in first round - Albert BRYAN, Jr. (Democratic Party) 38.1%, Kenneth MAPP (independent) 33.5%, Adlah "Foncie" DONASTORG, Jr. (independent) 16.5%, other 11.9%; percent of vote in second round- Albert BRYAN, Jr. (Democratic Party) 54.5%, Kenneth MAPP (independent) 45.2%, other 0.3%

Legislative branch: *description:* unicameral Legislature of the Virgin Islands (15 seats; senators directly elected in single- and multi-seat constituencies by simple majority popular vote to serve 2-year terms)
the Virgin Islands directly elects 1 delegate to the US House of Representatives by simple majority vote to serve a 2-year term
elections: Legislature of the Virgin Islands last held on 8 November 2022 (next to be held on 5 November 2024) Delegate to the US House of Representatives last held on 8 November 2022 (next to be held on 5 November 2024)
election results: Legislature of the Virgin Islands - percent of vote by party - NA; seats by party - Democratic Party 9, independent 6; composition - men 10, women 5, percent of women 33.3%
delegate to US House of Representatives - seat by party - Democratic Party 1
note: the Virgin Islands delegate to the US House of Representatives can vote when serving on a committee and when the House meets as the Committee of the Whole House, but not when legislation is submitted for a "full floor" House vote

Judicial branch: *highest court(s):* Supreme Court of the Virgin Islands (consists of the chief justice and 2 associate justices); note - court established by the US Congress in 2004 and assumed appellate jurisdiction in 2007
judge selection and term of office: justices appointed by the governor and confirmed by the Virgin Islands Senate; justices serve initial 10-year terms and upon reconfirmation, during the extent of good behavior; chief justice elected to position by peers for a 3-year term
subordinate courts: Superior Court (Territorial Court renamed in 2004); US Court of Appeals for the Third Circuit (has appellate jurisdiction over the District Court of the Virgin Islands; it is a territorial court and is not associated with a US federal judicial district); District Court of the Virgin Islands

Political parties: Democratic Party
Independent Citizens' Movement or ICM
Republican Party

International organization participation: AOSIS (observer), Interpol (subbureau), IOC, UPU, WFTU (NGOs)

Diplomatic representation in the US: none (territory of the US)

Diplomatic representation from the US: none (territory of the US)

Flag description: white field with a modified US coat of arms in the center between the large blue initials V and I; the coat of arms shows a yellow eagle holding an olive branch in its right talon and three arrows in the left with a superimposed shield of seven red and six white vertical stripes below a blue panel; white is a symbol of purity, the letters stand for the Virgin Islands

National anthem: *name:* "Virgin Islands March"
lyrics/music: multiple/Alton Augustus ADAMS, Sr.
note: adopted 1963; serves as a local anthem; as a territory of the US, "The Star-Spangled Banner" is official (see United States)

ECONOMY

Economic overview: high-income, tourism-based American territorial economy; severe COVID-19 economic disruptions; major rum distillery; high public debt; sluggish reopening of large oil refinery; environmentally susceptible to hurricanes; many informal industries

Real GDP (purchasing power parity): $4.895 billion (2021 est.)
$4.759 billion (2020 est.)
$4.852 billion (2019 est.)
note: data in 2021 dollars
comparison ranking: 188

Real GDP growth rate: 2.85% (2021 est.)
-1.92% (2020 est.)
2.93% (2019 est.)
note: annual GDP % growth based on constant local currency
comparison ranking: 114

Real GDP per capita: $46,200 (2021 est.)
$44,800 (2020 est.)
$45,500 (2019 est.)
note: data in 2021 dollars
comparison ranking: 52

GDP (official exchange rate): $4.444 billion (2021 est.)
note: data in current dollars at official exchange rate

Inflation rate (consumer prices): 1% (2016 est.)
2.6% (2015 est.)
comparison ranking: 20

GDP - composition, by end use: *household consumption:* 65.8% (2021 est.)
government consumption: 33.6% (2021 est.)
investment in fixed capital: 7.5% (2016 est.)
investment in inventories: 15% (2016 est.)
exports of goods and services: 91.7% (2021 est.)
imports of goods and services: -91.5% (2021 est.)
note: figures may not total 100% due to rounding or gaps in data collection

Agricultural products: fruit, vegetables, sorghum; Senepol cattle

Industries: tourism, watch assembly, rum distilling, construction, pharmaceuticals, electronics

Industrial production growth rate: 4.3% (2014 est.)
note: annual % change in industrial value added based on constant local currency
comparison ranking: 60

Labor force: 46,000 (2023 est.)
note: number of people ages 15 or older who are employed or seeking work
comparison ranking: 193

Unemployment rate: 12.09% (2023 est.)
12.67% (2022 est.)
13.93% (2021 est.)
note: % of labor force seeking employment
comparison ranking: 179

Youth unemployment rate (ages 15-24): *total:* 25.6% (2023 est.)
male: 23.1% (2023 est.)
female: 32.7% (2023 est.)
note: % of labor force ages 15-24 seeking employment
comparison ranking: total 41

Budget: *revenues:* $1.496 billion (2016 est.)
expenditures: $1.518 billion (2016 est.)

Public debt: 53.3% of GDP (2016 est.)
comparison ranking: 94

Taxes and other revenues: 28.9% (of GDP) (2016 est.)
comparison ranking: 27

Exports: $4.075 billion (2021 est.)
$1.62 billion (2020 est.)
$2.265 billion (2019 est.)
note: GDP expenditure basis - exports of goods and services in current dollars
comparison ranking: 146

Exports - partners: Haiti 14%, Guadeloupe 7%, Malaysia 7%, Martinique 7%, Barbados 7%, British Virgin Islands 5% (2019)

Exports - commodities: refined petroleum, jewelry, recreational boats, watches, rum (2019)

Imports: $4.065 billion (2021 est.)
$3.185 billion (2020 est.)
$4.139 billion (2019 est.)
note: GDP expenditure basis - imports of goods and services in current dollars
comparison ranking: 158

Imports - partners: India 18%, Algeria 14%, South Korea 9%, Argentina 9%, Sweden 7%, Brazil 5% (2019)

Imports - commodities: refined petroleum, crude petroleum, rubber piping, jewelry, beer (2019)

Exchange rates: the US dollar is used

ENERGY

Electricity access: *electrification - total population:* 100% (2022 est.)

Electricity: *installed generating capacity:* 326,000 kW (2022 est.)
consumption: 625.127 million kWh (2022 est.)
transmission/distribution losses: 50 million kWh (2022 est.)

comparison rankings: transmission/distribution losses 39; consumption 168; installed generating capacity 163

Electricity generation sources: *fossil fuels:* 97.4% of total installed capacity (2022 est.)
solar: 2.6% of total installed capacity (2022 est.)

Petroleum: *refined petroleum consumption:* 16,000 bbl/day (2022 est.)

Carbon dioxide emissions: 2.272 million metric tonnes of CO2 (2022 est.)
from petroleum and other liquids: 2.272 million metric tonnes of CO2 (2022 est.)
comparison ranking: total emissions 156

COMMUNICATIONS

Telephones - fixed lines: *total subscriptions:* 76,000 (2021 est.)
subscriptions per 100 inhabitants: 76 (2021 est.)
comparison ranking: total subscriptions 145

Telephones - mobile cellular: *total subscriptions:* 80,000 (2021 est.)
subscriptions per 100 inhabitants: 80 (2021 est.)
comparison ranking: total subscriptions 196

Telecommunication systems: *general assessment:* modern system with total digital switching, uses fiber-optic cable and microwave radio relay; good interisland and international connections; broadband access; expansion of FttP (Fiber to the Home) markets; LTE launches; regulatory development and expansion in several markets point to investment and focus on data (2020)
domestic: fixed-line 76 per 100 persons, with mobile-cellular 80 per 100 (2021)
international: country code - 1-340; landing points for the BSCS, St Thomas-ST Croix System, Southern Caribbean Fiber, Americas II, gCn, MAC, PAN-AM and SAC submarine cable connections to US, the Caribbean, Central and South America; satellite earth stations - NA (2020)

Broadcast media: about a dozen TV broadcast stations including 1 public TV station; multi-channel cable and satellite TV services are available; 24 radio stations

Internet country code: .vi

Internet users: *total:* 67,508 (2022 est.)
percent of population: 64.8% (2022 est.)
comparison ranking: total 196

TRANSPORTATION

Airports: 2 (2024)
comparison ranking: 209

Heliports: 3 (2024)

Roadways: *total:* 1,260 km (2008)
comparison ranking: total 180

Merchant marine: *total:* 2 (2023)
by type: general cargo 1, other 1
comparison ranking: total 177

Ports: *total ports:* 6 (2024)
large: 0
medium: 0
small: 3
very small: 3
ports with oil terminals: 3
key ports: Charlotte Amalie, Christiansted, Cruz Bay, Frederiksted, Limetree Bay, Port Alucroix

MILITARY AND SECURITY

Military and security forces: US Virgin Islands Police Department (VIPD)
US Virgin Islands Army National Guard (VING); US Virgin Islands Air National Guard (VIANG)

Military - note: defense is the responsibility of the US

W

WAKE ISLAND

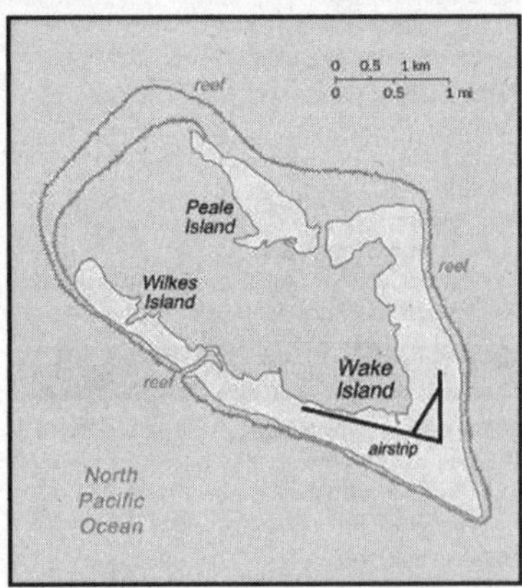

INTRODUCTION

Background: Early Micronesian and Polynesian settlers probably visited Wake Island, and oral legends tell of periodic voyages to the islands by people from the Marshall Islands. Wake Island was uninhabited when Spanish explorer Alvaro de Mendana de NEYRA became the first European to see it in 1568 and still had no inhabitants when English captain Samuel WAKE sailed by it in 1796. The United States Exploring Expedition visited the island in 1841, and the US annexed it in 1899 to use as a cable and refueling station for its newly acquired Pacific territories of Hawaii, the Philippines, and Guam. In the 1930s, Pan American Airways built facilities on Wake Island so that it could be used as a stopover for flights from the US to China. In 1941, the US began to install military assets on Wake Island, and Japan then captured the island and held it until the end of World War II. In 1946, commercial airlines resumed using Wake Island as a refueling stop.

In 1973, the Marshall Islands claimed Wake Island, based on the oral legends, although the US has not recognized these claims. In 1974, the US military took exclusive control of the island's airstrip and restricted visitors. In 1978, Bikini Islanders from the Marshall Islands, who were evacuated in the 1950s and 1960s because of US nuclear tests, considered rehoming on Wake Island, but the US military rejected that plan. Since the 1970s, the island has been important for missile defense testing. In 2009, Wake Island was included in the Pacific Remote Islands Marine National Monument.

GEOGRAPHY

Location: Oceania, atoll in the North Pacific Ocean, about two-thirds of the way from Hawaii to the Northern Mariana Islands

Geographic coordinates: 19 17 N, 166 39 E

Map references: Oceania

Area: *total:* 7 sq km
land: 6.5 sq km
water: 0 sq km
comparison ranking: total 243

Area - comparative: about 11 times the size of the National Mall in Washington, DC

Land boundaries: *total:* 0 km

Coastline: 19.3 km

Maritime claims: *territorial sea:* 12 nm
exclusive economic zone: 200 nm

Climate: tropical

Terrain: atoll of three low coral islands, Peale, Wake, and Wilkes, built up on an underwater volcano; central lagoon is former crater, islands are part of the rim

Elevation: *highest point:* unnamed location 8 m
lowest point: Pacific Ocean 0 m

Natural resources: none

Land use: *agricultural land:* 0% (2018 est.)
other: 100% (2018 est.)

Irrigated land: 0 sq km (2022)

Natural hazards: subject to occasional typhoons

Geography - note: strategic location in the North Pacific Ocean; emergency landing location for transpacific flights

PEOPLE AND SOCIETY

Population: *total:* (2018 est.) no indigenous inhabitants
note: approximately 100 military personnel and civilian contractors maintain and operate the airfield and communications facilities

ENVIRONMENT

Environment - current issues: potable water obtained through a catchment rainwater system and a desalinization plant for brackish ground water; hazardous wastes moved to an accumulation site for storage and eventual transport off site via barge

Climate: tropical

GOVERNMENT

Country name: *conventional long form:* none
conventional short form: Wake Island
etymology: although first discovered by British Captain William WAKE in 1792, the island is named after British Captain Samuel WAKE, who rediscovered the island in 1796

Dependency status: unincorporated unorganized territory of the US; administered from Washington, DC, by the Department of the Interior; activities in the atoll are currently conducted by the 11th US Air Force and managed from Pacific Air Force Support Center

Independence: none (territory of the US)

Legal system: US common law

Citizenship: see United States

Flag description: the flag of the US is used

ENERGY

Electricity access: *electrification - total population:* 100% (2021)

Petroleum: *refined petroleum consumption:* 8,000 bbl/day (2022 est.)

Carbon dioxide emissions: 1.221 million metric tonnes of CO_2 (2022 est.)
from petroleum and other liquids: 1.221 million metric tonnes of CO_2 (2022 est.)
comparison ranking: total emissions 168

Energy consumption per capita: (2019)

COMMUNICATIONS

Telecommunication systems: *general assessment:* satellite communications; 2 Defense Switched Network circuits off the Overseas Telephone System (OTS); located in the Hawaii area code - 808 (2018) (2018)

Broadcast media: American Armed Forces Radio and Television Service (AFRTS) provides satellite radio/TV broadcasts (2018)

TRANSPORTATION

Airports: 1 (2024)
comparison ranking: 225

Ports: *total ports:* 1 (2024)
large: 0
medium: 0
small: 0
very small: 1
ports with oil terminals: 1
key ports: Wake Island

Transportation - note: there are no commercial or civilian flights to and from Wake Island, except in direct support of island missions; emergency landing is available

MILITARY AND SECURITY

Military - note: defense is the responsibility of the US; the island serves as a trans-Pacific refueling stop for military aircraft and supports US Missile Defense Agency (MDA) testing activities; the US Air Force is responsible for overall administration and operation of the island facilities while the launch support facility is administered by the MDA (2024)

WALLIS AND FUTUNA

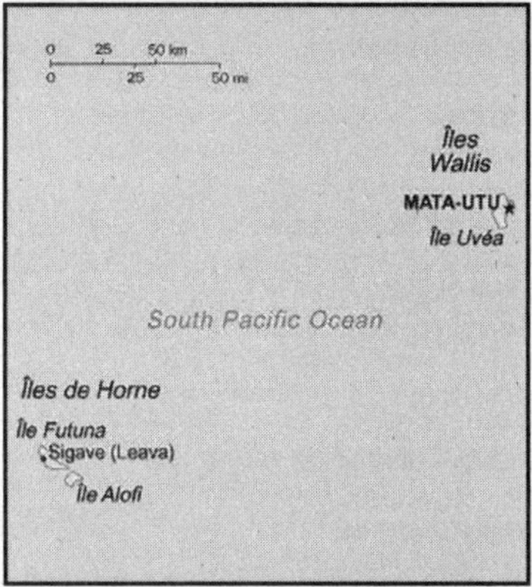

INTRODUCTION

Background: Around 800 B.C., the first settlers arrived on the islands of Wallis and Futuna, which are a natural midpoint between Fiji and Samoa. Around A.D. 1500, Tongans invaded Wallis, and a chiefdom system resembling Tonga's formal hierarchy developed on the island. Tongans attempted to settle Futuna but were repeatedly rebuffed. Samoans settled Futuna in the 1600s, and a slightly less centralized chiefdom system formed. Dutch explorers were the first Europeans to see the islands in 1616, followed intermittently by other Europeans, including British explorer Samuel WALLIS in 1767. French Catholic missionaries were the first Europeans to permanently settle Wallis and Futuna in 1837, and they converted most of the population of both islands by 1846. The missionaries and newly converted King LAVELUA of Uvea on Wallis asked France for a protectorate in 1842 following a local rebellion. France agreed, although the protectorate status would not be ratified until 1887. In 1888, King MUSULAMU of Alo and King TAMOLE of Sigave, both on Futuna, signed a treaty establishing a French protectorate; the Wallis and Futuna protectorate was integrated into the territory of New Caledonia the same year. France renegotiated the terms of the protectorate with the territory's three kings in 1910, expanding French authority. Wallis and Futuna was the only French colony to side with the Vichy regime during World War II, until the arrival of Free French and US troops in 1942. In 1959, inhabitants of the islands voted to separate from New Caledonia, becoming a French overseas territory in 1961. Despite the split, a significant Wallisian and Futunan community still lives in New Caledonia. In 2003, Wallis and Futuna became a French overseas collectivity. The islands joined the Pacific Islands Forum as an associate member in 2018, two years after France's other Pacific territories became full members of the organization.

GEOGRAPHY

Location: Oceania, islands in the South Pacific Ocean, about two-thirds of the way from Hawaii to New Zealand

Geographic coordinates: 13 18 S, 176 12 W

Map references: Oceania

Area: *total:* 142 sq km
land: 142 sq km
water: 0 sq km
note: includes Ile Uvea (Wallis Island), Ile Futuna (Futuna Island), Ile Alofi, and 20 islets
comparison ranking: total 221

Area - comparative: 1.5 times the size of Washington, DC

Land boundaries: *total:* 0 km

Coastline: 129 km

Maritime claims: *territorial sea:* 12 nm
exclusive economic zone: 200 nm

Climate: tropical; hot, rainy season (November to April); cool, dry season (May to October); rains 250-300 cm per year (80% humidity); average temperature 26.6 degrees Celsius

Terrain: volcanic origin; low hills

Elevation: *highest point:* Mont Singavi (on Futuna) 522 m
lowest point: Pacific Ocean 0 m

Natural resources: NEGL

Land use: *agricultural land:* 42.8% (2018 est.)
arable land: 7.1% (2018 est.)
permanent crops: 35.7% (2018 est.)
permanent pasture: 0% (2018 est.)
forest: 41.9% (2018 est.)
other: 15.3% (2018 est.)

Irrigated land: 0.6 sq km (2020)

Natural hazards: cyclones; tsunamis

Geography - note: both island groups have fringing reefs; Wallis contains several prominent crater lakes

PEOPLE AND SOCIETY

Population: *total:* 15,964
male: 8,201
female: 7,763 (2024 est.)
comparison rankings: female 220; male 220; total 220

Nationality: *noun:* Wallisian(s), Futunan(s), or Wallis and Futuna Islanders
adjective: Wallisian, Futunan, or Wallis and Futuna Islander

Ethnic groups: Polynesian

Languages: Wallisian (indigenous Polynesian language) 58.9%, Futunian 30.1%, French (official) 10.8%, other 0.2% (2003 est.)

Religions: Roman Catholic 99%, other 1%

Age structure: *0-14 years:* 19.8% (male 1,643/female 1,511)
15-64 years: 67.5% (male 5,535/female 5,247)
65 years and over: 12.7% (2024 est.) (male 1,023/female 1,005)

Dependency ratios: *total dependency ratio:* 57
youth dependency ratio: 36.6
elderly dependency ratio: 20.4
potential support ratio: 4.9 (2021)

Median age: *total:* 36.3 years (2024 est.)
male: 35.5 years
female: 37.3 years
comparison ranking: total 92

Population growth rate: 0.22% (2024 est.)
comparison ranking: 174

Birth rate: 11.8 births/1,000 population (2024 est.)
comparison ranking: 151

Death rate: 6 deaths/1,000 population (2024 est.)
comparison ranking: 153

Net migration rate: -3.6 migrant(s)/1,000 population (2024 est.)
comparison ranking: 189

Urbanization: *urban population:* 0% of total population (2023)
rate of urbanization: 0% annual rate of change (2020-25 est.)

Major urban areas - population: 1,000 MATA-UTU (capital) (2018)

Sex ratio: *at birth:* 1.05 male(s)/female
0-14 years: 1.09 male(s)/female
15-64 years: 1.05 male(s)/female
65 years and over: 1.02 male(s)/female
total population: 1.06 male(s)/female (2024 est.)

Infant mortality rate: *total:* 3.9 deaths/1,000 live births (2024 est.)
male: 3.8 deaths/1,000 live births
female: 3.9 deaths/1,000 live births
comparison ranking: total 188

Life expectancy at birth: *total population:* 81.1 years (2024 est.)
male: 78.2 years
female: 84.2 years
comparison ranking: total population 45

Total fertility rate: 1.71 children born/woman (2024 est.)
comparison ranking: 160

Gross reproduction rate: 0.83 (2024 est.)

Drinking water source: *improved: urban:* NA
rural: 99.1% of population
total: 99.1% of population
unimproved: urban: NA
rural: 0.9% of population
total: 0.9% of population (2020)

Sanitation facility access: *improved: urban:* NA
rural: 92.9% of population
total: 92.9% of population
unimproved: urban: NA
rural: 7.1% of population
total: 7.1% of population (2020 est.)

Currently married women (ages 15-49): 56% (2023)

ENVIRONMENT

Environment - current issues: deforestation (only small portions of the original forests remain) largely as a result of the continued use of wood as the main fuel source; as a consequence of cutting down the forests, the mountainous terrain of Futuna is particularly prone to erosion; there are no permanent settlements on Alofi because of the lack of natural freshwater resources; lack of soil fertility on the islands of Uvea and Futuna negatively impacts agricultural productivity

Climate: tropical; hot, rainy season (November to April); cool, dry season (May to October); rains 250-300 cm per year (80% humidity); average temperature 26.6 degrees Celsius

Land use: *agricultural land:* 42.8% (2018 est.)

arable land: 7.1% (2018 est.)
permanent crops: 35.7% (2018 est.)
permanent pasture: 0% (2018 est.)
forest: 41.9% (2018 est.)
other: 15.3% (2018 est.)

Urbanization: *urban population:* 0% of total population (2023)
rate of urbanization: 0% annual rate of change (2020-25 est.)

GOVERNMENT

Country name: *conventional long form:* Territory of the Wallis and Futuna Islands
conventional short form: Wallis and Futuna
local long form: Territoire des Iles Wallis et Futuna
local short form: Wallis et Futuna
former: Hoorn Islands is the former name of the Futuna Islands
etymology: Wallis Island is named after British Captain Samuel WALLIS, who discovered it in 1767; Futuna is derived from the native word "futu," which is the name of the fish-poison tree found on the island

Government type: parliamentary democracy (Territorial Assembly); overseas collectivity of France

Dependency status: overseas collectivity of France

Capital: *name:* Mata-Utu (on Ile Uvea)
geographic coordinates: 13 57 S, 171 56 W
time difference: UTC+12 (17 hours ahead of Washington, DC, during Standard Time)

Administrative divisions: 3 administrative precincts (circonscriptions, singular - circonscription) Alo, Sigave, Uvea

Independence: none (overseas collectivity of France)

National holiday: Bastille Day, 14 July (1789)

Legal system: French civil law

Constitution: *history:* 4 October 1958 (French Constitution)
amendments: French constitution amendment procedures apply

Citizenship: see France

Suffrage: 18 years of age; universal

Executive branch: *chief of state:* President Emmanuel MACRON (since 14 May 2017); represented by Administrator Superior Blaise GOURTAY (since 1 August 2023)
head of government: President of the Territorial Assembly Munipoese MULI'AKA'AKA (since 20 March 2022)
cabinet: Council of the Territory appointed by the administrator superior on the advice of the Territorial Assembly
elections/appointments: French president elected by absolute majority popular vote in 2 rounds if needed for a 5-year term (eligible for a second term); administrator superior appointed by the French president on the advice of the French Ministry of the Interior; the presidents of the Territorial Government and the Territorial Assembly elected by assembly members
note: there are 3 traditional kings with limited powers

Legislative branch: *description:* unicameral Territorial Assembly or Assemblee Territoriale (20 seats - Wallis 13, Futuna 7; members directly elected in multi-seat constituencies by party-list proportional representation vote to serve 5-year terms)
Wallis and Futuna indirectly elects 1 senator to the French Senate by an electoral college by absolute majority vote in 2 rounds if needed for a 6-year term, and directly elects 1 deputy to the French National Assembly by absolute majority vote for a 5-year term
elections:
Territorial Assembly - last held on 20 March 2022 (next to be held in March 2027)
French Senate - last held on 24 September 2023 (next to be held on 30 September 2026)
French National Assembly - last held on 12 and 19 June 2022 (next to be held in June 2027)
election results:
Territorial Assembly - percent of vote by party - NA; seats by party - 2 members are elected from the list Ofa mo'oni ki tou fenua and 2 members are elected from list Mauli fetokoniaki, 1 seat each from 16 other lists; composition - men NA, women NA, percent of women NA
French Senate representative - LR 1
French National Assembly representative - independent 1

Judicial branch: *highest court(s):* Court of Assizes or Cour d'Assizes (consists of 1 judge; court hears primarily serious criminal cases); note - appeals beyond the Court of Assizes are heard before the Court of Appeal or Cour d'Appel (in Noumea, New Caledonia)
judge selection and term of office: NA
subordinate courts: courts of first instance; labor court; note - justice generally administered under French law by the high administrator, but the 3 traditional kings administer customary law, and there is a magistrate in Mata-Utu

Political parties: Left Radical Party or PRG (formerly Radical Socialist Party or PRS and the Left Radical Movement or MRG)
Lua Kae Tahi (Giscardians)
Rally for Wallis and Futuna-The Republicans (Rassemblement pour Wallis and Futuna) or RPWF-LR
Socialist Party or PS
Taumu'a Lelei
Union Pour la Democratie Francaise or UDF

International organization participation: PIF (observer), SPC, UPU

Diplomatic representation in the US: none (overseas territory of France)

Diplomatic representation from the US: none (overseas collectivity of France)

Flag description: unofficial, local flag has a red field with four white isosceles triangles in the middle, representing the three native kings of the islands and the French administrator; the apexes of the triangles are oriented inward and at right angles to each other; the flag of France, outlined in white on two sides, is in the upper hoist quadrant
note: the design is derived from an original red banner with a white cross pattee that was introduced in the 19th century by French missionaries; the flag of France is used for official occasions

National symbol(s): red saltire (Saint Andrew's Cross) on a white square on a red field; national colors: red, white

National anthem: *note:* as a territory of France, "La Marseillaise" is official (see France)

ECONOMY

Economic overview: lower-middle-income, agrarian French dependency economy; heavily reliant on French subsidies; licenses fishing rights to Japan and South Korea; major remittances from New Caledonia; aging workforce; import-dependent; deforestation-fueled fragility

Inflation rate (consumer prices): 0.9% (2015) (2005)
comparison ranking: 15

Agricultural products: coconuts, breadfruit, yams, taro, bananas; pigs, goats; fish

Industries: copra, handicrafts, fishing, lumber

Budget: *revenues:* $32.54 million (2015 est.)
expenditures: $34.18 million (2015 est.)

Taxes and other revenues: 16.7% (of GDP) (2015 est.)
comparison ranking: 118

Exports - partners: France 48%, Singapore 12%, US 10%, Guatemala 9%, UK 4% (2022)
note: top five export partners based on percentage share of exports

Exports - commodities: integrated circuits, jewelry, cars, aircraft parts, polyacetals (2019)

Imports - partners: Fiji 38%, France 31%, NZ 8%, Iceland 6%, Australia 5% (2022)
note: top five import partners based on percentage share of imports

Imports - commodities: refined petroleum, beef products, poultry meats, engine parts, packaged medicines (2019)

Exchange rates: Comptoirs Francais du Pacifique francs (XPF) per US dollar -

Exchange rates: 110.347 (2023 est.)
113.474 (2022 est.)
100.88 (2021 est.)
104.711 (2020 est.)
110.347 (2019 est.)

COMMUNICATIONS

Telephones - fixed lines: *total subscriptions:* 3,000 (2021 est.)
subscriptions per 100 inhabitants: 26 (2021 est.)
comparison ranking: total subscriptions 209

Telephones - mobile cellular: *total subscriptions:* 0 (2018)
subscriptions per 100 inhabitants: 0 (2019)
comparison ranking: total subscriptions 225

Telecommunication systems: *general assessment:* 2G widespread; bandwidth is limited; mobile subscriber numbers are higher than fixed-line and better suited for islands; good mobile coverage in the capital cities and also reasonable coverage across more remote atolls; recent international interest in infrastructure development; increase in demand for mobile broadband as mobile services serve as primary source for Internet access; broadband satellite launched in 2019 to improve costs and capability (2020)
domestic: fixed-line teledensity 26 per 100 persons (2021)
international: country code - 681; landing point for the Tui-Samoa submarine cable network connecting Wallis & Futuna, Samoa and Fiji (2020)

Broadcast media: the publicly owned French Overseas Network (RFO), which broadcasts to France's overseas departments, collectivities, and territories, is carried on the RFO Wallis and Fortuna TV and radio stations (2019)

Internet country code: .wf

Internet users: *total:* 5,496 (2021 est.)
percent of population: 45.8% (2021 est.)
comparison ranking: total 222

TRANSPORTATION

Airports: 2 (2024)
comparison ranking: 199

Merchant marine: *total:* 1 (2023)
by type: general cargo 1
comparison ranking: total 183

Ports: *total ports:* 1 (2024)
large: 0
medium: 0
small: 0
very small: 1
ports with oil terminals: 0
key ports: Mata-Utu

MILITARY AND SECURITY

Military - note: defense is the responsibility of France

WEST BANK

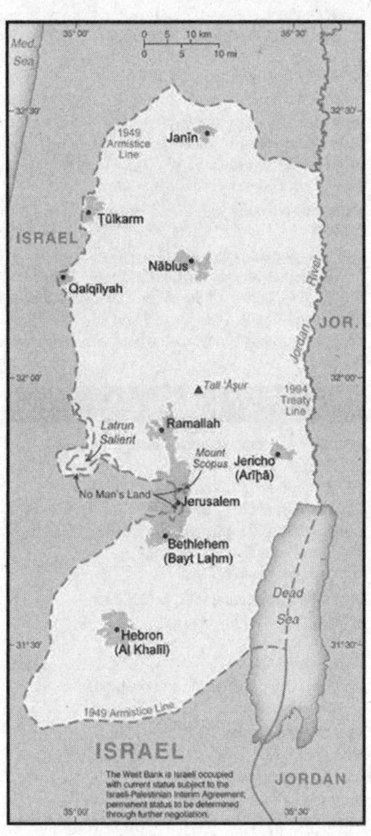

INTRODUCTION

Background: The landlocked West Bank – the larger of the two Palestinian territories – is home to some three million Palestinians. Inhabited since at least the 15th century B.C., the area currently known as the West Bank has been dominated by a succession of different powers. In the early 16th century, it was incorporated into the Ottoman Empire. The West Bank fell to British forces during World War I, becoming part of the British Mandate of Palestine. After the 1948 Arab-Israeli War, Transjordan (later renamed Jordan) captured the West Bank and annexed it in 1950; Israel then captured it in the Six-Day War in 1967. Under the Oslo Accords – a series of agreements that were signed between 1993 and 1999 – Israel transferred to the newly created Palestinian Authority (PA) security and civilian responsibility for the many Palestinian-populated areas of the West Bank, as well as the Gaza Strip.

In addition to establishing the PA as an interim government, the Oslo Accords divided the West Bank into three areas, with one fully managed by the PA (Area A), another fully managed by Israel (Area C), and a third with shared control (Area B) until a permanent agreement could be reached between the Palestine Liberation Organization (PLO) and Israel. In 2000, a violent *intifada*, or uprising, began across the Palestinian territories, and in 2001, negotiations for a permanent agreement between the PLO and Israel on final status issues stalled. Subsequent attempts to re-start direct negotiations have not resulted in progress toward determining final status of the area.

The PA last held national elections in 2006, when the Islamic Resistance Movement (HAMAS) won a majority of seats in the Palestinian Legislative Council (PLC). Fatah, the dominant Palestinian political faction in the West Bank, and HAMAS failed to maintain a unity government, leading to violent clashes between their respective supporters and to HAMAS's violent seizure of all PA military and governmental institutions in the Gaza Strip in 2007. In 2018, the Palestinian Constitutional Court dissolved the PLC. In recent years, Fatah and HAMAS have made several attempts at reconciliation, but the factions have been unable to implement agreements.

GEOGRAPHY

Location: Middle East, west of Jordan, east of Israel

Geographic coordinates: 32 00 N, 35 15 E

Map references: Middle East

Area: *total:* 5,860 sq km
land: 5,640 sq km
water: 220 sq km
note: includes West Bank, Latrun Salient, and the northwest quarter of the Dead Sea, but excludes Mt. Scopus; East Jerusalem and Jerusalem No Man's Land are also included only as a means of depicting the entire area occupied by Israel in 1967
comparison ranking: total 171

Area - comparative: slightly smaller than Delaware

Land boundaries: *total:* 478 km
border countries (2): Israel 330 km; Jordan 148 km

Coastline: 0 km (landlocked)

Maritime claims: none (landlocked)

Climate: temperate; temperature and precipitation vary with altitude, warm to hot summers, cool to mild winters

Terrain: mostly rugged, dissected upland in west, flat plains descending to Jordan River Valley to the east

Elevation: *highest point:* Khallat al Batrakh 1,020 m
lowest point: Dead Sea -431 m

Natural resources: arable land

Land use: *agricultural land:* 43.3% (2018 est.)
arable land: 7.4% (2018 est.)
permanent crops: 11% (2018 est.)
permanent pasture: 24.9% (2018 est.)
forest: 1.5% (2018 est.)
other: 55.2% (2018 est.)
note: includes Gaza Strip

Irrigated land: (2013) 151 sq km; note - includes Gaza Strip

Major lakes (area sq km): *salt water lake(s):* Dead Sea (shared with Jordan and Israel) - 1,020 sq km
note – endorheic hypersaline lake; 9.6 times saltier than the ocean; lake shore is 431 meters below sea level

Population distribution: the most populous Palestinian communities in the West Bank are located in the central ridge and western half of its territory; Jewish settlements are located throughout the West Bank, the most populous in the Seam Zone–between the 1949 Armistice Line and the separation barrier–and around Jerusalem

Natural hazards: droughts

Geography - note: landlocked; highlands are main recharge area for Israel's coastal aquifers; there are about 380 Israeli civilian sites, including about 213 settlements and 132 small outpost communities in the West Bank and 35 sites in East Jerusalem (2017)

PEOPLE AND SOCIETY

Population: *total:* 3,243,369
male: 1,648,450
female: 1,594,919 (2024 est.)
note: approximately 468,300 Israeli settlers live in the West Bank (2022); approximately 236,600 Israeli settlers live in East Jerusalem (2021)
comparison rankings: female 136; male 136; total 135

Nationality: *noun:* NA
adjective: NA

Ethnic groups: Palestinian Arab, Jewish, other

Languages: Arabic, Hebrew (spoken by Israeli settlers and many Palestinians), English (widely understood)
major-language sample(s):
كتاب حقائق العالم، المصدر الذي لا يمكن الاستغناء عنه للمعلومات الأساسية
(Arabic)

Religions: Muslim 80-85% (predominantly Sunni), Jewish 12-14%, Christian 1-2.5% (mainly Greek Orthodox), other, unaffiliated, unspecified <1% (2012 est.)

Age structure: *0-14 years:* 36.7% (male 609,497/ female 579,227)

15-64 years: 59.5% (male 979,719/female 949,746)
65 years and over: 3.9% (2024 est.) (male 59,234/female 65,946)

Dependency ratios: *total dependency ratio:* 74.3
youth dependency ratio: 68.2
elderly dependency ratio: 6.1
potential support ratio: 16.5 (2021 est.)
note: data represent Gaza Strip and the West Bank

Median age: *total:* 21.9 years (2024 est.)
male: 21.6 years
female: 22.1 years
comparison ranking: total 189

Population growth rate: 2.07% (2024 est.)
comparison ranking: 37

Birth rate: 27.8 births/1,000 population (2024 est.)
comparison ranking: 32

Death rate: 3.3 deaths/1,000 population (2024 est.)
comparison ranking: 223

Net migration rate: -3.8 migrant(s)/1,000 population (2024 est.)
comparison ranking: 191

Population distribution: the most populous Palestinian communities in the West Bank are located in the central ridge and western half of its territory; Jewish settlements are located throughout the West Bank, the most populous in the Seam Zone–between the 1949 Armistice Line and the separation barrier–and around Jerusalem

Urbanization: *urban population:* 77.6% of total population (2023)
rate of urbanization: 2.85% annual rate of change (2020-25 est.)
note: data represent Gaza Strip and the West Bank

Sex ratio: *at birth:* 1.06 male(s)/female
0-14 years: 1.05 male(s)/female
15-64 years: 1.03 male(s)/female
65 years and over: 0.9 male(s)/female
total population: 1.03 male(s)/female (2024 est.)

Maternal mortality ratio: 20 deaths/100,000 live births (2020 est.)
note: data represent Gaza Strip and the West Bank
comparison ranking: 125

Infant mortality rate: *total:* 15.1 deaths/1,000 live births (2024 est.)
male: 17.5 deaths/1,000 live births
female: 12.6 deaths/1,000 live births
comparison ranking: total 93

Life expectancy at birth: *total population:* 76.5 years (2024 est.)
male: 74.4 years
female: 78.8 years
comparison ranking: total population 108

Total fertility rate: 3.49 children born/woman (2024 est.)
comparison ranking: 34

Gross reproduction rate: 1.69 (2024 est.)

Contraceptive prevalence rate: 57.3% (2019/20)
note: includes Gaza Strip and the West Bank

Drinking water source: *improved: urban:* 98.9% of population
rural: 99% of population
total: 98.9% of population
unimproved: urban: 1.1% of population
rural: 1% of population
total: 1.1% of population (2020 est.)
note: includes Gaza Strip and the West Bank

Physician density: 3.25 physicians/1,000 population (2020)

Hospital bed density: 1.3 beds/1,000 population (2019)

Sanitation facility access: *improved: urban:* 99.9% of population
rural: 98.6% of population
total: 99.6% of population
unimproved: urban: 0.1% of population
rural: 1.4% of population
total: 0.4% of population (2020 est.)
note: note includes Gaza Strip and the West Bank

Children under the age of 5 years underweight: 2.1% (2019/20)
note: estimate is for Gaza Strip and the West Bank
comparison ranking: 101

Currently married women (ages 15-49): 62.4% (2023 est.)
note: data includes Gaza and the West Bank

Child marriage: *women married by age 15:* 0.7%
women married by age 18: 13.4% (2020 est.)
note: includes both the Gaza Strip and the West Bank

Education expenditures: 5.3% of GDP (2018 est.)
note: includes Gaza Strip and the West Bank
comparison ranking: 65

Literacy: *definition:* age 15 and over can read and write
total population: 97.5%
male: 98.8%
female: 96.2% (2020)
note: estimates are for Gaza and the West Bank

School life expectancy (primary to tertiary education): *total:* 13 years
male: 12 years
female: 14 years (2021)
note: data represent Gaza Strip and the West Bank

ENVIRONMENT

Environment - current issues: adequacy of freshwater supply; sewage treatment

Climate: temperate; temperature and precipitation vary with altitude, warm to hot summers, cool to mild winters

Urbanization: *urban population:* 77.6% of total population (2023)
rate of urbanization: 2.85% annual rate of change (2020-25 est.)
note: data represent Gaza Strip and the West Bank

Revenue from forest resources: 0% of GDP (2018 est.)
comparison ranking: 189

Air pollutants: *particulate matter emissions:* 30.82 micrograms per cubic meter (2019 est.)
carbon dioxide emissions: 3.23 megatons (2016 est.)
note: data represent combined total from the Gaza Strip and the West Bank.

Waste and recycling: *municipal solid waste generated annually:* 1.387 million tons (2016 est.)
municipal solid waste recycled annually: 6,935 tons (2013 est.)
percent of municipal solid waste recycled: 0.5% (2013 est.)
note: data represent combined total from the Gaza Strip and the West Bank.

Major lakes (area sq km): *salt water lake(s):* Dead Sea (shared with Jordan and Israel) - 1,020 sq km
note - endorheic hypersaline lake; 9.6 times saltier than the ocean; lake shore is 431 meters below sea level

Total water withdrawal: *municipal:* 200 million cubic meters (2020 est.)
industrial: 30 million cubic meters (2020 est.)
agricultural: 220 million cubic meters (2020 est.)
note: data represent combined total from the Gaza Strip and the West Bank.

Total renewable water resources: 840 million cubic meters (2020 est.)
note: data represent combined total from the Gaza Strip and the West Bank.

GOVERNMENT

Country name: *conventional long form:* none
conventional short form: West Bank
etymology: name refers to the location of the region of the British Mandate of Palestine that was occupied and administered by Jordan in 1948, as it is located on the far side (west bank) of the Jordan River in relation to Jordan proper; the designation was retained following the 1967 Six-Day War and the subsequent changes in administration

National heritage: *total World Heritage Sites:* 4 (all cultural)
selected World Heritage Site locales: Ancient Jericho/Tell es-Sultan; Birthplace of Jesus: Church of the Nativity and the Pilgrimage Route, Bethlehem; Hebron/Al-Khalil Old Town; Land of Olives and Vines – Cultural Landscape of Southern Jerusalem, Battir

ECONOMY

Real GDP (purchasing power parity): $27.418 billion (2023 est.)
$29.016 billion (2022 est.)
$27.878 billion (2021 est.)
note: data in 2021 dollars; entry includes West Bank and Gaza Strip
comparison ranking: 151

Real GDP growth rate: -5.51% (2023 est.)
4.08% (2022 est.)
7.01% (2021 est.)
note: annual GDP % growth based on constant local currency; entry includes West Bank and Gaza Strip
comparison ranking: 213

Real GDP per capita: $5,300 (2023 est.)
$5,800 (2022 est.)
$5,700 (2021 est.)
note: data in 2021 dollars; entry includes West Bank and Gaza Strip
comparison ranking: 176

GDP (official exchange rate): $17.396 billion (2023 est.)
note: data in current dollars at official exchange rate; entry includes West Bank and Gaza Strip

Inflation rate (consumer prices): 5.87% (2023 est.)
3.74% (2022 est.)
1.24% (2021 est.)
note: annual % change based on consumer prices; entry includes West Bank and Gaza Strip
comparison ranking: 122

GDP - composition, by sector of origin: *agriculture:* 5.7% (2022 est.)
industry: 17.4% (2022 est.)
services: 58.3% (2022 est.)
note: figures may not total 100% due to non-allocated consumption not captured in sector-reported data
comparison rankings: services 101; industry 156; agriculture 111

GDP - composition, by end use: *household consumption:* 101.6% (2023 est.)
government consumption: 20.2% (2023 est.)
investment in fixed capital: 24.8% (2023 est.)
investment in inventories: 1.5% (2023 est.)
exports of goods and services: 19.6% (2023 est.)
imports of goods and services: -66.9% (2023 est.)
note: figures may not total 100% due to rounding or gaps in data collection

Agricultural products: tomatoes, cucumbers, olives, poultry, milk, potatoes, sheep milk, eggplants, gourds

Industries: small-scale manufacturing, quarrying, textiles, soap, olive-wood carvings, and mother-of-pearl souvenirs

Industrial production growth rate: -8.57% (2023 est.)
note: annual % change in industrial value added based on constant local currency; entry includes West Bank and Gaza Strip
comparison ranking: 205

Labor force: 1.389 million (2022 est.)
note: number of people ages 15 or older who are employed or seeking work; entry includes West Bank and Gaza Strip
comparison ranking: 138

Unemployment rate: 24.42% (2022 est.)
26.39% (2021 est.)
25.9% (2020 est.)
note: % of labor force seeking employment; entry includes West Bank and Gaza Strip
comparison ranking: 204

Youth unemployment rate (ages 15-24): *total:* 36% (2022 est.)
male: 31.6% (2022 est.)
female: 56.7% (2022 est.)
note: % of labor force ages 15-24 seeking employment
comparison ranking: total 16

Population below poverty line: 29.2% (2016 est.)
note: % of population with income below national poverty line; entry includes West Bank and Gaza Strip

Gini Index coefficient - distribution of family income: 33.7 (2016 est.)
note: index (0-100) of income distribution; higher values represent greater inequality; entry includes West Bank and Gaza Strip
comparison ranking: 93

Household income or consumption by percentage share: *lowest 10%:* 2.9% (2016 est.)
highest 10%: 25.2% (2016 est.)
note: % share of income accruing to lowest and highest 10% of population; entry includes West Bank and Gaza Strip

Remittances: 21.84% of GDP (2023 est.)
21.13% of GDP (2022 est.)
20.77% of GDP (2021 est.)
note: personal transfers and compensation between resident and non-resident individuals/households/entities; entry includes West Bank and Gaza Strip

Budget: *revenues:* $3.803 billion (2020 est.)
expenditures: $5.002 billion (2020 est.)
note: includes Palestinian Authority expenditures in the Gaza Strip

Public debt: 24.4% of GDP (2014 est.)
comparison ranking: 176

Taxes and other revenues: 21.47% (of GDP) (2021 est.)
note: central government tax revenue as a % of GDP; entry includes West Bank and Gaza Strip
comparison ranking: 71

Current account balance: -$2.037 billion (2022 est.)
-$1.778 billion (2021 est.)
-$1.903 billion (2020 est.)
note: balance of payments - net trade and primary/secondary income in current dollars; entry includes West Bank and Gaza Strip
comparison ranking: 160

Exports: $3.533 billion (2022 est.)
$3.14 billion (2021 est.)
$2.385 billion (2020 est.)
note: balance of payments - exports of goods and services in current dollars; entry includes West Bank and Gaza Strip
comparison ranking: 150

Exports - partners: Israel 81%, Jordan 10%, UAE 2%, US 1%, Turkey 1% (2022)
note: top five export partners based on percentage share of exports; entry includes the West Bank and the Gaza Strip

Exports - commodities: building stone, scrap iron, plastic products, furniture, seats (2022)
note: top five export commodities based on value in dollars; entry includes the West Bank and the Gaza Strip

Imports: $12.257 billion (2022 est.)
$10.094 billion (2021 est.)
$8.065 billion (2020 est.)
note: balance of payments - imports of goods and services in current dollars; entry includes West Bank and Gaza Strip
comparison ranking: 114

Imports - partners: Israel 57%, Turkey 6%, Egypt 6%, Jordan 4%, China 4% (2022)
note: top five import partners based on percentage share of imports; entry includes the West Bank and the Gaza Strip

Imports - commodities: refined petroleum, electricity, animal food, cars, cement (2022)
note: top five import commodities based on value in dollars; entry includes the West Bank and the Gaza Strip

Reserves of foreign exchange and gold: $1.323 billion (2023 est.)
$896.9 million (2022 est.)
$872.541 million (2021 est.)
note: holdings of gold (year-end prices)/foreign exchange/special drawing rights in current dollars; entry includes West Bank and Gaza Strip
comparison ranking: 150

Exchange rates: new Israeli shekels (ILS) per US dollar -

Exchange rates: 3.36 (2022 est.)
3.23 (2021 est.)
3.442 (2020 est.)
3.565 (2019 est.)
3.591 (2018 est.)

ENERGY

Electricity access: *electrification - total population:* 100% (2022 est.)
note: includes the West Bank and the Gaza Strip

Electricity: *installed generating capacity:* 352,000 kW (2022 est.)
consumption: 6.746 billion kWh (2022 est.)
imports: 6.7 billion kWh (2022 est.)
transmission/distribution losses: 880.312 million kWh (2022 est.)
note: includes the West Bank and the Gaza Strip
comparison rankings: transmission/distribution losses 92; imports 38; consumption 118; installed generating capacity 159

Electricity generation sources: *fossil fuels:* 77.5% of total installed capacity (2022 est.)
solar: 22.4% of total installed capacity (2022 est.)
note: includes the West Bank and the Gaza Strip

Coal: *exports:* (2022 est.) less than 1 metric ton
note: includes the West Bank and the Gaza Strip

Petroleum: *refined petroleum consumption:* 29,000 bbl/day (2022 est.)
note: includes the West Bank and the Gaza Strip

Carbon dioxide emissions: 3.942 million metric tonnes of CO2 (2022 est.)
from petroleum and other liquids: 3.942 million metric tonnes of CO2 (2022 est.)
note: includes the West Bank and the Gaza Strip
comparison ranking: total emissions 142

Energy consumption per capita: 15.201 million Btu/person (2022 est.)
note: includes the West Bank and the Gaza Strip
comparison ranking: 140

COMMUNICATIONS

Telephones - fixed lines: *total subscriptions:* 458,000 (2022 est.)
subscriptions per 100 inhabitants: 9 (2021 est.)
note: entry includes the West Bank and the Gaza Strip
comparison ranking: total subscriptions 96

Telephones - mobile cellular: *total subscriptions:* 4.388 million (2022 est.)
subscriptions per 100 inhabitants: 78 (2021 est.)
note: entry includes the West Bank and the Gaza Strip
comparison ranking: total subscriptions 130

Telecommunication systems: *general assessment:* most telecommunications companies in the West Bank and Gaza import directly from international vendors; the major challenge they face are Israeli restrictions on telecommunication imports that are listed as "Dual Use" products; during a visit to the West Bank in July 2022, U.S. President Joe Biden announced that Israeli and Palestinian teams will work together to roll out an advanced infrastructure for 4G; currently, only 2G service is available in Gaza (2024)
domestic: fixed-line 9 per 100 and mobile-cellular subscriptions 78 per 100 (includes Gaza Strip) (2021)
international: country code 970 or 972; 1 international switch in Ramallah

Broadcast media: the Palestinian Authority operates 1 TV and 1 radio station; about 20 private TV and 40 radio stations; both Jordanian TV and satellite TV are accessible

Internet country code: .ps; note - IANA has designated .ps for the West Bank, same as Gaza Strip

Internet users: *total:* 3,938,199 (2021 est.)
percent of population: 80% (2021 est.)
note: includes the Gaza Strip
comparison ranking: total 111

Broadband - fixed subscriptions: *total:* 373,050 (2020 est.)
subscriptions per 100 inhabitants: 7 (2020 est.)
note: includes the Gaza Strip
comparison ranking: total 102

TRANSPORTATION

Airports: 1 (2024)
comparison ranking: 211

Heliports: 2 (2024)

Roadways: *total:* 4,686 km (2010)
paved: 4,686 km (2010)
note: includes Gaza Strip
comparison ranking: total 151

MILITARY AND SECURITY

Military and security forces: per the Oslo Accords, the Palestinian Authority (PA) is not permitted a conventional military but maintains security and police forces; PA security personnel have operated exclusively in the West Bank since HAMAS seized power in the Gaza Strip in 2007; PA forces include the National Security Forces, Presidential Guard, Civil Police, Civil Defense, Preventive Security Organization, the General Intelligence Organization, and the Military Intelligence Organization (2024)
note: the National Security Forces conduct gendarmerie-style security operations in circumstances that exceed the capabilities of the Civil Police; it is the largest branch of the PA security services and acts as the internal Palestinian security force; the Presidential Guard protects facilities and provides dignitary protection; the Preventive Security Organization is responsible for internal intelligence gathering and investigations related to internal security cases, including political dissent

Military expenditures: not available

Military and security service personnel strengths: the PA police and security forces have approximately 28,000 active personnel, including about 11,500 National Security Forces (2024)

Military equipment inventories and acquisitions: the security services are armed mostly with small arms and light weapons; in recent years, they have received small amounts of equipment from Jordan, Russia, and the US (2023)

Military - note: Palestinian Authority security forces maintain security control of 17.5% (called Area A) of the West Bank, as agreed by the Palestine Liberation Organization and Israel in the Oslo Accords; Israeli security forces maintain responsibility for the remaining 82.5% of the West Bank, including Area B (22.5%), where the Palestinian Authority has administrative control, and Area C (60%), where Israel maintains administrative control (2023)

TERRORISM

Terrorist group(s): Al-Aqsa Martyrs Brigade; HAMAS; Kahane Chai; Palestine Islamic Jihad; Palestine Liberation Front; Popular Front for the Liberation of Palestine
note: details about the history, aims, leadership, organization, areas of operation, tactics, targets, weapons, size, and sources of support of the group(s) appear(s) in the Terrorism reference guide

TRANSNATIONAL ISSUES

Refugees and internally displaced persons: *refugees (country of origin):* 901,000 (Palestinian refugees) (2022)

IDPs: 12,000 (includes persons displaced within the Gaza strip due to the intensification of the Israeli-Palestinian conflict since June 2014 and other Palestinian IDPs in the Gaza Strip and West Bank who fled as long ago as 1967, although confirmed cumulative data do not go back beyond 2006) (2022); note - data represent Gaza Strip and West Bank

WORLD

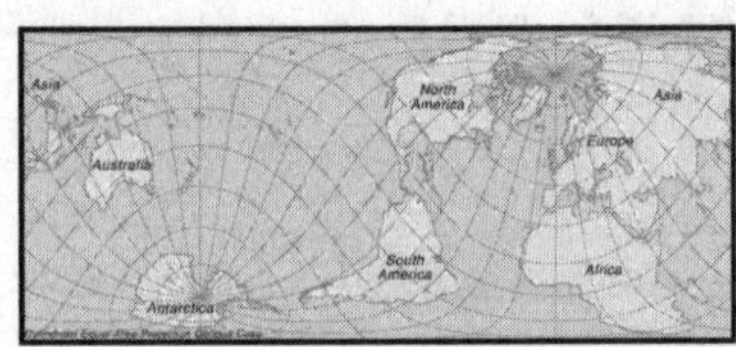

INTRODUCTION

Background: Globally, the 20th century was marked by: (a) two devastating World Wars; (b) the Great Depression of the 1930s; (c) the end of vast colonial empires; (d) rapid advances in science and technology; (e) the Cold War between the Western alliance and the Warsaw Pact nations; (f) a sharp rise in living standards in North America, Europe, and Japan; (g) increased concerns about environmental degradation including deforestation, energy and water shortages, declining biological diversity, and air pollution; and (h) the ultimate emergence of the US as the only world superpower. The planet's population continues to expand at a fast rate: from 1 billion in 1820 to 2 billion in 1930, 3 billion in 1960, 4 billion in 1974, 5 billion in 1987, 6 billion in 1999, 7 billion in 2012, and 8 billion in 2022. For the 21st century, the continued exponential growth in science and technology raises both hopes (e.g., advances in medicine and agriculture) and fears (e.g., development of even more lethal weapons of war).

GEOGRAPHY

Geographic overview: The surface of the Earth is approximately 70.9% water and 29.1% land. The former portion constitutes the World Ocean, the single largest feature of the planet and one that connects all places on the globe. The World Ocean is divided by the intervening continental landmasses into five major ocean basins, which are (in decreasing order of size) the Pacific, Atlantic, Indian, Southern, and Arctic. *The World Factbook* describes each of these five as oceans. Given the significant differences in direction and temperature of major ocean currents, as well as the effects of the major air masses above them, the Pacific and Atlantic Oceans are generally divided at the equator into the North and South Pacific Oceans and the North and South Atlantic Oceans, thus creating seven major water bodies – the so-called "Seven Seas."

About 97.5% of the Earth's water is saltwater. Of the 2.5% that is fresh, about two-thirds is frozen, mostly locked up in the Antarctic ice sheets and mountain glaciers worldwide. If all the surface ice on earth fully melted, the sea level would rise about 70 m (230 ft).

In a 100-year period, a water molecule spends 98 years in the ocean, 20 months as ice, about two weeks in lakes and rivers, and less than a week in the atmosphere. Groundwater can take 50 years to just traverse 1 km (0.6 mi).

Earth's land portion is divided into several large, discrete landmasses called continents. Depending on the convention used, the number of continents can vary from five to seven. The most common classification recognizes seven, which are (from largest to smallest) Asia, Africa, North America, South America, Antarctica, Europe, and Australia. Asia and Europe are sometimes lumped together into a Eurasian continent, resulting in six continents. Alternately, North and South America are sometimes grouped as simply the Americas, resulting in a continent total of six (or five, if the Eurasia designation is used).

North America is commonly understood to include Greenland and the Caribbean islands and to extend south to the Isthmus of Panama. The Ural Mountains and the Ural River are usually considered the easternmost part of Europe, the Caspian Sea is the limit to the southeast, and the Caucasus Mountains, the Black Sea, and the Mediterranean to the south. Portions of five countries – Azerbaijan, Georgia, Kazakhstan, Russia, and Turkey – fall within both Europe and Asia, but in every instance the larger section is in Asia. These countries are considered part of both continents. Armenia and Cyprus, which lie completely in Western Asia, are geopolitically European countries.

Asia usually incorporates all the islands of the Philippines, Malaysia, and Indonesia. The Pacific islands are often lumped with Australia into a "land mass" termed Oceania or Australasia. Africa's northeast extremity is frequently delimited at the Isthmus of Suez, but for geopolitical purposes, the Egyptian Sinai Peninsula is often included as part of Africa.

Although the above groupings are the most common, different continental dispositions are recognized or taught in certain parts of the world, with some more heavily based on cultural spheres than physical geographic considerations.

Based on the seven-continent model, and grouping islands with adjacent continents, Africa has the most countries with 54. Europe contains 49 countries and Asia 48, but these two continents share five countries: Azerbaijan, Georgia, Kazakhstan, Russia, and Turkey. North America consists of 23 sovereign states, Oceania has 16, and South America 12. In total, the United States recognizes 197 countries.

countries by continent: Africa (54): Algeria, Angola, Benin, Botswana, Burkina Faso, Burundi, Cabo Verde, Cameroon, Central African Republic, Chad, Comoros, Democratic Republic of the Congo, Republic of the Congo, Cote d'Ivoire, Djibouti, Egypt, Equatorial Guinea, Eritrea, Eswatini, Ethiopia, Gabon, The Gambia, Ghana, Guinea, Guinea-Bissau, Kenya, Lesotho, Liberia, Libya, Madagascar, Malawi, Mali, Mauritania, Mauritius, Morocco, Mozambique, Namibia, Niger, Nigeria, Rwanda,

Sao Tome and Principe, Senegal, Seychelles, Sierra Leone, Somalia, South Africa, South Sudan, Sudan, Tanzania, Togo, Tunisia, Uganda, Zambia, Zimbabwe

Europe (49): Albania, Andorra, Austria, Azerbaijan*, Belarus, Belgium, Bosnia and Herzegovina, Bulgaria, Croatia, Czech Republic, Denmark, Estonia, Finland, France, Georgia*, Germany, Greece, Holy See (Vatican City), Hungary, Iceland, Ireland, Italy, Kazakhstan*, Kosovo, Latvia, Liechtenstein, Lithuania, Luxembourg, Malta, Moldova, Monaco, Montenegro, Netherlands, North Macedonia, Norway, Poland, Portugal, Romania, Russia*, San Marino, Serbia, Slovakia, Slovenia, Spain, Sweden, Switzerland, Turkey*, Ukraine, United Kingdom (* indicates part of the country is also in Asia)

Asia (48): Afghanistan, Armenia, Azerbaijan*, Bahrain, Bangladesh, Bhutan, Brunei, Burma, Cambodia, China, Cyprus, Georgia*, India, Indonesia, Iran, Iraq, Israel, Japan, Jordan, Kazakhstan*, North Korea, South Korea, Kuwait, Kyrgyzstan, Laos, Lebanon, Malaysia, Maldives, Mongolia, Nepal, Oman, Pakistan, Philippines, Qatar, Russia*, Saudi Arabia, Singapore, Sri Lanka, Syria, Tajikistan, Thailand, Timor-Leste, Turkey*, Turkmenistan, United Arab Emirates, Uzbekistan, Vietnam, Yemen (* indicates part of the country is also in Europe)

North America (23): Antigua and Barbuda, The Bahamas, Barbados, Belize, Canada, Costa Rica, Cuba, Dominica, Dominican Republic, El Salvador, Grenada, Guatemala, Haiti, Honduras, Jamaica, Mexico, Nicaragua, Panama, Saint Kitts and Nevis, Saint Lucia, Saint Vincent and the Grenadines, Trinidad and Tobago, United States

Oceania (16): Australia, Cook Islands, Fiji, Kiribati, Marshall Islands, Federated States of Micronesia, Nauru, New Zealand, Niue, Palau, Papua New Guinea, Samoa, Solomon Islands, Tonga, Tuvalu, Vanuatu

South America (12): Argentina, Bolivia, Brazil, Chile, Colombia, Ecuador, Guyana, Paraguay, Peru, Suriname, Uruguay, Venezuela

Three of the states described above – France, Netherlands, and the United Kingdom – consist of smaller political entities that are referred to as countries. France considers French Polynesia an overseas country; the Kingdom of the Netherlands refers to all four of its constituent parts (Netherlands [proper], and the islands of Aruba, Curacao, and Sint Maarten) as countries; and the United Kingdom is composed of the countries of England, Wales, Scotland, and Northern Ireland. While not recognized as sovereign states, *The World Factbook* does include descriptive entries for the French and Dutch island "countries."

the World from space: Earth is the only planet in the solar system to have water in its three states of matter: liquid (oceans, lakes, and rivers), solid (ice), and gas (water vapor in clouds). From a distance, Earth would be the brightest of the eight planets in the solar system; this luminous effect would be because of the sunlight reflected by the planet's water.

Earth is also the only planet in the solar system known to be active with earthquakes and volcanoes due to plate tectonics; these events form the landscape, replenish carbon dioxide into the atmosphere, and erase impact craters caused by meteors.

Earth has a slight equatorial bulge – a difference between its equatorial and polar diameters – because of the centrifugal force from the planet rotating on its axis. The equatorial diameter is 12,756 km, but the polar diameter is 12,714 km; this results in the Earth's circumference at the equator being 40,075 km, while the polar circumference is 40,008 km.

the physical World: the Earth is composed of three layers: the outer lithosphere (with its crust and uppermost solid mantle), the mantle (the thickest layer, with distinct upper and lower layers), and the core (with an outer liquid core and inner solid core). Researchers have discovered that a transition zone (at a depth of 410-660 km, or 255-410 mi) between the upper and lower mantle may well be hydrous (water-bearing). But this hydrous rock would neither feel wet nor drip water. At that depth, high temperatures and pressures structurally transform a mineral called olivine into another mineral, ringwoodite, which can incorporate water, but not in a liquid, solid, or gas form. The high temperatures and pressures cause: 1) water molecules to split, creating hydroxide ions (hydrogen and oxygen atoms bound together), and 2) create structural changes in ringwoodite so that it is able to contain hydroxide ions. Ringwoodite can hold 1 to 3% of its weight in hydroxide ions. Considering that the 250 km-transition zone is about 7% of the Earth's mass (the crust is only about 1%), it could include at least as much (if not several times more) water than all the Earth's oceans.

Area: *total:* 510.072 million sq km
land: 148.94 million sq km
water: 361,899,999 sq km
note: 70.9% of the world's surface is water, 29.1% is land

Area - comparative: land area about 16 times the size of the US

Area - rankings: *top fifteen World Factbook entities ranked by size:* Pacific Ocean 155,557,000 sq km; Atlantic Ocean 76,762,000 sq km; Indian Ocean 68,556,000 sq km; Southern Ocean 20,327,000 sq km; Russia 17,098,242 sq km; Antarctica 14,200,000 sq km; Arctic Ocean 14,056,000 sq km; Canada 9,984,670 sq km; United States 9,826,675 sq km; China 9,596,960 sq km; Brazil 8,515,770 sq km; Australia 7,741,220 sq km; European Union 4,324,782 sq km; India 3,287,263 sq km; Argentina 2,780,400 sq km

top ten largest water bodies: Pacific Ocean 155,557,000 sq km; Atlantic Ocean 76,762,000 sq km; Indian Ocean 68,556,000 sq km; Southern Ocean 20,327,000 sq km; Arctic Ocean 14,056,000 sq km; Coral Sea 4,184,100 sq km; South China Sea 3,595,900 sq km; Caribbean Sea 2,834,000 sq km; Bering Sea 2,520,000 sq km; Mediterranean Sea 2,469,000 sq km

top ten largest landmasses: Asia 44,568,500 sq km; Africa 30,065,000 sq km; North America 24,473,000 sq km; South America 17,819,000 sq km; Antarctica 14,200,000 sq km; Europe 9,948,000 sq km; Australia 7,741,220 sq km; Greenland 2,166,086 sq km; New Guinea 785,753 sq km; Borneo 751,929 sq km

top ten largest islands: Greenland 2,166,086 sq km; New Guinea (Indonesia, Papua New Guinea) 785,753 sq km; Borneo (Brunei, Indonesia, Malaysia) 751,929 sq km; Madagascar 587,713 sq km; Baffin Island (Canada) 507,451 sq km; Sumatra (Indonesia) 472,784 sq km; Honshu (Japan) 227,963 sq km; Victoria Island (Canada) 217,291 sq km; Great Britain (United Kingdom) 209,331 sq km; Ellesmere Island (Canada) 196,236 sq km

top ten longest mountain ranges (land-based): Andes (Venezuela, Colombia, Ecuador, Peru, Bolivia, Chile, Argentina) 7,000 km; Rocky Mountains (Canada, US) 4,830 km; Great Dividing Range (Australia) 3,700 km; Transantarctic Mountains (Antarctica) 3,500 km; Kunlun Mountains (China) 3,000 km; Ural Mountains (Russia, Kazakhstan) 2,640 km; Atlas Mountains (Morocco, Algeria, Tunisia) 2,500 km; Appalachian Mountains (Canada, US) 2,400 km; Himalayas (Pakistan, Afghanistan, India, China, Nepal, Bhutan) 2,300 km; Altai Mountains (Kazakhstan, Russia, Mongolia) 2,000 km; note - lengths are approximate; if oceans are included, the Mid-Ocean Ridge is by far the longest mountain range at 40,389 km

top ten largest forested countries (sq km and percent of land): Russia 8,149,310 (49.8%); Brazil 4,935,380 (58.9%); Canada 3,470,690 (38.2%); United States 3,103,700 (33.9%); China 2,098,640 (22.3%); Democratic Republic of the Congo 1,522,670 (67.2%); Australia 1,250,590 (16.3%); Indonesia 903,250 (49.9%); Peru 738,054 (57.7%); India 708,600 (23.8%) (2016 est.)

top ten most densely forested countries (percent of land): Suriname (98.3%), Federated States of Micronesia (91.9%), Gabon (90%), Seychelles (88.4%), Palau (87.6%), Guyana (83.9%), Laos (82.1%), Solomon Islands (77.9%), Papua New Guinea (74.1%), Finland (73.1%) (2016 est.)

top ten largest (non-polar) deserts: Sahara (Algeria, Chad, Egypt, Libya, Mali, Mauritania, Niger, Western Sahara, Sudan, Tunisia) 9,200,000 sq km; Arabian (Saudi Arabia, Iraq, Jordan, Kuwait, Oman, Qatar, United Arab Emirates, Yemen) 2,330,000 sq km; Gobi (China, Mongolia) 1,295,000 sq km; Kalahari (Botswana, Namibia, South Africa) 900,000 sq km; Patagonian (Argentina) 673,000 sq km; Syrian (Syria, Iraq, Jordan, Saudi Arabia) 500,000 sq km; Chihuahuan (Mexico) 362,000 sq km; Kara-Kum (Turkmenistan) 350,000 sq km; Great Victoria (Australia) 348,750 sq km; Great Basin (United States) 343,169 sq km; note - if the two polar deserts are included, they would rank first and second: Antarctic Desert 14,200,000 sq km and Arctic Desert 13,900,000 sq km

ten smallest independent countries: Holy See (Vatican City) 0.44 sq km; Monaco 2 sq km; Nauru 21 sq km; Tuvalu 26 sq km; San Marino 61 sq km; Liechtenstein 160 sq km; Marshall Islands 181 sq km; Cook Islands 236 sq km; Niue 260 sq km; Saint Kitts and Nevis 261 sq km

Land boundaries: the land boundaries in *The World Factbook* total 279,035.5 km (not counting shared boundaries twice); two nations, China and Russia, each border 14 other countries

note 1: the precision of the total is somewhat misleading, since one cannot accurately measure every river meander along a boundary; a number rounded slightly higher – to 280,000 km – has been coordinated with and approved by the US State Department

note 2: 46 nations and other areas are landlocked, these include: Afghanistan, Andorra, Armenia, Austria, Azerbaijan, Belarus, Bhutan, Bolivia, Botswana, Burkina Faso, Burundi, Central African Republic, Chad, Czechia, Eswatini, Ethiopia, Holy See (Vatican City), Hungary, Kazakhstan, Kosovo, Kyrgyzstan, Laos, Lesotho, Liechtenstein, Luxembourg, Macedonia, Malawi, Mali, Moldova, Mongolia, Nepal, Niger, Paraguay, Rwanda, San Marino, Serbia, Slovakia, South Sudan, Switzerland, Tajikistan, Turkmenistan, Uganda, Uzbekistan, West Bank, Zambia, Zimbabwe; two of these, Liechtenstein and Uzbekistan, are doubly landlocked

note 3: worldwide, some one-quarter of interior (non-coastal) borders are rivers; South America with 43% leads the continents, followed by North America with 32%, Africa with 30%, Europe with 23%, and

Asia with 18%; Australia has no interior national river borders

Coastline: 356,000 km
note: 95 nations and other entities are islands that border no other countries, they include: American Samoa, Anguilla, Antigua and Barbuda, Aruba, Ashmore and Cartier Islands, The Bahamas, Bahrain, Baker Island, Barbados, Bermuda, Bouvet Island, British Indian Ocean Territory, British Virgin Islands, Cabo Verde, Cayman Islands, Christmas Island, Clipperton Island, Cocos (Keeling) Islands, Comoros, Cook Islands, Coral Sea Islands, Cuba, Curacao, Cyprus, Dominica, Falkland Islands (Islas Malvinas), Faroe Islands, Fiji, French Polynesia, French Southern and Antarctic Lands, Greenland, Grenada, Guam, Guernsey, Heard Island and McDonald Islands, Howland Island, Iceland, Isle of Man, Jamaica, Jan Mayen, Japan, Jarvis Island, Jersey, Johnston Atoll, Kingman Reef, Kiribati, Madagascar, Maldives, Malta, Marshall Islands, Mauritius, Mayotte, Federated States of Micronesia, Midway Islands, Montserrat, Nauru, Navassa Island, New Caledonia, New Zealand, Niue, Norfolk Island, Northern Mariana Islands, Palau, Palmyra Atoll, Paracel Islands, Philippines, Pitcairn Islands, Puerto Rico, Saint Barthelemy, Saint Helena, Saint Kitts and Nevis, Saint Lucia, Saint Pierre and Miquelon, Saint Vincent and the Grenadines, Samoa, Sao Tome and Principe, Seychelles, Singapore, Sint Maarten, Solomon Islands, South Georgia and the South Sandwich Islands, Spratly Islands, Sri Lanka, Svalbard, Taiwan, Tokelau, Tonga, Trinidad and Tobago, Turks and Caicos Islands, Tuvalu, Vanuatu, Virgin Islands, Wake Island, Wallis and Futuna

Maritime claims: *a variety of situations exist, but in general, most countries make the following claims measured from the mean low-tide baseline as described in the 1982 UN Convention on the Law of the Sea:* territorial sea - 12 nm, contiguous zone - 24 nm, and exclusive economic zone - 200 nm; additional zones provide for exploitation of continental shelf resources and an exclusive fishing zone; boundary situations with neighboring states prevent many countries from extending their fishing or economic zones to a full 200 nm

Climate: a wide equatorial band of hot and humid tropical climates is bordered north and south by subtropical temperate zones that separate two large areas of cold and dry polar climates
ten driest places on Earth (average annual precipitation): McMurdo Dry Valleys, Antarctica 0 mm (0 in)
Arica, Chile 0.76 mm (0.03 in)
Al Kufrah, Libya 0.86 mm (0.03 in)
Aswan, Egypt 0.86 mm (0.03 in)
Luxor, Egypt 0.86 mm (0.03 in)
Ica, Peru 2.29 mm (0.09 in)
Wadi Halfa, Sudan 2.45 mm (0.1 in)
Iquique, Chile 5.08 mm (0.2 in)
Pelican Point, Namibia 8.13 mm (0.32 in)
El Arab (Aoulef), Algeria 12.19 mm (0.48 in)
ten wettest places on Earth (average annual precipitation): Mawsynram, India 11,871 mm (467.4 in)
Cherrapunji, India 11,777 mm (463.7 in)
Tutunendo, Colombia 11,770 mm (463.4 in)
Cropp River, New Zealand 11,516 mm (453.4 in)
San Antonia de Ureca, Equatorial Guinea 10,450 mm (411.4 in)
Debundsha, Cameroon 10,299 mm (405.5 in)
Big Bog, US (Hawaii) 10,272 mm (404.4 in)
Mt Waialeale, US (Hawaii) 9,763 mm (384.4 in)
Kukui, US (Hawaii) 9,293 mm (365.9 in)
Emeishan, China 8,169 mm (321.6 in)
ten coldest places on Earth (lowest average monthly temperature): Verkhoyansk, Russia (Siberia) -47°C (-53°F) January
Oymyakon, Russia (Siberia) -46°C (-52°F) January
Eureka, Canada -38.4°C (-37.1°F) February
Isachsen, Canada -36°C (-32.8°F) February
Alert, Canada -34°C (-28°F) February
Kap Morris Jesup, Greenland -34°C (-29°F) March
Cornwallis Island, Canada -33.5°C (-28.3°F) February
Cambridge Bay, Canada -33.5°C (28.3°F) February
Ilirnej, Russia -33°C (-28°F) January
Resolute, Canada -33°C (-27.4°F) February
ten hottest places on Earth (highest average monthly temperature): Death Valley, US (California) 39°C (101°F) July Iranshahr, Iran 38.3°C (100.9°F) June
Ouallene, Algeria 38°C (100.4°F) July
Kuwait City, Kuwait 37.7°C (100°F) July
Medina, Saudi Arabia 36°C (97°F) July
Buckeye, US (Arizona) 34°C (93°F) July
Jazan, Saudi Arabia 33°C (91°F) June
Al Kufrah, Libya 31°C (87°F) July
Alice Springs, Australia 29°C (84°F) January
Tamanrasset, Algeria 29°C (84°F) June

Terrain: tremendous variation of terrain may be found on each of the continents, and a compilation of terrain extremes can be found in the World "Elevation" entry; the world's ocean floors also display extraordinary variation – check the "Bathymetry" and "Major surface currents" entries under each of the five ocean entries (Arctic, Atlantic, Indian, Pacific, and Southern) for further information on oceanic environs

Top ten world caves: compiled from "Geography - note(s)" under various country entries where more details may be found
largest cave: Son Doong in Phong Nha-Ke Bang National Park, Vietnam, is the world's largest cave (greatest cross sectional area) and is the largest known cave passage by volume; it currently measures a total of 38.5 million cu m (about 1.35 billion cu ft); it connects to Thung cave, but not yet officially – when recognized, it will add an additional 1.6 million cu m in volume
largest ice cave: the Eisriesenwelt (Ice Giants World) inside the Hochkogel mountain near Werfen, Austria, is the world's largest and longest ice cave system at 42 km (26 mi)
longest cave: Mammoth Cave in west-central Kentucky is the world's longest known cave system with more than 650 km (405 mi) of surveyed passageways
longest salt cave: the Malham Cave in Mount Sodom in Israel is the world's longest salt cave at 10 km (6 mi); its survey is not complete, so its recorded length will eventually increase
longest underwater cave: the Sac Actun cave system in Mexico is the longest underwater cave in the world at 348 km (216 mi), and the second longest cave worldwide
longest lava tube cave: Kazumura Cave on the island of Hawaii is the world's longest and deepest lava tube cave; it has been surveyed at 66 km (41 mi) long and 1,102 m (3,614 ft) deep
deepest cave: Veryovkina Cave in the country of Georgia is the world's deepest cave, plunging down 2,212 m (7,257 ft)
deepest underwater cave: the Hranice Abyss in Czechia is the world's deepest surveyed underwater cave at 404 m (1,325 ft); its survey is not complete, and it could be 800-1,200 m deep
largest cave chamber: the Miao Room in the Gebihe cave system in China's Ziyun Getu He Chuandong National Park has about 10.78 million cu m (380.7 million cu ft) of volume
largest bat cave: Bracken Cave outside San Antonio, Texas, is the world's largest bat cave; an estimated 20 million Mexican free-tailed bats roost in the cave from March to October, making it the world's largest known concentration of mammals
bonus "cave" - the world's largest sinkhole: the Xiaoxhai Tiankeng sinkhole in Chongqing Municipality, China is 660 m deep, with a volume of 130 million cu m

Elevation: *highest point:* Mount Everest 8,849 m
lowest point: Denman Glacier (Antarctica) more than -3,500 m (in the oceanic realm, Challenger Deep in the Mariana Trench is the lowest point, lying -10,924 m below the surface of the Pacific Ocean)
mean elevation: 840 m
top ten highest mountains (measured from sea level): Mount Everest (China-Nepal) 8,849 m; K2 (Pakistan) 8,611 m; Kanchenjunga (India-Nepal) 8,598 m; Lhotse (Nepal) 8,516 m; Makalu (China-Nepal) 8,463 m; Cho Oyu (China-Nepal) 8,201 m; Dhaulagiri (Nepal) 8,167 m; Manaslu (Nepal) 8,163 m; Nanga Parbat (Pakistan) 8,125 m; Anapurna (Nepal) 8,091 m; note - Mauna Kea (United States) is the world's tallest mountain as measured from base to summit; the peak of this volcanic colossus lies on the island of Hawaii, but its base begins more than 70 km offshore and at a depth of about 6,000 m; total height estimates range from 9,966 m to 10,203 m
top ten highest island peaks: Puncak Jaya (New Guinea) 4,884 m (Indonesia)*; Mauna Kea (Hawaii) 4,207 m (United States); Gunung Kinabalu (Borneo) 4,095 m (Malaysia)*; Yu Shan (Taiwan) 3,952 (Taiwan)*; Mount Kerinci (Sumatra) 3,805 m (Indonesia); Mount Erebus (Ross Island) 3,794 (Antarctica); Mount Fuji (Honshu) 3,776 m (Japan)*; Mount Rinjani (Lombok) 3,726 m (Indonesia); Aoraki-Mount Cook (South Island) 3,724 m (New Zealand)*; Pico de Teide (Tenerife) 3,718 m (Spain)*; note - * indicates the highest peak for that Factbook entry
highest point on each continent: Asia - Mount Everest (China-Nepal) 8,849 m; South America - Cerro Aconcagua (Argentina) 6,960 m; North America - Denali (Mount McKinley) (United States) 6,190 m; Africa - Kilimanjaro (Tanzania) 5,895 m; Europe - El'brus (Russia) 5,633 m; Antarctica - Vinson Massif 4,897 m; Australia - Mount Kosciuszko 2,229 m
highest capital on each continent: South America - La Paz (Bolivia) 3,640 m; Africa - Addis Ababa (Ethiopia) 2,355 m; Asia - Thimphu (Bhutan) 2,334 m; North America - Mexico City (Mexico) 2,240 m; Europe - Andorra la Vella (Andorra) 1,023 m; Australia - Canberra (Australia) 605 m
lowest point on each continent: Antarctica - Denman Glacier more than -3,500 m; Asia - Dead Sea (Israel-Jordan) -431 m; Africa - Lac Assal (Djibouti) -155 m; South America - Laguna del Carbon (Argentina) -105 m; North America - Death Valley (United States) -86 m; Europe - Caspian Sea (Azerbaijan-Kazakhstan-Russia) -28 m; Australia - Lake Eyre -15
lowest capital on each continent: Asia - Baku (Azerbaijan) -28 m; Europe - Amsterdam (Netherlands) -2 m; Africa - Banjul (Gambia); Bissau (Guinea-Bissau), Conakry (Guinea), Djibouti

(Djibouti), Libreville (Gabon), Male (Maldives), Monrovia (Liberia), Tunis (Tunisia), Victoria (Seychelles) 0 m; North America - Basseterre (Saint Kitts and Nevis), Kingstown (Saint Vincent and the Grenadines), Panama City (Panama), Port of Spain (Trinidad and Tobago), Roseau (Dominica), Saint John's (Antigua and Barbuda), Santo Domingo (Dominican Republic) 0 m; South America - Georgetown (Guyana) 0 m; Australia - Canberra (Australia) 605 m

Irrigated land: 3,242,917 sq km (2012 est.)

Major lakes (area sq km): *top ten largest natural lakes:* Caspian Sea (Azerbaijan, Iran, Kazakhstan, Russia, Turkmenistan) 374,000 sq km; Lake Superior (Canada, United States) 82,100 sq km; Lake Victoria (Kenya, Tanzania, Uganda) 62,940 sq km; Lake Huron (Canada, United States) 59,600 sq km; Lake Michigan (United States) 57,750 sq km; Lake Tanganyika (Burundi, Democratic Republic of the Congo, Tanzania, Zambia) 32,000 sq km; Great Bear Lake (Canada) 31,328 sq km; Lake Baikal (Russia) 31,500 sq km; Lake Malawi (Malawi, Mozambique, Tanzania) 22,490 sq km; Great Slave Lake (Canada) 28,568 sq km

note 1: the areas of the lakes are subject to seasonal variation; only the Caspian Sea is saline, the rest are fresh water

note 2: Lakes Huron and Michigan are technically a single lake because the flow of water between the Straits of Mackinac that connects the two lakes keeps their water levels at near-equilibrium; combined, Lake Huron-Michigan is the largest freshwater lake by surface area in the world

note 3: if ranked by water volume, the Caspian Sea would still be first, but it would be followed Lakes Baikal, Tanganyika, Superior, and Malawi; Lake Superior contains more water than the other four North American Great Lakes (Erie, Huron, Michigan, Ontario) combined

Major rivers (by length in km): *top ten longest rivers:* Nile (Africa) 6,650 km; Amazon (South America) 6,436 km; Yangtze (Asia) 6,300 km; Mississippi-Missouri (North America) 6,275 km; Yenisey-Angara (Asia) 5,539 km; Huang He/Yellow (Asia) 5,464 km; Ob- Irtysh (Asia) 5,410 km; Congo (Africa) 4,700 km; Amur (Asia) 4,444 km; Lena (Asia) 4,400 km

note: there are 21 countries without rivers: three in Africa (Comoros, Djibouti, Libya), one in the Americas (Bahamas), eight in Asia (Bahrain, Kuwait, Maldives, Oman, Qatar, Saudi Arabia, United Arab Emirates, Yemen), three in Europe (Malta, Monaco, Holy See), and six in Oceania (Kiribati, Marshall Islands, Nauru, Niue, Tonga, Tuvalu); these countries also do not have natural lakes

Major watersheds (area sq km): a watershed is a drainage basin on an area of land where precipitation collects and drains off into a common outlet, such as into a river, bay, or other body of water; oceans ultimately take in the drainage from 83% of all land area; the remaining 17% of the land drains into internal (endorheic) basins, e.g., the Caspian Sea

The World Factbook lists 51 different watersheds across 102 countries:
Asia - 18
Europe - 9
Africa- 9
North and Central America - 8
South America - 5
Australia - 2

all watersheds with an area of at least 500,000 sq km have been included, along with a number of smaller, regionally significant watersheds; together, these represent the surface hydrology water flows that are the world's primary sources of fresh water for individual consumption, industry, and agriculture

Major aquifers: aquifers are underground layers of water-bearing permeable rock formations; they include alluvial formations such as unconsolidated sand and gravel aquifers, sedimentary rock formations of sandstone and karst (carbonate rocks such as limestone) aquifers, as well as volcanic aquifers, and basement aquifers (igneous and metamorphic rocks that underlie sedimentary and volcanic rock sequences); groundwater from aquifers can be extracted using a water well

The World Factbook lists 37 major aquifers across 52 countries:
Africa - 13
Asia - 10
North America - 5
South America - 3
Europe - 4
Australia -2

although aquifers can vary in size, the major aquifers listed in *The Factbook* contain the bulk of the stored volume of groundwater; the fresh water held in these aquifers represents more than 30% of the world's fresh water; in the US, groundwater is primarily used for irrigation, and globally, 70% of groundwater withdrawn is used for agriculture; groundwater also supplies almost half of all drinking water worldwide

Population distribution: six of the world's seven continents are widely and permanently inhabited; Asia is the most populous continent with about 60% of the world's population (China and India together account for over 35%); Africa comes in second with over 15%, Europe has about 10%, North America 8%, South America almost 6%, and Oceania less than 1%; the harsh conditions on Antarctica prevent any permanent habitation

Natural hazards: large areas of the world are subject to severe weather (tropical cyclones) and natural disasters (earthquakes, landslides, tsunamis, volcanic eruptions)

volcanism: volcanism is a fundamental driver and consequence of plate tectonics, the physical process reshaping the Earth's lithosphere; the world is home to more than 1,500 potentially active volcanoes, with over 500 of these having erupted in historical times; an estimated 500 million people live near volcanoes; associated dangers include lava flows, lahars (mudflows), pyroclastic flows, ash clouds, ash fall, ballistic projectiles, gas emissions, landslides, earthquakes, and tsunamis; in the 1990s, the International Association of Volcanology and Chemistry of the Earth's Interior created a list of 16 "Decade Volcanoes" worthy of special study because of their great potential for destruction: Avachinsky- Koryaksky (Russia), Colima (Mexico), Etna (Italy), Galeras (Colombia), Mauna Loa (United States), Merapi (Indonesia), Nyiragongo (Democratic Republic of the Congo), Rainier (United States), Sakurajima (Japan), Santa Maria (Guatemala), Santorini (Greece), Taal (Philippines), Teide (Spain), Ulawun (Papua New Guinea), Unzen (Japan), Vesuvius (Italy); see second note under "Geography - note"

Volcano statistics: *countries with the most volcanoes (Holocene Epoch, the past 12,000 years):* United States (162), Japan (122), Indonesia (120), Russia (117), Chile (91); note - roughly 1,350 volcanoes have erupted over this time period; about 40-50 eruptions are ongoing at any one time; the frequency of volcanoes has not increased

longest erupting volcano: Santa Maria volcano in Guatemala has been constantly erupting since 22 June 1922; note - Captain Cook observed the Yasur volcano on Tanna Island in Vanuatu in 1774, and it has since been in constant activity but is not cited due to lack of a clear start date; research (tephra stratigraphy and radiocarbon dating) shows that activity may have begun on Yasur ca. A.D. 1270 and so has persisted for over 750 years

highest volcano (above sea level): Nevado Ojos del Salado (6,893 m; 22,615 ft) on the Chile-Argentina border is the world's highest volcano above sea level and the highest peak in Chile

highest volcano (from base): Mauna Kea (United States) is the world's tallest mountain as measured from base to summit; the peak of this volcanic colossus lies on the island of Hawaii, but its base begins more than 70 km offshore and at a depth of about 6,000 m; total height estimates range from 9,966 m to 10,203 m

Wonders of the World: The Seven Wonders of the Ancient World: The conquests of Alexander the Great (r. 336-323 B.C.) in the fourth century B.C. fostered the spread of Greek culture to the lands bordering the eastern Mediterranean and through much of the Middle East, ushering in what is today referred to as the Hellenistic Period (323-31 B.C.). Hellenistic sightseers compiled guidebooks focused on outstanding monuments in those parts of the world, including Persia, Egypt, and Babylon. Generally, seven sites were emphasized since that number was considered magical, perfect, and complete. Not all Wonders lists from ancient times agreed, but six sites consistently appeared (the massive Walls of Babylon sometimes substituted for the Lighthouse of Alexandria). The seven described below represent the "classic" Seven Wonders most often cited.

1.The Great Pyramid of Egypt

The oldest of the Seven Wonders, the Great Pyramid, is the only one that remains largely intact. Commissioned by the Pharaoh Khufu (r. ca. 2589-2566 B.C.), it is the largest of the three pyramids at Giza. It served as the ruler's tomb and was built over a period of about 20 years, concluding around 2560 B.C. The pyramid is estimated to have been 146.5 m tall when completed and was the tallest manmade structure in the world for over 3,800 years (until the 14th century A.D.). Most of the original limestone casing stones that formed the outer smooth surface of the pyramid are gone. Today, the pyramid's height is about 139 m.

2. The Hanging Gardens of Babylon

This is the only one of the ancient Seven Wonders for which a definitive location has never been established. No surviving Babylonian texts mention the Gardens, nor have any archeological remains been discovered in today's Iraq. According to tradition, the Gardens were a remarkable feat of engineering with an ascending series of mud-brick-tiered gardens containing a variety of trees, shrubs, and vines that, when viewed from below, resembled a leafy green mountain. The Gardens are frequently attributed to the Neo-Babylonian King Nebuchadnezzar II (r. 605-562 B.C.), who may have had them built for his Median wife Queen Amytis because she missed the green hills and valleys of her homeland.

3. The Temple of Artemis (Artemision) at Ephesus

This Greek temple at Ephesus (3 km southwest of Selcuk in present-day western Turkey) was dedicated to the goddess Artemis and was completely rebuilt twice: once after a 7th century B.C. flood and then after a 356 B.C. act of arson. In its final form, it was judged to be one of the Seven Wonders and survived for 600 years. The magnificent building was composed entirely of marble, with massive dimensions reported to be 130 m by 69 m, and included 127 columns, each some 18 m tall. The Temple was damaged in a Gothic raid in A.D. 268, and Christians finally closed it in the early-to-mid 5th century. The structure was dismantled in succeeding centuries, and today almost nothing of the temple remains.

4. The Mausoleum of Halicarnassus

Constructed in about 350 B.C., the Mausoleum of Halicarnassus was located on the site of the present-day city of Bodrum in southwestern Turkey. It was the tomb of Mausolus, a Persian ruler, and his wife – the term "mausoleum" is derived from his name. The structure stood about 45 m high and took some 20 years to complete. A series of earthquakes between the 12th and 15th centuries A.D. devastated the structure, which was the last of the original Seven Wonders to be destroyed.

5. The Colossus of Rhodes

This statue of the Greek sun god Helios, constructed to celebrate Rhodes' successful repulse of a siege, was made of iron tie bars to which brass or bronze plates were attached to form a skin. Contemporary descriptions list its height at about 70 cubits or some 33 m – approximately the same height as the Statue of Liberty from heel to top of head (34 m) – thus making it the tallest statue in the ancient world. Completed in about 280 B.C. at the entrance to the Rhodes harbor, the monument stood for only about 54 years until it toppled in an earthquake in 226 B.C. The impressive remains lay on the ground for over 800 years before finally being sold for scrap.

6. The Lighthouse (Pharos) of Alexandria

Completed around 275 B.C., the lighthouse stood on Pharos Island at the entrance to the Egyptian port city of Alexandria for some 1,600 years. Three earthquakes severely damaged it between A.D. 956 and 1323, when it was deactivated. The shape of the structure appeared on a number of ancient coins: a solid square base, which made up about half of the height, supported an octagonal middle section and a cylindrical top. The height of the structure is thought to have been at least 100 m and perhaps as high as 140 m. (The tallest lighthouse in the world today is the Jeddah Light in Saudi Arabia, which stands at 133 m.) At its apex stood a mirror that reflected sunlight during the day; a fire burned at night.

7. The Statue of Zeus at Olympia in Greece

The giant seated statue of the king of the Greek gods in the sanctuary of Olympia was completed by the Greek sculptor Phidias in approximately 435 B.C. Roughly 13 m tall, it was constructed of ivory plates and gold panels on a wooden framework, and the god's throne was ornamented with ebony, ivory, gold, and precious stones. With the rise of Christianity, the sanctuary at Olympia fell into disuse; the details of the statue's final destruction are unknown.

note: The Lighthouse of Alexandria may have been the last of the Wonders to be completed (ca. 275 B.C.), and the Colossus of Rhodes was the first to be destroyed in about 226 B.C., so the Seven Wonders existed at the same time for only about 50 years in the middle of the third century B.C.

The New Seven Wonders of the World: A private initiative to come up with a new list for seven of the world's wonders sprang up early in the new Millennium. Worldwide balloting – via internet or telephone – took place, covering a list of 200 existing monuments. Over 100 million votes were reportedly cast over a period of several years and the final list was announced on 7-7-2007. Even though the polling was unscientific, the seven "winners" were a worthy compilation of extraordinary Wonders to be found around the world. All seven of the New Wonders are inscribed as UNESCO World Heritage Sites and are frequently cited in the literature.

1. Chichen Itza,Yucatan, Mexico

This archeological site includes the impressive remains of a large pre-Columbian Mayan city that flourished from ca. A.D. 600-1100. Among the outstanding structures at the site are the massive Temple of the Warriors complex, an Observatory (El Caracol), the Great Ball Court, and the Sacred Cenote (sinkhole) where offerings were made. The most famous building, however, is the step-pyramid known as the Temple of Kukulcan that dominates the center of the site and serves as the symbol of Chichen Itza. The pyramidal structure is 24 m high; the crowning temple adds another 6 m. Although located in the dense jungles of Yucatan, it remains one of the most visited tourist sites in Mexico.

2.The Colosseum, Rome, Italy

The Roman Emperor Vespasian began construction on the Colosseum in A.D. 72, and his son Titus completed it in A.D. 80. Further modifications were made by Domitian (A.D. 81-96). The three emperors make up the Flavian Dynasty, thus providing the structure's alternate name, the Flavian Amphitheater. The massive structure is estimated to have seated, on average, about 65 thousand spectators and was most famously used for gladiatorial contests and public spectacles. Earthquakes and thieves destroyed much of the original structure, but it nonetheless remains an iconic symbol of Rome. The Colosseum is one of the most popular tourist attractions in the World.

3. Christ the Redeemer Statue, Rio de Janeiro, Brazil

Built between 1922 and 1931, the 30-meter-tall sculpture is reputed to be the largest Art Deco statue in the World. Its pedestal provides another 8 m in height and the arms stretch out to 28 m. Constructed of reinforced concrete and soapstone, the statue has become the cultural icon not only of Rio, but also of Brazil.

4. Great Wall, China

The name refers to a remarkable series of fortification systems that stretched across China's northern historical borders and served as protection against various nomadic peoples. An archeological survey revealed that the Wall and all its associated branches measures 21,196 km. The earliest of these walls date to the 7th century B.C.; certain stretches began to be linked in the 3rd century B.C., and successive dynasties added to or maintained various sections of the walls. The best-known and best-preserved portions of the wall are those built during the Ming Dynasty (1368-1644). Winding through amazingly varied terrain, the Great Wall is acknowledged as one of the most impressive architectural feats in history.

5. Machu Picchu, Cuzco Region, Peru

Perhaps the most spectacular archeological site in the Americas, the Inca citadel of Machu Picchu, situated on a 2,430 m Andean mountain ridge, is now thought to have been erected as an estate for the Inca Emperor Pachacuti (r. 1438-1471) and may have also served as a religious sanctuary. Built between about 1450 and 1460, it was abandoned approximately a century later, at the time of the Spanish conquest. Construction was carried out in the classic Inca style of polished, fitted, dry-stone walls. Some 750 people lived at this royal estate, most of them support staff to the nobility. The site is roughly divided into an agricultural sector (with myriad terraces for raising crops) and an urban sector. The latter is composed of an upper town (with temples) and a lower town (with warehouses). Some of the religious monuments include: the Intiwatana (a carved, ritual stone that served as a type of sundial and that is referred to as "The Hitching Post of the Sun"); the Torreon or Temple of the Sun, a small tower that likely served as a type of observatory; and the Intimachay, a sacred cave with a masonry entrance.

6. Petra, Ma'an, Jordan

Petra is believed to have been established in the 4th century B.C. as the capital of the Nabataean Kingdom, an entity that grew fabulously wealthy as the nexus of trade routes in the southern Levant. The kingdom retained its independence until the Roman Empire annexed it in A.D. 106. The city is famous for its stunning rock-cut architecture and its water conduit system, which allowed the Nabataeans to control and store the water supply in this desert region and create an artificial oasis. At its peak in the 1st century A.D., the city may have had a population of 20,000.

7.Taj Mahal, Agra, Uttar Pradesh, India

This gorgeous ivory-white mausoleum – described as "one of the universally admired masterpieces of the world's heritage" – was commissioned in 1632 by Shah Jahan (r. 1628-1658) as the final resting place for his favorite wife, Mumtaz Mahal. The building also houses the tomb of Shah Jahan himself. The Taj Mahal is the centerpiece of an entire 17-hectare complex that also includes a guest house, a mosque, and formal gardens. The entire project was not completed until about 1653. The Taj Mahal remains one of the most visited tourist sites in the world.

note: The Great Pyramid of Egypt, the only surviving Wonder of the ancient Seven, received an honorary status among the New Seven Wonders. Its inclusion enabled a Wonder to be listed for five of the six habitable continents (all but Australia).

Geography - note: *note 1:* the World is now thought to be about 4.55 billion years old, just about one-third of the 13.8-billion-year age estimated for the universe; the earliest widely accepted date for life appearing on Earth is 3.48 billion years ago

note 2: although earthquakes can strike anywhere at any time, the vast majority occur in three large zones of the Earth; the world's greatest earthquake belt, the Circum-Pacific Belt (popularly referred to as the Ring of Fire), is the zone of active volcanoes and earthquake epicenters bordering the Pacific Ocean; about 90% of the world's earthquakes (81% of the largest earthquakes) and some 75% of the world's volcanoes occur within the Ring of Fire; the belt extends northward from Chile, along the South American coast, through Central America, Mexico, the western US, southern Alaska and the Aleutian Islands, to Japan, the Philippines, Papua New Guinea, island groups in the southwestern Pacific, and New Zealand

the second prominent belt, the Alpide, extends from Java to Sumatra, northward along the mountains of Burma, then eastward through the Himalayas, the Mediterranean, and out into the Atlantic Ocean; it accounts for about 17% of the world's largest earthquakes; the third important belt follows the long Mid-Atlantic Ridge

note 3: information on the origin sites for many of the world's major food crops may be found in the "Geography - note" for the following countries: Argentina, Bolivia, Brazil, China, Ecuador, Ethiopia, Indonesia, Mexico, Papua New Guinea, Paraguay, Peru, and the United States

PEOPLE AND SOCIETY

Population: *total:* 8,057,236,243
male: 4,046,854,454
female: 4,010,381,789 (2024 est.)

Languages: *most-spoken language:* English 18.8%, Mandarin Chinese 13.8%, Hindi 7.5%, Spanish 6.9%, French 3.4%, Arabic 3.4%, Bengali 3.4%, Russian 3.2%, Portuguese 3.2%, Urdu 2.9% (2022 est.)
most-spoken first language: Mandarin Chinese 12.3%, Spanish 6%, English 5.1%, Arabic 5.1%, Hindi 3.5%, Bengali 3.3%, Portuguese 3%, Russian 2.1%, Japanese 1.7%, Punjabi, Western 1.3%, Javanese 1.1% (2018 est.)
note 1: the six UN languages - Arabic, Chinese (Mandarin), English, French, Russian, and Spanish (Castilian) - are the mother tongue or second language of about 49.6% of the world's population (2022), and are the official languages in more than half the states in the world; some 400 languages have more than a million first-language speakers (2018)
note 2: all told, there are estimated to be 7,168 living languages spoken in the world (2023); approximately 80% of these languages are spoken by less than 100,000 people; about 150 languages are spoken by fewer than 10 people; communities that are isolated from each other in mountainous regions often develop multiple languages; Papua New Guinea, for example, boasts about 840 separate languages (2018)
note 3: approximately 2,300 languages are spoken in Asia, 2,140, in Africa, 1,310 in the Pacific, 1,060 in the Americas, and 290 in Europe (2020)

Religions: Christian 31.1%, Muslim 24.9%, Hindu 15.2%, Buddhist 6.6%, folk religions 5.6%, Jewish <1%, other <1%, unaffiliated 15.6% (2020 est.)

Age structure: *0-14 years:* 24.5% (male 1,018,005,046/female 958,406,907)
15-64 years: 65.2% (male 2,658,595,672/female 2,592,930,538)
65 years and over: 10.3% (2024 est.) (male 370,253,736/female 459,044,344)

Dependency ratios: *total dependency ratio:* 54.1
youth dependency ratio: 39.3
elderly dependency ratio: 14.8
potential support ratio: 7 (2021 est.)

Median age: *total:* 31 years (2020 est.)
male: 30.3 years
female: 31.8 years

Population growth rate: 1.03% (2021 est.)
note: this rate results in about 154 net additions to the worldwide population every minute or 2.6 people every second

Birth rate: 17 births/1,000 population (2024 est.)
note: this rate results in about 260 worldwide births per minute or 4.3 births every second

Death rate: 7.9 deaths/1,000 population (2024 est.)
note: this rate results in about 121 worldwide deaths per minute or 2 deaths every second

Population distribution: six of the world's seven continents are widely and permanently inhabited; Asia is the most populous continent with about 60% of the world's population (China and India together account for over 35%); Africa comes in second with over 15%, Europe has about 10%, North America 8%, South America almost 6%, and Oceania less than 1%; the harsh conditions on Antarctica prevent any permanent habitation

Urbanization: *urban population:* 57.5% of total population (2023)
rate of urbanization: 1.73% annual rate of change (2020-25 est.)

Major urban areas - population: *ten largest urban agglomerations:* Tokyo (Japan) - 37,393,000; New Delhi (India) - 30,291,000; Shanghai (China) - 27,058,000; Sao Paulo (Brazil) - 22,043,000; Mexico City (Mexico) - 21,782,000; Dhaka (Bangladesh) - 21,006,000; Cairo (Egypt) - 20,901,000; Beijing (China) - 20,463,000; Mumbai (India) - 20,411,000; Osaka (Japan) - 19,165,000 (2020)
ten largest urban agglomerations, by continent:
Africa - Cairo (Egypt) - 20,901,000; Lagos (Nigeria) - 134,368,000; Kinshasha (DRC) - 14,342,000; Luanda (Angola) - 8,330,000; Dar Es Salaam (Tanzania) - 6,702,000; Khartoum (Sudan) - 5,829,000; Johannesburg (South Africa) - 5,783,000; Alexandria (Egypt) - 5,281,000; Abidjan (Cote d'Ivoire) - 5,203,000; Addis Ababa (Ethiopia) - 4,794,000
Asia - Tokyo (Japan) - 37,393,000; New Delhi (India) - 30,291,000; Shanghai (China) - 27,058,000; Dhaka (Bangladesh) - 21,006,000; Beijing (China) - 20,463,000; Mumbai (India) - 20,411,000; Osaka (Japan) - 19,165,000; Karachi (Pakistan) - 16,094,000; Chongqing (China) - 15,872,000; Istanbul (Turkey) - 15,190,000
Europe - Moscow (Russia) - 12,538,000; Paris (France) - 11,017,000; London (United Kingdom) - 9,304,000; Madrid (Spain) - 6,618,000; Barcelona (Spain) - 5,586,000, Saint Petersburg (Russia) - 5,468,000; Rome (Italy) - 4,257,000; Berlin (Germany) - 3,562,000; Athens (Greece) - 3,153,000; Milan (Italy) - 3,140,000
North America - Mexico City (Mexico) - 21,782,000; New York-Newark (United States) - 18,804,000; Los Angeles-Long Beach-Santa Ana (United States) - 12,447,000; Chicago (United States) - 8,865,000; Houston (United States) - 6,371,000; Dallas-Fort Worth (United States) - 6,301,000; Toronto (Canada) - 6,197,000; Miami (United States) - 6,122,000; Atlanta (United States) - 5,803,000; Philadelphia (United States) - 5,717,000
Oceania - Melbourne (Australia) - 4,968,000, Sydney (Australia) - 4,926,000; Brisbane (Australia) - 2,406,000; Perth (Australia) - 2,042,000; Auckland (New Zealand) - 1,607,000; Adelaide (Australia) - 1,336,000; Gold Coast-Tweed Head (Australia) - 699,000; Canberra (Australia) - 457,000; Newcastle-Maitland (Australia) - 450,000; Wellington (New Zealand) - 415,000
South America - Sao Paulo (Brazil) - 22,043,000; Buenos Aires (Argentina) - 15,154,000; Rio de Janeiro (Brazil) - 13,458,000; Bogota (Colombia) - 10,978,000; Lima (Peru) - 10,719,000; Santiago (Chile) - 6,767,000; Belo Horizonte (Brazil) - 6,084,000; Brasilia (Brazil) - 4,646,000; Porto Alegre (Brazil) - 4,137,000; Recife (Brazil) - 4,127,000 (2020)

Sex ratio: *at birth:* 1.05 male(s)/female
0-14 years: 1.05 male(s)/female
15-64 years: 1.03 male(s)/female
65 years and over: 0.81 male(s)/female
total population: 1.01 male(s)/female (2024 est.)

Maternal mortality ratio: 211 deaths/100,000 live births (2017 est.)

Infant mortality rate: *total:* 28.3 deaths/1,000 live births (2024 est.)

Life expectancy at birth: *total population:* 70.5 years (2020)
male: 68.4 years
female: 72.6 years

Total fertility rate: 2.42 children born/woman (2020 est.)

Drinking water source: *improved: urban:* 96.5% of population
rural: 84.7% of population
total: 91.1% of population
unimproved: urban: 3.5% of population
rural: 15.3% of population
total: 8.9% of population (2015 est.)

Sanitation facility access: *improved: urban:* 82.3% of population
rural: 50.5% of population
total: 67.7% of population
unimproved: urban: 17.7% of population
rural: 49.5% of population
total: 32.3% of population (2015 est.)

Currently married women (ages 15-49): 66.2% (2023 est.)

Child marriage: *women married by age 15:* 5%
women married by age 18: 18.7% (2022 est.)
men married by age 18: 2.8% (2021 est.)

Literacy: *definition:* age 15 and over can read and write
total population: 86.7%
male: 90.1%
female: 83.3% (2020)
note: more than three quarters of the world's 750 million illiterate adults are found in South Asia and sub-Saharan Africa; of all the illiterate adults in the world, almost two thirds are women (2016)

School life expectancy (primary to tertiary education): *total:* 13 years
male: 13 years
female: 13 years (2020)

ENVIRONMENT

Environment - current issues: large areas of the world are subject to overpopulation, industrial disasters, pollution (air, water, acid rain, toxic substances), loss of vegetation (overgrazing, deforestation, desertification), loss of biodiversity; soil degradation, soil depletion, erosion; ozone layer depletion; waste disposal; global warming becoming a greater concern

World biomes:Types of Biomes: A biome is a biogeographical designation describing a biological community of plants and animals that has formed in response to a physical environment and a shared regional climate. Biomes can extend over more than one continent. Different classification systems define different numbers of biomes. The World Factbook recognizes the following seven biomes used by NASA: tundra, coniferous forest, temperate deciduous forest, rainforest, grassland, shrubland, and desert.

Tundra biome: The tundra is the coldest of the biomes. It also receives low amounts of precipitation, making the tundra similar to a desert. Tundra comes from the Finnish word *tunturia,* meaning "treeless plain." Tundra is found in the regions just below the ice caps of the Arctic, extending across North America to Europe and to Siberia in Asia. Temperatures usually range between -40°C (-40 °F) and 18°C (64°F). The temperatures are so cold that there is a layer of permanently frozen ground below the surface, called permafrost. This permafrost is a defining characteristic of the tundra biome. In the tundra summers, the top layer of soil thaws only a few inches down, providing a growing surface for the roots of vegetation. This biome sees 150 to 250 mm (6 to 10 in) of rain per year. Vegetation in the tundra has adapted to the cold and the short growing season and consists of lichens, mosses, grasses, sedges, and shrubs, but almost no trees.

Coniferous Forest biome: The coniferous forest is sandwiched between the tundra to the north and the deciduous forest to the south. Coniferous forest regions have long, cold, snowy winters; warm, humid summers; well-defined seasons; and at least four to six frost-free months. The average temperature in winter ranges from -40°C (-40°F) to 20°C (68°F). The average summer temperatures are usually around 10°C (50°F). 300 to 900 mm (12 to 35 in) of rain per year can be expected in this biome. Vegetation consists of trees that produce cones and needles, which are called coniferous-evergreen trees. Some needles remain on the trees all year long. Some of the more common conifers are spruces, pines, and firs.

Temperate Deciduous Forest biome: Temperate deciduous forests are located in the mid-latitude areas, which means that they are found between the polar regions and the tropics. The deciduous forest regions are exposed to warm and cold air masses, which cause this area to have four seasons. Hot summers and cold winters are typical. The average daily temperatures range between -30°C (-22°F) and 30°C (86°F), with a yearly average of 10°C (50°F). On average, this biome receives 750 to 1,500 mm (30 to 59 in) of rain per year. Vegetation includes broadleaf trees (oaks, maples, beeches), shrubs, perennial herbs, and mosses.

Rainforest biome: The rainforest biome remains warm all year and stay frost-free. The average daily temperatures range from 20°C (68°F) to 25°C (77°F). Rainforests receive the most yearly rainfall of all of the biomes, and a typical year sees 2,000 to 10,000 mm (79 to 394 in) of rain. Vegetation typically includes vines, palm trees, orchids, and ferns. There are two types of rainforests: tropical rainforests are found closer to the equator, and temperate rainforests are found farther north near coastal areas. The majority of common houseplants come from the rainforest.

Grassland biome: Grasslands are open, continuous, and fairly flat areas of grass. Found on every continent except Antarctica, they are often located between temperate forests at high latitudes and deserts at subtropical latitudes. Depending on latitude, the annual temperature range can be -20°C (-4°F) to 30°C (86°F). Grasslands receive around 500 to 900 mm (20 to 35 in) of rain per year. Tropical grasslands have dry and wet seasons that remain warm all the time. Temperate grasslands have cold winters and warm summers with some rain. Vegetation is dominated by grasses but can include sedges and rushes, along with some legumes (clover) and herbs. A few trees may be found in this biome along the streams, but not many due to the lack of rainfall.

Shrubland biome: Shrublands include chaparral, woodland, and savanna, and are composed of shrubs or short trees. Many shrubs thrive on steep, rocky slopes, but there is usually not enough rain to support tall trees. Shrublands are located in west coastal regions between 30° and 40° North and South latitude and are usually found on the borders of deserts and grasslands. The summers are hot and dry with temperatures up to 38°C (100°F). Winters are cool and moist, with temperatures around -1 °C (30°F). Annual rainfall in the shrublands varies greatly, but 200 to 1,000 mm (8 to 40 in) of rain per year can be expected. Vegetation includes aromatic herbs (sage, rosemary, thyme, oregano), shrubs, acacia, chamise, grasses. Plants have adapted to fire caused by frequent lightning strikes in the summer.

Desert biome: The most important characteristic of a desert biome is that it receives very little rainfall, usually about 250 mm (10 in) of rain per year. During the day, desert temperatures rise to an average of 38°C (100°F). At night, desert temperatures fall to an average of -4°C (about 25°F). Vegetation is sparse, consisting of cacti, small bushes, and short grasses. Perennials survive for several years by becoming dormant and flourishing when water is available. Annuals are referred to as ephemerals because some can complete an entire life cycle in weeks. Since desert conditions are so severe, the plants that live there need to adapt to compensate. Some, such as cacti, store water in their stems and use it very slowly, while others, like bushes, conserve water by growing few leaves or by having large root systems to gather water.

Climate: a wide equatorial band of hot and humid tropical climates is bordered north and south by subtropical temperate zones that separate two large areas of cold and dry polar climates
ten driest places on Earth (average annual precipitation): McMurdo Dry Valleys, Antarctica 0 mm (0 in)
Arica, Chile 0.76 mm (0.03 in)
Al Kufrah, Libya 0.86 mm (0.03 in)
Aswan, Egypt 0.86 mm (0.03 in)
Luxor, Egypt 0.86 mm (0.03 in)
Ica, Peru 2.29 mm (0.09 in)
Wadi Halfa, Sudan 2.45 mm (0.1 in)
Iquique, Chile 5.08 mm (0.2 in)
Pelican Point, Namibia 8.13 mm (0.32 in)
El Arab (Aoulef), Algeria 12.19 mm (0.48 in)
ten wettest places on Earth (average annual precipitation): Mawsynram, India 11,871 mm (467.4 in)
Cherrapunji, India 11,777 mm (463.7 in)
Tutunendo, Colombia 11,770 mm (463.4 in)
Cropp River, New Zealand 11,516 mm (453.4 in)
San Antonia de Ureca, Equatorial Guinea 10,450 mm (411.4 in)
Debundsha, Cameroon 10,299 mm (405.5 in)
Big Bog, US (Hawaii) 10,272 mm (404.4 in)
Mt Waialeale, US (Hawaii) 9,763 mm (384.4 in)
Kukui, US (Hawaii) 9,293 mm (365.9 in)
Emeishan, China 8,169 mm (321.6 in)
ten coldest places on Earth (lowest average monthly temperature): Verkhoyansk, Russia (Siberia) -47°C (-53°F)
January
Oymyakon, Russia (Siberia) -46°C (-52°F) January
Eureka, Canada -38.4°C (-37.1°F) February
Isachsen, Canada -36°C (-32.8°F) February
Alert, Canada -34°C (-28°F) February
Kap Morris Jesup, Greenland -34°C (-29°F) March
Cornwallis Island, Canada -33.5°C (-28.3°F) February
Cambridge Bay, Canada -33.5°C (28.3°F) February
Ilirnej, Russia -33°C (-28°F) January
Resolute, Canada -33°C (-27.4°F) February
ten hottest places on Earth (highest average monthly temperature): Death Valley, US (California) 39°C (101°F) July
Iranshahr, Iran 38.3°C (100.9°F) June
Ouallene, Algeria 38°C (100.4°F) July
Kuwait City, Kuwait 37.7°C (100°F) July
Medina, Saudi Arabia 36°C (97°F) July
Buckeye, US (Arizona) 34°C (93°F) July
Jazan, Saudi Arabia 33°C (91°F) June
Al Kufrah, Libya 31°C (87°F) July
Alice Springs, Australia 29°C (84°F) January
Tamanrasset, Algeria 29°C (84°F) June

Urbanization: *urban population:* 57.5% of total population (2023)
rate of urbanization: 1.73% annual rate of change (2020-25 est.)

Major lakes (area sq km): *top ten largest natural lakes:* Caspian Sea (Azerbaijan, Iran, Kazakhstan, Russia, Turkmenistan) 374,000 sq km; Lake Superior (Canada, United States) 82,100 sq km; Lake Victoria (Kenya, Tanzania, Uganda) 62,940 sq km; Lake Huron (Canada, United States) 59,600 sq km; Lake Michigan (United States) 57,750 sq km; Lake Tanganyika (Burundi, Democratic Republic of the Congo, Tanzania, Zambia) 32,000 sq km; Great Bear Lake (Canada) 31,328 sq km; Lake Baikal (Russia) 31,500 sq km; Lake Malawi (Malawi, Mozambique, Tanzania) 22,490 sq km; Great Slave Lake (Canada) 28,568 sq km
note 1: the areas of the lakes are subject to seasonal variation; only the Caspian Sea is saline, the rest are fresh water
note 2: Lakes Huron and Michigan are technically a single lake because the flow of water between the Straits of Mackinac that connects the two lakes keeps their water levels at near-equilibrium; combined, Lake Huron-Michigan is the largest freshwater lake by surface area in the world
note 3: if ranked by water volume, the Caspian Sea would still be first, but it would be followed Lakes Baikal, Tanganyika, Superior, and Malawi; Lake Superior contains more water than the other four North American Great Lakes (Erie, Huron, Michigan, Ontario) combined

Major rivers (by length in km): *top ten longest rivers:* Nile (Africa) 6,650 km; Amazon (South America) 6,436 km; Yangtze (Asia) 6,300 km; Mississippi-Missouri (North America) 6,275 km; Yenisey-Angara (Asia) 5,539 km; Huang He/Yellow (Asia) 5,464 km; Ob- Irtysh (Asia) 5,410 km; Congo (Africa) 4,700 km; Amur (Asia) 4,444 km; Lena (Asia) 4,400 km
note: there are 21 countries without rivers: three in Africa (Comoros, Djibouti, Libya), one in the Americas (Bahamas), eight in Asia (Bahrain, Kuwait, Maldives, Oman, Qatar, Saudi Arabia, United Arab Emirates, Yemen), three in Europe (Malta, Monaco, Holy See), and six in Oceania (Kiribati, Marshall Islands, Nauru, Niue, Tonga, Tuvalu); these countries also do not have natural lakes

Major watersheds (area sq km): a watershed is a drainage basin on an area of land where precipitation collects and drains off into a common outlet, such as into a river, bay, or other body of water; oceans ultimately take in the drainage from 83% of all land area; the remaining 17% of the land drains into internal (endorheic) basins, e.g., the Caspian Sea
The World Factbook lists 51 different watersheds across 102 countries:
Asia - 18
Europe - 9
Africa- 9
North and Central America - 8
South America - 5
Australia - 2

all watersheds with an area of at least 500,000 sq km have been included, along with a number of smaller, regionally significant watersheds; together, these represent the surface hydrology water flows that are the world's primary sources of fresh water for individual consumption, industry, and agriculture

Major aquifers: aquifers are underground layers of water-bearing permeable rock formations; they include alluvial formations such as unconsolidated sand and gravel aquifers, sedimentary rock formations of sandstone and karst (carbonate rocks such as limestone) aquifers, as well as volcanic aquifers, and basement aquifers (igneous and metamorphic rocks that underlie sedimentary and volcanic rock sequences); groundwater from aquifers can be extracted using a water well

The World Factbook lists 37 major aquifers across 52 countries:
Africa - 13
Asia - 10
North America - 5
South America - 3
Europe - 4
Australia -2
although aquifers can vary in size, the major aquifers listed in *The Factbook* contain the bulk of the stored volume of groundwater; the fresh water held in these aquifers represents more than 30% of the world's fresh water; in the US, groundwater is primarily used for irrigation, and globally, 70% of groundwater withdrawn is used for agriculture; groundwater also supplies almost half of all drinking water worldwide

Total renewable water resources: 54 trillion cubic meters (2011 est.)

GOVERNMENT

Capital: *time difference:* there are 21 world entities (20 countries and 1 dependency) with multiple time zones: Australia, Brazil, Canada, Chile, Democratic Republic of Congo, Ecuador, France, Greenland (part of the Danish Kingdom), Indonesia, Kazakhstan, Kiribati, Mexico, Micronesia, Mongolia, Netherlands, New Zealand, Papua New Guinea, Portugal, Russia, Spain, United States

note 1: in some instances, the time zones pertain to portions of a country that lie overseas

note 2: in 1851, the British set their prime meridian (0° longitude) through the Royal Observatory at Greenwich, England; this meridian became the international standard in 1884 and thus the basis for the standard time zones of the world; today, GMT is officially known as Coordinated Universal Time (UTC) and is also referred to as "Zulu time"; UTC is the basis for all civil time, with the world divided into time zones expressed as positive or negative differences from UTC

note 3: each time zone is based on 15° starting from the prime meridian; in theory, there are 24 time zones based on the solar day, but there are now upward of 40 because of fractional hour offsets that adjust for various political and physical geographic realities; see the Standard Time Zones of the World map included with the World and Regional Maps

daylight saving time: some 67 countries – including most of the world's leading industrialized nations – use daylight savings time (DST) in at least a portion of the country; China, Japan, India, and Russia are major industrialized countries that do not use DST; Asia and Africa generally do not observe DST, and it is generally not observed near the equator, where sunrise and sunset times do not vary enough to justify it; some countries observe DST only in certain regions; only a minority of the world's population – about 20% – uses DST

Administrative divisions: 197 countries, 69 dependent areas and other entities

Dependent areas: Australia dependencies: Ashmore and Cartier Islands, Christmas Island, Cocos (Keeling) Islands, Coral Sea Islands, Heard Island and McDonald Islands, Norfolk Island (6)

France dependencies: Clipperton Island, French Polynesia, French Southern and Antarctic Lands, New Caledonia, Saint Barthelemy, Saint Martin, Saint Pierre and Miquelon, Wallis and Futuna (8)

New Zealand dependency: Tokelau (1)

Norway dependencies: Bouvet Island, Jan Mayen, Svalbard (3)

United Kingdom dependencies: Anguilla; Bermuda; British Indian Ocean Territory; British Virgin Islands; Cayman Islands; Falkland Islands; Gibraltar; Montserrat; Pitcairn Islands; Saint Helena, Ascension, and Tristan da Cunha; South Georgia and the South Sandwich Islands; Turks and Caicos Islands (12)

United States dependencies: American Samoa, Baker Island, Guam, Howland Island, Jarvis Island, Johnston Atoll, Kingman Reef, Midway Islands, Navassa Island, Northern Mariana Islands, Palmyra Atoll, Puerto Rico, Virgin Islands, Wake Island (14)

Legal system: *the legal systems of nearly all countries are modeled on elements of five main types:* civil law (including French law, the Napoleonic Code, Roman law, Roman-Dutch law, and Spanish law), common law (including English and US law), customary law, mixed or pluralistic law, and religious law (including Islamic sharia law); an additional type of legal system – international law – governs the conduct of independent nations in their relationships with one another

International law organization participation: all members of the UN are parties to the statute that established the International Court of Justice (ICJ) or World Court; states parties to the Rome Statute of the International Criminal Court (ICCt) are those countries that have ratified or acceded to the Rome Statute, the treaty that established the Court; as of May 2019, a total of 122 countries have accepted jurisdiction of the ICCt (see the reference guide on International Organizations and Groups for clarification on the differing mandates of the ICJ and ICCt)

Executive branch: *chief of state:* there are 27 countries with royal families in the world: most are in Asia (13) and Europe (10), three are in Africa, and one in Oceania; monarchies by continent are as follows: Asia (Bahrain, Bhutan, Brunei, Cambodia, Japan, Jordan, Kuwait, Malaysia, Oman, Qatar, Saudi Arabia, Thailand, United Arab Emirates); Europe (Belgium, Denmark, Liechtenstein, Luxembourg, Monaco, Netherlands, Norway, Spain, Sweden, United Kingdom); Africa (Eswatini, Lesotho, Morocco); Oceania (Tonga)

note 1: Andorra and the Holy See (Vatican) are also monarchies of a sort, but they are not ruled by royal houses; Andorra has two co-princes (the president of France and the bishop of Urgell) and the Holy See is ruled by an elected pope

note 2: the sovereign of Great Britain is also the monarch for 14 of the countries (including Australia, Canada, Jamaica, New Zealand) that make up the Commonwealth; that brings to 43 the total number of countries with some type of monarchies

Legislative branch: there are 230 political entities with legislative bodies; of these 144 are unicameral (a single "house") and 86 are bicameral (both upper and lower houses); note - 33 territories, possessions, or other special administrative units have their own governing bodies

Flag description: while a "World" flag does not exist, the flag of the United Nations (UN) – adopted on 7 December 1946 – has been used on occasion to represent the entire planet; technically, however, it only represents the international organization itself; the flag displays the official emblem of the UN in white on a blue background; the emblem design shows a world map in an azimuthal equidistant projection centered on the North Pole, with the image flanked by two olive branches crossed below; blue was selected as the color to represent peace, in contrast to the red usually associated with war; the map projection chosen includes all of the continents except Antarctica

note 1: the flags of 12 nations – Austria, Botswana, Georgia, Jamaica, Japan, Laos, Latvia, Micronesia, Nigeria, North Macedonia, Switzerland, and Thailand – have no top or bottom and may be flown with either long edge on top without any notice being taken

note 2: the most common colors found on national flags are as follows: red (including deep red; ~75%), white (~70%), and blue (including light blue; ~50%); these three colors are so prevalent that there are only two countries, Jamaica and Sri Lanka, that do not include one of them on their flag; the next three most popular colors are yellow/gold and green (both ~45%) and black (~30%)

note 3: flags composed of three colors are by far the most common type and, of those, the red-white-blue combination is the most widespread

National anthem: *name:* virtually every country has a national anthem; most (but not all) anthems have lyrics, which are usually in the national or most common language of the country; states with more than one national language may offer several versions of their anthem

note: the world's oldest national anthem is the "Het Wilhelmus" (The William) of the Netherlands, which dates to the 17th century; the first national anthem to be officially adopted (1795) was "La Marseillaise" (The Song of Marseille) of France; Japan claims to have the world's shortest national anthem, entitled "Kimigayo" (The Emperor's Reign), it consists of 11 measures of music (the lyrics are also the world's oldest, dating to the 10th century or earlier); the world's longest national anthem in terms of lyrics is that of Greece, "Ymnos eis tin Eleftherian" (Hymn to Liberty) with 158 stanzas – only two of which are used; the world's longest national anthem in terms of music is that of Uruguay, "Himno Nacional" (National Anthem of Uruguay) with 105 bars (almost five minutes) – generally only the first verse and chorus are sung; both Denmark and New Zealand have two official national anthems

National heritage: *total World Heritage Sites:* 1,199 (933 cultural, 227 natural, 39 mixed) (2023)

note: a summary of every country's UNESCO World Heritage Sites (i.e., country-specific "Wonders") may be found in individual country "National heritage" entries; a Wonders of the World field may be found under World > Geography > "Wonders of the World"

ECONOMY

Real GDP (purchasing power parity): $165.804 trillion (2023 est.)
$160.74 trillion (2022 est.)
$155.603 trillion (2021 est.)
note: data in 2021 dollars

Real GDP growth rate: 2.72% (2023 est.)
3.09% (2022 est.)
6.26% (2021 est.)
note: annual GDP % growth based on constant local currency

Real GDP per capita: $20,700 (2023 est.)
$20,200 (2022 est.)
$19,700 (2021 est.)
note: data in 2021 dollars

GDP (official exchange rate): $105.435 trillion (2023 est.)
note: data in current dollars at official exchange rate

Inflation rate (consumer prices): 5.8% (2023 est.)
7.99% (2022 est.)
3.45% (2021 est.)
note: annual % change based on consumer prices

GDP - composition, by sector of origin: *agriculture:* 4.1% (2023 est.)
industry: 26.4% (2023 est.)
services: 61.8% (2022 est.)
note: figures may not total 100% due to non-allocated consumption not captured in sector-reported data

GDP - composition, by end use: *household consumption:* 55.3% (2022 est.)
government consumption: 16.5% (2022 est.)
investment in fixed capital: 26.1% (2022 est.)
investment in inventories: 1.4% (2022 est.)
exports of goods and services: 29.3% (2023 est.)
imports of goods and services: -28.7% (2023 est.)
note: figures may not total 100% due to rounding or gaps in data collection

Agricultural products: the whole range of agricultural products
top ten agricultural products by global production tonnage: sugarcane, maize, wheat, rice, milk, oil palm fruit, potatoes, soybeans, cassava, vegetables (2022)

Industries: dominated by the onrush of technology, especially in computers, robotics, telecommunications, and medicines and medical equipment; most of these advances take place in OECD nations; only a small portion of non-OECD countries have succeeded in rapidly adjusting to these technological forces; the accelerated development of new technologies is complicating already grim environmental problems

Industrial production growth rate: 1.95% (2023 est.)
note: annual % change in industrial value added based on constant local currency

Labor force: 3.628 billion (2023 est.)
note: number of people ages 15 or older who are employed or seeking work

Unemployment rate: 4.96% (2023 est.)
5.26% (2022 est.)
6.03% (2021 est.)
note: % of labor force seeking employment

Youth unemployment rate (ages 15-24): *total:* 13.8% (2023 est.)
male: 13.4% (2023 est.)
female: 15.4% (2023 est.)
note: % of labor force ages 15-24 seeking employment

Gini Index coefficient - distribution of family income: (2012)

Remittances: 0.82% of GDP (2023 est.)
0.8% of GDP (2022 est.)
0.78% of GDP (2021 est.)
note: personal transfers and compensation between resident and non-resident individuals/households/entities

Budget: *revenues:* $21.68 trillion (2017 est.)
expenditures: $23.81 trillion (2017 est.)

Public debt: 67.2% of GDP (2017 est.)

Taxes and other revenues: 14.68% (of GDP) (2022 est.)
note: central government tax revenue as a % of GDP

Exports: $31.132 trillion (2023 est.)
$31.696 trillion (2022 est.)
$28.359 trillion (2021 est.)
note: balance of payments - exports of goods and services in current dollars

Exports - commodities: the whole range of industrial and agricultural goods and services
top ten commodities by share of world trade: crude petroleum, refined petroleum, integrated circuits, natural gas, cars, broadcasting equipment, garments, gold, packaged medicine, vehicle parts/accessories (2022)

Imports: $30.184 trillion (2023 est.)
$30.874 trillion (2022 est.)
$27.27 trillion (2021 est.)
note: balance of payments - imports of goods and services in current dollars

Imports - commodities: the whole range of industrial and agricultural goods and services
top ten - share of world trade: see listing for exports

ENERGY

Electricity access: *electrification - total population:* 91.4% (2022 est.)
electrification - urban areas: 97.7%
electrification - rural areas: 84%

Electricity: *installed generating capacity:* 8.483 billion kW (2022 est.)
consumption: 26.587 trillion kWh (2022 est.)
exports: 805.371 billion kWh (2022 est.)
imports: 811.992 billion kWh (2022 est.)
transmission/distribution losses: 2.064 trillion kWh (2022 est.)

Electricity generation sources: *fossil fuels:* 61.2% of total installed capacity (2022 est.)
nuclear: 9% of total installed capacity (2022 est.)
solar: 4.5% of total installed capacity (2022 est.)
wind: 7.3% of total installed capacity (2022 est.)
hydroelectricity: 15% of total installed capacity (2022 est.)
geothermal: 0.3% of total installed capacity (2022 est.)
biomass and waste: 2.6% of total installed capacity (2022 est.)

Nuclear energy: Number of operational nuclear reactors: 416 (2023)

Number of nuclear reactors under construction: 59

Net capacity of operational nuclear reactors: 374.67GW (2023)

Coal: *production:* 9.279 billion metric tons (2022 est.)
consumption: 9.456 billion metric tons (2022 est.)
exports: 1.445 billion metric tons (2022 est.)
imports: 1.416 billion metric tons (2022 est.)
proven reserves: 1.141 trillion metric tons (2022 est.)

Petroleum: *total petroleum production:* 99.478 million bbl/day (2023 est.)
refined petroleum consumption: 99.845 million bbl/day (2022 est.)
crude oil estimated reserves: 1.697 trillion barrels (2021 est.)

Natural gas: *production:* 4.108 trillion cubic meters (2022 est.)
consumption: 4.052 trillion cubic meters (2022 est.)
exports: 1.288 trillion cubic meters (2022 est.)
imports: 1.274 trillion cubic meters (2022 est.)
proven reserves: 206.683 trillion cubic meters (2021 est.)

Carbon dioxide emissions: 38.502 billion metric tonnes of CO2 (2022 est.)
from coal and metallurgical coke: 18.399 billion metric tonnes of CO2 (2022 est.)
from petroleum and other liquids: 12.242 billion metric tonnes of CO2 (2022 est.)
from consumed natural gas: 7.862 billion metric tonnes of CO2 (2022 est.)

Energy consumption per capita: 75.306 million Btu/person (2022 est.)

COMMUNICATIONS

Telephones - fixed lines: *total subscriptions:* 840.736 million (2022 est.)
subscriptions per 100 inhabitants: 11 (2022 est.)

Telephones - mobile cellular: *total subscriptions:* 8.361 billion (2022 est.)
subscriptions per 100 inhabitants: 108 (2022 est.)

Telecommunication systems: *general assessment:* Information, Communications, and Technology (ICT) is tied to economic growth; business, trade, and foreign direct investment are all based on effective sources of ICT, and development of ICT flourishes with a vigorous economy, open trade, and sound regulation; some 2020 estimates point to a digital economy worth $11.5 trillion globally, equivalent to 15.5% of global GDP (with ICT growing 2.5 times faster than global GDP over the past 15 years); 2020 reports indicate about 7.7 billion global mobile broadband subscriptions, rising from 3.3 billion in five years, and over 1.1 billion fixed broadband subscribers, up from 830 million in 2015
international: economic impact - telecommunications has been and continues to be one of the world's fastest growing markets; countries and firms are transitioning from analog to digital broadcasting, increasing automation capabilities and applications, adopting more high-definition technologies, and converting to digital channels
broadcasting typically refers to transmission of information to all devices in a network without any acknowledgment by the receivers; data-processing parts and accessories includes many supporting elements to broadcasting equipment, such as monitors, keyboards, printers, etc.

Internet users: *total:* 5.3 billion (2022 est.)
percent of population: 66% (2022 est.)
top ten countries by Internet usage (in millions): 854 China; 560 India; 293 United States; 171 Indonesia; 149 Brazil; 123 Nigeria; 119 Japan; 116 Russia; 96 Bangladesh; 88 Mexico (2023)

Broadband - fixed subscriptions: *total:* 1.33 billion (2021 est.) note - the number of fixed broadband

subscriptions has been higher than that of fixed telephony since 2017
subscriptions per 100 inhabitants: 18 (2022 est.)

Communications - note: *note 1:* the development of formal postal systems may be traced back thousands of years; the earliest documented organized courier service for the dissemination of written dispatches was set up by the pharaohs of Ancient Egypt (ca. 2400 B.C.); the invention of a true postal system organized for delivery of post to citizens is credited to Ancient Persia (6th century B.C.); other credible early postal services are those of Ancient India (Mauryan Empire, 4th century B.C.) and Ancient China (Han Dynasty, 3rd century B.C.)
note 2: data centers consist of a dedicated space within a building or a group of buildings used to house computing resources and other components, such as telecommunications and storage systems; the ongoing worldwide boom in data generation is responsible for the mushrooming of data centers; the three largest data center facilities by area as of the first half of 2022 are:
1. the China Telecom data center located in the Inner Mongolia Information Park, Hohhot, China, reportedly covers 1 million sq m (10.7 million sq ft); the largest Internet data center in the world, it has over 50% market share in China, with an extensive network of over 400 data centers located in prime regions in mainland China and overseas markets
2. the China Mobile data center located in the Inner Mongolia Information Park, Hohhot, China, covers 720,000 sq m (7.7 million sq ft); it is one of the world's biggest cloud-computing data centers
3. the Citadel data center owned by US-based Switch, in Reno, Nevada, covers 670,000 sq m (7.2 million sq ft); called the world's largest technology ecosystem, the facility runs on 100% renewable (solar and wind) energy (2021)

TRANSPORTATION

Airports: 45,527 (2024)

Heliports: 20,316 (2024)

Railways: *total:* 1,148,186 km (2013)

Waterways: 2,293,412 km (2017)
top ten longest rivers: Nile (Africa) 6,693 km; Amazon (South America) 6,436 km; Mississippi-Missouri (North America) 6,238 km; Yenisey-Angara (Asia) 5,981 km; Ob-Irtysh (Asia) 5,569 km; Yangtze (Asia) 5,525 km; Yellow (Asia) 4,671 km; Amur (Asia) 4,352 km; Lena (Asia) 4,345 km; Congo (Africa) 4,344 km
note 1: rivers are not necessarily navigable along the entire length; if measured by volume, the Amazon is the largest river in the world, responsible for about 20% of the Earth's freshwater entering the ocean
note 2: there are 20 countries without rivers: 3 in Africa (Comoros, Djibouti, Libya); 1 in the Americas (Bahamas); 8 in Asia (Bahrain, Kuwait, Maldives, Oman, Qatar, Saudi Arabia, United Arab Emirates, Yemen); 3 in Europe (Malta, Monaco, Holy See), 5 in Oceania (Kiribati, Marshall Islands, Nauru, Tonga, Tuvalu); these countries also do not have natural lakes
top ten largest natural lakes (by surface area): Caspian Sea (Azerbaijan, Iran, Kazakhstan, Russia, Turkmenistan) 372,960 sq km; Lake Superior (Canada, United States) 82,414 sq km; Lake Victoria (Kenya, Tanzania, Uganda) 69,490 sq km; Lake Huron (Canada, United States) 59,596 sq km; Lake Michigan (United States) 57,441 sq km; Lake Tanganyika (Burundi, Democratic Republic of the Congo, Tanzania, Zambia) 32,890 sq km; Great Bear Lake (Canada) 31,800 sq km; Lake Baikal (Russia) 31,494 sq km; Lake Nyasa (Malawi, Mozambique, Tanzania) 30,044 sq km; Great Slave Lake (Canada) 28,400 sq km
note 1: the areas of the lakes are subject to seasonal variation; only the Caspian Sea is saline, the rest are fresh water
note 2: Lakes Huron and Michigan are technically a single lake because the flow of water between the Straits of Mackinac that connects the two lakes keeps their water levels at near-equilibrium; combined, Lake Huron-Michigan is the largest freshwater lake by surface area in the world
note 3: the deepest lake in the world (1,620 m), and also the largest freshwater lake by volume (23,600 cu km), is Lake Baikal in Russia

Merchant marine: *total:* 103,577 (2023)
by type: bulk carrier 13,141, container ship 5,815, general cargo 19,918, oil tanker 11,604, other 53,099

MILITARY AND SECURITY

Military expenditures: 2.3% of GDP (2023 est.)
2.2% of GDP (2022 est.)
2.3% of GDP (2021 est.)
2.4% of GDP (2020 est.)
2.2% of GDP (2019 est.)

Military and security service personnel strengths: approximately 20 million active-duty military personnel worldwide (2023)
note: the largest militaries in the world based on personnel numbers belong to China, India, the US, North Korea, and Russia

Military equipment inventories and acquisitions: the US is the world's leading arms exporter (2023)

Military deployments: as of January 2024, there were approximately 65,000 personnel deployed on UN peacekeeping missions worldwide (2024)

SPACE

Space agency/agencies: more than 70 countries have national space agencies (2024)

Space launch site(s): more than 30 countries have existing or planned commercial or government space launch sites (2024)
note: there were approximately 220 attempted space launches worldwide in 2023; as of December 2023, there were over 11,000 satellites in orbit, of which about 9,000 were still active

TRANSNATIONAL ISSUES

Refugees and internally displaced persons: the UN High Commissioner for Refugees (UNHCR) estimated that as of mid-year 2023 there were 110 million people forcibly displaced worldwide; this includes 62.5 million IDPs, 36.4 million refugees, 6.1 million asylum seekers, 5.3 million others in need of international protection; the UNHCR estimates there are currently more than 4.4 million stateless persons as of year-end 2022 (the true number is estimated to be significantly higher)

Trafficking in persons: *tier rating:*

Tier 2 Watch List: (32 countries) Algeria, Benin, Burkina Faso, Central African Republic, Chad, Republic of Congo, Curaçao, Dominican Republic, Equatorial Guinea, Fiji, Gabon, Guinea-Bissau, Hong Kong, Kuwait, Kyrgyzstan, Laos, Lebanon, Liberia, Madagascar, Maldives, Mali, Malta, Marshall Islands, Nepal, Niger, Rwanda, Serbia, Solomon Islands, Tajikistan, Uruguay, Vanuatu, Zimbabwe (2024)

Tier 3: (21 countries) Afghanistan, Belarus, Brunei, Burma, Cambodia, People's Republic of China, Cuba, Djibouti, Eritrea, Iran, Democratic People's Republic of Korea, Macau, Nicaragua, Papua New Guinea, Russia, Sint Maarten, South Sudan, Sudan, Syria, Turkmenistan, Venezuela (2024)

Illicit drugs: *cocaine:* worldwide coca cultivation in 2020 likely amounted to 373,000 hectares, potential pure cocaine production reached 2,100 metric tons in 2020
opiates: worldwide illicit opium poppy cultivation probably reached about 265,000 hectares in 2020, with potential opium production reaching 7,300 metric tons; Afghanistan is world's primary opium producer, accounting for 85% of the global supply; Southeast Asia was responsible for 7% of global opium; Latin America opium in 2020 was sufficient to produce about 61 metric tons of pure heroin (2015)

YEMEN

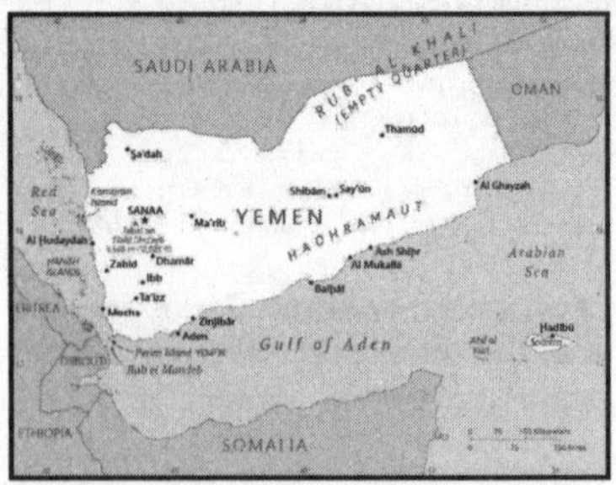

INTRODUCTION

Background: The Kingdom of Yemen (colloquially known as North Yemen) became independent from the Ottoman Empire in 1918 and in 1962 became the Yemen Arab Republic. The British, who had set up a protectorate area around the southern port of Aden in the 19th century, withdrew in 1967 from what became the People's Republic of Southern Yemen (colloquially known as South Yemen). Three years later, the southern government adopted a Marxist orientation and changed the country's name to the People's Democratic Republic of Yemen. The exodus of hundreds of thousands of Yemenis from the south to the north contributed to two decades of hostility between the states, which were formally unified as the Republic of Yemen in 1990. A southern secessionist movement and brief civil war in 1994 was quickly subdued. In 2000, Saudi Arabia and Yemen agreed to delineate their border. Fighting in the northwest between the government and the Houthis, a Zaydi Shia Muslim minority, continued intermittently from 2004 to 2010, and then again from 2014 to the present. The southern secessionist movement was revitalized in 2007.

Public rallies in Sana'a against then President Ali Abdallah SALIH – inspired by similar Arab Spring demonstrations in Tunisia and Egypt – slowly gained momentum in 2011, fueled by complaints over high unemployment, poor economic conditions, and corruption. Some protests resulted in violence, and the demonstrations spread to other major cities. The Gulf Cooperation Council (GCC) mediated the crisis with the GCC Initiative, an agreement in which the president would step down in exchange for immunity from prosecution. SALIH eventually agreed to step down and transfer some powers to Vice President Abd Rabuh Mansur HADI. After HADI's uncontested election victory in 2012, SALIH formally transferred all presidential powers. In accordance with the GCC Initiative, Yemen launched a National Dialogue Conference (NDC) in 2013 to discuss key constitutional, political, and social issues. HADI concluded the NDC in 2014 and planned to proceed with constitutional drafting, a constitutional referendum, and national elections.

The Houthis, perceiving their grievances were not addressed in the NDC, joined forces with SALIH and expanded their influence in northwestern Yemen, which culminated in a major offensive against military units and rival tribes and enabled their forces to overrun the capital, Sana'a, in 2014. In 2015, the Houthis surrounded key government facilities, prompting HADI and the cabinet to resign. HADI fled first to Aden – where he rescinded his resignation – and then to Oman before moving to Saudi Arabia and asking the GCC to intervene militarily in Yemen. Saudi Arabia assembled a coalition of Arab militaries and began airstrikes, and ground fighting continued through 2016. In 2016, the UN initiated peace talks that ended without agreement. Rising tensions between the Houthis and SALIH culminated in Houthi forces killing SALIH. In 2018, the Houthis and the Yemeni Government participated in UN-brokered peace talks, agreeing to a limited ceasefire and the establishment of a UN mission.

In 2019, Yemen's parliament convened for the first time since the conflict broke out in 2014. Violence then erupted between HADI's government and the pro-secessionist Southern Transitional Council (STC) in southern Yemen. HADI's government and the STC signed a power-sharing agreement to end the fighting, and in 2020, the signatories formed a new cabinet. In 2020 and 2021, fighting continued as the Houthis gained territory and also conducted regular UAV and missile attacks against targets in Saudi Arabia. In 2022, the UN brokered a temporary truce between the Houthis and the Saudi-led coalition. HADI and his vice-president resigned and were replaced by an eight-person Presidential Leadership Council. Although the truce formally expired in 2022, the parties nonetheless refrained from large-scale conflict through the end of 2023. Saudi Arabia, after the truce expired, continued to negotiate with the Yemeni Government and Houthis on a roadmap agreement that would include a permanent ceasefire and a peace process under UN auspices.

GEOGRAPHY

Location: Middle East, bordering the Arabian Sea, Gulf of Aden, and Red Sea, between Oman and Saudi Arabia

Geographic coordinates: 15 00 N, 48 00 E

Map references: Middle East

Area: *total:* 527,968 sq km
land: 527,968 sq km
water: 0 sq km
note: includes Perim, Socotra, the former Yemen Arab Republic (YAR or North Yemen), and the former People's Democratic Republic of Yemen (PDRY or South Yemen)
comparison ranking: total 52

Area - comparative: almost four times the size of Alabama; slightly larger than twice the size of Wyoming

Land boundaries: *total:* 1,601 km
border countries (2): Oman 294 km; Saudi Arabia 1,307 km

Coastline: 1,906 km

Maritime claims: *territorial sea:* 12 nm
contiguous zone: 24 nm
exclusive economic zone: 200 nm
continental shelf: 200 nm or to the edge of the continental margin

Climate: mostly desert; hot and humid along west coast; temperate in western mountains affected by seasonal monsoon; extraordinarily hot, dry, harsh desert in east

Terrain: narrow coastal plain backed by flat-topped hills and rugged mountains; dissected upland desert plains in center slope into the desert interior of the Arabian Peninsula

Elevation: *highest point:* Jabal an Nabi Shu'ayb 3,666 m
lowest point: Arabian Sea 0 m
mean elevation: 999 m

Natural resources: petroleum, fish, rock salt, marble; small deposits of coal, gold, lead, nickel, and copper; fertile soil in west

Land use: *agricultural land:* 44.5% (2018 est.)
arable land: 2.2% (2018 est.)
permanent crops: 0.6% (2018 est.)
permanent pasture: 41.7% (2018 est.)
forest: 1% (2018 est.)
other: 54.5% (2018 est.)

Irrigated land: 6,800 sq km (2012)

Population distribution: the vast majority of the population is found in the Asir Mountains (part of the larger Sarawat Mountain system), located in the far western region of the country

Natural hazards: sandstorms and dust storms in summer
volcanism: limited volcanic activity; Jebel at Tair (Jabal al-Tair, Jebel Teir, Jabal al-Tayr, Jazirat at-Tair) (244 m), which forms an island in the Red Sea, erupted in 2007 after awakening from dormancy; other historically active volcanoes include Harra of Arhab, Harras of Dhamar, Harra es-Sawad, and Jebel Zubair, although many of these have not erupted in over a century

Geography - note: strategic location on Bab el Mandeb, the strait linking the Red Sea and the Gulf of Aden, one of world's most active shipping lanes

PEOPLE AND SOCIETY

Population: *total:* 32,140,443
male: 16,221,139
female: 15,919,304 (2024 est.)
comparison rankings: female 47; male 47; total 48

Nationality: *noun:* Yemeni(s)
adjective: Yemeni

Ethnic groups: predominantly Arab; but also Afro-Arab, South Asian, European

Languages: Arabic (official)
major-language sample(s):
كتاب حقائق العالم، المصدر الذي لا يمكن الاستغناء عنه للمعلومات الأساسية
(Arabic)
note: a distinct Socotri language is widely used on Socotra Island and Archipelago; Mahri is still fairly widely spoken in eastern Yemen

Religions: Muslim 99.1% (official; virtually all are citizens, an estimated 65% are Sunni and 35% are Shia), other 0.9% (includes Jewish, Baha'i, Hindu, and Christian; many are refugees or temporary foreign residents) (2020 est.)

Age structure: *0-14 years:* 34.4% (male 5,622,998/female 5,430,285)
15-64 years: 62.2% (male 10,112,603/female 9,865,805)
65 years and over: 3.4% (2024 est.) (male 485,538/female 623,214)

Dependency ratios: *total dependency ratio:* 71.7
youth dependency ratio: 69.4
elderly dependency ratio: 4.7
potential support ratio: 19.9 (2021 est.)

Median age: *total:* 22 years (2024 est.)
male: 21.9 years
female: 22.2 years
comparison ranking: total 188

Population growth rate: 1.78% (2024 est.)
comparison ranking: 48

Birth rate: 23.4 births/1,000 population (2024 est.)
comparison ranking: 49

Death rate: 5.5 deaths/1,000 population (2024 est.)
comparison ranking: 182

Net migration rate: -0.2 migrant(s)/1,000 population (2024 est.)
comparison ranking: 108

Population distribution: the vast majority of the population is found in the Asir Mountains (part of the larger Sarawat Mountain system), located in the far western region of the country

Urbanization: *urban population:* 39.8% of total population (2023)
rate of urbanization: 3.71% annual rate of change (2015-20 est.)

Major urban areas - population: 3.292 million SANAA (capital), 1.080 million Aden, 941,000 Taiz, 772,000 Ibb (2023)

Sex ratio: *at birth:* 1.05 male(s)/female
0-14 years: 1.04 male(s)/female
15-64 years: 1.03 male(s)/female
65 years and over: 0.78 male(s)/female
total population: 1.02 male(s)/female (2024 est.)

Mother's mean age at first birth: 20.8 years (2013 est.)
note: data represents median age at first birth among women 25-49

Maternal mortality ratio: 183 deaths/100,000 live births (2020 est.)
comparison ranking: 49

Infant mortality rate: *total:* 44.6 deaths/1,000 live births (2024 est.)
male: 49.9 deaths/1,000 live births
female: 39 deaths/1,000 live births
comparison ranking: total 26

Life expectancy at birth: *total population:* 68.2 years (2024 est.)
male: 65.8 years
female: 70.6 years
comparison ranking: total population 191

Total fertility rate: 2.82 children born/woman (2024 est.)
comparison ranking: 54

Gross reproduction rate: 1.37 (2024 est.)

Contraceptive prevalence rate: 33.5% (2013)

Drinking water source: *improved: urban:* 98.5% of population
rural: 84.2% of population
total: 99.6% of population
unimproved: urban: 1.5% of population
rural: 15.8% of population
total: 10.4% of population (2020 est.)

Current health expenditure: 4.3% of GDP (2015)

Physician density: 0.53 physicians/1,000 population (2014)

Hospital bed density: 0.7 beds/1,000 population (2017)

Sanitation facility access: *improved: urban:* 83.5% of population
rural: 44.2% of population
total: 59.1% of population
unimproved: urban: 16.5% of population
rural: 55.8% of population
total: 40.9% of population (2020 est.)

Obesity - adult prevalence rate: 17.1% (2016)
comparison ranking: 120

Alcohol consumption per capita: *total:* 0.02 liters of pure alcohol (2019 est.)
beer: 0.02 liters of pure alcohol (2019 est.)
wine: 0 liters of pure alcohol (2019 est.)
spirits: 0 liters of pure alcohol (2019 est.)
other alcohols: 0 liters of pure alcohol (2019 est.)
comparison ranking: total 182

Tobacco use: *total:* 20.3% (2020 est.)
male: 32.5% (2020 est.)
female: 8.1% (2020 est.)
comparison ranking: total 85

Children under the age of 5 years underweight: 39.9% (2013)
comparison ranking: 1

Currently married women (ages 15-49): 60.4% (2023 est.)

Literacy: *definition:* age 15 and over can read and write
total population: 70.1%
male: 85.1%
female: 55% (2015)

ENVIRONMENT

Environment - current issues: limited natural freshwater resources; inadequate supplies of potable water; overgrazing; soil erosion; desertification

Environment - international agreements: *party to:* Biodiversity, Climate Change, Climate Change-Kyoto Protocol, Desertification, Endangered Species, Environmental Modification, Hazardous Wastes, Law of the Sea, Marine Dumping-London Protocol, Nuclear Test Ban, Ozone Layer Protection, Wetlands
signed, but not ratified: Climate Change-Paris Agreement, Comprehensive Nuclear Test Ban

Climate: mostly desert; hot and humid along west coast; temperate in western mountains affected by seasonal monsoon; extraordinarily hot, dry, harsh desert in east

Urbanization: *urban population:* 39.8% of total population (2023)
rate of urbanization: 3.71% annual rate of change (2015-20 est.)

Food insecurity: *widespread lack of access: due to conflict, poverty, floods, high food and fuel prices* - in 2023, a partial analysis in government-controlled areas, where approximately 25 percent of the population in acute food insecurity resides, shows that the situation remains dire; despite some improvements in security, the economic crisis and localized conflicts continue, fueled by persistent political instability, while insufficient external revenues and elevated global commodity prices on imported food limits food security (2023)

Revenue from forest resources: 0.04% of GDP (2018 est.)
comparison ranking: 130

Revenue from coal: 0% of GDP (2018 est.)
comparison ranking: 65

Air pollutants: *particulate matter emissions:* 41.61 micrograms per cubic meter (2019 est.)
carbon dioxide emissions: 10.61 megatons (2016 est.)
methane emissions: 8.03 megatons (2020 est.)

Waste and recycling: *municipal solid waste generated annually:* 4,836,820 tons (2011 est.)
municipal solid waste recycled annually: 386,946 tons (2016 est.)
percent of municipal solid waste recycled: 8% (2016 est.)

Total water withdrawal: *municipal:* 270 million cubic meters (2020 est.)
industrial: 70 million cubic meters (2020 est.)
agricultural: 3.24 billion cubic meters (2020 est.)

Total renewable water resources: 2.1 billion cubic meters (2020 est.)

GOVERNMENT

Country name: *conventional long form:* Republic of Yemen
conventional short form: Yemen
local long form: Al Jumhuriyah al Yamaniyah
local short form: Al Yaman
former: Yemen Arab Republic [Yemen (Sanaa) or North Yemen] and People's Democratic Republic of Yemen [Yemen (Aden) or South Yemen]
etymology: name derivation remains unclear but may come from the Arab term "yumn" (happiness) and be related to the region's classical name "Arabia Felix" (Fertile or Happy Arabia); the Romans referred to the rest of the peninsula as "Arabia Deserta" (Deserted Arabia)

Government type: in transition

Capital: *name:* Sanaa
geographic coordinates: 15 21 N, 44 12 E
time difference: UTC+3 (8 hours ahead of Washington, DC, during Standard Time)
etymology: the name is reputed to mean "well-fortified" in Sabaean, the South Arabian language that went extinct in Yemen in the 6th century A.D.

Administrative divisions: 22 governorates (muhafazat, singular - muhafazah); Abyan, 'Adan (Aden), Ad Dali', Al Bayda', Al Hudaydah, Al Jawf, Al Mahrah, Al Mahwit, Amanat al 'Asimah (Sanaa City), 'Amran, Arkhabil Suqutra (Socotra Archipelago), Dhamar, Hadramawt, Hajjah, Ibb, Lahij, Ma'rib, Raymah, Sa'dah, San'a' (Sanaa), Shabwah, Ta'izz

Independence: *22 May 1990 (Republic of Yemen was established with the merger of the Yemen Arab Republic [Yemen (Sanaa) or North Yemen] and the Marxist-dominated People's Democratic Republic of Yemen [Yemen (Aden) or South Yemen]); notable earlier dates:* North Yemen became independent on 1 November 1918 (from the Ottoman Empire) and became a republic with the overthrow of the theocratic Imamate on 27 September 1962; South Yemen became independent on 30 November 1967 (from the UK)

National holiday: Unification Day, 22 May (1990)

Legal system: mixed legal system of Islamic (sharia) law, Napoleonic law, English common law, and customary law

Constitution: *history:* adopted by referendum 16 May 1991 (following unification); note - after the National Dialogue ended in January 2015, a Constitutional Drafting Committee appointed by the president worked to prepare a new draft constitution

that was expected to be put to a national referendum before being adopted; however, the start of the current conflict in early 2015 interrupted the process
amendments: amended several times, last in 2009

International law organization participation: has not submitted an ICJ jurisdiction declaration; non-party state to the ICCt

Citizenship: *citizenship by birth:* no
citizenship by descent only: the father must be a citizen of Yemen; if the father is unknown, the mother must be a citizen
dual citizenship recognized: no
residency requirement for naturalization: 10 years

Suffrage: 18 years of age; universal

Executive branch: *chief of state:* Chairperson, Presidential Leadership Council Rashad Muhammad al-ALIMI, Dr. (since 19 April 2022)
head of government: Prime Minister Ahmad Awad Bin MUBAREK (since 5 February 2024)
cabinet: 24 members from northern and southern Yemen, with representatives from Yemen's major political parties
elections/appointments: formerly, the president was directly elected by absolute majority popular vote in 2 rounds if needed for a 7-year term (eligible for a second term); election last held on 21 February 2012 (next election NA); note - a special election was held on 21 February 2012 to remove Ali Abdallah SALIH under the terms of a Gulf Cooperation Council-mediated deal during the political crisis of 2011; vice president appointed by the president; prime minister appointed by the president
election results: Abd Rabuh Mansur HADI (GPC) elected consensus president
note: on 7 April 2022, President Abd Rabuh Mansur HADI announced his abdication, the dismissal of Vice President ALI MUHSIN al-Ahmar and the formation of a Presidential Leadership Council, an eight-member body chaired by former minister Rashad AL-ALIMI; on 19 April 2022, the Council was sworn in before Parliament and began assuming the responsibilities of the president and vice president and carrying out the political, security, and military duties of the government

Legislative branch: *description:* bicameral Parliament or Majlis consists of:
Shura Council or Majlis Alshoora (111 seats; members appointed by the president; member term is continuous); note – Shura Council serves in an advisory role to the president; it has no legislative responsibilities
House of Representatives or Majlis al Nuwaab (301 seats; members directly elected in single-seat constituencies by simple majority vote to serve 6-year terms)
elections: Shura Council - last appointments NA (next appointments NA)
House of Representatives - last held in April 2019 (next to be held in NA)
election results: percent of vote by party - GPC 58%, Islah 22.6%, YSP 3.8%, Unionist Party 1.9%, other 13.7%; seats by party - GPC 238, Islah 46, YSP 8, Nasserist Unionist Party 3, National Arab Socialist Ba'ath Party 2, independent 4; composition - men 245, women 0, percent of women 0%

Judicial branch: *highest court(s):* Supreme Court (consists of the court president, 2 deputies, and nearly 50 judges; court organized into constitutional, civil, commercial, family, administrative, criminal, military, and appeals scrutiny divisions)
judge selection and term of office: judges appointed by the Supreme Judicial Council, which is chaired by the president of the republic and includes 10 high-ranking judicial officers; judges serve for life with mandatory retirement at age 65
subordinate courts: appeal courts; district or first instance courts; commercial courts

Political parties: General People's Congress or GPC (3 factions: pro-Hadi, pro-Houthi, pro-Salih)
Nasserist Unionist People's Organization
National Arab Socialist Ba'ath Party
Southern Transitional Council or STC
Yemeni Reform Grouping or Islah
Yemeni Socialist Party or YSP

International organization participation: AFESD, AMF, CAEU, CD, EITI (temporarily suspended), FAO, G-77, IAEA, IBRD, ICAO, ICRM, IDA, IDB, IFAD, IFC, IFRCS, ILO, IMF, IMO, IMSO, Interpol, IOC, IOM, IPU, ISO, ITSO, ITU, ITUC (NGOs), LAS, MIGA, MINURSO, MINUSMA, MONUSCO, NAM, OAS (observer), OIC, OPCW, UN, UNAMID, UNCTAD, UNESCO, UNHCR, UNIDO, UNISFA, UNMHA, UNMIL, UNMIS, UNOCI, UNVIM, UNWTO, UPU, WCO, WFTU (NGOs), WHO, WIPO, WMO, WTO

Diplomatic representation in the US: *chief of mission:* Ambassador Mohammed Abdullah Mohammed AL-HADHRAMI (since 7 June 2022)
chancery: 2319 Wyoming Avenue NW, Washington, DC 20008
telephone: [1] (202) 965-4760
FAX: [1] (202) 337-2017
email address and website:
Information@yemenembassy.org
https://www.yemenembassy.org/

Diplomatic representation from the US: *chief of mission:* Ambassador Steven H. FAGIN (since 1 June 2022); note - the embassy closed in March 2015; Yemen Affairs Unit currently operates out of US Embassy Riyadh
embassy: previously - Sa'awan Street, Sanaa
mailing address: 6330 Sanaa Place, Washington DC 20521-6330
telephone: US Embassy Riyadh [966] 11-488-3800 previously - [967] 1 755-2000
FAX: US Embassy Riyadh [966] 11-488-7360
email address and website:
YemenEmergencyUSC@state.gov
https://ye.usembassy.gov/

Flag description: three equal horizontal bands of red (top), white, and black; the band colors derive from the Arab Liberation flag and represent oppression (black), overcome through bloody struggle (red), to be replaced by a bright future (white)
note: similar to the flag of Syria, which has two green stars in the white band, and of Iraq, which has an Arabic inscription centered in the white band; also similar to the flag of Egypt, which has a heraldic eagle centered in the white band

National symbol(s): golden eagle; national colors: red, white, black

National anthem: *name:* "al-qumhuriyatu l-muttahida" (United Republic)
lyrics/music: Abdullah Abdulwahab NOA'MAN/ Ayyoab Tarish ABSI
note: adopted 1990; the music first served as the anthem for South Yemen before unification with North Yemen in 1990

National heritage: *total World Heritage Sites:* 5 (4 cultural, 1 natural)
selected World Heritage Site locales: Old Walled City of Shibam (c); Old City of Sana'a (c); Historic Town of Zabid (c); Socotra Archipelago (n); Landmarks of the Ancient Kingdom of Saba, Marib (c)

ECONOMY

Economic overview: low-income Middle Eastern economy; infrastructure, trade, and economic institutions devastated by civil war; oil/gas-dependent but decreasing reserves; massive poverty, food insecurity, and unemployment; high inflation

Real GDP (purchasing power parity): $73.63 billion (2017 est.)
$78.28 billion (2016 est.)
$90.63 billion (2015 est.)
note: data are in 2017 dollars
comparison ranking: 106

Real GDP growth rate: 0.75% (2018 est.)
-5.07% (2017 est.)
-9.38% (2016 est.)
note: annual GDP % growth based on constant local currency
comparison ranking: 172

Real GDP per capita: $2,500 (2017 est.)
$2,700 (2016 est.)
$3,200 (2015 est.)
note: data are in 2017 dollars
comparison ranking: 204

GDP (official exchange rate): $21.606 billion (2018 est.)
note: data in current dollars at official exchange rate

Inflation rate (consumer prices): 24.7% (2017 est.)
-12.6% (2016 est.)
8.1% (2014 est.)
note: annual % change based on consumer prices
comparison ranking: 201

GDP - composition, by sector of origin: *agriculture:* 28.7% (2018 est.)
industry: 25.4% (2018 est.)
services: 41.8% (2018 est.)
note: figures may not total 100% due to non-allocated consumption not captured in sector-reported data
comparison rankings: services 186; industry 92; agriculture 11

GDP - composition, by end use: *household consumption:* 126.4% (2018 est.)
government consumption: 9.1% (2018 est.)
investment in fixed capital: 5.8% (2018 est.)
exports of goods and services: 8.8% (2018 est.)
imports of goods and services: -50.1% (2018 est.)
note: figures may not total 100% due to rounding or gaps in data collection

Agricultural products: mangoes/guavas, potatoes, onions, milk, sorghum, spices, watermelons, chicken, tomatoes, grapes (2022)
note: top ten agricultural products based on tonnage

Industries: crude oil production and petroleum refining; small-scale production of cotton textiles, leather goods; food processing; handicrafts; aluminum products; cement; commercial ship repair; natural gas production

Industrial production growth rate: -1.12% (2018 est.)
note: annual % change in industrial value added based on constant local currency
comparison ranking: 168

Labor force: 6.883 million (2023 est.)
note: number of people ages 15 or older who are employed or seeking work
comparison ranking: 69

Unemployment rate: 17.22% (2023 est.)
17.52% (2022 est.)
18.25% (2021 est.)
note: % of labor force seeking employment
comparison ranking: 194

Youth unemployment rate (ages 15-24): *total:* 32.7% (2023 est.)
male: 32.1% (2023 est.)
female: 38.4% (2023 est.)
note: % of labor force ages 15-24 seeking employment
comparison ranking: total 20

Population below poverty line: 48.6% (2014 est.)
note: % of population with income below national poverty line

Gini Index coefficient - distribution of family income: 36.7 (2014 est.)
note: index (0-100) of income distribution; higher values represent greater inequality
comparison ranking: 65

Household income or consumption by percentage share: *lowest 10%:* 3% (2014 est.)
highest 10%: 29.4% (2014 est.)
note: % share of income accruing to lowest and highest 10% of population

Remittances: 20.52% of GDP (2023 est.)
16.01% of GDP (2022 est.)
19.58% of GDP (2021 est.)
note: personal transfers and compensation between resident and non-resident individuals/households/entities

Budget: *revenues:* $2.207 billion (2019 est.)
expenditures: $3.585 billion (2019 est.)

Public debt: 74.5% of GDP (2017 est.)
comparison ranking: 47

Taxes and other revenues: 9% (of GDP) (2017 est.)
comparison ranking: 186

Current account balance: -$2.419 billion (2016 est.)
-$3.026 billion (2015 est.)
-$1.488 billion (2014 est.)
note: balance of payments - net trade and primary/secondary income in current dollars
comparison ranking: 164

Exports: $384.5 million (2017 est.)
$938.469 million (2016 est.)
$1.867 billion (2015 est.)
note: balance of payments - exports of goods and services in current dollars
comparison ranking: 193

Exports - partners: China 32%, Thailand 20%, India 12%, UAE 7%, Oman 5% (2022)
note: top five export partners based on percentage share of exports

Exports - commodities: crude petroleum, scrap iron, gold, fish, shellfish (2022)
note: top five export commodities based on value in dollars

Imports: $4.079 billion (2017 est.)
$8.256 billion (2016 est.)
$7.697 billion (2015 est.)
note: balance of payments - imports of goods and services in current dollars
comparison ranking: 157

Imports - partners: China 26%, UAE 14%, Turkey 10%, India 10%, Oman 4% (2022)
note: top five import partners based on percentage share of imports

Imports - commodities: wheat, raw iron bars, rice, garments, milk (2022)
note: top five import commodities based on value in dollars

Reserves of foreign exchange and gold: $1.251 billion (2022 est.)
$1.688 billion (2021 est.)
$969.613 million (2020 est.)
note: holdings of gold (year-end prices)/foreign exchange/special drawing rights in current dollars
comparison ranking: 133

Debt - external: $5.687 billion (2022 est.)
note: present value of external debt in current US dollars
comparison ranking: 50

Exchange rates: Yemeni rials (YER) per US dollar -

Exchange rates: 1,114.293 (2022 est.)
1,035.467 (2021 est.)
743.006 (2020 est.)
486.731 (2019 est.)
214.89 (2018 est.)

ENERGY

Electricity access: *electrification - total population:* 76% (2022 est.)
electrification - urban areas: 96.1%
electrification - rural areas: 65%

Electricity: *installed generating capacity:* 1.776 million kW (2022 est.)
consumption: 2.367 billion kWh (2022 est.)
transmission/distribution losses: 589.902 million kWh (2022 est.)
comparison rankings: transmission/distribution losses 84; consumption 145; installed generating capacity 124

Electricity generation sources: *fossil fuels:* 79.6% of total installed capacity (2022 est.)
solar: 20.4% of total installed capacity (2022 est.)

Coal: *consumption:* 165,000 metric tons (2022 est.)
imports: 165,000 metric tons (2022 est.)

Petroleum: *total petroleum production:* 15,000 bbl/day (2023 est.)
refined petroleum consumption: 60,000 bbl/day (2022 est.)
crude oil estimated reserves: 3 billion barrels (2021 est.)

Natural gas: *production:* 189.432 million cubic meters (2022 est.)
consumption: 189.432 million cubic meters (2022 est.)
proven reserves: 478.555 billion cubic meters (2021 est.)

Carbon dioxide emissions: 9.017 million metric tonnes of CO2 (2022 est.)
from coal and metallurgical coke: 373,000 metric tonnes of CO2 (2022 est.)
from petroleum and other liquids: 8.26 million metric tonnes of CO2 (2022 est.)
from consumed natural gas: 385,000 metric tonnes of CO2 (2022 est.)
comparison ranking: total emissions 109

Energy consumption per capita: 3.939 million Btu/person (2022 est.)
comparison ranking: 174

COMMUNICATIONS

Telephones - fixed lines: *total subscriptions:* 1.24 million (2021 est.)
subscriptions per 100 inhabitants: 4 (2021 est.)
comparison ranking: total subscriptions 65

Telephones - mobile cellular: *total subscriptions:* 15.178 million (2021 est.)
subscriptions per 100 inhabitants: 46 (2021 est.)
comparison ranking: total subscriptions 70

Telecommunication systems: *general assessment:* Yemen continues to provide an exceptionally challenging market for telcos; civil unrest has caused havoc and devastation across most parts of the country, while the threat of sanctions has also made it a challenging environment in which to operate; a large proportion of the population requires humanitarian assistance, and there is little disposable income for services upon which telcos can generate revenue; essential telecom infrastructure, such as mobile towers and fiber cabling, has often been targeted, destroyed, or damaged by the opposing sides in the ongoing conflict; these difficulties have proved to be a disincentive to telcos investing in infrastructure, with the result that the country lacks basic fixed-line infrastructure, and mobile services are based on outdated GSM; this has prevented the development of a mobile broadband sector, or the evolution of mobile data services; the ownership of telecommunication services, and the scrutiny of associated revenues and taxes, have become a political issue in Yemen; until telecom infrastructure can be improved across Yemen, and until civil unrest eases, there will be little progress for the sector (2022)
domestic: fixed-line teledensity is 4 per 100 but mobile cellular is 46 per 100 (2021)
international: country code - 967; landing points for the FALCON, SeaMeWe-5, Aden-Djibouti, and the AAE-1 international submarine cable connecting Europe, Africa, the Middle East, Asia and Southeast Asia; satellite earth stations - 3 Intelsat (2 Indian Ocean and 1 Atlantic Ocean), 1 Intersputnik (Atlantic Ocean region), and 2 Arabsat; microwave radio relay to Saudi Arabia and Djibouti (2020)

Broadcast media: state-run TV with 2 stations; state-run radio with 2 national radio stations and 5 local stations; stations from Oman and Saudi Arabia can be accessed

Internet country code: .ye

Internet users: *total:* 8,229,624 (2022 est.)
percent of population: 26.6% (2022 est.)
comparison ranking: total 73

Broadband - fixed subscriptions: *total:* 391,000 (2020 est.)
subscriptions per 100 inhabitants: 1 (2020 est.)
comparison ranking: total 98

TRANSPORTATION

National air transport system: *number of registered air carriers:* 2 (2020)
inventory of registered aircraft operated by air carriers: 8
annual passenger traffic on registered air carriers: 336,310 (2018)
annual freight traffic on registered air carriers: 3.27 million (2018) mt-km

Civil aircraft registration country code prefix: 7O

Airports: 36 (2024)
comparison ranking: 109

Heliports: 6 (2024)

Pipelines: 641 km gas, 22 km liquid petroleum gas, 1,370 km oil (2013)

Roadways: *total:* 71,300 km
paved: 6,200 km
unpaved: 65,100 km (2005)

comparison ranking: total 69

Merchant marine: *total:* 30 (2023)
by type: general cargo 2, oil tanker 1, other 27
comparison ranking: total 133

Ports: *total ports:* 10 (2024)
large: 1
medium: 2
small: 2
very small: 5
ports with oil terminals: 6
key ports: Aden, Al Ahmadi, Al Mukalla, Al Mukha, Ras Isa Marine Terminal

MILITARY AND SECURITY

Military and security forces: Republic of Yemen Government (ROYG) forces:

Ministry of Defense: Yemeni National Army, Air Force and Air Defense, Navy and Coastal Defense Forces, Border Guard, Strategic Reserve Forces (includes Special Forces and Presidential Protection Brigades, which are under the Ministry of Defense but responsible to the president), Popular Committee Forces (aka Popular Resistance Forces; government-backed tribal militia)

Ministry of Interior: Special Security Forces (paramilitary; formerly known as Central Security Forces), Political Security Organization (state security), National Security Bureau (intelligence), Counterterrorism Unit

Saudi-backed forces: paramilitary/militia border security brigades based largely on tribal or regional affiliation (based along the Saudi-Yemen border)

United Arab Emirates-backed forces include tribal and regionally based militia and paramilitary forces (concentrated in the southern governates): Southern Transitional Council (STC) forces, including the Security Belt Forces, the Shabwani and Hadrami "Elite" Forces, the Support and Backup Forces (aka Logistics and Support Forces), Facilities Protection Forces, and Anti-Terrorism Forces; Republican Forces; Joint Forces

Houthi (aka Ansarallah) forces: land, aerospace (air, missile), naval/coastal defense, presidential protection, special operations, internal security, and militia/tribal auxiliary forces (2023)
note 1: under the 2019 Riyadh Agreement, the STC forces were to be incorporated into Yemen's Ministries of Defense and Interior under the authority of the HADI government
note 2: a considerable portion–up to 70 percent by some estimates–of Yemen's military and security forces defected in whole or in part to former president SALAH and the Houthi opposition in 2011-2015

Military and security service personnel strengths: *information limited and widely varied; Yemen Government:* up to 300,000 estimated military, paramilitary, militia, and other security forces; UAE- and Saudi-backed forces: estimated 150-200,000 trained militia and paramilitary fighters; Houthis: up to 200,000 estimated fighters (2022)

Military equipment inventories and acquisitions: the inventory of the Yemeni Government forces consists primarily of Russian and Soviet-era equipment, although much of it has been lost in the current conflict; since the start of the civil war in 2014, it has received limited amounts of donated equipment from some Gulf States, including Saudi Arabia and UAE, as well as the US
Houthi forces are armed largely with weapons seized from Yemeni Government forces; they are also reported to have received military hardware from Iran (2023)

Military service age and obligation: 18 is the legal minimum age for voluntary military service; conscription abolished in 2001; 2-year service obligation (note - limited information since the start of the civil war in 2014) (2022)
note: as late as 2022, all parties to the ongoing conflict were implicated in child soldier recruitment and use; during the beginning of the truce in April 2022, the Houthis signed a plan with the UN to end the recruitment and use of child soldiers; Houthi leaders previously pledged to end the use of child soldiers in 2012, as did the Government of Yemen in 2014

Military - note: government forces under the Yemeni Ministry of Defense are responsible for territorial defense, but also have internal security functions; their main focus has been the Houthi separatists and protecting Yemen's maritime borders, which are susceptible to smuggling of arms, fighters, and other material support for the Houthis and terrorist groups operating in Yemen, including al-Qa'ida in the Arabian Peninsula (AQAP) and the Islamic State of Iraq and ash-Sham in Yemen (ISIS-Yemen)
in 2015, a Saudi-led coalition of Arab states (UAE, Qatar, Bahrain, Morocco, Sudan, Kuwait, Jordan and Egypt) intervened militarily in Yemen in support of the Republic of Yemen Government (ROYG) against the separatist Houthis; Saudi military forces conducted operations in Yemen and raised and equipped paramilitary/militia security forces in Yemen based largely on tribal or regional affiliation to deploy along the Saudi-Yemen border; UAE's participation in 2015 included several thousand ground troops, as well as supporting air and naval forces; UAE withdrew its main military force from Yemen in 2019, but has retained a smaller military presence while working with proxies in southern Yemen, most notably the Southern Transitional Council (STC); UAE has recruited, trained, and equipped tens of thousands of Yemeni fighters and formed them into dozens of militia and paramilitary units
in 2022, the RYOG and the Houthis signed a truce, halting military operations and establishing humanitarian measures; the former front lines of conflict, in some areas mirroring Yemen's pre -unification borders, remain static; AQAP and ISIS-Yemen have remained active in remote areas
in January 2024, the US Government designated the Houthis (aka Ansarallah) as a Specially Designated Global Terrorist group; the designation came after the Houthis began launching attacks against international maritime vessels in the Red Sea and Gulf of Aden, as well as military forces positioned in the area to defend the safety and security of commercial shipping (2024)

TERRORISM

Terrorist group(s): Islamic Revolutionary Guard Corps (IRGC)/Qods Force; Islamic State of Iraq and ash-Sham - Yemen; al-Qa'ida in the Arabian Peninsula (AQAP), Hizballah
note: details about the history, aims, leadership, organization, areas of operation, tactics, targets, weapons, size, and sources of support of the group(s) appear(s) in the Terrorism reference guide

TRANSNATIONAL ISSUES

Refugees and internally displaced persons: *refugees (country of origin):* 45,608 (Somalia), 17,812 (Ethiopia) (2023)
IDPs: 4.523 million (conflict in Sa'ada Governorate; clashes between al-Qa'ida in the Arabian Peninsula and government forces) (2022)

ZAMBIA

INTRODUCTION

Background: Bantu-speaking groups mainly from the Luba and Lunda Kingdoms in the Congo River Basin and from the Great Lakes region in East Africa settled in what is now Zambia beginning around A.D. 300, displacing and mixing with previous population groups in the region. The Mutapa Empire developed after the fall of Great Zimbabwe to the south in the 14th century and ruled the region, including large parts of Zambia, from the 14th to 17th century. The empire collapsed as a result of the growing slave trade and Portuguese incursions in the 16th and 17th centuries. The region was further influenced by migrants from the Zulu Kingdom to the south and the Luba and Lunda Kingdoms to the north, after invading colonial and African powers displaced local residents into the area around the Zambezi River, in what is now Zambia. In the 1880s, British companies began securing mineral and other economic concessions from local leaders. The companies eventually claimed control of the region and incorporated it as the protectorate of Northern Rhodesia in 1911. The UK took over administrative control from the British South Africa Company in 1924. During the 1920s and 1930s, advances in mining spurred British economic ventures and colonial settlement.

Northern Rhodesia's name was changed to Zambia upon independence from the UK in 1964, under independence leader and first President Kenneth KAUNDA. In the 1980s and 1990s, declining copper prices, economic mismanagement, and a prolonged drought hurt the economy. Elections in 1991 brought an end to one-party rule and propelled the Movement for Multiparty Democracy (MMD) into power. The subsequent vote in 1996, however, saw increasing harassment of opposition parties and abuse of state media and other resources. Administrative problems marked the election in 2001, with three parties filing a legal petition challenging the election of ruling party candidate Levy MWANAWASA. MWANAWASA was reelected in 2006 in an election that was deemed free and fair. Upon his death in 2008, he was succeeded by his vice president, Rupiah BANDA, who won a special presidential byelection later that year. BANDA and the MMD lost to Michael SATA and the Patriotic Front (PF) in the 2011 general elections. SATA, however, presided over a period of haphazard economic management and attempted to silence opposition to PF policies. SATA died in 2014 and was succeeded by his vice president, Guy SCOTT, who served as interim president until 2015, when Edgar LUNGU won the presidential byelection and completed SATA's term. LUNGU then won a full term in the 2016 presidential elections. Hakainde HICHILEMA was elected president in 2021.

GEOGRAPHY

Location: Southern Africa, east of Angola, south of the Democratic Republic of the Congo

Geographic coordinates: 15 00 S, 30 00 E

Map references: Africa

Area: *total:* 752,618 sq km
land: 743,398 sq km
water: 9,220 sq km
comparison ranking: total 40

Area - comparative: almost five times the size of Georgia; slightly larger than Texas

Land boundaries: *total:* 6,043.15 km
border countries (8): Angola 1,065 km; Botswana 0.15 km; Democratic Republic of the Congo 2,332 km; Malawi 847 km; Mozambique 439 km; Namibia 244 km; Tanzania 353 km; Zimbabwe 763 km

Coastline: 0 km (landlocked)

Maritime claims: none (landlocked)

Climate: tropical; modified by altitude; rainy season (October to April)

Terrain: mostly high plateau with some hills and mountains

Elevation: *highest point:* Mafinga Central 2,330 m
lowest point: Zambezi river 329 m
mean elevation: 1,138 m

Natural resources: copper, cobalt, zinc, lead, coal, emeralds, gold, silver, uranium, hydropower

Land use: *agricultural land:* 31.7% (2018 est.)
arable land: 4.8% (2018 est.)
permanent crops: 0% (2018 est.)
permanent pasture: 26.9% (2018 est.)
forest: 66.3% (2018 est.)
other: 2% (2018 est.)

Irrigated land: 1,560 sq km (2012)

Major lakes (area sq km): *fresh water lake(s):* Lake Tanganyika (shared with Democratic Republic of Congo, Tanzania, and Burundi) - 32,000 sq km; Lake Mweru (shared with Democratic Republic of Congo) - 4,350 sq km; Lake Bangweulu - 4,000-15,000 sq km seasonal variation

Major rivers (by length in km): Congo river source (shared with Angola, Republic of Congo, and Democratic Republic of Congo [m]) - 4,700 km; Zambezi river source (shared with Angola, Namibia, Botswana, Zimbabwe, and Mozambique [m]) - 2,740 km
note – [s] after country name indicates river source; [m] after country name indicates river mouth

Major watersheds (area sq km): Atlantic Ocean drainage: Congo (3,730,881 sq km)
Indian Ocean drainage: Zambezi (1,332,412 sq km)

Major aquifers: Upper Kalahari-Cuvelai-Upper Zambezi Basin

Population distribution: one of the highest levels of urbanization in Africa; high density in the central area, particularly around the cities of Lusaka, Ndola, Kitwe, and Mufulira as shown in this population distribution map

Natural hazards: periodic drought; tropical storms (November to April)

Geography - note: landlocked; the Zambezi forms a natural riverine boundary with Zimbabwe; Lake Kariba on the Zambia-Zimbabwe border forms the world's largest reservoir by volume (180 cu km; 43 cu mi)

PEOPLE AND SOCIETY

Population: *total:* 20,799,116
male: 10,407,253
female: 10,391,863 (2024 est.)
comparison rankings: female 64; male 63; total 63

Nationality: *noun:* Zambian(s)
adjective: Zambian

Ethnic groups: Bemba 21%, Tonga 13.6%, Chewa 7.4%, Lozi 5.7%, Nsenga 5.3%, Tumbuka 4.4%, Ngoni 4%, Lala 3.1%, Kaonde 2.9%, Namwanga 2.8%, Lunda (north Western) 2.6%, Mambwe 2.5%, Luvale 2.2%, Lamba 2.1%, Ushi 1.9%, Lenje 1.6%, Bisa 1.6%, Mbunda 1.2%, other 13.8%, unspecified 0.4% (2010 est.)

Languages: Bemba 33.4%, Nyanja 14.7%, Tonga 11.4%, Lozi 5.5%, Chewa 4.5%, Nsenga 2.9%, Tumbuka 2.5%, Lunda (North Western) 1.9%, Kaonde 1.8%, Lala 1.8%, Lamba 1.8%, English (official) 1.7%, Luvale 1.5%, Mambwe 1.3%, Namwanga 1.2%, Lenje 1.1%, Bisa 1%, other 9.7%, unspecified 0.2% (2010 est.)
note: Zambia is said to have over 70 languages, although many of these may be considered dialects; all of Zambia's major languages are members of the Bantu family; Chewa and Nyanja are mutually intelligible dialects

Religions: Protestant 75.3%, Roman Catholic 20.2%, other 2.7% (includes Muslim, Buddhist, Hindu, and Baha'i), none 1.8% (2010 est.)

Demographic profile: Zambia's poor, youthful population consists primarily of Bantu-speaking people representing nearly 70 different ethnicities. Zambia's high fertility rate continues to drive rapid population growth, averaging almost 3% annually between 2000 and 2010, and reaching over 3.3% in 2022. The country's total fertility rate has fallen by less than 1.5 children per woman during the last 30 years and still averages among the world's highest, almost 6 children per woman, largely because of the country's lack of access to family planning services, education for girls, and employment for women. Zambia also exhibits wide fertility disparities based on rural or urban location, education, and income. Poor, uneducated women from rural areas are more likely to marry young, to give birth early, and to have more children, viewing children as a sign of prestige and recognizing that not all of their children will live to adulthood. HIV/AIDS is prevalent in Zambia and contributes to its low life expectancy.

Zambian emigration is low compared to many other African countries and is comprised predominantly of the well-educated. The small amount of brain drain, however, has a major impact in Zambia because of its limited human capital and lack of educational infrastructure for developing skilled professionals in key fields. For example, Zambia has few schools for training doctors, nurses, and other health care workers. Its spending on education is low compared to other Sub-Saharan countries.

Age structure: *0-14 years:* 42.1% (male 4,418,980/female 4,337,187)
15-64 years: 55.1% (male 5,726,265/female 5,736,732)
65 years and over: 2.8% (2024 est.) (male 262,008/female 317,944)

Dependency ratios: *total dependency ratio:* 81.8
youth dependency ratio: 78.7
elderly dependency ratio: 3.2
potential support ratio: 31.6 (2021 est.)

Median age: *total:* 18.4 years (2024 est.)
male: 18.2 years
female: 18.6 years
comparison ranking: total 219

Population growth rate: 2.83% (2024 est.)
comparison ranking: 10

Birth rate: 34.1 births/1,000 population (2024 est.)
comparison ranking: 16

Death rate: 5.9 deaths/1,000 population (2024 est.)
comparison ranking: 160

Net migration rate: 0.1 migrant(s)/1,000 population (2024 est.)
comparison ranking: 76

Population distribution: one of the highest levels of urbanization in Africa; high density in the central area, particularly around the cities of Lusaka, Ndola, Kitwe, and Mufulira as shown in this population distribution map

Urbanization: *urban population:* 46.3% of total population (2023)
rate of urbanization: 4.15% annual rate of change (2020-25 est.)

Major urban areas - population: 3.181 million LUSAKA (capital), 763,000 Kitwe (2023)

Sex ratio: *at birth:* 1.03 male(s)/female
0-14 years: 1.02 male(s)/female
15-64 years: 1 male(s)/female
65 years and over: 0.82 male(s)/female
total population: 1 male(s)/female (2024 est.)

Mother's mean age at first birth: 19.2 years (2018 est.)
note: data represents median age at first birth among women 20-49

Maternal mortality ratio: 135 deaths/100,000 live births (2020 est.)
comparison ranking: 56

Infant mortality rate: *total:* 35.6 deaths/1,000 live births (2024 est.)
male: 38.9 deaths/1,000 live births
female: 32.1 deaths/1,000 live births
comparison ranking: total 37

Life expectancy at birth: *total population:* 66.9 years (2024 est.)
male: 65.2 years
female: 68.7 years
comparison ranking: total population 199

Total fertility rate: 4.42 children born/woman (2024 est.)
comparison ranking: 18

Gross reproduction rate: 2.18 (2024 est.)

Contraceptive prevalence rate: 49.6% (2018)

Drinking water source: *improved: urban:* 90.2% of population
rural: 56.6% of population
total: 71.6% of population
unimproved: urban: 9.8% of population
rural: 43.4% of population
total: 28.4% of population (2020 est.)

Current health expenditure: 5.6% of GDP (2020)

Physician density: 1.17 physicians/1,000 population (2018)

Hospital bed density: 2 beds/1,000 population

Sanitation facility access: *improved: urban:* 76.3% of population
rural: 31.9% of population
total: 51.7% of population
unimproved: urban: 23.7% of population
rural: 68.1% of population
total: 48.3% of population (2020 est.)

Obesity - adult prevalence rate: 8.1% (2016)
comparison ranking: 155

Alcohol consumption per capita: *total:* 3.82 liters of pure alcohol (2019 est.)
beer: 1.26 liters of pure alcohol (2019 est.)
wine: 0.04 liters of pure alcohol (2019 est.)
spirits: 0.36 liters of pure alcohol (2019 est.)
other alcohols: 2.16 liters of pure alcohol (2019 est.)
comparison ranking: total 98

Tobacco use: *total:* 14.4% (2020 est.)
male: 25.1% (2020 est.)
female: 3.7% (2020 est.)
comparison ranking: total 107

Children under the age of 5 years underweight: 11.8% (2018/19)
comparison ranking: 46

Currently married women (ages 15-49): 53.3% (2023 est.)

Child marriage: *women married by age 15:* 5.2%
women married by age 18: 29%
men married by age 18: 2.8% (2018 est.)

Education expenditures: 3.7% of GDP (2020)
comparison ranking: 131

Literacy: *definition:* age 15 and over can read and write English
total population: 86.7%
male: 90.6%
female: 83.1% (2018)

ENVIRONMENT

Environment - current issues: air pollution and resulting acid rain in the mineral extraction and refining region; chemical runoff into watersheds; loss of biodiversity; poaching seriously threatens rhinoceros, elephant, antelope, and large cat populations; deforestation; soil erosion; desertification; lack of adequate water treatment presents human health risks

Environment - international agreements: *party to:* Biodiversity, Climate Change, Climate Change-Kyoto Protocol, Climate Change-Paris Agreement, Comprehensive Nuclear Test Ban, Desertification, Endangered Species, Hazardous Wastes, Law of the Sea, Nuclear Test Ban, Ozone Layer Protection, Wetlands
signed, but not ratified: none of the selected agreements

Climate: tropical; modified by altitude; rainy season (October to April)

Urbanization: *urban population:* 46.3% of total population (2023)
rate of urbanization: 4.15% annual rate of change (2020-25 est.)

Food insecurity: *severe localized food insecurity: due to reduced incomes and localized shortfalls in cereal production* - cereal production declined to a below-average level in 2022 and along with the impact of rising food prices, the number of food insecure is foreseen to increase at the end of 2022 to levels above the 1.6 million people estimated in the first quarter of 2022 (2022)

Revenue from forest resources: 4.45% of GDP (2018 est.)
comparison ranking: 15

Revenue from coal: 0.04% of GDP (2018 est.)
comparison ranking: 33

Air pollutants: *particulate matter emissions:* 16.9 micrograms per cubic meter (2019 est.)
carbon dioxide emissions: 5.14 megatons (2016 est.)
methane emissions: 14.1 megatons (2020 est.)

Waste and recycling: *municipal solid waste generated annually:* 2,608,268 tons (2002 est.)

Major lakes (area sq km): *fresh water lake(s):* Lake Tanganyika (shared with Democratic Republic of Congo, Tanzania, and Burundi) - 32,000 sq km; Lake Mweru (shared with Democratic Republic of Congo) - 4,350 sq km; Lake Bangweulu - 4,000-15,000 sq km seasonal variation

Major rivers (by length in km): Congo river source (shared with Angola, Republic of Congo, and Democratic Republic of Congo [m]) - 4,700 km; Zambezi river source (shared with Angola, Namibia, Botswana, Zimbabwe, and Mozambique [m]) - 2,740 km
note – [s] after country name indicates river source; [m] after country name indicates river mouth

Major watersheds (area sq km): Atlantic Ocean drainage: Congo (3,730,881 sq km)

Indian Ocean drainage: Zambezi (1,332,412 sq km)

Major aquifers: Upper Kalahari-Cuvelai-Upper Zambezi Basin

Total water withdrawal: *municipal:* 290 million cubic meters (2020 est.)
industrial: 130 million cubic meters (2020 est.)
agricultural: 1.15 billion cubic meters (2020 est.)

Total renewable water resources: 104.8 billion cubic meters (2020 est.)

GOVERNMENT

Country name: *conventional long form:* Republic of Zambia
conventional short form: Zambia
former: Northern Rhodesia
etymology: name derived from the Zambezi River, which flows through the western part of the country and forms its southern border with neighboring Zimbabwe

Government type: presidential republic

Capital: *name:* Lusaka
geographic coordinates: 15 25 S, 28 17 E
time difference: UTC+2 (7 hours ahead of Washington, DC, during Standard Time)

etymology: named after a village called Lusaka, located at Manda Hill, near where Zambia's National Assembly building currently stands; the village was named after a headman (chief) LUSAKASA

Administrative divisions: 10 provinces; Central, Copperbelt, Eastern, Luapula, Lusaka, Muchinga, Northern, North-Western, Southern, Western

Independence: 24 October 1964 (from the UK)

National holiday: Independence Day, 24 October (1964)

Legal system: mixed legal system of English common law and customary law

Constitution: *history:* several previous; latest adopted 24 August 1991, promulgated 30 August 1991
amendments: proposed by the National Assembly; passage requires two-thirds majority vote by the Assembly in two separate readings at least 30 days apart; passage of amendments affecting fundamental rights and freedoms requires approval by at least one half of votes cast in a referendum prior to consideration and voting by the Assembly; amended 1996, 2015, 2016; note - in late 2020, an amendment which would have altered the structure of the constitution was defeated in the National Assembly

International law organization participation: has not submitted an ICJ jurisdiction declaration; accepts ICCt jurisdiction

Citizenship: *citizenship by birth:* only if at least one parent is a citizen of Zambia
citizenship by descent only: yes, if at least one parent was a citizen of Zambia
dual citizenship recognized: yes
residency requirement for naturalization: 5 years for those with an ancestor who was a citizen of Zambia, otherwise 10 years residency is required

Suffrage: 18 years of age; universal

Executive branch: *chief of state:* President Hakainde HICHILEMA (since 24 August 2021)
head of government: President Hakainde HICHILEMA (since 24 August 2021)
cabinet: Cabinet appointed by president from among members of the National Assembly
elections/appointments: president directly elected by absolute majority popular vote in 2 rounds if needed for a 5-year term (eligible for a second term); last held on 12 August 2021 (next to be held in 2026)
note - the president is both chief of state and head of government
election results:
2021: Hakainde HICHILEMA elected president; percent of the vote - Hakainde HICHILEMA (UPND) 57.9%, Edgar LUNGU (PF) 37.3%, other 4.8%
2016: Edgar LUNGU reelected president; percent of vote - Edgar LUNGU (PF) 50.4%, Hakainde HICHILEMA (UPND) 47.6%, other 2%

Legislative branch: *description:* unicameral National Assembly (167 seats statutory, 166 seats current; 156 members directly elected in single-seat constituencies by simple majority vote in 2 rounds if needed, and up to 8 appointed by the president; members serve 5-year terms); 3 ex-officio members elected by National Assembly membership
elections: last held on 12 August 2021 (next to be held in 2026)
election results: percent of vote by party - UPND 53.9%, PF 38.1%, PNUP 0.6%, independent 7.4%; seats by party - UPND 82, PF 62, PNUP 1, independent 11; composition - men 142, women 25, percentage women 15%

Judicial branch: *highest court(s):* Supreme Court (consists of the chief justice, deputy chief justice, and at least 11 judges);
Constitutional Court (consists of the court president, vice president, and 11 judges); note - the Constitutional Court began operation in June 2016
judge selection and term of office: Supreme Court and Constitutional Court judges appointed by the president of the republic upon the advice of the 9-member Judicial Service Commission, which is headed by the chief justice, and ratified by the National Assembly; judges normally serve until age 65
subordinate courts: Court of Appeal; High Court; Industrial Relations Court; subordinate courts (3 levels, based on upper limit of money involved); Small Claims Court; local courts (2 grades, based on upper limit of money involved)

Political parties: Alliance for Democracy and Development or ADD
Forum for Democracy and Development or FDD
Movement for Multiparty Democracy or MMD
Party of National Unity and Progress or PNUP
Patriotic Front or PF
United Party for National Development or UPND

International organization participation: ACP, AfDB, AU, C, COMESA, EITI (compliant country), FAO, G-77, IAEA, IBRD, ICAO, ICCt, ICRM, IDA, IFAD, IFC, IFRCS, ILO, IMF, Interpol, IOC, IOM, IPU, ISO (correspondent), ITSO, ITU, ITUC (NGOs), MIGA, MONUSCO, NAM, OPCW, PCA, SADC, UN, UNCTAD, UNDOF, UNESCO, UNHCR, UNIDO, UNISFA, UNMIL, UNMISS, UNOCI, UNWTO, UPU, WCO, WHO, WIPO, WMO, WTO

Diplomatic representation in the US: *chief of mission:* Ambassador Chibamba KANYAMA (since 30 June 2023)
chancery: 2200 R Street NW, Washington, DC 20008
telephone: [1] (202) 234-4009
FAX: [1] (202) 332-0826
email address and website:
info@zambiaembassy.org
https://www.zambiaembassy.org/

Diplomatic representation from the US: *chief of mission:* Ambassador Michael C. GONZALES (since 16 September 2022)
embassy: Eastern end of Kabulonga Road, Ibex Hill, Lusaka
mailing address: 2310 Lusaka Place, Washington DC 20521-2310
telephone: [260] (0) 211-357-000
FAX: [260] (0) 211-357-224
email address and website:
ACSLusaka@state.gov
https://zm.usembassy.gov/

Flag description: green field with a panel of three vertical bands of red (hoist side), black, and orange below a soaring orange eagle, on the outer edge of the flag; green stands for the country's natural resources and vegetation, red symbolizes the struggle for freedom, black the people of Zambia, and orange the country's mineral wealth; the eagle represents the people's ability to rise above the nation's problems

National symbol(s): African fish eagle; national colors: green, red, black, orange

National anthem: *name:* "Lumbanyeni Zambia" (Stand and Sing of Zambia, Proud and Free)
lyrics/music: multiple/Enoch Mankayi SONTONGA
note: adopted 1964; the melody, from the popular song "God Bless Africa," is the same as that of Tanzania but with different lyrics; the melody is also incorporated into South Africa's anthem

National heritage: *total World Heritage Sites:* 1 (natural)
selected World Heritage Site locales: Mosi-oa-Tunya/Victoria Falls

ECONOMY

Economic overview: lower middle-income Sub-Saharan economy; major copper exporter; high public debt is held mostly by China; systemic corruption; one of youngest and fastest growing labor forces; regional hydroelectricity exporter; extreme rural poverty

Real GDP (purchasing power parity): $76.493 billion (2023 est.)
$72.277 billion (2022 est.)
$68.672 billion (2021 est.)
note: data in 2021 dollars
comparison ranking: 105

Real GDP growth rate: 5.83% (2023 est.)
5.25% (2022 est.)
6.23% (2021 est.)
note: annual GDP % growth based on constant local currency
comparison ranking: 34

Real GDP per capita: $3,700 (2023 est.)
$3,600 (2022 est.)
$3,500 (2021 est.)
note: data in 2021 dollars
comparison ranking: 188

GDP (official exchange rate): $28.163 billion (2023 est.)
note: data in current dollars at official exchange rate

Inflation rate (consumer prices): 10.88% (2023 est.)
10.99% (2022 est.)
22.02% (2021 est.)
note: annual % change based on consumer prices
comparison ranking: 184

Credit ratings: Fitch rating: RD (2020)

Moody's rating: Ca (2020)

Standard & Poors rating: SD (2020)
note: The year refers to the year in which the current credit rating was first obtained.

GDP - composition, by sector of origin: *agriculture:* 2.8% (2023 est.)
industry: 36.1% (2023 est.)
services: 54.9% (2023 est.)
note: figures may not total 100% due to non-allocated consumption not captured in sector-reported data
comparison rankings: services 120; industry 41; agriculture 145

GDP - composition, by end use: *household consumption:* 35.6% (2022 est.)
government consumption: 14.3% (2022 est.)
investment in fixed capital: 25.1% (2022 est.)
investment in inventories: 1.9% (2022 est.)
exports of goods and services: 40.8% (2023 est.)
imports of goods and services: -39.1% (2023 est.)
note: figures may not total 100% due to rounding or gaps in data collection

Agricultural products: sugarcane, cassava, maize, milk, soybeans, vegetables, wheat, groundnuts, beef, sweet potatoes (2022)
note: top ten agricultural products based on tonnage

Industries: copper mining and processing, emerald mining, construction, foodstuffs, beverages, chemicals, textiles, fertilizer, horticulture

Industrial production growth rate: 1.73% (2023 est.)
note: annual % change in industrial value added based on constant local currency
comparison ranking: 119

Labor force: 7.051 million (2023 est.)
note: number of people ages 15 or older who are employed or seeking work
comparison ranking: 68

Unemployment rate: 5.91% (2023 est.)
5.99% (2022 est.)
5.2% (2021 est.)
note: % of labor force seeking employment
comparison ranking: 118

Youth unemployment rate (ages 15-24): *total:* 9.8% (2023 est.)
male: 9.7% (2023 est.)
female: 9.8% (2023 est.)
note: % of labor force ages 15-24 seeking employment
comparison ranking: total 137

Population below poverty line: 60% (2022 est.)
note: % of population with income below national poverty line

Gini Index coefficient - distribution of family income: 51.5 (2022 est.)
note: index (0-100) of income distribution; higher values represent greater inequality
comparison ranking: 8

Household income or consumption by percentage share: *lowest 10%:* 1.4% (2022 est.)
highest 10%: 39.1% (2022 est.)
note: % share of income accruing to lowest and highest 10% of population

Remittances: 0.89% of GDP (2023 est.)
0.83% of GDP (2022 est.)
1.08% of GDP (2021 est.)
note: personal transfers and compensation between resident and non-resident individuals/households/entities

Budget: *revenues:* $5.388 billion (2021 est.)
expenditures: $5.554 billion (2021 est.)
note: central government revenues and expenses (excluding grants/extrabudgetary units/social security funds) converted to US dollars at average official exchange rate for year indicated

Public debt: 71.41% of GDP (2021 est.)
note: central government debt as a % of GDP
comparison ranking: 52

Taxes and other revenues: 16.78% (of GDP) (2021 est.)
note: central government tax revenue as a % of GDP
comparison ranking: 117

Current account balance: $1.093 billion (2022 est.)
$2.63 billion (2021 est.)
$2.139 billion (2020 est.)
note: balance of payments - net trade and primary/secondary income in current dollars
comparison ranking: 54

Exports: $12.444 billion (2022 est.)
$11.728 billion (2021 est.)
$8.558 billion (2020 est.)
note: balance of payments - exports of goods and services in current dollars
comparison ranking: 105

Exports - partners: Switzerland 30%, China 18%, Democratic Republic of the Congo 10%, Pitcairn Islands 10%, UAE 7% (2022)
note: top five export partners based on percentage share of exports

Exports - commodities: raw copper, refined copper, gold, precious stones, iron alloys (2022)
note: top five export commodities based on value in dollars

Imports: $10.022 billion (2022 est.)
$7.691 billion (2021 est.)
$5.866 billion (2020 est.)
note: balance of payments - imports of goods and services in current dollars
comparison ranking: 124

Imports - partners: South Africa 26%, Equatorial Guinea 18%, China 14%, UAE 7%, Democratic Republic of the Congo 6% (2022)
note: top five import partners based on percentage share of imports

Imports - commodities: fertilizers, refined petroleum, trucks, copper ore, packaged medicine (2022)
note: top five import commodities based on value in dollars

Reserves of foreign exchange and gold: $2.968 billion (2022 est.)
$2.754 billion (2021 est.)
$1.203 billion (2020 est.)
note: holdings of gold (year-end prices)/foreign exchange/special drawing rights in current dollars
comparison ranking: 131

Exchange rates: Zambian kwacha (ZMK) per US dollar -

Exchange rates: 20.212 (2023 est.)
16.938 (2022 est.)
20.018 (2021 est.)
18.344 (2020 est.)
12.89 (2019 est.)

ENERGY

Electricity access: *electrification - total population:* 47.8% (2022 est.)
electrification - urban areas: 87%
electrification - rural areas: 14.5%

Electricity: *installed generating capacity:* 3.863 million kW (2022 est.)
consumption: 14.966 billion kWh (2022 est.)
exports: 2.152 billion kWh (2022 est.)
imports: 36.599 million kWh (2022 est.)
transmission/distribution losses: 2.392 billion kWh (2022 est.)
comparison rankings: transmission/distribution losses 128; imports 118; exports 54; consumption 84; installed generating capacity 101

Electricity generation sources: *fossil fuels:* 11.1% of total installed capacity (2022 est.)
solar: 0.7% of total installed capacity (2022 est.)
hydroelectricity: 87.8% of total installed capacity (2022 est.)
biomass and waste: 0.4% of total installed capacity (2022 est.)

Coal: *production:* 831,000 metric tons (2022 est.)
consumption: 823,000 metric tons (2022 est.)
exports: 200 metric tons (2022 est.)
imports: 300 metric tons (2022 est.)
proven reserves: 944.999 million metric tons (2022 est.)

Petroleum: *refined petroleum consumption:* 34,000 bbl/day (2022 est.)

Carbon dioxide emissions: 6.924 million metric tonnes of CO2 (2022 est.)
from coal and metallurgical coke: 1.857 million metric tonnes of CO2 (2022 est.)
from petroleum and other liquids: 5.068 million metric tonnes of CO2 (2022 est.)
comparison ranking: total emissions 126

Energy consumption per capita: 7.088 million Btu/person (2022 est.)
comparison ranking: 160

COMMUNICATIONS

Telephones - fixed lines: *total subscriptions:* 96,000 (2022 est.)
subscriptions per 100 inhabitants: (2022 est.) less than 1
comparison ranking: total subscriptions 135

Telephones - mobile cellular: *total subscriptions:* 19.838 million (2022 est.)
subscriptions per 100 inhabitants: 99 (2022 est.)
comparison ranking: total subscriptions 64

Telecommunication systems: *general assessment:* following elections held in August 2021, the new government immediately established a Ministry of Technology and Science to promote the use of ICT in developing economic growth and social inclusion; this focus on ICT, and on telecoms in particular, has been central to government strategies for some years; as part of the Smart Zambia initiative, investment has been made in data centers, a computer assembly plant, ICT training centers, and a Smart Education program; these efforts have been combined with the extension of broadband access and improved connectivity to international submarine cables; in turn, this has resulted in a considerable reduction in fixed-line and mobile access pricing for end-users; mobile network operators continue to invest in 3G and LTE-based services, the government contracted to upgrade the state-owned mobile infrastructure for 5G services; delays in holding spectrum have stymied the development of 5G thus far; in mid-2021 the regulator completed a consultation of auctioning low, medium, and high band spectrum for 5G, aiming to provide sufficient spectrum to meet the anticipated increase in data traffic in coming years; fixed-line broadband services remain underdeveloped (2022)
domestic: fixed-line teledensity less than 1 per 100 and mobile-cellular is 100 per 100 (2021)
international: country code - 260; multiple providers operate overland fiber optic routes via Zimbabwe/South Africa, Botswana/Namibia and Tanzania provide access to the major undersea cables

Broadcast media: according to the Independent Broadcast Authority, there are 137 radio stations and 47 television stations in Zambia; out of the 137 radio stations, 133 are private (categorized as either commercial or community radio stations), while 4 are public-owned; state-owned Zambia National Broadcasting Corporation (ZNBC) operates 2 television channels and 3 radio stations; ZNBC owns 75% shares in GoTV, 40% in MultiChoice, and 40% in TopStar Communications Company, all of which operate in-country
(2019)

Internet country code: .zm

Internet users: *total:* 3.99 million (2021 est.)
percent of population: 21% (2021 est.)

comparison ranking: total 109

Broadband - fixed subscriptions: *total:* 82,317 (2020 est.)
subscriptions per 100 inhabitants: 0.5 (2020 est.)
comparison ranking: total 131

TRANSPORTATION

National air transport system: *number of registered air carriers:* 3 (2020)
inventory of registered aircraft operated by air carriers: 6
annual passenger traffic on registered air carriers: 8,904 (2018)
annual freight traffic on registered air carriers: 75.08 million (2018) mt-km

Civil aircraft registration country code prefix: 9J

Airports: 119 (2024)
comparison ranking: 44

Heliports: 4 (2024)

Pipelines: 771 km oil (2013)

Railways: *total:* 3,126 km (2014)
narrow gauge: 3,126 km (2014) 1.067-m gauge
note: includes 1,860 km of the Tanzania-Zambia Railway Authority (TAZARA)
comparison ranking: total 57

Roadways: *total:* 67,671 km
paved: 10,150 km
unpaved: 57,520 km (2021)
comparison ranking: total 73

Waterways: 2,250 km (2010) (includes Lake Tanganyika and the Zambezi and Luapula Rivers)
comparison ranking: 39

Merchant marine: *total:* 2 (2023)
by type: general cargo 1, oil tanker 1
comparison ranking: total 178

MILITARY AND SECURITY

Military and security forces: Zambia Defense Force (ZDF): Zambia Army, Zambia Air Force, Zambia National Service; Defense Force Medical Service

Ministry of Home Affairs and Internal Security: Zambia Police (includes a paramilitary battalion) (2024)
note 1: the Zambia National Service is a support organization that also does public work projects; its main objectives revolve around land development, agriculture, industries, youth skills training as well as arts, sports and culture
note 2: the Zambia Army comprises the Regular Force, the Home Guard, and the Territorial reserve

Military expenditures: 1.4% of GDP (2023 est.)
1.2% of GDP (2022 est.)
1.3% of GDP (2021 est.)
1.3% of GDP (2020 est.)
1.3% of GDP (2019 est.)
comparison ranking: 99

Military and security service personnel strengths: approximately 17,000 active troops (15,000 Army; 2,000 Air) (2024)

Military equipment inventories and acquisitions: the ZDF's inventory is largely comprised of Chinese, Russian, and Soviet-era armaments with small quantities of Western-origin equipment (2024)

Military service age and obligation: 18-25 years of age (17 with parental consent) for voluntary military service for men and women; no conscription; 12-year enlistment period (7 years active, 5 in the Reserves) (2023)
note: Zambia had military conscription from 1975-1980

Military deployments: 930 Central African Republic (MINUSCA) (2024)

Military - note: the Zambia Defense Forces (ZDF) are responsible for preserving the country's sovereignty and territorial integrity; it also has some domestic security responsibilities in cases of national emergency; border security and support to African and UN peacekeeping operations are priorities; the ZDF is part of the Southern Africa Development Community (SADC) Standby Force and participates in multinational training exercises; it has received training assistance from China and the US
the ZDF traces its roots to the Northern Rhodesia Regiment, which was raised by the British colonial government to fight in World War II; the ZDF was established in 1964 from units of the dissolved Federation of Rhodesia and Nyasaland armed forces; it participated in a number of regional conflicts during the 1970s and 1980s; Zambia actively supported independence movements such as the Union for the Total Liberation of Angola (UNITA), the Zimbabwe African People's Union (ZAPU), the African National Congress of South Africa (ANC), and the South-West Africa People's Organization (SWAPO) (2024)

TRANSNATIONAL ISSUES

Refugees and internally displaced persons: *refugees (country of origin):* 8,436 (Burundi) (2023); 62,660 (Democratic Republic of the Congo) (refugees and asylum seekers) (2024)

Illicit drugs: transshipment point for moderate amounts of methaqualone, small amounts of heroin, and cocaine bound for southern Africa and possibly Europe; a poorly developed financial infrastructure coupled with a government commitment to combating money laundering make it an unattractive venue for money launderers; major consumer of cannabis

ZIMBABWE

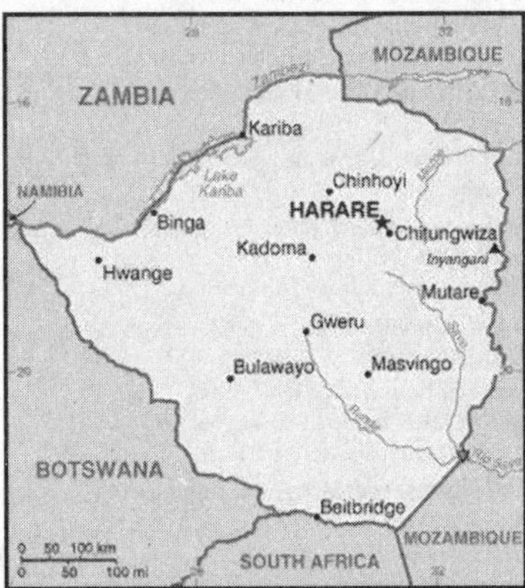

INTRODUCTION

Background: The hunter-gatherer San people first inhabited the area that eventually became Zimbabwe. Farming communities migrated to the area around A.D. 500 during the Bantu expansion, and Shona-speaking societies began to develop in the Limpopo valley and Zimbabwean highlands around the 9th century. These societies traded with Arab merchants on the Indian Ocean coast and organized under the Kingdom of Mapungubwe in the 11th century. A series of powerful trade-oriented Shona states succeeded Mapungubwe, including the Kingdom of Zimbabwe (ca. 1220-1450), Kingdom of Mutapa (ca. 1450-1760), and the Rozwi Empire. The Rozwi Empire expelled Portuguese colonists from the Zimbabwean plateau, but the Ndebele clan of Zulu King MZILIKAZI eventually conquered the area in 1838 during the era of conflict and population displacement known as the Mfecane.

In the 1880s, colonists arrived with the British South Africa Company (BSAC) and obtained a written concession for mining rights from Ndebele King LOBENGULA. The king later disavowed the concession and accused the BSAC agents of deceit. The BSAC annexed Mashonaland and then conquered Matabeleland during the First Matabele War of 1893-1894, establishing company rule over the territory. In 1923, the UK annexed BSAC holdings south of the Zambezi River, which became the British colony of Southern Rhodesia. The 1930 Land Apportionment Act restricted Black land ownership and established rules that would favor the White minority for decades. A new constitution in 1961 further cemented White minority rule.

In 1965, the government under White Prime Minister Ian SMITH unilaterally declared its independence from the UK. London did not recognize Rhodesia's independence and demanded more voting rights for the Black majority in the country. International diplomacy and an uprising by Black Zimbabweans led to biracial elections in 1979 and independence (as Zimbabwe) in 1980. Robert MUGABE, who led the uprising and became the nation's first prime minister, was the country's only ruler (as president since 1987) from independence until 2017. In the mid-1980s, the government tortured and killed thousands of civilians in a crackdown on dissent known as the Gukurahundi campaign. Economic mismanagement and chaotic implementation of land redistribution policies periodically crippled the economy. General elections in 2002, 2008, and 2013 were severely flawed and widely condemned but allowed MUGABE to remain president. In 2017, Vice President Emmerson MNANGAGWA became president after a military intervention that forced MUGABE to resign, and MNANGAGWA cemented power by sidelining rival Grace MUGABE (Robert MUGABE's wife). In 2018, MNANGAGWA won the presidential election, and he has maintained the government's longstanding practice of violently disrupting protests and politicizing institutions. Economic conditions remain dire under MNANGAGWA.

GEOGRAPHY

Location: Southern Africa, between South Africa and Zambia

Geographic coordinates: 20 00 S, 30 00 E

Map references: Africa

Area: *total:* 390,757 sq km
land: 386,847 sq km
water: 3,910 sq km
comparison ranking: total 62

Area - comparative: about four times the size of Indiana; slightly larger than Montana

Land boundaries: *total:* 3,229 km
border countries (4): Botswana 834 km; Mozambique 1,402 km; South Africa 230 km; Zambia 763 km

Coastline: 0 km (landlocked)

Maritime claims: none (landlocked)

Climate: tropical; moderated by altitude; rainy season (November to March)

Terrain: mostly high plateau with higher central plateau (high veld); mountains in east

Elevation: *highest point:* Inyangani 2,592 m
lowest point: junction of the Runde and Save Rivers 162 m
mean elevation: 961 m

Natural resources: coal, chromium ore, asbestos, gold, nickel, copper, iron ore, vanadium, lithium, tin, platinum group metals

Land use: *agricultural land:* 42.5% (2018 est.)
arable land: 10.9% (2018 est.)
permanent crops: 0.3% (2018 est.)
permanent pasture: 31.3% (2018 est.)
forest: 39.5% (2018 est.)
other: 18% (2018 est.)

Irrigated land: 1,740 sq km (2012)

Major rivers (by length in km): Zambezi (shared with Zambia [s]), Angola, Namibia, Botswana, and Mozambique [m]) - 2,740 km; Limpopo (shared with South Africa [s], Botswana, and Mozambique [m]) - 1,800 km
note – [s] after country name indicates river source; [m] after country name indicates river mouth

Major watersheds (area sq km): Indian Ocean drainage: Zambezi (1,332,412 sq km)

Internal (endorheic basin) drainage: Okavango Basin (863,866 sq km)

Major aquifers: Upper Kalahari-Cuvelai-Upper Zambezi Basin

Population distribution: Aside from major urban agglomerations in Harare and Bulawayo, population distribution is fairly even, with slightly greater overall numbers in the eastern half as shown in this population distribution map

Natural hazards: recurring droughts; floods and severe storms are rare

Geography - note: landlocked; the Zambezi forms a natural riverine boundary with Zambia; in full flood (February-April) the massive Victoria Falls on the river forms the world's largest curtain of falling water; Lake Kariba on the Zambia-Zimbabwe border forms the world's largest reservoir by volume (180 cu km; 43 cu mi)

PEOPLE AND SOCIETY

Population: *total:* 17,150,352
male: 8,343,790
female: 8,806,562 (2024 est.)
comparison rankings: female 72; male 72; total 72

Nationality: *noun:* Zimbabwean(s)
adjective: Zimbabwean

Ethnic groups: African 99.6% (predominantly Shona; Ndebele is the second largest ethnic group), other (includes Caucasian, Asiatic, mixed race) 0.4% (2022 est.)

Languages: Shona (official, most widely spoken) 80.9%, Ndebele (official, second most widely spoken) 11.5%, English (official, traditionally used for official business) 0.3%, 13 minority languages (official; includes Chewa, Chibarwe, Kalanga, Koisan, Nambya, Ndau, Shangani, sign language, Sotho, Tonga, Tswana, Venda, and Xhosa) 7%, other 0.3% (2022 est.)
note: data represent population by mother tongue

Religions: Apostolic Sect 40.3%, Pentecostal 17%, Protestant 13.8%, other Christian 7.8%, Roman Catholic 6.4%, African traditionalist 5%, other 1.5% (includes Muslim, Jewish, Hindu), none 8.3% (2022 est.)

Demographic profile: Zimbabwe's progress in reproductive, maternal, and child health has stagnated in recent years. According to a 2010 Demographic and Health Survey, contraceptive use, the number of births attended by skilled practitioners, and child mortality have either stalled or somewhat deteriorated since the mid-2000s. Zimbabwe's total fertility rate has remained fairly stable at about 4 children per woman for the last two decades, although an uptick in the urban birth rate in recent years has caused a slight rise in the country's overall fertility rate. Zimbabwe's HIV prevalence rate dropped from approximately 29% to 15% since 1997 but remains among the world's highest and continues to suppress the country's life expectancy rate. The proliferation of HIV/AIDS information and prevention programs and personal experience with those suffering or dying from the disease have helped to change sexual behavior and reduce the epidemic.
Historically, the vast majority of Zimbabwe's migration has been internal – a rural-urban flow. In terms of international migration, over the last 40 years Zimbabwe has gradually shifted from being a destination country to one of emigration and, to a lesser degree, one of transit (for East African illegal migrants traveling to South Africa). As a British colony, Zimbabwe attracted significant numbers of permanent immigrants from the UK and other European countries, as well as temporary economic migrants from Malawi, Mozambique, and Zambia. Although Zimbabweans have migrated to South Africa since the beginning of the 20th century to work as miners, the first major exodus from the country occurred in the years before and after independence in 1980. The outward migration was politically and racially influenced; a large share of the white population of European origin chose to leave rather than live under a new black-majority government.
In the 1990s and 2000s, economic mismanagement and hyperinflation sparked a second, more diverse wave of emigration. This massive outmigration – primarily to other southern African countries, the UK, and the US – has created a variety of challenges, including brain drain, illegal migration, and human smuggling and trafficking. Several factors have pushed highly skilled workers to go abroad, including unemployment, lower wages, a lack of resources, and few opportunities for career growth.

Age structure: *0-14 years:* 38.3% (male 3,315,075/female 3,254,643)
15-64 years: 57.8% (male 4,758,120/female 5,152,773)
65 years and over: 3.9% (2024 est.) (male 270,595/female 399,146)

Dependency ratios: *total dependency ratio:* 79.4
youth dependency ratio: 73.4
elderly dependency ratio: 6
potential support ratio: 16.6 (2021 est.)

Median age: *total:* 21.2 years (2024 est.)
male: 20.3 years
female: 22 years
comparison ranking: total 194

Population growth rate: 1.91% (2024 est.)
comparison ranking: 44

Birth rate: 28.8 births/1,000 population (2024 est.)
comparison ranking: 29

Death rate: 6.5 deaths/1,000 population (2024 est.)
comparison ranking: 136

Net migration rate: -3.2 migrant(s)/1,000 population (2024 est.)
comparison ranking: 184

Population distribution: Aside from major urban agglomerations in Harare and Bulawayo, population distribution is fairly even, with slightly greater overall numbers in the eastern half as shown in this population distribution map

Urbanization: *urban population:* 32.5% of total population (2023)
rate of urbanization: 2.41% annual rate of change (2020-25 est.)

Major urban areas - population: 1.578 million HARARE (capital) (2023)

Sex ratio: *at birth:* 1.03 male(s)/female
0-14 years: 1.02 male(s)/female
15-64 years: 0.92 male(s)/female
65 years and over: 0.68 male(s)/female
total population: 0.95 male(s)/female (2024 est.)

Mother's mean age at first birth: 20.3 years (2015 est.)
note: data represents median age at first birth among women 25-49

Maternal mortality ratio: 357 deaths/100,000 live births (2020 est.)
comparison ranking: 26

Infant mortality rate: *total:* 33.4 deaths/1,000 live births (2024 est.)
male: 37 deaths/1,000 live births
female: 29.6 deaths/1,000 live births
comparison ranking: total 39

Life expectancy at birth: *total population:* 67.2 years (2024 est.)
male: 65.6 years
female: 68.8 years
comparison ranking: total population 198

Total fertility rate: 3.47 children born/woman (2024 est.)
comparison ranking: 36

Gross reproduction rate: 1.71 (2024 est.)

Contraceptive prevalence rate: 66.8% (2015)

Drinking water source: *improved: urban:* 97.9% of population
rural: 66.9% of population
total: 76.9% of population
unimproved: urban: 2.1% of population
rural: 33.1% of population
total: 23.1% of population (2020 est.)

Current health expenditure: 3.4% of GDP (2020)

Physician density: 0.2 physicians/1,000 population (2020)

Hospital bed density: 1.7 beds/1,000 population (2011)

Sanitation facility access: *improved: urban:* 96.1% of population
rural: 49% of population
total: 64.2% of population
unimproved: urban: 3.9% of population
rural: 51% of population
total: 35.8% of population (2017 est.)

Obesity - adult prevalence rate: 15.5% (2016)
comparison ranking: 126

Alcohol consumption per capita: *total:* 3.11 liters of pure alcohol (2019 est.)
beer: 1.2 liters of pure alcohol (2019 est.)
wine: 0.05 liters of pure alcohol (2019 est.)
spirits: 0.39 liters of pure alcohol (2019 est.)
other alcohols: 1.47 liters of pure alcohol (2019 est.)
comparison ranking: total 110

Tobacco use: *total:* 11.7% (2020 est.)
male: 21.8% (2020 est.)
female: 1.5% (2020 est.)
comparison ranking: total 125

Children under the age of 5 years underweight: 9.7% (2019)
comparison ranking: 57

Currently married women (ages 15-49): 61.6% (2023 est.)

Child marriage: *women married by age 15:* 5.4%
women married by age 18: 33.7%
men married by age 18: 1.9% (2019 est.)

Education expenditures: 3.9% of GDP (2018 est.)
comparison ranking: 123

Literacy: *definition:* any person age 15 and above who completed at least grade 3 of primary education
total population: 89.7%
male: 88.3%
female: 90.9% (2021)

School life expectancy (primary to tertiary education): *total:* 11 years
male: 12 years
female: 11 years (2013)

ENVIRONMENT

Environment - current issues: deforestation; soil erosion; land degradation; air and water pollution; the black rhinoceros herd - once the largest concentration of the species in the world - has been significantly reduced by poaching; poor mining practices have led to toxic waste and heavy metal pollution

Environment - international agreements: *party to:* Biodiversity, Climate Change, Climate Change-Kyoto Protocol, Climate Change-Paris Agreement, Comprehensive Nuclear Test Ban, Desertification, Endangered Species, Hazardous Wastes, Law of the Sea, Ozone Layer Protection, Wetlands
signed, but not ratified: none of the selected agreements

Climate: tropical; moderated by altitude; rainy season (November to March)

Urbanization: *urban population:* 32.5% of total population (2023)
rate of urbanization: 2.41% annual rate of change (2020-25 est.)

Food insecurity: *widespread lack of access: due to high food prices* - based on a government assessment, an estimated 3.8 million people are expected to be in need of humanitarian assistance between January and March 2023; this number is higher than the level estimated in the first quarter of 2022; the downturn in food security conditions is largely on account of poor food access resulting from prevailing high food prices and reduced incomes owing to the effects of an economic downturn; a decline in cereal production in 2022 has also aggravated conditions (2023)

Revenue from forest resources: 1.61% of GDP (2018 est.)
comparison ranking: 39

Revenue from coal: 0.4% of GDP (2018 est.)
comparison ranking: 15

Air pollutants: *particulate matter emissions:* 13.08 micrograms per cubic meter (2019 est.)
carbon dioxide emissions: 10.98 megatons (2016 est.)
methane emissions: 12.1 megatons (2020 est.)

Waste and recycling: *municipal solid waste generated annually:* 1,449,752 tons (2015 est.)
municipal solid waste recycled annually: 231,960 tons (2005 est.)
percent of municipal solid waste recycled: 16% (2005 est.)

Major rivers (by length in km): Zambezi (shared with Zambia [s]), Angola, Namibia, Botswana, and Mozambique [m]) - 2,740 km; Limpopo (shared with South Africa [s], Botswana, and Mozambique [m]) - 1,800 km
note – [s] after country name indicates river source; [m] after country name indicates river mouth

Major watersheds (area sq km): Indian Ocean drainage: Zambezi (1,332,412 sq km)

Internal (endorheic basin) drainage: Okavango Basin (863,866 sq km)

Major aquifers: Upper Kalahari-Cuvelai-Upper Zambezi Basin

Total water withdrawal: *municipal:* 650 million cubic meters (2020 est.)
industrial: 80 million cubic meters (2020 est.)
agricultural: 3.04 billion cubic meters (2020 est.)

Total renewable water resources: 20 billion cubic meters (2020 est.)

GOVERNMENT

Country name: *conventional long form:* Republic of Zimbabwe
conventional short form: Zimbabwe
former: Southern Rhodesia, Rhodesia, Zimbabwe-Rhodesia
etymology: takes its name from the Kingdom of Zimbabwe (13th-15th century) and its capital of Great Zimbabwe, the largest stone structure in pre-colonial southern Africa

Government type: presidential republic

Capital: *name:* Harare
geographic coordinates: 17 49 S, 31 02 E
time difference: UTC+2 (7 hours ahead of Washington, DC, during Standard Time)
etymology: named after a village of Harare at the site of the present capital; the village name derived from a Shona chieftain, NE-HARAWA, whose name meant "he who does not sleep"

Administrative divisions: 8 provinces and 2 cities* with provincial status; Bulawayo*, Harare*, Manicaland, Mashonaland Central, Mashonaland East, Mashonaland West, Masvingo, Matabeleland North, Matabeleland South, Midlands

Independence: 18 April 1980 (from the UK)

National holiday: Independence Day, 18 April (1980)

Legal system: mixed legal system of English common law, Roman-Dutch civil law, and customary law

Constitution: *history:* previous 1965 (at Rhodesian independence), 1979 (Lancaster House Agreement), 1980 (at Zimbabwean independence); latest final draft completed January 2013, approved by referendum 16 March 2013, approved by Parliament 9 May 2013, effective 22 May 2013
amendments: proposed by the Senate or by the National Assembly; passage requires two-thirds majority vote by the membership of both houses of Parliament and assent of the president of the republic; amendments to constitutional chapters on fundamental human rights and freedoms and on agricultural lands also require approval by a majority of votes cast in a referendum; amended many times, last in 2017

International law organization participation: has not submitted an ICJ jurisdiction declaration; non-party state to the ICCt

Citizenship: *citizenship by birth:* no
citizenship by descent only: the father must be a citizen of Zimbabwe; in the case of a child born out of wedlock, the mother must be a citizen
dual citizenship recognized: no
residency requirement for naturalization: 5 years

Suffrage: 18 years of age; universal

Executive branch: *chief of state:* President Emmerson Dambudzo MNANGAGWA (since 4 September 2023)
head of government: Vice President Constantino CHIWENGA (since 11 September 2023)
cabinet: Cabinet appointed by president, responsible to National Assembly
elections/appointments: each presidential candidate nominated with a nomination paper signed by at least 10 registered voters (at least 1 candidate from each province) and directly elected by absolute majority popular vote in 2 rounds if needed for a 5-year term (no term limits); election last held on 23 August 2023 (next to be held in 2028); co-vice presidents drawn from party leadership
election results:
2023: Emmerson MNANGAGWA reelected president in first round; percent of vote - Emmerson MNANGAGWA (ZANU-PF) 52.6%, Nelson CHAMISA (MDC-T) 44%, Wilbert MUBAIWA (NPC) 1.2%, other 2.2%
2018: Emmerson MNANGAGWA elected president in first round; percent of vote - Emmerson MNANGAGWA (ZANU-PF) 50.7%, Nelson CHAMISA (MDC-T) 44.4%, Thokozani KHUPE (MDC-N) 0.9%, other 4%

Legislative branch: *description:* bicameral Parliament consists of:
Senate (80 seats; 60 members directly elected in multi-seat constituencies - 6 seats in each of the 10 provinces - by proportional representation vote, 16 indirectly elected by the regional governing councils,

18 reserved for the National Council Chiefs, and 2 reserved for members with disabilities; members serve 5-year terms)
National Assembly (280 seats; 210 members directly elected in single-seat constituencies by simple majority vote and 60 seats reserved for women directly elected by proportional representation vote and 10 additional seats reserved for candidates aged between 21 and 35 directly elected by proportional representation, members serve 5-year terms)
elections:
Senate - last held for elected member on 23 August 2023 (next to be held in 2028)
National Assembly - last held on 23 August 2023 (next to be held in 2028); note - a byelection was held on 11 November 2023 due to the death of a candidate during the August general election; a special byelection was held on 9 December 2023 after nine opposition lawmakers were removed from their seats and disqualified from running again; another byelection was held on 3 February 2024 for six open seats
election results:
Senate - percent of vote by party - NA; seats by party - ZANU-PF 33, CCC- 27, Chiefs 18, people with disabilities 2; composition - men 36, women 35, percentage of women 49.3%
National Assembly - percent of vote by party - NA; seats by party - ZANU-PF 190, CCC-93; composition - men 192, women 75, percentage women 28.1%; total Parliament percentage women 32.5%

Judicial branch: *highest court(s):* Supreme Court (consists of the chief justice and 4 judges); Constitutional Court (consists of the chief and deputy chief justices and 9 judges)
judge selection and term of office: Supreme Court judges appointed by the president upon recommendation of the Judicial Service Commission, an independent body consisting of the chief justice, Public Service Commission chairman, attorney general, and 2-3 members appointed by the president; judges normally serve until age 65 but can elect to serve until age 70; Constitutional Court judge appointment NA; judges serve nonrenewable 15-year terms
subordinate courts: High Court; Labor Court; Administrative Court; regional magistrate courts; customary law courts; special courts

Political parties: Citizens Coalition for Change
Movement for Democratic Change or MDC-T
National People's Congress or NPC
Zimbabwe African National Union-Patriotic Front or ZANU-PF
Zimbabwe African Peoples Union or ZAPU

International organization participation: ACP, AfDB, ATMIS, AU, COMESA, FAO, G-15, G-77, IAEA, IBRD, ICAO, ICRM, IDA, IFAD, IFC, IFRCS, ILO, IMF, IMO, Interpol, IOC, IOM, IPU, ISO, ITSO, ITU, ITUC (NGOs), MIGA, NAM, OPCW, PCA, SADC, UN, UNAMID, UNCTAD, UNESCO, UNIDO, UNISFA, UNMIL, UNMISS, UNOCI, UNSOM, UNWTO, UPU, WCO, WFTU (NGOs), WHO, WIPO, WMO, WTO

Diplomatic representation in the US: *chief of mission:* Ambassador Tadeous Tafirenyika CHIFAMBA (since 7 July 2021)
chancery: 1608 New Hampshire Avenue NW, Washington, DC 20009
telephone: [1] (202) 332-7100
FAX: [1] (202) 483-9326
email address and website:
general@zimembassydc.org
https://zimembassydc.org/

Diplomatic representation from the US: *chief of mission:* Ambassador (vacant); Chargé d'Affaires Elaine M. FRENCH (since August 2022)
embassy: 2 Lorraine Drive, Bluffhill, Harare
mailing address: 2180 Harare Place, Washington DC 20521-2180
telephone: [263] 867-701-1000
FAX: [263] 24-233-4320
email address and website:
consularharare@state.gov
https://zw. usembassy.gov/

Flag description: seven equal horizontal bands of green (top), yellow, red, black, red, yellow, and green with a white isosceles triangle edged in black with its base on the hoist side; a yellow Zimbabwe bird representing the long history of the country is superimposed on a red five-pointed star in the center of the triangle, which symbolizes peace; green represents agriculture, yellow mineral wealth, red the blood shed to achieve independence, and black stands for the native people

National symbol(s): Zimbabwe bird symbol, African fish eagle, flame lily; national colors: green, yellow, red, black, white

National anthem: *name:* "Kalibusiswe Ilizwe leZimbabwe" [Northern Ndebele language] "Simudzai Mureza WeZimbabwe" [Shona] (Blessed Be the Land of Zimbabwe)
lyrics/music: Solomon MUTSWAIRO/Fred Lecture CHANGUNDEGA
note: adopted 1994

National heritage: *total World Heritage Sites:* 5 (3 cultural, 2 natural)
selected World Heritage Site locales: Mana Pools National Park, Sapi, and Chewore Safari Areas (n); Great Zimbabwe National Monument (c); Khami Ruins National Monument (c); Mosi-oa-Tunya/ Victoria Falls (n); Matobo Hills (c)

ECONOMY

Economic overview: low income Sub-Saharan economy; political instability and endemic corruption have prevented reforms and stalled debt restructuring; new Zimbabwe Gold (ZiG) currency latest effort to combat ongoing hyperinflation; reliant on natural resource extraction, agriculture and remittances

Real GDP (purchasing power parity): $58.583 billion (2023 est.)
$55.817 billion (2022 est.)
$52.399 billion (2021 est.)
note: data in 2021 dollars
comparison ranking: 115

Real GDP growth rate: 4.96% (2023 est.)
6.52% (2022 est.)
8.47% (2021 est.)
note: annual GDP % growth based on constant local currency
comparison ranking: 57

Real GDP per capita: $3,500 (2023 est.)
$3,400 (2022 est.)
$3,300 (2021 est.)
note: data in 2021 dollars
comparison ranking: 190

GDP (official exchange rate): $26.538 billion (2023 est.)
note: data in current dollars at official exchange rate

Inflation rate (consumer prices): 104.71% (2022 est.)
98.55% (2021 est.)
557.2% (2020 est.)
note: annual % change based on consumer prices
comparison ranking: 217

GDP - composition, by sector of origin: *agriculture:* 27% (2023 est.)
industry: 46.9% (2023 est.)
services: 18.5% (2023 est.)
note: figures may not total 100% due to non-allocated consumption not captured in sector-reported data
comparison rankings: services 215; industry 17; agriculture 16

GDP - composition, by end use: *household consumption:* 77.7% (2022 est.)
government consumption: 16.7% (2022 est.)
investment in fixed capital: 11.3% (2022 est.)
investment in inventories: 3.3% (2022 est.)
exports of goods and services: 28% (2022 est.)
imports of goods and services: -37% (2022 est.)
note: figures may not total 100% due to rounding or gaps in data collection

Agricultural products: sugarcane, maize, beef, milk, cassava, wheat, bananas, vegetables, tobacco, cotton (2022)
note: top ten agricultural products based on tonnage

Industries: mining (coal, gold, platinum, copper, nickel, tin, diamonds, clay, numerous metallic and nonmetallic ores), steel, wood products, cement, chemicals, fertilizer, clothing and footwear, foodstuffs, beverages

Industrial production growth rate: 5.5% (2022 est.)
note: annual % change in industrial value added based on constant local currency
comparison ranking: 47

Labor force: 6.561 million (2023 est.)
note: number of people ages 15 or older who are employed or seeking work
comparison ranking: 71

Unemployment rate: 8.76% (2023 est.)
10.09% (2022 est.)
9.54% (2021 est.)
note: % of labor force seeking employment
comparison ranking: 155

Youth unemployment rate (ages 15-24): *total:* 14.3% (2023 est.)
male: 13.2% (2023 est.)
female: 15.6% (2023 est.)
note: % of labor force ages 15-24 seeking employment
comparison ranking: total 97

Population below poverty line: 38.3% (2019 est.)
note: % of population with income below national poverty line

Gini Index coefficient - distribution of family income: 50.3 (2020 est.)
note: index (0-100) of income distribution; higher values represent greater inequality
comparison ranking: 12

Household income or consumption by percentage share: *lowest 10%:* 2.5% (2017 est.)
highest 10%: 34.8% (2017 est.)
note: % share of income accruing to lowest and highest 10% of population

Remittances: 11.74% of GDP (2023 est.)
11.27% of GDP (2022 est.)
9.07% of GDP (2021 est.)
note: personal transfers and compensation between resident and non-resident individuals/households/ entities

Budget: *revenues:* $17 million (2018 est.)

expenditures: $23 million (2018 est.)

Public debt: 82.3% of GDP (2017 est.)
comparison ranking: 36

Taxes and other revenues: 7.21% (of GDP) (2018 est.)
note: central government tax revenue as a % of GDP
comparison ranking: 196

Current account balance: $1.096 billion (2020 est.)
$920.472 million (2019 est.)
-$1.38 billion (2018 est.)
note: balance of payments - net trade and primary/secondary income in current dollars
comparison ranking: 53

Exports: $7.65 billion (2022 est.)
$6.462 billion (2021 est.)
$5.263 billion (2020 est.)
note: GDP expenditure basis - exports of goods and services in current dollars
comparison ranking: 126

Exports - partners: UAE 57%, South Africa 17%, China 7%, Belgium 4%, Mozambique 2% (2022)
note: top five export partners based on percentage share of exports

Exports - commodities: gold, nickel, tobacco, iron alloys, diamonds (2022)
note: top five export commodities based on value in dollars

Imports: $10.126 billion (2022 est.)
$7.964 billion (2021 est.)
$5.489 billion (2020 est.)
note: GDP expenditure basis - imports of goods and services in current dollars
comparison ranking: 122

Imports - partners: South Africa 39%, China 15%, Singapore 12%, UAE 6%, Mozambique 4% (2022)
note: top five import partners based on percentage share of imports

Imports - commodities: refined petroleum, fertilizers, trucks, soybean oil, electricity (2022)
note: top five import commodities based on value in dollars

Reserves of foreign exchange and gold: $115.53 million (2023 est.)
$598.622 million (2022 est.)
$838.78 million (2021 est.)
note: holdings of gold (year-end prices)/foreign exchange/special drawing rights in current dollars
comparison ranking: 186

Exchange rates: Zimbabwean dollars (ZWD) per US dollar -

Exchange rates: 3,509.172 (2023 est.)
374.954 (2022 est.)
88.552 (2021 est.)
51.329 (2020 est.)
16.446 (2019 est.)
note: ongoing hyperinflation rendered Zimbabwean dollar essentially worthless; introduction of Zimbabwe Gold (ZiG) as new currency effective April 2024

ENERGY

Electricity access: *electrification - total population:* 50.1% (2022 est.)
electrification - urban areas: 89%
electrification - rural areas: 33.7%

Electricity: *installed generating capacity:* 2.487 million kW (2022 est.)
consumption: 8.884 billion kWh (2022 est.)
exports: 438.591 million kWh (2022 est.)
imports: 2.2 billion kWh (2022 est.)
transmission/distribution losses: 1.81 billion kWh (2022 est.)
comparison rankings: transmission/distribution losses 122; imports 59; exports 80; consumption 109; installed generating capacity 115

Electricity generation sources: *fossil fuels:* 32.7% of total installed capacity (2022 est.)
solar: 0.3% of total installed capacity (2022 est.)
hydroelectricity: 65.8% of total installed capacity (2022 est.)
biomass and waste: 1.1% of total installed capacity (2022 est.)

Coal: *production:* 3.877 million metric tons (2022 est.)
consumption: 4.479 million metric tons (2022 est.)
exports: 434,000 metric tons (2022 est.)
imports: 2,000 metric tons (2022 est.)
proven reserves: 502 million metric tons (2022 est.)

Petroleum: *total petroleum production:* 800 bbl/day (2023 est.)
refined petroleum consumption: 29,000 bbl/day (2022 est.)

Carbon dioxide emissions: 13.871 million metric tonnes of CO_2 (2022 est.)
from coal and metallurgical coke: 9.7 million metric tonnes of CO_2 (2022 est.)
from petroleum and other liquids: 4.171 million metric tonnes of CO_2 (2022 est.)
comparison ranking: total emissions 98

Energy consumption per capita: 11.726 million Btu/person (2022 est.)
comparison ranking: 146

COMMUNICATIONS

Telephones - fixed lines: *total subscriptions:* 291,000 (2022 est.)
subscriptions per 100 inhabitants: 2 (2022 est.)
comparison ranking: total subscriptions 110

Telephones - mobile cellular: *total subscriptions:* 14.301 million (2022 est.)
subscriptions per 100 inhabitants: 88 (2022 est.)
comparison ranking: total subscriptions 72

Telecommunication systems: *general assessment:* Zimbabwe's telcos continue to be affected by the country's poor economy; this has been exacerbated by the significant economic difficulties related to the pandemic; revenue has also been under pressure from a number of recent regulatory measures and additional taxes imposed by the cash-strapped government; inflation has become so high that year-on-year revenue comparisons since 2019 have been difficult to assess meaningfully; the three MNOs continue to invest in network upgrades, partly supported by government efforts and cash released from the Universal Service Fund; as a result of these investments, LTE networks have expanded steadily, though services remain concentrated in urban areas; international bandwidth has improved since fiber links to several submarine cables were established via neighboring countries; the expansion of 3G and LTE-based mobile broadband services has meant that most of the population has access to the internet; the government has started a national broadband scheme aimed at delivering a 1Mb/s service nationally by 2030; investment in fixed broadband infrastructure has also resulted in a slow but steady growth in the number of DSL connections, and also fiber subscriptions; during 2021, most growth in the fixed broadband segment has been with fiber connections (2022)
domestic: fixed-line teledensity is 2 per 100 and mobile-cellular is 89 per 100 (2021)
international: country code - 263; fiber-optic connections to neighboring states provide access to international networks via undersea cable; satellite earth stations - 2 Intelsat; 5 international digital gateway exchanges

Broadcast media: government owns all local radio and TV stations; foreign shortwave broadcasts and satellite TV are available to those who can afford antennas and receivers; in rural areas, access to TV broadcasts is extremely limited; analog TV only, no digital service (2017)

Internet country code: .zw

Internet users: *total:* 5.6 million (2021 est.)
percent of population: 35% (2021 est.)
comparison ranking: total 84

Broadband - fixed subscriptions: *total:* 203,461 (2020 est.)
subscriptions per 100 inhabitants: 1 (2020 est.)
comparison ranking: total 120

TRANSPORTATION

National air transport system: *number of registered air carriers:* 2 (2020)
inventory of registered aircraft operated by air carriers: 12
annual passenger traffic on registered air carriers: 285,539 (2018)
annual freight traffic on registered air carriers: 670,000 (2018) mt-km

Civil aircraft registration country code prefix: Z

Airports: 144 (2024)
comparison ranking: 37

Heliports: 5 (2024)

Pipelines: 270 km refined products (2013)

Railways: *total:* 3,427 km (2014)
narrow gauge: 3,427 km (2014) 1.067-m gauge (313 km electrified)
comparison ranking: total 55

Roadways: *total:* 97,267 km
paved: 18,481 km
unpaved: 78,786 km (2023)
comparison ranking: total 50

Waterways: 223 km (2022) some navigation possible on Lake Kariba (223 km)
comparison ranking: 104

MILITARY AND SECURITY

Military and security forces: Zimbabwe Defense Forces (ZDF): Zimbabwe National Army (ZNA), Air Force of Zimbabwe (AFZ)

Ministry of Home Affairs: Zimbabwe Republic Police (2024)

Military expenditures: 0.3% of GDP (2023 est.)
0.5% of GDP (2022 est.)
0.8% of GDP (2021 est.)
0.5% of GDP (2020 est.)
2.6% of GDP (2019 est.)
comparison ranking: 163

Military and security service personnel strengths: information varies; approximately 30,000 active-duty troops, including about 4,000 Air Force personnel (2023)

Military equipment inventories and acquisitions: the ZDF inventory is comprised mostly of Soviet-era and older Chinese armaments; since the early 2000s, Zimbabwe has been under an arms embargo from the EU, as well as targeted sanctions from Australia, Canada, New Zealand, the UK, and the US (2024)

Military service age and obligation: 18-22 years of age for voluntary military service for men and women (18-24 for officer cadets; 18-30 for technical/ specialist personnel); no conscription (2023)

Military - note: the ZDF's primary responsibilities are protecting the country's sovereignty and territory and securing its borders; it also has a considerable role in domestic security and has continued to be active in the country's politics since the 2017 military-assisted political transition; the ZDF is part of the Southern Africa Development Community (SADC) Standby Force and provided troops for the SADC military deployment to Mozambique, from 2021-2024; Zimbabwe has defense ties with China and Russia
the ZDF was formed after independence from the former Rhodesian Army and the two guerrilla forces that opposed it during the Rhodesian Civil War (aka "Bush War") of the 1970s, the Zimbabwe African National Liberation Army (ZANLA) and the Zimbabwe People's Revolutionary Army (ZIPRA); the ZDF intervened in the Mozambique Civil War (1983-1992), the Democratic Republic of Congo during the Second Congo War (1998-2003), and the Angolan Civil War (1975-2002) during the late 1990s (2024)

SPACE

Space agency/agencies: Zimbabwe National Geospatial and Space Agency (ZINGSA; established in 2019 and officially launched in 2021; under the Ministry of Higher and Tertiary Education, Science and Technology Development) (2024)

Space program overview: has a nascent program with the goal of utilizing space technologies in economic development; particularly interested in remote sensing capabilities to assist with monitoring or managing agriculture and food security, climate change, disease outbreaks, environmental hazards and disasters, and natural resources, as well as weather forecasting; part of a joint project (BIRDS-5) with Japan, which seeks to promote the first steps towards creating an indigenous space program by designing, building, testing, launching, and operating the first satellites for participating countries (2024)
note: further details about the key activities, programs, and milestones of the country's space program, as well as government spending estimates on the space sector, appear in the Space Programs reference guide

TRANSNATIONAL ISSUES

Refugees and internally displaced persons: *refugees (country of origin)*: 9,931 (Mozambique) (2023); 12,293 (Democratic Republic of Congo) (refugees and asylum seekers) (2024)

Trafficking in persons: tier rating: Tier 2 Watch List — the government did not demonstrate overall increasing efforts to eliminate trafficking compared with the previous reporting period, therefore Zimbabwe was downgraded to Tier 2 Watch List; for more details, go to: https://www.state.gov/reports/2024-trafficking-in-persons-report/zimbabwe/

Illicit drugs: transit point for cannabis and South Asian heroin, methaqualone, and methamphetamines en route to South Africa

APPENDIX A: ABBREVIATIONS

ABEDA	Arab Bank for Economic Development in Africa
ACP Group	African, Caribbean, and Pacific Group of States
ADB	Asian Development Bank
AfDB	African Development Bank
AFESD	Arab Fund for Economic and Social Development
AG	Australia Group
Air Pollution	Convention on Long-Range Transboundary Air Pollution
Air Pollution-Nitrogen Oxides	Protocol to the 1979 Convention on Long-Range Transboundary Air Pollution Concerning the Control of Emissions of Nitrogen Oxides or Their Transboundary Fluxes
Air Pollution-Persistent Organic Pollutants	Protocol to the 1979 Convention on Long-Range Transboundary Air Pollution on Persistent Organic Pollutants
Air Pollution-Sulphur 85	Protocol to the 1979 Convention on Long-Range Transboundary Air Pollution on the Reduction of Sulphur Emissions or Their Transboundary Fluxes by at Least 30%
Air Pollution-Sulphur 94	Protocol to the 1979 Convention on Long-Range Transboundary Air Pollution on Further Reduction of Sulphur Emissions
Air Pollution-Volatile Organic Compounds	Protocol to the 1979 Convention on Long-Range Transboundary Air Pollution Concerning the Control of Emissions of Volatile Organic Compounds or Their Transboundary Fluxes
AMF	Arab Monetary Fund
AMISOM	African Union Mission in Somalia
AMU	Arab Maghreb Union
Antarctic Marine Living Resources	Convention on the Conservation of Antarctic Marine Living Resources
Antarctic Seals	Convention for the Conservation of Antarctic Seals
Antarctic-Environmental Protocol	Protocol on Environmental Protection to the Antarctic Treaty
ANZUS	Australia-New Zealand-United States Security Treaty
AOSIS	Alliance of Small Island States
APEC	Asia-Pacific Economic Cooperation
Arabsat	Arab Satellite Communications Organization
ARF	ASEAN Regional Forum
ASEAN	Association of Southeast Asian Nations
ATMIS	African Union Transition Mission in Somalia
AU	African Union
Autodin	Automatic Digital Network
BA	Baltic Assembly
bbl/day	barrels per day
BCIE	Central American Bank for Economic Integration
BDEAC	Central African States Development Bank
Benelux	Benelux Union
BGN	United States Board on Geographic Names
BIMSTEC	Bay of Bengal Initiative for Multi-sectoral Technical and Economic Cooperation
Biodiversity	Convention on Biological Diversity
BIS	Bank for International Settlements
BRICS	(Brazil, Russia, India, China, and South Africa)
BSEC	Black Sea Economic Cooperation Zone
°C	degree(s) Celsius, degree(s) centigrade
C	Commonwealth
CACM	Central American Common Market
CAEU	Council of Arab Economic Unity
CAN	Andean Community
Caricom	Caribbean Community and Common Market
CB	citizen's band mobile radio communications
CBSS	Council of the Baltic Sea States
CCC	Customs Cooperation Council
CD	Community of Democracies
CDB	Caribbean Development Bank
CE	Council of Europe
CEI	Central European Initiative
CELAC	Community of Latin America and Caribbean States

CEMA	Council for Mutual Economic Assistance
CEMAC	Economic and Monetary Community of Central Africa
CEPGL	Economic Community of the Great Lakes Countries
CERN	European Organization for Nuclear Research
CIA	Central Intelligence Agency
CICA	Conference of Interaction and Confidence-Building Measures in Asia
c.i.f.	cost, insurance, and freight
CIS	Commonwealth of Independent States
CITES	see Endangered Species
Climate Change	United Nations Framework Convention on Climate Change
Climate Change-Kyoto Protocol	Kyoto Protocol to the United Nations Framework Convention on Climate Change
COCOM	Coordinating Committee on Export Controls
COMESA	Common Market for Eastern and Southern Africa
Comsat	Communications Satellite Corporation
CP	Colombo Plan
CPLP	Comunidade dos Paises de Lingua Portuguesa
CSN	South American Community of Nations became UNASUL - Union of South American Nations
CSTO	Collective Security Treaty Organization
CTBTO	Preparatory Commission for the Nuclear-Test-Ban Treaty Organization
CY	calendar year
D-8	Developing Eight
DC	developed country
DDT	dichloro-diphenyl-trichloro-ethane
Desertification	United Nations Convention to Combat Desertification in Those Countries Experiencing Serious Drought and/or Desertification, Particularly in Africa
DIA	United States Defense Intelligence Agency
DSN	Defense Switched Network
DST	daylight savings time
DWT	deadweight ton
EAC	East African Community
EADB	East African Development Bank
EAEC	Eurasian Economic Community
EAPC	Euro-Atlantic Partnership Council
EAS	East Asia Summit
EBRD	European Bank for Reconstruction and Development
EC	European Community or European Commission
ECA	Economic Commission for Africa
ECB	European Central Bank
ECE	Economic Commission for Europe
ECLAC	Economic Commission for Latin America and the Caribbean
ECO	Economic Cooperation Organization
ECOMIG	ECOWAS Mission in The Gambia
ECOSOC	Economic and Social Council
ECOWAS	Economic Community of West African States
ECSC	European Coal and Steel Community
EE	Eastern Europe
EEC	European Economic Community
EEZ	exclusive economic zone
EFTA	European Free Trade Association
EIB	European Investment Bank
EITI	Extractive Industry Transparency Initiative
EMU	European Monetary Union
Endangered Species	Convention on the International Trade in Endangered Species of Wild Flora and Fauna (CITES)
Entente	Council of the Entente
Environmental Modification	Convention on the Prohibition of Military or Any Other Hostile Use of Environmental Modification Techniques
ESA	European Space Agency
ESCAP	Economic and Social Commission for Asia and the Pacific
ESCWA	Economic and Social Commission for Western Asia

est.	estimate
EU	European Union
EUFOR	European Union Force in Bosnia and Herzegovina
Euratom	European Atomic Energy Community
Eutelsat	European Telecommunications Satellite Organization
EUTM	European Union Training Mission (military force deployed to provide advice, operational training, and education to security forces in Bosnia-Herzegovina, Central African Republic, Mali, and Somalia)
Ex-Im	Export-Import Bank of the United States
°F	degree(s) Fahrenheit
FAO	Food and Agriculture Organization
FATF	Financial Action Task Force
FAX	facsimile
FLS	Front Line States
f.o.b.	free on board
FOC	flags of convenience
FSU	former Soviet Union
ft	foot
FttP	FttP: Fiber to the Home (FttP) is a pure fiber-optic cable connection running from an Internet Service Provider (ISP) directly to the user's home or business
FY	fiscal year
FZ	Franc Zone
G-10	Group of 10
G-11	Group of 11
G-15	Group of 15
G-20	Group of 20
G-24	Group of 24
G-3	Group of 3
G-5	Group of 5
G-6	Group of 6
G-7	Group of 7
G-77	Group of 77
G-8	Group of 8
G-9	Group of 9
GATT	General Agreement on Tariffs and Trade; now WTO
GCC	Gulf Cooperation Council
GCN	Global Caribbean Network
GCTU	General Confederation of Trade Unions
GDP	gross domestic product
GMT	Greenwich Mean Time
GNP	gross national product
GRT	gross register ton
GSM	global system for mobile cellular communications
GUAM	Organization for Democracy and Economic Development; acronym for member states - Georgia, Ukraine, Azerbaijan, Moldova
GWP	gross world product
Hazardous Wastes	Basel Convention on the Control of Transboundary Movements of Hazardous Wastes and Their Disposal
HF	high-frequency
HIV/AIDS	human immunodeficiency virus/acquired immune deficiency syndrome
IADB	Inter-American Development Bank
IAEA	International Atomic Energy Agency
IANA	Internet Assigned Numbers Authority
IBRD	International Bank for Reconstruction and Development (World Bank)
ICAO	International Civil Aviation Organization
ICC	International Chamber of Commerce
ICCt	International Criminal Court
ICJ	International Court of Justice (World Court)
ICRC	International Committee of the Red Cross
ICRM	International Red Cross and Red Crescent Movement
ICSID	International Center for Settlement of Investment Disputes
ICTR	International Criminal Tribunal for Rwanda

ICTY	International Criminal Tribunal for the former Yugoslavia
IDA	International Development Association
IDB	Islamic Development Bank
IDP	Internally Displaced Person
IEA	International Energy Agency
IFAD	International Fund for Agricultural Development
IFC	International Finance Corporation
IFRCS	International Federation of Red Cross and Red Crescent Societies
IGAD	Inter-Governmental Authority on Development
IHO	International Hydrographic Organization
ILO	International Labor Organization
IMF	International Monetary Fund
IMO	International Maritime Organization
IMSO	International Mobile Satellite Organization
in	inch
Inmarsat	International Maritime Satellite Organization
InOC	Indian Ocean Commission
Intelsat	International Telecommunications Satellite Organization
Interpol	International Criminal Police Organization
Intersputnik	International Organization of Space Communications
IOC	International Olympic Committee
IOM	International Organization for Migration
IPU	Inter-Parliamentary Union
ISO	International Organization for Standardization
ISP	Internet Service Provider
ITC	International Trade Center
ITSO	International Telecommunications Satellite Organization
ITU	International Telecommunication Union
ITUC	International Trade Union Confederation, the successor to ICFTU (International Confederation of Free Trade Unions) and the WCL (World Confederation of Labor)
kg	kilogram
kHz	kilohertz
km	kilometer
kW	kilowatt
kWh	kilowatt-hour
LAES	Latin American and Caribbean Economic System
LAIA	Latin American Integration Association
LAS	League of Arab States
Law of the Sea	United Nations Convention on the Law of the Sea (LOS)
LDC	less developed country
LLDC	least developed country
LNG	liquefied natural gas
London Convention	see Marine Dumping
LOS	see Law of the Sea
m	meter
Marecs	Maritime European Communications Satellite
Marine Dumping	Convention on the Prevention of Marine Pollution by Dumping Wastes and Other Matter
Marine Life Conservation	Convention on Fishing and Conservation of Living Resources of the High Seas
MARPOL	see Ship Pollution
Medarabtel	Middle East Telecommunications Project of the International Telecommunications Union
Mercosur	Southern Cone Common Market
MFO	Multinational Force & Observers--Sinai
MHz	megahertz
mi	mile
MICAH	International Civilian Support Mission in Haiti
MIGA	Multilateral Investment Guarantee Agency
MINURCAT	United Nations Mission in the Central African Republic and Chad
MINURSO	United Nations Mission for the Referendum in Western Sahara
MINUSCA	United Nations Multidimensional Integrated Stabilization Mission in the Central African Republic
MINUSMA	United Nations Multidimensional Integrated Stabilization Mission in Mali

MINUSTAH	United Nations Stabilization Mission in Haiti
mm	millimeter
MONUSCO	United Nations Organization Stabilization Mission in the Democratic Republic of the Congo
mt	metric ton
Mt.	Mount
NA	not available
NAFTA	North American Free Trade Agreement
NAM	Nonaligned Movement
NATO	North Atlantic Treaty Organization
NC	Nordic Council
NEA	Nuclear Energy Agency
NEGL	negligible
NGA	National Geospatial-Intelligence Agency
NGO	nongovernmental organization
NIB	Nordic Investment Bank
NIC	newly industrializing country
NIE	newly industrializing economy
NIS	new independent states
nm	nautical mile
NMT	Nordic Mobile Telephone
NSG	Nuclear Suppliers Group
Nuclear Test Ban	Treaty Banning Nuclear Weapons Tests in the Atmosphere, in Outer Space, and Under Water
NZ	New Zealand
OAPEC	Organization of Arab Petroleum Exporting Countries
OAS	Organization of American States
OAU	Organization of African Unity; see African Union
ODA	official development assistance
OECD	Organization for Economic Cooperation and Development
OECS	Organization of Eastern Caribbean States
OHCHR	Office of the United Nations High Commissioner for Human Rights
OIC	Organization of the Islamic Conference
OIF	International Organization of the French-speaking World
OOF	other official flows
OPANAL	Agency for the Prohibition of Nuclear Weapons in Latin America and the Caribbean
OPCW	Organization for the Prohibition of Chemical Weapons
OPEC	Organization of Petroleum Exporting Countries
OSCE	Organization for Security and Cooperation in Europe
Ozone Layer Protection	Montreal Protocol on Substances That Deplete the Ozone Layer
PCA	Permanent Court of Arbitration
PFP	Partnership for Peace
PIF	Pacific Islands Forum
PPP	purchasing power parity
Quad	Quadrilateral Security Dialogue
Ramsar	see Wetlands
RG	Rio Group
SAARC	South Asian Association for Regional Cooperation
SACEP	South Asia Co-operative Environment Program
SACU	Southern African Customs Union
SADC	Southern African Development Community
SAFE	South African Far East Cable
SCO	Shanghai Cooperation Organization
SECI	Southeast European Cooperative Initiative
SELEC	Convention of the Southeast European Law Enforcement Centers (successor to SECI)
SHF	super-high-frequency
Ship Pollution	Protocol of 1978 Relating to the International Convention for the Prevention of Pollution From Ships, 1973 (MARPOL)
SICA	Central American Integration System
Sparteca	South Pacific Regional Trade and Economic Cooperation Agreement
SPC	Secretariat of the Pacific Communities
SPF	South Pacific Forum
sq km	square kilometer

sq mi square mile
TAT Trans-Atlantic Telephone
TEU Twenty-Foot Equivalent Unit, a unit of measure for containerized cargo capacity
Tropical Timber 83 International Tropical Timber Agreement, 1983
Tropical Timber 94 International Tropical Timber Agreement, 1994
UAE United Arab Emirates
UDEAC Central African Customs and Economic Union
UHF ultra-high-frequency
UK United Kingdom
UN United Nations
UN-AIDS Joint United Nations Program on HIV/AIDS
UNAMA United Nations Assistance Mission in Afghanistan
UNAMID African Union/United Nations Hybrid Operation in Darfur
UNASUR Union of South American Nations
UNCLOS United Nations Convention on the Law of the Sea, also known as LOS
UNCTAD United Nations Conference on Trade and Development
UNDCP United Nations Drug Control Program
UNDEF United Nations Democracy Fund
UNDOF United Nations Disengagement Observer Force
UNDP United Nations Development Program
UNEP United Nations Environment Program
UNESCO United Nations Educational, Scientific, and Cultural Organization
UNFICYP United Nations Peacekeeping Force in Cyprus
UNFPA United Nations Population Fund
UN-Habitat United Nations Center for Human Settlements
UNHCR United Nations High Commissioner for Refugees
UNHRC United Nations Human Rights Council
UNICEF United Nations Children's Fund
UNICRI United Nations Interregional Crime and Justice Research Institute
UNIDIR United Nations Institute for Disarmament Research
UNIDO United Nations Industrial Development Organization
UNIFIL United Nations Interim Force in Lebanon
UNISFA United Nations Interim Force for Abyei
UNITAR United Nations Institute for Training and Research
UNMIK United Nations Interim Administration Mission in Kosovo
UNMIL United Nations Mission in Liberia
UNMIS United Nations Mission in the Sudan
UNMISS United Nations Mission in South Sudan
UNMIT United Nations Integrated Mission in Timor-Leste
UNMOGIP United Nations Military Observer Group in India and Pakistan
UNOCI United Nations Operation in Cote d'Ivoire
UNODC United Nations Office of Drugs and Crime
UNOPS United Nations Office of Project Services
UNRISD United Nations Research Institute for Social Development
UNRWA United Nations Relief and Works Agency for Palestine Refugees in the Near East
UNSC United Nations Security Council
UNSOM United Nations Assistance Mission in Somalia
UNSSC United Nations System Staff College
UNTSO United Nations Truce Supervision Organization
UNU United Nations University
UNWTO World Tourism Organization
UPU Universal Postal Union
US United States
USSR Union of Soviet Socialist Republics (Soviet Union); used for information dated before 25 December 1991
UTC Coordinated Universal Time
UV ultraviolet
VHF very-high-frequency
VSAT very small aperture terminal
WADB West African Development Bank
WAEMU West African Economic and Monetary Union

WCL	World Confederation of Labor
WCO	World Customs Organization
Wetlands	Convention on Wetlands of International Importance Especially As Waterfowl Habitat
WEU	Western European Union
WFP	World Food Program
WFTU	World Federation of Trade Unions
Whaling	International Convention for the Regulation of Whaling
WHO	World Health Organization
WIPO	World Intellectual Property Organization
WMO	World Meteorological Organization
WP	Warsaw Pact
WTO	World Trade Organization
ZC	Zangger Committee

APPENDIX T: TERRORIST ORGANIZATIONS

This listing includes the 60+ terrorist groups designated by the US State Department as Foreign Terrorist Organizations (FTOs), as well as an additional 10 non-designated, self-proclaimed branches and affiliates of the Islamic State of Iraq and ash-Sham (ISIS) FTO. The information provided includes details on each cited group's history, goals, leadership, organization, areas of operation, tactics, weapons, size, and sources of support.

Abdallah Azzam Brigades (AAB)

aka – AAB, Ziyad al-Jarrah Battalions of the Abdallah Azzam Brigades; Yusuf al-'Uyayri Battalions of the Abdallah Azzam Brigades; Marwan Hadid Brigades; Marwan Hadid Brigade; Abdullah Azzam Brigades in the Land of Al Sham
history – formed around 2005 as a Sunni jihadist group with ties to al-Qa'ida; named after the influential jihadist ideologue Abdallah Yusuf Azzam; formally announced its presence in a 2009 video statement while claiming responsibility for a rocket attack against Israel; in 2013, became involved in the Syrian War where it fought against Iranian-backed forces, particularly Hizballah; in 2019 announced that it was disbanding; had been largely dormant for years prior to the announcement
goals – rid the Middle East of Western influence, disrupt Israel's economy and its efforts to establish security, and erode Shia Muslim influence in Lebanon
leadership and organization – Sirajeddin ZURAYQAT (var: Surajuddin Zureiqat, Siraj al-Din Zreqat, Siraj al-Din Zuraiqat) was AAB's spiritual leader, spokesman, and commander; was divided into regionally based branches
areas of operation – was based in Lebanon and operated chiefly in Lebanon; was also active in Gaza and Syria
targets, tactics, and weapons – principal targets were Shia Muslims, the Shia terrorist group Hizballah, and Israel; was responsible for several car and suicide bombing attacks against Shia Muslims in Beirut, Lebanon, including twin suicide bombs that detonated outside the Iranian Embassy in Beirut, Lebanon—killing 22 and injuring at least 140; claimed responsibility for numerous rocket attacks against Israel and Lebanon; members were typically armed with small arms, light machine guns, grenades, rockets, and improvised explosive devices
strength – not available; it was estimated to be down to a few dozen members in 2021
financial and other support – funding support is unknown but probably received donations from sympathizers and engaged in smuggling contraband, including weapons
designation – placed on the US Department of State's list of Foreign Terrorist Organizations on 30 May 2012

Abu Sayyaf Group (ASG)

aka – al-Harakat al Islamiyya (the Islamic Movement); al-Harakat-ul al-Islamiyah; Bearer of the Sword; Father of the Executioner; Father of the Swordsman; International Harakatu'l Al-Islamia; Lucky 9; Islamic State in the Philippines; Mujahideen Commando Freedom Fighters
history – formed in 1991 when it split from the Moro Islamic Liberation Front; has carried out dozens of attacks in the Philippines; linked to al-Qa'ida in the 1990s and 2000s; in recent years, the group has focused on local violence and criminal activity, especially kidnap-for-ransom operations; some factions have declared allegiance to the Islamic State and have had a large role in the operations of ISIS-East Asia (ISIS-EA) in the Philippines, including the attack on Marawi City in 2017; ASG fighters affiliated with ISIS-EA were reportedly linked to suicide attacks in 2019 and 2020 in Jolo, Sulu province; the commander of an ASG faction, Hatib Hajan SAWADJAAN, was the acting leader of ISIS-EA until his reported death in mid-2020; continued to be active in 2024, despite considerable losses in members and leaders to counter-terrorism operations by Philippine security forces
goals – stated goal is to establish an independent Islamic state in the Muslim-majority provinces of the southern Philippines
leadership and organization – leadership fragmented; loosely structured and family/clan/network-based; factions tend to coalesce around individual leaders; Sulu-based Radullan SAHIRON (aka Kahal Mohammad) reportedly became the leader in 2017; SAHIRON has not pledged allegiance to ISIS
areas of operation – the southern Philippines, especially Basilan, Jolo, and Tawi-Tawi islands and their surrounding waters, as well as Mindanao; also has been active in Malaysia
targets, tactics, and weapons – targets military and security personnel, facilities, and checkpoints; also attacks civilian targets, such as churches, markets, and ferry boats; conducted the country's deadliest terrorist attack when it bombed a ferry boat in Manila Bay in 2004, killing 116 people; two suicide bombers affiliated with both ASG and ISIS-EA killed 23 people and wound more than 100 at a cathedral; known for kidnapping civilians, particularly foreigners, for ransom and has killed hostages when ransoms were not paid; tactics include car bombings, ambushes, complex assaults involving dozens of fighters, beheadings, and assassinations, as well as possible suicide bombings; has conducted acts of piracy in local waters; weapons include small arms, light and heavy machine guns, mortars, landmines, and improvised explosive devices
strength – assessed in 2023 to have less than 100 armed fighters
financial and other support – funded primarily through kidnapping-for-ransom operations and extortion; makes financial appeals on social media; may receive funding from external sources, including remittances from overseas Philippine workers and Middle East-based sympathizers; has received training and other assistance from other regional terrorist groups; has received weapons and ammunition from corrupt local government officials or through smuggling
designation – placed on the US Department of State's list of Foreign Terrorist Organizations on 8 October 1997

Al-Aqsa Martyrs Brigade (AAMB)

aka – al-Aqsa Martyrs Battalion; al-Aqsa Brigades; Martyr Yasser Arafat; Kata'ib Shuhada al-Aqsa; The Brigades; al-Aqsa Intifada Martyrs' Group; Martyrs of al-Aqsa Group
history – emerged at the outset of the second intifada in September 2000 as a loosely-organized armed wing of Yasser ARAFAT's Fatah faction in the West Bank; in 2002, some members splintered from Fatah while others remained loyal; the group carried out suicide attacks against Israeli targets between 2001-2007; most of the group's leaders have been captured or killed by Israel; following an agreement between Israel and the Palestinian Authority (PA) after the HAMAS takeover of Gaza in 2007, Israel pardoned some AAMB fighters in return for an agreement to disarm; after a trial period, those that disarmed were absorbed into PA security forces while those that refused were targeted by PA security forces; still others formed splinter groups such as the Al-Aqsa Martyrs Brigades-Nidal al-Amoudi Division and the Popular Resistance Committees in Gaza; some factions participated in operations against Israeli targets through the 2010s, including the "Stabbing Intifada" of 2015-16, as well as periodic rocket attacks in 2017-2018; publicly claimed that it participated in the October 2023 attack on Israel from Gaza and was active in 2024 against Israeli security and military forces in both Gaza and the West Bank

goals – drive Israeli military forces and settlers from Jerusalem, the West Bank, and the Gaza Strip and establish a Palestinian state
leadership and organization – not available; most of the group's original leaders have been captured or killed by Israel; typically has operated as a collection of loosely organized cells with their own leaders and independent operational agendas, although the group reportedly formed a Joint Operations Room with Katibat Jenin (the Jenin branch of Palestine Islamic Jihad) in the West Bank in early 2022
areas of operation – Israel, Gaza, and the West Bank; has members in Palestinian refugee camps in Lebanon
targets, tactics, and weapons – has conducted military-style assaults, rocket attacks, bombings, ambushes, and suicide operations against Israeli military and security personnel and civilians; claimed first female suicide bombing inside Israel in 2002 and a double bombing in Tel Aviv in 2003 that killed more than 20 civilians; since 2010, has launched numerous rocket attacks against Israel, including more than 500 rockets during Israeli military operations in Gaza in 2012; since 2023, has conducted combat operations against Israeli military forces in Gaza; fighters typically armed with small arms, light and heavy machine guns, mortars, improvised explosive devices, rockets, and rocket propelled grenades
strength – estimated in 2022 to have a few hundred members
financial and other support – Iran has provided AAMB with funds and guidance, mostly through Hizballah facilitators; has cooperated with other terrorist groups throughout its existence, including HAMAS, the Popular Front for the Liberation of Palestine (PFLP), and Palestinian Islamic Jihad (PIJ)
designation –placed on the US Department of State's list of Foreign Terrorist Organizations on 27 March 2002

al-Ashtar Brigades (AAB)
aka – Saraya al-Ashtar; the military arm of the al-Wafa Islamic movement
history – is an Iranian-backed Shia militant group established in 2013 with the aim of overthrowing the ruling Sunni family in Bahrain; in 2018, formally adopted Iran's Islamic Revolutionary Guard Corps branding in its logo and flag and reaffirmed the group's loyalty to Tehran; has not claimed any attacks in recent years, but was reportedly active in 2024
goals – foment an insurgency against the ruling Sunni family of Bahrain and, ultimately, replace it with a Shia-based government; also seeks to expel US and other Western military forces from Bahrain
leadership and organization – Qassim Abdullah Ali AHMED (aka Qassim al Muamen); operates in cells
areas of operation – based in Bahrain; its leaders and some members are located in Iran
targets, tactics, and weapons – has claimed more than 20 attacks targeting local security forces in Bahrain; has plotted to attack oil pipelines; also has promoted violence against the British, Saudi Arabian, and US governments; claimed a drone attack on Israel in 2024; methods include shootings and bombings; equipped with small arms and explosives, including improvised explosive devices
strength – not available
funding and other support – receives funding, training, and weapons support from the Iranian Revolutionary Guard Corps; has also allied itself with Iranian-backed Iraqi Shia militants and with Lebanese Hizballah for financial and logistic support
designation – placed on the US Department of State's list of Foreign Terrorist Organizations on 11 July 2018

al-Mourabitoun
aka – Al-Murabitun; al-Mulathamun Battalion; al-Mulathamun Brigade; al-Muwaqqi'un bil-Dima; Those Signed in Blood Battalion (or Brigade); Signatories in Blood; Those who Sign in Blood; Witnesses in Blood; Signed-in-Blood Battalion; Masked Men Brigade; Khaled Abu al-Abbas Brigade; al-Mulathamun Masked Ones Brigade; al-Murabitoun; The "Sentinels" or "Guardians"
history – was part of al-Qa'ida in the Islamic Maghreb (AQIM) but split from AQIM in 2012 over leadership disputes; merged with the Mali-based Movement for Unity and Jihad in West Africa to form al-Murabitoun in August 2013; some members split from the group in mid-2015 and declared allegiance to the Islamic State, which acknowledged the pledge in October 2016, creating the Islamic State in the Greater Sahara; in late 2015, al-Mulathamun/al-Mourabitoun announced a re-merger with AQIM and in 2017, joined a coalition of al-Qa'ida-affiliated groups operating in the Sahel region known as Jama'at Nusrat al-Islam wal-Muslimin (JNIM); the group remained active in 2023
goals – replace regional governments with an Islamic state; expel Western influence
leadership and organization – unclear; possibly Hamza Tabankort; operations guided by a governing shura council but details on the sub-structure are not available; operates under the JNIM banner
areas of operation – based primarily in North and West Africa; conducts operations primarily in Mali; has operated in Algeria, Burkina Faso, Libya, and Niger
targets, tactics, and weapons – primarily targets Western interests in the Sahel but also regional military forces, including Malian, French (until their withdrawal in 2022), and UN; known for high-profile attacks with small arms and explosives against civilian targets frequented or run by Westerners, including restaurants, hotels, mines, and energy facilities; in 2013, claimed responsibility for taking over 800 people hostage during a four-day siege at the Tiguentourine gas plant in southeastern Algeria, resulting in the deaths of 39 civilians; has claimed responsibility for suicide car bombings at military bases in Niger and Mali, including a suicide car bombing attack on a military camp in Gao, Mali in 2017 that killed at least 60 and wounded more than 100; armed with small arms, machine guns, landmines, mortars, and explosives, including ground and vehicle-borne improvised explosive devices
strength – not available; dated information suggests a few hundred
financial and other support – engages in kidnappings for ransom and smuggling activities; receives support through its connections to other terrorist organizations in the region; acquired weapons from Libya, battlefield captures, and seized stockpiles from local militaries
designation – placed on the US Department of State's list of Foreign Terrorist Organizations on 19 December 2013

al-Qa'ida (AQ)
aka – al-Qa'eda; al-Qaeda; Qa'idat al-Jihad (The Base for Jihad); formerly Qa'idat Ansar Allah (The Base of the Supporters of God); the Islamic Army; Islamic Salvation Foundation; The Base; The Group for the Preservation of the Holy Sites; The Islamic Army for the Liberation of the Holy Places; the World Islamic Front for Jihad Against Jews and Crusaders; the Usama Bin Ladin Network; the Usama Bin Ladin Organization; al-Jihad; the Jihad Group; Egyptian al-Jihad; Egyptian Islamic Jihad; New Jihad
history – formed under Usama BIN LADIN (UBL) circa 1988 and now one of the largest and longest-operating jihadist organizations in the world; helped finance, recruit, transport, and train fighters for the Afghan resistance against the former Soviet Union in the 1980s; in the 1990s, was based in Sudan and then Afghanistan, where it planned and staged attacks; merged with al-Jihad (Egyptian Islamic Jihad) in June 2001; developed a reputation for carrying out large-scale, mass casualty attacks against civilians; has lost dozens of mid- and senior-level operatives to counterterrorism efforts, including UBL in May 2011, which has disrupted operations but the group continues to recruit, plan, inspire, and conduct attacks; has established affiliated organizations in the Middle East, Africa, and Asia, and its contemporary strength is primarily in these affiliates; tied to the Taliban in Afghanistan and remained active there into 2024

goals – eject Western influence from the Islamic world, unite the worldwide Muslim community, overthrow governments perceived as un-Islamic, and ultimately, establish a pan-Islamic caliphate under a strict Salafi Muslim interpretation of sharia; direct, enable, and inspire individuals to conduct attacks, recruit, disseminate propaganda, and raise funds on behalf of the group around the world; destabilize local economies and governments by attacking security services, government targets, and civilian targets; maintain its traditional safe haven in Afghanistan; establish and maintain additional safehavens elsewhere
leadership and organization – Iran-based Sayf al-'Adl reportedly the group's current de facto leader; Ayman al-ZAWAHIRI, who was selected to lead following UBL's death, was killed in 2022; has a leadership council ("majlis al-shura"); al-Qa'ida reportedly maintains branches for military, security, political, religious, financial, and media affairs; affiliates have separate emirs (leaders) and organizational structures that vary by region
areas of operation – based in South Asia (core members in Afghanistan, Iran, Pakistan); uses Afghanistan as an ideological and logistical hub to mobilize and recruit new fighters while covertly rebuilding its external operations capability; employs an affiliate or proxy model, which includes al-Qa'ida in the Arabian Peninsula (Yemen), al-Qa'ida in the Islamic Maghreb (North Africa and the Sahel), Hurras al-Din (Syria), al-Shabaab (Somalia), and al-Qa'ida in the Indian Subcontinent (Afghanistan, Bangladesh, India, and Pakistan); has supporters, sympathizers, and associates worldwide; maintains a strong online presence and individuals inspired by AQ's ideology may conduct operations without direction from its central leadership; opportunistically enters (or secures the allegiance of participants in) local conflicts
targets, tactics, and weapons – considers its enemies to be Shia Muslims, US and Western interests, so-called "apostate" governments (such as Saudi Arabia) perceived to be supporting the US and the West, and the Islamic State; leader ZAWAHIRI has encouraged followers to attack European (particularly British and French), Israeli, NATO, Russian, and US targets, specifically military bases and forces; targets have included embassies, restaurants, hotels, airplanes, trains, and tourists sites; employs a combination of guerrilla warfare hit-and-run and terrorist tactics against security and military forces; known for use of suicide bombers, car bombs, explosive-laden boats, and airplanes; conducted the September 11, 2001 attacks on the US, which involved 19 operatives hijacking and crashing four US commercial jets—two into the World Trade Center in New York City, one into the Pentagon, and the last into a field in Shanksville, Pennsylvania—killing nearly 3,000 people
strength – as of 2024, it was estimated to have about 400 fighters in Afghanistan; the organization remained a focal point of inspiration for a worldwide network of affiliated groups and other sympathetic terrorist organizations, such as the Islamic Movement of Uzbekistan, Islamic Jihad Union, Lashkar i Jhangvi, Harakat ul-Mujahideen, the Haqqani Network, and Tehrik-e Taliban Pakistan
financial and other support –primarily depends on donations from like-minded supporters and from individuals, primarily in the Gulf States; uses social media platforms to solicit donations and has been channeled funds through cyberfinancing campaigns; has received some funds from kidnapping for ransom operations; historically has acquired money from Islamic charitable organizations; also recruits followers through social media
designation – placed on the US Department of State's list of Foreign Terrorist Organizations on 8 October 1999
note – has some ideological and tactical similarities with the Islamic State of Iraq and ash-Sham (ISIS) and the groups typically operate in the same conflict zones, but the relationship is mostly adversarial, and they compete for resources and recruits, and often clash militarily

al-Qa'ida in the Arabian Peninsula (AQAP)
aka – al-Qa'ida in the South Arabian Peninsula; al-Qa'ida in Yemen; al-Qa'ida of Jihad Organization in the Arabian Peninsula; al-Qa'ida Organization in the Arabian Peninsula; Tanzim Qa'idat al-Jihad fi Jazirat al-Arab; AQY; Ansar al-Shari'a; Sons of Abyan; Sons of Hadramawt; Sons of Hadramawt Committee; Civil Council of Hadramawt; National Hadramawt Council
history – formed in January 2009 when the now-deceased leader of al-Qa'ida (AQ) in Yemen, Nasir AL-WAHISHI, publicly announced that Yemeni and Saudi al-Qa'ida operatives were working together under the banner of AQAP; the announcement signaled the rebirth of an AQ franchise that previously carried out attacks in Saudi Arabia; beginning in 2014-2015, AQAP was able to take advantage of Yemen's civil war and expand operations in the country, controlling a large portion of the southern part of the Yemen by 2016; after 2017, the group began losing territory, fighters, and leaders to internal dissensions, desertions to ISIS, and casualties from clashes with Yemeni and international security forces, the Houthis, and ISIS; nevertheless, as of 2024 the group continued to persist as a local and regional threat
goals – establish a caliphate and a government/society based on sharia in the Arabian Peninsula and the wider Middle East; support the broader goals of AQ's central leadership
leadership and organization – led by Saad bin Atef al-Awlaki (aka Abu al-Laith); has a leadership council ("majlis al-shura") comprised of lieutenant commanders who are responsible for overall political direction and military operations; organized in branches or wings for military operations, political, propaganda (recruitment), religious issues (for justifying attacks from a theological perspective while offering spiritual guidance), and security; typically operates in a decentralized manner that allows individual cells to operate independently
areas of operation – operates primarily in southern and central Yemen; probably has a limited presence in Saudi Arabia
targets, tactics, and weapons – chiefly targets Security Belt Forces and other groups affiliated with the United Arab Emirates and Saudi Arabia in the Shabwa and Abyan governorates, as well as the Houthis in the Bayda governorate; also targets Yemeni Government officials, oil facilities, merchant ships, and Shia Muslims; has targeted Western interests, including embassies, diplomats, business people, tourists, and both commercial airliners, and has regularly called for attacks against Western interests and regional partners in the group's media releases; claimed the small arms attack in Feb 2020 that resulted in the deaths of three US military personnel in Florida, as well as an attack in Paris in 2015 that killed 12 civilians at the office of a magazine publisher; has waged open warfare with Islamic State elements in Yemen since 2018; employs guerrilla-style and terrorist tactics, including ambushes, complex assaults, assassinations, snipers, bombings, and suicide attacks; equipped with small arms, machine guns, artillery, rockets, landmines, anti-tank missiles, armored combat vehicles, man-portable air defense systems (MANPADs), armed unmanned aerial vehicles (drones), and improvised explosive devices, including car bombs, road side bombs, and suicide vests
strength – estimated in 2024 to have up to 4,000 fighters
financial and other support – receives funding from theft, robberies, oil and gas revenue, kidnapping-for-ransom operations, and donations from like-minded supporters; for nearly a year after seizing the city of Mukallah in April 2015, had access millions of dollars from port fees and funds stolen from the central bank; many of its weapons have been seized from the Yemeni military; recruits through social media, print, and digital means
designation – placed on the US Department of State's list of Foreign Terrorist Organizations on 19 January 2010

al-Qa'ida in the Indian Subcontinent (AQIS)
aka – al-Qaeda in the Indian Subcontinent; Qaedat al-Jihad in the Indian Subcontinent, Qaedat al-Jihad, Jamaat Qaidat al-Jihad fi'shibhi al-Qarrat al-Hindiya,
history – al-Qa'ida leader Dr. Ayman al-ZAWAHIRI announced AQIS's inception in a video address in September 2014; the group claimed responsibility for a September 2014 attack on a naval dockyard in Karachi in an attempt to seize a Pakistani warship; since the assault, the group has conducted a limited number of small attacks on civilians, but has not publicly claimed any attacks since 2017, although some members fought in Afghanistan with the Taliban; suffered some losses to counter-terrorism operations in 2020-2022; in September and October 2021, the group released two propaganda videos specifically targeting India and Kashmir, and in mid-2022 threatened to conduct suicide bombings in several Indian cities; has ties to designated terrorist groups Lashkare Tayyiba (LeT) and Tehrik-e-Taliban Pakistan (TTP); active in 2024

goals – establish an Islamic caliphate in the Indian subcontinent; support the broader goals of al-Qai'da's central leadership
leadership and organization – Usama MAHMOOD (alt. Osama MEHMOOD; aka Abu Zar); has a shura council, which, like other AQ affiliates, probably includes subordinates and branches/wings for military/security, intelligence, religious, propaganda, political matters, and recruitment; reportedly has regional branches for Bangladesh, India, and Pakistan; Ansar al-Islam in Bangladesh has claimed to be the official wing of AQIS in Bangladesh
areas of operation – based primarily in Afghanistan with some activity in Pakistan, India, and Bangladesh
targets, tactics, and weapons – military and security personnel, political parties, foreigners, foreign aid workers, academics, students, and secular bloggers; has engaged in suicide bombings, small-arms attacks, ambushes, and assassinations; has used small arms and improvised explosive devices, as well as crude weapons such as machetes; claimed responsibility for the 2016 machete murders of two editors of a human rights magazine in Dhaka, Bangladesh
membership – estimated in 2024 to have up to 400 members
financial and other support – likely receives financial and material support from AQ senior leadership; also engages in kidnapping-for-ransom, extortion, and general criminal activity to raise funds
designation – placed on the US Department of State's list of Foreign Terrorist Organizations on 1 July 2016

al-Qaida in the Islamic Maghreb (AQIM)

aka – GSPC; Le Groupe Salafiste Pour la Predication et le Combat; Salafist Group for Preaching and Combat; Salafist Group for Call and Combat; Tanzim al-Qa'ida fi Bilad alMaghrib al-Islamiya
history – formed in 1998 in Algeria under Hassan HATTAB, when he split from the Armed Islamic Group (GIA); was known as the Salafist Group for Preaching and Combat (GSPC) until rebranding itself as AQIM in September 2006; has since undergone various schisms and rapprochements; in 2011, a Mauritanian-led group broke away, calling itself the Movement for Unity and Jihad in West Africa (MUJWA); in 2012, the Veiled Men Battalion split off and rebranded itself the al-Mulathamun Battalion; al-Mulathamun and MUJWA merged to form al-Mourabitoun in 2013; in late 2015, AQIM reincorporated al-Murabitoun and in 2017, the Mali Branch of AQIM and al-Murabitoun joined the Mali-based al-Qa'ida coalition Jama'at Nasr al-Islam wal-Muslimin (JNIM); continued to be active through 2023 despite pressure from regional and international counterterrorism operations, particularly in using North Africa as a support zone for assisting JNIM operations in Mali and the Sahel, including operating transnational financial networks to move and share funds
goals – overthrow "apostate" African regimes and establish a regional Islamic state across all of North and West Africa; support the broader goals of al-Qai'da's central leadership
leadership and organization – Abu Obaida al-ANNABI (aka Abu Ubaydah Yusuf al-Anabi, Yazid Mubarak); has a 14-member shura council comprised of regional commanders and the heads of the political, military, judicial, and media committees; locally organized into "battalions" and "brigades," which may range in size from a few dozen to several hundred fighters at any given time
areas of operation – has historically operated in the coastal areas of northern Algeria and in Libya and Tunisia, but counterterrorism efforts have forced it largely into the Sahel region, including Mali; has conducted attacks in Algeria, Burkina Faso, Cote d'Ivoire, and Mali
targets, tactics, and weapons – local and international military and security forces using both terrorist and guerrilla warfare tactics; employs improvised explosive devices, suicide bombers, as well as light weapons, machine guns, mortars, rockets, and landmines; also attacks "soft" civilian targets such as hotels, resorts, and restaurants that cater to Westerners and tourists with small arms, explosives, and suicide bombers; known for assassinations and kidnappings
strength – estimated in 2022 to have up to 1,000 fighters
financial and other support – engages in kidnappings-for-ransom and other criminal activities, particularly extorting drug trafficking groups and others; arms largely acquired from Libyan stockpiles, battlefield captures, or via illicit regional arms markets
designation – GSPC was designated as a Foreign Terrorist Organization on 27 March 2002; the Department of State amended the GSPC designation on 20 February 2008, after the GSPC officially joined with al-Qa'ida in September 2006 and became AQIM

al-Shabaab (AS)

aka – the Harakat Shabaab al-Mujahidin (HSM); al-Shabab; Shabaab; the Youth; Mujahidin al-Shabaab Movement; Mujahideen Youth Movement; Mujahidin Youth Movement; al-Hijra, Al Hijra, Muslim Youth Center, MYC, Pumwani Muslim Youth, Pumwani Islamist Muslim Youth Center
history – descended from Al-Ittihad Al-Islami, a Somali terrorist group whose leaders fought in Afghanistan in the 1990s and formed circa 2003; has operated as a core al-Qa'ida affiliate since 2012; was the militant wing of the former Somali Islamic Courts Council that took over parts of Somalia in 2006; since the end of 2006, has engaged in an insurgency against the Government of Somalia and supporting foreign military forces and a campaign of violence against Somali civilians; responsible for numerous high-profile bombings and shootings throughout Somalia, and more than 3,000 civilian deaths since 2015; has influence in large areas of rural Somalia through coercion, control over local economies and commercial transit points; provides rudimentary government services in areas under its control, including rule of law through sharia courts, sharia-based institutions and schools, funding, services, security, and food; in July 2022, it launched an incursion into Ethiopia with several hundred fighters; continued to conduct attacks in Somalia in 2024, particularly in the central and southern regions, as well as the capital, Mogadishu; also was engaged in heavy fighting with the Somali military, which claimed to have re-taken considerable amounts of territory from the group
goals – discredit, destabilize, and overthrow the Federal Government of Somalia; establish Islamic rule in Somalia and the border regions of Somalia-Kenya and southern Ethiopia; drive out Western influence
leadership and organization – led by Ahmad DIRIYE (aka Abu UBEYDAH/UBAIDAH, Abu Ubaidah DIREYE, Ahmad UMAR) since September 2014; DIRIYE reportedly directs both an executive council and a shura (or consultative) council; the executive council runs the group's operations and is made up of committees, ministries, departments, or wings, including for finance, intelligence and security (Amniyat), media/propaganda, politics, education, judicial matters, religion, logistics, explosives (Sanaaca), and military operations (Jabhat), as well as regional commanders or shadow governors in areas that al-Shabaab controls; each regional division has sub-offices or wings, including for police/security and taxation; has shown the ability to mobilize and coordinate significant numbers of fighters for large-scale ground attacks; in 2024, had reportedly formed a pan-East African force of foreign fighters known as Muhajirin
areas of operation – holds large swathes of southern and central Somalia; active in Mogadishu and northern Somalia; has conducted operations in Ethiopia, Kenya, and Uganda; mounted armed incursions into Ethiopia in 2022 and 2007
targets, tactics, and weapons – Somali Government officials, military units, police, and civilians, international aid workers, journalists, foreign troops (including US, African Union), and neighboring countries contributing to military stabilization operations in Somalia, particularly Kenya and Uganda; has attacked hotels, schools, military bases, police stations, shopping areas, and telecommunications towers in Kenya; has clashed with an Islamic State faction operating in northern Somalia; methods include assassinations, drive-by shootings, ambushes, suicide bombings, hostage taking, armed drone attacks, indiscriminate attacks on civilians, roadside improvised explosive devices (IEDs), mortar and rocket-propelled

grenade (RPG) attacks, and complex ground assaults, including some involving multiple suicide bombers, followed by an assault by members carrying small arms and explosives; in 2022 and 2023, for example, it conducted two ground assaults involving vehicle-mounted bombs and hundreds of militants on international military peacekeeper bases that killed more than 50 troops in each incident; has placed vehicle-mounted bombs in high-density urban areas, including attacks in Mogadishu in October 2022, December 2019, and October 2017 that together killed over 700 civilians; typically armed with small arms, light and heavy machine guns (including truck-mounted machine guns), landmines, mortars, RPGs, IEDs, man-portable air defense systems, and unmanned aerial vehicles/drones
strength – estimated in 2024 to have 7,000-12,000 fighters
financial and other support – obtains funds primarily through extortion of businesses, taxation, and zakat (religious donations) collections from the local populations, robbery, and remittances and other money transfers from the Somali diaspora (although these funds are not always intended to support al-Shabaab members); estimated that the group generates $100-$150 million annually; probably receives training, arms, and bomb-making materials from other al-Qa'ida branches; has captured arms, ammunition, and other materiel from regional and Somali military forces; also purchases arms and ammunition through black markets; operates military training camps in areas it occupies
designation – placed on the US Department of State's list of Foreign Terrorist Organizations on 18 March 2008

Ansar al-Dine (AAD)
aka – Ansar Dine; Ansar al-Din; Ancar Dine; Ansar ul-Din; Ansar Eddine; Defenders of the Faith
history – formed in November 2011 as a Tuareg rebel group under Iyad Ag Ghali and in mid-2012 began an association with al-Qai'da in the Islamic Maghrib (AQIM), in part because of their shared desire to implement Islamic law in Mali; was among the terrorist groups to take over northern Mali following the March 2012 coup that toppled the Malian Government; proceeded to destroy UNESCO World Heritage sites and enforce a severe interpretation of Islam upon the civilian population living in the areas under their control; beginning in 2013, French and African military forces forced AAD and its allies out of the population centers they had seized, severely weakening AAD, although the group made a comeback in 2015-2016; in 2017, joined Jama'ah Nusrah al-Islam wal-Muslimin (Group for the Support of Islam and Muslims, JNIM), a coalition of al-Qa'ida-linked groups in Mali that formed the same year; active in 2024
goals – replace the Malian government with an Islamic state
leadership and organization – led by its founder Iyad Ag GHALI (aka Abu al-FADEL), who also leads JNIM; reportedly has regionally based branches; operates under the JNIM banner
areas of operation – operates mostly in central and northern Mali
targets, tactics, and weapons – targets Malian military and security forces, as well as supporting Russian security personnel; also targeted French and UN military troops prior to their departure in 2022 and 2023, respectively; uses a mix of insurgent/guerrilla warfare hit-and-run and terrorist tactics, including ambushes, complex ground assaults involving dozens of fighters, road side bombs, rocket attacks, assassinations, kidnappings, and car and suicide bombings; fighters are armed with small arms, light and heavy machine guns, rocket-propelled grenades, landmines, mortars, rockets, trucks mounting machine guns (aka "technicals"), and explosives, including improvised explosive devices
strength – not available
financial and other support – cooperates with and has received support from al-Qa'ida since its inception; also reportedly receives funds from foreign donors and through smuggling; has utilized arms and equipment captured from the Malian Army or received from former Libyan military stockpiles; has taken advantage of trans-Saharan smuggling routes to resupply from illicit markets in Libya and elsewhere in the region
designation – placed on the US Department of State's list of Foreign Terrorist Organizations on 22 March 2013

Ansar al-Islam (AAI)
aka – Ansar al-Sunna; Ansar al-Sunna Army; Devotees of Islam; Followers of Islam in Kurdistan; Helpers of Islam; Jaish Ansar al-Sunna; Jund al-Islam; Kurdish Taliban; Kurdistan Supporters of Islam; Partisans of Islam; Soldiers of God; Soldiers of Islam; Supporters of Islam in Kurdistan
history – founded in December 2001 with support from al-Qa'ida; originated in the Iraqi Kurdistan region with the merger of two Kurdish terrorist factions, Jund al-Islam and a splinter group of the Islamic Movement of Kurdistan; from 2003 to 2011, conducted attacks against a wide range of targets in Iraq, including government and security forces, as well as US and Coalition troops; in the summer of 2014, a faction of AAI pledged allegiance to ISIS and the two factions reportedly have fought each other; after 2014, most activity has been in Syria where AAI has fought against Syrian regime forces, although it claimed a bombing attack against members of a Shia militia in Iraq in late 2019; active in Syria in 2024
goals – expel Western interests from Iraq and, ultimately, establish an Iraqi state operating according to its interpretation of sharia; similar goals in Syria
leadership and organization – led by Amir Shaykh Abu Hashim Muhammad bin Abdul Rahman al-IBRAHIM; likely has a cell-based structure
areas of operation – active in central and western Iraq and in Syria (leadership assessed to be in Syria)
targets, tactics, and weapons – historically targeted Iraqi security and police forces, citizens, politicians, and Shia militia forces for assassinations, bombings, and executions; targets Syrian government forces and pro-Syrian regime militias with guerrilla-style hit-and-run assaults and terrorist attacks; equipped with small arms, light and heavy machine guns, rocket-propelled grenades, mortars, and explosives, including improvised explosive devices
strength – estimated in 2023 to have less than 300 fighters
financial and other support – receives assistance from a loose network of associates in Europe and the Middle East
designation – placed on the US Department of State's list of Foreign Terrorist Organizations on 22 March 2004

Ansar al-Shari'a groups in Libya (ASL)
aka – Ansar al-Shari'a in Benghazi; Ansar al-Sharia in Darnah; Ansar al-Shariah Brigade; Ansar al-Shari'a Brigade; Katibat Ansar al-Sharia in Benghazi; Ansar al-Shariah-Benghazi; Al-Raya Establishment for Media Production; Ansar al-Sharia; Soldiers of the Sharia; Ansar al-Shariah; Supporters of Islamic Law; Partisans of Islamic Law; Supporters of Islamic Law in Darnah, Ansar al-Sharia Brigade in Darnah; Ansar al-Sharia in Derna
history – consists of Ansar al-Shari'a in Benghazi (AAS-B) and Ansar al-Sharia in Darnah (AAS-D); AAS-B and AAS-D were formed in 2011 following the fall of the QADHAFI regime as Sunni Muslim Salafist armed groups with links to al-Qa'ida; at their peak in 2013, held territory and operated branches in Benghazi, Darnah, Sirte, Ajdabiya, and Nawfalia; promoted charitable work to gain popular support from local communities; in 2014, began fighting against the Libyan National Army (LNA) under General HIFTER and the Islamic State in Libya (ISIS-Libya) and by 2015 had lost most of their territory and suffered heavy losses; in May 2017, AAS-B announced its dissolution due to battle losses, as well as defections to ISIS-Libya; AAS-D's status as of 2023 was unclear
goals – a strict implementation of sharia in Libya
leadership and organization – unknown; AAS-B's last known emir (leader) was Abu Khalid al-MADANI; the last known emir of AAS-D was founder Abu Sufian Ibrahim Ahmed Hamuda Bin QUMU who defected to ISIS in 2014; organizations are also unknown, but AAS-B reportedly had two main divisions, one dedicated to military affairs and one to charitable work

areas of operation – operated mostly in eastern Libya, particularly Benghazi and Darnah
targets, tactics, and weapons – targeted Libyan political and security officials and Westerners for kidnappings, executions, bombings, and assassinations; AAS-B participated in the 2012 attacks on US diplomatic facilities in Benghazi, for example; also conducted guerrilla warfare hit-and-run and terrorist attacks against Libyan security forces, LNA militias, and other terrorist groups using small arms and light weapons, rockets, mortars, anti-tank guided missiles, anti-aircraft artillery and missiles, improvised explosive devices and suicide bombings
strength – not available
financial and other support – obtained funds from al-Qa'ida in the Islamic Maghreb, witting and unwitting Islamic charities, donations from sympathizers, and criminal activities; raided Libyan military bases for weapons and ammunition
designation – AAS-B and AAS-D were placed on the US Department of State's list of Foreign Terrorist Organizations on 13 January 2014

Ansar al-Shari'a in Tunisia (AAS-T)
aka – Al-Qayrawan Media Foundation; Supporters of Islamic Law; Ansar al-Sharia in Tunisia; Ansar al-Shari'ah; Ansar al-Shari'ah in Tunisia; Ansar al-Sharia
history – formed in April 2011 as a Sunni Salafi-jihadist militant organization linked to al-Qa'ida; combined community service, proselytization, and violence to promote its ideology and goals; in 2014, multiple AAS-T leaders swore loyalty to the Islamic State and many left the group to fight in Syria; has not claimed any attacks in recent years, and its status is unclear
goals – expand its influence in Tunisia and, ultimately, replace the Tunisian Government with one operating according to Islamic law
leadership and organization – leadership unclear; was reportedly a decentralized movement that gave considerable autonomy to local groups or cells and loosely organized into northern, central, and southern branches; included a media wing known as al-Bayariq Media (The Banners Media)
areas of operation – headquartered in Tunisia; has also operated in Libya
targets, tactics, and weapons – attacked Tunisian military and security personnel with small arms and rocket-propelled grenades; also targeted Tunisian politicians, religious sites, and groups and places representing Western influence, such as tourists and tourist sites, with assassinations and bombings; organized riots and violent demonstrations against the Tunisian government; members are typically armed with small arms and other light weapons, as well as explosives, including improvised explosive devices
strength – not available
financial and other support – precise sources of financial support are not available but believed to come from Tunisian charities, private donors, and smuggling contraband
designation – placed on the US Department of State's list of Foreign Terrorist Organizations on 13 January 2014

Army of Islam (AOI)
aka – Jaysh al-Islam; Jaish al-Islam; JAI
history – formed around 2005 as a Salafi Sunni Muslim splinter from HAMAS; subscribes to Salafist ideology of global jihad blended with the traditional model of armed Palestinian resistance; traditionally focused on attacking Israel and Egypt; in September 2015, ISIS claimed that the Army of Islam had pledged allegiance to ISIS and declared itself as part of the Islamic State's Sinai Province but the group denied the claim; it has not claimed responsibility for any attacks in recent years, but was considered active as of 2022
goals – establish a regional Islamic emirate
leadership and organization – led by Mumtaz DUGHMUSH; group organization not available
areas of operation – Egypt, Gaza, Israel
targets, tactics, and weapons – has targeted the Egyptian and Israeli governments and their citizens, as well as American, British, and New Zealand citizens; has a history of conducting rocket attacks against Israel, kidnapping civilians, and attacking Christians; conducted a bombing attack on a Coptic Christian church in Egypt in 2011 that killed 25 and wounded 100; equipped with small arms, bombs, light and heavy machine guns, mortars, rockets, and improvised explosives devices
strength – estimated in 2022 to number a few hundred fighters
financial and other support – generates funding through criminal activities conducted primarily in Gaza, including kidnappings for ransom; also receives funds from foreign sympathizers and organizations
designation – placed on the US Department of State's list of Foreign Terrorist Organizations on 19 May 2011

Asa'ib Ahl al-Haqq (AAH)
aka – Ahl al-Kahf; Band of the Righteous; Bands of Right; Islamic Shia Resistance in Iraq; Khazali Faction/Network; Khazali Special Groups Network; League of Righteousness
history – is an Iraqi Shia militia and political group that split off from Jaysh al-Mahdi in 2006; fought US military forces in Iraq from 2006 until the US withdrawal in 2011 and has continued attack planning against US and coalition interests following Operation Iraqi Freedom; following the rise of the Islamic State of Iraq and ash-Sham (ISIS) in 2013, fought alongside the Iraqi military as part of the Popular Mobilization Committee and Affiliated Forces (PMC or PMF) militia forces (aka Popular Mobilization Units or PMU) until ISIS's territorial defeat in 2017; fought in support of the ASAD regime in Syria from 2011 until at least 2017 where it claimed the loss of about 700 fighters; in 2017, AAH's affiliated political party (Al Sadiqun Bloc) was approved by the Iraqi electoral commission to run in the national election; in 2018, Al Sadiqun joined the Al Fatah Alliance (Victory), a political coalition primarily comprised of parties affiliated with Iranian-backed Shia militias; in late 2019, it participated in an assault on the US Embassy compound in Baghdad; largely follows the directives of Iran's IRGC Qods Force and has vowed revenge on the US for the death of the Iranian Qods Force commander in early 2020; active as of 2024, including indirect fire attacks on US facilities in Iraq, typically using front names or proxy groups
goals – maintain a Shia-controlled government in Iraq, promote Iran's political and religious influence in Iraq, and expel the remaining US military presence
leadership and organization – led by Qays al-KHAZALI; maintains a paramilitary force inside the PMC/PMF that is divided into three brigades (the 41st, 42nd, and 43rd PMC brigades) representing geographic sectors of Iraq; reportedly models itself after Lebanese Hizballah
note – following the onset of the Hamas-Israel war in the Gaza Strip in October 2023, an umbrella group called the Islamic Resistance in Iraq (IRI or al-Haya al-Tansiqiya lil-Muqawama al-Iraqiya) announced its formation by claiming responsibility for an October 2023 failed drone strike on an US military base in northern Iraq; the IRI is a coalition of all Iran-backed Shiite militias operating in Iraq, including designated terrorist groups AAH and Kataib Hezbollah (KH), operating in solidarity with HAMAS in its 2023-2024 war with Israel; since its establishment, the IRI has claimed responsibility for dozens of attacks on US elements in Iraq and Syria; it has also claimed responsibility for more than 100 attacks on Israel
area(s) of operation – based in Iraq; has deployed fighters to Syria
targets, tactics, and weapons – targets foreign military forces, US interests, ISIS, and Sunni Muslims; from 2006 to 2011, claimed to have conducted more than 6,000 attacks against US and Coalition forces using small arms, road side bombs, car bombs, and mortars; has carried out

abductions, executions, and targeted killings of Sunni Muslims; has killed civilian protesters and used mass gatherings to protest domestic and international political decisions; has fought as a paramilitary/irregular force in Syria and alongside the Iraqi military; armed with a variety of weapons, including small arms, machine guns, rocket-propelled grenades, mortars, rockets, artillery, armed unmanned aerial vehicles/drones, improvised explosive devices, and armored vehicles
strength – estimated in 2023 to have 10-15,000 members
financial and other support – receives funding, logistical support, training, and weapons from the Iranian Revolutionary Guard Force-Qods Force and Lebanese Hizballah; solicits donations online and through a pro-Iran television channel; also raises funds through legitimate business enterprises, as well as criminal activities, including kidnappings-for-ransom, smuggling, and taxing/extortion of economic activities in areas where the group is dominant; AAH's official status provides some members government salaries and access to state resources
designation – placed on the US Department of State's list of Foreign Terrorist Organizations on 10 January 2020

Asbat al-Ansar (AAA)
aka – Band of Helpers; Band of Partisans; League of Partisans; League of the Followers; God's Partisans; Gathering of Supporters; Partisan's League; Esbat al-Ansar; Isbat al-Ansar; Osbat al-Ansar; Usbat al-Ansar; Usbat ul-Ansar
history – emerged in the early 1990s in Lebanon under the late Shaykh Hisham SHRAID, a Palestinian refugee and preacher; until the 2000s, was known for assassinating Lebanese religious leaders and government officials, as well as bombing venues it deemed un-Islamic and representing Western influence, such as nightclubs, theaters, and liquor stores; from 2005 to 2011, some members fought against US and Coalition forces in Iraq; has links to al-Qa'ida and other Sunni terrorist groups; has not claimed responsibility for any attacks in recent years, but remained active as of 2023
goals – overthrow the Lebanese Government, rid Lebanon of Western influence; destroy Israel and establish an Islamic state in the Levant; oppose Christian, secular, and Shia Muslim institutes operating in the Levant
leadership and organization – not available
areas of operation – primary base of operations is the Ayn al-Hilwah Palestinian refugee camp near Sidon in southern Lebanon; has been reluctant to involve itself in operations in Lebanon in recent years, in part because of concerns of losing its safe haven in the camp
targets, tactics, and weapons – until the mid-2000s, operatives conducted small-scale bombing and shooting attacks in Lebanon against Christian, secular, and Shia Muslim figures and institutions, elements of foreign influence inside the country, and Lebanese government officials, such as judges; has also plotted against foreign diplomatic targets; weapons include small arms, rocket-propelled grenades, and improvised explosive devices
strength – estimated in 2021 to have a few hundred members
financial resources – receives donations from sympathizers and through international Sunni extremist networks
designation – placed on the US Department of State's list of Foreign Terrorist Organizations on 27 March 2002

Boko Haram (BH)
aka – Nigerian Taliban; Jama'atu Ahlus-Sunnah Lidda'Awati Wal Jihad; Jama'atu Ahlis Sunna Lidda'awati wal-Jihad; Jama'atu Ahlus-Sunnah (JAS); People Committed to the Prophet's Teachings for Propagation and Jihad; Sunni Group for Preaching and Jihad
history – formed in 2002 under the late Muslim cleric Mohammed YUSUF; in 2009, launched an insurgency and campaign of terror against the Nigerian Government, its security forces, and civilians; by 2015, had captured territory roughly the size of Belgium in northeastern Nigeria; since 2015, the Nigerian military has dislodged Boko Haram from almost all of the territory it previously controlled, although the group continued to operate in Nigeria, as well as in Cameroon, Chad, and Niger; in 2015, the group declared allegiance to the Islamic State in Iraq and al-Sham (ISIS) and began calling itself ISIS in West Africa (ISIS-WA); following an ISIS decision regarding a change in leadership in 2016, the group split into two factions with one group continuing its activities under the original Boko Haram leader, Abubakar bin Muhammad SHEKAU, and the other continuing as ISIS-WA; in recent years, has been engaged in fighting with ISIS-WA, as well as the Nigerian military and regional military forces under the Multinational Joint Task Force (MNJTF); fighting had resulted in the loss of territory and heavy casualties, including battlefield losses, defections to ISIS-WA, desertions, and surrenders to government forces; continued conducting attacks and maintained a limited safehaven in northeast Nigeria into 2024; since 2009, violence associated with Boko Haram and ISIS-WA has killed an estimated 40,000 people, mostly civilians, and displaced as many as 3 million
goals – establish an Islamic state in Nigeria based on Islamic law
leadership and organization – reportedly led by Bakura MODOU although some accounts have the group divided into two factions, each operating in separate areas with different leaders; previously, the group had a shura council and regionally based cells/commands, which operated with some autonomy; under the shura were departments for logistics, propaganda, training and education, finance, weapons procurement, recruitment, and legal/religious issues
areas of operation – most active in northeastern Nigeria (Borno State); also operates in northern Cameroon, southeastern Niger, and areas of Chad near Lake Chad; police have arrested suspected Boko Haram members in Chad's capital, N'Djamena
targets, tactics, and weapons – targets tourists and other foreigners (particularly businessmen), wealthy civilians, and government leaders to kidnap for ransom or kill; conducts shootings and suicide bombing attacks against government buildings, military installations, police stations, schools, markets, places of worship and entertainment, and sometimes entire villages; has kidnapped thousands of civilians, including children, many of whom are either forced or indoctrinated into fighting with the group or conducting suicide bombings; some female captives are subjected to forced labor and sexual servitude; conducts an insurgency combining guerrilla warfare and terrorist tactics against military and security forces; uses small arms, light and heavy machine guns, landmines, mortars, rockets, armored vehicles, trucks mounted with machine guns (aka "technicals"), improvised explosive devices, car bombs, and suicide bombings;
strength – unclear; estimated in 2023 to have up to 2,000 members; the group has taken heavy losses from casualties, defections, desertions, and surrenders
financial and other support – largely self-financed through criminal activities such as looting, extortion, kidnapping-for-ransom, bank robberies, cattle rustling, and assassinations for hire; has seized vehicles, weapons, ammunition, and other supplies from the Nigerian and Nigerien militaries and has acquired other arms from the regional black market
designation – placed on the US Department of State's list of Foreign Terrorist Organizations on 14 November 2013

Communist Party of the Philippines/New People's Army (CPP/NPA)
aka – Communist Party of the Philippines; CPP; New People's Army; NPA; Bagong Hukbong Bayan or BHB; Communist Party of the Philippines-New People's Army-National Democratic Front or CPP-NPA-NDF
history – CPP formed in 1968 and followed in 1969 by the creation of its armed/military wing, the NPA; since 1971, has waged a Maoist-based insurgency and terrorist campaign against the Philippine Government that has resulted in about 40,000 civilian and combatant deaths; from 2016 to 2019, several attempts were made to establish a cease-fire and peace deal between the CPP/NPA and the Philippine Government without success; talks typically broke down when each side accused the other of initiating attacks or violating cease-fires; CPP/NPA attacks and clashes

between the group and Philippine security forces continued in the years following the breakdown in talks in 2019; 2023 saw an estimated 250 fatalities amongst civilians, CPP/NPA fighters, and government security personnel; in November 2023, the CPP/NPA and the Philippine Government agreed to restart talks, but as of 2024 Philippine security forces continued to conduct operations against the group
goals – destabilize the Philippines' economy to inspire the populace to revolt; ultimately wants to overthrow the government and install a Maoist-based regime; opposes the US military and commercial presence in the Philippines
leadership and organization – unclear following the death of its long-time leader Jose Maria SISON in December 2022; highest leadership body is its 26-member Central Committee, which reported to SISON; organized in "fronts" or regions but operates in cells and platoons at the local level; overt political wing is known as the National Democratic Front
areas of operation – in 2023, the CPP claimed its armed wing was present in about 70 of the country's 82 provinces; however, its operations and clashes with government forces were occurring in only a few rural areas, including northern Mindanao, southern Luzon, and parts of the Visayas; some of the group's leaders, including its negotiating panel, live in exile in the Netherlands
targets, tactics, and weapons – targets military and security forces, government officials and facilities, local infrastructure (including power facilities, telecommunication towers, and bridges), foreign enterprises, and businesses that refuse to pay "revolutionary taxes"; follows a Maoist-inspired protracted guerrilla warfare strategy; uses guerrilla tactics, including ambushes, bombings, assassinations, raids on military and security posts, and kidnapping security personnel; also has attacked local infrastructure, plantations, mines, foreign enterprises, and US personnel and interests (has not attacked a US citizen or facility since 2001, however); employs small arms, light weapons, grenades, improvised explosive devices, and landmines; has employed city-based assassination squads at times
strength – estimated in 2024 to have about 1,500 full-time combatants (from a peak of about 25,000 armed members in the late 1980s)
financial and other support – raises funds through theft and extortion, including extracting "revolutionary taxes" from local businesses; probably also receives donations from sympathizers in the Philippines, Europe, and elsewhere; arms and ammunition largely stolen or captured from Philippine military and security forces or acquired on the black market
designation –placed on the US Department of State's list of Foreign Terrorist Organizations on 9 August 2002

Continuity Irish Republican Army (CIRA)
aka – Continuity Army Council; Continuity IRA; Republican Sinn Fein
history – terrorist splinter group that became operational in 1986 as the clandestine armed wing of Republican Sinn Fein, following its split from Sinn Fein; "Continuity" refers to the group's belief that it is carrying on the original goal of the Irish Republican Army (IRA) of forcing the British out of Northern Ireland; rejects ceasefires, weapons decommissioning, and all peace accords, including the Belfast Agreement and the 1998 Good Friday Agreement; cooperates with the larger Real IRA (RIRA), a US-designated terrorist group; in June 2017, released a statement claiming it would disband and decommission some of its arms over the following three months, describing the conflict as a "futile war"; however, some members have since claimed responsibility for several attacks, and the group remained active as of 2023
goals – disrupt the Northern Ireland peace process, remove British rule in Northern Ireland and, ultimately, unify Ireland
leadership and organization – operations are guided by its Irish Continuity Army Council
areas of operation – has been active in Belfast and the border areas of Northern Ireland
targets, tactics, and weapons – targets the British military, Northern Ireland security forces, and Loyalist paramilitary groups; has carried out bombings, assassinations, hijackings, extortion operations, and robberies; on occasion, has provided advance warning to police of its attacks; members are typically equipped with small arms and explosives
strength – estimated in 2022 to have fewer than 50 members; police counterterrorism operations have reduced the group's strength considerably
financial and other support – receives donations from local and international sympathizers, but the majority of funds are obtained through criminal activity, including bank robberies, extortion, and smuggling
designation – placed on the US Department of State's list of Foreign Terrorist Organizations on 13 July 2004

HAMAS
aka – HAMAS is the acronym for Harakat al-Muqawama al-Islamiya (Islamic Resistance Movement); Izz al-Din al Qassam (Qassim) Battalions; Izz al-Din al Qassam (or Qassim) Brigades; Izz al-Din al Qassam (or Qassim) Forces; Students of Ayyash; Student of the Engineer; Yahya Ayyash Units
history – established in 1987 at the onset of the first Palestinian uprising, or Intifada, as an outgrowth of the Palestinian branch of the Muslim Brotherhood; prior to 2005 conducted numerous attacks against Israel, including more than 50 suicide bombings; in addition to its anti-Israel stance, used a network of *Dawa* or social services that included charities, schools, clinics, youth camps, fundraising, and political activities to help build grassroots support amongst Palestinians in Gaza; won the Palestinian Legislative Council elections in 2006, giving it control of significant Palestinian Authority (PA) ministries in Gaza; expelled the PA and its dominant political faction Fatah in a violent takeover in 2007; since 2007, it has remained the de facto ruler of Gaza and has engaged in sporadic rocket attacks, border clashes, organized protests, and periodic targeted attacks against Israeli citizens, including a suicide bombing in 2016; it fought significant conflicts with Israel in 2008-2009, 2012, 2014, and 2021, typically involving HAMAS rocket attacks against Israel and Israeli air and artillery counter-strikes on HAMAS targets in Gaza, as well as Israeli military ground incursions; in October 2023 it conducted a surprise ground attack into Israel, supported by rockets and armed drones, killing large numbers of Israelis and foreigners, mostly civilians, and sparking another war with Israel that continued into 2024
goals – ideology combines Palestinian nationalism with Islamic fundamentalism; seeks to maintain control of the Gaza Strip to facilitate Palestinian nationalist aims; the group's charter calls for establishing an Islamic Palestinian state in place of Israel and rejects all agreements made between the Palestine Liberation Organization and Israel
leadership and organization – not available; previous leader (Yahya SINWAR) killed in October 2024; has a shura council as its central consultative body; has smaller shura/executive committees to supervise political activities, military operations, social services, finances, and media relations; military wing (the 'Izz al-Din al-Qassam Brigades) organized into approximately six "brigades," special forces (Nukhba Special Forces), and various paramilitary units
areas of operation – has controlled Gaza since 2007 and has a presence in the West Bank; also has a presence in the Palestinian refugee camps in Lebanon and key regional capitals such as Doha, Qatar, and Cairo
targets, tactics, and weapons – targets Israeli military forces and civilians, as well as Islamic State and other Salafist armed group members based in Gaza; has conducted suicide bombings (carried out a suicide attack on a bus in Jerusalem in 2016 that killed 20 people), improvised explosive attacks, shootings, and rocket launches; fired more than 4,000 rockets at Israel during both the 50-day conflict in 2014 and the 11-day conflict in 2021; weapons include small arms, light and heavy machine guns, rockets (some with ranges of up to 200kms), mortars, rocket-propelled grenades, man-portable air defense systems, anti-tank missiles, armed unmanned aerial vehicles/drones, and improvised explosive devices (IEDs), including balloons armed with IEDs or designed to start fires; has also engaged in cyber espionage and computer network exploitation operations
strength – estimates prior to the war in 2023 ranged from 20,000 to 40,000 armed combatants

financial and other support – the military wing receives funding, weapons, and training from Iran and procures additional weapons from the regional black market; weapons are typically supplied through tunnels under the border with Sinai and/or through maritime smuggling routes; also raises funds in some Gulf countries as well as through business taxation, donations from Palestinian expatriates, international investments, and through its own charity organizations
designation – placed on the US Department of State's list of Foreign Terrorist Organizations on 8 October 1997

Haqqani Network (HQN)
aka – Haqqani Taliban Network, Afghanistan Mujahidin
history – formed in the late 1980s during the then-Soviet Union's occupation of Afghanistan; founder, Jalaluddin HAQQANI, established a relationship with Usama BIN LADIN in the mid-1980s and joined the Taliban in 1995; helped the Taliban capture the capital, Kabul, in 1996; after the fall of the Taliban to US and allied forces in 2001, HAQQANI retreated to Pakistan where, under the leadership of his son, Sirajuddin HAQQANI (Jalaluddin HAQQANI reportedly died in 2018), continued to conduct an insurgency in Afghanistan against the Afghan Government and its security forces, Afghan civilians, and foreign military forces; insurgency continued until the collapse of the Afghan Government in August 2021; semi-autonomous component of the Afghan Taliban and a close ally of al-Qa'ida; cooperates with other regional terrorist groups, including the Islamic Movement of Uzbekistan and Lashkar e-Tayyiba; following the Taliban takeover of Afghanistan, it secured control of the de facto ministries of interior, intelligence, and immigration and largely controlled the country's internal security
goals – prior to August 2021, expel foreign military forces from Afghanistan and replace the Afghan Government with an Islamic state operating according to a strict Salafi Muslim interpretation of sharia under the Afghan Taliban
leadership and organization – operational commander is Sirajuddin HAQQANI, who leads the group through its Peshawar Shura, which features both military and political wings and consists of Haqqani family members along with veteran commanders trusted by the family; during the insurgency, it operated under Taliban command and control but maintained significant autonomy and regional influence in its area of operations in southeast Afghanistan; beginning in 2015, HAQQANI was the deputy leader of the Afghan Taliban, and as of 2024 was the acting interior minister for the de facto Taliban government
areas of operation – Afghanistan; Pakistan (leadership historically maintained a power base around Pakistan's tribal areas and a presence in Pakistan's settled areas)
targets, tactics, and weapons – employed insurgency-type tactics, including coordinated small-arms assaults coupled with the use of mortars and rockets, rocket-propelled grenades, improvised explosive devices, suicide attacks, and car/truck bombs against Afghan Government security forces, US military, and other coalition troops; also targeted Afghan civilians and foreigners with kidnappings, bombings, and suicide attacks; attacked government buildings, hotels, embassies, markets, and schools; conducted some of Afghanistan's most deadly bombings, including truck bomb attacks in Kabul in 2017 and 2018 that killed more than 250 civilians; in 2019, conducted multiple attacks in Kabul that killed 100 people and injured more than 500; equipped with small arms, light and heavy machine guns, mortars, rockets, rocket-propelled grenades, and improvised explosive devices
strength – estimated in 2022 to have 3-5,000 fighters, although some size estimates were as high as 10,000; during combat operations against the Afghan Government, the group's numbers likely fluctuated based on time of year and battlefield operations
financial and other support – in addition to the funding it received as part of the broader Afghan Taliban, received some assistance from donors in Pakistan and the Gulf; most funds are from taxing local commerce, extortion, smuggling, kidnapping-for-ransom, and other licit and illicit business ventures; recruits, trains, raises funds, resupplies, and plans operations in the tribal areas of Pakistan; reportedly receives weapons smuggled in from Iran and Pakistan
designation – placed on the US Department of State's list of Foreign Terrorist Organizations on 19 September 2012

Harakat Sawa'd Misr (HASM)
aka – HASM Movement; Arms of Egypt Movement; HASSAM; HASAM; Harakah Sawa'id Misr; Movement of Egypt's Arms
history – formed in 2015; the group is in part composed of alienated Muslim Brotherhood (MB) members who view violence rather than dialogue as a more effective means to overthrow the Egyptian Government and operate independent of MB; in 2016, the group claimed responsibility for the assassination of a senior Egyptian security official, as well as the attempted assassination of Egypt's former Grand Mufti; following a January 2017 shootout with Egyptian security forces in Cairo, HASM declared a jihad against the Egyptian Government; later in 2017, it claimed an ambush attack that killed more than 50 Egyptian security forces and an attack on Burma's embassy in Cairo; in January 2019, it conducted a car bomb attack targeting security forces in Giza, which it claimed killed or wounded 10 soldiers; in August of the same year, it was held responsible (but denied responsibility) for a car bomb attack on a government health institute in Cairo, killing at least 20 people and injuring dozens; continued to be active in 2022
goals – overthrow the Egyptian Government and replace it with an Islamic regime
leadership and organization – Yahya al-Sayyid Ibrahim MUSA and Alaa Ali Mohammed al-SAMAHI (both based in Turkey); organization is not available, but probably operates in small, loosely connected cells and networks
areas of operation – Egypt (some leaders in Turkey)
targets, tactics, and weapons – primarily Egyptian security officials and other government-affiliated targets; typical attacks include ambushes, shootings, and bombings, including car bombings; employs improvised explosive devices and small arms
strength – not available
financial and other support – not available
designation – placed on the US Department of State's list of Foreign Terrorist Organizations on 14 January 2021

Harakat ul-Jihad-i-Islami (HUJI)
aka – Movement of Islamic Holy War; Harkat-ul-Jihad-al Islami; Harkat-al-Jihad-ul Islami; Harkat-ul-Jehad-al-Islami; Harakat ul Jihad-e-Islami; Harakat-ul Jihad Islami
history – formed in 1980 in Afghanistan to fight against the former Soviet Union; following the Soviet withdrawal in 1989, redirected its efforts to the cause of Muslims in the Indian state of Jammu and Kashmir; also supplied fighters to the Taliban in Afghanistan to fight Afghan, Coalition, and US forces; has experienced internal splits, and a portion of the group aligned with al-Qa'ida; largely inactive and has not publicly claimed any attacks since 2015; status unclear
goals – annexation of the state of Jammu and Kashmir into Pakistan and establishment of Islamic rule in Afghanistan, India, and Pakistan
leadership and organization – leadership not available; organization not available
areas of operation – historically extended throughout South Asia with operations focused on Afghanistan, India, and Pakistan; also active in Bangladesh
targets, tactics, and weapons – targeted Pakistani military, security, and police personnel, as well as Indian security forces in the Kashmir region and Indian Government officials; also targeted Hindu and Western civilians; most significant attack was the bombing of the New Delhi High Court

in 2011, which killed 11 people and injured 76; claimed the bombing was intended to force India to repeal the death sentence of a HUJI member; attacks typically involved the use of small arms, grenades, and improvised explosive devices
strength – not available
financial and other support – not available
designation – placed on the US Department of State's list of Foreign Terrorist Organizations on 6 August 2010

Harakat ul-Jihad-i-Islami/Bangladesh (HUJI-B)

aka – Harakat ul Jihad e Islami Bangladesh; Harkatul Jihad al Islam; Harkatul Jihad; Harakat ul Jihad al Islami; Harkat ul Jihad al Islami; Harkat-ul-Jehad-al-Islami; Harakat ul Jihad Islami Bangladesh; Islami Dawat-e-Kafela; IDEK
history – formed in 1992 by a group of former Bangladeshi Afghan veterans wanting to establish Islamist rule in Bangladesh; HUJI-B leaders signed the February 1998 *fatwa* sponsored by Usama BIN LADEN that declared US civilians legitimate targets; in October 2005, Bangladeshi authorities banned the group; has connections to al-Qa'ida and Pakistani terrorist groups advocating similar objectives, including HUJI and Lashkar e-Tayyiba; activities have waned in recent years but remained active as of 2023
goals – install an Islamic state in Bangladesh; draws inspiration from al-Qaida and the Afghan Taliban
leadership and organization – leadership unclear; Bangladeshi authorities executed former leader Mufti Abdul HANNAN and two of his associates in 2017 for a 2004 grenade attack on the British High Commissioner in Sylhet, Bangladesh; most of HUJI-B's other leadership have been in Bangladeshi custody for years
areas of operation – headquartered in Bangladesh and mostly active in the southeast; maintains a network of madrassas and training camps in Bangladesh; also active in India; members have reportedly fought in Burma
targets, tactics, and weapons – conducts low-level bombing attacks against Bangladeshi officials and Westerners; also targets activists, bloggers, academics, religious minorities, and political rallies; most lethal attack occurred in 2004, when operatives lobbed grenades during a political rally in Dhaka, killing 24 and injuring about 400 others; attackers typically use small arms, hand grenades, and various explosives, including petrol bombs and improvised explosive devices
strength – not available
financial and other support – garners donations from sympathetic individuals and organizations; probably also garners funds from criminal activities, including piracy, smuggling, and arms running
designation – placed on the US Department of State's list of Foreign Terrorist Organizations on 5 March 2008

Harakat ul-Mujahidin (HUM)

aka – Harakat ul-Ansar; HUA; Jamiat ul-Ansar; JUA; al-Faran; al-Hadid; al-Hadith; Harakat ul-Mujahidin; Ansar ul Ummah
history – formed in 1985 under Maulana Fazlur Rahman KHALIL in the Pakistani state of Punjab as an anti-Soviet jihadist group that splintered from Harakat ul-Jihad-i-Islami (HUJI); operated terrorist training camps in eastern Afghanistan until US air strikes destroyed them in 2001; a significant portion of the group defected to Jaysh-e-Mohammed after 2000; in 2003, began using the name Jamiat ul-Ansar; Pakistan banned the group the same year; has long been an ally of al-Qa'ida and has links to other terrorist groups in the region, including Lashkar-e-Taiba, Jaish-e-Muhammad, and Lashkar-e-Jhangvi; activities have waned in recent years; status unclear; has not claimed responsibility for any attacks since 2018
goals – annex the Indian Union Territory of Jammu and Kashmir into Pakistan
leadership and organization – Badr MUNIR has led the group since 2005; organization unavailable
areas of operation – operates primarily in Afghanistan and in the Indian state of Jammu and Kashmir; also operates in Muzaffarabad in Pakistan-administered Azad Kashmir and in other cities in Pakistan
targets, tactics, and weapons – conducted numerous attacks against Indian troops, government officials, and civilians in the state of Jammu and Kashmir, as well as in India's northeastern states, especially between 2005 and 2013; also attacked Western targets, such as the 2002 suicide car bombing of a bus carrying French workers in Karachi, Pakistan, that killed 15 and wounded 20; uses various attack methods, including suicide bombings, airplane hijackings, kidnappings, and assassinations; typically used small arms, grenades, and improvised explosive devices
strength – estimated in 2021 to have only a small number of cadres active
financial and other support – receives donations from wealthy supporters in Pakistan
designation – placed on the US Department of State's list of Foreign Terrorist Organizations on 8 October 1997

Hay'at Tahrir al-Sham (HTS)/al-Nusrah Front (ANF)

aka – Jabhat al-Nusrah; Jabhet al-Nusrah; The Victory Front; al-Nusrah Front for the People of the Levant; al-Nusrah Front in Lebanon; Jabhat al-Nusra li-Ahl al-Sham min Mujahedi al-Sham fi Sahat al-Jihad; Support Front for the People of the Levant; Jabhat Fath al-Sham; Jabhat Fath al Sham; Jabhat Fatah al-Sham; Jabhat Fateh al-Sham; Front for the Conquest of Syria; the Front for liberation of al Sham; Front for the Conquest of Syria/the Levant; Front for the Liberation of the Levant; Conquest of the Levant Front; Fatah al-Sham Front; Fateh al-Sham Front; Hay'at Tahrir al-Sham; Hay'et Tahrir al-Sham; Hayat Tahrir al-Sham; HTS; Assembly for the Liberation of Syria; Assembly for Liberation of the Levant; Liberation of al-Sham Commission; Liberation of the Levant Organization; Tahrir al-Sham; Tahrir al-Sham Hay'at
history – formed circa late 2011 as the al-Nusrah Front (Jabhat al-Nusrah) when former al-Qa'ida in Iraq (AQI) leader Abu Bakr al-BAGHDADI sent Syrian militant Abu Muhammad al-JAWLANI (var: al-GOLANI, al-JOLANI) to organize al-Qa'ida cells in Syria; split from AQI in early 2013 and became an independent entity; operated as Jabhat Fateh al-Sham briefly in 2016; in 2017, joined with four smaller Syrian Islamist factions (Harakat Nur al Din al Zenki, Liwa al Haqq, Ansar al Din, and Jaysh al Sunna) and created Hay'at Tahrir al-Sham (HTS, "Assembly for the Liberation of the Levant") as a vehicle to advance its position in Syria; since 2017, additional groups and individuals have joined; as of 2024, HTS was the dominate militant group in northwest Syria and the de facto authority in the Iblib de-escalation zone where it continued to defend against attacks from Syrian Government forces and its allies and consolidate its position; maintained a tense relationship with al-Qa'ida affiliate in Syria Hurras al-Din (HAD) and has refused efforts to resolve differences; has reportedly detained or killed some HAD leaders; has openly clashed with the Islamic State of Iraq and ash-Sham (ISIS) and detained ISIS members seeking to use Idlib as a safehaven
goals – unify under its banner the various anti-ASAD jihadist groups operating in Syria and consolidate its control over the Idlib region; ultimately oust Syrian President Bashar al-ASAD's regime and replace it with a Sunni Islamic state
leadership and organization – led by an overall commander (Abu Muhammad al-JAWLANI) assisted by a small consultative council ("majlis-ash-shura"); has branches or ministries for political, religious, military, financial, civilian services, media, administrative affairs, and security services; operational structure varies from clandestine cells to paramilitary/semi-conventional military units organized as battalions and brigades; claims to have 10 brigades, each with its own infantry, armor, fire support, and logistics units; reportedly operates a commando unit known as the "Red Bands" or "Band of Deaths" that is responsible for conducting raids behind regime front lines; presides over a collection of other armed factions
areas of operation – most territory held by the group is in Syria's Idlib province in the country's northwest, plus small parts of western Aleppo province

targets, tactics, and weapons – primarily attacks Syrian Government and pro-regime forces (including Iranian-backed) and other Syrian insurgent groups, including ISIS, as well as some minorities and civilians; engages in conventional and guerrilla-style attacks using small arms and other light weapons, artillery, rockets, landmines, anti-tank missiles, armored combat vehicles, armed unmanned aerial systems, and surface-to-air missiles; also known for using terrorist tactics, including assassinations and suicide attacks incorporating car bombs and explosive vests
strength – assessed in 2024 to have 7-12,000 fighters, including subordinate factions
financial and other support – largely self-financed; derives funding from smuggling, extortion, taxes and fines on local populations and at border crossings it controls, plus some donations from external Gulf-based donors; taxes imposed on local populations include income, business, and services and utilities such as access to electricity, water, and bread; also raises funds through control of the import and distribution of fuel through a front company; has conducted kidnappings-for-ransom operations in the past; maintains training camps and provides some logistical support to like-minded groups; has also reportedly received military training from private foreign contractors
designation – placed on the US Department of State's list of Foreign Terrorist Organizations on 15 May 2014; on 31 May 2018, the Department of State amended the designation of al-Nusrah Front to include Hay'at Tahrir al-Sham (HTS) and other aliases

Hizballah
aka – the Party of God; Hezbollah; Islamic Jihad; Islamic Jihad Organization; Revolutionary Justice Organization; Organization of the Oppressed on Earth; Islamic Jihad for the Liberation of Palestine; Organization of Right Against Wrong; Ansar Allah; Followers of the Prophet Muhammed; Lebanese Hizballah; Lebanese Hezbollah; LH; Foreign Relations Department; External Security Organization; Foreign Action Unit; Hizballah International; Special Operations Branch; External Services Organization; External Security Organization of Hezbollah
history – formed in 1982 following the Israeli invasion of Lebanon as a Shia militant group that takes its ideological inspiration from the Iranian revolution and the teachings of the late Ayatollah KHOMEINI; generally follows the religious guidance of the Iranian Supreme Leader, which since 1989 has been Ali Hoseini-KHAMENEI; closely allied with Iran and the two often work together on shared initiatives, although Hizballah also acts independently in some cases; shares a close relationship with the Syrian ASAD regime and has provided assistance – including thousands of fighters – to regime forces in the Syrian civil war; since the early 1990s, has evolved into a business and political enterprise and become a state within a state in Lebanon with strong influence in Lebanon's Shia community; actively participates in Lebanon's political system and runs social programs, such as hospitals and schools; has seats in Lebanon's parliament and has had members appointed to the Lebanese Government's ministries; military capabilities continue to expand and have the characteristics of both a paramilitary and a conventional military force; fought a month-long war with Israel in 2006 and continues to prepare for large-scale conflict with Israel; from 2019-2023, engaged in periodic tit-for-tat hostile exchanges with Israel, typically involving Hizballah missile or rocket attacks, followed by Israeli air strikes; following the terrorist group HAMAS's attack on Israel in October 2023 and subsequent Israeli invasion of Gaza, Hizballah has sought to demonstrate solidarity with HAMAS by launching barrages of missiles, rockets, and armed drones into northern Israel; these attacks continued into 2024 and have been countered by strikes from Israel on Hizballah targets in Lebanon
goals – accrue military resources and political power and defend its position of strength in Lebanon; seeks to expel Western influence from Lebanon and the greater Middle East, destroy the state of Israel, and establish Islamic rule in Lebanon and the Palestinian territories
leadership and organization – Naim QASSEM; former leader (secretary general) Shaykh Sayyid Hasan NASRALLAH, who had led the group since 1992, was killed by an Israeli airstrike in September 2024; prior to NASRALLAH's death the secretary general had led with two deputies through a seven-seat Shura Council; the Council has five subordinate specialized assemblies: the Executive, Judicial, Parliamentary, Political, and Jihad Councils; each assembly oversees several sub-entities that handle Hizballah's affairs in various sectors; for example, the Jihad/Military council reportedly has two wings, the Islamic Resistance (combat operations) and the Security Organ (external and internal security operations): Islamic Resistance is organized into territorial commands and units of infantry, artillery, rockets, coastal defense, and commandos/special forces (Unit 1800 or Radwan Force); Hizballah also has Lebanese militia "brigades" which serve as auxiliary forces; the Security Organ has two sub-branches: the Islamic Jihad Organization (External Security Organization, aka Unit 910) for external operations, including the group's international terrorist operations, recruitment, fundraising, intelligence gathering, and support to Shia militias abroad; and the Party Security Organ is responsible for internal security; has a youth movement known as the al-Mahdi Scouts
areas of operation – headquartered in the southern suburbs of Beirut with a significant presence in the Bekaa Valley and southern Lebanon; however, operates around the world, and operatives and financiers have been arrested or detained in Africa, Asia, Europe, the Middle East, South America, and North America; deployed thousands of fighters to support the ASAD Government during the Syrian civil war and continues to maintain a presence there
targets, tactics, and weapons – targets Israeli security forces, civilians, and interests; Jews; US and Western military forces and other symbols of American/Western influence in the Middle East; entities in Syria combatting the ASAD regime, particularly Islamic State and al-Qa'ida affiliated forces; historically used a variety of guerrilla-style hit-and-run and terrorist tactics, particularly kidnappings and suicide vehicle bombings; some of its most devastating attacks involved the use of car/truck bombs, such as the 1983 attacks on the US Embassy, the US Marine barracks, and a French military base in Beirut, which killed over 300 civilians and military personnel; has conducted attacks on Israeli and Jewish targets abroad, including the 1992 bombing of the Israeli Embassy in Argentina and the 1994 suicide bombing of a Jewish community center in Argentina, which killed more than 100 and wounded more than 500 others; since the 2000s, has developed elements of a more traditional state-like conventional military force and demonstrated considerable military capabilities in the 2006 conflict with Israel and during the Syrian civil war; forces are equipped with small arms, light and heavy machineguns, mortars, landmines, improvised explosive devises, artillery, armored combat vehicles, rockets, antiaircraft guns, ballistic missiles, anti-ship cruise missiles, armed unmanned aerial vehicles/drones, man-portable air defense systems, and antitank guided missiles; the group is estimated to have as many as 150,000 missiles and rockets of various types and ranges
strength – estimated in 2024 to have up to 50,000 armed combatants, divided between full-time and reserve personnel; in 2021, NASRALLAH claimed the group had 100,000 trained fighters
financial and other support – receives most of its funding, training, and weapons, as well as political, diplomatic, and organizational aid, from Iran; in 2019, funding from Iran was estimated at more than $700 million per year, although economic sanctions since 2020 may have constrained Iran's ability to finance the group; Syria also furnishes training, weapons, and diplomatic and political support; has developed a network of training camps in Lebanon and runs most of its own military training; receives additional funding in the form of legal businesses, international criminal enterprises (including smuggling, narcotics trafficking, and money laundering), and donations from the Shia in Lebanon and Lebanese diaspora communities worldwide
designation – placed on the US Department of State's list of Foreign Terrorist Organizations on 8 October 1997

Hizbul Mujahideen (HM)
aka – Hizb-ul-Mujahideen; Party of Mujahideen; Party of Holy Warriors
history – formed in 1989 and is one of the largest and oldest militant separatist groups fighting against Indian rule in the state of Jammu and Kashmir; reportedly operated in Afghanistan through the mid-1990s and trained alongside the Afghan Hizb-e-Islami Gulbuddin until the Taliban takeover; made up primarily of ethnic Kashmiris and has conducted operations jointly with other Kashmiri militant groups; active in 2022

goals – supports the liberation of the territory of Jammu and Kashmir from Indian control and its accession to Pakistan, although some cadres are pro-independence
leadership and organization – led by Syed SALAHUDDIN (aka Mohammad Yusuf SHAH); reportedly organized in five regionally-based divisions; probably operates in small loosely connected networks and cells
areas of operation – headquartered in Pakistan but conducts operations primarily in India, particularly the Indian Union Territory of Jammu and Kashmir
targets, tactics, and weapons – focuses attacks on Indian security forces and politicians in the state of Jammu and Kashmir; most attacks involved small arms and grenades, although it has also utilized improvised explosive devices, including vehicle-mounted
strength – specific numbers not available, but information from 2020 suggested a cadre of up to 1,500 fighters
financial and other support – specific sources of support are not clear, but probably originate in Pakistan, as well as from local fundraising
designation – placed on the US Department of State's list of Foreign Terrorist Organizations on 17 August 2017

Hurras al-Din

aka – Tanzim Hurras al-Din; Tandhim Hurras al-Din; Hurras al-Deen; Houras al-Din; HAD; al-Qa'ida in Syria (AQS); Guardians of the Religion Organization; Sham al-Ribat
history – publicly announced itself in February 2018 as an al-Qa'ida affiliate after its members broke away from al-Nusrah Front (subsequently rebranded as Hayat Tahrir al-Sham, or HTS) because HTS publicly cut ties with al-Qa'ida; maintains allied or cooperative relationships with several extremist elements in Syria, including Jamaat Ansar al-Islam, the Turkestan Islamic Party (TIP), Sham al-Islam, and Ansar al-Tawhid; viewed as the leading force behind the "Incite the Believers" jihadist alliance in Syria, which conducts battlefield operations against Syrian Government forces in northern Syria; since 2020, has had a tense relationship HTS/al-Nusrah Front, which controls Syria's northwestern province of Iblib, that has involved assassinations, open clashes, competition for recruits, and arrests of its members by HTS; rejected the March 2020 Russian-Turkish ceasefire agreement in Idlib and has since conducted attacks on Russian, Syrian, and Turkish forces; an aggressive, wide-scale campaign by HTS to detain HAD members since 2020 has hampered the group's ability to conduct operations and prompted some members to defect from the group; remained active in 2024 but was overshadowed by HTS
goals – oust Syrian President Bashar al-ASAD's regime and replace it with a Sunni Islamic State; likely adheres to al-Qa'ida's chief objectives of neutralizing Israeli and US influence within the Middle East, specifically within the Levant
leadership and organization – led by Samir HIJAZI (aka Abu Hamamm al-Shami, Faruq al-Suri, Mohammed Abu Khalid al-Suri); has a shura council; as of 2020, claimed to be comprised of 16 jihadist factions; sub-structure not available, but operational units probably organized into cells and "battalions"
areas of operation – mostly in the Syrian provinces of Idlib and Latakia, with a small presence in Dara'a
targets, tactics, and weapons – primarily attacks Syrian Government and pro-regime forces; has also conducted armed assaults against Turkish and Russian military forces active in Syria; potentially responsible for the kidnapping of aid workers in northwestern Syria; has encouraged violent attacks against Israeli and Western targets in its propaganda releases; employs insurgent-type tactics; has conducted assassinations and car bombings; armed largely with small arms, bombs, explosives (including vehicle mounted improvised explosive devices), mortars, machine guns, and trucks mounting machine guns (aka "technicals")
strength – estimated in 2024 have 1,500-2,000 members, including foreigners and associated armed factions; since 2020, the group has suffered considerable losses during its conflict with HTS
financial and other support – appeals for donations under the auspices of supporting its efforts against the Syrian Government; leverages social media platforms to call for financial assistance, public support, and recruits; active in training operatives at a number of unspecified training camps in Syria
designation – placed on the US Department of State's list of Foreign Terrorist Organizations on 5 September 2019

Indian Mujahedeen (IM)

aka – Indian Mujahidin; Islamic Security Force-Indian Mujahideen (ISF-IM)
history – formed as an ultra-conservative Islamic movement circa 2004 from remnants of the radical youth organization Students Islamic Movement of India; responsible for dozens of bomb attacks throughout India since 2005 and the deaths of hundreds of civilians; maintains ties to other terrorist entities including Pakistan-based Lashkar e-Tayyiba, Jaish-e-Mohammed, and Harakat ul-Jihad Islami; outlawed in India in 2010; by 2016, was increasingly linked to the Islamic State of Iraq and ash-Sham (ISIS); that year, six IM operatives were identified in an ISIS propaganda video threatening attacks on India, and an IM cell linked to ISIS was reportedly plotting attacks on multiple targets in India; Indian authorities claimed they disrupted bombing plots by the group in 2015 and 2017 and have apprehended dozens of suspected IM operatives; has not publicly claimed any attacks in recent years
goals – establish Islamic rule in India; stated goal is to carry out terrorist operations against Indians for their perceived oppression of Muslims
leadership and organization – not available; Indian security services have captured or killed a number of alleged leaders of the group, including co-founder Yasin BHATKAL, who was arrested in 2018; organization not available but probably operates in small, loosely connected networks and cells
areas of operation – India; also reportedly active in Nepal and Pakistan
targets, tactics, and weapons – known for carrying out multiple coordinated bombings in crowded areas against Indian and Western civilian and economic targets, including restaurants and commercial centers; in 2008, was responsible for 16 synchronized bomb blasts in crowded urban centers, including an attack in Delhi that killed 30 people and an attack at a local hospital in Ahmedabad that killed 38 (note - in 2022, an Indian court sentenced 38 individuals to death for the attack in Aghmedabad); in 2010, bombed a popular German bakery frequented by tourists in Pune, India, killing 17 and wounding more than 60 people; attackers typically have used improvised explosive devices
strength – not available
financial and other support – probably receives funding and support from other terrorist organizations, as well as from unspecified donors in Pakistan and the Middle East
designation – placed on the US Department of State's list of Foreign Terrorist Organizations on 19 September 2011

Islamic Jihad Union (IJU)

aka – Islamic Jihad Group; IJG; Islomiy Jihod Ittihodi; al-Djihad al-Islami; Dzhamaat Modzhakhedov; Islamic Jihad Group of Uzbekistan; Jamiat al-Jihad al-Islami; Jamiyat; The Jamaat Mojahedin; The Kazakh Jama'at; The Libyan Society
history – emerged in 2002 as a splinter movement of the Islamic Movement of Uzbekistan (IMU) after internal splits over goals; originally known as the Islamic Jihad Group but was renamed Islamic Jihad Union in 2005; committed to overthrowing the government of Uzbekistan, but has been active in other areas outside Central Asia, particularly Afghanistan, but also Pakistan, Syria, and Europe; pledged allegiance to the Afghan Taliban

in August 2015 and participated in Taliban attacks on the Afghan city of Kunduz, as well as Afghan military bases; continued to maintain a presence in Afghanistan following 2021 Taliban takeover; participated in the Syrian conflict as part of a coalition of al-Qa'ida-linked terrorist groups
goals – overthrow the Uzbek government and replace it with an Islamic state; support al-Qa'ida's overall goals, including efforts to create an Islamic State in Syria
leadership and organization – Ilimbek MAMATOV; probably operates in a loose network of cells
areas of operation – Afghanistan, Syria, Turkey, Uzbekistan, and Europe
targets, tactics, and weapons – targets international and Afghan military and security forces in Afghanistan and Syrian regime forces using a variety of guerrilla warfare and terrorist tactics; has attacked security checkpoints, law enforcement facilities, market places, and foreign embassies in Uzbekistan, often with suicide bombers; in 2007, an IJU cell in Germany (known as the "Sauerland Cell") attempted to construct and detonate a series of car bombs to carry out a mass attack, but the militants were arrested before they could carry out the attack and were ultimately convicted; fighters are armed with small arms, light and heavy machine guns, rocket-propelled grenades, antiaircraft weapons, and various explosives including improvised explosive devices and car bombs
strength – estimated in 2023 to have 200-250 members in Afghanistan
financial and other support – specific sources of support are not available but probably receives assistance from allied terrorist groups and sympathetic donors
designation – placed on the US Department of State's list of Foreign Terrorist Organizations on 17 June 2005

Islamic Movement of Uzbekistan (IMU)
aka – Islamic Party of Uzbekistan; Islamskaia partiia Turkestana;, byvshee Islamskoe dvizhenie Uzbekistana; Islamic Movement of Turkistan
history – formed in the early 1990s as a Sunni Muslim armed group in Uzbekistan's part of the Ferghana Valley, where the Uzbek, Kyrgyz, and Tajik borders converge; moved to Pakistan after the US-led invasion of Afghanistan in 2001; operated primarily along the Afghanistan-Pakistan border and in northern Afghanistan, where it fought against international forces despite its goal of setting up an Islamic state in Uzbekistan; was allied to al-Qa'ida, the Afghan Taliban, and Tehrik-i-Taliban Pakistan, and frequently conducted joint operations with those organizations; in 2011, some fighters broke off to fight separately alongside the Taliban against the Afghan Government under the name Khatiba Imam al-Bukhari, which had fighters in both Afghanistan and Syria as of 2022; in 2015, a significant faction, including the IMU's top leadership, pledged loyalty to the Islamic State of Iraq and ash-Sham (ISIS) and began cooperating with ISIS-Khorasan (ISIS-K); numerous IMU members, including its leader, were subsequently reported to have been killed in clashes with their former Taliban allies; operational tempo has decreased in recent years, but the group was active into 2024
goals – overthrow the Uzbek Government and establish an Islamic state
leadership and organization – Samatov MAMASOLI (aka Abu Ali); probably structured as a network of cells
areas of operation – Afghanistan, Pakistan, Syria, Turkey, and Central Asia
targets, tactics, and weapons – targeted military and security forces and government facilities using guerrilla warfare and terrorist tactics, including ambushes, assassinations, ground assaults, indirect fire attacks, kidnappings, and suicide bombings; in 2010 the IMU claimed responsibility for an ambush that killed 25 Tajik troops in Tajikistan; in 2014, it claimed responsibility for an attack on Karachi's international airport that resulted in the deaths of at least 39 people, as well as a 2012 attack on a Pakistani prison that freed nearly 400 prisoners (both attacks conducted jointly with the Tehrik-i-Taliban Pakistan terrorist group); also has attacked government and allied foreign military forces in Afghanistan, as well as security forces in Pakistan; typically used small arms and light weapons, mortars, rockets, and various explosives, including car bombs and suicide vests
strength – unclear; reportedly about 700 in 2021, including family members
financial and other support – receives support from a large Uzbek diaspora, allied terrorist organizations, and sympathizers from Europe, Central and South Asia, and the Middle East; also engages in narcotics trafficking and conducts kidnappings for ransom
designation – placed on the US Department of State's list of Foreign Terrorist Organizations on 25 September 2000

Islamic Revolutionary Guard Corps (IRGC)/Qods Force
aka – Islamic Revolutionary Guards, Pasdaran (Guards), Revolutionary Guards, Sepah (Corps), Sepah-e Pasdaran-e Enghelab-e Eslami; Quds ("Jerusalem") Force
history – formed in May 1979 in the immediate aftermath of Shah Mohammad Reza PAHLAVI's fall, as leftists, nationalists, and Islamists jockeyed for power; while the interim prime minister controlled the government and state institutions, such as the army, followers of Ayatollah Ruhollah KHOMEINI organized counterweights, including the IRGC, to protect the Islamic revolution; the IRGC's command structure bypassed the elected president and went directly to KHOMEINI; the Iran-Iraq War (1980–88) transformed the IRGC into more of a conventional fighting force with its own ground, air, naval, and special forces, plus control over Iran's strategic missile and rocket forces; the IRGC is highly institutionalized and a parallel military force to Iran's regular armed forces (Artesh); is heavily involved in internal security and have significant influence in the political and economic spheres of Iranian society, as well as Iran's foreign policy; its special operations forces are known as the Qods Force which specializes in foreign missions, providing advice, funding, guidance, material support, training, and weapons to militants in countries such as Afghanistan, Bahrain, Lebanon, Iraq, Syria, and Yemen, as well as extremist groups, including al-Ashtar Brigades, Asa'ib Ahl al-Haqq, HAMAS, Hizballah, Kata'ib Hizballah, and Palestine Islamic Jihad
goals – protect Iran's Islamic revolution and the state; spread Iranian/Shia influence; provide internal security, including border control, law enforcement, and suppressing domestic opposition; influence Iran's politics, economy, and foreign policy
leadership and organization – General Hossein SALAMI is the commander of the IRGC; Brigadier General Ismail QAANI is the commander of the Qods Force; organized along the lines of a traditional conventional military force with Ground Forces, Navy (includes marines), Aerospace Force (includes the strategic missile forces), Cyber Command, Qods Force (special operations), and Basij Paramilitary Forces (aka Popular Mobilization Army); the IRGC ground forces are deployed throughout Iran in all 31 provinces and Tehran and include a broad mix of armored, infantry, mechanized, and commando units, which are postured to counter internal unrest or a ground invasion; the IRGC also has branches for intelligence, counterintelligence, and security; the Qods Force is reportedly divided into branches focusing on intelligence/espionage, finance, politics, sabotage, and special operations, as well as regionally-focused directorates; the Basij is a volunteer paramilitary group under the IRGC with local organizations across the country which augment internal security
areas of operation – headquartered in Tehran; active throughout Iran and the Middle East region, as well as Afghanistan, Gaza, Iraq, Lebanon, Syria, and Yemen; has a worldwide capability to commit attacks if Iranian leadership deems it appropriate; in recent years, Qods Force planning for terror attacks has been uncovered and disrupted in a number of countries worldwide, including Albania, Bahrain, Belgium, Bosnia, Bulgaria, Denmark, France, Germany, Kenya, Turkey, and the US
targets, tactics, and weapons – targets US, Israeli, Saudi, and UAE interests, as well as Iranian dissident groups; has the capability to fight conventionally and conduct a wide-range of terrorist-type attacks; armed as a conventional military with typical ground, air, and naval platforms and weapons; the IRGC-QF also has active and growing cyberwarfare capabilities; also makes extensive use of proxy and partner forces such as Hizballah, Shia militias in Iraq, and the Houthis in Yemen; has provided a wide range of arms to proxy/partner forces, including small arms, rockets,

rocket-propelled grenades, air defense systems, coastal defense cruise missiles, improvised explosive devises (IEDs), anti-aircraft weapons, armor-piercing explosively formed projectiles, and armed unmanned aerial vehicles (UAVs)/drones
strength – IRGC: estimated in 2023 to have up to 190,000 personnel, including 5-15,000 in the Qods Force; Basij Paramilitary Forces: estimated 100,000 full-time, uniformed personnel; the Basij reportedly can mobilize several hundred thousand additional personnel when required
financial and other support – receives a portion of the Iranian defense budget, by some estimates as much as 50%; IRGC-linked companies control up to 20% of Iran's economy; Qods Force also exerts control over strategic industries, commercial services, and black-market enterprises, and has engaged in large-scale illicit finance schemes and money laundering
designation – placed on the US Department of State's list of Foreign Terrorist Organizations on 15 April 2019

Islamic State of Iraq and ash-Sham – Democratic Republic of the Congo (ISIS-DRC)

aka – Allied Democratic Forces (ADF); Madina Tawheed wal Mujahideen ("the City of Monotheism and Holy Warriors"); Islamic State of Iraq and ash-Sham – Central Africa (ISIS-CA); Islamic State's Central Africa Province (ISCAP); Wilayat Central Africa; Wilayah Central Africa
history – first mentioned as "ISIS-Central Africa" in an August 2018 speech by then-ISIS leader al-BAGHDADI; claimed its first attack against the Democratic Republic of the Congo (DRC) military near the border with Uganda in April 2019; has its origins in the DRC-based militant group Allied Democratic Forces (ADF), which was founded in 1995 with the stated goal of overthrowing the Ugandan Government but shifted in the late 1990s to carrying out attacks against civilians, military forces, and UN peacekeepers in the DRC; many of ADF's early members came from Uganda's Salafist movement; online posts by some ADF members in 2016 and 2017 referred to their group as Madina Tawheed wal Mujahideen ("the City of Monotheism and Holy Warriors") and displayed an ISIS-like flag; ISIS-DRC has been notorious for its brutal violence against Congolese citizens and regional military forces, with attacks killing approximately 5,000 civilians between 2014 and 2021, including more than 1,000 in 2021 and nearly 850 in 2020; in 2020 and 2022, it launched assaults on two prisons in eastern DRC that resulted in the escape of approximately 2,000 prisoners, including several hundred ISIS/ADF fighters and sympathizers; the group implemented its first suicide bombing in Goma in 2022 and has subsequently conducted several more; since 2022, it has continued conducting attacks and been engaged in fighting with DRC and international military forces; the group continued to be active in 2024
goals – implement ISIS's strict interpretation of sharia and establish an Islamic state in central Africa
leadership and organization – Seka Musa BALUKU, who presides over a shura/executive council of senior leaders, including a military commander; military wing reportedly has sub-commanders for intelligence, operations, training, finances, logistics, and medical services
areas of operation – DRC, primarily in the Nord Kivu and Ituri provinces; also active in Uganda; has emerged as a regional conduit for facilitating funds transfers to ISIS cells in East Africa
targets, tactics, and weapons – Congolese civilians, particularly Christians, and military/security forces, as well as UN personnel; has attacked churches and schools; methods include insurgent-type tactics, direct ground assaults, small-scale attacks, indiscriminate killings, ambushes, assassinations, kidnappings, and suicide bombings; ADF was sanctioned in 2014 by the US Department of the Treasury and the UN under the UN Security Council's DRC sanctions regime for its violence and atrocities; uses small arms, machine guns, improvised explosive devices, rocket-propelled grenades, mortars, and unmanned aerial vehicles (UAVs)/drones
strength – assessed in 2024 to have 1,500-2,000 fighters
financial and other support – reportedly receives some funding from control of mines and the export of minerals, as wells as from ISIS-Core through a web of financial mechanisms running through Kenya, Somalia, South Africa and Uganda; arms include seized weapons and ammunition from the DRC military
designation – placed on the US Department of State's list of Foreign Terrorist Organizations on 10 March 2021

Islamic State of Iraq and ash-Sham - East Asia (ISIS-EA) in the Philippines

aka – ISIS in the Philippines (ISIS-P); ISIL Philippines; ISIL in the Philippines; IS Philippines (ISP); Islamic State in the Philippines; Islamic State in Iraq and Syria in Southeast Asia; ISIS-East Asia; IS-EA; Dawlah Islamiyah; Dawlatul Islamiyah Waliyatul Masrik; Dawlatul Islamiyah Waliyatul Mashriq; IS East Asia Division; ISIS Branch in the Philippines; ISIS "Philippines province"
history – Islamic militants in the Philippines initially pledged allegiance to ISIS in 2014, however the group officially formed in 2016 with now-deceased leader Isnilon HAPILON as the first amir; ISIS media claimed its first attack in the Philippines against Philippine soldiers on Mindanao Island in March 2016; in May 2017, ISIS-EA and fighters from associated jihadist groups stormed and captured the city of Marawi on Mindanao; five months of subsequent fighting for the city between the militants and the Philippine military resulted in nearly 900 militants and more than 160 Philippine soldiers killed; over 300,000 residents were forced to flee the area during the fighting; in 2018, the group conducted the first ever suicide attack in the Philippines; ISIS-EA has since claimed several additional suicide and other high-profile bombings, including two suicide bombings undertaken by females within one hour of one another in August of 2020 in the capital of Sulu province; remained active as of 2024 with low-level attacks and clashes with Philippine security forces
goals – create an Islamic state in the southern Philippines and across Southeast Asia adhering to ISIS's strict interpretation of sharia
leadership and organization – Esmael Abdulmalik (aka Abu Turaife) has been touted by pro-ISIS media channels as the emir in 2024; ISIS-EA is comprised of a decentralized, loose network of groups with varying levels of allegiance and ties to ISIS, including the Abu Sayaf Group (ASG), the Maute Group (aka Daulah Islamiyah Fi Ranao, Islamic State of Lanao, Abu Zacaria Group), Ansar al-Khilafah Philippines (AKP), and a faction of the Bangsamoro Islamic Freedom Fighters (BIFF); these groups operate autonomously and maintain their own leaders and organizational structures
areas of operation – southern Philippines
targets, tactics, and weapons – targets Philippine security forces and non-Muslim civilians; has attacked government-related targets, military bases and security checkpoints, churches, internet cafés, resorts, and street festivals; employs insurgent-type tactics, including armed assaults, mortar attacks, suicide bombers, and road-side bombs; weapons include small arms, improvised explosive devices, light and heavy machine guns, rocket-propelled grenades, mortars, and hand grenades
strength – estimated in 2022 to have up to 500 combatants
financial and other support – receives some financial assistance from ISIS-core, but mostly relies on criminal activities such as kidnappings for ransom and extortion; maintains training camps in remote areas under its control and acquires weapons through smuggling and captured or black market purchases of Philippine military arms; receives some media support from ISIS-core
designation – placed on the US Department of State's list of Foreign Terrorist Organizations on 28 February 2018

Islamic State of Iraq and ash-Sham – Mozambique (ISIS-M)

aka – Ansar al-Sunna; Helpers of Tradition; Ahl al-Sunna wal-Jamaa (ASWJ); Adherents to the Traditions and the Community; al-Shabaab in Mozambique; Islamic State Central Africa province; Wilayah Central Africa; Ansaar Kalimat Allah; Supporters of the Word of Allah, "Mashababos"
history – based on a domestic terrorist group known as Ansar al-Sunna (aka al-Shabaab, among other names) that has conducted an insurgency against the Mozambique Government since 2017, and ISIS publicly recognized as an affiliate in June 2019; since 2017, violence associated with the group has led to the deaths of approximately 5,000 civilians, security force members, and suspected ISIS-M militants, and displaced

approximately 1 million persons in northern Mozambique (as of 2024); the group was responsible for orchestrating a series of large-scale and sophisticated attacks resulting in the capture of the port of Mocimboa da Praia, Cabo Delgado Province in August 2020, which it held for a year; in March 2021, it seized the northern Mozambican town of Palma, holding it for four days while killing dozens of civilians and security personnel; during the attack, the group targeted the local airfield, an army barracks, several banks, and a food storage warehouse; in 2021-2022, several African countries sent military troops to assist the Mozambique Government's efforts to defeat the group; these military operations have resulted in setbacks to ISIS-M, including considerable casualties and the destruction of some bases and training camps; nevertheless, the group continued to be active in 2024 and was showing signs of resurgence
goals – implement ISIS's strict interpretation of sharia and establish an Islamic state
leadership and organization – led by Abu Yasir HASSAN; organizational information limited but reportedly has regional commands; operates mostly in semi-autonomous cells, although the group has shown the ability to mass fighters for specific attacks
areas of operation – northern Mozambique; primarily Cabo Delgado province; has also conducted attacks in Nampula and Niassa provinces; has conducted cross-border attacks in Tanzania
targets, tactics, and weapons – has attacked army barracks, police stations, security checkpoints, government buildings, banks, churches, and gas stations, and captured entire villages and towns; attacks characterized by ambushes and direct assaults on government security forces and foreign private security contractors, murders of gas industry workers and contractors, indiscriminate killings of civilians, including women and children, beheadings, kidnappings, and looting and burning out villages; in April 2020, the group killed more than 50 young men in a village for reportedly resisting recruitment; has been accused of wholesale abductions of women and girls; armed with small arms, machine guns, improvised explosives, mortars, and rocket-propelled grenades (RPG); has also used motorboats to conduct raids on coastal villages
strength – unclear; had an estimated 1,200 fighters in 2022 but has since reportedly incurred heavy casualties from multinational military operations; as of 2024, was estimated to have less than 250 fighters
financial and other support – unclear, although the group has targeted banks; the area's natural resources, including gas, gems, timber, and wildlife present opportunities for fund-raising; in addition, the group has taken control of food supplies in areas under its control; weapons typically captured from government security forces
designation – placed on the US Department of State's list of Foreign Terrorist Organizations on 10 March 2021

Islamic State of Iraq and ash-Sham - Sinai Province (ISIS-SP)
aka – Islamic State-Sinai Province (IS-SP); ISIS-Sinai Province; ISIS-Sinai; ISIL Sinai Province (ISIL-SP); The State of Sinai; Wilayat Sinai; Islamic State in the Sinai; Ansar Bayt al-Maqdes; Ansar Beit al-Maqdis; Jamaat Ansar Beit al-Maqdis; Jamaat Ansar Beit al-Maqdis fi Sinaa; Ansar Jerusalem; Supporters of Jerusalem; Supporters of the Holy Place; Allies of the Holy House
history – began as Ansar Bayt al-Maqdis (ABM), which rose to prominence in 2011 following the uprisings in Egypt; ABM was responsible for attacks against Egyptian and Israeli government and security elements and against tourists in Egypt; in November 2014, ABM officially declared allegiance to ISIS; has since conducted a bloody insurgency against Egyptian security forces under the ISIS banner and become one of the most deadly of the ISIS affiliates; the Egyptian Government deployed thousands of military troops and other security personnel to the Sinai to suppress the insurgency; as of 2023, the group continued to conduct attacks, although the scale of the insurgency had declined
goals – spread the Islamic caliphate by eliminating the Egyptian government, destroying Israel, and establishing an Islamic emirate in the Sinai
leadership and organization – current leader not available; reportedly has sections or branches for security, military affairs, bomb-making, and media operations
areas of operation – Egypt; operations are conducted primarily in the Sinai Peninsula, but its reach periodically extends to Cairo, the Egyptian Nile Valley, and Gaza
targets, tactics, and weapons – mainly targets Egyptian security forces, particularly checkpoints, convoys, and bases; conducts ambushes, assassinations, complex attacks involving dozens of attackers, car and suicide bombings, kidnappings, public executions, and road side bombings attacks; conducted large armed assaults on a military base in 2018 and on the Egyptian city of Sheikh Zuweid in 2014; both attacks included dozens of fighters with small arms, light and heavy machine guns, rocket-propelled grenades, mortars, car bombs, and suicide bombers; also targets Egyptian Government facilities and officials, oil pipelines and other infrastructure, tourists, religious minorities, government-allied tribes, places of worship, and airliners; two of its most deadly attacks were the 2017 assault by suicide bombers and gunmen on an Egyptian Sufi mosque that killed more than 300 and the 2015 bombing of a Russian airliner from the Egyptian resort town of Sharm el-el-Sheikh, which killed all 231 on board
strength – estimated in 2022 to have less than 1,000 fighters
financial and other support – receives funding from external actors, including core ISIS, and from smuggling; weapons reportedly are smuggled in from Gaza, Sudan, and Libya
designation – placed on the US Department of State's list of Foreign Terrorist Organizations on 9 April 2014

Islamic State of Iraq and ash-Sham - West Africa (ISIS-WA)
aka – Islamic State West Africa Province (ISWAP); Islamic State of Iraq and the Levant-West Africa (ISIL-WA); Islamic State of Iraq and Syria West Africa Province; ISIS West Africa Province; ISIS-West Africa (ISIS-WA); Wilayat Gharb Ifriqiyya
history – formed in 2015-2016 when a faction of Boko Haram broke off and pledged allegiance to ISIS; the split occurred primarily because of the indiscriminate violence Boko Haram inflicted on Muslims; since its founding, has waged an insurgency against the Nigerian Government, overrunning dozens of military bases and killing hundreds of soldiers; by 2019, reportedly controlled hundreds of square miles of territory in the Lake Chad region where it governed according to a strict interpretation of Islamic law and attempted to cultivate support among local civilians by focusing on filling gaps in governance; claimed additional attacks against Nigerian and regional military forces in 2021-2024; during the same period, it was also engaged in fighting with Boko Haram and had reportedly far outstripped Boko Haram in size and capacity; between 2009 and 2023, jihadist violence associated with Boko Haram and ISIS-WA had killed an estimated 35-40,000 people, mostly civilians, and displaced as many as 3 million persons
goals – implement ISIS's strict interpretation of sharia and replace regional governments with an Islamic state
leadership and organization – not available; Abu Musab al-BARNAWI reportedly killed in 2021 by Nigerian military; group is led by a shura council; has military and regional commanders/leaders; probably operates in small units and cells that mass for larger operations
areas of operation – Nigeria (primarily the northeast, but as of 2024 had reportedly spread to other regions of the country, including in and around the capital Abuja; greater Lake Chad region (including southeast Niger, northern Cameroon, and areas of Chad near Lake Chad)
targets, tactics, and weapons – seeks to de-legitimize the Nigerian Government by focusing its attacks on security forces, state-sponsored civilian defense groups, government targets, infrastructure, and individuals who collaborate with the government; attacks military bases and mobile columns; in 2018-2019, it overran more than 20 military bases in northeastern Nigeria, including one assault that resulted in the deaths of some 100 soldiers; in 2022, it claimed responsibility for an attack on a prison in Nigeria's capital Abuja which freed nearly 900 inmates including 60 of its members; employs ambushes, complex ground assaults, hit-and-run attacks, targeted killings, road side bombs, and kidnappings of security

forces personnel; has also conducted attacks against Boko Haram and engaged in the kidnapping and murder of aid workers and Christians, as well as civilians who aid the Nigerian military; fighters typically equipped with small arms, light and heavy machine guns, vehicle mounted weapons, rocket-propelled grenades, mines, rockets, improvised explosive devices (including vehicle-mounted), armored vehicles (including tanks), and unmanned aerial vehicles
strength – estimated in 2024 to have 4-7,000 active fighters
financial and other support – receives some funding from core ISIS and local sources, including kidnappings-for-ransom, other criminal activities, taxation, extortion, and some farming activities; has captured a considerable number of vehicles, weapons, and ammunition from the Nigerian military; maintains training camps and has publicly advertised a "Caliphate Cadet School" featuring children between 8-16 years old undergoing indoctrination and military-style training; has links to ISIS-Greater Sahara
designation – placed on the US Department of State's list of Foreign Terrorist Organizations on 28 February 2018

Islamic State of Iraq and ash-Sham in Bangladesh (ISB)
aka – ISIS-Bangladesh, Caliphate in Bangladesh; Caliphate's Soldiers in Bangladesh; Soldiers of the Caliphate in Bangladesh; Khalifa's Soldiers in Bengal; Islamic State Bangladesh; Islamic State in Bangladesh; Islamic State in Bengal; Dawlatul Islam Bengal; ISIB; Abu Jandal al-Bangali; Jammat-ul Mujahadeen-Bangladesh; JMB; Neo-JMB; New JMB
history – formed in 2014-15 out of ISIS's desire to expand to the Indian Subcontinent; consists of individuals who defected from Jamaat-ul-Mujahideen Bangladesh and Jund at-Tawhid wal-Khilafah and pledged allegiance to ISIS; has killed dozens in mostly smaller attacks, including a US citizen, and wounded more than 200 since its formation; active as of 2023
goals – protect Muslims in Bangladesh from perceived injustices and, ultimately, establish an Islamic caliphate in the Indian subcontinent
leadership and organization – led by Mahadi Hasan Jon; probably operates in a cell-based network
areas of operation – operates in major cities throughout Bangladesh
targets and tactics – primarily targets military and security personnel but also activists, bloggers, academics, religious minorities, and foreigners (particularly Westerners); has attacked restaurants, places of worship, government buildings, and crowds of civilians, typically with small arms, grenades, and improvised explosives devices, including suicide bombers; most deadly attack was a 2016 armed assault on a bakery in Dhaka, where the attackers used small arms, grenades, and machetes to kill 24 people
strength – at least several dozen members as of 2022
financial and other support – has received some support from ISIS; other funding sources not available
designation – placed on the US Department of State's list of Foreign Terrorist Organizations on 28 February 2018

Islamic State of Iraq and ash-Sham in Libya (ISIS-L)
aka – ISIS-Libya, Islamic State-Libya; IS-Libya; Islamic State of Iraq and the Levant in Libya (ISIL-L); Wilayat Barqa; Wilayat Fezzan; Wilayat Tripolitania; Wilayat Tarablus; Wilayat al-Tarabulus; Desert Army; Jaysh al-Sahraa
history – formed in 2014 when then ISIS leader Abu Bakr al-BAGHDADI dispatched operatives from Syria to establish a branch; claimed responsibility for its first operation, a suicide attack on a hotel in Tripoli, in January 2015; from 2015 to 2016, grew to as many as 6,000 fighters, established a stronghold in Sirte, and expanded operations into Libya's oil producing region; from late 2016 to 2017, was driven from Sirte into the desert by Libyan forces, with assistance from the US military, while suffering heavy losses in personnel; since 2018, has altered its strategy to what it described as a *nikayah* (war of attrition) of guerrilla warfare and traditional terrorist tactics with small bands of fighters operating out of ungoverned spaces in Libya and conducting attacks throughout the country; claimed several small-scale attacks against local military and security services in 2020-2021 despite losses to government counterterrorism operations; although weakened, the group in 2024 retained some operational capability and was involved in providing logistics support to ISIS groups in the Sahel and in operational activities such as conducting kidnappings for ransom, including of traffickers
goals – prevent the formation of a reunified Libyan state, secure control over the country's oil resources and, ultimately, establish an Islamic caliphate in Libya
leadership and organization – leadership not available; when ISIS-L held territory, its structure included three regionally-based provinces (*wilayat*) with defined state-like departments (*diwans*) and a hierarchal chain of command; operates in cells that are geographically dispersed
areas of operation – unable to control any population centers, but continues to have some mobile desert camps in rural central and southern Libya; assessed to retain an undetermined number of dormant cells in some coastal cities
targets, tactics, and weapons – targets military and security forces, oil infrastructure, and entities or individuals associated with Libya's competing governments; targets include oil facilities, security checkpoints and police stations, and symbolic state targets such as Libya's electoral commission headquarters and the Ministry of Foreign Affairs; also kidnaps local notables for potential prisoner exchanges or ransom; attacks typically are hit-and-run and conducted with small arms and suicide bombers; weapons mostly include small arms, rocket-propelled grenades, mortars, light and heavy machine guns, landmines, and improvised explosive devices
strength – estimated in 2024 to have 300-500 fighters
financial and other support – ISIS core has provided ad hoc financial support; additional funding comes from arms smuggling, taxes on illicit trade routes, kidnappings for ransom, and external sources, such as enterprises run by sympathizers, especially in western Libya; has acquired weapons through captured Libyan military stockpiles and smuggling networks
designation – placed on the US Department of State's list of Foreign Terrorist Organizations on 20 May 2016

Islamic State of Iraq and ash-Sham in the Greater Sahara (ISIS-GS)
aka – ISIS in the Greater Sahara; Islamic State in the Greater Sahel; Islamic State of the Greater Sahel or ISGS; Islamic State's Sahel Province or ISSP; ISIS in the Islamic Sahel; ISIS in the Sahel or ISIS-Sahel
history – emerged in May 2015 when Adnan Abu Walid al-SAHRAWI and his followers split from the al-Qaida-affiliated group al-Murabitoun and pledged allegiance to ISIS; ISIS acknowledged the group in October 2016; has carried out attacks in the Sahel region, including one on a joint US-Nigerien military force operating near the Mali-Niger border in October 2017; since February 2018, has clashed repeatedly with French military forces and allied local militias operating under the French-sponsored counterterrorism operation known as Operation Barkhane, as well as Nigerien, Malian, and Burkinabe troops; for example, conducted attacks against Nigerien and Malian military bases in late 2019 that killed 89 and 54 soldiers, respectively; after a period of some reported cooperation, ISIS-GS has engaged in fighting in with the local al-Qa'ida-aligned coalition known as Jama'at Nusrat al-Islam wal-Muslimin (JNIM) over territory, including control of gold extraction areas and access to buyers, since 2020; as of 2024, it had gained strength and ground in Mali and northern Benin and was actively engaged in clashes with government security forces and JNIM
goals – replace regional governments with an Islamic state; reportedly has not developed a cohesive, ideologically driven narrative but instead tries to adapt its message to what can garner the most support from local communities

leadership and organization – Mohamed Ibrahim al-Salem al-Shafi'i (aka Aba al-Saharawi or al-Sahrawi); probably operates in small mobile, geographically dispersed cells or groups with varying levels of autonomy that consolidate for operations
areas of operation – mostly concentrated in the Mali-Niger border region but also operates in Burkina Faso and northern Benin
targets, tactics, and weapons – targets local military and security forces, foreign military forces (French, UN, US), ethnic groups, local government officials, humanitarian workers, and schools; since 2018, has forced the closure of an estimated 2,000 schools in the region with threats, attacks, and murders of teachers and administrators; employs insurgency-type tactics against military and security forces, including ambushes, targeted killings, hit-and-run attacks, mortar attacks, road side bombs, car and truck bombs, suicide bombers, and direct assaults; ISIS-GS fighters attacking Malian and Nigerien military bases in 2019 used assault rifles, light machine guns, motorcycles, trucks mounting machine guns (aka "technicals"), mortars, and suicide bombers
strength – estimated in 2024 to have up to 2-3,000 fighters
financial and other support – specific sources not available, but probably originates from smuggling activities, local donations and taxation, attacks on gold mines, kidnapping for ransom, theft, and from other groups operating in the region; most of its weapons probably originate from the black market or are captured after attacks on local security forces; has also engaged in the smuggling of weapons, mostly from facilitation networks in southern Libya; has links with ISIS-West Africa
designation – placed on the US Department of State's list of Foreign Terrorist Organizations on 23 May 2018

Islamic State of Iraq and ash-Sham (ISIS)
aka – al-Qa'ida in Iraq; al-Qa'ida Group of Jihad in Iraq; al-Qa'ida Group of Jihad in the Land of the Two Rivers; al-Qa'ida in Mesopotamia; al-Qa'ida in the Land of the Two Rivers; al-Qa'ida of Jihad in Iraq; al-Qa'ida of Jihad Organization in the Land of the Two Rivers; al-Qa'ida of the Jihad in the Land of the Two Rivers; al-Tawhid; Jam'at al-Tawhid Wa'al-Jihad; Tanzeem Qa'idat al Jihad/Bilad al Raafidaini; Tanzim Qa'idat al-Jihad fi Bilad al-Rafidayn; The Monotheism and Jihad Group; The Organization Base of Jihad/Country of the Two Rivers; The Organization Base of Jihad/Mesopotamia; The Organization of al-Jihad's Base in Iraq; The Organization of al-Jihad's Base in the Land of the Two Rivers; The Organization of al-Jihad's Base of Operations in Iraq; The Organization of al-Jihad's Base of Operations in the Land of the Two Rivers; The Organization of Jihad's Base in the Country of the Two Rivers; al-Zarqawi Network; Islamic State of Iraq; Islamic State of Iraq and al-Sham; Islamic State of Iraq and Syria; ad-Dawla al-Islamiyya fi al-'Iraq wa-sh-Sham; Daesh; Dawla al Islamiya; Al-Furqan Establishment for Media Production; Islamic State; ISIL; ISIS; ISIS-Core; Amaq News Agency; Al Hayat Media Center; Al-Hayat Media Center; Al Hayat
history – formed in the 1990s under the name al-Tawhid wal-Jihad by Jordanian militant Abu Mus'ab al-ZARQAWI to oppose the presence of Western military forces in the Middle East and the West's support for, and the existence of, Israel; in late 2004, ZARQAWI pledged allegiance to al-Qa'ida (AQ) and the group became known as al-Qa'ida in Iraq (AQI); ZARQAWI led AQI against US and Coalition Forces in Iraq until his death in June 2006; in October 2006, renamed itself the Islamic State in Iraq; in 2013, adopted the moniker ISIS to express regional ambitions and expanded operations to Syria where it established control of a large portion of eastern Syria; in June 2014, then ISIS leader Abu Bakr al-BAGHDADI declared a worldwide Islamic caliphate with its capital in Raqqa, Syria; by 2015, held an area in Iraq and Syria with an estimated population of between 8 and 12 million, including the Iraqi city of Mosul; imposed a brutal version of Islamic law in the areas under its control and became known for brutality against perceived enemies, including the murder of large numbers of civilians, its large contingent of foreign fighters, and a substantial social media presence; by the end of 2017, had lost control of its largest population centers in both Iraq and Syria, including Mosul and Raqqa, to US and allied military forces; lost its final piece of territory in Baghuz, Syria in March 2019; has since transitioned to an insurgency, reverting to guerrilla warfare and more traditional terrorist tactics, developing sleeper cells, and assimilating into the broader population in Iraq and Syria where it continued to maintain a considerable presence and conduct operations as of 2024
goals – replace the world order with a global Islamic state based in Iraq and Syria, expand its branches and networks globally, and rule according to ISIS's strict interpretation of Islamic law; in Iraq and Syria, it seeks to reestablish itself as a viable insurgency that is capable of seizing and controlling territory
leadership and organization – Abu Hafs al-Hashimi al-Quraishi (likely a nom de guerre) named leader in 2023 after predecessor killed; the top leader (emir) and a senior shura council determine the group's strategic direction and appoints the heads of provinces (*wilayat*); an "appointed (or delegated) committee" and up to 14 sub-bureaus or offices (*dawawin*) are reportedly charged with administrative duties, including security, explosives manufacturing, finances, religious matters, recruitment, military operations, training and education, media functions, resources and plunder, etc.; the group typically operates in small cells or groups of 15 or fewer in Iraq and Syria, but can organize in greater numbers for specific operations; outside of Iraq and Syria, ISIS-Core has adopted a flatter, more networked and decentralized structure, giving greater operational autonomy to its external branches, networks, and claimed provinces; ISIS-Core has relied on its General Directorate of Provinces (GDP) offices to provide funding and operational guidance for these branches, networks, and provinces; GDP offices include: the al-Furqan Office (West Africa and the Sahel); the Dhu al-Nurayn Office (North Africa and Sudan); al-Karrar Office (East, Central, and Southern Africa, and Yemen regions); the Afghanistan-based al-Siddiq Office (South, Central, and Southeast Asia); and the Iraq-based Bilad al-Rafidayn Office
areas of operation – ISIS-Core operations remain predominately in Iraq and Syria; has designated Iraq as a separate province with its own leader; operational in the rural and desert areas of central and northern Iraq, primarily within and near Sunni populations with some presence in major population areas (mostly the provinces of Anbar, Ninewa, Kirkuk, Salah ad Din, and Diyala; maintained safehavens in isolated areas such as the Hamrin Mountains of Kirkuk and the deserts of Anbar); in Syria, it continued to operate mainly in the central desert and across northern and eastern provinces, while top leaders likely remained in the western Idlib governorate; oversees about 20 external branches, networks, or wilayat (provinces, governorates)in more than 20 countries: Algeria, Azerbaijan, Bangladesh, the Caucasus (Russia), Central Africa (the Democratic Republic of the Congo, Mozambique), East Asia (Philippines, Indonesia), Greater Sahara (tri-border area of Burkina Faso, Mali, Niger), India, Libya, Khorasan (Afghanistan), Pakistan, Palestine (Israel), the Sahel (Mali), Sinai Peninsula (Egypt), Saudi Arabia, Somalia, Tunisia, Turkey, West Africa (northeastern Nigeria, southeastern Niger, northern Cameroon, areas of Chad around Lake Chad), and Yemen; local terrorist groups in other countries, such as Lebanon and Sudan, have pledged allegiance to ISIS; has supporters, sympathizers, and associates worldwide and has inspired or conducted attacks in Australia, Belgium, France, Germany, Iran, Maldives, Russia, Spain, Sri Lanka, Sweden, Tajikistan, Turkey, the UK, and the US; authorities in other countries, including, but not exclusive to, Austria, Brazil, Bulgaria, Canada, Greece, Israel, Italy, Jordan, Lebanon, Malaysia, and the Netherlands have arrested ISIS members or supporters or disrupted plots linked to ISIS; maintains a strong online presence and continuously calls for attacks against Western countries and their interests around the world; individuals inspired by its ideology may conduct operations without direction from the ISIS's central leadership
targets, tactics, and weapons – targets governments or groups that oppose its hardline Islamist ideology, including military forces and security services, government officials, perceived Sunni rivals, Westerners, and religious and ethnic minorities; typically targets security forces in Iraq and Syria, as well as tribal and civic leaders and other symbols of government; has also targeted infrastructure in Iraq, such as electrical towers; known for indiscriminate killings, mass executions, political assassinations, torture, kidnappings, rape and sexual slavery, forced marriages and religious conversions, conscripting children, publishing videos of beheadings, and using civilians as human shields; has engaged in the systematic destruction of antiquities, places of worship, monasteries, and other elements of the cultural heritage of ancient communities; attacks places of worship,

shopping centers and markets, tourist sites, hotels, concert venues, restaurants, train stations, nightclubs, government buildings, and infrastructure targets; attacks on civilians typically involve the use of small arms, vehicle bombs, explosive vests, and ramming vehicles into crowds of people; employs insurgent/guerrilla-style hit-and-run, and terrorist attacks against military and security forces that include the use of ambushes, snipers, complex ground/military assaults, mortar and rocket attacks, road side bombs, and suicide devices; possesses a wide variety of weapons, including small arms, light and heavy machine guns, rocket-propelled grenades, mortars, rockets, man-portable air defense systems (MANPADS), anti-tank guided missiles, and a variety of improvised explosive devices, including unmanned aerial vehicles (UAVs) armed with explosives
strength – estimated in 2024 to have 5-7,000 members in Iraq and Syria, most of whom were fighters
note: as of 2023, there were about 11,000 ISIS prisoners in Syrian Democratic Forces prisons, including approximately 2,000 foreign terrorist fighters of around 70 nationalities
financial and other support – raises funds through ad hoc criminal activities, particularly kidnapping for ransom, smuggling, and extortion activities; also receives funds through private donations, crowd-sourcing, online humanitarian appeals, and investments in legitimate businesses; prior to 2019, received virtually of its funding from oil sales, taxation, and selling confiscated goods within areas it controlled in Iraq and Syria; the group currently holds no territory, which has significantly reduced its ability to generate, store, and transfer revenue, but it continues to draw on financial reserves accrued when it controlled territory (estimated in 2020 at more than $100 million); ISIS has armed itself with weapons it has captured, purchased through local arms trafficking networks, and produced on its own; also recruits members, supporters, and sympathizers online through social media platforms
designation – predecessor organization al-Qa'ida in Iraq (AQI) was placed on the US Department of State's list of Foreign Terrorist Organizations on 17 December 2004

Islamic State of Iraq and ash-Sham: self-proclaimed ISIS branches, networks, and provinces (non-FTO designated)
note: this appendix provides short descriptions of identified or self-proclaimed ISIS branches, networks, and provinces that have not been designated by the US State Department as Foreign Terrorist Organizations
Islamic State of Iraq and ash-Sham – Algeria: the Islamic State declared the establishment of a province in Algeria (Wilayat al-Jazair) in November 2014; includes elements of a local terrorist organization known as Jund al-Khilafa; goal is to replace the Algerian Government with an Islamic state; targets security forces, local government figures, and Western interests; largely defunct due to heavy pressure from Algerian security forces, although ISIS core claimed responsibility for a February 2020 attack on a military base near the border with Mali; historically maintained an operational and recruitment presence mostly in the northeastern part of the country
Islamic State of Iraq and ash-Sham network in Azerbaijan: ISIS declared a new network in Azerbaijan in July of 2019, although it has not claimed responsibility for any attacks; additional details of the network unavailable
Islamic State of Iraq and ash-Sham – Caucasus Province: ISIS-Caucasus Province (ISIS-CP; aka Wilayat Qawqaz) was announced in June 2015; grew out of the former al-Qa'ida-affiliated Islamic Emirate of the Caucasus, which suffered from losses to Russian counterterrorism operations, leadership disputes, and defections to ISIS; claimed responsibility for its first attack against a Russian Army barracks in September 2015; claimed at least two attacks on local security forces in 2020, including a suicide bomber who blew himself up in the North Caucasus region of Karachay-Cherkessia, injuring six police officers; Russian security services conducted multiple operations against suspect ISIS militants in 2021; operates in the North Caucasus area of the Russian Federation between the Black Sea and Caspian Sea; typically conducts attacks against local security and military forces, as well as non-Muslim civilians, with small arms, improvised explosives, and knives
Islamic State of Iraq and ash-Sham – India: the Islamic State-India (aka ISI; Islamic State-Hind; Wilayah of Hind) was announced in May 2019 when ISIS claimed it had restructured the group's Khorasan Province and created separate provinces for ISIS-affiliated elements operating in India and Pakistan; the announcement followed an attack claimed by ISIS on Indian security forces in India-administered Kashmir; ISIS-India is reportedly dominated by Kashmiri jihadists and has conducted several additional low-scale attacks targeting Indian security forces in Kashmir; estimated in 2021 to have less than 200 members; presence was assessed as largely online as of 2023; ISIS-linked groups reportedly operating in India include Ansar-ut Tawhid fi Bilad al-Hind, Indian Mujahideen, and Junood-ul-Khilafa-Fil-Hind (aka Jundul Khilafa)
Islamic State of Iraq and ash-Sham – East Asia networks in Indonesia: comprises a loose network of ISIS affiliates, cells, and supporters throughout the country known as Jemaah Anshorut Daulau (JAD), which Aman ABDURRAHMAN (in prison) has led since 2015; goal is to replace the Indonesian Government with an Islamic state and implement ISIS's interpretation of sharia; known for attacking security forces and Christians; in 2019, a JAD member attempted to assassinate Indonesia's security minister and a local police chief; in 2018, staged simultaneous suicide bombings by families, including women and children, against three churches in Surabaya that killed more than 30 civilians; strength unknown, but maintains a clandestine operational presence across the country; local cells maintain their own structures and remain largely autonomous; JAD includes former members of the FTO-designated group Jemaah Ansharut Tauhid (JAT; aka Jemmah Ansharut Tauhid; Laskar 99), which disbanded in 2015 to join JAD (some members reportedly joined al-Qa'ida); has a relationship with the ISIS-affiliated East Indonesia Mujahideen (aka Mujahidin Indonesia Timor, or MIT), which Indonesian police linked to an assault on a village in Sulawesi in late 2020 that killed four; in 2021, Indonesian security forces disrupted planned attacks by JAD and killed the leader of MIT; in 2022, security forces arrested 15 JAD members of the group; JAD was active as of 2024; other ISIS-affiliated groups in Indonesia reportedly include Muhajirin Anshar Tauhid (MAT), Firqah Abu Hamzah (FAH), Jamaah Ansharul Khilafah (JAK), and some factions of Darul Islam/Negara Islam Indonesia (DI/NII)
Islamic State of Iraq and ash-Sham – Pakistan: ISIS announced in May 2019 that it restructured the group's Khorasan Province and created separate provinces for ISIS-affiliates operating in Pakistan; operates mostly in Balochistan and northern Sindh provinces and chiefly targets non-Muslims and the local Shia population, particularly the Hazaras; claimed several attacks Baluchistan in 2020 and early 2021; ISIS has claimed additional attacks in Pakistan, including a March 2022 suicide bombing on a Shia mosque in Peshawar that killed 64, but it is unclear if the attack was carried out by the Pakistan branch or ISIS-Khorasan
Islamic State of Iraq and ash-Sham – Somalia: formed in 2015-2016; splinter group of al-Shabaab and reportedly founded by former al-Shabaab commander Abdulqadir MUMIN (alt. Abdul Qadir Mumin); estimated in 2024 to have 300-500 fighters; operates primarily in the remote mountains of the Bari area of the semi-autonomous Puntland region; targets Somali Government and security forces, Puntland security forces, African Union peacekeepers, and al-Shabaab elements through low-level attacks using small arms and improvised explosive devices, as well as targeted assassinations; continued to be active into 2024; has reportedly gained prominence as a financial support hub for other ISIS groups in Africa
Islamic State of Iraq and ash-Sham cell in Sudan: fully operational since 2019 and headed by Abu Bakr al-Iraqi who was under orders from ISIS core to establish a logistical and financial base in the Sudan; in 2024, the cell was assessed to have 100-200 members, who act as facilitators for logistical movements and transactions
Islamic State of Iraq and ash-Sham network in Tunisia: a network of cells, supporters, and Islamic militant groups in Tunisia claiming allegiance to ISIS, including Jund al-Kilafah (JAK or "Soldiers of the Caliphate"); goal is to replace the Tunisian Government with an Islamic state and implement ISIS's strict interpretation of sharia; since 2015, the network has conducted periodic attacks against security forces and tourist sites frequented by Westerners, such as a resort in Sousse and a museum in Tunis; attacks have included suicide bombings, improvised explosive devices mounted on motorcycles, stabbings, targeted assassinations, and bank robberies; sporadic attacks continued through 2020; claimed an attack in February 2021

that killed 4 soldiers; Tunisian security forces in 2022 claimed it had destroyed at least two terrorist cells linked to ISIS; the network is mostly active in the mountainous region along the border with Algeria, particularly the Chaambi Mountains near the city of Kasserine

Islamic State of Iraq and ash-Sham –Turkey: publicly announced in July 2019 when ISIS released a video of a group of fighters in Turkey pledging allegiance to then-ISIS leader al-BAGHDADI and declaring a new province (wilayat) in Turkey; the speaker threatened both Turkey and the US while the fighters in the video were armed with assault rifles, grenades, light machine guns, and rocket-propelled grenade launchers; ISIS has long had a presence in Turkey, which previously served as a transit point for foreign fighters traveling to Syria to join the self-declared Islamic State caliphate and participate in the Syrian civil war; prior to the declaration of a province in Turkey, the Turkish government suspected ISIS of responsibility for numerous attacks, including suicide bombings at Ataturk Airport in June 2016 and at a wedding in August 2016, as well as a shooting at a nightclub in January 2017; since the collapse of the caliphate in early 2019, Turkey continues to be a regional transit hub for ISIS in its efforts to smuggle fighters, weapons, funding, and supplies into Syria; as of 2024, Turkish security forces continued to conduct counter-terrorism operations against ISIS and militants linked to the group

Islamic State of Iraq and ash-Sham – Yemen: publicly announced in April 2015 after a self-proclaimed ISIS affiliate calling itself "Wilayat Sana'a" claimed responsibility for a mosque bombing in Yemen that killed approximately 140 people; goal is to replace the Yemen Government and the Houthi rival government with an Islamic state and implement ISIS's strict interpretation of sharia; since 2015, has carried out hundreds of attacks against Yemeni security forces, Yemeni Government facilities and personnel, Houthi forces, Shia Muslims, and al-Qa'ida; attacks have included suicide bombers, car/truck bombs, road side bombs, ambushes, armed ground assaults, kidnappings, and targeted assassinations; operational primarily in south and central Yemen; reportedly has suffered heavy losses in fighting with the local al-Qa'ida affiliate (al-Qa'ida in the Arabian Pensinsula) and Houthi forces; the group also suffered from internal disputes and a reported lack of leadership; as of 2024, it was considerably degraded in capabilities and strength (estimated to be about 100 fighters) and was minimally active

Islamic State of Iraq and ash-Sham-Khorasan Province (ISIS-K)

aka – Islamic State of Iraq and Syria-Khorasan; Islamic State in Iraq and the Levant-Khurasan (ISIL-K); Islamic State Khurasan (IS, ISK, ISISK); Islamic State of Iraq and Levant in Khorasan Province (ISKP); Islamic State's Khorasan Province; ISIL-Khorasan; Wilayat al-Khorasan; Wilayat Khurasan; ISIL's South Asia Branch; South Asian Chapter of ISIL

history – formed in January 2015 primarily from former members of Tehrik-e Taliban Pakistan, the Afghan Taliban, and the Islamic Movement of Uzbekistan; ISIS appointed former Pakistani Taliban commander Hafiz Said KHAN as leader (later killed in a US military strike); frequently fought with the Afghan Taliban over control of territory and resources; also conducted an insurgency against the Afghan Government and foreign military forces; suffered heavy losses of fighters, leaders, and territory to Afghan and US counterterrorism operations, as well as to the Taliban, but retained the ability to orchestrate attacks, recruit, and replenish leadership positions; since the fall of the Afghan Government to the Taliban and the US/Coalition withdrawal in August 2021, has conducted dozens of attacks against the Taliban, including suicide bombings, assassinations, and ambushes on security checkpoints; in recent years, it has also claimed attacks against targets outside of Afghanistan, including a suicide bombing of a Shia mosque in Pakistan and a rocket strike on an Uzbek military border post, as well as a deadly assault on Russian concert hall in Moscow in March of 2024; the group is assessed to be one of ISIS's most lethal branches and the most serious terrorist threat in Afghanistan, as well as the wider region

goals – portrays itself as the primary rival to the Taliban and seeks to portray the Taliban as incapable of providing security in the country; also seeks to undermine the relationship between the Taliban and neighboring countries; ultimately seeks to establish an Islamic caliphate in Afghanistan, Pakistan, and parts of Central Asia, including Iran

leadership and organization – reportedly continues to be Sanaullah GHAFARI (aka Shahab al-Muhajir); operates in small cells; ISIS restructured the Khorasan Province in May 2019, when it announced the creation of separate provinces for India and Pakistan

areas of operation – Afghanistan and Pakistan; also has conducted attacks in Iran, Tajikistan, and Uzbekistan (note - "Khorasan" is a historical region that encompassed northeastern Iran, southern Turkmenistan, and northern Afghanistan)

targets, tactics, and weapons – targets the Taliban, the Haqqani Network, Shia Muslims (particularly the Hazaras community), followers of Sufi Islam, security and military personnel, and diplomatic and infrastructure targets; known for indiscriminate and large-scale attacks against civilians in both Afghanistan and Pakistan; in 2024, it conducted an attack on a civilian target in Russia; targets have included Shia religious sites, neighborhoods, and other gathering places, diplomatic facilities in Kabul, an Afghan prison, Kabul airport, a voter registration center, a television station, a hospital, a concert hall, and an election rally; in 2022, it claimed responsibility for a suicide bombing attack on a Shia mosque in Pakistan that killed 63 persons, and in August 2021, it conducted a bombing attack on the Kabul Airport that killed 13 US military personnel and 169 Afghan civilians; in March 2024, it claimed responsibility for an attack on a Moscow concert hall that left more than 140 people dead; it has employed a variety of terrorist tactics, including ambushes, assassinations, hit-and-run attacks/raids/military-style assaults, roadside bombings and other improvised explosive device (IEDs) operations, mortar/rocket attacks, suicide bombings, etc.; fighters have been typically armed with small arms, light and heavy machine guns, mortars, rockets, and various IEDs, including car bombs, road side bombs, and suicide vests

strength – estimated in 2024 have as many as 6,000 members

financial and other support – receives periodic funding from ISIS; raises additional funds locally from commerce, donations, taxes, ransoms, and extortion practices on individuals and businesses

designation – placed on the US Department of State's list of Foreign Terrorist Organizations on 14 January 2016

Jaish-e-Mohammed (JeM)

aka – the Army of Mohammed; Mohammed's Army; Tehrik ul-Furqaan; Khuddam-ul-Islam; Khudamul Islam; Kuddam e Islami; Jaish-i-Mohammed

history – founded in 2000 by former senior Harakat ul-Mujahideen leader Masood AZHAR upon his release from prison in India in exchange for 155 hijacked Indian Airlines passengers that JeM operatives were holding hostage; has claimed responsibility for multiple attacks in India-administered Kashmir, India, and Pakistan; after 2008, fought US and Coalition forces in Afghanistan until the Taliban came to power in 2021; maintains close relations with the Taliban and al-Qa'ida in Afghanistan; outlawed in Pakistan; has conducted several attacks against Indian security forces in Jammu and Kashmir since 2018, including a suicide bombing in the city of Pulwama that killed 40 security police in February 2019; active as of 2024

goals – drive India from the disputed region of Kashmir and establish Pakistani sovereignty

leadership and organization – led by Maulana Mohammed Masood AZHAR Alvi (aka Wali Adam Isah), with his brother and deputy, Mufti Abdul Rauf AZHAR Alvi, as well as a seven-member executive committee

areas of operation – based in Pakistan; operates in Afghanistan (training camps) and India (stages attacks in Indian Union Territory of Jammu and Kashmir)

targets, tactics, and weapons – attacks Indian military, security, and government officials, personnel, bases, and buildings; periodically attacks Pakistani government and security personnel; attempted to assassinate former Pakistani President Pervez MUSHARRAF in 2003; has assaulted

and kidnapped Christians and foreigners; typically employs small arms, light and heavy machine guns, rocket-propelled grenades, mines, improvised explosive devices, suicide bombers, and car bombs
strength – assessed in 2023 to have about 500 members
financial and other support – to avoid asset seizures by the Pakistani Government, JEM since 2007 has withdrawn funds from bank accounts and invested in legal businesses, such as commodity trading, real estate, and the production of consumer goods; also collects funds through donation requests, sometimes using charitable causes to solicit donations
designation – placed on the US Department of State's list of Foreign Terrorist Organizations on 26 December 2001

Jama'at Nusrat al-Islam wal-Muslimin (JNIM)
aka – Jamaat Nosrat al-Islam wal-Mouslimin; Group for the Support of Islam and Muslims; Group to Support Islam and Muslims; GSIM; GNIM; Nusrat al-Islam wal-Muslimeen
history – formed in 2017 when the Mali Branch of al-Qa'ida in the Islamic Maghreb (AQIM), al-Murabitoun, Ansar al-Dine, and the Macina Liberation Front (FLM; aka Katiba Macina or Macina Battalion/Brigade) agreed to work together as a coalition; describes itself as al-Qa'ida's official branch in Mali and has pledged allegiance to al-Qa'ida leader Ayman al-ZAWAHIRI and deceased AQIM emir Abdelmalek DROUKDEL; has conducted hundreds of attacks against local and international security troops, vowing to take "combat action against security forces, rather than attacks on the population" to preserve relations with local communities; has tried to displace the authority of local governments in the areas where it operates, including providing services through its own self-described non-profit organizations, conflict arbitration, policing, and community dispute resolution; while there have been periods of some reported cooperation and local truces, JNIM and the Islamic State of Iraq and ash-Sham in the Greater Sahara (ISIS-GS) elements have fought each other over territory in the region; the group continued to conduct attacks into 2024 and was recognized as one of al-Qa'ida's most active affiliates
goals – unite all terrorist groups in the Sahel, eliminate Western influence in the region, force out all international military forces, and establish an Islamic state centered on Mali
leadership and organization – led by Iyad ag Ghali (alt. Iyad Ag Ghaly; note - also the leader of Ansar al-Dine); JNIM portrays itself as broad alliance of jihadist groups; in recent years, it reportedly has developed from a loose coalition to a more developed formal structure with centralized leadership, regional commanders, and local commanders; has a dedicated media unit known as az-Zalaqah; coalition members and affiliates (such as Ansarul Islam) reportedly maintain their existing leadership and organizational structures; for example, the Macina Brigade (aka Katiba Macina), which has been assessed as JNIM's most important coalition member, has a decentralized chain of command with sub-units known as markaz (or "center"), each of which has a leader (amirou markaz), assisted by a military commander and an advisory shura council; each markaz exercises considerable local autonomy; some fighters are organized into battalions (katibas)
areas of operation – predominantly active in Mali but also conducts operations in Burkina Faso and Niger; stronghold is in northern and central Mali, although it has conducted operations and attacks over most of the country and has expanded its presence in Burkina Faso; groups affiliated with the coalition have conducted attacks in Benin, Cote d'Ivoire, and Togo; has lost ground to ISIS-GS in the tri-border region of Burkina Faso, Mali, and Niger
targets, tactics, and weapons – targets foreign and local military and security forces, as well as various non-state armed groups, including pro-government militias and rival jihadist militants; typically employs insurgent-type tactics, including hit and run attacks/raids, kidnappings, ambushes, improvised explosive devises, road-side bombings, and mortar attacks; has attacked military bases and outposts, security checkpoints, patrols, and convoys, as well as the French embassy in Burkina Faso with small arms, machine guns, rocket-propelled grenades, mortars, rockets, suicide bombers, and car bombs; also targets other symbols of the government's authority, including local leaders, civil servants, schools, teachers, and infrastructure, such as bridges, as well as foreign tourists with threats, assassinations, kidnappings, and bombings
strength – assessed in 2024 to have 5-6,000 fighters; in July 2024, it reportedly mustered more than 1,000 fighters in an attack on a Togolese military base
financial and other support – receives funding through kidnappings-for-ransom, cattle rustling, extortion, protection taxes on local residents, and from smugglers who pay a tax in exchange for safe transit through JNIM-controlled trafficking routes in Mali; has attacked gold mines in areas outside government control and used the profits to recruit new members and buy weapons; equipped with arms captured from local military forces and smuggled in from Libya
designation – placed on the US Department of State's list of Foreign Terrorist Organizations on 6 September 2018

Jama'atu Ansarul Muslimina Fi Biladis-Sudan (Ansaru)
aka – Ansarul Muslimina Fi Biladis Sudan; Vanguards for the Protection of Muslims in Black Africa; JAMBS; Jama'atu Ansaril Muslimina Fi Biladis Sudan
history – formed in January 2012 as a breakaway faction of Boko Haram in the aftermath of a January 2012 Boko Haram attack in the city of Kano, Nigeria, that resulted in the deaths of at least 180 people, mostly Muslims; the Ansaru faction objected to Boko Haram's attacks on fellow Muslims and killing non-Muslims who posed no threat to Muslims; claimed a kidnapping in 2013 and did not claim any further attacks until claiming responsibility for several in 2020, including two attacks on the Nigerian Army that resulted in the deaths of more than 60 Nigerian soldiers; the group announced its reemergence in late 2019; in January 2022, the group publicly announced that it had pledged loyalty to al-Qa'ida elements operating in the Sahel; active in 2023
goals – defend Muslims throughout Africa by fighting against the Nigerian Government and international interests; rid Nigeria of Western influence and establish an Islamic state in Nigeria
leadership and organization – reportedly led by Abu Usama ANSARI; previously was under Khalid al-BARNAWI until he was captured by the Nigerian Army in 2016; leads through a shura, but information on the group's organizational structure is otherwise not available; announced the creation of a new media outlet for the group in 2019 (Al Yaqut Media Center)
areas of operation – operates in the northwest and north central regions of Nigeria, particularly Kaduna State, including the Benin-Niger-Nigeria tri-border area; also has reportedly taken part in al-Qa'ida operations in the Sahel
targets, tactics, and weapons – targets Nigerian Government officials and security/military forces; also kidnaps and kills foreigners, especially Westerners and abducts individuals with ties to potential ransom payers; uses small arms, light weapons, and explosives to carry out coordinated attacks, including ambushes and hit-and-run assaults; reportedly cooperating with some armed gangs operating in northwest Nigeria, including providing weapons
strength – not available; has reportedly absorbed an undetermined number of former Boko Haram fighters
financial and other support – unclear, although some funding probably is generated from kidnappings for ransom; the group reportedly received training and weapons from al-Qa'ida elements in Mali, as well as arms from smugglers operating in the Sahel
designation – placed on the US Department of State's list of Foreign Terrorist Organizations on 14 November 2013

Jaysh al Adl (Jundallah)
aka – Jeysh al-adl, Army of Justice; Jaish ul-Adl, Jaish al-Adl, Jaish Aladl, Jeish al-Adl; Jundullah; Jondullah; Jundollah; Jondollah; Jondallah; Army of God (God's Army); Baloch Peoples Resistance Movement (BPRM); People's Resistance Movement of Iran (PMRI); Jonbesh-i Moqavemat-i-Mardom-i Iran; Popular Resistance Movement of Iran; Soldiers of God; Fedayeen-e-Islam; Former Jundallah of Iran
history – formed in 2002 under the name Jundallah as an anti-Iranian Sunni Muslim armed group; founder and then-leader Abdulmalik RIGI was captured and executed by Iranian authorities in 2010; has engaged in numerous attacks on Iranian civilians, government officials, and security personnel; adopted the name Jaysh al Adl in 2012 and has since claimed responsibility for attacks under that name; claimed multiple attacks against Iranian security forces in 2023 and 2024
goals – stated goals are to secure recognition of Balochi cultural, economic, and political rights from the Iranian government; procure greater autonomy for Balochis in Iran and Pakistan
leadership and organization – Abdolrahim Mullahzadeh (aka Salahuddin Farooqi); reportedly has branches based on regions of Iran and Pakistan where it is active; probably organized into cells; operates a media outlet known as the Telegram Channel
areas of operation – Afghanistan, Iran, and Pakistan; operates primarily in the province of Sistan va Baluchestan of southeastern Iran and the Baloch areas of Afghanistan and Pakistan (outlawed in Pakistan since January 2017); note: the Sistan-Baluchestan province is home to a large community of minority Sunni Muslims who complain of discrimination in Shia-dominated Iran
targets, tactics, and weapons – primarily targets Iranian security forces but also government officials and Shia civilians; attacks include hit-and-run raids, assaults, ambushes, kidnappings, assassinations, suicide bombings, and car bombings; has conducted several ambushes of Iranian security forces near the Pakistan border in recent years; one of its most deadly attacks was a February 2019 suicide car bombing of a bus carrying Islamic Revolutionary Guard Corps (IRGC) personnel that killed 27; it also claimed an attack which killed 11 Iranian police officers in December 2023; weapons include small arms, light weapons, and various improvised explosive devices such as suicide vests and car bombs
strength – limited, dated, and widely varied estimates range from a few hundred up to as many as 2,000 members
financial and other support – not available
designation – placed on the US Department of State's list of Foreign Terrorist Organizations on 4 November 2010

Jaysh Rijal al-Tariq al Naqshabandi (JRTN)
aka – Jaysh Rijal al-Tariq al-Naqshabandi; Army of the Men of the Naqshbandi Order; Armed Men of the Naqshabandi Order; Naqshbandi Army; Naqshabandi Army; Men of the Army of al-Naqshbandia Way; Jaysh Rajal al-Tariqah al-Naqshbandia; JRTN; JRN; AMNO
history – emerged in December 2006 as an Arab secular Ba'athist nationalistic armed group in response to SADDAM Husayn's execution; consisted largely of Iraqi Sunni Muslims following Naqshabandi Sufi Islam ideals; between 2006 and the 2011 withdrawal of US forces from Iraq, claimed responsibility for numerous attacks on US bases and personnel; in 2014, elements joined forces with ISIS in opposition to the Iraqi government and assisted with the taking of Mosul, but fissures later emerged between the two factions; some elements splintered off, but the majority of JRTN was subsumed by ISIS; current status unavailable; has not claimed responsibility for any attacks since 2016
goals – end external influence in Iraq and, ultimately, overthrow the Iraqi Government to install a secular Ba'athist state within the internationally recognized borders of Iraq
leadership and organization – Izzat Ibrahim al-DOURI, former vice president of SADDAM Husayn's Revolutionary Council, led JRTN with former Ba'ath Party officials and military personnel under SADDAM; information on the organization not available
areas of operation – Iraq; historically had a heavy presence in Salah ad Din, Ninawa, Tikrit, Kirkuk, Mosul, and Al Hawija regions and in the north
strength – not available
targets, tactics, and weapons – targeted Iraqi Government military and security forces and Iraqi Kurds who belong to any of the separatist Kurdish groups; also targeted US military personnel from 2006 to 2011; used small arms, light and heavy machine guns, artillery rockets, various improvised explosive devices, including road side and vehicle-borne bombs
financial resources – received funding from former members of the SADDAM regime, major tribal figures in Iraq, and contributions from Gulf-based sympathizers
designation – placed on the US Department of State's list of Foreign Terrorist Organizations on 30 September 2015

Jemaah Islamiya (JI)
aka – Jemaa Islamiyah, Jema'a Islamiyah, Jemaa Islamiyya, Jema'a Islamiyya, Jemaa Islamiyyah, Jema'a Islamiyyah, Jemaah Islamiah, Jema'ah Islamiyah, Jemaah Islamiyyah, Jema'ah Islamiyyah, Jama'a Assalafiyah Lidda'wa Wal Jihad, Islamic Congregation, Salafi Group for Call and Holy War, Jemaah Islamia, al-Qa'ida Indonesia
history – has roots in the Darul Islam movement that emerged in Indonesia in the 1940s to resist the country's post-colonial government, which it viewed as too secular; JI's earliest efforts to organize date back to the late 1960s and early 1970 under co-founders Abu Bukar BA'ASYIR and Abdullah SUNGKAR; sent fighters to Afghanistan in the 1980s during the war with the Soviets to train; gained international notoriety in 2002 for the suicide bombing of a nightclub on the resort island of Bali that killed more than 200 people; outlawed by the Indonesian Government in 2007; since 2002 and into 2022, Indonesian authorities have killed or captured several hundred JI operatives, including several senior leaders; remains active in recruiting and cultivating support through religious boarding schools, mosques, print publications, the internet, media outlets, and charitable organizations that are fronts for the organization; trying to use political influence to press for Islamic law in Indonesia while clandestinely building a paramilitary force; has sent fighters to Iraq, the Philippines, and Syria for training and battlefield experience; affiliated with al-Qa'ida and has ties with the Abu Sayaf Group in the Philippines; Indonesian security forces captured stockpiles of weapons and ammunition and broke up a training camp in 2021; has not claimed responsibility for any attacks since 2016, but was active into 2024, and the Indonesian Government continued to conduct law enforcement and counter-terrorism operations against the group; in June 2024, senior JI leaders declared in a video that they were disbanding the organization
goals – stated goal is to create an Islamic state comprising Malaysia, Singapore, Indonesia, and the southern Philippines
leadership and organization – current leadership not available; has a shura council, a paramilitary wing, and regional units known as *mantiqi*, which are responsible for administration and operations; each *mantiqi* is divided into smaller districts known as *wakalah*
areas of operation – operates throughout Indonesia; reportedly strongest in Java; has operated in the Philippines, Malaysia, and Singapore
targets, tactics, and weapons – targets Christians and Western interests, particularly tourist sites such as nightclubs and hotels; the majority of its victims have been civilians; attackers historically used small arms and improvised explosive devices, including car bombs and suicide vests
strength – estimated in 2022 to have up to 6,000 members
financial and other support – fundraises through membership donations and criminal and business activities, including cultivating palm oil plantations; has received financial, ideological, and logistical support from Middle Eastern contacts and Islamic charities and organizations; collects

cash remittances from Indonesians abroad; members have received weapons and explosives training in Afghanistan, Iraq, Pakistan, the Philippines, and Syria
designation – placed on the US Department of State's list of Foreign Terrorist Organizations on 23 October 2002

Kata'ib Hizballah (KH)
aka – Hizballah Brigades; Hizballah Brigades in Iraq; Hizballah Brigades-Iraq; Kata'ib Hezbollah; Khata'ib Hezbollah; Khata'ib Hizballah; Khattab Hezballah; Hizballah Brigades-Iraq of the Islamic Resistance in Iraq; Islamic Resistance in Iraq; Kata'ib Hizballah Fi al-Iraq; Katibat Abu Fathel al-A'abas; Katibat Zayd Ebin Ali; Katibut Karbalah; Brigades (or Battalions) of the Party of God
history – formed in 2007 from several predecessor networks and former members of the Badr Organization as an Iraqi Shia militia and political organization; fought against US and Coalition forces from 2007 to 2011 and earned a reputation for conducting lethal bombing and rocket attacks; sent fighters to Syria to fight alongside Lebanese Hizballah and Syrian government forces beginning in 2012; fought in Iraq against the Islamic State of Iraq and ash-Sham (ISIS) as a member of the Popular Mobilization Committee and Affiliated Forces (PMC or PMF), an umbrella group of mostly Shia militia groups; was accused of extrajudicial killings and abductions of Iraqi Sunni Muslims during this period; in 2018, its affiliated political party (Independent Popular Gathering) joined the Al Fatah (Victory) Alliance, a political coalition primarily comprised of parties affiliated with Iranian-backed Shia militias; in 2019 and early 2020, conducted several attacks against US military bases and participated in an assault on the US Embassy in Baghdad; also involved in attacking and abducting anti-government protesters in Baghdad; has continued to be active into 2024, including attacks on US forces; typically uses front names or proxy groups to obfuscate its involvement in attacks; has strong ties to the Iranian Revolutionary Guard Corps (IRGC) and recognizes Ayatollah KHAMENEI, the Supreme Leader of Iran, as its spiritual leader
goals – overthrow the Iraqi Government to install a government based on Shia Muslim laws and precepts; eliminate US influence in Iraq
leadership and organization – led by a shura council, with individuals reportedly selected by the IRGC; secretary general of the council is Ahmad Mohsen Faraj al-HAMIDAWI (aka Abu Hussein, Abu Zalata, Abu Zeid); shura council members are responsible for special military operations, military/paramilitary forces, funding and logistics, civil affairs, media, social/cultural affairs, and administration; KH fighters comprise three brigades of the PMC's paramilitary forces (aka Popular Mobilization Forces, PMF), the 45th, 46th, and 47th; has a political party created in 2021 called Huqooq (Rights) Movement
note – following the onset of the Hamas-Israel war in the Gaza Strip in October 2023, an umbrella group called the Islamic Resistance in Iraq (IRI or al-Haya al-Tansiqiya lil-Muqawama al-Iraqiya) announced its formation by claiming responsibility for an October 2023 failed drone strike on an US military base in northern Iraq; the IRI is a coalition of all Iran-backed Shiite militias operating in Iraq, including designated terrorist groups KH and Asa'ib Ahl al-Haqq (AAH), operating in solidarity with HAMAS in its 2023-2024 war with Israel; since its establishment, the IRI has claimed responsibility for dozens of attacks on US elements in Iraq and Syria; it has also claimed responsibility for more than 100 attacks on Israel
areas of operation – headquartered in Baghdad; also active in Ninawa, Al Anbar, Babil, and throughout Iraq's southern governorates, including Al Basrah, Maysan, Dhi Qar, and Wasit; has participated in the Syrian civil war since 2012 (remained active in Syria in 2022)
targets, tactics, and weapons – targets ISIS fighters, Sunni Muslim civilians, rival Shia factions, and US personnel and interests; employs both guerrilla-style and terrorist tactics, including hit-and-run assaults, ambushes, mortar and rocket attacks, roadside bombs, car bombs, targeted killings/assassinations, sniping, and abductions; has been accused of torturing and executing Sunni civilians, as well as looting and burning Sunni homes; fighters are equipped with small arms, machine guns, rockets (including large-caliber, up to 240mm), mortars, man-portable air defense systems (MANPADs), improvised explosive devices, rocket-propelled grenades, anti-aircraft guns, artillery, recoilless rifles, light tactical vehicles (Humvees), truck-mounted weapons (aka "technicals"), armed unmanned aerial vehicles (aka drones), and armored vehicles; reportedly has been involved in the training of Shia militants in other Gulf countries
strength – estimated in 2023 to have as many as 30,000 members
financial and other support – receives funding, logistical support, intelligence, training, and weapons from the IRGC-Qods Force and Lebanese Hizballah; solicits donations online and through a pro-Iran television channel; also raises funds through criminal activities, including kidnappings-for-ransom, smuggling, and taxing/extortion of activities in areas where the group is dominant; it also has legitimate business enterprises, such as property holdings and investments
designation – placed on the US Department of State's list of Foreign Terrorist Organizations on 2 July 2009

Kurdistan Workers Party (PKK)
aka – Kongra-Gel; the Kurdistan Freedom and Democracy Congress; the Freedom and Democracy Congress of Kurdistan; KADEK; Partiya Karkeran Kurdistan; the People's Defense Force; Halu Mesru Savunma Kuvveti; Kurdistan People's Congress; People's Congress of Kurdistan; KONGRAGEL, KGK
history – founded by Abdullah OCALAN in 1978 as a Marxist-Leninist separatist organization comprised primarily of Turkish Kurds; launched a rural campaign of violence in 1984 which expanded to include urban terrorism in the early 1990s; fighting with Turkish security forces peaked in the mid-1990s with an estimated 40,000 casualties, the destruction of thousands of villages in the largely Kurdish southeast and east of Turkey, and the displacement of hundreds of thousands of Kurds; following his capture in 1999, OCALAN ordered members to refrain from violence and requested dialogue with the Turkish government; PKK foreswore violence until June 2004, when its militant wing took control, renounced the self-imposed cease-fire, and began conducting attacks from bases within Iraq; in 2009, the Turkish Government and the PKK resumed peace negotiations, but talks broke down after the PKK carried out an attack in July 2011 that left 13 Turkish soldiers dead; between 2012 and 2015, negotiations resumed but ultimately broke down owing partly to domestic political pressures and the war in Syria; since 2015, attacks and clashes with Turkish security forces have occurred largely in the country's rural southeast, northern Iraq, and northern Syria, and are estimated to have caused the deaths of as many as 7,000 PKK members, Turkish security forces personnel, and civilians; the group was active as of 2024
goals – advance Kurdish autonomy, political, and cultural rights in Turkey, Iran, Iraq, and Syria, and ultimately, establish an independent Kurdish state centered in southeastern Turkey
leadership and organization – OCALAN, currently serving life imprisonment in Turkey, is still the group's leader and figurehead, but day-to-day affairs and operations are run by Murat KARAYILAN and a three-man Executive Committee; the armed wing of the PKK is called the People's Defense Force (Hêzên Parastina Gel or HPG)
areas of operation – located primarily in northern Iraq (headquartered in the Qandil Mountains) and southeastern Turkey; affiliated groups operate in northwestern Syria, as well as in Iran
targets, tactics, and weapons – primarily attacks Turkish government personnel and security forces, including military patrols, convoys, security checkpoints, police stations, and government buildings; uses a mixture of guerrilla warfare and terrorist tactics, including armed assaults, hit-and-run attacks, kidnappings, grenade attacks, car bombs, remotely-detonated improvised explosive devices (IEDs), unmanned aerial vehicles (UAVs) mounting IEDs, and suicide bombers; for most of its history, the group has waged a rural insurgency, but the collapse of the peace process in 2015 led to a two-year campaign of urban violence before it resorted back to a rural-based insurgency; weapons include small arms, machine guns, grenades, mortars, man-portable air defense systems (MANPADs), UAVs, anti-tank weapons, and various improvised explosive devices

strength – estimated in 2022 to have at least 4,000 members
financial and other support – receives logistical and financial support from a large number of sympathizers among the Kurdish community in southeast Turkey, Syria, Iraq, and Iran, as well as the large Kurdish diaspora in Europe; additional sources of funding include criminal activity, such as narcotics smuggling and extortion
designation – placed on the US Department of State's list of Foreign Terrorist Organizations on 8 October 1997

Lashkar i Jhangvi (LJ)
aka – Lashkar-e-Jhangvi (LeJ), Lashkar-i-Jhangvi, Lashkar Jangvi, Army of the Jhangvi, Lashkar e Jhangvi al-Almi, LeJ al-Alami
history – formed around 1996 as a terrorist offshoot of the Sunni Deobandi sectarian group Sipah-i-Sahaba Pakistan; banned by the Pakistani Goverment in August 2001 as part of an effort to rein in sectarian violence, causing many LJ members to seek refuge in Afghanistan with the Taliban, with whom the group had existing ties; after the collapse of the Taliban in Afghanistan, members became active in aiding other terrorists, providing them with safe houses, false identities, and protection in Pakistani cities; linked to al-Qa'ida and Tehrik-e Taliban Pakistan (TTP), and reportedly cooperated with the Islamic State in a 2016 attack against a police training college in Quetta, Pakistan that killed more than 60; since 2017, has lost several senior leaders to Pakistani counter-terrorism operations and has not claimed responsibility for any attacks; as of 2020-21, the group reportedly had split into factions with one faction pledging allegiance to TTP; active as of 2023
goals – exterminate Shia Muslims and religious minorities; rid the region of Western influence and, ultimately, establish an Islamic state under sharia in Pakistan
leadership and organization – leadership not available; crackdowns by Pakistani security forces has reportedly fractured and decentralized the organization, leading to independent cells and factions
areas of operation – based primarily in Pakistan's Punjab province, the Federally Administered Tribal Areas, Karachi, and Balochistan; has carried out attacks in both Afghanistan and Pakistan
targets, tactics, and weapons – most known for violent attacks against Shia Muslims; has also targeted Sufi Muslims, non-Muslims, and Westerners; has attacked buses, markets, mosques, political rallies, and other venues where Shia Muslims congregate, as well as churches and hotels; has also conducted attacks on Pakistani officials and security personnel, including an attempted assassination of the Pakistani prime minister in 1999; tactics have included targeted killings, ambushes, suicide bombings, and vehicle bombings such as detonating a water tanker filled with explosives that killed or wounded more than 250 in Baluchistan, Pakistan in 2013; operatives typically armed with small arms and light weapons, grenades, improvised explosive devices, and suicide vests
strength – assessed in 2021 to have a few hundred members
financial and other support – funding comes from donors in Pakistan and the Middle East, particularly Saudi Arabia; engages in criminal activity, including extortion
designation – placed on the US Department of State's list of Foreign Terrorist Organizations on 30 January 2003

Lashkar-e Tayyiba (LeT)
aka – Jamaat-ud-Dawa, JuD; Lashkar-i-Taiba; al Mansooreen; Al Mansoorian; Army of the Pure; Army of the Pure and Righteous; Army of the Righteous; Lashkar e-Toiba; Paasban-e-Ahle-Hadis; Paasban-e-Kashmir; Paasban-i-Ahle-Hadith; Pasban-e-Ahle-Hadith; Pasban-e-Kashmir; Jama'at al-Dawa; Jamaat ud-Daawa; Jamaat ul-Dawah; Jamaat-ul-Dawa; Jama'at-i-Dawat; Jâmaiat-ud-Dawa; Jama'at-ud-Da'awah; Jama'at-ud-Da'awa; Jamaati-ud-Dawa; Idara Khidmate-Khalq; Falah-i-Insaniat Foundation; FiF; Falah-e-Insaniat Foundation; FalaheInsaniyat; Falah-i-Insaniyat; Falah Insania; Welfare of Humanity; Humanitarian Welfare Foundation; Human Welfare Foundation; Al-Anfal Trust; Tehrik-e-Hurmat-e-Rasool; TehrikeTahafuz Qibla Awwal; Al-Muhammadia Students; Al-Muhammadia Students Pakistan; AMS; Tehreek-e-Azadi-e-Kashmir; Kashmir Freedom Movement; Tehreek Azadi Jammu and Kashmir; Tehreek-e-Azadi Jammu and Kashmir; TAJK; Movement for Freedom of Kashmir; Tehrik-i-Azadi-i Kashmir; Tehreek-e-Azadi-e-Kashmir; TEK; Kashmir Freedom Movement ;Milli Muslim League; Milli Muslim League Pakistan; MML
history – formed in the late 1980s as the armed wing of Markaz ud Dawa ul-Irshad (MDI), a Pakistan-based extremist organization and charity originally formed to oppose the Soviet presence in Afghanistan; began attacking Indian troops and civilian targets in the state of Jammu and Kashmir in 1993; often operates under the guise of its charitable affiliates and other front organizations to avoid sanctions; combines with other groups like Jaish-e-Muhammad and Hizbul Mujahideen to mount anti-India attacks; linked to al-Qa'ida and has reportedly provided refuge and training to al-Qa'ida members in Pakistan; provided support to the Afghan Taliban prior to the Taliban takeover in 2021; continues to be active although the group has been banned in Pakistan and has faced pressure from the Pakistan Government to give up arms and integrate into Pakistan society
goals – annex the Indian Union Territory of Jammu and Kashmir to Pakistan and foment an Islamic insurgency in India; oust Western and Indian influence in Afghanistan; enhance its recruitment networks and paramilitary training in South Asia; and, ultimately, install Islamic rule throughout South Asia
leadership and organization – led by Hafiz Mohammad SAEED (currently imprisoned in Pakistan); has a robust infrastructure in Pakistan with district offices and departments (or wings) overseeing finances, charities, politics/government, foreign affairs, media and propaganda, social welfare programs, military operations (reportedly includes air and naval components), external affairs, education/students, ulema (clerics), and the building of mosques and madrassas; has zone/regional commanders; typically conducts military/terrorist operations in cells; activities are coordinated through numerous front organizations, including charities; set up a political party, the Milli Muslim League, in 2017
areas of operation – Afghanistan, India, and Pakistan
targets, tactics, and weapons – primarily focuses on Indian military and security, government, and civilian targets; has participated in attacks against Western interests in Afghanistan and called for the killing of non-Muslims and Westerners worldwide; typical attacks include hit-and-run raids, ambushes, grenade attacks, and bombings; most notorious attack was the November 2008 operation against two luxury hotels, a Jewish center, a train station, and a café in Mumbai, India that killed 166 people, including six Americans, and injured more than 300; attack was carried out by 10 gunmen armed with automatic weapons and grenades; operatives usually armed with assault rifles, machine guns, landmines, mortars, explosives, IEDs, and grenades, including rocket-propelled grenades
strength – estimated in 2022 to have up to 5,000 members
financial and other support – collects donations in Pakistan and the Gulf, as well as from other donors in the Middle East and the West; raises funds in Pakistan through charities, legitimate businesses, farming, and taxation; focuses recruitment on Pakistani nationals, but also recruits internationally
designation – placed on the US Department of State's list of Foreign Terrorist Organizations on 26 December 2001

Liberation Tigers of Tamil Eelam (LTTE)
aka – Ellalan Force, Tamil Tigers
history – formed circa 1975 and began an armed campaign against the Sri Lankan government to establish a Tamil homeland in 1983; started out as a guerrilla force but developed considerable conventional military capabilities, including air, artillery, and naval; employed an integrated

insurgent strategy targeting primarily Sri Lanka's key installations and senior political and military leaders; established and administered a de facto state (Tamil Eelam) with Kilinochchi as its administrative capital; provided state functions such as courts, a police force, a bank, a radio station (Voice of Tigers), a television station (National Television of Tamil Eelam), and boards for humanitarian assistance, health, and education; from 1983 until 2009, fighting between government forces and LTTE resulted in 300,000 internally displaced persons, a million Tamils leaving the country, and as many as 100,000 deaths; in early 2009, Sri Lankan forces captured the LTTE's key strongholds, including Kilinochchi, defeated the last LTTE fighting forces, killed its leader Velupillai PRABHAKARN, and declared military victory; approximately 12,000 members surrendered to Sri Lankan forces; LTTE has maintained an international network of sympathizers and financial support since its military defeat; remnants of the group continued to be still active in 2022, although the last fatality inflicted on Sri Lankan security forces was in 2014
goals – revive the movement to establish a Tamil homeland
leadership and organization – current leadership not available; previous structure included a central governing committee led by PRABHAKARAN that oversaw all LTTE activities; organization had political and military wings, as well as a women's wing; military was divided into conventionally organized brigades and regiments of infantry, artillery, air defense, anti-tank, mortars, and security forces; also included special units for naval (Sea Tigers), air (Air Tigers), and intelligence capabilities, as well as a unit of suicide bombers (Black Tigers)
areas of operation – was based in the northeastern part of Sri Lanka; since its defeat, supporters have been active in India, Malaysia, and Sri Lanka
targets, tactics, and weapons – targeted Sri Lankan Government, political, and security officials, and military forces, as well as transportation nodes and infrastructure; carried out a sustained military campaign against Sri Lankan military and security forces; employed a mix of conventional, guerrilla, and terrorist tactics, including ground assaults and numerous assassinations and suicide bombings; forces were armed with a variety of weapons, including small arms, machine guns, rocket-propelled grenades, anti-aircraft guns, anti-tank weapons, mortars, artillery, explosives, small naval craft, and light aircraft
strength – not available
financial and other support – financial network of support continued after the group's military defeat in 2009; employs charities as fronts to collect and divert funds for its activities
designation – placed on the US Department of State's list of Foreign Terrorist Organizations on 8 October 1997

National Liberation Army

aka – Ejercito de Liberacion Nacional; ELN
history – Colombian Marxist-Leninist group formed in 1964; reached its peak in the late 1990s, then suffered a marked period of decline, where it suffered from internal conflict and losses to both the Colombian security services and paramilitary forces that targeted leftist guerrilla groups; engaged in periodic negotiations with the Colombian Government throughout the 2000s and early 2010s while continuing to conduct attacks against security forces and the country's economic infrastructure; formal talks were started again in 2017 and continued into 2018; however, the government suspended the talks indefinitely following a January 2019 ELN car bomb attack on the National Police Academy in Bogota that killed 21 and wounded 68; has expanded its presence into some areas left by the FARC following that group's peace agreement with the Colombian Government in 2016, as well as neighboring Venezuela in order to escape Colombian security forces and exploit opportunities for illicit financing and recruitment; was also engaged in periodic fighting with FARC dissidents and other criminal groups over territory and drug trafficking routes, particularly near the Colombia-Venezuela border; in June 2023, the ELN and the Colombian Government had agreed to a 6-month ceasefire, which was extended for another 6 months in February 2024; and as part of the cease-fire, ELN had pledged to cease kidnappings for ransom
goals – defend Colombians who it believes to be victims of social, political, and economic injustices perpetrated by the Colombian government
leadership and organization – led by Eliecer Erlinto Chamorro (alt. Eliecer Herlinto Chamorro; aka "Antonio Garcia") since 2021; at the top of the organizational structure is the Central Command ("Comando Central" or COCE), which oversees all ELN political, military, financial, and international operations; under the COCE is a 23-member National Directorate that serves as the link between the COCE and the seven "War Fronts" (six regional and one urban-based front that operates in multiple large cities); each front has multiple subdivisions and subunits and operates with a significant degree of autonomy
areas of operation – operates mainly in the rural and mountainous areas of northern, northeastern, and southwestern Colombia, as well as the border regions with Venezuela; estimated to operate in at least 16 of Colombia's 32 departments, plus major cities, including Bogota; reportedly active in at least 8 of Venezuela's 23 states, particularly Amazonas, Apure, Bolivar, Guarico, Tachira, and Zulia
targets, tactics, and weapons – mostly attacks Colombia's military forces, security services, and economic infrastructure, in particular oil and gas pipelines and electricity pylons; typical tactics include mortaring police stations and military bases, placing explosive devices on pipelines, electric pylons, and near roads, and engaging in sniper attacks, roadblocks, and ambushes; conducts numerous kidnappings of civilians and members of the security services; for three days in February 2022, orchestrated an armed strike across significant portions of Colombia (as many as 10 departments) that included violent attacks and targeted killings, blocking highways, setting off explosions, burning vehicles, hanging the ELN flag on public buildings, and patrolling streets in villages and towns in areas where the group maintains a strong presence; fighters are equipped with small arms, rocket-propelled grenades, landmines, explosives, and mortars
strength – estimated in 2024 to have 5-6,000 members
financial and other support – draws funding from the narcotics trade, extortion of oil and gas companies, illegal mining (expansion into Venezuela has included taking control of mines, allowing the group to use the acquisition of gold and diamond deposits to help provide funding), and kidnapping-for-ransom payments
designation – placed on the US Department of State's list of Foreign Terrorist Organizations on 8 October 1997

Palestine Islamic Jihad (PIJ)

aka – PIJ-Shaqaqi Faction; PIJ-Shallah Faction; Islamic Jihad of Palestine; Islamic Jihad in Palestine; Abu Ghunaym Squad of the Hizballah Bayt al-Maqdis; Al-Quds Squads; Al-Quds Brigades; Saraya al-Quds; Al-Awdah Brigades; Harakat al-Jihad al-Islami al-Filastin
history – a Sunni Islamist group formed by militant Palestinians in Gaza in 1979 as an off-shoot of the Muslim Brotherhood in Egypt; has drawn inspiration from the Iranian revolution and receives support from Iran, Syria, and Lebanese Hizballah; is the smaller of the two main Palestinian militant groups in Gaza, the other being the ruling HAMAS group with which it cooperates, although the two have at times had a tense relationship because PIJ disagrees with HAMAS's strategy for confronting Israel; unlike HAMAS, PIJ has refused to negotiate with Israel and rejects a two-state solution; has been responsible for many attacks on Israeli targets since the 1990s including barrages of mortar and rocket strikes; participated with HAMAS in its ground and air attack from Gaza on Israel in October 2023; as of 2024, was engaged in significant fighting with the Israeli military
goals – committed to the destruction of Israel and to the creation of an Islamic state in historic Palestine, an area that covers present-day Israel, Gaza, and the West Bank
leadership and organization – led by Ziyad al-NAKHALLAH and an eight-member leadership council (al-Maktab al-Am or General Bureau); has a 15-member political council, which represents PIJ members in Gaza, the West Bank, Israeli prisons, and abroad; also has an armed wing,

known as the al-Quds (Jerusalem) Brigades, which has subordinate regional military commands, "brigades," or "battalions" that are comprised of cells and smaller units; in 2021-2022 reportedly had established several new "brigades" or "battalions" representing cities in the West Bank
areas of operation – Israel, the Gaza Strip, and the West Bank; maintains a presence in Lebanon and Syria and offices in Tehran, Iran
targets, tactics, and weapons – targets Israeli civilians and military personnel with bombings, small arms attacks on military patrols, and mortar and rocket attacks; most rocket attacks have struck southern Israel, but the group has developed longer-range versions capable of reaching further into Israel, including Tel Aviv; armed with small arms and light weapons, artillery rockets, man-portable air defense systems (MANPADs), mortars, armed unmanned aerial vehicles (aka drones), antitank guided missiles, rockets, and improvised explosive devices; the group in the past targeted Israel with suicide bombings and abductions
strength – estimated in 2023 to have about 1,000 members
financial and other support – receives financial assistance, military training, and weapons primarily from Shia Muslim Iran in pursuit of their shared anti-Israel ideology; Hizballah provides safe harbor to PIJ leaders and representatives in Lebanon and probably facilitates Iran's support to PIJ; trains with HAMAS; maintains a tunnel network to smuggle goods, arms, and ammunition across borders
designation – placed on the US Department of State's list of Foreign Terrorist Organizations on 8 October 1997

Palestine Liberation Front – Abu Abbas Faction

aka – PLF; PLF-Abu Abbas; Palestine Liberation Front
history – initially founded in the 1960s and merged with several other Palestinian groups after the Six-Day War in 1967 but broke away in the late 1970s; by 1984, the PLF had split into three factions—all using the PLF name—with different leaders; Muhammad ZAYDAN, (aka Abu Abbas), established and led the most prominent and operationally active faction until his death in 2004; the PLF was responsible for the 1985 attack on the Italian cruise ship Achille Lauro and the murder of a US citizen on board; publicly agreed to abandon terrorism in the 1990s but was suspected of supporting terrorism against Israel by other Palestinian groups that decade and publicly claimed its own attacks on Israeli citizens and military personnel in the 2000s; has not claimed any attacks since 2010 (as of mid-2023)
goals – committed to establishing an independent Palestinian state
leadership and organization – led by Secretary General Dr. Wasil ABU YUSUF, a longtime member on the PLO's executive committee
areas of operation – maintains a presence in the Gaza Strip, Lebanon, Syria, and the West Bank
targets, tactics, and weapons – primarily targeted Israeli military and security personnel with occasional shootings and improvised explosive device (IED) attacks; weapons include small arms, artillery rockets, explosives, grenades, and mortars
strength – recent estimates not available; estimates in 2016 ranged from 50 to 500 members
financial and other support – not available
designation – placed on the US Department of State's list of Foreign Terrorist Organizations on 8 October 1997

Popular Front for the Liberation of Palestine - General Command (PFLP-GC)

aka – PFLP-GC, Al-Jibha Sha'biya lil-Tahrir Filistin-al-Qadiya al-Ama, Ahmed Jibril Militia
history – a Marxist-Nationalist and secular group that split from the Popular Front for the Liberation of Palestine (PFLP) in 1968, claiming it wanted to concentrate more on resistance and less on politics; carried out dozens of attacks in Europe and the Middle East during the 1970s and 1980s, including bombings of two Western airliners; was also was known for cross-border terrorist attacks into Israel using unusual means, such as hot-air balloons and motorized hang gliders; since the early 1990s, has supported Hizballah's attacks against Israel, trained members of other Palestinian terrorist groups, and smuggled weapons; between 2012 and 2015, claimed responsibility for several rocket attacks against Israel, as well as the bombing of a bus carrying civilians; fought alongside Syrian regime forces during the Syrian civil war until at least 2020; after 2015, did not claim any attacks until claiming responsibility for firing rockets against Israel in 2021; reportedly participated in the HAMAS-led attack on Israel in October 2023 which provoked a war between HAMAS and Israel that continued into 2024, and claimed an attack on Israeli settlers in the West Bank in 2024
goals – destroy Israel and remove Western influence from the Middle East, ultimately establishing a Marxist Palestinian state
leadership and organization – Talal NAJI (elected leader in July 2021 after the death of Ahmad JIBRIL, the group's leader and founder); overall organization not available, but has a military wing known as the Jihad Jibril Brigades
areas of operation – headquartered in Damascus, Syria; also maintains a presence in the Gaza Strip, Lebanon, and the West Bank
targets, tactics, and weapons – targets Israeli civilians and the military; also targeted paramilitary forces fighting against the Syrian ASAD regime from possibly 2011 until at least 2020; in the 1970s-1980s, it used innovative attack methods, including barometric bombs to destroy civilian aircraft and mail bombs; was also known for other more unusual means for conducting attacks—such as hot-air balloons and motorized hang-gliders—against what it perceived to be Israeli interests; since the 1990s, has used guerrilla tactics; weapons have typically included grenades, improvised explosive devices (IEDs), rockets, small arms, light machine guns, and suicide vests
strength – estimated in 2022 to have several hundred members
financial and other support – receives funds, logistical support, military training, and weapons from Iran and Syria, as well as the designated terrorist group Hizballah; garners payments in exchange for providing training to other armed groups, including HAMAS
designation – placed on the US Department of State's list of Foreign Terrorist Organizations on 8 October 1997

Popular Front for the Liberation of Palestine (PFLP)

aka – Halhul Gang; Halhul Squad; Palestinian Popular Resistance Forces; PPRF; Red Eagle Gang; Red Eagle Group; Red Eagles; Martyr Abu-Ali Mustafa Battalion
history – formed in December 1967 as an umbrella organization for Marxist and Arab nationalist groups after Israel seized the West Bank; became the second largest faction, and the main opposition force to Fatah, within the Palestine Liberation Organization (PLO); earned a reputation for large-scale international attacks in the 1960s and 1970s, including high-profile hijackings of Israeli and Western aircraft; has been in decline since the 1980s following the collapse of the Soviet Union which had been its chief benefactor, and the emergence of non-PLO groups such as HAMAS and Palestine Islamic Jihad; since the 2000s, has focused its attacks on Israel and launched multiple joint operations with other Palestinian militant groups but its operational tempo has been low; since June 2017, only one attack has been attributed to the group; in September 2019, four members were arrested by Israeli security services for detonating an improvised explosive device that resulted in several Israeli casualties; in 2022, the PLFP, along with HAMAS and the Palestinian Islamic Jihad, were attempting to take steps to create a National Liberation Front in an attempt to address divisions and to cooperate with and to rebuild the PLO; participated in the HAMAS-led attack on Israel in October 2023, which sparked a war between HAMAS, its allies, and Israel; fighting continued into 2024
goals – destroy the state of Israel and, ultimately, establish a secular, Marxist Palestinian state with Jerusalem as its capital

leadership and organization – official leader, General Secretary Ahmad SA'DAT, has been serving a 30-year prison sentence in Israel since 2006; Deputy Secretary General 'Abd-al-Rahim MALLUH (var: Abdul Rahim MALLOUH) oversees daily operations; MALLUH is also a member of the PLO's Executive Committee; has a Political Bureau and a military wing known as the Martyr Abu-Ali Mustafa Brigade
areas of operation – headquartered in the Gaza Strip; also operates in Israel, Lebanon, Syria, and the West Bank
targets, tactics, and weapons – since 2008, has claimed responsibility for numerous attacks on Israeli military forces in Gaza, as well as mortar shells and rockets fired from Gaza into Israel; members have been arrested by Israeli security forces for plotting to carry out kidnappings; in 2014, two members with axes, guns, and knives attacked a synagogue in West Jerusalem, killing five, including three Americans; in the early 2000s, the group carried out at least two suicide bombings and assassinated the Israeli Tourism Minister in retaliation for an Israeli airstrike that killed then PLFP leader Abu Ali Mustafa; fighters are equipped with small arms, light machine guns, artillery rockets, mortars, man-portable surface-to-air missiles, improvised weapons, and explosives, including improvised explosive devices and suicide vests
strength – not available
financial and other support – not available; historically received funds from the former Soviet Union and China; has claimed in draws support from Iran
designation – placed on the US Department of State's list of Foreign Terrorist Organizations on 8 October 1997

Real Irish Republican Army (RIRA)

aka – Real IRA; 32 County Sovereignty Committee; 32 County Sovereignty Movement; Irish Republican Prisoners Welfare Association; Real Oglaigh Na Heireann; Óglaigh na hÉireann (ÓNH); New Irish Republican Army (New IRA or NIRA)
established – formed in 1997 as the clandestine armed wing of the 32 County Sovereignty Movement, a political pressure group dedicated to removing British forces from Northern Ireland and unifying Ireland; claims to be the true descendent of the original Irish Republican Army; many members are former Provisional Irish Republican Army who left the organization after the group renewed its ceasefire in 1997 and brought extensive experience in terrorist tactics and bomb-making to RIRA; has historically sought to disrupt the Northern Ireland peace process and did not participate in the September 2005 weapons decommissioning; despite internal rifts and calls by some jailed members, including the group's founder Michael "Mickey" McKEVITT, for a cease-fire and disbandment, RIRA has pledged to continue conducting attacks; in 2012, RIRA merged with other small dissident republican groups to form the New IRA (NIRA); reportedly cooperates with the Continuity Irish Republican Army (CIRA); has claimed responsibility or been suspected in numerous bombing attempts and shootings since 2012; most recently, incidents have included placing a bomb under a police officer's car in Belfast in 2019, deploying an improvised explosive device (IED) at a passing police car in 2022, and the shooting of a police officer in 2023; the Police Service of Northern Ireland (PSNI) foiled a plot to set off a bomb during a visit by the US President in 2023 and has made arrests of RIRA/NIRA members as recently as 2024
goals – disrupt the Northern Ireland peace process, remove British rule in Northern Ireland and, ultimately, unify Ireland
leadership and organization – current leadership not available; reportedly has a command structure similar to the former Provisional IRA, with an "Army Council" consisting of a chief of staff and directors for training, operations, finance, and publicity; rank-and-file members operate in secret cells
areas of operation – UK and the Republic of Ireland
targets, tactics, and weapons – primarily targets police and other security personnel; tactics typically involve shootings and low-impact bombing attacks; weapons include small arms, mortars, and explosives, including IEDs and car bombs
strength – estimated in 2021 to have approximately 100 active members; may receive limited support from IRA hardliners and sympathizers who are dissatisfied with the IRA's ceasefire and with Sinn Fein's involvement in the peace process
financial and other support – receives funding from money laundering, smuggling, and other criminal activities; suspected of receiving funds from sympathizers in the US; has attempted to buy weapons from gun dealers in the US and the Balkans
designation – placed on the US Department of State's list of Foreign Terrorist Organizations on 16 May 2001

Revolutionary Armed Forces of Colombia – People's Army (FARC-EP)

aka – Fuerzas Armadas Revolucionarias de Colombia – Ejercito del Pueblo; FARC dissidents FARC – EP ; Revolutionary Armed Forces of Colombia dissidents FARC – EP; FARC – D/FARC – EP; Grupo Armado Organizado Residual FARC – EP; GAO-R FARC – EP; Residual Organized Armed Group FARC – EP; Central General Staff (Estado Mayor Central or EMC or FARC-EMC)
history – in 2016, the former Revolutionary Armed Forces of Colombia (FARC) signed a peace deal in which about 13,000 fighters gave up their weapons in exchange for numerous concessions from the Colombian Government, including development programs for rural areas and the opportunity for former guerrilla leaders to participate in local politics and avoid time in prison; however, a group of approximately 1,000 FARC "dissidents," led by Nestor Gregorio VERA Fernandez, commander of the FARC 1st Front, refused to lay down their arms; the group returned to fighting and eventually adopted the name FARC-EP; in late 2019, the Colombian Government began conducting military operations against FARC-EP; despite peace talks and a months-long cease-fire with the Colombian Government in late 2023 that extended well into 2024, the group was active in conducting attacks and fighting with Colombian security forces as of August 2024; the FARC-EP has also fought with a rival FARC dissident group and US-designated Foreign Terrorist Organization (FTO), Segunda Marquetalia, over control of revenue and territory
goals – the former FARC sought to install a Marxist-Leninist regime in Colombia through a violent revolution; the group seeks to unite all FARC dissidents and leftist guerrilla groups in Colombia
leadership and organization – leader Nestor Gregorio VERA Fernandez (aka Ivan MORDISCO); reportedly organized similarly to the former FARC with regionally based commands and subordinate "fronts" or "blocs" and "mobile columns," although some information points to a more fragmented command and control structure based in large part on alliances with disparate ex-FARC members and groups, as well as criminal organizations;
areas of operation – operates primarily in rural areas of southern and northeastern Colombia and has a presence in Venezuela (particularly Apure state); it also maintains alliances with ex-FARC individuals and groups in other parts of Colombia, particularly along narco-trafficking routes and areas that generate revenue; ex-FARC groups operate in many of the departments where the FARC previously operated, including along the borders with Venezuela, Brazil, and Ecuador
targets, tactics, and weapons – attacks Colombian Government, military, and police targets, as well as civilians and critical infrastructure, such as oil pipelines; tactics include armed assaults, assassinations, extortion operations, hostage-takings, and bombings; weapons include small arms, grenades, landmines, machine guns, mortars, grenades, and explosives, including improvised explosive devices (IEDs)
strength – estimated to have as many as 3,500 members as of 2024
financial and other support – generate funds through narcotics trafficking, extortion, illegal mining (typically gold), and other illicit economies; collects taxes from locals in areas it occupies

designation – placed on the US Department of State's list of FTOs on 30 November 2021; the designation followed the revocation of the designation of the Revolutionary Forces of Colombia (FARC) as an FTO; note – the former FARC has a political party (Comunes or "Together") that holds seats in the Colombian Congress

Revolutionary People's Liberation Party/Front (DHKP/C)
aka – Dev Sol; Dev Sol Armed Revolutionary Units; Dev Sol Silahli Devrimci Birlikleri; Dev Sol SDB; Devrimci Halk Kurtulus Partisi/Cephesi; Devrimci Sol; Revolutionary Left
history – formed in Turkey originally in 1978 as Devrimci Sol, or Dev Sol, a splinter faction of Dev Genc (Revolutionary Youth); renamed in 1994 after factional infighting; "Party" refers to the group's political activities and "Front" alludes to its militant operations; advocates a Marxist-Leninist ideology and opposes the US, NATO, and the Turkish establishment; reorganized after the death of its founder and leader Dursun KARATAS from cancer in 2008 and was reportedly in competition with the Kurdistan Workers' Party for influence in Turkey; since the late 1980s has primarily targeted Turkish security and military officials; in the 1990s began to conduct attacks against foreign—including US—interests; activities have declined in recent years, but the group remained active into 2024 with periodic small-scale attacks while continuing to be targeted by Turkish security forces
goals – espouses a Marxist-Leninist ideology and seeks to overthrow the Turkish Government and rid Turkey of "imperialist" foreign influences, such as NATO and the US
leadership and organization – current leadership not available; head of DHKP/C in Turkey, Gulten MATUR, arrested by Turkish authorities in November 2022; reportedly operates in small, clandestine cells
areas of operation – Turkey; presence in Europe, especially Germany and Greece; historically active in Syria
targets, tactics, and weapons – has targeted Turkish businessmen, civilians, police, politicians, and soldiers; has also attacked police and other government buildings, including an attempt to take a hostage in the Turkish Parliament in 2019 and a rocket attack against the Istanbul police headquarters in 2017; has also targeted foreign interests, especially US military and diplomatic personnel and facilities, such as opening fire on the US Consulate with small arms in 2015 and a suicide bombing attack against the US Embassy in 2013; typical tactics include assassinations, hostage taking, rocket attacks, suicide bombings, remotely detonated bombs, and car bombs; weapons include small arms, hand grenades, artillery rockets, and improvised explosive devices
strength – numbers inside Turkey not available; has a support network in Europe
financial and other support – finances its activities chiefly through donations and extortion; in Europe, it engages in fundraising, arms smuggling, and other criminal ventures to support its operations in Turkey
designation – placed on the US Department of State's list of Foreign Terrorist Organizations on 8 October 1997

Revolutionary Struggle (RS)
aka – Epanastatikos Aghonas; EA
history – EA (or RS) is a Marxist extremist group that emerged in 2003 following the arrests of members of two other Greek Marxist groups, 17 November (17N) and Revolutionary People's Struggle; first gained notoriety when it claimed responsibility for the September 2003 bombings at the Athens Courthouse during the trials of 17N members; after 2003, EA conducted numerous attacks against Greek and US targets in Greece but conducted its last successful attack in 2014; Greek authorities arrested the group's leaders—husband and wife Nikolaos MAZIOTIS and Pola ROUPA--in 2014 and 2017, respectively; the arrests, along with follow-on arrests of other EA members, disrupted the group's ability to conduct operations, although its remaining members have been linked to other anarchist groups in Greece
goals – disrupt the influence of globalization and international capitalism on Greek society and, ultimately, overthrow the Greek Government
leadership and organization – not available; organizational information not available
areas of operation – Greece, primarily in Athens and its suburbs
targets, tactics, and weapons – from 2003 to 2014, EA targeted Greek and US Government buildings, Greek police officers, the Athens Stock Exchange, and offices of major foreign corporations; EA was also linked to several Greek bank robberies, probably to help fund its operations; used small arms although most attacks involved explosives, including improvised explosive devices (IEDs), vehicle-borne IEDs, and parcel bombs; sometimes conducted attacks at night or in the early morning and called in bomb threats before attacks to limit casualties
strength – estimated to have fewer than two dozen members in 2022
financial and other support – unclear, but most likely supported itself through criminal activities, including bank robberies
designation – placed on the US Department of State's list of Foreign Terrorist Organizations on 18 May 2009

Segunda Marquetalia
aka – New Marquetalia; Second Marquetalia; La Nueva Marquetalia; FARC dissidents Segunda Marquetalia; Revolutionary Armed Forces of Colombia Dissidents Segunda Marquetalia; FARC-D Segunda Marquetalia; FARC-SM; Grupo Armado Organizado Residual Segunda Marquetalia; GAO-R Segunda Marquetalia;, Residual Organized Armed Group Segunda Marquetalia; Armed Organized Residual Group Segunda Marquetalia; note - "Marquetalia" is a reference to the town of Marquetalia, Colombia, that was the original stronghold of communist peasant militants who would later become the now former FARC
history – created in August 2019 by former commanders of the Revolutionary Armed Forces of Colombia (FARC) after they abandoned the 2016 peace accord between the FARC and the Colombian Government because of frustration over perceived lack of progress in implementing the terms of the accord; attempts to carry out the key functions of the state in the areas under its control, including taxation, security, and maintaining infrastructure; in July 2024, the group agreed to a unilateral cease-fire with the Colombian Government; however, it continued to fight with a rival FARC dissident group, FARC-People's Army (FARC-EP), over control of revenue and territory
goals – position itself as the natural successor of the former FARC and unite different groups that claim FARC heritage; the former FARC sought to install a Marxist-Leninist regime in Colombia through a violent revolution; the group seeks to unite or form alliances with armed leftist guerrilla organizations in Colombia, including ex-FARC members, the ELN (National Liberation Army), and the smaller EPL (People's Liberation Army)
leadership and organization – Luciano Marin ARANGO (aka Ivan MARQUEZ) (note - ARANGO was previously the FARC's second-in-command before demobilization, commander of the Caribbean bloc, and lead negotiator during the peace talks with the Colombian Government); has a central committee (aka central command), known as the National Directorate; claims to consist of a political wing (Partido Comunista Clandestino de Colombia or Clandestine Communist Party), as well as armed guerrilla forces and both armed and unarmed militia units; similar to the former FARC, it operates in "blocs" and "fronts"
areas of operation – based primarily in northeastern Colombia, near the border with Venezuela; also maintains a presence in other parts of the country, as well as inside Venezuela
targets, tactics, and weapons – has focused most of its attacks on Colombian Government and military targets, as well as critical infrastructure, such as oil pipelines; has also fought with rival FARC dissidents and other armed criminal groups; tactics have typically included armed assaults,

assassinations, bombings, extortion operations, grenade and mortar attacks, and hostage takings; armed generally with small arms, grenades, improvised explosive devices, machine guns, and mortars
strength – estimated to have up to 2,000 members in 2024
financial and other support – reportedly generates funds through narcotics trafficking, extortion, illegal mining (typically gold), and other illicit economies; collects taxes from locals in areas it occupies
designation – placed on the US Department of State's list of Foreign Terrorist Organizations on 30 November 2021; the designation followed the revocation of the designation of the Revolutionary Forces of Colombia (FARC) as an FTO; note – the former FARC has a political party (Comunes or "Together") that holds seats in the Colombian Congress

Shining Path (Sendero Luminoso, SL)
aka – Ejército Guerrillero Popular (People's Guerrilla Army); EGP; Ejército Popular de Liberación (People's Liberation Army); EPL; Partido Comunista del Peru (Communist Party of Peru); PCP; Partido Comunista del Peru en el Sendero Luminoso de Jose Carlos Mariategui (Communist Party of Peru on the Shining Path of Jose Carlos Mariategui); Socorro Popular del Peru (People's Aid of Peru); SPP; Militarizado Partido Comunista del Peru or MPCP; Militarized Communist Party of Peru; New Red Fraction (Nueva Fracción Roja – NFR; splinter group)
history – formed in the late 1960s as a breakaway faction of the Peruvian Communist Party by former university professor Abimael GUZMAN, whose teachings provided the basis of the group's militant Maoist doctrine; was one of the most ruthless terrorist groups in the Western Hemisphere at its height in the 1980s; conducted an insurgency against the Peruvian Government and waged a campaign of violence on civilians, particularly the rural peasantry; the conflict resulted in the deaths of an estimated 70,000 Peruvians between 1980 and 2000; in September 1992, Peruvian authorities captured GUZMAN, who died in prison in 2021; following his capture, membership declined and the remnants split into two factions; by 2014, one faction had largely been eliminated, while the other continued to operate; the group continues to try to reinvent itself, organize, and proselytize, particularly amongst university students and in rural areas, although most of its operations were in support of narcotrafficking; in recent years has called itself Militarizado Partido Comunista del Peru (the Militarized Communist Party of Peru); remnants of the group remained active into 2024
goals – generate revenue by providing security to narcotics traffickers and by growing coca to produce cocaine; historically aimed to replace existing Peruvian institutions with a peasant revolutionary regime
leadership and organization – Victor Quispe PALOMINO (aka Comrade Jose); organization not available
areas of operation – Peru; most active in the Valley of the Apurimac, Ene, and Mantaro Rivers (VRAEM), a vast jungle area near the Andes mountains and home to most of Peru's coca cultivation and production
targets, tactics, and weapons – primary targets in recent years have been Peruvian soldiers and police personnel running counter-narcotics and counter-terrorism operations against the group; also abducts and kills civilians; killed 16 civilians in an attack on a village as late as May 2021; typically uses guerrilla style hit-and-run tactics, including grenade attacks and snipers with long-range rifles; weapons include small arms and other light weapons, grenades, and other explosives, including improvised explosive devices
strength – estimated in 2023 to have less than 350 active members
financial resources – primarily funded by the illicit narcotics trade
designation – placed on the US Department of State's list of Foreign Terrorist Organizations on 8 October 1997

Tehrik-e-Taliban Pakistan (TTP)
aka – Pakistani Taliban; Tehreek-e-Taliban; Tehrik-e-Taliban; Tehrik-i-Taliban Pakistan; Tehrik-e Jihad Pakistan (TJP)
history – formed in 2007 to oppose Pakistani military efforts in the Federally Administered Tribal Areas (FATA); previously disparate tribal militants agreed to cooperate and eventually coalesced under the leadership of now-deceased leader Baitullah MEHSUD (var. MAHSUD); emerged as one of Pakistan's deadliest terrorist organizations; responsible for assaults on a Pakistani naval base in 2011, Karachi's international airport in 2014, and a military school in Peshawar that killed 150 people, mostly students, also in 2014; entered into peace talks with the Pakistani Government in 2014, but talks collapsed that same year; beginning around 2014, the group suffered from several years of internal conflict, fragmentation, public backlash for deadly attacks targeting civilians, and members defecting to ISIS's Khorasan branch in Afghanistan; however, in 2020-2022, the group demonstrated signs of resurgence, with more than 15 jihadist groups, including Jamat-ul-Ahrar (JuA), Hizb-ul-Ahrar (HuA), and the designated FTO Lashkar I Jhangvi (LJ), pledging allegiance to TTP (JuA and HuA had split off from TTP around 2014); at the same time, the group increased the number of attacks in Pakistan; TTP conducted peace talks with the Pakistan Government accompanied by a cease-fire in 2021; however, when the cease-fire ended in December 2021, the group increased its operations, conducting hundreds of attacks in 2022; operations in Pakistan continued to ramp up in 2023 and 2024, with more than 800 reported attacks the first half of 2024
goals – unite all the jihadist groups in Pakistan under one banner; push the Pakistani Government out of Khyber Pakhtunkwa Province (formerly known as the Federally Administered Tribal Areas) and establish strict Islamic law; ultimately, establish an Islamic caliphate over all of Pakistan; note - TTP has ties to and draws ideological guidance from al-Qa'ida (AQ)
leadership and organization – led by Mufti Noor Wali MEHSUD (aka Abu Mansur Asim); has a shura council with two regional committees covering seven zones of operation; however, because TTP is a coalition of more than 15 groups, as well as tribal factions, operational levels of cooperation may vary
areas of operation – based primarily in eastern Afghanistan; conducts operations in Pakistan
targets, tactics, and weapons – targets Pakistani Government officials and military, security, and police personnel, as well as pro-government tribal elders, Shia Muslims, educational figures, the general civilian population, and Westerners; previously targeted US military personnel in Afghanistan; claimed responsibility for a failed 2010 attempt to detonate an explosive device in New York City's Times Square; suspected of involvement in the 2007 assassination of former Pakistani Prime Minister Benazir BHUTTO; has attacked an airport, buses, churches, government buildings, homes of Pakistani officials, markets, hotels, military bases and convoys, mosques, public gatherings, schools, security checkpoints, and entire neighborhoods of Shia Muslims; tactics typically have involved ambushes, hit-and-run raids, small arms attacks, complex military-style assaults, kidnappings, assassinations, suicide bombings, and grenade, mortar, and rocket attacks; weapons include small arms, light and heavy machine guns, mortars, rockets, rocket-propelled grenades, and explosives, including remotely detonated improvised explosive devices (IEDs), suicide vests, and car bombs
strength – estimated in 2024 to have as many as 6,500 fighters
financial and other support – primarily recruits from the former FATA and finances its operations through donations, extortion, kidnappings-for-ransom, natural resource extraction, and other criminal activity, including arms and narcotics trafficking; has received equipment, ideological guidance, training, and weapons from AQ in Afghanistan; the Afghan Taliban is also reported to have provided support to TTP; Afghan Taliban rank and file and AQ members have reportedly assisted TTP forces in cross-border attacks
designation – placed on the US Department of State's list of Foreign Terrorist Organizations on 1 September 2010

REFERENCE MAPS

POLITICAL MAP OF AFRICA

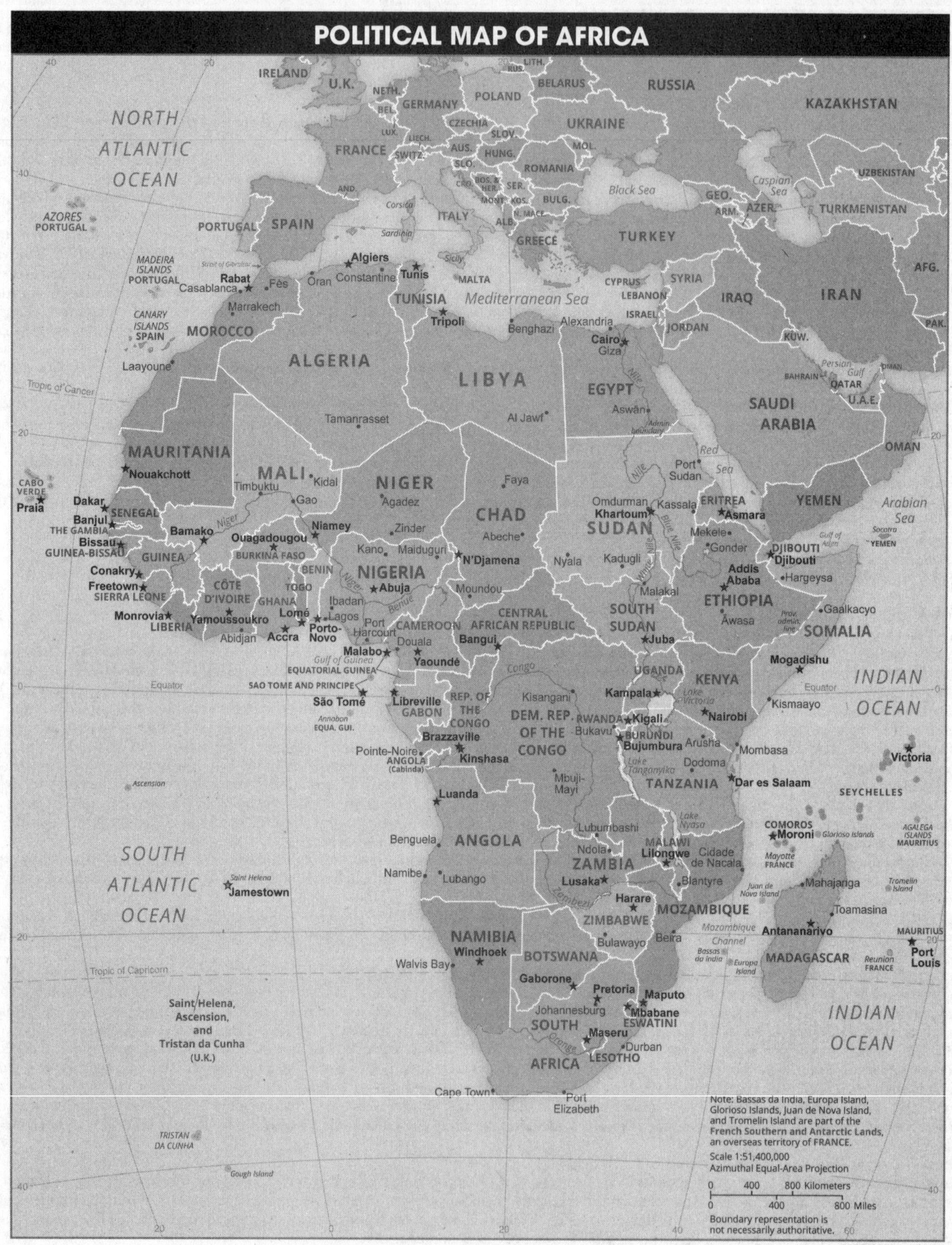

2020-00228-07 2-21

PHYSICAL MAP OF AFRICA

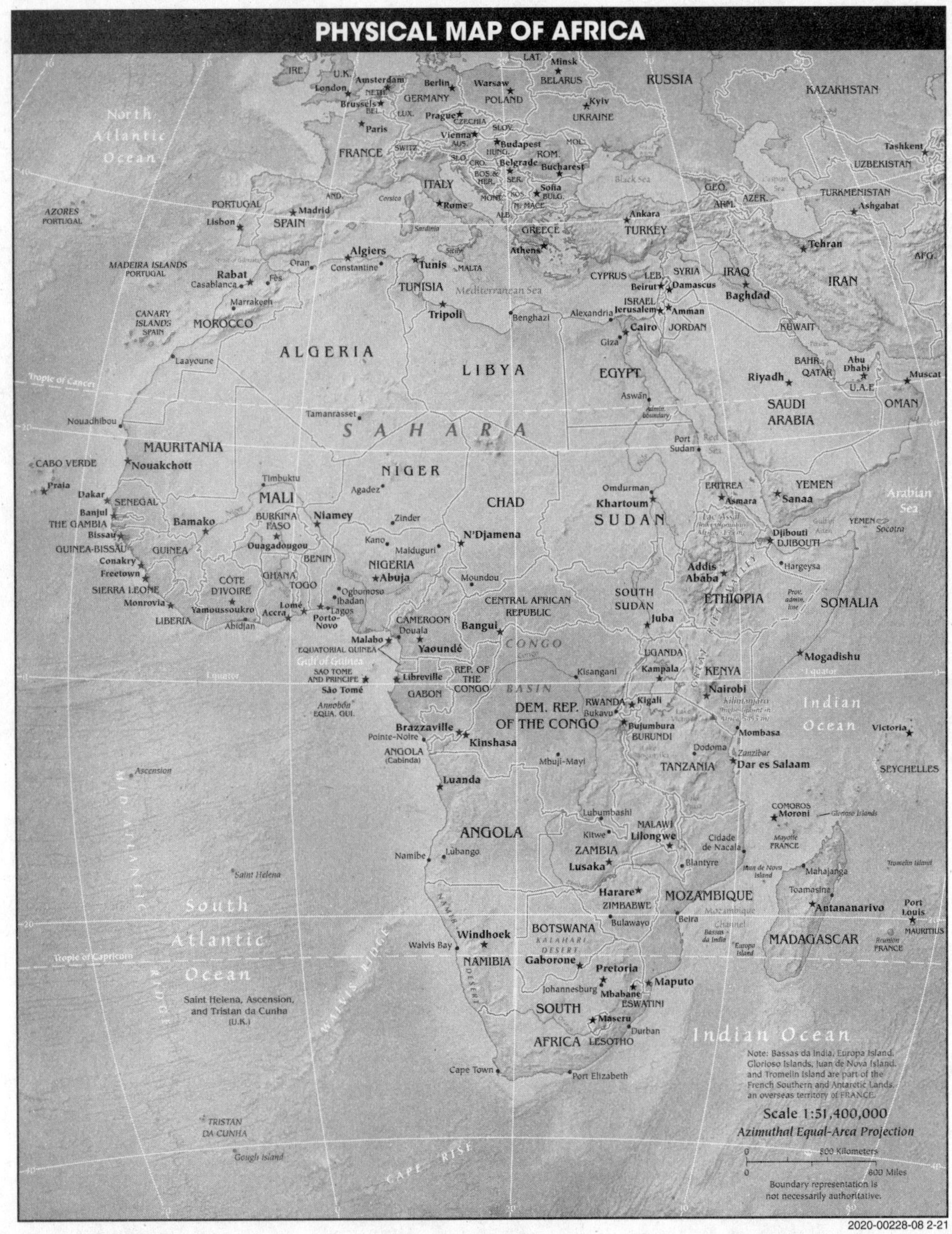

2020-00228-08 2-21

POLITICAL MAP OF ARCTIC REGION

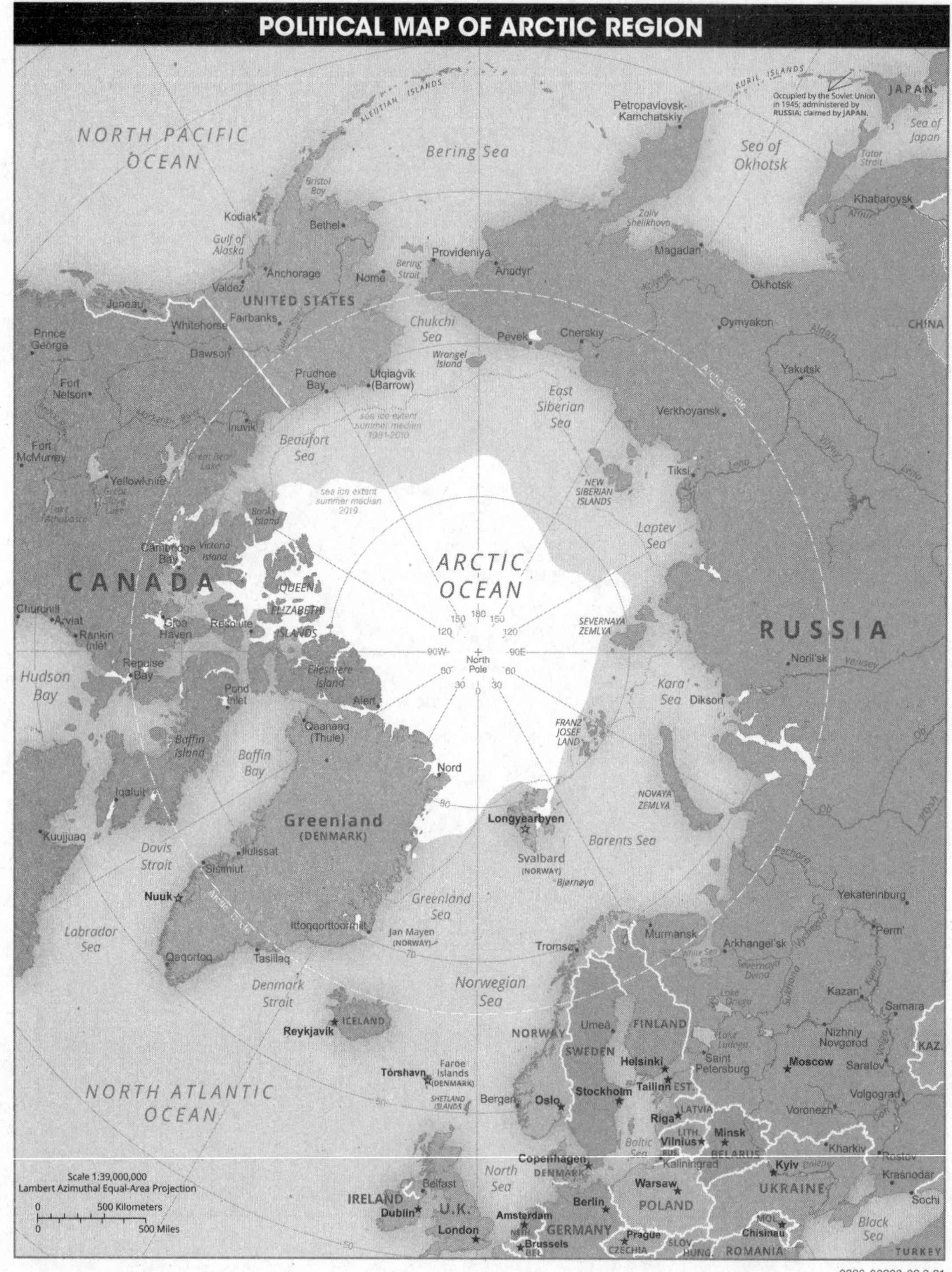

2020-00228-03 2-21

PHYSICAL MAP OF ARCTIC REGION

2020-00228-06 2-21

POLITICAL MAP OF ANTARCTIC REGION

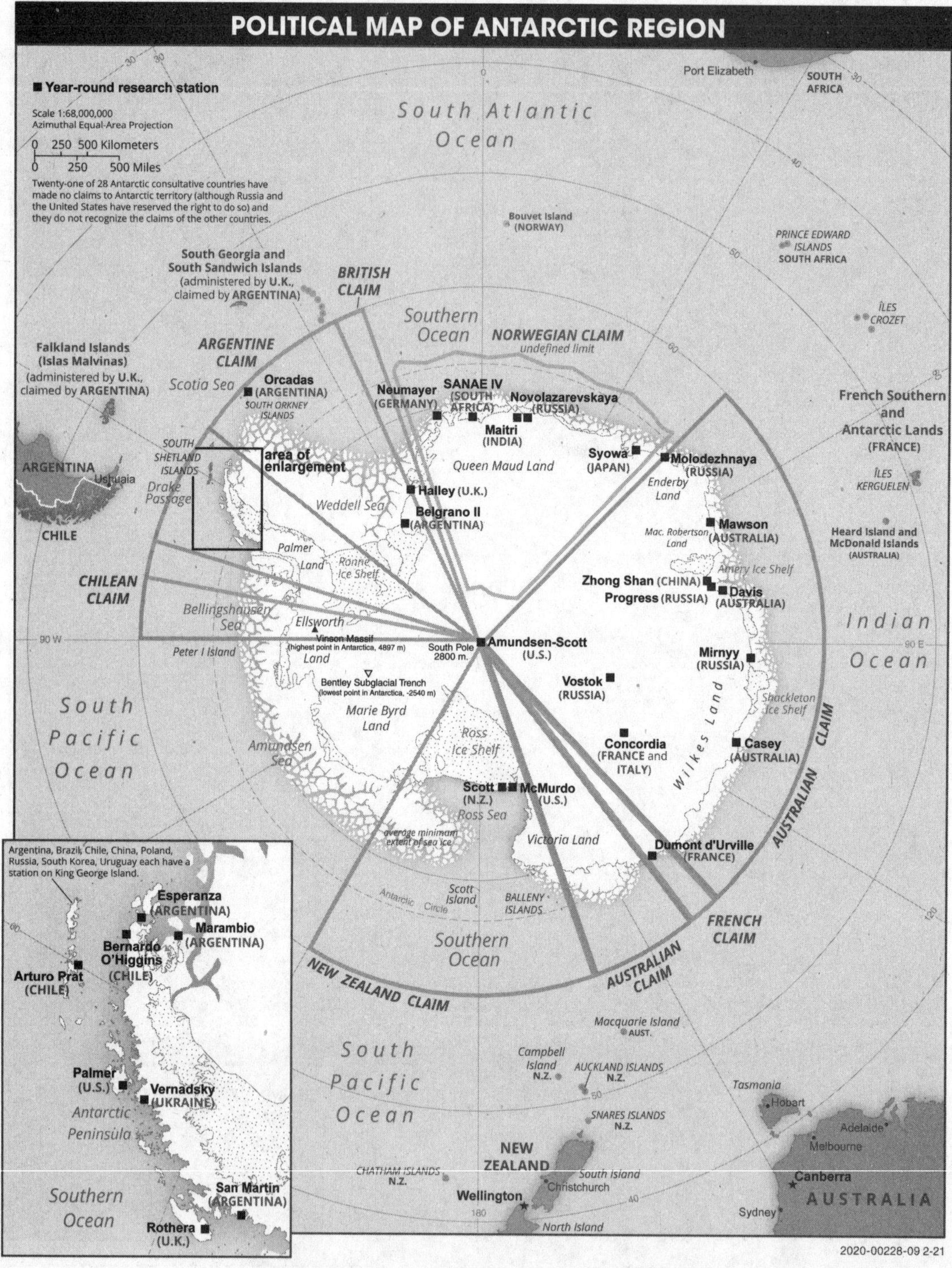

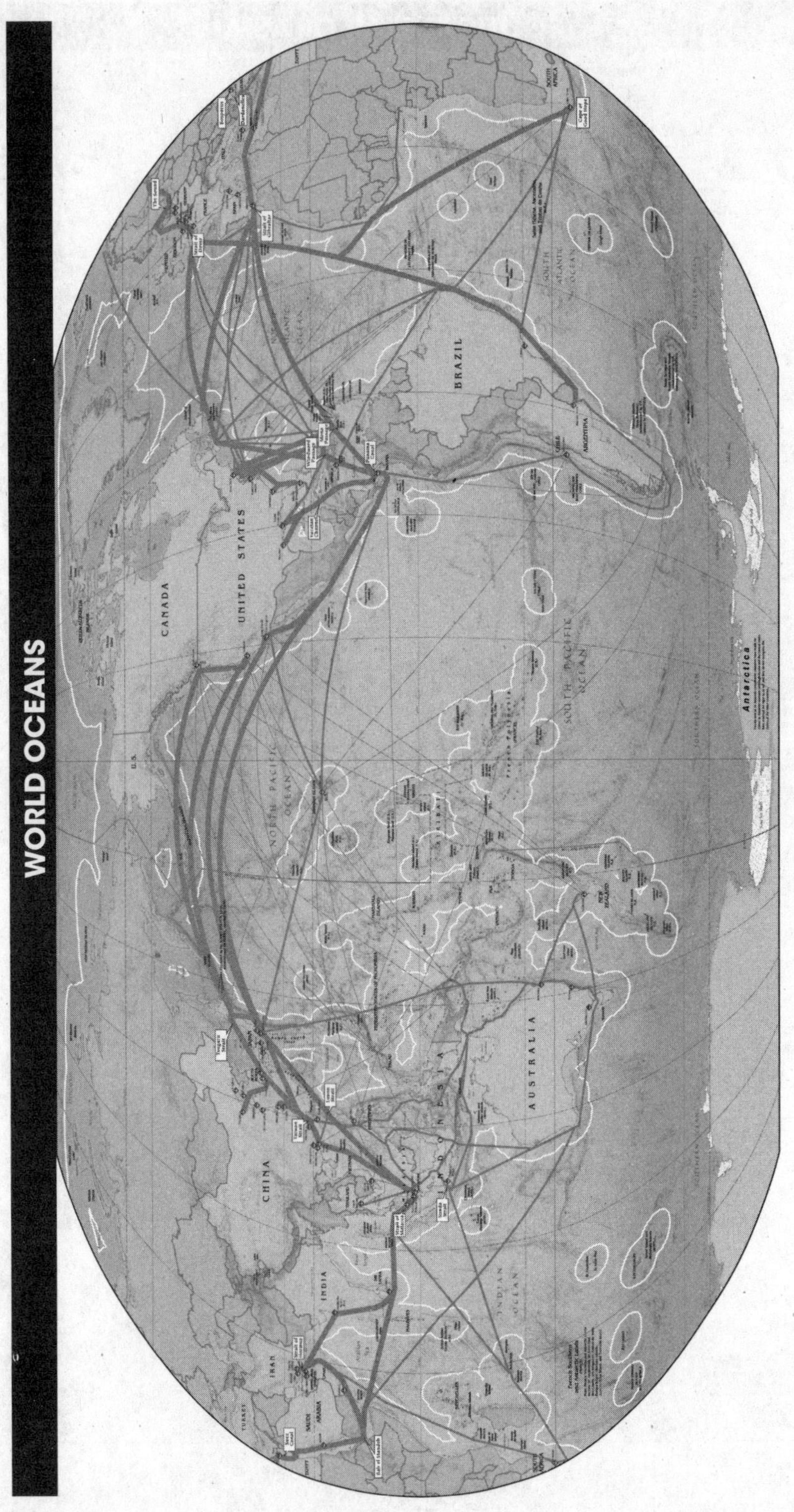
WORLD OCEANS
CANADA
UNITED STATES
BRAZIL
ARGENTINA
CHINA
INDIA
IRAN
SAUDI ARABIA
AUSTRALIA
NEW ZEALAND
NORTH PACIFIC OCEAN
SOUTH PACIFIC OCEAN
SOUTH ATLANTIC OCEAN
INDIAN OCEAN
Antarctica

POLITICAL MAP OF ASIA

PHYSICAL MAP OF ASIA

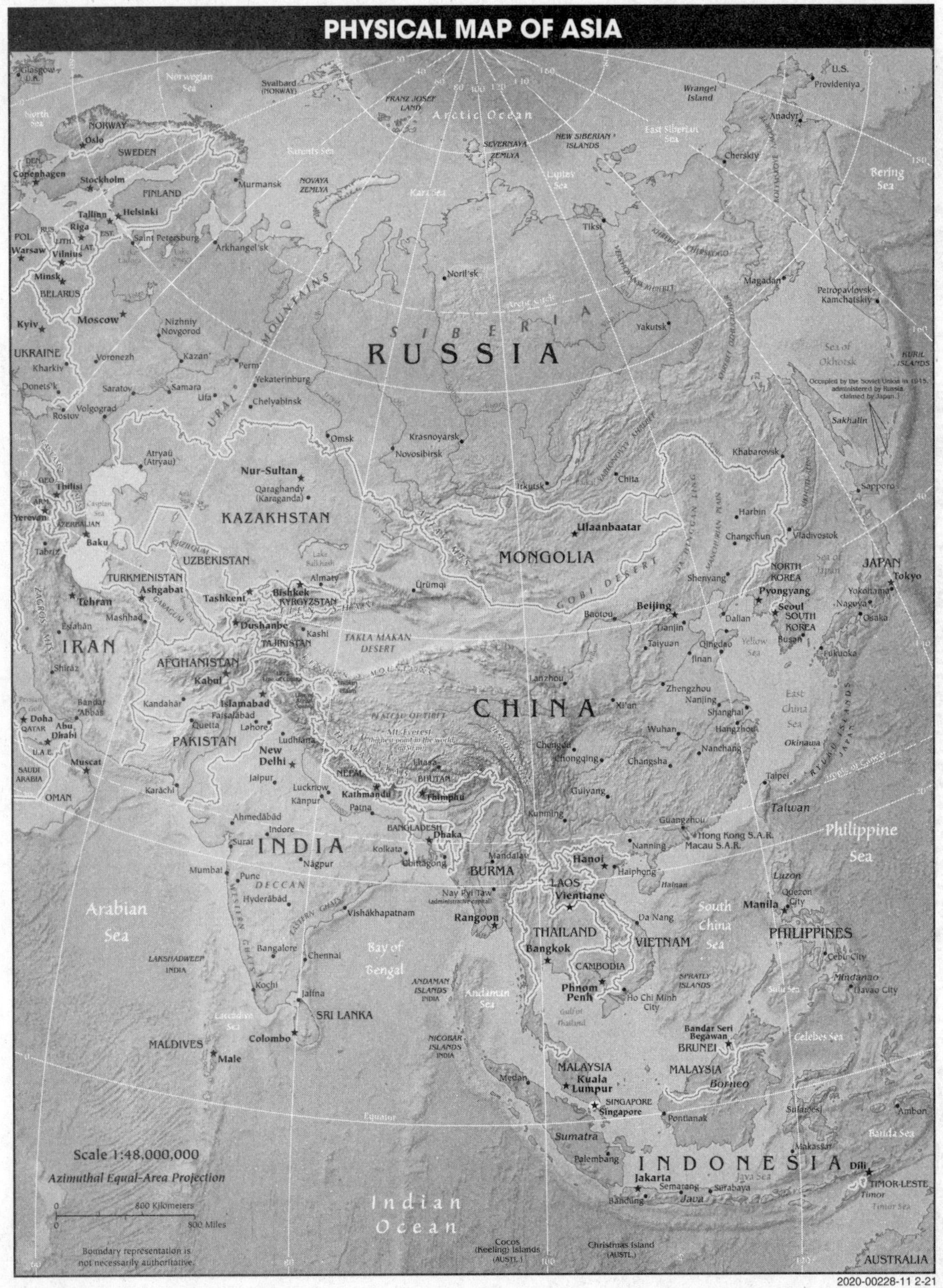

2020-00228-11 2-21

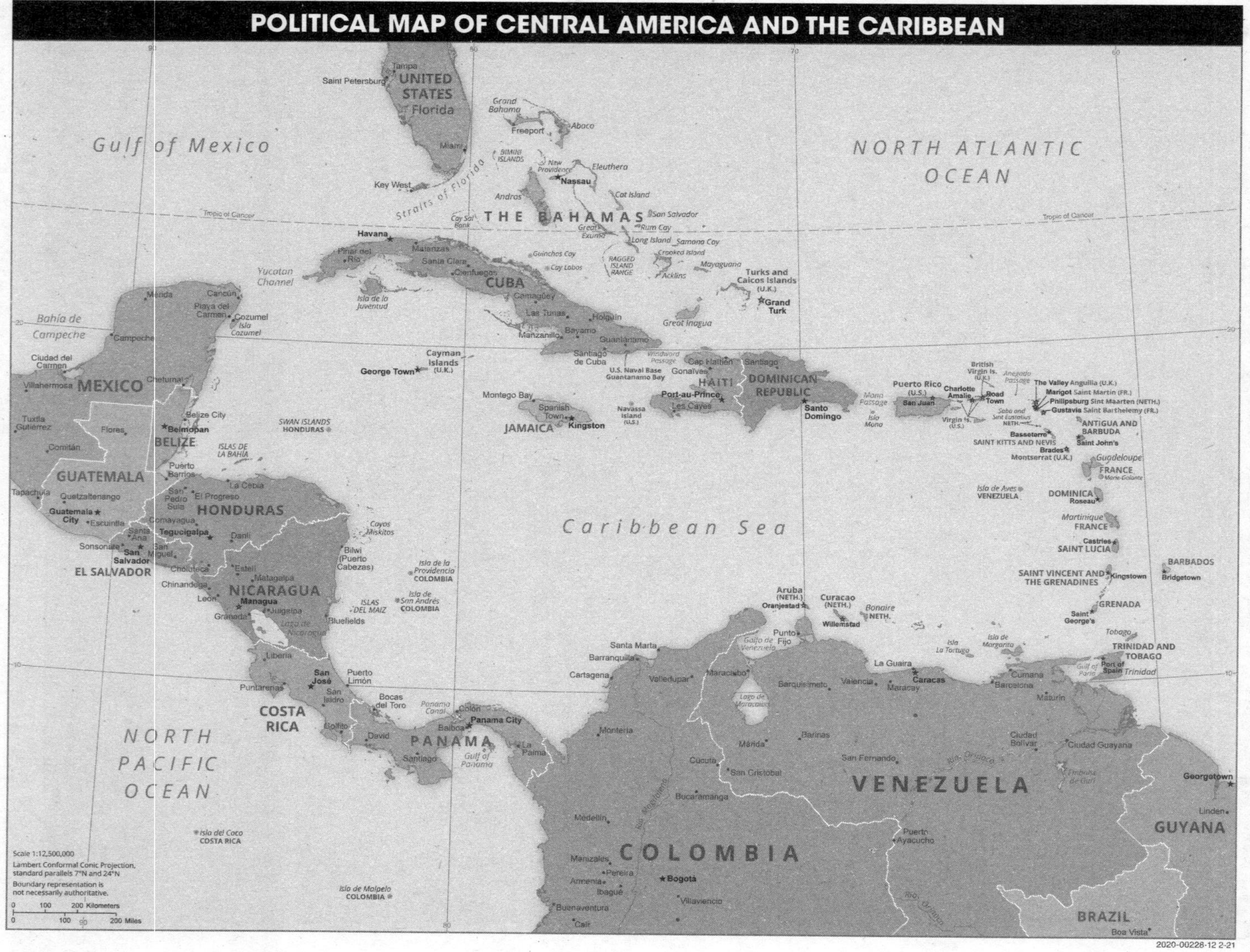

POLITICAL MAP OF CENTRAL AMERICA AND THE CARIBBEAN
NORTH ATLANTIC OCEAN
Gulf of Mexico
Caribbean Sea
NORTH PACIFIC OCEAN
UNITED STATES
Florida
THE BAHAMAS
CUBA
JAMAICA
HAITI
DOMINICAN REPUBLIC
MEXICO
BELIZE
GUATEMALA
HONDURAS
EL SALVADOR
NICARAGUA
COSTA RICA
PANAMA
COLOMBIA
VENEZUELA
GUYANA
BRAZIL
Havana
Nassau
Kingston
Port-au-Prince
Santo Domingo
San Juan
Belmopan
Guatemala City
Tegucigalpa
San Salvador
Managua
San José
Panama City
Bogota
Caracas
Georgetown
George Town
Cayman Islands (U.K.)
Turks and Caicos Islands (U.K.)
Grand Turk
Puerto Rico (U.S.)
TRINIDAD AND TOBAGO
Port of Spain
BARBADOS
Bridgetown
GRENADA
Saint George's
SAINT LUCIA
Castries
DOMINICA
Roseau
ANTIGUA AND BARBUDA
Saint John's
SAINT KITTS AND NEVIS
Basseterre
SAINT VINCENT AND THE GRENADINES
Kingstown
Aruba (NETH.)
Oranjestad
Curacao (NETH.)
Willemstad
Bonaire NETH.
Tropic of Cancer
Straits of Florida
Yucatan Channel
Scale 1:12,500,000
Lambert Conformal Conic Projection, standard parallels 7°N and 24°N
Boundary representation is not necessarily authoritative.
200 Kilometers
200 Miles
2020-00228-12 2-21

PHYSICAL MAP OF CENTRAL AMERICA AND THE CARIBBEAN

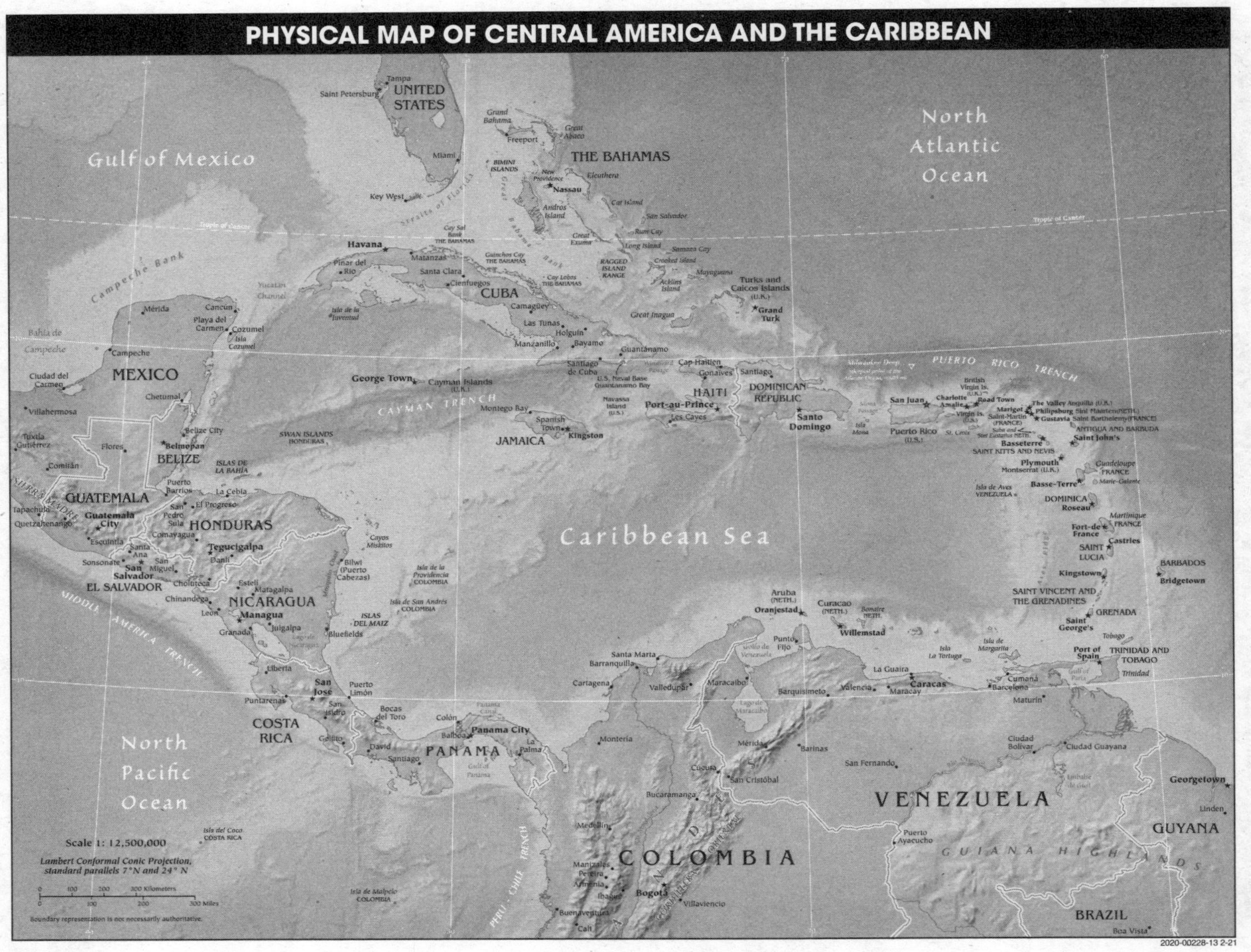

POLITICAL MAP OF EUROPE
Greenland
(DENMARK)
Greenland
Sea
Denmark
Strait
Jan Mayen
(NORWAY)
Norwegian Sea
Barents
Sea
Hammerfest
Tromsø
Murmansk
Kiruna
White Sea
Arkhangel'sk
Severnaya Dvina
ICELAND
Reykjavík
Arctic Circle
Luleå
Oulu
Lake
Onega
Umeå
FINLAND
Trondheim
SWEDEN
Gulf
of
Bothnia
Tórshavn
Faroe
Islands
(DEN.)
NORWAY
Tampere
Lake
Ladoga
SHETLAND
ISLANDS
Bergen
Gävle
Turku
Helsinki
Gulf of Finland
Saint Petersburg
RUSSIA
Rockall
U.K.
ORKNEY
ISLANDS
Oslo
Stockholm
ÅLAND
ISLANDS
Tallinn
ESTONIA
HEBRIDES
Stavanger
Volga
Moscow
NORTH
ATLANTIC
OCEAN
Aberdeen
Skagerrak
Göteborg
Gotland
Riga
LATVIA
Glasgow
Edinburgh
North
Sea
Kattegat
Baltic Sea
Öland
Vitsyebsk
Smolensk
LITHUANIA
Belfast
UNITED
DENMARK
Copenhagen
Malmö
Vilnius
Mahilyow
IRELAND
Dublin
Irish
Sea
Isle
of
Man
(U.K.)
Leeds
Kaliningrad
RUS.
Minsk
Bornholm
Gdańsk
BELARUS
Liverpool
Manchester
Hrodna
Homyel'
KINGDOM
Hamburg
Chernihiv
NETHERLANDS
Amsterdam
Birmingham
Bremen
Berlin
Poznań
Warsaw
Brest
Cardiff
The Hague
Łódź
Kyiv
Celtic
Sea
London
Rotterdam
Oder
POLAND
Zhytomyr
Dnieper
Essen
Leipzig
Wrocław
Vistula
Brussels
Cologne
Elbe
UKRAINE
English Channel
Lille
BELGIUM
Bonn
GERMANY
Kraków
L'viv
Vinnytsya
Guernsey (U.K.)
Jersey (U.K.)
Frankfurt
Prague
LUXEMBOURG
Luxembourg
CZECHIA
Chernivtsi
Seine
Paris
Brno
SLOVAKIA
Mykolayiv
Strasbourg
Stuttgart
Rhine
MOLDOVA
Munich
Danube
Bratislava
Iași
Chisinau
Odesa
Vienna
Budapest
Loire
LIECHTENSTEIN
Cluj-
Napoca
Nantes
AUSTRIA
HUNGARY
Zürich
Vaduz
FRANCE
Bern
ROMANIA
Bay of
Biscay
SWITZERLAND
Geneva
SLOVENIA
Ljubljana
Zagreb
Constanța
Bucharest
Bordeaux
Lyon
Milan
A Coruña
Turin
Po
Venice
Black
Sea
CROATIA
BOSNIA &
HERZEGOVINA
Belgrade
Danube
Varna
SERBIA
Genoa
SAN
MARINO
Bilbao
Toulouse
MONACO
Sarajevo
BULGARIA
Ligurian
Sea
Florence
Pristina
Sofia
Porto
Andorra
la Vella
Marseille
MONTENEGRO
KOSOVO
ANDORRA
ITALY
Adriatic
Sea
Podgorica
Skopje
Istanbul
Zaragoza
Corsica
NORTH
MACEDONIA
Rome
PORTUGAL
Madrid
Barcelona
Ajaccio
Tirana
VATICAN
CITY
Thessaloníki
Bursa
Tagus
ALBANIA
Lisbon
SPAIN
Naples
TURKEY
Balearic
Sea
Tyrrhenian
Sea
Valencia
Sardinia
Aegean
Sea
İzmir
GREECE
BALEARIC
ISLANDS
Cagliari
Sevilla
Ionian
Sea
Athens
Mediterranean Sea
Palermo
Gibraltar
(U.K.)
Málaga
Strait
of Sicily
Sicily
Rhodes
Strait of Gibraltar
Alboran
Sea
Ceuta
SPAIN
Melilla
SPAIN
Algiers
Tunis
Oran
Crete
Rabat
MALTA
Valletta
Mediterranean Sea
Casablanca
MOROCCO
ALGERIA
TUNISIA
300 Kilometers
300 Miles
Scale 1:19,300,000
Lambert Conformal Conic Projection,
standard parallels 40°N and 68°N
2020-00228-14 2-21

PHYSICAL MAP OF EUROPE

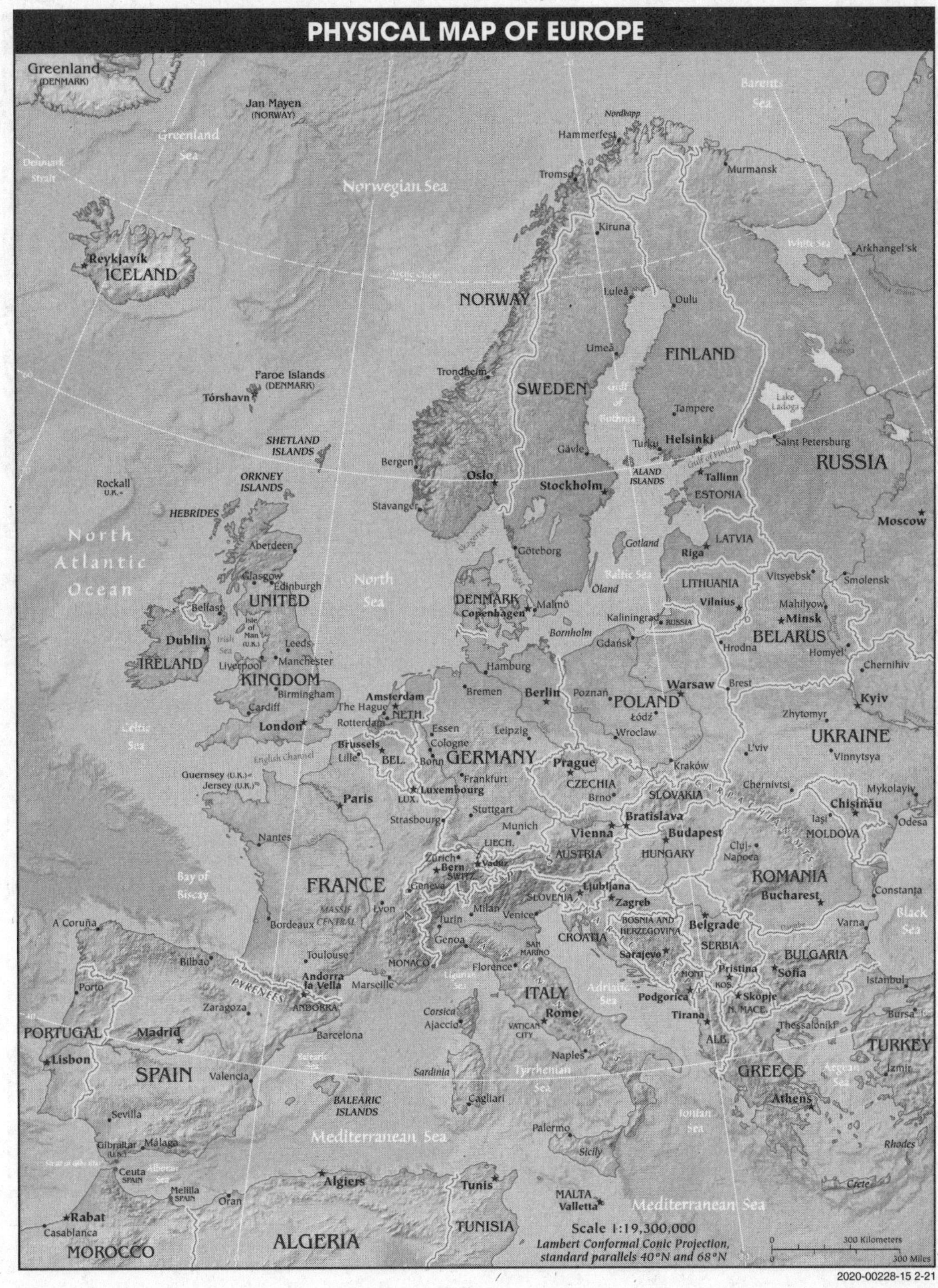

2020-00228-15 2-21

POLITICAL MAP OF MIDDLE EAST
ROMANIA
Bucharest
UKR.
Krasnodar
RUSSIA
KAZAKHSTAN
Sevastopol'
Constanța
SER.
Sofia
BULGARIA
Varna
Black Sea
Sochi
Groznyy
KAZAKHSTAN
Aqtaū (Aktau)
UZBEKISTAN
Nukus
N. MACE.
Sokhumi
Caspian Sea
Dasoguz
Amu Darya
Thessaloniki
Istanbul
Bosporus
Batumi
GEORGIA
Tbilisi
Bukhara
Samsun
Trabzon
Aegean Sea
Bursa
Dardanelles
Ankara
ARMENIA
AZERBAIJAN
Sumqayit
Baku
Yerevan
Türkmenbaşy
TURKMENISTAN
Turkmenabat
Erzurum
GREECE
Izmir
TURKEY
Balkanabat
Athens
Kayseri
Lake Van
Ashgabat
Denizli
Konya
Diyarbakir
Van
Tabrīz
Mary
Antalya
Lake Urmia
Rasht
Mersin
Adana
Gaziantep
Mashhad
Irákleio
Mosul
Zanjān
Crete
Aleppo
Dayr az Zawr
Erbil
Qazvīn
Tehran
Nicosia
Latakia
Herāt
CYPRUS
SYRIA
Kirkuk
Qom
Mediterranean Sea
LEBANON
Homs
Kermānshāh
Beirut
Damascus
Euphrates
Tigris
Arāk
Baghdad
AFG.
ISRAEL
Ar Ramādī
Eşfahān
IRAN
Bīrjand
Tel Aviv-Yafo
West Bank
IRAQ
Jerusalem
Amman
Yazd
LIBYA
Alexandria
Port Said
Dead Sea
Suez Canal
Gaza Strip
Ahvāz
Cairo
JORDAN
An Nāşirīyah
Kermān
Giza
Suez
Al Başrah
Ābādān
Zāhedān
SINAI
Al 'Aqabah
Shīrāz
PAK.
Kuwait City
KUWAIT
Bandar-e Būshehr
Gulf of Suez
Gulf of Aqaba
Tabūk
Bandar 'Abbās
Ḩafar al Bāţin
Asyūţ
Ḩā'il
Persian Gulf
EGYPT
Al Jubayl
Nile
Ad Dammām
Manama
Strait of Hormuz
OMAN
Luxor
Buraydah
Dhahran
BAHRAIN
Doha
Dubai
Gulf of Oman
QATAR
Abu Dhabi
Şuḩār
Aswān
Medina
Yanbu'
Riyadh
Al 'Ayn
SAUDI
Muscat
Tropic of Cancer
U.A.E.
'Ibrī
Admin. boundary
Tropic of Cancer
Ḩalā'ib
ARABIA
Jeddah
OMAN
Mecca
Red Sea
Port Sudan
Nile
Abhā
SUDAN
Şalālah
Jāzān
Al Ghayzah
Omdurman
ERITREA
Khartoum
Kassala
YEMEN
Asmara
Massawa
Sanaa
Arabian Sea
Al Ḩudaydah
Al Mukallā
El Obeid
White Nile
Blue Nile
Ta'izz
Mekele
Assab
Aden
YEMEN
Socotra
Ed Damazin
Lake Tana
Bab el Mandeb
Gulf of Aden
DJIBOUTI
Djibouti
Gonder
Boosaaso
Desē
Malakal
Berbera
SOUTH SUDAN
Addis Ababa
Dirē Dawa
Hargeysa
SOMALIA
ETHIOPIA
Awasa
Gaalkacyo
Scale 1:21,000,000
Lambert Conformal Conic Projection, standard parallels 12°N and 38°N
0 150 300 Kilometers
0 150 300 Miles
The United States recognized Jerusalem as Israel's capital in 2017 without taking a position on the specific boundaries of Israeli sovereignty.
The West Bank is Israeli occupied with current status subject to the Israeli-Palestinian Interim Agreement; permanent status to be determined through further negotiation.
The status of the Gaza Strip is a final status issue to be resolved through negotiations.
Boundary representation is not necessarily authoritative.
2020-00228-16 2-21

PHYSICAL MAP OF MIDDLE EAST

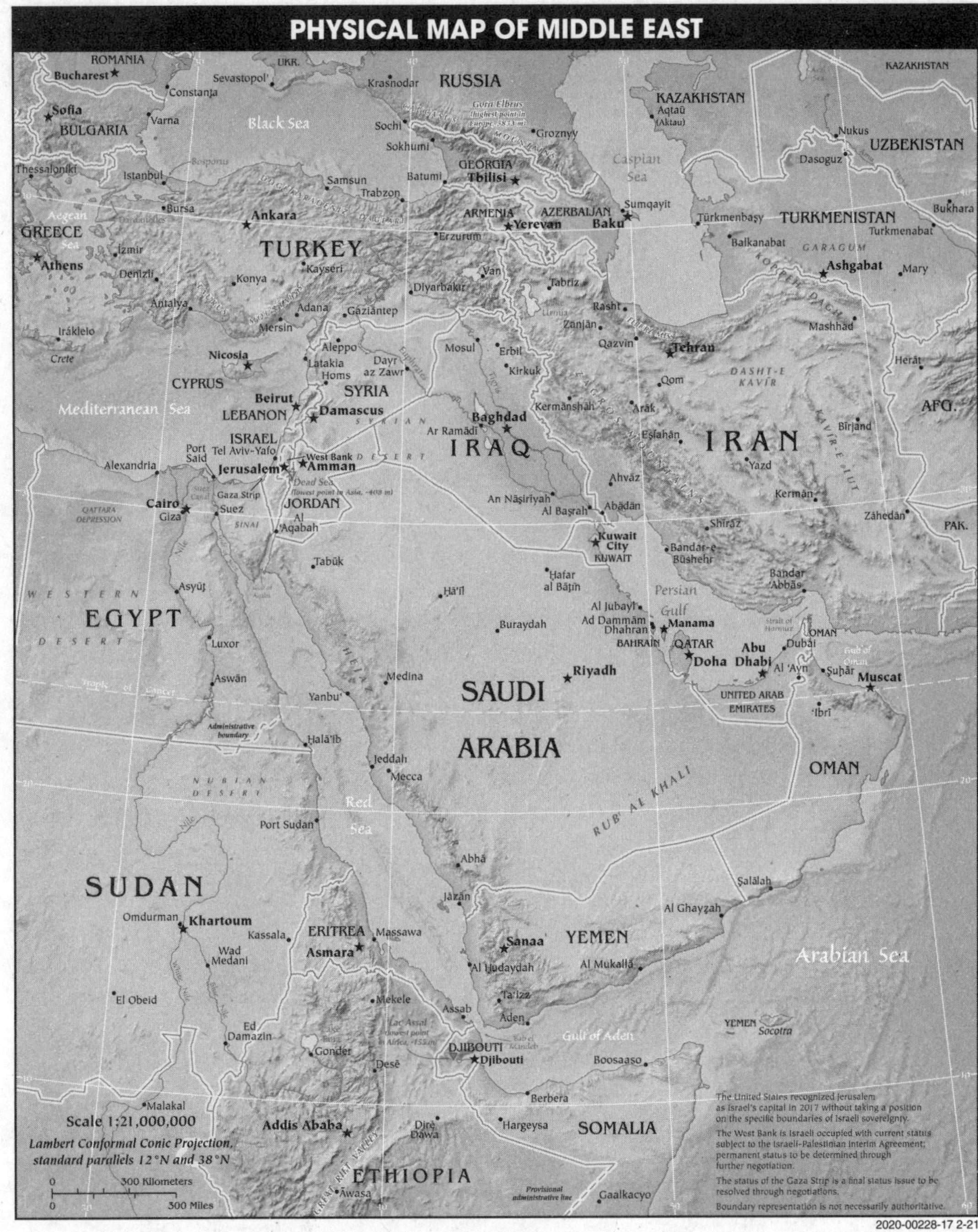

2020-00228-17 2-21

POLITICAL MAP OF NORTH AMERICA

2020-00228-18 2-21

PHYSICAL MAP OF NORTH AMERICA

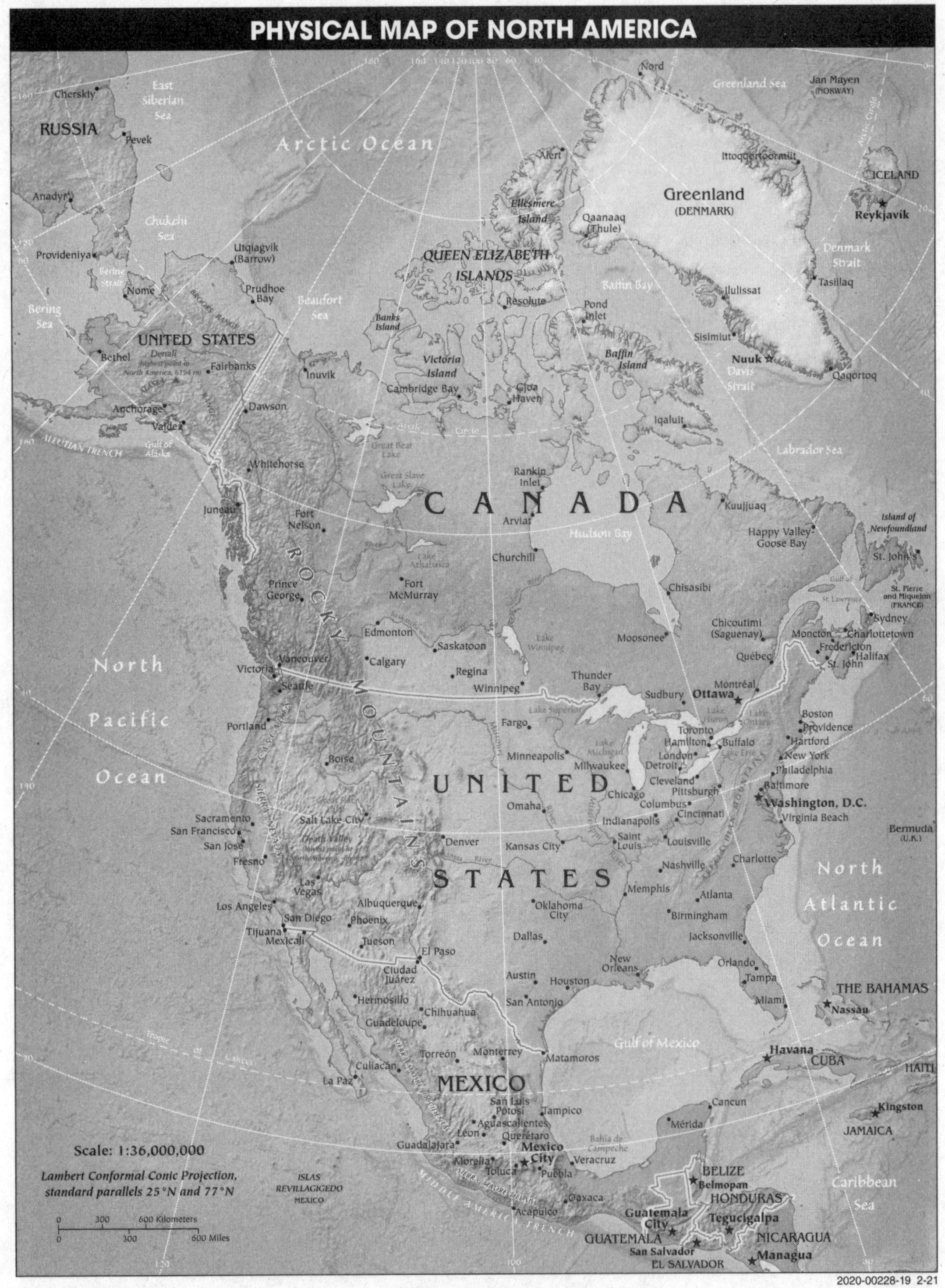

2020-00228-19 2-21

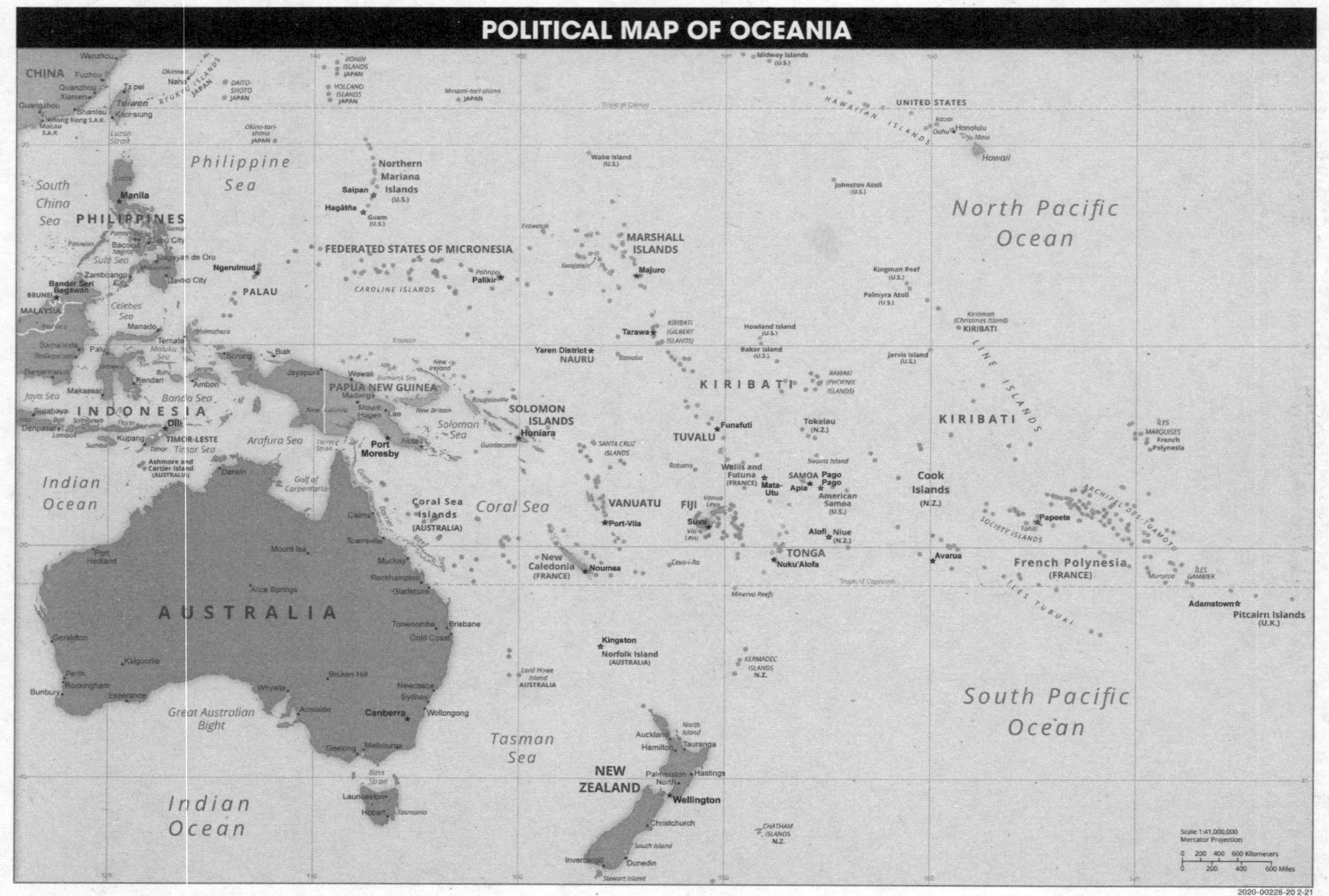
POLITICAL MAP OF OCEANIA
North Pacific Ocean
South Pacific Ocean
Indian Ocean
Philippine Sea
South China Sea
Coral Sea
Tasman Sea
Solomon Sea
Arafura Sea
Timor Sea
Banda Sea
Celebes Sea
Sulu Sea
Java Sea
Great Australian Bight
CHINA
Taiwan
PHILIPPINES
Manila
INDONESIA
MALAYSIA
BRUNEI
Bandar Seri Begawan
TIMOR-LESTE
Dili
Ashmore and Cartier Islands (AUSTRALIA)
PALAU
Ngerulmud
FEDERATED STATES OF MICRONESIA
Palikir
CAROLINE ISLANDS
Northern Mariana Islands (U.S.)
Saipan
Guam (U.S.)
Hagåtña
MARSHALL ISLANDS
Majuro
Wake Island (U.S.)
NAURU
Yaren District
KIRIBATI
Tarawa
TUVALU
Funafuti
PAPUA NEW GUINEA
Port Moresby
SOLOMON ISLANDS
Honiara
VANUATU
Port-Vila
New Caledonia (FRANCE)
Noumea
FIJI
Suva
TONGA
Nuku'alofa
SAMOA
Apia
American Samoa (U.S.)
Pago Pago
Wallis and Futuna (FRANCE)
Mata-Utu
Tokelau (N.Z.)
Niue (N.Z.)
Alofi
Cook Islands (N.Z.)
Avarua
French Polynesia (FRANCE)
Papeete
Pitcairn Islands (U.K.)
Adamstown
UNITED STATES
HAWAIIAN ISLANDS
Hawaii
Honolulu
Midway Islands (U.S.)
Johnston Atoll (U.S.)
Kingman Reef (U.S.)
Palmyra Atoll (U.S.)
Jarvis Island (U.S.)
Howland Island (U.S.)
Baker Island (U.S.)
LINE ISLANDS
Coral Sea Islands (AUSTRALIA)
Norfolk Island (AUSTRALIA)
Kingston
KERMADEC ISLANDS N.Z.
CHATHAM ISLANDS N.Z.
AUSTRALIA
Canberra
Sydney
Melbourne
Brisbane
Adelaide
Perth
Darwin
NEW ZEALAND
Wellington
Auckland
Christchurch
Dunedin
Scale 1:41,000,000
Mercator Projection
0 200 400 600 Kilometers
0 200 400 600 Miles
2020-00226-20 2-21

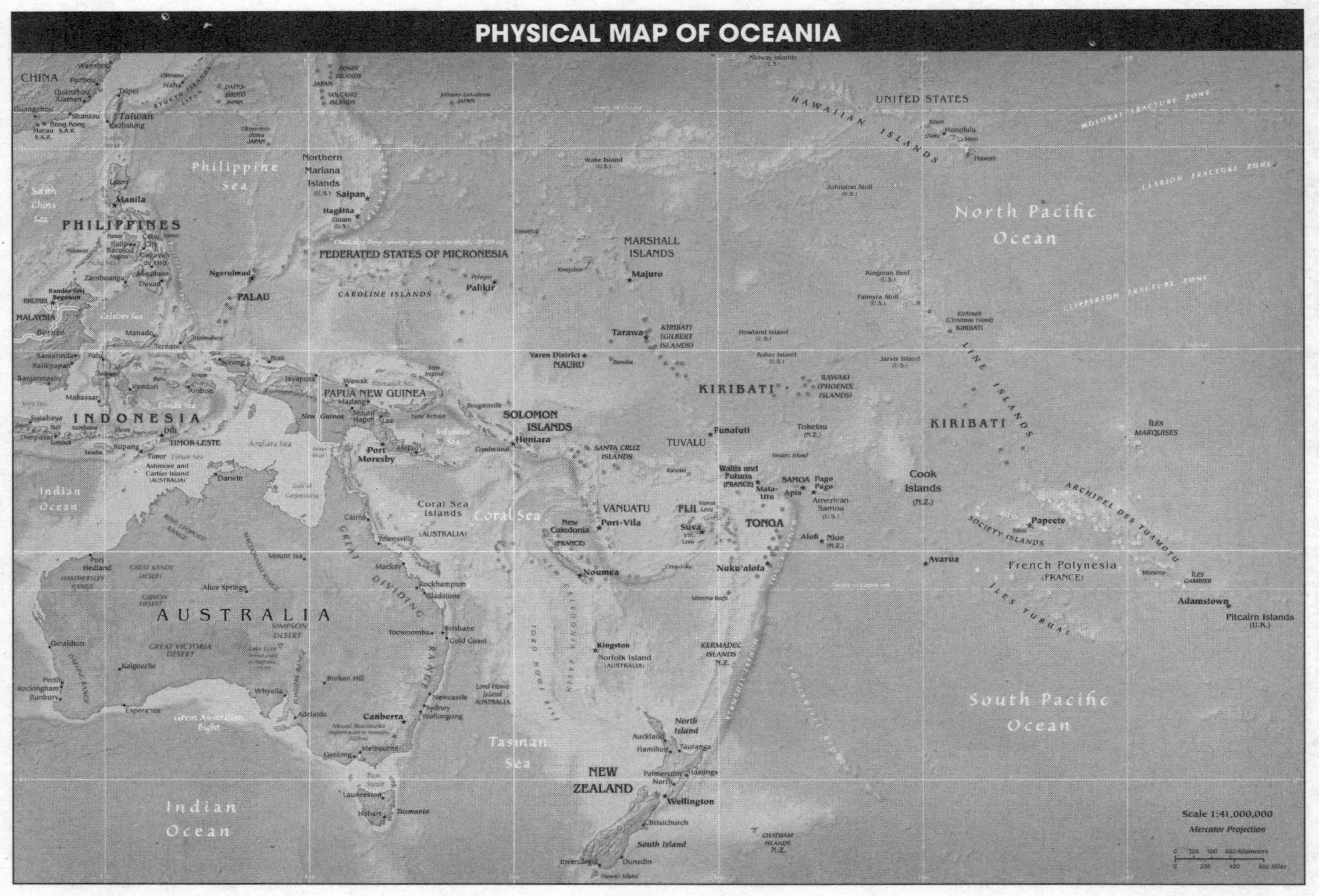
PHYSICAL MAP OF OCEANIA
CHINA
Taipei
Taiwan
PHILIPPINES
Manila
Philippine Sea
Northern Mariana Islands (U.S.)
Saipan
Hagåtña
Guam (U.S.)
FEDERATED STATES OF MICRONESIA
CAROLINE ISLANDS
Palikir
Ngerulmud
PALAU
MARSHALL ISLANDS
Majuro
Wake Island (U.S.)
UNITED STATES
HAWAIIAN ISLANDS
Honolulu
Johnston Atoll (U.S.)
North Pacific Ocean
Kingman Reef (U.S.)
Palmyra Atoll (U.S.)
Tarawa
KIRIBATI (GILBERT ISLANDS)
Howland Island (U.S.)
Baker Island (U.S.)
Jarvis Island (U.S.)
Yaren District
NAURU
KIRIBATI
RAWAKI (PHOENIX ISLANDS)
LINE ISLANDS
ÎLES MARQUISES
INDONESIA
Dili
TIMOR-LESTE
PAPUA NEW GUINEA
Port Moresby
SOLOMON ISLANDS
Honiara
SANTA CRUZ ISLANDS
TUVALU
Funafuti
Tokelau (N.Z.)
Wallis and Futuna (FRANCE)
Mata-Utu
SAMOA
Apia
Pago Pago
American Samoa (U.S.)
Cook Islands (N.Z.)
Indian Ocean
Darwin
Coral Sea Islands (AUSTRALIA)
Coral Sea
VANUATU
Port-Vila
New Caledonia (FRANCE)
FIJI
Suva
TONGA
Alofi
Niue (N.Z.)
ARCHIPEL DES TUAMOTU
SOCIETY ISLANDS
Papeete
Avarua
Noumea
Nuku'alofa
French Polynesia (FRANCE)
ÎLES GAMBIER
Adamstown
Pitcairn Islands (U.K.)
ÎLES TUBUAI
AUSTRALIA
GREAT DIVIDING RANGE
Alice Springs
Brisbane
Kingston
Norfolk Island (AUSTRALIA)
KERMADEC ISLANDS N.Z.
Canberra
Sydney
Melbourne
Adelaide
Perth
Tasman Sea
NEW ZEALAND
North Island
Auckland
Wellington
South Island
Christchurch
CHATHAM ISLANDS N.Z.
South Pacific Ocean
Indian Ocean
Tasmania
Hobart
Scale 1:41,000,000
Mercator Projection

POLITICAL MAP OF SOUTH AMERICA

2020-00228-23 2-21

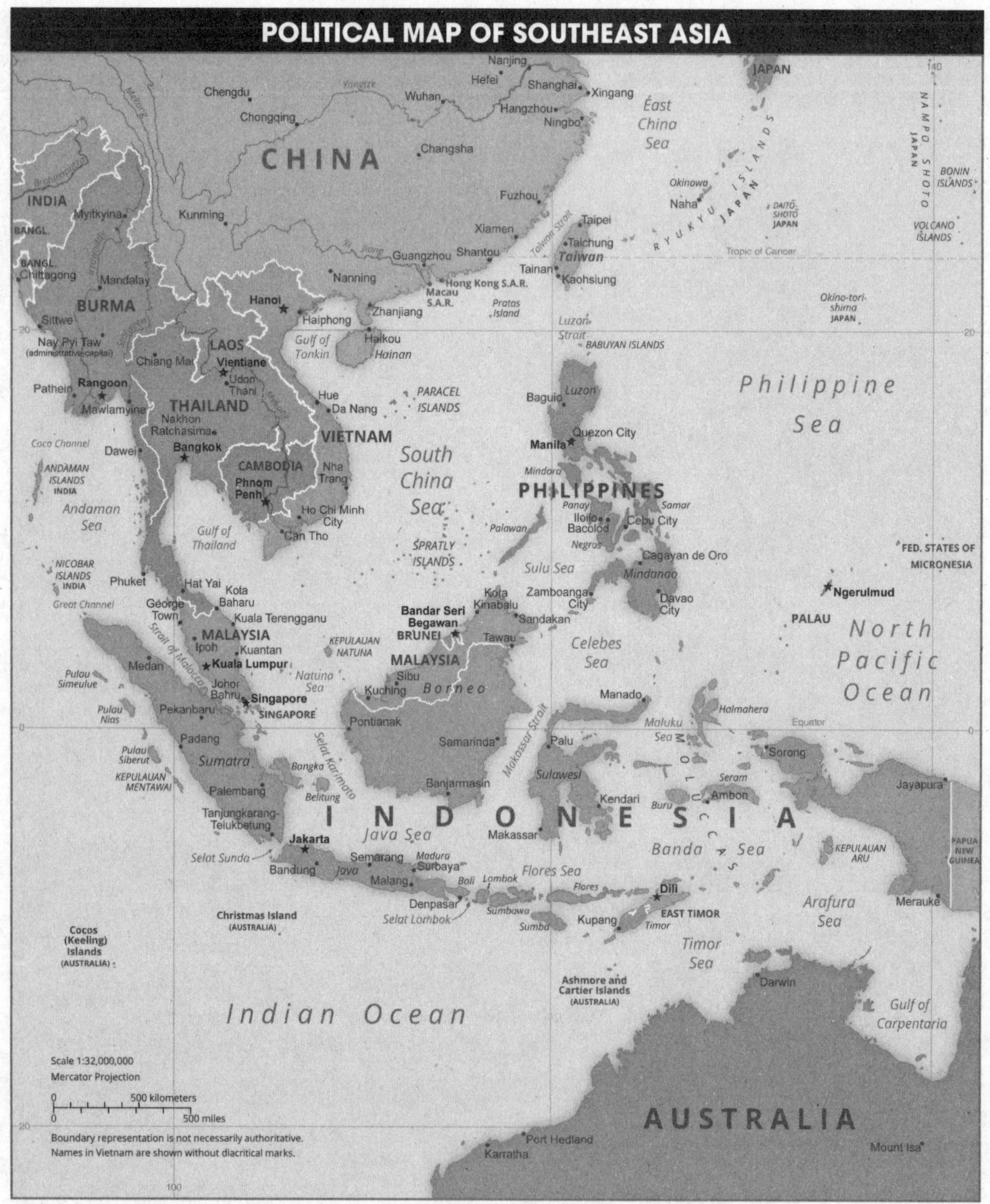
POLITICAL MAP OF SOUTHEAST ASIA
CHINA
Nanjing
Hefei
Shanghai
Xingang
Chengdu
Yangtze
Wuhan
Hangzhou
Ningbo
Chongqing
Changsha
East China Sea
JAPAN
NAMPO SHOTO JAPAN
BONIN ISLANDS
RYUKYU ISLANDS JAPAN
Okinawa
Naha
DAITŌ-SHOTŌ JAPAN
VOLCANO ISLANDS
Tropic of Cancer
INDIA
Brahmaputra
Myitkyina
Kunming
Fuzhou
Taipei
Taichung
Taiwan
Taiwan Strait
Tainan
Kaohsiung
Xiamen
Shantou
Guangzhou
Xi Jiang
BANGL.
Chittagong
Mandalay
Nanning
Hong Kong S.A.R.
Macau S.A.R.
Pratas Island
BURMA
Hanoi
Haiphong
Zhanjiang
Okino-tori-shima JAPAN
Sittwe
Nay Pyi Taw (administrative capital)
LAOS
Gulf of Tonkin
Haikou
Hainan
Luzon Strait
BABUYAN ISLANDS
Chiang Mai
Vientiane
Udon Thani
Pathein
Rangoon
THAILAND
Mawlamyine
Nakhon Ratchasima
Hue
Da Nang
PARACEL ISLANDS
Baguio
Luzon
Philippine Sea
VIETNAM
Quezon City
Manila
Coco Channel
Dawei
Bangkok
South China Sea
Mindoro
ANDAMAN ISLANDS INDIA
CAMBODIA
Phnom Penh
Nha Trang
PHILIPPINES
Andaman Sea
Ho Chi Minh City
Panay
Samar
Iloilo
Bacolod
Cebu City
Gulf of Thailand
Can Tho
Palawan
Negros
SPRATLY ISLANDS
Cagayan de Oro
FED. STATES OF MICRONESIA
NICOBAR ISLANDS INDIA
Phuket
Hat Yai
Kota Baharu
Sulu Sea
Mindanao
Ngerulmud
Great Channel
George Town
Kuala Terengganu
Kota Kinabalu
Zamboanga City
Davao City
PALAU
Bandar Seri Begawan
BRUNEI
Sandakan
MALAYSIA
Ipoh
Kuantan
KEPULAUAN NATUNA
Tawau
North Pacific Ocean
Strait of Malacca
Kuala Lumpur
MALAYSIA
Celebes Sea
Medan
Natuna Sea
Sibu
Pulau Simeulue
Johor Bahru
Singapore
SINGAPORE
Kuching
Borneo
Manado
Halmahera
Pulau Nias
Pekanbaru
Pontianak
Maluku Sea
Equator
Padang
Samarinda
Makassar Strait
Palu
Sorong
Pulau Siberut
Sumatra
Selat Karimata
Bangka
Sulawesi
MOLUCCAS
Seram
Jayapura
KEPULAUAN MENTAWAI
Palembang
Belitung
Banjarmasin
Kendari
Buru
Ambon
Tanjungkarang-Telukbetung
INDONESIA
Jakarta
Java Sea
Makassar
Banda Sea
KEPULAUAN ARU
PAPUA NEW GUINEA
Selat Sunda
Semarang
Madura
Surabaya
Bandung
Java
Malang
Bali
Lombok
Flores Sea
Flores
Dili
Denpasar
Selat Lombok
Sumbawa
Sumba
Kupang
EAST TIMOR
Timor
Arafura Sea
Merauke
Christmas Island (AUSTRALIA)
Cocos (Keeling) Islands (AUSTRALIA)
Timor Sea
Ashmore and Cartier Islands (AUSTRALIA)
Darwin
Indian Ocean
Gulf of Carpentaria
Scale 1:32,000,000
Mercator Projection
0 500 kilometers
0 500 miles
AUSTRALIA
Port Hedland
Karratha
Mount Isa
Boundary representation is not necessarily authoritative.
Names in Vietnam are shown without diacritical marks.
2020-00228-24 2-21

PHYSICAL MAP OF SOUTHEAST ASIA

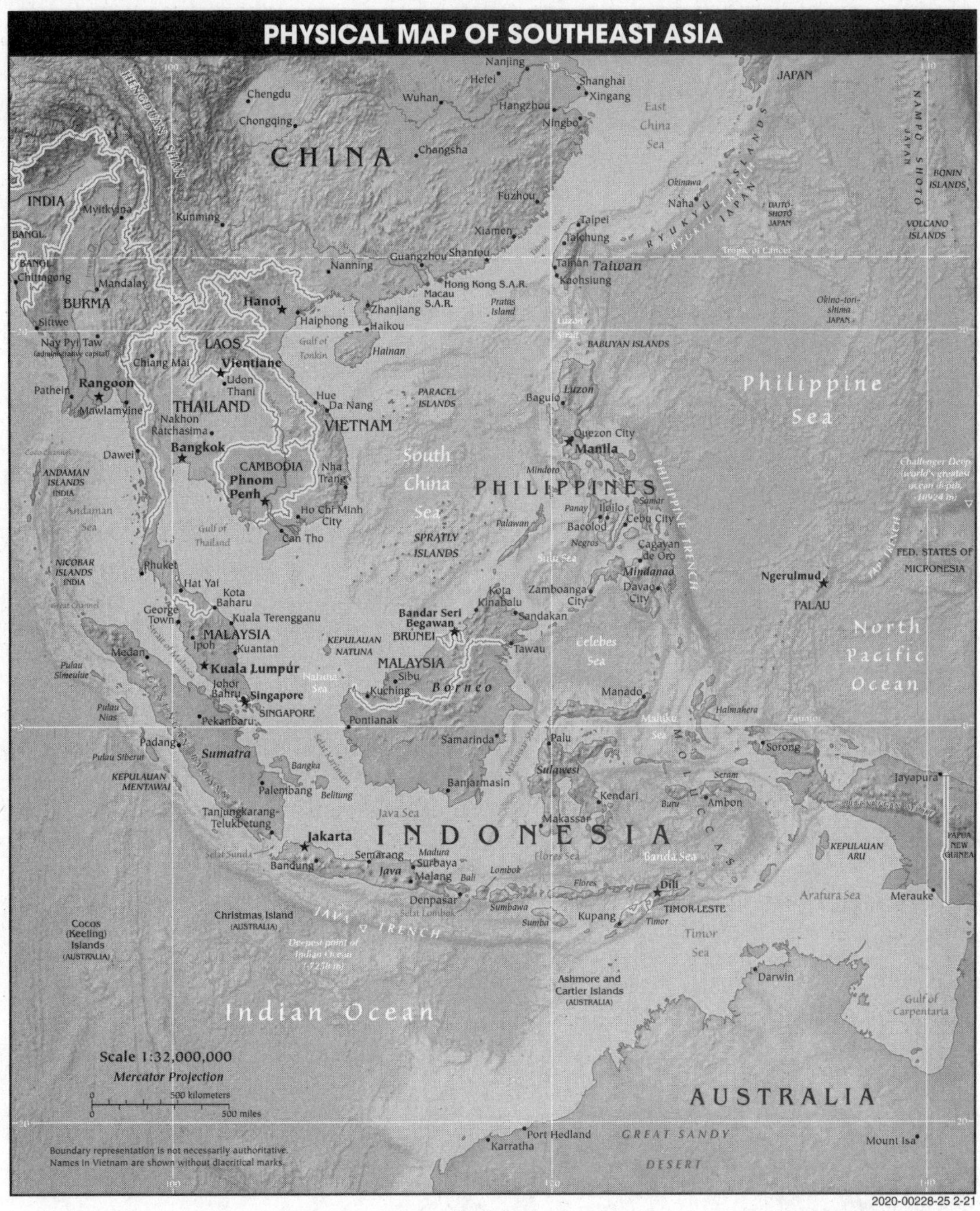

2020-00228-25 2-21

UNITED STATES

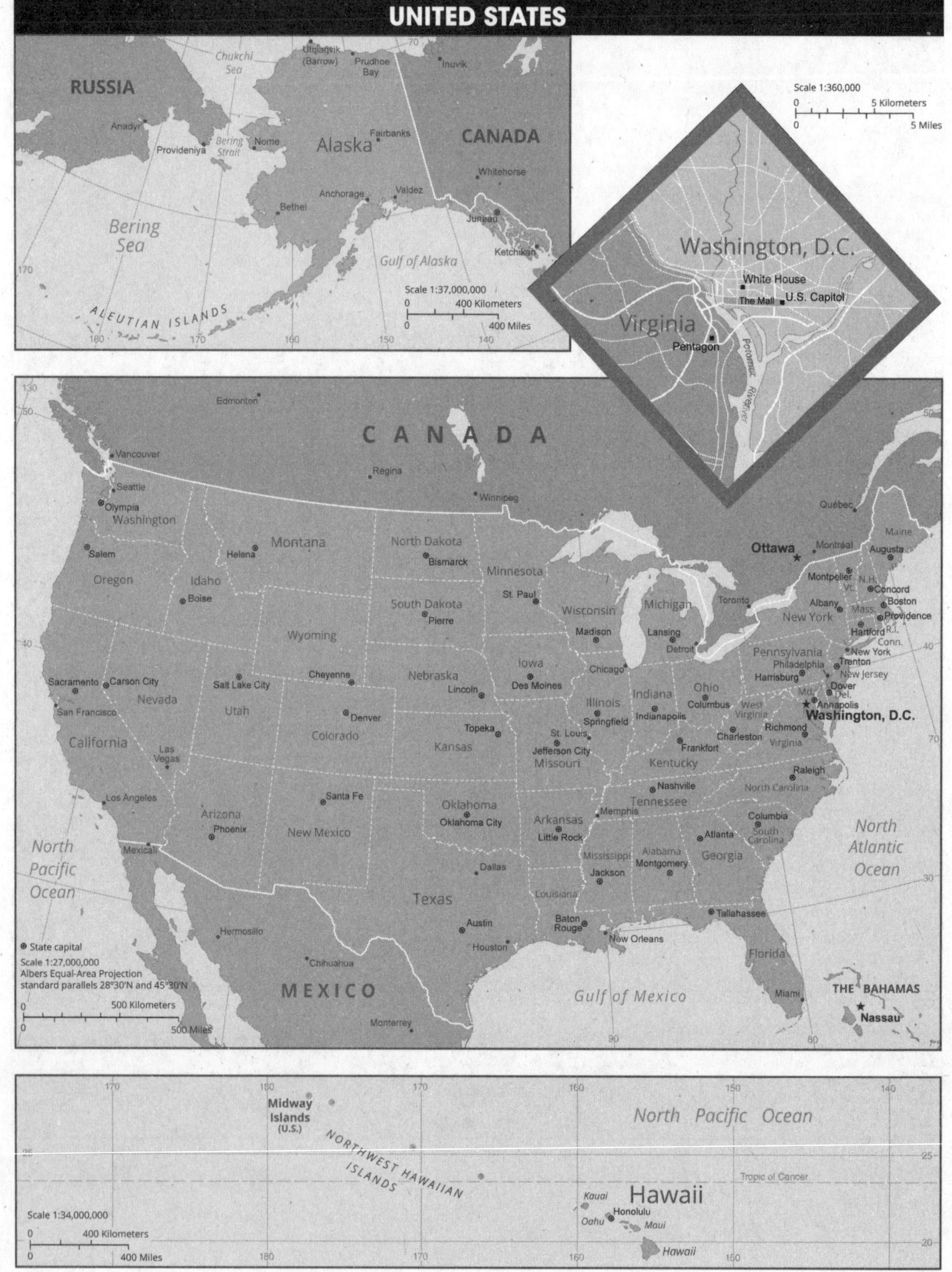

2020-00228-26 2-21

POLITICAL MAP OF THE WORLD

Political Map of the World
AUSTRALIA Independent state
Bermuda Dependency or area of special sovereignty
Sicily / AZORES Island / island group
National capital
Other capital
CANADA
UNITED STATES
NORTH PACIFIC OCEAN
NORTH ATLANTIC OCEAN
RUSSIA
CHINA
INDIA
BRAZIL
SOUTH ATLANTIC OCEAN
INDIAN OCEAN
AUSTRALIA
SOUTH PACIFIC OCEAN
SOUTHERN OCEAN
Antarctica

PHYSICAL MAP OF THE WORLD

Physical Map of the World
AUSTRALIA Independent state
Bermuda Dependency or area of special sovereignty
Sicily / AZORES Island / island group
National capital
Other capital
CANADA
UNITED STATES
RUSSIA
CHINA
INDIA
BRAZIL
AUSTRALIA
Antarctica

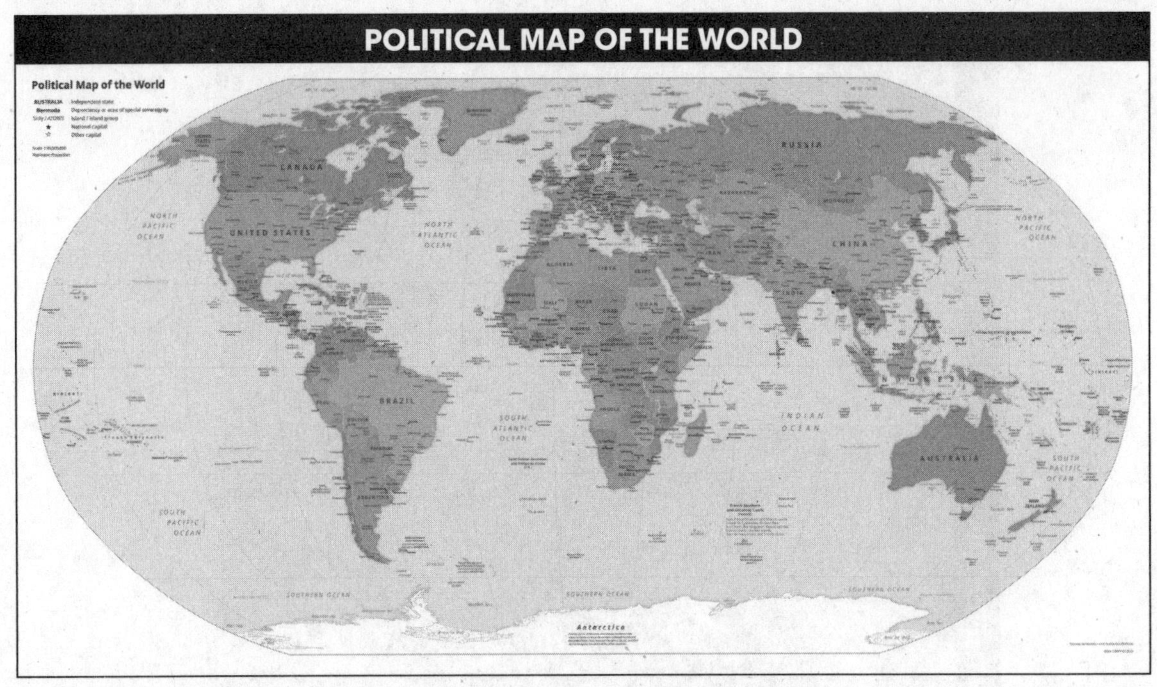

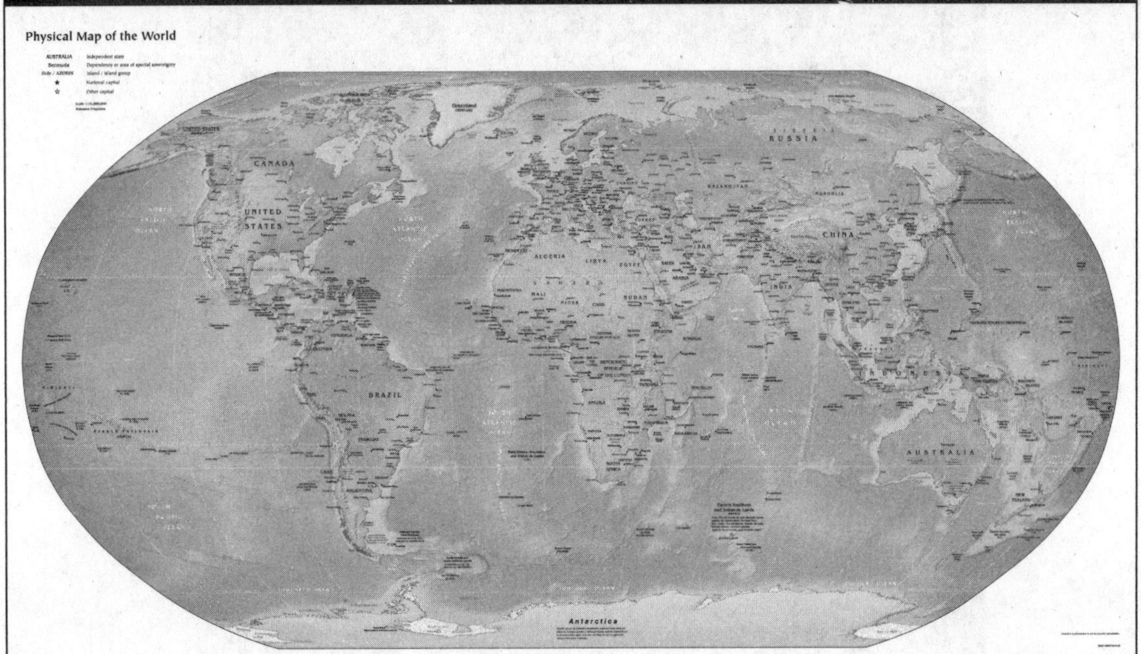

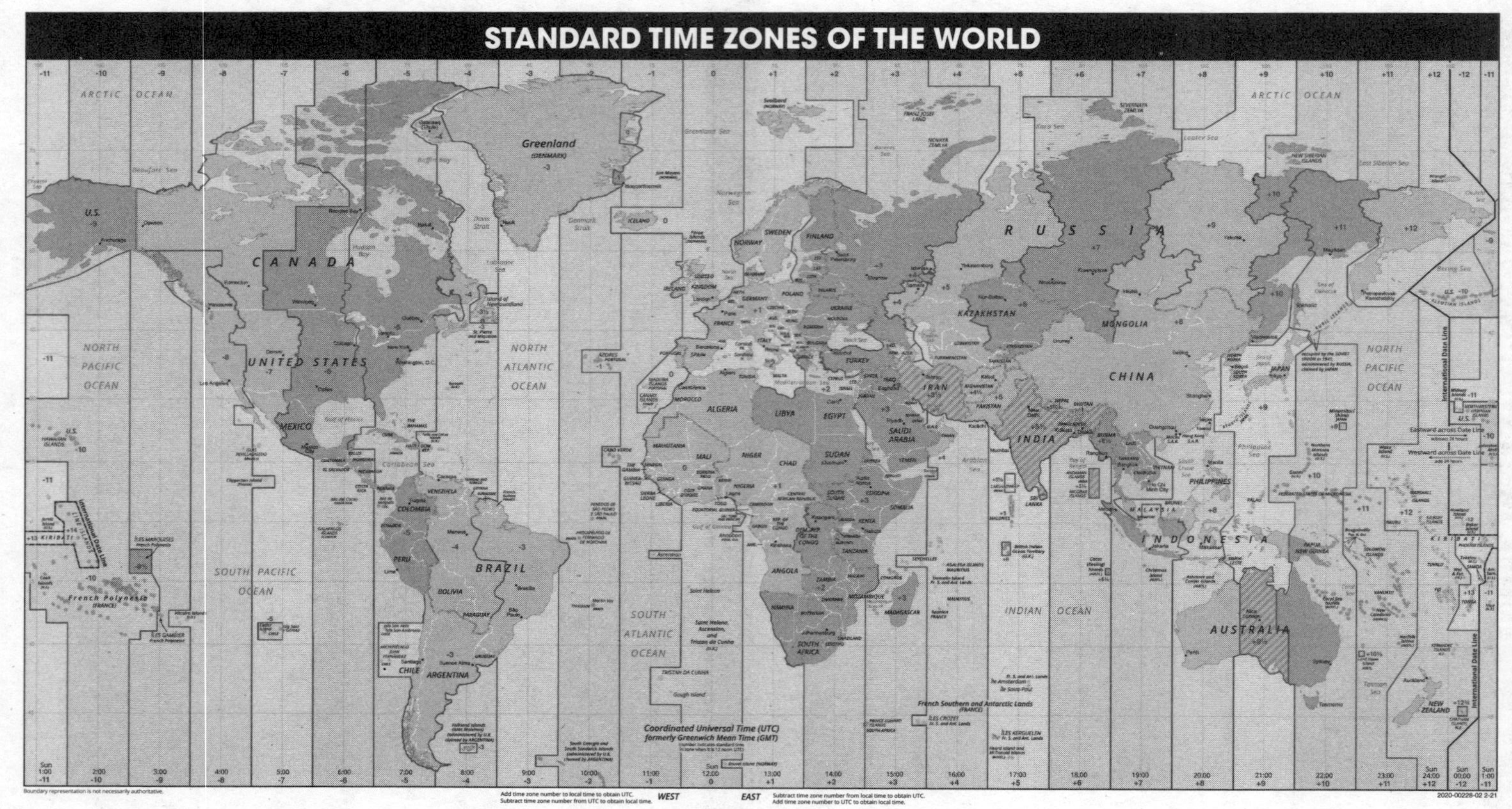
STANDARD TIME ZONES OF THE WORLD
ARCTIC OCEAN
NORTH PACIFIC OCEAN
SOUTH PACIFIC OCEAN
NORTH ATLANTIC OCEAN
SOUTH ATLANTIC OCEAN
INDIAN OCEAN
Greenland (DENMARK)
CANADA
UNITED STATES
MEXICO
BRAZIL
RUSSIA
CHINA
MONGOLIA
KAZAKHSTAN
INDIA
IRAN
SAUDI ARABIA
EGYPT
LIBYA
ALGERIA
SUDAN
AUSTRALIA
INDONESIA
PHILIPPINES
NEW ZEALAND
ARGENTINA
French Southern and Antarctic Lands (FRANCE)
Coordinated Universal Time (UTC) formerly Greenwich Mean Time (GMT)
Add time zone number to local time to obtain UTC. Subtract time zone number from UTC to obtain local time.
WEST
EAST
Subtract time zone number from local time to obtain UTC. Add time zone number to UTC to obtain local time.
International Date Line
Eastward across Date Line
Westward across Date Line
Boundary representation is not necessarily authoritative.
2020-00228-02 2-21

NOTES

NOTES

NOTES

NOTES

NOTES

NOTES

NOTES

NOTES

NOTES

NOTES